A Concordance to

THE COMPLETE POEMS AND PLAYS OF T. S. ELIOT

THE CORNELL CONCORDANCES

S. M. Parrish, *General Editor*

Supervisory Committee

M. H. Abrams

Donald D. Eddy

Alain Seznec

POEMS OF MATTHEW ARNOLD, *edited by Stephen Maxfield Parrish* (out of print)

POEMS OF W. B. YEATS, *edited by Stephen Maxfield Parrish*

POEMS OF EMILY DICKINSON, *edited by S. P. Rosenbaum*

WRITINGS OF WILLIAM BLAKE, *edited by David V. Erdman* (out of print)

BYRON'S *DON JUAN, edited by Charles W. Hagelman, Jr., and Robert J. Barnes*

THÉÂTRE ET POÉSIES DE JEAN RACINE, *edited by Bryant C. Freeman* (out of print)

BEOWULF, edited by J. B. Bessinger, Jr.

PLAYS OF W. B. YEATS, *edited by Eric Domville*

POEMS OF JONATHAN SWIFT, *edited by Michael Shinagel*

PLAYS OF WILLIAM CONGREVE, *edited by David Mann*

POEMS OF SAMUEL JOHNSON, *edited by Helen Harrold Naugle*

FABLES AND TALES OF JEAN DE LA FONTAINE, *edited by J. Allen Tyler*

POEMS OF OSIP MANDELSTAM, *edited by Demetrius J. Koubourlis*

POEMS OF SIR PHILIP SIDNEY, *edited by Herbert S. Donow*

PLAYS AND POEMS OF FEDERICO GARCÍA LORCA, *edited by Alice M. Pollin*

PASCAL'S *PENSÉES, edited by Hugh M. Davidson and Pierre H. Dubé*

COMPLETE WRITINGS OF GEORGE HERBERT, *edited by Mario A. Di Cesare and Rigo Mignani*

THE ANGLO-SAXON POETIC RECORDS, *edited by J. B. Bessinger, Jr.* (out of print)

POEMS OF BEN JONSON, *edited by Mario A. Di Cesare and Ephim Fogel*

PLAYS, POEMS, AND TRANSLATIONS OF CHRISTOPHER MARLOWE, *edited by Robert J. Fehrenbach, Lea Ann Boone, and Mario A. Di Cesare*

COMPLETE ENGLISH POEMS OF JOHN SKELTON, *edited by Alistair Fox and Gregory Waite*

COMPLETE POEMS OF E. E. CUMMINGS, *edited by Katharine Winters McBride*

THE COMPLETE POEMS AND PLAYS OF T. S. ELIOT, edited by J. L. Dawson, P. D. Holland, and D. J. McKitterick

A Concordance to

THE COMPLETE POEMS AND PLAYS OF T. S. ELIOT

Edited by

J. L. DAWSON

P. D. HOLLAND

D. J. McKITTERICK

Cornell University Press

ITHACA AND LONDON

First published 1995 by Cornell University Press.

Printed in the United States of America

♾ The paper in this book meets the minimum requirements of the American National Standard for Information Sciences–Permanence of Paper for Printed Library Materials, ANSI Z39.48-1984.

Library of Congress Cataloging-in-Publication Data

Dawson, J. L.
   A concordance to the complete poems and plays of T. S. Eliot / edited by J. L. Dawson, P. D. Holland, D. J. McKitterick.
      p.   cm. — (The Cornell concordances)
   Includes bibliographical references and index.
   ISBN 0-8014-1561-6 (cloth : alk. paper)
   1. Eliot, T. S. (Thomas Stearns), 1888–1965—Concordances. I. Holland, Peter, 1951–   . II. McKitterick, David. III. Eliot, T. S. (Thomas Stearns), 1888–1965. Complete poems and plays of T. S. Eliot. IV. Series.
PS3509.L43Z459   1995
821'.912—dc20   95-4884

Contents

Preface

The works of T. S. Eliot, who so rapidly became identified as one of the major English-language poets of the century, have appeared in various collected editions. For this concordance we have used as copy-text *The Complete Poems and Plays of T. S. Eliot*, published in England by Faber and Faber in 1969. British scholars immediately hailed this edition as the standard for all the works it includes, and we have deviated from it only to correct a few manifest errors, as recorded in the Technical Introduction.

There is still, in effect, no United States edition of comparable authority. *The Complete Poems and Plays, 1909–1950*, first published by Harcourt, Brace & World in 1952, continues to be widely used. But this edition necessarily excludes those works first published later (e.g., the plays *The Confidential Clerk* and *The Elder Statesman*) and the "Poems Written in Early Youth." We have not attempted any sort of collation of the text of our copy-text, the Faber edition, against either this American edition or the numerous volumes of individual works or groups of works published separately prior to the Faber edition of 1969, many of which continue in print. Yet, although this concordance is keyed to the page numbers of the Faber volume, readers of other editions will nonetheless be able to locate references by means of title and line number.

In 1971 Faber and Faber published *The Waste Land: A Facsimile and Transcript of the Original Drafts Including the Annotations of Ezra Pound*. This volume, following the rediscovery of the long-lost manuscript, showed the development of *The Waste Land* and enabled proper study of the role of Pound (the dedicatee of the poem and described by Eliot as "il miglior fabbro") and of the numerous passages Eliot cut from the printed text. This, by far the most scholarly edition yet published of any of Eliot's work, transformed critical understanding of the poem. We debated whether to concord it as well, but to do so would suggest that we ought also to concord the poems not included in *The Complete Poems and Plays*, particularly the many unpublished poems that have surfaced both before and since 1971.

Rumors of Eliot correcting in ink odd passages in poems in volumes he happened to encounter only confirmed our sense of the magnitude of the task of preparing a full-scale edited text of his work as well as the inappropriateness of undertaking any part of that work for a concordance at this stage. A variorum edition that expands the available corpus of Eliot's poetry collected in one volume and pays proper attention to the bibliographical complexities of the many manuscript and printed versions of that work is still awaited. But it is likely that even such a volume would itself be in need of subsequent revision as further unpublished work and further versions of already published work are uncovered. The end of such labor is many years off, and in the interim, the need for a concordance to what is still effectively the standard edition will remain.

In the slowly developing field of Eliot textual studies, a concordance such as this one is bound to be provisional. In the rapidly developing field of electronic texts, however, book-form publication of a concordance may seem outdated. But while a printed concordance cannot enable some of the kinds of linguistic analysis of literary data that scholars are undertaking, its availability and accessibility, its convenience in a book culture, continue to fulfill many academic needs in ways far better than any form of on-line data or diskette or CD-ROM. For, beyond the ease of straightforward reference tasks like search functions (where does "Because I do not hope to turn" come from?) and checking of quotations (is it "Hieronymo's mad againe" or "Hieronimo's mad again"?), printed concordances make possible the serendipity of scholarship, the critical chance of conjunction. To take just one example, our Index of Words Containing Hyphen or Apostrophe produces the intriguing juxtaposition of *god-given* and *god-shaken*.

One more substantial example is worth describing here. Once the text had been initially concorded and a word-frequency list prepared, we had to decide at what level of frequency we would place the inevitable cut-off point, beyond which we would remove words whose frequent usage would bulk the concordance out beyond the practicable limits of publication and whose concorded details were likely to be so rarely used and then for such specialized purposes that the suppression of these words could be adjudged reasonable. Our List of Omitted Words shows the consequence of that decision; placing the frequency level at 200 occurrences cuts the concordance by more than half. But it would have been unthinkable to omit *know* (677 occurrences), *think* (378), or *time* (357). The list of words over the 200-occurrence line that we decided to include becomes in itself a highly significant marker of Eliot's concerns; that exceptionally high incidence of *know*, for instance, outstrips such common words as *if* or *never*, suggesting something of Eliot's continual anxiety about epistemology, the possibility and limits of knowledge and knowability. The full litany of the nine frequently used words that we chose to include takes on its own potency: (in descending order of frequency) *know, think, time, like, see, say, want, good, man*.

It is not the task of a preface like this one to indicate the potential uses of the concordance. Although concordances are now produced by the labors of machines, they have a peculiar magic in their consequential revelations, a way of transforming our sense of the text. Words take on their own rhythms and potencies within any writer's work. The particularities of Eliot's vocabulary and usage are available in our concordance in ways others will uncover.

Creating computer-generated concordances is supposed to be a speedy operation, but this particular project has had a long history. Describing that history gives me the opportunity of acknowledging the help and support of many people.

The project began in 1970 when, as an undergraduate, I became fascinated by the possible applications of computers to literary study. Professor Roy Wisbey, then Head of the Literary and Linguistic Computing Centre at the University of Cambridge, encouraged me to create a concordance to an author for whom none existed. I quickly realized that there was no concordance to the work of T. S. Eliot and began marking up a copy and having it inputted. Like many undergraduates taking on such projects, I had no idea of the scale of the work and, in the pressure of exams, the concordance was left far behind.

A couple of years later, I was asked by David McKitterick, now Wren Librarian at Trinity College, Cambridge, and John Dawson of the Literary and Linguistic Computing Centre to join them in completing the same project, which they had taken much further, having made certain decisions about what to include and also having secured the invaluable support of Mrs. Valerie Eliot, the copyright holder in her late husband's work. All of us are most grateful to Mrs. Eliot for her kind permission to go ahead. We also subsequently discussed the concordance with Peter du Sautoy and Matthew Evans of Faber and Faber, both of whom were most helpful.

By this stage the text had been put into machine-readable form on paper tape. It is difficult now, in a time of widely available optical scanners and laser printers, to realize the tremendous labor involved in typing the text on such primitive machines. The staff of the Literary and Linguistic Computing Centre worked long hours and with exceptional accuracy to create the rolls of punched tape.

For a variety of reasons completion of the project was delayed and delayed. We are all most grateful to Mrs. Eliot, Faber and Faber, Cornell University Press, and, above all, Professor Stephen Parrish, for their continued support. Professor Parrish, as General Editor of The Cornell Concordances, has throughout displayed patience combined with tact, encouragement, and continual nudging. Without him, this concordance would never have been finished, let alone published. We owe him an especial debt.

I also thank both my collaborators; John Dawson, in particular, with his eagle-eyed proofreading both of the original text and of the whole concordance, line by line, and his suggestions for a number of additional indexes, has ensured a final version of exceptional usefulness.

PETER HOLLAND

Trinity Hall, Cambridge

Technical Introduction

"How's the book on Eliot, by the way?"
"It has a good twenty years to go."
—Simon Gray, *Butley*

Technical work on this concordance began in 1972 at the Literary and Linguistic Computing Centre in Cambridge, which used a computer called Titan (in essence a prototype Atlas II) with an operating system devised by the systems programming team at Cambridge. All the programs and data produced at the LLCC were typed onto punched paper tape, which was later read into the computer by optical means and then was ready for processing. By 1980 the typesetting facilities at Oxford were brought into play, and work had begun on developing the programs necessary to produce camera-ready copy of extremely high quality.

From the outset, various important (and far-reaching) decisions were taken. All poem titles and epigraphs, the notes on *The Waste Land*, and stage directions in the plays were to be ignored. Italic type was not specially marked. However, the French, German, and Spanish accents that appear in the text *were* included, coded in such a way that they could be represented by the limited computer alphabet available at the time. It was later decided to include poem titles and stage directions and to mark all italics in the text.

Format of Concordance

The concordance is essentially in Key Word in Context form, with each word being treated as a headword and printed centered in a line with its preceding and following context. Within the limitations of the line length, as much left and right context as possible is printed, with the proviso that whole words only are printed. A slash (/) is used to separate two of the original printed lines (and has been inserted in those sections of prose that have no natural line division, e.g., "Interlude" between the two parts of *Murder in the Cathedral*).

Multiple occurrences of the headword are printed in the order in which they appear in the original text, except that "Poems Written in Early Youth" appear after the other poems and before the plays. "Sweeney Agonistes," although in the form of a play, appears in its correct place in the poems.

The dedication "To My Wife," which precedes *The Elder Statesman*, has been included, even though it is substantially the same as the poem called "A Dedication to My Wife," and has been given the short title "ESd."

The references on the left-hand sides of all concordance lines are constructed as follows. For poems, the page number and short title are followed by the line number *within the whole poem*. For plays, the page number and short title are followed by the speaker name and the line number *on that page*.

Suffixes such as "m2" and "t" denote marginal words (stage directions, etc.) and title lines, respectively.

In the lists that follow the concordance, all words are printed entirely in lowercase letters, even proper names and words such as *I* and *I've*.

Hyphen and Apostrophe

Words consist of letters, hyphen, apostrophe, abbreviation period, and accents. Abbreviation period, apostrophe, and hyphen are sorted as though they were letters occurring in that order before *a* in the alphabet. So in the concordance, words appear in the following order: *c.i.f. c' cab-horse cat cat's cat-burglars cat-calls cataract cats*. A cross-referenced list of words that contain hyphen and apostrophe appears on pages 1234–1240.

Speaker Names

Within context lines, a change to a new speaker in the plays is marked with a sign such as {Wi}. The speaker names and abbreviations are given in the Speaker Abbreviation Index. The absence of a speaker name for the text that follows is denoted by { } and usually precedes a stage direction or a title.

Foreign Words

Foreign words, proper names, and abbreviations have been separated from the more usual forms of those words *only when they are homographs* of English words. No other homograph separation has been attempted. Words that differ only by a grave accent denoting a stress mark (e.g., *beloved, belovèd*) have been sorted separately in the concordance, Statistical Ranking List, and Reverse Index.

The French abbreviations *d', c', l', n', s'* and verbal affixes such as *-vous* and *-toi* have been separated for sorting purposes from the word to which they are joined. Thus the phrase *d'été* is sorted as the two words *d'* and *été* but always printed as one graphic form *d'été*.

The two phrases *co co rico* and *τὸ ἕν* are treated as single words, sorted as beginning with *co* and *to* respectively.

Accents

In the concordance *headwords,* which are printed in capitals, the letter À has been printed with its accent, even though it is customary in French to omit the accent. In the *contexts*, however, the grave accent has been omitted from the capitalized form of the word *à*. The only words affected by this are *À, BRIC-À-BRAC, DE-LÀ, JUSQU'À, LÀ, TÊTE-À-TÊTE, VOILÀ*. All other accents are printed on both lowercase and uppercase letters. Generally, accented words and words with an additional property such as *foreign word* or *proper name* follow plainer and unaccented forms of words. Thus, near the beginning of the concordance, we have the words

    A (2665)
    A (1) [Abbreviation]
    A (1) [Foreign word]
    À (16)

and on page 541 we have

LA (26)
LÀ (3)

Numbers

A separate list of lines containing numbers appears on page 1233.

Corrections to the Faber and Faber Edition

272 MC   11m *Edition reading* Dies Iræe *corrected to* Dies Iræ
51 Restaurant   11   *Edition reading* Ellé était *corrected to* Elle était
72 WL: Thund 345 · The line numbering printed in the edition does not agree with the number of lines actually printed, between lines 340 and 350. To make our line numbering match that of the edition, two of our lines have been numbered 345 (they are printed as divided in the edition). So we have

> 72 WL: Thund 344 But red sullen faces sneer and snarl
> 72 WL: Thund 345 From doors of mudcracked houses
> 72 WL: Thund 345 If there were water
> 72 WL: Thund 346 And no rock

Errata

The following page numbers are known to be incorrect in the concordance:

Rhapsody   Page 25 is labeled page 24.
Ash-Wed 3   Page 93 is labeled page 92.
Cor2 State   Page 130 is labeled page 129.
Space Time   Page 591 is labeled page 590.

Lists and Indexes

The concordance is preceded by a Short Title Index, a Speaker Abbreviation Index, and a List of Omitted Words. Four lists or indexes follow the concordance, each accompanied, if necessary, by an explanation of its form and use. These are the Reverse Index of Word Forms, Statistical Ranking List of Word Forms, Lines Containing Numbers, and Index of Words Containing Hyphen or Apostrophe.

Postscript

Although computers have no sense of humor, their output is sometimes amusing. See page 75 under the headword *bark*.

JOHN DAWSON

Wolfson College, Cambridge

Short Title Index

xv

Speaker Abbreviation Index

Sweeney Agonistes

{Ch}	Chorus	Chorus
{Do}	Doris	Doris
{Du}	Dusty	Dusty
{Kl}	Klip	Klipstein
{Kl&Kr}	Kl & Kr	Klipstein & Krumpacker
{Kr}	Krum	Krumpacker
{S}	Sweeney	Sweeney
{Sn}	Snow	Snow
{Sw}	Swarts	Swarts
{Tel}	phone	telephone
{W}	Wauch	Wauchope
{W&H}	Wa & Ho	Wauchope & Horsfall

Murder in the Cathedral

{Ch}	Chorus	Chorus of Women
{K1}	Knight1	First Knight
{K2}	Knight2	Second Knight
{K3}	Knight3	Third Knight
{K4}	Knight4	Fourth Knight
{3K}	Knights	The three Knights
{4K}	Knights	The four Knights
{M}	Mess	Messenger
{P1}	Priest1	First Priest
{P2}	Priest2	Second Priest
{P3}	Priest3	Third Priest
{3P}	Priests	The three Priests
{T}	Thomas	Archbishop Thomas Becket
{T1}	Tempt1	First Tempter
{T2}	Tempt2	Second Tempter
{T3}	Tempt3	Third Tempter
{T4}	Tempt4	Fourth Tempter
{4T}	Tempts	The four Tempters

The Family Reunion

{A}	Amy	Amy
{Ag}	Agatha	Agatha
{all}	All	All
{C}	Charles	Charles Piper
{Ch}	Chorus	Chorus (The Eumenides)
{D}	Denman	Denman
{Do}	Downing	Downing

{G}	Gerald	Gerald Piper
{H}	Harry	Harry, Lord Monchensey
{I}	Ivy	Ivy
{M}	Mary	Mary
{V}	Violet	Violet
{W}	Warburt	Dr. Warburton
{Wi}	Winch	Sergeant Winchell

The Cocktail Party

{A}	Alex	Alexander MacColgie Gibbs
{C}	Celia	Celia Coplestone
{CM}	Caterer	Caterer's Man
{E}	Edward	Edward Chamberlayne
{E&C}	Ed & Ce	Edward & Celia
{J}	Julia	Julia Shuttlethwaite
{L}	Lavinia	Lavinia Chamberlayne
{N}	Nurse	Nurse-Secretary
{P}	Peter	Peter Quilpe
{P&C}	Pe & Ce	Peter & Celia
{R}	Reilly	Sir Henry Harcourt-Reilly
{UG}	Reilly	Unidentified Guest

The Confidential Clerk

{C}	Colby	Colby Simpkins
{E}	Eggers	Eggerson
{K}	Kaghan	B. Kaghan
{L}	Lucasta	Lucasta Angel
{LE}	Lady E	Lady Elizabeth Mulhammer
{MG}	Guzzard	Mrs. Guzzard
{SC}	Claude	Sir Claude Mulhammer
*	note	footnote to page 457

The Elder Statesman

{C}	Charles	Charles Hemington
{ }	dedic	To my Wife
{G}	Gomez	Federico Gomez
{L}	Lambert	Lambert
{LC}	Ld Clav	Lord Claverton
{M}	Monica	Monica Claverton-Ferry
{MC}	Carghil	Mrs. Carghill
{Mi}	Michael	Michael Claverton-Ferry
{MP}	Piggott	Mrs. Piggott

List of Omitted Words

Words omitted from the concordance constitute 53.20% of all words contained in *The Complete Poems and Plays of T. S. Eliot*, and their omission thus shortens the concordance by more than half. The only words of frequency greater than 200 that have been concorded in full are:

good	233	man	228	think	378
know	677	say	314	time	357
like	346	see	321	want	256

Obviously, the choice of which words to concord in full, and which to omit, is based more on considerations of book size and cost than on any literary criteria. Good cases could be made for the retention of many of the omitted words; equally good cases could be made for the suppression of certain words that have been concorded in full. Researchers who require information about omitted words should address the Literary and Linguistic Computing Centre, University of Cambridge, Sidgwick Avenue, Cambridge CB3 9DA, UK. A small charge may be made for searching, sorting, and printing results.

a	2665	had	465	my	801
about	386	has	323	never	309
all	595	have	1161	no	627
always	263	he	749	not	1114
am	241	her	443	now	417
an	314	here	248	of	3114
and	3926	him	405	oh	222
are	665	his	485	on	563
as	699	how	252	one	431
at	751	i	4123	only	417
be	1014	i'm	404	or	540
been	406	i've	250	other	209
but	1248	if	528	our	261
by	374	in	2154	out	232
can	360	is	1756	shall	317
come	290	it	1440	she	446
could	220	it's	353	should	245
did	230	just	217	so	545
do	547	may	221	some	221
don't	395	me	908	than	216
for	1122	more	238	that	2085
from	477	much	200	that's	203
go	254	must	352	the	6940

List of Omitted Words

them	320	was	883	who	423
then	277	we	874	why	250
there	478	well	332	will	454
they	451	were	323	with	794
this	538	what	967	would	311
to	3838	when	519	you	3813
us	329	where	214	your	801
very	439	which	322		

CONCORDANCE

'ART (1)
236 Cat Morgan   12   can't but like Morgan, 'e's got a good 'art.'/I got knocked about on the Barbary
'AVE (1)
236 Cat Morgan   17   dead keen on old Morgan./So if you 'ave business with Faber — or Faber —/I'll give
'E'S (1)
236 Cat Morgan   12   enough;/'You can't but like Morgan, 'e's got a good 'art.'/I got knocked about on the
'IGH (1)
236 Cat Morgan   1   /I once was a Pirate what sailed the 'igh seas —/But now I've retired as a
'OUSE (1)
236 Cat Morgan   7   I'm allus content with a drink on the 'ouse/And a bit o' cold fish when I done me
'POTAMUS (2)
49 Hippopot   13   stir/To gather in its dividends./The 'potamus can never reach/The mango on the
50 Hippopot   25   can sleep and feed at once./I saw the 'potamus take wing/Ascending from the damp
'TILL (1)
589 Fable   92   took a knout/And flogged his mates 'till they grew good and friarly./Spirits from
'TIS (1)
595 Grad 14   5   one that we are ever loth to say./But 'tis a call we cannot disobey,/*Exeunt omnes*,
A (2665)
A (1) [*Abbreviation*]
535 ES   Gomez   15   /Or a woman — in this respect or that./*A* won't let me down in this relationship,/*B* won't
A (1) [*Foreign word*]
51 Restaurant   1   le Restaurant/Le garçon délabré qui n'a rien à faire/Que de se gratter les doigts et se
À (16)
46 Directeur   1   A.B.C.'s./Le Directeur/Malheur à la malheureuse Tamise/Qui coule si près du
46 Directeur   13   dessus bras dessous/Font des tours/A pas de loup./Dans un égout/Une petite fille/
47 Mél Adult   3   /En Angleterre, journaliste;/C'est à grands pas et en sueur/Que vous suivrez à
47 Mél Adult   4   pas et en sueur/Que vous suivrez à peine ma piste./En Yorkshire, conférencier;/A
47 Mél Adult   6   ma piste./En Yorkshire, conférencier;/A Londres, un peu banquier,/Vous me paierez
47 Mél Adult   8   /Vous me paierez bien la tête./C'est à Paris que je me coiffe/Casque noir de
47 Mél Adult   14   /J'erre toujours de-ci de-là/A divers coups de tra là là/De Damas jusqu'à
48 Lune Miel   1   /Ils ont vu les Pays-Bas, ils rentrent à Terre Haute;/Mais une nuit d'été, les voici à
48 Lune Miel   2   Haute;/Mais une nuit d'été, les voici à Ravenne,/A l'aise entre deux draps, chez deux
48 Lune Miel   3   une nuit d'été, les voici à Ravenne,/A l'aise entre deux draps, chez deux centaines
48 Lune Miel   12   /Prolonger leurs misères de Padoue à Milan/Où se trouve la Cène, et un restaurant
51 Restaurant   1   /Le garçon délabré qui n'a rien à faire/Que de se gratter les doigts et se pencher
51 Restaurant   6   lessive des gueux.'/(Bavard, baveux, à la croupe arrondie,/Je te prie, au moins, ne
51 Restaurant   15   de délire.'/Mais alors, vieux lubrique, à cet âge .../'Monsieur, le fait est dur./Il est
51 Restaurant   18   chien;/Moi j'avais peur, je l'ai quittée à mi-chemin./C'est dommage.'/Mais alors, tu as
75 WL: Thund   429   swallow/*Le Prince d'Aquitaine à la tour abolie*/These fragments I have shored
A.B.C.'S (1) [*Abbreviation*]
45 Cook Egg   33   multitudes/Droop in a hundred A.B.C.'s./Le Directeur/Malheur à la
A-LICKING (1)
227 Macavity   33   /You'll be sure to find him resting, or a-licking of his thumbs,/Or engaged in doing
A-TAKIN' (1)
236 Cat Morgan   3   /And that's how you find me a-takin' my ease/And keepin' the door in a
ABANDON (2)
341 FR   Amy   30   you this influence to persuade him/To abandon his duty, his family and his happiness?/
576 ES   Monica 25   /{M} Michael, Michael, you can't abandon your family/And your very self — it's
ABANDONED (3)
332 FR   Agatha   40   Oh, a dozen foolish ways, each one abandoned/For something more ingenious. You
379 CP   Celia   22   I thought that the future could be?/I abandoned the future before we began,/And
517 CC   Colby   13   and without ambitions./Now that I've abandoned *my* illusions and ambitions/All
ABANDONING (1)
213 Growltiger   43   the Chinks they swarmed aboard./Abandoning their sampans, and their pullaways
ABASED (1)
340 FR   Amy   24   have a husband:/Then I let him go. I abased myself./Did I show any weakness, any
ABBEYS (1)
587 Fable   4   the poor men,/And brought their abbeys tumbling at their backs,/There was a
ABBOT (3)
587 Fable   25   /When Christmas time was near the Abbot vowed/They'd eat their meal from ghosts
588 Fable   61   he had not eaten so much goose./The Abbot with proposing every toast/Had drank
589 Fable   73   know who reads this romance./The Abbot sat as pasted to his chair,/His eye became
ABBOT'S (1)
589 Fable   86   (such rascals are not rare)/That the Abbot's course lay nearer underground;/But the

ABDUCTED (1)
390 CP   Julia   16 were? Lavinia!/Don't tell me you were abducted! Tell us/I'm thrilled ... {}/[*The doorbell*
ABERRATION (1)
326 FR   Harry   27   /Some monstrous mistake and aberration/Of all men, of the world, which I
ABERRATIONS (1)
568 ES   Ld Clav   7   /Temporary failures, irreflective aberrations,/Reckless surrenders, unexplainable
ABIDE (1)
256 MC   Priests 27 for the sea to subside, in the night/Abide the coming of day, when the traveller
ABIDES (1)
187 FQ: DrySal 116   change, and smile: but the agony abides./Time the destroyer is time the preserver,
ABIDING (1)
243 MC   Chorus   14 Here is no continuing city, here is no abiding stay./Ill the wind, ill the time, uncertain
ABILITIES (2)
276 MC Knight1   29   speakers, who,/with their various abilities, and different points of view, will be
577 ES   Carghil 31 told me so./Now, Michael has great abilities for business./I saw that, and so does
ABILITY (1)
511 CC   Lady E   12   not good at figures. Your business ability/Comes, I suppose, from my side of the
ABLE (24)
588 Fable   44   know much about — as well's I'm able/I'll go through the account: They made a
604 Ode   10   has lost/We are still the less able to grieve,/With so much that of Harvard
244 MC   Chorus   16   /Unaccountably, and some not able to./We have all had our private terrors,/
276 MC Knight1   29   and different points of view, will be able/to lay before you the merits of this
278 MC Knight2   13 who had proved himself an extremely/able administrator — no one denies that —
279 MC Knight1   6   last word, for those who/have been able to follow his very subtle reasoning. We
279 MC Knight1   10 for its/loyalty to the Church, will be able to convince them. Richard Brito./{K4} The
322 FR   Harry   17 might surprise you;/I think I might be able to give you a shock./{Wi} There's been
396 CP   Lavinia 28   only a ghost to you,/You might be able to find the road back/To a time when you
418 CP   Celia   4 a good life./{C} I know I ought to be able to accept that/If I might still have it. Yet it
425 CP   Lavinia 29 the cocktails,/And the man won't be able to take the tray about,/So they'll go away
439 CP   Peter   29   not this time —/I simply shan't be able to./{E} But on your next visit?/{P} The next
449 CC   Eggers   21   my influence./I have never been able to make her like Miss Angel;/She becomes
462 CC   Colby   6 that up to this point/I haven't been able to feel very settled./And what you've had in
474 CC   Lucasta 35 understand music,/Not in order to be able to talk about it,/But ... partly, to enjoy it ...
485 CC   Lady E   16   But it made it all so simple!/To be able to think that one's earthly parents/Are only
493 CC   Lady E   22 with the light full on her:/I want to be able to watch her expression./{SC} But not in
506 CC   Guzzard 25   /{MG} You think that I might be able to help you?/{E} It seems just possible. A
510 CC   Eggers   6   still living/Mrs. Guzzard should be able to identify them./{LE} And will that prove
510 CC   Lady E   14 confirmation./{LE} And to my being able to adjust myself to it. {}/[*Re-enter* COLBY,
516 CC   Claude   30 musical ambitions —/Had you been able to fulfil them./Believe, if you like, that I am
574 ES   Ld Clav 22   /{LC} And what was Señor Gomez able to suggest?/{MC} Ah! That's the surprise
577 ES   Gomez   25   When he does come back/He'll be able to buy you out many times over./{MC}
580 ES   Carghil 22   pleases me most/Is that I shall be able to bring you news of Michael./And now
ABNORMAL (2)
414 CP   Celia   39 is most unusual./{C} It seemed to *me* abnormal./{R} We have yet to find what would
415 CP   Reilly   1   /For *you*, before we use the term 'abnormal'./Tell me what you mean by a sense
ABOARD (2)
213 Growltiger   42 of fireworks the Chinks they swarmed aboard./Abandoning their sampans, and their
232 Skimble   32   Mail/When Skimbleshanks is aboard./Oh it's very pleasant when you have
ABOLIE (1)
 75 WL: Thund 429   /*Le Prince d'Aquitaine à la tour abolie*/These fragments I have shored against my
ABOMINATIONS (1)
158 Rock 5   7 destroy it,/And have done with these abominations, the turpitudes of the Christians.'
ABOUND (1)
204 de la Mare   5   rove,/The kinkajou, the mangabey, abound/In the dark jungle of a mango grove,/
ABOUT (386)
ABOVE (12)
 21 Portrait   117   hand/With the smoke coming down above the housetops;/Doubtful, for a while/Not
 42 Swee Erect   5 and yelping seas./Display me Aeolus above/Reviewing the insurgent gales/Which
 54 Mr E Sun   15   shine the unoffending feet/And there above the painter set/The Father and the
 56 Swee Night   7   Plate,/Death and the Raven drift above/And Sweeney guards the hornèd gate./
 64 WL: Chess   97   sad light a carvèd dolphin swam./Above the antique mantel was displayed/As
 72 WL: Thund   333 and the sandy road/The road winding above among the mountains/Which are
158 Rock 5   1 impure heart: for the heart is deceitful above all things, and desperately wicked./
172 FQ: BurntN   58   to summer in the tree/We move above the moving tree/In light upon the figured
209 NamingCats   21   belong to more than one cat./But above and beyond there's still one name left

274 MC	Thomas	6	/I give my life/To the Law of God above the Law of Man./Unbar the door! unbar
335 FR	Harry	17	and I was left/Under the single eye above the desert./{Ag} Up and down, through
502 CC	Lucasta	20	care enough?/{L} No. You're either above caring,/Or else you're insensible — I

ABRITE (1)

51 Restaurant		9	—/C'est là, dans une averse, qu'on s'abrite./J'avais sept ans, elle était plus petite./Elle

ABROAD (20)

20 Portrait		88	and knees./'And so you are going abroad; and when do you return?/But that's a
196 FQ:	Little	180	forgotten/In other places, here and abroad,/And of one who died blind and quiet,/
249 MC	Tempt2	29	Monarchs also,/Waging war abroad, need fast friends at home./Private
267 MC	Knight1	34	French dominions./You sowed strife abroad, you reviled/The King to the King of
269 MC	Thomas	1	on foreign charity/I lingered abroad: seven years is no brevity./I shall not get
277 MC	Knight3	20	have to/spend the rest of our lives abroad. And even when reasonable/people come
319 FR	Warburt	17	mutual consent/And he went to live abroad. You were only a boy/When he died.
388 CP	Peter	19	*in with a latch-key]*/{P} You're going abroad?/{C} I don't know. Perhaps./{E} You're
414 CP	Celia	21	I share a flat/With a cousin: but she's abroad at the moment,/And my family want me
456 CC	Eggers	25	for her health. And when she's abroad/She is apt to buy a house. And then
506 CC	Eggers	8	it to Eggerson./{E} The father died abroad./Lady Elizabeth did not know the name
559 ES	Michael	3	to do with yourself?/{Mi} I want to go abroad./{LC} You want to go abroad?/Well,
559 ES	Ld Clav	4	to go abroad./{LC} You want to go abroad?/Well, that's not a bad idea. A few years
560 ES	Michael	9	/What I'd like is a chance to go abroad/As a partner in some interesting
560 ES	Ld Clav	31	natural enough/To want a few years abroad. It might be very good for you/To find
561 ES	Ld Clav	28	he must think over. But if he goes abroad/I want him to go in a very different
565 ES	Michael	21	I think of cutting loose, and going abroad./{MC} You must tell me all about it.
574 ES	Carghil	16	making a new start. He wants to go abroad!/And find his own way in the world.
574 ES	Michael	31	I spoke, Father, of my wish to get abroad,/You couldn't see my point of view.
578 ES	Monica	37	/It's not a question of your going abroad/But a question of the spirit which

ABRUPTLY (1)

298 FR	Charles	28	Sir./{C} I'm sorry to send for you so abruptly,/But I've a question I'd like to put to

ABSENCE (8)

268 MC	Knight3	12	one who transacts/His business in his absence, the business of the nation./{K1} These
272 MC	Chorus	25	than active shapes of hell;/Emptiness, absence, separation from God;/The horror of
272 MC	Chorus	27	/Which is no land, only emptiness, absence, the Void,/Where those who were men
290 FR	Amy	17	future happiness./Do not discuss his absence. Please behave only/As if nothing had
293 FR	Harry	19	to invent, please do so/In my absence. I shall be less embarrassing to you.
447 CC	Claude	25	making the appointment during her absence/You must say you had to leave under
448 CC	Claude	26	reasons for starting him during her absence/Are perfectly clear. But beyond that
559 ES	Michael	37	carrying on business in your absence./Why should I thank you for imposing

ABSENT (3)

117 SP	Dusty	13	What's that mean?/{Du} 'News of an absent friend'. — Pereira!/{Do} The Queen of
271 MC	Priests	33	Lord, to vespers! You must not be absent from vespers./You must not be absent
272 MC	Priests	1	absent from vespers./You must not be absent from the divine office. To vespers./Into

ABSENT-MINDED (1)

456 CC	Eggers	18	that I think I did touch on:/She's very absent-minded./{C} I hope you don't mean,/She

ABSOLUTE (5)

33 Conv	Gal	14	humorist,/The eternal enemy of the absolute,/Giving our vagrant moods the
181 FQ:	ECoker	162	if we do well, we shall/Die of the absolute paternal care/That will not leave us,
603 Spleen		16	of delay)/On the doorstep of the Absolute./Ode/THOMAS STEARNS ELIOT/
286 FR	Violet	21	all day and they dance all night/In the absolute *minimum* of clothes./{C} It's the
565 ES	Monica	1	/That my father should rest and have absolute quiet/Before every meal./{LC} But

ABSOLUTELY (5)

297 FR	Charles	11	/He's been with Harry ten years, he's absolutely discreet./He was with them on the
376 CP	Julia	33	you:/Anything that Alex makes is absolutely deadly./I could tell such tales of his
378 CP	Julia	10	a taxi./You know, you're looking absolutely famished./Good night, Edward. {}/
459 CC	Lady E	26	A primrose yellow/Would be absolutely baneful to Mr. Colby./He needs a
488 CC	Colby	22	to me ... there is nothing for me —/Absolutely nothing — for me to say about it./I

ABSOLUTION (1)

570 ES	Ld Clav	9	make a confession with no hope of absolution?/It was not her fault. We never

ABSOLVE (3)

268 MC	Knight3	27	/{K2} By you be this amended./{K3} Absolve them./{K1} Absolve them./{T} I do not
268 MC	Knight1	28	amended./{K3} Absolve them./{K1} Absolve them./{T} I do not deny/That this was
275 MC	Knight1	3	death,/My death for His death./{K1} Absolve all those you have excommunicated./

ABSORBED (2)

177 FQ:	ECoker	21	In a warm haze the sultry light/Is absorbed, not refracted, by grey stone./The
403 CP	Reilly	16	it, or they justify it/Because they are absorbed in the endless struggle/To think well

ABSORPTION (1)
463 CC   Claude   8   your military service,/And then your absorption in your music .../{C} You started by
ABSTENTION (1)
174 FQ: BurntN 127   /Is the same, not in movement/But abstention from movement; while the world
ABSTINENCE (1)
341 FR   Amy   21   only the stronger for all these years of abstinence./Thirty-five years ago you took my
ABSTRACT (2)
53 Whispers   29   in a drawing-room./And even the Abstract Entities/Circumambulate her charm;/
202 War Poetry   22   /Neither one for the other. But the abstract conception/Of private experience at its
ABSTRACTED (1)
449 CC   Eggers   22   her like Miss Angel;/She becomes abstracted, whenever I mention her./{SC} But
ABSTRACTION (1)
171 FQ: BurntN   6   /What might have been is an abstraction/Remaining a perpetual possibility/
ABSTRACTIONS (2)
327 FR   Harry   10   should like to believe./I was talking in abstractions: and you answered in abstractions./
327 FR   Harry   10   in abstractions: and you answered in abstractions./I have a private puzzle. Were they
ABSURD (6)
269 MC   Chorus   32   heaving of earth at nightfall, restless, absurd. I have heard/Laughter in the noises of
307 FR   Harry   18   erected, 'to please the children'./It's absurd that one's only memory of freedom/
393 CP   Lavinia   1   too seriously./And now I can see how absurd you are./{E} That is a very serious
489 CC   Claude   6   I didn't. For such a foolish reason./Absurd it sounds now. One child each —/That
496 CC   Lady E   7   Dervish dancing!/Really, Claude, how absurd you are!/Not that there isn't a lot to be
534 ES   Gomez   17   in forgery./{G} Forgery, Dick? An absurd suggestion!/Forgery, I can tell you, is a
ABSURDLY (1)
19 Portrait   33   my brain a dull tom-tom begins/Absurdly hammering a prelude of its own,/
ABUNDANT (1)
243 MC   Chorus   35   of dryness,/One year the apples are abundant,/Another year the plums are lacking./
ABUSE (1)
571 ES   Ld Clav   20   it's vain and selfish, we must not abuse it./That is where I failed. And the
ACANTHE (1)
48 Lune Miel   10   connue des amateurs/De chapitaux d'acanthe que tournoie le vent./Ils vont prendre le
ACCELERATOR (1)
540 ES   Gomez   27   /You never lifted your foot from the accelerator./{LC} We were in a hurry./{G} More
ACCENT (1)
354 CP   Celia   8   to./{C} Especially the Lithuanian accent./{J} Lithuanian? Lady Klootz?/{P} I
ACCENTS (1)
589 Fable   76   hair/And bade him come with him, in accents hollow./The friars could do nought but
ACCEPT (26)
196 FQ: Little   192   them/And those whom they opposed/Accept the constitution of silence/And are
271 MC Thomas   8   things had to come to you and you to accept them,/This is your share of the eternal
345 FR   Gerald   5   you are determined, Harry, we must accept it;/But it's a bad night, and you will have
405 CP   Reilly   7   *on his desk three times*]/{R} You must accept a rather unusual procedure:/I propose to
414 CP   Reilly   32   to be delusion,/But which we have to accept and go on from./And the second
418 CP   Celia   4   life./{C} I know I ought to be able to accept that/If I might still have it. Yet it leaves
421 CP   Julia   37   I myself am saying./{J} You must accept your limitations./— But how much
422 CP   Reilly   8   have chosen?/{R} They accept their destiny./{A} And *she* has made the
462 CC   Colby   10   believe that Lady Elizabeth/Can ever accept me as if I was her son?/{SC} As if you
462 CC   Claude   25   your own terms/Upon life, you must accept the terms it offers you./But tell me first
478 CC   Lucasta   4   in that event, Colby, you'll have to accept me/As your sister! Even if I am a
491 CC   Claude   17   from what I had intended./Could you accept us both in that way, Colby?/{C} I can
491 CC   Colby   22   /{C} It would be easier, I think,/To accept you both in the place of parents/If
501 CC   Lady E   22   step-daughter;/And shall be happy to accept Mr. Kaghan as a son-in-law./{L} Thank
503 CC   Lucasta   1   /We may understand each other. And accept the fact/That we're not necessary to each
503 CC   Lucasta   10   /{L} I shall be happy,/If you will accept me as a sister/For the happiness that
515 CC   Claude   40   if you think/I am not your father. I'll accept that./If you will stay with me. It shall
516 CC   Claude   32   like, that I am not your father:/I'll accept that. I put no claim upon you —/Except
516 CC   Colby   40   ambitions/And in the same way to accept their failure./You had your father before
536 ES   Gomez   40   I can trust —/And one who will accept both Culverwell and Gomez —/See
539 ES   Ld Clav   24   historical epitome./Though I cannot accept it as altogether accurate./The only thing I
540 ES   Gomez   38   suggestion!/Who's going to accept the unsupported statement/Of Federico
546 ES   Piggott   20   are exceptional/Though we never accept any guest who's incurable./You know,
546 ES   Piggott   23   want to come here to die!/We never accept them. Nor do we accept/Any guest who
546 ES   Piggott   23   /We never accept them. Nor do we accept/Any guest who *looks* incurable —/We
551 ES   Carghil   28   /My lawyer said: 'I advise you to accept',/'Because Mr. Ferry will be standing for

ACCEPTABLE (1)
474 CC   Colby   7   make the world outside it real/And acceptable, I think./{L} You sound awfully
ACCEPTANCE (1)
439 CP   Reilly   7   them/Into something new. Only by acceptance/Of the past will you alter its
ACCEPTED (13)
111 Xmas Trees   11   wonder/At the Feast as an event not accepted as a pretext;/So that the glittering
172 FQ: BurntN   32   at./There they were as our guests, accepted and accepting./So we moved, and they,
202 War Poetry   18   which may neither be ignored nor accepted,/A problem to be met with ambush
240 MC   Priest2 31   /In conference, meetings accepted, meetings refused,/Meetings unended
374 CP   Celia   26   are only temporary./You know I accepted the situation/Because a divorce would
425 CP   Lavinia   6   /{L} It's true, a great many more accepted/Than we thought would want to come.
425 CP   Lavinia 18   won't all come, out of those who accepted./You know we said, 'we can ask
437 CP   Reilly   31   of preparation./That way, which she accepted, led to this death./And if that is not a
475 CC   Colby   27   /Is that what you mean? I've just accepted you./{L} Oh, that's so wonderful, to be
475 CC   Lucasta 28   /{L} Oh, that's so wonderful, to be accepted!/No one has ever 'just accepted' me
475 CC   Lucasta 29   to be accepted!/No one has ever 'just accepted' me before./Of course the facts don't
477 CC   Lucasta 25   why you're shocked:/Claude has just accepted me like a debit item/Always in his cash
517 CC   Colby   9   not think of you/As my father: if I accepted that/I should be guilty towards you. I
ACCEPTING (5)
148 Rock 1   52   good deeds that lead to obscurity, accepting/With equal face those that bring
172 FQ: BurntN   32   they were as our guests, accepted and accepting./So we moved, and they, in a formal
466 CC   Claude   29   now what I meant when I spoke/Of accepting the terms life imposes upon you/Even
466 CC   Claude   30   upon you/Even to the point of accepting ... make-believe?/{C} I think I do. At
466 CC   Colby   34   ... something in me/Rebels against accepting such conditions./It would be so much
ACCEPTS (1)
538 ES   Gomez   18   are anonymous/Because the man who accepts responsibility/Isn't the man who made
ACCESSION (1)
220 Old Deut   4   /A long while before Queen Victoria's accession./Old Deuteronomy's buried nine
ACCIDENT (20)
261 MC Thomas   11   martyr, the blessed Stephen. Is it an accident, do you think,/that the day of the first
261 MC Thomas   24   is./A Christian martyrdom is never an accident, for Saints are not made by/accident.
261 MC Thomas   25   accident, for Saints are not made by/accident. Still less is a Christian martyrdom the
299 FRDowning   12   so./Much more likely to have been an accident./I mean, knowing her Ladyship,/I
301 FR   Chorus   30   column./We know about the railway accident/We know about the sudden thrombosis
311 FR   Harry   30   that I did/Has to do with me. The accident of a dreaming moment,/Of a dreaming
322 FR   Winch   31   arrived./Mr. John's had a bit of an accident/On the West Road, in the fog, coming
323 FR   Winch   9   /It's really nothing but a minor accident./{W} It's John has had the accident,
323 FR Warburt   10   accident./{W} It's John has had the accident, Lady Monchensey;/And Winchell tells
323 FR   Amy   17   doubt, will be all that he needs./{A} Accident? What sort of an accident?/{Wi}
323 FR   Amy   17   needs./{A} Accident? What sort of an accident?/{Wi} Coming along in the fog, my
326 FR   Ivy   36   Oh dear, I'm afraid *he*'s had an accident. {}/[*Exeunt* IVY *and* DENMAN]/{V}
327 FR   Ivy   30   It seems that Arthur too/Has had an accident. I don't think he's hurt,/But he says
328 FR   Gerald   3   was every bit as likely/To have an accident as John. And it wasn't John's fault,/I
328 FR   Charles   22   police stated that at the time of the/accident Mr. Piper was being pursued by a
337 FR   Agatha   1   a child, formed/To grow to maturity:/Accident is design/And design is accident/In a
337 FR   Agatha   2   /Accident is design/And design is accident/In a cloud of unknowing./O my child,
507 CC   Lady E   23   have been when Tony met with his accident./{MG} I was informed that the father
511 CC   Lady E   9   He died very suddenly. Of a fatal accident/When you were very young. That is
555 ES   Ld Clav 22   /{LC} I hope he's not had another accident./You know, after that last escapade of
ACCIDENTAL (4)
32 Hysteria   2   part of it, until her teeth were only accidental stars with a talent/for squad-drill. I
300 FRDowning   26   say I saw him,/I mean that I saw him accidental./You see, Sir, I was down in the
336 FR   Agatha   31   a moment of unconsciousness/In an accidental bed/Or under an elder tree/According
477 CC   Lucasta   4   eight years old/When she died of an 'accidental overdose'./Then Claude took me
ACCIDENTS (3)
325 FR   Ivy   27   /But John was the one that had the accidents,/Somehow, just because he *was* the
345 FR   Harry   10   fear that I am in any danger/Of such accidents as happen to Arthur and John:/Take
348 FR   Chorus   13   the machine,/We can usually avoid accidents?/We are insured against fire,/Against
ACCOMMODATING (1)
394 CP   Edward   36   be a support./Well, I tried to be accommodating. But, in future,/I shall behave, I
ACCOMMODATION (1)
498 CC   Eggers   20   taken in another one/As a temporary accommodation —/On suitable terms. But if she
ACCOMPANIED (2)
151 Rock 2   18   could set about imperial expansion/Accompanied by industrial development./
415 CP   Celia   11   never noticed that immorality/Was accompanied by a sense of sin:/At least, I have

ACCOMPLICE (1)
301 FR   Charles   15   /But I believe that an unconscious accomplice is desirable./{Ch} Why should we
ACCOMPLISHED (1)
429 CP   Edward   21   /{E} And what has your commission accomplished?/{A} We have just drawn up an
ACCORD (1)
251 MC   Tempt3   7   knew friendship/Can sooner know accord./{T} For a countryman/You wrap your
ACCORDANCE (1)
276 MC   Knight1   25   both sides of the case. That is in accordance with our long-established/principle
ACCORDING (8)
105 Song Sime   25   has eighty years and no to-morrow./According to thy word./They shall praise Thee
203 Indians   8   /(The warm or the cool hour, according to the climate)/Of foreign men, who
260 MC   Thomas   2   *of the second chapter of the Gospel according to Saint Luke.* In the/Name of the
336 FR   Agatha   33   accidental bed/Or under an elder tree/According to the phase/Of the determined
346 FRDowning   26   I mean:/We most of us seem to live according to circumstance,/But with people like
438 CP   Reilly   27   guilty too?/{R} If we all were judged according to the consequences/Of all our words
537 ES   Ld Clav   3   Dick, to give me reality!/{LC} But according to the description you have given/Of
559 ES   Michael 19   simply want to lead a life of my own,/According to my own ideas of good and bad,/
ACCOUNT (14)
222 Pekes Pols   m1   and the Pollicles/*Together with some Account of the Participation/of the Pugs and the*
588 Fable   45   as well's I'm able/I'll go through the account: They made a raid/On every bird and
343 FR   Harry   37   dangers/If I pursue it. I cannot account for this/But it is so, mother. Until I
409 CP   Reilly   14   to make the least sacrifice/On her account. This injured your vanity./You liked to
411 CP   Reilly   35   /{R} My secretary will send you my account./Go in peace. And work out your
467 CC   Claude   33   when we think we have settled our account/Life presents a new one, more difficult
477 CC   Lucasta 26   like a debit item/Always in his cash account. I don't like myself./I don't like the
492 CC   Colby   1   marry./You may be right. I can't take account of that./But now I want to know whose
534 ES   Gomez   30   an aeroplane ready:/And keep an account in a bank in Switzerland./The ones who
538 ES   Gomez   27   some mistake, Dick .../That would account for your leaving politics/And taking a
539 ES   Gomez   30   I don't propose to give you a detailed account/Of my own career. I've been very
541 ES   Gomez   22   For the matter of that,/My current account in Stockholm or Zürich/Would keep
551 ES   Ld Clav   8   behaviour./{LC} But we'd settled our account./What harm was done? I learned my
559 ES   Michael 15   /I want to be somebody on my own account./{LC} But what do you want to do?
ACCOUNTS (3)
346 FRDowning   28   there's something inside them/That accounts for what happens to them. You get a
390 CP   Julia   13   had a lapse of memory!/Then that accounts for the aunt — and the telegram./{L}
558 ES   Ld Clav 10   with you about it./{LC} That accounts for your coming down here so
ACCUMULATED (1)
111 Xmas Trees   29   meaning whichever is the last)/The accumulated memories of annual emotion/May
ACCURATE (1)
539 ES   Ld Clav 24   I cannot accept it as altogether accurate./The only thing I find surprising/In the
ACCUSE (2)
410 CP   Reilly   16   'no man could love her.'/You could accuse each other of your own faults,/And so
541 ES   Gomez   16   never have believed/That you would accuse an old friend of ... blackmail!/On the
ACCUSED (1)
538 ES   Ld Clav 16   as you had hoped./{LC} I was never accused of making a mistake./{G} No, in
ACCUSTOMED (1)
511 CC   Kaghan   18   you,/Lady Elizabeth. I've always been accustomed/To regard Mrs. Kaghan as my
ACHE (1)
310 FR   Mary   2   cold spring now is the time/For the ache in the moving root/The agony in the dark/
ACHIEVEMENT (1)
561 ES   Ld Clav   1   Michael! If you had some aim of high achievement,/Some dream of excellence, how
ACHILLES' (1)
19 Portrait   61   /You are invulnerable, you have no Achilles' heel./You will go on, and when you
ACIDS (1)
189 FQ: DrySal   196   fiddle with pentagrams/Or barbituric acids, or dissect/The recurrent image into
ACKNOWLEDGE (5)
282 MC   Chorus   6   Canterbury./Forgive us, O Lord, we acknowledge ourselves as type of the common
282 MC   Chorus   12   than we fear the love of God./We acknowledge our trespass, our weakness, our
282 MC   Chorus   12   trespass, our weakness, our fault; we acknowledge/That the sin of the world is upon
332 FR   Agatha   8   your father,/And my sister whom you acknowledge as your mother:/There is no
505 CC   Eggers   37   she could not, in the circumstances, acknowledge./That happens not infrequently,
ACKNOWLEDGED (2)
248 MC   Tempt2   22   rise! You, master of policy/Whom all acknowledged, should guide the state again./{T}
507 CC   Guzzard 27   careless./{MG} And that the heirs acknowledged no responsibility./The mother, I

ACONITE (1)
310 FR   Mary   7   are the ones that suffer least:/The aconite under the snow/And the snowdrop

ACQUAINTANCE (9)
119 SP   Klip   9   /{Kl} I'm very pleased to make your acquaintance/{Kr} Extremely pleased to become
301 FR   Gerald 22   her credit among her shabby genteel acquaintance./{V} Gerald is certain to make
482 CC   Lady E 35   society./Now, that already limits your acquaintance:/Because, what's surprising,
483 CC   Colby   4   the rarest./{C} That would limit my acquaintance to a very small number,/And I
505 CC   Guzzard 10   Colby./I am very happy to make his acquaintance./{SC} And I thought he might ...
541 ES   Gomez   8   even reach the ears of some of your acquaintance —/But you'd never know to
553 ES   Ld Clav 2   /And considering the brevity of our acquaintance,/You're surprisingly confident, I
553 ES   Carghil   6   /And although it's true that our acquaintance was brief,/Our relations were
569 ES   Charles 19   who, she says, claim a very long acquaintance —/I was thinking that if there's

ACQUAINTANCES (1)
380 CP   Celia   26   /But then, as he came to make more acquaintances,/I found him less interesting, and

ACQUAINTED (1)
119 SP   Krum   10   /{Kr} Extremely pleased to become acquainted/{Kl} Sam — I should say Loot Sam

ACQUIRE (2)
179 FQ: ECoker 98   /The only wisdom we can hope to acquire/Is the wisdom of humility: humility is
571 ES   Ld Clav   9   make of his admiration?/I led him to acquire tastes beyond his means:/So he became

ACQUIRED (1)
301 FR   Ivy 21   Charles with his confident vulgarity, acquired from worldly associates./{G} Ivy is

ACRE (1)
162 Rock 8   27 sins in Syria./But our King did well at Acre./And in spite of all the dishonour,/The

ACRES (1)
340 FR   Amy 15   /Except the walls, the furniture, the acres;/Leaving nothing — but what I could

ACRIMONY (2)
246 MC Tempt1 25   /Here I have come, forgetting all acrimony,/Hoping that your present gravity/
248 MC Tempt1   4   /I leave as I came, forgetting all acrimony,/Hoping that your present gravity/

ACROBATS (1)
218 Mung Rump   2   comedians, tight-rope walkers and acrobats/They had an extensive reputation.

ACROSS (25)
15 Prufrock   74   been a pair of ragged claws/Scuttling across the floors of silent seas./And the
19 Portrait   60   always sure that you feel,/Sure that across the gulf you reach your hand./You are
20 Portrait   81   song/With the smell of hyacinths across the garden/Recalling things that other
23 Preludes   39   soiled hands./His soul stretched tight across the skies/That fade behind a city block,/
23 Preludes   52   suffering thing./Wipe your hand across your mouth, and laugh;/The worlds
24 Rhapsody   61 nocturnal smells/That cross and cross across her brain.'/The reminiscence comes/Of
30 Cous Nancy   2   Nancy/Miss Nancy Ellicott/Strode across the hills and broke them,/Rode across
30 Cous Nancy   3 across the hills and broke them,/Rode across the hills and broke them —/The barren
54 Mr E Sun   3 /The sapient sutlers of the Lord/Drift across the window-panes./In the beginning was
134 Wind   9 Is a face that sweats with tears?/I saw the blackened river/The camp fire shake
134 Wind   11 fire shake with alien spears./Here, across death's other river/The Tartar horsemen
135 5FingerEx3   1   *in the Park*/The long light shakes across the lake,/The forces of the morning
136 5FingerEx3   3 the morning quake,/The dawn is slant across the lawn,/Here is no eft or mortal snake/
177 FQ: ECoker 15   is my end. Now the light falls/Across the open field, leaving the deep lane/
592 Grad 1   4   with a song upon our lips, sail we/Across the harbor bar — no chart to show/No
596 When we   1 'farewell'./Song/When we came home across the hill/No leaves were fallen from the
597 Before Mor   6   of yesterday/Their fragrance drifts across the room at dawn,/Fragrance of bloom
286 FR Gerald 37 the younger generation./I don't come across them very much now, myself;/But I must
311 FR   m 38 *to the window and pulls the curtains across*]/{H} They were here, I tell you. They are
332 FR Agatha 31   there is another kind,/I believe, across a whole Thibet of broken stones/That lie,
342 FR Agatha 38 found there./But Harry has been led across the frontier: he must follow;/For him the
356 CP   Peter   2   I never knew him at Oxford:/I came across him last year in California./{J} I've
415 CP   Celia 12   of sin:/At least, I have never come across it./I suppose it is wicked to hurt other
486 CC   Colby   1   hunting for!/{C} You may have come across the name before;/Although, as you say, it
534 ES   Gomez   4   anybody./In fact, I've never come across an official/Innocent enough to be

ACT (34)
85 Hollow Men 75   reality/Between the motion/And the act/Falls the Shadow/*For Thine is the Kingdom*
151 Rock 2   8   For love must be made real in act, as desire unites with desired; we have only
152 Rock 2   29 pride, for lechery, treachery, for every act of sin./And of all that was done that was
228 Gus   25 the cat out of the bag./I knew how to act with my back and my tail;/With an hour of
239 MC Chorus   6   in the cathedral. Some presage of an act/Which our eyes are compelled to witness,
245 MC Thomas 13 know and do not know, what it is to act or suffer./They know and do not know, that
245 MC Thomas 16 does the agent suffer/Nor the patient act. But both are fixed/In an eternal action, an
246 MC Thomas 20 /Meanwhile the substance of our first act/Will be shadows, and the strife with

255 MC Thomas	34	/Only by more sinful? Can I neither act nor suffer/Without perdition?/{T4} You
255 MC Tempt4	36	know and do not know, what it is to act or suffer./You know and do not know, that
255 MC Tempt4	39	does the agent suffer/Nor the patient act. But both are fixed/In an eternal action, an
259 MC Thomas	5	So must you./I shall no longer act or suffer, to the sword's end./Now my good
273 MC Thomas	33	as this world does,/To settle if an act be good or bad./You defer to the fact. For
273 MC Thomas	34	to the fact. For every life and every act/Consequence of good and evil can be
277 MC Knight1	31	completely disinterested. But/our act itself needs more justification than that; and
348 FR Chorus	17	plumbing,/But not against the act of God./We know various spells and
353 CP	1m 1	MEN/*The scene is laid in London*/Act One. Scene 1/*The drawing-room of the*
374 CP	1m 1	/No, it doesn't matter. {}/CURTAIN/Act One. Scene 2/*The same room: a quarter of*
384 CP	1m 1	now ... Good night. {}/CURTAIN/Act One. Scene 3/*The same room: late*
399 CP	1m 1	to fetch it up for me? {}/CURTAIN/Act Two/SIR HENRY
404 CP Edward	18	what you mean./{E} I can no longer act for myself./Coming to see you — that's the
424 CP	1m 1	— even in California. {}/CURTAIN/Act Three/*The drawing-room of the*
445 CC	1m 1	MULHAMMER/MRS. GUZZARD/Act One/*The Business Room on the first floor*
469 CC	1m 1	through the figures. {}/CURTAIN/Act Two/*The flat in the mews a few weeks later.*
493 CC	1m 1	LADY ELIZABETH]/CURTAIN/Act Three/*The Business Room, as in Act 1.*
493 CC	2m 1	/Act Three/*The Business Room, as in Act 1. Several mornings later.* SIR CLAUDE *is*/
523 ES	m 10	/MICHAEL CLAVERTON-FERRY/ACT ONE/*The drawing-room of Lord*
523 ES	m 12	*house. Four o'clock in the afternoon*/ACT TWO/*The Terrace at Badgley Court.*
523 ES	m 14	*Terrace at Badgley Court. Morning*/ACT THREE/*The Same. Late afternoon of the*
524 ES	1m 1	*Late afternoon of the following day*/Act One/*The drawing-room of* LORD
530 ES Ld Clav	18	simply waiting,/With no desire to act, yet a loathing of inaction./A fear of the
544 ES	1m 1	like at Badgley Court? {}/CURTAIN/Act Two/*The terrace of Badgley Court. A*
567 ES	1m 1	late for me, Monica? {}/CURTAIN/Act Three/*Same as Act Two. Late afternoon of*
567 ES	2m 1	{}/CURTAIN/Act Three/*Same as Act Two. Late afternoon of the following day.*

ACTED (5)

228 Gus	16	a Star of the highest degree —/He has acted with Irving, he's acted with Tree./And he
228 Gus	16	—/He has acted with Irving, he's acted with Tree./And he likes to relate his
460 CC Claude	25	beginning to remember./I must have acted on your guidance./{LE} I must explain to
494 CC Claude	14	to believe in facts;/And I've always acted as if I believed in them./I thought it was
551 ES Ld Clav	20	/I can't see how you could have acted as you did./{MC} Who can say whether a

ACTION (40)

147 Rock 1	6	dying!/The endless cycle of idea and action,/Endless invention, endless experiment,/
154 Rock 3	12	futile speculation and unconsidered action./Many are engaged in writing books and
155 Rock 3	60	of your mind and the glory of your action,/To arts and inventions and daring
173 FQ: BurntN	73	the practical desire,/The release from action and suffering, release from the inner/And
180 FQ: ECoker	110	cold the sense and lost the motive of action./And we all go with them, into the silent
187 FQ: DrySal	113	own past is covered by the currents of action,/But the torment of others remains an
188 FQ: DrySal	157	mind./At the moment which is not of action or inaction/You can receive this: "on
188 FQ: DrySal	160	the time of death" — that is the one action/(And the time of death is every moment)/
188 FQ: DrySal	163	/And do not think of the fruit of action./Fare forward./O voyagers, O seamen,/
190 FQ: DrySal	218	observance, discipline, thought and action./The hint half guessed, the gift half
190 FQ: DrySal	224	conquered, and reconciled,/Where action were otherwise movement/Of that which
190 FQ: DrySal	228	dæmonic, chthonic/Powers. And right action is freedom/From past and future also./
195 FQ: Little	162	as attachment to our own field of action/And comes to find that action of little
195 FQ: Little	163	field of action/And comes to find that action of little importance/Though never
197 FQ: Little	227	/Every poem an epitaph. And any action/Is a step to the block, to the fire, down
202 War Poetry	5	/Explosion breaks/In the path of an action merely typical/To create the universal,
203 Indians	19	home tell the same story of you:/Of action with a common purpose, action/None
203 Indians	19	/Of action with a common purpose, action/None the less fruitful if neither you nor
203 Indians	22	after death,/What is the fruit of action./To Walter de la Mare/The children who
240 MC Chorus	24	of scorn?/For us, the poor, there is no action,/But only to wait and to witness. {}/
245 MC Thomas	14	/They know and do not know, that action is suffering/And suffering is action.
245 MC Thomas	15	action is suffering/And suffering is action. Neither does the agent suffer/Nor the
245 MC Thomas	17	act. But both are fixed/In an eternal action, an eternal patience/To which all must
245 MC Thomas	20	may subsist, for the pattern is the action/And the suffering, that the wheel may
255 MC Tempt4	37	/You know and do not know, that action is suffering/And suffering action.
255 MC Tempt4	38	that action is suffering/And suffering action. Neither does the agent suffer/Nor the
255 MC Tempt4	40	act. But both are fixed/In an eternal action, an eternal patience/To which all must
270 MC Chorus	23	death-bringers; now is too late/For action, too soon for contrition./Nothing is
276 MC Chorus	3	/The terror by night that ends in daily action,/The terror by day that ends in sleep;/But
276 MC Knight1	20	to judge unfavourably/of our action. You are Englishmen, and therefore you
276 MC Knight1	27	to/put our case to you. I am a man of action and not of words. For that/reason I shall
280 MC Priest3	14	For the Church is stronger for this action,/Triumphant in adversity. It is fortified/

280 MC Priest3 32   round/Of thought, to justify your action to yourselves,/Weaving a fiction which
297 FR Agatha   4   a necessary move/In an unnecessary action,/Not for the good that it will do/But that
331 FR Harry   2   /And then I had no horror of my action,/I only felt the repetition of it/Over and
334 FR Agatha   7   /The young feel tired at the end of an action —/The old, at the beginning. It is as if/I
402 CP Edward   7   /{E} You talk as if I was capable of action:/If I were, I should not need to consult
448 CC Claude   38   your wife, to have had a son/Lost in action, and his grave unknown./{E} And you're
551 ES Carghil 23   that I would never have started an action/For breach of promise, if I'd really cared
551 ES Carghil 25   sentimental nonsense! One starts an action/Simply because one must do *something*./

ACTIONNAIRES (1)
 46 Directeur   7   /Du Spectateur/Empeste la brise./Les actionnaires/Réactionnaires/Du Spectateur/

ACTIONS (1)
417 CP Reilly   30   /Giving and taking, in the usual actions/What there is to give and take. They do

ACTIVE (4)
155 Rock 3   41   go./A colony of cavies or a horde of active marmots/Build better than they that
272 MC Chorus   24   the Void, more horrid than active shapes of hell;/Emptiness, absence,
413 CP Celia   16   I feel perfectly well./I could lead an active life — if there's anything to work for;/I
419 CP Reilly   30   /No one disappears. They lead very active lives/Very often, in the world./{C} How

ACTIVITY (2)
533 ES Ld Clav 26   won respect out there/By the sort of activity that lost you respect/Here in England?/
545 ES Ld Clav 7   terrorise us/And urge us on to futile activity,/And in the end, judge us still more

ACTOR (3)
229 Gus   38   he once walked on pat,/When some actor suggested the need for a cat./He once
569 ES Ld Clav 5   I be sure that she would love the actor/If she saw him, off the stage, without his
569 ES Ld Clav 12   him/For what he is, the broken-down actor./{M} I think I should only love you the

ACTORS (3)
290 FR Chorus   37   ill at ease,/Assembled like amateur actors who have not been assigned their parts?/
290 FR Chorus   38   assigned their parts?/Like amateur actors in a dream when the curtain rises, to find
363 CP Reilly   1   those who surround you, the masked actors;/All there is of you is your body/And the

ACTS (1)
276 MC Chorus   8   laid on the fire at daybreak,/These acts marked a limit to our suffering./Every

ACTUAL (5)
 89 Ash-Wed 1   18   is always and only place/And what is actual is actual only for one time/And only for
 89 Ash-Wed 1   18   and only place/And what is actual is actual only for one time/And only for one place
107 Animula   13   around a silver tray;/Confounds the actual and the fanciful,/Content with
190 FQ: DrySal   221   union/Of spheres of existence is actual,/Here the past and future/Are conquered,
336 FR Agatha   26   /In both, the incredible/Becomes the actual/Without our intention/Knowing what is

ACTUALLY (7)
409 CP Reilly   31   that your young friend/Had actually fallen in love with Miss Coplestone,/It
448 CC Claude   1 And by the way,/How much have you actually told him about her?/You remember, I
449 CC Eggers   35   her know, then, that Mr. Simpkins/Is actually your son?/{SC} That's where I'm in the
451 CC Eggers   24   ten minutes! I was horrified./But she actually liked it. Muriel *is* her name./He has a
460 CC Claude   34 /[*Exit* LADY ELIZABETH]/{SC} She actually went and changed her own ticket./It's
478 CC Lucasta 14   you to be sorry, thank you./Why, I'd actually thought of telling you before,/And I
485 CC Lady E   2   made me think so./But you know, I actually *liked* to believe/That I was a foundling

ACUTE (1)
490 CC Colby   12   to ... us./{C} I only wish it was more acute agony:/I don't know whether I've been

ACUTELY (2)
403 CP Edward   26   minutes/Before I felt, and still more acutely —/Indeed, acutely, perhaps, for the first
403 CP Edward   27   felt, and still more acutely —/Indeed, acutely, perhaps, for the first time,/The whole

AD-DRESS (4)
234 Ad-dress   17 and their habitat:/But *How would you ad-dress a Cat?*/So first, your memory I'll jog,/
235 Ad-dress   41   hold with that —/I say, you should ad-dress a Cat./But always keep in mind that he
235 Ad-dress   45   /I bow, and taking off my hat,/Ad-dress him in this form: O CAT!/But if he is
235 Ad-dress   69   and that is that:/And there's how you AD-DRESS A CAT./Cat Morgan Introduces

AD-DRESSING (1)
234 Ad-dress   t   /The Cat of the Railway Train.'/The Ad-dressing of Cats/You've read of several

ADAM (1)
253 MC Tempt4   28   power?/Man oppressed by sin, since Adam fell —/You hold the keys of heaven and

ADAM'S (1)
181 FQ: ECoker   157   to please/But to remind of our, and Adam's curse,/And that, to be restored, our

ADAPT (1)
512 CC Guzzard 24   have your son./We all of us have to adapt ourselves/To the wish that is granted.

ADAPTATION (1)
288 FR Agatha   27   door./He will find a new Wishwood. Adaptation is hard./{A} Nothing is changed,

ADAPTING (1)
462 CC   Claude 33   by a rather formal relationship/In adapting yourself to a new situation./{C} I'm
ADD (1)
279 MC Knight4 13   much to the/point. I have nothing to add along their particular lines of argument./
ADDED (2)
587 Fable   12   some old villainous baron died,/He added to their hoards — a deed which ne'er he/
557 ES Michael 30   for two years:/The interest was just added on to the capital./{LC} And how long
ADDITION (2)
185 FQ: DrySal 57   annunciation?/There is no end, but addition: the trailing/Consequence of further
186 FQ: DrySal 63   for renunciation./There is the final addition, the failing/Pride or resentment at
ADDRESS (13)
276 MC   m 18   *advance to the front of the stage and address the audience.*]/{K1} We beg you to give
345 FR   Harry 11   and John:/Take care of *them*. My address, mother,/Will be care of the bank in
357 CP   Julia 35 we won't probe into it./You have the address, and the telephone number?/I might run
419 CP   Reilly 36 make your preparations./Here is the address for you to give your friends; {}/[*Writes*
454 CC   Colby 27   has a good heart./{C} But does she address Sir Claude Mulhammer/As Claude? To
481 CC Lady E 32   I made you take a note of the address;/And I don't believe that you've been
498 CC   Eggers 2 be most surprising./And at the same address?/{LE} I don't know the address./Mrs.
498 CC Lady E 3 same address?/{LE} I don't know the address./Mrs. Guzzard of Teddington, that's all
511 CC Kaghan 17 I should like to know how I ought to address you,/Lady Elizabeth. I've always been
511 CC Lady E 21   any danger of confusion/You may address me as Aunt Elizabeth./{K} That's easier,
545 ES Monica 36   /We don't know how we ought to address you./Do we call you 'Matron'?/{MP}
546 ES Monica 34 to a nurse. When we see her/Do we address her as 'Nurse'?/{MP} Oh yes, that's
580 ES Gomez 3 Here's my business card/With the full address. You can always reach him there./But it
ADDRESSED (2)
42 Swee Erect 21   clawing at the pillow slip./Sweeney addressed full length to shave/Broadbottomed,
206 To my Wife 12   to read:/These are private words addressed to you in public./OLD POSSUM'S
ADDRESSES (1)
67 WL: Fire S 181 City directors;/Departed, have left no addresses./By the waters of Leman I sat down
ADDRESSING (1)
451 CC   Eggers 22 him once;/But do you know, he began addressing her as Muriel —/Within the first ten
ADEQUATE (1)
455 CC   Eggers 18   /He gives her an allowance — very adequate indeed,/Though she's always in debt.
ADJUST (2)
349 FR   All 12 I might understand./{all} But we must adjust ourselves to the moment: we must do the
510 CC Lady E 14   /{LE} And to my being able to adjust myself to it. {}/[*Re-enter* COLBY, *with*
ADJUSTS (1)
308 FR   Harry 6   never found its object;/And the eye adjusts itself to a twilight/Where the dead stone
ADMETUS (1)
209 NamingCats 11   some for the dames:/Such as Plato, Admetus, Electra, Demeter —/But all of them
ADMINISTRATION (1)
278 MC Knight2 16   /a union of spiritual and temporal administration, under the central/government. I
ADMINISTRATOR (1)
278 MC Knight2 13 had proved himself an extremely/able administrator — no one denies that — should
ADMIRABLE (1)
449 CC   Eggers 33 Elizabeth wants to adopt him —/An admirable solution — then what follows?/Will
ADMIRALTY (1)
226 Macavity   28   find a Treaty's gone astray,/Or the Admiralty lose some plans and drawings by the
ADMIRATION (3)
589 Fable   94 forth they did without,/And lived the admiration of the shire. We/Got the veracious
277 MC Knight3 22 — and personally I had a tremendous admiration for him —/you must have noted
571 ES Ld Clav 8   at Oxford;/What did I make of his admiration?/I led him to acquire tastes beyond
ADMIRE (4)
19 Portrait   37   us take the air, in a tobacco trance,/Admire the monuments,/Discuss the late events,
440 CP Lavinia 28 What you should have done was to admire my dress./{E} But I've already told you
571 ES Ld Clav 13   we ignore the fact that those who admire us/Will imitate our vices as well as our
571 ES Ld Clav 15   the qualities for which they did admire us!/And that again may nourish the
ADMIRED (4)
277 MC Knight2 39   /whose good qualities I very much admired, has throughout been/presented as the
472 CC Lucasta 33 B. I was sorry,/Very sorry for you. I admired your courage/In facing facts — or the
537 ES Gomez 24 /To see that I was flattered, and that I admired you./Everyone expected that I should
571 ES Ld Clav 7 Carghill and Lord Claverton./Freddy admired me, when we were at Oxford;/What did
ADMIRER (1)
563 ES Gomez 37 I should have been your most devoted admirer./{MC} *It's Not Too Late For You To*

ADMIRERS (1)
551 ES Carghil 2   want to forget/A single one of her admirers. Why, even a faithless lover/Is still, in

ADMIRES (1)
456 CC Eggers 1   French say./That's what Sir Claude admires about her./He said to me once, in a

ADMIT (11)
213 Growltiger 46 she was badly skeered;/I am sorry to admit it, but she quickly disappeared./She
309 FR Harry 6   seeing. They are much too clever/To admit you into *our* world. Yours is no better./
409 CP Reilly 33 I have no doubt,/Before you would admit it. Though perhaps you knew it/Before he
450 CC Eggers 10   you put it so convincingly,/I must admit there's a lot that *I* don't understand/
456 CC Eggers 13 a lady?/{E} Why, yes, indeed, I must admit she is./Most of her oddities are perfectly
471 CC Colby 34   And a very clever one./{C} I admit that at first I was very bewildered/By you
496 CC Eggers 25 with London,/Though she doesn't admit it. She misses my news/When I came
537 ES Ld Clav 33 came to *my* help./{LC} I certainly admit no responsibility,/None whatever, for
544 ES Ld Clav 14 wanting a fourth at bridge;/Still, I'll admit to a feeling of contentment/Already. I
545 ES Monica 10 own reproaches drove us?/{M} You admit that at the moment you find life pleasant,
558 ES Ld Clav 33 gone further than you're willing to admit./{Mi} Well, after all, she was the only one

ADMITTED (2)
567 ES Charles 11 me./On that last day in London, you admitted that you loved me,/But I wondered ...
570 ES Ld Clav 21   /In consequence of it all. He admitted as much,/Fred Culverwell .../{M} Fred

ADMONISHED (1)
188 FQ: DrySal 169 destination.'/So Krishna, as when he admonished Arjuna/On the field of battle./Not

ADMONITIONS (1)
290 FR Agatha 30   other's opacity/Neglecting all the admonitions/From the world around the corner

ADOLESCENCE (1)
578 ES Ld Clav 13 /When I think of your boyhood and adolescence,/And see how all the efforts aimed

ADOPT (11)
278 MC Knight2 30 with the measures/we have had to adopt, in order to set matters to rights, that you
360 CP Reilly 17 it sitting down./Breathe deeply, and adopt a relaxed position./There we are. Now for
449 CC Claude 12 he is an orphan,/She will want us to adopt him./{E} Adopt him! Yes, indeed,/That
449 CC Eggers 13 /She will want us to adopt him./{E} Adopt him! Yes, indeed,/That would be the
449 CC Eggers 32 /At which Lady Elizabeth wants to adopt him —/An admirable solution — then
478 CC Lucasta 2   white-headed boy./Perhaps he'll adopt you, and make you his heir/And you'll
488 CC Claude 32 him first — and that you'd want to adopt him./{LE} But of course I want to adopt
488 CC Lady E 33 him./{LE} But of course I want to adopt him, Claude!/That is, if one's allowed to
488 CC Lady E 34 Claude!/That is, if one's allowed to adopt one's own child./{SC} That's not what I
508 CC Guzzard 22 made;/But we could not afford to adopt the child,/Or continue to keep him, when
508 CC Guzzard 26 /Who were childless, and eager to adopt a child./They had taken a fancy to him.

ADOPTED (6)
278 MC Knight2 22 he ostentatiously and offensively adopted an ascetic/manner of life, he affirmed
480 CC Kaghan 29 that!/Never had any parents. Just adopted, from nowhere./That's why I want to
508 CC Guzzard 27 had taken a fancy to him. So they adopted him./Then they left Teddington, and
511 CC Lady E 10 very young. That is why you were adopted./{K} But what did he do? Was he a
570 ES Ld Clav 29 and the highest standing/In his adopted country. He even has sons/Following in
574 ES Carghil 2   /I've come to regard her as my adopted daughter./So much so, that it seems

ADOPTION (1)
537 ES Gomez 7 already, Dick; done many years ago:/Adoption tried, and grappled to my soul/With

ADOPTIVE (3)
510 CC Kaghan 23 your parents?/{K} Yes. They are. My adoptive parents./{MG} And did they at one
510 CC Eggers 28 suspicion./{E} Mr. Kaghan, are your adoptive parents living?/{K} In Kent. They
510 CC Eggers 35   Mr. Kaghan,/By putting your adoptive parents in touch/With Mrs. Guzzard.

ADORING (1)
581 ES Ld Clav 20 I wanted you to give your life to adoring/The man that I pretended to myself

ADORNED (1)
166 Rock 10 1 seen the house built, you have seen it adorned/By one who came in the night, it is

ADORNING (1)
164 Rock 9 10 like thoroughbreds ready for races,/Adorning themselves, and busy in the market,

ADULTERATED (1)
38 Gerontion 58 to keep it/Since what is kept must be adulterated?/I have lost my sight, smell, hearing,

ADULTÈRE (1)
47 Mél Adult t   /Et crève d'amour./Mélange Adultère de Tout/En Amérique, professeur;/En

ADVANCE (3)
222 Pekes Pols 19 happened to meet./They did not advance, or exactly retreat,/But they glared at
276 MC m 18 *having completed the murder, advance to the front of the stage and address the*
577 ES Michael 4 pays your passage .../{Mi} And an advance of salary./{C} Señor Gomez pays your

ADVANCED (1)
460 CC   Lady E   7   control is a different matter:/It's more advanced. But I wrote you all about it./{SC} It's
ADVANCEMENT (1)
258 MC   Thomas   10   all the ways/That lead to pleasure, advancement and praise./Delight in sense, in
ADVANCES (1)
161 Rock 7   32   turned upwards/In an age which advances progressively backwards?/VOICE OF
ADVANCING (1)
107 Animula   6   or falling, grasping at kisses and toys,/Advancing boldly, sudden to take alarm,/
ADVANTAGE (7)
21 Portrait   121   too soon .../Would she not have the advantage, after all?/This music is successful
251 MC   Tempt3   37   /For us, Church favour would be an advantage,/Blessing of Pope powerful
360 CP   Reilly   36   decide to be forgiving/And gain an advantage. If there's no other woman/And no
362 CP   Reilly   6   it —/Thus giving herself a permanent advantage./{E} It might turn out so, yet .../{UG}
400 CP   Reilly   24   illness./{R} Illness offers him a double advantage:/To escape from himself — and get
454 CC   Kaghan   8   /Never allow Lucasta the slightest advantage/Or she'll exploit it. You have to be
575 ES   Ld Clav   6   what I wanted./{LC} Yes, I see the advantage of a job created for you/By Señor
ADVANTAGES (3)
463 CC   Claude   5   it seemed to have such obvious advantages/That I had no doubts at the time —
507 CC   Guzzard   10   time,/And very poor. It offered two advantages./{E} And did you know the name of
548 ES   Ld Clav   20   She noticed that it seemed to offer the advantages/Which you have just mentioned. I
ADVENTURE (1)
365 CP   Julia   16   my spectacles:/*This* is what I call an adventure!/Tell me about him. You've been
ADVENTURES (1)
456 CC   Eggers   28   /And very costly. I've had some rare adventures!/I remember long ago, saying to
ADVENTUROUS (1)
325 FR   Ivy   26   boys,/Arthur was always the more adventurous/But John was the one that had the
ADVERSITY (3)
152 Rock 2   37   neglect the Temple, and in time of adversity they will decry it./What life have you
242 MC   Priest1   19   /Was but confirmed by bitter adversity./I saw him as Chancellor, flattered by
280 MC   Priest3   15   for this action,/Triumphant in adversity. It is fortified/By persecution:
ADVICE (15)
247 MC   Tempt1   37   eat the best dinners./Take a friend's advice. Leave well alone,/Or your goose may be
293 FR   Amy   5   always found them forthcoming with advice/Which I have never taken. Now it is your
293 FR   Amy   10   woman./They can give me no further advice when I'm dead./{I} Oh, dear Amy!/No
303 FR   Mary   29   world?/Cousin Agatha, I want your advice./{Ag} I should have thought/You had
304 FR   Mary   6   /But I really wish that I'd taken your advice/And tried for a fellowship, seven years
304 FR   Mary   8   seven years ago./Now I want your advice, because there's no one else to ask,/And
338 FR   Harry   1   more than with the rest of you./My advice has come from quite a different quarter,/
363 CP   Reilly   25   to be the fool you are./That's the best advice that *I* can give you./{E} But how can I
381 CP   Celia   1   own age./{C} I don't think I care for advice from you, Edward:/You are not entitled
454 CC   Kaghan   7   had enough for one day. Take my advice, Colby./Never allow Lucasta the slightest
460 CC   Lady E   13   glad to find/That you've taken my advice./{SC} Your advice? About what?/{LE}
460 CC   Claude   14   you've taken my advice./{SC} Your advice? About what?/{LE} To engage Mr.
482 CC   Kaghan   2   you so much. You give such good advice. {}/[*Exeunt* KAGHAN *and* LUCASTA]/
538 ES   Gomez   30   of course didn't have to take your advice .../I've made a point, you see, of
580 ES   Carghil   19   out to Australia,/On my doctor's advice. And on my way back/Señor Gomez has
ADVISE (7)
16 Prufrock   114   swell a progress, start a scene or two,/Advise the prince; no doubt, an easy tool,/
319 FR   Warburt   37   Agatha. I never dared before./{W} I advise you strongly, not to ask your aunt —/I
525 ES   Charles   13   to guess what you want to buy/And advise you to buy it./{M} But why not stop to
547 ES   Piggott   27   there's always croquet. But I don't advise croquet/Until you know enough about
551 ES   Carghil   28   out of court./My lawyer said: 'I advise you to accept','Because Mr. Ferry will
565 ES   Carghil   22   tell me all about it. Perhaps I could advise you./We'll leave you now, Richard. Au
569 ES   Charles   24   least, I think I know the best man to advise you./{LC} Blackmail? Yes, I've heard
ADVISED (3)
389 CP   Lavinia   21   he is right to go./{L} Oh, so you advised him?/{P} She knew nothing about it./{C}
402 CP   Edward   14   about the symptoms./Two people advised me recently,/Almost in the same words,
412 CP   Celia   27   was Julia ... Mrs. Shuttlethwaite/Who advised me to come to you. — But I've met you
AEOLUS (1)
42 Swee Erect   5   snarled and yelping seas./Display me Aeolus above/Reviewing the insurgent gales/
AERIAL (1)
188 FQ: DrySal   148   /At nightfall, in the rigging and the aerial,/Is a voice descanting (though not to the

AEROPLANE (3)

127	Cor1 March	19	and fuses,/13,000 aeroplanes,/24,000 aeroplane engines,/50,000 ammunition
286	FR Gerald	19	knows where —/{G} Dividends from aeroplane shares./{V} They bathe all day and
534	ES Gomez	29	The prudent ones/Always have an aeroplane ready:/And keep an account in a

AEROPLANES (1)

127	Cor1 March	18	projectiles, mines and fuses,/13,000 aeroplanes,/24,000 aeroplane engines,/50,000

ÆSOP'S (1)

588	Fable	46	a raid/On every bird and beast in Æsop's fable/To fill out their repast, and pies

AESTIVALE (1)

48	Lune Miel	4	deux centaines de punaises;/La sueur aestivale, et une forte odeur de chienne./Ils

AETHEREAL (1)

74	WL: Thund	415	confirms a prison/Only at nightfall, aethereal rumours/Revive for a moment a

AFAR (2)

161	Rock 7	m33	/VOICE OF THE UNEMPLOYED (*afar off*):/*In this land/There shall be one*
261	MC Thomas	2	things: they went forth to journey afar, to suffer by land/and sea, to know torture,

AFFAIR (4)

242	MC Mess	4	not the kiss of peace./A patched up affair, if you ask my opinion./And if you ask
370	CP Edward	13	And what interrupted this interesting affair? { }/[*Enter* ALEX *in shirtsleeves and an*
370	CP Edward	34	/This might have become an ordinary affair/Like any other. As the fever cooled/You
405	CP Reilly	22	that —/Your freedom. That is my affair. { }/[LAVINIA *is shown in by the*

AFFAIRS (4)

279	MC Knight2	1	in bringing about the state of/affairs that you approve. We have served your
328	FR Charles	32	hard on him./{C} In my time, these affairs were kept out of the papers;/But
495	CC Lady E	10	interested/In anything but financial affairs;/And that you needed me chiefly as a
496	CC Eggers	23	/You're losing touch with public affairs.'/The fact is, she misses the contact with

AFFECTION (4)

174	FQ: BurntN	101	sensual with deprivation/Cleansing affection from the temporal./Neither plenitude
186	FQ: DrySal	93	/Fruition, fulfilment, security or affection,/Or even a very good dinner, but the
334	FR Harry	21	/Of you, and of all of us. Family affection/Was a kind of formal obligation, a
542	ES Gomez	8	lonely man, Dick, with a craving for affection./All I want is as much of your

AFFECTIONATE (3)

143	Lines OM	9	over the archèd tongue/Is more affectionate than hate,/More bitter than the
385	CP Reilly	11	that you are not strangers./The affectionate ghosts: the grandmother,/The lively
562	ES Michael	10	been very fond of you —/I've a very affectionate nature, really,/But ... { }/[*Enter*

AFFINA (1)

75	WL: Thund	427	down/*Poi s'ascose nel foco che gli affina/Quando fiam uti chelidon* — O swallow

AFFIRM (3)

97	Ash-Wed 5	32	terrified and cannot surrender/And affirm before the world and deny between the
281	MC Chorus	12	it were so, they would not exist./They affirm Thee in living; all things affirm Thee in
281	MC Chorus	12	/They affirm Thee in living; all things affirm Thee in living; the bird in the air, both

AFFIRMATION (1)

160	Rock 7	15	of the dead, denial of this world, affirmation of rites with forgotten meanings/In

AFFIRMED (2)

202	War Poetry	25	which we call 'poetry',/May be affirmed in verse./To the Indians who Died in
278	MC Knight2	23	adopted an ascetic/manner of life, he affirmed immediately that there was a higher/

AFFIRMING (1)

241	MC Mess	30	/He comes in pride and sorrow, affirming all his claims,/Assured, beyond doubt,

AFFLICTED (1)

244	MC Chorus	13	had various scandals,/We have been afflicted with taxes,/We have had laughter and

AFFLICTION (2)

133	Eyes	6	the eyes but not the tears/This is my affliction./This is my affliction/Eyes I shall not
133	Eyes	7	tears/This is my affliction./This is my affliction/Eyes I shall not see again/Eyes of

AFFORD (7)

285	FR Ivy	17	go south in the winter, if I could afford it,/Not freeze, as I do, in Bayswater, by a
298	FR Charles	1	him./And as for my means, we can't afford to be squeamish/In taking hold of
313	FR Ivy	12	once, in Cornwall,/When I could afford a garden; and I took several prizes/With
414	CP Celia	16	live in the country,/Now they can't afford to have a place in town./It's all they can
508	CC Guzzard	22	were made;/But we could not afford to adopt the child,/Or continue to keep
513	CC Colby	22	He's had his foster-parents,/So he can afford another relationship./Let my mother rest
534	ES Gomez	28	In my country, Dick,/Politicians can't afford mistakes. The prudent ones/Always have

AFRAID (71)

15	Prufrock	86	coat, and snicker,/And in short, I was afraid./And would it have been worth it, after
119	SP Klip	34	— er — you haven't quite got it/(I'm afraid I didn't quite catch your name —/But I'm
120	SP Krum	2	I mean anything *coarse* —/But I'm afraid we couldn't stand the pace./What about
219	Mung Rump	26	that was broken with sorrow:/'I'm afraid you must wait and have dinner

223	Pekes Pols	48	some of the neighbours were so much afraid/That they started to ring up the Fire
588	Fable	43	to table./The menus of that time I am afraid/I don't know much about — as well's I'm
244 MC	Chorus	22	death alone/In a void apart. We/Are afraid in a fear which we cannot know, which
245 MC	Priest2	8	cooked and eaten./Whatever you are afraid of, in your craven apprehension,/Let me
276 MC	Knight3	33	Baron William de Traci./{K3} I am afraid I am not anything like such an
287 FR	Mary	9	you must ask someone else./I'm afraid that I don't deserve the compliment:/I
295 FR	Harry	26	drowsiness;/Then I recovered. I am afraid of sleep:/A condition in which one can be
296 FR	Harry	12	them/Or at least, made me cease to be afraid of them./I will go and have my bath. {}/
301 FR	Charles	24	useless out of the army./{C} Violet is afraid that her status as Amy's sister will be
304 FR	Mary	16	you so seldom come here? You're not afraid of her,/But I think you must have wanted
315 FR	Chorus	30	WARBURTON, HARRY]/{Ch} I am afraid of all that has happened, and of all that is
316 FR	Chorus	3	bird sits on the broken chimney. I am afraid./{I} This is a most undignified terror, and
322 FR	Harry	10	Do you know or don't you?/I'm not afraid of you./{Wi} I should hope not, my Lord.
325 FR	Gerald	13	know at once./{G} I am really more afraid of the shock for Amy;/But I think that
326 FR	Ivy	36	Mr. Arthur./{I} Arthur! Oh dear, I'm afraid he's had an accident. {}/[Exeunt IVY and
330 FR	Agatha	15	needed to connect them./You may be afraid that I would not understand you,/You
330 FR	Agatha	16	not understand you,/You may also be afraid of being understood,/Try not to regard it
336 FR	Harry	14	/And you shall not think that I am afraid to see you./This time, you are real, this
358 CP	Julia	24	come to dinner on Friday?/No, I'm afraid my good Mrs. Batten/Would give me
358 CP	Alex	26	And now I must be going./{A} I'm afraid I ought to be going./{P} Celia —/May I
359 CP	Edward	31	off at last. {}/[Exit]/{E} I'm sorry. I'm afraid I don't know your name./{UG} I ought
365 CP	Julia	3	kind of a plastic sort of frame —/I'm afraid I don't remember the colour,/But I'd
367 CP	Peter	6	the others did,/Though I'm rather afraid of Julia Shuttlethwaite./{E} Julia is
377 CP	Celia	7	Yes, who was that man? I was rather afraid of him;/He has some sort of power./{E} I
386 CP	Edward	36	is really a ludicrous situation./{E} I'm afraid I can't see the humorous side of it./{C}
389 CP	Celia	37	goes to answer it]/{C} Oh, I'm afraid that all this sounds rather silly/But ... {}/
404 CP	Edward	14	had time to be surprised:/I am not afraid of the death of the body,/But this death is
412 CP	Celia	33	to waste your time. And I'm awfully afraid/That you'll think that I am wasting it
417 CP	Celia	5	/{C} I cannot argue./It's not that I'm afraid of being hurt again:/Nothing again can
418 CP	Celia	17	— which belongs to that life./Oh, I'm afraid this sounds like raving!/Or just
421 CP	Julia	24	not understand innocence./She will be afraid of nothing; she will not even know/That
421 CP	Julia	25	/That there is anything there to be afraid of./She is too humble. She will pass
432 CP	Peter	1	We're all very typical./{P} No, I'm afraid .../{CM} Sir Henry Harcourt-Reilly!/{J}
432 CP	Julia	6	you know him already, you won't be afraid of him./You know, I was afraid of him at
432 CP	Julia	7	be afraid of him./You know, I was afraid of him at first:/He looks so forbidding .../
432 CP	Peter	38	I was just about to explain —/I'm afraid I can't find parts for anybody/In this film
433 CP	Alex	27	of her./When you came in, Peter. I'm afraid you can't have Celia./{P} Oh ... Is she
449 CC	Eggers	20	that once or twice, perhaps .../But I'm afraid you overrate my influence./I have never
450 CC	Colby	29	Good afternoon,/Mr. Eggerson. I was afraid I'd miss you./{E} I'm off in half an hour,
452 CC	Colby	38	of your responsibilities?/{C} No, I'm afraid I didn't know that./{E} You mustn't give
469 CC	Lucasta	23	of course, several times,/But I'm afraid I never really listened to the music:/I just
472 CC	Colby	2	wait to see what happened./You're afraid of what would happen if you left things
472 CC	Colby	3	/You jump — because you're afraid of being pushed./I think that you're
474 CC	Lucasta	20	I can think of putting it./{L} How afraid one is of ... being hurt!/{C} It's not the
479 CC	Lucasta	27	the threshold./{L} As if you weren't as afraid of her as anybody!/{K} Well, at least, I've
479 CC	Kaghan	31	start:/I saw that it was necessary. I'm afraid Colby/Has made a good impression;
483 CC	Lady E	24	a photograph in a silver frame./I'm afraid I shall have to instruct you, Colby./
488 CC	Claude	10	—/If it is a coincidence. But I'm afraid, Elizabeth,/What has happened is that,
488 CC	Claude	19	different/From what you expect. I'm afraid, Colby,/It seems to me that we must let
502 CC	Colby	2	/{C} Have I come too soon?/I'm afraid I got impatient of waiting./{L} Colby!
504 CC	Claude	25	Mrs. Guzzard. I must apologise:/I'm afraid there has been some domestic
517 CC	Eggers	39	stipend is small —/Very small, I'm afraid. Not enough to live on./We'll have to
527 ES	Monica	36	will be of any use to anybody,/I'm afraid. Poor Michael! Mother spoilt him/And
528 ES	Monica	36	postponing our marriage./{M} I'm afraid ... not a very long time, Charles./It's
542 ES	Gomez	32	Than when I'm out of sight. You'll be afraid of whispers,/The reflection in the mirror
545 ES	Piggott	24	/Isn't this a glorious morning!/I'm afraid you'll think I've been neglecting you;/So
549 ES	Ld Clav	5	Don't you know me yet?/{LC} I'm afraid not./{MC} There were the three of us —
553 ES	Carghil	30	Would you like to read them?/I'm afraid I can't show you the originals;/They're in
554 ES	Piggott	34	/She was well-known at one time. I'm afraid her name/Means nothing at all to the
555 ES	Piggott	8	you again/Just let me know. I'm afraid it's the penalty/Of being famous. {}/
555 ES	Monica	19	drive. He says he must see you./I'm afraid that something unpleasant has happened.
555 ES	Monica	25	/{M} Why, Father, should you be afraid of that?/This shows how bad your nerves
568 ES	Ld Clav	30	and his love will save him./I'm afraid that I've never loved anyone, really./No,
569 ES	Monica	15	you better./There's nothing I'm afraid of learning about Charles,/There's
569 ES	Monica	16	about Charles,/There's nothing I'm afraid of learning about you./{C} I was

569 ES   Ld Clav   31   you to get your company/I'm afraid the law can't touch them./{C} Then why
580 ES   Carghil   15   MICHAEL *and* GOMEZ]/{MC} I'm afraid this seems awfully sudden to you,
AFRICA (2)
203 Indians   t   in verse./To the Indians who Died in Africa/A man's destination is his own village,/
488 CC   Lady E   3   Tony was killed, as you know, in Africa,/And I had lost the name. Mrs. Guzzard.
AFRIQUE (1)
47 Mél   Adult   17   mon jour de fête/Dans une oasis d'Afrique/Vêtu d'une peau de girafe./On
AFTER (118)
15 Prufrock   79   here beside you and me./Should I, after tea and cakes and ices,/Have the strength
15 Prufrock   87   /And would it have been worth it, after all,/After the cups, the marmalade, the tea,
15 Prufrock   88   would it have been worth it, after all,/After the cups, the marmalade, the tea,/Among
16 Prufrock   99   all.'/And would it have been worth it, after all,/Would it have been worth while,/After
16 Prufrock   101   all,/Would it have been worth while,/After the sunsets and the dooryards and the
16 Prufrock   102   dooryards and the sprinkled streets,/After the novels, after the teacups, after the
16 Prufrock   102   the sprinkled streets,/After the novels, after the teacups, after the skirts that trail along
16 Prufrock   102   /After the novels, after the teacups, after the skirts that trail along the floor —/And
19 Portrait   55   world/To be wonderful and youthful, after all.'/The voice returns like the insistent
21 Portrait   121   .../Would she not have the advantage, after all?/This music is successful with a 'dying
31 Apollinax   18   /'He is a charming man' — 'But after all what did he mean?' —/'His pointed
38 Gerontion   33   draughty house/Under a windy knob./After such knowledge, what forgiveness? Think
70 WL: Fire S   297   and my heart/Under my feet. After the event/He wept. He promised "a new
72 WL: Thund   322   tall as you./What the Thunder said/After the torchlight red on sweaty faces/After
72 WL: Thund   323   the torchlight red on sweaty faces/After the frosty silence in the gardens/After the
72 WL: Thund   324   After the frosty silence in the gardens/After the agony in stony places/The shouting
95 Ash-Wed 4   29   thousand whispers from the yew/And after this our exile/If the lost word is lost, if the
106 Song Sime   34   my own life and the lives of those after me,/I am dying in my own death and the
106 Song Sime   35   my own death and the deaths of those after me./Let thy servant depart,/Having seen
107 Animula   31   dusty room;/Living first in the silence after the viaticum./Pray for Guiterriez, avid of
129 Cor2 State   34   feather stirred by the small wind after noon/There the cyclamen spreads its
158 Rock 5   8   for silence: seeking every one after his own elevation, and dodging his
165 Rock 9   38   you shall see the Temple completed:/After much striving, after many obstacles;/For
165 Rock 9   38   completed:/After much striving, after many obstacles;/For the work of creation
173 FQ: BurntN   94   of disaffection/Time before and time after/In a dim light: neither daylight/Investing
174 FQ: BurntN 108   the cold wind/That blows before and after time,/Wind in and out of unwholesome
174 FQ: BurntN 110   lungs/Time before and time after./Eructation of unhealthy souls/Into the
175 FQ: BurntN 137   of yew be curled/Down on us? After the kingfisher's wing/Has answered light
175 FQ: BurntN 142   is only living/Can only die. Words, after speech, reach/Into the silence. Only by the
175 FQ: BurntN 151   there/Before the beginning and after the end./And all is always now. Words
176 FQ: BurntN 178   waste sad time/Stretching before and after./East Coker/In my beginning is my end. In
182 FQ: ECoker 195   moment/Isolated, with no before and after,/But a lifetime burning in every moment/
193 FQ: Little   83   /At the recurrent end of the unending/After the dark dove with the flickering tongue/
194 FQ: Little   108   /Of meeting nowhere, no before and after,/We trod the pavement in a dead patrol./I
203 Indians   21   you nor we/Know, until the judgment after death,/What is the fruit of action./To
218 Mung Rump   13   find one of your winter vests,/Or after supper one of the girls/Suddenly missed
588 Fable   52   a viand made of turtle eggs,/And after that a great pie made of plover,/And
589 Fable   89   rebuking all such scandal./But after this the monks grew most devout,/And
592 Grad 3   2   as lightning-winged clouds that fly/After a summer tempest, when some haste/
594 Grad 11   3   pass/Into the unknown world — class after class,/O queen of schools — a momentary
602 Humoresque   m   all true lovers seek!'/Humouresque/(AFTER J. LAFORGUE)/One of my
246 MC   Priest1   15   unmolested./{P1} But do they follow after?/{T} For a little time the hungry hawk/Will
254 MC   Tempt4   10   /But think, Thomas, think of glory after death./When king is dead, there's another
265 MC   Priest1   25   with us./Your men shall be looked after also./Dinner before business. Do you like
265 MC   Knight1   28   your pork/First, and dine upon it after./{K2} We must see the Archbishop./{K3}
266 MC   Thomas   25   /{T} This is not true./Both before and after I received the ring/I have been a loyal /
267 MC   Knight1   28   /They are too well known. But after dissension/Had ended, in France, and you
279 MC   Knight4   40   you can give, upon/one who was, after all, a great man./{K1} Thank you, Brito, I
280 MC   Priest1   9   now guide us, protect us, direct us?/After what journey through what further dread/
285 FR   2m   1   England/PART I/*The drawing-room, after tea. An afternoon in late March.*/Scene I/
286 FR   Gerald   9   prudence;/And your servants look after you very much better./{A} My servants are
288 FR   Amy   6   Amy,/And open your presents?/{A} After dinner:/That is the best time./{I} It is the
288 FR   Agatha   14   going to be rather painful for Harry/After eight years and all that has happened/To
292 FR   Amy   18   /Would you like to have them in after dinner/Or wait till tomorrow? I am sure
293 FR   Harry   25   to *you*?/You will understand less after I have explained it./All that I could hope
296 FR   Gerald   36   /That he should be asked. He looked after all the boys/When they were children. I'll
298 FR   Charles   25   Downing./It's good to see you again, after all these years./You're well, I hope?/{Do}

298 FR	Charles	31	about his Lordship./You've looked after his Lordship for over ten years .../{Do}
299 FR	Downing	3	Quite natural, if I may say so, Sir,/After what happened./{C} Quite so, quite./
302 FR	Amy	19	suppose. I hope Harry will feel better/After his rest upstairs. {}/[*Exeunt, except*
304 FR	Agatha	11	than I do. I want to get away./{Ag} After seven years?/{M} Oh, you don't
307 FR	Harry	8	were punished for being out at night/After being put to bed. But at least they never
307 FR	Harry	12	back from school/For the holidays, after the formal reception/And the family
313 FR	Violet	4	*them together*]/{V} Very well, I think, after such a long journey;/You know what a
313 FR	Charles	24	have a sobering effect upon him./After all, you're the head of the family./{A}
317 FR	2m	1	OF PART I/PART II/*The library, after dinner.*/Scene I/HARRY, WARBURTON/
325 FR	Charles	22	Oh, but Arthur's a brilliant driver./After all the experience he's had at Brooklands,/
334 FR	Harry	24	its neglect. One had that part to play./After such training, I could endure, these ten
340 FR	Amy	27	/I even asked you back, for visits, after he was gone,/So that there might be no
346 FR	Downing	18	Miss, when you come to look at it:/After all these years that I've been with him/I
347 FR	Ivy	16	VIOLET]/{I} I wonder why he sent it, after telephoning./Shall I read it to you? I was
347 FR	Ivy	20	returns hurrah love Arthur.'/I mean, after what we know of what did happen,/Do
349 FR	Ivy	8	in the dark./{I} I shall have to stay till after the funeral: will my ticket to London still
369 CP	Edward	39	once or twice dined together./{E} And after that/Did she ever introduce you to her
370 CP	Edward	4	interests./{E} And what happened after that?/{P} Oh, nothing happened./But I
372 CP	Edward	38	if you don't mind,/Please *shut the door after you*, so that it latches./{A} Remember,
377 CP	Julia	25	we are all in need of a stimulant/After this disaster. Now I'll propose a health./
379 CP	Celia	23	the future before we began,/And after that I lived in a present/Where time was
385 CP	Reilly	17	you say to them, or they to you/After the first ten minutes? You would find it
390 CP	Julia	34	/I can see that she is quite worn out/After her anxiety about her aunt —/Who, you'll
390 CP	Julia	36	has quite recovered, Alex —/And after that long journey on the old Great
392 CP	Lavinia	13	you do about it?/I only remembered after I had left./{E} I telephoned to everyone I
398 CP	Edward	11	python. The octopus./Must I become after all what you would make me?/{L} Well,
399 CP	Nurse	22	ring, I show the others out;/And only after they have left the house..../{R} Quite right,
413 CP	Reilly	9	no one to blame but myself./{R} And after that, the prologue to my treatment/Is to
426 CP	Edward	3	will do. I'm too tired to bother./{E} After they're all gone, we will have some
427 CP	Alex	15	I did try to get you on the telephone/After lunch, but my secretary couldn't get
429 CP	Alex	7	some of the converts —/Who, after all, prefer not to be slaughtered —/To
430 CP	Peter	9	a party —/She's coming on later, after the Gunnings —/So I said, I really must
437 CP	Reilly	16	astonishment/Of the first five minutes after a violent death./If this strains your
461 CC	Claude	25	of prudence./As we arranged. But after two months —/And as my wife insists
465 CC	Claude	1	for a long time a secret reproach:/But after his death, and then it was too late,/I knew
467 CC	Colby	2	often happen./And the reconcilement, after his death,/That perfects the relation. You
493 CC	Claude	27	to be conspicuous,/Poor boy!/{SC} After all, it was he who insisted/On this ...
498 CC	Eggers	13	made a profession/Of ... looking after other people's children?/In a manner of
501 CC	Eggers	35	them wait downstairs/And come back after Mrs. Guzzard has left?/{SC} That's not a
527 ES	Charles	18	which you're taking him? And what after that?/{M} There are several good reasons
529 ES	Ld Clav	30	Just remember:/Every day, year after year, over my breakfast,/I have looked at
530 ES	Ld Clav	22	/In a railway station on a branch line,/After the last train, after all the other passengers
530 ES	Ld Clav	22	on a branch line,/After the last train, after all the other passengers/Have left, and the
532 ES	m	4	/A pleasant-spoken gentleman. {}/[*after reading the note*]./{LC} I'll see him in the
535 ES	Gomez	26	simple. I come back to England/After thirty-five years. Can you imagine/What it
544 ES	Ld Clav	11	far, so good./I'll feel more confidence after a fortnight —/After fourteen days of
544 ES	Ld Clav	12	more confidence after a fortnight —/After fourteen days of people not staring/Or
545 ES	Piggott	28	understand/My not coming in directly after breakfast:/He's led a busy life, too.' But I
547 ES	Monica	17	decants for every newcomer./Perhaps after what she considers proper courtesies,/She
548 ES	Piggott	1	apologise for the lack of excitement:/After all, peace and quiet is our *raison d'être*./
548 ES	4m	14	/*herself and takes out her knitting.*/[*after a pause*]./{MC} I hope I'm not disturbing
548 ES	Carghil	30	to you./Dear me, it's astonishing, after all these years;/And you don't even
554 ES	Carghil	16	feel they *need* me!/{MC} You do look after us well, Mrs. Piggott:/You're so
555 ES	Ld Clav	23	not had another accident./You know, after that last escapade of his,/I've lived in
558 ES	Michael	34	you're willing to admit./{Mi} Well, after all, she was the only one/Who was at all
560 ES	Michael	1	/In the grave? If you're still conscious after death,/I bet it will be a surprised state of
564 ES	Gomez	24	we, Richard?/{G} I expect that was after I had left England./{MC} Of course, that
564 ES	Carghil	25	/{MC} Of course, that explains it. After Oxford/I suppose you went back to ...
565 ES	Monica	7	/Will you come back in the morning? After breakfast?/{LC} Yes, come tomorrow
572 ES	Ld Clav	1	natural death/And had been run over after he was dead./It was only a corpse that we
582 ES	Ld Clav	18	/I leave Monica to you. Look after her, Charles,/Now and always. I shall take

AFTERNOON (34)

15 Prufrock	75	the floors of silent seas./And the afternoon, the evening, sleeps so peacefully!/
18 Portrait	1	the smoke and fog of a December afternoon/You have the scene arrange itself —
18 Portrait	3	seem to do —/With 'I have saved this afternoon for you';/And four wax candles in the

19 Portrait		57	/Of a broken violin on an August afternoon:/'I am always sure that you
21 Portrait		114	Well! and what if she should die some afternoon,/Afternoon grey and smoky, evening
21 Portrait		115	if she should die some afternoon,/Afternoon grey and smoky, evening yellow and
24 Rhapsody		43	lighted shutters,/And a crab one afternoon in a pool,/An old crab with barnacles
31 Apollinax		17	dry and passionate talk devoured the afternoon./'He is a charming man' — 'But after
32 Hysteria		10	stopped,/some of the fragments of the afternoon might be collected, and I
177 FQ: ECoker		16	/Shuttered with branches, dark in the afternoon,/Where you lean against a bank while
191 FQ: Little		8	/A glare that is blindness in the early afternoon./And glow more intense than blaze of
197 FQ: Little		238	So, while the light fails/On a winter's afternoon, in a secluded chapel/History is now
216 Jellicles		26	hours,/They're quiet enough in the afternoon,/Reserving their terpsichorean powers
221 Old Deut		33	/Of the Fox and French Horn for his afternoon sleep;/And when the men say:
285 FR	2m	1	I/*The drawing-room, after tea. An afternoon in late March.*/Scene I/AMY, IVY,
360 CP	Edward	5	/She'd gone when I came in, this afternoon./She left a note to say that she was
384 CP	2m	1	Act One. Scene 3/*The same room: late afternoon of the next day.* EDWARD *alone. He*
424 CP	3m	1	*London flat. Two years later.*/*A late afternoon in July.* A CATERER'S MAN *is*
445 CC	3m	1	/*London house. Early afternoon.* SIR CLAUDE *writing at desk. Enter/*
448 CC	Claude	21	on how she takes to him. This afternoon/She will only learn that you have
450 CC	Colby	28	what you wanted, Sir Claude. Good afternoon,/Mr. Eggerson. I was afraid I'd miss
502 CC	Lucasta	6	apologise for my behaviour/The other afternoon./{C} Apologise?/{SC} I've told her./
523 ES	m 11		*London house. Four o'clock in the afternoon/*ACT TWO/*The Terrace at Badgley*
523 ES	m 15		/ACT THREE/*The Same. Late afternoon of the following day/*Act One/*The*
524 ES	2m	1	*London house. Four o'clock in the afternoon.*/[*Voices in the hall*]/{C} Is your father
524 ES	Monica	6	you said you could give me the whole afternoon./{C} But I couldn't say what I wanted
525 ES	Charles	2	/I arranged to be free for the whole afternoon/On the plain understanding .../{M}
525 ES	Charles	5	I said that I was free for the whole afternoon,/That meant you were to give *me* the
525 ES	Charles	6	meant you were to give *me* the whole afternoon./I couldn't say what I wanted to, in a
529 ES	Ld Clav	20	have you been doing?/{LC} Good afternoon, Charles. You might have guessed,
529 ES	Ld Clav	34	years ago, to-day, at this hour of the afternoon./If I've been looking at this
547 ES	Piggott	8	Don't let him stay out late/In the afternoon, Miss Claverton-Ferry./And
565 ES	Ld Clav	4	I/Must continue our discussion. This afternoon, Michael./{M} No, I think you've had
567 ES	2m	1	/Act Three/*Same as Act Two. Late afternoon of the following day*. MONICA *seated*/

AFTERNOONS (1)

14 Prufrock	50	/Have known the evenings, mornings, afternoons,/I have measured out my life with

AFTERSIGHT (1)

194 FQ: Little	130	of the tribe/And urge the mind to aftersight and foresight,/Let me disclose the

AFTERTHOUGHT (1)

552 ES	Carghill	17	of us./{MC} That 'both of us'/Was an afterthought, Richard. A lucky escape/You

AFTERWARDS (7)

29 Aunt Helen		9	handsomely provided for,/But shortly afterwards the parrot died too./The Dresden
425 CP	Edward	26	/Will be going on to the Gunnings afterwards,/To make room for those who come
471 CC	Colby	37	B./{L} Oh, by me ... and B./{C} Only afterwards,/When I had seen you a number of
474 CC	Colby	22	mind/But the sense of desolation afterwards./{L} I know what you mean. Then
503 CC	Eggers	24	B. come up now?/{E} Better wait till afterwards./{SC} Quite right, Eggerson./{L}
549 ES	Carghill	21	And the three of us talked you over afterwards —/Effie and Maud and I. What a
564 ES	Carghill	23	and I became great friends/Not long afterwards, didn't we, Richard?/{G} I expect

AGAIN (131)

63 WL: Burial	75	men,/'Or with his nails he'll dig it up again!/'You! hypocrite lecteur! — mon
65 WL: Chess	120	What is the wind doing?'/Nothing again nothing./'Do/'You know nothing? Do
69 WL: Fire S	254	to folly and/Paces about her room again, alone,/She smoothes her hair with
89 Ash-Wed 1	1	/Because I do not hope to turn again/Because I do not hope/Because I do not
89 Ash-Wed 1	9	reign?/Because I do not hope to know again/The infirm glory of the positive hour/
89 Ash-Wed 1	15	and springs flow, for there is nothing again/Because I know that time is always time/
89 Ash-Wed 1	23	voice/Because I cannot hope to turn again/Consequently I rejoice, having to
90 Ash-Wed 1	30	explain/Because I do not hope to turn again/Let these words answer/For what is done,
90 Ash-Wed 1	32	/For what is done, not to be done again/May the judgement not be too heavy
98 Ash-Wed 6	1	/Although I do not hope to turn again/Although I do not hope/Although I do
104 Journ Magi	33	ago, I remember,/And I would do it again, but set down/This set down/This: were
118 SP	m 17	Cards are queer! {}/(*Whistle again*.)/{Do} Is that Sam?/{Du} Of course it's
125 SA Sweeney	1	up?/{Du} Cheer him up?/{S} Well here again that don't apply/But I've gotta use words
125 SA Sweeney	18	/You're either or neither/I tell you again it don't apply/Death or life or life or
133 Eyes	8	is my affliction/Eyes I shall not see again/Eyes of decision/Eyes I shall not see
150 Rock 1 m	109	*in 'The Times'.*/Chant of WORKMEN *again.*/*The river flows, the seasons turn/*The
165 Rock 9	30	us to create/And employ our creation again in His service/Which is already His service
179 FQ: ECoker	73	does not matter./It was not (to start again) what one had expected./What was to be
181 FQ: ECoker	136	I have said before. I shall say it again./Shall I say it again? In order to arrive

181 FQ: ECoker	137	I shall say it again./Shall I say it again? In order to arrive there,/To arrive where
182 FQ: ECoker	173	sound, substantial flesh and blood —/Again, in spite of that, we call this Friday good.
182 FQ: ECoker	189	has been lost/And found and lost again and again: and now, under conditions/
182 FQ: ECoker	189	lost/And found and lost again and again: and now, under conditions/That seem
191 FQ: Little	25	you would find the hedges/White again, in May, with voluptuary sweetness./It
195 FQ: Little	171	of thing shall be well./If I think, again, of this place,/And of people, not wholly
201 Def Island	18	ways but the weapons/and those again for whom the paths of glory are/the lanes
222 Pekes Pols	6	yet once in a way,/Or now and again, they join in to the fray/And they/Bark
224 Mr Mistoff	13	defy examination/And deceive you again./The greatest magicians have something
226 Macavity	10	air —/But I tell you once and once again, *Macavity's not there!*/Macavity's a ginger
229 Gus	39	He once played a Tiger — could do it again —/Which an Indian Colonel pursued
233 Skimble	64	brown tail/Which says: 'I'll see you again!/You'll meet without fail on the Midnight
235 Ad-dress	36	lout,/He'll answer any hail or shout./Again I must remind you that/A Dog's a Dog
592 Grad 2	5	they fully understand/That though again they see their fatherland/They there shall
593 Grad 8	3	be our lot,/We shall desire to see again the spot/Which, whatsoever we have been
598 Circe	7	the dead. —/We shall not come here again./Panthers rise from their lairs/In the forest
240 MC Chorus	23	you?/Shall the Son of Man be born again in the litter of scorn?/For us, the poor,
242 MC Priest1	2	King, that is another matter./{P1} But again, is it war or peace?/{M} Peace, but not the
242 MC Mess	13	man/Whom in this life I shall not see again./I have this, I assure you, on the highest
242 MC Priest2	31	Our lord has come back to his own again./We have had enough of waiting, from
247 MC Thomas	15	generation/The same things happen again and again./Men learn little from others'
247 MC Thomas	15	/The same things happen again and again./Men learn little from others' experience./
247 MC Tempt1	24	the good times past, that are come again/I am your man./{T} Not in this train/
248 MC Tempt2	22	acknowledged, should guide the state again./{T} Your meaning?/{T2} The
258 MC Thomas	4	shall not come in this kind again./The last temptation is the greatest
260 MC Thomas	10	for the salvation of men, and/offer again to God His Body and Blood in sacrifice,
262 MC Thomas	1	not think I shall ever preach to you again; and because/it is possible that in a short
269 MC Thomas	2	/I shall not get those seven years back again./Never again, you must make no doubt,/
269 MC Thomas	3	those seven years back again./Never again, you must make no doubt,/Shall the sea
275 MC Chorus	27	let the spring not come./Can I look again at the day and its common things, and see
285 FR	5	cuckoo will be gone before I am out again./O Sun, that was once so warm, O Light
286 FR Gerald	6	for me,/I'd just as soon be a subaltern again/To be back in the East. An incomparable
289 FR Gerald	9	I've no doubt./Let him marry again and carry on at Wishwood./{A} Thank
292 FR Ivy	37	to your mother/Time and time again: she's done nothing about it/Because she
292 FR Violet	39	your coming./{V} And time and time again I have spoken to your mother/About the
295 FR Amy	37	country. When you see Wishwood/Again by day, all will be the same again./I beg
295 FR Amy	37	/Again by day, all will be the same again./I beg you to go now and rest before
298 FR Charles	25	Downing./It's good to see you again, after all these years./You're well, I hope?/
299 FR Downing	16	/{Do} Oh yes, she did, every now and again./But in my opinion, it is those that talk/
308 FR Harry	21	to the point of departure/And start again as if nothing had happened,/Isn't that all
311 FR Harry	17	instant of inattention/They are roused again, the sleepless hunters/That will not let me
313 FR Gerald	15	I see./It's good to have him back again, isn't it?/We must make him feel at home.
314 FR Warburt	10	than you can remember/To see you again. But you can't have forgotten/The day
325 FR Violet	32	him I would never go out with him again./Not that I wanted to go with him at all
330 FR Harry	2	be what he always was;/Arthur again be sober, though not for very long;/And
334 FR Agatha	11	income daily:/And I am old, to start again to make my living./{H} But you are not
337 FR Harry	18	You must go./{H} Shall we ever meet again?/{Ag} Shall we ever meet again?/And who
337 FR Agatha	19	meet again?/{Ag} Shall we ever meet again?/And who will meet again? Meeting is for
337 FR Agatha	20	ever meet again?/And who will meet again? Meeting is for strangers./Meeting is for
337 FR Harry	23	moment of clarity, and now I feel dull again./I only know that I made a decision/
338 FR Harry	8	must just believe me,/Until I come again./{A} But why are you going?/{H} I can
340 FR Amy	1	/{A} I was a fool, to ask you again to Wishwood;/But I thought, thirty-five
343 FR Agatha	7	and I,/My dear, may very likely meet again/In our wanderings in the neutral territory/
343 FR Harry	38	this/But it is so, mother. Until I come again./{A} If you go now, I shall never see you
344 FR Amy	1	If you go now, I shall never see you again. {}/[*Meanwhile* VIOLET, GERALD *and*
345 FR Harry	4	So I shall say good-bye, until we meet again./{G} Well, if you are determined, Harry,
353 CP Peter	7	/{P} You'll have to tell us all over again, Alex./{A} I never tell the same story
357 CP Julia	21	may come back and be called away again./I understand these tough old women —/
359 CP Julia	30	people's business./Well, good-bye again. I'm off at last. {}/[*Exit*]/{E} I'm sorry. I'm
364 CP Edward	16	you want her./{E} I want to see her again — here./{UG} You shall see her again —
364 CP Reilly	17	again — here./{UG} You shall see her again — here./{E} Do you mean to say that you
364 CP Edward	30	*goes to the door*]/{E} So it's you again, Julia! {}/[*Enter* JULIA *and* PETER]/{J}
369 CP Peter	24	came to know Celia./{P} I saw her again a few days later/Alone at a concert. And I
376 CP m	7	{}/[*Returns to kitchen. The bell rings again.* EDWARD *goes to front door, and is*/
383 CP Edward	2	Julia: what is it now?/Your spectacles again ... where did you leave them?/Or have we

383 CP	Celia	9	/I shall never go into your kitchen again. { }/[*Exit* EDWARD. *He returns with the*
389 CP	Celia	30	/Don't put me off. I may not see you again./What I want to say is this: I should like
391 CP	Julia	13	no use to me./I'm not coming back again *this* evening./{L} Stop! I want you to
395 CP	Edward	37	of understanding./{E} So here we are again. Back in the trap,/With only one
397 CP	Edward	29	/And then had to unwrap everything again/To find what you wanted. And I never
399 CP	Reilly	2	like to run over my instructions again./You understand, of course, that it is
402 CP	Edward	16	I ought to see a doctor./They said — again, in almost the same words —/That I was
403 CP	Edward	25	made me into./We had not been alone again for fifteen minutes/Before I felt, and still
404 CP	Edward	29	to the sanatorium?/I can't go home again. And at my club/They won't let you keep
413 CP	Celia	2	/If you simply tell me to go away again./{R} Most of my patients begin, Miss
417 CP	Celia	5	/It's not that I'm afraid of being hurt again:/Nothing again can either hurt or heal./I
417 CP	Celia	6	afraid of being hurt again:/Nothing again can either hurt or heal./I have thought at
419 CP	Celia	14	to your sanatorium, and come back again —/I don't mean to say they weren't much
425 CP	Lavinia	30	the tray about,/So they'll go away again. Anyway, at that stage/There's nothing
434 CP	Alex	16	other/Will never be fit for normal life again./But Celia Coplestone, she was taken./
435 CP	Peter	9	/And then I thought about her again. More and more./At first I did not want
439 CP	Edward	23	I'll be going./{E} Shall we see you again, Peter,/Before you leave England?/{L} Do
452 CC	Kaghan	7	cash from the money-box./Bankrupt again! So I thought I'd better bring her/And
452 CC	Eggers	12	/{L} Eggy, I've lost my job!/{E} Again, Miss Angel?/{L} Yes, again! And serve
452 CC	Lucasta	13	job!/{E} Again, Miss Angel?/{L} Yes, again! And serve them right!/{E} You have
452 CC	Lucasta	34	sure they both suit you./{L} Snubbed again! I suppose I asked for it./That's what
457 CC	Claude	22	/Where is she? Oh, she's gone out again. { }/[*Goes to the window and looks down*
463 CC	Colby	28	returns to take possession:/And I am again the disappointed organist,/And for a
466 CC	Claude	27	me hear you play./I shan't mention it again. I'll wait until you ask me./Do you
470 CC	Lucasta	15	I'm not people. Will you play to me again/And teach me about music?/{C} Yes, of
479 CC	Lucasta	40	/{L} You're always free to think again./{K} Marriage is a gamble. But I'm a born
492 CC	Colby	16	the moment, I never want to touch it again./But there's another reason. I must
525 ES	Charles	33	it all before./{C} And you'll hear it again. You think I'm going to tell you/Once
526 ES	Charles	6	that you've said so, you must say it again,/For I need so much assurance! Are you
534 ES	Ld Clav	8	in England,/It might land you in gaol again?/{G} That's true enough,/Except for a
536 ES	Gomez	6	a gap — and you can't jump back again./I parted from myself by a sudden effort,/
539 ES	Gomez	2	to be an impressive figurehead./But again, you've retired at sixty. Why at sixty?/
539 ES	Gomez	22	Well, now, I'm beginning to be thirsty again. { }/[*Pours himself whisky*]/{LC} An
542 ES	Gomez	40	be getting impatient./I'll see you soon again./{LC} Not very soon, I think./I am going
543 ES	Gomez	6	present. It's been an elixir/To see you again, and assure myself/That we can begin just
548 ES	Monica	5	I don't believe she'll be bothering us again:/I could see from her expression when she
555 ES	Piggott	7	she's gone now. If she bothers you again/Just let me know. I'm afraid it's the
555 ES	Monica	12	{M} I saw Mrs. Piggott bothering you again/So I hurried to your rescue. You look
557 ES	Ld Clav	3	come to the point. You're in trouble again./We'll ignore, if you please, the question
565 ES	Ld Clav	36	would teach? Come, I'll start to learn again./Michael and I shall go to school
571 ES	Ld Clav	16	which they did admire us!/And that again may nourish the faults that they were
579 ES	Michael	2	no difference./You'll be seeing me again./{M} But who will you be/When I see you
579 ES	Monica	4	But who will you be/When I see you again? Whoever you are then/I shall always
579 ES	Michael	19	that just depends./I could look in again. If there's any point in it./Personally, I
579 ES	Ld Clav	24	sooner the better./We may never meet again, Michael./{Mi} I don't see why not./{G}
580 ES	Michael	9	/But I'll send you a card, now and again,/Just to let you know I'm flourishing./
580 ES	Carghil	23	And now that we've found each other again,/We must always keep in touch. But you'd

AGAINE (1)

75 WL: Thund	431		then Ile fit you. Hieronymo's mad againe./Datta. Dayadhvam. Damyata./Shantih

AGAINST (55)

13 Prufrock	2		and I,/When the evening is spread out against the sky/Like a patient etherised upon a
23 Preludes	29		soul was constituted;/They flickered against the ceiling./And when all the world
39 Gerontion	69		Bear/In fractured atoms. Gull against the wind, in the windy straits/Of Belle
75 WL: Thund	430		*abolie*/These fragments I have shored against my ruins/Why then Ile fit you.
96 Ash-Wed 5	8		/And the light shone in darkness and/Against the Word the unstilled world still
129 Cor2 State	23		a joint committee to protest against the reduction of orders./Meanwhile the
129 Cor2 State	26		croak in the marshes./Fireflies flare against the faint sheet lightning/What shall I
149 Rock 1	m94		*group of* WORKMEN *is silhouetted against the dim sky. From farther/away, they are*
177 FQ: ECoker	17		in the afternoon,/Where you lean against a bank while a van passes,/And the deep
178 FQ: ECoker	62		in constellated wars/Scorpion fights against the Sun/Until the Sun and Moon go
230 Bust Jones	14		to the *Senior Educational*/And it is against the rules/For any one Cat to belong
603 Spleen	10		in the alley;/Dejection unable to rally/Against this dull conspiracy./And Life, a little
605 Narcissus	5		/Your shadow leaping behind the fire against the red rock:/I will show you his bloody
243 MC Priest2	1		on a rock, we can feel a firm foothold/Against the perpetual wash of tides of balance
244 MC Chorus	6		beer and cider,/Gathered wood against the winter,/Talked at the corner of the

246 MC Thomas	12	Fearing for the King's name, warning against treason,/Made them hold their hands.
248 MC Tempt2	19	not too pleasant memories/In balance against other, earlier/And weightier ones: those
249 MC Tempt2	35	/{T2} Hungry hatred/Will not strive against intelligent self-interest./{T} You forget
249 MC Tempt2	38	curbing of petty privilege./{T2} Against the barons/Is King's cause, churl's
252 MC Tempt3	12	/Church and people have good cause against the throne./{T} If the Archbishop
253 MC Tempt4	18	of the fiend./Barons are employable against each other;/Greater enemies must kings
256 MC Chorus	7	the sky. And the earth presses up against our feet./What is the sickly smell, the
258 MC Thomas	21	/In England, and waged war with him against Toulouse,/I beat the barons at their own
264 MC Priest1	2	*did sit, and did witness falsely against me.*/A day that was always most dear to
266 MC Knights	14	You are the Archbishop in revolt against the King; in rebellion to the King and
267 MC Knight1	36	of France, to the Pope,/Raising up against him false opinions./{K2} Yet the King,
269 MC Thomas	12	I, Becket from Cheapside,/It is not against me, Becket, that you strive./It is not
273 MC Priests	27	like beasts. You would bar the door/Against the lion, the leopard, the wolf or the
273 MC Priests	29	the wolf or the boar,/Why no more/Against beasts with the souls of damned men,
273 MC Priests	29	beasts with the souls of damned men, against men/Who would damn themselves to
277 MC Knight3	11	you come to the/point, it does go against the grain to kill an Archbishop,
288 FR Agatha	22	real past. Wandering in the tropics/Or against the painted scene of the Mediterranean,/
297 FR Violet	34	to express my emphatic protest/Both against your purpose and the means you are
300 FR Downing	11	Sir./That was just my complaint against my Lady./It's my opinion that man and
300 FR Downing	16	him alone./And there's my complaint against these ocean liners/With all their
304 FR Mary	1	have known you'd throw that up against me./I know I wasn't one of your
304 FR Mary	19	if I'd had the moral courage,/Even against a will like hers. I know very well/Why
314 FR Warburt	37	an incurable cancer./How he fought against it! I never saw a man/More anxious to
316 FR Ivy	4	terror, and I must struggle against it.{G} I am used to tangible danger, but
341 FR Amy	36	/And now at the moment of success against failure,/When I felt assured of his
348 FR Chorus	14	avoid accidents,/We are insured against fire,/Against larceny and illness,/Against
348 FR Chorus	15	accidents,/We are insured against fire,/Against larceny and illness,/Against defective
348 FR Chorus	16	fire,/Against larceny and illness,/Against defective plumbing,/But not against the
348 FR Chorus	17	/Against defective plumbing,/But not against the act of God./We know various spells
348 FR Chorus	21	Divination and chiromancy,/Specifics against insomnia,/Lumbago, and the loss of
455 CC Eggers	28	And I have my garden/To protect me against Mrs. E. That's my joke./{C} Well, I've
466 CC Colby	34	you. But … something in me/Rebels against accepting such conditions./It would be
467 CC Colby	15	what I said just now/About rebelling against the terms/That life has imposed./{SC}
508 CC Eggers	4	/For a mother who has been hoping against hope/To find her son. Put yourself in
512 CC Guzzard	38	when realised, sometimes turn/Against those who have made them. {}/[*To*
551 ES Carghll	35	I think you'd be awarded.'/Effie was against it — she wanted you exposed./But I
558 ES Michael	30	there was one thing he brought up against me,/That I'd been too familiar with one
572 ES Charles	12	/{C} And Mrs. Carghill:/What has she against you?/{LC} I was her first lover./I would
573 ES Ld Clav	19	I feel sure they are conspiring against me./I see Mrs. Carghill coming./{M} Let
577 ES Charles	14	through you,/His lifelong grievance against your father?/Remember, you put

AGAMEMNON (1)

57 Swee Night	38	sang within the bloody wood/When Agamemnon cried aloud/And let their liquid

AGATHA (34)

284 FR	m	2	IVY, VIOLET, *and* AGATHA, *her younger sisters*/COL. THE
285 FR	4m	1	/Scene I/AMY, IVY, VIOLET, AGATHA, GERALD, CHARLES, MARY/
287 FR Amy		32	shudder in a vacant room./Only Agatha seems to discover some meaning in
288 FR Violet		17	painful?/{V} Gerald! you know what Agatha means./{A} I mean painful, because
288 FR Amy		28	is hard./{A} Nothing is changed, Agatha, at Wishwood./Everything is kept as it
289 FR Amy		10	/{A} Thank you, Gerald. Though Agatha means/As a rule, a good deal more than
292 FR Harry		14	Violet, Uncle Gerald, Uncle Charles. Agatha./{A} We are very glad to have you back,
293 FR Harry		19	I shall be less embarrassing to you. Agatha?/{Ag} I think, Harry, that having got so
297 FR Amy		2	/It should be myself. What does Agatha think?/{Ag} It seems a necessary move/
302 FR	m	13	Arthur or John. {}/[*Enter* AMY *and* AGATHA]/{A} It is very annoying. They both
302 FR	m	19	his rest upstairs. {}/[*Exeunt, except* AGATHA]/Scene II/AGATHA/[*Enter* MARY
303 FR	2m	1	/[*Exeunt, except* AGATHA]/Scene II/AGATHA/[*Enter* MARY *with flowers*]/{M}
303 FR Mary		29	like a man of the world?/Cousin Agatha, I want your advice./{Ag} I should have
316 FR	m	8	*and passes through to dinner. Enter* AGATHA]/{Ag} The eye is on this house/The
319 FR Harry		10	whispering aunts: Ivy and Violet —/Agatha never came then. Where was my father?/
319 FR Harry		36	close. If you won't tell me,/I must ask Agatha. I never dared before./{W} I advise you
323 FR	m	7	*followed severally by* VIOLET, IVY, AGATHA, GERALD *and* CHARLES.]/{A}
328 FR Violet		28	{V} This is just what I expected. But if Agatha/Is going to moralise about it, I shall
330 FR	2m	1	CHORUS]/Scene II/HARRY, AGATHA/{H} John will recover, be what he
336 FR	1m	23	I will follow. {}/[*The curtains close.* AGATHA *goes to the window, in a*
337 FR Harry		38	Oh, mother,/This is not to do with Agatha, any more than with the rest of you./My
338 FR Amy		14	liked to explain./{A} Why should Agatha know, and I not be allowed to?/{H} I do

338 FR	Harry	15	to?/{H} I do not know whether Agatha knows/Or how much she knows. Any
340 FR	2m	1	angels. {}/[*Exit*]/Scene III/AMY, AGATHA/{A} I was a fool, to ask you again to
340 FR	Amy	3	time might have made a change in Agatha —/It has made enough in *me.*
342 FR	Mary	19	/Can you not stop him? Cousin Agatha, stop him!/You do not know what I
342 FR	Mary	28	me,/But Harry must not go. Cousin Agatha!/{Ag} Here the danger, here the death,
344 FR	Amy	3	going? What is the matter?/{A} Ask Agatha./{G} Why, what's the matter? Where is
344 FR	Amy	5	matter? Where is he going?/{A} Ask Agatha./{V} I cannot understand at all. Why is
344 FR	Amy	7	at all. Why is he leaving?/{A} Ask Agatha./{V} Really, it sometimes seems to me/
347 FR	Amy	30	/To know what has happened./{A} Agatha! Mary! come!/The clock has stopped in
347 FR	m	32	has stopped in the dark! {}/[*Exeunt* AGATHA *and* MARY. *Pause. Enter*
349 FR	1m	13	{}/[*Exeunt*]/[*Enter, from one door*, AGATHA *and* MARY, *and set a small*
349 FR	3m	13	*she sets on the table. Exit* DENMAN. AGATHA/*and* MARY *walk slowly in single*

AGATHA'S (1)

327 FR	Violet	7	We must learn to suffer more./{V} Agatha's remarks are invariably pointed./{H}

AGE (21)

71 WL: DWater	317	and fell/He passed the stages of his age and youth/Entering the whirlpool./Gentile
74 WL: Thund	404	of a moment's surrender/Which an age of prudence can never retract/By this, and
161 Rock 7	32	and palms turned upwards/In an age which advances progressively backwards?/
163 Rock 8	42	the call of a wandering preacher./Our age is an age of moderate virtue/And of
163 Rock 8	42	a wandering preacher./Our age is an age of moderate virtue/And of moderate vice/
179 FQ: ECoker	76	autumnal serenity/And the wisdom of age? Had they deceived us,/Or deceived
194 FQ: Little	131	/Let me disclose the gifts reserved for age/To set a crown upon your lifetime's effort./
271 MC Thomas	16	them, droning by the fire,/When age and forgetfulness sweeten memory/Only like
287 FR Charles	15	{C} She's a nice girl; but it's a difficult age for her./I suppose she must be getting on for
311 FR Harry	31	a dreaming moment,/Of a dreaming age, when I was someone else/Thinking of
320 FR Harry	39	know my father at about my present age?/{W} Why, yes, Harry, of course I did./{H}
345 FR Amy	19	yourself. {}/[*Exit* HARRY]/{A} At my age, I only just begin to apprehend the truth/
345 FR Charles	36	know. I suppose I'm getting old:/Old age came softly up to now. I felt safe enough;/
380 CP Edward	39	have a man ... nearer your own age./{C} I don't think I care for advice from
505 CC Eggers	30	so many years — when you get to my age/The past and the future both seem very
529 ES Monica	7	of himself/When he was your age — when he started like you,/With the same
535 ES Gomez	29	years? I was twenty-five —/The same age as you — when I went away,/Thousands of
542 ES Ld Clav	22	was I responsible?/We were the same age. You were a free moral agent./You pretend
562 ES Carghil	21	so like your father/When he was your age. He's the picture of you, Richard,/As you
576 ES Gomez	5	we can well imagine you at ... what age were you?/{MC} Just eighteen./{LC} Now,
583 ES Monica	23	out a blessing on the living./{M} Age and decrepitude can have no terrors for me,

ÂGE (1)

51 Restaurant	15	/Mais alors, vieux lubrique, à cet âge .../'Monsieur, le fait est dur./Il est venu,

AGÈD (2)

89 Ash-Wed 1	6	towards such things/(Why should the agèd eagle stretch its wings?)/Why should I
92 Ash-Wed 3	11	repair,/Or the toothed gullet of an agèd shark./At the first turning of the third stair

AGENCY (1)

458 CC Lady E	16	your ticket?/{LE} I went to the agency and got them to change it./I can't

AGENT (5)

245 MC Thomas	15	suffering is action. Neither does the agent suffer/Nor the patient act. But both are
255 MC Tempt4	38	suffering action. Neither does the agent suffer/Nor the patient act. But both are
343 FR Amy	28	/With the solicitor, the broker, agent? Why should I?/It is no concern of the
542 ES Ld Clav	22	the same age. You were a free moral agent./You pretend that I taught you expensive
577 ES Ld Clav	39	you know very well./Michael's a free agent. So if he chooses/To place himself in your

AGENT'S (1)

68 WL: Fire S	232	carbuncular, arrives,/A small house agent's clerk, with one bold stare,/One of the

AGENTS (2)

227 Macavity	41	Griddlebone)/Are nothing more than agents for the Cat who all the time/Just controls
272 MC Chorus	20	/More than fury in the hall./The agents of hell disappear, the human, they shrink

AGES (1)

430 CP Peter	15	my looking in so early./It does seem ages since I last saw any of you!/And how are

AGES' (1)

201 Def Island	9	—/contributing their share to the ages' pavement/of British bone on the sea floor/

AGITATE (1)

429 CP Edward	2	/{E} And the agitators;/How do they agitate?/{A} By convincing the heathen/That the

AGITATORS (2)

428 CP Alex	35	of the matter./There are also foreign agitators,/Stirring up trouble .../{L} Why don't
429 CP Edward	1	are very deep waters./{E} And the agitators;/How do they agitate?/{A} By

AGO (56)

62 WL:	Burial	35	/'You gave me hyacinths first a year ago;/'They called me the hyacinth girl.'/— Yet
104 Journ	Magi	32	satisfactory./All this was a long time ago, I remember,/And I would do it again, but
149 Rock 1		76	some of the things that were long ago done,/That you may take heart. Make
225 Mr	Mistoff	54	was asleep in the hall./And not long ago this phenomenal Cat/Produced *seven*
598 Circe		14	the eyes/Of men whom we knew long ago./On a Portrait/Among a crowd of tenuous
258 MC	Thomas	9	in which our lives begin./Thirty years ago, I searched all the ways/That lead to
289 FR	Charles	14	his wife —/That was just about a year ago, wasn't it?/Do you think that I ought to
303 FR	Agatha	19	thought of asking him a little while ago./{M} Well, there's something to be said for
304 FR	Mary	7	tried for a fellowship, seven years ago./Now I want your advice, because there's
315 FR	Violet	21	older/Than on her birthday ten years ago./{G} Is there any use in waiting for Arthur
325 FR	Violet	31	always on his head./{V} But a year ago, Arthur took me out in his car,/And I told
326 FR	Harry	30	live/Since I came home, a few hours ago, to Wishwood./{V} I will make no
330 FR	Harry	19	is./At the beginning, eight years ago,/I felt, at first, that sense of separation,/Of
340 FR	Amy	4	made enough in *me*. Thirty-five years ago/You took my husband from me. Now you
341 FR	Amy	22	years of abstinence./Thirty-five years ago you took my husband from me/And now
355 CP	Julia	30	wedding. Oh, so many years ago! {}/[*To the* UNIDENTIFIED GUEST]/{J}
368 CP	Peter	31	Celia./I met her here, about a year ago./{E} At one of Lavinia's amateur
373 CP	Edward	3	Celia Coplestone in? ... How long ago? .../No, it doesn't matter. {}/CURTAIN/Act
374 CP	Edward	4	/And I tried to get you a short while ago./{C} If there had happened to be anyone
375 CP	Edward	29	/He made his way in, a little while ago,/And insisted on cooking me something for
381 CP	Edward	29	I see that my life was determined long ago/And that the struggle to escape from it/Is
408 CP	Reilly	39	when you came to me two months ago/I was dissatisfied with your explanation/Of
409 CP	Edward	3	enquiries./{E} It was two months ago/That your breakdown began! and I never
430 CP	Peter	6	night —/I left Los Angeles three days ago./I saw Sheila Paisley at lunch to-day/And
435 CP	Julia	5	... take up this career?/{J} Two years ago./{P} Two years ago! I tried to forget about
435 CP	Peter	6	/{J} Two years ago./{P} Two years ago! I tried to forget about her,/Until I began to
439 CP	Lavinia	2	she said good-bye to us, two years ago./{E} Your responsibility is nothing to mine,
455 CC	Colby	4	wonder./I nearly did, a moment ago./Then I'd have been certain I'd lost my
456 CC	Eggers	29	rare adventures!/I remember long ago, saying to Mrs. E.,/When we'd bought our
466 CC	Colby	36	struck by what you said, a little while ago,/When you spoke of never having
476 CC	Lucasta	9	In one way, it matters. A little while ago/You said, very cleverly, that when we first
489 CC	Claude	2	/I ought to have told you, years ago./I told you about Lucasta, and you told me/
505 CC	Eggers	32	seem very brief —/But long enough ago for the question to be possible./Lady
506 CC	Eggers	26	/{E} It seems just possible. A few days ago,/As I said, Lady Elizabeth learned your
516 CC	Claude	18	a tale we had —/So very long ago! — when we shared our ambitions/And
517 CC	Eggers	28	organist we had/Died two months ago. We've been looking for another./{C} Do
519 CC	Guzzard	1	/Had *our* wishes twenty-five years ago;/But we failed to observe, when we had our
526 ES	Charles	18	I'm not the same person as a moment ago./What do the words mean now — *I* and
526 ES	Monica	22	/That we entered only a few minutes ago./Here's an armchair, there's the table;/
529 ES	Ld Clav	34	out what I was doing/Twenty years ago, to-day, at this hour of the afternoon./If
531 ES	Ld Clav	15	an inset, a portrait taken twenty years ago./In five years' time, it will be the half of
536 ES	Gomez	9	/To the fact that Dick Ferry died long ago./I married a girl who didn't know a word of
537 ES	Gomez	6	done already, Dick; done many years ago:/Adoption tried, and grappled to my soul/
541 ES	Gomez	2	that happened so many years ago?/What damages you'd get! The Press
541 ES	Gomez	29	you pointedly reminded me a moment ago./Now it's my turn, perhaps, to do you a
542 ES	Ld Clav	1	you my friendship/So many years ago, I only gained in return/Your envy, spite
549 ES	Carghil	22	/Effie and Maud and I. What a time ago it seems!/It's surprising I remember it all so
550 ES	Ld Clav	11	You married, I suppose, many years ago?/{MC} Many years ago, the first time. That
550 ES	Carghil	12	many years ago?/{MC} Many years ago, the first time. That didn't last long./People
553 ES	Ld Clav	1	writes it./{LC} Considering how long ago it was when you knew me/And considering
557 ES	Ld Clav	31	on to the capital./{LC} And how long ago was that?/{Mi} Nearly two years./Time
562 ES	Carghil	30	/Since I knew him ever so many years ago,/Yet you're the image of what he was then./
565 ES	Ld Clav	33	And what a hypocrite!/A few minutes ago I was pleading with Michael/Not to try to
569 ES	Ld Clav	26	that word before,/Not so very long ago. When I asked him what he wanted./Oh no,
574 ES	Carghil	1	I almost married him,/Oh so long ago. So you see, Mr. Hemington,/I've come to
577 ES	Gomez	6	passage .../{G} Just as many years ago/His father paid mine./{C} This return of

AGON (1)

121 SA		t	to show us around. {}/Fragment of an Agon/SWEENEY. WAUCHOPE.

AGONISING (1)

466 CC	Claude	12	the maker, of which I spoke — an agonising ecstasy/Which makes life bearable.

AGONISTES (1)

115 S		t	/UNFINISHED POEMS/Sweeney Agonistes/*Fragments of an Aristophanic*

AGONY (15)

72 WL: Thund	324	frosty silence in the gardens/After the agony in stony places/The shouting and the
104 Journ Magi	39	this Birth was/Hard and bitter agony for us, like Death, our death./We
180 FQ: ECoker	133	lost, but requiring, pointing to the agony/Of death and birth./You say I am
187 FQ: DrySal	106	come to discover that the moments of agony/(Whether, or not, due to
187 FQ: DrySal	111	has. We appreciate this better/In the agony of others, nearly experienced,/Involving
187 FQ: DrySal	116	/People change, and smile: but the agony abides./Time the destroyer is time the
282 MC Chorus	13	that the blood of the martyrs and the agony of the saints/Is upon our heads./Lord,
310 FR Mary	3	/For the ache in the moving root/The agony in the dark/The slow flow throbbing the
329 FR Chorus	3	and presses hard on the future./The agony in the curtained bedroom, whether of
342 FR Agatha	30	not elsewhere;/Elsewhere no doubt is agony, renunciation,/But birth and life. Harry
438 CP Lavinia	3	Perhaps she had been through greater agony beforehand./I mean — I know nothing of
490 CC Claude	10	this situation must be more of an agony/To you, than it can be even to ... us./{C} I
490 CC Colby	12	us./{C} I only wish it was more acute agony:/I don't know whether I've been suffering
490 CC Colby	15	I only feel ... numb./If there's agony, it's part of a total agony/Which I can't
490 CC Colby	15	/If there's agony, it's part of a total agony/Which I can't begin to feel yet. I'm

AGREE (12)

277 MC Knight1	28	I have to say./{K1} I think we will all agree that William de Traci has/spoken well and
278 MC Knight2	27	orders were incompatible./You will agree with me that such interference by an
289 FR Amy	12	to betray,/I am bound to say that I agree with you./{C} I never wrote to him when
298 FR Violet	13	own methods. {}/[*Rises*]/{V} I do not agree./I think there should be witnesses. I intend
363 CP Edward	37	of incalculable value./{E} Stop! I agree that much of what you've said/Is true
449 CC Claude	15	Yes, quite ideal./{SC} I'm glad you agree. Your support will be helpful./{E} I'm sure
452 CC Lucasta	31	Angel,/Just to annoy me. Don't you agree/That Lucasta suits me better?/{C} I'm sure
497 CC Eggers	36	.../{LE} *Two* Mrs. Guzzards?/{E} I agree, it is a most uncommon name,/But
498 CC Eggers	1	/{LE} And both in Teddington?/{E} I agree, that would be most surprising./And at
510 CC Eggers	3	{}/[*Exit* COLBY]/{E} And now, if you agree, Lady Elizabeth,/We can ask Mr. Kaghan
564 ES Gomez	3	It will never be too late. Don't you agree, Dick?/— This young lady I take to be
579 ES Ld Clav	23	and I see no way to stop you,/Then I agree with you, the sooner the better./We may

AGREEABLE (1)

582 ES Ld Clav	16	of persons/And situations not very agreeable./You two ought to have a little time

AGREED (3)

356 CP Julia	23	/I said so to Lavinia. She agreed with me./She said: 'I wish you'd try.'
421 CP Reilly	14	just now/That she would go far, you agreed with me./{J} Oh yes, she will go far. And
527 ES Charles	3	engaged yet./{C} Aren't we? We're agreed that we're in love with each other,/And,

AGREES (2)

321 FR Winch	35	you, no, my Lord;/I don't find port agrees with the rheumatism./{W} For God's
501 CC Claude	36	/{SC} That's not a bad idea. If Colby agrees./{L} I trust you, Eggy. And I want to

AGUE (1)

52 Whispers	14	knew the anguish of the marrow/The ague of the skeleton;/No contact possible to

AH (14)

19 Portrait	44	one in her fingers while she talks./'Ah, my friend, you do not know, you do not
367 CP Alex	35	to know her? {}/[*Enter* ALEX]/{A} Ah, there you are, Edward! Do you know why
368 CP Alex	3	both shut it when you go out./{A} Ah, but you're coming with me, Edward./I
368 CP Alex	12	want much, and I'll get it myself./{A} Ah, in that case I know what I'll do./I'm going
368 CP Alex	23	cooking./I couldn't think of it./{A} Ah, but that's my special gift —/Concocting a
372 CP Alex	18	just sent them from the country./{A} Ah, so the aunt/Really exists. A substantial
384 CP Reilly	26	yesterday that my wife left me./{UG} Ah, but we die to each other daily./What we
390 CP Alex	38	And I suppose she's famished./{A} Ah, in that case I know what I'll do .../{J} No,
429 CP Alex	32	multiply./{L} And the Christians?/{A} Ah, the Christians! Now, I think I ought to tell
445 CC Claude	1	*at desk. Enter*/EGGERSON./{SC} Ah, there you are, Eggerson! Punctual as
450 CC Claude	26	SIMPKINS *with briefcase*]/{SC} Ah, Colby, I was just saying to Eggerson/It was
497 CC Eggers	9	Mrs. Guzzard, of Teddington./{E} Ah, indeed!/I shouldn't have expected her name
541 ES Gomez	35	to take it. {}/[*Exit* LAMBERT]/{G} Ah, the pre-arranged interruption/To terminate
574 ES Carghil	23	Señor Gomez able to suggest?/{MC} Ah! That's the surprise for which I've come to

AH-H-H (1)

116 SP Dusty	38	bye./I'm sure, that's very kind of *you.*/Ah-h-h/{Do} Now I'm going to cut the cards for

AHEAD (5)

73 WL: Thund	361	you and I together/But when I look ahead up the white road/There is always
335 FR Agatha	21	of disinfectant,/Looking straight ahead, passing barred windows./Up and down.
386 CP Celia	23	/Julia was delayed, and sent me on ahead./{E} It seems very odd. And not like
452 CC Kaghan	8	better bring her/And come upstairs ahead, to ease the shock for Colby./But as
570 ES Ld Clav	15	completely indifferent to whatever lay ahead of her./{M} It is time to break the silence!

AI (2)

51 Restaurant	11	petite./Elle était toute mouillée, je lui ai donné des primevères.'/Les taches de son gilet
51 Restaurant	18	un gros chien;/Moi j'avais peur, je l'ai quittée à mi-chemin./C'est dommage.'/Mais

AID (3)

593 Grad 7	6	the cause to victory,/That with their aid the flag is raised on high./Sometime in
327 FR Harry	13	/I could cheat them perhaps with the aid of Dr. Warburton —/Or any other doctor,
581 ES Charles	5	to welcome him/And give all the aid we can. But it's both of you together/Make

AILANTHUS (1)

184 FQ: DrySal	12	in the nursery bedroom,/In the rank ailanthus of the April dooryard,/In the smell of

AILMENTS (1)

314 FR Violet	15	was always the same with your minor ailments/And children's epidemics: you would

AIM (6)

178 FQ: ECoker	56	under feet/And hollyhocks that aim too high/Red into grey and tumble down/
190 FQ: DrySal	230	future also./For most of us, this is the aim/Never here to be realised;/Who are only
235 Ad-dress	66	/And so in time you reach your aim,/And finally call him by his NAME./So this
278 MC Knight2	6	the key to the problem./The King's aim has been perfectly consistent. During the
542 ES Gomez	16	/It's most unkind of you. My only aim/Is to renew our friendship. Don't you
561 ES Ld Clav	1	reality./Oh Michael! If you had some aim of high achievement,/Some dream of

AIMED (2)

516 CC Colby	9	/It doesn't matter about success —/I aimed too high before — beyond my capacity./I
578 ES Ld Clav	14	/And see how all the efforts aimed at your good/Only succeeded in defeating

AIMING (2)

409 CP Reilly	36	for as long as you could,/That he was aiming at a higher social distinction/Than the
506 CC Eggers	22	her./{E} That is exactly what we are aiming at./We have a clue — or what appears to

AIMLESS (1)

27 Morning	8	a passer-by with muddy skirts/An aimless smile that hovers in the air/And

AIMS (5)

212 Growltiger	3	up to Oxford he pursued his evil aims,/Rejoicing in his title of 'The Terror of the
240 MC Chorus	21	planning and guessing,/Having their aims which turn in their hands in the pattern of
278 MC Knight2	4	soberly: what/were the Archbishop's aims? and what are King Henry's aims? In/the
278 MC Knight2	4	aims? and what are King Henry's aims? In/the answer to these questions lies the
577 ES Charles	13	confidence,/Michael, in a man who aims to gratify, through you,/His lifelong

AIN'T (2)

236 Cat Morgan	9	o' cold fish when I done me patrol./I ain't got much polish, me manners is gruff,/But
236 Cat Morgan	14	the Barbary Coast,/And me voice it ain't no sich melliferous horgan;/But yet I can

AIR (41)

19 Portrait	36	definite 'false note.'/— Let us take the air, in a tobacco trance,/Admire the
21 Portrait	113	chatter like an ape./Let us take the air, in a tobacco trance —/Well! and what if she
27 Morning	8	/An aimless smile that hovers in the air/And vanishes along the level of the roofs./
33 Conv Gal	16	moods the slightest twist!/With your air indifferent and imperious/At a stroke our
64 WL: Chess	89	the sense in odours; stirred by the air/That freshened from the window, these
73 WL: Thund	366	you?/What is that sound high in the air/Murmur of maternal lamentation/Who are
73 WL: Thund	372	and reforms and bursts in the violet air/Falling towers/Jerusalem Athens Alexandria
73 WL: Thund	382	a blackened wall/And upside down in air were towers/Tolling reminiscent bells, that
90 Ash-Wed 1	35	to fly/But merely vans to beat the air/The air which is now thoroughly small and
90 Ash-Wed 1	36	/But merely vans to beat the air/The air which is now thoroughly small and dry/
92 Ash-Wed 3	4	banister/Under the vapour in the fetid air/Struggling with the devil of the stairs who
135 5FingerEx1	1	*to a Persian Cat*/The songsters of the air repair/To the green fields of Russell Square./
140 Usk	10	/Where the grey light meets the green air/The hermit's chapel, the pilgrim's prayer./
141 Rannoch	4	soar. Substance crumbles, in the thin air/Moon cold or moon hot. The road winds in/
160 Rock 7	12	and shot with darkness/As the air of temperate seas is pierced by the still dead
172 FQ: BurntN	27	the autumn heat, through the vibrant air,/And the bird called, in response to/The
174 FQ: BurntN	112	of unhealthy souls/Into the faded air, the torpid/Driven on the wind that sweeps
192 FQ: Little	58	ash the burnt roses leave./Dust in the air suspended/Marks the place where a story
192 FQ: Little	63	hope and despair,/This is the death of air./There are flood and drouth/Over the eyes
196 FQ: Little	202	/The dove descending breaks the air/With flame of incandescent terror/Of which
201 Def Island	12	death, fight the power of darkness in air/and fire/and of those who have followed
226 Macavity	9	the basement, you may look up in the air —/But I tell you once and once again,
602 Humoresque	9	grimace;/Half bullying, half imploring air,/Mouth twisted to the latest tune;/His
256 MC Chorus	6	restless movement of feet. And the air is heavy and thick./Thick and heavy the sky.
257 MC Chorus	26	/Sweet and cloying through the dark air/Falls the stifling scent of despair;/The forms
257 MC Chorus	28	/The forms take shape in the dark air:/Puss-purr of leopard, footfall of padding
257 MC Chorus	32	feet, swing and wing through the dark air./O Thomas Archbishop, save us, save us/
263 MC Chorus	7	colder the night./Still and stifling the air: but a wind is stored up in the East./The
263 MC Chorus	22	may/Burst over the stream, and the air is clear and high,/And voices trill at

270 MC Chorus   5   soil and criticised the worm. In the air/Flirted with the passage of the kite, I have
275 MC Chorus   21   we hear the CHORUS./{C} Clear the air! clean the sky! wash the wind! take stone
276 MC Chorus   17   world that is wholly foul./Clear the air! clean the sky! wash the wind! take the stone
281 MC Chorus   12   affirm Thee in living; the bird in the air, both the hawk and the finch; the beast on
287 FR   Amy   38   from Marseilles,/He would come by air to Paris, and so to London,/And hoped to
300 FR Downing 28   in the Tourist,/And I took a bit of air before I went to bed,/And you could see the
335 FR Agatha   6   down a concrete corridor/In a dead air. Only feet walking/And sharp heels scraping.
336 FR   Harry   8   feel a kind of stirring underneath the air?/Do you? don't you? a communication, a
458 CC Lady E   13   And besides,/I didn't come by air. I arrived at Victoria./{SC} Do you mean to
458 CC Lady E   23   with me,/And she can't go by air — she says it makes her sea-sick;/So we took
526 ES Charles   32   will come. With his calm possessive air/And his kindly welcome, which is always a
580 ES Gomez   4   takes some days, you know, even by air mail./{M} Take the card, Charles. If I write
AIR (1) [*Foreign word*]
  47 Mél Adult   12   /Surexcité par Emporheben/Au grand air de Bergsteigleben;/J'erre toujours de-ci de-là/
AIRPORT (2)
447 CC Claude   4   Elizabeth,/Coming back from the airport, about Colby./I think, you ought to give
457 CC Eggers   13   *at his watch*]/{E} I'll arrive at the airport with minutes to spare,/And besides,
AIRS (1)
216 Jellicles   11   black eyes;/They like to practise their airs and graces/And wait for the Jellicle Moon
AISE (1)
  48 Lune Miel   3   nuit d'été, les voici à Ravenne,/A l'aise entre deux draps, chez deux centaines de
AJAR (1)
218 Mung Rump   7   bear./If the area window was found ajar/And the basement looked like a field of
ALARM (1)
107 Animula   6   /Advancing boldly, sudden to take alarm,/Retreating to the corner of arm and
ALARMED (2)
548 ES Monica   8   about the grounds. Don't look so alarmed!/If you spy any guest who seems to be
553 ES Carghil   12   we belong together .../Now, don't get alarmed. But you touched my soul —/Pawed it,
ALARMING (1)
451 CC Colby   1   about her,/But that's rather alarming./{E} Mr. Kaghan is prejudiced./He's
ALAS (2)
  83 Hollow Men   4   together/Headpiece filled with straw. Alas!/Our dried voices, when/We whisper
587 Fable   15   if they had been kept by a kind fairy./Alas! no fairy visited their host,/Oh, no; much
ALBANIA (1)
372 CP   Alex   12   /Never, even when travelling in Albania,/Have I made such a supper out of so
ALBERT (4)
  66 WL: Chess   147   more can't I, I said, and think of poor Albert,/He's been in the army four years, he
  66 WL: Chess   155   pick and choose if you can't./But if Albert makes off, it won't be for lack of telling./
  66 WL: Chess   163   You *are* a proper fool, I said./Well, if Albert won't leave you alone, there it is, I said,/
  66 WL: Chess   166   ITS TIME/Well, that Sunday Albert was home, they had a hot gammon,/And
ALBERT'S (1)
  65 WL: Chess   142   UP PLEASE ITS TIME/Now Albert's coming back, make yourself a bit
ALBUM (2)
182 FQ: ECoker 201   /(The evening with the photograph album)./Love is most nearly itself/When here
315 FR Chorus   36   in the nursery, mutilated/The family album, rendered ludicrous/The tenants' dinner,
ALCOHOL (1)
375 CP Edward   20   .../Oh, from Jugoslavia ... prunes and alcohol?/No, really, Alex, I don't want
ALDER (1)
600 Moonflower   4   bird, a snowy owl,/Slips from the alder tree./Whiter the flowers, Love, you hold,/
ALDERMAN (1)
511 CC Lucasta 35   in the City./{L} When you're an alderman, you'll be Sir Barney Kaghan!/{LE}
ALE (3)
150 Rock 1   105   /*To two women one half pint of bitter*/Ale. *In this land*/*No man has hired us.*/*Our life is*
161 Rock 7   36   /*To two women one half pint of bitter*/Ale..../CHORUS:/What does the world say, does
588 Fable   54   which perhaps held several kegs/Of ale, and cheese which they kept under cover./
ALERT (1)
320 FR Warburt   6   that although your mother/Is still so alert, so vigorous of mind,/Although she seems
ALEX (59)
353 CP   Peter   7   You'll have to tell us all over again, Alex./{A} I never tell the same story twice./{J}
359 CP Edward   5   Oh ... yes ... thank you. Good-bye, Alex,/It was nice of you to come. {}/[*Exeunt*
359 CP   m   6   It was nice of you to come. {}/[*Exeunt* ALEX *and* CELIA]/[*To the* UNIDENTIFIED
367 CP   m   35   did you come to know her? {}/[*Enter* ALEX]/{A} Ah, there you are, Edward! Do you
367 CP Edward   36   I'd like to know first how you *got* in, Alex./{A} Why, I came and found that the door
368 CP Edward   7   /{E} That's very thoughtful of you, Alex, I'm sure;/But I rather *want* to be alone,
368 CP Edward   20   I shan't disturb you./{E} My dear Alex,/There'll be nothing in the larder worthy of

370 CP	m	14	this interesting affair? {}/[*Enter* ALEX *in shirtsleeves and an apron*]/{A}
372 CP	m	9	It's very good of you. {}/[*Enter* ALEX, *with his jacket on*]/{A} Oh, Edward! I've
372 CP	Edward	37	Good night, Peter,/And good night, Alex. Oh, and if you don't mind,/Please *shut the*
373 CP	m	2	my work will be ruined. {}/[*Exeunt* ALEX *and* PETER]/[EDWARD *picks up the*
375 CP	Edward	12	/Hello ... oh, hello! ... No. I mean yes, Alex;/Yes, of course ... it was marvellous./I've
375 CP	Edward	17	be rather indigestible? .../Oh, no, Alex, don't bring me any cheese;/I've got some
375 CP	Edward	21	... prunes and alcohol?/No, really, Alex, I don't want anything./I'm very tired.
375 CP	Edward	22	/I'm very tired. Thanks awfully, Alex./Good night./{C} What on earth was that
375 CP	Edward	25	earth was that about?/{E} That was Alex./{C} I know it was Alex./But what was he
375 CP	Celia	26	/{E} That was Alex./{C} I know it was Alex./But what was he talking of?/{E} I had
376 CP	Edward	27	knows./{E} It's something that Alex came and prepared for me./He *would* do
376 CP	Julia	33	have warned you:/Anything that Alex makes is absolutely deadly./I could tell
387 CP	Peter	17	telegram .../{P} No, not to me,/But to Alex. She told him to come here/And to bring
388 CP	Peter	3	overnight?/{P} Why, it's a man Alex put me in touch with/And we settled
388 CP	Peter	5	we settled everything this morning./Alex is a wonderful person to know,/Because,
388 CP	Peter	27	to Julia./{P} And the one you sent to Alex./{L} I don't know what you mean./
388 CP	Peter	33	/And is *she* coming?/{P} Yes, and Alex./{L} Then I shall ask *them* for an
390 CP	m	17	EDWARD *goes to answer it. Enter* ALEX]/{A} Has Lavinia arrived?/{E} Yes./{A}
390 CP	Julia	29	/{A} But what is the mystery?/{J} Alex, *don't* be inquisitive./Lavinia has had a
390 CP	Julia	35	be glad to hear, has quite recovered, Alex —/And after that long journey on the old
390 CP	Julia	39	case I know what I'll do .../{J} No, Alex./We must leave them alone, and let
391 CP	Julia	9	Celia. {}/[*Exit* CELIA]/{J} And now, Alex, you and I should be going./{E} Are you
391 CP	Julia	15	the telegram? What do you think, Alex?/{A} No, Julia, *we* can't explain the
391 CP	Julia	24	feel free ... and yet I started it .../{J} Alex, do you think we could explain *anything*?/
391 CP	m	33	Good-bye! {}/[*Exeunt* JULIA, ALEX *and* PETER]/{L} I must say, you don't
399 CP	2m	25	in. {}/[*Exit* NURSE-SECRETARY]/[ALEX *enters almost immediately*]/{A} When is
400 CP	m	34	/{R} Yes, when they've gone. {}/[*Exit* ALEX *by side door*]/[EDWARD *is shown in by*
401 CP	Edward	9	of a man who did not know you./Yet Alex is so plausible. And his recommendations/
412 CP	Julia	22	/{R} Yes, when she's gone./{J} Will Alex be here?/{R} Yes, he'll be here. {}/[*Exit*
421 CP	Julia	38	/— But how much longer will Alex keep us waiting?/{R} He should be here by
422 CP	m	5	tray in now, Miss Barraway. {}/[*Enter* ALEX]/{A} Well! Well! and how have we got
426 CP	Julia	38	/I've got a surprise: I've brought Alex with me!/He only got back this morning
427 CP	m	5	/But what's become of him? {}/[*Enter* ALEX]/{E} Well, Alex!/Where on earth do you
427 CP	Edward	5	of him? {}/[*Enter* ALEX]/{E} Well, Alex!/Where on earth do you turn up from?/{A}
427 CP	Lavinia	13	and Lavinia./{L} How are you, Alex?/{A} I did try to get you on the telephone/
427 CP	Julia	20	well enough for that./{J} But tell us, Alex./What were you doing in this strange place
430 CP	Peter	16	saw any of you!/And how are you, Alex? And dear old Julia!/{L} So you've just
430 CP	Peter	24	are saffron./{P} Your monkeys, Alex? I always said/That Alex knew everybody.
430 CP	Peter	25	monkeys, Alex? I always said/That Alex knew everybody. But I didn't know/That
430 CP	Peter	36	to the movies?/{L} Occasionally./{P} Alex knows./Did you see my last picture, Alex?/
430 CP	Peter	37	knows./Did you see my last picture, Alex?/{A} I knew about it, but I didn't see it./
431 CP	Peter	4	be a good place to make one./— Alex knows all about Pan-Am-Eagle:/It was he
431 CP	Julia	9	Is he your connection in California, Alex?/{A} Yes, we have sometimes obliged each
432 CP	m	28	myself. Oh, I forgot — {}/[*Turning to* ALEX]/{L} I rather assumed that you knew
433 CP	Julia	24	any directory. You can tell them now, Alex./{L} What does Julia mean?/{A} I was
433 CP	Julia	34	dead./{J} You had better tell them, Alex,/The means that you bring back from
436 CP	Lavinia	21	I want to say to you./While Alex was telling us what had happened to Celia/
439 CP	Peter	33	much./Good-bye, Julia. Good-bye, Alex. Good-bye, Sir Henry. {}/[*Exit*]/{J} ... And
440 CP	Lavinia	1	... I am glad you came ... I am glad Alex told us .../And Peter had to know .../{E}
440 CP	Julia	15	get on better without us. You too, Alex./{L} We don't *want* you to go!/{A} We
440 CP	Julia	19	be unexpected./{J} Now, Henry. Now, Alex. We're going to the Gunnings. {}/[*Exeunt*
440 CP	m	19	{}/[*Exeunt* JULIA, REILLY *and* ALEX]/{L} Edward, how am I looking?/{E}

ALEX'S (3)

377 CP	Edward	27	/{E} No, I can't. But I won't drink to Alex's./{J} Oh, it isn't Alex's. Come, I give you/
377 CP	Julia	28	I won't drink to Alex's./{J} Oh, it isn't Alex's. Come, I give you/Lavinia's aunt! You
411 CP	Lavinia	3	has just taken over, is a friend of Alex's./I could go down with you, and then

ALEXANDER (2)

352 CP	m	5	/CELIA COPLESTONE/ALEXANDER MACCOLGIE GIBBS/PETER
353 CP	4m	1	/COPLESTONE, PETER QUILPE, ALEXANDER MACCOLGIE GIBBS,/*and an*

ALEXANDER'S (1)

359 CP	Julia	28	lucky it was my umbrella,/And not Alexander's — *he's* so inquisitive!/But *I* never

ALEXANDRIA (1)

73 WL: Thund		374	air/Falling towers/Jerusalem Athens Alexandria/Vienna London/Unreal/A woman

ALFRED (7)

13 Prufrock	t	Observations/The Love Song of J. Alfred Prufrock/Let us go then, you and I,/
44 Cook Egg	14	in Heaven/For I shall meet Sir Alfred Mond./We two shall lie together, lapt/In
510 CC Guzzard	22	my name?/{MG} Were Mr. and Mrs. Alfred Kaghan your parents?/{K} Yes. They
557 ES Ld Clav	8	my job./{LC} The position that Sir Alfred Walter made for you./{Mi} I'd stuck it
558 ES Michael	5	discharged?/{Mi} Well, partly. Sir Alfred did come to hear about it,/And so he
558 ES Ld Clav	29	list of your shortcomings?/Or did Sir Alfred make other unflattering criticisms?/{Mi}
574 ES Michael	34	me here in London? With another Sir Alfred/Who'd constitute himself custodian of

ALFRED'S (1)

558 ES Ld Clav	12	have your version first./I dare say Sir Alfred's will be rather different./And what else

ALGAE (1)

184 FQ: DrySal	21	to our curiosity/The more delicate algae and the sea anemone./It tosses up our

ALGY (1)

550 ES Carghil	15	to make another'./How true that is! Algy was a weakling,/But simple he was — not

ALI (1)

136 5FingerEx5	t	for *Cuscuscaraway and Mirza Murad Ali Beg*/How unpleasant to meet Mr. Eliot!/With

ALIBI (1)

227 Macavity	37	and suavity./He always has an alibi, and one or two to spare:/At whatever time

ALIEN (2)

104 Journ Magi	42	here, in the old dispensation,/With an alien people clutching their gods./I should be
134 Wind	10	river/The camp fire shake with alien spears./Here, across death's other river/

ALIKE (2)

195 FQ: Little	152	are three conditions which often look alike/Yet differ completely, flourish in the same
577 ES Carghil	29	Señor Gomez!/You're very much alike in some ways —/So I understand business.

ALIVE (17)

65 WL: Chess	126	are pearls that were his eyes./'Are you alive, or not? Is there nothing in your head?'/
125 SA Sweeney	4	to say./He didn't know if he was alive/and the girl was dead/He didn't know if
125 SA Sweeney	6	dead/He didn't know if the girl was alive/and he was dead/He didn't know if they
125 SA Sweeney	8	/He didn't know if they were both alive/or both were dead/If he was alive then the
125 SA Sweeney	10	alive/or both were dead/If he was alive then the milkman wasn't/and the
125 SA Sweeney	12	rent-collector wasn't/And if they were alive then he was dead./There wasn't any joint/
126 SA Chorus	6	waiting for you./And perhaps you're alive/And perhaps you're dead/Hoo ha ha/Hoo
287 FR Amy	26	/That is the reason. I keep Wishwood alive/To keep the family alive, to keep them
287 FR Amy	27	Wishwood alive/To keep the family alive, to keep them together,/To keep me alive,
287 FR Amy	28	to keep them together,/To keep me alive, and I live to keep them./You none of you
320 FR Warburt	9	/Her indomitable will, that keeps her alive./I needn't go into technicalities/At the
435 CP Peter	24	that seemed possible, while Celia was alive./I wanted it, believed in it, for Celia./And,
435 CP Peter	27	what mattered was, that Celia was alive./And now it's all worthless. Celia's not
435 CP Peter	28	And now it's all worthless. Celia's not alive./{L} No, it's not all worthless, Peter.
506 CC Eggers	15	day. This son, Mrs. Guzzard,/If he is alive, must be a grown man./I believe you have
528 ES Charles	5	to strangers./{C} But he's most alive when he's among people/Managing,
536 ES Gomez	35	/My mother — I dare say she's still alive,/But she must be very old. And she must

ALL (595)

ALL-POWERFUL (1)

251 MC Tempt3	19	situation./King in England is not all-powerful;/King is in France, squabbling in

ALLAYED (1)

52 Whispers	16	skeleton;/No contact possible to flesh/Allayed the fever of the bone./Grishkin is nice:

ALLEMAGNE (1)

47 Mél Adult	10	/Casque noir de jemenfoutiste./En Allemagne, philosophe/Surexcité par

ALLEY (4)

65 WL: Chess	115	Think.'/I think we are in rats' alley/Where the dead men lost their bones./
172 FQ: BurntN	34	in a formal pattern,/Along the empty alley, into the box circle,/To look down into the
603 Spleen	8	and tea!/Children and cats in the alley;/Dejection unable to rally/Against this dull
474 CC Colby	17	/Unexpectedly. Walking down an alley/I should become aware of someone

ALLIANCE (2)

251 MC Tempt3	5	mended./Sooner shall enmity turn to alliance./The enmity that never knew friendship/
280 MC Priest3	25	an oasis in the desert sun,/Go seek alliance with the heathen Saracen,/To share his

ALLOW (9)

173 FQ: BurntN	86	endure./Time past and time future/Allow but a little consciousness./To be
252 MC Tempt3	11	for King's undoing?/{T3} Kings will allow no power but their own;/Church and
279 MC Knight4	34	kept himself from us long enough to allow our righteous/anger to cool. That was just
454 CC Kaghan	8	day. Take my advice, Colby./Never allow Lucasta the slightest advantage/Or she'll
501 CC Eggers	26	you want *us* at your meeting./{E} Allow me. May I make a suggestion?/Though
534 ES Gomez	26	doing well for themselves./I wouldn't allow either of my sons/To go into politics. In
542 ES Gomez	7	to you from Cuba/If your doctors allow you a smoke now and then./I'm a lonely

554 ES   Piggott 22 Claverton was comfortable:/We can't allow him to tire himself with talking./What he
571 ES   Charles 23   mustn't persecute you./We can't allow that. What hold have they upon you?/
ALLOWANCE (2)
455 CC   Eggers   18 won't stick to them./He gives her an allowance — very adequate indeed,/Though
476 CC   Lucasta 37   Claude gave her money, a regular allowance;/But it wouldn't have mattered how
ALLOWANCES (2)
287 FR   Gerald   3   Besides, you've got to make allowances:/We haven't left them such an easy
508 CC   Eggers   3   Far from it. You must make allowances/For a mother who has been hoping
ALLOWED (9)
212 Growltiger   18 foreign name and race no quarter was allowed./The Persian and the Siamese regarded
587 Fable   27 fiend must stay at home — no ghosts allowed/At this exclusive feast. From over sea/
589 Fable   70 sorely/Such slippery folk should be allowed about,/For often they drop in at
338 FR   Amy   14   should Agatha know, and I not be allowed to?/{H} I do not know whether Agatha
347 FR   Ivy   28   look so peculiar? I think I might be allowed/To know what has happened./{A}
476 CC   Colby   2   tell you./At least, not yet. I'm not allowed to tell./And that's about my parents./
488 CC   Lady E   34 adopt him, Claude!/That is, if one's allowed to adopt one's own child./{SC} That's
530 ES   Monica   5   You would soon fill them up if we allowed you to!/That's my business to prevent.
582 ES   Monica   21 far, will you?/You know you're not allowed to stop out late/At this season. It's
ALLOWING (1)
321 FR   Warburt   4   Of course there are differences:/But, allowing for the changes in fashion/And your
ALLOWS (2)
 69 WL: Fire S   251   of her departed lover;/Her brain allows one half-formed thought to pass:/'Well
205 de la Mare   27   /The whispered incantation which allows/Free passage to the phantoms of the
ALLUS (1)
236 Cat Morgan   7 Devonshire cream in a bowl;/But I'm allus content with a drink on the 'ouse/And a
ALLUSION (1)
575 ES   Ld Clav   30   future son-in-law/Understand that allusion. I have told them the story/In
ALMANACH (1)
180 FQ: ECoker   108 And dark the Sun and Moon, and the Almanach de Gotha/And the Stock Exchange
ALMIGHTY (1)
275 MC Thomas   20   I owe shall now be paid./{T} Now to Almighty God, to the Blessed Mary ever Virgin,
ALMOST (25)
 16 Prufrock   118   but a bit obtuse;/At times, indeed, almost ridiculous —/Almost, at times, the Fool.
 16 Prufrock   119 At times, indeed, almost ridiculous —/Almost, at times, the Fool./I grow old ... I grow
129 Cor2 State   41   /Mother/May we not be some time, almost now, together,/If the mactations,
184 FQ: DrySal   6   once solved, the brown god is almost forgotten/By the dwellers in cities —
222 Pekes Pols   12 on the occasion of which I shall speak/Almost nothing had happened for nearly a week
278 MC Knight2   15 King's wishes, we should have had an almost ideal State:/a union of spiritual and
279 MC Knight1   5 about. It/seems to me that he has said almost the last word, for those who/have been
304 FR   Mary   29 died: I believed that Cousin Amy —/I almost believed it — had killed her by willing./
308 FR   Harry   34   flickering at the corner of my eye,/Almost whispering just out of earshot —/And
357 CP   Celia   4 old ladies alone in the country,/And almost impossible to get a nurse./{J} Is that her
399 CP   Nurse   8 waiting-room;/And you will see him almost at once./{R} I shall see him at once. And
399 CP   2m   25   /[ALEX enters almost immediately]/{A} When is
402 CP   Edward   15   /Two people advised me recently,/Almost in the same words, that I ought to see a
402 CP   Edward   16 to see a doctor./They said — again, in almost the same words —/That I was on the
402 CP   Reilly   21   is a term I never use:/It can mean almost anything./{E} And since then, I have
420 CP   Celia   9 decision:/I must tell you that. Oh, I almost forgot —/May I ask what your fee is?/
439 CP   Peter   17 be waiting,/And the experts — I'd almost forgotten them./I realise that I can't get
440 CP   Edward   22 am I looking?/{E} Very well./I might almost say, your best. But you always look your
459 CC   Lady E   3   aura.'/I remember people's auras almost better than their faces./What did you say
489 CC   Claude   4 About your own ... misfortune. And I almost told you/About Colby. I didn't. For
528 ES   Monica   37 ... not a very long time, Charles./It's almost certain that the winter in Jamaica/Will
532 ES   Gomez   32 We're as thick as thieves, you might almost say./Don't you know me, Dick?/{LC}
542 ES   Gomez   26   /{G} Neatly argued, and almost convincing:/Don't you wish you could
559 ES   Ld Clav   8   or at least correspondents/Almost everywhere. Australia — no./The men I
573 ES   Carghill   39   /And there was a moment when I almost married him,/Oh so long ago. So you
ALMS (1)
151 Rock 2   6 look in vain towards foreign lands for alms to be more or the urn to be filled./Your
ALOFT (1)
 33 Conv Gal   4   /Or an old battered lantern hung aloft/To light poor travellers to their distress.'/
ALONE (112)
 24 Rhapsody   59 of dust and eau de Cologne,/She is alone/With all the old nocturnal smells/That
 66 WL: Chess   163 I said./Well, if Albert won't leave you alone, there it is, I said,/What you get married
 69 WL: Fire S   254   and/Paces about her room again, alone,/She smoothes her hair with automatic

84 Hollow Men	47	/In death's other kingdom/Waking alone/At the hour when we are/Trembling with
125 SA Sweeney	15	wasn't any joint/For when you're alone/When you're alone like he was alone/
125 SA Sweeney	16	/For when you're alone/When you're alone like he was alone/You're either or neither/
125 SA Sweeney	16	alone/When you're alone like he was alone/You're either or neither/I tell you again it
125 SA Chorus	31	KRUMPACKER/{Ch} When you're alone in the middle of the night and/you wake
125 SA Chorus	33	and a hell of a fright/When you're alone in the middle of the bed and/you wake
148 Rock 1	49	/I have trodden the winepress alone, and I know/That it is hard to be really
152 Rock 2	31	good and ill deeds belong to a man alone, when he stands alone on the other side of
152 Rock 2	31	to a man alone, when he stands alone on the other side of death,/But here upon
152 Rock 2	41	/Even the anchorite who meditates alone,/For whom the days and nights repeat the
162 Rock 8	7	Edom?/He has trodden the wine-press alone./There came one who spoke of the shame
213 Growltiger	29	forepeak of the vessel Growltiger sate alone,/Concentrating his attention on the Lady
599 On a Port	4	/She stands at evening in the room alone./Not like a tranquil carved goddess of
239 MC Chorus	25	/And we are content if we are left alone./We try to keep our households in order;/
242 MC Priest1	28	/Wishing subjection to God alone./Had the King been greater, or had he
244 MC Chorus	20	death, when we see birth and death alone/In a void apart. We/Are afraid in a fear
247 MC Tempt1	37	/Take a friend's advice. Leave well alone,/Or your goose may be cooked and eaten
248 MC Tempt2	33	/Only to those giving love to God alone./Shall he who held the solid substance/
250 MC Thomas	1	the keys/Of heaven and hell, supreme alone in England,/Who bind and loose, with
252 MC Thomas	14	has good cause to trust none but God alone./I ruled once as Chancellor/And men like
252 MC Thomas	29	/But if I break, I must break myself alone. {}/[Enter FOURTH TEMPTER]/{T4}
266 MC Knight1	10	the King./We must speak with you alone. {}/[to PRIESTS]/{T} Leave us then alone.
266 MC Thomas	11	{}/[to PRIESTS]/{T} Leave us then alone./Now what is the matter?/{K1} This is the
268 MC Thomas	20	own/And bid me sit in Canterbury, alone?/I would wish him three crowns rather
276 MC Chorus	15	to supernatural vermin,/It is not we alone, it is not the house, it is not the city that is
280 MC Priest1	12	strength? The Church lies bereft,/Alone, desecrated, desolated, and the heathen
294 FR Harry	28	to escape/By violence, but one is still alone/In an over-crowded desert, jostled by
295 FR Harry	5	attentive./That night I slept heavily, alone./{A} Harry!/{C} You mustn't indulge such
300 FRDowning	15	/I dare say. She wouldn't leave him alone./And there's my complaint against these
300 FRDowning	34	for near half an hour/He stayed there alone, looking over the rail./Her Ladyship must
311 FR Harry	15	I remember them/They leave me alone: when I forget them/Only for an instant of
317 FR Warburt	1	/{W} I'm glad of a few minutes alone with you, Harry./In fact, I had another
319 FR Warburt	14	Then, has only left a cautery./Leave it alone. You know that your mother/And your
327 FR Harry	19	can't understand me. It's not being alone/That is the horror — to be alone with the
327 FR Harry	20	alone/That is the horror — to be alone with the horror./What matters is the
332 FR Agatha	17	A man and a woman/Married, alone in a lonely country house together,/For
333 FR Agatha	36	You may learn hereafter,/Moving alone through flames of ice, chosen/To resolve
340 FR Agatha	8	did I get? thirty years of solitude,/Alone, among women, in a women's college,/
343 FR Amy	22	you will all leave me!/An old woman alone in a damned house./I will let the walls
356 CP Julia	21	said:/'If I could only get Edward alone/And have a really serious conversation!'/I
357 CP Celia	3	to say?/It's dreadful for old ladies alone in the country,/And almost impossible to
357 CP Julia	40	course./I am going to make you dine alone with me/On Friday, and talk to me about
358 CP Edward	8	But you asked me to dine with you alone./{J} Yes, alone!/Without Lavinia! You'll
358 CP Julia	9	me to dine with you alone./{J} Yes, alone!/Without Lavinia! You'll like the other
366 CP Edward	29	already;/And I did rather want to be alone./But what's it all about?/{P} I want your
368 CP Alex	4	/I thought, Edward may be all alone this evening,/And I know that he hates to
368 CP Alex	5	that he hates to spend an evening alone,/So you're going to come out and have
368 CP Edward	8	I'm sure;/But I rather want to be alone, this evening./{A} But you've got to have
368 CP Alex	17	nice little dinner/Which you can have alone. And then we'll leave you./Meanwhile,
369 CP Peter	25	/{P} I saw her again a few days later/Alone at a concert. And I was alone./I've
369 CP Peter	25	later/Alone at a concert. And I was alone./I've always gone to concerts alone —/At
369 CP Peter	26	alone./I've always gone to concerts alone —/At first, because I knew no one to go
369 CP Peter	28	/And later, I found I preferred to go alone./But a girl like Celia, it seemed very
369 CP Peter	31	/In a society column, to find her there alone./Anyway, we got into conversation/And I
369 CP Peter	33	And I found that she went to concerts alone/And to look at pictures. So we often met/
372 CP Peter	31	of your time,/And you want to be alone. Give my love to Lavinia/When she comes
374 CP 2m	1	quarter of an hour later. EDWARD is alone, playing/Patience. The doorbell rings, and
374 CP Celia	1	and he goes to answer it./{C} Are you alone? {}/[EDWARD returns with CELIA]/{E}
374 CP Edward	14	to try to understand it, I want to be alone./{C} I should have thought it was
384 CP 2m	1	afternoon of the next day. EDWARD alone. He goes to/answer the doorbell./{E} Oh ...
384 CP Edward	5	/{E} I take it that as you have come alone/You have been unsuccessful./{UG} Not at
391 CP Julia	1	.../{J} No, Alex./We must leave them alone, and let Lavinia rest./Now we'll all go
396 CP Lavinia	6	talking to me when we had to be alone./{E} I've often wondered why you married
397 CP Edward	5	/What is hell? Hell is oneself,/Hell is alone, the other figures in it/Merely projections.
397 CP Edward	7	nothing to escape to. One is always alone./{L} Edward, what are you talking about?

399 CP		3m	1	/*several weeks later.* SIR HENRY *alone at his desk. He presses an/electric button.*
403 CP	Edward	25	had made me into./We had not been alone again for fifteen minutes/Before I felt, and
403 CP	Edward	39	live in/Except on her terms. I must be alone,/But not in the same world. So I want you
404 CP	Edward	2	me/Into your sanatorium. I could be alone there? {}/[*House-telephone rings*]/[*into*
404 CP	Reilly	4	EDWARD]/{R} Yes, you could be alone there./{E} I wonder/If you have
411 CP	Lavinia	5	leave you there/If you want to be alone .../{E} But I can't go away!/I have a case
414 CP	Celia	8	me aware/That I've always been alone. That one always is alone./Not simply the
414 CP	Celia	8	always been alone. That one always is alone./Not simply the ending of one
414 CP	Celia	25	/{C} No ... it isn't that I *want* to be alone,/But that everyone's alone — or so it
414 CP	Celia	26	*want* to be alone,/But that everyone's alone — or so it seems to me./They make
416 CP	Celia	26	unloving and unlovable?/Then one *is* alone, and if one is alone/Then lover and
416 CP	Celia	26	/Then one *is* alone, and if one is alone/Then lover and belovèd are equally unreal
426 CP	Lavinia	19	shall be quite free./{L} And we can be alone./I love that house being so remote./{E}
462 CC	Claude	29	/You know I've deliberately left you alone,/And so far we've discussed only current
463 CC	Claude	2	so she made me feel. I never saw you alone./And then when I sent you both over to
464 CC	Claude	20	you feel at all like that/When you are alone with your music?/{C} Just the same./All
465 CC	Claude	28	piano. The best./And when you are alone at your piano, in the evening,/I believe
466 CC	Claude	10	anyone to see them!/But when I am alone, and look at one thing long enough,/I
470 CC	Colby	12	play to other people,/And when I'm alone I can't forget/That it's only myself to
473 CC	Colby	26	through the gate,/And there I am ... alone, in my 'garden'./Alone, that's the thing.
473 CC	Colby	27	there I am ... alone, in my 'garden'./Alone, that's the thing. That's why it's not real./
473 CC	Colby	34	I retire to mine./But he doesn't feel alone there. And when he comes out/He has
474 CC	Colby	4	But what do you want?/{C} Not to be alone there./If I were religious, God would walk
474 CC	Colby	10	you?/{C} It's simply the fact of being alone there/That makes it unreal./{L} Can no
477 CC	Lucasta	38	in that garden/Where you like to be alone with yourself?/Or perhaps you think it
525 ES	Charles	26	you know that I shan't have a minute alone with you./{M} You've already had several
525 ES	Monica	27	You've already had several minutes alone with me/Which you've wasted in
527 ES	Charles	16	/How long will you be imprisoned, alone with your father/In that very expensive
527 ES	Monica	22	reasons?/{M} First, his terror of being alone./In the life he's led, he's never had to be
527 ES	Monica	23	the life he's led, he's never had to be alone./And when he's been at home in the
536 ES	Ld Clav	24	/{LC} I'm sure I do,/I've always been alone./{G} Oh, loneliness —Everybody knows
536 ES	Gomez	30	have lost *yourself*/That you are quite alone./{LC} I'm waiting to hear/Why you
543 ES	Monica	18	/{M} Father, can't you bear to be alone with me?/If you can't bear to dine alone
543 ES	Monica	19	with me?/If you can't bear to dine alone with me tonight,/What will it be like at
544 ES	Monica	2	/Isn't it, Father? They've let us alone;/The people in the dining-room show no
545 ES	Monica	13	looks rather dominating,/Has left us alone./{LC} Yes, but remember/What she said.
545 ES	Ld Clav	15	said. She said: 'I'm going to leave you alone!/You want perfect peace: that's what
547 ES	Monica	18	proper courtesies,/She will leave us alone. {}/[*Re-enter* MRS. PIGGOTT]/{MP} I
554 ES	Carghil	7	she'll take the hint/And leave us alone tomorrow./Good morning, Mrs. Piggott!/
567 ES		3m	1	*of the following day.* MONICA *seated/alone. Enter* CHARLES./{C} Well, Monica, here
582 ES	Charles	30	for a walk./{C} He wanted to leave us alone together!/{M} Yes, he wanted to leave us
582 ES	Monica	31	/{M} Yes, he wanted to leave us alone together./And yet, Charles, though we've
582 ES	Monica	32	/And yet, Charles, though we've been alone to-day/Only a few minutes, I've felt all the
582 ES	Charles	35	what you're going to say!/We *were* alone together, in some mysterious fashion,/

ALONG (25)

13 Prufrock	24	time/For the yellow smoke that slides along the street/Rubbing its back upon the
15 Prufrock	67	makes me so digress?/Arms that lie along a table, or wrap about a shawl./And
16 Prufrock	102	the teacups, after the skirts that trail along the floor —/And this, and so much more?
23 Preludes	35	the street hardly understands;/Sitting along the bed's edge, where/You curled the
24 Rhapsody	2	on a Windy Night/Twelve o'clock./Along the reaches of the street/Held in a lunar
24 Rhapsody	39	and pocketed a toy that was running along the quay,/I could see nothing behind that
27 Morning	2	plates in basement kitchens,/And along the trampled edges of the street/I am
27 Morning	9	that hovers in the air/And vanishes along the level of the roofs./The Boston
54 Mr E Sun	25	of the devout/Burn invisible and dim./Along the garden-wall the bees/With hairy
56 Swee Night	3	down to laugh,/The zebra stripes along his jaw/Swelling to maculate giraffe./The
69 WL: Fire S	258	crept by me upon the waters'/And along the Strand, up Queen Victoria Street./O
162 Rock 8	19	to the kites of Syria/Or sea-strewn along the routes;/Many left their souls in Syria,/
172 FQ: BurntN	34	moved, and they, in a formal pattern,/Along the empty alley, into the box circle,/To
172 FQ: BurntN	54	long forgotten wars./The dance along the artery/The circulation of the lymph/
212 Growltiger	12	the silly goose,/When the rumour ran along the shore: GROWLTIGER'S ON THE
598 Circe	10	/In the forest which thickens below,/Along the garden stairs/The sluggish python
247 MC Tempt1	10	/Shall float as sweet as blossoms. Ice along the ditches/Mirror the sunlight. Love in
279 MC Knight4	13	to the/point. I have nothing to add along their particular lines of argument./What I
322 FR	Winch	27	disturb her Ladyship./So I slipped along on my bike. Mostly walking,/What with
322 FR	Winch	32	On the West Road, in the fog, coming along/At a pretty smart pace, I fancy, ran into a

323 FR	Winch	18	sort of an accident?/{Wi} Coming along in the fog, my Lady,/And he must have
358 CP	Peter	28	to be going./{P} Celia —/May I walk along with you?/{C} No, I'm sorry, Peter;/I've
366 CP	Julia	13	fly. I've kept the taxi waiting./Come along, Peter./{P} I hope you won't mind/If I
405 CP	Reilly	16	your case/So to speak, as you went along. A barrister/Ought to know his brief
454 CC	Kaghan	11	/I'll show you how it's done. Come along, Lucasta,/I'm going to make a day of it,

ALONZO (1)

| 209 NamingCats | | 6 | use daily,/Such as Peter, Augustus, Alonzo or James,/Such as Victor or Jonathan, |

ALOOF (2)

| 223 Pekes Pols | | 38 | the Pugs and the Poms held no longer aloof,/But some from the balcony, some from |
| 225 Mr Mistoff | | 42 | /His manner is vague and aloof,/You would think there was nobody shyer |

ALORS (2)

| 51 Restaurant | | 15 | de puissance et de délire.'/Mais alors, vieux lubrique, à cet âge .../'Monsieur, le |
| 51 Restaurant | | 20 | à mi-chemin./C'est dommage.'/Mais alors, tu as ton vautour!/Va t'en te décrotter les |

ALOUD (2)

| 57 Swee Night | | 38 | wood/When Agamemnon cried aloud/And let their liquid siftings fall/To stain |
| 135 5FingerEx2 | | 4 | a green cloud/Natural forces shriek'd aloud,/Screamed, rattled, muttered endlessly./ |

ALPS (1)

| 45 Cook Egg | | 30 | /Buried beneath some snow-deep Alps./Over buttered scones and crumpets/ |

ALREADY (46)

14 Prufrock		49	reverse./For I have known them all already, known them all —/Have known the
14 Prufrock		55	presume?/And I have known the eyes already, known them all —/The eyes that fix
15 Prufrock		62	presume?/And I have known the arms already, known them all —/Arms that are
66 WL: Chess		160	bring it off, she said./(She's had five already, and nearly died of young George.)/The
91 Ash-Wed 2		7	contained/In the bones (which were already dry) said chirping:/Because of the
165 Rock 9		31	creation again in His service/Which is already His service in creating./For Man is
177 FQ: ECoker		7	ashes, and ashes to the earth/Which is already flesh, fur and faeces,/Bone of man and
182 FQ: ECoker	185	/By strength and submission, has already been discovered/Once or twice, or
239 MC Chorus		5	tribulation/With which we are not already familiar? There is no danger/For us, and
253 MC Tempt4		23	are closed to you/Except the way already chosen./But what is pleasure, kingly
254 MC Tempt4		9	this be?/{T4} Save what you know already, ask nothing of me./But think, Thomas,
290 FR Agatha		25	preparation/Of that which is already prepared/Men tighten the knot of
297 FR Gerald		20	to know/Any more than he knows already./And even if he knew, it's very much
303 FR Mary		11	surely./I hear that Harry has arrived already/And he was the only one that was
317 FR Harry		16	things that are going to happen/Have already happened./{W} That is in a sense true,/
319 FR Harry		1	me/Is either something that I know already/Or unimportant, or else untrue./But I
336 FR Harry		19	I should escape you —/No! you were already here before I arrived./Now I see at last
358 CP Julia		7	You dine with me on Friday./I've already chosen the people you're to meet./{E}
366 CP Edward		28	/{E} I seem to have been disturbed already;/And I did rather want to be alone./But
371 CP Edward		15	you remember./Remember! I say it's already a memory./{P} But I must see Celia at
400 CP Reilly		17	by anyone except his wife./{R} I had already impressed upon her/That she was not to
416 CP Reilly		34	to go home./{R} Compassion may be already a clue/Towards finding your own way
424 CP Lavinia		13	/And your clerk told me you had already left./But all I rang up for was to
432 CP Julia		6	met before./{J} Then if you know him already, you won't be afraid of him./You know,
433 CP Peter		18	to. And now I could help her./I've already spoken to Bela about her,/And I want
433 CP Alex		39	order. A very austere one./And as she already had experience of nursing .../{L} Yes,
440 CP Edward		29	was to admire my dress./{E} But I've already told you how much I like it./{L} But so
475 CC Colby		1	understand *you.*/{C} I believe you do already,/Better than ... other people. And I want
475 CC Colby		34	know most of what there is to say/Already, either from what I've told you/Or from
482 CC Lady E		35	need intellectual society./Now, that already limits your acquaintance:/Because,
483 CC Colby		18	typewriter./{C} It is a typewriter./I've already begun to work here. At the moment/I'm
491 CC Lady E		13	should we not be happy,/All of us? Already, Claude,/I feel as if this brought us
491 CC Colby		25	on such a mixture/Of fiction and fact. Already, it's been hard/For me, who have never
499 CC Claude		9	*the door*]/{SC} Good Lord, she's here already! Well ... Come in! {}/[*Enter* LUCASTA]/
525 ES Monica		22	a good deal more than two words already./And besides, my father doesn't amble./
525 ES Monica		27	a minute alone with you./{M} You've already had several minutes alone with me/
526 ES Monica		15	me/And I am changing you./{M} Already/How much of me is you?/{C} And how
534 ES Gomez		2	/How can one corrupt those who are already corrupted?/I can swear that I've never
535 ES Gomez		1	you come?/{G} You've asked me that already!/To see you, Dick. A natural desire!/For
537 ES Gomez		6	while to be trustworthy?/{G} It's done already, Dick; done many years ago:/Adoption
542 ES Ld Clav		24	tastes:/If you had not had those tastes already/You would hardly have welcomed my
544 ES Ld Clav		15	I'll admit to a feeling of contentment/Already. I only hope that it will last —/The
571 ES Monica		26	Father, you should tell *us* what they already know./Why should you wish to conceal
573 ES Carghil		36	days!/But I feel like a mother to her already./You may say that I just missed being
575 ES Gomez		19	ancient history./Michael knows it already. I've told him myself./I thought he'd
576 ES Monica		1	/{M} I am satisfied with what I know already, Mrs. Carghill,/About you./{MC} But I

ALSO (44)

72 WL: Thund	348	/And no rock/If there were rock/And also water/And water/A spring/A pool among
84 Hollow Men	31	/In death's dream kingdom/Let me also wear/Such deliberate disguises/Rat's coat,
106 Song Sime	33	a sword shall pierce thy heart,/Thine also)./I am tired with my own life and the lives
111 Xmas Trees	25	to the children/(And here I remember also with gratitude/St. Lucy, her carol, and her
111 Xmas Trees	31	into a great joy/Which shall be also a great fear, as on the occasion/When fear
184 FQ: DrySal	16	about us;/The sea is the land's edge also, the granite/Into which it reaches, the
189 FQ: DrySal	178	who conduct them./Repeat a prayer also on behalf of/Women who have seen their
189 FQ: DrySal	183	del tuo figlio,/Queen of Heaven./Also pray for those who were in ships, and/
190 FQ: DrySal	229	is freedom/From past and future also./For most of us, this is the aim/Never here
192 FQ: Little	37	There are other places/Which also are the world's end, some at the sea jaws,/
604 Ode	14	years that efface and destroy/Give us also the vision to see/What we owe for the
242 MC Priest2	35	Our Lord is at one with the Pope, and also the King of France./We can lean on a rock,
249 MC Tempt2	28	Yes! men must manœuvre. Monarchs also,/Waging war abroad, need fast friends at
254 MC Tempt4	26	than kings to compel you./You have also thought, sometimes at your prayers,/
261 MC Thomas	5	ask that, remember/then that He said also, 'Not as the world gives, give I unto you.'/
261 MC Thomas	8	peace as the world/gives./Consider also one thing of which you have probably
261 MC Thomas	14	and in the Passion of Our Lord; so also, in a smaller figure, we/both rejoice and
264 MC Priest1	24	*holy day.*/{P1} As for the people, so also for himself, he offereth for sins./He lays
265 MC Priest1	25	us./Your men shall be looked after also./Dinner before business. Do you like roast
270 MC Chorus	19	in the councils of princes/Is woven also in our veins, our brains,/Is woven like a
295 FR Harry	28	can be caught for the last time./And also waking. She is nearer than ever./The
296 FR Agatha	2	/They will be clear later. I am also convinced/That you only hold a fragment
297 FR Gerald	22	he shouldn't know that we knew it also./Why not let sleeping dogs lie?/{C} All the
303 FR Agatha	15	to keep the dinner back .../{Ag} And also Dr. Warburton. At least, Amy has invited
330 FR Agatha	16	would not understand you,/You may also be afraid of being understood,/Try not to
336 FR Agatha	1	stage: relief from what happened/Is also relief from that unfulfilled craving/
385 CP Reilly	4	must sometimes be broken. We must also remember/That at every meeting we are
385 CP Reilly	25	like to forget./{UG} And persons also. But you must not forget them./You must
385 CP Edward	27	as strangers./{E} Then I myself must also be a stranger./{UG} And to yourself as
386 CP Reilly	13	may ask it./{E} Who are you?/{UG} I also am a stranger. {}/[*Exit. A pause.*
402 CP Reilly	29	kinds of patient. And there are also patients/For whom a sanatorium is the
418 CP Reilly	34	better./Both ways are necessary. It is also necessary/To make a choice between them./
428 CP Alex	35	to the heart of the matter./There are also foreign agitators,/Stirring up trouble .../{L}
439 CP Reilly	37	moment./{R} Julia, you are right. It is also right/That the Chamberlaynes should now
466 CC Claude	20	can find some unity./Then there are also the men of genius./There are others, it
473 CC Colby	33	retires to his garden — literally,/And also in the same sense that I retire to mine./But
505 CC Eggers	21	you surmised, with Mr. Simpkins./It also concerns a problem of paternity./{LE} Or
514 CC Guzzard	39	to have a child:/That much is true. I also was expecting one./That you did not know.
515 CC Guzzard	10	I thought — why not?/My husband also had died. I was left very poor./If I let you
515 CC Guzzard	23	ambitions for Colby./I am sacrificing also my previous sacrifice./This is even greater
559 ES Michael	31	you wished to be Lord Claverton/Also, to hold your own with Mother's family —
568 ES Ld Clav	27	meanness and cowardice,/But also situations which are simply ridiculous,/
570 ES Ld Clav	31	in their father's footsteps/Who are also successful. What would *he* have been/If he
582 ES Ld Clav	2	me,/For the *me* he rejected, I reject also./I've been freed from the self that pretends

ALTAR (7)

165 Rock 9	41	stone, the visible crucifix,/The dressed altar, the lifting light,/Light/Light/The visible
166 Rock 10	27	that we have kindled,/The light of altar and of sanctuary;/Small lights of those
167 Rock 10	44	our eyes./And when we have built an altar to the Invisible Light, we may set thereon
271 MC Priests	21	They are coming back, armed. To the altar, to the altar./{T} All my life they have been
271 MC Priests	21	back, armed. To the altar, to the altar./{T} All my life they have been coming,
271 MC Priests	27	/You will be killed. Come to the altar./Make haste, my Lord. Don't stop here
339 FR Harry	9	/A stony sanctuary and a primitive altar,/The heat of the sun and the icy vigil,/A

ALTAR-SMOKE (1)

594 Grad 9	2	the sanctuaries of the soul/Incense of altar-smoke shall rise to thee/From spotless

ALTARS (1)

155 Rock 3	45	swept the floors and garnished the altars./Where there is no temple there shall be

ALTER (4)

308 FR Mary	28	do for yourself./What you need to alter is something inside you/Which you can
327 FR Harry	16	/But this is too real for your words to alter./Oh, there *must* be another way of talking/
410 CP Reilly	39	this phrase,/And in forgetting it will alter the condition./{L} Edward, there *is* that
439 CP Reilly	8	by acceptance/Of the past will you alter its meaning./{J} Henry, I think it is time

ALTERED (3)
192 FQ: Little   36   is beyond the end you figured/And is altered in fulfilment. There are other places/
306 FR   Mary   3   to you, I am sure,/We must seem very altered./{H} You have hardly changed at all —/
308 FR   Harry 30   inside me, you think, that can be altered!/And here, indeed! where I have felt
ALTERNATE (1)
154 Rock 3   11   you power of choice, and you only alternate/Between futile speculation and
ALTERNATELY (1)
256 MC   m 29   PRIESTS *and* TEMPTERS *alternately./*{C} Is it the owl that calls, or a signal
ALTERNATIVE (2)
307 FR   Harry 31 know:/The sudden extinction of every alternative,/The unexpected crash of the iron
420 CP   Julia   36   question the decision/What possible alternative can you imagine?/{R} None./{J} Very
ALTHOUGH (18)
  49 Hippopot   3   /Rests on his belly in the mud;/Although he seems so firm to us/He is merely
  98 Ash-Wed 6   1   withered apple-seed./O my people./Although I do not hope to turn again/Although
  98 Ash-Wed 6   2 Although I do not hope to turn again/Although I do not hope/Although I do not
  98 Ash-Wed 6   3 to turn again/Although I do not hope/Although I do not hope to turn/Wavering
193 FQ: Little   101   voice cry: 'What! are *you* here?'/Although we were not. I was still the same,/
222 Pekes Pols   4   goes./And the Pugs and the Poms, although most people say/That they do not like
222 Pekes Pols   25   all over the Park./Now the Peke, although people may say what they please,/Is
592 Grad 4   1   their passing may no more be traced./Although the path be tortuous and slow,/
592 Grad 4   2   the path be tortuous and slow,/Although it bristle with a thousand fears,/To
309 FR   Mary 15 sense I don't know you very well,/Although I remember you better than you
320 FR Warburt   5   to you./I must tell you, Harry, that although your mother/Is still so alert, so
320 FR Warburt   7 /Is still so alert, so vigorous of mind,/Although she seems as vital as ever —/It is only
417 CP   Celia   8   at moments that the ecstasy is real/Although those who experience it may have no
450 CC   Claude   6   I don't know/About you, Eggerson, although we worked together/For nearly thirty
465 CC   Colby 33   my own feelings you have expressed,/Although the medium is different. I know/I
473 CC   Colby 23 you know, it's not quite real to me —/Although it's as real to me as ... this world./But
486 CC   Colby   2   have come across the name before;/Although, as you say, it is an uncommon one./
553 ES   Carghil   6   progress year by year, Richard./And although it's true that our acquaintance was
ALTOGETHER (4)
365 CP   Julia   33   singing songs all the time?/There's altogether too much mystery/About this place
482 CC   Lady E   7   to have dropped the use of surnames altogether./But, Colby, I hope you won't mind a
539 ES   Gomez 17   /That your marriage had not been altogether happy./And as for your son — from
539 ES   Ld Clav 24 epitome./Though I cannot accept it as altogether accurate./The only thing I find
ALWAYS (263)
AM (241)
AMATEUR (4)
290 FR Chorus 37   fretful, ill at ease,/Assembled like amateur actors who have not been assigned
290 FR Chorus 38   not been assigned their parts?/Like amateur actors in a dream when the curtain
368 CP   Edward 32   a year ago./{E} At one of Lavinia's amateur Thursdays?/{P} A Thursday. Why do
368 CP   Peter   33   /{P} A Thursday. Why do you say amateur?/{E} Lavinia's attempts at starting a
AMATEURS (1)
  48 Lune Miel   9   /En Classe, basilique connue des amateurs/De chapitaux d'acanthe que tournoie
AMAZE (2)
  34 Figlia   23   /Sometimes these cogitations still amaze/The troubled midnight and the noon's
583 ES   Monica 25   me,/Not even death can dismay or amaze me/Fixed in the certainty of love
AMAZEMENT (1)
111 Xmas Trees 12   /So that the glittering rapture, the amazement/Of the first-remembered Christmas
AMAZING (5)
223 Pekes Pols   53   gave a great yawn, and his jaws were amazing;/And when he looked out through the
403 CP   Reilly   3 for your dreams,/You would produce amazing dreams, to oblige me./I could make
457 CC   Eggers 32 *can* have happened?/{E} It's perfectly amazing. Let *me* go down to meet her./{SC}
460 CC   Eggers 36 ticket./It's something unheard of./{E} Amazing, isn't it!/{SC} If this is what the doctor
497 CC   Eggers 16 own child was entrusted./{E} What an amazing coincidence!/{SC} That's what it is,/
AMBIGUOUS (1)
542 ES   Gomez 34   mirror of the face behind you,/The ambiguous smile, the distant salutation,/The
AMBITION (7)
258 MC Thomas 17   /Were all things equally desirable./Ambition comes when early force is spent/And
258 MC Thomas 19   we find no longer all things possible./Ambition comes behind and unobservable./Sin
266 MC Knight1 31   not think it is like to do./Saving your ambition is what you mean,/Saving your pride,
369 CP   Edward 17   and fashion./Lavinia always had the ambition/To establish herself in two worlds at
446 CC   Claude 14   form. He won't forget/That his great ambition was to be an organist,/Just as I can't
515 CC Guzzard 26   a small thing/For me, to see my life's ambition come to nothing?/When I gave up my
560 ES   Ld Clav 33   what inspired you was no positive ambition/But only the desire to escape./{Mi} I'm

AMBITIONS (13)

38 Gerontion	35	/And issues, deceives with whispering ambitions,/Guides us by vanities. Think now/
604 Ode	7	blessings bestow,/From the hopes and ambitions that sprang at thy feet/To the
388 CP Celia	13	have a chance,/I hope, to realise your ambitions./I shall miss you./{P} It's nice of you
389 CP Lavinia	5	have a chance/At last, to realise your ambitions./You're going together?/{P} We're
492 CC Claude	29	Oh yes. To say something of my early ambitions/To be a potter. Not that the
515 CC Guzzard	22	you the truth/I am sacrificing my ambitions for Colby./I am sacrificing also my
516 CC Claude	18	very long ago! — when we shared our ambitions/And shared our disappointment. And
516 CC Claude	29	way of your fulfilling your musical ambitions —/Had you been able to fulfil them./
516 CC Colby	39	/I was content to have had the same ambitions/And in the same way to accept their
517 CC Colby	12	illusions/About himself, and without ambitions./Now that I've abandoned *my*
517 CC Colby	13	that I've abandoned *my* illusions and ambitions/All that's left is love. But not on false
529 ES Monica	8	you,/With the same hopes, the same ambitions —/And of his disappointments./{C}
551 ES Carghil	30	Parliament:/His father has political ambitions for him./If he's lost a breach of

AMBLE (1)

525 ES Monica	23	/And besides, my father doesn't amble./You're not at all respectful./{C} I try to

AMBLING (1)

525 ES Charles	21	Before I've said two words he'll come ambling in .../{M} You've said a good deal more

AMBUSH (2)

202 War Poetry	19	accepted,/A problem to be met with ambush and stratagem,/Enveloped or scattered
348 FR Chorus	32	is the meaning of happening?/What ambush lies beyond the heather/And behind the

AMEN (2)

260 MC Thomas	3	of the Son, and of the Holy Ghost. Amen./Dear children of God, my sermon this
262 MC Thomas	5	of the Son, and of the Holy Ghost. Amen./Part II/{C} Does the bird sing in the

AMENDED (1)

268 MC Knight2	26	were suspended./{K2} By you be this amended./{K3} Absolve them./{K1} Absolve

AMENDS (1)

20 Portrait	69	my hat: how can I make a cowardly amends/For what she has said to me?/You will

AMENITIES (1)

547 ES Piggott	21	I ought to tell you more/About the amenities which Badgley Court/Can offer to

AMERICA (2)

388 CP Edward	37	we talk about?/{E} Peter's going to America./{P} Yes, and I would have rung you
563 ES Ld Clav	4	He comes from some place in Central America./{MC} How romantic! I'd love to meet

AMERICAN (6)

119 SP Wauch	5	want you to meet two friends of ours,/American gentlemen here on business./Meet
291 FR Violet	5	helping Lady Bumpus, at the Vicar's American Tea./{Ch} Yet we are here at Amy's
470 CC Lucasta	24	I invited you .../{L} To go to see that American Musical!/{C} Well, I'd heard you say
470 CC Lucasta	30	/{L} Because you don't like them —/American Musicals. Do you think it's any
533 ES Gomez	21	a highly respected citizen/Of a central American republic: San Marco./It's as hard to
570 ES Ld Clav	26	/He's Federico Gomez, the Central American,/A man who's made a fortune by his

AMÉRIQUE (1)

47 Mél Adult	1	/Mélange Adultère de Tout/En Amérique, professeur;/En Angleterre,

AMITY (2)

247 MC Templ1	3	/Now that the King and you are in amity,/Clergy and laity may return to gaiety,/
301 FR Chorus	20	do we huddle together/In a horrid amity of misfortune? why should we be

AMMONITE (1)

158 Rock 5	2	the Horonite and Tobiah the Ammonite and Geshem the Arabian: were

AMMUNITION (1)

127 Cor1 March	20	/24,000 aeroplane engines,/50,000 ammunition waggons,/now 55,000 army

AMONG (57)

15 Prufrock	89	the cups, the marmalade, the tea,/Among the porcelain, among some talk of you
15 Prufrock	89	the tea,/Among the porcelain, among some talk of you and me,/Would it have
18 Portrait	1	us, and drown./Portrait of a Lady/Among the smoke and fog of a December
18 Portrait	11	his soul/Should be resurrected only among friends/Some two or three, who will not
18 Portrait	15	/— And so the conversation slips/Among velleities and carefully caught regrets/
19 Portrait	29	friendships — life, what *cauchemar!*/Among the windings of the violins/And the
20 Portrait	92	much to learn.'/My smile falls heavily among the bric-à-brac./'Perhaps you can write
31 Apollinax	2	the United States/His laughter tinkled among the teacups./I thought of Fragilion, that
31 Apollinax	3	I thought of Fragilion, that shy figure among the birch-trees,/And of Priapus in the
37 Gerontion	16	gutter./I an old man,/A dull head among windy spaces./Signs are taken for
37 Gerontion	23	be eaten, to be divided, to be drunk/Among whispers; by Mr. Silvero/With caressing
37 Gerontion	26	next room;/By Hakagawa, bowing among the Titians;/By Madame de Tornquist,
50 Hippopot	31	/And him shall heavenly arms enfold,/Among the saints he shall be seen/Performing
56 Swee Night	t	Are controversial, polymath./Sweeney Among the Nightingales/Apeneck Sweeney
69 WL: Fire S	246	by Thebes below the wall/And walked among the lowest of the dead.)/Bestows one

72 WL: Thund	333	sandy road/The road winding above among the mountains/Which are mountains of
72 WL: Thund	351	water/And water/A spring/A pool among the rock/If there were the sound of water
73 WL: Thund	385	exhausted wells./In this decayed hole among the mountains/In the faint moonlight,
94 Ash-Wed 4	7	of eternal dolour/Who moved among the others as they walked,/Who then
96 Ash-Wed 5	19	No time to rejoice for those who walk among noise and deny the voice/Will the veiled
98 Ash-Wed 6	29	not to care/Teach us to sit still/Even among these rocks,/Our peace in His will/And
99 Ash-Wed 6	31	/Our peace in His will/And even among these rocks/Sister, mother/And spirit of
129 Cor2 State	36	droops over the lintel/O mother (not among these busts, all correctly inscribed)/I a
129 Cor2 State	37	all correctly inscribed)/I a tired head among these heads/Necks strong to bear them/
155 Rock 3	43	the LORD./Shall we lift up our feet among perpetual ruins?/I have loved the beauty
162 Rock 8	11	Hermit, scourging with words./And among his hearers were a few good men,/Many
164 Rock 9	6	quavering lowly, whispering faintly,/Among a few flickering scattered lights?/They
166 Rock 10	10	eyes to plumb. Come/Ye out from among those who prize the serpent's golden
172 FQ: BurntN	63	their pattern as before/But reconciled among the stars./At the still point of the turning
185 FQ: DrySal	60	itself the emotionless/Years of living among the breakage/Of what was believed in as
187 FQ: DrySal	127	if that is what Krishna meant —/Among other things — or one way of putting
588 Fable	48	puddings,/And jellies, pasties, cakes among the good things./A mighty peacock
599 On a Port	1	we knew long ago./On a Portrait/Among a crowd of tenuous dreams, unknown/
605 Narcissus	22	had been a tree,/Twisting its branches among each other/And tangling its roots among
605 Narcissus	23	each other/And tangling its roots among each other./Then he knew that he had
242 MC Priest1	23	despising, always isolated,/Never one among them, always insecure;/His pride always
244 MC Chorus	27	and assured of your fate, unaffrayed among the shades, do you realise what you ask,
244 MC Chorus	28	of fate, the small folk who live among small things,/The strain on the brain of
250 MC Thomas	5	/To condemn kings, not serve among their servants,/Is my open office. No!
252 MC Thomas	20	doves/Now take the shape of a wolf among wolves?/Pursue your treacheries as you
261 MC Thomas	17	rejoice, that another soul is/numbered among the Saints in Heaven, for the glory of
263 MC Chorus	13	there not peace upon earth, goodwill among men?/The peace of this world is always
263 MC Chorus	15	men keep the peace of God./And war among men defiles this world, but death in the
296 FR Charles	25	this notion grow in his mind,/Living among strangers, with no one to talk to./I
296 FR Amy	32	believe that a few days at Wishwood/Among his own family, is all that he needs./{G}
301 FR Gerald	22	concerned for herself, and her credit among her shabby genteel acquaintance./{V}
311 FR Harry	32	/Thinking of something else, puts me among you./I tell you, it is not me you are
335 FR Harry	24	/{H} To and fro, dragging my feet/Among inner shadows in the smoky wilderness,/
340 FR Agatha	8	I get? thirty years of solitude,/Alone, among women, in a women's college,/Trying
363 CP Reilly	12	you really feel./What you really are among other people./Most of the time we have
376 CP Edward	22	of that before./{E} The man who fell among thieves was luckier than I:/He was left at
429 CP Julia	15	dine out on eating Christians —/Even among pagans!/{A} Not on the *whole* story./{E}
434 CP Alex	12	And then, the insurrection broke out/Among the heathen, of which I was telling you./
464 CC Claude	11	/For me, they are life itself. To be among such things,/If it is an escape, is escape
528 ES Charles	5	/{C} But he's most alive when he's among people/Managing, manœuvring, cajoling
547 ES Ld Clav	14	there's a Mrs. Piggott/There may be, among the guests, something worse than Mrs.
547 ES Piggott	23	/When there are enough young people among us/We dance in the evening. At the

AMONGST (3)

72 WL: Thund	336	were water we should stop and drink/Amongst the rock one cannot stop or think/
72 WL: Thund	338	in the sand/If there were only water amongst the rock/Dead mountain mouth of
427 CP Alex	38	become the pretext/For general unrest amongst the natives./{E} But how do the

AMOUNT (1)

403 CP Reilly	10	/And you would go on, doing such amount of mischief/As lay within your power —

AMOUR (1)

46 Directeur	22	Spectateur/Conservateur/Et crève d'amour./Mélange Adultère de Tout/En

AMSTERDAM (1)

450 CC Claude	23	I'll leave you./I must telephone to Amsterdam, and possibly to Paris./But when

AMUSE (1)

194 FQ: Little	139	/Of laughter at what ceases to amuse./And last, the rending pain of

AMUSED (1)

454 CC Colby	35	amuses him./{C} Well, perhaps I'll be amused./But it did make my head spin — all

AMUSES (1)

454 CC Eggers	34	And do you know —/I think it amuses him./{C} Well, perhaps I'll be amused./

AMUSING (1)

44 Cook Egg	19	my Bride;/Her anecdotes will be more amusing/Than Pipit's experience could provide./

AMY (37)

284 FR	m 2	/THE FAMILY REUNION/Persons/AMY, DOWAGER LADY MONCHENSEY,
285 FR	4m 1	*An afternoon in late March.*/Scene I/AMY, IVY, VIOLET, AGATHA, GERALD,
285 FR Agatha	13	Wishwood was always a cold place, Amy./{I} I have always told Amy she should go
285 FR Ivy	14	place, Amy./{I} I have always told Amy she should go south in the winter./Were I

285 FR	Charles	24	at all. We are country-bred people./Amy has been too long used to our ways/Living
286 FR	Violet	14	never,/Even could I do it as well as Amy:/England's bad enough, I would never go
287 FR	Gerald	22	said the better./{G} That reminds me, Amy,/When are the boys all due to arrive?/{A} I
288 FR	Ivy	4	will you have your birthday cake, Amy,/And open your presents?/{A} After
293 FR	Ivy	11	advice when I'm dead./{I} Oh, dear Amy!/No one wants you to die, I'm sure!/Now
296 FR	Gerald	33	is all that he needs./{G} Nevertheless, Amy, there's something in Violet's suggestion./
297 FR	Violet	32	us nowhere,/And which I am sure Amy would disapprove of —/I only wish to
302 FR	m	13	no news of Arthur or John. {}/[*Enter* AMY *and* AGATHA]/{A} It is very annoying.
303 FR	Agatha	15	And also Dr. Warburton. At least, Amy has invited him./{M} Dr. Warburton? I
304 FR	Mary	15	know perfectly well,/What Cousin Amy wants, she usually gets./Why do *you* so
304 FR	Mary	28	when *she* died: I believed that Cousin Amy —/I almost believed it — had killed her by
304 FR	Agatha	34	only one Harry asked to his wedding:/Amy did not know that. I was sorry for her;/I
313 FR	Violet	26	yet?/{V} Neither of them is here yet, Amy. {}/[*Enter* AMY, *with* DR.
313 FR	m	27	of them is here yet, Amy. {}/[*Enter* AMY, *with* DR. WARBURTON]/{A} It is
315 FR	m	29	bring me the same honour. {}/[*Exeunt* AMY, DR. WARBURTON, HARRY]/{Ch} I
323 FR	m	7	you? Is it Arthur or John? {}/[*Enter* AMY, *followed severally by* VIOLET, IVY,
323 FR	Gerald	26	of luck./{G} I'll go down and see him, Amy, and come back and report to you./{A} I
323 FR	Charles	34	Much better leave it to Warburton, Amy./Extremely fortunate for us that he's here./
325 FR	m	4	be very tired. {}/[*Exeunt* HARRY *and* AMY]/{V} I really do not understand Harry's
325 FR	Gerald	13	am really more afraid of the shock for Amy;/But I think that Warburton understands
326 FR	Gerald	7	is reckless./{G} I wonder how much Amy knows about Arthur?/{C} More than she
328 FR	Gerald	30	to be awkward, explaining this to Amy./{I} Poor Arthur! I'm sure that you're
337 FR	m	30	must go./{Ag} You must go. {}/[*Enter* AMY]/{A} What are you saying to Harry? He
340 FR	2m	1	the bright angels. {}/[*Exit*]/Scene III/AMY, AGATHA/{A} I was a fool, to ask you
341 FR	Agatha	1	it is my son./{Ag} I know one thing, Amy:/That you have never changed. And
342 FR	Mary	4	MARY/{M} Excuse me, Cousin Amy. I have just seen Denman./She came to tell
343 FR	m	31	the wind and rain do that. {}/[*While* AMY *has been speaking*, HARRY *has entered*,
344 FR	Violet	11	unaccountable./What *has* happened, Amy?/{A} Harry is going away — to become a
345 FR	Gerald	29	you can leave me./{G} Oh, certainly, Amy./{V} I do not understand/A single thing
345 FR	m	31	thing that's happened. {}/[*Exeunt* AMY, VIOLET, GERALD]/{C} It's very odd,/
347 FR	Ivy	18	was wondering/Whether to show it to Amy or not. {}/[*Reads*]/{I} 'Regret delayed
347 FR	Ivy	21	of what did happen,/Do you think Amy ought to see it?/{V} No, certainly not./You
347 FR	Violet	25	not understand, so how could you? Amy is not well;/And she is resting./{I} Oh, I'm

AMY'S (6)

284 FR	m	6	/HARRY, LORD MONCHENSEY, *Amy's eldest son*/DOWNING, *his servant and*
285 FR	Ivy	15	go south in the winter./Were I in Amy's position, I would go south in the winter./
285 FR	Charles	23	stewed bad Indian tea./{C} That's not Amy's style at all. We are country-bred people./
289 FR	Gerald	5	/I must say, this isn't cheerful for Amy's birthday/Or for Harry's homecoming.
291 FR	Chorus	6	Tea./{Ch} Yet we are here at Amy's command, to play an unread part in
301 FR	Charles	24	/{C} Violet is afraid that her status as Amy's sister will be diminished./{Ch} We all of

AN (314)

ANÆSTHESIA (1)

294 FR	Harry	21	of light and darkness;/The partial anæsthesia of suffering without feeling/And

ANALYSIS (1)

364 CP	Edward	9	I am./And what is the use of all your analysis/If I am to remain always lost in the

ANATHEMA (1)

268 MC	Knight2	9	/{K2} Binding with the chains of anathema./{K3} Using every means in your

ANCESTORS' (1)

201 Def	Island	17	in triumph, changing nothing/of their ancestors' ways but the weapons/and those

ANCESTRY (1)

485 CC	Lady E	18	reincarnate. And that one's real ancestry/Is one's previous existences. Of course,

ANCHORITE (1)

152 Rock 2		41	not lived in praise of GOD./Even the anchorite who meditates alone,/For whom the

ANCIENT (7)

23 Preludes		53	and laugh;/The worlds revolve like ancient women/Gathering fuel in vacant lots./
94 Ash-Wed 4		18	years, restoring/With a new verse the ancient rhyme. Redeem/The time. Redeem/The
141 Rannoch		6	hot. The road winds in/Listlessness of ancient war,/Languor of broken steel,/Clamour
160 Rock 7		14	of life,/And they came to the withered ancient look of a child that has died of
605 Narcissus		26	/Writhing in his own clutch, his ancient beauty/Caught fast in the pink tips of
294 FR	Harry	3	/The unspoken voice of sorrow in the ancient bedroom/At three o'clock in the
575 ES	Gomez	18	/You're wasting your time, rehearsing ancient history./Michael knows it already. I've

AND (3926)

ANECDOTES (2)

44 Cook Egg		19	Borgia shall be my Bride;/Her anecdotes will be more amusing/Than Pipit's
228 Gus		14	them, if someone else pays,/With anecdotes drawn from his palmiest days./For he

ANEMONE (1)
184 FQ: DrySal   21   /The more delicate algae and the sea anemone./It tosses up our losses, the torn seine,/
ANEW (2)
590 Time Space   13   the eglantine./So let us haste to pluck anew/Nor mourn to see them pine,/And though
590 Space Time   13   eglantine./But let us haste to pluck anew/Nor mourn to see them pine,/And though
ANFRACTUOUS (1)
42 Swee Erect   3   unstilled Cyclades,/Paint me the bold anfractuous rocks/Faced by the snarled and
ANGEL (6)
111 Xmas Trees   6   the candle is a star, and the gilded angel/Spreading its wings at the summit of the
111 Xmas Trees   8   tree/Is not only a decoration, but an angel./The child wonders at the Christmas Tree:
259 MC Thomas   6   to the sword's end./Now my good Angel, whom God appoints/To be my guardian,
398 CP Edward   8   And then you came back, you/The angel of destruction — just as I felt sure./In a
478 CC Kaghan   38   intuitions! I'm your guardian angel,/Colby, to protect you from Lucasta./{L}
479 CC Lucasta   1   Lucasta./{L} You're *my* guardian angel at the moment, B./You're to take me out
ANGEL (23) [*Proper name*]
444 CC   m 6   /B. KAGHAN/LUCASTA ANGEL/LADY ELIZABETH
449 CC Eggers   21   never been able to make her like Miss Angel;/She becomes abstracted, whenever I
449 CC Claude   23   But she knew about Lucasta — Miss Angel, from the start./That was one difficulty.
449 CC Claude   27   think she takes much notice of Miss Angel./She just doesn't see her. And Miss Angel
449 CC Claude   28   /She just doesn't see her. And Miss Angel/Will soon be getting married, I expect./
452 CC   m 11   the sidelines. {}/[*Enter* LUCASTA ANGEL]/{L} Eggy, I've lost my job!/{E} Again,
452 CC Eggers   12   I've lost my job!/{E} Again, Miss Angel?/{L} Yes, again! And serve them right!/
452 CC Eggers   25   other of you./{E} Mr. Simpkins, Miss Angel. As you know, Miss Angel,/Mr. Simpkins
452 CC Eggers   25   Miss Angel. As you know, Miss Angel,/Mr. Simpkins has taken over my duties./
452 CC Lucasta 30   Lucasta./It's only Eggy calls me Miss Angel,/Just to annoy me. Don't you agree/That
452 CC Lucasta 35   of being cursed with a name like Angel./I'm thinking of changing it. But, Colby,/
453 CC Eggers   2   do. I always say/That if you give Miss Angel an inch/She'll take an ell./{L} L. for
453 CC Eggers   19   leave Mrs. Eggerson out of this, Miss Angel./{L} That's what he always says, Colby,/
454 CC Colby   23   But you never warned me about Miss Angel./What about *her*?/{E} Oh, Miss Angel./
454 CC Eggers   25   Angel./What about *her*?/{E} Oh, Miss Angel./She's rather flighty. But she has a good
455 CC Colby   7   /But tell me about Lu ... Miss Angel/What's her connection with this
455 CC Colby   29   Well, I've never met anyone like Miss Angel./{E} You'll get used to her, Mr. Simpkins.
455 CC Colby   36   /Can be quite so unusual as Miss Angel./{E} O yes, Mr. Simpkins, much more
482 CC Lady E   10   friendly/With Mr. Kaghan and Miss Angel./I can see you've lived a rather sheltered
500 CC Eggers   1   your brother./{E} Half-brother, Miss Angel./{SC} Yes, half-brother./{L} What do you
501 CC Eggers   28   must take the occasion/To wish Miss Angel every happiness./And I'm sure she will be
501 CC Eggers   31   a heart of gold. So have you, Miss Angel./We have this very important interview,/
503 CC Eggers   19   /{E} And now may I interrupt, Miss Angel?/Why shouldn't you and Mr. Kaghan
ANGELES (1)
430 CP Peter   6   New York last night —/I left Los Angeles three days ago./I saw Sheila Paisley at
ANGELIC (1)
260 MC Thomas   24   of/War? Does it seem to you that the angelic voices were mistaken, and/that the
ANGELS (3)
50 Hippopot   27   the damp savannas,/And quiring angels round him sing/The praise of God, in
260 MC Thomas   22   Does/it seem strange to you that the angels should have announced Peace,/when
339 FR Harry   22   given./I must follow the bright angels. {}/[*Exit*]/Scene III/AMY, AGATHA/{A}
ANGELUS (1)
189 FQ: DrySal 187   the sound of the sea bell's/Perpetual angelus./To communicate with Mars, converse
ANGER (2)
253 MC Tempt4   15   /Is still more stubborn than king's anger./Kings have public policy, barons private
279 MC Knight4 35   long enough to allow our righteous/anger to cool. That was just what he did not
ANGEVIN (1)
251 MC Tempt3   25   land for Norman/Sovereignty. Let the Angevin/Destroy himself, fighting in Anjou./He
ANGLE (2)
150 Rock 1   101   *untilled/Where the plough rests, at an angle/To the furrow. In this land/There shall be*
508 CC Eggers   15   approach the question from another angle,/And ask Mrs. Guzzard what became of
ANGLES (1)
254 MC Tempt4   27   prayers,/Sometimes hesitating at the angles of stairs,/And between sleep and waking,
ANGLETERRE (1)
47 Mél Adult   2   de Tout/En Amérique, professeur;/En Angleterre, journaliste;/C'est à grands pas et en
ANGRY (3)
428 CP Julia   6   /And in a *couchette*. She was very angry/When I told her the creature ought to be
531 ES Lambert 37   want to see him. Said you'd be very angry/If you heard that he'd gone away without
561 ES Monica   23   has happened? Why do you look so angry?/I know that Michael must be in great

ANGUISH (1)
52 Whispers   13   beyond experience,/He knew the anguish of the marrow/The ague of the
ANIMAL (1)
271 MC Chorus   2   flesh of nature,/Mastered by the animal powers of spirit,/Dominated by the lust
ANIMALS (1)
109 Marina   12   /Those who suffer the ecstasy of the animals, meaning/Death/Are become
ANIMULA (1)
107 Animula   t   depart,/Having seen thy salvation./Animula/'Issues from the hand of God, the
ANJOU (2)
251 MC Tempt3   20   /King is in France, squabbling in Anjou;/Round him waiting hungry sons./We are
251 MC Tempt3   26   Angevin/Destroy himself, fighting in Anjou./He does not understand us, the English
ANN (1)
142 Cape Ann   t   pass/No concurrence of bone./Cape Ann/O quick quick quick, quick hear the
ANNIVERSARY (2)
496 CC Eggers   37   season,/When we're getting near the anniversary./{SC} The anniversary? Of your
496 CC Claude   38   near the anniversary./{SC} The anniversary? Of your son's death?/{E} Of the
ANNOUNCED (2)
260 MC Thomas   22   to you that the angels should have announced Peace,/when ceaselessly the world
504 CC Claude   26   incompetence./You should have been announced./{MG} I believe I was punctual./But
ANNOUNCEMENT (1)
499 CC Lucasta   18   such a support./In any case, I've an announcement to make,/And I might as well
ANNOUNCING (1)
511 CC Lady E   36   /{LE} And I'm very glad you're announcing your engagement./Lucasta, I shall
ANNOY (1)
452 CC Lucasta   31   Eggy calls me Miss Angel,/Just to annoy me. Don't you agree/That Lucasta suits
ANNOYANCE (1)
513 CC Colby   16   I wanted was relief/From the nagging annoyance of knowing there's a fact/That one
ANNOYED (1)
447 CC Claude   24   /But if she appears to be puzzled, or annoyed/At my making the appointment during
ANNOYING (2)
302 FR Amy   13   AMY *and* AGATHA]/{A} It is very annoying. They both promised to be here/In
302 FR Amy   14   /In good time for dinner. It is very annoying./Now they can hardly arrive in time to
ANNUAL (2)
111 Xmas Trees   29   last)/The accumulated memories of annual emotion/May be concentrated into a
129 Cor2 State   13   of one pound ten a week rising by annual increments of five shillings/To two
ANNUITY (2)
357 CP Edward   17   /{E} No, I think she put it all into an annuity./{J} So it's very unselfish of Lavinia/Yet
357 CP Julia   39   be *your* maiden aunt —/Living on an annuity, of course./I am going to make you dine
ANNUNCIATION (3)
185 FQ: DrySal   56   unprayable/Prayer at the calamitous annunciation?/There is no end, but addition: the
186 FQ: DrySal   68   /Clamour of the bell of the last annunciation./Where is the end of them, the
186 FQ: DrySal   86   barely prayable/Prayer of the one Annunciation./It seems, as one becomes older,/
ANONYMOUS (1)
538 ES Gomez   17   /{G} No, in England mistakes are anonymous/Because the man who accepts
ANOTHER (139)
20 Portrait   76   was murdered at a Polish dance,/Another bank defaulter has confessed./I keep
52 Whispers   9   luxuries./Donne, I suppose, was such another/Who found no substitute for sense,/To
64 WL: Chess   81   which a golden Cupidon peeped out/(Another hid his eyes behind his wing)/Doubled
73 WL: Thund   362   up the white road/There is always another one walking beside you/Gliding wrapt
104 Journ Magi   43   their gods./I should be glad of another death./A Song for Simeon/Lord, the
109 Marina   26   canvas rotten/Between one June and another September./Made this unknowing, half
124 SA Sweeney   27   get pinched in the end/But that's another story too./This went on for a couple of
163 Rock 8   30   lives,/The broken faith in one place or another,/There was something left that was
178 FQ: ECoker   48   Dung and death./Dawn points, and another day/Prepares for heat and silence. Out
179 FQ: ECoker   97   fear of possession,/Of belonging to another, or to others, or to God./The only
183 FQ: ECoker   207   We must be still and still moving/Into another intensity/For a further union, a deeper
186 FQ: DrySal   88   one becomes older,/That the past has another pattern, and ceases to be a mere
194 FQ: Little   121   /And next year's words await another voice./But, as the passage now presents
195 FQ: Little   167   /To become renewed, transfigured, in another pattern./Sin is Behovely, but/All shall
203 Indians   13   is home to one man/And exile to another. Where a man dies bravely/At one with
226 Macavity   24   rifled,/Or when the milk is missing, or another Peke's been stifled,/Or the greenhouse
230 Bust Jones   30   Bustopher's day —/At one club or another he's found./It can be no surprise that
240 MC Chorus   10   streams/And the poor shall wait for another decaying October./Why should the
240 MC Chorus   14   /But wait in barren orchards for another October?/Some malady is coming upon
240 MC Priest2   33   unended or endless/At one place or another in France?/{P3} I see nothing quite

242 MC	Mess	1	kingdom:/But as for our King, that is another matter./{P1} But again, is it war or
243 MC	Chorus	34	is good,/One year is a year of rain,/Another a year of dryness,/One year the apples
244 MC	Chorus	1	/One year the apples are abundant,/Another year the plums are lacking./Yet we
246 MC	Thomas	7	of their prevision/I sent my letters on another day,/Had fair crossing, found at
252 MC	Tempt3	24	at your door./And I well hope, before another spring/The King will show his regard
254 MC	Tempt4	11	death./When king is dead, there's another king,/And one more king is another
254 MC	Tempt4	12	another king,/And one more king is another reign./King is forgotten, when another
254 MC	Tempt4	13	reign./King is forgotten, when another shall come:/Saint and Martyr rule from
254 MC	Tempt4	22	grace,/And think of your enemies, in another place./{T} I have thought of these
261 MC	Thomas	16	has martyred them; we rejoice, that another soul is/numbered among the Saints in
262 MC	Thomas	2	that in a short time you may have yet another martyr,/and that one perhaps not the
262 MC	Thomas	4	words that I say, and think of them at another time. In the Name/of the Father, and of
265 MC	Priest1	1	/{P1} To-day, what is to-day? but another day, the dusk of the year./{P2} To-day,
265 MC	Priest2	2	the year./{P2} To-day, what is to-day? Another night, and another dawn./{P3} What
265 MC	Priest3	2	what is to-day? Another night, and another dawn./{P3} What day is the day that we
265 MC	Priest3	5	hope from. One moment/Weighs like another. Only in retrospection, selection,/We
271 MC	Thomas	11	This is one moment,/But know that another/Shall pierce you with a sudden painful
278 MC	Knight2	33	social justice can be secured. At another time, you would/condemn an
279 MC	Knight1	7	one more speaker, who has I think another point of view/to express. If there are
281 MC	Priest3	6	ascend/To God, who has given us another Saint in Canterbury. {}/[while a Te
288 FR	Agatha	33	I mean that at Wishwood he will find another Harry./The man who returns will have
289 FR	Amy	18	/If he wants to talk about it, that's another matter;/But I don't believe he will. He
293 FR	Harry	17	/Or if you want to pretend that I am another person —/A person that you have
306 FR	Harry	21	I might escape from one life to another,/And it may be all one life, with no
307 FR	Mary	22	of older people —They lived in another world, which did not touch me./Just
308 FR	Harry	2	/{H} What I see/May be one dream or another; if there is nothing else/The most real is
308 FR	Mary	14	awful it must be./But in this world another hope keeps springing/In an unexpected
310 FR	Harry	37	sure/That every corridor only led to another,/Or to a blank wall; that I kept moving/
311 FR	Harry	6	a sweet and bitter smell/From another world. I know it, I know it!/More
314 FR	Harry	20	to health;/Is only incubation of another malady./{W} You mustn't take such a
314 FR	Warburt	25	/To do away with one disease or another./Now I've had forty years' experience/
314 FR	Warburt	28	/We're all of us ill in one way or another:/We call it health when we find no
317 FR	Warburt	2	alone with you, Harry./In fact, I had another reason for coming this evening/Than
319 FR	Harry	6	him mentioned, but in some way or another/We felt that he was always here./But
320 FR	Warburt	16	off at any moment./If she had been another woman/She would not have lived until
327 FR	Harry	14	/Or any other doctor, who would be another Warburton,/If you decided to set
327 FR	Harry	15	Warburton,/If you decided to set another doctor on me./But this is too real for
327 FR	Harry	17	words to alter./Oh, there *must* be another way of talking/That would get us
330 FR	Harry	24	numbness came to cover it — that is another —/That was the second hell of not
332 FR	Agatha	30	God, that kind. Perhaps there is another kind,/I believe, across a whole Thibet of
334 FR	Harry	26	upon me;/And I returned to find another one made ready —/The book laid out,
341 FR	Amy	20	what you would make for him/Is another. I call it failure. Your fury for
342 FR	Agatha	17	/It is inexplicable, the resolution is in another./{M} Oh, but it is the danger comes
342 FR	Mary	18	Oh, but it is the danger comes from another!/Can you not stop him? Cousin Agatha,
343 FR	Agatha	2	side,/For him, danger and safety have another meaning./*They* have made this clear.
349 FR	2m	13	*and set a small portable table./From another door, enter* DENMAN *carrying a*
355 CP	Julia	27	*with a tray*]/{J} Edward, give me another of those delicious olives./What's that?
356 CP	Julia	17	host,/But just try to pretend you're another guest/At Lavinia's party. There are so
357 CP	Edward	6	/{J} Is that her Aunt Laura?/{E} No; another aunt/Whom you wouldn't know. Her
360 CP	Reilly	9	{UG} This is an occasion./May I take another drink?/{E} Whisky?/{UG} Gin./{E}
360 CP	Reilly	29	—/None that I know of./{UG} Or another woman/Of whom she thought she had
360 CP	Reilly	33	no doubt it's all for the best./With another man, she might have made a mistake/
360 CP	Reilly	34	/And want to come back to you. If another woman,/She might decide to be
360 CP	Reilly	39	that she won't come back at all./If another man, then you'd want to re-marry/To
361 CP	Reilly	1	world that somebody wanted you;/If another woman, you might have to marry her
362 CP	Edward	11	thought I should be any happier/With another person. Why speak of love?/We were
369 CP	Alex	11	goes *that* surprise. I must think of another./{P} Not very often./And when I did, I
370 CP	Alex	16	Lavinia hates curry./{A} There goes another surprise, then. I must think./I didn't
370 CP	Edward	36	/You would have found that she was another woman/And that you were another
370 CP	Edward	37	another woman/And that you were another man. I congratulate you/On a timely
371 CP	Edward	8	have happened to you with Celia/In another six months' time. There it is./You can
372 CP	Edward	20	proof./{E} No, no ... I mean, this is another aunt./{A} I understand. The real aunt.
372 CP	Alex	28	simmering./Don't leave it longer than another ten minutes./Now I'll be going, and I'll
378 CP	Celia	28	/Because your wife has left you for another man?/I shall soon put that right,
382 CP	Celia	13	always thrilled me,/And it became another voice — no, not a voice:/What I heard

382 CP	Celia	26	Of what I had thought you were. I see another person,/I see you as a person whom I
384 CP	Reilly	21	That is one consideration./And another is this: it is a serious matter/To bring
395 CP	Lavinia	29	soon get over it/And find yourself another little part to play,/With another face, to
395 CP	Lavinia	30	another little part to play,/With another face, to take people in./{E} One of the
396 CP	Edward	33	yourself responsible for me:/It's only another kind of contempt./And I do not want
401 CP	Edward	6	person:/But I dismissed that as just another symptom./Well, I should have known
405 CP	Reilly	5	the exception./I have recently had another patient/Whose situation is much the
405 CP	Edward	11	—/I will not discuss my case before another patient./{R} On the contrary. That is
408 CP	Reilly	35	revelations/About each of you, to one another,/Have not been of anything that you
410 CP	Lavinia	11	be just enough to make us loathe one another./{R} See it rather as the bond which
418 CP	Reilly	20	then I feel just hopeless./{R} There *is* another way, if you have the courage./The first
431 CP	Peter	25	so as to reproduce it./Then we build another Boltwell in California./{J} But what is
432 CP	Julia	3	Harcourt-Reilly!/{J} Oh, I forgot! I'd another surprise for you. {}/[*Enter* REILLY]/{J}
433 CP	Peter	20	casting director./I've got an idea for another film./Can you tell me where she is? I
439 CP	Julia	10	makes a choice, of one kind or another,/And then must take the consequences.
440 CP	Alex	17	don't *want* you to go!/{A} We have another engagement./{R} And on this occasion I
447 CC	Claude	31	a quick decision/Because he'd had another very tempting offer./Something like
454 CC	Lucasta	14	this crisis/Has been too much for me. Another time, Colby./I'll ring you up, and let
458 CC	Eggers	31	.../{E} And at the same time, he had another tempting offer:/So we had to make a
475 CC	Colby	17	.../{C} Is, beginning to understand another person./{L} Oh Colby, now that we
478 CC	Lucasta	3	make you his heir/And you'll marry another Lady Elizabeth./But in that event,
489 CC	Claude	8	And mine I couldn't lose. But if I had another/I thought you might think — 'and how
492 CC	Colby	17	want to touch it again./But there's another reason. I must remind you/About your
497 CC	Eggers	34	say so. Of course, we might discover/Another Mrs. Guzzard .../{LE} *Two* Mrs.
498 CC	Eggers	19	baby./{E} She might have taken in another one/As a temporary accommodation —
498 CC	Eggers	33	we must try to trace./{E} If there was another child/Then we must try to trace it.
499 CC	Claude	14	in this meeting, Lucasta./Won't it do another time?/{L} I came to apologise/To
499 CC	Lucasta	16	/To Colby. No matter. It'll do another time./Oh, I'm glad you're here, Eggy!
508 CC	Eggers	15	/Let us approach the question from another angle,/And ask Mrs. Guzzard what
513 CC	Colby	22	his foster-parents,/So he can afford another relationship./Let my mother rest in
517 CC	Eggers	28	months ago. We've been looking for another./{C} Do you think that they would give
518 CC	Eggers	5	/I think you'll come to find you've another vocation./We worked together every
518 CC	Guzzard	39	have all had your wish/In one form or another. You and I, Sir Claude,/Had *our* wishes
532 ES	Ld Clav	35	/Why do you come back with another name?/{G} You've changed your name
535 ES	Gomez	30	away,/Thousands of miles away, to another climate,/To another language, other
535 ES	Gomez	31	of miles away, to another climate,/To another language, other standards of behaviour,
535 ES	Gomez	32	of behaviour,/To fabricate for myself another personality/And to take another name.
535 ES	Gomez	33	another personality/And to take another name. Think what that means —/To
535 ES	Gomez	34	Think what that means —/To take another name. {}/[*Gets up and helps himself to*
538 ES	Gomez	21	you made it/You simply get moved to another post/Where at least you can't make
539 ES	Gomez	7	/You should have been good for another five years/At least. Why did they let
539 ES	Ld Clav	10	I had had a stroke./And I might have another./{G} Yes. You might have another./But
539 ES	Gomez	11	another./{G} Yes. You might have another./But I wonder what brought about this
539 ES	Gomez	39	.../{G} A worldly success, Dick. In another sense/We're both of us failures. But
542 ES	Gomez	1	say your caller/Could hang on for another quarter of an hour./{LC} Before you go
547 ES	Piggott	1	our nurses 'Nurse' reassures them/In another respect./{LC} I follow you perfectly./
550 ES	Carghil	14	/You're more than likely to make another'./How true that is! Algy was a
555 ES	Ld Clav	22	walking./{LC} I hope he's not had another accident./You know, after that last
561 ES	Ld Clav	13	the coward —/I should merely be another twenty years in dying./{Mi} Very well: if
562 ES	Carghil	37	it. But who's this coming?/It's another new guest here. He's waving to us./Do
567 ES	Charles	17	engaged to you for ever./{C} There's another shopping expedition we must make!/
571 ES	Ld Clav	37	in the road/And I did not stop. Then another man ran over him./A lorry driver. He
574 ES	Michael	34	/You got me here in London? With another Sir Alfred/Who'd constitute himself
577 ES	Charles	1	to invoke it./And, Michael, here's another point to think of:/Señor Gomez has

ANOTHER'S (1)

193 FQ: Little	100	a double part, and cried/And heard another's voice cry: 'What! are *you* here?'/

ANS (1)

51 Restaurant	10	averse, qu'on s'abrite./J'avais sept ans, elle était plus petite./Elle était toute

ANSWER (26)

90 Ash-Wed 1	31	hope to turn again/Let these words answer/For what is done, not to be done again/
148 Rock 1	40	/The Rock. Who will perhaps answer our doubtings./The Rock. The Watcher.
155 Rock 3	54	you love each other?'/What will you answer? 'We all dwell together/To make money
235 Ash-dress	35	/He's such an easy-going lout,/He'll answer any hail or shout./Again I must remind
268 MC Knight1	15	therefore if you will be content/To answer in the King's presence. Therefore were
269 MC Knight1	24	man, in the King's name./{K1} Or answer with your bodies./{K2} Enough of

278 MC Knight2   5   what are King Henry's aims? In/the answer to these questions lies the key to the
323 FR Warburt 31   /At this time of night, I would not answer for the consequences/I am going myself.
349 FR Chorus   5   questions/There is no conceivable answer./We have suffered far more than a
363 CP Edward 28   'My wife has gone away'?/And they answer 'Where?' and I say 'I don't know';/And
363 CP Edward 32   what are you going to do?'/And I answer 'Nothing'. They will think me mad/Or
364 CP Reilly 19   is not worth the trouble of an answer./But if I bring her back it must be on
364 CP Edward 29 her. { }/[*The doorbell rings*]/{E} I must answer the door. { }/[EDWARD *goes to the*
374 CP   3m   1   *The doorbell rings, and he goes to* answer *it.*/{C} Are you alone? { }/[EDWARD
375 CP Edward 11   the telephone. I suppose I must answer it./Hello ... oh, hello! ... No. I mean yes,
376 CP Celia   2   *in an apron.*]/{C} You'd better answer the door, Edward./It's the best thing to
382 CP Edward 38   the telephone./I suppose I had better answer it./{C} Yes, better answer it./{E} Hello!
382 CP Celia 39 I had better answer it./{C} Yes, better answer it./{E} Hello! ... Oh, Julia: what is it
384 CP   3m   1   *day.* EDWARD *alone. He goes to/answer the doorbell.*/{E} Oh ... good evening. { }/
389 CP   m 37 *doorbell rings, and* EDWARD *goes to* answer *it*]/{C} Oh, I'm afraid that all this sounds
390 CP   m 17   *doorbell rings.* EDWARD *goes to* answer *it.* Enter ALEX]/{A} Has Lavinia
394 CP Lavinia 39   /Now who could have taught you to answer back like that?/{E} I have had quite
504 CC Lucasta   5   /But there seems to be nobody to answer the door./I've just let someone in. It's
512 CC Guzzard 19   /{MG} I have been asked here to answer strange questions —/And now it is my
513 CC Colby 13   /To which I can only give a strange answer./Sir Claude is right: I wished to know
580 ES Monica   6 I write to you, Michael,/Will you ever answer?/{Mi} Oh of course, Monica./You know

ANSWERED (5)
149 Rock 1   m94   *sky. From farther/away, they are* answered *by voices of the* UNEMPLOYED./*No*
175 FQ: BurntN 138   us? After the kingfisher's wing/Has answered light to light, and is silent, the light is
327 FR Harry 10 I was talking in abstractions: and you answered in abstractions./I have a private
410 CP Reilly 31   /What can we do?/{R} You have answered your own question,/Though you do
411 CP Lavinia 31   not concerned./{L} I think you have answered my question too./They had to tell us,

ANSWERS (2)
411 CP   3m 36 *house-telephone rings. He/gets up and* answers *it.*]/{R} Yes? ... Yes. Come in. { }/[*Enter*
437 CP Lavinia   3   has made a point, Henry./{L} ... if it answers my question./{R} *Ere Babylon was dust*

ANT-HILL (1)
434 CP   Alex 25   have been crucified/Very near an ant-hill./{L} But Celia! ... Of all people .../{E}

ANTÉRIEURE (1)
 51 Restaurant 29 loin,/Le repassant aux étapes de sa vie antérieure./Figurez-vous donc, c'était un sort

ANTHONY (1)
366 CP   Julia 11 come straight to you, instead of to St. Anthony./And now I must fly. I've kept the taxi

ANTI-CLIMAX (2)
419 CP Celia 13   to the sanatorium./{C} Oh, what an anti-climax! I have known people/Who have
504 CC Lucasta   4   /{L} I'm sorry to come back. It's an anti-climax./But there seems to be nobody to

ANTIQUE (4)
 64 WL: Chess 97   a carvèd dolphin swam./Above the antique mantel was displayed/As though a
 66 WL: Chess 156   to be ashamed, I said, to look so antique./(And her only thirty-one.)/I can't help
 92 Ash-Wed 3   16 green/Enchanted the maytime with an antique flute./Blown hair is sweet, brown hair
196 FQ: Little 189   restore old policies/Or follow an antique drum./These men, and those who

ANTWERP (1)
 37 Gerontion   9 owner,/Spawned in some estaminet of Antwerp,/Blistered in Brussels, patched and

ANVIL (1)
241 MC Priest3 21 To grow between the hammer and the anvil?/{P2} Tell us,/Are the old disputes at an

ANXIETIES (1)
544 ES Monica 26   you as other than occupied/With anxieties from which you were longing to

ANXIETY (1)
390 CP   Julia 34   that she is quite worn out/After her anxiety about her aunt —/Who, you'll be glad

ANXIOUS (8)
185 FQ: DrySal 41   older/Than time counted by anxious worried women/Lying awake,
289 FR   Amy 37 very much easier/And is why I was so anxious you should all be here./She never would
300 FR Downing   3 I don't know, Sir./But he seemed very anxious about my Lady./Tried to keep her in
314 FR Warburt 38   against it! I never saw a man/More anxious to live./{H} Not at all extraordinary./It
323 FR Winch   2 mustn't be moved./But Dr. Owen was anxious that you should have a look at him./
348 FR Warburt   3   hasn't been worrying?/I'm anxious to relieve her mind. Why, what's the
428 CP Edward 32   boring you?/{E} No indeed: we are anxious to learn the solution./{A} I'm not sure
467 CC   Claude 18 /{SC} It's my own fault./I was always anxious to avoid the mistakes/My father made

ANY (177)
 20 Portrait   71   she has said to me?/You will see me any morning in the park/Reading the comics
 21 Portrait   106 leave it now to fate./You will write, at any rate./Perhaps it is not too late./I shall sit
 38 Gerontion   52   show purposelessly/And it is not by any concitation/Of the backward devils./I
105 Song Sime 12   honour and ease./There went never any rejected from my door./Who shall

117 SP	Doris	36	I do./Well I'm not going to draw any more,/You cut for luck. You cut for luck./It
123 SAWa & Ho		5	*palmleaf/Or under the bamboo tree?/Any old tree will do for me/Any old wood is just*
123 SAWa & Ho		6	*tree?/Any old tree will do for me/Any old wood is just as good/Any old isle is just*
123 SAWa & Ho		7	*do for me/Any old wood is just as good/Any old isle is just my style/Any fresh egg/Any*
123 SAWa & Ho		8	*as good/Any old isle is just my style/Any fresh egg/Any fresh egg/And the sound of*
123 SAWa & Ho		9	*old isle is just my style/Any fresh egg/Any fresh egg/And the sound of the coral sea./*
123 SA Kl & Kr		17	*what to do/We won't have to catch any trains/And we won't go home when it rains/*
124 SA Sweeney		13	/{S} I knew a man once did a girl in./Any man might do a girl in/Any man has to,
124 SA Sweeney		14	a girl in./Any man might do a girl in/Any man has to, needs to, wants to/Once in a
125 SA Sweeney		13	alive then he was dead./There wasn't any joint/There wasn't any joint/For when
125 SA Sweeney		14	/There wasn't any joint/There wasn't any joint/For when you're alone/When you're
164 Rock 9		12	good of themselves, ready for any festivity,/Doing themselves very well./Let us
186 FQ: DrySal		97	/In a different form, beyond any meaning/We can assign to happiness. I have
188 FQ: DrySal		140	the past/Into different lives, or into any future;/You are not the same people who
188 FQ: DrySal		142	left that station/Or who will arrive at any terminus,/While the narrowing rails slide
188 FQ: DrySal		150	murmuring shell of time, and not in any language)/'Fare forward, you who think
192 FQ: Little		42	/If you came this way,/Taking any route, starting from anywhere,/At any time
192 FQ: Little		43	route, starting from anywhere,/At any time or at any season,/It would always be
192 FQ: Little		43	from anywhere,/At any time or at any season,/It would always be the same: you
197 FQ: Little		227	/Every poem an epitaph. And any action/Is a step to the block, to the fire,
212 Growltiger		16	lurks on foreign ships,/And woe to any Cat with whom Growltiger came to grips!/
214 RTTugger		8	is a Curious Cat —/And there isn't any call for me to shout it:/For he will do/As he
214 RTTugger		19	is a Curious Cat —/And it isn't any use for you to doubt it:/For he will do/As
214 RTTugger		26	wants a feast;/When there isn't any fish then he won't eat rabbit./If you offer
215 RTTugger		36	is a Curious Cat —/And there isn't any need for me to spout it:/For he will do/As
221 Old Deut		38	woken —/I'll have the police if there's any uproar' —/And out they all shuffle, without
224 Mr Mistoff		27	on the narrowest rail./He can pick any card from a pack,/He is equally cunning
224 Mr Mistoff		31	only hunting for mice./He can play any trick with a cork/Or a spoon and a bit of
226 Macavity		22	/And his footprints are not found in any file of Scotland Yard's./And when the
230 Bust Jones		15	/And it is against the rules/For any one Cat to belong both to that/And the
235 Ad-dress		35	such an easy-going lout,/He'll answer any hail or shout./Again I must remind you that
587 Fable		19	had been walled up for his crimes;/At any rate, he sometimes came to dinner,/
589 Fable		74	his chair,/His eye became the size of any dollar,/The ghost then took him roughly by
589 Fable		79	him rudely by the collar,/And before any one could say 'O jiminy!'/The pair had
242 MC	Mess	6	Archbishop/Is not the man to cherish any illusions,/Or yet to diminish the least of his
246 MC	Priest2	4	good Archbishop/Is likely to arrive at any moment?/The crowds in the streets will be
251 MC Thomas		10	meaning in as dark generality/As any courtier./{T3} This is the simple fact!/You
277 MC Knight3		24	up at the end —/they won't give *us* any glory. No, we have done for ourselves,
279 MC Knight2		2	merit/your applause; and if there is any guilt whatever in the matter, you/must
279 MC Knight1		8	point of view/to express. If there are any who are still unconvinced, I think that/
280 MC Knight1		4	and do/nothing that might provoke any public outbreak. {}/[*Exeunt* KNIGHTS]/
287 FR	Mary	10	the compliment:/I don't belong to any generation. {}/[*Exit*]/{V} Really, Gerald, I
297 FR	Charles	15	might have pushed her over?/{C} In any case, I shouldn't blame Harry./I might have
297 FR	Gerald	20	so, we don't want Downing to know/Any more than he knows already./And even if
298 FR	Agatha	9	—/{Ag} I have no objection,/Any more than I object to asking Dr.
300 FRDowning		23	him./I don't mean to say that he had any orders —/His Lordship is always most
300 FR	Charles	38	Downing,/I don't think we need you any more./{G} Oh, Downing,/Is there anything
302 FR	Chorus	3	we may think well of ourselves./And any explanation will satisfy:/We only ask to be
304 FR	Mary	5	timid girls./I don't see you any differently now;/But I really wish that I'd
304 FR	Mary	10	and because you don't belong here/Any more than I do. I want to get away./{Ag}
304 FR	Mary	27	to me/Because she couldn't bear to let any project go;/And even when *she* died: I
305 FR	Agatha	7	help you: but you must not run away./Any time before now, it would have shown
306 FR	Mary	36	carefully prepared;/There was never any time to invent our own enjoyments./But
309 FR	Mary	9	of understanding you —/But in any case, I must get ready for dinner./{H} No,
311 FR	Harry	29	I was not the same person./I was not any person. Nothing that I did/Has to do with
315 FR	Gerald	22	birthday ten years ago./{G} Is there any use in waiting for Arthur and John?/{A} We
317 FR Warburt		19	what you know/Or do not know, at any moment/May make an endless difference to
318 FR	Harry	23	not with the past./{H} Oh, is there any difference!/How can we be concerned with
320 FR Warburt		15	A sudden shock/Might send her off at any moment./If she had been another woman/
325 FR	Charles	9	/{C} Well, there's no sort of use in any of us going —/On a night like this — it's a
327 FR	Harry	14	with the aid of Dr. Warburton —/Or any other doctor, who would be another
333 FR	Agatha	13	were in some way mine!/And that in any case I should have no other child./{H} And
337 FR	Harry	38	/This is not to do with Agatha, any more than with the rest of you./My advice
338 FR	Harry	16	knows/Or how much she knows. Any knowledge she may have —/It was not I
338 FR	Harry	29	have chosen this way, had there been any other!/It is at once the hardest thing, and

340 FR	Amy	25	him go. I abased myself./Did I show	any	weakness, any self-pity?/I forced myself to
340 FR	Amy	25	myself./Did I show any weakness,	any	self-pity?/I forced myself to the purposes of
342 FR	Amy	9	weakling as his father/In the hands of	any	unscrupulous woman./I have no influence
343 FR	Harry	32	/To worry about: not that John is	any	worry —/The destined and the perfect
345 FR	Harry	9	/You need not fear that I am in	any	danger/Of such accidents as happen to
345 FR	Amy	26	way;/I prefer your company to that of	any	of the others/Just to help me to the next
346 FR	Downing	21	me/Very long now. I can't give you	any	reasons./But to show you what I mean,
355 CP	Julia	18	room./Now I want to relax, Are there	any	more cocktails?/{P} But do go on. Edward
357 CP	Edward	1	you an aunt too?/{E} No, I haven't	any	aunt. But I might go away./{C} But,
357 CP	Julia	16	Lavinia./I quite understand. Are there	any	prospects?/{E} No, I think she put it all into
362 CP	Edward	10	granted./I never thought I should be	any	happier/With another person. Why speak
363 CP	Reilly	16	Who are you now?/You don't know	any	more than I do,/But rather less. You are
368 CP	Alex	25	a toothsome meal out of nothing./Any	scraps you have will do. I learned that in
369 CP	Peter	4	I met Celia./She was different from	any	girl I'd ever known/And not easy to talk to,
370 CP	Edward	1	introduce you to her family/Or to	any	of her friends?/{P} No, but once or twice
370 CP	Alex	14	an apron]/{A} Edward, I can't find	any	curry powder./{E} There isn't any curry
370 CP	Edward	15	any curry powder./{E} There isn't	any	curry powder. Lavinia hates curry./{A}
370 CP	Alex	17	I must think./I didn't expect to find	any	mangoes,/But I *did* count upon curry
370 CP	Edward	35	have become an ordinary affair/Like	any	other. As the fever cooled/You would have
371 CP	Peter	30	only hold to the memory/I can bear	any	future. But I must find out/The truth about
375 CP	Edward	17	.../Oh, no, Alex, don't bring me	any	cheese;/I've got some cheese ... No, not
380 CP	Celia	23	this is ridiculous! I never gave Peter/Any	reason to suppose I cared for him./I
381 CP	Celia	2	Edward:/You are not entitled to take	any	interest/Now, in *my* future. I only hope
381 CP	Edward	25	/{E} No — not happy: or, if there is	any	happiness,/Only the happiness of knowing/
386 CP	Edward	17	have you come?/I expect Lavinia at	any	moment./You must not be here. Why have
388 CP	Edward	30	/{E} Of course I haven't sent	any	telegrams./{L} This is some of Julia's
390 CP	Lavinia	25	from Dedham./Edward, have *you*	any	friends in Dedham?/{E} No, *I* have no
392 CP	Lavinia	24	to happen./Trust her not to miss	any	awkward situation!/And what did you tell
393 CP	Edward	37	in —/And they didn't come through	any	of *your* friends —/You suddenly found it
399 CP	Reilly	4	course, that it is important/To avoid	any	meeting?/{N} You made that clear, Sir
400 CP	Reilly	4	time./Tell me now, did you have	any	difficulty/In convincing him I was the man
400 CP	Alex	15	/Besides, he was ready to consult	any	doctor/Recommended by anyone except his
402 CP	Reilly	2	Do you suppose that things would be	any	better — now?/{E} I don't know, I'm sure.
403 CP	Reilly	4	oblige me./I could make you dream	any	kind of dream I suggested,/And it would
403 CP	Edward	36	she has made me incapable/Of having	any	existence of my own./That is what she has
404 CP	Edward	21	I am in your hands./I cannot take	any	further responsibility./{R} Many patients
405 CP	Edward	34	concerns us./{E} I am not going to	any	sanatorium./I am going to a hotel. And I
409 CP	Reilly	39	towards her/Were different from	any	you had aroused in him —/It was a shock.
410 CP	Reilly	14	could always say: 'he could not love	any	woman;'/*You* could always say: 'no man
410 CP	Reilly	36	/The best of a bad job is all	any	of us make of it —/Except of course, the
413 CP	Celia	18	I am being persecuted;/I don't hear	any	voices, I have no delusions —/Except that
415 CP	Celia	35	one feel sinful!/And yet I can't find	any	other word for it./It must be some kind of
424 CP	Caterer	1	*from side door./{CM}* Have you	any	further orders for us, Madam?/{L} You
428 CP	Alex	33	/{A} I'm not sure that there *is*	any	solution./But even this does not bring us to
429 CP	Edward	17	Not on the *whole* story./{E} And have	any	of the English residents been murdered?/{A}
430 CP	Peter	15	/It does seem ages since I last saw	any	of you!/And how are you, Alex? And dear
430 CP	Peter	26	But I didn't know/That he knew	any	monkeys./{J} But give us your news;/Give
431 CP	Peter	22	mansion in England!/At least, of	any	that are still inhabited./We've got a team of
433 CP	Julia	24	/{J} Not in the directory,/Or in	any	directory. You can tell them now, Alex./{L}
435 CP	Reilly	17	Mr. Quilpe —/Which is the most that	any	of us can ask for./{P} And what a *métier!*
436 CP	Lavinia	32	knew her./I suspect that you did. In	any	case you knew *about* her./Yet I thought
438 CP	Reilly	12	evil always at his shoulder/Suffered	any	less from hunger, damp, exposure,/Bowel
439 CP	Julia	36	for it./Their guests may be arriving at	any	moment./{R} Julia, you are right. It is also
446 CC	Claude	36	watching./{SC} But there won't be	any	birds — none worth watching./{E} I don't
455 CC	Eggers	14	made himself responsible for her./In	any	case, he's behaved like a father —/A very
456 CC	Colby	12	But is Lady Elizabeth very unusual/In	any	other way, besides being a lady?/{E} Why,
457 CC	Eggers	2	her passport./But let's not be crossing	any	bridges/Until we come to them. That's what
457 CC	Lady E	25	/{LE} No, Gertrude, I haven't had	any	lunch,/And I don't want it now. Just bring
461 CC	Eggers	7	in the garden./And I'll slip up to town	any	day, if you want me./In fact, Mrs. E. said: 'I
466 CC	Claude	19	religious people —/I've never known	any	— can find some unity./Then there are also
467 CC	Colby	30	I don't want my position/To be, in	any	way, a make-believe./{SC} It shan't be.
470 CC	Lucasta	30	American Musicals. Do you think it's	any	compliment/To invite a woman to
472 CC	Colby	7	something in your life/To rob you of	any	sense of security./{L} And I'm sure you
474 CC	Lucasta	39	contact with a world/More real than	any	*I've* ever lived in./And I'd like to

480 CC	Kaghan	29	You didn't know that!/Never had	any parents. Just adopted, from nowhere./
481 CC	Kaghan	11	We can't dine till eight;/Not at	any restaurant that *you* like./— For a change,
482 CC	Lady E	24	intelligent and kind./I'm not making	any malicious suggestions:/But they are rather
484 CC	Colby	4	As for other relatives,/I never knew	any, when I was a child./I suppose I've never
486 CC	Lady E	22	Guzzard/And Mr. Guzzard — have	any children?/{C} They had no children of their
488 CC	Claude	14	to see him as your son,/And then —	any name you heard would have seemed the
489 CC	Claude	10	more?'/You might have suspected	any number of children!/That seems grotesque
491 CC	Lady E	7	only *yours*./Why should we make	any further enquiries?/Let us regard him as
492 CC	Claude	32	anything at all/About ceramics ... or	any other art./No, I don't think I shall be in a
499 CC	Claude	6	to her./Don't let her think that *I* have	any doubts:/You are putting the questions on
499 CC	Lucasta	18	here, Eggy! You're such a support./In	any case, I've an announcement to make,/And I
500 CC	Lucasta	30	world,/And he might vanish into it at	any moment —/At just the moment when you
503 CC	Lucasta	7	a sister, than we could have been/In	any other form of relationship./{C} I want you
503 CC	Lucasta	32	and sister —/Or so I hope. Yes, in	any event,/Good-bye, Colby. {}/[*Exit*
506 CC	Eggers	11	had forgotten it./She was not, in	any case, in a position/In which she could have
507 CC	Eggers	1	you can help us —/Do you know of	any other Mrs. Guzzard?/{MG} None./{E}
507 CC	Eggers	5	a more delicate question:/Did you, at	any time, take in a child —/A child, that is, of
508 CC	Eggers	7	a similar way,/Wouldn't you grasp at	any straw/That offered hope of finding him?/
511 CC	Lucasta	2	You don't need to talk that language	any longer:/Just say you're embarrassed./{K}
511 CC	Lady E	20	mother./{LE} Then in order to avoid	any danger of confusion/You may address me
512 CC	Claude	10	*imposture*./{SC} I don't think there is	any confusion now:/I'm sure that my wife is
525 ES	Charles	20	your father simply can't bear it/That	any man but he should have you to himself,/
526 ES	Charles	36	granted/That you don't really care for	any company but his!/{M} You're not to assume
527 ES	Charles	34	say,/For your brother's never been of	any use to you./{M} And never will be of any
527 ES	Monica	35	use to you./{M} And never will be of	any use to anybody,/I'm afraid. Poor Michael!
528 ES	Charles	2	your going with your father./Is there	any better reason than his fear of solitude?/{M}
528 ES	Charles	16	wondered whether there was	any .../Private self to preserve./{M} There *is* a
531 ES	Ld Clav	2	left cards/And if I was going to have	any visitors./{M} Father, you simply want to
531 ES	Ld Clav	12	established liturgy/Of the Press on	any conspicuous retirement./My obituary, if I
534 ES	Gomez	38	/Dick, don't tell me that there isn't	any whisky in the house?/{LC} I can provide
541 ES	Gomez	4	at it./Besides, you can't think I've	any desire/To appear in public as Frederick
541 ES	Gomez	26	apology./Blackmail! On the contrary/Any time you're in a tight corner/My entire
546 ES	Piggott	20	exceptional/Though we never accept	any guest who's incurable./You know, we've
546 ES	Piggott	24	never accept them. Nor do we accept/Any guest who *looks* incurable —/We make
547 ES	Piggott	31	like being beaten,/And that spoils	any sport, in my opinion./{M} Thank you, Mrs.
548 ES	Monica	9	Don't look so alarmed!/If you spy	any guest who seems to be stalking you/Put
550 ES	Carghil	36	— 'he doesn't understand women./Any woman who trusted *him* would soon find
552 ES	Ld Clav	35	always looked it./{LC} I've no longer	any part to play, Maisie./{MC} There'll always
558 ES	Michael	7	very shocked./Said he couldn't retain	any man on his staff/Who'd taken to gambling.
560 ES	Ld Clav	16	/I will help you to make a start in	any business/You may find for yourself — if, on
560 ES	Michael	28	needn't worry/About that girl — or	any other./But I want to get out. I'm fed up
569 ES	Charles	20	—/I was thinking that if there's	any question of blackmail,/I've seen something
579 ES	Michael	19	/I could look in again. If there's	any point in it./Personally, I think that when
579 ES	Gomez	35	more clearly./{G} Not that I deserve	any credit for it./We can only regard it as a

ANYBODY (18)

276 MC	Knight1	24	and therefore will not judge	anybody without/hearing both sides of the case.
289 FR	Ivy	24	have been shocking,/Especially to lose	anybody in *that* way —/Swept off the deck in
314 FR	Amy	4	/And he's known you longer than	anybody, Harry./When he heard that you were
346 FR	Downing	19	I understand his Lordship better than	anybody/And I have a kind of feeling that his
346 FR	Downing	32	want me long, and he won't want	anybody./{Ag} And, Downing, if his behaviour
365 CP	Julia	1	for them everywhere I've been./Has	anybody found them? You can tell if they're
409 CP	Lavinia	12	husband has never been in love with	anybody./{R} And were not prepared to make
409 CP	Reilly	17	/That you had never been in love with	anybody;/Which made you suspect that you
418 CP	Celia	14	For me, now, to try to make a life with	*anybody*!/I couldn't give anyone the kind of love
428 CP	Edward	23	cooked them myself .../{E} And did	anybody eat them/When you cooked them?/{A}
432 CP	Peter	38	—/I'm afraid I can't find parts for	anybody/In *this* film — it's not my business;/
446 CC	Eggers	39	sure Mr. Simpkins will find them if	anybody./{SC} Well, we'll leave that for the
453 CC	Kaghan	23	about me?/{K} It's no use telling	anybody about you:/Nobody'd ever believe in
474 CC	Lucasta	30	You don't seem to me/To need	anybody./{C} That's quite untrue./{L} But
479 CC	Lucasta	27	As if you weren't as afraid of her as	anybody!/{K} Well, at least, I've always
503 CC	Lucasta	18	something to you. But you don't *need*	anybody./{E} And now may I interrupt, Miss
527 ES	Monica	35	/{M} And never will be of any use to	anybody,/I'm afraid. Poor Michael! Mother
534 ES	Gomez	3	/I can swear that I've never corrupted	anybody./In fact, I've never come across an

ANYONE (40)

117 SP	Doris	20	read the cards,/It's not a thing that	anyone can do./{Du} Yes I know you've a touch
589 Fable		83	could be found,/The monks, when	anyone questioned, would declare/St. Peter'd

291 FR	Gerald	27	do you see them?/{G} No, I don't see anyone about./{H} No, no, not there. Look
294 FR	Harry	35	her?/{H} You would never imagine anyone could sink so quickly./I had always
297 FR	Amy	1	/I'd trust Warburton's opinion./{A} If anyone speaks to Dr. Warburton/It should be
324 FR	Harry	18	very much difference/To him or to anyone else. If he was ever really conscious,/I
325 FR	Ivy	16	that matters/Is not to let her see that anyone is worried./We must carry on as if
338 FR	Harry	5	/But at present, I cannot explain it to anyone:/I do not know the words in which to
359 CP	Edward	21	mattered —/I shouldn't have minded anyone else, {}/[*The doorbell rings*. EDWARD
367 CP	Alex	38	And so I thought I'd slip in and see if anyone was with you./{P} Julia must have left it
368 CP	Alex	10	dinner. Are you going out?/Is there anyone here to get dinner for you?/{E} No, I
374 CP	Celia	5	ago./{C} If there had happened to be anyone with you/I was going to say I'd come
380 CP	Edward	36	—/I have never been in love with anyone but you,/And perhaps I still am. But
400 CP	Alex	16	consult any doctor/Recommended by anyone except his wife./{R} I had already
402 CP	Edward	9	I should not need to consult you/Or anyone else. I came here as a patient./If you
406 CP	Edward	25	to a sanatorium?/I have never known anyone in my life/With fewer mental
407 CP	Lavinia	37	know about it./I wonder if there was anyone who didn't know./{R} There was one, in
408 CP	Edward	20	you. You could not have chosen/Anyone I was less likely to suspect./And then he
414 CP	Celia	13	longer seems worth while to *speak* to anyone!/{R} And what about your parents?/{C}
418 CP	Celia	15	a life with *any*body!/I couldn't give anyone the kind of love —/I wish I could —
445 CC	Claude	4	/But you know my wife wouldn't like anyone to meet her/At Northolt, but you. And I
450 CC	Claude	1	something one's ignorant of/About anyone, however well one knows them;/And
455 CC	Eggers	22	/And I think he can manage her. If anyone can./{C} But is she likely to be a
455 CC	Colby	29	my joke./{C} Well, I've never met anyone like Miss Angel./{E} You'll get used to
464 CC	Claude	18	strange. I have never talked of this to anyone./Never until now. Do you feel at all like
466 CC	Claude	9	room./It isn't that I don't want anyone to see them!/But when I am alone, and
469 CC	Colby	29	this is the first time I've played to anyone .../{L} Don't be such a fraud. You know
470 CC	Colby	7	I mean that I've not played/To anyone, since I came to the conclusion/That I
473 CC	Colby	17	is a garden somewhere for you —/For anyone who wants one as much as you do./{L}
475 CC	Colby	3	/Does one ever come to understand anyone?/{L} I think you're being very
480 CC	Colby	13	/You've got as level a head as anyone,/And you never get involved in anything
484 CC	Lady E	31	had three obsessions, and I never told anyone./I wonder if *you* had the same
485 CC	Lady E	23	that we are nearer to God than to anyone./— Where did you live, as a child?/{C}
500 CC	Lucasta	28	doesn't need me,/He doesn't need anyone. He's fascinating,/But he's
517 CC	Colby	24	church?/{C} That is what I want. If anyone will take me./{E} If so, I happen to
531 ES	Lambert	34	see you./I told him you never saw anyone, my Lord,/But by previous
537 ES	Gomez	15	/{G} I was just about as different as anyone could be/From the sort of men you'd
567 ES	Monica	23	in me?/{M} Oh Charles! How could anyone blackmail Father?/Father, of all people
568 ES	Ld Clav	30	him./I'm afraid that I've never loved anyone, really./No, I do love my Monica — but
568 ES	Ld Clav	33	child/If you've never been honest with anyone older,/On terms of equality. To one's

ANYONE'S (1)

512 CC	Guzzard	13	That is as much to my interest as anyone's./But will your wife be satisfied,/When

ANYTHING (91)

120 SP	Krum	1	too gay for us/Don't think I mean anything *coarse* —/But I'm afraid we couldn't
211 Old Gumbie		27	/She sits upon the window-sill, or anything that's smooth and flat:/She sits and
214 RTTugger		11	do/As he do do/And there's no doing anything about it!/The Rum Tum Tugger is a
214 RTTugger		22	do/As he do do/And there's no doing anything about it!/The Rum Tum Tugger is a
215 RTTugger		39	do/As he do do/And there's no doing anything about it!/The Song of the Jellicles/
223 Pekes·Pols		55	the bars of the area,/You never saw anything fiercer or hairier./And what with the
232 Skimble		24	patrol/And he'd know at once if anything occurred./He will watch you without
233 Skimble		44	to remind him./For Skimble won't let anything go wrong./And when you creep into
233 Skimble		60	he summons the police/If there's anything they ought to know about:/When you
243 MC	Chorus	22	a doom on the world./We do not wish anything to happen./Seven years we have lived
261 MC	Thomas	31	of God, and who no/longer desires anything for himself, not even the glory of being
275 MC	Chorus	28	of falling blood?/We did not wish anything to happen./We understood the private
276 MC	Knight3	33	de Traci./{K3} I am afraid I am not anything like such an experienced/speaker as my
277 MC	Knight3	4	'Hear! hear!'] *We* are not getting anything out of this./We have much more to
298 FR	Charles	2	to be squeamish/In taking hold of anything that comes to hand./If you are
300 FR	Gerald	40	any more./{G} Oh, Downing,/Is there anything wrong with his Lordship's car?/{Do}
301 FR	Downing	7	her always ready./Would there be anything more, Sir?/{G} Thank you, Downing;/
305 FR	Harry	29	same positions./I was looking to see if anything was changed,/But if so, I can't find it./
317 FR	Harry	8	is probably going to be useless,/Or if anything, make matters rather more difficult./
321 FR	Harry	20	not real?/That would be worse than anything that has happened./What if *you* saw
329 FR	Chorus	24	about it,/There is nothing to do about anything,/And now it is nearly time for the news
343 FR	Mary	15	course it was much too late/Then, for anything to come for me: I should have known
354 CP	Peter	6	*are* a good mimic. You never miss anything./{A} She never misses anything unless
354 CP	Alex	7	miss anything./{A} She never misses anything unless she wants to./{C} Especially the

359 CP	Edward	11	rather have whisky?/{UG} Gin./{E} Anything in it?/{UG} A drop of water./{E} I
360 CP	Edward	12	drink?/{E} Whisky?/{UG} Gin./{E} Anything in it?/{UG} Nothing but water./And I
363 CP	Edward	7	drinking?/Whisky?/{UG} Gin./{E} Anything with it?/{UG} Water./{E} To what
366 CP	Julia	10	them but for you./The next time I lose *anything*, Edward,/I'll come straight to you,
367 CP	Edward	11	about yourself and Celia?/Have you anything in common, do you think?/{P} It
372 CP	Edward	34	what I've told you./{E} I shall not say anything about it to Lavinia./{P} Thank you,
375 CP	Edward	14	... it was marvellous./I've never tasted anything like it .../Yes, that's very interesting.
375 CP	Edward	21	/No, really, Alex, I don't want anything./I'm very tired. Thanks awfully, Alex./
376 CP	Julia	33	My dear, I should have warned you:/Anything that Alex makes is absolutely deadly./
378 CP	Celia	21	you care about/Is to avoid a break — anything unpleasant!/No, it can't be that. I
380 CP	Celia	18	/To justify yourself. There was never anything/Between me and Peter./{E} Wasn't
387 CP	Celia	1	Edward./I couldn't have laughed at anything, yesterday;/But I've learnt a lot in
387 CP	Edward	7	I wish I could. I wish I understood anything./I'm completely in the dark./{C} But
391 CP	Edward	10	/{E} Are you sure you haven't left anything, Julia?/{J} Left anything? Oh, you
391 CP	Julia	11	haven't left anything, Julia?/{J} Left anything? Oh, you mean my spectacles./No,
391 CP	Julia	24	Alex, do you think we could explain *anything*?/{A} I think not, Julia. She must find
391 CP	Julia	31	/Good-bye. I believe ... I haven't left anything. {}/[*Enter* PETER]/{P} I've got a taxi,
391 CP	Edward	36	I've had much opportunity/To seem anything. But of course I'm glad to see you./{L}
396 CP	Lavinia	19	at least be horrid to you —/Anything but nothing, which is all you seem to
402 CP	Reilly	21	term I never use:/It can mean almost anything./{E} And since then, I have realised/
408 CP	Edward	22	about Celia!/I have never heard anything so utterly ludicrous:/This is the best
408 CP	Reilly	36	to one another,/Have not been of anything that you confided to me./The
409 CP	Lavinia	5	noticed it./{L} You wouldn't notice anything. You never noticed *me*./{R} Now, I
411 CP	Lavinia	17	be economical./Edward, have you anything else to ask him/Before we go?/{E} Yes,
411 CP	Edward	33	made their decision./{E} Have you anything else to say to us, Sir Henry?/{R} No.
413 CP	Celia	16	/I could lead an active life — if there's anything to work for;/I don't imagine that I am
413 CP	Celia	34	me, that could be put right./I'd do anything you told me, to get back to normality./
415 CP	Celia	15	I haven't hurt *her*./I wasn't taking anything away from her —/Anything she
415 CP	Celia	16	taking anything away from her —/Anything she wanted. I may have been a fool:/
415 CP	Celia	22	mean that it was ever mentioned!/But anything wrong, from our point of view,/Was
415 CP	Celia	38	by the fear/That it is more real than anything I believed in./{R} What is more real
415 CP	Reilly	39	in./{R} What is more real than anything you believed in?/{C} It's not the feeling
416 CP	Celia	1	believed in?/{C} It's not the feeling of anything I've ever *done*,/Which I might get
416 CP	Celia	2	/Which I might get away from, or of anything in me/I could get rid of — but of
418 CP	Celia	12	do without everything,/Put up with anything, if I might cherish it./In fact, I think it
419 CP	Reilly	8	hell/Till you become incapable of anything else./Now — do you feel quite sure?/
421 CP	Julia	25	she will not even know/That there is anything there to be afraid of./She is too
421 CP	Reilly	29	/{R} When I express confidence in anything/You always raise doubts; when I am
421 CP	Reilly	31	/Then you see no reason for anything but confidence./{J} That's one way in
424 CP	Lavinia	6	/You can get in and out. Is there anything you need/That you can't find in the
424 CP	Caterer	9	{CM} Nothing, Madam./Will there be anything more you require?/{L} Nothing more, I
432 CP	Edward	23	{R} Might I have a glass of water?/{E} Anything with it?/{R} Nothing, thank you./{L}
435 CP	Peter	2	a mistake./Julia! Why don't *you* say anything?/{J} You gave her those two years, as
435 CP	Peter	14	her just now; but I never thought/Of anything like this. I suppose I didn't know her,/
461 CC	Eggers	4	better be off now. Mr. Simpkins —/If anything *should* turn up unexpected/And you
469 CC	Lucasta	2	—/Not that *my* opinion counts for anything:/You know that. But I'd like to learn
475 CC	Lucasta	36	Sir Claude./{L} Claude hasn't told me anything about you;/He doesn't tell me much. '
477 CC	Colby	35	I'm not shocked. Not by you,/Not by anything you think. It's to do with myself./{L}
478 CC	Lucasta	27	But .../{L} I don't believe there's anything to explain/That could explain anything
478 CC	Lucasta	28	to explain/That could explain anything away. I shall never/Never forget that
480 CC	Colby	14	/And you never get involved in anything risky./You like to pretend to other
480 CC	Colby	17	I don't believe you ever gamble/On anything that isn't a certainty./{K} Well, there's
492 CC	Claude	31	/Of the Potters' Company know anything at all/About ceramics ... or any other
494 CC	Lady E	29	I know you don't think I understand anything,/And perhaps I don't. But I wish you
495 CC	Lady E	10	that you were not interested/In anything but financial affairs;/And that you
495 CC	Lady E	13	believe,/For married people to take anything for granted./{SC} That was a very
501 CC	Claude	14	Perhaps you are right. I'm not sure of anything./Perhaps, as you say, I've
526 ES	Monica	37	his!/{M} You're not to assume that anything I've said to you/Has given you the
527 ES	Monica	28	sitting — someone/Not occupied with anything that can't be interrupted./Someone to
534 ES	Gomez	20	/No, forgery, or washing cheques, or anything of that nature,/Is certain to be found
536 ES	Gomez	12	to learn English, wasn't interested/In anything that happened four thousand miles
545 ES	Piggott	30	But I hope you're happy?/Is there anything you need that hasn't been provided?/
546 ES	Piggott	11	You see, we've studied to avoid/Anything like a nursing-home atmosphere./We
548 ES	Monica	3	[*Exit*]/{M} I hope she won't remember anything else./{LC} She'll come back to tell us
557 ES	Michael	20	a good deal more capital/To make anything of it. If I could have borrowed more/I

| 568 ES | Ld Clav | 6 | things not crimes, Monica,/Beyond anything of which the law takes cognisance:/ |
| 578 ES | Ld Clav | 16 | defeating each other,/How can I feel anything but sorrow and compunction?/{M} Oh |

ANYWAY (14)

117 SP	Dusty	7	*just* as well be Sweeney/{Du} Well anyway it's very queer./{Do} Here's the four of
326 FR	Violet	4	him somewhere in Chiswick, I think./Anyway, the district was unfamiliar/And I had
355 CP	Peter	19	do go on. Edward wasn't listening anyway./{J} No, he wasn't listening, but he's
369 CP	Peter	32	column, to find her there alone./Anyway, we got into conversation/And I found
376 CP	Celia	6	helpless/And had to do something. Anyway, I'm *staying*/And I'm not going to hide.
395 CP	Lavinia	7	find that you have a mind to speak./Anyway, I'm prepared to take you as you are./
412 CP	Celia	34	/That you'll think that I am wasting it anyway./I suppose most people, when they
425 CP	Lavinia	30	tray about,/So they'll go away again. Anyway, at that stage/There's nothing whatever
434 CP	Edward	28	natives/Who would have died anyway./{A} Yes, the patients died anyway;/
434 CP	Alex	29	anyway./{A} Yes, the patients died anyway;/Being tainted with the plague, they
469 CC	Colby	6	much teaching;/Not at this stage, anyway. All you need at first/Is to hear more
471 CC	Colby	27	thought I'd get a false impression anyway./You preferred it to be one of your own
500 CC	Lucasta	19	he tell me? Perhaps he was about to./Anyway, I *knew* there had been some mistake./
560 ES	Michael	19	about the nature of the business./{Mi} Anyway, I'm determined to get out of England./

ANYWHERE (9)

192 FQ: Little	42	way,/Taking any route, starting from anywhere,/At any time or at any season,/It
294 FR	Harry	18	direction, for no direction/Leads anywhere but round and round in that vapour
308 FR	Mary	29	inside you/Which you can change anywhere — here, as well as elsewhere./{H}
314 FR	Amy	1	them up,/So it's no use to telephone anywhere. Harry!/Haven't you seen Dr.
357 CP	Julia	32	somewhere./{E} She lives in Essex./{J} Anywhere near Colchester? Lavinia loves
416 CP	Celia	40	was not there/And perhaps is not anywhere? But if not anywhere,/Why do I feel
416 CP	Celia	40	perhaps is not anywhere? But if not anywhere,/Why do I feel guilty at not having
530 ES	Ld Clav	13	thing he wants is to take a train for anywhere!/No, I've not the slightest longing for
548 ES	Carghil	31	even recognise me! I'd know you anywhere./But then, we've all seen your portrait

APART (9)

57 Swee Night	34	indistinct/Converses at the door apart,/The nightingales are singing near/The
136 5FingerEx4	10	/(They regard him as something apart)/While on his palate fine he presses/The
244 MC	Chorus	21	see birth and death alone/In a void apart. We/Are afraid in a fear which we cannot
312 FR	m	9	them. {}/[*He rushes forward and tears apart the curtains: but the embrasure is empty*.]/
313 FR	Violet	3	who could have pulled those curtains apart? {}/[*Pulls them together*]/{V} Very well, I
319 FR	Harry	5	and I know very well/That I was kept apart from him, till he went away./We never
367 CP	Edward	28	if one is interested in Celia./Apart, of course, from its literary merit/Which I
451 CC	Colby	16	very helpful/And very good company apart from business./{E} Oh yes, Mr. Kaghan is
496 CC	Eggers	29	I've so much to do, in Joshua Park —/Apart from the garden — that I've not an idle

APATHY (1)

| 174 FQ: BurntN | 106 | fancies and empty of meaning/Tumid apathy with no concentration/Men and bits of |

APE (3)

21 Portrait	112	bear,/Cry like a parrot, chatter like an ape./Let us take the air, in a tobacco trance —/
257 MC	Chorus	30	of padding bear,/Palm-pat of nodding ape, square hyaena waiting/For laughter,
270 MC	Chorus	11	descending/To the horror of the ape. Have I not known, not known/What was

APENECK (1)

| 56 Swee Night | 1 | /Sweeney Among the Nightingales/Apeneck Sweeney spreads his knees/Letting his |

APHYLLOUS (1)

| 308 FR | Harry | 8 | stone is seen to be batrachian,/The aphyllous branch ophidian./{M} You bring your |

APOLLINAIRE (2)

| 48 Lune Miel | 8 | /Moins d'une lieue d'ici est Saint Apollinaire/En Classe, basilique connue des |
| 48 Lune Miel | 16 | Suisse et traversé la France./Et Saint Apollinaire, raide et ascétique,/Vieille usine |

APOLLINAX (3)

31 Apollinax	t	/The army of unalterable law./Mr. Apollinax/When Mr. Apollinax visited the
31 Apollinax	1	law./Mr. Apollinax/When Mr. Apollinax visited the United States/His laughter
31 Apollinax	13	of surf./I looked for the head of Mr. Apollinax rolling under a chair/Or grinning

APOLOGISE (9)

345 FR	Harry	2	You must get used to it;/Meanwhile, I apologise for my bad manners./But if you *could*
359 CP	Edward	13	/{UG} A drop of water./{E} I want to apologise for this evening./The fact is, I tried to
499 CC	Lucasta	15	it do another time?/{L} I came to apologise/To Colby. No matter. It'll do another
502 CC	Lucasta	5	But I did come to see you./I came to apologise for my behaviour/The other
502 CC	Colby	7	behaviour/The other afternoon./{C} Apologise? I've told her./{C} But why
502 CC	Colby	9	I've told her./{C} But why should you apologise?/{L} Oh, because I knew/That I must
504 CC	Claude	24	Good morning, Mrs. Guzzard. I must apologise:/I'm afraid there has been some
545 ES	Piggott	25	been neglecting you;/So I've come to apologise and explain./I've been in such a rush,
547 ES	Piggott	37	must learn the best walks./I won't apologise for the lack of excitement:/After all,

APOLOGY (1)
541 ES   Gomez   24   my life./Really, Dick, you owe me an apology./Blackmail! On the contrary/Any time
APOSTLE (3)
264 MC   m   7   PRIEST, *with a banner of St. John the Apostle borne before him.*]/{P2} Since St.
264 MC   Priest2   7   a day: and the day of St. John the Apostle./*In the midst of the congregation he*
264 MC   Priest3   14   *before him.*]/{P3} Since St. John the Apostle a day: and the day of the Holy
APOSTLES (3)
151 Rock 2   3   being built upon the foundation/Of apostles and prophets, Christ Jesus Himself the
151 Rock 2   16   settled all the inconvenient saints,/Apostles, martyrs, in a kind of Whipsnade,/
275 MC   Thomas   20   the blessed John the Baptist, the holy apostles Peter and Paul, to the blessed martyr
APPAL (1)
583 ES   Monica   24   for me,/Loss and vicissitude cannot appal me,/Not even death can dismay or amaze
APPAREL (1)
117 SP   Dusty   10   of money, or a present/Of wearing apparel, or a party'./That's queer too./{Do}
APPARENT (2)
334 FR   Harry   29   other people seemed so strong, their apparent strength/Stifled my decision. Now I
338 FR   Harry   22   I fled. Now I know/That the last apparent refuge, the safe shelter,/That is where
APPARITION (1)
437 CP   Reilly   7   *own image walking in the garden./That apparition, sole of men, he saw./For know there*
APPEAL (4)
276 MC   Knight1   23   feelings, I/share them. Nevertheless, I appeal to your sense of honour. You/are
278 MC   Knight2   1   is this really the case? I am going/to appeal not to your emotions but to your reason.
517 CC   Eggers   27   parish, in Joshua Park —/If it should appeal to you. The organist we had/Died two
574 ES   Carghil   18   very natural./So I thought, why not appeal to Señor Gomez?/He's a wealthy man,
APPEAR (11)
 83 Hollow Men   21   death's dream kingdom/These do not appear:/There, the eyes are/Sunlight on a
219 Mung Rump   24   and greens,/And the cook would appear from behind the scenes/And say in a
232 Skimble   11   frantic to a man —/Then Skimble will appear and he'll saunter to the rear:/He's been
265 MC   Priest3   8   particulars/The eternal design may appear. {}/[*Enter the* FOUR KNIGHTS. *The*
301 FR   Chorus   28   /To the universal bondage./We like to appear in the newspapers/So long as we are in
336 FR   m 12   not the same ... {}/[*The* EUMENIDES *appear*]/{H} and this time/You cannot think that
338 FR   Agatha   36   taking the opposite direction/Will appear to run away./{A} I was speaking to
524 ES   Charles   23   utterly unknown/And the waiters all appear to be avoiding his eye./{M} We're getting
541 ES   Gomez   5   you can't think I've any desire/To appear in public as Frederick Culverwell?/No,
551 ES   Carghil   32   suit/Some people won't want to appear as his supporters.'/He said: 'What his
573 ES   Ld Clav   5   realise/The magnitude of things that appear to them petty;/It's harder to confess the
APPEARANCE (4)
111 Xmas Trees   17   or turkey/And the expected awe on its appearance,/So that the reverence and the
212 Growltiger   5   of the Thames'./His manners and appearance did not calculate to please;/His coat
594 Grad 10   3   that which now we know;/But only in appearance t'will be so./That which has made it
421 CP   Reilly   22   {R} Will she be frightened/By the first appearance of projected spirits?/{J} Henry, you
APPEARANCES (1)
329 FR   Chorus   15   deception/The keeping up of appearances/The making the best of a bad job/
APPEARED (2)
260 MC   Thomas   12   that a multitude of the heavenly host appeared before the/shepherds at Bethlehem,
552 ES   Ld Clav   3   only a year or so/Before your name appeared in very large letters/In Shaftesbury
APPEARS (7)
211 Old Gumbie   38   well-ordered households depend, it appears./Growltiger's Last Stand/
216 Jellicles   17   and a jig./Until the Jellicle Moon appears/They make their toilette and take their
592 Grad 4   3   fears,/To hopeful eye of youth it still appears/A lane by which the rose and hawthorn
361 CP   Edward   22   /A good deal more about us than appears —/I think your speculations rather
420 CP   1m 19   diligence. {}/[NURSE-SECRETARY *appears at door. Exit* CELIA. REILLY *dials on*/
447 CC   Claude   24   can't argue with guidance./But if she appears to be puzzled, or annoyed/At my
506 CC   Eggers   23   aiming at./We have a clue — or what appears to be a clue./That is why Sir Claude has
APPEASING (1)
172 FQ: BurntN   53   blood/Sings below inveterate scars/Appeasing long forgotten wars./The dance
APPELLE (1)
 51 Restaurant   5   soleil, et de la pluie;/C'est ce qu'on appelle le jour de lessive des gueux.'/(Bavard,
APPENDICITIS (1)
546 ES   Piggott   8   I fell in love with him/During an appendicitis operation!/I was a theatre nurse.
APPETENCY (1)
174 FQ: BurntN   128   movement; while the world moves/In appetency, on its metalled ways/Of time past
APPETITE (1)
453 CC   Lucasta   33   B., you're a beast. I've a very small appetite./But the point is, that I'm penniless./

APPETITES (1)
28 Boston ET 4 faintly in the street,/Wakening the appetites of life in some/And to others bringing
APPLAUSE (3)
148 Rock 1 54 face those that bring ignominy,/The applause of all or the love of none./All men are
243 MC Chorus 20 us to perish in quiet./You come with applause, you come with rejoicing, but you
279 MC Knight2 2 served your interests; we merit/your applause; and if there is any guilt whatever in
APPLE (3)
187 FQ: DrySal 119 cows and chicken coops,/The bitter apple and the bite in the apple./And the ragged
187 FQ: DrySal 119 /The bitter apple and the bite in the apple./And the ragged rock in the restless
588 Fable 56 in took four pages,/His mouth an apple held, his skull held sausages./Over their
APPLE-BLOSSOM (1)
246 MC Tempt1 38 viols in the hall,/Laughter and apple-blossom floating on the water,/Singing at
APPLE-SEED (1)
97 Ash-Wed 5 35 spitting from the mouth the withered apple-seed./O my people./Although I do not
APPLE-TREE (2)
138 New Hamp 12 swing,/Spring, sing,/Swing up into the apple-tree./Virginia/Red river, red river,/Slow
197 FQ: Little 250 waterfall/And the children in the apple-tree/Not known, because not looked for/
APPLES (2)
239 MC Chorus 10 into sombre November/And the apples were gathered and stored, and the land
243 MC Chorus 35 a year of dryness,/One year the apples are abundant,/Another year the plums
APPLICATIONS (1)
546 ES Piggott 21 /You know, we've been deluged with applications/From people who want to come
APPLIED (1)
472 CC Lucasta 30 do something different./And so you applied for Eggerson's position,/And made up
APPLY (4)
124 SA Sweeney 35 did he do! what did he do?/That don't apply./Talk to live men about what they do./He
125 SA Sweeney 1 up?/{S} Well here again that don't apply/But I've gotta use words when I talk to
125 SA Sweeney 18 or neither/I tell you again it don't apply/Death or life or life or death/Death is life
517 CC Colby 37 am the Vicar's Warden./{C} I'd like to apply./{E} The stipend is small —/Very small,
APPOINTED (7)
129 Cor2 State 12 I cry?/Arthur Edward Cyril Parker is appointed telephone operator/At a salary of one
129 Cor2 State 16 leave a year./A committee has been appointed to nominate a commission of
129 Cor2 State 18 the Water Supply./A commission is appointed/For Public Works, chiefly the
129 Cor2 State 20 the fortifications./A commission is appointed/To confer with a Volscian
129 Cor2 State 23 and javelin-makers and smiths/Have appointed a joint committee to protest against
201 Def Island 7 /the islands/and the memory of those appointed to the grey/ships — battleship,
440 CP Reilly 11 to see these people./{R} It is your appointed burden. And as for the party,/I am
APPOINTING (1)
447 CC Claude 14 rather inconvenient/When it comes to appointing a successor./Makes it very difficult
APPOINTMENT (10)
365 CP Reilly 9 *my heart entirely.*/You will keep our appointment?/{E} I shall keep it. {}/[*Sings*]./
399 CP 4m 1 NURSE-SECRETARY *enters, with Appointment/Book.*/{R} About those three
399 CP Nurse 6 made that clear, Sir Henry:/The first appointment at eleven o'clock./He is to be
400 CP Alex 1 /{A} When is Chamberlayne's appointment?/{R} At eleven o'clock,/The
400 CP Alex 7 /At having to wait four days for the appointment./{R} It was necessary to delay his
400 CP Reilly 8 /{R} It was necessary to delay his appointment/To lower his resistance. But what I
447 CC Claude 25 or annoyed/At my making the appointment during her absence,/You must say
482 CC Lady E 3 Were those young people here by appointment?/Or did they come in
504 CC Claude 2 wouldn't be like her/To be late for an appointment. She always mentioned it/If *I* was
531 ES Lambert 35 anyone, my Lord,/But by previous appointment. He said he knew that,/So he had
APPOINTMENTS (1)
399 CP Reilly 1 /*Book.*/{R} About those three appointments this morning, Miss Barraway:/I
APPOINTS (1)
259 MC Thomas 6 /Now my good Angel, whom God appoints/To be my guardian, hover over the
APPRECIATE (8)
187 FQ: DrySal 110 such permanence as time has. We appreciate this better/In the agony of others,
407 CP Reilly 15 of each other/Will prepare you to appreciate what I have to say to you./I do not
469 CC Lucasta 4 /I wish you would teach me how to appreciate it./{C} I don't think that you'll need
478 CC Lucasta 33 I think that now/I'm just beginning to appreciate B./{C} Lucasta, wait! {}/[*Enter* B.
499 CC Lucasta 36 But for Colby/I'd never have come to appreciate B./{SC} But Colby! Lucasta, if I'd
501 CC Lucasta 23 /{L} Thank you. I'm sure he'll appreciate *that*./But that reminds me. He's
535 ES Ld Clav 4 can trust./{LC} You really trust me? I appreciate the compliment./{G} Which you're
573 ES Ld Clav 7 in/Than the crime that everyone can appreciate./For the crime is in relation to the

APPREHEND (2)
189 FQ: DrySal 204 /And clings to that dimension. But to apprehend/The point of intersection of the
345 FR Amy 19 /{A} At my age, I only just begin to apprehend the truth/About things too late to
APPREHENSION (2)
245 MC Priest2 8 you are afraid of, in your craven apprehension,/Let me ask you at the least to put
311 FR Harry 3 feel it?/{M} What, Harry?/{H} That apprehension deeper than all sense,/Deeper than
APPREHENSIVE (1)
421 CP Reilly 30 /You always raise doubts; when I am apprehensive/Then you see no reason for
APPROACH (5)
54 Mr E Sun 17 the Paraclete./The sable presbyters approach/The avenue of penitence;/The young
186 FQ: DrySal 96 but missed the meaning,/And approach to the meaning restores the experience
361 CP Reilly 28 stranger./But let me tell you, that to approach the stranger/Is to invite the
447 CC Eggers 7 /{E} How would you like me to approach the subject?/{SC} Of course, she
508 CC Eggers 15 oil on these troubled waters?/Let us approach the question from another angle,/And
APPROACHING (3)
148 Rock 1 39 respectful distance./For I perceive approaching/The Rock. Who will perhaps
185 FQ: DrySal 33 /And the wailing warning from the approaching headland/Are all sea voices, and
493 CC Claude 19 the first questions./He's very good at approaching a subject/In a roundabout way.
APPROPRIATE (2)
324 FR Harry 37 feeling about John/That you consider appropriate. Only, that's not the language/That
575 ES Gomez 24 is just what I should be! And most appropriate,/Isn't it, Dick, when we recall/That
APPROPRIATED (1)
275 MC Knight3 5 Restore to the King the money you appropriated./{K1} Renew the obedience you
APPROVAL (5)
195 FQ: Little 145 for exercise of virtue./Then fools' approval stings, and honour stains./From
278 MC Knight2 29 ours. So far, I know that I have/your approval: I read it in your faces. It is only with
449 CC Claude 17 {SC} You mustn't overdo it! But your approval matters./You know she thinks the
453 CC Lucasta 36 remember you're only my fiancé on approval./Can I have some money, Eggy?/{E}
573 ES Charles 31 I'm glad my name meets with your approval, Mrs. Carghill./{MC} And let me
APPROVE (2)
232 Skimble 26 /And it's certain that he doesn't approve/Of hilarity and riot, so the folk are very
279 MC Knight2 1 about the state of/affairs that you approve. We have served your interests; we
APPROVED (1)
518 CC Colby 20 very glad indeed — if Mrs. Eggerson approved./{E} There'll be no one so pleased as
APPROXIMATE (1)
164 Rock 9 23 sleet and hail of verbal imprecisions,/Approximate thoughts and feelings, words that
APRIL (3)
19 Portrait 52 go on drinking tea./'Yet with these April sunsets, that somehow recall/My buried
61 WL: Burial 1 Waste Land/The Burial of the Dead/April is the cruellest month, breeding/Lilacs out
184 FQ: DrySal 12 bedroom,/In the rank ailanthus of the April dooryard,/In the smell of grapes on the
APRON (4)
370 CP m 14 {}/[Enter ALEX *in shirtsleeves and an apron*]/{A} Edward, I can't find any curry
376 CP m 2 *repeatedly. Re-enter CELIA, in an apron.*]/{C} You'd better answer the door,
377 CP Julia 1 /Now, my dear, you give me that apron/And we'll see what I can do. You stay
377 CP m 19 devil's that? {}/[*Re-enter JULIA, in apron, with a tray and three glasses*]/{J} I've had
APT (4)
141 Rannoch 8 steel,/Clamour of confused wrong, apt/In silence. Memory is strong/Beyond the
325 FR Gerald 20 about Arthur:/He's much more apt than John to get into trouble./{C} Oh, but
456 CC Eggers 26 health. And when she's abroad/She is apt to buy a house. And then goes away/And
556 ES Monica 5 is like when he's frightened./He's apt to be sullen and quick to take offence./So I
AQUITAINE (2)
75 WL: Thund 429 — O swallow swallow/*Le Prince d'Aquitaine à la tour abolie*/These fragments I have
280 MC Priest3 29 date-tree;/Or sit and bite your nails in Aquitaine./In the small circle of pain within the
ARABIAN (1)
158 Rock 5 2 the Ammonite and Geshem the Arabian: were doubtless men of public spirit
ARBOREAL (1)
52 Whispers 26 sleek Brazilian jaguar/Does not in its arboreal gloom/Distil so rank a feline smell/As
ARBOUR (1)
173 FQ: BurntN 89 the rose-garden,/The moment in the arbour where the rain beat,/The moment in the
ARCADE (1)
346 FR Charles 3 /By the bull-dog in the Burlington Arcade./What if every moment were like that, if
ARCH-DUKE'S (1)
61 WL: Burial 13 when we were children, staying at the arch-duke's,/My cousin's, he took me out on a

ARCHBISHOP (51)

238 MC		m	6	CATHEDRAL/A MESSENGER/ARCHBISHOP THOMAS BECKET/FOUR
238 MC		m	13	PRIESTS/FOUR KNIGHTS/ARCHBISHOP THOMAS BECKET/
239 MC	Chorus		19	summer is over/Seven years since the Archbishop left us,/He who was always kind to
240 MC	Priest1		27	summer is over./Seven years since the Archbishop left us./{P2} What does the
240 MC	Priest2		28	left us./{P2} What does the Archbishop do, and our Sovereign Lord the
241 MC	Mess		13	you, without circumlocution:/The Archbishop is in England, and is close outside
241 MC	Priest1		17	What, is the exile ended, is our Lord Archbishop/Reunited with the King? what
242 MC	Mess		5	/And if you ask me, I think the Lord Archbishop/Is not the man to cherish any
242 MC	Mess		10	is common knowledge that when the Archbishop/Parted from the King, he said to
242 MC	Priest1		17	prognostic. {}/[*Exit*]/{P1} I fear for the Archbishop, I fear for the Church,/I know that
242 MC	Priest2		33	December to dismal December./The Archbishop shall be at our head, dispelling
243 MC	Priest2		2	is beneath our feet. Let us meet the Archbishop with cordial thanksgiving:/Our
243 MC	Priest2		3	cordial thanksgiving:/Our lord, our Archbishop returns. And when the Archbishop
243 MC	Priest2		3	Archbishop returns. And when the Archbishop returns/Our doubts are dispelled.
243 MC	Priest2		6	the Archbishop's man. Let us give the Archbishop welcome!/{P3} For good or ill, let
243 MC	Chorus		18	grey grey grey./O Thomas, return, Archbishop; return, return to France./Return.
244 MC	Chorus		24	which none understands. O Thomas Archbishop,/O Thomas our Lord, leave us and
244 MC	Chorus		26	doom on the house, the doom on the Archbishop, the doom on the world./
244 MC	Chorus		27	Archbishop, the doom on the world./Archbishop, secure and assured of your fate,
244 MC	Chorus		30	the doom of the world?/O Thomas, Archbishop, leave us, leave us, leave sullen
244 MC	Chorus		30	and set sail for France. Thomas our Archbishop still our Archbishop even in France.
244 MC	Chorus		30	Thomas our Archbishop still our Archbishop even in France. Thomas
244 MC	Chorus		30	Archbishop even in France. Thomas Archbishop, set the white sail between the grey
245 MC	Priest2		3	/Do you not know that the good Archbishop/Is likely to arrive at any moment?/
245 MC	Priest2		10	give a hearty welcome to our good Archbishop. {}/[*Enter* THOMAS]/{T} Peace.
248 MC	Tempt2		25	you resigned/When you were made Archbishop — that was a mistake/On your part
252 MC	Thomas		9	of a new constellation./{T} And if the Archbishop cannot trust the King,/How can he
252 MC	Thomas		13	cause against the throne./{T} If the Archbishop cannot trust the Throne,/He has
258 MC	Chorus		1	wing through the dark air./O Thomas Archbishop, save us, save us, save yourself that
260 MC		2m	1	the swords' points. {}/Interlude/THE ARCHBISHOP/*preaches in the Cathedral on*
261 MC	Thomas		39	our martyr of Canterbury,/the blessed Archbishop Elphege; because it is fitting, on
264 MC	Priest1		3	day that was always most dear to the Archbishop Thomas./And he kneeled down and
265 MC	Knight1		15	last night,/Having business with the Archbishop./{K2} Urgent business./{K3} From
265 MC	Priest1		22	are about to go to dinner./The good Archbishop would be vexed/If we did not offer
265 MC	Knight2		29	upon it after./{K2} We must see the Archbishop./{K3} Go, tell the Archbishop/We
265 MC	Knight3		30	see the Archbishop./{K3} Go, tell the Archbishop/We have no need of his hospitality./
266 MC	Knights		14	This is the matter./{3K} You are the Archbishop in revolt against the King; in
266 MC	Knights		15	and the law of the land;/You are the Archbishop who was made by the King; whom
270 MC	Chorus		26	humiliation./I have consented, Lord Archbishop, have consented./Am torn away,
271 MC	Chorus		6	ecstasy of waste and shame,/O Lord Archbishop, O Thomas Archbishop, forgive us,
271 MC	Chorus		6	/O Lord Archbishop, O Thomas Archbishop, forgive us, forgive us, pray for us
277 MC	Knight3		11	it does go against the grain to kill an Archbishop, especially/when you have been
277 MC	Knight3		21	/people come to see that the Archbishop *had* to be put out of the/way — and
277 MC	Knight2		38	spirit of fair play. Now the worthy Archbishop,/whose good qualities I very much
278 MC	Knight2		14	unite/the offices of Chancellor and Archbishop. Had Becket concurred/with the
278 MC	Knight2		20	at the King's instance, had been made Archbishop, he/resigned the office of
278 MC	Knight2		27	with me that such interference by an Archbishop/offends the instincts of a people like
278 MC	Knight2		34	another time, you would/condemn an Archbishop by vote of Parliament and execute
279 MC	Knight4		15	the form of a question: *Who killed/the Archbishop?* As you have been eye-witnesses of
279 MC	Knight4		18	by the last speaker. While the late Archbishop/was Chancellor, no one, under the
279 MC	Knight4		22	needed. From the moment he/became Archbishop, he completely reversed his policy;

ARCHBISHOP'S (5)

238 MC		m	9	/ATTENDANTS/*The scene is the Archbishop's Hall, on December 2nd*, 1170/
238 MC		m	16	/*The first scene is in the Archbishop's Hall,/the second scene is in the*
243 MC	Priest2		6	a glad face for his welcome./I am the Archbishop's man. Let us give the Archbishop
265 MC	Priest1		20	men are outside./{P1} You know the Archbishop's hospitality./We are about to go to
278 MC	Knight2		4	to consider soberly: what/were the Archbishop's aims? and what are King Henry's

ARCHÈD (1)

| 143 Lines OM | | | 8 | the tooth of wit/The hissing over the archèd tongue/Is more affectionate than hate,/ |

ARCTIC (1)

| 160 Rock 7 | | | 12 | pierced by the still dead breath of the Arctic Current;/And they came to an end, a |

ARDOUR (1)

| 190 FQ: DrySal | | | 209 | taken, in a lifetime's death in love,/Ardour and selflessness and self-surrender./For |

ARE (665)
AREA (5)
27 Morning   4   /Sprouting despondently at area gates./The brown waves of fog toss up to
218 Mung Rump   7   of cats can very well bear./If the area window was found ajar/And the basement
223 Pekes Pols   54   he looked out through the bars of the area,/You never saw anything fiercer or hairier./
348 FR   Chorus 24   our understanding/Is a very restricted area./Except for a limited number/Of strictly
474 CC   Lucasta 25   would find yourself in a devastated area —/A bomb-site ... willow-herb ... a dirty
AREN'T (10)
313 FR   Violet   1 CHARLES/{V} Good evening, Mary: aren't you dressed yet?/How do you think that
324 FR   Violet   10   might have had something to say./Aren't you sorry for your brother? Aren't you
324 FR   Violet   10   /Aren't you sorry for your brother? Aren't you aware/Of what is going on? and
366 CP   Julia   1   the greatest mystery./Peter! Why aren't you looking for them?/Look on the
415 CP   Celia   8 don't feel as if I was immoral:/In fact, aren't the people one thinks of as immoral/Just
527 ES   Charles   3   place, we're not engaged yet./{C} Aren't we? We're agreed that we're in love with
527 ES   Charles   6 enough to constitute an engagement?/Aren't you sure that you want to marry me?/
548 ES   Carghil 25   /You are the great Lord Claverton, aren't you?/Somebody said you were coming
562 ES   Carghil 17   be your brother, Michael./I'm right, aren't I?/{Mi} Yes, you're right./But .../{MC}
565 ES   Gomez   19   /You're in business in London, aren't you?/{Mi} Not a holiday, no. I've been in
ARGENTINE (1)
219 Mung Rump   23 up that they wouldn't get thinner/On Argentine joint, potatoes and greens,/And the
ARGOS (1)
329 FR   Chorus 20   nothing of exorcism/And whether in Argos or England/There are certain inflexible
ARGUE (5)
273 MC Thomas 32 me reckless, desperate and mad./You argue by results, as this world does,/To settle if
381 CP   Edward 37   speak,/Who never talks, who cannot argue;/And who in some men may be the
417 CP   Celia   4 illusion/If we rest in it./{C} I cannot argue./It's not that I'm afraid of being hurt
447 CC   Claude 23   believing in her judgment:/We could argue about that. You can't argue with
447 CC   Claude 23   We could argue about that. You can't argue with guidance./But if she appears to be
ARGUED (1)
542 ES   Gomez   26   my companionship./{G} Neatly argued, and almost convincing:/Don't you wish
ARGUMENT (5)
13 Prufrock   8   /Streets that follow like a tedious argument/Of insidious intent/To lead you to an
277 MC Knight1 30 very important point. The gist of his/argument is this: that we have been completely
279 MC Knight4 13   to add along their particular lines of argument./What I have to say may be put in the
341 FR   Agatha 26   or a son/We have no ground for argument./{A} Who set you up to judge? what,
378 CP   Edward 17   thankful./And yet, the effect of all his argument/Was to make me see that I wanted
ARIADNE'S (1)
42 Swee Erect   7   the insurgent gales/Which tangle Ariadne's hair/And swell with haste the
ARID (1)
74 WL: Thund 424 I sat upon the shore/Fishing, with the arid plain behind me/Shall I at least set my
ARIEL (1)
101   t /And let my cry come unto Thee./ARIEL POEMS/Journey of the Magi/'A cold
ARIETTES (1)
19 Portrait   30   the windings of the violins/And the ariettes/Of cracked cornets/Inside my brain a
ARISEN (1)
379 CP   Edward 19   leaving, this would never have arisen./What future had you ever thought there
ARISTOCRATIC (1)
564 ES   Carghil 19   /I do like Spaniards. They're so aristocratic./But it's very strange that we never
ARISTOPHANIC (1)
115 S   m /Sweeney Agonistes/*Fragments of an Aristophanic Melodrama*/Fragment of a Prologue
ARJUNA (1)
188 FQ: DrySal 169 /So Krishna, as when he admonished Arjuna/On the field of battle./Not fare well,/But
ARM (6)
107 Animula   7   alarm,/Retreating to the corner of arm and knee,/Eager to be reassured, taking
109 Marina   18 less clear and clearer/The pulse in the arm, less strong and stronger —/Given or lent?
153 Rock 2   53 /Let the work not delay, time and the arm not waste;/Let the clay be dug from the pit,
178 FQ: ECoker 33   eche other by the hand or the arm/Whiche betokeneth concorde. Round and
250 MC Thomas 16   with the King —/I *was* the King, his arm, his better reason./But what was once
276 MC Chorus 17 from the stone, take the skin from the arm, take the muscle from the bone, and wash
ARMCHAIR (3)
469 CC   3m   1 *seated at the piano;/LUCASTA in an armchair. The concluding bars of a piece of music*
493 CC   Claude 23   not in this chair! She must have an armchair .../{LE} Not such a low one. Leave
526 ES   Monica 23   only a few minutes ago./Here's an armchair, there's the table;/There's the door ...

ARMED (2)
213 Growltiger   40   of their lives —/For the foe was armed with toasting forks and cruel carving
271 MC   Priests   21 time to waste. They are coming back, armed. To the altar, to the altar./{T} All my life
ARMIES (2)
253 MC   Tempt4   33   king:/Uncertain mastery of melting armies,/War, plague, and revolution,/New
281 MC   Chorus   21   shall not depart from it/Though armies trample over it, though sightseers come
ARMS (14)
14 Prufrock   44   pin —/(They will say: 'But how his arms and legs are thin!')/Do I dare/Disturb the
15 Prufrock   62   I presume?/And I have known the arms already, known them all —/Arms that are
15 Prufrock   63   the arms already, known them all —/Arms that are braceleted and white and bare/
15 Prufrock   67   a dress/That makes me so digress?/Arms that lie along a table, or wrap about a
34 Figlia   20   and many hours:/Her hair over her arms and her arms full of flowers./And I
34 Figlia   20   /Her hair over her arms and her arms full of flowers./And I wonder how they
50 Hippopot   30   him clean/And him shall heavenly arms enfold,/Among the saints he shall be seen/
56 Swee Night   2 Sweeney spreads his knees/Letting his arms hang down to laugh,/The zebra stripes
62 WL: Burial   38 late, from the hyacinth garden,/Your arms full, and your hair wet, I could not/Speak,
222 Pekes Pols   16   /He'd slipped into the Wellington Arms for a drink —/And no one at all was
605 Narcissus   10   passing each other/And of his arms crossed over his breast./When he walked
322 FR   Winch 36   his bearings. We've got him at the Arms —/Mr. John, I mean. By a bit of luck/Dr.
323 FR   Winch 23   Road./{A} Where is he?/{Wi} At the Arms, my Lady,/Of course, he hasn't come
519 CC   m 22 of meaning it. {}/[LUCASTA *puts her arms around* SIR CLAUDE]/{SC} Don't leave
ARMY (4)
30 Cous Nancy   13   Waldo, guardians of the faith,/The army of unalterable law./Mr. Apollinax/When
66 WL: Chess   148 think of poor Albert,/He's been in the army four years, he wants a good time,/And if
127 Cor1 March   21   ammunition waggons,/now 55,000 army waggons,/11,000 field kitchens,/1,150 field
301 FR   Violet 23 some blunder, he is useless out of the army./{C} Violet is afraid that her status as
AROSE (1)
193 FQ: Little   87   three districts whence the smoke arose/I met one walking, loitering and hurried/
AROUND (12)
23 Preludes   49 I am moved by fancies that are curled/Around these images, and cling:/The notion of
42 Swee Erect   24   temperament/And wipes the suds around his face./(The lengthened shadow of a
107 Animula   12   on the floor/And running stags around a silver tray;/Confounds the actual and
120 SP   Krum   8 Britisher/A guy like Sam to show you around./Sam of course is at *home* in London,/
120 SP   Krum 10   /And he's promised to show us around. {}/Fragment of an Agon/SWEENEY.
149 Rock 1   71   tropics,/The desert is not only around the corner,/The desert is squeezed in the
177 FQ: ECoker   28 the little drum/And see them dancing around the bonfire/The association of man and
598 Circe   1   flowers of dawn./Circe's Palace/Around her fountain which flows/With the
290 FR   Agatha 31 all the admonitions/From the world around the corner/The wind's talk in the dry
496 CC   Eggers 36 Pretty well./She's always low-spirited, around this season,/When we're getting near the
519 CC   m 22 it. {}/[LUCASTA *puts her arms around* SIR CLAUDE]/{SC} Don't leave me,
546 ES   Piggott 27 you go in to lunch/Just take a glance around the dining-room:/Nobody looks ill!
AROUSE (1)
205 de la Mare   23   /When the nocturnal traveller can arouse/No sleeper by his call; or when by
AROUSED (1)
409 CP   Reilly 39 her/Were different from any you had aroused in him —/It was a shock. You had
ARRANGE (5)
18 Portrait   2   afternoon/You have the scene arrange itself — as it will seem to do —/With 'I
313 FR   Ivy   8 birthday./{I} Mary, my dear,/Did you arrange these flowers? Just let me change them./
445 CC   Claude   6   send Colby./That's not the way to arrange their first meeting,/On her return from
492 CC   Claude 10 /But we must see Mrs. Guzzard. I'll arrange to get her here./{LE} And I think you
504 CC   Claude 19 LUCASTA]/{SC} I wish you could arrange the servants' time-table better./This is a
ARRANGED (5)
360 CP   Edward   4 warning, of course;/Just when she'd arranged a cocktail party./She'd gone when I
362 CP   Reilly 29   with everything about you/Arranged to support you in the role you have
425 CP   Edward 11 them./{E} Perhaps we ought to have arranged to have two parties/Instead of one./{L}
461 CC   Claude 25 now, as a matter of prudence./As we arranged. But after two months —/And as my
525 ES   Charles 2 leaving London, with your father:/I arranged to be free for the whole afternoon/On
ARRANGEMENT (1)
449 CC   Eggers 30 /{E} And so I hope. A most suitable arrangement./But will you tell me this: if it
ARRANGEMENTS (1)
493 CC   Claude   4   meeting,/To decide on the seating arrangements beforehand./I don't think you
ARRANGING (2)
361 CP   Reilly 39   critic, the patient misunderstander/Arranging life a little better than you like it,/
424 CP   3m   1   *in July.* A CATERER'S MAN *is arranging a buffet/table.* LAVINIA *enters from*

ARRAS (1)
177 FQ: ECoker   13   trots/And to shake the tattered arras woven with a silent motto./In my
ARREST (2)
173 FQ: BurntN   66   point, there the dance is,/But neither arrest nor movement. And do not call it fixity,/
250 MC Thomas   13   of God,/In confident ignorance, but arrest disorder,/Make it fast, breed fatal disease,
ARRESTED (1)
571 ES   Ld Clav   38   /A lorry driver. He stopped and was arrested,/But was later discharged. It was
ARRESTING (1)
305 FR   Harry   34   done that. It's very unnatural,/This arresting of the normal change of things:/But
ARRIVAL (2)
447 CC   Claude   6   /Of whom she is to meet on her arrival./{E} How would you like me to approach
461 CC   Claude   29   for both of us./{SC} Her sudden arrival was very disconcerting:/As you gather,
ARRIVE (15)
181 FQ: ECoker   137   again./Shall I say it again? In order to arrive there,/To arrive where you are, to get
181 FQ: ECoker   138   it again? In order to arrive there,/To arrive where you are, to get from where you are
181 FQ: ECoker   140   there is no ecstasy./In order to arrive at what you do not know/You must go
181 FQ: ECoker   144   the way of dispossession./In order to arrive at what you are not/You must go
188 FQ: DrySal   142   who left that station/Or who will arrive at any terminus,/While the narrowing
197 FQ: Little   243   the end of all our exploring/Will be to arrive where we started/And know the place for
246 MC Priest2   4   that the good Archbishop/Is likely to arrive at any moment?/The crowds in the streets
287 FR   Gerald   23   Amy,/When are the boys all due to arrive?/{A} I do not want the clock to stop in
287 FR   Amy   39   and so to London,/And hoped to arrive in the course of the evening./{V} Harry
302 FR   Amy   15   very annoying./Now they can hardly arrive in time to dress./I do not understand
394 CP   Lavinia   16   wanted you to meet,/You didn't arrive until just as they were leaving./{E} Well,
410 CP   Reilly   26   of desires. A prey/To the devils who arrive at their plenitude of power/When they
430 CP   Lavinia   4   Hullo, everybody!/{L} When did you arrive?/{P} I flew over from New York last night
456 CC   Colby   39   /{C} Perhaps she won't even arrive by this plane./{E} Oh, that could happen.
457 CC   Eggers   13   time. {}/[*Looks at his watch*]/{E} I'll arrive at the airport with minutes to spare,/And
ARRIVED (17)
40 Burb Blei   3   at a small hotel;/Princess Volupine arrived,/They were together, and he fell./
103 Journ Magi   30   no information, so we continued/And arrived at evening, not a moment too soon/
278 MC Knight2   38   unnecessary. But, if you have now/arrived at a just subordination of the
303 FR   Mary   11   ... ten surely./I hear that Harry has arrived already/And he was the only one that
305 FR   Mary   21   very early. I thought you had just arrived./Did you have a comfortable journey?/
319 FR   Harry   29   I suppose, the day on which the news arrived./{W} You overinterpret./I am sure that
322 FR   Winch   30   told me he was here, and that you'd arrived./Mr. John's had a bit of an accident/On
336 FR   Harry   19   —/No! you were already here before I arrived./Now I see at last that I am following
337 FR   Amy   30   are you saying to Harry? He has only arrived,/And you tell him to go?/{Ag} He shall
386 CP   Celia   15   *door*.]/{E} Celia!/{C} Has Lavinia arrived?/{E} Celia! Why have you come?/I
390 CP   Alex   18   *it. Enter* ALEX]/{A} Has Lavinia arrived?/{E} Yes./{A} Welcome back, Lavinia!/
393 CP   Edward   3   is a very serious conclusion/To have arrived at in ... how many? ... thirty-two hours./
399 CP   Nurse   20   I need not let you know that she has arrived./Then, when you ring, I show the others
458 CC   Lady E   9   What's surprising, Eggerson? I've arrived, that's all./{E} I was just starting for
458 CC   Lady E   13   And besides,/I didn't come by air. I arrived at Victoria./{SC} Do you mean to say
481 CC   Lady E   16   evening, Lucasta./Have you just arrived, or are you just leaving?/{L} We're on
487 CC   Lady E   35   Oh, I forgot/In my excitement: you arrived the very moment/When the truth
ARRIVES (6)
68 WL: Fire S   231   /He, the young man carbuncular, arrives,/A small house agent's clerk, with one
266 MC Thomas   3   foreseen may be unexpected/When it arrives. It comes when we are/Engrossed with
399 CP   Nurse   11   into the other room/Just as usual. She arrives at a quarter past;/But you may keep her
399 CP   Nurse   16   telephone through/The moment she arrives. I leave her there/Until you ring three
422 CP   Reilly   1   /{R} Miss Barraway, when Mr. Gibbs arrives .../Oh, very good. {}/[*To* JULIA]/{R}
498 CC   Claude   37   will be here shortly./And when she arrives I will summon Colby./I wanted you here
ARRIVING (1)
439 CP   Julia   36   be ready for it./Their guests may be arriving at any moment./{R} Julia, you are
ARROGANT (1)
258 MC Thomas   36   /Senseless self-slaughter of a lunatic,/Arrogant passion of a fanatic./I know that
ARROGATED (1)
275 MC Knight2   4   /{K2} Resign the powers you have arrogated./{K3} Restore to the King the money
ARRONDIE (1)
51 Restaurant   6   gueux.'/(Bavard, baveux, à la croupe arrondie,/Je te prie, au moins, ne bave pas dans
ARROW (1)
142 Cape Ann   9   Follow the flight/Of the dancing arrow, the purple martin. Greet/In silence the

ARROWS (2)

606 Narcissus	34	his flesh was in love with the burning arrows/He danced on the hot sand/Until the
606 Narcissus	36	/He danced on the hot sand/Until the arrows came./As he embraced them his white

ART (11)

180 FQ: ECoker	105	of letters./The generous patrons of art, the statesmen and the rulers,/Distinguished
181 FQ: ECoker	152	/The sharp compassion of the healer's art/Resolving the enigma of the fever chart./Our
205 de la Mare	31	measure is refined;/By conscious art practised with natural ease;/By the delicate,
240 MC Priest3	34	I see nothing quite conclusive in the art of temporal government,/But violence,
367 CP Peter	22	sarcastic:/Celia was interested in the art of the film./{E} As a possible profession?/{P}
459 CC Lady E	9	frail./I must give you lessons in the art of health./Where is your home, Mr. Colby?/
463 CC Colby	30	a moment the thing I cannot do,/The art that I could never excel in,/Seems the one
464 CC Claude	8	—/In either case, an inferior art./For me, they are neither 'use' nor
492 CC Claude	32	at all/About ceramics ... or any other art./No, I don't think I shall be in a reminiscent
496 CC Claude	4	with *me*:/Health cures. And modern art — so long as it was modern —/And dervish
552 ES Carghil	5	Avenue./{MC} Yes, I had my art./Don't you remember what a hit I made/

ARTAXERXES (1)

157 Rock 4	6	Nisan,/He served the wine to the king Artaxerxes,/And he grieved for the broken city,

ARTERY (2)

172 FQ: BurntN	54	forgotten wars./The dance along the artery/The circulation of the lymph/Are figured
301 FR Chorus	32	thrombosis/And the slowly hardening artery./We like to be thought well of by others/

ARTFUL (3)

128 Cor1 March	47	sausage,/It'll come in handy. He's artful. Please, will you/Give us a light?/Light/
214 RTTugger	31	larder shelf./The Rum Tum Tugger is artful and knowing,/The Rum Tum Tugger
469 CC Lucasta	16	/{L} Colby, I didn't know you were so artful!/So the things I liked were the right ones

ARTHUR (36)

129 Cor2 State	12	several committees./What shall I cry?/Arthur Edward Cyril Parker is appointed
287 FR Amy	34	I cannot find./— I am only certain of Arthur and John,/Arthur in London, John in
287 FR Amy	35	I am only certain of Arthur and John,/Arthur in London, John in Leicestershire:/They
291 FR Amy	11	way to come./John at least, if not Arthur. Hark, there is someone coming:/Yes, it
302 FR Amy	11	taken it to be./{A} Ivy! Violet! has Arthur or John come yet?/{I} There is no news
302 FR Ivy	12	come yet?/{I} There is no news of Arthur or John. {}/[*Enter* AMY *and* AGATHA]
303 FR Mary	13	was the only one that was uncertain./Arthur or John may be late, of course./We may
303 FR Mary	25	is coming./I shall have to sit between Arthur and John./Which is worse, thinking of
307 FR Harry	3	/From which we fought the Indians, Arthur and John./{M} It was the cave where we
307 FR Harry	6	/To raise the evil spirits./{H} Arthur and John./Of course we were punished
313 FR Charles	19	late. {}/[*Exit*]/{C} Now we only want Arthur and John/I'm glad that you'll all be
313 FR Amy	25	head of the family./{A} Violet! Has Arthur or John come yet?/{V} Neither of them
315 FR Gerald	22	/{G} Is there any use in waiting for Arthur and John?/{A} We might as well go in to
319 FR Harry	19	/{H} But now I do remember. Not Arthur or John,/They were too young. But now
320 FR Warburt	33	—/You know as well as I do that Arthur and John/Have been a great
320 FR Warburt	36	— but he's not exactly brilliant,/And Arthur has always been rather irresponsible./
323 FR Amy	6	Harry!/Who's there with you? Is it Arthur or John? {}/[*Enter* AMY, *followed*
325 FR Gerald	19	presents./{G} But *I*'m worried about Arthur:/He's much more apt than John to get
325 FR Ivy	26	I remember, when they were boys,/Arthur was always the more adventurous/But
325 FR Violet	31	on his head./{V} But a year ago, Arthur took me out in his car,/And I told him I
326 FR Gerald	7	wonder how much Amy knows about Arthur?/{C} More than she cares to mention, I
326 FR Denman	35	give his name, Miss; but it's Mr. Arthur./{I} Arthur! Oh dear, I'm afraid *he*'s had
326 FR Ivy	36	name, Miss; but it's Mr. Arthur./{I} Arthur! Oh dear, I'm afraid *he*'s had an
327 FR Ivy	26	the matter./{I} Somebody, look for Arthur in the evening paper./That was Arthur,
327 FR Ivy	27	in the evening paper./That was Arthur, ringing up from London:/The
327 FR Ivy	29	his voice was very queer. It seems that Arthur too/Has had an accident. I don't think
328 FR Gerald	2	in that. {}/[*Exit*]/{G} Well, I said that Arthur was every bit as likely/To have an
328 FR Gerald	5	/I don't believe. John is unlucky,/But Arthur is definitely reckless./{V} I think these
328 FR Charles	12	*Brother in Motor Smash*/The Hon. Arthur Gerald Charles Piper, younger brother
328 FR Ivy	31	explaining this to Amy./{I} Poor Arthur! I'm sure that you're being much too
330 FR Harry	2	will recover, be what he always was;/Arthur again be sober, though not for very
343 FR Harry	31	{H} But, mother, you will always have Arthur and John/To worry about: not that John
345 FR Harry	10	/Of such accidents as happen to Arthur and John:/Take care of *them*. My
347 FR Ivy	15	/Look. Here's a telegram come from Arthur; {}/[*Enter* GERALD *and* VIOLET]/{I} I
347 FR Ivy	19	many happy returns hurrah love Arthur.'/I mean, after what we know of what
349 FR Gerald	9	forward with pleasure to dealing with Arthur and John in the morning./{V} We must

ARTHUR'S (3)

303 FR Mary	27	to say to John,/Or having to listen to Arthur's chatter/When he thinks he is behaving
313 FR Charles	22	the influence of their elder brother./Arthur's a bit irresponsible, you know;/You
325 FR Charles	21	John to get into trouble./{C} Oh, but Arthur's a brilliant driver./After all the

ARTICLES (1)
531 ES   Charles   6   in the papers./{C} And the leading articles saying 'we are confident/That his
ARTIST (4)
164 Rock 9   17   /Out of the formless stone, when the artist unites himself with stone,/Spring always
495 CC   Lady E   17   did *you* want?/{LE} To inspire an artist. Don't laugh./{SC} I'm not laughing./So
495 CC   Claude   19 So what you wanted was to inspire an artist!/{LE} Or to inspire a poet. I thought Tony
495 CC   Lady E   30   to forget/Colby. But Colby is an artist./{SC} A musician./I am a disappointed
ARTIST'S (1)
164 Rock 9   20   is living or lifeless/Joined with the artist's eye, new life, new form, new colour./Out
ARTISTIC (1)
459 CC   Lady E   8   most people think./You should be artistic. But you look rather frail./I must give
ARTISTS (1)
367 CP   Peter   13   deal in common./We're both of us artists./{E} I never thought of that./What arts
ARTS (2)
155 Rock 3   61   and the glory of your action,/To arts and inventions and daring enterprises,/To
367 CP   Edward   15 /{E} I never thought of that./What arts do you practise?/{P} You won't have seen
AS (699)
AS (1) [*Foreign word*]
51 Restaurant   20   /C'est dommage.'/Mais alors, tu as ton vautour!/Va t'en te décrotter les rides du
ASCEND (2)
172 FQ: BurntN   57 lymph/Are figured in the drift of stars/Ascend to summer in the tree/We move above
281 MC   Priest3 5   /Remember us./{P3} Let our thanks ascend/To God, who has given us another Saint
ASCENDED (1)
64 WL: Chess   90   freshened from the window, these ascended/In fattening the prolonged
ASCENDING (1)
50 Hippopot   26 at once./I saw the 'potamus take wing/Ascending from the damp savannas,/And
ASCENDS (1)
181 FQ: ECoker 164 but prevents us everywhere./The chill ascends from feet to knees,/The fever sings in
ASCENT (1)
173 FQ: BurntN   68 movement from nor towards,/Neither ascent nor decline. Except for the point, the still
ASCETIC (1)
278 MC Knight2   22   and offensively adopted an ascetic/manner of life, he affirmed immediately
ASCÉTIQUE (1)
48 Lune Miel   16 France./Et Saint Apollinaire, raide et ascétique,/Vieille usine désaffectée de Dieu, tient
ASCOSE (1)
75 WL: Thund   427 down falling down falling down/*Poi s'ascose nel foco che gli affina*/*Quando fiam uti*
ASH (2)
192 FQ: Little   56   and nowhere. Never and always./Ash on an old man's sleeve/Is all the ash the
192 FQ: Little   57 /Ash on an old man's sleeve/Is all the ash the burnt roses leave./Dust in the air
ASH-WEDNESDAY (1)
87 Ash-Wed   t   *ends*/*Not with a bang but a whimper.*/Ash-Wednesday/Because I do not hope to turn
ASHAMED (8)
66 WL: Chess   156 be for lack of telling./You ought to be ashamed, I said, to look so antique./(And her
151 Rock 2   7   not fitly framed together, you sit ashamed and wonder whether and how you
477 CC   Lucasta 21   mistress./Claude has always been ashamed of me:/Now *you're* ashamed of me. I
477 CC   Lucasta 22   been ashamed of me:/Now *you're* ashamed of me. I thought you'd understand./
501 CC   Lucasta 13 /I'm very conventional. And I'm not ashamed of it./{SC} Perhaps you are right. I'm
502 CC   Lucasta 14 /In the way I thought you were. I was ashamed/Of what I was telling you, and so I
551 ES   Carghil 5   /Besides a woman has nothing to be ashamed of:/A man is always trying to forget/
580 ES   Monica   33   himself, the unhappy self that he's ashamed of./I'm sure he loves us./{LC} Monica
ASHES (3)
177 FQ: ECoker   6   old timber to new fires,/Old fires to ashes, and ashes to the earth/Which is already
177 FQ: ECoker   6   to new fires,/Old fires to ashes, and ashes to the earth/Which is already flesh, fur
276 MC Chorus   6 broom,/The night-time heaping of the ashes,/The fuel laid on the fire at daybreak,/
ASIA (1)
189 FQ: DrySal   202 perplexity/Whether on the shores of Asia, or in the Edgware Road./Men's curiosity
ASIDE (1)
140 Usk   4 hart behind the white well./Glance aside, not for lance, do not spell/Old
ASK (82)
13 Prufrock   11 overwhelming question.../Oh, do not ask, 'What is it?'/Let us go and make our visit./
118 SP   Dusty   7   got to know what you want to ask them/{Do} You've got to know what you
155 Rock 3   58 prepared for him who knows how to ask questions./O weariness of men who turn
233 Skimble   41   the guard looks in politely and will ask you very brightly/'Do you like your
593 Grad 7   4 labor for the good until they die,/And ask no other guerdon than to know/That they
242 MC   Mess   4 of peace./A patched up affair, if you ask my opinion./And if you ask me, I think the

242	MC	Mess	5	if you ask my opinion./And if you ask me, I think the Lord Archbishop/Is not the
242	MC	Mess	8	the least of his pretensions./If you ask my opinion, I think that this peace/Is
244	MC	Chorus	25	frame of existence, leave us; do not ask us/To stand to the doom on the house, the
244	MC	Chorus	27	the shades, do you realise what you ask, do you realise what it means/To the small
245	MC	Priest2	9	in your craven apprehension,/Let me ask you at the least to put on pleasant faces,/
254	MC	Tempt4	9	/{T4} Save what you know already, ask nothing of me./But think, Thomas, think of
255	MC	Thomas	21	/What do you offer? what do you ask?/{T4} I offer what you desire. I ask/What
255	MC	Tempt4	22	ask?/{T4} I offer what you desire. I ask/What you have to give. Is it too much?/For
261	MC	Thomas	4	What then did He mean? If you ask that, remember/then that He said also, 'Not
266	MC	Knight2	34	your insolence and greed./Won't you ask us to pray to God for you, in your need?/
278	MC	Knight2	3	in by/emotional clap-trap. I therefore ask you to consider soberly: what/were the
287	FR	Mary	8	the younger generation, you must ask someone else./I'm afraid that I don't
289	FR	Amy	30	she been drinking?/{A} I would never ask him./{I} These things are much better not
296	FR	Gerald	34	/Why not ring up Warburton, and ask him to join us?/He's an old friend of the
297	FR	Charles	25	{}/[Rings the bell]/{C} That I'd like to ask Downing./He shan't know why I'm asking.
302	FR	Chorus	4	any explanation will satisfy:/We only ask to be reassured/About the noises in the
303	FR	Mary	18	/For uncertain numbers. Why did she ask him?/{Ag} She only thought of asking him a
304	FR	Mary	8	advice, because there's no one else to ask,/And because you are strong, and because
306	FR	Harry	11	{H} There was something/I wanted to ask you. I don't know yet./All these years I'd
319	FR	Harry	36	close. If you won't tell me,/I must ask Agatha. I never dared before./{W} I advise
319	FR	Warburt	37	/{W} I advise you strongly, not to ask your aunt —/I mean, there is nothing she
322	FR	Winch	7	years. How is her Ladyship,/If I may ask, my Lord?/{H} Why do you keep asking/
331	FR	Harry	16	If I knew, then I should not have to ask./You know what I want to know, and that
340	FR	Amy	1	AMY, AGATHA/{A} I was a fool, to ask you again to Wishwood;/But I thought,
342	FR	Mary	21	is in great danger, I know that, don't ask me,/You would not believe me, but I tell
344	FR	Amy	3	Harry going? What is the matter?/{A} Ask Agatha./{G} Why, what's the matter?
344	FR	Amy	5	the matter? Where is he going?/{A} Ask Agatha./{V} I cannot understand at all.
344	FR	Amy	7	at all. Why is he leaving?/{A} Ask Agatha./{V} Really, it sometimes seems to
356	CP	Julia	19	are so many questions/I want to ask you. It's a golden opportunity/Now
363	CP	Edward	31	that she is coming back'./And they ask 'But what are you going to do?'/And I
364	CP	Edward	3	that I could describe her/If I had to ask the police to search for her./I'm sure I don't
364	CP	Reilly	21	one condition:/That you promise to ask her no questions/Of where she has been./{E}
364	CP	Edward	23	/Of where she has been./{E} I will not ask them./And yet — it seems to me — when we
382	CP	Celia	34	was simply making use of you./And I ask you to forgive me./{E} You ... ask me to
382	CP	Edward	35	I ask you to forgive me./{E} You ... ask me to forgive you!/{C} Yes, for two things.
385	CP	Reilly	22	obliterate/The last five years./{UG} I ask you to forget nothing./To try to forget is to
385	CP	Reilly	29	/When you see your wife, you must ask no questions/And give no explanations. I
386	CP	Reilly	2	not prepared to explain to you/I must ask you not to speak of me to her;/And she will
386	CP	Edward	10	by the service staircase./{E} May I ask one question?/{UG} You may ask it./{E}
386	CP	Reilly	11	I ask one question?/{UG} You may ask it./{E} Who are you?/{UG} I also am a
388	CP	Lavinia	34	/{P} Yes, and Alex./{L} Then I shall ask them for an explanation./Meanwhile, I
390	CP	Lavinia	7	your telegram./{L} But where, may I ask, was this telegram sent from?/{J} Why, from
392	CP	Edward	4	I said it./Well, here I am./{E} I am to ask no questions./{L} And I know I am to give
392	CP	Lavinia	7	give no explanations./{L} And I am to ask no questions. And yet ... why not?/{E} I
399	CP	Reilly	25	{N} Mr. Gibbs is here, Sir Henry./{R} Ask him to come straight in. {}/[Exit
401	CP	Reilly	16	as well sit down./You were going to ask a question./{E} When you came to my flat/
405	CP	Edward	35	/I am going to a hotel. And I shall ask you, Lavinia,/To be so good as to send me
408	CP	Reilly	29	/About my patients. You must not ask me to reveal it —/That is a matter of
411	CP	Lavinia	17	/Edward, have you anything else to ask him/Before we go?/{E} Yes, I have./But it's
411	CP	Lavinia	22	there is something I would like you to ask./{E} It's about the future of ... the others./I
420	CP	Celia	10	that. Oh, I almost forgot —/May I ask what your fee is?/{R} I have told my
425	CP	Lavinia	19	accepted./You know we said, 'we can ask twenty more/Because they will be going to
433	CP	Peter	12	you./But there's someone I wanted to ask about,/Who did really want to get into
435	CP	Peter	12	wanted to know/And did not dare to ask. It took all my courage/To ask you about
435	CP	Peter	13	to ask. It took all my courage/To ask you about her just now; but I never thought
435	CP	Reilly	17	/Which is the most that any of us can ask for./{P} And what a métier! I've tried to
437	CP	Reilly	18	your credulity, Mrs. Chamberlayne,/I ask you only to entertain the suggestion/That a
454	CC	Eggers	1	matters himself./You will have to ask Sir Claude. But I'll speak to him/When I
461	CC	Eggers	15	Mrs. E. keeps saying:/'Why don't you ask him out to dinner one Sunday?'/But I say:
461	CC	Eggers	16	one Sunday?'/But I say: 'We couldn't ask him to come/All the way to Joshua Park, at
464	CC	Colby	23	/Into terms of music. But may I ask,/With this passion for ... ceramics, how did
466	CC	Claude	27	mention it again. I'll wait until you ask me./Do you understand now what I meant
481	CC	Lady E	38	mention my name, Mr. Kaghan,/And ask for the table in the left hand corner:/It has
498	CC	Claude	25	/{SC} But Eggerson, you really can't ask me to believe/That she took two babies, and
507	CC	Eggers	4	or elsewhere?/Now I must ask a more delicate question:/Did you, at any

508	CC	Eggers	16	the question from another angle,/And ask Mrs. Guzzard what became of the child/She
510	CC	Eggers	4	if you agree, Lady Elizabeth,/We can ask Mr. Kaghan about his parents;/And if Mr.
512	CC	Guzzard	20	questions —/And now it is my turn to ask them./I should like to gratify everyone's
513	CC	Guzzard	3	are the wisest wisher here:/I shall not ask you whether you are satisfied/To be the wife
513	CC	Guzzard	10	daughter./{MG} Now, Colby, I must ask *you* now, have you had your wish?/{SC}
515	CC	Guzzard	17	child is yours',/I feared you would ask for the birth certificate./You never did. And
517	CC	Claude	3	Now I know mine./{SC} I shall never ask you to think of me as a father;/All I ask you
517	CC	Claude	4	you to think of me as a father;/All I ask you is — to regard me as a friend./{C} But
519	CC	Lady E	13	/And not knowing what one should ask of other people,/One does make mistakes!
529	ES	Monica	15	of being envious./It's all we can ask if compassion and wistfulness .../And
556	ES	Monica	27	you know what you've come to ask of Father/And Father knows that you want

ASKED (36)

66	WL:	Chess	167	they had a hot gammon,/And they asked me in to dinner, to get the beauty of it hot
68	WL:	Fire S	212	/C.i.f. London: documents at sight,/Asked me in demotic French/To luncheon at
296	FR	Gerald	36	perfectly natural/That he should be asked. He looked after all the boys/When they
304	FR	Agatha	33	ever met her,/The only one Harry asked to his wedding:/Amy did not know that. I
328	FR	Charles	23	at the rate of 66 miles an hour. When asked why he/did not stop when signalled by the
340	FR	Amy	27	to the purposes of Wishwood;/I even asked you back, for visits, after he was gone,/So
358	CP	Edward	8-	people you're to meet./{E} But you asked me to dine with you alone./{J} Yes, alone!
368	CP	Peter	30	where did you leave off?/{P} You asked me how I came to know Celia./I met her
369	CP	Edward	14	to talk to her./{E} You and Celia were asked for different purposes./Your role was to
377	CP	Edward	14	I could believe he was./{E} Because I asked him to./{C} Because you asked him to!/
377	CP	Celia	15	I asked him to./{C} Because you asked him to!/Then he *must* be the Devil! He
379	CP	Celia	29	in it till to-day,/And then, when Julia asked about Lavinia/And it came to me that
386	CP	Celia	19	you come here?/{C} Because Lavinia asked me./{E} Because Lavinia asked you!/{C}
386	CP	Edward	20	asked me./{E} Because Lavinia asked you!/{C} Well, not directly. Julia had a
406	CP	Lavinia	10	/{L} What do you mean? I asked to be sent/And you took me there. If that
425	CP	Edward	5	them./{E} Well, you deserve it. — We asked too many people./{L} It's true, a great
425	CP	Lavinia	14	never satisfactory./Everyone who's asked to either party/Suspects that the other
435	CP	Peter	11	to know about Celia/And so I never asked. Then I wanted to know/And did not
448	CC	Claude	2	told him about her?/You remember, I asked you to prepare him a little;/There are
452	CC	Lucasta	20	it. And then he got suspicious/And asked for things I'm sure he didn't want —/Just
452	CC	Lucasta	34	you./{L} Snubbed again! I suppose I asked for it./That's what comes of being cursed
453	CC	Lucasta	18	Mrs. Eggerson;/That's why he's never asked me out to lunch./{E} We will leave Mrs.
467	CC	Colby	38	in the City/Tomorrow morning. You asked me to prepare/Some figures for you. I've
469	CC	Lucasta	21	invites me,/And no one has ever asked me to a concert./I've been to the Opera,
482	CC	Colby	5	/{C} I'd invited Lucasta. She had asked me to play to her./{LE} You call her
487	CC	Claude	10	help than Eggerson./I couldn't have asked Eggerson to write a speech for me./Oh, by
497	CC	Claude	6	are we expecting her?/{SC} I have asked her to come. Lady Elizabeth/Is sure that
497	CC	Claude	31	the facts. And that is why/I have asked Mrs. Guzzard here. *She* doesn't know
505	CC	Claude	6	friend —/For very many years. So I asked him to be present./I hope you don't
506	CC	Eggers	24	be a clue./That is why Sir Claude has asked you to be present./{MG} You think that I
508	CC	Claude	1	her son. I know he is *my* son./And I asked you here so that you might tell her so./{E}
512	CC	Guzzard	19	Mrs. Guzzard./{MG} I have been asked here to answer strange questions —/And
535	ES	Gomez	1	But why have you come?/{G} You've asked me that already!/To see you, Dick. A
541	ES	Lambert	31	me, my Lord, but Miss Monica asked me/To remind you there's a trunk call
544	ES	Monica	7	really *is* a chambermaid:/For when I asked about morning coffee/She said 'I'm not
569	ES	Ld Clav	26	before,/Not so very long ago. When I asked him what he wanted./Oh no, he said, I

ASKING (16)

118	SP	Dusty	9	you want to know/{Du} It's no use asking them too much/{Do} It's no use asking
118	SP	Doris	10	them too much/{Do} It's no use asking more than once/{Du} Sometimes they're
261	MC	Thomas	38	of God, of the martyrs of/the past, asking you to remember especially our martyr
297	FR	Charles	26	Downing./He shan't know why I'm asking. {}/[*Enter* DENMAN]/{C} Denman,
298	FR	Agatha	9	objection,/Any more than I object to asking Dr. Warburton?/I only see that this is all
303	FR	Agatha	19	ask him?/{Ag} She only thought of asking him a little while ago./{M} Well, there's
322	FR	Harry	8	ask, my Lord?/{H} Why do you keep asking/About her Ladyship? Do you know or
322	FR	Winch	13	see, my Lord, I had good reason for asking .../{H} Well, do you want me to produce
326	FR	Violet	37	/{V} When it's Ivy that he's asking for, I expect the worst./{Ag} Whatever
327	FR	Violet	35	tell his mother./{V} What's the use of asking for an evening paper?/You know as well
386	CP	Celia	22	not directly. Julia had a telegram/Asking her to come, and to bring me with her./
425	CP	Lavinia	10	/To hear we'd given a party without asking them./{E} Perhaps we ought to have
462	CC	Claude	26	/But tell me first — I've a reason for asking —/How do you like your work? You
463	CC	Colby	9	in your music .../{C} You started by asking me how I found this work./{SC} Yes,
488	CC	Claude	6	now to piece it together./You've been asking Colby about his family .../{LE} And
510	CC	Kaghan	31	they keep bees. But why are you asking?/{LE} Because, Barnabas, it seems you

ASKS (1)

251 MC Tempt3   36   —/To gain from you, your Lordship asks./For us, Church favour would be an

ASLEEP (11)

13 Prufrock   22   Curled once about the house, and fell asleep./And indeed there will be time/For the
15 Prufrock   77   peacefully!/Smoothed by long fingers,/Asleep ... tired ... or it malingers,/Stretched on
167 Rock 10   37   who are up in the night and fall asleep as the rocket is fired; and the day is long
210 Old Gumbie   7   /And when all the family's in bed and asleep,/She tucks up her skirts to the basement
225 Mr Mistoff   53   the garden for hours,/While he was asleep in the hall./And not long ago this
226 Macavity   16   snake;/And when you think he's half asleep, he's always wide awake./Macavity,
233 Skimble   55   there to catch a flea./You were fast asleep at Crewe and so you never knew/That he
326 FR   Harry 9   {}/[*Enter* HARRY]/{H} Mother is asleep, I think: it's strange how the old/Can
348 FR   Chorus 10   resembles what happens when we are asleep./We understand the ordinary business of
548 ES   Monica 11   /And pretend you're pretending to be asleep./If they think you *are* asleep they'll do
548 ES   Monica 12   to be asleep./If they think you *are* asleep they'll do something to wake you,/But if

ASPARAGUS (1)

228 Gus   3   to have told you before,/Is really Asparagus. That's such a fuss/To pronounce,

ASPECT (1)

175 FQ: BurntN 169   and undesiring/Except in the aspect of time/Caught in the form of limitation/

ASPHALT (2)

155 Rock 3   35   people:/Their only monument the asphalt road/And a thousand lost golf balls'./
193 FQ: Little   86   leaves still rattled on like tin/Over the asphalt where no other sound was/Between

ASPIRED (2)

382 CP   Celia 30   —/No, not *wanted* — something I aspired to —/Something that I desperately
465 CC   Colby 35   have become a great organist,/As I aspired to be. I'm not an executant;/I'm only a

ASSAIL (1)

175 FQ: BurntN 158   or merely chattering,/Always assail them. The Word in the desert/Is most

ASSAULTS (1)

68 WL: Fire S   239   if undesired./Flushed and decided, he assaults at once;/Exploring hands encounter no

ASSEMBLED (3)

218 Mung Rump   21   in conversation./When the family assembled for Sunday dinner,/With their minds
223 Pekes Pols   46   Now when these bold heroes together assembled,/The traffic all stopped, and the
290 FR   Chorus 37   impatient, fretful, ill at ease,/Assembled like amateur actors who have not

ASSERT (1)

479 CC Kaghan   25   interfering. Be firm with her, Colby;/Assert your right to a little privacy./Now's the

ASSERTED (1)

14 Prufrock   43   /My necktie rich and modest, but asserted by a simple pin —/(They will say: 'But

ASSERTION (1)

251 MC Tempt3   14   the King. You look only/To blind assertion in isolation./That is a mistake./{T} O

ASSET (1)

451 CC Eggers   35   Your music will certainly be a great asset/With Lady Elizabeth. I envy you that./I've

ASSIGN (1)

186 FQ: DrySal   98   form, beyond any meaning/We can assign to happiness. I have said before/That the

ASSIGNED (1)

290 FR   Chorus 37   amateur actors who have not been assigned their parts?/Like amateur actors in a

ASSISTANCE (1)

538 ES Ld Clav 7   to have forgotten:/I came to your assistance when you were released./{G} Yes, and

ASSOCIATE (2)

298 FR   Ivy   6   /{V} I do object./{I} And I wish to associate myself with my sister/In her objections
331 FR   Harry 5   over. When I was outside,/I could associate nothing of it with myself,/Though

ASSOCIATES (2)

301 FR   Ivy   21   vulgarity, acquired from worldly associates./{G} Ivy is only concerned for herself,
531 ES Ld Clav 24   are mildly grieved,/And our closest associates, the small minority/Of those who

ASSOCIATION (1)

177 FQ: ECoker   29   them dancing around the bonfire/The association of man and woman/In daunsinge,

ASSUME (4)

23 Preludes   47   of a blackened street/Impatient to assume the world./I am moved by fancies that
163 Rock 8   45   the Cross/Because they will never assume it./Yet nothing is impossible, nothing,/
395 CP Edward   15   is very interesting:/But you seem to assume that you've done all the changing —/
526 ES Monica   37   company but his!/{M} You're not to assume that anything I've said to you/Has given

ASSUMED (5)

193 FQ: Little   99   Both intimate and unidentifiable./So I assumed a double part, and cried/And heard
332 FR Agatha   7   /{Ag} The dead man whom you have assumed to be your father,/And my sister whom
432 CP Lavinia 28   — {}/[*Turning to* ALEX]/{L} I rather assumed that you knew each other —/I don't
515 CC Guzzard 7   news to you./You saw the child. You assumed that it was yours;/And you were so
558 ES Michael 32   too familiar with one of the girls./He assumed it had gone a good deal further than it

ASSUMING (1)
498 CC   Eggers   8   Mrs. Guzzards in Teddington./But assuming, for the moment, only one Mrs.
ASSUMPTION (1)
395 CP   Lavinia   35   you/Has always been your placid assumption/That I wasn't worth the trouble of
ASSURANCE (6)
 68 WL: Fire S   233   bold stare,/One of the low on whom assurance sits/As a silk hat on a Bradford
187 FQ: DrySal 103   /The backward look behind the assurance/Of recorded history, the backward
241 MC   Priest1 26   or war?/{P1} Does he come/In full assurance, or only secure/In the power of
241 MC   Priest1 28   of Rome, the spiritual rule,/The assurance of right, and the love of the people?/
395 CP   Edward   32   you/Has always been your perfect assurance/That you understood me better than I
526 ES   Charles   7   must say it again,/For I need so much assurance! Are you sure you're not mistaken?/
ASSURE (9)
124 SA   Snow   11   Let Mr. Sweeney continue his story./I assure you, Sir, we are very interested./{S} I
242 MC   Mess   14   life I shall not see again./I have this, I assure you, on the highest authority;/There are
379 CP   Celia   5   /{C} Edward, if I go now,/Will you assure me that everything is right,/That you do
394 CP   Edward   37   But, in future,/I shall behave, I assure you, very differently./{L} Bravo! Edward.
457 CC   Eggers   10   You'll come to find that I'm right, I assure you. {}/[*Enter* SIR CLAUDE]/{SC}
486 CC   Colby   29   interesting about my background —/I assure you there isn't./{LE} It may be more
518 CC   Eggers   22   so pleased as Mrs. E.;/Of that I can assure you./{MG} Mr. Eggerson,/I cannot see
533 ES   Gomez   36   right places, pays many times over./I assure you it does./{LC} In other words/You
543 ES   Gomez   6   been an elixir/To see you again, and assure myself/That we can begin just where we
ASSURED (9)
 23 Preludes   45   /And evening newspapers, and eyes/Assured of certain certainties,/The conscience of
152 Rock 2   23   the Word of GOD:/The British race assured of a mission/Performed it, but left much
241 MC   Mess   31   and sorrow, affirming all his claims,/Assured, beyond doubt, of the devotion of the
244 MC   Chorus   27   on the world./Archbishop, secure and assured of your fate, unaffrayed among the
285 FR   Amy   9   clocks could be trusted, tomorrow assured/And time would not stop in the dark!/
307 FR   Mary   24   very difficult to bear./They are always assured that you ought to be happy/At the very
338 FR   Harry   39   has just recovered sanity,/And not yet assured in possession, that is when/One begins
341 FR   Amy   37   of success against failure,/When I felt assured of his settlement and happiness,/You
515 CC   Guzzard 12   the child was yours,/My son was assured of a proper start in life —/That I knew.
ASTHMATIC (1)
583 ES   Charles   6   words are so inadequate./Yet, like the asthmatic struggling for breath,/So the lover
ASTONISHING (2)
548 ES   Carghil   30   here talking to you./Dear me, it's astonishing, after all these years;/And you don't
562 ES   Carghil   27   I'm Mrs. John Carghill./Richard! It's astonishing about your children:/Monica hardly
ASTONISHMENT (2)
587 Fable   24   he sat the prior on the steeple,/To the astonishment of all the people./When Christmas
437 CP   Reilly   15   Coplestone whose face showed the astonishment/Of the first five minutes after a
ASTRAY (1)
226 Macavity   27   Foreign Office find a Treaty's gone astray,/Or the Admiralty lose some plans and
ASUNDER (1)
194 FQ: Little 136   fruit/As body and soul begin to fall asunder./Second, the conscious impotence of
AT (751)
ATE (1)
258 MC   Thomas   25   matched their finger-nails./While I ate out of the King's dish/To become servant of
ATHENS (1)
 73 WL: Thund 374   violet air/Falling towers/Jerusalem Athens Alexandria/Vienna London/Unreal/A
ATLANTIS (1)
448 CC   Claude   10   of Revelation? And the Wisdom of Atlantis?/{E} Well, to tell the truth, Sir Claude,
ATMOSPHERE (3)
 18 Portrait   6   of light upon the ceiling overhead,/An atmosphere of Juliet's tomb/Prepared for all the
528 ES   Monica   30   place. A *convalescent* home/With the atmosphere of an hotel —/Nothing about it to
546 ES   Piggott   11   avoid/Anything like a nursing-home atmosphere./We don't want our guests to think
ATOMS (1)
 39 Gerontion   69   of the shuddering Bear/In fractured atoms. Gull against the wind, in the windy
ATONE (3)
 91 Ash-Wed 2   18   gown./Let the whiteness of bones atone to forgetfulness./There is no life in them.
416 CP   Celia   5   outside of myself;/And I feel I must ... *atone* — is that the word?/Can you treat a patient
467 CC   Colby   5   I only wish/That I had something to atone for!/There's something lacking, between
ATONEMENT (1)
466 CC   Colby   38   it was too late. And you spoke of atonement./Even your failure to understand
ATONING (1)
465 CC   Claude   3   was right. And all my life/I have been atoning. To a dead father,/Who had always

ATTACH (1)
309 FR   Mary   23   you think,/But what you feel. You attach yourself to loathing/As others do to
ATTACHMENT (2)
195 FQ: Little   154   flourish in the same hedgerow:/Attachment to self and to things and to persons,
195 FQ: Little   162   Thus, love of a country/Begins as attachment to our own field of action/And
ATTACK (1)
267 MC   m 25   No! here and now! {}/[*They make to attack him, but the priests and attendants return*
ATTACKED (2)
152 Rock 2   35   for it is forever decaying within and attacked from without;/For this is the law of
175 FQ: BurntN 159   them. The Word in the desert/Is most attacked by voices of temptation,/The crying
ATTAINMENTS (1)
159 Rock 6   11   need to be told that even such modest attainments/As you can boast in the way of
ATTAINTING (1)
269 MC Knight1   8   madman, whom nothing deters/From attainting his servants and ministers./{T} It is
ATTEMPT (2)
182 FQ: EColer 176   to learn to use words, and every attempt/Is a wholly new start, and a different
349 FR   Mary   18   delayed/{M} It cannot be diverted/An attempt to divert it/Only implicates others/At
ATTEMPTS (2)
368 CP   Edward 34   do you say amateur?/{E} Lavinia's attempts at starting a salon,/Where I
578 ES   Ld Clav 7   mistake upon mistake,/The mistaken attempts to correct mistakes/By methods which
ATTEND (2)
202 War Poetry   8   This is a meeting/On which we attend/Of forces beyond control by experiment
579 ES   Michael 9   up to London./Señor Gomez will attend to my needs for that climate./And you
ATTENDANT (2)
 16 Prufrock   112   Hamlet, nor was meant to be;/Am an attendant lord, one that will do/To swell a
265 MC   m 33   /We will find our own dinner. {}/[*to attendant*]./{P1} Go, tell His Lordship./{K4} How
ATTENDANTS (3)
238 MC   m 8   BECKET/FOUR TEMPTERS/ATTENDANTS/*The scene is the Archbishop's*
238 MC   m 15   OF WOMEN OF CANTERBURY/ATTENDANTS/*The first scene is in the*
267 MC   m 25   *make to attack him, but the priests and attendants return and quietly interpose*
ATTENDED (1)
424 CP   Lavinia 18   parties/In the last two years. And I've attended *all* of them./I hope you're not too
ATTENDING (1)
554 ES   Piggott 15   breath of life to me, Mrs. Carghill,/Attending to my guests. I like to feel they *need*
ATTENTION (7)
 32 Hysteria   11   be collected, and I concentrated/my attention with careful subtlety to this end./
 38 Gerontion   37   Think now/She gives when our attention is distracted/And what she gives, gives
213 Growltiger   30   sate alone,/Concentrating his attention on the Lady GRIDDLEBONE./And
276 MC Knight1   18   /{K1} We beg you to give us your attention for a few/moments. We know that you
290 FR   Agatha 23   careful devotion/Thus with precise attention/To detail, interfering preparation/Of
292 FR   Charles 32   you;/Your cellar could do with a little attention./{I} And you'll really have to find a
482 CC   Lady E 12   them paying you a good deal of attention./You see, you're rather a curiosity/To
ATTENTIONS (1)
245 MC Thomas   36   more than grateful for all your kind attentions./These are small matters. Little rest in
ATTENTIVE (2)
263 MC   Chorus 8   /The starved crow sits in the field, attentive; and in the wood/The owl rehearses
295 FR   Harry   4   sympathetic/And the doctor very attentive./That night I slept heavily, alone./{A}
ATTENUATED (1)
 18 Portrait   16   and carefully caught regrets/Through attenuated tones of violins/Mingled with remote
ATTITUDES (1)
111 Xmas Trees   1   of Christmas Trees/There are several attitudes towards Christmas,/Some of which we
ATTRACT (1)
581 ES   Charles 6   of you together/Make the force to attract him: you and Monica combined./{LC} I
ATTRACTED (1)
549 ES   Carghil 24   I remember it all so clearly./You attracted me, you know, at the very first
ATTRACTION (2)
290 FR   Agatha 34   /The inclination of the moon/The attraction of the dark passage/The paw under
572 ES   Ld Clav 19   other,/Yet she had a peculiar physical attraction/Which no other woman has had. And
ATTRACTIVE (1)
396 CP   Lavinia 8   me./{L} Well, you really were rather attractive, you know;/And you kept on *saying*
ATTRIBUTE (2)
537 ES   Ld Clav 14   your influence./{LC} You cannot attribute your ... misfortune to *my* influence./
542 ES   Ld Clav 20   spite and hatred. That is why you attribute/Your downfall to me. But how was I
ATTRITION (1)
187 FQ: DrySal 115   /Unqualified, unworn by subsequent attrition./People change, and smile: but the

AU (4)

47 Mél	Adult	12	/Surexcité par Emporheben/Au grand air de Bergsteigleben;/J'erre toujours
51 Restaurant		7	à la croupe arrondie,/Je te prie, au moins, ne bave pas dans la soupe)./'Les
51 Restaurant		12	/Les taches de son gilet montent au chiffre de trente-huit./'Je la chatouillais, pour
565 ES	Carghil	23	you./We'll leave you now, Richard. Au revoir, Monica./And Señor Gomez, I shall

AUCTIONED (1)

553 ES	Carghil	38	in want, you could have these letters auctioned.'/Yes, I'll bring the photostats

AUCUNE (1)

24 Rhapsody		51	/'Regard the moon,/La lune ne garde aucune rancune,/She winks a feeble eye,/She

AUDIENCE (2)

276 MC		m 18	*the front of the stage and address the audience.*]/{K1} We beg you to give us your
457 CC	note 16&	25	*intended to be heard distinctly by an audience in the theatre.*/{LE} Just open that case,

AUGHT (1)

213 Growltiger		33	/Growltiger had no eye or ear for aught but Griddlebone,/And the Lady seemed

AUGUST (1)

19 Portrait		57	out-of-tune/Of a broken violin on an August afternoon:/'I am always sure that you

AUGUSTUS (1)

209 NamingCats		6	the family use daily,/Such as Peter, Augustus, Alonzo or James,/Such as Victor or

AUNT (54)

29 Aunt Helen		t	is the *Boston Evening Transcript.*'/Aunt Helen/Miss Helen Slingsby was my
29 Aunt Helen		1	/Miss Helen Slingsby was my maiden aunt,/And lived in a small house near a
292 FR	Harry	14	happy returns of the day, mother./Aunt Ivy, Aunt Violet, Uncle Gerald, Uncle
292 FR	Harry	14	returns of the day, mother./Aunt Ivy, Aunt Violet, Uncle Gerald, Uncle Charles.
319 FR	Warburt	37	I advise you strongly, not to ask your aunt —/I mean, there is nothing she could tell
356 CP	Edward	36	know until I hear from her./If her aunt is very ill, she may be gone some time./{C}
356 CP	Julia	40	Go away yourself!/{J} Have you an aunt too?/{E} No, I haven't any aunt. But I
357 CP	Edward	1	an aunt too?/{E} No, I haven't any aunt. But I might go away./{C} But, Edward ...
357 CP	Julia	5	to get a nurse./{J} Is that her Aunt Laura?/{E} No; another aunt/Whom you
357 CP	Edward	6	that her Aunt Laura?/{E} No; another aunt/Whom you mustn't know. Her mother's
357 CP	Julia	9	rather a recluse./{J} Her favourite aunt?/{E} Her aunt's favourite niece. And she's
357 CP	Julia	24	I feel as if I knew/All about that aunt in Hampshire./{E} Hampshire?/{J} Didn't
357 CP	Julia	38	Now you must let me be *your* maiden aunt —/Living on an annuity, of course./I am
359 CP	Alex	4	/You'll have better news of Lavinia's aunt./{E} Oh ... yes ... thank you. Good-bye,
372 CP	Edward	16	You used all those eggs! Lavinia's aunt/Has just sent them from the country./{A}
372 CP	Alex	18	from the country./{A} Ah, so the aunt/Really exists. A substantial proof./{E} No,
372 CP	Edward	20	/{E} No, no ... I mean, this is another aunt./{A} I understand. The real aunt. But
372 CP	Alex	21	aunt./{A} I understand. The real aunt. But you'll be grateful./There are very few
374 CP	Celia	19	everyone./{C} It was obvious that the aunt was a pure invention/On the spur of the
377 CP	Julia	29	Alex's. Come, I give you/Lavinia's aunt! You might have guessed it./{E&C}
377 CP	Ed & Ce	30	have guessed it./{E&C} Lavinia's aunt./{J} Now, the next question/Is, what's to be
387 CP	Peter	27	party to-day./So I don't suppose her aunt can have died./{E} What aunt?/{P} The
387 CP	Edward	28	her aunt can have died./{E} What aunt?/{P} The aunt you told us about./But
387 CP	Peter	29	have died./{E} What aunt?/{P} The aunt you told us about./But Edward — you
390 CP	Julia	3	to come. And how is the dear aunt?/{L} So far as I know, she is very well,
390 CP	Julia	13	memory!/Then that accounts for the aunt — and the telegram./{L} Well, perhaps I
390 CP	Julia	34	worn out/After her anxiety about her aunt —/Who, you'll be glad to hear, has quite
392 CP	Edward	26	did you tell them?/{E} I invented an aunt/Who was ill in the country, and had sent
392 CP	Lavinia	30	could deceive Julia./But how did the aunt come to live in Essex?/{E} Julia compelled
446 CC	Eggers	23	best. While he's still living/With his aunt in Teddington, and coming up daily/Just
463 CC	Claude	1	were a child, you belonged to your aunt,/Or so she made me feel. I never saw you
483 CC	Colby	37	this your mother?/{C} No, that is my aunt. I never knew my mother./She died when I
484 CC	Colby	11	up by a governess?/{C} No. By my aunt./{LE} And did you loathe her? No, of
485 CC	Lady E	32	small one./{LE} But you had your aunt. And she was devoted to you,/I have no
485 CC	Colby	35	/Is it Simpkins?/{C} No, a married aunt./A widow. Her name is Mrs. Guzzard./
486 CC	Colby	3	one./You couldn't have known my aunt./{LE} No. I never met ... your aunt./But
486 CC	Lady E	4	aunt./{LE} No. I never met ... your aunt./But the name is familiar. How old are
486 CC	Lady E	12	Guzzard. And you always called her 'aunt'?/{C} Why not? She was my aunt./{LE}
486 CC	Colby	13	her 'aunt'?/{C} Why not? She was my aunt./{LE} And as for your mother —/Mrs.
486 CC	Colby	16	— which makes Mrs. Guzzard my aunt./{LE} And are you quite sure that Mrs.
486 CC	Colby	20	it?/That is not the kind of story my aunt would invent./{LE} Not if she *is* your aunt.
486 CC	Lady E	21	would invent./{LE} Not if she *is* your aunt. Did Mrs. Guzzard/And Mr. Guzzard —
497 CC	Claude	12	/And he mentioned the name of his aunt, Mrs. Guzzard./Now she's convinced that
500 CC	Claude	9	awaiting Mrs. Guzzard — Colby's aunt./{L} Colby's aunt? You make my brain
500 CC	Lucasta	10	Guzzard — Colby's aunt./{L} Colby's aunt? You make my brain reel./{SC} I ought to
509 CC	Colby	13	/Who died? Don't you remember, Aunt Sarah,/My finding a rattle and a

511 CC   Lady E   21   of confusion/You may address me as Aunt Elizabeth./{K} That's easier, certainly./
511 CC   Kaghan   27   /{K} But, Lady Elizabeth —/I mean, Aunt Elizabeth: if I call you Aunt Elizabeth/
511 CC   Kaghan   27   /I mean, Aunt Elizabeth: if I call you Aunt Elizabeth/Would you mind very much
512 CC   Kaghan   34   /{K} *B.* — if you don't mind, Aunt Elizabeth./{LE} *B.* — and I'm sure we
513 CC   Colby   12   /{C} That is a very strange question, Aunt Sarah:/To which I can only give a strange
514 CC   Guzzard 15   your mother; but I chose to be your aunt./So you may have your wish, and have no
518 CC   Colby   32   to Waterloo?/{C} Get you a taxi? Yes, Aunt Sarah;/But I should see you home./{MG}
519 CC   Kaghan   18   including both of you,/Claude ... and Aunt Elizabeth./You know, Claude, both

AUNT'S (2)
357 CP   Edward   10   /{J} Her favourite aunt?/{E} Her aunt's favourite niece. And she's rather difficult.
485 CC   Lady E   33   you,/I have no doubt. What is your aunt's name?/Is it Simpkins?/{C} No, a married

AUNTS (6)
30 Cous Nancy   9   all the modern dances;/And her aunts were not quite sure how they felt about it,
44 Cook Egg   6   /Her grandfather and great great aunts,/Supported on the mantelpiece/An
204 de la Mare   22   /At witches' sabbath of the maiden aunts;/When the nocturnal traveller can arouse/
293 FR   Amy   4   at Wishwood./{A} You see your aunts and uncles are very helpful, Harry./I have
319 FR   Harry   9   a vacuum/Surrounded by whispering aunts: Ivy and Violet —/Agatha never came
319 FR   Harry   24   the low conversation of triumphant aunts./It is the conversations not overheard,/

AURA (1)
459 CC   Lady E   2   is./I remember saying: 'He has a good aura.'/I remember people's auras almost better

AURAS (1)
459 CC   Lady E   3   a good aura.'/I remember people's auras almost better than their faces./What did

AURONT (1)
48 Lune Miel   15   pourboires, et rédige son bilan./Ils auront vu la Suisse et traversé la France./Et

AUS (1)
61 WL: Burial   12   hour./Bin gar keine Russin, stamm' aus Litauen, echt deutsch./And when we were

AUSPICIOUS (2)
313 FR   Gerald   16   make him feel at home. And most auspicious/That he could be here for his
459 CC   Lady E   6   /{LE} Thirteen letters. That's very auspicious —/Contrary to what most people

AUSTERE (2)
433 CP   Alex   38   /{A} She had joined an order. A very austere one./And as she already had experience
567 ES   Monica   25   people the most scrupulous,/The most austere. It's quite impossible./Father with a

AUSTRALIA (2)
559 ES   Ld Clav   8   correspondents/Almost everywhere. Australia — no./The men I know there are all in
580 ES   Carghil 18   own:/Next autumn, I'm going out to Australia,/On my doctor's advice. And on my

AUTHORITY (3)
242 MC   Mess   14   have this, I assure you, on the highest authority;/There are several opinions as to what
313 FR   Ivy   13   With my delphiniums. I was rather an authority./{G} Good evening, Mary. You've
528 ES   Monica   9   thing meeting people/When you're in authority, with authority's costume,/When the

AUTHORITY'S (1)
528 ES   Monica   9   /When you're in authority, with authority's costume,/When the man that people

AUTOMATIC (2)
24 Rhapsody   38   butter.'/So the hand of the child, automatic,/Slipped out and pocketed a toy that
69 WL: Fire S   255   alone,/She smoothes her hair with automatic hand,/And puts a record on the

AUTOMATISM (1)
294 FR   Harry   22   And partial observation of one's own automatism/While the slow stain sinks deeper

AUTUMN (9)
34 Figlia   17   hand./She turned away, but with the autumn weather/Compelled my imagination
147 Rock 1   5   seasons,/O world of spring and autumn, birth and dying!/The endless cycle of
172 FQ: BurntN   27   pressure, over the dead leaves,/In the autumn heat, through the vibrant air,/And the
184 FQ: DrySal   13   /In the smell of grapes on the autumn table,/And the evening circle in the
185 FQ: DrySal   52   wailing,/The silent withering of autumn flowers/Dropping their petals and
240 MC   Chorus   12   the summer bring consolation/For autumn fires and winter fogs?/What shall we do
329 FR   Chorus   9   little pain/The chopping of wood in autumn/And the singing in the kitchen/And the
332 FR   Agatha   34   /{H} I have known neither./{Ag} The autumn came too soon, not soon enough./The
580 ES   Carghil 18   a little piece of news of my own:/Next autumn, I'm going out to Australia,/On my

AUTUMNAL (1)
179 FQ: ECoker   75   forward to,/Long hoped for calm, the autumnal serenity/And the wisdom of age? Had

AUX (3)
47 Mél Adult   20   girafe./On montrera mon cénotaphe/Aux côtes brûlantes de Mozambique./Lune de
48 Lune Miel   14   et un restaurant pas cher./Lui pense aux pourboires, et rédige son bilan./Ils auront
51 Restaurant   29   l'emporta très loin,/Le repassant aux étapes de sa vie antérieure./Figurez-vous

AVAIS (2)
51 Restaurant   10   là, dans une averse, qu'on s'abrite./J'avais sept ans, elle était plus petite./Elle était
51 Restaurant   18   nous peloter, un gros chien;/Moi j'avais peur, je l'ai quittée à mi-chemin./C'est

AVARICE (2)
152 Rock 2   28   suffer the consequence:/For sloth, for avarice, gluttony, neglect of the Word of GOD,/
163 Rock 8   36   of a few,/Part faith of many./Not avarice, lechery, treachery,/Envy, sloth,
AVENGE (1)
264 MC   Priest3 19   /And there was no man to bury them. Avenge, O Lord,/The blood of thy saints. In
AVENUE (2)
54 Mr E Sun   18   /The sable presbyters approach/The avenue of penitence;/The young are red and
552 ES Ld Clav   4   in very large letters/In Shaftesbury Avenue./{MC} Yes, I had my art./Don't you
AVERSE (1)
51 Restaurant   9   sur les ronces —/C'est là, dans une averse, qu'on s'abrite./J'avais sept ans, elle était
AVERT (1)
257 MC Chorus   23   terror has soiled us, which none can avert, none can avoid, flowing under our feet
AVID (1)
108 Animula   32   the viaticum./Pray for Guiterriez, avid of speed and power,/For Boudin, blown to
AVOID (15)
85 Hollow Men   59   places/We grope together/And avoid speech/Gathered on this beach of the
96 Ash-Wed 5   18   here/No place of grace for those who avoid the face/No time to rejoice for those who
257 MC Chorus   23   us, which none can avert, none can avoid, flowing under our feet and over the sky;/
304 FR   Mary   17   /But I think you must have wanted to avoid collision./I suppose I could have gone, if
335 FR   Harry   25   in the smoky wilderness,/Trying to avoid the clasping branches/And the giant
338 FR   Harry   28   to run away, but to pursue,/Not to avoid being found, but to seek./I would not
348 FR   Chorus 13   to work the machine,/We can usually avoid accidents,/We are insured against fire,/
378 CP   Celia   21   So the one thing you care about/Is to avoid a break — anything unpleasant!/No, it
399 CP   Reilly   4   of course, that it is important/To avoid any meeting?/{N} You made that clear,
410 CP   Reilly 17   of your own faults,/And so could avoid understanding each other./Now, you have
417 CP   Reilly 28   by the common routine,/Learn to avoid excessive expectation,/Become tolerant of
419 CP   Reilly   3   — and communion./Both ways avoid the final desolation/Of solitude in the
467 CC   Claude 18   own fault./I was always anxious to avoid the mistakes/My father made with me.
511 CC   Lady E 20   as my mother./{LE} Then in order to avoid any danger of confusion/You may
546 ES   Piggott 10   Court. You see, we've studied to avoid/Anything like a nursing-home
AVOIDING (4)
243 MC Chorus   24   we have lived quietly,/Succeeded in avoiding notice,/Living and partly living./There
320 FR Warburt   13   heart's very feeble./With care, and avoiding all excitement/She may live several
329 FR Chorus   18   together, all are recorded./There is no avoiding these things/And we know nothing of
524 ES Charles   23   /And the waiters all appear to be avoiding his eye./{M} We're getting off the point
AWAIT (2)
194 FQ: Little   121   language/And next year's words await another voice./But, as the passage now
386 CP   Reilly   5   I promise./{UG} And now you must await your visitors./{E} Visitors? What visitors?/
AWAITED (1)
68 WL: Fire S   230   scene, and foretold the rest —/I too awaited the expected guest./He, the young man
AWAITING (2)
213 Growltiger   35   baritone,/Disposed to relaxation, and awaiting no surprise —/But the moonlight
500 CC   Claude   9   reason for this meeting today./We're awaiting Mrs. Guzzard — Colby's aunt./{L}
AWAKE (9)
166 Rock 10   7   World?/The great snake lies ever half awake, at the bottom of the pit of the world,
185 FQ: DrySal   42   by anxious worried women/Lying awake, calculating the future,/Trying to
226 Macavity   16   he's half asleep, he's always wide awake./Macavity, Macavity, there's no one like
293 FR   Harry   40   be unendurable/If you were wide awake. You do not know/The noxious smell
324 FR   Harry   33   don't understand what it is to be awake,/To be living on several planes at once/
332 FR   Agatha   36   and wind had not shaken your father/Awake yet. I found him thinking/How to get rid
346 FR Charles   4   moment were like that, if one were awake?/You both seem to know more about
348 FR   Chorus   10   not like what happens when we are awake, because it too closely resembles what
417 CP   Celia   14   A state one does not know/When awake. But what, or whom I loved,/Or what in
AWAKENED (1)
110 Marina   32   my speech for that unspoken,/The awakened, lips parted, the hope, the new ships./
AWAKENS (1)
166 Rock 10   8   curled/In folds of himself until he awakens in hunger and moving his head to right
AWARDED (2)
256 MC Tempts   14   at the children's party,/The prize awarded for the English Essay,/The scholar's
551 ES Carghil   34   /Is twice as much as I think you'd be awarded.'/Effie was against it — she wanted
AWARE (19)
27 Morning   3   the trampled edges of the street/I am aware of the damp souls of housemaids/
29 Aunt Helen   7   undertaker wiped his feet —/He was aware that this sort of thing had occurred
32 Hysteria   1   /Hysteria/As she laughed I was aware of becoming involved in her laughter and
69 WL: Fire S   250   looks a moment in the glass,/Hardly aware of her departed lover;/Her brain allows

605 Narcissus	9	high cliffs/When the wind made him	aware of his limbs smoothly passing each other/
605 Narcissus	14	rhythm./By the river/His eyes were	aware of the pointed corners of his eyes/And his
605 Narcissus	15	corners of his eyes/And his hands	aware of the pointed tips of his fingers./Struck
246 MC Thomas	6	me in bitterest hate./By God's grace	aware of their prevision/I sent my letters on
324 FR Violet	10	sorry for your brother? Aren't you	aware/Of what is going on? and what it means
361 CP Reilly	34	some relief/Of which you're not	aware. It will come to you slowly:/When you
367 CP Edward	2	two things;/But I don't pretend I was	aware of everything./{P} Oh, I'm very glad that
414 CP Celia	7	that what has happened has made me	aware/That I've always been alone. That one
474 CC Colby	18	down an alley/I should become	aware of someone walking with me./That's the
486 CC Lady E	31	be more interesting/Than you are	aware of. Colby ... { }/[*A knock on the door*]/
503 CC Claude	37	now! It's surprising,/I hadn't been	aware how the time was passing,/What with
504 CC Lady E	34	have more in common than you are	aware of./{MG} I suppose you mean Colby?/
505 CC Guzzard	39	Mrs. Guzzard./{MG} So I am	aware. I have known it to happen./{E} — Who
528 ES Monica	25	—/Father is much iller than he is	aware of:/It may be, he will never return from
536 ES Gomez	4	a step up the ladder,/So you weren't	aware of becoming a different person:/But

AWARENESS (5)

111 Xmas Trees	21	the fatigue, the tedium,/The	awareness of death, the consciousness of failure,
194 FQ: Little	142	/Of motives late revealed, and the	awareness/Of things ill done and done to others'
409 CP Reilly	28	/And were always humiliated by the	awareness/That you had forced him into this
413 CP Celia	38	two things:/What is the first?/{C} An	awareness of solitude./But that sounds so flat. I
582 ES Charles	38	begun to belong together,/And that	awareness .../{M} Was a shield protecting both

AWAY (90)

34 Figlia	17	and shake of the hand./She turned	away, but with the autumn weather/Compelled
94 Ash-Wed 4	13	the years that walk between, bearing/	Away the fiddles and the flutes, restoring/One
96 Ash-Wed 5	26	children at the gate/Who will not go	away and cannot pray:/Pray for those who
98 Ash-Wed 6	23	voices shaken from the yew-tree drift	away/Let the other yew be shaken and reply./
103 Journ Magi	12	cursing and grumbling/And running	away, and wanting their liquor and women,/
103 Journ Magi	25	sky./And an old white horse galloped	away in the meadow./Then we came to a tavern
128 Corl March	46	out loud, *crumpets.*)/Don't throw	away that sausage,/It'll come in handy. He's
135 5FingerEx1	10	day delay?/*When* will Time flow	away?/*Lines to a Yorkshire Terrier*/In a brown
149 Rock 1	m94	*against the dim sky. From farther*/	*away, they are answered by voices of the*
153 Rock 2	51	his motor cycle,/And daughters ride	away on casual pillions./Much to cast down,
174 FQ: BurntN	131	day,/The black cloud carries the sun	away./Will the sunflower turn to us, will the
180 FQ: ECoker	118	imposing façade are all being rolled	away —/Or as, when an underground train, in
212 Growltiger	27	he too had stol'n	away —/In the yard behind the Lion he was
214 RTTugger	30	in it right up to the ears,/If you put it	away on the larder shelf./The Rum Tum Tugger
220 Old Deut	20	dogs and the herdsmen will turn them	away./The cars and the lorries run over the
222 Pekes Pols	14	or a Peke)./The big Police Dog was	away from his beat —/I don't know the reason,
224 Mr Mistoff	17	Mistoffelees' Conjuring Turn./Presto!/	Away we go!/And we all say: OH!/Well I never!/
227 Macavity	32	been Macavity!' — but he's a mile	away./You'll be sure to find him resting, or
590 Space Time	7	are free,/For time is time, and runs	away,/Though sages disagree./The flowers I sent
604 Ode	11	so much that of Harvard we carry	away/In the place of the life that we leave./And
257 MC Chorus	13	milk in summer,/Our labour taken	away from us,/Our sins made heavier upon us./
267 MC Knight2	20	delay,/Before the old fox is off and	away./{T} What you have to say/By the King's
270 MC Chorus	27	have consented./Am torn	away, subdued, violated,/United to the spiritual
295 FR Harry	19	it is just the cancer/That eats	away the self. I knew how you would take it./
296 FR Harry	11	was not there,/Which they explained	away, but you explained them/Or at least, made
304 FR Mary	10	/Any more than I do. I want to get	away./{Ag} After seven years?/{M} Oh, you
305 FR Agatha	6	to help you: but you must not run	away./Any time before now, it would have
307 FR Harry	36	hope taken from you,/Or to fling it	away, to join the legion of the hopeless/
309 FR Harry	3	/Explaining would only set me farther	away from you./There is only one way for you
314 FR Warburt	25	making some great discovery/To do	away with one disease or another./Now I've had
319 FR Harry	5	was kept apart from him, till he went	away./We never heard him mentioned, but in
335 FR Agatha	5	then I was only my own feet walking/	Away, down a concrete corridor/In a dead air.
338 FR Harry	27	know/That my business is not to run	away, but to pursue,/Not to avoid being found,
338 FR Amy	33	am not safe here./{A} So you *will* run	away./{Ag} In a world of fugitives/The person
338 FR Agatha	36	opposite direction/Will appear to run	away./{A} I was speaking to Harry./{H} It is
344 FR Amy	12	happened, Amy?/{A} Harry is going	away — to become a missionary./{H} But ...!/
346 FR Mary	12	to leave his Lordship/While you are	away?/{Do} Oh, certainly, Miss;/I'll never leave
356 CP Julia	20	a golden opportunity/Now Lavinia's	away. I've always said:/'If I could only get
356 CP Julia	30	believe that's the reason why she went	away —/So that I could make you talk. Perhaps
356 CP Celia	34	not in the pantry./{C} Will she be	away for some time, Edward?/{E} I really don't
356 CP Celia	37	how will you manage while she is	away?/{E} I really don't know. I may go away
356 CP Edward	38	/{E} I really don't know. I may go	away myself./{C} Go away yourself!/{J} Have
356 CP Celia	39	know. I may go away myself./{C} Go	away yourself!/{J} Have you an aunt too?/{E}

357	CP	Edward	1	I haven't any aunt. But I might go away./{C} But, Edward ... what was I going to
357	CP	Julia	20	But really, Edward,/Lavinia may be away for weeks,/Or she may come back and be
357	CP	Julia	21	/Or she may come back and be called away again./I understand these tough old
362	CP	Edward	12	were used to each other. So her going away/At a moment's notice, without
363	CP	Edward	27	say to my friends, 'My wife has gone away'?/And they answer 'Where?' and I say 'I
378	CP	Celia	38	nervous breakdown./Edward, if I go away now/Will you promise me to see a very
388	CP	Celia	18	shall be going to concerts./I am going away too. {}/[LAVINIA *lets herself in with a*
388	CP	Edward	21	Perhaps./{E} You're both going away! {}/[*Enter* LAVINIA]/{L} Who's going
388	CP	Lavinia	22	{}/[*Enter* LAVINIA]/{L} Who's going away? Well, Celia. Well, Peter./I didn't expect
389	CP	Peter	8	together./Celia told us she was going away,/But I don't know where./{L} You don't
389	CP	Celia	23	it./{C} But now that I may be going away — somewhere —/I should like to say
392	CP	Lavinia	39	/The point is, that since I've been away/I see that I've taken you much too
396	CP	Lavinia	26	be some way out for you/If I went away. I thought that if I died/To you, I who
396	CP	Edward	36	for me/Which will only keep me away from myself./{L} You're complicating
401	CP	Edward	13	the use!/I suppose I might as well go away at once./{R} No. If you please, sit down,
401	CP	Reilly	15	Chamberlayne./You are not going away, so you might as well sit down./You were
411	CP	Edward	6	want to be alone .../{E} But I can't go away!/I have a case coming on next Monday./
413	CP	Celia	2	offended/If you simply tell me to go away again./{R} Most of my patients begin,
415	CP	Celia	15	hurt *her*./I wasn't taking anything away from her —/Anything she wanted. I may
416	CP	Celia	2	I've ever *done*,/Which I might get away from, or of anything in me/I could get rid
424	CP	Edward	15	{}/[*smiling*]./{E} That you hadn't run away?/{L} Now Edward, that's unfair!/You
425	CP	Lavinia	30	to take the tray about,/So they'll go away again. Anyway, at that stage/There's
426	CP	Lavinia	16	no more committees./{L} Can we get away soon?/{E} By the end of next week/I shall
434	CP	Peter	34	understand at all. But then I've been away/For two years, and I don't know what
456	CC	Eggers	26	is apt to buy a house. And then goes away/And forgets all about it. That can be
478	CC	Lucasta	28	explain/That could explain anything away. I shall never/Never forget that look on
488	CC	Claude	39	/{SC} I'd never want to take your son away from you./Perhaps you have a son. But it
491	CC	Lady E	4	to me./Claude! I don't want to take away from you/The son you thought was yours.
515	CC	Guzzard	3	could be born. You were very far away;/I sent you a message, which never
526	ES	Charles	13	words seem to come/From very far away. Yet very near. You are changing me/And
531	ES	Lambert	38	angry/If you heard that he'd gone away without your seeing him./{LC} What sort
535	ES	Gomez	27	/What it would be like to have been away from home/For thirty-five years? I was
535	ES	Gomez	29	/The same age as you — when I went away,/Thousands of miles away, to another
535	ES	Gomez	30	I went away,/Thousands of miles away, to another climate,/To another language,
536	ES	Gomez	12	that happened four thousand miles away,/Only believed what the parish priest told
543	ES	Ld Clav	2	Not very soon, I think./I am going away./{G} So I've been informed./I have friends
547	ES	Piggott	36	on the shore or in the hills,/Quite away from the motor roads. You must learn the
549	ES	Carghil	28	was said 'you'd be throwing yourself away./Mark my words' Effie said, 'if you chose
559	ES	Michael	20	/Of right and wrong. I want to go far away/To some country where no one has heard
559	ES	Ld Clav	25	to repudiate your family,/To throw away the whole of your inheritance?/{Mi} What
561	ES	Ld Clav	3	help you!/Even though it carried you away from me forever/To suffer the
565	ES	Michael	15	staying at the George — it's not far away./{MC} Then I'd like to walk a little way
568	ES	Ld Clav	1	Where have you been?/{LC} Not far away. Standing under the great beech tree./{M}
572	ES	Ld Clav	34	an occasion/On which I ran away. Very well./I shan't run away now — run
572	ES	Ld Clav	35	I ran away. Very well./I shan't run away now — run away from *them*./It is through
572	ES	Ld Clav	35	well./I shan't run away now — run away from *them*./It is through this meeting that
578	ES	Michael	27	/And once, Mother snatched a book away from you/And tossed it into the fire. How

AWE (3)

111	Xmas	Trees	17	the goose or turkey/And the expected awe on its appearance,/So that the reverence
306	FR	Mary	30	so much older. We were rather in awe of you —/At least, I was./{H} Why were we
464	CC	Claude	32	/When I was young. And yet I was in awe of him./I was wrong, in both. I loathed this

AWEFULL (1)

222	Pekes	Pols	t	careful of Old Deuteronomy!'/Of the Awefull Battle of the Pekes and the Pollicles/

AWFUL (10)

74	WL:	Thund	403	friend, blood shaking my heart/The awful daring of a moment's surrender/Which an
118	SP	Dusty	5	you pick them up/{Du} There's an awful lot in the way you feel/{Do} Sometimes
277	MC	Knight3	19	to happen; and/there is going to be an awful row; and at the best we shall have to/
304	FR	Mary	30	her by willing./Doesn't that sound awful? I know that it does./Did you ever meet
308	FR	Mary	13	it,/And I can well imagine how awful it must be./But in this world another hope
334	FR	Harry	37	thought were private shadows. O that awful privacy/Of the insane mind! Now I can
335	FR	Harry	31	judicial sun/Of the final eye, and the awful evacuation/Cleanses./I was not there, you
366	CP	Peter	36	I felt I could bear it no longer./That awful party! I'm sorry, Edward;/Of course in
472	CC	Lucasta	37	why! And now I think I know./It's awful for a man to have to give up,/A career
565	ES	Monica	28	present. {}/[*Exit*]/{M} Father, those awful people. We mustn't stay here./I want you

AWFULLY (11)

277 MC	Knight3	14	why it was; and for/my part I am awfully sorry about it. We realised this was our
369 CP	Peter	2	I wouldn't say that./But Lavinia was awfully kind to me/And I owe her a great deal.
375 CP	Edward	22	anything./I'm very tired. Thanks awfully, Alex./Good night./{C} What on earth
383 CP	Edward	28	Julia! are you there? .../Well, I'm awfully sorry to have kept you waiting;/But we
388 CP	Celia	8	to say good-bye./{C} Well, Peter, I'm awfully glad, for your sake,/Though of course
412 CP	Celia	33	want to waste your time. And I'm awfully afraid/That you'll think that I am
469 CC	Lucasta	1	*the curtain rises.*/{L} *I* think you play awfully well, Colby —/Not that *my* opinion
469 CC	Lucasta	18	were the right ones to like?/Still, I'm awfully ignorant. Can you believe/That I've
474 CC	Lucasta	8	acceptable, I think./{L} You sound awfully religious./Is there no other way of
556 ES	Michael	30	together. {}/[*Exit*]/{Mi} You know, it's awfully hard to explain things to *you.*/You've
580 ES	Carghil	15	GOMEZ]/{MC} I'm afraid this seems awfully sudden to you, Richard;/It isn't so

AWKWARD (4)

589 Fable		71	about,/For often they drop in at awkward moments,/As everybody'll know who
328 FR	Gerald	30	it, I shall scream./{G} It's going to be awkward, explaining this to Amy./{I} Poor
392 CP	Lavinia	24	to happen./Trust her not to miss any awkward situation!/And what did you tell
493 CC	Claude	16	to cross-examine a witness./It's very awkward. We don't want to start/By offending

AXE'S (1)

259 MC	Thomas	2	/Crime, wrong, oppression and the axe's edge,/Indifference, exploitation, you, and

AXLE-TREE (1)

172 FQ:	BurntN	50	sapphires in the mud/Clot the bedded axle-tree./The trilling wire in the blood/Sings

AXLETREE (1)

40 Burb	Blei	9	loved him well./The horses, under the axletree/Beat up the dawn from Istria/With

AY (1)

226 Macavity		26	broken, and the trellis past repair —/Ay, there's the wonder of the thing! *Macavity's*

B (2) [*Abbreviation*]
511 CC Kaghan 28　　mind very much calling me ... just 'B'?/{LE} Certainly, if you prefer that, Barnabas.
535 ES Gomez 16 won't let me down in this relationship,/*B* won't let me down in some other connection./
B. **(41)** [*Abbreviation*]
444 CC　　m 5　/EGGERSON/COLBY SIMPKINS/B. KAGHAN/LUCASTA ANGEL/LADY
450 CC Colby 38　I've no idea how I ought to behave./B. Kaghan has told me something about her,/
451 CC Colby 15　why it should be so different./I like B. Kaghan. I've found him very helpful/And
451 CC Eggers 21　can't you make me laugh/The way B. Kaghan did?' She's only met him once;/But
451 CC　　m 39　meeting her. {}/[*A loud knock. Enter* B. KAGHAN]/{K} Enter B. Kaghan. Hello
452 CC Kaghan 1　　*Enter* B. KAGHAN]/{K} Enter B. Kaghan. Hello Colby!/And hello Eggers! I'm
453 CC Lucasta 22 Mrs. Eggerson. He never fails to rise./B.! What have you told Colby about me?/{K}
453 CC Lucasta 33　to keep her fed between meals./{L} B., you're a beast. I've a very small appetite./
453 CC Lucasta 36　a week's salary in lieu of notice./{L} B., remember you're only my fiancé on
454 CC Colby 21　on either point, none at all./{C} And B. Kaghan has always seemed to me sane./{E} I
471 CC Colby 35　I was very bewildered/By you ... and B./{L} Oh, by me ... and B./{C} Only afterwards,
471 CC Lucasta 36　you ... and B./{L} Oh, by me ... and B./{C} Only afterwards,/When I had seen you a
472 CC Lucasta 32　/And be someone like Claude ... or B. I was sorry,/Very sorry for you. I admired
475 CC Colby 35　I've told you/Or from what I've told B.; or from Sir Claude./{L} Claude hasn't told
475 CC Lucasta 37　/He doesn't tell me much. And as for B. —/I'd much rather hear it from yourself./{C}
476 CC Lucasta 15　giving that impression./That's where B. has been such a help to me —/He fosters the
476 CC Lucasta 21　had been his mistress, palmed off on B./{C} I never thought of such a thing!/{L} You
476 CC Lucasta 25　have thought it./I don't know about B. He's very generous./I don't think he'd have
478 CC Lucasta 32 some self-respect./Well, there's always B. I think that now/I'm just beginning to
478 CC Lucasta 33　now/I'm just beginning to appreciate B./{C} Lucasta, wait! {}/[*Enter* B. KAGHAN]/
478 CC　　m 35　　　B./{C} Lucasta, wait! {}/[*Enter* B. KAGHAN]/{K} Enter B. Kaghan./To see the
478 CC Kaghan 35　　{}/[*Enter* B. KAGHAN]/{K} Enter B. Kaghan./To see the new flat. And here's
479 CC Lucasta 1　*my* guardian angel at the moment, B./You're to take me out to dinner. And I'm
479 CC Lucasta 8　racket/So far as I'm concerned, B. And as for Lizzie,/You'd better not get in *her*
499 CC Lucasta 21　take much time. I'm going to marry B./{SC} To marry B.! But I thought that was all
499 CC Claude 22　I'm going to marry B./{SC} To marry B.! But I thought that was all settled./{L} Yes,
499 CC Lucasta 29　that you wanted me to marry B./Made me determined that I wouldn't. Just to
499 CC Lucasta 36　/I'd never have come to appreciate B./{SC} But Colby! Lucasta, if I'd suspected this
500 CC Lucasta 25 He made me see what I really wanted./B. makes me feel safe. And that's what I want./
500 CC Lucasta 33　depend upon other people, either./B. needs me. He's been hurt by life, just as I
501 CC Lucasta 6　suited because we're both common./B. knows you think him common. And so he
501 CC Claude 15　as you say, I've misunderstood B.,/And I've never thought that I understood
503 CC Lucasta 13　/I shall be happy. I'm going to marry B./I know you like B./{C} I'm very fond of him;/
503 CC Lucasta 14　going to marry B./I know you like B./{C} I'm very fond of him;/And I'm glad to
503 CC Colby 23　/{C} Of course I'd like them ... Can't B. come up now?/{E} Better wait till afterwards.
504 CC Lucasta 18　show her up, Lucasta?/{L} I'll make B. do it. {}/[*Exit* LUCASTA]/{SC} I wish you
509 CC Claude 28　for some reason;/So we call him B./{MG} A very good name./He ought to be
510 CC Claude 18　you tell her, Sir Claude?/{SC} No, B. It was Mrs. Guzzard who revealed it./This is
512 CC Kaghan 34　/{LE} I shall see to that, Barnabas./{K} *B.* — if you don't mind, Aunt Elizabeth./{LE} B.
512 CC Lady E 35　you don't mind, Aunt Elizabeth./{LE} B. — and I'm sure we shall become great
513 CC Colby 21　or a mother —/It's different for B. He's had his foster-parents,/So he can afford
BABBLE (2)
206 To my Wife 7　thoughts without need of speech/And babble the same speech without need of
522 ES dedic 7　*thoughts without need of speech/And babble the same speech without need of meaning:*/
BABBLING (1)
245 MC Priest2 2　/You are foolish, immodest and babbling women./Do you not know that the
BABES (2)
264 MC Priest3 15　Innocents./*Out of the mouth of very babes, O God.*/As the voice of many waters, of
264 MC Priest3 21　weeping./Out of the mouth of very babes, O God! {}/[THE PRIESTS *stand*
BABIES (3)
498 CC Eggers 9　/Could there not have been two babies?/{LE} *Two* babies, Eggerson?/{E} I was
498 CC Lady E 10　not have been two babies?/{LE} *Two* babies, Eggerson?/{E} I was only suggesting/
498 CC Claude 26　ask me to believe/That she took two babies, and got them mixed./{LE} That seems to
BABY (4)
73 WL: Thund 379　music on those strings/And bats with baby faces in the violet light/Whistled, and beat
498 CC Claude 15　{SC} You're suggesting that she ran a baby farm./That's most unlikely, nowadays./
498 CC Claude 18　/Often. I never saw more than one baby./{E} She might have taken in another one/
498 CC Claude 23　of the other one./{SC} But *this* baby was Colby./{LE} Of course it was Colby./
BABYLON (1)
437 CP Reilly 4　... if it answers my question./{R} *Ere Babylon was dust/The magus Zoroaster, my dead*

BACHELOR (3)

385 CP	Reilly	12	ghosts: the grandmother,/The lively bachelor uncle at the Christmas party,/The
479 CC	Kaghan	13	time./I've come to inspect the new bachelor quarters,/And to wish Colby luck. I've
479 CC	Kaghan	22	to drink it,/To Colby, and a happy bachelor life!/Which depends, of course, on

BACK (152)

13 Prufrock		15	/The yellow fog that rubs its back upon the window-panes,/The yellow
13 Prufrock		19	that stand in drains,/Let fall upon its back the soot that falls from chimneys,/Slipped
14 Prufrock		25	slides along the street/Rubbing its back upon the window-panes;/There will be
14 Prufrock		39	dare?' and, 'Do I dare?'/Time to turn back and descend the stair,/With a bald spot in
16 Prufrock		95	Lazarus, come from the dead,/Come back to tell you all, I shall tell you all' —/If one,
17 Prufrock		127	the white hair of the waves blown back/When the wind blows the water white and
20 Portrait		90	hardly know when you are coming back,/You will find so much to learn.'/My smile
22 Preludes		25	from the bed,/You lay upon your back, and waited;/You dozed, and watched the
23 Preludes		30	ceiling./And when all the world came back/And the light crept up between the
24 Rhapsody		44	/An old crab with barnacles on his back,/Gripped the end of a stick which I held
62 WL: Burial		37	hyacinth girl.'/— Yet when we came back, late, from the hyacinth garden,/Your
62 WL: Burial		53	blank, is something he carries on his back,/Which I am forbidden to see. I do not
65 WL: Chess		142	ITS TIME/Now Albert's coming back, make yourself a bit smart./He'll want to
67 WL: Fire S		185	I speak not loud or long./But at my back in a cold blast I hear/The rattle of the
67 WL: Fire S		196	foot only, year to year./But at my back from time to time I hear/The sound of
68 WL: Fire S		215	/At the violet hour, when the eyes and back/Turn upward from the desk, when the
105 Song Sime		5	the death wind,/Like a feather on the back of my hand./Dust in sunlight and memory
151 Rock 2		7	of the waters like a lantern set on the back of a tortoise./And some say: 'How can we
162 Rock 8		22	in moral corruption;/Many came back well broken,/Diseased and beggared,
187 FQ: DrySal		131	down, the way forward is the way back./You cannot face it steadily, but this thing
221 Old Deut		35	more,'/Then the landlady from her back parlour will peep/And say: 'Now then, out
221 Old Deut		36	say: 'Now then, out you go, by the back door,/For Old Deuteronomy mustn't be
228 Gus		12	at their club/(Which takes place at the back of the neighbouring pub)/He loves to
228 Gus		25	the bag./I knew how to act with my back and my tail;/With an hour of rehearsal, I
230 Bust Jones		8	trousers/Or such an impeccable back./In the whole of St. James's the smartest of
235 Ad-dress		32	him underneath the chin/Or slap his back or shake his paw,/And he will gambol and
242 MC Priest2		31	lord is returned. Our lord has come back to his own again./We have had enough of
256 MC Chorus		8	is the sticky dew that forms on the back of my hand?/{4T} Man's life is a cheat and
261 MC Thomas		28	them and to lead them, to bring them back to His ways. It is/never the design of man;
266 MC Knights		17	jack,/You wore his favours on your back,/You had your honours all from his hand;
268 MC Knight2		2	peace, and all dispute ended/Sent you back to your See as you demanded./{K3} And
269 MC Thomas		2	/I shall not get those seven years back again./Never again, you must make no
271 MC Priests		21	No time to waste. They are coming back, armed. To the altar, to the altar./{T} All
281 MC Chorus		14	Even with the hand to the broom, the back bent in laying the fire, the knee bent in
281 MC Chorus		15	and sweepers of Canterbury,/The back bent under toil, the knee bent under sin,
286 FR Gerald		7	as soon be a subaltern again/To be back in the East. An incomparable climate/For
288 FR Agatha		15	and all that has happened/To come back to Wishwood./{G} Why, painful?/{V}
288 FR Agatha		26	the old pony,/And thought to creep back through the little door./He will find a new
291 FR Amy		25	here,/And who all want to see you back, Harry./{H} Look there, look there: do you
292 FR Harry		10	/Why should they wait until I came back to Wishwood?/There were a thousand
292 FR Amy		15	/{A} We are very glad to have you back, Harry./Now we shall all be together for
293 FR Ivy		13	to die, I'm sure!/Now that Harry's back, is the time to think of living./{H} Time
295 FR Harry		1	/I expected to find her when I went back to the cabin./Later, I became excited, I
303 FR Mary		14	/We may have to keep the dinner back .../{Ag} And also Dr. Warburton. At least,
306 FR Harry		12	All these years I'd been longing to get back/Because I thought I never should. I
307 FR Harry		11	/{H} Not then. But later, coming back from school/For the holidays, after the
308 FR Mary		16	/You hoped for something, in coming back to Wishwood,/Or you would not have
313 FR Gerald		15	Harry, I see./It's good to have him back again, isn't it?/We must make him feel at
314 FR Warburt		9	doesn't get younger./It takes me back longer than you can remember/To see you
314 FR Warburt		11	forgotten/The day when you came back from school with measles/And we had
317 FR Harry		23	/Everything has always been referred back to mother./When we were children, before
318 FR Harry		5	before we had begun./When we came back, for the school holidays,/They were not
323 FR Gerald		26	down and see him, Amy, and come back and report to you./{A} I must see for
323 FR Warburt		32	/I am going myself. I will come back and report to you./{A} I must see for
324 FR Warburt		7	We can put your bicycle/On the back of my car. {}/[*Exeunt* WARBURTON *and*
325 FR Violet		36	/And you feel so conspicuous, lolling back/And so near the street, and everyone
331 FR Harry		7	I thought foolishly/That when I got back to Wishwood, as I had left it,/Everything
337 FR	m	8	crooked made straight. {}/[*She moves back into the room*]/{Ag} What have I been
340 FR Amy		27	of Wishwood;/I even asked you back, for visits, after he was gone,/So that there
346 FR Downing		7	Mr. Charles:/His Lordship sent me back because he remembered/He thinks he left

348 FR	Chorus	8	walk out of a door, and find ourselves back in the same room./We do not like the
355 CP	Julia	17	{J} No, we'll wait until Edward comes back into the room./Now I want to relax, Are
357 CP	Julia	21	be away for weeks,/Or she may come back and be called away again./I understand
360 CP	Reilly	34	made a mistake/And want to come back to you. If another woman,/She might
360 CP	Reilly	38	ground for hope that she won't come back at all./If another man, then you'd want to
361 CP	Edward	3	to marry her./{E} But I want my wife back./{UG} That's the natural reaction./It's
362 CP	Edward	15	she had gone/And was not coming back — well, I can't understand it./Nobody
363 CP	Edward	29	/And they say, 'But when will she be back?'/And I reply 'I don't know that she *is*
363 CP	Edward	30	reply 'I don't know that she *is* coming back'./And they ask 'But what are you going to
364 CP	Edward	5	I saw her last. And yet I want her back./And I *must* get her back, to find out what
364 CP	Edward	6	I want her back./And I *must* get her back, to find out what has happened/During the
364 CP	Reilly	20	of an answer./But if I bring her back it must be on one condition:/That you
366 CP	Peter	15	come with you, Julia? On the way back/I remembered something I had to say to
371 CP	Edward	11	am I to do?/{E} Nothing. Wait. Go back to California./{P} But I must see Celia./{E}
372 CP	Peter	32	my love to Lavinia/When she comes back ... but, if you don't mind,/I'd rather you
374 CP	Edward	2	/{E} Celia! Why have you come back?/I said I would telephone as soon as I
374 CP	Celia	6	with you/I was going to say I'd come back for my umbrella ... ./I must say you don't
375 CP	Edward	4	not like that at all./Lavinia is coming back./{C} Lavinia coming back!/Do you mean
375 CP	Celia	5	is coming back./{C} Lavinia coming back!/Do you mean to say that she's laid a trap
376 CP	Edward	9	*say:*]/{E} Julia!/What have you come back for? {}/[*Enter* JULIA]/{J} I've had an
377 CP	Edward	4	has happened?/{E} Lavinia is coming back, I think./{C} You think! Don't you know?/
377 CP	Edward	11	/And he said he would bring Lavinia back, tomorrow./{C} But why should that man
377 CP	Celia	12	should that man want to bring her back —/Unless he is the Devil! I could believe
377 CP	Celia	17	How did he persuade you to want her back? {}/[*A popping noise is heard from the*
378 CP	Edward	18	to make me see that I wanted her back./{C} That's the Devil's method! So you
378 CP	Celia	19	Devil's method! So you want Lavinia back!/Lavinia! So the one thing you care about/
379 CP	Celia	6	you do not mean to have Lavinia back/And that you do mean to gain your
380 CP	Edward	21	there? *He* thought so./He came back this evening to talk to me about it./{C} But
384 CP	Reilly	22	is a serious matter/To bring someone back from the dead./{E} From the dead?/That
385 CP	Edward	33	I shall go./{E} Stop! Will you come back with her?/{UG} No, I shall not come with
390 CP	Alex	20	arrived?/{E} Yes./{A} Welcome back, Lavinia!/When I got your telegram .../{L}
391 CP	Julia	2	and let Lavinia rest./Now we'll all go back to *my* house. Peter, call a taxi. {}/[*Exit*
391 CP	Julia	13	they're no use to me./I'm not coming back again *this* evening./{L} Stop! I want you to
394 CP	Edward	23	is how you see me, why did you come back?/{L} Frankly, I don't know. I was warned
394 CP	Lavinia	39	who could have taught you to answer back like that?/{E} I have had quite enough
395 CP	Edward	37	/{E} So here we are again. Back in the trap,/With only one difference,
396 CP	Lavinia	28	/You might be able to find the road back/To a time when you were real — for you
398 CP	Edward	7	doubts to enter? And then you came back, you/The angel of destruction — just as I
400 CP	Alex	33	out by the service staircase/And come back when they've gone./{R} Yes, when they've
401 CP	Edward	36	me to blame you for bringing my wife back,/I suppose. You seemed to be trying to
402 CP	Reilly	1	/{R} If I had not brought your wife back, Mr. Chamberlayne,/Do you suppose that
402 CP	Reilly	39	the immediate situation/And then go back as far as I find necessary./You see, your
403 CP	Edward	23	now why I wanted my wife to come back./It was because of what she had made me
410 CP	Lavinia	29	can we do/When we can go neither back nor forward? Edward!/What can we do?/
412 CP	Julia	7	a moment, and slipped in by the back way./I only came to tell you, I am sure she
412 CP	Julia	20	wait in the next room,/And come back when she's gone./{R} Yes, when she's
413 CP	Celia	34	/I'd do anything you told me, to get back to normality./{R} We must find out about
419 CP	Celia	14	been to your sanatorium, and come back again —/I don't mean to say they weren't
419 CP	Reilly	21	there:/Those who go do not come back as these did./{C} It sounds like a prison.
419 CP	Reilly	24	go. But I said they did not come back/In the sense in which your friends came
419 CP	Reilly	25	the sense in which your friends came back./I did not say they stayed there./{C} What
420 CP	Reilly	25	an eye on them./{R} To send them back: what have they to go back to?/To the
420 CP	Reilly	25	send them back: what have they to go back to?/To the stale food mouldering in the
427 CP	Julia	1	brought Alex with me!/He only got back this morning from somewhere —/One of
427 CP	Alex	9	you won't have heard of/Yet. Got back this morning. I heard about your party/
433 CP	Julia	35	them, Alex,/The news that you bring back from Kinkanja./{L} Kinkanja? What was
445 CC	Claude	22	to the City this morning,/But he'll be back, I hope, before you leave./{E} And how's
447 CC	Claude	4	to say to Lady Elizabeth,/Coming back from the airport, about Colby./I think,
450 CC	Claude	22	have to repeat it./But he should be back by now. And then I'll leave you./I must
450 CC	Claude	27	to Eggerson/It was time you were back. Was your morning satisfactory?/{C} I've
450 CC	Claude	31	you now. But when Eggerson comes back/With Lady Elizabeth, I will rejoin you. {}/
456 CC	Eggers	3	of confidence —/He'd just come back from a public luncheon —/'Eggerson', he
456 CC	Eggers	33	travel *I* want is up to the City/And back to Joshua Park in the evening,/And once a
461 CC	Colby	11	know that I have you always at my back/If I get into trouble. But I hope/That I
462 CC	Claude	28	not changing the subject: I'm coming back to it./You know I've deliberately left you

487 CC	Lady E	29	that Providence has brought you back to me,/And you, Claude, and Eggerson
501 CC	Eggers	35	let them wait downstairs/And come back after Mrs. Guzzard has left?/{SC} That's
503 CC	Lucasta	31	we're always changing./When I come back, we'll be brother and sister —/Or so I
504 CC	Lucasta	4	LUCASTA]/{L} I'm sorry to come back. It's an anti-climax./But there seems to be
505 CC	Eggers	29	in Teddington./And now we must go back, many years:/Well, not so many years —
515 CC	Guzzard	28	gave up something I could never have back./Don't you understand that this revelation
519 CC	Claude	5	Have they gone? Is Colby coming back?/{LE} My poor Claude! {}/[LUCASTA
526 ES	Monica	9	/On silent feet, and stood behind my back/Quietly, a long time, a long long time/
526 ES	Monica	21	meanings are different. Look! We're back in the room/That we entered only a few
532 ES	Ld Clav	35	Fred Culverwell!/Why do you come back with another name?/{G} You've changed
535 ES	Gomez	25	/{G} That's perfectly simple. I come back to England/After thirty-five years. Can
536 ES	Gomez	6	jumping a gap — and you can't jump back again./I parted from myself by a sudden
540 ES	Gomez	17	the moonlight night/We drove back to Oxford. *You* were driving./{LC} That
548 ES	Ld Clav	4	anything else./{LC} She'll come back to tell us more about the peace and quiet./
562 ES	Carghil	13	think you'd still be here./I came back to have a quiet read of your letters;/But
564 ES	Carghil	26	it. After Oxford/I suppose you went back to ... where is your home?/{G} The
564 ES	Carghil	28	republic of San Marco./{MC} Went back to San Marco./Señor Gomez, if it's true
565 ES	Monica	7	so close at hand/Will you come back in the morning? After breakfast?/{LC}
571 ES	Ld Clav	34	has always haunted me./I was driving back to Oxford. We had two girls with us./It
574 ES	Michael	36	of my morals/And send you back reports. Some sort of place/Where
577 ES	Gomez	24	he's got flair. When he does come back/He'll be able to buy you out many times
580 ES	Carghil	19	my doctor's advice. And on my way back/Señor Gomez has invited me to visit San
580 ES	Monica	28	learn his lesson./I believe he'll come back. If it's all a failure/Homesickness, I'm sure,
580 ES	Monica	29	I'm sure, will bring him back to us;/If he prospers, that will give him
581 ES	Ld Clav	1	better./And when he comes back, if he does come back,/I know that you
581 ES	Ld Clav	1	when he comes back, if he does come back,/I know that you and Charles will do what
582 ES	Charles	27	us/And had turned and was looking back at us/With a glance of farewell./{M} I can't

BACK-CHAT (1)

228 Gus		23	speeches by heart./I'd extemporize back-chat, I knew how to gag,/And I knew how

BACKBONE (2)

184 FQ: DrySal		19	the horseshoe crab, the whale's backbone;/The pools where it offers to our
250 MC Tempt3		33	We care for the country./We are the backbone of the nation./We, not the plotting

BACKGROUND (7)

394 CP	Edward	33	/You wanted me to supply a public background/For your kind of public life. You
464 CC	Claude	10	—/That is, decoration as a background for living;/For me, they are life
475 CC	Colby	24	if you mean, wondered about your ... background:/No. I've been curious to know
480 CC	Kaghan	32	solidest companies:/Because I've no background — no background at all./That's
480 CC	Kaghan	32	/Because I've no background — no background at all./That's one thing I like about
484 CC	Lady E	19	/Yet we must have *some* similarity of background./{C} But you had parents. And no
486 CC	Colby	28	nothing very interesting about my background —/I assure you there isn't./{LE} It

BACKS (1)

587 Fable		4	their abbeys tumbling at their backs,/There was a village founded by some

BACKSTAIRS (1)

266 MC Knights		19	who was the tradesman's son: the backstairs brat who was born in Cheapside;/

BACKWARD (6)

38 Gerontion		53	it is not by any concitation/Of the backward devils./I would meet you upon this
43 Swee Erect		32	/The epileptic on the bed/Curves backward, clutching at her sides./The ladies of
52 Whispers		4	creatures under ground/Leaned backward with a lipless grin./Daffodil bulbs
187 FQ: DrySal		103	that is probably quite ineffable:/The backward look behind the assurance/Of
187 FQ: DrySal		104	the assurance/Of recorded history, the backward half-look/Over the shoulder, towards
196 FQ: Little		184	the dying?/It is not to ring the bell backward/Nor is it an incantation/To summon

BACKWARDS (1)

161 Rock 7		32	an age which advances progressively backwards?/VOICE OF THE UNEMPLOYED

BACON (1)

210 Old Gumbie		24	peas,/And a *beautiful* fry of lean bacon and cheese./I have a Gumbie Cat in

BAD (31)

62 WL: Burial		44	Sosostris, famous clairvoyante,/Had a bad cold, nevertheless/Is known to be the wisest
65 WL: Chess		111	be savagely still./'My nerves are bad to-night. Yes, bad. Stay with me./'Speak to
65 WL: Chess		111	/'My nerves are bad to-night. Yes, bad. Stay with me. 'Speak to me. Why do you
194 FQ: Little		118	others, as I pray you to forgive/Both bad and good. Last season's fruit is eaten/And
234 Ad-dress		10	/And some are good and some are bad/And some are better, some are worse —/
273 MC Thomas		33	does,/To settle if an act be good or bad./You defer to the fact. For every life and
285 FR	Violet	22	cold tea —/The strong cold stewed bad Indian tea./{C} That's not Amy's style at
286 FR	Violet	15	I do it as well as Amy:/England's bad enough, I would never go south,/Simply to
286 FR	Charles	23	the harm:/There's nothing on earth so bad for the young./All that a civilised person

296 FR	Gerald	15	us!/I never thought it would be as	bad as this./{V} There is only one thing to be
322 FR	Winch	40	wrong but some nasty cuts/And a	bad concussion; says he'll come round/In the
327 FR	Ivy	28	from London:/The connection was so	bad, I could hardly hear him,/And his voice was
329 FR	Chorus	16	appearances/The making the best of a	bad job/All twined and tangled together, all are
345 FR	Harry	2	to it;/Meanwhile, I apologise for my	bad manners./But if *you could* understand you
345 FR	Gerald	6	Harry, we must accept it;/But it's a	bad night, and you will have to be careful./
410 CP	Edward	33	Lavinia, we must make the best of a	bad job./That is what he means./{R} When you
410 CP	Reilly	36	Mr. Chamberlayne,/The best of a	bad job is all any of us make of it —/Except of
415 CP	Celia	23	from our point of view,/Was either	bad form, or was psychological./And bad form
415 CP	Celia	24	bad form, or was psychological./And	bad form always led to disaster/Because the
415 CP	Celia	27	myself —/But when everything's	bad form, or mental kinks,/You either become
415 CP	Celia	28	or mental kinks,/You either become	bad form, and cease to care,/Or else, if you care,
432 CP	Reilly	10	dear Julia,/You are giving me a very	bad introduction —/Supposing that an
452 CC	Lucasta	18	least, not till yesterday./Then, just by	bad luck, the boss did want a letter/And I
470 CC	Colby	20	/You'll very quickly realise how	bad my playing is./{L} Really, Colby, you do
477 CC	Lucasta	39	/Or perhaps you think it would be	bad for your prospects/Now that you're
479 CC	Kaghan	30	to pursue you./{K} Yes, I made a	bad impression at the start:/I saw that it was
501 CC	Claude	36	Guzzard has left?/{SC} That's not a	bad idea. If Colby agrees./{L} I trust you, Eggy.
555 ES	Monica	26	be afraid of that?/This shows how	bad your nerves have been./He only ran into a
556 ES	Michael	16	/About two miles from here. Not a	bad little place./{LC} Why are you staying
559 ES	Ld Clav	5	want to go abroad?/Well, that's not a	bad idea. A few years out of England/In one of
559 ES	Michael	19	to my own ideas of good and	bad,/Of right and wrong. I want to go far away/

BADE (1)

589 Fable		76	took him roughly by the hair/And bade him come with him, in accents hollow./

BADGLEY (15)

523 ES		m 13	*afternoon/ACT TWO/The Terrace at*	Badgley Court. Morning/ACT THREE/The
528 ES	Monica	26	/It may be, he will never return from	Badgley Court./But Selby wants him to have
529 ES	Monica	1	Selby said, 'as if you were going'./But	Badgley Court's so near your constituency!/You
532 ES	Charles	24	look forward to seeing you both at	Badgley Court/In a week or two. {}/[Enter
543 ES	Monica	20	me tonight,/What will it be like at	Badgley Court? {}/CURTAIN/Act Two/*The*
544 ES		2m 1	{}/CURTAIN/Act Two/*The terrace of*	Badgley Court. A bright sunny morning, several
545 ES	Ld Clav	16	/You want perfect peace: that's what	Badgley Court is for.'/I thought that very
546 ES	Piggott	10	But you mustn't call me 'Matron'/At	Badgley Court. You see, we've studied to avoid/
547 ES	Piggott	21	you more/About the amenities which	Badgley Court/Can offer to guests of the
563 ES	Gomez	12	I heard you'd chosen to come to	Badgley Court/I said to my doctor, 'Well, what
564 ES	Carghil	29	Gomez, if it's true you're staying at	Badgley Court,/I warn you — I'm going to
569 ES	Charles	33	should you submit?/Why not leave	Badgley and escape from them?/{LC} Because
581 ES	Monica	11	I'm convinced of: you must leave	Badgley Court./{C} Monica is right. You should
581 ES	Monica	32	I have come to know you/Here, at	Badgley Court. And I love you the more/
582 ES	Ld Clav	13	a while./This is your first visit to us at	Badgley Court,/Charles, and not at all what you

BADLY (5)

213 Growltiger		45	she gave a screech, for she was	badly skeered;/I am sorry to admit it, but she
279 MC	Knight4	21	tranquillity,/and justice that it so	badly needed. From the moment he/became
392 CP	Lavinia	12	I forgot all about it!/I let you down	badly. What did you do about it?/I only
472 CC	Colby	5	frightened./Perhaps you've been very	badly hurt, at some time./Or at least, there may
526 ES	Charles	4	right! The moment I'd said it/I was	badly frightened. For I didn't *know* you loved

BAEDEKER (1)

40 Burb Blei		t	brain in a dry season./Burbank with a Baedeker: Bleistein with a Cigar/Burbank

BAFFLEMENT (1)

226 Macavity		3	who can defy the Law./He's the bafflement of Scotland Yard, the Flying

BAG (3)

228 Gus		24	I knew how to let the cat out of the bag./I knew how to act with my back and my
366 CP	Edward	5	Are you quite sure they're not in your bag?/{J} Why no, of course not: that's where I
383 CP	Edward	4	all over?/Have you looked in your bag? ... Well, don't snap my head off .../You're

BAGGY (1)

212 Growltiger		6	/His coat was torn and seedy, he was baggy at the knees;/One ear was somewhat

BAGMEN (1)

232 Skimble		19	From the driver and the guards to the bagmen playing cards/He will supervise them

BAILEY (1)

209 NamingCats		7	as Victor or Jonathan, George or Bill Bailey —/All of them sensible everyday names./

BAILHACHE (1)

39 Gerontion		67	operations, will the weevil/Delay? De Bailhache, Fresca, Mrs. Cammel, whirled/

BAILING (1)

186 FQ: DrySal		75	/We have to think of them as forever bailing,/Setting and hauling, while the North

BAITED (1)
253 MC Tempt4   5 shall be said at last./Hooks have been baited with morsels of the past./Wantonness is
BAKED (1)
193 FQ: Little   96   /Both one and many; in the brown baked features/The eyes of a familiar compound
BAKERIES (1)
127 Corl March   23   /11,000 field kitchens,/1,150 field bakeries./What a time that took. Will it be he
BAKING (1)
210 Old Gumbie   22   trying,/She sets to work with her baking and frying./She makes them a
BALANCE (2)
243 MC Priest2   1 Against the perpetual wash of tides of balance of forces of barons and landholders./
248 MC Tempt2   19   these not too pleasant memories/In balance against other, earlier/And weightier
BALANCED (1)
546 ES   Piggott   37   /Our system is very delicately balanced:/For me to be simply 'Mrs. Piggott'/
BALCONY (1)
223 Pekes Pols   39   no longer aloof,/But some from the balcony, some from the roof,/Joined in/To the
BALD (3)
  14 Prufrock   40   back and descend the stair,/With a bald spot in the middle of my hair —/(They will
  15 Prufrock   82 I have seen my head (grown slightly bald) brought in upon a platter,/I am no
603 Spleen   11 this dull conspiracy./And Life, a little bald and gray,/Languid, fastidious, and bland,/
BALL (3)
  15 Prufrock   92 /To have squeezed the universe into a ball/To roll it towards some overwhelming
216 Jellicles   4 bright —/Jellicles come to the Jellicle Ball./Jellicle Cats are black and white,/Jellicle
217 Jellicles   36 /For the Jellicle Moon and the Jellicle Ball./Mungojerrie and Rumpelteazer/
BALLOON (1)
  33 Conv Gal   3 I confess)/It may be Prester John's balloon/Or an old battered lantern hung aloft/
BALLS (2)
  52 Whispers   5 lipless grin./Daffodil bulbs instead of balls/Stared from the sockets of the eyes!/He
155 Rock 3   36   road/And a thousand lost golf balls'./CHORUS:/We build in vain unless the
BALMY (1)
212 Growltiger   23 the barge at Molesey lay./All in the balmy moonlight it lay rocking on the tide —/
BALTIC (2)
354 CP   Alex   11 Belgian./{A} Her father belonged to a Baltic family —/One of the *oldest* Baltic families
354 CP   Alex   12 to a Baltic family —/One of the *oldest* Baltic families/With a branch in Sweden and
BAM (3)
122 SAWa & Ho   21 *live as two/Two live as three/Under the bam/Under the boo/Under the bamboo tree./*
122 SAWa & Ho   27 *sound is the sound of the sea/Under the bam/Under the boo/Under the bamboo tree/*
122 SAWa & Ho   33   */Wear palmleaf drapery/Under the bam/Under the boo/Under the bamboo tree./Tell*
BAMBOO (8)
122 SAWa & Ho   15   AS BONES/{W&H} *Under the bamboo/Bamboo bamboo/Under the bamboo tree*
122 SAWa & Ho   16   BONES/{W&H} *Under the bamboo/Bamboo bamboo/Under the bamboo tree/Two*
122 SAWa & Ho   16 */{W&H} Under the bamboo/Bamboo bamboo/Under the bamboo tree/Two live as one/*
122 SAWa & Ho   17 *bamboo/Bamboo bamboo/Under the bamboo tree/Two live as one/One live as two/Two*
122 SAWa & Ho   23 *the bam/Under the boo/Under the bamboo tree./Where the breadfruit fall/And the*
122 SAWa & Ho   29 *the bam/Under the boo/Under the bamboo tree/Where the Gauguin maids/In the*
122 SAWa & Ho   35 *the bam/Under the boo/Under the bamboo tree./Tell me in what part of the wood/*
123 SAWa & Ho   4 *banyan, palmleaf/Or under the bamboo tree?/Any old tree will do for me/Any old*
BANAL (1)
601 Nocturne   6   failing, strikes some tune/Banal, and out of pity for their fate/Behind the
BANANAS (1)
  56 Swee Night   20   gapes;/The waiter brings in oranges/Bananas figs and hothouse grapes;/The silent
BAND (2)
587 Fable   8   was a monastery/Inhabited by a band of friars merry./They were possessors of
438 CP Edward 24 responsibility/Is greater than that of a band of half-crazed savages./{L} Oh, Edward, I
BANDICOOT (1)
212 Growltiger   15 Growltiger's rage;/Woe to the bristly Bandicoot, that lurks on foreign ships,/And woe
BANEFUL (1)
459 CC   Lady E 26 primrose yellow/Would be absolutely baneful to Mr. Colby./He needs a light mauve. I
BANG (1)
  86 Hollow Men   98 *is the way the world ends/Not with a bang but a whimper./*Ash-Wednesday/Because I
BANGKOK (1)
213 Growltiger   56 day of celebration was commanded in Bangkok./The Rum Tum Tugger/The Rum
BANISTER (1)
  92 Ash-Wed 3   3 below/The same shape twisted on the banister/Under the vapour in the fetid air/

BANK (8)

20 Portrait	76	murdered at a Polish dance,/Another bank defaulter has confessed./I keep my
67 WL: Fire S	174	of leaf/Clutch and sink into the wet bank. The wind/Crosses the brown land,
67 WL: Fire S	188	/Dragging its slimy belly on the bank/While I was fishing in the dull canal/On a
159 Rock 6	4	/It is hard for those who live near a Bank/To doubt the security of their money./It is
177 FQ: ECoker	17	afternoon,/Where you lean against a bank while a van passes,/And the deep lane
345 FR Harry	12	address, mother,/Will be care of the bank in London until you hear from me./
534 ES Gomez	30	ready:/And keep an account in a bank in Switzerland./The ones who don't get
538 ES Gomez	38	/And went into the City. Director of a bank/And chairman of companies. You looked

BANKERS (1)

180 FQ: ECoker	104	the vacant,/The captains, merchant bankers, eminent men of letters./The generous

BANKRUPT (1)

452 CC Kaghan	7	pry some cash from the money-box./Bankrupt again! So I thought I'd better bring

BANKS (1)

186 FQ: DrySal	77	the North East lowers/Over shallow banks unchanging and erosionless/Or drawing

BANNER (3)

263 MC	1m 27	{}/[*Enter the* FIRST PRIEST *with a banner of St. Stephen borne before him.*/*The lines*
264 MC	m 7	[*Enter the* SECOND PRIEST, *with a banner of St. John the Apostle borne before him.*]
264 MC	m 14	/[*Enter the* THIRD PRIEST, *with a banner of the Holy Innocents borne before him.*]/

BANNERS (2)

264 MC	m 22	PRIESTS *stand together with the banners behind them*]/{P1} Since the Holy
265 MC	m 9	{}/[*Enter the* FOUR KNIGHTS. *The banners disappear*]/{K1} Servants of the King./

BANQUET (1)

530 ES Monica	29	how you grumbled/At the farewell banquet, with the tributes from the staff,/The

BANQUIER (1)

47 Mél Adult	6	conférencier;/A Londres, un peu banquier,/Vous me paierez bien la tête./C'est à

BANYAN (2)

122 SAWa & Ho	31	*tree*/*Where the Gauguin maids*/*In the banyan shades*/*Wear palmleaf drapery*/*Under the*
123 SAWa & Ho	3	*to flirt with me?*/*Under the breadfruit, banyan, palmleaf*/*Or under the bamboo tree?*/*Any*

BAPTISED (1)

508 CC Guzzard	38	to show that the child had been baptised/When it came to us; but we could not

BAPTISM (1)

509 CC Guzzard	2	/So we had it given conditional baptism./{E} What name did you give him?/

BAPTIST (1)

275 MC Thomas	20	ever Virgin, to the blessed John the Baptist, the holy apostles Peter and Paul, to the

BAPTIZED (1)

54 Mr E Sun	11	a gesso ground/The nimbus of the Baptized God./The wilderness is cracked and

BAR (10)

69 WL: Fire S	260	I can sometimes hear/Beside a public bar in Lower Thames Street,/The pleasant
592 Grad 1	4	our lips, sail we/Across the harbor bar — no chart to show/No light to warn of
599 On a Port	13	thought she stands./The parrot on his bar, a silent spy,/Regards her with a patient
273 MC Priests	10	THOMAS *and* PRIESTS]/{3P} Bar the door. Bar the door/The door is barred./
273 MC Priests	10	*and* PRIESTS]/{3P} Bar the door. Bar the door/The door is barred./We are safe.
273 MC Priests	26	of Christ,/But like beasts. You would bar the door/Against the lion, the leopard, the
393 CP Lavinia	33	it was I who made you work at the Bar .../{E} You nagged me because I didn't get
569 ES Charles	21	something of it in my practice at the bar./I'm sure I could help./{M} Oh Father, do
577 ES Carghil	37	at the door./Richard, you must not bar his way. That would be shameful./{LC} I
577 ES Ld Clav	38	would be shameful./{LC} I cannot bar his way, as you know very well./Michael's a

BARBAROUS (1)

64 WL: Chess	99	scene/The change of Philomel, by the barbarous king/So rudely forced; yet there the

BARBARY (1)

236 Cat Morgan	13	'art.'/I got knocked about on the Barbary Coast,/And me voice it ain't no sich

BARBITURIC (1)

189 FQ: DrySal	196	cards, fiddle with pentagrams/Or barbituric acids, or dissect/The recurrent image

BARE (2)

15 Prufrock	63	that are braceleted and white and bare/(But in the lamplight, downed with light
143 Lines OM	7	from the friendly tree./When I lay bare the tooth of wit/The hissing over the

BARELY (1)

186 FQ: DrySal	85	to Death its God. Only the hardly, barely prayable/Prayer of the one

BARGAIN (1)

456 CC Eggers	5	/And I'm perfectly satisfied with the bargain.'/Of course it's true that her family

BARGE (3)

40 Burb Blei	11	Istria/With even feet. Her shuttered barge/Burned on the water all the day./But this
212 Growltiger	1	was a Bravo Cat, who travelled on a barge:/In fact he was the roughest cat that ever
212 Growltiger	22	tender moon was shining bright, the barge at Molesey lay./All in the balmy

BARGES (2)

69 WL: Fire S	268	/The river sweats/Oil and tar/The barges drift/With the turning tide/Red sails/
69 WL: Fire S	273	swing on the heavy spar./The barges wash/Drifting logs/Down Greenwich

BARITONE (1)

213 Growltiger	34	Lady seemed enraptured by his manly baritone,/Disposed to relaxation, and awaiting

BARK (25)

222 Pekes Pols	8	they join in to the fray/And they/Bark bark bark bark/Bark bark BARK BARK/
222 Pekes Pols	8	join in to the fray/And they/Bark bark bark bark/Bark bark BARK BARK/Until
222 Pekes Pols	8	in to the fray/And they/Bark bark bark bark/Bark bark BARK BARK/Until you
222 Pekes Pols	8	to the fray/And they/Bark bark bark bark/Bark bark BARK BARK/Until you can
222 Pekes Pols	9	fray/And they/Bark bark bark bark/Bark bark BARK BARK/Until you can hear
222 Pekes Pols	9	/And they/Bark bark bark bark/Bark bark BARK BARK/Until you can hear them all
222 Pekes Pols	9	they/Bark bark bark bark/Bark bark BARK BARK/Until you can hear them all over
222 Pekes Pols	9	bark bark bark/Bark bark BARK BARK/Until you can hear them all over the
222 Pekes Pols	22	their hind feet,/And started to/Bark bark bark bark/Bark bark BARK BARK/
222 Pekes Pols	22	their hind feet,/And started to/Bark bark bark bark/Bark bark BARK BARK/Until
222 Pekes Pols	22	hind feet,/And started to/Bark bark bark bark/Bark bark BARK BARK/Until you
222 Pekes Pols	22	feet,/And started to/Bark bark bark bark/Bark bark BARK BARK/Until you could
222 Pekes Pols	23	/And started to/Bark bark bark bark/Bark bark BARK BARK/Until you could hear
222 Pekes Pols	23	started to/Bark bark bark bark/Bark bark BARK BARK/Until you could hear them
222 Pekes Pols	23	to/Bark bark bark bark/Bark bark BARK BARK/Until you could hear them all
222 Pekes Pols	23	bark bark bark/Bark bark BARK BARK/Until you could hear them all over the
223 Pekes Pols	43	the roof,/Joined in/To the din/With a/Bark bark bark bark/Bark bark BARK BARK/
223 Pekes Pols	43	/Joined in/To the din/With a/Bark bark bark bark/Bark bark BARK BARK/Until
223 Pekes Pols	43	in/To the din/With a/Bark bark bark bark/Bark bark BARK BARK/Until you
223 Pekes Pols	43	in/To the din/With a/Bark bark bark bark/Bark bark BARK BARK/Until you could
223 Pekes Pols	44	the din/With a/Bark bark bark bark/Bark bark BARK BARK/Until you could hear
223 Pekes Pols	44	din/With a/Bark bark bark bark/Bark bark BARK BARK/Until you could hear them
223 Pekes Pols	44	a/Bark bark bark bark/Bark bark BARK BARK/Until you could hear them all
223 Pekes Pols	44	bark bark bark/Bark bark BARK BARK/Until you could hear them all over the
234 Ad-dress	21	pretend they like to fight;/They often bark, more seldom bite;/But yet a Dog is, on the

BARKING (1)

158 Rock 5	6	dogs, full of enterprise, sniffing and barking: they say, 'This house is a nest of

BARN (1)

270 MC Chorus	13	in the passage,/In the mews in the barn in the byre in the market-place/In our

BARNABAS (24)

509 CC Guzzard	4	give him?/{MG} We named the child Barnabas./{LE} Barnabas? There's never been
509 CC Lady E	5	We named the child Barnabas./{LE} Barnabas? There's never been such a name/In
509 CC Guzzard	11	had been married in the church of St. Barnabas./{C} Barnabas Kaghan. Is he the little
509 CC Colby	12	in the church of St. Barnabas./{C} Barnabas Kaghan. Is he the little cousin/Who
509 CC Lady E	19	of that./But I believe that Colby is Barnabas./{SC} No, Elizabeth, Barnabas is
509 CC Claude	20	is Barnabas./{SC} No, Elizabeth, Barnabas is Barnabas./I must explain this, Mrs.
509 CC Claude	20	/{SC} No, Elizabeth, Barnabas is Barnabas./I must explain this, Mrs. Guzzard./I
509 CC Claude	24	you upstairs —/Whose name is Barnabas Kaghan./{LE} Barnabas?/{SC} Yes,
509 CC Lady E	25	name is Barnabas Kaghan./{LE} Barnabas?/{SC} Yes, Elizabeth. He sometimes
509 CC Lady E	31	be proud of it./{LE} How old is this Barnabas?/{SC} About twenty-eight, I think./
509 CC Lady E	37	so confused. What with Colby being Barnabas —/I mean, not Barnabas. And Mr.
509 CC Lady E	38	Colby being Barnabas —/I mean, not Barnabas. And Mr. Kaghan/Being Barnabas. I
509 CC Lady E	39	Barnabas. And Mr. Kaghan/Being Barnabas. I suppose I'll get used to it./{C} But
510 CC Lady E	16	to be prepared for a surprise./{LE} Barnabas! Is your name Barnabas?/{K} Why,
510 CC Lady E	16	/{LE} Barnabas! Is your name Barnabas?/{K} Why, yes, it is. Did you tell her,
510 CC Claude	19	Guzzard who revealed it./This is Mr. Barnabas Kaghan —/Mrs. Guzzard. And ... my
510 CC Lady E	32	why are you asking?/{LE} Because, Barnabas, it seems you are my son./{E} You will
511 CC Lady E	6	There is no doubt whatever about it, Barnabas./I am your mother./{K} But who was
511 CC Lady E	29	'B'?/{LE} Certainly, if you prefer that, Barnabas./{L} Why is it that you don't like the
511 CC Lucasta	30	is it that you don't like the name of Barnabas?/{K} I don't want people calling me
512 CC Guzzard	16	Kaghans will supply,/To recognise Barnabas Kaghan as her son? {}/[*To* LADY
512 CC Guzzard	26	painful process,/As I know. And you, Barnabas Kaghan,/Are you satisfied to find
512 CC Lady E	33	you know./{LE} I shall see to that, Barnabas./{K} *B.* — if you don't mind, Aunt
513 CC Guzzard	4	you are satisfied/To be the wife of Barnabas Kaghan,/The daughter-in-law of

BARNACLES (1)

24 Rhapsody	44	afternoon in a pool,/An old crab with barnacles on his back,/Gripped the end of a

BARNEY (4)

511 CC Kaghan	31	/{K} I don't want people calling me 'Barney' —/Barney Kaghan! Kaghan's all right./
511 CC Kaghan	32	want people calling me 'Barney' —/Barney Kaghan! Kaghan's all right./But Barney

| 511 CC | Kaghan | 33 | Kaghan! Kaghan's all right./But Barney Kaghan — it sounds rather flashy:/It |
| 511 CC | Lucasta | 35 | you're an alderman, you'll be Sir Barney Kaghan!/{LE} And I'm very glad you're |

BARON (3)

587 Fable		11	dairy;/Whenever some old villainous baron died,/He added to their hoards — a deed
253 MC	Tempt4	32	your heel./King, emperor, bishop, baron, king:/Uncertain mastery of melting
276 MC	Knight1	32	first, my neighbour in/the country: Baron William de Traci./{K3} I am afraid I am

BARON'S (1)

| 252 MC | Tempt3 | 4 | bishop's court,/Of king's court over baron's court./{T} Which I helped to found./ |

BARONS (12)

229 MC	Chorus	22	well if he should return./King rules or barons rule;/We have suffered various
241 MC	Priest3	2	frequent malversation./King rules or barons rule:/The strong man strongly and the
243 MC	Priest2	1	wash of tides of balance of forces of barons and landholders./The rock of God is
249 MC	Thomas	36	self-interest./{T} You forget the barons. Who will not forget/Constant curbing
249 MC	Tempt2	38	of petty privilege./{T2} Against the barons/Is King's cause, churl's cause,
251 MC	Tempt3	27	does not understand us, the English barons./We are the people./{T} To what does
251 MC	Thomas	33	what have you —/If you do speak for barons —/{T3} For a powerful party/Which has
253 MC	Tempt4	14	turn, broken and crushed./As for barons, envy of lesser men/Is still more
253 MC	Tempt4	16	anger./Kings have public policy, barons private profit,/Jealousy raging
253 MC	Tempt4	18	raging possession of the fiend./Barons are employable against each other;/
258 MC	Thomas	22	with him against Toulouse,/I beat the barons at their own game. I/Could then despise
260 MC	Thomas	29	at peace with its/neighbours, the barons at peace with the King, the householder

BARRAWAY (5)

399 CP	Reilly	1	appointments this morning, Miss Barraway:/I should like to run over my
399 CP	Reilly	23	left the house..../{R} Quite right, Miss Barraway. That's all for the moment./{N} Mr.
421 CP	Reilly	39	be here by now. I'll speak to Miss Barraway. {}/[*Takes up house-telephone*]/{R}
422 CP	Reilly	1	/[*Takes up house-telephone*]/{R} Miss Barraway, when Mr. Gibbs arrives .../Oh, very
422 CP	Reilly	4	You may bring the tray in now, Miss Barraway. {}/[*Enter* ALEX]/{A} Well! Well! and

BARRED (3)

589 Fable		65	most always do./The doors, though barred and bolted most securely,/Gave way —
273 MC	Priests	11	the door. Bar the door/The door is barred./We are safe. We are safe./They dare not
335 FR	Agatha	21	/Looking straight ahead, passing barred windows./Up and down. Until the chain

BARRELS (1)

| 213 Growltiger | | 31 | his raffish crew were sleeping in their barrels and their bunks —/As the Siamese came |

BARREN (3)

30 Cous Nancy		4	the hills and broke them —/The barren New England hills —/Riding to hounds/
240 MC	Chorus	14	do in the heat of summer/But wait in barren orchards for another October?/Some
275 MC	Chorus	24	in the past; and I wander in a land of barren boughs: if I break them, they bleed; I

BARRISTER (2)

| 405 CP | Reilly | 16 | /So to speak, as you went along. A barrister/Ought to know his brief before he |
| 576 ES | Gomez | 34 | confidential .../{G} Be careful, Mr. Barrister./You ought to know something about |

BARRISTERS (1)

| 493 CC | Claude | 14 | /We mustn't look like a couple of barristers/Ready to cross-examine a witness./It's |

BARS (3)

24 Rhapsody		68	in corridors/And cocktail smells in bars./The lamp said,/'Four o'clock,/Here is the
223 Pekes Pols		54	/And when he looked out through the bars of the area,/You never saw anything fiercer
469 CC		3m 1	*in an armchair. The concluding bars of a piece of music are/heard as the curtain*

BASE (1)

| 42 Swee Erect | | 22 | /Broadbottomed, pink from nape to base,/Knows the female temperament/And |

BASED (1)

| 49 Hippopot | | 8 | True Church can never fail/For it is based upon a rock./The hippo's feeble steps |

BASEMENT (5)

27 Morning		1	/They are rattling breakfast plates in basement kitchens,/And along the trampled
210 Old Gumbie		8	asleep,/She tucks up her skirts to the basement to creep./She is deeply concerned with
218 Mung Rump		8	area window was found ajar/And the basement looked like a field of war,/If a tile or
223 Pekes Pols		50	/When suddenly, up from a small basement flat,/Why who should stalk out but
226 Macavity		9	*not there!*/You may seek him in the basement, you may look up in the air —/But I

BASEMENTS (1)

| 155 Rock 3 | | 49 | while the rent is paid,/Subsiding basements where the rat breeds/Or sanitary |

BASILIQUE (1)

| 48 Lune Miel | | 9 | d'ici est Saint Apollinaire/En Classe, basilique connue des amateurs/De chapitaux |

BASIN (1)

| 233 Skimble | | 39 | make a breeze./There's a funny little basin you're supposed to wash your face in/And |

BASIS (2)

| 446 CC | Claude | 21 | /If we started on a purely business basis./{E} No doubt that's best. While he's still |
| 462 CC | Claude | 4 | We can put matters onto a permanent basis./{C} I must confess, that up to this point/I |

BASKERVILLE (1)
136 5FingerEx4   4   *him*)/With his musical sound/And his Baskerville Hound/Which, just at a word from
BASKET (1)
549 ES   Carghil   14   punt/On the river — and we had a tea basket/With some lovely little cakes — I've
BASTARD (2)
477 CC   Lucasta   23   /Little you know what it's like to be a bastard/And wanted by nobody. I know why
478 CC   Lucasta   31   Claude and my mother./I may be a bastard, but I have some self-respect./Well,
BAT (1)
224 Mr Mistoff   5   All his/Inventions are off his own bat./There's no such Cat in the metropolis;/He
BAT'S (1)
129 Cor2 State   47   /Come with the sweep of the little bat's wing, with the small flare of the firefly or
BATFLIGHT (1)
166 Rock 10   22   /The twilight over stagnant pools at batflight,/Moon light and star light, owl and
BATH (9)
43 Swee Erect   41   of good./But Doris, towelled from the bath,/Enters padding on broad feet,/Bringing
55 Mr E Sun   30   ham to ham/Stirring the water in his bath./The masters of the subtle schools/Are
124 SA Sweeney   16   a girl in/Well he kept her there in a bath/With a gallon of lysol in a bath/{Sw} These
124 SA Sweeney   17   in a bath/With a gallon of lysol in a bath/{Sw} These fellows always get pinched in
129 Cor2 State   3   /The Companions of the Bath, the Knights of the British Empire, the
295 FR   Amy   39   /Get Downing to draw you a hot bath,/And you will feel better./{Ag} There are
296 FR   Harry   13   afraid of them./I will go and have my bath. {}/[*Exit*]/{G} God preserve us!/I never
446 CC   Eggers   33   a garden of his own. And yes, a bird bath!/{SC} A bird bath? In the mews? What's
446 CC   Claude   34   And yes, a bird bath!/{SC} A bird bath? In the mews? What's the point of that?/
BATHE (1)
286 FR   Violet   20   from aeroplane shares./{V} They bathe all day and they dance all night/In the
BATHING (1)
547 ES   Piggott   25   /And it's still too early for the bathing pool./But several of our guests are keen
BATHS (1)
300 FRDowning   17   ocean liners/With all their swimming baths and gymnasiums/There's not even a place
BATRACHIAN (1)
308 FR   Harry   7   /Where the dead stone is seen to be batrachian,/The aphyllous branch ophidian./
BATS (7)
73 WL: Thund 379   whisper music on those strings/And bats with baby faces in the violet light/Whistled,
204 de la Mare   21   moonlight dance,/Dogs cower, flitter bats, and owls range/At witches' sabbath of the
355 CP   Julia   1   I ever met who could hear the cry of bats./{P} Hear the cry of bats?/{J} He could hear
355 CP   Peter   2   the cry of bats./{P} Hear the cry of bats?/{J} He could hear the cry of bats./{C} But
355 CP   Julia   3   of bats?/{J} He could hear the cry of bats./{C} But how do you know he could hear
355 CP   Celia   4   do you know he could hear the cry of bats?/{J} Because he said so. And I believed
355 CP   Julia   12   island for him/Where there were no bats./{A} And is he still there?/Julia is really a
BATTEN (1)
358 CP   Julia   24   Friday?/No, I'm afraid my good Mrs. Batten/Would give me notice. And now I must
BATTENED (1)
213 Growltiger   44   and their pullaways and junks,/They battened down the hatches on the crew within
BATTERED (1)
33 Conv Gal   4   be Prester John's balloon/Or an old battered lantern hung aloft/To light poor
BATTERSON (5)
550 ES   Ld Clav   2   more./{LC} Your name was Maisie Batterson./{MC} Oh, Richard, you're only
570 ES   Ld Clav   34   in the Midlands./As for Maisie Batterson .../{M} Maisie Batterson?/Who is
570 ES   Monica   35   for Maisie Batterson .../{M} Maisie Batterson?/Who is Maisie Batterson?/{LC} She
570 ES   Monica   36   {M} Maisie Batterson?/Who is Maisie Batterson?/{LC} She no longer exists./Nor the
571 ES   Ld Clav   2   /But Freddy Culverwell and Maisie Batterson,/And Dick Ferry too, and Richard
BATTLE (2)
188 FQ: DrySal 170   he admonished Arjuna/On the field of battle./Not fare well,/But fare forward,
222 Pekes Pols   t   of Old Deuteronomy!'/Of the Awefull Battle of the Pekes and the Pollicles/*Together*
BATTLESHIP (2)
201 Def Island   8   those appointed to the grey/ships — battleship, merchantman, trawler —/
406 CP   Edward   27   than you;/You're stronger than a ... battleship. That's what drove me mad./I am the
BAVARD (1)
51 Restaurant   6   appelle le jour de lessive des gueux.'/(Bavard, baveux, à la croupe arrondie,/Je te prie,
BAVE (1)
51 Restaurant   7   arrondie,/Je te prie, au moins, ne bave pas dans la soupe)./'Les saules trempés, et
BAVEUX (1)
51 Restaurant   6   le jour de lessive des gueux.'/(Bavard, baveux, à la croupe arrondie,/Je te prie, au
BAY-BUSH (1)
142 Cape Ann   7   the quail, the bob-white/Dodging by bay-bush. Follow the feet/Of the walker, the

BAYSWATER (1)
285 FR   Ivy   18   could afford it,/Not freeze, as I do, in Bayswater, by a gas-fire counting shillings./{V}
BE (1014)
BEACH (4)
16 Prufrock   123   flannel trousers, and walk upon the beach./I have heard the mermaids singing, each
24 Rhapsody   25   things;/A twisted branch upon the beach/Eaten smooth, and polished/As if the
85 Hollow Men   60   /And avoid speech/Gathered on this beach of the tumid river/Sightless, unless/The
185 FQ: DrySal   55   /The prayer of the bone on the beach, the unprayable/Prayer at the calamitous
BEACHES (1)
184 FQ: DrySal   17   the granite/Into which it reaches, the beaches where it tosses/Its hints of earlier and
BEAK (1)
315 FR   Chorus 33   of the future darken the past, the beak and claws have desecrated/History.
BEAMS (2)
149 Rock 1   86   *will build with new stone/Where the beams are rotten/We will build with new timbers/*
167 Rock 10   43   forming at the ends of our fingers and beams of our eyes./And when we have built an
BEAR (25)
21 Portrait   111   ... dance, dance/Like a dancing bear,/Cry like a parrot, chatter like an ape./Let
39 Gerontion   68   /Beyond the circuit of the shuddering Bear/In fractured atoms. Gull against the wind,
66 WL: Chess   146   get a nice set,/He said, I swear, I can't bear to look at you./And no more can't I, I
129 Cor2 State   38   among these heads/Necks strong to bear them/Noses strong to break the wind/
135 5FingerEx1   5   desires/And the quick eyes of Woolly Bear./There is no relief but in grief./O when will
172 FQ: BurntN   45   go, said the bird: human kind/Cannot bear very much reality./Time past and time
186 FQ: DrySal   80   be unpayable/For a haul that will not bear examination./There is no end of it, the
218 Mung Rump   6   than a couple of cats can very well bear./If the area window was found ajar/And
239 MC   Chorus 8   the cathedral. We are forced to bear witness./Since golden October declined
257 MC   Chorus 29   of leopard, footfall of padding bear,/Palm-pat of nodding ape, square hyaena
271 MC   Thomas 19   will seem unreal./Human kind cannot bear very much reality. {}/[*Enter* PRIESTS]/
278 MC Knight2   35   a traitor, and no one would have to bear the burden of/being called murderer. And
295 FR   Harry   22   happened,/Because you could not bear it. So you must believe/That I suffer from
304 FR   Mary   27   held on to me/Because she couldn't bear to let any project go;/And even when *she*
307 FR   Mary   23   Just now, I find them very difficult to bear./They are always assured that you ought to
366 CP   Peter   35   /{P} This evening I felt I could bear it no longer./That awful party! I'm sorry,
371 CP   Peter   30   I can only hold to the memory/I can bear any future. But I must find out/The truth
381 CP   Celia   23   /But what will your life be? I cannot bear to think of it./Oh, Edward! Can you be
396 CP   Lavinia 24   are for yourself. And that's hard to bear./I thought that there might be some way
397 CP   Lavinia 9   /Talking to yourself. Could you bear, for a moment,/To think about *me*?/{E} It
411 CP   Reilly 29   your conscience/But to learn how to bear the burdens on your conscience./With the
525 ES   Charles 19   /And because your father simply can't bear it/That any man but he should have you to
543 ES   Monica 18   a dinner party./{M} Father, can't you bear to be alone with me?/If you can't bear to
543 ES   Monica 19   bear to be alone with me?/If you can't bear to dine alone with me tonight,/What will it
554 ES   Carghil 5   /She never stops talking. Can you bear it?/If I go at once, perhaps she'll take the
BEARABLE (1)
466 CC   Claude 13   agonising ecstasy/Which makes life bearable. It's all I have./I suppose it takes the
BEARD (1)
212 Growltiger   26   at Hampton he had gone to wet his beard;/And his bosun, TUMBLEBRUTUS, he
BEARING (3)
94 Ash-Wed 4   12   Here are the years that walk between, bearing/Away the fiddles and the flutes,
128 Cor1 March   36   the sacrifice./Now come the virgins bearing urns, urns containing/Dust/Dust/Dust
554 ES   Carghil 4   /— Oh, there's Mrs. Piggott!/She's bearing down on us. Isn't she frightful!/She
BEARINGS (1)
322 FR   Winch   36   the country/And stopped to take his bearings. We've got him at the Arms —/Mr.
BEARS (1)
67 WL: Fire S   177   softly, till I end my song./The river bears no empty bottles, sandwich papers,/Silk
BEAST (13)
157 Rock 4   14   consumed with fire;/No place for a beast to pass./There were enemies without to
177 FQ: ECoker   8   fur and faeces,/Bone of man and beast, cornstalk and leaf./Houses live and die:
194 FQ: Little   119   season's fruit is eaten/And the fullfed beast shall kick the empty pail./For last year's
214 RTTugger   23   it!/The Rum Tum Tugger is a curious beast:/His disobliging ways are a matter of
588 Fable   46   They made a raid/On every bird and beast in Æsop's fable/To fill out their repast,
247 MC Tempt1   32   Lordship is too proud!/The safest beast is not the one that roars most loud,/This
274 MC Thomas   9   beasts as men. We have fought the beast/And have conquered. We have only to
274 MC Knights   19   down Daniel for the mark of the beast./Are you washed in the blood of the
274 MC Knights   21   Are you marked with the mark of the beast?/Come down Daniel to the lions' den,/
281 MC Chorus   12   air, both the hawk and the finch; the beast on the earth, both the wolf and the lamb;/
310 FR   Mary   23   of sacrifice/For the tree and the beast, and the fish/Thrashing itself upstream:/

| 428 CP | Julia | 4 | monkey,/The horrid little beast — stole my ticket to Mentone/And I had |
| 453 CC | Lucasta | 33 | fed between meals./{L} B., you're a beast. I've a very small appetite./But the point |

BEASTS (9)

178 FQ:	ECoker	46	of man and woman/And that of beasts. Feet rising and falling./Eating and
269 MC	Chorus	33	have heard/Laughter in the noises of beasts that make strange noises: jackal, jackass,
273 MC	Priests	24	not as men come, but/Like maddened beasts. They come not like men, who/Respect
273 MC	Priests	26	kneel to the Body of Christ,/But like beasts. You would bar the door/Against the
273 MC	Priests	29	or the boar,/Why not more/Against beasts with the souls of damned men, against
273 MC	Priests	30	men/Who would damn themselves to beasts. My Lord! My Lord!/{T} You think me
274 MC	Thomas	9	or by resistance,/Not to fight with beasts as men. We have fought the beast/And
275 MC	Chorus	22	The land is foul, the water is foul, our beasts and ourselves defiled with blood./A rain
281 MC	Chorus	16	the drone of summer, the voices of beasts and of birds, praise Thee./We thank Thee

BEAT (11)

22 Preludes		9	from vacant lots;/The showers beat/On broken blinds and chimney-pots,/And
31 Apollinax		16	/With seaweed in its hair./I heard the beat of centaur's hoofs over the hard turf/As his
40 Burb Blei		10	well./The horses, under the axletree/Beat up the dawn from Istria/With even feet.
73 WL:	Thund	380	faces in the violet light/Whistled, and beat their wings/And crawled head downward
90 Ash-Wed 1		35	wings to fly/But merely vans to beat the air/The air which is now thoroughly
173 FQ:	BurntN	89	moment in the arbour where the rain beat,/The moment in the draughty church at
222 Pekes Pols		14	big Police Dog was away from his beat —/I don't know the reason, but most
223 Pekes Pols		60	*when the Police Dog returned to his beat,/There wasn't a single one left in the street./*
240 MC	Chorus	7	from the sea,/Ruinous spring shall beat at our doors,/Root and shoot shall eat our
258 MC	Thomas	22	war with him against Toulouse,/I beat the barons at their own game. I/Could then
451 CC	Eggers	10	he has a heart of gold. But not to beat about the bush,/He's rather a rough

BEATEN (1)

| 547 ES | Piggott | 30 | are one or two who don't like being beaten,/And that spoils any sport, in my |

BEATING (3)

70 WL:	Fire S	280	leialala/Elizabeth and Leicester/Beating oars/The stern was formed/A gilded
74 WL:	Thund	421	have responded,/Gaily, when invited, beating obedient/To controlling hands/I sat
103 Journ Magi		23	a running stream and a water-mill beating the darkness,/And three trees on the low

BEATS (2)

| 24 Rhapsody | | 9 | /Every street lamp that I pass/Beats like a fatalistic drum,/And through the |
| 61 WL: | Burial | 22 | heap of broken images, where the sun beats, and the dead tree gives no shelter, the |

BEAUTIFUL (4)

210 Old Gumbie		24	of bread and dried peas,/And a *beautiful* fry of lean bacon and cheese./I have a
495 CC	Lady E	21	he wrote me poems. And he was so beautiful./I know now that poets don't look like
553 ES	Carghil	23	worth keeping./Only a few. But very beautiful!/It was Effie said, when the break
563 ES	Gomez	30	revue./{G} If Maisie Montjoy was as beautiful to look at/As Mrs. Carghill, I can well

BEAUTY (7)

38 Gerontion		56	heart was removed therefrom/To lose beauty in terror, terror in inquisition./I have
66 WL:	Chess	167	they asked me in to dinner, to get the beauty of it hot —/HURRY UP PLEASE ITS
155 Rock 3		44	perpetual ruins?/I have loved the beauty of Thy House, the peace of Thy
164 Rock 9		24	the perfect order of speech, and the beauty of incantation./LORD, shall we not
173 FQ:	BurntN	97	/Turning shadow into transient beauty/With slow rotation suggesting
605 Narcissus		26	in his own clutch, his ancient beauty/Caught fast in the pink tips of his new
605 Narcissus		27	Caught fast in the pink tips of his new beauty./Then he had been a young girl/Caught

BECAME (19)

589 Fable		74	sat as pasted to his chair,/His eye became the size of any dollar,/The ghost then
605 Narcissus		17	/He could not live men's ways, but became a dancer before God/If he walked in
606 Narcissus		33	/And he felt drunken and old./So he became a dancer to God./Because his flesh was
239 MC	Chorus	10	gathered and stored, and the land became brown sharp points of death in a waste
278 MC	Knight2	21	/resigned the office of Chancellor, he became more priestly than the/priests, he
279 MC	Knight4	22	badly needed. From the moment he/became Archbishop, he completely reversed his
279 MC	Knight4	25	This egotism grew upon him, until it/became at last an undoubted mania. I have
295 FR	Harry	2	I went back to the cabin./Later, I became excited, I think I made enquiries;/The
382 CP	Celia	13	that had always thrilled me,/And it became another voice — no, not a voice:/What
486 CC	Lady E	7	twenty-five./{LE} Twenty-five. What became of your father?/{C} Well ... I didn't have
498 CC	Eggers	22	if she did that,/We must enquire what became of the other one./{SC} But *this* baby
498 CC	Lady E	28	And now we must find out/What became of your child, Claude./{SC} What
498 CC	Claude	29	of your child, Claude./{SC} What became of *my* child!/The mother of *my* child
508 CC	Eggers	16	angle,/And ask Mrs. Guzzard what became of the child/She took in, which may
533 ES	Gomez	4	you took your wife's name/And became Mr. Richard Claverton-Ferry;/And
537 ES	Gomez	13	went up to Oxford/And then what I became under your influence./{LC} You cannot
563 ES	Carghil	26	you see, Señor Gomez, when we first became friends —/Lord Claverton and I — I
564 ES	Carghil	22	at Oxford/And Richard and I became great friends/Not long afterwards,

571 ES	Ld Clav	10	tastes beyond his means:/So he became a forger. And so he served his term./

BECAUSE (134)

89	Ash-Wed 1	1	*bang but a whimper.*/Ash-Wednesday/Because I do not hope to turn again/Because I
89	Ash-Wed 1	2	/Because I do not hope to turn again/Because I do not hope/Because I do not hope to
89	Ash-Wed 1	3	to turn again/Because I do not hope/Because I do not hope to turn/Desiring this
89	Ash-Wed 1	9	vanished power of the usual reign?/Because I do not hope to know again/The
89	Ash-Wed 1	11	/The infirm glory of the positive hour/Because I do not think/Because I know I shall
89	Ash-Wed 1	12	positive hour/Because I do not think/Because I know I shall not know/The one
89	Ash-Wed 1	14	/The one veritable transitory power/Because I cannot drink/There, where trees
89	Ash-Wed 1	16	flow, for there is nothing again/Because I know that time is always time/And
89	Ash-Wed 1	23	blessèd face/And renounce the voice/Because I cannot hope to turn again/
90	Ash-Wed 1	30	I too much discuss/Too much explain/Because I do not hope to turn again/Let these
90	Ash-Wed 1	34	judgement not be too heavy upon us/Because these wings are no longer wings to fly/
91	Ash-Wed 2	8	were already dry) said chirping:/Because of the goodness of this Lady/And
91	Ash-Wed 2	9	of the goodness of this Lady/And because of her loveliness, and because/She
91	Ash-Wed 2	9	/And because of her loveliness, and because/She honours the Virgin in meditation,/
111	Xmas Trees	33	/When fear came upon every soul:/Because the beginning shall remind us of the
155	Rock 3	53	city?/Do you huddle close together because you love each other?'/What will you
163	Rock 8	45	men will not lay down the Cross/Because they will never assume it./Yet nothing
182	FQ: ECoker	178	start, and a different kind of failure/Because one has only learnt to get the better of
190	FQ: DrySal	233	be realised;/Who are only undefeated/Because we have gone on trying;/We, content at
198	FQ: Little	251	children in the apple-tree/Not known, because not looked for/But heard, half-heard, in
212	Growltiger	20	Siamese regarded him with fear —/Because it was a Siamese had mauled his
231	Bust Jones	35	every day:/But he's so well preserved because he's observed/All his life a routine, so
606	Narcissus	34	old./So he became a dancer to God./Because his flesh was in love with the burning
261	MC Thomas	20	a good Christian who/has been killed because he is a Christian: for that would be
261	MC Thomas	39	/the blessed Archbishop Elphege; because it is fitting, on Christ's birth/day, to
261	MC Thomas	40	is that Peace which He brought; and because,/dear children, I do not think I shall
262	MC Thomas	1	I shall ever preach to you again; and because/it is possible that in a short time you
286	FR Charles	29	lost their sense of taste and smell/Because of their cocktails and cigarettes. {}/
288	FR Agatha	18	Agatha means./{Ag} I mean painful, because everything is irrevocable,/Because the
288	FR Agatha	19	because everything is irrevocable,/Because the past is irremediable,/Because the
288	FR Agatha	20	/Because the past is irremediable,/Because the future can only be built/Upon the
292	FR Ivy	38	again: she's done nothing about it/Because she preferred to wait for your coming./
294	FR Harry	27	I talk in general terms/Because the particular has no language. One
295	FR Harry	22	that it couldn't have happened,/Because you could not bear it. So you must
296	FR Agatha	4	of the explanation./It is only because of what you do not understand/That
304	FR Mary	8	years ago./Now I want your advice, because there's no one else to ask,/And because
304	FR Mary	9	there's no one else to ask,/And because you are strong, and because you don't
304	FR Mary	9	ask,/And because you are strong, and because you don't belong here/Any more than I
304	FR Mary	27	he married, she still held on to me/Because she couldn't bear to let any project go;/
306	FR Harry	13	years I'd been longing to get back/Because I thought I never should. I thought it
306	FR Mary	28	I was only a cousin/Kept here because there was nothing else to do with me./I
314	FR Violet	17	you would never stay in bed/Because you were convinced that you would
325	FR Ivy	28	that had the accidents,/Somehow, just because he *was* the slow one./He was always the
330	FR Harry	23	or gives a knowledge of eternity,/Because it feels eternal while it lasts. That is one
341	FR Agatha	7	voracious for what you cannot have/Because you repel it./{A} I prepared the
341	FR Amy	9	the situation/For us to be reconciled, because of Harry,/Because of his mistakes,
341	FR Amy	10	us to be reconciled, because of Harry,/Because of his mistakes, because of his
341	FR Amy	10	of Harry,/Because of his mistakes, because of his unhappiness,/Because of the
341	FR Amy	11	mistakes, because of his unhappiness,/Because of the misery that he has left behind
341	FR Amy	12	misery that he has left behind him,/Because of the waste. I wanted to obliterate/His
346	FRDowning	7	Charles:/His Lordship sent me back because he remembered/He thinks he left his
348	FR Chorus	9	do not like the maze in the garden, because it too closely resembles the maze in the
348	FR Chorus	10	what happens when we are awake, because it too closely resembles what happens
355	CP Julia	5	he could hear the cry of bats?/{J} Because he said so. And I believed him./{C} But
358	CP Julia	35	you very soon. Now don't all go/Just because I'm going. Good-bye, Edward./{E}
359	CP Edward	16	only the people I couldn't put off/Because I couldn't get at them in time;/And I
361	CP Reilly	7	inconvenient, having to lie about it/Because you can't tell the truth on the
362	CP Reilly	25	a person./It's always happening, because one is an object/As well as a person.
365	CP Julia	4	the colour,/But I'd know them, because one lens is missing. {}/[*Sings*]./{UG} *As*
369	CP Peter	27	gone to concerts alone —/At first, because I knew no one to go with,/And later, I
369	CP Peter	30	girl like Celia, it seemed very strange,/Because I thought of her merely as a name/In a
374	CP Celia	27	/You know I accepted the situation/Because a divorce would ruin your career;/And
377	CP Edward	14	the Devil! I could believe he was./{E} Because I asked him to./{C} Because you asked

377 CP	Celia	15	was./{E} Because I asked him to./{C} Because you asked him to!/Then he *must* be the
378 CP	Celia	28	you think the world will laugh at you/Because your wife has left you for another man?
386 CP	Celia	19	here. Why have you come here?/{C} Because Lavinia asked me./{E} Because Lavinia
386 CP	Edward	20	/{C} Because Lavinia asked me./{E} Because Lavinia asked you!/{C} Well, not
387 CP	Peter	35	I've done nothing./{P} I'm so glad./Because I've changed my mind. I mean, I've
388 CP	Peter	6	/Alex is a wonderful person to know,/Because, you see, he knows everybody,
390 CP	Julia	10	course./{L} And why from Essex?/{J} Because you've been in Essex./{L} Because I've
390 CP	Lavinia	11	/{J} Because you've been in Essex./{L} Because I've been in Essex!/{J} Lavinia! Don't
392 CP	Lavinia	9	There is one thing I ought to know,/Because of other people/And what to do about
393 CP	Edward	34	at the Bar .../{E} You nagged me because I didn't get enough work/And said that
396 CP	Lavinia	23	of people being sorry for me./{L} Yes, because they can never be so sorry for you/As
400 CP	Alex	20	foresight. Now, he's quite triumphant/Because he thinks he's stolen a march on her./
403 CP	Reilly	16	Or they do not see it, or they justify it/Because they are absorbed in the endless
403 CP	Edward	24	wanted my wife to come back./It was because of what she had made me into./We had
405 CP	Reilly	20	up. I shall go to a hotel./{R} It is just because you are not free, Mr. Chamberlayne,/
407 CP	Edward	1	Edward. You do know that./{E} Only because you've told me so often./I'd like to see
413 CP	Celia	29	there's something wrong with me —/Because, if there isn't, then there's something
415 CP	Celia	25	/And bad form always led to disaster/Because the people one knew disapproved of it./
418 CP	Reilly	22	first I could describe in familiar terms/Because you have seen it, as we all have seen it,/
420 CP	Reilly	29	his own meanness/From himself, because it is known to the other./It's not the
425 CP	Lavinia	20	we said, 'we can ask twenty more/Because they will be going to the Gunnings
436 CP	Lavinia	24	disturb you/Or the fact that she died because she would not leave/A few dying
437 CP	Reilly	25	what sort of death? *I* could not know;/Because it was for her to choose the way of life/
437 CP	Reilly	39	a *thing*./I'd say she suffered more, because more conscious/Than the rest of us. She
438 CP	Reilly	34	decision./As for Miss Coplestone, because you think her death was waste/You
438 CP	Reilly	35	was waste/You blame yourselves, and because you blame yourselves/You think her life
447 CC	Claude	31	that I had to make a quick decision/Because he'd had another very tempting offer./
452 CC	Kaghan	5	Colby./{E} How so Mr. Kaghan?/{K} Because Lucasta's with me! The usual
455 CC	Eggers	17	in his flesh,/Always losing her jobs, because she won't stick to them./He gives her an
458 CC	Lady E	21	why did you change your plans?/{LE} Because of Mildred Deverell./She's been having
465 CC	Claude	9	That your father had been right./{SC} Because I came to see/That I should never have
469 CC	Lucasta	25	people,/And to be seen there! And because you feel out of it/If you never go to the
470 CC	Lucasta	29	very clear./But why not with me?/{L} Because you don't like them —/American
471 CC	Lucasta	20	simple./{L} Then I wish you'd tell me./Because *I* don't know./{C} The first time we met
472 CC	Colby	1	you think it was self-defence?/{C} Because you couldn't wait to see what
472 CC	Colby	3	things to themselves./You jump — because you're afraid of being pushed./I think
474 CC	Lucasta	36	it,/But ... partly, to enjoy it ... and because of what it stands for./You know, I'm a
477 CC	Lucasta	28	forced myself to be;/And I liked you because you didn't like that person either,/And
479 CC	Lucasta	29	managed to escape her./{L} Only because she's never wanted to pursue you./{K}
480 CC	Kaghan	32	boards of all the solidest companies:/Because I've no background — no background
481 CC	Lady E	19	at the flat/Now that you've moved in. Because you can't tell/Whether a scheme of
482 CC	Lady E	36	that already limits your acquaintance:/Because, what's surprising, well-bred people/
484 CC	Lady E	2	brothers or sisters — and I was lonely/Because they were so numerous — and so
489 CC	Lady E	40	a son, and would do well by him —/Because you *did* care for the girl, didn't you?/
495 CC	Lady E	21	a poet. I thought Tony was a poet./Because he wrote me poems. And he was so
499 CC	Lucasta	32	was why I took an interest/In Colby. Because you thought he was too good for me./
501 CC	Lucasta	5	*you* think so:/*You* think we're suited because we're both common./B. knows you
501 CC	Lucasta	7	so he pretends/To be very common, because he knows you think so./*You* gave us
502 CC	Lucasta	10	why should you apologise?/{L} Oh, because I knew/That I must have
510 CC	Lady E	32	bees. But why are you asking?/{LE} Because, Barnabas, it seems you are my son./{E}
513 CC	Colby	27	never known and couldn't know now,/Because he would have died before I was born/
516 CC	Claude	26	other evidence, that you were my son,/Because you described my own experience,
518 CC	Eggers	2	lessons? —/As a temporary measure; because, Mr. Simpkins —/I hope you won't
525 ES	Charles	19	And you're leaving London./And because your father simply can't bear it/That
525 ES	Charles	40	me? But I'm selfish/In saying that, because I think —/I think you're tormenting
526 ES	Monica	2	as well./{M} You're right. I am. Because I *am* in love with you./{C} So I was
537 ES	Gomez	23	you made friends with me/Because it flattered *you* — tickled your love of
538 ES	Gomez	18	in England mistakes are anonymous/Because the man who accepts responsibility/
540 ES	Gomez	11	of your ... worldly success?/{G} No, because I know the value of the coinage/I pay
551 ES	Carghil	26	nonsense! One starts an action/Simply because one must do *something*./Well, perhaps I
551 ES	Carghil	29	lawyer said: 'I advise you to accept',/'Because Mr. Ferry will be standing for
555 ES	Monica	15	better. But I'm all the more distressed/Because I have some ... not very good news for
558 ES	Michael	3	your son that gets me into debt./Just because of your name they insist on giving
558 ES	Michael	22	knew the job had been made for me/Because I was your son. They considered me
559 ES	Michael	28	you took it. And Mother knew./First, because it gave you the opportunity/Of retiring

562 ES   Carghil   20   right./But .../{MC} How did I know? Because you're so like your father/When he was
569 ES   Ld Clav   34   Badgley and escape from them?/{LC} Because they are not real, Charles. They are
581 ES   Ld Clav   18   mark out a narrow path for Michael?/Because I wanted to perpetuate myself in him./
581 ES   Ld Clav   20   want to keep you to myself, Monica?/Because I wanted you to give your life to
581 ES   Monica   33   Court. And I love you the more/Because I love Charles./{LC} Yes, my dear./
582 ES   Charles   37   Michael, and despite those people,/Because somehow we'd begun to belong

BECKET (14)

238 MC   m   6   /ARCHBISHOP THOMAS BECKET/FOUR TEMPTERS/
238 MC   m 13   /ARCHBISHOP THOMAS BECKET/CHORUS OF WOMEN OF
246 MC Tempt1   30   out of favour?/Old Tom, gay Tom, Becket of London,/Your Lordship won't forget
269 MC Thomas   11   higher than I or the King./It is not I, Becket from Cheapside,/It is not against me,
269 MC Thomas   12   from Cheapside,/It is not against me, Becket, that you strive./It is not Becket who
269 MC Thomas   13   me, Becket, that you strive./It is not Becket who pronounces doom,/But the Law of
274 MC Knights 16   Come. Force him./{4K} Where is Becket, the traitor to the King?/Where is
274 MC Knights 17   the traitor to the King?/Where is Becket, the meddling priest?/Come down Daniel
274 MC Knights 24   Daniel and join in the feast./Where is Becket the Cheapside brat?/Where is Becket the
274 MC Knights 25   Becket the Cheapside brat?/Where is Becket the faithless priest?/Come down Daniel
278 MC Knight2 12   system./He therefore intended that Becket, who had proved himself an extremely/
278 MC Knight2 14   of Chancellor and Archbishop. Had Becket concurred/with the King's wishes, we
278 MC Knight2 17   under the central/government. I knew Becket well, in various official relations; and I/
278 MC Knight2 20   what happened? The moment/that Becket, at the King's instance, had been made

BECOME (47)

109 Marina   14   of the animals, meaning/Death/Are become unsubstantial, reduced by a wind,/A
119 SP   Krum   10   /{Kr} Extremely pleased to become acquainted/{Kl} Sam — I should say
194 FQ: Little 124   and peregrine/Between two worlds become much like each other,/So I find words I
195 FQ: Little 167 self which, as it could, loved them,/To become renewed, transfigured, in another
256 MC Tempts 16   the statesman's decoration./All things become less real, man passes/From unreality to
258 MC Thomas 26   /While I ate out of the King's dish/To become servant of God was never my wish./
261 MC Thomas 26   the effect of a man's will to/become a Saint, as a man by willing and
261 MC Thomas 26   a man by willing and contriving may become a ruler/of men. A martyrdom is always
261 MC Thomas 29   for the true martyr is he who has become the/instrument of God, who has lost his
271 MC Priests 29   talking. It is not right./What shall become of us, my Lord, if you are killed; what
271 MC Priests 29   my Lord, if you are killed; what shall become of us?/{T} Peace! be quiet! remember
273 MC Thomas 37   blended/So good and evil in the end become confounded./It is not in time that my
278 MC Knight2 37   temperate/measures as these would become unnecessary. But, if you have now/
316 FR   Agatha 13   separated/May the knot that was tied/Become unknotted/May the crossed bones/In
334 FR   Harry 31   my decision. Now I see/I might even become fonder of my mother —/More
344 FR   Amy   12   Amy?/{A} Harry is going away — to become a missionary./{H} But ...!/{C} A
354 CP   Alex   15   lovely daughters:/I wonder what's become of them now./{J} Lady Klootz was very
370 CP   Edward 34   are. In a little while/This might have become an ordinary affair/Like any other. As
398 CP   Edward 11   The python. The octopus./Must I become after all what you would make me?/{L}
415 CP   Celia 28   form, or mental kinks,/You either become bad form, and cease to care,/Or else, if
417 CP   Reilly 2   having found it?/{R} Disillusion can become itself an illusion/If we rest in it./{C} I
417 CP   Reilly 29   /Learn to avoid excessive expectation,/Become tolerant of themselves and others,/
419 CP   Reilly 8   have been in./{R} It isn't hell/Till you become incapable of anything else./Now — do
427 CP   Julia   4   him to tell us all about it./But what's become of him? {}/[*Enter* ALEX]/{E} Well,
427 CP   Alex   37   so sure./At least, the monkeys have become the pretext/For general unrest amongst
431 CP   Julia 27   is your question, Peter?/Have you become an expert on decaying houses?/{P} Oh
437 CP   Reilly 38   —/And reluctance of the body to become a *thing*./I'd say she suffered more,
462 CC   Claude 15   type of person —/Then you *will* become her son, in her eyes. She's like that./
465 CC   Claude 10   came to see/That I should never have become a first-rate potter./I didn't have it in me.
465 CC   Colby 34   different. I know/I should never have become a great organist,/As I aspired to be. I'm
470 CC   Colby   8   to the conclusion/That I should never become a musician./{L} Did you find it a strain,
474 CC   Colby 18   Walking down an alley/I should become aware of someone walking with me./
477 CC   Lucasta 33   else sees me/As I really am, I might become myself./{C} Oh Lucasta, I'm not
482 CC   Lady E 9   /I feared it was possible you might become too friendly/With Mr. Kaghan and
485 CC   Lady E 18   the means that we have to employ/To become reincarnate. And that one's real
488 CC   Claude 30   plans —/I'd hoped that you would become fond of Colby,/And that he might come
503 CC   Lucasta 5   perhaps — who knows? —/We might become more necessary to each other,/As a
512 CC   Lady E 35   /{LE} B. — and I'm sure we shall become great friends./{E} I'm sure we all wish
516 CC   Colby 12   of getting to the top —/That is, to become the organist of a cathedral./But my
517 CC   Colby 11   you. I like you too much./You've become a man without illusions/About himself,
517 CC   Eggers 23   Simpkins, that what you desire/Is to become the organist of some parish church?/{C}
533 ES   Gomez 22   republic: San Marco./It's as hard to become a respected citizen/Out there, as it is
539 ES   Gomez 34   have got my First,/And I might have become the history master/In a school like that

551 ES   Carghil   38   career,/And then you wouldn't have become Lord Claverton./So perhaps I laid the
560 ES   Michael   8   much pleasanter/You will find life become, once I'm out of the country./What I'd
569 ES   Ld Clav   3   /And speak as ourselves. So I'd become an idol/To Monica. She worshipped me
583 ES   Monica   17   there./In becoming no one, he has become himself./He is only my father now, and
BECOMES (9)
182 FQ: ECoker 193   from. As we grow older/The world becomes stranger, the pattern more complicated
186 FQ: DrySal   87   one Annunciation./It seems, as one becomes older,/That the past has another
186 FQ: DrySal   91   notions of evolution,/Which becomes, in the popular mind, a means of
241 MC   Mess   37   of its tail,/A single hair of which becomes a precious relic./He is at one with the
336 FR   Agatha   26   is formed./In both, the incredible/Becomes the actual/Without our intention/
419 CP   Celia   27   not say they stayed there./{C} What becomes of them?/{R} They choose, Miss
449 CC   Eggers   22 able to make her like Miss Angel;/She becomes abstracted, whenever I mention her./
553 ES   Carghil 37   Only a few friends./Effie said: 'If he becomes a famous man/And you should be in
569 ES   Ld Clav   1   the longer we pretend/The harder it becomes to drop the pretence,/Walk off the
BECOMING (9)
 32 Hysteria   1   /As she laughed I was aware of becoming involved in her laughter and/being
202 War Poetry   24   experience at its greatest intensity/Becoming universal, which we call 'poetry',/
361 CP   Reilly   37 your independence;/Finding your life becoming cosier and cosier/Without the
463 CC   Colby   17   /I mean, about myself. As if I was becoming/A different person. Just as, I suppose,
463 CC   Colby   23   the other person/That I feel myself becoming — though he fascinates me./And yet
496 CC   Eggers   22   a week:/But now she says: 'You're becoming such a countryman!/You're losing
536 ES   Gomez   4   the ladder,/So you weren't aware of becoming a different person:/But where *I*
582 ES   Ld Clav   4   that pretends to be someone;/And in becoming no one, I begin to live./It is worth
583 ES   Monica   17   tree. It is quiet and cold there./In becoming no one, he has become himself./He is
BED (19)
 22 Preludes   24 rooms./You tossed a blanket from the bed,/You lay upon your back, and waited;/You
 26 Rhapsody   76   a ring on the stair./Mount./The bed is open; the tooth-brush hangs on the wall,/
 42 Swee Erect   19   to hip/Pushing the framework of the bed/And clawing at the pillow slip./Sweeney
 43 Swee Erect   31   shriek subsides./The epileptic on the bed/Curves backward, clutching at her sides./
 63 WL: Burial   73 /'Or has the sudden frost disturbed its bed?/'O keep the Dog far hence, that's friend to
 68 WL: Fire S   226   /On the divan are piled (at night her bed)/Stockings, slippers, camisoles, and stays./I
 69 WL: Fire S   244   all/Enacted on this same divan or bed;/I who have sat by Thebes below the wall/
125 SA   Chorus   33   you're alone in the middle of the bed and/you wake like someone hit you in the
150 Rock 1   115 *bread/They shall not die in a shortened bed/And a narrow sheet. In this street/There is no*
204 de la Mare   12   shall it be,/At not quite time for bed? .../Or when the lawn/Is pressed by unseen
210 Old Gumbie   7   begun./And when all the family's in bed and asleep,/She tucks up her skirts to the
300 FRDowning   28   I took a bit of air before I went to bed,/And you could see the corner of the upper
307 FR   Harry   8 being out at night/After being put to bed. But at least they never knew/Where we had
314 FR   Warburt   12   we had such a time to keep you in bed./You didn't like being ill in the holidays./{I}
314 FR   Violet   16   epidemics: you would never stay in bed/Because you were convinced that you
336 FR   Agatha   31   of unconsciousness/In an accidental bed/Or under an elder tree/According to the
361 CP   Reilly   35 wake in the morning, when you go to bed at night,/That you are beginning to enjoy
362 CP   Reilly   37   doctor and the surgeon,/In going to bed in the nursing home,/In talking to the
422 CP   Julia   17   /May the moon herself influence the bed. {}/[*They drink*]/{A} The words for those
BED'S (1)
 23 Preludes   35 hardly understands;/Sitting along the bed's edge, where/You curled the papers from
BEDDED (1)
172 FQ: BurntN   50   and sapphires in the mud/Clot the bedded axle-tree./The trilling wire in the blood/
BEDROOM (7)
184 FQ: DrySal   11 His rhythm was present in the nursery bedroom,/In the rank ailanthus of the April
218 Mung Rump   11   the drawers were pulled out from the bedroom chests,/And you couldn't find one of
294 FR   Harry   3   voice of sorrow in the ancient bedroom/At three o'clock in the morning. I am
315 FR   Chorus   35   /History. Shamed/The first cry in the bedroom, the noise in the nursery, mutilated/
329 FR   Chorus   3   future./The agony in the curtained bedroom, whether of birth or of dying,/Gathers
340 FR   Amy   20   /Of the chilly pretences in the silent bedroom,/Forcing sons upon an unwilling
483 CC   Lady E   27   /May I remove it? Surely your bedroom/Is the proper place for photographic
BEDS (2)
240 MC   Chorus   9 ears,/Disastrous summer burn up the beds of our streams/And the poor shall wait for
544 ES   Monica   4 dining-room show no curiosity;/The beds are comfortable, the hot water is hot,/They
BEDSIDE (1)
228 Gus   29   in character parts./I have sat by the bedside of poor Little Nell;/When the Curfew
BEE (2)
590 Time Space   11   the vine,/Were withered ere the wild bee flew/To suck the eglantine./So let us haste
590 Space Time   11   the vine/Were withered ere the wild bee flew/To suck the eglantine./But let us haste

BEECH (3)

568 ES	Ld Clav	1	far away. Standing under the great beech tree./{M} Why under the beech tree?/{LC}
568 ES	Monica	2	great beech tree./{M} Why under the beech tree?/{LC} I feel drawn to that spot./No
583 ES	Monica	16	far to return to us./He is under the beech tree. It is quiet and cold there./In

BEEN (406)

BEER (2)

22 Preludes	15	consciousness/Of faint stale smells of beer/From the sawdust-trampled street/With all
244 MC Chorus	5	heard the masses,/We have brewed beer and cider,/Gathered wood against the

BEES (2)

54 Mr E Sun	25	and dim./Along the garden-wall the bees/With hairy bellies pass between/The
510 CC Kaghan	31	near Sevenoaks/Where they keep bees. But why are you asking?/{LE} Because,

BEETLE (3)

270 MC Chorus	7	the wren. I have felt/The horn of the beetle, the scale of the viper, the mobile hard
382 CP Celia	19	heart, your blood;/And saw only a beetle the size of a man/With nothing more
382 CP Celia	21	what comes out/When you tread on a beetle./{E} Perhaps that is what I am./Tread on

BEETLES' (1)

211 Old Gumbie	36	to do —/And she's even created a Beetles' Tattoo./So for Old Gumbie Cats let us

BEETROOT (1)

473 CC Colby	35	he comes out/He has marrows, or beetroot, or peas ... for Mrs. Eggerson./{L} Are

BEFALL (1)

221 Old Deut	41	/Must never be broken, whatever befall:/And the Oldest Inhabitant croaks: 'Well,

BEFORE (182)

14 Prufrock		34	for a hundred visions and revisions,/Before the taking of a toast and tea./In the
20 Portrait		84	night comes down; returning as before/Except for a slight sensation of being ill
29 Aunt Helen		7	that this sort of thing had occurred before./The dogs were handsomely provided
62 WL: Burial		65	exhaled,/And each man fixed his eyes before his feet./Flowed up the hill and down
67 WL: Fire S		192	/And on the king my father's death before him./White bodies naked on the low
97 Ash-Wed 5		32	and cannot surrender/And affirm before the world and deny between the rocks/In
105 Song Sime		17	foreign faces and the foreign swords./Before the time of cords and scourges and
105 Song Sime		19	and lamentation/Grant us thy peace./Before the stations of the mountain of
105 Song Sime		20	of the mountain of desolation,/Before the certain hour of maternal sorrow,/
111 Xmas Trees		27	carol, and her crown of fire):/So that before the end, the eightieth Christmas/(By
117 SP	Doris	30	/Oh good heavens what'll I do?/Just before a party too!/{Du} Well it needn't be
119 SP	Klip	23	/{Kl} No we never been here before/{Kr} We hit this town last night for the
123 SA	2m	13	/SNOW AND SWARTS AS BEFORE/{Kl&Kr} *My little island girl/My*
124 SA	Doris	4	please don't talk,/I cut the cards before you came/And I drew the coffin/{Sw}
152 Rock 2		32	was done by those who have gone before you./And all that is ill you may repair if
158 Rock 5		10	with the gift of silence, and doze before he sleeps./But we are encompassed with
161 Rock 7		23	their negative being;/Bestial as always before, carnal, self-seeking as always before,
161 Rock 7		23	before, carnal, self-seeking as always before, selfish and purblind as ever before,/Yet
161 Rock 7		23	before, selfish and purblind as ever before,/Yet always struggling, always
161 Rock 7		26	happened that has never happened before: though we know not just when, or why,
161 Rock 7		27	no god; and this has never happened before/That men both deny gods and worship
172 FQ: BurntN		62	and the boar/Pursue their pattern as before/But reconciled among the stars./At the
173 FQ: BurntN		94	/Here is a place of disaffection/Time before and time after/In a dim light: neither
174 FQ: BurntN		108	whirled by the cold wind/That blows before and after time,/Wind in and out of
174 FQ: BurntN		110	and out of unwholesome lungs/Time before and time after./Eructation of unhealthy
175 FQ: BurntN		151	and the beginning were always there/Before the beginning and after the end./And all
176 FQ: BurntN		178	the waste sad time/Stretching before and after./East Coker/In my beginning is
179 FQ: ECoker		68	to that destructive fire/Which burns before the ice-cap reigns./That was a way of
181 FQ: ECoker		136	I am repeating/Something I have said before. I shall say it again./Shall I say it again?
182 FQ: ECoker		195	the intense moment/Isolated, with no before and after,/But a lifetime burning in every
185 FQ: DrySal		46	is all deception,/The future futureless, before the morning watch/When time stops and
186 FQ: DrySal		98	can assign to happiness. I have said before/That the past experience revived in the
188 FQ: DrySal		147	'the past is finished'/Or 'the future is before us'./At nightfall, in the rigging and the
193 FQ: Little		80	water and fire./In the uncertain hour before the morning/Near the ending of
193 FQ: Little		90	towards me like the metal leaves/Before the urban dawn wind unresisting./And
194 FQ: Little		108	time/Of meeting nowhere, no before and after,/We trod the pavement in a
220 Old Deut		4	and famous in rhyme/A long while before Queen Victoria's accession./Old
228 Gus		2	His name, as I ought to have told you before,/Is really Asparagus. That's such a fuss/
230 Bust Jones		23	*Pothunter's* succulent bones;/And just before noon's not a moment too soon/To drop
235 Ad-dress		47	next door,/Whom I have often met before/(He comes to see me in my flat)/I greet
235 Ad-dress		52	—/But we've not got so far as names./Before a Cat will condescend/To treat you as a
587 Fable		1	Fable for Feasters/In England, long before that royal Mormon/King Henry VIII
587 Fable		13	— a deed which ne'er he/Had done before — their fortune multiplied,/As if they

589 Fable		79	pulled him rudely by the collar,/And before any one could say 'O jiminy!'/The pair
593 Grad 5		2	dowered than those which came before,/Summons — who knows what time may
593 Grad 6		2	is to be more great/Than those before, her sons must make her so,/And we are
595 Grad 13		4	to warn them, and a friend to bless/Before they leave thy care for lands unseen;/
597 Before Mor		t	faded, and the leaves were brown./Before Morning/While all the East was weaving
605 Narcissus		17	live men's ways, but became a dancer before God/If he walked in city streets/He
241 MC	Mess	14	is close outside the city./I was sent before in haste/To give you notice of his
252 MC	Thomas	21	your treacheries as you have done before:/No one shall say that I betrayed a king./
252 MC	Tempt3	24	wait at your door./And I well hope, before another spring/The King will show his
252 MC	Thomas	26	then break, this thought has come before,/The desperate exercise of failing power./
252 MC	Tempt4	35	/Had I been expected, I had been here before./I always precede expectation./{T} Who
253 MC	Tempt4	2	but have never seen my face./To meet before was never time or place./{T} Say what
254 MC	Tempt4	18	/Think of pilgrims, standing in line/Before the glittering jewelled shrine,/From
260 MC	Thomas	12	of the heavenly host appeared before the/shepherds at Bethlehem, saying
263 MC	Chorus	20	turn the same earth/He has turned before, the bird shall sing the same song./When
263 MC	1m	27	*with a banner of St. Stephen borne before him./The lines sung are in italics.*]/{P1}
264 MC	m	7	*a banner of St. John the Apostle borne before him.*]/{P2} Since St. Stephen a day: and
264 MC	m	14	*a banner of the Holy Innocents borne before him.*]/{P3} Since St. John the Apostle a
265 MC	Priest1	24	If we did not offer you entertainment/Before your business. Please dine with us./Your
265 MC	Priest1	26	shall be looked after also./Dinner before business. Do you like roast pork?/{K1}
265 MC	Knight1	27	you like roast pork?/{K1} Business before dinner. We will roast your pork/First,
266 MC	Thomas	25	his King./{T} This is not true./Both before and after I received the ring/I have been
267 MC	Knight2	20	we say it now?/{K2} Without delay,/Before the old fox is off and away./{T} What
269 MC	Thomas	21	from my tomb?/To submit my cause before God's throne. {}/[*Exit*]/{K4} Priest!
276 MC	Knight1	30	points of view, will be able/to lay before you the merits of this extremely complex
279 MC	Knight4	26	evidence/to the effect that before he left France he clearly prophesied, in
279 MC	Knight4	37	I say more? I think, with these facts before/you, you will unhesitatingly render a
281 MC	Priest2	3	with all the saints and martyrs gone before you,/Remember us./{P3} Let our thanks
285 FR	Amy	5	be over/And the cuckoo will be gone before I am out again./O Sun, that was once so
286 FR	Charles	25	needs/Is a glass of dry sherry or two before dinner./The modern young people don't
293 FR	Amy	8	going/And to make no changes before your return./Now it's for you to manage.
294 FR	Harry	7	the noxious smell and the sorrow before morning,/In which all past is present, all
295 FR	Charles	13	/When I wake, as I do now, early before morning./I understand these feelings
295 FR	Amy	38	again./I beg you to go now and rest before dinner./Get Downing to draw you a hot
296 FR	Ivy	19	—/I have heard of such cases before — that people in his condition/Often
300 FR	Downing	28	in the Tourist,/And I took a bit of air before I went to bed,/And you could see the
305 FR	Agatha	7	but you must not run away./Any time before now, it would have shown courage/And
311 FR	Harry	7	it, I know it!/More potent than ever before, a vapour dissolving/All other worlds,
311 FR	Harry	18	will not let me sleep. At the moment before sleep/I always see their claws distended/
315 FR	Amy	24	well go in to dinner./They may come before we finish. Will you take me in, Doctor?/I
317 FR	Harry	24	to mother./When we were children, before we went to school,/The rule of conduct
318 FR	Harry	4	That was why/We all felt like failures, before we had begun./When we came back, for
319 FR	Harry	36	me,/I must ask Agatha. I never dared before./{W} I advise you strongly, not to ask
327 FR	Charles	39	Stop, I think I bought a lunch edition/Before I left St. Pancras. If I did, it's in my
330 FR	Harry	3	long;/And everything will go on as before. These mild surprises/Should be in the
330 FR	Harry	30	same emotion/Or lack of emotion, as before: the same loathing/Diffused, I not a
332 FR	Agatha	13	not always so. There were many years/Before she succeeded in making terms with
333 FR	Harry	16	that would have seemed meaningless before./Everything tends towards reconciliation/
336 FR	Harry	10	/Direct to the brain ... but not just as before,/Not quite like, not the same ... {}/[*The*
336 FR	Harry	19	you —/No! you were already here before I arrived./Now I see at last that I am
343 FR	Mary	16	known it;/It was all over, I believe, before it began;/But I deceived myself. It takes
344 FR	Charles	15	our family!/And why in such a hurry? Before you make up your mind .../{V} You can't
354 CP	Julia	28	her./{J} Well, one can't be too careful/Before one tells a story./{A} Delia Verinder?/
357 CP	Julia	12	/{J} I never heard of her being ill before./{E} No, she's always very strong. That's
365 CP	Edward	22	*You* don't know?/{E} I never saw him before in my life./{J} But how did he come here?
376 CP	Julia	21	Samaritans? I never heard of that before./{E} The man who fell among thieves was
378 CP	Celia	6	follow you/In about ten minutes? Before I go, there's something/I want to say to
379 CP	Celia	22	could be?/I abandoned the future before we began,/And after that I lived in a
381 CP	Edward	14	desire for all that was most desirable,/Before you are contented with what you can
381 CP	Edward	15	contented with what you can desire;/Before you know what is left to be desired;/And
382 CP	Celia	5	/And yet I understand as I never did before./I think — I believe — you are being
382 CP	Celia	7	are being yourself/As you never were before, with me./Twice you have changed since
382 CP	Celia	27	see you as a person whom I never saw before./The man I saw before, he was only a
382 CP	Celia	28	I never saw before./The man I saw before, he was only a projection —/I see that
386 CP	Celia	34	been found out in. I never saw you so before./This is really a ludicrous situation./{E}

389 CP	Peter	1	/And come in to say good-bye before I left./{L} And Celia's going too? Was
396 CP	Lavinia	30	have been real/At some other time, before you ever knew me:/Perhaps only when
398 CP	Edward	5	O God, if I could return to yesterday/Before I thought that I had made a decision./
401 CP	Edward	5	/{E} It came into my mind/Before I entered the door, that you might be the
401 CP	Edward	31	chair comfortable./{E} You knew,/Before I began to tell you, what had happened?/
402 CP	Reilly	32	first find out what is wrong with you/Before we decide what to do with you./{E} I
403 CP	Edward	26	been alone again for fifteen minutes/Before I felt, and still more acutely —/Indeed,
404 CP	Reilly	37	You might say, a long journey./But before I treat a patient like yourself/I need to
405 CP	Edward	11	conduct —/I will not discuss my case before another patient./{R} On the contrary.
405 CP	Reilly	17	A barrister/Ought to know his brief before he enters the court./{E} I am at least free
405 CP	Reilly	30	dishonourable trick./{R} Honesty before honour, Mr. Chamberlayne./Sit down,
409 CP	Reilly	33	took you some time, I have no doubt,/Before you would admit it. Though perhaps you
409 CP	Reilly	34	admit it. Though perhaps you knew it/Before he did. You pretended to yourself,/I
411 CP	Lavinia	18	have you anything else to ask him/Before we go?/{E} Yes, I have./But it's difficult
412 CP	Celia	27	to come to you. — But I've met you before,/Haven't I, somewhere? ... Oh, of course.
413 CP	Reilly	35	/{R} We must find out about you, before we decide/What *is* normality. You say
415 CP	Reilly	1	find what would be normal/For *you*, before we use the term 'abnormal'./Tell me
417 CP	Reilly	34	that brings together/For casual talk before the fire/Two people who know they do
425 CP	Lavinia	4	first time you've paid me a compliment/*Before* a party? And that's when one needs them./
432 CP	Edward	5	delighted to see him. But we *have* met before./{J} Then if you know him already, you
434 CP	Edward	21	they found the traces of it./{E} But before that .../{A} It was difficult to tell./But
439 CP	Edward	24	/{E} Shall we see you again, Peter,/Before you leave England?/{L} Do try to come
440 CP	Julia	14	I think, Henry,/That we should leave before the party begins./They will get on better
445 CC	Claude	22	morning,/But he'll be back, I hope, before you leave./{E} And how's he getting on?
447 CC	Claude	2	the present. As we have a little time/Before you start for Northolt — the car will be
448 CC	Eggers	16	like to know —/If you don't mind — before I go to meet her./How soon do you
455 CC	Eggers	2	used to it. You'll be calling me Eggers/Before you know it!/{C} I shouldn't wonder./I
460 CC	Lady E	20	Leroux./Don't you remember, I said before I left:/'Trust my guidance for once, and
461 CC	Claude	30	gather, such a thing never happened before./So the meeting didn't go quite the way
461 CC	Colby	36	she really think/That she had seen me before?/{SC} Impossible to tell./The point is that
462 CC	Claude	3	it./So I feel pretty confident that, before long,/We can put matters onto a
463 CC	Colby	15	kind of self-confidence/I've never had before. Yet at the same time/It's rather
465 CC	Colby	40	it came to him;/But when I played before other people/I was always conscious that
469 CC	Lucasta	28	/That nobody has ever played to me before?/{C} And this is the first time I've played
475 CC	Lucasta	29	/No one has ever 'just accepted' me before./Of course the facts don't matter, in a
476 CC	Lucasta	13	And it's always succeeded with people before:/I got into the habit of giving that
476 CC	Lucasta	39	he'd given her:/It was always spent before the end of the quarter/On gin and
478 CC	Lucasta	14	I'd actually thought of telling you before,/And I postponed telling you, just for the
480 CC	Lucasta	21	a better judge of character/Yourself, before you said that of Colby./{K} Oh, I'm a
486 CC	Colby	1	You may have come across the name before;/Although, as you say, it is an
488 CC	Claude	26	see now I might as well have told you before,/But I'd hoped — and now it seems a
490 CC	Claude	2	Very much. I had never/Been in love before./{LE} Very well then./That is the way it
492 CC	Colby	23	/{C} I was looking at your notes —/Before you brought me into the conversation —
494 CC	Lady E	27	You've never talked like this to me before!/Why haven't you? I don't suppose I
505 CC	Eggers	33	to be possible./Lady Elizabeth, before her marriage/Had a child .../{LE} A son./
513 CC	Colby	27	now,/Because he would have died before I was born/Or before I could remember;
513 CC	Colby	28	would have died before I was born/Or before I could remember; whom I could get to
515 CC	Guzzard	3	/As I have just said, my sister died/Before the child could be born. You were very
516 CC	Colby	9	about success —/I aimed too high before — beyond my capacity./I thought I
517 CC	Colby	1	their failure./You had your father before you, as a model;/You knew your
518 CC	Eggers	17	to find your feet/In Joshua Park, before you settled on lodgings;/We have a spare
525 ES	Charles	21	but he should have you to himself,/Before I've said two words he'll come ambling
525 ES	Monica	32	it is you want to say. I've heard it all before./{C} And you'll hear it again. You think
525 ES	Charles	35	else to say that I haven't said before,/That will give you a shock. I believe *you*
526 ES	Monica	11	Quietly, a long time, a long long time/Before I felt its presence./{C} Your words seem
529 ES	Ld Clav	36	book, to-day,/Not over breakfast, but before tea,/It's the empty pages that I've been
530 ES	Ld Clav	15	I've left —/Only fear of the emptiness before me./If I had the energy to work myself to
530 ES	Ld Clav	25	waiting for/In a cold and empty room before an empty grate?/For no one. For
534 ES	Gomez	33	in gaol and not very comfortable,/Or before a firing squad./You don't know what
538 ES	Gomez	35	me./You were given a ministry before you were fifty:/That should have led you
540 ES	Gomez	8	the morning/Has to make up his face before he looks in the mirror./{LC} Isn't that
542 ES	Ld Clav	2	for another quarter of an hour./{LC} Before you go — what is it that you want?/{G}
543 ES	Monica	15	you out./You must go and rest now, before dinner./{LC} Yes, I'll go and rest now. I
547 ES	Piggott	4	fly. I've so much on my hands!/But before I go, just let me tuck you up .../You must
552 ES	Ld Clav	3	to remember, it was only a year or so/Before your name appeared in very large letters/

556 ES	Michael	25	a holiday, exactly./Oh. I said that before, didn't I?/{M} I wish you'd stop being so
556 ES	Michael	32	up your mind that I was to blame/Before you knew the facts. The first thing I
564 ES	Carghil	20	it's very strange that we never met before./You were a friend of Richard's at
565 ES	Monica	2	should rest and have absolute quiet/Before every meal./{LC} But Michael and I/
569 ES	Ld Clav	25	Blackmail? Yes, I've heard that word before,/Not so very long ago. When I asked him
575 ES	Gomez	21	he'd better learn the facts from me/Before he heard your distorted version./But,
578 ES	Ld Clav	3	something to say to you,/Michael, before you go. I shall never repudiate you/
579 ES	Carghil	13	/— No sooner had I put my proposal before him/Than he had it all planned out! It
583 ES	Monica	9	you from the beginning of the world./Before you and I were born, the love was always

BEFOREHAND (5)

346 FR	Downing	29	get a feeling of it./So I seem to know beforehand, when something's going to happen,
438 CP	Lavinia	3	she had been through greater agony beforehand./I mean — I know nothing of her
471 CC	Colby	3	{C} And perhaps you'll let me tell you beforehand/About the programme — or the
493 CC	Claude	4	decide on the seating arrangements beforehand./I don't think you and I should be
497 CC	Eggers	1	I know what's on her mind, for days beforehand./But here I am, talking about

BEFOULED (1)

| 337 FR | Harry | 25 | /Which your words echo. I am still befouled,/But I know there is only one way out |

BEG (5)

136	5FingerEx5	t	*Cuscuscaraway and Mirza Murad Ali Beg*/How unpleasant to meet Mr. Eliot!/With his
276 MC	Knight1	18	*and address the audience.*]/{K1} We beg you to give us your attention for a few/
295 FR	Amy	38	by day, all will be the same again./I beg you to go now and rest before dinner./Get
322 FR	Winch	4	be the same if it was my birthday —/I beg pardon, I'm forgetting./If it was my
401 CP	Edward	11	have always been satisfactory./I beg your pardon. But he *is* a blunderer./I should

BEGAN (17)

588	Fable	63	t' have of grape juice./The lights began to burn distinctly blue,/As in ghost
329 FR	Chorus	2	to hear it./And whatever happens began in the past, and presses hard on the
343 FR	Mary	16	it;/It was all over, I believe, before it began;/But I deceived myself. It takes so many
364 CP	Edward	24	And yet — it seems to me — when we began to talk/I was not sure I wanted her; and
379 CP	Celia	22	be?/I abandoned the future before we began,/And after that I lived in a present/Where
393 CP	Edward	36	more people:/But when the briefs began to come in —/And they didn't come
401 CP	Edward	31	comfortable./{E} You knew,/Before I began to tell you, what had happened?/{R} That
403 CP	Edward	32	/When I thought she had left me, I began to dissolve,/To cease to exist. That was
409 CP	Edward	4	months ago/That your breakdown began! and I never noticed it./{L} You wouldn't
410 CP	Reilly	2	no one had ever loved you./Then you began to fear that no one *could* love you./{E}
435 CP	Peter	7	I tried to forget about her,/Until I began to think myself a success/And got a little
451 CC	Eggers	22	met him once;/But do you know, he began addressing her as Muriel —/Within the
464 CC	Claude	34	I loathed this occupation/Until I began to feel my power in it./The life changed
488 CC	Claude	12	is that, brooding on the past,/You began to think of Colby as what your son
488 CC	Claude	13	your son would be,/And then you began to see him as your son,/And then — any
535 ES	Gomez	10	/{L} Ice? Yes, my Lord. {}/[*Exit*]/{G} I began to say: when I say 'trust'/I use the term as
558 ES	Michael	26	nothing to do./Even the office boys began to sneer at me./I wonder I stood it as

BEGGARED (1)

| 162 | Rock 8 | 23 | came back well broken,/Diseased and beggared, finding/A stranger at the door in |

BEGIN (28)

14	Prufrock	59	on the wall,/Then how should I begin/To spit out all the butt-ends of my days
15	Prufrock	69	I then presume?/And how should I begin?/Shall I say, I have gone at dusk through
194	FQ: Little	136	of shadow fruit/As body and soul begin to fall asunder,/Second, the conscious
258 MC	Thomas	8	sin/Is the way in which our lives begin./Thirty years ago, I searched all the ways/
263 MC	Chorus	5	a shoot, not a breath./Do the days begin to lengthen?/Longer and darker the day,
306 FR	Harry	19	other memories,/Earlier, forgotten, begin to return/Out of my childhood. I can't
324 FR	Warburt	5	Monchensey;/This is not the time to begin to doubt me./Come, Winchell. We can
334 FR	Harry	20	but that was impossible./I only now begin to have some understanding/Of you, and
341 FR	Agatha	4	/But at least I wanted to. Now I must begin./There is nothing more difficult. But you
345 FR	Amy	19	HARRY]/{A} At my age, I only just begin to apprehend the truth/About things too
368 CP	Alex	28	dishes. Don't say a word./I shall begin at once. {}/[*Exit to kitchen*]/{E} Well,
402 CP	Reilly	38	in my childhood .../{R} I always begin from the immediate situation/And then go
410 CP	Reilly	6	it was *my* fault./{R} And now you begin to see, I hope,/How much you have in
413 CP	Reilly	3	away again./{R} Most of my patients begin, Miss Coplestone,/By telling me exactly
413 CP	Celia	15	my trouble is interesting;/But I shan't begin that way. I feel perfectly well./I could lead
428 CP	Alex	1	do the monkeys create unrest?/{A} To begin with, the monkeys are very destructive .../
435 CP	Lavinia	31	you to the point/At which you *must* begin. You were saying just now/That you
440 CP	Lavinia	35	will soon be over./{L} I wish it would begin./{E} There's the doorbell./{L} Oh, I'm
448 CC	Eggers	13	/He's highly educated. He'll soon begin to grasp them./No, I haven't told him
461 CC	Claude	27	upon your being Mr. Colby —/I shall begin to call you Colby with everyone./{C} I'm
467 CC	Colby	8	always will have, with your father./I begin to see how I have always thought of you

469 CC	Colby	8	/When you know what you like, and	begin to know it well,/Then you will want to
471 CC	Lucasta	8	yourself, and explained them./We'll	begin my education at once./{C} I suspect that
472 CC	Lucasta	14	/In unexpected ways. And then you	begin/To discover differences inside the likeness.
475 CC	Lucasta	18	person./{L} Oh Colby, now that we	begin to understand,/I'd like you to know a
490 CC	Colby	16	part of a total agony/Which I can't	begin to feel yet. I'm simply indifferent./And all
543 ES	Gomez	7	again, and assure myself/That we can	begin just where we left off. {}/[*Exit* GOMEZ]/
582 ES	Ld Clav	4	someone;/And in becoming no one, I	begin to live./It is worth while dying, to find out

BEGINNER (1)

582 ES	Ld Clav	10	— remember, my dear,/I am only a	beginner in the practice of loving —/Well, that

BEGINNING (47)

54 Mr E Sun		4	Drift across the window-panes./In the	beginning was the Word./In the beginning was
54 Mr E Sun		5	the beginning was the Word./In the	beginning was the Word./Superfetation of τὸ ἕν,
111 Xmas Trees		33	came upon every soul:/Because the	beginning shall remind us of the end/And the
150 Rock 1		117	*narrow sheet. In this street/There is no*	*beginning, no movement, no peace and no end/But*
150 Rock 1		120	*without haste/We would build the*	*beginning and the end of this street./We build the*
160 Rock 7		1	must first build the Temple./In the	beginning GOD created the world. Waste and
175 FQ: BurntN		149	/Or say that the end precedes the	beginning,/And the end and the beginning were
175 FQ: BurntN		150	the beginning,/And the end and the	beginning were always there/Before the
175 FQ: BurntN		151	were always there/Before the	beginning and after the end./And all is always
177 FQ: ECoker		1	before and after./East Coker/In my	beginning is my end. In succession/Houses rise
177 FQ: ECoker		14	woven with a silent motto./In my	beginning is my end. Now the light falls/Across
178 FQ: ECoker		51	am here/Or there, or elsewhere. In my	beginning./What is the late November doing/
182 FQ: ECoker		181	say it. And so each venture/Is a new	beginning, a raid on the inarticulate/With
183 FQ: DrySal		211	and the porpoise. In my end is my	beginning./The Dry Salvages/I do not know
185 FQ: DrySal		48	swell, that is and was from the	beginning,/Clangs/The bell./Where is there an
197 FQ: Little		216	by either fire or fire./What we call the	beginning is often the end/And to make an end
197 FQ: Little		217	end/And to make an end is to make a	beginning./The end is where we start from. And
197 FQ: Little		226	and every sentence is an end and a	beginning,/Every poem an epitaph. And any
197 FQ: Little		247	left to discover/Is that which was the	beginning;/At the source of the longest river/
242 MC	Mess	9	peace/Is nothing like an end, or like a	beginning./It is common knowledge that when
264 MC	Priest2	9	*his mouth./*That which was from the	beginning, which we have heard,/Which we
277 MC	Knight3	25	about that. So, as I said at the	beginning, please give us/at least the credit for
330 FR	Harry	19	exactly what their meaning is./At the	beginning, eight years ago,/I felt, at first, that
333 FR	Harry	19	/That is the completion which at the	beginning/Would have seemed the ruin./Perhaps
334 FR	Agatha	5	vision. This is like an end./{Ag} And a	beginning. Harry, my dear,/I feel very tired, as
334 FR	Agatha	8	end of an action —/The old, at the	beginning. It is as if/I had been living all these
335 FR	Agatha	37	This is the next moment. This is the	beginning./We do not pass twice through the
345 FR	Charles	33	/{C} It's very odd,/But I am	beginning to feel, just beginning to feel/That
345 FR	Charles	33	odd,/But I am beginning to feel, just	beginning to feel/That there is something I
361 CP	Reilly	36	you go to bed at night,/That you are	beginning to enjoy your independence;/Finding
381 CP	Edward	11	met myself as a middle-aged man/	Beginning to know what it is to feel old./That is
410 CP	Edward	3	that no one *could* love you./{E} I'm	beginning to feel very sorry for you, Lavinia./
420 CP	Julia	22	not need to tell me. I knew from the	beginning./{R} It's the other ones I am worried
436 CP	Edward	6	harder to recover, and make a new	beginning./It's not so hard for you. You're
440 CP	Edward	7	/I think, that every moment is a fresh	beginning;/And Julia, that life is only keeping
446 CC	Claude	6	the hang of things,/And I think he's	beginning to take a keen interest./{E} And
456 CC	Eggers	35	/And to think that was only the	beginning of my travels!/It's been a very
460 CC	Claude	24	Colby./{SC} Oh, I see./Yes, now I am	beginning to remember./I must have acted on
470 CC	Lucasta	40	to want to educate me;/And now I'm	beginning to believe that I want it./{C} Well, I'm
475 CC	Colby	17	that comes about, perhaps .../{C} Is,	beginning to understand another person./{L} Oh
478 CC	Lucasta	33	always B. I think that now/I'm just	beginning to appreciate B./{C} Lucasta, wait! {}/
481 CC	Colby	2	We need you where you are./{C} I'm	beginning to believe you've a pretty shrewd
488 CC	Claude	5	the name. Mrs. Guzzard./{SC} I'm	beginning now to piece it together./You've been
504 CC	Claude	20	better./This is a most unfortunate	beginning./{LE} She's been making progress,/The
516 CC	Claude	20	And you described your feelings/On	beginning to learn the ways of business;/The
539 ES	Gomez	22	him not to go too far./Well, now, I'm	beginning to be thirsty again. {}/[*Pours himself*
583 ES	Monica	8	words./{M} I've loved you from the	beginning of the world./Before you and I were

BEGINNINGS (1)

21 Portrait		97	wondering frequently of late/(But our	beginnings never know our ends!)/Why we have

BEGINS (7)

18 Portrait		18	/Mingled with remote cornets/And	begins./'You do not know how much they mean
19 Portrait		32	/Inside my brain a dull tom-tom	begins/Absurdly hammering a prelude of its
195 FQ: Little		162	as the past. Thus, love of a country/	Begins as attachment to our own field of action/
326 FR	Harry	26	of waste in an orderly universe./But it	begins to seem just part of some huge disaster,/
338 FR	Harry	40	in possession, that is when/One	begins to seem the maddest to other people./It is

440 CP   Julia   14 That we should leave before the party begins./They will get on better without us. You
464 CC   Claude 36 changed me, as it is changing you:/It begins as a kind of make-believe/And the
BEGUN (9)
 63 WL: Burial   72   last year in your garden,/'Has it begun to sprout? Will it bloom this year?/'Or
210 Old Gumbie   6   the Gumbie Cat's work is but hardly begun./And when all the family's in bed and
210 Old Gumbie   18   the Gumbie Cat's work is but hardly begun./As she finds that the mice will not ever
211 Old Gumbie   30   the Gumbie Cat's work is but hardly begun./She thinks that the cockroaches just
318 FR   Harry   4 We all felt like failures, before we had begun./When we came back, for the school
435 CP   Lavinia 29   all worthless, Peter. You've only just begun./I mean, this only brings you to the point
440 CP   Lavinia 37   the doorbell./{L} Oh, I'm glad. It's begun. {}/CURTAIN/THE CONFIDENTIAL
483 CC   Colby   18   /{C} It is a typewriter./I've already begun to work here. At the moment/I'm
582 ES   Charles 37 those people,/Because somehow we'd begun to belong together,/And that awareness
BEHALF (2)
189 FQ: DrySal 178   them./Repeat a prayer also on behalf of/Women who have seen their sons or
499 CC   Claude   7 /You are putting the questions on behalf of my wife./{E} I understand, Sir Claude:
BEHAVE (5)
260 MC Thomas 16 Beloved, as the World sees, this is to behave in a strange/fashion. For who in the
290 FR   Amy   17 /Do not discuss his absence. Please behave only/As if nothing had happened in the
302 FR   Chorus   7 not have been open./Why do we all behave as if the door might suddenly open, the
394 CP   Edward 37   But, in future,/I shall behave, I assure you, very differently./{L}
450 CC   Colby   37 much:/So I've no idea how I ought to behave./B. Kaghan has told me something
BEHAVED (4)
299 FR Downing 40   could see that he was nervous./He behaved as if he thought something might
367 CP   Peter   4   that you didn't notice:/I must have behaved rather better than I thought./If you
455 CC   Eggers 14   responsible for her./In any case, he's behaved like a father —A very generous man,
562 ES   Monica   4 I say to you?/However Michael has behaved, Father,/Whatever Father has said,
BEHAVES (1)
 84 Hollow Men 35 staves/In a field/Behaving as the wind behaves/No nearer —/Not that final meeting/In
BEHAVING (2)
 84 Hollow Men 35   crowskin, crossed staves/In a field/Behaving as the wind behaves/No nearer —/
303 FR   Mary   28 Arthur's chatter/When he thinks he is behaving like a man of the world?/Cousin
BEHAVIOUR (11)
189 FQ: DrySal 189   converse with spirits,/To report the behaviour of the sea monster,/Describe the
247 MC Thomas 27   /{T} Not in this train/Look to your behaviour. You were safer/Think of penitence
325 FR   Violet   5   I really do not understand Harry's behaviour./{Ag} I think it is as well to leave
344 FR   Violet   10   only sane person in this house./Your behaviour all seems to me quite unaccountable./
346 FR   Agatha 33   anybody./{Ag} And, Downing, if his behaviour seems unaccountable/At times, you
360 CP   Edward 31 She had nothing to complain of in my behaviour./{UG} Then no doubt it's all for the
408 CP   Lavinia 32   professional etiquette/About your behaviour to-day./{R} A point well taken./But
500 CC   Lucasta 16   What I do understand/Is Colby's behaviour. If he knew it./{SC} He knew it./{L}
502 CC   Lucasta 5   see you./I came to apologise for my behaviour/The other afternoon./{C} Apologise?/
535 ES   Gomez   31 another language, other standards of behaviour,/To fabricate for myself another
551 ES   Carghil 7   trying to forget/His own shabby behaviour./{LC} But we'd settled our account./
BEHAVIOUR'S (1)
210 Old Gumbie 10   with the ways of the mice —/Their behaviour's not good and their manners not
BEHIND (47)
 16 Prufrock   122   trousers rolled./Shall I part my hair behind? Do I dare to eat a peach?/I shall wear
 23 Preludes   40   tight across the skies/That fade behind a city block,/Or trampled by insistent
 24 Rhapsody   40 along the quay,/I could see nothing behind that child's eye./I have seen eyes in the
 45 Cook Egg   26   world I bought/To eat with Pipit behind the screen?/The red-eyed scavengers are
 61 WL: Burial   28 /Your shadow at morning striding behind you/Or your shadow at evening rising to
 64 WL: Chess   81   peeped out/(Another hid his eyes behind his wing)/Doubled the flames of
 67 WL: Fire S   190   dull canal/On a winter evening round behind the gashouse/Musing upon the king my
 74 WL: Thund   424   the shore/Fishing, with the arid plain behind me/Shall I at least set my lands in order?
 94 Ash-Wed 4   23   in white and blue/Between the yews, behind the garden god,/Whose flute is
107 Animula   23 up the small soul in the window seat/Behind the *Encyclopaedia Britannica.*/Issues
140 Usk   3   or/Hope to find/The white hart behind the white well./Glance aside, not for
172 FQ: BurntN   40 out of heart of light,/And they were behind us, reflected in the pool./Then a cloud
180 FQ: ECoker 121 slowly fades into silence/And you see behind every face the mental emptiness deepen/
187 FQ: DrySal 103   quite ineffable:/The backward look behind the assurance/Of recorded history, the
188 FQ: DrySal 143   the narrowing rails slide together behind you;/And on the deck of the drumming
188 FQ: DrySal 145   /Watching the furrow that widens behind you,/You shall not think 'the past is
191 FQ: Little   30 you leave the rough road/And turn behind the pig-sty to the dull façade/And the
196 FQ: Little   211 Love./Love is the unfamiliar Name/Behind the hands that wove/The intolerable
212 Growltiger   28 he too had stol'n away —/In the yard behind the Lion he was prowling for his prey./

216 Jellicles	19	and take their repose:/Jellicles wash	behind their ears,/Jellicles dry between their
219 Mung Rump	24	/And the cook would appear from	behind the scenes/And say in a voice that was
233 Skimble	43	weak or strong?'/But Skimble's just	behind him and was ready to remind him./For
594 Grad 10	4	That which has made it great, not left	behind,/The same school in the future shall we
601 Nocturne	7	/Banal, and out of pity for their fate/	Behind the wall I have some servant wait,/Stab,
605 Narcissus	5	at daybreak, or/Your shadow leaping	behind the fire against the red rock:/I will show
258 MC Thomas	19	all things possible./Ambition comes	behind and unobservable./Sin grows with doing
264 MC m	22	*stand together with the banners behind them*]/{P1} Since the Holy Innocents a
272 MC Chorus	23	of Death, God's silent servant,/And	behind the face of Death the Judgement/And
272 MC Chorus	24	the face of Death the Judgement/And	behind the Judgement the Void, more horrid
292 FR Harry	6	they were coming./In Italy, from	behind the nightingale's thicket,/The eyes stared
292 FR Harry	8	at me, and corrupted that song./	Behind the palm trees in the Grand Hotel/They
331 FR Harry	12	torture,/The shadow of something	behind our meagre childhood,/Some origin of
341 FR Amy	11	/Because of the misery that he has left	behind him,/Because of the waste. I wanted to
348 FR Chorus	33	ambush lies beyond the heather/And	behind the Standing Stones?/Beyond the
349 FR Chorus	1	/Beyond the Heaviside Layer/And	behind the smiling moon?/And what is being
350 FR Mary	10	is written/On the under side of things/	Behind the smiling mirror/And behind the
350 FR Mary	11	things/Behind the smiling mirror/And	behind the smiling moon/Follow follow/{Ag}
381 CP Edward	17	you could desire/What desire has left	behind. But you cannot understand./How could
437 CP Reilly	14	this room,/I saw the image, standing	behind her chair,/Of a Celia Coplestone whose
473 CC Lucasta	3	you can retire/And lock the gate	behind you./{C} And lock the gate behind me?/
473 CC Colby	4	behind you./{C} And lock the gate	behind me?/Are you sure that you haven't your
493 CC Lady E	7	/{LE} On the other side, with the light	behind me:/But won't you be sitting at the desk
493 CC Claude	10	be better/To put Eggerson there,	behind the desk./You see, I want him to be a
499 CC Eggers	3	/I do feel more at ease when I'm	behind a desk:/It's second nature./{SC} And put
526 ES Monica	9	so softly/On silent feet, and stood	behind my back/Quietly, a long time, a long
542 ES Gomez	33	reflection in the mirror of the face	behind you,/The ambiguous smile, the distant
570 ES Ld Clav	14	without interest in the life that lay	behind her/And completely indifferent to

BEHOLD (1)

164 Rock 9	1	will./O GOD, help us./Son of Man, behold with thine eyes, and hear with thine ears/

BEHOLDEST (1)

437 CP Reilly	9	*of life and death:/One that which thou beholdest; but the other/Is underneath the grave,*

BEHOVELY (1)

195 FQ: Little	168	in another pattern./Sin is Behovely, but/All shall be well, and/All manner

BEIN' (1)

365 CP Reilly	6	*I was drinkin' gin and water,/And me bein' the One Eyed Riley,/Who came in but the*

BEING (104)

20 Portrait	85	before/Except for a slight sensation of being ill at ease/I mount the stairs and turn the
32 Hysteria	2	involved in her laughter and/being part of it, until her teeth were only
37 Gerontion	2	I am, an old man in a dry month,/Being read to by a boy, waiting for rain./I was
49 Hippopot	20	week we hear rejoice/The Church, at being one with God./The hippopotamus's day/
111 Xmas Trees	4	commercial,/The rowdy (the pubs being open till midnight),/And the childish —
149 Rock 1	75	will show you the things that are now being done,/And some of the things that were
151 Rock 2	2	the saints, of the household of GOD, being built upon the foundation/Of apostles and
152 Rock 2	26	and always decaying, and always being restored./For every ill deed in the past we
158 Rock 5	8	/And they write innumerable books; being too vain and distracted for silence:
161 Rock 7	22	saved in spite of their negative being;/Bestial as always before, carnal,
175 FQ: BurntN	171	of limitation/Between un-being and being./Sudden in a shaft of sunlight/Even while
180 FQ: ECoker	118	/And the bold imposing façade are all being rolled away —/Or as, when an
188 FQ: DrySal	158	receive this: "on whatever sphere of being/The mind of a man may be intent/At the
192 FQ: Little	52	for, when living,/They can tell you, being dead: the communication/Of the dead is
193 FQ: Little	102	still the same,/Knowing myself yet being someone other —/And he a face still
195 FQ: Little	157	the others as death resembles life,/Being between two lives — unflowering,
245 MC Priest2	33	December,/Your Lordship now being used to a better climate./Your Lordship
251 MC Tempt3	40	fight for liberty. You, my Lord,/In being with us, would fight a good stroke/At
261 MC Thomas	31	for himself, not even the glory of being a/martyr. So thus as on earth the Church
261 MC Thomas	36	Godhead from which they draw their/being./I have spoken to you to-day, dear
274 MC Thomas	4	call that decision/To which my whole being gives entire consent./I give my life/To the
276 MC Knight	21	fair/play: and when you see one man being set upon by four, then your/sympathies
277 MC Knight1	26	please give us/at least the credit for being completely disinterested in this business./I
278 MC Knight2	36	one would have to bear the burden of/being called murderer. And at a later time still,
286 FR Gerald	36	the sense of responsibility./{G} You're being very hard on the younger generation./I
305 FR Mary	32	Your mother insisted/On everything being kept the same as when you left it./{H} I
307 FR Harry	7	John./Of course we were punished for being out at night/After being put to bed. But at
307 FR Harry	8	punished for being out at night/After being put to bed. But at least they never knew/

307 FR	Mary	26	when you are wholly conscious/Of	being a misfit, of being superfluous./But why
307 FR	Mary	26	wholly conscious/Of being a misfit, of	being superfluous./But why should I talk about
314 FR	Warburt	13	to keep you in bed./You didn't like	being ill in the holidays./{I} It *was* unpleasant,
317 FR	Harry	26	mother;/Misconduct was simply	being unkind to mother;/What was wrong was
321 FR	Warburt	5	for the changes in fashion/And your	being clean-shaven, very much like you./And
327 FR	Agatha	2	is always more: we cannot rest in	being/The impatient spectators of malice or
327 FR	Harry	19	/You can't understand me. It's not	being alone/That is the horror — to be alone
328 FR	Charles	22	time of the/accident Mr. Piper was	being pursued by a patrol, and was/travelling at
328 FR	Ivy	31	/{I} Poor Arthur! I'm sure that you're	being much too hard on him./{C} In my time,
330 FR	Harry	9	can resist the influence/Of Wishwood,	being unconscious, living in gentle motion/Of
330 FR	Agatha	16	you,/You may also be afraid of	being understood,/Try not to regard it as an
330 FR	Harry	25	—/That was the second hell of not	being there,/The degradation of being parted
330 FR	Harry	26	not being there,/The degradation of	being parted from my self,/From the self which
336 FR	Agatha	23	had occupied.]/{Ag} A curse comes to	being/As a child is formed./In both, the
338 FR	Harry	28	away, but to pursue,/Not to avoid	being found, but to seek./I would not have
346 FR	Downing	30	happen,/And it seems quite natural,	being his Lordship./And that's why I say now, I
349 FR	Chorus	2	the smiling moon?/And what is	being done to us?/And what are we, and what
357 CP	Julia	12	Lavinia./{J} I never heard of her	being ill before./{E} No, she's always very
362 CP	Reilly	33	a moment/You have the experience of	being an object/At the mercy of a malevolent
367 CP	Peter	21	people together./{P} Now you're only	being sarcastic:/Celia was interested in the art of
379 CP	Celia	18	/You can stand there and talk about	being fair to *me*!/{E} But for Lavinia leaving,
382 CP	Celia	6	before./I think — I believe — you are	being yourself/As you never were before, with
387 CP	Celia	5	/I can see you at last as a human	being./Can't you see me that way too, and
396 CP	Edward	22	for me!/I have had enough of people	being sorry for me./{L} Yes, because they can
397 CP	Lavinia	34	divided to know what you want./But,	being divided, you will tend to compromise,/
409 CP	Reilly	37	/Than the honour conferred by	being *your* lover./When you had to face the fact
413 CP	Celia	17	to work for;/I don't imagine that I am	being persecuted;/I don't hear any voices, I have
414 CP	Celia	3	of an illusion/In the ordinary way, or	being ditched./Of course that's something that's
415 CP	Celia	6	sense?/{C} Well ... I suppose it's	being immoral —/And I don't feel as if I was
417 CP	Celia	5	argue./It's not that I'm afraid of	being hurt again:/Nothing again can either hurt
426 CP	Lavinia	20	we can be alone./I love that house	being so remote./{E} That's why we took it. And
434 CP	Alex	30	/{A} Yes, the patients died anyway;/	Being tainted with the plague, they were not
435 CP	Lavinia	35	needs./Peter, please don't think I'm	being unkind .../{P} No, I don't think you're
435 CP	Peter	36	.../{P} No, I don't think you're	being unkind, Lavinia;/And I know that you're
436 CP	Julia	17	not concerned with yourself/But just	being an eye. You will come to think of Celia/
438 CP	Lavinia	40	I shall go on blaming myself/For	being so unkind to her ... so spiteful./I shall go
452 CC	Lucasta	35	I asked for it./That's what comes of	being cursed with a name like Angel./I'm
453 CC	Lucasta	8	not married./{L} Then I don't mind	being seen with you in public./You may take me
456 CC	Colby	12	unusual/In any other way, besides	being a lady?/{E} Why, yes, indeed, I must
461 CC	Claude	26	—/And as my wife insists upon your	being Mr. Colby —/I shall begin to call you
462 CC	Claude	17	That you really are her son, instead of	being mine./She has always lived in a world of
470 CC	Lucasta	33	That's not a compliment:/That's just	being ... patronising. But if you invite me/To
472 CC	Colby	3	You jump — because you're afraid of	being pushed./I think that you're brave — and I
473 CC	Colby	37	/{L} Are you laughing at me?/{C} I'm	being very serious./What I mean is, my garden's
474 CC	Colby	10	real to you?/{C} It's simply the fact of	being alone there/That makes it unreal./{L} Can
474 CC	Lucasta	20	putting it./{L} How afraid one is of ...	being hurt!/{C} It's not the hurting that one
475 CC	Lucasta	4	anyone?/{L} I think you're	being very discouraging:/Are you doing it
476 CC	Lucasta	36	/Always living in seedy lodgings/And	being turned out when the neighbours
480 CC	Kaghan	26	Now Colby/Doesn't really care about	being respectable —/He was born and bred to
484 CC	Lady E	38	know it./Of course, I was terrified of	being ugly,/And of being feeble-minded: though
485 CC	Lady E	1	I was terrified of being ugly,/And of	being feeble-minded: though my family made
490 CC	Colby	36	/At the time when I was born, your	being my mother —/If you are my mother —
491 CC	Lady E	8	enquiries?/Let us regard him as	being *our* son:/It won't be the same as what we
491 CC	Colby	34	with those ghosts, one indignant/At	being cheated of his — or her — parenthood,/
496 CC	Eggers	21	ladies! She used to complain/At my	being up in London five or six days a week:/But
506 CC	Eggers	28	name;/And the name struck her as	being familiar./{MG} Indeed? It is not a very
509 CC	Lady E	37	getting so confused. What with Colby	being Barnabas —/I mean, not Barnabas. And
509 CC	Lady E	39	not Barnabas. And Mr. Kaghan/Being	Barnabas. I suppose I'll get used to it./{C}
510 CC	Lady E	14	to confirmation./{LE} And to my	being able to adjust myself to it. {}/[*Re-enter*
512 CC	Kaghan	29	/{K} It's very much better than	being a foundling —/If I can live up to it. And
513 CC	Colby	37	I could in some way perpetuate/By	being the person he would have liked to be,/
527 ES	Charles	4	in love with each other,/And, there	being no legal impediment/Isn't that enough to
527 ES	Monica	22	What reasons?/{M} First, his terror of	being alone./In the life he's led, he's never had
528 ES	Monica	4	is exactly the opposite:/It's his fear of	being exposed to strangers./{C} But he's most
529 ES	Monica	14	people/Are unaware or unashamed of	being envious./It's all we can ask if compassion

547 ES	Piggott	30	there are one or two who don't like	being beaten,/And that spoils any sport, in my
552 ES	Carghil	31	/And the difference between	being an elder statesman/And posing
555 ES	Piggott	9	know. I'm afraid it's the penalty/Of	being famous. {}/[*Enter* MONICA]/{MP} Oh,
556 ES	Monica	26	didn't I?/{M} I wish you'd stop	being so polite to each other./Michael, you
556 ES	Michael	33	facts. The first thing I remember/Is	being blamed for something I hadn't done./I
558 ES	Michael	2	their bills, and then I forget them./It's	being your son that gets me into debt./Just
558 ES	Ld Clav	4	your debts: are they the cause of your	being discharged?/{Mi} Well, partly. Sir Alfred
558 ES	Michael	19	quiet. I can tell you, it's no joke/Being	the son of a famous public man./You
559 ES	Michael	30	from politics, not without dignity,/Being	no longer wanted. And you wished to be
573 ES	Carghil	37	/You may say that I just missed	being her mother!/I've known her father for a
575 ES	Gomez	23	by that insinuation/About my not	being custodian of Michael's morals./That is

BEINGS (3)

334 FR	Harry	35	in a war of phantoms,/Not by human	beings — they have no more power than I./The
569 ES	Ld Clav	37	tormented me, to be only human	beings,/Malicious, petty, and I see myself
570 ES	Charles	17	ghosts!/{C} But these are only human	beings, who can be dealt with./{M} Or only

BEL (1)

| 51 Restaurant | | 31 | pénible;/Cependant, ce fut jadis un | bel homme, de haute taille./Whispers of |

BELA (7)

431 CP	Peter	5	he who introduced me to the great	Bela./{J} And who is the great Bela?/{P} Why,
431 CP	Julia	6	great Bela./{J} And who is the great	Bela?/{P} Why, Bela Szogody —/He's my boss. I
431 CP	Peter	7	And who is the great Bela?/{P} Why,	Bela Szogody —/He's my boss. I thought
431 CP	Peter	11	obliged each other./{P} Well, it was	Bela sent me over/Just for a week. And I have
431 CP	Peter	29	written the script of this film,/And	Bela is very pleased with it./He thought I should
433 CP	Peter	18	could help her./I've already spoken to	Bela about her,/And I want to introduce her to
439 CP	Alex	21	/{A} It is your film./And I know that	Bela expects great things of it./{P} So now I'll be

BELGIAN (1)

| 354 CP | Peter | 10 | Lady Klootz?/{P} I thought she was | Belgian./{A} Her father belonged to a Baltic |

BELIEF (2)

| 280 MC | Priest3 | 35 | hell of make-believe/Which never is | belief: this is your fate on earth/And we must |
| 404 CP | Reilly | 22 | /{R} Many patients come in that | belief./{E} And now will you send me to the |

BELIEVE (127)

159 Rock	6	3	have never known a Christian,/To	believe these tales of Christian persecution./It is
159 Rock	6	7	who live near a Police Station/To	believe in the triumph of violence./Do you think
220 Old Deut		16	may be wandering, but I confess/I	*believe* it is Old Deuteronomy!'/Old
276 MC	Knight1	20	are Englishmen, and therefore you	believe in fair/play: and when you see one man
277 MC	Knight3	1	Reginald Fitz Urse would lead you to/believe.	But there is one thing I should like to
289 FR	Amy	19	it, that's another matter;/But I don't	believe he will. He will wish to forget it./I do not
295 FR	Harry	22	you could not bear it. So you must	believe/That I suffer from delusions. It is not
296 FR	Charles	27	the wish to get rid of her/Makes him	believe he did. He cannot trust his good fortune.
296 FR	Charles	28	He cannot trust his good fortune./I	believe that all he needs is someone to talk to,/
296 FR	Amy	31	are not the right person./I prefer to	believe that a few days at Wishwood/Among his
301 FR	Charles	15	/{C} Of which you disapprove./But I	believe that an unconscious accomplice is
310 FR	Mary	19	of joy/But joy is a kind of pain/I	believe the moment of birth/Is when we have
310 FR	Mary	21	when we have knowledge of death/I	believe the season of birth/Is the season of
314 FR	Warburt	35	first patient, now —/You wouldn't	believe it, ladies — was a murderer,/Who
314 FR	Harry	40	all extraordinary./It is really harder to	believe in murder/Than to believe in cancer.
315 FR	Harry	1	harder to believe in murder/Than to	believe in cancer. Cancer is here:/The lump, the
323 FR	Amy	33	/{A} I must see for myself. I do not	believe you./{C} Much better leave it to
327 FR	Harry	8	pointed./{H} Do you think that I	believe what I said just now?/That was only
327 FR	Harry	9	/That was only what I should like to	believe./I was talking in abstractions: and you
328 FR	Gerald	4	And it wasn't John's fault,/I don't	believe. John is unlucky,/But Arthur is
332 FR	Agatha	31	kind. Perhaps there is another kind,/I	believe, across a whole Thibet of broken stones/
338 FR	Harry	7	what makes it harder. You must just	believe me,/Until I come again./{A} But why are
342 FR	Amy	7	been always trying to make myself	believe/That he was not such a weakling as his
342 FR	Mary	22	that, don't ask me,/You would not	believe me, but I tell you I know./You must
343 FR	Agatha	3	And I who have seen them must	believe them./{M} Oh! ... so ... *you* have seen
343 FR	Mary	16	have known it;/It was all over, I	believe, before it began;/But I deceived myself.
344 FR	Harry	34	explain, but you would none of you	believe it;/If you believed it, still you would not
353 CP	Celia	22	tired of hearing *you* tell it./I don't	believe everyone here knows it. {}/[*To the*
354 CP	Celia	1	listener for you, Julia;/And I don't	believe that Edward knows it./{E} I may have
355 CP	Celia	6	he was so ... harmless, how could you	believe him?/He might have imagined it./{J} My
356 CP	Julia	30	serious. Lavinia takes me seriously./I	believe that's the reason why she went away —/
377 CP	Edward	6	think! Don't you know?/{E} No, but I	believe it. That man who was here —/{C} Yes,
377 CP	Celia	13	—/Unless he is the Devil! I could	believe he was./{E} Because I asked him to./{C}
381 CP	Celia	20	understand./And, Edward, please	believe that whatever happens/I shall not loathe

382 CP	Celia	6	as I never did before./I think — I believe — you are being yourself/As you never
389 CP	Celia	20	I don't doubt that either./{C} And I believe he is right to go./{L} Oh, so you advised
390 CP	Julia	32	sent us telegrams:/And now I don't believe she really wants us./I can see that she is
391 CP	Julia	31	Did I say you'd see me?/Good-bye. I believe ... I haven't left anything. {}/[Enter
392 CP	Lavinia	11	about that party./I suppose you won't believe I forgot all about it!/I let you down
396 CP	Lavinia	10	that you were in love with me —/I believe you were trying to persuade yourself you
402 CP	Reilly	11	go elsewhere./{R} You have reason to believe that you are very ill?/{E} I should have
402 CP	Edward	34	had a case like mine:/I have ceased to believe in my own personality./{R} Oh, dear yes;
406 CP	Reilly	16	They return refreshed;/And if they believe it to be a sanatorium/That is good
407 CP	Reilly	39	Chamberlayne,/Tried to make me believe that it was this discovery/Precipitated
412 CP	Julia	13	reluctant:/Only diffident. She cannot believe/That you will take her seriously./{R}
412 CP	Reilly	25	Coplestone? ... Won't you sit down?/I believe you are a friend of Mrs. Shuttlethwaite./
413 CP	Celia	32	/That would be terrible. So I'd rather believe/There is something wrong with me, that
435 CP	Peter	18	/{P} And what a *métier*! I've tried to believe in it/So that I might believe in myself./I
435 CP	Peter	19	tried to believe in it/So that I might believe in myself./I thought I had ideas to make
436 CP	Peter	8	naturally good./{P} I'm sorry. I don't believe I've taken in/All that you've been
436 CP	Julia	38	more observant than you think./I believe that she has forced you to a show-down.
440 CP	Lavinia	23	Edward, that spoils it. No woman can believe/That she always looks her best. You're
447 CC	Claude	34	once:/If so, she is certain to come to believe/That she chose him herself. By the way,
449 CC	Eggers	19	the world of your opinion./{E} Well, I believe that once or twice, perhaps .../But I'm
453 CC	Eggers	12	on a gas ring .../{E} You mustn't believe a word she says./{L} *Mr.* Simpkins is
453 CC	Lucasta	13	she says./{L} *Mr.* Simpkins is going to believe all I say,/*Mr.* Eggerson. And I know
453 CC	Kaghan	24	anybody about you:/Nobody'd ever believe in your existence/Until they met you.
457 CC	Colby	7	/But there's one thing I do believe, Mr. Eggerson:/That *you* have a kind
461 CC	Claude	32	quite the way I'd intended;/And yet I believe that it's all for the best./It went off very
462 CC	Colby	9	life upon a deception./Do you really believe that Lady Elizabeth/Can ever accept me
462 CC	Claude	13	her son would have been —/And I believe she will: though I'm perfectly convinced,
462 CC	Claude	16	it wouldn't surprise me if she came to believe/That you really are her son, instead of
465 CC	Claude	29	alone at your piano, in the evening,/I believe you will go through the private door/
469 CC	Lucasta	18	/Still, I'm awfully ignorant. Can you believe/That I've never been to a concert in my
470 CC	Lucasta	40	me;/And now I'm beginning to believe that I want it./{C} Well, I'm going to
471 CC	Lucasta	15	not quite the reason./{L} Oh, so you believe that I like you?/I didn't know that you
472 CC	Lucasta	10	I haven't either./{L} There, I don't believe you./What did I think till now? Oh, it's
475 CC	Colby	1	/And I'd like to understand *you*./{C} I believe you do already,/Better than ... other
476 CC	Lucasta	5	parents./{L} Oh, I see./Well, I can't believe that matters./But I can tell you all about
477 CC	Lucasta	19	disappointed./I suppose that's all. I believe you're most shocked/Than if I'd told
478 CC	Lucasta	27	breaking a promise. But .../{L} I don't believe there's anything to explain/That could
480 CC	Colby	16	people/That you're a gambler. I don't believe you ever gamble/On anything that isn't a
481 CC	Colby	2	where you are./{C} I'm beginning to believe you've a pretty shrewd insight/Into
481 CC	Lady E	33	a note of the address;/And I don't believe that you've been there yet./{K} Why no,
483 CC	Lady E	9	the colour scheme really suited you./I believe it does. The walls; and the curtains;/And
483 CC	Lady E	30	I going to say? Oh, I know./Do you believe in reincarnation?/{C} No, I don't.
483 CC	Lady E	32	about it./{LE} I can't say that *I* believe in it. I did, for a time. I studied the .
485 CC	Lady E	2	so./But you know, I actually *liked* to believe/That I was a foundling — or do I mean
485 CC	Lady E	6	want to belong there. I refused to believe/That my father could have been an
485 CC	Lady E	8	been an ordinary earl!/And I couldn't believe that my mother *was* my mother./These
485 CC	Lady E	14	/That seemed to explain it all. I don't believe it now./That was only a phase. But it
486 CC	Colby	37	/{C} That's tomorrow night, I believe./{LE} Yes it is./But you know that I'll
487 CC	Lady E	27	a coincidence./Perhaps I ought not to believe it yet,/Perhaps it is wrong of me to feel
487 CC	Claude	32	But Elizabeth, what has led you to believe/That Colby is your son?/{LE} Oh, I
491 CC	Colby	19	what I feel at the moment:/And yet I believe I shall always feel the same./{SC} Well?/
492 CC	Lady E	5	Claude! I am terribly sorry for you./I believe that if I had known of your ... delusion/I
494 CC	Lady E	9	like him to be mine,/But for you to believe that he is yours!/So I hope Mrs.
494 CC	Lady E	11	will say he is your son/And I needn't believe her. I don't believe in facts./You do.
494 CC	Lady E	11	son/And I needn't believe her. I don't believe in facts./You do. That is the difference
494 CC	Claude	13	I'm not so sure of that. I've tried to believe in facts;/And I've always acted as if I
495 CC	Lady E	12	as a hostess./It's a great mistake, I do believe,/For married people to take anything for
495 CC	Lady E	37	... obedience to the facts./{LE} I believe that was what *I* was trying to do./It's
497 CC	Claude	21	I told her the truth. But she cannot believe it./{LE} Claude, that's not quite right.
498 CC	Claude	25	Eggerson, you really can't ask me to believe/That she took two babies, and got them
502 CC	Lucasta	16	/What I thought I got. But I couldn't believe it!/It isn't like you, to despise people:/
504 CC	Guzzard	27	should have been announced./{MG} I believe I was punctual./But I didn't mind
506 CC	Eggers	16	/If he is alive, must be a grown man./I believe you have had no children of your own;/
509 CC	Lady E	19	is living. I was sure of that./But I believe that Colby is Barnabas./{SC} No,
510 CC	Claude	11	/If that's the right expression./{SC} I believe, Elizabeth,/That you have found your

510 CC	Kaghan	25	at one time live in Teddington?/{K} I	believe they did. But why are you interested?/
510 CC	Guzzard	26	interested?/{MG} Lady Elizabeth, I	believe that this is your son./If so, I am cleared
514 CC	Claude	25	child was never born./{SC} I don't	believe it. I simply can't believe it./Mrs.
514 CC	Claude	25	/{SC} I don't believe it. I simply can't	believe it./Mrs. Guzzard, you are inventing this
514 CC	Claude	33	Eggerson. Quite well./{SC} I shall not	believe it. I'll not believe those records./You
514 CC	Claude	33	/{SC} I shall not believe it. I'll not	believe those records./You pretend to have
515 CC	Colby	32	that the facts were otherwise./{C} I	believe you. I must believe you:/This gives me
515 CC	Colby	32	otherwise./{C} I believe you. I must	believe you:/This gives me freedom./{SC} But,
515 CC	Claude	36	it can't be true! —/But I see you	believe it. You want to believe it./Well, believe
515 CC	Claude	36	/But I see you believe it. You want to	believe it./Well, believe it, then. But don't let it
515 CC	Claude	37	it. You want to believe it./Well,	believe it, then. But don't let it make a
516 CC	Claude	31	—/Had you been able to fulfil them./	Believe, if you like, that I am not your father:/
518 CC	Guzzard	27	I think, have had a wish realised./— I	believe that this interview can now be
519 CC	Claude	23	me, Lucasta./Eggerson! Do *you* really	believe her? {}/[EGGERSON *nods*]/CURTAIN/
525 ES	Charles	36	before,/That will give you a shock. I	believe *you* love *me.*/{M} Oh, what a
526 ES	Charles	5	you loved me —/I merely wanted to	believe it. And I've made you say so!/But now
529 ES	Monica	17	Charles! are mixed with envy:/I do	believe that he is fond of you./So you must
542 ES	Gomez	27	/Don't you wish you could	believe it?/{LC} And what if I decline/To give
548 ES	Monica	5	the peace and quiet./{M} I don't	believe she'll be bothering us again:/I could see
548 ES	Carghil	28	topic of conversation./But I couldn't	believe that it would really happen!/And now
551 ES	Carghil	11	the lesson./{MC} You refuse to	believe that I was really in love with you!/Well,
551 ES	Carghil	12	natural that you shouldn't want to	believe it./But you think, or try to think, that if
552 ES	Carghil	27	conscience was clear./At bottom, I	believe you're still the same silly Richard/You
561 ES	Ld Clav	5	/Or shiver in the northern night.	Believe me, Michael:/Those who flee from their
561 ES	Michael	16	hero/If you were in my place. I don't	believe you would./*You* didn't suffer from the
564 ES	Carghil	11	/{Mi} How do you do./{MC} I don't	believe you've known Lord Claverton/As long
580 ES	Monica	28	Michael may learn his lesson./I	believe he'll come back. If it's all a failure/
581 ES	Ld Clav	22	to myself that I was,/So that I could	believe in my own pretences./I've only just now

BELIEVED (19)

38	Gerontion	40	the craving. Gives too late/What's not	believed in, or if still believed,/In memory only,
38	Gerontion	40	late/What's not believed in, or if still	believed,/In memory only, reconsidered passion.
185 FQ: DrySal		61	among the breakage/Of what was	believed in as the most reliable —/And therefore
304 FR	Mary	28	project go;/And even when *she* died: I	believed that Cousin Amy —/I almost believed
304 FR	Mary	29	believed that Cousin Amy —/I almost	believed it — had killed her by willing./Doesn't
332 FR	Agatha	32	lie, fang up, a lifetime's march. I have	believed this./{H} I have known neither./{Ag}
344 FR	Harry	35	would none of you believe it;/If you	believed it, still you would not understand./You
355 CP	Julia	5	of bats?/{J} Because he said so. And I	believed him./{C} But if he was so ... harmless,
415 CP	Celia	38	/That it is more real than anything I	believed in./{R} What is more real than
415 CP	Reilly	39	What is more real than anything you	believed in?/{C} It's not the feeling of anything
416 CP	Reilly	7	a state of mind?/{R} What had you	believed were your relations with this man?/{C}
435 CP	Peter	25	while Celia was alive./I wanted it,	believed in it, for Celia./And, of course, I
483 CC	Lady E	34	doctrine./But I was going to say, *if* I	believed in it/I should have said that we had
485 CC	Lady E	13	took up the Wisdom of the East/And	believed, for a while, in reincarnation./That
494 CC	Claude	14	in facts;/And I've always acted as if I	believed in them./I thought it was facts that my
494 CC	Claude	15	/I thought it was facts that my father	believed in;/I thought that what he cared for
516 CC	Colby	38	But it is very different./As long as I	believed that you were my father/I was content
536 ES	Gomez	13	four thousand miles away,/Only	believed what the parish priest told her./I made
541 ES	Gomez	15	/And then you ... well, I'd never have	believed/That you would accuse an old friend of

BELIEVES (7)

309 FR	Mary	27	he is paralysed/Or like the man who	believes that he is blind/While he still sees the
400 CP	Alex	22	she can't get at him — then, he	believes,/She will be very penitent. He's enjoying
447 CC	Eggers	21	your business genius./But it's true she	believes she has what she calls 'guidance'./{SC}
476 CC	Lucasta	16	—/He fosters the impression. He half	believes in it./But he knows all about me, and
500 CC	Lady E	5	my son./{LE} That is what Sir Claude	believes. Claude, let me explain./{SC} No, I'll
500 CC	Claude	7	some misunderstanding./My wife	believes that Colby is *her* son./That is the
573 ES	Ld Clav	6	harder to confess the sin that no one	believes in/Than the crime that everyone can

BELIEVING (4)

210 Old Gumbie		21	is sure it is due to irregular diet/And	believing that nothing is done without trying,/
224 Mr Mistoff		29	dice;/He is always deceiving you into	believing/That he's only hunting for mice./
364 CP	Reilly	15	for wanting her/Is the best reason for	believing that you want her./{E} I want to see
447 CC	Claude	22	/{SC} Guidance. That's worse than	believing in her judgment:/We could argue

BELITTLE (1)

| 149 Rock 1 | | 69 | mind./Second, you neglect and | belittle the desert./The desert is not remote in |

BELL (16)

28 Boston ET	6	/I mount the steps and ring the	bell, turning/Wearily, as one would turn to nod
40 Burb Blei	6	sea/Passed seaward with the passing	bell/Slowly: the God Hercules/Had left him,
128 Corl March	44	Cyril to church. And they rang a	bell/And he said right out loud, *crumpets.*)/
174 FQ: BurntN	130	past and time future./Time and the	bell have buried the day,/The black cloud
185 FQ: DrySal	37	of the silent fog/The tolling	bell/Measures time not our time, rung by the
185 FQ: DrySal	50	was from the beginning,/Clangs/The	bell./Where is there an end of it, the soundless
186 FQ: DrySal	68	to the undeniable/Clamour of the	bell of the last annunciation./Where is the end
196 FQ: Little	184	than the dying?/It is not to ring the	bell backward/Nor is it an incantation/To
212 Growltiger	26	since had disappeared,/For to the	Bell at Hampton he had gone to wet his beard;/
228 Gus	30	was rung, then I swung on the	bell./In the Pantomime season I never fell flat,/
595 Grad 14	3	/A word that echoes like a funeral	bell/And one that we are ever loth to say./But
297 FR	m 25	there's a question or two {}/[*Rings the bell*]/{C}	That I'd like to ask Downing./He shan't
376 CP	m 7	to hide. {}/[*Returns to kitchen. The bell rings again.* EDWARD *goes to front door,*
386 CP	m 14	EDWARD *moves about restlessly. The bell rings, and he goes to the front door.*]/{E}
405 CP	m 7	the same as your own. {}/[*Presses the bell on his desk three times*]/{R} You must accept
534 ES	m 39	I can provide whisky. {}/[*Presses the bell*]/{LC} But why have you come?/{G} You've

BELL'S (1)

189 FQ: DrySal	186	reach them the sound of the sea	bell's/Perpetual angelus./To communicate with

BELLADONNA (1)

62 WL: Burial	49	that were his eyes. Look!)/Here is	Belladonna, the Lady of the Rocks,/The lady of

BELLE (1)

39 Gerontion	70	the wind, in the windy straits/Of	Belle Isle, or running on the Horn./White

BELLIED (1)

92 Ash-Wed 3	13	the third stair/Was a slotted window	bellied like the fig's fruit/And beyond the

BELLIES (1)

54 Mr E Sun	26	the garden-wall the bees/With hairy	bellies pass between/The staminate and

BELLOW (1)

220 Old Deut	19	on market day;/The bullocks may	bellow, the sheep they may bleat,/But the dogs

BELLS (5)

70 WL: Fire S	288	/Carried down stream/The peal of	bells/White towers/Weialala leia/Wallala leialala
73 WL: Thund	383	in air were towers/Tolling reminiscent	bells, that kept the hours/And voices singing out
134 Wind	2	/The wind sprang up and broke the	bells/Swinging between life and death/Here, in
147 Rock 1	25	Sundays./In the City, we need no	bells:/Let them waken the suburbs./I journeyed
161 Rock 7	30	disowned, the tower overthrown, the	bells upturned, what have we to do/But stand

BELLY (5)

49 Hippopot	2	hippopotamus/Rests on his	belly in the mud;/Although he seems so firm to
67 WL: Fire S	188	the vegetation/Dragging its slimy	belly on the bank/While I was fishing in the dull
605 Narcissus	25	had been a fish/With slippery white	belly held tight in his own fingers,/Writhing in
272 MC Chorus	13	horror/Than when tearing in the	belly./Still the horror, but more horror/Than
281 MC Chorus	12	worm in the soil and the worm in the	belly./Therefore man, whom Thou hast made to

BELONG (14)

152 Rock 2	31	inheritance./For good and ill deeds	belong to a man alone, when he stands alone on
194 FQ: Little	120	the empty pail./For last year's words	belong to last year's language/And next year's
209 NamingCats	20	else Jellylorum —/Names that never	belong to more than one cat./But above and
230 Bust Jones	15	against the rules/For any one Cat to	belong both to that/And the *Joint Superior*
602 Humoresque	23	some star/A hero! — Where would he	belong?/But, even at that, what mask *bizarre!*/
287 FR Mary	10	don't deserve the compliment:/I don't	belong to any generation. {}/[*Exit*]/{V} Really,
291 FR Amy	24	one to see you but our servants who	belong here,/And who all want to see you back,
303 FR Mary	7	greenhouse flowers/Which do not	belong here, which do not know/The wind and
304 FR Mary	9	are strong, and because you don't	belong here/Any more than I do. I want to get
306 FR Mary	29	nothing else to do with me./I didn't	belong here. It was different for you./And you
485 CC Lady E	6	that may be,/I didn't want to	belong there. I refused to believe/That my father
526 ES Charles	34	/That I mustn't stay too long, for you	belong to him./He seems so placidly to take it
553 ES Carghil	11	/It's simply that I feel that we	belong together .../Now, don't get alarmed. But
582 ES Charles	37	/Because somehow we'd begun to	belong together,/And that awareness .../{M}

BELONGED (4)

354 CP Alex	11	she was Belgian./{A} Her father	belonged to a Baltic family —/One of the *oldest*
463 CC Claude	1	/{SC} When you were a child, you	belonged to your aunt,/Or so she made me feel.
495 CC Lady E	27	— and then, too late, I discovered/He	belonged to the world I wanted to escape from./
513 CC Colby	32	than his success —/By objects that	belonged to him, and faded photographs/In

BELONGING (1)

179 FQ: ECoker	97	frenzy, their fear of possession,/Of	belonging to another, or to others, or to God./

BELONGS (1)

418 CP Celia	16	of love —/I wish I could — which	belongs to that life./Oh, I'm afraid this sounds

BELOVED (3)
260 MC Thomas 16   Passion and Death upon/the Cross. Beloved, as the World sees, this is to behave in a
261 MC Thomas 19   of God and for the/salvation of men./Beloved, we do not think of a martyr simply as
385 CP Reilly 13   uncle at the Christmas party,/The beloved nursemaid — those who enfolded/Your
BELOVÈD (1)
416 CP Celia 27   and if one is alone/Then lover and belovèd are equally unreal/And the dreamer is
BELOVED'S (1)
567 ES Monica 6   Mrs. Piggott/Should have heard my beloved's voice/And I couldn't, just when I had
BELOW (13)
42 Swee Erect 14   withered root of knots of hair/Slitted below and gashed with eyes,/This oval O
50 Hippopot 35   kist,/While the True Church remains below/Wrapt in the old miasmal mist./Dans le
69 WL: Fire S 245   or bed;/I who have sat by Thebes below the wall/And walked among the lowest of
92 Ash-Wed 3 2   of the second stair/I turned and saw below/The same shape twisted on the banister/
92 Ash-Wed 3 8   stair/I left them twisting, turning below;/There were no more faces and the stair
103 Journ Magi 22   down to a temperate valley,/Wet, below the snow line, smelling of vegetation,/
172 FQ: BurntN 52   /The trilling wire in the blood/Sings below inveterate scars/Appeasing long forgotten
172 FQ: BurntN 61   leaf/And hear upon the sodden floor/Below, the boarhound and the boar/Pursue
193 FQ: Little 84   with the flickering tongue/Had passed below the horizon of his homing/While the dead
592 Grad 1 5   /No light to warn of rocks which lie below,/But let us yet put forth courageously./As
598 Circe 9   their lairs/In the forest which thickens below,/Along the garden stairs/The sluggish
248 MC Tempt1 8   /I'll remember you at kissing-time below the stairs./{T} Leave-well-alone, the
255 MC Tempt4 14   to be high in heaven./And see far off below you, where the gulf is fixed,/Your
BEN'SON (1)
230 Bust Jones 21   /In the season of venison he gives his ben'son/To the *Pothunter's* succulent bones;/
BEND (3)
174 FQ: BurntN 133   to us, will the clematis/Stray down, bend to us; tendril and spray/Clutch and cling?/
252 MC Tempt4 30   done, Thomas, your will is hard to bend./And with me beside you, you shall not
322 FR Winch 34   ran into a lorry/Drawn up round the bend. We'll have the driver up for this:/Says he
BENDING (3)
40 Burb Blei 14   or such was Bleistein's way:/A saggy bending of the knees/And elbows, with the
254 MC Tempt4 20   /From generation to generation/Bending the knee in supplication,/Think of the
273 MC Chorus 7   in my last fear./Dust I am, to dust am bending,/From the final doom impending/Help
BENDS (1)
240 MC Chorus 3   a little fortune,/And the labourer bends to his piece of earth, earth-colour, his
BENEATH (11)
14 Prufrock 53   the voices dying with a dying fall/Beneath the music from a farther room./So how
45 Cook Egg 30   the eagles and the trumpets?/Buried beneath some snow-deep Alps./Over buttered
52 Whispers 2   possessed by death/And saw the skull beneath the skin;/And breastless creatures under
135 5FingerEx1 3   To the green fields of Russell Square./Beneath the trees there is no ease/For the dull
181 FQ: ECoker 151   /That questions the distempered part;/Beneath the bleeding hands we feel/The sharp
596 When we 6   flowers still,/No withered petals lay beneath;/But still the wild roses in your wreath/
601 Nocturne 4   Juliet, in the usual debate/Of love, beneath a bored but courteous moon;/The
243 MC Priest2 2   and landholders./The rock of God is beneath our feet. Let us meet the Archbishop
249 MC Tempt2 4   set down the great, protect the poor,/Beneath the throne of God can man do more?/
253 MC Tempt4 25   pleasure, kingly rule,/Or rule of men beneath a king,/With craft in corners, stealthy
331 FR Agatha 38   public duties./He hid his strength beneath unusual weakness,/The diffidence of a
BENEFICENT (1)
74 WL: Thund 407   /Or in memories draped by the beneficent spider/Or under seals broken by the
BENEFIT (1)
561 ES Michael 20   always made so much of, for my benefit:/I wonder whether *you* have always lived
BENEFITS (1)
593 Grad 7 1   future centuries bestow/A legacy of benefits — may we/In future years be found
BENEVOLENCE (1)
576 ES Charles 27   you think Señor Gomez is inspired by benevolence —/{Mi} I told you he'd come to
BENIGNANT (1)
544 ES Ld Clav 20   /It comes less often./I hope this benignant sunshine/And warmth will last for a
BENT (7)
94 Ash-Wed 4 24   garden god,/Whose flute is breathless, bent her head and signed but spoke no word/
98 Ash-Wed 6 14   weak spirit quickens to rebel/For the bent golden-rod and the lost sea smell/Quickens
281 MC Chorus 14   with the hand to the broom, the back bent in laying the fire, the knee bent in cleaning
281 MC Chorus 14   back bent in laying the fire, the knee bent in cleaning the hearth, we, the scrubbers
281 MC Chorus 15   sweepers of Canterbury,/The back bent under toil, the knee bent under sin, the
281 MC Chorus 15   /The back bent under toil, the knee bent under sin, the hands to the face under fear,
281 MC Chorus 15   hands to the face under fear, the head bent under grief,/Even in us the voices of

BEQUEATHING (1)
179 FQ: ECoker   78   themselves, the quiet-voiced elders,/Bequeathing us merely a receipt for deceit?/The
BEREFT (1)
280 MC   Priest1   11   /Your strength? The Church lies bereft,/Alone, desecrated, desolated, and the
BERGSTEIGLEBEN (1)
47 Mél   Adult   12   par Emporheben/Au grand air de Bergsteigleben;/J'erre toujours de-ci de-là/A
BERTH (2)
233 Skimble   35   written up on the door./And the berth is very neat with a newly folded sheet/And
233 Skimble   45   /And when you creep into your cosy berth/And pull up the counterpane,/You ought
BESEECHING (1)
196 FQ: Little   201   of the motive/In the ground of our beseeching./The dove descending breaks the air/
BESIDE (11)
15 Prufrock   78   /Stretched on the floor, here beside you and me./Should I, after tea and
69 WL: Fire S   260   /O City city, I can sometimes hear/Beside a public bar in Lower Thames Street,/
73 WL: Thund   359   /Who is the third who walks always beside you?/When I count, there are only you
73 WL: Thund   362   /There is always another one walking beside you/Gliding wrapt in a brown mantle,
210 Old Gumbie   15   and sunny spots./All day she sits beside the hearth or in the sun or on my hat:/
601 Nocturne   2   to importune/Guitar and hat in hand, beside the gate/With Juliet, in the usual debate/
252 MC Tempt4   31   will is hard to bend./And with me beside you, you shall not lack a friend./{T} Who
383 CP   Edward   5   off .../You're sure, in the kitchen? Beside the champagne bottle?/You're quite
426 CP   Lavinia   7   /So just stretch out./{L} You must sit beside me,/Then I can relax./{E} This is the best
493 CC   Claude   6   be near together./Will you sit there, beside the desk?/{LE} On the other side, with
519 CC   m   7   *crosses to* SIR CLAUDE *and kneels beside him*]/{K} You know, Claude, I think we all
BESIDES (23)
287 FR   Gerald   3   you were,/Charles, as I remember. Besides, you've got to make allowances:/We
363 CP   Edward   22   waiting is the one thing impossible./Besides, don't you see that it makes me
366 CP   Julia   24   to Edward. I'm not helpless yet./And besides, I like to manage the machine myself —/
391 CP   Julia   12   mean my spectacles./No, they're here. Besides, they're no use to me./I'm not coming
400 CP   Alex   15   doctor, as well as the right shops./Besides, he was ready to consult any doctor/
404 CP   Edward   32   the courage to go to a hotel,/And besides, I need more shirts — you can get my
431 CP   Peter   31   should see the original Boltwell;/And besides, he thought that as I'm English/I ought
431 CP   Peter   33   know the best way to handle a duke./Besides that, we've got the casting director:/He's
434 CP   Alex   3   there are various endemic diseases/Besides, of course, those brought by Europeans,
440 CP   Lavinia   30   much has happened since then. And besides,/One sometimes likes to hear the same
447 CC   Claude   17   to have a hand in the choosing;/And besides, she is convinced that she, of all people,/
451 CC   Eggers   30   that you're a man of culture;/And besides, she's very musical./{C} Thank you for
456 CC   Colby   12   very unusual/In any other way, besides being a lady?/{E} Why, yes, indeed, I
457 CC   Eggers   14   airport with minutes to spare,/And besides, there's the Customs. That'll take her a
458 CC   Lady E   12   /But quite unnecessary. And besides,/I didn't come by air. I arrived at
458 CC   Eggers   36   Than I am, to be a confidential clerk./Besides, he's very musical./{LE} Musical?/Isn't
461 CC   Eggers   2   I wouldn't have missed it./And besides, as I told you, I've done some shopping.
498 CC   Claude   17   /That's most unlikely, nowadays./Besides, I should have noticed it. I visited her
525 ES   Monica   23   more than two words already./And besides, my father doesn't amble./You're not at
533 ES   Gomez   8   people do change their names;/And besides, my wife's name is a good deal more
541 ES   Gomez   4   get! The Press wouldn't look at it./Besides, you can't think I've any desire/To
551 ES   Carghil   5   — women live on memories./Besides a woman has nothing to be ashamed of:
554 ES   Carghil   27   have to cope with both of us at once./Besides, I ought to do my breathing exercises. {}
BEST (46)
179 FQ: ECoker   83   their eyes. There is, it seems to us,/At best, only a limited value/In the knowledge
601 Nocturne   10   ground —/The hero smiles; in my best mode oblique/Rolls toward the moon a
247 MC Tempt1   36   man!/The easy man lives to eat the best dinners./Take a friend's advice. Leave well
254 MC Tempt4   37   you./And men shall only do their best to forget you./And later is worse, when
258 MC Thomas   34   history/Will seem to most of you at best futility,/Senseless self-slaughter of a lunatic,
260 MC Thomas   30   peaceful gains, the swept hearth, his best wine for a friend/at the table, his wife
277 MC Knight3   19   going to be an awful row; and at the best we shall have to/spend the rest of our lives
288 FR   Amy   7   /{A} After dinner:/That is the best time./{I} It is the first time/You have not
294 FR   Agatha   12   matters./{Ag} Nevertheless, Harry, best tell us as you can:/Talk in your own
329 FR   Chorus   16   up of appearances/The making the best of a bad job/All twined and tangled
338 FR   Harry   4   and what I must do,/And that it is the best thing for everybody./But at present, I
341 FR   Amy   28   /Gives *you* the power to know what is best for Harry?/What gave you this influence to
360 CP   Reilly   32   /{UG} Then no doubt it's all for the best./With another man, she might have made a
363 CP   Reilly   25   to be the fool you are./That's the best advice that *I* can give you./{E} But how can
364 CP   Reilly   15   give a reason for wanting her/Is the best reason for believing that you want her./{E}
376 CP   Celia   3   answer the door, Edward./It's the best thing to do. Don't lose your head./You see,
378 CP   Edward   15   tried to persuade me it was all for the best/That Lavinia had gone; that I ought to be

383 CP	Edward	15	it was a half-bottle?/It's one of my best: and I have no half-bottles./Well, I hoped
408 CP	Edward	23	so utterly ludicrous:/This is the best joke that ever happened./{L} I never knew
410 CP	Edward	33	said./{E} Lavinia, we must make the best of a bad job./That is what he means./{R}
410 CP	Reilly	36	you find, Mr. Chamberlayne,/The best of a bad job is all any of us make of it —/
417 CP	Celia	38	understand them./{C} Is that the best life?/{R} It is a good life. Though you will
420 CP	Reilly	7	/That is the only reason./{R} It is the best reason./{C} But I know it is I who have
426 CP	Edward	9	me,/Then I can relax./{E} This is the best moment/Of the whole party./{L} Oh no,
426 CP	Lavinia	12	whole party./{L} Oh no, Edward./The best moment is the moment it's over;/And then
431 CP	Peter	32	as I'm English/I ought to know the best way to handle a duke./Besides that, we've
435 CP	Julia	3	/{J} You gave her those two years, as best you could./{P} When did she ... take up this
440 CP	Edward	22	Very well./I might almost say, your best. But you always look your best./{L} Oh,
440 CP	Edward	22	your best. But you always look your best./{L} Oh, Edward, that spoils it. No woman
440 CP	Lavinia	24	can believe/That she always looks her best. You're rather transparent,/You know,
440 CP	Lavinia	26	cheer me up./To say I always look my best can only mean the worst./{E} I never shall
446 CC	Eggers	22	business basis./{E} No doubt that's best. While he's still living/With his aunt in
448 CC	Eggers	8	say that!/Though I've done my best to gain his confidence./I did mention her
457 CC	Colby	9	That you always contrive to think the best of everyone./{E} You'll come to find that
461 CC	Claude	32	/And yet I believe that it's all for the best./It went off very well. It's very obvious/
462 CC	Claude	19	in a world of make-believe,/And the best one can do is to guide her delusions/In the
465 CC	Claude	15	/To be a second-rate potter? To be, at best,/A competent copier, possessed by the
465 CC	Claude	27	that you shall have a good piano. The best./And when you are alone at your piano, in
466 CC	Claude	21	others, it seems to me, who have at best to live/In two worlds — each a kind of
467 CC	Colby	25	done for me;/And I want to do my best to justify your kindness/By the work I do./
481 CC	Lady E	39	in the left hand corner:/It has the best waitress. Good night./{L} Good night./{K}
516 CC	Claude	35	/I want us to make the best of it, together./{C} No, Sir Claude. I hate to
522 ES	dedic	8	*you I dedicate this book, to return as best I can/With words a little part of what you*
528 ES	Charles	33	to suggest recovery./{C} This is your best reason, and the most depressing;/For this
547 ES	Piggott	36	the motor roads. You must learn the best walks./I won't apologise for the lack of
569 ES	Charles	24	him./{C} At least, I think I know the best man to advise you./{LC} Blackmail? Yes,

BESTIAL (1)

161 Rock 7		23	saved in spite of their negative being;/Bestial as always before, carnal, self-seeking as

BESTOW (2)

593 Grad 6		6	estate/As shall on future centuries bestow/A legacy of benefits — may we/In future
604 Ode		6	/Of the hopes that thy blessings bestow,/From the hopes and ambitions that

BESTOWS (1)

69 WL: Fire S		247	among the lowest of the dead.)/Bestows one final patronising kiss,/And gropes

BET (1)

560 ES	Michael	2	If you're still conscious after death,/I bet it will be a surprised state of consciousness./

BETHLEHEM (1)

260 MC	Thomas	13	host appeared before the/shepherds at Bethlehem, saying 'Glory to God in the highest,

BETOKENETH (1)

178 FQ: ECoker		34	other by the hand or the arm/Whiche betokeneth concorde. Round and round the fire

BETRAY (2)

289 FR	Amy	11	a good deal more than she cares to betray,/I am bound to say that I agree with you.
296 FR	Ivy	20	— that people in his condition/Often betray the most immoderate resentment/At such

BETRAYAL (1)

418 CP	Celia	8	—/No, not a surrender — more like a betrayal./You see, I think I really had a vision

BETRAYED (4)

154 Rock 3		4	generation of enlightened men,/Betrayed in the mazes of your ingenuities,/Sold
252 MC	Thomas	22	done before:/No one shall say that I betrayed a king./{T3} Then, my Lord, I shall
266 MC	Knights	23	swindled, lied; broke his oath and betrayed his King./{T} This is not true./Both
379 CP	Celia	36	like a dream./Perhaps it was I who betrayed my own dream/All the while; and to

BETRAYS (1)

49 Hippopot		18	sea./At mating time the hippo's voice/Betrays inflexions hoarse and odd,/But every

BETTER (111)

155 Rock 3		42	or a horde of active marmots/Build better than they that build without the LORD./
155 Rock 3		51	numbered doors/Or a house a little better than your neighbour's;/When the
182 FQ: ECoker		178	Because one has only learnt to get the better of words/For the thing one no longer has
187 FQ: DrySal		110	as time has. We appreciate this better/In the agony of others, nearly
229 Gus		41	/And he thinks that he still can, much better than most,/Produce blood-curdling noises
234 Ad-dress		11	good and some are bad/And some are better, some are worse —/But all may be
245 MC	Thomas	12	be, in their exaltation./They speak better than they know, and beyond your
245 MC	Priest2	25	us, my Lord, you would have had a better welcome/If we had been sooner prepared
245 MC	Priest2	29	seven years of emptiness,/Have better prepared our hearts for your coming,/
245 MC	Priest2	33	/Your Lordship now being used to a better climate./Your Lordship will find your

249 MC	Tempt2	6	the laws,/Rule for the good of the better cause,/Dispensing justice make all even,/
250 MC	Thomas	16	King —/I *was* the King, his arm, his better reason./But what was once exaltation/
286 FR	Charles	2	winter./But a single man like me is better off in London:/A man can be very cosy at
286 FR	Gerald	9	servants look after you very much better./{A} My servants are perfectly competent,
287 FR	Gerald	2	/And some first-class shots — better than you were,/Charles, as I remember.
287 FR	Amy	21	us drop the subject. The less said the better./{G} That reminds me, Amy,/When are
289 FR	Ivy	31	ask him./{I} These things are much better not enquired into./She may have done it
295 FR	Charles	14	morning./I understand these feelings better than you know —/But *you* have no
295 FR	Amy	40	you a hot bath,/And you will feel better./{Ag} There are certain points I do not
297 FR	Gerald	21	/And even if he knew, it's very much better/That he shouldn't know that we knew it
298 FR	Agatha	11	this is all quite irrelevant;/We had better leave Charles to talk to Downing/And
302 FR	Amy	18	I suppose. I hope Harry will feel better/After his rest upstairs. {}/[*Exeunt, except*
309 FR	Harry	6	you into *our* world. Yours is no better./They have seen to that: it is part of the
309 FR	Mary	15	very well,/Although I remember you better than you think,/And what is the real you.
322 FR	Winch	25	my Lord, I'm sorry./I thought I'd better have a word with you quiet,/Rather than
323 FR	Charles	34	I do not believe you./{C} Much better leave it to Warburton, Amy./Extremely
328 FR	Gerald	10	been more in the later editions./You'd better read it to us. {}/[*reads*]./{C} '*Peer's*
331 FR	Harry	27	always known it. And that will be better./{Ag} I will try to tell you. I hope I have
342 FR	Mary	26	/I will stay or I will go, whichever is better;/I do not care what happens to me,/But
346 FR	Downing	19	him/I think I understand his Lordship better than anybody;/And I have a kind of
359 CP	Alex	4	Edward. I do hope/You'll have better news of Lavinia's aunt./{E} Oh ... yes ...
361 CP	Edward	21	unless you know my wife/A good deal better than I thought, or unless you know/A
361 CP	Reilly	39	/Arranging life a little better than you like it,/Preferring not quite the
362 CP	Reilly	1	/Or making your friends like her better than you;/And, turning the past over and
367 CP	Peter	4	notice:/I must have behaved rather better than I thought./If you didn't notice, I
371 CP	Edward	14	Celia./{E} Will it be the same Celia?/Better be content with the Celia you remember./
374 CP	Celia	21	have been prepared with something better, for Julia;/But it doesn't really matter.
376 CP	Celia	2	CELIA, *in an apron*.]/{C} You'd better answer the door, Edward./It's the best
379 CP	Celia	34	to tell you./Perhaps the dream was better. It seemed the real reality,/And if this is
380 CP	Celia	31	of person you are —/Well, you had better have her./{E} It's not like that./It is not
382 CP	Edward	38	Damn the telephone./I suppose I had better answer it./{C} Yes, better answer it./{E}
382 CP	Celia	39	I had better answer it./{C} Yes, better answer it./{E} Hello! ... Oh, Julia: what is
388 CP	Peter	16	to say so;/But you'll find someone better, to go about with./{C} I don't think that I
392 CP	Lavinia	28	you./{L} Really, Edward! You had better have told the truth:/Nothing less than the
395 CP	Edward	16	I haven't yet found it a change for the better./But doesn't it occur to you that possibly/
395 CP	Edward	33	assurance/That you understood me better than I understood myself./{L} And the
396 CP	Edward	1	his corner of the cage./Well, it's a better way of passing the evening/Than listening
400 CP	Reilly	25	To escape from himself — and get the better of his wife./{A} Not to escape from her?/
401 CP	Edward	7	symptom./Well, I should have known better than to come here/On the
401 CP	Edward	38	be trying to persuade me/That I was better off without her. But didn't you realise/
402 CP	Reilly	2	you suppose that things would be any better — now?/{E} I don't know, I'm sure. They
406 CP	Edward	38	/You always know of something better./{L} It's only that I have a more practical
418 CP	Celia	32	its own duty./{C} Which way is better?/{R} Neither way is better./Both ways are
418 CP	Reilly	33	way is better?/{R} Neither way is better./Both ways are necessary. It is also
419 CP	Celia	15	don't mean to say they weren't much better for it —/That's why I came to you. But
419 CP	Reilly	37	*on a slip of paper*]/{R} You had better let your family know at once./I will send
433 CP	Julia	34	out of it./{E} Celia dead./{J} You had better tell them, Alex,/The news that you bring
435 CP	Peter	23	it was going to lead to something better,/And that seemed possible, while Celia
440 CP	Julia	15	the party begins./They will get on better without us. You too, Alex./{L} We don't
445 CC	Eggers	27	say that!/Mr. Simpkins is far better qualified than I was/To be your
447 CC	Claude	18	convinced that she, of all people,/Is a better judge of character than I am./{E} Oh, I
448 CC	Claude	3	/There are some things you could say better than I could,/And ways in which you
448 CC	Claude	5	ways in which you could reassure him/Better than I. He's more at ease with you/Than
450 CC	Claude	17	don't understand me — a good deal better/Than I should care to think, perhaps./{E}
452 CC	Kaghan	7	/Bankrupt again! So I thought I'd better bring her/And come upstairs ahead, to
452 CC	Lucasta	32	you agree/That Lucasta suits me better?/{C} I'm sure they both suit you./{L}
459 CC	Lady E	3	/I remember people's auras almost better than their faces./What did you say his
461 CC	Eggers	3	I've done some shopping./But I'd better be off now. Mr. Simpkins —/If anything
463 CC	Claude	34	what you are saying/Much better than you think. It's my own experience/
466 CC	Colby	31	think I do. At least, I understand *you* better/In learning to understand the conditions/
470 CC	Colby	10	As a matter of fact, I think I played better./I can't bring myself to play to other
471 CC	Colby	6	the themes, so you'll recognise them./Better still, I'll play you the gramophone
472 CC	Lucasta	12	it,/That as one gets to know a person better/One finds them in some ways very like
475 CC	Colby	2	*you.*/{C} I believe you do already,/Better than ... other people. And I want to
475 CC	Colby	8	/All one can do is to understand them better,/To keep up with them; so that as the

475 CC	Lucasta	15	call change .../{L} Is understanding	better	what one really is./And the reason why
479 CC	Lucasta	9	B. And as for Lizzie,/You'd	better	not get in *her* way when she's hunting./
479 CC	Kaghan	19	success to the flat. Lucasta too:/Much	better	for you than cocktails, Lucasta./{L} You
480 CC	Lucasta	20	of character./{L} You'd need to be a	better	judge of character/Yourself, before you
481 CC	Kaghan	5	head for business./Maybe you're a	better	financier than I am!/That's why we ought
487 CC	Claude	14	need a good piano. You'll play all the	better	./{LE} Claude!/{SC} What is it, Elizabeth?/
489 CC	Claude	12	But it influenced me./And I found a	better	reason for keeping silent./I came to see
490 CC	Colby	31	am your son./Then it's merely a fact.	Better	not know/Than to know the fact and
491 CC	Lady E	10	we had wanted —/But in some ways	better	! And prevent us both/From making
493 CC	Claude	9	too formal. I thought it would be	better	/To put Eggerson there, behind the desk./
494 CC	Lady E	32	perhaps I might come to understand	better	./What did you want to do?/{SC} To be a
502 CC	Colby	28	don't know./Perhaps you know me	better	than I know myself./But now that you
503 CC	Eggers	24	them ... Can't B. come up now?/{E}	Better	wait till afterwards./{SC} Quite right,
504 CC	Claude	19	could arrange the servants' time-table	better	./This is a most unfortunate beginning./
512 CC	Kaghan	29	Mulhammer?/{K} It's very much	better	than being a foundling —/If I can live up
512 CC	Eggers	36	/{E} I'm sure we all wish for nothing	better	./{MG} Wishes, when realised, sometimes
515 CC	Claude	38	/To our relations. Or, perhaps, for the	better	?/Perhaps we'll be happier together if you
519 CC	Lady E	14	make mistakes! But I mean to do	better	./Claude, we've got to try to understand
527 ES	Charles	20	why I should go with him./{C}	Better	reasons than for marrying me?/What
528 ES	Charles	2	going with your father./Is there any	better	reason than his fear of solitude?/{M} The
532 ES	Ld Clav	6	left too many papers about there./I'd	better	see him here./{L} Very good, my Lord./
542 ES	Gomez	37	Dick:/You *didn't stop*! Well, I'd	better	be going./I hope I haven't outstayed my
544 ES	Monica	1	*and* MONICA./{M} Well, so far, it's	better	than you expected,/Isn't it, Father?
549 ES	Ld Clav	20	/The more you remind me of, the	better	I'll remember./{MC} And the three of us
555 ES	Monica	14	tired, Father./She ought to know	better	. But I'm all the more distressed/Because I
559 ES	Ld Clav	10	cities:/An outdoor life would suit you	better	./How would you like to go to Western
563 ES	Gomez	14	doctor, 'Well, what about it?/What	better	recommendation could I have?'/So he
569 ES	Monica	13	{M} I think I should only love you the	better	, Father,/The more I knew about you. I
569 ES	Monica	14	about you. I should understand you	better	./There's nothing I'm afraid of learning
570 ES	Ld Clav	20	/{LC} ... And yet they've both done	better	for themselves/In consequence of it all.
575 ES	Gomez	20	I've told him myself./I thought he'd	better	learn the facts from me/Before he heard
576 ES	Gomez	20	There's time for that later./{G} Much	better	to wait until we get there./The nature of
577 ES	Gomez	11	pleasant/To repay an old debt. And	better	late than never./{C} I see your point of
579 ES	Ld Clav	23	Then I agree with you, the sooner the	better	./We may never meet again, Michael./{Mi}
580 ES	Carghil	24	must always keep in touch. But you'd	better	rest now./You're looking rather tired. I'll
580 ES	Ld Clav	37	you are right to hope for something	better	./And when he comes back, if he does

BETTING (1)

476 CC	Lucasta	40	the end of the quarter/On gin and	betting	, I should guess./And I knew how she

BETWEEN (85)

23 Preludes	31	came back/And the light crept up	between	the shutters/And you heard the
53 Whispers	31	her charm;/But our lot crawls	between	dry ribs/To keep our metaphysics
54 Mr E Sun	26	the bees/With hairy bellies pass	between	/The staminate and pistillate,/Blest
68 WL: Fire S	218	/I Tiresias, though blind, throbbing	between	two lives,/Old man with wrinkled
85 Hollow Men	72	*pear/At five o'clock in the morning.*/Between	the idea/And the reality/Between the
85 Hollow Men	74	/Between the idea/And the reality/Between	the motion/And the act/Falls the
85 Hollow Men	78	Shadow/*For Thine is the Kingdom*/Between	the conception/And the creation/
85 Hollow Men	80	the conception/And the creation/Between	the emotion/And the response/Falls
85 Hollow Men	84	/Falls the Shadow/*Life is very long*/Between	the desire/And the spasm/Between the
85 Hollow Men	86	/Between the desire/And the spasm/Between	the potency/And the existence/Between
85 Hollow Men	88	the potency/And the existence/Between	the essence/And the descent/Falls the
94 Ash-Wed 4	1	speak the word only./Who walked	between	the violet and the violet/Who walked
94 Ash-Wed 4	2	the violet and the violet/Who walked	between	/The various ranks of varied green/
94 Ash-Wed 4	12	vos/Here are the years that walk	between	, bearing/Away the fiddles and the
94 Ash-Wed 4	14	restoring/One who moves in the time	between	sleep and waking, wearing/White light
94 Ash-Wed 4	23	silent sister veiled in white and blue/Between	the yews, behind the garden god,/
96 Ash-Wed 5	22	thee,/Those who are torn on the horn	between	season and season, time and time,
96 Ash-Wed 5	22	season and season, time and time,	between	/Hour and hour, word and word, power
97 Ash-Wed 5	29	I done unto thee./Will the veiled sister	between	the slender/Yew trees pray for those
97 Ash-Wed 5	32	And affirm before the world and deny	between	the rocks/In the last desert between the
97 Ash-Wed 5	33	between the rocks/In the last desert	between	the last blue rocks/The desert in the
98 Ash-Wed 6	4	I do not hope to turn/Wavering	between	the profit and the loss/In this brief
98 Ash-Wed 6	6	cross/The dreamcrossed twilight	between	birth and dying/(Bless me father)
98 Ash-Wed 6	18	the blind eye creates/The empty forms	between	the ivory gates/And smell renews the
98 Ash-Wed 6	20	earth/This is the time of tension	between	dying and birth/The place of solitude
98 Ash-Wed 6	22	of solitude where three dreams cross/Between	blue rocks/But when the voices shaken

BEWITCHED (1)
377 CP   Celia   16   he *must* be the Devil! He must have bewitched you./How did he persuade you to
BEYOND (35)
 39 Gerontion   68   Fresca, Mrs. Cammel, whirled/Beyond the circuit of the shuddering Bear/In
 52 Whispers   12   seize and clutch and penetrate;/Expert beyond experience,/He knew the anguish of the
 92 Ash-Wed 3   10   like an old man's mouth drivelling, beyond repair,/Or the toothed gullet of an agèd
 92 Ash-Wed 3   14   window bellied like the fig's fruit/And beyond the hawthorn blossom and a pasture
 92 Ash-Wed 3   20   third stair,/Fading, fading; strength beyond hope and despair/Climbing the third
110 Marina   30   life/Living to live in a world of time beyond me; let me/Resign my life for this life,
141 Rannoch   10   apt/In silence. Memory is strong/Beyond the bone. Pride snapped,/Shadow of
160 Rock 7   5   rather than nothing: crying for life beyond life, for ecstasy not of the flesh./Waste
186 FQ: DrySal   97   the experience/In a different form, beyond any meaning/We can assign to
192 FQ: Little   35   you had no purpose/Or the purpose is beyond the end you figured/And is altered in
192 FQ: Little   53   /Of the dead is tongued with fire beyond the language of the living./Here, the
195 FQ: Little   160   not less of love but expanding/Of love beyond desire, and so liberation/From the
202 War Poetry   9   /On which we attend/Of forces beyond control by experiment —/Of Nature
209 NamingCats   21   to more than one cat./But above and beyond there's still one name left over,/And that
599 On a Port   12   eyes keep their secrets hid from us,/Beyond the circle of our thought she stands./
241 MC   Mess   31   affirming all his claims,/Assured, beyond doubt, of the devotion of the people,/
245 MC Thomas   12   speak better than they know, and beyond your understanding./They know and do
255 MC Tempt4   16   in timeless torment,/Parched passion, beyond expiation./{T} No!/Who are you,
273 MC Chorus   1   /Not what we call death, but what beyond death is not death,/We fear, we fear.
279 MC Knight4   33   he had deliberately exasperated/us beyond human endurance, he could still have
294 FR   Agatha   14   to debate/Whether it may be too far beyond our understanding./{H} The sudden
305 FR   Agatha   12   /The decision will be made by powers beyond us/Which now and then emerge. You
342 FR   Agatha   32   life. Harry has crossed the frontier/Beyond which safety and danger have a
348 FR   Chorus   32   of happening?/What ambush lies beyond the heather/And behind the Standing
348 FR   Chorus   34   /And behind the Standing Stones?/Beyond the Heaviside Layer/And behind the
361 CP   Reilly   32   bottle./It is to start a train of events/Beyond your control. So let me continue./I will
410 CP   Reilly   23   you this:/It would have been a horror beyond your imagining,/For you would have
438 CP   Reilly   28   /Of all our words and deeds, beyond the intention/And beyond our limited
438 CP   Reilly   29   and deeds, beyond the intention/And beyond our limited understanding/Of ourselves
448 CC   Claude   27   her absence/Are perfectly clear. But beyond that point/I haven't yet explained my
516 CC   Colby   9   success —/I aimed too high before — beyond my capacity./I thought I didn't want to
560 ES   Ld Clav 21   there reasons for your wanting to go/Beyond what you've told me? It isn't ...
568 ES   Ld Clav   6   are many things not crimes, Monica,/Beyond anything of which the law takes
571 ES   Ld Clav   9   /I led him to acquire tastes beyond his means:/So he became a forger. And
583 ES   Charles   4   I love you to the limits of speech, and beyond./It's strange that words are so
BICYCLE (1)
324 FR Warburt   6   /Come, Winchell. We can put your bicycle/On the back of my car. {}/[*Exeunt*
BID (1)
268 MC Thomas   20   me and keep me from my own/And bid me sit in Canterbury, alone?/I would wish
BIEN (1)
 47 Mél Adult   7   un peu banquier,/Vous me paierez bien la tête./C'est à Paris que je me coiffe/
BIG (2)
216 Jellicles   14   slowly,/Jellicle Cats are not too big;/Jellicle Cats are roly-poly,/They know how
222 Pekes Pols   14   a long time for a Pol or a Peke)./The big Police Dog was away from his beat —/I
BIKE (1)
322 FR   Winch   27   Ladyship./So I slipped along on my bike. Mostly walking,/What with the fog so
BILAN (1)
 48 Lune Miel   14   pense aux pourboires, et rédige son bilan./Ils auront vu la Suisse et traversé la
BILL (2)
557 ES   Michael 36   /{Mi} Oh, ordinary debts:/My tailor's bill, for instance./{LC} I expected that./It was
562 ES   Carghil 26   name of Maisie Montjoy/Topped the bill in revue. Now I'm Mrs. John Carghill./
BILL (2) [*Proper name*]
 66 WL: Chess   170   UP PLEASE ITS TIME/Goonight Bill. Goonight Lou. Goonight May. Goonight./
209 NamingCats   7   as Victor or Jonathan, George or Bill Bailey —/All of them sensible everyday
BILLS (1)
558 ES   Michael   1   own fault./They won't send in their bills, and then I forget them./It's being your son
BIN (1)
 61 WL: Burial   12   drank coffee, and talked for an hour./Bin gar keine Russin, stamm' aus Litauen, echt
BIND (5)
250 MC Thomas   2   hell, supreme alone in England,/Who bind and loose, with power from the Pope,/
253 MC Tempt4   30   the keys of heaven and hell./Power to bind and loose: bind, Thomas, bind,/King and
253 MC Tempt4   30   and hell./Power to bind and loose: bind, Thomas, bind,/King and bishop under

253 MC Tempt4	30		to bind and loose: bind, Thomas, bind,/King and bishop under your heel./King,
350 FR Agatha	6		/Where the meshes we have woven/Bind us to each other/Follow follow/{M} A

BINDING (2)

155 Rock 3		63	greatness thoroughly discredited,/Binding the earth and the water to your service,/
268 MC Knight2	9		the legality of his coronation./{K2} Binding with the chains of anathema./{K3}

BIOGRAPHY (1)

189 FQ: DrySal	192		/Observe disease in signatures, evoke/Biography from the wrinkles of the palm/And

BIRCH-TREES (1)

31 Apollinax	3		Fragilion, that shy figure among the birch-trees,/And of Priapus in the shrubbery/

BIRD (18)

95 Ash-Wed 4	25		/But the fountain sprang up and the bird sang down/Redeem the time, redeem the
171 FQ: BurntN	21		Shall we follow?/Quick, said the bird, find them, find them,/Round the corner.
172 FQ: BurntN	28	heat, through the vibrant air,/And the bird called, in response to/The unheard music
172 FQ: BurntN	42	and the pool was empty./Go, said the bird, for the leaves were full of children,/Hidden
172 FQ: BurntN	44		laughter./Go, go, go, said the bird: human kind/Cannot bear very much
588 Fable	46	account: They made a raid/On every bird and beast in Æsop's fable/To fill out their
600 Moonflower	3	mist crawls in from sea;/A great white bird, a snowy owl,/Slips from the alder tree./
254 MC Tempt4	29		early in the morning,/When the bird cries, have thought of further scorning./
254 MC Tempt4	31		turns,/The nest is rifled, and the bird mourns;/That the shrine shall be pillaged,
263 MC Chorus	1	Ghost. Amen./Part II/{C} Does the bird sing in the South?/Only the sea-bird cries,
263 MC Chorus	20	same earth/He has turned before, the bird shall sing the same song./When the leaf is
269 MC Chorus	33		the laugh of the loon, the lunatic bird. I have seen/Grey necks twisting, rat tails
281 MC Chorus	12		all things affirm Thee in living; the bird in the air, both the hawk and the finch; the
316 FR Chorus	3		perhaps it was never there./And the bird sits on the broken chimney. I am afraid./{I}
333 FR Agatha	34		of your unhappy family,/Its bird sent flying through the purgatorial flame./
446 CC Eggers	33	want a garden of his own. And yes, a bird bath!/{SC} A bird bath? In the mews?
446 CC Claude	34	his own. And yes, a bird bath!/{SC} A bird bath? In the mews? What's the point of
446 CC Eggers	35		/{E} He told me he was very fond of bird watching./{SC} But there won't be any

BIRD'S (1)

263 MC Chorus	25		been done, what wrong/Shall the bird's song cover, the green tree cover, what

BIRDS (3)

281 MC Chorus	16		summer, the voices of beasts and of birds, praise Thee./We thank Thee for Thy
446 CC Claude	36		/{SC} But there won't be any birds — none worth watching./{E} I don't
446 CC Eggers	38	read a letter in *The Times* about wild birds seen in London:/And I'm sure Mr.

BIRTH (32)

98 Ash-Wed 6	6		/The dreamcrossed twilight between birth and dying/(Bless me father) though I do
98 Ash-Wed 6	20	the time of tension between dying and birth/The place of solitude where three dreams
104 Journ Magi	36		/This: were we led all that way for/Birth or Death? There was a Birth, certainly,/
104 Journ Magi	36	way for/Birth or Death? There was a Birth, certainly,/We had evidence and no doubt.
104 Journ Magi	37		evidence and no doubt. I had seen birth and death,/But had thought they were
104 Journ Magi	38	had thought they were different; this Birth was/Hard and bitter agony for us, like
105 Song Sime	21	hour of maternal sorrow,/Now at this birth season of decease,/Let the Infant, the still
108 Animula	37		for us now and at the hour of our birth./Marina/What seas what shores what grey
122 SA Sweeney	1		three things/{Do} What things?/{S} Birth, and copulation, and death./That's all,
122 SA Sweeney	3	all, that's all, that's all, that's all,/Birth, and copulation, and death./{Do} I'd be
122 SA Sweeney	6		I'd be bored./{S} You'd be bored./Birth, and copulation, and death./{Do} I'd be
122 SA Sweeney	9		I'd be bored./{S} You'd be bored./Birth, and copulation, and death./That's all the
122 SA Sweeney	11	facts when you come to brass tacks:/Birth, and copulation, and death./I've been
147 Rock 1	5		/O world of spring and autumn, birth and dying!/The endless cycle of idea and
180 FQ: ECoker	134	pointing to the agony/Of death and birth./You say I am repeating/Something I have
244 MC Chorus	20		not of one but of many,/A fear like birth and death, when we see birth and death
244 MC Chorus	20	fear like birth and death, when we see birth and death alone/In a void apart. We/Are
257 MC Chorus	25		us, more pang, more pain than birth or death./Sweet and cloying through the
260 MC Thomas	8	Day we do this in celebration of His Birth. So that at/the same moment we rejoice in
260 MC Thomas	15	the year that we/celebrate at once the Birth of Our Lord and His Passion and Death
261 MC Thomas	10		celebrate at once Our Lord's/Birth and His Death: but on the next day we
261 MC Thomas	12	follows immediately the day of the Birth/of Christ? By no means. Just as we rejoice
261 MC Thomas	14	we rejoice and mourn at once, in the/Birth and in the Passion of Our Lord; so also, in
261 MC Thomas	39	because it is fitting, on Christ's birth/day, to remember what is that Peace
263 MC Chorus	12	in the East./What, at the time of the birth of Our Lord, at Christmastide,/Is there
310 FR Mary	19	kind of pain/I believe the moment of birth/Is when we have knowledge of death/I
310 FR Mary	21	of death/I believe the season of birth/Is the season of sacrifice/For the tree and
329 FR Chorus	3	in the curtained bedroom, whether of birth or of dying,/Gathers in to itself all the
333 FR Agatha	31		and struggle/In its dark instinctive birth, to come to consciousness/And so find
342 FR Agatha	31	no doubt is agony, renunciation,/But birth and life. Harry has crossed the frontier/

514 CC Guzzard   21   this statement?/{MG} Registration of birth. To Herbert and Sarah Guzzard/A son./
515 CC Guzzard   17   yours',/I feared you would ask for the birth certificate./You never did. And so it went

BIRTHDAY (10)
288 FR   Ivy   4   all./{I} And when will you have your birthday cake, Amy,/And open your presents?/
289 FR   Gerald   5   must say, this isn't cheerful for Amy's birthday/Or for Harry's homecoming. Make
313 FR   Violet   6   to be here in time/For his mother's birthday./{I} Mary, my dear,/Did you arrange
313 FR   Gerald   17   he could be here for his mother's birthday./{M} I must go and change. I came in
315 FR   Violet   21   that she was a day older/Than on her birthday ten years ago./{G} Is there any use in
317 FR   Warburt   3   simply in honour of your mother's birthday./I wanted a private conversation with
319 FR   Warburt   40   you know;/You will have to have the birthday celebration,/And your brothers will be
321 FR   Winch   26   my Lord,/I was thinking it was your birthday, not her Ladyship's./{H} Her
322 FR   Winch   3   Sir./It'd be the same if it was my birthday —I beg pardon, I'm forgetting./If it
349 FR   2m   13   *door, enter* DENMAN *carrying a birthday cake with/lighted candles, which she sets*

BIRTHS (1)
244 MC Chorus   11   and partly living./We have seen births, deaths and marriages,/We have had

BISCUITS (1)
377 CP   Edward   37   not at all hungry./I shall have a few biscuits./{J} But you, Celia?/You must come and

BISECTING (1)
160 Rock 7   19   in what we call history: transecting, bisecting the world of time, a moment in time

BISHOP (3)
589 Fable   82   everywhere,/But not a shred of Bishop could be found,/The monks, when
253 MC Tempt4   31   loose: bind, Thomas, bind,/King and bishop under your heel./King, emperor, bishop,
253 MC Tempt4   32   under your heel./King, emperor, bishop, baron, king:/Uncertain mastery of

BISHOP'S (1)
252 MC Tempt3   3   jurisdiction/Of king's court over bishop's court,/Of king's court over baron's

BISHOPS (3)
246 MC Thomas   2   enemies restless about us./Rebellious bishops, York, London, Salisbury,/Would have
249 MC Thomas   32   with decorum./{T} You forget the bishops/Whom I have laid under
268 MC Thomas   22   rather than one,/And as for the bishops, it is not my yoke/That is laid upon

BIT (18)
 16 Prufrock   117   /Full of high sentence, but a bit obtuse;/At times, indeed, almost ridiculous
 65 WL: Chess   142   coming back, make yourself a bit smart./He'll want to know what you done
119 SP   Klip   16   Cap and Sam./{Kl} Yes we did our bit, as you folks say,/I'll tell the world we got
224 Mr Mistoff   32   trick with a cork/Or a spoon and a bit of fish-paste;/If you look for a knife or a
236 Cat Morgan   8   with a drink on the 'ouse/And a bit o' cold fish when I done me patrol./I ain't
277 MC Knight3   13   Church traditions. So if/we seemed a bit rowdy, you will understand why it was; and
300 FRDowning   28   down in the Tourist,/And I took a bit of air before I went to bed,/And you could
313 FR   Charles   22   of their elder brother./Arthur's a bit irresponsible, you know;/You should have a
322 FR   Winch   31   that you'd arrived./Mr. John's had a bit of an accident/On the West Road, in the fog,
322 FR   Winch   37   the Arms —/Mr. John, I mean. By a bit of luck/Dr. Owen was there, and looked him
323 FR   Winch   25   round yet./Dr. Owen was there, by a bit of luck./{G} I'll go down and see him, Amy,
326 FR   Harry   25   own life as an isolated ruin,/A casual bit of waste in an orderly universe./But it begins
328 FR   Gerald   2 {G} Well, I said that Arthur was every bit as likely/To have an accident as John. And it
346 FR   Agatha   35   mustn't worry about that./He is every bit as sane as you or I,/He sees the world as
390 CP   Julia   2   to be late./But your telegram was a bit unexpected./I dropped everything to come.
473 CC Lucasta   12   that I'm even a person:/Nothing but a bit of living matter/Floating on the surface of
479 CC Kaghan   36   must change the colours./It's all a bit too dim. You need something brighter./But
563 ES   Gomez   25   Mrs. John Carghill./{G} We seem a bit weak on the surnames, Dick!/{MC} Well,

BITE (3)
187 FQ: DrySal 119   coops,/The bitter apple and the bite in the apple./And the ragged rock in the
234 Ad-dress   21   fight;/They often bark, more seldom bite;/But yet a Dog is, on the whole,/What you
280 MC Priest3   29   fountain by the date-tree;/Or sit and bite your nails in Aquitaine./In the small circle

BITERS (1)
223 Pekes Pols   34   Scottish cousins are snappers and biters,/And every dog-jack of them notable

BITES (1)
253 MC Tempt4   39   at last breath,/No sons, no empire, he bites broken teeth./You hold the skein: wind,

BITING (1)
246 MC Tempt1   33   /Friendship should be more than biting Time can sever./What, my Lord, now

BITS (2)
174 FQ: BurntN 107   with no concentration/Men and bits of paper, whirled by the cold wind/That
471 CC Lucasta   7   records./{L} I'd rather you played me bits yourself, and explained them./We'll begin

BITTEN (3)
 15 Prufrock   91   it have been worth while,/To have bitten off the matter with a smile,/To have
 31 Apollinax   22   /I remember a slice of lemon, and a bitten macaroon./Hysteria/As she laughed I was
 37 Gerontion   6   in the salt marsh, heaving a cutlass,/Bitten by flies, fought./My house is a decayed

BITTER (11)
104	Journ Magi	39	different; this Birth was/Hard and bitter agony for us, like Death, our death./We
143	Lines OM	10	/Is more affectionate than hate,/More bitter than the love of youth,/And inaccessible
150	Rock 1	104	*men,/To two women one half pint of bitter/Ale. In this land/No man has hired us./Our*
161	Rock 7	35	*men,/To two women one half pint of bitter/Ale....*/CHORUS:/What does the world
187	FQ: DrySal	119	negroes, cows and chicken coops,/The bitter apple and the bite in the apple./And the
194	FQ: Little	135	offering no promise/But bitter tastelessness of shadow fruit/As body and
242	MC Priest1	19	prosperity/Was but confirmed by bitter adversity./I saw him as Chancellor,
243	MC Chorus	17	rotten the year;/Evil the wind, and bitter the sea, and grey the sky, grey grey grey./
244	MC Chorus	30	sail between the grey sky and the bitter sea, leave us, leave us for France./{P2}
263	MC Chorus	10	hollow note of death./What signs of a bitter spring?/The wind stored up in the East./
311	FR Harry	5	In that it is indescribable, a sweet and bitter smell/From another world. I know it, I

BITTEREST (1)
| 246 | MC Thomas | 5 | to meet me/Some who hold me in bitterest hate./By God's grace aware of their |

BITTERLY (2)
| 425 | CP Lavinia | 9 | to come/But all the same would be bitterly offended/To hear we'd given a party |
| 489 | CC Claude | 16 | came./And now I regret the decision bitterly./I ought to have told you that I had a |

BITTERNESS (1)
| 341 | FR Amy | 34 | without him, at Wishwood,/Years of bitterness and disappointment./What share had |

BIZARRE (1)
| 602 | Humoresque | 24 | belong?/But, even at that, what mask *bizarre!*/Spleen/Sunday: this satisfied procession/ |

BLACK (18)
17	Prufrock	128	the wind blows the water white and black./We have lingered in the chambers of the
73	WL: Thund	377	/Unreal/A woman drew her long black hair out tight/And fiddled whisper music
74	WL: Thund	396	limp leaves/Waited for rain, while the black clouds/Gathered far distant, over
129	Cor2 State	5	Legion of Honour,/The Order of the Black Eagle (1st and 2nd class),/And the Order
135	5FingerEx2	3	And the tree was crookt and dry./In a black sky, from a green cloud/Natural forces
138	New Hamp	5	/Between the green tip and the root./Black wing, brown wing, hover over;/Twenty
138	New Hamp	9	me over, light-in-leaves;/Golden head, black wing,/Cling, swing,/Spring, sing,/Swing
164	Rock 9	4	a House of Sorrow;/We must walk in black and go sadly, with longdrawn faces,/We
174	FQ: BurntN	131	and the bell have buried the day,/The black cloud carries the sun away./Will the
216	Jellicles	5	*to the Jellicle Ball.*/Jellicle Cats are black and white,/Jellicle Cats are rather small;/
216	Jellicles	10	faces,/Jellicle Cats have bright black eyes;/They like to practise their airs and
216	Jellicles	21	their toes./Jellicle Cats are white and black,/Jellicle Cats are of moderate size;/Jellicles
216	Jellicles	29	of the Jellicle Moon./Jellicle Cats are black and white,/Jellicle Cats (as I said) are
224	Mr Mistoff	23	/He is quiet and small, he is black/From his ears to the tip of his tail;/He can
230	Bust Jones	6	the street/In his coat of fastidious black:/No commonplace mousers have such
335	FR Agatha	3	in the distance tiny voices/And then a black raven flew over./And then I was only my
372	CP Alex	26	/All you should want is a cup of black coffee/And a little dry toast. I've left it
457	CC Lady E	29	how to make tea properly./A cup of black coffee. Is Sir Claude at home?/I'll speak

BLACKAMOORS (1)
| 280 | MC Priest3 | 21 | shipwreck on the sullen coasts/Where blackamoors make captive Christian men;/Go |

BLACKBURNIAN (1)
| 142 | Cape Ann | 5 | at noon. Leave to chance/The Blackburnian warbler, the shy one. Hail/With |

BLACKENED (4)
23	Preludes	46	certainties,/The conscience of a blackened street/Impatient to assume the world.
73	WL: Thund	381	And crawled head downward down a blackened wall/And upside down in air were
134	Wind	7	else/When the surface of the blackened river/Is a face that sweats with tears?/
134	Wind	9	sweats with tears?/I saw across the blackened river/The camp fire shake with alien

BLACKMAIL (7)
541	ES Gomez	16	you would accuse an old friend of ... blackmail!/On the contrary, I dare say I could
541	ES Gomez	25	Dick, you owe me an apology./Blackmail! On the contrary/Any time you're in
567	ES Charles	21	what I could do to help him./If it's blackmail, and that's very much what it looks
567	ES Monica	23	/{M} Oh Charles! How could anyone blackmail Father?/Father, of all people the most
569	ES Charles	20	that if there's any question of blackmail,/I've seen something of it in my
569	ES Ld Clav	25	the best man to advise you./{LC} Blackmail? Yes, I've heard that word before,/
569	ES Ld Clav	30	she's a rich woman./If people merely blackmail you to get your company/I'm afraid

BLAME (11)
297	FR Charles	15	her over?/{C} In any case, I shouldn't blame Harry./I might have done the same thing
401	CP Edward	36	opinion./{E} It's not for me to blame you for bringing my wife back,/I
413	CP Reilly	7	they think that someone else is to blame./{C} I at least have no one to blame but
413	CP Celia	8	to blame./{C} I at least have no one to blame but myself./{R} And after that, the
428	CP Alex	13	And do not want them killed. So they blame the Government/For the damage that the
438	CP Reilly	35	you think her death was waste/You blame yourselves, and because you blame
438	CP Reilly	35	blame yourselves, and because you blame yourselves/You think her life was wasted.

490 CC   Colby   34   /But you chose not to be. I don't blame you for that:/God forbid! but we must
556 ES   Michael 31   made up your mind that I was to blame/Before you knew the facts. The first thing
556 ES   Michael 34   /I never got over that. If you always blame a person/It's natural he should end by
557 ES   Ld Clav   4   ignore, if you please, the question of blame:/Which will spare you the necessity of

BLAMED (1)
556 ES   Michael 33   The first thing I remember/Is being blamed for something I hadn't done./I never got

BLAMING (2)
438 CP   Lavinia   39   you are./{L} Yet I know I shall go on blaming myself/For being so unkind to her ... so
557 ES   Ld Clav   5   /Which will spare you the necessity of blaming someone else./Just tell me what's

BLANCHED (1)
191 FQ: Little   15   covenant. Now the hedgerow/Is blanched for an hour with transitory blossom/

BLAND (2)
220 Old Deut   9   /At the sight of that placid and bland physiognomy,/When he sits in the sun on
603 Spleen   12   and gray,/Languid, fastidious, and bland,/Waits, hat and gloves in hand,/

BLANK (2)
62 WL: Burial   53   merchant, and this card,/Which is blank, is something he carries on his back,/
310 FR   Harry   38   corridor only led to another,/Or to a blank wall; that I kept moving/Only so as not to

BLANKET (1)
22 Preludes   24   furnished rooms./You tossed a blanket from the bed,/You lay upon your back,

BLASPHEMING (1)
267 MC Thomas   6   said so urgent, is it only/Scolding and blaspheming?/{K1} That was only/Our

BLAST (1)
67 WL: Fire S   185   or long./But at my back in a cold blast I hear/The rattle of the bones, and chuckle

BLAVATSKY (1)
44 Cook Egg   22   not want Pipit in Heaven:/Madame Blavatsky will instruct me/In the Seven Sacred

BLAZE (3)
191 FQ: Little   9   /And glow more intense than blaze of branch, or brazier,/Stirs the dumb
291 FR   Harry   19   Denman./{H} How can you sit in this blaze of light for all the world to look at?/If you
531 ES   Monica   4   gloom!/You know you've retired in a blaze of glory —/You've read every word about

BLAZING (1)
223 Pekes Pols   52   /His eyes were like fireballs fearfully blazing,/He gave a great yawn, and his jaws

BLEAT (1)
220 Old Deut   19   may bellow, the sheep they may bleat,/But the dogs and the herdsmen will turn

BLEED (2)
275 MC Chorus   24   barren boughs: if I break them, they bleed; I wander in a land of dry stones: if I
275 MC Chorus   24   of dry stones: if I touch them they bleed./How how can I ever return, to the soft

BLEEDING (1)
181 FQ: ECoker   151   the distempered part;/Beneath the bleeding hands we feel/The sharp compassion of

BLEISTEIN (1)
40 Burb Blei   t   season./Burbank with a Baedeker: Bleistein with a Cigar/Burbank crossed a little

BLEISTEIN'S (1)
40 Burb Blei   13   all the day./But this or such was Bleistein's way:/A saggy bending of the knees/

BLENDED (1)
273 MC Thomas   36   as in time results of many deeds are blended/So good and evil in the end become

BLESS (5)
98 Ash-Wed 6   7   twilight between birth and dying/(Bless me father) though I do not wish to wish
594 Grad 13   3   A guide to warn them, and a friend to bless/Before they leave thy care for lands
267 MC Knights   13   The King!/{K3} The King!/{3K} God bless him!/{T} Then let your new coat of loyalty
277 MC Knight3   17   will turn out. King Henry — God bless him — will have to/say, for reasons of
422 CP   Reilly   20   a journey./{R} Protector of travellers/Bless the road./{A} Watch over her in the desert.

BLESSED (8)
158 Rock 5   10   return to his hearth at nightfall: to be blessed with the gift of silence, and doze before
261 MC Thomas   11   martyrdom/of His first martyr, the blessed Stephen. Is it an accident, do you think,/
261 MC Thomas   39   our martyr of Canterbury,/the blessed Archbishop Elphege; because it is
275 MC Thomas   20   /{T} Now to Almighty God, to the Blessed Mary ever Virgin, to the blessed John
275 MC Thomas   20   the Blessed Mary ever Virgin, to the blessed John the Baptist, the holy apostles Peter
275 MC Thomas   20   holy apostles Peter and Paul, to the blessed martyr Denys, and to all the Saints, I
282 MC Chorus   18   upon us./Lord, have mercy upon us./Blessed Thomas, pray for us. {}/THE FAMILY
289 FR   Amy   21   family:/You can call it nothing but a blessed relief./{V} *I* call it providential./{I} Yet it

BLESSÈD (2)
89 Ash-Wed 1   21   are as they are and/I renounce the blessèd face/And renounce the voice/Because I
98 Ash-Wed 6   25   the other yew be shaken and reply./Blessèd sister, holy mother, spirit of the

BLESSING (5)
92 Ash-Wed 2   50   a tree in the cool of the day, with the blessing of sand,/Forgetting themselves and
251 MC Tempt3   38   favour would be an advantage,/Blessing of Pope powerful protection/In the

282	MC Chorus	5	we thank Thee/Who hast given such blessing to Canterbury./Forgive us, O Lord, we
282	MC Chorus	8	door and sit by the fire;/Who fear the blessing of God, the loneliness of the night of
583	ES Charles	22	strange./The dead has poured out a blessing on the living./{M} Age and decrepitude

BLESSINGS (1)

| 604 | Ode | 6 | in the strength/Of the hopes that thy blessings bestow,/From the hopes and |

BLEST (1)

| 55 | Mr E Sun | 28 | between/The staminate and pistillate,/Blest office of the epicene./Sweeney shifts from |

BLIMP'S (1)

| 230 | Bust Jones | 18 | season/He is found, not at *Fox's*, but *Blimp's*;/But he's frequently seen at the gay |

BLIND (10)

18	Portrait	22	not love it ... you knew? you are not blind!/How keen you are!)/To find a friend who
68	WL: Fire S	218	throbbing waiting,/I Tiresias, though blind, throbbing between two lives,/Old man
98	Ash-Wed 6	17	quail and the whirling plover/And the blind eye creates/The empty forms between the
196	FQ: Little	181	and abroad,/And of one who died blind and quiet,/Why should we celebrate/These
251	MC Tempt3	14	Henry the King. You look only/To blind assertion in isolation./That is a mistake./
256	MC Tempts	18	to unreality./This man is obstinate, blind, intent/On self-destruction,/Passing from
292	FR Ivy	36	to rack and ruin,/And he's nearly half blind. I've spoken to your mother/Time and
309	FR Mary	27	like the man who believes that he is blind/While he still sees the sunlight. I know
407	CP Lavinia	35	/{L} Really, Edward! Even if I'd been blind/There were plenty of people to let me
418	CP Reilly	28	until you get there;/You will journey blind. But the way leads towards possession/Of

BLINDED (1)

| 275 | MC Chorus | 23 | with blood./A rain of blood has blinded my eyes. Where is England? where is |

BLINDLY (1)

| 160 | Rock 7 | 3 | struggled in torment towards GOD/Blindly and vainly, for man is a vain thing, and |

BLINDNESS (1)

| 191 | FQ: Little | 8 | in a watery mirror/A glare that is blindness in the early afternoon./And glow |

BLINDS (2)

| 22 | Preludes | 10 | lots;/The showers beat/On broken blinds and chimney-pots,/And at the corner of |
| 291 | FR Amy | 23 | in town, where you have to close the blinds./There is no one to see you but our |

BLISS (2)

| 52 | Whispers | 20 | bust/Gives promise of pneumatic bliss./The couched Brazilian jaguar/Compels the |
| 272 | MC Thomas | 5 | be spared./I have had a tremor of bliss, a wink of heaven, a whisper,/And I would |

BLISTERED (1)

| 37 | Gerontion | 10 | in some estaminet of Antwerp,/Blistered in Brussels, patched and peeled in |

BLOCK (2)

| 23 | Preludes | 40 | the skies/That fade behind a city block,/Or trampled by insistent feet/At four and |
| 197 | FQ: Little | 228 | And any action/Is a step to the block, to the fire, down the sea's throat/Or to |

BLOOD (38)

49	Hippopot	4	so firm to us/He is merely flesh and blood./Flesh and blood is weak and frail,/
49	Hippopot	5	is merely flesh and blood./Flesh and blood is weak and frail,/Susceptible to nervous
50	Hippopot	29	/The praise of God, in loud hosannas./Blood of the Lamb shall wash him clean/And
74	WL: Thund	402	what have we given?/My friend, blood shaking my heart/The awful daring of a
107	Animula	28	good,/Denying the importunity of the blood,/Shadow of its own shadows, spectre in
143	Lines OM	5	the enemy/Writhing in the essential blood/Or dangling from the friendly tree./When
159	Rock 6	27	was not crucified once for all,/The blood of the martyrs not shed once for all,/The
159	Rock 6	31	shall be Martyrs and Saints./And if blood of Martyrs is to flow on the steps/We
167	Rock 10	39	to sleep,/Controlled by the rhythm of blood and the day and the night and the
172	FQ: BurntN	51	axle-tree./The trilling wire in the blood/Sings below inveterate scars/Appeasing
182	FQ: ECoker	169	and the smoke is briars./The dripping blood our only drink,/The bloody flesh our only
182	FQ: ECoker	172	we are sound, substantial flesh and blood —/Again, in spite of that, we call this
601	Nocturne	9	and the lady sinks into a swoon./Blood looks effective on the moonlit ground —/
606	Narcissus	37	surrendered itself to the redness of blood, and satisfied him./Now he is green, dry
260	MC Thomas	10	and/offer again to God His Body and Blood in sacrifice, oblation and satisfaction/for
264	MC Priest3	18	/They sang as it were a new song./The blood of thy saints have they shed like water,/
264	MC Priest3	20	to bury them. Avenge, O Lord,/The blood of thy saints. In Rama, a voice heard,
266	MC Knights	20	crawled upon the King; swollen with blood and swollen with pride./Creeping out of
274	MC Knights	20	of the beast./Are you washed in the blood of the Lamb?/Are you marked with the
274	MC Thomas	32	am a priest,/A Christian, saved by the blood of Christ,/Ready to suffer with my blood.
274	MC Thomas	33	of Christ,/Ready to suffer with my blood./This is the sign of the Church always,/
274	MC Thomas	35	of the Church always,/The sign of blood. Blood for blood./His blood given to buy
274	MC Thomas	35	Church always,/The sign of blood. Blood for blood./His blood given to buy my
274	MC Thomas	35	always,/The sign of blood. Blood for blood./His blood given to buy my life,/My
274	MC Thomas	36	sign of blood. Blood for blood./His blood given to buy my life,/My blood given to
275	MC Thomas	1	/His blood given to buy my life,/My blood given to pay for His death,/My death for
275	MC Chorus	22	our beasts and ourselves defiled with blood./A rain of blood has blinded my eyes.

275 MC Chorus 23   defiled with blood./A rain of blood has blinded my eyes. Where is England?
275 MC Chorus 27 things, and see them all smeared with blood, through a curtain of falling blood?/We
275 MC Chorus 27   blood, through a curtain of falling blood?/We did not wish anything to happen./
281 MC Chorus 17   /We thank Thee for Thy mercies of blood, for Thy redemption by blood. For the
281 MC Chorus 17   of blood, for Thy redemption by blood. For the blood of Thy martyrs and saints/
281 MC Chorus 17 for Thy redemption by blood. For the blood of Thy martyrs and saints/Shall enrich
281 MC Chorus 19   wherever a martyr has given his blood for the blood of Christ,/There is holy
281 MC Chorus 19   a martyr has given his blood for the blood of Christ,/There is holy ground, and the
282 MC Chorus 13 the world is upon our heads; that the blood of the martyrs and the agony of the saints
310 FR   Harry   9 in the wood./{H} Spring is an issue of blood/A season of sacrifice/And the wail of the
382 CP   Celia 18 /And listened for your heart, your blood;/And saw only a beetle the size of a man/
BLOOD-CURDLING (1)
229 Gus   42 can, much better than most,/Produce blood-curdling noises to bring on the Ghost./
BLOODY (3)
57 Swee Night   37   Sacred Heart,/And sang within the bloody wood/When Agamemnon cried aloud/
182 FQ: ECoker 170 dripping blood our only drink,/The bloody flesh our only food:/In spite of which we
605 Narcissus   6   the red rock:/I will show you his bloody cloth and limbs/And the gray shadow
BLOOM (5)
18 Portrait   12 two or three, who will not touch the bloom/That is rubbed and questioned in the
19 Portrait   41   our bocks./Now that lilacs are in bloom/She has a bowl of lilacs in her room/And
63 WL: Burial   72 /'Has it begun to sprout? Will it bloom this year?/'Or has the sudden frost
191 FQ: Little 16 with transitory blossom/Of snow, a bloom more sudden/Than that of summer,
597 Before Mor   7   the room at dawn,/Fragrance of bloom and fragrance of decay,/Fresh flowers,
BLOOMED (1)
596 When we   5   cobweb down./The hedgerow bloomed with flowers still,/No withered petals
BLOOMING (1)
105 Song Sime   1 /Lord, the Roman hyacinths are blooming in bowls and/The winter sun creeps
BLOOMSBURY (1)
236 Cat Morgan   4   my ease/And keepin' the door in a Bloomsbury Square./I'm partial to partridges,
BLOSSOM (2)
92 Ash-Wed 3   14 fig's fruit/And beyond the hawthorn blossom and a pasture scene/The broadbacked
191 FQ: Little 15 blanched for an hour with transitory blossom/Of snow, a bloom more sudden/Than
BLOSSOM- (1)
138 New Hamp   2   voices in the orchard/Between the blossom- and the fruit-time:/Golden head,
BLOSSOMS (2)
247 MC Tempt1   10 in the branches/Shall float as sweet as blossoms. Ice along the ditches/Mirror the
303 FR   Mary   5 I had rather wait for our windblown blossoms,/Such as they are, than have these
BLOW (1)
349 FR   5m 13   *clockwise./At each revolution they blow out a few candles, so that their last/words*
BLOWING (1)
195 FQ: Little 151 kind of valediction,/And faded on the blowing of the horn./There are three conditions
BLOWN (6)
17 Prufrock   127 /Combing the white hair of the waves blown back/When the wind blows the water
92 Ash-Wed 3   17   the maytime with an antique flute./Blown hair is sweet, brown hair over the mouth
92 Ash-Wed 3   17 is sweet, brown hair over the mouth blown,/Lilac and brown hair;/Distraction,
108 Animula   33   of speed and power,/For Boudin, blown to pieces,/For this one who made a great
193 FQ: Little 89 walking, loitering and hurried/As if blown towards me like the metal leaves/Before
325 FR   Violet 35 an open car/Is so undignified: you're blown about so,/And you feel so conspicuous,
BLOWS (2)
17 Prufrock   128 the waves blown back/When the wind blows the water white and black./We have
174 FQ: BurntN 108 paper, whirled by the cold wind/That blows before and after time,/Wind in and out of
BLUE (10)
92 Ash-Wed 3   15 scene/The broadbacked figure drest in blue and green/Enchanted the maytime with an
94 Ash-Wed 4   4   of varied green/Going in white and blue, in Mary's colour,/Talking of trivial things/
94 Ash-Wed 4   10 dry rock and made firm the sand/In blue of larkspur, blue of Mary's colour,/
94 Ash-Wed 4   10   firm the sand/In blue of larkspur, blue of Mary's colour,/Sovegna vos/Here are
94 Ash-Wed 4   22 /The silent sister veiled in white and blue/Between the yews, behind the garden god,/
97 Ash-Wed 5   33 /In the last desert between the last blue rocks/The desert in the garden the garden
98 Ash-Wed 6   22 where three dreams cross/Between blue rocks/But when the voices shaken from the
213 Growltiger 36 shone reflected from a hundred bright blue eyes./And closer still and closer the
223 Pekes Pols 37 their pipers in order,/Playing *When the Blue Bonnets Came Over the Border.*/Then the
588 Fable   63 /The lights began to burn distinctly blue,/As in ghost stories lights most always do./
BLUE-NAILED (1)
41 Burb Blei   26 /Princess Volupine extends/A meagre, blue-nailed, phthisic hand/To climb the

BLUNDER (1)
301 FR   Violet   23   /{V} Gerald is certain to make some blunder, he is useless out of the army./{C} Violet
BLUNDERER (1)
401 CP   Edward 11   /I beg your pardon. But he *is* a blunderer./I should like to know ... but what is
BLUNTNESS (1)
250 MC Tempt3 35   parasites/About the King. Excuse my bluntness:/I am a rough straightforward
BOAR (2)
172 FQ: BurntN 61   floor/Below, the boarhound and the boar/Pursue their pattern as before/But
273 MC Priests 27   the lion, the leopard, the wolf or the boar,/Why not more/Against beasts with the
BOAR'S (1)
588 Fable   55   which they kept under cover./Last, a boar's head, which to bring in took four pages,/
BOARDING-HOUSE (1)
406 CP   Edward 34   /Then I'll go and be ill in a suburban boarding-house./{L} That would never suit you,
BOARDS (1)
480 CC Kaghan 31   to be a power in the City,/On the boards of all the solidest companies:/Because
BOARHOUND (2)
108 Animula   36   his own way./Pray for Floret, by the boarhound slain between the yew trees,/Pray for
172 FQ: BurntN 61   upon the sodden floor/Below, the boarhound and the boar/Pursue their pattern as
BOARS (1)
588 Fable   34 with holy water,/The turkeys, capons, boars, they were to eat,/He even soakt the
BOAST (2)
159 Rock 6   12 such modest attainments/As you can boast in the way of polite society/Will hardly
236 Cat Morgan 15 yet I can state, and I'm not one to boast,/That some of the gals is dead keen on old
BOAT (3)
74 WL: Thund 418   Coriolanus/DA/*Damyata:* The boat responded/Gaily, to the hand expert with
186 FQ: DrySal 66   pass for devotionless,/In a drifting boat with a slow leakage,/The silent listening to
297 FR   Charles 12   discreet./He was with them on the boat. He might be of use./{I} Charles! you don't
BOATMAN (1)
41 Burb Blei   24   the lot./Money in furs. The boatman smiles,/Princess Volupine extends/A
BOB-WHITE (1)
142 Cape Ann   6 shrill whistle the note of the quail, the bob-white/Dodging by bay-bush. Follow the
BOBTAIL (1)
137 5FingerEx5   9 unpleasant to meet Mr. Eliot!/With a bobtail cur/In a coat of fur/And a porpentine
BOCKS (1)
19 Portrait   40   sit for half an hour and drink our bocks./Now that lilacs are in bloom/She has a
BODIES (6)
31 Apollinax   11   under coral islands/Where worried bodies of drowned men drift down in the green
67 WL: Fire S 193 my father's death before him./White bodies naked on the low damp ground/And
162 Rock 8   18 rapacious and lustful./Many left their bodies to the kites of Syria/Or sea-strewn along
188 FQ: DrySal 166   who come to port, and you whose bodies/Will suffer the trial and judgement of the
206 To my Wife   5   breathing in unison/Of lovers whose bodies smell of each other/Who think the same
269 MC Knight1 24   name./{K1} Or answer with your bodies./{K2} Enough of words./{4K} We come
BODILY (1)
167 Rock 10   44   thereon little lights for which our bodily vision is made./And we thank Thee that
BODY (19)
33 Conv Gal   10   moonshine; music which we seize/To body forth our own vacuity.'/She then: 'Does
34 Figlia   11   would have left/As the soul leaves the body torn and bruised,/As the mind deserts the
34 Figlia   12   and bruised,/As the mind deserts the body it has used./I should find/Some way
152 Rock 2   43   of GOD,/Prays for the Church, the Body of Christ incarnate./And now you live
165 Rock 9   32   creating./For Man is joined spirit and body,/And therefore must serve as spirit and
165 Rock 9   33 And therefore must serve as spirit and body./Visible and invisible, two worlds meet in
165 Rock 9   36   His Temple;/You must not deny the body./Now you shall see the Temple completed:
173 FQ: BurntN 82   in the weakness of the changing body,/Protects mankind from heaven and
194 FQ: Little 127   I should revisit/When I left my body on a distant shore./Since our concern was
194 FQ: Little 136 bitter tastelessness of shadow fruit/As body and soul begin to fall asunder./Second, the
602 Humoresque 3   yet tired of the game —/But weak in body as in head,/(A jumping-jack has such a
260 MC Thomas 10   of men, and/offer again to God His Body and Blood in sacrifice, oblation and
273 MC Priests 25   the sanctuary, who kneel to the Body of Christ,/But like beasts. You would bar
289 FR   Ivy 26   storm,/And never even to recover the body./{C} 'Well-known Peeress Vanishes from
343 FR   Amy 29 Why should I?/It is no concern of the body in the tomb/To bother about the upkeep.
363 CP   Reilly   2   actors;/All there is of you is your body/And the 'you' is withdrawn. May I
404 CP   Edward 14   /I am not afraid of the death of the body,/But this death is terrifying. The death of
434 CP   Alex   19   survived. And then they found her body,/Or at least, they found the traces of it./
437 CP   Reilly 38   together —/And reluctance of the body to become a *thing.*/I'd say she suffered

BOILED (1)
376 CP   Edward 15   eggs:/I wanted one for breakfast. A boiled egg./It's the only thing I know how to

BOILER (2)
369 CP   Alex   7   /{A} Edward, have you a double boiler?/{E} I suppose there must be a double
369 CP   Edward 8 /{E} I suppose there must be a double boiler:/Isn't there one in every kitchen?/{A} I

BOLD (7)
  42 Swee Erect   3   the unstilled Cyclades,/Paint me the bold anfractuous rocks/Faced by the snarled
  68 WL: Fire S 232 /A small house agent's clerk, with one bold stare,/One of the low on whom assurance
180 FQ: ECoker 118   trees, the distant panorama/And the bold imposing façade are all being rolled away
223 Pekes Pols 46   all over the Park./Now when these bold heroes together assembled,/The traffic all
268 MC Thomas 36   that *is* the King's command, I will be bold/To say: seven years were my people
274 MC Thomas 29   /{T} It is the just man who/Like a bold lion, should be without fear./I am here./No
299 FRDowning 27   irresponsible, Sir./If I may make so bold, Sir,/I always thought that a very few

BOLDLY (1)
107 Animula   6   at kisses and toys,/Advancing boldly, sudden to take alarm,/Retreating to the

BOLOGOLOMSKY (1)
430 CP   Peter 20   saw me off./You remember Princess Bologolomsky/In the old days? We dined the

BOLOGOLOMSKYS (1)
430 CP   Peter 19   York./{P} Yes, from New York./The Bologolomskys saw me off./You remember

BOLSTERED (1)
393 CP   Lavinia 30   only passivity;/You only wanted to be bolstered, encouraged..../{E} Encouraged? To

BOLT (1)
256 MC   Priests 30   made fast, is the door under lock and bolt?/{4T} Is it rain that taps at the window, is it

BOLTED (1)
589 Fable   65   do./The doors, though barred and bolted most securely,/Gave way — my

BOLTWELL (9)
431 CP   Peter 13 hands full/I'm going down tonight, to Boltwell./{J} To stay with the Duke?/{P} And do
431 CP   Peter 17   of English life/And we want to use Boltwell./{J} But I understood that Boltwell/Is
431 CP   Julia   18   Boltwell./{J} But I understood that Boltwell/Is in a very decayed condition./{P}
431 CP   Peter 25   reproduce it./Then we build another Boltwell in California./{J} But what is your
431 CP   Peter 30 /He thought I should see the original Boltwell;/And besides, he thought that as I'm
433 CP   Julia   4   do it./{J} But, Peter;/If you're taking Boltwell to California/Why can't you take me?/
433 CP   Peter   6   you take me?/{P} We're not taking Boltwell./We reconstruct a Boltwell./{J} Very
433 CP   Peter   7 not taking Boltwell./We reconstruct a Boltwell./{J} Very well, then:/Why not
439 CP   Julia   13 /Peter chose a way that leads him to Boltwell:/And he's got to go there .../{P} I see

BOMB-SITE (1)
474 CC Lucasta 26   yourself in a devastated area —/A bomb-site ... willow-herb ... a dirty public

BOMBALURINA (1)
209 NamingCats 19   Quaxo, or Coricopat,/Such as Bombalurina, or else Jellylorum —/Names that

BOND (4)
  44 Cook Egg   16   lapt/In a five per cent. Exchequer Bond./I shall not want Society in Heaven,/
410 CP   Reilly 12   one another./{R} See it rather as the bond which holds you together./While still in a
490 CC Lady E 27   different?/There should always be a bond between mother and son,/No matter how
537 ES   Gomez 10   there should always have been this bond between us?/{LC} It has never crossed my

BONDAGE (1)
301 FR Chorus 27   exception/To the universal bondage./We like to appear in the newspapers/

BONE (11)
  52 Whispers   16   to flesh/Allayed the fever of the bone./Grishkin is nice: her Russian eye/Is
141 Rannoch   10 silence. Memory is strong/Beyond the bone. Pride snapped,/Shadow of pride is long,
141 Rannoch   12   in the long pass/No concurrence of bone./Cape Ann/O quick quick quick, quick
177 FQ: ECoker   8 Which is already flesh, fur and faeces,/Bone of man and beast, cornstalk and leaf./
185 FQ: DrySal 55   drifting wreckage,/The prayer of the bone on the beach, the unprayable/Prayer at the
201 Def Island 10 share to the ages' pavement/of British bone on the sea floor/and of those who, in
247 MC Templ1 38 goose may be cooked and eaten to the bone./{T} You come twenty years too late./{T1}
276 MC Chorus 17   the arm, take the muscle from the bone, and wash them. Wash the stone, wash the
276 MC Chorus 17 wash them. Wash the stone, wash the bone, wash the brain, wash the soul, wash them
294 FR   Harry 24   the flesh and discolouring the bone —/This is what matters, but it is
335 FR   Harry 15 of putrescent embraces/On dissolving bone. In and out, the movement/Until the chain

BONE'S (1)
186 FQ: DrySal 85   sea and the drifting wreckage,/The bone's prayer to Death its God. Only the

BONES (16)
  65 WL: Chess 116   alley/Where the dead men lost their bones./'What is that noise?'/The wind under the
  67 WL: Fire S 186 in a cold blast I hear/The rattle of the bones, and chuckle spread from ear to ear./A
  67 WL: Fire S 194 naked on the low damp ground/And bones cast in a little low dry garret,/Rattled by
  71 WL: DWater316 loss./A current under sea/Picked his bones in whispers. As he rose and fell/He passed

74 WL: Thund	390	windows, and the door swings,/Dry bones can harm no one./Only a cock stood on
91 Ash-Wed 2	5	of my skull. And God said/Shall these bones live? shall these/Bones live? And that
91 Ash-Wed 2	6	said/Shall these bones live? shall these/Bones live? And that which had been contained/
91 Ash-Wed 2	7	that which had been contained/in the bones (which were already dry) said chirping:/
91 Ash-Wed 2	18	in a white gown./Let the whiteness of bones atone to forgetfulness./There is no life in
91 Ash-Wed 2	23	for only/The wind will listen. And the bones sang chirping/With the burden of the
92 Ash-Wed 2	48	all love ends./Under a juniper-tree the bones sang, scattered and shining/We are glad
122 SA	2m 15	/SWARTS AS TAMBO. SNOW AS BONES/{W&H} *Under the bamboo/Bamboo*
124 SA Snow	20	pinched in the end./What about them bones on Epsom Heath?/I seen that in the
230 Bust Jones	1	/Bustopher Jones is *not* skin and bones —/In fact, he's remarkably fat./He
230 Bust Jones	22	ben'son/To the *Pothunter's* succulent bones;/And just before noon's not a moment
316 FR Agatha	14	/Become unknotted/May the crossed bones/In the filled-up well/Be at last

BONFIRE (1)

177 FQ: ECoker	28	/And see them dancing around the bonfire/The association of man and woman/In

BONNETS (2)

223 Pekes Pols	37	pipers in order,/Playing *When the Blue Bonnets Came Over the Border./*Then the Pugs
603 Spleen	3	procession/Of definite Sunday faces;/Bonnets, silk hats, and conscious graces/In

BONUS (1)

129 Cor2 State	14	/To two pounds ten a week; with a bonus of thirty shillings at Christmas/And one

BOO (3)

122 SAWa & Ho	22	live as three/Under the bam/Under the boo/Under the bamboo tree./Where the breadfruit
122 SAWa & Ho	28	of the sea/Under the bam/Under the boo/Under the bamboo tree/Where the Gauguin
122 SAWa & Ho	34	drapery/Under the bam/Under the boo/Under the bamboo tree./Tell me in what part

BOOK (15)

187 FQ: DrySal	130	/Pressed between yellow leaves of a book that has never been opened./And the way
207	t	to you in public./OLD POSSUM'S BOOK OF PRACTICAL CATS/The Naming
334 FR Harry	27	find another one made ready —/The book laid out, lines underscored, and the
399 CP 5m	1	*enters, with Appointment/Book.*/{R} About those three appointments this
418 CP Reilly	1	/And the other life will be only like a book/You have read once, and lost. In a world
448 CC Claude	10	in Light from the East./{SC} And the Book of Revelation? And the Wisdom of
522 ES dedic	8	of meaning:/To you I dedicate this book, to return as best I can/With words a little
529 ES Ld Clav	21	been doing. Don't you recognise this book?/{M} It's your engagement book./{LC}
529 ES Monica	22	this book?/{M} It's your engagement book./{LC} Yes, I've been brooding over it./{M}
529 ES Monica	24	But what a time for your engagement book!/You know what the doctors said:
529 ES Ld Clav	31	my breakfast,/I have looked at this book — or one just like it —/You know I keep
529 ES Ld Clav	33	together;/I could look in the right book, and find out what I was doing/Twenty
529 ES Ld Clav	35	I've been looking at this engagement book, to-day,/Not over breakfast, but before
578 ES Michael	26	sitting there with your nose in a book./And once, Mother snatched a book away
578 ES Michael	27	a book./And once, Mother snatched a book away from you/And tossed it into the fire.

BOOKING (1)

530 ES Ld Clav	23	other passengers/Have left, and the booking office is closed/And the porters have

BOOKS (4)

154 Rock 3	13	action./Many are engaged in writing books and printing them,/Many desire to see
156 Rock 3	68	/Engaged in printing as many books as possible,/Plotting of happiness and
158 Rock 5	8	others./And they write innumerable books; being too vain and distracted for silence:
309 FR Mary	18	doesn't come from tutors/Or from books, or from thinking, or from observation:/

BOOT (1)

239 MC Chorus	12	While the labourer kicks off a muddy boot and stretches his hand to the fire,/The New

BOOZE (1)

125 SA Sweeney	25	do/We're gona sit here and drink this booze/We're gona sit here and have a tune/

BORDEAUX (2)

119 SP Krum	19	Sam?/What about that poker game in Bordeaux?/Yes Miss Dorrance you get Sam/To
119 SP Krum	21	Sam/To tell about that poker game in Bordeaux./{Du} Do you know London well,

BORDER (3)

24 Rhapsody	19	opens on her like a grin./You see the border of her dress/Is torn and stained with
223 Pekes Pols	37	*When the Blue Bonnets Came Over the Border./*Then the Pugs and the Poms held no
342 FR Agatha	36	/Of tempting them over the border? No one could, no one who knows./No

BORE (2)

70 WL: Fire S	293	/'Trams and dusty trees./Highbury bore me. Richmond and Kew/Undid me. By
214 RTTugger	12	it!/The Rum Tum Tugger is a terrible bore:/When you let him in, then he wants to be

BORED (7)

68 WL: Fire S	236	he guesses,/The meal is ended, she is bored and tired,/Endeavours to engage her in
111 Xmas Trees	20	forgotten in later experience,/In the bored habituation, the fatigue, the tedium,/The
122 SA Doris	4	copulation, and death./{Do} I'd be bored./{S} You'd be bored./Birth, and
122 SA Sweeney	5	/{Do} I'd be bored./{S} You'd be bored./Birth, and copulation, and death./{Do}

122 SA	Doris	7	copulation, and death./{Do} I'd be bored./{S} You'd be bored./Birth, and
122 SA	Sweeney	8	/{Do} I'd be bored./{S} You'd be bored./Birth, and copulation, and death./That's
601 Nocturne		4	in the usual debate/Of love, beneath a bored but courteous moon;/The conversation

BORGIA (1)

44 Cook Egg		18	not want Society in Heaven,/Lucretia Borgia shall be my Bride;/Her anecdotes will be

BORING (1)

428 CP	Alex	31	the real problem. I hope I'm not boring you?/{E} No indeed: we are anxious to

BORN (19)

122 SA	Sweeney	12	and copulation, and death./I've been born, and once is enough./You don't remember,
151 Rock 2		5	in a ruined house?/Where many are born to idleness, to frittered lives and squalid
197 FQ: Little		232	depart, and we go with them./We are born with the dead:/See, they return, and bring
240 MC Chorus		23	you?/Shall the Son of Man be born again in the litter of scorn?/For us, the
266 MC Knights		19	son: the backstairs brat who was born in Cheapside;/This is the creature that
333 FR	Agatha	2	time;/You would not have been born in that event: I stopped him./I can take no
480 CC	Kaghan	1	/{K} Marriage is a gamble. But I'm a born gambler/And I've put my shirt ... no, not
480 CC	Kaghan	27	about being respectable —He was born and bred to it. I wasn't, Colby./Do you
483 CC	Colby	38	my mother./She died when I was born./{LE} She died when you were born./Have
484 CC	Lady E	1	born./{LE} She died when you were born./Have you other near relatives? Brothers
489 CC	Claude	20	sister,/Who died when he was born. Mrs. Guzzard brought him up,/And I
489 CC	Lady E	25	were you, Claude,/When Colby was born?/{SC} Where was I? In Canada./My father
490 CC	Colby	33	it means nothing./At the time I was born, you might have been my mother,/But you
490 CC	Colby	36	consequences./At the time when I was born, your being my mother —/If you are my
513 CC	Colby	27	he would have died before I was born/Or before I could remember; whom I
514 CC Guzzard		24	of death. The child was never born./{SC} I don't believe it. I simply can't
515 CC Guzzard		3	sister died/Before the child could be born. You were very far away;/I sent you a
571 ES Ld Clav		16	may nourish the faults that they were born with./And Maisie loved me, with whatever
583 ES Monica		9	of the world./Before you and I were born, the love was always there/That brought us

BORNE (3)

263 MC	1m	27	PRIEST *with a banner of St. Stephen borne before him.*/*The lines sung are in italics.*]/
264 MC	m	7	*with a banner of St. John the Apostle borne before him.*]/{P2} Since St. Stephen a day:
264 MC	m	14	*with a banner of the Holy Innocents borne before him.*]/{P3} Since St. John the

BORROW (2)

21 Portrait		109	serving tea to friends.'/And I must borrow every changing shape/To find
253 MC Tempt4		10	the man who has been his friend./Borrow use cautiously, employ/Your services as

BORROWED (2)

557 ES Michael		20	make anything of it. If I could have borrowed more/I might have pulled it off./{LC}
557 ES Ld Clav		22	more/I might have pulled it off./{LC} Borrowed? From whom?/Not ... from the firm?/

BOSS (2)

431 CP	Peter	8	/{P} Why, Bela Szogody —/He's my boss. I thought everyone knew *his* name./{J} Is
452 CC Lucasta		18	yesterday./Then, just by bad luck, the boss did want a letter/And I couldn't find it.

BOSTON (4)

28 Boston ET		t	along the level of the roofs./The Boston Evening Transcript/The readers of the
28 Boston ET		1	Evening Transcript/The readers of the *Boston Evening Transcript*/Sway in the wind like
28 Boston ET		5	life in some/And to others bringing the *Boston Evening Transcript*,/I mount the steps and
28 Boston ET		9	/And I say, 'Cousin Harriet, here is the *Boston Evening Transcript*.'/Aunt Helen/Miss

BOSUN (1)

212 Growltiger		27	he had gone to wet his beard;/And his bosun, TUMBLEBRUTUS, he too had stol'n

BOTH (95)

23 Preludes		38	yellow soles of feet/In the palms of both soiled hands./His soul stretched tight
34 Figlia		15	light and deft,/Some way we both should understand,/Simple and faithless as
70 WL: Fire S		285	Red and gold/The brisk swell/Rippled both shores/Southwest wind/Carried down
96 Ash-Wed 5		16	land,/For those who walk in darkness/Both in the day time and in the night time/The
119 SP	Wauch	3	you permit me —/I think you girls both know Captain Horsfall —/We want you to
125 SA Sweeney		8	was dead/He didn't know if they were both alive/or both were dead/If he was alive
125 SA Sweeney		9	didn't know if they were both alive/or both were dead/If he was alive then the
161 Rock 7		28	has never happened before/That men both deny gods and worship gods, professing
171 FQ: BurntN		2	/Time present and time past/Are both perhaps present in time future/And time
173 FQ: BurntN		77	concentration/Without elimination, both a new world/And the old made explicit,
193 FQ: Little		96	I had known, forgotten, half recalled/Both one and many; in the brown baked
193 FQ: Little		98	eyes of a familiar compound ghost/Both intimate and unidentifiable./So I assumed
194 FQ: Little		118	/By others, as I pray you to forgive/Both bad and good. Last season's fruit is eaten/
219 Mung Rump		33	you have sworn that it mightn't be both?/And when you heard a dining-room
230 Bust Jones		15	the rules/For any one Cat to belong both to that/And the *Joint Superior Schools.*/
234 Ad-dress		13	described in verse./You've seen them both at work and games,/And learnt about their
588 Fable		49	things./A mighty peacock standing on both legs/With difficulty kept from toppling

245 MC	Thomas	16	agent suffer/Nor the patient act. But both are fixed/In an eternal action, an eternal
255 MC	Tempt4	39	agent suffer/Nor the patient act. But both are fixed/In an eternal action, an eternal
260 MC	Thomas	17	/fashion. For who in the World will both mourn and rejoice at once and/for the
261 MC	Thomas	15	Lord; so also, in a smaller figure, we/both rejoice and mourn in the death of martyrs.
266 MC	Thomas	25	his King./{T} This is not true./Both before and after I received the ring/I have
276 MC	Knight1	25	not judge anybody without/hearing both sides of the case. That is in accordance
281 MC	Chorus	8	in the storm; in all of Thy creatures, both the hunters and the hunted./For all things
281 MC	Chorus	12	Thee in living; the bird in the air, both the hawk and the finch; the beast on the
281 MC	Chorus	12	and the finch; the beast on the earth, both the wolf and the lamb; the worm in the soil
287 FR	Amy	36	John in Leicestershire:/They should both be here in good time for dinner./Harry
297 FR	Violet	34	wish to express my emphatic protest/Both against your purpose and the means you
302 FR	Amy	13	/{A} It is very annoying. They both promised to be here/In good time for
302 FR	Amy	17	what could have gone wrong/With both of them, coming from different directions./
314 FR	Warburt	7	to come./{W} I dare say we've both changed a good deal, Harry./A country
336 FR	Agatha	25	to being/As a child is formed./In both, the incredible/Becomes the actual/
346 FR	Charles	5	like that, if one were awake?/You both seem to know more about this than I do. {}
353 CP	Celia	13	no tigers./{C} Oh do stop wrangling,/Both of you. It's your turn, Julia./Do tell us
355 CP	Julia	33	know the Vincewells./{J} Oh, they're both dead now. But I wanted to know./If they'd
366 CP	Julia	26	Good-bye then./And thank you — both of you — very much. {}/[Exit]/{P} I hope
367 CP	Peter	13	had a great deal in common./We're both of us artists./{E} I never thought of that./
367 CP	Peter	18	But it's more the cinema that interests both of us./{E} A common interest in the
368 CP	Edward	2	open./{E} Never mind;/So long as you both shut it when you go out./{A} Ah, but
370 CP	Peter	30	experience/In which we were both unaware of ourselves./In your terms,
377 CP	Julia	34	early, to go to a restaurant./You must both come home with me./{E} No, I'm sorry,
388 CP	Edward	21	I don't know. Perhaps./{E} You're both going away! {}/[Enter LAVINIA]/{L}
389 CP	Lavinia	3	that what I heard?/I congratulate you. To Hollywood, of course?/How exciting
405 CP	Reilly	31	Mr. Chamberlayne./Sit down, please, both of you. Mrs. Chamberlayne,/Your
407 CP	Reilly	6	interesting discussion?/I say you are both too ill. There are several symptoms/Which
407 CP	Reilly	13	you, Lavinia./{R} I congratulate you both on your perspicacity./Your sympathetic
407 CP	Reilly	20	/Yet never quite successful. You have both of you pretended/To be consulting me;
407 CP	Reilly	21	you pretended/To be consulting me; both, tried to impose upon me/Your own
407 CP	Reilly	29	that. All that you have told me —/Both of you — was true enough: you described
409 CP	Reilly	6	me./{R} Now, I want to point out to both of you/How much you have in common.
418 CP	Reilly	34	is better?/{R} Neither way is better./Both ways are necessary. It is also necessary/To
419 CP	Reilly	3	means loneliness — and communion./Both ways avoid the final desolation/Of solitude
432 CP	Julia	16	to interrupt Julia .../{J} But you're both interrupting!/{R} Who is interrupting now?
439 CP	Peter	32	you./I really do want to see you both, very much./Good-bye, Julia. Good-bye,
448 CC	Eggers	34	/{E} I'm sure it's been a grief to both of you/That you've never had children./
449 CC	Claude	25	And there are others./For one, they're both of them women./{E} True./{SC} But I
452 CC	Colby	33	suits me better?/{C} I'm sure they both suit you./{L} Snubbed again! I suppose I
458 CC	Lady E	17	it./I can't understand why you're both so surprised./You know I'm a very
461 CC	Colby	28	I'm sure that will make it easier for both of us./{SC} Her sudden arrival was very
463 CC	Claude	3	you alone./And then when I sent you both over to Canada/In the war — that was
464 CC	Claude	33	I was in awe of him./I was wrong, in both. I loathed this occupation/Until I began to
474 CC	Colby	1	to do with each other —/Well, they're both unreal. But for Eggerson/His garden is a
481 CC	Lucasta	7	to be in business together./{L} You're both very good at paying compliments;/But I
482 CC	Lady E	14	/You see, you're rather a curiosity/To both of them — you're not the sort of person/
482 CC	Colby	22	what is it you object to?/They're both intelligent ... and kind./{LE} Oh, I don't
490 CC	Colby	22	never can be filled. Never./I like you both, I could even come to love you —/But as
491 CC	Lady E	10	in some ways better! And prevent us both/From making unreasonable claims upon
491 CC	Claude	17	I had intended./Could you accept us both in that way, Colby?/{C} I can only say
491 CC	Colby	22	be easier, I think,/To accept you both in the place of parents/If neither of you
491 CC	Colby	36	the imputation/Of false parenthood. Both mocked at./{SC} Then what do you want,
495 CC	Claude	36	been a second-rate organist./We have both chosen ... obedience to the facts./{LE} I
497 CC	Lady E	38	things have happened./{LE} And both in Teddington?/{E} I agree, that would be
501 CC	Lucasta	5	/You think we're suited because we're both common./B. knows you think him
503 CC	Colby	17	my brother-in-law./I shall need you, both of you, Lucasta!/{L} We'll mean something
505 CC	Eggers	31	get to my age/The past and the future both seem very brief —/But long enough ago
517 CC	Colby	7	of father and son/Unless it works both ways. For you to regard me —/As you
519 CC	Kaghan	17	you .../I mean, I'm including both of you,/Claude ... and Aunt Elizabeth./
519 CC	Kaghan	19	Aunt Elizabeth./You know, Claude, both Lucasta and I/Would like to mean
532 ES	Charles	24	sir./And look forward to seeing you both at Badgley Court/In a week or two. {}/
532 ES	Ld Clav	28	And please remember/That we both want to see you, whenever you can come/If
532 ES	Monica	30	Father. {}/[To CHARLES]/{M} We both want to see you. {}/[Exeunt MONICA and
534 ES	Gomez	36	politics./Stay out of politics, and play both parties:/What you don't get from one you

536 ES	Gomez	40	can trust —/And one who will accept both Culverwell and Gomez —/See Culverwell
540 ES	Gomez	1	success, Dick. In another sense/We're both of us failures. But even so,/I'd rather be
548 ES	Carghil	24	to her father./I was watching you both in the dining-room last night./You are the
550 ES	Ld Clav	33	/Which I should have thought we both preferred to leave buried./{MC} There
551 ES	Carghil	16	past./You're wrong, you know. It's both pain and pleasure/To talk about the past
552 ES	Ld Clav	15	what a lucky escape/It had been, for both of us./{MC} That 'both of us'/Was an
552 ES	Carghil	16	had been, for both of us./{MC} That 'both of us'/Was an afterthought, Richard. A
554 ES	Carghil	26	find it a strain/To have to cope with both of us at once./Besides, I ought to do my
560 ES	Michael	14	/With an opportunity of profits both ways./{LC} This is what I will do for you,
570 ES	Ld Clav	20	in your life?/{LC} ... And yet they've both done better for themselves/In consequence
578 ES	Ld Clav	10	our failure/To understand each other, both misunderstood you/In our divergent ways.
581 ES	Charles	5	/And give all the aid we can. But it's both of you together/Make the force to attract
582 ES	Monica	39	.../{M} Was a shield protecting both of us .../{C} So that now we are conscious

BOTHER (8)

343 FR	Amy	30	concern of the body in the tomb/To bother about the upkeep. Let the wind and rain
375 CP	Edward	37	*room*]/{E} For heaven's sake, don't bother! {}/[*Exit* CELIA]/{E} Suppose someone
426 CP	Lavinia	2	right./That will do. I'm too tired to bother./{E} After they're all gone, we will have
426 CP	Lavinia	24	now. {}/[*The doorbell rings*]/{L} Oh, bother!/Now who would come so early? I
452 CC	Lucasta	22	all filed somewhere, I'm sure, so why bother?/But who's this, Eggy? Is it Colby
458 CC	Claude	33	quick decision./{SC} I didn't want to bother you, during your treatment .../{E} And
459 CC	Claude	17	closer at hand —/You know what a bother it's been for Eggerson —/So I'm having
532 ES	Monica	19	worthless./{M} You ought not to bother with such people now, Father./If you

BOTHERED (2)

233 Skimble		48	very nice/To know that you won't be bothered by mice —/You can leave all that to
560 ES	Michael	4	profit and loss/And wondering why it bothered about such trifles./{LC} So you want

BOTHERING (2)

548 ES	Monica	5	quiet./{M} I don't believe she'll be bothering us again:/I could see from her
555 ES	Monica	12	fly. {}/[*Exit*]/{M} I saw Mrs. Piggott bothering you again/So I hurried to your rescue.

BOTHERS (1)

555 ES	Piggott	7	/Well, she's gone now. If she bothers you again/Just let me know. I'm afraid

BOTTLE (5)

361 CP	Reilly	30	new force,/Or let the genie out of the bottle./It is to start a train of events/Beyond
383 CP	Edward	5	in the kitchen? Beside the champagne bottle?/You're quite sure? ... Very well, hold on
383 CP	m	10	*He returns with the spectacles and a bottle*]/{E} She was right for once./{C} She is
383 CP	Celia	12	/But why bring an empty champagne bottle?/{E} It isn't empty. It may be a little flat
457 CC	Lady E	17	out of it./Unwrap that — It's a bottle of medicine./Now, Parkman, will you

BOTTLES (2)

67 WL: Fire S		177	my song./The river bears no empty bottles, sandwich papers,/Silk handkerchiefs,
156 Rock 3		69	of happiness and flinging empty bottles,/Turning from your vacancy to fevered

BOTTOM (6)

27 Morning		6	toss up to me/Twisted faces from the bottom of the street,/And tear from a passer-by
166 Rock 10		7	snake lies ever half awake, at the bottom of the pit of the world, curled/In folds
362 CP	Reilly	30	sometimes, when you come to the bottom step/There is one step more than your
366 CP	Julia	3	Where was I sitting?/Just turn out the bottom of that sofa —/No, this chair. Look
433 CP	Peter	32	{A} Dead./{P} Dead. That knocks the bottom out of it./{E} Celia dead./{J} You had
552 ES	Carghil	27	So your conscience was clear./At bottom, I believe you're still the same silly

BOTTOMS (1)

16 Prufrock		121	old ... I grow old .../I shall wear the bottoms of my trousers rolled./Shall I part my

BOUDIN (1)

108 Animula		33	avid of speed and power,/For Boudin, blown to pieces,/For this one who

BOUGHS (1)

275 MC Chorus		24	past; and I wander in a land of barren boughs: if I break them, they bleed; I wander in

BOUGHT (4)

45 Cook Egg		25	me./But where is the penny world I bought/To eat with Pipit behind the screen?/The
327 FR	Charles	38	evening's paper./{C} Stop, I think I bought a lunch edition/Before I left St. Pancras.
456 CC	Eggers	30	ago, saying to Mrs. E.,/When we'd bought our house in Joshua Park/(On a
530 ES	Ld Clav	36	/Oh the grudging contributions/That bought this piece of silver! The inadequate levy/

BOUND (2)

268 MC Thomas		31	I/Who can loose whom the Pope has bound./Let them go to him, upon whom
289 FR	Amy	12	more than she cares to betray,/I am bound to say that I agree with you./{C} I never

BOUNDER (1)

231 Bust Jones		33	He's a twenty-five pounder, or I am a bounder,/And he's putting on weight every day:

BOURGEONS (1)

51 Restaurant		8	la soupe)./'Les saules trempés, et des bourgeons sur les ronces —/C'est là, dans une

BOW (2)

| 109 Marina | | 2 | what islands/What water lapping the bow/And scent of pine and the woodthrush |
| 235 Ad-dress | | 44 | in mind that he/Resents familiarity./I bow, and taking off my hat,/Ad-dress him in |

BOWED (1)

| 230 Bust Jones | | 11 | we're all of us proud to be nodded or bowed to/By Bustopher Jones in white spats!/ |

BOWEL (1)

| 438 CP | Reilly | 13 | less from hunger, damp, exposure,/Bowel trouble, and the fear of lions,/Cold of the |

BOWELS (3)

270 MC	Chorus	2	prawn; and they live and spawn in my bowels, and my bowels dissolve in the light of
270 MC	Chorus	2	live and spawn in my bowels, and my bowels dissolve in the light of dawn. I have
270 MC	Chorus	14	in the market-place/In our veins our bowels our skulls as well/As well as in the

BOWING (1)

| 37 Gerontion | | 26 | in the next room;/By Hakagawa, bowing among the Titians;/By Madame de |

BOWL (4)

19 Portrait		42	that lilacs are in bloom/She has a bowl of lilacs in her room/And twists one in her
171 FQ: BurntN		17	purpose/Disturbing the dust on a bowl of rose-leaves/I do not know./Other
236 Cat Morgan		6	I favour that Devonshire cream in a bowl;/But I'm allus content with a drink on the
424 CP	m	4	*about the room critically and moves a bowl of flowers.]/[Re-enter* CATERER'S MAN

BOWLS (1)

| 105 Song Sime | | 1 | the Roman hyacinths are blooming in bowls and/The winter sun creeps by the snow |

BOWSPRIT (1)

| 109 Marina | | 22 | sleep, where all the waters meet./Bowsprit cracked with ice and paint cracked |

BOX (1)

| 172 FQ: BurntN | | 34 | /Along the empty alley, into the box circle,/To look down into the drained pool./ |

BOXES (3)

67 WL: Fire S		178	papers,/Silk handkerchiefs, cardboard boxes, cigarette ends/Or other testimony of
446 CC	Eggers	30	if I might make a suggestion: window boxes!/He's expressed such an interest in my
446 CC	Eggers	32	I think he ought to have window boxes./Some day, he'll want a garden of his

BOY (17)

37 Gerontion		2	in a dry month,/Being read to by a boy, waiting for rain./I was neither at the hot
115 SP	Dusty	21	{Du} *I* like Sam/Yes and Sam's a nice boy too./He's a funny fellow/{Do} He *is* a funny
148 Rock 1		m46	inborn./*Enter the* ROCK, *led by a* BOY:/THE ROCK:/The lot of man is ceaseless
288 FR	Agatha	35	who returns will have to meet/The boy who left. Round by the stables,/In the
295 FR	Charles	10	need to revert to it. Remember, my boy,/I understand, your life together made it
319 FR	Warburt	17	went to live abroad. You were only a boy/When he died. You would not remember./
341 FR	Amy	14	the years when he had been a happy boy at Wishwood;/For his future success./{Ag}
386 CP	Celia	32	my laughing./You look like a little boy who's been sent for/To the headmaster's
395 CP	Lavinia	19	Oh, Edward, when you were a little boy,/I'm sure you were always getting yourself
464 CC	Claude	1	potter!/{SC} A potter. When I was a boy/I loved to shape things. I loved form and
478 CC	Lucasta	1	that you're Claude's white-headed boy./Perhaps he'll adopt you, and make you his
486 CC	Colby	24	/That is to say, they had had one little boy/Who died when I was very young indeed./I
493 CC	Lady E	26	won't want to be conspicuous,/Poor boy!/{SC} After all, it was he who insisted/On
508 CC	Guzzard	20	/{MG} We parted with it. A dear little boy./I was happy to have him while the
537 ES	Gomez	20	you found in me —/A scholarship boy from an unknown grammar school./I didn't
577 ES	Carghil	33	/He's simply been suffering, poor boy, from frustration./He's been waiting all this
578 ES	Ld Clav	12	/When I think of the happy little boy who was Michael,/When I think of your

BOY-SCOUTS (1)

| 211 Old Gumbie | | 34 | /A troop of well-disciplined helpful boy-scouts,/With a purpose in life and a good |

BOYHOOD (1)

| 578 ES | Ld Clav | 13 | was Michael,/When I think of your boyhood and adolescence,/And see how all the |

BOYS (6)

287 FR	Gerald	23	That reminds me, Amy,/When are the boys all due to arrive?/{A} I do not want the
296 FR	Gerald	36	be asked. He looked after all the boys/When they were children. I'll have a word
325 FR	Ivy	25	/{I} Yet I remember, when they were boys,/Arthur was always the more adventurous/
534 ES	Gomez	35	serious politics is like!/I said to my boys: 'Never touch politics./Stay out of politics,
535 ES	Gomez	17	/But, as I've always said to my boys:'When you come to the point where you
558 ES	Michael	26	I'd nothing to do./Even the office boys began to sneer at me./I wonder I stood it

BRACE (1)

| 277 MC | Knight3 | 10 | not a drinking man/ordinarily — to brace myself up for it. When you come to the/ |

BRACELETED (1)

| 15 Prufrock | | 63 | known them all —/Arms that are braceleted and white and bare/(But in the |

BRADFORD (1)

| 68 WL: Fire S | | 234 | assurance sits/As a silk hat on a Bradford millionaire./The time is now |

BRAIN (12)

19 Portrait	32	ariettes/Of cracked cornets/Inside my brain a dull tom-tom begins/Absurdly
24 Rhapsody	61	smells/That cross and cross across her brain.'/The reminiscence comes/Of sunless dry
39 Gerontion	75	of the house,/Thoughts of a dry brain in a dry season./Burbank with a
69 WL: Fire S	251	aware of her departed lover;/Her brain allows one half-formed thought to pass:/
135 5FingerEx1	4	the trees there is no ease/For the dull brain, the sharp desires/And the quick eyes of
599 On a Port	2	dreams, unknown/To us of restless brain and weary feet,/Forever hurrying, up and
244 MC Chorus	29	among small things,/The strain on the brain of the small folk who stand to the doom
276 MC Chorus	17	the stone, wash the bone, wash the brain, wash the soul, wash them wash them! {}/
280 MC Priest3	23	makes numb the hand, makes dull the brain;/Find an oasis in the desert sun,/Go seek
336 FR Harry	10	communication, a scent/Direct to the brain ... but not just as before,/Not quite like,
348 FR Chorus	9	too closely resembles the maze in the brain./We do not like what happens when we
500 CC Lucasta	10	/{L} Colby's aunt? You make my brain reel./{SC} I ought to have made things

BRAINLESS (1)

574 ES Carghil	13	you've always thought me utterly brainless,/But I have an idea or two, now and

BRAINS (3)

244 MC Chorus	23	/And our hearts are torn from us, our brains unskinned like the layers of an onion,
270 MC Chorus	19	/Is woven also in our veins, our brains,/Is woven like a pattern of living worms/
577 ES Gomez	24	head is well screwed on./He's got brains, he's got flair. When he does come back/

BRAMBLE (1)

179 FQ: ECoker	91	/But all the way, in a dark wood, in a bramble,/On the edge of a grimpen, where is no

BRANCH (6)

24 Rhapsody	25	/A crowd of twisted things;/A twisted branch upon the beach/Eaten smooth, and
140 Usk	1	river./Usk/Do not suddenly break the branch, or/Hope to find/The white hart behind
191 FQ: Little	9	/And glow more intense than blaze of branch, or brazier,/Stirs the dumb spirit: no
308 FR Harry	8	seen to be batrachian,/The aphyllous branch ophidian./{M} You bring your own
354 CP Alex	13	of the *oldest* Baltic families/With a branch in Sweden and one in Denmark./There
530 ES Ld Clav	21	room/In a railway station on a branch line,/After the last train, after all the

BRANCHES (7)

57 Swee Night	31	/Outside the window, leaning in,/Branches of wistaria/Circumscribe a golden
61 WL: Burial	19	/What are the roots that clutch, what branches grow/Out of this stony rubbish? Son
129 Cor2 State	33	repose of noon, set under the upper branches of noon's widest tree/Under the breast
177 FQ: ECoker	16	leaving the deep lane/Shuttered with branches, dark in the afternoon,/Where you
605 Narcissus	22	that he had been a tree,/Twisting its branches among each other/And tangling its
247 MC Tempt1	9	has come in winter. Snow in the branches/Shall float as sweet as blossoms. Ice
335 FR Harry	25	/Trying to avoid the clasping branches/And the giant lizard. To and fro./

BRANDY (1)

43 Swee Erect	44	/Bringing sal volatile/And a glass of brandy neat./A Cooking Egg/Pipit sate upright

BRAS (2)

46 Directeur	11	/Du Spectateur/Conservateur/Bras dessus bras dessous/Font des tours/A pas
46 Directeur	11	Spectateur/Conservateur/Bras dessus bras dessous/Font des tours/A pas de loup./

BRASS (1)

122 SA Sweeney	10	/That's all the facts when you come to brass tacks:/Birth, and copulation, and death./

BRAT (2)

266 MC Knights	19	the tradesman's son: the backstairs brat who was born in Cheapside;/This is the
274 MC Knights	24	feast./Where is Becket the Cheapside brat?/Where is Becket the faithless priest?/Come

BRAVE (1)

472 CC Colby	4	of being pushed./I think that you're brave — and I think that you're frightened./

BRAVELY (1)

203 Indians	13	exile to another. Where a man dies bravely/At one with his destiny, that soil is his./

BRAVERY (1)

249 MC Tempt2	23	and the glory./{T} No!/{T2} Yes! Or bravery will be broken,/Cabined in Canterbury,

BRAVO (2)

212 Growltiger	1	Last Stand/GROWLTIGER was a Bravo Cat, who travelled on a barge:/In fact he
394 CP Lavinia	38	I assure you, very differently./{L} Bravo! Edward. This is surprising./Now who

BRAW (1)

223 Pekes Pols	34	is a dour Yorkshire tyke,/And his braw Scottish cousins are snappers and biters,/

BRAZIER (1)

191 FQ: Little	9	more intense than blaze of branch, or brazier,/Stirs the dumb spirit: no wind, but

BRAZILIAN (2)

52 Whispers	21	of pneumatic bliss./The couched Brazilian jaguar/Compels the scampering
52 Whispers	25	has a maisonnette;/The sleek Brazilian jaguar/Does not in its arboreal gloom/

BREACH (3)
551 ES	Carghil	24	never have started an action/For breach of promise, if I'd really cared for you./
551 ES	Carghil	31	ambitions for him./If he's lost a breach of promise suit/Some people won't want
560 ES	Michael	26	a fool/As to get myself involved in a breach of promise suit/Or somebody's divorce.

BREAD (4)
136 5FingerEx3		7	the morning shine,/I have had the Bread and Wine,/Let the feathered mortals take
136 5FingerEx3		10	which is their mortal due,/Pinching bread and finger too,/Easier had than squirming
150 Rock 1		114	*the field is tilled/And the wheat is bread/They shall not die in a shortened bed/And a*
210 Old Gumbie		23	/She makes them a mouse-cake of bread and dried peas,/And a *beautiful* fry of

BREADFRUIT (2)
122 SAWa & Ho		24	*boo/Under the bamboo tree./Where the breadfruit fall/And the penguin call/And the*
123 SAWa & Ho		3	*you want to flirt with me?/Under the breadfruit, banyan, palmleaf/Or under the*

BREAK (18)
117 SP	Doris	38	for luck. You cut for luck./It might break the spell. You cut for luck./{Du} The
129 Cor2 State		39	strong to bear them/Noses strong to break the wind/Mother/May we not be some
140 Usk		1	river, river./Usk/Do not suddenly break the branch, or/Hope to find/The white
175 FQ: BurntN		153	Words strain,/Crack and sometimes break, under the burden,/Under the tension,
177 FQ: ECoker		11	generation/And a time for the wind to break the loosened pane/And to shake the
252 MC Thomas		26	for your loyalty./{T} To make, then break, this thought has come before,/The
252 MC Thomas		29	Samson in Gaza did no more./But if I break, I must break myself alone. {}/[*Enter*
252 MC Thomas		29	did no more./But if I break, I must break myself alone. {}/[*Enter* FOURTH
271 MC	Priests	26	My Lord, they are coming. They will break through presently./You will be killed.
273 MC	Priests	13	are safe. We are safe./They dare not break in./They cannot break in. They have not
273 MC	Priests	14	/They dare not break in./They cannot break in. They have not the force./We are safe
275 MC	Chorus	24	in a land of barren boughs: if I break them, they bleed; I wander in a land of
362 CP	Reilly	5	saw it first, and had the courage to break it —/Thus giving herself a permanent
378 CP	Celia	21	thing you care about/Is to avoid a break — anything unpleasant!/No, it can't be
453 CC	Lucasta	29	crisis./{L} Yes, Eggy, will you break the sad news to Claude?/Meanwhile,
515 CC	Guzzard	6	to see me;/And I found that I had to break the news to you./You saw the child. You
553 ES	Carghil	24	beautiful!/It was Effie said, when the break came,/'They'll be worth a fortune to you,
570 ES	Monica	16	lay ahead of her./{M} It is time to break the silence! Let us share your ghosts!/{C}

BREAKAGE (1)
185 FQ: DrySal		60	/Years of living among the breakage/Of what was believed in as the most

BREAKDOWN (7)
378 CP	Celia	37	mean, you're on the edge of a nervous breakdown./Edward, if I go away now/Will you
397 CP	Lavinia	14	think you're on the edge of a nervous breakdown!/{E} Don't say that!/{L} I must say
402 CP	Edward	17	/That I was on the edge of a nervous breakdown./I didn't know it then myself — but
402 CP	Reilly	20	a doctor could see it./{R} 'Nervous breakdown' is a term I never use:/It can mean
407 CP	Reilly	40	what you called your nervous breakdown./{L} But it's true! I was completely
409 CP	Edward	4	{E} It was two months ago/That your breakdown began! and I never noticed it./{L}
413 CP	Reilly	6	quite sure/They have had a nervous breakdown — that is what they call it —/And

BREAKFAST (12)
27 Morning		1	at the Window/They are rattling breakfast plates in basement kitchens,/And
68 WL: Fire S		222	The typist home at teatime, clears her breakfast, lights/Her stove, and lays out food in
589 Fable		90	most devout,/And lived on milk and breakfast food entirely;/Each morn from four to
363 CP	Edward	39	I saw her this morning when we had breakfast/I no longer remember what my wife is
372 CP	Edward	24	nowadays./{E} But what about my breakfast?/{A} Don't worry about breakfast./All
372 CP	Alex	25	my breakfast?/{A} Don't worry about breakfast./All you should want is a cup of black
376 CP	Edward	15	half a dozen eggs:/I wanted one for breakfast. A boiled egg./It's the only thing I
529 ES	Ld Clav	30	/Every day, year after year, over my breakfast,/I have looked at this book — or one
529 ES	Ld Clav	36	engagement book, to-day,/Not over breakfast, but before tea,/It's the empty pages
544 ES	Monica	5	is hot,/They give us a very tolerable breakfast;/And the chambermaid really *is* a
545 ES	Piggott	28	/My not coming in directly after breakfast:/He's led a busy life, too.' But I hope
565 ES	Monica	7	you come back in the morning? After breakfast?/{LC} Yes, come tomorrow morning./

BREAKING (3)
195 FQ: Little		149	measure, like a dancer.'/The day was breaking. In the disfigured street/He left me,
310 FR	Mary	5	throbbing the trunk/The pain of the breaking bud./These are the ones that suffer
478 CC	Colby	26	explain,/And now I'm going to. I'm breaking a promise. But .../{L} I don't believe

BREAKS (8)
185 FQ: DrySal		31	/The menace and caress of wave that breaks on water,/The distant rote in the granite
192 FQ: Little		33	of meaning/From which the purpose breaks only when it is fulfilled/If at all. Either
196 FQ: Little		202	our beseeching./The dove descending breaks the air/With flame of incandescent terror
202 War Poetry		4	the merely individual/Explosion breaks/In the path of an action merely typical/
226 Macavity		6	/He's broken every human law, he breaks the law of gravity./His powers of
335 FR	Agatha	22	/Up and down. Until the chain breaks./{H} To and fro, dragging my feet/

335 FR Harry 27 lizard. To and fro./Until the chain breaks./The chain breaks,/The wheel stops, and
335 FR Harry 28 fro./Until the chain breaks./The chain breaks,/The wheel stops, and the noise of

BREAST (3)
127 Cor1 March 32 the dove's wing, hidden in the turtle's breast,/Under the palmtree at noon, under the
129 Cor2 State 34 of noon's widest tree/Under the breast feather stirred by the small wind after
605 Narcissus 10 /And of his arms crossed over his breast./When he walked over the meadows/He

BREASTLESS (1)
52 Whispers 3 saw the skull beneath the skin;/And breastless creatures under ground/Leaned

BREASTS (2)
32 Hysteria 9 ...' I decided that if the shaking of her breasts could be stopped,/some of the fragments
68 WL: Fire S 219 lives,/Old man with wrinkled female breasts, can see/At the violet hour, the evening

BREATH (8)
109 Marina 15 unsubstantial, reduced by a wind,/A breath of pine, and the woodsong fog/By this
160 Rock 7 12 seas is pierced by the still dead breath of the Arctic Current;/And they came to
253 MC Tempt4 38 Old King shall know it, when at last breath,/No sons, no empire, he bites broken
263 MC Chorus 4 the old: not a stir, not a shoot, not a breath./Do the days begin to lengthen?/Longer
280 MC Priest3 23 seas confined with ice/Where the dead breath makes numb the hand, makes dull the
508 CC Claude 19 very sensible suggestion, Eggerson./A breath of sanity. Thank you for that./{MG} We
554 ES Piggott 14 sacrifice yourself for us./{MP} It's the breath of life to me, Mrs. Carghill,/Attending to
583 ES Charles 6 /Yet, like the asthmatic struggling for breath,/So the lover must struggle for words./

BREATHE (1)
360 CP Reilly 17 it slowly ... and drink it sitting down./Breathe deeply, and adopt a relaxed position./

BREATHED (1)
270 MC Chorus 5 I have lain on the floor of the sea and breathed with the breathing of the sea-anemone,

BREATHES (1)
239 MC Chorus 11 water and mud,/The New Year waits, breathes, waits, whispers in darkness./While the

BREATHING (6)
206 To my Wife 4 the repose of our sleepingtime,/The breathing in unison/Of lovers whose bodies
270 MC Chorus 5 floor of the sea and breathed with the breathing of the sea-anemone, swallowed with
324 FR Harry 19 /I should be glad for him to have a breathing spell:/But John's ordinary day isn't
324 FR Harry 20 ordinary day isn't much more than breathing./{I} Really, Harry! how can you be so
522 ES dedic 4 *the repose of our sleepingtime,/The breathing in unison/Of lovers .../Who think the*
554 ES Carghil 27 us at once./Besides, I ought to do my breathing exercises. {}/[*Exit*]/{MP} As a matter

BREATHLESS (1)
94 Ash-Wed 4 24 behind the garden god,/Whose flute is breathless, bent her head and signed but spoke

BRED (3)
242 MC Priest1 18 for the Church,/I know that the pride bred of sudden prosperity/Was but confirmed
480 CC Kaghan 27 being respectable —/He was born and bred to it. I wasn't, Colby./Do you know, I was
482 CC Lady E 32 when I first saw you,/'He is very well bred'. I knew nothing about you,/But one

BREED (2)
250 MC Thomas 14 but arrest disorder,/Make it fast, breed fatal disease,/Degrade what they exalt.
340 FR Amy 16 /Leaving nothing — but what I could breed for myself,/What I could plant here.

BREEDING (4)
61 WL: Burial 1 the Dead/April is the cruellest month, breeding/Lilacs out of the dead land, mixing/
417 CP Reilly 36 they do not understand each other,/Breeding children whom they do not understand
482 CC Lady E 30 you ought to mix with people of breeding./I said to myself, when I first saw you,/
482 CC Lady E 33 need to know, if one knows what breeding is./And, second, you need intellectual

BREEDS (2)
141 Rannoch 2 the crow starves, here the patient stag/Breeds for the rifle. Between the soft moor/And
155 Rock 3 49 /Subsiding basements where the rat breeds/Or sanitary dwellings with numbered

BREEZE (2)
233 Skimble 38 a button that you turn to make a breeze./There's a funny little basin you're
596 When we 3 the trees;/The gentle fingers of the breeze/Had torn no quivering cobweb down./

BRENTFORD (1)
213 Growltiger 55 strand./Rats were roasted whole at Brentford, and at Victoria Dock,/And a day of

BREVITY (2)
269 MC Thomas 1 /I lingered abroad: seven years is no brevity./I shall not get those seven years back
553 ES Ld Clav 2 you knew me/And considering the brevity of our acquaintance,/You're surprisingly

BREWED (1)
244 MC Chorus 5 the feasts, heard the masses,/We have brewed beer and cider,/Gathered wood against

BRIAR (1)
184 FQ: DrySal 26 and many voices./The salt is on the briar rose,/The fog is in the fir trees./The sea

BRIARS (1)
181 FQ: ECoker 168 the flame is roses, and the smoke is briars./The dripping blood our only drink,/The

BRIC-À-BRAC (1)
20 Portrait   92   /My smile falls heavily among the bric-à-brac./'Perhaps you can write to me.'/My
BRICK (2)
149 Rock 1   82   *hands and machines/And clay for new* *brick/And lime for new mortar/Where the bricks*
154 Rock 3   26   of rusty iron,/In a street of scattered brick where the goat climbs,/Where My Word is
BRICKS (2)
149 Rock 1   80   *vacant places/We will build with new* *bricks/There are hands and machines/And clay*
149 Rock 1   84   */And lime for new mortar/Where the* *bricks are fallen/We will build with new stone/*
BRIDE (1)
44 Cook Egg   18   Heaven,/Lucretia Borgia shall be my Bride;/Her anecdotes will be more amusing/
BRIDGE (5)
40 Burb Blei   1   with a Cigar/Burbank crossed a little bridge/Descending at a small hotel;/Princess
62 WL: Burial   62   dawn,/A crowd flowed over London Bridge, so many,/I had not thought death had
74 WL: Thund   426   least set my lands in order?/London Bridge is falling down falling down falling down
518 CC   Colby   12   And a canonry!/{C} We'll cross that bridge when we come to it, Eggers./Oh, I'm
544 ES Ld Clav   13   picture papers, or wanting a fourth at bridge;/Still, I'll admit to a feeling of
BRIDGES (2)
184 FQ: DrySal   5   a problem confronting the builder of bridges./The problem once solved, the brown
457 CC Eggers   2   /But let's not be crossing any bridges/Until we come to them. That's what *I*
BRIEF (7)
98 Ash-Wed 6   5   between the profit and the loss/In this brief transit where the dreams cross/The
191 FQ: Little   5   is brightest, with frost and fire,/The brief sun flames the ice, on pond and ditches,/In
324 FR   Harry   16   very much difference to John./A brief vacation from the kind of consciousness/
405 CP   Reilly   17   along. A barrister/Ought to know his brief before he enters the court./{E} I am at least
505 CC Eggers   31   past and the future both seem very brief —/But long enough ago for the question
552 ES Ld Clav   20   My conscience was clear./A brief infatuation, ended in the only way possible
553 ES Carghil   6   it's true that our acquaintance was brief,/Our relations were intense enough, I
BRIEFCASE (1)
450 CC   m 26   {}/[*Enter* COLBY SIMPKINS *with briefcase*]/{SC} Ah, Colby, I was just saying to
BRIEFLY (2)
279 MC Knight4   17   course of events. I am obliged, very briefly, to go over/the ground traversed by the
571 ES Ld Clav   29   hate you?/{LC} I will tell you very briefly/And simply. As for Frederick
BRIEFS (1)
393 CP Edward   36   to meet more people:/But when the briefs began to come in —/And they didn't
BRIGADE (1)
223 Pekes Pols   49   /That they started to ring up the Fire Brigade./When suddenly, up from a small
BRIGHT (14)
67 WL: Fire S   199   in the spring./O the moon shone bright on Mrs. Porter/And on her daughter/
94 Ash-Wed 4   17   new years walk, restoring/Through a bright cloud of tears, the years, restoring/With a
166 Rock 10   18   Light Invisible, we praise Thee!/Too bright for mortal vision./O Greater Light, we
212 Growltiger   22   at play,/The tender moon was shining bright, the barge at Molesey lay./All in the
213 Growltiger   36   shone reflected from a hundred bright blue eyes./And closer still and closer the
216 Jellicles   3   *come all:/The Jellicle Moon is shining* *bright —/Jellicles come to the Jellicle Ball./*
216 Jellicles   7   small;/Jellicle Cats are merry and bright,/And pleasant to hear when they
216 Jellicles   10   have cheerful faces,/Jellicle Cats have bright black eyes;/They like to practise their airs
217 Jellicles   33   hall./If it happens the sun is shining bright/You would say they had nothing to do at
233 Skimble   37   of light — you can make it dark or bright;/There's a button that you turn to make
233 Skimble   51   of the night he is always fresh and bright;/Every now and then he has a cup of tea/
308 FR   Harry   3   else/The most real is what I fear. The bright colour fades/Together with the
339 FR   Harry   22   enough given./I must follow the bright angels. {}/[*Exit*]/Scene III/AMY,
544 ES   2m   1   Two/*The terrace of Badgley Court. A* *bright sunny morning, several days later./Enter*
BRIGHTER (3)
600 Moonflower   7   white mist on the sea;/Have you no brighter tropic flowers/With scarlet life, for me?
360 CP   Reilly   23   /{E} No./{UG} Then look at the brighter side./You say you don't know where
479 CC Kaghan   36   all a bit too dim. You need something brighter./But otherwise, it looks pretty
BRIGHTEST (1)
191 FQ: Little   4   and tropic./When the short day is brightest, with frost and fire,/The brief sun
BRIGHTLY (1)
233 Skimble   41   looks in politely and will ask you very brightly/'Do you like your morning tea weak or
BRIGHTNESS (1)
91 Ash-Wed 2   11   Virgin in meditation,/We shine with brightness. And I who am here dissembled/
BRILLIANCE (1)
107 Animula   9   taking pleasure/In the fragrant brilliance of the Christmas tree,/Pleasure in the

BRILLIANT (3)

320 FR	Warburt	35	very steady — but he's not exactly brilliant;/And Arthur has always been rather
325 FR	Charles	21	into trouble./{C} Oh, but Arthur's a brilliant driver./After all the experience he's had
325 FR	Gerald	24	not likely to get into trouble./{G} A brilliant driver, but more reckless./{I} Yet I

BRING (52)

62 WL:	Burial	58	see dear Mrs. Equitone,/Tell her I bring the horoscope myself:/One must be so
66 WL:	Chess	159	a long face,/It's them pills I took, to bring it off, she said./(She's had five already,
67 WL:	Fire S	197	of horns and motors, which shall bring/Sweeney to Mrs. Porter in the spring./O
147 Rock 1		18	cycles of Heaven in twenty centuries/Bring us farther from GOD and nearer to the
148 Rock 1		53	accepting/With equal face those that bring ignominy,/The applause of all or the love
151 Rock 2		9	/We wait on corners, with nothing to bring but the songs we can sing which nobody
164 Rock 9		25	of incantation./LORD, shall we not bring these gifts to Your service?/Shall we not
164 Rock 9		26	gifts to Your service?/Shall we not bring to Your service all our powers/For life,
179 FQ: ECoker		66	plains/Whirled in a vortex that shall bring/The world to that destructive fire/Which
197 FQ: Little		233	with the dead:/See, they return, and bring us with them./The moment of the rose
229 Gus		42	/Produce blood-curdling noises to bring on the Ghost./And he once crossed the
588 Fable		55	cover./Last, a boar's head, which to bring in took four pages,/His mouth an apple
240 MC	Chorus	11	October./Why should the summer bring consolation/For autumn fires and winter
261 MC	Thomas	28	/to warn them and to lead them, to bring them back to His ways. It is/now the
290 FR	Amy	8	to fit herself to Harry,/But only to bring Harry down to her own level./A restless
308 FR	Mary	9	aphyllous branch ophidian./{M} You bring your own landscape/No more real than
310 FR	Harry	34	I say it,/That does not matter. You bring me news/Of a door that opens at the end
315 FR	Warburt	29	/And I hope that next year will bring me the same honour. {}/[*Exeunt* AMY,
319 FR	Harry	27	heard, with the sidewise looks,/That bring death into the heart of a child./*That* was
323 FR	Warburt	15	like this. You can trust Owen./We'll bring him up tomorrow; and a few days' rest,/
346 FR	Charles	1	Pall Mall./I thought that life could bring no further surprises;/But I remember now,
364 CP	Reilly	20	the trouble of an answer./But if I bring her back it must be on one condition:/
375 CP	Edward	17	indigestible? .../Oh, no, Alex, don't bring me any cheese;/I've got some cheese ...
377 CP	Edward	11	of you had left,/And he said he would bring Lavinia back, tomorrow./{C} But why
377 CP	Celia	12	{C} But why should that man want to bring her back —/Unless he is the Devil! I could
383 CP	Celia	12	/{C} She is always right./But why bring an empty champagne bottle?/{E} It isn't
384 CP	Reilly	22	is this: it is a serious matter/To bring someone back from the dead./{E} From
385 CP	Edward	36	why,/But I think I should like you to bring her yourself./{UG} Yes, I know you
386 CP	Celia	22	telegram/Asking her to come, and to bring me with her./Julia was delayed, and sent
387 CP	Peter	18	She told him to come here/And to bring me with him. He'll be here in a minute./
387 CP	Celia	23	she telegraphed to Julia to come and bring me with her./{E} I wonder whom else
395 CP	Edward	1	quite enough humiliation/Lately, to bring me to the point/At which humiliation
422 CP	Reilly	4	up. {}/[*Into telephone*]/{R} You may bring the tray in now, Miss Barraway. {}/[*Enter*
424 CP	Lavinia	2	orders for us, Madam?/{L} You could bring in the trolley with the glasses/And leave
428 CP	Alex	34	*is* any solution./But even this does not bring us to the heart of the matter./There are
433 CP	Julia	35	tell them, Alex,/The news that you bring back from Kinkanja./{L} Kinkanja? What
445 CC	Claude	2	as always./I'm sorry to have to bring you up to London/All the way from
452 CC	Kaghan	7	again! So I thought I'd better bring her/And come upstairs ahead, to ease the
457 CC	Lady E	26	lunch,/And I don't want it now. Just bring me some tea./Nothing with it. No, I
470 CC	Colby	11	of fact, I think I played better./I can't bring myself to play to other people,/And when
479 CC	Kaghan	15	I've always been lucky,/And I always bring luck to other people./{C} Will you have a
496 CC	Claude	15	/{SC} I'm sorry, Eggerson, to bring you up to London/At such short notice./
496 CC	Eggers	18	It's true, I haven't much nowadays to bring me;/But Mrs. E. wishes I'd come up
503 CC	Lucasta	11	the happiness that relationship may bring us/In twenty or thirty or forty years' time.
504 CC	Eggers	15	explain to Mrs. Guzzard/And then bring her up./{SC} No, I want you here,
510 CC	Colby	1	Isn't this the moment/For me to bring him up? And Lucasta?/{E} An excellent
532 ES	Monica	22	a trunk call./Come, Charles. Will you bring my coat?/{C} I'll say goodbye, sir./And
535 ES	Ld Clav	6	LAMBERT]/{LC} Lambert, will you bring in the whisky. And soda./{L} Very good,
554 ES	Carghil	1	have these letters auctioned.'/Yes, I'll bring the photostats tomorrow morning,/And
558 ES	Ld Clav	28	it as long as I did./{LC} And does this bring us to the end of the list of your
580 ES	Carghil	22	me most/Is that I shall be able to bring you news of Michael./And now that we've
580 ES	Monica	29	a failure/Homesickness, I'm sure, will bring him back to us;/If he prospers, that will

BRINGING (10)

28 Boston ET		5	of life in some/And to others bringing the *Boston Evening Transcript,*/I
43 Swee Erect		43	bath,/Enters padding on broad feet,/Bringing sal volatile/And a glass of brandy neat.
74 WL: Thund		394	flash of lightning. Then a damp gust/Bringing rain/Ganga was sunken, and the limp
103 Journ Magi		10	the terraces,/And the silken girls bringing sherbet./Then the camel men cursing
240 MC	Chorus	6	the quiet seasons:/Winter shall come bringing death from the sea,/Ruinous spring
243 MC	Chorus	20	come with rejoicing, but you come bringing death into Canterbury:/A doom on the
278 MC	Knight2	40	/step. We have been instrumental in bringing about the state of/affairs that you

383 CP   Edward   30   ... No, I found them./... Yes, she's bringing them now ... Good night. {}/
401 CP   Edward   36   /{E} It's not for me to blame you for bringing my wife back,/I suppose. You seemed
415 CP   Celia   19   of view of your family?/{C} Well, my bringing up was pretty conventional —/I had
BRINGS (9)
56 Swee Night   19   the window-sill and gapes;/The waiter brings in oranges/Bananas figs and hothouse
68 WL: Fire S   221   hour that strives/Homeward, and brings the sailor home from sea,/The typist
147 Rock 1   8   invention, endless experiment,/Brings knowledge of motion, but not of
147 Rock 1   11   of the Word./All our knowledge brings us nearer to our ignorance,/All our
147 Rock 1   12   to our ignorance,/All our ignorance brings us nearer to death,/But nearness to death
250 MC Thomas   22   my present purpose./{T} No purpose brings surprise./{T3} Well, my Lord,/I am no
367 CP   Edward   20   in the moving pictures/Frequently brings young people together./{P} Now you're
417 CP   Reilly   33   separates/And with the evening that brings together/For casual talk before the fire/
435 CP   Lavinia 30   only just begun./I mean, this only brings you to the point/At which you *must*
BRISE (1)
46 Directeur   6   /Du Spectateur/Empeste la brise./Les actionnaires/Réactionnaires/Du
BRISK (1)
70 WL: Fire S   284   /A gilded shell/Red and gold/The brisk swell/Rippled both shores/Southwest wind
BRISTLE (1)
592 Grad 4   2   be tortuous and slow,/Although it bristle with a thousand fears,/To hopeful eye of
BRISTLY (1)
212 Growltiger   15   faced Growltiger's rage;/Woe to the bristly Bandicoot, that lurks on foreign ships,/
BRITAIN (1)
201 Def Island   19   glory are/the lanes and the streets of Britain:/to say, to the past and the future
BRITANNICA (1)
107 Animula   23   window seat/Behind the *Encyclopaedia Britannica.*/Issues from the hand of time the
BRITISH (4)
129 Cor2 State   3   of the Bath, the Knights of the British Empire, the Cavaliers,/O Cavaliers! of
152 Rock 2   23   versions of the Word of GOD:/The British race assured of a mission/Performed it,
201 Def Island   10   their share to the ages' pavement/of British bone on the sea floor/and of those who,
222 Pekes Pols   26   may say what they please,/Is no British Dog, but a Heathen Chinese./And so all
BRITISHER (1)
120 SP   Krum   7   Specially when you got a real live Britisher/A guy like Sam to show you around./
BRITO (3)
279 MC Knight1   9   unconvinced, I think that/Richard Brito, coming as he does of a family
279 MC Knight1   10   be able to convince them. Richard Brito./{K4} The speakers who have preceded
280 MC Knight1   1   all, a great man./{K1} Thank you, Brito, I think that there is no more to be/said;
BRITTANY (1)
280 MC Priest3   19   sunset reddens the last grey rock/Of Brittany, or the Gates of Hercules./Go venture
BROAD (1)
43 Swee Erect   42   from the bath,/Enters padding on broad feet,/Bringing sal volatile/And a glass of
BROAD-BACKED (1)
49 Hippopot   1   de Byzance./The Hippopotamus/The broad-backed hippopotamus/Rests on his belly
BROADBACKED (1)
92 Ash-Wed 3   15   blossom and a pasture scene/The broadbacked figure drest in blue and green/
BROADBOTTOMED (1)
42 Swee Erect   22   addressed full length to shave/Broadbottomed, pink from nape to base,/
BROC (1)
246 MC Thomas   9   Had fair crossing, found at Sandwich/Broc, Warenne, and the Sheriff of Kent,/Those
BROKE (8)
30 Cous Nancy   2   Ellicott/Strode across the hills and broke them,/Rode across the hills and broke
30 Cous Nancy   3   broke them,/Rode across the hills and broke them —/The barren New England hills —
116 SP   Doris   18   Say what you like: say I'm ill,/Say I broke my leg on the stairs/Say we've had a fire/
134 Wind   2   four o'clock/The wind sprang up and broke the bells/Swinging between life and death/
266 MC Knights   23   The man who cheated, swindled, lied; broke his oath and betrayed his King./{T} This
314 FR   Amy   6   were going to be here for dinner/He broke an important engagement to come./{W} I
335 FR   Harry   16   out, the movement/Until the chain broke, and I was left/Under the single eye above
434 CP   Alex   11   then?/{A} And then, the insurrection broke out/Among the heathen, of which I was
BROKEN (38)
19 Portrait   57   like the insistent out-of-tune/Of a broken violin on an August afternoon:/'I am
22 Preludes   10   vacant lots;/The showers beat/On broken blinds and chimney-pots,/And at the
24 Rhapsody   30   of its skeleton,/Stiff and white./A broken spring in a factory yard,/Rust that clings
61 WL: Burial   22   guess, for you know only/A heap of broken images, where the sun beats,/And the
67 WL: Fire S   173   /The Fire Sermon/The river's tent is broken; the last fingers of leaf/Clutch and sink
70 WL: Fire S   303   connect/Nothing with nothing./The broken fingernails of dirty hands./My people
74 WL: Thund   408   the beneficent spider/Or under seals broken by the lean solicitor/In our empty rooms

74 WL: Thund	416	rumours/Revive for a moment a broken Coriolanus/DA/*Damyata:* The boat
83 Hollow Men	9	wind in dry grass/Or rats' feet over broken glass/In our dry cellar/Shape without
83 Hollow Men	23	/There, the eyes are/Sunlight on a broken column/There, is a tree swinging/And
84 Hollow Men	51	Lips that would kiss/Form prayers to broken stone./The eyes are not here/There are
84 Hollow Men	56	dying stars/In this hollow valley/This broken jaw of our lost kingdoms/In this last of
135 5FingerEx1	8	creaking heart cease?/When will the broken chair give ease?/Why will the summer
141 Rannoch	7	of ancient war,/Languor of broken steel,/Clamour of confused wrong, apt/
154 Rock 3	24	stupor?/There shall be left the broken chimney,/The peeled hull, a pile of rusty
157 Rock 4	7	Artaxerxes,/And he grieved for the broken city, Jerusalem;/And the King gave him
162 Rock 8	22	corruption;/Many came back well broken,/Diseased and beggared, finding/A
163 Rock 8	29	And in spite of all the dishonour,/The broken standards, the broken lives,/The broken
163 Rock 8	29	dishonour,/The broken standards, the broken lives,/The broken faith in one place or
163 Rock 8	30	standards, the broken lives,/The broken faith in one place or another,/There was
184 FQ: DrySal	23	seine,/The shattered lobsterpot, the broken oar/And the gear of foreign dead men.
191 FQ: Little	27	journey,/If you came at night like a broken king,/If you came by day not knowing
219 Mung Rump	25	the scenes/And say in a voice that was broken with sorrow:/'I'm afraid you must wait
221 Old Deut	41	feline's gastronomy/Must never be broken, whatever befall:/And the Oldest
226 Macavity	6	there's no one like Macavity,/He's broken every human law, he breaks the law of
226 Macavity	25	stifled,/Or the greenhouse glass is broken, and the trellis past repair —/Ay, there's
249 MC Tempt2	23	/{T} No!/{T2} Yes! Or bravery will be broken,/Cabined in Canterbury, realmless ruler,
253 MC Tempt4	13	trap to snap/Having served your turn, broken and crushed./As for barons, envy of
253 MC Tempt4	35	and revolution,/New conspiracies, broken pacts;/To be master or servant within an
253 MC Tempt4	39	breath,/No sons, no empire, he bites broken teeth./You hold the skein: wind,
254 MC Tempt4	34	light ladies' ornament,/The sanctuary broken, and its stores/Swept into the laps of
257 MC Priests	4	the stair in the day, and slip on a broken step./{4T} A man may sit at meat, and
282 MC Chorus	2	the prayer in forgotten places by the broken imperial column,/From such ground
316 FR Chorus	3	never there./And the bird sits on the broken chimney. I am afraid./{I} This is a most
332 FR Agatha	31	/I believe, across a whole Thibet of broken stones/That lie, fang up, a lifetime's
385 CP Reilly	4	convention/Which must sometimes be broken. We must also remember/That at every
474 CC Lucasta	24	would stop. And the walls would be broken./And you would find yourself in a
551 ES Carghil	21	Who can say whether a heart's been broken/Once it's been repaired? But I know

BROKEN-DOWN (1)

569 ES Ld Clav	12	you know him/For what he is, the broken-down actor./{M} I think I should only

BROKEN-HEARTED (1)

551 ES Ld Clav	19	them./{LC} If you had really been broken-hearted/I can't see how you could have

BROKER (1)

343 FR Amy	28	calculations/With the solicitor, the broker, agent? Why should I?/It is no concern

BRONZE (2)

127 Corl March	1	/Coriolan/Triumphal March/Stone, bronze, stone, steel, stone, oakleaves, horses'
128 Corl March	40	/Dust/Dust of dust, and now/Stone, bronze, stone, steel, stone, oakleaves, horses'

BROODING (4)

488 CC Claude	11	/What has happened is that, brooding on the past,/You began to think of
529 ES Ld Clav	23	book./{LC} Yes, I've been brooding over it./{M} But what a time for your
543 ES m	8	CLAVERTON *sits for a few minutes brooding. A knock. Enter* MONICA.]/{M} Who
573 ES Ld Clav	2	from a morbid conscience,/From brooding over faults I might well have

BROOK (1)

204 de la Mare	1	Mare/The children who explored the brook and found/A desert island with a sandy

BROOKLANDS (1)

325 FR Charles	22	/After all the experience he's had at Brooklands, *He*'s not likely to get into trouble./

BROOM (2)

276 MC Chorus	5	in the market-place, the hand on the broom,/The night-time heaping of the ashes,/
281 MC Chorus	14	in deed./Even with the hand to the broom, the back bent in laying the fire, the knee

BROTHER (14)

149 Rock 1	73	you,/The desert is in the heart of your brother./The good man is the builder, if he
313 FR Charles	21	/They need the influence of their elder brother./Arthur's a bit irresponsible, you know;
324 FR Violet	10	to say./Aren't you sorry for your brother? Aren't you aware/Of what is going on?
328 FR Charles	11	read it to us. {}/[*reads*]./{C} 'Peer's Brother in Motor Smash/The Hon. Arthur
328 FR Charles	12	Arthur Gerald Charles Piper, younger brother of Lord/Monchensey, who ran into and
499 CC Claude	38	I would have explained. Colby is your brother./{E} Half-brother, Miss Angel./{SC}
502 CC Lucasta	31	sense I've been told that you're my brother;/Which makes it more difficult to know
502 CC Lucasta	34	one so hard to understand/As one's brother .../{C} Or sister .../{L} What's so
502 CC Lucasta	38	/It may be that understanding, as a brother and a sister,/Will come, in time.
503 CC Lucasta	6	more necessary to each other,/As a brother and a sister, than we could have been/In
503 CC Lucasta	31	changing./When I come back, we'll be brother and sister —/Or so I hope. Yes, in any
562 ES Carghil	16	of course:/And this must be your brother, Michael./I'm right, aren't I?/{Mi} Yes,

578 ES   Monica   17   Michael, remember, you're my only brother/And I'm your only sister. You never
578 ES   Monica   21   /How much it means to me to have a brother./{Mi} Why of course, Monica. You
BROTHER'S (2)
67 WL: Fire S   191   gashouse/Musing upon the king my brother's wreck/And on the king my father's
527 ES   Charles   34   Sisters, I should say,/For your brother's never been of any use to you./{M}
BROTHER-IN-LAW (1)
503 CC   Colby   16   /And I'm glad to think he'll be my brother-in-law./I shall need you, both of you,
BROTHERS (11)
284 FR   m   3   *and* THE HON. CHARLES PIPER, *brothers of her deceased husband*/MARY,
320 FR   Warburt   1   the birthday celebration,/And your brothers will be here. Won't you let me tell you/
321 FR   Warburt   15   has happened/To either of your brothers./{H} Nothing can have happened/To
321 FR   Harry   17   can have happened/To either of my brothers. Nothing can happen —/If Sergeant
321 FR   Warburt   23   may have happened to one of your brothers. {}/[*Enter* WINCHELL]/{Wi} Good
354 CP   Alex   30   /Was she the one who had three brothers?/{J} How many brothers? Two, I think.
354 CP   Julia   31   had three brothers?/{J} How many brothers? Two, I think./{A} No, there were
484 CC   Lady E   2   born./Have you other near relatives? Brothers or sisters?/{C} No brothers or sisters.
484 CC   Colby   3   relatives? Brothers or sisters?/{C} No brothers or sisters. No. As for other relatives,/I
484 CC   Lady E   27   child, having no relatives —/No brothers or sisters — and I was lonely/Because
527 ES   Charles   32   you./It's a pity that you haven't had brothers and sisters/To share the burden.
BROUGHT (31)
15 Prufrock   82   seen my head (grown slightly bald) brought in upon a platter,/I am no prophet —
587 Fable   4   and money from the poor men,/And brought their abbeys tumbling at their backs,/
243 MC   Priest3   13   all the daughters of music shall be brought low./{C} Here is no continuing city,
261 MC   Thomas   40   what is that Peace which He brought; and because,/dear children, I do not
265 MC   Knight1   13   far to-day, but matters urgent/Have brought us from France. We rode hard,/Took
277 MC   Knight3   12   especially/when you have been brought up in good Church traditions. So if/we
301 FR   Violet   12   as they were —/Except for having brought Downing into it:/Of which I
301 FR   Chorus   20   why should we be implicated, brought in and brought together?/{I} I do not
301 FR   Chorus   20   we be implicated, brought in and brought together?/{I} I do not trust Charles with
374 CP   Edward   24   all our difficulties?/{E} It has only brought to light the real difficulties./{C} But
402 CP   Reilly   1   to make a decision?/{R} If I had not brought your wife back, Mr. Chamberlayne,/Do
410 CP   Reilly   24   would have been left with what you brought with you:/The shadow of desires of
412 CP   Julia   3   downstairs./{J} I know that, Henry. I brought her here myself./{R} Oh? You didn't let
412 CP   Reilly   11   Was she reluctant?/Was that why you brought her?/{J} Oh no, not reluctant:/Only
426 CP   Julia   38   forgetting!/I've got a surprise: I've brought Alex with me!/He only got back this
434 CP   Alex   3   diseases/Besides, of course, those brought by Europeans,/And where the
460 CC   Claude   39   Well, Eggerson,/I seem to have brought you up to London for nothing./{E} Oh,
484 CC   Lady E   10   And I loathed them all./Were you brought up by a governess?/{C} No. By my
485 CC   Lady E   28   close to London./{LE} Still, you were brought up, like me, in the country./
487 CC   Lady E   29   sure,/But it seems that Providence has brought you back to me,/And you, Claude, and
487 CC   Lady E   37   Mrs. Guzzard!/Claude, Colby was brought up by a Mrs. Guzzard./{SC} I know
489 CC   Claude   20   when he was born. Mrs. Guzzard brought him up,/And I provided for his
491 CC   Lady E   14   us? Already, Claude,/I feel as if this brought us closer together./{SC} I should be
492 CC   Colby   23   looking at your notes —/Before you brought me into the conversation —/And I
507 CC   Guzzard   16   not have taken him./But he was brought to me by a third party,/Through whom
531 ES   Lambert   36   He said he knew that,/So he had brought this note. He said that when you read it
533 ES   Ld Clav   12   finished my sentence./{LC} What has brought you to England?/{G} Call it
539 ES   Gomez   12   have another./But I wonder what brought about this ... stroke;/And I wonder
554 ES   Piggott   29   I flew to your rescue/(That's why I've brought your morning tipple myself/Instead of
558 ES   Michael   30   /{Mi} Well, there was one thing he brought up against me,/That I'd been too
583 ES   Monica   10   born, the love was always there/That brought us together./Oh Father, Father!/I could
BROW (2)
136 5FingerEx5   3   his features of clerical cut,/And his brow so grim/And his mouth so prim/And his
226 Macavity   13   him, for his eyes are sunken in./His brow is deeply lined with thought, his head is
BROWN (21)
15 Prufrock   64   in the lamplight, downed with light brown hair!)/Is it perfume from a dress/That
17 Prufrock   130   wreathed with seaweed red and brown/Till human voices wake us, and we
27 Morning   5   despondently at area gates./The brown waves of fog toss up to me/Twisted faces
56 Swee Night   17   stocking up;/The silent man in mocha brown/Sprawls at the window-sill and gapes;/
56 Swee Night   21   grapes;/The silent vertebrate in brown/Contracts and concentrates, withdraws;/
62 WL: Burial   61   these days./Unreal City,/Under the brown fog of a winter dawn,/A crowd flowed
67 WL: Fire S   175   the wet bank. The wind/Crosses the brown land, unheard. The nymphs are departed.
68 WL: Fire S   208   forc'd./Tereu/Unreal City/Under the brown fog of a winter noon/Mr. Eugenides, the
73 WL: Thund   363   beside you/Gliding wrapt in a brown mantle, hooded/I do not know whether a
92 Ash-Wed 3   17   an antique flute./Blown hair is sweet, brown hair over the {mouth blown,/Lilac and

92 Ash-Wed 3	18	hair over the mouth blown,/Lilac and brown hair;/Distraction, music of the flute,
135 5FingerEx2	1	*/Lines to a Yorkshire Terrier/*In a brown field stood a tree/And the tree was
135 5FingerEx2	8	/Yet the field was cracked and brown/And the tree was cramped and dry./
138 New Hamp	5	green tip and the root./Black wing, brown wing, hover over;/Twenty years and the
172 FQ: BurntN	36	pool./Dry the pool, dry concrete, brown edged,/And the pool was filled with
184 FQ: DrySal	2	but I think that the river/Is a strong brown god — sullen, untamed and intractable,/
184 FQ: DrySal	6	bridges./The problem once solved, the brown god is almost forgotten/By the dwellers
193 FQ: Little	96	recalled/Both one and many; in the brown baked features/The eyes of a familiar
233 Skimble	63	out!/He gives you a wave of his long brown tail/Which says: 'I'll see you again!/
596 When we	8	/Were faded, and the leaves were brown./Before Morning/While all the East was
239 MC Chorus	10	and stored, and the land became brown sharp points of death in a waste of water

BROWNED (1)

54 Mr E Sun	12	God./The wilderness is cracked and browned/But through the water pale and thin/

BRUISED (2)

32 Hysteria	4	in the dark caverns of her throat, bruised by/the ripple of unseen muscles. An
34 Figlia	11	/As the soul leaves the body torn and bruised,/As the mind deserts the body it has

BRÛLANTES (1)

47 Mél Adult	20	montrera mon cénotaphe/Aux côtes brûlantes de Mozambique./Lune de Miel/Ils ont

BRUMMELL (1)

230 Bust Jones	10	smartest of names is/The name of this Brummell of Cats;/And we're all of us proud to

BRUSH (1)

64 WL: Chess	108	stair./Under the firelight, under the brush, her hair/Spread out in fiery points/

BRUSHED (1)

581 ES Ld Clav	27	in defiance of reason,/I have been brushed by the wing of happiness./And I am

BRUSSELS (1)

37 Gerontion	10	estaminet of Antwerp,/Blistered in Brussels, patched and peeled in London./The

BUBBLE (1)

594 Grad 11	5	of schools — a momentary gleam,/A bubble on the surface of the stream,/A drop of

BUCKO (1)

212 Growltiger	25	to show his sentimental side./His bucko mate, GRUMBUSKIN, long since had

BUD (1)

310 FR Mary	5	the trunk/The pain of the breaking bud./These are the ones that suffer least:/The

BUDDING (1)

191 FQ: Little	17	sudden/Than that of summer, neither budding nor fading,/Not in the scheme of

BUFFALO (1)

204 de la Mare	4	ground,/For here the water buffalo may rove,/The kinkajou, the mangabey,

BUFFET (1)

424 CP 3m	1	A CATERER'S MAN *is arranging a buffet/table.* LAVINIA *enters from side door./*

BUG (1)

129 Cor2 State	47	small flare of the firefly or lightning bug,/'Rising and falling, crowned with dust', the

BUILD (25)

149 Rock 1	74	/The good man is the builder, if he build what is good./I will show you the things
149 Rock 1	80	*chanting./In the vacant places/We will build with new bricks/There are hands and*
149 Rock 1	85	*/Where the bricks are fallen/We will build with new stone/Where the beams are rotten/*
149 Rock 1	87	*/Where the beams are rotten/We will build with new timbers/Where the word is*
149 Rock 1	89	*/Where the word is unspoken/We will build with new speech/There is work together/A*
150 Rock 1	111	*have no time to waste./If men do not build/How shall they live?/When the field is tilled/*
150 Rock 1	120	*delay, without haste/We would build the beginning and the end of this street./We*
150 Rock 1	121	*and the end of this street./We build the meaning:/A Church for all/And a job for*
151 Rock 2	6	hives,/And those who would build and restore turn out the palms of their
153 Rock 2	52	pillions./Much to cast down, much to build, much to restore;/Let the work not delay,
154 Rock 3	18	but not the House of GOD./Will you build me a house of plaster, with corrugated
155 Rock 3	37	lost golf balls'./CHORUS:/We build in vain unless the LORD build with us./
155 Rock 3	37	/We build in vain unless the LORD build with us./Can you keep the City that the
155 Rock 3	42	cavies or a horde of active marmots/Build better than they that build without the
155 Rock 3	42	marmots/Build better than they that build without the LORD./Shall we lift up our
157 Rock 4	1	Stranger./There are those who would build the Temple,/And those who prefer that
157 Rock 4	18	the wall./So they built as men must build/With the sword in one hand and the
159 Rock 6	32	is to flow on the steps/We must first build the steps;/And if the Temple is to be cast
159 Rock 6	34	is to be cast down/We must first build the Temple./In the beginning GOD
166 Rock 10	5	of the future? Is one church all we can build?/Or shall the Visible Church go on to
250 MC Thomas	9	falcons./{T} Temporal power, to build a good world,/To keep order, as the world
280 MC Priest1	12	desolated, and the heathen shall build on the ruins,/Their world without God. I
411 CP Edward	24	of ... the others./I don't want to build on other people's ruins./{L} Exactly. And
422 CP Reilly	13	[*They raise their glasses*]/{R} Let them build the hearth/Under the protection of the

431 CP   Peter 25 decay, so as to reproduce it./Then we build another Boltwell in California./{J} But
BUILDED (2)
151 Rock 2   7 wonder whether and how you may be builded together for a habitation of GOD in the
158 Rock 5   10 are not in the City./The man who has builded during the day would return to his
BUILDER (2)
149 Rock 1   74 of your brother./The good man is the builder, if he build what is good./I will show
184 FQ: DrySal   5 /Then only a problem confronting the builder of bridges./The problem once solved,
BUILDING (10)
151 Rock 2   7 be more or the urn to be filled./Your building not fitly framed together, you sit
152 Rock 2   26 ripe./And the Church must be forever building, and always decaying, and always
152 Rock 2   35 gain it./The Church must be forever building, for it is forever decaying within and
154 Rock 3   17 not the Word of GOD,/Much is your building, but not the House of GOD./Will you
167 Rock 10   43 We thank Thee who hast moved us to building, to finding, to forming at the ends of
177 FQ: ECoker   5 or a by-pass./Old stone to new building, old timber to new fires,/Old fires to
177 FQ: ECoker   9 live and die: there is a time for building/And a time for living and for
257 MC Chorus   21 pieces,/Gathering faggots at nightfall,/Building a partial shelter,/For sleeping, and
422 CP   Alex   12 to the libation./{A} The words for the building of the hearth. {}/[*They raise their*
462 CC   Colby   8 had in mind still seems to me/Like building my life upon a deception./Do you
BUILT (10)
151 Rock 2   2 of the household of GOD, being built upon the foundation/Of apostles and
151 Rock 2   4 chief cornerstone./But you, have you built well, that you now sit helpless in a ruined
151 Rock 2   11 less useful than dung'./You, have you built well, have you forgotten the cornerstone?/
157 Rock 4   2 prefer that the Temple should not be built./In the days of Nehemiah the Prophet/
157 Rock 4   18 hands to rebuilding the wall./So they built as men must build/With the sword in one
166 Rock 10   1 Light./You have seen the house built, you have seen it adorned/By one who
167 Rock 10   44 of our eyes./And when we have built an altar to the Invisible Light, we may set
201 Def Island   1 of the Islands/Let these memorials of built stone — music's/enduring instrument, of
288 FR Agatha   20 /Because the future can only be built/Upon the real past. Wandering in the
464 CC Claude   27 /My father — your grandfather — built up this business/Starting from nothing. It
BULBS (1)
52 Whispers   5 backward with a lipless grin./Daffodil bulbs instead of balls/Stared from the sockets of
BULL (1)
298 FR Charles   22 there's nothing to do but take the bull by the horns,/And this is one. {}/[*Knock:*
BULL-DOG (1)
346 FR Charles   3 that I am always surprised/By the bull-dog in the Burlington Arcade./What if
BULLBAT (1)
142 Cape Ann   10 purple martin. Greet/In silence the bullbat. All are delectable. Sweet sweet sweet/
BULLFINCH (1)
258 MC Thomas   13 and philosophy, curiosity,/The purple bullfinch in the lilac tree,/The tiltyard skill, the
BULLOCKS (1)
220 Old Deut   19 the High Street on market day;/The bullocks may bellow, the sheep they may bleat,/
BULLYING (2)
602 Humoresque   9 in a comic, dull grimace;/Half bullying, half imploring air,/Mouth twisted to
528 ES Charles   6 /Managing, manœuvring, cajoling or bullying —/At all of which he's a master.
BUMPUS (1)
291 FR   Violet   5 /{V} I should have been helping Lady Bumpus, at the Vicar's American Tea./{Ch} Yet
BUNGLED (1)
333 FR Agatha   4 a little common sense,/He would have bungled it./I did not want to kill *you*!/You to be
BUNKS (2)
213 Growltiger   31 sleeping in their barrels and their bunks —/As the Siamese came creeping in their
213 Growltiger   44 the hatches on the crew within their bunks./Then Griddlebone she gave a screech,
BURBANK (3)
40 Burb Blei   t of a dry brain in a dry season./Burbank with a Baedeker: Bleistein with a Cigar
40 Burb Blei   1 a Baedeker: Bleistein with a Cigar/Burbank crossed a little bridge/Descending at a
41 Burb Blei   31 rump and pared his claws?/Thought Burbank, meditating on/Time's ruins, and the
BURDEN (10)
91 Ash-Wed 2   24 And the bones sang chirping/With the burden of the grasshopper, saying/Lady of
107 Animula   16 and what the servants say./The heavy burden of the growing soul/Perplexes and
175 FQ: BurntN   153 and sometimes break, under the burden,/Under the tension, slip, slide, perish,/
271 MC Thomas   9 them,/This is your share of the eternal burden,/The perpetual glory. This is one
278 MC Knight2   35 and no one would have to bear the burden of/being called murderer. And at a later
334 FR Agatha   14 the word mean?/There's relief from a burden that I carried,/And exhaustion at the
334 FR Agatha   17 /The burden's yours now, yours/The burden of all the family. And I am a little
440 CP   Reilly   11 these people./{R} It is your appointed burden. And as for the party,/I am sure it will
494 CC Claude   21 to him was life. To me, it was a burden./You can't communicate an inspiration,/

527 ES   Charles   33   had brothers and sisters/To share the burden. Sisters, I should say,/For your brother's
BURDEN'S (1)
334 FR   Agatha   16   at the moment of relief./The burden's yours now, yours/The burden of all the
BURDENS (1)
411 CP   Reilly   29   /But to learn how to bear the burdens on your conscience./With the future of
BUREAU (1)
214 RTTugger   16   like to get about./He likes to lie in the bureau drawer,/But he makes such a fuss if he
BURIAL (1)
60 WL: Burial   t   shroud./The Waste Land/The Burial of the Dead/April is the cruellest month,
BURIED (6)
  19 Portrait   53   sunsets, that somehow recall/My buried life, and Paris in the Spring,/I feel
  45 Cook Egg   30   are the eagles and the trumpets?/Buried beneath some snow-deep Alps./Over
174 FQ: BurntN 130   time future./Time and the bell have buried the day,/The black cloud carries the sun
220 Old Deut   5   accession./Old Deuteronomy's buried nine wives/And more — I am tempted to
525 ES   Monica   29   seriously, Charles,/Father's sure to be buried in the library/And he won't think of
550 ES   Ld Clav   33   thought we both preferred to leave buried./{MC} There you're wrong, Richard.
BURLINGTON (1)
346 FR   Charles   3   surprised/By the bull-dog in the Burlington Arcade./What if every moment were
BURN (4)
  54 Mr E Sun   24   /Where the souls of the devout/Burn invisible and dim./Along the garden-wall
588 Fable   63   of grape juice./The lights began to burn distinctly blue,/As in ghost stories lights
240 MC   Chorus   9   eyes and our ears,/Disastrous summer burn up the beds of our streams/And the poor
332 FR   Agatha   28   of pointed light/When you want to burn. When you stretch out your hand/To the
BURNED (2)
  40 Burb Blei   12   /With even feet. Her shuttered barge/Burned on the water all the day./But this or
  64 WL: Chess   95   /Huge sea-wood fed with copper/Burned green and orange, framed by the
BURNING (8)
  70 WL: Fire S   308   /la la/To Carthage then I came/Burning burning burning burning/O Lord Thou
  70 WL: Fire S   308   la/To Carthage then I came/Burning burning burning burning/O Lord Thou pluckest
  70 WL: Fire S   308   then I came/Burning burning burning burning/O Lord Thou pluckest me out/
  70 WL: Fire S   308 then I came/Burning burning burning burning/O Lord Thou pluckest me out/O Lord
  70 WL: Fire S   311   me out/O Lord Thou pluckest/burning/Death by Water/Phlebas the
182 FQ: ECoker 196   no before and after,/But a lifetime burning in every moment/And not the lifetime
606 Narcissus   34 /Because his flesh was in love with the burning arrows/He danced on the hot sand/
294 FR   Harry   31   /For a momentary rest on the burning wheel/That cloudless night in the
BURNISHED (1)
  64 WL: Chess   77   of Chess/The Chair she sat in, like a burnished throne,/Glowed on the marble, where
BURNS (1)
179 FQ: ECoker   68   world to that destructive fire/Which burns before the ice-cap reigns./That was a way
BURNT (2)
171 FQ: BurntN   t Thy great glory!/FOUR QUARTETS/Burnt Norton/Time present and time past/Are
192 FQ: Little   57   an old man's sleeve/Is all the ash the burnt roses leave./Dust in the air suspended/
BURNT-OUT (1)
  22 Preludes   4   in passageways./Six o'clock./The burnt-out ends of smoky days./And now a gusty
BURROW (1)
155 Rock 3   32   and tennis flannels/The rabbit shall burrow and the thorn revisit,/The nettle shall
BURST (3)
213 Growltiger   42   Mongolian horde;/With a frightful burst of fireworks the Chinks they swarmed
263 MC   Chorus   22   on the tree, when the elder and may/Burst over the stream, and the air is clear and
398 CP   Lavinia   3   if you were human/You would burst out laughing. But you won't./{E} O God,
BURSTS (1)
  73 WL: Thund 372   mountains/Cracks and reforms and bursts in the violet air/Falling towers/Jerusalem
BURY (2)
180 FQ: ECoker 112   funeral, for there is no one to bury./I said to my soul, be still, and let the dark
264 MC   Priest3   19   like water,/And there was no man to bury them. Avenge, O Lord,/The blood of thy
BURYING (1)
268 MC Knight3   3 your See as you demanded./{K3} And burying the memory of your transgressions/
BUSH (1)
451 CC   Eggers   10   of gold. But not to beat about the bush,/He's rather a rough diamond. Very free
BUSINESS (66)
119 SP   Wauch   5 of ours,/American gentlemen here on business./Meet Mr. Klipstein. Meet Mr.
182 FQ: ECoker 191   is only the trying. The rest is not our business./Home is where one starts from. As we
187 FQ: DrySal 135   are settled/To fruit, periodicals and business letters/(And those who saw them off
189 FQ: DrySal 175   those who are in ships, those/Whose business has to do with fish, and/Those
236 Cat Morgan   17   keen on old Morgan./So if you 'ave business with Faber — or Faber —/I'll give you

250	MC	Tempt3	29	lord who minds his own business./It is we country lords who know the
265	MC	Knight1	15	yesterday, landed last night,/Having business with the Archbishop./{K2} Urgent
265	MC	Knight2	16	with the Archbishop./{K2} Urgent business./{K3} From the King./{K2} By the
265	MC	Priest1	24	offer you entertainment/Before your business. Please dine with us./Your men shall be
265	MC	Priest1	26	be looked after also./Dinner before business. Do you like roast pork?/{K1} Business
265	MC	Knight1	27	Do you like roast pork?/{K1} Business before dinner. We will roast your pork
266	MC	Thomas	7	/{T} You are welcome, whatever your business may be./You say, from the King?/{K1}
267	MC	Thomas	4	help you!/{T} But, gentlemen, your business/Which you said so urgent, is it only/
268	MC	Knight3	12	servants, every one who transacts/His business in his absence, the business of the
268	MC	Knight3	12	/His business in his absence, the business of the nation./{K1} These are the facts./
277	MC	Knight3	26	being completely disinterested in this business./I think that is about all I have to say./
292	FR	Amy	22	to call tomorrow/On some legal business, a question about taxes —/But I think
293	FR	Amy	6	I have never taken. Now it is your business./I have only struggled to keep
316	FR	Agatha	18	and the otter/Be about their proper business/The eye of the day time/And the eye of
321	FR	Warburt	36	For God's sake, Winchell, tell us your business./His Lordship isn't very well this
322	FR	Warburt	21	Heaven's sake, Winchell,/Tell us your business./{Wi} It's about Mr. John./{H} John!/
338	FR	Harry	27	/{H} And now I know/That my business is not to run away, but to pursue,/Not
347	FR	Ivy	19	or not. {}/[*Reads*]/{I} 'Regret delayed business in town many happy returns see you
348	FR	Chorus	11	asleep./We understand the ordinary business of living,/We know how to work the
359	CP	Julia	29	/But *I* never poke into other people's business./Well, good-bye again. I'm off at last.
411	CP	Reilly	28	problem. {}/[*To* EDWARD]/{R} Your business is not to clear your conscience/But to
433	CP	Peter	1	anybody/In *this* film — it's not my business;/And that's not the way we do it./{J}
445	CC	2m	1	/MRS. GUZZARD/Act One/*The Business Room on the first floor of* SIR
446	CC	Claude	21	quickly/If we started on a purely business basis./{E} No doubt that's best. While
447	CC	Eggers	20	/She has too much respect for your business genius./But it's true she believes she
451	CC	Colby	16	/And very good company apart from business. {}/[*Enter* LADY ELIZABETH
458	CC	Claude	4	must look as if we'd been engaged in business. {}/[*Enter* LADY ELIZABETH
460	CC	Claude	32	and rest./I'm in the middle of some business with Mr. .../{LE} Colby! {}/[*Exit*
462	CC	Claude	30	so far we've discussed only current business,/Thinking that you might find it easier/
464	CC	Claude	27	— your grandfather — built up this business/Starting from nothing. It was *his*
472	CC	Lucasta	31	/And made up your mind to go into business/And be someone like Claude ... or B. I
480	CC	Kaghan	6	Colby,/You and I ought to be in business together./I'm a good guesser. But I
481	CC	Colby	3	things that have nothing to do with business./{K} And you have a very sound head
481	CC	Kaghan	4	And you have a very sound head for business./Maybe you're a better financier than I
481	CC	Kaghan	6	I am!/That's why we ought to be in business together./{L} You're both very good at
489	CC	Claude	27	Canada./My father had sent me on a business tour/To learn about his overseas
493	CC	2m	1	/CURTAIN/Act Three/*The Business Room, as in Act* 1. *Several mornings*
497	CC	Eggers	3	ourselves!/And we've more important business, I imagine./{SC} Eggerson, I'm
500	CC	Lucasta	35	I know you think of him/Simply as a business man. As you thought of me/Simply as
511	CC	Lady E	12	He was not good at figures. Your business ability/Comes, I suppose, from my side
516	CC	Claude	20	/On beginning to learn the ways of business;/The exhilaration of finding you could
530	ES	Monica	6	up if we allowed you to!/That's my business to prevent. You know I'm to protect
534	ES	Ld Clav	6	It would seem then that most of your business/Has been of such a nature that, if
534	ES	Gomez	11	I wouldn't dream/Of carrying on such business if I lived in England./I have the same
539	ES	Ld Clav	27	/Is that in the midst of the engrossing business/Of the nature of which dark hints have
544	ES	Monica	9	the one for elevens's,/That's Nurse's business'./{LC} So far, so good./I'll feel more
550	ES	Ld Clav	24	of equipment./I trust that the business was very successful .../I mean, that he
557	ES	Michael	13	I want to find some more speculative business./{LC} I dare say you've tried a little
559	ES	Michael	37	/A representative carrying on business in your absence./Why should I thank
560	ES	Michael	10	/As a partner in some interesting business./But I might be expected to put up
560	ES	Ld Clav	12	up some capital./{LC} What sort of business have you in mind?/{Mi} Oh, I don't
560	ES	Ld Clav	16	/I will help you to make a start in any business/You may find for yourself — if, on
560	ES	Ld Clav	18	/I am satisfied about the nature of the business./{Mi} Anyway, I'm determined to get
565	ES	Gomez	19	sure./{G} Taking a holiday?/You're in business in London, aren't you?/{Mi} Not a
565	ES	Michael	20	/{Mi} Not a holiday, no. I've been in business in London,/But I think of cutting
576	ES	Gomez	21	wait until we get there./The nature of business in San Marco/Is easier explained in
577	ES	Charles	16	don't know, of the nature of whose business/You know nothing. All you can be
577	ES	Carghil	27	My late husband, Mr. Carghill, was a business man —/I wish you could have known
577	ES	Carghil	30	in some ways —/So I understand business. Mr. Carghill told me so./Now,
577	ES	Carghil	31	/Now, Michael has great abilities for business./I saw that, and so does Señor Gomez./
580	ES	Gomez	2	I'm glad you reminded me. Here's my business card/With the full address. You can

BUST (1)

52	Whispers		19	emphasis;/Uncorseted, her friendly bust/Gives promise of pneumatic bliss./The

BUSTLE (3)
210 Old Gumbie	5	Cat!/But when the day's hustle and bustle is done,/Then the Gumbie Cat's work is
210 Old Gumbie	17	Cat!/But when the day's hustle and bustle is done,/Then the Gumbie Cat's work is
211 Old Gumbie	29	Cat!/But when the day's hustle and bustle is done,/Then the Gumbie Cat's work is

BUSTOPHER (4)
230 Bust Jones	t	Firefrorefiddle, the Fiend of the Fell.'/Bustopher Jones: the Cat About Town/
230 Bust Jones	1	Jones: the Cat About Town/Bustopher Jones is *not* skin and bones —/In
230 Bust Jones	12	proud to be nodded or bowed to/By Bustopher Jones in white spats!/His visits are
231 Bust Jones	40	it shall be Spring in Pall Mall/While Bustopher Jones wears white spats!/

BUSTOPHER'S (1)
| 230 Bust Jones | 29 | mutton./So, much in this way, passes Bustopher's day —/At one club or another he's |

BUSTS (2)
| 129 Cor2 State | 29 | is the row of family portraits, dingy busts, all looking remarkably Roman,/ |
| 129 Cor2 State | 36 | the lintel/O mother (not among these busts, all correctly inscribed)/I a tired head |

BUSY (9)
164 Rock 9	10	for races,/Adorning themselves, and busy in the market, the forum,/And all other
232 Skimble	12	he'll saunter to the rear:/He's been busy in the luggage van!/He gives one flash of
233 Skimble	57	were sleeping all the while he was busy at Carlisle,/Where he greets the
301 FR Gerald	4	I only wondered/Why you've been busy about it tonight./{Do} Nothing wrong, Sir:
393 CP Edward	39	/That I should be always too busy or too tired/To be of use to you socially .../
400 CP Alex	31	show him up./{A} You will have a busy morning!/I will go out by the service
527 ES Lambert	14	/{M} Thank you, Lambert./{L} He's busy at the moment. But he won't be very long.
527 ES Monica	25	evening,/Even when he's reading, or busy with his papers/He needs to have someone
545 ES Piggott	29	in directly after breakfast:/He's led a busy life, too.' But I hope you're happy?/Is

BUT (1248)

BUTLER (4)
353 CP Peter	15	the wedding cake./{P} And how the butler found her in the pantry, rinsing her
394 CP Edward	12	/If you had hired me as your butler:/Some of your guests may have thought I
394 CP Edward	13	guests may have thought I *was* the butler./{L} And on several occasions, when
394 CP Edward	17	*they* can't have thought I was the butler./{L} Everything I tried only made matters

BUTT-ENDS (1)
| 15 Prufrock | 60 | how should I begin/To spit out all the butt-ends of my days and ways?/And how |

BUTTER (1)
| 24 Rhapsody | 37 | /And devours a morsel of rancid butter.'/So the hand of the child, automatic,/ |

BUTTERED (1)
| 45 Cook Egg | 31 | beneath some snow-deep Alps./Over buttered scones and crumpets/Weeping, |

BUTTERFLY (2)
| 590 Time Space | 7 | we ever pray/To live a century?/The butterfly that lives a day/Has lived eternity./The |
| 319 FR Harry | 22 | of unusual heat,/The day I lost my butterfly net;/I remember the silence, and the |

BUTTON (4)
233 Skimble	38	can make it dark or bright;/There's a button that you turn to make a breeze./There's
399 CP 4m	1	*at his desk. He presses an/electric button. The* NURSE-SECRETARY *enters, with*
412 CP m	24	*by side door]/*[REILLY *presses button.* NURSE-SECRETARY *shows in*
420 CP m	15	like yours/There is no fee. {}/[*Presses button*]/{C} You have been very kind./{R} Go in

BUY (8)
274 MC Thomas	36	Blood for blood./His blood given to buy my life,/My blood given to pay for His
445 CC Eggers	14	/And I thought, now's the moment to buy some new tools/So as not to lose a moment
456 CC Eggers	26	And when she's abroad/She is apt to buy a house. And then goes away/And forgets
525 ES Charles	12	—/Except to guess what you want to buy/And advise you to buy it./{M} But why not
525 ES Charles	13	you want to buy/And advise you to buy it./{M} But why not stop to tea?/{C} Very
541 ES Gomez	17	/On the contrary, I dare say I could buy you out/Several times over. San Marco's a
577 ES Gomez	25	he does come back/He'll be able to buy you out many times over./{MC} Richard, I
579 ES Michael	8	we can get a passage./And I must buy my kit. We're just going up to London./

BUZZING (1)
| 524 ES Monica | 19 | to want to have the waiters/All buzzing round you: and it reminds the girl/That |

BY (374)

BY-PASS (2)
| 161 Rock 7 | 37 | world stray in high-powered cars on a by-pass way?/VOICE OF THE |
| 177 FQ: ECoker | 4 | /Is an open field, or a factory, or a by-pass./Old stone to new building, old timber |

BY-STREET (1)
| 226 Macavity | 19 | of depravity./You may meet him in a by-street, you may see him in the square —/But |

BYE (4)
116 SP Dusty	36	phone through./Yes I'll tell her. Good bye. Goooood bye./I'm sure, that's very kind of
116 SP Dusty	36	/Yes I'll tell her. Good bye. Goooood bye./I'm sure, that's very kind of *you.*/Ah-h-h/
565 ES Gomez	27	some good talks/About old times. Bye bye for the present. {}/[*Exit]/*{M} Father,

565 ES   Gomez 27   good talks/About old times. Bye bye for the present. {}/[*Exit*]/{M} Father, those
BYRE (1)
270 MC Chorus 13   /In the mews in the barn in the byre in the market-place/In our veins our
BYZANCE (1)
  48 Lune Miel   18 pierres écroulantes la forme précise de Byzance./The Hippopotamus/The broad-backed

C.I.F. (1)
68 WL: Fire S	211		with a pocket full of currants/C.i.f. London: documents at sight,/Asked me in

C' (6)
47 Mél Adult	3	/En Angleterre, journaliste;/C'est à grands pas et en sueur/Que vous suivrez
47 Mél Adult	8	/Vous me paierez bien la tête./C'est à Paris que je me coiffe/Casque noir de
51 Restaurant	5	vent, du grand soleil, et de la pluie;/C'est ce qu'on appelle le jour de lessive des
51 Restaurant	9	et des bourgeons sur les ronces —/C'est là, dans une averse, qu'on s'abrite./J'avais
51 Restaurant	19	peur, je l'ai quittée à mi-chemin./C'est dommage.'/Mais alors, tu as ton vautour!/
51 Restaurant	30	sa vie antérieure./Figurez-vous donc, c'était un sort pénible;/Cependant, ce fut jadis

CAB-HORSE (1)
22 Preludes	12	at the corner of the street/A lonely cab-horse steams and stamps./And then the

CABBAGE (1)
230 Bust Jones	28	then he's lunched at the *Tomb*/On cabbage, rice pudding and mutton./So, much in

CABIN (1)
295 FR	Harry	1	to find her when I went back to the cabin./Later, I became excited, I think I made

CABINED (1)
249 MC Tempt2	24	/{T2} Yes! Or bravery will be broken,/Cabined in Canterbury, realmless ruler,/

CABMAN (1)
457 CC	Claude	23	She's having a conversation with the cabman./What can they be talking about? She's

CACTUS (1)
84 Hollow Men	40	kingdom/This is the dead land/This is cactus land/Here the stone images/Are raised,

CADENCES (1)
205 de la Mare	29	the mind?/By you; by those deceptive cadences/Wherewith the common measure is

CAGE (2)
212 Growltiger	13		weak canary, that fluttered from its cage;/Woe to the pampered Pekinese, that faced
395 CP	Edward	39	of each taking his corner of the cage./Well, it's a better way of passing the

CAJOLING (1)
528 ES	Charles	6	people/Managing, manœuvring, cajoling or bullying —/At all of which he's a

CAKE (10)
288 FR	Ivy	4	when will you have your birthday cake, Amy,/And open your presents?/{A} After
288 FR	Ivy	9	the first time/You have not had your cake and your presents at tea./{A} This is a very
325 FR	Ivy	18	nothing had happened,/And have the cake and presents./{G} But I'm worried about
349 FR 2m		13	*enter* DENMAN *carrying a birthday* cake *with/lighted candles, which she sets on the*
353 CP	Celia	14	about Lady Klootz and the wedding cake./{P} And how the butler found her in the
354 CP	Celia	21	on with the story about the wedding cake./{J} Well, but it really isn't my story./I
355 CP	Peter	16	on with the story about the wedding cake. { }/[EDWARD *leaves the room*]/{J} No,
356 CP	Celia	14	on with the story about the wedding cake./{J} Edward, do sit down for a moment./I
356 CP	Celia	16	Lady Klootz?/{C} And the wedding cake./{J} Wedding cake? I wasn't at her
358 CP	Julia	17	And the wedding cake./{J} Wedding cake? I wasn't at her wedding./Edward, it's been

CAKES (3)
15 Prufrock	79	you and me./Should I, after tea and cakes and ices,/Have the strength to force the
588 Fable	48	and puddings,/And jellies, pasties, cakes among the good things./A mighty
549 ES Carghil	15	a tea basket/With some lovely little cakes — I've forgotten what you called them,/

CALAMITOUS (1)
185 FQ: DrySal	56	beach, the unprayable/Prayer at the calamitous annunciation?/There is no end, but

CALAMITY (1)
326 FR	Harry	10	Can drop off to sleep in the middle of calamity/Like children, or like hardened

CALCULATE (1)
212 Growltiger	5	/His manners and appearance did not calculate to please;/His coat was torn and seedy,

CALCULATING (1)
185 FQ: DrySal	42	worried women/Lying awake, calculating the future,/Trying to unweave,

CALCULATION (1)
416 CP	Celia	16	/Seemed so right: not in terms of calculation/Of what was good for the persons

CALCULATIONS (2)
343 FR	Amy	27	/With wakeful nights and patient calculations/With the solicitor, the broker,
509 CC	Lady E	34	/{LE} Then I must be out in my calculations./{SC} That wouldn't surprise me./

CALIFORNIA (17)
356 CP	Peter	2	/I came across him last year in California./{J} I've always wanted to go to
356 CP	Julia	3	/{J} I've always wanted to go to California./Do tell us what you were doing in
356 CP	Julia	4	/Do tell us what you were doing in California./{C} Making a film./{P} Trying to
371 CP	Edward	11	to do?/{E} Nothing. Wait. Go back to California./{P} But I must see Celia./{E} Will it
387 CP	Peter	36	/That it's all no use. I'm going to California./{C} You're going to California!/{P}
387 CP	Celia	37	to California./{C} You're going to California!/{P} Yes, I have a new job./{E} And
389 CP	Peter	12	/{P} Yes, of course, I'm going to California./{L} Well, Celia, why don't you go to
389 CP	Lavinia	13	/{L} Well, Celia, why don't you go to California?/Everyone says it's a wonderful

397 CP	Lavinia	39	nothing to do/With Celia going to California?/{E} Celia? Going to California?/{L}
397 CP	Edward	40	to California?/{E} Celia? Going to California?/{L} Yes, with Peter./Really, Edward,
423 CP	Alex	3	know, I have connections — even in California. {}/CURTAIN/Act Three/*The*
431 CP	Julia	9	*his* name./{J} Is he your connection in California, Alex?/{A} Yes, we have sometimes
431 CP	Peter	25	it./Then we build another Boltwell in California./{J} But what is your position, Peter?/
431 CP	Julia	38	idea!/I've always wanted to go to California:/Couldn't you persuade your casting
432 CP	Julia	33	conversation./Peter's just over from California/Where he's something very
433 CP	Julia	4	Peter;/If you're taking Boltwell to California/Why can't you take me?/{P} We're
433 CP	Julia	11	/So good-bye to my hopes of seeing California./{P} You know you'd never come if

CALL (70)

43 Swee Erect		35	/Find themselves involved, disgraced,/Call witness to their principles/And deprecate
116 SP	Dusty	28	too —/Well I *hope* we shan't have to call a doctor/Doris just hates having a doctor/
122 SAWa & Ho		25	*the breadfruit fall/And the penguin call/And the sound is the sound of the sea/Under*
156 Rock 3		71	/For nation or race or what you call humanity;/Though you forget the way to
160 Rock 7		19	out of time, but in time, in what we call history: transecting, bisecting the world of
161 Rock 7		29	Money, and Power, and what they call Life, or Race, or Dialectic./The Church
163 Rock 8		41	that took men from home/At the call of a wandering preacher./Our age is an age
173 FQ: BurntN		66	arrest nor movement. And do not call it fixity,/Where past and future are
182 FQ: ECoker	173	blood —/Again, in spite of that, we call this Friday good./So here I am, in the
197 FQ: Little	216	by either fire or fire./What we call the beginning is often the end/And to make
202 War Poetry		24	/Becoming universal, which we call 'poetry',/May be affirmed in verse./To the
205 de la Mare		24	traveller can arouse/No sleeper by his call; or when by chance/An empty face peers
214 RTTugger		8	a Curious Cat —/And there isn't any call for me to shout it:/For he will do/As he do
225 Mr Mistoff		51	/And I have known the family to call/Him in from the garden for hours,/While he
228 Gus		4	a fuss/To pronounce, that we usually call him just Gus./His coat's very shabby, he's
234 Ad-dress		23	is, on the whole,/What you would call a simple soul./Of course I'm not including
235 Ad-dress		50	CAT!/I think I've heard them call him James —/But we've not got so far as
235 Ad-dress		67	time you reach your aim,/And finally call him by his NAME./So this is this, and that
593 Grad 5		1	into the future years./Great duties call — the twentieth century/More grandly
595 Grad 14		5	that we are ever loth to say./But 'tis a call we cannot disobey,/*Exeunt omnes*, with a
273 MC Chorus		1	nothing with nothing,/Not what we call death, but what beyond death is not death,/
274 MC Thomas		3	time that my decision is taken/If you call that decision/To which my whole being
276 MC Knight1		31	extremely complex problem. I/shall call upon our eldest member to speak first, my
277 MC Knight1		32	hear/our other speakers. I shall next call upon Hugh de Morville, who/has made a
289 FR	Amy	21	in front of the family:/You can call it nothing but a blessed relief./{V} *I* call it
289 FR	Violet	22	it nothing but a blessed relief./{V} *I* call it providential./{I} Yet it must have been
292 FR	Amy	21	Bevan — you remember — wants to call tomorrow/On some legal business, a
295 FR	Harry	18	a good deal deeper/Than what people call their conscience; it is just the cancer/That
299 FRDowning		37	his Lordship/Suffered from what they call a kind of repression./But what struck me ...
314 FR	Harry	19	some justification:/For what you call restoration to health/Is only incubation of
314 FR Warburt		29	all of us ill in one way or another:/We call it health when we find no symptom/Of
326 FR	Harry	21	that life ought to take,/That you call normal. What you call the normal/Is merely
326 FR	Harry	21	take,/That you call normal. What you call the normal/Is merely the unreal and the
326 FR	Denman	33	Excuse me, Miss Ivy. There's a trunk call for you./{I} A trunk call? for me? why, who
326 FR	Ivy	34	a trunk call for you./{I} A trunk call? for me? why, who can want me?/{D} He
341 FR	Amy	20	you would make for him/Is another. I call it failure. Your fury for possession/Is only
365 CP	Julia	16	I left my spectacles:/*This* is what I call an adventure!/Tell me about him. You've
378 CP	Edward	33	were suggested to me/By the man I call Riley — though his name is not Riley;/It
391 CP	Julia	2	we'll all go back to *my* house. Peter, call a taxi. {}/[*Exit* PETER]/{J} We'll have a
401 CP	Reilly	26	/{E} So this *is* a trap!/{R} Let's not call it a trap./But if it is a trap, then you cannot
405 CP	Edward	29	did not expect to meet *you*, Lavinia./I call this a very dishonourable trick./{R} Honesty
413 CP	Reilly	6	breakdown — that is what they call it —/And usually they think that someone
415 CP	Reilly	30	so you suppose you have what you call a 'kink'?/{C} But everything seemed so
454 CC	Eggers	16	seemed to me sane./{E} I should call him the very picture of sanity./{C} But you
454 CC	Colby	30	She does indeed./{C} And does she call Lady Elizabeth *Lizzie*?/{E} Well, not in her
454 CC	Eggers	32	I don't think she would. But she does call her Lizzie,/Sometimes, to Sir Claude. And
461 CC	Colby	13	But I hope/That I shan't have to call upon you often./{E} Oh, and I forgot ...
461 CC	Claude	27	being Mr. Colby —/I shall begin to call you Colby with everyone./{C} I'm sure that
475 CC	Colby	14	changing too. But perhaps what we call change .../{L} Is understanding better what
482 CC	Lady E	6	asked me to play to her./{LE} You call her Lucasta? Young people nowadays/Seem
482 CC	Colby	27	not your sort at all./{C} I shouldn't call them vulgar. Perhaps I'm vulgar too./But
505 CC	Eggers	16	/{E} Yes, that is what I should call it, Mrs. Guzzard./I take it, Sir Claude, I
509 CC	Claude	28	like the name, for some reason;/So we call him B./{MG} A very good name./He ought
511 CC	Kaghan	27	—/I mean, Aunt Elizabeth: if I call you Aunt Elizabeth/Would you mind very
532 ES	Monica	21	tell you that you have to take a trunk call./Come, Charles. Will you bring my coat?/

533 ES	Gomez	13	has brought you to England?/{G} Call it homesickness,/Curiosity, restlessness,
540 ES	Ld Clav	3	than yours./{LC} And what do you call failure?/{G} What do I call failure?/The
540 ES	Gomez	4	do you call failure?/{G} What do I call failure?/The worst kind of failure, in my
541 ES	Lambert	32	me/To remind you there's a trunk call coming through for you/In five minutes'
542 ES	Ld Clav	13	/{LC} This is preposterous!/Do you call it friendship to impose your company/On a
545 ES	Monica	37	how we ought to address you./Do we call you 'Matron'?/{MP} Oh no, not 'Matron'!/
546 ES	Piggott	4	I've always lived in what you might call/A medical milieu. My father was a specialist
546 ES	Piggott	9	was a theatre nurse. But you mustn't call me 'Matron'/At Badgley Court. You see,
546 ES	Piggott	17	I'm Mrs. Piggott./Just call me Mrs. Piggott. It's a short and simple
546 ES	Piggott	30	you. So you'll remember/Always to call me Mrs. Piggott, won't you?/{M} Yes, Mrs.
557 ES	Ld Clav	28	of your name. And what do you call good terms?/{Mi} I'd nothing at all to pay
561 ES	Michael	14	in dying./{Mi} Very well: if you like, call me a coward./I wonder whether you would
565 ES	Carghil	12	of mine/That it seems most natural to call you Michael./You don't mind, do you?/
574 ES	Carghil	3	/So much so, that it seems odd to call you Mr. Hemington:/I'm going to call you
574 ES	Carghil	4	call you Mr. Hemington:/I'm going to call you Charles!/{C} As you please, Mrs.

CALLED (16)

62 WL: Burial		36	me hyacinths first a year ago;/'They called me the hyacinth girl.'/— Yet when we
172 FQ: BurntN		28	through the vibrant air,/And the bird called, in response to/The unheard music hidden
226 Macavity		1	Cat/Macavity's a Mystery Cat: he's called the Hidden Paw —/For he's the master
278 MC Knight2		36	have to bear the burden of/being called murderer. And at a later time still, even
307 FR	Mary	1	/{M} The hollow tree in what we called the wilderness/{H} Down near the river.
333 FR	Agatha	6	What were you then? only a thing called 'life' —/Something that should have been
357 CP	Julia	21	weeks,/Or she may come back and be called away again./I understand these tough old
407 CP	Reilly	40	this discovery/Precipitated what you called your nervous breakdown./{L} But it's
427 CP	Julia	22	in this strange place —/What's it called?/{A} Kinkanja./{J} What were you doing/
486 CC	Lady E	12	/Was Mrs. Guzzard. And you always called her 'aunt'?/{C} Why not? She was my
509 CC	Lady E	7	father's./But how did he come to be called Colby?/{SC} But, Elizabeth, it isn't
525 ES	Monica	30	he won't think of leaving it until he's called for tea./So why not talk now? Though I
540 ES	Gomez	33	them) you didn't want *them*/To be called to give evidence. You just couldn't face it.
549 ES	Carghil	15	little cakes — I've forgotten what you called them,/And you made me try to punt, and
552 ES	Carghil	7	what a hit I made/With a number called *It's Not Too Late For You To Love Me*?/
558 ES	Michael	8	his staff/Who'd taken to gambling. Called me a gambler!/Said he'd communicate

CALLER (1)

541 ES	Gomez	38	you long, though I dare say your caller/Could hang on for another quarter of an

CALLING (7)

110 Marina		34	towards my timbers/And woodthrush calling through the fog/My daughter./The
197 FQ: Little		240	of this Love and the voice of this Calling/We shall not cease from exploration/
455 CC	Eggers	1	You'll soon get used to it. You'll be calling me Eggers/Before you know it!/{C} I
461 CC	Claude	23	/{SC} Well, Colby! I've been calling you Mr. Simpkins/In public, till now, as
511 CC	Kaghan	28	/Would you mind very much calling me ... just 'B'?/{LE} Certainly, if you
511 CC	Kaghan	31	of Barnabas?/{K} I don't want people calling me 'Barney' —/Barney Kaghan!
546 ES	Piggott	40	the guests in one respect;/And calling our nurses 'Nurse' reassures them/In

CALLOUS (1)

324 FR	Ivy	21	/{I} Really, Harry! how can you be so callous?/I always thought you were so fond of

CALLS (6)

256 MC Chorus		29	*alternately*./{C} Is it the owl that calls, or a signal between the trees?/{3P} Is the
447 CC	Eggers	21	it's true she believes she has what she calls 'guidance'./{SC} Guidance. That's worse
452 CC	Lucasta	30	Colby? I'm Lucasta./It's only Eggy calls me Miss Angel,/Just to annoy me. Don't
466 CC	Claude	16	wife's investigations/Into what she calls the life of the spirit/Are a kind of
556 ES		m 9	then, fetch him./Let's get this over. {}/[*calls*]/{M} Michael! {}/[*Enter* MICHAEL]/{LC}
561 ES	Michael	34	my own career:/And Father simply calls me a coward./{M} Father! You know that I

CALM (4)

74 WL: Thund		420	expert with sail and oar/The sea was calm, your heart would have responded/Gaily,
91 Ash-Wed 2		26	grasshopper, saying/Lady of silences/Calm and distressed/Torn and most whole/Rose
179 FQ: ECoker		75	looked forward to,/Long hoped for calm, the autumnal serenity/And the wisdom of
526 ES	Charles	32	And your father will come. With his calm possessive air/And his kindly welcome,

CAMARDE (1)

46 Directeur		17	un égout/Une petite fille/En guenilles/Camarde/Regarde/Le directeur/Du Spectateur/

CAMBRIDGE (1)

314 FR Warburt		23	I remember, when I was a student at Cambridge,/I used to dream of making some

CAMDEN (1)

174 FQ: BurntN		114	/Hampstead and Clerkenwell, Camden and Putney,/Highgate, Primrose and

CAME (120)

23 Preludes		30	the ceiling./And when all the world came back/And the light crept up between the
37 Gerontion		20	In the juvescence of the year/Came Christ the tiger/In depraved May,

62 WL: Burial	37	me the hyacinth girl.'/— Yet when we came back, late, from the hyacinth garden,/
70 WL: Fire S	307	/Nothing.'/la la/To Carthage then I came/Burning burning burning burning/O Lord
103 Journ Magi	21	this was all folly./Then at dawn we came down to a temperate valley,/Wet, below
103 Journ Magi	26	away in the meadow./Then we came to a tavern with vine-leaves over the lintel,
111 Xmas Trees	32	fear, as on the occasion/When fear came upon every soul:/Because the beginning
116 SP Dusty	24	I'm *so* sorry. I *am* so sorry/But Doris came home with a terrible chill/No, just a chill/
124 SA Doris	4	don't talk,/I cut the cards before you came/And I drew the coffin/{Sw} *You* drew the
124 SA Sweeney	29	on for a couple of months/Nobody came/And nobody went/But he took in the milk
139 Virginia	11	moving. Ever moving/Iron thoughts came with me/And go with me:/Red river, river,
154 Rock 3	1	in the forge./The Word of the LORD came unto me, saying:/O miserable cities of
160 Rock 7	13	of the Arctic Current;/And they came to an end, a dead end stirred with a flicker
160 Rock 7	14	stirred with a flicker of life,/And they came to the withered ancient look of a child
160 Rock 7	18	on the face of the deep./Then came, at a predetermined moment, a moment in
162 Rock 8	8	trodden the wine-press alone./There came one who spoke of the shame of Jerusalem/
162 Rock 8	22	sunken in moral corruption;/Many came back well broken,/Diseased and beggared,
162 Rock 8	25	/A stranger at the door in possession:/Came home cracked by the sun of the East/And
166 Rock 10	2	you have seen it adorned/By one who came in the night, it is now dedicated to GOD./
191 FQ: Little	21	unimaginable/Zero summer?/If you came this way,/Taking the route you would be
191 FQ: Little	24	would be likely to come from,/If you came this way in may time, you would find the
191 FQ: Little	27	same at the end of the journey,/If you came at night like a broken king,/If you came
191 FQ: Little	28	at night like a broken king,/If you came by day not knowing what you came for,/It
191 FQ: Little	28	came by day not knowing what you came for,/It would be the same, when you leave
192 FQ: Little	31	And what you thought you came for/Is only a shell, a husk of meaning/
192 FQ: Little	41	time,/Now and in England./If you came this way,/Taking any route, starting from
212 Growltiger	16	to any Cat with whom Growltiger came to grips!/But most to Cats of foreign race
213 Growltiger	32	and their bunks —/As the Siamese came creeping in their sampans and their junks./
218 Mung Rump	9	like a field of war,/If a tile or two came loose on the roof,/Which presently ceased
219 Mung Rump	35	smash/Or up from the pantry there came a loud crash/Or down from the library
219 Mung Rump	36	loud crash/Or down from the library came a loud *ping*/From a vase which was
223 Pekes Pols	28	when they heard the uproar,/Some came to the window, some came to the door;/
223 Pekes Pols	28	/Some came to the window, some came to the door;/There were surely a dozen,
223 Pekes Pols	37	order,/Playing *When the Blue Bonnets Came Over the Border*./Then the Pugs and the
587 Fable	19	his crimes;/At any rate, he sometimes came to dinner,/Whene'er the monks were
588 Fable	51	kept from toppling over,/Next came a viand made of turtle eggs,/And after
593 Grad 5	2	grandly dowered than those which came before,/Summons — who knows what
596 When we	1	with a last 'farewell'./Song/When we came home across the hill/No leaves were fallen
605 Narcissus	20	convulsive thighs and knees./So he came out under the rock./First he was sure that
606 Narcissus	36	on the hot sand/Until the arrows came./As he embraced them his white skin
248 MC Tempt1	4	not wait upon ceremony,/I leave as I came, forgetting all acrimony,/Hoping that your
277 MC Knight3	7	a/very good impression when we came in just now. The fact is that/we knew we
292 FR Harry	10	them./Why should they wait until I came back to Wishwood?/There were a
306 FR Harry	5	—/And I haven't seen you since you came down from Oxford./{M} Well, I must go
306 FR Harry	40	But what was the design?/It never came off. But do you remember/{M} The hollow
313 FR Mary	18	/{M} I must go and change. I came in very late. {}/[*Exit*]/{C} Now we only
314 FR Warburt	11	have forgotten/The day when you came back from school with measles/And we
315 FR Amy	27	we are the oldest inhabitants./As we came first, we will go first, in to dinner./{W}
318 FR Harry	5	before we had begun./When we came back, for the school holidays,/They were
319 FR Harry	10	Ivy and Violet —/Agatha never came then. Where was my father?/{W} Harry,
326 FR Harry	30	years that I have had to live/Since I came home, a few hours ago, to Wishwood./{V}
330 FR Harry	24	That is one hell./Then the numbness came to cover it — that is another —/That was
332 FR Agatha	21	then/An undergraduate at Oxford. I came/Once for a long vacation. I remember/A
332 FR Agatha	34	known neither./{Ag} The autumn came too soon, not soon enough./The rain and
342 FR Mary	2	Amy. I have just seen Denman./She came to tell me that Harry is leaving/Downing
345 FR Charles	36	I suppose I'm getting old:/Old age came softly up to now. I felt safe enough;/And
356 CP Peter	2	No, I never knew him at Oxford:/I came across him last year in California./{J} I've
360 CP Edward	5	a cocktail party./She'd gone when I came in, this afternoon./She left a note to say
365 CP Reilly	7	*me bein' the One Eyed Riley,/Who came in but the landlord's daughter/And she took*
367 CP Alex	37	first how you *got* in, Alex./{A} Why, I came and found that the door was open/And so
368 CP Peter	30	leave off?/{P} You asked me how I came to know Celia./I met her here, about a
369 CP Edward	23	/But you haven't told me how you came to know Celia./{P} I saw her again a few
376 CP Edward	1	/[*Exit* CELIA]/{E} Suppose someone came and found you in the kitchen? {}/
376 CP Edward	27	knows./{E} It's something that Alex came and prepared for me./He *would* do it.
379 CP Celia	30	Julia asked about Lavinia/And it came to me that Lavinia had left you/And that
380 CP Edward	21	/{E} Wasn't there? *He* thought so./He came back this evening to talk to me about it./
380 CP Celia	26	took him to concerts./But then, as he came to make more acquaintances,/I found him

387 CP	Celia	4	pleasant experience./Oh, I'm glad I came!/I can see you at last as a human being./
392 CP	Edward	15	I couldn't get everyone. And so a few came./{L} Who came?/{E} Just those who were
392 CP	Lavinia	16	And so a few came./{L} Who came?/{E} Just those who were here this evening
393 CP	Lavinia	9	sense of humour myself./That's what came of always giving in to you./{E} I was
398 CP	Edward	7	these doubts to enter? And then you came back, you/The angel of destruction — just
401 CP	Edward	4	/— Now, Mr. Chamberlayne?/{E} It came into my mind/Before I entered the door,
401 CP	Edward	17	to ask a question./{E} When you came to my flat/Had you been invited by my
402 CP	Edward	9	need to consult you/Or anyone else. I came here as a patient./If you take no interest in
403 CP	Reilly	11	As lay within your power — until you came to grief./Half of the harm that is done in
408 CP	Edward	21	less likely to suspect./And then he came to *me* to confide about Celia!/I have never
408 CP	Reilly	39	/Mrs. Chamberlayne, when you came to me two months ago/I was dissatisfied
410 CP	Reilly	22	sanatorium/In the state in which you came to me — I tell you this:/It would have
412 CP	Julia	8	slipped in by the back way./I only came to tell you, I am sure she is ready/To
413 CP	Celia	1	to see you. Well, I can't./I just came in desperation. And I shan't be offended/
419 CP	Celia	16	much better for it —/That's why I came to you. But they returned .../Well ... I
419 CP	Reilly	25	/In the sense in which your friends came back./I did not say they stayed there./{C}
433 CP	Alex	27	was about to speak of her/When you came in, Peter. I'm afraid you can't have Celia./
440 CP	Lavinia	1	it was over./I mean ... I am glad you came ... I am glad Alex told us .../And Peter had
445 CC	Eggers	24	heard nothing since the last time I came./{SC} Well, of course, Eggerson, you're
462 CC	Claude	16	/Why, it wouldn't surprise me if she came to believe/That you really are her son,
465 CC	Colby	7	You've still not explained why you came to think/That your father had been right./
465 CC	Claude	9	father had been right./{SC} Because I came to see/That I should never have become a
465 CC	Claude	18	uncreative?/I don't think so. For I came to see/That I had always known, at the
465 CC	Colby	39	/As the composer heard it when it came to him;/But when I played before other
470 CC	Colby	7	I've not played/To anyone, since I came to the conclusion/That I should never
471 CC	Colby	23	give a false impression./And then you came to see that you hadn't succeeded./{L} Oh,
483 CC	Lady E	7	them./{LE} They can be found./But I came to have a look at the flat/To see if the
486 CC	Claude	34	that you were here with Colby./So I came over instead of telephoning,/Just to give
489 CC	Claude	13	a better reason for keeping silent./I came to see how you longed for a son of your
489 CC	Claude	15	/And tell her then. And they never came./And now I regret the decision bitterly./I
494 CC	Claude	17	for was power and wealth;/And I came to see that what I had interpreted/In this
496 CC	Eggers	26	admit it. She misses my news/When I came home in the evening. And the late editions
497 CC	Claude	20	.../{LE} Now, Claude!/{SC} And she came to the conclusion that her child must be
499 CC	Lucasta	10	LUCASTA]/{L} Is this a meeting? I came to speak to Colby./I'm sorry./{SC} Colby
499 CC	Lucasta	15	/Won't it do another time?/{L} I came to apologise/To Colby. No matter. It'll do
500 CC	Claude	12	clear to you/At the time when he came here. But I didn't trust you/To keep a
500 CC	Lucasta	23	when I said I was your daughter!/I came to thank him for the shock he'd given me./
502 CC	Lucasta	5	about. But I did come to see you./I came to apologise for my behaviour/The other
508 CC	Guzzard	39	the child had been baptised/When it came to us; but we could not be sure./My
515 CC	Guzzard	5	reached you./On your return, you came at once to see me;/And I found that I had
537 ES	Gomez	22	either, but I was flattered./Later, I came to understand: you made friends with me/
537 ES	Ld Clav	29	And what is the conclusion that you came to?/{G} This is how it worked out, Dick.
537 ES	Gomez	32	devil/Inside you, Dick. He never came to *my* help./{LC} I certainly admit no
537 ES	Gomez	36	at Oxford, and left me to it./And so it came about that I was sent down/With the
538 ES	Ld Clav	7	thing you seem to have forgotten:/I came to your assistance when you were released.
553 ES	Carghil	24	/It was Effie said, when the break came,/'They'll be worth a fortune to you,
554 ES	Piggott	21	/Two of our very nicest guests!/I just came to see that Lord Claverton was
557 ES	Michael	16	gave me excellent tips./They always came off — the tips I didn't take./{LC} And the
562 ES	Carghil	13	I didn't think you'd still be here./I came back to have a quiet read of your letters;/
574 ES	Ld Clav	27	you this morning,/But you never came./{Mi} No, Father. I'll explain why./{LC}
575 ES	Michael	9	It's not created for me./Señor Gomez came to London to find a man to fill it,/And he
578 ES	Michael	24	in common./I remember, when I came home for the holidays/How it used to get
579 ES	Gomez	37	it as a stroke of good fortune/That I came to England at the very moment/When I

CAMEL (1)

103 Journ Magi	11	silken girls bringing sherbet./Then the camel men cursing and grumbling/And running

CAMELS (1)

103 Journ Magi	6	/The very dead of winter.'/And the camels galled, sore-footed, refractory,/Lying

CAMISOLES (1)

68 WL: Fire S	227	(at night her bed)/Stockings, slippers, camisoles, and stays./I Tiresias, old man with

CAMMEL (1)

39 Gerontion	67	/Delay? De Bailhache, Fresca, Mrs. Cammel, whirled/Beyond the circuit of the

CAMP (1)

134 Wind	10	/I saw across the blackened river/The camp fire shake with alien spears./Here, across

CAMPAIGNERS (1)

326 FR	Harry	11	/Like children, or like hardened campaigners. She looked/Very much as she

CAMPHOR (1)
371 CP	Edward	32	There's no memory you can wrap in camphor/But the moths will get in. So you want

CAN (360)
CAN'T (130)
66 WL: Chess	146	and get a nice set,/He said, I swear, I can't bear to look at you./And no more can't I,
66 WL: Chess	147	bear to look at you./And no more can't I, I said, and think of poor Albert,/He's
66 WL: Chess	154	/Others can pick and choose if you can't./But if Albert makes off, it won't be for
66 WL: Chess	158	antique./(And her only thirty-one.)/I can't help it, she said, pulling a long face,/It's
115 SP	Doris	12	He's no gentleman, Pereira:/You can't trust him!/{Du} Well that's true./He's no
115 SP	Dusty	14	that's true./He's no gentleman if you can't trust him/And *if* you can't trust him —/
115 SP	Dusty	15	if you can't trust him/And *if* you can't trust him —/Then you never know what
116 SP	Doris	4	right/{Do} But Pereira won't do./We can't have Pereira/{Du} Well what you going to
116 SP	Doris	14	ling/{Du} That's Pereira/{Do} Well can't you stop that horrible noise?/Pick up the
117 SP	Doris	17	it might be you/We're all hearts. You can't be sure./It just depends on what comes
214 RTTugger	17	/But he makes such a fuss if he can't get out./Yes the Rum Tum Tugger is a
232 Skimble	4	/We must find him or the train can't start.'/All the guards and all the porters
232 Skimble	8	very nimble/Then the Night Mail just can't go.'/At 11.42 then the signal's overdue/
236 Cat Morgan	12	says, and I guess that's enough;/'You can't but like Morgan, 'e's got a good 'art.'/I
589 Fable	68	—/That ghosts are fellows whom you *can't* keep out;/It is a thing to be lamented sorely
292 FR	Harry	2	/{H} No, no, not there. Look there!/Can't you see them? *You* don't see them, but I
293 FR	Gerald	30	of events./{G} Well, you can't say that nothing has happened to *me*./I
298 FR	Charles	1	for him./And as for my means, we can't afford to be squeamish/In taking hold of
300 FRDowning	19	/For a quiet smoke, where the women can't follow him./She wouldn't leave him out of
305 FR	Harry	30	if anything was changed,/But if so, I can't find it./{M} Your mother insisted/On
306 FR	Harry	20	to return/Out of my childhood. I can't explain./But I thought I might escape from
312 FR	Harry	5	not have listened/To your nonsense. Can't you help me?/You're of no use to me. I
314 FR	Warburt	10	remember/To see you again. But you can't have forgotten/The day when you came
315 FR	Violet	19	look at your mother!/Except that she can't get about now in winter/You wouldn't
319 FR	Warburt	39	she could tell you. But, Harry,/We can't sit here all the evening, you know;/You
322 FR	Harry	16	not .../{H} You mean you think I can't. But I might surprise you;/I think I might
324 FR	Harry	17	of consciousness/That John enjoys, can't make very much difference/To him or to
325 FR	Charles	11	nothing we could do that Warburton can't./If he's worse than Winchell said, then
327 FR	Harry	19	You don't understand me./You can't understand me. It's not being alone/That
334 FR	Harry	3	one wanted/Or in getting rid of what can't be got rid of/But in a different vision. This
344 FR	Violet	16	you make up your mind .../{V} You can't really think of *living* in a tropical climate!/
344 FR	Harry	36	still you would not understand./You can't know why I am going. You have not seen/
346 FRDowning	21	won't need me/Very long now. I can't give you any reasons./But to show you
347 FR	Ivy	27	she is resting./{I} Oh, I'm sorry. But can't you explain?/Why do you all look so
354 CP	Julia	27	No, I don't know her./{J} Well, one can't be too careful/Before one tells a story./{A}
355 CP	Julia	28	/What's that? Potato crisps? No, I can't endure them./Well, I started to tell you
361 CP	Reilly	7	having to lie about it/Because you can't tell the truth on the telephone./It will all
361 CP	Reilly	8	/It will all take time that you can't well spare;/But I put it to you .../{E} Don't
362 CP	Edward	15	/And was not coming back — well, I can't understand it./Nobody likes to be left with
364 CP	Reilly	14	been in the light./The fact that you can't give a reason for wanting her/Is the best
364 CP	Julia	33	left my glasses here,/And I simply can't see a thing without them./I've been
369 CP	Alex	10	Isn't there one in every kitchen?/{A} I can't find it./There goes *that* surprise. I must
370 CP	Peter	8	—/So ... contented, so ... at peace: I can't express it;/I had never imagined such quiet
370 CP	Alex	14	*and an apron*]/{A} Edward, I can't find any curry powder./{E} There isn't any
371 CP	Edward	23	{}/[*Into telephone*]/{E} Hello! ... I can't talk now .../Yes, there is ... Well then, I'll
377 CP	Edward	27	I'm going to propose?/{E} No, I can't. But I won't drink to Alex's./{J} Oh, it
378 CP	Celia	22	break — anything unpleasant!/No, it can't be that. I won't think it's that./I think it is
378 CP	Celia	24	surrender/To fatigue. And panic. You can't face the trouble./{E} No, it is not that. It is
380 CP	Edward	37	you,/And perhaps I still am. But this can't go on./It never could have been ... a
386 CP	Edward	29	God, what shall we talk about?/We can't sit here in silence./{C} Oh, I could./Just
386 CP	Edward	36	a ludicrous situation./{E} I'm afraid I can't see the humorous side of it./{C} I'm not
387 CP	Celia	6	can see you at last as a human being./Can't you see me that way too, and laugh about
387 CP	Celia	10	in the dark./{C} But it's all so simple./Can't you see that ... {}/[*The doorbell rings*]/{E}
391 CP	Alex	16	do you think, Alex?/{A} No, Julia, *we* can't explain the telegram./{L} I am sure that
391 CP	Edward	35	seem very pleased to see me./{E} I can't say that I've had much opportunity/To
394 CP	Edward	17	were leaving./{E} Well, at least, *they* can't have thought I was the butler./{L}
398 CP	Lavinia	13	unable to make you laugh,/And as I can't persuade you to see a doctor,/There's
400 CP	Alex	22	sent him to a sanatorium/Where she can't get at him — then, he believes,/She will be
404 CP	Edward	29	will you send me to the sanatorium?/I can't go home again. And at my club/They
411 CP	Edward	6	/If you want to be alone .../{E} But I can't go away!/I have a case coming on next
412 CP	Julia	19	uncommon./{J} Henry, get up./You can't be as tired as that. I shall wait in the next

412 CP	Celia	37	/For wanting to see you. Well, I can't./I just came in desperation. And I shan't
413 CP	Celia	14	is something to be done./{C} Well, I can't pretend that my trouble is interesting;/But
413 CP	Celia	26	mind./{C} Well, there are two things I can't understand,/Which you might consider
414 CP	Celia	16	they live in the country,/Now they can't afford to have a place in town./It's all they
414 CP	Celia	23	down and stay with them./But I just can't face it./{R} So you want to see no one?/{C}
415 CP	Celia	35	make one feel sinful!/And yet I can't find any other word for it./It must be
419 CP	Celia	22	/{C} It sounds like a prison. But they can't *all* stay there!/I mean, it would make the
424 CP	Lavinia	7	Is there anything you need/That you can't find in the kitchen?/{CM} Nothing,
425 CP	Lavinia	28	/{L} And if it's very crowded, they can't get at the cocktails,/And the man won't be
426 CP	Lavinia	25	who would come so early? I simply *can't* get up./{CM} Mrs. Shuttlethwaite!/{L} Oh,
428 CP	Lavinia	8	ought to be destroyed./{L} But can't they exterminate these monkeys/If they are
429 CP	Julia	14	dine out on those monkeys:/But one can't dine out on eating Christians —/Even
432 CP	Peter	38	just about to explain —/I'm afraid I can't find parts for anybody/In *this* film — it's
433 CP	Julia	5	taking Boltwell to California/Why can't you take me?/{P} We're not taking
433 CP	Alex	27	you came in, Peter. I'm afraid you can't have Celia./{P} Oh ... Is she married?/{A}
439 CP	Peter	18	almost forgotten them./I realise that I can't get out of it —/And what else can I do?/
446 CC	Claude	15	was to be an organist,/Just as I can't forget ... no matter./The great thing was to
447 CC	Claude	23	/We could argue about that. You can't argue with guidance./But if she appears to
449 CC	Claude	37	That's where I'm in the dark./I simply can't guess what her reaction would be./There's
451 CC	Eggers	20	says to me: 'Eggerson, why can't you make me laugh/The way B. Kaghan
458 CC	Lady E	17	agency and got them to change it./I can't understand why you're both so surprised.
458 CC	Lady E	23	the treatment with me,/And she can't go by air — she says it makes her sea-sick;
460 CC	Claude	9	from Zürich;/But you know that I can't decipher your writing./I like to have the
470 CC	Colby	11	of fact, I think I played better./I can't bring myself to play to other people,/And
470 CC	Colby	12	other people,/And when I'm alone I can't forget/That it's only myself to whom I'm
474 CC	Colby	13	/{L} Can no one else enter?/{C} It can't be done by issuing invitations:/They would
474 CC	Lucasta	27	... a dirty public square./But I can't imagine that happening to you./You seem
476 CC	Colby	1	yourself./{C} There's only one thing I can't tell you./At least, not yet. I'm not allowed
476 CC	Lucasta	5	my parents./{L} Oh, I see./Well, I can't believe that matters./But I can tell you all
477 CC	Colby	14	understand./I want to explain. But I can't, just yet./Oh, why did I ever come into this
481 CC	Kaghan	9	remarked that I was hungry./{K} You can't want dinner yet./It's only six o'clock. We
481 CC	Kaghan	10	dinner yet./It's only six o'clock. We can't dine till eight;/Not at any restaurant that
481 CC	Lady E	19	that you've moved in. Because you can't tell/Whether a scheme of decoration/Is
483 CC	Lady E	32	I've never thought about it./{LE} I can't say that *I* believe in it./I did, for a time. I
484 CC	Lady E	18	knew either of your parents,/You can't understand what loathing really is./Yet we
486 CC	Colby	27	him. I was told about him./But I can't help wondering why you are so interested:/
487 CC	Claude	2	written out/And then memorise it. I can't use notes:/It's got to sound spontaneous./
490 CC	Colby	16	it's part of a total agony/Which I can't begin to feel yet. I'm simply indifferent./
492 CC	Colby	1	want to marry./You may be right. I can't take account of that./But now I want to
492 CC	Colby	25	understand./'Reminiscent mood.' I can't develop that/Unless you can tell me —
494 CC	Claude	22	was life. To me, it was a burden./You can't communicate an inspiration,/Like that, by
498 CC	Claude	25	Colby./{SC} But Eggerson, you really can't ask me to believe/That she took two
502 CC	Lucasta	26	different from the rest of us/That we can't judge you. That's you, Colby./{C} That's
503 CC	Colby	23	/{C} Of course I'd like them ... Can't B. come up now?/{E} Better wait till
514 CC	Claude	25	born./{SC} I don't believe it. I simply can't believe it./Mrs. Guzzard, you are
515 CC	Claude	19	/{SC} This is horribly plausible. But it can't be true./{MG} Consider, Sir Claude.
515 CC	Claude	35	/If this should be true — of course it can't be true! —/But I see you believe it. You
517 CC	Claude	17	why I must leave you./{SC} Eggerson!/Can't you persuade him?/{LE} Yes. My poor
525 ES	Charles	19	/And because your father simply can't bear it/That any man but he should have
527 ES	Monica	28	/Not occupied with anything that can't be interrupted./Someone to make a
532 ES	Ld Clav	16	/From a man I used to know. I can't refuse to see him./Though from what I
534 ES	Gomez	28	In my country, Dick,/Politicians can't afford mistakes. The prudent ones/Always
536 ES	Gomez	6	/It was jumping a gap — and you can't jump back again./I parted from myself by
538 ES	Gomez	22	to another post/Where at least you can't make quite the same mistake./At the
541 ES	Gomez	4	wouldn't look at it./Besides, you can't think I've any desire/To appear in public
543 ES	Monica	18	having a dinner party./{M} Father, can't you bear to be alone with me?/If you can't
543 ES	Monica	19	you bear to be alone with me?/If you can't bear to dine alone with me tonight,/What
549 ES	Carghil	25	know, at the very first meeting —/I can't think why, but it's the way things happen./
551 ES	Ld Clav	20	you had really been broken-hearted/I can't see how you could have acted as you did./
553 ES	Carghil	30	you like to read them?/I'm afraid I can't show you the originals;/They're in my
554 ES	Piggott	22	Lord Claverton was comfortable:/We can't allow him to tire himself with talking./
555 ES	Ld Clav	29	tree./It might have been a man. But it can't be that,/Or he wouldn't be at large.
561 ES	Monica	25	Michael must be in great trouble,/So can't you help him?/{LC} I am trying to help
567 ES	Monica	27	with a guilty secret in his past!/I just can't imagine it. {}/[CLAVERTON *has entered*
568 ES	Ld Clav	34	terms of equality. To one's child one can't reveal oneself/While she is a child. And by

569 ES	Ld Clav	31	get your company/I'm afraid the law can't touch them./{C} Then why should you
571 ES	Charles	23	people mustn't persecute you./We can't allow that. What hold have they upon
576 ES	Monica	25	names./{M} Michael, Michael, you can't abandon your family/And your very self
582 ES	Monica	29	at us/With a glance of farewell./{M} I can't understand his going for a walk./{C} He

CANADA (4)

463 CC	Claude	3	then when I sent you both over to Canada/In the war — that was perhaps a
489 CC	Claude	26	was born?/{SC} Where was I? In Canada./My father had sent me on a business
514 CC	Guzzard	37	deceived yourself. When you went to Canada/My sister found that she was to have a
559 ES	Ld Clav	11	How would you like to go to Western Canada?/Or what about sheep farming in New

CANADIAN (1)

119 SP	Krum	12	say Loot Sam Wauchope/{Kr} Of the Canadian Expeditionary Force —/{Kl} The

CANAL (3)

67 WL: Fire S		189	bank/While I was fishing in the dull canal/On a winter evening round behind the
282 MC Chorus		10	fist in the tavern, the push into the canal,/Less than we fear the love of God./We
473 CC Lucasta		13	on the surface of the Regent's Canal./Floating, that's it./{C} You're very much

CANALETTO (1)

40 Burb Blei		19	protozoic slime/At a perspective of Canaletto./The smoky candle end of time/

CANARIES (1)

136 5FingerEx4		15	wants to know *him*)./He has 999 canaries/And round his head finches and fairies/

CANARY (1)

212 Growltiger		13	ON THE LOOSE!/Woe to the weak canary, that fluttered from its cage;/Woe to the

CANCER (6)

295 FR	Harry	18	call their conscience; it is just the cancer/That eats away the self. I knew how you
314 FR	Warburt	36	/Who suffered from an incurable cancer./How he fought against it! I never saw a
315 FR	Harry	1	believe in murder/Than to believe in cancer. Cancer is here:/The lump, the dull pain,
315 FR	Harry	1	in murder/Than to believe in cancer. Cancer is here:/The lump, the dull pain, the
315 FR	Harry	9	/The past unredeemable. But cancer, now,/That is something real./{W} Well,
315 FR	Warburt	12	/How did we get onto the subject of cancer?/I really don't know. — But now you're

CANDELABRA (1)

64 WL: Chess		82	Doubled the flames of sevenbranched candelabra/Reflecting light upon the table as/

CANDLE (4)

40 Burb Blei		20	perspective of Canaletto./The smoky candle end of time/Declines. On the Rialto
111 Xmas Trees		6	is not that of the child/For whom the candle is a star, and the gilded angel/Spreading
167 Rock 10		40	seasons./And we must extinguish the candle, put out the light and relight it;/Forever
256 MC Chorus		32	Does the torch flame in the hall, the candle in the room?/{3P} Does the watchman

CANDLE-FLAMES (1)

64 WL: Chess		91	ascended/In fattening the prolonged candle-flames,/Flung their smoke into the

CANDLES (4)

18 Portrait		4	this afternoon for you';/And four wax candles in the darkened room,/Four rings of
37 Gerontion		28	in the dark room/Shifting the candles; Fräulein von Kulp/Who turned in the
349 FR	3m	13	*carrying a birthday cake with/lighted candles, which she sets on the table. Exit*
349 FR	5m	13	*/At each revolution they blow out a few candles, so that their last/words are spoken in the*

CANINE (1)

234 Ad-dress		25	including Pekes,/And such fantastic canine freaks./The usual Dog about the Town/

CANNIBAL (5)

121 SA	Sweeney	2	DUSTY./{S} I'll carry you off/To a cannibal isle./{Do} You'll be the cannibal!/{S}
121 SA	Doris	3	To a cannibal isle./{Do} You'll be the cannibal!/{S} You'll be the missionary!/You'll
121 SA	Sweeney	6	/I'll gobble you up. I'll be the cannibal./{Do} You'll carry me off? To a
121 SA	Doris	7	/{Do} You'll carry me off? To a cannibal isle?/{S} I'll be the cannibal./{Do} I'll
121 SA	Sweeney	8	off? To a cannibal isle?/{S} I'll be the cannibal./{Do} I'll be the missionary./I'll

CANNON (1)

68 WL: Fire S		213	in demotic French/To luncheon at the Cannon Street Hotel/Followed by a weekend at

CANNOT (92)

19 Portrait		49	/And smiles at situations which it cannot see.'/I smile, of course,/And go on
61 WL: Burial		21	this stony rubbish? Son of man,/You cannot say, or guess, for you know only/A heap
72 WL: Thund		336	stop and drink/Amongst the rock one cannot stop or think/Sweat is dry and feet are in
72 WL: Thund		339	mountain mouth of carious teeth that cannot spit/Here one can neither stand nor lie
89 Ash-Wed 1		14	veritable transitory power/Because I cannot drink/There, where trees flower, and
89 Ash-Wed 1		23	/And renounce the voice/Because I cannot hope to turn again/Consequently I
96 Ash-Wed 5		26	at the gate/Who will not go away and cannot pray:/Pray for those who chose and
97 Ash-Wed 5		31	who offend her/And are terrified and cannot surrender/And affirm before the world
127 Cor1 March		17	/53,000 field and heavy guns,/I cannot tell how many projectiles, mines and
155 Rock 3		40	policemen directing the traffic/Cannot tell you why you come or where you go.
172 FQ: BurntN		45	Go, go, go, said the bird: human kind/Cannot bear very much reality./Time past and
173 FQ: BurntN		70	only say, *there* we have been: but I cannot say where./And I cannot say, how long,

173 FQ:	BurntN	71	been: but I cannot say where./And I cannot say, how long, for that is to place it in
173 FQ:	BurntN	84	heaven and damnation/Which flesh cannot endure./Time past and time future/
182 FQ:	ECoker	186	or several times, by men whom one cannot hope/To emulate — but there is no
182 FQ:	ECoker	198	one man only/But of old stones that cannot be deciphered./There is a time for the
186 FQ:	DrySal	71	wind's tail, where the fog cowers?/We cannot think of a time that is oceanless/Or of an
187 FQ:	DrySal	132	way forward is the way back./You cannot face it steadily, but this thing is sure,/
189 FQ:	DrySal	186	will not reject them/Or wherever cannot reach them the sound of the sea bell's/
196 FQ:	Little	187	summon the spectre of a Rose./We cannot revive old factions/We cannot restore
196 FQ:	Little	188	/We cannot revive old factions/We cannot restore old policies/Or follow an antique
196 FQ:	Little	213	shirt of flame/Which human power cannot remove./We only live, only suspire/
232 Skimble		30	with Skimbleshanks!/He's a Cat that cannot be ignored;/So nothing goes wrong on
590 Time Space		2	Space, as Sages say,/Are things which cannot be,/The sun which does not feel decay/
590 Space Time		2	time, as sages say,/Are things that cannot be,/The fly that lives a single day/Has
595 Grad 14		5	are ever loth to say./But 'tis a call we cannot disobey,/*Exeunt omnes*, with a last
244 MC	Chorus	22	We/Are afraid in a fear which we cannot know, which we cannot face, which none
244 MC	Chorus	22	fear which we cannot know, which we cannot face, which none understands,/And our
246 MC	Templ	36	summer's over/Or that the good time cannot last?/Fluting in the meadows, viols in the
251 MC	Tempt3	4	real/But real friendship, once ended, cannot be mended./Sooner shall enmity turn to
252 MC	Thomas	9	/{T} And if the Archbishop cannot trust the King,/How can he trust those
252 MC	Thomas	13	the throne./{T} If the Archbishop cannot trust the Throne,/He has good cause to
261 MC	Thomas	33	at once, in/a fashion that the world cannot understand; so in Heaven the Saints are/
271 MC	Thomas	19	They will seem unreal./Human kind cannot bear very much reality. {}/[*Enter*
273 MC	Priests	14	safe./They dare not break in./They cannot break in. They have not the force./We
276 MC	Chorus	14	/We are soiled by a filth that we cannot clean, united to supernatural vermin,/It
287 FR	Amy	33	some meaning in death/Which I cannot find./— I am only certain of Arthur or
293 FR	Harry	29	to whom nothing has ever happened/Cannot understand the unimportance of events.
296 FR	Charles	27	of her/Makes him believe he did. He cannot trust his good fortune./I believe that all
307 FR	Harry	30	hopelessness./{H} One thing you cannot know:/The sudden extinction of every
308 FR	Harry	37	dissolution. You do not know,/You cannot know, you cannot understand./{M} I
308 FR	Harry	37	do not know,/You cannot know, you cannot understand./{M} I think I could
315 FR	Harry	7	used to be/Or what he would be. He cannot realise/That everything is irrevocable,/
317 FR	Warburt	11	don't understand me./I'm sure you cannot know what is on my mind;/And as for
324 FR	Harry	15	/A minor trouble like a concussion/Cannot make very much difference to John./A
324 FR	Harry	35	on several planes at once/Though one cannot speak with several voices at once./I have
326 FR	Harry	28	/Of all men, of the world, which I cannot put in order./If you only knew the years
327 FR	Agatha	2	/That there is always more: we cannot rest in being/The impatient spectators of
336 FR	Harry	13	*appear*]/{H} and this time/I cannot think that I am surprised to see you.
338 FR	Harry	2	from quite a different quarter,/But I cannot explain that to you now. Only be sure/
338 FR	Harry	5	thing for everybody./But at present, I cannot explain it to anyone:/I do not know the
338 FR	Harry	11	going?/{H} I can only speak/And you cannot hear me. I can only speak/So you may
341 FR	Agatha	6	same:/Just as voracious for what you cannot have/Because you repel it./{A} I
342 FR	Agatha	33	have a different meaning,/And he cannot return. That is his privilege./For those
343 FR	Harry	37	from normal dangers/If I pursue it. I cannot account for this/But it is so, mother.
344 FR	Violet	6	is he going?/{A} Ask Agatha./{V} I cannot understand at all. Why is he leaving?/{A}
344 FR	Violet	32	never happened in our family./{V} I cannot understand it./{H} I never said that I
349 FR	Agatha	15	in coming/To complete fruition/It cannot be hurried/And it cannot be delayed/{M}
349 FR	Agatha	16	fruition/It cannot be hurried/And it cannot be delayed/{M} It cannot be diverted/An
349 FR	Mary	17	/And it cannot be delayed/{M} It cannot be diverted/An attempt to divert it/Only
370 CP	Peter	24	/With some secret excitement which I cannot share./{E} Do you think she has simply
378 CP	Celia	26	it is not that. It is not only that./{C} It cannot be simply a question of vanity:/That you
381 CP	Edward	17	/What desire has left behind. But you cannot understand./How could *you* understand
381 CP	Celia	23	loathing./But what will your life be? I cannot bear to think of it./Oh, Edward! Can
381 CP	Edward	37	does not speak,/Who never talks, who cannot argue;/And who in some men may be
384 CP	Reilly	20	life and in the lives of others/Which cannot be reversed. That is one consideration./
391 CP	Lavinia	20	machine, that goes on working,/And I cannot stop it; no, it's not like a machine —/Or
401 CP	Reilly	20	... Or did she *send* you?/{R} I cannot say that I had been invited;/And Mrs.
401 CP	Reilly	27	it a trap./But if it is a trap, then you cannot escape from it:/And so ... you might as
403 CP	Edward	34	That was what she had done to me!/I cannot live with her — that is now intolerable;/I
403 CP	Edward	35	with her — that is now intolerable;/I cannot live without her, for she has made me
403 CP	Edward	38	/She has made the world a place I cannot live in/Except on her terms. I must be
404 CP	Edward	21	of making. I am in your hands./I cannot take any further responsibility./{R}
408 CP	Reilly	27	did you know all this?/{R} That I cannot disclose./I have my own method of
412 CP	Julia	13	no, not reluctant:/Only diffident. She cannot believe/That you will take her seriously./
417 CP	Celia	4	itself an illusion/If we rest in it./{C} I cannot argue./It's not that I'm afraid of being
417 CP	Celia	17	be cured/Of a craving for something I cannot find/And of the shame of never finding

417 CP   Reilly   22 treatment must be your own choice:/I cannot choose for you. If that is what you wish,
418 CP   Reilly   26 issues from despair./The destination cannot be described;/You will know very little
419 CP   Reilly   19   But the friends you have in mind/Cannot have been to this sanatorium./I am very
422 CP   Reilly   29 /{R} There is one for whom the words cannot be spoken./{A} They can not be spoken
429 CP   Alex   24   /{E} Will it be made public?/{A} It cannot be, at present:/There are too many
438 CP   Edward   22 still feel/As your responsibility./{E} I cannot help the feeling/That, in some way, my
463 CC   Colby   29   /And for a moment the thing I cannot do,/The art that I could never excel in,/
497 CC   Claude   21   /So I told her the truth. But she cannot believe it./{LE} Claude, that's not quite
518 CC   Guzzard 24 assure you./{MG} Mr. Eggerson,/I cannot see eye to eye with you,/Having been,
537 ES   Ld Clav 14   under your influence./{LC} You cannot attribute your ... misfortune to *my*
539 ES   Ld Clav 24   historical epitome./Though I cannot accept it as altogether accurate./The
572 ES   Charles 31 /Confide them in whispers. They cannot harm you./{LC} Your reasoning's sound
577 ES   Ld Clav 38 way. That would be shameful./{LC} I cannot bar his way, as you know very well./
578 ES   Ld Clav   2 volition to contract his enslavement,/I cannot prevent him. I have something to say to
583 ES   Monica   24   terrors for me,/Loss and vicissitude cannot appal me,/Not even death can dismay or
CANOE (1)
70 WL: Fire S 295 knees/Supine on the floor of a narrow canoe.'/'My feet are at Moorgate, and my heart/
CANONRY (1)
518 CC   Eggers   11   /To a precentorship! And a canonry!/{C} We'll cross that bridge when we
CANTANKEROUSNESS (1)
418 CP   Celia   18 afraid this sounds like raving!/Or just cantankerousness ... still,/If there's no other way
CANTERBURY (14)
238 MC   m   3   I/A CHORUS OF WOMEN OF CANTERBURY/THREE PRIESTS OF THE
238 MC   m   14   /CHORUS OF WOMEN OF CANTERBURY/ATTENDANTS/*The first*
239 MC   Chorus   4 /For us, the poor, the poor women of Canterbury? what tribulation/With which we
243 MC   Chorus   20   but you come bringing death into Canterbury:/A doom on the house, a doom on
245 MC   Priest2 30 /Than seven days could make ready Canterbury./However, I will have fires laid in
245 MC   Thomas   37 /These are small matters. Little rest in Canterbury/With eager enemies restless about
249 MC   Tempt2   24   bravery will be broken,/Cabined in Canterbury, realmless ruler,/Self-bound servant
261 MC   Thomas   38 to remember especially our martyr of Canterbury,/the blessed Archbishop Elphege;
268 MC   Thomas   20 me from my own/And bid me sit in Canterbury, alone?/I would wish him three
270 MC   Chorus   21 worms/In the guts of the women of Canterbury./I have smelt them, the
275 MC   Chorus   23 is England? where is Kent? where is Canterbury?/O far far far far in the past; and I
281 MC   Priest3   6 who has given us another Saint in Canterbury. {}/[*while a* Te Deum *is sung in*
281 MC   Chorus   14 we, the scrubbers and sweepers of Canterbury,/The back bent under toil, the knee
282 MC   Chorus   5 Thee/Who hast given such blessing to Canterbury./Forgive us, O Lord, we
CANVAS (1)
109 Marina   25 remember./The rigging weak and the canvas rotten/Between one June and another
CAP (3)
119 SP   Krum   15 the war together/Klip and me and the Cap and Sam./{Kl} Yes we did our bit, as you
397 CP   Edward   31 never could teach you/How to put the cap on a tube of tooth-paste./{L} Very well,
574 ES   Carghil 12 suffered! So I put on my thinking cap./I know you've always thought me utterly
CAPABLE (3)
305 FR   Agatha   5 you;/Though you may not think me capable of such a feeling./I would like to help
402 CP   Edward   7 from ruin./{E} You talk as if I was capable of action:/If I were, I should not need
404 CP   Edward   20 you — that's the last decision/I was capable of making. I am in your hands./I
CAPACITY (6)
397 CP   Edward   23 —/At least, not in a professional capacity./{L} One can be practical, even in hell:/
403 CP   Reilly   21 shall we say, within your modest capacity./Try to explain what has happened
411 CP   Reilly   34 to us, Sir Henry?/{R} No. Not in this capacity. {}/[EDWARD *takes out his*
465 CC   Claude   13 do something for which he lacks the capacity?/Could a man be said to have a
516 CC   Colby   9 aimed too high before — beyond my capacity./I thought I didn't want to be an
571 ES   Ld Clav 17 /And Maisie loved me, with whatever capacity/For loving she had — self-centred and
CAPE (3)
56 Swee Night 11   seas;/The person in the Spanish cape/Tries to sit on Sweeney's knees/Slips and
56 Swee Night 25   paws;/She and the lady in the cape/Are suspect, thought to be in league;/
142 Cape Ann   t long pass/No concurrence of bone./Cape Ann/O quick quick quick, quick hear the
CAPER (1)
217 Jellicles   32 be a stormy night/They will practise a caper or two in the hall./If it happens the sun is
CAPES (1)
241 MC   Mess   33 the road and throwing down their capes,/Strewing the way with leaves and late
CAPITAL (7)
44 Cook Egg   13 of that kidney./I shall not want Capital in Heaven/For I shall meet Sir Alfred
152 Rock 2   21 /And everything, including capital/And several versions of the Word of
328 FR   Gerald   26 This is what the Communists make capital out of./{C} There's a little more. 'The

226 Macavity   21   respectable. (They say he cheats at cards.)/And his footprints are not found in any
232 Skimble   19   and the guards to the bagmen playing cards/He will supervise them all, more or less./
460 CC   Claude   10   your writing./I like to have the cards, just to know where you are/By reading
531 ES   Ld Clav   1   showy'./This would do for visiting cards — if people still left cards/And if I was
531 ES   Ld Clav   1   for visiting cards — if people still left cards/And if I was going to have any visitors./
564 ES   Carghil   36 /You've got to be the first to put your cards on the table!/{M} Father, I think you

CARE (36)

 90 Ash-Wed 1   38   and dryer than the will/Teach us to care and not to care/Teach us to sit still./Pray
 90 Ash-Wed 1   38   the will/Teach us to care and not to care/Teach us to sit still./Pray for us sinners
 98 Ash-Wed 6   27   ourselves with falsehood/Teach us to care and not to care/Teach us to sit still/Even
 98 Ash-Wed 6   27   falsehood/Teach us to care and not to care/Teach us to sit still/Even among these
115 SP   Doris   3   /{Do} What about Pereira?/I don't care./{Du} You don't care!/Who pays the rent?/
115 SP   Dusty   4   Pereira?/I don't care./{Du} You don't care!/Who pays the rent?/{Do} Yes he pays the
124 SA   Doris   8   the COFFIN very last card./I don't care for such conversation/A woman runs a
181 FQ: ECoker   156   obey the dying nurse/Whose constant care is not to please/But to remind of our, and
181 FQ: ECoker   162   we shall/Die of the absolute paternal care/That will not leave us, but prevents us
215 RTTugger   32   /The Rum Tum Tugger doesn't care for a cuddle;/But he'll leap on your lap in
594 Grad 11   2   flitting faces in a dream;/Out of thy care and tutelage we pass/Into the unknown
595 Grad 13   4   a friend to bless/Before they leave thy care for lands unseen;/And let thy motto be,
250 MC Tempt3   32   country needs./It is our country. We care for the country./We are the backbone of
286 FR   Charles   27   drinking,/Modern young people don't care what they're eating;/They've lost their sense
320 FR   Warburt   13   down. Her heart's very feeble./With care, and avoiding all excitement/She may live
324 FR   Violet   23   so fond of John./{V} And if you don't care what happens to John,/You might show
339 FR   Harry   11   heat of the sun and the icy vigil,/A care over lives of humble people,/The lesson of
342 FR   Mary   27   I will go, whichever is better;/I do not care what happens to me,/But Harry must not
345 FR   Harry   11   as happen to Arthur and John:/Take care of *them*. My address, mother,/Will be care
345 FR   Harry   12   of *them*. My address, mother,/Will be care of the bank in London until you hear from
345 FR   Mary   18   Mary./{M} Good-bye, Harry. Take care of yourself. {}/[*Exit* HARRY]/{A} At my
378 CP   Celia   20   back!/Lavinia! So the one thing you care about/Is to avoid a break — anything
381 CP   Celia   1   your own age./{C} I don't think I care for advice from you, Edward:/You are not
415 CP   Celia   28   either become bad form, and cease to care,/Or else, if you care, you must be kinky./
415 CP   Celia   29   and cease to care,/Or else, if you care, you must be kinky./{R} And so you
450 CC   Claude   18   — a good deal better/Than I should care to think, perhaps./{E} And do I infer/That
480 CC   Kaghan   26   Now Colby/Doesn't really care about being respectable —/He was born
489 CC   Lady E   40   do well by him —/Because you *did* care for the girl, didn't you?/{SC} Yes, I did
490 CC   Claude   1   the girl, didn't you?/{SC} Yes, I did care. Very much. I had never/Been in love
502 CC   Lucasta   18   like you, to despise people:/You don't care enough./{C} I don't care enough?/{L} No.
502 CC   Colby   19   /You don't care enough./{C} I don't care enough?/{L} No. You're either above
526 ES   Charles   36   it for granted/That you don't really care for any company but his!/{M} You're not
555 ES   Ld Clav   32   he has friends/Whom he wouldn't care for you or me to know about./{M} It's
559 ES   Michael   23   choose to —/No one would know or care what my name had been./{LC} So you are
574 ES   Ld Clav   7   some exciting news for us./Would you care to impart it?/{MC} It's about dear Michael.
576 ES   Michael   15   to find the man for./{Mi} I don't care about that. He's offered me the job/With a

CARED (7)

 29 Aunt Helen   3   small house near a fashionable square/Cared for by servants to the number of four./
370 CP   Peter   6   /But I thought that she really cared about me./And I was so happy when we
380 CP   Celia   23   gave Peter/Any reason to suppose I cared for him./I thought he had talent; I saw
494 CC   Claude   16   believed in;/I thought that what he cared for was power and wealth;/And I came to
506 CC   Eggers   1   /That is to say, placed out to be cared for/Till further notice by a foster-mother./
518 CC   Eggers   19   We should be most happy/If you cared to stop with us, until you were settled./{C}
551 ES   Carghil   24   /For breach of promise, if I'd really cared for you./What sentimental nonsense! One

CAREER (10)

374 CP   Celia   27   /Because a divorce would ruin your career;/And we thought that Lavinia would
394 CP   Edward   35   wished to be a hostess/For whom my career would be a support./Well, I tried to be
435 CP   Peter   4   /{P} When did she ... take up this career?/{J} Two years ago./{P} Two years ago! I
472 CC   Lucasta   38   awful for a man to have to give up,/A career that he's set his heart on, I'm sure:/But
538 ES   Gomez   31   a point, you see, of following your career./{LC} I am touched by your interest./{G}
539 ES   Gomez   19   /He's followed your undergraduate career/Without the protection of that prudent
539 ES   Ld Clav   29   himself so carefully about my career./{G} I don't propose to give you a
539 ES   Gomez   31   you a detailed account/Of my own career. I've been very successful./What would
551 ES   Carghil   37   carried on, it might have ended your career,/And then you wouldn't have become
561 ES   Michael   33   to leave England, and make my own career:/And Father simply calls me a coward./

CAREFUL (12)

 29 Aunt Helen   13   his knees —/Who had always been so careful while her mistress lived./Cousin Nancy/
 32 Hysteria   11   and I concentrated/my attention with careful subtlety to this end./Conversation

62 WL: Burial	59	the horoscope myself:/One must be so careful these days./Unreal City,/Under the
221 Old Deut	47	be tottery, I must go slow/And be careful of Old Deuteronomy!'/Of the Awefull
280 MC Knight1	3	quietly to your homes./Please be careful not to loiter in groups at street corners,
290 FR Agatha	22	thing to do./{Ag} Thus with most careful devotion/Thus with precise attention/To
345 FR Gerald	6	a bad night, and you will have to be careful./You're taking Downing with you?/{H}
354 CP Julia	27	know her./{J} Well, one can't be too careful/Before one tells a story./{A} Delia
419 CP Reilly	20	been to this sanatorium./I am very careful whom I send there:/Those who go do
514 CC Guzzard	3	and silent? A dead man, Colby./Be careful what you say./{C} A dead obscure man./
547 ES Piggott	5	me tuck you up .../You must be very careful at this time of year;/This early warm
576 ES Gomez	34	/Highly confidential .../{G} Be careful, Mr. Barrister./You ought to know

CAREFULLY (4)

18 Portrait	15	slips/Among velleities and carefully caught regrets/Through attenuated
267 MC Thomas	15	let your new coat of loyalty be worn/Carefully, so it get not soiled or torn./Have you
306 FR Mary	35	ready,/And the treats were always so carefully prepared;/There was never any time to
539 ES Ld Clav	29	been given,/He's informed himself so carefully about my career./{G} I don't propose

CARELESS (1)

| 507 CC Lady E | 26 | making a will./{LE} He was very careless./{MG} And that the heirs acknowledged |

CARES (3)

152 Rock 2	45	ribbon roads,/And no man knows or cares who is his neighbour/Unless his neighbour
289 FR Amy	11	/As a rule, a good deal more than she cares to betray,/I am bound to say that I agree
326 FR Charles	8	about Arthur?/{C} More than she cares to mention, I imagine. {}/[*Enter* HARRY]/

CARESS (2)

| 185 FQ: DrySal | 31 | whine in the rigging,/The menace and caress of wave that breaks on water,/The distant |
| 567 ES Monica | 8 | yearning/For the sound of it, for the caress that is in it!/Oh Charles, how I've wanted |

CARESSES (1)

| 68 WL: Fire S | 237 | tired,/Endeavours to engage her in caresses/Which still are unreproved, if |

CARESSING (1)

| 37 Gerontion | 24 | whispers; by Mr. Silvero/With caressing hands, at Limoges/Who walked all |

CARGAISON (1)

| 51 Restaurant | 27 | /Et les profits et les pertes, et la cargaison d'étain:/Un courant de sous-mer |

CARGHILL (29)

523 ES	m 8	GOMEZ/MRS. PIGGOTT/MRS. CARGHILL/MICHAEL
548 ES	2m 14	*newspaper over his face./Enter* MRS. CARGHILL. *She sits in a deckchair nearby,*
550 ES Carghil	10	now and here .../{MC} Is Mrs. John Carghill./{LC} You married, I suppose, many
550 ES Carghil	17	sly and slippery./Then I married Mr. Carghill. Twenty years older/Than me, he was.
550 ES Carghil	22	too hard. Have you never heard/Of Carghill Equipments? They make office
554 ES Piggott	10	/{MP} Good morning, Mrs. Carghill!/{MC} Dear Mrs. Piggott!/It seems to
554 ES Piggott	14	It's the breath of life to me, Mrs. Carghill,/Attending to my guests. I like to feel
554 ES Piggott	19	famous Lord Claverton. This is Mrs. Carghill./Two of our very nicest guests!/I just
554 ES Piggott	23	needs is *rest*! You're not going, Mrs. Carghill?/{MC} Oh, I knew that Lord Claverton
554 ES Piggott	31	to Nurse)/When I saw that Mrs. Carghill had caught you./You wouldn't know
562 ES	m 12	nature, really,/But ... {}/[*Enter* MRS. CARGHILL *with despatch-case*]/{MC}
562 ES Carghil	26	the bill in revue. Now I'm Mrs. John Carghill./Richard! It's astonishing about your
563 ES Carghil	24	/To Mrs. ... Mrs. .../{MC} Mrs. John Carghill./{G} We seem a bit weak on the
563 ES Gomez	31	was as beautiful to look at/As Mrs. Carghill, I can well understand/Her success on
565 ES	m 24	to your promise! {}/[*Exeunt* MRS. CARGHILL *and* MICHAEL]/{G} Well, Dick,
571 ES Ld Clav	1	Maisie Montjoy./There is Mrs. John Carghill, the wealthy widow./But Freddy
571 ES Ld Clav	6	very different/From Gomez, Mrs. Carghill and Lord Claverton./Freddy admired
572 ES Charles	11	why you were lonely./{C} And Mrs. Carghill:/What has she against you?/{LC} I was
573 ES Ld Clav	20	are conspiring against me./I see Mrs. Carghill coming./{M} Let us go./{LC} We will
573 ES	m 23	here. Let her join us. {}/[*Enter* MRS. CARGHILL]/{MC} I've been hunting high and
573 ES Monica	28	/{M} Mr. Charles Hemington. Mrs. Carghill./{C} How do you do./{MC} What a
573 ES Charles	31	name meets with your approval, Mrs. Carghill./{MC} And let me congratulate *you*,
574 ES Charles	5	you Charles!/{C} As you please, Mrs. Carghill./{LC} You said you had some exciting
574 ES Ld Clav	30	discussed your problems/With Mrs. Carghill and then with Señor Gomez./{Mi}
576 ES Monica	1	with what I know already, Mrs. Carghill,/About you./{MC} But I was very
576 ES Gomez	36	about the law of slander./Here's Mrs. Carghill, a reliable witness./{C} I know enough
577 ES Carghil	27	conversation./My late husband, Mr. Carghill, was a business man —/I wish you
577 ES Carghil	30	—/So I understand business. Mr. Carghill told me so./Now, Michael has great
580 ES	m 25	run and see them off. {}/[*Exit* MRS. CARGHILL]/{M} Oh Father, Father, I'm so

CARGO (1)

| 187 FQ: DrySal | 118 | the preserver,/Like the river with its cargo of dead negroes, cows and chicken coops, |

CARING (1)

| 502 CC Lucasta | 20 | enough?/{L} No. You're either above caring,/Or else you're insensible — I don't mean |

CARIOUS (1)
72 WL: Thund 339   the rock/Dead mountain mouth of carious teeth that cannot spit/Here one can
CARLISLE (1)
233 Skimble   57   sleeping all the while he was busy at Carlisle,/Where he greets the stationmaster with
CARNAL (1)
161 Rock 7   23   being;/Bestial as always before, carnal, self-seeking as always before, selfish and
CARNIVOROUS (1)
484 CC   Lady E 23   dove in an eagle's nest./They were so carnivorous. Always killing things and eating
CAROL (2)
111 Xmas Trees   26   also with gratitude/St. Lucy, her carol, and her crown of fire):/So that before the
451 CC   Eggers   38   in our voluntary choir/And at the carol service. But I wish I was musical./{C} I
CARRIED (8)
70 WL: Fire S   287 /Rippled both shores/Southwest wind/Carried down stream/The peal of bells/White
333 FR   Agatha 10   had happened, I knew I should have carried/Death in life, death through lifetime,
334 FR   Agatha 14   /There's relief from a burden that I carried,/And exhaustion at the moment of relief.
514 CC   Claude 18   incredible!/You couldn't have carried out such a deception/Over all these
514 CC   Claude 34   those records./You pretend to have carried out a deception/For twenty-five years?
534 ES   Ld Clav 7   /Has been of such a nature that, if carried on in England,/It might land you in gaol
551 ES   Carghil 37   way. I didn't want to ruin you./If I'd carried on, it might have ended your career,/
561 ES   Ld Clav 3   would I help you!/Even though it carried you away from me forever/To suffer the
CARRIES (2)
62 WL: Burial   53   card,/Which is blank, is something he carries on his back,/Which I am forbidden to
174 FQ: BurntN 131 have buried the day,/The black cloud carries the sun away./Will the sunflower turn to
CARRY (8)
121 SA   Sweeney 1   SNOW. DORIS. DUSTY./{S} I'll carry you off/To a cannibal isle./{Do} You'll be
121 SA   Doris   7   up. I'll be the cannibal./{Do} You'll carry me off? To a cannibal isle?/{S} I'll be the
192 FQ: Little   47   yourself, or inform curiosity/Or carry report. You are here to kneel/Where
604 Ode   11   /With so much that of Harvard we carry away/In the place of the life that we leave.
266 MC Knights   15   King; whom he set in your place to carry out his command./You are his servant, his
289 FR   Gerald   9   no doubt./Let him marry again and carry on at Wishwood./{A} Thank you, Gerald.
325 FR   Ivy   17   see that anyone is worried./We must carry on as if nothing had happened,/And have
414 CP   Celia   6   over it/More or less, or at least they carry on./No. I mean that what has happened
CARRYING (4)
349 FR   2m 13 /From another door, enter DENMAN carrying a birthday cake with/lighted candles,
524 ES   m 5   {}/[Enter MONICA and CHARLES carrying parcels]/{M} But you *must* stay to tea.
534 ES   Gomez 11 a false inference. I wouldn't dream/Of carrying on such business if I lived in England./I
559 FQ: Michael 37   of your existence,/A representative carrying on business in your absence./Why
CARS (6)
121 SA   Sweeney 23   no gramophones/There's no motor cars/No two-seaters, no six-seaters,/No Citroën
152 Rock 2   47   /But all dash to and fro in motor cars,/Familiar with the roads and settled
161 Rock 7   37   whole world stray in high-powered cars on a by-pass way?/VOICE OF THE
178 FQ: ECoker   60   the rolling stars/Simulates triumphal cars/Deployed in constellation wars/Scorpion
220 Old Deut   21   herdsmen will turn them away./The cars and the lorries run over the kerb,/And the
328 FR   Violet   6   reckless./{V} I think these racing cars ought to be prohibited. {}/[Re-enter
CART (1)
328 FR   Charles 14   into and demolished a roundsman's/cart in Ebury Street early on the morning of
CARTHAGE (1)
70 WL: Fire S   307 people who expect/Nothing.'/la la/To Carthage then I came/Burning burning burning
CARVED (1)
599 On a Port   5   in the room alone./Not like a tranquil carved goddess of stone/But evanescent, as if
CARVÈD (1)
64 WL: Chess   96   coloured stone,/In which sad light a carvèd dolphin swam./Above the antique
CARVEN (1)
167 Rock 10   31   from the polished stone,/The gilded carven wood, the coloured fresco./Our gaze is
CARVING (1)
213 Growltiger   40   armed with toasting forks and cruel carving knives./Then GILBERT gave the signal
CASE (27)
276 MC Knight1   25   without/hearing both sides of the case. That is in accordance with our
276 MC Knight1   27   I am not myself qualified to/put our case to you. I am a man of action and not of
277 MC Knight2   40 as the under dog. But is this really the case? I am going/to appeal not to your emotions
297 FR   Charles 15   have pushed her over?/{C} In any case, I shouldn't blame Harry./I might have
309 FR   Mary   9   of understanding you —/But in any case, I must get ready for dinner./{H} No, no,
333 FR   Agatha   13   in some way mine!/And that in any case I should have no other child./{H} And have
368 CP   Alex   12   and I'll get it myself./{A} Ah, in that case I know what I'll do./I'm going to give you
390 CP   Alex   38   she's famished./{A} Ah, in that case I know what I'll do .../{J} No, Alex./We

400 CP	Reilly	5	convincing him I was the man for his case?/{A} Difficulty? No! He was only impatient
402 CP	Edward	10	patient./If you take no interest in my case, I can go elsewhere./{R} You have reason
402 CP	Edward	23	realised/That mine is a very unusual case./{R} All cases are unique, and very similar
402 CP	Edward	33	/{E} I doubt if you have ever had a case like mine:/I have ceased to believe in my
405 CP	Reilly	1	always tell me./Indeed, it is often the case that my patients/Are only pieces of a total
405 CP	Edward	11	conduct —/I will not discuss my case before another patient./{R} On the
405 CP	Reilly	15	that you have been making up your case/So to speak, as you went along. A barrister
406 CP	Lavinia	3	That doesn't concern you./{L} In that case, Edward,/I don't think your clothes
406 CP	Reilly	31	right, Mr. Chamberlayne./You are no case for my sanatorium:/You are much too ill./
411 CP	Edward	7	...{E} But I can't go away!/I have a case coming on next Monday./{L} Then will you
420 CP	Reilly	14	there is no fee./{C} But .../{R} For a case like yours/There is no fee. {}/[*Presses*
436 CP	Lavinia	32	her./I suspect that you did. In any case you knew *about* her./Yet I thought your
455 CC	Eggers	14	himself responsible for her./In any case, he's behaved like a father —/A very
457 CC	Lady E	16	*in the theatre.*/{LE} Just open that case, I want something out of it./Unwrap that
464 CC	Claude	8	for use, or for decoration —/In either case, an inferior art./For me, they are neither
499 CC	Claude	5	/It's second nature./{SC} And put the case to her./Don't let her think that *I* have any
499 CC	Lucasta	18	Eggy! You're such a support./In any case, I've an announcement to make,/And I
506 CC	Eggers	11	had forgotten it./She was not, in any case, in a position/In which she could have
530 ES	m	32	*to a silver salver, still lying in its case*]./{LC} I don't know which impressed me

CASES (5)

64 WL: Chess	85	her jewels rose to meet it,/From satin cases poured in rich profusion./In vials of ivory
296 FR	Ivy	19	I understand —/I have heard of such cases before — that people in his condition/
358 CP	Julia	4	next election. And the secrets of your cases./{E} Most of my secrets are quite
402 CP	Reilly	24	mine is a very unusual case./{R} All cases are unique, and very similar to others./{E}
424 CP	Edward	22	solicitors/On quite straightforward cases. It's you who should be tired./{L} I'm not

CASH (3)

452 CC	Kaghan	6	catastrophe./She's come to pry some cash from the money-box./Bankrupt again! So I
477 CC	Lucasta	26	me like a debit item/Always in his cash account. I don't like myself./I don't like
552 ES	Carghil	25	/You got out of a tangle for a large cash payment/And no publicity. So your

CASQUE (1)

47 Mél Adult	9	la tête./C'est à Paris que je me coiffe/Casque noir de jemenfoutiste./En Allemagne,

CAST (6)

42 Swee Erect	2	/Paint me a cavernous waste shore/Cast in the unstilled Cyclades,/Paint me the
67 WL: Fire S	194	on the low damp ground/And bones cast in a little low dry garret,/Rattled by the
153 Rock 2	52	ride away on casual pillions./Much to cast down, much to build, much to restore;/Let
159 Rock 6	33	the steps;/And if the Temple is to be cast down/We must first build the Temple./In
241 MC Priest2	23	disputes at an end, is the wall of pride cast down/That divided them? Is it peace or
260 MC Thomas	19	by mourning, or/mourning will be cast out by joy; so it is only in these our

CASTING (3)

431 CP	Peter	33	a duke./Besides that, we've got the casting director:/He's looking for some typical
431 CP	Julia	39	/Couldn't you persuade your casting director/To take us all over? We're all
433 CP	Peter	19	/And I want to introduce her to our casting director./I've got an idea for another

CASTLE (1)

355 CP	Julia	10	sceptical. I stayed there once/At their castle in the North. How he suffered!/They had

CASUAL (3)

153 Rock 2	51	cycle,/And daughters ride away on casual pillions./Much to cast down, much to
326 FR	Harry	25	of my own life as an isolated ruin,/A casual bit of waste in an orderly universe./But it
417 CP	Reilly	34	the evening that brings together/For casual talk before the fire/Two people who

CAT (68)

24 Rhapsody	35	/The street-lamp said,'Remark the cat which flattens itself in the gutter,/Slips out
52 Whispers	23	marmoset/With subtle effluence of cat;/Grishkin has a maisonnette;/The sleek
135 5FingerEx1	t	Exercises/*Lines to a Persian Cat*/The songsters of the air repair/To the green
137 5FingerEx5	11	cur/In a coat of fur/And a porpentine cat/And a wopsical hat:/How unpleasant to
159 Rock 6	16	tooth of the dog and the talon of the cat./Why should men love the Church? Why
209 NamingCats	4	as mad as a hatter/When I tell you, a cat must have THREE DIFFERENT NAMES.
209 NamingCats	13	everyday names./But I tell you, a cat needs a name that's particular,/A name
209 NamingCats	20	that never belong to more than one cat./But above and beyond there's still one
209 NamingCats	24	research can discover —/But THE CAT HIMSELF KNOWS, and will never
209 NamingCats	25	will never confess./When you notice a cat in profound meditation,/The reason, I tell
210 Old Gumbie	t	singular Name./The Old Gumbie Cat/I have a Gumbie Cat in mind, her name is
210 Old Gumbie	1	Old Gumbie Cat/I have a Gumbie Cat in mind, her name is Jennyanydots;/Her
210 Old Gumbie	4	— and that's what makes a Gumbie Cat!/But when the day's hustle and bustle is
210 Old Gumbie	13	and tatting./I have a Gumbie Cat in mind, her name is Jennyanydots;/Her
210 Old Gumbie	16	— and that's what makes a Gumbie Cat!/But when the day's hustle and bustle is
210 Old Gumbie	25	bacon and cheese./I have a Gumbie Cat in mind, her name is Jennyanydots;/The

CATARRH (1)
457 CC Lady E 19 tells me that he suffers from chronic catarrh./{SC} Hello! What's that? {}/[*Opens*
CATASTROPHE (2)
275 MC Chorus 29 happen./We understood the private catastrophe,/The personal loss, the general
452 CC Kaghan 5 Because Lucasta's with me! The usual catastrophe./She's come to pry some cash from
CATASTROPHES (1)
329 FR Chorus 27 weather report/And the international catastrophes. {}/[*Exeunt* CHORUS]/Scene II/
CATCALLS (1)
291 FR Chorus 1 in the dress circle, the laughter and catcalls in the gallery?/{C} I might have been in
CATCH (4)
119 SP Klip 34 quite got it/(I'm afraid I didn't quite catch your name —/But I'm very pleased to
123 SA Kl & Kr 17 *worry what to do/We won't have to catch any trains/And we won't go home when it*
214 RTTugger 29 what he finds for himself;/So you'll catch him in it right up to the ears,/If you put it
233 Skimble 54 /Only stopping here and there to catch a flea./You were fast asleep at Crewe and
CATERER'S (4)
352 CP m 10 /A NURSE-SECRETARY/TWO CATERER'S MEN/*The scene is laid in London*
424 CP 3m 1 *later./A late afternoon in July.* A CATERER'S MAN *is arranging a buffet/table.*
424 CP m 5 *moves a bowl of flowers.*]/[*Re-enter* CATERER'S MAN *with trolley*]/{L} There, in
424 CP m 10 I think, till half past six. {}/[*Exit* CATERER'S MAN]/[EDWARD *lets himself in*
CATERWAUL (1)
216 Jellicles 8 /And pleasant to hear when they caterwaul./Jellicle Cats have cheerful faces,/
CATHEDRAL (12)
237 MC t in his mouth./MURDER IN THE CATHEDRAL/Characters/PART I/A
238 MC m 4 /THREE PRIESTS OF THE CATHEDRAL/A MESSENGER/
238 MC m 17 *Hall,/the second scene is in the Cathedral, on December 29th,* 1170/Part I/{C}
239 MC Chorus 1 I/{C} Here let us stand, close by the cathedral. Here let us wait./Are we drawn by
239 MC Chorus 3 that draws our feet/Towards the cathedral? What danger can be/For us, the
239 MC Chorus 6 /For us, and there is no safety in the cathedral. Some presage of an act/Which our
239 MC Chorus 8 has forced our feet/Towards the cathedral. We are forced to bear witness./Since
260 MC 3m 1 /THE ARCHBISHOP/*preaches in the Cathedral on Christmas Morning,* 1170/{T}
272 MC Priests 2 the divine office. To vespers./Into the Cathedral!/{T} Go to vespers, remember me at
272 MC m 10 *speak, the scene is changed to the cathedral.*]/[*while a* Dies Iræ *is sung in Latin by*
273 MC m 10 me, Lord, for death is near. {}/[*In the cathedral.* THOMAS *and* PRIESTS]/{3P} Bar
516 CC Colby 12 /That is, to become the organist of a cathedral./But my father was an unsuccessful
CATHERINE (1)
256 MC Tempts 12 unreal,/Unreal or disappointing:/The Catherine wheel, the pantomime cat,/The prizes
CATS (34)
135 5FingerEx2 10 cramped and dry./Pollicle dogs and cats all must/Jellicle cats and dogs all must/Like
135 5FingerEx2 11 Pollicle dogs and cats all must/Jellicle cats and dogs all must/Like undertakers, come
204 de la Mare 20 and intersect, and change;/When cats are maddened in the moonlight dance,/
207 t BOOK OF PRACTICAL CATS/The Naming of Cats/The Naming of
209 NamingCats t PRACTICAL CATS/The Naming of Cats/The Naming of Cats is a difficult matter,/
209 NamingCats 1 /The Naming of Cats/The Naming of Cats is a difficult matter,/It isn't just one of
211 Old Gumbie 37 a Beetles' Tattoo./So for Old Gumbie Cats let us now give three cheers —/On whom
212 Growltiger 17 came to grips!/But most to Cats of foreign race his hatred had been vowed;/
212 Growltiger 18 race his hatred had been vowed;/To Cats of foreign name and race no quarter was
216 Jellicles 1 it!/The Song of the Jellicles/*Jellicle Cats come out to-night,/Jellicle Cats come one*
216 Jellicles 2 *Jellicle Cats come out to-night,/Jellicle Cats come one come all:/The Jellicle Moon is*
216 Jellicles 5 *come to the Jellicle Ball.*/Jellicle Cats are black and white,/Jellicle Cats are rather
216 Jellicles 6 Cats are black and white,/Jellicle Cats are rather small;/Jellicle Cats are merry
216 Jellicles 7 /Jellicle Cats are rather small;/Jellicle Cats are merry and bright,/And pleasant to hear
216 Jellicles 9 to hear when they caterwaul./Jellicle Cats have cheerful faces,/Jellicle Cats have
216 Jellicles 10 Cats have cheerful faces,/Jellicle Cats have bright black eyes;/They like to
216 Jellicles 13 for the Jellicle Moon to rise./Jellicle Cats develop slowly,/Jellicle Cats are not too
216 Jellicles 14 /Jellicle Cats develop slowly,/Jellicle Cats are not too big;/Jellicle Cats are roly-poly,/
216 Jellicles 15 /Jellicle Cats are not too big;/Jellicle Cats are roly-poly,/They know how to dance a
216 Jellicles 21 dry between their toes./Jellicle Cats are white and black,/Jellicle Cats are of
216 Jellicles 22 Cats are white and black,/Jellicle Cats are of moderate size;/Jellicle Cats jump like a
216 Jellicles 24 jump like a jumping-jack,/Jellicle Cats have moonlit eyes;/They're quiet enough in
216 Jellicles 29 the light of the Jellicle Moon./Jellicle Cats are black and white,/Jellicle Cats (as I said)
216 Jellicles 30 Cats are black and white,/Jellicle Cats (as I said) are small;/If it happens to be a
218 Mung Rump 1 were a very notorious couple of cats./As knockabout clowns, quick-change
218 Mung Rump 6 more reputation than a couple of cats can very well bear./If the area window was
227 Macavity 39 THERE!/And they say that all the Cats whose wicked deeds are widely known/(I
228 Gus 7 in his youth, quite the smartest of Cats —/But no longer a terror to mice and to

230 Bust Jones   10   is/The name of this Brummell of Cats;/And we're all of us proud to be nodded or
231 Bust Jones   38   time'/Is the word for this stoutest of Cats./It must and it shall be Spring in Pall Mall/
234 Ad-dress   t   Railway Train.'/The Ad-dressing of Cats/You've read of several kinds of Cat,/And
234 Ad-dress   6   now have learned enough to see/That Cats are much like you and me/And other
235 Ad-dress   38   a Dog — A CAT'S A CAT./With Cats, some say, one rule is true:/*Don't speak till*
603 Spleen   8   Evening, lights, and tea!/Children and cats in the alley;/Dejection unable to rally/

CAUCHEMAR (1)
18 Portrait   28   /Without these friendships — life, what *cauchemar!*/Among the windings of the violins/

CAUGHT (8)
18 Portrait   15   slips/Among velleities and carefully caught regrets/Through attenuated tones of
175 FQ: BurntN   170   /Except in the aspect of time/Caught in the form of limitation/Between
193 FQ: Little   94   stranger in the waning dusk/I caught the sudden look of some dead master/
605 Narcissus   27   in his own clutch, his ancient beauty/Caught fast in the pink tips of his new beauty./
605 Narcissus   29   /Then he had been a young girl/Caught in the woods by a drunken old man/
295 FR   Harry   27   /A condition in which one can be caught for the last time./And also waking. She
426 CP   Julia   29   and here I am!/I seem *literally* to have caught you napping!/I know I'm much too
554 ES   Piggott   31   /When I saw that Mrs. Carghill had caught you./You wouldn't know that name, but

CAULKING (1)
110 Marina   28   garboard strake leaks, the seams need caulking./This form, this face, this life/Living to

CAUSE (20)
175 FQ: BurntN   167   /Love is itself unmoving,/Only the cause and end of movement,/Timeless, and
194 FQ: Little   111   wonder that I feel is easy,/Yet ease is cause of wonder. Therefore speak:/I may not
220 Old Deut   31   unreliable, but I can guess/That the cause of the trouble is Old Deuteronomy!'/Old
593 Grad 7   5   to know/That they have helpt the cause to victory,/That with their aid the flag is
249 MC Tempt2   6   laws,/Rule for the good of the better cause,/Dispensing justice make all even,/Is
249 MC Tempt2   39   /{T2} Against the barons/Is King's cause, churl's cause, Chancellor's cause./{T} No!
249 MC Tempt2   39   the barons/Is King's cause, churl's cause, Chancellor's cause./{T} No! shall I, who
249 MC Tempt2   39   cause, churl's cause, Chancellor's cause./{T} No! shall I, who keep the keys/Of
252 MC Tempt3   12   own;/Church and people have good cause against the throne./{T} If the Archbishop
252 MC Thomas   14   cannot trust the Throne,/He has good cause to trust none but God alone./I ruled once
258 MC Thomas   29   king./For those who serve the greater cause may make the cause serve them,/Still
258 MC Thomas   29   serve the greater cause may make the cause serve them,/Still doing right: and striving
258 MC Thomas   31   with political men/May make that cause political, not by what they do/But by
258 MC Thomas   38   strangest consequence from remotest cause./But for every evil, every sacrilege,/Crime,
269 MC Thomas   19   in malfeasance./{T} I submit my cause to the judgement of Rome./But if you kill
269 MC Thomas   21   rise from my tomb/To submit my cause before God's throne. {}/[*Exit*]/{K4} Priest!
275 MC Thomas   20   and to all the Saints, I commend my cause and that of the Church. {}/*While the*
360 CP   Reilly   30   /Of whom she thought she had cause to be jealous?/{E} She had nothing to
408 CP   Reilly   5   /But you failed to mention that the cause of your distress/Was the defection of your
558 ES   Ld Clav   4   /{LC} And your debts: are they the cause of your being discharged?/{Mi} Well,

CAUSES (1)
407 CP   Reilly   10   is an honest mind./That is one of the causes of their suffering./{L} No one can say my

CAUTERY (1)
319 FR Warburt   13   what festered/Then, has only left a cautery./Leave it alone. You know that your

CAUTIOUS (4)
16 Prufrock   116   Deferential, glad to be of use,/Politic, cautious, and meticulous;/Full of high sentence,
240 MC Chorus   2   in order;/The merchant, shy and cautious, tries to compile a little fortune,/And
480 CC Kaghan   5   thought of investing in./Colby's more cautious. You know, Colby,/You and I ought
530 ES Ld Clav   10   doctors, Charles; they tell me to be cautious,/To take life easily. Take life easily!/It's

CAUTIOUSLY (1)
253 MC Tempt4   10   who has been his friend./Borrow use cautiously, employ/Your services as long as you

CAVALIERS (2)
129 Cor2 State   3   the Knights of the British Empire, the Cavaliers,/O Cavaliers! of the Legion of
129 Cor2 State   4   the British Empire, the Cavaliers,/O Cavaliers! of the Legion of Honour,/The Order

CAVE (1)
307 FR   Mary   4   Arthur and John./{M} It was the cave where we met by moonlight/To raise the

CAVERNOUS (1)
42 Swee Erect   1   seven laws./Sweeney Erect/Paint me a cavernous waste shore/Cast in the unstilled

CAVERNS (1)
32 Hysteria   4   /recovery, lost finally in the dark caverns of her throat, bruised by/the ripple of

CAVIARE (1)
235 Ad-dress   57   you might now and then supply/Some caviare, or Strassburg Pie,/Some potted grouse,

CAVIES (1)
155 Rock 3   41   come or where you go./A colony of cavies or a horde of active marmots/Build better

CE (2)

51 Restaurant	5	du grand soleil, et de la pluie;/C'est ce qu'on appelle le jour de lessive des gueux.'/
51 Restaurant	31	c'était un sort pénible;/Cependant, ce fut jadis un bel homme, de haute taille./

CEASE (11)

135 5FingerEx1	7	grief./O when will the creaking heart cease?/When will the broken chair give ease?/
182 FQ: ECoker	203	most nearly itself/When here and now cease to matter./Old men ought to be explorers/
197 FQ: Little	241	the voice of this Calling/We shall not cease from exploration/And the end of all our
243 MC Priest3	11	of good or evil?/Until the grinders cease/And the door shall be shut in the street,/
254 MC Tempt4	36	parasites and whores./When miracles cease, and the faithful desert you./And men
296 FR Harry	12	explained them/Or at least, made me cease to be afraid of them./I will go and have
302 FR Chorus	9	the roof disappear,/And we should cease to be sure of what is real or unreal?/Hold
395 CP Edward	3	/You get to the point at which you cease to feel/And then you speak your mind./{L}
403 CP Edward	33	had left me, I began to dissolve,/To cease to exist. That was what she had done to
415 CP Celia	28	/You either become bad form, and cease to care,/Or else, if you care, you must be
417 CP Reilly	26	/The vision they have had, but they cease to regret it,/Maintain themselves by the

CEASED (2)

218 Mung Rump	10	loose on the roof,/Which presently ceased to be waterproof,/If the drawers were
402 CP Edward	34	have ever had a case like mine:/I have ceased to believe in my own personality./{R}

CEASELESS (3)

148 Rock 1	46	BOY:/THE ROCK:/The lot of man is ceaseless labour,/Or ceaseless idleness, which is
148 Rock 1	47	The lot of man is ceaseless labour,/Or ceaseless idleness, which is still harder,/Or
240 MC Priest2	30	King and the French King/In ceaseless intrigue, combinations,/In conference,

CEASELESSLY (1)

260 MC Thomas	23	should have announced Peace,/when ceaselessly the world has been stricken with War

CEASES (3)

186 FQ: DrySal	88	the past has another pattern, and ceases to be a mere sequence —/Or even
194 FQ: Little	139	the laceration/Of laughter at what ceases to amuse./And last, the rending pain of
395 CP Edward	2	me to the point/At which humiliation ceases to humiliate./You get to the point at

CEILING (3)

18 Portrait	5	room,/Four rings of light upon the ceiling overhead,/An atmosphere of Juliet's
23 Preludes	29	/They flickered against the ceiling./And when all the world came back/And
64 WL: Chess	93	/Stirring the pattern on the coffered ceiling./Huge sea-wood fed with copper/Burned

CÉLÉBRAI (1)

47 Mél Adult	16	là là/De Damas jusqu'à Omaha./Je célébrai mon jour de fête/Dans une oasis

CELEBRATE (4)

196 FQ: Little	182	died blind and quiet,/Why should we celebrate/These dead men more than the dying?/
260 MC Thomas	15	this same time of all the year that we/celebrate at once the Birth of Our Lord and His
261 MC Thomas	9	only do we at the feast of Christmas celebrate at once Our Lord's/Birth and His
261 MC Thomas	10	His Death: but on the next day we celebrate the martyrdom/of His first martyr, the

CELEBRATION (3)

213 Growltiger	56	and at Victoria Dock,/And a day of celebration was commanded in Bangkok./The
260 MC Thomas	8	/on this Christmas Day we do this in celebration of His Birth. So that at/the same
319 FR Warburt	40	/You will have to have the birthday celebration,/And your brothers will be here.

CELIA (82)

352 CP	m 4	(MRS. SHUTTLETHWAITE)/CELIA COPLESTONE/ALEXANDER
353 CP	3m 1	JULIA SHUTTLETHWAITE, CELIA/COPLESTONE, PETER QUILPE,
355 CP Julia	8	have imagined it./{J} My darling Celia,/You needn't be so sceptical. I stayed
358 CP Peter	27	I'm afraid *I* ought to be going./{P} Celia —/May I walk along with you?/{C} No,
358 CP Julia	33	I expect you on Friday, Edward. And Celia —/I must see you very soon. Now don't
359 CP Edward	2	Very well, good-bye./{E} Good-bye, Celia./{A} Good-bye, Edward. I do hope/You'll
359 CP	m 6	you to come. {}/[*Exeunt* ALEX *and* CELIA]/[*To the* UNIDENTIFIED GUEST]/
367 CP Peter	9	matter on her mind./{P} It's about Celia. Myself and Celia./{E} Why, what could
367 CP Peter	9	mind./{P} It's about Celia. Myself and Celia./{E} Why, what could there be about
367 CP Edward	10	could there be about yourself and Celia?/Have you anything in common, do you
367 CP Peter	22	/{P} Now you're only being sarcastic:/Celia was interested in the art of the film./{E}
367 CP Edward	27	—/Interesting if one is interested in Celia./Apart, of course, from its literary merit/
368 CP Peter	30	You asked me how I came to know Celia./I met her here, about a year ago./{E} At
369 CP Peter	3	owe her a great deal. And then I met Celia./She was different from any girl I'd ever
369 CP Edward	14	no chance to talk to her./{E} You and Celia were asked for different purposes./Your
369 CP Edward	23	told me how you came to know Celia./{P} I saw her again a few days later/Alone
369 CP Peter	29	I preferred to go alone./But a girl like Celia, it seemed very strange,/Because I thought
369 CP Peter	36	went together./And to be with Celia, that was something different/From
371 CP Edward	7	would have happened to you with Celia/In another six months' time. There it is./
371 CP Peter	12	back to California./{P} But I must see Celia./{E} Will it be the same Celia?/Better be
371 CP Edward	13	must see Celia./{E} Will it be the same Celia?/Better be content with the Celia you

371 CP	Edward	14	Celia?/Better be content with the Celia you remember./Remember! I say it's
371 CP	Peter	16	already a memory./{P} But I must see Celia at least to make her tell me/What has
371 CP	Edward	33	moths will get in. So you want to see Celia./I don't know why I should be taking all
372 CP	Peter	1	/What do you want me to do?/{P} See Celia for me./You know her in a different way
372 CP	Edward	7	disinterested./{E} Well, I will see Celia./{P} Thank you, Edward. It's very good of
373 CP	Edward	3	*and dials a number*]/{E} Is Miss Celia Coplestone in? ... How long ago? .../No, it
374 CP	m	2	alone? {}/[EDWARD *returns with* CELIA]/{E} Celia! Why have you come back?/I
374 CP	Edward	2	[EDWARD *returns with* CELIA]/{E} Celia! Why have you come back?/I said I would
375 CP	m	37	heaven's sake, don't bother! {}/[*Exit* CELIA]/{E} Suppose someone came and found
376 CP	m	2	*doorbell rings repeatedly. Re-enter* CELIA, *in an apron.*]/{C} You'd better answer
376 CP	m	11	/{J} I've had an inspiration! {}/[*Enter* CELIA *with saucepan*]/{C} Edward, it's ruined!/
376 CP	Julia	17	only thing I know how to cook./{J} Celia! I see you've had the same inspiration/
378 CP	Julia	1	shall have a few biscuits./{J} But you, Celia?/You must come and have a light supper
379 CP	Edward	12	else will be,/I promise you./{E} No, Celia./It has been very wonderful, and I'm very
383 CP	Edward	25	night, Edward./{E} Good night ... Celia. {}/[*Exit* CELIA]/{E} Oh! {}/[*He snatches*
383 CP	m	25	/{E} Good night ... Celia. {}/[*Exit* CELIA]/{E} Oh! {}/[*He snatches up the receiver*]
386 CP	Edward	14	*and he goes to the front door.*]/{E} Celia!/{C} Has Lavinia arrived?/{E} Celia! Why
386 CP	Edward	16	Celia!/{C} Has Lavinia arrived?/{E} Celia! Why have you come?/I expect Lavinia at
387 CP	Peter	19	with him. He'll be here in a minute./Celia! Have you heard from Lavinia too?/Or am
388 CP	Lavinia	22	/{L} Who's going away? Well, Celia. Well, Peter./I didn't expect to find either
389 CP	Lavinia	4	of course?/How exciting for you, Celia! Now you'll have a chance/At last, to
389 CP	Peter	8	/{P} We're not going together./Celia told us she was going away,/But I don't
389 CP	Lavinia	13	I'm going to California./{L} Well, Celia, why don't you go to California?/
389 CP	Lavinia	25	say good-bye — as friends./{L} Why, Celia, but haven't we always been friends?/I
391 CP	Edward	6	/Good-bye, Edward./{E} Good-bye, Celia./{C} Good-bye, Lavinia./{L} Good-bye,
391 CP	Lavinia	8	Good-bye, Lavinia./{L} Good-bye, Celia. {}/[*Exit* CELIA]/{J} And now, Alex, you
391 CP	m	8	Lavinia./{L} Good-bye, Celia. {}/[*Exit* CELIA]/{J} And now, Alex, you and I should
392 CP	Lavinia	2	thing to say./Like a schoolgirl. Like Celia. I don't know why I said it./Well, here I
397 CP	Lavinia	39	has the difference nothing to do/With Celia going to California?/{E} Celia? Going to
397 CP	Edward	40	/With Celia going to California?/{E} Celia? Going to California?/{L} Yes, with Peter.
408 CP	Edward	21	then he came to *me* to confide about Celia!/I have never heard anything so utterly
412 CP	m	24	NURSE-SECRETARY *shows in* CELIA]/{R} Miss Celia Coplestone? ... Won't
412 CP	Reilly	24	*shows in* CELIA]/{R} Miss Celia Coplestone? ... Won't you sit down?/I
420 CP	1m	19	*appears at door. Exit* CELIA. REILLY *dials on/house-telephone.*]/
421 CP	Julia	10	that. We shall see./It's the thought of Celia that weighs upon my mind./{R} Of Celia?/
421 CP	Reilly	11	that weighs upon my mind./{R} Of Celia?/{J} Of Celia./{R} But when I said just
421 CP	Julia	12	upon my mind./{R} Of Celia?/{J} Of Celia./{R} But when I said just now/That she
433 CP	Peter	16	of it/If she only got the chance. It's Celia Coplestone./She always wanted to. And
433 CP	Alex	27	in, Peter. I'm afraid you can't have Celia./{P} Oh ... Is she married?/{A} Not
433 CP	Lavinia	30	/{A} Not married, but dead./{L} Celia?/{A} Dead./{P} Dead. That knocks the
433 CP	Edward	33	That knocks the bottom out of it./{E} Celia dead./{J} You had better tell them, Alex,/
433 CP	Lavinia	36	Kinkanja./{L} Kinkanja? What was Celia doing in Kinkanja?/We heard that she had
434 CP	Alex	17	never be fit for normal life again./But Celia Coplestone, she was taken./When our
434 CP	Lavinia	26	/Very near an ant-hill./{L} But Celia! ... Of all people .../{E} And just for a
434 CP	Peter	36	and I don't know what happened/To Celia, during those two years./Two years!
434 CP	Peter	37	years./Two years! Thinking about Celia./{E} It's the waste that I resent./{P} You
435 CP	Peter	10	At first I did not want to know about Celia/And so I never asked. Then I wanted to
435 CP	Peter	24	/And that seemed possible, while Celia was alive./I wanted it, believed in it, for
435 CP	Peter	25	alive./I wanted it, believed in it, for Celia./And, of course, I wanted to do something
435 CP	Peter	26	course, I wanted to do something for Celia —/But what mattered was, that Celia was
435 CP	Peter	27	Celia —/But what mattered was, that Celia was alive./And now it's all worthless.
435 CP	Lavinia	32	saying just now/That you never knew Celia. We none of us did./What you've been
435 CP	Lavinia	33	you've been living on is an image of Celia/Which you made for yourself, to meet
436 CP	Peter	13	/And that isn't good enough for Celia./{J} You must have learned how to look at
436 CP	Julia	17	an eye. You will come to think of Celia/Like that, one day. And then you'll
437 CP	Lavinia	21	was telling us what had happened to Celia/I was looking at your face. And it seemed
438 CP	Reilly	15	standing behind her chair,/Of a Celia Coplestone whose face showed the
439 CP	Edward	15	if this was right — if this was right for Celia —/There must be something else that is
439 CP	Lavinia	5	Then I might not have misunderstood Celia./{R} You will have to live with these
439 CP	Julia	11	then must take the consequences. Celia chose/A way of which the consequence
439 CP	Lavinia	27	and me and Edward ... to talk about Celia./{P} Thanks very much. But not this time

CELIA'S (3)

369 CP	Edward	16	to be one of Lavinia's discoveries;/Celia's, to provide society and fashion./Lavinia
389 CP	Lavinia	2	to say good-bye before I left./{L} And Celia's going too? Was that what I heard?/I
435 CP	Peter	28	was alive./And now it's all worthless. Celia's not alive./{L} No, it's not all worthless,

CELLAR (4)

83 Hollow Men	10	rats' feet over broken glass/In our dry cellar/Shape without form, shade without
292 FR Charles	32	merchant to recommend you;/Your cellar could do with a little attention./{I} And
302 FR Chorus	5	be reassured/About the noises in the cellar/And the window that should not have
302 FR Chorus	8	open, the curtains be drawn,/The cellar make some dreadful disclosure, the roof

CÈNE (1)

48 Lune Miel	13	de Padoue à Milan/Où se trouve la Cène, et un restaurant pas cher./Lui pense aux

CÉNOTAPHE (1)

47 Mél Adult	19	peau de girafe./On montrera mon cénotaphe/Aux côtes brûlantes de Mozambique.

CENT. (1)

44 Cook Egg	16	shall lie together, lapt/In a five per cent. Exchequer Bond./I shall not want Society

CENTAINES (1)

48 Lune Miel	3	/A l'aise entre deux draps, chez deux centaines de punaises;/La sueur aestivale, et une

CENTAUR'S (1)

31 Apollinax	16	in its hair./I heard the beat of centaur's hoofs over the hard turf/As his dry

CENTRAL (4)

278 MC Knight2	16	temporal administration, under the central/government. I knew Becket well, in
533 ES Gomez	21	Is now a highly respected citizen/Of a central American republic: San Marco./It's as
563 ES Ld Clav	4	/{LC} He comes from some place in Central America./{MC} How romantic! I'd love
570 ES Ld Clav	26	exists./He's Federico Gomez, the Central American,/A man who's made a fortune

CENTRE (4)

96 Ash-Wed 5	9	world still whirled/About the centre of the silent Word./O my people, what
218 Mung Rump	4	Grove —/That was merely their centre of operation, for they were incurably
345 FR Charles	38	if the earth should open/Right to the centre, as I was about to cross Pall Mall./I
362 CP Reilly	39	matron, you are still the subject,/The centre of reality. But, stretched on the table,/

CENTRED (1)

320 FR Warburt	37	/Your mother's hopes are all centred on you./{H} Hopes? ... Tell me/Did you

CENTURIES (3)

147 Rock 1	17	/The cycles of Heaven in twenty centuries/Bring us farther from GOD and
201 Def Island	2	music's/enduring instrument, of many centuries of/patient cultivation of the earth, of
593 Grad 6	6	such proud estate/As shall on future centuries bestow/A legacy of benefits — may we

CENTURY (3)

590 Time Space	6	Love, should we ever pray/To live a century?/The butterfly that lives a day/Has lived
593 Grad 5	1	/Great duties call — the twentieth century/More grandly dowered than those
593 Grad 6	1	than were e'er of yore!/But if this century is to be more great/Than those before,

CEPENDANT (1)

51 Restaurant	31	donc, c'était un sort pénible;/Cependant, ce fut jadis un bel homme, de haute

CERAMICS (2)

464 CC Colby	24	may I ask,/With this passion for ... ceramics, how did it happen/That you never
492 CC Claude	32	know anything at all/About ceramics ... or any other art./No, I don't think I

CEREMONY (2)

246 MC Tempt1	24	You see, my Lord, I do not wait upon ceremony:/Here I have come, forgetting all
248 MC Tempt1	3	my Lord, I do not wait upon ceremony,/I leave as I came, forgetting all

CERTAIN (26)

13 Prufrock	4	upon a table;/Let us go, through certain half-deserted streets,/The muttering
23 Preludes	45	newspapers, and eyes/Assured of certain certainties,/The conscience of a
105 Song Sime	20	mountain of desolation,/Before the certain hour of maternal sorrow,/Now at this
232 Skimble	26	sees what you are thinking/And it's certain that he doesn't approve/Of hilarity and
241 MC Mess	29	/{M} You are right to express a certain incredulity./He comes in pride and
243 MC Chorus	15	ill the time, uncertain the profit, certain the danger./O late late late, late is the
249 MC Tempt2	11	Real power/Is purchased at price of a certain submission./Your spiritual power is
255 MC Tempt4	3	/About this man who played a certain part in history./{T} But what is there to
266 MC Thomas	1	/[to PRIESTS]./{T} However certain our expectation/The moment foreseen
287 FR Amy	34	/Which I cannot find./— I am only certain of Arthur and John,/Arthur in London,
296 FR Agatha	1	you will feel better./{Ag} There are certain points I do not yet understand:/They
301 FR Violet	23	genteel acquaintance./{V} Gerald is certain to make some blunder, he is useless out
329 FR Chorus	21	in Argos or England/There are certain inflexible laws/Unalterable, in the nature
333 FR Agatha	28	shall expiate, or whose, or why. It is certain/That the knowledge of it must precede
371 CP Peter	20	really feel the same/When we heard certain music? Or looked at certain pictures?/
371 CP Peter	20	we heard certain music? Or looked at certain pictures?/There was something real. But
381 CP Edward	8	one thing of which I am relatively certain/Is, that only since this morning/I have
409 CP Reilly	19	incapable/Of loving. To men of a certain type/The suspicion that they are
437 CP Reilly	19	suggestion/That a sudden intuition, in certain minds,/May tend to express itself at once
447 CC Claude	34	will take to him at once:/If so, she is certain to come to believe/That she chose him
455 CC Colby	5	a moment ago./Then I'd have been certain I'd lost my reason:/Her influence is

507 CC   Claude   32   understand, Colby?/{SC} Don't be certain yet, Elizabeth./{LE} There is no doubt
517 CC   Eggers   30   me a trial?/{E} Give you a trial? I'm certain./Good organists don't seem to want to
528 ES   Monica   37   a very long time, Charles./It's almost certain that the winter in Jamaica/Will never
534 ES   Gomez   21   or anything of that nature,/Is certain to be found out sooner or later./And
545 ES   Ld Clav 19   /With the privacy of others, which is certain to explode./{M} Hush, Father. I see her

CERTAINLY (23)

104 Journ Magi   36   /Birth or Death? There was a Birth, certainly,/We had evidence and no doubt. I had
119 SP   Klip 25   last night for the first time/{Kl} And I certainly hope it won't be the last time./{Do}
229 Gus   50   with his claws,/'Well, the Theatre's certainly not what it was./These modern
296 FR   Amy   30   a talk to him tomorrow./{A} Most certainly not, Charles, you are not the right
345 FR   Gerald 29   /Then you can leave me./{G} Oh, certainly, Amy./{V} I do not understand/A
346 FRDowning   13   /While you are away?/{Do} Oh, certainly, Miss,/I'll never leave him so long as
347 FR   Violet 22   think Amy ought to see it?/{V} No, certainly not./You do not know what has been
364 CP   Reilly 11   lost in the dark?/{UG} There is certainly no purpose in remaining in the dark/
367 CP   Edward   7   of Julia Shuttlethwaite./{E} Julia is certainly observant,/But I think she had some
385 CP   Edward 24   is to try to conceal./{E} There are certainly things I should like to forget./{UG}
408 CP   Reilly   3   if I have made a partial recovery./{R} Certainly, you were completely prostrated,/And
408 CP   Reilly   4   you were completely prostrated,/And certainly, you have somewhat recovered./But
451 CC   Eggers 35   be on my guard./{E} Your music will certainly be a great asset/With Lady Elizabeth. I
488 CC   Claude   9   Guzzard! It must be true./{SC} It is certainly a remarkable coincidence —/If it is a
498 CC   Eggers 34   child/Then we must try to trace it. Certainly, Sir Claude:/Our first step must be to
501 CC   Claude 17   thought that I understood *you*,/And I certainly fail to understand Colby./{LE} But
505 CC Guzzard   13   very soul of tact and discretion./{MG} Certainly, Sir Claude, if that is what you wish./
511 CC   Kaghan 22   as Aunt Elizabeth./{K} That's easier, certainly./{LE} And I shall wish to meet them./
511 CC   Lady E 29   very much calling me ... just 'B'?/{LE} Certainly, if you prefer that, Barnabas./{L} Why
537 ES   Ld Clav 33   He never came to *my* help./{LC} I certainly admit no responsibility,/None
560 ES   Michael 23   Oh, you mean on the road./Certainly not. I'm far too good a driver./{LC}
568 ES   Charles 13   wish to keep unknown?/{C} There are certainly things I would gladly forget, Sir,/Or
572 ES   Ld Clav 23   We should have been poor, we should certainly have quarrelled,/We should have been

CERTAINTIES (1)

23 Preludes   45   and eyes/Assured of certain certainties,/The conscience of a blackened street

CERTAINTY (2)

480 CC   Colby   17   ever gamble/On anything that isn't a certainty./{K} Well, there's something in that.
583 ES   Monica   26   can dismay or amaze me/Fixed in the certainty of love unchanging./I feel utterly

CERTIFICATE (1)

515 CC Guzzard   17   /I feared you would ask for the birth certificate./You never did. And so it went on./

CES (1)

67 WL: Fire S   202   wash their feet in soda water/Et O ces voix d'enfants, chantant dans la coupole!/

CET (1)

51 Restaurant   15   délire.'/Mais alors, vieux lubrique, à cet âge .../'Monsieur, le fait est dur./Il est venu,

CHAFF (1)

578 ES   Michael 30   a flirtation,/And my friends used to chaff me about my highbrow sister./But all the

CHAIN (4)

335 FR   Harry   16   In and out, the movement/Until the chain broke, and I was left/Under the single eye
335 FR   Agatha 22   windows./Up and down. Until the chain breaks./{H} To and fro, dragging my feet/
335 FR   Harry   27   the giant lizard. To and fro./Until the chain breaks./The chain breaks,/The wheel
335 FR   Harry   28   and fro./Until the chain breaks./The chain breaks,/The wheel stops, and the noise of

CHAINS (1)

268 MC Knight2   9   his coronation./{K2} Binding with the chains of anathema./{K3} Using every means in

CHAIR (11)

31 Apollinax   13   head of Mr. Apollinax rolling under a chair/Or grinning over a screen/With seaweed in
44 Cook Egg   1   Cooking Egg/Pipit sate upright in her chair/Some distance from where I was sitting;/
64 WL: Chess   77   — mon frère!'/A Game of Chess/The Chair she sat in, like a burnished throne,/
135 5FingerEx1   8   heart cease?/When will the broken chair give ease?/Why will the summer day
589 Fable   73   /The Abbot sat as pasted to his chair,/His eye became the size of any dollar,/
291 FR   Charles   2   in St. James's Street, in a comfortable chair rather nearer the fire./{I} I might have
366 CP   Julia   4   the bottom of that sofa —/No, this chair. Look under the cushion./{E} Are you
401 CP   Reilly   29   down./I think that you will find that chair comfortable./{E} You knew,/Before I
422 CP   Alex   15   of the stars./{A} Let them place a chair each side of it./{J} May the holy ones
437 CP   Reilly   14   /I saw the image, standing behind her chair,/Of a Celia Coplestone whose face showed
493 CC   Claude   23   her expression./{SC} But not in this chair! She must have an armchair .../{LE} Not

CHAIRMAN (3)

493 CC   Claude   11   /You see, I want him to be a sort of chairman./{LE} That's a good idea./{SC} On the
528 ES   Monica   13   wore a public label./And later, as chairman of public companies,/Always his
538 ES   Gomez   39   into the City. Director of a bank/And chairman of companies. You looked the part —

CHAIRMAN'S (1)
530 ES   Ld Clav   37   The inadequate levy/That made the Chairman's Price! And my fellow directors/
CHAIRMEN (1)
180 FQ: ECoker 106   rulers,/Distinguished civil servants, chairmen of many committees,/Industrial lords
CHAIRS (3)
107 Animula   4   between the legs of tables and of chairs,/Rising or falling, grasping at kisses and
305 FR   Harry   28   same pictures ... even the table,/The chairs, the sofa ... all in the same positions./I
493 CC   3m   1   *later.* SIR CLAUDE *is/moving chairs about. Enter* LADY ELIZABETH./{LE}
CHALLENGE (1)
193 FQ: Little   92   /That pointed scrutiny with which we challenge/The first-met stranger in the waning
CHALLENGED (2)
 31 Apollinax   20   something he said that I might have challenged.'/Of dowager Mrs. Phlaccus, and
328 FR Charles   18   reversed/into a shop-window. When challenged, Mr. Piper said:/"I thought it was all
CHAMBER (1)
164 Rock 9   14   very well./Let us mourn in a private chamber, learning the way of penitence,/And
CHAMBERLAYNE (27)
352 CP   m   2   PARTY/Persons/EDWARD CHAMBERLAYNE/JULIA (MRS.
352 CP   m   8   HARCOURT-REILLY/LAVINIA CHAMBERLAYNE/A
353 CP   3m   1   *flat. Early evening.*/EDWARD CHAMBERLAYNE, JULIA
384 CP   Reilly   2   GUEST]/{UG} Good evening, Mr. Chamberlayne./{E} Well. May I offer you some
401 CP   Reilly   1   *his papers]*./{R} Good morning, Mr. Chamberlayne./Please sit down. I won't keep
401 CP   Reilly   3   keep you a moment./— Now, Mr. Chamberlayne?/{E} It came into my mind/
401 CP   Reilly 14   /{R} No. If you please, sit down, Mr. Chamberlayne./You are not going away, so you
401 CP   Reilly 21   say that I had been invited;/And Mrs. Chamberlayne did not know that I was coming.
402 CP   Reilly   1   had not brought your wife back, Mr. Chamberlayne,/Do you suppose that things
402 CP   Reilly 27   /{R} You are very impetuous, Mr. Chamberlayne./There are several kinds of
404 CP   Reilly   7   You must have patience with me, Mr. Chamberlayne:/I learn a good deal by merely
405 CP   Reilly 20   It is just because you are not free, Mr. Chamberlayne,/That you have come to me. It is
405 CP   Reilly 30   /{R} Honesty before honour, Mr. Chamberlayne./Sit down, please, both of you.
405 CP   Reilly 31   /Sit down, please, both of you. Mrs. Chamberlayne,/Your husband wishes to enter a
406 CP   Reilly   8   /At least, for the moment. But, Mrs. Chamberlayne,/You have never visited my
406 CP   Reilly 30   going there./{R} You are right, Mrs. Chamberlayne./You are no case for my
407 CP   Reilly 38   There was one, in fact. But you, Mrs. Chamberlayne,/Tried to make me believe that it
408 CP   Reilly 39   obtained from outside sources./Mrs. Chamberlayne, when you came to me two
409 CP   Reilly   9   well-suited to each other./Mr. Chamberlayne, when you thought your wife
409 CP   Reilly 24   Edward./{R} So you say, Mrs. Chamberlayne./And now, let us turn to your
410 CP   Reilly 35   he means./{R} When you find, Mr. Chamberlayne,/The best of a bad job is all any
436 CP   Reilly 26   dying natives./{R} Who knows, Mrs. Chamberlayne,/The difference that made to the
436 CP   Reilly 34   was one of ... satisfaction!/{R} Mrs. Chamberlayne, I must be very transparent/Or
436 CP   Reilly 40   /Do you mind if I quote poetry, Mrs. Chamberlayne?/{L} Oh no, I should love to hear
437 CP   Reilly 17   /If this strains your credulity, Mrs. Chamberlayne,/I ask you only to entertain the
438 CP   Reilly   5   some insight on your part, Mrs. Chamberlayne;/But such experience can only be
438 CP   Reilly 31   we should all be condemned./Mrs. Chamberlayne, I often have to make a decision/
CHAMBERLAYNE'S (1)
400 CP   Alex   1   *almost immediately]*/{A} When is Chamberlayne's appointment?/{R} At eleven
CHAMBERLAYNES (2)
422 CP   Alex   7   /{J} Everything is in order./{A} The Chamberlaynes have chosen?/{R} They accept
439 CP   Reilly 38   you are right. It is also right/That the Chamberlaynes should now be giving a party./
CHAMBERLAYNES' (3)
353 CP   2m   1   One. Scene 1/*The drawing-room of the Chamberlaynes' London flat. Early evening.*/
424 CP   2m   1   /Act Three/*The drawing-room of the Chamberlaynes' London flat. Two years later.*/A
439 CP   Julia 34   ... And now the consequence of the Chamberlaynes' choice/Is a cocktail party. They
CHAMBERMAID (3)
544 ES Monica   6   us a very tolerable breakfast;/And the chambermaid really *is* a chambermaid:/For
544 ES Monica   6   /And the chambermaid really *is* a chambermaid:/For when I asked about morning
546 ES Monica 32   /We haven't seen her yet, but the chambermaid/Referred to a nurse. When we see
CHAMBERS (3)
 17 Prufrock   129   and black./We have lingered in the chambers of the sea/By sea-girls wreathed with
246 MC Templ1 39   /Singing at nightfall, whispering in chambers,/Fires devouring the winter season,/
424 CP Lavinia 12   /{L} Oh no. I did in fact ring up your chambers,/And your clerk told me you had
CHAMPAGNE (5)
353 CP   Peter 15   pantry, rinsing her mouth out with champagne./I like that story./{C} I love that
377 CP   Julia 21   high and low. But I found some champagne —/Only a half-bottle, to be sure,/
383 CP Edward   5   sure, in the kitchen? Beside the champagne bottle?/You're quite sure? ... Very
383 CP   Celia 12   always right./But why bring an empty champagne bottle?/{E} It isn't empty. It may be

426 CP   Edward   3   they're all gone, we will have some champagne,/Just ourselves. You lie down now,
CHANCE (16)
142 Cape Ann   4   /Of the goldfinch at noon. Leave to chance/The Blackburnian warbler, the shy one.
205 de la Mare   24   /No sleeper by his call; or when by chance/An empty face peers from an empty
220 Old Deut   23   —/So that nothing untoward may chance to disturb/Deuteronomy's rest when he
258 MC Thomas   27   never my wish./Servant of God has chance of greater sin/And sorrow, than the man
369 CP   Peter   13   very often./And when I did, I got no chance to talk to her./{E} You and Celia were
388 CP   Celia   12   fun, wasn't it! But now you'll have a chance,/I hope, to realise your ambitions./I shall
389 CP   Lavinia   4   for you, Celia! Now you'll have a chance/At last, to realise your ambitions./
394 CP   Lavinia   9   have those Thursdays, to give you the chance/Of talking to intellectual people .../{E}
402 CP   Reilly   6   only two —/Which you still have the chance of redeeming from ruin./{E} You talk as
421 CP   Julia   3   /All we could do was to give them the chance./And now, when they are stripped naked
430 CP   Peter   11   I really must crash in:/It's my only chance to see Edward and Lavinia./I'm only
433 CP   Peter   16   a success of it/If she only got the chance. It's Celia Coplestone./She always
481 CC   Lady E   26   will you get dinner?/Oh, I know. It's a chance to try that Herbal Restaurant/I
516 CC   Colby   11   an organist/When I found I had no chance of getting to the top —/That is, to
525 ES   Charles 16   to tea,/But you know I won't get a chance to talk to you./You know that. Now
560 ES   Michael   9   out of the country./What I'd like is a chance to go abroad/As a partner in some
CHANCELLOR (8)
242 MC   Priest1 20   by bitter adversity./I saw him as Chancellor, flattered by the King./Liked or
248 MC   Tempt2   38   hereafter./{T} Who then?/{T2} The Chancellor, King and Chancellor./King
248 MC   Tempt2   38   then?/{T2} The Chancellor, King and Chancellor./King commands. Chancellor richly
249 MC   Tempt2   1   and Chancellor./King commands. Chancellor richly rules./This is a sentence not
252 MC   Thomas   15   none but God alone./I ruled once as Chancellor/And men like you were glad to wait
278 MC   Knight2 14   that — should unite/the offices of Chancellor and Archbishop. Had Becket
278 MC   Knight2 21   Archbishop, he/resigned the office of Chancellor, he became more priestly than the/
279 MC   Knight4 19   While the late Archbishop/was Chancellor, no one, under the King, did more
CHANCELLOR'S (1)
249 MC   Tempt2   39   barons/Is King's cause, churl's cause, Chancellor's cause./{T} No! shall I, who keep
CHANCELLORSHIP (2)
248 MC   Tempt2   20   /And weightier ones: those of the Chancellorship./See how the late ones rise! You,
248 MC   Tempt2   24   again./{T} Your meaning?/{T2} The Chancellorship that you resigned/When you
CHANGE (36)
 64 WL: Chess   99   gave upon the sylvan scene/The change of Philomel, by the barbarous king/So
148 Rock 1   61   changes,/But one thing does not change./In all of my years, one thing does not
148 Rock 1   62   /In all of my years, one thing does not change./However you disguise it, this thing does
148 Rock 1   63   you disguise it, this thing does not change:/The perpetual struggle of Good and
187 FQ: DrySal   116   by subsequent attrition./People change, and smile: but the agony abides./Time
204 de la Mare   19   two worlds meet, and intersect, and change;/When cats are maddened in the
293 FR   Harry   14   /{H} Time and time and time, and change, no change!/You all of you try to talk as
293 FR   Harry   14   and time and time, and change, no change!/You all of you try to talk as if nothing
295 FR   Amy   34   so far/And making such haste, the change is too sudden for you./You are unused
305 FR   Agatha   15   not the easiest rôle. I must go and change for dinner. {}/[Exit]/{M} So you will not
305 FR   Harry   34   /This arresting of the normal change of things:/But it's very like her. What I
306 FR   Mary   2   up, I suppose,/Not noticing the change. But to you, I am sure,/We must seem
306 FR   Mary   6   Oxford./{M} Well, I must go and change for dinner./We do change — to that
306 FR   Mary   7   go and change for dinner./We do change — to that extent./{H} No, don't go just
308 FR   Mary   29   something inside you/Which you can change anywhere — here, as well as elsewhere./
313 FR   Ivy   8   you arrange these flowers? Just let me change them./You don't mind, do you? I know
313 FR   Mary   18   mother's birthday./{M} I must go and change. I came in very late. {}/[Exit]/{C} Now
340 FR   Amy   3   thought that time might have made a change in Agatha —/It has made enough in *me*.
384 CP   Reilly   10   /{UG} No. You will not be ready to change your mind/Until you recover from
384 CP   Reilly   12   I have come to tell you that you will change your mind,/But that it will not matter. It
384 CP   Edward   14   be too late./{E} I have half a mind to change my mind now/To show you that I am
384 CP   Edward   15   now/To show you that I am free to change it./{UG} You will change your mind, but
384 CP   Reilly   16   I am free to change it./{UG} You will change your mind, but you are not free./Your
395 CP   Edward   16   —/Though I haven't yet found it a change for the better./But doesn't it occur to
395 CP   Edward   25   what way have you changed?/{E} The change that comes/From seeing oneself through
458 CC   Eggers   15   /{E} Yes, how did you manage to change your ticket?/{LE} I went to the agency
458 CC   Lady E   16   I went to the agency and got them to change it./I can't understand why you're both
458 CC   Claude   20   that, Elizabeth./But why did you change your plans?/{LE} Because of Mildred
475 CC   Colby   10   changes/You can understand the change as soon as it happens,/Though you
475 CC   Colby   14   too. But perhaps what we call change .../{L} Is understanding better what one
479 CC   Kaghan   35   I'm not sure I like them. You must change the colours./It's all a bit too dim. You
481 CC   Kaghan   12   any restaurant that *you* like./— For a change, let's talk about Lucasta. {}/[rising]./{L}

533	ES	Gomez	7	/You know, where *I* live, people do change their names;/And besides, my wife's
569	ES	Ld Clav	2	drop the pretence,/Walk off the stage, change into our own clothes/And speak as
573	ES	Carghil	26	sure of it, Monica!/I can tell by the change in your expression to-day;/This must be
576	ES	Ld Clav	23	England./{LC} Perhaps you intend to change your name to Gomez?/{G} Oh no, Dick,

CHANGED (33)

180	FQ: ECoker	115	are extinguished, for the scene to be changed/With a hollow rumble of wings, with a
271	MC Thomas	18	has often been told/And often been changed in the telling. They will seem unreal./
272	MC	m 10	*the* CHORUS *speak, the scene is changed to the cathedral.*]/[*while a* Dies Iræ *is*
288	FR	Amy	28	Adaptation is hard./{A} Nothing is changed, Agatha, at Wishwood./Everything is
288	FR	Amy	32	to have destroyed./Nothing has been changed. I have seen to that./{Ag} Yes. I mean
292	FR	Amy	24	is all ready for you. Nothing has been changed./{H} Changed? nothing changed? how
292	FR	Harry	25	you. Nothing has been changed./{H} Changed? nothing changed? how can you say
292	FR	Harry	25	been changed./{H} Changed? nothing changed? how can you say that nothing is
292	FR	Harry	25	how can you say that nothing is changed?/You all look so withered and young./
305	FR	Harry	29	/I was looking to see if anything was changed,/But if so, I can't find it./{M} Your
306	FR	Harry	4	very altered./{H} You have hardly changed at all —And I haven't seen you since
314	FR	Warburt	7	to come./{W} I dare say we've both changed a good deal, Harry./A country
341	FR	Agatha	2	one thing, Amy:/That you have never changed. And perhaps I have not./I thought
381	CP	Edward	32	/That what is, is not, or could be changed./The self that can say 'I want this — or
382	CP	Celia	8	were before, with me./Twice you have changed since I have been looking at you./I
384	CP	Edward	9	/{E} Are you thinking that I may have changed my mind?/{UG} No. You will not be
385	CP	Reilly	1	which we knew them. And they have changed since then./To pretend that they and
387	CP	Peter	35	nothing./{P} I'm so glad./Because I've changed my mind. I mean, I've decided/That it's
395	CP	Edward	18	occur to you that possibly/I may have changed too?/{L} Oh, Edward, when you were a
395	CP	Lavinia	24	to grow too./In what way have you changed?/{E} The change that comes/From
458	CC	Claude	14	/{SC} Do you mean to say that you changed your ticket?/{E} Yes, how did you
460	CC	Claude	34	/{SC} She actually went and changed her own ticket./It's something unheard
464	CC	Claude	35	began to feel my power in it./The life changed me, as it is changing you:/It begins as a
475	CC	Lucasta	13	it./{L} I think I'm changing./I've changed quite a lot in the last two hours./{C}
503	CC	Lucasta	30	Lucasta whom Colby knew./We've changed since then: as you said, we're always
527	ES	Monica	9	so. But by that time/You may have changed your mind. Such things have happened.
533	ES	Gomez	1	back with another name?/{G} You've changed your name too, since I knew you./
536	ES	Gomez	2	you know more than you do./You've changed your name twice — by easy stages,/
536	ES	Gomez	5	a different person:/But where *I* changed my name, there was no social ladder./It
543	ES	Ld Clav	11	so you knew him?/{LC} Yes. He'd changed his name./{M} Then I suppose he
550	ES	Ld Clav	8	you didn't recognise me./{LC} You've changed your name, no doubt. And I've
550	ES	Ld Clav	8	your name, no doubt. And I've changed mine./Your name now and here .../
562	ES	Carghil	29	at all,/But Michael — your father has changed a good deal/Since I knew him ever so

CHANGELING (1)

| 485 | CC | Lady E | 3 | I was a foundling — or do I mean 'changeling'?/{C} I don't know which you mean./ |

CHANGES (6)

148	Rock 1	60	/The world turns and the world changes,/But one thing does not change./In all
293	FR	Amy	8	Wishwood going/And to make no changes before your return./Now it's for you to
305	FR	Mary	38	the more manifest./{M} Yes, nothing changes here,/And we just go on ... drying up, I
321	FR	Warburt	4	are differences:/But, allowing for the changes in fashion/And your being
475	CC	Colby	9	up with them; so that as the other changes/You can understand the change as
549	ES	Carghil	36	you./{MC} Time has wrought sad changes in me, Richard./I was very lovely once.

CHANGING (16)

21	Portrait	109	to friends.'/And I must borrow every changing shape/To find expression ... dance,
107	Animula	2	the simple soul'/To a flat world of changing lights and noise,/To light, dark, dry or
173	FQ: BurntN	82	future/Woven in the weakness of the changing body,/Protects mankind from heaven
201	Def Island	16	in defeat,/unalterable in triumph, changing nothing/of their ancestors' ways but
305	FR	Harry	36	have expected./It only makes the changing of people/All the more manifest./{M}
395	CP	Edward	15	to assume that you've done all the changing —Though I haven't yet found it a
452	CC	Lucasta	36	a name like Angel./I'm thinking of changing it. But, Colby,/Do you know that I'm
462	CC	Claude	28	don't find it uncongenial?/I'm not changing the subject: I'm coming back to it.
464	CC	Claude	35	in it./The life changed me, as it is changing you:/It begins as a kind of
475	CC	Lucasta	12	have predicted it./{L} I think I'm changing./I've changed quite a lot in the last
475	CC	Colby	14	last two hours./{C} And I think I'm changing too. But perhaps what we call change
479	CC	Kaghan	39	is, Lucasta,/I'd never have thought of changing my condition./{L} You're always free
503	CC	Lucasta	30	since then: as you said, we're always changing./When I come back, we'll be brother
516	CC	Claude	23	way in which you felt that you were changing?/That conversation would have
526	ES	Charles	13	very far away. Yet very near. You are changing me/And I am changing you./{M}
526	ES	Charles	14	near. You are changing me/And I am changing you./{M} Already/How much of me is

CHANNEL (1)
458 CC   Lady E   24   we took the night train, and did the Channel crossing./But who is this young man?
CHANNING-CHEETAH'S (1)
31 Apollinax   6   palace of Mrs. Phlaccus, at Professor Channing-Cheetah's/He laughed like an
CHANT (1)
150 Rock 1 m   109   *death/Unmentioned in 'The Times'./Chant of* WORKMEN *again./The river flows,*
CHANTANT (1)
67 WL: Fire S   202   in soda water/Et O ces voix d'enfants, chantant dans la coupole!/Twit twit twit/Jug jug
CHANTING (1)
149 Rock 1 m   79   *the voices of* WORKMEN *are heard chanting./In the vacant places/We will build with*
CHAP (1)
541 ES   Gomez   13   Do you need money?/{G} My dear chap, you are obtuse!/I said: 'Your secret is safe
CHAPEL (4)
73 WL: Thund   387   /Over the tumbled graves, about the chapel/There is the empty chapel, only the
73 WL: Thund   388   about the chapel/There is the empty chapel, only the wind's home./It has no
140 Usk   11   light meets the green air/The hermit's chapel, the pilgrim's prayer./Rannoch, by
197 FQ: Little   238   On a winter's afternoon, in a secluded chapel/History is now and England./With the
CHAPITAUX (1)
48 Lune Miel   10   basilique connue des amateurs/De chapiteaux d'acanthe que tournoie le vent./Ils
CHAPLAINS (1)
285 FR   Violet   20   the military widows and the English chaplains,/To the chilly deck-chair and the
CHAPTER (1)
260 MC Thomas   2   *The/fourteenth verse of the second chapter of the Gospel according to Saint Luke.* In
CHARACTER (7)
228 Gus   28   hearts,/Whether I took the lead, or in character parts./I have sat by the bedside of
234 Ad-dress   4   no interpreter/To understand their character./You now have learned enough to see/
447 CC   Claude   18   she, of all people,/Is a better judge of character than I am./{E} Oh, I wouldn't say
480 CC   Kaghan   19   Lucasta,/Colby is a good judge of character./{L} You'd need to be a better judge
480 CC   Lucasta   20 {L} You'd need to be a better judge of character/Yourself, before you said that of
535 ES   Gomez   23   take it, thank you./{G} A reformed character!/{LC} I should like to know why you
553 ES   Ld Clav   4   say,/About your understanding of my character./{MC} I've followed your progress
CHARACTERISTIC (1)
428 CP   Alex   17   /{A} It is unreasonable,/But characteristic. And that's not the worst of it./
CHARACTERS (4)
238 MC m   1   /MURDER IN THE CATHEDRAL/Characters/PART I/A CHORUS OF WOMEN
326 FR   Harry   14   — the usual family inquest/On the characters of all the junior members?/Or
444 CC m   1   /THE CONFIDENTIAL CLERK/Characters/SIR CLAUDE MULHAMMER/
523 ES m   1   *meaning/For you and me only./*Characters/MONICA CLAVERTON-FERRY/
CHARGE (6)
232 Skimble   17   by and large it is Skimble who's in charge/Of the Sleeping Car Express./From the
264 MC Priest1   5   voice:/Lord, lay not this sin to their charge./Princes moreover did sit. { }/[Introit of
293 FR   Violet   3   she is doing./It really needs a man in charge of things at Wishwood./{A} You see
453 CC   Eggers   38   money, Eggy?/{E} I'm no longer in charge/And that duty has *not* devolved on Mr.
505 CC   Eggers   40   it to happen./{E} — Who was taken charge of by the father./That is to say, placed
511 CC   Lady E   37   engagement./Lucasta, I shall take charge of your wedding./{L} We'd meant to be
CHARGES (1)
267 MC Thomas   23   Should be said in public. If you make charges,/Then in public I will refute them./{K1}
CHARGING (1)
103 Journ Magi   15   unfriendly/And the villages dirty and charging high prices:/A hard time we had of it./
CHARITABLE (1)
279 MC Knight4   39   while of/Unsound Mind. It is the only charitable verdict you can give, upon/one who
CHARITY (3)
267 MC Knight2   37   /{K2} Yet the King, out of his charity,/And urged by your friends, offered
268 MC Thomas   39   /Seven years a mendicant on foreign charity/I lingered abroad: seven years is no
281 MC Priest1   1   is hidden from us,/Pray for us of your charity./{P2} Now in the sight of God/
CHARLES (56)
284 FR m   3   GERALD PIPER, *and* THE HON. CHARLES PIPER, *brothers of her deceased*
285 FR 4m   1   VIOLET, AGATHA, GERALD, CHARLES, MARY/[DENMAN *enters to draw*
286 FR m   29   DENMAN *with sherry and whisky.* CHARLES *takes sherry and* GERALD
287 FR   Gerald   3   shots — better than you were,/Charles, as I remember. Besides, you've got to
287 FR   Violet   12   you're very tactless,/And I think that Charles might have been more considerate./{G}
290 FR m   36   (IVY, VIOLET, GERALD *and* CHARLES)./{Ch} Why do we feel embarrassed,
292 FR   Harry   14   Aunt Violet, Uncle Gerald, Uncle Charles. Agatha./{A} We are very glad to have
296 FR   Amy   30   tomorrow./{A} Most certainly not, Charles, you are not the right person./I prefer to
297 FR   Ivy   13   on the boat. He might be of use./{I} Charles! you don't really suppose/That he might

297 FR	Violet	30	him, please. {}/[Exit DENMAN]/{V} Charles, if you are determined upon this
298 FR	Agatha	11	quite irrelevant;/We had better leave Charles to talk to Downing/And pursue his own
301 FR	Violet	10	more. {}/[*Exit* DOWNING]/{V} Well, Charles, I must say, with your investigations,/
301 FR	Ivy	21	brought together?/{I} I do not trust Charles with his confident vulgarity, acquired
313 FR	2m	1	MARY, IVY, VIOLET, GERALD, CHARLES/{V} Good evening, Mary: aren't
316 FR	Violet	6	{V} It is the obtuseness of Gerald and Charles and that doctor, that gets on my nerves.
323 FR	m	7	IVY, AGATHA, GERALD *and* CHARLES.]/{A} Winchell! what are you here
328 FR	m	7	ought to be prohibited. {}/[*Re-enter* CHARLES, *with a newspaper*]/{C} Yes, there is
328 FR	Charles	12	*Smash*/The Hon. Arthur Gerald Charles Piper, younger brother of Lord/
344 FR	m	2	[*Meanwhile* VIOLET, GERALD *and* CHARLES *have entered*]/{C} Where is Harry
346 FR	Downing	6	Oh, excuse me, Miss, excuse me, Mr. Charles:/His Lordship sent me back because he
523 ES	m	3	/MONICA CLAVERTON-FERRY/CHARLES HEMINGTON/LAMBERT/
524 ES	m	5	to tea. {}/[*Enter* MONICA *and* CHARLES *carrying parcels*]/{M} But you *must*
525 ES	Monica	28	wasted in wrangling. But seriously, Charles,/Father's sure to be buried in the library
526 ES	Monica	8	mistaken?/{M} How did this come, Charles? It crept so softly/On silent feet, and
526 ES	Monica	29	Yes, Miss Monica./{M} I'm very glad, Charles,/That you *can* stay to tea. {}/[*Exit*
527 ES	Monica	7	that you want to marry me?/{M} Yes, Charles. I'm sure that I want to marry you/
528 ES	Monica	18	preserve./{M} There *is* a private self, Charles./I'm sure of that./{C} You've given two
528 ES	Monica	36	I'm afraid ... not a very long time, Charles./It's almost certain that the winter in
529 ES	Monica	16	and wistfulness .../And tenderness, Charles! are mixed with envy:/I do believe that
529 ES	Monica	18	/So you must come often. And Oh, Charles dear — {}/[*Enter* LORD
529 ES	Ld Clav	20	been doing?/{LC} Good afternoon, Charles. You might have guessed, Monica,/
530 ES	Ld Clav	10	it./They talk of rest, these doctors, Charles; they tell me to be cautious,/To take life
532 ES	Monica	22	you have to take a trunk call./Come, Charles. Will you bring my coat?/{C} I'll say
532 ES	Ld Clav	27	Gomez, my Lord./{LC} Goodbye, Charles. And please remember/That we both
532 ES	m	30	we, Monica?/{M} Yes, Father. {}/[*To* CHARLES]/{M} We *both* want to see you. {}/
532 ES	m	30	to see you. {}/[*Exeunt* MONICA *and* CHARLES]/[LAMBERT *shows in* GOMEZ]/
543 ES	Ld Clav	16	/{LC} Yes, I'll go and rest now. I wish Charles was dining with us./I wish we were
567 ES	3m	1	*day.* MONICA *seated*/*alone. Enter* CHARLES./{C} Well, Monica, here I am. I
567 ES	Monica	2	I hope you got my message./{M} Oh Charles, Charles, Charles, I'm so glad you've
567 ES	Monica	2	you got my message./{M} Oh Charles, Charles, Charles, I'm so glad you've come!/I've
567 ES	Monica	2	message./{M} Oh Charles, Charles, Charles, I'm so glad you've come!/I've been so
567 ES	Monica	9	of it, for the caress that is in it!/Oh Charles, how I've wanted you! And now I *need*
567 ES	Monica	23	him to confide in me?/{M} Oh Charles! How could anyone blackmail Father?/
568 ES	Ld Clav	11	/Has there been nothing in your life, Charles Hemington,/Which you wish to forget?
569 ES	Monica	15	nothing I'm afraid of learning about Charles,/There's nothing I'm afraid of learning
569 ES	Ld Clav	34	them?/{LC} Because they are not real, Charles. They are merely ghosts:/Spectres from
573 ES	Monica	28	fiancé. Do introduce him./{M} Mr. Charles Hemington. Mrs. Carghill./{C} How do
574 ES	Carghil	4	Mr. Hemington:/I'm going to call you Charles!/{C} As you please, Mrs. Carghill,/{LC}
580 ES	Monica	5	even by air mail./{M} Take the card, Charles. If I write to you, Michael,/Will you
581 ES	Ld Clav	2	does come back,/I know that you and Charles will do what you can/To make him feel
581 ES	Monica	33	I love you the more/Because I love Charles./{LC} Yes, my dear./Your love is for
581 ES	Ld Clav	35	my dear./Your love is for the real Charles, not a make-believe,/As was your love
582 ES	Ld Clav	14	first visit to us at Badgley Court,/Charles, and not at all what you were expecting.
582 ES	Ld Clav	18	leave Monica to you. Look after her, Charles,/Now and always. I shall take a stroll./
582 ES	Monica	32	to leave us alone together./And yet, Charles, though we've been alone to-day/Only a
583 ES	Monica	19	/And I am happy. Isn't it strange, Charles,/To be happy at this moment?/{C} It is

CHARM (4)

53	Whispers	30	Entities/Circumambulate her charm;/But our lot crawls between dry ribs/To
350 FR	Agatha	16	and round the circle/Completing the charm/So the knot be unknotted/The crossed be
562 ES	Carghil	35	of moving! It's marvellous./And the charm! He's inherited all of your charm,
562 ES	Carghil	35	the charm! He's inherited all of your charm, Richard./There's no denying it. But

CHARMING (4)

31	Apollinax	18	talk devoured the afternoon./'He is a charming man' — 'But after all what did he
548 ES	Carghil	22	so that *is* your daughter — that very charming girl?/And obviously devoted to her
555 ES	Piggott	2	*Me,*/Everybody was singing it once. A charming person,/I dare say, but not quite your
573 ES	Carghil	30	/{C} How do you do./{MC} What a charming name!/{C} I'm glad my name meets

CHART (2)

181 FQ:	ECoker	153	art/Resolving the enigma of the fever chart./Our only health is the disease/If we obey
592	Grad 1	4	sail we/Across the harbor bar — no chart to show/No light to warn of rocks which

CHASE (1)

214	RTTugger	6	you set him on a rat then he'd rather chase a mouse./Yes the Rum Tum Tugger is a

CHASING (1)

574 ES	Michael	32	my point of view. What's the use of chasing/Half round the world, for the same sort

CHATOUILLAIS (1)
51 Restaurant   13   au chiffre de trente-huit./'Je la chatouillais, pour la faire rire./J'éprouvais un
CHATTER (4)
21 Portrait   112   a dancing bear,/Cry like a parrot, chatter like an ape./Let us take the air, in a
69 WL: Fire S   262   of a mandoline/And a clatter and a chatter from within/Where fishmen lounge at
245 MC Priest2 24   not see you coming,/Engrossed by the chatter of these foolish women./Forgive us, my
303 FR   Mary   27   John,/Or having to listen to Arthur's chatter/When he thinks he is behaving like a
CHATTERING (1)
175 FQ: BurntN   157   voices/Scolding, mocking, or merely chattering,/Always assail them. The Word in the
CHAUFFEUR (1)
284 FR   m   7 *eldest son*/DOWNING, *his servant and chauffeur*/DR. WARBURTON/SERGEANT
CHAUFFEUR'S (1)
346 FR   m   5 {}/[*Enter* DOWNING, *hurriedly, in chauffeur's costume*]/{Do} Oh, excuse me, Miss,
CHE (2)
34 Figlia   t   — 'Are we then so serious?'/La Figlia Che Piange/Stand on the highest pavement of
75 WL: Thund   427   falling down/*Poi s'ascose nel foco che gli affina/Quando fiam uti chelidon* — O
CHEAP (2)
13 Prufrock   6 retreats/Of restless nights in one-night cheap hotels/And sawdust restaurants with
445 CC Eggers   19 a restaurant;/An excellent lunch, and cheap, for nowadays./But where's Mr.
CHEAPER (1)
433 CP   Julia   9 not reconstruct *me*? It's very much cheaper./Oh, dear, I can see you're determined
CHEAPSIDE (3)
266 MC Knights   19   the backstairs brat who was born in Cheapside;/This is the creature that crawled
269 MC Thomas   11 I or the King./It is not I, Becket from Cheapside,/It is not against me, Becket, that
274 MC Knights   24 join in the feast./Where is Becket the Cheapside brat?/Where is Becket the faithless
CHEAT (5)
256 MC Tempts   9 back of my hand?/{4T} Man's life is a cheat and a disappointment;/All things are
260 MC Thomas   25 promise was a disappointment and a cheat?/Reflect now, how Our Lord Himself
309 FR   Mary   20   /Even if, as you say, Wishwood is a cheat,/Your family a delusion — then it's *all* a
327 FR   Harry   13   Were they simply inside/I could cheat them perhaps with the aid of Dr.
407 CP   Reilly 16 not trouble myself with the common cheat,/Or with the insuperably, innocently dull:/
CHEATED (2)
266 MC Knights   23   a louse on your shirt,/The man who cheated, swindled, lied; broke his oath and
491 CC Colby   34 those ghosts, one indignant/At being cheated of his — or her — parenthood,/The
CHEATS (1)
226 Macavity   21 outwardly respectable. (They say he cheats at cards.)/And his footprints are not
CHECKED (1)
32 Hysteria   6 hurriedly spreading a pink and white checked cloth over the rusty/green iron table,
CHEEK (1)
577 ES Michael 20 I'll say that Hemington has plenty of cheek./Señor Gomez and I have talked things
CHEER (4)
124 SA Sweeney   38   sometimes/I'd give him a drink and cheer him up./{Do} Cheer him up?/{Du} Cheer
124 SA Doris   39   him a drink and cheer him up./{Do} Cheer him up?/{Du} Cheer him up?/{S} Well
124 SA Dusty   40   him up./{Do} Cheer him up?/{Du} Cheer him up?/{S} Well here again that don't
440 CP Lavinia   25   /You know, when you're trying to cheer me up./To say I always look my best can
CHEERFUL (3)
216 Jellicles   9   they caterwaul./Jellicle Cats have cheerful faces,/Jellicle Cats have bright black
289 FR Gerald   5 us all the hump./I must say, this isn't cheerful for Amy's birthday/Or for Harry's
459 CC Claude   24 I thought a primrose yellow would be cheerful./{LE} Just what I expected. A primrose
CHEERFUL-LIKE (1)
347 FRDowning   9 And not with me, so I could see them cheerful-like,/In a manner of speaking. There's
CHEERING (2)
245 MC Priest2 5   /The crowds in the streets will be cheering and cheering,/You go on croaking like
245 MC Priest2 5   in the streets will be cheering and cheering,/You go on croaking like frogs in the
CHEERS (1)
211 Old Gumbie   37 Gumbie Cats let us now give three cheers —/On whom well-ordered households
CHEESE (5)
210 Old Gumbie   24 And a *beautiful* fry of lean bacon and cheese./I have a Gumbie Cat in mind, her name
588 Fable   54 perhaps held several kegs/Of ale, and cheese which they kept under cover./Last, a
375 CP Edward   17   .../Oh, no, Alex, don't bring me any cheese;/I've got some cheese ... No, not
375 CP Edward   18   bring me any cheese;/I've got some cheese ... No, not Norwegian;/But I don't really
375 CP Edward   19   Norwegian;/But I don't really want cheese ... Slipper what? .../Oh, from Jugoslavia
CHEETAH (1)
31 Apollinax   21   Phlaccus, and Professor and Mrs. Cheetah/I remember a slice of lemon, and a

CHELIDON (1)
75 WL: Thund 428   *nel foco che gli affina*/*Quando fiam uti chelidon* — O swallow swallow/*Le Prince*
CHELTENHAM (1)
326 FR   Violet   2   to?/{V} He started out to take me to Cheltenham;/But I stopped him somewhere in
CHEMIST (1)
66 WL: Chess 161   nearly died of young George.)/The chemist said it would be all right, but I've never
CHEQUE-BOOK (1)
411 CP   m 35   capacity. {}/[EDWARD *takes out his cheque-book*. REILLY *raises his hand*]/{R} My
CHEQUES (1)
534 ES Gomez 20   conviction./No, forgery, or washing cheques, or anything of that nature,/Is certain
CHER (1)
48 Lune Miel   13   trouve la Cène, et un restaurant pas cher./Lui pense aux pourboires, et rédige son
CHERISH (4)
209 NamingCats 16   /Or spread out his whiskers, or cherish his pride?/Of names of this kind, I can
242 MC   Mess   6   Lord Archbishop/Is not the man to cherish any illusions,/Or yet to diminish the
418 CP   Celia 12   /Put up with anything, if I might cherish it./In fact, I think it would really be
551 ES Carghil 18   /These memories are painful — but I cherish them./{LC} If you had really been
CHERISHED (1)
464 CC Claude 40   to him. He knew, I am sure,/That I cherished for a long time a secret reproach:/But
CHESS (3)
64 WL: Chess   t   semblable, — mon frère!'/A Game of Chess/The Chair she sat in, like a burnished
65 WL: Chess 137   at four./And we shall play a game of chess,/Pressing lidless eyes and waiting for a
258 MC Thomas 14   tree,/The tiltyard skill, the strategy of chess,/Love in the garden, singing to the
CHEST (1)
295 FR Charles 12   my own past life that presses on my chest/When I wake, as I do now, early before
CHESTNUT (1)
37 Gerontion   21   tiger/In depraved May, dogwood and chestnut, flowering judas,/To be eaten, to be
CHESTNUTS (1)
24 Rhapsody   65   /And dust in crevices,/Smells of chestnuts in the streets,/And female smells in
CHESTS (1)
218 Mung Rump 11   were pulled out from the bedroom chests,/And you couldn't find one of your
CHEZ (1)
48 Lune Miel   3   à Ravenne,/A l'aise entre deux draps, chez deux centaines de punaises;/La sueur
CHICAGO (1)
40 Burb Blei   16   elbows, with the palms turned out,/Chicago Semite Viennese./A lustreless
CHICKEN (1)
187 FQ: DrySal 118   its cargo of dead negroes, cows and chicken coops,/The bitter apple and the bite in
CHIEF (1)
151 Rock 2   3   prophets, Christ Jesus Himself the chief cornerstone./But you, have you built well,
CHIEFLY (2)
129 Cor2 State 19   is appointed/For Public Works, chiefly the question of rebuilding the
495 CC Lady E 11   affairs;/And that you needed me chiefly as a hostess./It's a great mistake, I do
CHIEN (1)
51 Restaurant   17   dur./Il est venu, nous peloter, un gros chien;/Moi j'avais peur, je l'ai quittée à
CHIENNE (1)
48 Lune Miel   4   sueur aestivale, et une forte odeur de chienne./Ils restent sur le dos écartant les
CHIFFRE (1)
51 Restaurant   12   /Les taches de son gilet montent au chiffre de trente-huit./'Je la chatouillais, pour la
CHILD (75)
24 Rhapsody   38   of rancid butter.'/So the hand of the child, automatic,/Slipped out and pocketed a
111 Xmas Trees   5   childish — which is not that of the child/For whom the candle is a star, and the
111 Xmas Trees   9   only a decoration, but an angel./The child wonders at the Christmas Tree:/Let him
160 Rock 7   14   to the withered ancient look of a child that has died of starvation./Prayer wheels,
229 Gus   44   stage on a telegraph wire,/To rescue a child when a house was on fire./And he says:
257 MC Chorus   12   /The old without fire in winter,/The child without milk in summer,/Our labour taken
306 FR   Harry 23   me,/Were you ever happy here, as a child at Wishwood?/{M} Happy? not really,
307 FR   Mary   20   by the river./{M} But when I was a child I took everything for granted,/Including
319 FR   Harry 27   /That bring death into the heart of a child./*That* was the day he died. Of course./I
326 FR   Harry 12   she must have looked when she was a child./You've been holding a meeting — the
333 FR Agatha 13   in any case I should have no other child./{H} And have me. That is the way things
336 FR Agatha 24   /{Ag} A curse comes to being/As a child is formed./In both, the incredible/Becomes
336 FR Agatha 29   what is intended./A curse is like a child, formed/In a moment of unconsciousness/
336 FR Agatha 35   determined moon./A curse is like a child, formed/To grow to maturity:/Accident is
337 FR Agatha   4   /In a cloud of unknowing./O my child, my curse,/You shall be fulfilled:/The knot
396 CP Lavinia 31   me:/Perhaps only when you were a child./{E} I don't want you to make yourself

402 CP   Edward   37   indeed./{E} I remember, in my childhood .../{R} I always begin from the
402 CP   Reilly   40   necessary./You see, your memories of childhood —/I mean, in your present state of
467 CC   Colby   11   father who was missing in the years of childhood./Those years have gone forever. The
476 CC   Lucasta   34   Claude had ever liked her. Oh, that childhood —/Always living in seedy lodgings/
484 CC   Lady E   24   things and eating them./And yet our childhood must have been similar./These are
578 ES   Ld Clav   11   divergent ways. When I think of your childhood,/When I think of the happy little boy
CHILDISH (1)
111 Xmas Trees   5   being open till midnight),/And the childish — which is not that of the child/For
CHILDLESS (3)
332 FR   Agatha   18   house together,/For three years childless, learning the meaning/Of loneliness.
507 CC   Guzzard   9   in a child./My husband and I were childless ... at the time,/And very poor. It
508 CC   Guzzard   26   /{MG} We had neighbours/Who were childless, and eager to adopt a child./They had
CHILDREN (38)
61 WL: Burial   13   echt deutsch./And when we were children, staying at the arch-duke's,/My
66 WL: Chess   164   you get married for if you don't want children?/HURRY UP PLEASE ITS TIME/
96 Ash-Wed 5   25   Will the veiled sister pray/For children at the gate/Who will not go away and
105 Song Sime   13   house, where shall live my children's children/When the time of sorrow is come?/
111 Xmas Trees   24   to God and disrespectful to the children/(And here I remember also with
167 Rock 10   37   and ecstasy is too much pain./We are children quickly tired: children who are up in
167 Rock 10   37   pain./We are children quickly tired: children who are up in the night and fall asleep
172 FQ: BurntN   42   the bird, for the leaves were full of children,/Hidden excitedly, containing laughter.
176 FQ: BurntN   175   /There rises the hidden laughter/Of children in the foliage/Quick now, here, now,
197 FQ: Little   250   voice of the hidden waterfall/And the children in the apple-tree/Not known, because
204 de la Mare   1   of action./To Walter de la Mare/The children who explored the brook and found/A
603 Spleen   8   digression./Evening, lights, and tea!/Children and cats in the alley;/Dejection unable
260 MC Thomas   4   and of the Holy Ghost. Amen./Dear children of God, my sermon this Christmas
261 MC Thomas   1   /at the table, his wife singing to the children? Those men His disciples/knew no such
261 MC Thomas   37   /I have spoken to you to-day, dear children of God, of the martyrs of/the past,
262 MC Thomas   1   which He brought; and because,/dear children, I do not think I shall ever preach to
263 MC Chorus   23   high,/And voices trill at windows, and children tumble in front of the door,/What
296 FR   Gerald   37   after all the boys/When they were children. I'll have a word with him./He can talk
307 FR   Harry   17   /Had been erected, 'to please the children'./It's absurd that one's only memory of
317 FR   Harry   24   back to mother./When we were children, before we went to school,/The rule of
318 FR   Harry   16   make a deeper impression upon children/Than what they are told./{W} Stop,
326 FR   Harry   11   sleep in the middle of calamity/Like children, or like hardened campaigners. She
345 FR   Amy   22   /I always wanted too much for my children/More than life can give. And now I am
360 CP   Reilly   21   long married?/{E} Five years./{UG} Children?/{E} No./{UG} Then look at the
417 CP   Reilly   36   not understand each other,/Breeding children whom they do not understand/And
448 CC   Eggers   35   to both of you/That you've never had children./{SC} No worse, Eggerson,/Than for
486 CC   Lady E   22   /And Mr. Guzzard — have any children?/{C} They had no children of their
486 CC   Colby   23   have any children?/{C} They had no children of their own./That is to say, they had
489 CC   Claude   10   might have suspected any number of children!/That seems grotesque now. But it
489 CC   Claude   14   your own,/And I thought, I'll wait for children of *our* own,/And tell her then. And
491 CC   Claude   39   will want parents, for the sake of your children./{C} I don't feel, tonight, that I ever
498 CC   Eggers   13   /Of ... looking after other people's children?/In a manner of speaking, it's perfectly
506 CC   Eggers   16   man./I believe you have had no children of your own;/But I'm sure you can
519 CC   Lady E   15   we've got to try to understand our children./{K} And we should like to understand
534 ES   Gomez   24   /And by the way, I've several children,/All grown up, doing well for
536 ES   Gomez   14   the parish priest told her./I made my children learn English — it's useful;/I always
562 ES   Carghil   27   /Richard! It's astonishing about your children:/Monica hardly resembles you at all,/
581 ES   Ld Clav   16   did I always want to dominate my children?/Why did I mark out a narrow path for
CHILDREN'S (5)
105 Song Sime   13   my house, where shall live my children's children/When the time of sorrow is
138 New Hamp   1   shut)./Landscapes/New Hampshire/Children's voices in the orchard/Between the
256 MC Tempts   13   cat,/The prizes given at the children's party,/The prize awarded for the
314 FR   Violet   16   same with your minor ailments/And children's epidemics: you would never stay in
337 FR   Agatha   10   to stay for./Think of it as like a children's treasure hunt:/Here you have found a
CHILL (7)
116 SP   Dusty   24   /But Doris came home with a terrible chill/No, just a chill/Oh I *think* it's only a chill/
116 SP   Dusty   25   home with a terrible chill/No, just a chill/Oh I *think* it's only a chill/Yes indeed I
116 SP   Dusty   26   /No, just a chill/Oh I *think* it's only a chill/Yes indeed I hope so too —/Well I *hope*
174 FQ: BurntN   135   tendril and spray/Clutch and cling?/Chill/Fingers of yew be curled/Down on us?
181 FQ: ECoker   164   us, but prevents us everywhere./The chill ascends from feet to knees,/The fever sings
206 To my Wife   8   /No peevish winter wind shall chill/No sullen tropic sun shall wither/The roses
245 MC Priest2   32   laid in all your rooms/To take the chill off our English December,/Your Lordship

CHILLED (2)

| 38 Gerontion | 62 | /Protract the profit of their chilled delirium,/Excite the membrane, when the |
| 377 CP   Julia | 23 | to be sure,/And of course it isn't chilled. But it's so refreshing;/And I thought, we |

CHILLS (1)

| 105 Song Sime | 7 | in corners/Wait for the wind that chills towards the dead land./Grant us thy |

CHILLY (6)

107 Animula	3	noise,/To light, dark, dry or damp, chilly or warm;/Moving between the legs of
285 FR Violet	21	and the English chaplains,/To the chilly deck-chair and the strong cold tea —/The
340 FR Amy	20	What of the humiliation,/Of the chilly pretences in the silent bedroom,/Forcing
429 CP Julia	36	walked over my grave:/I'm feeling so chilly. Give me some gin./Not a cocktail. I'm
582 ES Monica	22	to stop out late/At this season. It's chilly at dusk./{LC} Yes, it's chilly at dusk. But
582 ES Ld Clav	23	It's chilly at dusk./{LC} Yes, it's chilly at dusk. But I'll be warm enough./I shall

CHIMERA (1)

| 175 FQ: BurntN | 161 | /The loud lament of the disconsolate chimera./The detail of the pattern is movement,/ |

CHIMES (1)

| 587 Fable | 22 | /To furnish all the milk — upset the chimes,/And once he sat the prior on the |

CHIMNEY (4)

154 Rock 3	24	stupor?/There shall be left the broken chimney,/The peeled hull, a pile of rusty iron,/
589 Fable	80	/The pair had vanisht swiftly up the chimney./Naturally every one searcht
296 FR Harry	9	you once explained the sobbing in the chimney/The evil in the dark closet, which they
316 FR Chorus	3	there./And the bird sits on the broken chimney. I am afraid./{I} This is a most

CHIMNEY-POTS (1)

| 22 Preludes | 10 | showers beat/On broken blinds and chimney-pots,/And at the corner of the street/A |

CHIMNEYS (2)

| 13 Prufrock | 19 | upon its back the soot that falls from chimneys,/Slipped by the terrace, made a |
| 257 MC   Chorus | 24 | over the sky;/Under doors and down chimneys, flowing in at the ear and the mouth |

CHIN (2)

| 14 Prufrock | 42 | my collar mounting firmly to the chin,/My necktie rich and modest, but asserted |
| 234 Ad-dress | 31 | in —/Just chuck him underneath the chin/Or slap his back or shake his paw,/And he |

CHINA (2)

| 464 CC   Claude | 6 | than a potter./Most people think of china or porcelain/As merely for use, or for |
| 467 CC   Claude | 35 | go now, and sit for a while with my china./{C} Excuse me, but I must remind you:/ |

CHINESE (3)

175 FQ: BurntN	145	or music reach/The stillness, as a Chinese jar still/Moves perpetually in its
222 Pekes Pols	26	/Is no British Dog, but a Heathen Chinese./And so all the Pekes, when they heard
223 Pekes Pols	31	/In their huffery-snuffery Heathen Chinese./But a terrible din is what Pollicles like,

CHINKS (1)

| 213 Growltiger | 42 | With a frightful burst of fireworks the Chinks they swarmed aboard./Abandoning |

CHIROMANCY (1)

| 348 FR   Chorus | 20 | forms of sorcery,/Divination and chiromancy,/Specifics against insomnia,/ |

CHIRP (2)

| 129 Cor2 State | 49 | small creatures,/The small creatures chirp thinly through the dust, through the night. |
| 339 FR   Harry | 15 | will not let me fall./Let the cricket chirp. John shall be the master./All I have is his. |

CHIRPING (2)

| 91 Ash-Wed 2 | 7 | bones (which were already dry) said chirping:/Because of the goodness of this Lady/ |
| 91 Ash-Wed 2 | 23 | wind will listen. And the bones sang chirping/With the burden of the grasshopper, |

CHISWICK (1)

| 326 FR   Violet | 3 | /But I stopped him somewhere in Chiswick, I think./Anyway, the district was |

CHOICE (8)

154 Rock 3	11	distrust./I have given you power of choice, and you only alternate/Between futile
196 FQ: Little	207	only hope, or else despair/Lies in the choice of pyre or pyre —/To be redeemed from
397 CP Edward	18	I go to a doctor, I shall make my own choice;/Not take one whom you choose. How
417 CP Reilly	21	form of treatment must be your own choice:/I cannot choose for you. If that is what
418 CP Reilly	35	It is also necessary/To make a choice between them./{C} Then I choose the
422 CP Alex	9	destiny./{A} And *she* has made the choice?/{R} She will be fetched this evening. {}/
439 CP Julia	10	*I* said something:/Everyone makes a choice, of one kind or another,/And then must
439 CP Julia	34	consequence of the Chamberlaynes' choice/Is a cocktail party. They must be ready

CHOIR (4)

193 FQ: Little	78	we forgot,/Of sanctuary and choir./This is the death of water and fire./In the
272 MC	m 11	/[*while a* Dies Iræ *is sung in Latin by a choir in the distance*]./{C} Numb the hand and
281 MC	m 7	[*while a* Te Deum *is sung in Latin by a choir in the distance*]./{C} We praise Thee, O
451 CC Eggers	37	/I've always sung in our voluntary choir/And at the carol service. But I wish I was

CHOOSE (16)

| 66 WL: Chess | 154 | on with it, I said./Others can pick and choose if you can't./But if Albert makes off, it |
| 184 FQ: DrySal | 9 | destroyer, reminder/Of what men choose to forget. Unhonoured, unpropitiated/ |

290 FR	Amy	5	undesirable society/Which she could choose herself. She never wanted/Harry's
324 FR	Harry	38	Only, that's not the language/That I choose to be talking. I will not talk yours./{A}
397 CP	Edward	19	own choice;/Not take one whom you choose. How do I know/That you wouldn't see
417 CP	Reilly	22	must be your own choice:/I cannot choose for you. If that is what you wish,/I can
418 CP	Reilly	31	is my duty?/{R} Whichever way you choose will prescribe its own duty./{C} Which
418 CP	Celia	36	a choice between them./{C} Then I choose the second./{R} It is a terrifying journey.
419 CP	Reilly	28	{C} What becomes of them?/{R} They choose, Miss Coplestone. Nothing is forced on
421 CP	Julia	5	stripped naked to their souls/And can choose, whether to put on proper costumes/Or
437 CP	Reilly	25	not know;/Because it was for her to choose the way of life/To lead to death, and,
437 CP	Reilly	27	and, without knowing the end/Yet choose the form of death. We know the death
478 CC	Lucasta	8	stronger than that,/And I will, if I choose. Oh, I'm sorry:/I suppose it's my mother
548 ES	Carghil	18	to find it so quickly./What made you choose it? {}/[*throwing down newspaper*]./{LC}
556 ES	Ld Clav	18	would be the sort of place that you'd choose for a holiday./{Mi} Well, this isn't a
559 ES	Michael	22	took a different name — and I might choose to —/No one would know or care what

CHOOSES (2)

| 375 CP | Celia | 2 | be the one to be divorced?/And if she chooses to give *you* the grounds .../{E} I see. But |
| 577 ES | Ld Clav | 39 | well./Michael's a free agent. So if he chooses/To place himself in your power, Fred |

CHOOSING (1)

| 447 CC | Claude | 16 | she ought to have a hand in the choosing;/And besides, she is convinced that |

CHOP-HOUSES (1)

| 147 Rock 1 | | 22 | too many churches,/And too few chop-houses. There I was told:/Let the vicars |

CHOPIN (1)

| 18 Portrait | | 10 | hair and finger-tips./'So intimate, this Chopin, that I think his soul/Should be |

CHOPPING (1)

| 329 FR | Chorus | 9 | and the wail of little pain/The chopping of wood in autumn/And the singing in |

CHORUS (12)

125 SA		m 31	to me and nothing to you. {}/FULL CHORUS: WAUCHOPE, HORSFALL,
148 Rock 1		m 38	town/Only for important weddings./CHORUS LEADER:/Silence! and preserve
155 Rock 3		m 37	road/And a thousand lost golf balls'./CHORUS:/We build in vain unless the LORD
161 Rock 7		m 37	*women one half pint of bitter*/*Ale*..../CHORUS:/What does the world say, does the
161 Rock 7		m 40	/*In this land*/*No man has hired us*..../CHORUS:/Waste and void. Waste and void.
238 MC		m 3	/Characters/PART I/A CHORUS OF WOMEN OF CANTERBURY/
238 MC		m 14	ARCHBISHOP THOMAS BECKET/CHORUS OF WOMEN OF CANTERBURY/
256 MC		m 29	/The sailor lay course by the sun? {}/CHORUS, PRIESTS *and* TEMPTERS
272 MC		m 10	{}/[*They drag him off. While the* CHORUS *speak, the scene is changed to the*
275 MC		m 21	*the* KNIGHTS *kill him, we hear the* CHORUS./{C} Clear the air! clean the sky!
290 FR		m 36	passage/The paw under the door. {}/CHORUS (IVY, VIOLET, GERALD *and*
329 FR		m 27	international catastrophes. {}/[*Exeunt* CHORUS]/Scene II/HARRY, AGATHA/{H}

CHORUSES (1)

| 145 Rock | | t | he is mad./Tell me if I am not glad!/Choruses from 'The Rock'/The Eagle soars in |

CHOSE (14)

96 Ash-Wed 5		21	for/Those who walk in darkness, who chose thee and oppose thee,/Those who are torn
96 Ash-Wed 5		27	and cannot pray:/Pray for those who chose and oppose/O my people, what have I
394 CP	Edward	31	I wanted,/But it wasn't the life you chose for me./You wanted your husband to be
437 CP	Reilly	27	of death. We know the death she chose./I did not know that she would die in this
439 CP	Julia	11	must take the consequences. Celia chose/A way of which the consequence was
439 CP	Julia	13	the consequence was Kinkanja./Peter chose a way that leads him to Boltwell:/And
447 CC	Claude	35	is certain to come to believe/That she chose him herself. By the way, don't forget/To
479 CC	Colby	34	done up./{C} It was Lady Elizabeth chose the decorations./{K} Then I'm not sure I
490 CC	Colby	34	might have been my mother,/But you chose not to be. I don't blame you for that:/
509 CC	Guzzard	10	you see who it is?/{MG} My husband chose the name./We had been married in the
514 CC	Guzzard	15	in peace./I *was* your mother; but I chose to be your aunt./So you may have your
528 ES	Monica	29	live a little longer./That's why Selby chose the place. A *convalescent* home/With the
548 ES	Ld Clav	19	*down newspaper*]./{LC} My daughter chose it./She noticed that it seemed to offer the
549 ES	Carghil	29	/Mark my words' Effie said, 'if you chose to follow *that* man/He'd give you the slip:

CHOSEN (12)

253 MC	Tempt4	23	closed to you/Except the way already chosen./But what is pleasure, kingly rule,/Or
333 FR	Agatha	36	/Moving alone through flames of ice, chosen/To resolve the enchantment under which
338 FR	Harry	29	found, but to seek./I would not have chosen this way, had there been any other!/It is
358 CP	Julia	7	dine with me on Friday./I've already chosen the people you're to meet./{E} But you
362 CP	Reilly	29	to support you in the role you have chosen,/Then sometimes, when you come to the
408 CP	Edward	19	congratulate you. You could not have chosen/Anyone I was less likely to suspect./And
422 CP	Alex	7	order./{A} The Chamberlaynes have chosen?/{R} They accept their destiny./{A} And
437 CP	Edward	33	happy?/{E} Do you mean that having chosen this form of death/She did not suffer as
459 CC	Lady E	23	Eggerson./What colour have you chosen, between you?/{SC} I thought a primrose

495 CC   Claude   36   a second-rate organist./We have both chosen ... obedience to the facts./{LE} I believe
563 ES   Gomez   12   cure too./And when I heard you'd chosen to come to Badgley Court/I said to my
568 ES   Ld Clav   39   to identify myself with the part/I had chosen to play. And the longer we pretend/The

CHRIST (9)
37 Gerontion   20   In the juvescence of the year/Came Christ the tiger/In depraved May, dogwood and
151 Rock 2   3   foundation/Of apostles and prophets, Christ Jesus Himself the chief cornerstone./But
152 Rock 2   43   /Prays for the Church, the Body of Christ incarnate./And now you live dispersed on
261 MC Thomas   13   immediately the day of the Birth/of Christ? By no means. Just as we rejoice and
273 MC Thomas   17   the house of prayer, the church of Christ,/The sanctuary, turned into a fortress./
273 MC Priests   25   sanctuary, who kneel to the Body of Christ,/But like beasts. You would bar the door
274 MC Thomas   32   /A Christian, saved by the blood of Christ,/Ready to suffer with my blood./This is
281 MC Chorus   19   has given his blood for the blood of Christ,/There is holy ground, and the sanctity
282 MC Chorus   16   heads./Lord, have mercy upon us./Christ, have mercy upon us./Lord, have mercy

CHRIST'S (2)
261 MC Thomas   39   Elphege; because it is fitting, on Christ's birth/day, to remember what is that
269 MC Thomas   14   pronounces doom,/But the Law of Christ's Church, the judgement of Rome./{K1}

CHRISTIAN (14)
159 Rock 6   2   /And who have never known a Christian,/To believe these tales of Christian
159 Rock 6   3   a Christian,/To believe these tales of Christian persecution./It is hard for those who
260 MC Thomas   19   out by joy; so it is only in these our Christian/mysteries that we can rejoice and
261 MC Thomas   19   think of a martyr simply as a good Christian who/has been killed because he is a
261 MC Thomas   20   who/has been killed because he is a Christian: for that would be solely to/mourn.
261 MC Thomas   21   do not think of him simply as a good Christian who has been/elevated to the
261 MC Thomas   24   our rejoicing is as the world's is./A Christian martyrdom is never an accident, for
261 MC Thomas   25   not made by/accident. Still less is a Christian martyrdom the effect of a man's will
274 MC Thomas   32   traitor to the King. I am a priest,/A Christian, saved by the blood of Christ,/Ready
280 MC Priest3   21   /Where blackamoors make captive Christian men;/Go to the northern seas
428 CP   Alex   18   the worst of it./Some of the tribes are Christian converts,/And, naturally, take a
428 CP   Alex   29   their crops from the monkeys/The Christian natives prosper exceedingly:/And that
434 CP   Alex   7   —/Three sisters at this station, in a Christian village;/And half the natives were
508 CC   Eggers   37   /{E} And the child, I suppose he had a Christian name?/{MG} There was nothing to

CHRISTIANS (6)
158 Rock 5   7   abominations, the turpitudes of the Christians.' And these are not justified, nor the
429 CP   Alex   5   only be removed by slaughtering the Christians./They have even been persuading
429 CP   Alex   9   of eating monkeys/They have even been eating Christians./{J} Who have eaten monkeys./{A}
429 CP   Julia   14   /But one can't dine out on eating Christians —/Even among pagans!/{A} Not on
429 CP   Lavinia   31   the monkeys multiply./{L} And the Christians?/{A} Ah, the Christians! Now, I think
429 CP   Alex   32   /{L} And the Christians?/{A} Ah, the Christians! Now, I think I ought to tell you/

CHRISTMAS (18)
107 Animula   9   /In the fragrant brilliance of the Christmas tree,/Pleasure in the wind, the
111 Xmas Trees   t   fog/My daughter./The Cultivation of Christmas Trees/There are several attitudes
111 Xmas Trees   1   /There are several attitudes towards Christmas,/Some of which we may disregard:/
111 Xmas Trees   9   an angel./The child wonders at the Christmas Tree:/Let him continue in the spirit
111 Xmas Trees   13   amazement/Of the first-remembered Christmas Tree,/So that the surprises, delight in
111 Xmas Trees   27   /So that before the end, the eightieth Christmas/(By 'eightieth' meaning whichever is
129 Cor2 State   14   with a bonus of thirty shillings at Christmas/And one week's leave a year./A
587 Fable   25   astonishment of all the people./When Christmas time was near the Abbot vowed/
588 Fable   57   his skull held sausages./Over their Christmas wassail the monks dozed,/A fine old
260 MC   3m   1   *preaches in the Cathedral on Christmas Morning*, 1170/{T} 'Glory to God in
260 MC Thomas   4   children of God, my sermon this Christmas morning will be a/very short one. I
260 MC Thomas   6   and mystery of our masses of Christmas Day. For whenever/Mass is said, we
260 MC Thomas   8   and Death of Our Lord; and/on this Christmas Day we do this in celebration of His
261 MC Thomas   9   /Not only do we at the feast of Christmas celebrate at once Our Lord's/Birth
263 MC Chorus   18   summer, an empty harvest./Between Christmas and Easter what work shall be done?/
264 MC Priest1   1   *lines sung are in italics.*]/{P1} Since Christmas a day: and the day of St. Stephen,
264 MC Priest1   22   Innocents a day: the fourth day from Christmas./{3P} *Rejoice we all, keeping holy*
385 CP   Reilly   12   /The lively bachelor uncle at the Christmas party,/The beloved nursemaid —

CHRISTMASTIDE (1)
263 MC Chorus   12   the time of the birth of Our Lord, at Christmastide,/Is there not peace upon earth,

CHRONIC (1)
457 CC   Lady E   19   /He tells me that he suffers from chronic catarrh./{SC} Hello! What's that? {}/

CHRONOMETERS (1)
185 FQ: DrySal   40   swell, a time/Older than the time of chronometers, older/Than time counted by

CHTHONIC (1)
190 FQ: DrySal   227   of movement —/Driven by dæmonic, chthonic/Powers. And right action is freedom/

CIGARETTE (4)
67 WL: Fire S   178 /Silk handkerchiefs, cardboard boxes, cigarette ends/Or other testimony of summer
150 Rock 1   103 *furrow. In this land/There shall be one cigarette to two men,/To two women one half pint*
161 Rock 7   34   *off):/In this land/There shall be one cigarette to two men,/To two women one half pint*
286 FR   m 30 That's what it comes to. {}/[*Lights a cigarette*]/{I} The younger generation/Are
CIGARETTE-CASE (1)
346 FRDowning   8 he remembered/He thinks he left his cigarette-case on the table./Oh, there it is.
CIGARETTES (2)
24 Rhapsody   67   smells in shuttered rooms,/And cigarettes in corridors/And cocktail smells in
286 FR Charles   29 smell/Because of their cocktails and cigarettes. {}/[*Enter* DENMAN *with sherry and*
CIGARS (1)
542 ES Gomez   6 tastes. Now it's my turn./I can have cigars sent direct to you from Cuba/If your
CINEMA (3)
367 CP   Peter 18 very good reviews./But it's more the cinema that interests both of us./{E} A common
430 CP   Alex   39 it, but I didn't see it./There is no cinema in Kinkanja./{P} Kinkanja? Where's
435 CP   Peter 21 had ideas to make a revolution/In the cinema, that no one could ignore —/And here I
CIRCE'S (1)
598 Circe   t withered flowers, flowers of dawn./Circe's Palace/Around her fountain which flows
CIRCLE (8)
172 FQ: BurntN   34 /Along the empty alley, into the box circle,/To look down into the drained pool./Dry
184 FQ: DrySal   14 on the autumn table,/And the evening circle in the winter gaslight./The river is within
599 On a Port   12 their secrets hid from us,/Beyond the circle of our thought she stands./The parrot on
280 MC Priest3   30 your nails in Aquitaine./In the small circle of pain within the skull/You still shall
291 FR Chorus   1   in the stalls, the titter in the dress circle, the laughter and catcalls in the gallery?/
348 FR Chorus   23   and the loss of money./But the circle of our understanding/Is a very restricted
348 FR Chorus   30 /What is happening outside of the circle?/And what is the meaning of happening?/
350 FR Agatha   15 /Of expiation/Round and round the circle/Completing the charm/So the knot be
CIRCLED (2)
213 Growltiger   37 closer still and closer the sampans circled round,/And yet from all the enemy there
249 MC Tempt2   26 of a powerless Pope,/The old stag, circled with hounds./{T} No!/{T2} Yes! men
CIRCLES (2)
56 Swee Night   5 jaw/Swelling to maculate giraffe./The circles of the stormy moon/Slide westward
178 FQ: ECoker   35   through the flames, or joined in circles,/Rustically solemn or in rustic laughter/
CIRCLING (1)
246 MC Thomas   17 hawk/Will only soar and hover, circling lower,/Waiting excuse, pretence,
CIRCUIT (2)
39 Gerontion   68 Mrs. Cammel, whirled/Beyond the circuit of the shuddering Bear/In fractured
147 Rock 1   2 /The Hunter with his dogs pursues his circuit./O perpetual revolution of configured
CIRCULAR (1)
335 FR Harry   13 endless drift/Of shrieking forms in a circular desert/Weaving with contagion of
CIRCULATING (1)
285 FR Violet   19 shillings./{V} Go south! to the English circulating libraries,/To the military widows and
CIRCULATION (1)
172 FQ: BurntN   55 wars./The dance along the artery/The circulation of the lymph/Are figured in the drift
CIRCUMAMBULATE (1)
53 Whispers   30 /And even the Abstract Entities/Circumambulate her charm;/But our lot crawls
CIRCUMLOCUTION (1)
241 MC Mess   12 /I am here to inform you, without circumlocution:/The Archbishop is in England,
CIRCUMSCRIBE (1)
57 Swee Night   32 leaning in,/Branches of wistaria/Circumscribe a golden grin;/The host with
CIRCUMSTANCE (3)
251 MC Tempt3   1 not depend/Upon ourselves, but upon circumstance./But circumstance is not
251 MC Tempt3   2   but upon circumstance./But circumstance is not undetermined./Unreal
346 FRDowning   26 most of us seem to live according to circumstance,/But with people like him, there's
CIRCUMSTANCES (5)
299 FR Charles   6 /We didn't learn very much about the circumstances;/We only knew what we read in
413 CP   Celia   20 /But oughtn't I first to tell you the circumstances?/I'd forgotten that you know
449 CC Claude   6 thinking of her missing child:/In the circumstances, that might make her jealous./I've
505 CC Eggers   37 a son/Whom she could not, in the circumstances, acknowledge./That happens not
508 CC Guzzard   13 straws! Colby is my son./{MG} In the circumstances, I ignore that remark./{E} May I
CISTERNS (1)
73 WL: Thund   384 /And voices singing out of empty cisterns and exhausted wells./In this decayed
CITIES (4)
103 Journ Magi   14 out, and the lack of shelters,/And the cities hostile and the towns unfriendly/And the
154 Rock 3   2 came unto me, saying:/O miserable cities of designing men,/O wretched generation

184 FQ: DrySal   7 is almost forgotten/By the dwellers in cities — ever, however, implacable,/Keeping his
559 ES Ld Clav   9 /The men I know there are all in the cities:/An outdoor life would suit you better./
CITIZEN (4)
533 ES   Gomez   20   you see,/Is now a highly respected citizen/Of a central American republic: San
533 ES   Gomez   22 /It's as hard to become a respected citizen/Out there, as it is here. With this
539 ES Ld Clav 26   I find surprising/In the respected citizen of San Marco/Is that in the midst of the
563 ES   Gomez   20   Federico Gomez,/The prominent citizen of San Marco./That's my name./{LC} So
CITIZENS (3)
151 Rock 2   2 /Thus your fathers were made/Fellow citizens of the saints, of the household of GOD.
592 Grad 2   6 their fatherland/They there shall be as citizens no more./We go; as lightning-winged
428 CP   Alex   38 don't you expel them?/{A} They are citizens of a friendly neighbouring state/Which
CITIZENSHIP (2)
151 Rock 2   13 not of relations of men to GOD./'Our citizenship is in Heaven'; yes, but that is the
151 Rock 2   13   that is the model and type for your citizenship upon earth./When your fathers fixed
CITROËN (1)
121 SA Sweeney   25 /No two-seaters, no six-seaters,/No Citroën no Rolls-Royce./Nothing to eat but the
CITY (33)
 23 Preludes   40   across the skies/That fade behind a city block,/Or trampled by insistent feet/At four
 62 WL: Burial   60 must be so careful these days./Unreal City,/Under the brown fog of a winter dawn,/A
 67 WL: Fire S 180   their friends, the loitering heirs of City directors;/Departed, have left no addresses.
 68 WL: Fire S 207 jug/So rudely forc'd./Tereu/Unreal City/Under the brown fog of a winter noon/Mr.
 69 WL: Fire S 259 Strand, up Queen Victoria Street./O City city, I can sometimes hear/Beside a public
 69 WL: Fire S 259   up Queen Victoria Street./O City city, I can sometimes hear/Beside a public bar in
 73 WL: Thund   371 by the flat horizon only/What is the city over the mountains/Cracks and reforms
105 Song Sime   9 /I have walked many years in this city,/Kept faith and fast, provided for the poor,/
127 Cor1 March   5 knew ourselves that day, or knew the City./This is the way to the temple, and we so
147 Rock 1   19 journeyed to London, to the timekept City,/Where the River flows, with foreign
147 Rock 1   25   they spend their Sundays./In the City, we need no bells:/Let them waken the
154 Rock 3   29 thousands travel daily to the timekept City;/Where My Word is unspoken,/In the land
155 Rock 3   38   build with us./Can you keep the City that the LORD keeps not with you?/A
155 Rock 3   52 says: 'What is the meaning of this city?/Do you huddle close together because you
157 Rock 4   7 /And he grieved for the broken city, Jerusalem;/And the King gave him leave to
157 Rock 4   9 to depart/That he might rebuild the city./So he went, with a few, to Jerusalem,/And
158 Rock 5   9 not in the home, they are not in the City./The man who has builded during the day
192 FQ: Little   38 /Or over a dark lake, in a desert or a city —/But this is the nearest, in place and time,
605 Narcissus   18 a dancer before God/If he walked in city streets/He seemed to tread on faces,
241 MC   Mess   13 is in England, and is close outside the city./I was sent before in haste/To give you
241 MC   Mess   35   of the season./The streets of the city will be packed to suffocation,/And I think
243 MC Chorus   14   low./{C} Here is no continuing city, here is no abiding stay./Ill the wind, ill the
276 MC Chorus   15 alone, it is not the house, it is not the city that is defiled,/But the world that is wholly
445 CC   Claude 21 be here?/{SC} I had to send him to the City this morning,/But he'll be back, I hope,
451 CC   Eggers   9 Mr. Simpkins. He'll be a power in the City!/And he has a heart of gold. But not to
456 CC   Eggers 32 /All the travel *I* want is up to the City/And back to Joshua Park in the evening,/
467 CC   Colby   37 you:/You have that meeting in the City/Tomorrow morning. You asked me to
480 CC Kaghan   30 why I want to be a power in the City,/On the boards of all the solidest
501 CC   Eggers 30 the most promising young men in the City,/And he has a heart of gold. So have you,
511 CC Kaghan   34 make the right impression in the City./{L} When you're an alderman, you'll be
531 ES Ld Clav 27 won't want my ghost/Walking in the City or sitting in the Lords./And I, who
538 ES   Gomez   28 /And taking a conspicuous job in the City/Where the Government could always
538 ES   Gomez   38 world of politics/And went into the City. Director of a bank/And chairman of
CIVIL (2)
180 FQ: ECoker 106   and the rulers,/Distinguished civil servants, chairmen of many committees,/
278 MC Knight2   19 qualified for the/highest rank of the Civil Service. And what happened? The moment
CIVILISED (1)
286 FR Charles 24 earth so bad for the young./All that a civilised person needs/Is a glass of dry sherry or
CLAIM (5)
461 CC   Claude 39 taken a fancy to you/And so she lays claim to you. That's very satisfactory./She's
515 CC Guzzard 25   the sacrifice I made/When I let you claim him. Do you think it is a small thing/For
516 CC   Claude 32 your father:/I'll accept that. I put no claim upon you —/Except the claim of our
516 CC   Claude 33 put no claim upon you —/Except the claim of our likeness to each other./We have
569 ES Charles 19 guests,/Two persons who, she says, claim a very long acquaintance —/I was
CLAIMS (3)
 39 Gerontion   71 /White feathers in the snow, the Gulf claims,/And an old man driven by the Trades/
241 MC   Mess   30 in pride and sorrow, affirming all his claims,/Assured, beyond doubt, of the devotion
491 CC   Lady E   11 us both/From making unreasonable claims upon you, Colby./It's a good idea! Why

CLAIRVOYANTE (1)
62 WL: Burial   43 *das Meer.*/Madame Sosostris, famous clairvoyante,/Had a bad cold, nevertheless/Is
CLAMOUR (2)
141 Rannoch   8 ancient war,/Languor of broken steel,/Clamour of confused wrong, apt/In silence.
186 FQ: DrySal   68 /The silent listening to the undeniable/Clamour of the bell of the last annunciation./
CLANGS (1)
185 FQ: DrySal   49   that is and was from the beginning,/Clangs/The bell./Where is there an end of it, the
CLAP-TRAP (1)
278 MC Knight2   3   and not to be taken in by/emotional clap-trap. I therefore ask you to consider
CLARENDON (1)
248 MC Tempt2   16 perhaps. I will remind you./We met at Clarendon, at Northampton,/And last at
CLARITY (1)
337 FR   Harry   23 have made a decision/In a moment of clarity, and now I feel dull again./I only know
CLASP (1)
 34 Figlia   4   weave the sunlight in your hair —/Clasp your flowers to you with a pained
CLASPED (1)
 23 Preludes   37   curled the papers from your hair,/Or clasped the yellow soles of feet/In the palms of
CLASPING (1)
335 FR   Harry   25   wilderness,/Trying to avoid the clasping branches/And the giant lizard. To and
CLASS (4)
129 Cor2 State   5 Order of the Black Eagle (1st and 2nd class),/And the Order of the Rising Sun./Cry cry
594 Grad 11   3   we pass/Into the unknown world — class after class,/O queen of schools — a
594 Grad 11   3 Into the unknown world — class after class,/O queen of schools — a momentary
602 Humoresque 17   /'Why don't you people get some class?/(Feebly contemptuous of nose),/'Your
CLASSE (1)
 48 Lune Miel   9   lieue d'ici est Saint Apollinaire/En Classe, basilique connue des amateurs/De
CLATTER (1)
 69 WL: Fire S 262   whining of a mandoline/And a clatter and a chatter from within/Where fishmen
CLAUDE (102)
444 CC   m   2   CLERK/Characters/SIR CLAUDE MULHAMMER/EGGERSON/
445 CC   2m   1   *Room on the first floor of* SIR CLAUDE MULHAMMER'S/*London house.*
445 CC   3m   1   /*London house. Early afternoon.* SIR CLAUDE *writing at desk. Enter*/EGGERSON.
445 CC   Eggers 8 from Switzerland./{E} Impossible, Sir Claude!/A very delicate situation —/Her first
445 CC   Eggers 26   you're irreplaceable .../{E} Oh, Sir Claude, you shouldn't say that!/Mr. Simpkins is
446 CC   Eggers 37 worth watching./{E} I don't know, Sir Claude. Only the other day/I read a letter in
447 CC   Eggers 19 I am./{E} Oh, I wouldn't say that, Sir Claude!/She has too much respect for your
448 CC   Eggers 11   /{E} Well, to tell the truth, Sir Claude, I only touched on these matters,/
450 CC   Colby 28 /{C} I've got what you wanted, Sir Claude. Good afternoon,/Mr. Eggerson. I was
450 CC   m   32   I will rejoin you. {}/[*Exit* SIR CLAUDE]/{C} I'm glad you don't have to leave
450 CC   Colby 36 little about Lady Elizabeth,/And Sir Claude himself hasn't told me very much:/So
451 CC   Eggers 4   listen to him. He understands Sir Claude,/And he's always been very grateful to
451 CC   Eggers 5 he's always been very grateful to Sir Claude,/As he ought to be. Sir Claude picked
451 CC   Eggers 6 to Sir Claude,/As he ought to be. Sir Claude picked him out/And gave him his start.
453 CC   Lucasta 29 Eggy, will you break the sad news to Claude?/Meanwhile, you'll have to raid the till
453 CC   Eggers 40 *not* devolved on Mr. Simpkins:/Sir Claude intends to deal with these matters
454 CC   Eggers 1 himself./You will have to ask Sir Claude. But I'll speak to him/When I return
454 CC   Colby 27 heart./{C} But does she address Sir Claude Mulhammer/As Claude? To his face?/
454 CC   Colby 28 address Sir Claude Mulhammer/As Claude? To his face?/{E} She does indeed./{C}
454 CC   Eggers 33 does call her Lizzie,/Sometimes, to Sir Claude. And do you know —/I think it amuses
455 CC   Eggers 15 father —/A very generous man, is Sir Claude./To tell the truth, she's something of a
456 CC   Eggers 1   as the French say./That's what Sir Claude admires about her./He said to me once,
456 CC   Eggers 15   get used to them. That's what Sir Claude said:/'Humour her, Eggerson,' he said,
457 CC   m   11 I'm right, I assure you. {}/[*Enter* SIR CLAUDE]/{SC} Hello! Still here? It's time you
457 CC   Lady E 29 properly./A cup of black coffee. Is Sir Claude at home?/I'll speak to him first./{SC}
459 CC   Lady E 1 interviewed/And recommended to Sir Claude? Of course it is./I remember saying: 'He
460 CC   Lady E 5   taught mind control?/{LE} No, Claude, he only teaches *thought* control./Mind
460 CC   Lady E 12 /By reading the postmark./{LE} But Claude, I'm glad to find/That you've taken my
461 CC   Eggers 22   you, Eggerson./{E} Good day, Claude. Good day, Mr. Simpkins. {}/[*Exit*
472 CC   Lucasta 32 go into business/And be someone like Claude ... or B. I was sorry,/Very sorry for you.
475 CC   Colby 35 Or from what I've told B.; or from Sir Claude./{L} Claude hasn't told me anything
475 CC   Lucasta 36 I've told B.; or from Sir Claude./{L} Claude hasn't told me anything about you;/He
476 CC   Lucasta 34 my mother. I never could see/How Claude had ever liked her. Oh, that childhood
476 CC   Lucasta 37 neighbours complained./Oh of course Claude gave her money, a regular allowance;/
477 CC   Lucasta 5 died of an 'accidental overdose'./Then Claude took me over. That was lucky./But I
477 CC   Lucasta 21 I'd told you I *was* Claude's mistress./Claude has always been ashamed of me:/Now

477 CC	Lucasta	25	nobody. I know why you're shocked:/Claude has just accepted me like a debit item/
478 CC	Lucasta	30	on your face/When I told you about Claude and my mother./I may be a bastard, but
483 CC	Colby	12	come from?/{C} It's an office desk. Sir Claude got it for me./I said I needed a desk in
486 CC	m	33	*door*]/{LE} Who's that? {}/[*Enter* SIR CLAUDE]/{SC} Elizabeth! I was told that you
487 CC	Lady E	15	piano. You'll play all the better./{LE} Claude!/{SC} What is it, Elizabeth?/{LE} I've
487 CC	Lady E	24	/It seems incredible, doesn't it, Claude?/And yet it would be still more
487 CC	Lady E	30	brought you back to me,/And you, Claude, and Eggerson have been the
487 CC	Lady E	31	been the instruments./I must be right. Claude, tell me I am right./{SC} But Elizabeth,
487 CC	Lady E	37	truth dawned on me. Mrs. Guzzard!/Claude, Colby was brought up by a Mrs.
488 CC	Lady E	15	have seemed the right one./{LE} Oh Claude, how can you be so sceptical!/We must
488 CC	Lady E	33	But of course I want to adopt him, Claude!/That is, if one's allowed to adopt one's
488 CC	Lady E	37	is *my* son./{LE} Quite impossible, Claude!/You have a daughter. Now you want a
489 CC	Lady E	24	is my son./{LE} But where were you, Claude,/When Colby was born?/{SC} Where
490 CC	Lady E	5	the way it must have happened./Oh, Claude, you know I'm rather weak in the head/
491 CC	Lady E	4	Colby! Something has come to me./Claude! I don't want to take away from you/
491 CC	Lady E	13	we not be happy,/All of us? Already, Claude,/I feel as if this brought us closer
492 CC	Lady E	4	we must see Mrs. Guzzard./{LE} Oh Claude! I am terribly sorry for you./I believe
492 CC	Lady E	38	/Come, Elizabeth./{LE} My poor Claude! {}/[*Exeunt* SIR CLAUDE *and* LADY
492 CC	1m	38	{LE} My poor Claude! {}/[*Exeunt* SIR CLAUDE *and* LADY ELIZABETH]/
493 CC	2m	1	in Act 1. *Several mornings later.* SIR CLAUDE *is/moving chairs about. Enter*
493 CC	Lady E	1	*Enter* LADY ELIZABETH./{LE} Claude, what are you doing?/{SC} Settling the
493 CC	Lady E	29	But perhaps you're right./{LE} Claude, I've been thinking things over and over
495 CC	Lady E	38	*I* was trying to do./It's very strange, Claude, but this is the first time/I have talked to
496 CC	Lady E	7	/{LE} Dervish dancing!/Really, Claude, how absurd you are!/Not that there
496 CC	Eggers	14	Eggerson./{E} Good morning, Sir Claude. And Lady Elizabeth!/{SC} I'm sorry,
496 CC	Eggers	17	short notice./{E} Don't say that, Sir Claude./It's true, I haven't much nowadays to
497 CC	Lady E	19	/Unless she is mistaken .../{LE} Now, Claude!/{SC} And she came to the conclusion
497 CC	Lady E	22	truth. But she cannot believe it./{LE} Claude, that's not quite right. Let me explain./I
497 CC	Lady E	23	me explain./I am convinced that Sir Claude is mistaken,/Or has been deceived, and
498 CC	Lady E	28	find out/What became of your child, Claude./{SC} What became of *my* child!/The
498 CC	Eggers	34	we must try to trace it. Certainly, Sir Claude:/Our first step must be to question Mrs.
499 CC	Eggers	2	sit at the desk?/{E} If you wish, Sir Claude./I do feel more at ease when I'm behind
499 CC	Eggers	8	of my wife./{E} I understand, Sir Claude: I understand completely. {}/[*A knock*
499 CC	Lucasta	23	was all settled./{L} Yes, of course, Claude. You thought everything settled./That
500 CC	Lady E	5	is my son./{LE} That is what Sir Claude believes. Claude, let me explain./{SC}
500 CC	Lady E	5	{LE} That is what Sir Claude believes. Claude, let me explain./{SC} No, I'll explain.
500 CC	Lucasta	37	to each other:/You thought so too, Claude, but for the wrong reasons,/And that
501 CC	Lady E	18	Colby./{LE} But you and I, Claude, can understand each other,/No matter
504 CC	Guzzard	28	I didn't mind waiting in the least, Sir Claude./I know that you are always much
505 CC	Guzzard	13	and discretion./{MG} Certainly, Sir Claude, if that is what you wish./But is the
505 CC	Eggers	17	call it, Mrs. Guzzard./I take it, Sir Claude, I should open the discussion?/{SC} If
506 CC	Eggers	24	appears to be a clue./That is why Sir Claude has asked you to be present./{MG} You
507 CC	Lady E	31	she was! What could I do?/{LE} Oh, Claude, you see? You understand, Colby?/{SC}
507 CC	Guzzard	37	a child of yours/And deceived Sir Claude by pretending it was his?/{SC} That is
510 CC	Kaghan	17	Why, yes, it is. Did you tell her, Sir Claude?/{SC} No, B. It was Mrs. Guzzard who
511 CC	Lady E	24	/{LE} And I shall wish to meet them./Claude, we must invite the Kaghans to dinner./
513 CC	Guzzard	6	Elizabeth,/And the daughter of Sir Claude Mulhammer./{SC} That is *my* concern
513 CC	Colby	14	I can only give a strange answer./Sir Claude is right: I wished to know the truth./
514 CC	Guzzard	9	/{MG} Colby is not your son, Sir Claude./{C} Who was my father, then?/{MG}
514 CC	Eggers	28	I'll examine the records myself, Sir Claude./Not that we doubt your word, Mrs.
514 CC	Guzzard	36	had no intention of deceiving you, Sir Claude,/Till you deceived yourself. When you
515 CC	Guzzard	20	it can't be true./{MG} Consider, Sir Claude. Would I tell you all this/Unless it was
516 CC	Colby	3	for your future./{C} Thank you, Sir Claude./You're a very generous man. But now I
516 CC	Colby	36	the best of it, together./{C} No, Sir Claude. I hate to hurt you/As I am hurting you.
517 CC	Lady E	18	persuade him?/{LE} Yes. My poor Claude!/Do try to help him, Eggerson./{E} I
518 CC	Guzzard	28	terminated./If you will excuse me, Sir Claude .../{SC} Excuse you? Yes./{MG} I shall
518 CC	Guzzard	35	/Do you mind if I take my leave, Sir Claude?/I'm no longer needed here. {}/[*Exit*
518 CC	Guzzard	39	one form or another. You and I, Sir Claude,/Had *our* wishes twenty-five years ago;/
519 CC	Lady E	6	Is Colby coming back?/{LE} My poor Claude! {}/[LUCASTA *crosses to* SIR
519 CC	m	7	Claude! {}/[LUCASTA *crosses to* SIR CLAUDE *and kneels beside him*]/{K} You
519 CC	Kaghan	7	*kneels beside him*]/{K} You know, Claude, I think we all made the same mistake —
519 CC	Lady E	11	I suppose that's true of you and me, Claude./Between not knowing what other
519 CC	Lady E	15	mistakes! But I mean to do better./Claude, we've got to try to understand our
519 CC	Kaghan	18	.../I mean, I'm including both of you,/Claude ... and Aunt Elizabeth./You know,
519 CC	Kaghan	19	... and Aunt Elizabeth./You know, Claude, both Lucasta and I/Would like to mean

519 CC   m 22   *puts her arms around* SIR CLAUDE]/{SC} Don't leave me, Lucasta./

CLAUDE'S (7)
455 CC   Eggers   12   I think her father was a friend of Sir Claude's,/And he's made himself responsible for
476 CC   Lucasta 20 /{C} What wasn't true?/{L} That I was Claude's mistress —/Or had been his mistress,
476 CC   Lucasta 30   You'll laugh when I tell you:/I'm only Claude's daughter./{C} His daughter!/{L} His
477 CC   Colby   7   remember ... too much./{C} You are Claude's daughter!/{L} Oh, there's no doubt of
477 CC   Lucasta 20   shocked/Than if I'd told you I *was* Claude's mistress./Claude has always been
478 CC   Lucasta   1   for your prospects/Now that you're Claude's white-headed boy./Perhaps he'll adopt
514 CC   Guzzard   1   son would you wish to be, Colby:/Sir Claude's — or the son of some other man/

CLAUSE (1)
519 CC   Guzzard   3   wishes,/That there was a time-limit clause in the contract./{SC} What's that? Oh.

CLAVERTON (25)
523 ES   m   5   HEMINGTON/LAMBERT/LORD CLAVERTON/FEDERICO GOMEZ/MRS.
529 ES   m 19   Oh, Charles dear — {}/[*Enter* LORD CLAVERTON]/{M} You've been very long in
533 ES   Gomez   5   Claverton-Ferry;/And finally, Lord Claverton. I've followed your example,/And
543 ES   m   8   we left off. {}/[*Exit* GOMEZ]/[LORD CLAVERTON *sits for a few minutes brooding.*
544 ES   3m 1   *several days later./Enter* LORD CLAVERTON *and* MONICA./{M} Well, so
545 ES   Piggott 22   /{MP} Good morning, Lord Claverton! Good morning, Miss Claverton!/
545 ES   Piggott 22   Lord Claverton! Good morning, Miss Claverton!/Isn't this a glorious morning!/I'm
545 ES   Piggott 27   last few days,/And I thought, 'Lord Claverton will understand/My not coming in
546 ES   Piggott 14   when they come like you, Miss Claverton./{M} Claverton-Ferry. Or Ferry: it's
548 ES   1m 14   hint. {}/[*Exit*]/*A moment later*, LORD CLAVERTON *spreads his newspaper over his*
548 ES   Carghil 25   last night./You are the great Lord Claverton, aren't you?/Somebody said you were
551 ES   Carghil 38   then you wouldn't have become Lord Claverton./So perhaps I laid the foundation of
554 ES   Piggott 18   you. You've been talking to Lord Claverton,/The famous Lord Claverton. This is
554 ES   Piggott 19   to Lord Claverton,/The famous Lord Claverton. This is Mrs. Carghill./Two of our
554 ES   Piggott 21   guests!/I just came to see that Lord Claverton was comfortable:/We can't allow him
554 ES   Carghil 24   Carghill?/{MC} Oh, I knew that Lord Claverton had come for a rest cure,/And it
554 ES   Piggott 36   you and I should remember her, Lord Claverton./That tune she was humming, *It's*
559 ES   Michael 21   where no one has heard the name of Claverton;/Or where, if I took a different name
559 ES   Michael 30   wanted. And you wished to be Lord Claverton/Also, to hold your own with
563 ES   Carghil 27   when we first became friends —/Lord Claverton and I — I was known by my stage
564 ES   Carghil 11   I don't believe you've known Lord Claverton/As long as I have, Señor Gomez./{G}
567 ES   m 27   in his past!/I just can't imagine it. {}/[CLAVERTON *has entered unobserved*]/{M} I
571 ES   Ld Clav   6   Gomez, Mrs. Carghill and Lord Claverton./Freddy admired me, when we were
573 ES   Charles 15   do you propose? How long, Lord Claverton,/Will you stay here and endure this
582 ES   m 24   enough./I shall not go far. {}/[*Exit* CLAVERTON]/{C} He's a very different man

CLAVERTON'S (2)
523 ES   m 11   ACT ONE/*The drawing-room of Lord Claverton's London house. Four o'clock in the*
524 ES   2m 1   One/*The drawing-room of* LORD CLAVERTON'S *London house. Four o'clock*

CLAVERTON-FERRY (8)
523 ES   m   2   *and me only./*Characters/MONICA CLAVERTON-FERRY/CHARLES
523 ES   m   9   /MRS. CARGHILL/MICHAEL CLAVERTON-FERRY/ACT ONE/*The*
533 ES   Gomez   4   name/And became Mr. Richard Claverton-Ferry;/And finally, Lord Claverton.
546 ES   Monica   15   come like you, Miss Claverton./{M} Claverton-Ferry. Or Ferry: it's shorter./{MP} So
546 ES   Piggott 16   it's shorter./{MP} So sorry. Miss Claverton-Ferry. I'm Mrs. Piggott./Just call me
547 ES   Piggott   8   stay out late/In the afternoon, Miss Claverton-Ferry./And remember, when you
547 ES   Piggott 20   /{MP} I really *am* neglectful!/Miss Claverton-Ferry, I ought to tell you more/
555 ES   Piggott 10   {}/[*Enter* MONICA]/{MP} Oh, Miss Claverton-Ferry!/I didn't see you coming. Now

CLAWING (1)
42 Swee Erect   20   the framework of the bed/And clawing at the pillow slip./Sweeney addressed

CLAWS (5)
15 Prufrock   73   /I should have been a pair of ragged claws/Scuttling across the floors of silent seas./
41 Burb Blei   30   /And flea'd his rump and pared his claws?/Thought Burbank, meditating on/Time's
229 Gus   49   say, as he scratches himself with his claws,/'Well, the Theatre's certainly not what it
311 FR   Harry   19   before sleep/I always see their claws distended/Quietly, as if they had never
315 FR   Chorus   33   future darken the past, the beak and claws have desecrated/History. Shamed/The

CLAY (3)
149 Rock 1   82   /*There are hands and machines/And clay for new brick/And lime for new mortar/*
153 Rock 2   54   time and the arm not waste;/Let the clay be dug from the pit, let the saw cut the
464 CC   Claude   30   the same devotion/That I gave to clay, and what could be done with it —/What I

CLEAN (5)
50 Hippopot   29   /Blood of the Lamb shall wash him clean/And him shall heavenly arms enfold,/
275 MC   Chorus   21   *hear the* CHORUS./{C} Clear the air! clean the sky! wash the wind! take stone from
276 MC   Chorus   14   are soiled by a filth that we cannot clean, united to supernatural vermin,/It is not

276 MC Chorus 17   that is wholly foul./Clear the air! clean the sky! wash the wind! take the stone
327 FR   Harry 21   /What matters is the filthiness. I can clean my skin,/Purify my life, void my mind,/

CLEAN-SHAVEN (1)
321 FR Warburt 5   changes in fashion/And your being clean-shaven, very much like you./And now,

CLEANED (1)
263 MC Chorus 16   renews it,/And the world must be cleaned in the winter, or we shall have only/A

CLEANING (1)
281 MC Chorus 14   in laying the fire, the knee bent in cleaning the hearth, we, the scrubbers and

CLEANSES (1)
335 FR   Harry 32   final eye, and the awful evacuation/Cleanses./I was not there, you were not there,

CLEANSING (1)
174 FQ: BurntN 101   the sensual with deprivation/Cleansing affection from the temporal./Neither

CLEAR (23)
24 Rhapsody   6   the floors of memory/And all its clear relations,/Its divisions and precisions./
109 Marina   17   in place/What is this face, less clear and clearer/The pulse in the arm, less
232 Skimble   14   eyes/And the signal goes 'All Clear!'/And we're off at last for the northern
258 MC Thomas 3   we are destroyed./{T} Now is my way clear, now is the meaning plain:/Temptation
263 MC Chorus 22   /Burst over the stream, and the air is clear and high,/And voices trill at windows, and
275 MC Chorus 21   *kill him, we hear the* CHORUS./{C} Clear the air! clean the sky! wash the wind! take
276 MC Chorus 17   /But the world that is wholly foul./Clear the air! clean the sky! wash the wind! take
295 FR Charles 16   yourself./Your conscience can be clear./{H} It goes a good deal deeper/Than what
296 FR Agatha 2 I do not yet understand:/They will be clear later. I am also convinced/That you only
343 FR Agatha 3   meaning./*They* have made this clear. And I who have seen them must believe
364 CP   Reilly 12   in the dark/Except long enough to clear from the mind/The illusion of having ever
378 CP Edward 14   Did he persuade me?/I have a very clear impression/That he tried to persuade me it
397 CP Edward 36   understand me. Have I not made it clear/That in future you will find me a different
399 CP   Nurse 5   any meeting?/{N} You made that clear, Sir Henry:/The first appointment at
411 CP   Reilly 28   /{R} Your business is not to clear your conscience/But to learn how to bear
448 CC Claude 27   him during her absence/Are perfectly clear. But beyond that point/I haven't yet
470 CC   Colby 27 not with you!/{C} You made that very clear./But why not with me?/{L} Because you
500 CC Claude 11   /{SC} I ought to have made things clear to you/At the time when he came here. But
542 ES Gomez 3   want?/{G} I've been trying to make clear that I only want your friendship!/Just as it
552 ES Ld Clav 19   embarrassment? My conscience was clear./A brief infatuation, ended in the only way
552 ES Carghil 22   /{MC} Your conscience was clear./I've very seldom heard people mention
552 ES Carghil 24 to observe that their consciences were clear./You got out of a tangle for a large cash
552 ES Carghil 26   no publicity. So your conscience was clear./At bottom, I believe you're still the same

CLEARED (3)
335 FR   Harry 30 noise of machinery,/And the desert is cleared, under the judicial sun/Of the final eye,
463 CC   Colby 25 I least expect it,/When my mind is cleared and empty, walking in the street/Or
510 CC Guzzard 27   that this is your son./If so, I am cleared from your unjust suspicion./{E} Mr.

CLEARER (1)
109 Marina   17 place/What is this face, less clear and clearer/The pulse in the arm, less strong and

CLEARLY (6)
279 MC Knight4 26 the effect that before he left France he clearly prophesied, in the/presence of numerous
346 FR Agatha 36 sane as you or I,/He sees the world as clearly as you or I see it,/It is only that he has
396 CP Lavinia 38   /But there is one point which I see clearly:/We are not to relapse into the kind of
549 ES Carghil 23   /It's surprising I remember it all so clearly./You attracted me, you know, at the
578 ES Ld Clav 4 /Though you repudiate me. I see now clearly/The many many mistakes I have made/
579 ES Carghil 34   /A friend of the family, can see more clearly./{G} Not that I deserve any credit for it./

CLEARS (1)
68 WL: Fire S 222   from sea,/The typist home at teatime, clears her breakfast, lights/Her stove, and lays

CLEMATIS (2)
129 Cor2 State 35 cyclamen spreads its wings, there the clematis droops over the lintel/O mother (not
174 FQ: BurntN 132 Will the sunflower turn to us, will the clematis/Stray down, bend to us; tendril and

CLEMENCY (1)
267 MC Knight2 38   /And urged by your friends, offered clemency,/Made a pact of peace, and all dispute

CLERGY (1)
247 MC Tempt1 4   that the King and you are in amity,/Clergy and laity may return to gaiety,/Mirth

CLERICAL (1)
136 5FingerEx5 2   meet Mr. Eliot!/With his features of clerical cut,/And his brow so grim/And his

CLERK (8)
68 WL: Fire S 232   arrives,/A small house agent's clerk, with one bold stare,/One of the low on
275 MC Thomas 11   in God's name,/Whether layman or clerk, shall you touch./This I forbid./{4K}
424 CP Lavinia 13   ring up your chambers,/And your clerk told me you had already left./But all I
443 CC   t /CURTAIN/THE CONFIDENTIAL CLERK/Characters/SIR CLAUDE

445 CC   Eggers   28   than I was/To be your confidential clerk./He was finding his feet, very quickly,/
458 CC   Eggers   35   /Than I am, to be a confidential clerk./Besides, he's very musical./{LE} Musical?/
467 CC   Claude   27   work I do./{SC} As my confidential clerk./{C} I'm really interested by the work I'm
505 CC   Claude   2   Mrs. Guzzard:/My confidential clerk. That is to say,/Colby's predecessor, who
CLERKENWELL (1)
174 FQ: BurntN 114   hills of London./Hampstead and Clerkenwell, Camden and Putney,/Highgate,
CLERKSHIP (1)
537 ES   Gomez   38   which you remember:/A miserable clerkship — which your father found for me,/
CLEVER (12)
224 Mr Mistoff   21   Well I never!/Was there ever/A Cat so clever/As Magical Mr. Mistoffelees!/He is quiet
225 Mr Mistoff   40   Well I never!/Was there ever/A Cat so clever/As Magical Mr. Mistoffelees!/His manner
225 Mr Mistoff   59   I never!/Did you ever/Know a Cat so clever/As Magical Mr. Mistoffelees!/Macavity:
309 FR   Harry   5   that is by seeing. They are much too clever/To admit you into *our* world. Yours is no
354 CP   Julia   39   Well then, harmless./{J} He was very clever at repairing clocks;/And he had a
366 CP   Julia   8   you, Edward;/That really was very clever of you;/I'd never have found them but for
416 CP   Celia   8   you'd guessed that, had you? That's clever of you./No, perhaps I made it obvious.
471 CC   Lucasta   33   /*That* was a compliment. And a very clever one./{C} I admit that at first I was very
476 CC   Lucasta   26   think he'd have minded. But he's very clever too;/And he guessed the truth from the
490 CC   Lady E   6   weak in the head/Though I try to be clever. Do try to help me./{SC} It could have
548 ES   Carghil   17   other guests have discovered it./It was clever of you to find it so quickly./What made
550 ES   Carghil   35   Richard. Effie always said —/What a clever girl she was! — 'he doesn't understand
CLEVERLY (1)
476 CC   Lucasta   10   A little while ago/You said, very cleverly, that when we first met/You saw I was
CLIENTS (1)
394 CP   Lavinia   5   /Of seeing nobody but solicitors and clients .../{E} And you were never very
CLIFFS (1)
605 Narcissus   8   once between the sea and the high cliffs/When the wind made him aware of his
CLIMATE (9)
203 Indians   8   or the cool hour, according to the climate)/Of foreign men, who fought in foreign
245 MC   Priest2   33   Lordship now being used to a better climate./Your Lordship will find your rooms in
286 FR   Gerald   7   be back in the East. An incomparable climate/For a man who can exercise a little
295 FR   Amy   35   for you./You are unused to our foggy climate/And the northern country. When you
344 FR   Violet   16   really think of *living* in a tropical climate!/{G} There's nothing wrong with a
344 FR   Gerald   17   There's nothing wrong with a tropical climate —/But you have to go in for some sort
389 CP   Lavinia   14   /Everyone says it's a wonderful climate:/The people who go there never want to
535 ES   Gomez   30   /Thousands of miles away, to another climate,/To another language, other standards
579 ES   Michael   9   will attend to my needs for that climate./And you see, he has friends in the
CLIMAX (1)
601 Nocturne   14   in tears are drowned: —'The perfect climax all true lovers seek!'/Humouresque/
CLIMB (3)
41 Burb Blei   27   meagre, blue-nailed, phthisic hand/To climb the waterstair. Lights, lights,/She
257 MC   Priests   4   drowned in a ditch./{3P} A man may climb the stair in the day, and slip on a broken
348 FR   Chorus   7   different landscape./We do not like to climb a stair, and find that it takes us down./We
CLIMBING (1)
92 Ash-Wed 3   21   strength beyond hope and despair/Climbing the third stair./Lord, I am not worthy/
CLIMBS (1)
154 Rock 3   26   of scattered brick where the goat climbs,/Where My Word is unspoken./2ND
CLING (3)
23 Preludes   49   are curled/Around these images, and cling:/The notion of some infinitely gentle/
138 New Hamp   10   /Golden head, black wing,/Cling, swing,/Spring, sing,/Swing up into the
174 FQ: BurntN 134   to us; tendril and spray/Clutch and cling?/Chill/Fingers of yew be curled/Down on
CLINGS (5)
24 Rhapsody   31   spring in a factory yard,/Rust that clings to the form that the strength has left/
52 Whispers   7   of the eyes!/He knew that thought clings round dead limbs/Tightening its lusts and
189 FQ: DrySal 204   searches past and future/And clings to that dimension. But to apprehend/The
303 FR   Mary   2   country,/Late and uncertain, clings to the south wall./The gardener had no
572 ES   Ld Clav   22   that the ghost of the man I was/Still clings to the ghost of the woman who was
CLINIC (1)
528 ES   Monica   31   —/Nothing about it to suggest the clinic —/Everything about it to suggest
CLIPPED (1)
41 Burb Blei   29   entertains Sir Ferdinand/Klein. Who clipped the lion's wings/And flea'd his rump
CLOCK (3)
29 Aunt Helen   10   the parrot died too./The Dresden clock continued ticking on the mantelpiece,/
287 FR   Amy   24   due to arrive?/{A} I do not want the clock to stop in the dark./If you want to know
347 FR   Amy   31   /{A} Agatha! Mary! come!/The clock has stopped in the dark! {}/[*Exeunt*

CLOCKS (3)

19 Portrait		39	/Correct our watches by the public clocks./Then sit for half an hour and drink our
285 FR	Amy	9	unfeared and the day expected/And clocks could be trusted, tomorrow assured/And
354 CP	Julia	39	/{J} He was very clever at repairing clocks;/And he had a remarkable sense of

CLOCKWISE (1)

349 FR	4m	13	*in single file round and round the table, clockwise./At each revolution they blow out a few*

CLOISTER (1)

271 MC	Priests	21	here. To the minster./Through the cloister. No time to waste. They are coming

CLOSE (13)

155 Rock 3		53	meaning of this city?/Do you huddle close together because you love each other?'/
177 FQ: ECoker		25	open field/If you do not come too close, if you do not come too close,/On a
177 FQ: ECoker		25	too close, if you do not come too close,/On a summer midnight, you can hear the
239 MC	Chorus	1	1170/Part I/{C} Here let us stand, close by the cathedral. Here let us wait./Are we
241 MC	Mess	13	/The Archbishop is in England, and is close outside the city./I was sent before in haste/
291 FR	Amy	23	/Not in town, where you have to close the blinds./There is no one to see you but
295 FR	Harry	31	Here, nearer than ever./They are very close here. I had not expected that./{A} Harry,
319 FR	Harry	35	when she kissed me,/I felt the trap close. If you won't tell me,/I must ask Agatha. I
336 FR	1m	23	no time. I will follow. {}/[*The curtains close. AGATHA goes to the window, in a*
340 FR	Amy	30	thought I did not know!/You may be close, but I always saw through *him*./And now
485 CC	Colby	27	In what county?/{C} It's very close to London./{LE} Still, you were brought
565 ES	Monica	6	to-day./Michael, as you're staying so close at hand/Will you come back in the
583 ES	Monica	14	{M} We will go to him together. He is close at hand,/Though he has gone too far to

CLOSED (4)

65 WL: Chess		136	hot water at ten./And if it rains, a closed car at four./And we shall play a game of
220 Old Deut		22	the villagers put up a notice: ROAD CLOSED —/So that nothing untoward may
253 MC Tempt4		22	to the end./All other ways are closed to you/Except the way already chosen./
530 ES Ld Clav		23	/Have left, and the booking office is closed/And the porters have gone. What am I

CLOSELY (4)

21 Portrait		104	were sure our feelings would relate/So closely! I myself can hardly understand./We
348 FR	Chorus	9	the maze in the garden, because it too closely resembles the maze in the brain./We do
348 FR	Chorus	10	when we are awake, because it too closely resembles what happens when we are
518 CC	Eggers	7	time, and I've watched you pretty closely./Mr. Simpkins! You'll be thinking of

CLOSER (5)

38 Gerontion		60	/How should I use them for your closer contact?/These with a thousand small
213 Growltiger		37	from a hundred bright blue eyes./And closer still and closer the sampans circled round,
213 Growltiger		37	bright blue eyes./And closer still and closer the sampans circled round,/And yet from
459 CC	Claude	16	London./But I want to have him closer at hand —/You know what a bother it's
491 CC	Lady E	14	Claude,/I feel as if this brought us closer together./{SC} I should be contented with

CLOSEST (1)

531 ES Ld Clav		24	folk are mildly grieved,/And our closest associates, the small minority/Of those

CLOSET (1)

296 FR	Harry	10	in the chimney/The evil in the dark closet, which they said was not there,/Which

CLOT (1)

172 FQ: BurntN		50	/Garlic and sapphires in the mud/Clot the bedded axle-tree./The trilling wire in

CLOTH (3)

32 Hysteria		6	spreading a pink and white checked cloth over the rusty/green iron table, saying: 'If
56 Swee Night		13	knees/Slips and pulls the table cloth/Overturns a coffee-cup,/Reorganised upon
605 Narcissus		6	red rock:/I will show you his bloody cloth and limbs/And the gray shadow on his

CLOTHES (4)

286 FR	Violet	21	all night/In the absolute *minimum* of clothes./{C} It's the cocktail-drinking does the
405 CP	Edward	36	To be so good as to send me on some clothes./{L} Oh, to what hotel?/{E} I don't know
406 CP	Lavinia	4	that case, Edward,/I don't think your clothes concern me either. {}/[*To REILLY*]/{L} I
569 ES Ld Clav		2	off the stage, change into our own clothes/And speak as ourselves. So I'd become

CLOUD (7)

94 Ash-Wed 4		17	walk, restoring/Through a bright cloud of tears, the years, restoring/With a new
135 5FingerEx2		3	and dry./In a black sky, from a green cloud/Natural forces shriek'd aloud,/Screamed,
172 FQ: BurntN		41	us, reflected in the pool./Then a cloud passed, and the pool was empty./Go, said
174 FQ: BurntN		131	bell have buried the day,/The black cloud carries the sun away./Will the sunflower
256 MC	Chorus	8	vapour? the dark green light from a cloud on a withered tree? The earth is heaving
310 FR	Mary	28	violent sun/Wet wings into the rain cloud/Harefoot over the moon?/{H} What have
337 FR	Agatha	3	is design/And design is accident/In a cloud of unknowing./O my child, my curse,/

CLOUDLESS (1)

294 FR	Harry	32	rest on the burning wheel/That cloudless night in the mid-Atlantic/When I

CLOUDS (2)

| 74 WL: Thund | 396 | /Waited for rain, while the black clouds/Gathered far distant, over Himavant./ |
| 592 Grad 3 | 1 | no more./We go; as lightning-winged clouds that fly/After a summer tempest, when |

CLOWN (1)

| 234 Ad-dress | 27 | the Town/Is much inclined to play the clown,/And far from showing too much pride/Is |

CLOWNS (1)

| 218 Mung Rump | 2 | couple of cats./As knockabout clowns, quick-change comedians, tight-rope |

CLOYING (1)

| 257 MC Chorus | 26 | pain than birth or death./Sweet and cloying through the dark air/Falls the stifling |

CLUB (8)

127 Cor1 March	25	it be he now? No,/Those are the golf club Captains, these the Scouts,/And now the
228 Gus	11	whenever he joins his friends at their club/(Which takes place at the back of the
230 Bust Jones	30	passes Bustopher's day —/At one club or another he's found./It can be no surprise
286 FR Charles	3	/A man can be very cosy at his club/Even in an English winter./{G} Well, as for
400 CP Alex	28	from her./{A} He is staying at his club./{R} Yes, that is where he wrote from. {}/
404 CP Edward	29	/I can't go home again. And at my club/They won't let you keep a room for more
411 CP Lavinia	8	/{L} Then will you stop at your club?/{E} No, they won't let me./I must leave
411 CP Edward	11	did you know/I was staying at the club?/{L} Really, Edward!/I have *some* sense of

CLUBS (2)

| 117 SP Doris | 2 | First is. What is?/{Do} The King of Clubs/{Du} That's Pereira/{Do} It might be |
| 230 Bust Jones | 3 | haunt pubs — he has eight or nine clubs,/For he's the St. James's Street Cat!/He's |

CLUE (5)

337 FR Agatha	11	treasure hunt:/Here you have found a clue, hidden in the obvious place./Delay, and it
416 CP Reilly	34	/{R} Compassion may be already a clue/Towards finding your own way out of the
506 CC Eggers	13	many years, she has been without a clue/Until the other day. This son, Mrs.
506 CC Eggers	23	what we are aiming at./We have a clue — or what appears to be a clue./That is
506 CC Eggers	23	a clue — or what appears to be a clue./That is why Sir Claude has asked you to

CLUMSY (1)

| 178 FQ: ECoker | 37 | in rustic laughter/Lifting heavy feet in clumsy shoes,/Earth feet, loam feet, lifted in |

CLUTCH (5)

52 Whispers	11	no substitute for sense,/To seize and clutch and penetrate;/Expert beyond experience,
61 WL: Burial	19	in the winter./What are the roots that clutch, what branches grow/Out of this stony
67 WL: Fire S	174	tent is broken; the last fingers of leaf/Clutch and sink into the wet bank. The wind/
174 FQ: BurntN	134	down, bend to us; tendril and spray/Clutch and cling?/Chill/Fingers of yew be curled
605 Narcissus	26	his own fingers,/Writhing in his own clutch, his ancient beauty/Caught fast in the

CLUTCHING (3)

43 Swee Erect	32	on the bed/Curves backward, clutching at her sides./The ladies of the corridor
54 Mr E Sun	20	/The young are red and pustular/Clutching piaculative pence./Under the
104 Journ Magi	42	dispensation,/With an alien people clutching their gods./I should be glad of another

CO CO RICO (2)

| 74 WL: Thund | 392 | /Only a cock stood on the rooftree/Co co rico co co rico/In a flash of lightning. |
| 74 WL: Thund | 392 | cock stood on the rooftree/Co co rico co co rico/In a flash of lightning. Then a damp |

CO-EXISTENCE (1)

| 175 FQ: BurntN | 148 | the note lasts,/Not that only, but the co-existence,/Or say that the end precedes the |

COACH-HOUSE (1)

| 288 FR Agatha | 36 | who left. Round by the stables,/In the coach-house, in the orchard,/In the plantation, |

COAL (1)

| 151 Rock 2 | 19 | development./Exporting iron, coal and cotton goods/And intellectual |

COALITION (1)

| 251 MC Tempt3 | 30 | what does this lead?/{T3} To a happy coalition/Of intelligent interests./{T} But what |

COARSE (1)

| 120 SP Krum | 1 | gay for us/Don't think I mean anything *coarse* —/But I'm afraid we couldn't stand the |

COAST (3)

236 Cat Morgan	13	/I got knocked about on the Barbary Coast,/And me voice it ain't no sich melliferous
246 MC Thomas	4	have intercepted our letters,/Filled the coast with spies and sent to meet me/Some who
282 MC Chorus	1	where the western seas gnaw at the coast of Iona,/To the death in the desert, the

COASTS (1)

| 280 MC Priest3 | 20 | /Go venture shipwreck on the sullen coasts/Where blackamoors make captive |

COAT (11)

14 Prufrock	42	hair is growing thin!')/My morning coat, my collar mounting firmly to the chin,/My
15 Prufrock	85	seen the eternal Footman hold my coat, and snicker,/And in short, I was afraid./
84 Hollow Men	33	wear/Such deliberate disguises/Rat's coat, crowskin, crossed staves/In a field/
137 5FingerEx5	10	Mr. Eliot!/With a bobtail cur/In a coat of fur/And a porpentine cat/And a

210 Old Gumbie		2	mind, her name is Jennyanydots;/Her coat is of the tabby kind, with tiger stripes and
212 Growltiger		6	did not calculate to please;/His coat was torn and seedy, he was baggy at the
226 Macavity		14	his head is highly domed;/His coat is dusty from neglect, his whiskers are
230 Bust Jones		6	as he walks down the street/In his coat of fastidious black:/No commonplace
236 Cat Morgan		10	manners is gruff,/But I've got a good coat, and I keep meself smart;/And everyone
267 MC Thomas		14	God bless him!/{T} Then let your new coat of loyalty be worn/Carefully, so it get not
532 ES Monica		22	/Come, Charles. Will you bring my coat?/{C} I'll say goodbye, sir./And look

COAT'S (1)

228 Gus		5	that we usually call him just Gus./His coat's very shabby, he's thin as a rake,/And he

COBWEB (1)

596 When we		4	of the breeze/Had torn no quivering cobweb down./The hedgerow bloomed with

COCK (1)

74 WL: Thund		391	/Dry bones can harm no one./Only a cock stood on the rooftree/Co co rico co co rico

COCKROACHES (1)

211 Old Gumbie		31	but hardly begun./She thinks that the cockroaches just need employment/To prevent

COCKTAIL (10)

24 Rhapsody		68	/And cigarettes in corridors/And cocktail smells in bars./The lamp said,/'Four
351 CP		t	—/May they rest in peace. {}/THE COCKTAIL PARTY/Persons/EDWARD
355 CP	Julia	24	fit to eat!/The only reason for a cocktail party/For a gluttonous old woman like
360 CP	Edward	4	of course;/Just when she'd arranged a cocktail party./She'd gone when I came in, this
387 CP	Peter	26	Lavinia intended/To have yesterday's cocktail party to-day./So I don't suppose her
391 CP	Julia	3	taxi. {}/[*Exit* PETER]/{J} We'll have a cocktail party at *my* house to-day./{C} Well, I'll
429 CP	Julia	37	so chilly. Give me some gin./Not a cocktail. I'm freezing — in July!/{CM} Mr.
432 CP	Julia	20	head's fairly spinning. I must have a cocktail. {}/[*To* REILLY]./{E} And will you
432 CP	Edward	21	REILLY]./{E} And will you have a cocktail?/{R} Might I have a glass of water?/{E}
439 CP	Julia	35	of the Chamberlaynes' choice/Is a cocktail party. They must be ready for it./Their

COCKTAIL-DRINKING (1)

286 FR	Charles	22	*minimum* of clothes./{C} It's the cocktail-drinking does the harm:/There's

COCKTAILS (7)

286 FR	Charles	29	of taste and smell/Because of their cocktails and cigarettes. {}/[*Enter* DENMAN
299 FRDowning		28	Sir,/I always thought that a very few cocktails/Went a long way with her Ladyship./
355 CP	Julia	18	I want to relax, Are there any more cocktails?/{P} But do go on. Edward wasn't
359 CP	Edward	8	go yet./Don't go yet. We'll finish the cocktails./Or would you rather have whisky?/
425 CP	Lavinia	28	it's very crowded, they can't get at the cocktails,/And the man won't be able to take
479 CC	Kaghan	3	/{K} I told Colby, never learn to mix cocktails,/If you don't want women always
479 CC	Kaghan	19	too:/Much better for you than cocktails, Lucasta./{L} You know I don't like

COFFEE (5)

14 Prufrock		51	/I have measured out my life with coffee spoons;/I know the voices dying with a
61 WL: Burial		11	into the Hofgarten,/And drank coffee, and talked for an hour./Bin gar keine
372 CP	Alex	26	/All you should want is a cup of black coffee/And a little dry toast. I've left it
457 CC	Lady E	29	to make tea properly./A cup of black coffee. Is Sir Claude at home?/I'll speak to him
544 ES	Monica	7	/For when I asked about morning coffee/She said 'I'm not the one for elevens's,/

COFFEE-CUP (1)

56 Swee Night		14	and pulls the table cloth/Overturns a coffee-cup,/Reorganised upon the floor/She

COFFEE-STANDS (1)

22 Preludes		18	all its muddy feet that press/To early coffee-stands./With the other masquerades/That

COFFERED (1)

64 WL: Chess		93	laquearia,/Stirring the pattern on the coffered ceiling./Huge sea-wood fed with copper

COFFIN (7)

117 SP	Dusty	27	The *two of spades*!/THAT'S THE COFFIN!!/{Do} THAT'S THE COFFIN?/Oh
117 SP	Doris	28	THE COFFIN!!/{Do} THAT'S THE COFFIN?/Oh good heavens what'll I do?/Just
118 SP	Doris	12	all./{Do} I'd like to know about that coffin./{Du} Well I never! What did I tell you?/
118 SP	Doris	31	/{Do} I'd like to know about that coffin. {}/KNOCK KNOCK KNOCK/
124 SA	Doris	5	before you came/And I drew the coffin/{Sw} *You* drew the coffin?/{Do} I drew
124 SA	Swarts	6	I drew the coffin/{Sw} *You* drew the coffin?/{Do} I drew the COFFIN very last card.
124 SA	Doris	7	*You* drew the coffin?/{Do} I drew the COFFIN very last card./I don't care for such

COGITATIONS (1)

34 Figlia		23	a gesture and a pose./Sometimes these cogitations still amaze/The troubled midnight

COGNISANCE (1)

568 ES	Ld Clav	6	anything of which the law takes cognisance:/Temporary failures, irreflective

COIFFE (1)

47 Mél Adult		8	bien la tête./C'est à Paris que je me coiffe/Casque noir de jemenfoutiste./En

COILING (1)

270 MC Chorus		10	heaved. I have seen/Rings of light coiling downwards, descending/To the horror of

COINAGE (1)
540 ES   Gomez   11   No, because I know the value of the coinage/I pay myself in./{LC} Indeed! How
COINCIDENCE (6)
118 SP   Dusty   17   *window.*)/{Du} Well I *never*/What a coincidence! Cards are queer! { }/(*Whistle again.*)
487 CC   Lady E   23   her./This couldn't possibly be a coincidence./It seems incredible, doesn't it,
487 CC   Lady E   26   still more incredible/If it were only a coincidence./Perhaps I ought not to believe it
488 CC   Claude   9   true./{SC} It is certainly a remarkable coincidence —/If it is a coincidence. But I'm
488 CC   Claude   10   a remarkable coincidence —/If it is a coincidence. But I'm afraid, Elizabeth,/What
497 CC   Eggers   16   was entrusted./{E} What an amazing coincidence!/{SC} That's what it is,/Unless she is
COKER (1)
177 FQ: ECoker   t   time/Stretching before and after./East Coker/In my beginning is my end. In succession
COL. (1) [*Abbreviation*]
284 FR m   3   *and* AGATHA, *her younger sisters*/COL. THE HON. GERALD PIPER, *and* THE
COLBY (158)
444 CC m   4   MULHAMMER/EGGERSON/COLBY SIMPKINS/B. KAGHAN/LUCASTA
445 CC   Claude   5   but you. And I couldn't send Colby./That's not the way to arrange their first
447 CC   Claude   4   Coming back from the airport, about Colby./I think, you ought to give her warning/
447 CC   Claude   28   /So she'll be sympathetic. And as for Colby —/Say that Mr. Simpkins was highly
448 CC   Claude   24   you have a young successor,/A Mr. Colby Simpkins./{E} Merely Mr. Simpkins./
449 CC   Claude   7   her jealousy./I've explained all this to you — Mr. Simpkins./{E} I see what you
450 CC m   26   waiting to introduce him. { }/[*Enter* COLBY SIMPKINS *with briefcase*]/{SC} Ah,
450 CC   Claude   26   SIMPKINS *with briefcase*]/{SC} Ah, Colby, I was just saying to Eggerson/It was time
452 CC   Kaghan   1   /{K} Enter B. Kaghan. Hello Colby!/And hello Eggers! I'm glad to find you
452 CC   Kaghan   3   glad to find you here./It's lucky for Colby./{E} How so Mr. Kaghan?/{K} Because
452 CC   Kaghan   8   upstairs ahead, to ease the shock for Colby./But as you're here, Eggers, I can just
452 CC   Lucasta   23   bother?/But who's this, Eggy? Is it Colby Simpkins?/Introduce him, one or the
452 CC   Lucasta   29   taking *me* over?/Did you know that, Colby? I'm Lucasta./It's only Eggy calls me
452 CC   Lucasta   36   /I'm thinking of changing it. But, Colby,/Do you know that I'm one of your
453 CC   Lucasta   5   /Go on, Eggy. Don't mind him, Colby./Colby, are you married?/{C} No, I'm not
453 CC   Lucasta   6   on, Eggy. Don't mind him, Colby./Colby, are you married?/{C} No, I'm not
453 CC   Lucasta   16   speak?/Eggy's really quite human, Colby./It's only that he's terrified of Mrs.
453 CC   Lucasta   20   /{L} That's what he always says, Colby,/When I mention Mrs. Eggerson. He
453 CC   Lucasta   22   fails to rise./B.! What have you told Colby about me?/{K} It's no use telling anybody
453 CC   Kaghan   27   /As your fiancé, to protect Colby from you./But first, let's cope with the
454 CC   Kaghan   6   I don't propose to leave you with Colby./He's had enough for one day. Take my
454 CC   Kaghan   7   enough for me. Take my advice, Colby./Never allow Lucasta the slightest
454 CC   Lucasta   14   been too much for me. Another time, Colby./I'll ring you up, and let you take me out
454 CC   Kaghan   16   { }/[*Exit* LUCASTA]/{K} Take it easy, Colby. You'll get used to her. { }/[*Exit*
458 CC   Claude   3   parlourmaid. She's coming up./{SC} Colby, sit at the desk, and pick up some papers.
459 CC   Claude   5   What did you say his name was?/{SC} Colby Simpkins. { }/[*counting on her fingers*]./
459 CC   Lady E   10   of health./Where is your home, Mr. Colby?/{C} Simpkins./{E} Mr. Colby Simpkins./
459 CC   Eggers   12   Mr. Colby?/{C} Simpkins./{E} Mr. Colby Simpkins./{LE} I prefer Colby./Where
459 CC   Lady E   13   Mr. Colby Simpkins./{LE} I prefer Colby./Where are you living?/{SC} His home's
459 CC   Lady E   21   of colour/For our spiritual life, Mr. Colby./Neither, I regret to say, does Eggerson./
459 CC   Lady E   26   /Would be absolutely baneful to Mr. Colby./He needs a light mauve. I shall see about
460 CC   Lady E   15   About what?/{LE} To engage Mr. Colby. I really am distressed!/This is not the
460 CC   Lady E   22   that young man?'/Well, that was Mr. Colby./{SC} Oh, I see./Yes, now I am beginning
460 CC   Lady E   26   /{LE} I must explain to you, Mr. Colby,/That I am to share you with my
460 CC   Lady E   33   of some business with Mr. .../{LE} Colby! { }/[*Exit* LADY ELIZABETH]/{SC} She
461 CC   Claude   23   { }/[*Exit* EGGERSON]/{SC} Well, Colby! I've been calling you Mr. Simpkins/In
461 CC   Claude   26   my wife insists upon your being Mr. Colby —/I shall begin to call you Colby with
461 CC   Claude   27   Mr. Colby —/I shall begin to call you Colby with everyone./{C} I'm sure that will
462 CC   Claude   37   now I want it to be different. It's odd, Colby./I didn't realise, till you started with me
468 CC   Claude   2   on my wife. Be patient with her, Colby./— Oh yes, that meeting. We must run
469 CC m   1   *flat in the mews a few weeks later.* COLBY *is seated at the piano;*/LUCASTA *in*
469 CC   Lucasta   1   /{L} *I* think you play awfully well, Colby —/Not that *my* opinion counts for
469 CC   Lucasta   16   them. You liked the right ones./{L} Colby, I didn't know you were so artful!/So the
470 CC   Lucasta   21   how bad my playing is./{L} Really, Colby, you do make difficulties!/But what
471 CC   Lucasta   10   it's you who are educating *me*./{L} Colby, you really are full of surprises!/I've never
475 CC   Lucasta   18   to understand another person./{L} Oh Colby, now that we begin to understand,/I'd
478 CC   Lucasta   4   Lady Elizabeth./But in that event, Colby, you'll have to accept me/As your sister!
478 CC   Lucasta   10   mother coming out in me./You know, Colby, I'm truly disappointed./I was sure, when
478 CC   Kaghan   39   intuitions! I'm your guardian angel,/Colby, to protect you from Lucasta./{L} You're
479 CC   Kaghan   3   And I'm dying for a drink./{K} I told Colby, never learn to mix cocktails,/If you don't
479 CC   Lucasta   7   he's got to have protection./{L} Colby doesn't need your protection racket/So
479 CC   Kaghan   14   new bachelor quarters,/And to wish Colby luck. I've always been lucky,/And I

479 CC	Kaghan	22	sherry./{K} You've got to drink it,/To	Colby, and a happy bachelor life!/Which
479 CC	Kaghan	24	always interfering. Be firm with her,	Colby;/Assert your right to a little privacy./
479 CC	Kaghan	31	I saw that it was necessary. I'm afraid	Colby/Has made a good impression; which he'll
479 CC	Kaghan	38	comfortable./If I was as snug as	Colby is, Lucasta,/I'd never have thought of
480 CC	Kaghan	5	/Colby's more cautious. You know,	Colby,/You and I ought to be in business
480 CC	Kaghan	19	in that. You know, Lucasta,/	Colby is a good judge of character./{L} You'd
480 CC	Lucasta	21	/Yourself, before you said that of	Colby./{K} Oh, I'm a good judge. Now, I'll tell
480 CC	Kaghan	23	the difference/Between ourselves and	Colby. You and me —/The one thing *we* want is
480 CC	Kaghan	25	is security/And respectability! Now	Colby/Doesn't really care about being
480 CC	Kaghan	27	/He was born and bred to it. I wasn't,	Colby./Do you know, I was a foundling? You
480 CC	Kaghan	38	we want the same things. But as for	Colby,/He's the sort of fellow who might chuck
482 CC	Lady E	8	the use of surnames altogether./But,	Colby, I hope you won't mind a gentle hint./I
483 CC	Lady E	24	I'm afraid I shall have to instruct you,	Colby./Photographic portraits — even in silver
484 CC	Lady E	30	were so commonplace./Do you know,	Colby, when I was a child/I had three
486 CC	Lady E	5	name is familiar. How old are you,	Colby?/{C} I'm twenty-five./{LE} Twenty-five.
486 CC	Lady E	31	interesting/Than you are aware of.	Colby ... {}/[*A knock on the door*]/{LE} Who's
486 CC	Claude	33	I was told that you were here with	Colby./So I came over instead of telephoning,/
487 CC	Claude	9	just in ways like this, Elizabeth,/That	Colby can be of greater help than Eggerson./I
487 CC	Claude	11	a speech for me./Oh, by the way,	Colby, how's the piano?/{C} It's a wonderful
487 CC	Lady E	20	proved. The truth has come out./It's	Colby. Colby is my lost child!/{SC} What? Your
487 CC	Lady E	20	The truth has come out./It's	Colby. Colby is my lost child!/{SC} What? Your child,
487 CC	Claude	33	what has led you to believe/That	Colby is your son?/{LE} Oh, I forgot/In my
487 CC	Lady E	37	on me. Mrs. Guzzard!/Claude,	Colby was brought up by a Mrs. Guzzard./{SC}
488 CC	Claude	6	piece it together./You've been asking	Colby about his family .../{LE} And when he
488 CC	Claude	12	on the past,/You began to think of	Colby as what your son would be,/And then
488 CC	Claude	19	/From what you expect. I'm afraid,	Colby,/It seems to me that we must let her
488 CC	Claude	30	that you would become fond of	Colby,/And that he might come to take the
488 CC	Claude	36	That's not what I meant. Elizabeth,/	Colby is *my* son./{LE} Quite impossible,
489 CC	Claude	1	/Perhaps you have a son. But it isn't	Colby./I ought to have told you, years ago./
489 CC	Claude	5	And I almost told you/About	Colby. I didn't. For such a foolish reason./
489 CC	Lady E	18	son./{LE} But why do you think that	Colby is your son?/{SC} Colby is the son of
489 CC	Claude	19	think that Colby is your son?/{SC}	Colby is the son of Mrs. Guzzard's sister,/Who
489 CC	Lady E	25	But where were you, Claude,/When	Colby was born?/{SC} Where was I? In Canada.
489 CC	Lady E	37	I was the mother and the child was	Colby;/And Mrs. Guzzard thought you would
490 CC	Lady E	8	But I'm sure it didn't./{LE} Oh,	Colby, doesn't your instinct tell you?/{SC} Yes,
490 CC	Lady E	26	be my parent./{LE} But a mother,	Colby, isn't that different?/There should always
491 CC	Lady E	3	a father and a mother./{LE} Stop,	Colby! Something has come to me./Claude! I
491 CC	Lady E	11	unreasonable claims upon you,	Colby./It's a good idea! Why should we not be
491 CC	Claude	17	you accept us both in that way,	Colby?/{C} I can only say what I feel at the
491 CC	Claude	37	at./{SC} Then what do you want,	Colby? What do you want?/Think of the future.
492 CC	Claude	9	/I would gladly have surrendered	Colby to you./But we must see Mrs. Guzzard.
492 CC	Claude	13	it./Let us say no more tonight. Now,	Colby,/Can you find some consolation at the
493 CC	Lady E	25	low one. Leave that in the corner/For	Colby. He won't want to be conspicuous,/Poor
494 CC	Lady E	2	night. I hardly slept at all./I wish that	Colby, somehow, might prove to be *your* son/
495 CC	Lady E	30	And so, I suppose, I wanted to forget/	Colby. But Colby is an artist./{SC} A musician./
495 CC	Lady E	30	I wanted to forget/	Colby. But Colby is an artist./{SC} A musician./I am a
495 CC	Claude	33	/I am a disappointed craftsman,/And	Colby is a disappointed composer./I should
496 CC	Lady E	11	Mrs. Guzzard tells us,/If it satisfies	Colby. Whatever happens/He shall be *our* son.
497 CC	Claude	11	to you./{SC} She'd been questioning	Colby about himself,/And he mentioned the
497 CC	Claude	20	the conclusion that her child must be	Colby,/So I told her the truth. But she cannot
497 CC	Lady E	24	/Or has been deceived, and that	Colby is my son./I feel sure he is. But I don't
497 CC	Claude	28	/{SC} That is perfectly correct. It is	Colby/Who is not satisfied with that solution./
498 CC	Claude	23	the other one./{SC} But *this* baby was	Colby./{LE} Of course it was Colby./{SC} But
498 CC	Lady E	24	was Colby./{LE} Of course it was	Colby./{SC} But Eggerson, you really can't ask
498 CC	Claude	37	/And when she arrives I will summon	Colby./I wanted you here first, to explain the
499 CC	Lucasta	10	Is this a meeting? I came to speak to	Colby./I'm sorry./{SC} Colby will be here./But
499 CC	Claude	12	to speak to Colby./I'm sorry./{SC}	Colby will be here./But you're not involved in
499 CC	Lucasta	16	time?/{L} I came to apologise/To	Colby. No matter. It'll do another time./Oh,
499 CC	Lucasta	32	That was why I took an interest/In	Colby. Because you thought he was too good
499 CC	Claude	33	he was too good for me./{SC} In	Colby!/{L} Why not? That's perfectly natural./
499 CC	Lucasta	35	perfectly natural./But I'm grateful to	Colby. But for Colby/I'd never have come to
499 CC	Lucasta	35	/But I'm grateful to	Colby. But for Colby/I'd never have come to appreciate B.
499 CC	Claude	37	have come to appreciate B./{SC} But	Colby! Lucasta, if I'd suspected this/I would
499 CC	Claude	38	this/I would have explained.	Colby is your brother./{E} Half-brother, Miss
500 CC	Claude	4	/{L} What do you mean?/{SC}	Colby is my son./{LE} That is what Sir Claude

500 CC	Claude	7	/My wife believes that Colby is *her* son./That is the reason for this
500 CC	Lucasta	27	give him —/Something that he needs. Colby doesn't need me,/He doesn't need
500 CC	Lucasta	38	that put me off. So I'm grateful to Colby./{SC} I don't know what's happened, but
501 CC	Claude	17	/And I certainly fail to understand Colby./{LE} But you and I, Claude, can
501 CC	Claude	36	left?/{SC} That's not a bad idea. If Colby agrees./{L} I trust you, Eggy. And I want
502 CC	m	1	*for the telephone*]/[*A knock. Enter* COLBY]/{C} Have I come too soon?/I'm afraid
502 CC	Lucasta	3	afraid I got impatient of waiting./{L} Colby! I've not come to interrupt your meeting./
502 CC	Lucasta	26	/That we can't judge you. That's you, Colby./{C} That's me, is it? I simply don't
503 CC	Lucasta	26	Quite right, Eggerson./{L} Good-bye, Colby./{C} Why do you say good-bye?/{L}
503 CC	Lucasta	28	you say good-bye?/{L} Good-bye to Colby as Lucasta knew him,/And good-bye to
503 CC	Lucasta	29	/And good-bye to the Lucasta whom Colby knew./We've changed since then: as you
503 CC	Lucasta	33	I hope. Yes, in any event,/Good-bye, Colby. {}/[*Exit* LUCASTA]/{C} Good-bye then,
504 CC	Guzzard	35	aware of./{MG} I suppose you mean Colby?/{LE} Yes. To do with Colby./{SC}
504 CC	Lady E	36	mean Colby?/{LE} Yes. To do with Colby./{SC} Elizabeth, you know we are to
505 CC	Guzzard	9	have heard about Mr. Eggerson from Colby./I am very happy to make his
505 CC	Guzzard	15	this meeting —/I suppose to do with Colby — so very confidential?/{E} Yes, that is
507 CC	Lady E	31	Claude, you see? You understand, Colby?/{SC} Don't be certain yet, Elizabeth./
507 CC	Lady E	34	/{LE} There is no doubt about it./Colby is my son./{MG} Your son, Lady
507 CC	Claude	39	My wife has convinced herself/That Colby is her son. I know he is *my* son./And I
508 CC	Lady E	12	training,/Should talk about straws! Colby is my son./{MG} In the circumstances, I
509 CC	Lady E	7	/But how did he come to be called Colby?/{SC} But, Elizabeth, it isn't Colby!/
509 CC	Claude	8	Colby?/{SC} But, Elizabeth, it isn't Colby!/Don't you see who it is?/{MG} My
509 CC	Guzzard	17	cousin/Who had died?/{MG} Yes, Colby, that is what I told you./{LE} So my child
509 CC	Lady E	19	I was sure of that./But I believe that Colby is Barnabas./{SC} No, Elizabeth,
509 CC	Lady E	37	/I'm getting so confused. What with Colby being Barnabas —/I mean, not Barnabas.
510 CC	m	2	suggestion, Mr. Simpkins. {}/[*Exit* COLBY]/{E} And now, if you agree, Lady
510 CC	m	15	to adjust myself to it. {}/[*Re-enter* COLBY, *with* KAGHAN *and* LUCASTA]/{C}
513 CC	Guzzard	9	/To be my daughter./{MG} Now, Colby,/I must ask *you* now, have you had your
513 CC	Claude	11	now, have you had your wish?/{SC} Colby only wanted to be sure of the truth./{C}
513 CC	Guzzard	39	Whose son would you wish to be, Colby:/Sir Claude's — or the son of some other
514 CC	Guzzard	2	man/Obscure and silent? A dead man, Colby./Be careful what you say./{C} A dead
514 CC	Guzzard	9	you./{SC} What do you mean?/{MG} Colby is not your son, Sir Claude./{C} Who was
514 CC	Claude	27	this fiction/In response to what Colby said he wanted./{E} I'll examine the
515 CC	Guzzard	22	/I am sacrificing my ambitions for Colby./I am sacrificing also my previous
515 CC	Claude	34	/This gives me freedom./{SC} But, Colby —/If this should be true — of course it
516 CC	Guzzard	14	organist./{MG} You should say, Colby, not very successful./{C} And I wish to
516 CC	Claude	16	I wish to follow my father./{SC} But, Colby:/Don't you remember a talk we had —/
518 CC	Guzzard	30	/{MG} I shall return to Teddington. Colby,/Will you get me a taxi to go to
518 CC	m	36	/I'm no longer needed here. {}/[*Exit* COLBY]/{SC} Mind? What do I mind?/{MG}
519 CC	Claude	5	What's happened? Have they gone? Is Colby coming back?/{LE} My poor Claude! {}/
519 CC	Kaghan	10	{E} Me, Mr. Kaghan?/{K} We wanted Colby to be something he wasn't./{LE} I

COLBY'S (7)

453 CC	Kaghan	25	in your existence/Until they met you. Colby's still reeling./It's going to be my
480 CC	Kaghan	5	/I've ever thought of investing in./Colby's more cautious. You know, Colby,/You
500 CC	Claude	9	/We're awaiting Mrs. Guzzard — Colby's aunt./{L} Colby's aunt? You make my
500 CC	Lucasta	10	Mrs. Guzzard — Colby's aunt./{L} Colby's aunt? You make my brain reel./{SC} I
500 CC	Lucasta	16	understand. What I do understand/Is Colby's behaviour. If he knew it./{SC} He knew
505 CC	Claude	3	/My confidential clerk. That is to say,/Colby's predecessor, who recently retired./Now
515 CC	Guzzard	27	nothing?/When I gave up my place as Colby's mother/I gave up something I could

COLCHESTER (1)

357 CP	Julia	32	She lives in Essex./{J} Anywhere near Colchester? Lavinia loves oysters./{E} No. In

COLD (24)

62 WL: Burial	44	famous clairvoyante,/Had a bad cold, nevertheless/Is known to be the wisest
67 WL: Fire S	185	not loud or long./But at my back in a cold blast I hear/The rattle of the bones, and
103 Journ Magi	1	POEMS/Journey of the Magi/'A cold coming we had of it,/Just the worst time of
141 Rannoch	5	crumbles, in the thin air/Moon cold or moon hot. The road winds in/
174 FQ: BurntN	107	Men and bits of paper, whirled by the cold wind/That blows before and after time,/
180 FQ: ECoker	110	the Directory of Directors,/And cold the sense and lost the motive of action./
183 FQ: ECoker	209	deeper communion/Through the dark cold and the empty desolation,/The wave cry,
191 FQ: Little	6	ice, on pond and ditches,/In windless cold that is the heart's heat,/Reflecting in a
194 FQ: Little	133	upon your lifetime's effort./First, the cold friction of expiring sense/Without
236 Cat Morgan	8	with a drink on the 'ouse/And a bit o' cold fish when I done me patrol./I ain't got
257 MC Tempts	5	A man may sit at meat, and feel the cold in his groin./{C} We have not been happy,
285 FR	Amy	12	fire. Will the spring never come? I am cold./{Ag} Wishwood was always a cold place,
285 FR	Agatha	13	cold./{Ag} Wishwood was always a cold place, Amy,/{I} I have always told Amy she

285 FR   Violet   21   the chilly deck-chair and the strong cold tea —/The strong cold stewed bad Indian
285 FR   Violet   22   and the strong cold tea —/The strong cold stewed bad Indian tea./{C} That's not
309 FR   Harry   39   know/How you should know it. Is the cold spring/Is the spring not an evil time, that
310 FR   Mary   1   excites us with lying voices?/{M} The cold spring now is the time/For the ache in the
315 FR Warburt   15   Wishwood./Wishwood was always a cold place, but healthy./It's only when I get an
332 FR   Agatha   24   summer day of unusual heat/For this cold country./{H} And then?/{Ag} There are
418 CP   Celia   5   I might still have it. Yet it leaves me cold./Perhaps that's just a part of my illness,/
438 CP   Reilly   14   /Bowel trouble, and the fear of lions,/Cold of the night and heat of the day, than we
502 CC Lucasta   22   mean insensitive!/But you're terribly cold. Or else you've some fire/To warm you,
530 ES Ld Clav   25   gone. What am I waiting for/In a cold and empty room before an empty grate?/
583 ES Monica   16   is under the beech tree. It is quiet and cold there./In becoming no one, he has become

COLD-HEARTED (1)
409 CP Lavinia   23   the fear of impotence./{L} You *are* cold-hearted, Edward./{R} So you say, Mrs.

COLDER (1)
263 MC Chorus   6   and darker the day, shorter and colder the night./Still and stifling the air: but a

COLLAPSED (1)
472 CC Lucasta   28   /And you felt that your life had all collapsed/And that you must learn to do

COLLAR (2)
 14 Prufrock   42   growing thin!')/My morning coat, my collar mounting firmly to the chin,/My necktie
589 Fable   78   /The spirit pulled him rudely by the collar,/And before any one could say 'O jiminy!'

COLLEAGUE (1)
509 CC Claude   22   /I have a very promising young colleague —/In fact, the young man who

COLLECTED (1)
 32 Hysteria   10   fragments of the afternoon might be collected, and I concentrated/my attention with

COLLECTING (1)
408 CP Reilly   28   disclose./I have my own method of collecting information/About my patients. You

COLLECTION (3)
466 CC Claude   24   day, perhaps,/I will show you my collection./{C} Thank you./{SC} And perhaps,
494 CC Lady E   40   make jugs and jars/Like those in your collection?/{SC} That's what I mean./{LE} But I
530 ES Ld Clav   39   hands in our pockets/To double this collection — it must be something showy'./This

COLLECTIVE (1)
202 War Poetry   1   on War Poetry/Not the expression of collective emotion/Imperfectly reflected in the

COLLEGE (3)
303 FR Agatha   31   than you wanted of that, when at college./{M} I might have known you'd throw
331 FR Agatha   23   /The efficient principal of a women's college —/That is the surface. There is a deeper/
340 FR Agatha   8   /Alone, among women, in a women's college,/Trying not to dislike women. Thirty

COLLEGES (1)
 44 Cook Egg   3   where I was sitting;/*Views of Oxford Colleges*/Lay on the table, with the knitting./

COLLISION (2)
304 FR   Mary   17   think you must have wanted to avoid collision./I suppose I could have gone, if I'd had
328 FR Charles   17   trying to extricate his car from the collision, Mr. Piper reversed/into a

COLOGNE (1)
 24 Rhapsody   58   rose,/That smells of dust and eau de Cologne,/She is alone/With all the old nocturnal

COLONEL (1)
229 Gus   40   could do it again —/Which an Indian Colonel pursued down a drain./And he thinks

COLONISTS (1)
592 Grad 2   1   let us yet put forth courageously./As colonists embarking from the strand/To seek

COLONNADE (1)
 61 WL: Burial   9   a shower of rain; we stopped in the colonnade,/And went on in sunlight, into the

COLONY (1)
155 Rock 3   41   why you come or where you go./A colony of cavies or a horde of active marmots/

COLOUR (11)
 83 Hollow Men   11   /Shape without form, shade without colour,/Paralysed force, gesture without motion;
 94 Ash-Wed 4   4   /Going in white and blue, in Mary's colour,/Talking of trivial things/In ignorance
 94 Ash-Wed 4   10   /In blue of larkspur, blue of Mary's colour,/Sovegna vos/Here are the years that
164 Rock 9   20   artist's eye, new life, new form, new colour./Out of the sea of sound the life of
240 MC Chorus   3   piece of earth, earth-colour, his own colour,/Preferring to pass unobserved./Now I
308 FR   Harry   3   most real is what I fear. The bright colour fades/Together with the unrecapturable
365 CP   Julia   3   —/I'm afraid I don't remember the colour,/But I'd know them, because one lens is
459 CC Lady E   20   not understand the importance of colour/For our spiritual life, Mr. Colby./
459 CC Lady E   23   I regret to say, does Eggerson./What colour have you chosen, between you?/{SC} I
464 CC Claude   2   to shape things. I loved form and colour/And I loved the material that the potter
483 CC Lady E   8   to have a look at the flat/To see if the colour scheme really suited you./I believe it

COLOURED (4)

64 WL: Chess	86	rich profusion./In vials of ivory and coloured glass/Unstopped, lurked her strange
64 WL: Chess	95	green and orange, framed by the coloured stone,/In which sad light a carvèd
167 Rock 10	29	/And lights directed through the coloured panes of windows/And light reflected
167 Rock 10	31	stone,/The gilded carven wood, the coloured fresco./Our gaze is submarine, our

COLOURS (3)

272 MC Chorus	31	for there are no objects, no tones,/No colours, no forms to distract, to divert the soul/
459 CC Lady E	19	done over./{LE} But all in the wrong colours, I'm sure. My husband/Does not
479 CC Kaghan	35	sure I like them. You must change the colours./It's all a bit too dim. You need

COLUMN (5)

83 Hollow Men	23	the eyes are/Sunlight on a broken column/There, is a tree swinging/And voices are
282 MC Chorus	2	places by the broken imperial column,/From such ground springs that which
301 FR Chorus	29	/So long as we are in the right column./We know about the railway accident/
369 CP Peter	31	of her merely as a name/In a society column, to find her there alone./Anyway, we
531 ES Ld Clav	14	in harness,/Would have occupied a column and a half/With an inset, a portrait

COM-MISSION-AIRE (1)

| 236 Cat Morgan | 2 | 'igh seas —/But now I've retired as a com-mission-aire:/And that's how you find me |

COMBAT (1)

| 343 FR Amy | 24 | I worry/To keep the tiles on the roof, combat the endless weather,/Resist the wind? |

COMBINATIONS (2)

| 68 WL: Fire S | 225 | window perilously spread/Her drying combinations touched by the sun's last rays,/On |
| 240 MC Priest2 | 30 | the French King/In ceaseless intrigue, combinations,/In conference, meetings accepted, |

COMBINED (1)

| 581 ES Charles | 6 | force to attract him: you and Monica combined./{LC} I shall not be here. You heard |

COMBING (1)

| 17 Prufrock | 127 | them riding seaward on the waves/Combing the white hair of the waves blown |

COME (290)

COMEDIANS (1)

| 218 Mung Rump | 2 | As knockabout clowns, quick-change comedians, tight-rope walkers and acrobats/ |

COMEDY (1)

| 570 ES Ld Clav | 38 | She no longer exists./Nor the musical comedy star, Maisie Montjoy./There is Mrs. |

COMES (42)

20 Portrait	84	right or wrong?/The October night comes down; returning as before/Except for a
22 Preludes	14	lighting of the lamps./The morning comes to consciousness/Of faint stale smells of
24 Rhapsody	62	across her brain.'/The reminiscence comes/Of sunless dry geraniums/And dust in
117 SP Doris	18	can't be sure./It just depends on what comes next./You've got to *think* when you read
117 SP Dusty	22	you've a touch with the cards/What comes next?/{Do} What comes next. It's the six.
117 SP Doris	23	cards/What comes next?/{Do} What comes next. It's the six./{Du} 'A quarrel. An
127 Cor1 March	12	our stools and our sausages./What comes first? Can you see? Tell us. It is/5,800,000
167 Rock 10	34	We see the light but see not whence it comes./O Light Invisible, we glorify Thee!/In
195 FQ: Little	163	to our own field of action/And comes to find that action of little importance/
235 Ad-dress	48	/Whom I have often met before/(He comes to see me in my flat)/I greet him with an
241 MC Mess	30	to express a certain incredulity./He comes in pride and sorrow, affirming all his
258 MC Thomas	17	all things equally desirable./Ambition comes when early force is spent/And when we
258 MC Thomas	19	longer all things possible./Ambition comes behind and unobservable./Sin grows with
266 MC Thomas	3	may be unexpected/When it arrives. It comes when we are/Engrossed with matters of
285 FR Amy	4	October to June,/And the swallow comes too soon and the spring will be over/And
286 FR Charles	30	GERALD *whisky*.]/{C} That's what it comes to. {}/[*Lights a cigarette*]/{I} The younger
289 FR Agatha	1	*jolly* corner./When the loop in time comes — and it does not come for everybody —
298 FR Charles	2	/In taking hold of anything that comes to hand./If you are interested in helping
309 FR Harry	31	yet you seem/Like someone who comes from a very long distance,/Or the distant
336 FR Agatha	23	*had occupied*.]/{Ag} A curse comes to being/As a child is formed./In both,
342 FR Mary	18	another./{M} Oh, but it is the danger comes from another!/Can you not stop him?
355 CP Julia	17	*room*]/{J} No, we'll wait until Edward comes back into the room./Now I want to relax,
372 CP Peter	32	Give my love to Lavinia/When she comes back ... but, if you don't mind,/I'd rather
382 CP Celia	20	nothing more inside it than what comes out/When you tread on a beetle./{E}
386 CP Reilly	7	What visitors?/{UG} Whoever comes. The strangers./As for myself, I shall take
395 CP Edward	25	you changed?/{E} The change that comes/From seeing oneself through the eyes of
447 CC Claude	14	but rather inconvenient/When it comes to appointing a successor./Makes it very
449 CC Eggers	31	/But will you tell me this: if it comes to the point/At which Lady Elizabeth
450 CC Claude	31	leave you now. But when Eggerson comes back/With Lady Elizabeth, I will rejoin
452 CC Lucasta	35	I suppose I asked for it./That's what comes of being cursed with a name like Angel./
454 CC Lucasta	5	propose to be on the scene when *she* comes./{K} And I don't propose to leave you
462 CC Claude	11	/{SC} As if you were her son? If she comes to think of you/As the kind of man that
465 CC Claude	26	of utter exhaustion and peace/Which comes in dying to give something life .../I intend

473 CC	Colby	34	doesn't feel alone there. And when he comes out/He has marrows, or beetroot, or peas
475 CC	Lucasta	16	one really is./And the reason why that comes about, perhaps .../{C} Is, beginning to
488 CC	Claude	17	I'm sorry, Elizabeth. If Mrs. Guzzard comes/To make her confession, it will be very
511 CC	Lady E	13	good at figures. Your business ability/Comes, I suppose, from my side of the family./
532 ES	Ld Clav	15	heard of this Señor Gomez/But he comes with a letter of introduction/From a man
544 ES	Ld Clav	19	one has grown to consciousness/It comes less often./I hope this benignant sunshine
563 ES	Ld Clav	4	Is he a foreigner?/{LC} He comes from some place in Central America./
580 ES	Ld Clav	36	/{LC} Monica my dear,/What you say comes home to me. I fear for Michael;/
581 ES	Ld Clav	1	for something better./And when he comes back, if he does come back,/I know that

COMETH (1)

162 Rock 8		6	have they defiled./Who is this that cometh from Edom?/He has trodden the

COMETS (1)

178 FQ: ECoker		64	/Until the Sun and Moon go down/Comets weep and Leonids fly/Hunt the heavens

COMFORT (2)

385 CP	Reilly	14	enfolded/Your childhood years in comfort, mirth, security —/If they returned,
541 ES	Gomez	23	or Zürich/Would keep me in comfort for the rest of my life./Really, Dick,

COMFORTABLE (7)

291 FR	Charles	2	have been in St. James's Street, in a comfortable chair rather nearer the fire./{I} I
305 FR	Mary	22	you had just arrived./Did you have a comfortable journey?/{H} Not very./But, at
401 CP	Reilly	29	/I think that you will find that chair comfortable./{E} You knew,/Before I began to
479 CC	Kaghan	37	/But otherwise, it looks pretty comfortable./If I was as snug as Colby is,
534 ES	Gomez	32	/Find themselves in gaol and not very comfortable,/Or before a firing squad./You
544 ES	Monica	4	show no curiosity;/The beds are comfortable, the hot water is hot,/They give us
554 ES	Piggott	21	came to see that Lord Claverton was comfortable:/We can't allow him to tire himself

COMFORTABLY (1)

550 ES	Ld Clav	25	successful .../I mean, that he left you comfortably provided for?/{MC} Well, Richard,

COMFY (1)

547 ES	Piggott	7	/There, now you look more comfy. Don't let him stay out late/In the

COMIC (1)

602 Humoresque		8	of face that we forget)/Pinched in a comic, dull grimace;/Half bullying, half

COMICS (1)

20 Portrait		72	any morning in the park/Reading the comics and the sporting page./Particularly I

COMING (77)

20 Portrait		90	/You hardly know when you are coming back,/You will find so much to learn.'/
21 Portrait		117	sitting pen in hand/With the smoke coming down above the housetops;/Doubtful,
61 WL: Burial		8	dried tubers./Summer surprised us, coming over the Starnbergersee/With a shower
65 WL: Chess		142	PLEASE ITS TIME/Now Albert's coming back, make yourself a bit smart./He'll
103 Journ Magi		1	POEMS/Journey of the Magi/'A cold coming we had of it,/Just the worst time of the
111 Xmas Trees		34	remind us of the end/And the first coming of the second coming./UNFINISHED
111 Xmas Trees		34	/And the first coming of the second coming./UNFINISHED POEMS/Sweeney
125 SA	Chorus	36	dream and/you've got the hoo-ha's coming to you./Hoo hoo hoo/You dreamt you
127 Cor1 March		8	did it matter, on such a day?/Are they coming? No, not yet. You can see some eagles.
127 Cor1 March		9	the trumpets./Here they come. Is he coming?/The natural wakeful life of our Ego is a
155 Rock 3		57	desert./O my soul, be prepared for the coming of the Stranger,/Be prepared for him
239 MC	Chorus	13	New Year waits, destiny waits for the coming./Who has stretched out his hand to the
240 MC	Chorus	15	for another October?/Some malady is coming upon us. We wait, we wait,/And the
241 MC	Mess	15	in haste/To give you notice of his coming, as much as possible,/That you may
245 MC	Priest2	23	Lord, forgive me, I did not see you coming,/Engrossed by the chatter of these
245 MC	Priest2	29	better prepared our hearts for your coming,/Than seven days could make ready
256 MC	Priests	27	sea to subside, in the night/Abide the coming of day, when the traveller may find his
260 MC	Thomas	9	at/the same moment we rejoice in His coming for the salvation of men, and/offer
270 MC	Chorus	12	I not known, not known/What was coming to be? It was here, in the kitchen, in the
271 MC	Priests	21	cloister. No time to waste. They are coming back, armed. To the altar, to the altar./
271 MC	Thomas	22	altar./{T} All my life they have been coming, these feet. All my life/I have waited.
271 MC	Priests	26	my will./{3P} My Lord, they are coming. They will break through presently./You
279 MC	Knight1	9	I think that/Richard Brito, coming as he does of a family distinguished for
291 FR	Amy	11	if not Arthur. Hark, there is someone coming:/Yes, it must be John. {}/[*Enter*
292 FR	Harry	5	sickly tropical night, I knew they were coming./In Italy, from behind the nightingale's
292 FR	Amy	17	have been looking forward to your coming:/Would you like to have them in after
292 FR	Ivy	38	Because she preferred to wait for your coming./{V} And time and time again I have
295 FR	Amy	33	you are very tired/And overwrought. Coming so far/And making such haste, the
302 FR	Amy	17	have gone wrong/With both of them, coming from different directions./Well, we must
303 FR	Mary	24	/I am very glad if Dr. Warburton is coming./I shall have to sit between Arthur and
307 FR	Harry	11	the secret./{H} Not then. But later, coming back from school/For the holidays,
308 FR	Mary	16	of it./You hoped for something, in coming back to Wishwood,/Or you would not

COMMEND (2)
275 MC Thomas 20 martyr Denys, and to all the Saints, I commend my cause and that of the Church. {}/
449 CC Eggers 16 /{E} I'm sure I shall be very happy to commend him./{SC} You mustn't overdo it! But
COMMENDABLE (1)
195 FQ: Little 172 this place,/And of people, not wholly commendable,/Of no immediate kin or
COMMENT (1)
 70 WL: Fire S 299 promised "a new start."/I made no comment. What should I resent?'/'On Margate
COMMENTS (1)
326 FR Violet 32 on what you say, Harry;/My comments are not always welcome in this
COMMERCE (2)
184 FQ: DrySal 4 untrustworthy, as a conveyor of commerce;/Then only a problem confronting
197 FQ: Little 222 diffident nor ostentatious,/An easy commerce of the old and the new,/The common
COMMERCIAL (1)
111 Xmas Trees 3 /The social, the torpid, the patently commercial,/The rowdy (the pubs being open
COMMISSION (5)
129 Cor2 State 16 has been appointed to nominate a commission of engineers/To consider the Water
129 Cor2 State 18 /To consider the Water Supply./A commission is appointed/For Public Works,
129 Cor2 State 20 of rebuilding the fortifications./A commission is appointed/To confer with a
129 Cor2 State 21 appointed/To confer with a Volscian commission/About perpetual peace: the
429 CP Edward 21 fit to eat./{E} And what has your commission accomplished?/{A} We have just
COMMISSIONS (3)
154 Rock 3 8 given you my Law, and you set up commissions,/I have given you lips, to express
432 CP Reilly 31 yes, we have met./{R} On several commissions./{J} We've been having such an
576 ES Michael 16 good screw, and some pickings in commissions./He's made a fortune there. San
COMMITTEE (5)
129 Cor2 State 16 /And one week's leave a year./A committee has been appointed to nominate a
129 Cor2 State 23 and smiths/Have appointed a joint committee to protest against the reduction of
129 Cor2 State 52 /What shall I cry?/We demand a committee, a representative committee, a
129 Cor2 State 52 demand a committee, a representative committee, a committee of investigation/
129 Cor2 State 52 a representative committee, a committee of investigation/RESIGN RESIGN
COMMITTEES (7)
129 Cor2 State 8 /The first thing to do is to form the committees:/The consultative councils, the
129 Cor2 State 9 consultative councils, the standing committees, select committees and
129 Cor2 State 9 the standing committees, select committees and sub-committees./One secretary
129 Cor2 State 10 /One secretary will do for several committees./What shall I cry?/Arthur Edward
180 FQ: ECoker 106 civil servants, chairmen of many committees,/Industrial lords and petty
426 CP Edward 15 no more parties./{E} And no more committees./{L} Can we get away soon?/{E} By
460 CC Lady E 29 /And then I shall tell you about my committees./I must go and rest now./{SC} Yes,
COMMODIOUS (1)
178 FQ: ECoker 31 matrimonie —/A dignified and commodious sacrament./Two and two,
COMMON (31)
 20 Portrait 80 and tired/Reiterates some worn-out common song/With the smell of hyacinths
155 Rock 3 65 the mountains,/Dividing the stars into common and preferred,/Engaged in devising the
194 FQ: Little 105 preceded./And so, compliant to the common wind,/Too strange to each other for
195 FQ: Little 175 of peculiar genius,/All touched by a common genius,/United in the strife which
197 FQ: Little 223 of the old and the new,/The common word exact without vulgarity,/The
203 Indians 19 same story of you:/Of action with a common purpose, action/None the less fruitful
205 de la Mare 30 deceptive cadences/Wherewith the common measure is refined;/By conscious art
602 Humoresque 6 deceasèd marionette/I rather liked: a common face,/(The kind of face that we forget)/
242 MC Mess 10 like an end, or like a beginning./It is common knowledge that when the Archbishop/
275 MC Chorus 27 /Can I look again at the day and its common things, and see them all smeared with
282 MC Chorus 6 acknowledge ourselves as type of the common man,/Of the men and women who shut
286 FR Gerald 8 /For a man who can exercise a little common prudence;/And your servants look
301 FR Chorus 18 the private shall be made public, the common photographer/Flashlight for the
331 FR Harry 32 you for strength. Now I think it is/A common pursuit of liberation./{Ag} Your father
333 FR Agatha 3 him./I can take no credit for a little common sense,/He would have bungled it./I did
367 CP Edward 11 and Celia?/Have you anything in common, do you think?/{P} It seemed to me we
367 CP Peter 12 seemed to me we had a great deal in common./We're both of us artists./{E} I never
367 CP Edward 19 that interests both of us./{E} A common interest in the moving pictures/
367 CP Peter 32 is, I thought we had a great deal in common/And I think she thought so too./{E}
402 CP Reilly 35 Oh, dear yes; this is serious. A very common malady./Very prevalent indeed./{E} I
407 CP Reilly 16 you./I do not trouble myself with the common cheat,/Or with the insuperably,
409 CP Reilly 7 both of you/How much you have in common. Indeed, I consider/That you are
410 CP Reilly 7 to see, I hope,/How much you have in common. The same isolation./A man who finds
410 CP Lavinia 10 It seems to me that what we have in common/Might be just enough to make us

417 CP   Reilly   27   regret it,/Maintain themselves by the common routine,/Learn to avoid excessive
501 CC   Lucasta   5   think we're suited because we're both common./B. knows you think him common.
501 CC   Lucasta   6   common./B. knows you think him common. And so he pretends/To be very
501 CC   Lucasta   7   And so he pretends/To be very common, because he knows you think so./*You*
504 CC   Lady E   34   I know about you:/We have more in common than you are aware of./{MG} I
506 CC   Guzzard 29   /{MG} Indeed? It is not a very common name./{E} That is what impressed her.
578 ES   Michael 23   never really seemed to have much in common./I remember, when I came home for
COMMONLY (1)
219 Mung Rump   37   a loud *ping*/From a vase which was commonly said to be Ming —/Then the family
COMMONPLACE (4)
230 Bust Jones   7   /In his coat of fastidious black:/No commonplace mousers have such well-cut
307 FR   Mary   27   /But why should I talk about my commonplace troubles?/They must seem very
484 CC   Lady E   29   feel an outcast. And yet they were so commonplace./Do you know, Colby, when I
495 CC   Lady E   28   I wanted to escape from./He was so commonplace! I wanted to forget him,/And so,
COMMUNICATE (3)
189 FQ: DrySal 188 of the sea bell's/Perpetual angelus./To communicate with Mars, converse with spirits,/
494 CC   Claude   22   To me, it was a burden./You can't communicate an inspiration,/Like that, by force
558 ES   Michael   9   Called me a gambler!/Said he'd communicate with you about it./{LC} That
COMMUNICATION (3)
192 FQ: Little   52   /They can tell you, being dead: the communication/Of the dead is tongued with fire
325 FR   Agatha   7   Harry to establish/If he can, some communication with his mother./{V} I do not
336 FR   Harry   9   the air?/Do you? don't you? a communication, a scent/Direct to the brain ...
COMMUNION (3)
164 Rock 9   15   /And then let us learn the joyful communion of saints./The soul of Man must
183 FQ: ECoker 208   /For a further union, a deeper communion/Through the dark cold and the
419 CP   Reilly   2   /Each way means loneliness — and communion./Both ways avoid the final
COMMUNISTS (1)
328 FR   Gerald   26   game with me.'"/{G} This is what the Communists make capital out of./{C} There's a
COMMUNITY (3)
152 Rock 2   39   /There is no life that is not in community,/And no community not lived in
152 Rock 2   40   life that is not in community,/And no community not lived in praise of GOD./Even
155 Rock 3   55   money from each other'? or 'This is a community'?/And the Stranger will depart and
COMPANIES (3)
480 CC   Kaghan 31   City,/On the boards of all the solidest companies:/Because I've no background — no
528 ES   Monica 13   /And later, as chairman of public companies,/Always his privacy has been
538 ES   Gomez   39   Director of a bank/And chairman of companies. You looked the part —/Cut out to
COMPANIONS (1)
129 Cor2 State   3   All flesh is grass: comprehending/The Companions of the Bath, the Knights of the
COMPANIONSHIP (1)
542 ES   Ld Clav 25   You would hardly have welcomed my companionship./{G} Neatly argued, and almost
COMPANY (16)
261 MC   Thomas 22   who has been/elevated to the company of the Saints: for that would be simply
345 FR   Amy   26   in a harmless way;/I prefer your company to that of any of the others/Just to
379 CP   Peter   36   that was something different/From company or solitude. And we sometimes had
451 CC   Colby   16   him very helpful/And very good company apart from business./{E} Oh yes, Mr.
451 CC   Eggers 17   /{E} Oh yes, Mr. Kaghan is very good company./He makes me laugh sometimes. I
483 CC   Colby   19   At the moment/I'm working on a company report./{LE} I hadn't reckoned on
486 CC   Claude 36   speech/At the dinner of the Potters' Company./{C} That's tomorrow night, I believe.
492 CC   Colby   18   /About your speech for the Potters' Company/Tomorrow night. I must get to work
492 CC   Claude 31   Not that the Members/Of the Potters' Company know anything at all/About ceramics
492 CC   Claude 35   things that would surprise the Potters' Company/If I told them what I was really
526 ES   Charles 36   /That you don't really care for any company but his!/{M} You're not to assume
542 ES   Gomez   9   /All I want is as much of your company,/So long as I stay here, as I can get./
542 ES   Ld Clav 13   you call it friendship to impose your company/On a man by threats? Why keep up
542 ES   Ld Clav 29   /To give you the pleasure of my company?/{G} Oh, I can wait, Dick. You'll
569 ES   Ld Clav 28   you/Except your friendship and your company./He's a very rich man. And she's a
569 ES   Ld Clav 30   merely blackmail you to get your company/I'm afraid the law can't touch them./
COMPARE (1)
255 MC   Tempt4   7   have thought of that too./What can compare with glory of Saints/Dwelling forever
COMPARED (1)
255 MC   Tempt4 11   earthly pride, that is not poverty/Compared with richness of heavenly grandeur?/
COMPARISONS (1)
294 FR   Harry   6   experience, but trying to give you/Comparisons in a more familiar medium. I am
COMPASSING (1)
49 Hippopot   10   /The hippo's feeble steps may err/In compassing material ends,/While the True

COMPASSION (4)

181 FQ: ECoker	152	the bleeding hands we feel/The sharp compassion of the healer's art/Resolving the
416 CP Reilly	34	in a forest, wanting to go home./{R} Compassion may be already a clue/Towards
529 ES Charles	11	/{C} Is that wistfulness,/Compassion, or ... envy?/{M} Envy is
529 ES Monica	15	of being envious./It's all we can ask if compassion and wistfulness .../And tenderness,

COMPASSIONATE (1)

| 334 FR Harry | 32 | fonder of my mother —/More compassionate at least — by understanding./ |

COMPEL (2)

| 194 FQ: Little | 104 | forming; yet the words sufficed/To compel the recognition they preceded./And so, |
| 254 MC Tempt4 | 25 | have more power than kings to compel you./You have also thought, sometimes |

COMPELLED (6)

34 Figlia	18	away, but with the autumn weather/Compelled my imagination many days,/Many
588 Fable	32	uninvited, then, of course,/I'll be compelled to keep them off by force.'/He
239 MC Chorus	7	presage of an act/Which our eyes are compelled to witness, has forced our feet/
310 FR Mary	26	/And what of the terrified spirit/Compelled to be reborn/To rise toward the
392 CP Edward	31	aunt come to live in Essex?/{E} Julia compelled me to make her live somewhere./{L} I
394 CP Lavinia	25	danger,/Yet something, or somebody, compelled me to come./And why did you want

COMPELS (2)

| 52 Whispers | 22 | bliss./The couched Brazilian jaguar/Compels the scampering marmoset/With subtle |
| 337 FR Agatha | 12 | place./Delay, and it is lost. Love compels cruelty/To those who do not |

COMPETENT (3)

286 FR Amy	10	better./{A} My servants are perfectly competent, Gerald./I can still see to that./{V}
381 CP Celia	3	in *my* future. I only hope you're competent/To manage your own. But if you are
465 CC Claude	16	second-rate potter? To be, at best,/A competent copier, possessed by the craving/To

COMPETITION (1)

| 182 FQ: ECoker | 187 | hope/To emulate — but there is no competition —/There is only the fight to recover |

COMPILE (1)

| 240 MC Chorus | 2 | merchant, shy and cautious, tries to compile a little fortune,/And the labourer bends |

COMPLACENCY (1)

| 136 5FingerEx3 | 14 | worm shall try/Our well-preserved complacency./*Lines to Ralph Hodgson Esqre.*/ |

COMPLAIN (3)

360 CP Edward	31	to be jealous?/{E} She had nothing to complain of in my behaviour./{UG} Then no
394 CP Edward	3	infuriating,/The way you *didn't* complain .../{L} It was you who complained/Of
496 CC Eggers	20	/Isn't that like the ladies! She used to complain/At my being up in London five or six

COMPLAINED (3)

394 CP Lavinia	1	be of use to you socially .../{L} I *never* complained./{E} No; and it was perfectly
394 CP Lavinia	4	complain .../{L} It was you who complained/Of seeing nobody but solicitors and
476 CC Lucasta	36	being turned out when the neighbours complained./Oh of course Claude gave her

COMPLAINT (2)

| 300 FRDowning | 11 | /{Do} Always, Sir./That was just my complaint against my Lady./It's my opinion |
| 300 FRDowning | 16 | leave him alone./And there's my complaint against these ocean liners/With all |

COMPLETE (6)

197 FQ: Little	225	word precise but not pedantic,/The complete consort dancing together)/Every
198 FQ: Little	255	here, now, always —/A condition of complete simplicity/(Costing not less than
271 MC Thomas	13	the figure of God's purpose is made complete./You shall forget these things, toiling
281 MC Chorus	11	not exist; and their denial is never complete, for if it were so, they would not exist./
349 FR Agatha	14	/{Ag} A curse is slow in coming/To complete fruition/It cannot be hurried/And it
529 ES Monica	25	/You know what the doctors said: complete relaxation/And to think about

COMPLETED (2)

| 165 Rock 9 | 37 | body./Now you shall see the Temple completed:/After much striving, after many |
| 276 MC | m 18 | wash them! {}/[*The* KNIGHTS, *having completed the murder, advance to the front of the* |

COMPLETELY (15)

195 FQ: Little	153	which often look alike/Yet differ completely, flourish in the same hedgerow:/
277 MC Knight3	26	give us/at least the credit for being completely disinterested in this business./I think
277 MC Knight1	30	/argument is this: that we have been completely disinterested. But/our act itself needs
279 MC Knight4	22	moment he/became Archbishop, he completely reversed his policy; he showed/
331 FR Harry	29	/{H} I have thought of you as the completely strong,/The liberated from the
353 CP Alex	1	GUEST./{A} You've missed the point completely, Julia:/There *were* no tigers. *That*
387 CP Edward	8	I wish I understood anything./I'm completely in the dark./{C} But it's all so
408 CP Lavinia	1	breakdown./{L} But it's true! I was completely prostrated;/Even if I have made a
408 CP Reilly	3	recovery./{R} Certainly, you were completely prostrated,/And certainly, you have
447 CC Claude	10	you know she regards you — well, completely/As one of the household./{E} That's
499 CC Eggers	8	understand, Sir Claude: I understand completely. {}/[*A knock on the door*]/{SC} Good
540 ES Gomez	32	with us (what were their names?/I've completely forgotten them) you didn't want
570 ES Ld Clav	14	of your mother, when she lay dying:/Completely without interest in the life that lay

570 ES Ld Clav 15   in the life that lay behind her/And completely indifferent to whatever lay ahead of
577 ES Charles 15   father?/Remember, you put yourself completely in the power/Of a man you don't
COMPLETING (1)
350 FR Agatha 16   expiation/Round and round the circle/Completing the charm/So the knot be
COMPLETION (2)
173 FQ: BurntN 79   old made explicit, understood/In the completion of its partial ecstasy,/The resolution
333 FR Harry 19   tree falls. And in the end/That is the completion which at the beginning/Would have
COMPLEX (1)
276 MC Knight1 30   you the merits of this extremely complex problem. I/shall call upon our eldest
COMPLIANT (1)
194 FQ: Little 105   recognition they preceded./And so, compliant to the common wind,/Too strange to
COMPLICATED (3)
182 FQ: ECoker 193   becomes stranger, the pattern more complicated/Of dead and living. Not the intense
227 Macavity 34   of his thumbs,/Or engaged in doing complicated long division sums./Macavity,
456 CC Eggers 27   /And forgets all about it. That can be complicated/And very costly. I've had some rare
COMPLICATING (1)
396 CP Lavinia 37   me away from myself./{L} You're complicating what is in fact very simple./But
COMPLICATIONS (2)
406 CP Edward 26   anyone in my life/With fewer mental complications than you;/You're stronger than a
429 CP Alex 25   /There are too many international complications./Eventually, there may be an
COMPLIMENT (15)
287 FR Mary 9   /I'm afraid that I don't deserve the compliment:/I don't belong to any generation. {}
304 FR Mary 23   wanted me for Harry —/Not such a compliment: she only wanted/To have a tame
393 CP Edward 26   course I didn't mind./I meant it as a compliment./{L} You meant it as a compliment!
393 CP Lavinia 27   a compliment./{L} You meant it as a compliment!/And you were so considerate,
425 CP Lavinia 3   it's the first time you've paid me a compliment/*Before* a party? And that's when
440 CP Edward 27   /{E} I never shall learn how to pay a compliment./{L} What you should have done
440 CP Lavinia 31   One sometimes likes to hear the same compliment twice./{E} And now for the party./
447 CC Eggers 12   of the household./{E} That's a great compliment./{SC} And well deserved; but rather
470 CC Lucasta 30   Musicals. Do you think it's any compliment/To invite a woman to something
470 CC Lucasta 32   *you* wouldn't like it? That's not a compliment:/That's just being ... patronising.
470 CC Lucasta 34   me/To something you like — that *is* a compliment./It shows you want to educate me./
471 CC Lucasta 32   that is, to know when you're paying a compliment./*That* was a compliment. And a
471 CC Lucasta 33   paying a compliment./*That* was a compliment. And a very clever one./{C} I admit
535 ES Ld Clav 4   You really trust me? I appreciate the compliment./{G} Which you're sure you
549 ES Carghil 2   /I wish you could have paid *me* that compliment, Richard./{LC} What!/{MC} Don't
COMPLIMENTARY (1)
314 FR Warburt 22   a pessimistic view/Which is hardly complimentary to my profession./But I
COMPLIMENTS (1)
481 CC Lucasta 7   /{L} You're both very good at paying compliments;/But I remarked that I was hungry.
COMPOSED (1)
 18 Portrait 21   rare and strange it is, to find/In a life composed so much, so much of odds and ends,/
COMPOSER (2)
465 CC Colby 39   I should like to have written,/As the composer heard it when it came to him;/But
495 CC Claude 33   /And Colby is a disappointed composer./I should have been a second-rate
COMPOSERS (1)
465 CC Colby 36   /I'm only a shadow of the great composers./Always, when I play to myself,/I
COMPOSES (1)
548 ES 2m 14   *She sits in a deckchair nearby, composes/herself and takes out her knitting./*
COMPOUND (1)
193 FQ: Little 97   baked features/The eyes of a familiar compound ghost/Both intimate and
COMPREHEND (1)
194 FQ: Little 112   wonder. Therefore speak:/I may not comprehend, may not remember.'/And he: 'I
COMPREHENDING (1)
129 Cor2 State 2   what shall I cry?/All flesh is grass: comprehending/The Companions of the Bath,
COMPREHENSION (1)
308 FR Mary 11   you contradict yourself:/That sudden comprehension of the death of hope/Of which
COMPROMISE (2)
397 CP Lavinia 34   /But, being divided, you will tend to compromise,/And your sort of compromise will
397 CP Lavinia 35   to compromise,/And your sort of compromise will be the old one./{E} You don't
COMPTON-SMITH (1)
291 FR Gerald 4   /{G} I might have been staying with Compton-Smith, down at his place in Dorset./
COMPULSION (1)
173 FQ: BurntN 74   release from the inner/And the outer compulsion, yet surrounded/By a grace of sense,

COMPUNCTION (2)
333 FR   Agatha   8 /Most people would not have felt that compunction/If they felt no other. But I wanted
578 ES Ld Clav   16   can I feel anything but sorrow and compunction?/{M} Oh Michael, remember,
CONCEAL (8)
187 FQ: DrySal 121   waters,/Waves wash over it, fogs conceal it;/On a halcyon day it is merely a
338 FR   Harry   12   only speak/So you may not think I conceal an explanation,/And to tell you that I
385 CP   Reilly 23   nothing./To try to forget is to try to conceal./{E} There are certainly things I should
568 ES Ld Clav 10 very next moment,/Episodes we try to conceal from the world./Has there been nothing
568 ES Charles 16   there's nothing I would ever wish to conceal from you./{LC} If there's nothing, truly
568 ES Ld Clav 20   /And if there is nothing that you conceal from *her*/However important you may
568 ES Ld Clav 22   important you may consider it/To conceal from the rest of the world — your soul
571 ES Monica 27   know./Why should you wish to conceal from those who love you/What is
CONCEALING (2)
361 CP   Edward 18   /By telling someone what I'd been concealing./I don't think I want to know who
407 CP   Reilly 33   /{R} You were lying to me/By concealing your relations with Miss Coplestone.
CONCEALMENT (1)
408 CP   Edward 10 to have been much more successful at concealment/Than I was. Now I wonder who it
CONCEIT (1)
471 CC   Colby 17   were so conceited./{C} No, it's not conceit — the reason that I'm thinking of./It's
CONCEITED (2)
380 CP   Celia   27 found him less interesting, and rather conceited./But why should we talk about Peter?
471 CC Lucasta 16 you?/I didn't know that you were so conceited./{C} No, it's not conceit — the reason
CONCEIVABLE (1)
349 FR   Chorus   5 and all of these questions/There is no conceivable answer./We have suffered far more
CONCEIVE (1)
330 FR   Harry   5   /John is the only one of us I can conceive/As settling down to make himself at
CONCENTRATED (3)
 32 Hysteria   10   afternoon might be collected, and I concentrated/my attention with careful subtlety
 91 Ash-Wed 2   21   so I would forget/Thus devoted, concentrated in purpose. And God said/
111 Xmas Trees   30 memories of annual emotion/May be concentrated into a great joy/Which shall be
CONCENTRATES (1)
 56 Swee Night   22 vertebrate in brown/Contracts and concentrates, withdraws;/Rachel *née*
CONCENTRATING (1)
213 Growltiger   30   of the vessel Growltiger sate alone,/Concentrating his attention on the Lady
CONCENTRATION (3)
167 Rock 10   38   or play./We tire of distraction or concentration, we sleep and are glad to sleep,/
173 FQ: BurntN   76   moving,/*Erhebung* without motion, concentration/Without elimination, both a new
174 FQ: BurntN 106   of meaning/Tumid apathy with no concentration/Men and bits of paper, whirled
CONCEPTION (2)
 85 Hollow Men   78   *Thine is the Kingdom*/Between the conception/And the creation/Between the
202 War Poetry   22   one for the other. But the abstract conception/Of private experience at its greatest
CONCERN (6)
194 FQ: Little 128 my body on a distant shore./Since our concern was speech, and speech impelled us/To
343 FR   Amy   29 broker, agent? Why should I?/It is no concern of the body in the tomb/To bother
406 CP   Edward   2 know — I mean to say,/That doesn't concern you./{L} In that case, Edward,/I don't
406 CP Lavinia   4   Edward,/I don't think your clothes concern me either. {}/[*To* REILLY]/{L} I
513 CC   Claude   7 Claude Mulhammer./{SC} That is *my* concern — that she shall be satisfied/To be my
515 CC Guzzard   1   /That you did not know. It did not concern you./As I have just said, my sister died/
CONCERNED (10)
189 FQ: DrySal 176   has to do with fish, and/Those concerned with every lawful traffic/And those
210 Old Gumbie   9   the basement to creep./She is deeply concerned with the ways of the mice —/Their
301 FR   Gerald 22   worldly associates./{G} Ivy is only concerned for herself, and her credit among her
318 FR Warburt   20   may be quite right, but what we are concerned with/Now, is your mother's
318 FR   Harry 24   there any difference!/How can we be concerned with the past/And not with the
395 CP Lavinia 22   holidays./You were always intensely concerned with yourself;/And if other people
411 CP   Reilly 30   the future of the others you are not concerned./{L} I think you have answered my
436 CP   Julia 16 for the films:/That is, when you're not concerned with yourself/But just being an eye.
447 CC   Claude 27   medical orders./She's always been concerned about your state of health,/So she'll
479 CC Lucasta   8 your protection racket/So far as I'm concerned, B. And as for Lizzie,/You'd better
CONCERNS (2)
405 CP   Reilly 33   that is a question which naturally concerns you./{E} I am not going to any
505 CC Eggers   21 surmised, with Mr. Simpkins./It also concerns a problem of paternity./{LE} Or of
CONCERT (6)
 18 Portrait   13 /That is rubbed and questioned in the concert room.'/— And so the conversation slips
369 CP   Peter   25 her again a few days later/Alone at a concert. And I was alone./I've always gone to

| 469 CC | Lucasta | 19 | you believe/That I've never been to a concert in my life?/I only go to shows when |

469 CC   Lucasta 19   you believe/That I've never been to a concert in my life?/I only go to shows when
469 CC   Lucasta 21   /And no one has ever asked me to a concert./I've been to the Opera, of course,
470 CC   Lucasta 22   /But what about taking me to a concert?/{C} Only the other day, I invited you ...
471 CC   Colby   1   I'm going to invite you to the next concert .../{L} The next that you want to go to
CONCERTS (6)
369 CP   Peter   26   And I was alone./I've always gone to concerts alone —At first, because I knew no
369 CP   Peter   33   /And I found that she went to concerts alone/And to look at pictures. So we
380 CP   Celia   25   that I could help him. I took him to concerts./But then, as he came to make more
388 CP   Celia   10   know how I depended on you for concerts,/And picture exhibitions — more than
388 CP   Celia   17   I don't think that I shall be going to concerts./I am going away too. {}/[LAVINIA
447 CC   Claude 37   very musical./She can take him to concerts. But don't overdo it!/{E} I'll remember
CONCITATION (1)
38 Gerontion   52   purposelessly/And it is not by any concitation/Of the backward devils./I would
CONCLUDING (1)
469 CC   3m   1 *piano;*/LUCASTA *in an armchair. The concluding bars of a piece of music are/heard as*
CONCLUSION (6)
38 Gerontion   49   Think at last/We have not reached conclusion, when I/Stiffen in a rented house.
92 Ash-Wed 2 41   End of the endless/Journey to no end/Conclusion of all that/Is inconclusible/Speech
393 CP   Edward   2   you are./{E} That is a very serious conclusion/To have arrived at in ... how many?
470 CC   Colby   7 played/To anyone, since I came to the conclusion/That I should never become a
497 CC   Claude 20   Claude!/{SC} And she came to the conclusion that her child must be Colby,/So I
537 ES   Ld Clav 29   over, later./{LC} And what is the conclusion that you came to?/{G} This is how it
CONCLUSIVE (1)
240 MC   Priest3 34   in France?/{P3} I see nothing quite conclusive in the art of temporal government,/
CONCOCTING (1)
368 CP   Alex   24   /{A} Ah, but that's my special gift —/Concocting a toothsome meal out of nothing./
CONCOCTION (1)
547 ES   Monica 15   /{M} Let's hope this was merely the concoction/Which she decants for every
CONCORD (1)
194 FQ: Little   107   each other for misunderstanding,/In concord at this intersection time/Of meeting
CONCORDE (1)
178 FQ: ECoker 34   hand or the arm/Whiche betokeneth concorde. Round and round the fire/Leaping
CONCRETE (2)
172 FQ: BurntN 36   the drained pool./Dry the pool, dry concrete, brown edged,/And the pool was filled
335 FR   Agatha   5   my own feet walking/Away, down a concrete corridor/In a dead air. Only feet
CONCUR (1)
503 CC   Eggers   22   is over?/I'm sure Mr. Simpkins will concur in this proposal./{C} Of course I'd like
CONCURRED (1)
278 MC Knight2 14   and Archbishop. Had Becket concurred/with the King's wishes, we should
CONCURRENCE (1)
141 Rannoch   12   of pride is long, in the long pass/No concurrence of bone./Cape Ann/O quick quick
CONCUSSION (3)
322 FR   Winch   40 wrong but some nasty cuts/And a bad concussion; says he'll come round/In the
323 FR   Warburt 12   him/And says it's nothing but a slight concussion,/But he mustn't be moved tonight.
324 FR   Harry   14   very serious./A minor trouble like a concussion/Cannot make very much difference
CONDEMN (2)
250 MC Thomas   5   to deal the doom of damnation,/To condemn kings, not serve among their servants,/
278 MC Knight2 34   secured. At another time, you would/condemn an Archbishop by vote of Parliament
CONDEMNED (2)
268 MC Thomas   24   them go to the Pope. It was he who condemned them./{K1} Through you they were
438 CP   Reilly   30 ourselves and others, we should all be condemned./Mrs. Chamberlayne, I often have
CONDESCEND (1)
235 Ad-dress   52 got so far as names./Before a Cat will condescend/To treat you as a trusted friend,/
CONDITION (11)
198 FQ: Little   255   /Quick now, here, now, always —/A condition of complete simplicity/(Costing not
295 FR   Harry   27   I recovered. I am afraid of sleep:/A condition in which one can be caught for the
296 FR   Ivy   19 such cases before — that people in his condition/Often betray the most immoderate
364 CP   Reilly   20   if I bring her back it must be on one condition:/That you promise to ask her no
410 CP   Reilly   39   /And in forgetting it will alter the condition./{L} Edward, there *is* that hotel in the
417 CP   Reilly   20 finding it./Can you cure me?/{R} The condition is curable./But the form of treatment
417 CP   Reilly   23   /I can reconcile you to the human condition,/The condition to which some who
417 CP   Reilly   24   you to the human condition,/The condition to which some who have gone as far
431 CP   Julia   19   that Boltwell/Is in a very decayed condition./{P} Exactly. It is. And that's why
479 CC   Kaghan   39   never have thought of changing my condition./{L} You're always free to think
564 ES   Gomez   33   /In his Oxford days./{G} On one condition:/That you tell me all about Dick when

CONDITIONAL (1)
509 CC Guzzard　2　　in such matters,/So we had it given conditional baptism./{E} What name did you
CONDITIONS (8)
182 FQ: ECoker 189　lost again and again: and now, under conditions/That seem unpropitious. But
195 FQ: Little　152　blowing of the horn./There are three conditions which often look alike/Yet differ
427 CP　　Alex　31　out on a tour of inspection/Of local conditions./{J} What about? Monkey nuts?/{A}
434 CP　　Alex　4　by Europeans,/And where the conditions are favourable to plague./{E} Go on.
466 CC　Colby　32　better/In learning to understand the conditions/Which life has imposed upon you.
466 CC　Colby　34　in me/Rebels against accepting such conditions./It would be so much simpler if you
467 CC　Claude　32　must simply wait to learn/What new conditions life will impose on us./Just when we
507 CC　Eggers　7　unknown to you —/Under such conditions?/{MG} Yes, I did take in a child./My
CONDUCT (9)
44 Cook Egg　24　Trances;/Piccarda de Donati will conduct me./But where is the penny world I
189 FQ: DrySal 177　every lawful traffic/And those who conduct them./Repeat a prayer also on behalf of
279 MC Knight4　29　every means of provocation;/from his conduct, step by step, there can be no inference/
294 FR　Harry　19　purpose, and without principle of conduct/In flickering intervals of light and
317 FR　Harry　25　before we went to school,/The rule of conduct was simply pleasing mother;/
405 CP Edward　10　/I consider this very unprofessional conduct —/I will not discuss my case before
498 CC　Claude　39　/And I thought I would like you to conduct the proceedings./Will you sit at the
505 CC　Claude　11　/{SC} And I thought he might ... conduct the proceedings:/He's the very soul of
561 ES Michael　19　to live up to. Those standards of conduct/You've always made so much of, for
CONFER (1)
129 Cor2 State　21　/A commission is appointed/To confer with a Volscian commission/About
CONFERENCE (1)
240 MC Priest2　31　ceaseless intrigue, combinations,/In conference, meetings accepted, meetings
CONFÉRENCIER (1)
47 Mél Adult　5　à peine ma piste./En Yorkshire, conférencier;/A Londres, un peu banquier,/
CONFERRED (1)
409 CP　Reilly　37　social distinction/Than the honour conferred by being *your* lover./When you had to
CONFESS (7)
33 Conv Gal　2　the moon!/Or possibly (fantastic, I confess)/It may be Prester John's balloon/Or an
209 NamingCats　24　HIMSELF KNOWS, and will never confess./When you notice a cat in profound
220 Old Deut　15　/My mind may be wandering, but I confess/I *believe* it is Old Deuteronomy!'/Old
462 CC　Colby　5　onto a permanent basis./{C} I must confess, that up to this point/I haven't been able
488 CC　Lady E　16　see this Mrs. Guzzard, and get her to confess it./{SC} I'm sorry, Elizabeth. If Mrs.
568 ES　Ld Clav　24　in his life,/To whom he is willing to confess everything —/And that includes, mind
573 ES　Ld Clav　6　appear to them petty;/It's harder to confess the sin that no one believes in/Than the
CONFESSED (1)
20 Portrait　　76　dance,/Another bank defaulter has confessed./I keep my countenance,/I remain
CONFESSION (4)
488 CC　Claude　18　If Mrs. Guzzard comes/To make her confession, it will be very different/From what
570 ES　Ld Clav　9　of the wrong response?/How make a confession with no hope of absolution?/It was
572 ES　Ld Clav　37　at last escape them./— I've made my confession to you, Monica:/That is the first step
573 ES　Ld Clav　12　of my misdeeds/But the fact of my confession. And to you, Monica,/To you, of all
CONFIDE (3)
408 CP Edward　21　suspect./And then he came to *me* to confide about Celia!/I have never heard
567 ES　Charles　22　Do you think I could persuade him to confide in me?/{M} Oh Charles! How could
572 ES　Charles　31　versions of their miserable stories,/Confide them in whispers. They cannot harm
CONFIDED (2)
408 CP　Reilly　36　/Have not been of anything that you confided to me./The information I have
506 CC　Eggers　33　/To whom her new-born child was confided./Of course she might be mistaken
CONFIDENCE (10)
421 CP　Reilly　29　she must suffer./{R} When I express confidence in anything/You always raise
421 CP　Reilly　31　you see no reason for anything but confidence./{J} That's one way in which I am so
446 CC　Eggers　2　we worked together./All he needs is confidence./{SC} And experience./With a young
448 CC　Eggers　8　/Though I've done my best to gain his confidence./I did mention her interest in Light
456 CC　Eggers　2　/He said to me once, in a moment of confidence —/He'd just come back from a
505 CC　Claude　5　the whole story:/He's been in my confidence — and I may say, my friend —/For
541 ES　Gomez　7　I might give it to a few friends, in confidence./It might even reach the ears of some
544 ES　Ld Clav　11　/{LC} So far, so good./I'll feel more confidence after a fortnight —/After fourteen
577 ES　Charles　12　point of view. Can you really feel confidence,/Michael, in a man who aims to
580 ES　Monica　30　us;/If he prospers, that will give him confidence —/It's only self-confidence that
CONFIDENT (5)
250 MC Thomas　13　controlled by the order of God,/In confident ignorance, but arrest disorder,/Make
301 FR　　Ivy　21　/{I} I do not trust Charles with his confident vulgarity, acquired from worldly

462 CC   Claude   3   she who proposed it./So I feel pretty confident that, before long,/We can put matters
531 ES   Charles   6   the leading articles saying 'we are confident/That his sagacious counsel will long
553 ES   Ld Clav   3   our acquaintance,/You're surprisingly confident, I must say,/About your
CONFIDENTIAL (10)
311 FR   Harry   34   me you are grinning at, not me your confidential looks/Incriminate, but that other
317 FR   Warburt   5   a private conversation with you/On a confidential matter./{H} I can imagine —/
443 CC   t   glad. It's begun. {}/CURTAIN/THE CONFIDENTIAL CLERK/Characters/SIR
445 CC   Eggers   28   qualified than I was/To be your confidential clerk./He was finding his feet, very
458 CC   Eggers   35   highly qualified/Than I am, to be a confidential clerk./Besides, he's very musical./
467 CC   Claude   27   /By the work I do./{SC} As my confidential clerk./{C} I'm really interested by
505 CC   Claude   2   is Mr. Eggerson, Mrs. Guzzard:/My confidential clerk. That is to say,/Colby's
505 CC   Guzzard   15   I suppose to do with Colby — so very confidential?/{E} Yes, that is what I should call
576 ES   Michael   31   of which is left very vague/{Mi} It's confidential, I tell you./{C} So I can imagine:/
576 ES   Charles   33   tell you./{C} So I can imagine:/Highly confidential .../{G} Be careful, Mr. Barrister./
CONFIGURED (1)
147 Rock 1   3   his circuit./O perpetual revolution of configured stars,/O perpetual recurrence of
CONFINED (1)
280 MC   Priest3   22   men;/Go to the northern seas confined with ice/Where the dead breath makes
CONFIRM (3)
510 CC   Eggers   36   /With Mrs. Guzzard. It's for them to confirm/That they took you, as a child, from
512 CC   Claude   12   Kaghan's ... mother, I am sure, will confirm it./{MG} That is as much to my interest
548 ES   Ld Clav   21   just mentioned. I am glad you can confirm them./{MC} Oh, so that *is* your
CONFIRMATION (3)
510 CC   Eggers   13   have found your son./{E} Subject to confirmation./{LE} And to my being able to
510 CC   Eggers   33   my son./{E} You will wish to obtain confirmation/Of this interesting discovery, Mr.
514 CC   Eggers   31   /You'll understand the need for exact confirmation./{MG} I understand that, Mr.
CONFIRMED (2)
242 MC   Priest1   19   bred of sudden prosperity/Was but confirmed by bitter adversity./I saw him as
269 MC   Knights   18   and treason./{3K} Priest! traitor, confirmed in malfeasance./{T} I submit my
CONFIRMS (1)
74 WL: Thund   414   his prison/Thinking of the key, each confirms a prison/Only at nightfall, aethereal
CONFOUNDED (1)
273 MC   Thomas   37   /So good and evil in the end become confounded./It is not in time that my death
CONFOUNDS (1)
107 Animula   13   running stags around a silver tray;/Confounds the actual and the fanciful,/Content
CONFRONT (1)
487 CC   Lady E   22   I must see this Mrs. Guzzard. I must confront her./This couldn't possibly be a
CONFRONTING (1)
184 FQ: DrySal   5   of commerce;/Then only a problem confronting the builder of bridges./The problem
CONFUSED (5)
64 WL: Chess   88   powdered, or liquid — troubled, confused/And drowned the sense in odours;
141 Rannoch   8   /Languor of broken steel,/Clamour of confused wrong, apt/In silence. Memory is
166 Rock 10   4   one more light set on a hill/In a world confused and dark and disturbed by portents of
495 CC   Lady E   24   —/Is that what I mean? I'm getting confused./I thought I was escaping from a
509 CC   Lady E   37   Yes, what year was it?/I'm getting so confused. What with Colby being Barnabas —/I
CONFUSING (1)
134 Wind   5   dream kingdom/The waking echo of confusing strife/Is it a dream or something else/
CONFUSION (6)
290 FR   Agatha   26   prepared/Men tighten the knot of confusion/Into perfect misunderstanding,/
511 CC   Lady E   20   Then in order to avoid any danger of confusion/You may address me as Aunt
512 CC   Lady E   7   suspicions!/I thought there had been a confusion — that's all./{MG} I feared there
512 CC   Guzzard   8   all./{MG} I feared there might be a confusion in your mind/Between the meaning of
512 CC   Guzzard   9   in your mind/Between the meaning of *confusion* and *imposture*./{SC} I don't think there
512 CC   Claude   10   /{SC} I don't think there is any confusion now:/I'm sure that my wife is
CONFUSIONS (2)
38 Gerontion   38   what she gives, gives with such supple confusions/That the giving famishes the craving.
224 Mr Mistoff   9   illusions/And creating eccentric confusions./At prestidigitation/And at
CONFUTE (1)
33 Conv Gal   17   /At a stroke our mad poetics to confute —'/And — 'Are we then so serious?'/La
CONGRATULATE (5)
370 CP   Edward   37   /And that you were another man. I congratulate you/On a timely escape./{P} I
389 CP   Lavinia   3   going too? Was that what I heard?/I congratulate you both. To Hollywood, of
407 CP   Reilly   13   say that of *you*, Lavinia./{R} I congratulate you both on your perspicacity./
408 CP   Edward   19   /Peter Quilpe! Really Lavinia!/I congratulate you. You could not have chosen/
573 ES   Carghill   32   Mrs. Carghill./{MC} And let me congratulate *you*, Mr. Hemington./You're a

CONGRATULATIONS (1)
371 CP   Peter   2 /{P} I should prefer to be spared/Your congratulations. I had to talk to someone./And
CONGREGATION (2)
264 MC   Priest2   8   John the Apostle./*In the midst of the congregation he opened his mouth.*/That which
264 MC   Priest2   13 we unto you./*In the midst of the congregation.* {}/[*Introit of St. John is heard*]/
CONIUNCTION (1)
178 FQ: ECoker   32 sacrament./Two and two, necessarye coniunction,/Holding eche other by the hand or
CONJOINED (1)
281 MC   Priest2   3 charity./{P2} Now in the sight of God/Conjoined with all the saints and martyrs gone
CONJURING (1)
224 Mr Mistoff   2 know Mr. Mistoffelees!/The Original Conjuring Cat —/(There can be no doubt about
224 Mr Mistoff   15   to learn/From Mr. Mistoffelees' Conjuring Turn./Presto!/Away we go!/And we
CONNECT (2)
 70 WL: Fire S   301 I resent?'/'On Margate Sands./I can connect/Nothing with nothing./The broken
330 FR   Agatha   14 /But a present is missing, needed to connect them./You may be afraid that I would
CONNECTED (1)
507 CC   Guzzard 14 /I understood the child was very well connected:/Otherwise, I should not have taken
CONNECTION (4)
327 FR   Ivy   28 Arthur, ringing up from London:/The connection was so bad, I could hardly hear him,
431 CP   Julia   9   knew *his* name./{J} Is he your connection in California, Alex?/{A} Yes, we
455 CC   Colby   8   about Lu ... Miss Angel:/What's her connection with this household?/{E} Well. A
535 ES   Gomez   16   /*B* won't let me down in some other connection./But, as I've always said to my boys:
CONNECTIONS (4)
390 CP   Edward   26 friends in Dedham?/{E} No, *I* have no connections in Dedham./{J} Well, it's all
423 CP   Alex   3   will speak them./You know, I have connections — even in California. {}/
456 CC   Eggers   6   /Of course it's true that her family connections/Have sometimes been useful. But
559 ES   Ld Clav 7   might set you on your feet./I have connections, or at least correspondents/Almost
CONNUE (1)
 48 Lune Miel   9 Saint Apollinaire/En Classe, basilique connue des amateurs/De chapitaux d'acanthe
CONQUER (3)
166 Rock 10   6 /Or shall the Visible Church go on to conquer the World?/The great snake lies ever
182 FQ: ECoker   184   of emotion. And what there is to conquer/By strength and submission, has
274 MC Thomas   10   have conquered. We have only to conquer/Now, by suffering. This is the easier
CONQUERED (4)
159 Rock 6   8   /Do you think that the Faith has conquered the World/And that lions no longer
173 FQ: BurntN   92 and future./Only through time time is conquered./Here is a place of disaffection/Time
190 FQ: DrySal   223   actual,/Here the past and future/Are conquered, and reconciled,/Where action were
274 MC Thomas   10   We have fought the beast/And have conquered. We have only to conquer/Now, by
CONQUEST (1)
593 Grad 5   5 deeds the distant years may see,/What conquest over pain and misery,/What heroes
CONSCIENCE (10)
 23 Preludes   46   /Assured of certain certainties,/The conscience of a blackened street/Impatient to
295 FR   Charles 16 no reason to reproach yourself./Your conscience can be clear./{H} It goes a good deal
295 FR   Harry   18   deeper/Than what people call their conscience; it is just the cancer/That eats away
295 FR   Harry   23   I suffer from delusions. It is not my conscience,/Not my mind, that is diseased, but
411 CP   Reilly   28 {R} Your business is not to clear your conscience/But to learn how to bear the burdens
411 CP   Reilly   29   how to bear the burdens on your conscience./With the future of the others you
552 ES   Ld Clav 19   should I feel embarrassment? My conscience was clear./A brief infatuation, ended
552 ES   Carghil 22   our mutual satisfaction./{MC} Your conscience was clear./I've very seldom heard
552 ES   Carghil 26   payment/And no publicity. So your conscience was clear./At bottom, I believe
573 ES   Ld Clav   1 You think that I suffer from a morbid conscience,/From brooding over faults I might
CONSCIENCES (2)
552 ES   Carghil 23   seldom heard people mention their consciences/Except to observe that their
552 ES   Carghil 24   /Except to observe that their consciences were clear./You got out of a tangle
CONSCIOUS (15)
110 Marina   27   /Made this unknowing, half conscious, unknown, my own./The garboard
173 FQ: BurntN   87   but a little consciousness./To be conscious is not to be in time/But only in time
180 FQ: ECoker 123   /Or when, under ether, the mind is conscious but conscious of nothing —/I said to
180 FQ: ECoker 123 under ether, the mind is conscious but conscious of nothing —/I said to my soul, be
192 FQ: Little   49 is more/Than an order of words, the conscious occupation/Of the praying mind, or
194 FQ: Little 137   begin to fall asunder./Second, the conscious impotence of rage/At human folly,
205 de la Mare   31   the common measure is refined;/By conscious art practised with natural ease;/By the
603 Spleen   3 Sunday faces;/Bonnets, silk hats, and conscious graces/In repetition that displaces/
281 MC Chorus   13   man, whom Thou hast made to be conscious of Thee, must consciously praise
307 FR   Mary   25   very moment when you are wholly conscious/Of being a misfit, of being

324 FR   Harry   18   to anyone else. If he was ever really conscious,/I should be glad for him to have a
437 CP   Reilly 39   say she suffered more, because more conscious/Than the rest of us. She paid the
466 CC   Colby   1   before other people/I was always conscious that what *they* heard/Was not what I
560 ES   Michael 1   it give you/In the grave? If you're still conscious after death,/I bet it will be a surprised
583 ES   Charles 1   both of us .../{C} So that now we are conscious of a new person/Who is you and me
CONSCIOUSLY (1)
281 MC   Chorus 13   made to be conscious of Thee, must consciously praise Thee, in thought and in word
CONSCIOUSNESS (8)
 22 Preludes   14   of the lamps./The morning comes to consciousness/Of faint stale smells of beer/From
111 Xmas Trees   21   tedium,/The awareness of death, the consciousness of failure,/Or in the piety of the
173 FQ: BurntN   86   past and time future/Allow but a little consciousness./To be conscious is not to be in
324 FR   Harry   16   /A brief vacation from the kind of consciousness/That John enjoys, can't make
333 FR   Agatha 31   its dark instinctive birth, to come to consciousness/And so find expurgation. It is
333 FR   Agatha 33   It is possible/You are the consciousness of your unhappy family,/Its bird
544 ES   Ld Clav 18   /And by the time one has grown to consciousness/It comes less often./I hope this
560 ES   Michael 2   /I bet it will be a surprised state of consciousness./Poor ghost! reckoning up its
CONSENT (4)
245 MC   Thomas 18   an eternal patience/To which all must consent that it may be willed/And which all
256 MC   Tempt4   1   an eternal patience/To which all must consent that it may be willed/And which all
274 MC   Thomas   4   To which my whole being gives entire consent./I give my life/To the Law of God
319 FR   Warburt 16   together:/They separated by mutual consent/And he went to live abroad. You were
CONSENTED (2)
270 MC   Chorus 26   to the last humiliation./I have consented, Lord Archbishop, have consented./
270 MC   Chorus 26   consented, Lord Archbishop, have consented./Am torn away, subdued, violated,/
CONSENTING (1)
270 MC   Chorus 25   but the shamed swoon/Of those consenting to the last humiliation./I have
CONSEQUENCE (8)
152 Rock 2   27   every ill deed in the past we suffer the consequence:/For sloth, for avarice, gluttony,
185 FQ: DrySal   58   is no end, but addition: the trailing/Consequence of further days and hours,/While
258 MC   Thomas 38   at all times draws/The strangest consequence from remotest cause./But for every
273 MC   Thomas 35   the fact. For every life and every act/Consequence of good and evil can be shown./
407 CP   Reilly 25   more than you meant to./This is the consequence of trying to lie to me./{L} I did not
439 CP   Julia   12   Celia chose/A way of which the consequence was Kinkanja./Peter chose a way
439 CP   Julia   34   Henry. {}/[*Exit*]/{J} ... And now the consequence of the Chamberlaynes' choice/Is a
570 ES   Ld Clav 21   both done better for themselves/In consequence of it all. He admitted as much,/
CONSEQUENCES (5)
323 FR   Warburt 31   of night, I would not answer for the consequences/I am going myself. I will come
438 CP   Reilly 27   If we all were judged according to the consequences/Of all our words and deeds,
439 CP   Julia   11   or another,/And then must take the consequences. Celia chose/A way of which the
490 CC   Colby   35   /God forbid! but we must take the consequences./At the time when I was born,
537 ES   Gomez   37   about that I was sent down/With the consequences which you remember:/A miserable
CONSEQUENTLY (1)
 89 Ash-Wed 1   24   /Because I cannot hope to turn again/Consequently I rejoice, having to construct
CONSERVATEUR (3)
 46 Directeur   4   si près du Spectateur./Le directeur/Conservateur/Du Spectateur/Empeste la brise./
 46 Directeur   10   /Réactionnaires/Du Spectateur/Conservateur/Bras dessus bras dessous/Font des
 46 Directeur   21   /Regarde/Le directeur/Du Spectateur/Conservateur/Et crève d'amour./Mélange
CONSERVATIVE (1)
456 CC   Eggers 10   He's rather a Socialist./I'm a staunch Conservative, myself./{C} But is Lady Elizabeth
CONSIDER (16)
 71 WL: DWater 321   turn the wheel and look to windward,/Consider Phlebas, who was once handsome and
129 Cor2 State   17   a commission of engineers/To consider the Water Supply./A commission is
188 FQ: DrySal   155   shore/While time is withdrawn, consider the future/And the past with an equal
261 MC   Thomas   8   but not peace as the world/gives./Consider also one thing of which you have
278 MC   Knight2   3   clap-trap. I therefore ask you to consider soberly: what/were the Archbishop's
279 MC   Knight4 17   at my putting it in this way. But/consider the course of events. I am obliged, very
324 FR   Harry   37   feeling about John/That you consider appropriate. Only, that's not the
397 CP   Edward 26   {E} I ought to know by now what you consider practical./Practical! I remember, on
405 CP   Edward 10   mean? Who is this other patient?/I consider this very unprofessional conduct —/I
409 CP   Reilly   7   much you have in common. Indeed, I consider/That you are exceptionally well-suited
413 CP   Celia   27   I can't understand,/Which you might consider symptoms. But first I must tell you/
515 CC   Guzzard 20   plausible. But it can't be true./{MG} Consider, Sir Claude. Would I tell you all this/
537 ES   Gomez   12   mind. Develop the point./{G} Well, consider what we were when we went up to
539 ES   Ld Clav 38   been in England./{LC} So, as you consider yourself a success .../{G} A worldly
556 ES   Ld Clav 22   expensive./{LC} You don't normally consider that a recommendation./Are you

568 ES Ld Clav 21   *her*/However important you may consider it/To conceal from the rest of the
CONSIDERATE (4)
287 FR   Violet 12   that Charles might have been more considerate./{G} I'm very sorry: but why was
300 FRDowning 24   —/His Lordship is always most considerate/About keeping me up. But when I
393 CP   Lavinia 28 it as a compliment!/And you were so considerate, people said;/And you thought you
554 ES   Carghil 17 after us well, Mrs. Piggott:/You're so considerate — and so understanding./{MP} But
CONSIDERATION (2)
324 FR   Violet 24   to John,/You might show some consideration to your mother./{A} I do not
384 CP   Reilly 20   cannot be reversed. That is one consideration./And another is this: it is a serious
CONSIDERED (1)
558 ES   Michael 22 for me/Because I was your son. They considered me superfluous;/They knew I
CONSIDERING (2)
553 ES Ld Clav 1   obituary, whoever writes it./{LC} Considering how long ago it was when you
553 ES Ld Clav 2   ago it was when you knew me/And considering the brevity of our acquaintance,/
CONSIDERS (2)
242 MC   Mess 16   as to what he meant,/But no one considers it a happy prognostic. {}/[*Exit*]/{P1} I
547 ES   Monica 17   newcomer./Perhaps after what she considers proper courtesies,/She will leave us
CONSIST (1)
334 FR   Harry 2   quite happy, as if happiness/Did not consist in getting what one wanted/Or in getting
CONSISTENT (2)
278 MC Knight2 6   /The King's aim has been perfectly consistent. During the reign of/the late Queen
361 CP   Reilly 38   cosier and cosier/Without the consistent critic, the patient misunderstander/
CONSOLATION (3)
105 Song Sime   23   and unspoken Word,/Grant Israel's consolation/To one who has eighty years and
240 MC Chorus 11   /Why should the summer bring consolation/For autumn fires and winter fogs?/
492 CC   Claude 14   Now, Colby,/Can you find some consolation at the piano?/{C} I don't think,
CONSORT (1)
197 FQ: Little   225   but not pedantic,/The complete consort dancing together)/Every phrase and
CONSPICUOUS (5)
325 FR   Violet 36   blown about so,/And you feel so conspicuous, lolling back/And so near the
328 FR   Charles 8   ... I'm glad to say/It's not very conspicuous .../{G} There'll have been more in
493 CC   Lady E 25   /For Colby. He won't want to be conspicuous,/Poor boy!/{SC} After all, it was he
531 ES Ld Clav 12   liturgy/Of the Press on any conspicuous retirement./My obituary, if I had
538 ES   Gomez 28 for your leaving politics/And taking a conspicuous job in the City/Where the
CONSPIRACIES (1)
253 MC Tempt4 35   /War, plague, and revolution,/New conspiracies, broken pacts;/To be master or
CONSPIRACY (1)
603 Spleen   10   unable to rally/Against this dull conspiracy./And Life, a little bald and gray,/
CONSPIRATORS (1)
301 FR Chorus 16 Why should we stand here like guilty conspirators, waiting for some revelation/When
CONSPIRED (1)
293 FR   Harry 18   person —/A person that you have conspired to invent, please do so/In my absence.
CONSPIRING (1)
573 ES Ld Clav 19   it./Meanwhile, I feel sure they are conspiring against me./I see Mrs. Carghill
CONSTANT (2)
181 FQ: ECoker 156 /If we obey the dying nurse/Whose constant care is not to please/But to remind of
249 MC Thomas 37   the barons. Who will not forget/Constant curbing of petty privilege./{T2}
CONSTANTLY (1)
159 Rock 6   21 Sin, and other unpleasant facts./They constantly try to escape/From the darkness
CONSTELLATED (1)
178 FQ: ECoker 61 Simulates triumphal cars/Deployed in constellated wars/Scorpion fights against the
CONSTELLATION (1)
252 MC Tempt3 8 forgotten./We expect the rise of a new constellation./{T} And if the Archbishop cannot
CONSTELLATIONS (1)
178 FQ: ECoker 43   /The time of the seasons and the constellations/The time of milking and the time
CONSTERNATION (1)
409 CP   Reilly 10 /You discovered, to your surprise and consternation,/That you were not really in love
CONSTITUENCY (1)
529 ES   Monica 1   /But Badgley Court's so near your constituency!/You can come down at weekends,
CONSTITUTE (2)
527 ES   Charles 5 legal impediment/Isn't that enough to constitute an engagement?/Aren't you sure that
574 ES   Michael 35   With another Sir Alfred/Who'd constitute himself custodian of my morals/And
CONSTITUTED (1)
23 Preludes   28 sordid images/Of which your soul was constituted;/They flickered against the ceiling./

CONSTITUTION (1)
196 FQ: Little   192   those whom they opposed/Accept the constitution of silence/And are folded in a single
CONSTITUTIONAL (1)
277 MC Knight1   33   made a special study of statecraft and constitutional law. Sir/Hugh de Morville./{K2} I
CONSTRUCT (1)
  89 Ash-Wed 1   24   /Consequently I rejoice, having to construct something/Upon which to rejoice/And
CONSULT (5)
344 FR   Violet   26   qualification!/I think you should consult the vicar .../{G} And don't forget/That
366 CP   Peter   19   Lavinia./It's something I want to consult him about,/And I could do it now./{J}
400 CP   Alex   15   right shops./Besides, he was ready to consult any doctor/Recommended by anyone
402 CP   Edward   8   action:/If I were, I should not need to consult you/Or anyone else. I came here as a
538 ES   Gomez   29   /Where the Government could always consult you/But of course didn't have to take
CONSULTATION (1)
362 CP   Reilly   36   /Or, take a surgical operation./In consultation with the doctor and the surgeon,/
CONSULTATIONS (2)
270 MC Chorus   16   of potentates/As well as in the consultations of powers./What is woven on the
424 CP Edward   21   tired?/{E} Oh no, a quiet day./Two consultations with solicitors/On quite
CONSULTATIVE (1)
129 Cor2 State   9   to do is to form the committees:/The consultative councils, the standing committees,
CONSULTING (2)
399 CP   2m   1   HENRY HARCOURT-REILLY'S *consulting room in London. Morning:/several*
407 CP   Reilly   21   have both of you pretended/To be consulting me; both, tried to impose upon me/
CONSUMED (2)
157 Rock 4   13   the king's pool,/Jerusalem lay waste, consumed with fire;/No place for a beast to
196 FQ: Little   215   remove./We only live, only suspire/Consumed by either fire or fire./What we call
CONSUMING (1)
465 CC   Claude   12   isn't it,/That a man should have a consuming passion/To do something for which
CONSUMMATION (3)
246 MC Thomas   22   /Heavier the interval than the consummation./All things prepare the event.
272 MC Thomas   7   denied; all things/Proceed to a joyful consummation./{3P} Seize him! force him! drag
349 FR   Mary   20   /Only implicates others/At the day of consummation/{Ag} A curse is a power/Not
CONTACT (4)
  38 Gerontion   60   should I use them for your closer contact?/These with a thousand small
  52 Whispers   15   marrow/The ague of the skeleton;/No contact possible to flesh/Allayed the fever of the
474 CC Lucasta   38   music!/When I see it as a means of contact with a world/More real than any *I've*
496 CC Eggers   24   affairs.'/The fact is, she misses the contact with London,/Though she doesn't
CONTAGION (1)
335 FR   Harry   14   in a circular desert/Weaving with contagion of putrescent embraces/On dissolving
CONTAINED (3)
  91 Ash-Wed 2   3   my liver and that which had been contained/In the hollow round of my skull. And
  91 Ash-Wed 2   6   /Bones live? And that which had been contained/In the bones (which were already dry)
171 FQ: BurntN   3   in time future/And time future contained in time past./If all time is eternally
CONTAINING (2)
128 Cor1 March   36   come the virgins bearing urns, urns containing/Dust/Dust/Dust of dust, and now/
172 FQ: BurntN   43   full of children,/Hidden excitedly, containing laughter./Go, go, go, said the bird:
CONTAMINATING (1)
331 FR   Harry   1   in a world not of persons/But only of contaminating presences./And then I had no
CONTAMINATION (1)
295 FR   Harry   29   waking. She is nearer than ever./The contamination has reached the marrow/And
CONTEMPLATING (1)
529 ES   Ld Clav   29   /{M} Thinking of nothing?/{LC} Contemplating nothingness. Just remember:/
CONTEMPLATION (2)
  91 Ash-Wed 2   17   is withdrawn/In a white gown, to contemplation, in a white gown./Let the
209 NamingCats   27   same:/His mind is engaged in a rapt contemplation/Of the thought, of the thought,
CONTEMPT (3)
268 MC Thomas   33   to him, upon whom redounds/Their contempt towards me, their contempt towards
268 MC Thomas   33   /Their contempt towards me, their contempt towards the Church shown./{K1} Be
396 CP Edward   33   for me:/It's only another kind of contempt./And I do not want you to explain me
CONTEMPTIBLE (2)
258 MC Thomas   33   the men who thought me most contemptible,/The raw nobility, whose manners
363 CP Edward   33   They will think me mad/Or simply contemptible./{UG} All to the good./You will
CONTEMPTUOUS (1)
602 Humoresque   18   you people get some class?/(Feebly contemptuous of nose),/'Your damned thin
CONTENDING (1)
193 FQ: Little   67   mouth,/Dead water and dead sand/Contending for the upper hand./The parched

CONTENT (9)
107 Animula   14   the actual and the fanciful,/Content with playing-cards and kings and
158 Rock 5   5   snakes that lie on mouldering stairs, content in the sunlight./And the others run
190 FQ: DrySal 234 /Because we have gone on trying;/We, content at the last/If our temporal reversion
236 Cat Morgan   7   cream in a bowl;/But I'm allus content with a drink on the 'ouse/And a bit o'
239 MC Chorus   25   left to our own devices,/And we are content if we are left alone./We try to keep our
268 MC Knight1 14   the facts./Say therefore if you will be content/To answer in the King's presence.
371 CP   Edward 14   Will it be the same Celia?/Better be content with the Celia you remember./
497 CC   Lady E 26   I don't want to know:/I am perfectly content to leave things as they are,/So that we
516 CC   Colby   39   that you were my father/I was content to have had the same ambitions/And in

CONTENTED (6)
295 FR   Harry   25   I have to live in./— I lay two days in contented drowsiness;/Then I recovered. I am
370 CP   Peter   8   when we were together —/So ... contented, so ... at peace: I can't express it;/I
381 CP   Edward 14   was most desirable,/Before you are contented with what you can desire;/Before you
417 CP   Reilly   32   and take. They do not repine;/Are contented with the morning that separates/And
491 CC   Claude 15   us closer together./{SC} I should be contented with such an understanding;/And
512 CC   Guzzard 17 LADY ELIZABETH]/{MG} Are you contented to have him as your son?/{SC} That

CONTENTMENT (3)
109 Marina   10   /Death/Those who sit in the sty of contentment, meaning/Death/Those who suffer
465 CC   Claude 24 But nothing *I* made ever gave me that contentment —/That state of utter exhaustion
544 ES   Ld Clav 14   bridge;/Still, I'll admit to a feeling of contentment/Already. I only hope that it will

CONTINUAL (1)
293 FR   Harry   37   nothing has happened, at most a continual impact/Of external events. You have

CONTINUE (10)
111 Xmas Trees 10   at the Christmas Tree:/Let him continue in the spirit of wonder/At the Feast as
124 SA   Snow   10   a terrible risk./{Sn} Let Mr. Sweeney continue his story./I assure you, Sir, we are very
124 SA   Snow   25   a terrible risk./{Sn} Let Mr. Sweeney continue his story./{S} This one didn't get
324 FR Warburt   1   go out./If you do, I must decline to continue to treat you./You are only delaying
361 CP   Reilly   32   /Beyond your control. So let me continue./I will say then, you experience some
508 CC   Guzzard 23   not afford to adopt the child,/Or continue to keep him, when the payments
515 CC   Guzzard 11   died. I was left very poor./If I let you continue to think the child was yours,/My son
531 ES   Charles   7   /That his sagacious counsel will long continue/To be at the disposal of the
549 ES   Ld Clav 19   me./Don't you remember?/{LC} Pray continue./The more you remind me of, the
565 ES   Ld Clav 4   meal./{LC} But Michael and I/Must continue our discussion. This afternoon,

CONTINUED (2)
 29 Aunt Helen   10   parrot died too./The Dresden clock continued ticking on the mantelpiece,/And the
103 Journ Magi   29 /But there was no information, so we continued/And arrived at evening, not a

CONTINUING (1)
243 MC Chorus   14   shall be brought low./{C} Here is no continuing city, here is no abiding stay./Ill the

CONTOUR (1)
382 CP   Celia   10 thought that I knew/And loved every contour; and as I looked/It withered, as if I had

CONTRACT (2)
519 CC   Guzzard 3   there was a time-limit clause in the contract./{SC} What's that? Oh. Good-bye,
578 ES   Ld Clav 1   Culverwell,/Of his own volition to contract his enslavement,/I cannot prevent him.

CONTRACTORS (1)
180 FQ: ECoker 107   /Industrial lords and petty contractors, all go into the dark,/And dark the

CONTRACTS (1)
 56 Swee Night   22   /The silent vertebrate in brown/Contracts and concentrates, withdraws;/Rachel

CONTRADICT (1)
308 FR   Mary   10 real than the other. And in a way you contradict yourself:/That sudden

CONTRADICTION (1)
528 ES   Charles 21   You've given two reasons,/One the contradiction of the other./Can there be a third?

CONTRARY (6)
300 FRDowning   14 too much of each other, Sir./Quite the contrary of the usual opinion,/I dare say. She
405 CP   Reilly   12   before another patient./{R} On the contrary. That is the only way/In which it can
437 CP   Reilly   35   Not at all what I mean. Rather the contrary./I'd say that she suffered all that we
459 CC   Lady E   7   letters. That's very auspicious —/Contrary to what most people think./You
541 ES   Gomez   17 an old friend of ... blackmail!/On the contrary, I dare say I could buy you out/Several
541 ES   Gomez   25   me an apology./Blackmail! On the contrary/Any time you're in a tight corner/My

CONTRIBUTING (1)
201 Def Island   9   battleship, merchantman, trawler —/contributing their share to the ages' pavement/

CONTRIBUTIONS (1)
530 ES   Ld Clav 35 thank them for that./Oh the grudging contributions/That bought this piece of silver!

CONTRITION (3)
270 MC	Chorus	23	is too late/For action, too soon for contrition./Nothing is possible but the shamed
581 ES	Ld Clav	14	now./It is the peace that ensues upon contrition/When contrition ensues upon
581 ES	Ld Clav	15	that ensues upon contrition/When contrition ensues upon knowledge of the truth./

CONTRIVE (3)
290 FR	Amy	16	at Wishwood/And I hope we can contrive his future happiness./Do not discuss his
382 CP	Edward	1	of mediocrity./The willing self can contrive the disaster/Of this unwilling
457 CC	Colby	9	And I'm convinced/That you always contrive to think the best of everyone./{E}

CONTRIVED (1)
38 Gerontion		34	/History has many cunning passages, contrived corridors/And issues, deceives with

CONTRIVING (1)
261 MC	Thomas	26	a Saint, as a man by willing and contriving may become a ruler/of men. A

CONTROL (8)
107 Animula		20	/And may and may not, desire and control./The pain of living and the drug of
202 War Poetry		9	On which we attend/Of forces beyond control by experiment —/Of Nature and the
232 Skimble		23	First and in the Third;/He establishes control by a regular patrol/And he'd know at
361 CP	Reilly	32	to start a train of events/Beyond your control. So let me continue./I will say then, you
460 CC	Lady E	1	a wonderful doctor who teaches mind control.'/So on I went to Zürich./{SC} So on
460 CC	Claude	4	the doctor in Lausanne taught mind control?/{LE} No, Claude, he only teaches
460 CC	Lady E	5	No, Claude, he only teaches *thought* control./Mind control is a different matter:/It's
460 CC	Lady E	6	only teaches *thought* control./Mind control is a different matter:/It's more

CONTROLLED (2)
167 Rock 10		39	we sleep and are glad to sleep,/Controlled by the rhythm of blood and the day
250 MC	Thomas	12	put their faith in worldly order/Not controlled by the order of God,/In confident

CONTROLLING (1)
74 WL: Thund		422	when invited, beating obedient/To controlling hands/I sat upon the shore/Fishing,

CONTROLS (1)
227 Macavity		42	for the Cat who all the time/Just controls their operations: the Napoleon of

CONTROVERSIAL (1)
55 Mr E Sun		32	The masters of the subtle schools/Are controversial, polymath./Sweeney Among the

CONVALESCENT (1)
528 ES	Monica	29	/That's why Selby chose the place. A *convalescent* home/With the atmosphere of an

CONVALESCENTS (2)
527 ES	Charles	17	father/In that very expensive hotel for convalescents/To which you're taking him? And
546 ES	Piggott	28	/Nobody looks ill! They're all convalescents,/Or resting, like you. So you'll

CONVENIENT (2)
385 CP	Reilly	3	and we are the same/Is a useful and convenient social convention/Which must
424 CP	Lavinia	5	There, in that corner. That's the most convenient;/You can get in and out. Is there

CONVENT (1)
57 Swee Night		36	The nightingales are singing near/The Convent of the Sacred Heart,/And sang within

CONVENTION (3)
374 CP	Celia	29	/Surely you don't hold to that silly convention/That the husband must always be
385 CP	Reilly	3	same/Is a useful and convenient social convention/Which must sometimes be broken.
538 ES	Gomez	20	who made the mistake./That's your convention. Or if it's known you made it/You

CONVENTIONAL (3)
400 CP	Reilly	3	/{R} At eleven o'clock,/The conventional hour. We have not much time./
415 CP	Celia	19	/{C} Well, my bringing up was pretty conventional —/I had always been taught to
501 CC	Lucasta	13	not a person of liberal views./I'm very conventional. And I'm not ashamed of it./{SC}

CONVERSATION (26)
18 Portrait		14	in the concert room.'/— And so the conversation slips/Among velleities and
33 Conv Gal		t	with careful subtlety to this end./Conversation Galante/I observe: 'Our
124 SA	Doris	8	very last card./I don't care for such conversation/A woman runs a terrible risk./{Sn}
137 5FingerEx5		5	grim/And his mouth so prim/And his conversation, so nicely/Restricted to What
180 FQ: ECoker		120	too long between stations/And the conversation rises and slowly fades into silence/
203 Indians		7	/Which return at the hour of conversation,/(The warm or the cool hour,
218 Mung Rump		20	to engage a friendly policeman in conversation./When the family assembled for
601 Nocturne		5	a bored but courteous moon;/The conversation failing, strikes some tune/Banal,
287 FR	Gerald	14	/I only meant to draw her into the conversation./{C} She's a nice girl; but it's a
303 FR	Mary	23	/Who meet very seldom, making conversation./I am very glad if Dr. Warburton
309 FR	Harry	12	/Something should have come of this conversation./{M} I am not a wise person,/And
317 FR	Warburt	4	mother's birthday./I wanted a private conversation with you/On a confidential matter.
319 FR	Harry	24	the hushed excitement/And the low conversation of triumphant aunts./It is the
321 FR	Harry	29	*is* real, Doctor./So let us resume the conversation. You, and I/And Winchell. Sit
356 CP	Julia	22	alone/And have a really *serious* conversation!'/I said so to Lavinia. She agreed
361 CP	Edward	15	it to *you*?/I know that I invited this conversation:/But I don't know who you are.

369 CP	Peter	32	her there alone./Anyway, we got into conversation/And I found that she went to
387 CP	Peter	30	/But Edward — you remember our conversation yesterday?/{E} Of course./{P} I
432 CP	Julia	32	We've been having such an interesting conversation./Peter's just over from California/
457 CC	Claude	23	*on the street*]/{SC} She's having a conversation with the cabman./What can they
490 CC	Colby	14	I've been suffering or not/During this conversation. I only feel ... numb./If there's
492 CC	Colby	23	—/Before you brought me into the conversation —/And I found one note I
516 CC	Claude	24	you felt that you were changing?/That conversation would have convinced me/With no
548 ES	Carghil	27	coming here —/It's been the topic of conversation./But I couldn't believe that it
549 ES	Ld Clav	34	don't you, Richard?/{LC} Not the conversation you have just repeated./That is
577 ES	Carghil	26	Richard, I think it's time *I* joined the conversation./My late husband, Mr. Carghill,

CONVERSATIONS (1)

| 319 FR | Harry | 25 | of triumphant aunts./It is the conversations not overheard,/Not intended to |

CONVERSE (1)

| 189 FQ: DrySal | 188 | angelus./To communicate with Mars, converse with spirits,/To report the behaviour |

CONVERSES (1)

| 57 Swee Night | 34 | /The host with someone indistinct/Converses at the door apart,/The nightingales |

CONVERT (3)

111 Xmas Trees	22	of failure,/Or in the piety of the convert/Which may be tainted with a
121 SA	Doris	10	/{Do} I'll be the missionary./I'll convert you!/{S} I'll convert *you*!/Into a stew./A
121 SA	Sweeney	11	missionary./I'll convert you!/{S} I'll convert *you*!/Into a stew./A nice little, white

CONVERTS (2)

| 428 CP | Alex | 18 | of it./Some of the tribes are Christian converts,/And, naturally, take a different view./ |
| 429 CP | Alex | 6 | even been persuading some of the converts —/Who, after all, prefer not to be |

CONVEYOR (1)

| 184 FQ: DrySal | 4 | frontier;/Useful, untrustworthy, as a conveyor of commerce;/Then only a problem |

CONVICTION (2)

| 163 Rock 8 | 47 | nothing,/To men of faith and conviction./Let us therefore make perfect our |
| 534 ES | Gomez | 19 | is a mug's game./I say that — with conviction./No, forgery, or washing cheques, or |

CONVINCE (2)

| 279 MC | Knight1 | 10 | /loyalty to the Church, will be able to convince them. Richard Brito./{K4} The |
| 405 CP | Reilly | 15 | and you have said enough/To convince me that you have been making up |

CONVINCED (15)

296 FR	Agatha	2	/They will be clear later. I am also convinced/That you only hold a fragment of the
297 FR	Violet	31	upon this investigation,/Which I am convinced is going to lead us nowhere,/And
309 FR	Mary	26	You deceive yourself/Like the man convinced that he is paralysed/Or like the man
314 FR	Violet	17	never stay in bed/Because you were convinced that you would never get well./{H}
447 CC	Claude	17	in the choosing;/And besides, she is convinced that she, of all people,/Is a better
457 CC	Colby	8	/That *you* have a kind heart. And I'm convinced/That you always contrive to think
462 CC	Claude	13	believe she will: though I'm perfectly convinced/That *her* son would have been a
472 CC	Lucasta	27	/But that's not the point. You'd convinced yourself;/And you felt that your life
497 CC	Claude	13	of his aunt, Mrs. Guzzard./Now she's convinced that Mrs. Guzzard/Of Teddington is
497 CC	Lady E	23	not quite right. Let me explain./I am convinced that Sir Claude is mistaken,/Or has
506 CC	Eggers	31	/Of Teddington! Lady Elizabeth is convinced/That it was a Mrs. Guzzard of
507 CC	Claude	38	That is just the point. My wife has convinced herself/That Colby is her son. I know
512 CC	Claude	11	/I'm sure that my wife is perfectly convinced;/And Mr. Kaghan's ... mother, I am
516 CC	Claude	24	/That conversation would have convinced me/With no other evidence, that you
581 ES	Monica	11	here to greet him./But one thing I'm convinced of: you must leave Badgley Court./

CONVINCING (3)

400 CP	Reilly	5	now, did you have any difficulty/In convincing him I was the man for his case?/{A}
429 CP	Alex	3	/How do they agitate?/{A} By convincing the heathen/That the slaughter of
542 ES	Gomez	26	/{G} Neatly argued, and almost convincing:/Don't you wish you could believe

CONVINCINGLY (1)

| 450 CC | Eggers | 9 | thirty-one./But now you put it so convincingly,/I must admit there's a lot that *I* |

CONVULSIVE (1)

| 605 Narcissus | 19 | streets/He seemed to tread on faces, convulsive thighs and knees./So he came out |

COOK (3)

219 Mung Rump	24	joint, potatoes and greens,/And the cook would appear from behind the scenes/And
368 CP	Alex	14	/You know, I'm rather a famous cook./I'm going straight to your kitchen now/
376 CP	Edward	16	egg./It's the only thing I know how to cook./{J} Celia! I see you've had the same

COOKED (4)

245 MC	Priest2	7	the treetops:/But frogs at least can be cooked and eaten./Whatever you are afraid of,
247 MC	Tempt1	38	well alone,/Or your goose may be cooked and eaten to the bone./{T} You come
428 CP	Alex	22	monkeys are extremely palatable:/I've cooked them myself .../{E} And did anybody eat
428 CP	Edward	24	And did anybody eat them/When you cooked them?/{A} Oh yes, indeed./I invented for

COOKING (9)

44 Cook Egg	t	/And a glass of brandy neat./A Cooking Egg/Pipit sate upright in her chair/
203 Indians	2	village,/His own fire, and his wife's cooking;/To sit in front of his own door at
368 CP Edward	21	nothing in the larder worthy of your cooking./I couldn't think of it./{A} Ah, but
375 CP Edward	30	in, a little while ago,/And insisted on cooking me something for supper;/And he said I
375 CP Edward	32	within ten minutes./I suppose it's still cooking./{C} You suppose it's still cooking!/I
375 CP Celia	33	cooking./{C} You suppose it's still cooking!/I thought I noticed a peculiar smell:/
375 CP Celia	35	a peculiar smell:/Of course it's still cooking — or doing *something*./I must go and
453 CC Lucasta	11	very hungry — living on a pittance —/Cooking a sausage on a gas ring .../{E} You
556 ES Michael	21	was very well recommended./Good cooking, for a country inn. And not at all

COOL (5)

91 Ash-Wed 2	2	sat under a juniper-tree/In the cool of the day, having fed to satiety/On my legs
92 Ash-Wed 2	50	to each other,/Under a tree in the cool of the day, with the blessing of sand,/
94 Ash-Wed 4	9	and made fresh the springs/Made cool the dry rock and made firm the sand/In
203 Indians	8	of conversation,/(The warm or the cool hour, according to the climate)/Of foreign
279 MC Knight4	35	to allow our righteous/anger to cool. That was just what he did not wish to

COOLED (2)

| 38 Gerontion | 63 | the membrane, when the sense has cooled,/With pungent sauces, multiply variety/ |
| 370 CP Edward | 35 | affair/Like any other. As the fever cooled/You would have found that she was |

COOPS (1)

| 187 FQ: DrySal | 118 | of dead negroes, cows and chicken coops,/The bitter apple and the bite in the |

COPE (2)

| 453 CC Kaghan | 28 | Colby from you./But first, let's cope with the financial crisis./{L} Yes, Eggy, will |
| 554 ES Carghil | 26 | he might find it a strain/To have to cope with both of us at once./Besides, I ought to |

COPIER (1)

| 465 CC Claude | 16 | potter? To be, at best,/A competent copier, possessed by the craving/To create, |

COPLESTONE (15)

352 CP	m	4	SHUTTLETHWAITE)/CELIA COPLESTONE/ALEXANDER
353 CP	4m	1	SHUTTLETHWAITE, CELIA/COPLESTONE, PETER QUILPE,
373 CP Edward	3	*and dials a number]*/{E} Is Miss Celia Coplestone in? ... How long ago? .../No, it
407 CP Reilly	33	concealing your relations with Miss Coplestone./{E} This is monstrous! My wife
409 CP Reilly	11	you were not really in love with Miss Coplestone .../{L} My husband has never been
409 CP Reilly	31	/Had actually fallen in love with Miss Coplestone,/It took you some time, I have no
412 CP Reilly	24	*shows in* CELIA]/{R} Miss Celia Coplestone? ... Won't you sit down?/I believe
413 CP Reilly	3	/{R} Most of my patients begin, Miss Coplestone,/By telling me exactly what is the
414 CP Reilly	37	You suffer from a sense of sin, Miss Coplestone?/This is most unusual./{C} It seemed
419 CP Reilly	28	of them?/{R} They choose, Miss Coplestone. Nothing is forced on them./Some
433 CP Peter	16	it/If she only got the chance. It's Celia Coplestone./She always wanted to. And now I
434 CP Alex	17	be fit for normal life again./But Celia Coplestone, she was taken./When our people
437 CP Reilly	13	*part no more!*/When I first met Miss Coplestone, in this room,/I saw the image,
437 CP Reilly	15	standing behind her chair,/Of a Celia Coplestone whose face showed the astonishment
438 CP Reilly	34	made the wrong decision./As for Miss Coplestone, because you think her death was

COPPER (1)

| 64 WL: Chess | 94 | ceiling./Huge sea-wood fed with copper/Burned green and orange, framed by the |

COPULATION (5)

122 SA Sweeney	1	/{Do} What things?/{S} Birth, and copulation, and death./That's all, that's all,
122 SA Sweeney	3	all, that's all, that's all,/Birth, and copulation, and death./{Do} I'd be bored./{S}
122 SA Sweeney	6	bored./{S} You'd be bored./Birth, and copulation, and death./{Do} I'd be bored./{S}
122 SA Sweeney	9	bored./{S} You'd be bored./Birth, and copulation, and death./That's all the facts when
122 SA Sweeney	11	you come to brass tacks:/Birth, and copulation, and death./I've been born, and once

CORAL (2)

| 31 Apollinax | 10 | old man of the sea's/Hidden under coral islands/Where worried bodies of drowned |
| 123 SAWa & Ho | 10 | /*Any fresh egg*/*And the sound of the coral sea.*/{Do} I don't like eggs; I never liked |

CORD (1)

| 247 MC Thomas | 19 | /The same time returns. Sever/The cord, shed the scale. Only/The fool, fixed in his |

CORDIAL (1)

| 243 MC Priest2 | 2 | feet. Let us meet the Archbishop with cordial thanksgiving:/Our lord, our Archbishop |

CORDS (1)

| 105 Song Sime | 17 | the foreign swords./Before the time of cords and scourges and lamentation/Grant us |

CORE (1)

| 427 CP Alex | 35 | /Though whether the monkeys are the core of the problem/Or merely a symptom, I am |

CORICOPAT (1)

| 209 NamingCats | 18 | /Such as Munkustrap, Quaxo, or Coricopat,/Such as Bombalurina, or else |

CORIOLAN (1)

| 127 Coriolan | t | /KNOCK/KNOCK/KNOCK/Coriolan/Triumphal March/Stone, bronze, |

CORIOLANUS (2)
| 44 Cook Egg | 11 | Sir Philip Sidney/And have talk with Coriolanus/And other heroes of that kidney./I |
| 74 WL: Thund | 416 | /Revive for a moment a broken Coriolanus/DA/*Damyata:* The boat responded/ |

CORK (1)
| 224 Mr Mistoff | 31 | for mice./He can play any trick with a cork/Or a spoon and a bit of fish-paste;/If you |

CORN (3)
28 Boston ET	2	/Sway in the wind like a field of ripe corn./When evening quickens faintly in the
178 FQ: ECoker	40	long since under earth/Nourishing the corn. Keeping time,/Keeping the rhythm in
243 MC Chorus	31	and partly living./Sometimes the corn has failed us,/Sometimes the harvest is

CORNER (20)
22 Preludes	11	blinds and chimney-pots,/And at the corner of the street/A lonely cab-horse steams
24 Rhapsody	21	stained with sand,/And you see the corner of her eye/Twists like a crooked pin.'/
39 Gerontion	73	man driven by the Trades/To a sleepy corner./Tenants of the house,/Thoughts of a dry
107 Animula	7	to take alarm,/Retreating to the corner of arm and knee,/Eager to be reassured,
118 SP Wauch	27	here./Wait till I put the car round the corner/We'll be right up/{Du} All right, come
149 Rock 1	71	/The desert is not only around the corner,/The desert is squeezed in the tube-train
171 FQ: BurntN	22	bird, find them, find them,/Round the corner. Through the first gate,/Into our first
244 MC Chorus	7	against the winter,/Talked at the corner of the fire,/Talked at the corners of
288 FR Agatha	38	/That led to the nursery, round the corner/Of the new wing, he will have to face
288 FR Agatha	40	him —/And it will not be a very *jolly* corner./When the loop in time comes — and it
290 FR Agatha	31	/From the world around the corner/The wind's talk in the dry holly-tree/The
300 FRDowning	29	I went to bed,/And you could see the corner of the upper deck./And I remember,
308 FR Harry	33	not looking,/Always flickering at the corner of my eye,/Almost whispering just out of
395 CP Edward	39	each other,/Instead of each taking his corner of the cage./Well, it's a better way of
412 CP Julia	6	/And went on in the taxi, round the corner;/Waited a moment, and slipped in by the
424 CP Lavinia	5	MAN *with trolley*]/{L} There, in that corner. That's the most convenient;/You can get
481 CC Lady E	38	/And ask for the table in the left hand corner:/It has the best waitress. Good night./{L}
493 CC Lady E	24	Not such a low one. Leave that in the corner/For Colby. He won't want to be
541 ES Gomez	26	contrary/Any time you're in a tight corner/My entire resources are at your disposal.
548 ES Carghil	15	/It's the sunniest and most sheltered corner,/And none of the other guests have

CORNERS (9)
13 Prufrock	17	/Licked its tongue into the corners of the evening,/Lingered upon the pools
24 Rhapsody	53	winks a feeble eye,/She smiles into corners./She smooths the hair of the grass./The
105 Song Sime	6	/Dust in sunlight and memory in corners/Wait for the wind that chills towards
151 Rock 2	9	labour is not required./We wait on corners, with nothing to bring but the songs we
605 Narcissus	14	/His eyes were aware of the pointed corners of his eyes/And his hands aware of the
244 MC Chorus	8	at the corner of the fire,/Talked at the corners of streets,/Talked not always in
253 MC Tempt4	26	of men beneath a king,/With craft in corners, stealthy stratagem,/To general grasp of
280 MC Knight1	3	careful not to loiter in groups at street corners, and do/nothing that might provoke any
293 FR Gerald	32	North-West Frontier —/Been in tight corners most of my life/And some pretty nasty

CORNERSTONE (2)
| 151 Rock 2 | 3 | Christ Jesus Himself the chief cornerstone./But you, have you built well, that |
| 151 Rock 2 | 11 | you built well, have you forgotten the cornerstone?/Talking of right relations of men, |

CORNETS (2)
| 18 Portrait | 17 | tones of violins/Mingled with remote cornets/And begins./'You do not know how |
| 19 Portrait | 31 | violins/And the ariettes/Of cracked cornets/Inside my brain a dull tom-tom begins/ |

CORNOUAILLE (1)
| 51 Restaurant | 26 | les cris des mouettes et la houle de Cornouaille,/Et les profits et les pertes, et la |

CORNSTALK (1)
| 177 FQ: ECoker | 8 | and faeces,/Bone of man and beast, cornstalk and leaf./Houses live and die: there is |

CORNWALL (3)
218 Mung Rump	5	rove./They were very well known in Cornwall Gardens, in Launceston Place and in
313 FR Ivy	11	know I had my own garden once, in Cornwall,/When I could afford a garden; and I
357 CP Julia	37	down and see Lavinia/On my way to Cornwall. But let's be sensible:/Now you must

CORONATION (1)
| 268 MC Knight1 | 8 | prince,/Denying the legality of his coronation./{K2} Binding with the chains of |

CORPSE (2)
| 63 WL: Burial | 71 | with me in the ships at Mylae!/'That corpse you planted last year in your garden,/ |
| 572 ES   Ld Clav | 2 | over after he was dead./It was only a corpse that we had run over/So neither of us |

CORRECT (3)
19 Portrait	39	monuments,/Discuss the late events,/Correct our watches by the public clocks./Then
497 CC Claude	28	him as *our* son./{SC} That is perfectly correct. It is Colby/Who is not satisfied with
578 ES Ld Clav	7	mistake,/The mistaken attempts to correct mistakes/By methods which proved to

CORRECTLY (2)
129 Cor2 State   36 /O mother (not among these busts, all correctly inscribed)/I a tired head among these
436 CP   Reilly 39   /{R} You state the position correctly, Julia./Do you mind if I quote poetry,
CORRESPONDENT (1)
580 ES   Michael   8   /You know I'm not much of a correspondent;/But I'll send you a card, now
CORRESPONDENTS (1)
559 ES   Ld Clav   7   feet./I have connections, or at least correspondents/Almost everywhere. Australia
CORRIDOR (7)
 43 Swee Erect   33   at her sides./The ladies of the corridor/Find themselves involved, disgraced,/
232 Skimble   21   them all, more or less./Down the corridor he paces and examines all the faces/Of
288 FR   Agatha   37   orchard,/In the plantation, down the corridor/That led to the nursery, round the
310 FR   Harry   35   /Of a door that opens at the end of a corridor,/Sunlight and singing; when I had felt
310 FR   Harry   37   when I had felt sure/That every corridor only led to another,/Or to a blank wall;
329 FR   Chorus   11   kitchen/And the steps at night in the corridor/The moment of sudden loathing/And
335 FR   Agatha   5   feet walking/Away, down a concrete corridor/In a dead air. Only feet walking/And
CORRIDORS (2)
 24 Rhapsody   67   in shuttered rooms,/And cigarettes in corridors/And cocktail smells in bars./The lamp
 38 Gerontion   34   has many cunning passages, contrived corridors/And issues, deceives with whispering
CORRUGATED (1)
154 Rock 3   18   you build me a house of plaster, with corrugated roofing,/To be filled with a litter of
CORRUPT (1)
534 ES   Gomez   2   a fault in your logic./How can one corrupt those who are already corrupted?/I can
CORRUPTED (3)
292 FR   Harry   7   thicket,/The eyes stared at me, and corrupted that song./Behind the palm trees in
534 ES   Gomez   2   one corrupt those who are already corrupted?/I can swear that I've never corrupted
534 ES   Gomez   3   corrupted?/I can swear that I've never corrupted anybody./In fact, I've never come
CORRUPTIBLE (1)
534 ES   Gomez   5   an official/Innocent enough to be corruptible./{LC} It would seem then that most
CORRUPTION (3)
162 Rock 8   21   in Syria,/Living on, sunken in moral corruption;/Many came back well broken,/
270 MC   Chorus   9   evasive flank of the fish./I have smelt/Corruption in the dish, incense in the latrine,
533 ES   Ld Clav 38   /You have been engaged in systematic corruption./{G} No, Dick, there's a fault in your
COSIER (2)
361 CP   Reilly 37   /Finding your life becoming cosier and cosier/Without the consistent critic,
361 CP   Reilly 37   Finding your life becoming cosier and cosier/Without the consistent critic, the patient
COSTING (1)
198 FQ: Little   256   /A condition of complete simplicity/(Costing not less than everything)/And all shall
COSTLY (1)
456 CC   Eggers   28   it. That can be complicated/And very costly. I've had some rare adventures!/I
COSTS (1)
328 FR   Charles 15   of January 1st, was/fined £50 and costs to-day, and forbidden to drive a car for
COSTUME (4)
334 FR   Harry   27   laid out, lines underscored, and the costume/Ready to be put on. But it is very odd:/
346 FR   m   5   DOWNING, *hurriedly, in chauffeur's costume*]/{Do} Oh, excuse me, Miss, excuse me,
528 ES   Monica   9   you're in authority, with authority's costume,/When the man that people see when
569 ES   Ld Clav   6   she saw him, off the stage, without his costume and makeup/And without his stage
COSTUMES (1)
421 CP   Julia   5   can choose, whether to put on proper costumes/Or huddle quickly into new disguises,/
COSY (3)
233 Skimble   45   /And when you creep into your cosy berth/And pull up the counterpane,/You
286 FR   Charles   3   off in London:/A man can be very cosy at his club/Even in an English winter./{G}
536 ES   Gomez   27   what that's like./Your loneliness — so cosy, warm and padded:/You're not isolated —
CÔTES (1)
 47 Mél Adult   20   /On montrera mon cénotaphe/Aux côtes brûlantes de Mozambique./Lune de Miel/
COTTAGERS (1)
212 Growltiger   9   world from one forbidding eye./The cottagers of Rotherhithe knew something of his
COTTON (1)
151 Rock 2   19   /Exporting iron, coal and cotton goods/And intellectual enlightenment/
COUCH (1)
411 CP   2m   36   *and* LAVINIA]/[REILLY *goes to the couch and lies down. The house-telephone rings.*
COUCHED (1)
 52 Whispers   21   promise of pneumatic bliss./The couched Brazilian jaguar/Compels the
COUCHETTE (1)
428 CP   Julia   6   to travel in a very slow train/And in a *couchette*. She was very angry/When I told her

COUGHS (1)

| 37 | Gerontion | 11 | and peeled in London./The goat coughs at night in the field overhead;/Rocks, |

COULD (220)

COULDN'T (43)

120 SP	Krum	2	anything *coarse* —/But I'm afraid we couldn't stand the pace./What about it Klip?/
218 Mung Rump		12	from the bedroom chests,/And you couldn't find one of your winter vests,/Or after
295 FR	Harry	21	/As something so dreadful that it couldn't have happened,/Because you could not
304 FR	Mary	27	she still held on to me/Because she couldn't bear to let any project go;/And even
355 CP	Julia	34	/If they'd been friends of yours, I couldn't tell the story./{P} Were they the parents
356 CP	Julia	27	she got locked in the lavatory/And couldn't get out. I know what you're thinking!/
359 CP	Edward	15	party:/These were only the people I couldn't put off/Because I couldn't get at them
359 CP	Edward	16	people I couldn't put off/Because I couldn't get at them in time;/And I didn't know
368 CP	Edward	22	the larder worthy of your cooking./I couldn't think of it./{A} Ah, but that's my
387 CP	Celia	1	not really laughing at *you*, Edward./I couldn't have laughed at anything, yesterday;/
392 CP	Edward	15	to everyone I knew was coming/But I couldn't get everyone. And so a few came./{L}
393 CP	Lavinia	18	we were planning our honeymoon,/I couldn't make you say where you wanted to go
418 CP	Celia	15	to try to make a life with *any*body!/I couldn't give anyone the kind of love —/I wish I
427 CP	Alex	15	/After lunch, but my secretary couldn't get through to you./Never mind, I said
431 CP	Julia	39	always wanted to go to California:/Couldn't you persuade your casting director/To
433 CP	Peter	21	film./Can you tell me where she is? I couldn't find her/In the telephone directory./{J}
445 CC	Claude	5	meet her/At Northolt, but you. And I couldn't send Colby./That's not the way to
452 CC	Lucasta	19	luck, the boss did want a letter/And I couldn't find it. And then he got suspicious/And
452 CC	Lucasta	21	want —/Just to make trouble! And I couldn't find one of them./But they're all filed
461 CC	Eggers	16	to dinner one Sunday?'/But I say: 'We couldn't ask him to come/All the way to Joshua
472 CC	Colby	1	it was self-defence?/{C} Because you couldn't wait to see what happened./You're
475 CC	Colby	11	as soon as it happens,/Though you couldn't have predicted it./{L} I think I'm
485 CC	Lady E	8	have been an ordinary earl!/And I couldn't believe that my mother *was* my
486 CC	Colby	3	you say, it is an uncommon one./You couldn't have known my aunt./{LE} No. I never
487 CC	Claude	10	be of greater help than Eggerson./I couldn't have asked Eggerson to write a speech
487 CC	Lady E	23	Guzzard. I must confront her./This couldn't possibly be a coincidence./It seems
489 CC	Claude	8	yours had been lost,/And mine I couldn't lose. But if I had another/I thought
492 CC	Colby	24	—/And I found one note I couldn't understand.'Reminiscent mood.' I
502 CC	Lucasta	16	expecting/What I thought I got. But I couldn't believe it!/It isn't like you, to despise
513 CC	Colby	26	/Whom I have never known and couldn't know now,/Because he would have
514 CC	Claude	18	this is perfectly incredible!/You couldn't have carried out such a deception/Over
524 ES	Charles	7	me the whole afternoon./{C} But I couldn't say what I wanted to say to you/Over
525 ES	Charles	7	to give *me* the whole afternoon./I couldn't say what I wanted to, in a restaurant;/
540 ES	Gomez	33	be called to give evidence. You just couldn't face it./Do you see now, Dick, why I
548 ES	Carghil	28	been the topic of conversation./But I couldn't believe that it would really happen!/
552 ES	Carghil	8	*Too Late For You To Love Me*?/I couldn't have put the feeling into it I did/But
558 ES	Michael	7	pretended to be very shocked./Said he couldn't retain any man on his staff/Who'd
558 ES	Michael	23	me superfluous;/They knew I couldn't be living on my pay;/They had a lot of
567 ES	Monica	4	/It was exasperating that they couldn't find me/When you telephoned this
567 ES	Monica	7	have heard my beloved's voice/And I couldn't, just when I had been yearning/For the
567 ES	Charles	12	me,/But I wondered ... I'm sorry, I couldn't help wondering/How much your words
568 ES	Ld Clav	17	nothing, truly nothing, that you couldn't tell Monica/Then all is well with you.
574 ES	Michael	32	of my wish to get abroad,/You couldn't see my point of view. What's the use of

COULE (1)

| 46 | Directeur | 2 | à la malheureuse Tamise/Qui coule si près du Spectateur./Le directeur/ |

COUNCIL (1)

| 517 CC | Eggers | 35 | try me .../{E} The Parochial Church Council will be only too pleased,/And I have |

COUNCILS (2)

| 129 Cor2 State | | 9 | the committees:/The consultative councils, the standing committees, select |
| 270 MC Chorus | | 18 | the loom of fate/What is woven in the councils of princes/Is woven also in our veins, |

COUNSEL (2)

| 253 MC Thomas | | 20 | must kings destroy./{T} What is your counsel?/{T4} Fare forward to the end./All |
| 531 ES | Charles | 7 | 'we are confident/That his sagacious counsel will long continue/To be at the disposal |

COUNT (5)

73 WL: Thund		360	walks always beside you?/When I count, there are only you and I together/But
127 Cor1 March		4	And so many eagles./How many? Count them. And such a press of people./We
148 Rock 1		51	useful, resigning/The things that men count for happiness, seeking/The good deeds
166 Rock 10		14	of Good and Evil;/Seek not to count the future waves of Time;/But be ye
370 CP	Alex	18	expect to find any mangoes,/But I *did* count upon curry powder. {}/[*Exit*]/{P} That is

COUNTED (1)

| 185 FQ: DrySal | | 41 | of chronometers, older/Than time counted by anxious worried women/Lying |

COUNTENANCE (1)
20 Portrait   77   defaulter has confessed./I keep my countenance,/I remain self-possessed/Except
COUNTERPANE (1)
233 Skimble   46   into your cosy berth/And pull up the counterpane,/You ought to reflect that it's very
COUNTESS (1)
20 Portrait   74   /Particularly I remark./An English countess goes upon the stage./A Greek was
COUNTING (3)
260 MC Thomas   29   peace with the King, the householder counting/over his peaceful gains, the swept
285 FR   Ivy   18   as I do, in Bayswater, by a gas-fire counting shillings./{V} Go south! to the English
459 CC   m   6   name was?/{SC} Colby Simpkins. {}/[*counting on her fingers*]./{LE} Thirteen letters.
COUNTRY (44)
128 Cor1 March   43   (And Easter Day, we didn't get to the country,/So we took young Cyril to church.
148 Rock 1   34   countryside, there it seemed/That the country now is only fit for picnics./And the
148 Rock 1   36   does not seem to be wanted/In country or in suburb; and in the town/Only for
178 FQ: ECoker   38   shoes,/Earth feet, loam feet, lifted in country mirth/Mirth of those long since under
195 FQ: Little   161   as well as the past. Thus, love of a country/Begins as attachment to our own field
203 Indians   12   destination is not his destiny/Every country is home to one man/And exile to
250 MC Tempt3   30   who minds his own business./It is we country lords who know the country/And we
250 MC Tempt3   30   /It is we country lords who know the country/And we who know what the country
250 MC Tempt3   31   country/And we who know what the country needs./It is our country. We care for the
250 MC Tempt3   32   what the country needs./It is our country. We care for the country./We are the
250 MC Tempt3   32   /It is our country. We care for the country./We are the backbone of the nation./
276 MC Knight1   32   to speak first, my neighbour in/the country: Baron William de Traci./{K3} I am
277 MC Knight3   6   four plain Englishmen/who put our country first. I dare say that we didn't make a/
279 MC Knight4   20   under the King, did more to weld the/country together, to give it the unity, the
279 MC Knight4   23   be utterly indifferent to the fate of the country, to be, in/fact, a monster of egotism.
284 FR   m 11   EUMENIDES/*The scene is laid in a country house in the North of England*/PART I/
292 FR   Gerald   28   tomorrow./You'll find you know the country as well as ever./There wasn't an inch of
295 FR   Amy   36   our foggy climate/And the northern country. When you see Wishwood/Again by
303 FR   Mary   1   spring is very late in this northern country,/Late and uncertain, clings to the south
314 FR Warburt   8   both changed a good deal, Harry./A country practitioner doesn't get younger./It
314 FR Warburt   8   years./{W} Indeed, yes./Even in a country practice. My first patient, now —/You
321 FR   Winch   33   when I saw you last, my Lord. But a country sergeant/Doesn't get younger. Thank
322 FR   Winch   35   /Says he doesn't know this part of the country/And stopped to take his bearings.
328 FR   Charles 19   Piper said:/"I thought it was all open country about here"—'/{G} Where?/{C} In
331 FR   Agatha   34   him —/An exceptionally cultivated country squire,/Reading, sketching, playing on
332 FR   Agatha   17   a woman/Married, alone in a lonely country. For three years
332 FR   Agatha   24   day of unusual heat/For this cold country./{H} And then?/{Ag} There are hours
357 CP   Celia   3   dreadful for old ladies alone in the country,/And almost impossible to get a nurse./
372 CP   Edward   17   aunt/Has just sent them from the country./{A} Ah, so the aunt/Really exists. A
392 CP   Edward   27   I invented an aunt/Who was ill in the country, and had sent for you./{L} Really,
414 CP   Celia   15   your parents?/{C} Oh, they live in the country,/Now they can't afford to have a place
414 CP   Celia   17   town./It's all they can do to keep the country house going:/But it's been in the family
427 CP   Alex   10   thought you might be leaving for the country,/I said, I must not miss the opportunity
430 CP   Peter   13   you see,/And I'm driving down to the country this evening,/So I knew you wouldn't
485 CC   Lady E   28   you were brought up, like me, in the country./Teddington. I seem to have heard of it.
505 CC   Claude   4 recently retired./Now he lives ... in the country. But he knows the whole story:/He's
510 CC   Kaghan   29   In Kent. They wanted to retire to the country./So I found them a little place near
533 ES   Gomez   9   is a good deal more normal/In my country, than Culverwell — and easier to
534 ES   Gomez   27   of my sons/To go into politics. In my country, Dick,/Politicians can't afford mistakes.
556 ES   Michael 21   recommended./Good cooking, for a country inn. And not at all expensive./{LC} You
559 ES   Michael 21   I want to go far away/To some country where no one has heard the name of
560 ES   Michael 8   find life become, once I'm out of the country./What I'd like is a chance to go abroad/
570 ES   Ld Clav 29   the highest standing/In his adopted country. He even has sons/Following in their
574 ES   Carghil 20   man, and very important,/In his own country. And a friend of Michael's father!/And
COUNTRY-BRED (1)
285 FR   Charles 23   That's not Amy's style at all. We are country-bred people./Amy has been too long
COUNTRY-KEEPING (1)
250 MC Tempt3   29   how to hold my estates in order,/A country-keeping lord who minds his own
COUNTRYMAN (2)
251 MC Thomas   8   /Can sooner know accord./{T} For a countryman/You wrap your meaning in as dark
496 CC   Eggers   22   she says: 'You're becoming such a countryman!/You're losing touch with public
COUNTRYSIDE (1)
148 Rock 1   33   /Of economic laws./In the pleasant countryside, there it seemed/That the country

COUNTS (1)

469 CC	Lucasta	2	well, Colby —/Not that *my* opinion counts for anything:/You know that. But I'd

COUNTY (2)

331 FR	Agatha	36	flute,/Something of an oddity to his county neighbours,/But not neglecting public
485 CC	Lady E	26	/{LE} Teddington? In what county?/{C} It's very close to London./{LE}

COUPLE (6)

124 SA	Sweeney	28	another story too./This went on for a couple of months/Nobody came/And nobody
218 Mung	Rump	1	Rumpelteazer were a very notorious couple of cats./As knockabout clowns,
218 Mung	Rump	6	really a little more reputation than a couple of cats can very well bear./If the area
292 FR	Gerald	30	know./But you'll have to see about a couple of new hunters./{C} And I've a new wine
479 CC	Kaghan	5	dropping in on you./And between a couple of man-eating tigers/Like you and Lizzie,
493 CC	Claude	14	other hand,/We mustn't look like a couple of barristers/Ready to cross-examine a

COUPLING (1)

178 FQ: ECoker		45	the time of harvest/The time of the coupling of man and woman/And that of

COUPOLE (1)

67 WL: Fire S		202	O ces voix d'enfants, chantant dans la coupole!/Twit twit twit/Jug jug jug jug jug jug/

COUPS (1)

47 Mél	Adult	14	/J'erre toujours de-ci de-là/A divers coups de tra là là/De Damas jusqu'à Omaha./Je

COURAGE (10)

38 Gerontion		44	a fear. Think/Neither fear nor courage saves us. Unnatural vices/Are fathered
299 FRDowning		14	Ladyship,/I don't think she had the courage./{C} Did she ever talk of suicide?/{Do}
304 FR	Mary	18	could have gone, if I'd had the moral courage,/Even against a will like hers. I know
305 FR	Agatha	7	time before now, it would have shown courage/And would have been right. Now, the
305 FR	Agatha	8	And would have been right. Now, the courage is only the moment/And the moment is
362 FR	Reilly	5	/That she saw it first, and had the courage to break it —/Thus giving herself a
404 CP	Edward	31	more than seven days;/I haven't the courage to go to a hotel,/And besides, I need
418 CP	Reilly	20	There *is* another way, if you have the courage./The first I could describe in familiar
435 CP	Peter	12	did not dare to ask. It took all my courage/To ask you about her just now; but I
472 CC	Lucasta	33	/Very sorry for you. I admired your courage/In facing facts — or the facts as you

COURAGEOUSLY (1)

592 Grad 1		6	lie below,/But let us yet put forth courageously./As colonists embarking from the

COURANT (1)

51 Restaurant		28	les pertes, et la cargaison d'étain:/Un courant de sous-mer l'emporta très loin,/Le

COURSE (104)

19 Portrait		50	which it cannot see.'/I smile, of course,/And go on drinking tea./'Yet with these
118 SP	Dusty	19	*again*.)/{Do} Is that Sam?/{Du} Of course it's Sam!/{Do} Of course, the Knave of
118 SP	Doris	20	/{Du} Of course it's Sam!/{Do} Of course, the Knave of Hearts *is* Sam!/{Du}
120 SP	Krum	9	like Sam to show you around./Sam of course is at *home* in London,/And he's
187 FQ: DrySal		124	it is always a seamark/To lay a course by: but in the sombre season/Or the
234 Ad-dress		24	you would call a simple soul./Of course I'm not including Pekes,/And such
588 Fable		31	he:/'If ghosts come uninvited, then, of course,/I'll be compelled to keep them off by
589 Fable		86	rascals are not rare)/That the Abbot's course lay nearer underground;/But the church
253 MC	Tempt4	37	or servant within an hour,/This is the course of temporal power./The Old King shall
256 MC	Priests	28	may find his way,/The sailor lay course by the sun? {}/CHORUS, PRIESTS *and*
279 MC Knight4		17	it in this way. But/consider the course of events. I am obliged, very briefly, to
287 FR	Amy	39	London,/And hoped to arrive in the course of the evening./{V} Harry was always the
295 FR	Charles	9	to your mother and yourself./Of course we know what really happened, we read
299 FR	Charles	8	what we read in the papers —/Of course, there was a great deal too much in the
303 FR	Mary	13	/Arthur or John may be late, of course./We may have to keep the dinner back ...
307 FR	Harry	7	evil spirits./{H} Arthur and John./Of course we were punished for being out at night/
318 FR Warburt		37	my father?/{W} Why, yes, of course, Harry, but I really don't see/What that
319 FR	Harry	28	a child./*That* was the day he died. Of course./{W} Why, yes, Harry, of course I did./{H} What did he look like then?
321 FR Warburt		1	present age?/{W} Why, yes, Harry, of course I did./{H} What did he look like then?
321 FR Warburt		3	like me?/{W} Very much like you. Of course there are differences:/But, allowing for
323 FR	Winch	24	is he?/{Wi} At the Arms, my Lady;/Of course, he hasn't come round yet./Dr. Owen
324 FR	Harry	12	it means to your mother?/{H} Oh, of course I'm sorry. But from what Winchell says/I
325 FR	Violet	34	to go with him at all —/Though of course he meant well — but I think an open car/
326 FR	Harry	20	deviation/From some imaginary course that life ought to take,/That you call
343 FR	Mary	14	mean it/Then, but I mean it now. Of course it was much too late/Then, for anything
343 FR	Harry	36	you need to worry about;/I have my course to pursue, and I am safe from normal
347 FRDowning		8	first. You soon get used to them./Of course, I knew they was to do with his
349 FR	Agatha	23	subject to reason/Each curse has its course/Its own way of expiation/Follow follow/
357 CP	Julia	39	aunt —/Living on an annuity, of course./I am going to make you dine alone with
360 CP	Edward	3	has left you?/{E} Without warning, of course;/Just when she'd arranged a cocktail
366 CP	Julia	6	not in your bag?/{J} Why no, of course not: that's where I keep them./Oh, here

366 CP	Julia	21	about,/And I could do it now./{J} Of course I don't mind./{P} Well, at least you must
366 CP	Peter	37	awful party! I'm sorry, Edward;/Of course it was really a very nice party/For
367 CP	Edward	28	if one is interested in Celia./Apart, of course, from its literary merit/Which I don't
372 CP	Alex	14	I found in your refrigerator. But of course/I was lucky to find half-a-dozen eggs./
375 CP	Edward	13	... No. I mean yes, Alex;/Yes, of course ... it was marvellous./I've never tasted
375 CP	Celia	35	thought I noticed a peculiar smell:/Of course it's still cooking — or doing *something*./I
376 CP	Edward	31	/{J} But you mustn't touch it./{E} Of course I shan't touch it./{J} My dear, I should
377 CP	Julia	23	/Only a half-bottle, to be sure,/And of course it isn't chilled. But it's so refreshing;/And
387 CP	Edward	31	our conversation yesterday?/{E} Of course./{P} I hope you've done nothing about it.
388 CP	Celia	9	glad, for your sake,/Though of course we ... I shall miss you;/You know how I
388 CP	Edward	30	you been sending telegrams?/{E} Of course I haven't sent any telegrams./{L} This is
389 CP	Lavinia	3	you both. To Hollywood, of course?/How exciting for you, Celia! Now you'll
389 CP	Peter	12	you are going, yourself?/{P} Yes, of course, I'm going to California./{L} Well, Celia,
390 CP	Julia	8	sent from?/{J} Why, from Essex, of course./{L} And why from Essex?/{J} Because
390 CP	Julia	31	had a lapse of memory,/And so, of course, she sent us telegrams:/And now I don't
391 CP	Edward	36	/To seem anything. But of course I'm glad to see you./{L} Yes, that was a
393 CP	Edward	25	/And you said 'I don't mind'./{E} Of course I didn't mind./I meant it as a
399 CP	Reilly	3	again./You understand, of course, that it is important/To avoid any
404 CP	Edward	34	sent on: whatever I shall need./But of course you mustn't tell her where I am./Is it far
410 CP	Reilly	37	all any of us make of it —/Except of course, the saints — such as those who go/To
412 CP	Julia	5	know you were seeing me first?/{J} Of course not. I dropped her at the door/And went
412 CP	Celia	28	/Haven't I, somewhere? ... Oh, of course./But I didn't know .../{R} There is
414 CP	Celia	4	ordinary way, or being ditched./Of course that's something that's always happening
421 CP	Julia	8	time, somewhere to start from./Oh, of course, they might just murder each other!/But I
431 CP	Peter	35	for some typical English faces —/Of course, only for minor parts —/And I'll help
434 CP	Alex	3	various endemic diseases/Besides, of course, those brought by Europeans,/And
435 CP	Peter	26	it, believed in it, for Celia./And, of course, I wanted to do something for Celia —/
445 CC	Claude	25	the last time I came./{SC} Well, of course, Eggerson, you're irreplaceable .../{E}
446 CC	Eggers	8	getting over his disappointment?/Of course, I never mentioned that:/It's only what
447 CC	Claude	8	me to approach the subject?/{SC} Of course, she knows you were wanting to retire,/
456 CC	Eggers	6	satisfied with the bargain.'/Of course it's true that her family connections/
456 CC	Eggers	31	in Joshua Park/(On a mortgage, of course) 'now we've settled down/All the travel *I*
458 CC	Claude	19	experienced traveller./{SC} Oh yes, of course we know that, Elizabeth./But why did
459 CC	Lady E	1	/And recommended to Sir Claude? Of course it is./I remember saying: 'He has a good
460 CC	Lady E	18	I must persuade you/To have a course of treatment with Dr. Rebmann —/No,
469 CC	Lucasta	22	a concert./I've been to the Opera, of course, several times,/But I'm afraid I never
470 CC	Colby	17	teach me about music?/{C} Yes, of course I will./But I'm sure that when you learn
472 CC	Lucasta	24	you'd never be a good musician —/Of course, *I* don't know whether you were right./
475 CC	Lucasta	30	has ever 'just accepted' me before./Of course the facts don't matter, in a sense./But
476 CC	Lucasta	37	the neighbours complained./Oh of course Claude gave her money, a regular
479 CC	Kaghan	23	bachelor life!/Which depends, of course, on preventing Lizzie/From always
484 CC	Lady E	12	/{LE} And did you loathe her? No, of course not./Or you wouldn't have her portrait.
484 CC	Lady E	38	a foundling, and didn't know it./Of course, I was terrified of being ugly,/And of
485 CC	Lady E	19	/Is one's previous existences. Of course, there's something in us,/In all of us,
488 CC	Lady E	33	you'd want to adopt him./{LE} But of course I want to adopt him, Claude!/That is, if
492 CC	Claude	12	as well. {}/[*rising*]./{SC} Oh, of course, Eggerson! He knows all about it./Let us
497 CC	Eggers	33	Simpkins to take,/If I may say so. Of course, we might discover/Another Mrs.
498 CC	Lady E	24	But *this* baby was Colby./{LE} Of course it was Colby./{SC} But Eggerson, you
499 CC	Claude	20	make it now. If you'll listen./{SC} Of course I'll listen. But we haven't much time./{L}
499 CC	Lucasta	23	that was all settled./{L} Yes, of course, Claude. You thought everything settled.
503 CC	Colby	23	will concur in this proposal./{C} Of course I'd like them ... Can't B. come up now?/
506 CC	Eggers	34	her new-born child was confided./Of course she might be mistaken about Teddington
512 CC	Lady E	22	gratify everyone's wishes./{LE} Oh, of course ... Yes, I'm sure ... I shall be very happy./
512 CC	Kaghan	30	—/If I can live up to it. And ... yes, of course,/If I can make it right with my parents./
515 CC	Claude	35	Colby —/If this should be true — of course it can't be true! —/But I see you believe
525 ES	Charles	10	don't like shopping with me .../{C} Of course I like shopping with you./But how can
535 ES	Gomez	35	*helps himself to whisky*]/{G} But of course you know!/Just enough to think you
537 ES	Gomez	27	It went the other way. You stayed the course, at least./I had plenty of time to think
538 ES	Gomez	30	could always consult you/But of course didn't have to take your advice .../I've
541 ES	Gomez	7	Dick, your secret's safe with me./Of course, I might give it to a few friends, in
546 ES	Piggott	1	/{MP} Oh no, not 'Matron'!/Of course, I *am* a matron in a sense —/No, I don't
546 ES	Piggott	4	But I was a Trained Nurse,/And of course I've always lived in what you might call/
547 ES	Piggott	27	our guests are keen on tennis,/And of course there's always croquet. But I don't advise
555 ES	Piggott	6	of hinting —/Tactfully, of course — that you should not be disturbed./
562 ES	Carghil	15	who you are! You're Monica, of course:/And this must be your brother, Michael.

564 ES	Carghil	18	to speak such perfect English?/Of course, I could tell from your looks that you
564 ES	Carghil	25	was after I had left England./{MC} Of course, that explains it. After Oxford/I suppose
572 ES	Ld Clav	16	was his way of putting it — and of course/Made it worth while for me not to marry
575 ES	Ld Clav	12	Yes, wasn't it extraordinary./{LC} Of course you're just the man that Señor Gomez
575 ES	Gomez	27	custodian of *my* morals:/Though of course you went a little *faster* than I did./{LC}
578 ES	Michael	22	to me to have a brother./{Mi} Why of course, Monica. You know I'm very fond of
578 ES	Monica	36	You must make your own life/Of course, just as I must make mine./It's not a
580 ES	Michael	7	/Will you ever answer?/{Mi} Oh of course, Monica./You know I'm not much of a

COURT (24)

118 SP	Dusty	3	/{Du} It's a funny thing how I draw court cards —/{Do} There's a lot in the way you
118 SP	Dusty	14	you?/Wasn't I saying I always draw court cards?/The Knave of Hearts! {}/(*Whistle*
155 Rock 3		33	/The nettle shall flourish on the gravel court,/And the wind shall say: 'Here were
250 MC	Tempt3	25	no politician./To idle or intrigue at court/I have no skill. I am no courtier./I know a
252 MC	Tempt3	3	the tyrannous jurisdiction/Of king's court over bishop's court,/Of king's court over
252 MC	Tempt3	3	/Of king's court over bishop's court,/Of king's court over baron's court./{T}
252 MC	Tempt3	4	court over bishop's court,/Of king's court over baron's court./{T} Which I helped to
252 MC	Tempt3	4	court,/Of king's court over baron's court./{T} Which I helped to found./{T3} Which
252 MC	Thomas	17	to wait at my door./Not only in the court, but in the field/And in the tilt-yard I
405 CP	Reilly	17	to know his brief before he enters the court./{E} I am at least free to leave. And I
523 ES	m	13	/ACT TWO/*The Terrace at Badgley Court. Morning*/ACT THREE/*The Same. Late*
528 ES	Monica	26	be, he will never return from Badgley Court./But Selby wants him to have every
532 ES	Charles	24	to seeing you both at Badgley Court/In a week or two. {}/[*Enter* LAMBERT]/
543 ES	Monica	20	/What will it be like at Badgley Court? {}/CURTAIN/Act Two/*The terrace of*
544 ES	2m	1	/Act Two/*The terrace of Badgley Court. A bright sunny morning, several days*
545 ES	Ld Clav	16	perfect peace: that's what Badgley Court is for.'/I thought that very ominous.
546 ES	Piggott	10	mustn't call me 'Matron'/At Badgley Court. You see, we've studied to avoid/
547 ES	Piggott	21	/About the amenities which Badgley Court/Can offer to guests of the younger
551 ES	Carghil	27	I shouldn't have settled out of court./My lawyer said: 'I advise you to accept',/
563 ES	Gomez	12	you'd chosen to come to Badgley Court/I said to my doctor, 'Well, what about it?
564 ES	Carghil	29	if it's true you're staying at Badgley Court,/I warn you — I'm going to
581 ES	Monica	11	convinced of: you must leave Badgley Court./{C} Monica is right. You should leave./
581 ES	Monica	32	come to know you/Here, at Badgley Court. And I love you the more/Because I love
582 ES	Ld Clav	13	This is your first visit to us at Badgley Court,/Charles, and not at all what you were

COURT'S (1)

| 529 ES | Monica | 1 | 'as if you were going'./But Badgley Court's so near your constituency!/You can |

COURTEOUS (1)

| 601 Nocturne | | 4 | debate/Of love, beneath a bored but courteous moon;/The conversation failing, |

COURTESIES (1)

| 547 ES | Monica | 17 | after what she considers proper courtesies,/She will leave us alone. {}/[*Re-enter* |

COURTIER (2)

| 250 MC | Tempt3 | 26 | at court/I have no skill. I am no courtier./I know a horse, a dog, a wench;/I |
| 251 MC | Thomas | 10 | meaning in as dark generality/As any courtier./{T3} This is the simple fact!/You have |

COURTIERS (1)

| 242 MC | Priest1 | 21 | by the King./Liked or feared by courtiers, in their overbearing fashion,/Despised |

COURTS (1)

| 280 MC | Priest3 | 27 | snatch/Forgetfulness in his libidinous courts,/Oblivion in the fountain by the |

COUSIN (15)

28 Boston ET		9	he at the end of the street,/And I say, 'Cousin Harriet, here is the *Boston Evening*
30 Cous Nancy		t	so careful while her mistress lived./Cousin Nancy/Miss Nancy Ellicott/Strode
284 FR	m	4	/MARY, *daughter of a deceased cousin of Lady Monchensey*/DENMAN, *a*
287 FR	Mary	7	does she think about it?/{M} Really, Cousin Gerald, if you want information/About
291 FR	Ivy	3	the fire./{I} I might have been visiting Cousin Lily at Sidmouth, if I had not had to
303 FR	Mary	29	is behaving like a man of the world?/Cousin Agatha, I want your advice./{Ag} I
304 FR	Mary	15	You know perfectly well,/What Cousin Amy wants, she usually gets./Why do
304 FR	Mary	28	even when *she* died: I believed that Cousin Amy —/I almost believed it — had
306 FR	Mary	27	/But there were reasons: I was only a cousin/Kept here because there was nothing else
342 FR	Mary	1	... {}/[*Enter* MARY]/{M} Excuse me, Cousin Amy. I have just seen Denman./She
342 FR	Mary	19	from another!/Can you not stop him? Cousin Agatha, stop him!/You do not know
342 FR	Mary	28	to me,/But Harry must not go. Cousin Agatha!/{Ag} Here the danger, here the
414 CP	Celia	21	/{C} I share a flat/With a cousin: but she's abroad at the moment,/And
509 CC	Colby	12	/{C} Barnabas Kaghan. Is he the little cousin/Who died? Don't you remember, Aunt
509 CC	Colby	15	/And your telling me I had had a little cousin/Who had died?/{MG} Yes, Colby, that is

COUSIN'S (1)

| 61 WL: Burial | | 14 | staying at the arch-duke's,/My cousin's, he took me out on a sled,/And I was |

COUSINS (1)
223 Pekes Pols   34   tyke,/And his braw Scottish cousins are snappers and biters,/And every
COVE (1)
204 de la Mare   2   found/A desert island with a sandy cove/(A hiding place, but very dangerous
COVENANT (1)
191 FQ: Little   14   is the spring time/But not in time's covenant. Now the hedgerow/Is blanched for an
COVER (6)
138 New Hamp   8   /To-day grieves, to-morrow grieves,/Cover me over, light-in-leaves;/Golden head,
588 Fable   54   ale, and cheese which they kept under cover./Last, a boar's head, which to bring in
263 MC Chorus   25   what wrong/Shall the bird's song cover, the green tree cover, what wrong/Shall
263 MC Chorus   25   the bird's song cover, the green tree cover, what wrong/Shall the fresh earth cover?
263 MC Chorus   26   what wrong/Shall the fresh earth cover? We wait, and the time is short/But
330 FR   Harry   24   one hell./Then the numbness came to cover it — that is another —/That was the
COVERED (1)
187 FQ: DrySal   113   than in our own./For our own past is covered by the currents of action,/But the
COVERING (2)
61 WL: Burial   5   spring rain./Winter kept us warm, covering/Earth in forgetful snow, feeding/A
250 MC Tempt2   8   to your fate./Your sin soars sunward, covering kings' falcons./{T} Temporal power, to
COVERS (1)
316 FR Agatha   9   {Ag} The eye is on this house/The eye covers it/There are three together/May the three
COVET (1)
531 ES Ld Clav   22   Who occupy positions that other men covet./When we go, a good many folk are
COW-PASTURE (1)
30 Cous Nancy   6   hills —/Riding to hounds/Over the cow-pasture./Miss Nancy Ellicott smoked/And
COWARD (4)
561 ES Ld Clav   12   /Knowing that my son had played the coward —/I should merely be another twenty
561 ES Michael   14   /{Mi} Very well: if you like, call me a coward./I wonder whether you would play the
561 ES Michael   34   career:/And Father simply calls me a coward./{M} Father! You know that I would
565 ES Ld Clav   31   from/Is myself, is the past. But what a coward I am,/To talk of escaping! And what a
COWARDICE (1)
568 ES Ld Clav   26   /Not only turpitude, meanness and cowardice,/But also situations which are simply
COWARDLY (1)
20 Portrait   69   /I take my hat: how can I make a cowardly amends/For what she has said to me?/
COWER (1)
204 de la Mare   21   in the moonlight dance,/Dogs cower, flitter bats, and owls range/At witches'
COWERED (1)
270 MC Chorus   6   kite, I have plunged with the kite and cowered with the wren. I have felt/The horn of
COWERS (1)
186 FQ: DrySal   70   /Into the wind's tail, where the fog cowers?/We cannot think of a time that is
COWS (2)
187 FQ: DrySal   118   river with its cargo of dead negroes, cows and chicken coops,/The bitter apple and
587 Fable   21   merry times./He stole the fatter cows and left the thinner/To furnish all the milk
COWSLIP (1)
270 MC Chorus   3   sweet pea, hyacinth, primrose and cowslip. I have seen/Trunk and horn, tusk and
CRAB (4)
24 Rhapsody   43   peer through lighted shutters,/And a crab one afternoon in a pool,/An old crab with
24 Rhapsody   44   crab one afternoon in a pool,/An old crab with barnacles on his back,/Gripped the
184 FQ: DrySal   19   creation:/The starfish, the horseshoe crab, the whale's backbone;/The pools where it
270 MC Chorus   2   I have tasted/The living lobster, the crab, the oyster, the whelk and the prawn; and
CRACK (2)
175 FQ: BurntN   153   /And all is always now. Words strain,/Crack and sometimes break, under the burden,/
224 Mr Mistoff   25   tail;/He can creep through the tiniest crack/He can walk on the narrowest rail./He
CRACKED (7)
19 Portrait   31   of the violins/And the ariettes/Of cracked cornets/Inside my brain a dull tom-tom
54 Mr E Sun   12   the Baptized God./The wilderness is cracked and browned/But through the water
73 WL: Thund   369   /Over endless plains, stumbling in cracked earth/Ringed by the flat horizon only/
109 Marina   22   where all the waters meet./Bowsprit cracked with ice and paint cracked with heat./I
109 Marina   22   /Bowsprit cracked with ice and paint cracked with heat./I made this, I have forgotten/
135 5FingerEx2   8   cretonne eiderdown,/Yet the field was cracked and brown/And the tree was cramped
162 Rock 8   25   at the door in possession:/Came home cracked by the sun of the East/And the seven
CRACKS (2)
24 Rhapsody   56   her memory./A washed-out smallpox cracks her face,/Her hand twists a paper rose,/
73 WL: Thund   372   /What is the city over the mountains/Cracks and reforms and bursts in the violet air/
CRAFT (1)
253 MC Tempt4   26   /Or rule of men beneath a king,/With craft in corners, stealthy stratagem,/To general

CRAFTSMAN (1)
495 CC   Claude   32   {SC} A musician./I am a disappointed craftsman,/And Colby is a disappointed

CRAMPED (1)
135 5FingerEx2   9   cracked and brown/And the tree was cramped and dry./Pollicle dogs and cats all

CRÂNE (1)
51 Restaurant   22   /Tiens, ma fourchette, décrasse-toi le crâne./De quel droit payes-tu des expériences

CRANK (1)
233 Skimble   40   supposed to wash your face in/And a crank to shut the window if you sneeze./Then

CRASH (4)
219 Mung Rump   35   up from the pantry there came a loud crash/Or down from the library came a loud
307 FR   Harry   32   of every alternative,/The unexpected crash of the iron cataract./You do not know
414 CP   Celia   1   mean simply/That there's been a crash: though indeed there has been./It isn't
430 CP   Peter   10   Gunnings —/So I said, I really must crash in:/It's my only chance to see Edward and

CRAVEN (1)
245 MC   Priest2   8   /Whatever you are afraid of, in your craven apprehension,/Let me ask you at the

CRAVING (5)
38 Gerontion   39   /That the giving famishes the craving. Gives too late/What's not believed in,
336 FR   Agatha   1   /Is also relief from that unfulfilled craving/Flattered in sleep, and deceived in
417 CP   Celia   17   meaningless, I want to be cured/Of a craving for something I cannot find/And of the
465 CC   Claude   16   /A competent copier, possessed by the craving/To create, when one is wholly
542 ES   Gomez   8   then./I'm a lonely man, Dick, with a craving for affection./All I want is as much of

CRAWLED (2)
73 WL: Thund   381   /Whistled, and beat their wings/And crawled head downward down a blackened wall
266 MC Knights   20   in Cheapside;/This is the creature that crawled upon the King; swollen with blood and

CRAWLING (1)
266 MC Knights   22   /Creeping out of the London dirt,/Crawling up like a louse on your shirt,/The man

CRAWLS (2)
53 Whispers   31   her charm;/But our lot crawls between dry ribs/To keep our
600 Moonflower   2   opens to the moth,/The mist crawls in from sea;/A great white bird, a snowy

CREAKING (1)
135 5FingerEx1   7   no relief but in grief./O when will the creaking heart cease?/When will the broken

CREAM (4)
125 SA   Chorus   35   hit you in the head/You've had a cream of a nightmare dream and you've got the
214 RTTugger   27   he won't eat rabbit./If you offer him cream then he sniffs and sneers,/For he only
235 Ad-dress   55   of esteem/Is needed, like a dish of cream;/And you might now and then supply/
236 Cat Morgan   6   grouse,/And I favour that Devonshire cream in a bowl;/But I'm allus content with a

CREATE (7)
14 Prufrock   28   /There will be time to murder and create,/And time for all the works and days of
165 Rock 9   29   LORD who created must wish us to create/And employ our creation again in His
202 War Poetry   6   path of an action merely typical/To create the universal, originate a symbol/Out of
281 MC Chorus   18   and saints/Shall enrich the earth, shall create the holy places./For wherever a saint has
427 CP   Edward   39   natives./{E} But how do the monkeys create unrest?/{A} To begin with, the monkeys
465 CC   Claude   17   copier, possessed by the craving/To create, when one is wholly uncreative?/I don't
513 CC   Colby   34   a likeness;/Whose image I could create in my own mind,/To live with that image.

CREATED (6)
160 Rock 7   1   the Temple./In the beginning GOD created the world. Waste and void. Waste and
165 Rock 9   29   of the senses?/The LORD who created must wish us to create/And employ our
211 Old Gumbie   36   a good deed to do —/And she's even created a Beetles' Tattoo./So for Old Gumbie
416 CP   Celia   24   horrible. Can we only love/Something created by our own imagination?/Are we all in
575 ES Ld Clav   6   {LC} Yes, I see the advantage of a job created for you/By Señor Gomez .../{Mi} It's
575 ES Michael   8   you/By Señor Gomez .../{Mi} It's not created for me./Señor Gomez came to London

CREATES (3)
98 Ash-Wed 6   17   the whirling plover/And the blind eye creates/The empty forms between the ivory
428 CP   Alex   30   natives prosper exceedingly:/And that creates friction between them and the others./
510 CC   Eggers   9   This Mr. Kaghan — is my son?/{E} It creates an inherent probability —/If that's the

CREATING (2)
165 Rock 9   31   /Which is already His service in creating./For Man is joined spirit and body,/
224 Mr Mistoff   9   performing surprising illusions/And creating eccentric confusions./At

CREATION (9)
85 Hollow Men   79   /Between the conception/And the creation/Between the emotion/And the response
164 Rock 9   16   /The soul of Man must quicken to creation./Out of the formless stone, when the
165 Rock 9   30   wish us to create/And employ our creation again in His service/Which is already
165 Rock 9   39   after many obstacles;/For the work of creation is never without travail;/The formed
184 FQ: DrySal   18   it tosses/Its hints of earlier and other creation:/The starfish, the horseshoe crab, the
228 Gus   19   him seven cat-calls./But his grandest creation, as he loves to tell,/Was Firefrorefiddle,

229 Gus   33   Whittington's Cat./But my grandest creation, as history will tell,/Was
465 CC   Claude 22   in the vision of some marvellous creation,/And I feel what the man must have
471 CC   Colby   28   preferred it to be one of your own creation/Rather than wait to see what
CREATURE (3)
266 MC Knights   20   was born in Cheapside;/This is the creature that crawled upon the King; swollen
381 CP   Edward 34   —/The self that wills — he is a feeble creature;/He has to come to terms in the end/
428 CP   Julia   7   was very angry/When I told her the creature ought to be destroyed./{L} But can't
CREATURES (8)
 52 Whispers   3   skull beneath the skin;/And breastless creatures under ground/Leaned backward with
129 Cor2 State   48   falling, crowned with dust', the small creatures,/The small creatures chirp thinly
129 Cor2 State   49   dust', the small creatures,/The small creatures chirp thinly through the dust, through
178 FQ: ECoker   54   the disturbance of the spring/And creatures of the summer heat,/And snowdrops
270 MC Chorus   1   light of dawn. I have eaten/Smooth creatures still living, with the strong salt taste of
281 MC Chorus   7   for Thy glory displayed in all the creatures of the earth,/In the snow, in the rain,
281 MC Chorus   8   the wind, in the storm; in all of Thy creatures, both the hunters and the hunted./For
294 FR   Harry   16   desert/In a thick smoke, many creatures moving/Without direction, for no
CREDIT (6)
277 MC Knight3   26   beginning, please give us/at least the credit for being completely disinterested in this
301 FR   Gerald 22   is only concerned for herself, and her credit among her shabby genteel acquaintance./
333 FR   Agatha   3   event: I stopped him./I can take no credit for a little common sense,/He would have
346 FRDowning   22   what I mean, though you'd hardly credit it,/I've always said, whatever happened to
558 ES   Michael 3   of your name they insist on giving credit./{LC} And your debts: are they the cause
579 ES   Gomez   35   clearly./{G} Not that I deserve any credit for it./We can only regard it as a stroke of
CREDULITY (1)
437 CP   Reilly 17   a violent death./If this strains your credulity, Mrs. Chamberlayne,/I ask you only to
CREEP (4)
210 Old Gumbie   8   tucks up her skirts to the basement to creep./She is deeply concerned with the ways of
224 Mr Mistoff   25   his ears to the tip of his tail;/He can creep through the tiniest crack/He can walk on
233 Skimble   45   let anything go wrong./And when you creep into your cosy berth/And pull up the
288 FR   Agatha 26   on the old pony,/And thought to creep back through the little door./He will find
CREEPING (4)
 45 Cook Egg   27   screen?/The red-eyed scavengers are creeping/From Kentish Town and Golder's
213 Growltiger   32   their bunks —/As the Siamese came creeping in their sampans and their junks./
254 MC Tempt4   16   Thomas, think of enemies dismayed,/Creeping in penance, frightened of a shade;/
266 MC Knights   21   with blood and swollen with pride./Creeping out of the London dirt,/Crawling up
CREEPS (1)
105 Song Sime   2   in bowls and/The winter sun creeps by the snow hills;/The stubborn season
CREPT (4)
 23 Preludes   31   all the world came back/And the light crept up between the shutters/And you heard
 67 WL: Fire S 187   chuckle spread from ear to ear./A rat crept softly through the vegetation/Dragging its
 69 WL: Fire S 257   on the gramophone.'This music crept by me upon the waters'/And along the
526 ES   Monica   8   /{M} How did this come, Charles? It crept so softly/On silent feet, and stood behind
CRETONNE (1)
135 5FingerEx2   7   dog was safe and warm/Under a cretonne eiderdown,/Yet the field was cracked
CRÈVE (1)
 46 Directeur   22   /Du Spectateur/Conservateur/Et crève d'amour./Mélange Adultère de Tout/En
CREVICES (1)
 24 Rhapsody   64   Of sunless dry geraniums/And dust in crevices,/Smells of chestnuts in the streets,/And
CREW (2)
213 Growltiger   31   GRIDDLEBONE./And his raffish crew were sleeping in their barrels and their
213 Growltiger   44   battened down the hatches on the crew within their bunks./Then Griddlebone she
CREWE (1)
233 Skimble   55   catch a flea./You were fast asleep at Crewe and so you never knew/That he was
CRICKET (2)
 61 WL: Burial   23   the dead tree gives no shelter, the cricket no relief,/And the dry stone no sound of
339 FR   Harry   15   me, and will not let me fall./Let the cricket chirp. John shall be the master./All I
CRIED (4)
 57 Swee Night   38   the bloody wood/When Agamemnon cried aloud/And let their liquid siftings fall/To
 64 WL: Chess   102   with inviolable voice/And still she cried, and still the world pursues,/'Jug Jug' to
193 FQ: Little   99   /So I assumed a double part, and cried/And heard another's voice cry: 'What! are
264 MC Priest1   4   Thomas./And he kneeled down and cried with a loud voice:/Lord, lay not this sin to
CRIES (2)
254 MC Tempt4   29   early in the morning,/When the bird cries, have thought of further scorning./That
263 MC Chorus   2   sing in the South?/Only the sea-bird cries, driven inland by the storm./What sign of

CRIME (7)

226 Macavity	4	/For when they reach the scene of crime — *Macavity's not there!*/Macavity,
226 Macavity	8	/And when you reach the scene of crime — *Macavity's not there!*/You may seek
227 Macavity	42	their operations: the Napoleon of Crime!/Gus: the Theatre Cat/Gus is the Cat at
259 MC Thomas	2	/But for every evil, every sacrilege,/Crime, wrong, oppression and the axe's edge,/
333 FR Agatha	26	written is not a story of detection,/Of crime and punishment, but of sin and expiation.
573 ES Ld Clav	7	sin that no one believes in/Than the crime that everyone can appreciate./For the
573 ES Ld Clav	8	that everyone can appreciate./For the crime is in relation to the law/And the sin is in

CRIME'S (1)

| 226 Macavity | 20 | see him in the square —/But when a crime's discovered, then *Macavity's not there!*/ |

CRIMES (4)

38 Gerontion	46	/Are forced upon us by our impudent crimes./These tears are shaken from the
213 Growltiger	52	to that drop,/At the end of all his crimes was forced to go ker-flip, ker-flop./Oh
587 Fable	18	who had been walled up for his crimes;/At any rate, he sometimes came to
568 ES Ld Clav	5	secrets./There are many things not crimes, Monica,/Beyond anything of which the

CRIMINAL (2)

| 226 Macavity | 2 | Hidden Paw —/For he's the master criminal who can defy the Law./He's the |
| 568 ES Ld Clav | 25 | includes, mind you, not only things criminal,/Not only turpitude, meanness and |

CRIMSON (1)

| 138 New Hamp | 3 | and the fruit-time:/Golden head, crimson head,/Between the green tip and the |

CRIS (1)

| 51 Restaurant | 26 | quinze jours noyé,/Oubliait les cris des mouettes et la houle de Cornouaille,/Et |

CRISIS (3)

15 Prufrock	80	strength to force the moment to its crisis?/But though I have wept and fasted, wept
453 CC Kaghan	28	/But first, let's cope with the financial crisis./{L} Yes, Eggy, will you break the sad
454 CC Lucasta	13	dying for my tea. The strain of this crisis/Has been too much for me. Another time,

CRISPS (3)

| 355 CP Julia | 28 | delicious olives./What's that? Potato crisps? No, I can't endure them./Well, I started |
| 358 CP Julia | 19 | been a delightful evening:/The potato crisps were really excellent./Now let me see. |

CRITIC (3)

148 Rock 1	44	what is to happen./The Witness. The Critic. The Stranger./The God-shaken, in whom
361 CP Reilly	38	and cosier/Without the consistent critic, the patient misunderstander/Arranging
545 ES Ld Clav	6	silent observer,/Severe and speechless critic, who can terrorise us/And urge us on to

CRITICAL (1)

| 265 MC Priest3 | 6 | /We say, that was the day. The critical moment/That is always now, and here. |

CRITICALLY (1)

| 424 CP m | 4 | [*Exit.* LAVINIA *looks about the room critically and moves a bowl of flowers.*]/ |

CRITICISE (1)

| 526 ES Monica | 38 | said to you/Has given you the right to criticise my father./In the first place, you don't |

CRITICISED (1)

| 270 MC Chorus | 5 | the sponge. I have lain in the soil and criticised the worm. In the air/Flirted with the |

CRITICISMS (1)

| 558 ES Ld Clav | 29 | did Sir Alfred make other unflattering criticisms?/{Mi} Well, there was one thing he |

CROAK (1)

| 129 Cor2 State | 25 | marches/And the frogs (O Mantuan) croak in the marshes./Fireflies flare against the |

CROAKING (2)

| 129 Cor2 State | 46 | in the stillness of noon, in the silent croaking night./Come with the sweep of the |
| 245 MC Priest2 | 6 | be cheering and cheering,/You go on croaking like frogs in the treetops:/But frogs at |

CROAKS (3)

220 Old Deut	11	vicarage wall,/The Oldest Inhabitant croaks: 'Well, of all .../Things ... Can it be ...
220 Old Deut	26	economy:/And the Oldest Inhabitant croaks: 'Well, of all .../Things ... Can it be ...
221 Old Deut	42	befall:/And the Oldest Inhabitant croaks: 'Well, of all .../Things ... Can it be ...

CROCHETING (1)

| 210 Old Gumbie | 12 | the matting,/She teaches them music, crocheting and tatting./I have a Gumbie Cat in |

CROCODILE (2)

| 121 SA Sweeney | 20 | /You see this egg/Well that's life on a crocodile isle./There's no telephones/There's no |
| 123 SA Doris | 12 | eggs;/And I don't like life on your crocodile isle. {}/SONG BY KLIPSTEIN AND |

CROOKED (4)

24 Rhapsody	22	see the corner of her eye/Twists like a crooked pin.'/The memory throws up high and
316 FR Agatha	24	/The crossed is uncrossed/And the crooked is made straight. {}/[*Exit to dinner*]/
337 FR Agatha	7	/The knot shall be unknotted/And the crooked made straight. {}/[*She moves back into*
350 FR Agatha	19	/The crossed be uncrossed/The crooked be made straight/And the curse be

CROOKT (1)

| 135 5FingerEx2 | 2 | field stood a tree/And the tree was crookt and dry./In a black sky, from a green |

CROPPED (1)

42 Swee Erect		15	and gashed with eyes,/This oval O cropped out with teeth:/The sickle motion from

CROPS (1)

428 CP	Alex	28	/And what with protecting their crops from the monkeys/The Christian natives

CROQUET (2)

547 ES	Piggott	27	tennis,/And of course there's always croquet. But I don't advise croquet/Until you
547 ES	Piggott	27	always croquet. But I don't advise croquet/Until you know enough about the other

CROSS (11)

24 Rhapsody		61	all the old nocturnal smells/That cross and cross across her brain.'/The
24 Rhapsody		61	old nocturnal smells/That cross and cross across her brain.'/The reminiscence comes
98 Ash-Wed 6		5	/In this brief transit where the dreams cross/The dreamcrossed twilight between birth
98 Ash-Wed 6		21	place of solitude where three dreams cross/Between blue rocks/But when the voices
163 Rock 8		44	vice/When men will not lay down the Cross/Because they will never assume it./Yet
260 MC Thomas		16	and His Passion and Death upon/the Cross. Beloved, as the World sees, this is to
274 MC Thomas		12	victory./Now is the triumph of the Cross, now/Open the door! I command it.
345 FR Charles		38	/Right to the centre, as I was about to cross Pall Mall./I thought that life could bring
479 CC Kaghan		26	moment for firmness. Don't let her cross the threshold./{L} As if you weren't as
492 CC Claude		34	I shall be in a reminiscent mood./Cross that out. It would only remind me/Of
518 CC Colby		12	And a canonry!/{C} We'll cross that bridge when we come to it, Eggers./

CROSS-EXAMINE (2)

493 CC Claude		15	like a couple of barristers/Ready to cross-examine a witness./It's very awkward. We
564 ES Carghil		30	Court,/I warn you — I'm going to cross-examine you/And make you tell me all

CROSSED (11)

40 Burb Blei		1	Bleistein with a Cigar/Burbank crossed a little bridge/Descending at a small
83 Hollow Men		13	without motion;/Those who have crossed/With direct eyes, to death's other
84 Hollow Men		33	disguises/Rat's coat, crowskin, crossed staves/In a field/Behaving as the wind
172 FQ: BurntN		30	shrubbery,/And the unseen eyebeam crossed, for the roses/Had the look of flowers
229 Gus		43	to bring on the Ghost./And he once crossed the stage on a telegraph wire,/To rescue
605 Narcissus		10	passing each other/And of his arms crossed over his breast./When he walked over
316 FR Agatha		14	was tied/Become unknotted/May the crossed bones/In the filled-up well/Be at last
316 FR Agatha		23	house/Till the knot is unknotted/The crossed is uncrossed/And the crooked is made
342 FR Agatha		31	/But birth and life. Harry has crossed the frontier/Beyond which safety and
350 FR Agatha		18	charm/So the knot be unknotted/The crossed be uncrossed/The crooked be made
537 ES Ld Clav		11	bond between us?/{LC} It has never crossed my mind. Develop the point./{G} Well,

CROSSES (2)

67 WL: Fire S		175	and sink into the wet bank. The wind/Crosses the brown land, unheard. The nymphs
519 CC	m	7	{LE} My poor Claude! {}/[LUCASTA *crosses to* SIR CLAUDE *and kneels beside him*]/

CROSSING (3)

246 MC Thomas		8	my letters on another day,/Had fair crossing, found at Sandwich/Broc, Warenne,
457 CC Eggers		2	or even her passport./But let's not be crossing any bridges/Until we come to them.
458 CC Lady E		24	the night train, and did the Channel crossing./But who is this young man? His face is

CROUCHED (1)

74 WL: Thund		398	distant, over Himavant./The jungle crouched, humped in silence./Then spoke the

CROUPE (1)

51 Restaurant		6	des gueux.'/(Bavard, baveux, à la croupe arrondie,/Je te prie, au moins, ne bave

CROW (2)

141 Rannoch		1	/Rannoch, by Glencoe/Here the crow starves, here the patient stag/Breeds for
263 MC Chorus		8	is stored up in the East./The starved crow sits in the field, attentive; and in the wood/

CROWD (4)

24 Rhapsody		24	memory throws up high and dry/A crowd of twisted things;/A twisted branch upon
62 WL: Burial		62	the brown fog of a winter dawn,/A crowd flowed over London Bridge, so many,/I
587 Fable		29	/He purchased at his own expense a crowd/Of relics from a Spanish saint — said he:
599 On a Port		1	long ago./On a Portrait/Among a crowd of tenuous dreams, unknown/To us of

CROWDED (3)

294 FR Harry		15	/{H} The sudden solitude in a crowded desert/In a thick smoke, many
425 CP Lavinia		28	the Gunnings./{L} And if it's very crowded, they can't get at the cocktails,/And the
547 ES Piggott		11	popular in the evenings. But not *too* crowded. {}/[*Exit*]/{LC} Much as I had feared.

CROWDING (1)

127 Corl March		6	way to the temple, and we so many crowding the way./So many waiting, how many

CROWDS (2)

62 WL: Burial		56	Man. Fear death by water./I see crowds of people, walking round in a ring./
245 MC Priest2		5	likely to arrive at any moment?/The crowds in the streets will be cheering and

355 CP	Julia	1	man I ever met who could hear the cry of bats./{P} Hear the cry of bats?/{J} He
355 CP	Peter	2	hear the cry of bats./{P} Hear the cry of bats?/{J} He could hear the cry of bats./
355 CP	Julia	3	the cry of bats?/{J} He could hear the cry of bats./{C} But how do you know he could
355 CP	Celia	4	how do you know he could hear the cry of bats?/{J} Because he said so. And I

CRYING (5)

62 WL: Burial	69	I saw one I knew, and stopped him, crying: 'Stetson!/'You who were with me in the
72 WL: Thund	325	in stony places/The shouting and the crying/Prison and palace and reverberation/Of
160 Rock 7	5	devils rather than nothing: crying for life beyond life, for ecstasy not of the
175 FQ: BurntN	160	attacked by voices of temptation,/The crying shadow in the funeral dance,/The loud
310 FR	Mary	8	under the snow/And the snowdrop crying for a moment in the wood./{H} Spring is

CRYPT (1)

274 MC	Priests	15	Up the stair. To the roof./To the crypt. Quick. Come. Force him./{4K} Where is

CUBA (1)

542 ES	Gomez	6	have cigars sent direct to you from Cuba/If your doctors allow you a smoke now

CUCKOO (1)

285 FR	Amy	5	and the spring will be over/And the cuckoo will be gone before I am out again./O

CUDDLE (1)

215 RTTugger	32	Rum Tum Tugger doesn't care for a cuddle;/But he'll leap on your lap in the middle

CULTIVATED (2)

331 FR	Agatha	34	or so I see him —/An exceptionally cultivated country squire,/Reading, sketching,
461 CC	Eggers	9	ring us up!/I'm sure he has a very cultivated voice.'/{C} Thank you very much, I

CULTIVATION (2)

111 Xmas Trees	t	through the fog/My daughter./The Cultivation of Christmas Trees/There are
201 Def Island	3	of many centuries of/patient cultivation of the earth, of English/verse/be

CULTURE (1)

451 CC	Eggers	29	She'll see at once that you're a man of culture;/And besides, she's very musical./{C}

CULVERWELL (14)

532 ES	Ld Clav	31	Mr. ... Gomez. You're a friend of Mr. Culverwell?/{G} We're as thick as thieves, you
532 ES	Ld Clav	34	Don't you know me, Dick?/{LC} Fred Culverwell!/Why do you come back with
533 ES	Gomez	9	more normal/In my country, than Culverwell — and easier to pronounce./{LC}
536 ES	Gomez	40	—/And one who will accept both Culverwell and Gomez —/See Culverwell as
537 ES	Gomez	1	both Culverwell and Gomez —/See Culverwell as Gomez — Gomez as Culverwell./I
537 ES	Gomez	1	Culverwell as Gomez — Gomez as Culverwell./I need you, Dick, to give me reality!
541 ES	Gomez	5	/To appear in public as Frederick Culverwell?/No, Dick, your secret's safe with
570 ES	Ld Clav	22	of it all. He admitted as much,/Fred Culverwell .../{M} Fred Culverwell?/Who is
570 ES	Monica	23	much,/Fred Culverwell .../{M} Fred Culverwell?/Who is Fred Culverwell?/{LC} He
570 ES	Monica	24	.../{M} Fred Culverwell?/Who is Fred Culverwell?/{LC} He no longer exists./He's
571 ES	Ld Clav	2	the wealthy widow./But Freddy Culverwell and Maisie Batterson,/And Dick
571 ES	Ld Clav	30	briefly/And simply. As for Frederick Culverwell,/He re-enters my life to make himself
575 ES	Ld Clav	16	of your morals;/His real name is Culverwell .../{G} My dear Dick,/You're
577 ES	Ld Clav	40	/To place himself in your power, Fred Culverwell,/Of his own volition to contract his

CULVERWELL'S (1)

572 ES	Ld Clav	7	stop!'/I knew the voice: it was Fred Culverwell's./{M} Poor Father! All your life!

CUNNING (3)

38 Gerontion	34	Think now/History has many cunning passages, contrived corridors/And
224 Mr Mistoff	28	any card from a pack,/He is equally cunning with dice;/He is always deceiving you
296 FR	Ivy	21	such a suggestion. They can be very cunning —/Their malady makes them so. They

CUP (3)

233 Skimble	52	bright;/Every now and then he has a cup of tea/With perhaps a drop of Scotch while
372 CP	Alex	26	breakfast./All you should want is a cup of black coffee/And a little dry toast. I've
457 CC	Lady E	29	yet how to make tea properly./A cup of black coffee. Is Sir Claude at home?/I'll

CUPBOARD (1)

477 CC	Lucasta	2	I was sent out. I've been locked in a cupboard!/I was only eight years old/When she

CUPIDON (1)

64 WL: Chess	80	fruited vines/From which a golden Cupidon peeped out/(Another hid his eyes

CUPS (1)

15 Prufrock	88	have been worth it, after all,/After the cups, the marmalade, the tea,/Among the

CUR (1)

137 5FingerEx5	9	to meet Mr. Eliot!/With a bobtail cur/In a coat of fur/And a porpentine cat/And a

CURABLE (1)

417 CP	Reilly	20	you cure me?/{R} The condition is curable./But the form of treatment must be your

CURB (1)

278 MC Knight2	9	thing needful was to restore order: to curb the excessive/powers of local government,

CURBING (1)

249 MC Thomas	37	barons. Who will not forget/Constant curbing of petty privilege./{T2} Against the

CURE (8)
379 CP	Edward	3	greater than the greatest doctor/To cure *this* illness./{C} Edward, if I go now,/Will
403 CP	Reilly	9	you would imagine it a marvellous cure;/And you would go on, doing such amount
407 CP	Reilly	22	diagnosis, and prescribe your own cure./But when you put yourselves into hands
417 CP	Celia	19	shame of never finding it./Can you cure me?/{R} The condition is curable./But the
533 ES	Gomez	17	take a long holiday,/Let's say a rest cure — that's what I've come for./You see, I'm
554 ES	Carghil	24	Lord Claverton had come for a rest cure,/And it struck me that he might find it a
563 ES	Gomez	10	here, were you?/You're here for a rest cure. I persuaded my doctor/That I was in need
563 ES	Gomez	11	doctor/That I was in need of a rest cure too./And when I heard you'd chosen to

CURED (2)
296 FR	Ivy	22	them so. They do not want to be cured/And they know what you are thinking./
417 CP	Celia	16	if that is all meaningless, I want to be cured/Of a craving for something I cannot find/

CURES (1)
496 CC	Claude	4	deep for discussion with *me*:/Health cures. And modern art — so long as it was

CURFEW (1)
228 Gus		30	bedside of poor Little Nell;/When the Curfew was rung, then I swung on the bell./In

CURIOSITY (7)
184 FQ: DrySal	20		/The pools where it offers to our curiosity/The more delicate algae and the sea
189 FQ: DrySal	203		Asia, or in the Edgware Road./Men's curiosity searches past and future/And clings to
192 FQ: Little	46		to verify,/Instruct yourself, or inform curiosity/Or carry report. You are here to kneel/
258 MC Thomas	12		in thought,/Music and philosophy, curiosity,/The purple bullfinch in the lilac tree,/
482 CC Lady E	13		of attention./You see, you're rather a curiosity/To both of them — you're not the sort
533 ES Gomez	14		to England?/{G} Call it homesickness,/Curiosity, restlessness, whatever you like./But
544 ES Monica	3		people in the dining-room show no curiosity;/The beds are comfortable, the hot

CURIOUS (9)
162 Rock 8	16		/Some went who were restless and curious,/Some were rapacious and lustful./
166 Rock 10	13		way and be ye separate./Be not too curious of Good and Evil;/Seek not to count the
214 RTTugger	1		Tugger/The Rum Tum Tugger is a Curious Cat:/If you offer him pheasant he
214 RTTugger	7		mouse./Yes the Rum Tum Tugger is a Curious Cat —/And there isn't any call for me
214 RTTugger	18		out./Yes the Rum Tum Tugger is a Curious Cat —/And it isn't any use for you to
214 RTTugger	23		about it!/The Rum Tum Tugger is a curious beast:/His disobliging ways are a matter
215 RTTugger	35		/Yes the Rum Tum Tugger is a Curious Cat —/And there isn't any need for me
599 On a Port	14		silent spy,/Regards her with a patient curious eye./Song/The moonflower opens to the
475 CC Colby	25		your ... background:/No. I've been curious to know what you *are*,/But not who you

CURL (2)
107 Animula	22		pain of living and the drug of dreams/Curl up the small soul in the window seat/
257 MC Chorus	32		The Lords of Hell are here./They curl round you, lie at your feet, swing and wing

CURLED (7)
13 Prufrock	22		that it was a soft October night,/Curled once about the house, and fell asleep./
23 Preludes	36		along the bed's edge, where/You curled the papers from your hair,/Or clasped the
23 Preludes	48		world./I am moved by fancies that are curled/Around these images, and cling:/The
24 Rhapsody	32		that the strength has left/Hard and curled and ready to snap./Half-past two,/The
166 Rock 10	7		at the bottom of the pit of the world, curled/In folds of himself until he awakens in
175 FQ: BurntN	136		and cling?/Chill/Fingers of yew be curled/Down on us? After the kingfisher's wing/
225 Mr Mistoff	45		been heard on the roof/When he was curled up by the fire./And he's sometimes been

CURRANTS (1)
68 WL: Fire S	210		/Unshaven, with a pocket full of currants/C.i.f. London: documents at sight,/

CURRENT (4)
71 WL: DWater	315		sea swell/And the profit and loss./A current under sea/Picked his bones in whispers./
160 Rock 7	12		by the still dead breath of the Arctic Current;/And they came to an end, a dead end
462 CC Claude	30		/And so far we've discussed only current business,/Thinking that you might find
541 ES Gomez	22		spread. For the matter of that,/My current account in Stockholm or Zürich/Would

CURRENTS (1)
187 FQ: DrySal	113		/For our own past is covered by the currents of action,/But the torment of others

CURRY (5)
230 Bust Jones	25		he's seen in a hurry there's probably curry/At the *Siamese* — or at the *Glutton*;/If he
370 CP	Alex	14	apron]/{A} Edward, I can't find any curry powder./{E} There isn't any curry powder.
370 CP	Edward	15	any curry powder./{E} There isn't any curry powder. Lavinia hates curry./{A} There
370 CP	Edward	15	isn't any curry powder. Lavinia hates curry./{A} There goes another surprise, then. I
370 CP	Alex	18	any mangoes,/But I *did* count upon curry powder. {}/[*Exit*]/{P} That is exactly what

CURSE (11)
181 FQ: ECoker	157		/But to remind of our, and Adam's curse,/And that, to be restored, our sickness
336 FR	Agatha	23	EUMENIDES *had occupied*.]/{Ag} A curse comes to being/As a child is formed./In
336 FR	Agatha	29	/Knowing what is intended./A curse is like a child, formed/In a moment of
336 FR	Agatha	35	the phase/Of the determined moon./A curse is like a child, formed/To grow to

337 FR   Agatha   4   cloud of unknowing./O my child, my curse,/You shall be fulfilled:/The knot shall be
349 FR   Agatha   13   *words are spoken in the dark.*]/{Ag} A curse is slow in coming/To complete fruition/It
349 FR   Agatha   21   /At the day of consummation/{Ag} A curse is a power/Not subject to reason/Each
349 FR   Agatha   23   a power/Not subject to reason/Each curse has its course/Its own way of expiation/
350 FR   Mary   8   us to each other/Follow follow/{M} A curse is written/On the under side of things/
350 FR   Agatha   20   crooked be made straight/And the curse be ended/By intercession/By pilgrimage/
429 CP   Alex   4   the slaughter of monkeys has put a curse on them/Which can only be removed by

CURSED (1)
452 CC   Lucasta 35   for it./That's what comes of being cursed with a name like Angel./I'm thinking of

CURSING (1)
103 Journ Magi   11   bringing sherbet./Then the camel men cursing and grumbling/And running away, and

CURTAIN (14)
275 MC   Chorus   27   all smeared with blood, through a curtain of falling blood?/We did not wish
290 FR   Chorus   38   amateur actors in a dream when the curtain rises, to find themselves dressed for a
373 CP   m   4   long ago? .../No, it doesn't matter. {}/CURTAIN/Act One. Scene 2/*The same room: a*
383 CP   m   30   bringing them now ... Good night. {}/CURTAIN/Act One. Scene 3/*The same room:*
398 CP   m   18   get the porter to fetch it up for me? {}/CURTAIN/Act Two/SIR HENRY
423 CP   m   3   connections — even in California. {}/CURTAIN/Act Three/*The drawing-room of*
440 CP   m   37   /{L} Oh, I'm glad. It's begun. {}/CURTAIN/THE CONFIDENTIAL CLERK/
468 CC   m   3   We must run through the figures. {}/CURTAIN/Act Two/*The flat in the mews a few*
469 CC   4m   1   *of a piece of music are/heard as the curtain rises.*/{L} *I* think you play awfully well,
492 CC   2m   38   CLAUDE *and* LADY ELIZABETH]/CURTAIN/Act Three/*The Business Room, as*
519 CC   2m   23   believe her? {}/[EGGERSON *nods*]/CURTAIN/THE ELDER STATESMAN/TO
543 ES   m   20   will it be like at Badgley Court? {}/CURTAIN/Act Two/*The terrace of Badgley*
566 ES   m   4   Is it too late for me, Monica? {}/CURTAIN/Act Three/*Same as Act Two. Late*
583 ES   m   28   of you. Now take me to my father. {}/CURTAIN

CURTAIN-CORD (1)
210 Old Gumbie   26   mind, her name is Jennyanydots;/The curtain-cord she likes to wind, and tie it into

CURTAINED (1)
329 FR   Chorus   3   hard on the future./The agony in the curtained bedroom, whether of birth or of

CURTAINS (12)
204 de la Mare   10   tea/And when the lamps are lit and curtains drawn/Demand some poetry, please.
285 FR   5m   1   /[DENMAN *enters to draw the curtains*]/{A} Not yet! I will ring for you. It is
285 FR   Amy   11   dark!/Put on the lights. But leave the curtains undrawn./Make up the fire. Will the
291 FR   Amy   18   matter?/{A} Harry, if you want the curtains drawn you should let me ring for
302 FR   Chorus   7   if the door might suddenly open, the curtains be drawn,/The cellar make some
311 FR   m   27   be all right./{H} Come out! {}/[*The curtains part, revealing the Eumenides in the*
311 FR   m   38   /[*She goes to the window and pulls the curtains across*]/{H} They were here, I tell you.
312 FR   m   9   [*He rushes forward and tears apart the curtains: but the embrasure is empty.*]/{M} Oh,
313 FR   Violet   3   /Why, who could have pulled those curtains apart? {}/[*Pulls them together*]/{V} Very
336 FR   1m   23   us lose no time. I will follow. {}/[*The curtains close. AGATHA goes to the window, in*
336 FR   2m   23   *a somnambular fashion,/and opens the curtains, disclosing the empty embrasure. She*
483 CC   Lady E   9   /I believe it does. The walls; and the curtains;/And most of the furniture. But, that

CURVES (1)
43 Swee Erect   32   subsides./The epileptic on the bed/Curves backward, clutching at her sides./The

CUSCUSCARAWAY (1)
136 5FingerEx5   t   wants to know *him*)./*Lines for Cuscuscaraway and Mirza Murad Ali Beg*/How

CUSHION (1)
366 CP   Julia   4   —/No, this chair. Look under the cushion./{E} Are you quite sure they're not in

CUSTODIAN (4)
574 ES   Michael 35   Sir Alfred/Who'd constitute himself custodian of my morals/And send you back
575 ES   Ld Clav 15   Gomez./He's unlikely to try to be custodian of your morals;/His real name is
575 ES   Gomez   23   that insinuation/About my not being custodian of Michael's morals./That is just what
575 ES   Gomez   26   when we recall/That you were once custodian of *my* morals:/Though of course you

CUSTOMS (1)
457 CC   Eggers   14   to spare,/And besides, there's the Customs. That'll take her a time,/From my

CUT (9)
116 SP   Doris   39   *you.*/Ah-h-h/{Do} Now I'm going to cut the cards for to-night./Oh guess what the
117 SP   Doris   37   I'm not going to draw any more,/You cut for luck. You cut for luck./It might break
117 SP   Doris   37   any more,/You cut for luck. You cut for luck./It might break the spell. You cut
117 SP   Doris   38   luck./It might break the spell. You cut for luck./{Du} The Knave of Spades./{Do}
124 SA   Doris   4   Oh Mr. Sweeney, please don't talk,/I cut the cards before you came/And I drew the
136 5FingerEx5   2   Eliot!/With his features of clerical cut,/And his brow so grim/And his mouth so
153 Rock 2   54   clay be dug from the pit, let the saw cut the stone,/Let the fire not be quenched in
536 ES   Gomez   19   don't know what it's like/To be so cut off! Homesickness!/Homesickness is a sickly

539 ES   Gomez   1 of companies. You looked the part —/Cut out to be an impressive figurehead./But
CUTLASS (1)
  37 Gerontion   5 knee deep in the salt marsh, heaving a cutlass,/Bitten by flies, fought./My house is a
CUTS (1)
322 FR   Winch   39 there's nothing wrong but some nasty cuts/And a bad concussion; says he'll come
CUTTING (1)
565 ES   Michael   21 in business in London,/But I think of cutting loose, and going abroad./{MC} You
CYCLADES (1)
  42 Swee Erect   2   waste shore/Cast in the unstilled Cyclades,/Paint me the bold anfractuous rocks/
CYCLAMEN (1)
129 Cor2 State   35   the small wind after noon/There the cyclamen spreads its wings, there the clematis
CYCLE (2)
147 Rock 1   6 autumn, birth and dying!/The endless cycle of idea and action,/Endless invention,
153 Rock 2   50 /But every son would have his motor cycle,/And daughters ride away on casual
CYCLES (1)
147 Rock 1   17   we have lost in information?/The cycles of Heaven in twenty centuries/Bring us
CYRIL (2)
128 Cor1 March   44 get to the country,/So we took young Cyril to church. And they rang a bell/And he
129 Cor2 State   12   /What shall I cry?/Arthur Edward Cyril Parker is appointed telephone operator/At

D' (12)

46 Directeur	22	Du Spectateur/Conservateur/Et crève d'amour./Mélange Adultère de Tout/En
47 Mél Adult	17	mon jour de fête/Dans une oasis d'Afrique/Vêtu d'une peau de girafe./On
47 Mél Adult	18	fête/Dans une oasis d'Afrique/Vêtu d'une peau de girafe./On montrera mon
48 Lune Miel	2	rentrent à Terre Haute;/Mais une nuit d'été, les voici à Ravenne,/A l'aise entre deux
48 Lune Miel	8	le drap pour mieux égratigner./Moins d'une lieue d'ici est Saint Apollinaire/En Classe,
48 Lune Miel	8	mieux égratigner./Moins d'une lieue d'ici est Saint Apollinaire/En Classe, basilique
48 Lune Miel	10	connue des amateurs/De chapitaux d'acanthe que tournoie le vent./Ils vont prendre
51 Restaurant	27	les profits et les pertes, et la cargaison d'étain:/Un courant de sous-mer l'emporta très
67 WL: Fire S	202	their feet in soda water/Et O ces voix d'enfants, chantant dans la coupole!/Twit twit
75 WL: Thund	429	— O swallow swallow/*Le Prince d'Aquitaine à la tour abolie*/These fragments I
524 ES Monica	11	/Instead of to one where the *maître d'hôtel*/And the waiters all seem to be your
548 ES Piggott	1	/After all, peace and quiet is our *raison d'être.*/Now I'll leave you to enjoy it. { }/[*Exit*]/

DA (3)

74 WL: Thund	400	in silence./Then spoke the thunder/DA/*Datta:* what have we given?/My friend,
74 WL: Thund	410	the lean solicitor/In our empty rooms/DA/*Dayadhvam:* I have heard the key/Turn in
74 WL: Thund	417	for a moment a broken Coriolanus/DA/*Damyata:* The boat responded/Gaily, to

DÆMONIC (1)

190 FQ: DrySal	227	no source of movement —/Driven by dæmonic, chthonic/Powers. And right action is

DAFFODIL (1)

52 Whispers	5	/Leaned backward with a lipless grin./Daffodil bulbs instead of balls/Stared from the

DAGUERREOTYPES (1)

44 Cook Egg	5	/Lay on the table, with the knitting./Daguerreotypes and silhouettes,/Her

DAHLIAS (1)

177 FQ: ECoker	22	not refracted, by grey stone./The dahlias sleep in the empty silence./Wait for the

DAILY (8)

154 Rock 3	29	the South/Whence thousands travel daily to the timekept City;/Where My Word is
164 Rock 9	8	sins and faults as they go about their daily occasions./Yet they walk in the street
202 War Poetry	2	emotion/Imperfectly reflected in the daily papers./Where is the point at which the
209 NamingCats	5	there's the name that the family use daily,/Such as Peter, Augustus, Alonzo or
276 MC Chorus	3	/The terror by night that ends in daily action,/The terror by day that ends in
334 FR Agatha	10	of earning my spiritual income daily:/And I am old, to start again to make my
384 CP Reilly	26	/{UG} Ah, but we die to each other daily./What we know of other people/Is only
446 CC Eggers	23	aunt in Teddington, and coming up daily/Just as I used to. And the flat in the

DAIRY (1)

587 Fable	10	/An orchard, and a vineyard, and a dairy;/Whenever some old villainous baron

DAMAGE (1)

428 CP Alex	14	they blame the Government/For the damage that the monkeys do./{E} That seems

DAMAGES (1)

541 ES Gomez	3	happened so many years ago?/What damages you'd get! The Press wouldn't look at

DAMAS (1)

47 Mél Adult	15	de-là/A divers coups de tra là là/De Damas jusqu'à Omaha./Je célébrai mon jour de

DAME (1)

455 CC Eggers	40	she really is a lady,/Rather a *grande dame*, as the French say./That's what Sir Claude

DAMES (1)

209 NamingCats	10	Some for the gentlemen, some for the dames:/Such as Plato, Admetus, Electra,

DAMN (3)

273 MC Priests	30	men, against men/Who would damn themselves to beasts. My Lord! My Lord!
375 CP Edward	11	{ }/[*The telephone rings*]/{E} Damn the telephone. I suppose I must answer
382 CP Edward	37	First ... { }/[*The telephone rings*]/{E} Damn the telephone./I suppose I had better

DAMNATION (5)

173 FQ: BurntN	83	/Protects mankind from heaven and damnation/Which flesh cannot endure./Time
250 MC Thomas	4	power?/Delegate to deal the doom of damnation,/To condemn kings, not serve
255 MC Thomas	27	/But real. You only offer/Dreams to damnation./{T4} You have often dreamt them./
255 MC Thomas	30	my soul's sickness,/Does not lead to damnation in pride?/I well know that these
397 CP Edward	12	me?/{E} It was only yesterday/That damnation took place. And now I must live

DAMNED (3)

602 Humoresque	19	contemptuous of nose),/'Your damned thin moonlight, worse than gas —/
273 MC Priests	29	more/Against beasts with the souls of damned men, against men/Who would damn
343 FR Amy	22	leave me!/An old woman alone in a damned house./I will let the walls crumble. Why

DAMP (8)

27 Morning	3	edges of the street/I am aware of the damp souls of housemaids/Sprouting
50 Hippopot	26	take wing/Ascending from the damp savannas,/And quiring angels round him
67 WL: Fire S	193	him./White bodies naked on the low damp ground/And bones cast in a little low dry
74 WL: Thund	393	/In a flash of lightning. Then a damp gust/Bringing rain/Ganga was sunken,
92 Ash-Wed 3	10	no more faces and the stair was dark,/Damp, jaggèd, like an old man's mouth
107 Animula	3	and noise,/To light, dark, dry or damp, chilly or warm;/Moving between the legs

126 SA	Chorus	3	at seven o'clock and it's/foggy and it's	damp and it's dawn and it's dark/And you wait
438 CP	Reilly	12	/Suffered any less from hunger,	damp, exposure,/Bowel trouble, and the fear of

DAMYATA (2)

74 WL: Thund	418	a moment a broken Coriolanus/DA/*Damyata:* The boat responded/Gaily, to the hand
75 WL: Thund	432	mad againe./Datta. Dayadhvam. Damyata./Shantih shantih shantih/The Hollow

DANCE (15)

20 Portrait	75	/A Greek was murdered at a Polish	dance,/Another bank defaulter has confessed./I
21 Portrait	110	changing shape/To find expression ...	dance, dance/Like a dancing bear,/Cry like a
21 Portrait	110	shape/To find expression ... dance,	dance/Like a dancing bear,/Cry like a parrot,
44 Cook Egg	8	on the mantelpiece/An *Invitation to the*	*Dance.*/I shall not want Honour in Heaven/For I
142 Cape Ann	3	/At dawn and dusk. Follow the	dance/Of the goldfinch at noon. Leave to
172 FQ: BurntN	54	/Appeasing long forgotten wars./The	dance along the artery/The circulation of the
173 FQ: BurntN	65	towards; at the still point, there the	dance is,/But neither arrest nor movement. And
173 FQ: BurntN	69	the still point,/There would be no	dance, and there is only the dance./I can only
173 FQ: BurntN	69	be no dance, and there is only the	dance./I can only say, *there* we have been: but I
175 FQ: BurntN	160	/The crying shadow in the funeral	dance,/The loud lament of the disconsolate
204 de la Mare	20	cats are maddened in the moonlight	dance,/Dogs cower, flitter bats, and owls range/
216 Jellicles	16	are roly-poly,/They know how to	dance a gavotte and a jig./Until the Jellicle
216 Jellicles	28	their terpsichorean powers/To	dance by the light of the Jellicle Moon./Jellicle
286 FR	Violet	20	/{V} They bathe all day and they	dance all night/In the absolute *minimum* of
547 ES	Piggott	24	enough young people among us/We	dance in the evening. At the moment there's no

DANCED (2)

30 Cous Nancy	8	/Miss Nancy Ellicott smoked/And	danced all the modern dances;/And her aunts
606 Narcissus	35	in love with the burning arrows/He	danced on the hot sand/Until the arrows came./

DANCER (3)

195 FQ: Little	148	you must move in measure, like a	dancer.'/The day was breaking. In the disfigured
605 Narcissus	17	not live men's ways, but became a	dancer before God/If he walked in city streets/
606 Narcissus	33	felt drunken and old./So he became a	dancer to God./Because his flesh was in love

DANCERS (1)

179 FQ: ECoker	101	houses are all gone under the sea./The	dancers are all gone under the hill./O dark dark

DANCES (1)

30 Cous Nancy	8	smoked/And danced all the modern	dances;/And her aunts were not quite sure how

DANCING (10)

21 Portrait	111	expression ... dance, dance/Like a	dancing bear,/Cry like a parrot, chatter like an
142 Cape Ann	9	water-thrush. Follow the flight/Of the	dancing arrow, the purple martin. Greet/In
177 FQ: ECoker	28	pipe and the little drum/And see them	dancing around the bonfire/The association of
178 FQ: ECoker	41	time,/Keeping the rhythm in their	dancing/As in their living in the living seasons/
180 FQ: ECoker	129	shall be the light, and the stillness the	dancing./Whisper of running streams, and
197 FQ: Little	225	not pedantic,/The complete consort	dancing together)/Every phrase and every
213 Growltiger	54	At Maidenhead and Henley there was	dancing on the strand./Rats were roasted whole
496 CC	Claude	5	long as it was modern —/And dervish	dancing./{LE} Dervish dancing!/Really, Claude,
496 CC	Lady E	6	/And dervish dancing./{LE} Dervish	dancing!/Really, Claude, how absurd you are!/
547 ES	Piggott	24	evening. At the moment there's no	dancing,/And it's still too early for the bathing

DANGER (19)

213 Growltiger	39	/The lovers sang their last duet, in	danger of their lives —/For the foe was armed
239 MC	Chorus	2	Here let us wait./Are we drawn by	danger? Is it the knowledge of safety, that draws
239 MC	Chorus	3	our feet/Towards the cathedral? What	danger can be/For us, the poor, the poor
239 MC	Chorus	5	are not already familiar? There is no	danger/For us, and there is no safety in the
243 MC	Chorus	15	time, uncertain the profit, certain the	danger./O late late late, late is the time, late too
269 MC	Knight2	16	life./{K2} Priest, you have spoken in	danger of the knife./{K3} Priest, you have
271 MC	Thomas	24	/And if I am worthy, there is no	danger./I have therefore only to make perfect
271 MC	Thomas	32	sought for but mine./And I am not in	danger: only near to death./{3P} My Lord, to
316 FR	Gerald	5	against it./{G} I am used to tangible	danger, but only to what I can understand./{V}
342 FR	Mary	18	is in another./{M} Oh, but it is the	danger comes from another!/Can you not stop
342 FR	Mary	21	seen and what I know!/He is in great	danger, I know that, don't ask me,/You would
342 FR	Mary	25	but elsewhere, everywhere, he is in	danger./I will stay or I will go, whichever is
342 FR	Agatha	29	not go. Cousin Agatha!/{Ag} Here the	danger, here the death, here, not elsewhere;/
342 FR	Agatha	32	the frontier/Beyond which safety and	danger have a different meaning,/And he
343 FR	Agatha	2	is now only on this side,/For him,	danger and safety have another meaning./*They*
345 FR	Harry	9	/You need not fear that I am in any	danger/Of such accidents as happen to Arthur
381 CP	Celia	22	sorry for you./It's only myself I am in	danger of loathing./But what will your life be? I
394 CP	Lavinia	24	I don't know. I was warned of the	danger,/Yet something, or somebody,
511 CC	Lady E	20	/{LE} Then in order to avoid any	danger of confusion/You may address me as

DANGEROUS (2)
204 de la Mare   3   sandy cove/(A hiding place, but very dangerous ground,/For here the water buffalo
295 FR   Charles   7   Harry!/{C} You mustn't indulge such dangerous fancies./It's only doing harm to your
DANGERS (1)
343 FR   Harry   36   to pursue, and I am safe from normal dangers/If I pursue it. I cannot account for this/
DANGLING (1)
143 Lines OM   6   /Writhing in the essential blood/Or dangling from the friendly tree./When I lay bare
DANIEL (6)
274 MC Knights   18   the meddling priest?/Come down Daniel to the lions' den,/Come down Daniel for
274 MC Knights   19   Daniel to the lions' den,/Come down Daniel for the mark of the beast./Are you
274 MC Knights   22   the mark of the beast?/Come down Daniel to the lions' den,/Come down Daniel
274 MC Knights   23   Daniel to the lions' den,/Come down Daniel and join in the feast./Where is Becket the
274 MC Knights   26   the faithless priest?/Come down Daniel to the lions' den,/Come down Daniel
274 MC Knights   27   Daniel to the lions' den,/Come down Daniel and join in the feast./{T} It is the just
DANS (8)
46 Directeur   14   /Font des tours/A pas de loup./Dans un égout/Une petite fille/En guenilles/
47 Mél Adult   17   Omaha./Je célébrai mon jour de fête/Dans une oasis d'Afrique/Vêtu d'une peau de
48 Lune Miel   18   désaffectée de Dieu, tient encore/Dans ses pierres écroulantes la forme précise de
51 Restaurant   t   below/Wrapt in the old miasmal mist./Dans le Restaurant/Le garçon délabré qui n'a
51 Restaurant   3   doigts et se pencher sur mon épaule:/'Dans mon pays il fera temps pluvieux,/Du vent,
51 Restaurant   7   /Je te prie, au moins, ne bave pas dans la soupe)./'Les saules trempés, et des
51 Restaurant   9   bourgeons sur les ronces —/C'est là, dans une averse, qu'on s'abrite./J'avais sept ans,
67 WL: Fire S   202   /Et O ces voix d'enfants, chantant dans la coupole!/Twit twit twit/Jug jug jug jug
DAPPLED (1)
167 Rock 10   42   thank Thee for our little light, this is dappled with shadow./We thank Thee who hast
DARE (22)
14 Prufrock   38   there will be time/To wonder, 'Do I dare?' and, 'Do I dare?'/Time to turn back and
14 Prufrock   38   /To wonder, 'Do I dare?' and, 'Do I dare?'/Time to turn back and descend the stair,/
14 Prufrock   45   how his arms and legs are thin!')/Do I dare/Disturb the universe?/In a minute there is
16 Prufrock   122   /Shall I part my hair behind? Do I dare to eat a peach?/I shall wear white flannel
83 Hollow Men   19   hollow men/The stuffed men./Eyes I dare not meet in dreams/In death's dream
273 MC   Priests   13   /We are safe. We are safe./They dare not break in./They cannot break in. They
277 MC Knight3   6   /who put our country first. I dare say that we didn't make a/very good
300 FRDowning   15   the contrary of the usual opinion,/I dare say. She wouldn't leave him alone./And
314 FR Warburt   7   important engagement to come./{W} I dare say we've both changed a good deal,
340 FR   Amy   22   sons upon an unwilling father?/Dare you think what that does to one? Try to
380 CP   Celia   8   only as a passing diversion./Oh, I dare say that you deceived yourself:/But that's
435 CP   Peter   12   Then I wanted to know/And did not dare to ask. It took all my courage/To ask you
466 CC Claude   18   Are a kind of substitute for religion./I dare say truly religious people —/I've never
499 CC Lucasta   31   that I wouldn't. Just to spite you,/I dare say. That was why I took an interest/In
536 ES Gomez   35   that's a good thing./My mother — I dare say she's still alive,/But she must be very
538 ES Gomez   26   have been more or less forgotten./I dare say you did make some mistake, Dick .../
541 ES Gomez   17   of ... blackmail!/On the contrary, I dare say I could buy you out/Several times over.
541 ES Gomez   38   Well, I shan't keep you long, though I dare say your caller/Could hang on for another
555 ES Piggott   3   singing it once. A charming person,/I dare say, but not quite your sort or mine./I
557 ES Ld Clav   14   more speculative business./{LC} I dare say you've tried a little private speculation.
558 ES Ld Clav   12   to let me have your version first./I dare say Sir Alfred's will be rather different./
573 ES Carghil   25   news for you!/But I suspect ... Dare I? Yes, I'm sure of it, Monica!/I can tell by
DARED (1)
319 FR   Harry   36   tell me,/I must ask Agatha. I never dared before./{W} I advise you strongly, not to
DARING (3)
74 WL: Thund   403   blood shaking my heart/The awful daring of a moment's surrender/Which an age
155 Rock 3   61   action,/To arts and inventions and daring enterprises,/To schemes of human
288 FR Agatha   25   nursery tea, the school holiday,/The daring feats on the old pony,/And thought to
DARK (46)
21 Portrait   101   gutters; we are really in the dark./'For everybody said so, all our friends,/
24 Rhapsody   10   drum,/And through the spaces of the dark/Midnight shakes the memory/As a
24 Rhapsody   48   sputtered,/The lamp muttered in the dark./The lamp hummed:/'Regard the moon,/
32 Hysteria   4   /recovery, lost finally in the dark caverns of her throat, bruised by/the ripple
37 Gerontion   27   /By Madame de Tornquist, in the dark room/Shifting the candles; Fräulein von
92 Ash-Wed 3   9   were no more faces and the stair was dark,/Damp, jaggèd, like an old man's mouth
107 Animula   3   of changing lights and noise,/To light, dark, dry or damp, chilly or warm;/Moving
126 SA Chorus   3   and it's damp and it's dawn and it's dark/And you wait for a knock and the turning
166 Rock 10   4   set on a hill/In a world confused and dark and disturbed by portents of fear./And
177 FQ: ECoker   16   deep lane/Shuttered with branches, dark in the afternoon,/Where you lean against a

179 FQ: ECoker	91	of the way/But all the way, in a dark wood, in a bramble,/On the edge of a
180 FQ: ECoker	102	dancers are all gone under the hill./O dark dark dark. They all go into the dark,/The
180 FQ: ECoker	102	are all gone under the hill./O dark dark dark. They all go into the dark,/The
180 FQ: ECoker	102	all gone under the hill./O dark dark dark. They all go into the dark,/The vacant
180 FQ: ECoker	102	dark dark dark. They all go into the dark,/The vacant interstellar spaces, the vacant
180 FQ: ECoker	107	and petty contractors, all go into the dark,/And dark the Sun and Moon, and the
180 FQ: ECoker	108	contractors, all go into the dark,/And dark the Sun and Moon, and the Almanach de
180 FQ: ECoker	113	/I said to my soul, be still, and let the dark come upon you/Which shall be the
183 FQ: ECoker	209	a deeper communion/Through the dark cold and the empty desolation,/The wave
189 FQ: DrySal	185	on the sand, in the sea's lips/Or in the dark throat which will not reject them/Or
191 FQ: Little	11	no wind, but pentecostal fire/In the dark time of the year. Between melting and
192 FQ: Little	38	end, some at the sea jaws,/Or over a dark lake, in a desert or a city —/But this is the
193 FQ: Little	83	end of the unending/After the dark dove with the flickering tongue/Had
204 de la Mare	6	the mangabey, abound/In the dark jungle of a mango grove,/And shadowy
233 Skimble	37	every sort of light — you can make it dark or bright;/There's a button that you turn
599 On a Port	11	lips, or move the slender hands;/Her dark eyes keep their secrets hid from us,/Beyond
251 MC Thomas	9	/You wrap your meaning in as dark generality/As any courtier./{T3} This is the
256 MC Chorus	8	is the sickly smell, the vapour? the dark green light from a cloud on a withered
257 MC Chorus	26	death./Sweet and cloying through the dark air/Falls the stifling scent of despair;/The
257 MC Chorus	28	despair;/The forms take shape in the dark air:/Puss-purr of leopard, footfall of
257 MC Chorus	32	your feet, swing and wing through the dark air./O Thomas Archbishop, save us, save
285 FR Amy	10	/And time would not stop in the dark!/Put on the lights. But leave the curtains
287 FR Amy	24	I do not want the clock to stop in the dark./If you want to know why I never leave
290 FR Agatha	34	of the moon/The attraction of the dark passage/The paw under the door. {}/
296 FR Harry	10	in the chimney/The evil in the dark closet, which they said was not there,/
310 FR Mary	3	in the moving root/The agony in the dark/The slow flow throbbing the trunk/The
333 FR Agatha	31	that sin may strain and struggle/In its dark instinctive birth, to come to consciousness/
347 FR Amy	31	come!/The clock has stopped in the dark! {}/[*Exeunt* AGATHA *and* MARY. *Pause.*
349 FR Chorus	7	loss —/We have lost our way in the dark./{I} I shall have to stay till after the
349 FR 6m	13	*that their last/words are spoken in the dark.*]/{Ag} A curse is slow in coming/To
364 CP Edward	10	/If I am to remain always lost in the dark?/{UG} There is certainly no purpose in
364 CP Reilly	11	no purpose in remaining in the dark/Except long enough to clear from the mind
387 CP Edward	8	anything./I'm completely in the dark./{C} But it's all so simple./Can't you see
449 CC Claude	36	son?/{SC} That's where I'm in the dark./I simply can't guess what her reaction
480 CC Kaghan	9	/But you'd never take a leap in the dark;/You'd keep me on the rails./{C} That's
539 ES Ld Clav	28	business/Of the nature of which dark hints have been given,/He's informed

DARKEN (1)

315 FR Chorus	33	settled./And the wings of the future darken the past, the beak and claws have

DARKENED (1)

18 Portrait	4	for you';/And four wax candles in the darkened room,/Four rings of light upon the

DARKER (1)

263 MC Chorus	6	days begin to lengthen?/Longer and darker the day, shorter and colder the night./

DARKNESS (28)

37 Gerontion	19	to speak a word,/Swaddled with darkness. In the juvescence of the year/Came
96 Ash-Wed 5	7	for the world;/And the light shone in darkness and/Against the Word the unstilled
96 Ash-Wed 5	15	the rain land,/For those who walk in darkness/Both in the day time and in the night
96 Ash-Wed 5	21	sister pray for/Those who walk in darkness, who chose thee and oppose thee,/
96 Ash-Wed 5	24	power and power, those who wait/In darkness? Will the veiled sister pray/For
103 Journ Magi	23	stream and a water-mill beating the darkness,/And three trees on the low sky./And
159 Rock 6	22	constantly try to escape/From the darkness outside and within/By dreaming of
160 Rock 7	1	Waste and void. Waste and void. And darkness was upon the face of the deep./And
160 Rock 7	4	to light and the shadow led them to darkness,/Worshipping snakes or trees,
160 Rock 7	6	Waste and void. Waste and void. And darkness on the face of the deep./And the Spirit
160 Rock 7	11	was ever surrounded and shot with darkness/As the air of temperate seas is pierced
160 Rock 7	17	Waste and void. Waste and void. And darkness on the face of the deep./Then came, at
161 Rock 7	40	Waste and void. Waste and void. And darkness on the face of the deep./Has the
167 Rock 10	45	is made./And we thank Thee that darkness reminds us of light./O Light Invisible,
173 FQ: BurntN	99	rotation suggesting permanence/Nor darkness to purify the soul/Emptying the
174 FQ: BurntN	116	and Ludgate. Not here/Not here the darkness, in this twittering world./Descend
174 FQ: BurntN	120	but that which is not world,/Internal darkness, deprivation/And destitution of all
179 FQ: ECoker	81	of dead secrets/Useless in the darkness into which they peered/Or from which
180 FQ: ECoker	114	come upon you/Which shall be the darkness of God. As, in a theatre,/The lights are
180 FQ: ECoker	116	rumble of wings, with a movement of darkness on darkness,/And we know that the
180 FQ: ECoker	116	with a movement of darkness on darkness,/And we know that the hills and the
180 FQ: ECoker	129	you are not ready for thought:/So the darkness shall be the light, and the stillness the

201 Def Island		12	gamble/with death, fight the power of darkness in air/and fire/and of those who have
239 MC Chorus		11	waits, breathes, waits, whispers in darkness./While the labourer kicks off a muddy
247 MC Templ1		2	the winter season,/Eating up the darkness, with wit and wine and wisdom!/Now
281 MC Chorus		10	even in that which denies Thee; the darkness declares the glory of light./Those who
294 FR Harry		20	/In flickering intervals of light and darkness;/The partial anæsthesia of suffering
438 FR Reilly		8	images. To speak about it/We talk of darkness, labyrinths, Minotaur terrors./But that

DARLING (3)

355 CP Julia		8	/He might have imagined it./{J} My darling Celia,/You needn't be so sceptical. I
567 ES Charles		10	you! And now I *need* you./{C} My darling, what I want is to know that you need
567 ES Charles		18	expedition we must make!/But my darling, since I got your letter this morning/

DARTS (1)

321 FR	m	28	/{H} Her Ladyship's! {}/*[He darts at* WINCHELL *and seizes him by the*

DAS (1)

62 WL: Burial		42	of light, the silence./*Oed' und leer das Meer.*/Madame Sosostris, famous

DASH (1)

152 Rock 2		47	makes too much disturbance,/But all dash to and fro in motor cars,/Familiar with the

DATE-TREE (1)

280 MC Priest3		28	/Oblivion in the fountain by the date-tree;/Or sit and bite your nails in

DATTA (2)

74 WL: Thund	401		in silence./Then spoke the thunder/DA/*Datta:* what have we given?/My friend, blood
75 WL: Thund	432		Ile fit you. Hieronymo's mad againe./Datta. Dayadhvam. Damyata./Shantih shantih

DAUGHTER (22)

67 WL: Fire S		200	bright on Mrs. Porter/And on her daughter/They wash their feet in soda water/Et
109 Marina		5	the fog/What images return/O my daughter./Those who sharpen the tooth of the
110 Marina		35	calling through the fog/My daughter./The Cultivation of Christmas Trees/
284 FR	m	4	*of her deceased husband*/MARY, *daughter of a deceased cousin of Lady*
365 CP Reilly		7	*Riley,/Who came in but the landlord's daughter/And she took my heart entirely.*/You
420 CP Reilly		17	been very kind./{R} Go in peace, my daughter./Work out your salvation with
476 CC Lucasta		30	when I tell you:/I'm only Claude's daughter./{C} His daughter!/{L} His daughter.
476 CC Colby		31	/I'm only Claude's daughter./{C} His daughter!/{L} His daughter. Oh, it's a sordid
476 CC Lucasta		32	daughter./{C} His daughter!/{L} His daughter. Oh, it's a sordid story./I hated my
477 CC Colby		7	... too much./{C} You are Claude's daughter!/{L} Oh, there's no doubt of that./I'm
488 CC Lady E		38	Quite impossible, Claude!/You have a daughter. Now you want a son./{SC} I'd never
500 CC Lucasta		22	been staggered when I said I was your daughter!/I came to thank him for the shock
510 CC Claude		20	Kaghan —/Mrs. Guzzard. And ... my daughter Lucasta./{K} But how did Mrs.
513 CC Guzzard		6	of Lady Elizabeth,/And the daughter of Sir Claude Mulhammer./{SC} That
513 CC Claude		8	— that she shall be satisfied/To be my daughter./{MG} Now, Colby,/I must ask *you*
548 ES Ld Clav		19	*[throwing down newspaper]*./{LC} My daughter chose it./She noticed that it seemed to
548 ES Carghil		22	them./{MC} Oh, so that *is* your daughter — that very charming girl?/And
564 ES Gomez		4	/— This young lady I take to be your daughter?/And this is your son?/{LC} This is my
564 ES Ld Clav		7	{LC} This is my son Michael,/And my daughter Monica./{M} How do you do./
574 ES Carghil		2	come to regard her as my adopted daughter./So much so, that it seems odd to call
575 ES Ld Clav		29	Fred, you're wasting *your* time:/My daughter and my future son-in-law/Understand
582 ES Ld Clav		6	out what life is./And I love you, my daughter, the more truly for knowing/That

DAUGHTER-IN-LAW (2)

304 FR Mary		24	she only wanted/To have a tame daughter-in-law with very little money,/A
513 CC Guzzard		5	be the wife of Barnabas Kaghan,/The daughter-in-law of Lady Elizabeth,/And the

DAUGHTERS (4)

153 Rock 2		51	son would have his motor cycle,/And daughters ride away on casual pillions./Much to
232 Skimble		5	all the porters and the stationmaster's daughters/They are searching high and low,/
243 MC Priest3		13	shall be shut in the street,/And all the daughters of music shall be brought low./{C}
354 CP Alex		14	/There were several very lovely daughters:/I wonder what's become of them

DAUNSINGE (1)

178 FQ: ECoker		30	association of man and woman/In daunsinge, signifying matrimonie —/A dignified

DAWLISH (1)

456 CC Eggers		34	/And once a year our holiday at Dawlish'./And to think that was only the

DAWN (18)

40 Burb Blei		10	horses, under the axletree/Beat up the dawn from Istria/With even feet. Her shuttered
62 WL: Burial		61	/Under the brown fog of a winter dawn,/A crowd flowed over London Bridge, so
103 Journ Magi		21	saying/That this was all folly./Then at dawn we came down to a temperate valley,/Wet,
126 SA Chorus		3	and it's/foggy and it's damp and it's dawn and it's dark/And you wait for a knock
136 5FingerEx3		3	The forces of the morning quake,/The dawn is slant across the lawn,/Here is no eft or
142 Cape Ann		3	fox-sparrow, vesper-sparrow/At dawn and dusk. Follow the dance/Of the
178 FQ: ECoker		48	and drinking. Dung and death./Dawn points, and another day/Prepares for
178 FQ: ECoker		49	for heat and silence. Out at sea the dawn wind/Wrinkles and slides. I am here/Or

185 FQ: DrySal	45	and the future,/Between midnight and dawn, when the past is all deception,/The future
193 FQ: Little	90	like the metal leaves/Before the urban dawn wind unresisting./And as I fixed upon the
204 de la Mare	15	return/Gently at twilight, gently go at dawn,/The sad intangible who grieve and yearn;
597 Before Mor	2	flowers at the window turned toward dawn,/Petal on petal, waiting for the day,/Fresh
597 Before Mor	4	flowers, withered flowers, flowers of dawn./This morning's flowers and flowers of
597 Before Mor	6	fragrance drifts across the room at dawn,/Fragrance of bloom and fragrance of
597 Before Mor	8	flowers, withered flowers, flowers of dawn./Circe's Palace/Around her fountain
265 MC Priest2	2	is to-day? Another night, and another dawn./{P3} What day is the day that we know
269 MC Chorus	34	rat tails twining, in the thick light of dawn. I have eaten/Smooth creatures still living,
270 MC Chorus	2	and my bowels dissolve in the light of dawn. I have smelt/Death in the rose, death in

DAWNED (1)

487 CC Lady E	36	the very moment/When the truth dawned on me. Mrs. Guzzard!/Claude, Colby

DAY (111)

40 Burb Blei	12	barge/Burned on the water all the day./But this or such was Bleistein's way:/A
49 Hippopot	21	one with God./The hippopotamus's day/Is passed in sleep; at night he hunts;/God
91 Ash-Wed 2	2	under a juniper-tree/In the cool of the day, having fed to satiety/On my legs my heart
92 Ash-Wed 2	50	other,/Under a tree in the cool of the day, with the blessing of sand,/Forgetting
96 Ash-Wed 5	16	who walk in darkness/Both in the day time and in the night time/The right time
107 Animula	17	soul/Perplexes and offends more, day by day;/Week by week, offends and
107 Animula	17	/Perplexes and offends more, day by day;/Week by week, offends and perplexes more
127 Cor1 March	5	/We hardly knew ourselves that day, or knew the City./This is the way to the
127 Cor1 March	7	waiting? what did it matter, on such a day?/Are they coming? No, not yet. You can see
128 Cor1 March	43	and how many trumpets!/(And Easter Day, we didn't get to the country,/So we took
135 5FingerEx1	9	chair give ease?/Why will the summer day delay?/*When* will Time flow away?/*Lines to*
158 Rock 5	10	/The man who has builded during the day would return to his hearth at nightfall: to be
167 Rock 10	36	we tire of light. We are glad when the day ends, when the play ends; and ecstasy is too
167 Rock 10	37	asleep as the rocket is fired; and the day is long for work or play./We tire of
167 Rock 10	39	by the rhythm of blood and the day and the night and the seasons./And we
174 FQ: BurntN	130	/Time and the bell have buried the day,/The black cloud carries the sun away./Will
178 FQ: ECoker	48	and death./Dawn points, and another day/Prepares for heat and silence. Out at sea the
187 FQ: DrySal	122	over it, fogs conceal it;/On a halcyon day it is merely a monument,/In navigable
191 FQ: Little	4	pole and tropic./When the short day is brightest, with frost and fire,/The brief
191 FQ: Little	28	like a broken king,/If you came by day not knowing what you came for,/It would
195 FQ: Little	149	move in measure, like a dancer.'/The day was breaking. In the disfigured street/He
202 War Poetry	13	only 'incidents'/In the effort to keep day and night together./It seems just possible
210 Old Gumbie	3	tiger stripes and leopard spots./All day she sits upon the stair or on the steps or on
210 Old Gumbie	15	likes the warm and sunny spots./All day she sits beside the hearth or in the sun or on
213 Growltiger	56	and at Victoria Dock,/And a day of celebration was commanded in Bangkok.
220 Old Deut	18	/He sits in the High Street on market day;/The bullocks may bellow, the sheep they
230 Bust Jones	29	much in this way, passes Bustopher's day —/At one club or another he's found./It
231 Bust Jones	34	/And he's putting on weight every day:/But he's so well preserved because he's
590 Time Space	7	a century?/The butterfly that lives a day/Has lived eternity./The flowers I gave thee
590 Space Time	3	cannot be,/The fly that lives a single day/Has lived as long as we./But let us live
597 Before Mor	3	dawn,/Petal on petal, waiting for the day,/Fresh flowers, withered flowers, flowers of
246 MC Thomas	7	prevision/I sent my letters on another day,/Had fair crossing, found at Sandwich/
256 MC Priests	27	in the night/Abide the coming of day, when the traveller may find his way,/The
257 MC Priests	4	{3P} A man may climb the stair in the day, and slip on a broken step./{4T} A man may
260 MC Thomas	6	mystery of our masses of Christmas Day. For whenever/Mass is said, we re-enact
260 MC Thomas	8	of Our Lord; and/on this Christmas Day we do this in celebration of His Birth. So
261 MC Thomas	10	/Birth and His Death: but on the next day we celebrate the martyrdom/of His first
261 MC Thomas	12	it an accident, do you think,/that the day of the first martyr follows immediately the
261 MC Thomas	12	first martyr follows immediately the day of the Birth/of Christ? By no means. Just as
261 MC Thomas	40	because it is fitting, on Christ's birth/day, to remember what is that Peace which He
263 MC Chorus	6	to lengthen?/Longer and darker the day, shorter and colder the night./Still and
264 MC Priest1	1	*are in italics*.]/{P1} Since Christmas a day: and the day of St. Stephen, First Martyr./
264 MC Priest1	1	/{P1} Since Christmas a day: and the day of St. Stephen, First Martyr./*Princes*
264 MC Priest1	3	*and did witness falsely against me*./A day that was always most dear to the
264 MC Priest2	7	*before him*.]/{P2} Since St. Stephen a day: and the day of St. John the Apostle./*In the*
264 MC Priest2	7	/{P2} Since St. Stephen a day: and the day of St. John the Apostle./*In the midst of the*
264 MC Priest3	14	/{P3} Since St. John the Apostle a day: and the day of the Holy Innocents./*Out of*
264 MC Priest3	14	St. John the Apostle a day: and the day of the Holy Innocents./*Out of the mouth of*
264 MC Priest1	22	*them*]/{P1} Since the Holy Innocents a day: the fourth day from Christmas./{3P}
264 MC Priest1	22	the Holy Innocents a day: the fourth day from Christmas./{3P} *Rejoice we all,*
264 MC Priests	23	/{3P} *Rejoice we all, keeping holy day*./{P1} As for the people, so also for himself,
264 MC Priests	26	/{3P} *Rejoice we all, keeping holy day*./{P1} To-day?/{P2} To-day, what is to-day?

264	MC	Priest2	28	/{P2} To-day, what is to-day? For the **day** is half gone./{P1} To-day, what is to-day?
265	MC	Priest1	1	To-day, what is to-day? but another **day**, the dusk of the year./{P2} To-day, what is
265	MC	Priest3	3	night, and another dawn./{P3} What **day** is the day that we know that we hope for or
265	MC	Priest3	3	another dawn./{P3} What day is the **day** that we know that we hope for or fear for?/
265	MC	Priest3	4	that we hope for or fear for?/Every **day** is the day we should fear from or hope
265	MC	Priest3	4	hope for or fear for?/Every day is the **day** we should fear from or hope from. One
265	MC	Priest3	6	selection,/We say, that was the **day**. The critical moment/That is always now,
275	MC	Chorus	26	with us, stop sun, hold season, let the **day** not come, let the spring not come./Can I
275	MC	Chorus	27	not come./Can I look again at the **day** and its common things, and see them all
276	MC	Chorus	4	ends in daily action,/The terror by **day** that ends in sleep;/But the talk in the
285	FR	Amy	8	for/And the night unfeared and the **day** expected/And clocks could be trusted,
286	FR	Violet	20	aeroplane shares./{V} They bathe all **day** and they dance all night/In the absolute
292	FR	Harry	13	why here?/Many happy returns of the **day**, mother./Aunt Ivy, Aunt Violet, Uncle
295	FR	Amy	37	When you see Wishwood/Again by **day**, all will be the same again./I beg you to go
298	FR	Downing	32	.../{Do} Eleven years, Sir, next Lady **Day**./{C} Eleven years, and you know him
314	FR	Warburt	11	But you can't have forgotten/The **day** when you came back from school with
315	FR	Violet	20	/You wouldn't think that she was a **day** older/Than on her birthday ten years ago./
316	FR	Agatha	19	their proper business/The eye of the **day** time/And the eye of the night time/Be
318	FR	Harry	12	guilty, and so we misbehaved/Next **day** at school, in order to be punished,/For
319	FR	Harry	21	But now I remember/A summer **day** of unusual heat,/The day I lost my butterfly
319	FR	Harry	22	/A summer day of unusual heat,/The **day** I lost my butterfly net;/I remember the
319	FR	Harry	28	into the heart of a child./*That* was the **day** he died. Of course./I mean, I suppose, the
319	FR	Harry	29	Of course./I mean, I suppose, the **day** on which the news arrived./{W} You
324	FR	Harry	20	a breathing spell:/But John's ordinary **day** isn't much more than breathing./{I} Really,
332	FR	Agatha	23	long vacation. I remember/A summer **day** of unusual heat/For this cold country./{H}
349	FR	Mary	20	divert it/Only implicates others/At the **day** of consummation/{Ag} A curse is a power/
349	FR	Mary	26	/Follow follow/{M} Not in the **day** time/And in the hither world/Where we
353	CP	Celia	14	tell us that story you told the other **day**, about Lady Klootz and the wedding cake./
384	CP	2m	1	*same room: late afternoon of the next* **day**. EDWARD *alone. He goes to/answer the*
397	CP	Edward	13	place. And now I must live with it/Day by **day**, hour by hour, for ever and ever./
397	CP	Edward	13	And now I must live with it/Day by **day**, hour by hour, for ever and ever./{L} I think
424	CP	Edward	20	not too tired?/{E} Oh no, a quiet **day**./Two consultations with solicitors/On quite
436	CP	Julia	18	come to think of Celia/Like that, one **day**. And then you'll understand her/And be
438	CP	Reilly	14	/Cold of the night and heat of the **day**, than we should?/{E} But if this was right —
446	CC	Eggers	33	ought to have window boxes./Some **day**, he'll want a garden of his own. And yes, a
446	CC	Eggers	37	know, Sir Claude. Only the other **day**/I read a letter in *The Times* about wild
454	CC	Kaghan	7	with Colby./He's had enough for one **day**. Take my advice, Colby./Never allow
454	CC	Kaghan	12	along, Lucasta,/I'm going to make a **day** of it, and take you out to tea./{L} I'm dying
459	CC	Lady E	30	get one's quiet hour. A quiet hour a **day**/Is most essential, Dr. Rebmann says./{SC}
461	CC	Eggers	7	garden./And I'll slip up to town any **day**, if you want me./In fact, Mrs. E. said: 'I
461	CC	Eggers	22	and thank you, Eggerson./{E} Good **day**, Sir Claude. Good day, Mr. Simpkins. {}/
461	CC	Eggers	22	/{E} Good day, Sir Claude. Good **day**, Mr. Simpkins. {}/[*Exit* EGGERSON]/{SC}
466	CC	Claude	23	/That's your son and me. Some **day**, perhaps,/I will show you my collection./{C}
470	CC	Colby	23	me to a concert?/{C} Only the other **day**, I invited you .../{L} To go to see that
488	CC	Claude	24	you./{SC} I should have told you one **day**./I've always loathed keeping such a thing
496	CC	Eggers	39	Of your son's death?/{E} Of the **day** we got the news. We don't often speak of it;
502	CC	Lucasta	39	/Will come, in time. Perhaps, one **day**/We may understand each other. And accept
504	CC	Claude	8	formidable./{SC} It's Parkman's **day** off. But where's the parlourmaid?/{L} I
506	CC	Eggers	14	been without a clue/Until the other **day**. This son, Mrs. Guzzard,/If he is alive, must
518	CC	Eggers	6	vocation./We worked together every **day**, you know,/For quite a little time, and I've
523	ES	m	15	*Same. Late afternoon of the following* **day**/Act One/*The drawing-room of* LORD
525	ES	Charles	18	father's retired/He's at home every **day**. And you're leaving London./And because
529	ES	Ld Clav	30	nothingness. Just remember:/Every **day**, year after year, over my breakfast,/I have
549	ES	Carghil	7	of us — Effie, Maudie and me./That **day** we spent on the river — I've never forgotten
556	ES	Michael	12	{}/[*A pause*]/{Mi} What a lovely **day**!/I'm glad you're here, to enjoy such
567	ES	2m	1	*Two. Late afternoon of the following* **day**. MONICA *seated/alone. Enter* CHARLES./
567	ES	Charles	11	know that you need me./On that last **day** in London, you admitted that you loved
575	ES	Carghil	39	the first time he looked at me!/Some **day**, Monica, I'll tell you all about it./{M} I am
582	ES	Monica	20	shall take a stroll./{M} At this time of **day**? You'll not go far, will you?/You know

DAY'S (3)

210	Old Gumbie		5	makes a Gumbie Cat!/But when the **day's** hustle and bustle is done,/Then the
210	Old Gumbie		17	makes a Gumbie Cat!/But when the **day's** hustle and bustle is done,/Then the
211	Old Gumbie		29	makes a Gumbie Cat!/But when the **day's** hustle and bustle is done,/Then the

DAYADHVAM (2)

74 WL: Thund	411	lean solicitor/In our empty rooms/DA/*Dayadhvam:* I have heard the key/Turn in the
75 WL: Thund	432	you. Hieronymo's mad againe./Datta. Dayadhvam. Damyata./Shantih shantih shantih

DAYBREAK (2)

605 Narcissus	4	shadow sprawling over the sand at daybreak, or/Your shadow leaping behind the
276 MC Chorus	7	the ashes,/The fuel laid on the fire at daybreak,/These acts marked a limit to our

DAYLIGHT (1)

173 FQ: BurntN	95	and time after/In a dim light: neither daylight/Investing form with lucid stillness/

DAYS (35)

14 Prufrock	29	/And time for all the works and days of hands/That lift and drop a question on
15 Prufrock	60	/To spit out all the butt-ends of my days and ways?/And how should I presume?/
22 Preludes	4	o'clock./The burnt-out ends of smoky days./And now a gusty shower wraps/The grimy
34 Figlia	18	/Compelled my imagination many days,/Many days and many hours:/Her hair
34 Figlia	19	my imagination many days,/Many days and many hours:/Her hair over her arms
62 WL: Burial	59	myself:/One must be so careful these days./Unreal City,/Under the brown fog of a
147 Rock 1	28	and there I was told:/We toil for six days, on the seventh we must motor/To
152 Rock 2	42	who meditates alone,/For whom the days and nights repeat the praise of GOD,/
157 Rock 4	3	the Temple should not be built./In the days of Nehemiah the Prophet/There was no
185 FQ: DrySal	58	the trailing/Consequence of further days and hours,/While emotion takes to itself
228 Gus	14	anecdotes drawn from his palmiest days./For he once was a Star of the highest
229 Gus	46	do not get trained/As we did in the days when Victoria reigned./They never get
590 Time Space	15	to see them pine,/And though our days of love be few/Yet let them be divine./Song
245 MC Priest2	30	hearts for your coming,/Than seven days could make ready Canterbury./However, I
263 MC Chorus	5	stir, not a shoot, not a breath./Do the days begin to lengthen?/Longer and darker the
285 FR Amy	2	/I have nothing to do but watch the days draw out,/Now that I sit in the house from
295 FR Harry	25	world I have to live in./— I lay two days in contented drowsiness;/Then I recovered.
296 FR Amy	31	person./I prefer to believe that a few days at Wishwood/Among his own family, is all
369 CP Peter	24	know Celia./{P} I saw her again a few days later/Alone at a concert. And I was alone./
400 CP Alex	7	only impatient/At having to wait four days for the appointment./{R} It was necessary
404 CP Edward	30	you keep a room for more than seven days;/I haven't the courage to go to a hotel,/
430 CP Peter	6	last night —/I left Los Angeles three days ago./I saw Sheila Paisley at lunch to-day/
430 CP Peter	21	Princess Bologolomsky/In the old days? We dined the other night/At the Saffron
496 CC Eggers	21	/At my being up in London five or six days a week;/But now she says: 'You're
497 CC Eggers	1	/Yet I know what's on her mind, for days beforehand./But here I am, talking about
506 CC Eggers	26	you?/{E} It seems just possible. A few days ago,/As I said, Lady Elizabeth learned
542 ES Gomez	4	/Just as it used to be in the old days/When you taught me expensive tastes.
544 ES 2m	1	*Court. A bright sunny morning, several days later./Enter* LORD CLAVERTON *and*
544 ES Ld Clav	12	after a fortnight —/After fourteen days of people not staring/Or offering picture
544 ES Ld Clav	21	/And warmth will last for a few days more./But this early summer, that's hardly
545 ES Piggott	26	I've been in such a rush, these last few days,/And I thought, 'Lord Claverton will
564 ES Carghil	32	me all about Richard/In his Oxford days./{G} On one condition:/That you tell me
573 ES Carghil	35	/Fancy! I've only known her two days!/But I feel like a mother to her already./
575 ES Carghil	38	father was simply *irresistible*/In those days. I melted the first time he looked at me!/
580 ES Gomez	4	reach him there./But it takes some days, you know, even by air mail./{M} Take the

DAYS' (1)

323 FR Warburt	15	bring him up tomorrow; and a few days' rest,/I've no doubt, will be all that he

DE (42)

24 Rhapsody	58	rose,/That smells of dust and eau de Cologne,/She is alone/With all the old
37 Gerontion	27	among the Titians;/By Madame de Tornquist, in the dark room/Shifting the
39 Gerontion	67	its operations, will the weevil/Delay? De Bailhache, Fresca, Mrs. Cammel, whirled/
44 Cook Egg	24	the Seven Sacred Trances;/Piccarda de Donati will conduct me./But where is the
46 Directeur	13	bras dessous/Font des tours/A pas de loup./Dans un égout/Une petite fille/En
47 Mél Adult	t	/Et crève d'amour./Mélange Adultère de Tout/En Amérique, professeur;/En
47 Mél Adult	9	à Paris que je me coiffe/Casque noir de jemenfoutiste./En Allemagne, philosophe/
47 Mél Adult	12	par Emporheben/Au grand air de Bergsteigleben;/J'erre toujours de-ci de-là/A
47 Mél Adult	14	toujours de-ci de-là/A divers coups de tra là là/De Damas jusqu'à Omaha./Je
47 Mél Adult	15	de-ci de-là/A divers coups de tra là là/De Damas jusqu'à Omaha./Je célébrai mon jour
47 Mél Adult	16	jusqu'à Omaha./Je célébrai mon jour de fête/Dans une oasis d'Afrique/Vêtu d'une
47 Mél Adult	18	une oasis d'Afrique/Vêtu d'une peau de girafe./On montrera mon cénotaphe/Aux
47 Mél Adult	20	mon cénotaphe/Aux côtes brûlantes de Mozambique./Lune de Miel/Ils ont vu les
48 Lune Miel	t	brûlantes de Mozambique./Lune de Miel/Ils ont vu les Pays-Bas, ils rentrent à
48 Lune Miel	3	entre deux draps, chez deux centaines de punaises;/La sueur aestivale, et une forte
48 Lune Miel	4	/La sueur aestivale, et une forte odeur de chienne./Ils restent sur le dos écartant les

48 Lune Miel	6	restent sur le dos écartant les genoux/De quatre jambes molles tout gonflées de
48 Lune Miel	6	quatre jambes molles tout gonflées de morsures./On relève le drap pour mieux
48 Lune Miel	10	Classe, basilique connue des amateurs/De chapitaux d'acanthe que tournoie le vent./Ils
48 Lune Miel	11	le vent./Ils vont prendre le train de huit heures/Prolonger leurs misères de
48 Lune Miel	12	de huit heures/Prolonger leurs misères de Padoue à Milan/Où se trouve la Cène, et un
48 Lune Miel	17	et ascétique,/Vieille usine désaffectée de Dieu, tient encore/Dans ses pierres
48 Lune Miel	18	pierres écroulantes la forme précise de Byzance./The Hippopotamus/The
51 Restaurant	2	délabré qui n'a rien à faire/Que de se gratter les doigts et se pencher sur mon
51 Restaurant	4	pluvieux,/Du vent, du grand soleil, et de la pluie;/C'est ce qu'on appelle le jour de
51 Restaurant	5	la pluie;/C'est ce qu'on appelle le jour de lessive des gueux.'/(Bavard, baveux, à la
51 Restaurant	12	ai donné des primevères.'/Les taches de son gilet montent au chiffre de trente-huit./
51 Restaurant	12	taches de son gilet montent au chiffre de trente-huit./'Je la chatouillais, pour la faire
51 Restaurant	14	la faire rire./J'éprouvais un instant de puissance et de délire.'/Mais alors, vieux
51 Restaurant	14	J'éprouvais un instant de puissance et de délire.'/Mais alors, vieux lubrique, à cet âge
51 Restaurant	23	ma fourchette, décrasse-toi le crâne./De quel droit payes-tu des expériences comme
51 Restaurant	26	les cris des mouettes et la houle de Cornouaille,/Et les profits et les pertes, et la
51 Restaurant	28	et la cargaison d'étain:/Un courant de sous-mer l'emporta très loin,/Le repassant
51 Restaurant	29	très loin,/Le repassant aux étapes de sa vie antérieure./Figurez-vous donc, c'était
51 Restaurant	31	ce fut jadis un bel homme, de haute taille./Whispers of Immortality/
127 Cor1 March	26	/And now the *société gymnastique de Poissy*/And now come the Mayor and the
180 FQ: ECoker	108	Sun and Moon, and the Almanach de Gotha/And the Stock Exchange Gazette, the
204 de la Mare	t	What is the fruit of action./To Walter de la Mare/The children who explored the
276 MC Knight1	32	in/the country: Baron William de Traci./{K3} I am afraid I am not anything
277 MC Knight1	28	I think we will all agree that William de Traci has/spoken well and has made a very
277 MC Knight1	32	speakers. I shall next call upon Hugh de Morville, who/has made a special study of
277 MC Knight1	34	and constitutional law. Sir/Hugh de Morville./{K2} I should like first to recur to a

DE-CI (1)

47 Mél Adult	13	air de Bergsteigleben;/J'erre toujours de-ci de-là/A divers coups de tra là là/De

DE-LÀ (1)

47 Mél Adult	13	Bergsteigleben;/J'erre toujours de-ci de-là/A divers coups de tra là là/De Damas

DEAD (76)

16 Prufrock	94	To say: 'I am Lazarus, come from the dead,/Come back to tell you all, I shall tell you
24 Rhapsody	12	the memory/As a madman shakes a dead geranium./Half-past one,/The street-lamp
52 Whispers	7	/He knew that thought clings round dead limbs/Tightening its lusts and luxuries./
60 WL: Burial	t	/The Waste Land/The Burial of the Dead/April is the cruellest month, breeding/
61 WL: Burial	2	month, breeding/Lilacs out of the dead land, mixing/Memory and desire, stirring/
61 WL: Burial	23	images, where the sun beats,/And the dead tree gives no shelter, the cricket no relief,/
62 WL: Burial	40	eyes failed, I was neither/Living nor dead, and I knew nothing,/Looking into the
62 WL: Burial	68	Woolnoth kept the hours/With a dead sound on the final stroke of nine./There I
65 WL: Chess	116	I think we are in rats' alley/Where the dead men lost their bones.'/What is that noise?'/
69 WL: Fire S	246	/And walked among the lowest of the dead.))/Bestows one final patronising kiss,/And
71 WL: DWater	312	/Phlebas the Phoenician, a fortnight dead,/Forgot the cry of gulls, and the deep sea
72 WL: Thund	328	mountains/He who was living is now dead/We who were living are now dying/With a
72 WL: Thund	339	were only water amongst the rock/Dead mountain mouth of carious teeth that
84 Hollow Men	39	/In the twilight kingdom/This is the dead land/This is cactus land/Here the stone
84 Hollow Men	43	they receive/The supplication of a dead man's hand/Under the twinkle of a fading
103 Journ Magi	5	deep and the weather sharp,/The very dead of winter.'/And the camels galled,
105 Song Sime	7	for the wind that chills towards the dead land./Grant us thy peace./I have walked
123 SA Doris	31	that's no life/Why I'd just as soon be dead./{S} That's what life is. Just is/{Do} What
125 SA Sweeney	5	know if he was alive/and the girl was dead/He didn't know if the girl was alive/and he
125 SA Sweeney	7	know if the girl was alive/and he was dead/He didn't know if they were both alive/or
125 SA Sweeney	9	if they were both alive/or both were dead/If he was alive then the milkman wasn't/
125 SA Sweeney	12	/And if they were alive then he was dead./There wasn't any joint/There wasn't any
126 SA Chorus	7	you're alive/And perhaps you're dead/Hoo ha ha/Hoo ha ha/Hoo/Hoo/Hoo {}/
160 Rock 7	12	temperate seas is pierced by the still dead breath of the Arctic Current;/And they
160 Rock 7	13	Current;/And they came to an end, a dead end stirred with a flicker of life,/And they
160 Rock 7	15	/Prayer wheels, worship of the dead, denial of this world, affirmation of rites
171 FQ: BurntN	26	/Moving without pressure, over the dead leaves,/In the autumn heat, through the
179 FQ: ECoker	80	/The wisdom only the knowledge of dead secrets/Useless in the darkness into which
182 FQ: ECoker	194	the pattern more complicated/Of dead and living. Not the intense moment/
184 FQ: DrySal	24	broken oar/And the gear of foreign dead men. The sea has many voices,/Many gods
187 FQ: DrySal	118	/Like the river with its cargo of dead negroes, cows and chicken coops,/The
192 FQ: Little	51	of the voice praying./And what the dead had no speech for, when living,/They can
192 FQ: Little	52	when living,/They can tell you, being dead: the communication/Of the dead is
192 FQ: Little	53	dead: the communication/Of the dead is tongued with fire beyond the language

193 FQ:	Little	66	/Over the eyes and in the mouth,/Dead water and dead sand/Contending for the
193 FQ:	Little	66	and in the mouth,/Dead water and dead sand/Contending for the upper hand./The
193 FQ:	Little	85	the horizon of his homing/While the dead leaves still rattled on like tin/Over the
193 FQ:	Little	94	/I caught the sudden look of some dead master/Whom I had known, forgotten,
194 FQ:	Little	109	and after,/We trod the pavement in a dead patrol./I said: 'The wonder that I feel is
195 FQ:	Little	158	between/The live and the dead nettle. This is the use of memory:/For
196 FQ:	Little	183	quiet,/Why should we celebrate/These dead men more than the dying?/It is not to ring
197 FQ:	Little	232	go with them./We are born with the dead:/See, they return, and bring us with them./
236 Cat	Morgan	16	one to boast,/That some of the gals is dead keen on old Morgan./So if you 'ave
598 Circe		6	/They sprang from the limbs of the dead. —/We shall not come here again./
602 Humoresque		1	/One of my marionettes is dead,/Though not yet tired of the game —/But
248 MC	Thomas	13	/Voices under sleep, waking a dead world,/So that the mind may not be whole
254 MC	Tempt4	11	of glory after death./When king is dead, there's another king,/And one more king
273 MC	Chorus	4	intercede for me, in my most need?/Dead upon the tree, my Saviour,/Let not be in
280 MC	Priest3	23	seas confined with ice/Where the dead breath makes numb the hand, makes dull
293 FR	Amy	10	give me no further advice when I'm dead./{I} Oh, dear Amy!/No one wants you to
308 FR	Harry	7	adjusts itself to a twilight/Where the dead stone is seen to be batrachian,/The
310 FR	Harry	12	full tide/Returning the ghosts of the dead/Those whom the winter drowned/Do not
310 FR	Harry	16	/Return to land in the spring?/Do the dead want to return?/{M} Pain is the opposite of
322 FR	Winch	6	God rest her soul,/She's been dead these ten years. How is her Ladyship,/If I
332 FR	Agatha	7	/{H} You tell me nothing./{Ag} The dead man whom you have assumed to be your
335 FR	Agatha	6	/Away, down a concrete corridor/In a dead air. Only feet walking/And sharp heels
343 FR	Mary	18	so many years/To learn that one is dead! So you must help me./I will go. But I
355 CP	Julia	33	the Vincewells./{J} Oh, they're both dead now. But I wanted to know./If they'd been
384 CP	Reilly	22	/To bring someone back from the dead./{E} From the dead?/That figure of speech
384 CP	Edward	23	back from the dead./{E} From the dead?/That figure of speech is somewhat ...
433 CP	Alex	29	Is she married?/{A} Not married, but dead./{L} Celia?/{A} Dead./{P} Dead. That
433 CP	Alex	31	Not married, but dead./{L} Celia?/{A} Dead./{P} Dead. That knocks the bottom out of
433 CP	Peter	32	but dead./{L} Celia?/{A} Dead./{P} Dead. That knocks the bottom out of it./{E}
433 CP	Edward	33	knocks the bottom out of it./{E} Celia dead./{J} You had better tell them, Alex,/The
437 CP	Reilly	5	*was dust/The magus Zoroaster, my dead child,/Met his own image walking in the*
449 CC	Claude	4	might say *mislaid,*/Since the father is dead, and there's no way of tracing it./Yes, I
465 CC	Claude	3	all my life/I have been atoning. To a dead father,/Who had always been right. I never
490 CC	Colby	38	— was a living fact./Now, it is a dead fact, and out of dead facts/Nothing living
490 CC	Colby	38	/Now, it is a dead fact, and out of dead facts/Nothing living can spring. Now, it is
514 CC	Guzzard	2	other man/Obscure and silent? A dead man, Colby./Be careful what you say./{C}
514 CC	Colby	4	/Be careful what you say./{C} A dead obscure man./{MG} You shall have your
514 CC	Guzzard	7	terms with it. You shall have a father/Dead, and unknown to you./{SC} What do you
536 ES	Gomez	34	me./{G} Perfectly simple./My father's dead long since — that's a good thing./My
536 ES	Gomez	36	be very old. And she must think I'm dead;/And as for my married sisters — I don't
572 ES	Ld Clav	1	/And had been run over after he was dead./It was only a corpse that we had run over
583 ES	Charles	22	/{C} It is not at all strange./The dead has poured out a blessing on the living./

DEADLY (3)

162 Rock 8		26	by the sun of the East/And the seven deadly sins in Syria./But our King did well at
376 CP	Julia	33	that Alex makes is absolutely deadly./I could tell such tales of his poisoning
557 ES	Michael	9	/{Mi} I'd stuck it for two years. And deadly dull it was./{LC} Every job is dull,

DEAF (1)

318 FR	Harry	33	been silent/Or talked to the stone deaf: and the others/Seem to hear something

DEAL (29)

250 MC	Thomas	4	to desire a punier power?/Delegate to deal the doom of damnation,/To condemn
277 MC	Knight3	9	for/myself, but I had drunk a good deal — I am not a drinking man/ordinarily —
279 MC	Knight1	4	us./{K1} Morville has given us a great deal to think about. It/seems to me that he has
289 FR	Amy	11	Agatha means/As a rule, a good deal more than she cares to betray,/I am bound
295 FR	Harry	17	can be clear./{H} It goes a good deal deeper/Than what people call their
299 FR	Charles	8	—/Of course, there was a great deal too much in the papers./Downing, do you
314 FR	Warburt	7	I dare say we've both changed a good deal, Harry./A country practitioner doesn't get
346 FR	Agatha	37	it,/It is only that he has seen a great deal more than that,/And we have seen them
361 CP	Edward	21	unless you know my wife/A good deal better than I thought, or unless you know/
361 CP	Edward	22	thought, or unless you know/A good deal more about us than appears —/I think
367 CP	Peter	12	/{P} It seemed to me we had a great deal in common./We're both of us artists./{E} I
367 CP	Peter	32	The point is, I thought we had a great deal in common/And I think she thought so
369 CP	Peter	3	kind to me/And I owe her a great deal. And then I met Celia./She was different
403 CP	Edward	19	am like that/I must have done a great deal of harm./{R} Oh, not so much as you
404 CP	Reilly	8	Mr. Chamberlayne:/I learn a good deal by merely observing you,/And letting you
404 CP	Reilly	38	like yourself/I need to know a great deal more about him,/Than the patient himself

407 CP   Reilly   24   like mine/You surrender a great deal more than you meant to./This is the
450 CC   Claude   17   they don't understand me — a good deal better/Than I should care to think,
453 CC   Eggers   40   Mr. Simpkins:/Sir Claude intends to deal with these matters himself./You will have
481 CC   Lady E   31   of person/Who needs to eat a great deal of salad./You remember, I made you take a
482 CC   Lady E   12   I've noticed them paying you a good deal of attention./You see, you're rather a
482 CC   Lady E   20   Well, older than you are,/And a good deal wiser in the ways of the world./{C} But,
483 CC   Colby   14   my room:/You see, I shall do a good deal of my work here./{LE} And what is that
525 ES   Monica   22   ambling in .../{M} You've said a good deal more than two words already./And besides,
533 ES   Gomez   8   besides, my wife's name is a good deal more normal/In my country, than
550 ES   Ld Clav   23   furniture./{LC} I've never had to deal with questions of equipment./I trust that
557 ES   Michael   19   reason./The fact is, I needed a good deal more capital/To make anything of it. If I
558 ES   Michael   32   girls./He assumed it had gone a good deal further than it had./{LC} Perhaps it had
562 ES   Carghil   29   — your father has changed a good deal/Since I knew him ever so many years ago,/
DEALING (1)
349 FR   Gerald   9   do not look forward with pleasure to dealing with Arthur and John in the morning./
DEALT (2)
368 CP   Edward   36   I entertained the minor guests/And dealt with the misfits, Lavinia's mistakes./But
570 ES   Charles   17   are only human beings, who can be dealt with./{M} Or only ghosts, who can be
DEAN (1)
246 MC   Thomas   11   my head from me/Only John, the Dean of Salisbury,/Fearing for the King's name,
DEAR (40)
 62 WL: Burial   57   in a ring./Thank you. If you see dear Mrs. Equitone,/Tell her I bring the
118 SP   Wauch   22   *the window*): Hello Sam!/{W} Hello dear/How many's up there?/{Du} Nobody's up
260 MC   Thomas   4   Son, and of the Holy Ghost. Amen./Dear children of God, my sermon this
261 MC   Thomas   37   /being./I have spoken to you to-day, dear children of God, of the martyrs of/the past,
262 MC   Thomas   1   which He brought; and because,/dear children, I do not think I shall ever preach
264 MC   Priest1   3   me./A day that was always most dear to the Archbishop Thomas./And he
293 FR   Ivy   11   further advice when I'm dead./{I} Oh, dear Amy!/No one wants you to die, I'm sure!/
313 FR   Ivy   7   his mother's birthday./{I} Mary, my dear,/Did you arrange these flowers? Just let me
326 FR   Ivy   36   but it's Mr. Arthur./{I} Arthur! Oh dear, I'm afraid *he*'s had an accident. {}/[*Exeunt*
334 FR   Agatha   5   /{Ag} And a beginning. Harry, my dear,/I feel very tired, as only the old feel./The
335 FR   Harry   35   is as true as what did happen/O my dear, and you walked through the little door/
343 FR   Agatha   7   and I, and Harry. You and I,/My dear, may very likely meet again/In our
353 CP   Alex   5   tree:/You and the Maharaja?/{A} My dear Julia!/It's perfectly hopeless. You haven't
368 CP   Edward   20   /And I shan't disturb you./{E} My dear Alex,/There'll be nothing in the larder
371 CP   Edward   6   And you don't understand./{E} My dear Peter, I have only been telling you/What
376 CP   Julia   32   {E} Of course I shan't touch it./{J} My dear, I should have warned you:/Anything that
377 CP   Julia   1   of his poisoning people./Now, my dear, you give me that apron/And we'll see what
390 CP   Julia   3   everything to come. And how is the dear aunt?/{L} So far as I know, she is very well,
402 CP   Reilly   35   in my own personality./{R} Oh, dear yes; this is serious. A very common
430 CP   Peter   16   of you!/And how are you, Alex? And dear old Julia!/{L} So you've just come from
431 CP   Peter   28   an expert on decaying houses?/{P} Oh dear no! I've written the script of this film,/And
432 CP   Reilly   9   /He looks so forbidding .../{R} My dear Julia,/You are giving me a very bad
432 CP   Julia   12   introduction was necessary./{J} My dear Henry, you are interrupting me./{L} If you
433 CP   Julia   10   *me*? It's very much cheaper./Oh, dear, I can see you're determined not to have
494 CC   Lady E   8   son: and so he could be *our* son./Oh dear, what do I want? I should like him to be
508 CC   Guzzard   20   for that./{MG} We parted with it. A dear little boy./I was happy to have him while
529 ES   Monica   18   must come often. And Oh, Charles dear — {}/[*Enter* LORD CLAVERTON]/{M}
540 ES   Gomez   37   to a Sunday newspaper?/{G} My dear Dick, what a preposterous suggestion!/
541 ES   Gomez   13   then? Do you need money?/{G} My dear chap, you are obtuse!/I said: 'Your secret is
548 ES   Carghil   30   now I'm sitting here talking to you./Dear me, it's astonishing, after all these years;/
554 ES   Carghil   11   Good morning, Mrs. Carghill!/{MC} Dear Mrs. Piggott!/It seems to me that you
562 ES   Carghil   32   he was then./Your father was a very dear friend of mine once./{Mi} Did he really
564 ES   Gomez   13   long as I have, Señor Gomez./{G} My dear lady, you're not old enough/To have
574 ES   Carghil   8   care to impart it?/{MC} It's about dear Michael./{LC} Oh? What about Michael?/
574 ES   Carghil   24   for which I've come to prepare you./Dear Michael is so happy — all his problems
575 ES   Gomez   17   real name is Culverwell .../{G} My dear Dick,/You're wasting your time, rehearsing
580 ES   Ld Clav   35   I'm sure he loves us./{LC} Monica my dear,/What you say comes home to me. I fear
581 ES   Ld Clav   34   Because I love Charles./{LC} Yes, my dear./Your love is for the real Charles, not a
582 ES   Ld Clav   9   for the first time — remember, my dear,/I am only a beginner in the practice of
583 ES   Charles   3   /Who is you and me together./Oh my dear,/I love you to the limits of speech, and
DEAREST (1)
389 CP   Lavinia   26   /I thought you were one of my dearest friends —/At least, in so far as a girl *can*

DEARS (4)

391 CP	Julia	28	way./{J} How right you are!/Well, my dears, I shall see you very soon./{E} *When* shall
426 CP	Julia	28	Julia! {}/[*Enter* JULIA]/{J} Well, my dears, and here I am!/I seem *literally* to have
426 CP	Julia	30	much too early; but the fact is, my dears,/That I have to go on to the Gunnings'
562 ES	Carghil	24	/That means nothing to you, my dears./It's a very long time since the name of

DEATH (124)

52 Whispers	1	/Webster was much possessed by death/And saw the skull beneath the skin;/And
56 Swee Night	7	westward toward the River Plate,/Death and the Raven drift above/And Sweeney
62 WL: Burial	55	I do not find/The Hanged Man. Fear death by water./I see crowds of people, walking
62 WL: Burial	63	Bridge, so many,/I had not thought death had undone so many./Sighs, short and
67 WL: Fire S	192	wreck/And on the king my father's death before him./White bodies naked on the
71 WL: DWater	t	out/O Lord Thou pluckest/burning/Death by Water/Phlebas the Phoenician, a
90 Ash-Wed 1	40	us sinners now and at the hour of our death/Pray for us now and at the hour of our
90 Ash-Wed 1	41	for us now and at the hour of our death./Lady, three white leopards sat under a
104 Journ Magi	36	were we led all that way for/Birth or Death? There was a Birth, certainly,/We had
104 Journ Magi	37	and no doubt. I had seen birth and death,/But had thought they were different; this
104 Journ Magi	39	/Hard and bitter agony for us, like Death, our death./We returned to our places,
104 Journ Magi	39	bitter agony for us, like Death, our death./We returned to our places, these
104 Journ Magi	43	gods./I should be glad of another death./A Song for Simeon/Lord, the Roman
105 Song Sime	4	stand./My life is light, waiting for the death wind,/Like a feather on the back of my
106 Song Sime	35	those after me,/I am dying in my own death and the deaths of those after me./Let thy
109 Marina	7	the tooth of the dog, meaning/Death/Those who glitter with the glory of the
109 Marina	9	glory of the hummingbird, meaning/Death/Those who sit in the sty of contentment,
109 Marina	11	sit in the sty of contentment, meaning/Death/Those who suffer the ecstasy of the
109 Marina	13	the ecstasy of the animals, meaning/Death/Are become unsubstantial, reduced by a
111 Xmas Trees	21	fatigue, the tedium,/The awareness of death, the consciousness of failure,/Or in the
122 SA Sweeney	1	things?/{S} Birth, and copulation, and death./That's all, that's all, that's all, that's all,/
122 SA Sweeney	3	that's all,/Birth, and copulation, and death./{Do} I'd be bored./{S} You'd be bored./
122 SA Sweeney	6	be bored./Birth, and copulation, and death./{Do} I'd be bored./{S} You'd be bored./
122 SA Sweeney	9	be bored./Birth, and copulation, and death./That's all the facts when you come to
122 SA Sweeney	11	tacks:/Birth, and copulation, and death./I've been born, and once is enough./You
124 SA Sweeney	1	is?/What's that life is?/{S} Life is death./I knew a man once did a girl in —/{Do}
125 SA Sweeney	19	neither/I tell you again it don't apply/Death or life or life or death/Death is life and
125 SA Sweeney	19	it don't apply/Death or life or life or death/Death is life and life is death/I gotta use
125 SA Sweeney	20	apply/Death or life or life or death/Death is life and life is death/I gotta use words
125 SA Sweeney	20	or life or death/Death is life and life is death/I gotta use words when I talk to you/But
134 Wind	3	the bells/Swinging between life and death/Here, in death's dream kingdom/This
147 Rock 1	12	/All our ignorance brings us nearer to death,/But nearness to death no nearer to GOD.
147 Rock 1	13	us nearer to death,/But nearness to death no nearer to GOD./Where is the Life we
150 Rock 1	107	*hired us./Our life is unwelcome, our death/Unmentioned in 'The Times'./Chant of*
152 Rock 2	31	he stands alone on the other side of death,/But here upon earth you have the reward
156 Rock 3	74	your door:/Life you may evade, but Death you shall not./You shall not deny the
159 Rock 6	18	her laws?/She tells them of Life and Death, and of all that they would forget./She is
178 FQ: ECoker	47	/Eating and drinking. Dung and death./Dawn points, and another day/Prepares
180 FQ: ECoker	134	requiring, pointing to the agony/Of death and birth./You say I am repeating/
186 FQ: DrySal	85	wreckage,/The bone's prayer to Death its God. Only the hardly, barely prayable
188 FQ: DrySal	160	of a man may be intent/At the time of death" — that is the one action/(And the time
188 FQ: DrySal	161	is the one action/(And the time of death is every moment)/Which shall fructify in
190 FQ: DrySal	208	given/And taken, in a lifetime's death in love,/Ardour and selflessness and
192 FQ: Little	62	the wainscot and the mouse./The death of hope and despair,/This is the death of
192 FQ: Little	63	death of hope and despair,/This is the death of air./There are flood and drouth/Over
193 FQ: Little	71	/Laughs without mirth./This is the death of earth./Water and fire succeed/The
193 FQ: Little	79	/Of sanctuary and choir./This is the death of water and fire./In the uncertain hour
195 FQ: Little	156	/Which resembles the others as death resembles life,/Being between two lives —
196 FQ: Little	197	— a symbol:/A symbol perfected in death./And all shall be well and/All manner of
201 Def Island	12	in man's newest form of gamble/with death, fight the power of darkness in air/and
203 Indians	21	we/Know, until the judgment after death,/What is the fruit of action./To Walter de
605 Narcissus	t	Harvard, to thine and to thee./The Death of Saint Narcissus/Come under the
239 MC Chorus	10	land became brown sharp points of death in a waste of water and mud,/The New
240 MC Chorus	6	seasons:/Winter shall come bringing death from the sea,/Ruinous spring shall beat at
243 MC Chorus	20	with rejoicing, but you come bringing death into Canterbury:/A doom on the house, a
244 MC Chorus	20	but of many,/A fear like birth and death, when we see birth and death alone/In a
244 MC Chorus	20	and death, when we see birth and death alone/In a void apart. We/Are afraid in a
254 MC Tempt4	1	wind/The thread of eternal life and death./You hold this power, hold it./{T}
254 MC Tempt4	10	think, Thomas, think of glory after death./When king is dead, there's another king,/

256 MC Chorus 35   the mastiff prowl by the gate?/{C} Death has a hundred hands and walks by a
257 MC Chorus 25   more pang, more pain than birth or death./Sweet and cloying through the dark air/
260 MC Thomas 7   is said, we re-enact the Passion and Death of Our Lord; and/on this Christmas Day
260 MC Thomas 15   of Our Lord and His Passion and Death upon/the Cross. Beloved, as the World
261 MC Thomas 4   disappointment, to suffer/death by martyrdom. What then did He mean?
261 MC Thomas 10   at once Our Lord's/Birth and His Death: but on the next day we celebrate the
261 MC Thomas 15   we/both rejoice and mourn in the death of martyrs. We mourn, for the sins/of the
263 MC Chorus 4   of the spring of the year?/Only the death of the old: not a stir, not a shoot, not a
263 MC Chorus 9   /The owl rehearses the hollow note of death./What signs of a bitter spring?/The wind
263 MC Chorus 15   among men defiles this world, but death in the Lord renews it,/And the world
270 MC Chorus 3   in the light of dawn. I have smelt/Death in the rose, death in the hollyhock, sweet
270 MC Chorus 3   dawn. I have smelt/Death in the rose, death in the hollyhock, sweet pea, hyacinth,
271 MC Chorus 4   /By the final utter uttermost death of spirit,/By the final ecstasy of waste and
271 MC Thomas 23   these feet. All my life/I have waited. Death will come only when I am worthy,/And if
271 MC Thomas 32   /And I am not in danger: only near to death./{3P} My Lord, to vespers! You must not
272 MC Chorus 22   only is here/The white flat face of Death, God's silent servant,/And behind the
272 MC Chorus 23   silent servant,/And behind the face of Death the Judgement/And behind the
273 MC Chorus 1   with nothing,/Not what we call death, but what beyond death is not death,/We
273 MC Chorus 1   what we call death, but what beyond death is not death,/We fear, we fear. Who shall
273 MC Chorus 1   death, but what beyond death is not death,/We fear, we fear. Who shall then plead
273 MC Chorus 9   doom impending/Help me, Lord, for death is near. {}/[In the cathedral. THOMAS
274 MC Thomas 1   confounded./It is not in time that my death shall be known;/It is out of time that my
275 MC Thomas 1   life,/My blood given to pay for His death,/My death for His death./{K1} Absolve all
275 MC Thomas 2   blood given to pay for His death,/My death for His death./{K1} Absolve all those you
275 MC Thomas 2   pay for His death,/My death for His death./{K1} Absolve all those you have
279 MC Knight4 30   except that he had determined upon a death by martyrdom. Even/at the last, he could
282 MC Chorus 2   seas gnaw at the coast of Iona,/To the death in the desert, the prayer in forgotten
287 FR Amy 30   you understand how old you are/And death will come to you as a mild surprise,/A
287 FR Amy 32   seems to discover some meaning in death/Which I cannot find./— I am only certain
290 FR Amy 10   /In life, she is less than a shadow in death./You might as well all of you know the
308 FR Mary 11   /That sudden comprehension of the death of hope/Of which you speak, I know you
310 FR Mary 20   birth/Is when we have knowledge of death/I believe the season of birth/Is the season
319 FR Harry 27   with the sidewise looks,/That bring death into the heart of a child./That was the day
333 FR Agatha 11   I knew I should have carried/Death in life, death through lifetime, death in
333 FR Agatha 11   I should have carried/Death in life, death through lifetime, death in my womb./I felt
333 FR Agatha 11   /Death in life, death through lifetime, death in my womb./I felt that you were in some
340 FR Amy 2   thought, thirty-five years is long, and death is an end,/And I thought that time might
342 FR Agatha 29   /{Ag} Here the danger, here the death, here, not elsewhere;/Elsewhere no doubt
343 FR Agatha 1   frontier: he must follow;/For him the death is now only on this side,/For him, danger
404 CP Edward 14   to be surprised:/I am not afraid of the death of the body,/But this death is terrifying.
404 CP Edward 15   of the death of the body,/But this death is terrifying. The death of the spirit —/
404 CP Edward 15   body,/But this death is terrifying. The death of the spirit —/Can you understand what
437 CP Reilly 8   know there are two worlds of life and death:/One that which thou beholdest; but the
437 CP Reilly 12   of all forms that think and live/Till death unite them and they part no more!/When I
437 CP Reilly 16   the first five minutes after a violent death./If this strains your credulity, Mrs.
437 CP Reilly 22   here was a woman under sentence of death./That was her destiny. The only question/
437 CP Reilly 24   only question/Then was, what sort of death? I could not know;/Because it was for her
437 CP Reilly 26   to choose the way of life/To lead to death, and, without knowing the end/Yet
437 CP Reilly 27   the end/Yet choose the form of death. We know the death she chose./I did not
437 CP Reilly 27   the form of death. We know the death she chose./I did not know that she would
437 CP Reilly 31   way, which she accepted, led to this death./And if that is not a happy death, what
437 CP Reilly 32   this death./And if that is not a happy death, what death is happy?/{E} Do you mean
437 CP Reilly 32   if that is not a happy death, what death is happy?/{E} Do you mean that having
437 CP Edward 33   mean that having chosen this form of death/She did not suffer as ordinary people
438 CP Reilly 34   Coplestone, because you think her death was waste/You blame yourselves, and
438 CP Reilly 38   —/And just as responsible for her death as you are./{L} Yet I know I shall go on
465 CC Claude 1   time a secret reproach:/But after his death, and then it was too late,/I knew that he
467 CC Colby 2   /And the reconcilement, after his death,/That perfects the relation. You have
496 CC Claude 38   /{SC} The anniversary? Of your son's death?/{E} Of the day we got the news. We
514 CC Guzzard 24   and her child?/{MG} Registration of death. The child was never born./{SC} I don't
530 ES Ld Clav 16   /If I had the energy to work myself to death/How gladly would I face death! But
530 ES Ld Clav 17   to death/How gladly would I face death! But waiting, simply waiting,/With no
560 ES Michael 1   grave? If you're still conscious after death,/I bet it will be a surprised state of
571 ES Ld Clav 40   /That the old man had died a natural death/And had been run over after he was dead.
583 ES Monica 25   vicissitude cannot appal me,/Not even death can dismay or amaze me/Fixed in the

DEATH'S (9)
83 Hollow Men	14	who have crossed/With direct eyes, to death's other Kingdom/Remember us — if at all
83 Hollow Men	20	/Eyes I dare not meet in dreams/In death's dream kingdom/These do not appear:/
84 Hollow Men	30	a fading star./Let me be no nearer/In death's dream kingdom/Let me also wear/Such
84 Hollow Men	46	of a fading star./Is it like this/In death's other kingdom/Waking alone/At the
85 Hollow Men	65	perpetual star/Multifoliate rose/Of death's twilight kingdom/The hope only/Of
133 Eyes	3	saw in tears/Through division/Here in death's dream kingdom/The golden vision
133 Eyes	11	I shall not see unless/At the door of death's other kingdom/Where, as in this,/The
134 Wind	4	between life and death/Here, in death's dream kingdom/The waking echo of
134 Wind	11	shake with alien spears./Here, across death's other river/The Tartar horsemen shake

DEATH-BRINGERS (2)
269 MC Chorus	27	{}/[*Exeunt*]/{C} I have smelt them, the death-bringers, senses are quickened/By subtile
270 MC Chorus	22	of Canterbury./I have smelt them, the death-bringers; now is too late/For action, too

DEATHS (3)
106 Song Sime	35	/I am dying in my own death and the deaths of those after me./Let thy servant depart,
151 Rock 2	5	idleness, to frittered lives and squalid deaths, embittered scorn in honeyless hives,/
244 MC Chorus	11	partly living./We have seen births, deaths and marriages,/We have had various

DEBATE (3)
601 Nocturne	3	the gate/With Juliet, in the usual debate/Of love, beneath a bored but courteous
294 FR Agatha	13	own language, without stopping to debate/Whether it may be too far beyond our
531 ES Charles	10	that your voice will be heard/In debate in the Upper House .../{LC} The

DEBIT (1)
477 CC Lucasta	25	/Claude has just accepted me like a debit item/Always in his cash account. I don't

DEBT (4)
455 CC Eggers	19	indeed,/Though she's always in debt. But you needn't worry/About her, Mr.
557 ES Michael	33	passes pretty quickly, when you're in debt./{LC} And have you other debts?/{Mi} Oh,
558 ES Michael	2	/It's being your son that gets me into debt./Just because of your name they insist on
577 ES Gomez	11	it's always pleasant/To repay an old debt. And better late than never./{C} I see your

DEBTS (4)
555 ES Ld Clav	34	It's probably money./{LC} If it's only debts/Once more, I expect I can put up with it./
557 ES Ld Clav	34	in debt./{LC} And have you other debts?/{Mi} Oh, ordinary debts:/My tailor's bill,
557 ES Michael	35	you other debts?/{Mi} Oh, ordinary debts:/My tailor's bill, for instance./{LC} I
558 ES Ld Clav	4	insist on giving credit./{LC} And your debts: are they the cause of your being

DECADENT (1)
286 FR Ivy	32	younger generation/Are undoubtedly decadent./{C} The younger generation/Are not

DECANTER (1)
422 CP 1m	11	*enters with a tray, a decanter and three glasses, and/exit.* REILLY

DECANTS (1)
547 ES Monica	16	was merely the concoction/Which she decants for every newcomer./Perhaps after what

DECAY (6)
139 Virginia	9	trees,/White trees, wait, wait,/Delay, decay. Living, living,/Never moving. Ever
175 FQ: BurntN	155	/Under the tension, slip, slide, perish,/Decay with imprecision, will not stay in place,/
590 Time Space	3	be,/The sun which does not feel decay/No greater is than we./So why, Love,
597 Before Mor	7	/Fragrance of bloom and fragrance of decay,/Fresh flowers, withered flowers, flowers
273 MC Thomas	20	not/As oak and stone; stone and oak decay,/Give no stay, but the Church shall
431 CP Peter	24	a team of experts over/To study the decay, so as to reproduce it./Then we build

DECAYED (4)
37 Gerontion	7	/Bitten by flies, fought./My house is a decayed house,/And the Jew squats on the
73 WL: Thund	385	cisterns and exhausted wells./In this decayed hole among the mountains/In the faint
431 CP Julia	19	understood that Boltwell/Is in a very decayed condition./{P} Exactly. It is. And that's
431 CP Peter	21	that's why we're interested./The most decayed noble mansion in England!/At least, of

DECAYING (4)
152 Rock 2	26	must be forever building, and always decaying, and always being restored./For every
152 Rock 2	35	be forever building, for it is forever decaying within and attacked from without;/For
240 MC Chorus	10	/And the poor shall wait for another decaying October./Why should the summer
431 CP Julia	27	Peter?/Have you become an expert on decaying houses?/{P} Oh dear no! I've written

DECEASE (1)
105 Song Sime	21	sorrow,/Now at this birth season of decease,/Let the Infant, the still unspeaking and

DECEASED (2)
284 FR m	3	CHARLES PIPER, *brothers of her deceased husband*/MARY, *daughter of a*
284 FR m	4	*husband*/MARY, *daughter of a deceased cousin of Lady Monchensey*/

DECEASÈD (1)
602 Humoresque	5	has such a frame)./But this deceasèd marionette/I rather liked: a common

DECEIT (1)
179 FQ: ECoker	78	/Bequeathing us merely a receipt for deceit?/The serenity only a deliberate hebetude,/

DECEITFUL (3)

92 Ash-Wed 3	6	the devil of the stairs who wears/The deceitful face of hope and of despair./At the
158 Rock 5	1	and impure heart: for the heart is deceitful above all things, and desperately
248 MC Tempt2	35	solid substance/Wander waking with deceitful shadows?/Power is present. Holiness

DECEITFULNESS (1)

| 227 Macavity | 36 | /There never was a Cat of such deceitfulness and suavity./He always has an |

DECEIVE (3)

224 Mr Mistoff	13	/He'll defy examination/And deceive you again./The greatest magicians have
309 FR Mary	25	a good that's misdirected. You deceive yourself/Like the man convinced that he
392 CP Lavinia	29	/Nothing less than the truth could deceive Julia./But how did the aunt come to live

DECEIVED (11)

179 FQ: ECoker	76	/And the wisdom of age? Had they deceived us,/Or deceived themselves, the
179 FQ: ECoker	77	of age? Had they deceived us,/Or deceived themselves, the quiet-voiced elders,/
272 MC Chorus	30	pretence,/Where the soul is no longer deceived, for there are no objects, no tones,/No
336 FR Agatha	2	craving/Flattered in sleep, and deceived in waking./You have a long journey./
343 FR Mary	17	over, I believe, before it began;/But I deceived myself. It takes so many years/To learn
380 CP Celia	8	diversion./Oh, I dare say that you deceived yourself:/But that's what it was, no
406 CP Reilly	19	my sort of sanatorium/Are not easily deceived./{L} Are you a devil/Or merely a
497 CC Lady E	24	Sir Claude is mistaken,/Or has been deceived, and that Colby is my son./I feel sure
507 CC Guzzard	37	that I kept a child of yours/And deceived Sir Claude by pretending it was his?/
514 CC Claude	19	years. And why *should* you have deceived me?/{E} Mrs. Guzzard, can you
514 CC Guzzard	37	of deceiving you, Sir Claude,/Till you deceived yourself. When you went to Canada/

DECEIVES (1)

| 38 Gerontion | 35 | contrived corridors/And issues, deceives with whispering ambitions,/Guides us |

DECEIVING (3)

179 FQ: ECoker	89	are only undeceived/Of that which, deceiving, could no longer harm./In the middle,
224 Mr Mistoff	29	cunning with dice;/He is always deceiving you into believing/That he's only
514 CC Guzzard	36	/{MG} I had no intention of deceiving you, Sir Claude,/Till you deceived

DECEMBER (7)

18 Portrait	1	Lady/Among the smoke and fog of a December afternoon/You have the scene
238 MC	m 9	/*The scene is the Archbishop's Hall, on December 2nd*, 1170/PART II/THREE
238 MC	m 17	*the second scene is in the Cathedral, on December 29th*, 1170/Part I/{C} Here let us
240 MC Chorus	22	in the pattern of time./Come, happy December, who shall observe you, who shall
242 MC Priest2	32	We have had enough of waiting, from December to dismal December./The
242 MC Priest2	32	of waiting, from December to dismal December./The Archbishop shall be at our
245 MC Priest2	32	/To take the chill off our English December,/Your Lordship now being used to a

DECENT (3)

155 Rock 3	34	/And the wind shall say: 'Here were decent godless people:/Their only monument
287 FR Gerald	1	/But I must say I've met some very decent specimens/And some first-class shots —
344 FR Gerald	21	often enough —/Some of them very decent fellows. A maligned profession./They're

DECEPTION (9)

171 FQ: BurntN	24	our first world, shall we follow/The deception of the thrush? Into our first world./
185 FQ: DrySal	45	and dawn, when the past is all deception,/The future futureless, before the
256 MC Tempts	20	/On self-destruction,/Passing from deception to deception,/From grandeur to
256 MC Tempts	20	/Passing from deception to deception,/From grandeur to grandeur to final
307 FR Mary	40	real,/However cruel, it may be a deception./{H} What I see/May be one dream or
329 FR Chorus	14	sorrow/The whisper, the transparent deception/The keeping up of appearances/The
462 CC Colby	8	to me/Like building my life upon a deception./Do you really believe that Lady
514 CC Claude	18	/You couldn't have carried out such a deception/Over all these years. And why *should*
514 CC Claude	34	/You pretend to have carried out a deception/For twenty-five years? It's quite

DECEPTIVE (1)

| 205 de la Mare | 29 | of the mind?/By you; by those deceptive cadences/Wherewith the common |

DECIDE (5)

360 CP Reilly	35	to you. If another woman,/She might decide to be forgiving/And gain an advantage.
402 CP Reilly	32	what is wrong with you/Before we decide what to do with you./{E} I doubt if you
413 CP Reilly	35	must find out about you, before we decide/What *is* normality. You say there are
431 CP Peter	36	for minor parts —/And I'll help him decide what faces are typical./{J} Peter, I've
493 CC Claude	4	when you have a difficult meeting,/To decide on the seating arrangements beforehand./

DECIDED (5)

32 Hysteria	9	to take their tea in the/garden ...' I decided that if the shaking of her breasts could
68 WL: Fire S	239	if undesired./Flushed and decided, he assaults at once;/Exploring hands
327 FR Harry	15	would be another Warburton,/If you decided to set another doctor on me./But this is
387 CP Peter	35	I've changed my mind. I mean, I've decided/That it's all no use. I'm going to
471 CC Colby	39	I had seen you a number of times,/I decided that was only your kind of self-defence./

DECIPHER (2)
460 CC   Claude   9   Zürich;/But you know that I can't decipher your writing./I like to have the cards,
513 CC   Colby   33   photographs/In which I should try to decipher a likeness;/Whose image I could create
DECIPHERED (1)
182 FQ: ECoker 198   only/But of old stones that cannot be deciphered./There is a time for the evening
DECISION (28)
133 Eyes   9   /Eyes I shall not see again/Eyes of decision/Eyes I shall not see unless/At the door
274 MC Thomas   2   be known;/It is out of time that my decision is taken/If you call that decision/To
274 MC Thomas   3   my decision is taken/If you call that decision/To which my whole being gives entire
305 FR   Agatha   11   for./At this moment, there is no decision to be made;/The decision will be made
305 FR   Agatha   12   there is no decision to be made;/The decision will be made by powers beyond us/
334 FR   Harry   30   their apparent strength/Stifled my decision. Now I see/I might even become fonder
337 FR   Harry   22   other./{H} I know that I have made a decision/In a moment of clarity, and now I feel
337 FR   Harry   24   dull again./I only know that I made a decision/Which your words echo. I am still
384 CP   Reilly   8   to remind you — you have made a decision./{E} Are you thinking that I may have
384 CP   Reilly   11   you recover from having made a decision./No. I have come to tell you that you
384 CP   Reilly   18   freedom was yesterday./You made a decision. You set in motion/Forces in your life
393 CP   Edward   19   .../{E} But I wanted *you* to make that decision./{L} But how could I tell where I
398 CP   Edward   5   /Before I thought that I had made a decision./What devil left the door on the latch/
401 CP   Edward   39   /That I was in no state to make a decision?/{R} If I had not brought your wife
404 CP   Edward   19   /Coming to see you — that's the last decision/I was capable of making. I am in your
411 CP   Lavinia   32   themselves, that they had made their decision./{E} Have you anything else to say to
412 CP   Julia   9   you, I am sure she is ready/To make a decision./{R} Was she reluctant?/Was that why
420 CP   Celia   8   But I know it is I who have made the decision:/I must tell you that. Oh, I almost
420 CP   Julia   35   is our destiny. Since you question the decision/What possible alternative can you
438 CP   Reilly   31   I often have to make a decision/Which may mean restoration or ruin to
438 CP   Reilly   33   sometimes I have made the wrong decision./As for Miss Coplestone, because you
447 CC   Claude   30   /And say that I had to make a quick decision/Because he'd had another very
458 CC   Eggers   32   offer:/So we had to make a quick decision./{SC} I didn't want to bother you,
489 CC   Claude   16   never came./And now I regret the decision bitterly./I ought to have told you that I
501 CC   Claude   1   I'm sure that you have made the right decision./{L} But the reasons why you think so
501 CC   Lady E   3   too, Lucasta, you have made a wise decision./{L} And I know very well why *you*
578 ES   Monica   38   of the spirit which inspired your decision:/If you wish to renounce your father
579 ES   Michael   20   I think that when one's come to a decision,/It's as well to say good-bye at once
DECISIONS (3)
14 Prufrock   48   /In a minute there is time/For decisions and revisions which a minute will
393 CP   Lavinia   14   /You mean, leaving all the practical decisions/That you should have made yourself. I
480 CC   Kaghan   8   But I sometimes guess wrong./I make decisions on the spur of the moment,/But you'd
DECK (3)
188 FQ: DrySal 144   slide together behind you;/And on the deck of the drumming liner/Watching the
289 FR   Ivy   25   anybody in *that* way —/Swept off the deck in the middle of a storm,/And never even
300 FRDowning 29   you could see the corner of the upper deck./And I remember, there I saw his Lordship
DECK-CHAIR (1)
285 FR   Violet   21   the English chaplains,/To the chilly deck-chair and the strong cold tea —/The
DECKCHAIR (1)
548 ES   2m 14   MRS. CARGHILL. *She sits in a deckchair nearby, composes/herself and takes out*
DECLARE (6)
196 FQ: Little   204   terror/Of which the tongues declare/The one discharge from sin and error./
589 Fable   83   when anyone questioned, would declare/St. Peter'd snatch to heaven their lord
255 MC Tempt4   2   the historical fact./When men shall declare that there was no mystery/About this
264 MC Priest2   12   that which we have seen and heard/Declare we unto you./*In the midst of the*
296 FR   Agatha   5   understand/That you feel the need to declare what you do./There is more to
549 ES   Carghil   11   one was it invited us to lunch?/I declare, I've utterly forgotten their names./And
DECLARED (1)
281 MC Chorus   10   /Only in Thy light, and Thy glory is declared even in that which denies Thee; the
DECLARES (1)
281 MC Chorus   10   that which denies Thee; the darkness declares the glory of light./Those who deny
DECLINE (4)
173 FQ: BurntN 68   from nor towards,/Neither ascent nor decline. Except for the point, the still point,/
220 Old Deut   8   /And the village is proud of him in his decline./At the sight of that placid and bland
324 FR Warburt   1   must not go out./If you do, I must decline to continue to treat you./You are only
542 ES   Ld Clav   28   could believe it?/{LC} And what if I decline/To give you the pleasure of my
DECLINED (1)
239 MC Chorus   9   to bear witness./Since golden October declined into sombre November/And the apples

DECLINES (2)
41 Burb Blei   21   /The smoky candle end of time/Declines. On the Rialto once./The rats are
57 Swee Night   28   /Therefore the man with heavy eyes/Declines the gambit, shows fatigue,/Leaves the
DECORATION (6)
111 Xmas Trees   8   at the summit of the tree/Is not only a decoration, but an angel./The child wonders at
256 MC Tempts   15   /The scholar's degree, the statesman's decoration./All things become less real, man
464 CC   Claude   7   or porcelain/As merely for use, or for decoration —/In either case, an inferior art./For
464 CC   Claude   9   /For me, they are neither 'use' nor 'decoration' —/That is, decoration as a
464 CC   Claude   10   'use' nor 'decoration' —/That is, decoration as a background for living;/For me,
481 CC   Lady E   20   you can't tell/Whether a scheme of decoration/Is *right*, until the place has been
DECORATIONS (1)
479 CC   Colby   34   /{C} It was Lady Elizabeth chose the decorations./{K} Then I'm not sure I like them.
DECORUM (1)
249 MC Tempt2   31   /Dignity still shall be dressed with decorum./{T} You forget the bishops/Whom I
DÉCRASSE (1)
51 Restaurant   22   rides du visage;/Tiens, ma fourchette, décrasse-toi le crâne./De quel droit payes-tu des
DECREPITUDE (1)
583 ES Monica   23   a blessing on the living./{M} Age and decrepitude can have no terrors for me,/Loss
DÉCROTTER (1)
51 Restaurant   21   alors, tu as ton vautour!/Va t'en te décrotter les rides du visage;/Tiens, ma
DECRY (1)
152 Rock 2   37   and in time of adversity they will decry it./What life have you if you have not life
DEDHAM (5)
390 CP   Alex   23   your telegram .../{L} Where from?/{A} Dedham./{L} Dedham is in Essex. So it was
390 CP   Lavinia 24   .../{L} Where from?/{A} Dedham./{L} Dedham is in Essex. So it was from Dedham./
390 CP   Lavinia 24   Dedham is in Essex. So it was from Dedham./Edward, have *you* any friends in
390 CP   Lavinia 25   /Edward, have *you* any friends in Dedham?/{E} No, *I* have no connections in
390 CP   Edward   26   /{E} No, *I* have no connections in Dedham./{J} Well, it's all delightfully
DEDICATE (1)
522 ES   dedic   8   *without need of meaning:/To you I dedicate this book, to return as best I can/With*
DEDICATED (1)
166 Rock 10   2   one who came in the night, it is now dedicated to GOD./It is now a visible church,
DEDICATION (2)
206 To my Wife   t   The inexplicable mystery of sound./A Dedication to my Wife/To whom I owe the
206 To my Wife   11   which is ours and ours only/But this dedication is for others to read:/These are
DEED (6)
152 Rock 2   27   always being restored./For every ill deed in the past we suffer the consequence:/For
211 Old Gumbie   35   /With a purpose in life and a good deed to do —/And she's even created a Beetles'
227 Macavity   38   or two to spare:/At whatever time the deed took place — MACAVITY WASN'T
587 Fable   12   died,/He added to their hoards — a deed which ne'er he/Had done before — their
258 MC Thomas   6   the greatest treason:/To do the right deed for the wrong reason./The natural vigour
281 MC Chorus   13   Thee, in thought and in word and in deed./Even with the hand to the broom, the
DEEDS (7)
91 Ash-Wed 2   12   I who am here dissembled/Proffer my deeds to oblivion, and my love/To the posterity
148 Rock 1   52   for happiness, seeking/The good deeds that lead to obscurity, accepting/With
152 Rock 2   31   have the inheritance./For good and ill deeds belong to a man alone, when he stands
227 Macavity   39   say that all the Cats whose wicked deeds are widely known/(I might mention
593 Grad 5   4   time may hold in store,/Or what great deeds the distant years may see,/What conquest
273 MC Thomas   36   /And as in time results of many deeds are blended/So good and evil in the end
438 CP   Reilly 28   consequences/Of all our words and deeds, beyond the intention/And beyond our
DEEP (18)
37 Gerontion   5   fought in the warm rain/Nor knee deep in the salt marsh, heaving a cutlass,/Bitten
71 WL: DWater 313   dead,/Forgot the cry of gulls, and the deep sea swell/And the profit and loss./A
103 Journ Magi   4   and such a long journey:/The ways deep and the weather sharp,/The very dead of
140 Usk   6   them sleep./'Gently dip, but not too deep',/Lift your eyes/Where the roads dip and
160 Rock 7   1   darkness was upon the face of the deep./And when there were men, in their
160 Rock 7   6   void. And darkness on the face of the deep./And the Spirit moved upon the face of the
160 Rock 7   17   void. And darkness on the face of the deep./Then came, at a predetermined moment, a
161 Rock 7   40   void. And darkness on the face of the deep./Has the Church failed mankind, or has
166 Rock 10   9   the Mystery of Iniquity is a pit too deep for mortal eyes to plumb. Come/Ye out
177 FQ: ECoker   15   falls/Across the open field, leaving the deep lane/Shuttered with branches, dark in the
177 FQ: ECoker   18   a bank while a van passes,/And the deep lane insists on the direction/Into the
209 NamingCats   31   /His ineffable effable/Effanineffable/Deep and inscrutable singular Name./The Old
260 MC Thomas   6   should meditate in your hearts the/deep meaning and mystery of our masses of
428 CP   Alex   40   You see, Lavinia,/These are very deep waters./{E} And the agitators;/How do

448 CC   Eggers   12   on these matters,/They're much too deep for me. And I thought, Mr. Simpkins,/
496 CC   Claude   3   that *your* interests/Were much too deep for discussion with *me*:/Health cures. And
545 ES   Ld Clav   2   /With myself, I suspect, very deep within myself/Has impelled me all my life
570 ES   Ld Clav   11   each other./And so we lived, with a deep silence between us,/And she died silently.

DEEPEN (1)
180 FQ: ECoker   121   every face the mental emptiness deepen/Leaving only the growing terror of

DEEPER (10)
183 FQ: ECoker   208   intensity/For a further union, a deeper communion/Through the dark cold and
294 FR   Harry   23   /While the slow stain sinks deeper through the skin/Tainting the flesh and
295 FR   Harry   17   can be clear./{H} It goes a good deal deeper/Than what people call their conscience;
311 FR   Harry   3   What, Harry?/{H} That apprehension deeper than all sense,/Deeper than the sense of
311 FR   Harry   4   apprehension deeper than all sense,/Deeper than the sense of smell, but like a smell/
318 FR   Harry   16   taken for granted/At home, make a deeper impression upon children/Than what
327 FR   Harry   23   always the filthiness, that lies a little deeper ... {}/[*Enter* IVY]/{I} Where is there an
331 FR   Agatha   24   —/That is the surface. There is a deeper/Organisation, which your question
360 CP   Reilly   37   no other man, then the reason may be deeper/And you've ground for hope that she
515 CC Guzzard   30   that this revelation/Drives the knife deeper and twists it in the wound?/I had very

DEEPLY (4)
190 FQ: DrySal   214   /Or the waterfall, or music heard so deeply/That it is not heard at all, but you are
210 Old Gumbie   9   skirts to the basement to creep./She is deeply concerned with the ways of the mice —/
226 Macavity   13   for his eyes are sunken in./His brow is deeply lined with thought, his head is highly
360 CP   Reilly   17   ... and drink it sitting down./Breathe deeply, and adopt a relaxed position./There we

DEFALCATION (1)
538 ES   Gomez   3   /Hence, as you have just reminded me/Defalcation and forgery. And then my stretch/

DEFAME (1)
254 MC Tempt4   39   men will not hate you/Enough to defame or to execrate you,/But pondering the

DEFAULTER (1)
20 Portrait   76   at a Polish dance,/Another bank defaulter has confessed./I keep my countenance,

DEFEAT (1)
201 Def Island   15   and France, those undefeated in defeat,/unalterable in triumph, changing

DEFEATED (1)
196 FQ: Little   195   the fortunate/We have taken from the defeated/What they had to leave us — a

DEFEATING (1)
578 ES   Ld Clav   15   at your good/Only succeeded in defeating each other,/How can I feel anything

DEFECTION (1)
408 CP   Reilly   6   the cause of your distress/Was the defection of your lover — who suddenly/For

DEFECTIVE (1)
348 FR   Chorus   16   /Against larceny and illness,/Against defective plumbing,/But not against the act of

DEFENCE (3)
68 WL: Fire S   240   once;/Exploring hands encounter no defence;/His vanity requires no response,/And
201 Def Island   t   are one./OCCASIONAL VERSES/Defence of the Islands/Let these memorials of
201 Def Island   5   /be joined with the memory of this defence of/the islands/and the memory of those

DEFER (1)
273 MC Thomas   34   settle if an act be good or bad./You defer to the fact. For every life and every act/

DEFERENTIAL (1)
16 Prufrock   115   the prince; no doubt, an easy tool,/Deferential, glad to be of use,/Politic, cautious,

DEFIANCE (1)
581 ES   Ld Clav   26   happy —/In spite of everything, in defiance of reason,/I have been brushed by the

DEFILED (4)
162 Rock 8   5   /And thy temple have they defiled./Who is this that cometh from Edom?/
162 Rock 8   9   of Jerusalem/And the holy places defiled;/Peter the Hermit, scourging with words.
275 MC Chorus   22   water is foul, our beasts and ourselves defiled with blood./A rain of blood has blinded
276 MC Chorus   15   not the house, it is not the city that is defiled,/But the world that is wholly foul./Clear

DEFILEMENT (1)
337 FR   Harry   26   I know there is only one way out of defilement —/Which leads in the end to

DEFILES (1)
263 MC Chorus   15   peace of God./And war among men defiles this world, but death in the Lord renews

DEFINITE (3)
19 Portrait   35   monotone/That is at least one definite 'false note.'/— Let us take the air, in a
603 Spleen   2   /Sunday: this satisfied procession/Of definite Sunday faces;/Bonnets, silk hats, and
385 CP   Reilly   37   Yes, I know you would. And for definite reasons/Which I am not prepared to

DEFINITELY (3)
286 FR   Violet   13   for me,/I would never go south, no, definitely never,/Even could I do it as well as
328 FR   Gerald   5   John is unlucky,/But Arthur is definitely reckless./{V} I think these racing cars
571 ES   Ld Clav   39   /But was later discharged. It was definitely shown/That the old man had died a

DEFINITION (1)
276 MC   Chorus   9   to our suffering./Every horror had its definition,/Every sorrow had a kind of end:/In
DEFT (1)
 34 Figlia   14   /Some way incomparably light and deft,/Some way we both should understand,/
DEFUNCTIVE (1)
 40 Burb Blei   5   /They were together, and he fell./Defunctive music under sea/Passed seaward
DEFY (2)
224 Mr Mistoff   12   /And at legerdemain/He'll defy examination/And deceive you again./The
226 Macavity   2   /For he's the master criminal who can defy the Law./He's the bafflement of Scotland
DEGRADATION (2)
294 FR   Harry   8   /In which all past is present, all degradation/Is unredeemable. As for what
330 FR   Harry   26   second hell of not being there,/The degradation of being parted from my self,/From
DEGRADE (1)
250 MC Thomas   15   /Make it fast, breed fatal disease,/Degrade what they exalt. Power with the King
DEGRADED (1)
380 CP   Celia   5   suppose that most women/Would feel degraded to find that a man/With whom they
DEGREE (4)
184 FQ: DrySal   3   and intractable,/Patient to some degree, at first recognised as a frontier;/Useful,
228 Gus   15   /For he once was a Star of the highest degree —/He has acted with Irving, he's acted
256 MC Tempts   15   for the English Essay,/The scholar's degree, the statesman's decoration./All things
407 CP   Reilly   7   must occur together, and to a marked degree,/To qualify a patient for *my* sanatorium:
DEJECTION (1)
603 Spleen   9   tea!/Children and cats in the alley;/Dejection unable to rally/Against this dull
DEL (1)
189 FQ: DrySal   181   forth, and not returning:/Figlia del tuo figlio,/Queen of Heaven./Also pray for
DÉLABRÉ (1)
 51 Restaurant   1   mist./Dans le Restaurant/Le garçon délabré qui n'a rien à faire/Que de se gratter les
DELAY (10)
 39 Gerontion   67   Suspend its operations, will the weevil/Delay? De Bailhache, Fresca, Mrs. Cammel,
135 5FingerEx1   9   give ease?/Why will the summer day delay?/*When* will Time flow away?/*Lines to a*
139 Virginia   9   Purple trees,/White trees, wait, wait,/Delay, decay. Living, living,/Never moving.
150 Rock 1   119   *speech, food without taste./Without delay, without haste/We would build the*
153 Rock 2   53   much to restore;/Let the work not delay, time and the arm not waste;/Let the clay
595 Grad 14   1   /So we are done; we may no more delay;/Thus is the end of every tale: 'Farewell',/
603 Spleen   15   tie and suit/(Somewhat impatient of delay)/On the doorstep of the Absolute./Ode/
267 MC Knight2   19   /Shall we say it now?/{K2} Without delay,/Before the old fox is off and away./{T}
337 FR   Agatha   12   a clue, hidden in the obvious place./Delay, and it is lost. Love compels cruelty/To
400 CP   Reilly   8   appointment./{R} It was necessary to delay his appointment/To lower his resistance.
DELAYED (3)
347 FR   Ivy   19   to Amy or not. {}/[*Reads*]/{I} 'Regret delayed business in town many happy returns
349 FR   Agatha   16   It cannot be hurried/And it cannot be delayed/{M} It cannot be diverted/An attempt
386 CP   Celia   23   and to bring me with her./Julia was delayed, and sent me on ahead./{E} It seems
DELAYING (2)
161 Rock 7   25   /Often halting, loitering, straying, delaying, returning, yet following no other way./
324 FR Warburt   2   continue to treat you./You are only delaying me. I shall return at once./{A} Well, I
DELECTABLE (1)
142 Cape Ann   10   Greet/In silence the bullbat. All are delectable. Sweet sweet sweet/But resign this
DELEGATE (1)
250 MC Thomas   4   /Descend to desire a punier power?/Delegate to deal the doom of damnation,/To
DELIA (3)
354 CP   Julia   23   isn't my story./I heard it first from Delia Verinder/Who was there when it
354 CP   Julia   25   GUEST]/{J} Do *you* know Delia Verinder?/{UG} No, I don't know her./{J}
354 CP   Alex   29   careful/Before one tells a story./{A} Delia Verinder?/Was she the one who had three
DELIBERATE (2)
 84 Hollow Men   32   kingdom/Let me also wear/Such deliberate disguises/Rat's coat, crowskin,
179 FQ: ECoker   79   receipt for deceit?/The serenity only a deliberate hebetude,/The wisdom only the
DELIBERATELY (3)
279 MC Knight4   32   our questions. And when he had deliberately exasperated/us beyond human
462 CC   Claude   29   I'm coming back to it./You know I've deliberately left you alone,/And so far we've
475 CC Lucasta   5   very discouraging:/Are you doing it deliberately?/{C} That's not what I meant./I
DELIBERATIONS (1)
 38 Gerontion   61   contact?/These with a thousand small deliberations/Protract the profit of their chilled
DELICATE (4)
184 FQ: DrySal   21   it offers to our curiosity/The more delicate algae and the sea anemone./It tosses up
205 de la Mare   32   art practised with natural ease;/By the delicate, invisible web you wove —/The

445 CC Eggers 9 /{E} Impossible, Sir Claude!/A very delicate situation —/Her first meeting with Mr.
507 CC Eggers 4 or elsewhere?/Now I must ask a more delicate question:/Did you, at any time, take in
DELICATELY (1)
546 ES Piggott 37 fully qualified./Our system is very delicately balanced:/For me to be simply 'Mrs.
DELICIOUS (2)
355 CP Julia 27 /{J} Edward, give me another of those delicious olives./What's that? Potato crisps? No,
481 CC Lady E 29 at half past six./They have the most delicious salads!/And I told you, Mr. Kaghan,
DELIGHT (6)
111 Xmas Trees 14 Christmas Tree,/So that the surprises, delight in new possessions/(Each one with its
206 To my Wife 1 my Wife/To whom I owe the leaping delight/That quickens my senses in our
258 MC Thomas 11 to pleasure, advancement and praise./Delight in sense, in learning and in thought,/
417 CP Celia 11 of loving/In the spirit, a vibration of delight/Without desire, for desire is fulfilled/In
417 CP Celia 13 desire, for desire is fulfilled/In the delight of loving. A state one does not know/
522 ES dedic 1 MY WIFE/*To whom I owe the leaping delight/That quickens my senses in our*
DELIGHTED (4)
432 CP Edward 5 Henry Harcourt-Reilly —/{E} We're delighted to see him. But we *have* met before./
518 CC Eggers 14 I'm sorry .../{E} Don't be sorry: I'm delighted./And by the way, a practical point:/If
531 ES Ld Clav 26 the place we filled/Are inwardly delighted. They won't want my ghost/Walking
565 ES Michael 17 to walk a little way with you./{Mi} Delighted, I'm sure./{G} Taking a holiday?/
DELIGHTFUL (5)
136 5FingerEx4 1 *Lines to Ralph Hodgson Esqre.*/How delightful to meet Mr. Hodgson!/(Everyone
136 5FingerEx4 8 /And tear you limb from limb./How delightful to meet Mr. Hodgson!/Who is
136 5FingerEx4 13 The juice of the gooseberry tart./How delightful to meet Mr. Hodgson!/(Everyone
136 5FingerEx4 18 fairies/In jubilant rapture skim./How delightful to meet Mr. Hodgson!/(Everyone
358 CP Julia 18 at her wedding./Edward, it's been a delightful evening:/The potato crisps were really
DELIGHTFULLY (1)
390 CP Julia 27 in Dedham./{J} Well, it's all delightfully mysterious./{A} But what is the
DÉLIRE (1)
51 Restaurant 14 un instant de puissance et de délire.'/Mais alors, vieux lubrique, à cet âge .../
DELIRIOUS (1)
154 Rock 3 23 forgotten/To idleness, labour, and delirious stupor?/There shall be left the broken
DELIRIUM (2)
38 Gerontion 62 /Protract the profit of their chilled delirium,/Excite the membrane, when the sense
370 CP Peter 10 /I had only experienced excitement, delirium,/Desire for possession. It was not like
DELIVER (1)
158 Rock 5 1 and the trowel in the other./O Lord, deliver me from the man of excellent intention
DELIVERED (1)
470 CC Lucasta 2 you told me/The piano was only delivered this week/And you had it tuned
DELPHINIUMS (1)
313 FR Ivy 13 and I took several prizes/With my delphiniums. I was rather an authority./{G}
DELUGED (1)
546 ES Piggott 21 incurable./You know, we've been deluged with applications/From people who
DELUSION (8)
272 MC Chorus 29 longer turn the mind/To distraction, delusion, escape into dream, pretence,/Where
309 FR Mary 21 Wishwood is a cheat,/Your family a delusion — then it's *all* a delusion,/Everything
309 FR Mary 21 family a delusion — then it's *all* a delusion,/Everything you feel — I don't mean
413 CP Celia 19 that the world I live in seems all a delusion!/But oughtn't I first to tell you the
414 CP Celia 29 I'm sure that they don't. Is that a delusion?/{R} A delusion is something we must
414 CP Reilly 30 they don't. Is that a delusion?/{R} A delusion is something we must return from./
414 CP Reilly 31 states of mind, which we take to be delusion,/But which we have to accept and go
492 CC Lady E 5 believe that if I had known of your ... delusion/I would never have undeceived you./
DELUSIONS (3)
295 FR Harry 23 you must believe/That I suffer from delusions. It is not my conscience,/Not my
413 CP Celia 18 /I don't hear any voices, I have no delusions —/Except that the world I live in
462 CC Claude 19 the best one can do is to guide her delusions/In the right direction./{C} It doesn't
DEMAND (2)
129 Cor2 State 52 night./O mother/What shall I cry?/We demand a committee, a representative
204 de la Mare 11 the lamps are lit and curtains drawn/Demand some poetry, please. Whose shall it be,
DEMANDED (2)
268 MC Knight2 2 /Sent you back to your See as you demanded./{K3} And burying the memory of
339 FR Harry 20 it was what I always wanted. Strength demanded/That seems too much, is just strength
DEMETER (1)
209 NamingCats 11 /Such as Plato, Admetus, Electra, Demeter —/But all of them sensible everyday
DEMOBBED (1)
65 WL: Chess 139 the door./When Lil's husband got demobbed, I said —/I didn't mince my words, I

DEMOLISHED (1)
328 FR   Charles 13   Lord/Monchensey, who ran into and demolished a roundsman's/cart in Ebury Street
DEMOTIC (1)
 68 WL: Fire S   212   documents at sight,/Asked me in demotic French/To luncheon at the Cannon
DEN (4)
233 Skimble   33   when you have found your little den/With your name written up on the door./
274 MC Knights   18   /Come down Daniel to the lions' den,/Come down Daniel for the mark of the
274 MC Knights   22   /Come down Daniel to the lions' den,/Come down Daniel and join in the feast./
274 MC Knights   26   /Come down Daniel to the lions' den,/Come down Daniel and join in the feast./
DENIAL (2)
160 Rock 7   15   /Prayer wheels, worship of the dead, denial of this world, affirmation of rites with
281 MC Chorus   11   if Thou didst not exist; and their denial is never complete, for if it were so, they
DENIED (3)
193 FQ: Little   75   and fire deride/The sacrifice that we denied./Water and fire shall rot/The marred
272 MC Thomas   6   a whisper,/And I would no longer be denied; all things/Proceed to a joyful
282 MC Chorus   4   renews the earth/Though it is forever denied. Therefore, O God, we thank Thee/Who
DENIES (2)
278 MC Knight2   13   /able administrator — no one denies that — should unite/the offices of
281 MC Chorus   10   glory is declared even in that which denies Thee; the darkness declares the glory of
DENMAN (16)
284 FR   m   5   *deceased cousin of Lady Monchensey*/DENMAN, *a parlourmaid*/HARRY, LORD
285 FR   5m   1   GERALD, CHARLES, MARY/[DENMAN *enters to draw the curtains*]/{A} Not
286 FR   m   29   cocktails and cigarettes. {}/[*Enter* DENMAN *with sherry and whisky.* CHARLES
291 FR   Amy   18   drawn you should let me ring for Denman./{H} How can you sit in this blaze of
297 FR   m   27   shan't know why I'm asking. {}/[*Enter* DENMAN]/{C} Denman, where is Downing? Is
297 FR   Charles 27   I'm asking. {}/[*Enter* DENMAN]/{C} Denman, where is Downing? Is he up with his
297 FR   m   30   have a word with him, please. {}/[*Exit* DENMAN]/{V} Charles, if you are determined
321 FR   m   9   you've been sleeping ... {}/[*Enter* DENMAN]/{D} It's Sergeant Winchell is here,
321 FR   m   13   troubled you./{H} I'll see him. {}/[*Exit* DENMAN]/{W} I wonder what he wants. I
321 FR   Harry 18   —/If Sergeant Winchell is real. But Denman saw him./But what if Denman saw
321 FR   Harry 19   But Denman saw him./But what if Denman saw him, and yet he was not real?/That
326 FR   m   33   welcome in this family. {}/[*Enter* DENMAN]/{D} Excuse me, Miss Ivy. There's a
326 FR   m   36   had an accident. {}/[*Exeunt* IVY *and* DENMAN]/{V} When it's Ivy that he's asking
342 FR   Mary   1   me, Cousin Amy. I have just seen Denman./She came to tell me that Harry is
349 FR   2m   13   *table./From another door, enter* DENMAN *carrying a birthday cake with*/
349 FR   3m   13   *which she sets on the table. Exit* DENMAN. AGATHA/*and* MARY *walk*
DENMARK (1)
354 CP   Alex   13   /With a branch in Sweden and one in Denmark./There were several very lovely
DENY (10)
 96 Ash-Wed 5   19   for those who walk among noise and deny the voice/Will the veiled sister pray for/
 97 Ash-Wed 5   32   /And affirm before the world and deny between the rocks/In the last desert
156 Rock 3   75   Death you shall not./You shall not deny the Stranger./There are those who would
161 Rock 7   28   happened before/That men both deny gods and worship gods, professing first
165 Rock 9   36   meet in His Temple;/You must not deny the body./Now you shall see the Temple
239 MC Chorus   16   /Stretch out his hand to the fire, and deny his master? who shall be warm/By the fire,
239 MC Chorus   17   who shall be warm/By the fire, and deny his master?/Seven years and the summer is
268 MC Thomas   29   /{K1} Absolve them./{T} I do not deny/That this was done through me. But it is
281 MC Chorus   11   declares the glory of light./Those who deny Thee could not deny, if Thou didst not
281 MC Chorus   11   light./Those who deny Thee could not deny, if Thou didst not exist; and their denial is
DENYING (3)
107 Animula   28   the warm reality, the offered good,/Denying the importunity of the blood,/Shadow
268 MC Knight1   8   who had crowned the young prince,/Denying the legality of his coronation./{K2}
562 ES Carghil   36   of your charm, Richard./There's no denying it. But who's this coming?/It's another
DENYS (1)
275 MC Thomas   20   Peter and Paul, to the blessed martyr Denys, and to all the Saints, I commend my
DEPART (8)
106 Song Sime   36   of those after me./Let thy servant depart,/Having seen thy salvation./Animula/
155 Rock 3   56   a community"?/And the Stranger will depart and return to the desert./O my soul, be
157 Rock 4   8   /And the King gave him leave to depart/That he might rebuild the city./So he
197 FQ: Little   231 start./We die with the dying:/See, they depart, and we go with them./We are born with
232 Skimble   2   11.39/When the Night Mail's ready to depart,/Saying 'Skimble where is Skimble has he
268 MC Knight1   35   /That you and your servants depart from this land./{T} If that *is* the King's
281 MC Chorus   20   ground, and the sanctity shall not depart from it/Though armies trample over it,
350 FR Agatha   23   /By pilgrimage/By those who depart/In several directions/For their own

DEPARTED (5)
67 WL: Fire S   175   land, unheard. The nymphs are departed./Sweet Thames, run softly, till I end
67 WL: Fire S   179   of summer nights. The nymphs are departed./And their friends, the loitering heirs
67 WL: Fire S   181   the loitering heirs of City directors;/Departed, have left no addresses./By the waters
69 WL: Fire S   250   in the glass,/Hardly aware of her departed lover;/Her brain allows one
350 FR   Agatha   26 their own redemption/And that of the departed —/May they rest in peace. {}/THE
DEPARTING (1)
594 Grad 13   1 distant lands and seas!/As thou to thy departing sons hast been/To those that follow
DEPARTURE (2)
308 FR   Harry   20 /The instinct to return to the point of departure/And start again as if nothing had
343 FR   m 31   HARRY *has entered, dressed for departure.*]/{H} But, mother, you will always
DEPEND (5)
211 Old Gumbie   38 —/On whom well-ordered households depend, it appears./Growltiger's Last Stand/
250 MC Tempt3   39   /Endurance of friendship does not depend/Upon ourselves, but upon circumstance.
311 FR   Mary   23 stay there./{M} Look at me. You can depend on me./Harry! Harry! It's all *right*, I tell
311 FR   Mary   25   It's all *right*, I tell you./If you will depend on me, it will be all right./{H} Come out!
500 CC Lucasta   32 you needed him most!/And he doesn't depend upon other people, either./B. needs me.
DEPENDED (1)
388 CP   Celia   10 ... I shall miss you;/You know how I depended on you for concerts,/And picture
DEPENDS (7)
117 SP   Doris   18 all hearts. You can't be sure./It just depends on what comes next./You've got to
320 FR Warburt   30 is yourself: the future of Wishwood/Depends on you. I don't like to say this;/But
344 FR   Gerald   29   need various inoculations —/That depends on where you're going./{C} Such a
448 CC   Claude   21 indeed whether — I reveal his identity/Depends on how she takes to him. This
468 CC   Claude   2 you. I've got them here./{SC} Much depends on my wife. Be patient with her, Colby.
479 CC   Kaghan   23   and a happy bachelor life!/Which depends, of course, on preventing Lizzie/From
579 ES Michael   18 then, Michael?/{Mi} Well, that just depends./I could look in again. If there's any
DEPLOYED (1)
178 FQ: ECoker   61 rolling stars/Simulates triumphal cars/Deployed in constellated wars/Scorpion fights
DEPOSITS (1)
535 ES   m 19   *this* LAMBERT *enters silently, deposits tray and exit*]/{LC} Won't you help
DEPRAVED (1)
37 Gerontion   21 of the year/Came Christ the tiger/In depraved May, dogwood and chestnut,
DEPRAVITY (1)
226 Macavity   18 a fiend in feline shape, a monster of depravity./You may meet him in a by-street,
DEPRECATE (1)
43 Swee Erect   36 `/Call witness to their principles/And deprecate the lack of taste/Observing that
DEPRESSED (1)
299 FRDowning   33 the voyage?/{Do} Well, you might say depressed, Sir./But you know his Lordship was
DEPRESSING (1)
528 ES   Charles   33 This is your best reason, and the most depressing;/For this situation may persist for a
DEPRIVATION (4)
174 FQ: BurntN 100   the soul/Emptying the sensual with deprivation/Cleansing affection from the
174 FQ: BurntN 120 which is not world,/Internal darkness, deprivation/And destitution of all property,/
282 MC Chorus   8 of God, the surrender required, the deprivation inflicted;/Who fear the injustice of
339 FR   Harry   8 worship in the desert, the thirst and deprivation,/A stony sanctuary and a primitive
DEPRIVE (1)
268 MC Thomas   19 and power. Why should he wish/To deprive my people of me and keep me from my
DEPRIVED (1)
241 MC   Mess   36 /And I think that his horse will be deprived of its tail,/A single hair of which
DEPTHS (1)
357 CP   Edward   33 Lavinia loves oysters./{E} No. In the *depths* of Essex./{J} Well, we won't probe into it./
DER (2)
61 WL: Burial   31 fear in a handful of dust./*Frisch weht der Wind/Der Heimat zu/Mein Irisch Kind/Wo*
61 WL: Burial   32 handful of dust./*Frisch weht der Wind/Der Heimat zu/Mein Irisch Kind/Wo weilest du?*/
DERIDE (2)
148 Rock 1   66   /The men you are in these times deride/What has been done of good, you find
193 FQ: Little   74 pasture and the weed./Water and fire deride/The sacrifice that we denied./Water and
DERISION (3)
105 Song Sime   27 in every generation/With glory and derision,/Light upon light, mounting the saints'
133 Eyes   15 while outlast the tears/And hold us in derision./The wind sprang up at four o'clock/
421 CP   Julia   27 scolding hills,/Through the valley of derision, like a child sent on an errand/In
DERIVED (1)
179 FQ: ECoker   84 only a limited value/In the knowledge derived from experience./The knowledge

DERVISH (3)

496 CC	Claude	5	— so long as it was modern —/And dervish dancing./{LE} Dervish dancing!/Really,
496 CC	Lady E	6	—/And dervish dancing./{LE} Dervish dancing!/Really, Claude, how absurd
496 CC	Lady E	9	to be learnt,/I don't doubt, from the dervish rituals./But it doesn't matter what Mrs.

DES (7)

46 Directeur	12	/Bras dessus bras dessous/Font des tours/A pas de loup./Dans un égout/Une
48 Lune Miel	9	/En Classe, basilique connue des amateurs/De chapitaux d'acanthe que
51 Restaurant	5	ce qu'on appelle le jour de lessive des gueux.'/(Bavard, baveux, à la croupe
51 Restaurant	8	dans la soupe)./'Les saules trempés, et des bourgeons sur les ronces —/C'est là, dans
51 Restaurant	11	était toute mouillée, je lui ai donné des primevères.'/Les taches de son gilet montent
51 Restaurant	23	le crâne./De quel droit payes-tu des expériences comme moi?/Tiens, voilà dix
51 Restaurant	26	quinze jours noyé,/Oubliait les cris des mouettes et la houle de Cornouaille,/Et les

DÉSAFFECTÉE (1)

| 48 Lune Miel | 17 | raide et ascétique,/Vieille usine désaffectée de Dieu, tient encore/Dans ses |

DESCANTING (1)

| 188 FQ: DrySal | 149 | the rigging and the aerial,/Is a voice descanting (though not to the ear,/The |

DESCEND (4)

14 Prufrock	39	'Do I dare?'/Time to turn back and descend the stair,/With a bald spot in the
174 FQ: BurntN	117	the darkness, in this twittering world./Descend lower, descend only/Into the world of
174 FQ: BurntN	117	this twittering world./Descend lower, descend only/Into the world of perpetual
250 MC Thomas	3	and loose, with power from the Pope,/Descend to desire a punier power?/Delegate to

DESCENDING (3)

40 Burb Blei	2	Cigar/Burbank crossed a little bridge/Descending at a small hotel;/Princess Volupine
196 FQ: Little	202	ground of our beseeching./The dove descending breaks the air/With flame of
270 MC Chorus	10	/Rings of light coiling downwards, descending/To the horror of the ape. Have I not

DESCENT (2)

| 85 Hollow Men | 89 | /Between the essence/And the descent/Falls the Shadow/*For Thine is the* |
| 250 MC Thomas | 18 | exaltation/Would now be only mean descent. {}/[*Enter* THIRD TEMPTER]/{T3} I |

DESCRIBE (4)

189 FQ: DrySal	190	the behaviour of the sea monster,/Describe the horoscope, haruspicate or scry,/
364 CP	Edward	2	like./I am not quite sure that I could describe her/If I had to ask the police to search
413 CP	Reilly	25	you for the moment:/Try first to describe your present state of mind./{C} Well,
418 CP	Reilly	21	have the courage./The first I could describe in familiar terms/Because you have

DESCRIBED (5)

234 Ad-dress	12	some are worse —/But all may be described in verse./You've seen them both at
407 CP	Reilly	29	/Both of you — was true enough: you described your feelings —/Or some of them —
418 CP	Reilly	26	despair./The destination cannot be described;/You will know very little until you
516 CC	Claude	19	shared our disappointment. And you described your feelings/On beginning to learn
516 CC	Claude	26	that you were my son,/Because you described my own experience, exactly./Does

DESCRIPTION (1)

| 537 ES | Ld Clav | 3 | me reality!/{LC} But according to the description you have given/Of trusting people, |

DESECRATED (2)

| 280 MC Priest1 | 12 | The Church lies bereft,/Alone, desecrated, desolated, and the heathen shall |
| 315 FR Chorus | 33 | the past, the beak and claws have desecrated/History. Shamed/The first cry in the |

DESECRATING (1)

| 275 MC Thomas | 17 | your spiritual lord,/Traitor to God in desecrating His Church./{K1} No faith do I owe |

DESERT (28)

64 WL: Chess	101	yet there the nightingale/Filled all the desert with inviolable voice/And still she cried,
91 Ash-Wed 2	13	and my love/To the posterity of the desert and the fruit of the gourd./It is this which
92 Ash-Wed 2	52	each other, united/In the quiet of the desert. This is the land which ye/Shall divide by
96 Ash-Wed 5	14	islands, not/On the mainland, in the desert or the rain land,/For those who walk in
97 Ash-Wed 5	33	deny between the rocks/In the last desert between the last blue rocks/The desert in
97 Ash-Wed 5	34	desert between the last blue rocks/The desert in the garden the garden in the desert/Of
97 Ash-Wed 5	34	desert in the garden the garden in the desert/Of drouth, spitting from the mouth the
149 Rock 1	69	/Second, you neglect and belittle the desert./The desert is not remote in southern
149 Rock 1	70	neglect and belittle the desert./The desert is not remote in southern tropics,/The
149 Rock 1	71	is not remote in southern tropics,/The desert is not only around the corner,/The desert
149 Rock 1	72	is not only around the corner,/The desert is squeezed in the tube-train next to you,/
149 Rock 1	73	in the tube-train next to you,/The desert is in the heart of your brother./The good
155 Rock 3	56	Stranger will depart and return to the desert./O my soul, be prepared for the coming
175 FQ: BurntN	158	/Always assail them. The Word in the desert/Is most attacked by voices of temptation,
192 FQ: Little	38	the sea jaws,/Or over a dark lake, in a desert or a city —/But this is the nearest, in
204 de la Mare	2	who explored the brook and found/A desert island with a sandy cove/(A hiding place,
254 MC Tempt4	36	/When miracles cease, and the faithful desert you./And men shall only do their best to
280 MC Priest3	24	dull the brain;/Find an oasis in the desert sun,/Go seek alliance with the heathen

282 MC	Chorus	2	the coast of Iona,/To the death in the desert, the prayer in forgotten places by the
294 FR	Harry	15	{H} The sudden solitude in a crowded desert/In a thick smoke, many creatures moving
294 FR	Harry	29	one is still alone/In an over-crowded desert, jostled by ghosts./It was only reversing
335 FR	Harry	13	drift/Of shrieking forms in a circular desert/Weaving with contagion of putrescent
335 FR	Harry	17	left/Under the single eye above the desert./{Ag} Up and down, through the stone
335 FR	Harry	30	and the noise of machinery,/And the desert is cleared, under the judicial sun/Of the
339 FR	Harry	8	side of despair./To the worship in the desert, the thirst and deprivation,/A stony
422 CP	Alex	21	the road./{A} Watch over her in the desert./Watch over her in the mountain./Watch
438 CP	Reilly	10	/Do you imagine that the Saint in the desert/With spiritual evil always at his shoulder/
480 CC	Kaghan	40	might chuck it all/And go to live on a desert island./But I hope you won't do that. We

DESERTS (1)

| 34 Figlia | | 12 | body torn and bruised,/As the mind deserts the body it has used./I should find/Some |

DESERVE (4)

287 FR	Mary	9	someone else./I'm afraid that I don't deserve the compliment:/I don't belong to any
425 CP	Edward	5	when one needs them./{E} Well, you deserve it. — We asked too many people./{L}
535 ES	Gomez	5	/{G} Which you're sure you deserve. But when I say 'trust' ... {}/[*Knock.*
579 ES	Gomez	35	can see more clearly./{G} Not that I deserve any credit for it./We can only regard it

DESERVED (1)

| 447 CC | Claude | 13 | a great compliment./{SC} And well deserved; but rather inconvenient/When it |

DESERVES (1)

| 412 CP | Julia | 16 | is not uncommon./{J} Or that she deserves to be taken seriously./{R} That is most |

DESICCATION (1)

| 174 FQ: BurntN | | 122 | /And destitution of all property,/Desiccation of the world of sense,/Evacuation |

DESIGN (8)

261 MC	Thomas	27	/of men. A martyrdom is always the design of God, for His love of men,/to warn
261 MC	Thomas	29	them back to His ways. It is/never the design of man; for the true martyr is he who has
265 MC	Priest3	8	now, in sordid particulars/The eternal design may appear. {}/[*Enter the* FOUR
306 FR	Harry	38	didn't seem like that. I was part of the design/As well as you. But what was the design?
306 FR	Harry	39	/As well as you. But what was the design?/It never came off. But do you remember
337 FR	Agatha	1	/To grow to maturity:/Accident is design/And design is accident/In a cloud of
337 FR	Agatha	2	to maturity:/Accident is design/And design is accident/In a cloud of unknowing./O
438 CP	Reilly	2	price/In suffering. That is part of the design./{L} Perhaps she had been through

DESIGNED (6)

54 Mr E Sun		10	/A painter of the Umbrian school/Designed upon a gesso ground/The nimbus of
205 de la Mare		26	whom, and by what means, was this designed?/The whispered incantation which
299 FRDowning		30	/She wasn't one of those that are *designed* for drinking:/It's natural for some and
306 FR	Mary	37	enjoyments./But perhaps it was all designed for you, not for us./{H} No, it didn't
481 CC	Lady E	22	in/By the person for whom it was designed./So I have to see you in it. Did you say
483 CC	Lady E	21	on reports and typewriters/When I designed this room./{C} It's the sort of room I

DESIGNING (2)

| 154 Rock 3 | | 2 | unto me, saying:/O miserable cities of designing men,/O wretched generation of |
| 341 FR | Amy | 32 | good? is it you or I?/Thirty-five years designing his life,/Eight years watching, without |

DESIRABLE (4)

175 FQ: BurntN		165	Desire itself is movement/Not in itself desirable;/Love is itself unmoving,/Only the
258 MC	Thomas	16	instrument,/Were all things equally desirable./Ambition comes when early force is
301 FR	Charles	15	that an unconscious accomplice is desirable./{Ch} Why should we stand here like
381 CP	Edward	13	lost/The desire for all that was most desirable,/Before you are contented with what

DESIRE (25)

61 WL: Burial		3	of the dead land, mixing/Memory and desire, stirring/Dull roots with spring rain./
85 Hollow Men		84	Shadow/*Life is very long*/Between the desire/And the spasm/Between the potency/And
107 Animula		20	'is and seems'/And may and may not, desire and control./The pain of living and the
151 Rock 2		8	For love must be made real in act, as desire unites with desired; we have only our
154 Rock 3		14	books and printing them,/Many desire to see their names in print,/Many read
173 FQ: BurntN		72	/The inner freedom from the practical desire,/The release from action and suffering,
175 FQ: BurntN		164	/As in the figure of the ten stairs./Desire itself is movement/Not in itself desirable;
195 FQ: Little		160	of love but expanding/Of love beyond desire, and so liberation/From the future as well
593 Grad 8		3	old, whatever be our lot,/We shall desire to see again the spot/Which, whatsoever
250 MC	Thomas	3	power from the Pope,/Descend to desire a punier power?/Delegate to deal the
255 MC	Tempt4	22	do you ask?/{T4} I offer what you desire. I ask/What you have to give. Is it too
370 CP	Peter	11	experienced excitement, delirium,/Desire for possession. It was not like that at all./
381 CP	Edward	13	when you feel that you have lost/The desire for all that was most desirable,/Before
381 CP	Edward	14	you are contented with what you can desire;/Before you know what is left to be
381 CP	Edward	16	you go on wishing that you could desire/What desire has left behind. But you
381 CP	Edward	17	wishing that you could desire/What desire has left behind. But you cannot
417 CP	Celia	12	spirit, a vibration of delight/Without desire, for desire is fulfilled/In the delight of

417 CP	Celia	12	of delight/Without desire, for	desire is fulfilled/In the delight of loving. A state
517 CC	Eggers	22	it true, Mr. Simpkins, that what you	desire/Is to become the organist of some parish
530 ES	Ld Clav	18	But waiting, simply waiting,/With no	desire to act, yet a loathing of inaction./A fear
530 ES	Ld Clav	19	/A fear of the vacuum, and no	desire to fill it./It's just like sitting in an empty
535 ES	Gomez	2	already!/To see you, Dick. A natural	desire!/For you're the only old friend I can
541 ES	Gomez	4	at it./Besides, you can't think I've any	desire/To appear in public as Frederick
545 ES	Ld Clav	18	talk like that/It indicates a latent	desire to interfere/With the privacy of others,
560 ES	Ld Clav	34	no positive ambition/But only the	desire to escape./{Mi} I'm not a fugitive./{LC}

DESIRED (3)

20 Portrait		82	things that other people have	desired./Are these ideas right or wrong?/The
151 Rock 2		8	made real in act, as desire unites with	desired; we have only our labour to give and
381 CP	Edward	15	/Before you know what is left to be	desired;/And you go on wishing that you could

DESIRES (6)

135 5FingerEx1		4	no ease/For the dull brain, the sharp	desires/And the quick eyes of Woolly Bear./
255 MC	Thomas	18	/Who are you, tempting with my own	desires?/Others have come, temporal tempters,/
261 MC	Thomas	31	in the will of God, and who no/longer	desires anything for himself, not even the glory
410 CP	Reilly	25	you brought with you:/The shadow of	desires of desires. A prey/To the devils who
410 CP	Reilly	25	with you:/The shadow of desires of	desires. A prey/To the devils who arrive at their
419 CP	Reilly	5	imagination, shuffling memories and	desires./{C} That is the hell I have been in./{R}

DESIRING (1)

89 Ash-Wed 1		4	hope/Because I do not hope to turn/Desiring	this man's gift and that man's scope/I

DESK (12)

68 WL: Fire S		216	eyes and back/Turn upward from the	desk, when the human engine waits/Like a taxi
399 CP		3m	1	*weeks later. SIR HENRY alone at his desk. He presses an/electric button. The*
405 CP		m	7	as your own. {}/[*Presses the bell on his desk three times*]/{R} You must accept a rather
445 CC		3m	1	*afternoon. SIR CLAUDE writing at desk. Enter/EGGERSON./{SC} Ah, there you*
458 CC	Claude	3	coming up./{SC} Colby, sit at the desk, and pick up some papers./We must look
483 CC	Colby	12	come from?/{C} It's an office desk. Sir Claude got it for me./I said I needed a
483 CC	Colby	13	Claude got it for me./I said I needed a	desk in my room:/You see, I shall do a good
493 CC	Claude	6	together./Will you sit there, beside the desk?/{LE} On the other side, with the light
493 CC	Lady E	8	me:/But won't you be sitting at the desk yourself?/{SC} No, that would look too
493 CC	Claude	10	/To put Eggerson there, behind the desk./You see, I want him to be a sort of
499 CC	Claude	1	the proceedings./Will you sit at the desk?/{E} If you wish, Sir Claude./I do feel more
499 CC	Eggers	3	feel more at ease when I'm behind a desk:/It's second nature./{SC} And put the case

DESKS (1)

566 ES	Ld Clav	1	/We'll sit side by side, at little desks/And suffer the same humiliations/At the

DESOLATED (1)

280 MC	Priest1	12	Church lies bereft,/Alone, desecrated, desolated, and the heathen shall build on the

DESOLATION (4)

105 Song Sime		19	the stations of the mountain of	desolation,/Before the certain hour of maternal
183 FQ: ECoker		209	Through the dark cold and the empty	desolation,/The wave cry, the wind cry, the vast
419 CP	Reilly	3	/Both ways avoid the final	desolation/Of solitude in the phantasmal world/
474 CC	Colby	22	that one would mind/But the sense of	desolation afterwards./{L} I know what you

DESPAIR (8)

92 Ash-Wed 3		6	/The deceitful face of hope and of	despair./At the second turning of the second
92 Ash-Wed 3		20	fading; strength beyond hope and	despair/Climbing the third stair./Lord, I am not
192 FQ: Little		62	the mouse./The death of hope and	despair,/This is the death of air./There are flood
196 FQ: Little		206	sin and error./The only hope, or else	despair/Lies in the choice of pyre or pyre —/To
226 Macavity		3	of Scotland Yard, the Flying Squad's	despair:/For when they reach the scene of crime
257 MC	Chorus	27	the dark air/Falls the stifling scent of	despair;/The forms take shape in the dark air:/
339 FR	Harry	7	/Somewhere on the other side of	despair./To the worship in the desert, the thirst
418 CP	Reilly	25	—/The kind of faith that issues from	despair./The destination cannot be described;/

DESPATCH-CASE (2)

562 ES		m	12	... {}/[*Enter MRS. CARGHILL with despatch-case*]/{MC} Richard! I didn't think
564 ES		m	35	Dick when you knew him. {}/[*pats her despatch-case*]./{MC} Secret for secret, Señor

DESPERATE (2)

252 MC	Thomas	27	this thought has come before,/The	desperate exercise of failing power./Samson in
273 MC	Thomas	31	My Lord!/{T} You think me reckless,	desperate and mad./You argue by results, as

DESPERATELY (2)

158 Rock 5		1	heart is deceitful above all things, and	desperately wicked./Sanballat the Horonite and
382 CP	Celia	31	I aspired to —/Something that I	desperately wanted to exist./It must happen

DESPERATION (2)

393 CP	Lavinia	22	first?/And I remember that finally in	desperation/I said: 'I suppose you'd as soon go
413 CP	Celia	1	see you. Well, I can't./I just came in	desperation. And I shan't be offended/If you

DESPISE (8)
246 MC Tempt1   29 good time past./Your Lordship won't despise an old friend out of favour?/Old Tom,
258 MC Thomas   23   at their own game. I/Could then despise the men who thought me most
480 CC Kaghan   34   I like about Lucasta:/She doesn't despise me./{L} Nobody could despise you./And
480 CC Lucasta 35 doesn't despise me./{L} Nobody could despise you./And what's more important, you
480 CC Lucasta 36   what's more important, you don't despise *me*./{K} Nobody could despise *you*,
480 CC Kaghan   37   don't despise *me*./{K} Nobody could despise *you*, Lucasta;/And we want the same
495 CC Claude   7   of importance. I thought you would despise me/If you knew what I'd really wanted
502 CC Lucasta 17 couldn't believe it!/It isn't like you, to despise people:/You don't care enough./{C} I
DESPISED (2)
242 MC Priest1 22   in their overbearing fashion,/Despised and despising, always isolated,/Never
464 CC Claude   31 I hoped I could do with it. I thought I despised him/When I was young. And yet I was
DESPISING (1)
242 MC Priest1 22   overbearing fashion,/Despised and despising, always isolated,/Never one among
DESPITE (1)
582 ES Charles 36   fashion,/Even with Michael, and despite those people,/Because somehow we'd
DESPONDENTLY (1)
 27 Morning   4 damp souls of housemaids/Sprouting despondently at area gates./The brown waves of
DESSOUS (1)
 46 Directeur   11   /Conservateur/Bras dessus bras dessous/Font des tours/A pas de loup./Dans un
DESSUS (1)
 46 Directeur   11   /Du Spectateur/Conservateur/Bras dessus bras dessous/Font des tours/A pas de
DESTINATION (6)
186 FQ: DrySal   74 is not liable/Like the past, to have no destination./We have to think of them as
188 FQ: DrySal 168 /Or whatever event, this is your real destination.'/So Krishna, as when he
203 Indians   1 Indians who Died in Africa/A man's destination is his own village,/His own fire, and
203 Indians   11   /Foreign to each other./A man's destination is not his destiny/Every country is
336 FR Harry   22 can be only one itinerary/And one destination. Let us lose no time. I will follow. {}/
418 CP Reilly   26 of faith that issues from despair./The destination cannot be described;/You will know
DESTINED (1)
343 FR Harry   33   not that John is any worry —/The destined and the perfect master of Wishwood,/
DESTINY (8)
203 Indians   11 other./A man's destination is not his destiny/Every country is home to one man/And
203 Indians   14 a man dies bravely/At one with his destiny, that soil is his./Let his village
239 MC Chorus   13 hand to the fire,/The New Year waits, destiny waits for the coming./Who has stretched
240 MC Chorus   17   who shall be martyrs and saints./Destiny waits in the hand of God, shaping the
240 MC Chorus   19 these things in a shaft of sunlight./Destiny waits in the hand of God, not in the
420 CP Julia   35 must always take risks./That is our destiny. Since you question the decision/What
422 CP Reilly   8 have chosen?/{R} They accept their destiny./{A} And *she* has made the choice?/{R}
437 CP Reilly   23   sentence of death./That was her destiny. The only question/Then was, what sort
DESTITUTION (2)
174 FQ: BurntN 121 /Internal darkness, deprivation/And destitution of all property,/Desiccation of the
257 MC Chorus   10 /We know of extortion and violence,/Destitution, disease,/The old without fire in
DESTROY (7)
157 Rock 4   15 pass./There were enemies without to destroy him,/And spies and self-seekers within,/
158 Rock 5   6 'This house is a nest of serpents, let us destroy it,/And have done with these
604 Ode   13 /And only the years that efface and destroy/Give us also the vision to see/What we
251 MC Tempt3   26 /Sovereignty. Let the Angevin/Destroy himself, fighting in Anjou./He does not
253 MC Tempt4   19 other;/Greater enemies must kings destroy./{T} What is your counsel?/{T4} Fare
258 MC Chorus   2 save yourself that we may be saved;/Destroy yourself and we are destroyed./{T}
339 FR Harry   17 harm can come to him./What would destroy me will be life for John,/I am
DESTROYED (4)
177 FQ: ECoker   3 crumble, are extended,/Are removed, destroyed, restored, or in their place/Is an open
258 MC Chorus   2 be saved;/Destroy yourself and we are destroyed./{T} Now is my way clear, now is the
288 FR Amy   31 mongrel setter/Which I had to have destroyed./Nothing has been changed. I have
428 CP Julia   7 I told her the creature ought to be destroyed./{L} But can't they exterminate these
DESTROYER (2)
184 FQ: DrySal   8 /Keeping his seasons and rages, destroyer, reminder/Of what men choose to
187 FQ: DrySal 117 smile: but the agony abides./Time the destroyer is time the preserver,/Like the river
DESTROYMENT (1)
211 Old Gumbie   32 prevent them from idle and wanton destroyment./So she's formed, from that lot of
DESTRUCTION (1)
398 CP Edward   8   you came back, you/The angel of destruction — just as I felt sure./In a moment,

DESTRUCTIVE (3)
179 FQ: ECoker   67   that shall bring/The world to that destructive fire/Which burns before the ice-cap
428 CP   Alex   1   To begin with, the monkeys are very destructive .../{J} You don't need to tell me that
428 CP   Julia   2   need to tell me that monkeys are destructive./I shall never forget Mary
DETACH (1)
438 CP   Reilly   20   one impediment:/You must try to detach yourself from what you still feel/As your
DETACHED (1)
502 CC Lucasta   13   I thought it was./You're much too ... detached, ever to be shocked/In the way I
DETACHMENT (1)
195 FQ: Little   154   to self and to things and to persons, detachment/From self and from things and
DETAIL (2)
175 FQ: BurntN 162   of the disconsolate chimera./The detail of the pattern is movement,/As in the
290 FR Agatha   24   /Thus with precise attention/To detail, interfering preparation/Of that which is
DETAILED (1)
539 ES   Gomez   30   /{G} I don't propose to give you a detailed account/Of my own career. I've been
DETAILS (1)
576 ES   Michael   19   you know?/{Mi} We didn't go into details. There's time for that later./{G} Much
DETAIN (2)
241 MC   Mess   39   /Who indeed would have liked to detain him in his kingdom:/But as for our King,
269 MC Knight4   22   Priest! monk! and servant! take, hold, detain,/Restrain this man, in the King's name./
DETECTION (1)
333 FR Agatha   25   we have written is not a story of detection,/Of crime and punishment, but of sin
DETERIORATING (1)
182 FQ: ECoker 182   /With shabby equipment always deteriorating/In the general mess of imprecision
DETERMINATION (1)
320 FR Warburt   18   would not have lived until now./Her determination has kept her going:/She has only
DETERMINED (10)
147 Rock 1   4   stars,/O perpetual recurrence of determined seasons,/O world of spring and
279 MC Knight4   30   be no inference/except that he had determined upon a death by martyrdom. Even/
297 FR   Violet   30   DENMAN]/{V} Charles, if you are determined upon this investigation,/Which I am
336 FR Agatha   34   tree/According to the phase/Of the determined moon./A curse is like a child,
345 FR Gerald   5   we meet again./{G} Well, if you are determined, Harry, we must accept it;/But it's a
381 CP Edward   29   of ecstasy./I see that my life was determined long ago/And that the struggle to
433 CP   Julia   10   cheaper./Oh, dear, I can see you're determined not to have me:/So good-bye to my
499 CC Lucasta   30   you wanted me to marry B./Made me determined that I wouldn't. Just to spite you,/I
560 ES Michael   19   of the business./{Mi} Anyway, I'm determined to get out of England./{LC}
573 ES Ld Clav   18   and time of liberation/Are, I think, determined. Let us say no more about it./
DETERS (1)
269 MC Knight1   7   /Insolent madman, whom nothing deters/From attainting his servants and
DEUM (1)
281 MC   m 7   Saint in Canterbury. {}/[*while a* Te Deum *is sung in Latin by a choir in the*
DEUTERONOMY (7)
220 Old Deut   t   at all to be done about that!/Old Deuteronomy/Old Deuteronomy's lived a long
220 Old Deut   16   but I confess/I *believe* it is Old Deuteronomy!'/Old Deuteronomy sits in the
220 Old Deut   17   /I *believe* it is Old Deuteronomy!'/Old Deuteronomy sits in the street,/He sits in the
220 Old Deut   31   /That the cause of the trouble is Old Deuteronomy!'/Old Deuteronomy lies on the
221 Old Deut   32   the trouble is Old Deuteronomy!'/Old Deuteronomy lies on the floor/Of the Fox and
221 Old Deut   37   you go, by the back door,/For Old Deuteronomy mustn't be woken —/I'll have the
221 Old Deut   47   I must go slow/And be careful of Old Deuteronomy!'/Of the Awefull Battle of the
DEUTERONOMY'S (3)
220 Old Deut   1   about that!/Old Deuteronomy/Old Deuteronomy's lived a long time;/He's a Cat
220 Old Deut   5   Queen Victoria's accession./Old Deuteronomy's buried nine wives/And more —
220 Old Deut   24   untoward may chance to disturb/Deuteronomy's rest when he feels so disposed/
DEUTSCH (1)
61 WL: Burial   12   Russin, stamm' aus Litauen, echt deutsch./And when we were children, staying at
DEUX (3)
48 Lune Miel   3   les voici à Ravenne,/A l'aise entre deux draps, chez deux centaines de punaises;/La
48 Lune Miel   3   /A l'aise entre deux draps, chez deux centaines de punaises;/La sueur aestivale,
182 FQ: ECoker 175   largely wasted, the years of *l'entre deux guerres* —/Trying to learn to use words, and
DEVASTATED (1)
474 CC Lucasta   25   /And you would find yourself in a devastated area —/A bomb-site ... willow-herb
DEVELOP (4)
216 Jellicles   13   the Jellicle Moon to rise./Jellicle Cats develop slowly,/Jellicle Cats are not too big;/
487 CC Claude   4   some headings./Just see if you can develop them for me/With a few striking
492 CC Colby   25   /'Reminiscent mood.' I can't develop that/Unless you can tell me —

537 ES   Ld Clav 11   /{LC} It has never crossed my mind. Develop the point./{G} Well, consider what we
DEVELOPED (1)
21 Portrait   98   know our ends!)/Why we have not developed into friends.'/I feel like one who
DEVELOPING (1)
155 Rock 3   64   your service,/Exploiting the seas and developing the mountains,/Dividing the stars
DEVELOPMENT (2)
151 Rock 2   18 expansion/Accompanied by industrial development./Exporting iron, coal and cotton
186 FQ: DrySal   89   to be a mere sequence —/Or even development: the latter a partial fallacy/
DEVERELL (2)
458 CC   Lady E   21   your plans?/{LE} Because of Mildred Deverell./She's been having the treatment with
459 CC   Lady E   38   whom should I meet but Mildred Deverell./She was going on to Zürich. So she
DEVIATION (1)
326 FR   Harry   19   /May be unimportant, a slight deviation/From some imaginary course that life
DEVICES (2)
239 MC   Chorus   24   /But mostly we are left to our own devices,/And we are content if we are left alone.
446 CC   Claude   19   /But so far, I've left him to his own devices:/I thought he would fall into this way of
DEVIL (8)
92 Ash-Wed 3   5   in the fetid air/Struggling with the devil of the stairs who wears/The deceitful face
377 CP   Celia   13   to bring her back —/Unless he is the Devil! I could believe he was./{E} Because I
377 CP   Celia   16   asked him to!/Then he *must* be the Devil! He must have bewitched you./How did
392 CP   Lavinia 22   puzzled by Julia. That woman is the devil./She knows by instinct when something's
398 CP   Edward   6   that I had made a decision./What devil left the door on the latch/For these doubts
406 CP   Lavinia 20 Are not easily deceived./{L} Are you a devil/Or merely a lunatic practical joker?/{E} I
537 ES   Gomez   31   never went too far. There's a prudent devil/Inside you, Dick. He never came to *my*
539 ES   Gomez   20   the protection of that prudent devil/Of yours, to tell him not to go too far./
DEVIL'S (2)
377 CP   Edward   18   *heard from the kitchen*]/{E} What the devil's that? {}/[*Re-enter* JULIA, *in apron, with*
378 CP   Celia   19 that I wanted her back./{C} That's the Devil's method! So you want Lavinia back!/
DEVILS (3)
38 Gerontion   53   by any concitation/Of the backward devils./I would meet you upon this honestly./I
160 Rock 7   5   snakes or trees, worshipping devils rather than nothing: crying for life
410 CP   Reilly   26   of desires of desires. A prey/To the devils who arrive at their plenitude of power/
DEVISED (1)
196 FQ: Little   209 redeemed from fire by fire./Who then devised the torment? Love./Love is the
DEVISING (1)
155 Rock 3   66   common and preferred,/Engaged in devising the perfect refrigerator,/Engaged in
DEVOLUTION (1)
242 MC   Priest1 27   /Loathing power given by temporal devolution,/Wishing subjection to God alone./
DEVOLVED (1)
453 CC   Eggers   39   in charge/And that duty has *not* devolved on Mr. Simpkins:/Sir Claude intends
DEVONSHIRE (1)
236 Cat Morgan   6 likewise to grouse,/And I favour that Devonshire cream in a bowl;/But I'm allus
DEVOTED (5)
91 Ash-Wed 2   21   be forgotten, so I would forget/Thus devoted, concentrated in purpose. And God
152 Rock 2   34   you must fight to keep with hearts as devoted as those of your fathers who fought to
485 CC   Lady E   32   But you had your aunt. And she was devoted to you,/I have no doubt. What is your
548 ES   Carghil 23   very charming girl?/And obviously devoted to her father./I was watching you both
563 ES   Gomez   37   /I should have been your most devoted admirer./{MC} *It's Not Too Late For*
DEVOTION (4)
186 FQ: DrySal   65   at failing powers,/The unattached devotion which might pass for devotionless,/In
241 MC   Mess   31 claims,/Assured, beyond doubt, of the devotion of the people,/Who receive him with
290 FR   Agatha   22   to do./{Ag} Thus with most careful devotion/Thus with precise attention/To detail,
464 CC   Claude   29 *his* passion./He loved it with the same devotion/That I gave to clay, and what could be
DEVOTIONLESS (1)
186 FQ: DrySal   65   devotion which might pass for devotionless,/In a drifting boat with a slow
DEVOUR (1)
166 Rock 10   8   and to left prepares for his hour to devour./But the Mystery of Iniquity is a pit too
DEVOURED (2)
31 Apollinax   17   turf/As his dry and passionate talk devoured the afternoon./'He is a charming man'
241 MC   Priest3   6 greed and lust of others,/The feeble is devoured by his own./{P1} Shall these things not
DEVOURING (1)
247 MC   Tempt1   1   whispering in chambers,/Fires devouring the winter season,/Eating up the
DEVOURS (2)
24 Rhapsody   37 in the gutter,/Slips out its tongue/And devours a morsel of rancid butter.'/So the hand
38 Gerontion   48   tiger springs in the new year. Us he devours. Think at last/We have not reached

DEVOUT (2)
54 Mr E Sun   23   Seraphim/Where the souls of the devout/Burn invisible and dim./Along the
589 Fable   89   /But after this the monks grew most devout,/And lived on milk and breakfast food
DEW (4)
590 Time Space   9   /The flowers I gave thee when the dew/Was trembling on the vine,/Were withered
590 Space Time   9   /The flowers I sent thee when the dew/Was trembling on the vine/Were withered
594 Grad 11   6   the surface of the stream,/A drop of dew upon the morning grass;/Thou dost not die
256 MC Chorus   8   of issue of hell. What is the sticky dew that forms on the back of my hand?/{4T}
DIAGNOSIS (1)
407 CP   Reilly 22   tried to impose upon me/Your own diagnosis, and prescribe your own cure./But
DIALECT (1)
194 FQ: Little   129   and speech impelled us/To purify the dialect of the tribe/And urge the mind to
DIALECTIC (1)
161 Rock 7   29   and what they call Life, or Race, or Dialectic./The Church disowned, the tower
DIALECTS (1)
344 FR   Gerald 24   to learn the language/And several dialects. It means a lot of preparation./{V} And
DIALS (2)
373 CP   m   3   *picks up the telephone, and dials a number]*/{E} Is Miss Celia Coplestone in?
420 CP   1m   19   *at door. Exit* CELIA. REILLY *dials on/house-telephone.]/[into telephone]./{R}
DIAMOND (1)
451 CC   Eggers 11   about the bush,/He's rather a rough diamond. Very free and easy ways;/And Lady
DIAMONDS (1)
117 SP   Doris 8   very queer./{Do} Here's the four of diamonds, what's that mean?/{Du} *(reading)* 'A
DICE (2)
129 Cor2 State   24   orders./Meanwhile the guards shake dice on the marches/And the frogs (O Mantuan)
224 Mr Mistoff   28   a pack,/He is equally cunning with dice;/He is always deceiving you into believing/
DICING (1)
103 Journ Magi   27   the lintel,/Six hands at an open door dicing for pieces of silver,/And feet kicking the
DICK (41)
228 Gus   32   fell flat,/And I once understudied Dick Whittington's Cat./But my grandest
532 ES   Gomez   33   almost say./Don't you know me, Dick?/{LC} Fred Culverwell!/Why do you come
533 ES   Gomez   2   we were up at Oxford, you were plain Dick Ferry./Then, when you married, you took
533 ES   Gomez   18   for./You see, I'm a widower, like you, Dick./So I'm pretty footloose. Gomez, you see,/
534 ES   Gomez   1   in systematic corruption./{G} No, Dick, there's a fault in your logic./How can one
534 ES   Gomez   17   to engage in forgery./{G} Forgery, Dick? An absurd suggestion!/Forgery, I can tell
534 ES   Gomez   27   /To go into politics. In my country, Dick,/Politicians can't afford mistakes. The
534 ES   Gomez   38   one you may get from the other'./Dick, don't tell me that there isn't any whisky in
535 ES   Gomez   2   asked me that already!/To see you, Dick. A natural desire!/For you're the only old
536 ES   Gomez   9   never woken up/To the fact that Dick Ferry died long ago./I married a girl who
536 ES   Gomez   18   are Indian thoughts./O God, Dick, *you* don't know what it's like/To be so
537 ES   Gomez   2   — Gomez as Culverwell./I need you, Dick, to give me reality!/{LC} But according to
537 ES   Gomez   6   be trustworthy?/{G} It's done already, Dick; done many years ago:/Adoption tried,
537 ES   Gomez   30   to?/{G} This is how it worked out, Dick. You liked to play the rake,/But you never
537 ES   Gomez   32   There's a prudent devil/Inside you, Dick. He never came to *my* help./{LC} I
538 ES   Gomez   26   dare say you did make some mistake, Dick .../That would account for your leaving
539 ES   Gomez   16   something of other vicissitudes./Dick, I was very very sorry when I heard/That
539 ES   Gomez   39   a success .../{G} A worldly success, Dick. In another sense/We're both of us
540 ES   Gomez   16   mean by saying you can trust me./{G} Dick, do you remember the moonlight night/We
540 ES   Gomez   25   you had been surprised/When I said 'Dick, you've run over somebody'/Wouldn't you
540 ES   Gomez   34   just couldn't face it./Do you see now, Dick, why I say I can trust you?/{LC} If you
540 ES   Gomez   37   to a Sunday newspaper?/{G} My dear Dick, what a preposterous suggestion!/Who's
541 ES   Gomez   6   public as Frederick Culverwell?/No, Dick, your secret's safe with me./Of course, I
541 ES   Gomez   24   for the rest of my life./Really, Dick, you owe me an apology./Blackmail! On
542 ES   Gomez   8   now and then./I'm a lonely man, Dick, with a craving for affection./All I want is
542 ES   Gomez   15   keep up the pretence?/{G} Threats, Dick! How can you speak of threats?/It's most
542 ES   Gomez   30   of my company?/{G} Oh, I can wait, Dick. You'll relent at last./You'll come to feel
542 ES   Gomez   36   the smoking room./Don't forget, Dick:/You *didn't stop*! Well, I'd better be going.
563 ES   Gomez   7   /[*Enter* GOMEZ]/{G} Good morning, Dick./{G} Good morning, Fred./{G} You
563 ES   Gomez   25   We seem a bit weak on the surnames, Dick!/{MC} Well, you see, Señor Gomez, when
564 ES   Gomez   3   never be too late. Don't you agree, Dick?/— This young lady I take to be your
564 ES   Gomez   14   not old enough/To have known Dick Ferry as long as I have./We were friends at
564 ES   Gomez   34   condition:/That you tell me all about Dick when you knew him. {}/[*pats her
565 ES   Gomez   25   *and* MICHAEL]/{G} Well, Dick, we've got to obey our doctors' orders./
571 ES   Ld Clav 3   and Maisie Batterson,/And Dick Ferry too, and Richard Ferry —/These are
575 ES   Gomez   17   name is Culverwell .../{G} My dear Dick,/You're wasting your time, rehearsing

575 ES	Gomez	22	he heard your distorted version./But, Dick, I was nettled by that insinuation/About
575 ES	Gomez	25	be! And most appropriate,/Isn't it, Dick, when we recall/That you were once
576 ES	Gomez	24	your name to Gomez?/{G} Oh no, Dick, there are plenty of other good names./{M}
579 ES	Gomez	31	/You'll be grateful to me in the end, Dick./{MC} A parent isn't always the right
580 ES	Gomez	12	write to Monica./{G} Well, good-bye Dick. And good-bye Monica./Good-bye, Mr. ...

DICK'S (1)

| 563 ES | Gomez | 36 | /Had I been in London, and in Dick's position/I should have been your most |

DID (230)

DIDN'T (102)

65 WL:	Chess	140	husband got demobbed, I said —/I didn't mince my words, I said to her myself,/
119 SP	Klip	34	you haven't quite got it/(I'm afraid I didn't quite catch your name —/But I'm very
124 SA	Sweeney	26	continue his story./{S} This one didn't get pinched in the end/But that's another
125 SA	Sweeney	4	here's what I was going to say./He didn't know if he was alive/and the girl was
125 SA	Sweeney	6	he was alive/and the girl was dead/He didn't know if the girl was alive/and he was
125 SA	Sweeney	8	the girl was alive/and he was dead/He didn't know if they were both alive/or both were
128 Cor1	March	43	many trumpets!/(And Easter Day, we didn't get to the country,/So we took young
277 MC	Knight3	6	our country first. I dare say that we didn't make a/very good impression when we
292 FR	Gerald	29	ever./There wasn't an inch of it you didn't know./But you'll have to see about a
299 FR	Charles	6	on the voyage from New York —/We didn't learn very much about the circumstances;
300 FR	Downing	5	her in when the weather was rough,/Didn't like to see her lean over the rail./He was
304 FR	Mary	20	well/Why she wanted to keep me. She didn't need me:/She would have done just as
306 FR	Mary	29	was nothing else to do with me./I didn't belong here. It was different for you./And
306 FR	Harry	38	for you, not for us./{H} No, it didn't seem like that. I was part of the design/
314 FR	Warburt	13	such a time to keep you in bed./You didn't like being ill in the holidays./{I} It *was*
322 FR	Winch	12	/{Wi} I should hope not, my Lord./I didn't mean to put myself forward./But you see,
357 CP	Julia	26	in Hampshire./{E} Hampshire?/{J} Didn't you say Hampshire?/{E} No, I didn't say
357 CP	Edward	27	Didn't you say Hampshire?/{E} No, I didn't say Hampshire./{J} Did you say
357 CP	Edward	29	Did you say Hampstead?/{E} No, I didn't say Hampstead./{J} But she must live
359 CP	Edward	17	I couldn't get at them in time;/And I didn't know that *you* were coming./I thought
367 CP	Peter	3	/{P} Oh, I'm very glad that you didn't notice:/I must have behaved rather better
367 CP	Peter	5	rather better than I thought./If you didn't notice, I don't suppose the others did,/
370 CP	Alex	17	another surprise, then. I must think./I didn't expect to find any mangoes,/But I *did*
372 CP	Peter	33	but, if you don't mind,/I'd rather you didn't tell *her* what I've told you./{E} I shall not
380 CP	Edward	10	/But that's what it was, no doubt./{E} I *didn't* take you as a passing diversion!/If you
388 CP	Lavinia	23	away? Well, Celia. Well, Peter./I didn't expect to find either of you here./{P&C}
393 CP	Edward	25	said 'I don't mind'./{E} Of course I didn't mind./I meant it as a compliment./{L}
393 CP	Edward	34	Bar .../{E} You nagged me because I didn't get enough work/And said that I ought
393 CP	Edward	37	briefs began to come in —/And they didn't come through any of *your* friends —/You
394 CP	Edward	3	was perfectly infuriating,/The way you *didn't* complain .../{L} It was you who complained
394 CP	Lavinia	16	particularly wanted you to meet,/You didn't arrive until just as they were leaving./{E}
401 CP	Edward	38	That I was better off without her. But didn't you realise/That I was in no state to
402 CP	Edward	18	the edge of a nervous breakdown./I didn't know it then myself — but if they saw it/I
404 CP	Edward	26	me?/{E} What else can I tell you?/You didn't want to hear about my early history./{R}
405 CP	Lavinia	27	come to talk about my husband:/I didn't say I was prepared to meet him./{E} And
407 CP	Lavinia	37	it./I wonder if there was anyone who didn't know./{R} There was one, in fact. But
412 CP	Reilly	4	her here myself./{R} Oh? You didn't let her know you were seeing me first?/{J}
412 CP	Celia	29	I, somewhere? ... Oh, of course./But I didn't know .../{R} There is nothing you need to
430 CP	Peter	25	/That Alex knew everybody. But I didn't know/That he knew any monkeys./{J}
430 CP	Alex	38	Alex?/{A} I knew about it, but I didn't see it./There is no cinema in Kinkanja./
435 CP	Peter	14	/Of anything like this. I suppose I didn't know her,/I didn't understand her. I
435 CP	Peter	15	this. I suppose I didn't know her,/I didn't understand her. I understand nothing./
439 CP	Peter	16	.../{P} I see what you mean./I wish I didn't have to. But the car will be waiting,/And
452 CC	Lucasta	20	/And asked for things I'm sure he didn't want —/Just to make trouble! And I
452 CC	Colby	38	responsibilities?/{C} No, I'm afraid I didn't know that./{E} You mustn't give way to
456 CC	Eggers	7	/Have sometimes been useful. But he didn't think of that:/He's not petty-minded —
456 CC	Eggers	21	/She has lapses of memory?/{E} I didn't mean that./No. She hasn't very much
458 CC	Lady E	13	But quite unnecessary. And besides,/I didn't come by air. I arrived at Victoria./{SC}
458 CC	Claude	33	had to make a quick decision./{SC} I didn't want to bother you, during your
461 CC	Claude	31	happened before./So the meeting didn't go quite the way I'd intended;/And yet I
462 CC	Claude	38	it to be different. It's odd, Colby./I didn't realise, till you started with me here,/That
465 CC	Claude	11	have become a first-rate potter./I didn't have it in me. It's strange, isn't it,/That I
465 CC	Claude	20	known, at the secret moments,/That I didn't have it in me. There are occasions/When
469 CC	Colby	15	you were very second-rate,/And you didn't like them. You liked the right ones./{L}
469 CC	Lucasta	16	You liked the right ones./{L} Colby, I didn't know you were so artful!/So the things I
470 CC	Colby	36	you want to educate me./{C} But I didn't know/That you wanted to be educated./

471 CC Lucasta 16   Oh, so you believe that I like you?/I didn't know that you were so conceited./{C} No,
472 CC Lucasta 36   the time, I found I *envied* you/And I didn't know why! And now I think I know./It's
477 CC Lucasta 28   to be;/And I liked you because you didn't like that person either,/And I thought
480 CC Kaghan 28   you know, I was a foundling? You didn't know that!/Never had any parents. Just
484 CC Lady E 35   first was, that I was very ugly/And didn't know it. Then, that I was feeble-minded/
484 CC Lady E 36   Then, that I was feeble-minded/And didn't know it. Finally,/That I was a foundling,
484 CC Lady E 37   Finally,/That I was a foundling, and didn't know it./Of course, I was terrified of
485 CC Lady E   6   mean./{LE} However that may be,/I didn't want to belong there. I refused to believe/
486 CC Colby   8   became of your father?/{C} Well ... I didn't have a father./You see ... I was an
489 CC Claude   5   I almost told you/About Colby. I didn't. For such a foolish reason./Absurd it
489 CC Lady E 40   —/Because you *did* care for the girl, didn't you?/{SC} Yes, I did care. Very much. I
490 CC Claude   7   could have happened. But I'm sure it didn't./{LE} Oh, Colby, doesn't your instinct
495 CC Claude   4   /Why have you never told me?/{SC} I didn't think/That you would be interested.
499 CC Lucasta 28   me!/And I haven't made it easier. I didn't try to./And knowing that you wanted me
500 CC Claude 12   /At the time when he came here. But I didn't trust you/To keep a secret. There were
500 CC Lucasta 18   he knew it./{SC} He knew it./{L} Why didn't he tell me? Perhaps he was about to./
504 CC Guzzard 28   /{MG} I believe I was punctual./But I didn't mind waiting in the least, Sir Claude./I
507 CC Guzzard 30   have established the paternity;/But I didn't know who she was! What could I do?/
516 CC Colby   10   — beyond my capacity./I thought I didn't want to be an organist/When I found I
526 ES Charles 4   said it/I was badly frightened. For I didn't *know* you loved me —/I merely wanted
536 ES Gomez   10   died long ago./I married a girl who didn't know a word of English,/Didn't want to
536 ES Gomez   11   who didn't know a word of English,/Didn't want to learn English, wasn't interested/
537 ES Gomez   17   of men you'd been at school with —/I didn't fit into your set, and I knew it./When you
537 ES Gomez   21   from an unknown grammar school./I didn't know either, but I was flattered./Later, I
538 ES Gomez   30   always consult you/But of course didn't have to take your advice .../I've made a
540 ES Gomez   30   /{G} More than in a hurry./You didn't want it to be known where we been./
540 ES Gomez   32   /I've completely forgotten them) you didn't want *them*/To be called to give evidence./
541 ES Gomez   10   it,/Or who knew the story and who didn't. I promise you./Rely upon me as the soul
542 ES Gomez   37   room./Don't forget, Dick:/You *didn't stop*! Well, I'd better be going./I hope I
543 ES Ld Clav 13   he wanted money?/{LC} No, he didn't want money./{M} Father, this interview
545 ES Ld Clav 1   it. Whereas I've often known/That I didn't enjoy it. Some dissatisfaction/With
550 ES Carghil 7   /I was Maisie Montjoy once. And you didn't recognise me./{LC} You've changed your
550 ES Carghil 12   Many years ago, the first time. That didn't last long./People sometimes say: 'Make
551 ES Carghil 36   you exposed./But I gave way. I didn't want to ruin you./If I'd carried on, it
555 ES Piggott 11   /{MP} Oh, Miss Claverton-Ferry!/I didn't see you coming. Now I must fly. {}/[*Exit*]/
555 ES Monica 17   Oh, indeed. What's the matter?/I didn't get far./I met Michael in the drive. He
556 ES Michael 25   exactly./Oh. I said that before, didn't I?/{M} I wish you'd stop being so polite
557 ES Michael 16   /They always came off — the tips I didn't take./{LC} And the ones you did take?/
561 ES Michael 17   place. I don't believe you would./*You* didn't suffer from the handicap that I've had./
562 ES Carghil 12   *with despatch-case*]/{MC} Richard! I didn't think you'd still be here./I came back to
564 ES Carghil 23   great friends/Not long afterwards, didn't we, Richard?/{G} I expect that was after I
567 ES Charles 13   /How much your words meant. You didn't seem to need me then./And you said we
572 ES Ld Clav 3   over/So neither of us killed him. But *I* didn't stop./And all my life I have heard, from
572 ES Ld Clav 6   sleeping,/A voice that whispered, 'you didn't stop!'/I knew the voice: it was Fred
576 ES Michael 19   duties to be? Do you know?/{Mi} We didn't go into details. There's time for that later.
578 ES Monica 20   /I took all that for granted. So I didn't know till now/How much it means to me

DIDST (1)

281 MC Chorus 11   deny Thee could not deny, if Thou didst not exist; and their denial is never

DIE (15)

 21 Portrait   114   —/Well! and what if she should die some afternoon,/Afternoon grey and smoky,
 21 Portrait   116   evening yellow and rose;/Should die and leave me sitting pen in hand/With the
150 Rock 1   115   /*And the wheat is bread/They shall not die in a shortened bed/And a narrow sheet. In this*
175 FQ: BurntN   142   but that which is only living/Can only die. Words, after speech, reach/Into the silence.
177 FQ: ECoker   9   cornstalk and leaf./Houses live and die: there is a time for building/And a time for
181 FQ: ECoker   162   /Wherein, if we do well, we shall/Die of the absolute paternal care/That will not
197 FQ: Little   230   stone: and that is where we start./We die with the dying:/See, they depart, and we go
593 Grad 7   3   try/To labor for the good until they die,/And ask no other guerdon than to know/
594 Grad 12   1   the morning grass;/Thou dost not die — for each succeeding year/Thy honor and
275 MC Thomas   7   /{T} For my Lord I am now ready to die,/That his Church may have peace and
280 MC Priest3   16   supreme, so long as men will die for it./Go, weak sad men, lost erring souls,
293 FR Ivy   12   Oh, dear Amy!/No one wants you to die, I'm sure!/Now that Harry's back, is the
384 CP Reilly   26   my wife left me./{UG} Ah, but we die to each other daily./What we know of other
437 CP Reilly   28   chose./I did not know that she would die in this way;/*She* did not know. So all that I
546 ES Piggott   22   people who want to come here to die!/We never accept them. Nor do we accept/

DIED (40)

29 Aunt Helen	4	to the number of four./Now when she	died there was silence in heaven/And silence at
29 Aunt Helen	9	for,/But shortly afterwards the parrot	died too./The Dresden clock continued ticking
66 WL: Chess	160	/(She's had five already, and nearly	died of young George.)/The chemist said it
160 Rock 7	14	ancient look of a child that has	died of starvation./Prayer wheels, worship of
195 FQ: Little	179	more, on the scaffold/And a few who	died forgotten/In other places, here and abroad,
196 FQ: Little	181	here and abroad,/And of one who	died blind and quiet,/Why should we celebrate/
203 Indians	t	affirmed in verse./To the Indians who	Died in Africa/A man's destination is his own
587 Fable	11	/Whenever some old villainous baron	died,/He added to their hoards — a deed which
304 FR Mary	28	let any project go;/And even when *she*	died: I believed that Cousin Amy —/I almost
319 FR Warburt	18	You were only a boy/When he	died. You would not remember./{H} But now I
319 FR Harry	28	heart of a child./*That* was the day he	died. Of course./I mean, I suppose, the day on
387 CP Peter	27	/So I don't suppose her aunt can have	died./{E} What aunt?/{P} The aunt you told us
396 CP Lavinia	26	you/If I went away. I thought that if I	died/To you, I who had been only a ghost to
434 CP Alex	15	Eventually, two of them escaped:/One	died in the jungle, and the other/Will never be
434 CP Edward	28	natives/Who would have	died anyway./{A} Yes, the patients died anyway;
434 CP Alex	29	died anyway./{A} Yes, the patients	died anyway;/Being tainted with the plague,
436 CP Lavinia	23	expression/That the way in which she	died did not disturb you/Or the fact that she
436 CP Lavinia	24	not disturb you/Or the fact that she	died because she would not leave/A few dying
436 CP Reilly	28	/Or the state of mind in which they	died?/{L} I'm willing to grant that. What struck
436 CP Lavinia	31	or horror/At the way in which she	died. I don't know if you knew her./I suspect
477 CC Lucasta	4	/I was only eight years old/When she	died of an 'accidental overdose'./Then Claude
483 CC Colby	38	aunt. I never knew my mother./She	died when I was born./{LE} She died when you
484 CC Lady E	1	/She died when I was born./{LE} She	died when you were born./Have you other near
486 CC Colby	25	say, they had had one little boy/Who	died when I was very young indeed./I don't
489 CC Claude	20	son of Mrs. Guzzard's sister,/Who	died when he was born. Mrs. Guzzard brought
489 CC Lady E	34	/Left on her hands. The father had	died/And she'd never been told the name of the
506 CC Eggers	3	/Unfortunately, the father	died suddenly .../{LE} He was run over. By a
506 CC Eggers	8	/Leave it to Eggerson./{E} The father	died abroad./Lady Elizabeth did not know the
507 CC Guzzard	24	I was informed that the father had	died/Without making a will./{LE} He was very
509 CC Colby	13	Kaghan. Is he the little cousin/Who	died? Don't you remember, Aunt Sarah,/My
509 CC Colby	16	me I had had a little cousin/Who had	died?/{MG} Yes, Colby, that is what I told you./
511 CC Lady E	9	/{K} But who was my father?/{LE} He	died very suddenly. Of a fatal accident/When
513 CC Colby	27	know now,/Because he would have	died before I was born/Or before I could
515 CC Guzzard	2	you./As I have just said, my sister	died/Before the child could be born. You were
515 CC Guzzard	10	— why not?/My husband also had	died. I was left very poor./If I let you continue
517 CC Eggers	28	appeal to you. The organist we had/	Died two months ago. We've been looking for
531 ES Ld Clav	13	retirement./My obituary, if I had	died in harness,/Would have occupied a column
536 ES Gomez	9	woken up/To the fact that Dick Ferry	died long ago./I married a girl who didn't know
570 ES Ld Clav	12	a deep silence between us,/And she	died silently. She had nothing to say to me./I
571 ES Ld Clav	40	shown/That the old man had	died a natural death/And had been run over

DIES (1)

203 Indians	13	/And exile to another. Where a man	dies bravely/At one with his destiny, that soil is

DIES (1) [*Foreign word*]

272 MC m	11	*is changed to the cathedral.*]/[*while a*	Dies Iræ *is sung in Latin by a choir in the*

DIET (1)

210 Old Gumbie	20	quiet,/She is sure it is due to irregular	diet/And believing that nothing is done without

DIEU (1)

48 Lune Miel	17	ascétique,/Vieille usine désaffectée de	Dieu, tient encore/Dans ses pierres écroulantes

DIFFER (1)

195 FQ: Little	153	conditions which often look alike/Yet	differ completely, flourish in the same

DIFFERENCE (14)

317 FR Warburt	20	at any moment/May make an endless	difference to the future./It's about your mother
318 FR Harry	23	with the past./{H} Oh, is there any	difference!/How can we be concerned with the
324 FR Harry	15	concussion/Cannot make very much	difference to John./A brief vacation from the
324 FR Harry	17	John enjoys, can't make very much	difference/To him or to anyone else. If he was
395 CP Edward	38	Back in the trap,/With only one	difference, perhaps — we can fight each other,/
397 CP Lavinia	38	person?/{L} Indeed. And has the	difference nothing to do/With Celia going to
436 CP Reilly	27	knows, Mrs. Chamberlayne,/The	difference that made to the natives who were
480 CC Kaghan	22	a good judge. Now, I'll tell you the	difference/Between ourselves and Colby. You
494 CC Lady E	12	believe in facts./You do. That is the	difference between us./{SC} I'm not so sure of
515 CC Claude	37	it, then. But don't let it make a	difference/To our relations. Or, perhaps, for the
516 CC Claude	1	will stay with me. It shall make no	difference/To my plans for your future./{C}
552 ES Carghil	31	as an elder statesman;/And the	difference between being an elder statesman/
573 ES Ld Clav	10	to the sinner./What has made the	difference in the last five minutes/Is not the
579 ES Michael	1	you and me?/{Mi} That makes no	difference./You'll be seeing me again./{M} But

DIFFERENCES (3)

321	FR	Warburt	3	much like you. Of course there are differences:/But, allowing for the changes in
472	CC	Lucasta	15	And then you begin/To discover differences inside the likeness./You may *feel*
484	CC	Lady E	25	similar./These are only superficial differences:/You must have been a lonely child,

DIFFERENT (70)

61	WL: Burial	27	rock),/And I will show you something different from either/Your shadow at morning
104	Journ Magi	38	and death,/But had thought they were different; this Birth was/Hard and bitter agony
182	FQ: ECoker	177	attempt/Is a wholly new start, and a different kind of failure/Because one has only
185	FQ: DrySal	29	/The sea howl/And the sea yelp, are different voices/Often together heard: the whine
186	FQ: DrySal	97	meaning restores the experience/In a different form, beyond any meaning/We can
188	FQ: DrySal	140	not escaping from the past/Into different lives, or into any future;/You are not
209	NamingCats	4	I tell you, a cat must have THREE DIFFERENT NAMES./First of all, there's the
594	Grad 10	2	shall return; and it will be to find/A different school from that which now we know;/
605	Narcissus	3	rock,/And I will show you something different from either/Your shadow sprawling
242	MC Priest1	30	weaker/Things had perhaps been different for Thomas./{P2} Yet our lord is
276	MC Knight1	29	who,/with their various abilities, and different points of view, will be able/to lay
290	FR Chorus	38	rises, to find themselves dressed for a different play, or having rehearsed the wrong
294	FR Harry	39	not like that./Everything is true in a different sense./I expected to find her when I
302	FR Amy	17	/With both of them, coming from different directions./Well, we must go and dress,
306	FR Mary	29	with me./I didn't belong here. It was different for you./And you seemed so much
333	FR Harry	15	things happen./Everything is true in a different sense,/A sense that would have seemed
334	FR Harry	4	of what can't be got rid of/But in a different vision. This is like an end./{Ag} And a
334	FR Harry	39	Now I can live in public./Liberty is a different kind of pain from prison./{Ag} I only
338	FR Harry	1	/My advice has come from quite a different quarter,/But I cannot explain that to
342	FR Agatha	32	which safety and danger have a different meaning,/And he cannot return. That
348	FR Chorus	6	of the same window, and see quite a different landscape./We do not like to climb a
356	CP Peter	10	They did a film/But they used a different scenario./{J} Not the one you wrote?/
369	CP Peter	4	deal. And then I met Celia./She was different from any girl I'd ever known/And not
369	CP Edward	14	her./{E} You and Celia were asked for different purposes./Your role was to be one of
369	CP Peter	36	to be with Celia, that was something different/From company or solitude. And we
372	CP Peter	2	See Celia for me./You know her in a different way from me/And you are so much
379	CP Celia	25	/Where the word 'happiness' had a different meaning/Or so it seemed./{E} I have
384	CP Reilly	4	water?/{UG} No, thank you. This is a different occasion./{E} I take it that as you have
395	CP Lavinia	12	always were./As for me, I'm rather a different person/Whom you must get to know./
397	CP Edward	37	/That in future you will find me a different person?/{L} Indeed. And has the
409	CP Reilly	39	that his feelings towards her/Were different from any you had aroused in him —/It
413	CP Celia	30	something wrong,/Or at least, very different from what it seemed to be,/With the
416	CP Reilly	13	I'm only typical./{R} There are different types. Some are rarer than others./{C}
428	CP Alex	19	converts,/And, naturally, take a different view./They trap the monkeys. And
446	CC Claude	13	The same disappointment/In a different form. He won't forget/That his great
449	CC Claude	3	of the child *she* lost./{SC} In a very different way, yes. You might say *mislaid*,/Since
451	CC Eggers	13	/But you, Mr. Simpkins, that's very different./{C} I don't know why it should be so
451	CC Colby	14	/{C} I don't know why it should be so different./I like B. Kaghan. I've found him very
451	CC Eggers	28	/But with you, as I said, it will be very different./She'll see at once that you're a man of
455	CC Eggers	34	/Lady Elizabeth, now, that's different./{C} At least, I don't suppose Lady
460	CC Lady E	6	*thought* control./Mind control is a different matter:/It's more advanced. But I
462	CC Claude	14	/That *her* son would have been a different type of person —/Then you *will*
462	CC Claude	37	me yet./{SC} But now I want it to be different. It's odd, Colby./I didn't realise, till
463	CC Colby	18	about myself. As if I was becoming/A different person. Just as, I suppose,/If you learn
463	CC Colby	21	it — you feel yourself to be/Rather a different person when you're talking it./I'm not
465	CC Claude	21	/When I am transported — a different person,/Transfigured in the vision of
465	CC Colby	33	expressed,/Although the medium is different. I know/I should never have become a
469	CC Colby	10	/And the various forms, and the different ways of playing it./{L} But suppose I
472	CC Colby	18	like mine./{C} In what way is it different?/{L} It's hard to explain./Perhaps it's
472	CC Lucasta	29	that you must learn to do something different./And so you applied for Eggerson's
473	CC Lucasta	1	that's more real./That's why you're different from the rest of us:/You have your
485	CC Lady E	11	romantic. But it goes to show/How different I felt myself to be/And then I took up
488	CC Claude	18	make her confession, it will be very different/From what you expect. I'm afraid,
490	CC Lady E	26	/{LE} But a mother, Colby, isn't that different?/There should always be a bond
502	CC Lucasta	25	either an egotist/Or something so different from the rest of us/That we can't judge
503	CC Lucasta	3	In the way we might have been. But a different way/That reveals itself in time. And
513	CC Colby	21	never had a father or a mother —/It's different for B. He's had his foster-parents,/So
516	CC Colby	37	/As I am hurting you. But it is very different./As long as I believed that you were
526	ES Monica	21	private world —/The meanings are different. Look! We're back in the room/That
533	ES Gomez	24	/Out there they respect you for rather different reasons./{LC} Do you mean that

536 ES   Gomez   4   /So you weren't aware of becoming a different person:/But where *I* changed my name,
537 ES   Gomez   15   *my* influence./{G} I was just about as different as anyone could be/From the sort of
546 ES   Piggott   35   her as 'Nurse'?/{MP} Oh yes, that's different./She is a real nurse, you know, fully
558 ES   Ld Clav   12   /I dare say Sir Alfred's will be rather different./And what else did he say?/{Mi} He
559 ES   Michael   22   of Claverton;/Or where, if I took a different name — and I might choose to —/No
561 ES   Ld Clav   29   abroad/I want him to go in a very different spirit/From that which he has just been
571 ES   Ld Clav   5   /People who might all have been very different/From Gomez, Mrs. Carghill and Lord
575 ES   Ld Clav   13   that Señor Gomez wants,/But in a different sense, and for different reasons/From
575 ES   Ld Clav   13   /But in a different sense, and for different reasons/From what you think. Let me
582 ES   Charles   25   /[*Exit* CLAVERTON]/{C} He's a very different man from the man he used to be./It's

DIFFERENTLY (5)
304 FR   Mary   5   timid girls./I don't see you any differently now;/But I really wish that I'd taken
370 CP   Peter   26   {P} You put it just wrong. I think of it differently./It is not her interest in *me* that I
393 CP   Edward   11   given in to me./It struck me very differently. As we're on the subject,/I thought
394 CP   Lavinia   20   something else. I shall treat you very differently/In future./{E} Thank you for the
394 CP   Edward   37   /I shall behave, I assure you, very differently./{L} Bravo! Edward. This is

DIFFICULT (22)
209 NamingCats   1   of Cats/The Naming of Cats is a difficult matter,/It isn't just one of your holiday
287 FR   Charles   15   /{C} She's a nice girl; but it's a difficult age for her./I suppose she must be
290 FR   Gerald   19   eight years./{G} That will be a little difficult./{V} Nonsense, Gerald!/You must see
303 FR   Mary   17   she might have told me;/It is very difficult, having to plan/For uncertain numbers.
307 FR   Mary   23   touch me./Just now, I find them very difficult to bear./They are always assured that
317 FR   Harry   8   if anything, make matters rather more difficult./But talk about it, if you like./{W} You
317 FR   Warburt   12   /And as for making matters more difficult —/It is much more difficult not to be
317 FR   Warburt   13   more difficult —/It is much more difficult not to be prepared/For something that
341 FR   Agatha   5   I must begin./There is nothing more difficult. But you are just the same:/Just as
355 CP   Julia   37   /He only made the situation more difficult./You know Tony Vincewell? You knew
357 CP   Edward   10   favourite niece. And she's rather difficult./When she's ill, she insists on having
385 CP   Reilly   8   /That will not be easy./{UG} It is very difficult./But it is perhaps still more difficult/To
385 CP   Reilly   9   difficult./But it is perhaps still more difficult/To keep up the pretence that you are
385 CP   Reilly   17   first ten minutes? You would find it difficult/To treat them as strangers, but still
385 CP   Reilly   18   treat them as strangers, but still more difficult/To pretend that you were not strange
411 CP   Edward   20   we go?/{E} Yes, I have./But it's difficult to say./{L} But I wish you would say it.
434 CP   Alex   22   of it./{E} But before that .../{A} It was difficult to tell./But from what we know of local
447 CC   Claude   15   appointing a successor./Makes it very difficult to replace you./She thinks she ought to
467 CC   Claude   34   /Life presents a new one, more difficult to pay./— I shall go now, and sit for a
493 CC   Claude   3   /It's important, when you have a difficult meeting,/To decide on the seating
502 CC   Lucasta   32   my brother;/Which makes it more difficult to know *what* you are./It may be
502 CC   Lucasta   36   .../{C} Or sister .../{L} What's so difficult/Is to recognise the limits of one's

DIFFICULTIES (6)
129 Cor2 State   t   *la haie? ILS LA FAISAIENT.*/Difficulties of a Statesman/CRY what shall I
374 CP   Celia   23   enough./Doesn't that settle all our difficulties?/{E} It has only brought to light the
374 CP   Edward   24   It has only brought to light the real difficulties./{C} But surely, these are only
401 CP   Reilly   34   the moment./Tell me first, about the difficulties/On which you want my professional
456 CC   Eggers   38   /Getting Lady Elizabeth out of her difficulties./{C} Perhaps she won't even arrive
470 CC   Lucasta   21   is./{L} Really, Colby, you do make difficulties!/But what about taking me to a

DIFFICULTY (4)
588 Fable   50   peacock standing on both legs/With difficulty kept from toppling over,/Next came a
400 CP   Reilly   4   time./Tell me now, did you have any difficulty/In convincing him I was the man for
400 CP   Alex   6   him I was the man for his case?/{A} Difficulty? No! He was only impatient/At
449 CC   Claude   24   Angel, from the start./That was one difficulty. And there are others./For one, they're

DIFFIDENCE (1)
331 FR   Agatha   39   beneath unusual weakness,/The diffidence of a solitary man:/Where he was

DIFFIDENT (2)
197 FQ: Little   221   support the others,/The word neither diffident nor ostentatious,/An easy commerce of
412 CP   Julia   13   her?/{J} Oh no, not reluctant:/Only diffident. She cannot believe/That you will take

DIFFUSED (1)
330 FR   Harry   31   emotion, as before: the same loathing/Diffused, I not a person, in a world not of

DIG (1)
63 WL: Burial   75   friend to men,/'Or with his nails he'll dig it up again!'/'You! hypocrite lecteur! — mon

DIGESTIVE (1)
221 Old Deut   40   shuffle, without a word spoken./The digestive repose of that feline's gastronomy/

DIGNIFIED (3)
171 FQ: BurntN   25 Into our first world./There they were, dignified, invisible,/Moving without pressure,
178 FQ: ECoker   31   signifying matrimonie —/A dignified and commodious sacrament./Two and
209 NamingCats   14 /A name that's peculiar, and more dignified,/Else how can he keep up his tail
DIGNITY (3)
164 Rock 9   27   service all our powers/For life, for dignity, grace and order,/And intellectual
249 MC Tempt2   31 home./Private policy is public profit;/Dignity still shall be dressed with decorum./{T}
559 ES Michael   29 /Of retiring from politics, not without dignity,/Being no longer wanted. And you
DIGRESS (2)
15 Prufrock   66   from a dress/That makes me so digress?/Arms that lie along a table, or wrap
33 Conv Gal   6 to their distress.'/She then: 'How you digress!'/And I then: 'Someone frames upon the
DIGRESSION (1)
603 Spleen   6 self-possession/By this unwarranted digression./Evening, lights, and tea!/Children
DILIGENCE (3)
411 CP   Reilly 36   And work out your salvation with diligence. {}/[*Exeunt* EDWARD *and* LAVINIA]
420 CP   Reilly 18   /Work out your salvation with diligence. {}/[NURSE-SECRETARY *appears at*
421 CP   Reilly 35 her/'Work out your salvation with diligence', I do not understand/What I myself
DIM (4)
54 Mr E Sun   24 souls of the devout/Burn invisible and dim./Along the garden-wall the bees/With hairy
149 Rock 1   m 94 WORKMEN *is silhouetted against the dim sky. From farther/away, they are answered*
173 FQ: BurntN   95   /Time before and time after/In a dim light: neither daylight/Investing form with
479 CC Kaghan   36 change the colours./It's all a bit too dim. You need something brighter./But
DIMENSION (1)
189 FQ: DrySal   204 past and future/And clings to that dimension. But to apprehend/The point of
DIMINISH (2)
242 MC   Mess   7 to cherish any illusions,/Or yet to diminish the least of his pretensions./If you ask
268 MC Thomas   17 /To uncrown the King's son, or to diminish/His honour and power. Why should he
DIMINISHED (1)
301 FR Charles 24 that her status as Amy's sister will be diminished./{Ch} We all of us make the
DIMINUENDO (1)
123 SA   m 22 /*For it won't be hours but years* {}/*diminuendo*/{Kl&Kr} *And the morning/And the*
DIMLY (1)
296 FR   Harry   9 /{H} I think I see what you mean,/Dimly — as you once explained the sobbing in
DIN (2)
223 Pekes Pols   32   Heathen Chinese./But a terrible din is what Pollicles like,/For your Pollicle Dog
223 Pekes Pols   41 some from the roof,/Joined in/To the din/With a/Bark bark bark bark/Bark bark
DINE (11)
588 Fable   39   the room in which they were to dine,/And watered everything except the wine./
265 MC Priest1 24   /Before your business. Please dine with us./Your men shall be looked after
265 MC Knight1   28 We will roast your pork/First, and dine upon it after./{K2} We must see the
357 CP   Julia 40 of course./I am going to make you dine alone with me/On Friday, and talk to me
358 CP   Julia   6 /{J} Well, you shan't escape. You dine with me on Friday./I've already chosen the
358 CP   Edward   8 to meet./{E} But you asked me to dine with you alone./{J} Yes, alone!/Without
429 CP   Julia 13 monkeys./I thought I was going to dine out on those monkeys:/But one can't dine
429 CP   Julia 14 out on those monkeys:/But one can't dine out on eating Christians —/Even among
481 CC Kaghan   10 yet./It's only six o'clock. We can't dine till eight;/Not at any restaurant that *you*
481 CC Lady E   28 have dinner early:/Most of its patrons dine at half past six./They have the most
543 ES Monica   19 be alone with me?/If you can't bear to dine alone with me tonight,/What will it be like
DINED (2)
369 CP   Peter 38 sometimes had tea/And once or twice dined together./{E} And after that/Did she ever
430 CP   Peter 21 Bologolomsky/In the old days? We dined the other night/At the Saffron Monkey.
DINGY (2)
22 Preludes   22   of all the hands/That are raising dingy shades/In a thousand furnished rooms./
129 Cor2 State   29 /Here is the row of family portraits, dingy busts, all looking remarkably Roman,/
DINING (1)
543 ES Ld Clav 16 go and rest now. I wish Charles was dining with us./I wish we were having a dinner
DINING-ROOM (4)
219 Mung Rump   34   be both?/And when you heard a dining-room smash/Or up from the pantry there
544 ES Monica   3   let us alone;/The people in the dining-room show no curiosity;/The beds are
546 ES Piggott 27 lunch/Just take a glance around the dining-room:/Nobody looks ill! They're all
548 ES Carghil 24 /I was watching you both in the dining-room last night./You are the great Lord
DINING-TABLE (1)
29 Aunt Helen   11   /And the footman sat upon the dining-table/Holding the second housemaid on

DINNER (49)

66 WL: Chess	167	gammon,/And they asked me in to dinner, to get the beauty of it hot —/HURRY
186 FQ: DrySal	94	or affection,/Or even a very good dinner, but the sudden illumination —/We had
218 Mung Rump	21	the family assembled for Sunday dinner,/With their minds made up that they
219 Mung Rump	26	/'I'm afraid you must wait and have dinner *tomorrow*!/For the joint has gone from
587 Fable	19	/At any rate, he sometimes came to dinner,/Whene'er the monks were having merry
265 MC Priest1	21	hospitality./We are about to go to dinner./The good Archbishop would be vexed/If
265 MC Priest1	26	/Your men shall be looked after also./Dinner before business. Do you like roast pork?
265 MC Knight1	27	like roast pork?/{K1} Business before dinner. We will roast your pork/First, and dine
265 MC Knight3	32	his hospitality./We will find our own dinner. {}/[*to attendant*]./{P1} Go, tell His
286 FR Charles	25	/Is a glass of dry sherry or two before dinner./The modern young people don't know
287 FR Amy	36	should both be here in good time for dinner./Harry telephoned to me from
288 FR Amy	6	/And open your presents?/{A} After dinner:/That is the best time./{I} It is the first
292 FR Amy	16	/Now we shall all be together for dinner./The servants have been looking forward
292 FR Amy	18	/Would you like to have them in after dinner/Or wait till tomorrow? I am sure you
295 FR Amy	38	/I beg you to go now and rest before dinner./Get Downing to draw you a hot bath,/
302 FR Amy	14	promised to be here/In good time for dinner. It is very annoying./Now they can
303 FR Agatha	9	I wonder how many we shall be for dinner./{M} Seven ... nine ... ten surely./I hear
303 FR Mary	14	of course./We may have to keep the dinner back .../{Ag} And also Dr. Warburton.
303 FR Mary	21	what is more formal than a family dinner?/An official occasion of uncomfortable
305 FR Agatha	15	easiest rôle./I must go and change for dinner. {}/[*Exit*]/{M} So you will not help me!/
306 FR Mary	6	/{M} Well, I must go and change for dinner./We do change — to that extent./{H} No,
309 FR Mary	9	/But in any case, I must get ready for dinner./{H} No, no, don't go! Please don't leave
314 FR Amy	5	that you were going to be here for dinner/He broke an important engagement to
315 FR Warburt	16	/It's only when I get an invitation to dinner/That I ever see your mother./{V} Yes,
315 FR Amy	23	John?/{A} We might as well go in to dinner./They may come before we finish. Will
315 FR Amy	27	we came first, we will go first, in to dinner./{W} With pleasure, Lady Monchensey,/
316 FR Chorus	1	rendered ludicrous/The tenants' dinner, the family picnic on the moors. Have
316 FR m	8	/[*Enter* MARY, *and passes through to* dinner. *Enter* AGATHA]/{Ag} The eye is on this
316 FR 1m	24	crooked is made straight. {}/[*Exit to* dinner]/END OF PART I/PART II/*The library*,
317 FR 2m	1	PART I/PART II/*The library, after* dinner./Scene I/HARRY, WARBURTON/{W}
358 CP Julia	23	repeat it./Why don't you *all* come to dinner on Friday?/No, I'm afraid my good Mrs.
368 CP Alex	6	So you're going to come out and have dinner with me./{E} That's very thoughtful of
368 CP Alex	9	/{A} But you've got to have some dinner. Are you going out?/Is there anyone here
368 CP Alex	10	going out?/Is there anyone here to get dinner for you?/{E} No, I shan't want much,
368 CP Alex	16	/And I shall prepare you a nice little dinner/Which you can have alone. And then
398 CP Lavinia	16	some eggs. But we must go out for dinner./Meanwhile, my luggage is in the hall
453 CC Lucasta	9	in public./You may take me out to dinner. A working girl like me/Is often very
461 CC Eggers	15	/'Why don't you ask him out to dinner one Sunday?'/But I say: 'We couldn't ask
479 CC Lucasta	2	moment, B./You're to take me out to dinner. And I'm dying for a drink./{K} I told
479 CC Lucasta	11	you've got to give me a very good dinner./{K} You shall be fed. All in good time./
481 CC Kaghan	9	I was hungry./{K} You can't want dinner yet./It's only six o'clock. We can't dine
481 CC Kaghan	24	were leaving?/{K} We're going out to dinner. Lucasta's very hungry./{LE} Hungry? At
481 CC Lady E	25	At six o'clock? Where will you get dinner?/Oh, I know. It's a chance to try that
481 CC Lady E	27	I recommended to you. You can have dinner early:/Most of its patrons dine at half
486 CC Claude	36	They're notes for my speech/At the dinner of the Potters' Company./{C} That's
492 CC Claude	20	Tomorrow night. Must I go to that dinner/Tomorrow night?/{C} I was looking at
511 CC Lady E	24	we must invite the Kaghans to dinner./{SC} By all means, Elizabeth./{K} But,
543 ES Monica	15	/You must go and rest now, before dinner./{LC} Yes, I'll go and rest now. I wish
543 ES Ld Clav	17	with us./I wish we were having a dinner party./{M} Father, can't you bear to be

DINNERS (1)

247 MC Tempt1	36	/The easy man lives to eat the best dinners./Take a friend's advice. Leave well

DIP (2)

140 Usk	6	Let them sleep./'Gently dip, but not too deep',/Lift your eyes/Where the
140 Usk	8	deep',/Lift your eyes/Where the roads dip and where the roads rise/Seek only there/

DIRECT (5)

83 Hollow Men	14	/Those who have crossed/With direct eyes, to death's other Kingdom/
280 MC Priest1	8	/Who shall now guide us, protect us, direct us?/After what journey through what
336 FR Harry	10	don't you? a communication, a scent/Direct to the brain ... but not just as before,/
437 CP Reilly	30	know. So all that I could do/Was to direct her in the way of preparation./That way,
542 ES Gomez	6	it's my turn./I can have cigars sent direct to you from Cuba/If your doctors allow

DIRECTED (2)

167 Rock 10	29	who meditate at midnight/And lights directed through the coloured panes of windows
434 CP Alex	1	a V.A.D. I remember./{A} She was directed to Kinkanja,/Where there are various

DIRECTEUR (3)

46 Directeur	t	/Droop in a hundred A.B.C.'s./Le Directeur/Malheur à la malheureuse Tamise/
46 Directeur	3	/Qui coule si près du Spectateur./Le directeur/Conservateur/Du Spectateur/Empeste
46 Directeur	19	/En guenilles/Camarde/Regarde/Le directeur/Du Spectateur/Conservateur/Et crève

DIRECTING (1)

155 Rock 3   39   not with you?/A thousand policemen directing the traffic/Cannot tell you why you

DIRECTION (10)

177 FQ: ECoker	18	/And the deep lane insists on the direction/Into the village, in the electric heat/
251 MC Tempt3	35	/Which has turned its eyes in your direction —/To gain from you, your Lordship
294 FR Harry	17	many creatures moving/Without direction, for no direction/Leads anywhere but
294 FR Harry	17	moving/Without direction, for no direction/Leads anywhere but round and round
294 FR Harry	30	/It was only reversing the senseless direction/For a momentary rest on the burning
338 FR Agatha	35	/The person taking the opposite direction/Will appear to run away./{A} I was
343 FR Agatha	5	/{Ag} We must all go, each in his own direction,/You, and I, and Harry. You and I,/
462 CC Claude	20	is to guide her delusions/In the right direction./{C} It doesn't seem quite honest./If
504 CC Lady E	21	been making progress, under my direction;/But she shouldn't have been singing./
567 ES Monica	28	/{M} I never expected you from *that* direction, Father!/I thought you were indoors.

DIRECTIONS (3)

302 FR Amy	17	both of them, coming from different directions./Well, we must go and dress, I
339 FR Harry	5	/I have not yet had the precise directions./Where does one go from a world of
350 FR Agatha	24	/By those who depart/In several directions/For their own redemption/And that

DIRECTLY (2)

386 CP Celia	21	Lavinia asked you!/{C} Well, not directly. Julia had a telegram/Asking her to
545 ES Piggott	28	will understand/My not coming in directly after breakfast:/He's led a busy life,

DIRECTOR (4)

431 CP Peter	33	/Besides that, we've got the casting director:/He's looking for some typical English
431 CP Julia	39	/Couldn't you persuade your casting director/To take us all over? We're all very
433 CP Peter	19	I want to introduce her to our casting director./I've got an idea for another film./Can
538 ES Gomez	38	of politics/And went into the City. Director of a bank/And chairman of companies.

DIRECTORS (3)

67 WL: Fire S	180	friends, the loitering heirs of City directors;/Departed, have left no addresses./By
180 FQ: ECoker	109	Exchange Gazette, the Directory of Directors,/And cold the sense and lost the
530 ES Ld Clav	37	the Chairman's Price! And my fellow directors/Saying 'we must put our hands in our

DIRECTORY (4)

180 FQ: ECoker	109	And the Stock Exchange Gazette, the Directory of Directors,/And cold the sense and
433 CP Peter	22	I couldn't find her/In the telephone directory./{J} Not in the directory,/Or in any
433 CP Julia	23	the telephone directory./{J} Not in the directory,/Or in any directory. You can tell
433 CP Julia	24	/{J} Not in the directory,/Or in any directory. You can tell them now, Alex./{L}

DIRT (1)

266 MC Knights   21   pride./Creeping out of the London dirt,/Crawling up like a louse on your shirt,/The

DIRTY (5)

64 WL: Chess	103	still the world pursues,/'Jug Jug' to dirty ears./And other withered stumps of time/
70 WL: Fire S	303	nothing./The broken fingernails of dirty hands./My people humble people who
103 Journ Magi	15	the towns unfriendly/And the villages dirty and charging high prices:/A hard time we
473 CC Lucasta	8	find it!/No, my only garden is ... a dirty public square/In a shabby part of London
474 CC Lucasta	26	—/A bomb-site ... willow-herb ... a dirty public square./But I can't imagine that

DISAFFECTION (1)

173 FQ: BurntN   93   time is conquered./Here is a place of disaffection/Time before and time after/In a dim

DISAGREE (1)

590 Space Time   8   is time, and runs away,/Though sages disagree./The flowers I sent thee when the dew/

DISAPPEAR (3)

265 MC m	9	*the* FOUR KNIGHTS. *The banners disappear*]/{K1} Servants of the King./{P1} And
272 MC Chorus	20	fury in the hall./The agents of hell disappear, the human, they shrink and dissolve/
302 FR Chorus	8	some dreadful disclosure, the roof disappear,/And we should cease to be sure of

DISAPPEARED (3)

212 Growltiger	25	GRUMBUSKIN, long since had disappeared,/For to the Bell at Hampton he had
213 Growltiger	46	I am sorry to admit it, but she quickly disappeared./She probably escaped with ease,
244 MC Chorus	15	and gossip,/Several girls have disappeared/Unaccountably, and some not able

DISAPPEARS (1)

419 CP Reilly   30   return, in a physical sense;/No one disappears. They lead very active lives/Very

DISAPPOINTED (6)

463 CC Colby	28	take possession:/And I am again the disappointed organist,/And for a moment the
477 CC Lucasta	18	/You ought to see your face! I'm disappointed./I suppose that's all. I believe
478 CC Lucasta	10	in me./You know, Colby, I'm truly disappointed./I was sure, when I told you all I
495 CC Claude	32	is an artist./{SC} A musician./I am a disappointed craftsman,/And Colby is a

495 CC Claude 33   craftsman,/And Colby is a disappointed composer./I should have been a
514 CC Guzzard 12   Guzzard./You are the son of a disappointed musician./{C} And who was my
DISAPPOINTING (1)
256 MC Tempts 11   /All things are unreal,/Unreal or disappointing:/The Catherine wheel, the
DISAPPOINTMENT (8)
256 MC Tempts   9 hand?/{4T} Man's life is a cheat and a disappointment;/All things are unreal,/Unreal
260 MC Thomas 25 mistaken, and/that the promise was a disappointment and a cheat?/Reflect now, how
261 MC Thomas   3   sea, to know torture, imprisonment, disappointment, to suffer/death by martyrdom.
320 FR Warburt 34   Arthur and John/Have been a great disappointment to your mother./John's very
341 FR   Amy 34 at Wishwood,/Years of bitterness and disappointment./What share had you in this?
446 CC Eggers   7 keen interest./{E} And getting over his disappointment?/Of course, I never mentioned
446 CC Claude 12   /He's like me, Eggerson. The same disappointment/In a different form. He won't
516 CC Claude 19 shared our ambitions/And shared our disappointment. And you described your
DISAPPOINTMENTS (1)
529 ES Monica   9   the same ambitions —/And of his disappointments./{C} Is that wistfulness,/
DISAPPROVE (4)
297 FR   Violet 32   /And which I am sure Amy would disapprove of —/I only wish to express my
301 FR   Violet 13 brought Downing into it:/Of which I disapprove./{C} Of which you disapprove./But I
301 FR   Charles 14 which I disapprove./{C} Of which you disapprove./But I believe that an unconscious
534 ES   Gomez 14   nothing in England that you would disapprove of./{LC} That's something, at least,
DISAPPROVED (1)
415 CP   Celia 25 disaster/Because the people one knew disapproved of it./I don't worry much about
DISARM (1)
249 MC Tempt2   5   the throne of God can man do more?/Disarm the ruffian, strengthen the laws,/Rule
DISASTER (6)
326 FR   Harry 16   /Engaged in foreseeing the minor disaster?/You go on trying to think of each
326 FR   Harry 26 begins to seem just part of some huge disaster,/Some monstrous mistake and
377 CP   Julia 25 all in need of a stimulant/After this disaster. Now I'll propose a health./Can you
382 CP   Edward   1   /The willing self can contrive the disaster/Of this unwilling partnership — but can
415 CP   Celia 24   /And bad form always led to disaster/Because the people one knew
472 CC Lucasta 22 know. When you first told me/What a disaster it was in your life/When you found that
DISASTROUS (1)
240 MC Chorus   9 shoot shall eat our eyes and our ears,/Disastrous summer burn up the beds of our
DISBELIEVE (1)
415 CP   Celia 20   —/I had always been taught to disbelieve in sin./Oh, I don't mean that it was
DISCHARGE (1)
196 FQ: Little   205 Of which the tongues declare/The one discharge from sin and error./The only hope, or
DISCHARGED (2)
558 ES Ld Clav   4   are they the cause of your being discharged?/{Mi} Well, partly. Sir Alfred did
571 ES Ld Clav 39   and was arrested,/But was later discharged. It was definitely shown/That the old
DISCIPLES (3)
260 MC Thomas 27   spoke of Peace. He said to His/disciples, 'Peace I leave with you, my peace I
261 MC Thomas   1   to the children? Those men His disciples/knew no such things: they went forth
261 MC Thomas   6 I unto you.'/So then, He gave to His disciples peace, but not peace as the world/
DISCIPLINE (1)
190 FQ: DrySal 218   and the rest/Is prayer, observance, discipline, thought and action./The hint half
DISCLOSE (2)
194 FQ: Little   131   to aftersight and foresight,/Let me disclose the gifts reserved for age/To set a crown
408 CP   Reilly 27 you know all this?/{R} That I cannot disclose./I have my own method of collecting
DISCLOSED (1)
227 Macavity   31 *not there*!/And when the loss has been disclosed, the Secret Service say:/'It *must* have
DISCLOSING (1)
336 FR   2m 23   *fashion,/and opens the curtains, disclosing the empty embrasure. She steps into/*
DISCLOSURE (2)
302 FR   Chorus   8   /The cellar make some dreadful disclosure, the roof disappear,/And we should
361 CP   Reilly 26 wanted was the luxury/Of an intimate disclosure to a stranger./Let me, therefore,
DISCOLOURING (1)
294 FR   Harry 24   the skin/Tainting the flesh and discolouring the bone —/This is what matters,
DISCONCERTING (1)
461 CC Claude 29 us./{SC} Her sudden arrival was very disconcerting:/As you gather, such a thing never
DISCONSOLATE (1)
175 FQ: BurntN 161 funeral dance,/The loud lament of the disconsolate chimera./The detail of the pattern
DISCONTENTED (1)
340 FR   Amy 18   him,/For the sake of the future, a discontented ghost,/In his own house. What of

DISCOURAGING (1)
475 CC Lucasta   4 anyone?/{L} I think you're being very discouraging:/Are you doing it deliberately?/{C}
DISCOVER (6)
187 FQ: DrySal 106 the primitive terror./Now, we come to discover that the moments of agony/(Whether,
197 FQ: Little   246   gate/When the last of earth left to discover/Is that which was the beginning;/At the
209 NamingCats   23   name that no human research can discover —/But THE CAT HIMSELF
287 FR   Amy   32 a vacant room./Only Agatha seems to discover some meaning in death/Which I cannot
472 CC Lucasta   15   ways. And then you begin/To discover differences inside the likeness./You
497 CC Eggers   33 /If I may say so. Of course, we might discover/Another Mrs. Guzzard .../{LE} *Two*
DISCOVERED (9)
182 FQ: ECoker 185   and submission, has already been discovered/Once or twice, or several times, by
226 Macavity   20   in the square —/But when a crime's discovered, then *Macavity's not there!*/He's
379 CP   Celia   31 you would be free — then I suddenly discovered/That the dream was not enough;
409 CP   Reilly   10 thought your wife had left you,/You discovered, to your surprise and consternation,/
409 CP   Reilly   26 your side of the problem./When you discovered that your young friend/(Though you
409 CP   Reilly   30 this position) —/When, I say, you discovered that your young friend/Had actually
495 CC Lady E   26   /In Tony — and then, too late, I discovered/He belonged to the world I wanted
548 ES Carghil   16 /And none of the other guests have discovered it./It was clever of you to find it so
574 ES Carghil   15 two, now and then./And in the end I discovered what Michael really wanted/For
DISCOVERIES (1)
369 CP Edward   15 /Your role was to be one of Lavinia's discoveries;/Celia's, to provide society and
DISCOVERS (1)
416 CP   Celia   32 an imaginary playmate/And suddenly discovers he is only a child/Lost in a forest,
DISCOVERY (5)
314 FR Warburt   24 I used to dream of making some great discovery/To do away with one disease or
393 CP Lavinia   4   hours./{L} Yes, a very important discovery,/Finding that you've spent five years
407 CP   Reilly   39 to make me believe that it was this discovery/Precipitated what you called your
487 CC Lady E   17   /{LE} I've just made a startling discovery!/All through a name — and intuition./
510 CC Eggers   34   confirmation/Of this interesting discovery, Mr. Kaghan,/By putting your
DISCREDITABLE (1)
571 ES Ld Clav   25 hold of those who know/Something discreditable, dishonourable .../{M} Then,
DISCREDITED (1)
155 Rock 3   62   of human greatness thoroughly discredited,/Binding the earth and the water to
DISCREET (1)
297 FR Charles   11 with Harry ten years, he's absolutely discreet./He was with them on the boat. He
DISCRETION (2)
505 CC Claude   12   /He's the very soul of tact and discretion./{MG} Certainly, Sir Claude, if that is
541 ES Gomez   11 you./Rely upon me as the soul of discretion./{LC} What do you want then? Do
DISCUSS (5)
 19 Portrait   38   trance,/Admire the monuments,/Discuss the late events,/Correct our watches by
 89 Ash-Wed 1   28 matters that with myself I too much discuss/Too much explain/Because I do not
290 FR   Amy   17 contrive his future happiness./Do not discuss his absence. Please behave only/As if
405 CP Edward   11 unprofessional conduct —/I will not discuss my case before another patient./{R} On
481 CC Lucasta   13 Lucasta. {}/[*rising*]./{L} If you want to discuss *me* ... {}/[*A knock at the door. Enter*
DISCUSSED (4)
405 CP   Reilly   13   is the only way/In which it can be discussed. You have told me nothing./You have
462 CC Claude   30   left you alone,/And so far we've discussed only current business,/Thinking that
574 ES Ld Clav   29 why./{LC} And I learn that you have discussed your problems/With Mrs. Carghill
577 ES Gomez   22 .../{G} As two men of the world, we discussed things very frankly;/And I can tell
DISCUSSION (5)
407 CP   Reilly   5 /{R} May I interrupt this interesting discussion?/I say you are both too ill. There are
447 CC Claude   9 wanting to retire,/As we had some discussion about replacing you./But you know
496 CC Claude   3 interests/Were much too deep for discussion with *me*:/Health cures. And modern
505 CC Eggers   17 take it, Sir Claude, I should open the discussion?/{SC} If you please, Eggerson./{E}
565 ES Ld Clav   4 But Michael and I/Must continue our discussion. This afternoon, Michael./{M} No, I
DISEASE (5)
181 FQ: ECoker 154 the fever chart./Our only health is the disease/If we obey the dying nurse/Whose
189 FQ: DrySal 191   haruspicate or scry,/Observe disease in signatures, evoke/Biography from the
250 MC Thomas   14   disorder,/Make it fast, breed fatal disease,/Degrade what they exalt. Power with
257 MC Chorus   10 extortion and violence,/Destitution, disease,/The old without fire in winter,/The
314 FR Warburt   25 great discovery/To do away with one disease or another./Now I've had forty years'
DISEASED (2)
162 Rock 8   23   /Many came back well broken,/Diseased and beggared, finding/A stranger at
295 FR   Harry   24 my conscience,/Not my mind, that is diseased, but the world I have to live in./— I lay

DISEASES (2)
339 FR   Harry   12 /The lesson of ignorance, of incurable diseases./Such things are possible. It is love and
434 CP   Alex   2   /Where there are various endemic diseases/Besides, of course, those brought by
DISEMBARK (1)
188 FQ: DrySal 153 harbour/Receding, or those who will disembark./Here between the hither and the
DISFIGURED (1)
195 FQ: Little   149 dancer.'/The day was breaking. In the disfigured street/He left me, with a kind of
DISGRACED (1)
 43 Swee Erect   34   corridor/Find themselves involved, disgraced,/Call witness to their principles/And
DISGUISE (2)
148 Rock 1   63 thing does not change./However you disguise it, this thing does not change:/The
420 CP   Reilly 28   in their minds./Each unable to disguise his own meanness/From himself,
DISGUISES (2)
 84 Hollow Men   32   /Let me also wear/Such deliberate disguises/Rat's coat, crowskin, crossed staves/In
421 CP   Julia   6 costumes/Or huddle quickly into new disguises,/They have, for the first time,
DISH (4)
235 Ad-dress   55 little token of esteem/Is needed, like a dish of cream;/And you might now and then
258 MC Thomas   25   /While I ate out of the King's dish/To become servant of God was never my
270 MC Chorus   9 fish./I have smelt/Corruption in the dish, incense in the latrine, the sewer in the
372 CP   Alex   23   in Montenegro/Who can have the dish that you'll be eating, nowadays./{E} But
DISHES (1)
368 CP   Alex   27   dried fish/I can make half a dozen dishes. Don't say a word./I shall begin at once.
DISHONEST (1)
418 CP   Celia 13 it./In fact, I think it would really be dishonest/For me, now, to try to make a life
DISHONOUR (1)
162 Rock 8   28 well at Acre./And in spite of all the dishonour,/The broken standards, the broken
DISHONOURABLE (2)
405 CP Edward 29 to meet *you*, Lavinia./I call this a very dishonourable trick./{R} Honesty before
571 ES Ld Clav 25 who know/Something discreditable, dishonourable .../{M} Then, Father, you should
DISHONOURED (1)
 57 Swee Night   40 liquid siftings fall/To stain the stiff dishonoured shroud./The Waste Land/The
DISILLUSION (1)
417 CP   Reilly   2 feel guilty at not having found it?/{R} Disillusion can become itself an illusion/If we
DISILLUSIONMENT (1)
516 CC Claude 34 other./We have undergone the same disillusionment:/I want us to make the best of it,
DISINFECTANT (1)
335 FR Agatha 20   hospital/Pervaded by a smell of disinfectant,/Looking straight ahead, passing
DISINTERESTED (4)
277 MC Knight3   3   think of it, we have been perfectly disinterested. [*The other*/KNIGHTS: 'Hear!
277 MC Knight3 26 least the credit for being completely disinterested in this business./I think that is
277 MC Knight1 30 is this: that we have been completely disinterested. But/our act itself needs more
372 CP   Peter   6 she would listen to you/As someone disinterested./{E} Well, I will see Celia./{P}
DISLIKE (1)
340 FR Agatha   9 in a women's college,/Trying not to dislike women. Thirty years in which to think./
DISLIKED (1)
484 CC Lady E   8   exactly how you felt./How I disliked my parents! I had a governess;/Several,
DISMAL (1)
242 MC Priest2 32 enough of waiting, from December to dismal December./The Archbishop shall be at
DISMAY (2)
242 MC Priest2 33   shall be at our head, dispelling dismay and doubt./He will tell us what we are
583 ES Monica 25 cannot appal me,/Not even death can dismay or amaze me/Fixed in the certainty of
DISMAYED (1)
254 MC Tempt4 15 /Think, Thomas, think of enemies dismayed,/Creeping in penance, frightened of a
DISMISS (1)
401 CP   Reilly 33 that is so. But all in good time./Let us dismiss that question for the moment./Tell me
DISMISSED (1)
401 CP Edward   6 you might be the same person:/But I dismissed that as just another symptom./Well, I
DISOBEY (1)
595 Grad 14   5 loth to say./But 'tis a call we cannot disobey,/*Exeunt omnes*, with a last 'farewell'./
DISOBLIGING (1)
214 RTTugger   24 Tum Tugger is a curious beast:/His disobliging ways are a matter of habit./If you
DISORDER (1)
250 MC Thomas 13 /In confident ignorance, but arrest disorder,/Make it fast, breed fatal disease,/
DISORDERED (1)
107 Animula   30 spectre in its own gloom,/Leaving disordered papers in a dusty room;/Living first

DISORDERLY (1)
211 Old Gumbie   33   /So she's formed, from that lot of disorderly louts,/A troop of well-disciplined
DISOWNED (1)
161 Rock 7   30   or Race, or Dialectic./The Church disowned, the tower overthrown, the bells
DISOWNING (1)
186 FQ: DrySal   91   in the popular mind, a means of disowning the past./The moments of happiness
DISPELLED (1)
243 MC Priest2   4   Archbishop returns/Our doubts are dispelled. Let us therefore rejoice,/I say rejoice,
DISPELLING (1)
242 MC Priest2   33 /The Archbishop shall be at our head, dispelling dismay and doubt./He will tell us
DISPELS (1)
604 Ode   3   shadow we wait, while thy presence dispels/Our vain hesitations and fears./And we
DISPENSATION (1)
104 Journ Magi   41 /But no longer at ease here, in the old dispensation,/With an alien people clutching
DISPENSED (1)
38 Gerontion   42   weak hands, what's thought can be dispensed with/Till the refusal propagates a
DISPENSING (1)
249 MC Tempt2   7 Rule for the good of the better cause,/Dispensing justice make all even,/Is thrive on
DISPERSE (1)
280 MC Knight1   2   be/said; and I suggest that you now disperse quietly to your homes./Please be
DISPERSED (1)
152 Rock 2   44 of Christ incarnate./And now you live dispersed on ribbon roads,/And no man knows
DISPLACES (1)
603 Spleen   4   conscious graces/In repetition that displaces/Your mental self-possession/By this
DISPLAY (1)
42 Swee Erect   5   by the snarled and yelping seas./Display me Aeolus above/Reviewing the
DISPLAYED (2)
64 WL: Chess   97 swam./Above the antique mantel was displayed/As though a window gave upon the
281 MC Chorus   7   praise Thee, O God, for Thy glory displayed in all the creatures of the earth,/In the
DISPLEASING (1)
111 Xmas Trees   24   may be tainted with a self-conceit/Displeasing to God and disrespectful to the
DISPOSAL (2)
531 ES Charles   8   will long continue/To be at the disposal of the Government in power'./And the
541 ES Gomez   27 /My entire resources are at your disposal./You were a generous friend to me
DISPOSE (3)
411 CP   Reilly 27   those telegrams?/{R} I think I will dispose of your husband's problem. {}/[*To*
498 CC   Claude   31 Mrs. Guzzard's sister./She wouldn't dispose of *him*. It's your child, Elizabeth,/
508 CC   Eggers   24   ended./{E} And how did you dispose of him?/{MG} We had neighbours/Who
DISPOSED (5)
182 FQ: ECoker   180 or the way in which/One is no longer disposed to say it. And so each venture/Is a new
212 Growltiger   24   on the tide —/And Growltiger was disposed to show his sentimental side./His
213 Growltiger   35   enraptured by his manly baritone,/Disposed to relaxation, and awaiting no
220 Old Deut   24 /Deuteronomy's rest when he feels so disposed/Or when he's engaged in domestic
976 MC Knight1   2 /moments. We know that you may be disposed to judge unfavourably/of our action.
DISPOSSESSION (2)
181 FQ: ECoker   143 possess/You must go by the way of dispossession./In order to arrive at what you are
331 FR Agatha   21 had to fight for many years to win my dispossession,/And many years to keep it. What
DISPUTE (1)
268 MC Knight2   1   /Made a pact of peace, and all dispute ended/Sent you back to your See as you
DISPUTED (1)
491 CC   Colby   27 known the feelings of a son,/To be disputed between two parents./But, if we
DISPUTES (1)
241 MC Priest2   23   the anvil?/{P2} Tell us,/Are the old disputes at an end, is the wall of pride cast
DISREGARD (1)
111 Xmas Trees   2 Christmas,/Some of which we may disregard:/The social, the torpid, the patently
DISRESPECTFUL (1)
111 Xmas Trees   24 a self-conceit/Displeasing to God and disrespectful to the children/(And here I
DISSATISFACTION (1)
545 ES Ld Clav   1   known/That I didn't enjoy it. Some dissatisfaction/With myself, I suspect, very deep
DISSATISFIED (1)
408 CP   Reilly 40   came to me two months ago/I was dissatisfied with your explanation/Of your
DISSECT (1)
189 FQ: DrySal   196   pentagrams/Or barbituric acids, or dissect/The recurrent image into pre-conscious
DISSEMBLED (1)
91 Ash-Wed 2   11   with brightness. And I who am here dissembled/Proffer my deeds to oblivion, and

DISSENSION (1)
267 MC Knight1 28 /They are too well known. But after dissension/Had ended, in France, and you were
DISSOLUTION (1)
308 FR Harry 36 too, in the nightly panic/Of dreaming dissolution. You do not know,/You cannot
DISSOLVE (4)
24 Rhapsody 5 /Whispering lunar incantations/Dissolve the floors of memory/And all its clear
270 MC Chorus 2 spawn in my bowels, and my bowels dissolve in the light of dawn. I have smelt/Death
272 MC Chorus 20 the human, they shrink and dissolve/Into dust on the wind, forgotten,
403 CP Edward 32 I thought she had left me, I began to dissolve,/To cease to exist. That was what she
DISSOLVED (1)
109 Marina 16 and the woodsong fog/By this grace dissolved in place/What is this face, less clear
DISSOLVING (2)
311 FR Harry 7 potent than ever before, a vapour dissolving/All other worlds, and me into it. O
335 FR Harry 15 contagion of putrescent embraces/On dissolving bone. In and out, the movement/
DISTANCE (8)
44 Cook Egg 2 /Pipit sate upright in her chair/Some distance from where I was sitting;/*Views of*
148 Rock 1 38 /Silence! and preserve respectful distance./For I perceive approaching/The Rock.
272 MC m 11 *Iræ is sung in Latin by a choir in the distance*]./{C} Numb the hand and dry the eyelid,
281 MC m 7 *Deum is sung in Latin by a choir in the distance*]./{C} We praise Thee, O God, for Thy
309 FR Harry 31 someone who comes from a very long distance,/Or the distant waterfall in the forest,/
310 FR Harry 32 someone who had come from a long distance./Whether I know what I am saying, or
327 FR Violet 36 /You know as well as I do, at this distance from London/Nobody's likely to have
335 FR Agatha 2 on the rose-garden:/And heard in the distance tiny voices/And then a black raven flew
DISTANT (13)
72 WL: Thund 327 /Of thunder of spring over distant mountains/He who was living is now
74 WL: Thund 397 while the black clouds/Gathered far distant, over Himavant./The jungle crouched,
84 Hollow Men 27 voices are/In the wind's singing/More distant and more solemn/Than a fading star./
109 Marina 19 and stronger —/Given or lent? more distant than stars and nearer than the eye/
180 FQ: ECoker 117 know that the hills and the trees, the distant panorama/And the bold imposing
185 FQ: DrySal 32 of wave that breaks on water,/The distant rote in the granite teeth,/And the wailing
194 FQ: Little 127 revisit/When I left my body on a distant shore./Since our concern was speech,
593 Grad 5 4 hold in store,/Or what great deeds the distant years may see,/What conquest over pain
593 Grad 8 1 flag is raised on high./Sometime in distant years when we are grown,/Gray-haired
593 Grad 8 5 we have been or done/Or to what distant lands we may have gone,/Through all
594 Grad 12 6 far and near/To spread thy name o'er distant lands and seas!/As thou to thy departing
309 FR Harry 32 from a very long distance,/Or the distant waterfall in the forest,/Inaccessible,
542 ES Gomez 34 you,/The ambiguous smile, the distant salutation,/The sudden silence when you
DISTEMPERED (1)
181 FQ: ECoker 150 plies the steel/That questions the distempered part;/Beneath the bleeding hands
DISTENDED (1)
311 FR Harry 19 before sleep/I always see their claws distended/Quietly, as if they had never stirred./
DISTIL (1)
53 Whispers 27 jaguar/Does not in its arboreal gloom/Distil so rank a feline smell/As Grishkin in a
DISTINCTION (1)
409 CP Reilly 36 /That he was aiming at a higher social distinction/Than the honour conferred by being
DISTINCTLY (2)
588 Fable 63 grape juice./The lights began to burn distinctly blue,/As in ghost stories lights most
457 CC note 16& 25 *off stage are not intended to be heard distinctly by an audience in the theatre.*/{LE} Just
DISTINGUISHED (3)
180 FQ: ECoker 106 of art, the statesmen and the rulers,/Distinguished civil servants, chairmen of many
279 MC Knight1 9 Brito, coming as he does of a family distinguished for its/loyalty to the Church, will
546 ES Piggott 7 And my husband/Was a distinguished surgeon. Do you know, I fell in
DISTORTED (1)
575 ES Gomez 21 facts from me/Before he heard your distorted version./But, Dick, I was nettled by
DISTRACT (1)
272 MC Chorus 31 no tones,/No colours, no forms to distract, to divert the soul/From seeing itself,
DISTRACTED (3)
38 Gerontion 37 now/She gives when our attention is distracted/And what she gives, gives with such
158 Rock 5 8 books; being too vain and distracted for silence: seeking every one after his
174 FQ: BurntN 104 /Over the strained time-ridden faces/Distracted from distraction by distraction/Filled
DISTRACTION (6)
92 Ash-Wed 3 19 mouth blown,/Lilac and brown hair;/Distraction, music of the flute, stops and steps
167 Rock 10 38 is long for work or play./We tire of distraction or concentration, we sleep and are
174 FQ: BurntN 104 time-ridden faces/Distracted from distraction by distraction/Filled with fancies
174 FQ: BurntN 104 faces/Distracted from distraction by distraction/Filled with fancies and empty of

190 FQ: DrySal 212   the moment in and out of time,/The distraction fit, lost in a shaft of sunlight,/The
272 MC Chorus 29   men can no longer turn the mind/To distraction, delusion, escape into dream,
DISTRAIT (1)
579 ES Carghil 16   to me, Richard?/You look very *distrait*. You ought to be excited!/{LC} Is this
DISTRESS (4)
 33 Conv Gal   5   aloft/To light poor travellers to their distress.'/She then: 'How you digress!'/And I
189 FQ: DrySal 201   of them especially/When there is distress of nations and perplexity/Whether on
408 CP   Reilly   5   to mention that the cause of your distress/Was the defection of your lover — who
541 ES Gomez 37   intrusion/Of the visitor in financial distress./Well, I shan't keep you long, though I
DISTRESSED (3)
 91 Ash-Wed 2   26   saying/Lady of silences/Calm and distressed/Torn and most whole/Rose of
460 CC   Lady E 15   To engage Mr. Colby. I really am distressed!/This is not the first sign that I've
555 ES Monica 14   to know better. But I'm all the more distressed/Because I have some ... not very good
DISTRICT (1)
326 FR   Violet   4   in Chiswick, I think./Anyway, the district was unfamiliar/And I had the greatest
DISTRICTS (2)
147 Rock 1   31   and read the papers./In industrial districts, there I was told/Of economic laws./In
193 FQ: Little   87   no other sound was/Between three districts whence the smoke arose/I met one
DISTRUST (1)
154 Rock 3   10 I have given you hearts, for reciprocal distrust./I have given you power of choice, and
DISTRUSTED (1)
304 FR Agatha 35   was sorry for her;/I could see that she distrusted me — she was frightened of the
DISTURB (7)
 14 Prufrock   46   arms and legs are thin!')/Do I dare/Disturb the universe?/In a minute there is time/
220 Old Deut   23   that nothing untoward may chance to disturb/Deuteronomy's rest when he feels so
599 On a Port   10   /No meditations glad or ominous/Disturb her lips, or move the slender hands;/
320 FR Warburt 22   is most essential/That nothing should disturb or excite her./{H} Well!/{W} I'm very
322 FR   Winch\ 26   /Rather than phone and perhaps disturb her Ladyship./So I slipped along on my
368 CP   Alex 19   Peter can go on talking/And I shan't disturb you./{E} My dear Alex,/There'll be
436 CP Lavinia 23   the way in which she died did not disturb you/Or the fact that she died because
DISTURBANCE (3)
152 Rock 2   46 Unless his neighbour makes too much disturbance,/But all dash to and fro in motor
178 FQ: ECoker   53   is the late November doing/With the disturbance of the spring/And creatures of the
240 MC Chorus   5   to pass unobserved./Now I fear disturbance of the quiet seasons:/Winter shall
DISTURBED (4)
 63 WL: Burial   73   this year?/'Or has the sudden frost disturbed its bed?/'O keep the Dog far hence,
166 Rock 10   4   hill/In a world confused and dark and disturbed by portents of fear./And what shall
366 CP Edward 28   you, Edward./{E} I seem to have been disturbed already;/And I did rather want to be
555 ES Piggott   6   of course — that you should not be disturbed./Well, she's gone now. If she bothers
DISTURBING (5)
171 FQ: BurntN 17   in your mind./But to what purpose/Disturbing the dust on a bowl of rose-leaves/I
366 CP   Peter 27   much. {}/[*Exit*]/{P} I hope I'm not disturbing you, Edward./{E} I seem to have
409 CP   Reilly 21   that they are incapable of loving/Is as disturbing to their self-esteem/As, in cruder
463 CC   Colby 16   Yet at the same time/It's rather disturbing. I don't mean the work:/I mean,
548 ES Carghil 14   /[*after a pause*]./{MC} I hope I'm not disturbing you. I always sit here./It's the
DISTURBS (1)
331 FR Agatha 25   /Organisation, which your question disturbs./{H} When I know, I know that in
DITCH (1)
257 MC Chorus   3   at night, and yet be drowned in a ditch./{3P} A man may climb the stair in the
DITCHED (1)
414 CP   Celia   3 illusion/In the ordinary way, or being ditched./Of course that's something that's
DITCHES (2)
191 FQ: Little   5 brief sun flames the ice, on pond and ditches,/In windless cold that is the heart's heat,
247 MC Templ1 10   as sweet as blossoms. Ice along the ditches/Mirror the sunlight. Love in the orchard
DIVAN (2)
 68 WL: Fire S 226 touched by the sun's last rays,/On the divan are piled (at night her bed)/Stockings,
 69 WL: Fire S 244 foresuffered all/Enacted on this same divan or bed;/I who have sat by Thebes below
DIVERGENT (1)
578 ES Ld Clav 11   both misunderstood you/In our divergent ways. When I think of your
DIVERS (1)
 47 Mél Adult   14   /J'erre toujours de-ci de-là/A divers coups de tra là là/De Damas jusqu'à
DIVERSION (2)
380 CP   Celia   7   /Had taken them only as a passing diversion./Oh, I dare say that you deceived
380 CP Edward 10   /{E} I *didn't* take you as a passing diversion!/If you want to speak of passing

DIVERSIONS (1)
380 CP Edward 11   /If you want to speak of passing diversions/How did you take Peter?/{C} Peter?
DIVERT (2)
272 MC Chorus 31   /No colours, no forms to distract, to divert the soul/From seeing itself, foully united
349 FR Mary   18   It cannot be diverted/An attempt to divert it/Only implicates others/At the day of
DIVERTED (2)
316 FR Agatha 21   time/And the eye of the night time/Be diverted from this house/Till the knot is
349 FR Mary   17   it cannot be delayed/{M} It cannot be diverted/An attempt to divert it/Only implicates
DIVIDE (1)
92 Ash-Wed 2   53   desert. This is the land which ye/Shall divide by lot. And neither division nor unity/
DIVIDED (6)
37 Gerontion   22   flowering judas,/To be eaten, to be divided, to be drunk/Among whispers; by Mr.
195 FQ: Little 176   genius,/United in the strife which divided them;/If I think of a king at nightfall,/
241 MC Priest2 24   is the wall of pride cast down/That divided them? Is it peace or war?/{P1} Does he
278 MC Knight2 8 /Stephen, the kingdom was very much divided. Our King saw that/the one thing
397 CP Lavinia 33   not try to press you./You're much too divided to know what you want./But, being
397 CP Lavinia 34   to know what you want./But, being divided, you will tend to compromise,/And your
DIVIDENDS (3)
49 Hippopot   12   need never stir/To gather in its dividends./The 'potamus can never reach/The
148 Rock 1   56   to invest their money/But most expect dividends./I say to you: *Make perfect your will.*/
286 FR Gerald 19   from heaven knows where —/{G} Dividends from aeroplane shares./{V} They
DIVIDING (1)
155 Rock 3   65   seas and developing the mountains,/Dividing the stars into common and preferred,/
DIVINATION (1)
348 FR Chorus 20   /And minor forms of sorcery,/Divination and chiromancy,/Specifics against
DIVINE (3)
590 Time Space 16   days of love be few/Yet let them be divine./Song/If space and time, as sages say,/
590 Space Time 16   flowers of life be few/Yet let them be divine./Standing upon the shore of all we know/
272 MC Priests 1   /You must not be absent from the divine office. To vespers./Into the Cathedral!/
DIVISION (3)
92 Ash-Wed 2   53   ye/Shall divide by lot. And neither division nor unity/Matters. This is the land. We
133 Eyes   2   /Eyes that last I saw in tears/Through division/Here in death's dream kingdom/The
227 Macavity   34   Or engaged in doing complicated long division sums./Macavity, Macavity, there's no
DIVISIONS (1)
24 Rhapsody   7   memory/And all its clear relations,/Its divisions and precisions./Every street lamp that
DIVORCE (3)
374 CP Celia   27   I accepted the situation/Because a divorce would ruin your career;/And we
560 ES Michael 27   breach of promise suit/Or somebody's divorce. No, you needn't worry/About that girl
572 ES Ld Clav 24   been unhappy, might have come to divorce;/But she hasn't forgotten or forgiven
DIVORCED (1)
375 CP Celia   1   husband must always be the one to be divorced?/And if she chooses to give *you* the
DIX (1)
51 Restaurant   24   expériences comme moi?/Tiens, voilà dix sous, pour la salle-de-bains./Phlébas, le
DO (547)
DOCK (1)
213 Growltiger 55   whole at Brentford, and at Victoria Dock,/And a day of celebration was
DOCKAGE (1)
186 FQ: DrySal 78   drawing their money, drying sails at dockage;/Not as making a trip that will be
DOCTOR (33)
116 SP Dusty   28   /Well I *hope* we shan't have to call a doctor/Doris just hates having a doctor/She
116 SP Dusty   29   call a doctor/Doris just hates having a doctor/She says will you ring up on Monday/
295 FR Harry   4   were extremely sympathetic/And the doctor very attentive./That night I slept heavily,
296 FR Violet 17   thing to be done:/Harry must see a doctor./{I} But I understand —/I have heard of
297 FR Amy   9   /{A} Very well./I will ring up the doctor myself. {}/[*Exit*]/{C} Meanwhile, I have
314 FR Ivy   31   must have had a very rich experience, Doctor,/In forty years./{W} Indeed, yes./Even in
315 FR Amy   24   before we finish. Will you take me in, Doctor?/I think we are very much the oldest
316 FR Violet   6   of Gerald and Charles and that doctor, that gets on my nerves./{C} If the matter
321 FR Winch   24   evening, my Lord. Good evening, Doctor./Many happy ... Oh, I'm sorry, my
321 FR Harry   28   *him by the shoulders*]/{H} He *is* real, Doctor./So let us resume the conversation. You,
323 FR Winch   8   sorry, my Lady, but I've just told the doctor,/It's really nothing but a minor accident.
323 FR Warburt 29   forbid it, Lady Monchensey./As your doctor, I forbid you to leave the house tonight./
327 FR Harry   14   of Dr. Warburton —/Or any other doctor, who would be another Warburton,/If
327 FR Harry   15   /If you decided to set another doctor on me./But this is too real for your
362 CP Reilly 36   operation./In consultation with the doctor and the surgeon,/In going to bed in the
378 CP Celia   39   you promise me to see a very great doctor/Whom I have heard of — and his name

379 CP	Edward	2	someone greater than the greatest doctor/To cure *this* illness./{C} Edward, if I go
397 CP	Lavinia	17	that!/{L} I must say it./I know ... of a doctor who I think could help you./{E} If I go
397 CP	Edward	18	think could help you./{E} If I go to a doctor, I shall make my own choice;/Not take
397 CP	Edward	21	*your* point of view? But I don't need a doctor./I am simply in hell. Where there are no
398 CP	Lavinia	13	/And as I can't persuade you to see a doctor,/There's nothing else at present that I
400 CP	Alex	14	of person/Who would know the right doctor, as well as the right shops./Besides, he
400 CP	Alex	15	/Besides, he was ready to consult any doctor/Recommended by anyone except his
402 CP	Edward	12	very ill?/{E} I should have thought a doctor could see that for himself./Or at least
402 CP	Edward	15	the same words, that I ought to see a doctor./They said — again, in almost the same
402 CP	Edward	19	saw it/I should have thought that a doctor could see it./{R} 'Nervous breakdown' is
458 CC	Eggers	29	medical orders, Lady Elizabeth:/The doctor made it very imperative .../{SC} Mr.
460 CC	Lady E	1	'Come to Zürich!/There's a wonderful doctor who teaches mind control.'/So on I went
460 CC	Claude	4	to Zürich./But I thought that the doctor in Lausanne taught mind control?/{LE}
460 CC	Claude	37	isn't it!/{SC} If this is what the doctor in Zürich has done for her,/I give him
550 ES	Carghil	26	for?/{MC} Well, Richard, my doctor could hardly have sent me *here*/If I
563 ES	Gomez	10	here for a rest cure. I persuaded my doctor/That I was in need of a rest cure too./
563 ES	Gomez	13	come to Badgley Court/I said to my doctor, 'Well, what about it?/What better

DOCTOR'S (1)

580 ES	Carghil	19	I'm going out to Australia,/On my doctor's advice. And on my way back/Señor

DOCTORS (8)

397 CP	Edward	22	am simply in hell. Where there are no doctors —/At least, not in a professional
529 ES	Monica	25	book!/You know what the doctors said: complete relaxation/And to think
530 ES	Ld Clav	10	you know it./They talk of rest, these doctors, Charles; they tell me to be cautious,/To
539 ES	Ld Clav	4	that I retired at the insistence of my doctors./{G} Oh yes, the usual euphemism./And
542 ES	Gomez	7	sent direct to you from Cuba/If your doctors allow you a smoke now and then./I'm a
546 ES	Piggott	25	—/We make that stipulation to all the doctors/Who send people here. When you go in
556 ES	Monica	2	I've made him understand/That the doctors want you to be free from worry./He
564 ES	Monica	38	rest now./— I must explain that the doctors were very insistent/That my father

DOCTORS' (1)

565 ES	Gomez	25	{G} Well, Dick, we've got to obey our doctors' orders./But while we're here, we must

DOCTRINE (1)

483 CC	Lady E	33	in it./I did, for a time. I studied the doctrine./But I was going to say, *if* I believed in

DOCUMENTS (3)

68 WL:	Fire S	211	pocket full of currants/C.i.f. London: documents at sight,/Asked me in demotic
266 MC	Thomas	6	will find/The papers in order, and the documents signed. {}/[*To* KNIGHTS]./{T} You
513 CC	Colby	29	could get to know/Only by report, by documents —/The story of his life, of his

DODGING (2)

142 Cape Ann		7	the note of the quail, the bob-white/Dodging by bay-bush. Follow the feet/Of the
158 Rock 5		8	every one after his own elevation, and dodging his emptiness./If humility and purity be

DOES (75)

33 Conv Gal		11	forth our own vacuity.'/She then: 'Does this refer to me?'/'Oh no, it is I who am
43 Swee Erect		40	/Mrs. Turner intimates/It does the house no sort of good./But Doris,
52 Whispers		26	/The sleek Brazilian jaguar/Does not in its arboreal gloom/Distil so rank a
148 Rock 1		35	is only fit for picnics./And the Church does not seem to be wanted/In country or in
148 Rock 1		61	and the world changes,/But one thing does not change./In all of my years, one thing
148 Rock 1		62	change./In all of my years, one thing does not change./However you disguise it, this
148 Rock 1		63	/However you disguise it, this thing does not change:/The perpetual struggle of
152 Rock 2		49	the roads and settled nowhere./Nor does the family even move about together,/But
161 Rock 7		37	*pint of bitter*/*Ale*..../CHORUS:/What does the world say, does the whole world stray
161 Rock 7		37	/CHORUS:/What does the world say, does the whole world stray in high-powered cars
179 FQ:	ECoker	72	words and meanings. The poetry does not matter./It was not (to start again) what
183 FQ:	ECoker	205	ought to be explorers/Here and there does not matter/We must be still and still
590 Time Space		3	which cannot be,/The sun which does not feel decay/No greater is than we./So
240 MC	Priest2	28	the Archbishop left us./{P2} What does the Archbishop do, and our Sovereign
241 MC	Priest1	25	divided them? Is it peace or war?/{P1} Does he come/In full assurance, or only secure/
245 MC	Thomas	15	/And suffering is action. Neither does the agent suffer/Nor the patient act. But
250 MC	Tempt3	39	is plain./Endurance of friendship does not depend/Upon ourselves, but upon
251 MC	Tempt3	27	himself, fighting in Anjou./He does not understand us, the English barons./We
251 MC	Thomas	29	/We are the people./{T} To what does this lead?/{T3} To a happy coalition/Of
255 MC	Thomas	30	Is there no way, in my soul's sickness,/Does not lead to damnation in pride?/I well
255 MC	Tempt4	38	/And suffering action. Neither does the agent suffer/Nor the patient act. But
256 MC	Chorus	32	is it wind that pokes at the door?/{C} Does the torch flame in the hall, the candle in
256 MC	Priests	33	the hall, the candle in the room?/{3P} Does the watchman walk by the wall?/{4T}
256 MC	Tempts	34	the watchman walk by the wall?/{4T} Does the mastiff prowl by the gate?/{C} Death
260 MC	Thomas	21	the meaning of this word 'peace'. Does/it seem strange to you that the angels

260 MC	Thomas	24	with War and the fear of/War? Does it seem to you that the angelic voices were
263 MC	Chorus	1	of the Holy Ghost. Amen./Part II/{C} Does the bird sing in the South?/Only the
273 MC	Thomas	32	/You argue by results, as this world does,/To settle if an act be good or bad./You
277 MC	Knight3	11	for it. When you come to the/point, it does go against the grain to kill an Archbishop,
279 MC	Knight1	9	that/Richard Brito, coming as he does of a family distinguished for its/loyalty to
286 FR	Charles	22	clothes./{C} It's the cocktail-drinking does the harm:/There's nothing on earth so bad
287 FR	Gerald	6	itself:/It's Mary's generation. What does she think about it?/{M} Really, Cousin
287 FR	Amy	19	gone as I intended./Harry's return does not make things easy for her/At the
289 FR	Agatha	1	the loop in time comes — and it does not come for everybody —/The hidden is
297 FR	Amy	2	Warburton/It should be myself. What does Agatha think?/{Ag} It seems a necessary
304 FR	Mary	30	that sound awful? I know that it does./Did you ever meet her? What was she
310 FR	Harry	34	I am saying, or why I say it,/That does not matter. You bring me news/Of a door
334 FR	Agatha	13	not unhappy, just now?/{Ag} What does the word mean?/There's relief from a
339 FR	Harry	6	yet had the precise directions./Where does one go from a world of insanity?/
340 FR	Amy	22	father?/Dare you think what that does to one? Try to think of it./I *would* have
363 CP	Edward	9	with it?/{UG} Water./{E} To what does this lead?/{UG} To finding out/What you
381 CP	Edward	27	of knowing/That the misery does not feed on the ruin of loveliness,/That the
381 CP	Edward	36	the obstinate, the tougher self; who does not speak,/Who never talks, who cannot
400 CP	Reilly	10	his resistance. But what I mean is,/Does he trust your judgement?/{A} Yes,
403 CP	Reilly	14	mean to do harm — but the harm does not interest them./Or they do not see it, or
416 CP	Reilly	29	his dreams./{R} And this man. What does he now seem like, to you?/{C} Like a child
417 CP	Celia	13	/In the delight of loving. A state one does not know/When awake. But what, or
428 CP	Alex	34	there *is* any solution./But even this does not bring us to the heart of the matter./
430 CP	Peter	15	mind my looking in so early./It does seem ages since I last saw any of you!/And
433 CP	Lavinia	25	can tell them now, Alex./{L} What does Julia mean?/{A} I was about to speak of
438 CP	Reilly	9	Minotaur terrors./But that world does not take the place of this one./Do you
452 CC	Lucasta	27	has taken over my duties./{L} And does he know that I'm one of his duties?/Have
454 CC	Colby	27	But she has a good heart./{C} But does she address Sir Claude Mulhammer/As
454 CC	Eggers	29	/As Claude? To his face?/{E} She does indeed./{C} And does she call Lady
454 CC	Colby	30	face?/{E} She does indeed./{C} And does she call Lady Elizabeth *Lizzie*?/{E} Well,
454 CC	Eggers	32	/No, I don't think she would. But she does call her Lizzie,/Sometimes, to Sir Claude.
456 CC	Eggers	24	when you least expect it./But she does forget things. And she likes to travel,/
459 CC	Lady E	20	wrong colours, I'm sure. My husband/Does not understand the importance of colour/
459 CC	Lady E	22	Mr. Colby./Neither, I regret to say, does Eggerson./What colour have you chosen,
475 CC	Colby	3	And I want to understand *you*./Does one ever come to understand anyone?/{L}
476 CC	Colby	8	parents:/At least, I'm going to./{C} Does that matter, either?/{L} In one way, it
483 CC	Lady E	9	scheme really suited you./I believe it does. The walls; and the curtains;/And most of
490 CC	Colby	18	/I've only been thinking: 'What does it matter/Whose son I am?' You don't
498 CC	Eggers	6	/And that I could swear to./{E} It does seem unlikely/That there should be two
516 CC	Claude	27	described my own experience, exactly./Does that mean nothing to you, the experience
519 CC	Lady E	14	one should ask of other people,/One does make mistakes! But I mean to do better./
524 ES	Charles	21	Well, tease me if you like. But a man does feel a fool/If he takes you to a place where
533 ES	Gomez	36	pays many times over./I assure you it does./{LC} In other words/You have been
535 ES	Gomez	13	of trusting people/In general. What does that mean? One trusts a man/Or a woman
535 ES		m 21	Won't you help yourself? {}/[GOMEZ *does so, liberally*]/{G} And what about you?/{LC}
545 ES	Monica	11	you find life pleasant,/That it really does seem quiet here and restful./Even the
558 ES	Ld Clav	28	I stood it as long as I did./{LC} And does this bring us to the end of the list of your
577 ES	Gomez	24	got brains, he's got flair. When he does come back/He'll be able to buy you out
577 ES	Carghil	32	for business./I saw that, and so does Señor Gomez./He's simply been suffering,
581 ES	Ld Clav	1	/And when he comes back, if he does come back,/I know that you and Charles

DOESN'T (45)

215 RT	Tugger	32	and knowing,/The Rum Tum Tugger doesn't care for a cuddle;/But he'll leap on your
230 Bust	Jones	3	—/In fact, he's remarkably fat./He doesn't haunt pubs — he has eight or nine
232 Skimble		26	are thinking/And it's certain that he doesn't approve/Of hilarity and riot, so the folk
289 FR	Gerald	7	him feel that what has happened doesn't matter./He's taken his medicine, I've no
299 FR	Charles	1	a little worried about his health./He doesn't seem to be ... quite himself./{Do} Quite
304 FR	Mary	30	it — had killed her by willing./Doesn't that sound awful? I know that it does./
309 FR	Mary	17	/But I see something now which doesn't come from tutors/Or from books, or
314 FR	Warburt	8	deal, Harry./A country practitioner doesn't get younger./It takes me back longer
321 FR	Winch	34	last, my Lord. But a country sergeant/Doesn't get younger. Thank you, no, my Lord;/
322 FR	Winch	35	have the driver up for this:/Says he doesn't know this part of the country/And
355 CP	Celia	15	/{C} There isn't much that Julia doesn't know./{P} Go on with the story about
370 CP	Peter	21	picture —/Like a film effect. She doesn't want to see me;/Makes excuses, not very
373 CP	Edward	4	in? ... How long ago? .../No, it doesn't matter. {}/CURTAIN/Act One. Scene 2/
374 CP	Celia	22	something better, for Julia;/But it doesn't really matter. They will know soon

374 CP	Celia	23	matter. They will know soon enough./Doesn't that settle all our difficulties?/{E} It has
395 CP	Edward	17	found it a change for the better./But doesn't it occur to you that possibly/I may have
400 CP	Reilly	27	/{A} Not to escape from her?/{R} He doesn't want to escape from her./{A} He is
406 CP	Edward	2	I don't know — I mean to say,/That doesn't concern you./{L} In that case, Edward,/I
438 CP	Lavinia	26	I knew what you were thinking!/Doesn't it help you, that I feel guilty too?/{R} If
449 CC	Claude	28	much notice of Miss Angel./She just doesn't see her. And Miss Angel/Will soon be
450 CC	Claude	13	my wife./{SC} And just as much/She doesn't know about you. And just as much/You
462 CC	Colby	21	delusions/In the right direction./{C} It doesn't seem quite honest./If we all have to live
471 CC	Colby	26	was I trying to give?/{C} That doesn't really matter. But, for some reason,/
473 CC	Colby	34	sense that I retire to mine./But he doesn't feel alone there. And when he comes out
475 CC	Lucasta	37	told me anything about you;/He doesn't tell me much. And as for B. —/I'd much
479 CC	Lucasta	7	he's got to have protection./{L} Colby doesn't need your protection racket/So far as
480 CC	Kaghan	26	/And respectability! Now Colby/Doesn't really care about being respectable —/
480 CC	Kaghan	34	one thing I like about Lucasta:/She doesn't despise me./{L} Nobody could despise
482 CC	Lady E	33	I knew nothing about you,/But one doesn't need to know, if one knows what
487 CC	Lady E	24	be a coincidence./It seems incredible, doesn't it, Claude?/And yet it would be still
490 CC	Lady E	8	I'm sure it didn't./{LE} Oh, Colby, doesn't your instinct tell you?/{SC} Yes, tell us
490 CC	Colby	24	/I am sorry. But that's why I say it doesn't matter/To me, which of you should be
496 CC	Lady E	10	doubt, from the dervish rituals./But it doesn't matter what Mrs. Guzzard tells us,/If it
496 CC	Eggers	25	the contact with London,/Though she doesn't admit it. She misses my news/When I
497 CC	Claude	31	/I have asked Mrs. Guzzard here. *She* doesn't know that./{E} A natural line for Mr.
500 CC	Lucasta	27	—/Something that he needs. Colby doesn't need me,/He doesn't need anyone. He's
500 CC	Lucasta	28	he needs. Colby doesn't need me,/He doesn't need anyone. He's fascinating,/But he's
500 CC	Lucasta	32	when you needed him most!/And he doesn't depend upon other people, either./B.
509 CC	Claude	27	has to sign his full name./But he doesn't like the name, for some reason;/So we
513 CC	Colby	15	wished to know the truth./What it is, doesn't matter. All I wanted was relief/From the
513 CC	Colby	17	of knowing there's a fact/That one doesn't know. But the fact itself/Is unimportant,
516 CC	Colby	8	mean?/{C} I want to be an organist./It doesn't matter about success —/I aimed too
525 ES	Monica	23	already./And besides, my father doesn't amble./You're not at all respectful./{C} I
550 ES	Carghil	35	—/What a clever girl she was! — 'he doesn't understand women./Any woman who
551 ES	Carghil	1	women/He has loved. But a woman doesn't want to forget/A single one of her

DOG (18)

56 Swee Night	9	hornèd gate./Gloomy Orion and the Dog/Are veiled; and hushed the shrunken seas;/
63 WL: Burial	74	frost disturbed its bed?/'O keep the Dog far hence, that's friend to men,/'Or with his
109 Marina	6	/Those who sharpen the tooth of the dog, meaning/Death/Those who glitter with the
135 5FingerEx2	6	rattled, muttered endlessly./Little dog was safe and warm/Under a cretonne
135 5FingerEx2	13	come to dust./Here a little dog I pause/Heaving up my prior paws,/Pause,
159 Rock 6	16	/You polish the tooth of the dog and the talon of the cat./Why should men
222 Pekes Pols	14	for a Pol or a Peke)./The big Police Dog was away from his beat —/I don't know
222 Pekes Pols	26	say what they please,/Is no British Dog, but a Heathen Chinese./And so all the
223 Pekes Pols	33	what Pollicles like,/For your Pollicle Dog is a dour Yorkshire tyke,/And his braw
223 Pekes Pols	60	like sheep./*And when the Police Dog returned to his beat,/There wasn't a single*
234 Ad-dress	19	I'll jog,/And say: A CAT IS NOT A DOG./Now Dogs pretend they like to fight;/
234 Ad-dress	22	bark, more seldom bite;/But yet a Dog is, on the whole,/What you would call a
234 Ad-dress	26	fantastic canine freaks./The usual Dog about the Town/Is much inclined to play
235 Ad-dress	37	I must remind you that/A Dog's a Dog — A CAT'S A CAT./With Cats, some say,
250 MC Tempt3	27	I am no courtier./I know a horse, a dog, a wench;/I know how to hold my estates in
276 MC Knight1	22	/sympathies are all with the under dog. I respect such feelings, I/share them.
277 MC Knight2	37	sympathies are always with the under dog./It is the English spirit of fair play. Now the
277 MC Knight2	40	been/presented as the under dog. But is this really the case? I am going/to

DOG'S (1)

| 235 Ad-dress | 37 | /Again I must remind you that/A Dog's a Dog — A CAT'S A CAT./With Cats, |

DOG-JACK (1)

| 223 Pekes Pols | 35 | are snappers and biters,/And every dog-jack of them notable fighters;/And so they |

DOGS (13)

29 Aunt Helen	8	of thing had occurred before./The dogs were handsomely provided for,/But shortly
69 WL: Fire S	276	Greenwich reach/Past the Isle of Dogs./Weialala leia/Wallala leialala/Elizabeth
135 5FingerEx2	10	tree was cramped and dry./Pollicle dogs and cats all must/Jellicle cats and dogs all
135 5FingerEx2	11	and cats all must/Jellicle cats and dogs all must/Like undertakers, come to dust./
147 Rock 1	2	of Heaven,/The Hunter with his dogs pursues his circuit./O perpetual revolution
158 Rock 5	6	/And the others run about like dogs, full of enterprise, sniffing and barking:
158 Rock 5	11	we are encompassed with snakes and dogs: therefore some must labour, and others
204 de la Mare	21	maddened in the moonlight dance,/Dogs cower, flitter bats, and owls range/At
220 Old Deut	20	the sheep they may bleat,/But the dogs and the herdsmen will turn them away./
234 Ad-dress	20	say: A CAT IS NOT A DOG./Now Dogs pretend they like to fight;/They often

285 FR	Charles	25	to our ways/Living with horses and dogs and guns/Ever to want to leave England in
297 FR	Gerald	23	we knew it also./Why not let sleeping dogs lie?/{C} All the same, there's a question or
329 FR	Chorus	7	/The mowing of hay in summer/The dogs and the old pony/The stumble and the wail

DOGWOOD (1)

37 Gerontion		21	Christ the tiger/In depraved May, dogwood and chestnut, flowering judas,/To be

DOIGTS (1)

51 Restaurant		2	n'a rien à faire/Que de se gratter les doigts et se pencher sur mon épaule:/'Dans mon

DOING (36)

65 WL: Chess		119	is that noise now? What is the wind doing?'/Nothing again nothing.'Do/'You know
164 Rock 9		13	of themselves, ready for any festivity,/Doing themselves very well./Let us mourn in a
178 FQ: ECoker		52	beginning./What is the late November doing/With the disturbance of the spring/And
214 RTTugger		11	will do/As he do do/And there's no doing anything about it!/The Rum Tum Tugger
214 RTTugger		22	will do/As he do do/And there's no doing anything about it!/The Rum Tum Tugger
215 RTTugger		39	will do/As he do do/And there's no doing anything about it!/The Song of the
227 Macavity		34	of his thumbs,/Or engaged in doing complicated long division sums./
258 MC Thomas		20	and unobservable./Sin grows with doing good. When I imposed the King's law/In
258 MC Thomas		30	may make the cause serve them,/Still doing right: and striving with political men/May
293 FR	Violet	2	Packell is too old to know what she is doing./It really needs a man in charge of things
295 FR	Charles	8	such dangerous fancies./It's only doing harm to your mother and yourself./Of
338 FR	Harry	3	Only be sure/That I know what I am doing, and what I must do,/And that it is the
342 FR	Agatha	15	that is not my spell, it is none of my doing:/I have only watched and waited. In this
348 FR	Chorus	27	/We do not know what we are doing;/And even, when you think of it,/We do
349 FR	Chorus	3	/And what are we, and what are we doing?/To each and all of these questions/There
349 FR	Mary	28	world/Where we know what we are doing/There is not its operation/Follow follow/
353 CP	Julia	3	the point./{J} Then what were you doing, up in a tree:/You and the Maharaja?/{A}
356 CP	Julia	4	California./Do tell us what you were doing in California./{C} Making a film./{P}
375 CP	Celia	35	/Of course it's still cooking — or doing *something*./I must go and investigate. {}/
403 CP	Reilly	10	cure;/And you would go on, doing such amount of mischief/As lay within
420 CP	Celia	4	I don't in the least know what I am doing/Or why I am doing it. There is nothing
420 CP	Celia	5	know what I am doing/Or why I am doing it. There is nothing else to do:/That is the
427 CP	Julia	21	/{J} But tell us, Alex./What were you doing in this strange place —/What's it called?/
427 CP	Julia	24	/{A} Kinkanja./{J} What were you doing/In Kinkanja? Visiting some Sultan?/You
433 CP	Lavinia	36	/{L} Kinkanja? What was Celia doing in Kinkanja?/We heard that she had
458 CC	Claude	1	ought we to be? What ought we to be doing? {}/[*at the open door*]./{E} She's speaking
463 CC	Colby	31	excel in,/Seems the one thing worth doing, the one thing/That I want to do. I have
467 CC	Colby	28	I'm really interested by the work I'm doing/And eager for more. I don't want my
475 CC	Lucasta	3	being very discouraging:/Are you doing it deliberately?/{C} That's not what I
493 CC	Lady E	1	/{LE} Claude, what are you doing?/{SC} Settling the places./It's important,
513 CC	Colby	38	he would have liked to be,/And by doing the things he had wanted to do./{MG}
529 ES	Monica	19	coming, Father. What have you been doing?/{LC} Good afternoon, Charles. You
529 ES	Ld Clav	21	guessed, Monica,/What I've been doing. Don't you recognise this book?/{M} It's
529 ES	Ld Clav	27	be easy./{LC} That is just what I was doing./{M} Thinking of nothing?/{LC}
529 ES	Ld Clav	33	right book, and find out what I was doing/Twenty years ago, to-day, at this hour of
534 ES	Gomez	25	I've several children,/All grown up, doing well for themselves./I wouldn't allow

DOINGS (1)

589 Fable		95	We/Got the veracious record of these doings/From an old manuscript found in the

DOLLAR (1)

589 Fable		74	chair,/His eye became the size of any dollar,/The ghost then took him roughly by the

DOLOUR (1)

94 Ash-Wed 4		6	and in knowledge of eternal dolour/Who moved among the others as they

DOLPHIN (1)

64 WL: Chess		96	stone,/In which sad light a carvèd dolphin swam./Above the antique mantel was

DOMED (1)

226 Macavity		13	lined with thought, his head is highly domed;/His coat is dusty from neglect, his

DOMESTIC (3)

220 Old Deut		25	so disposed/Or when he's engaged in domestic economy:/And the Oldest Inhabitant
504 CC	Claude	25	/I'm afraid there has been some domestic incompetence./You should have been
534 ES	Gomez	23	on./That wouldn't do for me. I'm too domestic./And by the way, I've several children,

DOMINATE (1)

581 ES	Ld Clav	16	the truth./Why did I always want to dominate my children?/Why did I mark out a

DOMINATED (1)

271 MC Chorus		3	by the animal powers of spirit,/Dominated by the lust of self-demolition,/By

DOMINATING (3)
304 FR   Mary   4   headmistress/Who knew the way of dominating timid girls./I don't see you any
525 ES   Monica   37   I believe *you* love *me.*/{M} Oh, what a dominating man you are!/Really, you must
545 ES   Monica   12   the matron, though she looks rather dominating,/Has left us alone./{LC} Yes, but
DOMINIONS (2)
267 MC Knight1   33   /Of stirring up trouble in the French dominions./You sowed strife abroad, you
559 ES   Ld Clav 6   years out of England/In one of the Dominions, might set you on your feet./I have
DOMMAGE (1)
51 Restaurant   19   peur, je l'ai quittée à mi-chemin./C'est dommage.'/Mais alors, tu as ton vautour!/Va
DON'T (395)
DONATI (1)
44 Cook Egg   24   Seven Sacred Trances;/Piccarda de Donati will conduct me./But where is the penny
DONC (1)
51 Restaurant   30   de sa vie antérieure./Figurez-vous donc, c'était un sort pénible;/Cependant, ce fut
DONE (80)
65 WL: Chess   143 smart./He'll want to know what you done with that money he gave you/To get
69 WL: Fire S   252 thought to pass:/'Well now that's done: and I'm glad it's over.'/When lovely
90 Ash-Wed 1   32   /Let these words answer/For what is done, not to be done again/May the judgement
90 Ash-Wed 1   32   answer/For what is done, not to be done again/May the judgement not be too
96 Ash-Wed 5   10   Word./O my people, what have I done unto thee./Where shall the word be found,
96 Ash-Wed 5   28   and oppose/O my people, what have I done unto thee./Will the veiled sister between
149 Rock 1   67   in these times deride/What has been done of good, you find explanations/To satisfy
149 Rock 1   75   you the things that are now being done,/And some of the things that were long
149 Rock 1   76   some of the things that were long ago done,/That you may take heart. Make perfect
152 Rock 2   25   much at home unsure./Of all that was done in the past, you eat the fruit, either rotten
152 Rock 2   30   every act of sin./And of all that was done that was good, you have the inheritance./
152 Rock 2   32   reward of the good and ill that was done by those who have gone before you./And
154 Rock 3   21   /A Cry from the East:/What shall be done to the shore of smoky ships?/Will you
158 Rock 5   7   serpents, let us destroy it,/And have done with these abominations, the turpitudes of
163 Rock 8   33   evenings./Only the faith could have done what was good of it;/Whole faith of a few,
194 FQ: Little   141 of re-enactment/Of all that you have done, and been; the shame/Of motives late
194 FQ: Little   143 and the awareness/Of things ill done and done to others' harm/Which once you
194 FQ: Little   143 the awareness/Of things ill done and done to others' harm/Which once you took for
210 Old Gumbie   5   when the day's hustle and bustle is done,/Then the Gumbie Cat's work is but
210 Old Gumbie   17   when the day's hustle and bustle is done,/Then the Gumbie Cat's work is but
210 Old Gumbie   21   diet/And believing that nothing is done without trying,/She sets to work with her
211 Old Gumbie   29   when the day's hustle and bustle is done,/Then the Gumbie Cat's work is but
219 Mung Rump   39   — And there's nothing at all to be done about that!/Old Deuteronomy/Old
236 Cat Morgan   8   'ouse/And a bit o' cold fish when I done me patrol./I ain't got much polish, me
587 Fable   13   hoards — a deed which ne'er he/Had done before — their fortune multiplied,/As if
593 Grad 8   4   /Which, whatsoever we have been or done/Or to what distant lands we may have
595 Grad 14   1   by, the word 'Progress!'/So we are done; we may no more delay;/Thus is the end of
252 MC Thomas   21   /Pursue your treacheries as you have done before:/No one shall say that I betrayed a
252 MC Tempt4   30   FOURTH TEMPTER]/{T4} Well done, Thomas, your will is hard to bend./And
255 MC Thomas   4   what is there to do? what is left to be done?/Is there no enduring crown to be won?/
263 MC Chorus   18   and Easter what work shall be done?/The ploughman shall go out in March
263 MC Chorus   24   the door,/What work shall have been done, what wrong/Shall the bird's song cover,
268 MC Thomas   30   them./{T} I do not deny/That this was done through me. But it is not I/Who can loose
277 MC Knight3   2   it at once. It is this: in what we have done, and whatever/you may think of us, we
277 MC Knight3   24   won't give *us* any glory. No, we have done for ourselves, there's/no mistake about
289 FR   Ivy   32   not enquired into./She may have done it in a fit of temper./{G} I never met her./
291 FR   Gerald   15   /{I} Welcome, Harry!/{G} Well done!/{V} Welcome home to Wishwood!/{C}
292 FR   Ivy   37   mother/Time and time again: she's done nothing about it/Because she preferred to
296 FR   Violet   16   this./{V} There is only one thing to be done:/Harry must see a doctor./{I} But I
297 FR   Charles 16   shouldn't blame Harry./I might have done the same thing once, myself./Nobody
304 FR   Mary   21   She didn't need me:/She would have done just as well with a hired servant/Or with
305 FR   Harry   33   you left it./{H} I wish she had not done that. It's very unnatural,/This arresting of
329 FR   Chorus   23   of music./There is nothing at all to be done about it,/There is nothing to do about
342 FR   Mary   24   leave./I do not know what must be done, what can be done,/Even here, but
342 FR   Mary   24   what must be done, what can be done,/Even here, but elsewhere, everywhere, he
349 FR   Chorus   2   the smiling moon?/And what is being done to us?/And what are we, and what are we
377 CP   Julia   32   the next question/Is, what's to be done. That's very simple./It's too late, or too
380 CP   Celia   2   /Humiliation — it's something I've done to myself./I am not sure even that you
387 CP   Peter   32   /{E} Of course./{P} I hope you've done nothing about it./{E} No, I've done
387 CP   Edward   33   done nothing about it./{E} No, I've done nothing./{P} I'm so glad./Because I've

395	CP	Edward	15	/But you seem to assume that you've done all the changing —/Though I haven't yet
398	CP	Edward	10	nothing but ruin./O God, what have I done? The python. The octopus./Must I become
403	CP	Reilly	12	came to grief./Half of the harm that is done in this world/Is due to people who want to
403	CP	Edward	19	/{E} If I am like that/I must have done a great deal of harm./{R} Oh, not so much
403	CP	Edward	33	cease to exist. That was what she had done to me!/I cannot live with her — that is
403	CP	Edward	37	of my own./That is what she has done to me in five years together!/She has made
413	CP	Reilly	13	as far as that, there is something to be done./{C} Well, I can't pretend that my trouble
416	CP	Celia	1	It's not the feeling of anything I've ever *done*,/Which I might get away from, or of
429	CP	Alex	19	eaten./When these people have done with a European/He is, as a rule, no
440	CP	Lavinia	28	/{L} What you should have done was to admire my dress./{E} But I've
448	CC	Eggers	8	you mustn't say that!/Though I've done my best to gain his confidence./I did
454	CC	Kaghan	11	off your hands./I'll show you how it's done. Come along, Lucasta,/I'm going to make
459	CC	Claude	18	—/So I'm having the flat in the mews done over./{LE} But all in the wrong colours,
460	CC	Claude	37	this is what the doctor in Zürich has done for her,/I give him full marks. Well,
461	CC	Eggers	2	it./And besides, as I told you, I've done some shopping./But I'd better be off now.
464	CC	Claude	30	I gave to clay, and what could be done with it —/What I hoped I could do with it.
467	CC	Colby	24	/{C} I'm very grateful for all you've done for me;/And I want to do my best to
474	CC	Colby	13	Can no one else enter?/{C} It can't be done by issuing invitations:/They would just
479	CC	Kaghan	33	I like the way you've had the place done up./{C} It was Lady Elizabeth chose the
494	CC	Claude	26	to my father's inspiration/If I had done what I wanted to do./{LE} You've never
515	CC	Guzzard	15	then I was frightened by what I had done./Though I had never said 'this child is
533	ES	Gomez	6	I've followed your example,/And done the same, in a modest way./You know,
537	ES	Gomez	6	my while to be trustworthy?/{G} It's done already, Dick; done many years ago:/
537	ES	Gomez	6	/{G} It's done already, Dick; done many years ago:/Adoption tried, and
548	ES	Monica	7	when she left/That she thought she'd done her duty by us for to-day./I'm going to
551	ES	Ld Clav	9	settled our account./What harm was done? I learned my lesson/And you learned
556	ES	Michael	33	being blamed for something I hadn't done./I never got over that. If you always blame
557	ES	Michael	27	/The only good the name has ever done me./{LC} On the strength of your name.
570	ES	Ld Clav	20	life?/{LC} ... And yet they've both done better for themselves/In consequence of it
579	ES	Michael	21	well to say good-bye at once and be done with it./{LC} Yes, if you're going, and I

DONNE (1)

| 52 | Whispers | 9 | /Tightening its lusts and luxuries./Donne, I suppose, was such another/Who found |

DONNÉ (1)

| 51 | Restaurant | 11 | /Elle était toute mouillée, je lui ai donné des primevères.'/Les taches de son gilet |

DOOM (12)

243	MC	Chorus	21	bringing death into Canterbury:/A doom on the house, a doom on yourself, a
243	MC	Chorus	21	Canterbury:/A doom on the house, a doom on yourself, a doom on the world./We do
243	MC	Chorus	21	on the house, a doom on yourself, a doom on the world./We do not wish anything to
244	MC	Chorus	26	us; do not ask us/To stand to the doom on the house, the doom on the
244	MC	Chorus	26	stand to the doom on the house, the doom on the Archbishop, the doom on the
244	MC	Chorus	26	the doom on the Archbishop, the doom on the world./Archbishop, secure and
244	MC	Chorus	29	of the small folk who stand to the doom of the house, the doom of their lord, the
244	MC	Chorus	29	stand to the doom of the house, the doom of their lord, the doom of the world?/O
244	MC	Chorus	29	the house, the doom of their lord, the doom of the world?/O Thomas, Archbishop,
250	MC	Thomas	4	a punier power?/Delegate to deal the doom of damnation,/To condemn kings, not
269	MC	Thomas	13	/It is not Becket who pronounces doom,/But the Law of Christ's Church, the
273	MC	Chorus	8	to dust am bending,/From the final doom impending/Help me, Lord, for death is

DOOR (89)

20	Portrait	86	the stairs and turn the handle of the door/And feel as if I had mounted on my hands
24	Rhapsody	17	towards you in the light of the door/Which opens on her like a grin./You see
26	Rhapsody	71	o'clock,/Here is the number on the door./Memory!/You have the key,/The little
26	Rhapsody	77	on the wall,/Put your shoes at the door, sleep, prepare for life.'/The last twist of
38	Gerontion	29	turned in the hall, one hand on the door. Vacant shuttles/Weave the wind. I have
57	Swee Night	34	someone indistinct/Converses at the door apart,/The nightingales are singing near/
65	WL: Chess	118	is that noise?'/The wind under the door./'What is that noise now? What is the wind
65	WL: Chess	138	and waiting for a knock upon the door./When Lil's husband got demobbed, I said
74	WL: Thund	389	home./It has no windows, and the door swings,/Dry bones can harm no one./Only
74	WL: Thund	412	I have heard the key/Turn in the door once and turn once only/We think of the
103	Journ Magi	27	over the lintel,/Six hands at an open door dicing for pieces of silver,/And feet kicking
105	Song Sime	12	went never any rejected from my door./Who shall remember my house, where
133	Eyes	11	/Eyes I shall not see unless/At the door of death's other kingdom/Where, as in
156	Rock 3	73	one who remembers the way to your door:/Life you may evade, but Death you shall
162	Rock 8	24	beggared, finding/A stranger at the door in possession:/Came home cracked by the
171	FQ: BurntN	13	which we did not take/Towards the door we never opened/Into the rose-garden. My
203	Indians	3	cooking;/To sit in front of his own door at sunset/And see his grandson, and his

214 RTTugger		14	always on the wrong side of every door,/And as soon as he's at home, then he'd
221 Old Deut		36	'Now then, out you go, by the back door,/For Old Deuteronomy mustn't be woken
223 Pekes Pols		28	to the window, some came to the door;/There were surely a dozen, more likely a
228 Gus		1	Cat/Gus is the Cat at the Theatre Door./His name, as I ought to have told you
233 Skimble		34	/With your name written up on the door./And the berth is very neat with a newly
235 Ad-dress		46	O CAT!/But if he is the Cat next door,/Whom I have often met before/(He comes
236 Cat Morgan		4	me a-takin' my ease/And keepin' the door in a Bloomsbury Square./I'm partial to
236 Cat Morgan		20	you make friends with the Cat at the door./MORGAN./POEMS WRITTEN IN
588 Fable		36	porter/Who stood outside the door from head to feet./To make a rather
243 MC Priest3		12	evil?/Until the grinders cease/And the door shall be shut in the street,/And all the
252 MC Thomas		16	men like you were glad to wait at my door./Not only in the court, but in the field/
252 MC Tempt3		23	my Lord, I shall not wait at your door./And I well hope, before another spring/
256 MC Priests		30	Is the window-bar made fast, is the door under lock and bolt?/{4T} Is it rain that
256 MC Tempts		31	window, is it wind that pokes at the door?/{C} Does the torch flame in the hall, that
263 MC Chorus		23	and children tumble in front of the door,/What work shall have been done, what
273 MC Priests		10	*and* PRIESTS]/{3P} Bar the door. Bar the door/The door is barred./We are
273 MC Priests		10	PRIESTS]/{3P} Bar the door. Bar the door/The door is barred./We are safe. We are
273 MC Priests		11	/{3P} Bar the door. Bar the door/The door is barred./We are safe. We are safe./They
273 MC Thomas		22	open, even to our enemies. Open the door!/{3P} My Lord! these are not men, these
273 MC Priests		26	/But like beasts. You would bar the door/Against the lion, the leopard, the wolf or
274 MC Thomas		7	above the Law of Man./Unbar the door! unbar the door!/We are not here to
274 MC Thomas		7	of Man./Unbar the door! unbar the door!/We are not here to triumph by fighting,
274 MC Thomas		13	triumph of the Cross, now/Open the door! I command it. OPEN THE DOOR! {}/
274 MC Thomas		13	the door! I command it. OPEN THE DOOR! {}/[*The door is opened. The* KNIGHTS
274 MC	m	14	it. OPEN THE DOOR! {}/[*The door is opened. The* KNIGHTS *enter, slightly*
282 MC Chorus		7	/Of the men and women who shut the door and sit by the fire;/Who fear the blessing
288 FR Agatha		26	to creep back through the little door./He will find a new Wishwood.
290 FR Agatha		35	the dark passage/The paw under the door. {}/CHORUS (IVY, VIOLET, GERALD
291 FR	m	14	{}/[HARRY *stops suddenly at the* door *and stares at the window*]/{I} Welcome,
302 FR Chorus		7	open./Why do we all behave as if the door might suddenly open, the curtains be
310 FR Harry		35	not matter. You bring me news/Of a door that opens at the end of a corridor,/
315 FR Chorus		31	/Of the things to come that sit at the door, as if they had been there always./And the
334 FR Agatha		40	/{Ag} I only looked through the little door/When the sun was shining on the
335 FR Harry		35	and you walked through the little door/And I ran to meet you in the rose-garden./
335 FR Agatha		38	do not pass twice through the same door/Or return to the door through which we
335 FR Agatha		39	the same door/Or return to the door through which we did not pass./I have
348 FR Chorus		8	/We do not like to walk out of a door, and find ourselves back in the same room.
349 FR	1m	13	thing. {}/[*Exeunt*]/[*Enter, from one* door, AGATHA *and* MARY, *and set a small*
349 FR	2m	13	*a small portable table.*/*From another* door, *enter* DENMAN *carrying a birthday cake*
359 CP	m	22	doorbell rings. EDWARD *goes to the* door, *saying:*]/{E} But she always turns up when
359 CP	m	23	when she's least wanted. {}/[*Opens the* door]/{E} Julia! {}/[*Enter* JULIA]/{J} Edward!
364 CP Edward		29	doorbell rings]/{E} I must answer the door. {}/[EDWARD *goes to the door*]/{E} So
364 CP	m	30	the door. {}/[EDWARD *goes to the door*]/{E} So it's you again, Julia! {}/[*Enter*
367 CP Alex		37	/{A} Why, I came and found that the door was open/And so I thought I'd slip in and
372 CP Edward		38	and if you don't mind,/Please *shut the* door *after you,* so that it latches./{A} Remember,
376 CP Celia		2	apron.]/{C} You'd better answer the door, Edward./It's the best thing to do. Don't
376 CP	m	7	rings again. EDWARD *goes to front* door, *and is/heard to say:*]/{E} Julia!/What have
386 CP	m	14	*The bell rings, and he goes to the front* door.]/{E} Celia!/{C} Has Lavinia arrived?/{E}
387 CP	m	12	/{E} There's Lavinia. {}/[*Goes to front* door]/{E} Peter! {}/[*Enter* PETER]/{P} Where's
397 CP Edward		1	yesterday morning./{E} There was a door/And I could not open it. I could not touch
398 CP Edward		6	made a decision./What devil left the door on the latch/For these doubts to enter?
400 CP	m	34	they've gone. {}/[*Exit* ALEX *by side* door]/[EDWARD *is shown in by*
401 CP Edward		2	into my mind/Before I entered the door, that you might be the same person:/But I
412 CP	m	2	Come in. {}/[*Enter* JULIA *by side* door]/{R} She's waiting downstairs./{J} I know
412 CP Julia		5	Of course not. I dropped her at the door/And went on in the taxi, round the corner;
412 CP	m	23	he'll be here. {}/[*Exit* JULIA *by side* door]/[REILLY *presses button.*
420 CP	1m	19	{}/[NURSE-SECRETARY *appears at* door. *Exit* CELIA. REILLY *dials on/*
420 CP	m	20	come in now. {}/[*Enter* JULIA *by side* door]/{R} She will go far, that one./{J} Very far,
424 CP	4m	1	/table. LAVINIA *enters from side* door./{CM} Have you any further orders for us,
424 CP	m	11	[EDWARD *lets himself in at the front* door]/{E} I'm in good time, I think. I hope you've
426 CP Julia		36	/I recognised one of their men at the door —/An old friend of mine, in fact. But I'm
457 CC	m	20	/{SC} Hello! What's that? {}/[*Opens* door *on to landing and listens*]/{SC} She's here,
458 CC	m	2	ought we to be doing? {}/[*at the open* door]./{E} She's speaking to the parlourmaid.
465 CC Claude		29	you will go through the private door/Into the real world, as I do, sometimes./
481 CC	m	14	to discuss *me* ... {}/[*A knock at the* door. *Enter* LADY ELIZABETH]/{LE} Oh,

486 CC		m	31	aware of. Colby ... {}/[*A knock on the door*]/{LE} Who's that? {}/[*Enter* SIR
496 CC		m	13	shall be *our* son. {}/[*A knock on the door. Enter* EGGERSON]/{SC} Good morning,
499 CC		m	9	completely. {}/[*A knock on the door*]/{SC} Good Lord, she's here already! Well
504 CC	Lucasta	5		seems to be nobody to answer the door./I've just let someone in. It's the Mrs.
526 ES	Monica	24		there's the table;/There's the door ... and I hear someone coming:/It's
577 ES	Carghil	36		has come knocking at the door./Richard, you must not bar his way. That
582 ES	Charles	26		/It's as if he had passed through some door unseen by us/And had turned and was

DOORBELL (10)

359 CP		m	22	have minded anyone else, {}/[*The doorbell rings*. EDWARD *goes to the door,*
364 CP		m	29	You will be here to meet her. {}/[*The doorbell rings*]/{E} I must answer the door. {}/
374 CP		3m	1	*is alone, playing*/*Patience. The doorbell rings, and he goes to answer it.*/{C} The
376 CP		m	2	*of Patience. He moves*/*a card. The doorbell rings repeatedly. Re-enter* CELIA, *in an*
384 CP		3m	1	*alone. He goes to*/*answer the doorbell.*/{E} Oh ... good evening. {}/[*Goes to*
387 CP		m	11	simple./Can't you see that ... {}/[*The doorbell rings*]/{E} There's Lavinia. {}/[*Goes to*
389 CP		m	37	/{C} Oh, not as in the past! {}/[*The doorbell rings, and* EDWARD *goes to answer it*]/
390 CP		m	17	Tell us/I'm thrilled ... {}/[*The doorbell rings*. EDWARD *goes to answer it.*
426 CP		m	24	/And you do need to rest now. {}/[*The doorbell rings*]/{L} Oh, bother!/Now who would
440 CP	Edward	36		I wish it would begin./{E} There's the doorbell./{L} Oh, I'm glad. It's begun. {}/

DOORS (9)

72 WL: Thund	345	red sullen faces sneer and snarl/From doors of mudcracked houses/If there were water
155 Rock 3	50	/Or sanitary dwellings with numbered doors/Or a house a little better than your
166 Rock 10	21	light that slants upon our western doors at evening,/The twilight over stagnant
589 Fable	65	stories lights most always do./The doors, though barred and bolted most securely,/
240 MC Chorus	7	sea,/Ruinous spring shall beat at our doors,/Root and shoot shall eat our eyes and
257 MC Chorus	24	our feet and over the sky;/Under doors and down chimneys, flowing in at the ear
273 MC Thomas	16	are safe. We are safe./{T} Unbar the doors! throw open the doors!/I will not have the
273 MC Thomas	16	/{T} Unbar the doors! throw open the doors!/I will not have the house of prayer, the
279 MC Knight4	36	still inflamed with wrath, that the doors/should be opened. Need I say more? I

DOORSTEP (1)

603 Spleen	16	impatient of delay)/On the doorstep of the Absolute./Ode/THOMAS

DOORWAY (1)

272 MC Chorus	18	the passage,/More than shadow in the doorway,/More than fury in the hall./The

DOORYARD (1)

184 FQ: DrySal	12	/In the rank ailanthus of the April dooryard,/In the smell of grapes on the autumn

DOORYARDS (1)

16 Prufrock	101	worth while,/After the sunsets and the dooryards and the sprinkled streets,/After the

DORIS (8)

43 Swee Erect		41	does the house no sort of good./But Doris, towelled from the bath,/Enters padding
115 SP		m	1	/Fragment of a Prologue/DUSTY. DORIS./{Du} How about Pereira?/{Do} What
116 SP	Dusty	24	/Oh I'm *so* sorry. I *am* so sorry/But Doris came home with a terrible chill/No, just a
116 SP	Dusty	29	I *hope* we shan't have to call a doctor/Doris just hates having a doctor/She says will
118 SP	Dusty	30	right up/{Du} All right, come up./(*to* DORIS): Cards are queer./{Do} I'd like to know
119 SP		m	1	/KNOCK/KNOCK/KNOCK/DORIS. DUSTY. WAUCHOPE. HORSFALL.
119 SP	Wauch	1	KRUMPACKER./{W} Hello Doris! Hello Dusty! How do you do!/How
121 SA		m	1	SWARTS. SNOW. DORIS. DUSTY./{S} I'll carry you off/To a

DORRANCE (1)

119 SP	Krum	20	poker game in Bordeaux?/Yes Miss Dorrance you get Sam/To tell about that poker

DORRANCE'S (1)

116 SP	Dusty	21	Hello are you there?/Yes this is Miss Dorrance's *flat* —/Oh Mr. Pereira is that you?

DORSET (1)

291 FR	Gerald	4	Compton-Smith, down at his place in Dorset./{V} I should have been helping Lady

DOS (1)

48 Lune Miel	5	odeur de chienne./Ils restent sur le dos écartant les genoux/De quatre jambes

DOST (1)

594 Grad 12	1	of dew upon the morning grass;/Thou dost not die — for each succeeding year/Thy

DOUBLE (5)

193 FQ: Little	99	and unidentifiable./So I assumed a double part, and cried/And heard another's
369 CP	Alex	7	her often?/{A} Edward, have you a double boiler?/{E} I suppose there must be a
369 CP	Edward	8	boiler?/{E} I suppose there must be a double boiler:/Isn't there one in every kitchen?/
400 CP	Reilly	24	his illness./{R} Illness offers him a double advantage:/To escape from himself —
530 ES	Ld Clav	39	put our hands in our pockets/To double this collection — it must be something

DOUBLED (1)

64 WL: Chess	82	hid his eyes behind his wing)/Doubled the flames of sevenbranched

DOUBT (35)

16 Prufrock	114	a scene or two,/Advise the prince; no doubt, an easy tool,/Deferential, glad to be of
104 Journ Magi	37	certainly,/We had evidence and no doubt. I had seen birth and death,/But had
159 Rock 6	5	for those who live near a Bank/To doubt the security of their money./It is hard for
214 RTTugger	19	Cat —/And it isn't any use for you to doubt it::/For he will do/As he do do/And
224 Mr Mistoff	3	Conjuring Cat —/(There can be no doubt about that)./Please listen to me and don't
589 Fable	66	way — my statement nobody can doubt,/Who knows the well known fact, as you
241 MC Mess	31	all his claims,/Assured, beyond doubt, of the devotion of the people,/Who
242 MC Priest2	33	be at our head, dispelling dismay and doubt./He will tell us what we are to do, he will
269 MC Thomas	3	/Never again, you must make no doubt,/Shall the sea run between the shepherd
289 FR Gerald	8	/He's taken his medicine, I've no doubt./Let him marry again and carry on at
323 FR Warburt	16	and a few days' rest,/I've no doubt, will be all that he needs./{A} Accident?
324 FR Warburt	5	/This is not the time to begin to doubt me./Come, Winchell. We can put your
342 FR Agatha	30	here, not elsewhere;/Elsewhere no doubt is agony, renunciation,/But birth and life.
360 CP Reilly	32	of in my behaviour./{UG} Then no doubt it's all for the best./With another man,
380 CP Celia	9	yourself:/But that's what it was, no doubt./{E} I *didn't* take you as a passing
389 CP Lavinia	17	about Peter .../{L} I have no doubt you do./{C} And why he is going .../{L} I
389 CP Lavinia	19	And why he is going .../{L} I don't doubt that either./{C} And I believe he is right
402 CP Edward	33	we decide what to do with you./{E} I doubt if you have ever had a case like mine:/I
409 CP Reilly	32	/It took you some time, I have no doubt,/Before you would admit it. Though
446 CC Eggers	22	on a purely business basis./{E} No doubt that's best. While he's still living/With his
449 CC Eggers	1	/{E} And you're thinking no doubt that Lady Elizabeth/Would be put in
454 CC Eggers	20	sane. And I think I am./{E} I have no doubt on either point, none at all./{C} And B.
477 CC Lucasta	8	Claude's daughter!/{L} Oh, there's no doubt of that./I'm sure he wished there had
484 CC Colby	20	/{C} But you had parents. And no doubt, many relatives./{LE} Oh, swarms of
485 CC Lady E	33	she was devoted to you,/I have no doubt. What is your aunt's name?/Is it
486 CC Colby	19	Why, Lady Elizabeth! Why should I doubt it?/That is not the kind of story my aunt
496 CC Lady E	9	there isn't a lot to be learnt,/I don't doubt, from the dervish rituals./But it doesn't
507 CC Lady E	33	yet, Elizabeth./{LE} There is no doubt about it./Colby is my son./{MG} Your
508 CC Lady E	10	should./{LE} There isn't a shadow of doubt in my mind./I'm surprised that you,
511 CC Lady E	6	is my mother .../{LE} There is no doubt whatever about it, Barnabas./I am your
514 CC Eggers	29	myself, Sir Claude./Not that we doubt your word, Mrs. Guzzard:/But in a
537 ES Gomez	19	to take me up at Oxford/I've no doubt your friends wondered what you found in
550 ES Ld Clav	8	/{LC} You've changed your name, no doubt. And I've changed mine./Your name now
559 ES Michael	32	lord it over them, in fact. Oh, I've no doubt/That the thought of passing on your
577 ES Charles	9	/{C} This return of past kindness/No doubt gives you pleasure?/{G} Yes, it's always

DOUBTFUL (1)

21 Portrait	118	coming down above the housetops;/Doubtful, for a while/Not knowing what to feel

DOUBTFULLY (1)

592 Grad 1	2	all we know/We linger for a moment doubtfully,/Then with a song upon our lips, sail

DOUBTINGS (1)

148 Rock 1	40	Rock. Who will perhaps answer our doubtings./The Rock. The Watcher. The

DOUBTLESS (1)

158 Rock 5	2	and Geshem the Arabian: were doubtless men of public spirit and zeal./Preserve

DOUBTS (5)

243 MC Priest2	4	when the Archbishop returns/Our doubts are dispelled. Let us therefore rejoice,/I
398 CP Edward	7	left the door on the latch/For these doubts to enter? And then you came back, you/
421 CP Reilly	30	in anything/You always raise doubts; when I am apprehensive/Then you see
463 CC Claude	6	obvious advantages/That I had no doubts at the time — that's five years;/And then
499 CC Claude	6	/Don't let her think that *I* have any doubts:/You are putting the questions on behalf

DOUR (1)

223 Pekes Pols	33	like,/For your Pollicle Dog is a dour Yorkshire tyke,/And his braw Scottish

DOUSED (1)

588 Fable	39	no wise precaution incomplete;/He doused the room in which they were to dine,/

DOVE (3)

193 FQ: Little	83	end of the unending/After the dark dove with the flickering tongue/Had passed
196 FQ: Little	202	/In the ground of our beseeching./The dove descending breaks the air/With flame of
484 CC Lady E	22	people!/I thought of myself as a dove in an eagle's nest./They were so

DOVE'S (2)

27 Cor1 March	32	indifferent./O hidden under the dove's wing, hidden in the turtle's breast,/Under
29 Cor2 State	32	the... Hidden under the... Where the dove's foot rested and locked for a moment,/A

DOVER (1)

244 MC Chorus	30	leave us, leave us, leave sullen Dover, and set sail for France. Thomas our

DOVES (1)

252 MC Thomas	19	/Shall I who ruled like an eagle over doves/Now take the shape of a wolf among

DOWAGER (2)

31 Apollinax	21	said that I might have challenged.'/Of dowager Mrs. Phlaccus, and Professor and Mrs.
284 FR	m 2	REUNION/Persons/AMY, DOWAGER LADY MONCHENSEY, IVY,

DOWERED (1)

593 Grad 5	2	the twentieth century/More grandly dowered than those which came before,/

DOWN (118)

20 Portrait	84	or wrong?/The October night comes down; returning as before/Except for a slight
21 Portrait	117	pen in hand/With the smoke coming down above the housetops;/Doubtful, for a
22 Preludes	1	/Preludes/The winter evening settles down/With smell of steaks in passageways./Six
31 Apollinax	11	worried bodies of drowned men drift down in the green silence,/Dropping from
56 Swee Night	2	his knees/Letting his arms hang down to laugh,/The zebra stripes along his jaw/
61 WL: Burial	16	Marie,/Marie, hold on tight. And down we went./In the mountains, there you feel
62 WL: Burial	66	before his feet./Flowed up the hill and down King William Street,/To where Saint
65 WL: Chess	133	am, and walk the street/'With my hair down, so. What shall we do tomorrow?/'What
67 WL: Fire S	182	/By the waters of Leman I sat down and wept .../Sweet Thames, run softly till
69 WL: Fire S	275	spar./The barges wash/Drifting logs/Down Greenwich reach/Past the Isle of Dogs./
70 WL: Fire S	287	both shores/Southwest wind/Carried down stream/The peal of bells/White towers/
73 WL: Thund	381	wings/And crawled head downward down a blackened wall/And upside down in air
73 WL: Thund	382	down a blackened wall/And upside down in air were towers/Tolling reminiscent
74 WL: Thund	426	in order?/London Bridge is falling down falling down falling down/*Poi s'ascose nel*
74 WL: Thund	426	London Bridge is falling down falling down falling down/*Poi s'ascose nel foco che gli*
74 WL: Thund	426	is falling down falling down falling down/*Poi s'ascose nel foco che gli affina/*
95 Ash-Wed 4	25	fountain sprang up and the bird sang down/Redeem the time, redeem the dream/The
103 Journ Magi	7	galled, sore-footed, refractory,/Lying down in the melting snow./There were times we
103 Journ Magi	21	was all folly./Then at dawn we came down to a temperate valley,/Wet, below the
104 Journ Magi	33	/And I would do it again, but set down/This set down/This: were we led all that
104 Journ Magi	34	do it again, but set down/This set down/This: were we led all that way for/Birth or
118 SP Dusty	25	/{Du} Nobody's up here/How many's down there?/{W} Four of us here./Wait till I put
153 Rock 2	52	away on casual pillions./Much to cast down, much to build, much to restore;/Let the
159 Rock 6	33	steps;/And if the Temple is to be cast down/We must first build the Temple./In the
163 Rock 8	44	moderate vice/When men will not lay down the Cross/Because they will never assume
171 FQ: BurntN	12	/Footfalls echo in the memory/Down the passage which we did not take/
172 FQ: BurntN	35	alley, into the box circle,/To look down into the drained pool./Dry the pool, dry
174 FQ: BurntN	133	turn to us, will the clematis/Stray down, bend to us; tendril and spray/Clutch and
175 FQ: BurntN	137	cling?/Chill/Fingers of yew be curled/Down on us? After the kingfisher's wing/Has
178 FQ: ECoker	57	too high/Red into grey and tumble down/Late roses filled with early snow?/
178 FQ: ECoker	63	the Sun/Until the Sun and Moon go down/Comets weep and Leonids fly/Hunt the
187 FQ: DrySal	131	opened./And the way up is the way down, the way forward is the way back./You
197 FQ: Little	228	/Is a step to the block, to the fire, down the sea's throat/Or to an illegible stone:
213 Growltiger	44	pullaways and junks,/They battened down the hatches on the crew within their
219 Mung Rump	36	the pantry there came a loud crash/Or down from the library came a loud *ping*/From a
229 Gus	40	—/Which an Indian Colonel pursued down a drain./And he thinks that he still can,
230 Bust Jones	5	/He's the Cat we all greet as he walks down the street/In his coat of fastidious black:/
232 Skimble	1	the Railway Cat/There's a whisper down the line at 11.39/When the Night Mail's
232 Skimble	21	will supervise them all, more or less./Down the corridor he paces and examines all
233 Skimble	56	knew/That he was walking up and down the station;/You were sleeping all the
588 Fable	42	been made,/The jovial epicures sat down to table./The menus of that time I am
596 When we	4	breeze/Had torn no quivering cobweb down./The hedgerow bloomed with flowers still,/
599 On a Port	3	weary feet,/Forever hurrying, up and down the street,/She stands at evening in the
605 Narcissus	16	the pointed tips of his fingers./Struck down by such knowledge/He could not live
241 MC Priest2	23	at an end, is the wall of pride cast down/That divided them? Is it peace or war?/
241 MC Mess	33	/Lining the road and throwing down their capes,/Strewing the way with leaves
248 MC Thomas	10	fancy,/So one thought goes whistling down the wind./The impossible is still
249 MC Tempt2	3	not taught in the schools./To set down the great, protect the poor,/Beneath the
257 MC Chorus	24	and over the sky;/Under doors and down chimneys, flowing in at the ear and the
264 MC Priest1	4	Archbishop Thomas./And he kneeled down and cried with a loud voice:/Lord, lay not
264 MC Priest1	25	himself, he offereth for sins./He lays down his life for the sheep./{3P} *Rejoice we all,*
274 MC Knights	18	is Becket, the meddling priest?/Come down Daniel to the lions' den,/Come down
274 MC Knights	19	down Daniel to the lions' den,/Come down Daniel for the mark of the beast./Are you
274 MC Knights	22	with the mark of the beast?/Come down Daniel to the lions' den,/Come down
274 MC Knights	23	down Daniel to the lions' den,/Come down Daniel and join in the feast./Where is
274 MC Knights	26	is Becket the faithless priest?/Come down Daniel to the lions' den,/Come down
274 MC Knights	27	down Daniel to the lions' den,/Come down Daniel and join in the feast./{T} It is the
280 MC Priest1	7	from what far place/Do you look down on us? You now in Heaven,/Who shall
288 FR Agatha	37	in the orchard,/In the plantation, down the corridor/That led to the nursery,

290 FR	Amy	8	to Harry,/But only to bring Harry down to her own level./A restless shivering
291 FR	Gerald	4	been staying with Compton-Smith, down at his place in Dorset./{V} I should have
299 FR	Downing	23	Sir./What I mean is, always up and down./Down in the morning, and up in the
299 FR	Downing	24	What I mean is, always up and down./Down in the morning, and up in the evening,/
300 FR	Downing	27	him accidental./You see, Sir, I was down in the Tourist,/And I took a bit of air
305 FR	Mary	21	/{M} How do you do, Harry./You are down very early. I thought you had just arrived.
306 FR	Harry	5	I haven't seen you since you came down from Oxford./{M} Well, I must go and
307 FR	Harry	2	in what we called the wilderness/{H} Down near the river. That was the stockade/
307 FR	Harry	14	/As soon as I could, and slipped down to the river/To find the old hiding place.
320 FR	Warburt	12	whole machine is weak/And running down. Her heart's very feeble./With care, and
321 FR	Harry	30	You, and I/And Winchell. Sit down, Winchell,/And have a glass of port. We
323 FR	Gerald	26	was there, by a bit of luck./{G} I'll go down and see him, Amy, and come back and
325 FR	Harry	4	I think, mother,/I shall make you lie down. You must be very tired. {}/[*Exeunt*
330 FR	Harry	6	one of us I can conceive/As settling down to make himself at home at Wishwood,/
335 FR	Agatha	5	was only my own feet walking/Away, down a concrete corridor/In a dead air. Only
335 FR	Agatha	18	eye above the desert./{Ag} Up and down, through the stone passages/Of an
335 FR	Agatha	22	passing barred windows./Up and down. Until the chain breaks./{H} To and fro,
345 FR	Amy	27	me to the next room. Where I can lie down./Then you can leave me./{G} Oh,
348 FR	Chorus	7	climb a stair, and find that it takes us down./We do not like to walk out of a door,
356 CP	Julia	15	the wedding cake./{J} Edward, do sit down for a moment./I know you're always the
357 CP	Julia	36	the telephone number?/I might run down and see Lavinia/On my way to Cornwall.
360 CP	Reilly	16	but sip it slowly … and drink it sitting down./Breathe deeply, and adopt a relaxed
362 CP	Reilly	32	your feet expected/And you come down with a jolt. Just for a moment/You have
366 CP	Peter	22	at least you must let me take you down in the lift./{J} No, you stop and talk to
386 CP	Edward	26	nothing to do but wait./Won't you sit down?/{C} Thank you. {}/[*Pause*]/{E} Oh, my
388 CP	Lavinia	35	I suppose we might as well sit down./What shall we talk about?/{E} Peter's
392 CP	Lavinia	12	believe I forgot all about it!/I let you down badly. What did you do about it?/I only
401 CP	Reilly	2	Mr. Chamberlayne./Please sit down. I won't keep you a moment./— Now,
401 CP	Reilly	14	at once./{R} No. If you please, sit down, Mr. Chamberlayne./You are not going
401 CP	Reilly	15	going away, so you might as well sit down./You were going to ask a question./{E}
401 CP	Reilly	28	it:/And so … you might as well sit down./I think that you will find that chair
405 CP	Reilly	31	honour, Mr. Chamberlayne./Sit down, please, both of you. Mrs. Chamberlayne,
411 CP	Lavinia	4	over, is a friend of Alex's./I could go down with you, and then leave you there/If you
411 CP		2m 36	/[REILLY *goes to the couch and lies* down. *The house-telephone rings. He/gets up and*
412 CP	Reilly	24	Celia Coplestone? … Won't you sit down?/I believe you are a friend of Mrs.
414 CP	Celia	22	/And my family want me to come down and stay with them./But I just can't face
426 CP	Edward	4	champagne,/Just ourselves. You lie down now, Lavinia/No one will be coming for
430 CP	Peter	13	for a week, you see,/And I'm driving down to the country this evening,/So I knew
431 CP	Peter	13	And I have my hands full/I've got going down tonight, to Boltwell./{J} To stay with the
456 CC	Eggers	31	of course) 'now we've settled down/All the travel *I* want is up to the City/And
457 CC		m 23	{}/[*Goes to the window and looks* down *on the street*]/{SC} She's having a
457 CC	Eggers	32	/{E} It's perfectly amazing. Let *me* go down to meet her./{SC} Where ought we to be?
474 CC	Colby	17	suddenly,/Unexpectedly. Walking down an alley/I should become aware of
478 CC	Lucasta	20	loneliness, then loneliness swoops down upon you;/When you think you're getting
479 CC	Kaghan	32	impression; which he'll have to live down./— I must say, I like the way you've had
483 CC		m 29	for photographic souvenirs. {}/[*She sits* down, *holding the portrait*]/{LE} What was I
487 CC	Claude	3	got to sound spontaneous. I've jotted down some headings./Just see if you can
504 CC	Eggers	14	Well, what shall I do?/{E} Let me go down and explain to Mrs. Guzzard/And then
529 ES	Monica	2	your constituency!/You can come down at weekends, even when the House is
530 ES	Ld Clav	2	I entered Parliament./I used to jot down notes of what I had to say to people:/
535 ES	Gomez	15	in this respect or that./*A* won't let me down in this relationship,/*B* won't let me down
535 ES	Gomez	16	in this relationship,/*B* won't let me down in some other connection./But, as I've
537 ES	Gomez	26	your tutor thought you'd be sent down./It went the other way. You stayed the
537 ES	Gomez	36	/And so it came about that I was sent down/With the consequences which you
548 ES		m 19	What made you choose it? {}/[*throwing* down *newspaper*]./{LC} My daughter chose it./
554 ES	Carghil	4	there's Mrs. Piggott!/She's bearing down on us. Isn't she frightful!/She never stops
556 ES	Ld Clav	14	You're glad I'm here? Did you drive down from London?/{Mi} I drove down last
556 ES	Michael	15	down from London?/{Mi} I drove down last night. I'm staying at a pub/About
558 ES	Ld Clav	10	/{LC} That accounts for your coming down here so precipitately —/In order to let me

DOWN-TURNED (1)

193 FQ: Little		91	unresisting./And as I fixed upon the down-turned face/That pointed scrutiny with

DOWNED (1)

15 Prufrock		64	white and bare/(But in the lamplight, downed with light brown hair!)/Is it perfume

DOWNFALL (1)

542 ES	Ld Clav	21	That is why you attribute/Your downfall to me. But how was I responsible?/We

DOWNING (28)

284 FR	m	7	MONCHENSEY, *Amy's eldest son*/DOWNING, *his servant and chauffeur*/DR.
295 FR	Amy	39	to go now and rest before dinner./Get Downing to draw you a hot bath,/And you will
297 FR	Charles	10	I have an idea. Why not question Downing?/He's been with Harry ten years, he's
297 FR	Gerald	19	get rid of./{G} Even so, we don't want Downing to know/Any more than he knows
297 FR	Charles	25	*the bell*]/{C} That I'd like to ask Downing./He shan't know why I'm asking. {}/
297 FR	Charles	27	DENMAN]/{C} Denman, where is Downing? Is he up with his Lordship?/{D} He's
298 FR	Agatha	11	We had better leave Charles to talk to Downing/And pursue his own methods. {}/
298 FR	Violet	15	And I wish to be present to hear what Downing says./I want to know at once, not be
298 FR	Agatha	19	with Violet./{Ag} I shall return/When Downing has left you. {}/[*Exit*]/{C} Well, I'm
298 FR	m	23	/And this is one. {}/[*Knock: and enter* DOWNING]/{C} Good evening, Downing./It's
298 FR	Charles	24	DOWNING]/{C} Good evening, Downing./It's good to see you again, after all
299 FR	Charles	5	what happened./{C} Quite so, quite./Downing, you were with them on the voyage
299 FR	Charles	9	a great deal too much in the papers./Downing, do you think that it might have been
299 FR	Charles	21	just for the effect./{C} I understand, Downing. Was she in good spirits?/{Do} Well,
300 FR	Charles	37	it./{C} Oh yes ... quite so. Thank you, Downing,/I don't think we need you any more./
300 FR	Gerald	39	think we need you any more./{G} Oh, Downing,/Is there anything wrong with his
301 FR	Gerald	8	anything more, Sir?/{G} Thank you, Downing;/Nothing more. {}/[*Exit* DOWNING]/
301 FR	m	9	Downing;/Nothing more. {}/[*Exit* DOWNING]/{V} Well, Charles, I must say,
301 FR	Violet	12	were —/Except for having brought Downing into it:/Of which I disapprove./{C} Of
342 FR	Mary	3	came to tell me that Harry is leaving:/Downing told her. He has got the car out./What
345 FR	Gerald	7	will have to be careful./You're taking Downing with you?/{H} Oh, yes, I'm taking
345 FR	Harry	8	with you?/{H} Oh, yes, I'm taking Downing./You need not fear that I am in any
346 FR	m	5	more about this than I do. {}/[*Enter* DOWNING, *hurriedly, in chauffeur's costume*]/
346 FR	Mary	11	/Miss Mary; good night, Sir./{M} Downing, will you promise never to leave his
346 FR	Agatha	33	he won't want anybody./{Ag} And, Downing, if his behaviour seems unaccountable
347 FR	Agatha	12	/{Ag} That will be all, thank you, Downing. We mustn't keep you;/His Lordship
347 FR	m	14	why you've been so long. {}/[*Exit* DOWNING. *Enter* IVY]/{I} Where is Downing
347 FR	Ivy	14	DOWNING. *Enter* IVY]/{I} Where is Downing going? where is Harry?/Look. Here's a

DOWNSTAIRS (8)

362 CP	Reilly	28	dressed for a party/And are going downstairs, with everything about you/
398 CP	Lavinia	17	/Meanwhile, my luggage is in the hall downstairs:/Will you get the porter to fetch it
412 CP	Reilly	2	*by side door*]/{R} She's waiting downstairs./{J} I know that, Henry. I brought
501 CC	Lucasta	24	/But that reminds me. He's waiting downstairs./I don't suppose you want *us* at your
501 CC	Eggers	34	in the family. Why not let them wait downstairs/And come back after Mrs. Guzzard
503 CC	Eggers	20	shouldn't you and Mr. Kaghan wait downstairs/And rejoin us when this interview is
509 CC	Colby	40	I'll get used to it./{C} But he's waiting downstairs! Isn't this the moment/For me to
531 ES	Lambert	32	me, my Lord. There's a gentleman downstairs/Is very insistent that he must see

DOWNWARD (1)

73 WL: Thund	381		beat their wings/And crawled head downward down a blackened wall/And upside

DOWNWARDS (1)

270 MC	Chorus	10	I have seen/Rings of light coiling downwards, descending/To the horror of the

DOZE (1)

158 Rock 5		10	be blessed with the gift of silence, and doze before he sleeps./But we are encompassed

DOZED (2)

23 Preludes		26	lay upon your back, and waited;/You dozed, and watched the night revealing/The
588 Fable		57	their Christmas wassail the monks dozed,/A fine old drink, though now gone out

DOZEN (4)

223 Pekes Pols		29	came to the door;/There were surely a dozen, more likely a score./And together they
332 FR	Agatha	40	he wish to murder her?/{Ag} Oh, a dozen foolish ways, each one abandoned/For
368 CP	Alex	27	a little dried fish/I can make half a dozen dishes. Don't say a word./I shall begin at
376 CP	Edward	14	the saucepan too./{E} *And* half a dozen eggs:/I wanted one for breakfast. A

DR. (25) [*Abbreviation*]

284 FR	m	8	*his servant and chauffeur*/DR. WARBURTON/SERGEANT
297 FR	Amy	1	opinion./{A} If anyone speaks to Dr. Warburton/It should be myself. What does
298 FR	Agatha	9	/Any more than I object to asking Dr. Warburton:/I only see that this is all quite
303 FR	Agatha	15	the dinner back .../{Ag} And also Dr. Warburton. At least, Amy has invited him./
303 FR	Mary	16	At least, Amy has invited him./{M} Dr. Warburton? I think she might have told me;
303 FR	Mary	24	conversation./I am very glad if Dr. Warburton is coming./I shall have to sit
313 FR	m	27	here yet, Amy. {}/[*Enter* AMY, *with* DR. WARBURTON]/{A} It is most vexing.
314 FR	Amy	2	anywhere. Harry!/Haven't you seen Dr. Warburton?/You know he's the oldest
315 FR	m	29	the same honour. {}/[*Exeunt* AMY, DR. WARBURTON, HARRY]/{Ch} I am
321 FR	Denman	11	see your Lordship very urgent,/And Dr. Warburton. He says it's very urgent/Or he
322 FR	Winch	29	been here sooner./I'd telephoned to Dr. Warburton's,/And they told me he was
322 FR	Winch	38	—/Mr. John, I mean. By a bit of luck/Dr. Owen was there, and looked him over;/Says

323 FR	Winch	2	likely, but he mustn't be moved./But Dr. Owen was anxious that you should have a
323 FR	Warburt	11	Monchensey;/And Winchell tells me Dr. Owen has seen him/And says it's nothing
323 FR	Winch	25	/Of course, he hasn't come round yet./Dr. Owen was there, by a bit of luck./{G} I'll go
327 FR	Harry	13	cheat them perhaps with the aid of Dr. Warburton —/Or any other doctor, who
348 FR	Mary	4	the trouble? {}/[*Enter* MARY]/{M} Dr. Warburton!/{W} Excuse me. {}/[*Exeunt*
459 CC	Lady E	31	A quiet hour a day/Is most essential, Dr. Rebmann says./{SC} Rebmann? I thought it
459 CC	Claude	32	/{SC} Rebmann? I thought it was a Dr. Leroux./{LE} Dr. Leroux is in Lausanne./I
459 CC	Lady E	33	I thought it was a Dr. Leroux./{LE} Dr. Leroux is in Lausanne./I have been in
459 CC	Lady E	34	/I have been in Zürich, under Dr. Rebmann./{SC} But you were going out to
459 CC	Claude	35	/{SC} But you were going out to Dr. Leroux/In Lausanne. What made you go to
460 CC	Lady E	18	/To have a course of treatment with Dr. Rebmann —/No, at your stage, I think,
460 CC	Lady E	19	—/No, at your stage, I think, with Dr. Leroux./Don't you remember, I said before
528 ES	Monica	24	is this:/I've only just been given it by Dr. Selby —/Father is much iller than he is

DRAG (2)

272 MC	Priests	8	/{3P} Seize him! force him! drag him!/{T} Keep your hands off!/{3P} To
272 MC	m	10	off!/{3P} To vespers! Hurry. {}/[*They drag him off. While the* CHORUS *speak, the*

DRAGGED (1)

290 FR	Amy	2	/To satisfy her vanity. That's why she dragged him/All over Europe and half round

DRAGGING (3)

67 WL: Fire S		188	crept softly through the vegetation/Dragging its slimy belly on the bank/While I
335 FR	Harry	23	the chain breaks./{H} To and fro, dragging my feet/Among inner shadows in the
364 CP	Julia	34	see a thing without them./I've been dragging Peter all over town/Looking for them

DRAGON'S (1)

157 Rock 4		11	a few, to Jerusalem,/And there, by the dragon's well, by the dung gate,/By the fountain

DRAIN (1)

229 Gus		40	an Indian Colonel pursued down a drain./And he thinks that he still can, much

DRAINED (1)

172 FQ: BurntN		35	the box circle,/To look down into the drained pool./Dry the pool, dry concrete, brown

DRAINS (2)

13 Prufrock		18	Lingered upon the pools that stand in drains,/Let fall upon its back the soot that falls
294 FR	Harry	1	/The noxious smell untraceable in the drains,/Inaccessible to the plumbers, that has its

DRAKE (1)

136 5FingerEx3		5	snake/But only sluggish duck and drake./I have seen the morning shine,/I have

DRAMATIC (1)

384 CP	Edward	24	/That figure of speech is somewhat ... dramatic,/As it was only yesterday that my wife

DRANK (2)

61 WL: Burial		11	in sunlight, into the Hofgarten,/And drank coffee, and talked for an hour./Bin gar
588 Fable		62	with proposing every toast/Had drank more than he ought t' have of grape juice.

DRAP (1)

48 Lune Miel		7	gonflées de morsures./On relève le drap pour mieux égratigner./Moins d'une lieue

DRAPED (1)

74 WL: Thund		407	in our obituaries/Or in memories draped by the beneficent spider/Or under seals

DRAPERY (1)

122 SAWa & Ho		32	/*In the banyan shades/Wear palmleaf drapery/Under the bam/Under the boo/Under the*

DRAPS (1)

48 Lune Miel		3	voici à Ravenne,/A l'aise entre deux draps, chez deux centaines de punaises;/La

DRAUGHTY (2)

38 Gerontion		31	I have no ghosts,/An old man in a draughty house/Under a windy knob./After
173 FQ: BurntN		90	the rain beat,/The moment in the draughty church at smokefall/Be remembered;

DRAW (9)

94 Ash-Wed 4		21	higher dream/While jewelled unicorns draw by the gilded hearse./The silent sister
117 SP	Doris	36	what'll I do./Well I'm not going to draw any more,/You cut for luck. You cut for
118 SP	Dusty	3	Snow/{Du} It's a funny thing how I draw court cards —/{Do} There's a lot in the
118 SP	Dusty	14	I tell you?/Wasn't I saying I always draw court cards?/The Knave of Hearts! {}/
261 MC	Thomas	35	light of the Godhead from which they draw their/being./I have spoken to you to-day,
285 FR	5m	1	MARY/[DENMAN *enters to draw the curtains*]/{A} Not yet! I will ring for
285 FR	Amy	2	nothing to do but watch the days draw out,/Now that I sit in the house from
287 FR	Gerald	14	why was she upset?/I only meant to draw her into the conversation./{C} She's a nice
295 FR	Amy	39	rest before dinner./Get Downing to draw you a hot bath,/And you will feel better./

DRAWER (1)

214 RTTugger		16	about./He likes to lie in the bureau drawer,/But he makes such a fuss if he can't get

DRAWERS (1)

218 Mung Rump		11	ceased to be waterproof,/If the drawers were pulled out from the bedroom

DRAWING (4)
186 FQ: DrySal   78 banks unchanging and erosionless/Or drawing their money, drying sails at dockage;/
197 FQ: Little   240   is now and England./With the drawing of this Love and the voice of this
242 MC   Priest1 25   feeding upon his own virtues,/Pride drawing sustenance from impartiality,/Pride
242 MC   Priest1 26   sustenance from impartiality,/Pride drawing sustenance from generosity,/Loathing
DRAWING-ROOM (6)
 53 Whispers   28 rank a feline smell/As Grishkin in a drawing-room./And even the Abstract Entities/
285 FR   2m 1 *in the North of England/PART I/The drawing-room, after tea. An afternoon in late*
353 CP   2m 1 *laid in London/Act One. Scene 1/The drawing-room of the Chamberlaynes' London*
424 CP   2m 1 *{}/CURTAIN/Act Three/The drawing-room of the Chamberlaynes' London*
523 ES   m 11   */ACT ONE/The drawing-room of Lord Claverton's London house.*
524 ES   2m 1 *of the following day/Act One/The drawing-room of* LORD CLAVERTON'S
DRAWINGS (1)
226 Macavity   28 Or the Admiralty lose some plans and drawings by the way,/There may be a scrap of
DRAWN (12)
 29 Aunt Helen   6   end of the street./The shutters were drawn and the undertaker wiped his feet —/He
 32 Hysteria   3   with a talent/for squad-drill. I was drawn in by short gasps, inhaled at each
204 de la Mare   10   when the lamps are lit and curtains drawn/Demand some poetry, please. Whose
228 Gus   14 if someone else pays,/With anecdotes drawn from his palmiest days./For he once was
239 MC   Chorus   2   cathedral. Here let us wait./Are we drawn by danger? Is it the knowledge of safety,
244 MC   Chorus   28   what it means/To the small folk drawn into the pattern of fate, the small folk
291 FR   Amy   18 /{A} Harry, if you want the curtains drawn you should let me ring for Denman./{H}
302 FR   Chorus   7 might suddenly open, the curtains be drawn,/The cellar make some dreadful
322 FR   Winch   34   smart pace, I fancy, ran into a lorry/Drawn up round the bend. We'll have the driver
323 FR   Winch   20   in rather a hurry./There was a lorry drawn up where it shouldn't be,/Outside of the
429 CP   Alex   22   accomplished?/{A} We have just drawn up an interim report./{E} Will it be made
568 ES   Ld Clav   3 Why under the beech tree?/{LC} I feel drawn to that spot./No matter. I heard what
DRAWS (3)
 56 Swee Night   16   upon the floor/She yawns and draws a stocking up;/The silent man in mocha
239 MC   Chorus   2 Is it the knowledge of safety, that draws our feet/Towards the cathedral? What
258 MC   Thomas   37   /I know that history at all times draws/The strangest consequence from remotest
DREAD (1)
280 MC   Priest1   9   what journey through what further dread/Shall we recover your presence? when
DREADED (1)
187 FQ: DrySal   108 Having hopes for the wrong things or dreaded the wrong things,/Is not the question)
DREADFUL (5)
295 FR   Harry   21   the single event/As something so dreadful that it couldn't have happened,/
302 FR   Chorus   8   be drawn,/The cellar make some dreadful disclosure, the roof disappear,/And we
357 CP   Celia   3   ... what was I going to say?/It's dreadful for old ladies alone in the country,/
359 CP   Edward   20 said she'd invited./But it's only that dreadful old woman who mattered —/I
365 CP   Julia   13 {}/[*Exit*]/{J} Edward, who *is* that dreadful man?/I've never been so insulted in my
DREAM (29)
 83 Hollow Men   20 I dare not meet in dreams/In death's dream kingdom/These do not appear:/There,
 84 Hollow Men   30   star./Let me be no nearer/In death's dream kingdom/Let me also wear/Such
 94 Ash-Wed 4   20   /The unread vision in the higher dream/While jewelled unicorns draw by the
 95 Ash-Wed 4   26   down/Redeem the time, redeem the dream/The token of the word unheard,
125 SA   Chorus   35 /You've had a cream of a nightmare dream and/you've got the hoo-ha's coming to
133 Eyes   3   /Through division/Here in death's dream kingdom/The golden vision reappears/I
134 Wind   4   life and death/Here, in death's dream kingdom/The waking echo of confusing
134 Wind   6 waking echo of confusing strife/Is it a dream or something else/When the surface of
594 Grad 11   1   we go./We go; like flitting faces in a dream;/Out of thy care and tutelage we pass/
271 MC   Thomas   17   sweeten memory/Only like a dream that has often been told/And often been
272 MC   Chorus   29 /To distraction, delusion, escape into dream, pretence,/Where the soul is no longer
290 FR   Chorus   38   their parts?/Like amateur actors in a dream when the curtain rises, to find themselves
308 FR   Harry   2   /{H} What I see/May be one dream or another; if there is nothing else/The
314 FR Warburt   24 was a student at Cambridge,/I used to dream of making some great discovery/To do
318 FR   Harry   31 for explanation —/But perhaps I only dream that I am talking/And shall wake to find
330 FR   Harry   29   together:/When I was inside the old dream, I felt all the same emotion/Or lack of
333 FR   Harry   21 ruin./Perhaps my life has only been a dream/Dreamt through me by the minds of
379 CP   Celia   28 I have heard of that experience./{C} A dream. I was happy in it till to-day,/And then,
379 CP   Celia   32   then I suddenly discovered/That the dream was not enough; that I wanted something
379 CP   Celia   34 wanted to run to tell you./Perhaps the dream was better. It seemed the real reality,/
379 CP   Celia   35 /And if this is reality, it is very like a dream./Perhaps it was I who betrayed my own
379 CP   Celia   36   it was I who betrayed my own dream/All the while; and to find I wanted/This
380 CP   Edward   14   was here this evening. *He* was in a dream/And now he is simply unhappy and

403 CP	Reilly	4	to oblige me./I could make you dream any kind of dream I suggested,/And it
403 CP	Reilly	4	/I could make you dream any kind of dream I suggested,/And it would only go to
417 CP	Celia	9	what happened is remembered like a dream/In which one is exalted by intensity of
432 CP	Reilly	15	been waiting for./{R} I should not dream of trying to interrupt Julia .../{J} But
534 ES	Gomez	10	for a false inference. I wouldn't dream/Of carrying on such business if I lived in
561 ES	Ld Clav	2	some aim of high achievement,/Some dream of excellence, how gladly would I help

DREAMCROSSED (1)

98 Ash-Wed 6		6	transit where the dreams cross/The dreamcrossed twilight between birth and dying/

DREAMER (1)

416 CP	Celia	28	belovèd are equally unreal/And the dreamer is no more real than his dreams./{R}

DREAMING (4)

159 Rock 6		23	the darkness outside and within/By dreaming of systems so perfect that no one will
308 FR	Harry	36	inside too, in the nightly panic/Of dreaming dissolution. You do not know,/You
311 FR	Harry	30	/Has to do with me. The accident of a dreaming moment,/Of a dreaming age, when I
311 FR	Harry	31	accident of a dreaming moment,/Of a dreaming age, when I was someone else/

DREAMS (10)

83 Hollow Men		19	stuffed men./Eyes I dare not meet in dreams/In death's dream kingdom/These do not
98 Ash-Wed 6		5	the loss/In this brief transit where the dreams cross/The dreamcrossed twilight
98 Ash-Wed 6		21	/The place of solitude where three dreams cross/Between blue rocks/But when the
107 Animula			/The pain of living and the drug of dreams/Curl up the small soul in the window
189 FQ: DrySal		198	—To explore the womb, or tomb, or dreams; all these are usual/Pastimes and drugs, and
599 On a Port		1	a Portrait/Among a crowd of tenuous dreams, unknown/To us of restless brain and
255 MC Thomas		27	worthless/But real. You only offer/Dreams to damnation./{T4} You have often
403 CP	Reilly	2	be largely fictitious; and as for your dreams,/You would produce amazing dreams,
403 CP	Reilly	3	dreams,/You would produce amazing dreams, to oblige me./I could make you dream
416 CP	Celia	28	the dreamer is no more real than his dreams./{R} And this man. What does he now

DREAMT (5)

117 SP	Doris	33	No it's mine. I'm sure it's mine./I dreamt of weddings all last night./Yes it's mine.
126 SA	Chorus	2	coming to you./Hoo hoo hoo/You dreamt you waked up at seven o'clock and it's/
255 MC	Tempt4	28	to damnation./{T4} You have often dreamt them./{T} Is there no way, in my soul's
333 FR	Harry	22	my life has only been a dream/Dreamt through me by the minds of others.
333 FR	Harry	23	the minds of others. Perhaps/I only dreamt I pushed her./{Ag} So I had supposed.

DRENCHT (1)

588 Fable		33	to keep them off by force.'/He drencht the gown he wore with holy water,/The

DRESDEN (1)

29 Aunt Helen		10	afterwards the parrot died too./The Dresden clock continued ticking on the

DRESS (7)

15 Prufrock		65	brown hair!)/Is it perfume from a dress/That makes me so digress?/Arms that lie
24 Rhapsody		19	like a grin./You see the border of her dress/Is torn and stained with sand,/And you
291 FR	Chorus	1	rustling in the stalls, the titter in the dress circle, the laughter and catcalls in the
302 FR	Amy	15	Now they can hardly arrive in time to dress./I do not understand what could have
302 FR	Amy	18	directions./Well, we must go and dress, I suppose. I hope Harry will feel better/
424 CP	Edward	25	glad/When it's all over./{E} I like the dress you're wearing:/I'm glad you put on that
440 CP	Lavinia	28	should have done was to admire my dress./{E} But I've already told you how much I

DRESSED (6)

165 Rock 9		41	formed stone, the visible crucifix,/The dressed altar, the lifting light,/Light/Light/The
249 MC	Tempt2	31	is public profit;/Dignity still shall be dressed with decorum./{T} You forget the
290 FR	Chorus	38	the curtain rises, to find themselves dressed for a different play, or having rehearsed
313 FR	Violet	1	/{V} Good evening, Mary: aren't you dressed yet?/How do you think that Harry is
343 FR	m	31	*been speaking,* HARRY *has entered, dressed for departure.*]/{H} But, mother, you will
362 CP	Reilly	27	it/As quickly as we can. When you've dressed for a party/And are going downstairs,

DREST (1)

92 Ash-Wed 3		15	pasture scene/The broadbacked figure drest in blue and green/Enchanted the maytime

DREW (4)

73 WL: Thund		377	/Vienna London/Unreal/A woman drew her long black hair out tight/And fiddled
124 SA	Doris	5	I cut the cards before you came/And I drew the coffin/{Sw} *You* drew the coffin?/{Do}
124 SA	Swarts	6	came/And I drew the coffin/{Sw} *You* drew the coffin?/{Do} I drew the COFFIN very
124 SA	Doris	7	/{Sw} *You* drew the coffin?/{Do} I drew the COFFIN very last card./I don't care

DRIED (5)

61 WL: Burial		7	snow, feeding/A little life with dried tubers./Summer surprised us, coming over
83 Hollow Men		5	filled with straw. Alas!/Our dried voices, when/We whisper together/Are
210 Old Gumbie		23	them a mouse-cake of bread and dried peas,/And a *beautiful* fry of lean bacon
368 CP	Alex	26	/With a handful of rice and a little dried fish/I can make half a dozen dishes. Don't
530 ES	Ld Clav	9	wears out the machine./{LC} They've dried up, Monica, and you know it./They talk

DRIFT (8)

31 Apollinax	11	worried bodies of drowned men drift down in the green silence,/Dropping from
54 Mr E Sun	3	/The sapient sutlers of the Lord/Drift across the window-panes./In the beginning
56 Swee Night	7	the River Plate,/Death and the Raven drift above/And Sweeney guards the hornèd
69 WL: Fire S	268	river sweats/Oil and tar/The barges drift/With the turning tide/Red sails/Wide/To
98 Ash-Wed 6	23	the voices shaken from the yew-tree drift away/Let the other yew be shaken and
172 FQ: BurntN	56	of the lymph/Are figured in the drift of stars/Ascend to summer in the tree/We
186 FQ: DrySal	84	is painless and motionless,/To the drift of the sea and the drifting wreckage,/The
335 FR Harry	12	under./{H} In and out, in an endless drift/Of shrieking forms in a circular desert/

DRIFTING (4)

69 WL: Fire S	274	on the heavy spar./The barges wash/Drifting logs/Down Greenwich reach/Past the
185 FQ: DrySal	54	/Where is there an end to the drifting wreckage,/The prayer of the bone on
186 FQ: DrySal	66	might pass for devotionless,/In a drifting boat with a slow leakage,/The silent
186 FQ: DrySal	84	/To the drift of the sea and the drifting wreckage,/The bone's prayer to Death

DRIFTS (1)

| 597 Before Mor | 6 | flowers of yesterday/Their fragrance drifts across the room at dawn,/Fragrance of |

DRILLED (1)

| 229 Gus | 47 | when Victoria reigned./They never get drilled in a regular troupe,/And they think they |

DRINK (25)

19 Portrait	40	clocks./Then sit for half an hour and drink our bocks./Now that lilacs are in bloom/
72 WL: Thund	335	there were water we should stop and drink/Amongst the rock one cannot stop or
89 Ash-Wed 1	14	transitory power/Because I cannot drink/There, where trees flower, and springs
124 SA Sweeney	38	and see me sometimes/I'd give him a drink and cheer him up./{Do} Cheer him up?/
125 SA Sweeney	25	we gotta do/We're gona sit here and drink this booze/We're gona sit here and have a
182 FQ: ECoker	169	is briars./The dripping blood our only drink,/The bloody flesh our only food:/In spite
222 Pekes Pols	16	into the Wellington Arms for a drink —/And no one at all was about on the
230 Bust Jones	24	a moment too soon/To drop in for a drink at the *Drones.*/When he's seen in a hurry
236 Cat Morgan	7	a bowl;/But I'm allus content with a drink on the 'ouse/And a bit o' cold fish when I
588 Fable	58	wassail the monks dozed,/A fine old drink, though now gone out of use —/His feet
355 CP Julia	26	like me/Is a really nice tit-bit. I can drink at home. {}/[EDWARD *returns with a*
360 CP Reilly	9	is an occasion./May I take another drink?/{E} Whisky?/{UG} Gin./{E} Anything in
360 CP Reilly	16	.../Strong ... but sip it slowly ... and drink it sitting down./Breathe deeply, and adopt
377 CP Edward	27	propose?/{E} No, I can't. But I won't drink to Alex's./{J} Oh, it isn't Alex's. Come, I
383 CP Edward	16	/Well, I hoped that you would drink a final glass with me./{C} What should we
383 CP Celia	17	glass with me./{C} What should we drink to?/{E} Whom shall we drink to?/{C} To
383 CP Edward	18	we drink to?/{E} Whom shall we drink to?/{C} To the Guardians./{E} To the
383 CP	m 22	you who spoke of guardians. {}/[*They drink*]/{C} It may be that even Julia is a
422 CP	m 17	herself influence the bed. {}/[*They drink*]/{A} The words for those who go upon a
422 CP	m 28	/Protect her in the silence. {}/[*They drink*]/{R} There is one for whom the words
425 CP Edward	24	come on to us later, roaring for drink./Well, let's hope that those who come to
426 CP Julia	32	*they* offer in the way of food and drink!/And I've had to miss my tea, and I'm
479 CC Lucasta	2	me out to dinner. And I'm dying for a drink./{K} I told Colby, never learn to mix
479 CC Kaghan	18	Yes, I'll have a glass of sherry,/To drink success to the flat. Lucasta too:/Much
479 CC Kaghan	21	I don't like sherry./{K} You've got to drink it,/To Colby, and a happy bachelor life!/

DRINKIN' (1)

| 365 CP   Reilly | 5 | is missing. {}/[*Sings*]./{UG} *As I was drinkin' gin and water,/And me bein' the One* |

DRINKING (9)

19 Portrait	51	see.'/I smile, of course,/And go on drinking tea./'Yet with these April sunsets, that
178 FQ: ECoker	47	Feet rising and falling./Eating and drinking. Dung and death./Dawn points, and
257 MC Chorus	22	shelter,/For sleeping, and eating and drinking and laughter./God gave us always
277 MC Knight3	9	had drunk a good deal — I am not a drinking man/ordinarily — to brace myself up
286 FR Charles	26	people don't know what they're drinking,/Modern young people don't care what
289 FR Violet	29	*missing.*/{V} Had she been drinking?/{A} I would never ask him./{I} These
299 FRDowning	30	one of those that are *designed* for drinking:/It's natural for some and unnatural
363 CP Edward	4	/{E} Oh, I'm sorry. What were you drinking?/Whisky?/{UG} Gin./{E} Anything
365 CP Julia	17	/Tell me about him. You've been *drinking* together!/So this is the kind of friend

DRINKS (1)

| 422 CP | 2m 11 | *three glasses, and/exit.* REILLY *pours drinks.*]/{R} And now we are ready to proceed to |

DRIP (2)

| 73 WL: Thund | 357 | hermit-thrush sings in the pine trees/Drip drop drip drop drop drop drop/But there |
| 73 WL: Thund | 357 | sings in the pine trees/Drip drop drip drop drop drop drop/But there is no water/ |

DRIPPING (1)

| 182 FQ: ECoker | 169 | is roses, and the smoke is briars./The dripping blood our only drink,/The bloody flesh |

DRIVE (3)
328 FR	Charles	15	and costs to-day, and forbidden to drive a car for the/next twelve months./While
555 ES	Monica	18	I didn't get far./I met Michael in the drive. He says he must see you./I'm afraid that
556 ES	Ld Clav	14	/{LC} You're glad I'm here? Did you drive down from London?/{Mi} I drove down

DRIVELLING (1)
| 92 Ash-Wed 3 | 10 | jaggèd, like an old man's mouth drivelling, beyond repair,/Or the toothed gullet |

DRIVEN (7)
39 Gerontion	72	the Gulf claims,/And an old man driven by the Trades/To a sleepy corner./
160 Rock 7	3	GOD is a seed upon the wind: driven this way and that, and finding no place
174 FQ: BurntN	113	souls/Into the faded air, the torpid/Driven on the wind that sweeps the gloomy hills
190 FQ: DrySal	227	has in it no source of movement —/Driven by dæmonic, chthonic/Powers. And
213 Growltiger	51	plank./He who a hundred victims had driven to that drop,/At the end of all his crimes
255 MC Thomas	33	future torment./Can sinful pride be driven out/Only by more sinful? Can I neither
263 MC Chorus	2	in the South?/Only the sea-bird cries, driven inland by the storm./What sign of the

DRIVER (7)
232 Skimble	19	the Sleeping Car Express./From the driver and the guards to the bagmen playing
322 FR	Winch	34	up round the bend. We'll have the driver up for this:/Says he doesn't know this
325 FR	Charles	21	/{C} Oh, but Arthur's a brilliant driver./After all the experience he's had at
325 FR	Gerald	24	to get into trouble./{G} A brilliant driver, but more reckless./{I} Yet I remember,
457 CC	Lady E	18	Now, Parkman, will you give it to the driver?/He tells me that he suffers from chronic
560 ES	Michael	23	/Certainly not. I'm far too good a driver./{LC} What then? That young woman?/
571 ES	Ld Clav	38	another man ran over him./A lorry driver. He stopped and was arrested,/But was

DRIVES (1)
| 515 CC | Guzzard | 30 | you understand that this revelation/Drives the knife deeper and twists it in the |

DRIVING (4)
430 CP	Peter	13	over for a week, you see,/And I'm driving down to the country this evening,/So I
540 ES	Gomez	17	/We drove back to Oxford? *You* were driving./{LC} That happened several times./{G}
555 ES	Ld Clav	20	has happened./{LC} Was he driving his car?/{M} No, he was walking./{LC} I
571 ES	Ld Clav	34	well, has always haunted me./I was driving back to Oxford. We had two girls with

DROIT (1)
| 51 Restaurant | 23 | décrasse-toi le crâne./De quel droit payes-tu des expériences comme moi?/ |

DRONE (1)
| 281 MC Chorus | 16 | of winter, the song of spring, the drone of summer, the voices of beasts and of |

DRONES (1)
| 230 Bust Jones | 24 | too soon/To drop in for a drink at the *Drones.*/When he's seen in a hurry there's |

DRONING (1)
| 271 MC Thomas | 15 | /You shall remember them, droning by the fire,/When age and forgetfulness |

DROOP (1)
| 45 Cook Egg | 33 | /Weeping, weeping multitudes/Droop in a hundred A.B.C.'s./Le Directeur/ |

DROOPS (1)
| 129 Cor2 State | 35 | spreads its wings, there the clematis droops over the lintel/O mother (not among |

DROP (17)
14 Prufrock	30	and days of hands/That lift and drop a question on your plate;/Time for you
73 WL: Thund	357	sings in the pine trees/Drip drop drip drop drop drop drop/But there is no
73 WL: Thund	357	sings in the pine trees/Drip drop drip drop drop drop drop/But there is no water/Who
73 WL: Thund	357	in the pine trees/Drip drop drip drop drop drop drop/But there is no water/Who is
73 WL: Thund	357	pine trees/Drip drop drip drop drop drop drop/But there is no water/Who is the
73 WL: Thund	357	trees/Drip drop drip drop drop drop drop/But there is no water/Who is the third who
213 Growltiger	51	a hundred victims had driven to that drop,/At the end of all his crimes was forced to
230 Bust Jones	24	noon's not a moment too soon/To drop in for a drink at the *Drones.*/When he's
233 Skimble	53	he has a cup of tea/With perhaps a drop of Scotch while he's keeping on the watch,
589 Fable	71	be allowed about,/For often they drop in at awkward moments,/As everybody'll
594 Grad 11	6	on the surface of the stream,/A drop of dew upon the morning grass;/Thou dost
287 FR	Amy	21	may still go right./Meanwhile, let us drop the subject. The less said the better./{G}
326 FR	Harry	10	I think: it's strange how the old/Can drop off to sleep in the middle of calamity/Like
358 CP	Julia	32	You can get *me* a taxi, and then I can drop you./I expect you on Friday, Edward. And
359 CP	Reilly	12	Gin./{E} Anything in it?/{UG} A drop of water./{E} I want to apologise for this
508 CC	Eggers	14	ignore that remark./{E} May I pour a drop of oil on these troubled waters?/Let us
569 ES	Ld Clav	1	we pretend/The harder it becomes to drop the pretence,/Walk off the stage, change

DROPPED (4)
390 CP	Julia	3	your telegram was a bit unexpected./I dropped everything to come. And how is the
412 CP	Julia	5	seeing me first?/{J} Of course not. I dropped her at the door/And went on in the
482 CC	Lady E	7	people nowadays/Seem to have dropped the use of surnames altogether./But,
549 ES	Carghil	17	and I got soaking wet/And nearly dropped the punt pole, and you all laughed at

DROPPING (3)

31 Apollinax	12	men drift down in the green silence,/Dropping from fingers of surf./I looked for the
185 FQ: DrySal	53	silent withering of autumn flowers/Dropping their petals and remaining
479 CC Kaghan	4	/If you don't want women always dropping in on you./And between a couple of

DROUTH (2)

| 97 Ash-Wed 5 | 35 | the garden the garden in the desert/Of drouth, spitting from the mouth the withered |
| 192 FQ: Little | 64 | the death of air./There are flood and drouth/Over the eyes and in the mouth,/Dead |

DROVE (4)

406 CP Edward	27	than a ... battleship. That's what drove me mad./I am the one who needs a
540 ES Gomez	17	remember the moonlight night/We drove back to Oxford? *You* were driving./{LC}
545 ES Ld Clav	9	errors into which his own reproaches drove us?/{M} You admit that at the moment
556 ES Michael	15	you drive down from London?/{Mi} I drove down last night. I'm staying at a pub/

DROWN (1)

| 17 Prufrock | 131 | /Till human voices wake us, and we drown./Portrait of a Lady/Among the smoke |

DROWNED (8)

31 Apollinax	11	coral islands/Where worried bodies of drowned men drift down in the green silence,/
62 WL: Burial	47	Here, said she,/Is your card, the drowned Phoenician Sailor,/(Those are pearls
64 WL: Chess	89	or liquid — troubled, confused/And drowned the sense in odours; stirred by the air/
213 Growltiger	47	with ease, I'm sure she was not drowned —/But a serried ring of flashing steel
601 Nocturne	13	/While female readers all in tears are drowned: —/'The perfect climax all true lovers
257 MC Chorus	3	walk with a lamp at night, and yet be drowned in a ditch./{3P} A man may climb the
310 FR Harry	13	of the dead/Those whom the winter drowned/Do not the ghosts of the drowned/
310 FR Harry	14	drowned/Do not the ghosts of the drowned/Return to land in the spring?/Do the

DROWSINESS (1)

| 295 FR Harry | 25 | live in./— I lay two days in contented drowsiness;/Then I recovered. I am afraid of |

DRUG (1)

| 107 Animula | 21 | control./The pain of living and the drug of dreams/Curl up the small soul in the |

DRUGS (1)

| 189 FQ: DrySal | 199 | all these are usual/Pastimes and drugs, and features of the press:/And always |

DRUM (3)

24 Rhapsody	9	lamp that I pass/Beats like a fatalistic drum,/And through the spaces of the dark/
177 FQ: ECoker	27	music/Of the weak pipe and the little drum/And see them dancing around the bonfire
196 FQ: Little	189	old policies/Or follow an antique drum./These men, and those who opposed them

DRUMMING (1)

| 188 FQ: DrySal | 144 | behind you;/And on the deck of the drumming liner/Watching the furrow that |

DRUNK (2)

| 37 Gerontion | 22 | /To be eaten, to be divided, to be drunk/Among whispers; by Mr. Silvero/With |
| 277 MC Knight3 | 9 | I'll only speak for/myself, but I had drunk a good deal — I am not a drinking man/ |

DRUNKEN (2)

| 605 Narcissus | 29 | young girl/Caught in the woods by a drunken old man/Knowing at the end the taste |
| 606 Narcissus | 32 | of his own smoothness,/And he felt drunken and old./So he became a dancer to |

DRY (32)

24 Rhapsody	23	pin.'/The memory throws up high and dry/A crowd of twisted things;/A twisted
24 Rhapsody	63	/The reminiscence comes/Of sunless dry geraniums/And dust in crevices,/Smells of
31 Apollinax	17	hoofs over the hard turf/As his dry and passionate talk devoured the afternoon.
37 Gerontion	1	/Here I am, an old man in a dry month,/Being read to by a boy, waiting for
39 Gerontion	75	/Tenants of the house,/Thoughts of a dry brain in a dry season./Burbank with a
39 Gerontion	75	house,/Thoughts of a dry brain in a dry season./Burbank with a Baedeker: Bleistein
53 Whispers	31	charm;/But our lot crawls between dry ribs/To keep our metaphysics warm./Mr.
61 WL: Burial	24	shelter, the cricket no relief,/And the dry stone no sound of water. Only/There is
67 WL: Fire S	194	ground/And bones cast in a little low dry garret,/Rattled by the rat's foot only, year
72 WL: Thund	337	one cannot stop or think/Sweat is dry and feet are in the sand/If there were only
72 WL: Thund	342	not even silence in the mountains/But dry sterile thunder without rain/There is not
73 WL: Thund	354	of water only/Not the cicada/And dry grass singing/But sound of water over a
74 WL: Thund	390	no windows, and the door swings,/Dry bones can harm no one./Only a cock stood
83 Hollow Men	8	Are quiet and meaningless/As wind in dry grass/Or rats' feet over broken glass/In our
83 Hollow Men	10	/Or rats' feet over broken glass/In our dry cellar/Shape without form, shade without
90 Ash-Wed 1	36	which is now thoroughly small and dry/Smaller and dryer than the will/Teach us to
91 Ash-Wed 2	7	/In the bones (which were already dry) said chirping:/Because of the goodness of
94 Ash-Wed 4	9	made fresh the springs/Made cool the dry rock and made firm the sand/In blue of
107 Animula	3	lights and noise,/To light, dark, dry or damp, chilly or warm;/Moving between
135 5FingerEx2	2	a tree/And the tree was crookt and dry./In a black sky, from a green cloud/Natural
135 5FingerEx2	9	brown/And the tree was cramped and dry./Pollicle dogs and cats all must/Jellicle cats
172 FQ: BurntN	36	/To look down into the drained pool./Dry the pool, dry concrete, brown edged,/And
172 FQ: BurntN	36	into the drained pool./Dry the pool, dry concrete, brown edged,/And the pool was

184 FQ: DrySal	t	In my end is my beginning./The Dry Salvages/I do not know much about gods;
216 Jellicles	20	wash behind their ears,/Jellicles dry between their toes./Jellicle Cats are white
606 Narcissus	38	and satisfied him./Now he is green, dry and stained/With the shadow in his mouth./
272 MC Chorus	11	*the distance*]./{C} Numb the hand and dry the eyelid,/Still the horror, but more horror/
275 MC Chorus	24	they bleed; I wander in a land of dry stones: if I touch them they bleed./How how
286 FR Charles	25	a civilised person needs/Is a glass of dry sherry or two before dinner./The modern
290 FR Agatha	32	the corner/The wind's talk in the dry holly-tree/The inclination of the moon/The
372 CP Alex	27	is a cup of black coffee/And a little dry toast. I've left it simmering./Don't leave it
382 CP Celia	15	heard was only the noise of an insect,/Dry, endless, meaningless, inhuman —/You

DRYER (1)

90 Ash-Wed 1	37	small and dry/Smaller and dryer than the will/Teach us to care and not to

DRYING (3)

68 WL: Fire S	225	of the window perilously spread/Her drying combinations touched by the sun's last
186 FQ: DrySal	78	erosionless/Or drawing their money, drying sails at dockage;/Not as making a trip
306 FR Mary	1	changes here,/And we just go on ... drying up, I suppose,/Not noticing the change.

DRYNESS (1)

243 MC Chorus	34	is a year of rain,/Another a year of dryness,/One year the apples are abundant,/

DU (8)

46 Directeur	2	malheureuse Tamise/Qui coule si près du Spectateur./Le directeur/Conservateur/Du
46 Directeur	5	/Le directeur/Conservateur/Du Spectateur/Empeste la brise./Les
46 Directeur	9	/Les actionnaires/Réactionnaires/Du Spectateur/Conservateur/Bras dessus bras
46 Directeur	20	/Camarde/Regarde/Le directeur/Du Spectateur/Conservateur/Et crève d'amour./
51 Restaurant	4	mon pays il fera temps pluvieux,/Du vent, du grand soleil, et de la pluie;/C'est ce
51 Restaurant	4	pays il fera temps pluvieux,/Du vent, du grand soleil, et de la pluie;/C'est ce qu'on
51 Restaurant	21	vautour!/Va t'en te décrotter les rides du visage;/Tiens, ma fourchette, décrasse-toi le
62 WL: Burial	34	*zu/Mein Irisch Kind/Wo weilest du?/*'You gave me hyacinths first a year ago;/

DUCK (2)

135 5FingerEx3	t	/Pause, and sleep endlessly./*Lines to a Duck in the Park*/The long light shakes across
136 5FingerEx3	5	eft or mortal snake/But only sluggish duck and drake./I have seen the morning shine,/

DUE (6)

136 5FingerEx3	9	take/That which is their mortal due,/Pinching bread and finger too,/Easier had
187 FQ: DrySal	107	moments of agony/(Whether, or not, due to misunderstanding,/Having hopes for the
210 Old Gumbie	20	not ever keep quiet,/She is sure it is due to irregular diet/And believing that nothing
287 FR Gerald	23	me, Amy,/When are the boys all due to arrive?/{A} I do not want the clock to
333 FR Agatha	1	something more ingenious. You were due in three months' time;/You would not have
403 CP Reilly	13	the harm that is done in this world/Is due to people who want to feel important./They

DUET (1)

213 Growltiger	39	a sound./The lovers sang their last duet, in danger of their lives —/For the foe was

DUG (1)

153 Rock 2	54	the arm not waste;/Let the clay be dug from the pit, let the saw cut the stone,/Let

DUGS (1)

68 WL: Fire S	228	/I Tiresias, old man with wrinkled dugs/Perceived the scene, and foretold the rest

DUKE (2)

431 CP Julia	14	to Boltwell./{J} To stay with the Duke?/{P} And do him a good turn./We're
431 CP Peter	32	to know the best way to handle a duke./Besides that, we've got the casting

DULL (17)

19 Portrait	32	/Of cracked cornets/Inside my brain a dull tom-tom begins/Absurdly hammering a
37 Gerontion	16	the peevish gutter./I an old man,/A dull head among windy spaces./Signs are taken
61 WL: Burial	4	mixing/Memory and desire, stirring/Dull roots with spring rain./Winter kept us
67 WL: Fire S	189	the bank/While I was fishing in the dull canal/On a winter evening round behind
135 5FingerEx1	4	the trees there is no ease/For the dull brain, the sharp desires/And the quick eyes
191 FQ: Little	30	/And turn behind the pig-sty to the dull façade/And the tombstone. And what you
602 Humoresque	8	that we forget)/Pinched in a comic, dull grimace;/Half bullying, half imploring air,/
603 Spleen	10	Dejection unable to rally/Against this dull conspiracy./And Life, a little bald and gray,
280 MC Priest3	23	breath makes numb the hand, makes dull the brain;/Find an oasis in the desert sun,/
312 FR Harry	2	you so imperceptive, have you such dull senses/That you could not see them? If I
315 FR Harry	2	cancer. Cancer is here:/The lump, the dull pain, the occasional sickness:/Murder a
330 FR Harry	7	at home at Wishwood,/Make a dull marriage, marry some woman stupider —/
337 FR Harry	23	In a moment of clarity, and now I feel dull again./I only know that I made a decision/
381 CP Edward	39	*guardian* —/But in men like me, the dull, the implacable,/The indomitable spirit of
407 CP Reilly	17	/Or with the insuperably, innocently dull:/My patients such as you are the
557 ES Michael	9	I'd stuck it for two years. And deadly dull it was./{LC} Every job is dull, nine-tenths
557 ES Ld Clav	10	deadly dull it was./{LC} Every job is dull, nine-tenths of the time .../{Mi} I need

DULLARD (1)

143 Lines OM	13	/Reflected from my golden eye/The dullard knows that he is mad./Tell me if I am

DUMB (1)
191 FQ: Little   10   blaze of branch, or brazier,/Stirs the dumb spirit: no wind, but pentecostal fire/In the
DUMFRIES (1)
233 Skimble   59   with elation./But you saw him at Dumfries, where he summons the police/If
DUNG (3)
151 Rock 2   10   in the end, on a heap less useful than dung'./You, have you built well, have you
157 Rock 4   11   there, by the dragon's well, by the dung gate,/By the fountain gate, by the king's
178 FQ: ECoker   47   and falling./Eating and drinking. Dung and death./Dawn points, and another day
DUPLICITY (1)
241 MC   Priest3   1   temporal government,/But violence, duplicity and frequent malversation./King rules
DUR (1)
51 Restaurant   16   à cet âge .../'Monsieur, le fait est dur./Il est venu, nous peloter, un gros chien;/
DURATION (1)
197 FQ: Little   235   moment of the yew-tree/Are of equal duration. A people without history/Is not
DURING (15)
158 Rock 5   10   in the City./The man who has builded during the day would return to his hearth at
278 MC   Knight2   6   aim has been perfectly consistent. During the reign of/the late Queen Matilda and
299 FR   Charles   32   /{C} And how was his Lordship, during the voyage?/{Do} Well, you might say
300 FR   Charles   21   leave him out of her sight./{C} During that evening, did you see him?/{Do} Oh
318 FR   Harry   8   make up to mother/For all the weeks during which she had not seen us/Except at
364 CP   Edward   7   back, to find out what has happened/During the five years that we've been married./I
385 CP   Reilly   1   /Is only our memory of the moments/During which we knew them. And they have
434 CP   Peter   36   don't know what happened/To Celia, during those two years./Two years! Thinking
446 CC   Eggers   1   /He was finding his feet, very quickly,/During the time we worked together./All he
447 CC   Claude   25   /At my making the appointment during her absence,/You must say you had to
448 CC   Claude   26   /{SC} The reasons for starting him during her absence/Are perfectly clear. But
458 CC   Claude   33   /{SC} I didn't want to bother you, during your treatment .../{E} And Mr. Simpkins
490 CC   Colby   14   whether I've been suffering or not/During this conversation. I only feel ... numb./If
535 ES   m   19   worth his while to be trustworthy'. { }/[*During this* LAMBERT *enters silently, deposits*
546 ES   Piggott   8   Do you know, I fell in love with him/During an appendicitis operation!/I was a
DUSK (6)
15 Prufrock   70   I begin?/Shall I say, I have gone at dusk through narrow streets/And watched the
142 Cape Ann   3   vesper-sparrow/At dawn and dusk. Follow the dance/Of the goldfinch at
193 FQ: Little   93   /The first-met stranger in the waning dusk/I caught the sudden look of some dead
265 MC   Priest1   1   what is to-day? but another day, the dusk of the year./{P2} To-day, what is to-day?
582 ES   Monica   22   out late/At this season. It's chilly at dusk./{LC} Yes, it's chilly at dusk. But I'll be
582 ES   Ld Clav   23   chilly at dusk./{LC} Yes, it's chilly at dusk. But I'll be warm enough./I shall not go
DUST (22)
24 Rhapsody   58   twists a paper rose,/That smells of dust and eau de Cologne,/She is alone/With all
24 Rhapsody   64   comes/Of sunless dry geraniums/And dust in crevices,/Smells of chestnuts in the
61 WL: Burial   30   /I will show you fear in a handful of dust./*Frisch weht der Wind/Der Heimat zu*/
105 Song Sime   6   a feather on the back of my hand./Dust in sunlight and memory in corners/Wait
128 Cor1 March   37   virgins bearing urns, urns containing/Dust/Dust/Dust of dust, and now/Stone,
128 Cor1 March   38   bearing urns, urns containing/Dust/Dust/Dust of dust, and now/Stone, bronze,
128 Cor1 March   39   urns, urns containing/Dust/Dust/Dust of dust, and now/Stone, bronze, stone,
128 Cor1 March   39   urns containing/Dust/Dust/Dust of dust, and now/Stone, bronze, stone, steel, stone,
129 Cor2 State   48   /'Rising and falling, crowned with dust', the small creatures,/The small creatures
129 Cor2 State   49   creatures chirp thinly through the dust, through the night./O mother/What shall I
135 5FingerEx2   12   all must/Like undertakers, come to dust./Here a little dog I pause/Heaving up my
147 Rock 1   18   farther from GOD and nearer to the Dust./I journeyed to London, to the timekept
171 FQ: BurntN   17   /But to what purpose/Disturbing the dust on a bowl of rose-leaves/I do not know./
176 FQ: BurntN   173   in a shaft of sunlight/Even while the dust moves/There rises the hidden laughter/Of
192 FQ: Little   58   /Is all the ash the burnt roses leave./Dust in the air suspended/Marks the place
192 FQ: Little   60   Marks the place where a story ended./Dust inbreathed was a house —/The wall, the
203 Indians   5   neighbour's grandson/Playing in the dust together./Scarred but secure, he has many
233 Skimble   36   sheet/And there's not a speck of dust on the floor./There is every sort of light —
272 MC   Chorus   21   human, they shrink and dissolve/Into dust on the wind, forgotten, unmemorable; only
273 MC   Chorus   7   /Help me, Lord, in my last fear./Dust I am, to dust am bending,/From the final
273 MC   Chorus   7   Lord, in my last fear./Dust I am, to dust am bending,/From the final doom
437 CP   Reilly   4   my question./{R} *Ere Babylon was* dust/The magus Zoroaster, my dead child,/Met
DUSTY (3)
70 WL: Fire S   292   leia/Wallala leialala/'Trams and dusty trees./Highbury bore me. Richmond and
107 Animula   30   /Leaving disordered papers in a dusty room;/Living first in the silence after the
226 Macavity   14   his head is highly domed;/His coat is dusty from neglect, his whiskers are uncombed./

DUSTY (4) [*Proper name*]

115 SP m		1	*Melodrama*/Fragment of a Prologue/DUSTY. DORIS./{Du} How about Pereira?/
119 SP m		1	/KNOCK/KNOCK/DORIS. DUSTY. WAUCHOPE. HORSFALL.
119 SP	Wauch	1	/{W} Hello Doris! Hello Dusty! How do you do!/How come? how come?
121 SA m		1	SWARTS. SNOW. DORIS. DUSTY./{S} I'll carry you off/To a cannibal

DUTIES (5)

593 Grad 5		1	look into the future years./Great duties call — the twentieth century/More
331 FR	Agatha	37	neighbours,/But not neglecting public duties./He hid his strength beneath unusual
452 CC	Eggers	26	/Mr. Simpkins has taken over my duties./{L} And does he know that I'm one of
452 CC	Lucasta	27	And does he know that I'm one of his duties?/Have you prepared him for taking *me*
576 ES	Ld Clav	18	for me!/{LC} And what are your duties to be? Do you know?/{Mi} We didn't go

DUTY (7)

277 MC	Knight3	14	about it. We realised this was our duty,/but all the same we had to work ourselves
334 FR	Harry	22	/Was a kind of formal obligation, a duty/Only noticed by its neglect. One had that
341 FR	Amy	30	to persuade him/To abandon his duty, his family and his happiness?/Who has
418 CP	Celia	30	like what I want. But what is my duty?/{R} Whichever way you choose will
418 CP	Reilly	31	way you choose will prescribe its own duty./{C} Which way is better?/{R} Neither way
453 CC	Eggers	39	/{E} I'm no longer in charge/And that duty has *not* devolved on Mr. Simpkins:/Sir
548 ES	Monica	7	left/That she thought she'd done her duty by us for to-day./I'm going to prowl about

DWELL (1)

155 Rock 3		54	other?'/What will you answer? 'We all dwell together/To make money from each

DWELLERS (1)

184 FQ: DrySal		7	brown god is almost forgotten/By the dwellers in cities — ever, however, implacable,/

DWELLING (1)

255 MC Tempt4		8	can compare with glory of Saints/Dwelling forever in presence of God?/What

DWELLINGS (1)

155 Rock 3		50	where the rat breeds/Or sanitary dwellings with numbered doors/Or a house a

DWELT (1)

281 MC Chorus		19	holy places./For wherever a saint has dwelt, wherever a martyr has given his blood for

DYE (1)

592 Grad 3		5	the sun stains with many a splendid dye,/Until their passing may no more be traced.

DYING (25)

14 Prufrock		52	with coffee spoons;/I know the voices dying with a dying fall/Beneath the music from
14 Prufrock		52	/I know the voices dying with a dying fall/Beneath the music from a farther
21 Portrait		122	all?/This music is successful with a 'dying fall'/Now that we talk of dying —/And
21 Portrait		123	a 'dying fall'/Now that we talk of dying —/And should I have the right to smile?/
72 WL: Thund		329	dead/We who were living are now dying/With a little patience/Here is no water but
84 Hollow Men		54	are no eyes here/In this valley of dying stars/In this hollow valley/This broken
98 Ash-Wed 6		6	twilight between birth and dying/(Bless me father) though I do not wish to
98 Ash-Wed 6		20	/This is the time of tension between dying and birth/The place of solitude where
106 Song Sime		35	and the lives of those after me,/I am dying in my own death and the deaths of those
147 Rock 1		5	of spring and autumn, birth and dying!/The endless cycle of idea and action,/
181 FQ: ECoker		155	health is the disease/If we obey the dying nurse/Whose constant care is not to
196 FQ: Little		183	/These dead men more than the dying?/It is not to ring the bell backward/Nor is
197 FQ: Little		230	is where we start./We die with the dying:/See, they depart, and we go with them./
329 FR	Chorus	3	bedroom, whether of birth or of dying,/Gathers in to itself all the voices of the
426 CP	Julia	34	my tea, and I'm simply ravenous/And dying of thirst. What can Parkinson's do for
434 CP	Alex	8	village/And half the natives were dying of pestilence./They must have been
434 CP	Alex	13	knew of it, but would not leave the dying natives./Eventually, two of them escaped:
436 CP	Lavinia	25	because she would not leave/A few dying natives./{R} Who knows, Mrs.
436 CP	Reilly	27	that made to the natives who were dying/Or the state of mind in which they died?/
454 CC	Lucasta	13	of it, and take you out to tea./{L} I'm dying for my tea. The strain of this crisis/Has
465 CC	Claude	26	exhaustion and peace/Which comes in dying to give something life .../I intend that you
479 CC	Lucasta	2	to take me out to dinner. And I'm dying for a drink./{K} I told Colby, never learn
561 ES	Ld Clav	13	merely be another twenty years in dying./{Mi} Very well: if you like, call me a
570 ES	Ld Clav	13	/I think of your mother, when she lay dying:/Completely without interest in the life
582 ES	Ld Clav	5	one, I begin to live./It is worth while dying, to find out what life is./And I love you,

E. (8) [*Abbreviation*]
445 CC	Eggers	16	I matched some material for Mrs. E.,/Which she's been wanting. So *she*'ll be
451 CC	Eggers	19	/Quite a humorist, he is. In fact, Mrs. E./Sometimes says to me: 'Eggerson, why can't
455 CC	Eggers	28	garden/To protect me against Mrs. E. That's my joke./{C} Well, I've never met
456 CC	Eggers	29	/I remember long ago, saying to Mrs. E.,/When we'd bought our house in Joshua
461 CC	Eggers	8	any day, if you want me./In fact, Mrs. E. said: 'I wish he'd ring us up!/I'm sure he has
461 CC	Eggers	14	often./{E} Oh, and I forgot ... Mrs. E. keeps saying:/'Why don't you ask him out to
496 CC	Eggers	19	nowadays to bring me;/But Mrs. E. wishes I'd come up oftener!/Isn't that like the
518 CC	Eggers	21	There'll be no one so pleased as Mrs. E.;/Of that I can assure you./{MG} Mr.

E'ER (1)
| 593 Grad 5 | | 6 | /What heroes greater than were e'er of yore!/But if this century is to be more |

EACH (89)
16 Prufrock		124	/I have heard the mermaids singing, each to each./I do not think that they will sing
16 Prufrock		124	heard the mermaids singing, each to each./I do not think that they will sing to me./I
32 Hysteria		3	drawn in by short gasps, inhaled at each momentary/recovery, lost finally in the
62 WL: Burial		65	and infrequent, were exhaled,/And each man fixed his eyes before his feet./Flowed
74 WL: Thund		413	turn once only/We think of the key, each in his prison/Thinking of the key, each
74 WL: Thund		414	in his prison/Thinking of the key, each confirms a prison/Only at nightfall,
92 Ash-Wed 2		49	to be scattered, we did little good to each other,/Under a tree in the cool of the day,
92 Ash-Wed 2		51	of sand,/Forgetting themselves and each other, united/In the quiet of the desert.
111 Xmas Trees		15	surprises, delight in new possessions/(Each one with its peculiar and exciting smell),/
129 Cor2 State		30	remarkably Roman,/Remarkably like each other, lit up successively by the flare/Of a
149 Rock 1		92	/*A Church for all*/*And a job for each*/*Every man to his work.*/*Now a group of*
150 Rock 1		123	/*A Church for all*/*And a job for each*/*Each man to his work.*/Thus your fathers
150 Rock 1		124	/*A Church for all*/*And a job for each*/*Each man to his work.*/Thus your fathers were
155 Rock 3		53	close together because you love each other?'/What will you answer? 'We all
155 Rock 3		55	dwell together/To make money from each other'? or 'This is a community'?/And the
182 FQ: ECoker		180	is no longer disposed to say it. And so each venture/Is a new beginning, a raid on the
194 FQ: Little		106	to the common wind,/Too strange to each other for misunderstanding,/In concord at
194 FQ: Little		124	two worlds become much like each other,/So I find words I never thought to
203 Indians		10	fought in foreign places,/Foreign to each other./A man's destination is not his
206 To my Wife		5	/Of lovers whose bodies smell of each other/Who think the same thoughts
222 Pekes Pols		20	or exactly retreat,/But they glared at each other, and scraped their hind feet,/And
588 Fable		60	—/His feet upon the table superposed/Each wisht he had not eaten so much goose./
589 Fable		91	on milk and breakfast food entirely;/Each morn from four to five one took a knout/
594 Grad 12		1	grass;/Thou dost not die — for each succeeding year/Thy honor and thy fame
605 Narcissus		9	aware of his limbs smoothly passing each other/And of his arms crossed over his
605 Narcissus		22	a tree,/Twisting its branches among each other/And tangling its roots among each
605 Narcissus		23	other/And tangling its roots among each other./Then he knew that he had been a
253 MC Tempt4		18	fiend./Barons are employable against each other;/Greater enemies must kings destroy.
290 FR Agatha		29	a pocket-torch of observation/Upon each other's opacity/Neglecting all the
300 FRDowning		13	and wife/Shouldn't see too much of each other, Sir./Quite the contrary of the usual
307 FR	Harry	37	by other men, though sometimes by each other./{M} I know what you mean. That is
326 FR	Harry	17	disaster?/You go on trying to think of each thing separately,/Making small things
332 FR	Agatha	40	her?/{Ag} Oh, a dozen foolish ways, each one abandoned/For something more
337 FR	Agatha	21	is for those who do not know each other./{H} I know that I have made a
343 FR	Agatha	5	seen them too!/{Ag} We must all go, each in his own direction,/You, and I, and
349 FR	Chorus	4	are we, and what are we doing?/To each and all of these questions/There is no
349 FR	5m	13	*and round the table, clockwise.*/*At each revolution they blow out a few candles, so*
349 FR	Agatha	23	is a power/Not subject to reason/Each curse has its course/Its own way of
350 FR	Agatha	6	the meshes we have woven/Bind us to each other/Follow follow/{M} A curse is written
362 CP	Edward	9	love her?/{E} Why, I thought we took each other for granted./I never thought I should
362 CP	Edward	12	Why speak of love?/We were used to each other. So her going away/At a moment's
384 CP	Reilly	26	wife left me./{UG} Ah, but we die to each other daily./What we know of other people
385 CP	Reilly	19	pretend that you were not strange to each other./{E} You can hardly expect me to
385 CP	Reilly	31	said the same to her./Don't strangle each other with knotted memories./Now I shall
395 CP	Edward	38	difference, perhaps — we can fight each other,/Instead of each taking his corner of
395 CP	Edward	39	— we can fight each other,/Instead of each taking his corner of the cage./Well, it's a
407 CP	Reilly	14	/Your sympathetic understanding of each other/Will prepare you to appreciate what
408 CP	Reilly	35	to remark that my revelations/About each of you, to one another,/Have not been of
409 CP	Reilly	8	you are exceptionally well-suited to each other./Mr. Chamberlayne, when you
410 CP	Reilly	16	could love her.'/You could accuse each other of your own faults,/And so could
410 CP	Reilly	17	/And so could avoid understanding each other./Now, you have only to reverse the
414 CP	Celia	27	noises, and think they are talking to each other;/They make faces, and think they
414 CP	Celia	28	faces, and think they understand each other./And I'm sure that they don't. Is that

416 CP	Celia	22	/But that we had merely made use of each other/Each for his purpose. That's
416 CP	Celia	23	had merely made use of each other/Each for his purpose. That's horrible. Can we
417 CP	Reilly	35	who know they do not understand each other,/Breeding children whom they do not
419 CP	Reilly	2	loneliness. You will not forget yours./Each way means loneliness — and communion./
420 CP	Reilly	28	thoughts mouldering in their minds./Each unable to disguise his own meanness/
421 CP	Julia	8	Oh, of course, they might just murder each other!/But I don't think they will do that.
422 CP	Alex	15	the stars./{A} Let them place a chair each side of it./{J} May the holy ones watch
431 CP	Alex	10	/{A} Yes, we have sometimes obliged each other./{P} Well, it was Bela sent me over/
432 CP	Lavinia	28	/{L} I rather assumed that you knew each other —/I don't know why I should. Mr.
462 CC	Claude	39	with me here,/That we hardly know each other at all./{C} I suppose there hasn't
466 CC	Claude	22	have at best to live/In two worlds — each a kind of make-believe./That's you and
473 CC	Colby	40	have nothing whatever to do with each other —/Well, they're both unreal. But for
483 CC	Lady E	35	I should have said that we had known each other/In some previous incarnation. — Is
489 CC	Claude	6	/Absurd it sounds now. One child each —/That seemed fair enough — though
490 CC	Lady E	28	/No matter how long they have lost each other./{C} No, Lady Elizabeth. The
500 CC	Lucasta	34	life, just as I have,/And we can help each other. Oh, I know you think of him/Simply
500 CC	Lucasta	36	/Simply as a nuisance. We're suited to each other:/You thought so too, Claude, but for
501 CC	Lady E	18	you and I, Claude, can understand each other,/No matter how late. And perhaps
503 CC	Lucasta	1	Perhaps, one day/We may understand each other. And accept the fact/That we're not
503 CC	Lucasta	2	the fact/That we're not necessary to each other/In the way we might have been. But
503 CC	Lucasta	5	/We might become more necessary to each other,/As a brother and a sister, than we
516 CC	Claude	33	—/Except the claim of our likeness to each other./We have undergone the same
527 ES	Charles	3	We're agreed that we're in love with each other,/And, there being no legal
536 ES	Gomez	3	name twice — by easy stages,/And each step was merely a step up the ladder,/So
556 ES	Monica	26	I wish you'd stop being so polite to each other./Michael, you know what you've
562 ES	Monica	6	has said, Michael,/You must forgive each other, you must love each other./{Mi}
562 ES	Monica	6	forgive each other, you must love each other./{Mi} I could have loved Father, if
563 ES	Carghil	16	sent me here./{MC} Oh, you've seen each other lately?/Richard, I think that you
568 ES	Ld Clav	18	is well with you. You're in love with each other —/I don't need to be told what I've
570 ES	Ld Clav	10	not her fault. We never understood each other./And so we lived, with a deep silence
572 ES	Ld Clav	18	/In fact, we were wholly unsuited to each other,/Yet she had a peculiar physical
572 ES	Ld Clav	33	sound enough. But it's irrelevant./Each of them remembers an occasion/On which
578 ES	Ld Clav	10	and I, in our failure/To understand each other, both misunderstood you/In our
578 ES	Ld Clav	15	good/Only succeeded in defeating each other,/How can I feel anything but sorrow
578 ES	Michael	32	don't meet often, but if we're fond of each other,/That needn't interfere with your life
580 ES	Carghil	23	Michael./And now that we've found each other again,/We must always keep in

EAGER (6)

107 Animula		8	to the corner of arm and knee,/Eager to be reassured, taking pleasure/In the
194 FQ: Little		113	not remember.'/And he: 'I am not eager to rehearse/My thoughts and theory
593 Grad 6		4	are of her sons, and we must go/With eager hearts to help mold well her fate,/And see
246 MC Thomas		1	Little rest in Canterbury/With eager enemies restless about us./Rebellious
467 CC	Colby	29	interested by the work I'm doing/And eager for more. I don't want my position/To be,
508 CC	Guzzard	26	neighbours/Who were childless, and eager to adopt a child./They had taken a fancy

EAGERNESS (1)

| 421 CP | Julia | 28 | like a child sent on an errand/In eagerness and patience. Yet she must suffer./{R} |

EAGLE (4)

89 Ash-Wed 1		6	such things/(Why should the agèd eagle stretch its wings?)/Why should I mourn/
129 Cor2 State		5	of Honour,/The Order of the Black Eagle (1st and 2nd class),/And the Order of the
147 Rock 1		1	glad!/Choruses from 'The Rock'/The Eagle soars in the summit of Heaven,/The
252 MC Thomas		19	many yield./Shall I who ruled like an eagle over doves/Now take the shape of a wolf

EAGLE'S (1)

| 484 CC | Lady E | 22 | /I thought of myself as a dove in an eagle's nest./They were so carnivorous. Always |

EAGLES (4)

45 Cook Egg		29	and Golder's Green;/Where are the eagles and the trumpets?/Buried beneath some
127 Cor1 March		3	And the trumpets. And so many eagles./How many? Count them. And such a
127 Cor1 March		8	No, not yet. You can see some eagles. And hear the trumpets./Here they come.
128 Cor1 March		42	is all we could see. But how many eagles! and how many trumpets!/(And Easter

EAR (8)

67 WL: Fire S		186	the bones, and chuckle spread from ear to ear./A rat crept softly through the
67 WL: Fire S		186	and chuckle spread from ear to ear./A rat crept softly through the vegetation/
188 FQ: DrySal		149	a voice descanting (though not to the ear,/The murmuring shell of time, and not in
212 Growltiger		7	seedy, he was baggy at the knees;/One ear was somewhat missing, no need to tell you
212 Growltiger		20	was a Siamese had mauled his missing ear./Now on a peaceful summer night, all
213 Growltiger		33	their junks./Growltiger had no eye or ear for aught but Griddlebone,/And the Lady
257 MC Tempts		2	/{4T} Come whispering through the ear, or a sudden shock on the skull./{C} A man

257 MC Chorus 24 and down chimneys, flowing in at the ear and the mouth and the eye./God is leaving

EARL (1)
485 CC   Lady E   7   father could have been an ordinary earl!/And I couldn't believe that my mother *was*

EARLIER (4)
184 FQ: DrySal 18 the beaches where it tosses/Its hints of earlier and other creation:/The starfish, the
248 MC Tempt2 19   memories/In balance against other, earlier/And weightier ones: those of the
267 MC Knight1 27   /{T} Now and here!/{K1} Of your earlier misdeeds I shall make no mention./They
306 FR   Harry 19   at the same time, other memories,/Earlier, forgotten, begin to return/Out of my

EARLY (25)
22 Preludes   18 /With all its muddy feet that press/To early coffee-stands./With the other masquerades
177 FQ: ECoker 23   in the empty silence./Wait for the early owl./In that open field/If you do not come
178 FQ: ECoker 58   tumble down/Late roses filled with early snow?/Thunder rolled by the rolling stars/
191 FQ: Little   8 mirror/A glare that is blindness in the early afternoon./And glow more intense than
585   t /MORGAN./POEMS WRITTEN IN EARLY YOUTH/A Fable for Feasters/In
254 MC Tempt4 28   /And between sleep and waking, early in the morning,/When the bird cries, have
258 MC Thomas 17   desirable./Ambition comes when early force is spent/And when we find no longer
295 FR Charles 13 my chest/When I wake, as I do now, early before morning./I understand these
305 FR   Mary 21 you do, Harry./You are down very early. I thought you had just arrived./Did you
328 FR Charles 14 a roundsman's/cart in Ebury Street early on the morning of January 1st, was/fined
353 CP   2m 1   *of the Chamberlaynes' London flat. Early evening.*/EDWARD CHAMBERLAYNE,
377 CP   Julia 33   very simple./It's too late, or too early, to go to a restaurant./You must both
404 CP Edward 26   /You didn't want to hear about my early history./{R} No, I did not want to hear
404 CP   Reilly 27 No, I did not want to hear about your *early* history./{E} And so will you send me to the
425 CP Edward 25 let's hope that those who come to us early/Will be going on to the Gunnings
426 CP Lavinia 25 Oh, bother!/Now who would come so early? I simply *can't* get up./{CM} Mrs.
426 CP   Julia 30   you napping!/I know I'm much too early; but the fact is, my dears,/That I have to
430 CP   Peter 14 you wouldn't mind my looking in so early./It does seem ages since I last saw any of
445 CC   3m 1   MULHAMMER'S/*London house. Early afternoon.* SIR CLAUDE *writing at desk.*
481 CC Lady E 27   to you. You can have dinner early:/Most of its patrons dine at half past six./
492 CC Claude 29 —/Oh yes. To say something of my early ambitions/To be a potter. Not that the
544 ES Ld Clav 22 will last for a few days more./But this early summer, that's hardly seasonable,/Is so
547 ES Piggott 6 very careful at this time of year;/This early warm weather can be very treacherous./
547 ES Piggott 25   there's no dancing,/And it's still too early for the bathing pool./But several of our
557 ES Ld Clav 1 into trouble./{LC} You started pretty early getting into trouble,/When you were

EARNING (1)
334 FR Agatha 10   years upon my capital,/Instead of earning my spiritual income daily:/And I am

EARS (9)
31 Apollinax   19   what did he mean?' —'His pointed ears.... He must be unbalanced.' —'There was
64 WL: Chess 103 the world pursues,/'Jug Jug' to dirty ears./And other withered stumps of time/Were
103 Journ Magi 19   /With the voices singing in our ears, saying/That this was all folly./Then at
164 Rock 9   1 with thine eyes, and hear with thine ears/And set thine heart upon all that I show
214 RTTugger 29 you'll catch him in it right up to the ears,/If you put it away on the larder shelf./The
216 Jellicles   19   repose:/Jellicles wash behind their ears,/Jellicles dry between their toes./Jellicle
224 Mr Mistoff 24 quiet and small, he is black/From his ears to the tip of his tail;/He can creep through
240 MC Chorus 8   and shoot shall eat our eyes and our ears,/Disastrous summer burn up the beds of
541 ES Gomez 8 in confidence./It might even reach the ears of some of your acquaintance —/But you'd

EARSHOT (1)
308 FR Harry 34 my eye,/Almost whispering just out of earshot —/And inside too, in the nightly panic/

EARTH (40)
61 WL: Burial 6   rain./Winter kept us warm, covering/Earth in forgetful snow, feeding/A little life with
73 WL: Thund 369 endless plains, stumbling in cracked earth/Ringed by the flat horizon only/What is
98 Ash-Wed 6 19   renews the salt savour of the sandy earth/This is the time of tension between dying
151 Rock 2   13   and type for your citizenship upon earth./When your fathers fixed the place of
152 Rock 2   32 the other side of death,/But here upon earth you have the reward of the good and ill
155 Rock 3   63 thoroughly discredited,/Binding the earth and the water to your service,/Exploiting
177 FQ: ECoker 6   /Old fires to ashes, and ashes to the earth/Which is already flesh, fur and faeces,/
178 FQ: ECoker 38   /Lifting heavy feet in clumsy shoes,/Earth feet, loam feet, lifted in country mirth/
178 FQ: ECoker 39 mirth/Mirth of those long since under earth/Nourishing the corn. Keeping time,/
181 FQ: ECoker 159 sickness must grow worse./The whole earth is our hospital/Endowed by the ruined
191 FQ: Little   12   /The soul's sap quivers. There is no earth smell/Or smell of living thing. This is the
193 FQ: Little   71   without mirth./This is the death of earth./Water and fire succeed/The town, the
197 FQ: Little   246   remembered gate/When the last of earth left to discover/Is that which was the
201 Def Island 3 centuries of/patient cultivation of the earth, of English/verse/be joined with the
602 Humoresque 16   last spring's,/'The newest style, on Earth, I swear.'/'Why don't you people get some
240 MC Chorus 3   the labourer bends to his piece of earth, earth-colour, his own colour,/Preferring

249 MC	Tempt2	8	justice make all even,/Is thrive on earth, and perhaps in heaven./{T} What means?/
255 MC	Tempt4	13	make yourself the lowest/On earth, to be high in heaven./And see far off
256 MC	Chorus	7	/Thick and heavy the sky. And the earth presses up against our feet./What is the
256 MC	Chorus	8	from a cloud on a withered tree? The earth is heaving to parturition of issue of hell.
260 MC	Thomas	1	'Glory to God in the highest, and on earth peace to men of good will.' *The*/
260 MC	Thomas	14	'Glory to God in the highest, and on/earth peace to men of good will'; at this same
261 MC	Thomas	32	glory of being a/martyr. So thus as on earth the Church mourns and rejoices at once,
263 MC	Chorus	13	/Is there not peace upon earth, goodwill among men?/The peace of this
263 MC	Chorus	19	go out in March and turn the same earth/He has turned before, the bird shall sing
263 MC	Chorus	26	tree cover, what wrong/Shall the fresh earth cover? We wait, and the time is short/But
269 MC	Chorus	32	the spoon. I have felt/The heaving of earth at nightfall, restless, absurd. I have heard/
280 MC	Priest3	17	men, lost erring souls, homeless in earth or heaven./Go where the sunset reddens
280 MC	Priest3	35	never is belief: this is your fate on earth/And we must think no further of you./
281 MC	Chorus	7	displayed in all the creatures of the earth,/In the snow, in the rain, in the wind, in
281 MC	Chorus	12	hawk and the finch; the beast on the earth, both the wolf and the lamb; the worm in
281 MC	Chorus	18	martyrs and saints/Shall enrich the earth, shall create the holy places./For wherever
282 MC	Chorus	3	springs that which forever renews the earth/Though it is forever denied. Therefore, O
286 FR	Charles	23	does the harm:/There's nothing on earth so bad for the young./All that a civilised
345 FR	Charles	37	/And now I don't feel safe. As if the earth should open/Right to the centre, as I was
375 CP	Celia	24	Alex./Good night./{C} What on earth was that about?/{E} That was Alex./{C} I
427 CP	Edward	6	ALEX]/{E} Well, Alex!/Where on earth do you turn up from?/{A} Where on
427 CP	Alex	7	do you turn up from?/{A} Where on earth? From the East. From Kinkanja —/An
458 CC	Claude	7	Elizabeth!/{SC} Elizabeth!/What on earth has happened?/{E} Lady Elizabeth! This is
487 CC	Claude	21	Your child, Elizabeth? What on earth makes you think so?/{LE} I must see this

EARTH-COLOUR (1)

240 MC	Chorus	3	labourer bends to his piece of earth, earth-colour, his own colour,/Preferring to pass

EARTHLY (5)

167 Rock 10		36	we glorify Thee!/In our rhythm of earthly life we tire of light. We are glad when
249 MC	Tempt2	12	submission./Your spiritual power is earthly perdition./Power is present, for him who
255 MC	Tempt4	9	forever in presence of God?/What earthly glory, of king or emperor,/What earthly
255 MC	Tempt4	10	glory, of king or emperor,/What earthly pride, that is not poverty/Compared
485 CC	Lady E	16	simple!/To be able to think that one's earthly parents/Are only the means that we

EASE (13)

20 Portrait		85	for a slight sensation of being ill at ease/I mount the stairs and turn the handle of
104 Journ Magi		41	these Kingdoms,/But no longer at ease here, in the old dispensation,/With an alien
105 Song Sime		11	/Have given and taken honour and ease./There went never any rejected from my
135 5FingerEx1		3	Square./Beneath the trees there is no ease/For the dull brain, the sharp desires/And
135 5FingerEx1		8	/When will the broken chair give ease?/Why will the summer day delay?/*When*
194 FQ: Little		111	'The wonder that I feel is easy,/Yet ease is cause of wonder. Therefore speak:/I may
205 de la Mare		31	conscious art practised with natural ease;/By the delicate, invisible web you wove —/
213 Growltiger		47	/She probably escaped with ease, I'm sure she was not drowned —/But a
236 Cat Morgan		3	that's how you find me a-takin' my ease/And keepin' the door in a Bloomsbury
290 FR	Chorus	36	embarrassed, impatient, fretful, ill at ease,/Assembled like amateur actors who have
448 CC	Claude	5	him/Better than I. He's more at ease with you/Than he is with me./{E} Oh, you
452 CC	Kaghan	8	her/And come upstairs ahead, to ease the shock for Colby./But as you're here,
499 CC	Eggers	3	wish, Sir Claude./I do feel more at ease when I'm behind a desk:/It's second nature.

EASIER (13)

136 5FingerEx3		11	due,/Pinching bread and finger too,/Easier had than squirming worm;/For I know,
274 MC	Thomas	11	/Now, by suffering. This is the easier victory./Now is the triumph of the Cross,
289 FR	Amy	36	/It will make the situation very much easier/And is why I was so anxious you should
359 CP	Edward	35	want to talk to somebody;/And it's easier to talk to a person you don't know./The
415 CP	Celia	3	mean by a sense of sin./{C} It's much easier to tell you what I don't mean:/I don't
461 CC	Colby	28	/{C} I'm sure that will make it easier for both of us./{SC} Her sudden arrival
462 CC	Claude	31	/Thinking that you might find it easier/To start by a rather formal relationship/
491 CC	Colby	21	the same./{SC} Well?/{C} It would be easier, I think,/To accept you both in the place
499 CC	Lucasta	28	found me!/And I haven't made it easier. I didn't try to./And knowing that you
511 CC	Kaghan	22	me as Aunt Elizabeth./{K} That's easier, certainly./{LE} And I shall wish to meet
533 ES	Gomez	9	my country, than Culverwell — and easier to pronounce./{LC} Have you lived out
542 ES	Gomez	31	relent at last./You'll come to feel easier when I'm with you/Than when I'm out of
576 ES	Gomez	22	nature of business in San Marco/Is easier explained in San Marco than in England./

EASIEST (1)

305 FR	Agatha	14	only watchers and waiters: not the easiest rôle./I must go and change for dinner. {}/

EASILY (8)

43 Swee Erect		38	taste/Observing that hysteria/Might easily be misunderstood;/Mrs. Turner intimates/
234 Ad-dress		30	/Is frequently undignified./He's very easily taken in —/Just chuck him underneath

279 MC Knight4	33	human endurance, he could still have easily escaped; he/could have kept himself from
406 CP Reilly	19	need my sort of sanatorium/Are not easily deceived./{L} Are you a devil/Or merely a
451 CC Eggers	18	me laugh sometimes. I don't laugh easily./Quite a humorist, he is. In fact, Mrs. E./
530 ES Ld Clav	11	tell me to be cautious,/To take life easily. Take life easily!/It's like telling a man he
530 ES Ld Clav	11	cautious,/To take life easily. Take life easily!/It's like telling a man he mustn't run for
571 ES Ld Clav	13	weakness in him?/Yes, I was./How easily we ignore the fact that those who admire

EAST (13)

154 Rock 3	20	/1ST MALE VOICE:/A Cry from the East:/What shall be done to the shore of smoky
162 Rock 8	25	Came home cracked by the sun of the East/And the seven deadly sins in Syria./But
177 FQ: ECoker	t	sad time/Stretching before and after./East Coker/In my beginning is my end. In
186 FQ: DrySal	76	/Setting and hauling, while the North East lowers/Over shallow banks unchanging
229 Gus	36	will tell how he once played a part in *East Lynne*./At a Shakespeare performance he
597 Before Mor	1	brown./Before Morning/While all the East was weaving red with gray,/The flowers at
263 MC Chorus	7	the air: but a wind is stored up in the East./The starved crow sits in the field,
263 MC Chorus	11	spring?/The wind stored up in the East./What, at the time of the birth of Our
286 FR Gerald	7	a subaltern again/To be back in the East. An incomparable climate/For a man who
368 CP Alex	25	you have will do. I learned that in the East./With a handful of rice and a little dried
427 CP Alex	7	from?/{A} Where on earth? From the East. From Kinkanja —/An island that you
448 CC Eggers	9	mention her interest in Light from the East./{SC} And the Book of Revelation? And
485 CC Lady E	12	then I took up the Wisdom of the East/And believed, for a while, in reincarnation.

EASTER (2)

| 128 Cor1 March | 43 | and how many trumpets!/(And Easter Day, we didn't get to the country,/So we |
| 263 MC Chorus | 18 | harvest./Between Christmas and Easter what work shall be done?/The |

EASTERN (2)

| 166 Rock 10 | 20 | we praise Thee for the less;/The eastern light our spires touch at morning,/The |
| 390 CP Julia | 36 | that long journey on the old Great Eastern,/Waiting at junctions. And I suppose |

EASTWARD (1)

| 592 Grad 3 | 3 | when some haste/North, South, and Eastward o'er the water's waste,/Some to the |

EASY (15)

16 Prufrock	114	two,/Advise the prince; no doubt, an easy tool,/Deferential, glad to be of use,/Politic,
194 FQ: Little	110	/I said: 'The wonder that I feel is easy,/Yet ease is cause of wonder. Therefore
197 FQ: Little	222	neither diffident nor ostentatious,/An easy commerce of the old and the new,/The
247 MC Tempt1	35	/When they were your friends. Be easy, man!/The easy man lives to eat the best
247 MC Tempt1	36	were your friends. Be easy, man!/The easy man lives to eat the best dinners./Take a
287 FR Gerald	4	/We haven't left them such an easy world to live in./Let the younger
287 FR Amy	19	/Harry's return does not make things easy for her/At the moment: but life may still go
304 FR Agatha	37	violent. And it could not have been easy,/Living with Harry. It's not what she did to
369 CP Peter	5	from any girl I'd ever known/And not easy to talk to, on that occasion./{E} Did you
385 CP Edward	7	wife as a stranger?/That will not be easy./{UG} It is very difficult./But it is perhaps
451 CC Eggers	11	a rough diamond. Very free and easy ways;/And Lady Elizabeth has never taken
454 CC Kaghan	16	{}/[*Exit* LUCASTA]/{K} Take it easy, Colby. You'll get used to her. {}/[*Exit*
529 ES Monica	26	Though I know that won't be easy./{LC} That is just what I was doing./{M}
536 ES Gomez	2	changed your name twice — by easy stages,/And each step was merely a step up
546 ES Piggott	18	It's a short and simple name/And easy to remember. But, as I was saying,/Guests

EASY-GOING (1)

| 235 Ad-dress | 34 | will gambol and guffaw./He's such an easy-going lout,/He'll answer any hail or shout./ |

EAT (19)

16 Prufrock	122	I part my hair behind? Do I dare to eat a peach?/I shall wear white flannel trousers,
45 Cook Egg	26	where is the penny world I bought/To eat with Pipit behind the screen?/The red-eyed
121 SA Doris	14	missionary stew./{Do} You wouldn't eat me!/{S} Yes I'd eat you!/In a nice little,
121 SA Sweeney	15	You wouldn't eat me!/{S} Yes I'd eat you!/In a nice little, white little, soft little,
121 SA Sweeney	26	Citroën, no Rolls-Royce./Nothing to eat but the fruit as it grows./Nothing to see but
152 Rock 2	25	/Of all that was done in the past, you eat the fruit, either rotten or ripe./And the
214 RTTugger	26	there isn't any fish then he won't eat rabbit./If you offer him cream then he sniffs
587 Fable	26	was near the Abbot vowed/They'd eat their meal from ghosts and phantoms free,
588 Fable	34	turkeys, capons, boars, they were to eat,/He even soakt the uncomplaining porter/
240 MC Chorus	8	at our doors,/Root and shoot shall eat our eyes and our ears,/Disastrous summer
247 MC Tempt1	36	Be easy, man!/The easy man lives to eat the best dinners./Take a friend's advice.
355 CP Julia	23	/What a host! And nothing fit to eat!/The only reason for a cocktail party/For a
375 CP Edward	31	for supper;/And he said I must eat it within ten minutes./I suppose it's still
377 CP Julia	20	/There's nothing in the place fit to eat:/I've looked high and low. But I found some
428 CP Alex	20	/They trap the monkeys. And they eat them./The young monkeys are extremely
428 CP Edward	23	them myself .../{E} And did anybody eat them/When you cooked them?/{A} Oh yes,
429 CP Alex	20	/He is, as a rule, no longer fit to eat./{E} And what has your commission
481 CC Lady E	31	the type of person/Who needs to eat a great deal of salad./You remember, I made

481 CC Lucasta 36   /{L} I'm so hungry, I could even eat a herbal salad./{LE} That's right. Just
EATEN (10)
  24 Rhapsody   26   /A twisted branch upon the beach/Eaten smooth, and polished/As if the world
  37 Gerontion   22   and chestnut, flowering judas,/To be eaten, to be divided, to be drunk/Among
 194 FQ: Little 118   bad and good. Last season's fruit is eaten/And the fullfed beast shall kick the empty
 588 Fable   60   superposed/Each wisht he had not eaten so much goose./The Abbot with
 245 MC Priest2 7   /But frogs at least can be cooked and eaten./Whatever you are afraid of, in your
 247 MC Templ1 38   /Or your goose may be cooked and eaten to the bone./{T} You come twenty years
 269 MC Chorus 34   in the thick light of dawn. I have eaten/Smooth creatures still living, with the
 429 CP   Julia 10   are eating Christians./{J} Who have eaten monkeys./{A} The native is not, I fear,
 429 CP   Alex 18   /{A} Yes, but they are not usually eaten./When these people have done with a
 434 CP   Alex 30   tainted with the plague, they were not eaten./{L} Oh, Edward, I'm so sorry — what a
EATING (11)
 178 FQ: ECoker 47   that of beasts. Feet rising and falling./Eating and drinking. Dung and death./Dawn
 235 Ad-dress   61   (I know a Cat, who makes a habit/Of eating nothing else but rabbit,/And when he's
 247 MC Templ1   2   /Fires devouring the winter season,/Eating up the darkness, with wit and wine and
 257 MC Chorus 22   a partial shelter,/For sleeping, and eating and drinking and laughter./God gave us
 286 FR Charles 27   young people don't care what they're eating;/They've lost their sense of taste and
 372 CP   Alex 23   /Who can have the dish that you'll be eating, nowadays./{E} But what about my
 428 CP   Alex 27   new recipes./But you see, what with eating the monkeys/And what with protecting
 429 CP   Alex   8   into heathendom. So, instead of eating monkeys/They are eating Christians./{J}
 429 CP   Alex   9   instead of eating monkeys/They are eating Christians./{J} Who have eaten monkeys.
 429 CP   Julia 14   monkeys:/But one can't dine out on eating Christians —/Even among pagans!/{A}
 484 CC Lady E 23   Always killing things and eating them./And yet our childhood must have
EATS (1)
 295 FR   Harry 19   conscience; it is just the cancer/That eats away the self. I knew how you would take
EAU (1)
  24 Rhapsody   58   a paper rose,/That smells of dust and eau de Cologne,/She is alone/With all the old
EBURY (2)
 328 FR Charles 14   demolished a roundsman's/cart in Ebury Street early on the morning of January
 328 FR Charles 21   about here"—/{G} Where?/{C} In Ebury Street. 'The police stated that at the time
ÉCARTANT (1)
  48 Lune Miel   5   de chienne./Ils restent sur le dos écartant les genoux/De quatre jambes molles
ECCENTRIC (1)
 224 Mr Mistoff   9   surprising illusions/And creating eccentric confusions./At prestidigitation/And at
ECHE (1)
 178 FQ: ECoker 33   two, necessarye coniunction,/Holding eche other by the hand or the arm/Whiche
ECHO (6)
 134 Wind   5   death's dream kingdom/The waking echo of confusing strife/Is it a dream or
 171 FQ: BurntN 11   which is always present./Footfalls echo in the memory/Down the passage which
 171 FQ: BurntN 14   /Into the rose-garden. My words echo/Thus, in your mind./But to what purpose/
 335 FR Agatha   8   sharp heels scraping. Over and under/Echo and noise of feet./I was only the feet, and
 337 FR   Harry 25   I made a decision/Which your words echo. I am still befouled,/But I know there is
 488 CC Lady E   7   *Teddington*, there was a faint echo —/And then Mrs. Guzzard! It must be
ECHOED (1)
 180 FQ: ECoker 132   /The laughter in the garden, echoed ecstasy/Not lost, but requiring, pointing
ECHOES (2)
 171 FQ: BurntN 19   of rose-leaves/I do not know./Other echoes/Inhabit the garden. Shall we follow?/
 595 Grad 14   3   of every tale: 'Farewell',/A word that echoes like a funeral bell/And one that we are
ECHT (1)
  61 WL: Burial 12   keine Russin, stamm' aus Litauen, echt deutsch./And when we were children,
ECONOMIC (1)
 147 Rock 1   32   districts, there I was told/Of economic laws./In the pleasant countryside,
ECONOMICAL (1)
 411 CP Lavinia 16   /{L} Then we can share a taxi, and be economical./Edward, have you anything else to
ECONOMIST (1)
 539 ES Gomez   13   I wonder whether you're the great economist/And financial wizard that you're
ECONOMY (1)
 220 Old Deut   25   /Or when he's engaged in domestic economy:/And the Oldest Inhabitant croaks:
ÉCROULANTES (1)
  48 Lune Miel   18   de Dieu, tient encore/Dans ses pierres écroulantes la forme précise de Byzance./The
ECSTASY (12)
 105 Song Sime   29   stair./Not for me the martyrdom, the ecstasy of thought and prayer,/Not for me the
 109 Marina   12   meaning/Death/Those who suffer the ecstasy of the animals, meaning/Death/Are
 160 Rock 7   5   crying for life beyond life, for ecstasy not of the flesh./Waste and void. Waste

167 Rock 10   36 the day ends, when the play ends; and ecstasy is too much pain./We are children
173 FQ: BurntN 79   /In the completion of its partial ecstasy,/The resolution of its partial horror./Yet
180 FQ: ECoker 132   /The laughter in the garden, echoed ecstasy/Not lost, but requiring, pointing to the
181 FQ: ECoker 139 must go by a way wherein there is no ecstasy./In order to arrive at what you do not
271 MC Chorus   5 uttermost death of spirit,/By the final ecstasy of waste and shame,/O Lord
332 FR   Harry   3 /And yielded to it./{H} There was no ecstasy./Tell me now, who were my parents?/
381 CP   Edward 28 /That the tedium is not the residue of ecstasy./I see that my life was determined long
417 CP   Celia   7 /I have thought at moments that the ecstasy is real/Although those who experience it
466 CC   Claude 12   of which I spoke — an agonising ecstasy/Which makes life bearable. It's all I
EDGE (7)
  23 Preludes   35 understands;/Sitting along the bed's edge, where/You curled the papers from your
179 FQ: ECoker 92 in a dark wood, in a bramble,/On the edge of a grimpen, where is no secure foothold,/
184 FQ: DrySal   16 is all about us;/The sea is the land's edge also, the granite/Into which it reaches, the
259 MC Thomas   2   wrong, oppression and the axe's edge,/Indifference, exploitation, you, and you,/
378 CP   Celia   37 you are mad —/I mean, you're on the edge of a nervous breakdown./Edward, if I go
397 CP   Lavinia 14   and ever./{L} I think you're on the edge of a nervous breakdown!/{E} Don't say
402 CP   Edward 17 the same words —/That I was on the edge of a nervous breakdown./I didn't know it
EDGED (1)
172 FQ: BurntN 36 /Dry the pool, dry concrete, brown edged,/And the pool was filled with water out of
EDGES (1)
  27 Morning   2   kitchens,/And along the trampled edges of the street/I am aware of the damp souls
EDGWARE (1)
189 FQ: DrySal 202   on the shores of Asia, or in the Edgware Road./Men's curiosity searches past
EDITION (1)
327 FR   Charles 38 /{C} Stop, I think I bought a lunch edition/Before I left St. Pancras. If I did, it's in
EDITIONS (2)
328 FR   Gerald   9 There'll have been more in the later editions./You'd better read it to us. {}/[*reads*]./
496 CC   Eggers 26 home in the evening. And the late editions/Of the papers that I picked up at
EDOM (1)
162 Rock 8   6 defiled./Who is this that cometh from Edom?/He has trodden the wine-press alone./
EDUCATE (2)
470 CC   Lucasta 35 a compliment./It shows you want to educate me./{C} But I didn't know/That you
470 CC   Lucasta 39 did I./But I wanted you to want to educate me;/And now I'm beginning to believe
EDUCATED (2)
448 CC   Eggers 13 I thought, Mr. Simpkins,/He's highly educated. He'll soon begin to grasp them./No, I
470 CC   Colby   37 I didn't know/That you wanted to be educated./{L} Neither did I./But I wanted you
EDUCATING (1)
471 CC   Colby   9 /{C} I suspect that it's you who are educating *me*./{L} Colby, you really are full of
EDUCATION (2)
471 CC   Lucasta 8 and explained them./We'll begin my education at once./{C} I suspect that it's you
489 CC   Claude 21   him up,/And I provided for his education./I have watched him grow. And Mrs.
EDUCATIONAL (1)
230 Bust Jones   13 /His visits are occasional to the *Senior Educational*/And it is against the rules/For any
EDWARD (118)
129 Cor2 State   12 committees./What shall I cry?/Arthur Edward Cyril Parker is appointed telephone
352 CP   m   2 /THE COCKTAIL PARTY/Persons/EDWARD CHAMBERLAYNE/JULIA
353 CP   3m   1   *London flat. Early evening.*/EDWARD CHAMBERLAYNE, JULIA
354 CP   Celia   1 you, Julia;/And I don't believe that Edward knows it./{E} I may have heard it, but I
355 CP   m   16 the story about the wedding cake. {}/[EDWARD *leaves the room*]/{J} No, we'll wait
355 CP   Julia   17   *the room*]/{J} No, we'll wait until Edward comes back into the room./Now I want
355 CP   Peter   19 any more cocktails?/{P} But do go on. Edward wasn't listening anyway./{J} No, he
355 CP   Julia   21   listening, but he's such a strain —/Edward without Lavinia! He's quite impossible!/
355 CP   m   27 nice tit-bit. I can drink at home. {}/[EDWARD *returns with a tray*]/{J} Edward, give
355 CP   Julia   27 {}/[EDWARD *returns with a tray*]/{J} Edward, give me another of those delicious
356 CP   Julia   15 the story about the wedding cake./{J} Edward, do sit down for a moment./I know
356 CP   Julia   21 I've always said:/'If I could only get Edward alone/And have a really *serious*
356 CP   Celia   34 /{C} Will she be away for some time, Edward?/{E} I really don't know until I hear
357 CP   Celia   2   aunt. But I might go away./{C} But, Edward ... what was I going to say?/It's
357 CP   Julia   19 Lavinia/Yet very like her. But really, Edward,/Lavinia may be away for weeks,/Or
358 CP   Julia   18   cake? I wasn't at her wedding./Edward, it's been a delightful evening:/The
358 CP   Julia   33   drop you./I expect you on Friday, Edward. And Celia —/I must see you very soon.
358 CP   Julia   35 go/Just because I'm going. Good-bye, Edward./{E} Good-bye, Julia. {}/[*Exeunt* JULIA
358 CP   Celia   37 JULIA *and* PETER]/{C} Good-bye, Edward./Shall I see you soon?/{E} Perhaps. I
359 CP   Alex   3 /{E} Good-bye, Celia./{A} Good-bye, Edward. I do hope/You'll have better news of
359 CP   m   22 anyone else, {}/[*The doorbell rings.* EDWARD *goes to the door, saying:*]/{E} But

359 CP	Julia	24	*door*]/{E} Julia! {}/[*Enter* JULIA]/{J} Edward! How lucky that it's raining!/It made
364 CP	m	30	*rings*]/{E} I must answer the door. {}/[EDWARD *goes to the door*]/{E} So it's you
364 CP	Julia	31	{}/[*Enter* JULIA *and* PETER]/{J} Edward, I'm so glad to find you./Do you know,
365 CP	Julia	13	*with One Eyed Riley?* {}/[*Exit*]/{J} Edward, who *is* that dreadful man?/I've never
366 CP	Julia	7	them./Oh, here they are! Thank you, Edward;/That really was very clever of you;/I'd
366 CP	Julia	10	you./The next time I lose *anything*, Edward,/I'll come straight to you, instead of to
366 CP	Peter	16	something I had to say to Edward .../{J} Oh, about Lavinia?/{P} No, not
366 CP	Julia	23	the lift./{J} No, you stop and talk to Edward. I'm not helpless yet./And besides, I
366 CP	Peter	27	/{P} I hope I'm not disturbing you, Edward./{E} I seem to have been disturbed
366 CP	Peter	36	longer./That awful party! I'm sorry, Edward;/Of course it was really a very nice
367 CP	Alex	35	/[*Enter* ALEX]/{A} Ah, there you are, Edward! Do you know why *I*'ve looked in?/{E}
368 CP	Alex	3	/{A} Ah, but you're coming with me, Edward./I thought, Edward may be all alone
368 CP	Alex	4	coming with me, Edward./I thought, Edward may be all alone this evening,/And I
369 CP	Alex	7	/{E} Did you see her often?/{A} Edward, have you a double boiler?/{E} I
370 CP	Alex	14	*in shirtsleeves and an apron*]/{A} I can't find any curry powder./{E}
372 CP	Peter	8	Well, I will see Celia./{P} Thank you, Edward. It's very good of you. {}/[*Enter* ALEX,
372 CP	Alex	9	ALEX, *with his jacket on*]/{A} Oh, Edward! I've prepared you such a treat!/I really
372 CP	Peter	30	going, and I'll take Peter with me./{P} Edward, I've taken too much of your time,/And
372 CP	Peter	35	about it to Lavinia./{P} Thank you, Edward. Good night./{E} Good night, Peter,/
373 CP	Alex	1	so that it latches./{A} Remember, Edward, not more than ten minutes,/Twenty
373 CP	m	3	{}/[*Exeunt* ALEX *and* PETER]/[EDWARD *picks up the telephone, and dials a*
374 CP	2m	1	*room: a quarter of an hour later.* EDWARD *is alone, playing/Patience. The*
374 CP	m	2	*to answer it.*/{C} Are you alone? {}/[EDWARD *returns with* CELIA]/{E} Celia!
374 CP	Celia	8	don't seem very pleased to see me./Edward, I understand what has happened/But I
376 CP	m	1	and found you in the kitchen? {}/[EDWARD *goes over to the table and inspects*
376 CP	Celia	2	/{C} You'd better answer the door, Edward./It's the best thing to do. Don't lose
376 CP	m	7	*to kitchen. The bell rings again.* EDWARD *goes to front door, and is/heard to*
376 CP	Celia	11	{}/[*Enter* CELIA *with saucepan*]/{C} Edward, it's ruined!/{E} What a good thing./{C}
376 CP	Julia	18	had the same inspiration/That I had. Edward must be fed./He's under such a strain.
376 CP	Julia	20	strain. We must keep his strength up./Edward! Don't you realise how lucky you are/
376 CP	Julia	24	than I can do. You stay and talk to Edward. {}/[*Exit* JULIA]/{C} But what has
377 CP	Julia	2	what I can do. You stay and talk to Edward. {}/[*Exit* JULIA]/{C} But what has
377 CP	Celia	3	JULIA]/{C} But what has happened, Edward? What has happened?/{E} Lavinia is
378 CP	Celia	7	go, there's something/I want to say to Edward./{J} About Lavinia?/Well, come on
378 CP	Julia	11	absolutely famished./Good night, Edward. {}/[*Exit* JULIA]/{C} Well, how did he
378 CP	Celia	29	man?/I shall soon put that right, Edward,/When you are free./{E} No, it is not
378 CP	Celia	36	about a man named Riley!/Really, Edward, I think you are mad —/I mean, you're
378 CP	Celia	38	on the edge of a nervous breakdown./Edward, if I go away now/Will you promise me
379 CP	Celia	4	doctor/To cure *this* illness./{C} Edward, if I go now,/Will you assure me that
379 CP	Celia	9	us?/That's all that matters. Truly, Edward,/If that is right, everything else will be,/
380 CP	Celia	17	know what you are talking about./Edward, this is really too crude a subterfuge/To
381 CP	Celia	1	think I care for advice from you, Edward:/You are not entitled to take any
381 CP	Celia	20	you. I could understand./And, Edward, please believe that whatever happens/I
381 CP	Celia	24	be? I cannot bear to think of it./Oh, Edward! Can you be happy with Lavinia?/{E}
382 CP	Celia	4	stronger partner./{C} I am not sure, Edward, that I understand you;/And yet I
382 CP	Celia	33	— but what, and where is it?/Edward, I see that I was simply making use of
383 CP	m	10	go into your kitchen again. {}/[*Exit* EDWARD. *He returns with the spectacles and*
383 CP	Celia	24	Give me the spectacles./Good night, Edward./{E} Good night ... Celia. {}/[*Exit*
384 CP	2m	1	*room: late afternoon of the next day.* EDWARD *alone. He goes to/answer the*
386 CP	m	14	also am a stranger. {}/[*Exit. A pause.* EDWARD *moves about restlessly. The bell*
386 CP	Celia	31	/{C} Oh, I could./Just looking at you. Edward, forgive my laughing./You look like a
386 CP	Celia	37	it./{C} I'm not really laughing at *you*, Edward./I couldn't have laughed at anything,
387 CP	Celia	21	/{C} I've just explained to Edward —/I only got here this moment myself
387 CP	Peter	30	/{P} The aunt you told us about./But Edward — you remember our conversation
388 CP	Lavinia	29	/{L} I don't know what you mean./Edward, have you been sending telegrams?/{E}
389 CP	Celia	32	me/As someone who wants you and Edward to be happy./{L} You are very kind, but
389 CP	m	37	in the past! {}/[*The doorbell rings, and* EDWARD *goes to answer it*]/{C} Oh, I'm afraid
389 CP	m	38	all this sounds rather silly!/But ... {}/[EDWARD *re-enters with* JULIA]/{J} There you
390 CP	m	17	/I'm thrilled ... {}/[*The doorbell rings.* EDWARD *goes to answer it. Enter* ALEX]/{A}
390 CP	Lavinia	25	is in Essex. So it was from Dedham./Edward, have *you* any friends in Dedham?/{E}
391 CP	Celia	5	now. Good-bye, Lavinia./Good-bye, Edward./{E} Good-bye, Celia./{C} Good-bye,
392 CP	Lavinia	28	and had sent for you./{L} Really, Edward! You had better have told the truth:/
392 CP	Lavinia	38	quite know what you mean./{L} Oh, Edward!/The point is, that since I've been away/
394 CP	Lavinia	38	you, very differently./{L} Bravo! Edward. This is surprising./Now who could
395 CP	Lavinia	19	/I may have changed too?/{L} Oh, Edward, when you were a little boy,/I'm sure

396 CP	Lavinia	17	you had no opinion of your own./Oh, Edward, I should like to be good to you —/Or
397 CP	Lavinia	8	to escape to. One is always alone./{L} Edward, what *are* you talking about?/Talking to
398 CP	Lavinia	2	/{L} Yes, with Peter./Really, Edward, if you were human/You would burst
398 CP	Lavinia	12	what you would make me?/{L} Well, Edward, as I am unable to make you laugh,/
400 CP	1m	35	gone. {}/[*Exit* ALEX *by side door*]/[EDWARD *is shown in by*
404 CP	m	4	*rings*]/[*into telephone*]/{R} Yes. {}/[*To* EDWARD]/{R} Yes, you could be alone there./
406 CP	Lavinia	3	doesn't concern you./{L} In that case, Edward,/I don't think your clothes concern me
406 CP	Lavinia	35	/{L} That would never suit you, Edward. Now I know of a hotel/In the New
406 CP	Lavinia	40	more practical mind/Than you have, Edward. You do know that./{E} Only because
407 CP	Lavinia	3	income-tax form./{L} Don't be silly, Edward. When I say practical,/I mean practical
407 CP	m	32	Let me take your husband first. {}/[*To* EDWARD]/{R} You were lying to me/By
407 CP	Lavinia	35	knew nothing about it./{L} Really, Edward! Even if I'd been blind/There were
409 CP	Lavinia	23	impotence./{L} You *are* cold-hearted, Edward./{R} So you say, Mrs. Chamberlayne./
410 CP	Lavinia	29	we can go neither back nor forward? Edward!/What can we do?/{R} You have
411 CP	Lavinia	1	it will alter the condition./{L} Edward, there *is* that hotel in the New Forest/If
411 CP	Lavinia	12	/I was staying at the club?/{L} Really, Edward!/I have *some* sense of responsibility./I
411 CP	Lavinia	17	can share a taxi, and be economical./Edward, have you anything else to ask him/
411 CP	m	28	of your husband's problem. {}/[*To* EDWARD]/{R} Your business is not to clear
411 CP	m	35	/{R} No. Not in this capacity. {}/[EDWARD *takes out his cheque-book.*
411 CP	1m	36	salvation with diligence. {}/[*Exeunt* EDWARD *and* LAVINIA]/[REILLY *goes to*
424 CP	m	11	six. {}/[*Exit* CATERER'S MAN]/[EDWARD *lets himself in at the front door*]/{E}
424 CP	Lavinia	16	That you hadn't run away?/{L} Now Edward, that's unfair!/You know that we've
425 CP	Lavinia	2	glad you put on that one./{L} Well, Edward!/Do you know it's the first time you've
426 CP	Lavinia	11	/Of the whole party./{L} Oh no, Edward./The best moment is the moment it's
427 CP	Alex	12	must not miss the opportunity/To see Edward and Lavinia./{L} How are you, Alex?/
429 CP	Julia	34	someone you know — or knew .../{J} Edward!/Somebody must have walked over my
430 CP	Peter	11	crash in:/It's my only chance to see Edward and Lavinia./I'm only over for a week,
434 CP	Lavinia	31	plague, they were not eaten./{L} Oh, Edward, I'm so sorry — what a feeble thing to
438 CP	Lavinia	25	band of half-crazed savages./{L} Oh, Edward, I knew! I knew what you were
439 CP	Lavinia	27	do us all good —/You and me and Edward ... to talk about Celia./{P} Thanks very
440 CP	Lavinia	20	JULIA, REILLY *and* ALEX]/{L} Edward, how am I looking?/{E} Very well./I
440 CP	Lavinia	23	you always look your best./{L} Oh, Edward, that spoils it. No woman can believe/

EFFABLE (1)

209 NamingCats	29	the thought of his name:/His ineffable effable/Effanineffable/Deep and inscrutable

EFFACE (1)

604 Ode	13	that we leave./And only the years that efface and destroy/Give us also the vision to see

EFFANINEFFABLE (1)

209 NamingCats	30	of his name:/His ineffable effable/Effanineffable/Deep and inscrutable singular

EFFECT (7)

261 MC	Thomas	25	Still less is a Christian martyrdom the effect of a man's will to/become a Saint, as a
279 MC	Knight4	26	I have unimpeachable evidence/to the effect that before he left France he clearly
299 FR	Downing	20	you take my meaning — just for the effect./{C} I understand, Downing. Was she in
313 FR	Charles	23	know;/You should have a sobering effect upon him./After all, you're the head of
370 CP	Peter	21	into some other picture —/Like a film effect. She doesn't want to see me;/Makes
378 CP	Edward	17	I ought to be thankful./And yet, the effect of all his argument/Was to make me see
393 CP	Lavinia	7	has no sense of humour;/And that the effect upon me was/That I lost all sense of

EFFECTIVE (1)

601 Nocturne	9	lady sinks into a swoon./Blood looks effective on the moonlit ground —/The hero

EFFICIENT (2)

218 Mung	Rump	18	gift of the gab./They were highly efficient cat-burglars as well, and remarkably
331 FR	Agatha	23	it. What people know me as,/The efficient principal of a women's college —/That

EFFIE (10)

549 ES	Carghil	6	/{MC} There were the three of us — Effie, Maudie and me./That day we spent on the
549 ES	Carghil	22	of us talked you over afterwards —/Effie and Maud and I. What a time ago it
549 ES	Carghil	27	I could follow round the world!'/But Effie it was — you know, Effie was very shrewd
549 ES	Carghil	27	world!'/But Effie it was — you know, Effie was very shrewd —/Effie it was said 'you'd
549 ES	Carghil	28	you know, Effie was very shrewd —/Effie it was said 'you'd be throwing yourself
549 ES	Carghil	29	yourself away./Mark my words' Effie said, 'if you chose to follow *that* man/He'd
550 ES	Carghil	34	/{MC} There you're wrong, Richard. Effie always said —/What a clever girl she was!
551 ES	Carghil	35	much as I think you'd be awarded.'/Effie was against it — she wanted you exposed./
553 ES	Carghil	24	Only a few. But very beautiful!/It was Effie said, when the break came,/'They'll be
553 ES	Carghil	37	people?/{MC} Only a few friends./Effie said: 'If he becomes a famous man/And

EFFLUENCE (1)

52 Whispers	23	the scampering marmoset/With subtle effluence of cat;/Grishkin has a maisonnette;/

EFFORT (3)
194 FQ: Little   132   /To set a crown upon your lifetime's effort./First, the cold friction of expiring sense/
202 War Poetry   13   emotions/Are only 'incidents'/In the effort to keep day and night together./It seems
536 ES   Gomez   7   /I parted from myself by a sudden effort,/You, so slowly and sweetly, that you've
EFFORTLESS (1)
272 MC   Chorus   26   from God;/The horror of the effortless journey, to the empty land/Which is
EFFORTS (1)
578 ES   Ld Clav   14   and adolescence,/And see how all the efforts aimed at your good/Only succeeded in
EFT (1)
136 5FingerEx3   4   is slant across the lawn,/Here is no eft or mortal snake/But only sluggish duck and
EGG (6)
 44 Cook Egg   t   a glass of brandy neat./A Cooking Egg/Pipit sate upright in her chair/Some
121 SA Sweeney   18   little, missionary stew./You see this egg/You see this egg/Well that's life on a
121 SA Sweeney   19   stew./You see this egg/You see this egg/Well that's life on a crocodile isle./There's
123 SA Wa&Ho   8   /Any old isle is just my style/Any fresh egg/Any fresh egg/And the sound of the coral sea.
123 SA Wa&Ho   9   just my style/Any fresh egg/Any fresh egg/And the sound of the coral sea./{Do} I don't
376 CP   Edward   15   /I wanted one for breakfast. A boiled egg./It's the only thing I know how to cook./{J}
EGG (1) [*Abbreviation*]
454 CC   Colby   17   used to her. { }/[*Exit* KAGHAN]/{C} Egg ... Mr. Eggerson!/{E} Yes, Mr. Simpkins?/
EGGERS (5) [*Abbreviation*]
452 CC   Kaghan   2   B. Kaghan. Hello Colby!/And hello Eggers! I'm glad to find you here./It's lucky for
452 CC   Kaghan   9   shock for Colby./But as you're here, Eggers, I can just relax./I'm going to enjoy the
455 CC   Eggers   1   get used to it. You'll be calling me Eggers/Before you know it!/{C} I shouldn't
518 CC   Colby   12   cross that bridge when we come to it, Eggers./Oh, I'm sorry .../{E} Don't be sorry: I'm
519 CC   Kaghan   8   made the same mistake —/All except Eggers .../{E} Me, Mr. Kaghan?/{K} We wanted
EGGERSON (63)
444 CC   m   3   /SIR CLAUDE MULHAMMER/EGGERSON/COLBY SIMPKINS/B.
445 CC   4m   1   SIR CLAUDE *writing at desk. Enter*/EGGERSON./{SC} Ah, there you are,
445 CC   Claude   1   /{SC} Ah, there you are, Eggerson! Punctual as always./I'm sorry to have
445 CC   Claude   25   last time I came./{SC} Well, of course, Eggerson, you're irreplaceable .../{E} Oh, Sir
446 CC   Claude   12   understand his feelings./He's like me, Eggerson. The same disappointment/In a
448 CC   Claude   36   never had children./{SC} No worse, Eggerson,/Than for you and your wife, to have
449 CC   Claude   10   must get to like him first:/And then, Eggerson, I am not unhopeful/That, under the
450 CC   Claude   6   there's a lot I don't know/About you, Eggerson, although we worked together/For
450 CC   Claude   26   /{SC} Ah, Colby, I was just saying to Eggerson/It was time you were back. Was your
450 CC   Colby   29   Sir Claude. Good afternoon,/Mr. Eggerson. I was afraid I'd miss you./{E} I'm off
450 CC   Claude   31   /{SC} I'll leave you now. But when Eggerson comes back/With Lady Elizabeth, I
451 CC   Eggers   20   fact, Mrs. E./Sometimes says to me: 'Eggerson, why can't you make me laugh/The
453 CC   Lucasta   14   is going to believe all I say,/Mr. Eggerson. And I know he'll be nice to me/When
453 CC   Lucasta   17   /It's only that he's terrified of Mrs. Eggerson;/That's why he's never asked me out
453 CC   Eggers   19   out to lunch./{E} We will leave Mrs. Eggerson out of this, Miss Angel./{L} That's
453 CC   Lucasta   21   says, Colby,/When I mention Mrs. Eggerson. He never fails to rise./B.! What have
454 CC   Colby   17   { }/[*Exit* KAGHAN]/{C} Egg ... Mr. Eggerson!/{E} Yes, Mr. Simpkins?/{C} You
455 CC   Colby   26   her./{C} But you have Mrs. Eggerson./{E} Yes, she's a great protection. And
456 CC   Eggers   4   back from a public luncheon —/'Eggerson,' he said, 'I wanted a lady,/And I'm
456 CC   Eggers   16   what Sir Claude said:/'Humour her, Eggerson,' he said, 'humour her.'/But she has
457 CC   Colby   7   there's one thing I do believe, Mr. Eggerson:/That *you* have a kind heart. And I'm
457 CC   Claude   21   *landing and listens*]/{SC} She's here, Eggerson! That's her voice./Where is she? Oh,
457 CC   Claude   31   to him first./{SC} Good heavens, Eggerson, what *can* have happened?/{E} I've
458 CC   Lady E   9   surprising./{LE} What's surprising, Eggerson? I've arrived, that's all./{E} I was just
458 CC   Lady E   11   That was very thoughtful of you, Eggerson,/But quite unnecessary. And besides,/I
459 CC   Claude   17   You know what a bother it's been for Eggerson —/So I'm having the flat in the mews
459 CC   Lady E   22   Colby./Neither, I regret to say, does Eggerson./What colour have you chosen,
460 CC   Claude   38   for her,/I give him full marks. Well, Eggerson,/I seem to have brought you up to
461 CC   Claude   21   going./{SC} Goodbye, and thank you, Eggerson./{E} Good day, Sir Claude. Good day,
461 CC   m   22   Good day, Mr. Simpkins. { }/[*Exit* EGGERSON]/{SC} Well, Colby! I've been
473 CC   Lucasta   31   garden?/What makes you think of Eggerson — of all people?/{C} Well, he retires
473 CC   Colby   35   or beetroot, or peas ... for Mrs. Eggerson./{L} Are you laughing at me?/{C} I'm
474 CC   Colby   1   —/Well, they're both unreal. But for Eggerson/His garden is a part of one single
487 CC   Claude   9   Colby can be of greater help than Eggerson./I couldn't have asked Eggerson to
487 CC   Claude   10   than Eggerson./I couldn't have asked Eggerson to write a speech for me./Oh, by the
487 CC   Lady E   30   back to me,/And you, Claude, and Eggerson have been the instruments./I must be
492 CC   Lady E   11   /{LE} And I think you ought to get Eggerson as well. { }/[*rising*]./{SC} Oh, of course,
492 CC   Claude   12   well. { }/[*rising*]./{SC} Oh, of course, Eggerson! He knows all about it./Let us say no

493 CC	Claude	10	I thought it would be better/To put Eggerson there, behind the desk./You see, I
493 CC	Claude	18	Guzzard. That's why I thought/That Eggerson should put the first questions./He's
496 CC		m 13	son. {}/[*A knock on the door.* Enter EGGERSON]/{SC} Good morning, Eggerson./
496 CC	Claude	13	EGGERSON]/{SC} Good morning, Eggerson./{E} Good morning, Sir Claude. And
496 CC	Claude	15	And Lady Elizabeth!/{SC} I'm sorry, Eggerson, to bring you up to London/At such
496 CC	Lady E	34	getting worse./{LE} — I hope Mrs. Eggerson is well?/{E} Pretty well./She's always
497 CC	Claude	4	important business, I imagine./{SC} Eggerson, I'm expecting Mrs. Guzzard./{E}
498 CC	Lady E	10	been two babies?/{LE} *Two* babies, Eggerson?/{E} I was only suggesting/That
498 CC	Claude	25	Of course it was Colby./{SC} But Eggerson, you really can't ask me to believe/
503 CC	Claude	25	wait till afterwards./{SC} Quite right, Eggerson./{L} Good-bye, Colby./{C} Why do
504 CC	Claude	16	her up./{SC} No, I want you here, Eggerson./Will you show her up, Lucasta?/{L}
504 CC	Claude	37	you know we are to leave that to Eggerson./This is Mr. Eggerson, Mrs. Guzzard:/
505 CC	Claude	1	to leave that to Eggerson./This is Mr. Eggerson, Mrs. Guzzard:/My confidential clerk.
505 CC	Guzzard	9	I mind?/I have heard about Mr. Eggerson from Colby./I am very happy to make
505 CC	Claude	18	the discussion?/{SC} If you please, Eggerson./{E} Then let's make a start./The
506 CC	Claude	7	/{SC} That's not relevant./Leave it to Eggerson./{E} The father died abroad./Lady
508 CC	Lady E	11	in my mind./I'm surprised that you, Eggerson, with your legal training,/Should talk
508 CC	Claude	18	That's a very sensible suggestion, Eggerson./A breath of sanity. Thank you for
514 CC	Guzzard	32	/{MG} I understand that, Mr. Eggerson. Quite well./{SC} I shall not believe it.
517 CC	Claude	19	/That's why I must leave you./{SC} Eggerson!/Can't you persuade him?/{LE} Yes.
517 CC	Lady E	19	My poor Claude!/Do try to help him, Eggerson./{E} I wouldn't venture./Mr. Simpkins
518 CC	Colby	20	/{C} I'd be very glad indeed — if Mrs. Eggerson approved./{E} There'll be no one so
518 CC	Guzzard	23	/Of that I can assure you./{MG} Mr. Eggerson,/I cannot see eye to eye with you,/
519 CC	Claude	23	/{SC} Don't leave me, Lucasta./Eggerson! Do *you* really believe her? {}/
519 CC		1m 23	Do *you* really believe her? {}/[EGGERSON *nods*]/CURTAIN/THE ELDER

EGGERSON'S (5)

458 CC	Claude	26	is familiar./{SC} This young man is Eggerson's successor./You know that
458 CC	Claude	27	Eggerson's successor./You know that Eggerson's been meaning to retire .../{E} Under
472 CC	Lucasta	30	different./And so you applied for Eggerson's position,/And made up your mind to
473 CC	Colby	28	it's not real./You know, I think that Eggerson's garden/Is more real than mine./{L}
473 CC	Lucasta	30	garden/Is more real than mine./{L} Eggerson's garden?/What makes you think of

EGGS (7)

123 SA	Doris	11	*of the coral sea.*/{Do} I don't like eggs; I never liked eggs;/And I don't like life on
123 SA	Doris	11	/{Do} I don't like eggs; I never liked eggs;/And I don't like life on your crocodile isle.
588 Fable		51	/Next came a viand made of turtle eggs,/And after that a great pie made of plover,/
372 CP	Alex	15	/I was lucky to find half-a-dozen eggs./{E} What! You used all those eggs!
372 CP	Edward	16	eggs./{E} What! You used all those eggs! Lavinia's aunt/Has just sent them from the
376 CP	Edward	14	saucepan too./{E} *And* half a dozen eggs:/I wanted one for breakfast. A boiled egg./
398 CP	Lavinia	16	in the kitchen./I know there are some eggs. But we must go out for dinner./

EGGY (9) [*Abbreviation*]

452 CC	Lucasta	11	{}/[*Enter* LUCASTA ANGEL]/{L} Eggy, I've lost my job!/{E} Again, Miss Angel?/
452 CC	Lucasta	15	unpunctual./{L} You're wrong, Eggy. It's rank injustice./Two months I'd gone
452 CC	Lucasta	23	sure, so why bother?/But who's this, Eggy? Is it Colby Simpkins?/Introduce him, one
452 CC	Lucasta	30	that, Colby? I'm Lucasta./It's only Eggy calls me Miss Angel,/Just to annoy me.
453 CC	Lucasta	5	an ell./{L} L. for Lucasta./Go on, Eggy. Don't mind him, Colby./Colby, are you
453 CC	Lucasta	29	cope with the financial crisis./{L} Yes, Eggy, will you break the sad news to Claude?/
453 CC	Lucasta	37	approval./Can I have some money, Eggy?/{E} I'm no longer in charge/And that
499 CC	Lucasta	17	time./Oh, I'm glad you're here, Eggy! You're such a support./In any case, I've
501 CC	Lucasta	37	idea. If Colby agrees./{L} I trust you, Eggy. And I want to make my peace with him./

EGGY'S (1) [*Abbreviation*]

453 CC	Lucasta	16	way. Why don't you let him speak?/Eggy's really quite human, Colby./It's only that

EGLANTINE (2)

590 Time Space		12	ere the wild bee flew/To suck the eglantine./So let us haste to pluck anew/Nor
590 Space Time		12	ere the wild bee flew/To suck the eglantine./But let us haste to pluck anew/Nor

EGO (1)

127 Cor1 March		10	/The natural wakeful life of our Ego is a perceiving./We can wait with our stools

EGOTISM (2)

279 MC Knight4		24	country, to be, in/fact, a monster of egotism. This egotism grew upon him, until it/
279 MC Knight4		24	be, in/fact, a monster of egotism. This egotism grew upon him, until it/became at last

EGOTIST (1)

502 CC	Lucasta	24	warms other people. You're either an egotist/Or something so different from the rest

ÉGOUT (1)

46 Directeur		14	des tours/A pas de loup./Dans un égout/Une petite fille/En guenilles/Camarde/

ÉGRATIGNER (1)

48 Lune Miel		7	/On relève le drap pour mieux égratigner./Moins d'une lieue d'ici est Saint

EH (2)

119 SP	Krum	18	/{Kr} What about that poker game? eh what Sam?/What about that poker game in
119 SP	Krum	28	we like London!/Do we like London!! Eh what Klip?/{Kl} Say, Miss — er — uh —

EIDERDOWN (1)

135 5FingerEx2		7	was safe and warm/Under a cretonne eiderdown,/Yet the field was cracked and brown

EIGHT (9)

230 Bust Jones		3	fat./He doesn't haunt pubs — he has eight or nine clubs,/For he's the St. James's
288 FR	Amy	12	to know. It will be the first time/For eight years that we have all been together./{Ag}
288 FR	Agatha	14	to be rather painful for Harry/After eight years and all that has happened/To come
290 FR	Amy	18	if nothing had happened in the last eight years./{G} That will be a little difficult./{V}
298 FR	Charles	35	too./*We* haven't seen him for nearly eight years;/And to tell the truth, now that
330 FR	Harry	19	their meaning is./At the beginning, eight years ago,/I felt, at first, that sense of
341 FR	Amy	33	I?/Thirty-five years designing his life,/Eight years watching, without him, at
477 CC Lucasta		3	been locked in a cupboard!/I was only eight years old/When she died of an 'accidental
481 CC Kaghan		10	It's only six o'clock. We can't dine till eight;/Not at any restaurant that *you* like./—

EIGHTEEN (1)

576 ES	Carghil	6	at ... what age were you?/{MC} Just eighteen./{LC} Now, Michael,/Señor Gomez

EIGHTIETH (2)

111 Xmas Trees		27	of fire):/So that before the end, the eightieth Christmas/(By 'eightieth' meaning
111 Xmas Trees		28	the end, the eightieth Christmas/(By 'eightieth' meaning whichever is the last)/The

EIGHTY (1)

105 Song Sime		24	Israel's consolation/To one who has eighty years and no to-morrow./According to

EITHER (36)

61 WL: Burial		27	show you something different from either/Your shadow at morning striding behind
125 SA Sweeney		17	you're alone like he was alone/You're either or neither/I tell you again it don't apply/
152 Rock 2		25	done in the past, you eat the fruit, either rotten or ripe./And the Church must be
190 FQ: DrySal		207	for the saint —/No occupation either, but something given/And taken, in a
192 FQ: Little		34	only when it is fulfilled/If at all. Either you had no purpose/Or the purpose is
196 FQ: Little		215	only live, only suspire/Consumed by either fire or fire./What we call the beginning is
605 Narcissus		3	show you something different from either/Your shadow sprawling over the sand at
260 MC Thomas		18	at once and/for the same reason? For either joy will be overborne by mourning, or/
293 FR	Charles	35	surprise me, Harry;/Or shock me, either./{H} You are all people/To whom nothing
319 FR	Harry	1	you./{H} What you have to tell me/Is either something that I know already/Or
321 FR Warburt		15	I hope nothing has happened/To either of your brothers./{H} Nothing can have
321 FR	Harry	17	/{H} Nothing can have happened/To either of my brothers. Nothing can happen —/If
388 CP	Lavinia	23	Well, Peter./I didn't expect to find either of you here./{P&C} But the telegram!/{L}
389 CP	Lavinia	19	he is going .../{L} I don't doubt that either./{C} And I believe he is right to go./{L}
394 CP	Edward	27	did you want me?/{E} I don't know either./You say you were trying to 'encourage'
406 CP	Lavinia	4	I don't think your clothes concern me either. {}/[*To* REILLY]/{L} I presume you will
410 CP	Reilly	21	/{L} Is that possible?/{R} If I had sent either of you to the sanatorium/In the state in
415 CP	Celia	23	wrong, from our point of view,/Was either bad form, or was psychological./And bad
415 CP	Celia	28	bad form, or mental kinks,/You either become bad form, and cease to care,/Or
417 CP	Celia	6	being hurt again:/Nothing again can either hurt or heal./I have thought at moments
425 CP	Lavinia	14	satisfactory./Everyone who's asked to either party/Suspects that the other one was
450 CC	Eggers	20	sure you understand Mr. Simpkins, either?/{SC} A timely reminder. You may have
454 CC	Eggers	20	I think I am./{E} I have no doubt on either point, none at all./{C} And B. Kaghan
464 CC	Claude	8	for use, or for decoration —/In either case, an inferior art./For me, they are
472 CC	Colby	9	sense of security./{C} No, I haven't either./{L} There, I don't believe you./What did
475 CC	Colby	34	most of what there is to say/Already, either from what I've told you/Or from what
476 CC	Colby	8	I'm going to./{C} Does that matter, either?/{L} In one way, it matters. A little while
477 CC Lucasta		28	because you didn't like that person either,/And I thought you'd come to see me as
484 CC	Lady E	17	a governess,/And if you never knew either of your parents,/You can't understand
500 CC Lucasta		32	he doesn't depend upon other people, either./B. needs me. He's been hurt by life, just
502 CC Lucasta		20	I don't care enough?/{L} No. You're either above caring,/Or else you're insensible —
502 CC Lucasta		24	fire/That warms other people. You're either an egotist/Or something so different from
507 CC Guzzard		13	of the mother?/{MG} I was not told either./I understood the child was very well
534 ES	Gomez	26	well for themselves./I wouldn't allow either of my sons/To go into politics. In my
537 ES	Gomez	21	grammar school./I didn't know either, but I was flattered./Later, I came to
541 ES	Gomez	20	— not all in my own name either —/Are pretty well spread. For the matter

ELATION (1)

233 Skimble		58	he greets the stationmaster with elation./But you saw him at Dumfries, where he

ELBOWS (1)

40 Burb Blei		15	/A saggy bending of the knees/And elbows, with the palms turned out,/Chicago

ELDER (7)

263 MC	Chorus	21	the leaf is out on the tree, when the elder and may/Burst over the stream, and the
313 FR	Charles	21	/They need the influence of their elder brother./Arthur's a bit irresponsible, you
336 FR	Agatha	32	/In an accidental bed/Or under an elder tree/According to the phase/Of the
521 ES	t		*nods*]/CURTAIN/THE ELDER STATESMAN/TO MY WIFE/*To*
552 ES	Carghil	30	posing/As what? I presume, as an elder statesman;/And the difference between
552 ES	Carghil	31	/And the difference between being an elder statesman/And posing successfully as an
552 ES	Carghil	32	/And posing successfully as an elder statesman/Is practically negligible. And

ELDERLY (2)

32 Hysteria		5	by/the ripple of unseen muscles. An elderly waiter with trembling hands/was
482 CC	Lady E	17	you up./I can speak more freely, as an elderly person./{C} But, Lady Elizabeth .../{LE}

ELDERS (1)

179 FQ: ECoker		77	deceived themselves, the quiet-voiced elders,/Bequeathing us merely a receipt for

ELDEST (2)

276 MC	Knight1	31	problem. I/shall call upon our eldest member to speak first, my neighbour in/
284 FR	m	6	LORD MONCHENSEY, *Amy's* eldest *son*/DOWNING, *his servant and chauffeur*

ELECTION (2)

339 FR	Harry	18	responsible for him. Why I have this election/I do not understand. It must have been
358 CP	Julia	4	Oh, you know what I mean./The next election. And the secrets of your cases./{E} Most

ELECTRA (1)

209 NamingCats		11	the dames:/Such as Plato, Admetus, Electra, Demeter —/But all of them sensible

ELECTRIC (2)

177 FQ: ECoker		19	the direction/Into the village, in the electric heat/Hypnotised. In a warm haze the
399 CP	4m	1	*alone at his desk. He presses an/electric button. The* NURSE-SECRETARY

ELEGANT (1)

65 WL: Chess		129	O that Shakespeherian Rag —/It's so elegant/So intelligent/'What shall I do now?

ELEPHANT (1)

270 MC	Chorus	7	the mobile hard insensitive skin of the elephant, the evasive flank of the fish./I have

ELEVATED (1)

261 MC	Thomas	22	as a good Christian who has been/elevated to the company of the Saints: for that

ELEVATION (1)

158 Rock 5		8	seeking every one after his own elevation, and dodging his emptiness./If

ELEVEN (4)

298 FR	Downing	32	Lordship for over ten years .../{Do} Eleven years, Sir, next Lady Day./{C} Eleven
298 FR	Charles	33	Eleven years, Sir, next Lady Day./{C} Eleven years, and you know him pretty well./
399 CP	Nurse	6	Sir Henry:/The first appointment at eleven o'clock./He is to be shown into the small
400 CP	Reilly	2	Chamberlayne's appointment?/{R} At eleven o'clock,/The conventional hour. We have

ELEVENS'S (1)

544 ES	Monica	8	coffee/She said 'I'm not the one for elevens's,/That's Nurse's business'./{LC} So far,

ELIMINATION (1)

173 FQ: BurntN		77	motion, concentration/Without elimination, both a new world/And the old

ELIOT (4)

136 5FingerEx5		1	*Ali Beg*/How unpleasant to meet Mr. Eliot!/With his features of clerical cut,/And his
137 5FingerEx5		8	But./How unpleasant to meet Mr. Eliot!/With a bobtail cur/In a coat of fur/And a
137 5FingerEx5		13	hat:/How unpleasant to meet Mr. Eliot!/(Whether his mouth be open or shut)./
604 Ode		m	Absolute./Ode/THOMAS STEARNS ELIOT/For the hour that is left us, Fair

ELIOT'S (1)

54 Mr E Sun		t	/To keep our metaphysics warm./Mr. Eliot's Sunday Morning Service/

ELIXIR (1)

543 ES	Gomez	5	/Goodbye for the present. It's been an elixir/To see you again, and assure myself/That

ELIZABETH (83)

70 WL: Fire S		279	Dogs./Weialala leia/Wallala leialala/Elizabeth and Leicester/Beating oars/The stern
444 CC	m	7	/LUCASTA ANGEL/LADY ELIZABETH MULHAMMER/MRS.
447 CC	Claude	3	think what you're to say to Lady Elizabeth,/Coming back from the airport, about
448 CC	Eggers	14	I haven't told him much about Lady Elizabeth./But there's one thing I should like to
449 CC	Eggers	1	you're thinking no doubt that Lady Elizabeth/Would be put in mind of the child *she*
449 CC	Eggers	32	it comes to the point/At which Lady Elizabeth wants to adopt him —/An admirable
450 CC	Claude	24	Paris./But when you return with Lady Elizabeth/I'll be ready waiting to introduce him.
450 CC	Claude	32	Eggerson comes back/With Lady Elizabeth, I will rejoin you. {}/[*Exit* SIR
450 CC	Colby	35	You've told me very little about Lady Elizabeth,/And Sir Claude himself hasn't told
451 CC	Eggers	3	/He's never hit it off with Lady Elizabeth./Don't listen to him. He understands
451 CC	Eggers	12	Very free and easy ways;/And Lady Elizabeth has never taken to him./But you, Mr.
451 CC	Eggers	26	the ladies, you know./But with Lady Elizabeth he wasn't so successful./She once
451 CC	Eggers	36	certainly be a great asset/With Lady Elizabeth. I envy you that./I've always sung in
454 CC	Eggers	4	meet Lizzie?/{E} I am meeting Lady Elizabeth at Northolt./{L} Well, I don't propose

454 CC	Colby	30	indeed./{C} And does she call Lady Elizabeth *Lizzie*?/{E} Well, not in her presence.
455 CC	Eggers	34	not on your shoulders./Lady Elizabeth, now, that's different./{C} At least, I
455 CC	Colby	35	/{C} At least, I don't suppose Lady Elizabeth/Can be quite so unusual as Miss
456 CC	Colby	11	Conservative, myself./{C} But is Lady Elizabeth very unusual/In any other way,
456 CC	Eggers	38	of Europe as I have,/Getting Lady Elizabeth out of her difficulties./{C} Perhaps she
457 CC	m	16	time,/From my experience. {}/LADY ELIZABETH MULHAMMER'S *voice off.*/*
457 CC	m	25	about? She's coming in! {}/LADY ELIZABETH MULHAMMER'S *voice off.*/
458 CC	1m	5	engaged in business. {}/[*Enter* LADY ELIZABETH MULHAMMER]/
458 CC	Eggers	5	/[*simultaneously*]./{E} Lady Elizabeth!/{SC} Elizabeth!/What on earth has
458 CC	Claude	6	/{E} Lady Elizabeth!/{SC} Elizabeth!/What on earth has happened?/{E}
458 CC	Eggers	8	on earth has happened?/{E} Lady Elizabeth! This is most surprising./{LE} What's
458 CC	Claude	19	/{SC} Oh yes, of course we know that, Elizabeth./But why did you change your plans?/
458 CC	Eggers	28	.../{E} Under medical orders, Lady Elizabeth:/The doctor made it very imperative
460 CC	m	33	Mr. .../{LE} Colby! {}/[*Exit* LADY ELIZABETH]/{SC} She actually went and
462 CC	Colby	9	/Do you really believe that Lady Elizabeth/Can ever accept me as if I was her
478 CC	Lucasta	3	heir/And you'll marry another Lady Elizabeth./But in that event, Colby, you'll have
479 CC	Colby	34	the place done up./{C} It was Lady Elizabeth chose the decorations./{K} Then I'm
481 CC	m	14	{}/[*A knock at the door. Enter* LADY ELIZABETH]/{LE} Oh, good evening./Good
481 CC	Lucasta	17	We're on the point of leaving, Lady Elizabeth./{LE} I've come over to have a look at
482 CC	Colby	18	as an elderly person./{C} But, Lady Elizabeth .../{LE} Well, older than you are,/And
482 CC	Colby	21	the ways of the world./{C} But, Lady Elizabeth, what is it you object to?/They're both
486 CC	Colby	19	was your mother?/{C} Why, Lady Elizabeth! Why should I doubt it?/That is not
486 CC	Claude	33	that? {}/[*Enter* SIR CLAUDE]/{SC} Elizabeth! I was told that you were here with
487 CC	Claude	8	I'll try./{SC} It's just in ways like this, Elizabeth,/That Colby can be of greater help
487 CC	Claude	16	better./{LE} Claude!/{SC} What is it, Elizabeth?/{LE} I've just made a startling
487 CC	Claude	21	my lost child!/{SC} What? Your child, Elizabeth? What on earth makes you think so?/
487 CC	Claude	32	Claude, tell me I am right./{SC} But Elizabeth, what has led you to believe/That
488 CC	Claude	10	/If it is a coincidence. But I'm afraid, Elizabeth,/What has happened is that, brooding
488 CC	Claude	17	get her to confess it./{SC} I'm sorry, Elizabeth. If Mrs. Guzzard comes/To make her
488 CC	Claude	35	child./{SC} That's not what I meant. Elizabeth,/Colby is *my* son./{LE} Quite
490 CC	Colby	29	have lost each other./{C} No, Lady Elizabeth. The position is the same/Or crueller.
492 CC	Claude	37	I was really remembering./Come, Elizabeth./{LE} My poor Claude! {}/[*Exeunt*
492 CC	1m	38	{}/[*Exeunt* SIR CLAUDE *and* LADY ELIZABETH]/CURTAIN/Act Three/*The*
493 CC	3m	1	*is*/*moving chairs about. Enter* LADY ELIZABETH./{LE} Claude, what are you
495 CC	Claude	16	too much for granted/About you, Elizabeth. What did *you* want?/{LE} To inspire
496 CC	Eggers	14	morning, Sir Claude. And Lady Elizabeth!/{SC} I'm sorry, Eggerson, to bring
497 CC	Claude	6	/{SC} I have asked her to come. Lady Elizabeth/Is sure that she knows the name of the
498 CC	Claude	31	dispose of *him*. It's your child, Elizabeth,/Whom we must try to trace./{E} If
504 CC	Claude	31	me introduce you to my wife./Lady Elizabeth Mulhammer./{LE} Good morning,
504 CC	Claude	37	/{LE} Yes. To do with Colby./{SC} Elizabeth, you know we are to leave that to
505 CC	Claude	23	of maternity./{SC} Don't interrupt, Elizabeth./{MG} I don't understand you./{E}
505 CC	Eggers	26	Guzzard./It is only recently that Lady Elizabeth/Heard your name mentioned, by Mr.
505 CC	Eggers	33	for the question to be possible./Lady Elizabeth, before her marriage/Had a child .../
506 CC	Eggers	9	/{E} The father died abroad./Lady Elizabeth did not know the name of the lady/
506 CC	Eggers	27	A few days ago,/As I said, Lady Elizabeth learned your name;/And the name
506 CC	Eggers	31	Mrs. Guzzard/Of Teddington! Lady Elizabeth is convinced/That it was a Mrs.
507 CC	Eggers	32	/{E} I am only suggesting, Lady Elizabeth,/There are other places that sound
507 CC Guzzard		35	Colby?/{SC} Don't be certain yet, Elizabeth,/{LE} There is no doubt about it./
509 CC	Claude	8	he come to be called Colby?/{SC} But, Elizabeth, it isn't Colby!/Don't you see who it
509 CC	Claude	20	that Colby is Barnabas./{SC} No, Elizabeth, Barnabas is Barnabas./I must explain
509 CC	Claude	26	Kaghan./{LE} Barnabas?/{SC} Yes, Elizabeth. He sometimes has to sign his full
510 CC	Eggers	3	/{E} And now, if you agree, Lady Elizabeth,/We can ask Mr. Kaghan about his
510 CC	Claude	11	the right expression./{SC} I believe, Elizabeth,/That you have found your son./{E}
510 CC Guzzard		26	why are you interested?/{MG} Lady Elizabeth, I believe that this is your son./If so, I
511 CC	Kaghan	5	/{K} Well, I am embarrassed./If Lady Elizabeth is my mother .../{LE} There is no
511 CC	Kaghan	18	how I ought to address you,/Lady Elizabeth. I've always been accustomed/To
511 CC	Lady E	21	/You may address me as Aunt Elizabeth./{K} That's easier, certainly./{LE}
511 CC	Claude	25	to dinner./{SC} By all means, Elizabeth./{K} But, Lady Elizabeth —/I mean,
511 CC	Kaghan	26	all means, Elizabeth./{K} But, Lady Elizabeth —/I mean, Aunt Elizabeth: if I call
511 CC	Kaghan	27	But, Lady Elizabeth —/I mean, Aunt Elizabeth: if I call you Aunt Elizabeth/Would
511 CC	Kaghan	27	Aunt Elizabeth: if I call you Aunt Elizabeth/Would you mind very much calling
512 CC Guzzard		2	I am glad to hear you say so, Lady Elizabeth./But are *you* satisfied?/{LE} Satisfied?
512 CC	m	17	Kaghan as her son? {}/[*To* LADY ELIZABETH]/{MG} Are you contented to have
512 CC Guzzard		28	to find yourself the son/Of Lady Elizabeth Mulhammer?/{K} It's very much

512 CC	Kaghan	34	/{K} *B.* — if you don't mind, Aunt Elizabeth./{LE} B. — and I'm sure we shall
512 CC		m 39	who have made them. {}/[*To* LADY ELIZABETH *and* KAGHAN]/{MG} Not, I
513 CC	Guzzard	5	/The daughter-in-law of Lady Elizabeth,/And the daughter of Sir Claude
519 CC	Kaghan	18	both of you,/Claude ... and Aunt Elizabeth./You know, Claude, both Lucasta

ELIZABETH'S (3)

457 CC	note 16&	25	MULHAMMER'S *voice off.**/* *Lady Elizabeth's words off stage are not intended to be*
506 CC	Guzzard	20	lost him. Not in the way/That Lady Elizabeth's child was lost./Let us hope that her
508 CC	Eggers	17	took in, which may have been Lady Elizabeth's./{SC} That's a very sensible

ELL (1)

| 453 CC | Eggers | 3 | Miss Angel an inch/She'll take an ell./{L} L. for Lucasta./Go on, Eggy. Don't |

ELLE (2)

| 51 Restaurant | | 10 | qu'on s'abrite./J'avais sept ans, elle était plus petite./Elle était toute mouillée, je |
| 51 Restaurant | | 11 | /J'avais sept ans, elle était plus petite./Elle était toute mouillée, je lui ai donné des |

ELLICOTT (2)

| 30 Cous Nancy | | 1 | lived./Cousin Nancy/Miss Nancy Ellicott/Strode across the hills and broke them,/ |
| 30 Cous Nancy | | 7 | /Over the cow-pasture./Miss Nancy Ellicott smoked/And danced all the modern |

ELPHEGE (1)

| 261 MC | Thomas | 39 | Canterbury,/the blessed Archbishop Elphege; because it is fitting, on Christ's birth/ |

ELSE (56)

134 Wind		6	strife/Is it a dream or something else/When the surface of the blackened river/Is
196 FQ: Little		206	from sin and error./The only hope, or else despair/Lies in the choice of pyre or pyre —
209 NamingCats		15	that's peculiar, and more dignified,/Else how can he keep up his tail perpendicular,/
209 NamingCats		19	Coricopat,/Such as Bombalurina, or else Jellylorum —/Names that never belong to
228 Gus		13	/He loves to regale them, if someone else pays,/With anecdotes drawn from his
235 Ad-dress		61	who makes a habit/Of eating nothing else but rabbit,/And when he's finished, licks his
287 FR	Mary	8	generation, you must ask someone else./I'm afraid that I don't deserve the
293 FR	Harry	16	/And yet you are talking of nothing else. Why not get to the point/Or if you want to
300 FR	Downing	36	all right then,/Mustn't she, Sir? or else he'd have known it./{C} Oh yes ... quite so.
304 FR	Mary	8	your advice, because there's no one else to ask,/And because you are strong, and
306 FR	Mary	28	/Kept here because there was nothing else to do with me./I didn't belong here. It was
308 FR	Harry	2	dream or another; if there is nothing else/The most real is what I fear. The bright
311 FR	Harry	31	a dreaming age, when I was someone else/Thinking of something else, puts me among
311 FR	Harry	32	someone else/Thinking of something else, puts me among you./I tell you, it is not me
318 FR	Harry	34	the others/Seem to hear something else than what I am saying./But if you want to
319 FR	Harry	2	I know already/Or unimportant, or else untrue./But I want to know more about my
324 FR	Harry	18	much difference/To him or to anyone else. If he was ever really conscious,/I should be
331 FR	Harry	6	of it with myself,/Though nothing else was real. I thought foolishly/That when I
346 FR	Downing	24	a kind of preparation for something else./I've no gift of language, but I'm sure of
359 CP	Edward	21	—/I shouldn't have minded anyone else, {}/[*The doorbell rings.* EDWARD *goes to*
379 CP	Celia	10	Edward,/If that is right, everything else will be,/I promise you./{E} No, Celia./It has
387 CP	Edward	24	me with her./{E} I wonder whom else Lavinia has invited./{P} Why, I got the
391 CP	Lavinia	21	—/Or if it's a machine, someone else is running it./But who? Somebody is always
394 CP	Lavinia	20	you wanted/You wanted something else. I shall treat you very differently/In future./
398 CP	Lavinia	14	you to see a doctor,/There's nothing else at present that I can do about it./I ought to
402 CP	Edward	9	not need to consult you/Or anyone else. I came here as a patient./If you take no
404 CP	Reilly	24	sanatorium?/{R} You have nothing else to tell me?/{E} What else can I tell you?/
404 CP	Edward	25	nothing else to tell me?/{E} What else can I tell you?/You didn't want to hear
411 CP	Lavinia	17	/Edward, have you anything else to ask him/Before we go?/{E} Yes, I have./
411 CP	Edward	33	their decision./{E} Have you anything else to say to us, Sir Henry?/{R} No. Not in this
413 CP	Reilly	7	/And usually they think that someone else is to blame./{C} I at least have no one to
415 CP	Celia	29	bad form, and cease to care,/Or else, if you care, you must be kinky./{R} And so
417 CP	Reilly	40	to the end. But you will want nothing else,/And the other life will be only like a book/
419 CP	Reilly	8	you become incapable of anything else./Now — do you feel quite sure?/{C} I want
420 CP	Celia	5	why I am doing it. There is nothing else to do:/That is the only reason./{R} It is the
425 CP	Lavinia	33	be seen at a party/Where everybody else is, to show they've been invited./That's
434 CP	Peter	40	than I do:/For *me*, it's everything else that's a waste./Two years! And it was all a
436 CP	Reilly	35	I must be very transparent/Or else you are very perceptive./{J} Oh, Henry!/
438 CP	Edward	16	for Celia —/There must be something else that is terribly wrong,/And the rest of us are
439 CP	Peter	19	that I can't get out of it —/And what else can I do?/{A} It is your film./And I know
446 CC	Claude	16	The great thing was to find something else/He could do, and do well. And I think he's
473 CC	Lucasta	19	/Where you hear a music that no one else could hear,/And the flowers have a scent
473 CC	Lucasta	20	the flowers have a scent that no one else could smell./{C} You may be right, up to a
474 CC	Lucasta	12	That makes it unreal./{L} Can no one else enter?/{C} It can't be done by issuing
474 CC	Lucasta	32	untrue./{L} But you've something else, that I haven't got:/Something of which the
477 CC	Lucasta	32	I thought, now, perhaps, if someone else sees me/As I really am, I might become

478 CC   Colby   25 mustn't go yet!/There's something else that I want to explain,/And now I'm going
494 CC   Claude 18   /In this way, was something else to *him* —/An idea, an inspiration. What he
502 CC   Lucasta 21 No. You're either above caring,/Or else you're insensible — I don't mean
502 CC   Lucasta 22   /But you're terribly cold. Or else you've some fire/To warm you, that isn't
525 ES   Charles 35 Well, you're right./But I've something else to say that I haven't said before,/That will
527 ES   Monica 26 his papers/He needs to have someone else in the room with him,/Reading too — or
548 ES   Monica   3 I hope she won't remember anything else./{LC} She'll come back to tell us more
557 ES   Ld Clav 5 you the necessity of blaming someone else./Just tell me what's happened./{Mi} Well,
558 ES   Ld Clav 13   will be rather different./And what else did he say?/{Mi} He took the usual line,/
561 ES   Monica 39 at, love within the light of which/All else is seen, the love within which/All other love

ELSEWHERE (7)
178 FQ: ECoker 51   and slides. I am here/Or there, or elsewhere. In my beginning./What is the late
308 FR   Mary   29 change anywhere — here, as well as elsewhere./{H} Something inside me, you think,
342 FR   Mary   25   what can be done,/Even here, but elsewhere, everywhere, he is in danger./I will
342 FR   Agatha 29 the danger, here the death, here, not elsewhere;/Elsewhere no doubt is agony,
342 FR   Agatha 30   here the death, here, not elsewhere;/Elsewhere no doubt is agony, renunciation,/But
402 CP   Edward 10 take no interest in my case, I can go elsewhere./{R} You have reason to believe that
507 CC   Eggers   3 Whether, I mean, in Teddington or elsewhere?/Now I must ask a more delicate

EMBARKING (1)
592 Grad 2   1 put forth courageously./As colonists embarking from the strand/To seek their

EMBARRASSED (3)
290 FR   Chorus 36   CHARLES)./{Ch} Why do we feel embarrassed, impatient, fretful, ill at ease,/
511 CC   Lucasta 3 language any longer:/Just say you're embarrassed./{K} Well, I am embarrassed./If
511 CC   Kaghan   4 you're embarrassed./{K} Well, I am embarrassed./If Lady Elizabeth is my mother ...

EMBARRASSING (3)
293 FR   Harry   19 do so/In my absence. I shall be less embarrassing to you. Agatha?/{Ag} I think,
361 CP   Reilly   5 {UG} That's the natural reaction./It's embarrassing, and inconvenient./It was
385 CP   Reilly 15 —/If they returned, would it not be embarrassing?/What would you say to them, or

EMBARRASSMENT (2)
552 ES   Carghil 18 /You thought, for you. You felt no embarrassment?/{LC} Why should I feel
552 ES   Ld Clav 19   /{LC} Why should I feel embarrassment? My conscience was clear./A

EMBITTERED (1)
151 Rock 2   5 to frittered lives and squalid deaths, embittered scorn in honeyless hives,/And those

EMBRACED (1)
606 Narcissus   37 sand/Until the arrows came./As he embraced them his white skin surrendered itself

EMBRACES (1)
335 FR   Harry   14 Weaving with contagion of putrescent embraces/On dissolving bone. In and out, the

EMBRASURE (3)
311 FR   m 27 *revealing the Eumenides in the window embrasure.*]/{H} Why do you show yourselves
312 FR   m 9   *and tears apart the curtains: but the embrasure is empty.*]/{M} Oh, Harry! {}/Scene
336 FR   2m 23   *the curtains, disclosing the empty embrasure. She steps into*/the place which the

EMERGE (1)
305 FR   Agatha 13   beyond us/Which now and then emerge. You and I, Mary,/Are only watchers

EMERGING (1)
569 ES   Ld Clav 38 /Malicious, petty, and I see myself emerging/From my spectral existence into

EMERSON (1)
43 Swee Erect   26 shadow of a man/Is history, said Emerson/Who had not seen the silhouette/Of

EMINENT (1)
180 FQ: ECoker 104 /The captains, merchant bankers, eminent men of letters./The generous patrons of

EMOTION (9)
85 Hollow Men   80   /And the creation/Between the emotion/And the response/Falls the Shadow/
111 Xmas Trees   29 The accumulated memories of annual emotion/May be concentrated into a great joy/
182 FQ: ECoker 184 of feeling,/Undisciplined squads of emotion. And what there is to conquer/By
185 FQ: DrySal   59 of further days and hours,/While emotion takes to itself the emotionless/Years of
202 War Poetry   1 /Not the expression of collective emotion/Imperfectly reflected in the daily
308 FR   Harry   4 /Together with the unrecapturable emotion,/The glow upon the world, that never
330 FR   Harry   29   the old dream, I felt all the same emotion/Or lack of emotion, as before: the same
330 FR   Harry   30 I felt all the same emotion/Or lack of emotion, as before: the same loathing/Diffused,
511 CC   Kaghan   1   /{K} I really don't know what emotion to register .../{L} You don't need to

EMOTIONAL (2)
278 MC Knight2   3 as I can see, and not to be taken in by/emotional clap-trap. I therefore ask you to
409 CP   Reilly   1   /Of your obvious symptoms of emotional strain/And so I made enquiries./{E} It

EMOTIONLESS (1)
185 FQ: DrySal   59 /While emotion takes to itself the emotionless/Years of living among the breakage

EMOTIONS (4)
202 War Poetry	11		is too large, or too small. Our emotions/Are only 'incidents'/In the effort to
278 MC Knight2	1		I am going/to appeal not to your emotions but to your reason. You are
324 FR	Harry	31	people can always show the suitable emotions —/And so far as they feel at all, their
324 FR	Harry	32	—/And so far as they feel at all, their emotions are suitable./They don't understand

EMPEROR (2)
253 MC Tempt4	32	and bishop under your heel./King, emperor, bishop, baron, king:/Uncertain
255 MC Tempt4	9	God?/What earthly glory, of king or emperor,/What earthly pride, that is not poverty

EMPESTE (1)
46 Directeur	6	/Conservateur/Du Spectateur/Empeste la brise./Les actionnaires/

EMPHASIS (1)
52 Whispers	18	her Russian eye/Is underlined for emphasis;/Uncorseted, her friendly bust/Gives

EMPHATIC (1)
297 FR	Violet	33	of —/I only wish to express my emphatic protest/Both against your purpose

EMPIRE (2)
129 Cor2 State	3	of the Bath, the Knights of the British Empire, the Cavaliers,/O Cavaliers! of the
253 MC Tempt4	39	it, when at last breath,/No sons, no empire, he bites broken teeth./You hold the

EMPLOY (3)
165 Rock 9	30	created must wish us to create/And employ our creation again in His service/Which
253 MC Tempt4	10	his friend./Borrow use cautiously, employ/Your services as long as you have to
485 CC Lady E	17	/Are only the means that we have to employ/To become reincarnate. And that one's

EMPLOYABLE (1)
253 MC Tempt4	18	possession of the fiend./Barons are employable against each other;/Greater enemies

EMPLOYING (1)
297 FR	Violet	34	your purpose and the means you are employing./{C} My purpose is, to find out

EMPLOYMENT (1)
211 Old Gumbie	31	thinks that the cockroaches just need employment/To prevent them from idle and

EMPORHEBEN (1)
47 Mél Adult	11	Allemagne, philosophe/Surexcité par Emporheben/Au grand air de Bergsteigleben;/

EMPORTA (1)
51 Restaurant	28	d'étain:/Un courant de sous-mer l'emporta très loin,/Le repassant aux étapes de sa

EMPTINESS (7)
158 Rock 5	8	his own elevation, and dodging his emptiness./If humility and purity be not in the
180 FQ: ECoker	121	you see behind every face the mental emptiness deepen/Leaving only the growing
245 MC Priest2	28	/Seven years of prayer, seven years of emptiness,/Have better prepared our hearts for
272 MC Chorus	25	horrid than active shapes of hell;/Emptiness, absence, separation from God;/The
272 MC Chorus	27	empty land/Which is no land, only emptiness, absence, the Void,/Where those who
416 CP Celia	3	in me/I could get rid of — but of emptiness, of failure/Towards someone, or
530 ES Ld Clav	15	the life I've left —/Only fear of the emptiness before me./If I had the energy to

EMPTY (34)
67 WL: Fire S	177	till I end my song./The river bears no empty bottles, sandwich papers,/Silk
73 WL: Thund	384	the hours/And voices singing out of empty cisterns and exhausted wells./In this
73 WL: Thund	388	graves, about the chapel/There is the empty chapel, only the wind's home./It has no
74 WL: Thund	409	broken by the lean solicitor/In our empty rooms/DA/*Dayadhvam:* I have heard the
85 Hollow Men	67	twilight kingdom/The hope only/Of empty men./*Here we go round the prickly pear/*
98 Ash-Wed 6	18	plover/And the blind eye creates/The empty forms between the ivory gates/And smell
103 Journ Magi	28	pieces of silver,/And feet kicking the empty wine-skins./But there was no
149 Rock 1	100	*unlit rooms./Only the wind moves/Over empty fields, untilled/Where the plough rests, at*
156 Rock 3	69	/Plotting of happiness and flinging empty bottles,/Turning from your vacancy to
161 Rock 7	31	what have we to do/But stand with empty hands and palms turned upwards/In an
164 Rock 9	5	faces,/We must go between empty walls, quavering lowly, whispering
172 FQ: BurntN	34	they, in a formal pattern,/Along the empty alley, into the box circle,/To look down
172 FQ: BurntN	41	a cloud passed, and the pool was empty./Go, said the bird, for the leaves were full
174 FQ: BurntN	105	by distraction/Filled with fancies and empty of meaning/Tumid apathy with no
177 FQ: ECoker	22	by grey stone./The dahlias sleep in the empty silence./Wait for the early owl./In that
183 FQ: ECoker	209	/Through the dark cold and the empty desolation,/The wave cry, the wind cry,
194 FQ: Little	119	/And the fullfed beast shall kick the empty pail./For last year's words belong to last
205 de la Mare	25	by his call; or when by chance/An empty face peers from an empty house;/By
205 de la Mare	25	chance/An empty face peers from an empty house;/By whom, and by what means,
263 MC Chorus	17	/A sour spring, a parched summer, an empty harvest./Between Christmas and Easter
272 MC Chorus	26	horror of the effortless journey, to the empty land/Which is no land, only emptiness,
312 FR	m	9	*the curtains: but the embrasure is empty*].]/{M} Oh, Harry! {}/Scene III/HARRY,
335 FR Agatha	19	stone passages/Of an immense and empty hospital/Pervaded by a smell of
336 FR	2m 23	*/and opens the curtains, disclosing the empty embrasure. She steps into/the place which*
383 CP Celia	12	She is always right./But why bring an empty champagne bottle?/{E} It isn't empty. It

383 CP   Edward   13   empty champagne bottle?/{E} It isn't empty. It may be a little flat —/But why did she
463 CC   Colby   25   it,/When my mind is cleared and empty, walking in the street/Or waking in the
467 CC   Colby   12   /Those years have gone forever. The empty years./Oh, I'm terribly sorry to be saying
529 ES   Ld Clav 37   over breakfast, but before tea,/It's the empty pages that I've been fingering —/The
530 ES   Ld Clav   1   that I've been fingering —/The first empty pages since I entered Parliament./I used
530 ES   Ld Clav   4   been wondering ... how many more empty pages?/{M} You would soon fill them up
530 ES   Ld Clav 20   to fill it./It's just like sitting in an empty waiting room/In a railway station on a
530 ES   Ld Clav 25   What am I waiting for/In a cold and empty room before an empty grate?/For no one.
530 ES   Ld Clav 25   /In a cold and empty room before an empty grate?/For no one. For nothing./{M} Yet

EMPTYING (1)
174 FQ: BurntN 100   /Nor darkness to purify the soul/Emptying the sensual with deprivation/

EMULATE (1)
182 FQ: ECoker 187   by men whom one cannot hope/To emulate — but there is no competition —/There

EN (8)
46 Directeur   16   loup./Dans un égout/Une petite fille/En guenilles/Camarde/Regarde/Le directeur/Du
47 Mél Adult   1   d'amour./Mélange Adultère de Tout/En Amérique, professeur;/En Angleterre,
47 Mél Adult   2   de Tout/En Amérique, professeur;/En Angleterre, journaliste;/C'est à grands pas et
47 Mél Adult   3   journaliste;/C'est à grands pas et en sueur/Que vous suivrez à peine ma piste./En
47 Mél Adult   5   /Que vous suivrez à peine ma piste./En Yorkshire, conférencier;/A Londres, un peu
47 Mél Adult   10   coiffe/Casque noir de jemenfoutiste./En Allemagne, philosophe/Surexcité par
48 Lune Miel   9   d'une lieue d'ici est Saint Apollinaire/En Classe, basilique connue des amateurs/De
51 Restaurant   21   /Mais alors, tu as ton vautour!/Va t'en te décrotter les rides du visage;/Tiens, ma

ENACTED (1)
69 WL: Fire S   244   /(And I Tiresias have foresuffered all/Enacted on this same divan or bed;/I who have

ENCHAINMENT (1)
173 FQ: BurntN   81   of its partial horror./Yet the enchainment of past and future/Woven in the

ENCHANTED (1)
92 Ash-Wed 3   16   figure drest in blue and green/Enchanted the maytime with an antique flute./

ENCHANTMENT (3)
179 FQ: ECoker   94   by monsters, fancy lights,/Risking enchantment. Do not let me hear/Of the
194 FQ: Little   134   friction of expiring sense/Without enchantment, offering no promise/But bitter
333 FR   Agatha 37   flames of ice, chosen/To resolve the enchantment under which we suffer./{H} Look,

ENCHANTMENTS (2)
140 Usk   5   aside, not for lance, do not spell/Old enchantments. Let them sleep./'Gently dip, but
348 FR   Chorus 18   of God./We know various spells and enchantments./And minor forms of sorcery,/

ENCLOSED (1)
64 WL: Chess   106   out, leaning, hushing the room enclosed./Footsteps shuffled on the stair./Under

ENCOMPASSED (1)
158 Rock 5   11   and doze before he sleeps./But we are encompassed with snakes and dogs: therefore

ENCORE (1)
48 Lune Miel   17   Vieille usine désaffectée de Dieu, tient encore/Dans ses pierres écroulantes la forme

ENCOUNTER (1)
68 WL: Fire S   240   he assaults at once;/Exploring hands encounter no defence;/His vanity requires no

ENCOURAGE (1)
394 CP   Edward 28   either./You say you were trying to 'encourage' me:/Then why did you always make

ENCOURAGED (4)
186 FQ: DrySal   90   the latter a partial fallacy/Encouraged by superficial notions of evolution,/
393 CP   Lavinia 30   /You only wanted to be bolstered, encouraged..../{E} Encouraged? To what?/{L}
393 CP   Edward 31   to be bolstered, encouraged..../{E} Encouraged? To what?/{L} To think well of
455 CC   Eggers 25   give her encouragement./I have never encouraged her./{C} But you have Mrs.

ENCOURAGEMENT (2)
455 CC   Eggers 24   nuisance?/{E} Not unless you give her encouragement./I have never encouraged her./
528 ES   Monica 27   /But Selby wants him to have every encouragement —/If he's hopeful, he's likely to

ENCOURAGING (1)
451 CC   Eggers   8   the most of it —/That I will say. An encouraging example/For you, Mr. Simpkins.

ENCYCLOPAEDIA (1)
107 Animula   23   soul in the window seat/Behind the *Encyclopaedia Britannica*./Issues from the hand

END (89)
20 Portrait   67   /Of one about to reach her journey's end./I shall sit here, serving tea to friends....'/I
24 Rhapsody   45   barnacles on his back,/Gripped the end of a stick which I held him./Half-past three,
28 Boston ET   8   /If the street were time and he at the end of the street,/And I say, 'Cousin Harriet,
29 Aunt Helen   5   silence in heaven/And silence at her end of the street./The shutters were drawn and
32 Hysteria   11   attention with careful subtlety to this end./Conversation Galante/I observe: 'Our
40 Burb Blei   20   of Canaletto./The smoky candle end of time/Declines. On the Rialto once./The
67 WL: Fire S   176   /Sweet Thames, run softly, till I end my song./The river bears no empty bottles,

67 WL: Fire S	183	.../Sweet Thames, run softly till I end my song,/Sweet Thames, run softly, for I
92 Ash-Wed 2	34	/Is now the Garden/Where all loves end/Terminate torment/Of love unsatisfied/The
92 Ash-Wed 2	39	/The greater torment/Of love satisfied/End of the endless/Journey to no end/
92 Ash-Wed 2	40	/End of the endless/Journey to no end/Conclusion of all that/Is inconclusible/
103 Journ Magi	17	/A hard time we had of it./At the end we preferred to travel all night,/Sleeping in
111 Xmas Trees	27	her crown of fire):/So that before the end, the eightieth Christmas/(By 'eightieth'
111 Xmas Trees	33	the beginning shall remind us of the end/And the first coming of the second coming./
124 SA Swarts	18	fellows always get pinched in the end./{Sn} Excuse me, they don't all get pinched
124 SA Snow	19	me, they don't all get pinched in the end./What about them bones on Epsom Heath?
124 SA Snow	23	/They *don't* all get pinched in the end./{Do} A woman runs a terrible risk./{Sn}
124 SA Sweeney	26	/{S} This one didn't get pinched in the end/But that's another story too./This went on
142 Cape Ann	11	sweet sweet/But resign this land at the end, resign it/To its true owner, the tough one,
150 Rock 1	117	*no movement, no peace and no end/But noise without speech, food without taste.*/
150 Rock 1	120	/*We would build the beginning and the end of this street./We build the meaning:/A*
151 Rock 2	10	hear sung;/Waiting to be flung in the end, on a heap less useful than dung'./You,
160 Rock 7	13	Arctic Current;/And they came to an end, a dead end stirred with a flicker of life,/
160 Rock 7	13	/And they came to an end, a dead end stirred with a flicker of life,/And they came
171 FQ: BurntN	10	been and what has been/Point to one end, which is always present./Footfalls echo in
172 FQ: BurntN	48	been and what has been/Point to one end, which is always present./Garlic and
175 FQ: BurntN	149	but the co-existence,/Or say that the end precedes the beginning,/And the end and
175 FQ: BurntN	150	end precedes the beginning,/And the end and the beginning were always there/Before
175 FQ: BurntN	151	/Before the beginning and after the end./And all is always now. Words strain,/
175 FQ: BurntN	167	is itself unmoving,/Only the cause and end of movement,/Timeless, and undesiring/
177 FQ: ECoker	1	/East Coker/In my beginning is my end. In succession/Houses rise and fall, crumble,
177 FQ: ECoker	14	a silent motto./In my beginning is my end. Now the light falls/Across the open field,
183 FQ: ECoker	211	/Of the petrel and the porpoise. In my end is my beginning./The Dry Salvages/I do not
185 FQ: DrySal	51	/Clangs/The bell./Where is there an end of it, the soundless wailing,/The silent
185 FQ: DrySal	54	motionless;/Where is there an end to the drifting wreckage,/The prayer of the
185 FQ: DrySal	57	calamitous annunciation?/There is no end, but addition: the trailing/Consequence of
186 FQ: DrySal	69	of the last annunciation./Where is the end of them, the fishermen sailing/Into the
186 FQ: DrySal	81	not bear examination./There is no end of it, the voiceless wailing,/No end to the
186 FQ: DrySal	82	no end of it, the voiceless wailing,/No end to the withering of withered flowers,/To the
191 FQ: Little	26	sweetness./It would be the same at the end of the journey,/If you came at night like a
192 FQ: Little	35	purpose/Or the purpose is beyond the end you figured/And is altered in fulfilment.
192 FQ: Little	37	places/Which also are the world's end, some at the sea jaws,/Or over a dark lake,
193 FQ: Little	82	of interminable night/At the recurrent end of the unending/After the dark dove with
197 FQ: Little	216	we call the beginning is often the end/And to make an end is to make a
197 FQ: Little	217	is often the end/And to make an end is to make a beginning./The end is where we
197 FQ: Little	218	an end is to make a beginning./The end is where we start from. And every phrase/
197 FQ: Little	226	Every phrase and every sentence is an end and a beginning,/Every poem an epitaph.
197 FQ: Little	242	not cease from exploration/And the end of all our exploring/Will be to arrive where
213 Growltiger	52	had driven to that drop,/At the end of all his crimes was forced to go ker-flip,
595 Grad 14	2	we may no more delay;/Thus is the end of every tale: 'Farewell',/A word that
606 Narcissus	30	a drunken old man/Knowing at the end the taste of his own whiteness/The horror of
241 MC Priest1	7	his own./{P1} Shall these things not end/Until the poor at the gate/Have forgotten
241 MC Priest2	23	Tell us,/Are the old disputes at an end, is the wall of pride cast down/That divided
242 MC Mess	9	that this peace/Is nothing like an end, or like a beginning./It is common
243 MC Priest3	10	the wheel turn./For who knows the end of good or evil?/Until the grinders cease/
246 MC Thomas	19	excuse, pretence, opportunity./End will be simple, sudden, God-given./
253 MC Tempt4	7	/His hardened hatred shall have no end./You know truly, the King will never trust/
253 MC Tempt4	21	counsel?/{T4} Fare forward to the end./All other ways are closed to you/Except
259 MC Thomas	5	no longer act or suffer, to the sword's end./Now my good Angel, whom God appoints
273 MC Thomas	37	are blended/So good and evil in the end become confounded./It is not in time that
276 MC Chorus	10	/Every sorrow had a kind of end./In life there is not time to grieve long./But
277 MC Knight3	23	what a good show he put up at the end —/they won't give *us* any glory. No, we
310 FR Harry	35	me news/Of a door that opens at the end of a corridor,/Sunlight and singing; when I
316 FR 2m	24	is made straight. {}/[*Exit to dinner*]/END OF PART I/PART II/*The library, after*
333 FR Harry	18	falls, as the tree falls. And in the end/That is the completion which at the
334 FR Harry	4	in a different vision. This is like an end./{Ag} And a beginning. Harry, my dear,/I
334 FR Agatha	7	old feel./The young feel tired at the end of an action —/The old, at the beginning.
337 FR Agatha	15	what you have learned/Mean the end of a relation, make it impossible./You did
337 FR Harry	27	of defilement —/Which leads in the end to reconciliation./And I know that I must
340 FR Amy	2	years is long, and death is an end,/And I thought that time might have made
381 CP Edward	35	/He has to come to terms in the end/With the obstinate, the tougher self; who
414 CP Celia	2	there has been./It isn't simply the end of an illusion/In the ordinary way, or being

417 CP	Reilly	40	know how good/Till you come to the end. But you will want nothing else,/And the
426 CP	Lavinia	13	over;/And then to remember, it's the end of the season/And no more parties./{E} And
426 CP	Edward	17	{L} Can we get away soon?/{E} By the end of next week/I shall be quite free./{L} And
437 CP	Reilly	26	to death, and, without knowing the end/Yet choose the form of death. We know the
445 CC	Eggers	15	/So as not to lose a moment at the end of the winter/And I matched some material
455 CC	Eggers	21	She'll marry Mr. Kaghan/In the end. He's a man who gets his own way,/And I
475 CC	Colby	7	not what I meant./I meant, there's no end to understanding a person./All one can do
476 CC	Lucasta	39	her:/It was always spent before the end of the quarter/On gin and betting, I should
507 CC	Eggers	21	/{E} Did the payments come to an end?/{MG} Very suddenly./{LE} That must have
545 ES	Ld Clav	8	us on to futile activity,/And in the end, judge us still more severely/For the errors
552 ES	Carghil	37	some sort of part for you/Right to the end. You'll still be playing a part/In your
556 ES	Michael	35	blame a person/It's natural he should end by getting into trouble./{LC} You started
558 ES	Ld Clav	28	/{LC} And does this bring us to the end of the list of your shortcomings?/Or did Sir
573 ES	Ld Clav	17	endure this persecution?/{LC} To the end. The place and time of liberation/Are, I
574 ES	Carghil	15	or two, now and then./And in the end I discovered what Michael really wanted/
579 ES	Gomez	26	/{Mi} I don't see why not./{G} At the end of five years he will get his first leave./{Mi}
579 ES	Gomez	31	going./You'll be grateful to me in the end, Dick./{MC} A parent isn't always the right

ENDEAVOURS (1)

68 WL: Fire S	237	meal is ended, she is bored and tired,/Endeavours to engage her in caresses/Which

ENDED (11)

68 WL: Fire S	236	propitious, as he guesses,/The meal is ended, she is bored and tired,/Endeavours to
189 FQ: DrySal	184	pray for those who were in ships, and/Ended their voyage on the sand, in the sea's lips
192 FQ: Little	59	/Marks the place where a story ended./Dust inbreathed was a house —/The
241 MC Priest1	17	to meet him./{P1} What, is the exile ended, is our Lord Archbishop/Reunited with
251 MC Tempt3	4	turn to real/But real friendship, once ended, cannot be mended./Sooner shall enmity
267 MC Knight1	29	well known. But after dissension/Had ended, in France, and you were endued/With
268 MC Knight2	1	/Made a pact of peace, and all dispute ended/Sent you back to your See as you
350 FR Agatha	20	be made straight/And the curse be ended/By intercession/By pilgrimage/By those
508 CC Guzzard	23	to keep him, when the payments ended./{E} And how did you dispose of him?/
551 ES Carghil	37	you./If I'd carried on, it might have ended your career,/And then you wouldn't have
552 ES Ld Clav	20	was clear./A brief infatuation, ended in the only way possible/To our mutual

ENDEMIC (1)

434 CP	Alex	2	to Kinkanja,/Where there are various endemic diseases/Besides, of course, those

ENDING (4)

185 FQ: DrySal	47	/When time stops and time is never ending;/And the ground swell, that is and was
193 FQ: Little	81	hour before the morning/Near the ending of interminable night/At the recurrent
252 MC Tempt3	2	/At once, for England and for Rome,/Ending the tyrannous jurisdiction/Of king's
414 CP Celia	9	one always is alone./Not simply the ending of one relationship,/Not even simply

ENDLESS (14)

73 WL: Thund	369	those hooded hordes swarming/Over endless plains, stumbling in cracked earth/
92 Ash-Wed 2	39	torment/Of love satisfied/End of the endless/Journey to no end/Conclusion of all
147 Rock 1	6	and autumn, birth and dying!/The endless cycle of idea and action,/Endless
147 Rock 1	7	/The endless cycle of idea and action,/Endless invention, endless experiment,/Brings
147 Rock 1	7	of idea and action,/Endless invention, endless experiment,/Brings knowledge of
154 Rock 3	7	worship,/I have given you speech, for endless palaver,/I have given you my Law, and
179 FQ: ECoker	99	Is the wisdom of humility: humility is endless./The houses are all gone under the sea./
240 MC Priest2	32	refused,/Meetings unended or endless/At one place or another in France?/{P3}
280 MC Priest3	31	/You still shall tramp and tread one endless round/Of thought, to justify your action
317 FR Warburt	20	know, at any moment/May make an endless difference to the future./It's about your
335 FR Harry	12	Over and under./{H} In and out, in an endless drift/Of shrieking forms in a circular
343 FR Amy	24	keep the tiles on the roof, combat the endless weather,/Resist the wind? fight with
382 CP Celia	15	was only the noise of an insect,/Dry, endless, meaningless, inhuman —/You might
403 CP Reilly	16	it/Because they are absorbed in the endless struggle/To think well of themselves./{E}

ENDLESSLY (2)

135 5FingerEx2	5	aloud,/Screamed, rattled, muttered endlessly./Little dog was safe and warm/Under
135 5FingerEx2	15	up my prior paws,/Pause, and sleep endlessly./*Lines to a Duck in the Park*/The long

ENDOWED (1)

181 FQ: ECoker	160	/The whole earth is our hospital/Endowed by the ruined millionaire,/Wherein, if

ENDS (15)

18 Portrait	21	so much, so much of odds and ends,/(For indeed I do not love it ... you knew?
21 Portrait	97	/(But our beginnings never know our ends!)/Why we have not developed into friends.'
22 Preludes	4	/Six o'clock./The burnt-out ends of smoky days./And now a gusty shower
49 Hippopot	10	steps may err/In compassing material ends,/While the True Church need never stir/To
67 WL: Fire S	178	cardboard boxes, cigarette ends/Or other testimony of summer nights. The
86 Hollow Men	95	Thine is the/*This is the way the world ends*/*This is the way the world ends*/*This is the*

86 Hollow Men	96	world ends/*This is the way the world ends/This is the way the world ends/Not with a*
86 Hollow Men	97	world ends/*This is the way the world ends/Not with a bang but a whimper./*
92 Ash-Wed 2	47	/For the Garden/Where all love ends./Under a juniper-tree the bones sang,
167 Rock 10	36	of light. We are glad when the day ends, when the play ends; and ecstasy is too
167 Rock 10	36	when the day ends, when the play ends; and ecstasy is too much pain./We are
167 Rock 10	43	building, to finding, to forming at the ends of our fingers and beams of our eyes./And
276 MC Chorus	3	partly living;/The terror by night that ends in daily action,/The terror by day that ends
276 MC Chorus	4	in daily action,/The terror by day that ends in sleep;/But the talk in the market-place,
278 MC Knight2	11	for/selfish and often for seditious ends, and to reform the legal system./He

ENDUED (1)

267 MC Knight1	29	/Had ended, in France, and you were endued/With your former privilege, how did

ENDURABLE (1)

336 FR Harry	16	time, you are outside me,/And just endurable. I know that you are ready,/Ready to

ENDURANCE (2)

250 MC Tempt3	39	forward./{T3} Purpose is plain./Endurance of friendship does not depend/Upon
279 MC Knight4	33	exasperated/us beyond human endurance, he could still have easily escaped; he

ENDURE (5)

173 FQ: BurntN	84	and damnation/Which flesh cannot endure./Time past and time future/Allow but a
273 MC Thomas	21	/Give no stay, but the Church shall endure./The Church shall be open, even to our
334 FR Harry	24	to play./After such training, I could endure, these ten years,/Playing a part that had
355 CP Julia	28	that? Potato crisps? No, I can't endure them./Well, I started to tell you about
573 ES Charles	16	Claverton,/Will you stay here and endure this persecution?/{LC} To the end. The

ENDURED (1)

362 CP Reilly	3	over,/You'll wonder only that you endured it for so long./And perhaps at times

ENDURING (3)

201 Def Island	2	memorials of built stone — music's/enduring instrument, of many centuries of/
202 War Poetry	21	/Enveloped or scattered./The enduring is not a substitute for the transient,/
255 MC Thomas	5	what is left to be done?/Is there no enduring crown to be won?/{T4} Yes, Thomas,

ENEMIES (6)

157 Rock 4	15	place for a beast to pass./There were enemies without to destroy him,/And spies and
246 MC Thomas	1	Little rest in Canterbury/With eager enemies restless about us./Rebellious bishops,
253 MC Tempt4	19	against each other;/Greater enemies must kings destroy./{T} What is your
254 MC Tempt4	15	the tomb./Think, Thomas, think of enemies dismayed,/Creeping in penance,
254 MC Tempt4	22	by God's grace,/And think of your enemies, in another place./{T} I have thought of
273 MC Thomas	22	Church shall be open, even to our enemies. Open the door!/{3P} My Lord! these

ENEMY (6)

33 Conv Gal	14	are the eternal humorist,/The eternal enemy of the absolute,/Giving our vagrant
143 Lines OM	4	not more still/Than when I smell the enemy/Writhing in the essential blood/Or
158 Rock 5	3	spirit and zeal./Preserve me from the enemy who has something to gain: and from the
213 Growltiger	38	circled round,/And yet from all the enemy there was not heard a sound./The lovers
256 MC Tempts	23	the wonder of his own greatness,/The enemy of society, enemy of himself./{3P} O
256 MC Tempts	23	own greatness,/The enemy of society, enemy of himself./{3P} O Thomas my Lord do

ENERGY (3)

407 CP Reilly	19	Taking infinite pains, exhausting their energy,/Yet never quite successful. You have
530 ES Monica	7	protect you/From your own restless energy — the inexhaustible/Sources of the
530 ES Ld Clav	16	the emptiness before me./If I had the energy to work myself to death/How gladly

ENERVATE (1)

54 Mr E Sun	8	at the mensual turn of time/Produced enervate Origen./A painter of the Umbrian

ENFANTS (1)

67 WL: Fire S	202	feet in soda water/Et O ces voix d'enfants, chantant dans la coupole!/Twit twit

ENFOLD (1)

50 Hippopot	30	clean/And him shall heavenly arms enfold,/Among the saints he shall be seen/

ENFOLDED (1)

385 CP Reilly	13	/The beloved nursemaid — those who enfolded/Your childhood years in comfort,

ENGAGE (5)

68 WL: Fire S	237	she is bored and tired,/Endeavours to engage her in caresses/Which still are
218 Mung Rump	20	were plausible fellows, and liked to engage a friendly policeman in conversation./
460 CC Lady E	15	Your advice? About what?/{LE} To engage Mr. Colby. I really am distressed!/This is
460 CC Lady E	21	left:/'Trust my guidance for once, and engage that young man?'/Well, that was Mr.
534 ES Ld Clav	16	for./I trust you've no need to engage in forgery./{G} Forgery, Dick? An

ENGAGED (17)

154 Rock 3	13	and unconsidered action./Many are engaged in writing books and printing them,/
155 Rock 3	66	the stars into common and preferred,/Engaged in devising the perfect refrigerator,/
156 Rock 3	67	in devising the perfect refrigerator,/Engaged in working out a rational morality,/
156 Rock 3	68	in working out a rational morality,/Engaged in printing as many books as possible,/

209 NamingCats   27   you, is always the same:/His mind is engaged in a rapt contemplation/Of the
220 Old Deut   25   he feels so disposed/Or when he's engaged in domestic economy:/And the Oldest
227 Macavity   34   resting, or a-licking of his thumbs,/Or engaged in doing complicated long division
326 FR   Harry   15   of all the junior members?/Or engaged in predicting the minor event,/Engaged
326 FR   Harry   16   in predicting the minor event,/Engaged in foreseeing the minor disaster?/You
458 CC   Claude   4   papers./We must look as if we'd been engaged in business. {}/[*Enter* LADY
504 CC   Guzzard 29   /I know that you are always much engaged./{SC} First, let me introduce you to my
527 ES   Monica   2   him;/In the second place, we're not engaged yet./{C} Aren't we? We're agreed that
533 ES   Ld Clav 38   /{LC} In other words/You have been engaged in systematic corruption./{G} No,
567 ES   Charles 14   me then./And you said we weren't engaged yet .../{M} We're engaged now./At least
567 ES   Monica   15   we weren't engaged yet .../{M} We're engaged now./At least *I'm* engaged. I'm
567 ES   Monica   16   /{M} We're engaged now./At least *I'm* engaged. I'm engaged to you for ever./{C}
567 ES   Monica   16   now./At least *I'm* engaged. I'm engaged to you for ever./{C} There's another
ENGAGEMENT (7)
314 FR   Amy   6   for dinner/He broke an important engagement to come./{W} I dare say we've both
440 CP   Alex   17   *want* you to go!/{A} We have another engagement./{R} And on this occasion I shall
511 CC   Lady E   36   I'm very glad you're announcing your engagement?/Lucasta, I shall take charge of
527 ES   Charles   5   /Isn't that enough to constitute an engagement?/Aren't you sure that you want to
529 ES   Monica   22   recognise this book?/{M} It's your engagement book./{LC} Yes, I've been brooding
529 ES   Monica   24   over it./{M} But what a time for your engagement book!/You know what the doctors
529 ES   Ld Clav 35   afternoon./If I've been looking at this engagement book, to-day,/Not over breakfast,
ENGINE (1)
68 WL: Fire S   216   from the desk, when the human engine waits/Like a taxi throbbing waiting,/I
ENGINEERS (1)
129 Cor2 State   16   to nominate a commission of engineers/To consider the Water Supply./A
ENGINES (1)
127 Cor1 March   19   /13,000 aeroplanes,/24,000 aeroplane engines,/50,000 ammunition waggons,/now
ENGLAND (42)
30 Cous Nancy   4   and broke them —/The barren New England hills —/Riding to hounds/Over the
192 FQ: Little   40   in place and time,/Now and in England./If you came this way,/Taking any
192 FQ: Little   55   intersection of the timeless moment/Is England and nowhere. Never and always./Ash
197 FQ: Little   239   a secluded chapel/History is now and England./With the drawing of this Love and the
587 Fable   1   YOUTH/A Fable for Feasters/In England, long before that royal Mormon/King
241 MC   Mess   13   circumlocution:/The Archbishop is in England, and is close outside the city./I was sent
250 MC   Thomas   1   /Of heaven and hell, supreme alone in England,/Who bind and loose, with power from
251 MC   Tempt3 19   in the present situation./King in England is not all-powerful;/King is in France,
251 MC   Tempt3 22   him waiting hungry sons./We are for England. We are in England./You and I, my
251 MC   Tempt3 22   sons./We are for England. We are in England./You and I, my Lord, are Normans./
251 MC   Tempt3 24   /You and I, my Lord, are Normans./England is a land for Norman/Sovereignty. Let
252 MC   Tempt3   1   fight a good stroke/At once, for England and for Rome,/Ending the tyrannous
258 MC   Thomas 21   When I imposed the King's law/In England, and waged war with him against
260 MC   Thomas 28   as we think of it: the kingdom of England at peace with its/neighbours, the
267 MC   Knight1 31   your gratitude?/You had fled from England, not exiled/Or threatened, mind you;
275 MC   Chorus 10   blood has blinded my eyes. Where is England? where is Kent? where is Canterbury?/
279 MC   Knight4 28   to live, and/that he would be killed in England. He used every means of provocation;/
284 FR   m   11   *laid in a country house in the North of England*/PART I/*The drawing-room, after tea.*
286 FR   Charles   1   dogs and guns/Ever to want to leave England in the winter./But a single man like me
309 FR   Harry   30   in useless travel;/You have staid in England, yet you seem/Like someone who
329 FR   Chorus   20   of exorcism/And whether in Argos or England/There are certain inflexible laws/
431 CP   Peter   21   /The most decayed noble mansion in England!/At least, of any that are still inhabited.
439 CP   Edward   24   see you again, Peter,/Before you leave England?/{L} Do try to come to see us./You
439 CP   Peter   31   visit?/{P} The next time I come to England, I promise you./I really do want to see
533 ES   Ld Clav 10   lived out there ever since ... you left England?/{G} Ever since I finished my sentence.
533 ES   Ld Clav 12   /{LC} What has brought you to England?/{G} Call it homesickness,/Curiosity,
533 ES   Ld Clav 27   activity that lost you respect/Here in England?/{G} Not at all, not at all./I think that
534 ES   Ld Clav   7   of such a nature that, if carried on in England,/It might land you in gaol again?/{G}
534 ES   Gomez   11   carrying on such business if I lived in England./I have the same standards of morality/
534 ES   Gomez   14   which I find myself./I do nothing in England that you would disapprove of./{LC}
535 ES   Gomez   25   perfectly simple. I come back to England/After thirty-five years. Can you
538 ES   Gomez   17   of making a mistake./{G} No, in England mistakes are anonymous/Because the
539 ES   Gomez   37   than I should ever have been in England./{LC} So, as you consider yourself a
559 ES   Ld Clav   5   not a bad idea. A few years out of England/In one of the Dominions, might set
560 ES   Michael 19   Anyway, I'm determined to get out of England./{LC} Michael! Are there reasons for
560 ES   Michael 29   But I want to get out. I'm fed up with England./{LC} I'm sure you don't mean that.
561 ES   Michael 33   What is there to say?/I want to leave England, and make my own career:/And Father

563 ES   Gomez   35   /{G} I lost touch with things in England./Had I been in London, and in Dick's
564 ES   Gomez   24   /{G} I expect that was after I had left England./{MC} Of course, that explains it. After
576 ES   Gomez   22   easier explained in San Marco than in England./{LC} Perhaps you intend to change
579 ES   Charles   6   Michael./{C} And when do you leave England?/{Mi} When we can get a passage./And
579 ES   Gomez   37   of good fortune/That I came to England at the very moment/When I could be

ENGLAND'S (1)
286 FR   Violet   15   /Even could I do it as well as Amy:/England's bad enough, I would never go south,/

ENGLISH (21)
 20 Portrait   74   page./Particularly I remark./An English countess goes upon the stage./A Greek
201 Def Island   3   of/patient cultivation of the earth, of English/verse/be joined with the memory of this
245 MC Priest2   32   your rooms/To take the chill off our English December,/Your Lordship now being
251 MC Tempt3   27   /He does not understand us, the English barons./We are the people./{T} To what
256 MC Tempts   14   party,/The prize awarded for the English Essay,/The scholar's degree, the
277 MC Knight2   38   always with the under dog./It is the English spirit of fair play. Now the worthy
285 FR   Violet   19   shillings./{V} Go south! to the English circulating libraries,/To the military
285 FR   Violet   20   /To the military widows and the English chaplains,/To the chilly deck-chair and
286 FR   Charles   4   be very cosy at his club/Even in an English winter./{G} Well, as for me,/I'd just as
429 CP   Edward   17   *whole* story./{E} And have any of the English residents been murdered?/{A} Yes, but
431 CP   Peter   16   a good turn./We're making a film of English life/And we want to use Boltwell./{J}
431 CP   Peter   31   /And besides, he thought that as I'm English/I ought to know the best way to handle
431 CP   Peter   34   /He's looking for some typical English faces —/Of course, only for minor parts
432 CP   Julia   35   in films./He's making a film of English life/And he's going to find parts for all
532 ES   Lambert   2   /By the looks of him. But talks good English./A pleasant-spoken gentleman. {}/[*after*
536 ES   Gomez   10   a girl who didn't know a word of English,/Didn't want to learn English, wasn't
536 ES   Gomez   11   word of English,/Didn't want to learn English, wasn't interested/In anything that
536 ES   Gomez   14   told her./I made my children learn English — it's useful;/I always talk to them in
536 ES   Gomez   15   — it's useful;/I always talk to them in English./But do they think in English? No, they
536 ES   Gomez   16   them in English./But do they think in English? No, they do not./They think in
564 ES   Carghil   17   how you come to speak such perfect English?/Of course, I could tell from your looks

ENGLISHMAN (1)
250 MC Tempt3   36   /I am a rough straightforward Englishman./{T} Proceed straight forward./{T3}

ENGLISHMEN (4)
276 MC Knight1   20   unfavourably/of our action. You are Englishmen, and therefore you believe in fair/
276 MC Knight1   24   to your sense of honour. You/are Englishmen, and therefore will not judge
277 MC Knight3   5   lose than to gain. We are four plain Englishmen/who put our country first. I dare
277 MC Knight2   36   Reginald Fitz Urse: that you are Englishmen,/and therefore your sympathies are

ENGROSSED (2)
245 MC Priest2   24   forgive me, I did not see you coming,/Engrossed by the chatter of these foolish
266 MC Thomas   4   it arrives. It comes when we are/Engrossed with matters of other urgency./On

ENGROSSING (1)
539 ES   Ld Clav   27   San Marco/Is that in the midst of the engrossing business/Of the nature of which dark

ENIGMA (1)
181 FQ: ECoker 153   of the healer's art/Resolving the enigma of the fever chart./Our only health is the

ENJOY (9)
361 CP   Reilly   36   at night,/That you are beginning to enjoy your independence;/Finding your life
430 CP   Peter   30   here in London./{P} You always did enjoy a leg-pull, Julia:/But you all know I'm
452 CC   Kaghan   10   Eggers, I can just relax./I'm going to enjoy the game from the sidelines. {}/[*Enter*
474 CC   Lucasta   36   able to talk about it,/But ... partly, to enjoy it ... and because of what it stands for./
544 ES   Monica   27   /Now I want to see you learning to enjoy yourself!/{LC} Perhaps I've never really
544 ES   Ld Clav   30   to do/Without knowing that they enjoy it. Whereas I've often known/That I
545 ES   Ld Clav   1   I've often known/That I didn't enjoy it. Some dissatisfaction/With myself, I
548 ES   Piggott   2   *raison d'être.*/Now I'll leave you to enjoy it. {}/[*Exit*]/{M} I hope she won't
556 ES   Michael   13   a lovely day!/I'm glad you're here, to enjoy such weather./{LC} You're glad I'm here?

ENJOYABLE (1)
356 CP   Peter   13   Not the one I wrote:/But I had a very enjoyable time./{C} Go on with the story about

ENJOYED (3)
354 CP   Julia   18   /You have too much vitality.' But she enjoyed herself. {}/[*To the* UNIDENTIFIED
469 CC   Lucasta   24   really listened to the music:/I just enjoyed going — to see the other people,/And
544 ES   Ld Clav   28   /{LC} Perhaps I've never really enjoyed living/As much as most people. At

ENJOYING (1)
400 CP   Alex   23   /She will be very penitent. He's enjoying his illness./{R} Illness offers him a

ENJOYMENTS (1)
306 FR   Mary   36   was never any time to invent our own enjoyments./But perhaps it was all designed for

ENJOYS (2)
215 RTTugger	34	your sewing,/For there's nothing he enjoys like a horrible muddle./Yes the Rum
324 FR	Harry	17	the kind of consciousness/That John enjoys, can't make very much difference/To him

ENLIGHTENED (2)
149 Rock 1	68	/To satisfy the rational and enlightened mind./Second, you neglect and
154 Rock 3	3	men,/O wretched generation of enlightened men,/Betrayed in the mazes of your

ENLIGHTENMENT (1)
151 Rock 2	20	and cotton goods/And intellectual enlightenment/And everything, including capital

ENMITY (2)
251 MC Tempt3	5	cannot be mended./Sooner shall enmity turn to alliance./The enmity that never
251 MC Tempt3	6	shall enmity turn to alliance./The enmity that never knew friendship/Can sooner

ENOUGH (61)
96 Ash-Wed 5	12	word/Resound? Not here, there is not enough silence/Not on the sea or on the islands,
122 SA Sweeney	12	death./I've been born, and once is enough./You don't remember, but I remember,/
122 SA Sweeney	14	remember, but I remember,/Once is enough. {}/SONG BY WAUCHOPE AND
166 Rock 10	16	But be ye satisfied that you have light/Enough to take your step and find your
216 Jellicles	25	Cats have moonlit eyes./They're quiet enough in the morning hours,/They're quiet
216 Jellicles	26	in the morning hours,/They're quiet enough in the afternoon,/Reserving their
234 Ad-dress	5	character./You now have learned enough to see/That Cats are much like you and
236 Cat Morgan	11	And everyone says, and I guess that's enough;/'You can't but like Morgan, 'e's got a
242 MC Priest2	32	back to his own again./We have had enough of waiting, from December to dismal
254 MC Tempt4	39	is worse, when men will not hate you/Enough to defame or to execrate you,/But
269 MC Knight2	25	Or answer with your bodies./{K2} Enough of words./{4K} We come for the King's
279 MC Knight4	34	/could have kept himself from us long enough to allow our righteous/anger to cool.
286 FR	Violet	15	I do it as well as Amy:/England's bad enough, I would never go south,/Simply to see
319 FR	Warburt	12	good probing for misery./There was enough once: but what festered/Then, has only
322 FR	Winch	18	you a shock./{Wi} There's been shock enough for one evening, my Lord:/That's what
331 FR	Harry	17	what I want to know, and that is enough:/Warburton told me that, though he did
332 FR	Agatha	34	The autumn came too soon, not soon enough./The rain and wind had not shaken
337 FR	Amy	34	to say he shall go?/I think I know well enough why you wish him to go./{Ag} I wish
339 FR	Harry	21	/That seems too much, is just strength enough given./I must follow the bright angels. {}
340 FR	Amy	4	a change in Agatha —/It has made enough in *me*. Thirty-five years ago/You took
344 FR	Gerald	20	/I've met with missionaries, often enough —/Some of them very decent fellows. A
345 FR	Charles	36	age came softly up to now. I felt safe enough;/And now I don't feel safe. As if the
363 CP	Edward	38	that much of what you've said/Is true enough. But that is not all./Since I saw her this
364 CP	Reilly	12	in remaining in the dark/Except long enough to clear from the mind/The illusion of
374 CP	Celia	22	really matter. They will know soon enough./Doesn't that settle all our difficulties?/
379 CP	Celia	32	discovered/That the dream was not enough; that I wanted something more/And I
380 CP	Celia	3	I am not sure even that you seem real enough/To humiliate me. I suppose that most
393 CP	Edward	34	You nagged me because I didn't get enough work/And said that I ought to meet
394 CP	Edward	40	back like that?/{E} I have had quite enough humiliation/Lately, to bring me to the
396 CP	Edward	22	say you are sorry for me!/I have had enough of people being sorry for me./{L} Yes,
405 CP	Reilly	14	the opportunity, and you have said enough/To convince me that you have been
407 CP	Reilly	29	told me —/Both of you — was true enough: you described your feelings —/Or some
410 CP	Lavinia	11	we have in common/Might be just enough to make us loathe one another./{R} See
413 CP	Reilly	24	explain myself./{R} I know quite enough about you for the moment:/Try first to
425 CP	Edward	23	were like./Their guests will get just enough to make them thirsty;/They'll come on
427 CP	Alex	19	warmest welcome./I know them well enough for that./{J} But tell us, Alex./What
436 CP	Peter	13	in myself:/And that isn't good enough for Celia./{J} You must have learned
454 CC	Kaghan	7	to leave you with Colby./He's had enough for one day. Take my advice, Colby./
465 CC	Claude	5	too young. And when I was mature enough/To understand him, he was not there./
466 CC	Claude	10	am alone, and look at one thing long enough,/I sometimes have that sense of
477 CC	Lucasta	6	over. That was lucky./But I was old enough to remember ... too much./{C} You are
477 CC	Lucasta	17	house!/Lucasta .../{L} I can see well enough you *are* shocked./You ought to see your
489 CC	Claude	7	One child each —/That seemed fair enough — though yours had been lost,/And
491 CC	Colby	31	of the other parents!/It's strange enough to have two parents —/But I should
502 CC	Lucasta	18	to despise people:/You don't care enough./{C} I don't care enough?/{L} No.
502 CC	Colby	19	don't care enough./{C} I don't care enough?/{L} No. You're either above caring,/Or
505 CC	Eggers	32	both seem very brief —/But long enough ago for the question to be possible./
517 CC	Eggers	39	small —/Very small, I'm afraid. Not enough to live on./We'll have to think of other
527 ES	Charles	5	being no legal impediment/Isn't that enough to constitute an engagement?/Aren't
534 ES	Gomez	5	come across an official/Innocent enough to be corruptible./{LC} It would seem
534 ES	Gomez	9	you in gaol again?/{G} That's true enough,/Except for a false inference. I wouldn't
536 ES	Gomez	1	/{G} But of course you know!/Just enough to think you know more than you do./
547 ES	Piggott	23	younger generation./When there are enough young people among us/We dance in

547 ES	Piggott	28	don't advise croquet/Until you know	enough about the other guests/To know whom
553 ES	Carghil	7	was brief,/Our relations were intense	enough, I think,/To have given me one or two
560 ES	Ld Clav	30	you don't mean that. But it's natural	enough/To want a few years abroad. It might be
564 ES	Gomez	13	/{G} My dear lady, you're not old	enough/To have known Dick Ferry as long as I
565 ES	Monica	5	Michael./{M} No, I think you've had	enough talk for to-day./Michael, as you're
572 ES	Ld Clav	32	you./{LC} Your reasoning's sound	enough. But it's irrelevant./Each of them
576 ES	Charles	37	a reliable witness./{C} I know	enough about the law of libel and slander/To
582 ES	Ld Clav	23	it's chilly at dusk. But I'll be warm	enough./I shall not go far. { }/[*Exit*

ENQUIRE (2)

402 CP	Edward	13	for himself./Or at least that he would	enquire about the symptoms./Two people
498 CC	Eggers	22	terms. But if she did that,/We must	enquire what became of the other one./{SC} But

ENQUIRED (1)

289 FR	Ivy	31	/{I} These things are much better not	enquired into./She may have done it in a fit of

ENQUIRIES (4)

295 FR	Harry	2	I became excited, I think I made	enquiries;/The purser and the steward were
409 CP	Reilly	2	of emotional strain/And so I made	enquiries./{E} It was two months ago/That your
491 CC	Lady E	7	/Why should we make any further	enquiries?/Let us regard him as being *our* son:/
506 CC	Eggers	12	/In which she could have instituted	enquiries./So, for many years, she has been

ENQUIRING (1)

136 5FingerEx3		13	and so should you/That soon the	enquiring worm shall try/Our well-preserved

ENRAPTURED (1)

213 Growltiger		34	Griddlebone,/And the Lady seemed	enraptured by his manly baritone,/Disposed to

ENRICH (1)

281 MC	Chorus	18	blood of Thy martyrs and saints/Shall	enrich the earth, shall create the holy places./

ENSLAVEMENT (1)

578 ES	Ld Clav	1	/Of his own volition to contract his	enslavement,/I cannot prevent him. I have

ENSUES (2)

581 ES	Ld Clav	14	feel at peace now./It is the peace that	ensues upon contrition/When contrition ensues
581 ES	Ld Clav	15	upon contrition/When contrition	ensues upon knowledge of the truth./Why did I

ENTER (101)

148 Rock 1 m		46	in whom is the truth inborn./*Enter the* ROCK, *led by a* BOY:/THE ROCK:/
240 MC m		26	/But only to wait and to witness. { }/[*Enter* PRIESTS]/{P1} Seven years and the
241 MC m		11	forgotten/That they had a friend? { }/[*Enter* MESSENGER]/{M} Servants of God, and
245 MC m		11	welcome to our good Archbishop. { }/[*Enter* THOMAS]/{T} Peace. And let them be, in
246 MC m		24	things prepare the event. Watch. { }/[*Enter* FIRST TEMPTER]/{T1} You see, my
248 MC m		15	may not be whole in the present. { }/[*Enter* SECOND TEMPTER]/{T2} Your
250 MC m		19	/Would now be only mean descent. { }/[*Enter* THIRD TEMPTER]/{T3} I am an
252 MC m		30	I break, I must break myself alone. { }/[*Enter* FOURTH TEMPTER]/{T4} Well done,
263 MC 1m		27	time is short/But waiting is long. { }/[*Enter the* FIRST PRIEST *with a banner of St.*
264 MC m		7	{ }/[*Introit of St. Stephen is heard*]/[*Enter the* SECOND PRIEST, *with a banner of*
264 MC m		14	{ }/[*Introit of St. John is heard*]/[*Enter the* THIRD PRIEST, *with a banner of the*
265 MC m		9	/The eternal design may appear. { }/[*Enter the* FOUR KNIGHTS. *The banners*
265 MC m		34	longer will you keep us waiting? { }/[*Enter* THOMAS]/[*to* PRIESTS]./{T} However
271 MC m		7	pray for you, out of your shame. { }/[*Enter* THOMAS]/{T} Peace, and be at peace
271 MC m		20	kind cannot bear very much reality. { }/[*Enter* PRIESTS]/[*severally*]./{3P} My Lord,
274 MC m		14	/[*The door is opened. The* KNIGHTS *enter, slightly tipsy*]/{3P} This way, my Lord!
286 FR m		29	of their cocktails and cigarettes. { }/[*Enter* DENMAN *with sherry and whisky.*
291 FR m		13	coming:/Yes, it must be John. { }/[*Enter* HARRY]/{A} Harry! { }/[HARRY *stops*
297 FR m		27	/He shan't know why I'm asking. { }/[*Enter* DENMAN]/{C} Denman, where is
298 FR m		23	horns,/And this is one. { }/[*Knock: and enter* DOWNING]/{C} Good evening, Downing.
302 FR m		13	There is no news of Arthur or John. { }/[*Enter* AMY *and* AGATHA]/{A} It is very
303 FR 3m		1	AGATHA]/Scene II/AGATHA]/[*Enter* MARY *with flowers*]/{M} The spring is
305 FR m		19	house *means* to keep us waiting. { }/[*Enter* HARRY]/{H} Waiting? For what?/{M}
313 FR m		27	Neither of them is here yet, Amy. { }/[*Enter* AMY, *with* DR. WARBURTON]/{A} It is
316 FR m		8	manage the situation. { }/[*Exeunt*]/[*Enter* MARY, *and passes through to dinner.*
316 FR m		8	MARY, *and passes through to dinner. Enter* AGATHA]/{Ag} The eye is on this house/
321 FR m		9	is, whether you've been sleeping ... { }/[*Enter* DENMAN]/{D} It's Sergeant Winchell is
321 FR m		24	happened to one of your brothers. { }/[*Enter* WINCHELL]/{Wi} Good evening, my
323 FR m		7	with you? Is it Arthur or John? { }/[*Enter* AMY, *followed severally by* VIOLET,
326 FR m		9	she cares to mention, I imagine. { }/[*Enter* HARRY]/{H} Mother is asleep, I think:
326 FR m		33	not always welcome in this family. { }/[*Enter* DENMAN]/{D} Excuse me, Miss Ivy.
327 FR m		24	filthiness, that lies a little deeper ... { }/[*Enter* IVY]/{I} Where is there an evening paper?/
337 FR m		30	that I must go./{Ag} You must go. { }/[*Enter* AMY]/{A} What are you saying to Harry?
342 FR m		1	take him from me,/You take him ... { }/[*Enter* MARY]/{M} Excuse me, Cousin Amy. I
346 FR m		5	to know more about this than I do. { }/[*Enter* DOWNING, *hurriedly, in chauffeur's*

347 FR	m 14	been so long. {}/[*Exit* DOWNING. *Enter* IVY]/{I} Where is Downing going? where
347 FR	m 16	a telegram come from Arthur; {}/[*Enter* GERALD *and* VIOLET]/{I} I wonder why
347 FR	m 32	AGATHA *and* MARY. *Pause. Enter* WARBURTON]/{W} Well! it's a filthy
348 FR	m 4	her mind. Why, what's the trouble? {}/[*Enter* MARY]/{M} Dr. Warburton!/{W} Excuse
349 FR	1m 13	must do the right thing. {}/[*Exeunt*]/[*Enter, from one door*, AGATHA *and* MARY,
349 FR	2m 13	*portable table.*/*From another door*, enter DENMAN *carrying a birthday cake with*/
359 CP	m 24	{}/[*Opens the door*]/{E} Julia! {}/[*Enter* JULIA]/{J} Edward! How lucky that it's
364 CP	m 31	*door*]/{E} So it's you again, Julia! {}/[*Enter* JULIA *and* PETER]/{J} Edward, I'm so
367 CP	m 35	How did you come to know her? {}/[*Enter* ALEX]/{A} Ah, there you are, Edward! Do
370 CP	m 14	interrupted this interesting affair? {}/[*Enter* ALEX *in shirtsleeves and an apron*]/{A}
372 CP	m 9	you, Edward. It's very good of you. {}/[*Enter* ALEX, *with his jacket on*]/{A} Oh,
376 CP	m 10	/What have you come back for? {}/[*Enter* JULIA]/{J} I've had an inspiration! {}/
376 CP	m 11	/{J} I've had an inspiration! {}/[*Enter* CELIA *with saucepan*]/{C} Edward, it's
384 CP	m 2	*doorbell.*/{E} Oh ... good evening. {}/[*Enter the* UNIDENTIFIED GUEST]/{UG}
387 CP	m 13	{}/[*Goes to front door*]/{E} Peter! {}/[*Enter* PETER]/{P} Where's Lavinia?/{E} Don't
388 CP	m 22	/{E} You're both going away! {}/[*Enter* LAVINIA]/{L} Who's going away? Well,
390 CP	m 17	*rings.* EDWARD *goes to answer it. Enter* ALEX]/{A} Has Lavinia arrived?/{E} Yes./
391 CP	m 32	I believe ... I haven't left anything. {}/[*Enter* PETER]/{P} I've got a taxi, Julia./{J}
398 CP	Edward 7	door on the latch/For these doubts to enter? And then you came back, you/The angel
405 CP	Reilly 32	/Your husband wishes to enter a sanatorium,/And that is a question
412 CP	m 2	it.]/{R} Yes? ... Yes. Come in. {}/[*Enter* JULIA *by side door*]/{R} She's waiting
420 CP	m 20	It is finished. You can come in now. {}/[*Enter* JULIA *by side door*]/{R} She will go far,
422 CP	m 5	the tray in now, Miss Barraway. {}/[*Enter* ALEX]/{A} Well! Well! and how have we
426 CP	m 28	Shuttlethwaite!/{L} Oh, it's Julia! {}/[*Enter* JULIA]/{J} Well, my dears, and here I
427 CP	m 5	it./But what's become of him? {}/[*Enter* ALEX]/{E} Well, Alex!/Where on earth do
430 CP	m 1	{CM} Mr. Quilpe!/{E} Now who ... {}/[*Enter* PETER]/{E} Why, it's Peter!/{L} Peter!/
432 CP	m 4	forgot! I'd another surprise for you. {}/[*Enter* REILLY]/{J} I want you to meet Sir
445 CC	3m 1	SIR CLAUDE *writing at desk. Enter*/EGGERSON./{SC} Ah, there you are,
450 CC	m 26	be ready waiting to introduce him. {}/[*Enter* COLBY SIMPKINS *with briefcase*]/{SC}
451 CC	m 39	for meeting her. {}/[*A loud knock. Enter* B. KAGHAN]/{K} Enter B. Kaghan. Hello
452 CC	Kaghan 1	*loud knock. Enter* B. KAGHAN]/{K} Enter B. Kaghan. Hello Colby!/And hello
452 CC	m 11	enjoy the game from the sidelines. {}/[*Enter* LUCASTA ANGEL]/{L} Eggy, I've lost
457 CC	m 11	to find that I'm right, I assure you. {}/[*Enter* SIR CLAUDE]/{SC} Hello! Still here? It's
458 CC	1m 5	as if we'd been engaged in business. {}/[*Enter* LADY ELIZABETH MULHAMMER]/
474 CC	Lucasta 12	makes it unreal./{L} Can no one else enter?/{C} It can't be done by issuing
478 CC	m 35	to appreciate B./{C} Lucasta, wait! {}/[*Enter* B. KAGHAN]/{K} Enter B. Kaghan./To
478 CC	Kaghan 35	wait! {}/[*Enter* B. KAGHAN]/{K} Enter B. Kaghan./To see the new flat. And
481 CC	m 14	discuss *me* ... {}/[*A knock at the door. Enter* LADY ELIZABETH]/{LE} Oh, good
486 CC	m 33	*on the door*]/{LE} Who's that? {}/[*Enter* SIR CLAUDE]/{SC} Elizabeth! I was told
493 CC	3m 1	SIR CLAUDE *is*/*moving chairs about. Enter* LADY ELIZABETH./{LE} Claude, what
496 CC	m 13	be *our* son. {}/[*A knock on the door. Enter* EGGERSON]/{SC} Good morning,
490 CC	m 10	here already! Well ... Come in! {}/[*Enter* LUCASTA]/{L} Is this a meeting? I came
502 CC	m 1	[*Reaches for the telephone*]/[*A knock. Enter* COLBY]/{C} Have I come too soon?/I'm
504 CC	m 4	If *I* was late when I went to see her. {}/[*Enter* LUCASTA]/{L} I'm sorry to come back.
504 CC	m 24	Well, are we ready? {}/[*A quiet knock. Enter* KAGHAN, *escorting* MRS. GUZZARD.
524 ES	m 5	really no point in my staying to tea. {}/[*Enter* MONICA *and* CHARLES *carrying*
526 ES	m 26	/It's Lambert with the tea ... {}/[*Enter* LAMBERT *with trolley*]/{M} and I shall
527 ES	m 11	That won't happen to me. {}/[*Knock. Enter* LAMBERT]/{L} Excuse me, Miss
529 ES	m 19	often. And Oh, Charles dear — {}/[*Enter* LORD CLAVERTON]/{M} You've been
531 ES	m 32	a ghost can be of men! {}/[*Knock. Enter* LAMBERT]/{L} Excuse me, my Lord.
532 ES	m 26	at Badgley Court/In a week or two. {}/[*Enter* LAMBERT]/{L} Mr. Gomez, my Lord./
535 ES	m 6	But when I say 'trust' ... {}/[*Knock. Enter* LAMBERT]/{LC} Lambert, will you bring
541 ES	m 31	turn, perhaps, to do you a kindness. {}/[*Enter* LAMBERT]/{L} Excuse me, my Lord, but
542 ES	Gomez 35	/The sudden silence when you enter the smoking room./Don't forget, Dick:/
543 ES	m 8	*for a few minutes brooding. A knock. Enter* MONICA.]/{M} Who was it, Father?/
544 ES	3m 1	*sunny morning, several days later. Enter* LORD CLAVERTON *and* MONICA./
545 ES	m 22	newspaper and start reading to me. {}/[*Enter* MRS. PIGGOTT]/{MP} Good morning,
548 ES	2m 14	*spreads his newspaper over his face. Enter* MRS. CARGHILL. *She sits in a deckchair*
554 ES	m 10	Piggott!/Isn't it a glorious morning! {}/[*Enter* MRS. PIGGOTT]/{MP} Good morning,
555 ES	m 10	it's the penalty/Of being famous. {}/[*Enter* MONICA]/{MP} Oh, Miss
556 ES	m 10	this over. {}/[*calls*]/{M} Michael! {}/[*Enter* MICHAEL]/{LC} Good morning,
562 ES	m 12	affectionate nature, really,/But ... {}/[*Enter* MRS. CARGHILL *with despatch-case*]/
563 ES	m 7	to us. You must introduce him. {}/[*Enter* GOMEZ]/{G} Good morning, Dick./{LC}
567 ES	3m 1	*following day.* MONICA *seated*/*alone. Enter* CHARLES./{C} Well, Monica, here I am.
573 ES	m 23	We will stay here. Let her join us. {}/[*Enter* MRS. CARGHILL]/{MC} I've been

574 ES   m 26   lamb. Let's all rejoice together. {}/[*Enter* GOMEZ *and* MICHAEL]/{LC} Well,
ENTERED (7)
343 FR   m 31   AMY *has been speaking,* HARRY *has entered, dressed for departure.*]/{H} But, mother,
344 FR   m 2   GERALD *and* CHARLES *have entered*]/{C} Where is Harry going? What is the
401 CP Edward   5   /{E} It came into my mind/Before I entered the door, that you might be the same
526 ES Monica   22   We're back in the room/That we entered only a few minutes ago./Here's an
530 ES Ld Clav   1   —/The first empty pages since I entered Parliament./I used to jot down notes of
561 ES   m 21   lived up to them. {}/[MONICA *has entered unobserved*]/{M} Michael! How can you
567 ES   m 27   imagine it. {}/[CLAVERTON *has entered unobserved*]/{M} I never expected you
ENTERING (1)
71 WL: DWater 318 passed the stages of his age and youth/Entering the whirlpool./Gentile or Jew/O you
ENTERPRISE (1)
158 Rock 5   6   the others run about like dogs, full of enterprise, sniffing and barking: they say, 'This
ENTERPRISES (1)
155 Rock 3   61   /To arts and inventions and daring enterprises,/To schemes of human greatness
ENTERS (8)
43 Swee Erect   42   /But Doris, towelled from the bath,/Enters padding on broad feet,/Bringing sal
285 FR   5m 1   CHARLES, MARY/[DENMAN *enters to draw the curtains*]/{A} Not yet! I will
399 CP   4m 1   *button. The* NURSE-SECRETARY *enters, with Appointment/Book./*{R} About those
399 CP   2m 25   NURSE-SECRETARY]/[ALEX *enters almost immediately*]/{A} When is
405 CP Reilly   17   /Ought to know his brief before he enters the court./{E} I am at least free to leave.
422 CP   1m 11   evening. {}/[NURSE-SECRETARY *enters with a tray, a decanter and three glasses,*
424 CP   4m 1   *is arranging a buffet/table.* LAVINIA *enters from side door./*{CM} Have you any
535 ES   m 19   {}/[*During this* LAMBERT *enters silently, deposits tray and exit*]/{LC}
ENTERTAIN (1)
437 CP Reilly   18   Chamberlayne,/I ask you only to entertain the suggestion/That a sudden
ENTERTAINED (1)
368 CP Edward   35   attempts at starting a salon,/Where I entertained the minor guests/And dealt with the
ENTERTAINMENT (1)
265 MC Priest1 23   be vexed/If we did not offer you entertainment/Before your business. Please dine
ENTERTAINS (1)
41 Burb Blei   28   the waterstair. Lights, lights,/She entertains Sir Ferdinand/Klein. Who clipped the
ENTHUSIASM (2)
156 Rock 3   70   from your vacancy to fevered enthusiasm/For nation or race or what you call
241 MC Mess   32   receive him with scenes of frenzied enthusiasm,/Lining the road and throwing
ENTIRE (2)
274 MC Thomas   4   /To which my whole being gives entire consent./I give my life/To the Law of
541 ES Gomez   27   /Any time you're in a tight corner/My entire resources are at your disposal./You were
ENTIRELY (2)
589 Fable   90   And lived on milk and breakfast food entirely;/Each morn from four to five one took
365 CP Reilly   8   *daughter/And she took my heart entirely./*You will keep our appointment?/{E} I
ENTITIES (1)
53 Whispers   29   /And even the Abstract Entities/Circumambulate her charm;/But our lot
ENTITLED (2)
235 Ad-dress   64   to waste the onion sauce.)/A Cat's entitled to expect/These evidences of respect./
381 CP Celia   2   from you, Edward:/You are not entitled to take any interest/Now, in *my* future.
ENTRE (2)
48 Lune Miel   3   d'été, les voici à Ravenne,/A l'aise entre deux draps, chez deux centaines de
182 FQ: ECoker 175   years largely wasted, the years of *l'entre deux guerres* —/Trying to learn to use
ENTRUSTED (2)
497 CC Claude   15   person/To whom her own child was entrusted./{E} What an amazing coincidence!/
510 CC Eggers   38   To whom, it seems, you had first been entrusted./{K} I really don't know what emotion
ENVELOPED (1)
202 War Poetry 20   be met with ambush and stratagem,/Enveloped or scattered./The enduring is not a
ENVIED (1)
472 CC Lucasta 35   them./And yet, all the time, I found I *envied* you/And I didn't know why! And now I
ENVIOUS (1)
529 ES Monica   14   /Are unaware or unashamed of being envious./It's all we can ask if compassion and
ENVY (9)
163 Rock 8   37   /Not avarice, lechery, treachery,/Envy, sloth, gluttony, jealousy, pride:/It was not
253 MC Tempt4   14   broken and crushed./As for barons, envy of lesser men/Is still more stubborn than
266 MC Knight1 32   is what you mean,/Saving your pride, envy and spleen./{K2} Saving your insolence
451 CC Eggers   36   a great asset/With Lady Elizabeth. I envy you that./I've always sung in our
529 ES Charles 11   Is that wistfulness,/Compassion, or ... envy?/{M} Envy is everywhere./Who is without
529 ES Monica   12   /Compassion, or ... envy?/{M} Envy is everywhere./Who is without envy? And

529 ES   Monica   13   Envy is everywhere./Who is without envy? And most people/Are unaware or
529 ES   Monica   16   tenderness, Charles! are mixed with envy:/I do believe that he is fond of you./So you
542 ES   Ld Clav   20   ago, I only gained in return/Your envy, spite and hatred. That is why you
ÉPAULE (1)
51 Restaurant   2   les doigts et se pencher sur mon épaule:/'Dans mon pays il fera temps pluvieux,/
EPICENE (1)
55 Mr E Sun   28   and pistillate,/Blest office of the epicene./Sweeney shifts from ham to ham/
EPICURES (1)
588 Fable   42   had been made,/The jovial epicures sat down to table./The menus of that
EPIDEMICS (1)
314 FR   Violet   16   your minor ailments/And children's epidemics: you would never stay in bed/Because
EPILEPTIC (1)
43 Swee Erect   31   Waiting until the shriek subsides./The epileptic on the bed/Curves backward, clutching
EPISODES (1)
568 ES   Ld Clav   10   we regret in the very next moment,/Episodes we try to conceal from the world./Has
EPITAPH (1)
197 FQ: Little   227   end and a beginning,/Every poem an epitaph. And any action/Is a step to the block,
EPITOME (1)
539 ES   Ld Clav   23   *whisky]*/{LC} An interesting historical epitome./Though I cannot accept it as
ÉPROUVAIS (1)
51 Restaurant   14   'Je la chatouillais, pour la faire rire./J'éprouvais un instant de puissance et de délire.'/
EPSOM (1)
124 SA   Snow   20   the end./What about them bones on Epsom Heath?/I seen that in the papers/You
EQUAL (5)
148 Rock 1   53   that lead to obscurity, accepting/With equal face those that bring ignominy,/The
188 FQ: DrySal   156   the future/And the past with an equal mind./At the moment which is not of
197 FQ: Little   235   the moment of the yew-tree/Are of equal duration. A people without history/Is not
210 Old Gumbie   14   mind, her name is Jennyanydots;/Her equal would be hard to find, she likes the warm
229 Gus   52   all very well,/But there's nothing to equal, from what I hear tell,/That moment of
EQUALITY (1)
568 ES   Ld Clav   34   with anyone older,/On terms of equality. To one's child one can't reveal oneself/
EQUALLY (6)
224 Mr Mistoff   28   can pick any card from a pack,/He is equally cunning with dice;/He is always
258 MC   Thomas   16   to the instrument,/Were all things equally desirable./Ambition comes when early
416 CP   Celia   27   is alone/Then lover and belovèd are equally unreal/And the dreamer is no more real
506 CC   Eggers   39   Guzzard —/Or if there are, they are equally uncommon./But, Mrs. Guzzard, this is
538 ES   Gomez   1   which you had fostered in me,/And, equally unfortunate, a talent for penmanship./
578 ES   Ld Clav   8   /By methods which proved to be equally mistaken./I see that your mother and I,
EQUIPMENT (2)
182 FQ: ECoker   182   raid on the inarticulate/With shabby equipment always deteriorating/In the general
550 ES   Ld Clav   23   never had to deal with questions of equipment./I trust that the business was very
EQUIPMENTS (1)
550 ES   Carghil   22   Have you never heard/Of Carghill Equipments? They make office furniture./{LC}
EQUITONE (1)
62 WL: Burial   57   ring./Thank you. If you see dear Mrs. Equitone,/Tell her I bring the horoscope myself:
ER (2)
119 SP   Klip   29   Eh what Klip?/{Kl} Say, Miss — er — uh — London's swell./We like London
119 SP   Klip   33   live here then?/{Kl} Well, no, Miss — er — you haven't quite got it/(I'm afraid I
ERE (4)
590 Time Space   11   trembling on the vine,/Were withered ere the wild bee flew/To suck the eglantine./So
590 Space Time   11   trembling on the vine/Were withered ere the wild bee flew/To suck the eglantine./But
604 Ode   2   is left us, Fair Harvard, with thee,/Ere we face the importunate years,/In thy
437 CP   Reilly   4   /{L} ... if it answers my question./{R} *Ere Babylon was dust/The magus Zoroaster, my*
ERECT (1)
42 Swee Erect   t   ruins, and the seven laws./Sweeney Erect/Paint me a cavernous waste shore/Cast in
ERECTED (1)
307 FR   Harry   17   and a neat summer-house/Had been erected, 'to please the children'./It's absurd that
ERHEBUNG (1)
173 FQ: BurntN   76   of sense, a white light still and moving,/*Erhebung* without motion, concentration/
EROSIONLESS (1)
186 FQ: DrySal   77   /Over shallow banks unchanging and erosionless/Or drawing their money, drying sails
ERR (1)
49 Hippopot   9   a rock./The hippo's feeble steps may err/In compassing material ends,/While the

ERRAND (2)
421 CP   Julia   27   of derision, like a child sent on an errand/In eagerness and patience. Yet she must
445 CC   Claude   3   /All the way from Joshua Park, on an errand like this./But you know my wife
ERRE (1)
47 Mél Adult   13   /Au grand air de Bergsteigleben;/J'erre toujours de-ci de-là/A divers coups de tra là
ERRING (1)
280 MC   Priest3   17   will die for it./Go, weak sad men, lost erring souls, homeless in earth or heaven./Go
ERROR (1)
196 FQ: Little   205   /The one discharge from sin and error./The only hope, or else despair/Lies in the
ERRORS (1)
545 ES   Ld Clav   9   judge us still more severely/For the errors into which his own reproaches drove us?/
ERUCTATION (1)
174 FQ: BurntN   111   lungs/Time before and time after./Eructation of unhealthy souls/Into the faded
ESCAPADE (1)
555 ES   Ld Clav   23   accident./You know, after that last escapade of his,/I've lived in terror of his
ESCAPE (35)
159 Rock 6   21   facts./They constantly try to escape/From the darkness outside and within/
272 MC   Chorus   29   the mind/To distraction, delusion, escape into dream, pretence,/Where the soul is
294 FR   Harry   27   has no language. One thinks to escape/By violence, but one is still alone/In an
306 FR   Harry   17   none of the shadows that I wanted to escape;/And at the same time, other memories,/
306 FR   Harry   21   I can't explain./But I thought I might escape from one life to another,/And it may be
306 FR   Harry   22   /And it may be all one life, with no escape. Tell me,/Were you ever happy here, as a
307 FR   Harry   13   /And the family festivities, I made my escape/As soon as I could, and slipped down to
327 FR   Harry   12   Were they simply outside,/I might escape somewhere, perhaps. Were they simply
336 FR   Harry   18   me here, where I thought I should escape you —/No! you were already here before
358 CP   Julia   6   uninteresting./{J} Well, you shan't escape. You dine with me on Friday./I've
370 CP   Edward   38   man. I congratulate you/On a timely escape./{P} I should prefer to be spared/Your
381 CP   Edward   30   long ago/And that the struggle to escape from it/Is only a make-believe, a
396 CP   Lavinia   5   that the gramophone was only your escape/From talking to me when we had to be
397 CP   Edward   6   projections. There is nothing to escape from/And nothing to escape to. One is
397 CP   Edward   7   to escape from/And nothing to escape to. One is always alone./{L} Edward,
400 CP   Reilly   25   offers him a double advantage:/To escape from himself — and get the better of his
400 CP   Alex   26   get the better of his wife./{A} Not to escape from her?/{R} He doesn't want to escape
400 CP   Reilly   27   from her?/{R} He doesn't want to escape from her./{A} He is staying at his club./
401 CP   Reilly   27   /But if it is a trap, then you cannot escape from it:/And so ... you might as well sit
464 CC   Claude   12   To be among such things,/If it is an escape, is escape into living,/Escape from a
464 CC   Claude   12   such things,/If it is an escape, is escape into living,/Escape from a sordid world
464 CC   Claude   13   If it is an escape, is escape into living,/Escape from a sordid world to a pure one./
478 CC   Lucasta   22   /And you know at last that there's no escape./Well, I'll be going./{C} You mustn't go
479 CC   Kaghan   28   Well, at least, I've always managed to escape her./{L} Only because she's never wanted
495 CC   Lady E   27   He belonged to the world I wanted to escape from./He was so commonplace! I wanted
544 ES   Monica   26   from which you were longing to escape;/Now I want to see you learning to enjoy
552 ES   Ld Clav   14   all./I thought, perhaps, what a lucky escape/It had been, for both of us./{MC} That
552 ES   Carghil   17   an afterthought, Richard. A lucky escape/You thought, for you. You felt no
560 ES   Ld Clav   5   /{LC} So you want me to help you to escape from your father!/{Mi} And to help my
560 ES   Ld Clav   34   ambition/But only the desire to escape./{Mi} I'm not a fugitive./{LC} No, not a
565 ES   Monica   29   We mustn't stay here./I want you to escape from them./{LC} What I want to escape
565 ES   Ld Clav   30   from them./{LC} What I want to escape from/Is myself, is the past. But what a
565 ES   Ld Clav   34   pleading with Michael/Not to try to escape from his own past failures:/I said I knew
569 ES   Charles   33   submit?/Why not leave Badgley and escape from them?/{LC} Because they are not
572 ES   Ld Clav   36   this meeting that I shall at last escape them./— I've made my confession to
ESCAPED (3)
213 Growltiger   47   quickly disappeared./She probably escaped with ease, I'm sure she was not
279 MC Knight4   33   endurance, he could still have easily escaped; he/could have kept himself from us
434 CP   Alex   14   natives./Eventually, two of them escaped:/One died in the jungle, and the other/
ESCAPES (1)
456 CC   Eggers   8   not petty-minded — though nothing escapes him./And such a generous heart! He's
ESCAPING (3)
188 FQ: DrySal   139   hours./Fare forward, travellers! not escaping from the past/Into different lives, or
495 CC   Lady E   25   I'm getting confused./I thought I was escaping from a world that I loathed/In Tony
565 ES   Ld Clav   32   But what a coward I am,/To talk of escaping! And what a hypocrite!/A few minutes
ESCORTING (1)
504 CC   m 24   {}/[*A quiet knock. Enter* KAGHAN, *escorting* MRS. GUZZARD. *Exit* KAGHAN]/

ESPECIALLY (5)

189 FQ: DrySal	200	/And always will be, some of them especially/When there is distress of nations and
261 MC Thomas	38	of/the past, asking you to remember especially our martyr of Canterbury,/the blessed
277 MC Knight3	11	the grain to kill an Archbishop, especially/when you have been brought up in
289 FR Ivy	24	/[I] Yet it must have been shocking,/Especially to lose anybody in *that* way —/Swept
354 CP Celia	8	anything unless she wants to./{C} Especially the Lithuanian accent./{J}

ESQRE. (1) [*Abbreviation*]

136 5FingerEx4		t complacency./*Lines to Ralph Hodgson Esqre.*/How delightful to meet Mr. Hodgson!/

ESSAY (1)

256 MC Tempts	14	/The prize awarded for the English Essay,/The scholar's degree, the statesman's

ESSENCE (1)

85 Hollow Men	88	/And the existence/Between the essence/And the descent/Falls the Shadow/*For*

ESSENTIAL (3)

143 Lines OM	5	I smell the enemy/Writhing in the essential blood/Or dangling from the friendly
320 FR Warburt	21	/And for that reason, it is most essential/That nothing should disturb or excite
459 CC Lady E	31	hour. A quiet hour a day/Is most essential, Dr. Rebmann says./{SC} Rebmann? I

ESSEX (11)

357 CP Edward	31	must live somewhere./{E} She lives in Essex./{J} Anywhere near Colchester? Lavinia
357 CP Edward	33	loves oysters./{E} No. In the *depths* of Essex./{J} Well, we won't probe into it./You
390 CP Julia	8	telegram sent from?/{J} Why, from Essex, of course./{L} And why from Essex?/{J}
390 CP Lavinia	9	Essex, of course./{L} And why from Essex?/{J} Because you've been in Essex./{L}
390 CP Julia	10	Essex?/{J} Because you've been in Essex./{L} Because I've been in Essex!/{J}
390 CP Lavinia	11	in Essex./{L} Because I've been in Essex!/{J} Lavinia! Don't say you've had a lapse
390 CP Lavinia	14	telegram./{L} Well, perhaps I was in Essex. I really don't know./{J} You don't know
390 CP Lavinia	24	from?/{A} Dedham./{L} Dedham is in Essex. So it was from Dedham./Edward, have
392 CP Lavinia	30	/But how did the aunt come to live in Essex?/{E} Julia compelled me to make her live
392 CP Lavinia	32	/{L} I see. So Julia made her live in Essex;/And made the telegrams come from
392 CP Lavinia	33	/And made the telegrams come from Essex./Well, I shall have to tell Julia the truth./I

EST (8)

47 Mél Adult	3	/En Angleterre, journaliste;/C'est à grands pas et en sueur/Que vous suivrez à
47 Mél Adult	8	/Vous me paierez bien la tête./C'est à Paris que je me coiffe/Casque noir de
48 Lune Miel	8	égratigner./Moins d'une lieue d'ici est Saint Apollinaire/En Classe, basilique
51 Restaurant	5	vent, du grand soleil, et de la pluie;/C'est ce qu'on appelle le jour de lessive des gueux.'
51 Restaurant	9	et des bourgeons sur les ronces —/C'est là, dans une averse, qu'on s'abrite./J'avais
51 Restaurant	16	à cet âge .../'Monsieur, le fait est dur./Il est venu, nous peloter, un gros chien;/
51 Restaurant	17	cet âge .../'Monsieur, le fait est dur./Il est venu, nous peloter, un gros chien;/Moi
51 Restaurant	19	peur, je l'ai quittée à mi-chemin./C'est dommage.'/Mais alors, tu as ton vautour!/

ESTABLISH (3)

278 MC Knight2	25	had/for so many years striven to establish; and that — God knows/why — the
325 FR Agatha	6	I think it is as well to leave Harry to establish/If he can, some communication with
369 CP Edward	18	/Lavinia always had the ambition/To establish herself in two worlds at once —/But

ESTABLISHED (2)

507 CC Guzzard	29	have got an order/If she could have established the paternity;/But I didn't know
531 ES Ld Clav	11	in the Upper House .../{LC} The established liturgy/Of the Press on any

ESTABLISHES (1)

232 Skimble	23	in the First and in the Third;/He establishes control by a regular patrol/And he'd

ESTAMINET (1)

37 Gerontion	9	sill, the owner,/Spawned in some estaminet of Antwerp,/Blistered in Brussels,

ESTATE (1)

593 Grad 6	5	see that she shall gain such proud estate/As shall on future centuries bestow/A

ESTATES (1)

250 MC Tempt3	28	dog, a wench;/I know how to hold my estates in order,/A country-keeping lord who

ESTEEM (1)

235 Ad-dress	54	a trusted friend,/Some little token of esteem/Is needed, like a dish of cream;/And you

ESTRANGED (1)

581 ES Ld Clav	3	can/To make him feel that he is not estranged from you./{C} We will indeed. We

ESTRANGEMENT (1)

117 SP Dusty	24	next. It's the six./{Du} 'A quarrel. An estrangement. Separation of friends'./{Do}

ET (18)

46 Directeur	22	/Du Spectateur/Conservateur/Et crève d'amour./Mélange Adultère de Tout/
47 Mél Adult	3	journaliste;/C'est à grands pas et en sueur/Que vous suivrez à peine ma piste./
48 Lune Miel	4	de punaises;/La sueur aestivale, et une forte odeur de chienne./Ils restent sur le
48 Lune Miel	13	à Milan/Où se trouve la Cène, et un restaurant pas cher./Lui pense aux
48 Lune Miel	14	pas cher./Lui pense aux pourboires, et rédige son bilan./Ils auront vu la Suisse et
48 Lune Miel	15	son bilan./Ils auront vu la Suisse et traversé la France./Et Saint Apollinaire, raide

48 Lune Miel	16	vu la Suisse et traversé la France./Et Saint Apollinaire, raide et ascétique,/Vieille
48 Lune Miel	16	la France./Et Saint Apollinaire, raide et ascétique,/Vieille usine désaffectée de Dieu,
51 Restaurant	2	à faire/Que de se gratter les doigts et se pencher sur mon épaule:/'Dans mon pays il
51 Restaurant	4	pluvieux,/Du vent, du grand soleil, et de la pluie;/C'est ce qu'on appelle le jour de
51 Restaurant	8	dans la soupe)./'Les saules trempés, et des bourgeons sur les ronces —/C'est là, dans
51 Restaurant	14	/J'éprouvais un instant de puissance et de délire.'/Mais alors, vieux lubrique, à cet
51 Restaurant	26	noyé,/Oubliait les cris des mouettes et la houle de Cornouaille,/Et les profits et les
51 Restaurant	27	mouettes et la houle de Cornouaille,/Et les profits et les pertes, et la cargaison
51 Restaurant	27	la houle de Cornouaille,/Et les profits et les pertes, et la cargaison d'étain:/Un courant
51 Restaurant	27	/Et les profits et les pertes, et la cargaison d'étain:/Un courant de sous-mer
67 WL: Fire S	202	/They wash their feet in soda water/Et O ces voix d'enfants, chantant dans la
128 Cor1 March	51	will you/Give us a light?/Light/Light/*Et les soldats faisaient la haie? ILS LA*

ÉTAIN (1)

51 Restaurant	27	profits et les pertes, et la cargaison d'étain:/Un courant de sous-mer l'emporta très

ÉTAIT (3)

51 Restaurant	10	qu'on s'abrite./J'avais sept ans, elle était plus petite./Elle était toute mouillée, je lui
51 Restaurant	11	sept ans, elle était plus petite./Elle était toute mouillée, je lui ai donné des
51 Restaurant	30	vie antérieure./Figurez-vous donc, c'était un sort pénible;/Cependant, ce fut jadis un

ÉTAPES (1)

51 Restaurant	29	l'emporta très loin,/Le repassant aux étapes de sa vie antérieure./Figurez-vous donc,

ÉTÉ (1)

48 Lune Miel	2	à Terre Haute;/Mais une nuit d'été, les voici à Ravenne,/A l'aise entre deux

ETERNAL (14)

15 Prufrock	85	greatness flicker,/And I have seen the eternal Footman hold my coat, and snicker,/
33 Conv Gal	13	who am inane.'/'You, madam, are the eternal humorist,/The eternal enemy of the
33 Conv Gal	14	madam, are the eternal humorist,/The eternal enemy of the absolute,/Giving our
94 Ash-Wed 4	6	/In ignorance and in knowledge of eternal dolour/Who moved among the others as
245 MC Thomas	17	patient act. But both are fixed/In an eternal action, an eternal patience/To which all
245 MC Thomas	17	both are fixed/In an eternal action, an eternal patience/To which all must consent that
254 MC Tempt4	1	wind, Thomas, wind/The thread of eternal life and death./You hold this power,
255 MC Tempt4	24	Is it too much?/For such a vision of eternal grandeur?/{T} Others offered real goods,/
255 MC Tempt4	40	patient act. But both are fixed/In an eternal action, an eternal patience/To which all
255 MC Tempt4	40	both are fixed/In an eternal action, an eternal patience/To which all must consent that
265 MC Priest3	8	Even now, in sordid particulars/The eternal design may appear. {}/[*Enter the* FOUR
271 MC Thomas	9	accept them,/This is your share of the eternal burden,/The perpetual glory. This is one
330 FR Harry	22	unredeemable, irrevocable —/It's eternal, or gives a knowledge of eternity,/
330 FR Harry	23	knowledge of eternity,/Because it feels eternal while it lasts. That is one hell./Then the

ETERNALLY (1)

171 FQ: BurntN	4	contained in time past./If all time is eternally present/All time is unredeemable./

ETERNITY (4)

590 Time Space	8	butterfly that lives a day/Has lived eternity./The flowers I gave thee when the dew/
276 MC Chorus	13	of life, this is out of time,/An instant eternity of evil and wrong./We are soiled by a
330 FR Harry	22	/It's eternal, or gives a knowledge of eternity,/Because it feels eternal while it lasts.
485 CC Lady E	22	Something we have been/From eternity. Something ... straight from God./That

ETHER (1)

180 FQ: ECoker	123	to think about;/Or when, under ether, the mind is conscious but conscious of

ETHERISED (1)

13 Prufrock	3	out against the sky/Like a patient etherised upon a table;/Let us go, through

ETIQUETTE (2)

408 CP Reilly	30	it —/That is a matter of professional etiquette./{L} I have not noticed much
408 CP Lavinia	31	I have not noticed much professional etiquette/About your behaviour to-day./{R} A

ÊTRE (1)

548 ES Piggott	1	all, peace and quiet is our *raison d'être.*/Now I'll leave you to enjoy it. {}/[*Exit*]/{M}

EUGENIDES (1)

68 WL: Fire S	209	the brown fog of a winter noon/Mr. Eugenides, the Smyrna merchant/Unshaven,

EUMENIDES (4)

284 FR	m 10	/SERGEANT WINCHELL/THE EUMENIDES/*The scene is laid in a country*
311 FR	m 27	{}/[*The curtains part, revealing the* Eumenides *in the window embrasure.*]/{H} Why
336 FR	m 12	Not quite like, not the same ... {}/[*The* EUMENIDES *appear*]/{H} and this time/You
336 FR	3m 23	*She steps into/the place which the* EUMENIDES *had occupied.*]/{Ag} A curse

EUPHEMISM (1)

539 ES Gomez	5	of my doctors./{G} Oh yes, the usual euphemism./And yet I wonder. It *is* surprising:/

EUROPE (3)

62 WL: Burial	45	/Is known to be the wisest woman in Europe,/With a wicked pack of cards. Here,
290 FR	Amy	3	That's why she dragged him/All over Europe and half round the world/To expensive
456 CC	Eggers	37	unusual privilege/To see as much of Europe as I have,/Getting Lady Elizabeth out

EUROPEAN (1)

429 CP	Alex	19	/When these people have done with a European/He is, as a rule, no longer fit to eat./

EUROPEANS (1)

434 CP	Alex	3	/Besides, of course, those brought by Europeans,/And where the conditions are

EVACUATION (2)

174 FQ: BurntN	123	/Desiccation of the world of sense,/Evacuation of the world of fancy,/Inoperancy
335 FR	Harry	31	sun/Of the final eye, and the awful evacuation/Cleanses./I was not there, you were

EVADE (1)

156 Rock 3	74	the way to your door:/Life you may evade, but Death you shall not./You shall not

EVADED (1)

279 MC Knight4	32	us reason: you have seen how he/evaded our questions. And when he had

EVANESCENT (1)

599 On a Port	6	tranquil carved goddess of stone/But evanescent, as if one should meet/A pensive

EVASION (1)

327 FR Agatha	6	fear. To rest in our own suffering/Is evasion of suffering. We must learn to suffer

EVASIVE (1)

270 MC Chorus	7	insensitive skin of the elephant, the evasive flank of the fish./I have smelt/

EVEN (89)

40 Burb Blei	11	/Beat up the dawn from Istria/With even feet. Her shuttered barge/Burned on the
53 Whispers	29	/As Grishkin in a drawing-room./And even the Abstract Entities/Circumambulate her
72 WL: Thund	341	stand nor lie nor sit/There is not even silence in the mountains/But dry sterile
72 WL: Thund	343	thunder without rain/There is not even solitude in the mountains/But red sullen
98 Ash-Wed 6	29	and not to care/Teach us to sit still/Even among these rocks,/Our peace in His will
99 Ash-Wed 6	31	rocks,/Our peace in His will/And even among these rocks/Sister, mother/And
152 Rock 2	41	not lived in praise of GOD./Even the anchorite who meditates alone,/For
152 Rock 2	49	settled nowhere./Nor does the family even move about together,/But every son would
159 Rock 6	11	still be?/Do you need to be told that even such modest attainments/As you can boast
161 Rock 7	42	the Church is no longer regarded, not even opposed, and men have forgotten/All gods
176 FQ: BurntN	173	being./Sudden in a shaft of sunlight/Even while the dust moves/There rises the
186 FQ: DrySal	89	ceases to be a mere sequence —/Or even development: the latter a partial fallacy/
186 FQ: DrySal	94	fulfilment, security or affection,/Or even a very good dinner, but the sudden
211 Old Gumbie	36	and a good deed to do —/And she's even created a Beetles' Tattoo./So for Old
588 Fable	35	capons, boars, they were to eat,/He even soakt the uncomplaining porter/But red sullen
602 Humoresque	24	— Where would he belong?/But, even at that, what mask *bizarre!*/Spleen/Sunday:
244 MC Chorus	30	our Archbishop still our Archbishop even in France. Thomas Archbishop, set the
249 MC Tempt2	7	cause,/Dispensing justice make all even,/Is thrive on earth, and perhaps in heaven./
261 MC Thomas	31	desires anything for himself, not even the glory of being a/martyr. So thus as on
265 MC Priest3	7	/That is always now, and here. Even now, in sordid particulars/The eternal
273 MC Thomas	22	endure./The Church shall be open, even to our enemies. Open the door!/{3P} My
277 MC Knight3	20	the rest of our lives abroad. And even when reasonable/people come to see that
278 MC Knight2	36	murderer. And at a later time still, even such temperate/measures as these would
279 MC Knight4	30	upon a death by martyrdom. Even/at the last, he could have given us reason:
281 MC Chorus	10	Thy light, and Thy glory is declared even in that which denies Thee; the darkness
281 MC Chorus	14	in thought and in word and in deed./Even with the hand to the broom, the back bent
281 MC Chorus	16	under fear, the head bent under grief,/Even in us the voices of seasons, the snuffle of
286 FR Charles	4	/A man can be very cosy at his club/Even in an English winter./{G} Well, as for me,/
286 FR Violet	14	never go south, no, definitely never,/Even could I do it as well as Amy:/England's
289 FR Ivy	26	in the middle of a storm,/And never even to recover the body./{C} 'Well-known
297 FR Gerald	19	somebody wants to get rid of./{G} Even so, we don't want Downing to know/Any
297 FR Gerald	21	more than he knows already./And even if he knew, it's very much better/That he
300 FRDowning	18	baths and gymnasiums/There's not even a place where a man can go/For a quiet
304 FR Mary	19	gone, if I'd had the moral courage,/Even against a will like hers. I know very well/
304 FR Mary	26	for her and Harry./Even when he married, she still held on to me/
304 FR Mary	28	bear to let any project go;/And even when *she* died: I believed that Cousin Amy
305 FR Harry	27	same hangings ... the same pictures ... even the table,/The chairs, the sofa ... all in the
306 FR Mary	34	it all seemed to be imposed upon us;/Even the nice things were laid out ready,/And
309 FR Mary	20	which I did not know I knew./Even if, as you say, Wishwood is a cheat,/Your
314 FR Warburt	34	/In forty years./{W} Indeed, yes./Even in a country practice. My first patient,
326 FR Harry	24	that in a way, so long as I could think/Even of my own life as an isolated ruin,/A
334 FR Harry	31	my decision. Now I see/I might even become fonder of my mother —/More
340 FR Amy	27	to the purposes of Wishwood;/I even asked you back, for visits, after he was

342 FR	Mary	25	must be done, what can be done,/Even here, but elsewhere, everywhere, he is in
348 FR	Chorus	28	do not know what we are doing;/And even, when you think of it,/We do not know
361 CP	Reilly	2	have to marry her —/You might even imagine that you wanted to marry her./{E}
371 CP	Peter	18	that/I shan't know the truth about even the memory./Did we really share these
372 CP	Alex	12	something out of nothing!/Never, even when travelling in Albania,/Have I made
380 CP	Celia	3	I've done to myself./I am not sure even that you seem real enough/To humiliate
383 CP	Celia	22	{}/[*They drink*]/{C} It may be that even Julia is a guardian./Perhaps she is *my*
397 CP	Lavinia	24	capacity./{L} One can be practical, even in hell:/And you know I am much more
407 CP	Lavinia	35	nothing about it./{L} Really, Edward! Even if I'd been blind/There were plenty of
408 CP	Lavinia	2	it's true! I was completely prostrated;/Even if I have made a partial recovery./{R}
412 CP	Celia	32	Shuttlethwaite./{C} That makes it even more perplexing. However,/I don't want to
414 CP	Celia	10	the ending of one relationship,/Not even simply finding that it never existed —/But
416 CP	Celia	19	us. If I could feel/As I did then, even now it would seem right./And then I found
416 CP	Celia	36	own way out of the forest./{C} But even if I find my way out of the forest/I shall be
421 CP	Julia	24	will be afraid of nothing; she will not even know/That there is anything there to be
423 CP	Alex	3	/You know, I have connections — even in California. {}/CURTAIN/Act Three/
428 CP	Alex	34	sure that there *is* any solution./But even this does not bring us to the heart of the
429 CP	Alex	6	the Christians./They have even been persuading some of the converts —/
429 CP	Julia	15	can't dine out on eating Christians —/Even among pagans!/{A} Not on the *whole*
456 CC	Colby	39	her difficulties./{C} Perhaps she won't even arrive by this plane./{E} Oh, that could
457 CC	Eggers	1	gets lost,/Or loses her ticket, or even her passport./But let's not be crossing any
466 CC	Claude	30	the terms life imposes upon you/Even to the point of accepting ... make-believe?/
466 CC	Colby	39	late. And you spoke of atonement./Even your failure to understand him,/Of which
473 CC	Lucasta	11	I've no garden./I hardly feel that I'm even a person:/Nothing but a bit of living
478 CC	Lucasta	5	have to accept me/As your sister! Even if I am a guttersnipe .../{C} You mustn't
481 CC	Lucasta	36	Lucasta?/{L} I'm so hungry, I could even eat a herbal salad./{LE} That's right. Just
483 CC	Lady E	25	Colby./Photographic portraits — even in silver frames —/Are much too intimate
490 CC	Claude	11	of an agony/To you, than it can be even to ... us./{C} I only wish it was more acute
490 CC	Colby	22	filled. Never./I like you both, I could even come to love you —/But as friends ... older
515 CC	Guzzard	24	also my previous sacrifice./This is even greater than the sacrifice I made/When I
527 ES	Monica	25	he's been at home in the evening,/Even when he's reading, or busy with his papers
529 ES	Monica	2	/You can come down at weekends, even when the House is sitting./And you can
540 ES	Gomez	1	sense/We're both of us failures. But even so,/I'd rather be my kind of failure than
541 ES	Gomez	8	a few friends, in confidence./It might even reach the ears of some of your
545 ES	Monica	12	does seem quiet here and restful./Even the matron, though she looks rather
548 ES	Carghil	31	after all these years;/And you don't even recognise me! I'd know you anywhere./But
551 ES	Carghil	2	/A single one of her admirers. Why, even a faithless lover/Is still, in her memory, a
558 ES	Michael	26	overworked, when I'd nothing to do./Even the office boys began to sneer at me./I
561 ES	Ld Clav	3	how gladly would I help you!/Even though it carried you away from me
570 ES	Ld Clav	29	standing/In his adopted country. He even has sons/Following in their father's
571 ES	Ld Clav	20	respect love always when we meet it;/Even when it's vain and selfish, we must not
578 ES	Michael	29	How I laughed!/You never seemed even to want a flirtation,/And my friends used
580 ES	Gomez	4	/But it takes some days, you know, even by air mail./{M} Take the card, Charles. If
582 ES	Ld Clav	1	/{LC} And Michael —/I love him, even for rejecting me,/For the *me* he rejected, I
582 ES	Charles	36	together, in some mysterious fashion,/Even with Michael, and despite those people,/
583 ES	Monica	25	and vicissitude cannot appal me,/Not even death can dismay or amaze me/Fixed in

EVENING (71)

13 Prufrock		2	/Let us go then, you and I,/When the evening is spread out against the sky/Like a
13 Prufrock		17	its tongue into the corners of the evening,/Lingered upon the pools that stand in
15 Prufrock		75	of silent seas./And the afternoon, the evening, sleeps so peacefully!/Smoothed by long
21 Portrait		115	/Afternoon grey and smoky, evening yellow and rose;/Should die and leave
22 Preludes		1	right to smile?/Preludes/The winter evening settles down/With smell of steaks in
23 Preludes		44	square fingers stuffing pipes,/And evening newspapers, and eyes/Assured of
28 Boston ET		t	the level of the roofs./The Boston Evening Transcript/The readers of the *Boston*
28 Boston ET		1	Transcript/The readers of the *Boston Evening Transcript*/Sway in the wind like a field
28 Boston ET		3	wind like a field of ripe corn./When evening quickens faintly in the street,/Wakening
28 Boston ET		5	/And to others bringing the *Boston Evening Transcript*,/I mount the steps and ring
28 Boston ET		9	'Cousin Harriet, here is the *Boston Evening Transcript*.'/Aunt Helen/Miss Helen
37 Gerontion		14	the kitchen, makes tea,/Sneezes at evening, poking the peevish gutter./I an old
61 WL: Burial		29	behind you/Or your shadow at evening rising to meet you;/I will show you fear
67 WL: Fire S		190	fishing in the dull canal/On a winter evening round behind the gashouse/Musing
68 WL: Fire S		220	can see/At the violet hour, the evening hour that strives/Homeward, and
103 Journ Magi		30	so we continued/And arrived at evening, not a moment too soon/Finding the
123 SA Kl & Kr		23	/{Kl&Kr} *And the morning/And the evening/And noontide/And night/Morning/*
123 SA Kl & Kr		27	*/And noontide/And night/Morning/Evening/Noontime/Night/*{Do} That's not life,

166 Rock 10	21	that slants upon our western doors at evening,/The twilight over stagnant pools at
182 FQ: ECoker	199	be deciphered./There is a time for the evening under starlight,/A time for the evening
182 FQ: ECoker	200	under starlight,/A time for the evening under lamplight/(The evening with the
182 FQ: ECoker	201	for the evening under lamplight/(The evening with the photograph album)./Love is
184 FQ: DrySal	14	grapes on the autumn table,/And the evening circle in the winter gaslight./The river is
599 On a Port	4	up and down the street,/She stands at evening in the room alone./Not like a tranquil
603 Spleen	7	/By this unwarranted digression./Evening, lights, and tea!/Children and cats in
246 MC Templt1	31	/Your Lordship won't forget that evening on the river/When the King, and you
287 FR Amy	39	hoped to arrive in the course of the evening./{V} Harry was always the most likely
298 FR Charles	24	*and enter* DOWNING]/{C} Good evening, Downing./It's good to see you again,
299 FRDowning	24	/Down in the morning, and up in the evening,/And *then* she used to get rather
300 FR Charles	21	him out of her sight./{C} During that evening, did you see him?/{Do} Oh yes, Sir, I'm
303 FR Mary	3	no garden-flowers to give me for this evening./{Ag} I always forget how late the
313 FR Violet	1	GERALD, CHARLES/{V} Good evening, Mary: aren't you dressed yet?/How do
313 FR Gerald	14	I was rather an authority./{G} Good evening, Mary. You've seen Harry, I see./It's
317 FR Warburt	2	I had another reason for coming this evening/Than simply in honour of your
318 FR Harry	29	talk./I don't know why, but just this evening/I feel an overwhelming need for
319 FR Warburt	39	But, Harry,/We can't sit here all the evening, you know;/You will have to have the
321 FR Winch	24	{}/[*Enter* WINCHELL]/{Wi} Good evening, my Lord. Good evening, Doctor./
321 FR Winch	24	/{Wi} Good evening, my Lord. Good evening, Doctor./Many happy ... Oh, I'm sorry,
322 FR Warburt	1	/His Lordship isn't very well this evening./{Wi} I understand, Sir./It'd be the same
322 FR Winch	18	There's been shock enough for one evening, my Lord:/That's what I've come about.
327 FR Ivy	24	... {}/[*Enter* IVY]/{I} Where is there an evening paper?/{G} Why, what's the matter./{I}
327 FR Ivy	26	/{I} Somebody, look for Arthur in the evening paper./That was Arthur, ringing up
327 FR Violet	35	/{V} What's the use of asking for an evening paper?/You know as well as I do, at this
341 FR Agatha	3	not./I thought that I had, until this evening./But at least I wanted to. Now I must
343 FR Mary	11	You remember what I said to you this evening?/I knew that I was right: you made me
353 CP	2m 1	*the Chamberlaynes' London flat. Early evening.*/EDWARD CHAMBERLAYNE,
358 CP Julia	18	/Edward, it's been a delightful evening:/The potato crisps were really excellent.
359 CP Edward	13	water./{E} I want to apologise for this evening./The fact is, I tried to put off this party:
366 CP Peter	35	{E} And what's your trouble?/{P} This evening I felt I could bear it no longer./That
368 CP Alex	4	Edward may be all alone this evening,/And I know that he hates to spend an
368 CP Alex	5	And I know that he hates to spend an evening alone,/So you're going to come out and
368 CP Edward	8	/But I rather *want* to be alone, this evening./{A} But you've got to have some
380 CP Edward	14	/{E} Peter Quilpe, who was here this evening. *He* was in a dream/And now he is
380 CP Edward	21	*He* thought so./He came back this evening to talk to me about it./{C} But this is
384 CP Edward	1	/answer the doorbell./{E} Oh ... good evening. {}/[*Enter the* UNIDENTIFIED
384 CP Reilly	2	GUEST]/{UG} Good evening, Mr. Chamberlayne./{E} Well. May I
391 CP Julia	13	me./I'm not coming back again *this* evening./{L} Stop! I want you to explain the
392 CP Edward	17	/{E} Just those who were here this evening .../{L} That's odd./{E} ... and one other.
396 CP Edward	1	/Well, it's a better way of passing the evening/Than listening to the gramophone./{L}
417 CP Reilly	33	morning that separates/And with the evening that brings together/For casual talk
422 CP Reilly	10	choice?/{R} She will be fetched this evening. {}/[NURSE-SECRETARY *enters with*
430 CP Peter	13	I'm driving down to the country this evening,/So I knew you wouldn't mind my
456 CC Eggers	33	City/And back to Joshua Park in the evening,/And once a year our holiday at
465 CC Claude	28	you are alone at your piano, in the evening,/I believe you will go through the
481 CC Lady E	14	LADY ELIZABETH]/{LE} Oh, good evening,/Good evening, Mr. Kaghan. Good
481 CC Lady E	15	/{LE} Oh, good evening./Good evening, Mr. Kaghan. Good evening, Lucasta./
481 CC Lady E	15	/Good evening, Mr. Kaghan. Good evening, Lucasta./Have you just arrived, or are
496 CC Eggers	26	my news/When I came home in the evening. And the late editions/Of the papers
527 ES Monica	24	/And when he's been at home in the evening,/Even when he's reading, or busy with
532 ES Ld Clav	31	*shows in* GOMEZ]/{LC} Good evening, Mr. ... Gomez. You're a friend of Mr.
547 ES Piggott	24	people among us/We dance in the evening. At the moment there's no dancing,/

EVENING'S (1)

327 FR Violet	37	London/Nobody's likely to have this evening's paper./{C} Stop, I think I bought a

EVENINGS (3)

14 Prufrock	50	known them all —/Have known the evenings, mornings, afternoons,/I have
163 Rock 8	32	than the tales/Of old men on winter evenings./Only the faith could have done what
547 ES Piggott	11	a television set./It's popular in the evenings. But not *too* crowded. {}/[*Exit*]/{LC}

EVENT (10)

70 WL: Fire S	297	my heart/Under my feet. After the event/He wept. He promised "a new start."/I
111 Xmas Trees	11	spirit of wonder/At the Feast as an event not accepted as a pretext;/So that the
188 FQ: DrySal	168	judgement of the sea,/Or whatever event, this is your real destination.'/So Krishna,
245 MC Priest2	26	we had been sooner prepared for the event./But your Lordship knows that seven
246 MC Thomas	23	consummation./All things prepare the event. Watch. {}/[*Enter* FIRST TEMPTER]/

295 FR	Harry	20	it./First of all, you isolate the single event/As something so dreadful that it couldn't
326 FR	Harry	15	/Or engaged in predicting the minor event,/Engaged in foreseeing the minor disaster?
333 FR	Agatha	2	would not have been born in that event: I stopped him./I can take no credit for a
478 CC	Lucasta	4	another Lady Elizabeth./But in that event, Colby, you'll have to accept me/As your
503 CC	Lucasta	32	sister —/Or so I hope. Yes, in any event,/Good-bye, Colby. {}/[*Exit* LUCASTA]/

EVENTS (6)

19 Portrait		38	the monuments,/Discuss the late events,/Correct our watches by the public
279 MC	Knight4	17	this way. But/consider the course of events. I am obliged, very briefly, to go over/the
293 FR	Harry	27	hope to make you understand/Is only events: not what has happened./And people to
293 FR	Harry	29	understand the unimportance of events./{G} Well, you can't say that nothing has
293 FR	Harry	38	most a continual impact/Of external events. You have gone through life in sleep,/
361 CP	Reilly	31	of the bottle./It is to start a train of events/Beyond your control. So let me continue.

EVENTUAL (1)

448 CC	Eggers	19	/You told me that was your eventual intention./{SC} When — or indeed

EVENTUALLY (2)

429 CP	Alex	26	many international complications./Eventually, there may be an official publication.
434 CP	Alex	14	would not leave the dying natives./Eventually, two of them escaped:/One died in

EVER (79)

65 WL:	Chess	134	we do tomorrow?/'What shall we ever do?'/'The hot water at ten./And if it rains,
139 Virginia		10	decay. Living, living,/Never moving. Ever moving/Iron thoughts came with me/And
160 Rock 7		11	of Good and Evil./But their light was ever surrounded and shot with darkness/As the
161 Rock 7		23	always before, selfish and purblind as ever before,/Yet always struggling, always
166 Rock 10		7	the World?/The great snake lies ever half awake, at the bottom of the pit of the
184 FQ:	DrySal	7	forgotten/By the dwellers in cities — ever, however, implacable,/Keeping his seasons
210 Old Gumbie		19	/As she finds that the mice will not ever keep quiet,/She is sure it is due to irregular
212 Growltiger		2	/In fact he was the roughest cat that ever roamed at large./From Gravesend up to
224 Mr Mistoff		20	all say: OH!/Well I never!/Was there ever/A Cat so clever/As Magical Mr.
225 Mr Mistoff		39	all say: OH!/Well I never!/Was there ever/A Cat so clever/As Magical Mr.
225 Mr Mistoff		58	all said: OH!/Well I never!/Did you ever/Know a Cat so clever/As Magical Mr.
590 Time Space		5	is than we./So why, Love, should we ever pray/To live a century?/The butterfly that
595 Grad 14		4	a funeral bell/And one that we are ever loth to say./But 'tis a call we cannot
604 Ode		5	and fears./And we turn as thy sons ever turn, in the strength/Of the hopes that thy
262 MC	Thomas	1	/dear children, I do not think I shall ever preach to you again; and because/it is
275 MC	Thomas	20	Almighty God, to the Blessed Mary ever Virgin, to the blessed John the Baptist, the
275 MC	Chorus	25	them they bleed./How how can I ever return, to the soft quiet seasons?/Night stay
286 FR	Charles	1	Living with horses and dogs and guns/Ever to want to leave England in the winter./
289 FR	Amy	35	not./I am very glad that none of you ever met her./It will make the situation very
292 FR	Gerald	28	find you know the country as well as ever./There wasn't an inch of it you didn't
293 FR	Harry	28	/And people to whom nothing has ever happened/Cannot understand the
295 FR	Harry	28	/And also waking. She is nearer than ever./The contamination has reached the
295 FR	Harry	30	are always near. Here, nearer than ever./They are very close here. I had not
299 FR	Charles	15	she had the courage./{C} Did you ever talk of suicide?/{Do} Oh yes, she did, every
304 FR	Mary	31	awful? I know that it does./Did you ever meet her? What was she like?/{Ag} I am the
304 FR	Agatha	32	she like?/{Ag} I am the only one who ever met her,/The only one Harry asked to his
306 FR	Harry	23	with no escape. Tell me,/Were you ever happy here, as a child at Wishwood?/{M}
311 FR	Harry	7	know it, I know it!/More potent than ever before, a vapour dissolving/All other
315 FR	Warburt	17	I get an invitation to dinner/That I ever see your mother./{V} Yes, look at your
320 FR	Warburt	7	mind,/Although she seems as vital as ever —/It is only the force of her personality,/
324 FR	Harry	18	/To him or to anyone else. If he was ever really conscious,/I should be glad for him
324 FR	Amy	27	am coming to think/How little I have ever known./But I think your remarks are much
337 FR	Harry	18	but ... You must go./{H} Shall we ever meet again?/{Ag} Shall we ever meet again?
337 FR	Agatha	19	we ever meet again?/{Ag} Shall we ever meet again?/And who will meet again?
340 FR	Agatha	6	What did I take? nothing that you ever had./What did I get? thirty years of
341 FR:	Agatha	25	what neither can have?/If neither has ever had a husband or a son/We have no
355 CP	Julia	1	sense of hearing —/The only man I ever met who could hear the cry of bats./{P}
356 CP	Julia	25	try.' And this is the first time/I've ever seen you without Lavinia/Except for the
364 CP	Reilly	13	from the mind/The illusion of having ever been in the light./The fact that you can't
369 CP	Peter	4	/She was different from any girl I'd ever known/And not easy to talk to, on that
369 CP	Edward	40	together./{E} And after that/Did she ever introduce you to her family/Or to any of
379 CP	Edward	20	have arisen./What future had you ever thought there could be?/{C} What had I
380 CP	Edward	34	love with Lavinia./I don't think I was ever really in love with her./If I have ever been
380 CP	Edward	35	ever really in love with her./If I have ever been in love — and I think that I have —/I
396 CP	Lavinia	30	/At some time or other, before you ever knew me:/Perhaps only when you were a
397 CP	Edward	13	with it/Day by day, hour by hour, for ever and ever./{L} I think you're on the edge of
397 CP	Edward	13	by day, hour by hour, for ever and ever./{L} I think you're on the edge of a nervous

402 CP	Edward	33	do with you./{E} I doubt if you have ever had a case like mine:/I have ceased to
408 CP	Edward	23	ludicrous:/This is the best joke that ever happened./{L} I never knew you had such a
410 CP	Reilly	1	You had come to see that no one had ever loved you./Then you began to fear that no
415 CP	Celia	21	in sin./Oh, I don't mean that it was ever mentioned!/But anything wrong, from our
416 CP	Celia	1	It's not the feeling of anything I've ever *done*,/Which I might get away from, or of
423 CP	Julia	1	the words are valid./{J} Shall we ever speak them?/{A} Others, perhaps, will
452 CC	Lucasta	17	on filing those papers/Which no one ever wanted — at least, not till yesterday./Then,
453 CC	Kaghan	24	telling anybody about you:/Nobody'd ever believe in your existence/Until they met
462 CC	Colby	10	believe that Lady Elizabeth/Can ever accept me as if I was her son?/{SC} As if
465 CC	Claude	24	when he made it./But nothing *I* made ever gave me that contentment —/That state of
469 CC	Lucasta	21	somebody invites me,/And no one has ever asked me to a concert./I've been to the
469 CC	Lucasta	28	And can you realise/That nobody has ever played to me before?/{C} And this is the
474 CC	Lucasta	39	with a world/More real than any I've ever lived in./And I'd like to understand *you.*/
475 CC	Colby	3	I want to understand *you.*/Does one ever come to understand anyone?/{L} I think
475 CC	Lucasta	29	to be accepted!/No one has ever 'just accepted' me before./Of course the
476 CC	Lucasta	34	I never could see/How Claude had ever liked her. Oh, that childhood —/Always
477 CC	Colby	15	But I can't, just yet./Oh, why did I ever come into this house!/Lucasta .../{L} I can
478 CC	Lucasta	18	/Nothing at all. It's far worse than ever./Just when you think you're on the point of
480 CC	Kaghan	4	the most exciting speculation/I've ever thought of investing in./Colby's more
480 CC	Colby	16	you're a gambler. I don't believe you ever gamble/On anything that isn't a certainty./
482 CC	Lady E	15	— you're not the sort of person/They ever meet in their kind of society./So naturally,
491 CC	Colby	40	/{C} I don't feel, tonight, that I ever want to marry./You may be right. I can't
502 CC	Lucasta	13	it was./You're much too ... detached, ever to be shocked/In the way I thought you
533 ES	Ld Clav	10	/{LC} Have you lived out there ever since ... you left England?/{G} Ever since I
533 ES	Gomez	11	ever since ... you left England?/{G} Ever since I finished my sentence./{LC} What
536 ES	Gomez	38	I don't suppose their husbands/Were ever told the story. *They* wouldn't want to see
539 ES	Gomez	37	man/In San Marco than I should ever have been in England./{LC} So, as you
557 ES	Michael	27	name:/The only good the name has ever done me./{LC} On the strength of your
562 ES	Carghil	30	a good deal/Since I knew him ever so many years ago,/Yet you're the image of
567 ES	Monica	16	*I'm* engaged. I'm engaged to you for ever./{C} There's another shopping expedition
568 ES	Charles	16	Monica,/But there's nothing I would ever wish to conceal from you./{LC} If there's
580 ES	Monica	6	If I write to you, Michael,/Will you ever answer?/{Mi} Oh of course, Monica./You

EVERY (67)

21 Portrait	109	tea to friends.'/And I must borrow every changing shape/To find expression ...
24 Rhapsody	8	relations,/Its divisions and precisions./Every street lamp that I pass/Beats like a
49 Hippopot	19	inflexions hoarse and odd,/But every week we hear rejoice/The Church, at
105 Song Sime	26	/They shall praise Thee and suffer in every generation/With glory and derision,/Light
111 Xmas Trees	32	the occasion/When fear came upon every soul:/Because the beginning shall remind
149 Rock 1	93	/*A Church for all*/*And a job for each*/*Every man to his work.*/Now a group of
152 Rock 2	27	and always being restored./For every ill deed in the past we suffer the
152 Rock 2	29	/For pride, for lechery, treachery, for every act of sin./And of all that was done that
153 Rock 2	50	family even move about together,/But every son would have his motor cycle,/And
158 Rock 5	8	and distracted for silence: seeking every one after his own elevation, and dodging
179 FQ: ECoker	86	and falsifies,/For the pattern is new in every moment/And every moment is a new and
179 FQ: ECoker	87	pattern is new in every moment/And every moment is a new and shocking/Valuation
180 FQ: ECoker	121	fades into silence/And you see behind every face the mental emptiness deepen/Leaving
182 FQ: ECoker	176	—/Trying to learn to use words, and every attempt/Is a wholly new start, and a
182 FQ: ECoker	196	and after,/But a lifetime burning in every moment/And not the lifetime of one man
188 FQ: DrySal	161	one action/(And the time of death is every moment)/Which shall fructify in the lives
189 FQ: DrySal	176	with fish, and/Those concerned with every lawful traffic/And those who conduct
197 FQ: Little	218	/The end is where we start from. And every phrase/And sentence that is right (where
197 FQ: Little	219	/And sentence that is right (where every word is at home,/Taking its place to
197 FQ: Little	226	complete consort dancing together)/Every phrase and every sentence is an end and a
197 FQ: Little	226	dancing together)/Every phrase and every sentence is an end and a beginning,/Every
197 FQ: Little	227	sentence is an end and a beginning,/Every poem an epitaph. And any action/Is a
203 Indians	12	A man's destination is not his destiny/Every country is home to one man/And exile to
214 RTTugger	14	out;/He's always on the wrong side of every door,/And as soon as he's at home, then
223 Pekes Pols	35	cousins are snappers and biters,/And every dog-jack of them notable fighters;/And so
223 Pekes Pols	59	and he gave a great leap —/And they every last one of them scattered like sheep./*And*
226 Macavity	6	no one like Macavity,/He's broken every human law, he breaks the law of gravity./
228 Gus	21	the Fell./'I have played', so he says, 'every possible part,/And I used to know seventy
231 Bust Jones	34	bounder,/And he's putting on weight every day;/But he's so well preserved because
233 Skimble	37	a speck of dust on the floor./There is every sort of light — you can make it dark or
233 Skimble	52	night he is always fresh and bright;/Every now and then he has a cup of tea/With
588 Fable	46	the account: They made a raid/On every bird and beast in Æsop's fable/To fill out

588 Fable	61	goose./The Abbot with proposing every toast/Had drank more than he ought t'
589 Fable	81	swiftly up the chimney./Naturally every one searcht everywhere,/But not a shred
595 Grad 14	2	no more delay;/Thus is the end of every tale: 'Farewell',/A word that echoes like a
259 MC Thomas	1	from remotest cause./But for every evil, every sacrilege,/Crime, wrong,
259 MC Thomas	1	remotest cause./But for every evil, every sacrilege,/Crime, wrong, oppression and
265 MC Priest3	4	we know that we hope for or fear for?/Every day is the day we should fear from or
268 MC Knight3	10	the chains of anathema./{K3} Using every means in your power to evince/The King's
268 MC Knight3	11	to evince/The King's faithful servants, every one who transacts/His business in his
273 MC Thomas	34	or bad./You defer to the fact. For every life and every act/Consequence of good
273 MC Thomas	34	defer to the fact. For every life and every act/Consequence of good and evil can be
276 MC Chorus	9	acts marked a limit to our suffering./Every horror had its definition,/Every sorrow
276 MC Chorus	10	/Every horror had its definition,/Every sorrow had a kind of end:/In life there is
279 MC Knight4	28	would be killed in England. He used every means of provocation;/from his conduct,
299 FRDowning	16	talk of suicide?/{Do} Oh yes, she did, every now and again./But in my opinion, it is
307 FR Harry	31	know:/The sudden extinction of every alternative,/The unexpected crash of the
310 FR Harry	37	singing; when I had felt sure/That every corridor only led to another,/Or to a
328 FR Gerald	2	/{G} Well, I said that Arthur was every bit as likely/To have an accident as John.
346 FR Charles	4	in the Burlington Arcade./What if every moment were like that, if one were awake?
346 FR Agatha	35	you mustn't worry about that./He is every bit as sane as you or I,/He sees the world
369 CP Edward	9	be a double boiler:/Isn't there one in every kitchen?/{A} I can't find it./There goes
382 CP Celia	10	and I thought that I knew/And loved every contour; and as I looked/It withered, as if
385 CP Reilly	5	We must also remember/That at every meeting we are meeting a stranger./{E} So
440 CP Edward	7	Henry has been saying,/I think, that every moment is a fresh beginning;/And Julia,
496 CC Eggers	31	really, now, I'm quite lost in London./Every time I come, I notice the traffic/Has got
501 CC Eggers	28	take the occasion/To wish Miss Angel every happiness./And I'm sure she will be
518 CC Eggers	6	vocation./We worked together every day, you know,/For quite a little time,
525 ES Charles	18	your father's retired/He's at home every day. And you're leaving London./And
528 ES Monica	27	Court./But Selby wants him to have every encouragement —/If he's hopeful, he's
529 ES Ld Clav	30	nothingness. Just remember:/Every day, year after year, over my breakfast,/I
531 ES Monica	5	in a blaze of glory —/You've read every word about you in the papers./{C} And
531 ES Charles	19	paragraph./{C} That's the reward/Of every public man./{LC} Say rather, the exequies/
547 ES Monica	16	the concoction/Which she decants for every newcomer./Perhaps after what she
553 ES Carghil	19	know what I do?/I read your letters every night./{LC} My letters!/{MC} Have you
557 ES Ld Clav	10	years. And deadly dull it was./{LC} Every job is dull, nine-tenths of the time .../{Mi}
565 ES Monica	2	rest and have absolute quiet/Before every meal./{LC} But Michael and I/Must

EVERYBODY (14)

21 Portrait	102	gutters; we are really in the dark./'For everybody said so, all our friends,/They all were
289 FR Agatha	1	comes — and it does not come for everybody —/The hidden is revealed, and the
292 FR Amy	20	sure you must be tired./You will find everybody here, and everything the same./Mr.
338 FR Harry	4	do,/And that it is the best thing for everybody./But at present, I cannot explain it to
388 CP Peter	6	to know,/Because, you see, he knows everybody, everywhere./So what I've really
396 CP Edward	14	thought you were in love with me./{E} Everybody told me that I was;/And they told
414 CP Celia	12	revelation about my relationship/With *everybody*. Do you know —/It no longer seems
425 CP Lavinia	33	likes to be seen at a party/Where everybody else is, to show they've been invited./
430 CP Peter	3	Why, it's Peter!/{L} Peter!/{P} Hullo, everybody!/{L} When did you arrive?/{P} I flew
430 CP Peter	25	Alex? I always said/That Alex knew everybody. But I didn't know/That he knew any
457 CC Colby	6	more, she has a good heart./{C} Everybody seems to be kind-hearted./But
536 ES Gomez	26	been alone./{G} Oh, loneliness —/Everybody knows what that's like./Your
549 ES Carghil	1	portrait in the papers/So often. And everybody knows *you*. But still,/I wish you
555 ES Piggott	2	*Not Too Late For You To Love Me*,/Everybody was singing it once. A charming

EVERYBODY'LL (1)

589 Fable	72	drop in at awkward moments,/As everybody'll know who reads this romance./The

EVERYDAY (4)

209 NamingCats	8	or Bill Bailey —/All of them sensible everyday names./There are fancier names if you
209 NamingCats	12	Demeter —/But all of them sensible everyday names./But I tell you, a cat needs a
406 CP Reilly	15	imagine that they need a respite/From everyday life. They return refreshed;/And if they
419 CP Celia	17	they returned .../Well ... I mean ... to everyday life./{R} True. But the friends you

EVERYONE (22)

136 5FingerEx4	2	delightful to meet Mr. Hodgson!/(Everyone wants to know *him*)/With his musical
136 5FingerEx4	14	delightful to meet Mr. Hodgson!/(Everyone wants to know *him*)./He has 999
136 5FingerEx4	19	delightful to meet Mr. Hodgson!/(Everyone wants to know *him*)./*Lines for*
222 Pekes Pols	1	/The Pekes and the Pollicles, everyone knows,/Are proud and implacable
236 Cat Morgan	11	coat, and I keep meself smart;/And everyone says, and I guess that's enough;/'You
325 FR Violet	37	back/And so near the street, and everyone staring;/And the pace he went at was
353 CP Celia	22	of hearing *you* tell it./I don't believe everyone here knows it. {}/[*To the*

366 CP	Peter	38	it was really a very nice party/For everyone but me. And that wasn't your fault./I
374 CP	Edward	18	/I suppose it was pretty obvious to everyone./{C} It was obvious that the aunt was
389 CP	Lavinia	14	why don't you go to California?/Everyone says it's a wonderful climate:/The
392 CP	Edward	14	after I had left./{E} I telephoned to everyone I knew was coming/But I couldn't get
392 CP	Edward	15	I knew was coming/But I couldn't get everyone. And so a few came./{L} Who came?/
425 CP	Lavinia	14	of one./{L} That's never satisfactory./Everyone who's asked to either party/Suspects
425 CP	Lavinia	32	whatever you can do about it:/And everyone likes to be seen at a party/Where
431 CP	Peter	8	Szogody —/He's my boss. I thought everyone knew *his* name./{J} Is he your
439 CP	Julia	10	think it is time that *I* said something:/Everyone makes a choice, of one kind or
457 CC	Colby	9	always contrive to think the best of everyone./{E} You'll come to find that I'm right,
461 CC	Claude	27	/I shall begin to call you Colby with everyone./{C} I'm sure that will make it easier
537 ES	Gomez	25	was flattered, and that I admired you./Everyone expected that I should get a First./I
563 ES	Carghil	28	name./There was a time, once, when everyone in London/Knew the name of Maisie
573 ES	Ld Clav	7	one believes in/Than the crime that everyone can appreciate./For the crime is in
574 ES	Michael	37	reports. Some sort of place/Where everyone would sneer at the fellow from

EVERYONE'S (2)

414 CP	Celia	26	isn't that I *want* to be alone,/But that everyone's alone — or so it seems to me./They
512 CC	Guzzard	21	to ask them./I should like to gratify everyone's wishes./{LE} Oh, of course ... Yes,

EVERYTHING (46)

152 Rock 2		21	/And intellectual enlightenment/And everything, including capital/And several
198 FQ: Little		256	simplicity/(Costing not less than everything))/And all shall be well and/All
588 Fable		40	which they were to dine,/And watered everything except the wine./So when all
288 FR	Agatha	18	means./{Ag} I mean painful, because everything is irrevocable,/Because the past is
288 FR	Amy	29	is changed, Agatha, at Wishwood./Everything is kept as it was when he left it,/
292 FR	Amy	20	/You will find everybody here, and everything the same./Mr. Bevan — you
294 FR	Harry	39	was unkillable. It was not like that./Everything is true in a different sense./I
305 FR	Mary	32	find it./{M} Your mother insisted/On everything being kept the same as when you left
307 FR	Mary	20	/{M} But when I was a child I took everything for granted,/Including the stupidity
309 FR	Mary	22	a delusion — then it's *all* a delusion,/Everything you feel — I don't mean what you
315 FR	Harry	8	he would be. He cannot realise/That everything is irrevocable,/The past
317 FR	Harry	23	.../{H} What about my mother?/Everything has always been referred back to
326 FR	Harry	18	small things important, so that everything/May be unimportant, a slight
330 FR	Harry	3	sober, though not for very long;/And everything will go on as before. These mild
331 FR	Harry	8	back to Wishwood, as I had left it,/Everything would fall into place. But *they*
333 FR	Harry	15	me. That is the way things happen./Everything is true in a different sense,/A sense
333 FR	Harry	17	have seemed meaningless before./Everything tends towards reconciliation/As the
340 FR	Amy	14	to live upon. You knew that you took everything/Except the walls, the furniture, the
358 CP	Julia	1	me/On Friday, and talk to me about everything./{E} Everything?/{J} Oh, you know
358 CP	Edward	2	and talk to me about everything./{E} Everything?/{J} Oh, you know what I mean./
358 CP	Julia	20	excellent./Now let me see. Have I got everything?/It's such a nice party, I hate to leave
362 CP	Reilly	28	party/And are going downstairs, with everything about you/Arranged to support you
367 CP	Edward	2	/But I don't pretend I was aware of everything./{P} Oh, I'm very glad that you
369 CP	Peter	21	were a failure./{P} You speak as if everything was finished./{E} Oh no, no,
369 CP	Edward	22	was finished./{E} Oh no, no, everything is left unfinished./But you haven't
379 CP	Celia	5	if I go now,/Will you assure me that everything is right,/That you do not mean to
379 CP	Celia	8	mean to gain your freedom,/And that everything is all right between us?/That's all that
379 CP	Celia	10	Truly, Edward,/If that is right, everything else will be,/I promise you./{E} No,
388 CP	Peter	4	put me in touch with/And we settled everything this morning./Alex is a wonderful
390 CP	Julia	3	was a bit unexpected./I dropped everything to come. And how is the dear aunt?/
394 CP	Lavinia	18	have thought I was the butler./{L} Everything I tried only made matters worse,/
397 CP	Edward	29	tissue paper/And then had to unwrap everything again/To find what you wanted. And
415 CP	Celia	31	have what you call a 'kink'?/{C} But everything seemed so right, at the time!/I've
418 CP	Celia	11	to live with it. I could do without everything,/Put up with anything, if I might
420 CP	Reilly	2	I need to take with me?/{R} Nothing./Everything you need will be provided for you,/
422 CP	Julia	6	Well! and how have we got on?/{J} Everything is in order./{A} The Chamberlaynes
434 CP	Peter	40	know more than I do:/For *me*, it's everything else that's a waste./Two years! And it
446 CC	Eggers	29	/When he has a piano. You think of everything./But if I might make a suggestion:
475 CC	Colby	32	know them./{C} I'd gladly tell you everything about myself;/But you know most of
490 CC	Claude	9	instinct tell you?/{SC} Yes, tell us everything that's in your mind./I know this
499 CC	Lucasta	23	Yes, of course, Claude. You thought everything settled./That was just the trouble.
528 ES	Monica	32	about it to suggest the clinic —/Everything about it to suggest recovery./{C}
568 ES	Ld Clav	24	life,/To whom he is willing to confess everything —/And that includes, mind you, not
576 ES	Michael	10	a term in prison?/{Mi} He told me everything. It was his experience/With you, that
579 ES	Carghil	12	Señor Gomez, how you manage *everything*!/— No sooner had I put my proposal
581 ES	Ld Clav	26	And now I feel happy —/In spite of everything, in defiance of reason,/I have been

EVERYTHING'S (1)
415 CP   Celia   27   about form, myself —/But when everything's bad form, or mental kinks,/You
EVERYWHERE (7)
181 FQ: ECoker 163 That will not leave us, but prevents us everywhere./The chill ascends from feet to
589 Fable   81 chimney./Naturally every one searcht everywhere,/But not a shred of Bishop could be
342 FR   Mary   25   be done,/Even here, but elsewhere, everywhere, he is in danger./I will stay or I will
364 CP   Julia 35 Peter all over town/Looking for them everywhere I've been./Has anybody found
388 CP   Peter   6   you see, he knows everybody, everywhere./So what I've really come for is to
529 ES Monica   12 /Compassion, or ... envy?/{M} Envy is everywhere./Who is without envy? And most
559 ES Ld Clav   8   or at least correspondents/Almost everywhere. Australia — no./The men I know
EVIDENCE (5)
104 Journ Magi   37 There was a Birth, certainly,/We had evidence and no doubt. I had seen birth and
279 MC Knight4   25   mania. I have unimpeachable evidence/to the effect that before he left France
512 CC Guzzard 15 wife be satisfied,/When she has the evidence the Kaghans will supply,/To recognise
516 CC Claude   25 have convinced me/With no other evidence, that you were my son,/Because you
540 ES Gomez   33 didn't want *them*/To be called to give evidence. You just couldn't face it./Do you see
EVIDENCES (1)
235 Ad-dress   65   /A Cat's entitled to expect/These evidences of respect./And so in time you reach
EVIL (16)
148 Rock 1   64 /The perpetual struggle of Good and Evil./Forgetful, you neglect your shrines and
159 Rock 6   20 they like to be soft./She tells them of Evil and Sin, and other unpleasant facts./They
160 Rock 7   10 to light, to knowledge of Good and Evil./But their light was ever surrounded and
162 Rock 8   12 a few good men,/Many who were evil,/And most who were neither./Like all men
166 Rock 10   13 /Be not too curious of Good and Evil;/Seek not to count the future waves of
212 Growltiger   3   up to Oxford he pursued his evil aims,/Rejoicing in his title of 'The Terror of
243 MC Priest3   10 /For who knows the end of good or evil?/Until the grinders cease/And the door shall
243 MC Chorus   17   late too late, and rotten the year;/Evil the wind, and bitter the sea, and grey the
259 MC Thomas   1   from remotest cause./But for every evil, every sacrilege,/Crime, wrong, oppression
273 MC Thomas   35 every act/Consequence of good and evil can be shown./And as in time results of
273 MC Thomas   37 many deeds are blended/So good and evil in the end become confounded./It is not in
276 MC Chorus   13 is out of time,/An instant eternity of evil and wrong./We are soiled by a filth that we
296 FR   Harry 10   the sobbing in the chimney/The evil in the dark closet, which they said was not
307 FR   Mary   5   we met by moonlight/To raise the evil spirits./{H} Arthur and John./Of course we
309 FR   Harry 40 Is the cold spring/Is the spring not an evil time, that excites us with lying voices?/{M}
438 CP   Reilly 11   the Saint in the desert/With spiritual evil always at his shoulder/Suffered any less
EVINCE (1)
268 MC Knight3   10 Using every means in your power to evince/The King's faithful servants, every one
EVISCERATE (1)
193 FQ: Little   68   for the upper hand./The parched eviscerate soil/Gapes at the vanity of toil,/
EVOKE (1)
189 FQ: DrySal 191 or scry,/Observe disease in signatures, evoke/Biography from the wrinkles of the palm/
EVOLUTION (1)
186 FQ: DrySal   90 /Encouraged by superficial notions of evolution,/Which becomes, in the popular mind,
EXACT (2)
197 FQ: Little   223 old and the new,/The common word exact without vulgarity,/The formal word
514 CC Eggers   31   /You'll understand the need for exact confirmation./{MG} I understand that,
EXACTLY (13)
222 Pekes Pols   19   to meet./They did not advance, or exactly retreat,/But they glared at each other,
320 FR Warburt   35 /John's very steady — but he's not exactly brilliant;/And Arthur has always been
330 FR   Harry 18 explanation./{H} I still have to learn exactly what their meaning is./At the beginning,
370 CP   Peter 19 curry powder. {}/[*Exit*]/{P} That is exactly what I want to know./She has simply
411 CP   Lavinia 25 to build on other people's ruins./{L} Exactly. And I have a question too./Sir Henry,
413 CP   Reilly   4 begin, Miss Coplestone,/By telling me exactly what is the matter with them,/And what
431 CP   Peter 20 /Is in a very decayed condition./{P} Exactly. It is. And that's why we're interested./
484 CC Lady E   7 to know your relatives!/I understand exactly how you felt./How I disliked my
506 CC Eggers   22 may be restored to her./{E} That is exactly what we are aiming at./We have a clue
516 CC Claude   26 you described my own experience, exactly./Does that mean nothing to you, the
528 ES Monica   3 of solitude?/{M} The second reason is exactly the opposite:/It's his fear of being
556 ES Michael   19   /{Mi} Well, this isn't a holiday exactly./But this hotel was very well
556 ES Michael   24   /{Mi} Well, this isn't a holiday, exactly./Oh. I said that before, didn't I?/{M} I
EXALT (1)
250 MC Thomas   15   fatal disease,/Degrade what they exalt. Power with the King —/I *was* the King,
EXALTATION (2)
245 MC Thomas   11 /{T} Peace. And let them be, in their exaltation./They speak better than they know,
250 MC Thomas   17 his better reason./But what was once exaltation/Would now be only mean descent. {}/

EXALTED (1)
417 CP   Celia   10   like a dream/In which one is exalted by intensity of loving/In the spirit, a
EXAMINATION (2)
186 FQ: DrySal   80   /For a haul that will not bear examination./There is no end of it, the voiceless
224 Mr Mistoff   12   /And at legerdemain/He'll defy examination/And deceive you again./The
EXAMINE (1)
514 CC   Eggers   28   to what Colby said he wanted./{E} I'll examine the records myself, Sir Claude./Not
EXAMINES (1)
232 Skimble   21   less./Down the corridor he paces and examines all the faces/Of the travellers in the
EXAMINING (1)
361 CP   Edward   13   /I have often used these terms in examining witnesses,/So I don't like them. May
EXAMPLE (2)
451 CC   Eggers   8   it —/That I will say. An encouraging example/For you, Mr. Simpkins. He'll be a
533 ES   Gomez   5   Lord Claverton. I've followed your example,/And done the same, in a modest way./
EXASPERATED (2)
195 FQ: Little   146   stains./From wrong to wrong the exasperated spirit/Proceeds, unless restored by
279 MC Knight4   32   And when he had deliberately exasperated/us beyond human endurance, he
EXASPERATING (1)
567 ES   Monica   4   worried, and rather frightened./It was exasperating that they couldn't find me/When
EXCEEDINGLY (1)
428 CP   Alex   29   /The Christian natives prosper exceedingly:/And that creates friction between
EXCEL (1)
463 CC   Colby   30   cannot do,/The art that I could never excel in,/Seems the one thing worth doing, the
EXCELLENCE (1)
561 ES   Ld Clav   2   of high achievement,/Some dream of excellence, how gladly would I help you!/Even
EXCELLENT (8)
158 Rock 5   1   /O Lord, deliver me from the man of excellent intention and impure heart: for the
330 FR   Harry   11   /At the right times; and be an excellent landlord./{Ag} What is in your mind,
358 CP   Julia   19   evening:/The potato crisps were really excellent./Now let me see. Have I got
445 CC   Eggers   19   store — they have a restaurant;/An excellent lunch, and cheap, for nowadays./But
464 CC   Claude   5   or a painter/Is something more excellent to be than a potter./Most people think
508 CC Guzzard   36   An odd name./They were excellent people. Nonconformists./{E} And the
510 CC   Eggers   2   bring him up? And Lucasta?/{E} An excellent suggestion, Mr. Simpkins. {}/[*Exit*
557 ES   Michael   15   /{Mi} Several of my friends gave me excellent tips./They always came off — the tips I
EXCEPT (30)
20 Portrait   79   countenance,/I remain self-possessed/Except when a street-piano, mechanical and
20 Portrait   85   comes down; returning as before/Except for a slight sensation of being ill at ease/
161 Rock 7   43   and men have forgotten/All gods except Usury, Lust and Power./O Father we
173 FQ: BurntN   68   towards,/Neither ascent nor decline. Except for the point, the still point,/There
175 FQ: BurntN   169   movement,/Timeless, and undesiring/Except in the aspect of time/Caught in the form
588 Fable   40   were to dine,/And watered everything except the wine./So when all preparations had
247 MC Thomas   14   do not know very much of the future/Except that from generation to generation/The
253 MC Tempt4   23   end./All other ways are closed to you/Except the way already chosen./But what is
279 MC Knight4   30   step by step, there can be no inference/except that he had determined upon a death by
288 FR   Amy   30   is kept as it was when he left it,/Except the old pony, and the mongrel setter/
301 FR   Violet   12   left matters much as they were —/Except for having brought Downing into it:/Of
302 FR   m   19   /After his rest upstairs. {}/[*Exeunt, except* AGATHA]/Scene II/AGATHA/[*Enter*
315 FR   Violet   19   /{V} Yes, look at your mother!/Except that she can't get about now in winter/
318 FR   Harry   9   during which she had not seen us/Except at half-term, and seeing us then/Only
340 FR   Amy   15   You knew that you took everything/Except the walls, the furniture, the acres;/
341 FR   Amy   13   /His past life, and have nothing except to remind him/Of the years when he had
348 FR   Chorus   25   /Is a very restricted area./Except for a limited number/Of strictly practical
356 CP   Julia   26   /I've ever seen you without Lavinia/Except for the time she got locked in the
364 CP   Reilly   12   no purpose in remaining in the dark/Except long enough to clear from the mind/The
400 CP   Alex   16   any doctor/Recommended by anyone except his wife./{R} I had already impressed
403 CP   Edward   39   the world a place I cannot live in/Except on her terms. I must be alone,/But not in
410 CP   Reilly   37   bad job is all any of us make of it —/Except of course, the saints — such as those
413 CP   Celia   19   any voices, I have no delusions —/Except that the world I live in seems all a
516 CC   Claude   33   that. I put no claim upon you —/Except the claim of our likeness to each other./
519 CC Kaghan   8   we all made the same mistake —/All except Eggers .../{E} Me, Mr. Kaghan?/{K} We
525 ES   Charles   12   one *talk* on a shopping expedition —/Except to guess what you want to buy/And
534 ES   Gomez   10   gaol again?/{G} That's true enough,/Except for a false inference. I wouldn't dream/
546 ES   Piggott   14   have guests who are perfectly well —/Except when they come like you, Miss
552 ES   Carghil   24   people mention their consciences/Except to observe that their consciences were
569 ES   Ld Clav   28   no, he said, I want nothing from you/Except your friendship and your company./He's

EXCEPTION (3)

157 Rock 4		4	Nehemiah the Prophet/There was no exception to the general rule./In Shushan the
301 FR	Chorus	26	the pretension/To be the uncommon exception/To the universal bondage./We like to
405 CP	Reilly	4	/Who is ill by himself, is rather the exception./I have recently had another patient/

EXCEPTIONAL (1)

546 ES	Piggott	19	saying,/Guests in perfect health are exceptional/Though we never accept any guest

EXCEPTIONALLY (3)

331 FR	Agatha	34	have lived — or so I see him —/An exceptionally cultivated country squire,/
409 CP	Reilly	8	Indeed, I consider/That you are exceptionally well-suited to each other./Mr.
410 CP	Edward	4	Lavinia./You know, you really are exceptionally unlovable,/And I never quite

EXCESSIVE (2)

278 MC	Knight2	9	was to restore order: to curb the excessive/powers of local government, which
417 CP	Reilly	28	the common routine,/Learn to avoid excessive expectation,/Become tolerant of

EXCHANGE (1)

180 FQ: ECoker		109	Almanach de Gotha/And the Stock Exchange Gazette, the Directory of Directors,/

EXCHANGED (1)

408 CP	Reilly	37	to me./The information I have exchanged between you/Was all obtained from

EXCHEQUER (1)

44 Cook Egg		16	lie together, lapt/In a five per cent. Exchequer Bond./I shall not want Society in

EXCITE (2)

38 Gerontion		63	the profit of their chilled delirium,/Excite the membrane, when the sense has
320 FR	Warburt	22	/That nothing should disturb or excite her./{H} Well!/{W} I'm very sorry for you,

EXCITED (4)

295 FR	Harry	2	back to the cabin./Later, I became excited, I think I made enquiries;/The purser
299 FR	Downing	25	/And *then* she used to get rather excited,/And, in a way, irresponsible, Sir./If I
579 ES	Carghil	16	look very *distrait*. You ought to be excited!/{LC} Is this good-bye then, Michael?/
580 ES	Carghil	21	invited me to visit San Marco./I'm so excited! But what pleases me most/Is that I shall

EXCITEDLY (1)

172 FQ: BurntN		43	leaves were full of children,/Hidden excitedly, containing laughter./Go, go, go, said

EXCITEMENT (6)

319 FR	Harry	23	remember the silence, and the hushed excitement/And the low conversation of
320 FR	Warburt	13	feeble./With care, and avoiding all excitement/She may live several years. A sudden
370 CP	Peter	10	happiness./I had only experienced excitement, delirium,/Desire for possession. It
370 CP	Peter	24	seems preoccupied/With some secret excitement which I cannot share./{E} Do you
487 CC	Lady E	35	is your son?/{LE} Oh, I forgot/In my excitement: you arrived the very moment/When
547 ES	Piggott	37	/I won't apologise for the lack of excitement:/After all, peace and quiet is our

EXCITES (1)

309 FR	Harry	40	/Is the spring not an evil time, that excites us with lying voices?/{M} The cold spring

EXCITING (6)

111 Xmas Trees		15	/(Each one with its peculiar and exciting smell),/The expectation of the goose or
389 CP	Lavinia	4	both. To Hollywood, of course?/How exciting for you, Celia! Now you'll have a
480 CC	Kaghan	3	expression —/Lucasta's the most exciting speculation/I've ever thought of
558 ES	Michael	35	Who was at all nice to me. She wasn't exciting,/But it served to pass the time. It would
573 ES	Carghil	24	low for you, Richard!/I've some very exciting news for you!/But I suspect ... Dare I?
574 ES	Ld Clav	6	/{LC} You said you had some exciting news for us./Would you care to impart

EXCLUSIVE (1)

587 Fable		28	at home — no ghosts allowed/At this exclusive feast. From over sea/He purchased at

EXCOMMUNICATED (1)

275 MC	Knight1	3	/{K1} Absolve all those you have excommunicated./{K2} Resign the powers you

EXCOMMUNICATION (1)

249 MC	Thomas	33	the bishops/Whom I have laid under excommunication./{T2} Hungry hatred/Will not

EXCUSE (19)

124 SA	Snow	19	always get pinched in the end./{Sn} Excuse me, they don't all get pinched in the end.
246 MC	Thomas	18	and hover, circling lower,/Waiting excuse, pretence, opportunity./End will be
246 MC	Tempt1	27	that your present gravity/Will find excuse for my humble levity/Remembering all
248 MC	Tempt1	6	that your present gravity/Will find excuse for my humble levity./If you will
250 MC	Tempt3	35	plotting parasites/About the King. Excuse my bluntness:/I am a rough
326 FR	Denman	33	this family. {}/[*Enter* DENMAN]/{D} Excuse me, Miss Ivy. There's a trunk call for
342 FR	Mary	1	take him ... {}/[*Enter* MARY]/{M} Excuse me, Cousin Amy. I have just seen
346 FR	Downing	6	in *chauffeur's costume*]/{Do} Oh, excuse me, Miss, excuse me, Mr. Charles:/His
346 FR	Downing	6	*costume*]/{Do} Oh, excuse me, Miss, excuse me, Mr. Charles:/His Lordship sent me
348 FR	Warburt	5	MARY]/{M} Dr. Warburton!/{W} Excuse me. {}/[*Exeunt* MARY *and*
371 CP	Edward	22	reality ... {}/[*The telephone rings*]/{E} Excuse me a moment. {}/[*Into telephone*]/{E}
426 CP	Edward	22	And I'm really thankful/To have that excuse for not seeing people;/And you do need
445 CC	Eggers	11	Mr. Simpkins./But I was glad of the excuse for coming up to London:/I've spent the

467 CC	Colby	36	and sit for a while with my china./{C} Excuse me, but I must remind you:/You have
518 CC	Guzzard	28	can now be terminated./If you will excuse me, Sir Claude .../{SC} Excuse you? Yes./
518 CC	Claude	29	will excuse me, Sir Claude .../{SC} Excuse you? Yes./{MG} I shall return to
527 ES	Lambert	11	{}/[*Knock. Enter* LAMBERT]/{L} Excuse me, Miss Monica. His Lordship said to
531 ES	Lambert	32	{}/[*Knock. Enter* LAMBERT]/{L} Excuse me, my Lord. There's a gentleman
541 ES	Lambert	31	a kindness. {}/[*Enter* LAMBERT]/{L} Excuse me, my Lord, but Miss Monica asked

EXCUSES (1)

370 CP	Peter	22	She doesn't want to see me;/Makes excuses, not very plausible,/And when I do see

EXECRATE (1)

254 MC	Tempt4	39	not hate you/Enough to defame or to execrate you,/But pondering the qualities that

EXECUTANT (1)

465 CC	Colby	35	/As I aspired to be. I'm not an executant;/I'm only a shadow of the great

EXECUTE (1)

278 MC	Knight2	34	by vote of Parliament and execute him/formally as a traitor, and no one

EXEQUIES (1)

531 ES	Ld Clav	20	public man./{LC} Say rather, the exequies/Of the failed successes, the successful

EXERCISE (3)

195 FQ:	Little	144	harm/Which once you took for exercise of virtue./Then fools' approval stings,
252 MC	Thomas	27	has come before,/The desperate exercise of failing power./Samson in Gaza did
286 FR	Gerald	8	climate/For a man who can exercise a little common prudence;/And your

EXERCISED (1)

278 MC	Knight2	10	local government, which were usually exercised for/selfish and often for seditious

EXERCISES (2)

135 5FingerEx		t	shake their spears./Five-Finger Exercises/*Lines to a Persian Cat*/The songsters
554 ES	Carghil	27	/Besides, I ought to do my breathing exercises. {}/[*Exit*]/{MP} As a matter of fact, I

EXEUNT (25)

595 Grad 14		6	say./But 'tis a call we cannot disobey,/*Exeunt omnes*, with a last 'farewell'./Song/When
269 MC		m 26	justice, we come with swords. {}/[*Exeunt*]/{C} I have smelt them, the
280 MC		m 4	might provoke any public outbreak. {}/[*Exeunt* KNIGHTS]/{P1} O father, father, gone
302 FR		m 19	feel better/After his rest upstairs. {}/[*Exeunt, except* AGATHA]/Scene II/AGATHA/
315 FR		m 29	will bring me the same honour. {}/[*Exeunt* AMY, DR. WARBURTON, HARRY]/
316 FR		m 7	think I could manage the situation. {}/[*Exeunt*]/[*Enter* MARY, *and passes through to*
324 FR		m 7	bicycle/On the back of my car. {}/[*Exeunt* WARBURTON *and* WINCHELL]/{V}
325 FR		m 4	lie down. You must be very tired. {}/[*Exeunt* HARRY *and* AMY]/{V} I really do not
326 FR		m 36	I'm afraid *he*'s had an accident. {}/[*Exeunt* IVY *and* DENMAN]/{V} When it's Ivy
329 FR		m 27	And the international catastrophes. {}/[*Exeunt* CHORUS]/Scene II/HARRY,
345 FR		m 31	/A single thing that's happened. {}/[*Exeunt* AMY, VIOLET, GERALD]/{C} It's
347 FR		m 32	/The clock has stopped in the dark! {}/[*Exeunt* AGATHA *and* MARY. *Pause. Enter*
348 FR		m 5	Dr. Warburton!/{W} Excuse me. {}/[*Exeunt* MARY *and* WARBURTON]/{Ch} We
349 FR		m 12	we must do the right thing. {}/[*Exeunt*]/[*Enter, from one door*, AGATHA *and*
358 CP		m 36	Edward./{E} Good-bye, Julia. {}/[*Exeunt* JULIA *and* PETER]/{C} Good-bye,
359 CP		m 6	Alex,/It was nice of you to come. {}/[*Exeunt* ALEX *and* CELIA]/[*To the*
373 CP		m 2	and my work will be ruined. {}/[*Exeunt* ALEX *and* PETER]/[EDWARD *picks*
391 CP		m 33	taxi, Julia./{J} Splendid! Good-bye! {}/[*Exeunt* JULIA, ALEX *and* PETER]/{L} I must
411 CP		1m 36	out your salvation with diligence. {}/[*Exeunt* EDWARD *and* LAVINIA]/[REILLY
440 CP		m 19	Alex. We're going to the Gunnings. {}/[*Exeunt* JULIA, REILLY *and* ALEX]/{L}
482 CC		m 2	much. You give such good advice. {}/[*Exeunt* KAGHAN *and* LUCASTA]/{LE} Were
492 CC		1m 38	Elizabeth./{LE} My poor Claude! {}/[*Exeunt* SIR CLAUDE *and* LADY
532 ES		m 30	/{M} We *both* want to see you. {}/[*Exeunt* MONICA *and* CHARLES]/
565 ES		m 24	I shall hold you to your promise! {}/[*Exeunt* MRS. CARGHILL *and* MICHAEL]/
580 ES		m 14	/{M} Good-bye Michael. {}/[*Exeunt* MICHAEL *and* GOMEZ]/{MC} I'm

EXHALED (1)

62 WL:	Burial	64	/Sighs, short and infrequent, were exhaled,/And each man fixed his eyes before his

EXHAUSTED (2)

73 WL:	Thund	384	singing out of empty cisterns and exhausted wells./In this decayed hole among the
91 Ash-Wed 2		30	of memory/Rose of forgetfulness/Exhausted and life-giving/Worried reposeful/

EXHAUSTING (1)

407 CP	Reilly	19	self-deceivers/Taking infinite pains, exhausting their energy,/Yet never quite

EXHAUSTION (2)

334 FR	Agatha	15	from a burden that I carried,/And exhaustion at the moment of relief./The
465 CC	Claude	25	contentment —/That state of utter exhaustion and peace/Which comes in dying to

EXHIBITING (1)

561 ES	Ld Clav	30	/From that which he has just been exhibiting./{M} Michael! Say something./{Mi}

EXHIBITIONS (1)

388 CP	Celia	11	on you for concerts,/And picture exhibitions — more than you realised./It *was*

EXHILARATING (1)
463 CC Colby 11   how do you find it?/{C} In a way, exhilarating./To find there is something that I
EXHILARATION (1)
516 CC Claude 21   to learn the ways of business;/The exhilaration of finding you could handle/
EXILE (3)
 95 Ash-Wed 4 29   from the yew/And after this our exile/If the lost word is lost, if the spent word is
203 Indians 13   country is home to one man/And exile to another. Where a man dies bravely/At
241 MC Priest1 17   to meet him./{P1} What, is the exile ended, is our Lord Archbishop/Reunited
EXILED (1)
267 MC Knight1 31   /You had fled from England, not exiled/Or threatened, mind you; but in the hope
EXIST (7)
281 MC Chorus 9   and the hunted./For all things exist only as seen by Thee, only as known by
281 MC Chorus 9   only as known by Thee, all things exist/Only in Thy light, and Thy glory is
281 MC Chorus 11   could not deny, if Thou didst not exist; and their denial is never complete, for if it
281 MC Chorus 11   for if it were so, they would not exist./They affirm Thee in living; all things
382 CP Celia 31   that I desperately wanted to exist./It must happen somewhere — but what,
403 CP Edward 33   me, I began to dissolve,/To cease to exist. That was what she had done to me!/I
500 CC Claude 14   reasons for that/Which no longer exist. But I ought to have told you./{L} Well, I
EXISTED (2)
 74 WL: Thund 405 retract/By this, and this only, we have existed/Which is not to be found in our
414 CP Celia 10   /Not even simply finding that it never existed —/But a revelation about my
EXISTENCE (7)
 85 Hollow Men 87   spasm/Between the potency/And the existence/Between the essence/And the descent/
190 FQ: DrySal 221   the impossible union/Of spheres of existence is actual,/Here the past and future/Are
244 MC Chorus 25 in our humble and tarnished frame of existence, leave us; do not ask us/To stand to
403 CP Edward 36   made me incapable/Of having any existence of my own./That is what she has done
453 CC Kaghan 24   you:/Nobody'd ever believe in your existence/Until they met you. Colby's still
559 ES Michael 36   say,/A kind of prolongation of your existence,/A representative carrying on business
569 ES Ld Clav 39   myself emerging/From my spectral existence into something like reality./{M} But
EXISTENCES (1)
485 CC Lady E 19   one's real ancestry/Is one's previous existences. Of course, there's something in us,/
EXISTS (3)
372 CP Alex 19   country./{A} Ah, so the aunt/Really exists. A substantial proof./{E} No, no ... I
570 ES Ld Clav 25   Fred Culverwell?/{LC} He no longer exists./He's Federico Gomez, the Central
570 ES Ld Clav 37 Maisie Batterson?/{LC} She no longer exists./Nor the musical comedy star, Maisie
EXIT (65)
242 MC   m 16 one considers it a happy prognostic. {}/[*Exit*]/{P1} I fear for the Archbishop, I fear for
269 MC   m 21   my cause before God's throne. {}/[*Exit*]/{K4} Priest! monk! and servant! take, hold,
287 FR   m 10 /I don't belong to any generation. {}/[*Exit*]/{V} Really, Gerald, I must say you're very
296 FR   m 13 them./I will go and have my bath. {}/[*Exit*]/{G} God preserve us!/I never thought it
297 FR   m 9 /I will ring up the doctor myself. {}/[*Exit*]/{C} Meanwhile, I have an idea. Why not
297 FR   m 30 to have a word with him, please. {}/[*Exit* DENMAN]/{V} Charles, if you are
298 FR   m 19 return/When Downing has left you. {}/[*Exit*]/{C} Well, I'm very sorry/You all see it like
301 FR   m 9   you, Downing;/Nothing more. {}/[*Exit* DOWNING]/{V} Well, Charles, I must say,
305 FR   m 15 /I must go and change for dinner. {}/[*Exit*]/{M} So you will not help me!/Waiting,
313 FR   m 18 go and change. I came in very late. {}/[*Exit*]/{C} Now we only want Arthur and John/
316 FR   1m 24 /And the crooked is made straight. {}/[*Exit to dinner*]/END OF PART I/PART II/*The*
321 FR   m 13 have troubled you./{H} I'll see him. {}/[*Exit* DENMAN]/{W} I wonder what he wants. I
328 FR   m 1 There might be something in that. {}/[*Exit*]/{G} Well, I said that Arthur was every bit
339 FR   m 22 /I must follow the bright angels. {}/[*Exit*]/Scene III/AMY, AGATHA/{A} I was a
345 FR   m 18   Harry. Take care of yourself. {}/[*Exit* HARRY]/{A} At my age, I only just begin
347 FR   m 14 wondering why you've been so long. {}/[*Exit* DOWNING. *Enter* IVY]/{I} Where is
349 FR   3m 11   *candles, which she sets on the table. Exit* DENMAN. AGATHA/*and* MARY *walk*
359 CP   m 30 good-bye again. I'm off at last. {}/[*Exit*]/{E} I'm sorry. I'm afraid I don't know your
365 CP   m 12 *the matter with One Eyed Riley?* {}/[*Exit*]/{J} Edward, who *is* that dreadful man?/I've
366 CP   m 26 you — both of you — very much. {}/[*Exit*]/{P} I hope I'm not disturbing you, Edward.
368 CP   m 28 say a word./I shall begin at once. {}/[*Exit to kitchen*]/{E} Well, where did you leave
370 CP   m 18 But I *did* count upon curry powder. {}/[*Exit*]/{P} That is exactly what I want to know./
375 CP   m 37 For heaven's sake, don't bother! {}/[*Exit* CELIA]/{E} Suppose someone came and
377 CP   m 2 do. You stay and talk to Edward. {}/[*Exit* JULIA]/{C} But what has happened,
378 CP   m 11 famished./Good night, Edward. {}/[*Exit* JULIA]/{C} Well, how did he persuade you?
383 CP   m 10 never go into your kitchen again. {}/[*Exit* EDWARD. *He returns with the spectacles*
383 CP   m 25 Edward./{E} Good night ... Celia. {}/[*Exit* CELIA]/{E} Oh! {}/[*He snatches up the*
386 CP   m 14 you?/{UG} I also am a stranger. {}/[*Exit. A pause.* EDWARD *moves about restlessly.*
391 CP   m 2 to *my* house. Peter, call a taxi. {}/[*Exit* PETER]/{J} We'll have a cocktail party at

391 CP	m	8	Lavinia./{L} Good-bye, Celia. {}/[*Exit* CELIA]/{J} And now, Alex, you and I
399 CP	1m	25	/{R} Ask him to come straight in. {}/[*Exit* NURSE-SECRETARY]/[ALEX *enters*
400 CP	m	34	gone./{R} Yes, when they've gone. {}/[*Exit* ALEX *by side door*]/[EDWARD *is shown*
412 CP	m	23	be here?/{R} Yes, he'll be here. {}/[*Exit* JULIA *by side door*]/[REILLY *presses*
420 CP	1m	19	*appears at door. Exit* CELIA. REILLY *dials on*/
422 CP	2m	11	*tray, a decanter and three glasses, and*/*exit*. REILLY *pours drinks.*]/{R} And now we
424 CP	m	4	ready./{CM} Very good, Madam. {}/[*Exit*. LAVINIA *looks about the room critically*
424 CP	m	10	more, I think, till half past six. {}/[*Exit* CATERER'S MAN]/[EDWARD *lets*
439 CP	m	33	Alex. Good-bye, Sir Henry. {}/[*Exit*]/{J} ... And now the consequence of the
450 CC	m	32	Lady Elizabeth, I will rejoin you. {}/[*Exit* SIR CLAUDE]/{C} I'm glad you don't have
454 CC	m	15	and let you take me out to lunch. {}/[*Exit* LUCASTA]/{K} Take it easy, Colby. You'll
454 CC	m	16	easy, Colby. You'll get used to her. {}/[*Exit* KAGHAN]/{C} Egg ... Mr. Eggerson!/{E}
460 CC	m	33	business with Mr. .../{LE} Colby! {}/[*Exit* LADY ELIZABETH]/{SC} She actually
461 CC	m	22	Claude. Good day, Mr. Simpkins. {}/[*Exit* EGGERSON]/{SC} Well, Colby! I've been
503 CC	m	33	in any event,/Good-bye, Colby. {}/[*Exit* LUCASTA]/{C} Good-bye then, Lucasta./
504 CC	m	18	up, Lucasta?/{L} I'll make B. do it. {}/[*Exit* LUCASTA]/{SC} I wish you could arrange
504 CC	m	24	*escorting* MRS. GUZZARD. *Exit* KAGHAN]/{SC} Good morning, Mrs.
510 CC	m	2	suggestion, Mr. Simpkins. {}/[*Exit* COLBY]/{E} And now, if you agree, Lady
518 CC	m	36	Claude?/I'm no longer needed here. {}/[*Exit* COLBY]/{SC} Mind? What do I mind?/
519 CC	m	4	that? Oh. Good-bye, Mrs. Guzzard. {}/[*Exit* MRS. GUZZARD]/{SC} What's happened?
526 ES	m	30	Charles,/That you *can* stay to tea. {}/[*Exit* LAMBERT]/{M} — Now we're in the
527 ES	m	14	moment. But he won't be very long. {}/[*Exit*]/{C} Don't you understand that you're
532 ES	m	9	/{M} Yes, thank you, Lambert. {}/[*Exit* LAMBERT]/{C} I ought to be going./{M}
535 ES	m	9	some ice./{L} Ice? Yes, my Lord. {}/[*Exit*]/{G} I began to say: when I say 'trust'/I use
535 ES	m	19	*enters silently, deposits tray and exit*]/{LC} Won't you help yourself? {}/[GOMEZ
541 ES	m	34	time./{LC} I'll be ready to take it. {}/[*Exit* LAMBERT]/{G} Ah, the pre-arranged
543 ES	m	7	we can begin just where we left off. {}/[*Exit* GOMEZ]/[LORD CLAVERTON *sits for*
547 ES	m	11	the evenings. But not *too* crowded. {}/[*Exit*]/{LC} Much as I had feared. But I'm not
548 ES	m	2	/Now I'll leave you to enjoy it. {}/[*Exit*]/{M} I hope she won't remember anything
548 ES	m	13	they'll have to take the hint. {}/[*Exit*]/*A moment later*, LORD CLAVERTON
554 ES	m	27	ought to do my breathing exercises. {}/[*Exit*]/{MP} As a matter of fact, I flew to your
555 ES	m	11	see you coming. Now I must fly. {}/[*Exit*]/{M} I saw Mrs. Piggott bothering you
556 ES	m	29	to the point if I leave you together. {}/[*Exit*]/{Mi} You know, it's awfully hard to
565 ES	m	27	old times. Bye bye for the present. {}/[*Exit*]/{M} Father, those awful people. We
580 ES	m	25	tired. I'll run and see them off. {}/[*Exit* MRS. CARGHILL]/{M} Oh Father,
582 ES	m	24	be warm enough./I shall not go far. {}/[*Exit* CLAVERTON]/{C} He's a very different

EXORCISED (1)

| 570 ES | Monica | 18 | with./{M} Or only ghosts, who can be exorcised!/Who are they, and what do they |

EXORCISM (1)

| 329 FR | Chorus | 19 | these things/And we know nothing of exorcism/And whether in Argos or England/ |

EXOTIC-LOOKING (1)

| 563 ES | Carghil | 3 | a very good figure/And he's rather exotic-looking. Is he a foreigner?/{LC} He |

EXPANDING (1)

| 195 FQ: Little | | 159 | /For liberation — not less of love but expanding/Of love beyond desire, and so |

EXPANSION (1)

| 151 Rock 2 | | 17 | /Then they could set about imperial expansion/Accompanied by industrial |

EXPECT (21)

70 WL: Fire S		304	/My people humble people who expect/Nothing.'/la la/To Carthage then I came/
148 Rock 1		56	ready to invest their money/But most expect dividends./I say to you: *Make perfect*
235 Ad-dress		64	the onion sauce.)/A Cat's entitled to expect/These evidences of respect./And so in
252 MC Tempt3		8	/But time past is time forgotten./We expect the rise of a new constellation./{T} And if
257 MC Chorus		7	women, we know what we must expect and not expect./We know of oppression
257 MC Chorus		7	know what we must expect and not expect./We know of oppression and torture,/We
326 FR	Violet	37	When it's Ivy that he's asking for, I expect the worst./{Ag} Whatever you have
358 CP	Julia	33	*me* a taxi, and then I can drop you./I expect you on Friday, Edward. And Celia —/I
370 CP	Alex	17	surprise, then. I must think./I didn't expect to find any mangoes,/But I *did* count
385 CP	Edward	20	to each other./{E} You can hardly expect me to obliterate/The last five years./{UG}
386 CP	Edward	17	/{E} Celia! Why have you come?/I expect Lavinia at any moment./You must not
388 CP	Lavinia	23	Well, Celia. Well, Peter./I didn't expect to find either of you here./{P&C} But the
405 CP	Edward	28	to meet him./{E} And I did not expect to meet *you*, Lavinia. I call this a very
449 CC	Claude	29	Angel/Will soon be getting married, I expect./{E} And so I hope. A most suitable
455 CC	Eggers	32	that's what I always say./But I don't expect you'll have to see much of her:/That
456 CC	Eggers	23	sometimes remembers when you least expect it./But she does forget things. And she
463 CC	Colby	24	yet from time to time, when I least expect it,/When my mind is cleared and empty,
488 CC	Claude	19	will be very different/From what you expect. I'm afraid, Colby,/It seems to me that

532 ES Ld Clav 18   of the man who introduces him/I expect he wants money. Or to sell me something
555 ES Ld Clav 35   /{LC} If it's only debts/Once more, I expect I can put up with it./But where is he?/
564 ES Gomez 24   afterwards, didn't we, Richard?/{G} I expect that was after I had left England./{MC}

EXPECTATION (5)
111 Xmas Trees 16   its peculiar and exciting smell),/The expectation of the goose or turkey/And the
252 MC Tempt4 36   been here before./I always precede expectation./{T} Who are you?/{T4} As you do
266 MC Thomas 1   PRIESTS]./{T} However certain our expectation/The moment foreseen may be
417 CP Reilly 28   routine,/Learn to avoid excessive expectation,/Become tolerant of themselves and
531 ES Charles 9   the Government in power'./And the expectation that your voice will be heard/In

EXPECTED (26)
 68 WL: Fire S 230   foretold the rest —/I too awaited the expected guest./He, the young man carbuncular,
111 Xmas Trees 17   of the goose or turkey/And the expected awe on its appearance,/So that the
179 FQ: ECoker 73   was not (to start again) what one had expected./What was to be the value of the long
250 MC Thomas 20   {T3} I am an unexpected visitor./{T} I expected you./{T3} But not in this guise, or for
252 MC Thomas 32   not lack a friend./{T} Who are you? I expected/Three visitors, not four./{T4} Do not
252 MC Tempt4 35   to receive one more./Had I been expected, I had been here before./I always
285 FR Amy 8   /And the night unfeared and the day expected/And clocks could be trusted,
295 FR Harry 1   is true in a different sense./I expected to find her when I went back to the
295 FR Harry 31   /They are very close here. I had not expected that./{A} Harry, Harry, you are very
305 FR Harry 35   it's very like her. What I might have expected./It only makes the changing of people/
308 FR Mary 25   what you say/Only proves that you expected Wishwood/To be your real self, to do
328 FR Violet 28   read that./{V} This is just what I expected. But if Agatha/Is going to moralise
347 FRDowning 3   /We was off tonight. In fact, I half expected it,/So I had the car all ready. You
361 CP Edward 16   know who you are. This is not what I expected./I only wanted to relieve my mind/By
362 CP Reilly 31   /There is one step more than your feet expected/And you come down with a jolt. Just
459 CC Lady E 25   would be cheerful./{LE} Just what I expected. A primrose yellow/Would be
489 CC Claude 31   should she invent it? The child was expected./{LE} In order to get money from you,
497 CC Eggers 10   /{E} Ah, indeed!/I shouldn't have expected her name to be known to you./{SC}
537 ES Gomez 25   and that I admired you./Everyone expected that I should get a First./I suppose
544 ES Monica 1   /{M} Well, so far, it's better than you expected,/Isn't it, Father? They've let us alone;/
557 ES Ld Clav 37   /My tailor's bill, for instance./{LC} I expected that./It was just the same at Oxford./
558 ES Michael 16   my tutor at Oxford./'Not what we expected from the son of your father'/And that
560 ES Michael 11   interesting business./But I might be expected to put up some capital./{LC} What
567 ES Monica 28   *has entered unobserved*]/{M} I never expected you from *that* direction, Father!/I
572 ES Ld Clav 5   from time to time,/When I least expected, between waking and sleeping,/A voice
574 ES Ld Clav 26   /{LC} Well, Michael, you know I expected you this morning,/But you never came.

EXPECTING (8)
497 CC Claude 4   I imagine./{SC} Eggerson, I'm expecting Mrs. Guzzard./{E} Indeed! Mrs.
497 CC Eggers 5   Mrs. Guzzard! And why are we expecting her?/{SC} I have asked her to come.
502 CC Lucasta 15   what I was telling you, and so I was expecting/What I thought I got. But I couldn't
503 CC Eggers 35   /{E} And now, how soon are we expecting Mrs. Guzzard? {}/[*looking at his*
504 CC Lucasta 7   It's the Mrs. Guzzard/Whom you are expecting. She looks rather formidable./{SC} It's
514 CC Guzzard 39   a child:/That much is true. I also was expecting one./That you did not know. It did
563 ES Gomez 9   morning, Fred./{G} You weren't expecting me to join you here, were you?/You're
582 ES Ld Clav 14   Charles, and not at all what you were expecting./I am sorry you have had to see so

EXPECTS (1)
439 CP Alex 21   It is your film./And I know that Bela expects great things of it./{P} So now I'll be

EXPEDITION (3)
525 ES Charles 8   And then you took me on a shopping expedition .../{M} If you don't like shopping
525 ES Charles 11   /But how can one *talk* on a shopping expedition —/Except to guess what you want to
567 ES Charles 17   ever./{C} There's another shopping expedition we must make!/But my darling, since

EXPEDITIONARY (1)
119 SP Krum 12   Wauchope/{Kr} Of the Canadian Expeditionary Force —/{Kl} The Loot has told

EXPEDITIONS (1)
427 CP Julia 2   somewhere —/One of his mysterious expeditions,/And we're going to get him to tell

EXPEL (1)
428 CP Lavinia 37   up trouble .../{L} Why don't you expel them?/{A} They are citizens of a friendly

EXPELLED (1)
557 ES Ld Clav 2   getting into trouble,/When you were expelled from your prep school for stealing./But

EXPENSE (1)
587 Fable 29   over sea/He purchased at his own expense a crowd/Of relics from a Spanish saint

EXPENSES (1)
420 CP Reilly 3   for you,/And you will have no expenses at the sanatorium./{C} I don't in the

EXPENSIVE (6)

290 FR	Amy	4	Europe and half round the world/To expensive hotels and undesirable society/Which
527 ES	Charles	17	alone with your father/In that very expensive hotel for convalescents/To which
537 ES	Gomez	39	which your father found for me,/And expensive tastes — which you had fostered in
542 ES	Gomez	5	in the old days/When you taught me expensive tastes. Now it's my turn./I can have
542 ES	Ld Clav	23	agent./You pretend that I taught you expensive tastes:/If you had not had those tastes
556 ES	Michael	21	for a country inn. And not at all expensive./{LC} You don't normally consider

EXPERIENCE (42)

44 Cook Egg		20	will be more amusing/Than Pipit's experience could provide./I shall not want Pipit
52 Whispers		12	clutch and penetrate;/Expert beyond experience,/He knew the anguish of the marrow
111 Xmas Trees		19	gaiety/May not be forgotten in later experience,/In the bored habituation, the
179 FQ: ECoker		84	value/In the knowledge derived from experience./The knowledge imposes a pattern,
186 FQ: DrySal		95	sudden illumination —/We had the experience but missed the meaning,/And
186 FQ: DrySal		96	approach to the meaning restores the experience/In a different form, beyond any
187 FQ: DrySal		99	I have said before/That the past experience revived in the meaning/Is not the
187 FQ: DrySal		100	revived in the meaning/Is not the experience of one life only/But of many
187 FQ: DrySal		114	/But the torment of others remains an experience/Unqualified, unworn by subsequent
202 War Poetry		11	and the Spirit. Mostly the individual/Experience is too large, or too small. Our
202 War Poetry		23	the abstract conception/Of private experience at its greatest intensity/Becoming
247 MC Thomas		16	again./Men learn little from others' experience./But in the life of one man, never/
294 FR	Harry	5	I am not speaking/Of my own experience, but trying to give you/Comparisons
307 FR	Mary	38	I know what you mean. That is an experience/I have not had. Nevertheless,
308 FR	Mary	39	with people who have not had your experience./{H} If I tried to explain, you could
309 FR	Mary	16	what is the real you. I haven't much experience,/But I see something now which
314 FR	Warburt	26	or another./Now I've had forty years' experience/I've left off thinking in terms of the
314 FR	Ivy	31	/{I} You must have had a very rich experience, Doctor,/In forty years./{W} Indeed,
325 FR	Charles	22	a brilliant driver./After all the experience he's had at Brooklands,/*He*'s not
361 CP	Reilly	33	let me continue./I will say then, you experience some relief/Of which you're not
362 CP	Reilly	33	jolt. Just for a moment/You have the experience of being an object/At the mercy of a
363 CP	Reilly	36	survive humiliation./And that's an experience of incalculable value./{E} Stop! I
370 CP	Peter	29	/Some feeling, some indefinable experience/In which we were both unaware of
371 CP	Peter	4	you of something real —/My first experience of reality/And perhaps it is the last.
371 CP	Peter	28	I was saying, what is the reality/Of experience between two unreal people?/If I can
379 CP	Edward	27	so it seemed./{E} I have heard of that experience./{C} A dream. I was happy in it till
387 CP	Celia	3	hours./It wasn't a very pleasant experience./Oh, I'm glad I came!/I can see you
396 CP	Lavinia	11	on the verge of some wonderful experience/And then it never happened. I
417 CP	Celia	8	ecstasy is real/Although those who experience it may have no reality./For what
433 CP	Alex	39	austere one./And as she already had experience of nursing .../{L} Yes, she had been a
438 CP	Reilly	6	part, Mrs. Chamberlayne;/But such experience can only be hinted at/In myths and
446 CC	Claude	3	/All he needs is confidence./{SC} And experience./With a young man, some
457 CC	Eggers	15	That'll take her a time,/From my experience. {}/LADY ELIZABETH
463 CC	Claude	34	better than you think. It's my own experience/That you are repeating./{C} Your
463 CC	Colby	36	you are repeating./{C} Your own experience?/{SC} Yes, I did not want to be a
516 CC	Claude	26	son,/Because you described my own experience, exactly./Does that mean nothing to
516 CC	Claude	27	/Does that mean nothing to you, the experience we shared?/Heaven knows — and
533 ES	Gomez	33	to pay pretty heavily;/But I learnt by experience whom to pay;/And a little money
535 ES	Gomez	11	when I say 'trust'/I use the term as experience has taught me./It's nonsense to talk
561 ES	Ld Clav	7	always lose the race./I know this from experience. When you reach your goal,/Your
565 ES	Ld Clav	35	own past failures:/I said I knew from experience. Do I understand the meaning/Of the
576 ES	Michael	10	He told me everything. It was his experience/With you, that made him so

EXPERIENCED (6)

187 FQ: DrySal		111	better/In the agony of others, nearly experienced,/Involving ourselves, than in our
276 MC Knight3		33	afraid I am not anything like such an experienced/speaker as my old friend Reginald
308 FR	Mary	12	Of which you speak, I know you have experienced it,/And I can well imagine how
370 CP	Peter	10	such quiet happiness./I had only experienced excitement, delirium,/Desire for
404 CP	Edward	11	of what you do not say./{E} I once experienced the extreme of physical pain,/And
458 CC	Lady E	18	so surprised./You know I'm a very experienced traveller./{SC} Oh yes, of course we

EXPÉRIENCES (1)

51 Restaurant		23	le crâne./De quel droit payes-tu des expériences comme moi?/Tiens, voilà dix sous,

EXPERIMENT (2)

147 Rock 1		7	and action,/Endless invention, endless experiment,/Brings knowledge of motion, but
202 War Poetry		9	attend/Of forces beyond control by experiment —/Of Nature and the Spirit. Mostly

EXPLAINED (12)
293 FR   Harry   25   /You will understand less after I have explained it./All that I could hope to make you
296 FR   Harry   9   you mean,/Dimly — as you once explained the sobbing in the chimney/The evil in
296 FR   Harry   11   they said was not there,/Which they explained away, but you explained them/Or at
296 FR   Harry   11   /Which they explained away, but you explained them/Or at least, made me cease to be
387 CP   Celia   21   /Or am I interrupting?/{C} I've just explained to Edward —/I only got here this
448 CC   Claude   28   But beyond that point/I haven't yet explained my plans to you./Why I've never told
449 CC   Claude   7   that might make her jealous./I've explained all this to Colby — Mr. Simpkins./{E}
465 CC   Colby   7   he was not there./{C} You've still not explained why you came to think/That your
471 CC   Lucasta   7   you played me bits yourself, and explained them./We'll begin my education at
499 CC   Claude   38   if I'd suspected this/I would have explained. Colby is your brother./{E}
575 ES   Carghil   34   /{MC} Oh, Richard!/Have you explained to them our intimacy too?/{LC} I
576 ES   Gomez   22   of business in San Marco/Is easier explained in San Marco than in England./{LC}
EXPLAINING (3)
309 FR   Harry   2   explain, you could never understand:/Explaining would only make a worse
309 FR   Harry   3   only make a worse misunderstanding;/Explaining would only set me farther away
328 FR   Gerald   30   scream./{G} It's going to be awkward, explaining this to Amy./{I} Poor Arthur! I'm
EXPLAINS (1)
564 ES   Carghil   25   left England./{MC} Of course, that explains it. After Oxford/I suppose you went
EXPLANATION (10)
296 FR   Agatha   3   /That you only hold a fragment of the explanation./It is only because of what you do
302 FR   Chorus   3   may think well of ourselves./And any explanation will satisfy;/We only ask to be
318 FR   Harry   30   /I feel an overwhelming need for explanation —/But perhaps I only dream that I
330 FR   Agatha   17   understood,/Try not to regard it as an explanation./{H} I still have to learn exactly
338 FR   Harry   12   /So you may not think I conceal an explanation,/And to tell you that I would have
362 CP   Edward   13   away/At a moment's notice, without explanation,/Only a note to say that she had
388 CP   Lavinia   34   Alex./{L} Then I shall ask *them* for an explanation./Meanwhile, I suppose we might as
406 CP   Edward   22   joker?/{E} I incline to the second explanation/Without the qualification 'lunatic'./
408 CP   Reilly   40   ago/I was dissatisfied with your explanation/Of your obvious symptoms of
575 ES   Ld Clav   31   allusion. I have told them the story/In explanation of our ... intimacy/Which they
EXPLANATIONS (4)
149 Rock 1   67   has been done of good, you find explanations/To satisfy the rational and
385 CP   Reilly   30   must ask no questions/And give no explanations. I have said the same to her./Don't
392 CP   Lavinia   5   /{L} And I know I am to give no explanations./{E} And I am to give no
392 CP   Edward   6   explanations./{E} And I am to give no explanations./{L} And I am to ask no questions.
EXPLICIT (1)
173 FQ: BurntN   78   both a new world/And the old made explicit, understood/In the completion of its
EXPLODE (1)
545 ES   Ld Clav   19   privacy of others, which is certain to explode./{M} Hush, Father. I see her coming
EXPLOIT (1)
454 CC   Kaghan   9   the slightest advantage/Or she'll exploit it. You have to be tough with her;/She's
EXPLOITATION (1)
259 MC Thomas   3   and the axe's edge,/Indifference, exploitation, you, and you,/And you, must all
EXPLOITING (1)
155 Rock 3   64   earth and the water to your service,/Exploiting the seas and developing the
EXPLOITS (1)
204 de la Mare   9   treasure-trove)/Recount their exploits at the nursery tea/And when the lamps
EXPLORATION (1)
197 FQ: Little   241   this Calling/We shall not cease from exploration/And the end of all our exploring/
EXPLORE (2)
189 FQ: DrySal   198   into pre-conscious terrors —/To explore the womb, or tomb, or dreams; all these
405 CP   Reilly   3   of a total situation/Which I have to explore. The single patient/Who is ill by himself,
EXPLORED (1)
204 de la Mare   1   Walter de la Mare/The children who explored the brook and found/A desert island
EXPLORERS (1)
182 FQ: ECoker   204   cease to matter./Old men ought to be explorers/Here and there does not matter/We
EXPLORING (2)
 68 WL: Fire S   240   and decided, he assaults at once;/Exploring hands encounter no defence;/His
197 FQ: Little   242   exploration/And the end of all our exploring/Will be to arrive where we started/
EXPLOSION (1)
202 War Poetry   4   point at which the merely individual/Explosion breaks/In the path of an action
EXPORT (1)
560 ES   Michael   13   /{Mi} Oh, I don't know. Import and export,/With an opportunity of profits both
EXPORTING (1)
151 Rock 2   19   by industrial development./Exporting iron, coal and cotton goods/And

EXPOSED (3)
301 FR   Chorus   17   revelation/When the hidden shall be exposed, and the newsboy shall shout in the
528 ES   Monica   4   the opposite:/It's his fear of being exposed to strangers./{C} But he's most alive
551 ES   Carghil 35   Effie was against it — she wanted you exposed./But I gave way. I didn't want to ruin

EXPOSURE (1)
438 CP   Reilly   12   Suffered any less from hunger, damp, exposure,/Bowel trouble, and the fear of lions,/

EXPRESS (8)
154 Rock 3   9 commissions,/I have given you lips, to express friendly sentiments,/I have given you
232 Skimble   18   who's in charge/Of the Sleeping Car Express./From the driver and the guards to the
241 MC   Mess   29   of the people?/{M} You are right to express a certain incredulity./He comes in pride
279 MC Knight1   8   has I think another point of view/to express. If there are any who are still
297 FR   Violet   33 would disapprove of —/I only wish to express my emphatic protest/Both against your
370 CP   Peter   8 So ... contented, so ... at peace: I can't express it;/I had never imagined such quiet
421 CP   Reilly   29   Yet she must suffer./{R} When I express confidence in anything/You always raise
437 CP   Reilly   20   in certain minds,/May tend to express itself at once in a picture./That happens

EXPRESSED (2)
446 CC   Eggers   31   a suggestion: window boxes!/He's expressed such an interest in my garden/That I
465 CC   Colby   32   /That it's my own feelings you have expressed,/Although the medium is different. I

EXPRESSION (11)
21 Portrait   100   turning shall remark/Suddenly, his expression in a glass./My self-possession gutters;
21 Portrait   110 borrow every changing shape/To find expression ... dance, dance/Like a dancing bear,
202 War Poetry   1   /A Note on War Poetry/Not the expression of collective emotion/Imperfectly
436 CP   Lavinia 22   your face. And it seemed from your expression/That the way in which she died did
436 CP   Lavinia 33   knew *about* her./Yet I thought your expression was one of ... satisfaction!/{R} Mrs.
474 CC   Lucasta 29   only in your music —/That's just its expression. You don't seem to me/To need
480 CC   Kaghan   2   put my shirt ... no, not quite the right expression —/Lucasta's the most exciting
493 CC   Lady E   22 on her:/I want to be able to watch her expression./{SC} But not in this chair! She must
510 CC   Eggers   10   probability —/If that's the right expression./{SC} I believe, Elizabeth,/That you
548 ES   Monica   6   us again:/I could see from her expression when she left/That she thought she'd
573 ES   Carghil 26   /I can tell by the change in your expression to-day;/This must be your fiancé. Do

EXPURGATION (1)
333 FR   Agatha   32 to come to consciousness/And so find expurgation. It is possible/You are the

EXQUISITE (1)
33 Conv Gal   8 'Someone frames upon the keys/That exquisite nocturne, with which we explain/The

EXTEMPORIZE (1)
228 Gus   23   know seventy speeches by heart./I'd extemporize back-chat, I knew how to gag,/And

EXTENDED (1)
177 FQ: ECoker   2   /Houses rise and fall, crumble, are extended,/Are removed, destroyed, restored, or

EXTENDS (1)
41 Burb Blei   25   boatman smiles,/Princess Volupine extends/A meagre, blue-nailed, phthisic hand/

EXTENSIVE (1)
218 Mung Rump   3   walkers and acrobats/They had an extensive reputation. They made their home in

EXTENT (1)
306 FR   Mary   7 for dinner./We do change — to that extent./{H} No, don't go just yet./{M} Are you

EXTERMINATE (1)
428 CP   Lavinia   8   to be destroyed./{L} But can't they exterminate these monkeys/If they are a pest?/

EXTERNAL (1)
293 FR   Harry   38   at most a continual impact/Of external events. You have gone through life in

EXTINCTION (1)
307 FR   Harry   31 thing you cannot know:/The sudden extinction of every alternative,/The unexpected

EXTINGUISH (1)
167 Rock 10   40   night and the seasons./And we must extinguish the candle, put out the light and

EXTINGUISHED (1)
180 FQ: ECoker 115   God. As, in a theatre,/The lights are extinguished, for the scene to be changed/With

EXTORTION (1)
257 MC   Chorus   9   oppression and torture,/We know of extortion and violence,/Destitution, disease,/

EXTRAORDINARY (2)
314 FR   Harry   39   /More anxious to live./{H} Not at all extraordinary./It is really harder to believe in
575 ES   Gomez   11   I'm just the man./{G} Yes, wasn't it extraordinary./{LC} Of course you're just the

EXTREME (2)
404 CP   Edward   11 do not say./{E} I once experienced the extreme of physical pain,/And now I know there
514 CC   Eggers   30   Guzzard:/But in a matter of such extreme importance/You'll understand the need

EXTREMELY (6)
119 SP   Krum   10   to make your acquaintance/{Kr} Extremely pleased to become acquainted/{Kl}
276 MC Knight1   30   /to lay before you the merits of this extremely complex problem. I/shall call upon

278 MC Knight2   12   Becket, who had proved himself an extremely/able administrator — no one denies
295 FR   Harry   3   /The purser and the steward were extremely sympathetic/And the doctor very
323 FR   Charles   35   better leave it to Warburton, Amy./Extremely fortunate for us that he's here./We
428 CP   Alex   21   eat them./The young monkeys are extremely palatable:/I've cooked them myself ...
EXTRICATE (1)
328 FR   Charles   17   /next twelve months./While trying to extricate his car from the collision, Mr. Piper
EYE (36)
24 Rhapsody   21   sand,/And you see the corner of her eye/Twists like a crooked pin.'/The memory
24 Rhapsody   40   could see nothing behind that child's eye./I have seen eyes in the street/Trying to peer
24 Rhapsody   52   aucune rancune,/She winks a feeble eye,/She smiles into corners./She smooths the
40 Burb Blei   17   Viennese./A lustreless protrusive eye/Stares from the protozoic slime/At a
52 Whispers   17   bone./Grishkin is nice: her Russian eye/Is underlined for emphasis;/Uncorseted, her
98 Ash-Wed 6   17   and the whirling plover/And the blind eye creates/The empty forms between the ivory
109 Marina   19   distant than stars and nearer than the eye/Whispers and small laughter between leaves
143 Lines OM   12   the young./Reflected from my golden eye/The dullard knows that he is mad./Tell me
164 Rock 9   20   or lifeless/Joined with the artist's eye, new life, new form, new colour./Out of the
212 Growltiger   8   a hostile world from one forbidding eye./The cottagers of Rotherhithe knew
213 Growltiger   33   and their junks./Growltiger had no eye or ear for aught but Griddlebone,/And the
220 Old Deut   14   ... No! ... Yes! .../Ho! hi!/Oh, my eye!/My mind may be wandering, but I confess/
220 Old Deut   29   ... No! ... Yes! .../Ho! hi!/Oh, my eye!/My sight's unreliable, but I can guess/That
221 Old Deut   45   ... Yes! ... No! .../Ho! hi!/Oh, my eye!/My legs may be tottery, I must go slow/
589 Fable   74   Abbot sat as pasted to his chair,/His eye became the size of any dollar,/The ghost
592 Grad 4   3   with a thousand fears,/To hopeful eye of youth it still appears/A lane by which the
599 On a Port   14   /Regards her with a patient curious eye./Song/The moonflower opens to the moth,/
601 Nocturne   11   /Rolls toward the moon a frenzied eye profound,/(No need of 'Love forever?' —
257 MC Chorus   24   in at the ear and the mouth and the eye./God is leaving us, God is leaving us, more
308 FR   Harry   6   that never found its object;/And the eye adjusts itself to a twilight/Where the dead
308 FR   Harry   33   /Always flickering at the corner of my eye,/Almost whispering just out of earshot —/
316 FR   Agatha   8   *to dinner. Enter* AGATHA]/{Ag} The eye is on this house/The eye covers it/There are
316 FR   Agatha   9   /{Ag} The eye is on this house/The eye covers it/There are three together/May the
316 FR   Agatha   19   /Be about their proper business/The eye of the day time/And the eye of the night
316 FR   Agatha   20   /The eye of the day time/And the eye of the night time/Be diverted from this
330 FR   Harry   27   the self which persisted only as an eye, seeing./All this last year, I could not fit
335 FR   Agatha   9   of feet./I was only the feet, and the eye/Seeing the feet: the unwinking eye/Fixing
335 FR   Agatha   10   the eye/Seeing the feet: the unwinking eye/Fixing the movement. Over and under./{H}
335 FR   Harry   17   broke, and I was left/Under the single eye above the desert./{Ag} Up and down,
335 FR   Harry   31   under the judicial sun/Of the final eye, and the awful evacuation/Cleanses./I was
420 CP   Julia   24   /{J} Nonsense, Henry. *I* shall keep an eye on them./{R} To send them back: what have
436 CP   Julia   15   /When you look at them with an eye for the films:/That is, when you're not
436 CP   Julia   17   with yourself/But just being an eye. You will come to think of Celia/Like that,
518 CC Guzzard   24   /{MG} Mr. Eggerson,/I cannot see eye to eye with you,/Having been, myself, the
518 CC Guzzard   24   Mr. Eggerson,/I cannot see eye to eye with you,/Having been, myself, the wife of
524 ES   Charles   23   waiters all appear to be avoiding his eye./{M} We're getting off the point .../{C}
EYE-WITNESSES (1)
279 MC Knight4   15   /*the Archbishop?* As you have been eye-witnesses of this lamentable/scene, you may
EYEBEAM (1)
172 FQ: BurntN   30   in the shrubbery,/And the unseen eyebeam crossed, for the roses/Had the look of
EYED (2)
365 CP   Reilly   6   *gin and water,/And me bein' the One Eyed Riley,/Who came in but the landlord's*
365 CP   Reilly   12   *toory-iley,/What's the matter with One Eyed Riley?* {}/[*Exit*]/{J} Edward, who *is* that
EYELID (1)
272 MC Chorus   11   /{C} Numb the hand and dry the eyelid,/Still the horror, but more horror/Than
EYES (62)
14 Prufrock   55   I presume?/And I have known the eyes already, known them all —/The eyes that
14 Prufrock   56   eyes already, known them all —/The eyes that fix you in a formulated phrase,/And
23 Preludes   44   pipes,/And evening newspapers, and eyes/Assured of certain certainties,/The
24 Rhapsody   41   behind that child's eye./I have seen eyes in the street/Trying to peer through lighted
34 Figlia   6   /With a fugitive resentment in your eyes:/But weave, weave the sunlight in your
42 Swee Erect   14   of hair/Slitted below and gashed with eyes,/This oval O cropped out with teeth:/The
52 Whispers   6   of balls/Stared from the sockets of the eyes!/He knew that thought clings round dead
57 Swee Night   27   league;/Therefore the man with heavy eyes/Declines the gambit, shows fatigue,/Leaves
62 WL: Burial   39   hair wet, I could not/Speak, and my eyes failed, I was neither/Living nor dead, and I
62 WL: Burial   48   Sailor,/(Those are pearls that were his eyes. Look!)/Here is Belladonna, the Lady of
62 WL: Burial   65   were exhaled,/And each man fixed his eyes before his feet./Flowed up the hill and
64 WL: Chess   81   Cupidon peeped out/(Another hid his eyes behind his wing)/Doubled the flames of

FABER (2)
236 Cat Morgan   17 Morgan./So if you 'ave business with Faber — or Faber —/I'll give you this tip, and it's
236 Cat Morgan   17 if you 'ave business with Faber — or Faber —/I'll give you this tip, and it's worth a lot
FABLE (2)
587 Fable   t WRITTEN IN EARLY YOUTH/A Fable for Feasters/In England, long before that
588 Fable   46 raid/On every bird and beast in Æsop's fable/To fill out their repast, and pies and
FABRICATE (1)
535 ES   Gomez   32   other standards of behaviour,/To fabricate for myself another personality/And to
FAÇADE (2)
180 FQ: ECoker   118   panorama/And the bold imposing façade are all being rolled away —/Or as, when
191 FQ: Little   30 /And turn behind the pig-sty to the dull façade/And the tombstone. And what you
FACE (55)
 14 Prufrock   27 be time, there will be time/To prepare a face to meet the faces that you meet;/There will be
 24 Rhapsody   56 /A washed-out smallpox cracks her face,/Her hand twists a paper rose,/That smells of
 42 Swee Erect   24   /And wipes the suds around his face./(The lengthened shadow of a man/Is
 66 WL: Chess   158 /I can't help it, she said, pulling a long face,/It's them pills I took, to bring it off, she
 89 Ash-Wed 1   21 as they are and/I renounce the blessèd face/And renounce the voice/Because I cannot
 92 Ash-Wed 3   6 of the stairs who wears/The deceitful face of hope and of despair./At the second
 96 Ash-Wed 5   18 place of grace for those who avoid the face/No time to rejoice for those who walk among
109 Marina   17   grace dissolved in place/What is this face, less clear and clearer/The pulse in the arm,
110 Marina   29 seams need caulking./This form, this face, this life/Living to live in a world of time
134 Wind   8 the surface of the blackened river/Is a face that sweats with tears?/I saw across the
148 Rock 1   53   to obscurity, accepting/With equal face those that bring ignominy,/The applause of
151 Rock 2   7 Spirit, the Spirit which moved on the face of the waters like a lantern set on the back of
160 Rock 7   1 and void. And darkness was upon the face of the deep./And when there were men, in
160 Rock 7   6 Waste and void. And darkness on the face of the deep./And the Spirit moved upon the
160 Rock 7   7 deep./And the Spirit moved upon the face of the water./And men who turned towards
160 Rock 7   17 Waste and void. And darkness on the face of the deep./Then came, at a predetermined
161 Rock 7   40 Waste and void. And darkness on the face of the deep./Has the Church failed mankind,
180 FQ: ECoker 121 into silence/And you see behind every face the mental emptiness deepen/Leaving only
187 FQ: DrySal 132 forward is the way back./You cannot face it steadily, but this thing is sure,/That time is
193 FQ: Little   91 /And as I fixed upon the down-turned face/That pointed scrutiny with which we
193 FQ: Little 103 yet being someone other —/And he a face still forming; yet the words sufficed/To
205 de la Mare   25 his call; or when by chance/An empty face peers from an empty house;/By whom, and
233 Skimble   39   basin you're supposed to wash your face in/And a crank to shut the window if you
602 Humoresque   6 marionette/I rather liked: a common face,/(The kind of face that we forget)/Pinched in
602 Humoresque   7 liked: a common face,/(The kind of face that we forget)/Pinched in a comic, dull
604 Ode   2 left us, Fair Harvard, with thee,/Ere we face the importunate years,/In thy shadow we
243 MC   Priest2   5 rejoice,/I say rejoice, and show a glad face for his welcome./I am the Archbishop's man.
244 MC   Chorus   22 we cannot know, which we cannot face, which none understands,/And our hearts are
253 MC   Tempt4   1 /You know me, but have never seen my face./To meet before was never time or place./{T}
272 MC   Chorus   22   only is here/The white flat face of Death, God's silent servant,/And behind
272 MC   Chorus   23 God's silent servant,/And behind the face of Death the Judgement/And behind the
281 MC   Chorus   15 knee bent under sin, the hands to the face under fear, the head bent under grief,/Even
288 FR   Agatha   39 corner/Of the new wing, he will have to face him —/And it will not be a very *jolly* corner./
312 FR   Harry   6 me?/You're of no use to me. I must face them./I must fight them. But they are stupid./
378 CP   Celia   24 /To fatigue. And panic. You can't face the trouble./{E} No, it is not that. It is not
382 CP   Celia   9 been looking at you./I looked at your face: and I thought that I knew/And loved every
385 CP   Reilly   26 you must not forget them./You must face them all, but meet them as strangers./{E}
395 CP   Lavinia 30   little part to play,/With another face, to take people in./{E} One of the most
409 CP   Reilly   38 by being *your* lover./When you had to face the fact that his feelings towards her/Were
414 CP   Celia   23 and stay with them./But I just can't face it./{R} So you want to see no one?/{C} No ...
436 CP   Edward   3 about yourself/That you don't like to face: well, just remember/That some men have to
436 CP   Lavinia 22 to Celia/I was looking at your face. And it seemed from your expression/That
436 CP   Lavinia 30 struck me, though,/Was that your face showed no surprise or horror/At the way in
437 CP   Reilly   15 her chair,/Of a Celia Coplestone whose face showed the astonishment/Of the first five
439 CP   Lavinia 40 for these last five minutes,/How I could face my guests. I wish it was over./I mean ... I am
454 CC   Colby   28   Mulhammer/As Claude? To his face?/{E} She does indeed./{C} And does she call
458 CC   Lady E   25 /But who is this young man? His face is familiar./{SC} This young man is
477 CC   Lucasta 18 *are* shocked./You ought to see your face! I'm disappointed./I suppose that's all. I
478 CC   Lucasta 29 never/Never forget that look on your face/When I told you about Claude and my
530 ES   Ld Clav 17 myself to death/How gladly would I face death! But waiting, simply waiting,/With no
540 ES   Gomez   8 in the morning/Has to make up his face before he looks in the mirror./{LC} Isn't that
540 ES   Gomez   33 to give evidence. You just couldn't face it./Do you see now, Dick, why I say I can
542 ES   Gomez   33 /The reflection in the mirror of the face behind you,/The ambiguous smile, the

490 CC   Colby   31   I am your son./Then it's merely a fact. Better not know/Than to know the fact and
490 CC   Colby   32   Better not know/Than to know the fact and know it means nothing./At the time I
490 CC   Colby   37   /If you are my mother — was a living fact./Now, it is a dead fact, and out of dead facts/
490 CC   Colby   38   — was a living fact./Now, it is a dead fact, and out of dead facts/Nothing living can
491 CC   Colby   25   not on such a mixture/Of fiction and fact. Already, it's been hard/For me, who have
496 CC   Eggers   24   losing touch with public affairs.'/The fact is, she misses the contact with London,/
503 CC   Lucasta   1 understand each other. And accept the fact/That we're not necessary to each other/In the
509 CC   Claude   23 very promising young colleague —/In fact, the young man who showed you upstairs —/
513 CC   Colby   16   annoyance of knowing there's a fact/That one doesn't know. But the fact itself/Is
513 CC   Colby   17 a fact/That one doesn't know. But the fact itself/Is unimportant, once one knows it./
534 ES   Gomez   4 that I've never corrupted anybody./In fact, I've never come across an official/Innocent
536 ES   Gomez   9   that you've never woken up/To the fact that Dick Ferry died long ago./I married a
546 ES   Piggott   3 I'm a married woman —/A widow in fact. But I was a Trained Nurse,/And of course
554 ES   Piggott   28 exercises. {}/[*Exit*]/{MP} As a matter of fact, I flew to your rescue/(That's why I've
557 ES   Michael   19 {Mi} Not so well, for some reason./The fact is, I needed a good deal more capital/To
559 ES   Michael   32   family —/To lord it over them, in fact. Oh, I've no doubt/That the thought of
571 ES   Ld Clav   13 /Yes, I was./How easily we ignore the fact that those who admire us/Will imitate our
572 ES   Ld Clav   18   while for me not to marry her./In fact, we were wholly unsuited to each other,/Yet
573 ES   Ld Clav   12 heinousness of my misdeeds/But the fact of my confession. And to you, Monica,/To
576 ES   Ld Clav   9 told you his story./Did he include the fact that he served a term in prison?/{Mi} He told
FACTIONS (1)
196 FQ: Little   187   of a Rose./We cannot revive old factions/We cannot restore old policies/Or follow
FACTORY (2)
24 Rhapsody   30 /Stiff and white./A broken spring in a factory yard,/Rust that clings to the form that the
177 FQ: ECoker   4 or in their place/Is an open field, or a factory, or a by-pass./Old stone to new building,
FACTS (17)
122 SA   Sweeney   10   copulation, and death./That's all the facts when you come to brass tacks:/Birth, and
159 Rock 6   20 of Evil and Sin, and other unpleasant facts./They constantly try to escape/From the
268 MC Knight1   13   of the nation./{K1} These are the facts./Say therefore if you will be content/To
279 MC Knight4   37   Need I say more? I think, with these facts before/you, you will unhesitatingly render a
407 CP   Reilly   30   of them — omitting the important facts./Let me take your husband first. {}/[*To*
472 CC   Lucasta   34 you. I admired your courage/In facing facts — or the facts as you saw them./And yet, all
472 CC   Lucasta   34 your courage/In facing facts — or the facts as you saw them./And yet, all the time, I
475 CC   Lucasta   30   accepted' me before./Of course the facts don't matter, in a sense./But now we've got
490 CC   Colby   38 /Now, it is a dead fact, and out of dead facts/Nothing living can spring. Now, it is too
494 CC   Lady E   11 I needn't believe her. I don't believe in facts./You do. That is the difference between us./
494 CC   Claude   13 so sure of that. I've tried to believe in facts;/And I've always acted as if I believed in
494 CC   Claude   15 if I believed in them./I thought it was facts that my father believed in;/I thought that
495 CC   Claude   36   have both chosen ... obedience to the facts./{LE} I believe that was what *I* was trying to
497 CC   Claude   30 with that solution./He insists upon the facts. And that is why/I have asked Mrs. Guzzard./
515 CC   Guzzard   31   /I had very much rather that the facts were otherwise./{C} I believe you. I must
556 ES   Michael   32   I was to blame/Before you knew the facts. The first thing I remember/Is being blamed
575 ES   Gomez   20 myself./I thought he'd better learn the facts from me/Before he heard your distorted
FADE (3)
23 Preludes   40   stretched tight across the skies/That fade behind a city block,/Or trampled by insistent
149 Rock 1 m   79 work of the humble. Listen./*The lights fade; in the semi-darkness the voices of*
474 CC   Lucasta   23   you mean. Then the flowers would fade/And the music would stop. And the walls
FADED (6)
174 FQ: BurntN   112   of unhealthy souls/Into the faded air, the torpid/Driven on the wind that
187 FQ: DrySal   128   the same thing:/That the future is a faded song, a Royal Rose or a lavender spray/Of
195 FQ: Little   151 left me, with a kind of valediction,/And faded on the blowing of the horn./There are three
596 When we   8 But the wild roses in your wreath/Were faded, and the leaves were brown./Before
370 CP   Peter   20 what I want to know./She has simply faded — into some other picture —/Like a film
513 CC   Colby   32 /By objects that belonged to him, and faded photographs/In which I should try to
FADES (2)
180 FQ: ECoker   120 /And the conversation rises and slowly fades into silence/And you see behind every face
308 FR   Harry   3 real is what I fear. The bright colour fades/Together with the unrecapturable
FADING (5)
84 Hollow Men   28   distant and more solemn/Than a fading star./Let me be no nearer/In death's dream
84 Hollow Men   44 man's hand/Under the twinkle of a fading star./Is it like this/In death's other
92 Ash-Wed 3   20 steps of the mind over the third stair,/Fading, fading; strength beyond hope and despair
92 Ash-Wed 3   20 the mind over the third stair,/Fading, fading; strength beyond hope and despair/
191 FQ: Little   17 that of summer, neither budding nor fading,/Not in the scheme of generation./Where is
FAECES (1)
177 FQ: ECoker   7 earth/Which is already flesh, fur and faeces,/Bone of man and beast, cornstalk and leaf.

FAGGOTS (1)
257 MC Chorus 20 together the pieces,/Gathering faggots at nightfall,/Building a partial shelter,/

FAIL (4)
 49 Hippopot   7 /While the True Church can never fail/For it is based upon a rock./The hippo's
228 Gus   26 an hour of rehearsal, I never could fail./I'd a voice that would soften the hardest of
233 Skimble   65 'I'll see you again!/You'll meet without fail on the Midnight Mail/The Cat of the Railway
501 CC Claude 17 that I understood *you*;/And I certainly fail to understand Colby./{LE} But you and I,

FAILED (9)
 20 Portrait   63 can say: at this point many a one has failed./But what have I, but what have I, my
 62 WL: Burial   39 wet, I could not/Speak, and my eyes failed, I was neither/Living nor dead, and I knew
161 Rock 7   41 the face of the deep./Has the Church failed mankind, or has mankind failed the
161 Rock 7   41 failed mankind, or has mankind failed the Church?/When the Church is no longer
243 MC Chorus   31 partly living./Sometimes the corn has failed us,/Sometimes the harvest is good,/One
408 CP Reilly   5 have somewhat recovered./But you failed to mention that the cause of your distress/
519 CC Guzzard   2 wishes twenty-five years ago;/But we failed to observe, when we had our wishes,/That
531 ES Ld Clav   21 /{LC} Say rather, the exequies/Of the failed successes, the successful failures,/Who
571 ES Ld Clav   21 we must not abuse it./That is where I failed. And the memory frets me./{C} But all the

FAILING (5)
186 FQ: DrySal   63 /There is the final addition, the failing/Pride or resentment at failing powers,/The
186 FQ: DrySal   64 the failing/Pride or resentment at failing powers,/The unattached devotion which
601 Nocturne   5 courteous moon;/The conversation failing, strikes some tune/Banal, and out of pity
252 MC Thomas   27 come before,/The desperate exercise of failing power./Samson in Gaza did no more./But
460 CC Lady E   17 sign that I've noticed/Of your memory failing. I must persuade you/To have a course of

FAILS (2)
197 FQ: Little   237 timeless moments. So, while the light fails/On a winter's afternoon, in a secluded chapel
453 CC Lucasta   21 I mention Mrs. Eggerson. He never fails to rise./B.! What have you told Colby about

FAILURE (16)
111 Xmas Trees   21 of death, the consciousness of failure,/Or in the piety of the convert/Which may
182 FQ: ECoker   177 new start, and a different kind of failure/Because one has only learnt to get the
341 FR Amy   20 would make for him/Is another. I call it failure. Your fury for possession/Is only the
341 FR Amy   36 now at the moment of success against failure,/When I felt assured of his settlement and
369 CP Edward   20 is why, I think, her Thursdays were a failure./{P} You speak as if everything was
416 CP Celia   3 could get rid of — but of emptiness, of failure/Towards someone, or something, outside
466 CC Colby   39 you spoke of atonement./Even your failure to understand him,/Of which you spoke —
513 CC Colby   30 /The story of his life, of his success or failure .../Perhaps his failure more than his
513 CC Colby   31 of his success or failure .../Perhaps his failure more than his success —/By objects that
516 CC Colby   40 /And in the same way to accept their failure./You had your father before you, as a
540 ES Gomez   2 But even so,/I'd rather be my kind of failure than yours./{LC} And what do you call
540 ES Ld Clav   3 than yours./{LC} And what do you call failure?/{G} What do I call failure?/The worst
540 ES Gomez   4 do you call failure?/{G} What do I call failure?/The worst kind of failure, in my opinion,/
540 ES Gomez   5 do I call failure?/The worst kind of failure, in my opinion,/Is the man who has to
578 ES Ld Clav   9 /I see that your mother and I, in our failure/To understand each other, both
580 ES Monica   28 /I believe he'll come back. If it's all a failure/Homesickness, I'm sure, will bring him

FAILURES (6)
318 FR Harry   4 That was why/We all felt like failures, before we had begun./When we came
531 ES Ld Clav   21 /Of the failed successes, the successful failures,/Who occupy positions that other men
540 ES Gomez   1 In another sense/We're both of us failures. But even so,/I'd rather be my kind of
561 ES Ld Clav   9 and grandeur,/You will find your past failures waiting there to greet you./You're all I
565 ES Ld Clav   34 /Not to try to escape from his own past failures:/I said I knew from experience. Do I
568 ES Ld Clav   7 the law takes cognisance:/Temporary failures, irreflective aberrations,/Reckless

FAINT (4)
 22 Preludes   15 morning comes to consciousness/Of faint stale smells of beer/From the
 73 WL: Thund   386 hole among the mountains/In the faint moonlight, the grass is singing/Over the
129 Cor2 State   26 the marshes./Fireflies flare against the faint sheet lightning/What shall I cry?/Mother
488 CC Lady E   7 he mentioned *Teddington*, there was a faint echo —/And then Mrs. Guzzard! It must be

FAINTLY (3)
 28 Boston ET   3 of ripe corn./When evening quickens faintly in the street,/Wakening the appetites of life
161 Rock 7 m   38 OF THE UNEMPLOYED (*more faintly*):/In this land/No man has hired us..../
164 Rock 9   5 walls, quavering lowly, whispering faintly,/Among a few flickering scattered lights?/

FAIR (9)
604 Ode   1 ELIOT/For the hour that is left us, Fair Harvard, with thee,/Ere we face the
604 Ode   16 for the future, the present, and past,/Fair Harvard, to thine and to thee./The Death of
246 MC Thomas   8 /I sent my letters on another day,/Had fair crossing, found at Sandwich/Broc, Warenne,
276 MC Knight1   20 and therefore you believe in fair/play: and when you see one man being set
277 MC Knight2   38 the under dog./It is the English spirit of fair play. Now the worthy Archbishop,/whose

379 CP	Edward	16	I should have known/That it wasn't fair to you./{C} It wasn't fair to *me*!/You can
379 CP	Celia	17	That it wasn't fair to you./{C} It wasn't fair to *me*!/You can stand there and talk about
379 CP	Celia	18	can stand there and talk about being fair to *me*!/{E} But for Lavinia leaving, this would
489 CC	Claude	7	now. One child each —/That seemed fair enough — though yours had been lost,/And

FAIRE (2)

| 51 Restaurant | 1 | /Le garçon délabré qui n'a rien à faire/Que de se gratter les doigts et se pencher sur |
| 51 Restaurant | 13 | trente-huit.'Je la chatouillais, pour la faire rire./J'éprouvais un instant de puissance et |

FAIRER (1)

| 494 CC | Lady E | 4 | Really, I do!/It would be so much fairer. If he is mine —/As I am sure he is — then |

FAIRIES (2)

| 107 Animula | 15 | and kings and queens,/What the fairies do and what the servants say./The heavy |
| 136 5FingerEx4 | 16 | /And round his head finches and fairies/In jubilant rapture skim./How delightful |

FAIRLY (1)

| 432 CP | Julia | 20 | than interrupting./Now my head's fairly spinning. I must have a cocktail. {}/[*To* |

FAIRY (2)

| 587 Fable | 14 | /As if they had been kept by a kind fairy./Alas! no fairy visited their host,/Oh, no; |
| 587 Fable | 15 | had been kept by a kind fairy./Alas! no fairy visited their host,/Oh, no; much worse than |

FAISAIENT (2)

| 128 Cor1 March | 51 | us a light?/Light/Light/*Et les soldats faisaient la haie? ILS LA FAISAIENT.*/ |
| 128 Cor1 March | 51 | /*Et les soldats faisaient la haie? ILS LA FAISAIENT.*/Difficulties of a Statesman/CRY |

FAIT (1)

| 51 Restaurant | 16 | lubrique, à cet âge ...'Monsieur, le fait est dur./Il est venu, nous peloter, un gros |

FAITH (16)

30 Cous Nancy	12	/Matthew and Waldo, guardians of the faith,/The army of unalterable law./Mr.
105 Song Sime	10	walked many years in this city,/Kept faith and fast, provided for the poor,/Have given
159 Rock 6	8	of violence./Do you think that the Faith has conquered the World/And that lions no
159 Rock 6	13	polite society/Will hardly survive the Faith to which they owe their significance?/Men!
163 Rock 8	30	the broken lives,/The broken faith in one place or another,/There was
163 Rock 8	33	old men on winter evenings./Only the faith could have done what was good of it;/Whole
163 Rock 8	34	have done what was good of it;/Whole faith of a few,/Part faith of many./Not avarice,
163 Rock 8	35	good of it;/Whole faith of a few,/Part faith of many./Not avarice, lechery, treachery,/
163 Rock 8	40	that unmade them./Remember the faith that took men from home/At the call of a
163 Rock 8	47	is impossible, nothing,/To men of faith and conviction./Let us therefore make
180 FQ: ECoker	126	be love of the wrong thing; there is yet faith/But the faith and the love and the hope are
180 FQ: ECoker	127	wrong thing; there is yet faith/But the faith and the love and the hope are all in the
250 MC Tempt1	17	knows order./Those who put their faith in worldly order/Not controlled by the order
275 MC Knight1	18	in desecrating His Church./{K1} No faith do I owe to a renegade,/And what I owe
418 CP	Reilly	24	second is unknown, and so requires faith —/The kind of faith that issues from
418 CP	Reilly	25	and so requires faith —/The kind of faith that issues from despair./The destination

FAITHFUL (3)

254 MC Tempt4	36	whores./When miracles cease, and the faithful desert you./And men shall only do their
266 MC Thomas	28	I am at his command,/As his most faithful vassal in the land./{K1} Saving your
268 MC Knight3	11	in your power to evince/The King's faithful servants, every one who transacts/His

FAITHLESS (3)

34 Figlia	16	both should understand,/Simple and faithless as a smile and shake of the hand./She
274 MC Knights	25	Cheapside brat?/Where is Becket the faithless priest?/Come down Daniel to the lions'
551 ES	Carghil	2	single one of her admirers. Why, even a faithless lover/Is still, in her memory, a kind of

FAKIR (1)

| 226 Macavity | 7 | /His powers of levitation would make a fakir stare,/And when you reach the scene of |

FALCONS (1)

| 250 MC Tempt2 | 8 | sin soars sunward, covering kings' falcons./{T} Temporal power, to build a good |

FALL (12)

13 Prufrock	19	the pools that stand in drains,/Let fall upon its back the soot that falls from
14 Prufrock	52	/I know the voices dying with a dying fall/Beneath the music from a farther room./So
21 Portrait	122	/This music is successful with a 'dying fall'/Now that we talk of dying —/And should I
57 Swee Night	39	cried aloud/And let their liquid siftings fall/To stain the stiff dishonoured shroud./The
122 SAWa & Ho	24	*the bamboo tree./Where the breadfruit fall/And the penguin call/And the sound is the*
167 Rock 10	37	children who are up in the night and fall asleep as the rocket is fired; and the day is
177 FQ: ECoker	2	my end. In succession/Houses rise and fall, crumble, are extended,/Are removed,
194 FQ: Little	136	fruit/As body and soul begin to fall asunder./Second, the conscious impotence of
325 FR	Ivy	29	the slow one./He was always the one to fall off the pony,/Or out of a tree — and always
331 FR	Harry	8	as I had left it,/Everything would fall into place. But *they* prevent it./I still have to
339 FR	Harry	14	waits and wants me, and will not let me fall./Let the cricket chirp. John shall be the
446 CC	Claude	20	to his own devices:/I thought he would fall into this way of life more quickly/If we started

FALLACY (1)

186 FQ: DrySal		89	even development: the latter a partial fallacy/Encouraged by superficial notions of

FALLEN (3)

149 Rock 1		84	*for new mortar/Where the bricks are fallen/We will build with new stone/Where the*
596 When we		2	home across the hill/No leaves were fallen from the trees;/The gentle fingers of the
409 CP	Reilly	31	that your young friend/Had actually fallen in love with Miss Coplestone,/It took you

FALLING (8)

73 WL: Thund		373	and reforms and bursts in the violet air/Falling towers/Jerusalem Athens Alexandria/
74 WL: Thund		426	my lands in order?/London Bridge is falling down falling down falling down/*Poi*
74 WL: Thund		426	order?/London Bridge is falling down falling down falling down/*Poi s'ascose nel foco*
74 WL: Thund		426	Bridge is falling down falling down falling down/*Poi s'ascose nel foco che gli affina/*
107 Animula		5	legs of tables and of chairs,/Rising or falling, grasping at kisses and toys,/Advancing
129 Cor2 State		48	the firefly or lightning bug,/'Rising and falling, crowned with dust', the small creatures,/
178 FQ: ECoker		46	/And that of beasts. Feet rising and falling./Eating and drinking. Dung and death./
275 MC Chorus		27	with blood, through a curtain of falling blood?/We did not wish anything to

FALLS (9)

13 Prufrock		19	/Let fall upon its back the soot that falls from chimneys,/Slipped by the terrace, made
20 Portrait		92	will find so much to learn.'/My smile falls heavily among the bric-à-brac./'Perhaps you
85 Hollow Men		76	the motion/And the act/Falls the Shadow/*For Thine is the Kingdom/*
85 Hollow Men		82	the emotion/And the response/Falls the Shadow/*Life is very long/*Between the
85 Hollow Men		90	/Between the essence/And the descent/Falls the Shadow/*For Thine is the Kingdom/*For
177 FQ: ECoker		14	my beginning is my end. Now the light falls/Across the open field, leaving the deep lane/
257 MC Chorus		27	Sweet and cloying through the dark air/Falls the stifling scent of despair;/The forms take
333 FR	Harry	18	towards reconciliation/As the stone falls, as the tree falls. And in the end/That is the
333 FR	Harry	18	/As the stone falls, as the tree falls. And in the end/That is the completion which

FALSE (10)

19 Portrait		35	monotone/That is at least one definite 'false note.'/— Let us take the air, in a tobacco
267 MC Knight1		36	to the Pope,/Raising up against him false opinions./{K2} Yet the King, out of his
471 CC	Colby	22	/You were trying very hard to give a false impression./And then you came to see that
471 CC	Lucasta	24	/{L} Oh, so I was trying to give a false impression?/What sort of impression was I
471 CC	Colby	27	for some reason,/You thought I'd get a false impression anyway./You preferred it to be
476 CC	Lucasta	11	met/You saw I was trying to give a false impression./I want to tell you now, why I
491 CC	Colby	36	other indignant at the imputation/Of false parenthood. Both mocked at./{SC} Then
517 CC	Colby	14	/All that's left is love. But not on false pretences:/That's why I must leave you./
534 ES	Gomez	10	/{G} That's true enough,/Except for a false inference. I wouldn't dream/Of carrying on
569 ES Ld Clav		8	Monica!/I've had your love under false pretences./Now, I'm tired of keeping up

FALSEHOOD (1)

98 Ash-Wed 6		26	/Suffer us not to mock ourselves with falsehood/Teach us to care and not to care/Teach

FALSELY (1)

264 MC Priest1		2	*moreover did sit, and did witness falsely against me./*A day that was always most

FALSIFIES (1)

179 FQ: ECoker		85	/The knowledge imposes a pattern, and falsifies,/For the pattern is new in every moment/

FAME (2)

212 Growltiger		9	of Rotherhithe knew something of his fame;/At Hammersmith and Putney people
594 Grad 12		2	succeeding year/Thy honor and thy fame shall but increase/Forever, and may

FAMILIAR (10)

152 Rock 2		48	/But all dash to and fro in motor cars,/Familiar with the roads and settled nowhere./Nor
193 FQ: Little		97	the brown baked features/The eyes of a familiar compound ghost/Both intimate and
204 de la Mare		17	who grieve and yearn;/When the familiar scene is suddenly strange/Or the well
239 MC Chorus		5	/With which we are not already familiar? There is no danger/For us, and there is
294 FR	Harry	6	to give you/Comparisons in a more familiar medium. I am the old house/With the
418 CP	Reilly	21	courage./The first I could describe in familiar terms/Because you have seen it, as we all
458 CC	Lady E	25	who is this young man? His face is familiar./{SC} This young man is Eggerson's
486 CC	Lady E	5	met ... your aunt./But the name is familiar. How old are you, Colby?/{C} I'm
506 CC	Eggers	28	/And the name struck her as being familiar./{MG} Indeed? It is not a very common
558 ES	Michael	31	up against me./That I'd been too familiar with one of the girls./He assumed it had

FAMILIARITY (1)

235 Ad-dress		43	always keep in mind that he/Resents familiarity./I bow, and taking off my hat,/

FAMILIES (1)

354 CP	Alex	12	family —/One of the *oldest* Baltic families/With a branch in Sweden and one in

FAMILY (57)

129 Cor2 State		29	cry?/Mother mother/Here is the row of family portraits, dingy busts, all looking
152 Rock 2		49	and settled nowhere./Nor does the family even move about together,/But every son
209 NamingCats		5	/First of all, there's the name that the family use daily,/Such as Peter, Augustus, Alonzo
218 Mung Rump		15	her Woolworth pearls:/Then the family would say: 'It's that horrible cat!/It was

218	Mung Rump	21	policeman in conversation./When the family assembled for Sunday dinner,/With their
219	Mung Rump	28	from the oven — like that!'/Then the family would say: 'It's that horrible cat!/It was
219	Mung Rump	38	commonly said to be Ming —/Then the family would say: 'Now which was which cat?/It
225	Mr Mistoff	51	magical powers:/And I have known the family to call/Him in from the garden for hours,/
279	MC Knight1	9	/Richard Brito, coming as he does of a family distinguished for its/loyalty to the Church,
283	FR	t	/Blessed Thomas, pray for us. {}/THE FAMILY REUNION/Persons/AMY,
287	FR Amy	27	I keep Wishwood alive/To keep the family alive, to keep them together,/To keep me
289	FR Amy	20	/I do not mince matters in front of the family:/You can call it nothing but a blessed
289	FR Amy	38	/She never would have been one of the family,/She never wished to be one of the family,/
289	FR Amy	39	/She never wished to be one of the family,/She only wanted to keep him to herself/To
296	FR Amy	32	few days at Wishwood/Among his own family, is all that he needs./{G} Nevertheless,
296	FR Gerald	35	to join us?/He's an old friend of the family, it's perfectly natural/That he should be
303	FR Mary	21	/For what is more formal than a family dinner?/An official occasion of
304	FR Agatha	35	me — she was frightened of the family,/She wanted to fight them — with the
307	FR Harry	13	after the formal reception/And the family festivities, I made my escape/As soon as I
309	FR Mary	21	as you say, Wishwood is a cheat,/Your family a delusion — then it's *all* a delusion,/
313	FR Charles	24	him./After all, you're the head of the family./{A} Violet! Has Arthur or John come yet?/
314	FR Amy	3	/You know he's the oldest friend of the family,/And he's known you longer than
315	FR Chorus	36	the noise in the nursery, mutilated/The family album, rendered ludicrous/The tenants'
316	FR Chorus	1	ludicrous/The tenants' dinner, the family picnic on the moors. Have torn/The roof
320	FR Warburt	32	/And have always been a party to the family secrets —/You know as well as I do that
326	FR Harry	13	been holding a meeting — the usual family inquest/On the characters of all the junior
326	FR Violet	32	are not always welcome in this family. {}/[*Enter* DENMAN]/{D} Excuse me,
328	FR Charles	27	of./{C} There's a little more. 'The Piper family ...' no, we needn't read that./{V} This is
333	FR Agatha	33	are the consciousness of your unhappy family,/Its bird sent flying through the
334	FR Agatha	17	yours now, yours/The burden of all the family. And I am a little frightened./{H} You,
334	FR Harry	21	understanding/Of you, and of all of us. Family affection/Was a kind of formal obligation,
338	FR Amy	25	There is no one here!/No one, but your family!/{H} And now I know/That my business is
341	FR Amy	30	persuade him/To abandon his duty, his family and his happiness?/Who has planned his
344	FR Charles	14	that's never happened in our family!/And why in such a hurry? Before you
344	FR Charles	31	a thing/Has never happened in our family./{V} I cannot understand it./{H} I never
354	CP Alex	11	/{A} Her father belonged to a Baltic family —/One of the *oldest* Baltic families/With a
369	CP Edward	40	that/Did she ever introduce you to her family/Or to any of her friends?/{P} No, but once
414	CP Celia	18	house going:/But it's been in the family so long, they won't leave it./{R} And you
414	CP Celia	22	she's abroad at the moment,/And my family want me to come down and stay with
415	CP Reilly	18	And what is the point of view of your family?/{C} Well, my bringing up was pretty
419	CP Reilly	37	*of paper*]/{R} You had better let your family know at once./I will send a car for you at
456	CC Eggers	6	bargain.'/Of course it's true that her family connections/Have sometimes been useful.
464	CC Claude	26	never made it your profession?/{SC} Family pressure, in the first place./My father —
485	CC Lady E	1	of being feeble-minded: though my family made me think so./But you know, I
488	CC Claude	6	/You've been asking Colby about his family .../{LE} And when he mentioned
501	CC Lady E	11	—/That's why I never got on with my family./{L} Well, I'm not a person of liberal views.
501	CC Eggers	34	to greet the happy pair./It's all in the family. Why not let them wait downstairs/And
509	CC Lady E	6	There's never been such a name/In my family. Or, I'm sure, in his father's./But how did
511	CC Lady E	13	/Comes, I suppose, from my side of the family./But he was in a very good regiment —/
538	ES Gomez	13	your father's money/And your wife's family influence, you got on in politics./Shall we
559	ES Ld Clav	24	So you are ready to repudiate your family,/To throw away the whole of your
559	ES Michael	31	/Also, to hold your own with Mother's family —/To lord it over them, in fact. Oh, I've
561	ES Monica	37	no vocabulary/For love within a family, love that's lived in/But not looked at, love
562	ES Carghil	14	letters;/But how nice to find a little family party!/I know who you are! You're
576	ES Monica	25	Michael, you can't abandon your family/And your very self — it's a kind of suicide.
578	ES Monica	39	wish to renounce your father and your family/What is left between you and me?/{Mi}
579	ES Carghil	34	Sometimes an outsider,/A friend of the family, can see more clearly./{G} Not that I

FAMILY'S (1)

210	Old Gumbie	7	is but hardly begun./And when all the family's in bed and asleep,/She tucks up her skirts

FAMISHED (2)

378	CP Julia	10	/You know, you're looking absolutely famished./Good night, Edward. {}/[*Exit* JULIA]/
390	CP Julia	37	at junctions. And I suppose she's famished./{A} Ah, in that case I know what I'll do

FAMISHES (1)

38	Gerontion	39	such supple confusions/That the giving famishes the craving. Gives too late/What's not

FAMOUS (10)

62	WL: Burial	43	*und leer das Meer.*/Madame Sosostris, famous clairvoyante,/Had a bad cold,
220	Old Deut	3	lived many lives in succession./He was famous in proverb and famous in rhyme/A long
220	Old Deut	3	/He was famous in proverb and famous in rhyme/A long while before Queen
228	Gus	10	his prime;/Though his name was quite famous, he says, in its time./And whenever he

230 Bust Jones   20   at the gay *Stage and Screen*/Which is famous for winkles and shrimps./In the season of
368 CP   Alex 14 little surprise:/You know, I'm rather a famous cook./I'm going straight to your kitchen
553 ES   Carghil 37 few friends./Effie said: 'If he becomes a famous man/And you should be in want, you
554 ES Piggott 19 been talking to Lord Claverton,/The famous Lord Claverton. This is Mrs. Carghill./
555 ES Piggott   9   I'm afraid it's the penalty/Of being famous. {}/[*Enter* MONICA]/{MP} Oh, Miss
558 ES Michael 19 tell you, it's no joke/Being the son of a famous public man./You don't know what I

FANATIC (1)
258 MC Thomas 36   of a lunatic,/Arrogant passion of a fanatic./I know that history at all times draws/

FANCIER (1)
209 NamingCats   9   sensible everyday names./There are fancier names if you think they sound sweeter,/

FANCIES (4)
23 Preludes   48   to assume the world./I am moved by fancies that are curled/Around these images, and
174 FQ: BurntN 105   distraction by distraction/Filled with fancies and empty of meaning/Tumid apathy with
295 FR Charles   7   You mustn't indulge such dangerous fancies./It's only doing harm to your mother and
485 CC Lady E   9   *was* my mother./These were foolish fancies. I was a silly girl,/And very romantic. But

FANCIFUL (1)
107 Animula   13   tray;/Confounds the actual and the fanciful,/Content with playing-cards and kings

FANCY (8)
174 FQ: BurntN 123   of sense,/Evacuation of the world of fancy,/Inoperancy of the world of spirit;/This is
179 FQ: ECoker 93   foothold,/And menaced by monsters, fancy lights,/Risking enchantment. Do not let me
599 On a Port   8   in some wood-retreat,/An immaterial fancy of one's own./No meditations glad or
248 MC Thomas   9   /{T} Leave-well-alone, the springtime fancy,/So one thought goes whistling down the
322 FR   Winch 33 coming along/At a pretty smart pace, I fancy, ran into a lorry/Drawn up round the bend.
461 CC   Claude 38 to tell./The point is that she's taken a fancy to you/And so she lays claim to you. That's
508 CC Guzzard 27   to adopt a child./They had taken a fancy to him. So they adopted him./Then they left
573 ES   Carghil 35   /I take a great interest in her future./Fancy! I've only known her two days!/But I feel

FANES (1)
594 Grad 9   3   shall rise to thee/From spotless fanes of lucid purity,/O school of ours! The

FANG (1)
332 FR   Agatha 32   Thibet of broken stones/That lie, fang up, a lifetime's march. I have believed this./

FANGED (1)
598 Circe   4   that no man knows./Their petals are fanged and red/With hideous streak and stain;/

FANTASTIC (2)
33 Conv Gal   2   friend the moon!/Or possibly (fantastic, I confess)/It may be Prester John's
234 Ad-dress   25   I'm not including Pekes,/And such fantastic canine freaks./The usual Dog about the

FAR (53)
63 WL: Burial   74   disturbed its bed?/'O keep the Dog far hence, that's friend to men,/'Or with his nails
74 WL: Thund 397 rain, while the black clouds/Gathered far distant, over Himavant./The jungle crouched,
190 FQ: DrySal 236 temporal reversion nourish/(Not too far from the yew-tree)/The life of significant soil./
234 Ad-dress   28 much inclined to play the clown,/And far from showing too much pride/Is frequently
235 Ad-dress   51 call him James —/But we've not got so far as names./Before a Cat will condescend/To
594 Grad 5   5   /May worthier sons be thine, from far and near/To spread thy name o'er distant
255 MC Tempt4 14 earth, to be high in heaven./And see far off below you, where the gulf is fixed,/Your
265 MC Priest1 11 us./You are welcome. Have you ridden far?/{K1} Not far to-day, but matters urgent/
265 MC Knight1 12   Have you ridden far?/{K1} Not far to-day, but matters urgent/Have brought us
275 MC Chorus 24 where is Kent? where is Canterbury?/O far far far far in the past; and I wander in a land
275 MC Chorus 24 is Kent? where is Canterbury?/O far far far far in the past; and I wander in a land of
275 MC Chorus 24 is Kent? where is Canterbury?/O far far far far in the past; and I wander in a land of
275 MC Chorus 24 where is Canterbury?/O far far far far in the past; and I wander in a land of barren
278 MC Knight2 28 the instincts of a people like ours. So far, I know that I have/your approval: I read it in
280 MC Priest1   6 us,/How shall we find you, from what far place/Do you look down on us? You now in
293 FR   Agatha 20 /{Ag} I think, Harry, that having got so far —/If you want no pretences, let us have no
294 FR   Agatha 14 to debate/Whether it may be too far beyond our understanding./{H} The sudden
295 FR   Amy 33 tired/And overwrought. Coming so far/And making such haste, the change is too
324 FR   Harry 32 show the suitable emotions —/And so far as they feel at all, their emotions are suitable./
349 FR Chorus   6 conceivable answer./We have suffered far more than a personal loss —/We have lost our
389 CP Lavinia 27 of my dearest friends —/At least, in so far as a girl *can* be a friend/Of a woman so much
390 CP Lavinia   4   And how is the dear aunt?/{L} So far as I know, she is very well, thank you./{J} She
402 CP   Reilly 39   situation/And then go back as far as I find necessary./You see, your memories of
404 CP Edward 35 you mustn't tell her where I am./Is it far to go?/{R} You might say, a long journey./But
413 CP   Reilly 13 as they had imagined./When I get as far as that, there is something to be done./{C}
417 CP   Reilly 24   to which some who have gone as far as you/Have succeeded in returning. They may
420 CP   Reilly 20 JULIA *by side door*]/{R} She will go far, that one./{J} Very far, I think./You do not
420 CP   Julia 21 /{R} She will go far, that one./{J} Very far, I think./You do not need to tell me. I knew
421 CP   Reilly 14   I said just now/That she would go far, you agreed with me./{J} Oh yes, she will go

421 CP   Julia   15 agreed with me./{J} Oh yes, she will go far. And we know where she is going./But what
445 CC   Eggers   27   shouldn't say that!/Mr. Simpkins is far better qualified than I was/To be your
446 CC   Claude   19   I shall tell him about myself./But so far, I've left him to his own devices:/I thought he
462 CC   Claude   30 I've deliberately left you alone,/And so far we've discussed only current business,/
478 CC   Lucasta 18   there's nothing,/Nothing at all. It's far worse than ever./Just when you think you're
479 CC   Lucasta   8 doesn't need your protection racket/So far as I'm concerned, B. And as for Lizzie,/You'd
482 CC   Lady E   37   well-bred people/Are sometimes far from intellectual;/And — what's less
491 CC   Claude   16 understanding;/And indeed, it's not so far from what I had intended./Could you accept
508 CC   Eggers   3 as a personal reflection,/Mrs. Guzzard. Far from it. You must make allowances/For a
513 CC   Guzzard   1 you. {}/[*To* LUCASTA]/{MG} Nor, so far as I can judge, with you./Perhaps you are the
515 CC   Guzzard   3 the child could be born. You were very far away;/I sent you a message, which never
526 ES   Charles 13 Your words seem to come/From very far away. Yet very near. You are changing me/
537 ES   Gomez   31 play the rake,/But you never went too far. There's a prudent devil/Inside you, Dick. He
539 ES   Gomez   21   /Of yours, to tell him not to go too far./Well, now, I'm beginning to be thirsty again.
544 ES   Monica   1   *and* MONICA./{M} Well, so far, it's better than you expected,/Isn't it, Father?
544 ES   Ld Clav 10   /That's Nurse's business'./{LC} So far, so good./I'll feel more confidence after a
555 ES   Monica   17   What's the matter?/{M} I didn't get far./I met Michael in the drive. He says he must
559 ES   Michael 20 bad,/Of right and wrong. I want to go far away/To some country where no one has
560 ES   Michael 23   mean on the road./Certainly not. I'm far too good a driver./{LC} What then? That
565 ES   Michael 15   /I'm staying at the George — it's not far away./{MC} Then I'd like to walk a little way
568 ES   Ld Clav   1   Where have you been?/{LC} Not far away. Standing under the great beech tree./
582 ES   Monica   20 /{M} At this time of day? You'll not go far, will you?/You know you're not allowed to
582 ES   Ld Clav 24 But I'll be warm enough./I shall not go far. {}/[*Exit* CLAVERTON]/{C} He's a very
583 ES   Monica   15 close at hand,/Though he has gone too far to return to us./He is under the beech tree. It

FARCE (1)
291 FR   Chorus   6 play an unread part in some monstrous farce, ridiculous in some nightmare pantomime./

FARE (7)
107 Animula   26   selfish, misshapen, lame,/Unable to fare forward or retreat,/Fearing the warm reality,
188 FQ: DrySal 139 the sleepy rhythm of a hundred hours./Fare forward, travellers! not escaping from the
188 FQ: DrySal 151 shell of time, and not in any language)/'Fare forward, you who think that you are
188 FQ: DrySal 164 And do not think of the fruit of action./Fare forward./O voyagers, O seamen,/You who
188 FQ: DrySal 171   Arjuna/On the field of battle./Not fare well,/But fare forward, voyagers./Lady,
188 FQ: DrySal 172 the field of battle./Not fare well,/But fare forward, voyagers./Lady, whose shrine
253 MC   Tempt4   21   /{T} What is your counsel?/{T4} Fare forward to the end./All other ways are

FAREWELL (5)
595 Grad 14   2 delay;/Thus is the end of every tale: 'Farewell',/A word that echoes like a funeral bell/
595 Grad 14   6 disobey,/*Exeunt omnes*, with a last 'farewell'./Song/When we came home across the
248 MC   Templ1   3 have to be paid for at higher prices./Farewell, my Lord, I do not wait upon ceremony,
530 ES   Monica   29 You know how you grumbled/At the farewell banquet, with the tributes from the staff,/
582 ES   Charles 28 looking back at us/With a glance of farewell./{M} I can't understand his going for a

FARM (1)
498 CC   Claude   15 You're suggesting that she ran a baby farm./That's most unlikely, nowadays./Besides, I

FARMING (2)
559 ES   Ld Clav 12   Canada?/Or what about sheep farming in New Zealand?/{Mi} Sheep farming?
559 ES   Michael 13 farming in New Zealand?/{Mi} Sheep farming? Good Lord, no./That's not my idea. I

FARTHER (5)
14 Prufrock   53 a dying fall/Beneath the music from a farther room./So how should I presume?/And I
147 Rock 1   18 of Heaven in twenty centuries/Bring us farther from GOD and nearer to the Dust./I
149 Rock 1 m   94 *is silhouetted against the dim sky. From farther/away, they are answered by voices of the*
188 FQ: DrySal 154   /Here between the hither and the farther shore/While time is withdrawn, consider
309 FR   Harry   3   /Explaining would only set me farther away from you./There is only one way for

FASCINATES (1)
463 CC   Colby   23 I feel myself becoming — though he fascinates me./And yet from time to time, when I

FASCINATING (1)
500 CC   Lucasta 28 need me,/He doesn't need anyone. He's fascinating,/But he's undependable. He has his

FASHION (9)
179 FQ: ECoker   70   study in a worn-out poetical fashion,/Leaving one still with the intolerable
602 Humoresque   15 spectres, set him there;/'The snappiest fashion since last spring's,/'The newest style, on
242 MC   Priest1 21   by courtiers, in their opprobrious fashion,/Despised and despising, always
260 MC   Thomas   17 sees, this is to behave in a strange/fashion. For who in the World will both mourn
261 MC   Thomas   33 mourns and rejoices at once, in/a fashion that the world cannot understand; so in
321 FR   Warburt   4   /But, allowing for the changes in fashion/And your being clean-shaven, very much
336 FR   1m 23 *goes to the window, in a somnambular fashion,/and opens the curtains, disclosing the*
369 CP   Edward   16   /Celia's, to provide society and fashion./Lavinia always had the ambition/To
582 ES   Charles 35 alone together, in some mysterious fashion,/Even with Michael, and despite those

FASHIONABLE (1)
  29 Aunt Helen   2 aunt,/And lived in a small house near a fashionable square/Cared for by servants to the
FAST (8)
 105 Song Sime   10 many years in this city,/Kept faith and fast, provided for the poor,/Have given and taken
 233 Skimble   55   and there to catch a flea./You were fast asleep at Crewe and so you never knew/That
 605 Narcissus   27 own clutch, his ancient beauty/Caught fast in the pink tips of his new beauty./Then he
 247 MC Tempt1   30   /{T1} Not at this gait!/If you go so fast, others may go faster./Your Lordship is too
 249 MC Tempt2   29   also,/Waging war abroad, need fast friends at home./Private policy is public
 250 MC Thomas   14 ignorance, but arrest disorder,/Make it fast, breed fatal disease,/Degrade what they exalt.
 256 MC Priests   30 the trees?/{3P} Is the window-bar made fast, is the door under lock and bolt?/{4T} Is it
 296 FR   Agatha   6 do./There is more to understand: hold fast to that/As the way to freedom./{H} I think I
FASTED (1)
  15 Prufrock   81 its crisis?/But though I have wept and fasted, wept and prayed,/Though I have seen my
FASTER (4)
 136 5FingerEx4   6 word from his master/Will follow you faster and faster/And tear you limb from limb./
 136 5FingerEx4   6 his master/Will follow you faster and faster/And tear you limb from limb./How
 247 MC Tempt1   30 gait!/If you go so fast, others may go faster./Your Lordship is too proud!/The safest
 575 ES Gomez   27 /Though of course you went a little *faster* than I did./{LC} On that point, Fred, you're
FASTIDIOUS (2)
 230 Bust Jones   6 he walks down the street/In his coat of fastidious black:/No commonplace mousers have
 603 Spleen   12 Life, a little bald and gray,/Languid, fastidious, and bland,/Waits, hat and gloves in
FAT (1)
 230 Bust Jones   2 and bones —/In fact, he's remarkably fat./He doesn't haunt pubs — he has eight or nine
FATAL (2)
 250 MC Thomas   14 but arrest disorder,/Make it fast, breed fatal disease,/Degrade what they exalt. Power
 511 CC Lady E   9   /{LE} He died very suddenly. Of a fatal accident/When you were very young. That is
FATALISTIC (1)
  24 Rhapsody   9   street lamp that I pass/Beats like a fatalistic drum,/And through the spaces of the
FATE (10)
  21 Portrait   105 understand./We must leave it now to fate./You will write, at any rate./Perhaps it is not
 593 Grad 6   4 With eager hearts to help mold well her fate,/And see that she shall gain such proud estate
 601 Nocturne   6 tune/Banal, and out of pity for their fate/Behind the wall I have some servant wait,/
 244 MC Chorus   27   secure and assured of your fate, unaffrayed among the shades, do you realise
 244 MC Chorus   28 the small folk drawn into the pattern of fate, the small folk who live among small things,/
 247 MC Tempt1   40 too late./{T1} Then I leave you to your fate./I leave you to the pleasures of your higher
 250 MC Tempt2   7 No! Go./{T2} Then I leave you to your fate./Your sin soars sunward, covering kings'
 270 MC Chorus   17 powers./What is woven on the loom of fate/What is woven in the councils of princes/Is
 279 MC Knight4   23 /himself to be utterly indifferent to the fate of the country, to be, in/fact, a monster of
 280 MC Priest3   35 /Which never is belief: this is your fate on earth/And we must think no further of
FATHER (150)
  54 Mr E Sun   16 /And there above the painter set/The Father and the Paraclete./The sable presbyters
  98 Ash-Wed 6   7   between birth and dying/(Bless me father) though I do not wish to wish these things/
 162 Rock 8   1 gods except Usury, Lust and Power./O Father we welcome your words,/And we will take
 241 MC Priest1   9 gate/Have forgotten their friend, their Father in God, have forgotten/That they had a
 260 MC Thomas   3 *to Saint Luke.* In the/Name of the Father, and of the Son, and of the Holy Ghost.
 262 MC Thomas   5 at another time. In the Name/of the Father, and of the Son, and of the Holy Ghost.
 280 MC Priest1   5 }/[*Exeunt* KNIGHTS]/{P1} O father, father, gone from us, lost to us,/How shall
 280 MC Priest1   5 }/[*Exeunt* KNIGHTS]/{P1} O father, father, gone from us, lost to us,/How shall we find
 318 FR   Harry   36   useful. Do you remember my father?/{W} Why, yes, of course, Harry, but I
 319 FR   Harry   3 /But I want to know more about my father./I hardly remember him, and I know very
 319 FR   Harry   10   never came then. Where was my father?/{W} Harry, there's no good probing for
 319 FR Warburt   15 You know that your mother/And your father were never very happy together:/They
 320 FR   Harry   39 Hopes? ... Tell me/Did you know my father at about my present age?/{W} Why, yes,
 321 FR   Harry   31 a glass of port. We were talking of my father./{Wi} Always at your jokes, I see. You
 325 FR   Amy   1 talk yours./{A} You looked like your father/When you said that./{H} I think, mother,/I
 331 FR   Harry   14 now I want you to tell me about my father./{Ag} What do you want to know about
 331 FR   Agatha   15 What do you want to know about your father?/{H} If I knew, then I should not have to
 331 FR   Agatha   33   pursuit of liberation./{Ag} Your father might have lived — or so I see him —/An
 332 FR   Agatha   5 now, who were my parents?/{Ag} Your father and your mother./{H} You tell me nothing.
 332 FR   Agatha   7 whom you have assumed to be your father,/And my sister whom you acknowledge as
 332 FR   Agatha   35 rain and wind had not shaken your father/Awake yet. I found him thinking/How to
 340 FR   Amy   21   /Forcing sons upon an unwilling father?/Dare you think what that does to one?
 342 FR   Amy   8 /That he was not such a weakling as his father/In the hands of any unscrupulous woman./
 354 CP   Alex   11 /{P} I thought she was Belgian./{A} Her father belonged to a Baltic family —/One of the
 449 CC   Claude   4 yes. You might say *mislaid,*/Since the father is dead, and there's no way of tracing it./

455 CC	Eggers	12	may have gathered;/But I think her	father	was a friend of Sir Claude's,/And he's
455 CC	Eggers	14	her./In any case, he's behaved like a	father	—/A very generous man, is Sir Claude./To
464 CC	Claude	27	Family pressure, in the first place./My	father	— your grandfather — built up this
464 CC	Claude	38	it real./That's not the whole story. My	father	knew I hated it:/That was a grief to him.
465 CC	Claude	3	my life/I have been atoning. To a dead	father,/	Who had always been right. I never
465 CC	Colby	8	why you came to think/That your	father	had been right./{SC} Because I came to see/
466 CC	Colby	35	be so much simpler if you *weren't* my	father!	/I was struck by what you said, a little
466 CC	Colby	37	spoke of never having understood your	father/	Until it was too late. And you spoke of
467 CC	Colby	1	spoke — that was a relationship/Of	father	and son. It must often happen./And the
467 CC	Colby	4	been his son/And he is still your	father.	I only wish/That I had something to atone
467 CC	Colby	7	have, and always will have, with your	father./	I begin to see how I have always thought
467 CC	Colby	10	provider:/Rather as a patron than a	father	—/The father who was missing in the years
467 CC	Colby	11	as a patron than a father —/The	father	who was missing in the years of childhood./
467 CC	Claude	19	anxious to avoid the mistakes/My	father	made with me. And yet I seem/To have
484 CC	Lady E	14	knew your parents .../But was your	father	living?/{C} I never knew my father./{LE}
484 CC	Colby	15	father living?/{C} I never knew my	father./	{LE} Then, if you never had a governess,/
485 CC	Lady E	7	there. I refused to believe/That my	father	could have been an ordinary earl!/And I
486 CC	Lady E	7	Twenty-five. What became of your	father?/	{C} Well ... I didn't have a father./You see
486 CC	Colby	8	father?/{C} Well ... I didn't have a	father./	You see ... I was an illegitimate child./{LE}
489 CC	Claude	27	/{SC} Where was I? In Canada./My	father	had sent me on a business tour/To learn
489 CC	Lady E	34	she had a child/Left on her hands. The	father	had died/And she'd never been told the
491 CC	Colby	2	/And I wish that I could have had a	father	and a mother./{LE} Stop, Colby!
494 CC	Claude	15	in them./I thought it was facts that my	father	believed in;/I thought that what he cared
505 CC	Eggers	40	{E}— Who was taken charge of by the	father./	That is to say, placed out to be cared for/
506 CC	Eggers	3	by a foster-mother./Unfortunately, the	father	died suddenly .../{LE} He was run over. By
506 CC	Eggers	8	/Leave it to Eggerson./{E} The	father	died abroad./Lady Elizabeth did not know
507 CC	Eggers	11	{E} And did you know the name of the	father/	Or of the mother?/{MG} I was not told
507 CC	Guzzard	24	/{MG} I was informed that the	father	had died/Without making a will./{LE} He
511 CC	Kaghan	8	am your mother./{K} But who was my	father?/	{LE} He died very suddenly. Of a fatal
513 CC	Guzzard	19	You had no preference? Between a	father	and a mother?/{C} I've never had a father
513 CC	Colby	20	and a mother?/{C} I've never had a	father	or a mother —/It's different for B. He's
513 CC	Colby	23	/Let my mother rest in peace. As for a	father	—/I have the idea of a father./It's only just
513 CC	Colby	24	As for a father —/I have the idea of a	father./	It's only just come to me. I should like a
513 CC	Colby	25	only just come to me. I should like a	father/	Whom I have never known and couldn't
514 CC	Guzzard	6	to terms with it. You shall have a	father/	Dead, and unknown to you./{SC} What do
514 CC	Colby	10	son, Sir Claude./{C} Who was my	father,	then?/{MG} Herbert Guzzard./You are
515 CC	Claude	40	together if you think/I am not your	father.	I'll accept that./If you will stay with me. It
516 CC	Colby	4	man. But now I know who was my	father/	I must follow my father — so that I may
516 CC	Colby	5	who was my father/I must follow my	father	— so that I may come to know him./{SC}
516 CC	Colby	13	the organist of a cathedral./But my	father	was an unsuccessful organist./{MG} You
516 CC	Colby	15	/{C} And I wish to follow my	father./	{SC} But, Colby:/Don't you remember a
516 CC	Claude	31	/Believe, if you like, that I am not your	father./	I'll accept that. I put no claim upon you
516 CC	Colby	38	As long as I believed that you were my	father/	I was content to have had the same
517 CC	Colby	1	to accept their failure./You had your	father	before you, as a model;/You knew your
517 CC	Claude	3	shall never ask you to think of me as a	father;/	All I ask you is — to regard me as a
517 CC	Colby	6	your son./There can be no relation of	father	and son/Unless it works both ways. For
517 CC	Colby	9	when I could not think of you/As my	father:	if I accepted that/I should be guilty
524 ES	Charles	1	/[*Voices in the hall*]/{C} Is your	father	at home to-day?/{M} You'll see him at tea./
525 ES	Charles	1	you're leaving London, with your	father:/	I arranged to be free for the whole day.
525 ES	Charles	19	leaving London./And because your	father	simply can't bear it/That any man but he
525 ES	Monica	23	two words already./And besides, my	father	doesn't amble./You're not at all
526 ES	Charles	32	in the public world./{C} And your	father	will come. With his calm possessive air/
526 ES	Monica	38	/Has given you the right to criticise my	father./	In the first place, you don't understand
527 ES	Charles	16	you be imprisoned, alone with your	father/	In that very expensive hotel for
527 ES	Monica	37	Poor Michael! Mother spoilt him/And	Father	was too severe — so they're always at
528 ES	Charles	1	reasons for your going with your	father./	Is there any better reason than his fear of
528 ES	Monica	12	but the public personage./In politics	Father	wore a public label./And later, as
528 ES	Monica	25	only just been given it by Dr. Selby —/	Father	is much iller than he is aware of:/It may
529 ES	Monica	3	is sitting./And you can take me out, if	Father	can spare me./But he'll simply love having
529 ES	Monica	19	{M} You've been very long in coming,	Father.	What have you been doing?/{LC} Good
531 ES	Monica	3	I was going to have any visitors./{M}	Father,	you simply want to revel in gloom!/You
532 ES	Monica	19	not to bother with such people now,	Father./	If you haven't got rid of him in twenty
532 ES	Monica	30	vicinity. Don't we, Monica?/{M} Yes,	Father.	{}/[*To* CHARLES]/{M} We *both* want to
537 ES	Gomez	38	/A miserable clerkship — which your	father	found for me,/And expensive tastes —
543 ES	Monica	8	*Enter* MONICA.]/{M} Who was it,	Father?/	{LC} A man I used to know./{M} Oh, so

543 ES Monica   14 /{LC} No, he didn't want money./{M} Father, this interview has worn you out./You
543 ES Monica   18   we were having a dinner party./{M} Father, can't you bear to be alone with me?/If
544 ES Monica   2 it's better than you expected,/Isn't it, Father? They've let us alone;/The people in the
545 ES Monica   20 which is certain to explode./{M} Hush, Father. I see her coming from the house./Take
546 ES Piggott   5 you might call/A medical milieu. My father was a specialist/In pharmacology. And my
548 ES Carghil   23   girl?/And obviously devoted to her father./I was watching you both in the
551 ES Carghil   30   will be standing for Parliament:/His father has political ambitions for him./If he's lost
555 ES Monica   13 hurried to your rescue. You look tired, Father./She ought to know better. But I'm all the
555 ES Monica   25 his running over somebody./{M} Why, Father, should you be afraid of that?/This shows
556 ES Michael   11   Michael./{Mi} Good morning, Father. {}/[A pause]/{Mi} What a lovely day!/I'm
556 ES Monica   27 you know what you've come to ask of Father/And Father knows that you want
556 ES Monica   28   you've come to ask of Father/And Father knows that you want something from him.
558 ES Michael   16 what we expected from the son of your father'/And that sort of thing. It's for your sake,
560 ES Ld Clav   5 me to help you to escape from your father!/{Mi} And to help my father to be rid of
560 ES Michael   6 from your father!/{Mi} And to help my father to be rid of *me*./You simply don't know
561 ES Michael   18 from the handicap that I've had./Your father was rich, but was no one in particular,/So
561 ES Monica   22 /{M} Michael! How can you speak to Father like that?/Father! What has happened?
561 ES Monica   23   can you speak to Father like that?/Father! What has happened? Why do you look so
561 ES Michael   34   and make my own career:/And Father simply calls me a coward./{M} Father!
561 ES Monica   35 Father simply calls me a coward./{M} Father! You know that I would give my life for
562 ES Monica   4 you?/However Michael has behaved, Father,/Whatever Father has said, Michael,/You
562 ES Monica   5 has behaved, Father,/Whatever Father has said, Michael,/You must forgive each
562 ES Michael   7 each other./{Mi} I could have loved Father, if he'd wanted love,/But he never did,
562 ES Carghil   20   I know? Because you're so like your father/When he was your age. He's the picture of
562 ES Carghil   29   you at all,/But Michael — your father has changed a good deal/Since I knew him
562 ES Carghil   32 the image of what he was then./Your father was a very dear friend of mine once./{Mi}
564 ES Monica   37   to put your cards on the table!/{M} Father, I think you should take your rest now./—
565 ES Monica   1 doctors were very insistent/That my father should rest and have absolute quiet/Before
565 ES Carghil   11 in the neighbourhood, Michael?/Your father is such an old friend of mine/That it seems
565 ES Monica   28   Bye bye for the present. {}/[Exit]/{M} Father, those awful people. We mustn't stay here.
567 ES Charles   19   your letter this morning/About your father and Michael, and those people from his
567 ES Monica   23 Charles! How could anyone blackmail Father?/Father, of all people the most
567 ES Monica   24 How could anyone blackmail Father?/Father, of all people the most scrupulous,/The
567 ES Monica   26 The most austere. It's quite impossible./Father with a guilty secret in his past!/I just can't
567 ES Monica   28 never expected you from *that* direction, Father!/I thought you were indoors. Where have
569 ES Ld Clav   11 a little love in your heart/Still, for your father, when you know him/For what he is, the
569 ES Monica   13 think I should only love you the better, Father,/The more I knew about you. I should
569 ES Monica   23 the bar./I'm sure I could help./{M} Oh Father, do let him./{C} At least, I think I know
571 ES Monica   26   dishonourable .../{M} Then, Father, you should tell *us* what they already
572 ES Monica   8   it was Fred Culverwell's./{M} Poor Father! All your life! And no one to share it with;/
572 ES Ld Clav   14 /I would have married her — but my father prevented that:/Made it worth while for her
573 ES Carghil   38   being her mother!/I've known her father for a very long time,/And there was a
574 ES Carghil   20 country. And a friend of Michael's father!/And I found him only too ready to help./
574 ES Michael   28   /But you never came./{Mi} No, Father. I'll explain why./{LC} And I learn that
574 ES Michael   31   Señor Gomez./{Mi} When I spoke, Father, of my wish to get abroad,/You couldn't
575 ES Carghil   37 /{MC} The romance of my life./Your father was simply *irresistible*/In those days. I
577 ES Gomez   7   .../{G} Just as many years ago/His father paid mine./{C} This return of past kindness
577 ES Charles   14 /His lifelong grievance against your father?/Remember, you put yourself completely
578 ES Monica   39 decision:/If you wish to renounce your father and your family/What is left between you
580 ES Monica   26 {}/[Exit MRS. CARGHILL]/{M} Oh Father, Father, I'm so sorry!/But perhaps,
580 ES Monica   26 MRS. CARGHILL]/{M} Oh Father, Father, I'm so sorry!/But perhaps, perhaps,
580 ES Monica   32 that Michael is lacking./Oh Father, it's not you and me he rejects,/But
581 ES Monica   10 it is as well./{M} What do you mean, Father? You'll be here to greet him./But one thing
581 ES Monica   30 love for the man he really is./{M} Oh Father, I've always loved you,/But I love you
581 ES Monica   37 your love for me./{M} But not now, Father!/It's the real you I love — the man you
582 ES Ld Clav   7 is someone you love more than your father —/That you love and are loved. And now
583 ES Monica   11   there/That brought us together./Oh Father, Father!/I could speak to you now./{C} Let
583 ES Monica   11 /That brought us together./Oh Father, Father!/I could speak to you now./{C} Let me go
583 ES Monica   18 he has become himself./He is only my father now, and Michael's./And I am happy. Isn't
583 ES Monica   28 I am a part of you. Now take me to my father. {}/CURTAIN

FATHER'S (9)
67 WL: Fire S 192 brother's wreck/And on the king my father's death before him./White bodies naked on
332 FR Agatha   14 with Wishwood,/Until she took your father's place, and reached the point where/
494 CC Claude   25   one./I might have been truer to my father's inspiration/If I had done what I wanted
509 CC Lady E   6 name/In my family. Or, I'm sure, in his father's./But how did he come to be called Colby?

525 ES   Charles   17 to you./You know that. Now that your father's retired/He's at home every day. And
525 ES   Monica   29   in wrangling. But seriously, Charles,/Father's sure to be buried in the library/And he
536 ES   Gomez   34   to trust me./{G} Perfectly simple./My father's dead long since — that's a good thing./
538 ES   Gomez   12   —/Or so it seemed — and with your father's money/And your wife's family influence,
570 ES   Ld Clav   30   He even has sons/Following in their father's footsteps/Who are also successful. What

FATHERED (1)
  38 Gerontion   45 courage saves us. Unnatural vices/Are fathered by our heroism. Virtues/Are forced upon

FATHERLAND (1)
592 Grad 2   5   /That though again they see their fatherland/They there shall be as citizens no

FATHERS (4)
151 Rock 2   1 *each*/*Each man to his work.*/Thus your fathers were made/Fellow citizens of the saints, of
151 Rock 2   14   citizenship upon earth./When your fathers fixed the place of GOD,/And settled all
152 Rock 2   33   repentance, expiating the sins of your fathers;/And all that was good you must fight to
152 Rock 2   34   with hearts as devoted as those of your fathers who fought to gain it./The Church must

FATIGUE (3)
  57 Swee Night   28 heavy eyes/Declines the gambit, shows fatigue,/Leaves the room and reappears/Outside
111 Xmas Trees   20   /In the bored habituation, the fatigue, the tedium,/The awareness of death, the
378 CP   Celia   24   it is just a moment of surrender/To fatigue. And panic. You can't face the trouble./

FATTENING (1)
  64 WL: Chess   91   from the window, these ascended/In fattening the prolonged candle-flames,/Flung

FATTER (1)
587 Fable   21   were having merry times./He stole the fatter cows and left the thinner/To furnish all the

FAULT (12)
282 MC   Chorus   12   our trespass, our weakness, our fault; we acknowledge/That the sin of the world is
288 FR   Amy   2 be late./{A} This time, it will not be his fault./We are very lucky to have Harry at all./{I}
306 FR   Mary   25 always seemed that it must be my own fault,/And never to be happy was always to be
328 FR   Gerald   3 accident as John. And it wasn't John's fault,/I don't believe. John is unlucky,/But Arthur
366 CP   Peter   38 everyone but me. And that wasn't your fault./I don't suppose you noticed the situation./
410 CP   Edward   5   quite knew why. I thought it was *my* fault./{R} And now you begin to see, I hope,/How
467 CC   Claude   17   life has imposed./{SC} It's my own fault./I was always anxious to avoid the mistakes/
524 ES   Monica   9 Over luncheon .../{M} That's your own fault./You should have taken me to some other
534 ES   Gomez   1   corruption./{G} No, Dick, there's a fault in your logic./How can one corrupt those
557 ES   Michael   39 the same at Oxford./{Mi} It's their own fault./They won't send in their bills, and then I
570 ES   Ld Clav   10   no hope of absolution?/It was not her fault. We never understood each other./And so
572 ES   Charles   27   you see that they were as much at fault as you/And that they know it? That's why

FAULTS (4)
164 Rock 9   8 grief they should feel/For their sins and faults as they go about their daily occasions./Yet
410 CP   Reilly   16   could accuse each other of your own faults,/And so could avoid understanding each
571 ES   Ld Clav   16   us!/And that again may nourish the faults that they were born with./And Maisie loved
573 ES   Ld Clav   2   conscience,/From brooding over faults I might well have forgotten./You think that

FAVOUR (4)
236 Cat Morgan   6 to partridges, likewise to grouse,/And I favour that Devonshire cream in a bowl;/But I'm
246 MC   Templ1   29   won't despise an old friend out of favour?/Old Tom, gay Tom, Becket of London,/
246 MC   Templ1   35 /What, my Lord, now that you recover/Favour with the King, shall we say that summer's
251 MC   Templ3   37   your Lordship asks./For us, Church favour would be an advantage,/Blessing of Pope

FAVOURABLE (1)
434 CP   Alex   4   /And where the conditions are favourable to plague./{E} Go on./{A} It seems

FAVOURITE (3)
304 FR   Mary   2   me./I know I wasn't one of your favourite students:/I only saw you as a hard
357 CP   Julia   9   sister/And rather a recluse./{J} Her favourite aunt?/{E} Her aunt's favourite niece.
357 CP   Edward   10 /{J} Her favourite aunt?/{E} Her aunt's favourite niece. And she's rather difficult./When

FAVOURS (1)
266 MC Knights   17   his tool, and his jack,/You wore his favours on your back,/You had your honours all

FEAR (47)
  38 Gerontion   43   with/Till the refusal propagates a fear. Think/Neither fear nor courage saves us.
  38 Gerontion   44   propagates a fear. Think/Neither fear nor courage saves us. Unnatural vices/Are
  61 WL: Burial   30   rising to meet you;/I will show you fear in a handful of dust./*Frisch weht der Wind*/
  62 WL: Burial   55 to see. I do not find/The Hanged Man. Fear death by water./I see crowds of people,
111 Xmas Trees   31 a great joy/Which shall be also a great fear, as on the occasion/When fear came upon
111 Xmas Trees   32 a great fear, as on the occasion/When fear came upon every soul:/Because the beginning
166 Rock 10   4 and dark and disturbed by portents of fear./And what shall we say of the future? Is one
179 FQ: ECoker   96 old men, but rather of their folly,/Their fear of fear and frenzy, their fear of possession,/
179 FQ: ECoker   96   but rather of their folly,/Their fear of fear and frenzy, their fear of possession,/Of
179 FQ: ECoker   96   /Their fear of fear and frenzy, their fear of possession,/Of belonging to another, or to
212 Growltiger   19   and the Siamese regarded him with fear —/Because it was a Siamese had mauled his

240 MC	Chorus	5	/Preferring to pass unobserved./Now I fear disturbance of the quiet seasons:/Winter shall
242 MC	Priest1	17	it a happy prognostic. {}/[*Exit*]/{P1} I fear for the Archbishop, I fear for the Church,/I
242 MC	Priest1	17	/[*Exit*]/{P1} I fear for the Archbishop, I fear for the Church,/I know that the pride bred of
244 MC	Chorus	19	our secret fears./But now a great fear is upon us, a fear not of one but of many,/
244 MC	Chorus	19	/But now a great fear is upon us, a fear not of one but of many,/A fear like birth and
244 MC	Chorus	20	us, a fear not of one but of many,/A fear like birth and death, when we see birth and
244 MC	Chorus	22	/In a void apart. We/Are afraid in a fear which we cannot know, which we cannot
244 MC	Chorus	24	onion, our selves are lost lost/In a final fear which none understands. O Thomas
260 MC	Thomas	23	has been stricken with War and the fear of/War? Does it seem to you that the angelic
265 MC	Priest3	3	day that we know that we hope for or fear for?/Every day is the day we should fear from
265 MC	Priest3	4	for?/Every day is the day we should fear from or hope from. One moment/Weighs like
273 MC	Chorus	2	what beyond death is not death,/We fear, we fear. Who shall then plead for me,/Who
273 MC	Chorus	2	beyond death is not death,/We fear, we fear. Who shall then plead for me,/Who intercede
273 MC	Chorus	6	Thy labour;/Help me, Lord, in my last fear./Dust I am, to dust am bending,/From the
274 MC	Thomas	29	/Like a bold lion, should be without fear./I am here./No traitor to the King. I am a
281 MC	Chorus	15	under sin, the hands to the face under fear, the head bent under grief,/Even in us the
282 MC	Chorus	8	shut the door and sit by the fire;/Who fear the blessing of God, the loneliness of the
282 MC	Chorus	9	the deprivation inflicted;/Who fear the injustice of men less than the justice of
282 MC	Chorus	10	men less than the justice of God;/Who fear the hand at the window, the fire in the
282 MC	Chorus	11	the push into the canal,/Less than we fear the love of God./We acknowledge our
305 FR	Agatha	9	the moment/And the moment is only fear and pride. I see more than this,/More than I
308 FR	Harry	3	is nothing else/The most real is what I fear. The bright colour fades/Together with the
327 FR	Agatha	5	private worlds/Of make-believe and fear. To rest in our own suffering/Is evasion of
345 FR	Harry	9	I'm taking Downing./You need not fear that I am in any danger/Of such accidents as
349 FR	Charles	11	I shall send a wire in the morning./{C} I fear that my mind is not what it was — or was it?
409 CP	Reilly	22	their self-esteem/As, in cruder men, the fear of impotence./{L} You *are* cold-hearted,
410 CP	Reilly	2	had ever loved you./Then you began to fear that no one *could* love you./{E} I'm
415 CP	Celia	37	at the same time, I'm frightened by the fear/That it is more real than anything I believed
429 CP	Alex	11	eaten monkeys./{A} The native is not, I fear, very logical./{J} I wondered where you were
437 CP	Reilly	37	she suffered all that we should suffer/In fear and pain and loathing — all these together —
438 CP	Reilly	13	exposure,/Bowel trouble, and the fear of lions,/Cold of the night and heat of the
528 ES	Charles	2	/Is there any better reason than his fear of solitude?/{M} The second reason is exactly
528 ES	Monica	4	reason is exactly the opposite:/It's his fear of being exposed to strangers./{C} But he's
530 ES	Ld Clav	15	longing for the life I've left —/Only fear of the emptiness before me./If I had the
530 ES	Ld Clav	19	to act, yet a loathing of inaction./A fear of the vacuum, and no desire to fill it./It's
580 ES	Ld Clav	36	/What you say comes home to me. I fear for Michael;/Nevertheless, you are right to

FEARED (5)

242 MC	Priest1	21	flattered by the King./Liked or feared by courtiers, in their overbearing fashion,/
482 CC	Lady E	9	I hope you won't mind a gentle hint./I feared it was possible you might become too
512 CC	Guzzard	8	been a confusion — that's all./{MG} I feared there might be a confusion in your mind/
515 CC	Guzzard	17	I had never said 'this child is yours',/I feared you would ask for the birth certificate./
547 ES	Ld Clav	12	crowded. {}/[*Exit*]/{LC} Much as I had feared. But I'm not going to say/Nothing could be

FEARFULLY (1)

223 Pekes Pols		52	/His eyes were like fireballs fearfully blazing,/He gave a great yawn, and his

FEARING (2)

107 Animula		27	/Unable to fare forward or retreat,/Fearing the warm reality, the offered good,/
246 MC	Thomas	12	me/Only John, the Dean of Salisbury,/Fearing for the King's name, warning against

FEARS (3)

592 Grad 4		2	/Although it bristle with a thousand fears,/To hopeful eye of youth it still appears/A
604 Ode		4	dispels/Our vain hesitations and fears./And we turn as thy sons ever turn, in the
244 MC	Chorus	18	/Our particular shadows, our secret fears./But now a great fear is upon us, a fear not

FEAST (6)

111 Xmas Trees		11	continue in the spirit of wonder/At the Feast as an event not accepted as a pretext;/So
214 RTTugger		25	offer him fish then he always wants a feast;/When there isn't any fish then he won't eat
587 Fable		28	— no ghosts allowed/At this exclusive feast. From over sea/He purchased at his own
261 MC	Thomas	9	never thought./Not only do we at the feast of Christmas celebrate at once Our Lord's/
274 MC	Knights	23	/Come down Daniel and join in the feast./Where is Becket the Cheapside brat?/
274 MC	Knights	27	/Come down Daniel and join in the feast./{T} It is the just man who/Like a bold lion,

FEASTERS (1)

587 Fable		t	IN EARLY YOUTH/A Fable for Feasters/In England, long before that royal

FEASTS (1)

244 MC	Chorus	4	and partly living./We have kept the feasts, heard the masses,/We have brewed beer

FEATHER (2)

105 Song Sime		5	waiting for the death wind,/Like a feather on the back of my hand./Dust in sunlight
129 Cor2 State		34	of noon's widest tree/Under the breast feather stirred by the small wind after noon/There

FEATHERED (1)
136 5FingerEx3   8 have had the Bread and Wine,/Let the feathered mortals take/That which is their mortal
FEATHERS (1)
 39 Gerontion   71   Isle, or running on the Horn./White feathers in the snow, the Gulf claims,/And an old
FEATS (1)
288 FR   Agatha   25   tea, the school holiday,/The daring feats on the old pony,/And thought to creep back
FEATURES (3)
136 5FingerEx5   2 unpleasant to meet Mr. Eliot!/With his features of clerical cut,/And his brow so grim/
189 FQ: DrySal   199   are usual/Pastimes and drugs, and features of the press:/And always will be, some of
193 FQ: Little   96   one and many; in the brown baked features/The eyes of a familiar compound ghost/
FED (7)
 64 WL: Chess   94 on the coffered ceiling./Huge sea-wood fed with copper/Burned green and orange, framed
 91 Ash-Wed 2   2   /In the cool of the day, having fed to satiety/On my legs my heart my liver and
338 FR   Harry   21 my life has been a flight/And phantoms fed upon me while I fled. Now I know/That the
376 CP   Julia   18   /That I had. Edward must be fed./He's under such a strain. We must keep his
453 CC   Kaghan   32   with Lucasta/Is how to keep her fed between meals./{L} B., you're a beast. I've a
479 CC   Kaghan   12 a very good dinner./{K} You shall be fed. All in good time./I've come to inspect the
560 ES   Michael   29 or any other./But I want to get out. I'm fed up with England./{LC} I'm sure you don't
FEDERICO (4)
523 ES   m   6 /LAMBERT/LORD CLAVERTON/FEDERICO GOMEZ/MRS. PIGGOTT/MRS.
541 ES   Gomez   1 accept the unsupported statement/Of Federico Gomez of San Marco/About something
563 ES   Gomez   19 {LC} Oh. This is .../{G} Your old friend Federico Gomez,/The prominent citizen of San
570 ES   Ld Clav   26   /{LC} He no longer exists./He's Federico Gomez, the Central American,/A man
FEE (3)
420 CP   Celia   10 almost forgot —/May I ask what your fee is?/{R} I have told my secretary/That there is
420 CP   Reilly   12 have told my secretary/That there is no fee./{C} But .../{R} For a case like yours/There is
420 CP   Reilly   15 .../{R} For a case like yours/There is no fee. {}/[*Presses button*]/{C} You have been very
FEEBLE (6)
 24 Rhapsody   52 ne garde aucune rancune,/She winks a feeble eye,/She smiles into corners./She smooths
 49 Hippopot   9   it is based upon a rock./The hippo's feeble steps may err/In compassing material
241 MC   Priest3   6   the greed and lust of others,/The feeble is devoured by his own./{P1} Shall these
320 FR   Warburt   12 /And running down. Her heart's very feeble./With care, and avoiding all excitement/
381 CP   Edward   34   that' —/The self that wills — he is a feeble creature;/He has to come to terms in the
434 CP   Lavinia   31   Oh, Edward, I'm so sorry — what a feeble thing to say!/But you know what I mean./
FEEBLE-MINDED (4)
354 CP   Alex   35 {J} Oh, you mean *that* one./{A} He was feeble-minded./{J} Oh, not feeble-minded:/He
354 CP   Julia   36 /{A} He was feeble-minded./{J} Oh, not feeble-minded:/He was only harmless./{A} Well
484 CC   Lady E   35 /And didn't know it. Then, that I was feeble-minded/And didn't know it. Finally,/That
485 CC   Lady E   1   terrified of being ugly,/And of being feeble-minded: though my family made me think
FEEBLY (1)
602 Humoresque   18 'Why don't you people get some class?/(Feebly contemptuous of nose),/'Your damned
FEED (3)
 49 Hippopot   24   way —/The Church can sleep and feed at once./I saw the 'potamus take wing/
311 FR   Harry   37 You thought I was: let your necrophily/Feed upon that carcase. They will not go./{M}
381 CP   Edward   27 of knowing/That the misery does not feed on the ruin of loveliness,/That the tedium is
FEEDING (2)
 61 WL: Burial   6   covering/Earth in forgetful snow, feeding/A little life with dried tubers./Summer
242 MC   Priest1   24   always insecure;/His pride always feeding upon his own virtues,/Pride drawing
FEEL (113)
 19 Portrait   54 buried life, and Paris in the Spring,/I feel immeasurably at peace, and find the world/
 19 Portrait   59   /My feelings, always sure that you feel,/Sure that across the gulf you reach your
 20 Portrait   87 and turn the handle of the door/And feel as if I had mounted on my hands and knees./
 21 Portrait   99 we have not developed into friends.'/I feel like one who smiles, and turning shall remark
 21 Portrait   119   for a while/Not knowing what to feel or if I understand/Or whether wise or foolish,
 61 WL: Burial   17 we went./In the mountains, there you feel free./I read, much of the night, and go south
118 SP   Dusty   5   There's an awful lot in the way you feel/{Do} Sometimes they'll tell you nothing at all/
164 Rock 9   7 their own sorrow, the grief they should feel/For their sins and faults as they go about
181 FQ: ECoker   151   part;/Beneath the bleeding hands we feel/The sharp compassion of the healer's art/
194 FQ: Little   110 dead patrol./I said: 'The wonder that I feel is easy,/Yet ease is cause of wonder.
590 Time Space   3   cannot be,/The sun which does not feel decay/No greater is than we./So why, Love,
242 MC   Priest2   36 France./We can lean on a rock, we can feel a firm foothold/Against the perpetual wash of
257 MC   Tempts   5 step./{4T} A man may sit at meat, and feel the cold in his groin./{C} We have not been
279 MC Knight4   16   of this lamentable/scene, you may feel some surprise at my putting it in this way. But
289 FR   Gerald   6 for Harry's homecoming. Make him feel at home, I say!/Make him feel that what has
289 FR   Gerald   7   him feel at home, I say!/Make him feel that what has happened doesn't matter./He's

290 FR	Chorus	36	*and* CHARLES)./{Ch} Why do we feel embarrassed, impatient, fretful, ill at ease,/
295 FR	Amy	40	to draw you a hot bath,/And you will feel better./{Ag} There are certain points I do not
296 FR	Agatha	5	what you do not understand/That you feel the need to declare what you do./There is
302 FR	Amy	18	and dress, I suppose. I hope Harry will feel better/After his rest upstairs. {}/[*Exeunt*,
309 FR	Harry	11	don't leave me/Just at this moment. I feel it is important./Something should have come
309 FR	Mary	22	then it's *all* a delusion,/Everything you feel — I don't mean what you think,/But what
309 FR	Mary	23	mean what you think,/But what you feel. You attach yourself to loathing/As others do
311 FR	Harry	1	and light./Stop!/What is that? do you feel it?/{M} What, Harry?/{H} That apprehension
313 FR	Gerald	16	back again, isn't it?/We must make him feel at home. And most auspicious/That he could
318 FR	Harry	11	make her more unhappy, and made us/Feel more guilty, and so we misbehaved/Next day
318 FR	Harry	13	be punished,/For punishment made us feel less guilty. Mother/Never punished us, but
318 FR	Harry	14	/Never punished us, but made us feel guilty./I think that the things that are taken
318 FR	Harry	30	don't know why, but just this evening/I feel an overwhelming need for explanation —/But
324 FR	Harry	32	suitable emotions —/And so far as they feel at all, their emotions are suitable./They don't
325 FR	Violet	36	you're blown about so,/And you feel so conspicuous, lolling back/And so near the
333 FR	Harry	39	suffer./{H} Look, I do not know why,/I feel happy for a moment, as if I had come home./
334 FR	Harry	1	home./It is quite irrational, but now/I feel quite happy, as if happiness/Did not consist
334 FR	Agatha	6	And a beginning. Harry, my dear,/I feel very tired, as only the old feel./The young feel
334 FR	Agatha	6	dear,/I feel very tired, as only the old feel./The young feel tired at the end of an action
334 FR	Agatha	7	tired, as only the old feel./The young feel tired at the end of an action —/The old, at
336 FR	Harry	8	quiet place./Why is it so quiet?/Do you feel a kind of stirring underneath the air?/Do you?
337 FR	Harry	23	/In a moment of clarity, and now I feel dull again./I only know that I made a decision
345 FR	Charles	33	It's very odd,/But I am beginning to feel, just beginning to feel/That there is something
345 FR	Charles	33	am beginning to feel, just beginning to feel/That there is something I *could* understand, if
345 FR	Charles	37	I felt safe enough,/And now I don't feel safe. As if the earth should open/Right to the
357 CP	Julia	23	tough old women —/I'm one myself. I feel as if I knew/All about that aunt in
362 CP	Reilly	4	so long./And perhaps at times you will feel a little jealous/That she saw it first, and had
362 CP	Reilly	22	/You thought you were. You no longer feel quite human./You're suddenly reduced to the
363 CP	Reilly	11	/What you really are. What you really feel./What you really are among other people./
371 CP	Peter	19	share these interests? Did we really feel the same/When we heard certain music? Or
379 CP	Edward	39	/{E} There is no reason why you should feel humiliated .../{C} Oh, don't think that you
380 CP	Celia	5	I suppose that most women/Would feel degraded to find that a man/With whom they
381 CP	Edward	11	man/Beginning to know what it is to feel old./That is the worst moment, when you feel
381 CP	Edward	12	/That is the worst moment, when you feel that you have lost/The desire for all that was
381 CP	Edward	18	could *you* understand what it is to feel old?/{C} But I want to understand you. I
381 CP	Celia	21	/I shall not loathe you. I shall only feel sorry for you./It's only myself I am in danger
391 CP	Lavinia	23	is always interfering .../I don't feel free ... and yet I started it .../{J} Alex, do you
394 CP	Edward	29	me:/Then why did you always make me feel insignificant?/I may not have known what life
395 CP	Edward	3	get to the point at which you cease to feel/And then you speak your mind./{L} That will
403 CP	Reilly	8	/{R} Precisely. And I could make you feel important,/And you would imagine it a
403 CP	Reilly	13	world/Is due to people who want to feel important./They don't mean to do harm —
410 CP	Edward	3	*could* love you./{E} I'm beginning to feel very sorry for you, Lavinia./You know, you
413 CP	Celia	15	/But I shan't begin that way. I feel perfectly well./I could lead an active life — if
415 CP	Celia	7	it's being immoral —/And I don't feel as if I was immoral:/In fact, aren't the people
415 CP	Celia	34	see why mistakes should make one feel sinful!/And yet I can't find any other word
416 CP	Celia	5	or something, outside of myself;/And I feel I must ... *atone* — is that the word?/Can you
416 CP	Celia	18	/But for the new person, *us*. If I could feel/As I did then, even now it would seem right./
417 CP	Celia	1	But if not anywhere,/Why do I feel guilty at not having found it?/{R} Disillusion
418 CP	Celia	7	that's just a part of my illness,/But I feel it would be a kind of surrender —/No, not a
418 CP	Celia	19	... still,/If there's no other way ... then I feel just hopeless./{R} There *is* another way, if you
419 CP	Reilly	9	of anything else./Now — do you feel quite sure?/{C} I want your second way./So
438 CP	Reilly	20	to detach yourself from what you still feel/As your responsibility./{E} I cannot help the
438 CP	Lavinia	26	thinking!/Doesn't it help you, that I feel guilty too?/{R} If we all were judged
446 CC	Eggers	28	piano./{E} A piano? Yes, I'm sure he'll feel at home/When he has a piano. You think of
451 CC	Colby	39	I wish I was musical./{C} I still don't feel very well prepared for meeting her. {}/[*A loud*
462 CC	Claude	3	sure it was she who proposed it./So I feel pretty confident that, before long,/We can put
462 CC	Colby	6	up to this point/I haven't been able to feel very settled./And what you've had in mind
463 CC	Claude	2	to your aunt,/Or so she made me feel. I never saw you alone./And then when I sent
463 CC	Colby	20	/So that you can think in it — you feel yourself to be/Rather a different person when
463 CC	Colby	23	sure that I like the other person/That I feel myself becoming — though he fascinates me./
464 CC	Claude	19	to anyone./Never until now. Do you feel at all like that/When you are alone with your
464 CC	Claude	34	this occupation/Until I began to feel my power in it./The life changed me, as it is
465 CC	Claude	23	of some marvellous creation,/And I feel what the man must have felt when he made it.
469 CC	Lucasta	25	And to be seen there! And because you feel out of it/If you never go to the Opera, in the
472 CC	Lucasta	16	inside the likeness./You may *feel* insecure, in some ways —/But your insecurity

473 CC Lucasta 11 my mother. I've no garden./I hardly feel that I'm even a person:/Nothing but a bit of
473 CC Colby 34 that I retire to mine./But he doesn't feel alone there. And when he comes out/He has
484 CC Lady E 29 — and so uncongenial./They made me feel an outcast. And yet they were so
487 CC Lady E 28 it yet,/Perhaps it is wrong of me to feel so sure,/But it seems that Providence has
490 CC Colby 14 or not/During this conversation. I only feel ... numb./If there's agony, it's part of a total
490 CC Colby 16 of a total agony/Which I can't begin to feel yet. I'm simply indifferent./And all the time
491 CC Lady E 14 happy,/All of us? Already, Claude,/I feel as if this brought us closer together./{SC} I
491 CC Colby 18 way, Colby?/{C} I can only say what I feel at the moment:/And yet I believe I shall
491 CC Colby 19 /And yet I believe I shall always feel the same./{SC} Well?/{C} It would be easier, I
491 CC Colby 40 the sake of your children./{C} I don't feel, tonight, that I ever want to marry./You may
492 CC Claude 28 what? Reminiscent of what?/'Tonight I feel in a reminiscent mood' —/Oh yes. To say
496 CC Lady E 1 very stupid./You always made me feel that I wasn't worth talking to./{SC} And you
496 CC Claude 2 to./{SC} And you always made me feel that *your* interests/Were much too deep for
497 CC Lady E 25 deceived, and that Colby is my son./I feel sure he is. But I don't want to know:/I am
499 CC Eggers 3 desk?/{E} If you wish, Sir Claude./I do feel more at ease when I'm behind a desk:/It's
500 CC Lucasta 25 see what I really wanted./B. makes me feel safe. And that's what I want./And somehow
524 ES Charles 21 tease me if you like. But a man does feel a fool/If he takes you to a place where he's
542 ES Gomez 31 You'll relent at last./You'll come to feel easier when I'm with you/Than when I'm out
544 ES Ld Clav 11 business'./{LC} So far, so good./I'll feel more confidence after a fortnight —/After
552 ES Carghil 11 you sing it./{MC} And what did you feel?/{LC} Nothing at all. I remember my surprise
552 ES Ld Clav 19 embarrassment?/{LC} Why should I feel embarrassment? My conscience was clear./A
553 ES Carghil 11 idolise your memory./It's simply that I feel that we belong together .../Now, don't get
554 ES Piggott 15 /Attending to my guests. I like to feel they *need* me!/{MC} You do look after us
568 ES Ld Clav 3 /{M} Why under the beech tree?/{LC} I feel drawn to that spot./No matter. I heard what
573 ES Ld Clav 19 us say no more about it./Meanwhile, I feel sure they are conspiring against me./I see
573 ES Carghil 36 I've only known her two days!/But I feel like a mother to her already./You may say
577 ES Charles 12 I see your point of view. Can you really feel confidence,/Michael, in a man who aims to
578 ES Ld Clav 16 in defeating each other,/How can I feel anything but sorrow and compunction?/{M}
581 ES Ld Clav 3 will do what you can/To make him feel that he is not estranged from you./{C} We will
581 ES Ld Clav 13 leave./{LC} This may surprise you: I feel at peace now./It is the peace that ensues upon
581 ES Ld Clav 25 /But how few of us do! And now I feel happy —/In spite of everything, in defiance of
583 ES Monica 27 in the certainty of love unchanging./I feel utterly secure/In you; I am a part of you.

FEELING (15)
182 FQ: ECoker 183 /In the general mess of imprecision of feeling,/Undisciplined squads of emotion. And
294 FR Harry 21 partial ansthesia of suffering without feeling/And partial observation of one's own
305 FR Agatha 5 may not think me capable of such a feeling./I would like to help you: but you must
324 FR Harry 36 at once./I have all of the rightminded feeling about John/That you consider
346 FRDowning 20 than anybody;/And I have a kind of feeling that his Lordship won't need me/Very long
346 FRDowning 28 for what happens to them. You get a feeling of it./So I seem to know beforehand, when
346 FRDowning 31 /And that's why I say now, I have a feeling/That he won't want me long, and he won't
370 CP Peter 29 to share some perception,/Some feeling, some indefinable experience/In which we
403 CP Reilly 6 vanity/With the temporary stimulus of feeling interesting./{E} But I am obsessed by the
416 CP Celia 1 you believed in?/{C} It's not the feeling of anything I've ever *done*,/Which I might
429 CP Julia 36 must have walked over my grave:/I'm feeling so chilly. Give me some gin./Not a
438 CP Edward 22 responsibility./{E} I cannot help the feeling/That, in some way, my responsibility/Is
495 CC Lady E 39 first time/I have talked to you, without feeling very stupid./You always made me feel that
544 ES Ld Clav 14 a fourth at bridge;/Still, I'll admit to a feeling of contentment/Already. I only hope that
552 ES Carghil 8 *To Love Me*?/I couldn't have put the feeling into it I did/But for what I'd gone

FEELINGS (12)
19 Portrait 59 always sure that you understand/My feelings, always sure that you feel,/Sure that
21 Portrait 103 all our friends,/They all were sure our feelings would relate/So closely! I myself can
164 Rock 9 23 /Approximate thoughts and feelings, words that have taken the place of
164 Rock 9 23 have taken the place of thoughts and feelings,/There spring the perfect order of speech,
276 MC Knight1 22 all with the under dog. I respect such feelings, I/share them. Nevertheless, I appeal to
295 FR Charles 14 before morning./I understand these feelings better than you know —/But *you* have no
407 CP Reilly 29 was true enough: you described your feelings —/Or some of them — omitting the
409 CP Reilly 38 /When you had to face the fact that his feelings towards her/Were different from any you
446 CC Claude 11 music./Yes, I think so. I understand his feelings./He's like me, Eggerson. The same
465 CC Colby 32 you've been talking,/That it's my own feelings you have expressed,/Although the
491 CC Colby 26 /For me, who have never known the feelings of a son,/To be disputed between two
516 CC Claude 19 And you described your feelings/On beginning to learn the ways of

FEELS (2)
220 Old Deut 24 disturb/Deuteronomy's rest when he feels so disposed/Or when he's engaged in
330 FR Harry 23 a knowledge of eternity,/Because it feels eternal while it lasts. That is one hell./Then

FEET (52)

22 Preludes	7	scraps/Of withered leaves about your feet/And newspapers from vacant lots;/The
22 Preludes	17	street/With all its muddy feet that press/To early coffee-stands./With the
23 Preludes	37	hair,/Or clasped the yellow soles of feet/In the palms of both soiled hands./His soul
23 Preludes	41	a city block,/Or trampled by insistent feet/At four and five and six o'clock;/And short
29 Aunt Helen	6	drawn and the undertaker wiped his feet —/He was aware that this sort of thing had
40 Burb Blei	11	up the dawn from Istria/With even feet. Her shuttered barge/Burned on the water all
42 Swee Erect	9	the perjured sails./Morning stirs the feet and hands/(Nausicaa and Polypheme)./
43 Swee Erect	42	the bath,/Enters padding on broad feet,/Bringing sal volatile/And a glass of brandy
54 Mr E Sun	14	and thin/Still shine the unoffending feet/And there above the painter set/The Father
62 WL: Burial	65	/And each man fixed his eyes before his feet./Flowed up the hill and down King William
67 WL: Fire S	201	/And on her daughter/They wash their feet in soda water/Et O ces voix d'enfants,
70 WL: Fire S	296	on the floor of a narrow canoe.'/'My feet are at Moorgate, and my heart/Under my
70 WL: Fire S	297	at Moorgate, and my heart/Under my feet. After the event/He wept. He promised "a
72 WL: Thund	337	cannot stop or think/Sweat is dry and feet are in the sand/If there were only water
83 Hollow Men	9	/As wind in dry grass/Or rats' feet over broken glass/In our dry cellar/Shape
103 Journ Magi	28	door dicing for pieces of silver,/And feet kicking the empty wine-skins./But there was
109 Marina	20	laughter between leaves and hurrying feet/Under sleep, where all the waters meet./
116 SP Dusty	33	mind if I ring off now/She's got her feet in mustard and water/I said I'm giving her
142 Cape Ann	7	/Dodging by bay-bush. Follow the feet/Of the walker, the water-thrush. Follow the
155 Rock 3	43	the LORD./Shall we lift up our feet among perpetual ruins?/I have loved the
178 FQ: ECoker	37	or in rustic laughter/Lifting heavy feet in clumsy shoes,/Earth feet, loam feet, lifted
178 FQ: ECoker	38	heavy feet in clumsy shoes,/Earth feet, loam feet, lifted in country mirth/Mirth of
178 FQ: ECoker	38	feet in clumsy shoes,/Earth feet, loam feet, lifted in country mirth/Mirth of those long
178 FQ: ECoker	46	of man and woman/And that of beasts. Feet rising and falling./Eating and drinking.
178 FQ: ECoker	55	heat,/And snowdrops writhing under feet/And hollyhocks that aim too high/Red into
181 FQ: ECoker	164	us everywhere./The chill ascends from feet to knees,/The fever sings in mental wires./If
204 de la Mare	14	Or when the lawn/Is pressed by unseen feet, and ghosts return/Gently at twilight, gently
222 Pekes Pols	20	at each other, and scraped their hind feet,/And started to/Bark bark bark bark/Bark
588 Fable	36	stood outside the door from head to feet./To make a rather lengthy story shorter,/He
588 Fable	59	though now gone out of use —/His feet upon the table superposed/Each wisht he had
599 On a Port	2	/To us of restless brain and weary feet/Forever hurrying, up and down the street,/
604 Ode	7	hopes and ambitions that sprang at thy feet/To the thoughts of the past as we go./Yet for
239 MC Chorus	2	the knowledge of safety, that draws our feet/Towards the cathedral? What danger can be/
239 MC Chorus	7	compelled to witness, has forced our feet/Towards the cathedral. We are forced to bear
243 MC Priest2	2	/The rock of God is beneath our feet. Let us meet the Archbishop with cordial
256 MC Chorus	6	the street./I hear restless movement of feet. And the air is heavy and thick./Thick and
256 MC Chorus	7	And the earth presses up against our feet./What is the sickly smell, the vapour? the
257 MC Chorus	23	none can avoid, flowing under our feet and over the sky;/Under doors and down
257 MC Chorus	32	here./They curl round you, lie at your feet, swing and wing through the dark air./O
271 MC Thomas	22	my life they have been coming, these feet. All my life/I have waited. Death will come
335 FR Agatha	4	flew over./And then I was only my own feet walking/Away, down a concrete corridor/In a
335 FR Agatha	6	a concrete corridor/In a dead air. Only feet walking/And sharp heels scraping. Over and
335 FR Agatha	8	Over and under/Echo and noise of feet./I was only the feet, and the eye/Seeing the
335 FR Agatha	9	/Echo and noise of feet./I was only the feet, and the eye/Seeing the feet: the unwinking
335 FR Agatha	10	only the feet, and the eye/Seeing the feet: the unwinking eye/Fixing the movement.
335 FR Harry	23	breaks./{H} To and fro, dragging my feet/Among inner shadows in the smoky
362 CP Reilly	31	step/There is one step more than your feet expected/And you come down with a jolt.
445 CC Eggers	29	confidential clerk./He was finding his feet, very quickly,/During the time we worked
518 CC Eggers	16	the position, you'd want to find your feet/In Joshua Park, before you settled on
526 ES Monica	9	Charles? It crept so softly/On silent feet, and stood behind my back/Quietly, a long
559 ES Ld Clav	6	the Dominions, might set you on your feet./I have connections, or at least
560 ES Ld Clav	32	be very good for you/To find your feet. But I shouldn't like to think/That what

FELINE (2)

53 Whispers	27	in its arboreal gloom/Distil so rank a feline smell/As Grishkin in a drawing-room./And
226 Macavity	18	one like Macavity,/For he's a fiend in feline shape, a monster of depravity./You may

FELINE'S (1)

221 Old Deut	40	spoken./The digestive repose of that feline's gastronomy/Must never be broken,

FELL (11)

13 Prufrock	22	/Curled once about the house, and fell asleep./And indeed there will be time/For the
40 Burb Blei	4	arrived,/They were together, and he fell./Defunctive music under sea/Passed seaward
71 WL: DWater	316	his bones in whispers. As he rose and fell/He passed the stages of his age and youth/
228 Gus	20	/Was Firefrorefiddle, the Fiend of the Fell.'/'I have played', so he says, 'every possible
228 Gus	31	bell./In the Pantomime season I never fell flat,/And I once understudied Dick
229 Gus	34	/Was Firefrorefiddle, the Fiend of the Fell.'/Then, if someone will give him a toothful of

229 Gus	55	/As Firefrorefiddle, the Fiend of the Fell.'/Bustopher Jones: the Cat About Town/
253 MC Tempt4	28	/Man oppressed by sin, since Adam fell —/You hold the keys of heaven and hell./
376 CP Edward	22	heard of that before./{E} The man who fell among thieves was luckier than I:/He was left
408 CP Reilly	7	suddenly/For the first time in his life, fell in love with someone,/And with someone of
546 ES Piggott	7	distinguished surgeon. Do you know, I fell in love with him/During an appendicitis

FELLED (1)

307 FR Harry	16	was gone,/The tree had been felled, and a neat summer-house/Had been

FELLOW (8)

115 SP Dusty	22	and Sam's a nice boy too./He's a funny fellow/{Do} He *is* a funny fellow/He's like a fellow
115 SP Doris	23	He's a funny fellow/{Do} He *is* a funny fellow/He's like a fellow once I knew./*He* could
115 SP Doris	24	/{Do} He *is* a funny fellow/He's like a fellow once I knew./*He* could make you laugh./
151 Rock 2	2	*his work./*Thus your fathers were made/Fellow citizens of the saints, of the household of
480 CC Kaghan	39	But as for Colby,/He's the sort of fellow who might chuck it all/And go to live on a
530 ES Ld Clav	37	made the Chairman's Price! And my fellow directors/Saying 'we must put our hands in
569 ES Charles	18	what Monica has told me about your fellow guests,/Two persons who, she says, claim a
574 ES Michael	37	/Where everyone would sneer at the fellow from London,/The limey remittance man

FELLOWS (4)

124 SA Swarts	18	a gallon of lysol in a bath/{Sw} These fellows always get pinched in the end./{Sn} Excuse
218 Mung Rump	20	occupation./They were plausible fellows, and liked to engage a friendly policeman
589 Fable	68	as you do surely —/That ghosts are fellows whom you *can't* keep out;/It is a thing to
344 FR Gerald	21	enough —/Some of them very decent fellows. A maligned profession./They're

FELLOWSHIP (2)

304 FR Mary	7	I'd taken your advice/And tried for a fellowship, seven years ago./Now I want your
343 FR Mary	20	it is much too late/Now, to try to get a fellowship?/{A} So you will all leave me!/An old

FELT (34)

30 Cous Nancy	9	her aunts were not quite sure how they felt about it,/But they knew that it was modern./
606 Narcissus	32	horror of his own smoothness,/And he felt drunken and old./So he became a dancer to
269 MC Chorus	31	of putrid flesh in the spoon. I have felt/The heaving of earth at nightfall, restless,
270 MC Chorus	6	kite and cowered with the wren. I have felt/The horn of the beetle, the scale of the viper,
305 FR Mary	2	I knew that Harry had returned/That I felt the strength to go. I know I must go./But
308 FR Harry	31	/And here, indeed! where I have felt them near me,/Here and here and here —
310 FR Harry	36	/Sunlight and singing; when I had felt sure/That every corridor only led to another,/
318 FR Harry	4	I remember. That was why/We all felt like failures, before we had begun./When we
319 FR Harry	7	but in some way or another/We felt that he was always here./But when we would
319 FR Harry	35	now. That night, when she kissed me,/I felt the trap close. If you won't tell me,/I must ask
330 FR Harry	20	is./At the beginning, eight years ago,/I felt, at first, that sense of separation,/Of isolation
330 FR Harry	29	/When I was inside the old dream, I felt all the same emotion/Or lack of emotion, as
331 FR Harry	3	I had no horror of my action,/I only felt the repetition of it/Over and over. When I was
333 FR Agatha	7	that should have been *mine*, as I felt then./Most people would not have felt that
333 FR Agatha	8	felt then./Most people would not have felt that compunction/If they felt no other. But I
333 FR Agatha	9	not have felt that compunction/If they felt no other. But I wanted you!/If that had
333 FR Agatha	12	through lifetime, death in my womb./I felt that you were in some way mine!/And that in
341 FR Amy	37	of success against failure,/When I felt assured of his settlement and happiness,/You
345 FR Charles	36	old:/Old age came softly up to now. I felt safe enough;/And now I don't feel safe. As if
366 CP Peter	35	what's your trouble?/{P} This evening I felt I could bear it no longer./That awful party!
374 CP Celia	10	/It did not seem like you. So I felt I must see you./Tell me it's all right, and then
398 CP Edward	8	/The angel of destruction — just as I felt sure./In a moment, at your touch, there is
403 CP Edward	26	alone again for fifteen minutes/Before I felt, and still more acutely —/Indeed, acutely,
465 CC Claude	23	/And I feel what the man must have felt when he made it./But nothing *I* made ever
465 CC Colby	31	as I do, sometimes./{C} Indeed, I have felt, while you've been talking,/That it's my own
469 CC Lucasta	27	in the season./Though I've always felt out of it. And can you realise/That nobody
472 CC Lucasta	28	You'd convinced yourself;/And you felt that your life had all collapsed/And that you
484 CC Lady E	7	/I understand exactly how you felt./How I disliked my parents! I had a
485 CC Lady E	11	But it goes to show/How different I felt myself to be/And then I took up the Wisdom
516 CC Claude	23	/And the way in which you felt that you were changing?/That conversation
526 ES Monica	11	a long time, a long long time/Before I felt its presence./{C} Your words seem to come/
552 ES Ld Clav	13	my surprise/At finding that I felt nothing at all./I thought, perhaps, what a
552 ES Carghil	18	escape/You thought, for you. You felt no embarrassment?/{LC} Why should I feel
582 ES Monica	33	alone to-day/Only a few minutes, I've felt all the time .../{C} I know what you're going

FEMALE (4)

24 Rhapsody	66	/Smells of chestnuts in the streets,/And female smells in shuttered rooms,/And cigarettes
42 Swee Erect	23	pink from nape to base,/Knows the female temperament/And wipes the suds around
68 WL: Fire S	219	two lives,/Old man with wrinkled female breasts, can see/At the violet hour, the
601 Nocturne	13	forever?' — 'Love next week?')/While female readers all in tears are drowned: —/'The

FERA (1)
51 Restaurant   3   sur mon épaule:/'Dans mon pays il fera temps pluvieux,/Du vent, du grand soleil, et
FERDINAND (1)
41 Burb Blei   28   Lights, lights,/She entertains Sir Ferdinand/Klein. Who clipped the lion's wings/
FERRY (7)
533 ES   Gomez   2   up at Oxford, you were plain Dick Ferry./Then, when you married, you took your
536 ES   Gomez   9   never woken up/To the fact that Dick Ferry died long ago./I married a girl who didn't
546 ES   Monica   15   Claverton./{M} Claverton-Ferry. Or Ferry: it's shorter./{MP} So sorry. Miss
551 ES   Carghil   29   'I advise you to accept','Because Mr. Ferry will be standing for Parliament:/His father
564 ES   Gomez   14   not old enough/To have known Dick Ferry as long as I have./We were friends at
571 ES   Ld Clav   3   and Maisie Batterson,/And Dick Ferry too, and Richard Ferry —/These are my
571 ES   Ld Clav   3   /And Dick Ferry too, and Richard Ferry —/These are my ghosts. They were people
FESTERED (1)
319 FR Warburt   12   /There was enough once: but what festered/Then, has only left a cautery./Leave it
FESTIVITIES (1)
307 FR   Harry   13   the formal reception/And the family festivities, I made my escape/As soon as I could,
FESTIVITY (1)
164 Rock 9   12   good of themselves, ready for any festivity,/Doing themselves very well./Let us
FETCH (2)
398 CP   Lavinia   18   downstairs:/Will you get the porter to fetch it up for me? {}/CURTAIN/Act Two/SIR
556 ES   Ld Clav   7   hope you'll be patient./{LC} Well then, fetch him./Let's get this over. {}/[*calls*]/{M}
FETCHED (1)
422 CP   Reilly   10   has made the choice?/{R} She will be fetched this evening. {}/[NURSE-SECRETARY
FÊTE (1)
47 Mél Adult   16   Omaha./Je célébrai mon jour de fête/Dans une oasis d'Afrique/Vêtu d'une peau de
FETID (1)
92 Ash-Wed 3   4   the banister/Under the vapour in the fetid air/Struggling with the devil of the stairs
FEVER (4)
52 Whispers   16   contact possible to flesh/Allayed the fever of the bone./Grishkin is nice: her Russian
181 FQ: ECoker 153   art/Resolving the enigma of the fever chart./Our only health is the disease/If we
181 FQ: ECoker 165   chill ascends from feet to knees,/The fever sings in mental wires./If to be warmed, then
370 CP   Edward   35   ordinary affair/Like any other. As the fever cooled/You would have found that she was
FEVERED (1)
156 Rock 3   70   bottles,/Turning from your vacancy to fevered enthusiasm/For nation or race or what
FEW (38)
147 Rock 1   22   we have too many churches,/And too few chop-houses. There I was told:/Let the vicars
157 Rock 4   10   rebuild the city./So he went, with a few, to Jerusalem,/And there, by the dragon's
162 Rock 8   11   words./And among his hearers were a few good men,/Many who were evil,/And most
163 Rock 8   34   what was good of it;/Whole faith of a few,/Part faith of many./Not avarice, lechery,
164 Rock 9   6   lowly, whispering faintly,/Among a few flickering scattered lights?/They would put
195 FQ: Little 179   men, and more, on the scaffold/And a few who died forgotten/In other places, here and
590 Time Space   15   pine,/And though our days of love be few/Yet let them be divine./Song/If space and
590 Space Time   15   pine,/And though the flowers of life be few/Yet let them be divine./Standing upon the
276 MC Knight1   18   beg you to give us your attention for a few/moments. We know that you may be
296 FR   Amy   31   right person./I prefer to believe that a few days at Wishwood/Among his own family, is
299 FRDowning   28   bold, Sir,/I always thought that a very few cocktails/Went a long way with her Ladyship.
317 FR Warburt   1   WARBURTON/{W} I'm glad of a few minutes alone with you, Harry./In fact, I had
323 FR Warburt   15   /We'll bring him up tomorrow; and a few days' rest,/I've no doubt, will be all that he
326 FR   Harry   30   I have had to live/Since I came home, a few hours ago, to Wishwood./{V} I will make no
349 FR   5m   13   /*At each revolution they blow out a few candles, so that their last/words are spoken in*
360 CP   Reilly   18   position./There we are. Now for a few questions./How long married?/{E} Five years.
369 CP   Peter   24   to know Celia./{P} I saw her again a few days later/Alone at a concert. And I was
372 CP   Alex   13   /Have I made such a supper out of so few materials/As I found in your refrigerator. But
372 CP   Alex   22   But you'll be grateful./There are very few peasants in Montenegro/Who can have the
377 CP   Edward   37   I'm not at all hungry./I shall have a few biscuits./{J} But you, Celia?/You must come
392 CP   Edward   15   /But I couldn't get everyone. And so a few came./{L} Who came?/{E} Just those who
436 CP   Lavinia   25   she died because she would not leave/A few dying natives./{R} Who knows, Mrs.
469 CC   2m   1   /*Act Two/The flat in the mews a few weeks later.* COLBY *is seated at the piano;*/
487 CC   Claude   5   if you can develop them for me/With a few striking phrases. It should last about ten
506 CC   Eggers   26   help you?/{E} It seems just possible. A few days ago,/As I said, Lady Elizabeth learned
526 ES   Monica   22   in the room/That we entered only a few minutes ago./Here's an armchair, there's the
541 ES   Gomez   7   with me./Of course, I might give it to a few friends, in confidence./It might even reach the
543 ES   m   8   /[LORD CLAVERTON *sits for a few minutes brooding. A knock. Enter* MONICA.]/
544 ES   Ld Clav   21   sunshine/And warmth will last for a few days more./But this early summer, that's
545 ES   Piggott   26   /I've been in such a rush, these last few days,/And I thought, 'Lord Claverton will

553 ES   Carghil   22 me letters?/Oh, not very many. Only a few worth keeping./Only a few. But very
553 ES   Carghil   23   Only a few worth keeping./Only a few. But very beautiful!/It was Effie said, when
553 ES   Carghil   36 letters/To many people?/{MC} Only a few friends./Effie said: 'If he becomes a famous
559 ES   Ld Clav   5 abroad?/Well, that's not a bad idea. A few years out of England/In one of the
560 ES   Ld Clav   31 that. But it's natural enough/To want a few years abroad. It might be very good for you/
565 ES   Ld Clav   33 of escaping! And what a hypocrite!/A few minutes ago I was pleading with Michael/Not
581 ES   Ld Clav   25 love is. We all think we know,/But how few of us do! And now I feel happy —/In spite of
582 ES   Monica   33 though we've been alone to-day/Only a few minutes, I've felt all the time .../{C} I know

FEWER (1)
406 CP   Edward   26 never known anyone in my life/With fewer mental complications than you;/You're

FIAM (1)
 75 WL: Thund   428 *s'ascose nel foco che gli affina/Quando fiam uti chelidon* — O swallow swallow/*Le Prince*

FIANCÉ (3)
453 CC   Kaghan   27 going to be my responsibility,/As your fiancé, to protect Colby from you./But first, let's
453 CC   Lucasta   36   /{L} B., remember you're only my fiancé on approval./Can I have some money,
573 ES   Carghil   27 expression to-day;/This must be your fiancé. Do introduce him./{M} Mr. Charles

FICTION (6)
280 MC   Priest3   33 your action to yourselves,/Weaving a fiction which unravels as you weave,/Pacing
491 CC   Colby   23 neither of you could be. If it was pure fiction —/One can live on a fiction — but not on
491 CC   Colby   24 it was pure fiction —/One can live on a fiction — but not on such a mixture/Of fiction
491 CC   Colby   25 fiction — but not on such a mixture/Of fiction and fact. Already, it's been hard/For me,
514 CC   Claude   26 /Mrs. Guzzard, you are inventing this fiction/In response to what Colby said he wanted.
568 ES   Ld Clav   36 grown/You've woven such a web of fiction about you!/I've spent my life in trying to

FICTITIOUS (1)
403 CP   Reilly   2   state of mind —/Would be largely fictitious; and as for your dreams,/You would

FIDDLE (1)
189 FQ: DrySal   195   the inevitable/With playing cards, fiddle with pentagrams/Or barbituric acids, or

FIDDLED (1)
 73 WL: Thund   378 drew her long black hair out tight/And fiddled whisper music on those strings/And bats

FIDDLES (1)
 94 Ash-Wed 4   13 that walk between, bearing/Away the fiddles and the flutes, restoring/One who moves in

FIDUCIARY (1)
455 CC   Eggers   9 this household?/{E} Well. A kind of fiduciary relationship./No, I don't think that's

FIELD (17)
 28 Boston ET   2   *Transcript*/Sway in the wind like a field of ripe corn./When evening quickens faintly
 37 Gerontion   11   /The goat coughs at night in the field overhead;/Rocks, moss, stonecrop, iron,
 84 Hollow Men   34 coat, crowskin, crossed staves/In a field/Behaving as the wind behaves/No nearer —/
127 Cor1 March   16 guns,/28,000 trench mortars,/53,000 field and heavy guns,/I cannot tell how many
127 Cor1 March   22 /now 55,000 army waggons,/11,000 field kitchens,/1,150 field bakeries./What a time
127 Cor1 March   23 waggons,/11,000 field kitchens,/1,150 field bakeries./What a time that took. Will it be
135 5FingerEx2   1   *to a Yorkshire Terrier*/In a brown field stood a tree/And the tree was crookt and
135 5FingerEx2   8 /Under a cretonne eiderdown,/Yet the field was cracked and brown/And the tree was
150 Rock 1   113 *not build/How shall they live?/When the field is tilled/And the wheat is bread/They shall not*
177 FQ: ECoker   4 restored, or in their place/Is an open field, or a factory, or a by-pass./Old stone to new
177 FQ: ECoker   15 Now the light falls/Across the open field, leaving the deep lane/Shuttered with
177 FQ: ECoker   24 /Wait for the early owl./In that open field/If you do not come too close, if you do not
188 FQ: DrySal   170 as when he admonished Arjuna/On the field of battle./Not fare well,/But fare forward,
195 FQ: Little   162   /Begins as attachment to our own field of action/And comes to find that action of
218 Mung Rump   8 ajar/And the basement looked like a field of war,/If a tile or two came loose on the
252 MC Thomas   17 door./Not only in the court, but in the field/And in the tilt-yard I made many yield./Shall
263 MC Chorus   8 in the East./The starved crow sits in the field, attentive; and in the wood/The owl

FIELD-MOUSE (1)
177 FQ: ECoker   12 /And to shake the wainscot where the field-mouse trots/And to shake the tattered arras

FIELDS (2)
135 5FingerEx1   2 songsters of the air repair/To the green fields of Russell Square./Beneath the trees there is
149 Rock 1   100 *Only the wind moves/Over empty fields, untilled/Where the plough rests, at an angle/*

FIEND (6)
226 Macavity   18   no one like Macavity,/For he's a fiend in feline shape, a monster of depravity./You
228 Gus   20 loves to tell,/Was Firefrorefiddle, the Fiend of the Fell./'I have played', so he says,
229 Gus   34 will tell,/Was Firefrorefiddle, the Fiend of the Fell.'/Then, if someone will give him
229 Gus   55 I made history/As Firefrorefiddle, the Fiend of the Fell.'/Bustopher Jones: the Cat
587 Fable   27 from ghosts and phantoms free,/The fiend must stay at home — no ghosts allowed/At
253 MC Tempt4   17 /Jealousy raging possession of the fiend./Barons are employable against each other;/

FIERCE (1)
213 Growltiger   41 /Then GILBERT gave the signal to his fierce Mongolian horde;/With a frightful burst of

FIERCER (1)
223 Pekes Pols   55   of the area,/You never saw anything fiercer or hairier./And what with the glare of his
FIERY (1)
65 WL: Chess   109 under the brush, her hair/Spread out in fiery points/Glowed into words, then would be
FIFTEEN (1)
403 CP Edward   25 into./We had not been alone again for fifteen minutes/Before I felt, and still more acutely
FIFTY (1)
538 ES   Gomez   35 were given a ministry before you were fifty:/That should have led you to the very top!/
FIG'S (1)
92 Ash-Wed 3   13 /Was a slotted window bellied like the fig's fruit/And beyond the hawthorn blossom and
FIGHT (15)
152 Rock 2   34   /And all that was good you must fight to keep with hearts as devoted as those of
182 FQ: ECoker 188 is no competition —/There is only the fight to recover what has been lost/And found
201 Def Island   12   newest form of gamble/with death, fight the power of darkness in air/and of
234 Ad-dress   20 DOG./Now Dogs pretend they like to fight;/They often bark, more seldom bite;/But yet
251 MC Tempt3 39   of Pope powerful protection/In the fight for liberty. You, my Lord,/In being with us,
251 MC Tempt3 40 You, my Lord,/In being with us, would fight a good stroke/At once, for England and for
256 MC Priests 24   /{3P} O Thomas my Lord do not fight the intractable tide,/Do not sail the
274 MC Thomas   9 by stratagem, or by resistance,/Not to fight with beasts as men. We have fought the
304 FR Agatha 36 frightened of the family,/She wanted to fight them — with the weapons of the weak,/
312 FR   Harry   7 no use to me. I must face them./I must fight them. But they are stupid./How can one
312 FR   Harry   8   But they are stupid./How can one fight with stupidity?/Yet I must speak to them. {}/
331 FR Agatha 21 me. I know that much./{Ag} I had to fight for many years to win my dispossession,/
343 FR   Amy 25 the endless weather,/Resist the wind? fight with increasing taxes/And unpaid rents and
395 CP Edward 38 only one difference, perhaps — we can fight each other,/Instead of each taking his corner
463 CC   Colby 32 one thing/That I want to do. I have to fight that person./{SC} I understand what you are
FIGHTERS (1)
223 Pekes Pols   35   /And every dog-jack of them notable fighters;/And so they stepped out, with their
FIGHTING (3)
222 Pekes Pols   5 most people say/That they do not like fighting, yet once in a way,/Or now and again,
251 MC Tempt3 26   Let the Angevin/Destroy himself, fighting in Anjou./He does not understand us, the
274 MC Thomas   8 door!/We are not here to triumph by fighting, by stratagem, or by resistance,/Not to
FIGHTS (1)
178 FQ: ECoker 62   in constellated wars/Scorpion fights against the Sun/Until the Sun and Moon go
FIGLIA (2)
34 Figlia   t /And — 'Are we then so serious?'/La Figlia Che Piange/Stand on the highest pavement
189 FQ: DrySal 181   /Setting forth, and not returning:/Figlia del tuo figlio,/Queen of Heaven./Also pray
FIGLIO (1)
189 FQ: DrySal 181 forth, and not returning:/Figlia del tuo figlio,/Queen of Heaven./Also pray for those who
FIGS (1)
56 Swee Night   20 /The waiter brings in oranges/Bananas figs and hothouse grapes;/The silent vertebrate in
FIGURE (7)
31 Apollinax   3   /I thought of Fragilion, that shy figure among the birch-trees,/And of Priapus in
92 Ash-Wed 3   15 and a pasture scene/The broadbacked figure drest in blue and green/Enchanted the
175 FQ: BurntN 163 of the pattern is movement,/As in the figure of the ten stairs./Desire itself is movement/
261 MC Thomas 14   of Our Lord; so also, in a smaller figure, we/both rejoice and mourn in the death of
271 MC Thomas 13 with a sudden painful joy/When the figure of God's purpose is made complete./You
384 CP Edward 24 the dead./{E} From the dead?/That figure of speech is somewhat ... dramatic,/As it
563 ES   Carghil   2   How interesting! He's a very good figure/And he's rather exotic-looking. Is he a
FIGURED (4)
172 FQ: BurntN 56   /The circulation of the lymph/Are figured in the drift of stars/Ascend to summer in
172 FQ: BurntN 59   the moving tree/In light upon the figured leaf/And hear upon the sodden floor/
192 FQ: Little   35 /Or the purpose is beyond the end you figured/And is altered in fulfilment. There are
553 ES Carghil 26   to you, Maisie.'/They would have figured at the trial, I suppose,/If there had been a
FIGUREHEAD (1)
539 ES   Gomez   1 the part —/Cut out to be an impressive figurehead./But again, you've retired at sixty.
FIGURES (4)
397 CP Edward   5 Hell is oneself,/Hell is alone, the other figures in it/Merely projections. There is nothing
468 CC   Colby   1   You asked me to prepare/Some figures for you. I've got them here./{SC} Much
468 CC   Claude   3 that meeting. We must run through the figures. {}/CURTAIN/Act Two/*The flat in the*
511 CC   Lady E 12 a financier?/{LE} He was not good at figures. Your business ability/Comes, I suppose,
FIGUREZ (1)
51 Restaurant   30   aux étapes de sa vie antérieure./Figurez-vous donc, c'était un sort pénible;/

FILE (2)

226 Macavity		22	And his footprints are not found in any file of Scotland Yard's./And when the larder's
349 FR	4m	13	/and MARY *walk slowly in single file round and round the table, clockwise.*/At each

FILED (1)

452 CC Lucasta	22	find one of them./But they're all filed somewhere, I'm sure, so why bother?/But

FILING (1)

452 CC Lucasta	16	injustice./Two months I'd gone on filing those papers/Which no one ever wanted —

FILL (4)

588 Fable	47	bird and beast in Æsop's fable/To fill out their repast, and pies and puddings,/And
530 ES Monica	5	empty pages?/{M} You would soon fill them up if we allowed you to!/That's my
530 ES Ld Clav	19	/A fear of the vacuum, and no desire to fill it./It's just like sitting in an empty waiting
575 ES Michael	9	came to London to find a man to fill it,/And he thinks I'm just the man./{G} Yes,

FILLE (1)

46 Directeur	15	pas de loup./Dans un égout/Une petite fille/En guenilles/Camarde/Regarde/Le

FILLED (10)

64 WL: Chess	101	rudely forced; yet there the nightingale/Filled all the desert with inviolable voice/And still
83 Hollow Men	4	men/Leaning together/Headpiece filled with straw. Alas!/Our dried voices, when/
151 Rock 2	6	for alms to be more or the urn to be filled./Your building not fitly framed together,
154 Rock 3	19	plaster, with corrugated roofing,/To be filled with a litter of Sunday newspapers?/1ST
172 FQ: BurntN	37	brown edged,/And the pool was filled with water out of sunlight,/And the lotos
174 FQ: BurntN	105	from distraction by distraction/Filled with fancies and empty of meaning/Tumid
178 FQ: ECoker	58	into grey and tumble down/Late roses filled with early snow?/Thunder rolled by the
246 MC Thomas	4	/Would have intercepted our letters,/Filled the coast with spies and sent to meet me/
490 CC Colby	21	a child,/There's a gap that never can be filled. Never./I like you both, I could even come
531 ES Ld Clav	25	who really understand the place we filled/Are inwardly delighted. They won't want

FILLED-UP (1)

316 FR Agatha	15	/May the crossed bones/In the filled-up well/Be at last straightened/May the

FILLING (1)

407 CP Edward	2	told me so often./I'd like to see *you* filling up an income-tax form./{L} Don't be silly,

FILM (13)

356 CP	Celia	5	were doing in California./{C} Making a film./{P} Trying to make a film./{J} Oh, what film
356 CP	Peter	6	Making a film./{P} Trying to make a film./{J} Oh, what film was it? I wonder if I've
356 CP	Julia	7	{P} Trying to make a film./{J} Oh, what film was it? I wonder if I've seen it./{P} No, you
356 CP	Peter	9	fact/It was never produced. They did a film/But they used a different scenario./{J} Not
367 CP	Peter	22	/Celia was interested in the art of the film./{E} As a possible profession?/{P} She might
370 CP	Peter	21	— into some other picture —/Like a film effect. She doesn't want to see me;/Makes
431 CP	Peter	16	do him a good turn./We're making a film of English life/And we want to use Boltwell./
431 CP	Peter	28	dear no! I've written the script of this film,/And Bela is very pleased with it./He thought
432 CP	Julia	35	very important in films./He's making a film of English life/And he's going to find parts
433 CP	Peter	1	I can't find parts for anybody/In *this* film — it's not my business;/And that's not the
433 CP	Peter	20	director./I've got an idea for another film./Can you tell me where she is? I couldn't find
435 CP	Peter	22	/And here I am, making a second-rate film!/But I thought it was going to lead to
439 CP	Alex	20	/And what else can I do?/{A} It is your film./And I know that Bela expects great things of

FILMS (3)

432 CP	Julia	34	he's something very important in films./He's making a film of English life/And he's
433 CP	Peter	14	about,/Who did really want to get into films,/And I always thought she could make a
436 CP	Julia	15	you look at them with an eye for the films:/That is, when you're not concerned with

FILTH (1)

276 MC Chorus	14	of evil and wrong./We are soiled by a filth that we cannot clean, united to supernatural

FILTHINESS (2)

327 FR	Harry	21	with the horror./What matters is the filthiness. I can clean my skin,/Purify my life, void
327 FR	Harry	23	my life, void my mind,/But always the filthiness, that lies a little deeper ... {}/[*Enter* IVY]/

FILTHY (2)

280 MC Priest3	26	with the heathen Saracen,/To share his filthy rites, and try to snatch/Forgetfulness in his
347 FR Warburt	32	WARBURTON]/{W} Well! it's a filthy night to be out in./That's why I've been so

FINAL (13)

62 WL: Burial	68	the hours/With a dead sound on the final stroke of nine./There I saw one I knew, and
69 WL: Fire S	247	the lowest of the dead.)/Bestows one final patronising kiss,/And gropes his way,
84 Hollow Men	37	wind behaves/No nearer —/Not that final meeting/In the twilight kingdom/This is the
186 FQ: DrySal	63	the fittest for renunciation./There is the final addition, the failing/Pride or resentment at
244 MC Chorus	24	an onion, our selves are lost lost/In a final fear which none understands. O Thomas
256 MC Tempts	21	/From grandeur to grandeur to final illusion,/Lost in the wonder of his own
271 MC Chorus	4	by the lust of self-demolition,/By the final utter uttermost death of spirit,/By the final
271 MC Chorus	5	utter uttermost death of spirit,/By the final ecstasy of waste and shame,/O Lord
273 MC Chorus	8	I am, to dust am bending,/From the final doom impending/Help me, Lord, for death is

335 FR	Harry	31	is cleared, under the judicial sun/Of the final eye, and the awful evacuation/Cleanses./I
383 CP	Edward	16	/Well, I hoped that you would drink a final glass with me./{C} What should we drink to?
419 CP	Reilly	3	and communion./Both ways avoid the final desolation/Of solitude in the phantasmal
581 ES	Ld Clav	8	me say to him/That this might be a final good-bye./I am sure of it now. Perhaps it is

FINALLY (6)

32 Hysteria		4	at each momentary/recovery, lost finally in the dark caverns of her throat, bruised
235 Ad-dress		67	so in time you reach your aim,/And finally call him by his NAME./So this is this, and
393 CP	Lavinia	22	other place first?/And I remember that finally in desperation/I said: 'I suppose you'd as
448 CC	Claude	22	/She will only learn that you have finally retired/And that you have a young
484 CC	Lady E	36	was feeble-minded/And didn't know it. Finally,/That I was a foundling, and didn't know
533 ES	Gomez	5	Mr. Richard Claverton-Ferry;/And finally, Lord Claverton. I've followed your

FINANCIAL (4)

453 CC	Kaghan	28	from you./But first, let's cope with the financial crisis./{L} Yes, Eggy, will you break the
495 CC	Lady E	10	were not interested/In anything but financial affairs;/And that you needed me chiefly
539 ES	Gomez	14	you're the great economist/And financial wizard that you're supposed to be./And
541 ES	Gomez	37	unwelcome intrusion/Of the visitor in financial distress./Well, I shan't keep you long,

FINANCIER (4)

463 CC	Claude	37	/{SC} Yes, I did not want to be a financier./{C} What did you want to do?/{SC}
481 CC	Kaghan	5	for business./Maybe you're a better financier than I am!/That's why we ought to be in
494 CC	Claude	23	that, by force of will. He was a great financier —/And I am merely a successful one./I
511 CC	Kaghan	11	/{K} But what did he do? Was he a financier?/{LE} He was not good at figures. Your

FINANCIERS (1)

495 CC	Lady E	23	that poets don't look like poets:/And financiers, it seems, don't look like potters —/Is

FINCH (1)

281 MC	Chorus	12	bird in the air, both the hawk and the finch; the beast on the earth, both the wolf and

FINCHES (1)

136 5FingerEx4		16	has 999 canaries/And round his head finches and fairies/In jubilant rapture skim./How

FIND (151)

18 Portrait		20	And how, how rare and strange it is, to find/In a life composed so much, so much of odds
18 Portrait		24	are not blind!/How keen you are!)/To find a friend who has these qualities,/Who has,
19 Portrait		54	/I feel immeasurably at peace, and find the world/To be wonderful and youthful,
20 Portrait		91	when you are coming back,/You will find so much to learn.'/My smile falls heavily
21 Portrait		110	must borrow every changing shape/To find expression ... dance, dance/Like a dancing
34 Figlia		13	deserts the body it has used./I should find/Some way incomparably light and deft,/
43 Swee Erect		34	at her sides./The ladies of the corridor/Find themselves involved, disgraced,/Call witness
62 WL: Burial		54	/Which I am forbidden to see. I do not find/The Hanged Man. Fear death by water./I see
140 Usk		2	suddenly break the branch, or/Hope to find/The white hart behind the white well./Glance
149 Rock 1		67	/What has been done of good, you find explanations/To satisfy the rational and
166 Rock 10		16	light/Enough to take your step and find your foothold./O Light Invisible, we praise
171 FQ: BurntN		21	Shall we follow?/Quick, said the bird, find them, find them,/Round the corner. Through
171 FQ: BurntN		21	follow?/Quick, said the bird, find them, find them,/Round the corner. Through the first
191 FQ: Little		24	came this way in may time, you would find the hedges/White again, in May, with
194 FQ: Little	125		become much like each other,/So I find words I never thought to speak/In streets I
195 FQ: Little	163		our own field of action/And comes to find that action of little importance/Though never
210 Old Gumbie		14	/Her equal would be hard to find, she likes the warm and sunny spots./All day
218 Mung Rump		12	the bedroom chests,/And you couldn't find one of your winter vests,/Or after supper one
225 Mr Mistoff		36	and then it is *gawn*!/But you'll find it next week lying out on the lawn./And we
226 Macavity		27	*there*!/And when the Foreign Office find a Treaty's gone astray,/Or the Admiralty lose
227 Macavity		33	but he's a mile away./You'll be sure to find him resting, or a-licking of his thumbs,/Or
232 Skimble		4	he gone to hunt the thimble?/We must find him or the train can't start.'/All the guards
234 Ad-dress		7	and me/And other people whom we find/Possessed of various types of mind./For
236 Cat Morgan		3	com-mission-aire:/And that's how you find me a-takin' my ease/And keepin' the door in
594 Grad 10		1	/We shall return; and it will be to find/A different school from that which now we
594 Grad 10		5	/The same school in the future shall we find/As this from which as pupils now we go./We
245 MC	Priest2	34	to a better climate./Your Lordship will find your rooms in order as you left them./{T}
245 MC	Thomas	35	And will try to leave them in order as I find them./I am more than grateful for all your
246 MC	Templ	27	/Hoping that your present gravity/Will find excuse for my humble levity/Remembering
248 MC	Templ	6	/Hoping that your present gravity/Will find excuse for my humble levity./If you will
255 MC	Templ4	1	that you lacked/Will only try to find the historical fact./When men shall declare
256 MC	Priests	27	coming of day, when the traveller may find his way,/The sailor lay course by the sun? {}/
258 MC	Thomas	18	when early force is spent/And when we find no longer all things possible./Ambition
265 MC	Knight3	32	have no need of his hospitality./We will find our own dinner. {}/[*to attendant*]./{P1} Go,
266 MC	Thomas	5	of other urgency./On my table you will find/The papers in order, and the documents
272 MC	Thomas	4	me at your prayers./They shall find the shepherd here; the flock shall be spared./I
280 MC	Priest1	6	gone from us, lost to us,/How shall we find you, from what far place/Do you look down

280 MC	Priest3	24	numb the hand, makes dull the brain;/Find an oasis in the desert sun,/Go seek alliance
287 FR	Amy	33	meaning in death/Which I cannot find./— I am only certain of Arthur and John,/
288 FR	Agatha	27	back through the little door./He will find a new Wishwood. Adaptation is hard./{A}
288 FR	Agatha	33	Yes. I mean that at Wishwood he will find another Harry./The man who returns will
290 FR	Chorus	38	in a dream when the curtain rises, to find themselves dressed for a different play, or
292 FR	Amy	20	I am sure you must be tired./You will find everybody here, and everything the same./
292 FR	Gerald	28	We must have a ride tomorrow./You'll find you know the country as well as ever./There
292 FR	Ivy	33	attention./{I} And you'll really have to find a successor to old Hawkins./It's really high
295 FR	Harry	1	true in a different sense./I expected to find her when I went back to the cabin./Later, I
297 FR	Charles	35	are employing./{C} My purpose is, to find out what's wrong with Harry:/Until we know
305 FR	Harry	30	was changed,/But if so, I can't find it./{M} Your mother insisted/On everything
307 FR	Harry	15	and slipped down to the river/To find the old hiding place. The wilderness was
307 FR	Mary	23	which did not touch me./Just now, I find them very difficult to bear./They are always
308 FR	Harry	19	/Now that I am here I know I shall not find it./The instinct to return to the point of
314 FR	Warburt	29	or another:/We call it health when we find no symptom/Of illness. Health is a relative
318 FR	Harry	32	that I am talking/And shall wake to find that I have been silent/Or talked to the stone
321 FR	Winch	35	Thank you, no, my Lord;/I don't find port agrees with the rheumatism./{W} For
331 FR	Harry	9	But *they* prevent it./I still have to find out what their meaning is./Here I have been
331 FR	Harry	26	know, I know that in some way I shall find/That I have always known it. And that will
333 FR	Agatha	32	birth, to come to consciousness/And so find expurgation. It is possible/You are the
334 FR	Harry	26	imposed upon me;/And I returned to find another one made ready —/The book laid
348 FR	Chorus	7	/We do not like to climb a stair, and find that it takes us down./We do not like to walk
348 FR	Chorus	8	do not like to walk out of a door, and find ourselves back in the same room./We do not
355 CP	Julia	11	North. How he suffered!/They had to find an island for him/Where there were no bats./
363 CP	Reilly	23	/{UG} It will do you no harm to find yourself ridiculous./Resign yourself to be the
363 CP	Reilly	35	/{UG} All to the good./You will find that you survive humiliation./And that's an
364 CP	Edward	6	her back./And I *must* get her back, to find out what has happened/During the five years
364 CP	Edward	8	years that we've been married./I must find out who she is, to find out who I am./And
364 CP	Edward	8	married./I must find out who she is, to find out who I am./And what is the use of all
364 CP	Julia	31	PETER]/{J} Edward, I'm so glad to find you./Do you know, I must have left my
369 CP	Alex	10	there one in every kitchen?/{A} I can't find it./There goes *that* surprise. I must think of
369 CP	Peter	31	as a name/In a society column, to find her there alone./Anyway, we got into
370 CP	Alex	14	*and an apron*]/{A} Edward, I can't find any curry powder./{E} There isn't any curry
370 CP	Alex	17	then. I must think./I didn't expect to find any mangoes,/But I *did* count upon curry
371 CP	Peter	30	/I can bear any future. But I must find out/The truth about the past, for the sake of
372 CP	Alex	15	But of course/I was lucky to find half-a-dozen eggs./{E} What! You used all
379 CP	Celia	37	my own dream/All the while; and to find I wanted/This world as well as that ... well,
380 CP	Celia	5	most women/Would feel degraded to find that a man/With whom they thought they
385 CP	Reilly	17	/After the first ten minutes? You would find it difficult/To treat them as strangers, but
388 CP	Peter	16	{P} It's nice of you to say so;/But you'll find someone better, to go about with./{C} I don't
388 CP	Lavinia	23	Celia. Well, Peter../I didn't expect to find either of you here./{P&C} But the telegram!/
391 CP	Alex	25	/{A} I think not, Julia. She must find out for herself:/That's the only way./{J} How
395 CP	Lavinia	6	mind./{L} That will be a novelty/To find that you have a mind to speak./Anyway, I'm
395 CP	Lavinia	29	never mind, you'll soon get over it/And find yourself another little part to play,/With
396 CP	Lavinia	28	a ghost to you,/You might be able to find the road back/To a time when you were real
397 CP	Edward	30	had to unwrap everything again/To find what you wanted. And I never could teach
397 CP	Edward	37	made it clear/That in future you will find me a different person?/{L} Indeed. And has
401 CP	Reilly	22	would be there, and whom I should find with you./{E} But you had seen my wife?/{R}
401 CP	Reilly	29	as well sit down./I think that you will find that chair comfortable./{E} You knew,/
402 CP	Reilly	31	the worst place possible./We must first find out what is wrong with you/Before we decide
402 CP	Reilly	39	situation./And then go back as far as I find necessary./You see, your memories of
410 CP	Reilly	35	/That is what he means./{R} When you find, Mr. Chamberlayne,/The best of a bad job is
413 CP	Reilly	35	to get back to normality./{R} We must find out about you, before we decide/What *is*
414 CP	Celia	36	— but the only word for it/That I can find, is a sense of sin./{R} You suffer from a sense
414 CP	Reilly	40	to *me* abnormal./{R} We have yet to find what would be normal/For *you*, before we
415 CP	Celia	35	make one feel sinful!/And yet I can't find any other word for it./It must be some kind
416 CP	Celia	36	way out of the forest./{C} But even if I find my way out of the forest/I shall be left with
416 CP	Celia	38	Of the treasure I went into the forest to find/And never found, and which was not there/
417 CP	Celia	17	/Of a craving for something I cannot find/And of the shame of never finding it./Can
424 CP	Lavinia	7	anything you need/That you can't find in the kitchen?/{CM} Nothing, Madam./Will
432 CP	Julia	36	a film of English life/And he's going to find parts for all of us. Think of it!/{P} But, Julia,
432 CP	Peter	38	about to explain —/I'm afraid I can't find parts for anybody/In *this* film — it's not my
433 CP	Peter	21	you tell me where she is? I couldn't find her/In the telephone directory./{J} Not in the
436 CP	Edward	2	This is where you start from./If you find out now, Peter, things about yourself/That
446 CC	Claude	16	... no matter./The great thing was to find something else/He could do, and do well.

446 CC	Claude	27	then it must be furnished./I'm trying to find him a really good piano./{E} A piano? Yes,
446 CC	Eggers	39	/And I'm sure Mr. Simpkins will find them if anybody./{SC} Well, we'll leave that
452 CC	Kaghan	2	Colby!/And hello Eggers! I'm glad to find you here./It's lucky for Colby./{E} How so
452 CC	Lucasta	19	boss did want a letter/And I couldn't find it. And then he got suspicious/And asked for
452 CC	Lucasta	21	/Just to make trouble! And I couldn't find one of them./But they're all filed somewhere,
457 CC	Eggers	10	best of everyone./{E} You'll come to find that I'm right, I assure you. {}/[*Enter* SIR
460 CC	Lady E	12	/{LE} But Claude, I'm glad to find/That you've taken my advice./{SC} Your
461 CC	Eggers	5	*should* turn up unexpected/And you find yourself non-plussed, you must get me on the
462 CC	Claude	27	do you like your work? You don't find it uncongenial?/I'm not changing the subject:
462 CC	Claude	31	business,/Thinking that you might find it easier/To start by a rather formal
463 CC	Claude	10	found this work./{SC} Yes, how do you find it?/{C} In a way, exhilarating./To find there is
463 CC	Colby	12	find it?/{C} In a way, exhilarating./To find there is something that I can do/So remote
466 CC	Claude	19	people —/I've never known any — can find some unity./Then there are also the men of
469 CC	Colby	7	at first/Is to hear more music. And to find out what you like./When you know what you
470 CC	Lucasta	9	never become a musician./{L} Did you find it a strain, then, playing to me?/{C} As a
473 CC	Colby	6	secret garden/Somewhere, if you could find it?/{L} If I could find it!/No, my only garden
473 CC	Lucasta	7	if you could find it?/{L} If I could find it!/No, my only garden is ... a dirty public
474 CC	Lucasta	25	would be broken./And you would find yourself in a devastated area —/A bomb-site
475 CC	Colby	23	world/To me, you know, in which I find myself./But if you mean, wondered about
478 CC	Kaghan	37	And here's Lucasta./I knew I should find she'd got in first!/Trust Kaghan's intuitions!
483 CC	Colby	5	number,/And I don't know where to find them./{LE} They can be found./But I came to
492 CC	Claude	14	more tonight. Now, Colby,/Can you find some consolation at the piano?/{C} I don't
498 CC	Lady E	27	be what happened. And now we must find out/What became of your child, Claude./
508 CC	Eggers	5	who has been hoping against hope/To find her son. Put yourself in her position./If you
512 CC	Guzzard	27	Barnabas Kaghan,/Are you satisfied to find yourself the son/Of Lady Elizabeth
518 CC	Eggers	5	as an organist./I think you'll come to find you've another vocation./We worked
518 CC	Eggers	16	If you took the position, you'd want to find your feet/In Joshua Park, before you settled
529 ES	Ld Clav	33	/I could look in the right book, and find out what I was doing/Twenty years ago,
534 ES	Gomez	13	of morality/As the society in which I find myself./I do nothing in England that you
534 ES	Gomez	32	/The ones who don't get out in time/Find themselves in gaol and not very comfortable,
539 ES	Ld Clav	25	altogether accurate./The only thing I find surprising/In the respected citizen of San
545 ES	Ld Clav	3	myself/Has impelled me all my life to find justification/Not so much to the world —
545 ES	Monica	10	{M} You admit that at the moment you find life pleasant,/That it really does seem quiet
548 ES	Carghil	17	discovered it./It was clever of you to find it so quickly./What made you choose it? {}/
550 ES	Carghil	36	woman who trusted *him* would soon find that out'./A man may prefer to forget all the
554 ES	Carghil	25	cure,/And it struck me that he might find it a strain/To have to cope with both of us at
557 ES	Michael	13	stimulating./{LC} Well?/{Mi} I want to find some more speculative business./{LC} I dare
560 ES	Michael	8	how very much pleasanter/You will find life become, once I'm out of the country./
560 ES	Ld Clav	17	make a start in any business/You may find for yourself — if, on investigation,/I am
560 ES	Ld Clav	32	It might be very good for you/To find your feet. But I shouldn't like to think/That
561 ES	Ld Clav	9	of success and grandeur,/You will find your past failures waiting there to greet you./
562 ES	Carghil	14	read of your letters;/But how nice to find a little family party!/I know who you are!
567 ES	Monica	4	/It was exasperating that they couldn't find me/When you telephoned this morning. That
569 ES	Ld Clav	10	those pretences,/But I hope that you'll find a little love in your heart/Still, for your
574 ES	Carghil	17	new start. He wants to go abroad!/And find his own way in the world. That's very
575 ES	Michael	9	me./Señor Gomez came to London to find a man to fill it,/And he thinks I'm just the
576 ES	Ld Clav	14	/The position which he'd come to find the man for./{Mi} I don't care about that.
582 ES	Ld Clav	5	begin to live./It is worth while dying, to find out what life is./And I love you, my
583 ES	Charles	13	speak to you now./{C} Let me go and find him./{M} We will go to him together. He is

FINDING (18)

69 WL	Fire S	248	patronising kiss,/And gropes his way, finding the stairs unlit .../She turns and looks a
103 Journ	Magi	31	at evening, not a moment too soon/Finding the place; it was (you may say)
160 Rock 7		3	the wind: driven this way and that, and finding no place of lodgement and germination./
162 Rock 8		23	well broken,/Diseased and beggared, finding/A stranger at the door in possession:/
167 Rock 10		43	who hast moved us to building, to finding, to forming at the ends of our fingers and
331 FR	Harry	10	their meaning is./Here I have been finding/A misery long forgotten, and a new
361 CP	Reilly	37	beginning to enjoy your independence;/Finding your life becoming cosier and cosier/
363 CP	Reilly	10	/{E} To what does this lead?/{UG} To finding out/What you really are. What you really
393 CP	Lavinia	5	/{L} Yes, a very important discovery,/Finding that you've spent five years of your life/
414 CP	Celia	10	of one relationship,/Not even simply finding that it never existed —/But a revelation
416 CP	Reilly	35	may be already a clue/Towards finding your own way out of the forest./{C} But
417 CP	Celia	18	cannot find/And of the shame of never finding it./Can you cure me?/{R} The condition is
445 CC	Eggers	29	/To be your confidential clerk./He was finding his feet, very quickly,/During the time we
508 CC	Eggers	8	at any straw/That offered hope of finding him?/{MG} Perhaps I should./{LE} There
509 CC	Colby	14	Don't you remember, Aunt Sarah,/My finding a rattle and a jingle-bell,/And your telling

516 CC   Claude   21   ways of business;/The exhilaration of finding you could handle/Matters you would have
550 ES   Ld Clav   32   you should take the first opportunity,/Finding me here, to revive old memories/Which I
552 ES   Ld Clav   13   at all. I remember my surprise/At finding that I felt nothing at all./I thought,
FINDS (6)
210 Old Gumbie   19   Cat's work is but hardly begun./As she finds that the mice will not ever keep quiet,/She is
214 RTTugger   28   and sneers,/For he only likes what he finds for himself;/So you'll catch him in it right up
410 CP   Reilly   8   The same isolation./A man who finds himself incapable of loving/And a woman
410 CP   Reilly   9   incapable of loving/And a woman who finds that no man can love her./{L} It seems to me
472 CC   Lucasta   13   one gets to know a person better/One finds them in some ways very like oneself,/In
562 ES   Monica   1   the love within which/All other love finds speech./This love is silent./What can I say to
FINE (4)
119 SP   Klip   30   uh — London's swell./We like London fine./{Kr} Perfectly slick./{Du} Why don't you
120 SP   Klip   6   London's a swell place,/London's a fine place to come on a visit —/{Kr} Specially
136 5FingerEx4   11   something apart)/While on his palate fine he presses/The juice of the gooseberry tart./
588 Fable   58   Christmas wassail the monks dozed,/A fine old drink, though now gone out of use —/His
FINED (1)
328 FR   Charles   15   on the morning of January 1st, was/fined £50 and costs to-day, and forbidden to drive
FINGER (1)
136 5FingerEx3   10   is their mortal due,/Pinching bread and finger too,/Easier had than squirming worm;/For
FINGER-NAILS (1)
258 MC Thomas   24   nobility, whose manners matched their finger-nails./While I ate out of the King's dish/To
FINGER-TIPS (1)
18 Portrait   9   the Preludes, through his hair and finger-tips./'So intimate, this Chopin, that I think
FINGERING (1)
529 ES   Ld Clav   37   tea,/It's the empty pages that I've been fingering —/The first empty pages since I entered
FINGERNAILS (2)
70 WL: Fire S   303   /Nothing with nothing./The broken fingernails of dirty hands./My people humble
159 Rock 6   15   and retiring;/Women! polish your fingernails:/You polish the tooth of the dog and
FINGERS (13)
15 Prufrock   76   sleeps so peacefully!/Smoothed by long fingers,/Asleep ... tired ... or it malingers,/
19 Portrait   43   lilacs in her room/And twists one in her fingers while she talks./'Ah, my friend, you do not
23 Preludes   43   five and six o'clock;/And short square fingers stuffing pipes,/And evening newspapers,
31 Apollinax   12   in the green silence,/Dropping from fingers of surf./I looked for the head of Mr.
67 WL: Fire S   173   /The river's tent is broken; the last fingers of leaf/Clutch and sink into the wet bank.
167 Rock 10   43   finding, to forming at the ends of our fingers and beams of our eyes./And when we have
175 FQ: BurntN 136   and spray/Clutch and cling?/Chill/Fingers of yew be curled/Down on us? After the
189 FQ: DrySal 193   wrinkles of the palm/And tragedy from fingers; release omens/By sortilege, or tea leaves,
596 When we   3   were fallen from the trees;/The gentle fingers of the breeze/Had torn no quivering
605 Narcissus   15   hands aware of the pointed tips of his fingers./Struck down by such knowledge/He
605 Narcissus   25   white belly held tight in his own fingers,/Writhing in his own clutch, his ancient
272 MC Chorus 15   more horror/Than when twisting in the fingers,/Than when splitting in the skull./More
459 CC   m   6   Colby Simpkins. {}/[*counting on her fingers*]./{LE} Thirteen letters. That's very
FINISH (2)
315 FR   Amy   24   in to dinner./They may come before we finish. Will you take me in, Doctor?/I think we
359 CP   Edward   8   /{E} Don't go yet./Don't go yet. We'll finish the cocktails./Or would you rather have
FINISHED (6)
142 Cape Ann   13   tough one, the sea-gull./The palaver is finished./Lines for an Old Man/The tiger in the
188 FQ: DrySal 146   you,/You shall not think 'the past is finished'/Or 'the future is before us'./At nightfall,
235 Ad-dress   62   nothing else but rabbit,/And when he's finished, licks his paws/So's not to waste the
369 CP   Peter   21   /{P} You speak as if everything was finished./{E} Oh no, no, everything is left
420 CP   Reilly   19   /[*into telephone*]./{R} It is finished. You can come in now. {}/[*Enter* JULIA
533 ES   Gomez   11   ... you left England?/{G} Ever since I finished my sentence./{LC} What has brought you
FIR (1)
185 FQ: DrySal 27   is on the briar rose,/The fog is in the fir trees./The sea howl/And the sea yelp, are
FIRE (48)
67 WL: Fire S   t   ladies, good night, good night./The Fire Sermon/The river's tent is broken; the last
111 Xmas Trees 26   /St. Lucy, her carol, and her crown of fire):/So that before the end, the eightieth
116 SP   Doris 19   my leg on the stairs/Say we've had a fire/{Du} Hello Hello are you there?/Yes this is
134 Wind   10   across the blackened river/The camp fire shake with alien spears./Here, across death's
153 Rock 2   55   pit, let the saw cut the stone,/Let the fire not be quenched in the forge./The Word of
157 Rock 4   13   /Jerusalem lay waste, consumed with fire;/No place for a beast to pass./There were
178 FQ: ECoker 34   concorde. Round and round the fire/Leaping through the flames, or joined in
179 FQ: ECoker 67   bring/The world to that destructive fire/Which burns before the ice-cap reigns./That
191 FQ: Little   4   short day is brightest, with frost and fire,/The brief sun flames the ice, on pond and
191 FQ: Little   10   dumb spirit: no wind, but pentecostal fire/In the dark time of the year. Between melting

192 FQ: Little	53	/Of the dead is tongued with fire beyond the language of the living./Here, the
193 FQ: Little	72	/This is the death of earth./Water and fire succeed/The town, the pasture and the weed./
193 FQ: Little	74	the pasture and the weed./Water and fire deride/The sacrifice that we denied./Water
193 FQ: Little	76	sacrifice that we denied./Water and fire shall rot/The marred foundations we forgot,/
193 FQ: Little	79	choir./This is the death of water and fire./In the uncertain hour before the morning/
195 FQ: Little	147	unless restored by that refining fire/Where you must move in measure, like a
196 FQ: Little	208	pyre or pyre —/To be redeemed from fire by fire./Who then devised the torment? Love./
196 FQ: Little	208	or pyre —/To be redeemed from fire by fire./Who then devised the torment? Love./Love
196 FQ: Little	215	live, only suspire/Consumed by either fire or fire./What we call the beginning is often
196 FQ: Little	215	suspire/Consumed by either fire or fire./What we call the beginning is often the end/
197 FQ: Little	228	any action/Is a step to the block, to the fire, down the sea's throat/Or to an illegible stone:
198 FQ: Little	260	are in-folded/Into the crowned knot of fire/And the fire and the rose are one./
198 FQ: Little	261	/Into the crowned knot of fire/And the fire and the rose are one./OCCASIONAL
201 Def Island	13	fight the power of darkness in air/and fire/and of those who have followed their
203 Indians	2	destination is his own village,/His own fire, and his wife's cooking;/To sit in front of his
223 Pekes Pols	49	afraid/That they started to ring up the Fire Brigade./When suddenly, up from a small
225 Mr Mistoff	45	the roof/When he was curled up by the fire./And he's sometimes been heard by the fire/
225 Mr Mistoff	46	/And he's sometimes been heard by the fire/When he was about on the roof —/(At least
229 Gus	44	/To rescue a child when a house was on fire./And he says: 'Now, these kittens, they do not
605 Narcissus	5	or/Your shadow leaping behind the fire against the red rock:/I will show you his
239 MC Chorus	12	boot and stretches his hand to the fire,/The New Year waits, destiny waits for the
239 MC Chorus	14	/Who has stretched out his hand to the fire and remembered the Saints at All Hallows,/
239 MC Chorus	16	who shall/Stretch out his hand to the fire, and deny his master? who shall be warm/By
239 MC Chorus	17	his master? who shall be warm/By the fire, and deny his master?/Seven years and the
244 MC Chorus	7	the winter,/Talked at the corner of the fire,/Talked at the corners of streets,/Talked not
257 MC Chorus	11	/Destitution, disease,/The old without fire in winter,/The child without milk in summer,/
271 MC Thomas	15	shall remember them, droning by the fire,/When age and forgetfulness sweeten memory
276 MC Chorus	7	of the ashes,/The fuel laid on the fire at daybreak,/These acts marked a limit to our
281 MC Chorus	14	the broom, the back bent in laying the fire, the knee bent in cleaning the hearth, we, the
282 MC Chorus	7	who shut the door and sit by the fire;/Who fear the blessing of God, the loneliness
282 MC Chorus	10	/Who fear the hand at the window, the fire in the thatch, the fist in the tavern, the push
285 FR Amy	12	the curtains undrawn./Make up the fire. Will the spring never come? I am cold./{Ag}
291 FR Charles	2	in a comfortable chair rather nearer the fire./{I} I might have been visiting Cousin Lily at
348 FR Chorus	14	accidents,/We are insured against fire,/Against larceny and illness,/Against
417 CP Reilly	34	together/For casual talk before the fire/Two people who know they do not
502 CC Lucasta	22	terribly cold. Or else you've some fire/To warm you, that isn't the same kind of fire/
502 CC Lucasta	23	warm you, that isn't the same kind of fire/That warms other people. You're either an
578 ES Michael	28	away from you/And tossed it into the fire. How I laughed!/You never seemed even to

FIREBALLS (1)

223 Pekes Pols	52	RUMPUSCAT./His eyes were like fireballs fearfully blazing,/He gave a great yawn,

FIRED (1)

167 Rock 10	37	the night and fall asleep as the rocket is fired; and the day is long for work or play./We

FIREFLIES (1)

129 Cor2 State	26	(O Mantuan) croak in the marshes./Fireflies flare against the faint sheet lightning/

FIREFLY (1)

129 Cor2 State	47	bat's wing, with the small flare of the firefly or lightning bug,/'Rising and falling,

FIREFROREFIDDLE (3)

228 Gus	20	creation, as he loves to tell,/Was Firefrorefiddle, the Fiend of the Fell./'I have
229 Gus	34	creation, as history will tell,/Was Firefrorefiddle, the Fiend of the Fell.'/Then, if
229 Gus	55	of mystery/When I made history/As Firefrorefiddle, the Fiend of the Fell.'/Bustopher

FIRELIGHT (1)

64 WL: Chess	108	shuffled on the stair./Under the firelight, under the brush, her hair/Spread out in

FIRES (7)

177 FQ: ECoker	5	to new building, old timber to new fires,/Old fires to ashes, and ashes to the earth/
177 FQ: ECoker	6	building, old timber to new fires,/Old fires to ashes, and ashes to the earth/Which is
181 FQ: ECoker	167	freeze/And quake in frigid purgatorial fires/Of which the flame is roses, and the smoke is
240 MC Chorus	12	bring consolation/For autumn fires and winter fogs?/What shall we do in the
245 MC Priest2	31	Canterbury./However, I will have fires laid in all your rooms/To take the chill off
247 MC Templ1	1	at nightfall, whispering in chambers,/Fires devouring the winter season,/Eating up the
553 ES Carghil	18	reading somewhere:/*Where their fires are not quenched.* Do you know what I do?/I

FIREWORKS (1)

213 Growltiger	42	horde;/With a frightful burst of fireworks the Chinks they swarmed aboard./

FIRING (1)

534 ES Gomez	33	and not very comfortable,/Or before a firing squad./You don't know what serious

FIRM (5)

49 Hippopot	3	belly in the mud;/Although he seems so firm to us/He is merely flesh and blood./Flesh and
94 Ash-Wed 4	9	/Made cool the dry rock and made firm the sand/In blue of larkspur, blue of Mary's
242 MC Priest2	36	/We can lean on a rock, we can feel a firm foothold/Against the perpetual wash of tides
479 CC Kaghan	24	Lizzie/From always interfering. Be firm with her, Colby;/Assert your right to a little
557 ES Ld Clav	23	From whom?/Not ... from the firm?/{Mi} I went to a lender,/A man whom a

FIRMLY (1)

14 Prufrock	42	/My morning coat, my collar mounting firmly to the chin,/My necktie rich and modest,

FIRMNESS (1)

479 CC Kaghan	26	a little privacy./Now's the moment for firmness. Don't let her cross the threshold./{L} As

FIRST (138)

62 WL: Burial	35	*weilest du?*/'You gave me hyacinths first a year ago;/'They called me the hyacinth girl.'
92 Ash-Wed 3	1	land. We have our inheritance./At the first turning of the second stair/I turned and saw
92 Ash-Wed 3	12	toothed gullet of an agèd shark./At the first turning of the third stair/Was a slotted
107 Animula	31	papers in a dusty room;/Living first in the silence after the viaticum./Pray for
111 Xmas Trees	34	shall remind us of the end/And the first coming of the second coming./
116 SP Doris	40	cards for to-night./Oh guess what the first is/{Du} First is. What is?/{Do} The King of
117 SP Dusty	1	/Oh guess what the first is/{Du} First is. What is?/{Do} The King of Clubs/{Du}
119 SP Krum	24	{Kr} We hit this town last night for the first time/{Kl} And I certainly hope it won't be the
127 Cor1 March	12	stools and our sausages./What comes first? Can you see? Tell us. It is/5,800,000 rifles
129 Cor2 State	8	Sun./Cry cry what shall I cry?/The first thing to do is to form the committees:/The
159 Rock 6	32	is to flow on the steps/We must first build the steps;/And if the Temple is to be
159 Rock 6	34	the Temple is to be cast down/We must first build the Temple./In the beginning GOD
161 Rock 7	28	gods and worship gods, professing first Reason,/And then Money, and Power, and
171 FQ: BurntN	22	them,/Round the corner. Through the first gate,/Into our first world, shall we follow/
171 FQ: BurntN	23	corner. Through the first gate,/Into our first world, shall we follow/The deception of the
171 FQ: BurntN	24	/The deception of the thrush? Into our first world./There they were, dignified, invisible,/
184 FQ: DrySal	3	intractable,/Patient to some degree, at first recognised as a frontier;/Useful,
194 FQ: Little	133	set a crown upon your lifetime's effort./First, the cold friction of expiring sense/Without
197 FQ: Little	244	we started/And know the place for the first time./Through the unknown, remembered
209 NamingCats	3	your holiday games;/You may think at first I'm as mad as a hatter/When I tell you, a cat
209 NamingCats	5	have THREE DIFFERENT NAMES./First of all, there's the name that the family use
232 Skimble	22	all the faces/Of the travellers in the First and in the Third;/He establishes control by a
234 Ad-dress	18	/*How would you ad-dress a Cat?*/So first, your memory I'll jog,/And say: A CAT IS
605 Narcissus	21	knees./So he came out under the rock./First he was sure that he had been a tree,/
238 MC m	16	/ATTENDANTS/*The first scene is in the Archbishop's Hall,/the second*
246 MC Thomas	20	/Meanwhile the substance of our first act/Will be shadows, and the strife with
246 MC m	24	prepare the event. Watch. {}/[*Enter* FIRST TEMPTER]/{T1} You see, my Lord, I do
249 MC Tempt2	17	be the month?/{T2} The last from the first./{T} What shall we give for it?/{T2} Pretence
261 MC Thomas	11	day we celebrate the martyrdom/of His first martyr, the blessed Stephen. Is it an accident,
261 MC Thomas	12	do you think,/that the day of the first martyr follows immediately the day of the
263 MC 1m	27	short/But waiting is long. {}/[*Enter the* FIRST PRIEST *with a banner of St. Stephen*
264 MC Priest1	1	a day: and the day of St. Stephen, First Martyr./*Princes moreover did sit, and did*
265 MC Knight1	28	before dinner. We will roast your pork/First, and dine upon it after./{K2} We must see
276 MC Knight1	31	call upon our eldest member to speak first, my neighbour in/the country: Baron William
277 MC Knight3	6	plain Englishmen/who put our country first. I dare say that we didn't make a/very good
277 MC Knight2	35	/Hugh de Morville./{K2} I should like first to recur to a point that was very/well put by
278 MC Knight2	39	remember that it is we who took the first/step. We have been instrumental in bringing
288 FR Ivy	8	/That is the best time./{I} It is the first time/You have not had your cake and your
288 FR Amy	11	/As you ought to know. It will be the first time/For eight years that we have all been
292 FR Harry	3	I see them,/And they see me. This is the first time that I have seen them./In the Java
295 FR Harry	20	the self. I knew how you would take it./First of all, you isolate the single event/As
311 FR Harry	27	do you show yourselves now for the first time?/When I knew her, I was not the same
314 FR Warburt	34	yes./Even in a country practice. My first patient, now —/You wouldn't believe it,
315 FR Amy	27	are the oldest inhabitants./As we came first, we will go first, in to dinner./{W} With
315 FR Amy	27	/As we came first, we will go first, in to dinner./{W} With pleasure, Lady
315 FR Chorus	35	have desecrated/History. Shamed/The first cry in the bedroom, the noise in the nursery,
330 FR Harry	20	the beginning, eight years ago,/I felt, at first, that sense of separation,/Of isolation
332 FR Agatha	16	her, and she supported Wishwood./At first it was a vacancy. A man and a woman/
335 FR Agatha	40	which we did not pass./I have seen the first stage: relief from what happened/Is also relief
336 FR Harry	4	/{H} Not yet! not yet! this is the first time that I have been free/From the ring of
344 FR Gerald	19	training;/The medical knowledge is the first thing./I've met with missionaries, often
347 FR Downing	7	have given you a turn!/They did me, at first. You soon get used to them./Of course, I
354 CP Julia	23	but it really isn't my story./I heard it first from Delia Verinder/Who was there when it
356 CP Julia	24	said: 'I wish you'd try.' And this is the first time/I've ever seen you without Lavinia/

362 CP	Reilly	5	will feel a little jealous/That she saw it first, and had the courage to break it —/Thus
367 CP	Edward	36	*I've* looked in?/{E} I'd like to know first how you *got* in, Alex./{A} Why, I came and
369 CP	Peter	27	always gone to concerts alone —/At first, because I knew no one to go with,/And later,
371 CP	Peter	4	telling you of something real —/My first experience of reality/And perhaps it is the
382 CP	Celia	36	to forgive *you!*/{C} Yes, for two things. First ... {}/[*The telephone rings*]/{E} Damn the
385 CP	Reilly	17	say to them, or they to you/After the first ten minutes? You would find it difficult/To
393 CP	Lavinia	21	you suggested some other place first?/And I remember that finally in desperation/
397 CP	Edward	20	do I know/That you wouldn't see him first, and tell him all about me/From *your* point
399 CP	Nurse	6	You made that clear, Sir Henry:/The first appointment at eleven o'clock./He is to be
401 CP	Reilly	34	that question for the moment./Tell me first, about the difficulties/On which you want my
402 CP	Reilly	31	is the worst place possible./We must first find out what is wrong with you/Before we
403 CP	Edward	27	—/Indeed, acutely, perhaps, for the first time,/The whole oppression, the unreality/Of
407 CP	Reilly	31	facts./Let me take your husband first. {}/[*To* EDWARD]/{R} You were lying to me
408 CP	Reilly	7	of your lover — who suddenly/For the first time in his life, fell in love with someone,/
408 CP	Reilly	25	such a sense of humour./{R} It is the first more hopeful symptom./{L} How did you
412 CP	Reilly	4	didn't let her know you were seeing me first?/{J} Of course not. I dropped her at the door/
413 CP	Celia	20	in seems all a delusion!/But oughtn't I first to tell you the circumstances?/I'd forgotten
413 CP	Reilly	25	about you for the moment:/Try first to describe your present state of mind./{C}
413 CP	Celia	27	you might consider symptoms. But first I must tell you/That I should really *like* to
413 CP	Reilly	37	say there are two things:/What is the first?/{C} An awareness of solitude./But that
418 CP	Reilly	21	way, if you have the courage./The first I could describe in familiar terms/Because
421 CP	Julia	7	into new disguises,/They have, for the first time, somewhere to start from./Oh, of course,
421 CP	Reilly	22	/{R} Will she be frightened/By the first appearance of projected spirits?/{J} Henry,
425 CP	Lavinia	3	Well, Edward!/Do you know it's the first time you've paid me a compliment/*Before a*
432 CP	Julia	7	him./You know, I was afraid of him at first:/He looks so forbidding .../{R} My dear Julia,
435 CP	Peter	10	about her again. More and more./At first I did not want to know about Celia/And so I
437 CP	Reilly	13	*them and they part no more!*/When I first met Miss Coplestone, in this room,/I saw the
437 CP	Reilly	16	face showed the astonishment/Of the first five minutes after a violent death./If this
445 CC	2m	1	/Act One/*The Business Room on the first floor of* SIR CLAUDE MULHAMMER'S/
445 CC	Claude	6	/That's not the way to arrange their first meeting,/On her return from Switzerland./
445 CC	Eggers	10	/A very delicate situation —/Her first meeting with Mr. Simpkins./But I was glad
449 CC	Claude	9	mean./{SC} She must get to like him first:/And then, Eggerson, I am not unhopeful/
451 CC	Eggers	23	addressing her as Muriel —/Within the first ten minutes! I was horrified./But she actually
453 CC	Kaghan	28	fiancé, to protect Colby from you./But first, let's cope with the financial crisis./{L} Yes,
454 CC	Colby	36	it did make my head spin — all those first names/The first time I met her. I'm not used to it./{E} You'll
454 CC	Colby	37	head spin — all those first names/The first time I met her. I'm not used to it./{E} You'll
457 CC	Lady E	30	Sir Claude at home?/I'll speak to him first./{SC} Good heavens, Eggerson, what *can*
460 CC	Lady E	16	I really am distressed!/This is not the first sign that I've noticed/Of your memory
462 CC	Claude	26	the terms it offers you./But tell me first — I've a reason for asking —/How do you
464 CC	Claude	26	/{SC} Family pressure, in the first place./My father — your grandfather — built
469 CC	Colby	6	at this stage, anyway. All you need at first/Is to hear more music. And to find out what
469 CC	Colby	29	to me before?/{C} And this is the first time I've played to anyone .../{L} Don't be
470 CC	Lucasta	4	Still, I'm flattered/To be your first visitor in this flat/And to be the first to hear
470 CC	Lucasta	5	first visitor in this flat/And to be the first to hear you play *this* piano./{C} That's not
471 CC	Colby	21	tell me./Because *I* don't know./{C} The first time we met/You were trying very hard to
471 CC	Colby	34	a very clever one./{C} I admit that I was very bewildered/By you ... and B./{L}
472 CC	Lucasta	21	/There's one thing I know. When you first told me/What a disaster it was in your life/
476 CC	Lucasta	10	/You said, very cleverly, that when we first met/You saw I was trying to give a false
476 CC	Lucasta	27	And he guessed the truth from the very first moment./{C} But what is there to know?/{L}
478 CC	Kaghan	37	/I knew I should find she'd got in first!/Trust Kaghan's intuitions! I'm your
482 CC	Lady E	30	And I should like to know./{LE} In the first place, you ought to mix with people of
482 CC	Lady E	31	of breeding./I said to myself, when I first saw you,/'He is very well bred'. I knew
484 CC	Lady E	34	/{C} What were they?/{LE} The first was, that I was very ugly/And didn't know it.
488 CC	Claude	32	own child,/If you got to know him first — and that you'd want to adopt him./{LE}
492 CC	Claude	3	know whose son I am./{SC} Then the first thing is: we must see Mrs. Guzzard./{LE} Oh
493 CC	Claude	18	thought/That Eggerson should put the first questions./He's very good at approaching a
495 CC	Lady E	38	It's very strange, Claude, but this is the first time/I have talked to you, without feeling
498 CC	Eggers	35	to trace it. Certainly, Sir Claude:/Our first step must be to question Mrs. Guzzard./{SC}
498 CC	Claude	38	will summon Colby./I wanted you here first, to explain the situation:/And I thought I
501 CC	Eggers	27	me. May I make a suggestion?/Though first of all I must take the occasion/To wish Miss
504 CC	Claude	30	you are always much engaged./{SC} First, let me introduce you to my wife./Lady
510 CC	Eggers	38	Guzzard,/To whom, it seems, you had first been entrusted./{K} I really don't know what
527 ES	Monica	1	the right to criticise my father./In the first place, you don't understand him;/In the
527 ES	Monica	22	for marrying me?/What reasons?/{M} First, his terror of being alone./In the life he's led,
530 ES	Ld Clav	1	pages that I've been fingering —/The first empty pages since I entered Parliament./I

537 ES   Gomez   25 /Everyone expected that I should get a First./I suppose your tutor thought you'd be sent
539 ES   Gomez   33 never met you? I should have got my First,/And I might have become the history
545 ES   Ld Clav   4   /Not so much to the world — first of all to myself./What is this self inside us,
549 ES   Carghil   24 attracted me, you know, at the very first meeting —/I can't think why, but it's the way
550 ES   Carghil   12 years ago?/{MC} Many years ago, the first time. That didn't last long./People sometimes
550 ES   Ld Clav   31 understand/Is why you should take the first opportunity,/Finding me here, to revive old
555 ES   Piggott   5   you, so I thought/That I'd take the first opportunity of hinting —/Tactfully, of
556 ES   Michael   32 blame/Before you knew the facts. The first thing I remember/Is being blamed for
558 ES   Ld Clav   11 —/In order to let me have your version first./I dare say Sir Alfred's will be rather
558 ES   Michael   21 suffered, working in that office./In the first place, they all knew the job had been made
559 ES   Michael   28   why you took it. And Mother knew./First, because it gave you the opportunity/Of
563 ES   Carghil   26 Well, you see, Señor Gomez, when we first became friends —/Lord Claverton and I — I
564 ES   Carghil   36   Señor Gomez!/You've got to be the first to put your cards on the table!/{M} Father, I
572 ES   Ld Clav   13   has she against you?/{LC} I was her first lover./I would have married her — but my
572 ES   Ld Clav   38 confession to you, Monica:/That is the first step taken towards my freedom,/And
575 ES   Carghil   38 *irresistible*/In those days. I melted the first time he looked at me!/Some day, Monica, I'll
579 ES   Gomez   26 At the end of five years he will get his first leave./{Mi} Well ... there's nothing more to
582 ES   Ld Clav   9   that I love Michael,/I think, for the first time — remember, my dear,/I am only a
582 ES   Ld Clav   13 shall leave you for a while./This is your first visit to us at Badgley Court,/Charles, and not
FIRST-CLASS (1)
287 FR   Gerald   2 some very decent specimens/And some first-class shots — better than you were,/Charles,
FIRST-MET (1)
193 FQ: Little   93 scrutiny with which we challenge/The first-met stranger in the waning dusk/I caught the
FIRST-RATE (1)
465 CC   Claude   10 see/That I should never have become a first-rate potter./I didn't have it in me. It's
FIRST-REMEMBERED (1)
111 Xmas Trees   13   rapture, the amazement/Of the first-remembered Christmas Tree,/So that the
FISH (8)
189 FQ: DrySal 175 those/Whose business has to do with fish, and/Those concerned with every lawful
214 RTTugger   25 are a matter of habit./If you offer him fish then he always wants a feast;/When there
214 RTTugger   26 wants a feast;/When there isn't any fish then he won't eat rabbit./If you offer him
236 Cat Morgan   8 a drink on the 'ouse/And a bit o' cold fish when I done me patrol./I ain't got much
605 Narcissus   24   /Then he knew that he had been a fish/With slippery white belly held tight in his
270 MC Chorus   7 of the elephant, the evasive flank of the fish./I have smelt/Corruption in the dish, incense
310 FR   Mary   23   /For the tree and the beast, and the fish/Thrashing itself upstream:/And what of the
368 CP   Alex   26 With a handful of rice and a little dried fish/I can make half a dozen dishes. Don't say a
FISH-PASTE (1)
224 Mr Mistoff   32   with a cork/Or a spoon and a bit of fish-paste;/If you look for a knife or a fork/And
FISHERMEN (1)
186 FQ: DrySal   69   /Where is the end of them, the fishermen sailing/Into the wind's tail, where the
FISHING (2)
67 WL: Fire S 189 its slimy belly on the bank/While I was fishing in the dull canal/On a winter evening
74 WL: Thund 424 controlling hands/I sat upon the shore/Fishing, with the arid plain behind me/Shall I at
FISHMEN (1)
69 WL: Fire S 263   and a chatter from within/Where fishmen lounge at noon: where the walls/Of
FIST (1)
282 MC Chorus   10 the window, the fire in the thatch, the fist in the tavern, the push into the canal,/Less
FIT (12)
75 WL: Thund 431 shored against my ruins/Why then Ile fit you. Hieronymo's mad againe./Datta.
148 Rock 1   34 it seemed/That the country now is only fit for picnics./And the Church does not seem to
190 FQ: DrySal 212   in and out of time,/The distraction fit, lost in a shaft of sunlight,/The wild thyme
289 FR   Ivy   32   into./She may have done it in a fit of temper./{G} I never met her./{A} I am very
290 FR   Amy   7   old friends;/She never wanted to fit herself to Harry,/But only to bring Harry
330 FR   Harry   28 seeing./All this last year, I could not fit myself together:/When I was inside the old
355 CP   Julia   23   going./What a host! And nothing fit to eat!/The only reason for a cocktail party/
377 CP   Julia   20   /There's nothing in the place fit to eat:/I've looked high and low. But I found
429 CP   Alex   20 a European/He is, as a rule, no longer fit to eat./{E} And what has your commission
434 CP   Alex   16 the jungle, and the other/Will never be fit for normal life again./But Celia Coplestone,
440 CP   Edward   9 /And somehow, the two ideas seem to fit together./{L} But all the same ... I don't want
537 ES   Gomez   17 you'd been at school with —/I didn't fit into your set, and I knew it./When you started
FITLY (1)
151 Rock 2   7 the urn to be filled./Your building not fitly framed together, you sit ashamed and
FITTEST (1)
185 FQ: DrySal   62 the most reliable —/And therefore the fittest for renunciation./There is the final

FITTING (1)
261 MC Thomas 39 Archbishop Elphege; because it is fitting, on Christ's birth/day, to remember what is
FITZ (3)
276 MC Knight3 34 /speaker as my old friend Reginald Fitz Urse would lead you to/believe. But there is
277 MC Knight2 36 very/well put by our leader, Reginald Fitz Urse: that you are Englishmen,/and therefore
279 MC Knight4 12 to say nothing/of our leader, Reginald Fitz Urse, have all spoken very much to the/point.
FIVE (21)
23 Preludes 42 trampled by insistent feet/At four and five and six o'clock;/And short square fingers
44 Cook Egg 16 /We two shall lie together, lapt/In a five per cent. Exchequer Bond./I shall not want
66 WL: Chess 160 to bring it off, she said./(She's had five already, and nearly died of young George.)/
85 Hollow Men 71 /*Here we go round the prickly pear*/*At five o'clock in the morning.*/Between the idea/And
129 Cor2 State 13 a week rising by annual increments of five shillings/To two pounds ten a week; with a
203 Indians 17 village in the Midlands,/And one in the Five Rivers, may have the same graveyard./Let
589 Fable 91 food entirely;/Each morn from four to five one took a knout/And flogged his mates 'till
360 CP Edward 20 few questions./How long married?/{E} Five years./{UG} Children?/{E} No./{UG} Then
364 CP Edward 7 out what has happened/During the five years that we've been married./I must find
385 CP Edward 21 hardly expect me to obliterate/The last five years./{UG} I ask you to forget nothing./To
393 CP Lavinia 5 discovery,/Finding that you've spent five years of your life/With a man who has no
403 CP Edward 37 /That is what she has done to me in five years together!/She has made the world a
437 CP Reilly 16 showed the astonishment/Of the first five minutes after a violent death./If this strains
439 CP Lavinia 39 And I have been thinking, for these last five minutes,/How I could face my guests. I wish
463 CC Claude 6 I had no doubts at the time — that's five years;/And then your school, and your
496 CC Eggers 21 to complain/At my being up in London five or six days a week:/But now she says: 'You're
531 ES Ld Clav 16 a portrait taken twenty years ago./In five years' time, it will be the half of that;/In ten
539 ES Gomez 7 should have been good for another five years/At least. Why did they let you retire?/
541 ES Lambert 33 a trunk call coming through for you/In five minutes' time./{LC} I'll be ready to take it. {}/
573 ES Ld Clav 10 has made the difference in the last five minutes/Is not the heinousness of my
579 ES Gomez 26 I don't see why not./{G} At the end of five years he will get his first leave./{Mi} Well ...
FIVE-FINGER (1)
135 5FingerEx t Tartar horsemen shake their spears./Five-Finger Exercises/*Lines to a Persian Cat*/The
FIX (1)
14 Prufrock 56 known them all —/The eyes that fix you in a formulated phrase,/And when I am
FIXED (8)
62 WL: Burial 65 were exhaled,/And each man fixed his eyes before his feet./Flowed up the hill
151 Rock 2 14 upon earth./When your fathers fixed the place of GOD,/And settled all the
193 FQ: Little 91 urban dawn wind unresisting./And as I fixed upon the down-turned face/That pointed
245 MC Thomas 16 suffer/Nor the patient act. But both are fixed/In an eternal action, an eternal patience/To
247 MC Thomas 20 cord, shed the scale. Only/The fool, fixed in his folly, may think/He can turn the wheel
255 MC Tempt4 14 see far off below you, where the gulf is fixed,/Your persecutors, in timeless torment,/
255 MC Tempt4 39 suffer/Nor the patient act. But both are fixed/In an eternal action, an eternal patience/To
583 ES Monica 26 even death can dismay or amaze me/Fixed in the certainty of love unchanging./I feel
FIXING (1)
335 FR Agatha 11 eye/Seeing the feet: the unwinking eye/Fixing the movement. Over and under./{H} In
FIXITY (1)
173 FQ: BurntN 66 nor movement. And do not call it fixity,/Where past and future are gathered.
FLAG (1)
593 Grad 7 6 to victory,/That with their aid the flag is raised on high./Sometime in distant years
FLAGONS (1)
588 Fable 53 that a great pie made of plover,/And flagons which perhaps held several kegs/Of ale,
FLAGS (1)
127 Cor1 March 3 horses' heels/Over the paving./And the flags. And the trumpets. And so many eagles./
FLAIR (1)
577 ES Gomez 24 screwed on./He's got brains, he's got flair. When he does come back/He'll be able to
FLAME (7)
167 Rock 10 41 must quench, forever relight the flame./Therefore we thank Thee for our little
181 FQ: ECoker 168 in frigid purgatorial fires/Of which the flame is roses, and the smoke is briars./The
196 FQ: Little 203 dove descending breaks the air/With flame of incandescent terror/Of which the tongues
196 FQ: Little 212 that wove/The intolerable shirt of flame/Which human power cannot remove./We
198 FQ: Little 259 thing shall be well/When the tongues of flame are in-folded/Into the crowned knot of fire/
256 MC Chorus 32 pokes at the door?/{C} Does the torch flame in the hall, the candle in the room?/{3P}
333 FR Agatha 34 bird sent flying through the purgatorial flame./Indeed it is possible. You may learn
FLAMES (5)
64 WL: Chess 82 his eyes behind his wing)/Doubled the flames of sevenbranched candelabra/Reflecting
178 FQ: ECoker 35 and round the fire/Leaping through the flames, or joined in circles,/Rustically solemn or
191 FQ: Little 5 with frost and fire,/The brief sun flames the ice, on pond and ditches,/In windless

332 FR   Agatha   29   you stretch out your hand/To the flames. They only come once,/Thank God, that
333 FR   Agatha   36   learn hereafter,/Moving alone through flames of ice, chosen/To resolve the enchantment
FLANDERS (1)
201 Def Island   15   who have followed their forebears/to Flanders and France, those undefeated in defeat,/
FLANK (1)
270 MC   Chorus   7   skin of the elephant, the evasive flank of the fish./I have smelt/Corruption in the
FLANNEL (1)
 16 Prufrock   123 dare to eat a peach?/I shall wear white flannel trousers, and walk upon the beach./I have
FLANNELS (1)
155 Rock 3   31   /In the land of lobelias and tennis flannels/The rabbit shall burrow and the thorn
FLARE (3)
129 Cor2 State   26   croak in the marshes./Fireflies flare against the faint sheet lightning/What shall I
129 Cor2 State   30   each other, lit up successively by the flare/Of a sweaty torchbearer, yawning./O hidden
129 Cor2 State   47   of the little bat's wing, with the small flare of the firefly or lightning bug,/'Rising and
FLARES (1)
 20 Portrait   94   can write to me.'/My self-possession flares up for a second;/*This* is as I had reckoned./
FLASH (2)
 74 WL: Thund   393 the rooftree/Co co rico co co rico/In a flash of lightning. Then a damp gust/Bringing
232 Skimble   13 busy in the luggage van!/He gives one flash of his glass-green eyes/And the signal goes
FLASHING (1)
213 Growltiger   48   not drowned —/But a serried ring of flashing steel Growltiger did surround./The
FLASHLIGHT (1)
301 FR   Chorus   19   public, the common photographer/Flashlight for the picture papers: why do we
FLASHY (1)
511 CC   Kaghan   33 But Barney Kaghan — it sounds rather flashy:/It wouldn't make the right impression in
FLAT (25)
 73 WL: Thund   370   in cracked earth/Ringed by the flat horizon only/What is the city over the
107 Animula   2 the hand of God, the simple soul'/To a flat world of changing lights and noise,/To light,
116 SP   Dusty   21 you there?/Yes this is Miss Dorrance's *flat* —/Oh Mr. Pereira is that you? how do you
211 Old Gumbie   27   or anything that's smooth and flat:/She sits and sits and sits and sits — and
214 RTTugger   3 him in a house he would much prefer a flat,/If you put him in a flat then he'd rather have
214 RTTugger   4 much prefer a flat,/If you put him in a flat then he'd rather have a house./If you set him
223 Pekes Pols   50   suddenly, up from a small basement flat,/Why who should stalk out but the GREAT
228 Gus   31 /In the Pantomime season I never fell flat,/And I once understudied Dick Whittington's
235 Ad-dress   48 met before/(He comes to see me in my flat)/I greet him with an OOPSA CAT!/I think
272 MC   Chorus   22 unmemorable; only is here/The white flat face of Death, God's silent servant,/And
353 CP   2m   1   of the Chamberlaynes' London *flat. Early evening.*/EDWARD
383 CP   Edward   13   /{E} It isn't empty. It may be a little flat —/But why did she say that it was a
401 CP   Edward   17 a question./{E} When you came to my flat/Had you been invited by my wife as a guest/
413 CP   Celia   39   of solitude./But that sounds so flat. I don't mean simply/That there's been a
414 CP   Celia   20 And you live in London?/{C} I share a flat/With a cousin: but she's abroad at the
424 CP   2m   1   of the Chamberlaynes' London *flat. Two years later./A late afternoon in July.* A
446 CC   Eggers   24   up daily/Just as I used to. And the flat in the mews?/How soon will that be ready for
459 CC   Claude   18   for Eggerson —/So I'm having the flat in the mews done over./{LE} But all in the
462 CC   Claude   1 it for granted that you should have the flat —/By tomorrow she'll be sure it was she who
469 CC   2m   1   figures. {}/CURTAIN/Act Two/*The flat in the mews a few weeks later.* COLBY is
470 CC   Lucasta   4 flattered/To be your first visitor in this flat/And to be the first to hear you play *this*
478 CC   Kaghan   36 /{K} Enter B. Kaghan./To see the new flat. And here's Lucasta./I knew I should find
479 CC   Kaghan   18 glass of sherry,/To drink success to the flat. Lucasta too:/Much better for you than
481 CC   Lady E   18   I've come over to have a look at the flat/Now that you've moved in. Because you can't
483 CC   Lady E   7 found./But I came to have a look at the flat/To see if the colour scheme really suited you./
FLATTENS (1)
 24 Rhapsody   35   said,/'Remark the cat which flattens itself in the gutter,/Slips out its tongue/
FLATTER (1)
403 CP   Reilly   5 I suggested,/And it would only go to flatter your vanity/With the temporary stimulus
FLATTERED (7)
242 MC   Priest1   20   adversity./I saw him as Chancellor, flattered by the King./Liked or feared by
336 FR   Agatha   2 also relief from that unfulfilled craving/Flattered in sleep, and deceived in waking./You
470 CC   Lucasta   3   you had it tuned yesterday. Still, I'm flattered/To be your first visitor in this flat/And
477 CC   Lucasta   31 /That was new to me. I suppose I was flattered./And I thought, now, perhaps, if
537 ES   Gomez   21 school./I didn't know either, but I was flattered./Later, I came to understand: you made
537 ES   Gomez   23 you made friends with me/Because it flattered *you* — tickled your love of power/To see
537 ES   Gomez   24   your love of power/To see that I was flattered, and that I admired you./Everyone
FLEA (1)
233 Skimble   54 Only stopping here and there to catch a flea./You were fast asleep at Crewe and so you

FLEA'D (1)
41 Burb Blei   30   Who clipped the lion's wings/And flea'd his rump and pared his claws?/Thought
FLED (2)
267 MC Knight1 31 did you show your gratitude?/You had fled from England, not exiled/Or threatened,
338 FR   Harry 21 /And phantoms fed upon me while I fled. Now I know/That the last apparent refuge,
FLEE (1)
561 ES Ld Clav 6 night. Believe me, Michael:/Those who flee from their past will always lose the race./I
FLEEING (1)
105 Song Sime 16 to the goat's path, and the fox's home,/Fleeing from the foreign faces and the foreign
FLESH (15)
49 Hippopot   4   he seems so firm to us/He is merely flesh and blood./Flesh and blood is weak and
49 Hippopot   5   to us/He is merely flesh and blood./Flesh and blood is weak and frail,/Susceptible to
52 Whispers   15 of the skeleton;/No contact possible to flesh/Allayed the fever of the bone./Grishkin is
129 Cor2 State   2 a Statesman/CRY what shall I cry?/All flesh is grass: comprehending/The Companions
160 Rock 7   5 life beyond life, for ecstasy not of the flesh./Waste and void. Waste and void. And
173 FQ: BurntN 64 still point of the turning world. Neither flesh nor fleshless;/Neither from nor towards; at
173 FQ: BurntN 84   from heaven and damnation/Which flesh cannot endure./Time past and time future/
177 FQ: ECoker   7 and ashes to the earth/Which is already flesh, fur and faeces,/Bone of man and beast,
182 FQ: ECoker 170   blood our only drink,/The bloody flesh our only food:/In spite of which we like to
182 FQ: ECoker 172   think/That we are sound, substantial flesh and blood —/Again, in spite of that, we call
606 Narcissus   34 became a dancer to God./Because his flesh was in love with the burning arrows/He
269 MC Chorus 31   I have tasted/The savour of putrid flesh in the spoon. I have felt/The heaving of
271 MC Chorus   1   violated,/United to the spiritual flesh of nature,/Mastered by the animal powers of
294 FR   Harry 24 deeper through the skin/Tainting the flesh and discolouring the bone —/This is what
455 CC Eggers 16 truth, she's something of a thorn in his flesh,/Always losing her jobs, because she won't
FLESHLESS (1)
173 FQ: BurntN 64 of the turning world. Neither flesh nor fleshless;/Neither from nor towards; at the still
FLETCHERS (1)
129 Cor2 State   22   /About perpetual peace: the fletchers and javelin-makers and smiths/Have
FLEW (6)
213 Growltiger 53   was joy in Wapping when the news flew through the land;/At Maidenhead and
590 Time Space 11   vine,/Were withered ere the wild bee flew/To suck the eglantine./So let us haste to
590 Space Time 11 the vine/Were withered ere the wild bee flew/To suck the eglantine./But let us haste to
335 FR Agatha   3   tiny voices/And then a black raven flew over./And then I was only my own feet
430 CP   Peter   5   /{L} When did you arrive?/{P} I flew over from New York last night —/I left Los
554 ES Piggott 28   {}/[*Exit*]/{MP} As a matter of fact, I flew to your rescue/(That's why I've brought your
FLICKER (3)
15 Prufrock   84 have seen the moment of my greatness flicker,/And I have seen the eternal Footman hold
160 Rock 7   13   to an end, a dead end stirred with a flicker of life,/And they came to the withered
174 FQ: BurntN 102 /Neither plenitude nor vacancy. Only a flicker/Over the strained time-ridden faces/
FLICKERED (1)
23 Preludes   29 which your soul was constituted;/They flickered against the ceiling./And when all the
FLICKERING (4)
164 Rock 9   6   whispering faintly,/Among a few flickering scattered lights?/They would put upon
193 FQ: Little   83 unending/After the dark dove with the flickering tongue/Had passed below the horizon
294 FR   Harry 20 and without principle of conduct/In flickering intervals of light and darkness;/The
308 FR   Harry 33 — wherever I am not looking,/Always flickering at the corner of my eye,/Almost
FLIES (1)
37 Gerontion   6 salt marsh, heaving a cutlass,/Bitten by flies, fought./My house is a decayed house,/And
FLIGHT (3)
142 Cape Ann   8 walker, the water-thrush. Follow the flight/Of the dancing arrow, the purple martin.
338 FR   Harry 18 this year,/This last year, I have been in flight/But always in ignorance of invisible
338 FR   Harry 20 Now I know that all my life has been a flight/And phantoms fed upon me while I fled.
FLIGHTY (1)
454 CC Eggers 26 *her*?/{E} Oh, Miss Angel./She's rather flighty. But she has a good heart./{C} But does
FLING (2)
34 Figlia   5   to you with a pained surprise —/Fling them to the ground and turn/With a fugitive
307 FR   Harry 36 is to have hope taken from you,/Or to fling it away, to join the legion of the hopeless/
FLINGING (1)
156 Rock 3   69 as possible,/Plotting of happiness and flinging empty bottles,/Turning from your
FLIRT (1)
123 SAWa & Ho 2 *in what part of the wood/Do you want to flirt with me?/Under the breadfruit, banyan,*
FLIRTATION (1)
578 ES Michael 29   /You never seemed even to want a flirtation,/And my friends used to chaff me about

FLIRTED (1)
270 MC Chorus   6 soil and criticised the worm. In the air/Flirted with the passage of the kite, I have
FLITTER (1)
204 de la Mare   21 in the moonlight dance,/Dogs cower, flitter bats, and owls range/At witches' sabbath of
FLITTING (1)
594 Grad 11   1 which as pupils now we go./We go; like flitting faces in a dream;/Out of thy care and
FLOAT (1)
247 MC Templ1   10 in winter. Snow in the branches/Shall float as sweet as blossoms. Ice along the ditches/
FLOATING (3)
246 MC Templ1   38 the hall,/Laughter and apple-blossom floating on the water,/Singing at nightfall,
473 CC Lucasta   13   /Nothing but a bit of living matter/Floating on the surface of the Regent's Canal./
473 CC Lucasta   14 on the surface of the Regent's Canal./Floating, that's it./{C} You're very much a
FLOCK (1)
272 MC Thomas   4 /They shall find the shepherd here; the flock shall be spared./I have had a tremor of bliss,
FLOGGED (1)
589 Fable   92   four to five one took a knout/And flogged his mates 'till they grew good and friarly./
FLOOD (1)
192 FQ: Little   64   /This is the death of air./There are flood and drouth/Over the eyes and in the mouth,
FLOOR (11)
15 Prufrock   78 ... or it malingers,/Stretched on the floor, here beside you and me./Should I, after tea
16 Prufrock   102   after the skirts that trail along the floor —/And this, and so much more? —/It is
56 Swee Night   15 a coffee-cup,/Reorganised upon the floor/She yawns and draws a stocking up;/The
70 WL: Fire S   295   I raised my knees/Supine on the floor of a narrow canoe.'/'My feet are at
107 Animula   11 sea;/Studies the sunlit pattern on the floor/And running stags around a silver tray;/
172 FQ: BurntN   60 figured leaf/And hear upon the sodden floor/Below, the boarhound and the boar/Pursue
201 Def Island   10 pavement/of British bone on the sea floor/and of those who, in man's newest form of
221 Old Deut   32   /Old Deuteronomy lies on the floor/Of the Fox and French Horn for his
233 Skimble   36 /And there's not a speck of dust on the floor./There is every sort of light — you can make
270 MC Chorus   5 hoof, in odd places;/I have lain on the floor of the sea and breathed with the breathing
445 CC   2m 1 Act One/*The Business Room on the first floor of* SIR CLAUDE MULHAMMER'S/
FLOORS (3)
15 Prufrock   74 of ragged claws/Scuttling across the floors of silent seas./And the afternoon, the
24 Rhapsody   5   lunar incantations/Dissolve the floors of memory/And all its clear relations,/Its
155 Rock 3   45 of Thy sanctuary,/I have swept the floors and garnished the altars./Where there is no
FLORET (1)
108 Animula   36 one who went his own way./Pray for Floret, by the boarhound slain between the yew
FLOTATIONS (1)
147 Rock 1   20 /Where the River flows, with foreign flotations./There I was told: we have too many
FLOURISH (3)
155 Rock 3   33 and the thorn revisit,/The nettle shall flourish on the gravel court,/And the wind shall
195 FQ: Little   153 often look alike/Yet differ completely, flourish in the same hedgerow:/Attachment to self
382 CP Edward   2 unwilling partnership — but can only flourish/In submission to the rule of the stronger
FLOURISHING (1)
580 ES Michael   10 and again,/Just to let you know I'm flourishing./{LC} Yes, write to Monica./{G} Well,
FLOW (7)
19 Portrait   47   twisting the lilac stalks)/'You let it flow from you, you let it flow,/And youth is cruel,
19 Portrait   47 /'You let it flow from you, you let it flow,/And youth is cruel, and has no more
89 Ash-Wed 1   15 /There, where trees flower, and springs flow, for there is nothing again/Because I know
135 5FingerEx1   10 the summer day delay?/*When* will Time flow away?/*Lines to a Yorkshire Terrier*/In a
139 Virginia   2 /Virginia/Red river, red river,/Slow flow heat is silence/No will is still as a river/Still.
159 Rock 6   31 Saints./And if blood of Martyrs is to flow on the steps/We must first build the steps;/
310 FR   Mary   4 root/The agony in the dark/The slow flow throbbing the trunk/The pain of the
FLOWED (2)
62 WL: Burial   62 brown fog of a winter dawn,/A crowd flowed over London Bridge, so many,/I had not
62 WL: Burial   66 each man fixed his eyes before his feet./Flowed up the hill and down King William Street,
FLOWER (1)
89 Ash-Wed 1   15   I cannot drink/There, where trees flower, and springs flow, for there is nothing
FLOWERING (1)
37 Gerontion   21 depraved May, dogwood and chestnut, flowering judas,/To be eaten, to be divided, to be
FLOWERS (31)
34 Figlia   4 the sunlight in your hair —/Clasp your flowers to you with a pained surprise —/Fling
34 Figlia   20 hair over her arms and her arms full of flowers./And I wonder how they should have
123 SA Kl & Kr   19 *home when it rains/We'll gather hibiscus flowers/For it won't be minutes but hours/For it*
172 FQ: BurntN   31 crossed, for the roses/Had the look of flowers that are looked at./There they were as our
185 FQ: DrySal   52   /The silent withering of autumn flowers/Dropping their petals and remaining

186 FQ: DrySal   82 /No end to the withering of withered flowers,/To the movement of pain that is painless
590 Time Space   9 that lives a day/Has lived eternity./The flowers I gave thee when the dew/Was trembling
590 Space Time   9 away,/Though sages disagree./The flowers I sent thee when the dew/Was trembling
590 Space Time   15 to see them pine,/And though the flowers of life be few/Yet let them be divine./
596 When we   5 down./The hedgerow bloomed with flowers still,/No withered petals lay beneath;/But
597 Before Mor   2 East was weaving red with gray,/The flowers at the window turned toward dawn,/Petal
597 Before Mor   4 on petal, waiting for the day,/Fresh flowers, withered flowers, flowers of dawn./This
597 Before Mor   4 for the day,/Fresh flowers, withered flowers, flowers of dawn./This morning's flowers
597 Before Mor   4 day,/Fresh flowers, withered flowers, flowers of dawn./This morning's flowers and
597 Before Mor   5 flowers of dawn./This morning's flowers and flowers of yesterday/Their fragrance
597 Before Mor   5 of dawn./This morning's flowers and flowers of yesterday/Their fragrance drifts across
597 Before Mor   8 bloom and fragrance of decay,/Fresh flowers, withered flowers, flowers of dawn./
597 Before Mor   8 of decay,/Fresh flowers, withered flowers, flowers of dawn./Circe's Palace/Around
597 Before Mor   8 decay,/Fresh flowers, withered flowers, flowers of dawn./Circe's Palace/Around her
598 Circe   3 /With the voice of men in pain,/Are flowers that no man knows./Their petals are
600 Moonflower   5 /Slips from the alder tree./Whiter the flowers, Love, you hold,/Than the white mist on
600 Moonflower   7 on the sea;/Have you no brighter tropic flowers/With scarlet life, for me?/Nocturne/
241 MC   Mess   34 /Strewing the way with leaves and late flowers of the season./The streets of the city will
303 FR   3m   1   II/AGATHA/[*Enter* MARY *with flowers*]/{M} The spring is very late in this
303 FR   Mary   6 as they are, than have these greenhouse flowers/Which do not belong here, which do not
313 FR   Ivy   8 Mary, my dear,/Did you arrange these flowers? Just let me change them./You don't
313 FR   Ivy   9 mind, do you? I know so much about flowers;/Flowers have always been my passion./
313 FR   Ivy   10 you? I know so much about flowers;/Flowers have always been my passion./You know
424 CP   m   4 *the room critically and moves a bowl of flowers*]./[*Re-enter* CATERER'S MAN *with*
473 CC Lucasta   20 that no one else could hear,/And the flowers have a scent that no one else could smell./
474 CC Lucasta   23 /{L} I know what you mean. Then the flowers would fade/And the music would stop.

FLOWING (2)
257 MC Chorus   23 which none can avert, none can avoid, flowing under our feet and over the sky;/Under
257 MC Chorus   24 sky;/Under doors and down chimneys, flowing in at the ear and the mouth and the eye./

FLOWS (3)
147 Rock 1   20 to the timekept City,/Where the River flows, with foreign flotations./There I was told:
150 Rock 1   109   *of* WORKMEN *again./The river flows, the seasons turn/The sparrow and starling*
598 Circe   1   Palace/Around her fountain which flows/With the voice of men in pain,/Are flowers

FLUENTLY (1)
463 CC   Colby   19 you learn to speak a foreign language fluently,/So that you can think in it — you feel

FLUNG (2)
64 WL: Chess   92 fattening the prolonged candle-flames,/Flung their smoke into the laquearia,/Stirring the
151 Rock 2   10   wants to hear sung;/Waiting to be flung in the end, on a heap less useful than dung'./

FLUSHED (1)
68 WL: Fire S   239   still are unreproved, if undesired./Flushed and decided, he assaults at once;/

FLUTE (4)
92 Ash-Wed 3   16   the maytime with an antique flute./Blown hair is sweet, brown hair over the
92 Ash-Wed 3   19 brown hair;/Distraction, music of the flute, stops and steps of the mind over the third
94 Ash-Wed 4   24 yews, behind the garden god,/Whose flute is breathless, bent her head and signed but
331 FR Agatha   35   /Reading, sketching, playing on the flute,/Something of an oddity to his county

FLUTES (1)
94 Ash-Wed 4   13   bearing/Away the fiddles and the flutes, restoring/One who moves in the time

FLUTING (3)
246 MC Tempt1   37 over/Or that the good time cannot last?/Fluting in the meadows, viols in the hall,/
269 MC Chorus   29 /By subtile forebodings; I have heard/Fluting in the night-time, fluting and owls, have
269 MC Chorus   29 I have heard/Fluting in the night-time, fluting and owls, have seen at noon/Scaly wings

FLUTTERED (1)
212 Growltiger   13 LOOSE!/Woe to the weak canary, that fluttered from its cage;/Woe to the pampered

FLY (8)
90 Ash-Wed 1   34   these wings are no longer wings to fly/But merely vans to beat the air/The air which
98 Ash-Wed 6   9 the granite shore/The white sails still fly seaward, seaward flying/Unbroken wings/And
178 FQ: ECoker   64 go down/Comets weep and Leonids fly/Hunt the heavens and the plains/Whirled in a
590 Space Time   3 say,/Are things that cannot be,/The fly that lives a single day/Has lived as long as we./
592 Grad 3   1 We go; as lightning-winged clouds that fly/After a summer tempest, when some haste/
366 CP   Julia   12 of to St. Anthony./And now I must fly. I've kept the taxi waiting./Come along, Peter./
547 ES Piggott   3 you perfectly./{MP} And now I must fly. I've so much on my hands!/But before I go,
555 ES Piggott   11 /I didn't see you coming. Now I must fly. {}/[*Exit*]/{M} I saw Mrs. Piggott bothering you

FLYING (3)

98 Ash-Wed 6	9	white sails still fly seaward, seaward flying/Unbroken wings/And the lost heart stiffens
226 Macavity	3	the bafflement of Scotland Yard, the Flying Squad's despair:/For when they reach the
333 FR Agatha	34	of your unhappy family,/Its bird sent flying through the purgatorial flame./Indeed it is

FOCO (1)

75 WL: Thund	427	down falling down/*Poi s'ascose nel foco che gli affina*/*Quando fiam uti chelidon* — O

FOE (2)

213 Growltiger	40	duet, in danger of their lives —/For the foe was armed with toasting forks and cruel
213 Growltiger	49	Growltiger did surround./The ruthless foe pressed forward, in stubborn rank on rank;/

FOES (1)

222 Pekes Pols	2	/Are proud and implacable passionate foes;/It is always the same, wherever one goes./

FŒTUS (1)

31 Apollinax	7	/He laughed like an irresponsible fœtus./His laughter was submarine and

FOG (15)

13 Prufrock	15	/Talking of Michelangelo./The yellow fog that rubs its back upon the window-panes,/
18 Portrait	1	of a Lady/Among the smoke and fog of a December afternoon/You have the scene
27 Morning	5	at area gates./The brown waves of fog toss up to me/Twisted faces from the bottom
62 WL: Burial	61	days./Unreal City,/Under the brown fog of a winter dawn,/A crowd flowed over
68 WL: Fire S	208	/Tereu/Unreal City/Under the brown fog of a winter noon/Mr. Eugenides, the Smyrna
109 Marina	3	the woodthrush singing through the fog/What images return/O my daughter./Those
109 Marina	15	/A breath of pine, and the woodsong fog/By this grace dissolved in place/What is this
110 Marina	34	/And woodthrush calling through the fog/My daughter./The Cultivation of Christmas
185 FQ: DrySal	27	/The salt is on the briar rose,/The fog is in the fir trees./The sea howl/And the sea
185 FQ: DrySal	36	/And under the oppression of the silent fog/The tolling bell/Measures time not our time,
186 FQ: DrySal	70	sailing/Into the wind's tail, where the fog cowers?/We cannot think of a time that is
313 FR Amy	28	can have happened?/I suppose it's the fog that is holding them up,/So it's no use to
322 FR Winch	28	bike. Mostly walking,/What with the fog so thick, or I'd have been here sooner./I'd
322 FR Winch	32	an accident/On the West Road, in the fog, coming along/At a pretty smart pace, I fancy,
323 FR Winch	18	an accident?/{Wi} Coming along in the fog, my Lady,/And he must have been in rather a

FOGGY (2)

126 SA Chorus	3	you waked up at seven o'clock and it's/foggy and it's damp and it's dawn and it's dark/
295 FR Amy	35	sudden for you./You are unused to our foggy climate/And the northern country. When

FOGS (2)

187 FQ: DrySal	121	the restless waters,/Waves wash over it, fogs conceal it;/On a halcyon day it is merely a
240 MC Chorus	12	/For autumn fires and winter fogs?/What shall we do in the heat of summer/But

FOLD (1)

269 MC Thomas	4	sea run between the shepherd and his fold./{K1} The King's justice, the King's majesty,/

FOLDED (4)

94 Ash-Wed 4	15	sleep and waking, wearing/White light folded, sheathed about her, folded./The new years
94 Ash-Wed 4	15	White light folded, sheathed about her, folded./The new years walk, restoring/Through a
196 FQ: Little	193	the constitution of silence/And are folded in a single party./Whatever we inherit from
233 Skimble	35	And the berth is very neat with a newly folded sheet/And there's not a speck of dust on

FOLDS (1)

166 Rock 10	8	of the pit of the world, curled/In folds of himself until he awakens in hunger and

FOLIAGE (1)

176 FQ: BurntN	175	the hidden laughter/Of children in the foliage/Quick now, here, now, always —/

FOLK (6)

232 Skimble	27	approve/Of hilarity and riot, so the folk are very quiet/When Skimble is about and on
589 Fable	70	to be lamented sorely/Such slippery folk should be allowed about,/For often they
244 MC Chorus	28	you realise what it means/To the small folk drawn into the pattern of fate, the small folk
244 MC Chorus	28	into the pattern of fate, the small folk who live among small things,/The strain on
244 MC Chorus	29	/The strain on the brain of the small folk who stand to the doom of the house, the
531 ES Ld Clav	23	men covet./When we go, a good many folk are mildly grieved,/And our closest

FOLKS (1)

119 SP Klip	16	Sam./{Kl} Yes we did our bit, as you folks say,/I'll tell the world we got the Hun on the

FOLLOW (31)

13 Prufrock	8	with oyster-shells:/Streets that follow like a tedious argument/Of insidious intent
136 5FingerEx4	6	just at a word from his master/Will follow you faster and faster/And tear you limb
142 Cape Ann	3	vesper-sparrow/At dawn and dusk. Follow the dance/Of the goldfinch at noon. Leave
142 Cape Ann	7	the bob-white/Dodging by bay-bush. Follow the feet/Of the walker, the water-thrush.
142 Cape Ann	8	feet/Of the walker, the water-thrush. Follow the flight/Of the dancing arrow, the
171 FQ: BurntN	20	echoes/Inhabit the garden. Shall we follow?/Quick, said the bird, find them, find them,
171 FQ: BurntN	23	first gate,/Into our first world, shall we follow/The deception of the thrush? Into our first
196 FQ: Little	189	/We cannot restore old policies/Or follow an antique drum./These men, and those
594 Grad 13	2	departing sons hast been/To those that follow may'st thou be no less;/A guide to warn
246 MC Priest1	15	/We are unmolested./{P1} But do they follow after?/{T} For a little time the hungry hawk
247 MC Thomas	28	You were safer/Think of penitence and follow your master./{T1} Not at this gait!/If you

279 MC	Knight1	6	word, for those who/have been able to follow his very subtle reasoning. We have,/
285 FR	Ivy	16	I would go south in the winter./I would follow the sun, not wait for the sun to come here./
300 FR	Downing	19	a quiet smoke, where the women can't follow him./She wouldn't leave him out of her
336 FR	Harry	22	destination. Let us lose no time. I will follow. {}/[*The curtains close.* AGATHA *goes to*
339 FR	Harry	22	is just strength enough given./I must follow the bright angels. {}/[*Exit*]/Scene III/
342 FR	Agatha	38	been led across the frontier: he must follow;/For him the death is now only on this
349 FR	Agatha	25	has its course/Its own way of expiation/Follow follow/{M} Not in the day time/And in
349 FR	Agatha	25	/Its own way of expiation/Follow follow/{M} Not in the day time/And in the hither
350 FR	Mary	2	we are doing/There is not its operation/Follow follow/{Ag} But in the night time/And in
350 FR	Mary	2	/There is not its operation/Follow follow/{Ag} But in the night time/And in the
350 FR	Agatha	7	we have woven/Bind us to each other/Follow follow/{M} A curse is written/On the
350 FR	Agatha	7	woven/Bind us to each other/Follow follow/{M} A curse is written/On the under side of
350 FR	Mary	12	mirror/And behind the smiling moon/Follow follow/{Ag} This way the pilgrimage/Of
350 FR	Mary	12	/And behind the smiling moon/Follow follow/{Ag} This way the pilgrimage/Of
378 CP	Celia	5	you, Julia./I think I will, if I may follow you/In about ten minutes? Before I go,
516 CC	Colby	5	now I know who was my father/I must follow my father — so that I may come to know
516 CC	Colby	15	not very successful./{C} And I wish to follow my father./{SC} But, Colby:/Don't you
547 ES	Ld Clav	2	them/In another respect./{LC} I follow you perfectly./{MP} And now I must fly.
549 ES	Carghil	26	happen./I said 'there's a man I could follow round the world!'/But Effie it was — you
549 ES	Carghil	29	my words' Effie said, 'if you chose to follow *that* man/He'd give you the slip: he's not to

FOLLOWED (10)

68 WL: Fire S		214	luncheon at the Cannon Street Hotel/Followed by a weekend at the Metropole./At the
160 Rock 7		4	of lodgement and germination./They followed the light and the shadow, and the light
190 FQ: DrySal		217	These are only hints and guesses,/Hints followed by guesses; and the rest/Is prayer,
201 Def Island		14	in air/and fire/and of those who have followed their forebears/to Flanders and France,
323 FR	m	7	Is it Arthur or John? {}/[*Enter* AMY, *followed severally by* VIOLET, IVY, AGATHA,
336 FR	Harry	18	and I am going with you./You followed me here, where I thought I should escape
491 CC	Colby	28	between two parents./But, if we followed your suggestion,/I know, I know I
533 ES	Gomez	5	/And finally, Lord Claverton. I've followed your example,/And done the same, in a
539 ES	Gomez	19	from what I've heard about *him*,/He's followed your undergraduate career/Without the
553 ES	Carghil	5	of my character./{MC} I've followed your progress year by year, Richard./

FOLLOWING (6)

161 Rock 7		25	straying, delaying, returning, yet following no other way./But it seems that
336 FR	Harry	20	I arrived./Now I see at last that I am following you,/And I know that there can be only
523 ES	m	15	/*The Same. Late afternoon of the following day*/Act One/*The drawing-room of*
538 ES	Gomez	31	advice .../I've made a point, you see, of following your career./{LC} I am touched by your
567 ES	2m	1	*Same as Act Two. Late afternoon of the following day.* MONICA *seated/alone. Enter*
570 ES	Ld Clav	30	his adopted country. He even has sons/Following in their father's footsteps/Who are also

FOLLOWS (2)

261 MC	Thomas	12	think,/that the day of the first martyr follows immediately the day of the Birth/of
449 CC	Eggers	33	—/An admirable solution — then what follows?/Will you let her know, then, that Mr.

FOLLY (6)

69 WL: Fire S		253	over.'/When lovely woman stoops to folly and/Paces about her room again, alone,/She
103 Journ Magi		20	in our ears, saying/That this was all folly./Then at dawn we came down to a temperate
179 FQ: ECoker		95	wisdom of old men, but rather of their folly,/Their fear of fear and frenzy, their fear of
194 FQ: Little		138	impotence of rage/At human folly, and the laceration/Of laughter at what
247 MC	Thomas	20	the scale. Only/The fool, fixed in his folly, may think/He can turn the wheel on which
308 FR	Harry	22	if nothing had happened,/Isn't that all folly? It's like the hollow tree,/Not there./{M} But

FOND (11)

324 FR	Ivy	22	callous?/I always thought you were so fond of John./{V} And if you don't care what
446 CC	Eggers	35	of that?/{E} He told me he was very fond of bird watching./{SC} But there won't be
488 CC	Claude	30	—/I'd hoped that you would become fond of Colby,/And that he might come to take
503 CC	Colby	15	B./I know you like B./{C} I'm very fond of him;/And I'm glad to think he'll be my
512 CC	Kaghan	32	can make it right with my parents./I'm fond of them, you know./{LE} I shall see to that,
529 ES	Monica	17	mixed with envy:/I do believe that he is fond of you./So you must come often. And Oh,
547 ES	Monica	32	Thank you, Mrs. Piggott. But I'm very fond of walking/And I'm told there are very good
562 ES	Michael	9	me./You know I've always been very fond of you —/I've a very affectionate nature,
578 ES	Michael	22	of course, Monica. You know I'm very fond of you/Though we never really seemed to
578 ES	Michael	31	highbrow sister./But all the same, I was fond of you, and always shall be./We don't meet
578 ES	Michael	32	be./We don't meet often, but if we're fond of each other,/That needn't interfere with

FONDER (1)

334 FR	Harry	31	Now I see/I might even become fonder of my mother —/More compassionate at

FONT (1)

46 Directeur		12	Conservateur/Bras dessus bras dessous/Font des tours/A pas de loup./Dans un égout/

FOOD (6)
68 WL: Fire S   223   lights/Her stove, and lays out food in tins./Out of the window perilously spread/
150 Rock 1   118   *and no end/But noise without speech, food without taste./Without delay, without haste/*
182 FQ: ECoker 170   only drink,/The bloody flesh our only food:/In spite of which we like to think/That we
589 Fable   90   /And lived on milk and breakfast food entirely;/Each morn from four to five one
420 CP   Reilly 26   have they to go back to?/To the stale food mouldering in the larder,/The stale thoughts
426 CP   Julia   32 you know what *they* offer in the way of food and drink!/And I've had to miss my tea, and

FOOL (11)
16 Prufrock   119   ridiculous —/Almost, at times, the Fool./I grow old ... I grow old .../I shall wear the
66 WL: Chess   162   never been the same./You *are* a proper fool, I said./Well, if Albert won't leave you alone,
247 MC Thomas   20   /The cord, shed the scale. Only/The fool, fixed in his folly, may think/He can turn the
340 FR   Amy   1   III/AMY, AGATHA/{A} I was a fool, to ask you again to Wishwood;/But I
363 CP   Reilly 24   ridiculous./Resign yourself to be the fool you are./That's the best advice that *I* can give
371 CP   Edward 35   all this trouble/To protect you from the fool you are./What do you want me to do?/{P}
415 CP   Celia 16   she wanted. I may have been a fool:/But I don't mind at all having been a fool./
415 CP   Celia 17   /But I don't mind at all having been a fool./{R} And what is the point of view of your
524 ES   Charles 21 me if you like. But a man does feel a fool/If he takes you to a place where he's utterly
560 ES   Michael 25 young woman?/{Mi} I'm not such a fool/As to get myself involved in a breach of
568 ES   Ld Clav 28 ridiculous,/When he has played the fool (as who has not?) —/Then he loves that

FOOLISH (7)
21 Portrait   120   or if I understand/Or whether wise or foolish, tardy or too soon .../Would she not have
245 MC   Priest2 2   way to talk at such a juncture!/You are foolish, immodest and babbling women./Do you
245 MC   Priest2 24 /Engrossed by the chatter of these foolish women./Forgive us, my Lord, you would
332 FR   Agatha 40 wish to murder her?/{Ag} Oh, a dozen foolish ways, each one abandoned/For something
485 CC   Lady E   9 my mother *was* my mother./These were foolish fancies. I was a silly girl,/And very
489 CC   Claude   5 you/About Colby. I didn't. For such a foolish reason./Absurd it sounds now. One child
571 ES   Ld Clav 18 /For loving she had — self-centred and foolish —/But we should respect love always

FOOLISHLY (1)
331 FR   Harry   6   nothing else was real. I thought foolishly/That when I got back to Wishwood, as I

FOOLS' (1)
195 FQ: Little 145   you took for exercise of virtue./Then fools' approval stings, and honour stains./From

FOOT (3)
67 WL: Fire S   195   low dry garret,/Rattled by the rat's foot only, year to year./But at my back from time
129 Cor2 State   32 Hidden under the... Where the dove's foot rested and locked for a moment,/A still
540 ES   Gomez   27 for a second?/You never lifted your foot from the accelerator./{LC} We were in a

FOOTFALL (2)
257 MC Chorus   29   in the dark air:/Puss-purr of leopard, footfall of padding bear,/Palm-pat of nodding
272 MC Chorus   17   when splitting in the skull./More than footfall in the passage,/More than shadow in the

FOOTFALLS (1)
171 FQ: BurntN 11   to one end, which is always present./Footfalls echo in the memory/Down the passage

FOOTHOLD (3)
166 Rock 10   16   to take your step and find your foothold./O Light Invisible, we praise Thee!/Too
179 FQ: ECoker 92   edge of a grimpen, where is no secure foothold,/And menaced by monsters, fancy
242 MC   Priest2 36 can lean on a rock, we can feel a firm foothold/Against the perpetual wash of tides of

FOOTLOOSE (1)
533 ES   Gomez   19 widower, like you, Dick./So I'm pretty footloose. Gomez, you see,/Is now a highly

FOOTMAN (2)
15 Prufrock   85   flicker,/And I have seen the eternal Footman hold my coat, and snicker,/And in
29 Aunt Helen   11   ticking on the mantelpiece,/And the footman sat upon the dining-table/Holding the

FOOTPRINTS (1)
226 Macavity   22 (They say he cheats at cards.)/And his footprints are not found in any file of Scotland

FOOTSTEPS (2)
64 WL: Chess   107   leaning, hushing the room enclosed./Footsteps shuffled on the stair./Under the
570 ES   Ld Clav 30 has sons/Following in their father's footsteps/Who are also successful. What would *he*

FOR (1122)

FORBID (4)
275 MC Thomas   12   or clerk, shall you touch./This I forbid./{4K} Traitor! traitor! traitor!/{T} You,
323 FR   Warburt 28 for myself. Order the car at once./{W} I forbid it, Lady Monchensey./As your doctor, I
323 FR   Warburt 29 Lady Monchensey./As your doctor, I forbid you to leave the house tonight./There is
490 CC   Colby   35 to be. I don't blame you for that:/God forbid! but we must take the consequences./At the

FORBIDDEN (2)
62 WL: Burial   54   he carries on his back,/Which I am forbidden to see. I do not find/The Hanged Man.
328 FR   Charles 15 was/fined £50 and costs to-day, and forbidden to drive a car for the/next twelve

FORBIDDING (2)
212 Growltiger   8 scowled upon a hostile world from one forbidding eye./The cottagers of Rotherhithe
432 CP   Julia   8 I was afraid of him at first:/He looks so forbidding .../{R} My dear Julia,/You are giving
FORC'D (1)
68 WL: Fire S   205 twit/Jug jug jug jug jug jug/So rudely forc'd./Tereu/Unreal City/Under the brown fog
FORCE (12)
15 Prufrock   80   cakes and ices,/Have the strength to force the moment to its crisis?/But though I have
83 Hollow Men   12 form, shade without colour,/Paralysed force, gesture without motion;/Those who have
119 SP   Krum   12 /{Kr} Of the Canadian Expeditionary Force —/{Kl} The Loot has told us a lot about
588 Fable   32 /I'll be compelled to keep them off by force.'/He drench the gown he wore with holy
258 MC Thomas   17 desirable./Ambition comes when early force is spent/And when we find no longer all
272 MC   Priests   8 joyful consummation./{3P} Seize him! force him! drag him!/{T} Keep your hands off!/
273 MC   Priests   14   cannot break in. They have not the force./We are safe. We are safe./{T} Unbar the
274 MC   Priests   15 the roof./To the crypt. Quick. Come. Force him./{4K} Where is Becket, the traitor to
320 FR Warburt   8 seems as vital as ever —/It is only the force of her personality,/Her indomitable will,
361 CP   Reilly   29 to invite the unexpected, release a new force,/Or let the genie out of the bottle./It is to
494 CC   Claude   23   an inspiration,/Like that, by force of will. He was a great financier —/And I
581 ES   Charles   6 But it's both of you together/Make the force to attract him: you and Monica combined./
FORCED (11)
38 Gerontion   46 fathered by our heroism. Virtues/Are forced upon us by our impudent crimes./These
64 WL: Chess   100   by the barbarous king/So rudely forced; yet there the nightingale/Filled all the
213 Growltiger   50 /Growltiger to his vast surprise was forced to walk the plank./He who a hundred
213 Growltiger   52 drop,/At the end of all his crimes was forced to go ker-flip, ker-flop./Oh there was joy in
239 MC Chorus   7 our eyes are compelled to witness, has forced our feet/Towards the cathedral. We are
239 MC Chorus   8 our feet/Towards the cathedral. We are forced to bear witness./Since golden October
340 FR   Amy   26 I show any weakness, any self-pity?/I forced myself to the purposes of Wishwood;/I
409 CP   Reilly   29   by the awareness/That you had forced him into this position) —/When, I say, you
419 CP   Reilly   28 choose, Miss Coplestone. Nothing is forced on them./Some of them return, in a
436 CP   Julia   38 than you think./I believe that she has forced you to a show-down./{R} You state the
477 CC Lucasta   27 like myself./I don't like the person I've forced myself to be;/And I liked you because you
FORCES (5)
135 5FingerEx2   4 black sky, from a green cloud/Natural forces shriek'd aloud,/Screamed, rattled,
135 5FingerEx3   2 long light shakes across the lake,/The forces of the morning quake,/The dawn is slant
202 War Poetry   9 is a meeting/On which we attend/Of forces beyond control by experiment —/Of
243 MC   Priest2   1 perpetual wash of tides of balance of forces of barons and landholders./The rock of
384 CP   Reilly   19   made a decision. You set in motion/Forces in your life and in the lives of others/
FORCING (1)
340 FR   Amy   21 chilly pretences in the silent bedroom,/Forcing sons upon an unwilling father?/Dare you
FOREBEARS (1)
201 Def Island   14 /and of those who have followed their forebears/to Flanders and France, those
FOREBODINGS (1)
269 MC Chorus   28   senses are quickened/By subtile forebodings; I have heard/Fluting in the
FOREIGN (17)
105 Song Sime   16 and the fox's home,/Fleeing from the foreign faces and the foreign swords./Before the
105 Song Sime   16 /Fleeing from the foreign faces and the foreign swords./Before the time of cords and
147 Rock 1   20   City,/Where the River flows, with foreign flotations./There I was told: we have too
151 Rock 2   6 of their hands, or look in vain towards foreign lands for alms to be more or the urn to be
184 FQ: DrySal   24   the broken oar/And the gear of foreign dead men. The sea has many voices,/
203 Indians   9 cool hour, according to the climate))/Of foreign men, who fought in foreign places,/
203 Indians   9 climate))/Of foreign men, who fought in foreign places,/Foreign to each other./A man's
203 Indians   10 men, who fought in foreign places,/Foreign to each other./A man's destination is not
212 Growltiger   15 to the bristly Bandicoot, that lurks on foreign ships,/And woe to any Cat with whom
212 Growltiger   17 came to grips!/But most to Cats of foreign race his hatred had been vowed;/To Cats
212 Growltiger   18 his hatred had been vowed;/To Cats of foreign name and race no quarter was allowed./
226 Macavity   27   *Macavity's not there!*/And when the Foreign Office find a Treaty's gone astray,/Or the
592 Grad 2   2 strand/To seek their fortunes on some foreign shore/Well know they lose what time shall
268 MC Thomas   39 and pain./Seven years a mendicant on foreign charity/I lingered abroad: seven years is
428 CP   Alex   35 the heart of the matter./There are also foreign agitators,/Stirring up trouble .../{L} Why
463 CC   Colby   19 as, I suppose,/If you learn to speak a foreign language fluently,/So that you can think
532 ES Lambert   1 /{LC} What sort of a person?/{L} A foreign person/By the looks of him. But talks
FOREIGNER (1)
563 ES   Carghil   3 /And he's rather exotic-looking. Is he a foreigner?/{LC} He comes from some place in
FOREPEAK (1)
213 Growltiger   29 he was prowling for his prey./In the forepeak of the vessel Growltiger sate alone,/

FORESEEING (1)
326 FR   Harry   16 predicting the minor event,/Engaged in foreseeing the minor disaster?/You go on trying
FORESEEN (1)
266 MC Thomas   2   certain our expectation/The moment foreseen may be unexpected/When it arrives. It
FORESIGHT (2)
194 FQ: Little   130 /And urge the mind to aftersight and foresight,/Let me disclose the gifts reserved for
400 CP   Alex   19 my name to him./{A} With your usual foresight. Now, he's quite triumphant/Because he
FOREST (9)
598 Circe   9   /Panthers rise from their lairs/In the forest which thickens below,/Along the garden
309 FR   Harry   32 distance,/Or the distant waterfall in the forest,/Inaccessible, half-heard./And I hear your
406 CP   Lavinia   36   Now I know of a hotel/In the New Forest .../{E} How like you, Lavinia./You always
411 CP   Lavinia   1 Edward, there *is* that hotel in the New Forest/If you want to go there. The proprietor/
416 CP   Celia   30 Like a child who has wandered into a forest/Playing with an imaginary playmate/And
416 CP   Celia   33 discovers he is only a child/Lost in a forest, wanting to go home./{R} Compassion may
416 CP   Reilly   35   finding your own way out of the forest./{C} But even if I find my way out of the
416 CP   Celia   36   But even if I find my way out of the forest/I shall be left with the inconsolable memory
416 CP   Celia   38 memory/Of the treasure I went into the forest to find/And never found, and which was
FORESUFFERED (1)
 69 WL: Fire S   243   of indifference./(And I Tiresias have foresuffered all/Enacted on this same divan or
FORETOLD (1)
 68 WL: Fire S   229 wrinkled dugs/Perceived the scene, and foretold the rest —/I too awaited the expected
FOREVER (18)
152 Rock 2   26 rotten or ripe./And the Church must be forever building, and always decaying, and
152 Rock 2   35 fought to gain it./The Church must be forever building, for it is forever decaying within
152 Rock 2   35   must be forever building, for it is forever decaying within and attacked from
167 Rock 10   41 candle, put out the light and relight it;/Forever must quench, forever relight the flame./
167 Rock 10   41   and relight it;/Forever must quench, forever relight the flame./Therefore we thank
186 FQ: DrySal   75   /We have to think of them as forever bailing,/Setting and hauling, while the
594 Grad 12   3 honor and thy fame shall but increase/Forever, and may stronger words than these/
599 On a Port   3 /To us of restless brain and weary feet,/Forever hurrying, up and down the street,/She
601 Nocturne   12   eye profound,/(No need of 'Love forever?' — 'Love next week?')/While female
245 MC Thomas   22   that the wheel may turn and still/Be forever still./{P2} O my Lord, forgive me, I did
255 MC Tempt4   8 compare with glory of Saints/Dwelling forever in presence of God?/What earthly glory,
256 MC Tempt4   4   that the wheel may turn and still/Be forever still./{C} There is no rest in the house.
272 MC Chorus   32 soul/From seeing itself, foully united forever, nothing with nothing,/Not what we call
280 MC Priest3   34 which unravels as you weave,/Pacing forever in the hell of make-believe/Which never is
282 MC Chorus   3 /From such ground springs that which forever renews the earth/Though it is forever
282 MC Chorus   4   forever renews the earth/Though it is forever denied. Therefore, O God, we thank
467 CC   Colby   12 of childhood./Those years have gone forever. The empty years./Oh, I'm terribly sorry
561 ES Ld Clav   3   though it carried you away from me forever/To suffer the monotonous sun of the
FORGE (1)
153 Rock 2   55   /Let the fire not be quenched in the forge./The Word of the LORD came unto me,
FORGER (1)
571 ES Ld Clav   10   beyond his means:/So he became a forger. And so he served his term./Was I
FORGERY (6)
534 ES Ld Clav   16 for./I trust you've no need to engage in forgery./{G} Forgery, Dick? An absurd
534 ES   Gomez   17   no need to engage in forgery./{G} Forgery, Dick? An absurd suggestion!/Forgery, I
534 ES   Gomez   18 Forgery, Dick? An absurd suggestion!/Forgery, I can tell you, is a mug's game./I say
534 ES   Gomez   20   /I say that — with conviction./No, forgery, or washing cheques, or anything of that
538 ES   Gomez   3   just reminded — me/Defalcation and forgery. And then my stretch/Which gave me time
577 ES   Charles 18 /Is that he served a prison sentence for forgery./{G} Well, Michael, what do you say to all
FORGET (45)
 89 Ash-Wed 1   27 mercy upon us/And I pray that I may forget/These matters that with myself I too much
 91 Ash-Wed 2   20   /And would be forgotten, so I would forget/Thus devoted, concentrated in purpose.
156 Rock 3   72 what you call humanity;/Though you forget the way to the Temple,/There is one who
159 Rock 6   18 and Death, and of all that they would forget./She is tender where they would be hard,
184 FQ: DrySal   9   reminder/Of what men choose to forget. Unhonoured, unpropitiated/By
602 Humoresque   7   face,/(The kind of face that we forget)/Pinched in a comic, dull grimace;/Half
246 MC Tempt1   31 of London,/Your Lordship won't forget that evening on the river/When the King,
249 MC Thomas   32   be dressed with decorum./{T} You forget the bishops/Whom I have laid under
249 MC Thomas   36   intelligent self-interest./{T} You forget the barons. Who will not forget/Constant
249 MC Thomas   36 You forget the barons. Who will not forget/Constant curbing of petty privilege./{T2}
254 MC Tempt4   37   /And men shall only do their best to forget you./And later is worse, when men will not
271 MC Thomas   14 purpose is made complete./You shall forget these things, toiling in the household,/You
289 FR   Amy   19 I don't believe he will. He will wish to forget it./I do not mince matters in front of the

291 FR	Amy	22	at by eyes through a window?/{A} You forget, Harry, that you are at Wishwood,/Not in
303 FR	Agatha	4	give me for this evening./{Ag} I always forget how late the spring is, here./{M} I had
311 FR	Harry	15	them/They leave me alone: when I forget them/Only for an instant of inattention/
344 FR	Gerald	27	consult the vicar .../{G} And don't forget/That you'll need various inoculations —/
362 CP	Reilly	26	is an object/As well as a person. But we forget about it/As quickly as we can. When
385 CP	Reilly	22	/The last five years./{UG} I ask you to forget nothing./To try to forget is to try to
385 CP	Reilly	23	I ask you to forget nothing./To try to forget is to try to conceal./{E} There are certainly
385 CP	Edward	24	are certainly things I should like to forget./{UG} And persons also. But you must not
385 CP	Reilly	25	And persons also. But you must not forget them./You must face them all, but meet
410 CP	Reilly	38	who go/To the sanatorium — you will forget this phrase,/And in forgetting it will alter
418 CP	Celia	10	I don't know what it is. I don't want to forget it./I want to live with it. I could do without
419 CP	Reilly	1	But those who take the other/Can forget their loneliness. You will not forget yours./
419 CP	Reilly	1	forget their loneliness. You will not forget yours./Each way means loneliness — and
428 CP	Julia	3	monkeys are destructive./I shall never forget Mary Mallington's monkey,/The horrid
435 CP	Peter	6	years ago./{P} Two years ago! I tried to forget about her,/Until I began to think myself a
446 CC	Claude	13	/In a different form. He won't forget/That his great ambition was to be an
446 CC	Claude	15	was to be an organist,/Just as I can't forget ... no matter./The great thing was to find
447 CC	Claude	35	chose him herself. By the way, don't forget/To let her know that he's very musical./She
456 CC	Eggers	24	when you least expect it./But she does forget things. And she likes to travel,/Mostly for
470 CC	Colby	12	people,/And when I'm alone I can't forget/That it's only myself to whom I'm playing./
477 CC	Lucasta	11	him/Of something he would prefer to forget. {}/[*A pause*]/{L} But why don't you say
478 CC	Lucasta	29	anything away. I shall never/Never forget that look on your face/When I told you
495 CC	Lady E	28	/He was so commonplace! I wanted to forget him,/And so, I suppose, I wanted to forget/
495 CC	Lady E	29	him,/And so, I suppose, I wanted to forget/Colby. But Colby is an artist./{SC} A
542 ES	Gomez	36	you enter the smoking room./Don't forget, Dick:/You *didn't stop*! Well, I'd better be
550 ES	Carghil	37	find that out'./A man may prefer to forget all the women/He has loved. But a woman
551 ES	Carghil	1	loved. But a woman doesn't want to forget/A single one of her admirers. Why, even a
551 ES	Carghil	6	ashamed of:/A man is always trying to forget/His own shabby behaviour./{LC} But we'd
558 ES	Michael	1	won't send in their bills, and then I forget them./It's being your son that gets me into
568 ES	Ld Clav	12	Hemington,/Which you wish to forget? Which you wish to keep unknown?/{C}
568 ES	Charles	13	are certainly things I would gladly forget, Sir,/Or rather, which I wish had never
568 ES	Ld Clav	37	you!/I've spent my life in trying to forget myself,/In trying to identify myself with the

FORGETFUL (3)

61 WL: Burial	6	kept us warm, covering/Earth in forgetful snow, feeding/A little life with dried
148 Rock 1	65	perpetual struggle of Good and Evil./Forgetful, you neglect your shrines and
154 Rock 3	22	smoky ships?/Will you leave my people forgetful and forgotten/To idleness, labour, and

FORGETFULNESS (4)

91 Ash-Wed 2	18	/Let the whiteness of bones atone to forgetfulness./There is no life in them. As I am
91 Ash-Wed 2	29	most whole/Rose of memory/Rose of forgetfulness/Exhausted and life-giving/Worried
271 MC Thomas	16	droning by the fire,/When age and forgetfulness sweeten memory/Only like a dream
280 MC Priest3	27	share his filthy rites, and try to snatch/Forgetfulness in his libidinous courts,/Oblivion in

FORGETS (1)

456 CC	Eggers	27	buy a house. And then goes away/And forgets all about it. That can be complicated/And

FORGETTING (9)

92 Ash-Wed 2	51	of the day, with the blessing of sand,/Forgetting themselves and each other, united/In
187 FQ: DrySal	101	only/But of many generations — not forgetting/Something that is probably quite
246 MC Tempt1	25	upon ceremony:/Here I have come, forgetting all acrimony,/Hoping that your present
247 MC Thomas	7	that are past. I remember/Not worth forgetting./{T1} And of the new season./Spring
248 MC Tempt1	4	wait upon ceremony,/I leave as I came, forgetting all acrimony,/Hoping that your present
322 FR Winch	4	was my birthday —/I beg pardon, I'm forgetting./If it was my mother's. God rest her
410 CP Reilly	39	— you will forget this phrase,/And in forgetting it will alter the condition./{L} Edward,
426 CP Julia	37	/An old friend of mine, in fact. But I'm forgetting!/I've got a surprise: I've brought Alex
551 ES Carghil	4	a kind of testimonial./Men live by forgetting — women live on memories./Besides a

FORGIVE (11)

194 FQ: Little	117	be forgiven/By others, as I pray you to forgive/Both bad and good. Last season's fruit is
245 MC Priest2	23	still/Be forever still./{P2} O my Lord, forgive me, I did not see you coming,/Engrossed
245 MC Priest2	25	by the chatter of these foolish women./Forgive us, my Lord, you would have had a
271 MC Chorus	6	Archbishop, O Thomas Archbishop, forgive us, forgive us, pray for us that we may
271 MC Chorus	6	O Thomas Archbishop, forgive us, pray for us that we may pray for you,
282 MC Chorus	6	hast given such blessing to Canterbury./Forgive us, O Lord, we acknowledge ourselves as
382 CP Celia	34	making use of you./And I ask you to forgive me./{E} You ... ask me to forgive *you*!/{C}
382 CP Edward	35	to forgive me./{E} You ... ask me to forgive *you*!/{C} Yes, for two things. First ... {}/
386 CP Celia	31	I could./Just looking at you. Edward, forgive my laughing./You look like a little boy
562 ES Monica	6	Father has said, Michael,/You must forgive each other, you must love each other./
569 ES Charles	17	about you./{C} I was thinking, Sir — forgive the suspicion —/From what Monica has

FORGIVEN (2)
194 FQ: Little   116 be./So with your own, and pray they be forgiven/By others, as I pray you to forgive/Both
572 ES   Ld Clav 25 to divorce;/But she hasn't forgotten or forgiven me./{C} This man, and this woman, who
FORGIVENESS (1)
38 Gerontion   33   knob./After such knowledge, what forgiveness? Think now/History has many
FORGIVING (1)
360 CP   Reilly 35   woman,/She might decide to be forgiving/And gain an advantage. If there's no
FORGOT (12)
71 WL: DWater313   the Phoenician, a fortnight dead,/Forgot the cry of gulls, and the deep sea swell/
193 FQ: Little   77 shall rot/The marred foundations we forgot,/Of sanctuary and choir./This is the death
593 Grad 8   6   all the years will ne'er have been forgot./For in the sanctuaries of the soul/Incense
376 CP   Edward   29 *would* do it. Three Good Samaritans./I forgot all about it./{J} But you mustn't touch it./
392 CP   Lavinia 11 party./I suppose you won't believe I forgot all about it!/I let you down badly. What
420 CP   Celia   9   /I must tell you that. Oh, I almost forgot —/May I ask what your fee is?/{R} I have
432 CP   Julia   3   Sir Henry Harcourt-Reilly!/{J} Oh, I forgot! I'd another surprise for you. {}/[*Enter*
432 CP   Lavinia 27   /Of my husband and myself. Oh, I forgot — {}/[*Turning to* ALEX]/{L} I rather
457 CC   Lady E 27   me some tea./Nothing with it. No, I forgot:/You haven't learned yet how to make tea
461 CC   Eggers 14 to call upon you often./{E} Oh, and I forgot ... Mrs. E. keeps saying:/'Why don't you
487 CC   Lady E 34   /That Colby is your son?/{LE} Oh, I forgot/In my excitement: you arrived the very
504 CC   Lady E 10   singing in the pantry./{LE} Oh, I forgot. It's Gertrude's quiet hour./I've been
FORGOTTEN (40)
91 Ash-Wed 2   19   /There is no life in them. As I am forgotten/And would be forgotten, so I would
91 Ash-Wed 2   20 them. As I am forgotten/And would be forgotten, so I would forget/Thus devoted,
109 Marina   23 cracked with heat./I made this, I have forgotten/And remember./The rigging weak and
111 Xmas Trees 19   reverence and the gaiety/May not be forgotten in later experience,/In the bored
151 Rock 2   11   /You, have you built well, have you forgotten the cornerstone?/Talking of right
154 Rock 3   22 Will you leave my people forgetful and forgotten/To idleness, labour, and delirious
158 Rock 5   5   who sit in a house of which the use is forgotten: are like snakes that lie on mouldering
160 Rock 7   15 of this world, affirmation of rites with forgotten meanings/In the restless wind-whipped
161 Rock 7   42   not even opposed, and men have forgotten/All gods except Usury, Lust and Power.
172 FQ: BurntN 53 below inveterate scars/Appeasing long forgotten wars./The dance along the artery/The
184 FQ: DrySal   6   once solved, the brown god is almost forgotten/By the dwellers in cities — ever,
193 FQ: Little   95   dead master/Whom I had known, forgotten, half recalled/Both one and many; in the
194 FQ: Little   114   thoughts and theory which you have forgotten./These things have served their
195 FQ: Little   179   on the scaffold/And a few who died forgotten/In other places, here and abroad,/And
241 MC   Priest1   9   end/Until the poor at the gate/Have forgotten their friend, their Father in God, have
241 MC   Priest1   9 their friend, their Father in God, have forgotten/That they had a friend? {}/[*Enter*
248 MC   Tempt2   15 TEMPTER]/{T2} Your Lordship has forgotten me, perhaps. I will remind you./We met
252 MC   Tempt3   7 helped to found./But time past is time forgotten./We expect the rise of a new
254 MC   Tempt4   13 one more king is another reign./King is forgotten, when another shall come:/Saint and
272 MC   Chorus   21   and dissolve/Into dust on the wind, forgotten, unmemorable; only is here/The white
282 MC   Chorus   2   the death in the desert, the prayer in forgotten places by the broken imperial column,/
306 FR   Harry   19   same time, other memories,/Earlier, forgotten, begin to return/Out of my childhood. I
314 FR   Warburt 10 /To see you again. But you can't have forgotten/The day when you came back from
331 FR   Harry   11 Here I have been finding/A misery long forgotten, and a new torture,/The shadow of
375 CP   Edward   28 what was he talking of?/{E} I had quite forgotten./He made his way in, a little while ago,/
413 CP   Celia   21 I first to tell you the circumstances?/I'd forgotten that you know nothing about me;/And
425 CP   Edward   22 that's what we said at the time;/But I'd forgotten what the Gunnings' parties were like./
439 CP   Peter   17 waiting,/And the experts — I'd almost forgotten them./I realise that I can't get out of it
489 CC   Lady E 36   of the mother;/And the mother had forgotten the name of Mrs. Guzzard,/And I was
506 CC   Eggers 10   had taken the child. Or rather, had forgotten it./She was not, in any case, in a
538 ES   Ld Clav   6 there's just one thing you seem to have forgotten:/I came to your assistance when you
538 ES   Gomez   25 /Until your own have been more or less forgotten./I dare say you did make some mistake,
540 ES   Gomez   32   were their names?/I've completely forgotten them) you didn't want *them*/To be
549 ES   Carghil   7 day we spent on the river — I've never forgotten it —/The turning point of all my life!/
549 ES   Carghil   11   us to lunch?/I declare, I've utterly forgotten their names./And you gave us lunch —
549 ES   Carghil   12 names./And you gave us lunch — I've forgotten what hotel —/But such a good lunch —
549 ES   Carghil   15   /With some lovely little cakes — I've forgotten what you called them,/And you made
553 ES   Carghil   21   /{LC} My letters!/{MC} Have you forgotten that you wrote me letters?/Oh, not very
572 ES   Ld Clav 25 have come to divorce;/But she hasn't forgotten or forgiven me./{C} This man, and this
573 ES   Ld Clav   2 brooding over faults I might well have forgotten./You think that I'm sickening, when
FORK (1)
225 Mr Mistoff   33 fish-paste;/If you look for a knife or a fork/And you think it is merely misplaced —/You
FORKS (1)
213 Growltiger   40 —/For the foe was armed with toasting forks and cruel carving knives./Then GILBERT

FORM (27)

24	Rhapsody	31	a factory yard,/Rust that clings to the form that the strength has left/Hard and curled
83	Hollow Men	11	glass/In our dry cellar/Shape without form, shade without colour,/Paralysed force,
84	Hollow Men	51	with tenderness/Lips that would kiss/Form prayers to broken stone./The eyes are not
110	Marina	29	leaks, the seams need caulking./This form, this face, this life/Living to live in a world
129	Cor2 State	8	shall I cry?/The first thing to do is to form the committees:/The consultative councils,
164	Rock 9	20	with the artist's eye, new life, new form, new colour./Out of the sea of sound the life
173	FQ: BurntN	96	a dim light: neither daylight/Investing form with lucid stillness/Turning shadow into
175	FQ: BurntN	143	reach/Into the silence. Only by the form, the pattern,/Can words or music reach/The
175	FQ: BurntN	170	in the aspect of time/Caught in the form of limitation/Between un-being and being./
186	FQ: DrySal	97	restores the experience/In a different form, beyond any meaning/We can assign to
201	Def Island	11	/and of those who, in man's newest form of gamble/with death, fight the power of
235	Ad-dress	45	taking off my hat,/Ad-dress him in this form: O CAT!/But if he is the Cat next door,/
279	MC Knight4	14	/What I have to say may be put in the form of a question: *Who killed/the Archbishop?*
407	CP Edward	2	like to see *you* filling up an income-tax form./{L} Don't be silly, Edward. When I say
415	CP Celia	23	from our point of view,/Was either bad form, or was psychological./And bad form always
415	CP Celia	24	form, or was psychological./And bad form always led to disaster/Because the people
415	CP Celia	26	of it./I don't worry much about form, myself —/But when everything's bad form,
415	CP Celia	27	myself —/But when everything's bad form, or mental kinks,/You either become bad
415	CP Celia	28	mental kinks,/You either become bad form, and cease to care,/Or else, if you care, you
417	CP Reilly	21	/{R} The condition is curable./But the form of treatment must be your own choice:/I
437	CP Reilly	27	knowing the end/Yet choose the form of death. We know the death she chose./I
437	CP Edward	33	Do you mean that having chosen this form of death/She did not suffer as ordinary
446	CC Claude	13	same disappointment/In a different form. He won't forget/That his great ambition
464	CC Claude	2	a boy/I loved to shape things. I loved form and colour/And I loved the material that the
464	CC Claude	16	longed for./I want a world where the form is the reality,/Of which the substantial is
503	CC Lucasta	7	than we could have been/In any other form of relationship./{C} I want you to be happy./
518	CC Guzzard	39	You have all had your wish/In one form or another. You and I, Sir Claude,/Had *our*

FORMAL (7)

172	FQ: BurntN	33	accepting./So we moved, and they, in a formal pattern,/Along the empty alley, into the
197	FQ: Little	224	word exact without vulgarity,/The formal word precise but not pedantic,/The
303	FR Mary	21	having an outsider;/For what is more formal than a family dinner?/An official occasion
307	FR Harry	12	from school/For the holidays, after the formal reception/And the family festivities, I
334	FR Harry	22	of us. Family affection/Was a kind of formal obligation, a duty/Only noticed by its
462	CC Claude	32	might find it easier/To start by a rather formal relationship/In adapting yourself to a new
493	CC Claude	9	yourself?/{SC} No, that would look too formal. I thought it would be better/To put

FORMALLY (1)

278	MC Knight2	35	by vote of Parliament and execute him/formally as a traitor, and no one would have to

FORME (1)

48	Lune Miel	18	encore/Dans ses pierres écroulantes la forme précise de Byzance./The Hippopotamus/

FORMED (6)

70	WL: Fire S	281	Leicester/Beating oars/The stern was formed/A gilded shell/Red and gold/The brisk
165	Rock 9	40	creation is never without travail;/The formed stone, the visible crucifix,/The dressed
211	Old Gumbie	33	idle and wanton destroyment./So she's formed, from that lot of disorderly louts,/A troop
336	FR Agatha	24	A curse comes to being/As a child is formed./In both, the incredible/Becomes the
336	FR Agatha	29	is intended./A curse is like a child, formed/In a moment of unconsciousness/In an
336	FR Agatha	35	moon./A curse is like a child, formed/To grow to maturity:/Accident is design/

FORMER (2)

267	MC Knight1	30	and you were endued/With your former privilege, how did you show your
463	CC Colby	26	street/Or waking in the night, then the former person,/The person I used to be, returns to

FORMIDABLE (1)

504	CC Lucasta	7	you are expecting. She looks rather formidable./{SC} It's Parkman's day off. But

FORMING (2)

167	Rock 10	43	moved us to building, to finding, to forming at the ends of our fingers and beams of
193	FQ: Little	103	someone other —/And he a face still forming; yet the words sufficed/To compel the

FORMLESS (1)

164	Rock 9	17	must quicken to creation./Out of the formless stone, when the artist unites himself with

FORMS (10)

64	WL: Chess	105	time/Were told upon the walls; staring forms/Leaned out, leaning, hushing the room
98	Ash-Wed 6	18	/And the blind eye creates/The empty forms between the ivory gates/And smell renews
164	Rock 9	18	himself with stone,/Spring always new forms of life, from the soul of man that is joined
256	MC Chorus	8	of hell. What is the sticky dew that forms on the back of my hand?/{4T} Man's life is
257	MC Chorus	28	/Falls the stifling scent of despair;/The forms take shape in the dark air:/Puss-purr of
272	MC Chorus	31	no objects, no tones,/No colours, no forms to distract, to divert the soul/From seeing
335	FR Harry	13	out, in an endless drift/Of shrieking forms in a circular desert/Weaving with

348 FR   Chorus   19   spells and enchantments./And minor forms of sorcery,/Divination and chiromancy,/
437 CP   Reilly   11   *where do inhabit/The shadows of all forms that think and live/Till death unite them and*
469 CC   Colby   10   about its structure/And the various forms, and the different ways of playing it./{L}
FORMULATED (2)
14 Prufrock   56   them all —/The eyes that fix you in a formulated phrase,/And when I am formulated,
14 Prufrock   57   a formulated phrase,/And when I am formulated, sprawling on a pin,/When I am
FORTE (1)
48 Lune Miel   4   de punaises;/La sueur aestivale, et une forte odeur de chienne./Ils restent sur le dos
FORTH (5)
33 Conv Gal   10   music which we seize/To body forth our own vacuity.'/She then: 'Does this refer
189 FQ: DrySal   180   seen their sons or husbands/Setting forth, and not returning:/Figlia del tuo figlio,/
589 Fable   93   good and friarly./Spirits from that time forth they did without,/And lived the admiration
592 Grad 1   6   which lie below,/But let us yet put forth courageously./As colonists embarking from
261 MC Thomas   2   /knew no such things: they went forth to journey afar, to suffer by land/and sea, to
FORTHCOMING (2)
293 FR   Amy   5   Harry./I have always found them forthcoming with advice/Which I have never
507 CC Guzzard   20   long, that is to say, as the money was forthcoming./{E} Did the payments come to an
FORTIFICATIONS (1)
129 Cor2 State   19   chiefly the question of rebuilding the fortifications./A commission is appointed/To
FORTIFIED (1)
280 MC Priest3   15   action,/Triumphant in adversity. It is fortified/By persecution: supreme, so long as men
FORTIFY (1)
212 Growltiger   11   shuddered at his name./They would fortify the hen-house, lock up the silly goose,/
FORTNIGHT (2)
71 WL: DWater 312   by Water/Phlebas the Phoenician, a fortnight dead,/Forgot the cry of gulls, and the
544 ES   Ld Clav 11   good./I'll feel more confidence after a fortnight —/After fourteen days of people not
FORTRESS (1)
273 MC Thomas   18   of Christ,/The sanctuary, turned into a fortress./The Church shall protect her own, in her
FORTUNATE (2)
196 FQ: Little   194   party./Whatever we inherit from the fortunate/We have taken from the defeated/What
323 FR   Charles 35   it to Warburton, Amy./Extremely fortunate for us that he's here./We must put
FORTUNE (8)
108 Animula   34   pieces,/For this one who made a great fortune,/And that one who went his own way./
587 Fable   13   ne'er he/Had done before — their fortune multiplied,/As if they had been kept by a
240 MC Chorus   2   and cautious, tries to compile a little fortune,/And the labourer bends to his piece of
296 FR   Charles 27   he did. He cannot trust his good fortune./I believe that all he needs is someone to
553 ES   Carghil 25   the break came,/'They'll be worth a fortune to you, Maisie.'/They would have figured
570 ES   Ld Clav 27   American,/A man who's made a fortune by his own peculiar methods,/A man of
576 ES   Michael 17   pickings in commissions./He's made a fortune there. San Marco for me!/{LC} And what
579 ES   Gomez   36   can only regard it as a stroke of good fortune/That I came to England at the very
FORTUNES (2)
592 Grad 2   2   from the strand/To seek their fortunes on some foreign shore/Well know they
551 ES   Carghil 39   perhaps I laid the foundation of your fortunes!/{LC} And perhaps at the same time of
FORTY (3)
314 FR   Warburt 26   one disease or another./Now I've had forty years' experience/I've left off thinking in
314 FR   Ivy   32   had a very rich experience, Doctor,/In forty years./{W} Indeed, yes./Even in a country
503 CC Lucasta   12   may bring us/In twenty or thirty or forty years' time./I shall be happy. I'm going to
FORUM (1)
164 Rock 9   10 themselves, and busy in the market, the forum,/And all other secular meetings./Thinking
FORWARD (18)
107 Animula   26   misshapen, lame,/Unable to fare forward or retreat,/Fearing the warm reality, the
160 Rock 7   4 and the shadow, and the light led them forward to light and the shadow led them to
179 FQ: ECoker   74 was to be the value of the long looked forward to,/Long hoped for calm, the autumnal
187 FQ: DrySal   131   the way up is the way down, the way forward is the way back./You cannot face it
188 FQ: DrySal   139   rhythm of a hundred hours./Fare forward, travellers! not escaping from the past/
188 FQ: DrySal   151 of time, and not in any language)/'Fare forward, you who think that you are voyaging;/
188 FQ: DrySal   164 do not think of the fruit of action./Fare forward./O voyagers, O seamen,/You who come
188 FQ: DrySal   172 field of battle./Not fare well,/But fare forward, voyagers./Lady, whose shrine stands on
213 Growltiger   49 did surround./The ruthless foe pressed forward, in stubborn rank on rank;/Growltiger to
250 MC Thomas   37   Englishman./{T} Proceed straight forward./{T3} Purpose is plain./Endurance of
253 MC Tempt4   21   /{T} What is your counsel?/{T4} Fare forward to the end./All other ways are closed to
292 FR   Amy   17   /The servants have been looking forward to your coming:/Would you like to have
312 FR   m 9 Yet I must speak to them. {}/[*He rushes forward and tears apart the curtains: but the*
322 FR   Winch   12   my Lord./I didn't mean to put myself forward./But you see, my Lord, I had good
349 FR   Gerald   9   still be valid?/{G} I do not look forward with pleasure to dealing with Arthur and

410 CP	Lavinia	29	do/When we can go neither back nor forward? Edward!/What can we do?/{R} You
530 ES	Monica	27	nothing./{M} Yet you've been looking forward/To this very time! You know how you
532 ES	Charles	24	/{C} I'll say goodbye, sir./And look forward to seeing you both at Badgley Court/In a

FOSTER-MOTHER (1)

| 506 CC | Eggers | 2 | to be cared for/Till further notice by a foster-mother./Unfortunately, the father died |

FOSTER-PARENTS (1)

| 513 CC | Colby | 21 | —/It's different for B. He's had his foster-parents,/So he can afford another |

FOSTERED (1)

| 537 ES | Gomez | 39 | And expensive tastes — which you had fostered in me,/And, equally unfortunate, a talent |

FOSTERS (1)

| 476 CC | Lucasta | 16 | B. has been such a help to me —/He fosters the impression. He half believes in it./But |

FOUGHT (7)

37 Gerontion		4	rain./I was neither at the hot gates/Nor fought in the warm rain/Nor knee deep in the salt
37 Gerontion		6	heaving a cutlass,/Bitten by flies, fought./My house is a decayed house,/And the
152 Rock 2		34	as devoted as those of your fathers who fought to gain it./The Church must be forever
203 Indians		9	to the climate)/Of foreign men, who fought in foreign places,/Foreign to each other./A
274 MC Thomas		9	to fight with beasts as men. We have fought the beast/And have conquered. We have
307 FR Harry		3	That was the stockade/From which we fought the Indians, Arthur and John./{M} It was
314 FR Warburt		37	from an incurable cancer./How he fought against it! I never saw a man/More

FOUL (4)

147 Rock 1		30	or Maidenhead./If the weather is foul we stay at home and read the papers./In
275 MC Chorus		22	from stone and wash them./The land is foul, the water is foul, our beasts and ourselves
275 MC Chorus		22	them./The land is foul, the water is foul, our beasts and ourselves defiled with blood./
276 MC Chorus		16	is defiled,/But the world that is wholly foul./Clear the air! clean the sky! wash the wind!

FOULLY (1)

| 272 MC Chorus | | 32 | to divert the soul/From seeing itself, foully united forever, nothing with nothing,/Not |

FOUND (69)

52 Whispers		10	I suppose, was such another/Who found no substitute for sense,/To seize and clutch
74 WL: Thund		406	we have existed/Which is not to be found in our obituaries/Or in memories draped by
96 Ash-Wed 5		11	unto thee./Where shall the word be found, where will the word/Resound? Not here,
182 FQ: ECoker		189	fight to recover what has been lost/And found and lost again and again: and now, under
204 de la Mare		1	children who explored the brook and found/A desert island with a sandy cove/(A
218 Mung Rump		7	very well bear./If the area window was found ajar/And the basement looked like a field
226 Macavity		22	at cards.)/And his footprints are not found in any file of Scotland Yard's./And when
230 Bust Jones		18	reason, when game is in season/He is found, not at *Fox's*, but *Blimp's*;/But he's
230 Bust Jones		30	day —/At one club or another he's found./It can be no surprise that under our eyes/
233 Skimble		33	/Oh it's very pleasant when you have found your little den/With your name written up
587 Fable		2	that royal Mormon/King Henry VIII found out that monks were quacks,/And took
589 Fable		82	/But not a shred of Bishop could be found,/The monks, when anyone questioned,
589 Fable		96	these doings/From an old manuscript found in the ruins./If Time and Space, as Sages
593 Grad 7		2	benefits — may we/In future years be found with those who try/To labor for the good
241 MC Priest3		20	proud men?/{P3} What peace can be found/To grow between the hammer and the
246 MC Thomas		8	on another day,/Had fair crossing, found at Sandwich/Broc, Warenne, and the
251 MC Tempt3		18	O my King!/{T3} Other friends/May be found in the present situation./King in England is
252 MC Thomas		5	baron's court./{T} Which I helped to found./{T3} Which you helped to found./But time
252 MC Tempt3		6	to found./{T3} Which you helped to found./But time past is time forgotten./We expect
293 FR Amy		5	are very helpful, Harry./I have always found them forthcoming with advice/Which I
307 FR Mary		10	/Where we had been./{M} They never found the secret./{H} Not then. But later, coming
308 FR Harry		5	/The glow upon the world, that never found its object;/And the eye adjusts itself to a
332 FR Agatha		36	not shaken your father/Awake yet. I found him thinking/How to get rid of your
337 FR Agatha		11	treasure hunt:/Here you have found a clue, hidden in the obvious place./Delay,
338 FR Harry		28	but to pursue,/Not to avoid being found, but to seek./I would not have chosen this
342 FR Agatha		37	has the least suspicion of what is to be found there./But Harry has been led across the
353 CP Peter		15	wedding cake./{P} And how the butler found her in the pantry, rinsing her mouth out
365 CP Julia		1	everywhere I've been./Has anybody found them? You can tell if they're mine —/Some
366 CP Julia		9	was very clever of you;/I'd never have found them but for you./The next time I lose
367 CP Alex		37	you *got* in, Alex./{A} Why, I came and found that the door was open/And so I thought
369 CP Peter		28	I knew no one to go with,/And later, I found I preferred to go alone./But a girl like
369 CP Peter		33	we got into conversation,/And I found that she went to concerts alone/And to
370 CP Edward		36	As the fever cooled/You would have found that she was another woman/And that you
372 CP Alex		14	a supper out of so few materials/As I found in your refrigerator. But of course/I was
376 CP Edward		1	/{E} Suppose someone came and found you in the kitchen? {}/[EDWARD *goes*
376 CP Celia		5	did leave my umbrella;/And I'll say I found you here starving and helpless/And had to
377 CP Julia		21	to eat:/I've looked high and low. But I found some champagne —/Only a half-bottle, to
380 CP Celia		27	came to make more acquaintances,/I found him less interesting, and rather conceited./

383 CP   Edward   29   we ... I had to hunt for them ... No, I found them./... Yes, she's bringing them now ...
386 CP   Celia   34   and is not quite sure/What he's been found out in. I never saw you so before./This is
393 CP   Edward   38   any of *your* friends —/You suddenly found it inconvenient/That I should be always too
395 CP   Edward   16   the changing —/Though I haven't yet found it a change for the better./But doesn't it
416 CP   Celia   20   now it would seem right./And then I found we were only strangers/And that there had
416 CP   Celia   39   I went into the forest to find/And never found, and which was not there/And perhaps is
417 CP   Celia   1   /Why do I feel guilty at not having found it?/{R} Disillusion can become itself an
434 CP   Alex   19   —/Those who survived. And then they found her body,/Or at least, they found the traces
434 CP   Alex   20   they found her body,/Or at least, they found the traces of it./{E} But before that .../{A} It
446 CC   Claude   17   could do, and do well. And I think he's found it,/Just as I did. I shall tell him about
451 CC   Colby   15   be so different./I like B. Kaghan. I've found him very helpful/And very good company
463 CC   Colby   9   .../{C} You started by asking me how I found this work./{SC} Yes, how do you find it?/
472 CC   Lucasta 23   a disaster it was in your life/When you found that you'd never be a good musician —/Of
472 CC   Lucasta 35   you saw them./And yet, all the time, I found I *envied* you/And I didn't know why! But
483 CC   Lady E   6   where to find them./{LE} They can be found./But I came to have a look at the flat/To
489 CC   Claude   12   now. But it influenced me./And I found a better reason for keeping silent./I came to
492 CC   Colby   24   me into the conversation —/And I found one note I couldn't understand./
499 CC   Lucasta 27   I know what a nuisance you've always found me!/And I haven't made it easier. I didn't
510 CC   Claude   12   I believe, Elizabeth,/That you have found your son./{E} Subject to confirmation./
510 CC   Kaghan   30   wanted to retire to the country./So I found them a little place near Sevenoaks/Where
514 CC   Guzzard 38   When you went to Canada/My sister found that she was to have a child:/That much is
515 CC   Guzzard   6   you came at once to see me;/And I found that I had to break the news to you./You
516 CC   Colby   11   I didn't want to be an organist/When I found I had no chance of getting to the top —/
534 ES   Gomez   21   of that nature,/Is certain to be found out sooner or later./And then what
537 ES   Gomez   19   doubt your friends wondered what you found in me —/A scholarship boy from an
537 ES   Gomez   38   clerkship — which your father found for me,/And expensive tastes — which you
569 ES   Ld Clav 36   me/Though it was not till lately that I found the living persons/Whose ghosts tormented
574 ES   Carghil 21   a friend of Michael's father!/And I found him only too ready to help./{LC} And what
575 ES   Ld Clav 32   of our ... intimacy/Which they found puzzling./{MC} Oh, Richard!/Have you
580 ES   Carghil 23   news of Michael./And now that we've found each other again,/We must always keep in
581 ES   Ld Clav 28   I am happy, Monica, that you have found a man/Whom you can love for the man he
FOUNDATION (2)
151 Rock 2   2   of GOD, being built upon the foundation/Of apostles and prophets, Christ
551 ES   Carghil 39   Lord Claverton./So perhaps I laid the foundation of your fortunes!/{LC} And perhaps
FOUNDATIONS (1)
193 FQ: Little   77   /Water and fire shall rot/The marred foundations we forgot,/Of sanctuary and choir./
FOUNDED (1)
587 Fable   5   at their backs,/There was a village founded by some Norman/Who levied on all
FOUNDLING (4)
480 CC   Kaghan   28   I wasn't, Colby./Do you know, I was a foundling? You didn't know that!/Never had any
484 CC   Lady E   37   didn't know it. Finally,/That I was a foundling, and didn't know it./Of course, I was
485 CC   Lady E   3   I actually *liked* to believe/That I was a foundling — or do I mean 'changeling'?/{C} I
512 CC   Kaghan   29   /{K} It's very much better than being a foundling —/If I can live up to it. And ... yes, of
FOUNTAIN (5)
 95 Ash-Wed 4   25   and signed but spoke no word/But the fountain sprang up and the bird sang down/
 98 Ash-Wed 6   25   Blessèd sister, holy mother, spirit of the fountain, spirit of the garden,/Suffer us not to
157 Rock 4   12   dragon's well, by the dung gate,/By the fountain gate, by the king's pool,/Jerusalem lay
598 Circe   1   of dawn./Circe's Palace/Around her fountain which flows/With the voice of men in
280 MC   Priest3 28   in his libidinous courts,/Oblivion in the fountain by the date-tree;/Or sit and bite your
FOUNTAINS (1)
 94 Ash-Wed 4   8   walked,/Who then made strong the fountains and made fresh the springs/Made cool
FOUR (25)
 18 Portrait   4   saved this afternoon for you';/And four wax candles in the darkened room,/Four
 18 Portrait   5   wax candles in the darkened room,/Four rings of light upon the ceiling overhead,/An
 23 Preludes   42   block,/Or trampled by insistent feet/At four and five and six o'clock;/And short square
 26 Rhapsody   70   cocktail smells in bars./The lamp said,/'Four o'clock,/Here is the number on the door./
 29 Aunt Helen   3   Cared for by servants to the number of four./Now when she died there was silence in
 65 WL: Chess   136   at ten./And if it rains, a closed car at four./And we shall play a game of chess,/Pressing
 66 WL: Chess   148   of poor Albert,/He's been in the army four years, he wants a good time,/And if you
117 SP   Doris   8   anyway it's very queer./{Do} Here's the four of diamonds, what's that mean?/{Du}
118 SP   Wauch   26   up here/How many's down there?/{W} Four of us here./Wait till I put the car round the
134 Wind   t   us in derision./The wind sprang up at four o'clock/The wind sprang up at four o'clock/
134 Wind   1   at four o'clock/The wind sprang up at four o'clock/The wind sprang up and broke the
169 4 Quartets   t   give Thee thanks for Thy great glory!/FOUR QUARTETS/Burnt Norton/Time
588 Fable   55   a boar's head, which to bring in took four pages,/His mouth an apple held, his skull

589 Fable 91   food entirely;/Each morn from four to five one took a knout/And flogged his
238 MC   m 7   THOMAS BECKET/FOUR TEMPTERS/ATTENDANTS/*The scene*
238 MC   m 12   1170/PART II/THREE PRIESTS/FOUR KNIGHTS/ARCHBISHOP THOMAS
252 MC Thomas 33 are you? I expected/Three visitors, not four./{T4} Do not be surprised to receive one
265 MC   m 9   design may appear. {}/[*Enter the* FOUR KNIGHTS. *The banners disappear*]/{K1}
276 MC Knight1 21   you see one man being set upon by four, then your/sympathies are all with the under
277 MC Knight3 5 much more to lose than to gain. We are four plain Englishmen/who put our country first.
400 CP   Alex 7   was only impatient/At having to wait four days for the appointment./{R} It was
491 CC   Colby 32 have two parents —/But I should have four! What about those others?/I should have to
523 ES   m 11   *of Lord Claverton's London house. Four o'clock in the afternoon*/ACT TWO/*The*
524 ES   2m 1   CLAVERTON'S *London house. Four o'clock in the afternoon.*/[*Voices in the hall*]/
536 ES   Gomez 12 interested/In anything that happened four thousand miles away,/Only believed what
FOURCHETTE (1)
  51 Restaurant 22 décrotter les rides du visage;/Tiens, ma fourchette, décrasse-toi le crâne./De quel droit
FOURTEEN (1)
544 ES   Ld Clav 12   confidence after a fortnight —/After fourteen days of people not staring/Or offering
FOURTEENTH (1)
260 MC Thomas   2   earth peace to men of good will.' The/*fourteenth verse of the second chapter of the Gospel*
FOURTH (3)
252 MC   m 30   I must break myself alone. {}/[*Enter* FOURTH TEMPTER]/{T4} Well done, Thomas,
264 MC   Priest1 22   Since the Holy Innocents a day: the fourth day from Christmas./{3P} *Rejoice we all,*
544 ES   Ld Clav 13   offering picture papers, or wanting a fourth at bridge;/Still, I'll admit to a feeling of
FOX (2)
221 Old Deut 33 Deuteronomy lies on the floor/Of the Fox and French Horn for his afternoon sleep;/
267 MC Knight2 20   /{K2} Without delay,/Before the old fox is off and away./{T} What you have to say/By
FOX'S (2)
105 Song Sime 15   will take to the goat's path, and the fox's home,/Fleeing from the foreign faces and
230 Bust Jones 18 game is in season/He is found, not at *Fox's*, but *Blimp's*;/But he's frequently seen at the
FOX-SPARROW (1)
142 Cape Ann   2   the song-sparrow,/Swamp-sparrow, fox-sparrow, vesper-sparrow/At dawn and dusk.
FRACTURED (1)
  39 Gerontion 69   the circuit of the shuddering Bear/In fractured atoms. Gull against the wind, in the
FRACTURES (1)
167 Rock 10   33   look upward/And see the light that fractures through unquiet water./We see the light
FRAGILION (1)
  31 Apollinax   3   among the teacups./I thought of Fragilion, that shy figure among the birch-trees,/
FRAGMENT (3)
115 SP   t   *of an Aristophanic Melodrama*/Fragment of a Prologue/DUSTY. DORIS./{Du}
121 SA   t   he's promised to show us around. {}/Fragment of an Agon/SWEENEY.
296 FR Agatha   3   also convinced/That you only hold a fragment of the explanation./It is only because of
FRAGMENTS (3)
  32 Hysteria 10 breasts could be stopped,/some of the fragments of the afternoon might be collected,
  75 WL: Thund 430   *d'Aquitaine à la tour abolie*/These fragments I have shored against my ruins/Why
115 S   m   POEMS/Sweeney Agonistes/*Fragments of an Aristophanic Melodrama*/
FRAGRANCE (3)
597 Before Mor 6 flowers and flowers of yesterday/Their fragrance drifts across the room at dawn,/
597 Before Mor 7   drifts across the room at dawn,/Fragrance of bloom and fragrance of decay,/
597 Before Mor 7   at dawn,/Fragrance of bloom and fragrance of decay,/Fresh flowers, withered
FRAGRANT (1)
107 Animula   9 to be reassured, taking pleasure/In the fragrant brilliance of the Christmas tree,/Pleasure
FRAIL (2)
  49 Hippopot   5   blood./Flesh and blood is weak and frail,/Susceptible to nervous shock;/While the
459 CC   Lady E 8 should be artistic. But you look rather frail./I must give you lessons in the art of health./
FRAME (4)
602 Humoresque 4 as in head,/(A jumping-jack has such a frame)./But this deceasèd marionette/I rather
244 MC Chorus 25   us be, in our humble and tarnished frame of existence, leave us; do not ask us/To
365 CP   Julia 2 mine —/Some kind of a plastic sort of frame —/I'm afraid I don't remember the colour,/
483 CC   Lady E 23 {LE} And I see a photograph in a silver frame./I'm afraid I shall have to instruct you,
FRAMED (2)
  64 WL: Chess 95 with copper/Burned green and orange, framed by the coloured stone,/In which sad light
151 Rock 2   7 urn to be filled./Your building not fitly framed together, you sit ashamed and wonder

525 ES   Charles   2   with your father:/I arranged to be free for the whole afternoon/On the plain
525 ES   Charles   5 stop to tea./{C} When I said that I was free for the whole afternoon,/That meant you
527 ES   Monica   8   that I want to marry you/When I'm free to do so. But by that time/You may have
542 ES   Ld Clav   22   /We were the same age. You were a free moral agent./You pretend that I taught you
556 ES   Monica   2   /That the doctors want you to be free from worry./He won't make a scene. But I
577 ES   Ld Clav   39 as you know very well./Michael's a free agent. So if he chooses/To place himself in
FREED (1)
582 ES   Ld Clav   3 *me* he rejected, I reject also./I've been freed from the self that pretends to be someone;/
FREEDOM (10)
173 FQ: BurntN   72 for that is to place it in time./The inner freedom from the practical desire,/The release
190 FQ: DrySal   228 chthonic/Powers. And right action is freedom/From past and future also./For most of
195 FQ: Little   165 may be servitude,/History may be freedom. See, now they vanish,/The faces and
296 FR   Agatha   7   hold fast to that/As the way to freedom./{H} I think I see what you mean,/Dimly
307 FR   Harry   18 /It's absurd that one's only memory of freedom/Should be a hollow tree in a wood by the
379 CP   Celia   7 /And that you do mean to gain your freedom,/And that everything is all right between
384 CP   Reilly   17 but you are not free./Your moment of freedom was yesterday./You made a decision.
405 CP   Reilly   22   It is for me to give you that —/Your freedom. That is my affair. {}/[LAVINIA *is*
515 CC   Colby   33 you. I must believe you:/This gives me freedom./{SC} But, Colby —/If this should be
572 ES   Ld Clav   38 /That is the first step taken towards my freedom,/And perhaps the most important. I
FREELY (1)
482 CC   Lady E   17 want to take you up./I can speak more freely, as an elderly person./{C} But, Lady
FREEZE (2)
181 FQ: ECoker   166 wires./If to be warmed, then I must freeze/And quake in frigid purgatorial fires/Of
285 FR   Ivy   18 in the winter, if I could afford it,/Not freeze, as I do, in Bayswater, by a gas-fire
FREEZING (2)
191 FQ: Little   11 time of the year. Between melting and freezing/The soul's sap quivers. There is no earth
429 CP   Julia   37 Give me some gin./Not a cocktail. I'm freezing — in July!/{CM} Mr. Quilpe!/{E} Now
FRENCH (5)
 68 WL: Fire S   212   at sight,/Asked me in demotic French/To luncheon at the Cannon Street Hotel/
221 Old Deut   33   lies on the floor/Of the Fox and French Horn for his afternoon sleep;/And when
240 MC   Priest2 29 Pope/With the stubborn King and the French King/In ceaseless intrigue, combinations,/
267 MC   Knight1 33   the hope/Of stirring up trouble in the French dominions./You sowed strife abroad, you
455 CC   Eggers   40 is a lady,/Rather a *grande dame*, as the French say./That's what Sir Claude admires
FRENZIED (2)
601 Nocturne   11   oblique/Rolls toward the moon a frenzied eye profound,/(No need of 'Love
241 MC   Mess   32 people,/Who receive him with scenes of frenzied enthusiasm,/Lining the road and
FRENZY (1)
179 FQ: ECoker   96 of their folly,/Their fear of fear and frenzy, their fear of possession,/Of belonging to
FREQUENT (2)
241 MC   Priest3   1   /But violence, duplicity and frequent malversation./King rules or barons
408 CP   Reilly   16 who?/{R} Mr. Peter Quilpe/Was a frequent guest./{E} Peter Quilpe./Peter Quilpe!
FREQUENTLY (4)
 20 Portrait   96 had reckoned./'I have been wondering frequently of late/(But our beginnings never know
230 Bust Jones   19   not at *Fox's*, but *Blimp's*;/But he's frequently seen at the gay *Stage and Screen*/
234 Ad-dress   29 far from showing too much pride/Is frequently undignified./He's very easily taken in
367 CP   Edward   20   interest in the moving pictures/Frequently brings young people together./{P}
FRÈRE (1)
 63 WL: Burial   76   lecteur! — mon semblable, — mon frère!'/A Game of Chess/The Chair she sat in, like
FRESCA (1)
 39 Gerontion   67 will the weevil/Delay? De Bailhache, Fresca, Mrs. Cammel, whirled/Beyond the circuit
FRESCO (1)
167 Rock 10   31 /The gilded carven wood, the coloured fresco./Our gaze is submarine, our eyes look
FRESH (8)
 94 Ash-Wed 4   8 made strong the fountains and made fresh the springs/Made cool the dry rock and
123 SAWa & Ho   8 *as good/Any old isle is just my style/Any fresh egg/Any fresh egg/And the sound of the coral*
123 SAWa & Ho   9 *isle is just my style/Any fresh egg/Any fresh egg/And the sound of the coral sea./*{Do} I
233 Skimble   51 In the watches of the night he is always fresh and bright;/Every now and then he has a
597 Before Mor   4 /Petal on petal, waiting for the day,/Fresh flowers, withered flowers, flowers of dawn./
597 Before Mor   8   of bloom and fragrance of decay,/Fresh flowers, withered flowers, flowers of dawn./
263 MC   Chorus   26 green tree cover, what wrong/Shall the fresh earth cover? We wait, and the time is short;/
440 CP   Edward   7 saying,/I think, that every moment is a fresh beginning;/And Julia, that life is only
FRESHENED (1)
 64 WL: Chess   90 sense in odours; stirred by the air/That freshened from the window, these ascended/In
FRETFUL (1)
290 FR   Chorus   36   do we feel embarrassed, impatient, fretful, ill at ease,/Assembled like amateur actors

FRETS (1)
571 ES Ld Clav 21 That is where I failed. And the memory frets me./{C} But all the same, these two people
FRIARLY (1)
589 Fable 92   his mates 'till they grew good and friarly./Spirits from that time forth they did
FRIARS (2)
587 Fable   8 a monastery/Inhabited by a band of friars merry./They were possessors of rich lands
589 Fable 77 come with him, in accents hollow./The friars could do nought but gape and stare,/The
FRICTION (2)
194 FQ: Little 133   your lifetime's effort./First, the cold friction of expiring sense/Without enchantment,
428 CP   Alex 30 prosper exceedingly:/And that creates friction between them and the others./And that's
FRIDAY (5)
182 FQ: ECoker 173 —/Again, in spite of that, we call this Friday good./So here I am, in the middle way,
358 CP   Julia   1 to make you dine alone with me/On Friday, and talk to me about everything./{E}
358 CP   Julia   6 shan't escape. You dine with me on Friday./I've already chosen the people you're to
358 CP   Julia 23 /Why don't you *all* come to dinner on Friday?/No, I'm afraid my good Mrs. Batten/
358 CP   Julia 33 then I can drop you./I expect you on Friday, Edward. And Celia —/I must see you
FRIEND (46)
 18 Portrait 24 blind!/How keen you are!)/To find a friend who has these qualities,/Who has, and
 19 Portrait 44 in her fingers while she talks./'Ah, my friend, you do not know, you do not know/What
 20 Portrait 64 /But what have I, but what have I, my friend,/To give you, what can you receive from
 33 Conv Gal   1 Galante/I observe: 'Our sentimental friend the moon!/Or possibly (fantastic, I confess)
 63 WL: Burial 74 bed?/'O keep the Dog far hence, that's friend to men,/'Or with his nails he'll dig it up
 74 WL: Thund 402 /DA/*Datta:* what have we given?/My friend, blood shaking my heart/The awful daring
117 SP   Dusty 13 that mean?/{Du} 'News of an absent friend'. — Pereira!/{Do} The Queen of Hearts! —
117 SP   Dusty 31 Well it needn't be yours, it may mean a friend./{Do} No it's mine. I'm sure it's mine./I
158 Rock 5   3 has something to gain: and from the friend who has something to lose./Remembering
235 Ad-dress 53 condescend/To treat you as a trusted friend,/Some little token of esteem/Is needed, like
594 Grad 13   3 no less;/A guide to warn them, and a friend to bless/Before they leave thy care for lands
241 MC Priest1   9 poor at the gate/Have forgotten their friend, their Father in God, have forgotten/That
241 MC Priest1 10 God, have forgotten/That they had a friend? {}/[*Enter* MESSENGER]/{M} Servants of
246 MC Tempt1 29 /Your Lordship won't despise an old friend out of favour?/Old Tom, gay Tom, Becket
252 MC Tempt4 31 me beside you, you shall not lack a friend./{T} Who are you? I expected/Three
253 MC Tempt4   9 trust/Twice, the man who has been his friend./Borrow use cautiously, employ/Your
260 MC Thomas 30 the swept hearth, his best wine for a friend/at the table, his wife singing to the
276 MC Knight3 34 such an experienced/speaker as my old friend Reginald Fitz Urse would lead you to/
296 FR   Gerald 35 and ask him to join us?/He's an old friend of the family, it's perfectly natural/That he
298 FR   Charles 34 /And I'm sure that you've been a good friend to him, too./*We* haven't seen him for nearly
314 FR   Amy   3 Warburton?/You know he's the oldest friend of the family,/And he's known you longer
320 FR Warburt 31 /But you know that I am a very old friend,/And have always been a party to the
365 CP   Julia 18 *drinking* together!/So this is the kind of friend you have/When Lavinia is out of the way!
389 CP Lavinia 27 —/At least, in so far as a girl *can* be a friend/Of a woman so much older than herself./
409 CP   Reilly 26 /When you discovered that your young friend/(Though you knew, in your heart, that he
409 CP   Reilly 30 I say, you discovered that your young friend/Had actually fallen in love with Miss
411 CP Lavinia   3   /Who has just taken over, is a friend of Alex's./I could go down with you, and
412 CP   Reilly 25 you sit down?/I believe you are a friend of Mrs. Shuttlethwaite./{C} Yes, it was
426 CP   Julia 37 one of their men at the door —/An old friend of mine, in fact. But I'm forgetting!/I've got
432 CP Lavinia 26 Henry Harcourt-Reilly. Peter's an old friend/Of my husband and myself. Oh, I forgot —
455 CC   Eggers 12 gathered;/But I think her father was a friend of Sir Claude's,/And he's made himself
505 CC   Claude   5 in my confidence — and I may say, my friend —/For very many years. So I asked him to
517 CC   Claude   4 /All I ask you is — to regard me as a friend. —/{C} But you would still think of me as
532 ES Ld Clav 31 Good evening, Mr. ... Gomez. You're a friend of Mr. Culverwell?/{G} We're as thick as
535 ES   Gomez   3 natural desire!/For you're the only old friend I can trust./{LC} You really trust me? I
536 ES   Gomez 39 want to see me./No, I need one old friend, a friend whom I can trust —/And one who
536 ES   Gomez 39 to see me./No, I need one old friend, a friend whom I can trust —/And one who will
541 ES   Gomez 16 believed/That you would accuse an old friend of ... blackmail!/On the contrary, I dare say
541 ES   Gomez 28 at your disposal./You were a generous friend to me once/As you pointedly reminded me
557 ES Michael 25   I went to a lender,/A man whom a friend of mine recommended./He gave me good
562 ES Carghil 32 was then./Your father was a very dear friend of mine once./{Mi} Did he really look like
563 ES   Gomez 19 us./{LC} Oh. This is .../{G} Your old friend Federico Gomez,/The prominent citizen of
564 ES Carghil 21 that we never met before./You were a friend of Richard's at Oxford/And Richard and I
565 ES Carghil 11 Michael?/Your father is such an old friend of mine/That it seems most natural to call
574 ES Carghil 20 important/In his own country. And a friend of Michael's father!/And I found him only
579 ES Carghil 34 problems. Sometimes an outsider,/A friend of the family, can see more clearly./{G} Not
FRIEND'S (1)
247 MC Tempt1 37   lives to eat the best dinners./Take a friend's advice. Leave well alone,/Or your goose

542 ES   Gomez   3   to make clear that I only want your friendship!/Just as it used to be in the old days/
542 ES   Ld Clav   13   This is preposterous!/Do you call it friendship to impose your company/On a man by
542 ES   Gomez   17   of you. My only aim/Is to renew our friendship. Don't you understand?/{LC} I see that
542 ES   Ld Clav   18   /{LC} I see that when I gave you my friendship/So many years ago, I only gained in
569 ES   Ld Clav   28   I want nothing from you/Except your friendship and your company./He's a very rich

FRIENDSHIPS (1)
 18 Portrait   28   that I say this to you —/Without these friendships — life, what *cauchemar!*/Among the

FRIGHT (2)
125 SA   Chorus   32   /you wake in a sweat and a hell of a fright/When you're alone in the middle of the bed
300 FR Downing   6   her lean over the rail./He was in a rare fright, once or twice./But you know, it is just my

FRIGHTEN (1)
299 FR Downing   19   my way of thinking/She only did it to frighten people./If you take my meaning — just

FRIGHTENED (16)
 61 WL: Burial   15   he took me out on a sled,/And I was frightened. He said, Marie,/Marie, hold on tight.
254 MC   Tempt4   16   dismayed,/Creeping in penance, frightened of a shade;/Think of pilgrims, standing
304 FR   Agatha   35   see that she distrusted me — she was frightened of the family,/She wanted to fight them
334 FR   Agatha   17   of all the family. And I am a little frightened./{H} You, frightened! I can hardly
334 FR   Harry   18   And I am a little frightened./{H} You, frightened! I can hardly imagine it./I wish I had
415 CP   Celia   37   /Yet, at the same time, I'm frightened by the fear/That it is more real than
418 CP   Celia   38   It is a terrifying journey./{C} I am not frightened/But glad. I suppose it is a lonely way?/
421 CP   Reilly   21   way of illumination?/{R} Will she be frightened/By the first appearance of projected
472 CC   Colby   4   you're brave — and I think that you're frightened./Perhaps you've been very badly hurt,
515 CC Guzzard   15   future could he have?/And then I was frightened by what I had done./Though I had
526 ES   Charles   4   The moment I'd said it/I was badly frightened. For I didn't *know* you loved me —/I
531 ES   Ld Clav   30   me smile/To think that men should be frightened of ghosts./If they only knew how
531 ES   Ld Clav   31   of ghosts./If they only knew how frightened a ghost can be of men! { }/[*Knock.*
556 ES   Monica   3 won't make a scene. But I can see he's frightened./And you know what Michael is like
556 ES   Monica   4   know what Michael is like when he's frightened./He's apt to be sullen and quick to take
567 ES   Monica   3 come!/I've been so worried, and rather frightened./It was exasperating that they couldn't

FRIGHTENING (4)
413 CP   Celia   31   world itself — and that's much more frightening!/That would be terrible. So I'd rather
455 CC   Colby   6   my reason:/Her influence is perfectly frightening./But tell me about Lu ... Miss Angel:/
553 ES   Carghil   15   lingers./And I've touched yours./It's frightening to think that we're still together/And
553 ES   Carghil   16   that we're still together/And more frightening to think that we may *always* be

FRIGHTFUL (2)
213 Growltiger   42   to his fierce Mongolian horde;/With a frightful burst of fireworks the Chinks they
554 ES   Carghil   4   /She's bearing down on us. Isn't she frightful!/She never stops talking. Can you bear

FRIGID (1)
181 FQ: ECoker   167   then I must freeze/And quake in frigid purgatorial fires/Of which the flame is

FRISCH (1)
 61 WL: Burial   31 will show you fear in a handful of dust./*Frisch weht der Wind/Der Heimat zu/Mein Irisch*

FRITTERED (1)
151 Rock 2   5   /Where many are born to idleness, to frittered lives and squalid deaths, embittered

FRO (3)
152 Rock 2   47   much disturbance,/But all dash to and fro in motor cars,/Familiar with the roads and
335 FR   Harry   23   Until the chain breaks./{H} To and fro, dragging my feet/Among inner shadows in
335 FR   Harry   26   branches/And the giant lizard. To and fro./Until the chain breaks./The chain breaks,/

FROGS (3)
129 Cor2 State   25   shake dice on the marches/And the frogs (O Mantuan) croak in the marshes./Fireflies
245 MC   Priest2   6 and cheering,/You go on croaking like frogs in the treetops:/But frogs at least can be
245 MC   Priest2   7   croaking like frogs in the treetops:/But frogs at least can be cooked and eaten./Whatever

FROM (477)

FRONT (8)
203 Indians   3   fire, and his wife's cooking;/To sit in front of his own door at sunset/And see his
263 MC   Chorus   23 trill at windows, and children tumble in front of the door,/What work shall have been
276 MC   m   18   completed the murder, advance to the *front of the stage and address the audience.*]/{K1}
289 FR   Amy   20   to forget it./I do not mince matters in front of the family:/You can call it nothing but a
376 CP   m   7   *bell rings again.* EDWARD *goes to front door, and is/heard to say:*]/{E} Julia!/What
386 CP   m   14   *The bell rings, and he goes to the front door.*]/{E} Celia!/{C} Has Lavinia arrived?/
387 CP   m   12 *rings*]/{E} There's Lavinia. { }/[*Goes to front door*]/{E} Peter! { }/[*Enter* PETER]/{P}
424 CP   m   11   /[EDWARD *lets himself in at the front door*]/{E} I'm in good time, I think. I hope

FRONTIER (4)
184 FQ: DrySal   3 to some degree, at first recognised as a frontier;/Useful, untrustworthy, as a conveyor of
293 FR   Gerald   31   as a youngster on the North-West Frontier —/Been in tight corners most of my life/
342 FR   Agatha   31   birth and life. Harry has crossed the frontier/Beyond which safety and danger have a

342 FR   Agatha   38   /But Harry has been led across the frontier: he must follow;/For him the death is now

FROST (3)
  63 WL: Burial   73 it bloom this year?/'Or has the sudden frost disturbed its bed?/'O keep the Dog far
191 FQ: Little   4 /When the short day is brightest, with frost and fire,/The brief sun flames the ice, on
544 ES   Ld Clav   23 seasonable,/Is so often a harbinger of frost on the fruit trees./{M} Oh, let's make the

FROSTY (1)
  72 WL: Thund   323   red on sweaty faces/After the frosty silence in the gardens/After the agony in

FRUCTIFY (1)
188 FQ: DrySal   162 of death is every moment)/Which shall fructify in the lives of others:/And do not think of

FRUIT (10)
  91 Ash-Wed 2   13 /To the posterity of the desert and the fruit of the gourd./It is this which recovers/My
  92 Ash-Wed 3   13 a slotted window bellied like the fig's fruit/And beyond the hawthorn blossom and a
121 SA   Sweeney   26 Rolls-Royce./Nothing to eat but the fruit as it grows./Nothing to see but the palmtrees
152 Rock 2   25 that was done in the past, you eat the fruit, either rotten or ripe./And the Church must
187 FQ: DrySal   135   and the passengers are settled/To fruit, periodicals and business letters/(And those
188 FQ: DrySal   163 lives of others:/And do not think of the fruit of action./Fare forward. O voyagers, O
194 FQ: Little   118 /Both bad and good. Last season's fruit is eaten/And the fullfed beast shall kick the
194 FQ: Little   135 /But bitter tastelessness of shadow fruit/As body and soul begin to fall asunder./
203 Indians   22 the judgment after death,/What is the fruit of action./To Walter de la Mare/The
544 ES   Ld Clav   23 /Is so often a harbinger of frost on the fruit trees./{M} Oh, let's make the most of this

FRUIT-TIME (1)
138 New Hamp   2 orchard/Between the blossom- and the fruit-time:/Golden head, crimson head,/Between

FRUITED (1)
  64 WL: Chess   79 /Held up by standards wrought with fruited vines/From which a golden Cupidon

FRUITFUL (1)
203 Indians   20 common purpose, action/None the less fruitful if neither you nor we/Know, until the

FRUITION (2)
186 FQ: DrySal   93   — not the sense of well-being,/Fruition, fulfilment, security or affection,/Or even
349 FR   Agatha   14 A curse is slow in coming/To complete fruition/It cannot be hurried/And it cannot be

FRUITS (1)
  49 Hippopot   15 /The mango on the mango-tree;/But fruits of pomegranate and peach/Refresh the

FRUSTRATION (1)
577 ES   Carghil   33 simply been suffering, poor boy, from frustration./He's been waiting all this time for

FRY (1)
210 Old Gumbie   24 bread and dried peas,/And a *beautiful* fry of lean bacon and cheese./I have a Gumbie

FRYING (1)
210 Old Gumbie   22 /She sets to work with her baking and frying./She makes them a mouse-cake of bread

FUEL (2)
  23 Preludes   54 revolve like ancient women/Gathering fuel in vacant lots./Rhapsody on a Windy Night/
276 MC   Chorus   7 night-time heaping of the ashes,/The fuel laid on the fire at daybreak,/These acts

FUGITIVE (4)
  34 Figlia   6 them to the ground and turn/With a fugitive resentment in your eyes:/But weave,
560 ES   Michael   35 the desire to escape./{Mi} I'm not a fugitive./{LC} No, not a fugitive from justice —/
560 ES   Ld Clav   36 {Mi} I'm not a fugitive./{LC} No, not a fugitive from justice —/Only a fugitive from
560 ES   Ld Clav   37 not a fugitive from justice —/Only a fugitive from reality./Oh Michael! If you had

FUGITIVES (1)
338 FR   Agatha   34 you *will* run away./{Ag} In a world of fugitives/The person taking the opposite direction

FULFIL (1)
516 CC   Claude   30 ambitions —/Had you been able to fulfil them./Believe, if you like, that I am not your

FULFILLED (3)
192 FQ: Little   33 the purpose breaks only when it is fulfilled/If at all. Either you had no purpose/Or
337 FR   Agatha   5 /O my child, my curse,/You shall be fulfilled:/The knot shall be unknotted/And the
417 CP   Celia   12 of delight/Without desire, for desire is fulfilled/In the delight of loving. A state one does

FULFILLING (1)
516 CC   Claude   29 I put no obstruction/In the way of your fulfilling your musical ambitions —/Had you

FULFILMENT (2)
186 FQ: DrySal   93 not the sense of well-being,/Fruition, fulfilment, security or affection,/Or even a very
192 FQ: Little   36 the end you figured/And is altered in fulfilment. There are other places/Which also are

FULL (17)
  16 Prufrock   117 use,/Politic, cautious, and meticulous;/Full of high sentence, but a bit obtuse;/At times,
  34 Figlia   20 /Her hair over her arms and her arms full of flowers./And I wonder how they should
  42 Swee Erect   21 at the pillow slip./Sweeney addressed full length to shave/Broadbottomed, pink from
  62 WL: Burial   38 from the hyacinth garden,/Your arms full, and your hair wet, I could not/Speak, and
  68 WL: Fire S   210 merchant/Unshaven, with a pocket full of currants/C.i.f. London: documents at
125 SA   m 31 nothing to me and nothing to you. {}/FULL CHORUS: WAUCHOPE, HORSFALL,

158 Rock 5   6   /And the others run about like dogs, full of enterprise, sniffing and barking: they say,
172 FQ: BurntN   42 /Go, said the bird, for the leaves were full of children,/Hidden excitedly, containing
230 Bust Jones   27   — or at the *Glutton*;/If he looks full of gloom then he's lunched at the *Tomb*/On
241 MC   Priest1   26 it peace or war?/{P1} Does he come/In full assurance, or only secure/In the power of
310 FR   Harry   11   of sacrifice/And the wail of the new full tide/Returning the ghosts of the dead/Those
431 CP   Peter   12 /Just for a week. And I have my hands full/I'm going down tonight, to Boltwell./{J} To
460 CC   Claude   38 in Zürich has done for her,/I give him full marks. Well, Eggerson,/I seem to have
471 CC   Lucasta   10 educating *me*./{L} Colby, you really are full of surprises!/I've never met a man so ignorant
493 CC   Lady E   21   her?/{LE} Over there, with the light full on her:/I want to be able to watch her
509 CC   Claude   26 Elizabeth. He sometimes has to sign his full name./But he doesn't like the name, for some
580 ES   Gomez   3 me. Here's my business card/With the full address. You can always reach him there./But

FULLFED (1)
194 FQ: Little   119   Last season's fruit is eaten/And the fullfed beast shall kick the empty pail./For last

FULLY (2)
592 Grad 2   4 not restore,/And when they leave they fully understand/That though again they see their
546 CC   Piggott   36   /She is a real nurse, you know, fully qualified./Our system is very delicately

FUN (3)
388 CP   Celia   12   — more than you realised./It *was* fun, wasn't it! But now you'll have a chance,/I
478 CC   Lucasta   15   I postponed telling you, just for the fun of it:/I thought, when I tell him, it will be so
558 ES   Michael   24 be living on my pay;/They had a lot of fun with me — sometimes they'd pretend/That I

FUNERAL (5)
175 FQ: BurntN 160 temptation,/The crying shadow in the funeral dance,/The loud lament of the
180 FQ: ECoker 111 And we all go with them, into the silent funeral,/Nobody's funeral, for there is no one to
180 FQ: ECoker 112 them, into the silent funeral,/Nobody's funeral, for there is no one to bury./I said to my
595 Grad 14   3 'Farewell',/A word that echoes like a funeral bell/And one that we are ever loth to say./
349 FR   Ivy   8   /{I} I shall have to stay till after the funeral: will my ticket to London still be valid?/

FUNNY (4)
115 SP   Dusty   22 /Yes and Sam's a nice boy too./He's a funny fellow/{Do} He *is* a funny fellow/He's like a
115 SP   Doris   23 too./He's a funny fellow/{Do} He *is* a funny fellow/He's like a fellow once I knew./*He*
118 SP   Dusty   3 /{Do} Or it might be Snow/{Du} It's a funny thing how I draw court cards —/{Do}
233 Skimble   39 you turn to make a breeze./There's a funny little basin you're supposed to wash your

FUR (2)
137 5FingerEx5 10 Eliot!/With a bobtail cur/In a coat of fur/And a porpentine cat/And a wopsical hat:/
177 FQ: ECoker   7 to the earth/Which is already flesh, fur and faeces,/Bone of man and beast, cornstalk

FURNISH (1)
587 Fable   22 the fatter cows and left the thinner/To furnish all the milk — upset the chimes,/And once

FURNISHED (2)
 22 Preludes   23 are raising dingy shades/In a thousand furnished rooms./You tossed a blanket from the
446 CC   Claude   26   to do the walls. And then it must be furnished./I'm trying to find him a really good

FURNITURE (4)
340 FR   Amy   15 took everything/Except the walls, the furniture, the acres;/Leaving nothing — but what
362 CP   Reilly   40   on the table,/You are a piece of furniture in a repair shop/For those who
483 CC   Lady E   10   and the curtains;/And most of the furniture. But, that writing-table!/Where did that
550 ES   Carghil   22   Equipments? They make office furniture./{LC} I've never had to deal with

FURROW (2)
150 Rock 1   102   *the plough rests, at an angle/To the furrow. In this land/There shall be one cigarette to*
188 FQ: DrySal   145 of the drumming liner/Watching the furrow that widens behind you,/You shall not

FURS (1)
 41 Burb Blei   24 Jew is underneath the lot./Money in furs. The boatman smiles,/Princess Volupine

FURTHER (15)
183 FQ: ECoker 208   moving/Into another intensity/For a further union, a deeper communion/Through the
185 FQ: DrySal   58 addition: the trailing/Consequence of further days and hours,/While emotion takes to
254 MC   Tempt4   29 /When the bird cries, have thought of further scorning./That nothing lasts, but the
280 MC   Priest1   9 us?/After what journey through what further dread/Shall we recover your presence?
280 MC   Priest3   36 fate on earth/And we must think no further of you./{P1} O my lord/The glory of
293 FR   Amy   10 an old woman./They can give me no further advice when I'm dead./{I} Oh, dear Amy!/
346 FR   Charles   1 Mall./I thought that life could bring no further surprises;/But I remember now, that I am
404 CP   Edward   21 I am in your hands./I cannot take any further responsibility./{R} Many patients come in
424 CP   Caterer   1   *from side door./*{CM} Have you any further orders for us, Madam?/{L} You could
478 CC   Lucasta   21 think you're getting out, you're getting further in,/And you know at last that there's no
491 CC   Lady E   7 only *yours*./Why should we make any further enquiries?/Let us regard him as being *our*
506 CC   Eggers   2 is to say, placed out to be cared for/Till further notice by a foster-mother./Unfortunately,
522 ES   dedic   10 *mean what they say, but some have a further meaning/For you and me only.*/Characters/
558 ES   Michael   32 /He assumed it had gone a good deal further than it had./{LC} Perhaps it had gone
558 ES   Ld Clav   33 than it had./{LC} Perhaps it had gone further than you're willing to admit./{Mi} Well,

FURY (3)
187 FQ: DrySal 125   in the sombre season/Or the sudden fury, is what it always was./I sometimes wonder if
272 MC   Chorus 19   shadow in the doorway,/More than fury in the hall./The agents of hell disappear, the
341 FR   Amy 20   him/Is another. I call it failure. Your fury for possession/Is only the stronger for all
FUSES (1)
127 Cor1 March 17   tell how many projectiles, mines and fuses,/13,000 aeroplanes,/24,000 aeroplane
FUSS (3)
214 RTTugger 17   bureau drawer,/But he makes such a fuss if he can't get out./Yes the Rum Tum Tugger
228 Gus   3   /Is really Asparagus. That's such a fuss/To pronounce, that we usually call him just
345 FR   Harry 1   /Just now? I only want, please,/As little fuss as possible. You must get used to it;/
FUT (1)
51 Restaurant 31   c'était un sort pénible;/Cependant, ce fut jadis un bel homme, de haute taille./Whispers
FUTILE (2)
154 Rock 3   12   and you only alternate/Between futile speculation and unconsidered action./
545 ES   Ld Clav 7   who can terrorise us/And urge us on to futile activity,/And in the end, judge us still more
FUTILITY (1)
258 MC Thomas 34   /Will seem to most of you at best futility,/Senseless self-slaughter of a lunatic,/
FUTURE (65)
162 Rock 8   2   words,/And we will take heart for the future,/Remembering the past./The heathen are
166 Rock 10   5   of fear./And what shall we say of the future? Is one church all we can build?/Or shall
166 Rock 10   14   Good and Evil;/Seek not to count the future waves of Time;/But be ye satisfied that you
171 FQ: BurntN   2   past/Are both perhaps present in time future/And time future contained in time past./If
171 FQ: BurntN   3   present in time future/And time future contained in time past./If all time is
172 FQ: BurntN   46 very much reality./Time past and time future/What might have been and what has been/
173 FQ: BurntN   67   do not call it fixity,/Where past and future are gathered. Neither movement from nor
173 FQ: BurntN   81   /Yet the enchainment of past and future/Woven in the weakness of the changing
173 FQ: BurntN   85   cannot endure./Time past and time future/Allow but a little consciousness./To be
173 FQ: BurntN   91   remembered; involved with past and future./Only through time time is conquered./
174 FQ: BurntN 129 its metalled ways/Of time past and time future./Time and the bell have buried the day,/
185 FQ: DrySal   42   women/Lying awake, calculating the future,/Trying to unweave, unwind, unravel/And
185 FQ: DrySal   44   /And piece together the past and the future,/Between midnight and dawn, when the
185 FQ: DrySal   46   when the past is all deception,/The future futureless, before the morning watch/
186 FQ: DrySal   73 ocean not littered with wastage/Or of a future that is not liable/Like the past, to have no
187 FQ: DrySal 128   of putting the same thing:/That the future is a faded song, a Royal Rose or a lavender
188 FQ: DrySal 140 the past/Into different lives, or into any future;/You are not the same people who left that
188 FQ: DrySal 147 not think 'the past is finished' or 'the future is before us'./At nightfall, in the rigging
188 FQ: DrySal 155 /While time is withdrawn, consider the future/And the past with an equal mind./At the
189 FQ: DrySal 203   /Men's curiosity searches past and future/And clings to that dimension. But to
190 FQ: DrySal 222   existence is actual,/Here the past and future/Are conquered, and reconciled,/Where
190 FQ: DrySal 229 right action is freedom/From past and future also./For most of us, this is the aim/Never
195 FQ: Little   161   desire, and so liberation/From the future as well as the past. Thus, love of a country/
201 Def Island   20   of Britain:/to say, to the past and the future generations/of our kin and of our speech,
593 Grad 4   6   know!/Would we might look into the future years./Great duties call — the twentieth
593 Grad 6   6   gain such proud estate/As shall on future centuries bestow/A legacy of benefits —
593 Grad 7   2   /A legacy of benefits — may we/In future years be found with those who try/To labor
594 Grad 10   5 not left behind,/The same school in the future shall we find/As this from which as pupils
604 Ode   15 the vision to see/What we owe for the future, the present, and past,/Fair Harvard, to
247 MC Thomas 13 /{T} We do not know very much of the future/Except from generation to
255 MC Thomas 32 temptations/Mean present vanity and future torment./Can sinful pride be driven out/
288 FR   Agatha 20   the past is irremediable,/Because the future can only be built/Upon the real past.
290 FR   Amy 12 you know the truth/For the sake of the future. There can be no grief/And no regret and
290 FR   Amy 14   it if I could. For the sake of the future:/Harry is to take command at Wishwood/
290 FR   Amy 16   /And I hope we can contrive his future happiness./Do not discuss his absence.
315 FR   Chorus 32   the past is about to happen, and the future was long since settled./And the wings of
315 FR   Chorus 33 long since settled./And the wings of the future darken the past, the beak and claws have
317 FR Warburt 20 /May make an endless difference to the future./It's about your mother .../{H} What about
318 FR Warburt 21 Now, is your mother's happiness in the future,/For the time she has to live: not with the
318 FR   Harry 25   with the past/And not with the future? or with the future/And not with the past?
318 FR   Harry 25 /And not with the future? or with the future/And not with the past? What I'm telling
320 FR Warburt 29   has to live./The other is yourself: the future of Wishwood/Depends on you. I don't like
329 FR   Chorus   1   remains in the room, waiting for the future to hear it./And whatever happens began in
329 FR   Chorus   2   in the past, and presses hard on the future./The agony in the curtained bedroom,
329 FR   Chorus   4 of the past, and projects them into the future./The treble voices on the lawn/The mowing
330 FR   Agatha 13 the past and what you mean about the future;/But a present is missing, needed to
332 FR   Agatha 26   when there seems to be no past or future,/Only a present moment of pointed light/

340 FR	Amy	18	years I kept him,/For the sake of the future, a discontented ghost,/In his own house.
341 FR	Amy	15	a happy boy at Wishwood;/For his future success./{Ag} Success is relative:/It is what
371 CP	Peter	30	hold to the memory/I can bear any future. But I must find out/The truth about the
379 CP	Edward	20	this would never have arisen./What future had you ever thought there could be?/{C}
379 CP	Celia	21	be?/{C} What had I thought that the future could be?/I abandoned the future before we
379 CP	Celia	22	the future could be?/I abandoned the future before we began,/And after that I lived in a
381 CP	Celia	3	to take any interest/Now, in *my* future. I only hope you're competent/To manage
394 CP	Lavinia	21	else. I shall treat you very differently/In future./{E} Thank you for the warning. But tell
394 CP	Edward	36	I tried to be accommodating. But, in future,/I shall behave, I assure you, very
397 CP	Edward	37	me. Have I not made it clear/That in future you will find me a different person?/{L}
411 CP	Edward	23	like you to ask./{E} It's about the future of ... the others./I don't want to build on
411 CP	Reilly	30	burdens on your conscience./With the future of the others you are not concerned./{L} I
491 CC	Claude	38	What do you want?/Think of the future. When you marry/You will want parents,
505 CC	Eggers	31	you get to my age/The past and the future both seem very brief —/But long enough
515 CC	Guzzard	14	/If I said the child was mine, what future could he have?/And then I was frightened
516 CC	Claude	2	no difference/To my plans for your future./{C} Thank you, Sir Claude./You're a very
573 ES	Carghil	34	Monica./I take a great interest in her future./Fancy! I've only known her two days!/But
575 ES	Ld Clav	29	*your* time:/My daughter and my future son-in-law/Understand that allusion. I

FUTURELESS (1)

185 FQ:	DrySal	46	the past is all deception,/The future futureless, before the morning watch/When time

GAB (1)
218 Mung Rump 17   had a very unusual gift of the gab./They were highly efficient cat-burglars as
GAG (1)
228 Gus   23   back-chat, I knew how to gag,/And I knew how to let the cat out of the
GAIETY (2)
111 Xmas Trees 18   /So that the reverence and the gaiety/May not be forgotten in later experience,/
247 MC Tempt1 . 4 amity,/Clergy and laity may return to gaiety,/Mirth and sportfulness need not walk
GAILY (2)
74 WL: Thund 419 /DA/*Damyata:* The boat responded/Gaily, to the hand expert with sail and oar/The
74 WL: Thund 421 your heart would have responded/Gaily, when invited, beating obedient/To
GAIN (9)
152 Rock 2   34 those of your fathers who fought to gain it./The Church must be forever building,
158 Rock 5   3 the enemy who has something to gain: and from the friend who has something to
182 FQ: ECoker 190 unpropitious. But perhaps neither gain nor loss./For us, there is only the trying.
593 Grad 6   5 well her fate,/And see that she shall gain such proud estate/As shall on future
251 MC Tempt3 36 its eyes in your direction —/To gain from you, your Lordship asks./For us,
277 MC Knight3 5 /We have much more to lose than to gain. We are four plain Englishmen/who put
360 CP   Reilly 36 She might decide to be forgiving/And gain an advantage. If there's no other woman/
379 CP   Celia 7 back/And that you do mean to gain your freedom,/And that everything is all
448 CC   Eggers 8 that!/Though I've done my best to gain his confidence./I did mention her interest
GAINED (1)
542 ES Ld Clav 19 friendship/So many years ago, I only gained in return/Your envy, spite and hatred.
GAINS (1)
260 MC Thomas 30   counting/over his peaceful gains, the swept hearth, his best wine for a
GAIT (1)
247 MC Tempt1 29 follow your master./{T1} Not at this gait!/If you go so fast, others may go faster./
GALANTE (1)
33 Conv Gal   t subtlety to this end./Conversation Galante/I observe: 'Our sentimental friend the
GALES (1)
42 Swee Erect   6   above/Reviewing the insurgent gales/Which tangle Ariadne's hair/And swell
GALLED (1)
103 Journ Magi 6 very dead of winter.'/And the camels galled, sore-footed, refractory,/Lying down in
GALLERY (2)
228 Gus   18 his success on the Halls,/Where the Gallery once gave him seven cat-calls./But his
291 FR Chorus 1 circle, the laughter and catcalls in the gallery?/{C} I might have been in St. James's
GALLON (1)
124 SA Sweeney 17 he kept her there in a bath/With a gallon of lysol in a bath/{Sw} These fellows
GALLOPED (1)
103 Journ Magi 25 the low sky./And an old white horse galloped away in the meadow./Then we came to
GALLOWGATE (1)
233 Skimble   61 to know about:/When you get to Gallowgate there you do not have to wait —/
GALS (1)
236 Cat Morgan 16 not one to boast,/That some of the gals is dead keen on old Morgan./So if you 'ave
GAMBIT (1)
57 Swee Night 28 the man with heavy eyes/Declines the gambit, shows fatigue,/Leaves the room and
GAMBLE (3)
201 Def Island 11 those who, in man's newest form of gamble/with death, fight the power of darkness
480 CC Kaghan 1 free to think again./{K} Marriage is a gamble. But I'm a born gambler/And I've put
480 CC Colby 16 a gambler. I don't believe you ever gamble/On anything that isn't a certainty./{K}
GAMBLER (4)
480 CC Kaghan 1 Marriage is a gamble. But I'm a born gambler/And I've put my shirt ... no, not quite
480 CC Colby 12 /You only pretend that you're a gambler./You've got as level a head as anyone,/
480 CC Colby 16 pretend to other people/That you're a gambler. I don't believe you ever gamble/On
558 ES Michael 8 taken to gambling. Called me a gambler!/Said he'd communicate with you
GAMBLING (1)
558 ES Michael 8 any man on his staff/Who'd taken to gambling. Called me a gambler!/Said he'd
GAMBOL (1)
235 Ad-dress   33 back or shake his paw,/And he will gambol and guffaw./He's such an easy-going
GAME (12)
64 WL: Chess   t — mon semblable, — mon frère!'/A Game of Chess/The Chair she sat in, like a
65 WL: Chess 137 car at four./And we shall play a game of chess,/Pressing lidless eyes and waiting
119 SP   Krum 18 the run/{Kr} What about that poker game?/eh what Sam?/What about that poker
119 SP   Krum 19 eh what Sam?/What about that poker game in Bordeaux?/Yes Miss Dorrance you get
119 SP   Krum 21 you get Sam/To tell about that poker game in Bordeaux./{Du} Do you know London
230 Bust Jones 17 *Schools.*/For a similar reason, when game is in season/He is found, not at *Fox's,* but

602 Humoresque   2   is dead,/Though not yet tired of the game —/But weak in body as in head,/(A
258 MC Thomas   22   /I beat the barons at their own game. I/Could then despise the men who
328 FR Charles   25   he said: "I/thought you were having a game with me."'/{G} This is what the
376 CP   m 1   *goes over to the table and inspects his game of Patience. He moves/a card. The doorbell*
452 CC Kaghan   10   can just relax./I'm going to enjoy the game from the sidelines. {}/[*Enter* LUCASTA
534 ES Gomez   18   /Forgery, I can tell you, is a mug's game./I say that — with conviction./No,
GAMES (2)
209 NamingCats   2   /It isn't just one of your holiday games;/You may think at first I'm as mad as a
234 Ad-dress   13   /You've seen them both at work and games,/And learnt about their proper names,/
GAMMON (1)
66 WL: Chess   166   Albert was home, they had a hot gammon,/And they asked me in to dinner, to
GANGA (1)
74 WL: Thund   395   Then a damp gust/Bringing rain/Ganga was sunken, and the limp leaves/Waited
GAOL (2)
534 ES Ld Clav   8   on in England,/It might land you in gaol again?/{G} That's true enough,/Except for
534 ES Gomez   32   get out in time/Find themselves in gaol and not very comfortable,/Or before a
GAP (2)
490 CC Colby   21   without parents, as a child,/There's a gap that never can be filled. Never./I like you
536 ES Gomez   6   no social ladder./It was jumping a gap — and you can't jump back again./I parted
GAPE (1)
589 Fable   77   /The friars could do nought but gape and stare,/The spirit pulled him rudely by
GAPES (2)
56 Swee Night   18   brown/Sprawls at the window-sill and gapes;/The waiter brings in oranges/Bananas
193 FQ: Little   69   hand./The parched eviscerate soil/Gapes at the vanity of toil,/Laughs without
GAPING (1)
31 Apollinax   5   /And of Priapus in the shrubbery/Gaping at the lady in the swing./In the palace of
GAR (1)
61 WL: Burial   12   coffee, and talked for an hour./Bin gar keine Russin, stamm' aus Litauen, echt
GARAGE (1)
297 FR Denman   28   his Lordship?/{D} He's out in the garage, Sir, with his Lordship's car./{C} Tell
GARBOARD (1)
110 Marina   28   conscious, unknown, my own./The garboard strake leaks, the seams need caulking./
GARÇON (1)
51 Restaurant   1   miasmal mist./Dans le Restaurant/Le garçon délabré qui n'a rien à faire/Que de se
GARDE (1)
24 Rhapsody   51   /'Regard the moon,/La lune ne garde aucune rancune,/She winks a feeble eye,/
GARDEN (44)
20 Portrait   81   With the smell of hyacinths across the garden/Recalling things that other people have
32 Hysteria   8   wish to take their/tea in the garden, if the lady and gentleman wish to take
32 Hysteria   9   wish to take their tea in the/garden ...' I decided that if the shaking of her
34 Figlia   2   pavement of the stair —/Lean on a garden urn —/Weave, weave the sunlight in
62 WL: Burial   37   we came back, late, from the hyacinth garden,/Your arms full, and your hair wet, I
63 WL: Burial   71   corpse you planted last year in your garden,/'Has it begun to sprout? Will it bloom
92 Ash-Wed 2   33   reposeful/The single Rose/Is now the Garden/Where all loves end/Terminate torment/
92 Ash-Wed 2   46   speech/Grace to the Mother/For the Garden/Where all love ends./Under a
94 Ash-Wed 4   23   blue/Between the yews, behind the garden god,/Whose flute is breathless, bent her
97 Ash-Wed 5   34   the last blue rocks/The desert in the garden the garden in the desert/Of drouth,
97 Ash-Wed 5   34   rocks/The desert in the garden the garden in the desert/Of drouth, spitting from
98 Ash-Wed 6   25   spirit of the fountain, spirit of the garden,/Suffer us not to mock ourselves with
171 FQ: BurntN   20   not know./Other echoes/Inhabit the garden. Shall we follow?/Quick, said the bird,
180 FQ: ECoker   132   wild strawberry,/The laughter in the garden, echoed ecstasy/Not lost, but requiring,
225 Mr Mistoff   52   the family to call/Him in from the garden for hours,/While he was asleep in the
598 Circe   10   which thickens below,/Along the garden stairs/The sluggish python lies;/The
258 MC Thomas   15   the strategy of chess,/Love in the garden, singing to the instrument,/Were all
292 FR   Ivy   35   man was pensioned./He's let the rock garden go to rack and ruin,/And he's nearly half
313 FR   Ivy   11   my passion./You know I had my own garden once, in Cornwall,/When I could afford
313 FR   Ivy   12   in Cornwall,/When I could afford a garden; and I took several prizes/With my
348 FR Chorus   9   room./We do not like the maze in the garden, because it too closely resembles the
437 CP Reilly   6   */Met his own image walking in the garden./That apparition, sole of men, he saw./For*
445 CC Eggers   13   The number of things one needs for a garden!/And I thought, now's the moment to
446 CC Eggers   31   /He's expressed such an interest in my garden/That I think he ought to have window
446 CC Eggers   33   boxes./Some day, he'll want a garden of his own. And yes, a bird bath!/{SC} A
455 CC Eggers   27   a great protection. And I have my garden/To protect me against Mrs. E. That's
461 CC Eggers   6   I'm not in the house, I'll be out in the garden./And I'll slip up to town any day, if you
461 CC Eggers   19   think about it in the Spring/When the garden will really be a treat to look at.'/Well, I'll

473 CC	Lucasta	2	the rest of us:/You have your secret garden; to which you can retire/And lock the
473 CC	Colby	5	sure that you haven't your own secret garden/Somewhere, if you could find it?/{L} If I
473 CC	Lucasta	8	it?/{L} If I could find it!/No, my only garden is ... a dirty public square/In a shabby
473 CC	Lucasta	10	/For a time, with my mother. I've no garden./I hardly feel that I'm even a person:/
473 CC	Colby	16	a person./I'm sure that there is a garden somewhere for you —/For anyone who
473 CC	Lucasta	18	one as much as you do./{L} And *your* garden is a garden/Where you hear a music that
473 CC	Lucasta	18	as you do./{L} And *your* garden is a garden/Where you hear a music that no one else
473 CC	Colby	26	gate,/And there I am ... alone, in my 'garden'./Alone, that's the thing. That's why it's
473 CC	Colby	28	/You know, I think that Eggerson's garden/Is more real than mine./{L} Eggerson's
473 CC	Lucasta	30	more real than mine./{L} Eggerson's garden?/What makes you think of Eggerson —
473 CC	Colby	32	all people?/{C} Well, he retires to his garden — literally,/And also in the same sense
474 CC	Colby	2	both unreal. But for Eggerson/His garden is a part of one single world./{L} But
474 CC	Colby	5	were religious, God would walk in my garden/And that would make the world outside
477 CC	Lucasta	37	don't you shut yourself up in that garden/Where you like to be alone with
496 CC	Eggers	29	do, in Joshua Park —/Apart from the garden — that I've not an idle moment./And
555 ES	Monica	37	/{M} I told him he must wait in the garden/Until I had prepared you. I've made him

GARDEN'S (1)
| 473 CC | Colby | 38 | very serious./What I mean is, my garden's no less unreal to me/Than the world |

GARDEN-FLOWERS (1)
| 303 FR | Mary | 3 | the south wall./The gardener had no garden-flowers to give me for this evening./{Ag} |

GARDEN-WALL (1)
| 54 Mr E Sun | 25 | /Burn invisible and dim./Along the garden-wall the bees/With hairy bellies pass |

GARDENER (1)
| 303 FR | Mary | 3 | clings to the south wall./The gardener had no garden-flowers to give me for |

GARDENING (1)
| 445 CC | Eggers | 12 | /I've spent the morning shopping! Gardening tools./The number of things one |

GARDENS (2)
| 72 WL: Thund | 323 | faces/After the frosty silence in the gardens/After the agony in stony places/The |
| 218 Mung Rump | 5 | were very well known in Cornwall Gardens, in Launceston Place and in |

GARLIC (1)
| 172 FQ: BurntN | 49 | to one end, which is always present./Garlic and sapphires in the mud/Clot the |

GARNISHED (1)
| 155 Rock 3 | 45 | /I have swept the floors and garnished the altars./Where there is no temple |

GARRET (1)
| 67 WL: Fire S | 194 | /And bones cast in a little low dry garret,/Rattled by the rat's foot only, year to |

GAS (2)
| 602 Humoresque | 19 | damned thin moonlight, worse than gas —/'Now in New York' — and so it goes./ |
| 453 CC | Lucasta | 11 | a pittance —/Cooking a sausage on a gas ring .../{E} You mustn't believe a word she |

GAS-FIRE (1)
| 285 FR | Ivy | 18 | freeze, as I do, in Bayswater, by a gas-fire counting shillings./{V} Go south! to the |

GASHED (1)
| 42 Swee Erect | 14 | of knots of hair/Slitted below and gashed with eyes,/This oval O cropped out with |

GASHOUSE (1)
| 67 WL: Fire S | 190 | On a winter evening round behind the gashouse/Musing upon the king my brother's |

GASLIGHT (1)
| 184 FQ: DrySal | 14 | /And the evening circle in the winter gaslight./The river is within us, the sea is all |

GASPS (1)
| 32 Hysteria | 3 | squad-drill. I was drawn in by short gasps, inhaled at each momentary/recovery, lost |

GASTRONOMY (1)
| 221 Old Deut | 40 | /The digestive repose of that feline's gastronomy/Must never be broken, whatever |

GATE (13)
56 Swee Night	8	/And Sweeney guards the hornèd gate./Gloomy Orion and the Dog/Are veiled;
96 Ash-Wed 5	25	veiled sister pray/For children at the gate/Who will not go away and cannot pray:/
157 Rock 4	11	by the dragon's well, by the dung gate,/By the fountain gate, by the king's pool,/
157 Rock 4	12	by the dung gate,/By the fountain gate, by the king's pool,/Jerusalem lay waste,
171 FQ: BurntN	22	/Round the corner. Through the first gate,/Into our first world, shall we follow/The
197 FQ: Little	245	/Through the unknown, remembered gate/When the last of earth left to discover/Is
601 Nocturne	2	/Guitar and hat in hand, beside the gate/With Juliet, in the usual debate/Of love,
241 MC	Priest1	8	things not end/Until the poor at the gate/Have forgotten their friend, their Father in
256 MC	Tempts	34	/{4T} Does the mastiff prowl by the gate?/{C} Death has a hundred hands and walks
473 CC	Lucasta	3	to which you can retire/And lock the gate behind you./{C} And lock the gate behind
473 CC	Colby	4	the gate behind you./{C} And lock the gate behind me?/Are you sure that you haven't
473 CC	Colby	25	/I turn the key, and walk through the gate,/And there I am ... alone, in my 'garden'./
474 CC	Colby	15	/I should not hear the opening of the gate./They would simply ... be there suddenly,/

GATES (6)
27 Morning	4	/Sprouting despondently at area gates./The brown waves of fog toss up to me/
37 Gerontion	3	for rain./I was neither at the hot gates/Nor fought in the warm rain/Nor knee
54 Mr E Sun	21	pence./Under the penitential gates/Sustained by staring Seraphim/Where the
98 Ash-Wed 6	18	/The empty forms between the ivory gates/And smell renews the salt savour of the
139 Virginia	7	/Heard once? Still hills/Wait. Gates wait. Purple trees,/White trees, wait, wait,
280 MC Priest3	19	the last grey rock/Of Brittany, or the Gates of Hercules./Go venture shipwreck on the

GATHER (3)
49 Hippopot	12	the True Church need never stir/To gather in its dividends./The 'potamus can never
123 SA Kl & Kr	19	*we won't go home when it rains/We'll gather hibiscus flowers/For it won't be minutes*
461 CC Claude	30	was very disconcerting:/As you gather, such a thing never happened before./So

GATHERED (6)
74 WL: Thund	397	for rain, while the black clouds/Gathered far distant, over Himavant./The
85 Hollow Men	60	/We grope together/And avoid speech/Gathered on this beach of the tumid river/
173 FQ: BurntN	67	it fixity,/Where past and future are gathered. Neither movement from nor towards,/
239 MC Chorus	10	November/And the apples were gathered and stored, and the land became
244 MC Chorus	6	/We have brewed beer and cider,/Gathered wood against the winter,/Talked at
455 CC Eggers	11	money of her own, as you may have gathered;/But I think her father was a friend of

GATHERING (2)
23 Preludes	54	worlds revolve like ancient women/Gathering fuel in vacant lots./Rhapsody on a
257 MC Chorus	20	living,/Picking together the pieces,/Gathering faggots at nightfall,/Building a

GATHERS (1)
329 FR Chorus	4	whether of birth or of dying,/Gathers in to itself all the voices of the past, and

GAUGUIN (1)
122 SAWa & Ho	30	*boo/Under the bamboo tree/Where the Gauguin maids/In the banyan shades/Wear*

GAVE (32)
24 Rhapsody	27	smooth, and polished/As if the world gave up/The secret of its skeleton,/Stiff and
62 WL: Burial	35	*Irisch Kind/Wo weilest du?/*'You gave me hyacinths first a year ago;/'They called
64 WL: Chess	98	was displayed/As though a window gave upon the sylvan scene/The change of
65 WL: Chess	143	what you done with that money he gave you/To get yourself some teeth. He did, I
157 Rock 4	8	broken city, Jerusalem;/And the King gave him leave to depart/That he might rebuild
160 Rock 7	20	is no time, and that moment of time gave the meaning./Then it seemed as if men
213 Growltiger	41	cruel carving knives./Then GILBERT gave the signal to his fierce Mongolian horde;/
213 Growltiger	45	their bunks./Then Griddlebone she gave a screech, for she was badly skeered;/I am
223 Pekes Pols	53	like fireballs fearfully blazing,/He gave a great yawn, and his jaws were amazing;/
223 Pekes Pols	58	warning./He looked at the sky and he gave a great leap —/And they every last one of
228 Gus	18	on the Halls,/Where the Gallery once gave him seven cat-calls./But his grandest
589 Fable	66	barred and bolted most securely,/Gave way — my statement nobody can doubt,/
590 Time Space	9	day/Has lived eternity./The flowers I gave thee when the dew/Was trembling on the
257 MC Chorus	23	and drinking and laughter./God gave us always some reason, some hope; but
261 MC Thomas	6	gives, give I unto you.'/So then, He gave to His disciples peace, but not peace as the
341 FR Amy	29	know what is best for Harry?/What gave you this influence to persuade him/To
380 CP Celia	22	it./{C} But this is ridiculous! I never gave Peter/Any reason to suppose I cared for
435 CP Julia	3	Why don't *you* say anything?/{J} You gave her those two years, as best you could./{P}
451 CC Eggers	7	to be. Sir Claude picked him out/And gave him his start. And he's made the most of it
464 CC Claude	30	it with the same devotion/That I gave to clay, and what could be done with it —/
465 CC Claude	24	he made it./But nothing *I* made ever gave me that contentment —/That state of utter
476 CC Lucasta	37	complained./Oh of course Claude gave her money, a regular allowance;/But it
501 CC Lucasta	8	because he knows you think so./*You* gave us our parts. And we've shown that we can
515 CC Guzzard	27	ambition come to nothing?/When I gave up my place as Colby's mother/I gave up
515 CC Guzzard	28	gave up my place as Colby's mother/I gave up something I could never have back./
538 ES Gomez	4	forgery. And then my stretch/Which gave me time to think it all out./{LC} That's the
542 ES Ld Clav	18	understand?/{LC} I see that when I gave you my friendship/So many years ago, I
549 ES Carghil	12	forgotten their names./And you gave us lunch — I've forgotten what hotel —/
551 ES Carghil	36	it — she wanted you exposed./But I gave way. I didn't want to ruin you./If I'd
557 ES Michael	15	/{Mi} Several of my friends gave me excellent tips./They always came off —
557 ES Michael	26	a friend of mine recommended./He gave me good terms, on the strength of my
559 ES Michael	28	And Mother knew./First, because it gave you the opportunity/Of retiring from

GAVOTTE (1)
216 Jellicles	16	roly-poly,/They know how to dance a gavotte and a jig./Until the Jellicle Moon

GAWN (1)
225 Mr Mistoff	35	have seen it one moment, and then it is *gawn!*/But you'll find it next week lying out on

GAY (5)
119 SP Klip	36	all the same) —/London's a little too gay for us/Yes I'll say a little too gay./{Kr} Yes
119 SP Klip	37	too gay for us/Yes I'll say a little too gay./{Kr} Yes London's a little too gay for us/

119 SP	Krum	38	gay./{Kr} Yes London's a little too gay for us/Don't think I mean anything *coarse*
230 Bust	Jones	19	/But he's frequently seen at the gay *Stage and Screen*/Which is famous for
246 MC	Templ1	30	old friend out of favour?/Old Tom, gay Tom, Becket of London,/Your Lordship

GAZA (1)

252 MC	Thomas	28	exercise of failing power./Samson in Gaza did no more./But if I break, I must break

GAZE (1)

167 Rock 10		32	wood, the coloured fresco./Our gaze is submarine, our eyes look upward/And

GAZETTE (1)

180 FQ: ECoker	109		de Gotha/And the Stock Exchange Gazette, the Directory of Directors,/And cold

GEAR (1)

184 FQ: DrySal	24		lobsterpot, the broken oar/And the gear of foreign dead men. The sea has many

GENERAL (7)

157 Rock 4		4	/There was no exception to the general rule./In Shushan the palace, in the
182 FQ: ECoker	183		always deteriorating/In the general mess of imprecision of feeling,/
253 MC	Tempt4	27	in corners, stealthy stratagem,/To general grasp of spiritual power?/Man
276 MC	Chorus	1	catastrophe,/The personal loss, the general misery,/Living and partly living;/The
294 FR	Harry	26	unspeakable,/Untranslatable: I talk in general terms/Because the particular has no
427 CP	Alex	38	have become the pretext/For general unrest amongst the natives./{E} But how
535 ES	Gomez	13	nonsense to talk of trusting people/In general. What does that mean? One trusts a

GENERALITY (1)

251 MC	Thomas	9	/You wrap your meaning in as dark generality/As any courtier./{T3} This is the

GENERATION (19)

105 Song Sime		26	shall praise Thee and suffer in every generation/With glory and derision,/Light upon
154 Rock 3		3	cities of designing men,/O wretched generation of enlightened men,/Betrayed in the
177 FQ: ECoker	10		building/And a time for living and for generation/And a time for the wind to break the
191 FQ: Little	18		nor fading,/Not in the scheme of generation./Where is the summer, the
247 MC	Thomas	14	much of the future/Except that from generation to generation/The same things
247 MC	Thomas	14	future/Except that from generation to generation/The same things happen again and
254 MC	Tempt4	19	the glittering jewelled shrine,/From generation to generation/Bending the knee in
254 MC	Tempt4	19	jewelled shrine,/From generation to generation/Bending the knee in supplication,/
286 FR	Ivy	31	{}/[*Lights a cigarette*]/{I} The younger generation/Are undoubtedly decadent./{C} The
286 FR	Charles	33	decadent./{C} The younger generation/Are not what we were. Haven't the
286 FR	Gerald	36	being very hard on the younger generation./I don't come across them very much
287 FR	Gerald	5	easy world to live in./Let the younger generation speak for itself:/It's Mary's
287 FR	Gerald	6	speak for itself:/It's Mary's generation. What does she think about it?/{M}
287 FR	Mary	8	want information/About the younger generation, you must ask someone else./I'm
287 FR	Mary	10	the compliment:/I don't belong to any generation. {}/[*Exit*]/{V} Really, Gerald, I must
342 FR	Amy	12	she has some spell/That works from generation to generation./{M} Is Harry really
342 FR	Amy	12	spell/That works from generation to generation./{M} Is Harry really going?/{Ag} He
547 ES	Piggott	22	/Can offer to guests of the younger generation./When there are enough young
554 ES	Piggott	35	/Means nothing at all to the younger generation,/But you and I should remember her,

GENERATIONS (2)

187 FQ: DrySal	101		of one life only/But of many generations — not forgetting/Something that is
201 Def Island	20		/to say, to the past and the future generations/of our kin and of our speech, that

GENEROSITY (1)

242 MC	Priest1	26	/Pride drawing sustenance from generosity,/Loathing power given by temporal

GENEROUS (7)

180 FQ: ECoker	105		bankers, eminent men of letters./The generous patrons of art, the statesmen and the
455 CC	Eggers	15	he's behaved like a father —A very generous man, is Sir Claude./To tell the truth,
456 CC	Eggers	9	nothing escapes him./And such a generous heart! He's rather a Socialist./I'm a
467 CC	Colby	9	of you —As a kind of protector, a generous provider:/Rather as a patron than a
476 CC	Lucasta	25	it./I don't know about B. He's very generous./I don't think he'd have minded. But
516 CC	Colby	4	Thank you, Sir Claude./You're a very generous man. But now I know who was my
541 ES	Gomez	28	are at your disposal./You were a generous friend to me once/As you pointedly

GENIE (1)

361 CP	Reilly	30	release a new force,/Or let the genie out of the bottle./It is to start a train of

GENIUS (4)

195 FQ: Little	174		kin or kindness,/But some of peculiar genius,/All touched by a common genius,/
195 FQ: Little	175		genius,/All touched by a common genius,/United in the strife which divided them;/
447 CC	Eggers	20	too much respect for your business genius./But it's true she believes she has what
466 CC	Claude	20	unity./Then there are also the men of genius./There are others, it seems to me, who

GENOUX (1)

48 Lune Miel		5	/Ils restent sur le dos écartant les genoux/De quatre jambes molles tout gonflées

GENTEEL (1)

301 FR	Gerald	22	and her credit among her shabby genteel acquaintance./{V} Gerald is certain to

GENTILE (1)
71 WL: DWater 319   and youth/Entering the whirlpool./Gentile or Jew/O you who turn the wheel and
GENTLE (4)
23 Preludes   50   cling:/The notion of some infinitely gentle/Infinitely suffering thing./Wipe your
596 When we   3   leaves were fallen from the trees;/The gentle fingers of the breeze/Had torn no
330 FR   Harry   9   being unconscious, living in gentle motion/Of horses, and right visits to the
482 CC   Lady E   8   /But, Colby, I hope you won't mind a gentle hint./I feared it was possible you might
GENTLEMAN (7)
32 Hysteria   7   iron table, saying: 'If the lady and gentleman wish to take their/tea in the garden,
32 Hysteria   8   their/tea in the garden, if the lady and gentleman wish to take their tea in the/garden
115 SP   Doris   11   What about Pereira?/{Do} He's no gentleman, Pereira:/You can't trust him!/{Du}
115 SP   Dusty   14   him!/{Du} Well that's true./He's no gentleman if you can't trust him/And *if* you
115 SP   Dusty   18   nice to Pereira./{Du} Now Sam's a gentleman through and through./{Do} I like
531 ES   Lambert 32   /{L} Excuse me, my Lord. There's a gentleman downstairs/Is very insistent that he
532 ES   Lambert   3   good English./A pleasant-spoken gentleman. {}/[*after reading the note*]./{LC} I'll
GENTLEMEN (3)
119 SP   Wauch   5   meet two friends of ours,/American gentlemen here on business./Meet Mr.
209 NamingCats   10   they sound sweeter,/Some for the gentlemen, some for the dames:/Such as Plato,
267 MC   Thomas   4   pray that God may help you!/{T} But, gentlemen, your business/Which you said so
GENTLY (3)
140 Usk   6   /Old enchantments. Let them sleep./'Gently dip, but not too deep',/Lift your eyes/
204 de la Mare   15   by unseen feet, and ghosts return/Gently at twilight, gently go at dawn,/The sad
204 de la Mare   15   and ghosts return/Gently at twilight, gently go at dawn,/The sad intangible who
GEORGE (3)
66 WL: Chess   160   five already, and nearly died of young George.)/The chemist said it would be all right,
209 NamingCats   7   James,/Such as Victor or Jonathan, George or Bill Bailey —/All of them sensible
565 ES   Michael 15   No, I don't mind./I'm staying at the George — it's not far away./{MC} Then I'd like
GERALD (21)
284 FR   m   3   *her younger sisters*/COL. THE HON. GERALD PIPER, *and* THE HON. CHARLES
285 FR   4m   1   I/AMY, IVY, VIOLET, AGATHA, GERALD, CHARLES, MARY/[DENMAN
286 FR   Amy   10   My servants are perfectly competent, Gerald./I can still see to that./{V} Well, as for
286 FR   m   29   *whisky.* CHARLES *takes sherry and* GERALD *whisky.*]/{C} That's what it comes to.
287 FR   Mary   7   think about it?/{M} Really, Cousin Gerald, if you want information/About the
287 FR   Violet   11   any generation. {}/[*Exit*]/{V} Really, Gerald, I must say you're very tactless,/And I
288 FR   Violet   17   to Wishwood./{G} Why, painful?/{V} Gerald! you know what Agatha means./{Ag} I
289 FR   Amy   10   on at Wishwood./{A} Thank you, Gerald. Though Agatha means/As a rule, a
290 FR   Violet   20   will be a little difficult./{A} Nonsense, Gerald!/You must see for yourself it's the only
290 FR   m   36   door. {}/CHORUS (IVY, VIOLET, GERALD *and* CHARLES)./{Ch} Why do we
292 FR   Harry   14   mother./Aunt Ivy, Aunt Violet, Uncle Gerald, Uncle Charles. Agatha./{A} We are very
301 FR   Violet   23   her shabby genteel acquaintance./{V} Gerald is certain to make some blunder, he is
313 FR   2m   1   /HARRY, MARY, IVY, VIOLET, GERALD, CHARLES/{V} Good evening,
316 FR   Violet   6   /{V} It is the obtuseness of Gerald and Charles and that doctor, that gets
323 FR   m   7   *by* VIOLET, IVY, AGATHA, GERALD *and* CHARLES.]/{A} Winchell! what
325 FR   Ivy   15   *that.*/{I} You are quite right, Gerald, the one thing that matters/Is not to let
328 FR Charles   12   *in Motor Smash*/The Hon. Arthur Gerald Charles Piper, younger brother of Lord/
344 FR   m   2   you again. {}/[*Meanwhile* VIOLET, GERALD *and* CHARLES *have entered*]/{C}
345 FR   Amy   24   give. And now I am punished for it./Gerald! you are the stupidest person in this
345 FR   m   31   {}/[*Exeunt* AMY, VIOLET, GERALD]/{C} It's very odd,/But I am
347 FR   m   16   telegram come from Arthur; {}/[*Enter* GERALD *and* VIOLET]/{I} I wonder why he
GERANIUM (1)
24 Rhapsody   12   memory/As a madman shakes a dead geranium./Half-past one,/The street-lamp
GERANIUMS (1)
24 Rhapsody   63   reminiscence comes/Of sunless dry geraniums/And dust in crevices,/Smells of
GERMINATION (1)
160 Rock 7   3   finding no place of lodgement and germination./They followed the light and the
GERONTION (1)
37 Gerontion   t   and the noon's repose./Poems/Gerontion/Here I am, an old man in a dry
GERTRUDE (1)
457 CC   Lady E   25   *voice off.**/{LE} No, Gertrude, I haven't had any lunch,/And I don't
GERTRUDE'S (1)
504 CC   Lady E   10   in the pantry./{LE} Oh, I forgot. It's Gertrude's quiet hour./I've been giving her
GESHEM (1)
158 Rock 5   2   and Tobiah the Ammonite and Geshem the Arabian: were doubtless men of
GESSO (1)
54 Mr E Sun   10   the Umbrian school/Designed upon a gesso ground/The nimbus of the Baptized God./

GESTURE (3)

34 Figlia	22	been together!/I should have lost a gesture and a pose./Sometimes these cogitations
42 Swee Erect	11	hands/(Nausicaa and Polypheme)./Gesture of orang-outang/Rises from the sheets
83 Hollow Men	12	without colour,/Paralysed force, gesture without motion;/Those who have

GET (137)

66 WL: Chess	144	done with that money he gave you/To get yourself some teeth. He did, I was there./
66 WL: Chess	145	there./You have them all out, Lil, and get a nice set,/He said, I swear, I can't bear to
66 WL: Chess	153	TIME/If you don't like it you can get on with it, I said./Others can pick and
66 WL: Chess	164	alone, there it is, I said,/What you get married for if you don't want children?/
66 WL: Chess	167	/And they asked me in to dinner, to get the beauty of it hot —/HURRY UP
119 SP Krum	20	in Bordeaux?/Yes Miss Dorrance you get Sam/To tell about that poker game in
124 SA Swarts	18	in a bath/{Sw} These fellows always get pinched in the end./{Sn} Excuse me, they
124 SA Snow	19	end./{Sn} Excuse me, they don't all get pinched in the end./What about them bones
124 SA Snow	23	seen it in the papers/They *don't* all get pinched in the end./{Do} A woman runs a
124 SA Sweeney	26	continue his story./{S} This one didn't get pinched in the end/But that's another story
128 Cor1 March	43	trumpets!/(And Easter Day, we didn't get to the country,/So we took young Cyril to
181 FQ: ECoker	138	there,/To arrive where you are, to get from where you are not,/You must go by a
182 FQ: ECoker	178	failure/Because one has only learnt to get the better of words/For the thing one no
214 RTTugger	15	as he's at home, then he'd like to get about./He likes to lie in the bureau drawer,/
214 RTTugger	17	/But he makes such a fuss if he can't get out./Yes the Rum Tum Tugger is a Curious
218 Mung Rump	22	minds made up that they wouldn't get thinner/On Argentine joint, potatoes and
229 Gus	45	says: 'Now, these kittens, they do not get trained/As we did in the days when Victoria
229 Gus	47	when Victoria reigned./They never get drilled in a regular troupe,/And they think
233 Skimble	61	they ought to know about:/When you get to Gallowgate there you do not have to wait
233 Skimble	62	/For Skimbleshanks will help you to get out!/He gives you a wave of his long brown
602 Humoresque	17	I swear.'/'Why don't you people get some class?/(Feebly contemptuous of nose),/
267 MC Thomas	15	of loyalty be worn/Carefully, so it get not soiled or torn./Have you something to
269 MC Thomas	2	seven years is no brevity./I shall not get those seven years back again./Never again,
293 FR Harry	16	are talking of nothing else. Why not get to the point/Or if you want to pretend that I
295 FR Amy	39	you to go now and rest before dinner./Get Downing to draw you a hot bath,/And you
296 FR Charles	26	/I suspect it is simply that the wish to get rid of her/Makes him believe he did. He
296 FR Charles	29	all he needs is someone to talk to,/To get it off his mind. I'll have a talk to him
297 FR Charles	18	/Until there's somebody he wants to get rid of./{G} Even so, we don't want Downing
299 FRDowning	25	in the evening,/And *then* she used to get rather excited,/And, in a way, irresponsible,
304 FR Mary	10	here/Any more than I do. I want to get away./{Ag} After seven years?/{M} Oh, you
306 FR Harry	12	/All these years I'd been longing to get back/Because I thought I never should. I
306 FR Harry	16	my memory,/I think. It seems I shall get rid of nothing./Of none of the shadows that
309 FR Mary	9	you —/But in any case, I must get ready for dinner./{H} No, no, don't go!
314 FR Warburt	8	Harry./A country practitioner doesn't get younger./It takes me back longer than you
314 FR Violet	17	were convinced that you would never get well./{H} Not, I think, without some
315 FR Warburt	12	not talk of such matters./How did we get onto the subject of cancer?/I really don't
315 FR Warburt	16	place, but healthy./It's only when I get an invitation to dinner/That I ever see your
315 FR Violet	19	at your mother!/Except that she can't get about now in winter/You wouldn't think
321 FR Winch	34	Lord. But a country sergeant/Doesn't get younger. Thank you, no, my Lord;/I don't
324 FR Amy	26	I do not know very much:/And as I get older, I am coming to think/How little I
325 FR Gerald	20	/He's much more apt than John to get into trouble./{C} Oh, but Arthur's a brilliant
325 FR Charles	23	had at Brooklands,/*He's* not likely to get into trouble./{G} A brilliant driver, but more
327 FR Harry	18	be another way of talking/That would get us somewhere. You don't understand me./
332 FR Agatha	37	yet. I found him thinking/How to get rid of your mother. What simple plots!/He
340 FR Agatha	7	that you ever had./What did I get? thirty years of solitude,/Alone, among
343 FR Mary	20	it is much too late/Now, to try to get a fellowship?/{A} So you will all leave me!/
345 FR Harry	1	/As little fuss as possible. You must get used to it;/Meanwhile, I apologise for my
346 FRDowning	28	for what happens to them. You get a feeling of it./So I seem to know
347 FRDowning	5	/I wondered when his Lordship would get round to seeing them —/And so you've seen
347 FRDowning	7	turn!/They did me, at first. You soon get used to them./Of course, I knew they was to
356 CP Julia	21	I've always said:/'If I could only get Edward alone/And have a really *serious*
356 CP Julia	27	locked in the lavatory/And couldn't get out. I know what you're thinking!/I know
357 CP Celia	4	country,/And almost impossible to get a nurse./{J} Is that her Aunt Laura?/{E} No;
358 CP Julia	32	You come with me, Peter:/You can get *me* a taxi, and then I can drop you./I expect
359 CP Edward	16	I couldn't put off/Because I couldn't get at them in time;/And I didn't know that *you*
364 CP Edward	6	And yet I want her back./And I *must* get her back, to find out what has happened/
368 CP Alex	10	going out?/Is there anyone here to get dinner for you?/{E} No, I shan't want much,
368 CP Edward	11	/{E} No, I shan't want much, and I'll get it myself./{A} Ah, in that case I know what
371 CP Edward	33	wrap in camphor/But the moths will get in. So you want to see Celia./I don't know
374 CP Edward	4	as soon as I could:/And I tried to get you a short while ago./{C} If there had

392 CP	Edward	15	I knew was coming/But I couldn't	get	everyone. And so a few came./{L} Who
393 CP	Edward	34	/{E} You nagged me because I didn't	get	enough work/And said that I ought to meet
395 CP	Edward	3	humiliation ceases to humiliate./You	get	to the point at which you cease to feel/And
395 CP	Lavinia	13	a different person/Whom you must	get	to know./{E} This is very interesting:/But
395 CP	Lavinia	28	for you./But never mind, you'll soon	get	over it/And find yourself another little part
398 CP	Lavinia	18	is in the hall downstairs:/Will you	get	the porter to fetch it up for me? {}/
400 CP	Alex	22	him to a sanatorium/Where she can't	get	at him — then, he believes,/She will be very
400 CP	Reilly	25	/To escape from himself — and	get	the better of his wife./{A} Not to escape
404 CP	Edward	32	besides, I need more shirts — you can	get	my wife/To have my things sent on:
412 CP	Julia	18	That is most uncommon./{J} Henry,	get	up./You can't be as tired as that. I shall wait
413 CP	Reilly	13	as they had imagined./When I	get	as far as that, there is something to be done.
413 CP	Celia	34	right./I'd do anything you told me, to	get	back to normality./{R} We must find out
414 CP	Celia	5	/To all sorts of people, and they	get	over it/More or less, or at least they carry
416 CP	Celia	2	I've ever *done*,/Which I might	get	away from, or of anything in me/I could get
416 CP	Celia	3	from, or of anything in me/I could	get	rid of — but of emptiness, of failure/
418 CP	Reilly	27	/You will know very little until you	get	there;/You will journey blind. But the way
424 CP	Lavinia	6	That's the most convenient;/You can	get	in and out. Is there anything you need/That
425 CP	Edward	23	parties were like./Their guests will	get	just enough to make them thirsty;/They'll
425 CP	Lavinia	28	And if it's very crowded, they can't	get	at the cocktails,/And the man won't be able
426 CP	Lavinia	16	And no more committees./{L} Can we	get	away soon?/{E} By the end of next week/I
426 CP	Lavinia	25	would come so early? I simply *can't*	get	up./{CM} Mrs. Shuttlethwaite!/{L} Oh, it's
427 CP	Julia	3	expeditions,/And we're going to	get	him to tell us all about it./But what's
427 CP	Alex	14	How are you, Alex?/{A} I did try to	get	you on the telephone/After lunch, but my
427 CP	Alex	15	lunch, but my secretary couldn't	get	through to you./Never mind, I said — to
433 CP	Peter	14	to ask about,/Who did really want to	get	into films,/And I always thought she could
439 CP	Peter	18	forgotten them./I realise that I can't	get	out of it —/And what else can I do?/{A} It is
440 CP	Julia	15	before the party begins./They will	get	on better without us. You too, Alex./{L} We
449 CC	Claude	9	I see what you mean./{SC} She must	get	to like him first:/And then, Eggerson, I am
454 CC	Kaghan	16	/{K} Take it easy, Colby. You'll	get	used to her. {}/[*Exit* KAGHAN]/{C} Egg ...
455 CC	Eggers	1	I'm not used to it./{E} You'll soon	get	used to it. You'll be calling me Eggers/
455 CC	Eggers	30	anyone like Miss Angel./{E} You'll	get	used to her, Mr. Simpkins./Time works
456 CC	Eggers	15	are perfectly harmless./You'll soon	get	used to them. That's what Sir Claude said:/
459 CC	Lady E	30	sleeping-car it is quite impossible:/To	get	one's quiet hour. A quiet hour a day/Is most
461 CC	Eggers	5	find yourself non-plussed, you must	get	me on the phone./If I'm not in the house, I'll
461 CC	Colby	12	I have you always at my back/If I	get	into trouble. But I hope/That I shan't have
471 CC	Colby	27	for some reason,/You thought I'd	get	a false impression anyway./You preferred it
479 CC	Lucasta	9	And as for Lizzie,/You'd better not	get	in *her* way when she's hunting./But all that
480 CC	Colby	14	a head as anyone,/And you never	get	involved in anything risky./You like to
481 CC	Lady E	25	At six o'clock? Where will you	get	dinner?/Oh, I know. It's a chance to try that
488 CC	Lady E	16	/We must see this Mrs. Guzzard, and	get	her to confess it./{SC} I'm sorry, Elizabeth.
489 CC	Lady E	32	child was expected./{LE} In order to	get	money from you, perhaps./No, I shouldn't
492 CC	Claude	10	see Mrs. Guzzard. I'll arrange to	get	her here./{LE} And I think you ought to get
492 CC	Lady E	11	here./{LE} And I think you ought to	get	Eggerson as well. {}/[*rising*]./{SC} Oh, of
492 CC	Colby	19	Company/Tomorrow night. I must	get	to work on it./{SC} Tomorrow night. Must I
499 CC	Lucasta	26	solution/From your point of view. To	get	me off your hands./Oh, I know what a
501 CC	Claude	38	make my peace with him./{SC} We'll	get	him now. {}/[*Reaches for the telephone*]/[A
505 CC	Eggers	30	/Well, not so many years — when you	get	to my age/The past and the future both
509 CC	Lady E	39	/Being Barnabas. I suppose I'll	get	used to it./{C} But he's waiting downstairs!
511 CC	Kaghan	16	/For a time, at least./{K} Well, I must	get	used to that./But I should like to know how
513 CC	Colby	28	I could remember; whom I could	get	to know/Only by report, by documents —/
518 CC	Guzzard	31	to Teddington. Colby,/Will you	get	me a taxi to go to Waterloo?/{C} Get you a
518 CC	Colby	32	get me a taxi to go to Waterloo?/{C}	Get	you a taxi? Yes, Aunt Sarah;/But I should
524 ES	Charles	14	where I'm really well known/And	get	well served. And when *you're* with me/It
525 ES	Charles	16	stop to tea,/But you know I won't	get	a chance to talk to you./You know that.
534 ES	Gomez	31	in Switzerland./The ones who don't	get	out in time/Find themselves in gaol and not
534 ES	Gomez	37	play both parties/What you don't	get	from one you may get from the other'./Dick,
534 ES	Gomez	37	you don't get from one you may	get	from the other'./Dick, don't tell me that
537 ES	Gomez	25	you./Everyone expected that I should	get	a First./I suppose your tutor thought you'd
538 ES	Gomez	9	I know the reason:/You wanted to	get	rid of me. I shall tell you why presently./
538 ES	Gomez	21	if it's known you made it/You simply	get	moved to another post/Where at least you
541 ES	Gomez	3	years ago?/What damages you'd	get	! The Press wouldn't look at it./Besides, you
542 ES	Gomez	10	/So long as I stay here, as I can	get	./And the more I get, the longer I may stay./
542 ES	Gomez	11	here, as I can get./And the more I	get	, the longer I may stay./{LC} This is
553 ES	Carghil	12	we belong together .../Now, don't	get	alarmed. But you touched my soul —/
555 ES	Monica	17	What's the matter?/{M} I didn't	get	far./I met Michael in the drive. He says he

556 ES	Ld Clav	8	/{LC} Well then, fetch him./Let's get this over. {}/[*calls*]/{M} Michael! {}/[*Enter*
556 ES	Monica	29	something from him./Perhaps you'll get to the point if I leave you together. {}/[*Exit*]/
560 ES	Michael	19	/{Mi} Anyway, I'm determined to get out of England./{LC} Michael! Are there
560 ES	Michael	26	/{Mi} I'm not such a fool/As to get myself involved in a breach of promise suit/
560 ES	Michael	29	girl — or any other./But I want to get out. I'm fed up with England./{LC} I'm sure
569 ES	Ld Clav	30	/If people merely blackmail you to get your company/I'm afraid the law can't
573 ES	Carghil	33	/You're a very lucky man, to get a girl like Monica./I take a great interest in
574 ES	Michael	31	When I spoke, Father, of my wish to get abroad,/You couldn't see my point of view.
576 ES	Gomez	20	/{G} Much better to wait until we get there./The nature of business in San Marco/
578 ES	Michael	25	home for the holidays/How it used to get on my nerves, when I saw you/Always
579 ES	Michael	7	leave England?/{Mi} When we can get a passage./And I must buy my kit. We're
579 ES	Gomez	26	/{G} At the end of five years he will get his first leave./{Mi} Well ... there's nothing

GETS (9)

304 FR	Mary	15	What Cousin Amy wants, she usually gets./Why do *you* so seldom come here? *You*'re
316 FR	Violet	6	and Charles and that doctor, that gets on my nerves./{C} If the matter were left in
357 CP	Edward	14	strong. That's why when she's ill/She gets into a panic./{J} And sends for Lavinia./I
411 CP	3m	36	*down. The house-telephone rings. He/gets up and answers it.*]/{R} Yes? ... Yes. Come
455 CC	Eggers	21	Kaghan/In the end. He's a man who gets his own way,/And I think he can manage
456 CC	Eggers	40	that could happen. She sometimes gets lost,/Or loses her ticket, or even her
472 CC	Lucasta	12	Oh, it's strange, isn't it,/That as one gets to know a person better/One finds them in
535 ES	m	34	means —/To take another name. {}/[*Gets up and helps himself to whisky*]/{G} But of
558 ES	Michael	2	I forget them./It's being your son that gets me into debt./Just because of your name

GETTING (26)

277 MC	Knight3	4	KNIGHTS: 'Hear! hear!'] *We* are not getting anything out of this./We have much
277 MC	Knight3	16	up to it. And, as I said,/*we* are not getting a penny out of this. We know perfectly
287 FR	Charles	16	age for her./I suppose she must be getting on for thirty?/She ought to be married,
326 FR	Violet	5	/And I had the greatest trouble in getting home./I am sure he meant well. But I do
334 FR	Harry	2	as if happiness/Did not consist in getting what one wanted/Or in getting rid of
334 FR	Harry	3	in getting what one wanted/Or in getting rid of what can't be got rid of/But in a
345 FR	Charles	35	that I want to know. I suppose I'm getting old:/Old age came softly up to now. I
347 FR	Warburt	34	/But I'm glad to say that John is getting on nicely;/It wasn't so serious as
395 CP	Lavinia	20	a little boy,/I'm sure you were always getting yourself measured/To prove how you
445 CC	Eggers	23	before you leave./{E} And how's he getting on? Swimmingly, I'm sure,/As I've heard
446 CC	Claude	5	necessary./But I'm satisfied that he's getting the hang of things,/And I think he's
446 CC	Eggers	7	to take a keen interest./{E} And getting over his disappointment?/Of course, I
449 CC	Claude	29	see her. And Miss Angel/Will soon be getting married, I expect./{E} And so I hope. A
456 CC	Eggers	38	/To see as much of Europe as I have,/Getting Lady Elizabeth out of her difficulties./
478 CC	Lucasta	21	upon you;/When you think you're getting out, you're getting further in,/And you
478 CC	Lucasta	21	you think you're getting out, you're getting further in,/And you know at last that
495 CC	Lady E	24	potters —/Is that what I mean? I'm getting confused./I thought I was escaping from
496 CC	Claude	33	so much worse./{SC} Yes, it's always getting worse./{LE} — I hope Mrs. Eggerson is
496 CC	Eggers	37	around this season,/When we're getting near the anniversary./{SC} The
509 CC	Lady E	37	me./{LE} Yes, what year was it?/I'm getting so confused. What with Colby being
516 CC	Colby	11	/When I found I had no chance of getting to the top —/That is, to become the
524 ES	Monica	24	to be avoiding his eye./{M} We're getting off the point .../{C} You've got me off
542 ES	Gomez	39	welcome?/Your telephone pal may be getting impatient./I'll see you soon again./{LC}
556 ES	Michael	35	a person/It's natural he should end by getting into trouble./{LC} You started pretty
557 ES	Ld Clav	1	trouble./{LC} You started pretty early getting into trouble,/When you were expelled
579 ES	Michael	11	line/Who he thinks can be helpful in getting reservations./{MC} It's wonderful, Señor

GHOST (15)

193 FQ:	Little	97	/The eyes of a familiar compound ghost/Both intimate and unidentifiable./So I
229	Gus	42	blood-curdling noises to bring on the Ghost./And he once crossed the stage on a
587	Fable	16	no; much worse than that, they had a ghost./Some wicked and heretical old sinner/
588	Fable	64	began to burn distinctly blue,/As in ghost stories lights most always do./The doors,
589	Fable	75	eye became the size of any dollar,/The ghost then took him roughly by the hair/And
260 MC	Thomas	3	and of the Son, and of the Holy Ghost. Amen./Dear children of God, my
262 MC	Thomas	5	and of the Son, and of the Holy Ghost. Amen./Part II/{C} Does the bird sing in
340 FR	Amy	18	the sake of the future, a discontented ghost,/In his own house. What of the
396 CP	Lavinia	27	I died/To you, I who had been only a ghost to you,/You might be able to find the
531 ES	Ld Clav	26	delighted. They won't want my ghost/Walking in the City or sitting in the
531 ES	Ld Clav	28	/And I, who recognise myself as a ghost/Shan't want to be seen there. It makes me
531 ES	Ld Clav	31	/If they only knew how frightened a ghost can be of men! {}/[*Knock. Enter*
560 ES	Michael	3	surprised state of consciousness./Poor ghost! reckoning up its profit and loss/And
572 ES	Ld Clav	21	she knows it./And she knows that the ghost of the man I was/Still clings to the ghost
572 ES	Ld Clav	22	of the man I was/Still clings to the ghost of the woman who was Maisie./We

GHOSTS (22)

38 Gerontion		30	shuttles/Weave the wind. I have no ghosts,/An old man in a draughty house/Under
204 de la Mare		14	lawn/Is pressed by unseen feet, and ghosts return/Gently at twilight, gently go at
587 Fable		26	vowed/They'd eat their meal from ghosts and phantoms free,/The fiend must stay
587 Fable		27	/The fiend must stay at home — no ghosts allowed/At this exclusive feast. From
588 Fable		31	from a Spanish saint — said he:/'If ghosts come uninvited, then, of course,/I'll be
589 Fable		68	known fact, as you do surely —/That ghosts are fellows whom you *can't* keep out;/It
294 FR	Harry	29	/In an over-crowded desert, jostled by ghosts./It was only reversing the senseless
310 FR	Harry	12	of the new full tide/Returning the ghosts of the dead/Those whom the winter
310 FR	Harry	14	whom the winter drowned/Do not the ghosts of the drowned/Return to land in the
336 FR	Harry	5	that I have been free/From the ring of ghosts with joined hands, from the pursuers,/
347 FRDowning		4	had the car all ready. You mean them ghosts, Miss!/I wondered when his Lordship
385 CP	Reilly	11	are not strangers./The affectionate ghosts: the grandmother,/The lively bachelor
491 CC	Colby	30	always be haunted/By the miserable ghosts of the other parents!/It's strange enough
491 CC	Colby	33	/I should have to live with those ghosts, one indignant/At being cheated of his —
531 ES	Ld Clav	30	that men should be frightened of ghosts./If they only knew how frightened a
569 ES	Ld Clav	34	are not real, Charles. They are merely ghosts:/Spectres from my past. They've always
569 ES	Ld Clav	37	that I found the living persons/Whose ghosts tormented me, to be only human beings,/
570 ES	Monica	1	like reality./{M} But what did the ghosts mean? All these years/You've kept them
570 ES	Ld Clav	6	/Or that she would be jealous of the ghosts who haunted me./And I'm still of that
570 ES	Monica	16	to break the silence! Let us share your ghosts!/{C} But these are only human beings,
570 ES	Monica	18	who can be dealt with./{M} Or only ghosts, who can be exorcised!/Who are they,
571 ES	Ld Clav	4	and Richard Ferry —/These are my ghosts. They were people with good in them,/

GIANT (1)

335 FR	Harry	26	avoid the clasping branches/And the giant lizard. To and fro./Until the chain breaks.

GIBBS (5)

352 CP	m	5	/ALEXANDER MACCOLGIE GIBBS/PETER QUILPE/AN
353 CP	4m	1	ALEXANDER MACCOLGIE GIBBS,/*and an* UNIDENTIFIED GUEST./{A}
399 CP	Nurse	24	That's all for the moment./{N} Mr. Gibbs is here, Sir Henry./{R} Ask him to come
422 CP	Reilly	1	/{R} Miss Barraway, when Mr. Gibbs arrives .../Oh, very good. {}/[*To* JULIA]/
432 CP	Lavinia	29	know why I should. Mr. MacColgie Gibbs./{A} Indeed, yes, we have met./{R} On

GIDDING (1)

191 FQ: Little		t	/The life of significant soil./Little Gidding/Midwinter spring is its own season/

GIFT (7)

89 Ash-Wed 1		4	not hope to turn/Desiring this man's gift and that man's scope/I no longer strive to
158 Rock 5		10	at nightfall: to be blessed with the gift of silence, and doze before he sleeps./But we
190 FQ: DrySal		219	and action./The hint half guessed, the gift half understood, is Incarnation./Here the
218 Mung Rump		17	and Rumpelteazer had a very unusual gift of the gab./They were highly efficient
346 FRDowning		25	for something else./I've no gift of language, but I'm sure of what I mean:/
368 CP	Alex	23	of it./{A} Ah, but that's my special gift —/Concocting a toothsome meal out of
538 ES	Gomez	33	touched by your interest./{G} I have a gift for friendship./I rejoiced in your success.

GIFTS (3)

164 Rock 9		25	/LORD, shall we not bring these gifts to Your service?/Shall we not bring to
194 FQ: Little		131	and foresight,/Let me disclose the gifts reserved for age/To set a crown upon your
577 ES	Carghil	35	for opportunity/To make use of his gifts; and now, opportunity —/Opportunity has

GILBERT (1)

213 Growltiger		41	forks and cruel carving knives./Then GILBERT gave the signal to his fierce

GILDED (4)

70 WL: Fire S		282	Beating oars/The stern was formed/A gilded shell/Red and gold/The brisk swell/
94 Ash-Wed 4		21	/While jewelled unicorns draw by the gilded hearse./The silent sister veiled in white
111 Xmas Trees		6	whom the candle is a star, and the gilded angel/Spreading its wings at the summit
167 Rock 10		31	reflected from the polished stone,/The gilded carven wood, the coloured fresco./Our

GILET (1)

51 Restaurant		12	des primevères.'/Les taches de son gilet montent au chiffre de trente-huit./'Je la

GIN (8)

229 Gus		35	if someone will give him a toothful of gin,/He will tell how he once played a part in
359 CP	Reilly	10	would you rather have whisky?/{UG} Gin./{E} Anything in it?/{UG} A drop of water./
360 CP	Reilly	11	another drink?/{E} Whisky?/{UG} Gin./{E} Anything in it?/{UG} Nothing but
363 CP	Reilly	6	were you drinking?/Whisky?/{UG} Gin./{E} Anything with it?/{UG} Water./{E} To
365 CP	Reilly	5	{}/[*Sings*]./{UG} *As I was drinkin'* gin and water,/And me bein' the One Eyed Riley,/
384 CP	Edward	3	/{E} Well. May I offer you some gin and water?/{UG} No, thank you. This is a
429 CP	Julia	36	/I'm feeling so chilly. Give me some gin./Not a cocktail. I'm freezing — in July!/
476 CC	Lucasta	40	before the end of the quarter/On gin and betting, I should guess./And I knew

GINGER (1)

226 Macavity		11	*Macavity's not there*!/Macavity's a ginger cat, he's very tall and thin;/You would

GIRAFE (1)

47 Mél Adult   18   oasis d'Afrique/Vêtu d'une peau de girafe./On montrera mon cénotaphe/Aux côtes

GIRAFFE (1)

56 Swee Night   4   along his jaw/Swelling to maculate giraffe./The circles of the stormy moon/Slide

GIRL (24)

62 WL: Burial	36	ago;/'They called me the hyacinth girl.'/— Yet when we came back, late, from the
123 SA Kl & Kr	13	AS BEFORE/{Kl&Kr} *My little island girl/My little island girl/I'm going to stay with*
123 SA Kl & Kr	14	*My little island girl/My little island girl/I'm going to stay with you/And we won't*
124 SA Sweeney	2	is death./I knew a man once did a girl in —/{Do} Oh Mr. Sweeney, please don't
124 SA Sweeney	12	/{S} I knew a man once did a girl in./Any man might do a girl in/Any man
124 SA Sweeney	13	did a girl in./Any man might do a girl in/Any man has to, needs to, wants to/Once
124 SA Sweeney	15	to, wants to/Once in a lifetime, do a girl in/Well he kept her there in a bath/With a
125 SA Sweeney	5	didn't know if he was alive/and the girl was dead/He didn't know if the girl was
125 SA Sweeney	6	girl was dead/He didn't know if the girl was alive/and he was dead/He didn't know
605 Narcissus	28	beauty./Then he had been a young girl/Caught in the woods by a drunken old man
257 MC Chorus	16	the young man mutilated,/The torn girl trembling by the mill-stream./And
287 FR Charles	15	into the conversation./{C} She's a nice girl; but it's a difficult age for her./I suppose she
369 CP Peter	4	met Celia./She was different from any girl I'd ever known/And not easy to talk to, on
369 CP Peter	29	I found I preferred to go alone./But a girl like Celia, it seemed very strange,/Because I
389 CP Lavinia	27	friends —/At least, in so far as a girl *can* be a friend/Of a woman so much older
453 CC Lucasta	9	take me out to dinner. A working girl like me/Is often very hungry — living on a
485 CC Lady E	9	were foolish fancies. I was a silly girl,/And very romantic. But it goes to show/
489 CC Lady E	40	him —/Because you *did* care for the girl, didn't you?/{SC} Yes, I did care. Very
524 ES Monica	19	round you: and it reminds the girl/That she's not the only one who's been
536 ES Gomez	10	Dick Ferry died long ago./I married a girl who didn't know a word of English,/Didn't
548 ES Carghil	22	your daughter — that very charming girl?/And obviously devoted to her father./I was
550 ES Carghil	35	Effie always said —/What a clever girl she was! — 'he doesn't understand women./
560 ES Michael	28	No, you needn't worry/About that girl — or any other./But I want to get out. I'm
573 ES Carghil	33	/You're a very lucky man, to get a girl like Monica./I take a great interest in her

GIRLS (8)

103 Journ Magi	10	on slopes, the terraces,/And the silken girls bringing sherbet./Then the camel men
119 SP Wauch	3	will you permit me —/I think you girls both know Captain Horsfall —/We want
218 Mung Rump	13	vests,/Or after supper one of the girls/Suddenly missed her Woolworth pearls:/
244 MC Chorus	15	have had laughter and gossip,/Several girls have disappeared/Unaccountably, and
304 FR Mary	4	knew the way of dominating timid girls./I don't see you any differently now;/But I
540 ES Gomez	31	it to be known where we'd been./The girls who were with us (what were their names?/
558 ES Michael	31	I'd been too familiar with one of the girls./He assumed it had gone a good deal
571 ES Ld Clav	34	driving back to Oxford. We had two girls with us./It was late at night. A secondary

GIST (1)

277 MC Knight1   29   has made a very important point. The gist of his/argument is this: that we have been

GIVE (98)

20 Portrait	65	I, but what have I, my friend,/To give you, what can you receive from me?/Only
66 WL: Chess	149	wants a good time,/And if you don't give it him, there's others will, I said./Oh is
66 WL: Chess	151	I'll know who to thank, she said, and give me a straight look./HURRY UP PLEASE
124 SA Sweeney	38	to come and see me sometimes/I'd give him a drink and cheer him up./{Do} Cheer
128 Cor1 March	48	in handy. He's artful. Please, will you/Give us a light?/Light/Light/*Et les soldats*
135 5FingerEx1	8	cease?/When will the broken chair give ease?/Why will the summer day delay?/
151 Rock 2	8	desired; we have only our labour to give and our labour is not required./We wait on
167 Rock 10	46	us of light./O Light Invisible, we give Thee thanks for Thy great glory!/FOUR
209 NamingCats	17	pride;/Of names of this kind, I can give you a quorum,/Such as Munkustrap,
211 Old Gumbie	37	/So for Old Gumbie Cats let us now give three cheers —/On whom well-ordered
229 Gus	35	of the Fell.'/Then, if someone will give him a toothful of gin,/He will tell how he
236 Cat Morgan	18	with Faber — or Faber —/I'll give you this tip, and it's worth a lot more:/
604 Ode	14	only the years that efface and destroy/Give us also the vision to see/What we owe for
241 MC Mess	15	the city./I was sent before in haste/To give you notice of his coming, as much as was
242 MC Priest2	34	will tell us what we are to do, he will give us our orders, instruct us./Our Lord is at
243 MC Priest2	6	/I am the Archbishop's man. Let us give the Archbishop welcome!/{P3} For good or
245 MC Priest2	10	least to put on pleasant faces,/And give a hearty welcome to our good Archbishop.
249 MC Thomas	18	last from the first./{T} What shall we give for it?/{T2} Pretence of priestly power./{T}
249 MC Thomas	20	of priestly power./{T} Why should we give it?/{T2} For the power and the glory./{T}
255 MC Tempt4	23	you desire. I ask/What you have to give. Is it too much/For such a vision of eternal
260 MC Thomas	27	'Peace I leave with you, my peace I give unto you.' Did He/mean peace as we think
261 MC Thomas	5	He said also, 'Not as the world gives, give I unto you.'/So then, He gave to His
273 MC Thomas	21	oak and stone; stone and oak decay,/Give no stay, but the Church shall endure./The
274 MC Thomas	5	my whole being gives entire consent./I give my life/To the Law of God above the Law

276	MC	Knight1	18	*the audience.*]/{K1} We beg you to give us your attention for a few/moments. We
277	MC	Knight3	24	he put up at the end —/they won't give *us* any glory. No, we have done for
277	MC	Knight3	25	So, as I said at the beginning, please give us/at least the credit for being completely
279	MC	Knight4	20	more to weld the/country together, to give it the unity, the stability, order, tranquillity,
279	MC	Knight4	39	is the only charitable verdict you can give, upon/one who was, after all, a great man./
289	FR	Gerald	4	about./You seem to be wanting to give us all the hump./I must say, this isn't
293	FR	Amy	10	I am an old woman./They can give me no further advice when I'm dead./{I}
294	FR	Harry	5	/Of my own experience, but trying to give you/Comparisons in a more familiar
303	FR	Mary	3	gardener had no garden-flowers to give me for this evening./{Ag} I always forget
322	FR	Harry	17	you;/I think I might be able to give you a shock./{Wi} There's been shock
326	FR	Denman	35	who can want me?/{D} He wouldn't give his name, Miss; but it's Mr. Arthur./{I}
345	FR	Amy	23	for my children/More than life can give. And now I am punished for it./Gerald!
346	FR	Downing	21	won't need me/Very long now. I can't give you any reasons./But to show you what I
355	CP	Julia	27	*returns with a tray*]/{J} Edward, give me another of those delicious olives./
358	CP	Julia	25	afraid my good Mrs. Batten/Would give me notice. And now I must be going./{A}
363	CP	Reilly	25	are./That's the best advice that *I* can give you./{E} But how can I wait, not knowing
364	CP	Reilly	14	in the light./The fact that you can't give a reason for wanting her/Is the best reason
368	CP	Alex	13	case I know what I'll do./I'm going to give you a little surprise:/You know, I'm rather
372	CP	Peter	31	your time,/And you want to be alone. Give my love to Lavinia/When she comes back
375	CP	Celia	2	to be divorced?/And if she chooses to give *you* the grounds .../{E} I see. But it is not
377	CP	Julia	1	poisoning people./Now, my dear, you give me that apron/And we'll see what I can do.
377	CP	Julia	28	Alex's./{J} Oh, it isn't Alex's. Come, I give you/Lavinia's aunt! You might have
383	CP	Celia	23	/Perhaps she is *my* guardian. Give me the spectacles./Good night, Edward./
385	CP	Reilly	30	wife, you must ask no questions/And give no explanations. I have said the same to
392	CP	Lavinia	5	no questions./{L} And I know I am to give no explanations./{E} And I am to give no
392	CP	Edward	6	give no explanations./{E} And I am to give no explanations./{L} And I am to ask no
394	CP	Lavinia	9	trouble/To have those Thursdays, to give you the chance/Of talking to intellectual
405	CP	Reilly	21	you have come to see. It is for me to give you that —/Your freedom. That is my
412	CP	Celia	36	to see you,/Are obviously ill, or can give good reasons/For wanting to see you. Well,
417	CP	Reilly	31	in the usual actions/What there is to give and take. They do not repine;/Are
418	CP	Celia	15	make a life with *any*body!/I couldn't give anyone the kind of love —/I wish I could
419	CP	Reilly	36	/Here is the address for you to give your friends; {}/[*Writes on a slip of paper*]/
421	CP	Julia	3	take the risk./All we could do was to give them the chance./And now, when they are
427	CP	Alex	18	guest/Is the one to whom they give the warmest welcome./I know them well
429	CP	Julia	36	over my grave:/I'm feeling so chilly. Give me some gin./Not a cocktail. I'm freezing
430	CP	Julia	27	/That he knew any monkeys./{J} But give us your news;/Give us your news of the
430	CP	Julia	28	monkeys./{J} But give us your news;/Give us your news of the world, Peter./We lead
447	CC	Claude	5	about Colby./I think, you ought to give her warning/Of whom she is to meet on her
452	CC	Eggers	39	I didn't know that./{E} You mustn't give way to her, Mr. Simpkins./I never do. I
453	CC	Eggers	2	/I never do. I always say/That if you give Miss Angel an inch/She'll take an ell./{L}
455	CC	Eggers	24	to be a nuisance?/{E} Not unless you give her encouragement./I have never
457	CC	Lady E	18	of medicine./Now, Parkman, will you give it to the driver?/He tells me that he suffers
459	CC	Lady E	9	But you look rather frail./I must give you lessons in the art of health./Where is
460	CC	Claude	38	doctor in Zürich has done for her,/I give him full marks. Well, Eggerson,/I seem to
465	CC	Claude	26	and peace/Which comes in dying to give something life .../I intend that you shall
471	CC	Colby	22	we met/You were trying very hard to give a false impression./And then you came to
471	CC	Lucasta	24	succeeded./{L} Oh, so I was trying to give a false impression?/What sort of impression
471	CC	Lucasta	25	sort of impression was I trying to give?/{C} That doesn't really matter. But, for
472	CC	Lucasta	37	know./It's awful for a man to have to give up,/A career that he's set his heart on, I'm
476	CC	Lucasta	11	we first met/You saw I was trying to give a false impression./I want to tell you now,
479	CC	Lucasta	11	that I'm hungry,/And you've got to give me a very good dinner./{K} You shall be
482	CC	Kaghan	2	/{K} And thank you so much. You give such good advice. {}/[*Exeunt* KAGHAN
486	CC	Claude	35	over instead of telephoning,/Just to give him these notes. They're notes for my
500	CC	Lucasta	26	somehow or other, I've something to give him —/Something that he needs. Colby
509	CC	Eggers	3	baptism./{E} What name did you give him?/{MG} We named the child Barnabas./
513	CC	Colby	13	Aunt Sarah:/To which I can only give a strange answer./Sir Claude is right: I
517	CC	Colby	29	/{C} Do you think that they would give me a trial?/{E} Give you a trial? I'm certain.
517	CC	Eggers	30	that they would give me a trial?/{E} Give you a trial? I'm certain./Good organists
524	ES	Monica	6	understood/When you said you could give me the whole afternoon./{C} But I couldn't
525	ES	Charles	6	afternoon,/That meant you were to give *me* the whole afternoon./I couldn't say
525	ES	Charles	36	that I haven't said before,/That will give you a shock. I believe *you* love *me*./{M}
537	ES	Gomez	2	as Culverwell./I need you, Dick, to give me reality!/{LC} But according to the
539	ES	Gomez	30	my career./{G} I don't propose to give you a detailed account/Of my own career.
540	ES	Gomez	33	you didn't want *them*/To be called to give evidence. You just couldn't face it./Do you
541	ES	Gomez	7	safe with me./Of course, I might give it to a few friends, in confidence./It might

542 ES	Ld Clav	29	it?/{LC} And what if I decline/To give you the pleasure of my company?/{G} Oh, I
544 ES	Monica	5	the hot water is hot,/They give us a very tolerable breakfast;/And the
549 ES	Carghil	30	'if you chose to follow *that* man/He'd give you the slip: he's not to be trusted./That
549 ES	Carghil	40	by which you knew me. It would give me such a thrill/To hear you speak my
559 ES	Michael	39	what satisfaction, I wonder, will it give you/In the grave? If you're still conscious
561 ES	Monica	35	/{M} Father! You know that I would give my life for you./Oh, how silly that phrase
580 ES	Monica	30	back to us;/If he prospers, that will give him confidence —/It's only self-confidence
581 ES	Charles	5	shall be ready to welcome him/And give all the aid we can. But it's both of you
581 ES	Ld Clav	20	Monica?/Because I wanted you to give your life to adoring/The man that I

GIVEN (44)

74 WL: Thund	401	the thunder/DA/*Datta:* what have we given?/My friend, blood shaking my heart/The
105 Song Sime	11	and fast, provided for the poor,/Have given and taken honour and ease./There went
109 Marina	19	the arm, less strong and stronger —/Given or lent? more distant than stars and
154 Rock 3	6	of your proper inventions:/I have given you hands which you turn from worship,/
154 Rock 3	7	which you turn from worship,/I have given you speech, for endless palaver,/I have
154 Rock 3	8	speech, for endless palaver,/I have given you my Law, and you set up commissions,
154 Rock 3	9	and you set up commissions,/I have given you lips, to express friendly sentiments,/I
154 Rock 3	10	to express friendly sentiments,/I have given you hearts, for reciprocal distrust./I have
154 Rock 3	11	hearts, for reciprocal distrust./I have given you power of choice, and you only
159 Rock 6	28	for all,/The lives of the Saints not given once for all:/But the Son of Man is
190 FQ: DrySal	207	/No occupation either, but something given/And taken, in a lifetime's death in love,/
218 Mung Rump	4	of operation, for they were incurably given to rove./They were very well known in
242 MC Priest1	27	from generosity,/Loathing power given by temporal devolution,/Wishing
256 MC Tempts	13	wheel, the pantomime cat,/The prizes given at the children's party,/The prize awarded
274 MC Thomas	36	of blood. Blood for blood./His blood given to buy my life,/My blood given to pay for
275 MC Thomas	1	blood given to buy my life,/My blood given to pay for His death,/My death for His
279 MC Knight1	4	share it with us./{K1} Morville has given us a great deal to think about. It/seems to
279 MC Knight4	31	Even/at the last, he could have given us reason: you have seen how he/evaded
281 MC Priest3	6	our thanks ascend/To God, who has given us another Saint in Canterbury. {}/[*while a*
281 MC Chorus	19	has dwelt, wherever a martyr has given his blood for the blood of Christ,/There is
282 MC Chorus	5	O God, we thank Thee/Who hast given such blessing to Canterbury./Forgive us,
339 FR	Harry	21	too much, is just strength enough given./I must follow the bright angels. {}/[*Exit*]/
341 FR	Amy	35	share had you in this? what have you given?/And now at the moment of success
347 FR Downing	6	seen them too! They must have given you a turn!/They did me, at first. You
393 CP	Edward	10	/{E} I was unaware that you'd always given in to me./It struck me very differently. As
393 CP	Edward	12	/I thought that it was I who had given in to *you*./{L} I know what you mean by
394 CP	Edward	11	people .../{E} You would have given me about as much opportunity/If you had
424 CP	Lavinia	17	that's unfair!/You know that we've given *several* parties/In the last two years. And
425 CP	Lavinia	10	be bitterly offended/To hear we'd given a party without asking them./{E} Perhaps
453 CC	Kaghan	31	till for me. I'm starving./{K} I've just given her lunch. The problem with Lucasta/Is
466 CC	Colby	5	hear is an inferior rendering./So I've given up trying to play to other people:/I am
469 CC	Colby	13	things, when you hear them./I've given you a test. Several of the pieces/That I've
476 CC	Lucasta	38	have mattered how much he'd given her:/It was always spent before the end of
500 CC	Lucasta	23	came to thank him for the shock he'd given me./He made me see what I really wanted.
509 CC	Guzzard	2	in such matters,/So we had it given conditional baptism./{E} What name did
522 ES	dedic	9	*words a little part of what you have given me./The words mean what they say, but*
526 ES	Monica	38	that anything I've said to you/Has given you the right to criticise my father./In the
528 ES	Charles	20	Charles./I'm sure of that./{C} You've given two reasons,/One the contradiction of the
528 ES	Monica	24	reason is this:/I've only just been given it by Dr. Selby —/Father is much iller
537 ES	Ld Clav	3	according to the description you have given/Of trusting people, how do you propose/
538 ES	Gomez	35	one thing has puzzled me./You were given a ministry before you were fifty:/That
539 ES	Ld Clav	28	nature of which dark hints have been given,/He's informed himself so carefully about
553 ES	Carghil	8	were intense enough, I think,/To have given me one or two insights into you./No,
559 ES	Michael	1	never have happened/If only I'd been given some interesting work!/{LC} And what do

GIVES (20)

18 Portrait	25	has these qualities,/Who has, and gives/Those qualities upon which friendship
38 Gerontion	37	Guides us by vanities. Think now/She gives when our attention is distracted/And what
38 Gerontion	38	attention is distracted/And what she gives, gives with such supple confusions/That
38 Gerontion	38	is distracted/And what she gives, gives with such supple confusions/That the
38 Gerontion	39	/That the giving famishes the craving. Gives too late/What's not believed in, or if still
38 Gerontion	41	memory only, reconsidered passion. Gives too soon/Into weak hands, what's
52 Whispers	20	/Uncorseted, her friendly bust/Gives promise of pneumatic bliss./The couched
61 WL: Burial	23	the sun beats,/And the dead tree gives no shelter, the cricket no relief,/And the
230 Bust Jones	21	shrimps./In the season of venison he gives his ben'son/To the *Pothunter's* succulent
232 Skimble	13	been busy in the luggage van!/He gives one flash of his glass-green eyes/And the

233 Skimble	63		will help you to get out!/He gives you a wave of his long brown tail/Which
261 MC Thomas	5		that He said also, 'Not as the world gives, give I unto you.'/So then, He gave to His
261 MC Thomas	7		peace, but not peace as the world/gives./Consider also one thing of which you
274 MC Thomas	4		decision/To which my whole being gives entire consent./I give my life/To the Law
330 FR	Harry	22	irrevocable —/It's eternal, or gives a knowledge of eternity,/Because it feels
341 FR	Amy	28	you up to judge? what, if you please,/Gives *you* the power to know what is best for
455 CC	Eggers	18	because she won't stick to them./He gives her an allowance — very adequate indeed,
463 CC	Colby	14	remote from my previous interests./It gives me, in a way, a kind of self-confidence/I've
515 CC	Colby	33	I believe you. I must believe you:/This gives me freedom./{SC} But, Colby —/If this
577 ES	Charles	9	return of past kindness/No doubt gives you pleasure?/{G} Yes, it's always pleasant

GIVING (17)

33 Conv Gal	15		/The eternal enemy of the absolute,/Giving our vagrant moods the slightest twist!/
38 Gerontion	39		with such supple confusions/That the giving famishes the craving. Gives too late/
116 SP	Dusty	34	feet in mustard and water/I said I'm giving her mustard and water/All right,
248 MC	Tempt2	33	gladness?/{T2} Sadness/Only to those giving love to God alone./Shall he who held the
362 CP	Reilly	6	had the courage to break it —/Thus giving herself a permanent advantage./{E} It
393 CP	Lavinia	9	myself./That's what came of always giving in to you./{E} I was unaware that you'd
393 CP	Lavinia	13	to *you*./{L} I know what you mean by giving in to *me*:/You mean, leaving all the
416 CP	Celia	14	others./{C} Oh, I thought that I was giving him so much!/And he to me — and the
416 CP	Celia	15	so much!/And he to me — and the giving and the taking/Seemed so right: not in
416 CP	Celia	21	/And that there had been neither giving nor taking/But that we had merely made
417 CP	Reilly	30	tolerant of themselves and others,/Giving and taking, in the usual actions/What
430 CP	Peter	8	to-day/And she told me you were giving a party —/She's coming on later, after
432 CP	Reilly	10	.../{R} My dear Julia,/You are giving me a very bad introduction —/Supposing
439 CP	Reilly	38	the Chamberlaynes should now be giving a party./{L} And I have been thinking,
476 CC	Lucasta	14	people before:/I got into the habit of giving that impression./That's where B. has
504 CC	Lady E	11	It's Gertrude's quiet hour./I've been giving her lessons in recollection./But she
558 ES	Michael	3	because of your name they insist on giving credit./{LC} And your debts: are they the

GLAD (53)

16 Prufrock	115		no doubt, an easy tool,/Deferential, glad to be of use,/Politic, cautious, and
69 WL: Fire S	252		pass:/'Well now that's done: and I'm glad it's over.'/When lovely woman stoops to
92 Ash-Wed 2	49		sang, scattered and shining/We are glad to be scattered, we did little good to each
104 Journ Magi	43		clutching their gods./I should be glad of another death./A Song for Simeon/
143 Lines OM	14		that he is mad./Tell me if I am not glad!/Choruses from 'The Rock'/The Eagle
167 Rock 10	36		of earthly life we tire of light. We are glad when the day ends, when the play ends;
167 Rock 10	38		or concentration, we sleep and are glad to sleep,/Controlled by the rhythm of
599 On a Port	9		fancy of one's own./No meditations glad or ominous/Disturb her lips, or move the
243 MC	Priest2	5	rejoice,/I say rejoice, and show a glad face for his welcome./I am the
252 MC Thomas	16		as Chancellor/And men like you were glad to wait at my door./Not only in the court,
289 FR	Amy	34	/{G} I never met her./{A} I am very glad you did not./I am very glad that none of
289 FR	Amy	35	I am very glad you did not./I am very glad that none of you ever met her./It will make
292 FR	Amy	15	Charles. Agatha./{A} We are very glad to have you back, Harry./Now we shall all
303 FR	Mary	24	making conversation./I am very glad if Dr. Warburton is coming./I shall have to
306 FR	Mary	9	No, don't go just yet./{M} Are you glad to be at home?/{H} There was something/I
313 FR	Charles	20	we only want Arthur and John/I'm glad that you'll all be together, Harry;/They
317 FR	Warburt	1	I/HARRY, WARBURTON/{W} I'm glad of a few minutes alone with you, Harry./In
324 FR	Harry	19	was ever really conscious,/I should be glad for him to have a breathing spell:/But
328 FR	Charles	7	/{C} Yes, there is a paragraph ... I'm glad to say/It's not very conspicuous .../{G}
345 FR	Amy	21	that is to be old./Nevertheless, I am glad if I can come to know them./I always
347 FR	Warburt	34	so long, going and coming./But I'm glad to say that John is getting on nicely;/It
364 CP	Julia	31	*and* PETER]/{J} Edward, I'm so glad to find you./Do you know, I must have left
367 CP	Peter	3	aware of everything./{P} Oh, I'm very glad that you didn't notice:/I must have
387 CP	Celia	4	a very pleasant experience./Oh, I'm glad I came!/I can see you at last as a human
387 CP	Peter	34	/{E} No, I've done nothing./{P} I'm so glad./Because I've changed my mind. I mean,
388 CP	Celia	8	/{C} Well, Peter, I'm awfully glad, for your sake,/Though of course we ... I
390 CP	Julia	35	about her aunt —/Who, you'll be glad to hear, has quite recovered, Alex —/And
391 CP	Edward	36	/To seem anything. But of course I'm glad to see you./{L} Yes, that was a silly thing to
406 CP	Reilly	7	he needs it more than I did./{R} I am glad that you have come to see it in that light —
418 CP	Celia	39	journey./{C} I am not frightened/But glad. I suppose it is a lonely way?/{R} No
424 CP	Lavinia	23	not tired yet. But I know that I'll be glad/When it's all over./{E} I like the dress
425 CP	Edward	1	I like the dress you're wearing:/I'm glad you put on that one./{L} Well, Edward!/Do
440 CP	Lavinia	1	I wish it was over./I mean ... I am glad you came ... I am glad Alex told us .../And
440 CP	Lavinia	1	I mean ... I am glad you came ... I am glad Alex told us .../And Peter had to know .../
440 CP	Lavinia	37	/{E} There's the doorbell./{L} Oh, I'm glad. It's begun. {}/CURTAIN/THE
445 CC	Eggers	11	with Mr. Simpkins./But I was glad of the excuse for coming up to London:/

449 CC	Claude	15	solution. Yes, quite ideal./{SC} I'm glad you agree. Your support will be helpful./
450 CC	Colby	33	you. {}/[*Exit* SIR CLAUDE]/{C} I'm glad you don't have to leave just yet./I'm rather
452 CC	Kaghan	2	Hello Colby!/And hello Eggers! I'm glad to find you here./It's lucky for Colby./{E}
460 CC	Lady E	12	the postmark./{LE} But Claude, I'm glad to find/That you've taken my advice./{SC}
470 CC	Lucasta	15	neither solitude nor ... people./{L} I'm glad I'm not people. Will you play to me again/
499 CC	Lucasta	17	matter. It'll do another time./Oh, I'm glad you're here, Eggy! You're such a support./
503 CC	Colby	16	B./{C} I'm very fond of him;/And I'm glad to think he'll be my brother-in-law./I shall
511 CC	Lady E	36	Barney Kaghan!/{LE} And I'm very glad you're announcing your engagement./
512 CC	Guzzard	2	have a church wedding./{MG} I am glad to hear you say so, Lady Elizabeth./But are
518 CC	Colby	20	until you were settled./{C} I'd be very glad indeed — if Mrs. Eggerson approved./{E}
526 ES	Monica	29	/{L} Yes, Miss Monica./{M} I'm very glad, Charles,/That you *can* stay to tea. {}/[*Exit*
548 ES	Ld Clav	21	Which you have just mentioned. I am glad you can confirm them./{MC} Oh, so that *is*
556 ES	Michael	13	*pause*]/{Mi} What a lovely day!/I'm glad you're here, to enjoy such weather./{LC}
556 ES	Ld Clav	14	to enjoy such weather./{LC} You're glad I'm here? Did you drive down from
567 ES	Monica	2	Oh Charles, Charles, Charles, I'm so glad you've come!/I've been so worried, and
573 ES	Charles	31	What a charming name!/{C} I'm glad my name meets with your approval, Mrs.
580 ES	Gomez	2	you let me write to you?/{G} Oh, I'm glad you reminded me. Here's my business card/

GLADLY (5)

475 CC	Colby	32	you might as well know them./{C} I'd gladly tell you everything about myself;/But you
492 CC	Claude	9	what was going to happen,/I would gladly have surrendered Colby to you./But we
530 ES	Ld Clav	17	energy to work myself to death/How gladly would I face death! But waiting, simply
561 ES	Ld Clav	2	/Some dream of excellence, how gladly would I help you!/Even though it carried
568 ES	Charles	13	{C} There are certainly things I would gladly forget, Sir,/Or rather, which I wish had

GLADNESS (1)

| 248 MC | Thomas | 31 | /{T} To the man of God what gladness?/{T2} Sadness/Only to those giving |

GLANCE (3)

140 Usk		4	/The white hart behind the white well./Glance aside, not for lance, do not spell/Old
546 ES	Piggott	27	When you go in to lunch/Just take a glance around the dining-room:/Nobody looks
582 ES	Charles	28	and was looking back at us/With a glance of farewell./{M} I can't understand his

GLARE (2)

| 191 FQ: | Little | 8 | heat,/Reflecting in a watery mirror/A glare that is blindness in the early afternoon./ |
| 223 Pekes | Pols | 56 | fiercer or hairier./And what with the glare of his eyes and his yawning,/The Pekes |

GLARED (1)

| 222 Pekes | Pols | 20 | advance, or exactly retreat,/But they glared at each other, and scraped their hind feet, |

GLASS (13)

21 Portrait		100	remark/Suddenly, his expression in a glass./My self-possession gutters; we are really
43 Swee	Erect	44	feet,/Bringing sal volatile/And a glass of brandy neat./A Cooking Egg/Pipit sate
64 WL:	Chess	78	/Glowed on the marble, where the glass/Held up by standards wrought with
64 WL:	Chess	86	/In vials of ivory and coloured glass/Unstoppered, lurked her strange synthetic
69 WL:	Fire S	249	/She turns and looks a moment in the glass,/Hardly aware of her departed lover;/Her
83 Hollow	Men	9	in dry grass/Or rats' feet over broken glass/In our dry cellar/Shape without form,
226 Macavity		25	Peke's been stifled,/Or the greenhouse glass is broken, and the trellis past repair —/Ay,
286 FR	Charles	25	/All that a civilised person needs/Is a glass of dry sherry or two before dinner./The
321 FR	Harry	31	Sit down, Winchell,/And have a glass of port. We were talking of my father./
383 CP	Edward	16	I hoped that you would drink a final glass with me./{C} What should we drink to?/
432 CP	Reilly	22	have a cocktail?/{R} Might I have a glass of water?/{E} Anything with it?/{R}
479 CC	Colby	16	to other people./{C} Will you have a glass of sherry?/{K} Yes, I'll have a glass of
479 CC	Kaghan	17	a glass of sherry?/{K} Yes, I'll have a glass of sherry,/To drink success to the flat.

GLASS-GREEN (1)

| 232 Skimble | | 13 | luggage van!/He gives one flash of his glass-green eyes/And the signal goes 'All Clear!' |

GLASSES (6)

364 CP	Julia	32	/Do you know, I must have left my glasses here,/And I simply can't see a thing
365 CP	Julia	37	it. But that reminds me/About my glasses. That's the greatest mystery./Peter! Why
377 CP		m 19	JULIA, *in apron, with a tray and three glasses*]/{J} I've had an inspiration!/There's
422 CP		1m 11	*enters with a tray, a decanter and three glasses, and/exit.* REILLY *pours drinks.*]/{R}
422 CP		m 13	of the hearth. {}/[*They raise their glasses*]/{R} Let them build the hearth/Under the
424 CP	Lavinia	2	could bring in the trolley with the glasses/And leave them ready./{CM} Very good,

GLAZEN (1)

| 30 Cous | Nancy | 11 | knew that it was modern./Upon the glazen shelves kept watch/Matthew and Waldo, |

GLEAM (1)

| 594 Grad | 11 | 4 | /O queen of schools — a momentary gleam,/A bubble on the surface of the stream,/A |

GLENCOE (1)

| 141 Rannoch | | t | the pilgrim's prayer./Rannoch, by Glencoe/Here the crow starves, here the patient |

GLI (1)

| 75 WL: | Thund | 427 | falling down/*Poi s'ascose nel foco che gli affina*/*Quando fiam uti chelidon* — O swallow |

GLIDE (1)
204 de la Mare   7 a mango grove,/And shadowy lemurs glide from tree to tree —/The guardians of some
GLIDING (1)
73 WL: Thund 363   another one walking beside you/Gliding wrapt in a brown mantle, hooded/I do
GLITTER (2)
64 WL: Chess   84 Reflecting light upon the table as/The glitter of her jewels rose to meet it,/From satin
109 Marina   8   the dog, meaning/Death/Those who glitter with the glory of the hummingbird,
GLITTERED (1)
172 FQ: BurntN 39   rose, quietly, quietly,/The surface glittered out of heart of light,/And they were
GLITTERING (2)
111 Xmas Trees 12 not accepted as a pretext;/So that the glittering rapture, the amazement/Of the
254 MC Tempt4 18 pilgrims, standing in line/Before the glittering jewelled shrine,/From generation to
GLOOM (4)
52 Whispers   26   jaguar/Does not in its arboreal gloom/Distil so rank a feline smell/As Grishkin
107 Animula   29 of its own shadows, spectre in its own gloom,/Leaving disordered papers in a dusty
230 Bust Jones   27   or at the *Glutton*;/If he looks full of gloom then he's lunched at the *Tomb*/On
531 ES Monica   3   Father, you simply want to revel in gloom!/You know you've retired in a blaze of
GLOOMY (2)
56 Swee Night   9 And Sweeney guards the hornèd gate./Gloomy Orion and the Dog/Are veiled; and
174 FQ: BurntN 113 /Driven on the wind that sweeps the gloomy hills of London./Hampstead and
GLORIFY (1)
167 Rock 10   35   it comes./O Light Invisible, we glorify Thee!/In our rhythm of earthly life we
GLORIOUS (2)
545 ES Piggott 23 morning, Miss Claverton!/Isn't this a glorious morning!/I'm afraid you'll think I've
554 ES Carghil   9   morning, Mrs. Piggott!/Isn't it a glorious morning! {}/[*Enter* MRS. PIGGOTT]/
GLORY (24)
89 Ash-Wed 1   10   not hope to know again/The infirm glory of the positive hour/Because I do not
105 Song Sime   27 and suffer in every generation/With glory and derision,/Light upon light, mounting
109 Marina   8 /Death/Those who glitter with the glory of the hummingbird, meaning/Death/
155 Rock 3   60   the grandeur of your mind and the glory of your action,/To arts and inventions and
162 Rock 8   15 in all places,/Some went from love of glory,/Some went who were restless and curious,
167 Rock 10   46   we give Thee thanks for Thy great glory!/FOUR QUARTETS/Burnt Norton/Time
201 Def Island   18 those again for whom the paths of glory are/the lanes and the streets of Britain:/to
594 Grad 12   4   words than these/Proclaim the glory so that all may hear;/May worthier sons
248 MC Tempt2   27 my Lord,/Power obtained grows to glory,/Life lasting, a permanent possession./A
249 MC Tempt2   21 give it?/{T2} For the power and the glory./{T} No!/{T2} Yes! Or bravery will be
254 MC Tempt4   10 of me./But think, Thomas, think of glory after death./When king is dead, there's
255 MC Tempt4   7 of that too./What can compare with glory of Saints/Dwelling forever in presence of
255 MC Tempt4   9 in presence of God?/What earthly glory, of king or emperor,/What earthly pride,
260 MC Thomas   1   *on Christmas Morning*, 1170/{T} 'Glory to God in the highest, and on earth peace
260 MC Thomas   13 the/shepherds at Bethlehem, saying 'Glory to God in the highest, and on/earth peace
261 MC Thomas   17 among the Saints in Heaven, for the glory of God and for the/salvation of men./
261 MC Thomas   31 anything for himself, not even the glory of being a/martyr. So thus as on earth the
271 MC Thomas   10 of the eternal burden,/The perpetual glory. This is one moment,/But know that
277 MC Knight3   24 at the end —/they won't give *us* any glory. No, we have done for ourselves, there's/
280 MC Priest1   38 further of you./{P1} O my lord/The glory of whose new state is hidden from us,/
281 MC Chorus   7 /{C} We praise Thee, O God, for Thy glory displayed in all the creatures of the earth,/
281 MC Chorus   10   exist/Only in Thy light, and Thy glory is declared even in that which denies Thee;
281 MC Chorus   10 denies Thee; the darkness declares the glory of light./Those who deny Thee could not
531 ES Monica   4 You know you've retired in a blaze of glory —/You've read every word about you in
GLOVES (1)
603 Spleen   13 fastidious, and bland,/Waits, hat and gloves in hand,/Punctilious of tie and suit/
GLOW (2)
191 FQ: Little   9 blindness in the early afternoon./And glow more intense than blaze of branch, or
308 FR Harry   5 with the unrecapturable emotion,/The glow upon the world, that never found its
GLOW-WORM (1)
166 Rock 10   24   and star light, owl and moth light,/Glow-worm glowlight on a grassblade./O Light
GLOWED (2)
64 WL: Chess   78   she sat in, like a burnished throne,/Glowed on the marble, where the glass/Held up
65 WL: Chess   110   her hair/Spread out in fiery points/Glowed into words, then would be savagely
GLOWLIGHT (1)
166 Rock 10   24   owl and moth light,/Glow-worm glowlight on a grassblade./O Light Invisible, we
GLUTTON (1)
230 Bust Jones   26   curry/At the *Siamese* — or at the *Glutton*;/If he looks full of gloom then he's

GLUTTONOUS (1)

| 355 CP | Julia | 25 | only reason for a cocktail party/For a gluttonous old woman like me/Is a really nice |

GLUTTONY (2)

| 152 Rock 2 | | 28 | consequence:/For sloth, for avarice, gluttony, neglect of the Word of GOD,/For |
| 163 Rock 8 | | 37 | lechery, treachery,/Envy, sloth, gluttony, jealousy, pride:/It was not these that |

GNAW (1)

| 282 MC Chorus | | 1 | over it;/From where the western seas gnaw at the coast of Iona,/To the death in the |

GO (254)

GOAL (2)

| 594 Grad 9 | | 5 | /Between, as we press onward to the goal,/Shall not have power to quench the |
| 561 ES Ld Clav | | 7 | experience. When you reach your goal,/Your imagined paradise of success and |

GOAT (2)

| 37 Gerontion | | 11 | patched and peeled in London./The goat coughs at night in the field overhead;/ |
| 154 Rock 3 | | 26 | a street of scattered brick where the goat climbs,/Where My Word is unspoken./ |

GOAT'S (1)

| 105 Song Sime | | 15 | sorrow is come?/They will take to the goat's path, and the fox's home,/Fleeing from |

GOBBLE (1)

| 121 SA Sweeney | | 6 | my little seven stone missionary!/I'll gobble you up. I'll be the cannibal./{Do} You'll |

GOD (102)

40 Burb Blei	7	with the passing bell/Slowly: the God Hercules/Had left him, that had loved him
49 Hippopot	20	rejoice/The Church, at being one with God./The hippopotamus's day/Is passed in
49 Hippopot	23	/Is passed in sleep; at night he hunts;/God works in a mysterious way —/The Church
50 Hippopot	28	angels round him sing/The praise of God, in loud hosannas./Blood of the Lamb
54 Mr E Sun	11	ground/The nimbus of the Baptized God./The wilderness is cracked and browned/
89 Ash-Wed 1	26	/Upon which to rejoice/And pray to God to have mercy upon us/And I pray that I
91 Ash-Wed 2	4	In the hollow round of my skull. And God said/Shall these bones live? shall these/
91 Ash-Wed 2	21	concentrated in purpose. And God said/Prophesy to the wind, to the wind
94 Ash-Wed 4	23	/Between the yews, behind the garden god,/Whose flute is breathless, bent her head
107 Animula	1	/Animula/'Issues from the hand of God, the simple soul'/To a flat world of
111 Xmas Trees	24	with a self-conceit/Displeasing to God and disrespectful to the children/(And here
147 Rock 1	13	/But nearness to death no nearer to GOD./Where is the Life we have lost in living?/
147 Rock 1	18	centuries/Bring us farther from GOD and nearer to the Dust./I journeyed to
151 Rock 2	2	of the saints, of the household of GOD, being built upon the foundation/Of
151 Rock 2	7	builded together for a habitation of GOD in the Spirit, the Spirit which moved on
151 Rock 2	12	of men, but not of relations of men to GOD./'Our citizenship is in Heaven'; yes, but
151 Rock 2	14	/When your fathers fixed the place of GOD,/And settled all the inconvenient saints,/
152 Rock 2	22	/And several versions of the Word of GOD:/The British race assured of a mission/
152 Rock 2	28	gluttony, neglect of the Word of GOD,/For pride, for lechery, treachery, for
152 Rock 2	40	no community not lived in praise of GOD./Even the anchorite who meditates alone,/
152 Rock 2	42	days and nights repeat the praise of GOD,/Prays for the Church, the Body of Christ
154 Rock 3	16	is your reading, but not the Word of GOD,/Much is your building, but not the
154 Rock 3	17	is your building, but not the House of GOD./Will you build me a house of plaster,/
155 Rock 3	59	/O weariness of men who turn from GOD/To the grandeur of your mind and the
160 Rock 7	1	build the Temple./In the beginning GOD created the world. Waste and void. Waste
160 Rock 7	2	they struggled in torment towards GOD/Blindly and vainly, for man is a vain
160 Rock 7	3	man is a vain thing, and man without GOD is a seed upon the wind: driven this way
161 Rock 7	27	why, or how, or where./Men have left GOD not for other gods, they say, but for no
161 Rock 7	27	for other gods, they say, but for no god; and this has never happened before/That
163 Rock 8	49	us therefore make perfect our will./O GOD, help us./Son of Man, behold with thine
164 Rock 9	3	is this that has said: the House of GOD is a House of Sorrow;/We must walk in
164 Rock 9	7	lights?/They would put upon GOD their own sorrow, the grief they should
166 Rock 10	2	in the night, it is now dedicated to GOD./It is now a visible church, one more light
179 FQ: ECoker	97	to another, or to others, or to God./The only wisdom we can hope to acquire/
180 FQ: ECoker	114	you/Which shall be the darkness of God. As, in a theatre,/The lights are
184 FQ: DrySal	2	think that the river/Is a strong brown god — sullen, untamed and intractable,/Patient
184 FQ: DrySal	6	/The problem once solved, the brown god is almost forgotten/By the dwellers in cities
186 FQ: DrySal	85	/The bone's prayer to Death its God. Only the hardly, barely prayable/Prayer of
605 Narcissus	17	ways, but became a dancer before God/If he walked in city streets/He seemed to
606 Narcissus	33	and old./So he became a dancer to God./Because his flesh was in love with the
240 MC Chorus	17	saints./Destiny waits in the hand of God, shaping the still unshapen/I have seen
240 MC Chorus	19	sunlight./Destiny waits in the hand of God, not in the hands of statesmen/Who do,
241 MC Priest1	9	forgotten their friend, their Father in God, have forgotten/That they had a friend? {}/
241 MC Mess	11	MESSENGER]/{M} Servants of God, and watchers of the temple,/I am here to
242 MC Priest1	28	devolution,/Wishing subjection to God alone./Had the King been greater, or had
243 MC Priest2	2	barons and landholders./The rock of God is beneath our feet. Let us meet the

248 MC Thomas   31   no madness./{T} To the man of God what gladness?/{T2} Sadness/Only to those
248 MC Tempt2   33   Sadness/Only to those giving love to God alone./Shall he who held the solid
249 MC Tempt2   4   the poor,/Beneath the throne of God can man do more?/Disarm the ruffian,
250 MC Thomas   12   order/Not controlled by the order of God,/In confident ignorance, but arrest
252 MC Thomas   14   /He has good cause to trust none but God alone./I ruled once as Chancellor/And men
255 MC Tempt4   8   Saints/Dwelling forever in presence of God?/What earthly glory, of king or emperor,/
257 MC Chorus   23   and eating and drinking and laughter./God gave us always some reason, some hope;
257 MC Chorus   25   at the ear and the mouth and the eye./God is leaving us, God is leaving us, more pang,
257 MC Chorus   25   mouth and the eye./God is leaving us, God is leaving us, more pang, more pain than
258 MC Thomas   26   the King's dish/To become servant of God was never my wish./Servant of God has
258 MC Thomas   27   God was never my wish./Servant of God has chance of greater sin/And sorrow, than
259 MC Thomas   6   end./Now my good Angel, whom God appoints/To be my guardian, hover over
260 MC Thomas   1   *Morning, 1170*/{T} 'Glory to God in the highest, and on earth peace to men
260 MC Thomas   4   Holy Ghost. Amen./Dear children of God, my sermon this Christmas morning will be
260 MC Thomas   10   salvation of men, and/offer again to God His Body and Blood in sacrifice, oblation
260 MC Thomas   13   at Bethlehem, saying 'Glory to God in the highest, and on/earth peace to men
261 MC Thomas   17   the Saints in Heaven, for the glory of God and for the/salvation of men./Beloved, we
261 MC Thomas   27   A martyrdom is always the design of God, for His love of men,/to warn them and to
261 MC Thomas   30   he who has become the/instrument of God, who has lost his will in the will of God,
261 MC Thomas   30   who has lost his will in the will of God, and who no/longer desires anything for
261 MC Thomas   37   to you to-day, dear children of God, of the martyrs of/the past, asking you to
263 MC Chorus   14   unless men keep the peace of God./And war among men defiles this world,
264 MC Priest3   15   /*Out of the mouth of very babes, O God*./As the voice of many waters, of thunder, of
264 MC Priest3   21   /Out of the mouth of very babes, O God! {}/[THE PRIESTS *stand together with the*
266 MC Knight2   34   greed./Won't you ask us to pray to God for you, in your need?/{K3} Yes, we'll pray
267 MC Knights   3   for you!/{3K} Yes, we'll pray that God may help you!/{T} But, gentlemen, your
267 MC Knights   13   /{K2} The King!/{K3} The King!/{3K} God bless him!/{T} Then let your new coat of
272 MC Chorus   25   /Emptiness, absence, separation from God;/The horror of the effortless journey, to the
274 MC Thomas   6   consent./I give my life/To the Law of God above the Law of Man./Unbar the door!
275 MC Thomas   17   me as your spiritual lord,/Traitor to God in desecrating His Church./{K1} No faith
275 MC Thomas   20   now be paid./{T} Now to Almighty God, to the Blessed Mary ever Virgin, to the
277 MC Knight3   17   /things will turn out. King Henry — God bless him — will have to/say, for reasons
278 MC Knight2   25   years striven to establish; and that — God knows/why — the two orders were
280 MC Priest1   13   on the ruins,/Their world without God. I see it. I see it./{P3} No. For the Church
281 MC Priest2   2   your charity./{P2} Now in the sight of God/Conjoined with all the saints and martyrs
281 MC Priest3   6   us./{P3} Let our thanks ascend/To God, who has given us another Saint in
281 MC Chorus   7   *the distance*]./{C} We praise Thee, O God, for Thy glory displayed in all the creatures
282 MC Chorus   4   it is forever denied. Therefore, we thank Thee/Who hast given such
282 MC Chorus   8   by the fire;/Who fear the blessing of God, the loneliness of the night of God, the
282 MC Chorus   8   of God, the loneliness of the night of God, the surrender required, the deprivation
282 MC Chorus   9   of men less than the justice of God;/Who fear the hand at the window, the fire
282 MC Chorus   11   canal,/Less than we fear the love of God./We acknowledge our trespass, our
296 FR Gerald   14   go and have my bath. {}/[*Exit*]/{G} God preserve us!/I never thought it would be as
317 FR Harry   15   that is very likely to happen./{H} O God, man, the things that are going to happen/
322 FR Winch   5   I'm forgetting./If it was my mother's. God rest her soul,/She's been dead these ten
332 FR Agatha   30   flames. They only come once,/Thank God, that kind. Perhaps there is another kind,/I
348 FR Chorus   17   plumbing,/But not against the act of God./We know various spells and
386 CP Edward   28   {C} Thank you. {}/[*Pause*]/{E} Oh, my God, what shall we talk about?/We can't sit
398 CP Edward   4   out laughing. But you won't./{E} O God, O God, if I could return to yesterday/
398 CP Edward   4   But you won't./{E} O God, O God, if I could return to yesterday/Before I
398 CP Edward   10   touch, there is nothing but ruin./O God, what have I done? The python. The
474 CC Colby   5   to be alone there./If I were religious, God would walk in my garden/And that would
485 CC Lady E   22   eternity. Something ... straight from God./That means that we are nearer to God
485 CC Lady E   23   /That means that we are nearer to God than to anyone./— Where did you live, as
490 CC Colby   35   not to be. I don't blame you for that:/God forbid! but we must take the consequences.
536 ES Gomez   18   their thoughts are Indian thoughts./O God, Dick, *you* don't know what it's like/To be

GOD'S (7)

246 MC Thomas   6   who hold me in bitterest hate./By God's grace aware of their prevision/I sent my
254 MC Tempt4   21   /Think of the miracles, by God's grace,/And think of your enemies, in
269 MC Thomas   21   my tomb/To submit my cause before God's throne. {}/[*Exit*]/{K4} Priest! monk! and
271 MC Thomas   13   sudden painful joy/When the figure of God's purpose is made complete./You shall
272 MC Chorus   22   is here/The white flat face of Death, God's silent servant,/And behind the face of
275 MC Thomas   10   and shame;/But none of my people, in God's name,/Whether layman or clerk, shall
321 FR Warburt   36   agrees with the rheumatism./{W} For God's sake, Winchell, tell us your business./His

GOD-GIVEN (1)
246 MC Thomas 19 /End will be simple, sudden, God-given./Meanwhile the substance of our
GOD-SHAKEN (1)
148 Rock 1 45 The Critic. The Stranger./The God-shaken, in whom is the truth inborn./*Enter*
GODDESS (1)
599 On a Port 5 alone./Not like a tranquil carved goddess of stone/But evanescent, as if one
GODHEAD (1)
261 MC Thomas 35 as we/see them, but in the light of the Godhead from which they draw their/being./I
GODLESS (1)
155 Rock 3 34 the wind shall say: 'Here were decent godless people:/Their only monument the
GODS (7)
104 Journ Magi 42 /With an alien people clutching their gods./I should be glad of another death./A Song
161 Rock 7 27 /Men have left GOD not for other gods, they say, but for no god; and this has
161 Rock 7 28 happened before/That men both deny gods and worship gods, professing first Reason,
161 Rock 7 28 men both deny gods and worship gods, professing first Reason,/And then Money,
161 Rock 7 43 opposed, and men have forgotten/All gods except Usury, Lust and Power./O Father
184 FQ: DrySal 1 Salvages/I do not know much about gods; but I think that the river/Is a strong
184 FQ: DrySal 25 men. The sea has many voices,/Many gods and many voices./The salt is on the briar
GOES (29)
20 Portrait 74 I remark./An English countess goes upon the stage./A Greek was murdered at
222 Pekes Pols 3 /It is always the same, wherever one goes./And the Pugs and the Poms, although
232 Skimble 14 of his glass-green eyes/And the signal goes 'All Clear!'/And we're off at last for the
232 Skimble 31 that cannot be ignored;/So nothing goes wrong on the Northern Mail/When
602 Humoresque 20 —/'Now in New York' — and so it goes./Logic a marionette's, all wrong/Of
248 MC Thomas 10 the springtime fancy,/So one thought goes whistling down the wind./The impossible is
293 FR Violet 1 to your mother/About the waste that goes on in the kitchen./Mrs. Packell is too old
295 FR Harry 17 /Your conscience can be clear./{H} It goes a good deal deeper/Than what people call
311 FR m 38 Harry! There is no one here. {}/[*She goes to the window and pulls the curtains across*]/
336 FR 1m 23 {}/[*The curtains close. AGATHA goes to the window, in a somnambular fashion,*/
359 CP m 22 {}/[*The doorbell rings. EDWARD goes to the door, saying:*]/{E} But she always
364 CP m 30 I must answer the door. {}/[EDWARD *goes to the door*]/{E} So it's you again, Julia! {}/
369 CP Alex 11 kitchen?/{A} I can't find it./There goes *that* surprise. I must think of another./{P}
370 CP Alex 16 Lavinia hates curry./{A} There goes another surprise, then. I must think./I
374 CP 3m 1 /*Patience. The doorbell rings, and he goes to answer it.*/{C} Are you alone? {}/
376 CP m 1 you in the kitchen? {}/[EDWARD *goes over to the table and inspects his game of*
376 CP m 7 *The bell rings again.* EDWARD *goes to front door, and is/heard to say:*]/{E}
384 CP 2m 1 *of the next day.* EDWARD *alone. He goes to/answer the doorbell.*/{E} Oh ... good
386 CP m 14 *about restlessly. The bell rings, and he goes to the front door.*]/{E} Celia!/{C} Has
387 CP m 12 *rings*]/{E} There's Lavinia. {}/[*Goes to front door*]/{E} Peter! {}/[*Enter*
389 CP m 37 {}/[*The doorbell rings, and* EDWARD *goes to answer it*]/{C} Oh, I'm afraid that all this
390 CP m 17 ... {}/[*The doorbell rings.* EDWARD *goes to answer it. Enter* ALEX]/{A} Has Lavinia
391 CP Lavinia 19 /I started some machine, that goes on working,/And I cannot stop it; no, it's
411 CP 2m 36 EDWARD *and* LAVINIA]/[REILLY *goes to the couch and lies down. The*
456 CC Eggers 26 /She is apt to buy a house. And then goes away/And forgets all about it. That can be
457 CC m 23 is she? Oh, she's gone out again. {}/[*Goes to the window and looks down on the street*]
467 CC Colby 14 terribly sorry to be saying this;/But it goes to explain what I said just now/About
485 CC Lady E 10 a silly girl,/And very romantic. But it goes to show/How different I felt myself to be/
561 ES Ld Clav 28 /Which he must think over. But if he goes abroad/I want him to go in a very different
GOING (148)
20 Portrait 88 my hands and knees./'And so you are going abroad; and when do you return?/But
94 Ash-Wed 4 4 /The various ranks of varied green/Going in white and blue, in Mary's colour,/
103 Journ Magi 13 and women,/And the night-fires going out, and the lack of shelters,/And the
115 SP Dusty 16 —/Then you never know what he's going to do./{Do} No it wouldn't do to be too
116 SP Dusty 5 have Pereira/{Du} Well what you going to do?/{Tel} Ting a ling ling/Ting a ling
116 SP Dusty 10 that's Pereira/{Du} Well what you going to do?/{Tel} Ting a ling ling/Ting a ling
116 SP Doris 39 kind of *you.*/Ah-h-h/{Do} Now I'm going to cut the cards for to-night./Oh guess
117 SP Doris 36 heavens what'll I do./Well I'm not going to draw any more,/You cut for luck. You
123 SA Kl & Kr 15 *island girl*/*My little island girl*/*I'm going to stay with you*/*And we won't worry what*
125 SA Sweeney 3 I talk to you./But here's what I was going to say./He didn't know if he was alive/and
277 MC Knight3 19 meant this to happen; and/there is going to be an awful row; and at the best we
277 MC Knight2 40 dog. But is this really the case? I am going/to appeal not to your emotions but to
288 FR Agatha 13 we have all been together./{Ag} It is going to be rather painful for Harry/After eight
293 FR Amy 7 only struggled to keep Wishwood going/And to make no changes before your
297 FR Violet 31 /Which I am convinced is going to lead us nowhere,/And which I am sure
311 FR Harry 10 like that! Stop! Try to stop it!/I am going. Oh why, now? Come out!/Come out!

314 FR	Amy	5	Harry./When he heard that you were	going to be here for dinner/He broke an
317 FR	Harry	7	—/Though I think it is probably	going to be useless,/Or if anything, make
317 FR	Harry	15	/{H} O God, man, the things that are	going to happen/Have already happened./{W}
320 FR	Warburt	18	now./Her determination has kept her	going:/She has only lived for your return to
323 FR	Warburt	32	not answer for the consequences/I am	going myself. I will come back and report to
324 FR	Violet	11	brother? Aren't you aware/Of what is	going on? and what it means to your mother?/
325 FR	Charles	9	there's no sort of use in any of us	going —/On a night like this — it's a good three
328 FR	Violet	29	just what I expected. But if Agatha/Is	going to moralise about it, I shall scream./{G}
328 FR	Gerald	30	about it, I shall scream./{G} It's	going to be awkward, explaining this to Amy./
336 FR	Harry	17	/Ready to leave Wishwood, and I am	going with you./You followed me here, where I
338 FR	Amy	9	I come again./{A} But why are you	going?/{H} I can only speak/And you cannot
339 FR	Amy	3	to understand./{A} Where are you	going?/{H} I shall have to learn. That is still
342 FR	Mary	13	to generation./{M} Is Harry really	going?/{Ag} He is going./But that is not my
342 FR	Agatha	14	/{M} Is Harry really going?/{Ag} He is	going./But that is not my spell, it is none of my
344 FR	Charles	2	have entered]/{C} Where is Harry	going? What is the matter?/{A} Ask Agatha./{G}
344 FR	Gerald	4	Why, what's the matter? Where is he	going?/{A} Ask Agatha./{V} I cannot
344 FR	Amy	12	has happened, Amy?/{A} Harry is	going away — to become a missionary./{H} But
344 FR	Gerald	29	—/That depends on where you're	going./{C} Such a thing/Has never happened in
344 FR	Harry	33	it./{H} I never said that I was	going to be a missionary./I would explain, but
344 FR	Harry	36	/You can't know why I am going. You have not seen/What I have seen. Oh
346 FR	Downing	16	You may think it laughable, what I'm	going to say —/But it's not really strange, Miss,
346 FR	Downing	29	know beforehand, when something's	going to happen,/And it seems quite natural,
347 FR	Ivy	14	Enter IVY]/{I} Where is Downing	going? where is Harry?/Look. Here's a telegram
347 FR	Violet	23	not./You do not know what has been	going on, Ivy./And if you did, you would not
347 FR	Warburt	33	out in./That's why I've been so long,	going and coming,/But I'm glad to say that
355 CP	Julia	22	/Leaving it to me to keep things	going./What a host! And nothing fit to eat!/The
357 CP	Celia	2	away./{C} But, Edward ... what was I	going to say?/It's dreadful for old ladies alone in
357 CP	Julia	40	Living on an annuity, of course./I am	going to make you dine alone with me/On
358 CP	Julia	12	that's all settled./And now I must be	going./{E} Must you be going?/{P} But won't
358 CP	Edward	13	I must be going./{E} Must you be	going?/{P} But won't you tell the story about
358 CP	Julia	25	give me notice. And now I must be	going./{A} I'm afraid I ought to be going./{P}
358 CP	Alex	26	be going./{A} I'm afraid I ought to be	going./{P} Celia —/May I walk along with you?/
358 CP	Julia	35	Now don't all go/Just because I'm	going. Good-bye, Edward./{E} Good-bye, Julia.
359 CP	Reilly	32	know your name./{UG} I ought to be	going./{E} Don't go yet./I very much want to
362 CP	Reilly	8	turn out so, yet .../{UG} Are you	going to say, you love her?/{E} Why, I thought
362 CP	Edward	12	/We were used to each other. So her	going away/At a moment's notice, without
362 CP	Reilly	28	you've dressed for a party/And are	going downstairs, with everything about you/
362 CP	Reilly	37	with the doctor and the surgeon,/In	going to bed in the nursing home,/In talking to
363 CP	Edward	31	/And they ask 'But what are you	going to do?'/And I answer 'Nothing'. They will
366 CP	Peter	32	all about?/{P} I want your help./I was	going to telephone and try to see you later;/But
368 CP	Alex	6	to spend an evening alone,/So you're	going to come out and have dinner with me./{E}
368 CP	Alex	9	got to have some dinner. Are you	going out?/Is there anyone here to get dinner for
368 CP	Alex	13	in that case I know what I'll do./I'm	going to give you a little surprise:/You know,
368 CP	Alex	15	know, I'm rather a famous cook./I'm	going straight to your kitchen now/And I shall
372 CP	Alex	29	than another ten minutes./Now I'll be	going, and I'll take Peter with me./{P} Edward,
374 CP	Celia	6	to be anyone with you/I was	going to say I'd come back for my umbrella ... ./
374 CP	Edward	13	know what has happened, or what is	going to happen;/And to try to understand it, I
376 CP	Celia	7	Anyway, I'm staying/And I'm not	going to hide. {}/[Returns to kitchen. The bell
377 CP	Julia	26	/Can you guess whose health I'm	going to propose?/{E} No, I can't. But I won't
387 CP	Peter	36	I've decided/That it's all no use. I'm	going to California./{C} You're going to
387 CP	Celia	37	I'm going to California./{C} You're	going to California!/{P} Yes, I have a new job./
388 CP	Celia	17	with./{C} I don't think that I shall be	going to concerts./I am going away too. {}/
388 CP	Celia	18	that I shall be going to concerts./I am	going away too. {}/[LAVINIA lets herself in
388 CP	Peter	19	herself in with a latch-key]/{P} You're	going abroad?/{C} I don't know. Perhaps./{E}
388 CP	Edward	21	know. Perhaps./{E} You're both	going away! {}/[Enter LAVINIA]/{L} Who's
388 CP	Lavinia	22	away! {}/[Enter LAVINIA]/{L} Who's	going away? Well, Celia. Well, Peter./I didn't
388 CP	Edward	37	/What shall we talk about?/{E} Peter's	going to America./{P} Yes, and I would have
389 CP	Lavinia	2	before I left./{L} And Celia's	going too? Was that what I heard?/I
389 CP	Lavinia	6	last, to realise your ambitions./You're	going together?/{P} We're not going together./
389 CP	Peter	7	/You're going together?/{P} We're not	going together./Celia told us she was going
389 CP	Peter	8	going together./Celia told us she was	going away,/But I don't know where./{L} You
389 CP	Lavinia	11	/And do you know where you are	going, yourself?/{P} Yes, of course, I'm going to
389 CP	Peter	12	yourself?/{P} Yes, of course, I'm	going to California./{L} Well, Celia, why don't
389 CP	Celia	18	no doubt you do./{C} And why he is	going .../{L} I don't doubt that either./{C} And I
389 CP	Celia	23	about it./{C} But now that I may be	going away — somewhere —/I should like to

391	CP	Julia	9	And now, Alex, you and I should be going./{E} Are you sure you haven't left
392	CP	Lavinia	23	knows by instinct when something's going to happen./Trust her not to miss any
397	CP	Lavinia	39	difference nothing to do/With Celia going to California?/{E} Celia? Going to
397	CP	Edward	40	Celia going to California?/{E} Celia? Going to California?/{L} Yes, with Peter./
401	CP	Reilly	15	Mr. Chamberlayne./You are not going away, so you might as well sit down./You
401	CP	Reilly	16	you might as well sit down./You were going to ask a question./{E} When you came to
405	CP	Edward	34	naturally concerns you./{E} I am not going to any sanatorium./I am going to a hotel.
405	CP	Edward	35	not going to any sanatorium./I am going to a hotel. And I shall ask you, Lavinia,/
406	CP	Edward	29	needs a sanatorium —/But I'm not going there./{R} You are right, Mr.
411	CP	Lavinia	14	*some* sense of responsibility./I was going to leave some shirts there for you./{E} It
413	CP	Celia	22	about me;/And with what I've been going through, these last weeks,/I somehow
414	CP	Celia	17	they can do to keep the country house going:/But it's been in the family so long, they
421	CP	Julia	15	will go far. And we know where she is going./But what do we know of the terrors of
425	CP	Lavinia	20	ask twenty more/Because they will be going to the Gunnings instead'./{E} I know,
425	CP	Edward	26	those who come to us early/Will be going on to the Gunnings afterwards,/To make
427	CP	Julia	3	his mysterious expeditions,/And we're going to get him to tell us all about it./But
429	CP	Julia	13	with your monkeys./I thought I was going to dine out on those monkeys:/But one
431	CP	Peter	13	a week. And I have my hands full/I'm going down tonight, to Boltwell./{J} To stay
432	CP	Julia	36	making a film of English life/And he's going to find parts for all of us. Think of it!/{P}
435	CP	Peter	23	second-rate film!/But I thought it was going to lead to something better,/And that
436	CP	Peter	11	been talking,/One thought has been going round and round in my head —/That I've
439	CP	Peter	22	great things of it./{P} So now I'll be going./{E} Shall we see you again, Peter,/Before
440	CP	Julia	19	/{J} Now, Henry. Now, Alex. We're going to the Gunnings. {}/[*Exeunt* JULIA,
452	CC	Kaghan	10	here, Eggers, I can just relax./I'm going to enjoy the game from the sidelines. {}/
453	CC	Lucasta	13	a word she says./{L} *Mr.* Simpkins is going to believe all I say,/*Mr.* Eggerson. And I
453	CC	Kaghan	26	they met you. Colby's still reeling./It's going to be my responsibility,/As your fiancé, to
454	CC	Lucasta	3	I return from Northolt./{L} You're going to meet Lizzie?/{E} I am meeting Lady
454	CC	Kaghan	12	it's done. Come along, Lucasta,/I'm going to make a day of it, and take you out to
457	CC	Eggers	12	It's time you were off./{E} I'm just going. There's plenty of time. {}/[*Looks at his*
459	CC	Claude	35	Dr. Rebmann./{SC} But you were going out to Dr. Leroux/In Lausanne. What
459	CC	Lady E	39	I meet but Mildred Deverell./She was going on to Zürich. So she said: 'Come to
461	CC	Eggers	20	be a treat to look at.'/Well, I'll be going./{SC} Goodbye, and thank you,
469	CC	Lucasta	24	listened to the music:/I just enjoyed going — to see the other people,/And to be seen
471	CC	Colby	1	to believe that I want it./{C} Well, I'm going to invite you to the next concert .../{L}
476	CC	Lucasta	7	all about *my* parents:/At least, I'm going to./{C} Does that matter, either?/{L} In
478	CC	Lucasta	23	that there's no escape./Well, I'll be going./{C} You mustn't go yet!/There's
478	CC	Colby	26	that I want to explain,/And now I'm going to. I'm breaking a promise. But .../{L} I
481	CC	Kaghan	24	you say you were leaving?/{K} We're going out to dinner. Lucasta's very hungry./
483	CC	Lady E	29	*holding the portrait*]/{LE} What was I going to say? Oh, I know./Do you believe in
483	CC	Lady E	34	time. I studied the doctrine./But I was going to say, *if* I believed in it/I should have
492	CC	Claude	8	me,/If I could have known what was going to happen,/I would surely have
499	CC	Lucasta	21	/{L} It won't take much time. I'm going to marry B./{SC} To marry B.! But I
503	CC	Lucasta	13	years' time./I shall be happy. I'm going to marry B./I know you like B./{C} I'm
524	ES	Charles	3	see him at tea./{C} But if I'm not going to have you to myself/There's really no
525	ES	Charles	33	you'll hear it again. You think I'm going to tell you/Once more, that I'm in love
528	ES	Charles	1	you spoke of several reasons for your going with your father./Is there any better
528	ES	Monica	39	/Selby said, 'as if you were going'./But Badgley Court's so near your
531	ES	Ld Clav	2	if people still left cards/And if I was going to have any visitors./{M} Father, you
532	ES	Charles	10	/[*Exit* LAMBERT]/{C} I ought to be going./{M} Let *us* go into the library. And then
540	ES	Gomez	38	a preposterous suggestion!/Who's going to accept the unsupported statement/Of
542	ES	Gomez	37	/You *didn't stop*! Well, I'd better be going./I hope I haven't outstayed my welcome?/
543	ES	Ld Clav	2	/{LC} Not very soon, I think./I am going away./{G} So I've been informed./I have
545	ES	Ld Clav	15	/What she said. She said: 'I'm going to leave you alone!/You want perfect
547	ES	Ld Clav	12	Much as I had feared. But I'm not going to say/Nothing could be worse. Where
548	ES	Monica	8	done her duty by us for to-day./I'm going to prowl about the grounds. Don't look
554	ES	Piggott	23	/What he needs is *rest*! You're not going, Mrs. Carghill?/{MC} Oh, I knew that
564	ES	Carghil	30	at Badgley Court,/I warn you — I'm going to cross-examine you/And make you tell
565	ES	Michael	21	/But I think of cutting loose, and going abroad./{MC} You must tell me all about
574	ES	Carghil	4	odd to call you Mr. Hemington:/I'm going to call you Charles!/{C} As you please,
578	ES	Monica	37	mine./It's not a question of your going abroad/But a question of the spirit which
579	ES	Michael	8	/And I must buy my kit. We're just going up to London./Señor Gomez will attend
579	ES	Ld Clav	22	be done with it./{LC} Yes, if you're going, and I see no way to stop you,/Then I
579	ES	Michael	29	at all./{Mi} Then we might as well be going./{G} Yes, we might as well be going.
579	ES	Gomez	30	going./{G} Yes, we might as well be going./You'll be grateful to me in the end, Dick.
580	ES	Carghil	18	news of my own:/Next autumn, I'm going out to Australia,/On my doctor's advice.

582 ES	Monica	29	farewell./{M} I can't understand his going for a walk./{C} He wanted to leave us
582 ES	Charles	34	all the time .../{C} I know what you're going to say!/We *were* alone together, in some

GOLD (6)

50 Hippopot		32	shall be seen/Performing on a harp of gold./He shall be washed as white as snow,/By
69 WL: Fire S		265	splendour of Ionian white and gold./The river sweats/Oil and tar/The barges
70 WL: Fire S		283	was formed/A gilded shell/Red and gold/The brisk swell/Rippled both shores/
254 MC Tempt4		32	the shrine shall be pillaged, and the gold spent,/The jewels gone for light ladies'
451 CC	Eggers	10	in the City!/And he has a heart of gold. But not to beat about the bush,/He's
501 CC	Eggers	31	in the City,/And he has a heart of gold. So have you, Miss Angel./We have this

GOLDEN (9)

57 Swee Night		32	/Branches of wistaria/Circumscribe a golden grin;/The host with someone indistinct/
64 WL: Chess		80	with fruited vines/From which a golden Cupidon peeped out/(Another hid his
133 Eyes		4	/Here in death's dream kingdom/The golden vision reappears/I see the eyes but not
138 New Hamp		3	the blossom- and the fruit-time:/Golden head, crimson head,/Between the green
138 New Hamp		9	/Cover me over, light-in-leaves:/Golden head, black wing,/Cling, swing,/Spring,
143 Lines OM		12	by the young./Reflected from my golden eye/The dullard knows that he is mad./
166 Rock 10		10	among those who prize the serpent's golden eyes,/The worshippers, self-given
239 MC Chorus		9	We are forced to bear witness./Since golden October declined into sombre November
356 CP	Julia	19	questions/I want to ask you. It's a golden opportunity/Now Lavinia's away. I've

GOLDEN-ROD (1)

98 Ash-Wed 6		14	spirit quickens to rebel/For the bent golden-rod and the lost sea smell/Quickens to

GOLDER'S (1)

45 Cook Egg		28	are creeping/From Kentish Town and Golder's Green;/Where are the eagles and the

GOLDFINCH (1)

142 Cape Ann		4	and dusk. Follow the dance/Of the goldfinch at noon. Leave to chance/The

GOLF (2)

127 Corl March		25	Will it be he now? No,/Those are the golf club Captains, these the Scouts,/And now
155 Rock 3		36	the asphalt road/And a thousand lost golf balls'./CHORUS:/We build in vain unless

GOMEZ (45)

523 ES	m	6	/LORD CLAVERTON/FEDERICO GOMEZ/MRS. PIGGOTT/MRS. CARGHILL
532 ES	Ld Clav	14	/I've never heard of this Señor Gomez/But he comes with a letter of
532 ES	Lambert	26	two. {}/[*Enter* LAMBERT]/{L} Mr. Gomez, my Lord./{LC} Goodbye, Charles. And
532 ES	m	31	CHARLES]/[LAMBERT *shows in* GOMEZ]/{LC} Good evening, Mr. ... Gomez.
532 ES	Ld Clav	31	GOMEZ]/{LC} Good evening, Mr. ... Gomez. You're a friend of Mr. Culverwell?/{G}
533 ES	Gomez	19	you, Dick,/So I'm pretty footloose. {}/[GOMEZ *does so, liberally*]/{G} And what about
535 ES	m	21	/{LC} Won't you help yourself? {}/[GOMEZ *does so, liberally*]/{G} And what about
536 ES	Gomez	40	who will accept both Culverwell and Gomez —/See Culverwell as Gomez — Gomez
537 ES	Gomez	1	and Gomez —/See Culverwell as Gomez — Gomez as Culverwell./I need you,
537 ES	Gomez	1	—/See Culverwell as Gomez — Gomez as Culverwell./I need you, Dick, to give
541 ES	Gomez	1	unsupported statement/Of Federico Gomez of San Marco/About something that
543 ES	m	7	begin just where we left off. {}/[*Exit* GOMEZ]/[LORD CLAVERTON *sits for a few*
563 ES	m	7	us. You must introduce him. {}/[*Enter* GOMEZ]/{G} Good morning, Dick./{LC} Good
563 ES	Gomez	19	is .../{G} Your old friend Federico Gomez,/The prominent citizen of San Marco./
563 ES	Carghil	26	Dick!/{MC} Well, you see, Señor Gomez, when we first became friends —/Lord
563 ES	Carghil	34	never see me?/That's a pity, Señor Gomez./{G} I lost touch with things in England.
564 ES	Carghil	2	/That made my reputation, Señor Gomez./{G} It will never be too late. Don't you
564 ES	Carghil	12	Claverton/As long as I have, Señor Gomez./{G} My dear lady, you're not old
564 ES	Carghil	29	Went back to San Marco./Señor Gomez, if it's true you're staying at Badgley
564 ES	Carghil	35	/{MC} Secret for secret, Señor Gomez!/You've got to be the first to put your
565 ES	Carghil	24	Au revoir, Monica./And Señor Gomez, I shall hold you to your promise! {}/
570 ES	Ld Clav	26	He no longer exists./He's Federico Gomez, the Central American,/A man who's
571 ES	Ld Clav	6	all have been very different/From Gomez, Mrs. Carghill and Lord Claverton./
574 ES	Carghil	18	I thought, which did not appeal to Señor Gomez?/He's a wealthy man, and very
574 ES	Ld Clav	22	to help./{LC} And what was Señor Gomez able to suggest?/{MC} Ah! That's the
574 ES	m	26	Let's all rejoice together. {}/[*Enter* GOMEZ *and* MICHAEL]/{LC} Well, Michael,
574 ES	Ld Clav	30	Mrs. Carghill and then with Señor Gomez./{Mi} When I spoke, Father, of my wish
575 ES	Michael	3	be your son. That's what Señor Gomez sees./He understands my point of view,
575 ES	Ld Clav	7	of a job created for you/By Señor Gomez .../{Mi} It's not created for me./Señor
575 ES	Michael	9	.../{Mi} It's not created for me./Señor Gomez came to London to find a man to fill it,/
575 ES	Ld Clav	12	course you're just the man that Señor Gomez wants,/But in a different sense, and for
575 ES	Ld Clav	14	what you think. Let me tell you about Gomez./He's unlikely to try to be custodian of
576 ES	Ld Clav	8	eighteen./{LC} Now, Michael,/Señor Gomez says he has told you his story./Did he
576 ES	Ld Clav	23	you intend to change your name to Gomez?/{G} Oh no, Dick, there are plenty of
576 ES	Charles	27	suicide./{C} Michael, you think Señor Gomez is inspired by benevolence —/{Mi} I told
577 ES	Charles	2	another point to think of:/Señor Gomez has offered you a post in San Marco,/

577 ES	Charles	3	you a post in San Marco,/Señor	Gomez pays your passage .../{Mi} And an
577 ES	Charles	5	And an advance of salary./{C} Señor	Gomez pays your passage .../{G} Just as many
577 ES	Michael	21	has plenty of cheek./Señor	Gomez and I have talked things over,
577 ES	Carghil	28	you could have known him, Señor	Gomez!/You're very much alike in some ways
577 ES	Carghil	32	/I saw that, and so does Señor	Gomez./He's simply been suffering, poor boy,
579 ES	Michael	9	We're just going up to London./Señor	Gomez will attend to my needs for that climate.
579 ES	Carghil	12	/{MC} It's wonderful, Señor	Gomez, how you manage *everything*!/— No
580 ES	m	14	Michael. {}/[*Exeunt* MICHAEL *and*	GOMEZ]/{MC} I'm afraid this seems awfully
580 ES	Carghil	20	advice. And on my way back/Señor	Gomez has invited me to visit San Marco./I'm

GONA (4)

125 SA	Sweeney	25	all gotta do what we gotta do/We're	gona sit here and drink this booze/We're gona
125 SA	Sweeney	26	sit here and drink this booze/We're	gona sit here and have a tune/We're gona stay
125 SA	Sweeney	27	gona sit here and have a tune/We're	gona stay and we're gona go/And somebody's
125 SA	Sweeney	27	a tune/We're gona stay and we're	gona go/And somebody's gotta pay the rent/

GONE (50)

15 Prufrock		70	should I begin?/Shall I say, I have	gone at dusk through narrow streets/And
152 Rock 2		32	ill that was done by those who have	gone before you./And all that is ill you may
179 FQ: ECoker		100	humility is endless./The houses are all	gone under the sea./The dancers are all gone
179 FQ: ECoker		101	under the sea./The dancers are all	gone under the hill./O dark dark dark. They all
190 FQ: DrySal		233	are only undefeated/Because we have	gone on trying;/We, content at the last/If our
212 Growltiger		26	/For to the Bell at Hampton he had	gone to wet his beard;/And his bosun,
219 Mung Rump		27	dinner *tomorrow*!/For the joint has	gone from the oven — like that!'/Then the
226 Macavity		27	the Foreign Office find a Treaty's	gone astray,/Or the Admiralty lose some plans
232 Skimble		3	'Skimble where is Skimble has he	gone to hunt the thimble?/We must find him or
588 Fable		58	dozed,/A fine old drink, though now	gone out of use —/His feet upon the table
593 Grad 8		5	Or to what distant lands we may have	gone,/Through all the years will ne'er have been
243 MC	Chorus	29	has been minor injustice./Yet we have	gone on living,/Living and partly living./
244 MC	Chorus	2	the plums are lacking./Yet we have	gone on living,/Living and partly living./We
254 MC	Tempt4	33	and the gold spent,/The jewels	gone for light ladies' ornament,/The sanctuary
257 MC	Chorus	17	mill-stream./And meanwhile we have	gone on living,/Living and partly living,/Picking
264 MC	Priest2	28	what is to-day? For the day is half	gone./{P1} To-day, what is to-day? but another
280 MC	Priest1	5	KNIGHTS]/{P1} O father, father,	gone from us, lost to us,/How shall we find you,
281 MC	Priest2	3	with all the saints and martyrs	gone before you,/Remember us./{P3} Let our
285 FR	Amy	5	will be over/And the cuckoo will be	gone before I am out again./O Sun, that was
287 FR	Amy	18	So she should have been, if things had	gone as I intended./Harry's return does not
293 FR	Harry	38	impact/Of external events. You have	gone through life in sleep,/Never woken to the
302 FR	Amy	16	/I do not understand what could have	gone wrong/With both of them, coming from
304 FR	Mary	18	collision./I suppose I could have	gone, if I'd had the moral courage,/Even against
307 FR	Harry	15	old hiding place. The wilderness was	gone,/The tree had been felled, and a neat
340 FR	Amy	27	you back, for visits, after he was	gone,/So that there might be no ugly rumours./
356 CP	Edward	36	her./If her aunt is very ill, she may be	gone some time./{C} And how will you manage
360 CP	Edward	5	she'd arranged a cocktail party./She'd	gone when I came in, this afternoon./She left a
360 CP	Edward	7	me;/But I don't know where she's	gone./{UG} This is an occasion./May I take
360 CP	Reilly	24	/You say you don't know where she's	gone?/{E} No, I do not./{UG} Do you know
362 CP	Edward	14	/Only a note to say that she had	gone/And was not coming back — well, I can't
363 CP	Edward	27	I say to my friends, 'My wife has	gone away'?/And they answer 'Where?' and I
369 CP	Peter	26	concert. And I was alone./I've always	gone to concerts alone —/At first, because I
378 CP	Edward	16	was all for the best/That Lavinia had	gone; that I ought to be thankful./And yet, the
400 CP	Alex	33	/And come back when they've	gone./{R} Yes, when they've gone. {}/[*Exit*
400 CP	Reilly	34	they've gone./{R} Yes, when they've	gone. {}/[*Exit* ALEX *by side door*]/[EDWARD
412 CP	Julia	20	room,/And come back when she's	gone./{R} Yes, when she's gone./{J} Will Alex be
412 CP	Reilly	21	when she's gone./{R} Yes, when she's	gone./{J} Will Alex be here?/{R} Yes, he'll be
417 CP	Reilly	24	condition to which some who have	gone as far as you/Have succeeded in returning.
426 CP	Edward	3	tired to bother./{E} After they're all	gone, we will have some champagne,/Just
452 CC	Lucasta	16	It's rank injustice./Two months I'd	gone on filing those papers/Which no one ever
457 CC	Claude	22	her voice./Where is she? Oh, she's	gone out again. {}/[*Goes to the window and*
467 CC	Colby	12	years of childhood./Those years have	gone forever. The empty years./Oh, I'm terribly
519 CC	Claude	5	/{SC} What's happened? Have they	gone? Is Colby coming back?/{LE} My poor
530 ES	Ld Clav	24	office is closed/And the porters have	gone. What am I waiting for/In a cold and
531 ES	Lambert	38	be very angry/If you heard that he'd	gone away without your seeing him./{LC} What
552 ES	Carghil	9	feeling into it I did/But for what I'd	gone through. Did you hear me sing it?/{LC}
555 ES	Piggott	7	should not be disturbed./Well, she's	gone now. If she bothers you again/Just let me
558 ES	Michael	32	one of the girls./He assumed it had	gone a good deal further than it had./{LC}
558 ES	Ld Clav	33	than it had./{LC} Perhaps it had	gone further than you're willing to admit./{Mi}
583 ES	Monica	15	He is close at hand,/Though he has	gone too far to return to us./He is under the

GONFLÉES (1)

48 Lune Miel	6	genoux/De quatre jambes molles tout gonflées de morsures./On relève le drap pour

GOOD (233)

43 Swee Erect	40	intimates/It does the house no sort of good./But Doris, towelled from the bath,/Enters
66 WL: Chess	148	in the army four years, he wants a good time,/And if you don't give it him, there's
66 WL: Chess	172	/Ta ta. Goonight. Goonight./Good night, ladies, good night, sweet ladies,
66 WL: Chess	172	Goonight./Good night, ladies, good night, sweet ladies, good night, good
66 WL: Chess	172	night, ladies, good night, sweet ladies, good night, good night./The Fire Sermon/The
66 WL: Chess	172	good night, sweet ladies, good night, good night./The Fire Sermon/The river's tent is
92 Ash-Wed 2	49	are glad to be scattered, we did little good to each other,/Under a tree in the cool of
107 Animula	27	/Fearing the warm reality, the offered good,/Denying the importunity of the blood,/
116 SP Dusty	36	you'll phone through./Yes I'll tell her. Good bye. Goooood bye./I'm sure, that's very
117 SP Doris	29	/{Do} THAT'S THE COFFIN?/Oh good heavens what'll I do?/Just before a party
117 SP Doris	35	/Yes it's mine. I know it's mine./Oh good heavens what'll I do./Well I'm not going
123 SAWa & Ho	6	*will do for me/Any old wood is just as good/Any old isle is just my style/Any fresh egg/*
148 Rock 1	52	men count for happiness, seeking/The good deeds that lead to obscurity, accepting/
148 Rock 1	64	not change:/The perpetual struggle of Good and Evil./Forgetful, you neglect your
149 Rock 1	67	times deride/What has been done of good, you find explanations/To satisfy the
149 Rock 1	74	is in the heart of your brother./The good man is the builder, if he build what is
149 Rock 1	74	man is the builder, if he build what is good./I will show you the things that are now
152 Rock 2	30	sin./And of all that was done that was good, you have the inheritance./For good and
152 Rock 2	31	good, you have the inheritance./For good and ill deeds belong to a man alone, when
152 Rock 2	32	earth you have the reward of the good and ill that was done by those who have
152 Rock 2	34	sins of your fathers;/And all that was good you must fight to keep with hearts as
159 Rock 6	23	so perfect that no one will need to be good./But the man that is will shadow/The man
160 Rock 7	9	and the Higher Religions were good/And led men from light to light, to
160 Rock 7	10	from light to light, to knowledge of Good and Evil./But their light was ever
162 Rock 8	11	/And among his hearers were a few good men,/Many who were evil,/And most who
163 Rock 8	33	the faith could have done what was good of it;/Whole faith of a few,/Part faith of
164 Rock 9	12	all other secular meetings./Thinking good of themselves, ready for any festivity,/
166 Rock 10	13	be ye separate./Be not too curious of Good and Evil;/Seek not to count the future
182 FQ: ECoker	173	in spite of that, we call this Friday good./So here I am, in the middle way, having
186 FQ: DrySal	94	security or affection,/Or even a very good dinner, but the sudden illumination —/We
194 FQ: Little	118	as I pray you to forgive/Both bad and good. Last season's fruit is eaten/And the
210 Old Gumbie	10	of the mice —/Their behaviour's not good and their manners not nice;/So when she
211 Old Gumbie	35	/With a purpose in life and a good deed to do —/And she's even created a
234 Ad-dress	10	sane and some are mad/And some are good and some are bad/And some are better,
236 Cat Morgan	10	me manners is gruff,/But I've got a good coat, and I keep meself smart;/And
236 Cat Morgan	12	'You can't but like Morgan, 'e's got a good 'art.'/I got knocked about on the Barbary
588 Fable	48	/And jellies, pasties, cakes among the good things./A mighty peacock standing on
589 Fable	92	/And flogged his mates 'till they grew good and friarly./Spirits from that time forth
593 Grad 7	3	with those who try/To labor for the good until they die,/And ask no other guerdon
243 MC Priest3	7	the Archbishop welcome!/{P3} For good or ill, let the wheel turn./The wheel has
243 MC Priest3	8	been still, these seven years, and no good./For ill or good, let the wheel turn./For
243 MC Priest3	9	seven years, and no good./For ill or good, let the wheel turn./For who knows the
243 MC Priest3	10	turn./For who knows the end of good or evil?/Until the grinders cease/And the
243 MC Chorus	32	failed us,/Sometimes the harvest is good,/One year is a year of rain,/Another year
245 MC Priest2	3	women./Do you not know that the good Archbishop/Is likely to arrive at any
245 MC Priest2	10	/And give a hearty welcome to our good Archbishop. {}/[Enter THOMAS]/{T}
246 MC Templ1	28	humble levity/Remembering all the good time past./Your Lordship won't despise an
246 MC Templ1	36	say that summer's over/Or that the good time cannot last?/Fluting in the meadows,
247 MC Templ1	22	he turns./{T1} My Lord, a nod is as good as a wink./A man will often love what he
247 MC Templ1	24	often love what he spurns./For the good times past, that are come again/I am your
249 MC Templ2	6	strengthen the laws,/Rule for the good of the better cause,/Dispensing justice
250 MC Thomas	9	/{T} Temporal power, to build a good world,/To keep order, as the world knows
251 MC Templ3	40	Lord,/In being with us, would fight a good stroke/At once, for England and for
252 MC Templ3	12	their own;/Church and people have good cause against the throne./{T} If the
252 MC Thomas	14	cannot trust the Throne,/He has good cause to trust none but God alone./I ruled
258 MC Thomas	20	unobservable./Sin grows with doing good. When I imposed the King's law/In
259 MC Thomas	6	or suffer, to the sword's end./Now my good Angel, whom God appoints/To be my
260 MC Thomas	1	highest, and on earth peace to men of good will.' *The/fourteenth verse of the second*
260 MC Thomas	14	highest, and on/earth peace to men of good will'; at this same time of all the year that
261 MC Thomas	19	do not think of a martyr simply as a good Christian who/has been killed because he
261 MC Thomas	21	We do not think of him simply as a good Christian who has been/elevated to the
265 MC Priest1	22	/We are about to go to dinner./The good Archbishop would be vexed/If we did not

273	MC	Thomas	33	this world does,/To settle if an act be good or bad./You defer to the fact. For every
273	MC	Thomas	35	life and every act/Consequence of good and evil can be shown./And as in time
273	MC	Thomas	37	results of many deeds are blended/So good and evil in the end become confounded./It
277	MC	Knight3	7	I dare say that we didn't make a/very good impression when we came in just now. The
277	MC	Knight3	9	speak for/myself, but I had drunk a good deal — I am not a drinking man/
277	MC	Knight3	12	/when you have been brought up in good Church traditions. So if/we seemed a bit
277	MC	Knight3	23	him —/you must have noted what a good show he put up at the end —/they won't
277	MC	Knight2	39	Now the worthy Archbishop,/whose good qualities I very much admired, has
287	FR	Amy	36	/They should both be here in good time for dinner./Harry telephoned to me
289	FR	Amy	11	Though Agatha means/As a rule, a good deal more than she cares to betray,/I am
295	FR	Harry	17	conscience can be clear./{H} It goes a good deal deeper/Than what people call their
296	FR	Charles	27	believe he did. He cannot trust his good fortune./I believe that all he needs is
297	FR	Agatha	5	In an unnecessary action,/Not for the good that it will do/But that nothing may be left
298	FR	Charles	24	/[Knock: and enter DOWNING]/{C} Good evening, Downing./It's good to see you
298	FR	Charles	25	/{C} Good evening, Downing./It's good to see you again, after all these years./
298	FR	Charles	34	well./And I'm sure that you've been a good friend to him, too./We haven't seen him
299	FR	Charles	21	I understand, Downing. Was she in good spirits?/{Do} Well, always about the same,
301	FR	Downing	1	car?/{Do} Oh no, Sir, she's in good running order:/I see to that./{G} I only
302	FR	Amy	14	They both promised to be here/In good time for dinner. It is very annoying./Now
309	FR	Mary	25	an infatuation/That's wrong, a good that's misdirected. You deceive yourself/
313	FR	Violet	1	VIOLET, GERALD, CHARLES/{V} Good evening, Mary: aren't you dressed yet?/
313	FR	Gerald	14	I was rather an authority./{G} Good evening, Mary. You've seen Harry, I see./
313	FR	Gerald	15	Mary. You've seen Harry, I see./It's good to have him back again, isn't it?/We must
314	FR	Warburt	7	/{W} I dare say we've both changed a good deal, Harry./A country practitioner
319	FR	Warburt	11	was my father?/{W} Harry, there's no good probing for misery./There was enough
321	FR	Winch	24	{}/[Enter WINCHELL]/{Wi} Good evening, my Lord. Good evening,
321	FR	Winch	24	/{Wi} Good evening, my Lord. Good evening, Doctor./Many happy ... Oh, I'm
322	FR	Winch	13	forward./But you see, my Lord, I had good reason for asking .../{H} Well, do you
324	FR	Warburt	4	trust you?/{W} You have trusted me a good many years, Lady Monchensey;/This is
325	FR	Charles	10	going —/On a night like this — it's a good three miles;/There's nothing we could do
341	FR	Amy	31	his happiness?/Who has planned his good? is it you or I?/Thirty-five years designing
346	FR	Downing	9	the table./Oh, there it is. Thank you. Good night, Miss; good night,/Miss Mary; good
346	FR	Downing	9	it is. Thank you. Good night, Miss; good night,/Miss Mary; good night, Sir./{M}
346	FR	Downing	10	night, Miss; good night,/Miss Mary; good night, Sir./{M} Downing, will you promise
354	CP	Celia	4	the only person to tell it./She's such a good mimic./{J} Am I a good mimic?/{P} You
354	CP	Julia	5	/She's such a good mimic./{J} Am I a good mimic?/{P} You are a good mimic. You
354	CP	Peter	6	{J} Am I a good mimic?/{P} You are a good mimic. You never miss anything./{A} She
358	CP	Julia	24	dinner on Friday?/No, I'm afraid my good Mrs. Batten/Would give me notice. And
361	CP	Edward	21	time, unless you know my wife/A good deal better than I thought, or unless you
361	CP	Edward	22	than I thought, or unless you know/A good deal more about us than appears —/I
363	CP	Reilly	34	simply contemptible./{UG} All to the good./You will find that you survive
367	CP	Peter	17	my novel,/Though it had some very good reviews./But it's more the cinema that
367	CP	Peter	31	I can judge it,/And I think it's very good. But that's not the point./The point is, I
372	CP	Peter	8	/{P} Thank you, Edward. It's very good of you. {}/[Enter ALEX, with his jacket
372	CP	Peter	35	to Lavinia./{P} Thank you, Edward. Good night./{E} Good night, Peter,/And good
372	CP	Edward	36	Thank you, Edward. Good night./{E} Good night, Peter,/And good night, Alex. Oh,
372	CP	Edward	37	night./{E} Good night, Peter,/And good night, Alex. Oh, and if you don't mind,/
374	CP	Celia	20	spur of the moment, and not a very good one./You should have been prepared with
375	CP	Edward	23	/I'm very tired. Thanks awfully, Alex./Good night./{C} What on earth was that about?
376	CP	Edward	12	/{C} Edward, it's ruined!/{E} What a good thing./{C} But it's ruined the saucepan
376	CP	Julia	21	how lucky you are/To have two Good Samaritans? I never heard of that before./
376	CP	Edward	28	for me./He would do it. Three Good Samaritans./I forgot all about it./{J} But
378	CP	Julia	11	you're looking absolutely famished./Good night, Edward. {}/[Exit JULIA]/{C} Well,
383	CP	Celia	24	my guardian. Give me the spectacles./Good night, Edward./{E} Good night ... Celia.
383	CP	Edward	25	spectacles./Good night, Edward./{E} Good night ... Celia. {}/[Exit CELIA]/{E} Oh! {}/
383	CP	Edward	30	/... Yes, she's bringing them now ... Good night. {}/CURTAIN/Act One. Scene 3/
384	CP	Edward	1	to/answer the doorbell./{E} Oh ... good evening. {}/[Enter the UNIDENTIFIED
384	CP	Reilly	2	the UNIDENTIFIED GUEST]/{UG} Good evening, Mr. Chamberlayne./{E} Well.
396	CP	Lavinia	3	to the gramophone./{L} We have very good records;/But I always suspected that you
396	CP	Lavinia	17	own./Oh, Edward, I should like to be good to you —/Or if that's impossible, at least
401	CP	Reilly	1	looking up from his papers]./{R} Good morning, Mr. Chamberlayne./Please sit
401	CP	Reilly	32	/{R} That is so, that is so. But all in good time./Let us dismiss that question for the
404	CP	Reilly	8	with me, Mr. Chamberlayne:/I learn a good deal by merely observing you,/And letting
405	CP	Edward	36	I shall ask you, Lavinia,/To be so good as to send me on some clothes./{L} Oh, to
406	CP	Reilly	17	believe it to be a sanatorium/That is good reason for not sending them to one./The

412 CP	Celia	36	see you,/Are obviously ill, or can give	good reasons/For wanting to see you. Well, I
416 CP	Celia	17	in terms of calculation/Of what was	good for the persons we had been/But for the
417 CP	Reilly	39	/{C} Is that the best life?/{R} It is a	good life. Though you will not know how good/
417 CP	Reilly	39	life. Though you will not know how	good/Till you come to the end. But you will
418 CP	Reilly	3	/Violence, stupidity, greed ... it is a	good life./{C} I know I ought to be able to
422 CP	Reilly	2	when Mr. Gibbs arrives .../Oh, very	good. {}/[To JULIA]/{R} He's on his way up. {}/
424 CP	Caterer	4	/And leave them ready./{CM} Very	good, Madam. {}/[Exit. LAVINIA looks about
424 CP	Edward	11	in at the front door]/{E} I'm in	good time, I think. I hope you've not been
431 CP	Peter	3	look into this./Perhaps it would be a	good place to make one./— Alex knows all
431 CP	Peter	15	stay with the Duke?/{P} And do him a	good turn./We're making a film of English life/
436 CP	Edward	7	not so hard for you. You're naturally	good./{P} I'm sorry. I don't believe I've taken in
436 CP	Peter	13	interested in myself:/And that isn't	good enough for Celia./{J} You must have
439 CP	Lavinia	26	/You know, I think it would do us all	good —/You and me and Edward ... to talk
446 CC	Claude	27	/I'm trying to find him a really	good piano./{E} A piano? Yes, I'm sure he'll feel
450 CC	Claude	17	/That they don't understand me — a	good deal better/Than I should care to think,
450 CC	Colby	28	I've got what you wanted, Sir Claude.	Good afternoon,/Mr. Eggerson. I was afraid I'd
451 CC	Colby	16	I've found him very helpful/And very	good company apart from business./{E} Oh yes,
451 CC	Eggers	17	/{E} Oh yes, Mr. Kaghan is very	good company./He makes me laugh sometimes.
454 CC	Eggers	26	/She's rather flighty. But she has a	good heart./{C} But does she address Sir Claude
457 CC	Eggers	5	a lady!/And what's more, she has a	good heart./{C} Everybody seems to be
457 CC	Claude	31	at home?/I'll speak to him first./{SC}	Good heavens, Eggerson, what can have
459 CC	Lady E	2	it is./I remember saying: 'He has a	good aura.'/I remember people's auras almost
461 CC	Eggers	22	and thank you, Eggerson./{E}	Good day, Sir Claude. Good day, Mr.
461 CC	Eggers	22	Eggerson./{E} Good day, Sir Claude.	Good day, Mr. Simpkins. {}/[Exit
462 CC	Colby	23	in a world of make-believe,/Is that	good for us? Or a kindness to her?/{SC} If you
464 CC	Claude	14	and painting — I have some	good things —/But they haven't this ...
465 CC	Claude	27	life .../I intend that you shall have a	good piano. The best./And when you are alone
470 CC	Colby	19	that won't take you long — and hear	good performers,/You'll very quickly realise
472 CC	Lucasta	23	you found that you'd never be a	good musician —/Of course, I don't know
477 CC	Lucasta	9	he wished there had been. He's been	good to me/In his way. But I'm always a
479 CC	Lucasta	11	/And you've got to give me a very	good dinner./{K} You shall be fed. All in good
479 CC	Kaghan	12	dinner./{K} You shall be fed. All in	good time./I've come to inspect the new
479 CC	Kaghan	32	I'm afraid Colby/Has made a	good impression; which he'll have to live down./
480 CC	Kaghan	7	to be in business together./I'm a	good guesser. But I sometimes guess wrong./I
480 CC	Kaghan	19	that. You know, Lucasta,/Colby is a	good judge of character./{L} You'd need to be a
480 CC	Kaghan	22	you said that of Colby./{K} Oh, I'm a	good judge. Now, I'll tell you the difference/
481 CC	Lucasta	7	together./{L} You're both very	good at paying compliments;/But I remarked
481 CC	Lady E	14	LADY ELIZABETH]/{LE} Oh,	good evening/Good evening, Mr. Kaghan.
481 CC	Lady E	15	/{LE} Oh, good evening./	Good evening, Mr. Kaghan. Good evening,
481 CC	Lady E	15	evening./Good evening, Mr. Kaghan.	Good evening, Lucasta./Have you just arrived,
481 CC	Lady E	39	hand corner:/It has the best waitress.	Good night./{L} Good night./{K} And thank
482 CC	Lucasta	1	has the best waitress. Good night./{L}	Good night./{K} And thank you so much. You
482 CC	Kaghan	2	thank you so much. You give such	good advice. {}/[Exeunt KAGHAN and
482 CC	Lady E	12	/And I've noticed them paying you a	good deal of attention./You see, you're rather a
482 CC	Lady E	20	/{LE} Well, older than you are,/And a	good deal wiser in the ways of the world./{C}
483 CC	Colby	14	in my room:/You see, I shall do a	good deal of my work here./{LE} And what is
487 CC	Colby	13	On such an instrument. It's much too	good for me./{SC} You need a good piano.
487 CC	Claude	14	too good for me./{SC} You need a	good piano. You'll play all the better./{LE}
491 CC	Lady E	12	claims upon you, Colby./It's a	good idea! Why should we not be happy,/All of
493 CC	Lady E	12	be a sort of chairman./{LE} That's a	good idea./{SC} On the other hand,/We mustn't
493 CC	Claude	19	put the first questions./He's very	good at approaching a subject/In a roundabout
496 CC	Claude	13	the door. Enter EGGERSON]/{SC}	Good morning, Eggerson./{E} Good morning,
496 CC	Eggers	14	/{SC} Good morning, Eggerson./{E}	Good morning, Sir Claude. And Lady
499 CC	Claude	9	{}/[A knock on the door]/{SC}	Good Lord, she's here already! Well ... Come
499 CC	Lucasta	32	Because you thought he was too	good for me./{SC} In Colby!/{L} Why not?
504 CC	Claude	24	GUZZARD. Exit KAGHAN]/{SC}	Good morning, Mrs. Guzzard. I must
504 CC	Lady E	32	/Lady Elizabeth Mulhammer./{LE}	Good morning, Mrs. Guzzard./You don't know
509 CC	Guzzard	29	/So we call him B./{MG} A very	good name./He ought to be proud of it./{LE}
511 CC	Lady E	12	Was he a financier?/{LE} He was not	good at figures. Your business ability/Comes, I
511 CC	Lady E	14	of the family./But he was in a very	good regiment —/For a time, at least./{K} Well,
517 CC	Eggers	31	/{E} Give you a trial? I'm certain./	Good organists don't seem to want to come to
517 CC	Colby	32	/{C} But I've told you, I'm not a very	good organist!/{E} Don't say that, Mr.
525 ES	Monica	22	come ambling in .../{M} You've said a	good deal more than two words already./And
527 ES	Monica	19	what after that?/{M} There are several	good reasons why I should go with him./{C}
529 ES	Ld Clav	20	What have you been doing?/{LC}	Good afternoon, Charles. You might have

531 ES Ld Clav 23   that other men covet./When we go, a good many folk are mildly grieved,/And our
532 ES Lambert   2   person/By the looks of him. But talks good English./A pleasant-spoken gentleman. {}/
532 ES Lambert   7   /I'd better see him here./{L} Very good, my Lord./Shall I take the trolley, Miss
532 ES Ld Clav 31   [LAMBERT *shows in* GOMEZ]/{LC} Good evening, Mr. ... Gomez. You're a friend
533 ES Gomez   8   /And besides, my wife's name is a good deal more normal/In my country, than
535 ES Lambert   7   in the whisky. And soda./{L} Very good, my Lord./{G} And some ice./{L} Ice? Yes,
536 ES Gomez   34   father's dead long since — that's a good thing./My mother — I dare say she's still
538 ES Gomez   11   had plenty of money, and you made a good marriage —/Or so it seemed — and with
539 ES Gomez   7   It *is* surprising:/You should have been good for another five years/At least. Why did
541 ES Gomez   18   out/Several times over. San Marco's a good place/To make money in — though not to
544 ES Ld Clav 10   Nurse's business'./{LC} So far, so good./I'll feel more confidence after a fortnight
545 ES Piggott 22   me. {}/[*Enter* MRS. PIGGOTT]/{MP} Good morning, Lord Claverton! Good
545 ES Piggott 22   Good morning, Lord Claverton! Good morning, Miss Claverton!/Isn't this a
547 ES Monica   33   walking/And I'm told there are very good walks in this neighbourhood./{MP} There
549 ES Carghil 13   forgotten what hotel —/But such a good lunch — and we all went in a punt/On the
553 ES Carghil 32   I have photostats/Which are quite as good, I'm told. And I like to read them/In your
554 ES Carghil   8   hint/And leave us alone tomorrow./Good morning, Mrs. Piggott!/Isn't it a glorious
554 ES Piggott 10   {}/[*Enter* MRS. PIGGOTT]/{MP} Good morning, Mrs. Carghill!/{MC} Dear Mrs.
555 ES Monica   15   /Because I have some ... not very good news for you./{LC} Oh, indeed. What's the
556 ES Ld Clav 10   Michael! {}/[*Enter* MICHAEL]/{LC} Good morning, Michael./{Mi} Good morning,
556 ES Michael 11   /{LC} Good morning, Michael./{Mi} Good morning, Father. {}/[*A pause*]/{Mi} What
556 ES Michael 21   hotel was very well recommended./Good cooking, for a country inn. And not at all
557 ES Michael 19   some reason./The fact is, I needed a good deal more capital/To make anything of it.
557 ES Michael 26   of mine recommended./He gave me good terms, on the strength of my name:/The
557 ES Michael 27   on the strength of my name:/The only good the name has ever done me./{LC} On the
557 ES Ld Clav 28   of your name. And what do you call good terms?/{Mi} I'd nothing at all to pay for
558 ES Michael 32   of the girls./He assumed it had gone a good deal further than it had./{LC} Perhaps it
559 ES Michael 13   in New Zealand?/{Mi} Sheep farming? Good Lord, no./That's not my idea. I want to
559 ES Michael 19   own,/According to my own ideas of good and bad,/Of right and wrong. I want to go
560 ES Michael 23   the road./Certainly not. I'm far too good a driver./{LC} What then? That young
560 ES Ld Clav 31   a few years abroad. It might be very good for you/To find your feet. But I shouldn't
562 ES Carghil 29   Michael — your father has changed a good deal/Since I knew him ever so many years
563 ES Carghil   2   /{MC} How interesting! He's a very good figure/And he's rather exotic-looking. Is
563 ES Gomez   7   him. {}/[*Enter* GOMEZ]/{G} Good morning, Dick./{LC} Good morning,
563 ES Ld Clav   8   /{G} Good morning, Dick./{LC} Good morning, Fred./{G} You weren't
565 ES Gomez   26   while we're here, we must have some good talks/About old times. Bye bye for the
571 ES Ld Clav   4   are my ghosts. They were people with good in them,/People who might all have been
576 ES Michael 16   He's offered me the job/With a jolly good screw, and some pickings in commissions./
576 ES Gomez   24   Oh no, Dick, there are plenty of other good names./{M} Michael, Michael, you can't
578 ES Ld Clav 14   see how all the efforts aimed at your good/Only succeeded in defeating each other,/
579 ES Gomez   36   /We can only regard it as a stroke of good fortune/That I came to England at the

GOOD-BYE (47)

28   Boston ET   7   /Wearily, as one would turn to nod good-bye to La Rochefoucauld,/If the street
345 FR   Harry   4   be quite happy about it,/So I shall say good-bye, until we meet again./{G} Well, if you
345 FR   Harry   13   in London until you hear from me./Good-bye, mother./{A} Good-bye, Harry./{H}
345 FR   Amy   14   from me./Good-bye, mother./{A} Good-bye, Harry./{H} Good-bye./{Ag}
345 FR   Harry   15   mother./{A} Good-bye, Harry./{H} Good-bye./{Ag} Good-bye./{H} Good-bye,
345 FR   Agatha   16   Harry./{H} Good-bye./{Ag} Good-bye./{H} Good-bye, Mary./{M}
345 FR   Harry   17   /{H} Good-bye./{Ag} Good-bye./{H} Good-bye, Mary./{M} Good-bye, Harry. Take
345 FR   Mary   18   Good-bye./{H} Good-bye, Mary./{M} Good-bye, Harry. Take care of yourself. {}/[*Exit*
358 CP   Julia   35   don't all go/Just because I'm going. Good-bye, Edward./{E} Good-bye, Julia. {}/
358 CP   Edward   36   I'm going. Good-bye, Edward./{E} Good-bye, Julia. {}/[*Exeunt* JULIA *and*
358 CP   Celia   37   {}/[*Exeunt* JULIA *and* PETER]/{C} Good-bye, Edward./Shall I see you soon?/{E}
359 CP   Celia   1   Perhaps you don't know? Very well, good-bye./{E} Good-bye, Celia./{A} Good-bye,
359 CP   Edward   2   don't know? Very well, good-bye./{E} Good-bye, Celia./{A} Good-bye, Edward. I do
359 CP   Alex   3   good-bye./{E} Good-bye, Celia./{A} Good-bye, Edward. I do hope/You'll have
359 CP   Edward   5   aunt./{E} Oh ... yes ... thank you. Good-bye, Alex,/It was nice of you to come. {}/
359 CP   Julia   30   into other people's business./Well, good-bye again. I'm off at last. {}/[*Exit*]/{E} I'm
366 CP   Julia   25   myself —/In a lift I can meditate. Good-bye then./And thank you — both of you
388 CP   Peter   7   /So what I've really come for is to say good-bye./{C} Well, Peter, I'm awfully glad, for
389 CP   Peter   1   you up tomorrow/And come in to say good-bye before I left./{L} And Celia's going
389 CP   Celia   24   — somewhere —/I should like to say good-bye — as friends./{L} Why, Celia, but
391 CP   Celia   4   house to-day./{C} Well, I'll go now. Good-bye, Lavinia./Good-bye, Edward./{E}
391 CP   Celia   5   Well, I'll go now. Good-bye, Lavinia./Good-bye, Edward./{E} Good-bye, Celia./{C}
391 CP   Edward   6   Lavinia./Good-bye, Edward./{E} Good-bye, Celia./{C} Good-bye, Lavinia./{L}

120 SP	Krum	7	on a visit —/{Kr} Specially when you	got	a real live Britisher/A guy like Sam to show
125 SA	Chorus	36	of a nightmare dream and/you've	got	the hoo-ha's coming to you./Hoo hoo hoo/
210	Old Gumbie	11	manners not nice;/So when she has	got	them lined up on the matting,/She teaches
235	Ad-dress	51	them call him James —/But we've not	got	so far as names./Before a Cat will
236	Cat Morgan	9	fish when I done me patrol./I ain't	got	much polish, me manners is gruff,/But I've
236	Cat Morgan	10	polish, me manners is gruff,/But I've	got	a good coat, and I keep meself smart;/And
236	Cat Morgan	12	/'You can't but like Morgan, 'e's	got	a good 'art.'/I got knocked about on the
236	Cat Morgan	13	like Morgan, 'e's got a good 'art.'/I	got	knocked about on the Barbary Coast,/And
589	Fable	95	lived the admiration of the shire. We/	Got	the veracious record of these doings/From
287 FR	Gerald	3	as I remember. Besides, you've	got	to make allowances:/We haven't left them
293 FR	Agatha	20	/{Ag} I think, Harry, that having	got	so far —/If you want no pretences, let us
322 FR	Winch	36	stopped to take his bearings. We've	got	him at the Arms —/Mr. John, I mean. By a
327 FR	Ivy	31	he's hurt,/But he says that he hasn't	got	the use of his car,/And he missed the last
331 FR	Harry	7	real. I thought foolishly/That when I	got	back to Wishwood, as I had left it,/
334 FR	Harry	3	/Or in getting rid of what can't be	got	rid of/But in a different vision. This is like
342 FR	Mary	3	is leaving:/Downing told her. He has	got	the car out./What is the matter?/{A} That
356 CP	Julia	26	Lavinia/Except for the time she	got	locked in the lavatory/And couldn't get out.
358 CP	Julia	20	excellent./Now let me see. Have I	got	everything?/It's such a nice party, I hate to
358 CP	Celia	30	you?/{C} No, I'm sorry, Peter;/I've	got	to take a taxi./{J} You come with me, Peter:/
365 CP	Edward	30	you I've no idea who he is/Or how he	got	there./{J} But what did you talk about/Or
367 CP	Edward	36	in?/{E} I'd like to know first how you	got	in, Alex./{A} Why, I came and found that the
368 CP	Alex	9	be alone, this evening./{A} But you've	got	to have some dinner. Are you going out?/Is
369 CP	Peter	13	{P} Not very often./And when I did, I	got	no chance to talk to her./{E} You and Celia
369 CP	Peter	32	to find her there alone./Anyway, we	got	into conversation/And I found that she
375 CP	Edward	18	Alex, don't bring me any cheese;/I've	got	some cheese ... No, not Norwegian;/But I
383 CP	Edward	3	you leave them?/Or have we ... have I	got	to hunt all over?/Have you looked in your
387 CP	Celia	22	just explained to Edward —/I only	got	here this moment myself —/That she
387 CP	Peter	25	else Lavinia has invited./{P} Why, I	got	the impression that Lavinia intended/To
390 CP	Julia	6	recovery./I said so to myself, when I	got	your telegram./{L} But where, may I ask,
390 CP	Alex	21	/{A} Welcome back, Lavinia!/When I	got	your telegram .../{L} Where from?/{A}
391 CP	Peter	32	anything. {}/[Enter PETER]/{P} I've	got	a taxi, Julia./{J} Splendid! Good-bye! {}/
422 CP	Alex	5	/{A} Well! Well! and how have we	got	on?/{J} Everything is in order./{A} The
426 CP	Julia	38	mine, in fact. But I'm forgetting!/I've	got	a surprise: I've brought Alex with me!/He
427 CP	Julia	1	I've brought Alex with me!/He only	got	back this morning from somewhere —/One
427 CP	Alex	9	that you won't have heard of./Yet	Got	back this morning. I heard about your
431 CP	Peter	23	of any that are still inhabited./We've	got	a team of experts over/To study the decay,
431 CP	Peter	33	to handle a duke./Besides that, we've	got	the casting director:/He's looking for some
433 CP	Peter	16	could make a success of it/If she only	got	the chance. It's Celia Coplestone./She
433 CP	Peter	20	her to our casting director./I've	got	an idea for another film./Can you tell me
434 CP	Alex	18	she was taken./When our people	got	there, they questioned the villagers —/Those
435 CP	Peter	8	I began to think myself a success/And	got	a little more self-confidence;/And then I
439 CP	Julia	14	that leads him to Boltwell:/And he's	got	to go there .../{P} I see what you mean./I
450 CC	Colby	28	your morning satisfactory?/{C} I've	got	what you wanted, Sir Claude. Good
452 CC	Lucasta	19	/And I couldn't find it. And then he	got	suspicious/And asked for things I'm sure he
458 CC	Lady E	16	ticket?/{LE} I went to the agency and	got	them to change it./I can't understand why
459 CC	Lady E	37	to Zürich?/{LE} Why, I'd no sooner	got	to Lausanne/Than whom should I meet but
468 CC	Colby	1	to prepare/Some figures for you. I've	got	them here./{SC} Much depends on my wife.
472 CC	Lucasta	40	world that you've lost:/You've still	got	your inner world — a world that's more
474 CC	Lucasta	32	you've something else, that I haven't	got:/	Something of which the music is a ...
475 CC	Lucasta	31	matter, in a sense./But now we've	got	to this point — you might as well know
476 CC	Lucasta	14	succeeded with people before:/I	got	into the habit of giving that impression./
478 CC	Kaghan	37	Lucasta./I knew I should find she'd	got	in first!/Trust Kaghan's intuitions! I'm your
479 CC	Kaghan	6	tigers/Like you and Lizzie, he's	got	to have protection./{L} Colby doesn't need
479 CC	Lucasta	11	now is, that I'm hungry,/And you've	got	to give me a very good dinner./{K} You
479 CC	Kaghan	21	know I don't like sherry./{K} You've	got	to drink it,/To Colby, and a happy bachelor
480 CC	Colby	13	that you're a gambler./You've	got	as level a head as anyone,/And you never
483 CC	Colby	12	/{C} It's an office desk. Sir Claude	got	it for me./I said I needed a desk in my
487 CC	Claude	3	memorise it. I can't use notes:/It's	got	to sound spontaneous. I've jotted down
488 CC	Claude	32	the place of your own child,/If you	got	to know him first — and that you'd want to
496 CC	Eggers	32	time I come, I notice the traffic/Has	got	so much worse./{SC} Yes, it's always getting
496 CC	Eggers	39	your son's death?/{E} Of the day we	got	the news. We don't often speak of it;/Yet I
498 CC	Claude	26	believe/That she took two babies, and	got	them mixed./{LE} That seems to be what
501 CC	Lady E	11	of liberal views —/That's why I never	got	on with my family./{L} Well, I'm not a
502 CC	Colby	2	Have I come too soon?/I'm afraid I	got	impatient of waiting./{L} Colby! I've not
502 CC	Lucasta	16	so I was expecting/What I thought I	got.	But I couldn't believe it!/It isn't like you, to

507 CC Guzzard 28 /The mother, I suppose, could have got an order/If she could have established the
519 CC Lady E 15 I mean to do better./Claude, we've got to try to understand our children./{K} And
524 ES Charles 25 getting off the point .../{C} You've got me off *my* point .../I was trying to explain ...
532 ES Monica 20 people now, Father./If you haven't got rid of him in twenty minutes/I'll send
538 ES Gomez 13 And your wife's family influence, you got on in politics./Shall we say that you did very
539 ES Gomez 33 If I had never met you? I should have got my First,/And I might have become the
549 ES Carghil 16 /And you made me try to punt, and I got soaking wet/And nearly dropped the punt
552 ES Carghil 25 that their consciences were clear./You got out of a tangle for a large cash payment/
556 ES Michael 34 for something I hadn't done./I never got over that. If you always blame a person/It's
564 ES Carghil 36 for secret, Señor Gomez!/You've got to be the first to put your cards on the table!
565 ES Gomez 25 MICHAEL]/{G} Well, Dick, we've got to obey our doctors' orders./But while we're
567 ES Charles 1 Well, Monica, here I am. I hope you got my message./{M} Oh Charles, Charles,
567 ES Charles 18 must make!/But my darling, since I got your letter this morning/About your father
574 ES Michael 34 world, for the same sort of job/You got me here in London? With another Sir Alfred
577 ES Gomez 24 head is well screwed on./He's got brains, he's got flair. When he does come
577 ES Gomez 24 well screwed on./He's got brains, he's got flair. When he does come back/He'll be able
580 ES Carghil 17 sudden. We talked it all over./But I've got a little piece of news of my own:/Next
GOTHA (1)
180 FQ: ECoker 108 Sun and Moon, and the Almanach de Gotha/And the Stock Exchange Gazette, the
GOTTA (5)
125 SA Sweeney 2 here again that don't apply/But I've gotta use words when I talk to you./But here's
125 SA Sweeney 21 death/Death is life and life is death/I gotta use words when I talk to you/But if you
125 SA Sweeney 24 to me and nothing to you/We all gotta do what we gotta do/We're gona sit here
125 SA Sweeney 24 to you/We all gotta do what we gotta do/We're gona sit here and drink this
125 SA Sweeney 28 and we're gona go/And somebody's gotta pay the rent/{Do} I know who/{S} But
GOURD (1)
91 Ash-Wed 2 13 of the desert and the fruit of the gourd./It is this which recovers/My guts the
GOVERNESS (3)
484 CC Lady E 8 /How I disliked my parents! I had a governess;/Several, in fact. And I loathed them
484 CC Lady E 10 them all./Were you brought up by a governess?/{C} No. By my aunt./{LE} And did
484 CC Lady E 16 father./{LE} Then, if you never had a governess,/And if you never knew either of your
GOVERNMENT (6)
240 MC Priest3 34 quite conclusive in the art of temporal government,/But violence, duplicity and
278 MC Knight2 10 to curb the excessive/powers of local government, which were usually exercised for/
278 MC Knight2 17 administration, under the central/government. I knew Becket well, in various
428 CP Alex 13 want them killed. So they blame the Government/For the damage that the monkeys
531 ES Charles 8 continue/To be at the disposal of the Government in power'./And the expectation
538 ES Gomez 29 job in the City/Where the Government could always consult you/But of
GOVERNOR (1)
427 CP Alex 29 sultans./I have been staying with the Governor./Three of us have been out on a tour
GOVERNS (2)
206 To my Wife 3 our wakingtime/And the rhythm that governs the repose of our sleepingtime,/The
522 ES dedic 3 *in our wakingtime/And the rhythm that governs the repose of our sleepingtime,/The*
GOWN (3)
91 Ash-Wed 2 17 The Lady is withdrawn/In a white gown, to contemplation, in a white gown./Let
91 Ash-Wed 2 17 gown, to contemplation, in a white gown./Let the whiteness of bones atone to
588 Fable 33 them off by force.'/He drencht the gown he wore with holy water,/The turkeys,
GRACE (7)
92 Ash-Wed 2 45 without word and/Word of no speech/Grace to the Mother/For the Garden/Where all
96 Ash-Wed 5 18 right place are not here/No place of grace for those who avoid the face/No time to
109 Marina 16 pine, and the woodsong fog/By this grace dissolved in place/What is this face, less
164 Rock 9 27 all our powers/For life, for dignity, grace and order,/And intellectual pleasures of
173 FQ: BurntN 75 compulsion, yet surrounded/By a grace of sense, a white light still and moving,/
246 MC Thomas 6 hold me in bitterest hate./By God's grace aware of their prevision/I sent my letters
254 MC Tempt4 21 /Think of the miracles, by God's grace,/And think of your enemies, in another
GRACES (2)
216 Jellicles 11 /They like to practise their airs and graces/And wait for the Jellicle Moon to rise./
603 Spleen 3 /Bonnets, silk hats, and conscious graces/In repetition that displaces/Your mental
GRAIN (1)
277 MC Knight3 11 to the/point, it does go against the grain to kill an Archbishop, especially/when you
GRAMMAR (2)
537 ES Gomez 20 /A scholarship boy from an unknown grammar school./I didn't know either, but I was
570 ES Ld Clav 33 Only a schoolmaster/In an obscure grammar school somewhere in the Midlands./

GRAMOPHONE (4)

69 WL: Fire S	256	hand,/And puts a record on the	gramophone./'This music crept by me upon the
396 CP	Edward	2	the evening/Than listening to the	gramophone./{L} We have very good records;/
396 CP	Lavinia	5	you really hated music/And that the	gramophone was only your escape/From
471 CC	Colby	6	them./Better still, I'll play you the	gramophone records./{L} I'd rather you played

GRAMOPHONES (1)

121 SA	Sweeney	22	isle./There's no telephones/There's no	gramophones/There's no motor cars/No

GRAND (1)

292 FR	Harry	8	song./Behind the palm trees in the	Grand Hotel/They were always there. But I did

GRAND (3) [*Foreign word*]

47 Mél Adult	12	/Surexcité par Emporheben/Au	grand air de Bergsteigleben;/J'erre toujours
51 Restaurant	4	il fera temps pluvieux,/Du vent, du	grand soleil, et de la pluie;/C'est ce qu'on
601 Nocturne	1	scarlet life, for me?/Nocturne/Romeo,	*grand sérieux*, to importune/Guitar and hat in

GRANDE (1)

455 CC	Eggers	40	told you, she really is a lady,/Rather a	*grande dame*, as the French say./That's what Sir

GRANDEST (2)

228 Gus	19	once gave him seven cat-calls./But his	grandest creation, as he loves to tell,/Was
229 Gus	33	Dick Whittington's Cat./But my	grandest creation, as history will tell,/Was

GRANDEUR (6)

155 Rock 3	60	of men who turn from GOD/To the	grandeur of your mind and the glory of your
255 MC	Tempt4	11	/Compared with richness of heavenly	grandeur?/Seek the way of martyrdom, make
255 MC	Tempt4	24	too much?/For such a vision of eternal	grandeur?/{T} Others offered real goods,
256 MC	Tempts	21	from deception to deception,/From	grandeur to grandeur to final illusion,/Lost in
256 MC	Tempts	21	to deception,/From grandeur to	grandeur to final illusion,/Lost in the wonder of
561 ES	Ld Clav	8	imagined paradise of success and	grandeur,/You will find your past failures

GRANDFATHER (2)

44 Cook Egg	6	/Daguerreotypes and silhouettes,/Her	grandfather and great great aunts,/Supported
464 CC	Claude	27	in the first place./My father — your	grandfather — built up this business/Starting

GRANDLY (1)

593 Grad 5	2	call — the twentieth century/More	grandly dowered than those which came before,

GRANDMOTHER (1)

385 CP	Reilly	11	strangers./The affectionate ghosts: the	grandmother,/The lively bachelor uncle at the

GRANDS (1)

47 Mél Adult	3	/En Angleterre, journaliste;/C'est à	grands pas et en sueur/Que vous suivrez à peine

GRANDSON (2)

203 Indians	4	of his own door at sunset/And see his	grandson, and his neighbour's grandson/Playing
203 Indians	4	see his grandson, and his neighbour's	grandson/Playing in the dust together./Scarred

GRANITE (4)

98 Ash-Wed 6	8	/From the wide window towards the	granite shore/The white sails still fly seaward,
110 Marina	33	ships./What seas what shores what	granite islands towards my timbers/And
184 FQ: DrySal	16	us;/The sea is the land's edge also, the	granite/Into which it reaches, the beaches where
185 FQ: DrySal	32	on water,/The distant rote in the	granite teeth,/And the wailing warning from the

GRANT (6)

105 Song Sime	8	that chills towards the dead land./Grant us thy peace./I have walked many years
105 Song Sime	18	cords and scourges and lamentation/Grant us thy peace./Before the stations of the
105 Song Sime	23	still unspeaking and unspoken Word,/Grant Israel's consolation/To one who has
106 Song Sime	31	/Not for me the ultimate vision./Grant me thy peace./(And a sword shall pierce
436 CP	Lavinia	29	in which they died?/{L} I'm willing to	grant that. What struck me, though,/Was that
573 ES	Charles	14	Monica,/To you, of all people./{C} I	grant you all that./But what do you propose?

GRANTED (15)

268 MC	Knight3	5	and your possessions./All was	granted for which you sued:/Yet how, I repeat,
285 FR	Amy	6	so warm, O Light that was taken for	granted/When I was young and strong, and sun
307 FR	Mary	20	I was a child I took everything for	granted,/Including the stupidity of older people
318 FR	Harry	15	that the things that are taken for	granted/At home, make a deeper impression
362 CP	Edward	9	I thought we took each other for	granted./I never thought I should be any
363 CP	Reilly	13	of the time we take ourselves for	granted,/As we have to, and live on a little
413 CP	Celia	23	last weeks,/I somehow took it for	granted that I needn't explain myself./{R} I
462 CC	Claude	1	very satisfactory./She's taken it for	granted that you should have the flat —/By
495 CC	Claude	6	More than that./I took it for	granted that what you wanted/Was a husband
495 CC	Lady E	9	wanted to be./{LE} And I took it for	granted that you were not interested/In
495 CC	Lady E	13	married people to take anything for	granted./{SC} That was a very intelligent
495 CC	Claude	15	/Perhaps I have taken too much for	granted/About you, Elizabeth. What did *you*
512 CC	Guzzard	25	to adapt ourselves/To the wish that is	granted. That can be a painful process,/As I
526 ES	Charles	35	/He seems so placidly to take it for	granted/That you don't really care for any
578 ES	Monica	20	the same friends./I took all that for	granted. So I didn't know till now/How much it

GRAPE (1)
588 Fable   62   drank more than he ought t' have of grape juice./The lights began to burn distinctly
GRAPES (3)
56 Swee Night   20   in oranges/Bananas figs and hothouse grapes;/The silent vertebrate in brown/
56 Swee Night   24   /Rachel *née* Rabinovitch/Tears at the grapes with murderous paws;/She and the lady
184 FQ: DrySal   13   of the April dooryard,/In the smell of grapes on the autumn table,/And the evening
GRAPPLED (1)
537 ES Gomez   7   many years ago:/Adoption tried, and grappled to my soul/With hoops of steel, and all
GRASP (3)
253 MC Tempt4   27   stealthy stratagem,/To general grasp of spiritual power?/Man oppressed by sin,
448 CC Eggers   13   highly educated. He'll soon begin to grasp them./No, I haven't told him much about
508 CC Eggers   7   son, in a similar way,/Wouldn't you grasp at any straw/That offered hope of finding
GRASPED (1)
319 FR Harry   8 always here./But when we would have grasped for him, there was only a vacuum/
GRASPING (1)
107 Animula   5 tables and of chairs,/Rising or falling, grasping at kisses and toys,/Advancing boldly,
GRASS (7)
24 Rhapsody   54   corners./She smooths the hair of the grass./The moon has lost her memory./A
73 WL: Thund   354 of water only/Not the cicada/And dry grass singing/But sound of water over a rock/
73 WL: Thund   386 mountains/In the faint moonlight, the grass is singing/Over the tumbled graves, about
83 Hollow Men   8 quiet and meaningless/As wind in dry grass/Or rats' feet over broken glass/In our dry
129 Cor2 State   2   /CRY what shall I cry?/All flesh is grass: comprehending/The Companions of the
594 Grad 11   6   /A drop of dew upon the morning grass;/Thou dost not die — for each succeeding
309 FR Harry   36   the moderate usual noises/In the grass and leaves, of life persisting,/Which
GRASSBLADE (1)
166 Rock 10   24   light,/Glow-worm glowlight on a grassblade./O Light Invisible, we worship Thee!/
GRASSHOPPER (1)
91 Ash-Wed 2   24   sang chirping/With the burden of the grasshopper, saying/Lady of silences/Calm and
GRASSHOPPERS (1)
382 CP Celia   17   your legs together —/Or however grasshoppers do it. I looked,/And listened for
GRATE (1)
530 ES Ld Clav   25   and empty room before an empty grate?/For no one. For nothing./{M} Yet you've
GRATEFUL (11)
245 MC Thomas   36   order as I find them./I am more than grateful for all your kind attentions./These are
372 CP Alex   21   The real aunt. But you'll be grateful./There are very few peasants in
379 CP Edward   13   been very wonderful, and I'm very grateful,/And I think you are a very rare person.
421 CP Julia   33   am so useful to you./You ought to be grateful./{R} And when I say to one like her/
436 CP Peter   9   /All that you've been saying. But I'm grateful all the same./You know, all the time
451 CC Eggers   5   Claude,/And he's always been very grateful to Sir Claude,/As he ought to be. Sir
462 CC Colby   34   to a new situation./{C} I'm very grateful to you, for that:/It is indeed a new and
467 CC Colby   24   mustn't think of that./{C} I'm very grateful for all you've done for me;/And I want
499 CC Lucasta   35   not? That's perfectly natural./But I'm grateful to Colby. But for Colby/I'd never have
500 CC Lucasta   38   reasons,/And that put me off. So I'm grateful to Colby./{SC} I don't know what's
579 ES Gomez   31   we might as well be going./You'll be grateful to me in the end, Dick./{MC} A parent
GRATIFY (2)
512 CC Guzzard   21   my turn to ask them./I should like to gratify everyone's wishes./{LE} Oh, of course ...
577 ES Charles   13   /Michael, in a man who aims to gratify, through you,/His lifelong grievance
GRATIFYING (1)
559 ES Michael   34   on your name and title/To a son, was gratifying. But it wasn't for *my* sake!/I was just
GRATITUDE (3)
111 Xmas Trees   25   /(And here I remember also with gratitude/St. Lucy, her carol, and her crown of
267 MC Knight1   30   privilege, how did you show your gratitude?/You had fled from England, not
268 MC Knight3   6 Yet how, I repeat, did you show your gratitude?/{K1} Suspending those who had
GRATTER (1)
51 Restaurant   2 délabré qui n'a rien à faire/Que de se gratter les doigts et se pencher sur mon épaule:/
GRAVE (4)
429 CP Julia   35 Somebody must have walked over my grave:/I'm feeling so chilly. Give me some gin./
437 CP Reilly   10   *but the other/Is underneath the grave, where do inhabit/The shadows of all forms*
448 CC Claude   38   had a son/Lost in action, and his grave unknown./{E} And you're thinking no
560 ES Michael   1   I wonder, will it give you/In the grave? If you're still conscious after death,/I bet
GRAVEL (1)
155 Rock 3   33 revisit,/The nettle shall flourish on the gravel court,/And the wind shall say: 'Here were
GRAVES (1)
73 WL: Thund   387 the grass is singing/Over the tumbled graves, about the chapel/There is the empty

GRAVESEND (1)

212 Growltiger	3	cat that ever roamed at large./From Gravesend up to Oxford he pursued his evil

GRAVEYARD (1)

203 Indians	17	in the Five Rivers, may have the same graveyard./Let those who go home tell the same

GRAVITY (3)

226 Macavity	6	human law, he breaks the law of gravity./His powers of levitation would make a
246 MC Tempt1	26	acrimony,/Hoping that your present gravity/Will find excuse for my humble levity/
248 MC Tempt1	5	acrimony,/Hoping that your present gravity/Will find excuse for my humble levity./If

GRAY (5)

597 Before Mor	1	all the East was weaving red with gray,/The flowers at the window turned toward
603 Spleen	11	conspiracy./And Life, a little bald and gray,/Languid, fastidious, and bland,/Waits, hat
605 Narcissus	1	/Come under the shadow of this gray rock —/Come in under the shadow of this
605 Narcissus	2	—/Come in under the shadow of this gray rock,/And I will show you something
605 Narcissus	7	his bloody cloth and limbs/And the gray shadow on his lips./He walked once

GRAY-HAIRED (1)

593 Grad 8	2	in distant years when we are grown/Gray-haired and old, whatever be our lot,/We

GREAT (61)

15 Prufrock	83	/I am no prophet — and here's no great matter;/I have seen the moment of my
44 Cook Egg	6	and silhouettes,/Her grandfather and great great aunts,/Supported on the mantelpiece
44 Cook Egg	6	/Her grandfather and great great aunts,/Supported on the mantelpiece/An
108 Animula	34	to pieces,/For this one who made a great fortune,/And that one who went his own
111 Xmas Trees	30	emotion/May be concentrated into a great joy/Which shall be also a great fear, as on
111 Xmas Trees	31	into a great joy/Which shall be also a great fear, as on the occasion/When fear came
166 Rock 10	7	go on to conquer the World?/The great snake lies ever half awake, at the bottom
167 Rock 10	46	we give Thee thanks for Thy great glory!/FOUR QUARTETS/Burnt Norton
222 Pekes Pols	m3	the Poms, and the Intervention/of the Great Rumpuscat/The Pekes and the Pollicles,
223 Pekes Pols	51	/Why who should stalk out but the GREAT RUMPUSCAT./His eyes were like
223 Pekes Pols	53	fireballs fearfully blazing,/He gave a great yawn, and his jaws were amazing;/And
223 Pekes Pols	58	/He looked at the sky and he gave a great leap —/And they every last one of them
588 Fable	52	made of turtle eggs,/And after that a great pie made of plover,/And flagons which
593 Grad 5	1	we might look into the future years./Great duties call — the twentieth century/More
593 Grad 5	4	what time may hold in store,/Or what great deeds the distant years may see,/What
593 Grad 6	1	yore!/But if this century is to be more great/Than those before, her sons must make
594 Grad 10	4	t'will be so./That which has made it great, not left behind,/The same school in the
600 Moonflower	3	moth,/The mist crawls in from sea;/A great white bird, a snowy owl,/Slips from the
244 MC Chorus	19	shadows, our secret fears./But now a great fear is upon us, a fear not of one but of
249 MC Tempt2	3	in the schools./To set down the great, protect the poor,/Beneath the throne of
279 MC Knight1	4	with us./{K1} Morville has given us a great deal to think about. It/seems to me that he
279 MC Knight4	40	give, upon/one who was, after all, a great man./{K1} Thank you, Brito, I think that
299 FR Charles	8	the papers —/Of course, there was a great deal too much in the papers./Downing, do
314 FR Warburt	24	/I used to dream of making some great discovery/To do away with one disease or
320 FR Warburt	34	do that Arthur and John/Have been a great disappointment to your mother./John's
342 FR Mary	21	I have seen and what I know!/He is in great danger, I know that, don't ask me,/You
346 FR Agatha	37	or I see it,/It is only that he has seen a great deal more than that,/And we have seen
367 CP Peter	12	think?/{P} It seemed to me we had a great deal in common./We're both of us artists./
367 CP Peter	32	/The point is, I thought we had a great deal in common/And I think she thought
369 CP Peter	3	awfully kind to me/And I owe her a great deal. And then I met Celia./She was
378 CP Celia	39	/Will you promise me to see a very great doctor/Whom I have heard of — and his
390 CP Julia	36	after that long journey on the old Great Eastern,/Waiting at junctions. And I
403 CP Edward	19	If I am like that/I must have done a great deal of harm./{R} Oh, not so much as you
404 CP Reilly	38	patient like yourself/I need to know a great deal more about him,/Than the patient
407 CP Reilly	24	into hands like mine/You surrender a great deal more than you meant to./This is the
420 CP Reilly	33	reflecting vanity./I have taken a great risk./{J} We must always take risks./That
425 CP Lavinia	6	too many people./{L} It's true, a great many more accepted/Than we thought
431 CP Peter	5	/It was he who introduced me to the great Bela./{J} And who is the great Bela?/{P}
431 CP Julia	6	to the great Bela./{J} And who is the great Bela?/{P} Why, Bela Szogody —/He's my
439 CP Alex	21	film./And I know that Bela expects great things of it./{P} So now I'll be going./{E}
446 CC Claude	14	form. He won't forget/That his great ambition was to be an organist,/Just as I
446 CC Claude	16	as I can't forget ... no matter./The great thing was to find something else/He could
447 CC Eggers	12	As one of the household./{E} That's a great compliment./{SC} And well deserved; but
451 CC Eggers	35	/{E} Your music will certainly be a great asset/With Lady Elizabeth. I envy you
455 CC Eggers	27	have Mrs. Eggerson./{E} Yes, she's a great protection. And I have my garden/To
465 CC Colby	34	I know/I should never have become a great organist,/As I aspired to be. I'm not an
465 CC Colby	36	executant;/I'm only a shadow of the great composers./Always, when I play to myself,
466 CC Colby	3	I play to myself./What I hear is a great musician's music,/What they hear is an

472 CC Lucasta 26   /And perhaps you could be a very great musician:/But that's not the point. You'd
481 CC Lady E   31 the type of person/Who needs to eat a great deal of salad./You remember, I made you
494 CC Claude   23 /Like that, by force of will. He was a great financier —/And I am merely a successful
495 CC Lady E   12 needed me chiefly as a hostess./It's a great mistake, I do believe,/For married people
512 CC Lady E   35 B. — and I'm sure we shall become great friends./{E} I'm sure we all wish for
539 ES Gomez   13 /And I wonder whether you're the great economist/And financial wizard that
548 ES Carghil 25 dining-room last night./You are the great Lord Claverton, aren't you?/Somebody
561 ES Monica   24 /I know that Michael must be in great trouble,/So can't you help him?/{LC} I am
564 ES Carghil 22 at Oxford/And Richard and I became great friends/Not long afterwards, didn't we,
568 ES Ld Clav   1   Not far away. Standing under the great beech tree./{M} Why under the beech tree?
570 ES Ld Clav 28 his own peculiar methods,/A man of great importance and the highest standing/In
573 ES Carghil 34 to get a girl like Monica./I take a great interest in her future./Fancy! I've only
577 ES Carghil 31 told me so./Now, Michael has great abilities for business./I saw that, and so

GREATER (14)
 92 Ash-Wed 2   37   torment/Of love unsatisfied/The greater torment/Of love satisfied/End of the
166 Rock 10   19 Thee!/Too bright for mortal vision./O Greater Light, we praise Thee for the less;/The
590 Time Space   4 The sun which does not feel decay/No greater is than we./So why, Love, should we
593 Grad 5   6   over pain and misery,/What heroes greater than were e'er of yore!/But if this
242 MC Priest1 29   to God alone./Had the King been greater, or had he been weaker/Things had
253 MC Tempt4   19 are employable against each other;/Greater enemies must kings destroy./{T} What
258 MC Thomas   27 wish./Servant of God has chance of greater sin/And sorrow, than the man who
258 MC Thomas   29 serves a king./For those who serve the greater cause may make the cause serve them,/
379 CP Edward   2 *is* Reilly!/{E} It would need someone greater than the greatest doctor/To cure *this*
438 CP Lavinia   3 /{L} Perhaps she had been through greater agony beforehand./I mean — I know
438 CP Edward   24 in some way, my responsibility/Is greater than that of a band of half-crazed
467 CC Claude   20 me. And yet I seem/To have made a greater mistake than he did./{C} I know that I'm
487 CC Claude   9 this, Elizabeth,/That Colby can be of greater help than Eggerson./I couldn't have
515 CC Guzzard 24 my previous sacrifice./This is even greater than the sacrifice I made/When I let you

GREATEST (8)
202 War Poetry 23   /Of private experience at its greatest intensity/Becoming universal, which we
224 Mr Mistoff 14   /And deceive you again./The greatest magicians have something to learn/
258 MC Thomas   5 kind again./The last temptation is the greatest treason:/To do the right deed for the
326 FR Violet   5 district was unfamiliar/And I had the greatest trouble in getting home./I am sure he
365 CP Julia   37 me/About my glasses. That's the greatest mystery./Peter! Why aren't you looking
372 CP Alex   11 that of all my triumphs/This is the greatest. To make something out of nothing!/
379 CP Edward   2 would need someone greater than the greatest doctor/To cure *this* illness./{C} Edward,
450 CC Claude   2 /And that may be something of the greatest importance./It's when you're sure you

GREATNESS (3)
 15 Prufrock   84 matter;/I have seen the moment of my greatness flicker,/And I have seen the eternal
155 Rock 3   62   enterprises,/To schemes of human greatness thoroughly discredited,/Binding the
256 MC Tempts   22   /Lost in the wonder of his own greatness,/The enemy of society, enemy of

GREED (3)
241 MC Priest3   5 /And the steadfast can manipulate the greed and lust of others,/The feeble is devoured
266 MC Knight2   33   /{K2} Saving your insolence and greed./Won't you ask us to pray to God for
418 CP Reilly   3 world of lunacy,/Violence, stupidity, greed ... it is a good life./{C} I know I ought to

GREEK (1)
 20 Portrait   75   countess goes upon the stage./A Greek was murdered at a Polish dance,/Another

GREEN (13)
 31 Apollinax   11   of drowned men drift down in the green silence,/Dropping from fingers of surf./I
 32 Hysteria   7   white checked cloth over the rusty/green iron table, saying: 'If the lady and
 45 Cook Egg   28 /From Kentish Town and Golder's Green;/Where are the eagles and the trumpets?/
 64 WL: Chess   95   sea-wood fed with copper/Burned green and orange, framed by the coloured stone,
 92 Ash-Wed 3   15 broadbacked figure drest in blue and green/Enchanted the maytime with an antique
 94 Ash-Wed 4   3 between/The various ranks of varied green/Going in white and blue, in Mary's
135 5FingerEx1   2 The songsters of the air repair/To the green fields of Russell Square./Beneath the trees
135 5FingerEx2   3   and dry./In a black sky, from a green cloud/Natural forces shriek'd aloud,/
138 New Hamp   4   head, crimson head,/Between the green tip and the root./Black wing, brown wing,
140 Usk   10 there/Where the grey light meets the green air/The hermit's chapel, the pilgrim's
606 Narcissus   38 blood, and satisfied him./Now he is green, dry and stained/With the shadow in his
256 MC Chorus   8 the sickly smell, the vapour? the dark green light from a cloud on a withered tree? The
263 MC Chorus   25 wrong/Shall the bird's song cover, the green tree cover, what wrong/Shall the fresh

GREENHOUSE (2)
226 Macavity   25 or another Peke's been stifled,/Or the greenhouse glass is broken, and the trellis past
303 FR Mary   6 /Such as they are, than have these greenhouse flowers/Which do not belong here,

GREENS (1)

219 Mung Rump	23	/On Argentine joint, potatoes and greens,/And the cook would appear from

GREENWICH (1)

69 WL: Fire S	275	/The barges wash/Drifting logs/Down Greenwich reach/Past the Isle of Dogs./

GREET (7)

142 Cape Ann	9	the dancing arrow, the purple martin. Greet/In silence the bullbat. All are delectable.
230 Bust Jones	5	Street Cat!/He's the Cat we all greet as he walks down the street/In his coat of
235 Ad-dress	49	/(He comes to see me in my flat)/I greet him with an OOPSA CAT!/I think I've
385 CP Edward	6	a stranger./{E} So you want me to greet my wife as a stranger?/That will not be
501 CC Eggers	33	/But I'm sure that we want to greet the happy pair./It's all in the family. Why
561 ES Ld Clav	9	your past failures waiting there to greet you./You're all I have to live for, Michael
581 ES Monica	10	you mean, Father? You'll be here to greet him./But one thing I'm convinced of: you

GREETS (1)

233 Skimble	58	he was busy at Carlisle,/Where he greets the stationmaster with elation./But you

GRETA (1)

354 CP Julia	17	a life she led! I used to say to her: 'Greta!/You have too much vitality.' But she

GREW (3)

589 Fable	89	scandal./But after this the monks grew most devout,/And lived on milk and
589 Fable	92	knout/And flogged his mates 'till they grew good and friarly./Spirits from that time
279 MC Knight4	24	a monster of egotism. This egotism grew upon him, until it/became at last an

GREY (13)

21 Portrait	115	die some afternoon,/Afternoon grey and smoky, evening yellow and rose;/
109 Marina	1	/Marina/What seas what shores what grey rocks and what islands/What water lapping
140 Usk	10	roads rise/Seek only there/Where the grey light meets the green air/The hermit's
177 FQ: ECoker	21	light/Is absorbed, not refracted, by grey stone./The dahlias sleep in the empty
178 FQ: ECoker	57	that aim too high/Red into grey and tumble down/Late roses filled with
201 Def Island	7	the memory of those appointed to the grey/ships — battleship, merchantman, trawler
243 MC Chorus	17	/Evil the wind, and bitter the sea, and grey the sky, grey grey grey./O Thomas, return,
243 MC Chorus	17	and bitter the sea, and grey the sky, grey grey grey./O Thomas, return, Archbishop;
243 MC Chorus	17	bitter the sea, and grey the sky, grey grey grey./O Thomas, return, Archbishop;
243 MC Chorus	17	the sea, and grey the sky, grey grey grey./O Thomas, return, Archbishop; return,
244 MC Chorus	30	set the white sail between the grey sky and the bitter sea, leave us, leave us for
269 MC Chorus	34	the loon, the lunatic bird. I have seen/Grey necks twisting, rat tails twining, in the
280 MC Priest3	18	/Go where the sunset reddens the last grey rock/Of Brittany, or the Gates of Hercules.

GRIDDLEBONE (4)

213 Growltiger	30	his attention on the Lady GRIDDLEBONE./And his raffish crew were
213 Growltiger	33	had no eye or ear for aught but Griddlebone,/And the Lady seemed enraptured
213 Growltiger	45	on the crew within their bunks./Then Griddlebone she gave a screech, for she was
227 Macavity	40	Mungojerrie, I might mention Griddlebone)/Are nothing more than agents for

GRIEF (8)

135 5FingerEx1	6	Woolly Bear./There is no relief but in grief./O when will the creaking heart cease?/
164 Rock 9	7	put upon GOD their own sorrow, the grief they should feel/For their sins and faults as
188 FQ: DrySal	137	the platform)/Their faces relax from grief into relief,/To the sleepy rhythm of a
281 MC Chorus	15	face under fear, the head bent under grief,/Even in us the voices of seasons, the
290 FR Amy	12	sake of the future. There can be no grief/And no regret and no remorse./I would
403 CP Reilly	11	your power — until you came to grief./Half of the harm that is done in this world
448 CC Eggers	34	thwarted./{E} I'm sure it's been a grief to both of you/That you've never had
464 CC Claude	39	father knew I hated it:/That was a grief to him. He knew, I am sure,/That I

GRIEVANCE (2)

524 ES Charles	29	you don't understand is that I have a grievance./On Monday you're leaving London,
577 ES Charles	14	to gratify, through you,/His lifelong grievance against your father?/Remember, you

GRIEVE (4)

34 Figlia	9	/So I would have had her stand and grieve,/So he would have left/As the soul leaves
204 de la Mare	16	go at dawn,/The sad intangible who grieve and yearn;/When the familiar scene is
604 Ode	10	has lost/We are still the less able to grieve,/With so much that of Harvard we carry
276 MC Chorus	11	of end:/In life there is not time to grieve long./But this, this is out of life, this is

GRIEVED (2)

157 Rock 4	7	wine to the king Artaxerxes,/And he grieved for the broken city, Jerusalem;/And the
531 ES Ld Clav	23	we go, a good many folk are mildly grieved,/And our closest associates, the small

GRIEVES (2)

138 New Hamp	7	years and the spring is over;/To-day grieves, to-morrow grieves,/Cover me over,
138 New Hamp	7	is over;/To-day grieves, to-morrow grieves,/Cover me over, light-in-leaves;/Golden

GRIM (1)

136 5FingerEx5	3	of clerical cut,/And his brow so grim/And his mouth so prim/And his

GRIMACE (1)
602 Humoresque   8   we forget)/Pinched in a comic, dull grimace;/Half bullying, half imploring air,/
GRIMPEN (1)
179 FQ: ECoker   92   wood, in a bramble,/On the edge of a grimpen, where is no secure foothold,/And
GRIMY (1)
22 Preludes   6   /And now a gusty shower wraps/The grimy scraps/Of withered leaves about your feet
GRIN (3)
24 Rhapsody   18   of the door/Which opens on her like a grin./You see the border of her dress/Is torn
52 Whispers   4   /Leaned backward with a lipless grin./Daffodil bulbs instead of balls/Stared from
57 Swee Night   32   of wistaria/Circumscribe a golden grin;/The host with someone indistinct/
GRINDERS (1)
243 MC Priest3   11   the end of good or evil?/Until the grinders cease/And the door shall be shut in the
GRINNING (2)
31 Apollinax   14   Apollinax rolling under a chair/Or grinning over a screen/With seaweed in its hair./
311 FR   Harry   34   you are looking at,/Not me you are grinning at, not me your confidential looks/
GRIPPED (1)
24 Rhapsody   45   old crab with barnacles on his back,/Gripped the end of a stick which I held him./
GRIPS (1)
212 Growltiger   16   Cat with whom Growltiger came to grips!/But most to Cats of foreign race his
GRISHKIN (3)
52 Whispers   17   to flesh/Allayed the fever of the bone./Grishkin is nice: her Russian eye/Is underlined
52 Whispers   24   /With subtle effluence of cat;/Grishkin has a maisonnette;/The sleek Brazilian
53 Whispers   28   gloom/Distil so rank a feline smell/As Grishkin in a drawing-room./And even the
GROANER (1)
185 FQ: DrySal   34   /Are all sea voices, and the heaving groaner/Rounded homewards, and the seagull:/
GROIN (1)
257 MC Tempts   5   sit at meat, and feel the cold in his groin./{C} We have not been happy, my Lord,
GROPE (1)
85 Hollow Men   58   /In this last of meeting places/We grope together/And avoid speech/Gathered on
GROPES (1)
69 WL: Fire S   248   one final patronising kiss,/And gropes his way, finding the stairs unlit .../She
GROS (1)
51 Restaurant   17   est dur./Il est venu, nous peloter, un gros chien;/Moi j'avais peur, je l'ai quittée à
GROSS (1)
269 MC Knight1   6   the King's majesty,/You insult with gross indignity;/Insolent madman, whom
GROTESQUE (1)
489 CC   Claude   11   any number of children!/That seems grotesque now. But it influenced me./And I
GROUND (15)
34 Figlia   5   a pained surprise —/Fling them to the ground and turn/With a fugitive resentment in
52 Whispers   3   skin;/And breastless creatures under ground/Leaned backward with a lipless grin./
54 Mr E Sun   10   school/Designed upon a gesso ground/The nimbus of the Baptized God./
67 WL: Fire S   193 /White bodies naked on the low damp ground/And bones cast in a little low dry garret,
185 FQ: DrySal   39   not our time, rung by the unhurried/Ground swell, a time/Older than the time of
185 FQ: DrySal   48   and time is never ending;/And the ground swell, that is and was from the
196 FQ: Little   201 the purification of the motive/In the ground of our beseeching./The dove descending
204 de la Mare   3   /(A hiding place, but very dangerous ground,/For here the water buffalo may rove,/
601 Nocturne   9   /Blood looks effective on the moonlit ground —/The hero smiles; in my best mode
270 MC Chorus   9   scent in the woodpath, while the ground heaved. I have seen/Rings of light
279 MC Knight4   18   obliged, very briefly, to go over/the ground traversed by the last speaker. While the
281 MC Chorus   20   for the blood of Christ,/There is holy ground, and the sanctity shall not depart from it
282 MC Chorus   3   broken imperial column,/From such ground springs that which forever renews the
341 FR Agatha   26   had a husband or a son/We have no ground for argument./{A} Who set you up to
360 CP   Reilly   38   the reason may be deeper/And you've ground for hope that she won't come back at
GROUNDS (2)
375 CP   Celia   2   /And if she chooses to give *you* the grounds .../{E} I see. But it is not like that at all.
548 ES Monica   8   to-day./I'm going to prowl about the grounds. Don't look so alarmed!/If you spy any
GROUP (1)
149 Rock 1 m   94   *each/Every man to his work./Now a group of* WORKMEN *is silhouetted against the*
GROUPS (1)
280 MC Knight1   3   /Please be careful not to loiter in groups at street corners, and do/nothing that
GROUSE (3)
214 RTTugger   2   him pheasant he would rather have grouse./If you put him in a house he would
235 Ad-dress   58   or Strassburg Pie,/Some potted grouse, or salmon paste —/He's sure to have his
236 Cat Morgan   5   /I'm partial to partridges, likewise to grouse,/And I favour that Devonshire cream in

GROVE (3)

204 de la Mare	6	/In the dark jungle of a mango grove,/And shadowy lemurs glide from tree to
218 Mung Rump	3	They made their home in Victoria Grove —/That was merely their centre of
218 Mung Rump	19	/They made their home in Victoria Grove. They had no regular occupation./They

GROW (12)

16 Prufrock	120	—/Almost, at times, the Fool./I grow old ... I grow old .../I shall wear the
16 Prufrock	120	at times, the Fool./I grow old ... I grow old .../I shall wear the bottoms of my
61 WL: Burial	19	the roots that clutch, what branches grow/Out of this stony rubbish? Son of man,/
181 FQ: ECoker	158	that, to be restored, our sickness must grow worse./The whole earth is our hospital/
182 FQ: ECoker	192	Home is where one starts from. As we grow older/The world becomes stranger, the
592 Grad 4	4	lane by which the rose and hawthorn grow./We hope it may be; would that we might
241 MC Priest3	21	/{P3} What peace can be found/To grow between the hammer and the anvil?/{P2}
296 FR Charles	24	/{C} He has probably let this notion grow in his mind,/Living among strangers, with
336 FR Agatha	36	/A curse is like a child, formed/To grow to maturity:/Accident is design/And
395 CP Lavinia	23	with yourself;/And if other people grow, well, you want to grow too./In what way
395 CP Lavinia	23	other people grow, well, you want to grow too./In what way have you changed?/{E}
489 CC Claude	22	for his education./I have watched him grow. And Mrs. Guzzard/Knows he is my son./

GROWING (5)

14 Prufrock	41	—/(They will say: 'How his hair is growing thin!')/My morning coat, my collar
107 Animula	16	servants say./The heavy burden of the growing soul/Perplexes and offends more, day
180 FQ: ECoker	122	emptiness deepen/Leaving only the growing terror of nothing to think about;/Or
195 FQ: Little	155	from things and from persons; and, growing between them, indifference/Which
578 ES Monica	19	much notice of me./When we were growing up we seldom had the same friends./I

GROWLTIGER (7)

212 Growltiger	1	it appears./Growltiger's Last Stand/GROWLTIGER was a Bravo Cat, who
212 Growltiger	16	/And woe to any Cat with whom Growltiger came to grips!/But most to Cats of
212 Growltiger	24	it lay rocking on the tide —/And Growltiger was disposed to show his
213 Growltiger	29	his prey./In the forepeak of the vessel Growltiger sate alone,/Concentrating his
213 Growltiger	33	in their sampans and their junks./Growltiger had no eye or ear for aught but
213 Growltiger	48	—/But a serried ring of flashing steel Growltiger did surround./The ruthless foe
213 Growltiger	50	forward, in stubborn rank on rank;/Growltiger to his vast surprise was forced to

GROWLTIGER'S (3)

212 Growltiger	t	households depend, it appears./Growltiger's Last Stand/GROWLTIGER was a
212 Growltiger	12	the rumour ran along the shore: GROWLTIGER'S ON THE LOOSE!/Woe to
212 Growltiger	14	to the pampered Pekinese, that faced Growltiger's rage;/Woe to the bristly Bandicoot,

GROWN (9)

15 Prufrock	82	prayed,/Though I have seen my head (grown slightly bald) brought in upon a platter,/I
231 Bust Jones	32	surprise that under our eyes/He has grown unmistakably round./He's a twenty-five
593 Grad 8	1	in distant years when we are grown/Gray-haired and old, whatever be our
315 FR Warburt	13	don't know. — But now you're all grown up/I haven't a patient left at Wishwood./
395 CP Lavinia	21	measured/To prove how you had grown since the last holidays./You were always
506 CC Eggers	15	Guzzard,/If he is alive, must be a grown man./I believe you have had no children
534 ES Gomez	25	by the way, I've several children,/All grown up, doing well for themselves./I wouldn't
544 ES Ld Clav	18	not noticed;/And by the time one has grown to consciousness/It comes less often./I
568 ES Ld Clav	35	she is a child. And by the time she's grown/You've woven such a web of fiction

GROWS (3)

121 SA Sweeney	26	/Nothing to eat but the fruit as it grows./Nothing to see but the palmtrees one
248 MC Tempt2	27	Think, my Lord,/Power obtained grows to glory,/Life lasting, a permanent
258 MC Thomas	20	comes behind and unobservable./Sin grows with doing good. When I imposed the

GRUDGING (1)

530 ES Ld Clav	35	—/All to thank them for that./Oh the grudging contributions/That bought this piece

GRUFF (1)

236 Cat Morgan	9	ain't got much polish, me manners is gruff,/But I've got a good coat, and I keep

GRUMBLE (1)

223 Pekes Pols	30	a score./And together they started to grumble and wheeze/In their huffery-snuffery

GRUMBLED (1)

530 ES Monica	28	To this very time! You know how you grumbled/At the farewell banquet, with the

GRUMBLING (1)

103 Journ Magi	11	/Then the camel men cursing and grumbling/And running away, and wanting

GRUMBUSKIN (1)

212 Growltiger	25	his sentimental side./His bucko mate, GRUMBUSKIN, long since had disappeared,/

GUARD (2)

233 Skimble	41	the window if you sneeze./Then the guard looks in politely and will ask you very
451 CC Colby	34	you are a musician./{C} I'll be on my guard./{E} Your music will certainly be a great

GUARDIAN (6)

259 MC	Thomas	7	Angel, whom God appoints/To be my	guardian, hover over the swords' points. {}/
381 CP	Edward	38	/And who in some men may be the	*guardian* —/But in men like me, the dull, the
383 CP	Celia	22	/{C} It may be that even Julia is a	guardian./Perhaps she is *my* guardian. Give me
383 CP	Celia	23	Julia is a guardian./Perhaps she is *my*	guardian. Give me the spectacles./Good night,
478 CC	Kaghan	38	/Trust Kaghan's intuitions! I'm your	guardian angel,/Colby, to protect you from
479 CC	Lucasta	1	you from Lucasta./{L} You're *my*	guardian angel at the moment, B./You're to

GUARDIANS (6)

30 Cous	Nancy	12	kept watch/Matthew and Waldo,	guardians of the faith,/The army of unalterable
204 de la Mare		8	lemurs glide from tree to tree —/The	guardians of some long-lost treasure-trove)/
383 CP	Celia	19	Whom shall we drink to?/{C} To the	Guardians./{E} To the Guardians?/{C} To the
383 CP	Edward	20	to?/{C} To the Guardians./{E} To the	Guardians?/{C} To the Guardians. It was you
383 CP	Celia	21	/{E} To the Guardians?/{C} To the	Guardians. It was you who spoke of guardians.
383 CP	Celia	21	Guardians. It was you who spoke of	guardians. {}/[*They drink*]/{C} It may be that

GUARDS (4)

56 Swee	Night	8	the Raven drift above/And Sweeney	guards the hornèd gate./Gloomy Orion and the
129 Cor2	State	24	reduction of orders./Meanwhile the	guards shake dice on the marches/And the frogs
232 Skimble		5	him or the train can't start.'/All the	guards and all the porters and the
232 Skimble		19	Car Express./From the driver and the	guards to the bagmen playing cards/He will

GUENILLES (1)

| 46 Directeur | | 16 | /Dans un égout/Une petite fille/En | guenilles/Camarde/Regarde/Le directeur/Du |

GUERDON (1)

| 593 Grad 7 | | 4 | good until they die,/And ask no other | guerdon than to know/That they have helpt the |

GUERRES (1)

| 182 FQ: ECoker | | 175 | wasted, the years of *l'entre deux guerres* —/Trying to learn to use words, and |

GUESS (12)

61 WL: Burial		21	Son of man,/You cannot say, or	guess, for you know only/A heap of broken
116 SP	Doris	40	to cut the cards for to-night./Oh	guess what the first is/{Du} First is. What is?/
209 NamingCats		22	that is the name that you never will	guess;/The name that no human research can
220 Old Deut		30	eye!/My sight's unreliable, but I can	guess/That the cause of the trouble is Old
236 Cat Morgan		11	smart;/And everyone says, and I	guess that's enough;/'You can't but like
330 FR	Agatha	13	What is in your mind, Harry?/I can	guess about the past and what you mean about
377 CP	Julia	26	Now I'll propose a health./Can you	guess whose health I'm going to propose?/{E}
427 CP	Alex	33	Monkey nuts?/{A} That was a nearer	guess than you think./No, not monkey nuts.
449 CC	Claude	37	where I'm in the dark./I simply can't	guess what her reaction would be./There's a lot
476 CC	Lucasta	40	quarter/On gin and betting, I should	guess./And I knew how she supplemented her
480 CC	Kaghan	7	/I'm a good guesser. But I sometimes	guess wrong./I make decisions on the spur of
525 ES	Charles	12	a shopping expedition —/Except to	guess what you want to buy/And advise you to

GUESSED (5)

190 FQ: DrySal		219	thought and action./The hint half	guessed, the gift half understood, is Incarnation.
377 CP	Julia	29	you/Lavinia's aunt! You might have	guessed it./{E&C} Lavinia's aunt./{J} Now, the
416 CP	Celia	8	with this man?/{C} Oh, you'd	guessed that, had you? That's clever of you./No,
476 CC	Lucasta	27	But he's very clever too;/And he	guessed the truth from the very first moment./
529 ES	Ld Clav	20	afternoon, Charles. You might have	guessed, Monica,/What I've been doing. Don't

GUESSER (1)

| 480 CC | Kaghan | 7 | to be in business together./I'm a good | guesser. But I sometimes guess wrong./I make |

GUESSES (3)

68 WL: Fire S		235	/The time is now propitious, as he	guesses,/The meal is ended, she is bored and
190 FQ: DrySal		216	music lasts. These are only hints and	guesses,/Hints followed by guesses; and the rest/
190 FQ: DrySal		217	hints and guesses,/Hints followed by	guesses; and the rest/Is prayer, observance,

GUESSING (1)

| 240 MC | Chorus | 20 | do, some well, some ill, planning and | guessing,/Having their aims which turn in their |

GUEST (18)

68 WL: Fire S		230	the rest —/I too awaited the expected	guest./He, the young man carbuncular, arrives,/
352 CP	m	7	QUILPE/AN UNIDENTIFIED	GUEST, *later identified as* SIR HENRY
353 CP	5m	1	GIBBS,/*and an* UNIDENTIFIED	GUEST./{A} You've missed the point
353 CP	m	23	it. {}/[*To the* UNIDENTIFIED	GUEST]/{C} You don't know it, do you?/{UG}
354 CP	m	19	herself. {}/[*To the* UNIDENTIFIED	GUEST]/{J} Did *you* know Lady Klootz?/{UG}
354 CP	m	25	{}/[*To the* UNIDENTIFIED	GUEST]/{J} Do *you* know Delia Verinder?/
355 CP	m	31	ago! {}/[*To the* UNIDENTIFIED	GUEST]/{J} Did *you* know the Vincewells?/
356 CP	Julia	17	But just try to pretend you're another	guest/At Lavinia's party. There are so many
359 CP	m	7	CELIA]/[*To the* UNIDENTIFIED	GUEST]/{E} Don't go yet./Don't go yet. We'll
384 CP	m	2	{}/[*Enter the* UNIDENTIFIED	GUEST]/{UG} Good evening, Mr.
401 CP	Edward	18	Had you been invited by my wife as a	guest/As I supposed? ... Or did she *send* you?/
408 CP	Reilly	16	/{R} Mr. Peter Quilpe/Was a frequent	guest./{E} Peter Quilpe./Peter Quilpe! Really

427 CP	Alex	17	to her —/Never mind: the unexpected guest/Is the one to whom they give the warmest
432 CP	Lavinia	14	Julia, Sir Henry,/You are the perfect guest we've been waiting for./{R} I should not
546 ES	Piggott	20	/Though we never accept any guest who's incurable./You know, we've been
546 ES	Piggott	24	accept them. Nor do we accept/Any guest who *looks* incurable —/We make that
548 ES	Monica	9	look so alarmed!/If you spy any guest who seems to be stalking you/Put your
562 ES	Carghil	37	who's this coming?/It's another new guest here. He's waving to us./Do you know

GUESTS (18)

172 FQ: BurntN		32	are looked at./There they were as our guests, accepted and accepting./So we moved,
368 CP	Edward	35	salon,/Where I entertained the minor guests/And dealt with the misfits, Lavinia's
394 CP	Edward	13	me as your butler:/Some of your guests may have thought I *was* the butler./{L}
425 CP	Edward	23	the Gunnings' parties were like./Their guests will get just enough to make them thirsty;
439 CP	Julia	36	They must be ready for it./Their guests may be arriving at any moment./{R}
439 CP	Lavinia	40	five minutes,/How I could face my guests. I wish it was over./I mean ... I am glad
546 ES	Piggott	12	atmosphere./We don't want our guests to think of themselves as ill,/Though we
546 ES	Piggott	13	as ill,/Though we never have guests who are perfectly well —/Except when
546 ES	Piggott	19	to remember. But, as I was saying,/Guests in perfect health are exceptional/Though
546 ES	Piggott	39	simply 'Mrs. Piggott'/Reassures the guests in one respect;/And calling our nurses
547 ES	Ld Clav	14	Piggott/There may be, among the guests, something worse than Mrs. Piggott./{M}
547 ES	Piggott	22	which Badgley Court/Can offer to guests of the younger generation./When there
547 ES	Piggott	26	the bathing pool./But several of our guests are keen on tennis,/And of course there's
547 ES	Piggott	28	you know enough about the other guests/To know whom *not* to play with. I'll
548 ES	Carghil	16	corner,/And none of the other guests have discovered it./It was clever of you to
554 ES	Piggott	15	me, Mrs. Carghill,/Attending to my guests. I like to feel they *need* me!/{MC} You do
554 ES	Piggott	20	Mrs. Carghill./Two of our very nicest guests!/I just came to see that Lord Claverton
569 ES	Charles	18	has told me about your fellow guests,/Two persons who, she says, claim a very

GUEUX (1)

51 Restaurant		5	ce qu'on appelle le jour de lessive des gueux.'/(Bavard, baveux, à la croupe arrondie,/

GUFFAW (1)

235 Ad-dress		33	his paw,/And he will gambol and guffaw./He's such an easy-going lout,/He'll

GUIDANCE (5)

447 CC	Eggers	21	she believes she has what she calls 'guidance'./{SC} Guidance. That's worse than
447 CC	Claude	22	has what she calls 'guidance'./{SC} Guidance. That's worse than believing in her
447 CC	Claude	23	about that. You can't argue with guidance./But if she appears to be puzzled, or
460 CC	Lady E	21	I said before I left:/'Trust my guidance for once, and engage that young man?'
460 CC	Claude	25	remember./I must have acted on your guidance./{LE} I must explain to you, Mr.

GUIDE (4)

594 Grad 13		3	that follow may'st thou be no less;/A guide to warn them, and a friend to bless/Before
248 MC Tempt2		22	/Whom all acknowledged, should guide the state again./{T} Your meaning?/{T2}
280 MC Priest1		8	You now in Heaven,/Who shall now guide us, protect us, direct us?/After what
462 CC	Claude	19	/And the best one can do is to guide her delusions/In the right direction./{C} It

GUIDE-BOOKS (1)

281 MC Chorus		21	over it, though sightseers come with guide-books looking over it;/From where the

GUIDES (1)

38 Gerontion		36	deceives with whispering ambitions,/Guides us by vanities. Think now/She gives

GUILT (1)

279 MC Knight2		2	/your applause; and if there is any guilt whatever in the matter, you/must share it

GUILTY (9)

301 FR	Chorus	16	/{Ch} Why should we stand here like guilty conspirators, waiting for some revelation/
318 FR	Harry	11	unhappy, and made us/Feel more guilty, and so we misbehaved/Next day at
318 FR	Harry	13	/For punishment made us feel less guilty. Mother/Never punished us, but made us
318 FR	Harry	14	/Never punished us, but made us feel guilty./I think that the things that are taken for
417 CP	Celia	1	But if not anywhere,/Why do I feel guilty at not having found it?/{R} Disillusion
438 CP	Lavinia	26	/Doesn't it help you, that I feel guilty too?/{R} If we all were judged according
517 CC	Colby	10	father: if I accepted that/I should be guilty towards you. I like you too much./You've
567 ES	Monica	26	It's quite impossible./Father with a guilty secret in his past!/I just can't imagine it. {}
568 ES	Ld Clav	4	matter. I heard what you said about guilty secrets./There are many things not crimes,

GUISE (1)

250 MC Tempt3		21	I expected you./{T3} But not in this guise, or for my present purpose./{T} No

GUITAR (1)

601 Nocturne		2	/Romeo, *grand sérieux*, to importune/Guitar and hat in hand, beside the gate/With

GUITERRIEZ (1)

108 Animula		32	silence after the viaticum./Pray for Guiterriez, avid of speed and power,/For

GULF (3)
19 Portrait	60	that you feel,/Sure that across the gulf you reach your hand./You are invulnerable,
39 Gerontion	71	Horn./White feathers in the snow, the Gulf claims,/And an old man driven by the
255 MC Tempt4	14	/And see far off below you, where the gulf is fixed,/Your persecutors, in timeless

GULL (1)
39 Gerontion	69	shuddering Bear/In fractured atoms. Gull against the wind, in the windy straits/Of

GULLET (1)
92 Ash-Wed 3	11	beyond repair,/Or the toothed gullet of an agèd shark./At the first turning of

GULLS (1)
71 WL: DWater	313	a fortnight dead,/Forgot the cry of gulls, and the deep sea swell/And the profit and

GUMBIE (11)
210 Old Gumbie	t	inscrutable singular Name./The Old Gumbie Cat/I have a Gumbie Cat in mind, her
210 Old Gumbie	1	Name./The Old Gumbie Cat/I have a Gumbie Cat in mind, her name is Jennyanydots;
210 Old Gumbie	4	and sits — and that's what makes a Gumbie Cat!/But when the day's hustle and
210 Old Gumbie	6	hustle and bustle is done,/Then the Gumbie Cat's work is but hardly begun./And
210 Old Gumbie	13	crocheting and tatting./I have a Gumbie Cat in mind, her name is Jennyanydots;
210 Old Gumbie	16	and sits — and that's what makes a Gumbie Cat!/But when the day's hustle and
210 Old Gumbie	18	hustle and bustle is done,/Then the Gumbie Cat's work is but hardly begun./As she
210 Old Gumbie	25	fry of lean bacon and cheese./I have a Gumbie Cat in mind, her name is Jennyanydots;
211 Old Gumbie	28	and sits — and that's what makes a Gumbie Cat!/But when the day's hustle and
211 Old Gumbie	30	hustle and bustle is done,/Then the Gumbie Cat's work is but hardly begun./She
211 Old Gumbie	37	created a Beetles' Tattoo./So for Old Gumbie Cats let us now give three cheers —/On

GUN (1)
158 Rock 5	4	Prophet: 'The trowel in hand, and the gun rather loose in the holster.'/Those who sit

GUNNINGS (5)
425 CP	Lavinia	20	/Because they will be going to the Gunnings instead'./{E} I know, that's what we
425 CP	Edward	26	to us early/Will be going on to the Gunnings afterwards,/To make room for those
425 CP	Edward	27	room for those who come from the Gunnings./{L} And if it's very crowded, they
430 CP	Peter	9	—/She's coming on later, after the Gunnings —/So I said, I really must crash in:/
440 CP	Julia	19	Now, Alex. We're going to the Gunnings. {}/[*Exeunt* JULIA, REILLY *and*

GUNNINGS' (2)
425 CP	Edward	22	the time;/But I'd forgotten what the Gunnings' parties were like./Their guests will
426 CP	Julia	31	my dears,/That I have to go on to the Gunnings' party —/And you know what *they*

GUNS (3)
127 Cor1 March	14	rifles and carbines,/102,000 machine guns,/28,000 trench mortars,/53,000 field and
127 Cor1 March	16	mortars,/53,000 field and heavy guns,/I cannot tell how many projectiles, mines
285 FR Charles	25	/Living with horses and dogs and guns/Ever to want to leave England in the

GUS (3)
228 Gus	t	operations: the Napoleon of Crime!/Gus: the Theatre Cat/Gus is the Cat at the
228 Gus	1	of Crime!/Gus: the Theatre Cat/Gus is the Cat at the Theatre Door./His name,
228 Gus	4	that we usually call him just Gus./His coat's very shabby, he's thin as a rake,

GUST (1)
74 WL: Thund	393	/In a flash of lightning. Then a damp gust/Bringing rain/Ganga was sunken, and the

GUSTY (1)
22 Preludes	5	ends of smoky days./And now a gusty shower wraps/The grimy scraps/Of

GUTS (2)
91 Ash-Wed 2	15	gourd./It is this which recovers/My guts the strings of my eyes and the indigestible
270 MC Chorus	21	like a pattern of living worms/In the guts of the women of Canterbury./I have smelt

GUTTER (2)
24 Rhapsody	35	the cat which flattens itself in the gutter,/Slips out its tongue/And devours a
37 Gerontion	14	at evening, poking the peevish gutter./I an old man,/A dull head among windy

GUTTERS (2)
21 Portrait	101	in a glass./My self-possession gutters; we are really in the dark./'For
23 Preludes	32	/And you heard the sparrows in the gutters,/You had such a vision of the street/As

GUTTERSNIPE (1)
478 CC Lucasta	5	me/As your sister! Even if I am a guttersnipe .../{C} You mustn't use such words!

GUY (1)
120 SP Krum	8	when you got a real live Britisher/A guy like Sam to show you around./Sam of

GUZZARD (77)
444 CC	m	8	MULHAMMER/MRS. GUZZARD/Act One/*The Business Room on*
485 CC	Colby	36	aunt./A widow. Her name is Mrs. Guzzard./{LE} Guzzard? Did you say Guzzard?
485 CC	Lady E	37	Her name is Mrs. Guzzard./{LE} Guzzard? Did you say Guzzard? An unusual
485 CC	Lady E	37	Guzzard./{LE} Guzzard? Did you say Guzzard? An unusual name./Guzzard, did you
485 CC	Lady E	38	you say Guzzard? An unusual name./Guzzard, did you say? The name means
485 CC	Lady E	39	name means something to me./Yes. Guzzard. *That* is the name I've been hunting

486 CC	Lady E	12	the only relative you knew/Was Mrs. Guzzard. And you always called her 'aunt'?/{C}
486 CC	Colby	16	.../{C} Her sister — which makes Mrs. Guzzard my aunt./{LE} And are you quite sure
486 CC	Lady E	21	Not if she *is* your aunt. Did Mrs. Guzzard/And Mr. Guzzard — have any
486 CC	Lady E	22	aunt. Did Mrs. Guzzard/And Mr. Guzzard — have any children?/{C} They had no
487 CC	Lady E	22	think so?/{LE} I must see this Mrs. Guzzard. I must confront her./This couldn't
487 CC	Lady E	36	/When the truth dawned on me. Mrs. Guzzard!/Claude, Colby was brought up by a
487 CC	Lady E	37	Colby was brought up by a Mrs. Guzzard./{SC} I know that. But why should
488 CC	Lady E	2	the other name, *Teddington:*/Mrs. Guzzard of Teddington. That was all I knew./
488 CC	Lady E	4	Africa,/And I had lost the name. Mrs. Guzzard./{SC} I'm beginning now to piece it
488 CC	Lady E	8	was a faint echo —/And then Mrs. Guzzard! It must be true./{SC} It is certainly a
488 CC	Lady E	16	be so sceptical!/We must see this Mrs. Guzzard, and get her to confess it./{SC} I'm
488 CC	Claude	17	it./{SC} I'm sorry, Elizabeth. If Mrs. Guzzard comes/To make her confession, it will
489 CC	Claude	20	/Who died when he was born. Mrs. Guzzard brought him up,/And I provided for
489 CC	Claude	22	/I have watched him grow. And Mrs. Guzzard/Knows he is my son./{LE} But where
489 CC	Lady E	30	the sister had a child?/Perhaps Mrs. Guzzard invented the story..../{SC} Why should
489 CC	Lady E	36	had forgotten the name of Mrs. Guzzard,/And I was the mother and the child
489 CC	Lady E	38	and the child was Colby;/And Mrs. Guzzard thought you would be happy/To think
492 CC	Claude	3	the first thing is: we must see Mrs. Guzzard./{LE} Oh Claude! I am terribly sorry
492 CC	Claude	10	Colby to you./But we must see Mrs. Guzzard. I'll arrange to get her here./{LE} And
493 CC	Claude	17	don't want to start/By offending Mrs. Guzzard. That's why I thought/That Eggerson
494 CC	Lady E	10	that he is yours!/So I hope Mrs. Guzzard will say he is your son/And I needn't
496 CC	Lady E	10	/But it doesn't matter what Mrs. Guzzard tells us,/If it satisfies Colby. Whatever
497 CC	Claude	4	/{SC} Eggerson, I'm expecting Mrs. Guzzard./{E} Indeed! Mrs. Guzzard! And why
497 CC	Eggers	5	Mrs. Guzzard./{E} Indeed! Mrs. Guzzard! And why are we expecting her?/{SC} I
497 CC	Claude	7	sure that she knows the name of Mrs. Guzzard./{LE} Mrs. Guzzard, of Teddington./
497 CC	Lady E	8	the name of Mrs. Guzzard./{LE} Mrs. Guzzard, of Teddington./{E} Ah, indeed!/I
497 CC	Claude	12	mentioned the name of his aunt. Mrs. Guzzard./Now she's convinced that Mrs.
497 CC	Claude	13	/Now she's convinced that Mrs. Guzzard/Of Teddington is the name of the
497 CC	Claude	31	And that is why/I have asked Mrs. Guzzard here. *She* doesn't know that./{E} A
497 CC	Eggers	34	we might discover/Another Mrs. Guzzard .../{LE} *Two* Mrs. Guzzards?/{E} I
498 CC	Lady E	4	/{LE} I don't know the address./Mrs. Guzzard of Teddington, that's all I know,/And
498 CC	Eggers	8	for the moment, only one Mrs. Guzzard,/Could there not have been two
498 CC	Eggers	12	only suggesting/That perhaps Mrs. Guzzard made a profession/Of ... looking after
498 CC	Eggers	35	first step must be to question Mrs. Guzzard./{SC} And that's what we are here for.
500 CC	Claude	9	meeting today./We're awaiting Mrs. Guzzard — Colby's aunt./{L} Colby's aunt?
501 CC	Eggers	35	downstairs/And come back after Mrs. Guzzard has left?/{SC} That's not a bad idea. If
503 CC	Eggers	35	now, how soon are we expecting Mrs. Guzzard? {}/[*looking at his watch*]./{SC} She
504 CC	Lucasta	6	/I've just let someone in. It's the Mrs. Guzzard/Whom we are expecting. She looks
504 CC	Eggers	14	Let me go down and explain to Mrs. Guzzard/And then bring her up./{SC} No, I
504 CC	m	24	*Enter* KAGHAN, *escorting* MRS. GUZZARD. *Exit* KAGHAN]/{SC} Good
504 CC	Claude	24	/{SC} Good morning, Mrs. Guzzard. I must apologise:/I'm afraid there has
504 CC	Lady E	32	/{LE} Good morning, Mrs. Guzzard./You don't know me, but I know
505 CC	Claude	1	Eggerson./This is Mr. Eggerson, Mrs. Guzzard./My confidential clerk. That is to say,/
505 CC	Eggers	16	Yes, that is what I should call it, Mrs. Guzzard./I take it, Sir Claude, I should open
505 CC	Eggers	25	you./{E} It's this way, Mrs. Guzzard./It is only recently that Lady Elizabeth
505 CC	Eggers	38	/That happens not infrequently, Mrs. Guzzard./{MG} So I am aware. I have known it
506 CC	Eggers	14	/Until the other day. This son, Mrs. Guzzard,/If he is alive, must be a grown man./I
506 CC	Eggers	30	/{E} That is what impressed her. Mrs. Guzzard/Of Teddington! Lady Elizabeth is
506 CC	Eggers	32	is convinced/That it was a Mrs. Guzzard of Teddington/To whom her new-born
506 CC	Eggers	38	not so many names that sound like Guzzard —/Or if there are, they are equally
506 CC	Eggers	40	are equally uncommon./But, Mrs. Guzzard, this is where you can help us —/Do
507 CC	Eggers	1	us —/Do you know of any other Mrs. Guzzard?/{MG} None./{E} Whether, I mean, in
508 CC	Eggers	3	this as a personal reflection,/Mrs. Guzzard. Far from it. You must make
508 CC	Eggers	16	from another angle,/And ask Mrs. Guzzard what became of the child/She took in,
509 CC	Claude	21	is Barnabas./I must explain this, Mrs. Guzzard./I have a very promising young
510 CC	Eggers	6	and Mrs. Kaghan are still living,/Mrs. Guzzard should be able to identify them./{LE}
510 CC	Claude	18	Sir Claude?/{SC} No, B. It was Mrs. Guzzard who revealed it./This is Mr. Barnabas
510 CC	Claude	20	is Mr. Barnabas Kaghan —/Mrs. Guzzard. And ... my daughter Lucasta./{K} But
510 CC	Kaghan	21	Lucasta./{K} But how did Mrs. Guzzard know my name?/{MG} Were Mr. and
510 CC	Eggers	36	adoptive parents in touch/With Mrs. Guzzard. It's for them to confirm/That they
510 CC	Eggers	37	they took you, as a child, from Mrs. Guzzard,/To whom, it seems, you had first been
512 CC	Lady E	6	wholly unfounded./{LE} Oh, Mrs. Guzzard, I had no suspicions!/I thought there
512 CC	Claude	18	That seems a strange question, Mrs. Guzzard./{MG} I have been asked here to
514 CC	Guzzard	11	was my father, then?/{MG} Herbert Guzzard./You are the son of a disappointed
514 CC	Claude	17	wish, and have no mother./{SC} Mrs. Guzzard, this is perfectly incredible!/You

514 CC   Eggers   20   you have deceived me?/{E} Mrs. Guzzard, can you substantiate this statement?/
514 CC   Guzzard   21   of birth. To Herbert and Sarah Guzzard/A son./{E} And what about your sister
514 CC   Claude   26   it. I simply can't believe it./Mrs. Guzzard, you are inventing this fiction/In
514 CC   Eggers   29   /Not that we doubt your word, Mrs. Guzzard:/But in a matter of such extreme
519 CC   Claude   4   What's that? Oh. Good-bye, Mrs. Guzzard. {}/[*Exit* MRS. GUZZARD]/{SC}
519 CC   m   4   Mrs. Guzzard. {}/[*Exit* MRS. GUZZARD]/{SC} What's happened? Have they

GUZZARD'S (4)
486 CC   Lady E   15   {LE} And as for your mother —/Mrs. Guzzard's sister, I suppose .../{C} Her sister —
486 CC   Lady E   17   And are you quite sure that Mrs. Guzzard's sister —/Who you say was your
489 CC   Claude   19   son?/{SC} Colby is the son of Mrs. Guzzard's sister,/Who died when he was born.
498 CC   Claude   30   /The mother of *my* child was Mrs. Guzzard's sister./She wouldn't dispose of *him*.

GUZZARDS (2)
497 CC   Lady E   35   Mrs. Guzzard .../{LE} *Two* Mrs. Guzzards?/{E} I agree, it is a most uncommon
498 CC   Eggers   7   /That there should be two Mrs. Guzzards in Teddington./But assuming, for the

GYMNASIUMS (1)
300 FRDowning   17   /With all their swimming baths and gymnasiums/There's not even a place where a

GYMNASTIQUE (1)
127 Cor1 March   26   these the Scouts,/And now the *société gymnastique de Poissy*/And now come the Mayor

HA (4)
126 SA   Chorus   8   alive/And perhaps you're dead/Hoo ha ha/Hoo ha ha/Hoo/Hoo/Hoo {}/KNOCK
126 SA   Chorus   8   /And perhaps you're dead/Hoo ha ha/Hoo ha ha/Hoo/Hoo/Hoo {}/KNOCK
126 SA   Chorus   9   perhaps you're dead/Hoo ha ha/Hoo ha ha/Hoo/Hoo/Hoo {}/KNOCK KNOCK
126 SA   Chorus   9   you're dead/Hoo ha ha/Hoo ha ha/Hoo/Hoo/Hoo {}/KNOCK KNOCK

HABIT (3)
214 RTTugger   24   /His disobliging ways are a matter of habit./If you offer him fish then he always
235 Ad-dress   60   taste./(I know a Cat, who makes a habit/Of eating nothing else but rabbit,/And
476 CC Lucasta   14   with people before:/I got into the habit of giving that impression./That's where B.

HABITAT (1)
234 Ad-dress   15   proper names,/Their habits and their habitat:/But/*How would you ad-dress a Cat?*/So

HABITATION (1)
151 Rock 2   7   you may be builded together for a habitation of GOD in the Spirit, the Spirit

HABITS (1)
234 Ad-dress   15   about their proper names,/Their habits and their habitat:/But/*How would you*

HABITUATION (1)
111 Xmas Trees   20   in later experience,/In the bored habituation, the fatigue, the tedium,/The

HAD (465)

HADN'T (6)
424 CP   Edward   15   you ... {}/[*smiling*]./{E} That you hadn't run away?/{L} Now Edward, that's
471 CC   Colby   23   /And then you came to see that you hadn't succeeded./{L} Oh, so I was trying to
483 CC   Lady E   20   working on a company report./{LE} I hadn't reckoned on reports and typewriters/
503 CC   Claude   37   to be here now! It's surprising,/I hadn't been aware how the time was passing,/
556 ES   Michael   33   /Is being blamed for something I hadn't done./I never got over that. If you
570 ES   Ld Clav   32   What would *he* have been/If he hadn't known me? Only a schoolmaster/In an

HAIE (1)
128 Cor1 March   51   /Light/Light/*Et les soldats faisaient la haie? ILS LA FAISAIENT.*/Difficulties of a

HAIL (3)
142 Cape Ann   5   Blackburnian warbler, the shy one. Hail/With shrill whistle the note of the quail,
164 Rock 9   22   mud of words, out of the sleet and hail of verbal imprecisions,/Approximate
235 Ad-dress   35   an easy-going lout,/He'll answer any hail or shout./Again I must remind you that/A

HAIR (24)
14 Prufrock   40   /With a bald spot in the middle of my hair —/(They will say: 'How his hair is growing
14 Prufrock   41   my hair —/(They will say: 'How his hair is growing thin!')/My morning coat, my
15 Prufrock   64   lamplight, downed with light brown hair!)/Is it perfume from a dress/That makes me
16 Prufrock   122   of my trousers rolled./Shall I part my hair behind? Do I dare to eat a peach?/I shall
17 Prufrock   127   on the waves/Combing the white hair of the waves blown back/When the wind
18 Portrait   9   /Transmit the Preludes, through his hair and finger-tips.'/So intimate, this Chopin,
23 Preludes   36   /You curled the papers from your hair,/Or clasped the yellow soles of feet/In the
24 Rhapsody   54   smiles into corners./She smooths the hair of the grass./The moon has lost her
31 Apollinax   15   over a screen/With seaweed in its hair./I heard the beat of centaur's hoofs over
34 Figlia   3   —/Weave, weave the sunlight in your hair —/Clasp your flowers to you with a pained
34 Figlia   7   But weave, weave the sunlight in your hair./So I would have had him leave,/So I
34 Figlia   20   /Many days and many hours:/Her hair over her arms and her arms full of flowers./
42 Swee Erect   7   gales/Which tangle Ariadne's hair/And swell with haste the perjured sails./
42 Swee Erect   13   steam./This withered root of knots of hair/Slitted below and gashed with eyes,/This
62 WL: Burial   38   garden,/Your arms full, and your hair wet, I could not/Speak, and my eyes failed,
64 WL: Chess   108   the firelight, under the brush, her hair/Spread out in fiery points/Glowed into
65 WL: Chess   133   as I am, and walk the street/'With my hair down, so. What shall we do tomorrow?/
69 WL: Fire S   255   room again, alone,/She smoothes her hair with automatic hand,/And puts a record on
73 WL: Thund   377   Unreal/A woman drew her long black hair out tight/And fiddled whisper music on
92 Ash-Wed 3   17   maytime with an antique flute./Blown hair is sweet, brown hair over the mouth blown,
92 Ash-Wed 3   17   flute./Blown hair is sweet, brown hair over the mouth blown,/Lilac and brown
92 Ash-Wed 3   18   the mouth blown,/Lilac and brown hair;/Distraction, music of the flute, stops and
589 Fable   75   ghost then took him roughly by the hair/And bade him come with him, in accents
241 MC   Mess   37   will be deprived of its tail,/A single hair of which becomes a precious relic./He is at

HAIRIER (1)
223 Pekes Pols   55   /You never saw anything fiercer or hairier./And what with the glare of his eyes and

HAIRY (1)
54 Mr E Sun   26   /Along the garden-wall the bees/With hairy bellies pass between/The staminate and

HAKAGAWA (1)
37 Gerontion   26   walked all night in the next room;/By Hakagawa, bowing among the Titians;/By

HALCYON (1)
187 FQ: DrySal   122   wash over it, fogs conceal it;/On a halcyon day it is merely a monument,/In

HALF (30)

19 Portrait	40	by the public clocks./Then sit for half an hour and drink our bocks./Now that
110 Marina	27	September./Made this unknowing, half conscious, unknown, my own./The
150 Rock 1	104	*to two men,/To two women one half pint of bitter/Ale. In this land/No man has*
161 Rock 7	35	*to two men,/To two women one half pint of bitter/Ale....*/CHORUS:/What does
166 Rock 10	7	the World?/The great snake lies ever half awake, at the bottom of the pit of the
190 FQ: DrySal	219	thought and action./The hint half guessed, the gift half understood, is
190 FQ: DrySal	219	action./The hint half guessed, the gift half understood, is Incarnation./Here the
193 FQ: Little	95	/Whom I had known, forgotten, half recalled/Both one and many; in the brown
226 Macavity	16	a snake;/And when you think he's half asleep, he's always wide awake./Macavity,
602 Humoresque	9	/Pinched in a comic, dull grimace;/Half bullying, half imploring air,/Mouth twisted
602 Humoresque	9	a comic, dull grimace;/Half bullying, half imploring air,/Mouth twisted to the latest
264 MC Priest2	28	what is to-day? For the day is half gone./{P1} To-day, what is to-day? but
290 FR Amy	3	she dragged him/All over Europe and half round the world/To expensive hotels and
292 FR Ivy	36	go to rack and ruin,/And he's nearly half blind. I've spoken to your mother/Time
300 FRDowning	33	/While I took my turn about, for near half an hour/He stayed there alone, looking
347 FRDowning	3	reason/We was off tonight. In fact, I half expected it,/So I had the car all ready. You
368 CP Alex	27	rice and a little dried fish/I can make half a dozen dishes. Don't say a word./I shall
376 CP Edward	14	it's ruined the saucepan too.{E} *And* half a dozen eggs:/I wanted one for breakfast. A
384 CP Edward	14	matter. It will be too late./{E} I have half a mind to change my mind now/To show
403 CP Reilly	12	power — until you came to grief./Half of the harm that is done in this world/Is
424 CP Lavinia	10	/{L} Nothing more, I think, till half past six. {}/[*Exit* CATERER'S MAN]/
426 CP Edward	5	/No one will be coming for at least half an hour;/So just stretch out./{L} You must
434 CP Alex	8	station, in a Christian village;/And half the natives were dying of pestilence./They
450 CC Eggers	30	was afraid I'd miss you./{E} I'm off in half an hour, Mr. Simpkins./{SC} I'll leave you
476 CC Lucasta	16	me —/He fosters the impression. He half believes in it./But he knows all about me,
481 CC Lady E	28	early:/Most of its patrons dine at half past six./They have the most delicious
531 ES Ld Clav	14	Would have occupied a column and a half/With an inset, a portrait taken twenty years
531 ES Ld Clav	16	ago./In five years' time, it will be the half of that;/In ten years' time, a paragraph./{C}
561 ES Ld Clav	27	trying to help him,/And to meet him half way. I have made him an offer/Which he
574 ES Michael	33	of view. What's the use of chasing/Half round the world, for the same sort of job/

HALF-A-DOZEN (1)

372 CP Alex 15	But of course/I was lucky to find half-a-dozen eggs./{E} What! You used all those

HALF-BOTTLE (2)

377 CP Julia 22	I found some champagne —/Only a half-bottle, to be sure,/And of course it isn't
383 CP Edward 14	—/But why did she say that it was a half-bottle?/It's one of my best: and I have no

HALF-BOTTLES (1)

383 CP Edward 15	/It's one of my best: and I have no half-bottles./Well, I hoped that you would drink

HALF-BROTHER (2)

500 CC Eggers 1	explained. Colby is your brother./{E} Half-brother, Miss Angel./{SC} Yes,
500 CC Claude 2	Half-brother, Miss Angel./{SC} Yes, half-brother./{L} What do you mean?/{SC}

HALF-CRAZED (1)

438 CP Edward 24	/Is greater than that of a band of half-crazed savages./{L} Oh, Edward, I knew! I

HALF-DESERTED (1)

13 Prufrock 4	a table;/Let us go, through certain half-deserted streets,/The muttering retreats/Of

HALF-FORMED (1)

69 WL: Fire S 251	departed lover;/Her brain allows one half-formed thought to pass:/'Well now that's

HALF-HEARD (2)

198 FQ: Little 252	because not looked for/But heard, half-heard, in the stillness/Between two waves of
309 FR Harry 33	waterfall in the forest,/Inaccessible, half-heard./And I hear your voice as in the

HALF-LOOK (1)

187 FQ: DrySal 104	/Of recorded history, the backward half-look/Over the shoulder, towards the

HALF-PAST (3)

24 Rhapsody 13	a madman shakes a dead geranium./Half-past one,/The street-lamp sputtered,/The
24 Rhapsody 33	/Hard and curled and ready to snap,/Half-past two,/The street-lamp said,/'Remark
24 Rhapsody 46	the end of a stick which I held him./Half-past three,/The lamp sputtered,/The lamp

HALF-TERM (1)

318 FR Harry 9	which she had not seen us/Except at half-term, and seeing us then/Only seemed to

HALL (11)

38 Gerontion 29	Fräulein von Kulp/Who turned in the hall, one hand on the door. Vacant shuttles/
217 Jellicles 32	will practise a caper or two in the hall./If it happens the sun is shining bright/You
225 Mr Mistoff 53	for hours,/While he was asleep in the hall./And not long ago this phenomenal Cat/
227 Macavity 29	/There may be a scrap of paper in the hall or on the stair —/But it's useless to
238 MC m 9	/*The scene is the Archbishop's Hall, on December 2nd, 1170*/PART II/THREE
238 MC m 16	/*The first scene is in the Archbishop's Hall,/the second scene is in the Cathedral, on*

246 MC Templ1   37   /Fluting in the meadows, viols in the hall,/Laughter and apple-blossom floating on
256 MC Chorus   32   door?/{C} Does the torch flame in the hall, the candle in the room?/{3P} Does the
272 MC Chorus   19   the doorway,/More than fury in the hall./The agents of hell disappear, the human,
398 CP   Lavinia   /Meanwhile, my luggage is in the hall downstairs:/Will you get the porter to fetch
524 ES   3m   1   *o'clock in the afternoon./[Voices in the hall]*/{C} Is your father at home to-day?/{M}

HALLOWS (1)
239 MC Chorus   14   fire and remembered the Saints at All Hallows,/Remembered the martyrs and saints

HALLS (1)
228 Gus   17   he likes to relate his success on the Halls,/Where the Gallery once gave him seven

HALLUCINATION (1)
415 CP   Celia   36   word for it./It must be some kind of hallucination;/Yet, at the same time, I'm

HALTING (1)
161 Rock 7   25   way that was lit by the light;/Often halting, loitering, straying, delaying, returning,

HAM (2)
55 Mr E Sun   29   of the epicene./Sweeney shifts from ham to ham/Stirring the water in his bath./The
55 Mr E Sun   29   epicene./Sweeney shifts from ham to ham/Stirring the water in his bath./The masters

HAMLET (1)
587 Fable   7   on all travelers his tax;/Nearby this hamlet was a monastery/Inhabited by a band of

HAMLET (1) [*Proper name*]
16 Prufrock   111   I meant, at all.'/No! I am not Prince Hamlet, nor was meant to be;/Am an attendant

HAMMER (1)
241 MC Priest3   21   can be found/To grow between the hammer and the anvil?/{P2} Tell us,/Are the old

HAMMERING (1)
19 Portrait   33 brain a dull tom-tom begins/Absurdly hammering a prelude of its own,/Capricious

HAMMERSMITH (1)
212 Growltiger   10   knew something of his fame;/At Hammersmith and Putney people shuddered at

HAMPSHIRE (5)
138 New Hamp   t   be open or shut)./Landscapes/New Hampshire/Children's voices in the orchard/
357 CP   Julia   24   as if I knew/All about that aunt in Hampshire./{E} Hampshire?/{J} Didn't you say
357 CP Edward 25   about that aunt in Hampshire./{E} Hampshire?/{J} Didn't you say Hampshire?/{E}
357 CP   Julia   26   /{E} Hampshire?/{J} Didn't you say Hampshire?/{E} No, I didn't say Hampshire./{J}
357 CP Edward 27   say Hampshire?/{E} No, I didn't say Hampshire./{J} Did you say Hampstead?/{E}

HAMPSTEAD (3)
174 FQ: BurntN 114   sweeps the gloomy hills of London./Hampstead and Clerkenwell, Camden and
357 CP   Julia   28   say Hampshire./{J} Did you say Hampstead?/{E} No, I didn't say Hampstead./
357 CP Edward 29   say Hampstead?/{E} No, I didn't say Hampstead./{J} But she must live somewhere./

HAMPTON (1)
212 Growltiger   26   had disappeared,/For to the Bell at Hampton he had gone to wet his beard;/And his

HAND (42)
19 Portrait   60   that across the gulf you reach your hand./You are invulnerable, you have no
21 Portrait   116 Should die and leave me sitting pen in hand/With the smoke coming down above the
23 Preludes   52   /Infinitely suffering thing./Wipe your hand across your mouth, and laugh;/The worlds
24 Rhapsody   38   a morsel of rancid butter.'/So the hand of the child, automatic,/Slipped out and
24 Rhapsody   57   smallpox cracks her face,/Her hand twists a paper rose,/That smells of dust
34 Figlia   16   faithless as a smile and shake of the hand./She turned away, but with the autumn
38 Gerontion   29   von Kulp/Who turned in the hall, one hand on the door. Vacant shuttles/Weave the
41 Burb Blei   26   /A meagre, blue-nailed, phthisic hand/To climb the waterstair. Lights, lights,/She
69 WL: Fire S 255 She smoothes her hair with automatic hand,/And puts a record on the gramophone./
74 WL: Thund 419   The boat responded/Gaily, to the hand expert with sail and oar/The sea was calm,
84 Hollow Men 43   /The supplication of a dead man's hand/Under the twinkle of a fading star./Is it
105 Song Sime   5   /Like a feather on the back of my hand./Dust in sunlight and memory in corners/
107 Animula   1   salvation./Animula/'Issues from the hand of God, the simple soul'/To a flat world of
107 Animula   24   *Britannica.*/Issues from the hand of time the simple soul/Irresolute and
157 Rock 4   19   must build/With the sword in one hand and the trowel in the other./O Lord,
158 Rock 5   4 Nehemiah the Prophet: 'The trowel in hand, and the gun rather loose in the holster.'/
178 FQ: ECoker 33   /Holding eche other by the hand or the arm/Whiche betokeneth concorde.
193 FQ: Little   67 dead sand/Contending for the upper hand./The parched eviscerate soil/Gapes at the
601 Nocturne   2   to importune/Guitar and hat in hand, beside the gate/With Juliet, in the usual
603 Spleen   13   and bland,/Waits, hat and gloves in hand,/Punctiliously of tie and suit/(Somewhat
239 MC Chorus   12   off a muddy boot and stretches his hand to the fire,/The New Year waits, destiny
239 MC Chorus   14   coming./Who has stretched out his hand to the fire and remembered the Saints at
239 MC Chorus   16   wait? and who shall/Stretch out his hand to the fire, and deny his master? who shall
240 MC Chorus   17   and saints./Destiny waits in the hand of God, shaping the still unshapen:/I have
240 MC Chorus   19 shaft of sunlight./Destiny waits in the hand of God, not in the hands of statesmen/
256 MC Chorus   8   dew that forms on the back of my hand?/{4T} Man's life is a cheat and a

266 MC Knights   18   /You had your honours all from his hand; from him you had the power, the seal and
272 MC Chorus   11   *a choir in the distance*]./{C} Numb the hand and dry the eyelid,/Still the horror, but
276 MC Chorus   5   /But the talk in the market-place, the hand on the broom,/The night-time heaping of
280 MC Priest3   23   the dead breath makes numb the hand, makes dull the brain;/Find an oasis in the
281 MC Chorus   14   in word and in deed./Even with the hand to the broom, the back bent in laying the
282 MC Chorus   10   than the justice of God;/Who fear the hand at the window, the fire in the thatch, the
298 FR Charles   2   taking hold of anything that comes to hand./If you are interested in helping Harry/
332 FR Agatha   28   to burn. When you stretch out your hand/To the flames. They only come once,/
411 CP   m 35   *his cheque-book*. REILLY *raises his hand*]/{R} My secretary will send you my
447 CC Claude   16   you./She thinks she ought to have a hand in the choosing;/And besides, she is
450 CC Claude   16   understand nobody,/But on the other hand never to be sure/That they don't
459 CC Claude   16   /But I want to have him closer at hand —/You know what a bother it's been for
481 CC Lady E   38   /And ask for the table in the left hand corner:/It has the best waitress. Good
493 CC Claude   13   That's a good idea./{SC} On the other hand,/We mustn't look like a couple of
565 ES Monica   6   /Michael, as you're staying so close at hand/Will you come back in the morning? After
583 ES Monica   14   will go to him together. He is close at hand,/Though he has gone too far to return to
HANDFUL (3)
 61 WL: Burial   30   to meet you;/I will show you fear in a handful of dust./*Frisch weht der Wind/Der*
368 CP   Alex   26   do. I learned that in the East./With a handful of rice and a little dried fish/I can make
434 CP Edward   27   ... Of all people .../{E} And just for a handful of plague-stricken natives/Who would
HANDICAP (1)
561 ES Michael   17   would./*You* didn't suffer from the handicap that I've had./Your father was rich,
HANDKERCHIEFS (1)
 67 WL: Fire S   178   empty bottles, sandwich papers,/Silk handkerchiefs, cardboard boxes, cigarette ends/
HANDLE (5)
 20 Portrait   86   ease/I mount the stairs and turn the handle of the door/And feel as if I had mounted
589 Fable   87   straightway put to his name the handle/Of Saint, thereby rebuking all such
397 CP Edward   2   not open it. I could not touch the handle./Why could I not walk out of my prison?
431 CP Peter   32   /I ought to know the best way to handle a duke./Besides that, we've got the
516 CC Claude   21   The exhilaration of finding you could handle/Matters you would have thought so
HANDLED (1)
264 MC Priest2   10   with our eyes, and our hands have handled/Of the word of life; that which we have
HANDLES (1)
464 CC Claude   3   I loved the material that the potter handles./Most people think that a sculptor or a
HANDS (43)
 14 Prufrock   29   time for all the works and days of hands/That lift and drop a question on your
 19 Portrait   45   /What life is, you who hold it in your hands';/(Slowly twisting the lilac stalks)/'You let
 20 Portrait   87   /And feel as if I had mounted on my hands and knees./'And so you are going
 22 Preludes   21   time resumes,/One thinks of all the hands/That are raising dingy shades/In a
 23 Preludes   38   of feet/In the palms of both soiled hands./His soul stretched tight across the skies/
 32 Hysteria   5   An elderly waiter with trembling hands/was hurriedly spreading a pink and white
 37 Gerontion   24   by Mr. Silvero/With caressing hands, at Limoges/Who walked all night in the
 38 Gerontion   42   passion. Gives too soon/Into weak hands, what's thought can be dispensed with/
 42 Swee Erect   9   sails./Morning stirs the feet and hands/(Nausicaa and Polypheme)./Gesture of
 68 WL: Fire S 240   he assaults at once;/Exploring hands encounter no defence;/His vanity requires
 70 WL: Fire S 303   /The broken fingernails of dirty hands./My people humble people who expect/
 74 WL: Thund   422   beating obedient/To controlling hands/I sat upon the shore/Fishing, with the
103 Journ Magi   27   with vine-leaves over the lintel,/Six hands at an open door dicing for pieces of
127 Cor1 March   30   no interrogation in his eyes/Or in the hands, quiet over the horse's neck,/And the eyes
149 Rock 1   81   *will build with new bricks/There are hands and machines/And clay for new brick/And*
149 Rock 1   95   /*No man has hired us/With pocketed hands/And lowered faces/We stand about in open*
151 Rock 2   6   restore turn out the palms of their hands, or look in vain towards foreign lands for
154 Rock 3   6   proper inventions:/I have given you hands which you turn from worship,/I have
157 Rock 4   17   /When he and his men laid their hands to rebuilding the wall./So they built as
161 Rock 7   31   have we to do/But stand with empty hands and palms turned upwards/In an age
181 FQ: ECoker 151   part;/Beneath the bleeding hands we feel/The sharp compassion of the
196 FQ: Little 211   is the unfamiliar Name/Behind the hands that wove/The intolerable shirt of flame/
599 On a Port   10   /Disturb her lips, or move the slender hands;/Her dark eyes keep their secrets hid from
605 Narcissus   15   pointed corners of his eyes/And his hands aware of the pointed tips of his fingers./
240 MC Chorus   19   waits in the hand of God, not in the hands of statesmen/Who do, some well, some
240 MC Chorus   21   /Having their aims which turn in their hands in the pattern of time./Come, happy
246 MC Thomas   13   treason,/Made them hold their hands. So for the time/We are unmolested./{P1}
256 MC Chorus   35   by the gate?/{C} Death has a hundred hands and walks by a thousand ways./{3P} He
264 MC Priest2   10   we have seen with our eyes, and our hands have handled/Of the word of life; that
272 MC Thomas   9   force him! drag him!/{T} Keep your hands off!/{3P} To vespers! Hurry. {}/[*They drag*

281 MC	Chorus	15	toil, the knee bent under sin, the hands to the face under fear, the head bent
316 FR	Charles	7	/{C} If the matter were left in my hands, I think I could manage the situation. {}/
336 FR	Harry	5	/From the ring of ghosts with joined hands, from the pursuers,/And come into a
342 FR	Amy	9	such a weakling as his father/In the hands of any unscrupulous woman./*I* have no
404 CP	Edward	20	I was capable of making. I am in your hands./I cannot take any further responsibility./
407 CP	Reilly	23	/But when you put yourselves into hands like mine/You surrender a great deal
431 CP	Peter	12	over/Just for a week. And I have my hands full/I'm going down tonight, to Boltwell./
454 CC	Kaghan	10	as nails. Now I'll take her off your hands./I'll show you how it's done. Come along,
489 CC	Lady E	34	that. But she had a child/Left on her hands. The father had died/And she'd never
499 CC	Lucasta	26	point of view. To get me off your hands./Oh, I know what a nuisance you've
530 ES	Ld Clav	38	directors/Saying 'we must put our hands in our pockets/To double this collection
547 ES	Piggott	3	now I must fly. I've so much on my hands!/But before I go, just let me tuck you up
566 ES	Ld Clav	3	suffer the same humiliations/At the hands of the same master. But have I still time?/

HANDSOME (1)
71 WL: DWater	321		/Consider Phlebas, who was once handsome and tall as you./What the Thunder

HANDSOMELY (1)
29 Aunt Helen		8	had occurred before./The dogs were handsomely provided for,/But shortly

HANDWRITING (1)
553 ES	Carghil	33	And I like to read them/In your own handwriting./{LC} And have you shown these

HANDY (1)
128 Corl	March	47	away that sausage,/It'll come in handy. He's artful. Please, will you/Give us a

HANG (3)
56 Swee Night		2	spreads his knees/Letting his arms hang down to laugh,/The zebra stripes along his
446 CC	Claude	5	/But I'm satisfied that he's getting the hang of things,/And I think he's beginning to
542 ES	Gomez	1	though I dare say your caller/Could hang on for another quarter of an hour./{LC}

HANGED (1)
62 WL: Burial		55	forbidden to see. I do not find/The Hanged Man. Fear death by water./I see crowds

HANGINGS (1)
305 FR	Harry	27	room is quite unchanged:/The same hangings ... the same pictures ... even the table,/

HANGMAN'S (1)
126 SA	Chorus	5	turning of a lock/for you know the hangman's waiting for you./And perhaps you're

HANGS (1)
26 Rhapsody		76	/The bed is open; the tooth-brush hangs on the wall,/Put your shoes at the door,

HAPPEN (34)
148 Rock 1		43	happened/And who sees what is to happen./The Witness. The Critic. The Stranger./
202 War Poetry		14	seems just possible that a poem might happen/To a very young man: but a poem is not
243 MC	Chorus	22	world./We do not wish anything to happen./Seven years we have lived quietly,/
247 MC	Thomas	15	to generation/The same things happen again and again./Men learn little from
275 MC	Chorus	28	blood?/We did not wish anything to happen./We understood the private catastrophe,
277 MC	Knight3	18	of state, that he never meant this to happen; and/there is going to be an awful row;
279 MC	Knight4	35	That was just what he did not wish to happen; he/insisted, while we were still inflamed
299 FR	Downing	40	as if he thought something might happen./{C} What sort of thing?/{Do} Well, I
315 FR	Chorus	32	there always./And the past is about to happen, and the future was long since settled./
317 FR	Warburt	14	/For something that is very likely to happen./{H} O God, man, the things that are
317 FR	Harry	15	man, the things that are going to happen/Have already happened./{W} That is in
321 FR	Harry	17	either of my brothers. Nothing can happen —/If Sergeant Winchell is real. But
333 FR	Harry	14	And have me. That is the way things happen./Everything is true in a different sense,/
335 FR	Harry	34	our phantasms/And what did not happen is as true as what did happen/O my
335 FR	Harry	34	did not happen is as true as what did happen/O my dear, and you walked through the
337 FR	Agatha	35	nothing. I only say what I know must happen./{A} You only say what you intended to
337 FR	Amy	36	You only say what you intended to happen./{H} Oh, mother,/This is not to do with
345 FR	Harry	10	in any danger/Of such accidents as happen to Arthur and John:/Take care of *them.*
346 FR	Downing	29	when something's going to happen,/And it seems quite natural, being his
347 FR	Ivy	20	after what we know of what did happen,/Do you think Amy ought to see it?/{V}
374 CP	Edward	13	has happened, or what is going to happen;/And to try to understand it, I want to
382 CP	Celia	32	I desperately wanted to exist./It must happen somewhere — but what, and where is it?
388 CP	Edward	2	have a new job./{E} And how did that happen, overnight?/{P} Why, it's a man Alex
392 CP	Lavinia	23	by instinct when something's going to happen./Trust her not to miss any awkward
456 CC	Eggers	40	by this plane./{E} Oh, that could happen. She sometimes gets lost,/Or loses her
464 CC	Colby	24	passion for ... ceramics, how did it happen/That you never made it your
467 CC	Colby	1	/Of father and son. It must often happen./And the reconcilement, after his death,/
472 CC	Colby	2	/You're afraid of what would happen if you left things to themselves./You
492 CC	Claude	8	could have known what was going to happen,/I would gladly have surrendered Colby
505 CC	Guzzard	39	So I am aware. I have known it to happen./{E} — Who was taken charge of by the
517 CC	Eggers	25	If anyone will take me./{E} If so, I happen to know of a vacancy/In my own

527 ES	Charles	10	things have happened./{C} That won't happen to me. {}/[*Knock. Enter* LAMBERT]/
548 ES	Carghil	28	I couldn't believe that it would really happen!/And now I'm sitting here talking to
549 ES	Carghil	25	think why, but it's the way things happen./I said 'there's a man I could follow

HAPPENED (81)

148 Rock 1		42	Stranger./He who has seen what has happened/And who sees what is to happen./The
161 Rock 7		26	way./But it seems that something has happened that has never happened before:
161 Rock 7		26	has happened that has never happened before: though we know not just
161 Rock 7		27	but for no god; and this has never happened before/That men both deny gods and
222 Pekes Pols		12	I shall speak/Almost nothing had happened for nearly a week/(And that's a long
222 Pekes Pols		18	the street/When a Peke and a Pollicle happened to meet./They did not advance, or
278 MC Knight2		19	rank of the Civil Service. And what happened? The moment/that Becket, at the
288 FR	Agatha	14	/After eight years and all that has happened/To come back to Wishwood./{G}
289 FR	Gerald	7	I say!/Make him feel that what has happened doesn't matter./He's taken his
290 FR	Amy	18	Please behave only/As if nothing had happened in the last eight years./{G} That will
293 FR	Harry	15	all of you try to talk as if nothing had happened,/And yet you are talking of nothing
293 FR	Harry	27	/Is only events: not what has happened./And people to whom nothing has
293 FR	Harry	28	people to whom nothing has ever happened/Cannot understand the unimportance
293 FR	Gerald	30	Well, you can't say that nothing has happened to *me*./I started as a youngster on the
293 FR	Harry	37	are all people/To whom nothing has happened, at most a continual impact/Of
295 FR	Charles	9	/Of course we know what really happened, we read it in the papers —/No need
295 FR	Harry	21	so dreadful that it couldn't have happened,/Because you could not bear it. So
299 FR Downing		3	if I may say so, Sir,/After what happened./{C} Quite so, quite./Downing, you
308 FR	Harry	21	/And start again as if nothing had happened,/Isn't that all folly? It's like the
313 FR	Amy	27	/{A} It is most vexing. What can have happened?/I suppose it's the fog that is holding
315 FR	Chorus	30	/{Ch} I am afraid of all that has happened, and of all that is to come;/Of the
317 FR	Harry	16	are going to happen/Have already happened./{W} That is in a sense true,/But
321 FR Warburt		14	what he wants. I hope nothing has happened/To either of your brothers./{H}
321 FR	Harry	16	your brothers./{H} Nothing can have happened/To either of my brothers. Nothing
321 FR	Harry	20	be worse than anything that has happened./What if *you* saw him, and .../{W}
321 FR Warburt		23	together./Something may have happened to one of your brothers. {}/[*Enter*
325 FR	Ivy	17	/We must carry on as if nothing had happened,/And have the cake and presents./{G}
333 FR	Agatha	10	other. But I wanted you!/If that had happened, I knew I should have carried/Death
335 FR	Agatha	40	seen the first stage: relief from what happened/Is also relief from that unfulfilled
344 FR	Violet	11	to me quite unaccountable./What *has* happened, Amy?/{A} Harry is going away — to
344 FR	Charles	14	But ...!/{C} A missionary! that's never happened in our family!/And why in such a
344 FR	Charles	31	going./{C} Such a thing/Has never happened in our family./{V} I cannot
345 FR	Violet	31	not understand/A single thing that's happened. {}/[*Exeunt* AMY, VIOLET,
346 FR Downing		23	credit it,/I've always said, whatever happened to his Lordship/Was just a kind of
347 FR	Ivy	29	I might be allowed/To know what has happened./{A} Agatha! Mary! come!/The clock
353 CP	Julia	9	{J} But I'm still waiting to know what happened./I know it started as a story about
354 CP	Julia	24	Verinder/Who was there when it happened. {}/[*To the* UNIDENTIFIED
364 CP	Edward	6	get her back, to find out what has happened/During the five years that we've been
370 CP	Edward	4	of intellectual interests./{E} And what happened after that?/{P} Oh, nothing happened.
370 CP	Peter	5	happened after that?/{P} Oh, nothing happened./But I thought that she really cared
371 CP	Edward	7	been telling you/What would have happened to you with Celia/In another six
371 CP	Peter	17	at least to make her tell me/What has happened, in her terms. Until I know that/I
374 CP	Celia	5	a short while ago./{C} If there had happened to be anyone with you/I was going to
374 CP	Celia	8	me./Edward, I understand what has happened/But I could not understand your
374 CP	Edward	12	can you say you understand what has happened?/*I* don't know what has happened, or
374 CP	Edward	13	has happened?/*I* don't know what has happened, or what is going to happen;/And to
375 CP	Celia	10	kind of a trap it is./{C} Then what has happened? {}/[*The telephone rings*]/{E} Damn
377 CP	Celia	3	{}/[*Exit* JULIA]/{C} But what has happened, Edward? What has happened?/{E}
377 CP	Celia	3	has happened, Edward? What has happened?/{E} Lavinia is coming back, I think./
396 CP	Lavinia	12	experience/And then it never happened. I wonder now/How you could have
401 CP	Edward	31	/Before I began to tell you, what had happened?/{R} That is so, that is so. But all in
403 CP	Reilly	22	capacity./Try to explain what has happened since I left you./{E} I see now why I
408 CP	Edward	23	/This is the best joke that ever happened./{L} I never knew you had such a
414 CP	Celia	7	carry on./No. I mean that what has happened has made me aware/That I've always
417 CP	Celia	9	it may have no reality./For what happened is remembered like a dream/In which
434 CP	Peter	35	two years, and I don't know what happened/To Celia, during those two years./
436 CP	Lavinia	21	/While Alex was telling us what had happened to Celia/I was looking at your face.
440 CP	Lavinia	30	much I like it./{L} But so much has happened since then. And besides,/One
457 CC	Claude	31	heavens, Eggerson, what *can* have happened?/{E} It's perfectly amazing. Let *me* go
458 CC	Claude	7	/{SC} Elizabeth!/What on earth has happened?/{E} Lady Elizabeth! This is most
461 CC	Claude	30	/As you gather, such a thing never happened before./So the meeting didn't go quite

471 CC	Colby	29	creation/Rather than wait to see what happened./I hope you don't mind: I know it
472 CC	Colby	1	Because you couldn't wait to see what happened./You're afraid of what would happen
488 CC	Claude	11	But I'm afraid, Elizabeth,/What has happened is that, brooding on the past,/You
490 CC	Lady E	4	then./That is the way it must have happened./Oh, Claude, you know I'm rather
490 CC	Claude	7	Do try to help me./{SC} It could have happened. But I'm sure it didn't./{LE} Oh,
497 CC	Eggers	37	name,/But stranger things have happened./{LE} And both in Teddington?/{E} I
498 CC	Lady E	27	mixed./{LE} That seems to be what happened. And now we must find out/What
500 CC	Claude	39	to Colby./{SC} I don't know what's happened, but nevertheless/I'm sure that you
519 CC	Claude	5	MRS. GUZZARD]/{SC} What's happened? Have they gone? Is Colby coming
527 ES	Monica	9	changed your mind. Such things have happened./{C} That won't happen to me. {}/
536 ES	Gomez	12	wasn't interested/In anything that happened four thousand miles away,/Only
537 ES	Ld Clav	34	/None whatever, for what happened to you later./{G} You led me on at
539 ES	Gomez	32	very successful./What would have happened to me, I wonder,/If I had never met
540 ES	Ld Clav	18	Oxford? *You* were driving./{LC} That happened several times./{G} One time in
541 ES	Gomez	2	of San Marco/About something that happened so many years ago?/What damages
555 ES	Monica	19	afraid that something unpleasant has happened./{LC} Was he driving his car?/{M}
557 ES	Ld Clav	6	someone else./Just tell me what's happened./{Mi} Well, I've lost my job./{LC} The
558 ES	Michael	36	to pass the time. It would never have happened/If only I'd been given some
561 ES	Monica	23	to Father like that?/Father! What has happened? Why do you look so angry?/I know
568 ES	Charles	14	Sir,/Or rather, which I wish had never happened./I can think of things you don't yet

HAPPENING (6)

271 MC	Thomas	30	remember where you are, and what is happening;/No life here is sought for but mine,/
348 FR	Chorus	30	know much about thinking./What is happening outside of the circle?/And what is the
348 FR	Chorus	31	circle?/And what is the meaning of happening?/What ambush lies beyond the
362 CP	Reilly	25	but no longer a person./It's always happening, because one is an object/As well as a
414 CP	Celia	4	course that's something that's always happening/To all sorts of people, and they get
474 CC	Lucasta	27	square./But I can't imagine that happening to you./You seem so secure, to me.

HAPPENS (16)

217 Jellicles		31	/Jellicle Cats (as I said) are small;/If it happens to be a stormy night/They will practise
217 Jellicles		33	a caper or two in the hall./If it happens the sun is shining bright/You would
294 FR	Harry	9	/Is unredeemable. As for what happens —/Of the past you can only see what is
324 FR	Violet	23	John./{V} And if you don't care what happens to John,/You might show some
329 FR	Chorus	2	the future to hear it./And whatever happens began in the past, and presses hard on
342 FR	Mary	27	is better;/I do not care what happens to me,/But Harry must not go. Cousin
346 FR	Downing	28	inside them/That accounts for what happens to them. You get a feeling of it./So I
348 FR	Chorus	10	in the brain./We do not like what happens when we are awake, because it too
348 FR	Chorus	10	because it too closely resembles what happens when we are asleep./We understand the
381 CP	Celia	20	Edward, please believe that whatever happens/I shall not loathe you. I shall only feel
437 CP	Reilly	21	itself at once in a picture./That happens to me, sometimes. So it was obvious/
475 CC	Colby	10	understand the change as soon as it happens,/Though you couldn't have predicted
488 CC	Claude	28	now it seems a silly thought .../What happens is so like what one had planned for,/
496 CC	Lady E	11	tells us,/If it satisfies Colby. Whatever happens/He shall be *our* son. {}/[*A knock on the*
505 CC	Eggers	38	the circumstances, acknowledge./That happens not infrequently, Mrs. Guzzard./{MG}
534 ES	Gomez	22	out sooner or later./And then what happens? You have to move on./That wouldn't

HAPPIER (2)

362 CP	Edward	10	/I never thought I should be any happier/With another person. Why speak of
515 CC	Claude	39	for the better?/Perhaps we'll be happier together if you think/I am not your

HAPPINESS (16)

148 Rock 1		51	/The things that men count for happiness, seeking/The good deeds that lead to
156 Rock 3		69	many books as possible,/Plotting of happiness and flinging empty bottles,/Turning
186 FQ: DrySal		92	disowning the past./The moments of happiness — not the sense of well-being,/
186 FQ: DrySal		98	any meaning/We can assign to happiness. I have said before/That the past
290 FR	Amy	16	And I hope we can contrive his future happiness./Do not discuss his absence. Please
318 FR	Warburt	21	with/Now, is your mother's happiness in the future,/For the time she has to
334 FR	Harry	1	but now/I feel quite happy, as if happiness/Did not consist in getting what one
341 FR	Amy	30	abandon his duty, his family and his happiness?/Who has planned his good? is it you
341 FR	Amy	37	I felt assured of his settlement and happiness,/You who took my husband, now
370 CP	Peter	9	it;/I had never imagined such quiet happiness./I had only experienced excitement,
379 CP	Celia	25	world of *ours*,/Where the word 'happiness' had a different meaning/Or so it
381 CP	Edward	25	No — not happy: or, if there is any happiness,/Only the happiness of knowing/That
381 CP	Edward	26	or, if there is any happiness,/Only the happiness of knowing/That the misery does not
501 CC	Eggers	28	occasion/To wish Miss Angel every happiness./And I'm sure she will be happy. Mr.
503 CC	Lucasta	11	you will accept me as a sister/For the happiness that relationship may bring us/In
581 ES	Ld Clav	27	/I have been brushed by the wing of happiness./And I am happy, Monica, that you

HAPPY (54)

240 MC	Chorus	22	hands in the pattern of time./Come, happy December, who shall observe you, who
242 MC	Mess	16	he meant,/But no one considers it a happy prognostic. {}/[*Exit*]/{P1} I fear for the
251 MC	Tempt3	30	{T} To what does this lead?/{T3} To a happy coalition/Of intelligent interests./{T} But
257 MC	Chorus	6	in his groin./{C} We have not been happy, my Lord, we have not been too happy./
257 MC	Chorus	6	my Lord, we have not been too happy./We are not ignorant women, we know
292 FR	Harry	13	them!/Why here? why here?/Many happy returns of the day, mother./Aunt Ivy,
306 FR	Harry	23	no escape. Tell me,/Were you ever happy here, as a child at Wishwood?/{M}
306 FR	Mary	24	here, as a child at Wishwood?/{M} Happy? not really, though I never knew why:/It
306 FR	Mary	26	be my own fault,/And never to be happy was always to be naughty./But there were
306 FR	Harry	32	/At least, I was./{H} Why were we not happy?/{M} Well, it all seemed to be imposed
307 FR	Mary	24	always assured that you ought to be happy/At the very moment when you are
318 FR	Harry	2	her suffer,/And whatever made her happy was what was virtuous —/Though never
318 FR	Harry	3	was virtuous —/Though never very happy, I remember. That was why/We all felt
319 FR Warburt		15	/And your father were never very happy together:/They separated by mutual
320 FR Warburt		28	One is your mother,/To make her happy for the time she has to live./The other is
321 FR	Winch	25	Lord. Good evening, Doctor./Many happy ... Oh, I'm sorry, my Lord,/I was
333 FR	Harry	39	/{H} Look, I do not know why,/I feel happy for a moment, as if I had come home./It
334 FR	Harry	1	quite irrational, but now/I feel quite happy, as if happiness/Did not consist in getting
341 FR	Amy	14	him/Of the years when he had been a happy boy at Wishwood;/For his future success.
345 FR	Harry		*could* understand you would be quite happy about it,/So I shall say good-bye, until
347 FR	Ivy	19	delayed business in town many happy returns see you tomorrow many happy
347 FR	Ivy	19	returns see you tomorrow many happy returns hurrah love Arthur.'/I mean,
370 CP	Peter	7	really cared about me./And I was so happy when we were together —/So ...
379 CP	Celia	28	that experience./{C} A dream. I was happy in it till to-day,/And then, when Julia
381 CP	Celia	24	think of it./Oh, Edward! Can you be happy with Lavinia?/{E} No — not happy: or, if
381 CP	Edward	25	be happy with Lavinia?/{E} No — not happy: or, if there is any happiness,/Only the
389 CP	Celia	32	who wants you and Edward to be happy./{L} You are very kind, but very
436 CP	Julia	19	her/And be reconciled, and be happy in the thought of her./{L} Sir Henry,
437 CP	Reilly	32	led to this death./And if that is not a happy death, what death is happy?/{E} Do you
437 CP	Reilly	32	is not a happy death, what death is happy?/{E} Do you mean that having chosen
449 CC	Eggers	16	be helpful./{E} I'm sure I shall be very happy to commend him./{SC} You mustn't
466 CC	Colby	6	to play to other people:/I am only happy when I play to myself./{SC} You shall
479 CC	Kaghan	22	got to drink it,/To Colby, and a happy bachelor life!/Which depends, of course,
489 CC	Lady E	38	Mrs. Guzzard thought you would be happy/To think you had a son, and would do
491 CC	Lady E	12	a good idea! Why should we not be happy,/All of us? Already, Claude,/I feel as if
501 CC	Lady E	22	as a ... step-daughter;/And shall be happy to accept Mr. Kaghan as a son-in-law./
501 CC	Eggers	29	happiness./And I'm sure she will be happy. Mr. Kaghan/Is one of the most
501 CC	Eggers	33	But I'm sure that we want to greet the happy pair./It's all in the family. Why not let
503 CC	Colby	8	of relationship./{C} I want you to be happy./{L} I shall be happy,/If you will accept
503 CC	Lucasta	9	I want you to be happy./{L} I shall be happy,/If you will accept me as a sister/For the
503 CC	Lucasta	13	thirty or forty years' time./I shall be happy. I'm going to marry B./I know you like
505 CC	Guzzard	10	Mr. Eggerson from Colby./I am very happy to make his acquaintance./{SC} And I
508 CC	Guzzard	21	parted with it. A dear little boy./I was happy to have him while the payments were
512 CC	Lady E	22	... Yes, I'm sure ... I shall be very happy./{MG} You wished for your son, and
515 CC	Guzzard	13	I knew. And it would make you so happy!/If I said the child was mine, what future
518 CC	Eggers	18	a spare room. We should be most happy/If you cared to stop with us, until you
539 ES	Gomez	17	marriage had not been altogether happy./And as for your son — from what I've
545 ES	Piggott	29	led a busy life, too.' But I hope you're happy?/Is there anything you need that hasn't
574 ES	Carghil	24	to prepare you./Dear Michael is so happy — all his problems are solved;/And he
578 ES	Ld Clav	12	your childhood,/When I think of the happy little boy who was Michael,/When I
581 ES	Ld Clav	25	But how few of us do! And now I feel happy —/In spite of everything, in defiance of
581 ES	Ld Clav	28	by the wing of happiness./And I am happy, Monica, that you have found a man/
583 ES	Monica	19	father now, and Michael's./And I am happy. Isn't it strange, Charles,/To be happy at
583 ES	Monica	20	happy. Isn't it strange, Charles,/To be happy at this moment?/{C} It is not at all

HARANGUING (1)

602 Humoresque		14	/With Limbo's other useless things/Haranguing spectres, set him there;/'The

HARBINGER (1)

544 ES	Ld Clav	23	that's hardly seasonable,/Is so often a harbinger of frost on the fruit trees./{M} Oh,

HARBOR (1)

592 Grad 1		4	song upon our lips, sail we/Across the harbor bar — no chart to show/No light to

HARBOUR (1)

188 FQ: DrySal		152	/You are not those who saw the harbour/Receding, or those who will disembark.

HARCOURT-REILLY (5)

352 CP	m	7	*later identified as* SIR HENRY HARCOURT-REILLY/LAVINIA
400 CP	Edward	35	/{E} Sir Henry Harcourt-Reilly — {}/[*Stops and stares at*
432 CP	Caterer	2	{P} No, I'm afraid .../{CM} Sir Henry Harcourt-Reilly!/{J} Oh, I forgot! I'd another
432 CP	Julia	4	/{J} I want you to meet Sir Henry Harcourt-Reilly —/{E} We're delighted to see
432 CP	Lavinia	26	Mr. Peter Quilpe?/Sir Henry Harcourt-Reilly. Peter's an old friend/Of my

HARCOURT-REILLY'S (1)

399 CP		2m	1 {}/CURTAIN/Act Two/SIR HENRY HARCOURT-REILLY'S *consulting room in*

HARD (34)

24 Rhapsody		32	to the form that the strength has left/Hard and curled and ready to snap./Half-past
31 Apollinax		16	the beat of centaur's hoofs over the hard turf/As his dry and passionate talk
103 Journ Magi		16	dirty and charging high prices:/A hard time we had of it./At the end we preferred
104 Journ Magi		39	they were different; this Birth was/Hard and bitter agony for us, like Death, our
148 Rock 1		50	alone, and I know/That it is hard to be really useful, resigning/The things
159 Rock 6		1	and others must hold the spears./It is hard for those who have never known
159 Rock 6		4	tales of Christian persecution./It is hard for those who live near a Bank/To doubt
159 Rock 6		6	the security of their money./It is hard for those who live near a Police Station/To
159 Rock 6		19	/She is tender where they would be hard, and hard where they like to be soft./She
159 Rock 6		19	tender where they would be hard, and hard where they like to be soft./She tells them of
210 Old Gumbie		14	is Jennyanydots;/Her equal would be hard to find, she likes the warm and sunny
247 MC Tempt1		34	master!/You were not used to be so hard upon sinners/When they were your friends.
252 MC Tempt4		30	/{T4} Well done, Thomas, your will is hard to bend./And with me beside you, you
265 MC Knight1		13	brought us from France. We rode hard,/Took ship yesterday, landed last night,/
270 MC Chorus		7	the scale of the viper, the mobile hard insensitive skin of the elephant, the evasive
286 FR	Gerald	36	responsibility./{G} You're being very hard on the younger generation./I don't come
288 FR	Agatha	27	find a new Wishwood. Adaptation is hard./{A} Nothing is changed, Agatha, at
304 FR	Mary	3	students:/I only saw you as a hard headmistress/Who knew the way of
328 FR	Ivy	31	I'm sure that you're being much too hard on him./{C} In my time, these affairs were
329 FR	Chorus	2	began in the past, and presses hard on the future./The agony in the curtained
338 FR	Harry	38	was speaking to Harry./{H} It is very hard, when one has just recovered sanity,/And
339 FR	Harry	1	the maddest to other people./It is hard for you too, mother, it is indeed harder,/
396 CP	Lavinia	24	/As you are for yourself. And that's hard to bear./I thought that there might be
436 CP	Edward	7	and make a new beginning./It's not so hard for you. You're naturally good./{P} I'm
454 CC	Kaghan	10	You have to be tough with her;/She's hard as nails. Now I'll take her off your hands./
471 CC	Colby	22	time we met/You were trying very hard to give a false impression./And then you
472 CC	Lucasta	19	In what way is it different?/{L} It's hard to explain./Perhaps it's something that
491 CC	Colby	25	/Of fiction and fact. Already, it's been hard/For me, who have never known the
502 CC	Lucasta	33	you are./It may be there's no one so hard to understand/As one's brother .../{C} Or
533 ES	Gomez	15	you like./But I've been a pretty hard worker all these years/And I thought,
533 ES	Gomez	22	republic: San Marco./It's as hard to become a respected citizen/Out there, as
550 ES	Carghil	21	had a weak heart./And he worked too hard. Have you never heard/Of Carghill
556 ES	Michael	30	{}/[*Exit*]/{Mi} You know, it's awfully hard to explain things to *you.*/You've always
573 ES	Ld Clav	4	when I'm just recovering!/It's hard to make other people realise/The

HARD-HEADED (1)

278 MC Knight2		1	emotions but to your reason. You are hard-headed/sensible people, as I can see, and

HARDENED (2)

253 MC Tempt4		7	is weakness. As for the King,/His hardened hatred shall have no end./You know
326 FR	Harry	11	of calamity/Like children, or like hardened campaigners. She looked/Very much

HARDENING (1)

301 FR	Chorus	32	sudden thrombosis/And the slowly hardening artery./We like to be thought well of

HARDER (7)

148 Rock 1		47	/Or ceaseless idleness, which is still harder,/Or irregular labour, which is not
314 FR	Harry	40	Not at all extraordinary./It is really harder to believe in murder/Than to believe in
338 FR	Harry	7	to explain it —/That is what makes it harder. You must just believe me,/Until I come
339 FR	Harry	1	hard for you too, mother, it is indeed harder,/Not to understand./{A} Where are you
436 CP	Edward	6	and learn them later/When it's harder to recover, and make a new beginning./
569 ES	Ld Clav	1	play. And the longer we pretend/The harder it becomes to drop the pretence,/Walk
573 ES	Ld Clav	6	things that appear to them petty;/It's harder to confess the sin that no one believes in/

HARDEST (2)

228 Gus		27	fail./I'd a voice that would soften the hardest of hearts,/Whether I took the lead, or in
338 FR	Harry	30	there been any other!/It is at once the hardest thing, and the only thing possible./Now

HARDLY (28)

20 Portrait		90	/But that's a useless question./You hardly know when you are coming back,/You
21 Portrait		104	would relate/So closely! I myself can hardly understand./We must leave it now to
23 Preludes		34	a vision of the street/As the street hardly understands;/Sitting along the bed's

69 WL: Fire S   250   and looks a moment in the glass,/Hardly aware of her departed lover;/Her brain
127 Cor1 March   5 them. And such a press of people./We hardly knew ourselves that day, or knew the
159 Rock 6   13 boast in the way of polite society/Will hardly survive the Faith to which they owe their
186 FQ: DrySal   85   prayer to Death its God. Only the hardly, barely prayable/Prayer of the one
210 Old Gumbie   6 /Then the Gumbie Cat's work is but hardly begun./And when all the family's in bed
210 Old Gumbie   18 /Then the Gumbie Cat's work is but hardly begun./As she finds that the mice will
211 Old Gumbie   30 /Then the Gumbie Cat's work is but hardly begun./She thinks that the cockroaches
298 FR Charles   4 interested in helping Harry/You can hardly object to the means./{V} I do object./{I}
302 FR   Amy   15   It is very annoying./Now they can hardly arrive in time to dress./I do not
306 FR   Harry   4 must seem very altered./{H} You have hardly changed at all —/And I haven't seen you
314 FR Warburt   22 take such a pessimistic view/Which is hardly complimentary to my profession./But I
319 FR   Harry   4   to know more about my father./I hardly remember him, and I know very well/
327 FR   Ivy   28 /The connection was so bad, I could hardly hear him,/And his voice was very queer.
334 FR   Harry   18 frightened./{H} You, frightened! I can hardly imagine it./I wish I had known — but
346 FRDowning   22 show you what I mean, though you'd hardly credit it,/I've always said, whatever
385 CP Edward   20   strange to each other./{E} You can hardly expect me to obliterate/The last five
402 CP Edward   3 I don't know, I'm sure. They could hardly be worse./{R} They might be much
462 CC Claude   39 till you started with me here,/That we hardly know each other at all./{C} I suppose
473 CC Lucasta   11   with my mother. I've no garden./I hardly feel that I'm even a person:/Nothing but
494 CC Lady E   1 and over —/All through the night. I hardly slept at all./I wish that Colby, somehow,
542 ES Ld Clav 25   had those tastes already/You would hardly have welcomed my companionship./{G}
544 ES Ld Clav 22   more./But this early summer, that's hardly seasonable,/Is so often a harbinger of
550 ES Carghil 26 {MC} Well, Richard, my doctor could hardly have sent me *here*/If I wasn't well off.
562 ES Carghil 28   about your children:/Monica hardly resembles you at all,/But Michael —
576 ES Charles 38   and slander/To know that you are hardly likely to invoke it./And, Michael, here's

HAREFOOT (1)
310 FR   Mary   29   sun/Wet wings into the rain cloud/Harefoot over the moon?/{H} What have we

HARK (1)
291 FR   Amy   11 to come./John at least, if not Arthur. Hark, there is someone coming:/Yes, it must be

HARM (14)
74 WL: Thund   390   and the door swings,/Dry bones can harm no one./Only a cock stood on the rooftree
179 FQ: ECoker 89 that which, deceiving, could no longer harm./In the middle, not only in the middle of
194 FQ: Little 143 Of things ill done and done to others' harm/Which once you took for exercise of
286 FR Charles 22 {C} It's the cocktail-drinking does the harm:/There's nothing on earth so bad for the
295 FR Charles   8   dangerous fancies./It's only doing harm to your mother and yourself./Of course
339 FR   Harry   16 be the master./All I have is his. No harm can come to him./What would destroy me
347 FRDowning   10 /In a manner of speaking. There's no harm in *them*,/I'll take my oath. Will that be all,
363 CP   Reilly 23 me ridiculous?/{UG} It will do you no harm to find yourself ridiculous./Resign
403 CP   Reilly 12 — until you came to grief./Half of the harm that is done in this world/Is due to people
403 CP   Reilly 14 important./They don't mean to do harm — but the harm does not interest them./
403 CP   Reilly 14   don't mean to do harm — but the harm does not interest them./Or they do not see
403 CP Edward 19 that/I must have done a great deal of harm./{R} Oh, not so much as you would like to
551 ES Ld Clav   9 But we'd settled our account./What harm was done? I learned my lesson/And you
572 ES Charles 31   them in whispers. They cannot harm you./{LC} Your reasoning's sound

HARMLESS (5)
345 FR   Amy   25   you are the most malicious in a harmless way;/I prefer your company to that of
354 CP   Julia   37 Oh, not feeble-minded:/He was only harmless./{A} Well then, harmless./{J} He was
354 CP   Alex   38 He was only harmless./{A} Well then, harmless./{J} He was very clever at repairing
355 CP   Celia   6 I believed him./{C} But if he was so ... harmless, how could you believe him?/He might
456 CC Eggers   14 is./Most of her oddities are perfectly harmless./You'll soon get used to them. That's

HARNESS (1)
531 ES Ld Clav 13   /My obituary, if I had died in harness,/Would have occupied a column and a

HARP (1)
50 Hippopot   32   he shall be seen/Performing on a harp of gold./He shall be washed as white as

HARPS (1)
264 MC Priest3 16 voice of many waters, of thunder, of harps,/They sang as it were a new song./The

HARRIET (1)
28 Boston ET   9 end of the street,/And I say, 'Cousin Harriet, here is the *Boston Evening Transcript*.'/

HARRY (96)
284 FR   m   6   /DENMAN, *a parlourmaid*/HARRY, LORD MONCHENSEY, *Amy's*
287 FR   Amy   37 both be here in good time for dinner./Harry telephoned to me from Marseilles,/He
288 FR Violet   1   in the course of the evening./{V} Harry was always the most likely to be late./{A}
288 FR   Amy   3 his fault./We are very lucky to have Harry at all./{I} And when will you have your
288 FR Agatha   13   It is going to be rather painful for Harry/After eight years and all that has
288 FR Agatha   23 painted scene of the Mediterranean,/Harry must often have remembered Wishwood

288 FR	Agatha	33	that at Wishwood he will find another Harry./The man who returns will have to meet/
290 FR	Amy	7	/She never wanted to fit herself to Harry,/But only to bring Harry down to her
290 FR	Amy	8	fit herself to Harry,/But only to bring Harry down to her own level./A restless
290 FR	Amy	15	if I could. For the sake of the future:/Harry is to take command at Wishwood/And I
291 FR	m	13	/Yes, it must be John. {}/[*Enter* HARRY]/{A} Harry! {}/[HARRY *stops*
291 FR	Amy	13	must be John. {}/[*Enter* HARRY]/{A} Harry! {}/[HARRY *stops suddenly at the door*
291 FR	m	14	{}/[*Enter* HARRY]/{A} Harry! {}/[HARRY *stops suddenly at the door and stares*
291 FR	Ivy	14	*stares at the window*]/{I} Welcome, Harry!/{G} Well done!/{V} Welcome home to
291 FR	Amy	18	/{C} Why, what's the matter?/{A} Harry, if you want the curtains drawn you
291 FR	Amy	22	through a window?/{A} You forget, Harry, that you are at Wishwood,/Not in town,
291 FR	Amy	25	/And who all want to see you back, Harry./{H} Look there, look there: do you see
292 FR	Amy	15	We are very glad to have you back, Harry./Now we shall all be together for dinner./
293 FR	Amy	4	aunts and uncles are very helpful, Harry./I have always found them forthcoming
293 FR	Agatha	20	to you. Agatha?/{Ag} I think, Harry, that having got so far —/If you want no
293 FR	Charles	34	there isn't much would surprise me, Harry;/Or shock me, either./{H} You are all
294 FR	Agatha	12	is what matters./{Ag} Nevertheless, Harry, best tell us as you can:/Talk in your own
295 FR	Amy	6	/That night I slept heavily, alone./{A} Harry!/{C} You mustn't indulge such dangerous
295 FR	Amy	32	here. I had not expected that./{A} Harry, Harry, you are very tired/And
295 FR	Amy	32	I had not expected that./{A} Harry, Harry, you are very tired/And overwrought.
296 FR	Violet	17	There is only one thing to be done:/Harry must see a doctor./{I} But I understand
296 FR	Gerald	38	have a word with him./He can talk to Harry, and Harry need have no suspicion./I'd
296 FR	Gerald	38	with him./He can talk to Harry, and Harry need have no suspicion./I'd trust
297 FR	Charles	11	question Downing?/He's been with Harry ten years, he's absolutely discreet./He
297 FR	Charles	15	/{C} In any case, I shouldn't blame Harry./I might have done the same thing once,
297 FR	Charles	35	is, to find out what's wrong with Harry:/Until we know that, we can do nothing
298 FR	Charles	3	hand./If you are interested in helping Harry/You can hardly object to the means./{V}
302 FR	Amy	18	must go and dress, I suppose. I hope Harry will feel better/After his rest upstairs. {}/
303 FR	Mary	11	Seven ... nine ... ten surely./I hear that Harry has arrived already/And he was the only
304 FR	Mary	22	with none. She only wanted me for Harry —/Not such a compliment: she only
304 FR	Mary	25	housekeeper-companion for her and Harry./Even when he married, she still held on
304 FR	Agatha	33	one who ever met her,/The only one Harry asked to his wedding:/Amy did not know
304 FR	Agatha	38	could not have been easy,/Living with Harry. It's not what she did to Harry,/That's
304 FR	Agatha	38	with Harry. It's not what she did to Harry,/That's important, I think, but what he
305 FR	Mary	1	/{M} But it wasn't till I knew that Harry had returned/That I felt the strength to
305 FR	m	19	*means* to keep us waiting. {}/[*Enter* HARRY]/{H} Waiting? For what?/{M} How do
305 FR	Mary	20	For what?/{M} How do you do, Harry./You are down very early. I thought you
311 FR	Mary	2	is that? do you feel it?/{H} What, Harry?/{H} That apprehension deeper than all
311 FR	Mary	24	Look at me. You can depend on me./Harry! Harry! It's all *right*, I tell you./If you will
311 FR	Mary	24	at me. You can depend on me./Harry! Harry! It's all *right*, I tell you./If you will
311 FR	Mary	38	that carcase. They will not go./{M} Harry! There is no one here. {}/[*She goes to the*
312 FR	Mary	10	*but the embrasure is empty*.]/{M} Oh, Harry! {}/Scene III/HARRY, MARY, IVY,
313 FR	2m	1	*is empty*.]/{M} Oh, Harry! {}/Scene III/HARRY, MARY, IVY, VIOLET, GERALD,
313 FR	Violet	2	dressed yet?/How do you think that Harry is looking?/Why, who could have pulled
313 FR	Gerald	14	Good evening, Mary. You've seen Harry, I see./It's good to have him back again,
313 FR	Charles	20	/I'm glad that you'll all be together, Harry;/They need the influence of their elder
314 FR	Amy	1	/So it's no use to telephone anywhere. Harry!/Haven't you seen Dr. Warburton?/You
314 FR	Amy	4	he's known you longer than anybody, Harry./When he heard that you were going to
314 FR	Warbur	7	say we've both changed a good deal, Harry./A country practitioner doesn't get
315 FR	m	29	[*Exeunt* AMY, DR. WARBURTON, HARRY]/{Ch} I am afraid of all that has
317 FR	4m	1	II/*The library, after dinner*./Scene I/HARRY, WARBURTON/{W} I'm glad of a
317 FR	Warburt	1	glad of a few minutes alone with you, Harry./In fact, I had another reason for coming
318 FR	Warburt	18	/Than what they are told./{W} Stop, Harry, you're mistaken./I mean, you don't
318 FR	Warburt	37	my father?/{W} Why, yes, of course, Harry, but I really don't see/What that has to
319 FR	Warburt	11	then. Where was my father?/{W} Harry, there's no good probing for misery./
319 FR	Warburt	38	is nothing she could tell you. But, Harry,/We can't sit here all the evening, you
320 FR	Warburt	5	wanted to talk to you./I must tell you, Harry, that although your mother/Is still so
320 FR	Warburt	24	{H} Well!/{W} I'm very sorry for you, Harry./I should have liked to spare you this,/
321 FR	Warburt	1	about my present age?/{W} Why, yes, Harry, of course I did./{H} What did he look
321 FR	Warburt	6	very much like you./And now, Harry, let's talk about yourself./{H} I never saw
321 FR	Warburt	22	/What if *you* saw him, and .../{W} Harry! Pull yourself together./Something may
323 FR	Amy	5	must explain to your mother .../{A} Harry! Harry!/Who's there with you? Is it
323 FR	Amy	5	explain to your mother .../{A} Harry! Harry!/Who's there with you? Is it Arthur or
324 FR	Violet	8	*and* WINCHELL]/{V} Well, Harry,/I think that you might have had
324 FR	Ivy	21	more than breathing./{I} Really, Harry! how can you be so callous?/I always
325 FR	m	4	You must be very tired. {}/[*Exeunt* HARRY *and* AMY]/{V} I really do not

325 FR   Agatha   6   /{Ag} I think it is as well to leave Harry to establish/If he can, some
326 FR   m   9   cares to mention, I imagine. {}/[*Enter* HARRY]/{H} Mother is asleep, I think: it's
326 FR   Violet   31   no observations on what you say, Harry;/My comments are not always welcome
327 FR   Agatha   1   /{Ag} Whatever you have learned, Harry, you must remember/That there is always
330 FR   2m   1   {}/[*Exeunt* CHORUS]/Scene II/HARRY, AGATHA/{H} John will recover, be
330 FR   Agatha   12   landlord./{Ag} What is in your mind, Harry?/I can guess about the past and what you
334 FR   Agatha   5   is like an end./{Ag} And a beginning. Harry, my dear,/I feel very tired, as only the old
337 FR   Amy   30   AMY]/{A} What are you saying to Harry? He has only arrived,/And you tell him to
338 FR   Amy   37   to run away./{A} I was speaking to Harry./{H} It is very hard, when one has just
341 FR   Amy   9   /For us to be reconciled, because of Harry,/Because of his mistakes, because of his
341 FR   Amy   28   the power to know what is best for Harry?/What gave you this influence to
342 FR   Mary   2   Denman./She came to tell me that Harry is leaving:/Downing told her. He has got
342 FR   Mary   13   from generation to generation./{M} Is Harry really going?/{Ag} He is going./But that
342 FR   Mary   28   do not care what happens to me,/But Harry must not go. Cousin Agatha!/{Ag} Here
342 FR   Agatha   31   renunciation,/But birth and life. Harry has crossed the frontier/Beyond which
342 FR   Agatha   38   of what is to be found there./But Harry has been led across the frontier: he must
343 FR   Agatha   6   in his own direction,/You, and I, and Harry. You and I,/My dear, may very likely
343 FR   m   31   {}/[*While* AMY *has been speaking,* HARRY *has entered, dressed for departure.*]/
344 FR   Charles   2   *have entered*]/{C} Where is Harry going? What is the matter?/{A} Ask
344 FR   Amy   12   /What *has* happened, Amy?/{A} Harry is going away — to become a missionary.
345 FR   Gerald   5   /{G} Well, if you are determined, Harry, we must accept it;/But it's a bad night,
345 FR   Amy   14   /Good-bye, mother./{A} Good-bye, Harry./{H} Good-bye./{Ag} Good-bye./{H}
345 FR   Mary   18   {H} Good-bye, Mary./{M} Good-bye, Harry. Take care of yourself. {}/[*Exit* HARRY]/
345 FR   m   18   Harry. Take care of yourself. {}/[*Exit* HARRY]/{A} At my age, I only just begin to
347 FR   Ivy   14   {I} Where is Downing going? where is Harry?/Look. Here's a telegram come from

HARRY'S (7)
287 FR   Amy   19   been, if things had gone as I intended./Harry's return does not make things easy for
289 FR   Gerald   6   cheerful for Amy's birthday/Or for Harry's homecoming. Make him feel at home, I
290 FR   Amy   6   choose herself. She never wanted/Harry's relations or Harry's old friends;/She
290 FR   Amy   6   She never wanted/Harry's relations or Harry's old friends;/She never wanted to fit
293 FR   Ivy   13   wants you to die, I'm sure!/Now that Harry's back, is the time to think of living./{H}
324 FR   Amy   29   are much more inappropriate/Than Harry's./{H} It's only when they see nothing/
325 FR   Violet   5   AMY]/{V} I really do not understand Harry's behaviour./{Ag} I think it is as well to

HART (1)
140 Usk   3   branch, or/Hope to find/The white hart behind the white well./Glance aside, not for

HARUSPICATE (1)
189 FQ: DrySal   190   sea monster,/Describe the horoscope, haruspicate or scry,/Observe disease in

HARVARD (3)
604 Ode   1   /For the hour that is left us, Fair Harvard, with thee,/Ere we face the
604 Ode   11   able to grieve,/With so much that of Harvard we carry away/In the place of the life
604 Ode   16   the future, the present, and past,/Fair Harvard, to thine and to thee./The Death of

HARVEST (4)
148 Rock 1   58   *will.*/I say: take no thought of the harvest,/But only of proper sowing./The world
178 FQ: ECoker   44   /The time of milking and the time of harvest/The time of the coupling of man and
243 MC   Chorus   32   the corn has failed us,/Sometimes the harvest is good,/One year is a year of rain,/
263 MC   Chorus   17   spring, a parched summer, an empty harvest./Between Christmas and Easter what

HAS (323)

HASN'T (9)
323 FR   Winch   24   At the Arms, my Lady;/Of course, he hasn't come round yet./Dr. Owen was there, by
327 FR   Ivy   31   think he's hurt,/But he says that he hasn't got the use of his car,/And he missed the
348 FR   Warburt   2   morning./I hope Lady Monchensey hasn't been worrying?/I'm anxious to relieve her
450 CC   Colby   36   Elizabeth,/And Sir Claude himself hasn't told me very much:/So I've no idea how I
456 CC   Eggers   22   /{E} I didn't mean that./No. She hasn't very much memory to lose,/Though she
462 CC   Colby   40   each other at all./{C} I suppose there hasn't been the opportunity./{SC} When you
475 CC   Lucasta   36   B.; or from Sir Claude./{L} Claude hasn't told me anything about you;/He doesn't
545 ES   Piggott   30   /Is there anything you need that hasn't been provided?/All you have to do is to
572 ES   Ld Clav   25   might have come to divorce;/But she hasn't forgotten or forgiven me./{C} This man,

HAST (4)
167 Rock 10   43   with shadow./We thank Thee who hast moved us to building, to finding, to
594 Grad 13   1   seas!/As thou to thy departing sons hast been/To those that follow may'st thou be
281 MC   Chorus   13   belly./Therefore man, whom Thou hast made to be conscious of Thee, must
282 MC   Chorus   5   O God, we thank Thee/Who hast given such blessing to Canterbury./Forgive

HASTE (8)
42 Swee Erect   8   tangle Ariadne's hair/And swell with haste the perjured sails./Morning stirs the feet
150 Rock 1   119   *without taste./Without delay, without haste/We would build the beginning and the end*

590 Time Space	13	flew/To suck the eglantine./So let us haste to pluck anew/Nor mourn to see them
590 Space Time	13	flew/To suck the eglantine./But let us haste to pluck anew/Nor mourn to see them
592 Grad 3	2	/After a summer tempest, when some haste/North, South, and Eastward o'er the
241 MC Mess	14	outside the city./I was sent before in haste/To give you notice of his coming, as much
271 MC Priests	28	be killed. Come to the altar./Make haste, my Lord. Don't stop here talking. It is
295 FR Amy	34	Coming so far/And making such haste, the change is too sudden for you./You

HAT (8)

20 Portrait	69	serving tea to friends....'/I take my hat: how can I make a cowardly amends?/For
68 WL: Fire S	234	low on whom assurance sits/As a silk hat on a Bradford millionaire./The time is now
137 5FingerEx5	12	And a porpentine cat/And a wopsical hat:/How unpleasant to meet Mr. Eliot!/
210 Old Gumbie	15	the hearth or in the sun or on my hat:/She sits and sits and sits and sits — and
225 Mr Mistoff	55	/Produced *seven kittens* right out of a hat!/And we all said: OH!/Well I never!/Did you
235 Ad-dress	44	familiarity./I bow, and taking off my hat,/Ad-dress him in this form: O CAT!/But if
601 Nocturne	2	*sérieux*, to importune/Guitar and hat in hand, beside the gate/With Juliet, in the
603 Spleen	13	fastidious, and bland,/Waits, hat and gloves in hand,/Punctilious of tie and

HATCHES (1)

| 213 Growltiger | 44 | and junks,/They battened down the hatches on the crew within their bunks./Then |

HATE (7)

143 Lines OM	9	tongue/Is more affectionate than hate,/More bitter than the love of youth,/And
246 MC Thomas	5	me/Some who hold me in bitterest hate./By God's grace aware of their prevision/I
254 MC Tempt4	38	And later is worse, when men will not hate you/Enough to defame or to execrate you,/
358 CP Julia	21	everything?/It's such a nice party, I hate to leave it./It's such a nice party, I'd like to
467 CC Colby	22	I'm hurting you and I know/That I hate myself for hurting you./{SC} You mustn't
516 CC Colby	36	of it, together./{C} No, Sir Claude. I hate to hurt you/As I am hurting you. But it is
571 ES Monica	28	/What is known so well to those who hate you?/{LC} I will tell you very briefly/And

HATED (3)

396 CP Lavinia	4	But I always suspected that you really hated music/And that the gramophone was only
464 CC Claude	38	not the whole story. My father knew I hated it:/That was a grief to him. He knew, I am
476 CC Lucasta	33	daughter. Oh, it's a sordid story./I hated my mother. I never could see/How

HATES (3)

116 SP Dusty	29	shan't have to call a doctor/Doris just hates having a doctor/She says will you ring up
368 CP Alex	5	this evening,/And I know that he hates to spend an evening alone,/So you're
370 CP Edward	15	There isn't any curry powder. Lavinia hates curry./{A} There goes another surprise,

HATRED (4)

212 Growltiger	17	/But most to Cats of foreign race his hatred had been vowed;/To Cats of foreign
249 MC Tempt2	34	excommunication./{T2} Hungry hatred/Will not strive against intelligent
253 MC Tempt4	7	As for the King,/His hardened hatred shall have no end./You know truly, the
542 ES Ld Clav	20	gained in return/Your envy, spite and hatred. That is why you attribute/Your

HATS (1)

| 603 Spleen | 3 | definite Sunday faces;/Bonnets, silk hats, and conscious graces/In repetition that |

HATTER (1)

| 209 NamingCats | 3 | may think at first I'm as mad as a hatter/When I tell you, a cat must have THREE |

HAUL (1)

| 186 FQ: DrySal | 80 | a trip that will be unpayable/For a haul that will not bear examination./There is no |

HAULING (1)

| 186 FQ: DrySal | 76 | them as forever bailing,/Setting and hauling, while the North East lowers/Over |

HAUNT (1)

| 230 Bust Jones | 3 | fact, he's remarkably fat./He doesn't haunt pubs — he has eight or nine clubs,/For |

HAUNTED (3)

491 CC Colby	29	/I know, I know I should always be haunted/By the miserable ghosts of the other
570 ES Ld Clav	6	would be jealous of the ghosts who haunted me./And I'm still of that opinion. How
571 ES Ld Clav	33	/He knows very well, has always haunted me./I was driving back to Oxford. We

HAUTE (2)

| 48 Lune Miel | 1 | vu les Pays-Bas, ils rentrent à Terre Haute;/Mais une nuit d'été, les voici à Ravenne, |
| 51 Restaurant | 31 | ce fut jadis un bel homme, de haute taille./Whispers of Immortality/Webster |

HAVE (1161)

HAVEN'T (43)

119 SP Klip	33	/{Kl} Well, no, Miss — er — you haven't quite got it/(I'm afraid I didn't quite
286 FR Charles	34	generation/Are not what we were. Haven't the stamina,/Haven't the sense of
286 FR Charles	35	what we were. Haven't the stamina,/Haven't the sense of responsibility./{G} You're
287 FR Gerald	4	you've got to make allowances:/We haven't left them such an easy world to live in./
298 FR Charles	35	been a good friend to him, too./*We* haven't seen him for nearly eight years;/And to
306 FR Harry	5	have hardly changed at all —/And I haven't seen you since you came down from
309 FR Mary	16	you think,/And what is the real you. I haven't much experience,/But I see something
314 FR Amy	2	no use to telephone anywhere. Harry!/Haven't you seen Dr. Warburton?/You know

315 FR	Warburt	14	— But now you're all grown up/I haven't a patient left at Wishwood./Wishwood
353 CP	Alex	6	Julia!/It's perfectly hopeless. You haven't been listening./{P} You'll have to tell us
357 CP	Edward	1	/{J} Have you an aunt too?/{E} No, I haven't any aunt. But I might go away./{C} But,
369 CP	Edward	23	everything is left unfinished./But you haven't told me how you came to know Celia./
388 CP	Edward	30	sending telegrams?/{E} Of course I haven't sent any telegrams./{L} This is some of
389 CP	Lavinia	25	— as friends./{L} Why, Celia, but haven't we always been friends?/I thought you
391 CP	Edward	10	be going./{E} Are you sure you haven't left anything, Julia?/{J} Left anything?
391 CP	Julia	31	see me?/Good-bye. I believe ... I haven't left anything. {}/[*Enter* PETER]/{P} I've
395 CP	Edward	16	done all the changing —/Though I haven't yet found it a change for the better./But
404 CP	Edward	31	a room for more than seven days;/I haven't the courage to go to a hotel,/And
412 CP	Celia	28	to you. — But I've met you before,/Haven't I, somewhere? ... Oh, of course./But I
415 CP	Celia	14	you know that you're hurting them. I haven't hurt *her.*/I wasn't taking anything away
448 CC	Eggers	14	He'll soon begin to grasp them./No, I haven't told him much about Lady Elizabeth./
448 CC	Claude	28	clear. But beyond that point/I haven't yet explained my plans to you./Why I've
457 CC	Lady E	25	*voice off.**/{LE} No, Gertrude, I haven't had any lunch,/And I don't want it
457 CC	Lady E	28	/Nothing with it. No, I forgot./You haven't learned yet how to make tea properly./
462 CC	Colby	6	I must confess, that up to this point/I haven't been able to feel very settled./And what
462 CC	Claude	24	us? Or a kindness to her?/{SC} If you haven't the strength to impose your own terms/
464 CC	Claude	15	I have some good things —/But they haven't this ... remoteness I have always longed
471 CC	Lucasta	31	/{L} Well, there's one thing you haven't learnt yet,/And that is, to know when
472 CC	Colby	9	— the sense of security./{C} No, I haven't either./{L} There, I don't believe you./
473 CC	Colby	5	behind me?/Are you sure that you haven't your own secret garden/Somewhere, if
474 CC	Lucasta	32	/{L} But you've something else, that I haven't got:/Something of which the music is a
475 CC	Colby	22	/{C} Must have wondered?/No, I haven't wondered. It's all a strange world/To
481 CC	Kaghan	34	yet./{K} Why no, as a matter of fact, I haven't./I've kept meaning to. Shall we go there,
494 CC	Lady E	28	talked like this to me before!/Why haven't you? I don't suppose I understand/And
496 CC	Eggers	18	Don't say that, Sir Claude./It's true, I haven't much nowadays to bring me;/But Mrs.
499 CC	Claude	20	/{SC} Of course I'll listen. But we haven't much time./{L} It won't take much time.
499 CC	Lucasta	28	you've always found me!/And I haven't made it easier. I didn't try to./And
525 ES	Charles	35	/But I've something else to say that I haven't said before,/That will give you a shock.
527 ES	Charles	32	it's been you./It's a pity that you haven't had brothers and sisters/To share the
532 ES	Monica	20	with such people now, Father./If you haven't got rid of him in twenty minutes/I'll
542 ES	Gomez	38	Well, I'd better be going./I hope I haven't outstayed my welcome?/Your telephone
546 ES	Monica	32	but please tell me one thing./We haven't seen her yet, but the chambermaid/
578 ES	Monica	34	life or mine./{M} Oh Michael, you haven't understood a single word/Of what I

HAVING (38)

89 Ash-Wed 1		24	to turn again/Consequently I rejoice, having to construct something/Upon which to
91 Ash-Wed 2		2	a juniper-tree/In the cool of the day, having fed to satiety/On my legs my heart my
106 Song Sime		37	after me./Let thy servant depart,/Having seen thy salvation./Animula/'Issues
116 SP	Dusty	29	have to call a doctor/Doris just hates having a doctor/She says will you ring up on
182 FQ: ECoker		174	/So here I am, in the middle way, having had twenty years —/Twenty years
187 FQ: DrySal		108	or not, due to misunderstanding,/Having hopes for the wrong things or dreaded
587 Fable		20	to dinner,/Whene'er the monks were having merry times./He stole the fatter cows
240 MC	Chorus	21	well, some ill, planning and guessing,/Having their aims which turn in their hands in
253 MC	Tempt4	13	/You would wait for trap to snap/Having served your turn, broken and crushed./
261 MC	Thomas	34	in Heaven the Saints are/most high, having made themselves most low, and are seen,
265 MC	Knight1	15	ship yesterday, landed last night,/Having business with the Archbishop./{K2}
276 MC	m	18	them wash them! {}/[*The* KNIGHTS, *having completed the murder, advance to the*
290 FR	Chorus	38	dressed for a different play, or having rehearsed the wrong parts,/Waiting for
293 FR	Agatha	20	Agatha?/{Ag} I think, Harry, that having got so far —/If you want no pretences,
301 FR	Violet	12	much as they were —/Except for having brought Downing into it:/Of which I
303 FR	Mary	17	have told me;/It is very difficult, having to plan/For uncertain numbers. Why did
303 FR	Mary	20	Well, there's something to be said for having an outsider;/For what is more formal
303 FR	Mary	27	thinking of what to say to John,/Or having to listen to Arthur's chatter/When he
328 FR	Charles	25	car, he said: "I/thought you were having a game with me."'/{G} This is what the
340 FR	Amy	12	unpardonable, to taunt me with not having it./Had you taken what I had, you
357 CP	Edward	11	difficult./When she's ill, she insists on having Lavinia./{J} I never heard of her being ill
361 CP	Reilly	6	inconvenient./It was inconvenient, having to lie about it/Because you can't tell the
364 CP	Reilly	13	to clear from the mind/The illusion of having ever been in the light./The fact that you
384 CP	Reilly	11	your mind/Until you recover from having made a decision./No. I have come to tell
400 CP	Alex	7	No! He was only impatient/At having to wait four days for the appointment./
403 CP	Edward	36	for she has made me incapable/Of having any existence of my own./That is what
415 CP	Celia	17	been a fool:/But I don't mind at all having been a fool./{R} And what is the point of
417 CP	Celia	1	anywhere,/Why do I feel guilty at not having found it?/{R} Disillusion can become
432 CP	Julia	32	several commissions./{J} We've been having such an interesting conversation./Peter's

437 CP Edward 33 is happy?/{E} Do you mean that having chosen this form of death/She did not
457 CC Claude 23 *looks down on the street*]/{SC} She's having a conversation with the cabman./What
458 CC Lady E 22 of Mildred Deverell./She's been having the treatment with me,/And she can't go
459 CC Claude 18 it's been for Eggerson —/So I'm having the flat in the mews done over./{LE} But
466 CC Colby 37 while ago,/When you spoke of never having understood your father/Until it was too
484 CC Lady E 26 /You must have been a lonely child, having no relatives —/No brothers or sisters —
518 CC Guzzard 25 /I cannot see eye to eye with you,/Having been, myself, the wife of an organist;/
529 ES Monica 4 can spare me./But he'll simply love having you to talk to!/{C} I know he's used to
543 ES Ld Clav 17 was dining with us./I wish we were having a dinner party./{M} Father, can't you

HAWK (2)
246 MC Thomas 16 after?/{T} For a little time the hungry hawk/Will only soar and hover, circling lower,/
281 MC Chorus 12 in living; the bird in the air, both the hawk and the finch; the beast on the earth, both

HAWKINS (1)
292 FR Ivy 33 really have to find a successor to old Hawkins./It's really high time the old man was

HAWTHORN (2)
92 Ash-Wed 3 14 like the fig's fruit/And beyond the hawthorn blossom and a pasture scene/The
592 Grad 4 4 appears/A lane by which the rose and hawthorn grow./We hope it may be; would that

HAY (1)
329 FR Chorus 6 voices on the lawn/The mowing of hay in summer/The dogs and the old pony/The

HAZE (1)
177 FQ: ECoker 20 electric heat/Hypnotised. In a warm haze the sultry light/Is absorbed, not refracted,

HE (749)

HE'D (21)
214 RTTugger 4 a flat,/If you put him in a flat then he'd rather have a house./If you set him on a
214 RTTugger 6 a rat,/If you set him on a rat then he'd rather chase a mouse./Yes the Rum Tum
214 RTTugger 15 /And as soon as he's at home, then he'd like to get about./He likes to lie in the
222 Pekes Pols 16 the reason, but most people think/He'd slipped into the Wellington Arms for a
231 Bust Jones 36 he's observed/All his life a routine, so he'd say./Or, to put it in rhyme: 'I shall last out
232 Skimble 24 control by a regular patrol/And he'd know at once if anything occurred./He will
300 FRDowning 36 right then,/Mustn't she, Sir? or else he'd have known it./{C} Oh yes ... quite so.
447 CC Claude 31 had to make a quick decision/Because he'd had another very tempting offer./
456 CC Eggers 3 once, in a moment of confidence —/He'd just come back from a public luncheon —/
461 CC Eggers 8 want me./In fact, Mrs. E. said: 'I wish he'd ring us up!/I'm sure he has a very
476 CC Lucasta 26 B. He's very generous./I don't think he'd have minded. But he's very clever too;/And
476 CC Lucasta 38 it wouldn't have mattered how much he'd given her:/It was always spent before the
500 CC Lucasta 23 /I came to thank him for the shock he'd given me./He made me see what I really
531 ES Lambert 38 you'd be very angry/If you heard that he'd gone away without your seeing him./{LC}
543 ES Ld Clav 11 /{M} Oh, so you knew him?/{LC} Yes. He'd changed his name./{M} Then I suppose he
549 ES Carghil 30 said, 'if you chose to follow *that* man/He'd give you the slip: he's not to be trusted./
558 ES Michael 9 gambling. Called me a gambler!/Said he'd communicate with you about it./{LC} That
562 ES Michael 7 /{Mi} I could have loved Father, if he'd wanted love,/But he never did, Monica, not
575 ES Gomez 20 I've told him myself./I thought he'd better learn the facts from me/Before he
576 ES Ld Clav 14 made him invent/The position which he'd come to find the man for./{Mi} I don't care
576 ES Michael 28 by benevolence —/{Mi} I told you he'd come to London looking for a man/For an

HE'LL (25)
63 WL: Burial 75 friend to men,/'Or with his nails he'll dig it up again!/'You! hypocrite lecteur! —
65 WL: Chess 143 back, make yourself a bit smart./He'll want to know what you done with that
215 RTTugger 33 Tugger doesn't care for a cuddle;/But he'll leap on your lap in the middle of your
224 Mr Mistoff 12 prestidigitation/And at legerdemain/He'll defy examination/And deceive you again./
229 Gus 49 just to jump through a hoop.'/And he'll say, as he scratches himself with his claws,/
232 Skimble 11 man —/Then Skimble will appear and he'll saunter to the rear:/He's been busy in the
235 Ad-dress 35 guffaw./He's such an easy-going lout,/He'll answer any hail or shout./Again I must
322 FR Winch 40 cuts/And a bad concussion; says he'll come round/In the morning, most likely,
325 FR Charles 12 If he's worse than Winchell said, then he'll let us know at once./{G} I am really more
387 CP Peter 18 come here/And to bring me with him. He'll be here in a minute./Celia! Have you heard
412 CP Reilly 23 gone./{J} Will Alex be here?/{R} Yes, he'll be here. {}/[*Exit* JULIA *by side door*]/
445 CC Claude 22 him to the City this morning,/But he'll be back, I hope, before you leave./{E} And
446 CC Eggers 28 piano./{E} A piano? Yes, I'm sure he'll feel at home/When he has a piano. You
446 CC Eggers 33 to have window boxes./Some day, he'll want a garden of his own. And yes, a bird
448 CC Eggers 13 Mr. Simpkins,/He's highly educated. He'll soon begin to grasp them./No, I haven't
451 CC Eggers 9 example/For you, Mr. Simpkins. He'll be a power in the City!/And he has a heart
453 CC Lucasta 14 all I say,/*Mr.* Eggerson. And I know he'll be nice to me/When you're out of the way.
478 CC Lucasta 2 Claude's white-headed boy./Perhaps he'll adopt you, and make you his heir/And
479 CC Kaghan 32 /Has made a good impression; which he'll have to live down./— I must say, I like the
501 CC Lucasta 23 a son-in-law./{L} Thank you. I'm sure he'll appreciate *that*./But that reminds me. He's

503 CC	Colby	16	fond of him;/And I'm glad to think he'll be my brother-in-law./I shall need you,
525 ES	Charles	21	to himself,/Before I've said two words he'll come ambling in .../{M} You've said a
529 ES	Monica	4	me out, if Father can spare me./But he'll simply love having you to talk to!/{C} I
577 ES	Gomez	25	got flair. When he does come back/He'll be able to buy you out many times over./
580 ES	Monica	28	may learn his lesson./I believe he'll come back. If it's all a failure/

HE'S (160)

66 WL:	Chess	148	I, I said, and think of poor Albert,/He's been in the army four years, he wants a
115 SP	Doris	11	/{Du} What about Pereira?/{Do} He's no gentleman, Pereira:/You can't trust
115 SP	Dusty	14	can't trust him!/{Du} Well that's true./He's no gentleman if you can't trust him/And *if*
115 SP	Dusty	16	him —/Then you never know what he's going to do./{Do} No it wouldn't do to be
115 SP	Dusty	22	Sam/Yes and Sam's a nice boy too./He's a funny fellow/{Do} He *is* a funny fellow/
115 SP	Doris	24	fellow/{Do} He *is* a funny fellow/He's like a fellow once I knew./*He* could make
120 SP	Krum	10	of course is at *home* in London,/And he's promised to show us around. {}/Fragment
128 Cor1	March	47	that sausage,/It'll come in handy. He's artful. Please, will you/Give us a light?/
214 RTT	ugger	14	let him in, then he wants to be out;/He's always on the wrong side of every door,/
214 RTT	ugger	15	side of every door,/And as soon as he's at home, then he'd like to get about./He
220 Old Deut		2	Old Deuteronomy's lived a long time;/He's a Cat who has lived many lives in
220 Old Deut		25	when he feels so disposed/Or when he's engaged in domestic economy:/And the
224 Mr Mistoff		30	deceiving you into believing/That he's only hunting for mice./He can play any
225 Mr Mistoff		46	he was curled up by the fire./And he's sometimes been heard by the fire/When he
226 Macavity		1	Cat/Macavity's a Mystery Cat: he's called the Hidden Paw —/For he's the
226 Macavity		2	he's called the Hidden Paw —/For he's the master criminal who can defy the Law./
226 Macavity		3	criminal who can defy the Law./He's the bafflement of Scotland Yard, the
226 Macavity		6	there's no one like Macavity,/He's broken every human law, he breaks the
226 Macavity		11	*not there!*/Macavity's a ginger cat, he's very tall and thin;/You would know him if
226 Macavity		16	like a snake;/And when you think he's half asleep, he's always wide awake./
226 Macavity		16	/And when you think he's half asleep, he's always wide awake./Macavity, Macavity,
226 Macavity		18	there's no one like Macavity,/For he's a fiend in feline shape, a monster of
226 Macavity		21	then *Macavity's not there!*/He's outwardly respectable. (They say he cheats
227 Macavity		32	/'It *must* have been Macavity!' — but he's a mile away./You'll be sure to find him
228 Gus		5	him just Gus./His coat's very shabby, he's thin as a rake,/And he suffers from palsy
228 Gus		16	degree —/He has acted with Irving, he's acted with Tree./And he likes to relate his
230 Bust Jones		2	is *not* skin and bones —/In fact, he's remarkably fat./He doesn't haunt pubs —
230 Bust Jones		4	— he has eight or nine clubs,/For he's the St. James's Street Cat!/He's the Cat we
230 Bust Jones		5	/For he's the St. James's Street Cat!/He's the Cat we all greet as he walks down the
230 Bust Jones		19	found, not at *Fox's*, but *Blimp's*;/But he's frequently seen at the gay *Stage and Screen*/
230 Bust Jones		25	in for a drink at the *Drones*./When he's seen in a hurry there's probably curry/At
230 Bust Jones		27	/If he looks full of gloom then he's lunched at the *Tomb*/On cabbage, rice
230 Bust Jones		30	day —/At one club or another he's found./It can be no surprise that under our
231 Bust Jones		33	/He has grown unmistakably round./He's a twenty-five pounder, or I am a bounder,/
231 Bust Jones		34	pounder, or I am a bounder,/And he's putting on weight every day:/But he's so
231 Bust Jones		35	he's putting on weight every day:/But he's so well preserved because he's observed/All
231 Bust Jones		35	/But he's so well preserved because he's observed/All his life a routine, so he'd say./
232 Skimble		7	'Skimble where is Skimble for unless he's very nimble/Then the Night Mail just can't
232 Skimble		12	appear and he'll saunter to the rear:/He's been busy in the luggage van!/He gives one
232 Skimble		30	play no pranks with Skimbleshanks!/He's a Cat that cannot be ignored;/So nothing
233 Skimble		53	/With perhaps a drop of Scotch while he's keeping on the watch,/Only stopping here
234 Ad-dress		30	much pride/Is frequently undignified./He's very easily taken in —/Just chuck him
235 Ad-dress		34	paw,/And he will gambol and guffaw./He's such an easy-going lout,/He'll answer any
235 Ad-dress		59	potted grouse, or salmon paste —/He's sure to have his personal taste./(I know a
235 Ad-dress		62	nothing else but rabbit,/And when he's finished, licks his paws/So's not to waste
289 FR	Gerald	8	what has happened doesn't matter./He's taken his medicine, I've no doubt./Let him
292 FR	Ivy	35	high time the old man was pensioned./He's let the rock garden go to rack and ruin,/
292 FR	Ivy	36	rock garden go to rack and ruin,/And he's nearly half blind. I've spoken to your
296 FR	Gerald	35	Warburton, and ask him to join us?/He's an old friend of the family, it's perfectly
297 FR	Charles	11	an idea. Why not question Downing?/He's been with Harry ten years, he's absolutely
297 FR	Charles	11	/He's been with Harry ten years, he's absolutely discreet./He was with them on
297 FR	Charles	17	once, myself./Nobody knows what he's likely to do/Until there's somebody he
297 FR	Denman	28	Is he up with his Lordship?/{D} He's out in the garage, Sir, with his Lordship's
314 FR	Amy	3	you seen Dr. Warburton?/You know he's the oldest friend of the family,/And he's
314 FR	Amy	4	the oldest friend of the family,/And he's known you longer than anybody, Harry./
320 FR	Warburt	35	mother./John's very steady — but he's not exactly brilliant;/And Arthur has
323 FR	Charles	35	Amy./Extremely fortunate for us that he's here./We must put ourselves under
325 FR	Charles	12	we could do that Warburton can't./If he's worse than Winchell said, then he'll let us
325 FR	Gerald	20	/{G} But *I'm* worried about Arthur:/He's much more apt than John to get into

325 FR	Charles	22	driver./After all the experience he's had at Brooklands,/*He*'s not likely to get
326 FR	Violet	37	DENMAN]/{V} When it's Ivy that he's asking for, I expect the worst./{Ag}
327 FR	Ivy	30	/Has had an accident. I don't think he's hurt,/But he says that he hasn't got the use
327 FR	Ivy	32	car,/And he missed the last train, so he's coming up tomorrow;/And he said there
355 CP	Julia	20	/{J} No, he wasn't listening, but he's such a strain —/Edward without Lavinia!
355 CP	Julia	21	a strain —/Edward without Lavinia! He's quite impossible!/Leaving it to me to keep
359 CP	Julia	28	my umbrella,/And not Alexander's — *he's* so inquisitive!/But *I* never poke into other
376 CP	Julia	19	/That I had. Edward must be fed./He's under such a strain. We must keep his
386 CP	Celia	34	study; and is not quite sure/What he's been found out in. I never saw you so
400 CP	Alex	19	/{A} With your usual foresight. Now, he's quite triumphant/Because he thinks he's
400 CP	Alex	20	quite triumphant/Because he thinks he's stolen a march on her./And when you've
400 CP	Alex	23	he believes,/She will be very penitent. He's enjoying his illness./{R} Illness offers him a
422 CP	Reilly	3	.../Oh, very good. {}/[*To* JULIA]/{R} He's on his way up. {}/[*Into telephone*]/{R} You
431 CP	Peter	8	great Bela?/{P} Why, Bela Szogody —/He's my boss. I thought everyone knew *his*
431 CP	Peter	34	that, we've got the casting director:/He's looking for some typical English faces —/
432 CP	Julia	34	just over from California/Where he's something very important in films./He's
432 CP	Julia	35	something very important in films./He's making a film of English life/And he's
432 CP	Julia	36	making a film of English life/And he's going to find parts for all of us. Think of it!
439 CP	Julia	14	a way that leads him to Boltwell:/And he's got to go there .../{P} I see what you mean./
446 CC	Claude	5	is necessary./But I'm satisfied that he's getting the hang of things,/And I think he's
446 CC	Claude	6	the hang of things,/And I think he's beginning to take a keen interest./{E} And
446 CC	Claude	12	I think so. I understand his feelings./He's like me, Eggerson. The same
446 CC	Claude	17	could do, and do well. And I think he's found it,/Just as I did. I shall tell him about
446 CC	Eggers	22	basis./{E} No doubt that's best. While he's still living/With his aunt in Teddington,
446 CC	Eggers	31	make a suggestion: window boxes!/He's expressed such an interest in my garden;
447 CC	Claude	36	don't forget/To let her know that he's musical./She can take him to concerts.
448 CC	Claude	5	you could reassure him/Better than I. He's more at ease with you/Than he is with me./
448 CC	Eggers	13	for me. And I thought, Mr. Simpkins,/He's highly educated. He'll soon begin to grasp
451 CC	Eggers	3	/{E} Mr. Kaghan is prejudiced./He's never hit it off with Lady Elizabeth./Don't
451 CC	Eggers	5	him. He understands Sir Claude,/And he's always been very grateful to Sir Claude,/As
451 CC	Eggers	7	him out/And gave him his start. And he's made the most of it —/That I will say. An
451 CC	Eggers	11	gold. But not to beat about the bush,/He's rather a rough diamond. Very free and
453 CC	Lucasta	17	quite human, Colby./It's only that he's terrified of Mrs. Eggerson;/That's why he's
453 CC	Lucasta	18	of Mrs. Eggerson;/That's why he's never asked me out to lunch./{E} We will
454 CC	Kaghan	7	propose to leave you with Colby./He's had enough for one day. Take my advice,
455 CC	Eggers	13	was a friend of Sir Claude's,/And he's made himself responsible for her./In any
455 CC	Eggers	14	responsible for her./In any case, he's behaved like a father —/A very generous
455 CC	Eggers	21	She'll marry Mr. Kaghan/In the end. He's a man who gets his own way,/And I think
456 CC	Eggers	8	useful. But he didn't think of that:/He's not petty-minded — though nothing
456 CC	Eggers	9	him./And such a generous heart! He's rather a Socialist./I'm a staunch
458 CC	Eggers	36	to be a confidential clerk./Besides, he's very musical./{LE} Musical?/Isn't this the
472 CC	Lucasta	38	man to have to give up,/A career that he's set his heart on, I'm sure:/But it's only the
476 CC	Lucasta	25	thought it./I don't know about B. He's very generous./I don't think he'd have
476 CC	Lucasta	26	/I don't think he'd have minded. But he's very clever too;/And he guessed the truth
477 CC	Lucasta	9	/I'm sure he wished there had been. He's been good to me/In his way. But I'm
479 CC	Kaghan	6	tigers/Like you and Lizzie, he's got to have protection./{L} Colby doesn't
480 CC	Kaghan	39	the same things. But as for Colby,/He's the sort of fellow who might chuck it all/
493 CC	Claude	19	should put the first questions:/He's very good at approaching a subject/In a
500 CC	Lucasta	28	need me,/He doesn't need anyone. He's fascinating,/But he's undependable. He has
500 CC	Lucasta	29	need anyone. He's fascinating,/But he's undependable. He has his own world,/And
500 CC	Lucasta	33	other people, either./B. needs me. He's been hurt by life, just as I have,/And we
501 CC	Lucasta	24	appreciate *that*./But that reminds me. He's waiting downstairs./I don't suppose you
505 CC	Claude	5	But he knows the whole story:/He's been in my confidence — and I may say,
505 CC	Claude	12	he might ... conduct the proceedings:/He's the very soul of tact and discretion./{MG}
509 CC	Colby	40	I suppose I'll get used to it./{C} But he's waiting downstairs! Isn't this the moment/
513 CC	Colby	21	or a mother —/It's different for B. He's had his foster-parents,/So he can afford
524 ES	Charles	22	fool/If he takes you to a place where he's utterly unknown/And the waiters all appear
525 ES	Charles	18	that. Now that your father's retired/He's at home every day. And you're leaving
525 ES	Monica	30	/And he won't think of leaving it until he's called for tea./So why not talk now?
527 ES	Lambert	14	him./{M} Thank you, Lambert./{L} He's busy at the moment. But he won't be very
527 ES	Monica	23	his terror of being alone./In the life he's led, he's never had to be alone./And when
527 ES	Monica	23	of being alone./In the life he's led, he's never had to be alone./And when he's been
527 ES	Monica	24	he's never had to be alone./And when he's been at home in the evening,/Even when
527 ES	Monica	25	at home in the evening,/Even when he's reading, or busy with his papers/He needs
528 ES	Charles	5	of being exposed to strangers./{C} But he's most alive when he's among people/

528 ES Charles   5   /{C} But he's most alive when he's among people/Managing, manœuvring,
528 ES Charles   7 cajoling or bullying —/At all of which he's a master. Strangers!/{M} You don't
528 ES Monica   28   to have every encouragement —/If he's hopeful, he's likely to live a little longer./
528 ES Monica   28   encouragement —/If he's hopeful, he's likely to live a little longer./That's why
529 ES Charles   5   having you to talk to!/{C} I know he's used to seeing me about./{M} I've seen him
539 ES Gomez   19   — from what I've heard about *him*,/He's followed your undergraduate career/
539 ES Ld Clav 29 of which dark hints have been given,/He's informed himself so carefully about my
540 ES Gomez   7 to keep on pretending to himself/That he's a success — the man who in the morning/
545 ES Piggott   29 not coming in directly after breakfast:/He's led a busy life, too.' But I hope you're
549 ES Carghil   30   *that* man/He'd give you the slip: he's not to be trusted./That man is hollow'.
551 ES Carghil   31   has political ambitions for him./If he's lost a breach of promise suit/Some people
555 ES Ld Clav 22 {M} No, he was walking./{LC} I hope he's not had another accident./You know, after
555 ES Ld Clav 30   /Or he wouldn't be at large. Perhaps he's in trouble/With some woman or other. I'm
556 ES Monica   3 /He won't make a scene. But I can see he's frightened./And you know what Michael is
556 ES Monica   4   you know what Michael is like when he's frightened./He's apt to be sullen and quick
556 ES Monica   5   Michael is like when he's frightened./He's apt to be sullen and quick to take offence./
562 ES Carghil   21   your father/When he was your age. He's the picture of you, Richard,/As you were
562 ES Carghil   35   It's marvellous./And the charm! He's inherited all of your charm, Richard./
562 ES Carghil   37   coming?/It's another new guest here. He's waving to us./Do you know him, Richard?
563 ES Carghil   2 used to know./{MC} How interesting! He's a very good figure/And he's rather
563 ES Carghil   3   He's a very good figure/And he's rather exotic-looking. Is he a foreigner?/
563 ES Carghil   6 How romantic! I'd love to meet him./He's coming to speak to us. You must introduce
569 ES Ld Clav 29   your friendship and your company./He's a very rich man. And she's a rich woman./
570 ES Ld Clav 26 Culverwell?/{LC} He no longer exists./He's Federico Gomez, the Central American,/A
574 ES Carghil   10 {LC} Oh? What about Michael?/{MC} He's told me all his story./You've cruelly
574 ES Carghil   19   why not appeal to Señor Gomez?/He's a wealthy man, and very important/In his
575 ES Michael   5   my point of view, if *you* don't./And he's offered me a job which is just what I
575 ES Ld Clav 15   think. Let me tell you about Gomez./He's unlikely to try to be custodian of your
576 ES Michael   15 man for./{Mi} I don't care about that. He's offered me the job/With a jolly good
576 ES Michael   17   and some pickings in commissions./He's made a fortune there. San Marco for me!/
577 ES Gomez   24   Michael's head is well screwed on./He's got brains, he's got flair. When he does
577 ES Gomez   24   is well screwed on./He's got brains, he's got flair. When he does come back/He'll be
577 ES Carghil   33 I saw that, and so does Señor Gomez./He's simply been suffering, poor boy, from
577 ES Carghil   34 suffering, poor boy, from frustration./He's been waiting all this time for opportunity/
580 ES Monica   33   /But himself, the unhappy self that he's ashamed of./I'm sure he loves us./{LC}
582 ES Charles   25   go far. {}/[*Exit* CLAVERTON]/{C} He's a very different man from the man he used

HEAD (32)

15 Prufrock   82   and prayed,/Though I have seen my head (grown slightly bald) brought in upon a
16 Prufrock   96   all' —/If one, settling a pillow by her head,/Should say: 'That is not what I meant at
31 Apollinax   13   from fingers of surf./I looked for the head of Mr. Apollinax rolling under a chair/Or
37 Gerontion   16   peevish gutter./I an old man,/A dull head among windy spaces./Signs are taken for
65 WL: Chess   126 alive, or not? Is there nothing in your head?'/But/O O O O that Shakespeherian Rag
73 WL: Thund   381   and beat their wings/And crawled head downward down a blackened wall/And
94 Ash-Wed 4   24   /Whose flute is breathless, bent her head and signed but spoke no word/But the
125 SA Chorus 34 /you wake like someone hit you in the head/You've had a cream of a nightmare dream
129 Cor2 State   37 busts, all correctly inscribed)/I a tired head among these heads/Necks strong to bear
136 5FingerEx4 16 /He has 999 canaries/And round his head finches and fairies/In jubilant rapture
138 New Hamp   3   blossom- and the fruit-time:/Golden head, crimson head,/Between the green tip and
138 New Hamp   3   the fruit-time:/Golden head, crimson head,/Between the green tip and the root./Black
138 New Hamp   9   me over, light-in-leaves;/Golden head, black wing,/Cling, swing,/Spring, sing,/
166 Rock 10   8 he awakens in hunger and moving his head to right and to left prepares for his hour to
226 Macavity   13 brow is deeply lined with thought, his head is highly domed;/His coat is dusty from
226 Macavity   15 whiskers are uncombed./He sways his head from side to side, with movements like a
588 Fable   36 /Who stood outside the door from head to feet./To make a rather lengthy story
588 Fable   55 they kept under cover./Last, a boar's head, which to bring in took four pages,/His
602 Humoresque 3   the game —/But weak in body as in head,/(A jumping-jack has such a frame)./But
242 MC Priest2 33   /The Archbishop shall be at our head, dispelling dismay and doubt./He will tell
246 MC Thomas 10   /Those who had sworn to have my head from me/Only John, the Dean of
281 MC Chorus 15 the hands to the face under fear, the head bent under grief,/Even in us the voices of
313 FR Charles   24 effect upon him./After all, you're the head of the family./{A} Violet! Has Arthur or
325 FR Ivy   30 /Or out of a tree — and always on his head./{V} But a year ago, Arthur took me out in
376 CP Celia   3 the best thing to do. Don't lose your head./You see, I really did leave my umbrella;/
383 CP Edward   4 in your bag? ... Well, don't snap my head off .../You're sure, in the kitchen? Beside
436 CP Peter   11 been going round and round in my head —/That I've only been interested in
454 CC Colby   36 I'll be amused./But it did make my head spin — all those first names/The first time

480 CC	Colby	13	a gambler./You've got as level a head as anyone,/And you never get involved in
481 CC	Kaghan	4	/{K} And you have a very sound head for business./Maybe you're a better
490 CC	Lady E	5	you know I'm rather weak in the head/Though I try to be clever. Do try to help
577 ES	Gomez	23	frankly;/And I can tell you, Michael's head is well screwed on./He's got brains, he's

HEAD'S (1)

| 432 CP | Julia | 20 | worse than interrupting./Now my head's fairly spinning. I must have a cocktail. {}/ |

HEADINGS (1)

| 487 CC | Claude | 3 | spontaneous. I've jotted down some headings./Just see if you can develop them for |

HEADLAND (1)

| 185 FQ: DrySal | 33 | warning from the approaching headland/Are all sea voices, and the heaving |

HEADMASTER (1)

| 558 ES | Michael | 15 | He took the usual line,/Just like the headmaster. And my tutor at Oxford./'Not |

HEADMASTER'S (1)

| 386 CP | Celia | 33 | a little boy who's been sent for/To the headmaster's study; and is not quite sure/What |

HEADMISTRESS (1)

| 304 FR | Mary | 3 | students:/I only saw you as a hard headmistress/Who knew the way of dominating |

HEADPIECE (1)

| 83 Hollow Men | 4 | are the stuffed men/Leaning together/Headpiece filled with straw. Alas!/Our dried |

HEADS (3)

129 Cor2	State	37	inscribed)/I a tired head among these heads/Necks strong to bear them/Noses strong
282 MC	Chorus	13	/That the sin of the world is upon our heads; that the blood of the martyrs and the
282 MC	Chorus	14	the agony of the saints/Is upon our heads./Lord, have mercy upon us./Christ, have

HEAL (1)

| 417 CP | Celia | 6 | /Nothing again can either hurt or heal./I have thought at moments that the |

HEALER (1)

| 187 FQ: DrySal | 133 | but this thing is sure,/That time is no healer: the patient is no longer here./When the |

HEALER'S (1)

| 181 FQ: ECoker | 152 | we feel/The sharp compassion of the healer's art/Resolving the enigma of the fever |

HEALTH (13)

181 FQ: ECoker	154	enigma of the fever chart./Our only health is the disease/If we obey the dying nurse/
298 FR	Charles	37	him,/We're a little worried about his health./He doesn't seem to be ... quite himself./
314 FR	Harry	19	/For what you call restoration to health/Is only incubation of another malady./
314 FR	Warburt	29	ill in one way or another:/We call it health when we find no symptom/Of illness.
314 FR	Warburt	30	when we find no symptom/Of illness. Health is a relative term./{I} You must have had
320 FR	Warburt	4	tell me./{W} It's about your mother's health that I wanted to talk to you./I must tell
377 CP	Julia	25	After this disaster. Now I'll propose a health./Can you guess whose health I'm going
377 CP	Julia	26	a health./Can you guess whose health I'm going to propose?/{E} No, I can't.
447 CC	Claude	27	been concerned about your state of health,/So she'll be sympathetic. And as for
456 CC	Eggers	25	she likes to travel,/Mostly for her health. And when she's abroad/She is apt to buy
459 CC	Lady E	9	/I must give you lessons in the art of health./Where is your home, Mr. Colby?/{C}
496 CC	Claude	4	too deep for discussion with *me*:/Health cures. And modern art — so long as it
546 ES	Piggott	19	But, as I was saying,/Guests in perfect health are exceptional/Though we never accept

HEALTHY (1)

| 315 FR | Warburt | 15 | was always a cold place, but healthy./It's only when I get an invitation to |

HEAP (2)

| 61 WL: Burial | 22 | say, or guess, for you know only/A heap of broken images, where the sun beats,/ |
| 151 Rock 2 | 10 | /Waiting to be flung in the end, on a heap less useful than dung'./You, have you built |

HEAPING (1)

| 276 MC | Chorus | 6 | hand on the broom,/The night-time heaping of the ashes,/The fuel laid on the fire at |

HEAR (66)

18 Portrait	8	unsaid./We have been, let us say, to hear the latest Pole/Transmit the Preludes,
49 Hippopot	19	hoarse and odd,/But every week we hear rejoice/The Church, at being one with
67 WL: Fire S	185	long./But at my back in a cold blast I hear/The rattle of the bones, and chuckle spread
67 WL: Fire S	196	/But at my back from time to time I hear/The sound of horns and motors, which
69 WL: Fire S	259	Street./O City city, I can sometimes hear/Beside a public bar in Lower Thames
121 SA Sweeney	29	the sea the other way,/Nothing to hear but the sound of the surf./Nothing at all
127 Cor1 March	8	yet. You can see some eagles. And hear the trumpets./Here they come. Is he
142 Cape Ann	1	Cape Ann/O quick quick quick, quick hear the song-sparrow,/Swamp-sparrow,
151 Rock 2	9	we can sing which nobody wants to hear sung;/Waiting to be flung in the end, on a
164 Rock 9	1	of Man, behold with thine eyes, and hear with thine ears/And set thine heart upon
172 FQ: BurntN	60	/In light upon the figured leaf/And hear upon the sodden floor/Below, the
177 FQ: ECoker	26	/On a summer midnight, you can hear the music/Of the weak pipe and the little
179 FQ: ECoker	94	/Risking enchantment. Do not let me hear/Of the wisdom of old men, but rather of
216 Jellicles	8	merry and bright,/And pleasant to hear when they caterwaul./Jellicle Cats have
222 Pekes Pols	10	bark BARK BARK/Until you can hear them all over the Park./Now on the

222 Pekes Pols		24	bark BARK BARK/Until you could hear them all over the Park./Now the Peke,
223 Pekes Pols		45	bark BARK BARK/Until you could hear them all over the Park./Now when these
229 Gus		52	there's nothing to equal, from what I hear tell,/That moment of mystery/When I
594 Grad 12		4	/Proclaim the glory so that all may hear;/May worthier sons be thine, from far and
256 MC Chorus		6	house. There is no rest in the street./I hear restless movement of feet. And the air is
275 MC	m	21	{}/*While the* KNIGHTS *kill him, we hear the* CHORUS./{C} Clear the air! clean the
277 MC Knight3		4	disinterested. [*The other*/KNIGHTS: 'Hear! hear!'] *We* are not getting anything out of
277 MC Knight3		4	[*The other*/KNIGHTS: 'Hear! hear!'] *We* are not getting anything out of this./
277 MC Knight1		31	justification than that; and you must hear/our other speakers. I shall next call upon
298 FR	Violet	15	remain./And I wish to be present to hear what Downing says./I want to know at
303 FR	Mary	11	/{M} Seven ... nine ... ten surely./I hear that Harry has arrived already/And he was
309 FR	Harry	34	forest,/Inaccessible, half-heard./And I hear your voice as in the silence/Between two
318 FR	Harry	34	stone deaf: and the others/Seem to hear something else than what I am saying./But
327 FR	Ivy	28	connection was so bad, I could hardly hear him,/And his voice was very queer. It
329 FR	Chorus	1	in the room, waiting for the future to hear it./And whatever happens began in the
338 FR	Harry	11	{H} I can only speak/And you cannot hear me. I can only speak/So you may not think
345 FR	Harry	12	care of the bank in London until you hear from me./Good-bye, mother./{A}
355 CP	Julia	1	/The only man I ever met who could hear the cry of bats./{P} Hear the cry of bats?/
355 CP	Peter	2	who could hear the cry of bats./{P} Hear the cry of bats?/{J} He could hear the cry
355 CP	Julia	3	{P} Hear the cry of bats?/{J} He could hear the cry of bats./{C} But how do you know
355 CP	Celia	4	/{C} But how do you know he could hear the cry of bats?/{J} Because he said so. And
356 CP	Edward	35	/{E} I really don't know until I hear from her./If her aunt is very ill, she may be
365 CP	Julia	26	know! And what's his name?/Did I hear him say his name was Riley?/{E} I don't
390 CP	Julia	35	her aunt —/Who, you'll be glad to hear, has quite recovered, Alex —/And after
404 CP	Edward	26	can I tell you?/You didn't want to hear about my early history./{R} No, I did not
404 CP	Reilly	27	history./{R} No, I did not want to hear about your *early* history./{E} And so will
413 CP	Celia	18	that I am being persecuted;/I don't hear any voices, I have no delusions —/Except
425 CP	Lavinia	10	same would be bitterly offended/To hear we'd given a party without asking them./
437 CP	Lavinia	1	/{L} Oh no, I should love to hear you speaking poetry .../{J} She has made a
440 CP	Lavinia	31	And besides,/One sometimes likes to hear the same compliment twice./{E} And now
465 CC	Colby	38	/Always, when I play to myself,/I hear the music I should like to have written,/As
466 CC	Colby	2	that what *they* heard/Was not what I hear when I play to myself./What I hear is a
466 CC	Colby	3	I hear when I play to myself./What I hear is a great musician's music,/What they hear
466 CC	Colby	4	a great musician's music,/What they hear is an inferior rendering./So I've given up
466 CC	Claude	26	perhaps, some time, you will let me hear you play./I shan't mention it again. I'll
469 CC	Colby	7	anyway. All you need at first/Is to hear more music. And to find out what you like.
469 CC	Colby	12	prefer the right things, when you hear them./I've given you a test. Several of the
470 CC	Lucasta	5	in this flat/And to be the first to hear you play *this* piano./{C} That's not what I
470 CC	Colby	19	/And that won't take you long — and hear good performers,/You'll very quickly
471 CC	Colby	4	programme — or the things I want to hear./I'll play you the themes, so you'll
473 CC	Lucasta	19	*your* garden is a garden/Where you hear a music that no one else could hear,/And
473 CC	Lucasta	19	hear a music that no one else could hear,/And the flowers have a scent that no one
474 CC	Colby	15	not see them coming./I should not hear the opening of the gate./They would simply
475 CC	Lucasta	38	And as for B. —/I'd much rather hear it from yourself./{C} There's only one thing
512 CC Guzzard		2	a church wedding./{MG} I am glad to hear you say so, Lady Elizabeth./But are *you*
525 ES	Charles	33	I've heard it all before./{C} And you'll hear it again. You think I'm going to tell you/
526 ES	Monica	24	the table;/There's the door ... and I hear someone coming:/It's Lambert with the tea
536 ES Ld Clav		31	are quite alone./{LC} I'm waiting to hear/Why you should need to trust me./{G}
550 ES	Carghil	1	me. It would give me such a thrill/To hear you speak my name once more./{LC} Your
552 ES	Carghil	9	for what I'd gone through. Did you hear me sing it?/{LC} Yes, I heard you sing it./
558 ES	Michael	5	Well, partly. Sir Alfred did come to hear about it,/And so he pretended to be very

HEARD (77)

16 Prufrock	124	and walk upon the beach./I have heard the mermaids singing, each to each./I do
23 Preludes	32	up between the shutters/And you heard the sparrows in the gutters,/You had such
31 Apollinax	16	a screen/With seaweed in its hair./I heard the beat of centaur's hoofs over the hard
74 WL: Thund	411	rooms/DA/*Dayadhvam:* I have heard the key/Turn in the door once and turn
139 Virginia	6	move/Only through the mocking-bird/Heard once? Still hills/Wait. Gates wait. Purple
149 Rock 1 m	79	*the voices of* WORKMEN *are heard chanting.*/*In the vacant places*/*We* will
185 FQ: DrySal	30	are different voices/Often together heard: the whine in the rigging,/The menace and
190 FQ: DrySal	214	lightning/Or the waterfall, or music heard so deeply/That it is not heard at all, but
190 FQ: DrySal	215	music heard so deeply/That it is not heard at all, but you are the music/While the
193 FQ: Little	100	a double part, and cried/And heard another's voice cry: 'What! are *you* here?'
198 FQ: Little	252	known, because not looked for/But heard, half-heard, in the stillness/Between two
213 Growltiger	38	yet from all the enemy there was not heard a sound./The lovers sang their last duet,
219 Mung Rump	34	it mightn't be both?/And when you heard a dining-room smash/Or up from the

223 Pekes Pols 27 /And so all the Pekes, when they heard the uproar,/Some came to the window,
225 Mr Mistoff 44 shyer —/But his voice has been heard on the roof/When he was curled up by the
225 Mr Mistoff 46 by the fire./And he's sometimes been heard by the fire/When he was about on the
225 Mr Mistoff 48 about on the roof —/(At least we all *heard* that somebody purred)/Which is
235 Ad-dress 50 with an OOPSA CAT!/I think I've heard them call him James —/But we've not got
244 MC Chorus 4 partly living./We have kept the feasts, heard the masses,/We have brewed beer and
264 MC m 6 *did sit.* {}/[*Introit of St. Stephen is heard*]/[*Enter the* SECOND PRIEST, *with a*
264 MC Priest2 9 from the beginning, which we have heard,/Which we have seen with our eyes, and
264 MC Priest2 11 of life; that which we have seen and heard/Declare we unto you./*In the midst of the*
264 MC m 13 *congregation.* {}/[*Introit of St. John is heard*]/[*Enter the* THIRD PRIEST, *with a*
264 MC Priest3 20 blood of thy saints. In Rama, a voice heard, weeping./Out of the mouth of very
269 MC Chorus 28 /By subtile forebodings; I have heard/Fluting in the night-time, fluting and
269 MC Chorus 32 at nightfall, restless, absurd. I have heard/Laughter in the noises of beasts that
296 FR Ivy 19 doctor./{I} But I understand —/I have heard of such cases before — that people in his
314 FR Amy 5 than anybody, Harry./When he heard that you were going to be here for dinner/
319 FR Harry 6 him, till he went away./We never heard him mentioned, but in some way or
319 FR Harry 26 not overheard,/Not intended to be heard, with the sidewise looks,/That bring death
328 FR Chorus 34 there is always listening, and more is heard than is spoken./And what is spoken
335 FR Agatha 2 was shining on the rose-garden:/And heard in the distance tiny voices/And then a
353 CP Reilly 24 know it, do you?/{UG} No, I've never heard it./{C} Here's one new listener for you,
354 CP Edward 2 that Edward knows it./{E} I may have heard it, but I don't remember it./{C} And
354 CP Julia 23 /{J} Well, but it really isn't my story./I heard it first from Delia Verinder/Who was
357 CP Julia 12 insists on having Lavinia./{J} I never heard of her being ill before./{E} No, she's
371 CP Peter 20 Did we really feel the same/When we heard certain music? Or looked at certain
376 CP m 8 EDWARD *goes to front door, and is/heard to say:*]/{E} Julia!/What have you come
376 CP Julia 21 have *two* Good Samaritans? I never heard of that before./{E} The man who fell
377 CP m 18 want her back? {}/[*A popping noise is heard from the kitchen*]/{E} What the devil's
379 CP Celia 1 see a very great doctor/Whom I have heard of — and his name *is* Reilly!/{E} It would
379 CP Edward 27 meaning/Or so it seemed./{E} I have heard of that experience./{C} A dream. I was
382 CP Celia 14 voice — no, not a voice:/What I have heard was only the noise of an insect,/Dry,
387 CP Peter 19 be here in a minute./Celia! Have you heard from Lavinia too?/Or am I interrupting?/
389 CP Lavinia 2 Celia's going too? Was that what I heard?/I congratulate you both. To Hollywood,
408 CP Edward 22 to confide about Celia!/I have never heard anything so utterly ludicrous:/This is the
427 CP Alex 8 —/An island that you won't have heard of/Yet. Got back this morning. I heard
427 CP Alex 9 of/Yet. Got back this morning. I heard about your party/And, as I thought you
433 CP Lavinia 37 was Celia doing in Kinkanja?/We heard that she had joined some nursing order ...
445 CC Eggers 24 on? Swimmingly, I'm sure,/As I've heard nothing since the last time I came./{SC}
457 CC note 16& 25 *words off stage are not intended to be heard distinctly by an audience in the theatre.*/
465 CC Colby 39 like to have written,/As the composer heard it when it came to him;/But when I played
466 CC Colby 1 I was always conscious that what *they* heard/Was not what I hear when I play to
469 CC 4m 1 *concluding bars of a piece of music are/heard as the curtain rises.*/{L} *I* think you play
470 CC Colby 25 that American Musical!/{C} Well, I'd heard you say you wanted to see it./{L} But not
485 CC Lady E 29 country./Teddington. I seem to have heard of it./Was it a large house?/{C} No, a very
488 CC Claude 14 your son,/And then — any name you heard would have seemed the right one./{LE}
504 CC Lucasta 9 the parlourmaid?/{L} I thought I heard someone singing in the pantry./{LE} Oh, I
505 CC Guzzard 9 /{MG} Why should I mind?/I have heard about Mr. Eggerson from Colby. I am
505 CC Eggers 27 It is only recently that Lady Elizabeth/Heard your name mentioned, by Mr. Simpkins./
525 ES Monica 32 well/What it is you want to say. I've heard it all before./{C} And you'll hear it again.
531 ES Charles 9 the expectation that your voice will be heard/In debate in the Upper House ...{LC}
531 ES Lambert 38 him. Said you'd be very angry/If you heard that he'd gone away without your seeing
532 ES Ld Clav 14 man by myself, Monica./I've never heard of this Señor Gomez/But he comes with a
539 ES Gomez 16 /Dick, I was very very sorry when I heard/That your marriage had not been
539 ES Gomez 18 as for your son — from what I've heard about *him*,/He's followed your
550 ES Carghil 21 he worked too hard. Have you never heard/Of Carghill Equipments? They make
552 ES Ld Clav 10 Did you hear me sing it?/{LC} Yes, I heard you sing it./{MC} And what did you feel?/
552 ES Carghil 23 conscience was clear./I've very seldom heard people mention their consciences/Except
559 ES Michael 21 /To some country where no one has heard the name of Claverton;/Or where, if I
563 ES Gomez 12 in need of a rest cure too./And when I heard you'd chosen to come to Badgley Court/I
567 ES Monica 6 That Mrs. Piggott/Should have heard my beloved's voice/And I couldn't, just
568 ES Ld Clav 4 feel drawn to that spot./No matter. I heard what you said about guilty secrets./There
569 ES Ld Clav 25 advise you./{LC} Blackmail? Yes, I've heard that word before,/Not so very long ago.
572 ES Ld Clav 4 *I* didn't stop./And all my life I have heard, from time to time,/When I least
575 ES Gomez 21 learn the facts from me/Before he heard your distorted version./But, Dick, I was
581 ES Ld Clav 7 /{LC} I shall not be here. You heard me say to him/That this might be a final

HEARERS (1)
162 Rock 8   11   with words./And among his hearers were a few good men,/Many who were
HEARING (5)
38 Gerontion   59   /I have lost my sight, smell, hearing, taste and touch:/How should I use
276 MC Knight1   25   will not judge anybody without/hearing both sides of the case. That is in
353 CP   Alex   18   love that story./{A} I'm never tired of hearing that story./{J} Well, you all seem to
353 CP   Celia   21   all know it?/But we're never tired of hearing *you* tell it./I don't believe everyone here
354 CP   Julia   40   /And he had a remarkable sense of hearing —/The only man I ever met who could
HEARS (1)
309 FR   Harry   35   the silence/Between two storms, one hears the moderate usual noises/In the grass and
HEARSE (1)
94 Ash-Wed 4   21   jewelled unicorns draw by the gilded hearse./The silent sister veiled in white and blue/
HEART (34)
38 Gerontion   55   this honestly./I that was near your heart was removed therefrom/To lose beauty in
57 Swee Night   36   near/The Convent of the Sacred Heart,/And sang within the bloody wood/When
62 WL: Burial   41   and I knew nothing,/Looking into the heart of light, the silence./*Oed' und leer das*
70 WL: Fire S   296   /'My feet are at Moorgate, and my heart/Under my feet. After the event/He wept.
74 WL: Thund   402   given?/My friend, blood shaking my heart/The awful daring of a moment's surrender
74 WL: Thund   420   sail and oar/The sea was calm, your heart would have responded/Gaily, when
91 Ash-Wed 2   3   having fed to satiety/On my legs my heart my liver and that which had been
98 Ash-Wed 6   11   flying/Unbroken wings/And the lost heart stiffens and rejoices/In the lost lilac and
106 Song Sime   32   peace./(And a sword shall pierce thy heart,/Thine also)./I am tired with my own life
135 5FingerEx1   7   but in grief./O when will the creaking heart cease?/When will the broken chair give
149 Rock 1   73   next to you,/The desert is in the heart of your brother./The good man is the
149 Rock 1   77   long ago done,/That you may take heart. Make perfect your will./Let me show you
158 Rock 5   1   man of excellent intention and impure heart: for the heart is deceitful above all things,
158 Rock 5   1   intention and impure heart: for the heart is deceitful above all things, and
158 Rock 5   9   /If humility and purity be not in the heart, they are not in the home: and if they are
162 Rock 8   2   your words,/And we will take heart for the future,/Remembering the past./The
164 Rock 9   2   hear with thine ears/And set thine heart upon all that I show thee./Who is this that
172 FQ: BurntN   39   quietly,/The surface glittered out of heart of light,/And they were behind us,
228 Gus   22   I used to know seventy speeches by heart./I'd extemporize back-chat, I knew how to
319 FR   Harry   27   looks,/That bring death into the heart of a child./*That* was the day he died. Of
365 CP   Reilly 8   *landlord's daughter*/*And she took my heart entirely.*/You will keep our appointment?/
382 CP   Celia   18   do it. I looked,/And listened for your heart, your blood;/And saw only a beetle the
409 CP   Reilly 27   friend/(Though you knew, in your heart, that he was not in love with you,/And
428 CP   Alex   34   /But even this does not bring us to the heart of the matter./There are also foreign
451 CC   Eggers 10   be a power in the City!/And he has a heart of gold. But not to beat about the bush,/
454 CC   Eggers 26   rather flighty. But she has a good heart./{C} But does she address Sir Claude
456 CC   Eggers 9   escapes him./And such a generous heart! He's rather a Socialist./I'm a staunch
457 CC   Eggers 5   /And what's more, she has a good heart./{C} Everybody seems to be kind-hearted./
457 CC   Colby   8   Mr. Eggerson:/That *you* have a kind heart. And I'm convinced/That you always
472 CC   Lucasta 38   to give up,/A career that he's set his heart on, I'm sure:/But it's only the outer world
501 CC   Eggers 31   young men in the City,/And he has a heart of gold. So have you, Miss Angel./We
550 ES   Carghil 20   Is he still living?/{MC} He had a weak heart./And he worked too hard. Have you never
569 ES   Ld Clav 10   that you'll find a little love in your heart/Still, for your father, when you know him/
570 ES   Ld Clav 7   still of that opinion. How open one's heart/When one is sure of the wrong response?/
HEART'S (3)
191 FQ: Little   6   ditches,/In windless cold that is the heart's heat,/Reflecting in a watery mirror/A
320 FR Warburt   12   is weak/And running down. Her heart's very feeble./With care, and avoiding all
551 ES   Carghil 21   did./{MC} Who can say whether a heart's been broken/Once it's been repaired?
HEARTH (6)
158 Rock 5   10   during the day would return to his hearth at nightfall: to be blessed with the gift of
210 Old Gumbie   15   spots./All day she sits beside the hearth or in the sun or on my hat:/She sits and
260 MC Thomas   30   /over his peaceful gains, the swept hearth, his best wine for a friend/at the table,
281 MC Chorus   14   the fire, the knee bent in cleaning the hearth, we, the scrubbers and sweepers of
422 CP   Alex   12   /{A} The words for the building of the hearth. {}/[*They raise their glasses*]/{R} Let them
422 CP   Reilly 13   *their glasses*]/{R} Let them build the hearth/Under the protection of the stars./{A}
HEARTS (12)
117 SP   Doris   14   — Pereira!/{Do} The Queen of Hearts! — Mrs. Porter!/{Du} Or it might be you
117 SP   Doris   17   /{Do} Or it might be you/We're all hearts. You can't be sure./It just depends on
118 SP   Dusty   15   draw court cards?/The Knave of Hearts! {}/(*Whistle outside of the window.*)/{Du}
118 SP   Doris   20   Sam!/{Do} Of course, the Knave of Hearts *is* Sam!/{Du} (*leaning out of the*
152 Rock 2   34   was good you must fight to keep with hearts as devoted as those of your fathers who
154 Rock 3   10   friendly sentiments,/I have given you hearts, for reciprocal distrust./I have given you

228 Gus   27 voice that would soften the hardest of hearts,/Whether I took the lead, or in character
593 Grad 6   4 her sons, and we must go/With eager hearts to help mold well her fate,/And see that
244 MC Chorus   23 which none understands,/And our hearts are torn from us, our brains unskinned
245 MC Priest2   29 emptiness,/Have better prepared our hearts for your coming,/Than seven days could
260 MC Thomas   5 only that you should meditate in your hearts the/deep meaning and mystery of our
262 MC Thomas   3 last. I would have you keep in your hearts/these words that I say, and think of them

HEARTY (1)
245 MC Priest2   10 to put on pleasant faces,/And give a hearty welcome to our good Archbishop. {}/

HEAT (13)
109 Marina   22 with ice and paint cracked with heat./I made this, I have forgotten/And
139 Virginia   2 /Red river, red river,/Slow flow heat is silence/No will is still as a river/Still. Will
139 Virginia   4 /No will is still as a river/Still. Will heat move/Only through the mocking-bird/
172 FQ: BurntN   27 over the dead leaves,/In the autumn heat, through the vibrant air,/And the bird
177 FQ: ECoker   19 /Into the village, in the electric heat/Hypnotised. In a warm haze the sultry
178 FQ: ECoker   49 points, and another day/Prepares for heat and silence. Out at sea the dawn wind/
178 FQ: ECoker   54 spring/And creatures of the summer heat,/And snowdrops writhing under feet/And
191 FQ: Little   6 /In windless cold that is the heart's heat,/Reflecting in a watery mirror/A glare that
240 MC Chorus   13 winter fogs?/What shall we do in the heat of summer/But wait in barren orchards for
319 FR   Harry   21 remember/A summer day of unusual heat,/The day I lost my butterfly net;/I
332 FR   Agatha   23 remember/A summer day of unusual heat/For this cold country./{H} And then?/{Ag}
339 FR   Harry   10 sanctuary and a primitive altar,/The heat of the sun and the icy vigil,/A care over
438 CP   Reilly   14 fear of lions,/Cold of the night and heat of the day, than we should?/{E} But if this

HEATH (1)
124 SA   Snow   20 /What about them bones on Epsom Heath?/I seen that in the papers/You seen it in

HEATHEN (8)
162 Rock 8   4 future,/Remembering the past./The heathen are come into thine inheritance,/And
222 Pekes Pols   26 they please,/Is no British Dog, but a Heathen Chinese./And so all the Pekes, when
223 Pekes Pols   31 and wheeze/In their huffery-snuffery Heathen Chinese./But a terrible din is what
280 MC Priest1   12 /Alone, desecrated, desolated, and the heathen shall build on the ruins,/Their world
280 MC Priest3   25 desert sun,/Go seek alliance with the heathen Saracen,/To share his filthy rites, and
428 CP   Alex   11 /The majority of the natives are heathen:/They hold these monkeys in peculiar
429 CP   Alex   3 they agitate?/{A} By convincing the heathen/That the slaughter of monkeys has put
434 CP   Alex   12 the insurrection broke out/Among the heathen, of which I was telling you./They knew

HEATHENDOM (1)
429 CP   Alex   8 to be slaughtered —/To relapse into heathendom. So, instead of eating monkeys/

HEATHER (1)
348 FR   Chorus   32 /What ambush lies beyond the heather/And behind the Standing Stones?/

HEAVED (1)
270 MC Chorus   9 in the woodpath, while the ground heaved. I have seen/Rings of light coiling

HEAVEN (22)
29 Aunt Helen   4 when she died there was silence in heaven/And silence at her end of the street./The
44 Cook Egg   9 *Dance.*/I shall not want Honour in Heaven/For I shall meet Sir Philip Sidney/And
44 Cook Egg   13 kidney./I shall not want Capital in Heaven/For I shall meet Sir Alfred Mond./We
44 Cook Egg   17 Bond./I shall not want Society in Heaven,/Lucretia Borgia shall be my Bride;/Her
44 Cook Egg   21 provide./I shall not want Pipit in Heaven:/Madame Blavatsky will instruct me/In
147 Rock 1   1 /The Eagle soars in the summit of Heaven,/The Hunter with his dogs pursues his
147 Rock 1   17 lost in information?/The cycles of Heaven in twenty centuries/Bring us farther
151 Rock 2   13 of men to GOD./'Our citizenship is in Heaven'; yes, but that is the model and type for
173 FQ: BurntN   83 body,/Protects mankind from heaven and damnation/Which flesh cannot
189 FQ: DrySal   182 /Figlia del tuo figlio,/Queen of Heaven./Also pray for those who were in ships,
589 Fable   84 would declare/St. Peter'd snatch to heaven their lord renowned,/Though the wicked
249 MC Tempt2   8 /Is thrive on earth, and perhaps in heaven./{T} What means?/{T2} Real power/Is
250 MC Thomas   1 /{T} No! shall I, who keep the keys/Of heaven and hell, supreme alone in England,/
253 MC Tempt4   29 Adam fell —/You hold the keys of heaven and hell./Power to bind and loose: bind,
255 MC Tempt4   13 the lowest/On earth, to be high in heaven./And see far off below you, where the
261 MC Thomas   17 soul is/numbered among the Saints in Heaven, for the glory of God and for the/
261 MC Thomas   33 the world cannot understand; so in Heaven the Saints are/most high, having made
272 MC Thomas   5 have had a tremor of bliss, a wink of heaven, a whisper,/And I would no longer be
280 MC Priest1   7 you look down on us? You now in Heaven,/Who shall now guide us, protect us,
280 MC Priest3   17 lost erring souls, homeless in earth or heaven./Go where the sunset reddens the last
286 FR   Violet   18 at home;/People with money from heaven knows where —/{G} Dividends from
516 CC   Claude   28 to you, the experience we shared?/Heaven knows — and you know — I put no

HEAVEN'S (2)
322 FR   Warburt 20 what I've come about./{W} For Heaven's sake, Winchell,/Tell us your business./
375 CP   Edward   37 {}/[*Starts to leave the room*]/{E} For heaven's sake, don't bother! {}/[*Exit CELIA*]/{E}

HEAVENLY (3)

50 Hippopot	30	shall wash him clean/And him shall heavenly arms enfold,/Among the saints he shall
255 MC Tempt4	11	poverty/Compared with richness of heavenly grandeur?/Seek the way of
260 MC Thomas	12	/just passed, that a multitude of the heavenly host appeared before the/shepherds at

HEAVENS (4)

117 SP Doris	29	THAT'S THE COFFIN?/Oh good heavens what'll I do?/Just before a party too!/
117 SP Doris	35	it's mine. I know it's mine./Oh good heavens what'll I do./Well I'm not going to
178 FQ: ECoker	65	weep and Leonids fly/Hunt the heavens and the plains/Whirled in a vortex that
457 CC Claude	31	/I'll speak to him first./{SC} Good heavens, Eggerson, what *can* have happened?/

HEAVIER (2)

246 MC Thomas	22	shadows, and the strife with shadows./Heavier the interval than the consummation./
257 MC Chorus	14	taken away from us,/Our sins made heavier upon us./We have seen the young man

HEAVILY (3)

20 Portrait	92	find so much to learn.'/My smile falls heavily among the bric-à-brac./'Perhaps you
295 FR Harry	5	very attentive./That night I slept heavily, alone./{A} Harry!/{C} You mustn't
533 ES Gomez	32	me./Sometimes I've had to pay pretty heavily;/But I learnt by experience whom to

HEAVING (5)

37 Gerontion	5	rain/Nor knee deep in the salt marsh, heaving a cutlass,/Bitten by flies, fought./My
135 5FingerEx2	14	to dust./Here a little dog I pause/Heaving up my prior paws,/Pause, and sleep
185 FQ: DrySal	34	headland/Are all sea voices, and the heaving groaner/Rounded homewards, and the
256 MC Chorus	8	cloud on a withered tree? The earth is heaving to parturition of issue of hell. What is
269 MC Chorus	32	flesh in the spoon. I have felt/The heaving of earth at nightfall, restless, absurd. I

HEAVISIDE (1)

348 FR Chorus	34	the Standing Stones?/Beyond the Heaviside Layer/And behind the smiling moon?

HEAVY (8)

57 Swee Night	27	be in league;/Therefore the man with heavy eyes/Declines the gambit, shows fatigue,/
69 WL: Fire S	272	sails/Wide/To leeward, swing on the heavy spar./The barges wash/Drifting logs/
90 Ash-Wed 1	33	again/May the judgement not be too heavy upon us/Because these wings are no
107 Animula	16	do and what the servants say./The heavy burden of the growing soul/Perplexes and
127 Cor1 March	16	trench mortars,/53,000 field and heavy guns,/I cannot tell how many projectiles,
178 FQ: ECoker	37	solemn or in rustic laughter/Lifting heavy feet in clumsy shoes,/Earth feet, loam
256 MC Chorus	6	movement of feet. And the air is heavy and thick./Thick and heavy the sky. And
256 MC Chorus	7	the air is heavy and thick./Thick and heavy the sky. And the earth presses up against

HEBETUDE (1)

179 FQ: ECoker	79	deceit?/The serenity only a deliberate hebetude,/The wisdom only the knowledge of

HEDGEROW (3)

191 FQ: Little	14	/But not in time's covenant. Now the hedgerow/Is blanched for an hour with
195 FQ: Little	153	differ completely, flourish in the same hedgerow:/Attachment to self and to things and
596 When we	5	torn no quivering cobweb down./The hedgerow bloomed with flowers still,/No

HEDGES (1)

191 FQ: Little	24	way in may time, you would find the hedges/White again, in May, with voluptuary

HEEL (3)

19 Portrait	61	invulnerable, you have no Achilles' heel./You will go on, and when you have
42 Swee Erect	18	the knees/Then straightens out from heel to hip/Pushing the framework of the bed/
253 MC Tempt4	31	bind,/King and bishop under your heel./King, emperor, bishop, baron, king:/

HEELS (3)

127 Cor1 March	1	stone, steel, stone, oakleaves, horses' heels/Over the paving./And the flags. And the
128 Cor1 March	40	stone, steel, stone, oakleaves, horses' heels/Over the paving./That is all we could see.
335 FR Agatha	7	air. Only feet walking/And sharp heels scraping. Over and under/Echo and noise

HEIMAT (1)

61 WL: Burial	32	of dust./*Frisch weht der Wind/Der Heimat zu/Mein Irisch Kind/Wo weilest du?/*'You

HEINOUSNESS (1)

573 ES Ld Clav	11	in the last five minutes/Is not the heinousness of my misdeeds/But the fact of my

HEIR (1)

478 CC Lucasta	2	he'll adopt you, and make you his heir/And you'll marry another Lady Elizabeth./

HEIRS (2)

67 WL: Fire S	180	/And their friends, the loitering heirs of City directors;/Departed, have left no
507 CC Guzzard	27	was very careless./{MG} And that the heirs acknowledged no responsibility./The

HELD (10)

24 Rhapsody	3	/Along the reaches of the street/Held in a lunar synthesis,/Whispering lunar
24 Rhapsody	45	/Gripped the end of a stick which I held him./Half-past three,/The lamp sputtered,/
64 WL: Chess	79	on the marble, where the glass/Held up by standards wrought with fruited
223 Pekes Pols	38	*Border.*/Then the Pugs and the Poms held no longer aloof,/But some from the
588 Fable	53	of plover,/And flagons which perhaps held several kegs/Of ale, and cheese which they
588 Fable	56	took four pages,/His mouth an apple held, his skull held sausages./Over their

588 Fable		56	/His mouth an apple held, his skull held sausages./Over their Christmas wassail the
605 Narcissus		25	been a fish/With slippery white belly held tight in his own fingers,/Writhing in his
248 MC	Tempt2	34	love to God alone./Shall he who held the solid substance/Wander waking with
304 FR	Mary	26	/Even when he married, she still held on to me/Because she couldn't bear to let

HELEN (2)

29 Aunt Helen		t	the *Boston Evening Transcript.*'/Aunt Helen/Miss Helen Slingsby was my maiden
29 Aunt Helen		1	*Transcript.*'/Aunt Helen/Miss Helen Slingsby was my maiden aunt,/And lived

HELL (17)

125 SA	Chorus	32	night and/you wake in a sweat and a hell of a fright/When you're alone in the middle
250 MC	Thomas	1	I, who keep the keys/Of heaven and hell, supreme alone in England,/Who bind and
253 MC	Tempt4	29	—/You hold the keys of heaven and hell./Power to bind and loose: bind, Thomas,
256 MC	Chorus	8	is heaving to parturition of issue of hell. What is the sticky dew that forms on the
257 MC	Chorus	31	laughter, laughter. The Lords of Hell are here./They curl round you, lie at your
272 MC	Chorus	20	than fury in the hall./The agents of hell disappear, the human, they shrink and
272 MC	Chorus	24	more horrid than active shapes of hell;/Emptiness, absence, separation from God;/
280 MC	Priest3	34	as you weave,/Pacing forever in the hell of make-believe/Which never is belief: this
330 FR	Harry	23	feels eternal while it lasts. That is one hell./Then the numbness came to cover it —
330 FR	Harry	25	is another —/That was the second hell of not being there,/The degradation of
397 CP	Edward	4	I not walk out of my prison?/What is hell? Hell is oneself,/Hell is alone, the other
397 CP	Edward	4	walk out of my prison?/What is hell? Hell is oneself,/Hell is alone, the other figures in
397 CP	Edward	5	prison?/What is hell? Hell is oneself,/Hell is alone, the other figures in it/Merely
397 CP	Edward	22	I don't need a doctor./I am simply in hell. Where there are no doctors —/At least, not
397 CP	Lavinia	24	/{L} One can be practical, even in hell:/And you know I am much more practical
419 CP	Celia	6	memories and desires./{C} That is the hell I have been in./{R} It isn't hell/Till you
419 CP	Reilly	7	is the hell I have been in./{R} It isn't hell/Till you become incapable of anything else./

HELLISH (1)

270 MC	Chorus	9	of sweet soap in the woodpath, a hellish sweet scent in the woodpath, while the

HELLO (16)

116 SP	Dusty	20	the stairs/Say we've had a fire/{Du} Hello Hello are you there?/Yes this is Miss
116 SP	Dusty	20	stairs/Say we've had a fire/{Du} Hello Hello are you there?/Yes this is Miss Dorrance's
118 SP	Dusty	21	/{Du} *(leaning out of the window)*: Hello Sam!/{W} Hello dear/How many's up
118 SP	Wauch	22	*out of the window)*: Hello Sam!/{W} Hello dear/How many's up there?/{Du}
119 SP	Wauch	1	KLIPSTEIN. KRUMPACKER./{W} Hello Doris! Hello Dusty! How do you do!/
119 SP	Wauch	1	KRUMPACKER./{W} Hello Doris! Hello Dusty! How do you do!/How come? how
371 CP	Edward	23	me a moment. {}/[*Into telephone*]/{E} Hello! ... I can't talk now .../Yes, there is ... Well
375 CP	Edward	12	telephone. I suppose I must answer it./Hello ... oh, hello! ... No. I mean yes, Alex;/Yes,
375 CP	Edward	12	suppose I must answer it./Hello ... oh, hello! ... No. I mean yes, Alex;/Yes, of course ...
383 CP	Edward	1	it./{C} Yes, better answer it./{E} Hello! ... Oh, Julia: what is it now?/Your
383 CP	Edward	27	{}/[*He snatches up the receiver*]/{E} Hello, Julia! are you there? .../Well, I'm awfully
400 CP	Reilly	30	{}/[*The house-telephone rings*]/{R} Hello! Yes, show him up./{A} You will have a
452 CC	Kaghan	1	B. KAGHAN]/{K} Enter B. Kaghan. Hello Colby!/And hello Eggers! I'm glad to find
452 CC	Kaghan	2	Enter B. Kaghan. Hello Colby!/And hello Eggers! I'm glad to find you here./It's
457 CC	Claude	11	you. {}/[*Enter SIR CLAUDE*]/{SC} Hello! Still here? It's time you were off./{E} I'm
457 CC	Claude	20	he suffers from chronic catarrh./{SC} Hello! What's that? {}/[*Opens door on to*

HELP (43)

66 WL:	Chess	158	/(And her only thirty-one.)/I can't help it, she said, pulling a long face,/It's them
163 Rock 8		49	make perfect our will./O GOD, help us./Son of Man, behold with thine eyes,
233 Skimble		62	to wait —/For Skimbleshanks will help you to get out!/He gives you a wave of his
593 Grad 6		4	and we must go/With eager hearts to help mold well her fate,/And see that she shall
267 MC	Knights	3	/{3K} Yes, we'll pray that God may help you!/{T} But, gentlemen, your business/
273 MC	Chorus	6	/Let not be in vain Thy labour;/Help me, Lord, in my last fear./Dust I am, to
273 MC	Chorus	9	/From the final doom impending/Help me, Lord, for death is near. {}/[*In the*
305 FR	Mary	3	But where? I want a job: and you can help me./{Ag} I am very sorry, Mary, I am very
305 FR	Agatha	6	of such a feeling./I would like to help you: but you must not run away./Any time
305 FR	Mary	16	dinner. {}/[*Exit*]/{M} So you will not help me!/Waiting, waiting, always waiting./I
312 FR	Harry	5	listened/To your nonsense. Can't you help me?/You're of no use to me. I must face
343 FR	Mary	10	two worlds./{M} Then you *will* help me!/You remember what I said to you this
343 FR	Mary	18	learn that one is dead! So you must help me./I will go. But I suppose it is much too
345 FR	Amy	27	to that of any of the others/Just to help me to the next room. Where I can lie down.
366 CP	Peter	31	what's it all about?/{P} I want your help./I was going to telephone and try to see
380 CP	Celia	25	he was lonely;/I thought that I could help him. I took him to concerts./But then, as
397 CP	Lavinia	17	... of a doctor who I think could help you./{E} If I go to a doctor, I shall make
431 CP	Peter	36	only for minor parts —/And I'll help him decide what faces are typical./{J} Peter,
433 CP	Peter	17	always wanted to. And now I could help her./I've already spoken to Bela about her,/
438 CP	Edward	22	/As your responsibility./{E} I cannot help the feeling/That, in some way, my

438 CP	Lavinia	26	what you were thinking!/Doesn't it help you, that I feel guilty too?/{R} If we all
476 CC	Lucasta	15	/That's where B. has been such a help to me —/He fosters the impression. He half
486 CC	Colby	27	him. I was told about him./But I can't help wondering why you are so interested:/
487 CC	Claude	9	/That Colby can be of greater help than Eggerson./I couldn't have asked
490 CC	Lady E	6	/Though I try to be clever. Do try to help me./{SC} It could have happened. But I'm
492 CC	Colby	15	don't think, tonight, the piano would help me:/At the moment, I never want to touch
500 CC	Lucasta	34	by life, just as I have,/And we can help each other. Oh, I know you think of him/
501 CC	Lady E	19	how late. And perhaps that will help us/To understand other people. I hope so./
506 CC	Guzzard	25	You think that I might be able to help you?/{E} It seems just possible. A few days
506 CC	Eggers	40	Mrs. Guzzard, this is where you can help us —/Do you know of any other Mrs.
517 CC	Lady E	19	{LE} Yes. My poor Claude!/Do try to help him, Eggerson./{E} I wouldn't venture./Mr.
535 ES	Ld Clav	20	*tray and exit*]/{LC} Won't you help yourself? {}/[GOMEZ *does so, liberally*]/
537 ES	Gomez	32	you, Dick. He never came to *my* help./{LC} I certainly admit no responsibility,/
560 ES	Ld Clav	5	such trifles./{LC} So you want me to help you to escape from your father!/{Mi} And
560 ES	Michael	6	escape from your father!/{Mi} And to help my father to be rid of *me*./You simply
560 ES	Ld Clav	16	what I will do for you, Michael./I will help you to make a start in any business/You
561 ES	Ld Clav	2	of excellence, how gladly would I help you!/Even though it carried you away from
561 ES	Monica	25	must be in great trouble,/So can't you help him?/{LC} I am trying to help him,/And to
561 ES	Ld Clav	26	you help him?/{LC} I am trying to help him,/And to meet him half way. I have
567 ES	Charles	12	I wondered ... I'm sorry, I couldn't help wondering/How much your words meant.
567 ES	Charles	20	trying to think what I could do to help him./If it's blackmail, and that's very much
569 ES	Charles	22	practice at the bar./I'm sure I could help./{M} Oh Father, do let him./{C} At least, I
574 ES	Carghil	21	/And I found him only too ready to help./{LC} And what was Señor Gomez able to

HELPED (2)

252 MC	Thomas	5	court over baron's court./{T} Which I helped to found./{T3} Which you helped to
252 MC	Tempt3	6	I helped to found./{T3} Which you helped to found./But time past is time forgotten.

HELPFUL (6)

211 Old	Gumbie	34	louts,/A troop of well-disciplined helpful boy-scouts,/With a purpose in life and a
293 FR	Amy	4	see your aunts and uncles are very helpful, Harry./I have always found them
449 CC	Claude	15	glad you agree. Your support will be helpful./{E} I'm sure I shall be very happy to
451 CC	Colby	15	I like B. Kaghan. I've found him very helpful/And very good company apart from
579 ES	Michael	11	shipping line/Who he thinks can be helpful in getting reservations./{MC} It's
579 ES	Gomez	38	at the very moment/When I could be helpful./{MC} It's truly providential!/{M}

HELPING (3)

291 FR	Violet	5	in Dorset./{V} I should have been helping Lady Bumpus, at the Vicar's American
298 FR	Charles	3	to hand./If you are interested in helping Harry/You can hardly object to the
545 ES	Piggott	34	be overjoyed to have the privilege of helping you!/{M} You're very kind ... Oh, I'm

HELPLESS (3)

151 Rock 2		4	have you built well, that you now sit helpless in a ruined house?/Where many are
366 CP	Julia	23	you stop and talk to Edward. I'm not helpless yet./And besides, I like to manage the
376 CP	Celia	5	I'll say I found you here starving and helpless/And had to do something. Anyway, I'm

HELPS (1)

535 ES		m 34	To take another name. {}/[*Gets up and helps himself to whisky*]/{G} But of course you

HELPT (1)

593 Grad 7		5	guerdon than to know/That they have helpt the cause to victory,/That with their aid

HEMINGTON (9)

523 ES		m 3	CLAVERTON-FERRY/CHARLES HEMINGTON/LAMBERT/LORD
568 ES	Ld Clav	11	been nothing in your life, Charles Hemington,/Which you wish to forget? Which
573 ES	Monica	28	Do introduce him./{M} Mr. Charles Hemington. Mrs. Carghill./{C} How do you do.
573 ES	Carghil	32	And let me congratulate *you*, Mr. Hemington./You're a very lucky man, to get a
574 ES	Carghil	1	him,/Oh so long ago. So you see, Mr. Hemington,/I've come to regard her as my
574 ES	Carghil	3	so, that it seems odd to call you Mr. Hemington:/I'm going to call you Charles!/{C}
577 ES	Michael	20	you say to all this?/{Mi} I'll say that Hemington has plenty of cheek./Señor Gomez
577 ES	Michael	21	Gomez and I have talked things over, Hemington .../{G} As two men of the world, we
580 ES	Gomez	13	good-bye Monica./Good-bye, Mr. ... Hemington./{M} Good-bye Michael. {}/[*Exeunt*

HEMISPHERE (1)

232 Skimble		16	for the northern part/Of the Northern Hemisphere!/You may say that by and large it is

HEN-HOUSE (1)

212 Growltiger		11	at his name./They would fortify the hen-house, lock up the silly goose,/When the

HENCE (2)

63 WL: Burial		74	its bed?/'O keep the Dog far hence, that's friend to men,/'Or with his nails
538 ES	Gomez	2	unfortunate, a talent for penmanship./Hence, as you have just reminded me/

HENLEY (1)

213 Growltiger		54	the land;/At Maidenhead and Henley there was dancing on the strand./Rats

HENRY (30)

587	Fable	2	long before that royal Mormon/King Henry VIII found out that monks were quacks,/
251	MC Tempt3	13	have no hope of reconciliation/With Henry the King. You look only/To blind
251	MC Thomas	16	in isolation./That is a mistake./{T} O Henry, O my King!/{T3} Other friends/May be
277	MC Knight3	17	well how/things will turn out. King Henry — God bless him — will have to/say, for
352	CP	m 7	GUEST, *later identified as* SIR HENRY HARCOURT-REILLY/LAVINIA
399	CP	2m 1	for me? {}/CURTAIN/Act Two/SIR HENRY HARCOURT-REILLY'S *consulting*
399	CP	3m 1	*Morning:/several weeks later.* SIR HENRY *alone at his desk. He presses an/*
399	CP	Nurse 5	/{N} You made that clear, Sir Henry:/The first appointment at eleven o'clock./
399	CP	Nurse 24	moment./{N} Mr. Gibbs is here, Sir Henry./{R} Ask him to come straight in. {}/[*Exit*
400	CP	Edward 35	*in by* NURSE-SECRETARY]/{E} Sir Henry Harcourt-Reilly — {}/[*Stops and stares at*
405	CP	Lavinia 25	patient./{E} Lavinia!/{L} Well, Henry!/I said I would come to talk about my
411	CP	Lavinia 26	And I have a question too./Sir Henry, was it you who sent those telegrams?/{R}
411	CP	Edward 33	you anything else to say to us, Sir Henry?/{R} No. Not in this capacity. {}/
412	CP	Julia 3	waiting downstairs./{J} I know that, Henry. I brought her here myself./{R} Oh? You
412	CP	Julia 18	/{R} That is most uncommon./{J} Henry, get up./You can't be as tired as that. I
420	CP	Julia 24	I am worried about./{J} Nonsense, Henry. *I* shall keep an eye on them./{R} To send
421	CP	Julia 23	appearance of projected spirits?/{J} Henry, you simply do not understand
432	CP	Caterer 2	/{P} No, I'm afraid .../{CM} Sir Henry Harcourt-Reilly!/{J} Oh, I forgot! I'd
432	CP	Julia 4	REILLY]/{J} I want you to meet Sir Henry Harcourt-Reilly —/{E} We're delighted
432	CP	Julia 12	was necessary./{J} My dear Henry, you are interrupting me./{L} If you can
432	CP	Lavinia 13	me./{L} If you can interrupt Julia, Sir Henry,/You are the perfect guest we've been
432	CP	Lavinia 26	I introduce Mr. Peter Quilpe/Sir Henry Harcourt-Reilly. Peter's an old friend/Of
436	CP	Lavinia 20	happy in the thought of her./{L} Sir Henry, there is something I want to say to you./
436	CP	Julia 36	else you are very perceptive./{J} Oh, Henry!/Lavinia is much more observant than
437	CP	Julia 2	poetry .../{J} She has made a point, Henry./{L} ... if it answers my question./{R} *Ere*
439	CP	Julia 9	the past will you alter its meaning./{J} Henry, I think it is time that *I* said something:/
439	CP	Peter 33	Julia. Good-bye, Alex. Good-bye, Sir Henry. {}/[*Exit*]/{J} ... And now the consequence
440	CP	Edward 6	much/That I understand yet! But Sir Henry has been saying,/I think, that every
440	CP	Julia 13	it will be a success./{J} And I think, Henry,/That we should leave before the party
440	CP	Julia 19	I shall not be unexpected./{J} Now, Henry. Now, Alex. We're going to the

HENRY'S (1)

278	MC Knight2	4	aims? and what are King Henry's aims? In/the answer to these questions

HER (443)

HERBAL (2)

481	CC Lady E	26	/Oh, I know. It's a chance to try that Herbal Restaurant/I recommended to you. You
481	CC Lucasta	36	/{L} I'm so hungry, I could even eat a herbal salad./{LE} That's right. Just mention

HERBERT (2)

514	CC Guzzard	11	/{C} Who was my father, then?/{MG} Herbert Guzzard./You are the son of a
514	CC Guzzard	21	/{MG} Registration of birth. To Herbert and Sarah Guzzard/A son./{E} And

HERCULES (2)

40	Burb Blei	7	with the passing bell/Slowly: the God Hercules/Had left him, that had loved him well.
280	MC Priest3	19	grey rock/Of Brittany, or the Gates of Hercules./Go venture shipwreck on the sullen

HERDSMEN (1)

220	Old Deut	20	they may bleat,/But the dogs and the herdsmen will turn them away./The cars and the

HERE (248)

HERE'S (12)

15	Prufrock	83	a platter,/I am no prophet — and here's no great matter;/I have seen the moment
117	SP Doris	8	Well anyway it's very queer./{Do} Here's the four of diamonds, what's that mean?/
117	SP Doris	12	or a party'./That's queer too./{Do} Here's the three. What's that mean?/{Du} 'News
117	SP Doris	25	Separation of friends'./{Do} Here's the two of spades./{Du} The *two of*
125	SA Sweeney	3	use words when I talk to you./But here's what I was going to say./He didn't know
347	FR Ivy	15	going? where is Harry?/Look. Here's a telegram come from Arthur; {}/[*Enter*
353	CP Celia	25	/{UG} No, I've never heard it./{C} Here's one new listener for you, Julia;/And I
478	CC Kaghan	36	B. Kaghan./To see the new flat. And here's Lucasta./I knew I should find she'd got in
526	ES Monica	23	we entered only a few minutes ago./Here's an armchair, there's the table;/There's
576	ES Gomez	36	something about the law of slander./Here's Mrs. Carghill, a reliable witness./{C}
577	ES Charles	1	likely to invoke it./And, Michael, here's another point to think of:/Señor Gomez
580	ES Gomez	2	/{G} Oh, I'm glad you reminded me. Here's my business card/With the full address.

HEREAFTER (2)

248	MC Tempt2	36	shadows?/Power is present. Holiness hereafter./{T} Who then?/{T2} The Chancellor,
333	FR Agatha	35	/Indeed it is possible. You may learn hereafter,/Moving alone through flames of ice,

HEREDITY (1)

485	CC Lady E	20	in us,/In all of us, which isn't just heredity,/But something unique. Something we

176 FQ: BurntN 174   while the dust moves/There rises the hidden laughter/Of children in the foliage/Quick
197 FQ: Little   249   of the longest river/The voice of the hidden waterfall/And the children in the
226 Macavity   1   a Mystery Cat: he's called the Hidden Paw —/For he's the master criminal
280 MC Priest1   38   lord/The glory of whose new state is hidden from us,/Pray for us of your charity./
289 FR Agatha   2   does not come for everybody —/The hidden is revealed, and the spectres show
301 FR Chorus   17   waiting for some revelation/When the hidden shall be exposed, and the newsboy shall
337 FR Agatha   11   hunt:/Here you have found a clue, hidden in the obvious place./Delay, and it is

HIDE (1)
376 CP   Celia   7   I'm *staying*/And I'm not going to hide. {}/[*Returns to kitchen. The bell rings*

HIDEOUS (1)
598 Circe   5 /Their petals are fanged and red/With hideous streak and stain;/They sprang from the

HIDING (2)
204 de la Mare   3 /A desert island with a sandy cove/(A hiding place, but very dangerous ground,/For
307 FR   Harry   15   down to the river/To find the old hiding place. The wilderness was gone,/The tree

HIERONYMO'S (1)
75 WL: Thund   431   against my ruins/Why then Ile fit you. Hieronymo's mad againe./Datta. Dayadhvam.

HIGH (18)
16 Prufrock   117   cautious, and meticulous;/Full of high sentence, but a bit obtuse;/At times,
24 Rhapsody   23   crooked pin.'/The memory throws up high and dry/A crowd of twisted things;/A
73 WL: Thund   366   other side of you?/What is that sound high in the air/Murmur of maternal lamentation
103 Journ Magi   15   /And the villages dirty and charging high prices:/A hard time we had of it./At the
178 FQ: ECoker   56   feet/And hollyhocks that aim too high/Red into grey and tumble down/Late roses
220 Old Deut   18   sits in the street,/He sits in the High Street on market day;/The bullocks may
232 Skimble   6   daughters/They are searching high and low,/Saying 'Skimble where is Skimble
593 Grad 7   6   with their aid the flag is raised on high./Sometime in distant years when we are
605 Narcissus   8   walked once between the sea and the high cliffs/When the wind made him aware of
255 MC Tempt4   13   yourself the lowest/On earth, to be high in heaven./And see far off below you,
261 MC Thomas   34   so in Heaven the Saints are/most high, having made themselves most low, and are
263 MC Chorus   22   the stream, and the air is clear and high,/And voices trill at windows, and children
292 FR   Ivy   34 a successor to old Hawkins./It's really high time the old man was pensioned./He's let
299 FRDowning   35   /Very uncommon that I saw him in high spirits./For what my judgment's worth, I
377 CP   Julia   21   in the place fit to eat:/I've looked high and low. But I found some champagne —/
516 CC   Colby   9   matter about success —/I aimed too high before — beyond my capacity./I thought I
561 ES   Ld Clav   1 /Oh Michael! If you had some aim of high achievement,/Some dream of excellence,
573 ES   Carghil   23   /{MC} I've been hunting high and low for you, Richard!/I've some very

HIGH-POWERED (1)
161 Rock 7   37   say, does the whole world stray in high-powered cars on a by-pass way?/VOICE

HIGHBROW (1)
578 ES   Michael   30   my friends used to chaff me about my highbrow sister./But all the same, I was fond of

HIGHBURY (1)
70 WL: Fire S   293   leialala/'Trams and dusty trees./Highbury bore me. Richmond and Kew/Undid

HIGHER (8)
94 Ash-Wed 4   20   Redeem/The unread vision in the higher dream/While jewelled unicorns draw by
160 Rock 7   9   were known of the light/Invented the Higher Religions; and the Higher Religions
160 Rock 7   9   the Higher Religions; and the Higher Religions were good/And led men from
248 MC Tempt1   1   /I leave you to the pleasures of your higher vices,/Which will have to be paid for
248 MC Tempt1   2   /Which will have to be paid for at higher prices./Farewell, my Lord, I do not wait
269 MC Thomas   10   I who insult the King,/And there is higher than I or the King./It is not I, Becket
278 MC Knight2   23   affirmed immediately that there was a higher/order than that which our King, and he
409 CP   Reilly   36 as you could,/That he was aiming at a higher social distinction/Than the honour

HIGHEST (8)
34 Figlia   1   /La Figlia Che Piange/Stand on the highest pavement of the stair —/Lean on a
228 Gus   15   days./For he once was a Star of the highest degree —/He has acted with Irving, he's
242 MC   Mess   14   /I have this, I assure you, on the highest authority;/There are several opinions as
260 MC Thomas   1   1170/{T} 'Glory to God in the highest, and on earth peace to men of good
260 MC Thomas   13   saying 'Glory to God in the highest, and on/earth peace to men of good
278 MC Knight2   19 known a man so well qualified for the/highest rank of the Civil Service. And what
438 CP   Reilly   1   /Than the rest of us. She paid the highest price/In suffering. That is part of the
570 ES   Ld Clav   28   /A man of great importance and the highest standing/In his adopted country. He

HIGHGATE (1)
174 FQ: BurntN 115   Clerkenwell, Camden and Putney,/Highgate, Primrose and Ludgate. Not here/Not

HIGHLY (7)
218 Mung Rump 18   unusual gift of the gab./They were highly efficient cat-burglars as well, and
226 Macavity   13 deeply lined with thought, his head is highly domed;/His coat is dusty from neglect,
447 CC   Claude   29   Colby —/Say that Mr. Simpkins was highly recommended,/And say that I had to

448 CC	Eggers	13	And I thought, Mr. Simpkins,/He's highly educated. He'll soon begin to grasp them.
458 CC	Eggers	34	/{E} And Mr. Simpkins is much more highly qualified/Than I am, to be a confidential
533 ES	Gomez	20	footloose. Gomez, you see,/Is now a highly respected citizen/Of a central American
576 ES	Charles	33	I tell you./{C} So I can imagine:/Highly confidential .../{G} Be careful, Mr.

HILARITY (1)

| 232 Skimble | | 27 | it's certain that he doesn't approve/Of hilarity and riot, so the folk are very quiet/ |

HILL (4)

62 WL: Burial		66	his eyes before his feet./Flowed up the hill and down King William Street,/To where
166 Rock 10		3	visible church, one more light set on a hill/In a world confused and dark and disturbed
179 FQ: ECoker		101	/The dancers are all gone under the hill./O dark dark dark. They all go into the
596 When we		1	Song/When we came home across the hill/No leaves were fallen from the trees;/The

HILLS (10)

30 Cous Nancy		2	Miss Nancy Ellicott/Strode across the hills and broke them,/Rode across the hills and
30 Cous Nancy		3	hills and broke them,/Rode across the hills and broke them —/The barren New
30 Cous Nancy		4	them —/The barren New England hills —/Riding to hounds/Over the cow-pasture.
105 Song Sime		2	/The winter sun creeps by the snow hills;/The stubborn season had made stand./My
139 Virginia		6	the mocking-bird/Heard once? Still hills/Wait. Gates wait. Purple trees,/White trees,
160 Rock 7		16	the restless wind-whipped sand, or the hills where the wind will not let the snow rest./
174 FQ: BurntN		113	on the wind that sweeps the gloomy hills of London./Hampstead and Clerkenwell,
180 FQ: ECoker		117	on darkness,/And we know that the hills and the trees, the distant panorama/And
421 CP	Julia	26	She will pass between the scolding hills,/Through the valley of derision, like a child
547 ES	Piggott	35	lovely walks, on the shore or in the hills,/Quite away from the motor roads. You

HIM (405)

HIMAVANT (1)

| 74 WL: Thund | | 397 | clouds/Gathered far distant, over Himavant./The jungle crouched, humped in |

HIMSELF (45)

151 Rock 2		3	apostles and prophets, Christ Jesus Himself the chief cornerstone./But you, have
164 Rock 9		17	formless stone, when the artist unites himself with stone,/Spring always new forms of
166 Rock 10		8	the pit of the world, curled/In folds of himself until he awakens in hunger and moving
209 NamingCats		24	can discover —/But THE CAT HIMSELF KNOWS, and will never confess./
214 RTTugger		28	/For he only likes what he finds for himself;/So you'll catch him in it right up to the
229 Gus		49	a hoop.'/And he'll say, as he scratches himself with his claws,/'Well, the Theatre's
236 Cat Morgan		t	A CAT./Cat Morgan Introduces Himself/I once was a Pirate what sailed the 'igh
251 MC Tempt3		26	Sovereignty. Let the Angevin/Destroy himself, fighting in Anjou./He does not
256 MC Tempts		23	/The enemy of society, enemy of himself./{3P} O Thomas my Lord do not fight
260 MC Thomas		26	a cheat?/Reflect now, how Our Lord Himself spoke of Peace. He said to His/
261 MC Thomas		31	who no/longer desires anything for himself, not even the glory of being a/martyr.
264 MC Priest1		24	/{P1} As for the people, so also for himself, he offereth for sins./He lays down his
278 MC Knight2		12	that Becket, who had proved himself an extremely/able administrator — no
279 MC Knight4		23	reversed his policy; he showed/himself to be utterly indifferent to the fate of the
279 MC Knight4		34	easily escaped; he/could have kept himself from us long enough to allow our
299 FR	Charles	1	health./He doesn't seem to be ... quite himself./{Do} Quite natural, if I may say so, Sir,
304 FR	Agatha	39	important, I think, but what he did to himself./{M} But it wasn't till I knew that Harry
315 FR	Harry	5	Your ordinary murderer/Regards himself as an innocent victim./To himself he is
315 FR	Harry	6	himself as an innocent victim./To himself he is still what he used to be/Or what he
330 FR	Harry	6	conceive/As settling down to make himself at home at Wishwood,/Make a dull
330 FR	Harry	8	woman stupider —/Stupider than himself. He can resist the influence/Of
400 CP	Reilly	25	a double advantage:/To escape from himself — and get the better of his wife./{A}
402 CP	Edward	12	thought a doctor could see that for himself./Or at least that he would enquire about
404 CP	Reilly	39	more about him,/Than the patient himself can always tell me./Indeed, it is often
405 CP	Reilly	4	The single patient/Who is ill by himself, is rather the exception./I have recently
410 CP	Reilly	8	The same isolation./A man who finds himself incapable of loving/And a woman who
420 CP	Reilly	29	to disguise his own meanness/From himself, because it is known to the other./It's
424 CP	m	11	CATERER'S MAN]/[EDWARD *lets himself in at the front door*]/{E} I'm in good time,
450 CC	Colby	36	Lady Elizabeth,/And Sir Claude himself hasn't told me very much:/So I've no
453 CC	Eggers	40	intends to deal with these matters himself./You will have to ask Sir Claude. But
455 CC	Eggers	13	friend of Sir Claude's,/And he's made himself responsible for her./In any case, he's
497 CC	Claude	11	She'd been questioning Colby about himself,/And he mentioned the name of his
517 CC	Colby	12	a man without illusions/About himself, and without ambitions./Now that I've
525 ES	Charles	20	any man but he should have you to himself,/Before I've said two words he'll come
529 ES	Monica	6	looking at you. He was thinking of himself/When he was your age — when he
535 ES	m	34	another name. {}/[*Gets up and helps himself to whisky*]/{G} But of course you know!/
539 ES	m	22	beginning to be thirsty again. {}/[*Pours himself whisky*]/{LC} An interesting historical
539 ES	Ld Clav	29	hints have been given,/He's informed himself so carefully about my career./{G} I
540 ES	Gomez	6	who has to keep on pretending to himself/That he's a success — the man who in

554 ES	Piggott	22	/We can't allow him to tire himself with talking./What he needs is *rest*!
571 ES	Ld Clav	31	/He re-enters my life to make himself a reminder/Of one occasion the memory
574 ES	Michael	35	another Sir Alfred/Who'd constitute himself custodian of my morals/And send you
577 ES	Ld Clav	40	free agent. So if he chooses/To place himself in your power, Fred Culverwell,/Of his
580 ES	Monica	33	it's not you and me he rejects,/But himself, the unhappy self that he's ashamed of./
583 ES	Monica	17	/In becoming no one, he has become himself./He is only my father now, and

HIND (1)
222 Pekes Pols		20	at each other, and scraped their hind feet,/And started to/Bark bark bark bark/

HINDHEAD (1)
147 Rock 1		29	on the seventh we must motor/To Hindhead, or Maidenhead./If the weather is

HINDRANCE (1)
194 FQ: Little		122	/But, as the passage now presents no hindrance/To the spirit unappeased and

HINT (4)
190 FQ: DrySal		219	discipline, thought and action./The hint half guessed, the gift half understood, is
482 CC	Lady E	8	I hope you won't mind a gentle hint./I feared it was possible you might become
548 ES	Monica	13	shamming they'll have to take the hint. {}/[*Exit*]/*A moment later*, LORD
554 ES	Carghil	6	If I go at once, perhaps she'll take the hint/And leave us alone tomorrow./Good

HINTED (1)
438 CP	Reilly	6	/But such experience can only be hinted at/In myths and images. To speak about

HINTING (1)
555 ES	Piggott	5	/That I'd take the first opportunity of hinting —/Tactfully, of course — that you

HINTS (4)
184 FQ: DrySal		18	the beaches where it tosses/Its hints of earlier and other creation:/The starfish,
190 FQ: DrySal		216	/While the music lasts. These are only hints and guesses,/Hints followed by guesses;
190 FQ: DrySal		217	These are only hints and guesses,/Hints followed by guesses; and the rest/Is
539 ES	Ld Clav	28	business/Of the nature of which dark hints have been given,/He's informed himself so

HIP (1)
42 Swee Erect		18	/Then straightens out from heel to hip/Pushing the framework of the bed/And

HIPPO'S (2)
49 Hippopot		9	fail/For it is based upon a rock./The hippo's feeble steps may err/In compassing
49 Hippopot		17	from over sea./At mating time the hippo's voice/Betrays inflexions hoarse and odd,

HIPPOPOTAMUS (2)
49 Hippopot		t	la forme précise de Byzance./The Hippopotamus/The broad-backed
49 Hippopot		1	Hippopotamus/The broad-backed hippopotamus/Rests on his belly in the mud;/

HIPPOPOTAMUS'S (1)
49 Hippopot		21	Church, at being one with God./The hippopotamus's day/Is passed in sleep; at night

HIRED (5)
149 Rock 1		94	*of the* UNEMPLOYED./*No man has hired us/With pocketed hands/And lowered faces/*
150 Rock 1		106	*of bitter/Ale. In this land/No man has hired us./Our life is unwelcome, our death/*
161 Rock 7		39	*faintly):/In this land/No man has hired us..../*CHORUS:/Waste and void. Waste
304 FR	Mary	21	would have done just as well with a hired servant/Or with none. She only wanted me
394 CP	Edward	12	as much opportunity/If you had hired me as your butler:/Some of your guests

HIS (485)

HISSING (1)
143 Lines OM		8	/When I lay bare the tooth of wit/The hissing over the archèd tongue/Is more

HISTORICAL (2)
255 MC Tempt4		1	you lacked/Will only try to find the historical fact./When men shall declare that
539 ES	Ld Clav	23	*himself whisky]/*{LC} An interesting historical epitome./Though I cannot accept it as

HISTORY (20)
38 Gerontion		34	what forgiveness? Think now/History has many cunning passages, contrived
43 Swee Erect		26	/(The lengthened shadow of a man/Is history, said Emerson/Who had not seen the
160 Rock 7		19	of time, but in time, in what we call history: transecting, bisecting the world of time,
187 FQ: DrySal		104	behind the assurance/Of recorded history, the backward half-look/Over the
195 FQ: Little		164	importance/Though never indifferent. History may be servitude,/History may be
195 FQ: Little		165	indifferent. History may be servitude,/History may be freedom. See, now they vanish,/
197 FQ: Little		235	of equal duration. A people without history/Is not redeemed from time, for history is
197 FQ: Little		236	/Is not redeemed from time, for history is a pattern/Of timeless moments. So,
197 FQ: Little		239	afternoon, in a secluded chapel/History is now and England./With the drawing
229 Gus		33	Cat./But my grandest creation, as history will tell,/Was Firefrorefiddle, the Fiend
229 Gus		54	moment of mystery/When I made history/As Firefrorefiddle, the Fiend of the
255 MC Tempt4		3	this man who played a certain part in history./{T} But what is there to do? what is left
258 MC Thomas		33	/What yet remains to show you of my history/Will seem to most of you at best futility,
258 MC Thomas		37	passion of a fanatic./I know that history at all times draws/The strangest
315 FR	Chorus	34	the beak and claws have desecrated/History. Shamed/The first cry in the bedroom,
404 CP	Edward	26	didn't want to hear about my early history./{R} No, I did not want to hear about

404 CP	Reilly	27	did not want to hear about your *early* history./{E} And so will you send me to the
538 ES	Gomez	10	let's look for a moment at *your* life history./You had plenty of money, and you
539 ES	Gomez	34	First,/And I might have become the history master/In a school like that from which
575 ES	Gomez	18	wasting your time, rehearsing ancient history./Michael knows it already. I've told him

HIT (4)

119 SP	Krum	24	we never been here before/{Kr} We hit this town last night for the first time/{Kl}
125 SA	Chorus	34	the bed and/you wake like someone hit you in the head/You've had a cream of a
451 CC	Eggers	3	Mr. Kaghan is prejudiced./He's never hit it off with Lady Elizabeth./Don't listen to
552 ES	Carghil	6	my art./Don't you remember what a hit I made/With a number called *It's Not Too*

HITHER (2)

| 188 FQ: DrySal | 154 | will disembark./Here between the hither and the farther shore/While time is |
| 349 FR | Mary | 27 | /{M} Not in the day time/And in the hither world/Where we know what we are doing |

HIVES (1)

| 151 Rock 2 | 5 | deaths, embittered scorn in honeyless hives,/And those who would build and restore |

HO (3)

220 Old Deut	13	Can it be ... really! ... No! ... Yes! .../Ho! hi!/Oh, my eye!/My mind may be
220 Old Deut	28	Can it be ... really! ... No! ... Yes! .../Ho! hi!/Oh, my eye!/My sight's unreliable, but I
221 Old Deut	44	Can it be ... really! ... Yes! ... No! .../Ho! hi!/Oh, my eye!/My legs may be tottery, I

HOARDS (1)

| 587 Fable | 12 | baron died,/He added to their hoards — a deed which ne'er he/Had done |

HOARSE (1)

| 49 Hippopot | 18 | the hippo's voice/Betrays inflexions hoarse and odd,/But every week we hear rejoice/ |

HODGSON (5)

136 5FingerEx4	t	complacency./*Lines to Ralph Hodgson Esqre.*/How delightful to meet Mr.
136 5FingerEx4	1	*Esqre.*/How delightful to meet Mr. Hodgson!/(Everyone wants to know *him*)/With
136 5FingerEx4	8	limb./How delightful to meet Mr. Hodgson!/Who is worshipped by all waitresses/
136 5FingerEx4	13	tart./How delightful to meet Mr. Hodgson!/(Everyone wants to know *him*)./He
136 5FingerEx4	18	skim./How delightful to meet Mr. Hodgson!/(Everyone wants to know *him*)./*Lines*

HOFGARTEN (1)

| 61 WL: Burial | 10 | /And went on in sunlight, into the Hofgarten,/And drank coffee, and talked for an |

HOLD (31)

15 Prufrock	85	/And I have seen the eternal Footman hold my coat, and snicker,/And in short, I was
19 Portrait	45	do not know/What life is, you who hold it in your hands';/(Slowly twisting the lilac
61 WL: Burial	16	frightened. He said, Marie,/Marie, hold on tight. And down we went./In the
69 WL: Fire S	264	where the walls/Of Magnus Martyr hold/Inexplicable splendour of Ionian white and
133 Eyes	15	/A little while outlast the tears/And hold us in derision./The wind sprang up at four
158 Rock 5	11	some must labour, and others must hold the spears./It is hard for those who have
235 Ad-dress	40	*you are spoken to.*/Myself, I do not hold with that —/I say, you should ad-dress a
593 Grad 5	3	— who knows what time may hold in store,/Or what great deeds the distant
600 Moonflower	5	tree./Whiter the flowers, Love, you hold,/Than the white mist on the sea;/Have you
246 MC Thomas	5	spies and sent to meet me/Some who hold me in bitterest hate./By God's grace aware
246 MC Thomas	13	warning against treason,/Made them hold their hands. So for the time/We are
250 MC Tempt3	28	horse, a dog, a wench;/I know how to hold my estates in order,/A country-keeping
253 MC Tempt4	29	by sin, since Adam fell —/You hold the keys of heaven and hell./Power to bind
253 MC Tempt4	40	no empire, he bites broken teeth./You hold the skein: wind, Thomas, wind/The thread
254 MC Tempt4	2	thread of eternal life and death./You hold this power, hold it./{T} Supreme, in this
254 MC Tempt4	2	life and death./You hold this power, hold it./{T} Supreme, in this land?/{T4}
269 MC Knight4	22	/{K4} Priest! monk! and servant! take, hold, detain,/Restrain this man, in the King's
275 MC Chorus	26	seasons?/Night stay with us, stop sun, hold season, let the day not come, let the spring
296 FR Agatha	3	I am also convinced/That you only hold a fragment of the explanation./It is only
296 FR Agatha	6	you do./There is more to understand: hold fast to that/As the way to freedom./{H} I
298 FR Charles	2	afford to be squeamish/In taking hold of anything that comes to hand./If you are
302 FR Chorus	10	to be sure of what is real or unreal?/Hold tight, hold tight, we must insist that the
302 FR Chorus	10	of what is real or unreal?/Hold tight, hold tight, we must insist that the world is what
371 CP Peter	29	two unreal people?/If I can only hold to the memory/I can bear any future. But I
374 CP Celia	29	want to leave you./Surely you don't hold to that silly convention/That the husband
383 CP Edward	6	/You're quite sure? ... Very well, hold on if you like;/We ... I'll look for them./{C}
428 CP Alex	12	of the natives are heathen:/They hold these monkeys in peculiar veneration/And
559 ES Michael	31	wished to be Lord Claverton/Also, to hold your own with Mother's family —/To lord
565 ES Carghil	24	Monica./And Señor Gomez, I shall hold you to your promise! {}/[*Exeunt* MRS.
571 ES Charles	23	you./We can't allow that. What hold have they upon you?/{LC} Only the hold
571 ES Ld Clav	24	have they upon you?/{LC} Only the hold of those who know/Something

HOLDING (5)

| 29 Aunt Helen | 12 | the footman sat upon the dining-table/Holding the second housemaid on his knees —/ |
| 178 FQ: ECoker | 33 | and two, necessarye coniunction,/Holding eche other by the hand or the arm/ |

313 FR	Amy	28	/I suppose it's the fog that is holding them up,/So it's no use to telephone
326 FR	Harry	13	when she was a child./You've been holding a meeting — the usual family inquest/
483 CC	m	29	souvenirs. {}/[*She sits down, holding the portrait*]/{LE} What was I going to

HOLDS (2)

224 Mr Mistoff		7	no such Cat in the metropolis;/He holds all the patent monopolies/For performing
410 CP	Reilly	12	/{R} See it rather as the bond which holds you together./While still in a state of

HOLE (1)

73 WL: Thund		385	and exhausted wells./In this decayed hole among the mountains/In the faint

HOLIDAY (10)

209 NamingCats		2	matter,/It isn't just one of your holiday games;/You may think at first I'm as
288 FR	Agatha	24	—/The nursery tea, the school holiday,/The daring feats on the old pony,/And
456 CC	Eggers	34	in the evening,/And once a year our holiday at Dawlish'./And to think that was only
533 ES	Gomez	16	thought, now's the time to take a long holiday,/Let's say a rest cure — that's what I've
556 ES	Ld Clav	18	sort of place that you'd choose for a holiday./{Mi} Well, this isn't a holiday exactly./
556 ES	Michael	19	for a holiday./{Mi} Well, this isn't a holiday exactly./But this hotel was very well
556 ES	Ld Clav	23	there long? For the whole of this holiday?/{Mi} Well, this isn't a holiday, exactly./
556 ES	Michael	24	of this holiday?/{Mi} Well, this isn't a holiday, exactly./Oh. I said that before, didn't I?
565 ES	Gomez	18	Delighted, I'm sure./{G} Taking a holiday?/You're in business in London, aren't
565 ES	Michael	20	in London, aren't you?/{Mi} Not a holiday, no. I've been in business in London,/

HOLIDAYS (6)

307 FR	Harry	12	coming back from school/For the holidays, after the formal reception/And the
314 FR	Warburt	13	in bed./You didn't like being ill in the holidays./{I} It *was* unpleasant, coming home to
318 FR	Harry	5	/When we came back, for the school holidays,/They were not holidays, but simply a
318 FR	Harry	6	the school holidays,/They were not holidays, but simply a time/In which we were
395 CP	Lavinia	21	how you had grown since the last holidays./You were always intensely concerned
578 ES	Michael	24	remember, when I came home for the holidays/How it used to get on my nerves, when

HOLINESS (1)

248 MC	Tempt2	36	deceitful shadows?/Power is present. Holiness hereafter./{T} Who then?/{T2} The

HOLLOW (12)

83 Hollow Men		t	/Shantih shantih shantih/The Hollow Men/We are the hollow men/We are the
83 Hollow Men		1	shantih/The Hollow Men/We are the hollow men/We are the stuffed men/Leaning
83 Hollow Men		17	as lost/Violent souls, but only/As the hollow men/The stuffed men./Eyes I dare not
84 Hollow Men		55	/In this valley of dying stars/In this hollow valley/This broken jaw of our lost
91 Ash-Wed 2		4	that which had been contained/In the hollow round of my skull. And God said/Shall
180 FQ: ECoker		116	for the scene to be changed/With a hollow rumble of wings, with a movement of
589 Fable		76	bade him come with him, in accents hollow./The friars could do nought but gape
263 MC	Chorus	9	in the wood/The owl rehearses the hollow note of death./What signs of a bitter
307 FR	Mary	1	off. But do you remember/{M} The hollow tree in what we called the wilderness/{H}
307 FR	Harry	19	only memory of freedom/Should be a hollow tree in a wood by the river./{M} But
308 FR	Harry	22	/Isn't that all folly? It's like the hollow tree,/Not there./{M} But surely, what
549 ES	Carghil	31	he's not to be trusted./That man is hollow'. That's what she said./Or did she say

HOLLY-TREE (1)

290 FR	Agatha	32	the corner/The wind's talk in the dry holly-tree/The inclination of the moon/The

HOLLYHOCK (1)

270 MC	Chorus	3	smelt/Death in the rose, death in the hollyhock, sweet pea, hyacinth, primrose and

HOLLYHOCKS (1)

178 FQ: ECoker		56	snowdrops writhing under feet/And hollyhocks that aim too high/Red into grey and

HOLLYWOOD (1)

389 CP	Lavinia	3	I heard?/I congratulate you both. To Hollywood, of course?/How exciting for you,

HOLSTER (1)

158 Rock 5		4	hand, and the gun rather loose in the holster.'/Those who sit in a house of which the

HOLY (14)

98 Ash-Wed 6		25	be shaken and reply./Blessèd sister, holy mother, spirit of the fountain, spirit of the
162 Rock 8		9	of the shame of Jerusalem/And the holy places defiled;/Peter the Hermit, scourging
588 Fable		33	/He drencht the gown he wore with holy water,/The turkeys, capons, boars, they
260 MC	Thomas	3	the Father, and of the Son, and of the Holy Ghost. Amen./Dear children of God, my
262 MC	Thomas	5	the Father, and of the Son, and of the Holy Ghost. Amen./Part II/{C} Does the bird
264 MC	m	14	THIRD PRIEST, *with a banner of the Holy Innocents borne before him.*]/{P3} Since St.
264 MC	Priest3	14	the Apostle a day: and the day of the Holy Innocents./*Out of the mouth of very*
264 MC	Priest1	22	*banners behind them*]/{P1} Since the Holy Innocents a day: the fourth day from
264 MC	Priests	23	/{3P} *Rejoice we all, keeping holy day.*/{P1} As for the people, so also for
264 MC	Priests	26	the sheep./{3P} *Rejoice we all, keeping holy day.*/{P1} To-day?/{P2} To-day, what is
275 MC	Thomas	20	to the blessed John the Baptist, the holy apostles Peter and Paul, to the blessed
281 MC	Chorus	18	Shall enrich the earth, shall create the holy places./For wherever a saint has dwelt,
281 MC	Chorus	20	for the blood of Christ,/There is holy ground, and the sanctity shall not depart

422 CP	Julia	16	a chair each side of it./{J} May the holy ones watch over the roof,/May the moon

HOME (56)

66 WL: Chess	166		TIME/Well, that Sunday Albert was home, they had a hot gammon,/And they asked
68 WL: Fire S	221		/Homeward, and brings the sailor home from sea,/The typist home at teatime,
68 WL: Fire S	222		the sailor home from sea,/The typist home at teatime, clears her breakfast, lights/Her
73 WL: Thund	388		is the empty chapel, only the wind's home./It has no windows, and the door swings,/
105 Song Sime	15		take to the goat's path, and the fox's home,/Fleeing from the foreign faces and the
116 SP	Dusty	24	sorry. I *am* so sorry/But Doris came home with a terrible chill/No, just a chill/Oh I
120 SP	Krum	9	show you around./Sam of course is at *home* in London,/And he's promised to show us
123 SA	Kl & Kr	18	*to catch any trains/And we won't go home when it rains/We'll gather hibiscus flowers/*
147 Rock 1	30		/If the weather is foul we stay at home and read the papers./In industrial
152 Rock 2	24		/Performed it, but left much at home unsure./Of all that was done in the past,
158 Rock 5	9		be not in the heart, they are not in the home: and if they are not in the home, they are
158 Rock 5	9		in the home: and if they are not in the home, they are not in the City./The man who
162 Rock 8	25		at the door in possession:/Came home cracked by the sun of the East/And the
163 Rock 8	40		the faith that took men from home/At the call of a wandering preacher./Our
182 FQ: ECoker	192		trying. The rest is not our business./Home is where one starts from. As we grow
197 FQ: Little	219		that is right (where every word is at home,/Taking its place to support the others,/
203 Indians	12		is not his destiny/Every country is home to one man/And exile to another. Where
203 Indians	18		the same graveyard./Let those who go home tell the same story of you:/Of action with
214 RTTugger	15		of every door,/And as soon as he's at home, then he'd like to get about./He likes to lie
218 Mung Rump	3		extensive reputation. They made their home in Victoria Grove —/That was merely
218 Mung Rump	19		a smash-and-grab./They made their home in Victoria Grove. They had no regular
587 Fable	27		phantoms free,/The fiend must stay at home — no ghosts allowed/At this exclusive
596 When we	1		a last 'farewell'./Song/When we came home across the hill/No leaves were fallen from
249 MC Tempt2	29		war abroad, need fast friends at home./Private policy is public profit;/Dignity
286 FR	Violet	17	—/You can keep out of their way at home;/People with money from heaven knows
289 FR	Gerald	6	homecoming. Make him feel at home, I say!/Make him feel that what has
291 FR	Violet	16	Harry!/{G} Well done!/{V} Welcome home to Wishwood!/{C} Why, what's the
306 FR	Mary	9	go just yet./{M} Are you glad to be at home?/{H} There was something/I wanted to
313 FR	Gerald	16	isn't it?/We must make him feel at home. And most auspicious/That he could be
314 FR	Ivy	14	/{I} It *was* unpleasant, coming home to have an illness./{V} It was always the
318 FR	Harry	16	things that are taken for granted/At home, make a deeper impression upon children/
326 FR	Violet	5	I had the greatest trouble in getting home./I am sure he meant well. But I do think
326 FR	Harry	30	that I have had to live/Since I came home, a few hours ago, to Wishwood./{V} I will
330 FR	Harry	6	/As settling down to make himself at home at Wishwood,/Make a dull marriage,
333 FR	Harry	39	happy for a moment, as if I had come home./It is quite irrational, but now/I feel quite
355 CP	Julia	26	/Is a really nice tit-bit. I can drink at home. {}/[EDWARD *returns with a tray*]/{J}
362 CP	Reilly	37	/In going to bed in the nursing home,/In talking to the matron, you are still the
377 CP	Julia	34	to a restaurant./You must both come home with me./{E} No, I'm sorry, Julia./I'm too
404 CP	Edward	29	send me to the sanatorium?/I can't go home again. And at my club/They won't let you
411 CP	Edward	15	It seems to me that I might as well go home./{L} Then we can share a taxi, and be
416 CP	Celia	33	a child/Lost in a forest, wanting to go home./{R} Compassion may be already a clue/
419 CP	Reilly	35	/{C} Tonight, by nine o'clock./{R} Go home then, and make your preparations./Here
446 CC	Eggers	28	A piano? Yes, I'm sure he'll feel at home/When he has a piano. You think of
457 CC	Lady E	29	cup of black coffee. Is Sir Claude at home?/I'll speak to him first./{SC} Good
459 CC	Lady E	10	in the art of health./Where is your home, Mr. Colby?/{C} Simpkins./{E} Mr. Colby
496 CC	Eggers	26	it. She misses my news/When I came home in the evening. And the late editions/Of
518 CC	Colby	33	Aunt Sarah;/But I should see you home./{MG} Home? Only to a taxi./Do you
518 CC Guzzard	34	/But I should see you home./{MG} Home? Only to a taxi./Do you mind if I take
524 ES	Charles	1	*in the hall*]/{C} Is your father at home to-day?/{M} You'll see him at tea./{C} But
525 ES	Charles	18	Now that your father's retired/He's at home every day. And you're leaving London./
527 ES	Monica	24	to be alone./And when he's been at home in the evening,/Even when he's reading,
528 ES	Monica	29	Selby chose the place. A *convalescent* home/With the atmosphere of an hotel —/
535 ES	Gomez	27	would be like to have been away from home/For thirty-five years? I was twenty-five —
564 ES	Carghil	26	you went back to ... where is your home?/{G} The republic of San Marco./{MC}
578 ES	Michael	24	common./I remember, when I came home for the holidays/How it used to get on my
580 ES	Ld Clav	36	my dear,/What you say comes home to me. I fear for Michael;/Nevertheless,

HOME'S (1)

459 CC	Claude	15	/Where are you living?/{SC} His home's outside London./But I want to have him

HOMECOMING (1)

289 FR	Gerald	6	for Amy's birthday/Or for Harry's homecoming. Make him feel at home, I say!/

HOMELESS (1)

280 MC Priest3	17		/Go, weak sad men, lost erring souls, homeless in earth or heaven./Go where the

HOMES (2)
155 Rock 3   46   there is no temple there shall be no homes,/Though you have shelters and
280 MC Knight1   2   that you now disperse quietly to your homes./Please be careful not to loiter in groups
HOMESICKNESS (4)
533 ES Gomez 13   brought you to England?/{G} Call it homesickness,/Curiosity, restlessness, whatever
536 ES Gomez 19   know what it's like/To be so cut off! Homesickness!/Homesickness is a sickly word./
536 ES Gomez 20   like/To be so cut off! Homesickness!/Homesickness is a sickly word./You don't
580 ES Monica 29   he'll come back. If it's all a failure/Homesickness, I'm sure, will bring him back to
HOMEWARD (1)
68 WL: Fire S 221   hour, the evening hour that strives/Homeward, and brings the sailor home from
HOMEWARDS (1)
185 FQ: DrySal 35   and the heaving groaner/Rounded homewards, and the seagull:/And under the
HOMING (1)
193 FQ: Little   84   /Had passed below the horizon of his homing/While the dead leaves still rattled on
HOMME (1)
51 Restaurant 31   /Cependant, ce fut jadis un bel homme, de haute taille./Whispers of
HON. (3) [*Abbreviation*]
284 FR   m 3   *her younger sisters*/COL. THE HON. GERALD PIPER, *and* THE HON.
284 FR   m 3   HON. GERALD PIPER, *and* THE HON. CHARLES PIPER, *brothers of her*
328 FR Charles 12   '*Peer's Brother in Motor Smash*/The Hon. Arthur Gerald Charles Piper, younger
HONEST (5)
407 CP Reilly   9   sanatorium:/And one of them is an honest mind./That is one of the causes of their
407 CP Lavinia 11   No one can say my husband has an honest mind./{E} And I could not honestly say
462 CC Colby   21   direction./{C} It doesn't seem quite honest./If we all have to live in a world of
568 ES Ld Clav 32   /It's impossible to be quite honest with your child/If you've never been
568 ES Ld Clav 33   with your child/If you've never been honest with anyone older,/On terms of equality.
HONESTLY (2)
38 Gerontion   54   devils./I would meet you upon this honestly./I that was near your heart was
407 CP Edward 12   an honest mind./{E} And I could not honestly say that of *you*, Lavinia./{R} I
HONESTY (1)
405 CP Reilly   30   this a very dishonourable trick./{R} Honesty before honour, Mr. Chamberlayne./Sit
HONEYLESS (1)
151 Rock 2   5   squalid deaths, embittered scorn in honeyless hives,/And those who would build
HONEYMOON (2)
393 CP Lavinia 17   —/When we were planning our honeymoon,/I couldn't make you say where you
397 CP Edward 27   /Practical! I remember, on our honeymoon,/You were always wrapping things
HONOR (1)
594 Grad 12   2   die — for each succeeding year/Thy honor and thy fame shall but increase/Forever,
HONOUR (10)
44 Cook Egg   9   *to the Dance.*/I shall not want Honour in Heaven/For I shall meet Sir Philip
105 Song Sime   11   for the poor,/Have given and taken honour and ease./There went never any rejected
129 Cor2 State   4   /O Cavaliers! of the Legion of Honour,/The Order of the Black Eagle (1st and
195 FQ: Little 145   /Then fools' approval stings, and honour stains./From wrong to wrong the
268 MC Thomas 18   the King's son, or to diminish/His honour and power. Why should he wish/To
276 MC Knight1 23   I appeal to your sense of honour. You/are Englishmen, and therefore will
315 FR Warburt 29   that next year will bring me the same honour. {}/[*Exeunt* AMY, DR.
317 FR Warburt   3   coming this evening/Than simply in honour of your mother's birthday./I wanted a
405 CP Reilly   30   trick./{R} Honesty before honour, Mr. Chamberlayne./Sit down, please,
409 CP Reilly   37   at a higher social distinction/Than the honour conferred by being *your* lover./When
HONOURS (3)
91 Ash-Wed 2   10   of her loveliness, and because/She honours the Virgin in meditation,/We shine
266 MC Knights 18   favours on your back,/You had your honours all from his hand; from him you had
268 MC Knight3   4   of your transgressions/Restored your honours and your possessions./All was granted
HOO (8)
126 SA Chorus   1   got the hoo-ha's coming to you./Hoo hoo hoo/You dreamt you waked up at
126 SA Chorus   1   got the hoo-ha's coming to you./Hoo hoo hoo/You dreamt you waked up at seven
126 SA Chorus   1   the hoo-ha's coming to you./Hoo hoo hoo/You dreamt you waked up at seven o'clock
126 SA Chorus   8   you're alive/And perhaps you're dead/Hoo ha ha/Hoo ha ha/Hoo/Hoo/Hoo {}/
126 SA Chorus   9   /And perhaps you're dead/Hoo ha ha/Hoo ha ha/Hoo/Hoo/Hoo {}/KNOCK
126 SA Chorus 10   you're dead/Hoo ha ha/Hoo ha ha/Hoo/Hoo/Hoo {}/KNOCK KNOCK KNOCK/
126 SA Chorus 11   dead/Hoo ha ha/Hoo ha ha/Hoo/Hoo/Hoo {}/KNOCK KNOCK KNOCK/
126 SA Chorus 12   /Hoo ha ha/Hoo ha ha/Hoo/Hoo/Hoo {}/KNOCK KNOCK KNOCK/KNOCK
HOO-HA'S (1)
125 SA Chorus 36   nightmare dream and/you've got the hoo-ha's coming to you./Hoo hoo hoo/You

HOODED (2)
| 73 WL: Thund | 363 | you/Gliding wrapt in a brown mantle, hooded/I do not know whether a man or a |
| 73 WL: Thund | 368 | maternal lamentation/Who are those hooded hordes swarming/Over endless plains, |

HOOF (1)
| 270 MC Chorus | 4 | I have seen/Trunk and horn, tusk and hoof, in odd places;/I have lain on the floor of |

HOOFS (1)
| 31 Apollinax | 16 | its hair./I heard the beat of centaur's hoofs over the hard turf/As his dry and |

HOOKS (1)
| 253 MC Tempt4 | 5 | to say./{T4} It shall be said at last./Hooks have been baited with morsels of the |

HOOP (1)
| 229 Gus | 48 | they are smart, just to jump through a hoop.'/And he'll say, as he scratches himself |

HOOPS (1)
| 537 ES Gomez | 8 | tried, and grappled to my soul/With hoops of steel, and all that sort of thing./We'll |

HOPE (89)
85 Hollow Men	66	rose/Of death's twilight kingdom/The hope only/Of empty men./*Here we go round the*
89 Ash-Wed 1	1	/Ash-Wednesday/Because I do not hope to turn again/Because I do not hope/
89 Ash-Wed 1	2	hope to turn again/Because I do not hope/Because I do not hope to turn/Desiring
89 Ash-Wed 1	3	I do not hope/Because I do not hope to turn/Desiring this man's gift and that
89 Ash-Wed 1	9	of the usual reign?/Because I do not hope to know again/The infirm glory of the
89 Ash-Wed 1	23	renounce the voice/Because I cannot hope to turn again/Consequently I rejoice,
90 Ash-Wed 1	30	/Too much explain/Because I do not hope to turn again/Let these words answer/For
92 Ash-Wed 3	6	stairs who wears/The deceitful face of hope and of despair./At the second turning of
92 Ash-Wed 3	20	stair,/Fading, fading; strength beyond hope and despair/Climbing the third stair./
98 Ash-Wed 6	1	/O my people./Although I do not hope to turn again/Although I do not hope/
98 Ash-Wed 6	2	hope to turn again/Although I do not hope/Although I do not hope to turn/Wavering
98 Ash-Wed 6	3	I do not hope/Although I do not hope to turn/Wavering between the profit and
110 Marina	32	/The awakened, lips parted, the hope, the new ships./What seas what shores
116 SP Dusty	27	I *think* it's only a chill/Yes indeed I hope so too —/Well I *hope* we shan't have to
116 SP Dusty	28	/Yes indeed I hope so too —/Well I *hope* we shan't have to call a doctor/Doris just
119 SP Klip	25	for the first time/{Kl} And I certainly hope it won't be the last time./{Do} You like
140 Usk	2	Do not suddenly break the branch, or/Hope to find/The white hart behind the white
179 FQ: ECoker	98	or to God./The only wisdom we can hope to acquire/Is the wisdom of humility:
180 FQ: ECoker	124	to my soul, be still, and wait without hope/For hope would be hope for the wrong
180 FQ: ECoker	125	be still, and wait without hope/For hope would be hope for the wrong thing; wait
180 FQ: ECoker	125	wait without hope/For hope would be hope for the wrong thing; wait without love/For
180 FQ: ECoker	127	/But the faith and the love and the hope are all in the waiting./Wait without
182 FQ: ECoker	186	times, by men whom one cannot hope/To emulate — but there is no competition
192 FQ: Little	62	and the mouse./The death of hope and despair,/This is the death of air./There
196 FQ: Little	206	from sin and error./The only hope, or else despair/Lies in the choice of pyre
593 Grad 4	5	the rose and hawthorn grow./We hope it may be; would that we might know!/
251 MC Tempt3	12	This is the simple fact!/You have no hope of reconciliation/With Henry the King.
252 MC Tempt3	24	not wait at your door./And I well hope, before another spring/The King will show
257 MC Chorus	23	gave us always some reason, some hope; but now a new terror has soiled us, which
265 MC Priest3	3	day is the day that we know that we hope for or fear for?/Every day is the day we
265 MC Priest3	4	day is the day we should fear from or hope from. One moment/Weighs like another.
267 MC Knight1	32	/Or threatened, mind you; but in the hope/Of stirring up trouble in the French
290 FR Amy	16	take command at Wishwood/And I hope we can contrive his future happiness./Do
293 FR Harry	26	I have explained it./All that I could hope to make you understand/Is only events:
298 FR Charles	26	after all these years./You're well, I hope?/{Do} Thank you, very well indeed, Sir./
302 FR Amy	18	we must go and dress, I suppose. I hope Harry will feel better/After his rest
307 FR Harry	33	iron cataract./You do not know what hope is, until you have lost it./You only know
307 FR Harry	34	it./You only know what it is not to hope:/You do not know what it is to have hope
307 FR Harry	35	/You do not know what it is to have hope taken from you,/Or to fling it away, to
308 FR Mary	11	comprehension of the death of hope/Of which you speak, I know you have
308 FR Mary	14	it must be./But in this world another hope keeps springing/In an unexpected place,
315 FR Warburt	29	pleasure, Lady Monchensey,/And I hope that next year will bring me the same
321 FR Warburt	14	/{W} I wonder what he wants. I hope nothing has happened/To either of your
322 FR Winch	11	/I'm not afraid of you./{Wi} I should hope not, my Lord./I didn't mean to put myself
331 FR Agatha	28	be better./{Ag} I will try to tell you. I hope I have the strength./{H} I have thought of
348 FR Warburt	2	have him up here in the morning./I hope Lady Monchensey hasn't been worrying?/
359 CP Alex	3	Celia./{A} Good-bye, Edward. I do hope/You'll have better news of Lavinia's aunt./
360 CP Reilly	38	be deeper/And you've ground for hope that she won't come back at all./If another
366 CP Peter	14	taxi waiting./Come along, Peter./{P} I hope you won't mind/If I don't come with you,
366 CP Peter	27	of you — very much. {}/[*Exit*]/{P} I hope I'm not disturbing you, Edward./{E} I
381 CP Celia	3	any interest/Now, in *my* future. I only hope you're competent/To manage your own.

387 CP	Peter	32	yesterday?/{E} Of course./{P} I hope you've done nothing about it./{E} No, I've
388 CP	Celia	13	it! But now you'll have a chance,/I hope, to realise your ambitions./I shall miss
410 CP	Reilly	6	/{R} And now you begin to see, I hope,/How much you have in common. The
424 CP	Edward	11	door]/{E} I'm in good time, I think. I hope you've not been worrying./{L} Oh no. I
424 CP	Lavinia	19	And I've attended *all* of them./I hope you're not too tired?/{E} Oh no, a quiet
425 CP	Edward	25	us later, roaring for drink./Well, let's hope that those who come to us early/Will be
428 CP	Alex	31	others./And that's the real problem. I hope I'm not boring you?/{E} No indeed: we are
440 CP	Lavinia	4	I think I understand .../{L} Then I hope you will explain it to me!/{E} Oh, it isn't
445 CC	Claude	22	City this morning,/But he'll be back, I hope, before you leave./{E} And how's he
447 CC	Claude	33	make too much of it./And I rather hope that she will take to him at once:/If so, she
449 CC	Eggers	30	married, I expect./{E} And so I hope. A most suitable arrangement./But will
456 CC	Colby	19	on:/She's very absent-minded./{C} I hope you don't mean,/She has lapses of
461 CC	Colby	12	at my back/If I get into trouble. But I hope/That I shan't have to call upon you often./
471 CC	Colby	30	than wait to see what happened./I hope you don't mind: I know it sounds
481 CC	Kaghan	1	go to live on a desert island./But I hope you won't do that. We need you where
482 CC	Lady E	8	of surnames altogether./But, Colby, I hope you won't mind a gentle hint./I feared it
494 CC	Lady E	10	you to believe that he is yours!/So I hope Mrs. Guzzard will say he is your son/And
496 CC	Lady E	34	it's always getting worse./{LE} — I hope Mrs. Eggerson is well?/{E} Pretty well./
501 CC	Lady E	20	help us/To understand other people. I hope so./Lucasta, I regard you as a ...
503 CC	Lucasta	32	we'll be brother and sister —/Or so I hope. Yes, in any event,/Good-bye, Colby. {}/
505 CC	Claude	7	years. So I asked him to be present./I hope you don't mind?/{MG} Why should I
506 CC	Guzzard	21	Elizabeth's child was lost./Let us hope that her son may be restored to her./{E}
508 CC	Eggers	4	mother who has been hoping against hope/To find her son. Put yourself in her
508 CC	Eggers	8	you grasp at any straw/That offered hope of finding him?/{MG} Perhaps I should./
518 CC	Eggers	3	measure; because, Mr. Simpkins —/I hope you won't take this as an impertinence —/
542 ES	Gomez	38	stop! Well, I'd better be going./I hope I haven't outstayed my welcome?/Your
544 ES	Ld Clav	15	of contentment./Already. I only hope that it will last —/The sense of wellbeing!
544 ES	Ld Clav	20	to consciousness/It comes less often./I hope this benignant sunshine/And warmth will
545 ES	Piggott	29	/He's led a busy life, too.' But I hope you're happy?/Is there anything you need
547 ES	Monica	15	worse than Mrs. Piggott./{M} Let's hope this was merely the concoction/Which she
548 ES	Monica	3	leave you to enjoy it. {}/[*Exit*]/{M} I hope she won't remember anything else./{LC}
548 ES	Carghil	14	her knitting./[*after a pause*]./{MC} I hope I'm not disturbing you. I always sit here./
555 ES	Ld Clav	22	car?/{M} No, he was walking./{LC} I hope he's not had another accident./You know,
556 ES	Monica	6	sullen and quick to take offence./So I hope you'll be patient./{LC} Well then, fetch
567 ES	Charles	1	/{C} Well, Monica, here I am. I hope you got my message./{M} Oh Charles,
569 ES	Ld Clav	10	of keeping up those pretences,/But I hope that you'll find a little love in your heart/
570 ES	Ld Clav	9	/How make a confession with no hope of absolution?/It was not her fault. We
580 ES	Ld Clav	37	/Nevertheless, you are right to hope for something better./And when he comes

HOPED (9)

179 FQ:	ECoker	75	of the long looked forward to,/Long hoped for calm, the autumnal serenity/And the
287 FR	Amy	39	air to Paris, and so to London,/And hoped to arrive in the course of the evening./{V}
308 FR	Mary	16	while we are unconscious of it./You hoped for something, in coming back to
308 FR	Harry	18	would not have come./{H} Whatever I hoped for/Now that I am here I know I shall
383 CP	Edward	16	and I have no half-bottles./Well, I hoped that you would drink a final glass with
464 CC	Claude	31	what could be done with it —/What I hoped I could do with it. I thought I despised
488 CC	Claude	27	as well have told you before,/But I'd hoped — and now it seems a silly thought .../
488 CC	Claude	30	a travesty of all one's plans —/I'd hoped that you would become fond of Colby,/
538 ES	Gomez	15	not, I suspect, as well as you had hoped./{LC} I was never accused of making a

HOPEFUL (3)

592 Grad 4		3	it bristle with a thousand fears,/To hopeful eye of youth it still appears/A lane by
408 CP	Reilly	25	of humour./{R} It is the first more hopeful symptom./{L} How did you know all
528 ES	Monica	28	have every encouragement —/If he's hopeful, he's likely to live a little longer./That's

HOPELESS (3)

307 FR	Harry	36	fling it away, to join the legion of the hopeless/Unrecognised by other men, though
353 CP	Alex	6	/{A} My dear Julia!/It's perfectly hopeless. You haven't been listening./{P} You'll
418 CP	Celia	19	there's no other way ... then I feel just hopeless./{R} There *is* another way, if you have

HOPELESSNESS (1)

307 FR	Mary	29	indeed to you./It's just ordinary hopelessness./{H} One thing you cannot know:/

HOPES (8)

116 SP	Dusty	31	says will you ring up on Monday/She hopes to be all right on Monday/I say do you
187 FQ:	DrySal	108	due to misunderstanding,/Having hopes for the wrong things or dreaded the
604 Ode		6	sons ever turn, in the strength/Of the hopes that thy blessings bestow,/From the
604 Ode		7	that thy blessings bestow,/From the hopes and ambitions that sprang at thy feet/To
320 FR	Warburt	37	rather irresponsible./Your mother's hopes are all centred on you./{H} Hopes? ... Tell
320 FR	Harry	38	hopes are all centred on you./{H} Hopes? ... Tell me/Did you know my father at

| 433 CP | Julia | 11 | not to have me:/So good-bye to my hopes of seeing California./{P} You know you'd |
| 529 ES | Monica | 8 | he started like you,/With the same hopes, the same ambitions —/And of his |

HOPING (3)

246 MC	Tempt1	26	I have come, forgetting all acrimony,/Hoping that your present gravity/Will find
248 MC	Tempt1	5	as I came, forgetting all acrimony,/Hoping that your present gravity/Will find
508 CC	Eggers	4	/For a mother who has been hoping against hope/To find her son. Put

HORDE (2)

| 155 Rock 3 | | 41 | where you go./A colony of cavies or a horde of active marmots/Build better than they |
| 213 Growltiger | | 41 | the signal to his fierce Mongolian horde;/With a frightful burst of fireworks the |

HORDES (1)

| 73 WL: Thund | 368 | lamentation/Who are those hooded hordes swarming/Over endless plains, stumbling |

HORGAN (1)

| 236 Cat Morgan | 14 | me voice it ain't no sich melliferous horgan;/But yet I can state, and I'm not one to |

HORIZON (2)

| 73 WL: Thund | 370 | in cracked earth/Ringed by the flat horizon only/What is the city over the |
| 193 FQ: Little | 84 | tongue/Had passed below the horizon of his homing/While the dead leaves |

HORN (6)

39 Gerontion		70	straits/Of Belle Isle, or running on the Horn./White feathers in the snow, the Gulf
96 Ash-Wed 5		22	thee,/Those who are torn on the horn between season and season, time and time,
195 FQ: Little		151	/And faded on the blowing of the horn./There are three conditions which often
221 Old Deut		33	on the floor/Of the Fox and French Horn for his afternoon sleep;/And when the
270 MC	Chorus	4	and cowslip. I have seen/Trunk and horn, tusk and hoof, in odd places;/I have lain
270 MC	Chorus	7	with the wren. I have felt/The horn of the beetle, the scale of the viper, the

HORNÈD (1)

| 56 Swee Night | 8 | drift above/And Sweeney guards the hornèd gate./Gloomy Orion and the Dog/Are |

HORNS (2)

| 67 WL: Fire S | 197 | time to time I hear/The sound of horns and motors, which shall bring/Sweeney to |
| 298 FR | Charles | 22 | nothing to do but take the bull by the horns,/And this is one. {}/[*Knock: and enter* |

HORONITE (1)

| 158 Rock 5 | 2 | and desperately wicked./Sanballat the Horonite and Tobiah the Ammonite and |

HOROSCOPE (2)

| 62 WL: Burial | 58 | Mrs. Equitone,/Tell her I bring the horoscope myself:/One must be so careful these |
| 189 FQ: DrySal | 190 | of the sea monster,/Describe the horoscope, haruspicate or scry,/Observe disease |

HORRIBLE (6)

116 SP	Doris	14	Pereira/{Do} Well can't you stop that horrible noise?/Pick up the receiver/{Du}
215 RTTugger		34	/For there's nothing he enjoys like a horrible muddle./Yes the Rum Tum Tugger is a
218 Mung Rump		15	/Then the family would say: 'It's that horrible cat!/It was Mungojerrie — or
219 Mung Rump		28	/Then the family would say: 'It's that horrible cat!/It was Mungojerrie — or
295 FR	Charles	11	your life together made it seem more horrible./There's a lot in my own past life that
416 CP	Celia	23	other/Each for his purpose. That's horrible. Can we only love/Something created

HORRIBLY (1)

| 515 CC | Claude | 19 | did. And so it went on./{SC} This is horribly plausible. But it can't be true./{MG} |

HORRID (4)

272 MC	Chorus	24	behind the Judgement the Void, more horrid than active shapes of hell;/Emptiness,
301 FR	Chorus	20	why do we huddle together/In a horrid amity of misfortune? why should we be
396 CP	Lavinia	18	—/Or if that's impossible, at least be horrid to you —/Anything but nothing, which is
428 CP	Julia	4	Mary Mallington's monkey,/The horrid little beast — stole my ticket to Mentone

HORRIFIED (1)

| 451 CC | Eggers | 23 | —/Within the first ten minutes! I was horrified./But she actually liked it. Muriel *is* her |

HORROR (14)

173 FQ: BurntN		80	ecstasy,/The resolution of its partial horror./Yet the enchainment of past and future/
606 Narcissus		31	the taste of his own whiteness/The horror of his own smoothness,/And he felt
270 MC	Chorus	11	downwards, descending/To the horror of the ape. Have I not known, not
272 MC	Chorus	12	the hand and dry the eyelid,/Still the horror, but more horror/Than when tearing in
272 MC	Chorus	12	the eyelid,/Still the horror, but more horror/Than when tearing in the belly./Still the
272 MC	Chorus	14	when tearing in the belly./Still the horror, but more horror/Than when twisting in
272 MC	Chorus	14	in the belly./Still the horror, but more horror/Than when twisting in the fingers,/Than
272 MC	Chorus	26	absence, separation from God;/The horror of the effortless journey, to the empty
276 MC	Chorus	9	marked a limit to our suffering./Every horror had its definition,/Every sorrow had a
327 FR	Harry	20	me. It's not being alone/That is the horror — to be alone with the horror./What
327 FR	Harry	20	is the horror — to be alone with the horror./What matters is the filthiness. I can
331 FR	Harry	2	presences./And then I had no horror of my action,/I only felt the repetition of
410 CP	Reilly	23	I tell you this:/It would have been a horror beyond your imagining,/For you would
436 CP	Lavinia	30	that your face showed no surprise or horror/At the way in which she died. I don't

HORSE (3)

103 Journ Magi	25	on the low sky./And an old white horse galloped away in the meadow./Then we
241 MC	Mess 36	to suffocation,/And I think that his horse will be deprived of its tail,/A single hair of
250 MC Tempt3	27	no skill. I am no courtier./I know a horse, a dog, a wench;/I know how to hold my

HORSE'S (1)

127 Cor1 March	30	eyes/Or in the hands, quiet over the horse's neck,/And the eyes watchful, waiting,

HORSEMEN (1)

134 Wind	12	across death's other river/The Tartar horsemen shake their spears./Five-Finger

HORSES (3)

40 Burb Blei	9	left him, that had loved him well./The horses, under the axletree/Beat up the dawn
285 FR Charles	25	long used to our ways/Living with horses and dogs and guns/Ever to want to leave
330 FR Harry	10	living in gentle motion/Of horses, and right visits to the right neighbours/

HORSES' (2)

127 Cor1 March	1	bronze, stone, steel, stone, oakleaves, horses' heels/Over the paving./And the flags.
128 Cor1 March	40	bronze, stone, steel, stone, oakleaves, horses' heels/Over the paving./That is all we

HORSESHOE (1)

184 FQ: DrySal	19	and other creation:/The starfish, the horseshoe crab, the whale's backbone;/The

HORSFALL (5)

119 SP	m 1	/DORIS. DUSTY. WAUCHOPE. HORSFALL. KLIPSTEIN. KRUMPACKER.
119 SP	Wauch 3	/I think you girls both know Captain Horsfall —/We want you to meet two friends of
121 SA	m 1	an Agon/SWEENEY. WAUCHOPE. HORSFALL. KLIPSTEIN. KRUMPACKER.
122 SA	1m 15	{}/SONG BY WAUCHOPE AND HORSFALL/SWARTS AS TAMBO. SNOW
125 SA	m 31	{}/FULL CHORUS: WAUCHOPE, HORSFALL, KLIPSTEIN, KRUMPACKER/

HOSANNAS (1)

50 Hippopot	28	him sing/The praise of God, in loud hosannas./Blood of the Lamb shall wash him

HOSPITAL (2)

181 FQ: ECoker	159	grow worse./The whole earth is our hospital/Endowed by the ruined millionaire,/
335 FR Agatha	19	passages/Of an immense and empty hospital/Pervaded by a smell of disinfectant,/

HOSPITALITY (2)

265 MC Priest1	20	/{P1} You know the Archbishop's hospitality./We are about to go to dinner./The
265 MC Knight3	31	Archbishop/We have no need of his hospitality./We will find our own dinner. {}/[to

HOST (5)

57 Swee Night	33	/Circumscribe a golden grin;/The host with someone indistinct/Converses at the
587 Fable	15	kind fairy./Alas! no fairy visited their host,/Oh, no; much worse than that, they had a
260 MC Thomas	12	that a multitude of the heavenly host appeared before the/shepherds at
355 CP Julia	23	it to me to keep things going./What a host! And nothing fit to eat!/The only reason
356 CP Julia	16	/I know you're always the perfect host,/But just try to pretend you're another

HOSTESS (2)

394 CP Edward	34	of public life. You wished to be a hostess/For whom my career would be a
495 CC Lady E	11	/And that you needed me chiefly as a hostess./It's a great mistake, I do believe,/For

HOSTILE (2)

103 Journ Magi	14	the lack of shelters,/And the cities hostile and the towns unfriendly/And the
212 Growltiger	8	tell you why,/And he scowled upon a hostile world from one forbidding eye./The

HOT (9)

37 Gerontion	3	waiting for rain./I was neither at the hot gates/Nor fought in the warm rain/Nor
65 WL: Chess	135	/'What shall we ever do?'/'The hot water at ten./And if it rains, a closed car at
66 WL: Chess	166	Sunday Albert was home, they had a hot gammon,/And they asked me in to dinner,
66 WL: Chess	167	me in to dinner, to get the beauty of it hot —/HURRY UP PLEASE ITS TIME/
141 Rannoch	5	in the thin air/Moon cold or moon hot. The road winds in/Listlessness of ancient
606 Narcissus	35	the burning arrows/He danced on the hot sand/Until the arrows came./As he
295 FR Amy	39	dinner./Get Downing to draw you a hot bath,/And you will feel better./{Ag} There
544 ES Monica	4	/The beds are comfortable, the hot water is hot,/They give us a very tolerable
544 ES Monica	4	beds are comfortable, the hot water is hot,/They give us a very tolerable breakfast;/

HOTEL (14)

40 Burb Blei	2	a little bridge/Descending at a small hotel;/Princess Volupine arrived,/They were
68 WL: Fire S	213	/To luncheon at the Cannon Street Hotel/Followed by a weekend at the Metropole.
292 FR Harry	8	/Behind the palm trees in the Grand Hotel/They were always there. But I did not *see*
404 CP Edward	31	days;/I haven't the courage to go to a hotel,/And besides, I need more shirts — you
405 CP Edward	19	/My mind is made up. I shall go to a hotel./{R} It is just because you are not free,
405 CP Edward	35	to any sanatorium./I am going to a hotel. And I shall ask you, Lavinia,/To be so
405 CP Lavinia	37	me on some clothes./{L} Oh, to what hotel?/{E} I don't know — I mean to say,/That
406 CP Reilly	13	/What was it?/{R} A kind of hotel. A retreat/For people who imagine that
406 CP Lavinia	35	suit you, Edward. Now I know of a hotel/In the New Forest .../{E} How like you,
411 CP Lavinia	1	condition./{L} Edward, there *is* that hotel in the New Forest/If you want to go there.
527 ES Charles	17	your father/In that very expensive hotel for convalescents/To which you're taking

528 ES   Monica   30   home/With the atmosphere of an hotel —/Nothing about it to suggest the clinic
549 ES   Carghil   12   gave us lunch — I've forgotten what hotel —/But such a good lunch — and we all
556 ES   Michael   20   this isn't a holiday exactly./But this hotel was very well recommended./Good
HÔTEL (1)
524 ES   Monica   11   /Instead of to one where the *maître d'hôtel*/And the waiters all seem to be your intimate
HOTELS (2)
13 Prufrock   6   /Of restless nights in one-night cheap hotels/And sawdust restaurants with
290 FR   Amy   4   half round the world/To expensive hotels and undesirable society/Which she could
HOTHOUSE (1)
56 Swee Night   20   brings in oranges/Bananas figs and hothouse grapes;/The silent vertebrate in brown
HOULE (1)
51 Restaurant   26   /Oubliait les cris des mouettes et la houle de Cornouaille,/Et les profits et les pertes,
HOUND (1)
136 5FingerEx4   4 his musical sound/And his Baskerville Hound/Which, just at a word from his master/
HOUNDS (2)
30 Cous Nancy   5   New England hills —/Riding to hounds/Over the cow-pasture./Miss Nancy
249 MC Tempt2   26   Pope,/The old stag, circled with hounds./{T} No!/{T2} Yes! men must
HOUR (35)
19 Portrait   40 the public clocks./Then sit for half an hour and drink our bocks./Now that lilacs are
61 WL: Burial   11   /And drank coffee, and talked for an hour./Bin gar keine Russin, stamm' aus
68 WL: Fire S   215   at the Metropole./At the violet hour, when the eyes and back/Turn upward
68 WL: Fire S   220   female breasts, can see/At the violet hour, the evening hour that strives/Homeward,
68 WL: Fire S   220   see/At the violet hour, the evening hour that strives/Homeward, and brings the
84 Hollow Men   48   other kingdom/Waking alone/At the hour when we are/Trembling with tenderness/
89 Ash-Wed 1   10   again/The infirm glory of the positive hour/Because I do not think/Because I know I
90 Ash-Wed 1   40   /Pray for us sinners now and at the hour of our death/Pray for us now and at the
90 Ash-Wed 1   41   our death/Pray for us now and at the hour of our death./Lady, three white leopards
96 Ash-Wed 5   23   and season, time and time, between/Hour and hour, word and word, power and
96 Ash-Wed 5   23   time and time, between/Hour and hour, word and word, power and power, those
105 Song Sime   20   of desolation,/Before the certain hour of maternal sorrow,/Now at this birth
108 Animula   37 yew trees,/Pray for us now and at the hour of our birth./Marina/What seas what
166 Rock 10   8   to right and to left prepares for his hour to devour./But the Mystery of Iniquity is a
191 FQ: Little   15 Now the hedgerow/Is blanched for an hour with transitory blossom/Of snow, a bloom
193 FQ: Little   80   of water and fire./In the uncertain hour before the morning/Near the ending of
203 Indians   7   many memories/Which return at the hour of conversation,/(The warm or the cool
203 Indians   8   conversation,/(The warm or the cool hour, according to the climate)/Of foreign men,
228 Gus   26   with my back and my tail;/With an hour of rehearsal, I never could fail./I'd a voice
604 Ode   1   STEARNS ELIOT/For the hour that is left us, Fair Harvard, with thee,/Ere
253 MC Tempt4   36   /To be master or servant within an hour,/This is the course of temporal power./The
294 FR   Harry   2   to the plumbers, that has its hour of the night; you do not know/The
300 FRDowning   33   took my turn about, for near half an hour/He stayed there alone, looking over the
328 FR   Charles   23   /travelling at the rate of 66 miles an hour. When asked why he/did not stop when
374 CP   2m   1   2/*The same room: a quarter of an hour later.* EDWARD *is alone, playing*/*Patience.*
397 CP   Edward   13   now I must live with it/Day by day, hour by hour, for ever and ever./{L} I think
397 CP   Edward   13   must live with it/Day by day, hour by hour, for ever and ever./{L} I think you're on
400 CP   Reilly   3   At eleven o'clock,/The conventional hour. We have not much time./Tell me now, did
426 CP   Edward   5   one will be coming for at least half an hour;/So just stretch out./{L} You must sit
450 CC   Eggers   30   I'd miss you./{E} I'm off in half an hour, Mr. Simpkins./{SC} I'll leave you now.
459 CC   Lady E   30   is quite impossible/To get one's quiet hour. A quiet hour a day/Is most essential, Dr.
459 CC   Lady E   30   /To get one's quiet hour. A quiet hour a day/Is most essential, Dr. Rebmann
504 CC   Lady E   10   Oh, I forgot. It's Gertrude's quiet hour./I've been giving her lessons in
529 ES   Ld Clav   34   /Twenty years ago, to-day, at this hour of the afternoon./If I've been looking at
542 ES   Gomez   1   hang on for another quarter of an hour./{LC} Before you go — what is it that you
HOURS (15)
34 Figlia   19   many days,/Many days and many hours:/Her hair over her arms and her arms full
62 WL: Burial   67 where Saint Mary Woolnoth kept the hours/With a dead sound on the final stroke of
73 WL: Thund   383   reminiscent bells, that kept the hours/And voices singing out of empty cisterns
123 SA Kl & Kr   20   *flowers/For it won't be minutes but hours/For it won't be hours but years* {}/
123 SA Kl & Kr   21   *be minutes but hours/For it won't be hours but years* {}/*diminuendo*/{Kl&Kr} *And the*
185 FQ: DrySal   58   /Consequence of further days and hours,/While emotion takes to itself the
188 FQ: DrySal   138   /To the sleepy rhythm of a hundred hours./Fare forward, travellers! not escaping
216 Jellicles   25 /They're quiet enough in the morning hours,/They're quiet enough in the afternoon,/
225 Mr Mistoff   52   to call/Him in from the garden for hours,/While he was asleep in the hall./And not
326 FR   Harry   30   had to live/Since I came home, a few hours ago, to Wishwood./{V} I will make no
332 FR   Agatha   26   /{H} And then?/{Ag} There are hours when there seems to be no past or future,/

364 CP	Reilly	27	We do not know yet. In twenty-four hours/She will come to you here. You will be
387 CP	Celia	2	/But I've learnt a lot in twenty-four hours./It wasn't a very pleasant experience./Oh,
393 CP	Edward	3	at in ... how many? ... thirty-two hours./{L} Yes, a very important discovery,/
475 CC	Lucasta	13	changed quite a lot in the last two hours./{C} And I think I'm changing too. But

HOUSE (64)

13 Prufrock		22	October night,/Curled once about the house, and fell asleep./And indeed there will be
29 Aunt Helen		2	my maiden aunt,/And lived in a small house near a fashionable square/Cared for by
37 Gerontion		7	a cutlass,/Bitten by flies, fought./My house is a decayed house,/And the Jew squats
37 Gerontion		7	flies, fought./My house is a decayed house,/And the Jew squats on the window sill,
38 Gerontion		31	no ghosts,/An old man in a draughty house/Under a windy knob./After such
38 Gerontion		50	conclusion, when I/Stiffen in a rented house. Think at last/I have not made this show
39 Gerontion		74	/To a sleepy corner./Tenants of the house,/Thoughts of a dry brain in a dry season./
43 Swee Erect		40	/Mrs. Turner intimates/It does the house no sort of good./But Doris, towelled from
68 WL: Fire S		232	man carbuncular, arrives,/A small house agent's clerk, with one bold stare,/One of
105 Song Sime		13	my door./Who shall remember my house, where shall live my children's children/
151 Rock 2		4	that you now sit helpless in a ruined house?/Where many are born to idleness, to
154 Rock 3		17	/Much is your building, but not the House of GOD./Will you build me a house of
154 Rock 3		18	House of GOD./Will you build me a house of plaster, with corrugated roofing,/To be
155 Rock 3		44	ruins?/I have loved the beauty of Thy House, the peace of Thy sanctuary,/I have
155 Rock 3		51	dwellings with numbered doors/Or a house a little better than your neighbour's;/
158 Rock 5		5	in the holster.'/Those who sit in a house of which the use is forgotten: are like
158 Rock 5		6	sniffing and barking: they say, 'This house is a nest of serpents, let us destroy it,/And
164 Rock 9		3	thee./Who is this that has said: the House of GOD is a House of Sorrow;/We must
164 Rock 9		3	that has said: the House of GOD is a House of Sorrow;/We must walk in black and
166 Rock 10		1	of Invisible Light./You have seen the house built, you have seen it adorned/By one
192 FQ: Little		60	a story ended./Dust inbreathed was a house —/The wall, the wainscot and the mouse.
205 de la Mare		25	/An empty face peers from an empty house;/By whom, and by what means, was this
214 RTTugger		3	have grouse./If you put him in a house he would much prefer a flat,/If you put
214 RTTugger		4	him in a flat then he'd rather have a house./If you set him on a mouse then he only
219 Mung Rump		32	weather./They would go through the house like a hurricane, and no sober person
229 Gus		44	wire,/To rescue a child when a house was on fire./And he says: 'Now, these
243 MC	Chorus	21	into Canterbury:/A doom on the house, a doom on yourself, a doom on the
244 MC	Chorus	26	ask us/To stand to the doom on the house, the doom on the Archbishop, the doom
244 MC	Chorus	29	folk who stand to the doom of the house, the doom of their lord, the doom of the
256 MC	Chorus	5	still./{C} There is no rest in the house. There is no rest in the street./I hear
273 MC	Thomas	17	open the doors!/I will not have the house of prayer, the church of Christ,/The
276 MC	Chorus	15	/It is not we alone, it is not the house, it is not the city that is defiled,/But the
284 FR	m	11	/The scene is laid in a country *house in the North of England*/PART I/*The*
285 FR	Amy	3	days draw out,/Now that I sit in the house from October to June,/And the swallow
294 FR	Harry	6	a more familiar medium. I am the old house/With the noxious smell and the sorrow
305 FR	Mary	18	waiting, always waiting./I think this house *means* to keep us waiting. { }/[*Enter*
316 FR	Chorus	2	moors. Have torn/The roof from the house, or perhaps it was never there./And the
316 FR	Agatha	8	AGATHA]/{Ag} The eye is on this house/The eye covers it/There are three together
316 FR	Agatha	21	the night time/Be diverted from this house/Till the knot is unknotted/The crossed is
323 FR	Warburt	29	your doctor, I forbid you to leave the house tonight./There is nothing you could do,
328 FR	Chorus	34	such thing as privacy./{Ch} In an old house there is always listening, and more is
332 FR	Agatha	11	see your mother as identified with this house —/It was not always so. There were many
332 FR	Agatha	17	/Married, alone in a lonely country house together,/For three years childless,
340 FR	Amy	19	a discontented ghost,/In his own house. What of the humiliation,/Of the chilly
343 FR	Amy	22	/An old woman alone in a damned house./I will let the walls crumble. Why should I
344 FR	Violet	9	That I am the only sane person in this house./Your behaviour all seems to me quite
391 CP	Julia	2	rest./Now we'll all go back to *my* house. Peter, call a taxi. { }/[*Exit* PETER]/{J}
391 CP	Julia	3	/{J} We'll have a cocktail party at *my* house to-day./{C} Well, I'll go now. Good-bye,
399 CP	Nurse	22	out;/And only after they have left the house..../{R} Quite right, Miss Barraway. That's
414 CP	Celia	17	all they can do to keep the country house going:/But it's been in the family so long,
426 CP	Lavinia	20	/{L} And we can be alone./I love that house being so remote./{E} That's why we took
445 CC	3m	1	MULHAMMER'S/*London house. Early afternoon.* SIR CLAUDE *writing at*
456 CC	Eggers	26	when she's abroad/She is apt to buy a house. And then goes away/And forgets all
456 CC	Eggers	30	to Mrs. E.,/When we'd bought our house in Joshua Park/(On a mortgage, of
461 CC	Eggers	6	get me on the phone./If I'm not in the house, I'll be out in the garden./And I'll slip up
477 CC	Colby	15	yet./Oh, why did I ever come into this house!/Lucasta .../{L} I can see well enough you
485 CC	Lady E	30	to have heard of it./Was it a large house?/{C} No, a very small one./{LE} But you
498 CC	Claude	17	I should have noticed it. I visited her house/Often. I never saw more than one baby./
523 ES	m	11	*of Lord Claverton's London house. Four o'clock in the afternoon*/ACT TWO/
524 ES	2m	1	*of* LORD CLAVERTON'S *London house. Four o'clock in the afternoon.*/[*Voices in*

529 ES Monica 2   down at weekends, even when the House is sitting./And you can take me out, if
531 ES Charles 10   will be heard/In debate in the Upper House .../{LC} The established liturgy/Of the
534 ES Gomez 38   me that there isn't any whisky in the house?/{LC} I can provide whisky. {}/[*Presses*
545 ES Monica 20   Father. I see her coming from the house./Take your newspaper and start reading

HOUSE-TELEPHONE (5)
400 CP   m 30   that is where he wrote from. {}/[*The house-telephone rings*]/{R} Hello! Yes, show him
404 CP   1m 3 sanatorium. I could be alone there? {}/[*House-telephone rings*]/[*into telephone*]/{R} Yes.
411 CP   2m 36 *goes to the couch and lies down. The house-telephone rings. He/gets up and answers*
420 CP   2m 2 *door. Exit* CELIA. REILLY *dials on/house-telephone.*]/[*into telephone*]./{R} It is
421 CP   m 39   speak to Miss Barraway. {}/[*Takes up house-telephone*]/{R} Miss Barraway, when Mr.

HOUSEHOLD (5)
151 Rock 2   2   /Fellow citizens of the saints, of the household of GOD, being built upon the
271 MC Thomas   14   shall forget these things, toiling in the household,/You shall remember them, droning
447 CC Claude 11   you — well, completely/As one of the household./{E} That's a great compliment./{SC}
448 CC Eggers 18   /Regularize his position in the household?/You told me that was your eventual
455 CC Colby   8   /What's her connection with this household?/{E} Well. A kind of fiduciary

HOUSEHOLDER (1)
260 MC Thomas   29   the barons at peace with the King, the householder counting/over his peaceful gains,

HOUSEHOLDS (2)
211 Old Gumbie 38   cheers —/On whom well-ordered households depend, it appears./Growltiger's
240 MC Chorus   1   we are left alone./We try to keep our households in order;/The merchant, shy and

HOUSEKEEPER-COMPANION (1)
304 FR   Mary   25   with very little money,/A housekeeper-companion for her and Harry./

HOUSEMAID (1)
29 Aunt Helen   12   the dining-table/Holding the second housemaid on his knees —/Who had always

HOUSEMAIDS (1)
27 Morning   3   /I am aware of the damp souls of housemaids/Sprouting despondently at area

HOUSES (5)
72 WL: Thund 345 and snarl/From doors of mudcracked houses/If there were water/And no rock/If there
177 FQ: ECoker   2   beginning my end. In succession/Houses rise and fall, crumble, are extended,/Are
177 FQ: ECoker   9   of man and beast, cornstalk and leaf./Houses live and die: there is a time for building/
179 FQ: ECoker 100 of humility: humility is endless./The houses are all gone under the sea./The dancers
431 CP   Julia 27   you become an expert on decaying houses?/{P} Oh dear no! I've written the script

HOUSETOPS (1)
21 Portrait   117   the smoke coming down above the housetops;/Doubtful, for a while/Not knowing

HOVER (3)
138 New Hamp   5   the root./Black wing, brown wing, hover over;/Twenty years and the spring is over;
246 MC Thomas 17   the hungry hawk/Will only soar and hover, circling lower,/Waiting excuse, pretence,
259 MC Thomas   7   God appoints/To be my guardian, hover over the swords' points. {}/Interlude/THE

HOVERS (1)
27 Morning   8   muddy skirts/An aimless smile that hovers in the air/And vanishes along the level of

HOW (252)

HOW'S (3)
425 CP Edward 39   now?/{L} Too much to the left./{E} How's that now?/{L} No, I meant the right./
445 CC Eggers 23   I hope, before you leave./{E} And how's he getting on? Swimmingly, I'm sure,/As
487 CC Claude 11   for me./Oh, by the way, Colby, how's the piano?/{C} It's a wonderful piano.

HOWEVER (13)
148 Rock 1   63   my years, one thing does not change./However you disguise it, this thing does not
184 FQ: DrySal   7   /By the dwellers in cities — ever, however, implacable,/Keeping his seasons and
245 MC Priest2 31   days could make ready Canterbury./However, I will have fires laid in all your rooms
266 MC Thomas   1   /[*Enter* THOMAS]/[*to* PRIESTS]./{T} However certain our expectation/The moment
279 MC Knight1   7   his very subtle reasoning. We have,/however, one more speaker, who has I think
307 FR   Mary   39   /I have not had. Nevertheless, however real,/However cruel, it may be a
307 FR   Mary   40   not had. Nevertheless, however real,/However cruel, it may be a deception./{H} What
382 CP   Celia   17   by scraping your legs together —/Or however grasshoppers do it. I looked,/And
412 CP   Celia   32   That makes it even more perplexing. However,/I don't want to waste your time. And
450 CC   Claude   1   one's ignorant of/About anyone, however well one knows them;/And that may be
485 CC   Lady E   5   I don't know which you mean./{LE} However that may be,/I didn't want to belong
562 ES   Monica   4   love is silent./What can I say to you?/However Michael has behaved, Father,/
568 ES   Ld Clav 21   is nothing that you conceal from *her*/However important you may consider it/To

HOWL (1)
185 FQ: DrySal 28   /The fog is in the fir trees./The sea howl/And the sea yelp, are different voices/

HUDDLE (3)

155 Rock 3	53	is the meaning of this city?/Do you huddle close together because you love each
301 FR Chorus	19	for the picture papers: why do we huddle together/In a horrid amity of
421 CP Julia	6	to put on proper costumes/Or huddle quickly into new disguises,/They have,

HUFFERY-SNUFFERY (1)

223 Pekes Pols	31	to grumble and wheeze/In their huffery-snuffery Heathen Chinese./But a

HUGE (3)

64 WL: Chess	94	the pattern on the coffered ceiling./Huge sea-wood fed with copper/Burned green
269 MC Chorus	30	at noon/Scaly wings slanting over, huge and ridiculous. I have tasted/The savour
326 FR Harry	26	it begins to seem just part of some huge disaster,/Some monstrous mistake and

HUGH (2)

277 MC Knight1	32	other speakers. I shall next call upon Hugh de Morville, who/has made a special
277 MC Knight1	34	statecraft and constitutional law. Sir/Hugh de Morville./{K2} I should like first to

HUIT (1)

48 Lune Miel	11	le vent./Ils vont prendre le train de huit heures/Prolonger leurs misères de Padoue à

HULL (1)

154 Rock 3	25	left the broken chimney,/The peeled hull, a pile of rusty iron,/In a street of scattered

HULLO (1)

430 CP Peter	3	/{E} Why, it's Peter!/{L} Peter!/{P} Hullo, everybody!/{L} When did you arrive?/{P}

HUMAN (21)

17 Prufrock	131	with seaweed red and brown/Till human voices wake us, and we drown./Portrait
68 WL: Fire S	216	Turn upward from the desk, when the human engine waits/Like a taxi throbbing
155 Rock 3	62	and daring enterprises,/To schemes of human greatness thoroughly discredited,/
172 FQ: BurntN	44	laughter./Go, go, go, said the bird: human kind/Cannot bear very much reality./
194 FQ: Little	138	the conscious impotence of rage/At human folly, and the laceration/Of laughter at
196 FQ: Little	213	/The intolerable shirt of flame/Which human power cannot remove./We only live,
209 NamingCats	23	never will guess;/The name that no human research can discover —/But THE CAT
226 Macavity	6	one like Macavity,/He's broken every human law, he breaks the law of gravity./His
271 MC Thomas	19	in the telling. They will seem unreal./Human kind cannot bear very much reality. {}/
272 MC Chorus	20	hall./The agents of hell disappear, the human, they shrink and dissolve/Into dust on
279 MC Knight4	33	deliberately exasperated/us beyond human endurance, he could still have easily
331 FR Harry	30	strong,/The liberated from the human wheel./So I looked to you for strength.
334 FR Harry	35	in a war of phantoms,/Not by human beings — they have no more power than
362 CP Reilly	22	you were. You no longer feel quite human./You're suddenly reduced to the status
387 CP Celia	5	glad I came!/I can see you at last as a human being./Can't you see me that way too,
398 CP Lavinia	2	Peter./Really, Edward, if you were human/You would burst out laughing. But you
417 CP Reilly	23	you wish,/I can reconcile you to the human condition,/The condition to which some
421 CP Julia	17	I don't know the process by which the human is/Transhumanised: what do we know/
453 CC Lucasta	16	you let him speak?/Eggy's really quite human, Colby./It's only that he's terrified of
569 ES Ld Clav	37	ghosts tormented me, to be only human beings,/Malicious, petty, and I see
570 ES Charles	17	your ghosts!/{C} But these are only human beings, who can be dealt with./{M} Or

HUMANITY (1)

156 Rock 3	71	/For nation or race or what you call humanity;/Though you forget the way to the

HUMBLE (8)

70 WL: Fire S	304	fingernails of dirty hands./My people humble people who expect/Nothing.'/la la/To
149 Rock 1	78	will./Let me show you the work of the humble. Listen./*The lights fade; in the*
152 Rock 2	33	may repair if you walk together in humble repentance, expiating the sins of your
244 MC Chorus	25	Lord, leave us and leave us be, in our humble and tarnished frame of existence, leave
246 MC Tempt1	27	gravity/Will find excuse for my humble levity/Remembering all the good time
248 MC Tempt1	6	gravity/Will find excuse for my humble levity./If you will remember me, my
339 FR Harry	11	and the icy vigil,/A care over lives of humble people,/The lesson of ignorance, of
421 CP Julia	26	there to be afraid of./She is too humble. She will pass between the scolding hills,

HUMILIATE (3)

380 CP Celia	1	.../{C} Oh, don't think that you can humiliate me!/Humiliation — it's something
380 CP Celia	4	even that you seem real enough/To humiliate me. I suppose that most women/
395 CP Edward	2	point/At which humiliation ceases to humiliate./You get to the point at which you

HUMILIATED (2)

379 CP Edward	39	is no reason why you should feel humiliated .../{C} Oh, don't think that you can
409 CP Reilly	28	in love with you,/And were always humiliated by the awareness/That you had

HUMILIATING (1)

379 CP Celia	38	/This world as well as that ... well, it's humiliating./{E} There is no reason why you

HUMILIATION (6)

270 MC Chorus	25	swoon/Of those consenting to the last humiliation./I have consented, Lord
340 FR Amy	19	ghost,/In his own house. What of the humiliation,/Of the chilly pretences in the silent
363 CP Reilly	35	good./You will find that you survive humiliation./And that's an experience of

380 CP	Celia	2	think that you can humiliate me!/Humiliation — it's something I've done to
394 CP	Edward	40	like that?/{E} I have had quite enough humiliation/Lately, to bring me to the point/At
395 CP	Edward	2	to bring me to the point/At which humiliation ceases to humiliate./You get to the

HUMILIATIONS (1)

566 ES	Ld Clav	2	at little desks/And suffer the same humiliations/At the hands of the same master.

HUMILITY (3)

158 Rock 5		9	and dodging his emptiness./If humility and purity be not in the heart, they are
179 FQ: ECoker		99	can hope to acquire/Is the wisdom of humility: humility is endless./The houses are all
179 FQ: ECoker		99	to acquire/Is the wisdom of humility: humility is endless./The houses are all gone

HUMMED (1)

24 Rhapsody		49	lamp muttered in the dark./The lamp hummed:/'Regard the moon,/La lune ne garde

HUMMING (1)

555 ES	Piggott	1	Lord Claverton./That tune she was humming, *It's Not Too Late For You To Love*

HUMMINGBIRD (1)

109 Marina		8	who glitter with the glory of the hummingbird, meaning/Death/Those who sit in

HUMORIST (2)

33 Conv Gal		13	inane.'/'You, madam, are the eternal humorist,/The eternal enemy of the absolute,/
451 CC	Eggers	19	I don't laugh easily./Quite a humorist, he is. In fact, Mrs. E./Sometimes says

HUMOROUS (1)

386 CP	Edward	36	/{E} I'm afraid I can't see the humorous side of it./{C} I'm not really laughing

HUMOUR (5)

393 CP	Lavinia	6	life/With a man who has no sense of humour;/And that the effect upon me was/That
393 CP	Lavinia	8	upon me was/That I lost all sense of humour myself./That's what came of always
408 CP	Lavinia	24	I never knew you had such a sense of humour./{R} It is the first more hopeful
456 CC	Eggers	16	to them. That's what Sir Claude said:/'Humour her, Eggerson,' he said, 'humour her.'/
456 CC	Eggers	16	/'Humour her, Eggerson,' he said, 'humour her.'/But she has one trait that I think I

HUMOURESQUE (1)

602 Humoresque		t	perfect climax all true lovers seek!'/Humouresque/(AFTER J. LAFORGUE)/One

HUMP (1)

289 FR	Gerald	4	seem to be wanting to give us all the hump./I must say, this isn't cheerful for Amy's

HUMPED (1)

74 WL: Thund		398	over Himavant./The jungle crouched, humped in silence./Then spoke the thunder/DA/

HUN (1)

119 SP	Klip	17	folks say,/I'll tell the world we got the Hun on the run/{Kr} What about that poker

HUNDRED (7)

14 Prufrock		32	and time for me,/And time yet for a hundred indecisions,/And for a hundred visions
14 Prufrock		33	for a hundred indecisions,/And for a hundred visions and revisions,/Before the taking
45 Cook Egg		33	weeping multitudes/Droop in a hundred A.B.C.'s./Le Directeur/Malheur à la
188 FQ: DrySal		138	into relief,/To the sleepy rhythm of a hundred hours./Fare forward, travellers! not
213 Growltiger		36	the moonlight shone reflected from a hundred bright blue eyes./And closer still and
213 Growltiger		51	forced to walk the plank./He who a hundred victims had driven to that drop,/At the
256 MC Chorus		35	prowl by the gate?/{C} Death has a hundred hands and walks by a thousand ways./

HUNG (1)

33 Conv Gal		4	balloon/Or an old battered lantern hung aloft/To light poor travellers to their

HUNGER (2)

166 Rock 10		8	folds of himself until he awakens in hunger and moving his head to right and to left
438 CP	Reilly	12	at his shoulder/Suffered any less from hunger, damp, exposure,/Bowel trouble, and the

HUNGRY (10)

246 MC Thomas		16	follow after?/{T} For a little time the hungry hawk/Will only soar and hover, circling
249 MC Tempt2		34	laid under excommunication./{T2} Hungry hatred/Will not strive against intelligent
251 MC Tempt3		21	in Anjou;/Round him waiting hungry sons./We are for England. We are in
377 CP	Edward	36	too tired to go out, and I'm not at all hungry./I shall have a few biscuits./{J} But you,
453 CC	Lucasta	10	A working girl like me/Is often very hungry — living on a pittance —/Cooking a
479 CC	Lucasta	10	/But all that matters now is, that I'm hungry,/And you've got to give me a very good
481 CC	Lucasta	8	/But I remarked that I was hungry./{K} You can't want dinner yet./It's
481 CC	Kaghan	24	going out to dinner. Lucasta's very hungry./{LE} Hungry? At six o'clock? Where
481 CC	Lady E	25	dinner. Lucasta's very hungry./{LE} Hungry? At six o'clock? Where will you get
481 CC	Lucasta	36	Shall we go there, Lucasta?/{L} I'm so hungry, I could even eat a herbal salad./{LE}

HUNT (5)

178 FQ: ECoker		65	down/Comets weep and Leonids fly/Hunt the heavens and the plains/Whirled in a
232 Skimble		3	where is Skimble has he gone to hunt the thimble?/We must find him or the train
337 FR	Agatha	10	of it as like a children's treasure hunt:/Here you have found a clue, hidden in the
383 CP	Edward	3	them?/Or have we ... have I got to hunt all over?/Have you looked in your bag? ...
383 CP	Edward	29	kept you waiting;/But we ... I had to hunt for them ... No, I found them./... Yes, she's

HUNTED (1)

| 281 | MC | Chorus | 8 | creatures, both the hunters and the hunted./For all things exist only as seen by |

HUNTER (1)

| 147 | Rock 1 | | 2 | soars in the summit of Heaven,/The Hunter with his dogs pursues his circuit./O |

HUNTERS (3)

281	MC	Chorus	8	in all of Thy creatures, both the hunters and the hunted./For all things exist only
292	FR	Gerald	30	have to see about a couple of new hunters./{C} And I've a new wine merchant to
311	FR	Harry	17	/They are roused again, the sleepless hunters/That will not let me sleep. At the

HUNTING (5)

224	Mr Mistoff		30	you into believing/That he's only hunting for mice./He can play any trick with a
479	CC	Lucasta	9	better not get in *her* way when she's hunting./But all that matters now is, that I'm
485	CC	Lady E	39	Guzzard. *That* is the name I've been hunting for!/{C} You may have come across the
487	CC	Lady E	39	son?/{LE} It's the name I've been hunting for all these years —/That, and the
573	ES	Carghil	23	MRS. CARGHILL]/{MC} I've been hunting high and low for you, Richard!/I've

HUNTS (1)

| 49 | Hippopot | | 22 | day/Is passed in sleep; at night he hunts;/God works in a mysterious way —/The |

HURRAH (1)

| 347 | FR | Ivy | 19 | you tomorrow many happy returns hurrah love Arthur.'/I mean, after what we |

HURRICANE (1)

| 219 | Mung Rump | | 32 | would go through the house like a hurricane, and no sober person could take his |

HURRIED (3)

193	FQ: Little		88	arose/I met one walking, loitering and hurried/As if blown towards me like the metal
349	FR	Agatha	15	/To complete fruition/It cannot be hurried/And it cannot be delayed/{M} It cannot
555	ES	Monica	13	Piggott bothering you again/So I hurried to your rescue. You look tired, Father./

HURRIEDLY (2)

| 32 | Hysteria | | 6 | waiter with trembling hands/was hurriedly spreading a pink and white checked |
| 346 | FR | m | 5 | this than I do. {}/[*Enter* DOWNING, *hurriedly, in chauffeur's costume*]/{Do} Oh, |

HURRY (11)

65	WL: Chess		141	mince my words, I said to her myself,/HURRY UP PLEASE ITS TIME/Now
66	WL: Chess		152	she said, and give me a straight look./HURRY UP PLEASE ITS TIME/If you don't
66	WL: Chess		165	for if you don't want children?/HURRY UP PLEASE ITS TIME/Well, that
66	WL: Chess		168	dinner, to get the beauty of it hot —/HURRY UP PLEASE ITS TIME/HURRY UP
66	WL: Chess		169	—/HURRY UP PLEASE ITS TIME/HURRY UP PLEASE ITS TIME/Goonight
230	Bust Jones		25	at the *Drones.*/When he's seen in a hurry there's probably curry/At the *Siamese* —
272	MC	Priests	10	your hands off!/{3P} To vespers! Hurry. {}/[*They drag him off. While the*
323	FR	Winch	19	/And he must have been in rather a hurry./There was a lorry drawn up where it
344	FR	Charles	15	in our family!/And why in such a hurry? Before you make up your mind .../{V}
540	ES	Ld Clav	28	the accelerator./{LC} We were in a hurry./{G} More than in a hurry./You didn't
540	ES	Gomez	29	were in a hurry./{G} More than in a hurry./You didn't want it to be known where

HURRYING (2)

| 109 | Marina | | 20 | small laughter between leaves and hurrying feet/Under sleep, where all the waters |
| 599 | On a Port | | 3 | restless brain and weary feet,/Forever hurrying, up and down the street,/She stands at |

HURT (10)

275	MC	Thomas	9	/Do with me as you will, to your hurt and shame;/But none of my people, in
327	FR	Ivy	30	had an accident. I don't think he's hurt,/But he says that he hasn't got the use of
415	CP	Celia	13	across it./I suppose it is wicked to hurt other people/If you know that you're
415	CP	Celia	14	that you're hurting them. I haven't hurt *her.*/I wasn't taking anything away from
417	CP	Celia	5	/It's not that I'm afraid of being hurt again:/Nothing again can either hurt or
417	CP	Celia	6	hurt again:/Nothing again can either hurt or heal./I have thought at moments that
472	CC	Colby	5	/Perhaps you've been very badly hurt, at some time./Or at least, there may have
474	CC	Lucasta	20	it./{L} How afraid one is of ... being hurt!/{C} It's not the hurting that one would
500	CC	Lucasta	33	people, either./B. needs me. He's been hurt by life, just as I have,/And we can help
516	CC	Colby	36	/{C} No, Sir Claude. I hate to hurt you/As I am hurting you. But it is very

HURTING (6)

415	CP	Celia	14	other people/If you know that you're hurting them. I haven't hurt *her.*/I wasn't taking
467	CC	Colby	21	than he did./{C} I know that I'm hurting you and I know/That I hate myself for
467	CC	Colby	22	and I know/That I hate myself for hurting you./{SC} You mustn't think of that./
474	CC	Colby	21	is of ... being hurt!/{C} It's not the hurting that one would mind/But the sense of
478	CC	Colby	6	such words! You don't know how it's hurting./{L} I could use words much stronger
516	CC	Colby	37	Claude. I hate to hurt you/As I am hurting you. But it is very different./As long as I

HUSBAND (24)

65	WL: Chess		139	a knock upon the door./When Lil's husband got demobbed, I said —/I didn't mince
284	FR	m	3	PIPER, *brothers of her deceased husband*/MARY, *daughter of a deceased cousin*
340	FR	Amy	5	Thirty-five years ago/You took my husband from me. Now you take my son./{Ag}
340	FR	Amy	23	*would* have sons, if I could not have a husband:/Then I let him go. I abased myself./

I (4123)
I (6) [*Foreign word*]

238 MC		m	2	CATHEDRAL/Characters/PART I/A CHORUS OF WOMEN OF
239 MC		m	1	*on December 29th*, 1170/Part I/{C} Here let us stand, close by the cathedral.
285 FR		1m	1	*house in the North of England*/PART I/*The drawing-room, after tea. An afternoon in*
285 FR		3m	1	*An afternoon in late March.*/Scene I/AMY, IVY, VIOLET, AGATHA, GERALD,
316 FR		2m	24	{}/[*Exit to dinner*]/END OF PART I/PART II/*The library, after dinner.*/Scene I/
317 FR		3m	1	II/*The library, after dinner.*/Scene I/HARRY, WARBURTON/{W} I'm glad of a

I'D (92)

118 SP	Doris		12	Sometimes they're no use at all./{Do} I'd like to know about that coffin./{Du} Well I
118 SP	Doris		31	/(*to* DORIS): Cards are queer./{Do} I'd like to know about that coffin. {}/KNOCK
121 SA	Sweeney		15	/{Do} You wouldn't eat me!/{S} Yes I'd eat you!/In a nice little, white little, soft
122 SA	Doris		4	and copulation, and death./{Do} I'd be bored./{S} You'd be bored./Birth, and
122 SA	Doris		7	and copulation, and death./{Do} I'd be bored./{S} You'd be bored./Birth, and
123 SA	Doris		31	That's not life, that's no life/Why I'd just as soon be dead./{S} That's what life is.
124 SA	Sweeney		38	used to come and see me sometimes/I'd give him a drink and cheer him up./{Do}
228 Gus			23	to know seventy speeches by heart./I'd extemporize back-chat, I knew how to gag,/
228 Gus			27	hour of rehearsal, I never could fail./I'd a voice that would soften the hardest of
286 FR	Gerald		6	English winter./{G} Well, as for me,/I'd just as soon be a subaltern again/To be back
296 FR	Gerald		39	and Harry need have no suspicion./I'd trust Warburton's opinion./{A} If anyone
297 FR	Charles		25	or two {}/[*Rings the bell*]/{C} That I'd like to ask Downing./He shan't know why
297 FR	Charles		29	with his Lordship's car./{C} Tell him I'd like to have a word with him, please. {}/[Exit
298 FR	Charles		29	you so abruptly,/But I've a question I'd like to put to you,/I'm sure you won't mind,
304 FR	Mary		6	differently now;/But I really wish that I'd taken your advice/And tried for a
304 FR	Mary		18	/I suppose I could have gone, if I'd had the moral courage,/Even against a will
306 FR	Harry		12	you. I don't know yet./All these years I'd been longing to get back/Because I thought I
322 FR	Winch		15	you?/{Wi} Oh no indeed, my Lord, I'd much rather not .../{H} You mean you think
322 FR	Winch		25	Yes, my Lord, I'm sorry./I thought I'd better have a word with you quiet,/Rather
322 FR	Winch		28	/What with the fog so thick, or I'd have been here sooner./I'd telephoned to Dr.
322 FR	Winch		29	thick, or I'd have been here sooner./I'd telephoned to Dr. Warburton's,/And they
323 FR	Warburt		13	/But he mustn't be moved tonight. I'd trust Owen/On a matter like this. You can
358 CP	Julia		22	hate to leave it./It's such a nice party, I'd like to repeat it./Why don't you *all* come to
361 CP	Edward		18	my mind/By telling someone what I'd been concealing./I don't think I want to
365 CP	Julia		4	I don't remember the colour,/But I'd know them, because one lens is missing. {}/
366 CP	Julia		9	/That really was very clever of you;/I'd never have found them but for you./The
367 CP	Edward		36	Do you know why *I've* looked in?/{E} I'd like to know first how you *got* in, Alex./{A}
367 CP	Alex		38	the door was open/And so I thought I'd slip in and see if anyone was with you./{P}
369 CP	Peter		4	Celia./She was different from any girl I'd ever known/And not easy to talk to, on that
372 CP	Peter		33	comes back ... but, if you don't mind,/I'd rather you didn't tell *her* what I've told you./
374 CP	Celia		6	anyone with you/I was going to say I'd come back for my umbrella ... ./I must say
407 CP	Edward		2	Only because you've told me so often./I'd like to see *you* filling up an income-tax form.
407 CP	Lavinia		35	about it./{L} Really, Edward! Even if I'd been blind/There were plenty of people to let
413 CP	Celia		21	I first to tell you the circumstances?/I'd forgotten that you know nothing about me;/
413 CP	Celia		32	/That would be terrible. So I'd rather believe/There is something wrong
413 CP	Celia		34	with me, that could be put right./I'd do anything you told me, to get back to
425 CP	Edward		22	that's what we said at the time;/But I'd forgotten what the Gunnings' parties were
432 CP	Julia		3	Harcourt-Reilly!/{J} Oh, I forgot! I'd another surprise for you. {}/[*Enter* REILLY]
437 CP	Reilly		36	all what I mean. Rather the contrary./I'd say she suffered all that we should
437 CP	Reilly		39	of the body to become a *thing*./I'd say she suffered more, because more
439 CP	Peter		17	will be waiting,/and the experts — I'd almost forgotten them./I realise that I can't
450 CC	Colby		29	/Mr. Eggerson. I was afraid I'd miss you./{E} I'm off in half an hour, Mr.
452 CC	Kaghan		7	/Bankrupt again! So I thought I'd better bring her/And come upstairs ahead,
452 CC	Lucasta		16	Eggy. It's rank injustice./Two months I'd gone on filing those papers/Which no one
455 CC	Colby		5	/I nearly did, a moment ago./Then I'd have been certain I'd lost my reason:/Her
455 CC	Colby		5	ago./Then I'd have been certain I'd lost my reason:/Her influence is perfectly
459 CC	Lady E		37	made you go to Zürich?/{LE} Why, I'd no sooner got to Lausanne/Than whom
461 CC	Eggers		3	you, I've done some shopping./But I'd better be off now. Mr. Simpkins —/If
461 CC	Claude		31	the meeting didn't go quite the way I'd intended;/And yet I believe that it's all for
469 CC	Lucasta		3	for anything:/You know that. But I'd like to learn about music./I wish you would
470 CC	Colby		25	see that American Musical!/{C} Well, I'd heard you say you wanted to see it./{L} But
471 CC	Lucasta		7	you the gramophone records./{L} I'd rather you played me bits yourself, and
471 CC	Colby		27	But, for some reason,/You thought I'd get a false impression anyway./You
474 CC	Lucasta		40	real than any *I've* ever lived in./And I'd like to understand *you*./{C} I believe you do
475 CC	Lucasta		19	now that we begin to understand,/I'd like you to know a little more about me./
475 CC	Colby		32	— you might as well know them./{C} I'd gladly tell you everything about myself;/But

475 CC	Lucasta	38	tell me much. And as for B. —/I'd much rather hear it from yourself./{C}
477 CC	Lucasta	20	I believe you're more shocked/Than if I'd told you I *was* Claude's mistress./Claude has
478 CC	Lucasta	14	you to be sorry, thank you./Why, I'd actually thought of telling you before,/And I
479 CC	Kaghan	39	/If I was as snug as Colby is, Lucasta,/I'd never have thought of changing my
482 CC	Colby	5	did they come in unexpectedly?/{C} I'd invited Lucasta. She had asked me to play to
488 CC	Claude	27	as well have told you before,/But I'd hoped — and now it seems a silly thought ...
488 CC	Claude	30	such a travesty of all one's plans —/I'd hoped that you would become fond of
488 CC	Claude	39	daughter. Now you want a son./{SC} I'd never want to take your son away from you.
495 CC	Claude	8	would despise me/If you knew what I'd really wanted to be./{LE} And I took it for
496 CC	Eggers	19	to bring me;/But Mrs. E. wishes I'd come up oftener!/Isn't that like the ladies!
499 CC	Lucasta	36	I'm grateful to Colby. But for Colby/I'd never have come to appreciate B./{SC} But
499 CC	Claude	37	B./{SC} But Colby! Lucasta, if I'd suspected this/I would have explained.
503 CC	Colby	23	concur in this proposal./{C} Of course I'd like them ... Can't B. come up now?/{E}
517 CC	Colby	37	*I* am the Vicar's Warden./{C} I'd like to apply./{E} The stipend is small —/
518 CC	Colby	20	with us, until you were settled./{C} I'd be very glad indeed — if Mrs. Eggerson
526 ES	Charles	3	you./{C} So I was right! The moment I'd said it/I was badly frightened. For I didn't
532 ES	Ld Clav	6	I've left too many papers about there./I'd better see him here./{L} Very good, my
540 ES	Gomez	2	both of us failures. But even so,/I'd rather be my kind of failure than yours./
541 ES	Gomez	9	—/But you'd never know to whom I'd told it,/Or who knew the story and who
541 ES	Gomez	15	safe with me',/And then you ... well, I'd never have believed/That you would accuse
542 ES	Gomez	37	forget, Dick:/You *didn't stop*! Well, I'd better be going./I hope I haven't outstayed
548 ES	Carghil	31	/And you don't even recognise me! I'd know you anywhere./But then, we've all seen
551 ES	Carghil	13	/But you think, or try to think, that if I'd really suffered/I shouldn't want to let you
551 ES	Carghil	24	an action/For breach of promise, if I'd really cared for you./What sentimental
551 ES	Carghil	37	way. I didn't want to ruin you./If I'd carried on, it might have ended your career,/
552 ES	Carghil	9	the feeling into it I did/But for what I'd gone through. Did you hear me sing it?/{LC}
555 ES	Piggott	5	to meet you, so I thought/That I'd take the first opportunity of hinting —/
557 ES	Michael	9	Sir Alfred Walter made for you./{Mi} I'd stuck it for two years. And deadly dull it
557 ES	Michael	29	what do you call good terms?/{Mi} I'd nothing at all to pay for two years:/The
558 ES	Michael	25	/That I was overworked, when I'd nothing to do./Even the office boys began to
558 ES	Michael	31	thing he brought up against me,/That I'd been too familiar with one of the girls./He
559 ES	Michael	1	It would never have happened/If only I'd been given some interesting work!/{LC} And
560 ES	Michael	9	once I'm out of the country./What I'd like is a chance to go abroad/As a partner in
563 ES	Carghil	5	America./{MC} How romantic! I'd love to meet him./He's coming to speak to
565 ES	Carghil	16	— it's not far away./{MC} Then I'd like to walk a little way with you./{Mi}
569 ES	Ld Clav	3	clothes/And speak as ourselves. So I'd become an idol/To Monica. She worshipped

I'LL (100)

66 WL:	Chess	151	said. Something o' that, I said./Then I'll know who to thank, she said, and give me a
116 SP	Dusty	36	Monday you'll phone through./Yes I'll tell her. Good bye. Goooood bye./I'm sure,
119 SP	Klip	17	Yes we did our bit, as you folks say,/I'll tell the world we got the Hun on the run/
119 SP	Klip	37	/London's a little too gay for us/Yes I'll say a little too gay./{Kr} Yes London's a
121 SA	Sweeney	1	SNOW. DORIS. DUSTY./{S} I'll carry you off/To a cannibal isle./{Do} You'll
121 SA	Sweeney	6	be my little seven stone missionary!/I'll gobble you up. I'll be the cannibal./{Do}
121 SA	Sweeney	6	stone missionary!/I'll gobble you up. I'll be the cannibal./{Do} You'll carry me off?
121 SA	Sweeney	8	carry me off? To a cannibal isle?/{S} I'll be the cannibal./{Do} I'll be the missionary./
121 SA	Doris	9	isle?/{S} I'll be the cannibal./{Do} I'll be the missionary./I'll convert you!/{S} I'll
121 SA	Doris	10	cannibal./{Do} I'll be the missionary./I'll convert you!/{S} I'll convert *you*!/Into a
121 SA	Sweeney	11	the missionary./I'll convert *you*!/{S} I'll convert *you*!/Into a stew./A nice little, white
221 Old Deut		38	Deuteronomy mustn't be woken —/I'll have the police if there's any uproar' —/And
233 Skimble		64	of his long brown tail/Which says: 'I'll see you again!/You'll meet without fail on
234 Ad-dress		18	*ad-dress a Cat?*/So first, your memory I'll jog,/And say: A CAT IS NOT A DOG./
236 Cat Morgan		18	business with Faber — or Faber —/I'll give you this tip, and it's worth a lot more:/
588 Fable		32	come uninvited, then, of course,/I'll be compelled to keep them off by force.'/He
588 Fable		45	much about — as well's I'm able/I'll go through the account: They made a raid/
248 MC	Tempt1	8	me, my Lord, at your prayers,/I'll remember you at kissing-time below the
277 MC	Knight3	8	we had taken on a pretty stiff job;/I'll only speak for/myself, but I had drunk a
296 FR	Charles	29	to talk to,/To get it off his mind. I'll have a talk to him tomorrow./{A} Most
296 FR	Gerald	37	all the boys/When they were children. I'll have a word with him./He can talk to Harry,
321 FR	Harry	13	he wouldn't have troubled you./{H} I'll see him. {}/[*Exit* DENMAN]/{W} I wonder
323 FR	Warburt	3	at him./{W} Quite right, quite right. I'll go and have a look at him./We must explain
323 FR	Gerald	26	Owen was there, by a bit of luck./{G} I'll go down and see him, Amy, and come back
328 FR	Charles	1	Pancras. If I did, it's in my overcoat./I'll see if it's there. There might be something in
346 FR	Downing	14	are away?/{Do} Oh, certainly, Miss;/I'll never leave him so long as he requires me./
347 FR	Downing	11	speaking. There's no harm in *them*,/I'll take my oath. Will that be all, Miss?/{Ag}
366 CP	Julia	11	next time I lose *anything*, Edward,/I'll come straight to you, instead of to St.

368 CP	Edward	11	you?/{E} No, I shan't want much, and I'll get it myself./{A} Ah, in that case I know
368 CP	Alex	12	/{A} Ah, in that case I know what I'll do./I'm going to give you a little surprise:/
371 CP	Edward	24	talk now .../Yes, there is ... Well then, I'll ring you/As soon as I can. {}/[To PETER]/
372 CP	Alex	29	than another ten minutes./Now I'll be going, and I'll take Peter with me./{P}
372 CP	Alex	29	ten minutes./Now I'll be going, and I'll take Peter with me./{P} Edward, I've taken
374 CP	Celia	11	you./Tell me it's all right, and then I'll go./{E} But how can you say you understand
376 CP	Celia	5	I really did leave my umbrella;/And I'll say I found you here starving and helpless/
377 CP	Julia	25	a stimulant/After this disaster. Now I'll propose a health./Can you guess whose
383 CP	Edward	7	Very well, hold on if you like;/We ... I'll look for them./{C} Yes, you look for them./I
390 CP	Alex	38	/{A} Ah, in that case I know what I'll do .../{J} No, Alex./We must leave them
391 CP	Celia	4	party at *my* house to-day./{C} Well, I'll go now. Good-bye, Lavinia./Good-bye,
406 CP	Edward	34	much too ill./{E} Much too ill?/Then I'll go and be ill in a suburban boarding-house./
421 CP	Reilly	39	/{R} He should be here by now. I'll speak to Miss Barraway. {}/[Takes up
424 CP	Lavinia	23	{L} I'm not tired yet. But I know that I'll be glad/When it's all over./{E} I like the
431 CP	Peter	36	course, only for minor parts —/And I'll help him decide what faces are typical./{J}
439 CP	Peter	22	expects great things of it./{P} So now I'll be going./{E} Shall we see you again, Peter,/
447 CC	Eggers	38	to concerts. But don't overdo it!/{E} I'll remember that. Music./{SC} And by the
450 CC	Claude	22	he should be back by now. And then I'll leave you./I must telephone to Amsterdam,
450 CC	Claude	25	when you return with Lady Elizabeth/I'll be ready waiting to introduce him. {}/[Enter
450 CC	Claude	31	in half an hour, Mr. Simpkins./{SC} I'll leave you now. But when Eggerson comes
451 CC	Colby	34	at once/That you are a musician./{C} I'll be on my guard./{E} If your music will
454 CC	Eggers	1	/You will have to ask Sir Claude. But I'll speak to him/When I return from Northolt./
454 CC	Kaghan	10	with her;/She's hard as nails. Now I'll take her off your hands./I'll show you how
454 CC	Kaghan	11	Now I'll take her off your hands./I'll show you how it's done. Come along,
454 CC	Lucasta	15	much for me. Another time, Colby./I'll ring you up, and let you take me out to
454 CC	Colby	35	it amuses him./{C} Well, perhaps I'll be amused./But it did make my head spin —
457 CC	Eggers	13	of time. {}/[Looks at his watch]/{E} I'll arrive at the airport with minutes to spare,/
457 CC	Lady E	30	black coffee. Is Sir Claude at home?/I'll speak to him first./{SC} Good heavens,
461 CC	Eggers	6	on the phone./If I'm not in the house, I'll be out in the garden./And I'll slip up to
461 CC	Eggers	7	house, I'll be out in the garden./And I'll slip up to town any day, if you want me./In
461 CC	Eggers	20	will really be a treat to look at.'/Well, I'll be going./{SC} Goodbye, and thank you,
466 CC	Claude	27	you play./I shan't mention it again. I'll wait until you ask me./Do you understand
471 CC	Colby	5	— or the things I want to hear./I'll play you the themes, so you'll recognise
471 CC	Colby	6	so you'll recognise them./Better still, I'll play you the gramophone records./{L} I'd
478 CC	Lucasta	23	at last that there's no escape./Well, I'll be going./{C} You mustn't go yet!/There's
479 CC	Kaghan	17	you have a glass of sherry?/{K} Yes, I'll have a glass of sherry,/To drink success to
480 CC	Kaghan	22	/{K} Oh, I'm a good judge. Now, I'll tell you the difference/Between ourselves and
487 CC	Claude	1	/{SC} Yes it is./But you know that I'll have to have my speech written out/And
487 CC	Colby	7	{}/[looking at the notes]./{C} I'll try./{SC} It's just in ways like this, Elizabeth,
489 CC	Claude	14	a son of your own,/And I thought, I'll wait for children of *our* own,/And tell her
492 CC	Claude	10	you./But we must see Mrs. Guzzard. I'll arrange to get her here./{LE} And I think
499 CC	Claude	20	it now. If you'll listen./{SC} Of course I'll listen. But we haven't much time./{L} It
500 CC	Claude	6	Claude, let me explain./{SC} No, I'll explain. There's been some
504 CC	Lucasta	18	/Will you show her up, Lucasta?/{L} I'll make B. do it. {}/[Exit LUCASTA]/{SC} I
509 CC	Lady E	39	Kaghan/Being Barnabas. I suppose I'll get used to it./{C} But he's waiting
514 CC	Eggers	28	to what Colby said he wanted./{E} I'll examine the records myself, Sir Claude./Not
514 CC	Claude	33	Quite well./{SC} I shall not believe it. I'll not believe those records./You pretend to
515 CC	Claude	40	you think/I am not your father./{SC} And/If you will stay with me. It shall
516 CC	Claude	32	if you like, that I am not your father:/I'll accept that. I put no claim upon you —/
532 ES	Ld Clav	4	{}/[after reading the note]./{LC} I'll see him in the library./No, stop. I've left too
532 ES	Monica	11	Let *us* go into the library. And then I'll see you off./{LC} I'm sorry to turn you out
532 ES	Ld Clav	13	you out of the room like this,/But I'll have to see this man by myself, Monica./I've
532 ES	Monica	21	got rid of him in twenty minutes/I'll send Lambert to tell you that you have to
532 ES	Charles	23	Charles. Will you bring my coat?/{C} I'll say goodbye, sir./And look forward to
541 ES	Ld Clav	34	for you/In five minutes' time./{LC} I'll be ready to take it. {}/[Exit LAMBERT]/{G}
542 ES	Gomez	40	pal may be getting impatient./I'll see you soon again./{LC} Not very soon, I
543 ES	Ld Clav	16	rest now, before dinner./{LC} Yes, I'll go and rest now. I wish Charles was dining
544 ES	Ld Clav	11	business'./{LC} So far, so good./I'll feel more confidence after a fortnight —/
544 ES	Ld Clav	14	or wanting a fourth at bridge;/Still, I'll admit to a feeling of contentment/Already. I
547 ES	Piggott	29	/To know whom *not* to play with. I'll mention no names,/But there are one or two
548 ES	Piggott	2	and quiet is our *raison d'être*./Now I'll leave you to enjoy it. {}/[Exit]/{M} I hope she
549 ES	Ld Clav	20	more you remind me of, the better I'll remember./{MC} And the three of us talked
554 ES	Carghil	1	have these letters auctioned.'/Yes, I'll bring the photostats tomorrow morning,/
562 ES	Carghil	23	once. You're not to introduce us,/I'll introduce myself. I'm Maisie Montjoy!/That
565 ES	Michael	9	come tomorrow morning./{Mi} Well, I'll come tomorrow morning./{MC} Are you

565 ES Ld Clav 36   /Of the lesson I would teach? Come, I'll start to learn again./Michael and I shall go
574 ES Michael 28   you never came./{Mi} No, Father. I'll explain why./{LC} And I learn that you have
575 ES Carghil 39   he looked at me!/Some day, Monica, I'll tell you all about it./{M} I am satisfied with
577 ES Michael 20   what do you say to all this?/{Mi} I'll say that Hemington has plenty of cheek./
580 ES Michael   9   I'm not much of a correspondent;/But I'll send you a card, now and again,/Just to let
580 ES Carghil 25   rest now./You're looking rather tired. I'll run and see them off. {}/[*Exit* MRS.
582 ES Ld Clav 23   /{LC} Yes, it's chilly at dusk. But I'll be warm enough./I shall not go far. {}/[*Exit*

I'M (404)
I'VE (250)
ICE (7)
109 Marina   22   waters meet./Bowsprit cracked with ice and paint cracked with heat./I made this, I
191 FQ: Little   5   and fire,/The brief sun flames the ice, on pond and ditches,/In windless cold that
247 MC Tempt1   10   /Shall float as sweet as blossoms. Ice along the ditches/Mirror the sunlight. Love
280 MC Priest3   22   Go to the northern seas confined with ice/Where the dead breath makes numb the
333 FR Agatha   36   /Moving alone through flames of ice, chosen/To resolve the enchantment under
535 ES Gomez   8   Very good, my Lord./{G} And some ice./{L} Ice? Yes, my Lord. {}/[*Exit*]/{G} I began
535 ES Lambert   9   my Lord./{G} And some ice./{L} Ice? Yes, my Lord. {}/[*Exit*]/{G} I began to say:
ICE-CAP (1)
179 FQ: ECoker   68   fire/Which burns before the ice-cap reigns./That was a way of putting it —
ICES (1)
15 Prufrock   79   me./Should I, after tea and cakes and ices,/Have the strength to force the moment to
ICI (1)
48 Lune Miel   8   mieux égratigner./Moins d'une lieue d'ici est Saint Apollinaire/En Classe, basilique
ICY (1)
339 FR Harry   10   altar,/The heat of the sun and the icy vigil,/A care over lives of humble people,/
IDEA (16)
85 Hollow Men   72   *o'clock in the morning.*/Between the idea/And the reality/Between the motion/And
147 Rock 1   6   birth and dying!/The endless cycle of idea and action,/Endless invention, endless
297 FR Charles 10   {}/[*Exit*]/{C} Meanwhile, I have an idea. Why not question Downing?/He's been
365 FR Edward   29   know his *name*?/{E} I tell you I've no idea who he is/Or how he got here./{J} But what
431 CP Julia   37   /{J} Peter, I've thought of a wonderful idea!/I've always wanted to go to California:/
433 CP Peter   20   to our casting director./I've got an idea for another film./Can you tell me where she
450 CC Colby   37   hasn't told me very much:/So I've no idea how I ought to behave./B. Kaghan has told
491 CC Lady E   12   claims upon you, Colby./It's a good idea! Why should we not be happy,/All of us?
493 CC Lady E   12   sort of chairman./{LE} That's a good idea./{SC} On the other hand,/We mustn't look
494 CC Claude   19   was something else to *him* —/An idea, an inspiration. What he wanted to
494 CC Claude   20   he wanted to transmit to me/Was that idea, that inspiration,/Which to him was life. To
501 CC Claude   36   has left?/{SC} That's not a bad idea. If Colby agrees./{L} I trust you, Eggy. And
513 CC Colby   24   in peace. As for a father —/I have the idea of a father./It's only just come to me. I
559 ES Ld Clav   5   to go abroad?/Well, that's not a bad idea. A few years out of England/In one of the
559 ES Michael 14   Good Lord, no./That's not my idea. I want to make money./I want to be
574 ES Carghil 14   me utterly brainless,/But I have an idea or two, now and then./And in the end I
IDEAL (3)
278 MC Knight2 15   wishes, we should have had an almost ideal State:/a union of spiritual and temporal
449 CC Eggers   14   would be the solution. Yes, quite ideal./{SC} I'm glad you agree. Your support
499 CC Lucasta 25   it so obvious/That this would be the ideal solution/From your point of view. To get
IDEAS (4)
20 Portrait   83   other people have desired./Are these ideas right or wrong?/The October night comes
435 CP Peter   20   believe in myself./I thought I had ideas to make a revolution/In the cinema, that
440 CP Edward   9   keeping on;/And somehow, the two ideas seem to fit together./{L} But all the same
559 ES Michael 19   life of my own,/According to my own ideas of good and bad,/Of right and wrong. I
IDENTIFICATION (1)
466 CC Claude   11   /I sometimes have that sense of identification/With the maker, of which I spoke
IDENTIFIED (2)
332 FR Agatha   11   then?/{Ag} You see your mother as identified with this house —/It was not always
352 CP   m   7   /AN UNIDENTIFIED GUEST, *later identified as* SIR HENRY
IDENTIFY (2)
510 CC Eggers   6   living/Mrs. Guzzard should be able to identify them./{LE} And will that prove that
568 ES Ld Clav 38   in trying to forget myself,/In trying to identify myself with the part/I had chosen to
IDENTITY (1)
448 CC Claude   20   — or indeed whether — I reveal his identity/Depends on how she takes to him. This
IDLE (3)
211 Old Gumbie 32   employment/To prevent them from idle and wanton destroyment./So she's formed,
250 MC Tempt3   25   /I am no trifler, and no politician./To idle or intrigue at court/I have no skill. I am no
496 CC Eggers   29   from the garden — that I've not an idle moment./And really, now, I'm quite lost in

IDLENESS (3)
148 Rock 1	47	man is ceaseless labour,/Or ceaseless idleness, which is still harder,/Or irregular
151 Rock 2	5	house?/Where many are born to idleness, to frittered lives and squalid deaths,
154 Rock 3	23	my people forgetful and forgotten/To idleness, labour, and delirious stupor?/There

IDOL (1)
569 ES Ld Clav	3	speak as ourselves. So I'd become an idol/To Monica. She worshipped the part I

IDOLISE (1)
553 ES Carghil	10	with you;/And you needn't think I idolise your memory./It's simply that I feel that

IF (528)

IGNOMINY (1)
148 Rock 1	53	/With equal face those that bring ignominy,/The applause of all or the love of

IGNORANCE (8)
94 Ash-Wed 4	6	colour,/Talking of trivial things/In ignorance and in knowledge of eternal dolour/
147 Rock 1	10	of silence;/Knowledge of words, and ignorance of the Word./All our knowledge
147 Rock 1	11	knowledge brings us nearer to our ignorance,/All our ignorance brings us nearer to
147 Rock 1	12	us nearer to our ignorance,/All our ignorance brings us nearer to death,/But
181 FQ: ECoker	141	must go by a way which is the way of ignorance./In order to possess what you do not
250 MC Thomas	13	by the order of God,/In confident ignorance, but arrest disorder,/Make it fast,
338 FR Harry	19	I have been in flight/But always in ignorance of invisible pursuers./Now I know
339 FR Harry	12	lives of humble people,/The lesson of ignorance, of incurable diseases./Such things are

IGNORANT (4)
257 MC Chorus	7	have not been too happy./We are not ignorant women, we know what we must expect
449 CC Claude	39	wife./There's always something one's ignorant of/About anyone, however well one
469 CC Lucasta	18	right ones to like?/Still, I'm awfully ignorant. Can you believe/That I've never been
471 CC Lucasta	11	of surprises!/I've never met a man so ignorant as you/Yet knowing so much that one

IGNORE (4)
435 CP Peter	21	/In the cinema, that no one could ignore —/And here I am, making a second-rate
508 CC Guzzard	13	my son./{MG} In the circumstances, I ignore that remark./{E} May I pour a drop of
557 ES Ld Clav	4	point. You're in trouble again./We'll ignore, if you please, the question of blame:/
571 ES Ld Clav	13	in him?/Yes, I was./How easily we ignore the fact that those who admire us/Will

IGNORED (2)
202 War Poetry	18	a situation,/One which may neither be ignored nor accepted,/A problem to be met with
232 Skimble	30	/He's a Cat that cannot be ignored;/So nothing goes wrong on the

II (5) *[Foreign word]*
238 MC	m 10	*Hall, on December 2nd,* 1170/PART II/THREE PRIESTS/FOUR KNIGHTS/
263 MC	m 1	and of the Holy Ghost. Amen./Part II/{C} Does the bird sing in the South?/Only the
303 FR	1m 1	{}/[*Exeunt, except* AGATHA]/Scene II/AGATHA/[*Enter* MARY *with flowers*]/{M}
317 FR	1m 1	*to dinner*]/END OF PART I/PART II/*The library, after dinner.*/Scene I/HARRY,
330 FR	1m 1	{}/[*Exeunt* CHORUS]/Scene II/HARRY, AGATHA/{H} John will recover,

III (2) *[Foreign word]*
313 FR	1m 1	*is empty.*]/{M} Oh, Harry! {}/Scene III/HARRY, MARY, IVY, VIOLET,
340 FR	1m 1	the bright angels. {}/[*Exit*]/Scene III/AMY, AGATHA/{A} I was a fool, to ask

IL (2)
51 Restaurant	3	sur mon épaule:/'Dans mon pays il fera temps pluvieux,/Du vent, du grand soleil,
51 Restaurant	17	à cet âge .../'Monsieur, le fait est dur./Il est venu, nous peloter, un gros chien;/Moi

ILE (1)
75 WL: Thund	431	shored against my ruins/Why then Ile fit you. Hieronymo's mad againe./Datta.

ILL (29)
20 Portrait	85	/Except for a slight sensation of being ill at ease/I mount the stairs and turn the handle
116 SP Doris	17	say?/{Do} Say what you like: say I'm ill,/Say I broke my leg on the stairs/Say we've
152 Rock 2	27	and always being restored./For every ill deed in the past we suffer the consequence:/
152 Rock 2	31	have the inheritance./For good and ill deeds belong to a man alone, when he stands
152 Rock 2	32	you have the reward of the good and ill that was done by those who have gone before
152 Rock 2	33	have gone before you./And all that is ill you may repair if you walk together in
194 FQ: Little	143	revealed, and the awareness/Of things ill done and done to others' harm/Which once
240 MC Chorus	20	statesmen/Who do, some well, some ill, planning and guessing,/Having their aims
243 MC Priest3	7	welcome!/{P3} For good or ill, let the wheel turn./The wheel has been still,
243 MC Priest3	9	these seven years, and no good./For ill or good, let the wheel turn./For who knows
243 MC Chorus	15	city, here is no abiding stay./Ill the wind, ill the time, uncertain the profit,
243 MC Chorus	15	here is no abiding stay./Ill the wind, ill the time, uncertain the profit, certain the
290 FR Chorus	36	feel embarrassed, impatient, fretful, ill at ease,/Assembled like amateur actors who
314 FR Warburt	13	you in bed./You didn't like being ill in the holidays./{I} It *was* unpleasant, coming
314 FR Warburt	28	of the laboratory./We're all of us ill in one way or another:/We call it health when
356 CP Edward	36	I hear from her./If her aunt is very ill, she may be gone some time./{C} And how
357 CP Edward	11	And she's rather difficult./When she's ill, she insists on having Lavinia./{J} I never

357 CP	Julia	12	Lavinia./{J} I never heard of her being ill before./{E} No, she's always very strong.
357 CP	Edward	13	very strong. That's why when she's ill/She gets into a panic./{J} And sends for
392 CP	Edward	27	/{E} I invented an aunt/Who was ill in the country, and had sent for you./{L}
402 CP	Reilly	11	reason to believe that you are very ill?/{E} I should have thought a doctor could see
405 CP	Reilly	4	to explore. The single patient/Who is ill by himself, is rather the exception./I have
406 CP	Reilly	32	my sanatorium:/You are much too ill./{E} Much too ill?/Then I'll go and be ill in a
406 CP	Edward	33	/You are much too ill./{E} Much too ill?/Then I'll go and be ill in a suburban
406 CP	Edward	34	/{E} Much too ill?/Then I'll go and be ill in a suburban boarding-house./{L} That
407 CP	Reilly	6	discussion?/I say you are both too ill. There are several symptoms/Which must
412 CP	Celia	36	they come to see you,/Are obviously ill, or can give good reasons/For wanting to see
546 ES	Piggott	12	our guests to think of themselves as ill,/Though we never have guests who are
546 ES	Piggott	28	the dining-room:/Nobody looks ill! They're all convalescents,/Or resting, like

ILL-BRED (1)

483 CC	Lady E	1	— intellectual people/Are often ill-bred. But that's not all./You need

ILLEGIBLE (1)

197 FQ: Little		229	fire, down the sea's throat/Or to an illegible stone: and that is where we start./We

ILLEGITIMATE (2)

486 CC	Colby	9	have a father./You see ... I was an illegitimate child./{LE} Oh yes. An illegitimate
486 CC	Lady E	10	an illegitimate child./{LE} Oh yes. An illegitimate child./So that the only relative you

ILLER (1)

528 ES	Monica	25	it by Dr. Selby —/Father is much iller than he is aware of:/It may be, he will never

ILLNESS (8)

314 FR	Ivy	14	unpleasant, coming home to have an illness./{V} It was always the same with your
314 FR	Warburt	30	health when we find no symptom/Of illness. Health is a relative term./{I} You must
348 FR	Chorus	15	against fire,/Against larceny and illness,/Against defective plumbing,/But not
379 FR	Edward	3	than the greatest doctor/To cure *this* illness./{C} Edward, if I go now,/Will you assure
400 CP	Alex	23	be very penitent. He's enjoying his illness./{R} Illness offers him a double
400 CP	Reilly	24	penitent. He's enjoying his illness./{R} Illness offers him a double advantage:/To
413 CP	Reilly	11	mistaken/About the nature of their illness, and lead them to see/That it's not so
418 CP	Celia	6	cold./Perhaps that's just a part of my illness,/But I feel it would be a kind of surrender

ILLUMINATION (3)

186 FQ: DrySal		94	a very good dinner, but the sudden illumination —/We had the experience but
421 CP	Julia	20	they must undergo/On the way of illumination?/{R} Will she be frightened/By the
581 ES	Ld Clav	23	pretences./I've only just now had the illumination/Of knowing what love is. We all

ILLUSION (4)

256 MC	Tempts	21	/From grandeur to grandeur to final illusion,/Lost in the wonder of his own
364 CP	Reilly	13	enough to clear the mind/The illusion of having ever been in the light./The
414 CP	Celia	2	has been./It isn't simply the end of an illusion/In the ordinary way, or being ditched./
417 CP	Reilly	2	/{R} Disillusion can become itself an illusion/If we rest in it./{C} I cannot argue./It's

ILLUSIONS (4)

224 Mr Mistoff		8	/For performing surprising illusions/And creating eccentric confusions./At
242 MC	Mess	6	/Is not the man to cherish any illusions,/Or yet to diminish the least of his
517 CC	Colby	11	much./You've become a man without illusions/About himself, and without ambitions.
517 CC	Colby	13	/Now that I've abandoned *my* illusions and ambitions/All that's left is love.

ILLUSTRATED (1)

418 CP	Reilly	23	have seen it, as we all have seen it,/Illustrated, more or less, in lives of those about

ILS (6)

48 Lune Miel		1	de Mozambique./Lune de Miel/Ils ont vu les Pays-Bas, ils rentrent à Terre
48 Lune Miel		1	/Lune de Miel/Ils ont vu les Pays-Bas, ils rentrent à Terre Haute;/Mais une nuit d'été,
48 Lune Miel		5	et une forte odeur de chienne./Ils restent sur le dos écartant les genoux/De
48 Lune Miel		11	d'acanthe que tournoie le vent./Ils vont prendre le train de huit heures/
48 Lune Miel		15	aux pourboires, et rédige son bilan./Ils auront vu la Suisse et traversé la France./Et
128 Cor1 March		51	/Light/*Et les soldats faisaient la haie? ILS LA FAISAIENT.*/Difficulties of a

IMAGE (7)

189 FQ: DrySal		197	acids, or dissect/The recurrent image into pre-conscious terrors —/To explore
435 CP	Lavinia	33	did./What you've been living on is an image of Celia/Which you made for yourself, to
437 CP	Reilly	6	*Zoroaster, my dead child,/Met his own image walking in the garden./That apparition*,
437 CP	Reilly	14	Coplestone, in this room,/I saw the image, standing behind her chair,/Of a Celia
513 CC	Colby	34	try to decipher a likeness;/Whose image I could create in my own mind,/To live
513 CC	Colby	35	in my own mind,/To live with that image. An ordinary man/Whose life I could in
562 ES	Carghil	31	so many years ago,/Yet you're the image of what he was then./Your father was a

IMAGES (6)

23 Preludes		27	night revealing/The thousand sordid images/Of which your soul was constituted;/
23 Preludes		49	fancies that are curled/Around these images, and cling:/The notion of some infinitely
61 WL: Burial		22	for you know only/A heap of broken images, where the sun beats,/And the dead tree

84 Hollow Men		41	/This is cactus land/Here the stone images/Are raised, here they receive/The
109 Marina		4	singing through the fog/What images return/O my daughter./Those who
438 CP	Reilly	7	can only be hinted at/In myths and images. To speak about it/We talk of darkness,

IMAGINARY (2)

| 326 FR | Harry | 20 | a slight deviation/From some imaginary course that life ought to take,/That |
| 416 CP | Celia | 31 | into a forest/Playing with an imaginary playmate/And suddenly discovers he |

IMAGINATION (3)

34 Figlia		18	the autumn weather/Compelled my imagination many days,/Many days and many
416 CP	Celia	24	love/Something created by our own imagination?/Are we all in fact unloving and
419 CP	Reilly	5	solitude in the phantasmal world/Of imagination, shuffling memories and desires./

IMAGINE (19)

294 FR	Harry	35	{V} Pushed her?/{H} You would never imagine anyone could sink so quickly./I had
308 FR	Mary	13	have experienced it,/And I can well imagine how awful it must be./But in this world
317 FR	Harry	6	/On a confidential matter./{H} I can imagine —/Though I think it is probably going
326 FR	Charles	8	{C} More than she cares to mention, I imagine. {}/[*Enter* HARRY]/{H} Mother is
334 FR	Harry	18	/{H} You, frightened! I can hardly imagine it./I wish I had known — but that was
361 CP	Reilly	2	have to marry her —/You might even imagine that you wanted to marry her./{E} But I
403 CP	Reilly	9	you feel important,/And you would imagine it a marvellous cure;/And you would go
406 CP	Reilly	14	of hotel. A retreat/For people who imagine that they need a respite/From everyday
413 CP	Celia	17	there's anything to work for;/I don't imagine that I am being persecuted;/I don't hear
420 CP	Julia	36	/What possible alternative can you imagine?/{R} None./{J} Very well then. We must
438 CP	Reilly	10	not take the place of this one./Do you imagine that the Saint in the desert/With
474 CC	Lucasta	27	... a dirty public square./But I can't imagine that happening to you./You seem so
497 CC	Eggers	3	And we've more important business, I imagine./{SC} Eggerson, I'm expecting Mrs.
525 ES	Monica	38	man you are!/Really, you must imagine you're a hypnotist./{C} Is this a time to
535 ES	Gomez	26	/After thirty-five years. Can you imagine/What it would be like to have been
553 ES	Carghil	9	insights into you./No, Richard, don't imagine that I'm still in love with you;/And you
567 ES	Monica	27	a guilty secret in his past!/I just can't imagine it. {}/[CLAVERTON *has entered*
576 ES	Gomez	5	so lovely now/That we can well imagine you at ... what age were you?/{MC} Just
576 ES	Charles	32	confidential, I tell you./{C} So I can imagine:/Highly confidential .../{G} Be careful,

IMAGINED (4)

355 CP	Celia	7	you believe him?/He might have imagined it./{J} My darling Celia,/You needn't
370 CP	Peter	9	peace: I can't express it;/I had never imagined such quiet happiness./I had only
413 CP	Reilly	12	it's not so interesting as they had imagined./When I get as far as that, there is
561 ES	Ld Clav	8	When you reach your goal,/Your imagined paradise of success and grandeur,/You

IMAGINING (1)

| 410 CP | Reilly | 23 | have been a horror beyond your imagining,/For you would have left with |

IMITATE (1)

| 571 ES | Ld Clav | 14 | fact that those who admire us/Will imitate our vices as well as our virtues —/Or |

IMMATERIAL (1)

| 599 On a Port | | 8 | lamia in some wood-retreat,/An immaterial fancy of one's own./No meditations |

IMMEASURABLY (1)

| 19 Portrait | | 54 | life, and Paris in the Spring,/I feel immeasurably at peace, and find the world/To |

IMMEDIATE (2)

| 195 FQ: Little | | 173 | not wholly commendable,/Of no immediate kin or kindness,/But some of |
| 402 CP | Reilly | 38 | .../{R} I always begin from the immediate situation/And then go back as far as |

IMMEDIATELY (3)

261 MC	Thomas	12	the day of the first martyr follows immediately the day of the Birth/of Christ? By
278 MC	Knight2	23	an ascetic/manner of life, he affirmed immediately that there was a higher/order than
399 CP	2m	25	/[ALEX *enters almost immediately*]/{A} When is Chamberlayne's

IMMENSE (1)

| 335 FR | Agatha | 19 | through the stone passages/Of an immense and empty hospital/Pervaded by a |

IMMODERATE (1)

| 296 FR | Ivy | 20 | his condition/Often betray the most immoderate resentment/At such a suggestion. |

IMMODEST (1)

| 245 MC | Priest2 | 2 | at such a juncture!/You are foolish, immodest and babbling women./Do you not |

IMMOLATIONS (1)

| 129 Cor2 | State | 42 | now, together,/If the mactations, immolations, oblations, impetrations,/Are now |

IMMORAL (3)

415 CP	Celia	6	sense?/{C} Well ... I suppose it's being immoral —/And I don't feel as if I was
415 CP	Celia	7	—/And I don't feel as if I was immoral:/In fact, aren't the people one thinks of
415 CP	Celia	8	aren't the people one thinks of as immoral/Just the people who we say have no

IMMORALITY (1)

| 415 CP | Celia | 10 | moral sense?/I've never noticed that immorality/Was accompanied by a sense of sin:/ |

IMMORTALITY (1)
52 Whispers   t   homme, de haute taille./Whispers of Immortality/Webster was much possessed by
IMPACT (2)
202 War Poetry   7   originate a symbol/Out of the impact? This is a meeting/On which we attend/
293 FR   Harry   37   has happened, at most a continual impact/Of external events. You have gone
IMPART (1)
574 ES   Ld Clav   7   news for us./Would you care to impart it?/{MC} It's about dear Michael./{LC}
IMPARTIALITY (1)
242 MC   Priest1   25   /Pride drawing sustenance from impartiality,/Pride drawing sustenance from
IMPATIENT (7)
23 Preludes   47   /The conscience of a blackened street/Impatient to assume the world./I am moved by
603 Spleen   15   Punctilious of tie and suit/(Somewhat impatient of delay)/On the doorstep of the
290 FR   Chorus   36   /{Ch} Why do we feel embarrassed, impatient, fretful, ill at ease,/Assembled like
327 FR   Agatha   3   more: we cannot rest in being/The impatient spectators of malice or stupidity./We
400 CP   Alex   6   case?/{A} Difficulty? No! He was only impatient/At having to wait four days for the
502 CC   Colby   2   I come too soon?/I'm afraid I got impatient of waiting./{L} Colby! I've not come
542 ES   Gomez   39   /Your telephone pal may be getting impatient./I'll see you soon again./{LC} Not
IMPECCABLE (1)
230 Bust Jones   8   such well-cut trousers/Or such an impeccable back./In the whole of St. James's the
IMPEDIMENT (3)
438 CP   Reilly   19   /{R} Let me free your mind from one impediment:/You must try to detach yourself
527 ES   Charles   4   each other,/And, there being no legal impediment/Isn't that enough to constitute an
568 ES   Ld Clav   31   do love my Monica — but there's the impediment:/It's impossible to be quite honest
IMPELLED (2)
194 FQ: Little   128   our concern was speech, and speech impelled us/To purify the dialect of the tribe/
545 ES   Ld Clav   3   suspect, very deep within myself/Has impelled me all my life to find justification/Not
IMPENDING (1)
273 MC   Chorus   8   am bending,/From the final doom impending/Help me, Lord, for death is near. {}/
IMPERATIVE (1)
458 CC   Eggers   29   Elizabeth:/The doctor made it very imperative .../{SC} Mr. Simpkins had very
IMPERATIVES (1)
107 Animula   19   offends and perplexes more/With the imperatives of 'is and seems'/And may and may
IMPERCEPTIVE (1)
312 FR   Harry   2   I tell you. They are here./Are you so imperceptive, have you such dull senses/That
IMPERFECTLY (1)
202 War Poetry   2   the expression of collective emotion/Imperfectly reflected in the daily papers./Where
IMPERIAL (2)
151 Rock 2   17   /Then they could set about imperial expansion/Accompanied by industrial
282 MC   Chorus   2   in forgotten places by the broken imperial column,/From such ground springs
IMPERIOUS (1)
33 Conv Gal   16   twist!/With your air indifferent and imperious/At a stroke our mad poetics to
IMPERTINENCE (1)
518 CC   Eggers   3   —/I hope you won't take this as an impertinence —/I don't see you spending a
IMPERTINENT (1)
471 CC   Colby   30   you don't mind: I know it sounds impertinent./{L} Well, there's one thing you
IMPETRATIONS (1)
129 Cor2 State   42   mactations, immolations, oblations, impetrations,/Are now observed/May we not be
IMPETUOUS (1)
402 CP   Reilly   27   observation?/{R} You are very impetuous, Mr. Chamberlayne./There are
IMPLACABLE (3)
184 FQ: DrySal   7   the dwellers in cities — ever, however, implacable,/Keeping his seasons and rages,
222 Pekes Pols   2   everyone knows,/Are proud and implacable passionate foes;/It is always the
381 CP   Edward   39   —/But in men like me, the dull, the implacable,/The indomitable spirit of
IMPLICATED (1)
301 FR   Chorus   20   of misfortune? why should we be implicated, brought in and brought together?/{I}
IMPLICATES (1)
349 FR   Mary   19   diverted/An attempt to divert it/Only implicates others/At the day of consummation/
IMPLICITLY (1)
400 CP   Alex   11   he trust your judgement?/{A} Yes, implicitly./It's not that he regards me as very
IMPLORING (1)
602 Humoresque   9   dull grimace;/Half bullying, half imploring air,/Mouth twisted to the latest tune;/
IMPORT (1)
560 ES   Michael   13   you in mind?/{Mi} Oh, I don't know. Import and export,/With an opportunity of

IMPORTANCE (6)

195 FQ:	Little	163	And comes to find that action of little importance/Though never indifferent. History
450 CC	Claude	2	that may be something of the greatest importance./It's when you're sure you
459 CC	Lady E	20	husband/Does not understand the importance of colour/For our spiritual life, Mr.
495 CC	Claude	7	what you wanted/Was a husband of importance. I thought you would despise me/If
514 CC	Eggers	30	/But in a matter of such extreme importance/You'll understand the need for
570 ES	Ld Clav	28	peculiar methods,/A man of great importance and the highest standing/In his

IMPORTANT (24)

148 Rock 1		37	in suburb; and in the town/Only for important weddings./CHORUS LEADER:/
277 MC	Knight1	29	has/spoken well and has made a very important point. The gist of his/argument is
304 FR	Agatha	39	It's not what she did to Harry,/That's important, I think, but what he did to himself./
309 FR	Harry	11	me/Just at this moment. I feel it is important./Something should have come of this
314 FR	Amy	6	to be here for dinner/He broke an important engagement to come./{W} I dare say
318 FR	Harry	27	the past? What I'm telling you/Is very important. Very important./You must let me
318 FR	Harry	27	telling you/Is very important. Very important./You must let me explain, and then
326 FR	Harry	18	thing separately,/Making small things important, so that everything/May be
393 CP	Lavinia	4	... thirty-two hours./{L} Yes, a very important discovery,/Finding that you've spent
399 CP	Reilly	3	/You understand, of course, that it is important/To avoid any meeting?/{N} You
403 CP	Reilly	8	Precisely. And I could make you feel important,/And you would imagine it a
403 CP	Reilly	13	/Is due to people who want to feel important./They don't mean to do harm — but
407 CP	Reilly	30	—/Or some of them — omitting the important facts./Let me take your husband first.
425 CP	Lavinia	15	/Suspects that the other one was more important./{E} That's true. You have a very
432 CP	Julia	34	California/Where he's something very important in films./He's making a film of
480 CC	Lucasta	36	could despise you./And what's more important, you don't despise *me*./{K} Nobody
493 CC	Claude	3	doing?/{SC} Settling the places./It's important, when you have a difficult meeting,/
497 CC	Eggers	3	about ourselves!/And we've more important business, I imagine./{SC} Eggerson,
501 CC	Eggers	32	you, Miss Angel./We have this very important interview,/But I'm sure that we want
539 ES	Gomez	36	/As it is, I'm somebody — a more important man/In San Marco than I should
568 ES	Ld Clav	21	that you conceal from *her*/However important you may consider it/To conceal from
572 ES	Ld Clav	39	my freedom,/And perhaps the most important. I know what you think./You think
574 ES	Carghil	19	/He's a wealthy man, and very important/In his own country. And a friend of
576 ES	Michael	29	to London looking for a man/For an important post on his staff —/{C} A post the

IMPORTUNATE (1)

604 Ode		2	Harvard, with thee,/Ere we face the importunate years,/In thy shadow we wait,

IMPORTUNE (1)

601 Nocturne		1	/Nocturne/Romeo, *grand sérieux*, to importune/Guitar and hat in hand, beside the

IMPORTUNITY (1)

107 Animula		28	reality, the offered good,/Denying the importunity of the blood,/Shadow of its own

IMPOSE (4)

407 CP	Reilly	21	/To be consulting me; both, tried to impose upon me/Your own diagnosis, and
462 CC	Claude	24	/{SC} If you haven't the strength to impose your own terms/Upon life, you must
467 CC	Claude	32	to learn/What new conditions life will impose on us./Just when we think we have
542 ES	Ld Clav	13	/Do you call it friendship to impose your company/On a man by threats?

IMPOSED (6)

258 MC	Thomas	20	/Sin grows with doing good. When I imposed the King's law/In England, and waged
306 FR	Mary	33	happy?/{M} Well, it all seemed to be imposed upon us;/Even the nice things were laid
334 FR	Harry	25	years,/Playing a part that had been imposed upon me;/And I returned to find
403 CP	Edward	29	unreality/Of the role she had always imposed upon me/With the obstinate,
466 CC	Colby	33	the conditions/Which life has imposed upon you. But ... something in me/
467 CC	Colby	16	against the terms/That life has imposed./{SC} It's my own fault./I was always

IMPOSES (2)

179 FQ:	ECoker	85	from experience./The knowledge imposes a pattern, and falsifies,/For the pattern
466 CC	Claude	29	I spoke/Of accepting the terms life imposes upon you/Even to the point of

IMPOSING (2)

180 FQ:	ECoker	118	the distant panorama/And the bold imposing façade are all being rolled away —/Or
559 ES	Michael	38	absence./Why should I thank you for imposing this upon me?/And what satisfaction,

IMPOSSIBLE (19)

16 Prufrock		104	/And this, and so much more? —/It is impossible to say just what I mean!/But as if a
163 Rock 8		46	will never assume it./Yet nothing is impossible, nothing,/To men of faith and
190 FQ:	DrySal	220	understood, is Incarnation./Here the impossible union/Of spheres of existence is
248 MC	Thomas	11	goes whistling down the wind./The impossible is still temptation./The impossible,
248 MC	Thomas	12	impossible is still temptation./The impossible, the undesirable,/Voices under sleep,
297 FR	Agatha	7	be left undone/On the margin of the impossible./{A} Very well./I will ring up the
334 FR	Harry	19	/I wish I had known — but that was impossible./I only now begin to have some
337 FR	Agatha	15	/Mean the end of a relation, make it impossible./You did not intend this, I did not

355 CP   Julia   21 /Edward without Lavinia! He's quite impossible!/Leaving it to me to keep things
357 CP   Celia   4   alone in the country,/And almost impossible to get a nurse./{J} Is that her Aunt
363 CP   Edward   21 {E} Wait!/But waiting is the one thing impossible./Besides, don't you see that it makes
396 CP   Lavinia 18 like to be good to you —/Or if that's impossible, at least be horrid to you —/
445 CC   Eggers   8 /On her return from Switzerland./{E} Impossible, Sir Claude!/A very delicate situation
459 CC   Lady E   29 rest now./In a sleeping-car it is quite impossible/To get one's quiet hour. A quiet
461 CC   Claude   37 /That she had seen me before?/{SC} Impossible to tell./The point is that she's taken
488 CC   Lady E   37   /Colby is *my* son./{LE} Quite impossible, Claude!/You have a daughter. Now
514 CC   Claude   35 /For twenty-five years? It's quite impossible./{MG} I had no intention of
567 ES   Monica   25   /The most austere. It's quite impossible./Father with a guilty secret in his
568 ES   Ld Clav 32 — but there's the impediment:/It's impossible to be quite honest with your child/If
IMPOSTURE (1)
512 CC   Guzzard   9 /Between the meaning of *confusion* and *imposture*./{SC} I don't think there is any
IMPOTENCE (2)
194 FQ: Little   137 to fall asunder./Second, the conscious impotence of rage/At human folly, and the
409 CP   Reilly   22   /As, in cruder men, the fear of impotence./{L} You *are* cold-hearted, Edward./
IMPRECISION (2)
175 FQ: BurntN 155 tension, slip, slide, perish,/Decay with imprecision, will not stay in place,/Will not stay
182 FQ: ECoker 183 deteriorating/In the general mess of imprecision of feeling,/Undisciplined squads of
IMPRECISIONS (1)
164 Rock 9   22   out of the sleet and hail of verbal imprecisions,/Approximate thoughts and
IMPRESSED (3)
400 CP   Reilly   17   except his wife./{R} I had already impressed upon her/That she was not to
506 CC   Eggers   30 very common name./{E} That is what impressed her. Mrs. Guzzard/Of Teddington!
530 ES   Ld Clav 32 *in its case*]./{LC} I don't know which impressed me more, the insincerity/Of what was
IMPRESSION (15)
277 MC Knight3   7 say that we didn't make a/very good impression when we came in just now. The fact
318 FR   Harry   16 for granted/At home, make a deeper impression upon children/Than what they are
378 CP   Edward   14 he persuade me?/I have a very clear impression/That he tried to persuade me it was
387 CP   Peter   25   has invited./{P} Why, I got the impression that Lavinia intended/To have
449 CC   Claude   11 I am not unhopeful/That, under the impression that he is an orphan,/She will want
471 CC   Colby   22 were trying very hard to give a false impression./And then you came to see that you
471 CC   Lucasta 24 /{L} Oh, so I was trying to give a false impression?/What sort of impression was I
471 CC   Lucasta 25 give a false impression?/What sort of impression was I trying to give?/{C} That
471 CC   Colby   27 reason,/You thought I'd get a false impression anyway./You preferred it to be one
476 CC   Lucasta 11 /You saw I was trying to give a false impression./I want to tell you now, why I tried
476 CC   Lucasta 14 /I got into the habit of giving that impression./That's where B. has been such a
476 CC   Lucasta 16 such a help to me —/He fosters the impression. He half believes in it./But he knows
479 CC   Kaghan   30 to pursue you./{K} Yes, I made a bad impression at the start:/I saw that it was
479 CC   Kaghan   32 I'm afraid Colby/Has made a good impression; which he'll have to live down./— I
511 CC   Kaghan   34 flashy:/It wouldn't make the right impression in the City./{L} When you're an
IMPRESSIVE (1)
539 ES   Gomez   1 looked the part —/Cut out to be an impressive figurehead./But again, you've retired
IMPRISONED (1)
527 ES   Charles 16 torturing me?/How long will you be imprisoned, alone with your father/In that very
IMPRISONMENT (1)
261 MC Thomas   3 by land/and sea, to know torture, imprisonment, disappointment, to suffer/death
IMPUDENT (1)
 38 Gerontion   46 Virtues/Are forced upon us by our impudent crimes./These tears are shaken from
IMPULSES (1)
568 ES   Ld Clav   8 /Reckless surrenders, unexplainable impulses,/Moments we regret in the very next
IMPURE (1)
158 Rock 5   1 the man of excellent intention and impure heart: for the heart is deceitful above all
IMPUTATION (1)
491 CC   Colby   35   /The other indignant at the imputation/Of false parenthood. Both mocked
IN (2154)
IN-FOLDED (1)
198 FQ: Little   259 well/When the tongues of flame are in-folded/Into the crowned knot of fire/And the
INACCESSIBLE (3)
143 Lines OM   11 bitter than the love of youth,/And inaccessible by the young./Reflected from my
294 FR   Harry   2   smell untraceable in the drains,/Inaccessible to the plumbers, that has its hour
309 FR   Harry   33 /Or the distant waterfall in the forest,/Inaccessible, half-heard./And I hear your voice
INACTION (2)
188 FQ: DrySal 157 the moment which is not of action or inaction/You can receive this: "on whatever
530 ES   Ld Clav 18   no desire to act, yet a loathing of inaction./A fear of the vacuum, and no desire to

INADEQUATE (2)
530 ES Ld Clav   36   /That bought this piece of silver! The inadequate levy/That made the Chairman's
583 ES Charles   5   beyond./It's strange that words are so inadequate./Yet, like the asthmatic struggling
INANE (1)
 33 Conv Gal   12   refer to me?'/'Oh no, it is I who am inane.'/'You, madam, are the eternal humorist,/
INAPPROPRIATE (1)
324 FR Amy   28   I think your remarks are much more inappropriate/Than Harry's./{H} It's only when
INARTICULATE (1)
182 FQ: ECoker 181   /Is a new beginning, a raid on the inarticulate/With shabby equipment always
INATTENTION (1)
311 FR Harry   16   I forget them/Only for an instant of inattention/They are roused again, the sleepless
INBORN (1)
148 Rock 1   45   God-shaken, in whom is the truth inborn./*Enter the* ROCK, *led by a* BOY:/THE
INBREATHED (1)
192 FQ: Little   60   the place where a story ended./Dust inbreathed was a house —/The wall, the
INCALCULABLE (1)
363 CP Reilly   36   /And that's an experience of incalculable value./{E} Stop! I agree that much
INCANDESCENT (1)
196 FQ: Little   203   breaks the air/With flame of incandescent terror/Of which the tongues
INCANTATION (3)
164 Rock 9   24   order of speech, and the beauty of incantation./LORD, shall we not bring these
196 FQ: Little   185 to ring the bell backward/Nor is it an incantation/To summon the spectre of a Rose./
205 de la Mare   27   was this designed?/The whispered incantation which allows/Free passage to the
INCANTATIONS (1)
 24 Rhapsody   4 in a lunar synthesis,/Whispering lunar incantations/Dissolve the floors of memory/And
INCAPABLE (6)
309 FR Mary   8 of the torment./{M} If you think I am incapable of understanding you —/But in any
403 CP Edward 35 live without her, for she has made me incapable/Of having any existence of my own./
409 CP Reilly   18   made you suspect that you were incapable/Of loving. To men of a certain type/
409 CP Reilly   20   type/The suspicion that they are incapable of loving/Is as disturbing to their
410 CP Reilly   8   isolation./A man who finds himself incapable of loving/And a woman who finds
419 CP Reilly   8   in./{R} It isn't hell/Till you become incapable of anything else./Now — do you feel
INCARNATE (1)
152 Rock 2   43   for the Church, the Body of Christ incarnate./And now you live dispersed on
INCARNATION (2)
190 FQ: DrySal 219   guessed, the gift half understood, is Incarnation./Here the impossible union/Of
483 CC Lady E 36 known each other/In some previous incarnation. — Is this your mother?/{C} No,
INCENSE (3)
594 Grad 9   2   /For in the sanctuaries of the soul/Incense of altar-smoke shall rise to thee/From
270 MC Chorus   9 /I have smelt/Corruption in the dish, incense in the latrine, the sewer in the incense,
270 MC Chorus   9 incense in the latrine, the sewer in the incense, the smell of sweet soap in the
INCH (2)
292 FR Gerald 29   as well as ever./There wasn't an inch of it you didn't know./But you'll have to
453 CC Eggers   2   say/That if you give Miss Angel an inch/She'll take an ell./{L} L. for Lucasta./Go
INCIDENTS (1)
202 War Poetry 12 or too small. Our emotions/Are only 'incidents'/In the effort to keep day and night
INCLINATION (1)
290 FR Agatha 33 wind's talk in the dry holly-tree/The inclination of the moon/The attraction of the
INCLINE (1)
406 CP Edward 22 merely a lunatic practical joker?/{E} I incline to the second explanation/Without the
INCLINED (1)
234 Ad-dress   27   usual Dog about the Town/Is much inclined to play the clown,/And far from
INCLUDE (1)
576 ES Ld Clav   9 says he has told you his story./Did he include the fact that he served a term in prison?/
INCLUDES (1)
568 ES Ld Clav 25   to confess everything —/And that includes, mind you, not only things criminal,/
INCLUDING (4)
152 Rock 2   21   enlightenment/And everything, including capital/And several versions of the
234 Ad-dress   24 call a simple soul./Of course I'm not including Pekes,/And such fantastic canine
307 FR Mary   21 a child I took everything for granted,/Including the stupidity of older people —/They
519 CC Kaghan 17 like to understand *you* .../I mean, I'm including both of you,/Claude ... and Aunt
INCOME (3)
334 FR Agatha 10   /Instead of earning my spiritual income daily:/And I am old, to start again to
477 CC Lucasta   1   I knew how she supplemented her income/When I was sent out. I've been locked
518 CC Eggers   1 think of other ways/Of making up an income. Piano lessons? —/As a temporary

INCOME-TAX (1)
407 CP   Edward   2   often./I'd like to see *you* filling up an income-tax form./{L} Don't be silly, Edward.
INCOMPARABLE (1)
286 FR   Gerald   7   again/To be back in the East. An incomparable climate/For a man who can
INCOMPARABLY (1)
 34 Figlia   14   it has used./I should find/Some way incomparably light and deft,/Some way we both
INCOMPATIBLE (1)
278 MC Knight2 26   knows/why — the two orders were incompatible./You will agree with me that such
INCOMPETENCE (1)
504 CC   Claude   25   afraid there has been some domestic incompetence./You should have been
INCOMPLETE (1)
588 Fable   38   shorter,/He left no wise precaution incomplete;/He doused the room in which they
INCONCLUSIBLE (1)
 92 Ash-Wed 2   42   to no end/Conclusion of all that/Is inconclusible/Speech without word and/Word
INCONSOLABLE (1)
416 CP   Celia   37   of the forest/I shall be left with the inconsolable memory/Of the treasure I went
INCONTESTABLE (1)
225 Mr Mistoff   49   that somebody purred)/Which is incontestable proof/Of his singular magical
INCONVENIENT (5)
151 Rock 2   15 the place of GOD,/And settled all the inconvenient saints,/Apostles, martyrs, in a kind
361 CP   Reilly   5   reaction./It's embarrassing, and inconvenient./It was inconvenient, having to lie
361 CP   Reilly   6   and inconvenient./It was inconvenient, having to lie about it/Because you
393 CP   Edward   38   friends —/You suddenly found it inconvenient/That I should be always too busy
447 CC   Claude   13   /{SC} And well deserved; but rather inconvenient/When it comes to appointing a
INCREASE (1)
594 Grad 12   2   /Thy honor and thy fame shall but increase/Forever, and may stronger words than
INCREASING (1)
343 FR   Amy   25   weather,/Resist the wind? fight with increasing taxes/And unpaid rents and tithes?
INCREDIBLE (4)
336 FR   Agatha   25   /As a child is formed./In both, the incredible/Becomes the actual/Without our
487 CC   Lady E   24   possibly be a coincidence./It seems incredible, doesn't it, Claude?/And yet it would
487 CC   Lady E   25   /And yet it would be still more incredible/If it were only a coincidence./Perhaps
514 CC   Claude   17   /{SC} Mrs. Guzzard, this is perfectly incredible!/You couldn't have carried out such a
INCREDULITY (1)
241 MC   Mess   29 {M} You are right to express a certain incredulity./He comes in pride and sorrow,
INCREMENTS (1)
129 Cor2 State   13   pound ten a week rising by annual increments of five shillings/To two pounds ten a
INCRIMINATE (1)
311 FR   Harry   35   at, not me your confidential looks/Incriminate, but that other person, if person/
INCUBATION (1)
314 FR   Harry   20   you call restoration to health/Is only incubation of another malady./{W} You mustn't
INCURABLE (4)
314 FR Warburt 36   a murderer,/Who suffered from an incurable cancer./How he fought against it! I
339 FR   Harry   12   people,/The lesson of ignorance, of incurable diseases./Such things are possible. It is
546 ES   Piggott   20   we never accept any guest who's incurable./You know, we've been deluged with
546 ES   Piggott   24   do we accept/Any guest who *looks* incurable —/We make that stipulation to all the
INCURABLY (1)
218 Mung Rump   4   centre of operation, for they were incurably given to rove./They were very well
INDECISION (1)
402 CP   Reilly   5 might have ruined three lives/By your indecision. Now there are only two —/Which
INDECISIONS (1)
 14 Prufrock   32   for me,/And time yet for a hundred indecisions,/And for a hundred visions and
INDEED (41)
 13 Prufrock   23   about the house, and fell asleep./And indeed there will be time/For the yellow smoke
 14 Prufrock   37   and go/Talking of Michelangelo./And indeed there will be time/To wonder, 'Do I
 16 Prufrock   118   sentence, but a bit obtuse;/At times, indeed, almost ridiculous —/Almost, at times,
 18 Portrait   22   so much of odds and ends,/(For indeed I do not love it ... you knew? you are not
116 SP   Dusty   27   a chill/Oh I *think* it's only a chill/Yes indeed I hope so too —/Well I *hope* we shan't
241 MC   Mess   39   and with the King of France,/Who indeed would have liked to detain him in his
298 FRDowning   27   I hope?/{Do} Thank you, very well indeed, Sir./{C} I'm sorry to send for you so
307 FR   Mary   28   troubles?/They must seem very trivial indeed to you./It's just ordinary hopelessness./
308 FR   Harry   31   think, that can be altered!/And here, indeed! where I have felt them near me,/Here
314 FR Warburt 33   Doctor,/In forty years./{W} Indeed, yes./Even in a country practice. My first
322 FR   Winch   15   to produce her for you?/{Wi} Oh no indeed, my Lord, I'd much rather not .../{H}
333 FR   Agatha   35   flying through the purgatorial flame./Indeed it is possible. You may learn hereafter,/

339 FR	Harry	1	/It is hard for you too, mother, it is indeed harder,/Not to understand./{A} Where
397 CP	Lavinia	38	will find me a different person?/{L} Indeed. And has the difference nothing to do/
402 CP	Reilly	36	very common malady./Very prevalent indeed./{E} I remember, in my childhood .../{R}
403 CP	Edward	27	Before I felt, and still more acutely —/Indeed, acutely, perhaps, for the first time,/The
405 CP	Reilly	1	the patient himself can always tell me./Indeed, it is often the case that my patients/Are
409 CP	Reilly	7	you/How much you have in common. Indeed, I consider/That you are exceptionally
414 CP	Celia	1	/That there's been a crash: though indeed there has been./It isn't simply the end of
428 CP	Alex	25	/When you cooked them?/{A} Oh yes, indeed./I invented for the natives several new
428 CP	Edward	32	I hope I'm not boring you?/{E} No indeed: we are anxious to learn the solution./{A}
432 CP	Alex	30	I should. Mr. MacColgie Gibbs./{A} Indeed, yes, we have met./{R} On several
448 CC	Claude	20	eventual intention./{SC} When — or indeed whether — I reveal his identity/Depends
449 CC	Eggers	13	us to adopt him./{E} Adopt him! Yes, indeed,/That would be the solution. Yes, quite
454 CC	Eggers	29	/As Claude? To his face?/{E} She does indeed./{C} And does she call Lady Elizabeth
455 CC	Eggers	18	her an allowance — very adequate indeed,/Though she's always in debt. But you
456 CC	Eggers	13	besides being a lady?/{E} Why, yes, indeed, I must admit she is./Most of her
462 CC	Colby	35	I'm very grateful to you, for that:/It is indeed a new and strange situation,/And
465 CC	Colby	31	/{C} Indeed, I have felt, while you've been talking,/
477 CC	Lucasta	36	It's to do with myself./{L} Yourself, indeed! Your precious self!/Why don't you shut
486 CC	Colby	25	boy/Who died when I was very young indeed./I don't remember him. I was told about
491 CC	Claude	16	with such an understanding;/And indeed, it's not so far from what I had intended.
497 CC	Eggers	5	I'm expecting Mrs. Guzzard./{E} Indeed! Mrs. Guzzard! And why are we
497 CC	Eggers	9	Guzzard, of Teddington./{E} Ah, indeed!/I shouldn't have expected her name to
506 CC	Guzzard	29	struck her as being familiar./{MG} Indeed? It is not a very common name./{E} That
518 CC	Colby	20	you were settled./{C} I'd be very glad indeed — if Mrs. Eggerson approved./{E}
540 ES	Ld Clav	13	of the coinage/I pay myself in./{LC} Indeed! How interesting!/I still don't know why
547 ES	Piggott	34	this neighbourhood./{MP} There are indeed. I can lend you a map./There are lovely
555 ES	Ld Clav	16	not very good news for you./{LC} Oh, indeed. What's the matter?/{M} I didn't get far./
575 ES	Ld Clav	35	them our intimacy too?/{LC} I have indeed./{MC} The romance of my life./Your
581 ES	Charles	4	not estranged from you./{C} We will indeed. We shall be ready to welcome him/And

INDEFINABLE (1)

370 CP	Peter	29	some perception,/Some feeling, some indefinable experience/In which we were both

INDEPENDENCE (1)

361 CP	Reilly	36	That you are beginning to enjoy your independence;/Finding your life becoming

INDESCRIBABLE (1)

311 FR	Harry	5	of smell, but like a smell/In that it is indescribable, a sweet and bitter smell/From

INDIAN (3)

229 Gus		40	— could do it again —/Which an Indian Colonel pursued down a drain./And he
285 FR	Violet	22	tea —/The strong cold stewed bad Indian tea./{C} That's not Amy's style at all. We
536 ES	Gomez	17	in Spanish, but their thoughts are Indian thoughts./O God, Dick, *you* don't know

INDIANS (2)

203 Indians		t	/May be affirmed in verse./To the Indians who Died in Africa/A man's destination
307 FR	Harry	3	stockade/From which we fought the Indians, Arthur and John./{M} It was the cave

INDICATES (1)

545 ES	Ld Clav	18	When people talk like that/It indicates a latent desire to interfere/With the

INDIFFERENCE (3)

68 WL: Fire S		242	response,/And makes a welcome of indifference./(And I Tiresias have foresuffered
195 FQ: Little		155	persons; and, growing between them, indifference/Which resembles the others as
259 MC Thomas		3	wrong, oppression and the axe's edge,/Indifference, exploitation, you, and you,/And

INDIFFERENT (6)

33 Conv Gal		16	the slightest twist!/With your air indifferent and imperious/At a stroke our mad
127 Cor1 March		31	the eyes watchful, waiting, perceiving, indifferent./O hidden under the dove's wing,
195 FQ: Little		164	of little importance/Though never indifferent. History may be servitude,/History
279 MC Knight4		23	he showed/himself to be utterly indifferent to the fate of the country, to be, in/
490 CC	Colby	16	I can't begin to feel yet. I'm simply indifferent./And all the time that you've been
570 ES	Ld Clav	15	that lay behind her/And completely indifferent to whatever lay ahead of her./{M} It

INDIGESTIBLE (2)

91 Ash-Wed 2		15	guts the strings of my eyes and the indigestible portions/Which the leopards reject.
375 CP	Edward	16	/Whether it mightn't be rather indigestible? .../Oh, no, Alex, don't bring me

INDIGNANT (2)

491 CC	Colby	33	have to live with those ghosts, one indignant/At being cheated of his — or her —
491 CC	Colby	35	— or her — parenthood,/The other indignant at the imputation/Of false

INDIGNATION (1)

267 MC Knight1		8	/{K1} That was only/Our indignation, as loyal subjects./{T} Loyal? to

INDIGNITY (1)

269 MC Knight1		6	King's majesty,/You insult with gross indignity;/Insolent madman, whom nothing

INDISTINCT (1)
57 Swee Night   33   a golden grin;/The host with someone indistinct/Converses at the door apart,/The
INDIVIDUAL (2)
202 War Poetry   3   is the point at which the merely individual/Explosion breaks/In the path of an
202 War Poetry   10   /Of Nature and the Spirit. Mostly the individual/Experience is too large, or too small.
INDOMITABLE (2)
320 FR Warburt   9   only the force of her personality,/Her indomitable will, that keeps her alive./I needn't
381 CP Edward   40   like me, the dull, the implacable,/The indomitable spirit of mediocrity./The willing self
INDOORS (1)
567 ES Monica   29   direction, Father!/I thought you were indoors. Where have you been?/{LC} Not far
INDUCE (1)
517 CC Colby   34   our organ!/{C} Well, if you could induce them to try me .../{E} The Parochial
INDULGE (1)
295 FR Charles   7   alone./{A} Harry!/{C} You mustn't indulge such dangerous fancies./It's only doing
INDUSTRIAL (3)
147 Rock 1   31   stay at home and read the papers./In industrial districts, there I was told/Of economic
151 Rock 2   18   imperial expansion/Accompanied by industrial development./Exporting iron, coal
180 FQ: ECoker 107   chairmen of many committees,/Industrial lords and petty contractors, all go
INEFFABLE (2)
187 FQ: DrySal 102   /Something that is probably quite ineffable:/The backward look behind the
209 NamingCats 29   of the thought of his name:/His ineffable effable/Effanineffable/Deep and
INEVITABLE (1)
189 FQ: DrySal 194   /By sortilege, or tea leaves, riddle the inevitable/With playing cards, fiddle with
INEXHAUSTIBLE (1)
530 ES Monica   7   From your own restless energy — the inexhaustible/Sources of the power that wears
INEXPLICABLE (3)
69 WL: Fire S   265   the walls/Of Magnus Martyr hold/Inexplicable splendour of Ionian white and
205 de la Mare   33   invisible web you wove —/The inexplicable mystery of sound./A Dedication to
342 FR Agatha   17   and waited. In this world/It is inexplicable, the resolution is in another./{M}
INFANT (1)
105 Song Sime   22   this birth season of decease,/Let the Infant, the still unspeaking and unspoken
INFATUATION (2)
309 FR Mary   24   to loathing/As others do to loving: an infatuation/That's wrong, a good that's
552 ES Ld Clav   20   My conscience was clear./A brief infatuation, ended in the only way possible/To
INFER (1)
450 CC Eggers   19   care to think, perhaps./{E} And do I infer/That you're not sure you understand Mr.
INFERENCE (2)
279 MC Knight4 29   conduct, step by step, there can be no inference/except that he had determined upon a
534 ES Gomez   10   That's true enough,/Except for a false inference. I wouldn't dream/Of carrying on such
INFERIOR (2)
464 CC Claude   8   or for decoration —/In either case, an inferior art./For me, they are neither 'use' nor
466 CC Colby   4   music,/What they hear is an inferior rendering./So I've given up trying to
INFINITE (1)
407 CP Reilly   19   as you are the self-deceivers/Taking infinite pains, exhausting their energy,/Yet
INFINITELY (2)
23 Preludes   50   and cling:/The notion of some infinitely gentle/Infinitely suffering thing./Wipe
23 Preludes   51   /The notion of some infinitely gentle/Infinitely suffering thing./Wipe your hand
INFIRM (1)
89 Ash-Wed 1   10   I do not hope to know again/The infirm glory of the positive hour/Because I do
INFLAMED (1)
279 MC Knight4 36   he/insisted, while we were still inflamed with wrath, that the doors/should be
INFLEXIBLE (1)
329 FR Chorus   21   Argos or England/There are certain inflexible laws/Unalterable, in the nature of
INFLEXIONS (1)
49 Hippopot   18   mating time the hippo's voice/Betrays inflexions hoarse and odd,/But every week we
INFLICTED (1)
282 MC Chorus   8   surrender required, the deprivation inflicted;/Who fear the injustice of men less than
INFLUENCE (11)
313 FR Charles   21   all be together, Harry;/They need the influence of their elder brother./Arthur's a bit
330 FR Harry   8   than himself. He can resist the influence/Of Wishwood, being unconscious,
341 FR Amy   29   is best for Harry?/What gave you this influence to persuade him/To abandon his duty,
342 FR Amy   10   any unscrupulous woman./*I* have no influence over him; *you* can try,/But you will
422 CP Julia   17   over the roof,/May the moon herself influence the bed. {}/[*They drink*]/{A} The words
449 CC Eggers   20   .../But I'm afraid you overrate my influence./I have never been able to make her
455 CC Colby   6   been certain I'd lost my reason:/Her influence is perfectly frightening./But tell me

517 CC   Eggers   36   be only too pleased,/And I have some influence. *I* am the Vicar's Warden./{C} I'd like
537 ES   Gomez   13   /And then what I became under your influence./{LC} You cannot attribute your ...
537 ES   Ld Clav   14   attribute your ... misfortune to *my* influence./{G} I was just about as different as
538 ES   Gomez   13   money/And your wife's family influence, you got on in politics./Shall we say

INFLUENCED (1)
489 CC   Claude   11   /That seems grotesque now. But it influenced me./And I found a better reason for

INFORM (2)
192 FQ: Little 46   here to verify,/Instruct yourself, or inform curiosity/Or carry report. You are here
241 MC   Mess   12   watchers of the temple,/I am here to inform you, without circumlocution:/The

INFORMATION (6)
103 Journ Magi   29   empty wine-skins./But there was no information, so we continued/And arrived at
147 Rock 1   16   is the knowledge we have lost in information?/The cycles of Heaven in twenty
287 FR   Mary   7   Really, Cousin Gerald, if you want information/About the younger generation, you
355 CP   Alex   14   he still there?/Julia is really a mine of information./{C} There isn't much that Julia
408 CP   Reilly   28   /I have my own method of collecting information/About my patients. You must not
408 CP   Reilly   37   that you confided to me./The information I have exchanged between you/Was

INFORMED (4)
400 CP   Alex   13   intelligent,/But he thinks I'm well informed: the sort of person/Who would know
507 CC Guzzard   24   met with his accident./{MG} I was informed that the father had died/Without
539 ES   Ld Clav   29   dark hints have been given,/He's informed himself so carefully about my career./
543 ES   Gomez   3   /I am going away./{G} So I've been informed./I have friends in the press — if not in

INFREQUENT (1)
 62 WL: Burial   64   undone so many./Sighs, short and infrequent, were exhaled,/And each man fixed

INFREQUENTLY (1)
505 CC   Eggers   38   acknowledge./That happens not infrequently, Mrs. Guzzard./{MG} So I am

INFURIATING (3)
394 CP   Edward   2   /{E} No; and it was perfectly infuriating,/The way you *didn't* complain .../{L}
395 CP   Edward   31   to take people in./{E} One of the most infuriating things about you/Has always been
395 CP   Lavinia   34   understood myself./{L} And the most infuriating thing about you/Has always been

INGENIOUS (1)
333 FR   Agatha   1   one abandoned/For something more ingenious. You were due in three months' time;/

INGENUITIES (1)
154 Rock 3   4   men,/Betrayed in the mazes of your ingenuities,/Sold by the proceeds of your proper

INGURGITATION (1)
270 MC   Chorus   5   of the sea-anemone, swallowed with ingurgitation of the sponge. I have lain in the

INHABIT (2)
171 FQ: BurntN 20   /I do not know./Other echoes/Inhabit the garden. Shall we follow?/Quick, said
437 CP   Reilly   10   *Is underneath the grave, where do inhabit/The shadows of all forms that think and*

INHABITANT (3)
220 Old Deut   11   sun on the vicarage wall,/The Oldest Inhabitant croaks: 'Well, of all .../Things ... Can
220 Old Deut   26   in domestic economy:/And the Oldest Inhabitant croaks: 'Well, of all .../Things ... Can
221 Old Deut   42   whatever befall:/And the Oldest Inhabitant croaks: 'Well, of all .../Things ... Can

INHABITANTS (1)
315 FR   Amy   26   present —/In fact we are the oldest inhabitants./As we came first, we will go first, in

INHABITED (2)
587 Fable   8   /Nearby this hamlet was a monastery/Inhabited by a band of friars merry./They were
431 CP   Peter   22   England!/At least, of any that are still inhabited./We've got a team of experts over/To

INHALED (1)
 32 Hysteria   3   I was drawn in by short gasps, inhaled at each momentary/recovery, lost finally

INHERENT (1)
510 CC   Eggers   9   — is my son?/{E} It creates an inherent probability —/If that's the right

INHERIT (2)
196 FQ: Little 194   folded in a single party./Whatever we inherit from the fortunate/We have taken from
280 MC   Priest1   10   Shall we recover your presence? when inherit/Your strength? The Church lies bereft,/

INHERITANCE (6)
 92 Ash-Wed 2 54   This is the land. We have our inheritance./At the first turning of the second
152 Rock 2   30   was done that was good, you have the inheritance./For good and ill deeds belong to a
162 Rock 8   4   past./The heathen are come into thine inheritance,/And thy temple have they defiled./
517 CC   Colby   2   you, as a model;/You knew your inheritance. Now I know mine./{SC} I shall
559 ES   Ld Clav   25   /To throw away the whole of your inheritance?/{Mi} What is my inheritance? As
559 ES   Michael   26   of your inheritance?/{Mi} What is my inheritance? As for your title,/I know why you

INHERITED (1)
562 ES   Carghil   35   It's marvellous./And the charm! He's inherited all of your charm, Richard./There's no

INHUMAN (1)
382 CP   Celia   15   an insect,/Dry, endless, meaningless, inhuman —/You might have made it by

INIQUITY (1)
166 Rock 10   9   hour to devour./But the Mystery of Iniquity is a pit too deep for mortal eyes to
INJURED (1)
409 CP   Reilly   14   least sacrifice/On her account. This injured your vanity./You liked to think of
INJUSTICE (3)
243 MC Chorus   28   and licence,/There has been minor injustice./Yet we have gone on living,/Living
282 MC Chorus   9   deprivation inflicted;/Who fear the injustice of men less than the justice of God;/
452 CC Lucasta 15   /{L} You're wrong, Eggy. It's rank injustice./Two months I'd gone on filing those
INLAND (1)
263 MC Chorus   2 South?/Only the sea-bird cries, driven inland by the storm./What sign of the spring of
INN (2)
376 CP   Edward   23   was luckier than I:/He was left at an inn./{J} Edward, how ungrateful./What's in that
556 ES   Michael 21   /Good cooking, for a country inn. And not at all expensive./{LC} You don't
INNER (4)
173 FQ: BurntN   72   for that is to place it in time./The inner freedom from the practical desire,/The
173 FQ: BurntN   73 action and suffering, release from the inner/And the outer compulsion, yet
335 FR   Harry   24 To and fro, dragging my feet/Among inner shadows in the smoky wilderness,/Trying
472 CC   Lucasta 40 that you've lost:/You've still got your inner world — a world that's more real./That's
INNOCENCE (1)
421 CP   Julia   23 Henry, you simply do not understand innocence./She will be afraid of nothing; she
INNOCENT (2)
315 FR   Harry   5   murderer/Regards himself as an innocent victim./To himself he is still what he
534 ES   Gomez   5 I've never come across an official/Innocent enough to be corruptible./{LC} It
INNOCENTLY (1)
407 CP   Reilly   17   cheat,/Or with the insuperably, innocently dull:/My patients such as you are the
INNOCENTS (3)
264 MC   m 14 PRIEST, *with a banner of the Holy Innocents borne before him.*]/{P3} Since St. John
264 MC   Priest3 14   a day: and the day of the Holy Innocents./*Out of the mouth of very babes*, O
264 MC   Priest1 22   *behind them*]/{P1} Since the Holy Innocents a day: the fourth day from
INNUMERABLE (1)
158 Rock 5   8   nor the others./And they write innumerable books; being too vain and
INOCULATIONS (1)
344 FR   Gerald   28 don't forget/That you'll need various inoculations —/That depends on where you're
INOPERANCY (1)
174 FQ: BurntN 124   /Evacuation of the world of fancy,/Inoperancy of the world of spirit;/This is the
INQUEST (1)
326 FR   Harry   13 holding a meeting — the usual family inquest/On the characters of all the junior
INQUISITION (1)
 38 Gerontion   56   /To lose beauty in terror, terror in inquisition./I have lost my passion: why should
INQUISITIVE (2)
359 CP   Julia   28   /And not Alexander's — *he's* so inquisitive!/But *I* never poke into other people's
390 CP   Julia   29   is the mystery?/{J} Alex, *don't* be inquisitive./Lavinia has had a lapse of memory,/
INSANE (1)
334 FR   Harry   38 shadows. O that awful privacy/Of the insane mind! Now I can live in public./Liberty is
INSANITY (1)
339 FR   Harry   6 /Where does one go from a world of insanity?/Somewhere on the other side of
INSCRIBED (1)
129 Cor2 State   36 (not among these busts, all correctly inscribed)/I a tired head among these heads/
INSCRUTABLE (1)
209 NamingCats 31   effable/Effanineffable/Deep and inscrutable singular Name./The Old Gumbie
INSECT (1)
382 CP   Celia   14 What I heard was only the noise of an insect,/Dry, endless, meaningless, inhuman —/
INSECURE (2)
242 MC   Priest1 23   /Never one among them, always insecure;/His pride always feeding upon his own
472 CC   Lucasta 16   inside the likeness./You may *feel* insecure, in some ways —/But your insecurity is
INSECURITY (1)
472 CC   Lucasta 17 insecure, in some ways —/But your insecurity is nothing like mine./{C} In what way
INSENSIBLE (1)
502 CC   Lucasta 21   either above caring,/Or else you're insensible — I don't mean insensitive!/But
INSENSITIVE (2)
270 MC Chorus   7 the scale of the viper, the mobile hard insensitive skin of the elephant, the evasive
502 CC   Lucasta 21 else you're insensible — I don't mean insensitive!/But you're terribly cold. Or else
INSET (1)
531 ES   Ld Clav 15   a column and a half/With an inset, a portrait taken twenty years ago./In five

INSIDE (11)

19 Portrait		32	/And the ariettes/Of cracked cornets/Inside my brain a dull tom-tom begins/Absurdly
308 FR	Mary	28	/What you need to alter is something inside you/Which you can change anywhere —
308 FR	Harry	30	as well as elsewhere./{H} Something inside me, you think, that can be altered!/And
308 FR	Harry	35	whispering just out of earshot —/And inside too, in the nightly panic/Of dreaming
327 FR	Harry	12	perhaps. Were they simply inside/I could cheat them perhaps with the aid
330 FR	Harry	29	not fit myself together:/When I was inside the old dream, I felt all the same emotion/
346 FR	Downing	27	people like him, there's something inside them/That accounts for what happens to
382 CP	Celia	20	the size of a man/With nothing more inside it than what comes out/When you tread
472 CC	Lucasta	15	you begin/To discover differences inside the likeness./You may *feel* insecure, in
537 ES	Gomez	32	went too far. There's a prudent devil/Inside you, Dick. He never came to *my* help./
545 ES	Ld Clav	5	first of all to myself./What is this self inside us, this silent observer,/Severe and

INSIDIOUS (1)

13 Prufrock		9	follow like a tedious argument/Of insidious intent/To lead you to an

INSIGHT (2)

438 CP	Reilly	5	last two years./{R} That shows some insight on your part, Mrs. Chamberlayne;/But
481 CC	Colby	2	to believe you've a pretty shrewd insight/Into things that have nothing to do with

INSIGHTS (1)

553 ES	Carghil	8	I think,/To have given me one or two insights into you./No, Richard, don't imagine

INSIGNIFICANCE (1)

403 CP	Edward	7	obsessed by the thought of my own insignificance./{R} Precisely. And I could make

INSIGNIFICANT (1)

394 CP	Edward	29	why did you always make me feel insignificant?/I may not have known what life I

INSINCERITY (1)

530 ES	Ld Clav	32	know which impressed me more, the insincerity/Of what was said about me, or of my

INSINUATION (1)

575 ES	Gomez	22	/But, Dick, I was nettled by that insinuation/About my not being custodian of

INSIST (2)

302 FR	Chorus	10	/Hold tight, hold tight, we must insist that the world is what we have always
558 ES	Michael	3	debt./Just because of your name they insist on giving credit./{LC} And your debts: are

INSISTED (4)

279 MC	Knight4	36	what he did not wish to happen; he/insisted, while we were still inflamed with wrath,
305 FR	Mary	31	if so, I can't find it./{M} Your mother insisted/On everything being kept the same as
375 CP	Edward	30	his way in, a little while ago,/And insisted on cooking me something for supper;/
493 CC	Claude	27	boy!/{SC} After all, it was he who insisted/On this ... investigation. But perhaps

INSISTENCE (1)

539 ES	Ld Clav	4	must have read that I retired at the insistence of my doctors./{G} Oh yes, the usual

INSISTENT (4)

19 Portrait		56	after all.'/The voice returns like the insistent out-of-tune/Of a broken violin on an
23 Preludes		41	behind a city block,/Or trampled by insistent feet/At four and five and six o'clock;/
531 ES	Lambert	33	a gentleman downstairs/Is very insistent that he must see you./I told him you
564 ES	Monica	38	explain that the doctors were very insistent/That my father should rest and have

INSISTS (4)

177 FQ: ECoker		18	while a van passes,/And the deep lane insists on the direction/Into the village, in the
357 CP	Edward	11	rather difficult./When she's ill, she insists on having Lavinia./{J} I never heard of
461 CC	Claude	26	after two months —/And as my wife insists upon your being Mr. Colby —/I shall
497 CC	Claude	30	is not satisfied with that solution./He insists upon the facts. And that is why/I have

INSOLENCE (1)

266 MC	Knight2	33	envy and spleen./{K2} Saving your insolence and greed./Won't you ask us to pray

INSOLENT (1)

269 MC	Knight1	7	/You insult with gross indignity;/Insolent madman, whom nothing deters/From

INSOMNIA (1)

348 FR	Chorus	21	and chiromancy,/Specifics against insomnia,/Lumbago, and the loss of money./

INSPECT (1)

479 CC	Kaghan	13	be fed. All in good time./I've come to inspect the new bachelor quarters,/And to wish

INSPECTION (1)

427 CP	Alex	30	of us have been out on a tour of inspection/Of local conditions./{J} What about?

INSPECTS (1)

376 CP		m	1	[EDWARD *goes over to the table and inspects his game of Patience. He moves/a card.*

INSPIRATION (8)

376 CP	Julia	10	for? {}/[*Enter* JULIA]/{J} I've had an inspiration! {}/[*Enter* CELIA *with saucepan*]/{C}
376 CP	Julia	17	/{J} Celia! I see you've had the same inspiration/That I had. Edward must be fed./
377 CP	Julia	19	*tray and three glasses*]/{J} I've had an inspiration!/There's nothing in the place fit to
494 CC	Claude	19	something else to *him* —/An idea, an inspiration. What he wanted to transmit to me/
494 CC	Claude	20	to transmit to me/Was that idea, that inspiration,/Which to him was life. To me, it

494 CC Claude 22 a burden./You can't communicate an inspiration,/Like that, by force of will. He was a
494 CC Claude 25 I might have been truer to my father's inspiration/If I had done what I wanted to do./
579 ES Carghil 14 had it all planned out! It really was an inspiration —/On my part, I mean. Are you

INSPIRE (3)
495 CC Lady E 17   What did *you* want?/{LE} To inspire an artist. Don't laugh./{SC} I'm not
495 CC Claude 19 laughing./So what you wanted was to inspire an artist!/{LE} Or to inspire a poet. I
495 CC Lady E 20   was to inspire an artist!/{LE} Or to inspire a poet. I thought Tony was a poet./

INSPIRED (4)
560 ES Ld Clav 33   I shouldn't like to think/That what inspired you was no positive ambition/But only
572 ES Charles 28   they know it? That's why they are inspired/With revenge — it's their means of
576 ES Charles 27 Michael, you think Señor Gomez is inspired by benevolence —/{Mi} I told you he'd
578 ES Monica 38 /But a question of the spirit which inspired your decision:/If you wish to renounce

INSTANCE (3)
278 MC Knight2 20   moment/that Becket, at the King's instance, had been made Archbishop, he/
412 CP Reilly 31 you need to know./I was there at the instance of Mrs. Shuttlethwaite./{C} That makes
557 ES Michael 36 ordinary debts:/My tailor's bill, for instance./{LC} I expected that./It was just the

INSTANT (2)
276 MC Chorus 13 is out of life, this is out of time,/An instant eternity of evil and wrong./We are soiled
311 FR Harry 16 alone: when I forget them/Only for an instant of inattention/They are roused again,

INSTANT (1) [*Foreign word*]
51 Restaurant 14   pour la faire rire./J'éprouvais un instant de puissance et de délire.'/Mais alors,

INSTEAD (12)
52 Whispers 5   with a lipless grin./Daffodil bulbs instead of balls/Stared from the sockets of the
334 FR Agatha 10 living all these years upon my capital,/Instead of earning my spiritual income daily:/
366 CP Julia 11   Edward,/I'll come straight to you, instead of to St. Anthony./And now I must fly.
395 CP Edward 39 perhaps — we can fight each other,/Instead of each taking his corner of the cage./
425 CP Edward 12 to have arranged to have two parties/Instead of one./{L} That's never satisfactory./
425 CP Lavinia 20   they will be going to the Gunnings instead'./{E} I know, that's what we said at the
429 CP Alex 8 —/To relapse into heathendom. So, instead of eating monkeys/They are eating
462 CC Claude 17 to believe/That you really are her son, instead of being mine./She has always lived in a
486 CC Claude 34 were here with Colby./So I came over instead of telephoning,/Just to give him these
494 CC Lady E 3 somehow, might prove to be *your* son/Instead of mine. Really, I do!/It would be so
524 ES Monica 11   taken me to some other restaurant/Instead of to one where the *maître d'hôtel*/And
554 ES Piggott 30 brought your morning tipple myself/Instead of leaving it, as usual, to Nurse)/When I

INSTINCT (4)
308 FR Harry 20 here I know I shall not find it./The instinct to return to the point of departure/And
392 CP Lavinia 23 woman is the devil./She knows by instinct when something's going to happen./
448 CC Claude 31 /Is, that she has a strong maternal instinct .../{E} I realise that./{SC} Which has
490 CC Lady E 8 didn't./{LE} Oh, Colby, doesn't your instinct tell you?/{SC} Yes, tell us everything

INSTINCTIVE (1)
333 FR Agatha 31 may strain and struggle/In its dark instinctive birth, to come to consciousness/And

INSTINCTS (1)
278 MC Knight2 28   by an Archbishop/offends the instincts of a people like ours. So far, I know

INSTITUTED (1)
506 CC Eggers 12 in a position/In which she could have instituted enquiries./So, for many years, she has

INSTITUTIONS (1)
155 Rock 3 47 homes,/Though you have shelters and institutions,/Precarious lodgings while the rent

INSTRUCT (4)
44 Cook Egg 22   in Heaven:/Madame Blavatsky will instruct me/In the Seven Sacred Trances;/
192 FQ: Little 46   notion. You are not here to verify,/Instruct yourself, or inform curiosity/Or carry
242 MC Priest2 34 are to do, he will give us our orders, instruct us./Our Lord is at one with the Pope,
483 CC Lady E 24 silver frame./I'm afraid I shall have to instruct you, Colby./Photographic portraits —

INSTRUCTIONS (2)
201 Def Island 22 up/our positions, in obedience to instructions./A Note on War Poetry/Not the
399 CP Reilly 2 /I should like to run over my instructions again./You understand, of course,

INSTRUMENT (4)
201 Def Island 2 of built stone — music's/enduring instrument, of many centuries of/patient
258 MC Thomas 15 /Love in the garden, singing to the instrument,/Were all things equally desirable./
261 MC Thomas 30 true martyr is he who has become the/instrument of God, who has lost his will in the
487 CC Colby 13 piano. I've never played/On such an instrument. It's much too good for me./{SC}

INSTRUMENTAL (1)
278 MC Knight2 40 who took the first/step. We have been instrumental in bringing about the state of/

INSTRUMENTS (1)
487 CC Lady E 30 Claude, and Eggerson have been the instruments./I must be right. Claude, tell me I

INSULATED (1)
536 ES   Gomez   28   /You're not isolated — merely insulated./It's only when you come to see that

INSULT (3)
269 MC Knight1   6   justice, the King's majesty,/You insult with gross indignity;/Insolent madman,
269 MC Thomas   9   and ministers./{T} It is not I who insult the King,/And there is higher than I or
407 CP   Reilly   27   /{R} You have come where the word 'insult' has no meaning;/And you must put up

INSULTED (2)
365 CP   Julia   14 that dreadful man?/I've never been so insulted in my life./It's very lucky that I left my
407 CP   Lavinia   26   to me./{L} I did not come here to be insulted./{R} You have come where the word

INSUPERABLY (1)
407 CP   Reilly   17   with the common cheat,/Or with the insuperably, innocently dull:/My patients such

INSURED (1)
348 FR   Chorus   14   can usually avoid accidents,/We are insured against fire,/Against larceny and illness,

INSURGENT (1)
42 Swee Erect   6   me Aeolus above/Reviewing the insurgent gales/Which tangle Ariadne's hair/

INSURRECTION (1)
434 CP   Alex   11   /{E} And then?/{A} And then, the insurrection broke out/Among the heathen, of

INTANGIBLE (1)
204 de la Mare   16   twilight, gently go at dawn,/The sad intangible who grieve and yearn;/When the

INTELLECTUAL (8)
151 Rock 2   20   iron, coal and cotton goods/And intellectual enlightenment/And everything,
164 Rock 9   28 life, for dignity, grace and order,/And intellectual pleasures of the senses?/The LORD
370 CP   Peter   3   of them/And about their lack of intellectual interests./{E} And what happened
394 CP   Lavinia   10   to give you the chance/Of talking to intellectual people .../{E} You would have given
482 CC   Lady E   34   breeding is./And, second, you need intellectual society./Now, that already limits
482 CC   Lady E   37   people/Are sometimes far from intellectual;/And — what's less surprising —
482 CC   Lady E   38   /And — what's less surprising — intellectual people/Are often ill-bred. But that's
483 CC   Lady E   2   ill-bred. But that's not all./You need intellectual, well-bred people/Of spirituality —

INTELLIGENT (7)
65 WL: Chess   130   Rag —/It's so elegant/So intelligent/'What shall I do now? What shall I
249 MC Tempt2   35 Hungry hatred/Will not strive against intelligent self-interest./{T} You forget the
251 MC Tempt3   31   lead?/{T3} To a happy coalition/Of intelligent interests./{T} But what have you —/If
400 CP   Alex   12   /It's not that he regards me as very intelligent,/But he thinks I'm well informed: the
482 CC   Colby   22 what is it you object to?/They're both intelligent ... and kind./{LE} Oh, I don't say
482 CC   Lady E   23 kind./{LE} Oh, I don't say they're not intelligent and kind./I'm not making any
495 CC   Claude   14   for granted./{SC} That was a very intelligent remark./Perhaps I have taken too

INTEND (5)
298 FR   Violet   14 /I think there should be witnesses. I intend to remain./And I wish to be present to
337 FR   Agatha   16   make it impossible./You did not intend this, I did not intend it,/No one intended,
337 FR   Agatha   16 /You did not intend this, I did not intend it,/No one intended, but ... You must go.
465 CC   Claude   27   in dying to give something life .../I intend that you shall have a good piano. The
576 ES   Ld Clav   23   than in England./{LC} Perhaps you intend to change your name to Gomez?/{G} Oh

INTENDED (10)
278 MC Knight2   12 reform the legal system./He therefore intended that Becket, who had proved himself
287 FR   Amy   18   have been, if things had gone as I intended./Harry's return does not make things
319 FR   Harry   26 the conversations not overheard,/Not intended to be heard, with the sidewise looks,/
336 FR   Agatha   28   our intention/Knowing what is intended./A curse is like a child, formed/In a
337 FR   Agatha   17   this, I did not intend it,/No one intended, but ... You must go./{H} Shall we ever
337 FR   Amy   36 happen./{A} You only say what you intended to happen./{H} Oh, mother,/This is not
387 CP   Peter   25   I got the impression that Lavinia intended/To have yesterday's cocktail party
457 CC note 16&   25   *Elizabeth's words off stage are not intended to be heard distinctly by an audience in*
461 CC   Claude   31   meeting didn't go quite the way I'd intended;/And yet I believe that it's all for the
491 CC   Claude   16 indeed, it's not so far from what I had intended./Could you accept us both in that way,

INTENDS (1)
453 CC   Eggers   40   on Mr. Simpkins:/Sir Claude intends to deal with these matters himself./You

INTENSE (3)
182 FQ: ECoker 194   /Of dead and living. Not the intense moment/Isolated, with no before and
191 FQ: Little   9   the early afternoon./And glow more intense than blaze of branch, or brazier,/Stirs
553 ES   Carghil   7   was brief,/Our relations were intense enough, I think,/To have given me one

INTENSELY (1)
395 CP   Lavinia   22   the last holidays./You were always intensely concerned with yourself;/And if other

INTENSITY (3)
183 FQ: ECoker 207   be still and still moving/Into another intensity/For a further union, a deeper
202 War Poetry   23   /Of private experience at its greatest intensity/Becoming universal, which we call
417 CP   Celia   10   a dream/In which one is exalted by intensity of loving/In the spirit, a vibration of

INTENT (3)
13 Prufrock	9	like a tedious argument/Of insidious intent/To lead you to an overwhelming
188 FQ: DrySal	159	of being/The mind of a man may be intent/At the time of death" — that is the one
256 MC Tempts	18	/This man is obstinate, blind, intent/On self-destruction,/Passing from

INTENTION (5)
158 Rock 5	1	deliver me from the man of excellent intention and impure heart: for the heart is
336 FR Agatha	27	/Becomes the actual/Without our intention/Knowing what is intended./A curse is
438 CP Reilly	28	all our words and deeds, beyond the intention/And beyond our limited
448 CC Eggers	19	/You told me that was your eventual intention./{SC} When — or indeed whether — I
514 CC Guzzard	36	It's quite impossible./{MG} I had no intention of deceiving you, Sir Claude,/Till you

INTERCEDE (1)
| 273 MC Chorus | 3 | Who shall then plead for me,/Who intercede for me, in my most need?/Dead upon |

INTERCEPTED (1)
| 246 MC Thomas | 3 | London, Salisbury,/Would have intercepted our letters,/Filled the coast with |

INTERCESSION (1)
| 350 FR Agatha | 21 | straight/And the curse be ended/By intercession/By pilgrimage/By those who depart |

INTEREST (17)
367 CP Edward	19	interests both of us./{E} A common interest in the moving pictures/Frequently
370 CP Edward	25	/{E} Do you think she has simply lost interest in you?/{P} You put it just wrong. I
370 CP Peter	27	I think of it differently./It is not her interest in *me* that I miss —/But those moments
370 CP Peter	31	/In your terms, perhaps, she's lost interest in me./{E} That is all very normal. If
381 CP Celia	2	/You are not entitled to take any interest/Now, in *my* future. I only hope you're
402 CP Edward	10	came here as a patient./If you take no interest in my case, I can go elsewhere./{R} You
403 CP Reilly	14	to do harm — but the harm does not interest them./Or they do not see it, or they
446 CC Claude	6	I think he's beginning to take a keen interest./{E} And getting over his
446 CC Eggers	31	boxes!/He's expressed such an interest in my garden/That I think he ought to
448 CC Eggers	9	gain his confidence./I did mention her interest in Light from the East./{SC} And the
499 CC Lucasta	31	/I dare say. That was why I took an interest/In Colby. Because you thought he was
512 CC Guzzard	13	it./{MG} That is as much to my interest as anyone's./But will your wife be
538 ES Ld Clav	32	career./{LC} I am touched by your interest./{G} I have a gift for friendship./I
540 ES Ld Clav	35	If you think that this story would interest the public/Why not sell your version to
557 ES Michael	30	at all to pay for two years:/The interest was just added on to the capital./{LC}
570 ES Ld Clav	14	she lay dying:/Completely without interest in the life that lay behind her/And
573 ES Carghil	34	get a girl like Monica./I take a great interest in her future./Fancy! I've only known

INTERESTED (13)
124 SA Snow	11	story./I assure you, Sir, we are very interested./{S} I knew a man once did a girl in./
298 FR Charles	3	that comes to hand./If you are interested in helping Harry/You can hardly
367 CP Peter	22	you're only being sarcastic:/Celia was interested in the art of the film./{E} As a
367 CP Edward	27	seen her poetry —/Interesting if one is interested in Celia./Apart, of course, from its
431 CP Peter	20	Exactly. It is. And that's why we're interested./The most decayed noble mansion in
436 CP Peter	12	in my head —/That I've only been interested in myself:/And that isn't good enough
467 CC Colby	28	my confidential clerk./{C} I'm really interested by the work I'm doing/And eager for
484 CC Colby	5	was a child./I suppose I've never been interested ... in relatives./{LE} You did not want
486 CC Colby	27	can't help wondering why you are so interested:/There's nothing very interesting
495 CC Claude	5	I didn't think/That you would be interested. More than that./I took it for granted
495 CC Lady E	9	took it for granted that you were not interested/In anything but financial affairs;/And
510 CC Kaghan	25	I believe they did. But why are you interested?/{MG} Lady Elizabeth, I believe that
536 ES Gomez	11	/Didn't want to learn English, wasn't interested/In anything that happened four

INTERESTING (19)
367 CP Edward	27	/{E} Yes, I've seen her poetry —/Interesting if one is interested in Celia./Apart,
370 CP Edward	13	.../{E} And what interrupted this interesting affair? {}/[*Enter* ALEX *in shirtsleeves*
375 CP Edward	15	anything like it .../Yes, that's very interesting. But I just wondered/Whether it
380 CP Celia	27	more acquaintances,/I found him less interesting, and rather conceited./But why
395 CP Edward	14	must get to know./{E} This is very interesting:/But you seem to assume that you've
403 CP Reilly	6	the temporary stimulus of feeling interesting./{E} But I am obsessed by the
407 CP Reilly	5	really matter./{R} May I interrupt this interesting discussion?/I say you are both too ill.
408 CP Edward	9	/{E} Really, Lavinia! This is very interesting./You seem to have been much more
413 CP Reilly	12	and lead them to see/That it's not so interesting as they had imagined./When I get as
413 CP Celia	14	I can't pretend that my trouble is interesting;/But I shan't begin that way. I feel
432 CP Julia	32	/{J} We've been having such an interesting conversation./Peter's just over from
486 CC Colby	28	so interested:/There's nothing very interesting about my background —/I assure
486 CC Lady E	30	you there isn't./{LE} It may be more interesting/Than you are aware of. Colby ... {}/
510 CC Eggers	34	wish to obtain confirmation/Of this interesting discovery, Mr. Kaghan,/By putting
539 ES Ld Clav	23	{}/[*Pours himself whisky*]/{LC} An interesting historical epitome./Though I cannot
540 ES Ld Clav	13	/I pay myself in./{LC} Indeed! How interesting!/I still don't know why you've come

559 ES   Michael   1 happened/If only I'd been given some interesting work!/{LC} And what do you now
560 ES   Michael   10   to go abroad/As a partner in some interesting business./But I might be expected to
563 ES   Carghil   2 It's a man I used to know./{MC} How interesting! He's a very good figure/And he's

INTERESTS (7)

251 MC   Tempt3   31   To a happy coalition/Of intelligent interests./{T} But what have you —/If you do
279 MC   Knight2   1   you approve. We have served your interests; we merit/your applause; and if there is
367 CP   Peter   18 reviews./But it's more the cinema that interests both of us./{E} A common interest in
370 CP   Peter   3 /And about their lack of intellectual interests./{E} And what happened after that?/{P}
371 CP   Peter   19 memory./Did we really share these interests? Did we really feel the same/When we
463 CC   Colby   13 I can do/So remote from my previous interests./It gives me, in a way, a kind of
496 CC   Claude   2   you always made me feel that *your* interests/Were much too deep for discussion

INTERFERE (2)

545 ES   Ld Clav   18 like that/It indicates a latent desire to interfere/With the privacy of others, which is
578 ES   Michael   33   fond of each other,/That needn't interfere with your life or mine./{M} Oh

INTERFERENCE (1)

278 MC   Knight2   27 /You will agree with me that such interference by an Archbishop/offends the

INTERFERING (3)

290 FR   Agatha   24 Thus with precise attention/To detail, interfering preparation/Of that which is already
391 CP   Lavinia   22 it./But who? Somebody is always interfering .../I don't feel free ... and yet I
479 CC   Kaghan   24 on preventing Lizzie/From always interfering. Be firm with her, Colby;/Assert your

INTERIM (1)

429 CP   Alex   22   /{A} We have just drawn up an interim report./{E} Will it be made public?/{A}

INTERLUDE (1)

260 MC   1m 1   hover over the swords' points. {}/Interlude/THE ARCHBISHOP/*preaches in the*

INTERMINABLE (1)

193 FQ: Little   81   the morning/Near the ending of interminable night/At the recurrent end of the

INTERNAL (1)

174 FQ: BurntN   120   world, but that which is not world,/Internal darkness, deprivation/And destitution

INTERNATIONAL (2)

329 FR   Chorus   27 listen to the weather report/And the international catastrophes. {}/[*Exeunt*
429 CP   Alex   25 be, at present:/There are too many international complications./Eventually, there

INTERPOSE (1)

267 MC   m 25   *and attendants return and quietly interpose themselves.*]/{T} Now and here!/{K1}

INTERPRETED (1)

494 CC   Claude   17 /And I came to see that what I had interpreted/In this way, was something else to

INTERPRETER (1)

234 Ad-dress   3   now is that/You should need no interpreter/To understand their character./You

INTERROGATION (1)

127 Cor1 March   29 /There he is now, look:/There is no interrogation in his eyes/Or in the hands, quiet

INTERRUPT (7)

407 CP   Reilly   5   things that really matter./{R} May I interrupt this interesting discussion?/I say you
432 CP   Lavinia   13   are interrupting me./{L} If you can interrupt Julia, Sir Henry,/You are the perfect
432 CP   Reilly   15   /{R} I should not dream of trying to interrupt Julia .../{J} But you're both
432 CP   Julia   18   now?/{J} Well, you shouldn't interrupt my interruptions:/That's really worse
502 CC   Lucasta   3 waiting./{L} Colby! I've not come to interrupt your meeting./I've been told what it's
503 CC   Eggers   19 *need* anybody./{E} And now may I interrupt, Miss Angel?/Why shouldn't you and
505 CC   Claude   23 /{LE} Or of maternity./{SC} Don't interrupt, Elizabeth./{MG} I don't understand

INTERRUPTED (2)

370 CP   Edward   13 such ... tranquillity .../{E} And what interrupted this interesting affair? {}/[*Enter*
527 ES   Monica   28 occupied with anything that can't be interrupted./Someone to make a remark to now

INTERRUPTING (5)

387 CP   Peter   20 you heard from Lavinia too?/Or am I interrupting?/{C} I've just explained to Edward
432 CP   Julia   12   /{J} My dear Henry, you are interrupting me./{L} If you can interrupt Julia,
432 CP   Julia   16   interrupt Julia .../{J} But you're both interrupting!/{R} Who is interrupting now?/{J}
432 CP   Reilly   17   you're both interrupting!/{R} Who is interrupting now?/{J} Well, you shouldn't
432 CP   Julia   19   /That's really worse than interrupting./Now my head's fairly spinning. I

INTERRUPTION (1)

541 ES   Gomez 35   /{G} Ah, the pre-arranged interruption/To terminate the unwelcome

INTERRUPTIONS (1)

432 CP   Julia   18 /{J} Well, you shouldn't interrupt my interruptions:/That's really worse than

INTERSECT (1)

204 de la Mare   19   to learn,/And two worlds meet, and intersect, and change;/When cats are maddened

186 FQ: DrySal	70	the end of them, the fishermen sailing/Into the wind's tail, where the fog cowers?/We
188 FQ: DrySal	137	platform)/Their faces relax from grief into relief,/To the sleepy rhythm of a hundred
188 FQ: DrySal	140	travellers! not escaping from the past/Into different lives, or into any future;/You are
188 FQ: DrySal	140	from the past/Into different lives, or into any future;/You are not the same people
189 FQ: DrySal	197	acids, or dissect/The recurrent image into pre-conscious terrors —/To explore the
198 FQ: Little	260	the tongues of flame are in-folded/Into the crowned knot of fire/And the fire and
210 Old Gumbie	26	she likes to wind, and tie it into sailor-knots./She sits upon the window-sill,
222 Pekes Pols	16	but most people think/He'd slipped into the Wellington Arms for a drink —/And no
224 Mr Mistoff	29	with dice;/He is always deceiving you into believing/That he's only hunting for mice./
233 Skimble	45	go wrong./And when you creep into your cosy berth/And pull up the
593 Grad 4	6	might know!/Would we might look into the future years./Great duties call — the
594 Grad 11	3	/Out of thy care and tutelage we pass/Into the unknown world — class after class,/O
601 Nocturne	8	servant wait,/Stab, and the lady sinks into a swoon./Blood looks effective on the
239 MC Chorus	9	/Since golden October declined into sombre November/And the apples were
243 MC Chorus	20	but you come bringing death into Canterbury:/A doom on the house, a doom
244 MC Chorus	28	it means/To the small folk drawn into the pattern of fate, the small folk who live
254 MC Tempt4	35	broken, and its stores/Swept into the laps of parasites and whores./When
272 MC Priests	2	from the divine office. To vespers./Into the Cathedral!/{T} Go to vespers,
272 MC Chorus	21	the human, they shrink and dissolve/Into dust on the wind, forgotten, unmemorable;
272 MC Chorus	29	mind/To distraction, delusion, escape into dream, pretence,/Where the soul is no
273 MC Thomas	18	of Christ,/The sanctuary, turned into a fortress./The Church shall protect her
282 MC Chorus	10	thatch, the fist in the tavern, the push into the canal,/Less than we fear the love of
287 FR Gerald	14	she upset?/I only meant to draw her into the conversation./{C} She's a nice girl; but
289 FR Ivy	31	things are much better not enquired into./She may have done it in a fit of temper./
290 FR Agatha	27	/Men tighten the knot of confusion/Into perfect misunderstanding,/Reflecting a
301 FR Violet	12	/Except for having brought Downing into it:/Of which I disapprove./{C} Of which
309 FR Harry	6	are much too clever/To admit you into our world. Yours is no better./They have
310 FR Mary	28	rise toward the violent sun/Wet wings into the rain cloud/Harefoot over the moon?/
311 FR Harry	8	dissolving/All other worlds, and me into it. O Mary!/Don't look at me like that!
319 FR Harry	27	the sidewise looks,/That bring death into the heart of a child./*That* was the day he
320 FR Warburt	10	will, that keeps her alive./I needn't go into technicalities/At the present moment. The
322 FR Winch	33	/At a pretty smart pace, I fancy, ran into a lorry/Drawn up round the bend. We'll
325 FR Gerald	20	/He's much more apt than John to get into trouble./{C} Oh, but Arthur's a brilliant
325 FR Charles	23	at Brooklands,/*He*'s not likely to get into trouble./{G} A brilliant driver, but more
328 FR Charles	13	of Lord/Monchensey, who ran into and demolished a roundsman's/cart in
328 FR Charles	18	from the collision, Mr. Piper reversed/into a shop-window. When challenged, Mr.
329 FR Chorus	4	voices of the past, and projects them into the future./The treble voices on the lawn/
331 FR Harry	8	as I had left it,/Everything would fall into place. But *they* prevent it./I still have to
336 FR Harry	6	hands, from the pursuers,/And come into a quiet place./Why is it so quiet?/Do you
336 FR 2m	23	*the empty embrasure. She steps into/the place which the* EUMENIDES *had*
337 FR m	8	made straight. {}/[*She moves back into the room*]/{Ag} What have I been saying? I
355 CP Julia	17	we'll wait until Edward comes back into the room./Now I want to relax, Are there
357 CP Edward	14	That's why when she's ill/She gets into a panic./{J} And sends for Lavinia./I quite
357 CP Edward	17	/{E} No, I think she put it all into an annuity./{J} So it's very unselfish of
357 CP Julia	34	of Essex./{J} Well, we won't probe into it./You have the address, and the telephone
359 CP Julia	29	he's so inquisitive!/But *I* never poke into other people's business./Well, good-bye
369 CP Peter	32	find her there alone./Anyway, we got into conversation/And I found that she went to
370 CP Peter	20	to know./She has simply faded — into some other picture —/Like a film effect.
371 CP m	23	*rings*]/{E} Excuse me a moment. {}/[*Into telephone*]/{E} Hello! ... I can't talk now .../
383 CP Celia	9	you look for them./I shall never go into your kitchen again. {}/[*Exit* EDWARD. *He*
396 CP Lavinia	39	I see clearly:/We are not to relapse into the kind of life we led/Until yesterday
399 CP Nurse	7	at eleven o'clock./He is to be shown into the small waiting-room;/And you will see
399 CP Nurse	10	second?/{N} The second one to be shown into the other room/Just as usual. She arrives at
399 CP Nurse	19	/{N} The third one to be shown into the small room;/And I need not let you
401 CP Edward	4	Now, Mr. Chamberlayne?/{E} It came into my mind/Before I entered the door, that
403 CP Edward	24	because of what she had made me into./We had not been alone again for fifteen
404 CP Edward	2	same world. So I want you to put me/Into your sanatorium. I could be alone there? {}/
404 CP 2m	3	there? {}/[*House-telephone rings*]/[*into telephone*]/{R} Yes. {}/[*To* EDWARD]/{R}
407 CP Reilly	23	cure./But when you put yourselves into hands like mine/You surrender a great deal
409 CP Reilly	29	awareness/That you had forced him into this position) —/When, I say, you
416 CP Celia	30	/{C} Like a child who has wandered into a forest/Playing with an imaginary
416 CP Celia	38	memory/Of the treasure I went into the forest to find/And never found, and
420 CP 3m	19	REILLY *dials on/house-telephone.*]/[*into telephone*]./{R} It is finished. You can come
421 CP Julia	6	proper costumes/Or huddle quickly into new disguises,/They have, for the first time,
422 CP m	4	JULIA]/{R} He's on his way up. {}/[*Into telephone*]/{R} You may bring the tray in

429 CP	Alex	8	not to be slaughtered —/To relapse into heathendom. So, instead of eating monkeys
431 CP	Peter	2	pictures?/Pan-Am-Eagle must look into this./Perhaps it would be a good place to
433 CP	Peter	14	ask about,/Who did really want to get into films,/And I always thought she could
439 CP	Reilly	7	with these memories and make them/Into something new. Only by acceptance/Of the
446 CC	Claude	20	own devices:/I thought he would fall into this way of life more quickly/If we started
461 CC	Colby	12	I have you always at my back/If I get into trouble. But I hope/That I shan't have to
464 CC	Claude	12	things,/If it is an escape, is escape into living,/Escape from a sordid world to a
464 CC	Colby	23	been speaking, I've been translating/Into terms of music. But may I ask,/With this
465 CC	Claude	30	you will go through the private door/Into the real world, as I do, sometimes./{C}
466 CC	Claude	16	/Just as my wife's investigations/Into what she calls the life of the spirit/Are a
472 CC	Lucasta	31	/And made up your mind to go into business/And be someone like Claude ... or
476 CC	Lucasta	14	succeeded with people before:/I got into the habit of giving that impression./That's
477 CC	Colby	15	just yet./Oh, why did I ever come into this house!/Lucasta ...{L} I can see well
481 CC	Colby	3	believe you've a pretty shrewd insight/Into things that have nothing to do with
492 CC	Colby	23	your notes —/Before you brought me into the conversation —/And I found one note I
500 CC	Lucasta	30	his own world,/And he might vanish into it at any moment —/At just the moment
532 ES	Monica	11	I ought to be going./{M} Let *us* go into the library. And then I'll see you off./{LC}
534 ES	Gomez	27	allow either of my sons/To go into politics. In my country, Dick,/Politicians
537 ES	Gomez	17	been at school with —/I didn't fit into your set, and I knew it./When you started
538 ES	Gomez	23	same mistake./At the worst, you go into opposition/And let the other people make
538 ES	Gomez	38	from the world of politics/And went into the City. Director of a bank/And chairman
545 ES	Ld Clav	9	us still more severely/For the errors into which his own reproaches drove us?/{M}
552 ES	Carghil	8	*Me*?/I couldn't have put the feeling into it I did/But for what I'd gone through. Did
553 ES	Carghil	8	/To have given me one or two insights into you./No, Richard, don't imagine that I'm
555 ES	Monica	27	your nerves have been./He only ran into a tree./{LC} Yes, a tree./It might have been
556 ES	Michael	35	/It's natural he should end by getting into trouble./{LC} You started pretty early
557 ES	Ld Clav	1	/{LC} You started pretty early getting into trouble,/When you were expelled from your
558 ES	Michael	2	them./It's being your son that gets me into debt./Just because of your name they insist
569 ES	Ld Clav	2	pretence,/Walk off the stage, change into our own clothes/And speak as ourselves. So
569 ES	Ld Clav	39	emerging/From my spectral existence into something like reality./{M} But what did
576 ES	Michael	19	be? Do you know?/{Mi} We didn't go into details. There's time for that later./{G}
578 ES	Michael	28	a book away from you/And tossed it into the fire. How I laughed!/You never seemed

INTOLERABLE (3)

179 FQ:	ECoker	71	fashion,/Leaving one still with the intolerable wrestle/With words and meanings.
196 FQ:	Little	212	/Behind the hands that wove/The intolerable shirt of flame/Which human power
403 CP	Edward	34	/I cannot live with her — that is now intolerable;/I cannot live without her, for she

INTRACTABLE (2)

184 FQ:	DrySal	2	brown god — sullen, untamed and intractable,/Patient to some degree, at first
256 MC	Priests	24	O Thomas my Lord do not fight the intractable tide,/Do not sail the irresistible

INTRIGUE (2)

240 MC	Priest2	30	and the French King/In ceaseless intrigue, combinations,/In conference, meetings
250 MC	Tempt3	25	trifler, and no politician./To idle or intrigue at court/I have no skill. I am no

INTRODUCE (15)

276 MC	Knight1	28	that/reason I shall do no more than introduce the other speakers, who,/with their
369 CP	Edward	40	/{E} And after that/Did she ever introduce you to her family/Or to any of her
405 CP	Reilly	8	unusual procedure:/I propose to introduce you to the other patient./{E} What do
432 CP	Lavinia	25	/{R} Nothing, thank you./{L} May I introduce Mr. Peter Quilpe?/Sir Henry
433 CP	Peter	19	to Bela about her,/And I want to introduce her to our casting director./I've got an
450 CC	Claude	25	Elizabeth/I'll be ready waiting to introduce him. {}/[*Enter* COLBY SIMPKINS
452 CC	Lucasta	24	this, Eggy? Is it Colby Simpkins?/Introduce him, one or the other of you./{E} Mr.
504 CC	Claude	30	much engaged./{SC} First, let me introduce you to my wife./Lady Elizabeth
554 ES	Piggott	18	understanding./{MP} But I ought to introduce you. You've been talking to Lord
562 ES	Carghil	22	/As you were once. You're not to introduce us,/I'll introduce myself. I'm Maisie
562 ES	Carghil	23	once. You're not to introduce us,/I'll introduce myself. I'm Maisie Montjoy!/That
563 ES	Carghil	6	coming to speak to us. You must introduce him. {}/[*Enter* GOMEZ]/{G} Good
563 ES	Carghil	17	/Richard, I think that you might introduce us./{LC} Oh. This is ...{G} Your old
563 ES	Ld Clav	22	/That's my name./{LC} So let me introduce you — by that name —/To Mrs. ...
573 ES	Carghil	27	to-day;/This must be your fiancé. Do introduce him./{M} Mr. Charles Hemington.

INTRODUCED (1)

431 CP	Peter	5	about Pan-Am-Eagle:/It was he who introduced me to the great Bela./{J} And who is

INTRODUCES (2)

236 Cat	Morgan	t	AD-DRESS A CAT./Cat Morgan Introduces Himself/I once was a Pirate what
532 ES	Ld Clav	17	what I remember of the man who introduces him/I expect he wants money. Or to

INTRODUCTION (3)
432 CP   Reilly   10   Julia,/You are giving me a very bad introduction —/Supposing that an introduction
432 CP   Reilly   11   introduction —/Supposing that an introduction was necessary./{J} My dear Henry,
532 ES   Ld Clav 15   Gomez/But he comes with a letter of introduction/From a man I used to know. I
INTROIT (2)
264 MC   m   6   charge./*Princes moreover did sit.* {}/[*Introit of St. Stephen is heard*]/[*Enter the*
264 MC   m   13   /*In the midst of the congregation.* {}/[*Introit of St. John is heard*]/[*Enter the* THIRD
INTRUSION (1)
541 ES   Gomez   36   /To terminate the unwelcome intrusion/Of the visitor in financial distress./
INTUITION (2)
437 CP   Reilly   19   the suggestion/That a sudden intuition, in certain minds,/May tend to express
487 CC   Lady E 18   discovery!/All through a name — and intuition./But it shall be proved. The truth has
INTUITIONS (1)
478 CC   Kaghan 38   find she'd got in first!/Trust Kaghan's intuitions! I'm your guardian angel,/Colby, to
INVARIABLY (1)
327 FR   Violet   7   more./{V} Agatha's remarks are invariably pointed./{H} Do you think that I
INVENT (6)
293 FR   Harry   18   /A person that you have conspired to invent, please do so/In my absence. I shall be
306 FR   Mary   36   /There was never any time to invent our own enjoyments./But perhaps it was
396 CP   Edward 35   me to myself./You're still trying to invent a personality for me/Which will only
486 CC   Colby   20   not the kind of story my aunt would invent./{LE} Not if she *is* your aunt. Did Mrs.
489 CC   Claude 31   the story..../{SC} Why should she invent it? The child was expected./{LE} In order
576 ES   Ld Clav 13   my predicament./{LC} And made him invent/The position which he'd come to find the
INVENTED (4)
160 Rock 7   9   the light and were known of the light/Invented the Higher Religions; and the Higher
392 CP   Edward 26   /And what did you tell them?/{E} I invented an aunt/Who was ill in the country,
428 CP   Alex   26   cooked them?/{A} Oh yes, indeed./I invented for the natives several new recipes./But
489 CC   Lady E 30   had a child?/Perhaps Mrs. Guzzard invented the story..../{SC} Why should she
INVENTING (1)
514 CC   Claude 26   believe it./Mrs. Guzzard, you are inventing this fiction/In response to what Colby
INVENTION (2)
147 Rock 1   7   cycle of idea and action,/Endless invention, endless experiment,/Brings
374 CP   Celia 19   was obvious that the aunt was a pure invention/On the spur of the moment, and not a
INVENTIONS (3)
154 Rock 3   5   /Sold by the proceeds of your proper inventions:/I have given you hands which you
155 Rock 3   61   the glory of your action,/To arts and inventions and daring enterprises,/To schemes
224 Mr Mistoff   5   listen to me and don't scoff. All his/Inventions are off his own bat./There's no such
INVEST (1)
148 Rock 1   55   the love of none./All men are ready to invest their money/But most expect dividends./I
INVESTIGATE (2)
227 Macavity   30   or on the stair —/But it's useless to investigate — *Macavity's not there!*/And when
375 CP   Celia 36   — or doing *something.*/I must go and investigate. {}/[*Starts to leave the room*]/{E} For
INVESTIGATION (4)
129 Cor2 State   52   committee, a committee of investigation/RESIGN RESIGN RESIGN/
297 FR   Violet   30   if you are determined upon this investigation,/Which I am convinced is going to
493 CC   Claude 28   all, it was he who insisted/On this ... investigation. But perhaps you're right./{LE}
560 ES   Ld Clav 17   /You may find for yourself — if, on investigation,/I am satisfied about the nature of
INVESTIGATIONS (2)
301 FR   Violet   10   Well, Charles, I must say, with your investigations,/You seem to have left matters
466 CC   Claude 15   the place of religion:/Just as my wife's investigations/Into what she calls the life of the
INVESTING (2)
173 FQ: BurntN   96   after/In a dim light: neither daylight/Investing form with lucid stillness/Turning
480 CC   Kaghan   4   speculation/I've ever thought of investing in./Colby's more cautious. You know,
INVESTMENTS (3)
343 FR   Amy   26   /And unpaid rents and tithes? nourish investments/With wakeful nights and patient
489 CC   Claude 28   tour/To learn about his overseas investments./{LE} Then how do you know that
541 ES   Gomez   20   in — though not to *keep* it in./My investments — not all in my own name either —
INVETERATE (1)
172 FQ: BurntN   52   trilling wire in the blood/Sings below inveterate scars/Appeasing long forgotten wars./
INVIOLABLE (1)
64 WL: Chess   101   nightingale/Filled all the desert with inviolable voice/And still she cried, and still the
INVISIBLE (12)
54 Mr E Sun   24   /Where the souls of the devout/Burn invisible and dim./Along the garden-wall the
165 Rock 9   34   serve as spirit and body./Visible and invisible, two worlds meet in Man;/Visible and
165 Rock 9   35   two worlds meet in Man;/Visible and invisible must meet in His Temple;/You must

165 Rock 9   44   /Light/Light/The visible reminder of Invisible Light./You have seen the house built,
166 Rock 10   17   step and find your foothold./O Light Invisible, we praise Thee!/Too bright for mortal
166 Rock 10   25   glowlight on a grassblade./O Light Invisible, we worship Thee!/We thank Thee for
167 Rock 10   35   but see not whence it comes./O Light Invisible, we glorify Thee!/In our rhythm of
167 Rock 10   44   when we have built an altar to the Invisible Light, we may set thereon the little
167 Rock 10   46   darkness reminds us of light./O Light Invisible, we give Thee thanks for Thy great
171 FQ: BurntN 25   world./There they were, dignified, invisible,/Moving without pressure, over the
205 de la Mare 32   with natural ease;/By the delicate, invisible web you wove —/The inexplicable
338 FR   Harry 19   in flight/But always in ignorance of invisible pursuers./Now I know that all my life
INVITATION (2)
 44 Cook Egg   8   /Supported on the mantelpiece/An *Invitation to the Dance.*/I shall not want Honour
315 FR Warburt 16   but healthy./It's only when I get an invitation to dinner/That I ever see your
INVITATIONS (1)
474 CC   Colby 13   enter?/{C} It can't be done by issuing invitations:/They would just have to come. And
INVITE (5)
361 CP   Reilly 29   that to approach the stranger/Is to invite the unexpected, release a new force,/Or let
470 CC Lucasta 31   Do you think it's any compliment/To invite a woman to something she would like/
470 CC Lucasta 33   just being ... patronising. But if you invite me/To something you like — that *is* a
471 CC   Colby   1   that I want it./{C} Well, I'm going to invite you to the next concert .../{L} The next
511 CC   Lady E 24   wish to meet them./Claude, we must invite the Kaghans to dinner./{SC} By all
INVITED (13)
 74 WL: Thund 421   would have responded/Gaily, when invited, beating obedient/To controlling hands/I
303 FR   Agatha 15   Dr. Warburton. At least, Amy has invited him./{M} Dr. Warburton? I think she
359 CP   Edward 19   names/Of all the people she said she'd invited./But it's only that dreadful old woman
361 CP   Edward 15   May I put it to *you*?/I know that I invited this conversation:/But I don't know who
387 CP   Edward 24   /{E} I wonder whom else Lavinia has invited./{P} Why, I got the impression that
401 CP   Edward 18   you came to my flat/Had you been invited by my wife as a guest/As I supposed? ...
401 CP   Reilly 20   you?/{R} I cannot say that I had been invited;/And Mrs. Chamberlayne did not know
425 CP Lavinia 33   else is, to show they've been invited./That's what makes it a success. Is that
433 CP   Peter 12   {P} You know you'd never come if we invited you./But there's someone I wanted to
470 CC   Colby 23   a concert?/{C} Only the other day, I invited you .../{L} To go to see that American
482 CC   Colby   5   they come in unexpectedly?/{C} I'd invited Lucasta. She had asked me to play to
549 ES Carghil 10   friends of yours/And which one was it invited us to lunch?/I declare, I've utterly
580 ES Carghil 20   on my way back/Señor Gomez has invited me to visit San Marco./I'm so excited!
INVITES (1)
469 CC Lucasta 20   /I only go to shows when somebody invites me,/And no one has ever asked me to a
INVOKE (1)
576 ES Charles 38   To know that you are hardly likely to invoke it./And, Michael, here's another point to
INVOLVED (7)
 32 Hysteria   1   she laughed I was aware of becoming involved in her laughter and/being part of it,
 43 Swee Erect 34   ladies of the corridor/Find themselves involved, disgraced,/Call witness to their
173 FQ: BurntN 91   church at smokefall/Be remembered; involved with past and future./Only through
438 CP   Edward 17   /And the rest of us are somehow involved in the wrong,/I should only speak for
480 CC   Colby 14   a head as anyone,/And you never get involved in anything risky./You like to pretend
499 CC Claude 13   Colby will be here./But you're not involved in this meeting, Lucasta./Won't it do
560 ES Michael 26   I'm not such a fool/As to get myself involved in a breach of promise suit/Or
INVOLVING (1)
187 FQ: DrySal 112   agony of others, nearly experienced,/Involving ourselves, than in our own./For our
INVULNERABLE (1)
 19 Portrait   61   gulf you reach your hand./You are invulnerable, you have no Achilles' heel./You
INWARDLY (1)
531 ES Ld Clav 26   understand the place we filled/Are inwardly delighted. They won't want my ghost/
IONA (1)
282 MC   Chorus 1   the western seas gnaw at the coast of Iona,/To the death in the desert, the prayer in
IONIAN (1)
 69 WL: Fire S 265   hold/Inexplicable splendour of Ionian white and gold./The river sweats/Oil and
IRÆ (1)
272 MC   m 11   *to the cathedral.*]/[*while a* Dies Iræ *is sung in Latin by a choir in the distance*]./
IRISCH (1)
 62 WL: Burial 33   *weht der Wind/Der Heimat zu/Mein Irisch Kind/Wo weilest du?/*'You gave me
IRON (6)
 32 Hysteria   7   checked cloth over the rusty/green iron table, saying: 'If the lady and gentleman
 37 Gerontion   12   overhead;/Rocks, moss, stonecrop, iron, merds./The woman keeps the kitchen,
139 Virginia   11   living,/Never moving. Ever moving/Iron thoughts came with me/And go with me:/
151 Rock 2   19   by industrial development./Exporting iron, coal and cotton goods/And intellectual

154 Rock 3   25   /The peeled hull, a pile of rusty iron,/In a street of scattered brick where the
307 FR   Harry   32   /The unexpected crash of the iron cataract./You do not know what hope is,
IRRATIONAL (1)
333 FR   Harry   40   as if I had come home./It is quite irrational, but now/I feel quite happy, as if
IRREFLECTIVE (1)
568 ES Ld·Clav   7 takes cognisance:/Temporary failures, irreflective aberrations,/Reckless surrenders,
IRREGULAR (2)
148 Rock 1   48   idleness, which is still harder,/Or irregular labour, which is not pleasant./I have
210 Old Gumbie   20   keep quiet,/She is sure it is due to irregular diet/And believing that nothing is done
IRRELEVANT (2)
298 FR   Agatha 10   /I only see that this is all quite irrelevant;/We had better leave Charles to talk
572 ES Ld Clav   32 reasoning's sound enough. But it's irrelevant./Each of them remembers an occasion
IRREMEDIABLE (1)
288 FR   Agatha 19   is irrevocable,/Because the past is irremediable,/Because the future can only be
IRREPLACEABLE (1)
445 CC   Claude 25   Well, of course, Eggerson, you're irreplaceable .../{E} Oh, Sir Claude, you
IRRESISTIBLE (2)
256 MC   Priests 25   the intractable tide,/Do not sail the irresistible wind; in the storm,/Should we not
575 ES   Carghil 37   of my life./Your father was simply *irresistible*/In those days. I melted the first time
IRRESOLUTE (1)
107 Animula   25 from the hand of time the simple soul/Irresolute and selfish, misshapen, lame,/Unable
IRRESPONSIBLE (4)
 31 Apollinax   7   /He laughed like an irresponsible fœtus./His laughter was submarine
299 FRDowning   26 to get rather excited,/And, in a way, irresponsible, Sir./If I may make so bold, Sir,/I
313 FR   Charles 22 of their elder brother./Arthur's a bit irresponsible, you know;/You should have a
320 FR   Warburt 36 /And Arthur has always been rather irresponsible./Your mother's hopes are all
IRREVOCABLE (3)
288 FR   Agatha 18 I mean painful, because everything is irrevocable,/Because the past is irremediable,/
315 FR   Harry   8 He cannot realise/That everything is irrevocable,/The past unredeemable. But cancer,
330 FR   Harry   21   /Of isolation unredeemable, irrevocable —/It's eternal, or gives a knowledge
IRRITABLE (1)
143 Lines OM   2 /The tiger in the tiger-pit/Is not more irritable than I./The whipping tail is not more
IRRUPTION (1)
278 MC Knight2   7   of/the late Queen Matilda and the irruption of the unhappy usurper/Stephen, the
IRVING (1)
228 Gus   16   highest degree —/He has acted with Irving, he's acted with Tree./And he likes to
IS (1756)
ISLAND (6)
123 SA Kl & Kr   13   AS BEFORE/{Kl&Kr} *My little island girl/My little island girl/I'm going to stay*
123 SA Kl & Kr   14 /{Kl&Kr} *My little island girl/My little island girl/I'm going to stay with you/And we*
204 de la Mare   2   the brook and found/A desert island with a sandy cove/(A hiding place, but
355 CP   Julia   11 How he suffered!/They had to find an island for him/Where there were no bats./{A}
427 CP   Alex   8   the East. From Kinkanja —/An island that you won't have heard of/Yet. Got
480 CC   Kaghan 40 chuck it all/And go to live on a desert island./But I hope you won't do that. We need
ISLANDS (6)
 31 Apollinax   10 man of the sea's/Hidden under coral islands/Where worried bodies of drowned men
 96 Ash-Wed 5   13   silence/Not on the sea or on the islands, not/On the mainland, in the desert or
109 Marina   1   shores what grey rocks and what islands/What water lapping the bow/And scent
110 Marina   33 /What seas what shores what granite islands towards my timbers/And woodthrush
201 Def Island   t   VERSES/Defence of the Islands/Let these memorials of built stone —
201 Def Island   6 the memory of this defence of/the islands/and the memory of those appointed to
ISLE (7)
 39 Gerontion   70 the wind, in the windy straits/Of Belle Isle, or running on the Horn./White feathers in
 69 WL: Fire S   276 logs/Down Greenwich reach/Past the Isle of Dogs./Weialala leia/Wallala leialala/
121 SA Sweeney   2 /{S} I'll carry you off/To a cannibal isle./{Do} You'll be the cannibal!/{S} You'll be
121 SA Doris   7 You'll carry me off? To a cannibal isle?/{S} I'll be the cannibal./{Do} I'll be the
121 SA Sweeney   20 this egg/Well that's life on a crocodile isle./There's no telephones/There's no
123 SAWa & Ho   7 */Any old wood is just as good/Any old isle is just my style/Any fresh egg/Any fresh egg/*
123 SA Doris   12 And I don't like life on your crocodile isle. {}/SONG BY KLIPSTEIN AND
ISN'T (60)
209 NamingCats   2   of Cats is a difficult matter,/It isn't just one of your holiday games;/You may
214 RTTugger   8 Tugger is a Curious Cat —/And there isn't any call for me to shout it:/For he will do/
214 RTTugger   19 Tugger is a Curious Cat —/And it isn't any use for you to doubt it:/For he will do/
214 RTTugger   26 he always wants a feast;/When there isn't any fish then he won't eat rabbit./If you
215 RTTugger   36 Tugger is a Curious Cat —/And there isn't any need for me to spout it:/For he will do/

228 Gus   9   a terror to mice and to rats./For he isn't the Cat that he was in his prime;/Though
289 FR   Gerald   5   give us all the hump./I must say, this isn't cheerful for Amy's birthday/Or for Harry's
293 FR   Charles   34   pretty nasty messes./{C} And there isn't much would surprise me, Harry;/Or shock
308 FR   Harry   22   again as if nothing had happened,/Isn't that all folly? It's like the hollow tree,/Not
313 FR   Gerald   15   see./It's good to have him back again, isn't it?/We must make him feel at home. And
322 FR   Warburt   1   tell us your business./His Lordship isn't very well this evening./{Wi} I understand,
324 FR   Harry   20   spell:/But John's ordinary day isn't much more than breathing./{I} Really,
354 CP   Julia   22   wedding cake./{J} Well, but it really isn't my story./I heard it first from Delia
355 CP   Celia   15   a mine of information./{C} There isn't much that Julia doesn't know./{P} Go on
369 CP   Edward   9   there must be a double boiler:/Isn't there one in every kitchen?/{A} I can't find
370 CP   Edward   15   find any curry powder./{E} There isn't any curry powder. Lavinia hates curry./{A}
377 CP   Julia   23   to be sure,/And of course it isn't chilled. But it's so refreshing;/And I
377 CP   Julia   28   But I won't drink to Alex's./{J} Oh, it isn't Alex's. Come, I give you/Lavinia's aunt!
383 CP   Edward   13   an empty champagne bottle?/{E} It isn't empty. It may be a little flat —/But why
413 CP   Celia   29   wrong with me —/Because, if there isn't, then there's something wrong,/Or at least,
414 CP   Celia   2   though indeed there has been./It isn't simply the end of an illusion/In the
414 CP   Celia   25   you want to see no one?/{C} No ... it isn't that I *want* to be alone,/But that
419 CP   Reilly   7   That is the hell I have been in./{R} It isn't hell/Till you become incapable of anything
425 CP   Lavinia   36   straight?/{E} Yes, it is./{L} No, it isn't. Do please straighten it./{E} Is it straight
436 CP   Peter   13   been interested in myself:/And that isn't good enough for Celia./{J} You must have
440 CP   Edward   5   you will explain it to me!/{E} Oh, it isn't much/That I understand yet! But Sir Henry
458 CC   Lady E   38   he's very musical./{LE} Musical?/Isn't this the young man I interviewed/And
460 CC   Eggers   36   something unheard of./{E} Amazing, isn't it!/{SC} If this is what the doctor in Zürich
465 CC   Claude   11   /I didn't have it in me. It's strange, isn't it,/That a man should have a consuming
466 CC   Claude   9   I keep my pieces in a private room./It isn't that I don't want anyone to see them!/But
472 CC   Lucasta   11   did I think till now? Oh, it's strange, isn't it,/That as one gets to know a person better
480 CC   Colby   17   you ever gamble/On anything that isn't a certainty./{K} Well, there's something in
485 CC   Lady E   20   something in us,/In all of us, which isn't just heredity,/But something unique.
486 CC   Colby   29   my background —I assure you there isn't./{LE} It may be more interesting/Than you
489 CC   Claude   1   you./Perhaps you have a son. But it isn't Colby./I ought to have told you, years ago.
490 CC   Lady E   26   parent./{LE} But a mother, Colby, isn't that different?/There should always be a
496 CC   Lady E   8   how absurd you are!/Not that there isn't a lot to be learnt,/I don't doubt, from the
496 CC   Eggers   20   Mrs. E. wishes I'd come up oftener!/Isn't that like the ladies! She used to complain/
502 CC   Lucasta   17   I got. But I couldn't believe it!/It isn't like you, to despise people:/You don't care
502 CC   Lucasta   23   you've some fire/To warm you, that isn't the same kind of fire/That warms other
508 CC   Lady E   10   /{MG} Perhaps I should./{LE} There isn't a shadow of doubt in my mind./I'm
509 CC   Claude   8   called Colby?/{SC} But, Elizabeth, it isn't Colby!/Don't you see who it is?/{MG} My
509 CC   Colby   40   to it./{C} But he's waiting downstairs! Isn't this the moment/For me to bring him up?
527 ES   Charles   5   And, there being no legal impediment/Isn't that enough to constitute an engagement?/
534 ES   Gomez   38   other'./Dick, don't tell me that there isn't any whisky in the house?/{LC} I can
537 ES   Gomez   9   thing./We'll come to that, very soon. Isn't it strange/That there should always have
538 ES   Gomez   19   the man who accepts responsibility/Isn't the man who made the mistake./That's
540 ES   Ld Clav   9   before he looks in the mirror./{LC} Isn't that the kind of pretence that you're
544 ES   Monica   2   so far, it's better than you expected,/Isn't it, Father? They've let us alone;/The people
545 ES   Piggott   23   Good morning, Miss Claverton!/Isn't this a glorious morning!/I'm afraid you'll
550 ES   Carghil   28   well off. Yes, I'm provided for./But isn't it strange that you and I/Should meet here
554 ES   Carghil   4   Piggott!/She's bearing down on us. Isn't she frightful!/She never stops talking. Can
554 ES   Carghil   9   /Good morning, Mrs. Piggott!/Isn't it a glorious morning! {}/[*Enter* MRS.
556 ES   Michael   19   choose for a holiday./{Mi} Well, this isn't a holiday exactly./But this hotel was very
556 ES   Michael   24   whole of this holiday?/{Mi} Well, this isn't a holiday, exactly./Oh. I said that before,
560 ES   Ld Clav   21   to go/Beyond what you've told me? It isn't ... manslaughter?/{Mi} Manslaughter? Why
575 ES   Gomez   25   I should be! And most appropriate,/Isn't it, Dick, when we recall/That you were
579 ES   Carghil   32   me in the end, Dick./{MC} A parent isn't always the right person, Richard,/To solve
580 ES   Carghil   16   awfully sudden to you, Richard;/It isn't so sudden. We talked it all over./But I've
583 ES   Monica   19   now, and Michael's./And I am happy. Isn't it strange, Charles,/To be happy at this

ISOLATE (1)
295 FR   Harry   20   you would take it./First of all, you isolate the single event/As something so

ISOLATED (4)
182 FQ: ECoker 195   and living. Not the intense moment/Isolated, with no before and after,/But a lifetime
242 MC   Priest1   22   /Despised and despising, always isolated,/Never one among them, always
326 FR   Harry   24   could think/Even of my own life as an isolated ruin,/A casual bit of waste in an orderly
536 ES   Gomez   28   cosy, warm and padded:/You're not isolated — merely insulated./It's only when you

ISOLATION (4)
251 MC   Tempt3   14   You look only/To blind assertion in isolation./That is a mistake./{T} O Henry, O my
330 FR   Harry   21   at first, that sense of separation,/Of isolation unredeemable, irrevocable —/It's

173 FQ: BurntN   79   understood/In the completion of its partial ecstasy,/The resolution of its partial
173 FQ: BurntN   80   its partial ecstasy,/The resolution of its partial horror./Yet the enchainment of past
174 FQ: BurntN 128   the world moves/In appetency, on its metalled ways/Of time past and time future./
175 FQ: BurntN 146 Chinese jar still/Moves perpetually in its stillness./Not the stillness of the violin, while
184 FQ: DrySal   18 it reaches, the beaches where it tosses/Its hints of earlier and other creation:/The
186 FQ: DrySal   85   /The bone's prayer to Death its God. Only the hardly, barely prayable/
187 FQ: DrySal 118 time the preserver,/Like the river with its cargo of dead negroes, cows and chicken
191 FQ: Little   1   /Little Gidding/Midwinter spring is its own season/Sempiternal though sodden
197 FQ: Little 220 (where every word is at home,/Taking its place to support the others,/The word neither
202 War Poetry   23   conception/Of private experience at its greatest intensity/Becoming universal, which
212 Growltiger   13   the weak canary, that fluttered from its cage;/Woe to the pampered Pekinese, that
228 Gus   10   name was quite famous, he says, in its time./And whenever he joins his friends at
605 Narcissus   22 sure that he had been a tree,/Twisting its branches among each other/And tangling its
605 Narcissus   23   among each other/And tangling its roots among each other./Then he knew that
241 MC   Mess   36   that his horse will be deprived of its tail,/A single hair of which becomes a
251 MC Tempt3   35   a powerful party/Which has turned its eyes in your direction —/To gain from you,
254 MC Tempt4   34 ornament,/The sanctuary broken, and its stores/Swept into the laps of parasites and
260 MC Thomas   28   kingdom of England at peace with its/neighbours, the barons at peace with the
275 MC Chorus   27   /Can I look again at the day and its common things, and see them all smeared
276 MC Chorus   9 to our suffering./Every horror had its definition,/Every sorrow had a kind of end:/
279 MC Knight1   9 he does of a family distinguished for its/loyalty to the Church, will be able to
294 FR   Harry   2 Inaccessible to the plumbers, that has its hour of the night; you do not know/The
308 FR   Harry   5   upon the world, that never found its object;/And the eye adjusts itself to a twilight
333 FR   Agatha   31   that sin may strain and struggle/In its dark instinctive birth, to come to
333 FR   Agatha   34   of your unhappy family,/Its bird sent flying through the purgatorial
334 FR   Harry   23 obligation, a duty/Only noticed by its neglect. One had that part to play./After
349 FR   Agatha   23 /Not subject to reason/Each curse has its course/Its own way of expiation/Follow
349 FR   Agatha   24 to reason/Each curse has its course/Its own way of expiation/Follow follow/{M}
350 FR   Mary   1 know what we are doing/There is not its operation/Follow follow/{Ag} But in the
367 CP Edward   28   in Celia./Apart, of course, from its literary merit/Which I don't pretend to
418 CP   Reilly   31   way you choose will prescribe its own duty./{C} Which way is better?/{R}
439 CP   Reilly   8 acceptance/Of the past will you alter its meaning./{J} Henry, I think it is time that *I*
469 CC   Colby   9 /Then you will want to learn about its structure/And the various forms, and the
474 CC Lucasta   29 Not only in your music —/That's just its expression. You don't seem to me/To need
481 CC Lady E   28 You can have dinner early:/Most of its patrons dine at half past six./They have the
526 ES Monica   11 time, a long long time/Before I felt its presence./{C} Your words seem to come/
530 ES   m   32   *to a silver salver, still lying in its case*]./{LC} I don't know which impressed me
533 ES   Gomez   31 law —/And seen that the law turned its right side to *me*./Sometimes I've had to pay
560 ES Michael   3   /Poor ghost! reckoning up its profit and loss/And wondering why it

ITSELF (20)
 18 Portrait   2   /You have the scene arrange itself — as it will seem to do —/With 'I have
 24 Rhapsody   35 said,/'Remark the cat which flattens itself in the gutter,/Slips out its tongue/And
175 FQ: BurntN 164 in the figure of the ten stairs./Desire itself is movement/Not in itself desirable;/Love
175 FQ: BurntN 165 /Desire itself is movement/Not in itself desirable;/Love is itself unmoving,/Only
175 FQ: BurntN 166 /Not in itself desirable;/Love is itself unmoving,/Only the cause and end of
182 FQ: ECoker 202   album)./Love is most nearly itself/When here and now cease to matter./Old
185 FQ: DrySal   59 and hours,/While emotion takes to itself the emotionless/Years of living among the
606 Narcissus   37   them his white skin surrendered itself to the redness of blood, and satisfied him./
272 MC Chorus   32 to divert the soul/From seeing itself, foully united forever, nothing with
277 MC Knight1   31 completely disinterested. But/our act itself needs more justification than that; and you
287 FR   Gerald   5 /Let the younger generation speak for itself:/It's Mary's generation. What does she
308 FR   Harry   6 found its object;/And the eye adjusts itself to a twilight/Where the dead stone is seen
310 FR   Mary   24 and the beast, and the fish/Thrashing itself upstream:/And what of the terrified spirit/
329 FR Chorus   4 of birth or of dying,/Gathers in itself all the voices of the past, and projects
413 CP   Celia   31 what it seemed to be,/With the world itself — and that's much more frightening!/That
417 CP   Reilly   2 found it?/{R} Disillusion can become itself an illusion/If we rest in it./{C} I cannot
437 CP   Reilly   20 in certain minds,/May tend to express itself at once in a picture./That happens to me,
464 CC Claude   11   for living;/For me, they are life itself. To be among such things,/If it is an
503 CC Lucasta   4   But a different way/That reveals itself in time. And perhaps — who knows? —/
513 CC   Colby   17 /That one doesn't know. But the fact itself/Is unimportant, once one knows it./{MG}

IVORY (2)
 64 WL: Chess   86 poured in rich profusion./In vials of ivory and coloured glass/Unstoppered, lurked
 98 Ash-Wed 6   18 creates/The empty forms between the ivory gates/And smell renews the salt savour of

IVY (15)

284 FR	m	2	LADY MONCHENSEY, IVY, VIOLET, *and* AGATHA, *her younger*
285 FR	4m	1	*in late March.*/Scene I/AMY, IVY, VIOLET, AGATHA, GERALD,
290 FR	m	36	paw under the door. {}/CHORUS (IVY, VIOLET, GERALD *and* CHARLES)./
292 FR	Harry	14	returns of the day, mother./Aunt Ivy, Aunt Violet, Uncle Gerald, Uncle Charles.
301 FR	Gerald	22	acquired from worldly associates./{G} Ivy is only concerned for herself, and her credit
302 FR	Amy	11	we have always taken it to be./{A} Ivy! Violet! has Arthur or John come yet?/{I}
313 FR	2m	1	{}/Scene III/HARRY, MARY, IVY, VIOLET, GERALD, CHARLES/{V}
319 FR	Harry	9	/Surrounded by whispering aunts: Ivy and Violet —/Agatha never came then.
323 FR	m	7	*followed severally by* VIOLET, IVY, AGATHA, GERALD *and* CHARLES.]/
326 FR	Denman	33	DENMAN]/{D} Excuse me, Miss Ivy. There's a trunk call for you./{I} A trunk
326 FR	m	36	*he's* had an accident. {}/[*Exeunt* IVY *and* DENMAN]/{V} When it's Ivy that
326 FR	Violet	37	IVY *and* DENMAN]/{V} When it's Ivy that he's asking for, I expect the worst./{Ag}
327 FR	m	24	that lies a little deeper ... {}/[*Enter* IVY]/{I} Where is there an evening paper?/{G}
347 FR	m	14	so long. {}/[*Exit* DOWNING. *Enter* IVY]/{I} Where is Downing going? where is
347 FR	Violet	23	do not know what has been going on, Ivy./And if you did, you would not understand

J. (2) [*Abbreviation*]
  13 Prufrock   t   Observations/The Love Song of J. Alfred Prufrock/Let us go then, you and I,/
 602 Humoresque m   lovers seek!'/Humouresque/(AFTER J. LAFORGUE)/One of my marionettes is
J' (4)
  47 Mél   Adult 13   /Au grand air de Bergsteigleben;/J'erre toujours de-ci de-là/A divers coups de tra
  51 Restaurant   10   là, dans une averse, qu'on s'abrite./J'avais sept ans, elle était plus petite./Elle était
  51 Restaurant   14   /'Je la chatouillais, pour la faire rire./J'éprouvais un instant de puissance et de délire.'
  51 Restaurant   18   nous peloter, un gros chien;/Moi j'avais peur, je l'ai quittée à mi-chemin./C'est
JACK (1)
 266 MC Knights 16 /You are his servant, his tool, and his jack,/You wore his favours on your back,/You
JACKAL (1)
 269 MC Chorus 33   of beasts that make strange noises: jackal, jackass, jackdaw; the scurrying noise of
JACKASS (1)
 269 MC Chorus 33   that make strange noises: jackal, jackass, jackdaw; the scurrying noise of mouse
JACKDAW (1)
 269 MC Chorus 33   make strange noises: jackal, jackass, jackdaw; the scurrying noise of mouse and
JACKET (1)
 372 CP   m   9   good of you. {}/[*Enter* ALEX, *with his jacket on*]/{A} Oh, Edward! I've prepared you
JACKKNIFES (1)
  42 Swee Erect   17   /The sickle motion from the thighs/Jackknifes upward at the knees/Then
JADIS (1)
  51 Restaurant   31   un sort pénible;/Cependant, ce fut jadis un bel homme, de haute taille./Whispers of
JAGGÈD (1)
  92 Ash-Wed 3 10   faces and the stair was dark,/Damp, jaggèd, like an old man's mouth drivelling,
JAGUAR (2)
  52 Whispers   21   bliss./The couched Brazilian jaguar/Compels the scampering marmoset/With
  52 Whispers   25   a maisonnette;/The sleek Brazilian jaguar/Does not in its arboreal gloom/Distil so
JAMAICA (1)
 528 ES   Monica 37 /It's almost certain that the winter in Jamaica/Will never take place. 'Make the
JAMBES (1)
  48 Lune Miel   6   le dos écartant les genoux/De quatre jambes molles tout gonflées de morsures./On
JAMES (2)
 209 NamingCats   6   /Such as Peter, Augustus, Alonzo or James,/Such as Victor or Jonathan, George or
 235 Ad-dress   50   /I think I've heard them call him James —/But we've not got so far as names./
JAMES'S (3)
 230 Bust Jones   4   eight or nine clubs,/For he's the St. James's Street Cat!/He's the Cat we all greet as
 230 Bust Jones   9   impeccable back./In the whole of St. James's the smartest of names is/The name of
 291 FR   Charles   2   gallery?/{C} I might have been in St. James's Street, in a comfortable chair rather
JANUARY (1)
 328 FR   Charles 14 Ebury Street early on the morning of January 1st, was/fined 50 and costs to-day,
JAR (1)
 175 FQ: BurntN 145   reach/The stillness, as a Chinese jar still/Moves perpetually in its stillness./Not
JARS (1)
 494 CC   Lady E 39   /You really mean, to make jugs and jars/Like those in your collection?/{SC} That's
JAVA (1)
 292 FR   Harry   4   time that I have seen them./In the Java Straits, in the Sunda Sea,/In the sweet
JAVELIN-MAKERS (1)
 129 Cor2 State   22   perpetual peace: the fletchers and javelin-makers and smiths/Have appointed a
JAW (2)
  56 Swee Night   3   to laugh,/The zebra stripes along his jaw/Swelling to maculate giraffe./The circles of
  84 Hollow Men 56   /In this hollow valley/This broken jaw of our lost kingdoms/In this last of meeting
JAWS (2)
 192 FQ: Little   37   are the world's end, some at the sea jaws,/Or over a dark lake, in a desert or a city
 223 Pekes Pols   53   /He gave a great yawn, and his jaws were amazing;/And when he looked out
JE (6)
  47 Mél   Adult   8   paierez bien la tête./C'est à Paris que je me coiffe/Casque noir de jemenfoutiste./En
  47 Mél   Adult 16   tra là là/De Damas jusqu'à Omaha./Je célébrai mon jour de fête/Dans une oasis
  51 Restaurant   7   baveux, à la croupe arrondie,/Je te prie, au moins, ne bave pas dans la soupe).
  51 Restaurant   11   plus petite./Elle était toute mouillée, je lui ai donné des primevères.'/Les taches de
  51 Restaurant   13   montent au chiffre de trente-huit./'Je la chatouillais, pour la faire rire./J'éprouvais
  51 Restaurant   18   un gros chien;/Moi j'avais peur, je l'ai quittée à mi-chemin./C'est dommage.'/
JEALOUS (6)
 360 CP   Reilly 30   she thought she had cause to be jealous?/{E} She had nothing to complain of in
 362 CP   Reilly   4 perhaps at times you will feel a little jealous/That she saw it first, and had the
 408 CP   Reilly   8   of whom you had reason to be jealous./{E} Really, Lavinia! This is very

449 CC	Claude	6	circumstances, that might make her jealous./I've explained all this to Colby — Mr.
474 CC	Lucasta	37	it stands for./You know, I'm a little jealous of your music!/When I see it as a means
570 ES	Ld Clav	6	understand/Or that she would be jealous of the ghosts who haunted me./And I'm

JEALOUSY (2)

163 Rock 8		37	treachery,/Envy, sloth, gluttony, jealousy, pride:/It was not these that made the
253 MC	Tempt4	17	public policy, barons private profit,/Jealousy raging possession of the fiend./Barons

JELLICLE (23)

135 5FingerEx2		11	dry./Pollicle dogs and cats all must/Jellicle cats and dogs all must/Like undertakers,
216 Jellicles		1	about it!/The Song of the Jellicles/*Jellicle Cats come out to-night,/Jellicle Cats*
216 Jellicles		2	/*Jellicle Cats come out to-night,/Jellicle Cats come one come all:/The Jellicle*
216 Jellicles		3	/*Jellicle Cats come one come all!/The Jellicle Moon is shining bright —/Jellicles come*
216 Jellicles		4	*shining bright —/Jellicles come to the Jellicle Ball.*/Jellicle Cats are black and white,/
216 Jellicles		5	—/*Jellicles come to the Jellicle Ball.*/Jellicle Cats are black and white,/Jellicle Cats
216 Jellicles		6	/Jellicle Cats are black and white,/Jellicle Cats are rather small;/Jellicle Cats are
216 Jellicles		7	white,/Jellicle Cats are rather small;/Jellicle Cats are merry and bright,/And pleasant
216 Jellicles		9	pleasant to hear when they caterwaul./Jellicle Cats have cheerful faces,/Jellicle Cats
216 Jellicles		10	/Jellicle Cats have cheerful faces,/Jellicle Cats have bright black eyes;/They like to
216 Jellicles		12	their airs and graces/And wait for the Jellicle Moon to rise./Jellicle Cats develop
216 Jellicles		13	wait for the Jellicle Moon to rise./Jellicle Cats develop slowly,/Jellicle Cats are not
216 Jellicles		14	to rise./Jellicle Cats develop slowly,/Jellicle Cats are not too big;/Jellicle Cats are
216 Jellicles		15	slowly,/Jellicle Cats are not too big;/Jellicle Cats are roly-poly,/They know how to
216 Jellicles		17	to dance a gavotte and a jig./Until the Jellicle Moon appears/They make their toilette
216 Jellicles		21	ears,/Jellicles dry between their toes./Jellicle Cats are white and black,/Jellicle Cats
216 Jellicles		22	/Jellicle Cats are white and black,/Jellicle Cats are of moderate size;/Jellicles jump
216 Jellicles		24	/Jellicles jump like a jumping-jack,/Jellicle Cats have moonlit eyes./They're quiet
216 Jellicles		28	powers/To dance by the light of the Jellicle Moon./Jellicle Cats are black and white,/
216 Jellicles		29	by the light of the Jellicle Moon./Jellicle Cats are black and white,/Jellicle Cats
216 Jellicles		30	/Jellicle Cats are black and white,/Jellicle Cats (as I said) are small;/If it happens
217 Jellicles		36	saving themselves to be right/For the Jellicle Moon and the Jellicle Ball./Mungojerrie
217 Jellicles		36	right/For the Jellicle Moon and the Jellicle Ball./Mungojerrie and Rumpelteazer/

JELLICLES (5)

216 Jellicles		t	anything about it!/The Song of the Jellicles/*Jellicle Cats come out to-night,/Jellicle*
216 Jellicles		4	/*The Jellicle Moon is shining bright —/Jellicles come to the Jellicle Ball.*/Jellicle Cats
216 Jellicles		19	their toilette and take their repose:/Jellicles wash behind their ears,/Jellicles dry
216 Jellicles		20	/Jellicles wash behind their ears,/Jellicles dry between their toes./Jellicle Cats are
216 Jellicles		23	/Jellicle Cats are of moderate size;/Jellicles jump like a jumping-jack,/Jellicle Cats

JELLIES (1)

588 Fable		48	repast, and pies and puddings,/And jellies, pasties, cakes among the good things./A

JELLYLORUM (1)

209 NamingCats		19	/Such as Bombalurina, or else Jellylorum —/Names that never belong to more

JEMENFOUTISTE (1)

47 Mél Adult		9	Paris que je me coiffe/Casque noir de jemenfoutiste./En Allemagne, philosophe/

JENNYANYDOTS (3)

210 Old Gumbie		1	a Gumbie Cat in mind, her name is Jennyanydots;/Her coat is of the tabby kind,
210 Old Gumbie		13	a Gumbie Cat in mind, her name is Jennyanydots;/Her equal would be hard to find,
210 Old Gumbie		25	a Gumbie Cat in mind, her name is Jennyanydots;/The curtain-cord she likes to

JERBOA (1)

269 MC	Chorus	33	the scurrying noise of mouse and jerboa; the laugh of the loon, the lunatic bird. I

JERUSALEM (5)

73 WL: Thund		374	bursts in the violet air/Falling towers/Jerusalem Athens Alexandria/Vienna London/
157 Rock 4		7	/And he grieved for the broken city, Jerusalem;/And the King gave him leave to
157 Rock 4		10	the city./So he went, with a few, to Jerusalem,/And there, by the dragon's well, by
157 Rock 4		13	the fountain gate, by the king's pool,/Jerusalem lay waste, consumed with fire;/No
162 Rock 8		8	came one who spoke of the shame of Jerusalem/And the holy places defiled;/Peter the

JESUS (1)

151 Rock 2		3	/Of apostles and prophets, Christ Jesus Himself the chief cornerstone./But you,

JEW (3)

37 Gerontion		8	house is a decayed house,/And the Jew squats on the window sill, the owner,/
41 Burb Blei		23	The rats are underneath the piles./The Jew is underneath the lot./Money in furs. The
71 WL: DWater		319	/Entering the whirlpool./Gentile or Jew/O you who turn the wheel and look to

JEWEL-CASE (1)

226 Macavity		23	/And when the larder's looted, or the jewel-case is rifled,/Or when the milk is missing,

JEWELLED (2)

94 Ash-Wed 4		21	vision in the higher dream/While jewelled unicorns draw by the gilded hearse./
254 MC	Tempt4	18	standing in line/Before the glittering jewelled shrine,/From generation to generation/

JEWELS (2)

| 64 WL: Chess | 84 | upon the table as/The glitter of her jewels rose to meet it,/From satin cases poured |
| 254 MC Tempt4 | 33 | be pillaged, and the gold spent,/The jewels gone for light ladies' ornament,/The |

JIG (1)

| 216 Jellicles | 16 | know how to dance a gavotte and a jig./Until the Jellicle Moon appears/They make |

JIMINY (1)

| 589 Fable | 79 | /And before any one could say 'O jiminy!'/The pair had vanisht swiftly up the |

JINGLE-BELL (1)

| 509 CC Colby | 14 | Sarah,/My finding a rattle and a jingle-bell,/And your telling me I had had a |

JIST (1)

| 236 Cat Morgan | 20 | and you'll spare yourself labour/If jist you make friends with the Cat at the door./ |

JOB (18)

149 Rock 1	92	*work together/A Church for all/And a job for each/Every man to his work./Now a group*
150 Rock 1	123	*the meaning:/A Church for all/And a job for each/Each man to his work./*Thus your
277 MC Knight3	8	knew we had taken on a pretty stiff job; I'll only speak for/myself, but I had drunk
305 FR Mary	3	know I must go./But where? I want a job: and you can help me./{Ag} I am very sorry,
329 FR Chorus	16	/The making the best of a bad job/All twined and tangled together, all are
388 CP Peter	1	to California!/{P} Yes, I have a new job./{E} And how did that happen, overnight?/
410 CP Edward	33	we must make the best of a bad job./That is what he means./{R} When you find,
410 CP Reilly	36	Mr. Chamberlayne,/The best of a bad job is all any of us make of it —/Except of
452 CC Lucasta	11	ANGEL]/{L} Eggy, I've lost my job!/{E} Again, Miss Angel?/{L} Yes, again!
538 ES Gomez	28	politics/And taking a conspicuous part in the City/Where the Government could
557 ES Michael	7	happened./{Mi} Well, I've lost my job./{LC} The position that Sir Alfred Walter
557 ES Ld Clav	10	And deadly dull it was./{LC} Every job is dull, nine-tenths of the time .../{Mi} I need
558 ES Michael	21	/In the first place, they all knew the job had been made for me/Because I was your
574 ES Michael	33	round the world, for the same sort of job/You got me here in London? With another
575 ES Michael	1	limey remittance man for whom a job was made./No! I want to go where I can
575 ES Michael	5	if *you* don't./And he's offered me a job which is just what I wanted./{LC} Yes, I see
575 ES Ld Clav	6	/{LC} Yes, I see the advantage of a job created for you/By Señor Gomez .../{Mi}
576 ES Michael	15	care about that. He's offered me the job/With a jolly good screw, and some pickings

JOBS (1)

| 455 CC Eggers | 17 | a thorn in his flesh,/Always losing her jobs, because she won't stick to them./He gives |

JOG (1)

| 234 Ad-dress | 18 | *a Cat?/*So first, your memory I'll jog,/And say: A CAT IS NOT A DOG./Now |

JOHN (50)

246 MC Thomas	11	sworn to have my head from me/Only John, the Dean of Salisbury,/Fearing for the
264 MC m	7	PRIEST, *with a banner of St. John the Apostle borne before him.*]/{P2} Since
264 MC Priest2	7	St. Stephen a day: and the day of St. John the Apostle./*In the midst of the*
264 MC m	13	of the congregation. {}/[*Introit of St. John is heard*]/[*Enter the* THIRD PRIEST, *with*
264 MC Priest3	14	*borne before him.*]/{P3} Since St. John the Apostle a day: and the day of the Holy
275 MC Thomas	20	Mary ever Virgin, to the blessed John the Baptist, the holy apostles Peter and
287 FR Amy	34	/— I am only certain of Arthur and John,/Arthur in London, John in Leicestershire:
287 FR Amy	35	Arthur and John,/Arthur in London, John in Leicestershire:/They should both be
291 FR Amy	10	is it?/{C} Nearly twenty to seven./{A} John should be here now, he has the shortest
291 FR Amy	11	now, he has the shortest way to come./John at least, if not Arthur. Hark, there is
291 FR Amy	12	is someone coming:/Yes, it must be John. {}/[*Enter* HARRY]/{A} Harry! {}/
302 FR Amy	11	it to be./{A} Ivy! Violet! has Arthur or John come yet?/{I} There is no news of Arthur
302 FR Ivy	12	yet?/{I} There is no news of Arthur or John. {}/[*Enter* AMY *and* AGATHA]/{A} It is
303 FR Mary	13	one that was uncertain./Arthur or John may be late, of course./We may have to
303 FR Mary	25	I shall have to sit between Arthur and John./Which is worse, thinking of what to say
303 FR Mary	26	is worse, thinking of what to say to John,/Or having to listen to Arthur's chatter/
307 FR Harry	3	we fought the Indians, Arthur and John./{M} It was the cave where we met by
307 FR Harry	6	raise the evil spirits./{H} Arthur and John./Of course we were punished for being out
313 FR Charles	19	/{C} Now we only want Arthur and John/I'm glad that you'll all be together, Harry;
313 FR Amy	25	the family./{A} Violet! Has Arthur or John come yet?/{V} Neither of them is here yet,
315 FR Gerald	22	any use in waiting for Arthur and John?/{A} We might as well go in to dinner./
319 FR Harry	19	now I do remember. Not Arthur or John,/They were too young. But now I
320 FR Warburt	33	know as well as I do that Arthur and John/Have been a great disappointment to your
322 FR Winch	22	us your business./{Wi} It's about Mr. John./{H} John!/{Wi} Yes, my Lord, I'm sorry./
322 FR Harry	23	/{Wi} It's about Mr. John./{H} John!/{Wi} Yes, my Lord, I'm sorry./I thought
322 FR Winch	37	We've got him at the Arms —/Mr. John, I mean. By a bit of luck/Dr. Owen was
323 FR Amy	6	/Who's there with you? Is it Arthur or John? {}/[*Enter* AMY, *followed severally by*
323 FR Warburt	10	but a minor accident./{W} It's John has had the accident, Lady Monchensey;/
324 FR Harry	15	Cannot make very much difference to John./A brief vacation from the kind of
324 FR Harry	17	from the kind of consciousness/That John enjoys, can't make very much difference/

324 FR	Ivy	22	/I always thought you were so fond of John./{V} And if you don't care what happens
324 FR	Violet	23	if you don't care what happens to John,/You might show some consideration to
324 FR	Harry	36	all of the rightminded feeling about John/That you consider appropriate. Only,
325 FR	Gerald	20	Arthur:/He's much more apt than John to get into trouble./{C} Oh, but Arthur's a
325 FR	Ivy	27	was always the more adventurous/But John was the one that had the accidents,/
328 FR	Gerald	3	bit as likely/To have an accident as John. And it wasn't John's fault,/I don't believe.
328 FR	Gerald	4	it wasn't John's fault,/I don't believe. John is unlucky,/But Arthur is definitely
330 FR	Harry	1	/Scene II/HARRY, AGATHA/{H} John will recover, be what he always was;/
330 FR	Harry	5	routine of normal life at Wishwood./John is the only one of us I can conceive/As
339 FR	Harry	15	not let me fall./Let the cricket chirp. John shall be the master./All I have is his. No
339 FR	Harry	17	would destroy me will be life for John,/I am responsible for him. Why I have this
343 FR	Harry	31	you will always have Arthur and John/To worry about: not that John is any
343 FR	Harry	32	and John/To worry about: not that John is any worry —/The destined and the
345 FR	Harry	10	accidents as happen to Arthur and John:/Take care of *them*. My address, mother,/
347 FR	Warburt	34	and coming./But I'm glad to say that John is getting on nicely;/It wasn't so serious as
349 FR	Gerald	9	pleasure to dealing with Arthur and John in the morning./{V} We must wait for the
550 ES	Carghil	10	name now and here .../{MC} Is Mrs. John Carghill./{LC} You married, I suppose,
562 ES	Carghil	26	the bill in revue. Now I'm Mrs. John Carghill./Richard! It's astonishing about
563 ES	Carghil	24	—/To Mrs. ... Mrs. .../{MC} Mrs. John Carghill./{G} We seem a bit weak on the
571 ES	Ld Clav	1	star, Maisie Montjoy./There is Mrs. John Carghill, the wealthy widow./But Freddy

JOHN'S (5)

33 Conv	Gal	3	(fantastic, I confess)/It may be Prester John's balloon/Or an old battered lantern hung
320 FR	Warburt	35	great disappointment to your mother./John's very steady — but he's not exactly
322 FR	Winch	31	was here, and that you'd arrived./Mr. John's had a bit of an accident/On the West
324 FR	Harry	20	for him to have a breathing spell:/But John's ordinary day isn't much more than
328 FR	Gerald	3	an accident as John. And it wasn't John's fault,/I don't believe. John is unlucky,/

JOIN (7)

222 Pekes	Pols	6	in a way,/Or now and again, they join in to the fray/And they/Bark bark bark
274 MC	Knights	23	lions' den,/Come down Daniel and join in the feast./Where is Becket the Cheapside
274 MC	Knights	27	lions' den,/Come down Daniel and join in the feast./{T} It is the just man who/Like
296 FR	Gerald	34	ring up Warburton, and ask him to join us?/He's an old friend of the family, it's
307 FR	Harry	36	from you,/Or to fling it away, to join the legion of the hopeless/Unrecognised by
563 ES	Gomez	9	/{G} You weren't expecting me to join you here, were you?/You're here for a rest
573 ES	Ld Clav	22	us go./{LC} We will stay here. Let her join us. {}/[*Enter* MRS. CARGHILL]/{MC} I've

JOINED (10)

164 Rock 9		18	of life, from the soul of man that is joined to the soul of stone;/Out of the
164 Rock 9		20	shapes of all that is living or lifeless/Joined with the artist's eye, new life, new form,
165 Rock 9		32	His service in creating./For Man is joined spirit and body,/And therefore must
178 FQ: ECoker		35	fire/Leaping through the flames, or joined in circles,/Rustically solemn or in rustic
201 Def	Island	5	of the earth, of English/verse/be joined with the memory of this defence of/the
223 Pekes	Pols	40	the balcony, some from the roof,/Joined in/To the din/With a/Bark bark bark
336 FR	Harry	5	free/From the ring of ghosts with joined hands, from the pursuers,/And come into
433 CP	Lavinia	37	in Kinkanja?/We heard that she had joined some nursing order .../{A} She had joined
433 CP	Alex	38	some nursing order .../{A} She had joined an order. A very austere one./And as she
577 ES	Carghil	26	/{MC} Richard, I think it's time *I* joined the conversation./My late husband, Mr.

JOINS (1)

228 Gus		11	he says, in its time./And whenever he joins his friends at their club/(Which takes place

JOINT (6)

125 SA	Sweeney	13	then he was dead./There wasn't any joint/There wasn't any joint/For when you're
125 SA	Sweeney	14	wasn't any joint/There wasn't any joint/For when you're alone/When you're alone
129 Cor2	State	23	and smiths/Have appointed a joint committee to protest against the reduction
219 Mung	Rump	23	wouldn't get thinner/On Argentine joint, potatoes and greens,/And the cook would
219 Mung	Rump	27	and have dinner *tomorrow*!/For the joint has gone from the oven — like that!'/Then
230 Bust	Jones	16	one Cat to belong both to that/And the *Joint Superior Schools.*/For a similar reason,

JOKE (3)

408 CP	Edward	23	so utterly ludicrous:/This is the best joke that ever happened./{L} I never knew you
455 CC	Eggers	28	protect me against Mrs. E. That's my joke./{C} Well, I've never met anyone like Miss
558 ES	Michael	18	things quiet. I can tell you, it's no joke/Being the son of a famous public man./

JOKER (1)

406 CP	Lavinia	21	a devil/Or merely a lunatic practical joker?/{E} I incline to the second explanation/

JOKES (1)

321 FR	Winch	32	of my father./{Wi} Always at your jokes, I see. You don't look a year older/Than

JOLLY (2)

288 FR	Agatha	40	to face him —/And it will not be a very *jolly* corner./When the loop in time comes — and
576 ES	Michael	16	that. He's offered me the job/With a jolly good screw, and some pickings in

JOLT (1)
362 CP   Reilly 32   expected/And you come down with a jolt. Just for a moment/You have the experience
JONATHAN (1)
209 NamingCats 7   Alonzo or James,/Such as Victor or Jonathan, George or Bill Bailey —/All of them
JONES (4)
230 Bust Jones   t   the Fiend of the Fell.'/Bustopher Jones: the Cat About Town/Bustopher Jones is
230 Bust Jones   1   the Cat About Town/Bustopher Jones is *not* skin and bones —/In fact, he's
230 Bust Jones 12   be nodded or bowed to/By Bustopher Jones in white spats!/His visits are occasional to
231 Bust Jones 40   Spring in Pall Mall/While Bustopher Jones wears white spats!/Skimbleshanks: the
JOSHUA (9)
445 CC   Claude   3   you up to London/All the way from Joshua Park, on an errand like this./But you
456 CC   Eggers 30   E.,/When we'd bought our house in Joshua Park/(On a mortgage, of course) 'now
456 CC   Eggers 33   *I* want is up to the City/And back to Joshua Park in the evening,/And once a year
461 CC   Eggers 17   ask him to come/All the way to Joshua Park, at this time of year!'/I said: 'Let's
496 CC   Eggers 28   Street./But I've so much to do, in Joshua Park —/Apart from the garden — that
517 CC   Eggers 26   of a vacancy/In my own parish, in Joshua Park —/If it should appeal to you. The
517 CC   Eggers 31   don't seem to want to come to Joshua Park./{C} But I've told you, I'm not a
518 CC   Eggers 10   your music. Why, Mr. Simpkins,/Joshua Park may be only a stepping-stone/To a
518 CC   Eggers 17   you'd want to find your feet/In Joshua Park, before you settled on lodgings;/We
JOSTLED (1)
294 FR   Harry 29   still alone/In an over-crowded desert, jostled by ghosts./It was only reversing the
JOT (1)
530 ES Ld Clav   2   since I entered Parliament./I used to jot down notes of what I had to say to people:/
JOTTED (1)
487 CC   Claude   3   /It's got to sound spontaneous. I've jotted down some headings./Just see if you can
JOUR (2)
47 Mél Adult   16   jusqu'à Omaha./Je célébrai mon jour de fête/Dans une oasis d'Afrique/Vêtu
51 Restaurant   5   de la pluie;/C'est ce qu'on appelle le jour de lessive des gueux.'/(Bavard, baveux, à la
JOURNALISTE (1)
47 Mél Adult   2   Amérique, professeur;/En Angleterre, journaliste;/C'est à grands pas et en sueur/Que
JOURNEY (18)
92 Ash-Wed 2   40   /Of love satisfied/End of the endless/Journey to no end/Conclusion of all that/Is
103 Journ Magi   t   cry come unto Thee./ARIEL POEMS/Journey of the Magi/'A cold coming we had of
103 Journ Magi   3   /Just the worst time of the year/For a journey, and such a long journey:/The ways
103 Journ Magi   3   year/For a journey, and such a long journey:/The ways deep and the weather sharp,/
191 FQ: Little   26   It would be the same at the end of the journey,/If you came at night like a broken
261 MC Thomas   2   no such things: they went forth to journey afar, to suffer by land/and sea, to know
272 MC Chorus   26   God;/The horror of the effortless journey, to the empty land/Which is no land,
280 MC Priest1   9   us, protect us, direct us?/After what journey through what further dread/Shall we
305 FR   Mary   22   arrived./Did you have a comfortable journey?/{H} Not very./But, at least, it did not
313 FR   Violet   4   Very well, I think, after such a long journey;/You know what a rush he had to be
336 FR   Agatha   3   deceived in waking./You have a long journey./{H} Not yet! not yet! this is the first
337 FR   Agatha   9   I was saying/That you have a long journey. You have nothing to stay for./Think of
390 CP   Julia   36   Alex —/And after that long journey on the old Great Eastern,/Waiting at
404 CP   Reilly   36   far to go?/{R} You might say, a long journey./But before I treat a patient like
418 CP   Reilly   28   little until you get there;/You will journey blind. But the way leads towards
418 CP   Reilly   37   the second./{R} It is a terrifying journey./{C} I am not frightened/But glad. I
421 CP   Julia   16   what do we know of the terrors of the journey?/You and I don't know the process by
422 CP   Alex   18   The words for those who go upon a journey./{R} Protector of travellers/Bless the
JOURNEY'S (1)
20 Portrait   67   sympathy/Of one about to reach her journey's end./I shall sit here, serving tea to
JOURNEYED (2)
147 Rock 1   19   from GOD and nearer to the Dust./I journeyed to London, to the timekept City,/
147 Rock 1   27   bells:/Let them waken the suburbs./I journeyed to the suburbs, and there I was told:/
JOURS (1)
51 Restaurant   25   Phlébas, le Phénicien, pendant quinze jours noyé,/Oubliait les cris des mouettes et la
JOVIAL (1)
588 Fable   42   all preparations had been made,/The jovial epicures sat down to table./The menus of
JOY (7)
111 Xmas Trees   30   /May be concentrated into a great joy/Which shall be also a great fear, as on the
213 Growltiger   53   to go ker-flip, ker-flop./Oh there was joy in Wapping when the news flew through the
260 MC Thomas   18   and/for the same reason? For either joy will be overborne by mourning, or/
260 MC Thomas   19   or/mourning will be cast out by joy; so it is only in these our Christian/mysteries
271 MC Thomas   12   pierce you with a sudden painful joy/When the figure of God's purpose is made
310 FR   Mary   17   to return?/{M} Pain is the opposite of joy/But joy is a kind of pain/I believe the

310 FR   Mary 18   /{M} Pain is the opposite of joy/But joy is a kind of pain/I believe the moment of

JOYFUL (2)

164 Rock 9   15   penitence,/And then let us learn the joyful communion of saints./The soul of Man

272 MC Thomas   7   be denied; all things/Proceed to a joyful consummation./{3P} Seize him! force him!

JUBILANT (1)

136 5FingerEx4 17   round his head finches and fairies/In jubilant rapture skim./How delightful to meet

JUDAS (1)

37 Gerontion   21   dogwood and chestnut, flowering judas,/To be eaten, to be divided, to be drunk/

JUDGE (12)

976 MC Knight1   2   know that you may be disposed to judge unfavourably/of our action. You are

276 MC Knight1 24   Englishmen, and therefore will not judge anybody without/hearing both sides of

341 FR   Amy 27 for argument./{A} Who set you up to judge? what, if you please,/Gives *you* the power

367 CP Edward 29   merit/Which I don't pretend to judge./{P} Well, I can judge it,/And I think it's

367 CP   Peter 30   pretend to judge./{P} Well, I can judge it,/And I think it's very good. But that's

447 CC Claude 18   that she, of all people,/Is a better judge of character than I am./{E} Oh, I wouldn't

480 CC Kaghan 19 You know, Lucasta,/Colby is a good judge of character./{L} You'd need to be a

480 CC Lucasta 20   /{L} You'd need to be a better judge of character/Yourself, before you said

480 CC Kaghan 22   that of Colby./{K} Oh, I'm a good judge. Now, I'll tell you the difference/Between

502 CC Lucasta 26   from the rest of us/That we can't judge you. That's you, Colby./{C} That's me, is

513 CC Guzzard   1   /{MG} Nor, so far as I can judge, with you./Perhaps you are the wisest

545 ES Ld Clav   8   on to futile activity,/And in the end, judge us still more severely/For the errors into

JUDGED (1)

438 CP   Reilly 27   I feel guilty too?/{R} If we all were judged according to the consequences/Of all our

JUDGEMENT (7)

90 Ash-Wed 1   33 is done, not to be done again/May the judgement not be too heavy upon us/Because

188 FQ: DrySal 167 whose bodies/Will suffer the trial and judgement of the sea,/Or whatever event, this is

269 MC Thomas 14 /But the Law of Christ's Church, the judgement of Rome./{K1} Priest, you have

269 MC Thomas 19   /{T} I submit my cause to the judgement of Rome./But if you kill me, I shall

272 MC Chorus 23   /And behind the face of Death the Judgement/And behind the Judgement the

272 MC Chorus 24 Death the Judgement/And behind the Judgement the Void, more horrid than active

400 CP   Reilly 10   what I mean is,/Does he trust your judgement?/{A} Yes, implicitly./It's not that he

JUDGMENT (2)

203 Indians   21 if neither you nor we/Know, until the judgment after death,/What is the fruit of

447 CC Claude 22   That's worse than believing in her judgment:/We could argue about that. You

JUDGMENT'S (1)

299 FRDowning 36 saw him in high spirits./For what my judgment's worth, I always said his Lordship/

JUDICIAL (1)

335 FR   Harry 30 /And the desert is cleared, under the judicial sun/Of the final eye, and the awful

JUG (8)

64 WL: Chess 103 she cried, and still the world pursues,/'Jug Jug' to dirty ears./And other withered

64 WL: Chess 103 cried, and still the world pursues,/'Jug Jug' to dirty ears./And other withered stumps of

67 WL: Fire S 204   dans la coupole!/Twit twit twit/Jug jug jug jug jug jug/So rudely forc'd./Tereu/

67 WL: Fire S 204   dans la coupole!/Twit twit twit/Jug jug jug jug jug jug/So rudely forc'd./Tereu/

67 WL: Fire S 204   la coupole!/Twit twit twit/Jug jug jug jug jug jug/So rudely forc'd./Tereu/Unreal

67 WL: Fire S 204   la coupole!/Twit twit twit/Jug jug jug jug jug jug/So rudely forc'd./Tereu/Unreal City/

67 WL: Fire S 204   /Twit twit twit/Jug jug jug jug jug jug/So rudely forc'd./Tereu/Unreal City/

67 WL: Fire S 204   /Twit twit twit/Jug jug jug jug jug jug/So rudely forc'd./Tereu/Unreal City/Under

JUGOSLAVIA (1)

375 CP Edward 20   cheese ... Slipper what? .../Oh, from Jugoslavia ... prunes and alcohol?/No, really,

JUGS (1)

494 CC Lady E 39   a potter!/You really mean, to make jugs and jars/Like those in your collection?/{SC}

JUICE (2)

136 5FingerEx4 12   on his palate fine he presses/The juice of the gooseberry tart./How delightful to

588 Fable   62 more than he ought t' have of grape juice./The lights began to burn distinctly blue,/

JUICY (1)

121 SA Sweeney 17   white little, soft little, tender little,/Juicy little, right little, missionary stew./You see

JULIA (66)

352 CP   m   3   /EDWARD CHAMBERLAYNE/JULIA (MRS. SHUTTLETHWAITE)/CELIA

353 CP   3m   1   /EDWARD CHAMBERLAYNE, JULIA SHUTTLETHWAITE, CELIA/

353 CP   Alex   1 You've missed the point completely, Julia:/There *were* no tigers. *That* was the point./

353 CP   Alex   5 /You and the Maharaja?/{A} My dear Julia!/It's perfectly hopeless. You haven't been

353 CP   Celia 13   /Both of you. It's your turn, Julia./Do tell us that story you told the other

353 CP   Celia 25 /{C} Here's one new listener for you, Julia;/And I don't believe that Edward knows it.

355 CP   Alex 14   no bats./{A} And is he still there?/Julia is really a mine of information./{C} There

355 CP   Celia 15   /{C} There isn't much that Julia doesn't know./{P} Go on with the story

358 CP	Edward	36	Good-bye, Edward./{E} Good-bye, Julia. {}/[*Exeunt* JULIA *and* PETER]/{C}
358 CP	m	36	/{E} Good-bye, Julia. {}/[*Exeunt* JULIA *and* PETER]/{C} Good-bye, Edward./
359 CP	Edward	23	least wanted. {}/[*Opens the door*]/{E} Julia! {}/[*Enter* JULIA]/{J} Edward! How lucky
359 CP	m	24	/[*Opens the door*]/{E} Julia! {}/[*Enter* JULIA]/{J} Edward! How lucky that it's
364 CP	Edward	30	*to the door*]/{E} So it's you again, Julia! {}/[*Enter* JULIA *and* PETER]/{J}
364 CP	m	31	/{E} So it's you again, Julia! {}/[*Enter* JULIA *and* PETER]/{J} Edward, I'm so glad to
366 CP	Peter	15	won't mind/If I don't come with you, Julia? On the way back/I remembered
367 CP	Peter	6	did,/Though I'm rather afraid of Julia Shuttlethwaite./{E} Julia is certainly
367 CP	Edward	7	afraid of Julia Shuttlethwaite./{E} Julia is certainly observant,/But I think she had
367 CP	Peter	39	in and see if anyone was with you./{P} Julia must have left it open./{E} Never mind;/So
374 CP	Celia	21	prepared with something better, for Julia;/But it doesn't really matter. They will
376 CP	Edward	8	*front door, and is*/*heard to say:*]/{E} Julia!/What have you come back for? {}/[*Enter*
376 CP	m	10	have you come back for? {}/[*Enter* JULIA]/{J} I've had an inspiration! {}/[*Enter*
377 CP	m	2	You stay and talk to Edward. {}/[*Exit* JULIA]/{C} But what has happened, Edward?
377 CP	m	19	{E} What the devil's that? {}/[*Re-enter* JULIA, *in apron, with a tray and three glasses*]/
377 CP	Edward	35	home with me./{E} I'm sorry, Julia./I'm too tired to go out, and I'm not at all
378 CP	Celia	4	Something very light./{C} Thank you, Julia./I think I will, if I may follow you/In
378 CP	m	11	/Good night, Edward. {}/[*Exit* JULIA]/{C} Well, how did he persuade you?/{E}
379 CP	Celia	29	in it till to-day,/And then, when Julia asked about Lavinia/And it came to me
383 CP	Edward	1	better answer it./{E} Hello! ... Oh, Julia: what is it now?/Your spectacles again ...
383 CP	Celia	22	/[*They drink*]/{C} It may be that even Julia is a guardian./Perhaps she is *my* guardian.
383 CP	Edward	27	*snatches up the receiver*]/{E} Hello, Julia! are you there? .../Well, I'm awfully sorry
386 CP	Celia	21	asked you!/{C} Well, not directly. Julia had a telegram/Asking her to come, and to
386 CP	Celia	23	to come, and to bring me with her./Julia was delayed, and sent me on ahead./{E} It
387 CP	Celia	23	myself —/That she telegraphed to Julia to come and bring me with her./{E} I
388 CP	Celia	26	telegram?/{C} The one you sent to Julia./{P} And the one you sent to Alex./{L} I
389 CP	m	38	/But ... {}/[EDWARD *re-enters with* JULIA]/{J} There you are, Lavinia. I'm sorry to
391 CP	Edward	10	you sure you haven't left anything, Julia?/{J} Left anything? Oh, you mean my
391 CP	Alex	16	What do you think, Alex?/{A} No, Julia, *we* can't explain the telegram./{L} I am
391 CP	Alex	25	explain *anything*?/{A} I think not, Julia. She must find out for herself:/That's the
391 CP	Peter	32	{}/[*Enter* PETER]/{P} I've got a taxi, Julia./{J} Splendid! Good-bye! {}/[*Exeunt*
391 CP	m	33	/{J} Splendid! Good-bye! {}/[*Exeunt* JULIA, ALEX *and* PETER]/{L} I must say,
392 CP	Lavinia	22	I think I know./But I'm puzzled by Julia. That woman is the devil/She knows by
392 CP	Lavinia	29	less than the truth could deceive Julia./But how did the aunt come to live in
392 CP	Edward	31	the aunt come to live in Essex?/{E} Julia compelled me to make her live somewhere.
392 CP	Lavinia	32	her live somewhere./{L} I see. So Julia made her live in Essex;/And made the
392 CP	Lavinia	34	from Essex./Well, I shall have to tell Julia the truth./I shall always tell the truth now.
412 CP	m	2	/{R} Yes? ... Yes. Come in. {}/[*Enter* JULIA *by side door*]/{R} She's waiting
412 CP	m	23	here?/{R} Yes, he'll be here. {}/[*Exit* JULIA *by side door*]/[REILLY *presses button.*
412 CP	Celia	26	Mrs. Shuttlethwaite./{C} Yes, it was Julia ... Mrs. Shuttlethwaite/Who advised me to
420 CP	m	20	You can come in now. {}/[*Enter* JULIA *by side door*]/{R} She will go far, that
422 CP	m	3	Gibbs arrives .../Oh, very good. {}/[*To* JULIA]/{R} He's on his way up. {}/[*Into*
426 CP	Lavinia	27	Mrs. Shuttlethwaite!/{L} Oh, it's Julia! {}/[*Enter* JULIA]/{J} Well, my dears, and
426 CP	m	28	/{L} Oh, it's Julia! {}/[*Enter* JULIA]/{J} Well, my dears, and here I am!/I
427 CP	Alex	27	tigers?/{A} There are no tigers, Julia,/In Kinkanja. And there are no sultans./I
430 CP	Peter	16	And how are you, Alex? And dear old Julia!/{L} So you've just come from New York./
430 CP	Peter	30	/{P} You always did enjoy a leg-pull, Julia:/But you all know I'm working for
432 CP	Reilly	9	looks so forbidding .../{R} My dear Julia,/You are giving me a very bad
432 CP	Lavinia	13	me./{L} If you can interrupt Julia, Sir Henry,/You are the perfect guest
432 CP	Reilly	15	not dream of trying to interrupt Julia .../{J} But you're both interrupting!/{R}
432 CP	Peter	37	for all of us. Think of it!/{P} But, Julia, I was just about to explain —/I'm afraid I
433 CP	Lavinia	25	tell them now, Alex./{L} What does Julia mean?/{A} I was just about to speak of her/
435 CP	Peter	2	/Two years! And it was all a mistake./Julia! Why don't *you* say anything?/{J} You
436 CP	Reilly	39	/{R} You state the position correctly, Julia./Do you mind if I quote poetry, Julia?
439 CP	Peter	33	see you both, very much./Good-bye, Julia. Good-bye, Alex. Good-bye, Sir Henry. {}/
439 CP	Reilly	37	may be arriving at any moment./{R} Julia, you are right. It is also right/That the
440 CP	Edward	8	moment is a fresh beginning;/And Julia, that life is only keeping on;/And
440 CP	m	19	going to the Gunnings. {}/[*Exeunt* JULIA, REILLY *and* ALEX]/{L} Edward, how

JULIA'S (2)

354 CP	Celia	3	it, but I don't remember it./{C} And Julia's the only person to tell it./She's such a
388 CP	Lavinia	31	any telegrams./{L} This is some of Julia's mischief./And is *she* coming?/{P} Yes,

JULIET (1)

601 Nocturne		3	and hat in hand, beside the gate/With Juliet, in the usual debate/Of love, beneath a

JULIET'S (1)

18 Portrait		6	ceiling overhead,/An atmosphere of Juliet's tomb/Prepared for all the things to be

JULY (2)
| 424 CP | | 3m | 1 | *Two years later./A late afternoon in July.* A CATERER'S MAN *is arranging a buffet* |
| 429 CP | Julia | 37 | | gin./Not a cocktail. I'm freezing — in July!/{CM} Mr. Quilpe!/{E} Now who ... {}/ |

JUMP (4)
216 Jellicles		23	Cats are of moderate size;/Jellicles jump like a jumping-jack,/Jellicle Cats have
229 Gus		48	And they think they are smart, just to jump through a hoop.'/And he'll say, as he
472 CC	Colby	3	if you left things to themselves./You jump — because you're afraid of being pushed./
536 ES	Gomez	6	was jumping a gap — and you can't jump back again./I parted from myself by a

JUMPING (1)
| 536 ES | Gomez | 6 | there was no social ladder./It was jumping a gap — and you can't jump back |

JUMPING-JACK (2)
| 216 Jellicles | | 23 | of moderate size;/Jellicles jump like a jumping-jack,/Jellicle Cats have moonlit eyes./ |
| 602 Humoresque | | 4 | —/But weak in body as in head,/(A jumping-jack has such a frame)./But this |

JUNCTIONS (1)
| 390 CP | Julia | 37 | on the old Great Eastern,/Waiting at junctions. And I suppose she's famished./{A} |

JUNCTURE (1)
| 245 MC | Priest2 | 1 | /{P2} What a way to talk at such a juncture!/You are foolish, immodest and |

JUNE (2)
| 109 Marina | | 26 | and the canvas rotten/Between one June and another September./Made this |
| 285 FR | Amy | 3 | I sit in the house from October to June,/And the swallow comes too soon and the |

JUNGLE (3)
74 WL: Thund		398	far distant, over Himavant./The jungle crouched, humped in silence./Then spoke
204 de la Mare		6	the mangabey, abound/In the dark jungle of a mango grove,/And shadowy lemurs
434 CP	Alex	15	two of them escaped:/One died in the jungle, and the other/Will never be fit for

JUNIOR (1)
| 326 FR | Harry | 14 | inquest/On the characters of all the junior members?/Or engaged in predicting the |

JUNIPER-TREE (2)
| 91 Ash-Wed 2 | | 1 | three white leopards sat under a juniper-tree/In the cool of the day, having fed to |
| 92 Ash-Wed 2 | | 48 | Garden/Where all love ends./Under a juniper-tree the bones sang, scattered and |

JUNKS (2)
| 213 Growltiger | | 32 | creeping in their sampans and their junks./Growltiger had no eye or ear for aught |
| 213 Growltiger | | 43 | sampans, and their pullaways and junks,/They battened down the hatches on the |

JURISDICTION (1)
| 252 MC | Tempt3 | 2 | and for Rome,/Ending the tyrannous jurisdiction/Of king's court over bishop's court,/ |

JURY (1)
| 276 MC | Knight1 | 26 | long-established/principle of Trial by Jury. I am not myself qualified to/put our case |

JUSQU'À (1)
| 47 Mél Adult | | 15 | A divers coups de tra là là/De Damas jusqu'à Omaha./Je célébrai mon jour de fête/ |

JUST (217)

JUSTICE (7)
249 MC	Tempt2	7	good of the better cause,/Dispensing justice make all even,/Is thrive on earth, and
269 MC	Knight1	5	and his fold./{K1} The King's justice, the King's majesty,/You insult with
269 MC	Knights	26	words./{4K} We come for the King's justice, we come with swords. {}/[*Exeunt*]/{C} I
278 MC	Knight2	33	is the only way in/which social justice can be secured. At another time, you
279 MC	Knight4	21	the stability, order, tranquillity,/and justice that it so badly needed. From the
282 MC	Chorus	9	fear the injustice of men less than the justice of God;/Who fear the hand at the
560 ES	Ld Clav	36	fugitive./{LC} No, not a fugitive from justice —/Only a fugitive from reality./Oh

JUSTIFICATION (3)
277 MC	Knight1	31	But/our act itself needs more justification than that; and you must hear/our
314 FR	Harry	18	well./{H} Not, I think, without some justification:/For what you call restoration to
545 ES	Ld Clav	3	/Has impelled me all my life to find justification/Not so much to the world — first

JUSTIFIED (1)
| 158 Rock 5 | | 7 | of the Christians.' And these are not justified, nor the others./And they write |

JUSTIFY (4)
280 MC	Priest3	32	one endless round/Of thought, to justify your action to yourselves,/Weaving a
380 CP	Celia	18	is really too crude a subterfuge/To justify yourself. There was never anything/
403 CP	Reilly	15	them./Or they do not see it, or they justify it/Because they are absorbed in the
467 CC	Colby	25	for me;/And I want to do my best to justify your kindness/By the work I do./{SC} As

JUSTLY (1)
| 409 CP | Reilly | 16 | Then you realised, what your wife has justly remarked,/That you had never been in |

JUVESCENCE (1)
| 37 Gerontion | | 19 | word,/Swaddled with darkness. In the juvescence of the year/Came Christ the tiger/In |

53 Whispers		32	our lot crawls between dry ribs/To keep our metaphysics warm./Mr. Eliot's Sunday
63 WL: Burial		74	the sudden frost disturbed its bed?/'O keep the Dog far hence, that's friend to men,/
152 Rock 2		34	all that was good you must fight to keep with hearts as devoted as those of your
155 Rock 3		38	the LORD build with us./Can you keep the City that the LORD keeps not with
202 War Poetry		13	/Are only 'incidents'/In the effort to keep day and night together./It seems just
209 NamingCats		15	and more dignified,/Else how can he keep up his tail perpendicular,/Or spread out his
210 Old Gumbie		19	she finds that the mice will not ever keep quiet,/She is sure it is due to irregular diet/
235 Ad-dress		42	should ad-dress a Cat./But always keep in mind that he/Resents familiarity./I bow,
236 Cat Morgan		10	gruff,/But I've got a good coat, and I keep meself smart;/And everyone says, and I
588 Fable		32	then, of course,/I'll be compelled to keep them off by force.'/He drencht the gown
589 Fable		68	ghosts are fellows whom you *can't* keep out;/It is a thing to be lamented sorely/
599 On a Port		11	the slender hands;/Her dark eyes keep their secrets hid from us,/Beyond the circle
240 MC	Chorus	1	content if we are left alone./We try to keep our households in order;/The merchant,
241 MC	Priest3	4	but one law, to seize the power and keep it,/And the steadfast can manipulate the
249 MC	Thomas	40	cause./{T} No! shall I, who keep the keys/Of heaven and hell, supreme
250 MC	Thomas	10	power, to build a good world,/To keep order, as the world knows order./Those
262 MC	Thomas	3	not the last. I would have you keep in your hearts/these words that I say, and
263 MC	Chorus	14	world is always uncertain, unless men keep the peace of God./And war among men
265 MC	Knight4	34	/{K4} How much longer will you keep us waiting? {}/[Enter THOMAS]/[to
268 MC	Thomas	19	wish/To deprive my people of me and keep me from my own/And bid me sit in
272 MC	Thomas	9	Seize him! force him! drag him!/{T} Keep your hands off!/{3P} To vespers! Hurry. {}
286 FR	Violet	17	see the vulgarest people —/You can keep out of their way at home;/People with
287 FR	Amy	26	leave Wishwood/That is the reason. I keep Wishwood alive/To keep the family alive,
287 FR	Amy	27	the reason. I keep Wishwood alive/To keep the family alive, to keep them together,/To
287 FR	Amy	27	alive/To keep the family alive, to keep them together,/To keep me alive, and I live
287 FR	Amy	28	alive, to keep them together,/To keep me alive, and I live to keep them./You
287 FR	Amy	28	/To keep me alive, and I live to keep them./You none of you understand how
290 FR	Amy	1	one of the family,/She only wanted to keep him to herself/To satisfy her vanity. That's
293 FR	Amy	7	business./I have only struggled to keep Wishwood going/And to make no changes
300 FR	Downing	4	anxious about my Lady./Tried to keep her in when the weather was rough,/Didn't
303 FR	Mary	14	be late, of course./We may have to keep the dinner back .../{Ag} And also Dr.
304 FR	Mary	20	I know very well/Why she wanted to keep me. She didn't need me:/She would have
305 FR	Mary	18	waiting./I think this house *means* to keep us waiting. {}/[Enter HARRY]/{H}
314 FR	Warburt	12	measles/And we had such a time to keep you in bed./You didn't like being ill in the
322 FR	Harry	8	I may ask, my Lord?/{H} Why do you keep asking/About her Ladyship? Do you know
331 FR	Agatha	22	my dispossession,/And many years to keep it. What people know me as,/The efficient
342 FR	Mary	23	me, but I tell you I know./You must keep him here, you must not let him leave./I do
343 FR	Amy	24	crumble. Why should I worry/To keep the tiles on the roof, combat the endless
347 FR	Agatha	12	all, thank you, Downing. We mustn't keep you;/His Lordship will be wondering why
355 CP	Julia	22	quite impossible!/Leaving it to me to keep things going./What a host! And nothing fit
365 CP	Reilly	9	*she took my heart entirely*/You will keep our appointment?/{E} I shall keep it. {}/
365 CP	Edward	10	will keep our appointment?/{E} I shall keep it. {}/[Sings]./{UG} *Tooryooly toory-iley*,/
366 CP	Julia	6	Why no, of course not: that's where I keep them./Oh, here they are! Thank you,
376 CP	Julia	19	/He's under such a strain. We must keep his strength up./Edward! Don't you realise
385 CP	Reilly	10	it is perhaps still more difficult/To keep up the pretence that you are not strangers./
396 CP	Edward	36	a personality for me/Which will only keep me away from myself./{L} You're
399 CP	Nurse	12	at a quarter past;/But you may keep her waiting./{R} Or she may keep me
399 CP	Reilly	13	keep her waiting./{R} Or she may keep me waiting;/But I think she will be
401 CP	Reilly	2	/Please sit down. I won't keep you a moment./— Now, Mr.
404 CP	Edward	30	And at my club/They won't let you keep a room for more than seven days;/I
414 CP	Celia	17	a place in town./It's all they can do to keep the country house going:/But it's been in
420 CP	Julia	24	about./{J} Nonsense, Henry. *I* shall keep an eye on them./{R} To send them back:
421 CP	Julia	38	/— But how much longer will Alex keep us waiting?/{R} He should be here by now.
453 CC	Kaghan	32	The problem with Lucasta/Is how to keep her fed between meals./{L} B., you're a
466 CC	Claude	8	play to yourself. And as for me,/I keep my pieces in a private room./It isn't that I
475 CC	Colby	9	do is to understand them better,/To keep up with them; so that as the other changes/
480 CC	Kaghan	10	never take a leap in the dark;/You'd keep me on the rails./{C} That's just nonsense./
500 CC	Claude	13	came here. But I didn't trust you/To keep a secret. There were reasons for that/
508 CC	Guzzard	23	to adopt the child,/Or continue to keep him, when the payments ended./{E} And
510 CC	Kaghan	31	place near Sevenoaks/Where they keep bees. But why are you asking?/{LE}
529 ES	Ld Clav	32	— or one just like it —/You know I keep the old ones on a shelf together;/I could
534 ES	Gomez	30	have an aeroplane ready:/And keep an account in a bank in Switzerland./The
540 ES	Gomez	6	in my opinion,/Is the man who has to keep on pretending to himself/That he's a
541 ES	Gomez	19	/To make money in — though not to *keep* it in./My investments — not all in my own
541 ES	Gomez	23	in Stockholm or Zürich/Would keep me in comfort for the rest of my life./

541 ES	Gomez	38	in financial distress./Well, I shan't keep you long, though I dare say your caller/
542 ES	Ld Clav	14	company/On a man by threats? Why keep up the pretence?/{G} Threats, Dick! How
558 ES	Michael	18	your sake, he says,/That he wants to keep things quiet. I can tell you, it's no joke/
568 ES	Ld Clav	12	wish to forget? Which you wish to keep unknown?/{C} There are certainly things I
580 ES	Carghil	24	each other again,/We must always keep in touch. But you'd better rest now./
581 ES	Ld Clav	19	myself in him./Why did I want to keep you to myself, Monica?/Because I wanted

KEEPERS (1)

159 Rock 6		9	World/And that lions no longer need keepers?/Do you need to be told that whatever

KEEPIN' (1)

236 Cat Morgan		4	you find me a-takin' my ease/And keepin' the door in a Bloomsbury Square./I'm

KEEPING (13)

178 FQ: ECoker		40	under earth/Nourishing the corn. Keeping time,/Keeping the rhythm in their
178 FQ: ECoker		41	/Nourishing the corn. Keeping time,/Keeping the rhythm in their dancing/As in their
184 FQ: DrySal		8	in cities — ever, however, implacable,/Keeping his seasons and rages, destroyer,
233 Skimble		53	perhaps a drop of Scotch while he's keeping on the watch,/Only stopping here and
264 MC	Priests	23	from Christmas./{3P} *Rejoice we all, keeping holy day.*/{P1} As for the people, so also
264 MC	Priests	26	life for the sheep./{3P} *Rejoice we all, keeping holy day.*/{P1} To-day?/{P2} To-day,
300 FRDowning		25	is always most considerate/About keeping me up. But when I say I saw him,/I
329 FR	Chorus	15	the transparent deception/The keeping up of appearances/The making the best
440 CP	Edward	8	beginning;/And Julia, that life is only keeping on;/And somehow, the two ideas seem
488 CC	Claude	25	told you one day./I've always loathed keeping such a thing from you./I see now I
489 CC	Claude	12	me./And I found a better reason for keeping silent./I came to see how you longed for
553 ES	Carghil	22	Oh, not very many. Only a few worth keeping./Only a few. But very beautiful!/It was
569 ES	Ld Clav	9	false pretences./Now, I'm tired of keeping up those pretences,/But I hope that

KEEPS (5)

37 Gerontion		13	stonecrop, iron, merds./The woman keeps the kitchen, makes tea,/Sneezes at
155 Rock 3		38	you keep the City that the LORD keeps not with you?/A thousand policemen
308 FR	Mary	14	be./But in this world another hope keeps springing/In an unexpected place, while
320 FR	Warburt	9	/Her indomitable will, that keeps her alive./I needn't go into technicalities/
461 CC	Eggers	14	often./{E} Oh, and I forgot ... Mrs. E. keeps saying:/'Why don't you ask him out to

KEGS (1)

588 Fable		53	flagons which perhaps held several kegs/Of ale, and cheese which they kept under

KEINE (1)

61 WL: Burial		12	and talked for an hour./Bin gar keine Russin, stamm' aus Litauen, echt deutsch.

KENSINGTON (1)

218 Mung Rump		5	Gardens, in Launceston Place and in Kensington Square —/They had really a little

KENT (3)

246 MC Thomas		9	/Broc, Warenne, and the Sheriff of Kent,/Those who had sworn to have my head
275 MC Chorus		23	my eyes. Where is England? where is Kent? where is Canterbury?/O far far far far in
510 CC Kaghan		29	your adoptive parents living?/{K} In Kent. They wanted to retire to the country./So I

KENTISH (1)

45 Cook Egg		28	scavengers are creeping/From Kentish Town and Golder's Green;/Where are

KEPT (28)

30 Cous Nancy		11	was modern./Upon the glazen shelves kept watch/Matthew and Waldo, guardians of
38 Gerontion		58	should I need to keep it/Since what is kept must be adulterated?/I have lost my sight,
61 WL: Burial		5	/Dull roots with spring rain./Winter kept us warm, covering/Earth in forgetful snow,
62 WL: Burial		67	/To where Saint Mary Woolnoth kept the hours/With a dead sound on the final
73 WL: Thund		383	towers/Tolling reminiscent bells, that kept the hours/And voices singing out of empty
105 Song Sime		10	I have walked many years in this city,/Kept faith and fast, provided for the poor,/
124 SA Sweeney		16	Once in a lifetime, do a girl in/Well he kept her there in a bath/With a gallon of lysol in
587 Fable		14	multiplied,/As if they had been kept by a kind fairy./Alas! no fairy visited their
588 Fable		50	standing on both legs/With difficulty kept from toppling over,/Next came a viand
588 Fable		54	kegs/Of ale, and cheese which they kept under cover./Last, a boar's head, which to
244 MC Chorus		4	/Living and partly living./We have kept the feasts, heard the masses,/We have
279 MC Knight4		34	have easily escaped; he/could have kept himself from us long enough to allow our
288 FR	Amy	29	Agatha, at Wishwood./Everything is kept as it was when he left it,/Except the old
305 FR	Mary	32	mother insisted/On everything being kept the same as when you left it./{H} I wish she
306 FR	Mary	28	were reasons: I was only a cousin/Kept here because there was nothing else to do
310 FR	Harry	38	to another,/Or to a blank wall; that I kept moving/Only so as not to stay still. Singing
319 FR	Harry	5	him, and I know very well/That I was kept apart from him, till he went away./We
320 FR	Warburt	18	until now./Her determination has kept her going:/She has only lived for your
328 FR	Charles	32	/{C} In my time, these affairs were kept out of the papers;/But nowadays, there's
340 FR	Amy	17	I could plant here. Seven years I kept him,/For the sake of the future, a
354 CP	Alex	33	wouldn't know the third one:/They kept him rather quiet./{J} Oh, you mean *that*
366 CP	Julia	12	Anthony./And now I must fly. I've kept the taxi waiting./Come along, Peter./{P} I

383 CP Edward 28   .../Well, I'm awfully sorry to have kept you waiting;/But we ... I had to hunt for
396 CP Lavinia 9   rather attractive, you know;/And you kept on *saying* that you were in love with me —
481 CC Kaghan 35   no, as a matter of fact, I haven't./I've kept meaning to. Shall we go there, Lucasta?/
507 CC Guzzard 36   Elizabeth?/Are you suggesting that I kept a child of yours/And deceived Sir Claude
533 ES Gomez 30   an unkind suggestion./I've always kept on the right side of the law —/And seen
570 ES Monica 2   ghosts mean? All these years/You've kept them to yourself. Did Mother know of

KER-FLIP (1)
213 Growltiger 52   end of all his crimes was forced to go ker-flip, ker-flop./Oh there was joy in Wapping

KER-FLOP (1)
213 Growltiger 52   his crimes was forced to go ker-flip, ker-flop./Oh there was joy in Wapping when the

KERB (1)
220 Old Deut 21   /The cars and the lorries run over the kerb,/And the villagers put up a notice: ROAD

KEW (1)
70 WL: Fire S 293   /Highbury bore me. Richmond and Kew/Undid me. By Richmond I raised my

KEY (6)
26 Rhapsody 73   on the door./Memory!/You have the key,/The little lamp spreads a ring on the stair./
74 WL: Thund 411   /DA/*Dayadhvam:* I have heard the key/Turn in the door once and turn once only/
74 WL: Thund 413   and turn once only/We think of the key, each in his prison/Thinking of the key,
74 WL: Thund 414   each in his prison/Thinking of the key, each confirms a prison/Only at nightfall,
278 MC Knight2 5   /the answer to these questions lies the key to the problem./The King's aim has been
473 CC Colby 25   They seem so unrelated./I turn the key, and walk through the gate,/And there I am

KEYS (3)
33 Conv Gal 7   I then: 'Someone frames upon the keys/That exquisite nocturne, with which we
249 MC Thomas 40   cause./{T} No! shall I, who keep the keys/Of heaven and hell, supreme alone in
253 MC Tempt4 29   sin, since Adam fell —/You hold the keys of heaven and hell./Power to bind and

KICK (1)
194 FQ: Little 119   is eaten/And the fullfed beast shall kick the empty pail./For last year's words

KICKING (1)
103 Journ Magi 28   dicing for pieces of silver,/And feet kicking the empty wine-skins./But there was no

KICKS (1)
239 MC Chorus 12   in darkness./While the labourer kicks off a muddy boot and stretches his hand

KIDNEY (1)
44 Cook Egg 12   Coriolanus/And other heroes of that kidney./I shall not want Capital in Heaven/For

KILL (4)
269 MC Thomas 20   to the judgement of Rome./But if you kill me, I shall rise from my tomb/To submit my
275 MC m 21   of the Church. {}/*While the* KNIGHTS *kill him, we hear the* CHORUS./{C} Clear the
277 MC Knight3 11   /point, it does go against the grain to kill an Archbishop, especially/when you have
333 FR Agatha 5   have bungled it./I did not want to kill *you*!/You to be killed! What were you then?

KILLED (10)
261 MC Thomas 20   as a good Christian who/has been killed because he is a Christian: for that would
271 MC Priests 27   break through presently./You will be killed. Come to the altar./Make haste, my Lord.
271 MC Priests 29   become of us, my Lord, if you are killed; what shall become of us?/{T} Peace! be
279 MC Knight4 14   be put in the form of a question: *Who killed/the Archbishop?* As you have been
279 MC Knight4 28   not long to live, and/that he would be killed in England. He used every means of
304 FR Mary 29   Amy —/I almost believed it — had killed her by willing./Doesn't that sound awful?
333 FR Agatha 6   /I did not want to kill *you*!/You to be killed! What were you then? only a thing called
428 CP Alex 13   veneration/And do not want them killed. So they blame the Government/For the
488 CC Lady E 3   That was all I knew./Then Tony was killed, as you know, in Africa,/And I had lost
572 ES Ld Clav 3   that we had run over/So neither of us killed him. But *I* didn't stop./And all my life I

KILLING (1)
484 CC Lady E 23   /They were so carnivorous. Always killing things and eating them./And yet our

KIN (2)
195 FQ: Little 173   commendable,/Of no immediate kin or kindness,/But some of peculiar genius,/
201 Def Island 21   past and the future generations/of our kin and of our speech, that we took up/our

KIND (64)
116 SP Dusty 37   Goooood bye./I'm sure, that's very kind of *you*./Ah-h-h/{Do} Now I'm going to cut
151 Rock 2 16   saints,/Apostles, martyrs, in a kind of Whipsnade,/Then they could set about
172 FQ: BurntN 44   /Go, go, go, said the bird: human kind/Cannot bear very much reality./Time past
182 FQ: ECoker 177   /Is a wholly new start, and a different kind of failure/Because one has only learnt to
195 FQ: Little 150   disfigured street/He left me, with a kind of valediction,/And faded on the blowing
209 NamingCats 17   or cherish his pride?/Of names of this kind, I can give you a quorum,/Such as
210 Old Gumbie 2   /Her coat is of the tabby kind, with tiger stripes and leopard spots./All
587 Fable 14   /As if they had been kept by a kind fairy./Alas! no fairy visited their host,/Oh,
602 Humoresque 7   /I rather liked: a common face,/(The kind of face that we forget)/Pinched in a comic,
239 MC Chorus 20   left us,/He who was always kind to his people./But it would not be well if he

245 MC Thomas   36   /I am more than grateful for all your kind attentions./These are small matters. Little
258 MC Thomas   4   /Temptation shall not come in this kind again./The last temptation is the greatest
271 MC Thomas   19   They will seem unreal./Human kind cannot bear very much reality. {}/[*Enter*
276 MC Chorus   10   had its definition,/Every sorrow had a kind of end:/In life there is not time to grieve
299 FRDowning   37   /Suffered from what they call a kind of repression./But what struck me ... more
310 FR   Mary   18   Pain is the opposite of joy/But joy is a kind of pain/I believe the moment of birth/Is
324 FR   Harry   16   to John./A brief vacation from the kind of consciousness/That John enjoys, can't
332 FR Agatha   30   only come once,/Thank God, that kind. Perhaps there is another kind,/I believe,
332 FR Agatha   30   that kind. Perhaps there is another kind,/I believe, across a whole Thibet of broken
334 FR   Harry   22   of all of us. Family affection/Was a kind of formal obligation, a duty/Only noticed
334 FR   Harry   39   live in public./Liberty is a different kind of pain from prison./{Ag} I only looked
336 FR   Harry   8   /Why is it so quiet?/Do you feel a kind of stirring underneath the air?/Do you?
346 FRDowning   20   better than anybody;/And I have a kind of feeling that his Lordship won't need me/
346 FRDowning   24   happened to his Lordship/Was just a kind of preparation for something else./I've no
365 CP   Julia   2   You can tell if they're mine —/Some kind of a plastic sort of frame —/I'm afraid I
365 CP   Julia   18   been *drinking* together!/So this is the kind of friend you have/When Lavinia is out of
369 CP   Peter   2   say that./But Lavinia was awfully kind to me/And I owe her a great deal. And
375 CP   Edward   9   ourselves. But I do not know/What kind of a trap it is./{C} Then what has
389 CP Lavinia   33   to be happy./{L} You are very kind, but very mysterious./I'm sure that we shall
394 CP   Edward   34   supply a public background/For your kind of public life. You wished to be a hostess/
396 CP   Edward   33   responsible for me:/It's only another kind of contempt./And I do not want you to
396 CP Lavinia   39   clearly:/We are not to relapse into the kind of life we led/Until yesterday morning./{E}
403 CP   Reilly   4   me./I could make you dream any kind of dream I suggested,/And it would only
406 CP   Reilly   13   not a sanatorium/What was it?/{R} A kind of hotel. A retreat/For people who imagine
415 CP   Celia   36   other word for it./It must be some kind of hallucination;/Yet, at the same time, I'm
418 CP   Celia   7   of my illness,/But I feel it would be a kind of surrender —/No, not a surrender —
418 CP   Celia   15   *any*body!/I couldn't give anyone the kind of love —/I wish I could — which belongs
418 CP   Reilly   25   and so requires faith —/The kind of faith that issues from despair./The
420 CP   Celia   16   *button*]/{C} You have been very kind./{R} Go in peace, my daughter./Work out
421 CP   Julia   19   what do we know?/Of the kind of suffering they must undergo/On the way
439 CP   Julia   10   /Everyone makes a choice, of one kind or another,/And then must take the
455 CC Eggers   9   with this household?/{E} Well. A kind of fiduciary relationship./No, I don't think
457 CC   Colby   8   Mr. Eggerson:/That *you* have a kind heart. And I'm convinced/That you always
462 CC Claude   12   If she comes to think of you/As the kind of man that her son would have been —/
463 CC   Colby   14   interests./It gives me, in a way, a kind of self-confidence/I've never had before.
464 CC Claude   36   as it is changing you:/It begins as a kind of make-believe/And the make-believing
466 CC Claude   17   she calls the life of the spirit/Are a kind of substitute for religion./I dare say truly
466 CC Claude   22   at best to live/In two worlds — each a kind of make-believe./That's you and me. Some
467 CC   Colby   9   I have always thought of you —/As a kind of protector, a generous provider:/Rather
471 CC   Colby   39   of times,/I decided that was only your kind of self-defence./{L} What made you think
477 CC Lucasta   29   you'd come to see me as the real kind of person/That I want to be. That I know I
482 CC   Lady E   15   sort of person/They ever meet in their kind of society./So naturally, they want to take
482 CC   Colby   22   to?/They're both intelligent ... and kind./{LE} Oh, I don't say they're not intelligent
482 CC   Lady E   23   I don't say they're not intelligent and kind./I'm not making any malicious
486 CC   Colby   20   should I doubt it?/That is not the kind of story my aunt would invent./{LE} Not if
502 CC Lucasta   23   fire/To warm you, that isn't the same kind of fire/That warms other people. You're
540 ES   Gomez   2   failures. But even so,/I'd rather be my kind of failure than yours./{LC} And what do
540 ES   Gomez   5   /{G} What do I call failure?/The worst kind of failure, in my opinion,/Is the man who
540 ES Ld Clav   9   in the mirror./{LC} Isn't that the kind of pretence that you're maintaining/In
545 ES   Monica   35   of helping you!/{M} You're very kind ... Oh, I'm sorry,/We don't know how we
551 ES Carghil   3   lover/Is still, in her memory, a kind of testimonial./Men live by forgetting —
559 ES Ld Clav   17   do? Where do you want to go?/What kind of a life do you think you want?/{Mi} I
559 ES Michael   36   was just your son — that is to say,/A kind of prolongation of your existence,/A
576 ES   Monica   26   family/And your very self — it's a kind of suicide./{C} Michael, you think Señor

KIND (1) [*Foreign word*]
 62 WL: Burial   33   *der Wind/Der Heimat zu/Mein Irisch Kind/Wo weilest du?*/'You gave me hyacinths first
KIND-HEARTED (1)
457 CC   Colby   6   heart./{C} Everybody seems to be kind-hearted./But there's one thing I do believe,
KINDLED (1)
166 Rock 10   26   thank Thee for the lights that we have kindled,/The light of altar and of sanctuary;/
KINDLY (1)
526 ES Charles   33   With his calm possessive air/And his kindly welcome, which is always a reminder/
KINDNESS (5)
195 FQ: Little   173   /Of no immediate kin or kindness,/But some of peculiar genius,/All
462 CC   Colby   23   /Is that good for us? Or a kindness to her?/{SC} If you haven't the

467 CC	Colby	25	I want to do my best to justify your kindness/By the work I do./{SC} As my
541 ES	Gomez	30	it's my turn, perhaps, to do you a kindness. {}/[*Enter* LAMBERT]/{L} Excuse me,
577 ES	Charles	8	paid mine./{C} This return of past kindness/No doubt gives you pleasure?/{G} Yes,

KINDS (3)

234 Ad-dress		1	of Cats/You've read of several kinds of Cat,/And my opinion now is that/You
402 CP	Reilly	28	Mr. Chamberlayne./There are several kinds of sanatoria/For several kinds of patient.
402 CP	Reilly	29	several kinds of sanatoria/For several kinds of patient. And there are also patients/For

KING (79)

62 WL: Burial	66	his feet./Flowed up the hill and down King William Street,/To where Saint Mary
64 WL: Chess	99	change of Philomel, by the barbarous king/So rudely forced; yet there the nightingale/
67 WL: Fire S	191	the gashouse/Musing upon the king my brother's wreck/And on the king my
67 WL: Fire S	192	king my brother's wreck/And on the king my father's death before him./White bodies
117 SP	Doris	2	is/{Du} First is. What is?/{Do} The King of Clubs/{Du} That's Pereira/{Do} It
157 Rock 4	6	Nisan,/He served the wine to the king Artaxerxes,/And he grieved for the broken
157 Rock 4	8	the broken city, Jerusalem;/And the King gave him leave to depart/That he might
162 Rock 8	27	seven deadly sins in Syria./But our King did well at Acre./And in spite of all the
191 FQ: Little	27	/If you came at night like a broken king,/If you came by day not knowing what you
195 FQ: Little	177	which divided them;/If I think of a king at nightfall,/Of three men, and more, on
587 Fable	2	long before that royal Mormon/King Henry VIII found out that monks were
229 MC Chorus	22	would not be well if he should return./King rules or barons rule;/We have suffered
240 MC Priest2	29	Lord the Pope/With the stubborn King and the French King/In ceaseless intrigue,
240 MC Priest2	29	the stubborn King and the French King/In ceaseless intrigue, combinations,/In
241 MC Priest3	2	duplicity and frequent malversation./King rules or barons rule:/The strong man
241 MC Priest1	18	Lord Archbishop/Reunited with the King? what reconciliation/Of two proud men?/
241 MC Mess	38	is at one with the Pope, and also the King of France,/Who indeed would have liked
242 MC Mess	1	him in his kingdom:/But as for our King, that is another matter./{P1} But again, is
242 MC Mess	11	when the Archbishop/Parted from the King, he said to the King,/My Lord, he said, I
242 MC Mess	11	/Parted from the King, he said to the King,/My Lord, he said, I leave you as a man/
242 MC Priest1	20	him as Chancellor, flattered by the King./Liked or feared by courtiers, in their
242 MC Priest1	29	subjection to God alone./Had the King been greater, or had he been weaker/
242 MC Priest2	35	is at one with the Pope, and also the King of France./We can lean on a rock, we can
246 MC Tempt1	32	that evening on the river/When the King, and you and I were all friends together?/
246 MC Tempt1	35	that you recover/Favour with the King, shall we say that summer's over/Or that
247 MC Tempt1	3	and wine and wisdom!/Now that the King and you are in amity,/Clergy and laity
247 MC Tempt1	33	loud,/This was not the way of the King our master!/You were not used to be so
248 MC Tempt2	38	/{T} Who then?/{T2} The Chancellor, King and Chancellor./King commands.
249 MC Tempt2	1	Chancellor, King and Chancellor./King commands. Chancellor richly rules./This is
250 MC Thomas	15	what they exalt. Power with the King —/I *was* the King, his arm, his better
250 MC Thomas	16	Power with the King —/I *was* the King, his arm, his better reason./But what was
250 MC Tempt3	35	not the plotting parasites/About the King. Excuse my bluntness:/I am a rough
251 MC Tempt3	13	of reconciliation/With Henry the King. You look only/To blind assertion in
251 MC Thomas	16	That is a mistake./{T} O Henry, O my King!/{T3} Other friends/May be found in the
251 MC Tempt3	19	be found in the present situation./King in England is not all-powerful;/King is in
251 MC Tempt3	20	/King in England is not all-powerful;/King is in France, squabbling in Anjou;/Round
252 MC Thomas	9	if the Archbishop cannot trust the King,/How can he trust those who work for
252 MC Thomas	22	/No one shall say that I betrayed a king./{T3} Then, my Lord, I shall not wait at
252 MC Tempt3	25	well hope, before another spring/The King will show his regard for your loyalty./{T}
253 MC Tempt4	6	/Wantonness is weakness. As for the King,/His hardened hatred shall have no end./
253 MC Tempt4	8	have no end./You know truly, the King will never trust/Twice, the man who has
253 MC Tempt4	25	kingly rule,/Or rule of men beneath a king,/With craft in corners, stealthy stratagem,/
253 MC Tempt4	31	bind and loose: bind, Thomas, bind,/King and bishop under your heel./King,
253 MC Tempt4	32	/King and bishop under your heel./King, emperor, bishop, baron, king:/Uncertain
253 MC Tempt4	32	heel./King, emperor, bishop, baron, king:/Uncertain mastery of melting armies,/
253 MC Tempt4	38	course of temporal power./The Old King shall know it, when at last breath,/No
254 MC Tempt4	11	think of glory after death./When king is dead, there's another king,/And one
254 MC Tempt4	11	/When king is dead, there's another king,/And one more king is another reign./King
254 MC Tempt4	12	there's another king,/And one more king is another reign./King is forgotten, when
254 MC Tempt4	13	/And one more king is another reign./King is forgotten, when another shall come:/
255 MC Tempt4	9	of God?/What earthly glory, of king or emperor,/What earthly pride, that is not
258 MC Thomas	28	sorrow, than the man who serves a king./For those who serve the greater cause may
260 MC Thomas	29	the barons at peace with the King, the householder counting/over his
265 MC Knight1	9	*disappear*]/{K1} Servants of the King./{P1} And known to us./You are welcome.
265 MC Knight3	17	{K2} Urgent business./{K3} From the King./{K2} By the King's order./{K1} Our men
266 MC Thomas	8	business may be./You say, from the King?/{K1} Most surely from the King./We
266 MC Knight1	9	the King?/{K1} Most surely from the King./We must speak with you alone. {}/[*to*

KINGDOMS (2)

84 Hollow Men		56	valley/This broken jaw of our lost kingdoms/In this last of meeting places/We
104 Journ Magi		40	/We returned to our places, these Kingdoms,/But no longer at ease here, in the

KINGFISHER'S (1)

175 FQ: BurntN		137	yew be curled/Down on us? After the kingfisher's wing/Has answered light to light,

KINGLY (1)

253 MC	Tempt4	24	already chosen./But what is pleasure, kingly rule,/Or rule of men beneath a king,/

KINGS (6)

107 Animula		14	/Content with playing-cards and kings and queens,/What the fairies do and what
250 MC	Thomas	5	the doom of damnation,/To condemn kings, not serve among their servants,/Is my
252 MC	Tempt3	11	who work for King's undoing?/{T3} Kings will allow no power but their own;/
253 MC	Tempt4	16	still more stubborn than king's anger./Kings have public policy, barons private profit,/
253 MC	Tempt4	19	each other;/Greater enemies must kings destroy./{T} What is your counsel?/{T4}
254 MC	Tempt4	25	Your thoughts have more power than kings to compel you./You have also thought,

KINGS' (1)

250 MC	Tempt2	8	/Your sin soars sunward, covering kings' falcons./{T} Temporal power, to build a

KINK (1)

415 CP	Reilly	30	suppose you have what you call a 'kink'?/{C} But everything seemed so right, at the

KINKAJOU (1)

204 de la Mare		5	here the water buffalo may rove,/The kinkajou, the mangabey, abound/In the dark

KINKANJA (11)

427 CP	Alex	7	on earth? From the East. From Kinkanja —/An island that you won't have
427 CP	Alex	23	strange place —/What's it called?/{A} Kinkanja./{J} What were you doing/In
427 CP	Julia	25	/{J} What were you doing/In Kinkanja? Visiting some Sultan?/You were
427 CP	Alex	28	/{A} There are no tigers, Julia,/In Kinkanja. And there are no sultans./I have been
430 CP	Alex	39	I didn't see it./There is no cinema in Kinkanja./{P} Kinkanja? Where's that? They
431 CP	Peter	1	/There is no cinema in Kinkanja./{P} Kinkanja? Where's that? They don't have
433 CP	Julia	35	/The news that you bring back from Kinkanja./{L} Kinkanja? What was Celia doing
433 CP	Lavinia	36	you bring back from Kinkanja./{L} Kinkanja? What was Celia doing in Kinkanja?/
433 CP	Lavinia	36	Kinkanja? What was Celia doing in Kinkanja?/We heard that she had joined some
434 CP	Alex	1	I remember./{A} She was directed to Kinkanja,/Where there are various endemic
439 CP	Julia	12	/A way of which the consequence was Kinkanja./Peter chose a way that leads him to

KINKS (1)

415 CP	Celia	27	everything's bad form, or mental kinks,/You either become bad form, and cease

KINKY (1)

415 CP	Celia	29	care,/Or else, if you care, you must be kinky./{R} And so you suppose you have what

KISS (3)

69 WL: Fire S		247	dead.)/Bestows one final patronising kiss,/And gropes his way, finding the stairs unlit
84 Hollow Men		50	with tenderness/Lips that would kiss/Form prayers to broken stone./The eyes are
242 MC	Mess	3	war or peace?/{M} Peace, but not the kiss of peace./A patched up affair, if you ask my

KISSED (1)

319 FR	Harry	34	/Yes, I see now. That night, when she kissed me,/I felt the trap close. If you won't tell

KISSES (1)

107 Animula		5	chairs,/Rising or falling, grasping at kisses and toys,/Advancing boldly, sudden to

KISSING-TIME (1)

248 MC	Tempt1	8	at your prayers,/I'll remember you at kissing-time below the stairs./{T}

KIST (1)

50 Hippopot		34	as snow,/By all the martyr'd virgins kist,/While the True Church remains below/

KIT (1)

579 ES	Michael	8	get a passage./And I must buy my kit. We're just going up to London./Señor

KITCHEN (14)

37 Gerontion		13	iron, merds./The woman keeps the kitchen, makes tea,/Sneezes at evening, poking
270 MC	Chorus	12	was coming to be? It was here, in the kitchen, in the passage,/In the mews in the barn
293 FR	Violet	1	/About the waste that goes on in the kitchen./Mrs. Packell is too old to know what
329 FR	Chorus	10	in autumn/And the singing in the kitchen/And the steps at night in the corridor/
368 CP	Alex	15	cook./I'm going straight to your kitchen now/And I shall prepare you a nice little
368 CP	m	28	word./I shall begin at once. {}/[*Exit to kitchen*]/{E} Well, where did you leave off?/{P}
369 CP	Edward	9	double boiler:/Isn't there one in every kitchen?/{A} I can't find it./There goes *that*
376 CP	Edward	1	someone came and found you in the kitchen? {}/[EDWARD *goes over to the table*
376 CP	m	7	I'm not going to hide. {}/[*Returns to kitchen. The bell rings again.* EDWARD *goes to*
377 CP	m	18	{}/[*A popping noise is heard from the kitchen*]/{E} What the devil's that? {}/[*Re-enter*
383 CP	Edward	5	my head off .../You're sure, in the kitchen? Beside the champagne bottle?/You're
383 CP	Celia	9	for them./I shall never go into your kitchen again. {}/[*Exit* EDWARD. *He returns*
398 CP	Lavinia	15	/I ought to go and have a look in the kitchen./I know there are some eggs. But we
424 CP	Lavinia	7	you need/That you can't find in the kitchen?/{CM} Nothing, Madam./Will there be

KITCHENS (2)

27 Morning		1	rattling breakfast plates in basement kitchens,/And along the trampled edges of the
127 Cor1 March		22	55,000 army waggons,/11,000 field kitchens,/1,150 field bakeries./What a time that

KITE (2)

270 MC Chorus		6	the air/Flirted with the passage of the kite, I have plunged with the kite and cowered
270 MC Chorus		6	of the kite, I have plunged with the kite and cowered with the wren. I have felt/The

KITES (1)

162 Rock 8		18	lustful./Many left their bodies to the kites of Syria/Or sea-strewn along the routes;/

KITTENS (2)

225 Mr Mistoff		55	this phenomenal Cat/Produced *seven kittens* right out of a hat!/And we all said: OH!/
229 Gus		45	was on fire./And he says: 'Now, these kittens, they do not get trained/As we did in the

KLEIN (1)

41 Burb Blei		29	lights,/She entertains Sir Ferdinand/Klein. Who clipped the lion's wings/And flea'd

KLIP (3)

119 SP	Krum	15	/{Kr} We were all in the war together/Klip and me and the Cap and Sam./{Kl} Yes we
119 SP	Krum	28	/Do we like London!! Eh what Klip?/{Kl} Say, Miss — er — uh — London's
120 SP	Krum	3	stand the pace./What about it Klip?/{Kl} You said it, Krum./London's a slick

KLIPSTEIN (6)

119 SP	m	1	WAUCHOPE. HORSFALL. KLIPSTEIN. KRUMPACKER./{W} Hello
119 SP	Wauch	6	here on business./Meet Mr. Klipstein. Meet Mr. Krumpacker./{Kl} How do
119 SP	Doris	26	last time./{Do} You like London, Mr. Klipstein?/{Kr} Do we like London? do we like
121 SA	m	1	WAUCHOPE. HORSFALL. KLIPSTEIN. KRUMPACKER. SWARTS.
123 SA	1m	13	on your crocodile isle. {}/SONG BY KLIPSTEIN AND KRUMPACKER/SNOW
125 SA	m	31	WAUCHOPE, HORSFALL, KLIPSTEIN, KRUMPACKER/{Ch} When

KLOOTZ (7)

353 CP	Celia	14	you told the other day, about Lady Klootz and the wedding cake./{P} And how the
354 CP	Julia	9	accent./{J} Lithuanian? Lady Klootz?/{P} I thought she was Belgian./{A} Her
354 CP	Julia	16	what's become of them now./{J} Lady Klootz was very lovely, once upon a time./What
354 CP	Julia	19	GUEST]/{J} Did *you* know Lady Klootz?/{UG} No, I never met her./{C} Go on
355 CP	Julia	29	/Well, I started to tell you about Lady Klootz./It was at the Vincewell wedding. Oh, so
358 CP	Peter	14	won't you tell the story about Lady Klootz?/{J} What Lady Klootz?/{C} And the
358 CP	Julia	15	about Lady Klootz?/{J} What Lady Klootz?/{C} And the wedding cake./{J} Wedding

KNAVE (3)

117 SP	Dusty	39	the spell. You cut for luck./{Du} The Knave of Spades./{Do} That'll be Snow/{Du}
118 SP	Dusty	15	I always draw court cards?/The Knave of Hearts! {}/(*Whistle outside of the*
118 SP	Doris	20	course it's Sam!/{Do} Of course, the Knave of Hearts *is* Sam!/{Du} (*leaning out of*

KNEE (5)

37 Gerontion		5	/Nor fought in the warm rain/Nor knee deep in the salt marsh, heaving a cutlass,/
107 Animula		7	/Retreating to the corner of arm and knee,/Eager to be reassured, taking pleasure/In
254 MC Tempt4		20	generation to generation/Bending the knee in supplication,/Think of the miracles, by
281 MC Chorus		14	the back bent in laying the fire, the knee bent in cleaning the hearth, we, the
281 MC Chorus		15	/The back bent under toil, the knee bent under sin, the hands to the face under

KNEEL (2)

192 FQ: Little		47	/Or carry report. You are here to kneel/Where prayer has been valid. And prayer
273 MC Priests		25	men, who/Respect the sanctuary, who kneel to the Body of Christ,/But like beasts.

KNEELED (1)

264 MC Priest1		4	to the Archbishop Thomas./And he kneeled down and cried with a loud voice:/

KNEELS (1)

519 CC	m	7	*crosses to* SIR CLAUDE *and kneels beside him*]/{K} You know, Claude, I

KNEES (10)

20 Portrait		87	as if I had mounted on my hands and knees./'And so you are going abroad; and when
29 Aunt Helen		12	Holding the second housemaid on his knees —/Who had always been so careful while
40 Burb Blei		14	way:/A saggy bending of the knees/And elbows, with the palms turned out,/
42 Swee Erect		17	the thighs/Jackknifes upward at the knees/Then straightens out from heel to hip/
56 Swee Night		1	/Apeneck Sweeney spreads his knees/Letting his arms hang down to laugh,/
56 Swee Night		12	cape/Tries to sit on Sweeney's knees/Slips and pulls the table cloth/Overturns a
70 WL: Fire S		294	/Undid me. By Richmond I raised my knees/Supine on the floor of a narrow canoe.'/
181 FQ: ECoker		164	/The chill ascends from feet to knees,/The fever sings in mental wires./If to be
212 Growltiger		6	torn and seedy, he was baggy at the knees;/One ear was somewhat missing, no need
605 Narcissus		19	tread on faces, convulsive thighs and knees./So he came out under the rock./First he

KNEW (122)

18 Portrait		22	/(For indeed I do not love it ... you knew? you are not blind!/How keen you are!)/
30 Cous Nancy		10	sure how they felt about it,/But they knew that it was modern./Upon the glazen
52 Whispers		7	from the sockets of the eyes!/He knew that thought clings round dead limbs/
52 Whispers		13	/Expert beyond experience,/He knew the anguish of the marrow/The ague of

62 WL: Burial	40	I was neither/Living nor dead, and I knew nothing,/Looking into the heart of light,
62 WL: Burial	69	final stroke of nine./There I saw one I knew, and stopped him, crying: 'Stetson!/'You
115 SP Doris	24	funny fellow/He's like a fellow once I knew./*He* could make you laugh./{Du} Sam can
124 SA Sweeney	2	What's that life is?/{S} Life is death./I knew a man once did a girl in —/{Do} Oh Mr.
124 SA Sweeney	12	you, Sir, we are very interested./{S} I knew a man once did a girl in./Any man might
127 Cor1 March	5	such a press of people./We hardly knew ourselves that day, or knew the City./This
127 Cor1 March	5	hardly knew ourselves that day, or knew the City./This is the way to the temple,
212 Growltiger	9	eye./The cottagers of Rotherhithe knew something of his fame;/At Hammersmith
228 Gus	23	by heart./I'd extemporize back-chat, I knew how to gag,/And I knew how to let the cat
228 Gus	24	back-chat, I knew how to gag,/And I knew how to let the cat out of the bag./I knew
228 Gus	25	how to let the cat out of the bag./I knew how to act with my back and my tail;/
233 Skimble	55	fast asleep at Crewe and so you never knew/That he was walking up and down the
598 Circe	14	at us with the eyes/Of men whom we knew long ago./On a Portrait/Among a crowd
605 Narcissus	24	its roots among each other./Then he knew that he had been a fish/With slippery
251 MC Tempt3	6	to alliance./The enmity that never knew friendship/Can sooner know accord./{T}
261 MC Thomas	2	the children? Those men His disciples/knew no such things: they went forth to journey
277 MC Knight3	8	came in just now. The fact is that/we knew we had taken on a pretty stiff job; I'll only
278 MC Knight2	17	under the central/government. I knew Becket well, in various official relations;
291 FR Harry	20	for all the world to look at?/If you knew how you looked, when I saw you through
292 FR Harry	5	/In the sweet sickly tropical night, I knew they were coming./In Italy, from behind
295 FR Harry	19	the cancer/That eats away the self. I knew how you would take it./First of all, you
297 FR Gerald	21	he knows already./And even if he knew, it's very much better/That he shouldn't
297 FR Gerald	22	/That he shouldn't know that we knew it also./Why not let sleeping dogs lie?/{C}
299 FR Charles	7	about the circumstances;/We only knew what we read in the papers —/Of course,
299 FR Charles	10	been suicide,/And that his Lordship knew it?/{Do} Unlikely, Sir, if I may say so./
304 FR Mary	4	saw you as a hard headmistress/Who knew the way of dominating timid girls./I don't
305 FR Mary	1	did to himself./{M} But it wasn't till I knew that Harry had returned/That I felt the
306 FR Mary	24	Happy? not really, though I never knew why:/It always seemed that it must be my
307 FR Harry	8	put to bed. But at least they never knew/Where we had been./{M} They never
309 FR Mary	19	/Something which I did not know I knew./Even if, as you say, Wishwood is a cheat,
311 FR Harry	28	now for the first time?/When I knew her, I was not the same person./I was not
326 FR Harry	29	I cannot put in order./If you only knew the years that I have had to live/Since I
331 FR Harry	16	to know about your father?/{H} If I knew, then I should not have to ask./*You* know
333 FR Agatha	10	I wanted you!/If that had happened, I knew I should have carried/Death in life, death
340 FR Amy	14	/Of something to live upon. You knew that you took everything/Except the walls,
343 FR Mary	12	what I said to you this evening?/I knew that I was right: you made me wait for
347 FR Downing	8	soon get used to them./Of course, I knew they was to do with his Lordship,/And
355 CP Julia	38	/You know Tony Vincewell? You knew him at Oxford?/{P} No, I never knew him
356 CP Peter	1	knew him at Oxford?/{P} No, I never knew him at Oxford:/I came across him last
357 CP Julia	23	—/I'm one myself. I feel as if I knew/All about that aunt in Hampshire./{E}
361 CP Reilly	25	as well as I know your wife;/And I knew that all you wanted was the luxury/Of an
369 CP Peter	27	concerts alone —/At first, because I knew no one to go with,/And later, I found I
382 CP Celia	9	at your face: and I thought that I knew/And loved every contour; and as I looked/
385 CP Reilly	1	of the moments/During which we knew them. And they have changed since then./
389 CP Peter	22	{L} Oh, so you advised him?/{P} She knew nothing about it./{C} But now that I may
392 CP Edward	14	left./{E} I telephoned to everyone I knew was coming/But I couldn't get everyone.
396 CP Lavinia	30	some time or other, before you ever knew me:/Perhaps only when you were a child.
401 CP Reilly	22	not know that I was coming./But I knew you would be there, and whom I should
401 CP Edward	30	find that chair comfortable./{E} You knew,/Before I began to tell you, what had
407 CP Edward	34	/{E} This is monstrous! My wife knew nothing about it./{L} Really, Edward!
408 CP Lavinia	24	joke that ever happened./{L} I never knew you had such a sense of humour./{R} It is
409 CP Reilly	27	that your young friend/(Though you knew, in your heart, that he was not in love
409 CP Reilly	33	would admit it. Though perhaps you knew it/Before he did. You pretended to
410 CP Edward	5	unlovable,/And I never quite knew why. I thought it was *my* fault./{R} And
415 CP Celia	25	led to disaster/Because the people one knew disapproved of it./I don't worry when
420 CP Julia	22	I think./{You do not need to tell me. I knew from the beginning./{R} It's the other ones
429 CP Alex	33	you/About someone you know — or knew .../{J} Edward!/Somebody must have
430 CP Peter	14	to the country this evening,/So I knew you wouldn't mind my looking in so
430 CP Peter	25	Alex? I always said/That Alex knew everybody. But I didn't know/That he
430 CP Peter	26	everybody. But I didn't know/That he knew any monkeys./{J} But give us your news;/
430 CP Alex	38	you see my last picture, Alex?/{A} I knew about it, but I didn't see it./There is no
431 CP Peter	8	—/He's my boss. I thought everyone knew *his* name./{J} Is he your connection in
432 CP Lavinia	28	ALEX]/{L} I rather assumed that you knew each other —/I don't know why I should.
434 CP Alex	13	of which I was telling you./They knew of it, but would not leave the dying
435 CP Lavinia	32	were saying just now/That you never knew Celia. We none of us did./What you've

436 CP	Lavinia	31	in which she died. I don't know if you knew her./I suspect that you did. In any case
436 CP	Lavinia	32	suspect that you did. In any case you knew *about* her./Yet I thought your expression
438 CP	Lavinia	25	savages./{L} Oh, Edward, I knew! I knew what you were thinking!/Doesn't
438 CP	Lavinia	25	savages./{L} Oh, Edward, I knew! I knew what you were thinking!/Doesn't it help
449 CC	Claude	23	whenever I mention her./{SC} But she knew about Lucasta — Miss Angel, from the
464 CC	Claude	38	That's not the whole story. My father knew I hated it:/That was a grief to him. He
464 CC	Claude	39	I hated it:/That was a grief to him. He knew, I am sure,/That I cherished for a long
465 CC	Claude	2	his death, and then it was too late,/I knew that he was right. And all my life/I have
477 CC	Lucasta	1	gin and betting, I should guess./And I knew how she supplemented her income/When I
478 CC	Kaghan	37	the new flat. And here's Lucasta./I knew I should find she'd got in first!/Trust
482 CC	Lady E	32	first saw you,'He is very well bred'. I knew nothing about you,/But one doesn't need
483 CC	Colby	37	/{C} No, that is my aunt. I never knew my mother./She died when I was born./
484 CC	Colby	4	No. As for other relatives,/I never knew any, when I was a child./I suppose I've
484 CC	Lady E	13	have her portrait. If you never knew your parents .../But was your father
484 CC	Colby	15	was your father living?/{C} I never knew my father./{LE} Then, if you never had a
484 CC	Lady E	17	had a governess,/And if you never knew either of your parents,/You can't
486 CC	Lady E	11	child./So that the only relative you knew/Was Mrs. Guzzard. And you always
488 CC	Lady E	2	of Teddington. That was all I knew./Then Tony was killed, as you know, in
495 CC	Claude	8	thought you would despise me/If you knew what I'd really wanted to be./{LE} And I
500 CC	Lucasta	16	/Is Colby's behaviour. If he knew it./{SC} He knew it./{L} Why didn't he tell
500 CC	Claude	17	behaviour. If he knew it./{SC} He knew it./{L} Why didn't he tell me? Perhaps he
500 CC	Lucasta	19	Perhaps he was about to./Anyway, I *knew* there had been some mistake./You don't
500 CC	Lucasta	21	all what I'm talking about!/But if he knew that he was your son/He must have been
502 CC	Lucasta	10	you apologise?/{L} Oh, because I knew/That I must have misunderstood your
503 CC	Lucasta	28	/{L} Good-bye to Colby as Lucasta knew him,/And good-bye to the Lucasta whom
503 CC	Lucasta	29	good-bye to the Lucasta whom Colby knew./We've changed since then: as you said,
515 CC	Guzzard	13	of a proper start in life —/That I knew. And it would make you so happy!/If I
517 CC	Colby	2	father before you, as a model;/You knew your inheritance. Now I know mine./{SC}
531 ES	Ld Clav	31	be frightened of ghosts./If they only knew how frightened a ghost can be of men! {}/
531 ES	Lambert	35	by previous appointment. He said he knew that,/So he had brought this note. He said
533 ES	Gomez	1	changed your name too, since I knew you./When we were up at Oxford, you
537 ES	Gomez	17	—/I didn't fit into your set, and I knew it./When you started to take me up at
540 ES	Gomez	24	over an old man in the road./{G} You knew it too. If you had been surprised/When I
541 ES	Gomez	10	know to whom I'd told it,/Or who knew the story and who didn't. I promise you./
543 ES	Monica	10	man I used to know./{M} Oh, so you knew him?/{LC} Yes. He'd changed his name./
549 ES	Carghil	40	— just once:/The name by which you knew me. It would give me such a thrill/To hear
550 ES	Carghil	4	stage name. The name by which you knew me./{LC} Well, then, Maisie Montjoy.
553 ES	Ld Clav	1	how long ago it was when you knew me/And considering the brevity of our
554 ES	Carghil	24	not going, Mrs. Carghill?/{MC} Oh, I knew that Lord Claverton had come for a rest
556 ES	Michael	32	mind that I was to blame/Before you knew the facts. The first thing I remember/Is
558 ES	Michael	21	that office./In the first place, they all knew the job had been made for me/Because I
558 ES	Michael	23	considered me superfluous;/They knew I couldn't be living on my pay;/They had
559 ES	Michael	27	I know why you took it. And Mother knew./First, because it gave you the
562 ES	Carghil	30	has changed a good deal/Since I knew him ever so many years ago,/Yet you're
563 ES	Carghil	29	time, once, when everyone in London/Knew the name of Maisie Montjoy in revue./
564 ES	Gomez	34	you tell me all about Dick when you knew him. {}/[*pats her despatch-case*]./{MC}
565 ES	Ld Clav	35	from his own past failures:/I said I knew from experience. Do I understand the
569 ES	Monica	14	you the better, Father,/The more I knew about you. I should understand you
570 ES	Ld Clav	3	know of them?/{LC} Your mother knew nothing about them. And I know/That I
570 ES	Ld Clav	4	about them. And I know/That I never knew your mother, as she never knew me./I
570 ES	Ld Clav	4	never knew your mother, as she never knew me./I thought that she would never
572 ES	Ld Clav	7	that whispered, 'you didn't stop!'/I knew the voice: it was Fred Culverwell's./{M}
572 ES	Monica	9	And no one to share it with;/I never knew how lonely you were/Or why you were

KNIFE (4)

26 Rhapsody		78	prepare for life.'/The last twist of the knife./Morning at the Window/They are rattling
225 Mr Mistoff		33	a bit of fish-paste;/If you look for a knife or a fork/And you think it is merely
269 MC	Knight2	16	you have spoken in danger of the knife./{K3} Priest, you have spoken treachery
515 CC	Guzzard	30	that this revelation/Drives the knife deeper and twists it in the wound?/I had

KNIGHTS (9)

129 Cor2	State	3	/The Companions of the Bath, the Knights of the British Empire, the Cavaliers,/O
238 MC		m 12	/PART II/THREE PRIESTS/FOUR KNIGHTS/ARCHBISHOP THOMAS
265 MC		m 9	may appear. {}/[*Enter the* FOUR KNIGHTS. *The banners disappear*]/{K1}
266 MC		m 7	and the documents signed. {}/[*To* KNIGHTS]./{T} You are welcome, whatever
274 MC		m 14	DOOR! {}/[*The door is opened. The* KNIGHTS *enter, slightly tipsy*]/{3P} This way,
275 MC		m 21	and that of the Church. {}/[*While the* KNIGHTS *kill him, we hear the* CHORUS./{C}

276 MC   m 18   soul, wash them wash them! {}/[*The* KNIGHTS, *having completed the murder,*
277 MC Knight3   4   perfectly disinterested. [*The other*/KNIGHTS: 'Hear! hear!'] *We* are not getting
280 MC   m   4   any public outbreak. {}/[*Exeunt* KNIGHTS]/{P1} O father, father, gone from us,
KNITTING (2)
44 Cook Egg   4   *Colleges*/Lay on the table, with the knitting./Daguerreotypes and silhouettes,/Her
548 ES   3m 14   *composes*/*herself and takes out her knitting.*/[*after a pause*]./{MC} I hope I'm not
KNIVES (1)
213 Growltiger 40   with toasting forks and cruel carving knives./Then GILBERT gave the signal to his
KNOB (1)
38 Gerontion   32   in a draughty house/Under a windy knob./After such knowledge, what forgiveness?
KNOCK (32)
65 WL: Chess   138   Pressing lidless eyes and waiting for a knock upon the door./When Lil's husband got
118 SP   32   I'd like to know about that coffin. {}/KNOCK KNOCK KNOCK/KNOCK
118 SP   32   know about that coffin. {}/KNOCK KNOCK KNOCK/KNOCK KNOCK
118 SP   32   that coffin. {}/KNOCK KNOCK KNOCK KNOCK/KNOCK KNOCK/
118 SP   33   {}/KNOCK KNOCK KNOCK KNOCK KNOCK KNOCK/KNOCK/
118 SP   33   KNOCK KNOCK KNOCK KNOCK KNOCK KNOCK/KNOCK/
118 SP   33   KNOCK/KNOCK KNOCK KNOCK/KNOCK KNOCK/KNOCK/
118 SP   34   /KNOCK KNOCK KNOCK/KNOCK/KNOCK/KNOCK/DORIS. DUSTY.
118 SP   35   KNOCK/KNOCK/KNOCK/KNOCK/KNOCK/DORIS. DUSTY.
118 SP   36   KNOCK/KNOCK/KNOCK/KNOCK/DORIS. DUSTY. WAUCHOPE.
126 SA   Chorus 4   and it's dark/And you wait for a knock and the turning of a lock/for you know
126 SA   13   ha ha/Hoo ha ha/Hoo/Hoo/Hoo {}/KNOCK KNOCK KNOCK/KNOCK
126 SA   13   ha ha/Hoo/Hoo/Hoo {}/KNOCK KNOCK KNOCK KNOCK
126 SA   13   /Hoo/Hoo/Hoo {}/KNOCK KNOCK KNOCK KNOCK KNOCK/
126 SA   14   /Hoo {}/KNOCK KNOCK KNOCK KNOCK KNOCK KNOCK/
126 SA   14   KNOCK KNOCK KNOCK KNOCK KNOCK KNOCK/KNOCK/
126 SA   15   /KNOCK KNOCK KNOCK/KNOCK/KNOCK/KNOCK/Coriolan/
126 SA   16   KNOCK KNOCK/KNOCK/KNOCK/KNOCK/Coriolan/Triumphal March
126 SA   17   KNOCK/KNOCK/KNOCK/KNOCK/KNOCK/Coriolan/Triumphal March/Stone,
298 FR   m 23   bull by the horns,/And this is one. {}/[*Knock: and enter* DOWNING]/{C} Good
451 CC   m 39   prepared for meeting her. {}/[*A loud knock. Enter* B. KAGHAN]/{K} Enter B.
481 CC   m 14   /{L} If you want to discuss *me* ... {}/[*A knock at the door. Enter* LADY ELIZABETH]/
486 CC   m 31   Than you are aware of. Colby ... {}/[*A knock on the door*]/{LE} Who's that? {}/[*Enter*
496 CC   m 13   happens/He shall be *our* son. {}/[*A knock on the door. Enter* EGGERSON]/{SC}
499 CC   m   9   Claude: I understand completely. {}/[*A knock on the door*]/{SC} Good Lord, she's here
502 CC   m   1   {}/[*Reaches for the telephone*]/[*A knock. Enter* COLBY]/{C} Have I come too
504 CC   m 24   /{SC} Well, are we ready? {}/[*A quiet knock. Enter* KAGHAN, *escorting* MRS.
527 ES   m 11   /{C} That won't happen to me. {}/[*Knock. Enter* LAMBERT]/{L} Excuse me, Miss
531 ES   m 32   frightened a ghost can be of men! {}/[*Knock. Enter* LAMBERT]/{L} Excuse me, my
535 ES   m   6   deserve. But when I say 'trust' ... {}/[*Knock. Enter* LAMBERT]/{LC} Lambert, will
543 ES   m   8   *sits for a few minutes brooding. A knock. Enter* MONICA.]/{M} Who was it,
KNOCKABOUT (1)
218 Mung Rump   2   a very notorious couple of cats./As knockabout clowns, quick-change comedians,
KNOCKED (1)
236 Cat Morgan 13   Morgan, 'e's got a good 'art.'/I got knocked about on the Barbary Coast,/And me
KNOCKING (1)
577 ES   Carghil 36   —/Opportunity has come knocking at the door./Richard, you must not
KNOCKS (1)
433 CP   Peter 32   /{L} Celia?/{A} Dead./{P} Dead. That knocks the bottom out of it./{E} Celia dead./{J}
KNOT (6)
198 FQ: Little 260   flame are in-folded/Into the crowned knot of fire/And the fire and the rose are one./
290 FR   Agatha 26   is already prepared/Men tighten the knot of confusion/Into perfect
316 FR   Agatha 12   /May the three be separated/May the knot that was tied/Become unknotted/May the
316 FR   Agatha 22   /Be diverted from this house/Till the knot is unknotted/The crossed is uncrossed/And
337 FR   Agatha   6   my curse,/You shall be fulfilled:/The knot shall be unknotted/And the crooked made
350 FR   Agatha 17   circle/Completing the charm/So the knot be unknotted/The crossed be uncrossed/
KNOTS (1)
42 Swee Erect   13   sheets in steam./This withered root of knots of hair/Slitted below and gashed with
KNOTTED (1)
385 CP   Reilly 31   to her./Don't strangle each other with knotted memories./Now I shall go./{E} Stop!
KNOUT (1)
589 Fable   91   morn from four to five one took a knout/And flogged his mates 'till they grew

KNOW (677)

14	Prufrock	52	out my life with coffee spoons;/I know the voices dying with a dying fall/Beneath
18	Portrait	19	cornets/And begins./'You do not know how much they mean to me, my friends,/
19	Portrait	44	she talks./'Ah, my friend, you do not know, you do not know/What life is, you who
19	Portrait	44	friend, you do not know, you do not know/What life is, you who hold it in your
20	Portrait	90	that's a useless question./You hardly know when you are coming back,/You will find
21	Portrait	97	of late/(But our beginnings never know our ends!)/Why we have not developed
61	WL: Burial	21	/You cannot say, or guess, for you know only/A heap of broken images, where the
65	WL: Chess	114	of? What thinking? What?/'I never know what you are thinking. Think.'/I think we
65	WL: Chess	122	/Nothing again nothing./'Do/'You know nothing? Do you see nothing? Do you
65	WL: Chess	143	yourself a bit smart./He'll want to know what you done with that money he gave
66	WL: Chess	151	Something o' that, I said./Then I'll know who to thank, she said, and give me a
73	WL: Thund	364	in a brown mantle, hooded/I do not know whether a man or a woman/— But who is
89	Ash-Wed 1	9	usual reign?/Because I do not hope to know again/The infirm glory of the positive
89	Ash-Wed 1	12	/Because I do not think/Because I know I shall not know/The one veritable
89	Ash-Wed 1	12	not think/Because I know I shall not know/The one veritable transitory power/
89	Ash-Wed 1	16	for there is nothing again/Because I know that time is always time/And place is
115	SP Dusty	8	men do/Some men don't and you know who/{Do} You can have Pereira/{Du}
115	SP Dusty	16	can't trust him —/Then you never know what he's going to do./{Do} No it
117	SP Dusty	21	thing that anyone can do./{Du} Yes I know you've a touch with the cards/What
117	SP Doris	34	all last night./Yes it's mine. I know it's mine./Oh good heavens what'll I do/
118	SP Dusty	7	you nothing at all/{Du} You've got to know what you want to ask them/{Do} You've
118	SP Doris	8	want to ask them/{Do} You've got to know what you want to know/{Du} It's no use
118	SP Doris	8	got to know what you want to know/{Du} It's no use asking them too much/
118	SP Doris	12	they're no use at all./{Do} I'd like to know about that coffin./{Du} Well I never!
118	SP Doris	31	Cards are queer./{Do} I'd like to know about that coffin. { }/KNOCK KNOCK
119	SP Wauch	3	permit me —/I think you girls both know Captain Horsfall —/We want you to meet
119	SP Dusty	22	game in Bordeaux./{Du} Do you know London well, Mr. Krumpacker?/{Kl} No
125	SA Sweeney	4	what I was going to say./He didn't know if he was alive/and the girl was dead/He
125	SA Sweeney	6	alive/and the girl was dead/He didn't know if the girl was alive/and he was dead/He
125	SA Sweeney	8	was alive/and he was dead/He didn't know if they were both alive/or both were dead/
125	SA Doris	29	somebody's gotta pay the rent/{Do} I know who/{S} But that's nothing to me and
126	SA Chorus	5	and the turning of a lock/for you know the hangman's waiting for you./And
136	5FingerEx3	12	had than squirming worm;/For I know, and so should you/That soon the
136	5FingerEx4	2	Mr. Hodgson!/(Everyone wants to know *him*)/With his musical sound/And his
136	5FingerEx4	14	Mr. Hodgson!/(Everyone wants to know *him*)./He has 999 canaries/And round his
136	5FingerEx4	19	Mr. Hodgson!/(Everyone wants to know *him*)./*Lines for Cuscuscaraway and Mirza*
148	Rock 1	49	trodden the winepress alone, and I know/That it is hard to be really useful,
161	Rock 7	26	never happened before: though we know not just when, or why, or how, or where./
171	FQ: BurntN	18	dust on a bowl of rose-leaves/I do not know./Other echoes/Inhabit the garden. Shall
180	FQ: ECoker	117	of darkness on darkness,/And we know that the hills and the trees, the distant
181	FQ: ECoker	140	/In order to arrive at what you do not know/You must go by a way which is the way
181	FQ: ECoker	146	you are not./And what you do not know is the only thing you know/And what you
181	FQ: ECoker	146	do not know is the only thing you know/And what you own is what you do not
184	FQ: DrySal	1	beginning./The Dry Salvages/I do not know much about gods; but I think that the
197	FQ: Little	244	be to arrive where we started/And know the place for the first time./Through the
203	Indians	21	the less fruitful if neither you nor we/Know, until the judgment after death,/What is
216	Jellicles	16	big/Jellicle Cats are roly-poly,/They know how to dance a gavotte and a jig./Until
222	Pekes Pols	15	was away from his beat —/I don't know the reason, but most people think/He'd
224	Mr Mistoff	1	street./Mr. Mistoffelees!/You ought to know Mr. Mistoffelees!/The Original Conjuring
225	Mr Mistoff	59	said: OH!/Well I never!/Did you ever/Know a Cat so clever/As Magical Mr.
226	Macavity	12	he's very tall and thin;/You would know him if you saw him, for his eyes are
228	Gus	22	'every possible part,/And I used to know seventy speeches by heart./I'd
232	Skimble	24	control by a regular patrol/And he'd know at once if anything occurred./He will
233	Skimble	48	ought to reflect that it's very nice/To know that you won't be bothered by mice —/
233	Skimble	60	/If there's anything they ought to know about:/When you get to Gallowgate there
235	Ad-dress	60	sure to have his personal taste./(I know a Cat, who makes a habit/Of eating
588	Fable	44	of that time I am afraid/I don't know much about — as well's I'm able/I'll go
589	Fable	72	awkward moments,/As everybody'll know who reads this romance./The Abbot sat
592	Grad 1	1	/Standing upon the shore of all we know/We linger for a moment doubtfully,/Then
592	Grad 2	3	fortunes on some foreign shore/Well know they lose what time shall not restore,/And
593	Grad 4	5	hope it may be; would that we might know!/Would we might look into the future
593	Grad 7	4	/And ask no other guerdon than to know/That they have helpt the cause to victory,
594	Grad 10	2	school from that which now we know;/But only in appearance t'will be so./That
242	MC Priest1	18	Archbishop, I fear for the Church,/I know that the pride bred of sudden prosperity/

244 MC Chorus	22	/Are afraid in a fear which we cannot know, which we cannot face, which none
245 MC Priest2	3	and babbling women./Do you not know that the good Archbishop/Is likely to
245 MC Thomas	12	/They speak better than they know, and beyond your understanding./They
245 MC Thomas	13	beyond your understanding./They know and do not know, what it is to act or
245 MC Thomas	13	/They know and do not know, what it is to act or suffer./They know
245 MC Thomas	14	know, what it is to act or suffer./They know and do not know, that action is suffering/
245 MC Thomas	14	act or suffer./They know and do not know, that action is suffering/And suffering is
247 MC Thomas	13	matches melancholy./{T} We do not know very much of the future/Except that from
250 MC Tempt3	27	/I have no skill. I am no courtier./I know a horse, a dog, a wench;/I know how to
250 MC Tempt3	28	/I know a horse, a dog, a wench;/I know how to hold my estates in order,/A
250 MC Tempt3	30	business./It is we country lords who know the country/And we who know what the
250 MC Tempt3	31	who know the country/And we who know what the country needs./It is our country.
251 MC Tempt3	7	never knew friendship/Can sooner know accord./{T} For a countryman/You wrap
252 MC Tempt4	38	{T} Who are you?/{T4} As you do not know me, I do not need a name,/And, as you
252 MC Tempt4	39	I do not need a name,/And, as you know me, that is why I come./You know me,
253 MC Tempt4	1	know me, that is why I come./You know me, but have never seen my face./To meet
253 MC Tempt4	8	hatred shall have no end./You know truly, the King will never trust/Twice, the
253 MC Tempt4	38	temporal power./The Old King shall know it, when at last breath,/No sons, no
254 MC Tempt4	7	here, Thomas, to tell you what you know./{T} How long shall this be?/{T4} Save
254 MC Tempt4	9	long shall this be?/{T4} Save what you know already, ask nothing of me./But think,
255 MC Thomas	31	not lead to damnation in pride?/I well know that these temptations/Mean present
255 MC Tempt4	36	suffer/Without perdition?/{T4} You know and do not know, what it is to act or
255 MC Tempt4	36	perdition?/{T4} You know and do not know, what it is to act or suffer./You know and
255 MC Tempt4	37	know, what it is to act or suffer./You know and do not know, that action is suffering,
255 MC Tempt4	37	act or suffer./You know and do not know, that action is suffering,/And suffering
257 MC Chorus	7	/We are not ignorant women, we know what we must expect and not expect./We
257 MC Chorus	8	we must expect and not expect./We know of oppression and torture,/We know of
257 MC Chorus	9	know of oppression and torture,/We know of extortion and violence,/Destitution,
258 MC Thomas	32	what they do/But by what they are. I know/What yet remains to show you of my
258 MC Thomas	37	/Arrogant passion of a fanatic./I know that history at all times draws/The
261 MC Thomas	3	afar, to suffer by land/and sea, to know torture, imprisonment, disappointment,
265 MC Priest3	3	/{P3} What day is the day that we know that we hope for or fear for?/Every day is
265 MC Priest1	20	/{K1} Our men are outside./{P1} You know the Archbishop's hospitality./We are
271 MC Thomas	11	glory. This is one moment,/But know that another/Shall pierce you with a
976 MC Knight1	2	attention for a few/moments. We know that you may be disposed to judge
277 MC Knight3	16	not getting a penny out of this. We know perfectly well how/things will turn out.
278 MC Knight2	28	of a people like ours. So far, I know that I have/your approval: I read it in
286 FR Charles	26	/The modern young people don't know what they're drinking,/Modern young
287 FR Amy	25	to stop in the dark./If you want to know why I never leave Wishwood/That is the
288 FR Amy	11	particular occasion/As you ought to know. It will be the first time/For eight years
288 FR Violet	17	/{G} Why, painful?/{V} Gerald! you know what Agatha means./{Ag} I mean painful,
289 FR Gerald	3	themselves./{G} I don't in the least know what you're talking about./You seem to
290 FR Amy	11	in death./You might as well all of you know the truth/For the sake of the future.
292 FR Gerald	28	a ride tomorrow./You'll find you know the country as well as ever./There wasn't
292 FR Gerald	29	/There wasn't an inch of it you didn't know./But you'll have to see about a couple of
293 FR Violet	2	the kitchen./Mrs. Packell is too old to know what she is doing./It really needs a man in
293 FR Harry	40	/If you were wide awake. You do not know/The noxious smell untraceable in the
294 FR Harry	2	has its hour of the night; you do not know/The unspoken voice of sorrow in the
295 FR Charles	9	mother and yourself./Of course we know what really happened, we read it in the
295 FR Charles	14	these feelings better than you know —/But you have no reason to reproach
296 FR Ivy	23	do not want to be cured/And they know what you are thinking./{C} He has
297 FR Gerald	19	Even so, we don't want Downing to know/Any more than he knows already./And
297 FR Gerald	22	very much better/That he shouldn't know that we knew it also./Why not let sleeping
297 FR Charles	26	I'd like to ask Downing./He shan't know why I'm asking. {}/[Enter DENMAN]/{C}
297 FR Charles	36	what's wrong with Harry:/Until we know that, we can do nothing for him./And as
298 FR Violet	16	to hear what Downing says./I want to know at once, not be told about it later./{I} And
298 FR Charles	33	Lady Day./{C} Eleven years, and you know him pretty well./And I'm sure that you've
299 FR Downing	34	you might say depressed, Sir./But you know his Lordship was always very quiet:/Very
300 FR Downing	2	sort of thing?/{Do} Well, I don't know, Sir./But he seemed very anxious about
300 FR Downing	7	a rare fright, once or twice./But you know, it is just my opinion, Sir,/That his
301 FR Chorus	30	as we are in the right column./We know about the railway accident/We know
301 FR Chorus	31	know about the railway accident/We know about the sudden thrombosis/And the
303 FR Mary	7	do not belong here, which do not know/The wind and rain, as I know them./{Ag}
303 FR Mary	8	do not know/The wind and rain, as I know them./{Ag} I wonder how many we shall
304 FR Mary	2	you'd throw that up against me./I know I wasn't one of your favourite students:/I

304 FR	Mary	13	you do understand. You only want to know/Whether I understand. You know
304 FR	Mary	14	to know/Whether I understand. You know perfectly well,/What Cousin Amy wants,
304 FR	Mary	19	/Even against a will like hers. I know very well/Why she wanted to keep me.
304 FR	Mary	30	willing./Doesn't that sound awful? I know that it does./Did you ever meet her? What
304 FR	Agatha	34	asked to his wedding:/Amy did not know that. I was sorry for her;/I could see that
305 FR	Mary	2	/That I felt the strength to go. I know I must go./But where? I want a job: and
306 FR	Harry	11	/I wanted to ask you. I don't know yet./All these years I'd been longing to get
307 FR	Harry	30	/{H} One thing you cannot know:/The sudden extinction of every
307 FR	Harry	33	of the iron cataract./You do not know what hope is, until you have lost it./You
307 FR	Harry	34	is, until you have lost it./You only know what it is not to hope:/You do not know
307 FR	Harry	35	what it is not to hope:/You do not know what it is to have hope taken from you,/
307 FR	Mary	38	sometimes by each other./{M} I know what you mean. That is an experience/I
308 FR	Mary	12	death of hope/Of which you speak, I know you have experienced it,/And I can well
308 FR	Harry	19	I hoped for/Now that I am here I know I shall not find it./The instinct to return
308 FR	Harry	36	/Of dreaming dissolution. You do not know,/You cannot know, you cannot
308 FR	Harry	37	You do not know,/You cannot know, you cannot understand./{M} I think I
309 FR	Mary	14	/And in the ordinary sense I don't know you very well,/Although I remember you
309 FR	Mary	19	/Something which I did not know I knew./Even if, as you say, Wishwood is
309 FR	Mary	28	blind/While he still sees the sunlight. I know that this is true./{H} I have spent many
309 FR	Harry	38	you are right, though I do not know/How you should know it. Is the cold
309 FR	Harry	39	I do not know/How you should know it. Is the cold spring/Is the spring not an
310 FR	Harry	33	come from a long distance./Whether I know what I am saying, or why I say it,/That
311 FR	Harry	6	bitter smell/From another world. I know it, I know it!/More potent than ever
311 FR	Harry	6	/From another world. I know it, I know it!/More potent than ever before, a
311 FR	Harry	12	are you? Let me see you,/Since I know you are there, I know you are spying on
311 FR	Harry	12	see you,/Since I know you are there, I know you are spying on me./Why do you play
313 FR	Violet	5	think, after such a long journey;/You know what a rush he had to be here in time/For
313 FR	Ivy	9	them./You don't mind, do you? I know so much about flowers;/Flowers have
313 FR	Ivy	11	have always been my passion./You know I had my own garden once, in Cornwall,/
313 FR	Charles	22	/Arthur's a bit irresponsible, you know;/You should have a sobering effect upon
314 FR	Amy	3	you seen Dr. Warburton?/You know he's the oldest friend of the family,/And
315 FR	Warburt	13	the subject of cancer?/I really don't know. — But now you're all grown up/I haven't
317 FR	Warburt	11	understand me./I'm sure you cannot know what is on my mind;/And as for making
317 FR	Warburt	18	your knowing it, and what you know/Or do not know, at any moment/May
317 FR	Warburt	19	it, and what you know/Or do not know, at any moment/May make an endless
318 FR	Warburt	19	you're mistaken./I mean, you don't know what I want to tell you./You may be quite
318 FR	Harry	29	and then you can talk./I don't know why, but just this evening/I feel an
319 FR	Harry	1	to tell me/Is either something that I know already/Or unimportant, or else untrue./
319 FR	Harry	3	or else untrue./But I want to know more about my father./I hardly remember
319 FR	Harry	4	father./I hardly remember him, and I know very well/That I was kept apart from him,
319 FR	Warburt	14	left a cautery./Leave it alone. You know that your mother/And your father were
319 FR	Warburt	39	/We can't sit here all the evening, you know;/You will have to have the birthday
320 FR	Warburt	27	were two reasons/Why you had to know. One is your mother,/To make her happy
320 FR	Warburt	31	you. I don't like to say this;/But you know that I am a very old friend,/And have
320 FR	Warburt	33	a party to the family secrets —/You know as well as I do that Arthur and John/
320 FR	Harry	39	you./{H} Hopes? ... Tell me/Did you know my father at about my present age?/{W}
321 FR	Warburt	8	is no portrait./{W} What I want to know is, whether you've been sleeping ... {}/
322 FR	Harry	9	asking/About her Ladyship? Do you know or don't you?/I'm not afraid of you./{Wi}
322 FR	Winch	35	the driver up for this:/Says he doesn't know this part of the country/And stopped to
324 FR	Amy	25	to your mother./{A} I do not know very much:/And as I get older, I am
325 FR	Charles	12	than Winchell said, then he'll let us know at once./{G} I am really more afraid of
327 FR	Violet	36	of asking for an evening paper?/You know as well as I do, at this distance from
329 FR	Chorus	19	is no avoiding these things/And we know nothing of exorcism/And whether in
331 FR	Agatha	15	my father./{Ag} What do you want to know about your father?/{H} If I knew, then I
331 FR	Harry	17	then I should not have to ask./*You* know what I want to know, and that is enough:/
331 FR	Harry	17	to ask./*You* know what I want to know, and that is enough:/Warburton told me
331 FR	Harry	19	he did not mean to./What I want to know is something I need to know,/And only
331 FR	Harry	19	I want to know is something I need to know,/And only you can tell me. I know that
331 FR	Harry	20	to know,/And only you can tell me. I know that much./{Ag} I had to fight for many
331 FR	Agatha	22	many years to keep it. What people know me as,/The efficient principal of a
331 FR	Harry	26	your question disturbs./{H} When I know, I know that in some way I shall find/
331 FR	Harry	26	disturbs./{H} When I know, I know that in some way I shall find/That I have
333 FR	Harry	38	which we suffer./{H} Look, I do not know why,/I feel happy for a moment, as if I
336 FR	Harry	16	are outside me,/And just endurable. I know that you are ready,/Ready to leave
336 FR	Harry	21	at last that I am following you,/And I know that there can be only one itinerary/And

337 FR	Agatha	14	love./What you have wished to know, what you have learned/Mean the end of
337 FR	Agatha	21	/Meeting is for those who do not know each other./{H} I know that I have made
337 FR	Harry	22	who do not know each other./{H} I know that I have made a decision/In a moment
337 FR	Harry	24	and now I feel dull again./I only know that I made a decision/Which your words
337 FR	Harry	26	words echo. I am still befouled,/But I know there is only one way out of defilement —
337 FR	Harry	28	in the end to reconciliation./And I know that I must go./{Ag} You must go. {}/
337 FR	Amy	34	are you to say he shall go?/I think I know well enough why you wish him to go./
337 FR	Agatha	35	{Ag} I wish nothing. I only say what I know must happen./{A} You only say what you
338 FR	Harry	3	that to you now. Only be sure/That I know what I am doing, and what I must do,/
338 FR	Harry	6	cannot explain it to anyone:/I do not know the words in which to explain it —/That is
338 FR	Amy	14	to explain./{A} Why should Agatha know, and I not be allowed to?/{H} I do not
338 FR	Harry	15	and I not be allowed to?/{H} I do not know whether Agatha knows/Or how much she
338 FR	Harry	20	of invisible pursuers./Now I know that all my life has been a flight/And
338 FR	Harry	21	fed upon me while I fled. Now I know/That the last apparent refuge, the safe
338 FR	Harry	26	one, but your family!/{H} And now I know/That my business is not to run away, but
340 FR	Amy	29	ugly rumours./You thought I did not know!/You may be close, but I always saw
341 FR	Agatha	1	*him.*/And now it is my son./{Ag} I know one thing, Amy:/That you have never
341 FR	Amy	28	if you please,/Gives *you* the power to know what is best for Harry?/What gave you
342 FR	Amy	6	/She has persuaded him: I do not know how./I have been always trying to make
342 FR	Mary	20	Agatha, stop him!/You do not know what I have seen and what I know!/He is
342 FR	Mary	20	know what I have seen and what I know!/He is in great danger, I know that, don't
342 FR	Mary	21	what I know!/He is in great danger, I know that, don't ask me,/You would not believe
342 FR	Mary	22	would not believe me, but I tell you I know./You must keep him here, you must not
342 FR	Mary	24	you must not let him leave./I do not know what must be done, what can be done,/
344 FR	Harry	36	you would not understand./You can't know why I am going. You have not seen/What
345 FR	Amy	21	I am glad if I can come to know them./I always wanted too much for my
345 FR	Charles	35	it./But I'm not sure that I want to know. I suppose I'm getting old:/Old age came
346 FR	Charles	5	if one were awake?/You both seem to know more about this than I do. {}/[*Enter*
346 FR	Downing	29	You get a feeling of it./So I seem to know beforehand, when something's going to
347 FR	Ivy	20	love Arthur.'/I mean, after what we know of what did happen,/Do you think Amy
347 FR	Violet	23	it?/{V} No, certainly not./You do not know what has been going on, Ivy./And if you
347 FR	Ivy	29	I think I might be allowed/To know what has happened./{A} Agatha! Mary!
348 FR	Chorus	12	the ordinary business of living,/We know how to work the machine,/We can usually
348 FR	Chorus	18	/But not against the act of God./We know various spells and enchantments./And
348 FR	Chorus	27	strictly practical purposes/We do not know what we are doing;/And even, when you
348 FR	Chorus	29	even, when you think of it,/We do not know much about thinking./What is happening
349 FR	Mary	28	/And in the hither world/Where we know what we are doing/There is not its
353 CP	Julia	9	story twice./{J} But I'm still waiting to know what happened./I know it started as a
353 CP	Julia	10	waiting to know what happened./I know it started as a story about tigers./{A} I
353 CP	Julia	19	that story./{J} Well, you all seem to know it./{C} Do we all know it?/But we're never
353 CP	Celia	20	all seem to know it./{C} Do we all know it?/But we're never tired of hearing *you*
353 CP	Celia	23	GUEST]/{C} You don't know it, do you?/{UG} No, I've never heard it./
354 CP	Julia	19	GUEST]/{J} Did *you* know Lady Klootz?/{UG} No, I never met her./
354 CP	Julia	25	GUEST]/{J} Do *you* know Delia Verinder?/{UG} No, I don't know
354 CP	Reilly	26	Delia Verinder?/{UG} No, I don't know her./{J} Well, one can't be too careful/
354 CP	Alex	32	there were three, but you wouldn't know the third one:/They kept him rather quiet.
355 CP	Celia	4	the cry of bats./{C} But how do you know he could hear the cry of bats?/{J} Because
355 CP	Celia	15	There isn't much that Julia doesn't know./{P} Go on with the story about the
355 CP	Julia	31	GUEST]/{J} Did *you* know the Vincewells?/{UG} No, I don't know
355 CP	Reilly	32	the Vincewells?/{UG} No, I don't know the Vincewells./{J} Oh, they're both dead
355 CP	Julia	33	both dead now. But I wanted to know./If they'd been friends of yours, I couldn't
355 CP	Julia	38	the situation more difficult./You know Tony Vincewell? You knew him at
356 CP	Julia	16	Edward, do sit down for a moment./I know you're always the perfect host,/But just
356 CP	Julia	27	the lavatory/And couldn't get out. I know what you're thinking!/I know you think
356 CP	Julia	28	out. I know what you're thinking!/I know you think I'm a silly old woman/But I'm
356 CP	Edward	35	some time, Edward?/{E} I really don't know until I hear from her./If her aunt is very
356 CP	Edward	38	while she is away?/{E} I really don't know. I may go away myself./{C} Go away
357 CP	Edward	7	another aunt/Whom you wouldn't know. Her mother's sister/And rather a recluse./
358 CP	Julia	3	/{E} Everything?/{J} Oh, you know what I mean./The next election. And the
358 CP	Edward	39	I see you soon?/{E} Perhaps. I don't know./{C} Perhaps you don't know? Very well,
359 CP	Celia	1	I don't know./{C} Perhaps you don't know? Very well, good-bye./{E} Good-bye,
359 CP	Edward	17	get at them in time;/And I didn't know that *you* were coming./I thought that
359 CP	Edward	31	[*Exit*]/{E} I'm sorry. I'm afraid I don't know your name./{UG} I ought to be going./{E}
359 CP	Edward	35	easier to talk to a person you don't know./The fact is, that Lavinia has left me./
360 CP	Edward	7	that she was leaving me;/But I don't know where she's gone./{UG} This is an

360 CP	Reilly	24	the brighter side./You say you don't know where she's gone?/{E} No, I do not./{UG}
360 CP	Reilly	26	gone?/{E} No, I do not./{UG} Do you know who the man is?/{E} There was no other
360 CP	Edward	28	was no other man —/None that I know of./{UG} Or another woman/Of whom
361 CP	Edward	15	like them. May I put it to *you*?/I know that I invited this conversation:/But I
361 CP	Edward	16	invited this conversation:/But I don't know who you are. This is not what I expected./
361 CP	Edward	19	concealing./I don't think I want to know who you are;/But, at the same time,
361 CP	Edward	20	are;/But, at the same time, unless you know my wife/A good deal better than I
361 CP	Edward	21	better than I thought, or unless you know/A good deal more about us than appears
361 CP	Reilly	24	speculations rather offensive./{UG} I know you as well as I know your wife;/And I
361 CP	Reilly	24	/{UG} I know you as well as I know your wife;/And I knew that all you
363 CP	Reilly	16	were. Who are you now?/You don't know any more than I do,/But rather less. You
363 CP	Edward	28	answer 'Where?' and I say 'I don't know';/And they say, 'But when will she be
363 CP	Edward	30	will she be back?'/And I reply 'I don't know that she *is* coming back'./And they ask
364 CP	Edward	4	to search for her./I'm sure I don't know what she was wearing/When I saw her
364 CP	Edward	18	/{E} Do you mean to say that you know where she is?/{UG} That question is not
364 CP	Reilly	27	your suggestion?/{UG} We do not know yet. In twenty-four hours/She will come
364 CP	Julia	32	I'm so glad to find you./Do you know, I must have left my glasses here,/And I
365 CP	Julia	4	I don't remember the colour,/But I'd know them, because one lens is missing. {}/
365 CP	Edward	20	out of the way! Who is he?/{E} *I* don't know./{J} *You* don't know?/{E} I never saw him
365 CP	Julia	21	is he?/{E} *I* don't know./{J} *You* don't know?/{E} I never saw him before in my life./{J}
365 CP	Edward	24	how did he come here?/{E} *I* don't know./{J} *You* don't know! And what's his
365 CP	Julia	25	here?/{E} *I* don't know./{J} *You* don't know! And what's his name?/Did I hear him say
365 CP	Edward	27	say his name was Riley?/{E} I don't know his name./{J} You don't know his *name*?/
365 CP	Julia	28	I don't know his name./{J} You don't know his *name*?/{E} I tell you I've no idea who
367 CP	Edward	34	so too./{E} How did you come to know her? {}/[*Enter* ALEX]/{A} Ah, there you
367 CP	Alex	35	Ah, there you are, Edward! Do you know why *I've* looked in?/{E} I'd like to know
367 CP	Edward	36	why *I've* looked in?/{E} I'd like to know first how you *got* in, Alex./{A} Why, I
368 CP	Alex	5	may be all alone this evening,/And I know that he hates to spend an evening alone,/
368 CP	Alex	12	get it myself./{A} Ah, in that case I know what I'll do./I'm going to give you a little
368 CP	Alex	14	to give you a little surprise:/You know, I'm rather a famous cook./I'm going
368 CP	Peter	30	off?/{P} You asked me how I came to know Celia./I met her here, about a year ago./
369 CP	Edward	23	you haven't told me how you came to know Celia./{P} I saw her again a few days later
370 CP	Peter	19	/{P} That is exactly what I want to know./She has simply faded — into some other
370 CP	Edward	32	is all very normal. If you could only know/How lucky you are. In a little while/This
371 CP	Peter	17	has happened, in her terms. Until I know that/I shan't know the truth about even
371 CP	Peter	18	her terms. Until I know that/I shan't know the truth about even the memory./Did we
371 CP	Edward	34	in. So you want to see Celia./{P} And I know why I should be taking all this trouble/To
372 CP	Peter	2	me to do?/{P} See Celia for me./You know her in a different way from me/And you
374 CP	Edward	13	what has happened?/*I* don't know what has happened, or what is going to
374 CP	Celia	22	But it doesn't really matter. They will know soon enough./Doesn't that settle all our
374 CP	Celia	26	surely, these are only temporary./You know I accepted the situation/Because a divorce
375 CP	Edward	8	have set it for ourselves. But I do not know/What kind of a trap it is./{C} Then what
375 CP	Celia	26	that about?/{E} I know it was Alex./{C} I know it was Alex./But what was he talking of?/
376 CP	Edward	16	A boiled egg./It's the only thing I know how to cook./{J} Celia! I see you've had
377 CP	Celia	5	I think./{C} You think! Don't you know?/{E} No, but I believe it. That man who
377 CP	Edward	9	has some sort of power./{E} I don't know who he is./But I had some talk with him,
378 CP	Julia	10	on quickly. And take a taxi./You know, you're looking absolutely famished./
380 CP	Celia	16	and bewildered./{C} I simply don't know what you are talking about./Edward, this
381 CP	Edward	11	as a middle-aged man/Beginning to know what it is to feel old./That is the worst
381 CP	Edward	15	with what you can desire;/Before you know what is left to be desired;/And you go on
384 CP	Reilly	27	we die to each other daily./What we know of other people/Is only our memory of the
385 CP	Edward	35	I shall not come with her./{E} I don't know why,/But I think I should like you to
385 CP	Reilly	37	to bring her yourself./{UG} Yes, I know you would. And for definite reasons/
388 CP	Peter	5	/Alex is a wonderful person to know,/Because, you see, he knows everybody,/
388 CP	Celia	10	of course we ... I shall miss you;/You know how I depended on you for concerts,/And
388 CP	Celia	20	/{P} You're going abroad?/{C} I don't know. Perhaps./{E} You're both going away! {}/
388 CP	Lavinia	28	the one you sent to Alex./{L} I don't know what you mean./Edward, have you been
389 CP	Peter	9	us she was going away,/But I don't know where./{L} You don't know where?/And
389 CP	Lavinia	10	I don't know where./{L} You don't know where?/And do you know where you are
389 CP	Lavinia	11	You don't know where?/And do you know where you are going, yourself?/{P} Yes, of
390 CP	Lavinia	4	how is the dear aunt?/{L} So far as I know, she is very well, thank you./{J} She must
390 CP	Lavinia	14	perhaps I was in Essex. I really don't know./{J} You don't know where you were?
390 CP	Julia	15	I really don't know./{J} You don't know where you were? Lavinia!/Don't tell me
390 CP	Alex	38	she's famished./{A} Ah, in that case I know what I'll do .../{J} No, Alex./We must
391 CP	Lavinia	18	could explain the telegram./I don't know why. But it seems to me that yesterday/I

392 CP	Lavinia	2	/Like a schoolgirl. Like Celia. I don't know why I said it./Well, here I am./{E} I am to
392 CP	Lavinia	5	I am to ask no questions./{L} And I know I am to give no explanations./{E} And I
392 CP	Edward	8	And yet ... why not?/{E} I don't know why not. So what are we to talk about?/
392 CP	Lavinia	9	/{L} There is one thing I ought to know, because of other people/And what to do
392 CP	Edward	19	odd./{E} ... and one other. I don't know who he was,/But *you* ought to know./{L}
392 CP	Edward	20	know who he was,/But *you* ought to know./{L} Yes, I think I know./But I'm puzzled
392 CP	Lavinia	21	*you* ought to know./{L} Yes, I think I know./But I'm puzzled by Julia. That woman is
392 CP	Edward	37	a lot of time in lying./{E} I don't quite know what you mean./{L} Oh, Edward!/The
393 CP	Lavinia	13	was I who had given in to *you*./{L} I know what you mean by giving in to *me*:/You
393 CP	Lavinia	33	/{L} To think well of yourself./You know it was I who made you work at the Bar ...
394 CP	Lavinia	24	you come back?/{L} Frankly, I don't know. I was warned of the danger,/Yet
394 CP	Edward	27	why did you want me?/{E} I don't know either./You say you were trying to
395 CP	Lavinia	13	person/Whom you must get to know./{E} This is very interesting:/But you seem
396 CP	Lavinia	8	you really were rather attractive, you know;/And you kept on *saying* that you were in
397 CP	Lavinia	17	{E} Don't say that!/{L} I must say it./I know ... of a doctor who I think could help you.
397 CP	Edward	19	take one whom you choose. How do I know/That you wouldn't see him first, and tell
397 CP	Lavinia	25	be practical, even in hell:/And you know I am much more practical than you are./
397 CP	Edward	26	practical than you are./{E} I ought to know by now what you consider practical./
397 CP	Lavinia	33	you./You're much too divided to know what you want./But, being divided, you
398 CP	Lavinia	16	go and have a look in the kitchen./I know there are some eggs. But we must go out
399 CP	Nurse	20	small room;/And I need not let you know that she has arrived./Then, when you
400 CP	Alex	14	the sort of person/Who would know the right doctor, as well as the right
401 CP	Edward	8	of a man who did not know you./Yet Alex is so plausible. And his
401 CP	Edward	12	But he *is* a blunderer./I should like to know ... but what is the use!/I suppose I might
401 CP	Reilly	21	/And Mrs. Chamberlayne did not know that I was coming./But I knew you would
402 CP	Edward	3	be any better — now?/{E} I don't know, I'm sure. They could hardly be worse./I
402 CP	Edward	18	of a nervous breakdown./I didn't know it then myself — but if they saw it/I
404 CP	Edward	12	extreme of physical pain,/And now I know there is suffering worse than that./It is
404 CP	Reilly	38	I treat a patient like yourself/I need to know a great deal more about him,/Than the
405 CP	Reilly	17	you went along. A barrister/Ought to know his brief before he enters the court./{E} I
406 CP	Edward	1	/{L} Oh, to what hotel?/{E} I don't know — I mean to say,/That doesn't concern
406 CP	Lavinia	35	would never suit you, Edward. Now I know of a hotel/In the New Forest .../{E} How
406 CP	Edward	38	How like you, Lavinia./You always know of something better./{L} It's only that I
406 CP	Lavinia	40	/Than you have, Edward. You do know that./{E} Only because you've told me so
407 CP	Lavinia	36	/There were plenty of people to let me know about it./I wonder if there was anyone
407 CP	Lavinia	37	if there was anyone who didn't know./{R} There was one, in fact. But you, Mrs.
408 CP	Lavinia	26	hopeful symptom./{L} How did you know all this?/{R} That I cannot disclose./I have
410 CP	Edward	4	feel very sorry for you, Lavinia./You know, you really are exceptionally unlovable,/
410 CP	Reilly	32	own question,/Though you do not know the meaning of what you have said./{E}
411 CP	Edward	10	leave tomorrow — but how did you know/I was staying at the club?/{L} Really,
412 CP	Julia	3	/{R} She's waiting downstairs./{J} I know that, Henry. I brought her here myself./
412 CP	Reilly	4	myself./{R} Oh? You didn't let her know you were seeing me first?/{J} Of course
412 CP	Celia	29	... Oh, of course./But I didn't know .../{R} There is nothing you need to know.
412 CP	Reilly	30	.../{R} There is nothing you need to know./I was there at the instance of Mrs.
413 CP	Celia	21	circumstances?/I'd forgotten that you know nothing about me;/And with what I've
413 CP	Reilly	24	that I needn't explain myself./{R} I know quite enough about you for the moment:/
414 CP	Celia	12	relationship/With *everybody*. Do you know —It no longer seems worth while to
415 CP	Celia	14	is wicked to hurt other people/If you know that you're hurting them. I haven't hurt
416 CP	Celia	9	I made it obvious. You don't need to know/About him, do you?/{R} No./{C} Perhaps
417 CP	Celia	13	delight of loving. A state one does not know/When awake. But what, or whom I loved,
417 CP	Celia	15	/Or what in me was loving, I do not know./And if that is all meaningless, I want to
417 CP	Reilly	35	talk before the fire/Two people who know they do not understand each other,/
417 CP	Reilly	39	It is a good life. Though you will not know how good/Till you come to the end. But
418 CP	Celia	4	greed ... it is a good life./{C} I know I ought to be able to accept that/If I
418 CP	Celia	10	a vision of something/Though I don't know what it is. I don't want to forget it./I want
418 CP	Reilly	27	cannot be described;/You will know very little until you get there;/You will
419 CP	Reilly	37	/{R} You had better let your family know at once./I will send a car for you at nine
420 CP	Celia	4	sanatorium./{C} I don't in the least know what I am doing/Or why I am doing it.
420 CP	Celia	8	/{R} It is the best reason./{C} But I know it is I who have made the decision:/I must
421 CP	Julia	15	/{J} Oh yes, she will go far. And we know where she is going./But what do we know
421 CP	Julia	16	where she is going./But what do we know of the terrors of the journey?/You and I
421 CP	Julia	17	of the journey?/You and I don't know the process by which the human is/
421 CP	Julia	18	is/Transhumanised: what do we know/Of the kind of suffering they must
421 CP	Julia	24	be afraid of nothing; she will not even know/That there is anything there to be afraid
423 CP	Alex	3	perhaps, will speak them./You know, I have connections — even in California.

424 CP	Lavinia	17	/{L} Now Edward, that's unfair!/You know that we've given *several* parties/In the last
424 CP	Lavinia	23	be tired./{L} I'm not tired yet. But I know that I'll be glad/When it's all over./{E} I
425 CP	Lavinia	3	that one./{L} Well, Edward!/Do you know it's the first time you've paid me a
425 CP	Lavinia	17	a very practical mind./{L} But you know, I don't think that you need worry:/They
425 CP	Lavinia	19	out of those who accepted./You know we said, 'we can ask twenty more/Because
425 CP	Edward	21	going to the Gunnings instead'./{E} I know, that's what we said at the time;/But I'd
426 CP	Julia	30	to have caught you napping!/I know I'm much too early; but the fact is, my
426 CP	Julia	32	to the Gunnings' party —/And you know what *they* offer in the way of food and
426 CP	Julia	35	can Parkinson's do for me?/Oh yes, I know this is a Parkinson party;/I recognised one
427 CP	Alex	19	they give the warmest welcome./I know them well enough for that./{J} But tell us,
429 CP	Alex	33	ought to tell you/About someone you know — or knew .../{J} Edward!/Somebody
430 CP	Peter	25	Alex knew everybody. But I didn't know/That he knew any monkeys./{J} But give
430 CP	Peter	31	did enjoy a leg-pull, Julia:/But you all know I'm working for Pan-Am-Eagle?/{E} No.
431 CP	Peter	32	that as I'm English/I ought to know the best way to handle a duke./Besides
432 CP	Julia	6	we *have* met before./{J} Then if you know him already, you won't be afraid of him./
432 CP	Julia	7	you won't be afraid of him./You know, I was afraid of him at first:/He looks so
432 CP	Lavinia	29	that you knew each other —/I don't know why I should. Mr. MacColgie Gibbs./{A}
433 CP	Peter	12	hopes of seeing California./{P} You know you'd never come if we invited you./But
434 CP	Alex	23	was difficult to tell./But from what we know of local practices/It would seem that she
434 CP	Lavinia	32	— what a feeble thing to say!/But you know what I mean./{E} And you know what
434 CP	Edward	33	you know what I mean./{E} And you know what I'm thinking./{P} I don't understand
434 CP	Peter	35	been away/For two years, and I don't know what happened/To Celia, during those
434 CP	Peter	39	It's the waste that I resent./{P} You know more than I do:/For *me*, it's everything
435 CP	Peter	10	and more./At first I did not want to know about Celia/And so I never asked. Then I
435 CP	Peter	11	so I never asked. Then I wanted to know/And did not dare to ask. It took all my
435 CP	Peter	14	anything like this. I suppose I didn't know her,/I didn't understand her. I understand
435 CP	Peter	37	you're being unkind, Lavinia;/And I know that you're right./{L} And perhaps what
436 CP	Peter	10	But I'm grateful all the same./You know, all the time that you've been talking,/One
436 CP	Lavinia	31	/At the way in which she died. I don't know if you knew her./I suspect that you did. In
437 CP	Reilly	8	*apparition, sole of men, he saw./For know there are two worlds of life and death:/One*
437 CP	Reilly	24	was, what sort of death? *I* could not know;/Because it was for her to choose the way
437 CP	Reilly	27	/Yet choose the form of death. We know the death she chose./I did not know that
437 CP	Reilly	28	know the death she chose./I did not know that she would die in this way;/*She* did
437 CP	Reilly	29	she would die in this way;/*She* did not know. So all that I could do/Was to direct her
438 CP	Lavinia	4	agony beforehand./I mean — I know nothing of her last two years./{R} That
438 CP	Lavinia	39	for her death as you are./{L} Yet I know I shall go on blaming myself/For being so
439 CP	Alex	21	can I do?/{A} It is your film./And I know that Bela expects great things of it./{P} So
439 CP	Lavinia	26	/{L} Do try to come to see us./You know, I think it would do us all good —/You
440 CP	Lavinia	2	glad Alex told us .../And Peter had to know .../{E} Now I think I understand .../{L}
440 CP	Lavinia	25	best. You're rather transparent,/You know, when you're trying to cheer me up./To
445 CC	Claude	4	Park, on an errand like this./But you know my wife wouldn't like anyone to meet her/
446 CC	Eggers	37	— none worth watching./{E} I don't know, Sir Claude. Only the other day/I read a
447 CC	Claude	10	about replacing you./But you know she regards you — well, completely/As
447 CC	Claude	36	By the way, don't forget/To let her know that he's very musical./She can take him
448 CC	Eggers	15	/But there's one thing I should like to know —/If you don't mind — before I go to
449 CC	Claude	18	it! But your approval matters./You know she thinks the world of your opinion./{E}
449 CC	Eggers	34	— then what follows?/Will you let her know, then, that Mr. Simpkins/Is actually your
450 CC	Claude	5	a matter of fact, there's a lot I don't know/About you, Eggerson, although we
450 CC	Claude	13	/{SC} And just as much/She doesn't know about you. And just as much/You don't
450 CC	Claude	14	you. And just as much/You don't know about me — I'm not so sure of that!/My
451 CC	Colby	14	that's very different./{C} I don't know why it should be so different./I like B.
451 CC	Eggers	22	She's only met him once;/But do you know, he began addressing her as Muriel —/
451 CC	Eggers	25	/He has a way with the ladies, you know./But with Lady Elizabeth he wasn't so
452 CC	Eggers	25	Mr. Simpkins, Miss Angel. As you know, Miss Angel,/Mr. Simpkins has taken
452 CC	Lucasta	27	over my duties./{L} And does he know that *I*'m one of his duties?/Have you
452 CC	Lucasta	29	him for taking *me* over?/Did you know that, Colby? I'm Lucasta./It's only Eggy
452 CC	Lucasta	37	of changing it. But, Colby,/Do you know that I'm one of your responsibilities?/{C}
452 CC	Colby	38	/{C} No, I'm afraid I didn't know that./{E} You mustn't give way to her,
453 CC	Lucasta	14	believe all I say,/Mr. Eggerson. And I know he'll be nice to me/When you're out of the
454 CC	Eggers	33	to Sir Claude. And do you know —/I think it amuses him./{C} Well,
455 CC	Eggers	2	be calling me Eggers/Before you know it!/{C} I shouldn't wonder./I nearly did, a
458 CC	Lady E	18	why you're both so surprised./You know I'm a very experienced traveller./{SC} Oh
458 CC	Claude	19	traveller./{SC} Oh yes, of course we know that, Elizabeth./But why did you change
458 CC	Claude	27	man is Eggerson's successor./You know that Eggerson's been meaning to retire .../
459 CC	Claude	17	to have him closer at hand —/You know what a bother it's been for Eggerson —/

460 CC	Claude	9	me postcards from Zürich;/But you know that I can't decipher your writing./I like
460 CC	Claude	10	/I like to have the cards, just to know where you are/By reading the postmark./
461 CC	Colby	11	very much, I will. It's reassuring/To know that I have you always at my back/If I get
462 CC	Claude	29	subject: I'm coming back to it./You know I've deliberately left you alone,/And so
462 CC	Claude	39	started with me here,/That we hardly know each other at all./{C} I suppose there
465 CC	Colby	33	/Although the medium is different. I know/I should never have become a great
467 CC	Colby	21	a greater mistake than he did./{C} I know that I'm hurting you and I know/That I
467 CC	Colby	21	{C} I know that I'm hurting you and I know/That I hate myself for hurting you./{SC}
469 CC	Lucasta	3	my opinion counts for anything:/You know that. But I'd like to learn about music./I
469 CC	Colby	8	to find out what you like./When you know what you like, and begin to know it well,/I
469 CC	Colby	8	you know what you like, and begin to know it well,/Then you will want to learn about
469 CC	Lucasta	16	the right ones./{L} Colby, I didn't know you were so artful!/So the things I liked
470 CC	Lucasta	1	.../{L} Don't be such a fraud. You know you told me/The piano was only delivered
470 CC	Colby	36	want to educate me./{C} But I didn't know/That you wanted to be educated./{L}
471 CC	Lucasta	16	so you believe that I like you?/I didn't know that you were so conceited./{C} No, it's
471 CC	Lucasta	20	I wish you'd tell me./Because I don't know./{C} The first time we met/You were
471 CC	Colby	30	happened./I hope you don't mind: I know it sounds impertinent./{L} Well, there's
471 CC	Lucasta	32	you haven't learnt yet,/And that is, to know when you're paying a compliment./That
472 CC	Lucasta	12	strange, isn't it,/That as one gets to know a person better/One finds them in some
472 CC	Lucasta	21	music stands for./There's one thing I know. When you first told me/What a disaster it
472 CC	Lucasta	24	a good musician —/Of course, I don't know whether you were right./For all I can tell,
472 CC	Lucasta	36	I found I envied you/And I didn't know why! And now I think I know./It's awful
472 CC	Lucasta	36	I didn't know why! And now I think I know./It's awful for a man to have to give up,/
473 CC	Colby	22	be right, up to a point./And yet, you know, it's not quite real to me —/Although it's
473 CC	Colby	28	thing. That's why it's not real./You know, I think that Eggerson's garden/Is more
474 CC	Lucasta	23	sense of desolation afterwards./{L} I know what you mean. Then the flowers would
474 CC	Lucasta	37	because of what it stands for./You know, I'm a little jealous of your music!/When I
475 CC	Lucasta	19	begin to understand,/I'd like you to know a little more about me./You must have
475 CC	Colby	23	It's all a strange world/To me, you know, in which I find myself./But if you mean,
475 CC	Colby	25	background:/No. I've been curious to know what you are,/But not who you are, in the
475 CC	Lucasta	31	got to this point — you might as well know them./{C} I'd gladly tell you everything
475 CC	Colby	33	you everything about yourself;/But you know most of what there is to say/Already,
476 CC	Lucasta	25	who wouldn't have thought it./I don't know about B. He's very generous./I don't
476 CC	Colby	28	first moment./{C} But what is there to know?/{L} You'll laugh when I tell you:/I'm
477 CC	Lucasta	23	thought you'd understand./Little you know what it's like to be a bastard/And wanted
477 CC	Lucasta	24	a bastard/And wanted by nobody. I know why you're shocked:/Claude has just
477 CC	Lucasta	30	of person/That I want to be. That I know I am./That was new to me. I suppose I
478 CC	Colby	6	mustn't use such words! You don't know how it's hurting./{L} I could use words
478 CC	Lucasta	10	my mother coming out in me./You know, Colby, I'm truly disappointed./I was
478 CC	Lucasta	22	you're getting further in,/And you know at last that there's no escape./Well, I'll be
479 CC	Lucasta	20	you than cocktails, Lucasta./{L} You know I don't like sherry./{K} You've got to
480 CC	Kaghan	5	in./Colby's more cautious. You know, Colby,/You and I ought to be in business
480 CC	Kaghan	18	Well, there's something in that. You know, Lucasta,/Colby is a good judge of
480 CC	Kaghan	28	bred to it. I wasn't, Colby./Do you know, I was a foundling? You didn't know that!
480 CC	Kaghan	28	know, I was a foundling? You didn't know that!/Never had any parents. Just
481 CC	Lady E	26	Where will you get dinner?/Oh, I know. It's a chance to try that Herbal
482 CC	Colby	29	do you think, is my sort?/I don't know, myself. And I should like to know./{LE}
482 CC	Colby	29	know, myself. And I should like to know./{LE} In the first place, you ought to mix
482 CC	Lady E	33	about you,/But one doesn't need to know, if one knows what breeding is./And,
483 CC	Colby	5	to a very small number,/And I don't know where to find them./{LE} They can be
483 CC	Lady E	29	/{LE} What was I going to say? Oh, I know./Do you believe in reincarnation?/{C} No,
484 CC	Lady E	6	in relatives./{LE} You did not want to know your relatives!/I understand exactly how
484 CC	Lady E	30	they were so commonplace./Do you know, Colby, when I was a child/I had three
484 CC	Lady E	35	was, that I was very ugly/And didn't know it. Then, that I was feeble-minded/And
484 CC	Lady E	36	that I was feeble-minded/And didn't know it. Finally,/That I was a foundling, and
484 CC	Lady E	37	/That I was a foundling, and didn't know it./Of course, I was terrified of being ugly,
485 CC	Lady E	2	my family made me think so./But you know, I actually liked to believe/That I was a
485 CC	Colby	4	or do I mean 'changeling'?/{C} I don't know which you mean./{LE} However that may
487 CC	Claude	1	I believe./{SC} Yes it is./But you know that I'll have to have my speech written
487 CC	Claude	38	up by a Mrs. Guzzard./{SC} I know that. But why should that make him your
488 CC	Lady E	3	I knew./Then Tony was killed, as you know, in Africa,/And I had lost the name. Mrs.
488 CC	Claude	20	/It seems to me that we must let her know the truth./{C} It seems to me ... there is
488 CC	Claude	32	place of your own child,/If you got to know him first — and that you'd want to adopt
489 CC	Lady E	29	investments./{LE} Then how do you know that the sister had a child?/Perhaps Mrs.
490 CC	Lady E	5	have happened./Oh, Claude, you know I'm rather weak in the head/Though I try

490 CC	Claude	10	us everything that's in your mind./I know this situation must be more of an agony/
490 CC	Colby	13	wish it was more acute agony:/I don't know whether I've been suffering or not/During
490 CC	Colby	31	/Then it's merely a fact. Better not know/Than to know the fact and know it means
490 CC	Colby	32	a fact. Better not know/Than to know the fact and know it means nothing./At
490 CC	Colby	32	not know/Than to know the fact and know it means nothing./At the time I was born,
491 CC	Lady E	5	son you thought was yours. And I know from what you said,/That you would
491 CC	Colby	29	But, if we followed your suggestion,/I know, I know I should always be haunted/By
491 CC	Colby	29	followed your suggestion,/I know, I know I should always be haunted/By the
492 CC	Colby	2	account of that./But now I want to know whose son I am./{SC} Then the first thing
492 CC	Claude	31	Members/Of the Potters' Company know anything at all/About ceramics ... or any
494 CC	Lady E	29	I don't suppose I understand/And I know you don't think I understand anything,/
495 CC	Lady E	22	me poems. And he was so beautiful./I know now that poets don't look like poets:/And
497 CC	Eggers	1	We don't often speak of it;/Yet I know what's on her mind, for days beforehand./
497 CC	Lady E	25	/I feel sure he is. But I don't want to know:/I am perfectly content to leave things as
497 CC	Claude	31	asked Mrs. Guzzard here. She doesn't know that./{E} A natural line for Mr. Simpkins
498 CC	Lady E	3	at the same address?/{LE} I don't know the address./Mrs. Guzzard of Teddington,
498 CC	Lady E	4	Guzzard of Teddington, that's all I know,/And that I could swear to./{E} It does
499 CC	Lucasta	27	view. To get me off your hands./Oh, I know what a nuisance you've always found me!/
500 CC	Lucasta	20	had been some mistake./You don't know at all what I'm talking about!/But if he
500 CC	Lucasta	34	/And we can help each other. Oh, I know you think of him/Simply as a business
500 CC	Claude	39	So I'm grateful to Colby./{SC} I don't know what's happened, but nevertheless/I'm
501 CC	Lucasta	4	have made a wise decision./{L} And I know very well why you think so:/You think
502 CC	Colby	27	/{C} That's me, is it? I simply don't know./Perhaps you know me better than I
502 CC	Colby	28	it? I simply don't know./Perhaps you know me better than I know myself./But now
502 CC	Colby	28	/Perhaps you know me better than I know myself./But now that you know what I
502 CC	Colby	29	I know myself./But now that you know what I am .../{L} Who you are,/In the
502 CC	Lucasta	32	/Which makes it more difficult to know what you are./It may be there's no one so
503 CC	Lucasta	14	be happy. I'm going to marry B./I know you like B./{C} I'm very fond of him;/And
504 CC	Guzzard	29	waiting in the least, Sir Claude./I know that you are always much engaged./{SC}
504 CC	Lady E	33	morning, Mrs. Guzzard./You don't know me, but I know about you:/We have more
504 CC	Lady E	33	Guzzard./You don't know me, but I know about you:/We have more in common
504 CC	Claude	37	do with Colby./{SC} Elizabeth, you know we are to leave that to Eggerson./This is
506 CC	Eggers	9	died abroad./Lady Elizabeth did not know the name of the lady/Who had taken the
507 CC	Eggers	1	is where you can help us —/Do you know of any other Mrs. Guzzard?/{MG} None./
507 CC	Eggers	11	two advantages./{E} And did you know the name of the father/Or of the mother?/
507 CC	Guzzard	30	established the paternity;/But I didn't know who she was! What could I do?/{LE} Oh,
507 CC	Claude	39	herself/That Colby is her son. I know he is my son./And I asked you here so
508 CC	Eggers	29	we lost sight of them./{E} But you know their name?/{MG} Yes, I know their
508 CC	Guzzard	30	you know their name?/{MG} Yes, I know their name:/Like mine, a somewhat
510 CC	Kaghan	21	/{K} But how did Mrs. Guzzard know my name?/{MG} Were Mr. and Mrs.
511 CC	Kaghan	1	first been entrusted./{K} I really don't know what emotion to register .../{L} You don't
511 CC	Kaghan	17	get used to that./But I should like to know how I ought to address you,/Lady
512 CC	Guzzard	26	That can be a painful process,/As I know. And you, Barnabas Kaghan,/Are you
512 CC	Kaghan	32	my parents./I'm fond of them, you know./{LE} I shall see to that, Barnabas./{K} B.
513 CC	Colby	14	/Sir Claude is right: I wished to know the truth./What it is, doesn't matter. All I
513 CC	Colby	17	there's a fact/That one doesn't know. But the fact itself/Is unimportant, once
513 CC	Colby	26	I have never known and couldn't know now,/Because he would have died before I
513 CC	Colby	28	could remember; whom I could get to know/Only by report, by documents —/The
515 CC	Guzzard	1	was expecting one./That you did not know. It did not concern you./As I have just
516 CC	Colby	4	a very generous man. But now I know who was my father/I must follow my
516 CC	Colby	5	my father — so that I may come to know him./{SC} What do you mean?/{C} I want
516 CC	Claude	28	we shared?/Heaven knows — and you know — I put no obstruction/In the way of
517 CC	Colby	2	/You knew your inheritance. Now I know mine./{SC} I shall never ask you to think
517 CC	Eggers	25	will take me./{E} If so, I happen to know of a vacancy/In my own parish, in Joshua
518 CC	Eggers	6	/We worked together every day, you know,/For quite a little time, and I've watched
519 CC	Kaghan	7	and kneels beside him]/{K} You know, Claude, I think we all made the same
519 CC	Kaghan	19	/Claude ... and Aunt Elizabeth./You know, Claude, both Lucasta and I/Would like
524 ES	Monica	17	/{M} It was a perfect lunch./But I know what men are — they like to show off./
525 ES	Charles	16	well then, I will stop to tea,/But you know I won't get a chance to talk to you./You
525 ES	Charles	17	get a chance to talk to you./You know that. Now that your father's retired/He's
525 ES	Charles	26	/{C} I try to be respectful;/But you know that I shan't have a minute alone with
525 ES	Monica	31	tea./So why not talk now? Though I know very well/What it is you want to say. I've
526 ES	Charles	4	it/I was badly frightened. For I didn't know you loved me —/I merely wanted to believe
526 ES	Monica	27	say, 'Lambert,/Please let his lordship know that tea is waiting'./{L} Yes, Miss
527 ES	Charles	31	then./And mostly it's been me./{C} I know it's been you./It's a pity that you haven't

529 ES	Charles	5	love having you to talk to!/{C} I know he's used to seeing me about./{M} I've
529 ES	Monica	25	time for your engagement book!/You know what the doctors said: complete
529 ES	Monica	26	to think about nothing. Though I know that won't be easy./{LC} That is just what
529 ES	Ld Clav	32	this book — or one just like it —/You know I keep the old ones on a shelf together;/I
530 ES	Monica	6	/That's my business to prevent. You know I'm to protect you/From your own
530 ES	Ld Clav	9	They've dried up, Monica, and you know it./They talk of rest, these doctors,
530 ES	Monica	28	forward/To this very time! You know how you grumbled/At the farewell
530 ES	Ld Clav	32	*still lying in its case*]./{LC} I don't know which impressed me more, the insincerity/
531 ES	Monica	4	simply want to revel in gloom!/You know you've retired in a blaze of glory —/
532 ES	Ld Clav	16	of introduction/From a man I used to know. I can't refuse to see him./Though from
532 ES	Gomez	33	you might almost say./Don't you know me, Dick?/{LC} Fred Culverwell!/Why do
533 ES	Gomez	7	done the same, in a modest way./You know, where *I* live, people do change their
534 ES	Gomez	34	/Or before a firing squad./You don't know what serious politics is like!/I said to my
535 ES	Ld Clav	24	character!/{LC} I should like to know why you need to trust *me*./{G} That's
535 ES	Gomez	35	*to whisky*]/{G} But of course you know!/Just enough to think you know more
536 ES	Gomez	1	you know!/Just enough to think you know more than you do./You've changed your
536 ES	Gomez	10	long ago./I married a girl who didn't know a word of English,/Didn't want to learn
536 ES	Gomez	18	thoughts./O God, Dick, *you* don't know what it's like/To be so cut off!
537 ES	Gomez	21	unknown grammar school./I didn't know either, but I was flattered./Later, I came
538 ES	Gomez	8	/{G} Yes, and paid my passage out. I know the reason:/You wanted to get rid of me. I
539 ES	Ld Clav	9	let you retire?/{LC} If you want to know, I had had a stroke./And I might have
540 ES	Gomez	11	... worldly success?/{G} No, because I know the value of the coinage/I pay myself in./
540 ES	Ld Clav	14	Indeed! How interesting!/I still don't know why you've come to see me/Or what you
540 ES	Gomez	20	/{G} One time in particular./You know quite well to which occasion I'm referring
541 ES	Gomez	9	acquaintance —/But you'd never know to whom I'd told it,/Or who knew the
543 ES	Ld Clav	9	was it, Father?/{LC} A man I used to know./{M} Oh, so you knew him?/{LC} Yes.
545 ES	Monica	36	very kind ... Oh, I'm sorry,/We don't know how we ought to address you./Do we call
546 ES	Piggott	7	/Was a distinguished surgeon. Do you know, I fell in love with him/During an
546 ES	Piggott	21	any guest who's incurable./You know, we've been deluged with applications/
546 ES	Piggott	36	different./She is a real nurse, you know, fully qualified./Our system is very
547 ES	Piggott	28	But I don't advise croquet/Until you know enough about the other guests/To know
547 ES	Piggott	29	enough about the other guests/To know whom *not* to play with. I'll mention no
548 ES	Carghil	31	And you don't even recognise me! I'd know you anywhere./But then, we've all seen
549 ES	Carghil	4	/{LC} What!/{MC} Don't you know me yet?/{LC} I'm afraid not./{MC} There
549 ES	Carghil	24	all so clearly./You attracted me, you know, at the very first meeting —I can't think
549 ES	Carghil	27	the world!'/But Effie it was — you know, Effie was very shrewd —/Effie it was said
550 ES	Carghil	4	only saying that to tease me./You know I meant my stage name. The name by
551 ES	Carghil	14	suffered/I shouldn't want to let you know who I am,/I shouldn't want to come and
551 ES	Carghil	16	about the past./You're wrong, you know. It's both pain and pleasure/To talk about
551 ES	Carghil	22	broken/Once it's been repaired? But I know what you mean./You mean that I would
553 ES	Carghil	18	*their fires are not quenched*. Do you know what I do?/I read your letters every night.
554 ES	Piggott	32	had caught you./You wouldn't know that name, but you might remember her/
555 ES	Piggott	8	If she bothers you again/Just let me know. I'm afraid it's the penalty/Of being
555 ES	Monica	14	You look tired, Father./She ought to know better. But I'm all the more distressed/
555 ES	Ld Clav	23	he's not had another accident./You know, after that last escapade of his,/I've lived
555 ES	Ld Clav	32	he wouldn't care for you or me to know about./{M} It's probably money./{LC} If
556 ES	Monica	4	I can see he's frightened./And you know what Michael is like when he's frightened.
556 ES	Monica	27	so polite to each other./Michael, you know what you've come to ask of Father/And
556 ES	Michael	30	leave you together. {}/[*Exit*]/{Mi} You know, it's awfully hard to explain things to *you*.
558 ES	Michael	20	of a famous public man./You don't know what I suffered, working in that office./In
559 ES	Ld Clav	9	Australia — no./The men I know there are all in the cities:/An outdoor life
559 ES	Michael	23	I might choose to —/No one would know or care what my name had been./{LC} So
559 ES	Michael	27	is my inheritance? As for your title,/I know why you took it. And Mother knew.
560 ES	Michael	7	to be rid of *me*./You simply don't know how very much pleasanter/You will find
560 ES	Michael	13	have you in mind?/{Mi} Oh, I don't know. Import and export,/With an opportunity
561 ES	Ld Clav	7	their past will always lose the race./I know this from experience. When you reach
561 ES	Monica	24	Why do you look so angry?/I know that Michael must be in great trouble,/So
561 ES	Monica	35	calls me a coward./{M} Father! You know that I would give my life for you./Oh,
562 ES	Michael	9	never did, Monica, not from me./You know I've always been very fond of you —/I've
562 ES	Carghil	15	nice to find a little family party!/I know who you are! You're Monica, of course:/
562 ES	Carghil	20	you're right./But ...{MC} How did I know? Because you're so like your father/When
562 ES	Carghil	38	guest here. He's waving to us./Do you know him, Richard?/{LC} It's a man I used to
563 ES	Ld Clav	1	Richard?/{LC} It's a man I used to know./{MC} How interesting! He's a very good
567 ES	Charles	10	/{C} My darling, what I want is to know that you need me./On that last day in
568 ES	Charles	15	/I can think of things you don't yet know about me, Monica,/But there's nothing I

239 MC	Chorus	2	/Are we drawn by danger? Is it the knowledge of safety, that draws our feet/
242 MC	Mess	10	or like a beginning./It is common knowledge that when the Archbishop/Parted
310 FR	Mary	20	the moment of birth/Is when we have knowledge of death/I believe the season of birth
330 FR	Harry	22	irrevocable —/It's eternal, or gives a knowledge of eternity,/Because it feels eternal
333 FR	Agatha	29	whose, or why. It is certain/That the knowledge of it must precede the expiation./It is
338 FR	Harry	16	knows/Or how much she knows. Any knowledge she may have —/It was not I who
344 FR	Gerald	19	for some sort of training;/The medical knowledge is the first thing./I've met with
363 CP	Reilly	14	/As we have to, and live on a little knowledge/About ourselves as we were. Who
420 CP	Reilly	30	it is known to the other./It's not the knowledge of the mutual treachery/But the
420 CP	Reilly	31	of the mutual treachery/But the knowledge that the other understands the
581 ES	Ld Clav	15	/When contrition ensues upon knowledge of the truth./Why did I always want

KNOWN (64)

14	Prufrock	49	a minute will reverse./For I have known them all already, known them all —/
14	Prufrock	49	/For I have known them all already, known them all —/Have known the evenings,
14	Prufrock	50	all already, known them all —/Have known the evenings, mornings, afternoons,/I
14	Prufrock	55	how should I presume?/And I have known the eyes already, known them all —/The
14	Prufrock	55	/And I have known the eyes already, known them all —/The eyes that fix you in a
15	Prufrock	62	how should I presume?/And I have known the arms already, known them all —/
15	Prufrock	62	/And I have known the arms already, known them all —/Arms that are braceleted and
62	WL: Burial	45	/Had a bad cold, nevertheless/Is known to be the wisest woman in Europe,/With
159	Rock 6	1	/It is hard for those who have never known persecution,/And who have never
159	Rock 6	2	persecution,/And who have never known a Christian,/To believe these tales of
160	Rock 7	8	turned towards the light and were known of the light/Invented the Higher
193	FQ: Little	95	of some dead master/Whom I had known, forgotten, half recalled/Both one and
198	FQ: Little	251	the children in the apple-tree/Not known, because not looked for/But heard,
204	de la Mare	18	scene is suddenly strange/Or the well known is what we have yet to learn,/And two
218	Mung Rump	5	given to rove./They were very well known in Cornwall Gardens, in Launceston
225	Mr Mistoff	51	singular magical powers:/And I have known the family to call/Him in from the
227	Macavity	39	Cats whose wicked deeds are widely known/(I might mention Mungojerrie, I might
589	Fable	67	can doubt,/Who knows the well known fact, as you do surely —/That ghosts are
265 MC	Priest1	10	/{K1} Servants of the King./{P1} And known to us./You are welcome. Have you
267 MC	Knight1	28	make no mention./They are too well known. But after dissension/Had ended, in
270 MC	Chorus	11	/To the horror of the ape. Have I not known, not known/What was coming to be? It
270 MC	Chorus	11	of the ape. Have I not known, not known/What was coming to be? It was here, in
274 MC	Thomas	1	is not in time that my death shall be known;/It is out of time that my decision
278 MC	Knight2	18	and I/may say that I have never known a man so well qualified for the/highest
281 MC	Chorus	9	exist only as seen by Thee, only as known by Thee, all things exist/Only in Thy
300 FR	Downing	36	/Mustn't she, Sir? or else he'd have known it./{C} Oh yes ... quite so. Thank you,
304 FR	Mary	1	when at college./{M} I might have known you'd throw that up against me./I know
314 FR	Amy	4	oldest friend of the family,/And he's known you longer than anybody, Harry./When
324 FR	Amy	27	to think/How little I have ever known./But I think your remarks are much
331 FR	Harry	27	way I shall find/That I have always known it. And that will be better./{Ag} I will try
332 FR	Harry	33	I have believed this./{H} I have known neither./{Ag} The autumn came too
333 FR	Agatha	27	/It is possible that you have not known what sin/You shall expiate, or whose, or
334 FR	Harry	19	I can hardly imagine it./I wish I had known — but that was impossible./I only now
343 FR	Mary	15	to come for me: I should have known it;/It was all over, I believe, before it
369 CP	Peter	4	was different from any girl I'd ever known/And not easy to talk to, on that
379 CP	Edward	15	But it was too late. And I should have known/That it wasn't fair to you./{C} It wasn't
394 CP	Edward	30	me feel insignificant?/I may not have known what life I wanted,/But it wasn't the life
401 CP	Edward	7	symptom./Well, I should have known better than to come here/On the
406 CP	Edward	25	*you* go to a sanatorium?/I have never known anyone in my life/With fewer mental
419 CP	Celia	13	/{C} Oh, what an anti-climax! I have known people/Who have been to your
420 CP	Reilly	29	meanness/From himself, because it is known to the other./It's not the knowledge of the
465 CC	Claude	19	For I came to see/That I had always known, at the secret moments,/That I didn't
466 CC	Claude	19	truly religious people —/I've never known any — can find some unity./Then there
483 CC	Lady E	35	in it/I should have said that we had known each other/In some previous
486 CC	Colby	3	uncommon one./You couldn't have known my aunt./{LE} No. I never met ... your
491 CC	Colby	26	been hard/For me, who have never known the feelings of a son,/To be disputed
492 CC	Lady E	5	sorry for you./I believe that if I had known of your ... delusion/I would never have
492 CC	Claude	8	/{SC} And as for me,/If I could have known what was going to happen,/I would
497 CC	Eggers	10	have expected her name to be known to you./{SC} She'd been questioning
505 CC	Guzzard	39	/{MG} So I am aware. I have known it to happen./{E} — Who was taken
513 CC	Colby	26	like a father/Whom I have never known and couldn't know now,/Because he
524 ES	Charles	13	the only place where I'm really well known/And get well served. And when *you're*
538 ES	Gomez	20	/That's your convention. Or if it's known you made it/You simply get moved to

540 ES   Gomez   30   in a hurry./You didn't want it to be known where we'd been./The girls who were
544 ES   Ld Clav 30   that they enjoy it. Whereas I've often known/That I didn't enjoy it. Some
545 ES   Piggott 31   you have to do is to make your wants known./Just ring through to my office. If I'm
563 ES   Carghil 27   —/Lord Claverton and I — I was known by my stage name./There was a time,
564 ES   Carghil 11   you do./{MC} I don't believe you've known Lord Claverton/As long as I have, Señor
564 ES   Gomez   14   lady, you're not old enough/To have known Dick Ferry as long as I have./We were
570 ES   Ld Clav 32   would *he* have been/If he hadn't known me? Only a schoolmaster/In an obscure
571 ES   Monica   28   from those who love you/What is known so well to those who hate you?/{LC} I
573 ES   Carghil 35   interest in her future./Fancy! I've only known her two days!/But I feel like a mother to
573 ES   Carghil 38   I just missed being her mother!/I've known her father for a very long time,/And
577 ES   Carghil 28   man —/I wish you could have known him, Señor Gomez!/You're very much

KNOWS (51)

42 Swee   Erect   23   pink from nape to base,/Knows the female temperament/And wipes the
143 Lines OM   13   from my golden eye/The dullard knows that he is mad./Tell me if I am not glad!/
152 Rock 2   45   on ribbon roads,/And no man knows or cares who is his neighbour/Unless his
155 Rock 3   58   Stranger,/Be prepared for him who knows how to ask questions./O weariness of
209 NamingCats   24   —/But THE CAT HIMSELF KNOWS, and will never confess./When you
222 Pekes Pols   1   /The Pekes and the Pollicles, everyone knows,/Are proud and implacable passionate
589 Fable   67   statement nobody can doubt,/Who knows the well known fact, as you do surely —/
593 Grad 5   3   which came before,/Summons — who knows what time may hold in store,/Or what
598 Circe   3   men in pain,/Are flowers that no man knows./Their petals are fanged and red/With
243 MC Priest3   10   or good, let the wheel turn./For who knows the end of good or evil?/Until the
245 MC Priest2   27   for the event./But your Lordship knows that seven years of waiting,/Seven years
250 MC Thomas   10   world,/To keep order, as the world knows order./Those who put their faith in
278 MC Knight2   25   striven to establish; and that — God knows/why — the two orders were
286 FR Violet   18   /People with money from heaven knows where —/{G} Dividends from aeroplane
297 FR Charles   17   the same thing once, myself./Nobody knows what he's likely to do/Until there's
297 FR Gerald   20   Downing to know/Any more than he knows already./And even if he knew, it's very
326 FR Gerald   7   /{G} I wonder how much Amy knows about Arthur?/{C} More than she cares
338 FR Harry   15   /{H} I do not know whether Agatha knows/Or how much she knows. Any
338 FR Harry   16   Agatha knows/Or how much she knows. Any knowledge she may have —/It was
342 FR Agatha   36   border? No one could, no one who knows./No one who has the least suspicion of
353 CP Celia   22   tell it./I don't believe everyone here knows it. {}/[*To the* UNIDENTIFIED GUEST]
354 CP Celia   1   /And I don't believe that Edward knows it./{E} I may have heard it, but I don't
376 CP Celia   26   What's in that saucepan?/{C} Nobody knows./{E} It's something that Alex came and
388 CP Peter   6   person to know,/Because, you see, he knows everybody, everywhere./So what I've
392 CP Lavinia   23   Julia. That woman is the devil./She knows by instinct when something's going to
430 CP Peter   36   movies?/{L} Occasionally./{P} Alex knows./Did you see my last picture, Alex?/{A} I
431 CP Peter   4   be a good place to make one./— Alex knows all about Pan-Am-Eagle:/It was he who
436 CP Reilly   26   leave/A few dying natives./{R} Who knows, Mrs. Chamberlayne,/The difference that
447 CC Claude   8   the subject?/{SC} Of course, she knows you were wanting to retire,/As we had
450 CC Claude   1   of/About anyone, however well one knows them;/And that may be something of the
470 CC Lucasta   32   something she would like/When she knows *you* wouldn't like it? That's not a
476 CC Lucasta   17   He half believes in it./But he knows all about me, and he knows/That what
476 CC Lucasta   17   it./But he knows all about me, and he knows/That what some men have thought
482 CC Lady E   33   /But one doesn't need to know, if one knows what breeding is./And, second, you need
489 CC Claude   23   him grow. And Mrs. Guzzard/Knows he is my son./{LE} But where were you,
492 CC Claude   12   /{SC} Oh, of course, Eggerson! He knows all about it./Let us say no more tonight.
497 CC Claude   7   come. Lady Elizabeth/Is sure that she knows the name of Mrs. Guzzard./{LE} Mrs.
501 CC Lucasta   6   because we're both common./B. knows you think him common. And so he
501 CC Lucasta   7   /To be very common, because he knows you think so./*You* gave us our parts.
503 CC Lucasta   4   itself in time. And perhaps — who knows? —/We might become more necessary to
505 CC Claude   4   Now he lives ... in the country. But he knows the whole story:/He's been in my
513 CC Colby   18   fact itself/Is unimportant, once one knows it./{MG} You had no preference?
516 CC Claude   28   the experience we shared?/Heaven knows — and you know — I put no obstruction
517 CC Eggers   21   venture./Mr. Simpkins is a man who knows his own mind./Is it true, Mr. Simpkins,
536 ES Gomez   26   /{G} Oh, loneliness —/Everybody knows what that's like./Your loneliness — so
549 ES Carghil   1   the papers/So often. And everybody knows *you*. But still,/I wish you could have paid
556 ES Monica   28   come to ask of Father/And Father knows that you want something from him./
571 ES Ld Clav   33   occasion the memory of which/He knows very well, has always haunted me./I was
572 ES Ld Clav   20   no other woman has had. And she knows it./And she knows that the ghost of the
572 ES Ld Clav   21   has had. And she knows it./And she knows that the ghost of the man I was/Still
575 ES Gomez   19   rehearsing ancient history./Michael knows it already. I've told him myself./I

KRISHNA (2)
187 FQ: DrySal 126   /I sometimes wonder if that is what Krishna meant —/Among other things — or
188 FQ: DrySal 169   this is your real destination.'/So Krishna, as when he admonished Arjuna/On the
KRUM (1)
120 SP   Klip   4 /What about it Klip?/{Kl} You said it, Krum./London's a slick place, London's a swell
KRUMPACKER (6)
119 SP   m   1   HORSFALL. KLIPSTEIN. KRUMPACKER./{W} Hello Doris! Hello
119 SP   Wauch   6   /Meet Mr. Klipstein. Meet Mr. Krumpacker./{Kl} How do you do/{Kr} How
119 SP   Dusty   22 {Du} Do you know London well, Mr. Krumpacker?/{Kl} No we never been here
121 SA   m   1   HORSFALL. KLIPSTEIN. KRUMPACKER. SWARTS. SNOW. DORIS.
123 SA   1m   13 isle. {}/SONG BY KLIPSTEIN AND KRUMPACKER/SNOW AND SWARTS AS
125 SA   m   31   HORSFALL, KLIPSTEIN, KRUMPACKER/{Ch} When you're alone in
KULP (1)
 37 Gerontion   28   /Shifting the candles; Fräulein von Kulp/Who turned in the hall, one hand on the

L. (1) [*Abbreviation*]
453 CC Lucasta   4   Angel an inch/She'll take an ell./{L} L. for Lucasta./Go on, Eggy. Don't mind him,
L' (4)
48 Lune Miel   3   une nuit d'été, les voici à Ravenne,/A l'aise entre deux draps, chez deux centaines de
51 Restaurant   18   un gros chien;/Moi j'avais peur, je l'ai quittée à mi-chemin./C'est dommage.'/Mais
51 Restaurant   28   d'étain:/Un courant de sous-mer l'emporta très loin,/Le repassant aux étapes de
182 FQ: ECoker 175   years largely wasted, the years of *l'entre deux guerres* —/Trying to learn to use
LA (26)
24 Rhapsody   51   lamp hummed:/'Regard the moon,/La lune ne garde aucune rancune,/She winks a
28 Boston ET   7   as one would turn to nod good-bye to La Rochefoucauld,/If the street were time and
34 Figlia   t   —'/And — 'Are we then so serious?'/La Figlia Che Piange/Stand on the highest
46 Directeur   1   A.B.C.'s./Le Directeur/Malheur à la malheureuse Tamise/Qui coule si près du
46 Directeur   6   Conservateur/Du Spectateur/Empeste la brise./Les actionnaires/Réactionnaires/Du
47 Mél Adult   7   peu banquier,/Vous me paierez bien la tête./C'est à Paris que je me coiffe/Casque
48 Lune Miel   4   chez deux centaines de punaises;/La sueur aestivale, et une forte odeur de
48 Lune Miel   13   de Padoue à Milan/Où se trouve la Cène, et un restaurant pas cher./Lui pense
48 Lune Miel   15   et rédige son bilan./Ils auront vu la Suisse et traversé la France./Et Saint
48 Lune Miel   15   /Ils auront vu la Suisse et traversé la France./Et Saint Apollinaire, raide et
48 Lune Miel   18   encore/Dans ses pierres écroulantes la forme précise de Byzance./The
51 Restaurant   4   /Du vent, du grand soleil, et de la pluie;/C'est ce qu'on appelle le jour de lessive
51 Restaurant   6   lessive des gueux.'/(Bavard, baveux, à la croupe arrondie,/Je te prie, au moins, ne bave
51 Restaurant   7   Je te prie, au moins, ne bave pas dans la soupe)./'Les saules trempés, et des bourgeons
51 Restaurant   13   montent au chiffre de trente-huit./'Je la chatouillais, pour la faire rire./J'éprouvais un
51 Restaurant   13   trente-huit./'Je la chatouillais, pour la faire rire./J'éprouvais un instant de puissance
51 Restaurant   24   moi?/Tiens, voilà dix sous, pour la salle-de-bains./Phlébas, le Phénicien, pendant
51 Restaurant   26   noyé,/Oubliait les cris des mouettes et la houle de Cornouaille,/Et les profits et les
51 Restaurant   27   /Et les profits et les pertes, et la cargaison d'étain:/Un courant de sous-mer
67 WL: Fire S   202   O ces voix d'enfants, chantant dans la coupole!/Twit twit twit/Jug jug jug jug jug
70 WL: Fire S   306   humble people who expect/Nothing.'/la la/To Carthage then I came/Burning burning
70 WL: Fire S   306   people who expect/Nothing.'/la la/To Carthage then I came/Burning burning
75 WL: Thund   429   swallow/*Le Prince d'Aquitaine à la tour abolie*/These fragments I have shored
128 Cor1 March   51   /Light/Light/*Et les soldats faisaient la haie? ILS LA FAISAIENT.*/Difficulties of a
128 Cor1 March   51   /*Et les soldats faisaient la haie? ILS LA FAISAIENT.*/Difficulties of a Statesman/
204 de la Mare   t   is the fruit of action./To Walter de la Mare/The children who explored the brook
LÀ (3)
47 Mél Adult   14   de-ci de-là/A divers coups de tra là là/De Damas jusqu'à Omaha./Je célébrai
47 Mél Adult   14   de-ci de-là/A divers coups de tra là là/De Damas jusqu'à Omaha./Je célébrai mon
51 Restaurant   9   des bourgeons sur les ronces —/C'est là, dans une averse, qu'on s'abrite./J'avais sept
LABEL (1)
528 ES Monica 12   /In politics Father wore a public label./And later, as chairman of public
LABOR (1)
593 Grad 7   3   years be found with those who try/To labor for the good until they die,/And ask no
LABORATORY (1)
314 FR Warburt   27   /I've left off thinking in terms of the laboratory./We're all of us ill in one way or
LABOUR (9)
148 Rock 1   46   ROCK:/The lot of man is ceaseless labour,/Or ceaseless idleness, which is still
148 Rock 1   48   which is still harder,/Or irregular labour, which is not pleasant./I have trodden
151 Rock 2   8   unites with desired; we have only our labour to give and our labour is not required./
151 Rock 2   8   have only our labour to give and our labour is not required./We wait on corners, with
154 Rock 3   23   forgetful and forgotten/To idleness, labour, and delirious stupor?/There shall be left
158 Rock 5   11   snakes and dogs: therefore some must labour, and others must hold the spears./It is
236 Cat Morgan   19   time, and you'll spare yourself labour/If jist you make friends with the Cat at
257 MC Chorus   13   child without milk in summer,/Our labour taken away from us,/Our sins made
273 MC Chorus   5   my Saviour,/Let not be in vain Thy labour;/Help me, Lord, in my last fear./Dust I
LABOURER (2)
239 MC Chorus   12   waits, whispers in darkness./While the labourer kicks off a muddy boot and stretches
240 MC Chorus   3   to compile a little fortune,/And the labourer bends to his piece of earth,
LABYRINTH (1)
422 CP   Alex   23   the mountain./Watch over her in the labyrinth./Watch over her by the quicksand./{J}
LABYRINTHS (1)
438 CP Reilly   8   speak about it/We talk of darkness, labyrinths, Minotaur terrors./But that world
LACERATION (1)
194 FQ: Little   138   of rage/At human folly, and the laceration/Of laughter at what ceases to amuse./

LACK (7)

43	Swee Erect	36	to their principles/And deprecate the lack of taste/Observing that hysteria/Might
66	WL: Chess	155	if Albert makes off, it won't be for lack of telling./You ought to be ashamed, I said,
103	Journ Magi	13	And the night-fires going out, and the lack of shelters,/And the cities hostile and the
252	MC Tempt4	31	with me beside you, you shall not lack a friend./{T} Who are you? I expected/
330	FR Harry	30	dream, I felt all the same emotion/Or lack of emotion, as before: the same loathing/
370	CP Peter	3	she spoke of them/And about their lack of intellectual interests./{E} And what
547	ES Piggott	37	best walks./I won't apologise for the lack of excitement:/After all, peace and quiet is

LACKED (1)

254	MC Tempt4	40	/But pondering the qualities that you lacked/Will only try to find the historical fact./

LACKING (3)

244	MC Chorus	1	/Another year the plums are lacking./Yet we have gone on living,/Living and
467	CC Colby	6	to atone for!/There's something lacking, between you and me,/That you had,
580	ES Monica	31	only self-confidence that Michael is lacking./Oh Father, it's not you and me he

LACKS (1)

465	CC Claude	13	/To do something for which he lacks the capacity?/Could a man be said to have

LADDER (2)

536	ES Gomez	3	each step was merely a step up the ladder,/So you weren't aware of becoming a
536	ES Gomez	5	my name, there was no social ladder./It was jumping a gap — and you can't

LADIES (7)

43	Swee Erect	33	backward, clutching at her sides./The ladies of the corridor/Find themselves involved,
66	WL: Chess	172	ta. Goonight. Goonight./Good night, ladies, good night, sweet ladies, good night,
66	WL: Chess	172	/Good night, ladies, good night, sweet ladies, good night, good night./The Fire Sermon
314	FR Warburt	35	now —/You wouldn't believe it, ladies — was a murderer,/Who suffered from an
357	CP Celia	3	I going to say?/It's dreadful for old ladies alone in the country,/And almost
451	CC Eggers	25	*is* her name./He has a way with the ladies, you know./But with Lady Elizabeth he
496	CC Eggers	20	come up oftener!/Isn't that like the ladies! She used to complain/At my being up in

LADIES' (1)

254	MC Tempt4	33	gold spent,/The jewels gone for light ladies' ornament,/The sanctuary broken, and its

LADY (103)

18	Portrait	t	wake us, and we drown./Portrait of a Lady/Among the smoke and fog of a December
31	Apollinax	5	in the shrubbery/Gaping at the lady in the swing./In the palace of Mrs.
32	Hysteria	7	rusty/green iron table, saying: 'If the lady and gentleman wish to take their/tea in the
32	Hysteria	8	to take their/tea in the garden, if the lady and gentleman wish to take their tea in the/
56	Swee Night	25	with murderous paws;/She and the lady in the cape/Are suspect, thought to be in
62	WL: Burial	49	eyes. Look!)/Here is Belladonna, the Lady of the Rocks,/The lady of situations./Here
62	WL: Burial	50	the Lady of the Rocks,/The lady of situations./Here is the man with three
91	Ash-Wed 2	1	us now and at the hour of our death./Lady, three white leopards sat under a
91	Ash-Wed 2	8	/Because of the goodness of this Lady/And because of her loveliness, and
91	Ash-Wed 2	16	/Which the leopards reject. The Lady is withdrawn/In a white gown, to
91	Ash-Wed 2	25	the burden of the grasshopper, saying/Lady of silences/Calm and distressed/Torn and
189	FQ: DrySal	173	fare well,/But fare forward, voyagers./Lady, whose shrine stands on the promontory,/
213	Growltiger	30	/Concentrating his attention on the Lady GRIDDLEBONE./And his raffish crew
213	Growltiger	34	for aught but Griddlebone,/And the Lady seemed enraptured by his manly baritone,/
601	Nocturne	8	have some servant wait,/Stab, and the lady sinks into a swoon./Blood looks effective
284	FR m	2	/Persons/AMY, DOWAGER LADY MONCHENSEY, IVY, VIOLET, *and*
284	FR m	4	*daughter of a deceased cousin of Lady Monchensey*/DENMAN, *a parlourmaid*/
291	FR Violet	5	/{V} I should have been helping Lady Bumpus, at the Vicar's American Tea./
298	FRDowning	32	years .../{Do} Eleven years, Sir, next Lady Day./{C} Eleven years, and you know him
300	FRDowning	3	But he seemed very anxious about my Lady./Tried to keep her in when the weather
300	FRDowning	11	was just my complaint against my Lady./It's my opinion that man and wife/
315	FR Warburt	28	first, in to dinner./{W} With pleasure, Lady Monchensey,/And I hope that next year
323	FR Winch	8	are you here for?/{Wi} I'm sorry, my Lady, but I've just told the doctor,/It's really
323	FR Warburt	10	/{Wi} It's John has had the accident, Lady Monchensey;/And Winchell tells me Dr.
323	FR Winch	18	/{Wi} Coming along in the fog, my Lady,/And he must have been in rather a hurry.
323	FR Winch	23	Where is he?/{Wi} At the Arms, my Lady;/Of course, he hasn't come round yet./Dr.
323	FR Warburt	28	Order the car at once./{W} I forbid it, Lady Monchensey./As your doctor, I forbid
323	FR Warburt	37	Warburton's orders./{W} I repeat, Lady Monchensey, that you must not go out./If
324	FR Warburt	4	have trusted me a good many years, Lady Monchensey;/This is not the time to begin
348	FR Warburt	2	him up here in the morning./I hope Lady Monchensey hasn't been worrying?/I'm
353	CP Celia	14	story you told the other day, about Lady Klootz and the wedding cake./{P} And
354	CP Julia	9	Lithuanian accent./{J} Lithuanian? Lady Klootz?/{P} I thought she was Belgian.
354	CP Julia	16	what's become of them now./{J} Lady Klootz was very lovely, once upon a time.
354	CP Julia	19	GUEST]/{J} Did *you* know Lady Klootz?/{UG} No, I never met her./{C}
355	CP Julia	29	them./Well, I started to tell you about Lady Klootz./It was at the Vincewell wedding.

358 CP	Peter	14	{P} But won't you tell the story about Lady Klootz?/{J} What Lady Klootz?/{C} And
358 CP	Julia	15	story about Lady Klootz?/{J} What Lady Klootz?/{C} And the wedding cake./{J}
444 CC	m	7	/B. KAGHAN/LUCASTA ANGEL/LADY ELIZABETH MULHAMMER/MRS.
447 CC	Claude	3	—/Let's think what you're to say to Lady Elizabeth,/Coming back from the airport,
448 CC	Eggers	14	/No, I haven't told him much about Lady Elizabeth./But there's one thing I should
449 CC	Eggers	1	And you're thinking no doubt that Lady Elizabeth/Would be put in mind of the
449 CC	Eggers	32	this: if it comes to the point/At which Lady Elizabeth wants to adopt him —/An
450 CC	Claude	24	to Paris./But when you return with Lady Elizabeth/I'll be ready waiting to
450 CC	Claude	32	But when Eggerson comes back/With Lady Elizabeth, I will rejoin you. {}/[Exit SIR
450 CC	Colby	35	/You've told me very little about Lady Elizabeth,/And Sir Claude himself hasn't
451 CC	Eggers	3	prejudiced./He's never hit it off with Lady Elizabeth./Don't listen to him. He
451 CC	Eggers	12	Very free and easy ways;/And Lady Elizabeth has never taken to him./But
451 CC	Eggers	26	with the ladies, you know./But with Lady Elizabeth he wasn't so successful./She
451 CC	Eggers	36	will certainly be a great asset/With Lady Elizabeth. I envy you that./I've always
454 CC	Eggers	4	to meet Lizzie?/{E} I am meeting Lady Elizabeth at Northolt./{L} Well, I don't
454 CC	Colby	30	does indeed./{C} And does she call Lady Elizabeth *Lizzie*?/{E} Well, not in her
455 CC	Eggers	34	not on your shoulders./Lady Elizabeth, now, that's different./{C} At
455 CC	Colby	35	/{C} At least, I don't suppose Lady Elizabeth/Can be quite so unusual as Miss
455 CC	Eggers	39	/{E} Well, as I told you, she really is a lady,/Rather a *grande dame*, as the French say./
456 CC	Eggers	4	—/'Eggerson', he said, 'I wanted a lady,/And I'm perfectly satisfied with the
456 CC	Colby	11	Conservative, myself./{C} But is Lady Elizabeth very unusual/In any other way,
456 CC	Colby	12	/In any other way, besides being a lady?/{E} Why, yes, indeed, I must admit she is./
456 CC	Eggers	38	as much of Europe as I have,/Getting Lady Elizabeth out of her difficulties./{C}
457 CC	Eggers	4	I'm sure you'll like her. She's *such* a lady!/And what's more, she has a good heart./
457 CC	m	16	her a time,/From my experience. {}/LADY ELIZABETH MULHAMMER'S *voice*
457 CC	note 16&	25	MULHAMMER'S *voice off.*/* *Lady Elizabeth's words off stage are not intended*
457 CC	m	25	be talking about? She's coming in! {}/LADY ELIZABETH MULHAMMER'S *voice*
458 CC	1m	5	been engaged in business. {}/[*Enter* LADY ELIZABETH MULHAMMER]/
458 CC	Eggers	5	/[*simultaneously*]./{E} Lady Elizabeth!/{SC} Elizabeth!/What on earth
458 CC	Eggers	8	/What on earth has happened?/{E} Lady Elizabeth! This is most surprising./{LE}
458 CC	Eggers	28	to retire .../{E} Under medical orders, Lady Elizabeth:/The doctor made it very
460 CC	m	33	with Mr. .../{LE} Colby! {}/[*Exit* LADY ELIZABETH]/{SC} She actually went
462 CC	Colby	9	deception./Do you really believe that Lady Elizabeth/Can ever accept me as if I was
478 CC	Lucasta	3	his heir/And you'll marry another Lady Elizabeth./But in that event, Colby, you'll
479 CC	Colby	34	had the place done up./{C} It was Lady Elizabeth chose the decorations./{K} Then
481 CC	m	14	me ... {}/[*A knock at the door. Enter* LADY ELIZABETH]/{LE} Oh, good evening./
481 CC	Lucasta	17	/{L} We're on the point of leaving, Lady Elizabeth./{LE} I've come over to have a
482 CC	Colby	18	freely, as an elderly person./{C} But, Lady Elizabeth .../{LE} Well, older than you
482 CC	Colby	21	in the ways of the world./{C} But, Lady Elizabeth, what is it you object to?/
486 CC	Colby	19	— really was your mother?/{C} Why, Lady Elizabeth! Why should I doubt it?/That is
490 CC	Colby	29	they have lost each other./{C} No, Lady Elizabeth. The position is the same/Or
492 CC	1m	38	{}/[*Exeunt* SIR CLAUDE *and* LADY ELIZABETH]/CURTAIN/Act Three/
493 CC	3m	1	is/moving chairs about. Enter LADY ELIZABETH]/{LE} Claude, what are
496 CC	Eggers	14	/{E} Good morning, Sir Claude. And Lady Elizabeth!/{SC} I'm sorry, Eggerson, to
497 CC	Claude	6	her?/{SC} I have asked her to come. Lady Elizabeth/Is sure that she knows the name
504 CC	Claude	31	let me introduce you to my wife./Lady Elizabeth Mulhammer./{LE} Good
505 CC	Eggers	26	Mrs. Guzzard./It is only recently that Lady Elizabeth/Heard your name mentioned,
505 CC	Eggers	33	ago for the question to be possible./Lady Elizabeth, before her marriage/Had a
506 CC	Eggers	9	/{E} The father died abroad./Lady Elizabeth did not know the name of
506 CC	Eggers	9	did not know the name of the lady/Who had taken the child. Or rather, had
506 CC	Guzzard	20	and lost him. Not in the way/That Lady Elizabeth's child was lost./Let us hope
506 CC	Eggers	27	possible. A few days ago,/As I said, Lady Elizabeth learned your name;/And the
506 CC	Eggers	31	her. Mrs. Guzzard/Of Teddington! Lady Elizabeth is convinced/That it was a Mrs.
506 CC	Eggers	36	Teddington./{E} I am only suggesting, Lady Elizabeth,/There are other places than
507 CC	Guzzard	35	it./Colby is my son./{MG} Your son, Lady Elizabeth?/Are you suggesting that I kept
508 CC	Eggers	17	/She took in, which may have been Lady Elizabeth's./{SC} That's a very sensible
510 CC	Eggers	3	COLBY]/{E} And now, if you agree, Lady Elizabeth,/We can ask Mr. Kaghan about
510 CC	Guzzard	26	But why are you interested?/{MG} Lady Elizabeth, I believe that this is your son./If
511 CC	Kaghan	5	/{K} Well, I am embarrassed./If Lady Elizabeth is my mother .../{LE} There is
511 CC	Kaghan	18	to know how I ought to address you,/Lady Elizabeth. I've always been accustomed/
511 CC	Kaghan	26	By all means, Elizabeth./{K} But, Lady Elizabeth —/I mean, Aunt Elizabeth: if I
512 CC	Guzzard	2	/{MG} I am glad to hear you say so, Lady Elizabeth./But are *you* satisfied?/{LE}
512 CC	m	17	Barnabas Kaghan as her son? {}/[*To* LADY ELIZABETH]/{MG} Are you contented
512 CC	Guzzard	28	satisfied to find yourself the son/Of Lady Elizabeth Mulhammer?/{K} It's very much
512 CC	m	39	those who have made them. {}/[*To* LADY ELIZABETH *and* KAGHAN]/{MG}

513 CC	Guzzard	5	Kaghan,/The daughter-in-law of Lady Elizabeth,/And the daughter of Sir Claude
564 ES	Gomez	4	you agree, Dick?/— This young lady I take to be your daughter?/And this is
564 ES	Gomez	13	as I have, Señor Gomez./{G} My dear lady, you're not old enough/To have known

LADYSHIP (6)

299 FR	Downing	13	an accident./I mean, knowing her Ladyship,/I don't think she had the courage./
299 FR	Downing	29	cocktails/Went a long way with her Ladyship./She wasn't one of those that are
300 FR	Downing	35	there alone, looking over the rail./Her Ladyship must have been all right then,/Mustn't
322 FR	Winch	6	been dead these ten years. How is her Ladyship,/If I may ask, my Lord?/{H} Why do
322 FR	Harry	9	Why do you keep asking/About her Ladyship? Do you know or don't you?/I'm not
322 FR	Winch	26	than phone and perhaps disturb her Ladyship./So I slipped along on my bike.

LADYSHIP'S (2)

321 FR	Winch	26	thinking it was your birthday, not her Ladyship's./{H} Her Ladyship's! { }/[*He darts at*
321 FR	Harry	27	birthday, not her Ladyship's./{H} Her Ladyship's! { }/[*He darts at* WINCHELL *and*

LAFORGUE (1)

602 Humoresque		m	seek!'/Humouresque/(AFTER J. LAFORGUE)/One of my marionettes is dead,/

LAID (12)

157 Rock 4		17	within,/When he and his men laid their hands to rebuilding the wall./So they
245 MC	Priest2	31	/However, I will have fires laid in all your rooms/To take the chill off our
249 MC	Thomas	33	You forget the bishops/Whom I have laid under excommunication./{T2} Hungry
268 MC	Thomas	23	the bishops, it is not my yoke/That is laid upon them, or mine to revoke./Let them go
276 MC	Chorus	7	heaping of the ashes,/The fuel laid on the fire at daybreak,/These acts marked
284 FR	m	11	/THE EUMENIDES/*The scene is laid in a country house in the North of England*/
306 FR	Mary	34	upon us;/Even the nice things were laid out ready,/And the treats were always so
334 FR	Harry	27	another one made ready —/The book laid out, lines underscored, and the costume/
352 CP	m	11	CATERER'S MEN/*The scene is laid in London*/Act One. Scene 1/*The*
375 CP	Celia	6	back!/Do you mean to say that she's laid a trap for us?/{E} No. If there is a trap, we
533 ES	Gomez	34	whom to pay;/And a little money laid out in the right manner/In the right places,
551 ES	Carghil	39	become Lord Claverton./So perhaps I laid the foundation of your fortunes!/{LC} And

LAIN (2)

270 MC	Chorus	5	tusk and hoof, in odd places;/I have lain on the floor of the sea and breathed with
270 MC	Chorus	5	ingurgitation of the sponge. I have lain in the soil and criticised the worm. In the

LAIRS (1)

598 Circe		8	here again./Panthers rise from their lairs/In the forest which thickens below,/Along

LAITY (1)

247 MC	Templ1	4	and you are in amity,/Clergy and laity may return to gaiety,/Mirth and

LAKE (2)

135 5FingerEx3		1	*Park*/The long light shakes across the lake,/The forces of the morning quake,/The
192 FQ: Little		38	some at the sea jaws,/Or over a dark lake, in a desert or a city —/But this is the

LAMB (4)

50 Hippopot		29	God, in loud hosannas./Blood of the Lamb shall wash him clean/And him shall
274 MC	Knights	20	/Are you washed in the blood of the Lamb?/Are you marked with the mark of the
281 MC	Chorus	12	on the earth, both the wolf and the lamb; the worm in the soil and the worm in the
574 ES	Carghil	25	/And he was so perplexed, poor lamb. Let's all rejoice together. { }/[*Enter*

LAMBERT (18)

523 ES	m	4	/CHARLES HEMINGTON/LAMBERT/LORD CLAVERTON/
526 ES	Monica	25	... and I hear someone coming:/It's Lambert with the tea ... { }/[*Enter* LAMBERT
526 ES	m	26	/It's Lambert with the tea ... { }/[*Enter* LAMBERT *with trolley*]/{M} and I shall say,
526 ES	Monica	26	*with trolley*]/{M} and I shall say, 'Please/Please let his lordship know that tea is
526 ES	m	30	/That you *can* stay to tea. { }/[*Exit* LAMBERT]/{M} — Now we're in the public
527 ES	m	11	won't happen to me. { }/[*Knock. Enter* LAMBERT]/{L} Excuse me, Miss Monica. His
527 ES	Monica	13	to wait tea for him./{M} Thank you, Lambert./{L} He's busy at the moment. But he
531 ES	m	32	ghost can be of men! { }/[*Knock. Enter* LAMBERT]/{L} Excuse me, my Lord. There's a
532 ES	Monica	9	Miss Monica?/{M} Yes, thank you, Lambert. { }/[*Exit* LAMBERT]/{C} I ought to be
532 ES	m	9	{M} Yes, thank you, Lambert. { }/[*Exit* LAMBERT]/{C} I ought to be going./{M} Let
532 ES	Monica	21	rid of him in twenty minutes/I'll send Lambert to tell you that you have to take a
532 ES	m	26	Court/In a week or two. { }/[*Enter* LAMBERT]/{L} Mr. Gomez, my Lord./{LC}
532 ES	m	31	/[*Exeunt* MONICA *and* CHARLES]/[LAMBERT *shows in* GOMEZ]/{LC} Good
535 ES	m	6	when I say 'trust' ... { }/[*Knock. Enter* LAMBERT]/{LC} Lambert, will you bring in
535 ES	Ld Clav	6	{ }/[*Knock. Enter* LAMBERT]/{LC} Lambert, will you bring in the whisky. And
535 ES	m	19	to be trustworthy'. { }/[*During this* LAMBERT *enters silently, deposits tray and*
541 ES	m	31	to do you a kindness. { }/[*Enter* LAMBERT]/{L} Excuse me, my Lord, but Miss
541 ES	m	34	/{LC} I'll be ready to take it. { }/[*Exit* LAMBERT]/{G} Ah, the pre-arranged

LAME (1)

107 Animula		25	soul/Irresolute and selfish, misshapen, lame,/Unable to fare forward or retreat,/

LAMENT (1)
175 FQ: BurntN 161   in the funeral dance,/The loud lament of the disconsolate chimera./The detail
LAMENTABLE (1)
279 MC Knight4   15   you have been eye-witnesses of this lamentable/scene, you may feel some surprise at
LAMENTATION (2)
73 WL: Thund 367   high in the air/Murmur of maternal lamentation/Who are those hooded hordes
105 Song Sime   17   the time of cords and scourges and lamentation/Grant us thy peace./Before the
LAMENTED (1)
589 Fable   69   you *can't* keep out;/It is a thing to be lamented sorely/Such slippery folk should be
LAMIA (1)
599 On a Port   7   as if one should meet/A pensive lamia in some wood-retreat,/An immaterial
LAMP (7)
24 Rhapsody   8   divisions and precisions./Every street lamp that I pass/Beats like a fatalistic drum,/
24 Rhapsody   47   I held him./Half-past three,/The lamp sputtered,/The lamp muttered in the dark.
24 Rhapsody   48   three,/The lamp sputtered,/The lamp muttered in the dark./The lamp hummed:/
24 Rhapsody   49   /The lamp muttered in the dark./The lamp hummed:/'Regard the moon,/La lune ne
26 Rhapsody   69   /And cocktail smells in bars./The lamp said,/'Four o'clock,/Here is the number on
26 Rhapsody   74   Memory!/You have the key,/The little lamp spreads a ring on the stair./Mount./The
257 MC Chorus   3   the skull./{C} A man may walk with a lamp at night, and yet be drowned in a ditch./
LAMPLIGHT (2)
15 Prufrock   64   and white and bare/(But in the lamplight, downed with light brown hair!)/Is it
182 FQ: ECoker 200   /A time for the evening under lamplight/(The evening with the photograph
LAMPS (2)
22 Preludes   13   stamps./And then the lighting of the lamps./The morning comes to consciousness/Of
204 de la Mare   10   at the nursery tea/And when the lamps are lit and curtains drawn/Demand some
LANCE (1)
140 Usk   4   the white well./Glance aside, not for lance, do not spell/Old enchantments. Let them
LAND (31)
59 Waste Land   t   stiff dishonoured shroud./The Waste Land/The Burial of the Dead/April is the
61 WL: Burial   2   breeding/Lilacs out of the dead land, mixing/Memory and desire, stirring/Dull
67 WL: Fire S   175   bank. The wind/Crosses the brown land, unheard. The nymphs are departed./Sweet
84 Hollow Men   39   the twilight kingdom/This is the dead land/This is cactus land/Here the stone images/
84 Hollow Men   40   /This is the dead land/This is cactus land/Here the stone images/Are raised, here
92 Ash-Wed 2   52   /In the quiet of the desert. This is the land which ye/Shall divide by lot. And neither
92 Ash-Wed 2   54   division nor unity/Matters. This is the land. We have our inheritance./At the first
96 Ash-Wed 5   14   the mainland, in the desert or the rain land,/For those who walk in darkness/Both in
105 Song Sime   7   the wind that chills towards the dead land./Grant us thy peace./I have walked many
142 Cape Ann   11   Sweet sweet sweet/But resign this land at the end, resign it/To its true owner, the
150 Rock 1   102   *at an angle/To the furrow. In this land/There shall be one cigarette to two men,/To*
150 Rock 1   105   *one half pint of bitter/Ale. In this land/No man has hired us./Our life is unwelcome,*
155 Rock 3   31   /Where My Word is unspoken,/In the land of lobelias and tennis flannels/The rabbit
161 Rock 7   33   UNEMPLOYED (*afar off*):/*In this land/There shall be one cigarette to two men,/To*
161 Rock 7   38   (*more faintly*):/*In this land/No man has hired us....*/CHORUS:/Waste
203 Indians   16   village remember./This was not your land, or ours: but a village in the Midlands,/
213 Growltiger   53   when the news flew through the land;/At Maidenhead and Henley there was
239 MC Chorus   10   were gathered and stored, and the land became brown sharp points of death in a
251 MC Tempt3   24   my Lord, are Normans./England is a land for Norman/Sovereignty. Let the Angevin/
254 MC Thomas   3   power, hold it./{T} Supreme, in this land?/{T4} Supreme, but for one./{T} That I do
261 MC Thomas   2   forth to journey afar, to suffer by land/and sea, to know torture, imprisonment,
266 MC Knights   14   to the King and the law of the land;/You are the Archbishop who was made by
266 MC Thomas   28   /As his most faithful vassal in the land./{K1} Saving your order! let your order
268 MC Knight1   35   and your servants depart from this land./{T} If that *is* the King's command, I will
272 MC Chorus   26   of the effortless journey, to the empty land/Which is no land, only emptiness, absence,
272 MC Chorus   27   to the empty land/Which is no land, only emptiness, absence, the Void,/Where
275 MC Chorus   22   stone from stone and wash them./The land is foul, the water is foul, our beasts and
275 MC Chorus   24   far far in the past; and I wander in a land of barren boughs: if I break them, they
275 MC Chorus   24   break them, they bleed; I wander in a land of dry stones: if I touch them they bleed./
310 FR   Harry   15   the ghosts of the drowned/Return to land in the spring?/Do the dead want to return?/
534 ES   Ld Clav   8   if carried on in England,/It might land you in gaol again?/{G} That's true enough,
LAND'S (1)
184 FQ: DrySal   16   the sea is all about us;/The sea is the land's edge also, the granite/Into which it
LANDED (1)
265 MC Knight1   14   We rode hard,/Took ship yesterday, landed last night,/Having business with the
LANDHOLDERS (1)
243 MC   Priest2   1   of balance of forces of barons and landholders./The rock of God is beneath our

LANDING (1)
457 CC   m 20   What's that? {}/[*Opens door on to landing and listens*]/{SC} She's here, Eggerson!
LANDLADY (1)
221 Old Deut   35   just time for one more,'/Then the landlady from her back parlour will peep/And
LANDLORD (1)
330 FR   Harry 11 At the right times; and be an excellent landlord./{Ag} What is in your mind, Harry?/I
LANDLORD'S (1)
365 CP   Reilly   7   *One Eyed Riley,/Who came in but the landlord's daughter/And she took my heart*
LANDS (7)
 74 WL: Thund 425   behind me/Shall I at least set my lands in order?/London Bridge is falling down
151 Rock 2   6   or look in vain towards foreign lands for alms to be more or the urn to be filled.
587 Fable   3   monks were quacks,/And took their lands and money from the poor men,/And
587 Fable   9   merry./They were possessors of rich lands and wide,/An orchard, and a vineyard,
593 Grad 8   5 have been or done/Or to what distant lands we may have gone,/Through all the years
594 Grad 12   6   near/To spread thy name o'er distant lands and seas!/As thou to thy departing sons
595 Grad 13   4 to bless/Before they leave thy care for lands unseen;/And let thy motto be, proud and
LANDSCAPE (2)
308 FR   Mary   9   ophidian./{M} You bring your own landscape/No more real than the other. And in
348 FR   Chorus   6   window, and see quite a different landscape./We do not like to climb a stair, and
LANDSCAPES (1)
138   t (Whether his mouth be open or shut)./Landscapes/New Hampshire/Children's voices
LANE (3)
177 FQ: ECoker 15   the open field, leaving the deep lane/Shuttered with branches, dark in the
177 FQ: ECoker 18   while a van passes,/And the deep lane insists on the direction/Into the village, in
592 Grad 4   4 hopeful eye of youth it still appears/A lane by which the rose and hawthorn grow./We
LANES (1)
201 Def Island   19   for whom the paths of glory are/the lanes and the streets of Britain:/to say, to the
LANGUAGE (11)
188 FQ: DrySal 150   shell of time, and not in any language)/'Fare forward, you who think that
192 FQ: Little   53   dead is tongued with fire beyond the language of the living./Here, the intersection of
194 FQ: Little   120 last year's words belong to last year's language/And next year's words await another
294 FR   Agatha 13   tell us as you can:/Talk in your own language, without stopping to debate/Whether
294 FR   Harry 27   terms/Because the particular has no language. One thinks to escape/By violence, but
324 FR   Harry 37   appropriate. Only, that's not the language/That I choose to be talking. I will not
344 FR   Gerald 23   But you'll have to learn the language/And several dialects. It means a lot of
346 FRDowning 25   for something else./I've no gift of language, but I'm sure of what I mean:/We
463 CC   Colby 19   /If you learn to speak a foreign language fluently,/So that you can think in it —
511 CC Lucasta   2   .../{L} You don't need to talk that language any longer:/Just say you're
535 ES   Gomez 31 away, to another climate,/To another language, other standards of behaviour,/To
LANGUID (1)
603 Spleen   12   /And Life, a little bald and gray,/Languid, fastidious, and bland,/Waits, hat and
LANGUOR (1)
141 Rannoch   7 winds in/Listlessness of ancient war,/Languor of broken steel,/Clamour of confused
LANTERN (3)
 16 Prufrock   105   just what I mean!/But as if a magic lantern threw the nerves in patterns on a screen:
 33 Conv Gal   4   John's balloon/Or an old battered lantern hung aloft/To light poor travellers to
151 Rock 2   7 moved on the face of the waters like a lantern set on the back of a tortoise./And some
LAP (1)
215 RTTugger   33   for a cuddle;/But he'll leap on your lap in the middle of your sewing,/For there's
LAPPING (1)
109 Marina   2   rocks and what islands/What water lapping the bow/And scent of pine and the
LAPS (1)
254 MC Tempt4 35   broken, and its stores/Swept into the laps of parasites and whores./When miracles
LAPSE (2)
390 CP   Julia 12   /{J} Lavinia! Don't say you've had a lapse of memory!/Then that accounts for the
390 CP   Julia 30   be inquisitive./Lavinia has had a lapse of memory,/And so, of course, she sent us
LAPSES (1)
456 CC   Colby 20   /{C} I hope you don't mean,/She has lapses of memory?/{E} I didn't mean that./No.
LAPT (1)
 44 Cook Egg   15   Mond./We two shall lie together, lapt/In a five per cent. Exchequer Bond./I shall
LAQUEARIA (1)
 64 WL: Chess   92   /Flung their smoke into the laquearia,/Stirring the pattern on the coffered
LARCENY (1)
348 FR   Chorus 15   /We are insured against fire,/Against larceny and illness,/Against defective plumbing,/

LARDER (3)
214 RTTugger   30   to the ears,/If you put it away on the larder shelf./The Rum Tum Tugger is artful and
368 CP   Edward   21   dear Alex,/There'll be nothing in the larder worthy of your cooking./I couldn't think
420 CP   Reilly   26   /To the stale food mouldering in the larder,/The stale thoughts mouldering in their
LARDER'S (1)
226 Macavity   23   file of Scotland Yard's./And when the larder's looted, or the jewel-case is rifled,/Or
LARGE (7)
202 War Poetry   11   the individual/Experience is too large, or too small. Our emotions/Are only
212 Growltiger   2   the roughest cat that ever roamed at large./From Gravesend up to Oxford he
232 Skimble   17   /You may say that by and large it is Skimble who's in charge/Of the
485 CC   Lady E   30   I seem to have heard of it./Was it a large house?/{C} No, a very small one./{LE} But
552 ES   Ld Clav   3   /Before your name appeared in very large letters/In Shaftesbury Avenue./{MC} Yes,
552 ES   Carghil   25   clear./You got out of a tangle for a large cash payment/And no publicity. So your
555 ES   Ld Clav   30   it can't be that,/Or he wouldn't be at large. Perhaps he's in trouble/With some
LARGELY (2)
182 FQ: ECoker   175   had twenty years —/Twenty years largely wasted, the years of *l'entre deux guerres*
403 CP   Reilly   2   present state of mind —/Would be largely fictitious; and as for your dreams,/You
LARKSPUR (1)
94 Ash-Wed 4   10   and made firm the sand/In blue of larkspur, blue of Mary's colour,/Sovegna vos/
LAST (92)
26 Rhapsody   78   the door, sleep, prepare for life.'/The last twist of the knife./Morning at the Window/
38 Gerontion   48   the new year. Us he devours. Think at last/We have not reached conclusion, when I/
38 Gerontion   50   I/Stiffen in a rented house. Think at last/I have not made this show purposelessly/
63 WL: Burial   71   at Mylae!/'That corpse you planted last year in your garden,/'Has it begun to
67 WL: Fire S   173   Sermon/The river's tent is broken; the last fingers of leaf/Clutch and sink into the wet
68 WL: Fire S   225   combinations touched by the sun's last rays,/On the divan are piled (at night her
85 Hollow Men   57   jaw of our lost kingdoms/In this last of meeting places/We grope together/And
97 Ash-Wed 5   33   and deny between the rocks/In the last desert between the last blue rocks/The
97 Ash-Wed 5   33   rocks/In the last desert between the last blue rocks/The desert in the garden the
111 Xmas Trees   28   'eightieth' meaning whichever is the last)/The accumulated memories of annual
117 SP   Doris   33   it's mine./I dreamt of weddings all last night./Yes it's mine. I know it's mine./Oh
119 SP   Krum   24   here before/{Kr} We hit this town last night for the first time/{Kl} And I certainly
119 SP   Klip   25   And I certainly hope it won't be the last time./{Do} You like London, Mr. Klipstein?
124 SA   Doris   7   coffin?/{Do} I drew the COFFIN very last card./I don't care for such conversation/A
133 Eyes   t   RESIGN/MINOR POEMS/Eyes that last I saw in tears/Eyes that last I saw in tears/
133 Eyes   1   Eyes that last I saw in tears/Eyes that last I saw in tears/Through division/Here in
186 FQ: DrySal   68   undeniable/Clamour of the bell of the last annunciation./Where is the end of them, the
190 FQ: DrySal   234   gone on trying;/We, content at the last/If our temporal reversion nourish/(Not too
194 FQ: Little   118   you to forgive/Both bad and good. Last season's fruit is eaten/And the fullfed beast
194 FQ: Little   120   beast shall kick the empty pail./For last year's words belong to last year's language/
194 FQ: Little   120   pail./For last year's words belong to last year's language/And next year's words
194 FQ: Little   140   at what ceases to amuse./And last, the rending pain of re-enactment/Of all
197 FQ: Little   246   remembered gate/When the last of earth left to discover/Is that which was
212 Growltiger   t   depend, it appears./Growltiger's Last Stand/GROWLTIGER was a Bravo Cat,
213 Growltiger   39   heard a sound./The lovers sang their last duet, in danger of their lives —/For the foe
223 Pekes Pols   59   gave a great leap —/And they every last one of them scattered like sheep./*And when*
231 Bust Jones   37   say./Or, to put it in rhyme: 'I shall last out my time'/Is the word for this stoutest of
232 Skimble   15   goes 'All Clear!'/And we're off at last for the northern part/Of the Northern
588 Fable   55   cheese which they kept under cover./Last, a boar's head, which to bring in took four
595 Grad 14   6   disobey,/*Exeunt omnes*, with a last 'farewell'./Song/When we came home
602 Humoresque   15   there;/'The snappiest fashion since last spring's,/'The newest style, on Earth, I
246 MC Tempt1   36   over/Or that the good time cannot last?/Fluting in the meadows, viols in the hall,/
248 MC Tempt2   17   at Clarendon, at Northampton,/And last at Montmirail, in Maine. Now that I have
249 MC Tempt2   17   What shall be the month?/{T2} The last from the first./{T} What shall we give for it?
253 MC Tempt4   4   come to say./{T4} It shall be said at last./Hooks have been baited with morsels of
253 MC Tempt4   38   /The Old King shall know it, when at last breath,/No sons, no empire, he bites broken
258 MC Thomas   5   shall not come in this kind again./The last temptation is the greatest treason:/To do
262 MC Thomas   3   martyr,/and that one perhaps not the last. I would have you keep in your hearts/these
265 MC Knight1   14   hard,/Took ship yesterday, landed last night,/Having business with the
270 MC Chorus   25   swoon/Of those consenting to the last humiliation./I have consented, Lord
273 MC Chorus   6   Thy labour;/Help me, Lord, in my last fear./Dust I am, to dust am bending,/From
279 MC Knight1   5   to me that he has said almost the last word, for those who/have been able to
279 MC Knight4   18   go over/the ground traversed by the last speaker. While the late Archbishop/was
279 MC Knight4   25   grew upon him, until it/became at last an undoubted mania. I have unimpeachable
279 MC Knight4   31   a death by martyrdom. Even/at the last, he could have given us reason: you have

280 MC	Priest3	18	/Go where the sunset reddens the last grey rock/Of Brittany, or the Gates of
290 FR	Amy	18	/As if nothing had happened in the last eight years./{G} That will be a little difficult.
295 FR	Harry	27	in which one can be caught for the last time./And also waking. She is nearer than
305 FR	Harry	24	/{H} Not very./But, at least, it did not last long. How are you, Mary?/{M} Oh, very
316 FR	Agatha	16	bones/In the filled-up well/Be at last straightened/May the weasel and the otter/
321 FR	Winch	33	a year older/Than when I saw you last, my Lord. But a country sergeant/Doesn't
327 FR	Ivy	32	the use of his car,/And he missed the last train, so he's coming up tomorrow;/And he
330 FR	Harry	28	only as an eye, seeing./All this last year, I could not fit myself together:/When I
336 FR	Harry	20	here before I arrived./Now I see at last that I am following you,/And I know that
338 FR	Harry	18	I who told her ... All this year,/This last year, I have been in flight/But always in
338 FR	Harry	22	me while I fled. Now I know/That the last apparent refuge, the safe shelter,/That is
343 FR	Harry	35	son. And as for me,/I am the last you need to worry about;/I have my course
349 FR	5m	13	*blow out a few candles, so that their last/words are spoken in the dark.*]/{Ag} A curse
356 CP	Peter	2	him at Oxford:/I came across him last year in California./{J} I've always wanted to
359 CP	Julia	30	/Well, good-bye again. I'm off at last. {}/[*Exit*]/{E} I'm sorry. I'm afraid I don't
364 CP	Edward	5	she was wearing/When I saw her last. And yet I want her back./And I *must* get
371 CP	Peter	5	of reality/And perhaps it is the last. And you don't understand./{E} My dear
385 CP	Edward	21	hardly expect me to obliterate/The last five years./{UG} I ask you to forget
387 CP	Celia	5	/Oh, I'm glad I came!/I can see you at last as a human being./Can't you see me that
389 CP	Lavinia	5	Celia! Now you'll have a chance/At last, to realise your ambitions./You're going
395 CP	Lavinia	21	prove how you had grown since the last holidays./You were always intensely
404 CP	Edward	19	/Coming to see you — that's the last decision/I was capable of making. I am in
413 CP	Celia	22	what I've been going through, these last weeks,/I somehow took it for granted that I
424 CP	Lavinia	18	that we've given *several* parties/In the last two years. And I've attended *all* of them./I
430 CP	Peter	5	/{P} I flew over from New York last night —/I left Los Angeles three days ago./I
430 CP	Peter	15	in so early./It does seem ages since I last saw any of you!/And how are you, Alex?
430 CP	Peter	37	/{P} Alex knows./Did you see my last picture, Alex?/{A} I knew about it, but I
438 CP	Lavinia	4	/I mean — I know nothing of her last two years./{R} That shows some insight on
439 CP	Lavinia	39	And I have been thinking, for these last five minutes,/How I could face my guests. I
445 CC	Eggers	24	sure,/As I've heard nothing since the last time I came./{SC} Well, of course,
475 CC	Lucasta	13	/I've changed quite a lot in the last two hours./{C} And I think I'm changing
478 CC	Lucasta	22	getting further in,/And you know at last that there's no escape./Well, I'll be going./
487 CC	Claude	5	With a few striking phrases. It should last about ten minutes./And then we'll go over it
530 ES	Ld Clav	13	he mustn't run for trains/When the last thing he wants is to take a train for
530 ES	Ld Clav	22	station on a branch line,/After the last train, after all the other passengers/Have
542 ES	Gomez	30	Oh, I can wait, Dick. You'll relent at last./You'll come to feel easier when I'm with
544 ES	Ld Clav	15	/Already. I only hope that it will last —/The sense of wellbeing! It's often with us
544 ES	Ld Clav	21	benignant sunshine/And warmth will last for a few days more./But this early summer,
545 ES	Piggott	26	/I've been in such a rush, these last few days,/And I thought, 'Lord Claverton
548 ES	Carghil	24	you both in the dining-room last night./You are the great Lord Claverton,
550 ES	Carghil	12	years ago, the first time. That didn't last long./People sometimes say: 'Make one
550 ES	Carghil	29	that you and I/Should meet here at last? Here, of all places!/{LC} Why not, of all
555 ES	Ld Clav	23	accident./You know, after that last escapade of his,/I've lived in terror of his
556 ES	Michael	15	from London?/{Mi} I drove down last night. I'm staying at a pub/About two miles
567 ES	Charles	11	is to know that you need me./On that last day in London, you admitted that you
572 ES	Ld Clav	36	is through this meeting that I shall at last escape them./— I've made my confession to
573 ES	Ld Clav	10	/What has made the difference in the last five minutes/Is not the heinousness of my

LASTING (1)

248 MC	Tempt2	28	/Power obtained grows to glory,/Life lasting, a permanent possession./A templed

LASTS (5)

175 FQ:	BurntN	147	stillness of the violin, while the note lasts,/Not that only, but the co-existence,/Or say
190 FQ:	DrySal	216	you are the music/While the music lasts. These are only hints and guesses,/Hints
254 MC	Tempt4	30	of further scorning./That nothing lasts, but the wheel turns,/The nest is rifled, and
330 FR	Harry	23	/Because it feels eternal while it lasts. That is one hell./Then the numbness came
544 ES	Monica	24	make the most of this weather while it lasts./I never remember you as other than

LATCH (1)

398 CP	Edward	6	/What devil left the door on the latch/For these doubts to enter? And then you

LATCH-KEY (1)

388 CP		m 19	{}/[LAVINIA *lets herself in with a latch-key*]/{P} You're going abroad?/{C} I don't

LATCHES (1)

372 CP	Edward	38	*shut the door after you*, so that it latches./{A} Remember, Edward, not more than

LATE (58)

19 Portrait		38	/Admire the monuments,/Discuss the late events,/Correct our watches by the public
20 Portrait		96	/'I have been wondering frequently of late/(But our beginnings never know our ends!)/
21 Portrait		107	at any rate./Perhaps it is not too late./I shall sit here, serving tea to friends.'/And

38	Gerontion	39	giving famishes the craving. Gives too late/What's not believed in, or if still believed,/
62	WL: Burial	37	girl.'/— Yet when we came back, late, from the hyacinth garden,/Your arms full,
178	FQ: ECoker	52	In my beginning./What is the late November doing/With the disturbance of
178	FQ: ECoker	58	high/Red into grey and tumble down/Late roses filled with early snow?/Thunder
194	FQ: Little	142	and been; the shame/Of motives late revealed, and the awareness/Of things ill
241	MC Mess	34	/Strewing the way with leaves and late flowers of the season./The streets of the city
243	MC Chorus	16	the profit, certain the danger./O late late late, late is the time, late too late, and
243	MC Chorus	16	the profit, certain the danger./O late late late, late is the time, late too late, and
243	MC Chorus	16	profit, certain the danger./O late late late, late is the time, late too late, and rotten the
243	MC Chorus	16	certain the danger./O late late late, late is the time, late too late, and rotten the
243	MC Chorus	16	/O late late late, late is the time, late too late, and rotten the year;/Evil the wind,
243	MC Chorus	16	late late late, late is the time, late too late, and rotten the year;/Evil the wind, and
247	MC Thomas	39	bone./{T} You come twenty years too late./{T1} Then I leave you to your fate./I leave
248	MC Tempt2	21	of the Chancellorship./See how the late ones rise! You, master of policy/Whom all
270	MC Chorus	22	them, the death-bringers; now is too late/For action, too soon for contrition./
278	MC Knight2	7	consistent. During the reign of/the late Queen Matilda and the irruption of the
279	MC Knight4	18	by the last speaker. While the late Archbishop/was Chancellor, no one, under
285	FR 2m	1	*after tea. An afternoon in late March.*/Scene I/AMY, IVY, VIOLET,
288	FR Violet	1	was always the most likely to be late./{A} This time, it will not be his fault./We
289	FR Charles	16	to mention it now?/It seems to me too late./{A} Much too late./If he wants to talk
289	FR Amy	17	It seems to me too late./{A} Much too late./If he wants to talk about it, that's another
303	FR Mary	1	*with flowers*]/{M} The spring is very late in this northern country,/Late and
303	FR Mary	2	is very late in this northern country,/Late and uncertain, clings to the south wall./
303	FR Agatha	4	evening./{Ag} I always forget how late the spring is, here./{Mg} I had rather wait for
303	FR Mary	13	uncertain./Arthur or John may be late, of course./We may have to keep the dinner
313	FR Mary	18	I must go and change. I came in very late. {}/[*Exit*]/{C} Now we only want Arthur and
343	FR Mary	14	it now. Of course it was much too late/Then, for anything to come for me: I
343	FR Mary	19	I will go. But I suppose it is much too late/Now, to try to get a fellowship?/{A} So you
345	FR Amy	20	apprehend the truth/About things too late to mend: and that is to be old./
377	CP Julia	33	be done. That's very simple./It's too late, or too early, to go to a restaurant./You
379	CP Edward	15	are a very rare person./But it was too late. And I should have known/That it wasn't
384	CP 2m	1	/Act One. Scene 3/*The same room: late afternoon of the next day.* EDWARD *alone.*
384	CP Reilly	13	that it will not matter. It will be too late./{E} I have half a mind to change my mind
390	CP Julia	1	you are, Lavinia! I'm sorry to be late./But your telegram was a bit unexpected./I
424	CP 3m	1	*London flat. Two years later.*/*A late afternoon in July.* A CATERER'S MAN *is*
465	CC Claude	1	after his death, and then it was too late,/I knew that he was right. And all my life/I
466	CC Colby	38	your father/Until it was too late. And you spoke of atonement./Even your
490	CC Colby	39	living can spring. Now, it is too late./I never wanted a parent till now —/I never
495	CC Lady E	26	I loathed/In Tony — and then, too late, I discovered/He belonged to the world I
496	CC Eggers	26	I came home in the evening. And the late editions/Of the papers that I picked up at
501	CC Lady E	19	each other,/No matter how late. And perhaps that will help us/To
504	CC Claude	2	be here. It wouldn't be like her/To be late for an appointment. She always mentioned
504	CC Claude	3	She always mentioned it/If *I* was late when I went to see her. {}/[*Enter*
523	ES m	15	*Morning*/ACT THREE/*The Same. Late afternoon of the following day*/Act One/*The*
547	ES Piggott	7	more comfy. Don't let him stay out late/In the afternoon, Miss Claverton-Ferry./
552	ES Carghil	7	/With a number called *It's Not Too Late For You To Love Me*?/I couldn't have put
555	ES Piggott	1	tune she was humming, *It's Not Too Late For You To Love Me,*/Everybody was
564	ES Carghil	1	devoted admirer./{MC} *It's Not Too Late For You To Love Me!* That's the song/That
564	ES Gomez	3	Señor Gomez./{G} It will never be too late. Don't you agree, Dick?/— This young lady
566	ES Ld Clav	4	/There is time for Michael. Is it too late for me, Monica? {}/CURTAIN/Act Three/
567	ES 2m	1	/Act Three/*Same as Act Two. Late afternoon of the following day.* MONICA
571	ES Ld Clav	35	We had two girls with us./It was late at night. A secondary road./I ran over an
577	ES Gomez	11	/To repay an old debt. And better late than never./{C} I see your point of view.
577	ES Carghil	27	time *I* joined the conversation./My late husband, Mr. Carghill, was a business man
582	ES Monica	21	know you're not allowed to stop out late/At this season. It's chilly at dusk./{LC} Yes,

LATELY (3)

395	CP Edward	1	I have had quite enough humiliation/Lately, to bring me to the point/At which
563	ES Carghil	16	/{MC} Oh, you've seen each other lately?/Richard, I think that you might
569	ES Ld Clav	36	been with me/Though it was not till lately that I found the living persons/Whose

LATENT (1)

545	ES Ld Clav	18	people talk like that/It indicates a latent desire to interfere/With the privacy of

LATER (29)

111	Xmas Trees	19	the gaiety/May not be forgotten in later experience,/In the bored habituation, the
254	MC Tempt4	38	only do their best to forget you./And later is worse, when men will not hate you/
278	MC Knight2	36	of/being called murderer. And at a later time still, even such temperate/measures as

295 FR	Harry	2	her when I went back to the cabin./Later, I became excited, I think I made
296 FR	Agatha	2	not yet understand:/They will be clear later. I am also convinced/That you only hold a
298 FR	Violet	16	to know at once, not be told about it later./{I} And I shall stay with Violet./{Ag} I
307 FR	Harry	11	found the secret./{H} Not then. But later, coming back from school/For the
328 FR	Gerald	9	.../{G} There'll have been more in the later editions./You'd better read it to us. {}/
352 CP	m	7	/AN UNIDENTIFIED GUEST, *later identified as* SIR HENRY
366 CP	Peter	32	going to telephone and try to see you later;/But this seemed an opportunity./{E} And
369 CP	Peter	24	Celia./{P} I saw her again a few days later/Alone at a concert. And I was alone./I've
369 CP	Peter	28	I knew no one to go with,/And later, I found I preferred to go alone./But a girl
374 CP	2m	1	*The same room: a quarter of an hour later.* EDWARD *is alone, playing/Patience. The*
399 CP	3m	1	*in London. Morning:/several weeks later.* SIR HENRY *alone at his desk. He presses*
424 CP	2m	1	*London flat. Two years later./A late afternoon in July.* A CATERER'S
425 CP	Edward	24	them thirsty;/They'll come on to us later, roaring for drink./Well, let's hope that
430 CP	Peter	9	giving a party —/She's coming on later, after the Gunnings —/So I said, I really
436 CP	Edward	5	/About themselves, and learn them later/When it's harder to recover, and make a
469 CC	2m	1	Two/*The flat in the mews a few weeks later.* COLBY *is seated at the piano;/*LUCASTA
493 CC	2m	1	*Room, as in Act 1. Several mornings later.* SIR CLAUDE *is/moving chairs about.*
528 ES	Monica	13	Father wore a public label./And later, as chairman of public companies,/Always
534 ES	Gomez	21	/Is certain to be found out sooner or later./And then what happens? You have to
537 ES	Gomez	22	know either, but I was flattered./Later, I came to understand: you made friends
537 ES	Gomez	28	plenty of time to think things over, later./{LC} And what is the conclusion that you
537 ES	Ld Clav	34	whatever, for what happened to you later./{G} You led me on at Oxford, and left me
544 ES	2m	1	*A bright sunny morning, several days later./Enter* LORD CLAVERTON *and*
548 ES	1m	14	to take the hint. {}/[*Exit*]/*A moment later,* LORD CLAVERTON *spreads his*
571 ES	Ld Clav	39	stopped and was arrested,/But was later discharged. It was definitely shown/That
576 ES	Michael	19	go into details. There's time for that later./{G} Much better to wait until we get

LATEST (2)

18 Portrait		8	/We have been, let us say, to hear the latest Pole/Transmit the Preludes, through his
602 Humoresque		10	imploring air,/Mouth twisted to the latest tune;/His who-the-devil-are-you stare;/

LATIN (2)

272 MC	m	11	*cathedral.*]/[*while a* Dies Iræ *is sung in Latin by a choir in the distance*]./{C} Numb the
281 MC	m	7	{}/[*while a* Te Deum *is sung in Latin by a choir in the distance*]./{C} We praise

LATRINE (1)

270 MC	Chorus	9	/Corruption in the dish, incense in the latrine, the sewer in the incense, the smell of

LATTER (1)

186 FQ: DrySal		89	—/Or even development: the latter a partial fallacy/Encouraged by superficial

LAUGH (14)

23 Preludes		52	your hand across your mouth, and laugh;/The worlds revolve like ancient women/
56 Swee Night		2	knees/Letting his arms hang down to laugh,/The zebra stripes along his jaw/Swelling
115 SP	Doris	25	once I knew./*He* could make you laugh./{Du} Sam can make you laugh:/Sam's all
116 SP	Dusty	1	you laugh./{Du} Sam can make you laugh:/Sam's all right/{Do} But Pereira won't
269 MC	Chorus	33	noise of mouse and jerboa; the laugh of the loon, the lunatic bird. I have seen/
378 CP	Celia	27	vanity:/That you think the world will laugh at you/Because your wife has left you for
387 CP	Celia	6	/Can't you see me that way too, and laugh about it?/{E} I wish I could. I wish I
398 CP	Lavinia	12	Edward, as I am unable to make you laugh,/And as I can't persuade you to see a
451 CC	Eggers	18	is very good company./He makes me laugh sometimes. I don't laugh easily./Quite a
451 CC	Eggers	18	makes me laugh sometimes. I don't laugh easily./Quite a humorist, he is. In fact,
451 CC	Eggers	20	'Eggerson, why can't you make me laugh/The way B. Kaghan did?' She's only met
476 CC	Lucasta	29	But what is there to know?/{L} You'll laugh when I tell you:/I'm only Claude's
494 CC	Claude	35	to do?/{SC} To be a potter./Don't laugh./{LE} I'm not laughing. I was only
495 CC	Lady E	17	/{LE} To inspire an artist. Don't laugh./{SC} I'm not laughing./So what you

LAUGHABLE (1)

346 FR	Downing	16	leave him./{Do} You may think it laughable, what I'm going to say —/But it's not

LAUGHED (5)

31 Apollinax		7	at Professor Channing-Cheetah's/He laughed like an irresponsible fœtus./His laughter
32 Hysteria		1	a bitten macaroon./Hysteria/As she laughed I was aware of becoming involved in
387 CP	Celia	1	at *you*, Edward./I couldn't have laughed at anything, yesterday;/But I've learnt a
549 ES	Carghil	17	dropped the punt pole, and you all laughed at me./Don't you remember?/{LC} Pray
578 ES	Michael	28	you/And tossed it into the fire. How I laughed!/You never seemed even to want a

LAUGHING (6)

386 CP	Celia	31	looking at you. Edward, forgive my laughing./You look like a little boy who's been
386 CP	Celia	37	side of it./{C} I'm not really laughing at *you*, Edward./I couldn't have
398 CP	Lavinia	3	were human/You would burst out laughing. But you won't./{E} O God, O God, if
473 CC	Lucasta	36	... for Mrs. Eggerson./{L} Are you laughing at me?/{C} I'm being very serious./
494 CC	Lady E	36	a potter./Don't laugh./{LE} I'm not laughing. I was only thinking/How strange to

495 CC   Claude   18   an artist. Don't laugh./{SC} I'm not laughing./So what you wanted was to inspire an
LAUGHS (1)
193 FQ: Little   70   soil/Gapes at the vanity of toil,/Laughs without mirth./This is the death of
LAUGHTER (17)
31 Apollinax   2   visited the United States/His laughter tinkled among the teacups./I thought
31 Apollinax   8   like an irresponsible fœtus./His laughter was submarine and profound/Like the
32 Hysteria   1   aware of becoming involved in her laughter and/being part of it, until her teeth
109 Marina   20   than the eye/Whispers and small laughter between leaves and hurrying feet/
172 FQ: BurntN   43   /Hidden excitedly, containing laughter./Go, go, go, said the bird: human kind/
176 FQ: BurntN   174   the dust moves/There rises the hidden laughter/Of children in the foliage/Quick now,
178 FQ: ECoker   36   circles,/Rustically solemn or in rustic laughter/Lifting heavy feet in clumsy shoes,/
180 FQ: ECoker   132   unseen and the wild strawberry,/The laughter in the garden, echoed ecstasy/Not lost,
194 FQ: Little   139   At human folly, and the laceration/Of laughter at what ceases to amuse./And last, the
244 MC   Chorus   14   afflicted with taxes,/We have had laughter and gossip,/Several girls have
246 MC   Tempt1   38   in the meadows, viols in the hall,/Laughter and apple-blossom floating on the
257 MC   Chorus   22   sleeping, and eating and drinking and laughter./God gave us always some reason,
257 MC   Chorus   31   ape, square hyaena waiting/For laughter, laughter, laughter. The Lords of Hell
257 MC   Chorus   31   square hyaena waiting/For laughter, laughter, laughter. The Lords of Hell are here./
257 MC   Chorus   31   waiting/For laughter, laughter, laughter. The Lords of Hell are here./They curl
269 MC   Chorus   33   restless, absurd. I have heard/Laughter in the noises of beasts that make
291 FR   Chorus   1   stalls, the titter in the dress circle, the laughter and catcalls in the gallery?/{C} I might
LAUNCESTON (1)
218 Mung Rump   5   well known in Cornwall Gardens, in Launceston Place and in Kensington Square —/
LAURA (1)
357 CP   Julia   5   to get a nurse./{J} Is that her Aunt Laura?/{E} No; another aunt/Whom you
LAUSANNE (4)
459 CC   Lady E   33   a Dr. Leroux./{LE} Dr. Leroux is in Lausanne./I have been in Zürich, under Dr.
459 CC   Claude   36   you were going out to Dr. Leroux/In Lausanne. What made you go to Zürich?/{LE}
459 CC   Lady E   37   /{LE} Why, I'd no sooner got to Lausanne/Than whom should I meet but
460 CC   Claude   4   /But I thought that the doctor in Lausanne taught mind control?/{LE} No,
LAVATORY (1)
356 CP   Julia   26   for the time she got locked in the lavatory/And couldn't get out. I know what
LAVENDER (1)
187 FQ: DrySal   128   is a faded song, a Royal Rose or a lavender spray/Of wistful regret for those who
LAVINIA (85)
352 CP   m   8   HENRY HARCOURT-REILLY/LAVINIA CHAMBERLAYNE/A
355 CP   Julia   21   he's such a strain —/Edward without Lavinia! He's quite impossible!/Leaving it to me
356 CP   Julia   23   *serious* conversation!'/I said so to Lavinia. She agreed with me./She said: 'I wish
356 CP   Julia   25   first time/I've ever seen you without Lavinia/Except for the time she got locked in
356 CP   Julia   29   woman/But I'm really very serious. Lavinia takes me seriously./I believe that's the
357 CP   Edward   11   /When she's ill, she insists on having Lavinia./{J} I never heard of her being ill before.
357 CP   Julia   15   gets into a panic./{J} And sends for Lavinia./I quite understand. Are there any
357 CP   Julia   18   annuity./{J} So it's very unselfish of Lavinia/Yet very like her. But really, Edward,/
357 CP   Julia   20   Yet very like her. But really, Edward,/Lavinia may be away for weeks,/Or she may
357 CP   Julia   32   Essex./{J} Anywhere near Colchester? Lavinia loves oysters./{E} No. In the *depths* of
358 CP   Julia   10   you alone./{J} Yes, alone!/Without Lavinia! You'll like the other people —/But
359 CP   Edward   18   that *you* were coming./I thought that Lavinia had told me the names/Of all the people
360 CP   Edward   1   you don't know./The fact is, that Lavinia has left me./{UG} Your wife has left
365 CP   Julia   19   is the kind of friend you have/When Lavinia is out of the way! Who is he?/{E} *I* don't
366 CP   Julia   17   to say to Edward .../{J} Oh, about Lavinia?/{P} No, not about Lavinia./It's
366 CP   Peter   18   Oh, about Lavinia?/{P} No, not about Lavinia./It's something I want to consult him
369 CP   Peter   2   at least./{P} I wouldn't say that./But Lavinia was awfully kind to me/And I owe her a
369 CP   Edward   17   to provide society and fashion./Lavinia always had the ambition/To establish
370 CP   Edward   15   /{E} There isn't any curry powder. Lavinia hates curry./{A} There goes another
372 CP   Peter   31   want to be alone. Give my love to Lavinia/When she comes back ... but, if you
372 CP   Edward   34   I shall not say anything about it to Lavinia./{P} Thank you, Edward. Good night./
374 CP   Celia   16   have thought it was perfectly simple./Lavinia has left you./{E} Yes, that *was* the
374 CP   Celia   28   your career;/And we thought that Lavinia would never want to leave you./Surely
375 CP   Edward   4   /{E} I see. But it is not like that at all./Lavinia is coming back./{C} Lavinia coming
375 CP   Celia   5   at all./Lavinia is coming back./{C} Lavinia coming back!/Do you mean to say that
377 CP   Edward   4   Edward? What has happened?/{E} Lavinia is coming back, I think./{C} You think!
377 CP   Edward   11   had left,/And he said he would bring Lavinia back, tomorrow./{C} But why should
378 CP   Julia   8   /I want to say to Edward./{J} About Lavinia?/Well, come on quickly. And take a
378 CP   Edward   16   me it was all for the best/That Lavinia had gone; that I ought to be thankful./

378 CP	Celia	19	the Devil's method! So you want Lavinia back!/Lavinia! So the one thing you
378 CP	Celia	20	method! So you want Lavinia back!/Lavinia! So the one thing you care about/Is to
379 CP	Celia	6	right,/That you do not mean to have Lavinia back/And that you do mean to gain
379 CP	Edward	19	about being fair to *me*!/{E} But for Lavinia leaving, this would never have arisen./
379 CP	Celia	29	/And then, when Julia asked about Lavinia/And it came to me that Lavinia had left
379 CP	Celia	30	about Lavinia/And it came to me that Lavinia had left you/And that you would be
380 CP	Celia	29	matters/Is, that you think you want Lavinia./And if that is the sort of person you
380 CP	Edward	33	that./It is not that I am in love with Lavinia./I don't think I was ever really in love
381 CP	Celia	5	/And never have been in love with Lavinia,/What is it that you want?/{E} I am not
381 CP	Celia	24	/Oh, Edward! Can you be happy with Lavinia?/{E} No — not happy: or, if there is any
386 CP	Celia	15	*to the front door.*]/{E} Celia!/{C} Has Lavinia arrived?/{E} Celia! Why have you
386 CP	Edward	17	Celia! Why have you come?/I expect Lavinia at any moment./You must not be here.
386 CP	Celia	19	have you come here?/{C} Because Lavinia asked me./{E} Because Lavinia asked
386 CP	Edward	20	Lavinia asked me./{E} Because Lavinia asked you!/{C} Well, not directly. Julia
386 CP	Edward	24	/{E} It seems very odd. And not like Lavinia./I suppose there is nothing to do but
387 CP	Edward	11	... {}/[*The doorbell rings*]/{E} There's Lavinia. {}/[*Goes to front door*]/{E} Peter! {}/
387 CP	Peter	13	Peter! {}/[*Enter* PETER]/{P} Where's Lavinia?/{E} Don't tell me that Lavinia/Sent
387 CP	Edward	14	Lavinia?/{E} Don't tell me that Lavinia/Sent you a telegram .../{P} No, not to
387 CP	Peter	19	a minute./Celia! Have you heard from Lavinia too?/Or am I interrupting?/{C} I've just
387 CP	Edward	24	me with her./{E} I wonder whom else Lavinia has invited./{P} Why, I got the
387 CP	Peter	25	/{P} Why, I got the impression that Lavinia intended/To have yesterday's cocktail
388 CP	m	19	to concerts./I am going away too. {}/[LAVINIA *lets herself in with a latch-key*]/{P}
388 CP	m	22	{E} You're both going away! {}/[*Enter* LAVINIA]/{L} Who's going away? Well, Celia.
389 CP	Celia	16	go there never want to leave it./{C} Lavinia, I think I understand about Peter .../{L}
389 CP	Celia	29	so much older than herself./{C} Lavinia,/Don't put me off. I may not see you
390 CP	Julia	1	*with* JULIA]/{J} There you are, Lavinia! I'm sorry to be late./But your telegram
390 CP	Julia	12	/{L} Because I've been in Essex!/{J} Lavinia! Don't say you've had a lapse of
390 CP	Julia	15	/{J} You don't know where you were? Lavinia!/Don't tell me you were abducted! Tell
390 CP	Alex	18	*to answer it. Enter* ALEX]/{A} Has Lavinia arrived?/{E} Yes./{A} Welcome back,
390 CP	Alex	20	arrived?/{E} Yes./{A} Welcome back, Lavinia!/When I got your telegram .../{L}
390 CP	Julia	30	/{J} Alex, *don't* be inquisitive./Lavinia has had a lapse of memory,/And so, of
391 CP	Julia	1	/We must leave them alone, and let Lavinia rest./Now we'll all go back to *my*
391 CP	Celia	4	/{C} Well, I'll go now. Good-bye, Lavinia./Good-bye, Edward./{E} Good-bye,
391 CP	Celia	7	/{E} Good-bye, Celia./{C} Good-bye, Lavinia./{L} Good-bye, Celia. {}/[*Exit* CELIA]/
405 CP	m	23	/Your freedom. That is my affair. {}/[LAVINIA *is shown in by the*
405 CP	Edward	24	/{R} But here is the other patient./{E} Lavinia!/{L} Well, Sir Henry!/I said I would
405 CP	Edward	28	{E} And I did not expect to meet *you*, Lavinia./I call this a very dishonourable trick./
405 CP	Edward	35	going to a hotel. And I shall ask you, Lavinia,/To be so good as to send me on some
406 CP	Edward	37	the New Forest .../{E} How like you, Lavinia./You always know of something better.
407 CP	Edward	12	I could not honestly say that of *you*, Lavinia./{R} I congratulate you both on your
408 CP	Edward	9	had reason to be jealous./{E} Really, Lavinia! This is very interesting./You seem to
408 CP	Edward	18	{E} Peter Quilpe./Peter Quilpe! Really Lavinia!/I congratulate you. You could not
410 CP	Edward	3	beginning to feel very sorry for you, Lavinia./You know, you really are exceptionally
410 CP	Edward	33	meaning of what you have said./{E} Lavinia, we must make the best of a bad job./
411 CP	1m	36	diligence. {}/[*Exeunt* EDWARD *and* LAVINIA]/[REILLY *goes to the couch and lies*
424 CP	4m	1	MAN *is arranging a buffet/table.* LAVINIA *enters from side door.*/{CM} Have
424 CP	m	4	/{CM} Very good, Madam. {}/[*Exit.* LAVINIA *looks about the room critically and*
426 CP	Edward	4	/Just ourselves. You lie down now, Lavinia/No one will be coming for at least half
427 CP	Alex	12	the opportunity/To see Edward and Lavinia./{L} How are you, Alex?/{A} I did try to
428 CP	Alex	39	we have just recognised. You see, Lavinia,/These are very deep waters./{E} And
430 CP	Peter	11	my only chance to see Edward and Lavinia./I'm only over for a week, you see,/And
435 CP	Peter	36	I don't think you're being unkind, Lavinia;/And I know that you're right./{L} And
436 CP	Edward	1	I've been talking about myself./{E} Lavinia is right. This is where you start from./If
436 CP	Julia	37	are very perceptive./{J} Oh, Henry!/Lavinia is much more observant than you think.
439 CP	Edward	3	responsibility is nothing to mine, Lavinia./{L} I'm not sure about that. If I had

LAVINIA'S (10)

356 CP	Julia	18	to pretend you're another guest/At Lavinia's party. There are many questions/I
356 CP	Julia	20	you. It's a golden opportunity/Now Lavinia's away. I've always said:/'If I could only
359 CP	Alex	4	I do hope/You'll have better news of Lavinia's aunt./{E} Oh ... yes ... thank you.
368 CP	Edward	32	here, about a year ago./{E} At one of Lavinia's amateur Thursdays?/{P} A Thursday.
368 CP	Edward	34	Why do you say amateur?/{E} Lavinia's attempts at starting a salon,/Where I
368 CP	Edward	36	guests/And dealt with the misfits, Lavinia's mistakes./But you were one of the
369 CP	Edward	15	purposes./Your role was to be one of Lavinia's discoveries;/Celia's, to provide society
372 CP	Edward	16	/{E} What! You used all those eggs! Lavinia's aunt/Has just sent them from the
377 CP	Julia	29	Oh, it isn't Alex's. Come, I give you/Lavinia's aunt! You might have guessed it./

377 CP Ed & Ce   30   You might have guessed it./{E&C} Lavinia's aunt./{J} Now, the next question/Is,
LAW (20)
30 Cous Nancy   13   of the faith,/The army of unalterable law./Mr. Apollinax/When Mr. Apollinax visited
152 Rock 2   36   attacked from without;/For this is the law of life; and you must remember that while
154 Rock 3   8   endless palaver,/I have given you my Law, and you set up commissions,/I have given
226 Macavity   2   the master criminal who can defy the Law./He's the bafflement of Scotland Yard, the
226 Macavity   6   Macavity,/He's broken every human law, he breaks the law of gravity./His powers of
226 Macavity   6   every human law, he breaks the law of gravity./His powers of levitation would
241 MC Priest3 4   man by caprice./They have but one law, to seize the power and keep it,/And the
258 MC Thomas   20   good. When I imposed the King's law/In England, and waged war with him
266 MC Knights 14   King; in rebellion to the King and the law of the land;/You are the Archbishop who
269 MC Thomas   14   who pronounces doom,/But the Law of Christ's Church, the judgement of
274 MC Thomas   6   entire consent./I give my life/To the Law of God above the Law of Man./Unbar the
274 MC Thomas   6   my life/To the Law of God above the Law of Man./Unbar the door! unbar the door!/
277 MC Knight1 33   study of statecraft and constitutional law. Sir/Hugh de Morville./{K2} I should like
533 ES   Gomez 30   always kept on the right side of the law —/And seen that the law turned its right
533 ES   Gomez 31   side of the law —/And seen that the law turned its right side to *me*./Sometimes I've
568 ES   Ld Clav 6   /Beyond anything of which the law takes cognisance:/Temporary failures,
569 ES   Ld Clav 31   to get your company/I'm afraid the law can't touch them./{C} Then why should you
573 ES   Ld Clav 8   /For the crime is in relation to the law/And the sin is in relation to the sinner./
576 ES   Gomez 35   ought to know something about the law of slander./Here's Mrs. Carghill, a reliable
576 ES   Charles 37   witness./{C} I know enough about the law of libel and slander/To know that you are
LAWFUL (1)
189 FQ: DrySal 176   fish, and/Those concerned with every lawful traffic/And those who conduct them./
LAWN (4)
136 5FingerEx3   3   quake,/The dawn is slant across the lawn,/Here is no eft or mortal snake/But only
204 de la Mare 13   quite time for bed? .../Or when the lawn/Is pressed by unseen feet, and ghosts
225 Mr Mistoff 36   find it next week lying out on the lawn./And we all say: OH!/Well I never!/Was
329 FR Chorus   5   the future./The treble voices on the lawn/The mowing of hay in summer/The dogs
LAWS (5)
41 Burb Blei   32   on/Time's ruins, and the seven laws./Sweeney Erect/Paint me a cavernous
147 Rock 1   32   there I was told/Of economic laws./In the pleasant countryside, there it
159 Rock 6   17   Church? Why should they love her laws?/She tells them of Life and Death, and of
249 MC Tempt2   5   /Disarm the ruffian, strengthen the laws,/Rule for the good of the better cause,/
329 FR Chorus 21   England/There are certain inflexible laws/Unalterable, in the nature of music./There
LAWYER (1)
551 ES Carghil 28   have settled out of court./My lawyer said: 'I advise you to accept',/'Because
LAWYER'S (1)
553 ES Carghil 31   show you the originals;/They're in my lawyer's safe. But I have photostats/Which are
LAWYERS (1)
551 ES Carghil 33   as his supporters.'/He said: 'What his lawyers are offering in settlement/Is twice as
LAY (18)
22 Preludes   25   tossed a blanket from the bed,/You lay upon your back, and waited;/You dozed,
44 Cook Egg   4   was sitting;/*Views of Oxford Colleges*/Lay on the table, with the knitting./
143 Lines OM   7   from the friendly tree./When I lay bare the tooth of wit/The hissing over the
157 Rock 4   13   gate, by the king's pool,/Jerusalem lay waste, consumed with fire;/No place for a
163 Rock 8   44   of moderate vice/When men will not lay down the Cross/Because they will never
187 FQ: DrySal 124   weather it is always a seamark/To lay a course by: but in the sombre season/Or the
212 Growltiger 22   shining bright, the barge at Molesey lay./All in the balmy moonlight it lay rocking
212 Growltiger 23   lay./All in the balmy moonlight it lay rocking on the tide —/And Growltiger was
589 Fable   86   are not rare)/That the Abbot's course lay nearer underground;/But the church
596 When we   6   with flowers still,/No withered petals lay beneath;/But the wild roses in your wreath/
256 MC Priests 28   traveller may find his way,/The sailor lay course by the sun? {}/CHORUS, PRIESTS
264 MC Priest1   5   and cried with a loud voice:/Lord, lay not this sin to their charge./*Princes*
276 MC Knight1 30   points of view, will be able/to lay before you the merits of this extremely
295 FR Harry   25   but the world I have to live in./— I lay two days in contented drowsiness;/Then I
403 CP Reilly 11   on, doing such amount of mischief/As lay within your power — until you came to
570 ES Ld Clav 13   me./I think of your mother, when she lay dying:/Completely without interest in the life
570 ES Ld Clav 14   without interest in the life that lay behind her/And completely indifferent to
570 ES Ld Clav 15   completely indifferent to whatever lay ahead of her./{M} It is time to break the
LAYER (1)
348 FR Chorus 34   Stones?/Beyond the Heaviside Layer/And behind the smiling moon?/And what
LAYERS (1)
244 MC Chorus   23   us, our brains unskinned like the layers of an onion, our selves are lost lost/In a

LAYING (1)
281 MC Chorus   14   hand to the broom, the back bent in laying the fire, the knee bent in cleaning the
LAYMAN (1)
275 MC Thomas   11   my people, in God's name,/Whether layman or clerk, shall you touch./This I forbid./
LAYS (3)
68 WL: Fire S   223   her breakfast, lights/Her stove, and lays out food in tins./Out of the window
264 MC Priest1   25   for himself, he offereth for sins./He lays down his life for the sheep./{3P} *Rejoice we*
461 CC Claude   39   she's taken a fancy to you/And so she lays claim to you. That's very satisfactory./She's
LAZARUS (1)
16 Prufrock   94   overwhelming question,/To say: 'I am Lazarus, come from the dead,/Come back to tell
LE (15)
46 Directeur   t   /Droop in a hundred A.B.C.'s./Le Directeur/Malheure à la malheureuse Tamise/
46 Directeur   3   /Qui coule si près du Spectateur./Le directeur/Conservateur/Du Spectateur/
46 Directeur   19   fille/En guenilles/Camarde/Regarde/Le directeur/Du Spectateur/Conservateur/Et
48 Lune Miel   5   forte odeur de chienne./Ils restent sur le dos écartant les genoux/De quatre jambes
48 Lune Miel   7   tout gonflées de morsures./On relève le drap pour mieux égratigner./Moins d'une
48 Lune Miel   10   /De chapitaux d'acanthe que tournoie le vent./Ils vont prendre le train de huit heures/
48 Lune Miel   11   que tournoie le vent./Ils vont prendre le train de huit heures/Prolonger leurs misères
51 Restaurant   t   /Wrapt in the old miasmal mist./Dans le Restaurant/Le garçon délabré qui n'a rien à
51 Restaurant   1   old miasmal mist./Dans le Restaurant/Le garçon délabré qui n'a rien à faire/Que de se
51 Restaurant   5   et de la pluie;/C'est ce qu'on appelle le jour de lessive des gueux.'/(Bavard, baveux, à
51 Restaurant   16   lubrique, à cet âge .../'Monsieur, le fait est dur./Il est venu, nous peloter, un gros
51 Restaurant   22   /Tiens, ma fourchette, décrasse-toi le crâne./De quel droit payes-tu des expériences
51 Restaurant   25   sous, pour la salle-de-bains./Phlébas, le Phénicien, pendant quinze jours noyé,/
51 Restaurant   29   de sous-mer l'emporta très loin,/Le repassant aux étapes de sa vie antérieure./
75 WL: Thund   429   *uti chelidon — O swallow swallow/Le Prince d'Aquitaine à la tour abolie/*These
LEAD (18)
13 Prufrock   10   argument/Of insidious intent/To lead you to an overwhelming question.../Oh, do
148 Rock 1   52   seeking/The good deeds that lead to obscurity, accepting/With equal face
228 Gus   28   hardest of hearts,/Whether I took the lead, or in character parts./I have sat by the
251 MC Thomas   29   are the people./{T} To what does this lead?/{T3} To a happy coalition/Of intelligent
255 MC Thomas   30   way, in my soul's sickness,/Does not lead to damnation in pride?/I well know that
258 MC Thomas   10   ago, I searched all the ways/That lead to pleasure, advancement and praise./
261 MC Thomas   28   His love of men,/to warn them and to lead them, to bring them back to His ways. It is/
276 MC Knight3 34   old friend Reginald Fitz Urse would lead you to/believe. But there is one thing I
297 FR Violet   31   /Which I am convinced is going to lead us nowhere,/And which I am sure Amy
338 FR Harry   31   the only thing possible./Now they will lead me. I shall be safe with them;/I am not safe
363 CP Edward   9   /{UG} Water./{E} To what does this lead?/{UG} To finding out/What you really are.
413 CP Reilly   11   /About the nature of their illness, and lead them to see/That it's not so interesting as
413 CP Celia   16   that way. I feel perfectly well./I could lead an active life — if there's anything to work
419 CP Reilly   30   sense;/No one disappears. They lead very active lives/Very often, in the world./
430 CP Julia   29   us your news of the world, Peter./We lead such a quiet life, here in London./{P} You
435 CP Peter   23   film!/But I thought it was going to lead to something better,/And that seemed
437 CP Reilly   26   for her to choose the way of life/To lead to death, and, without knowing the end/
559 ES Michael 18   you want?/{Mi} I simply want to lead a life of my own,/According to my own
LEADER (3)
148 Rock 1 m   38   for important weddings./CHORUS LEADER:/Silence! and preserve respectful
277 MC Knight2 36   a point that was very/well put by our leader, Reginald Fitz Urse: that you are
279 MC Knight4 12   preceded me, to say nothing/of our leader, Reginald Fitz Urse, have all spoken very
LEADING (1)
531 ES Charles   6   about you in the papers./{C} And the leading articles saying 'we are confident/That
LEADS (4)
294 FR Harry   18   /Without direction, for no direction/Leads anywhere but round and round in that
337 FR Harry   27   one way out of defilement —/Which leads in the end to reconciliation./And I know
418 CP Reilly   28   /You will journey blind. But the way leads towards possession/Of what you have
439 CP Julia   13   was Kinkanja./Peter chose a way that leads him to Boltwell:/And he's got to go there
LEAF (4)
67 WL: Fire S   173   tent is broken; the last fingers of leaf/Clutch and sink into the wet bank. The
172 FQ: BurntN   59   moving tree/In light upon the figured leaf/And hear upon the sodden floor/Below, the
177 FQ: ECoker   8   Bone of man and beast, cornstalk and leaf./Houses live and die: there is a time for
263 MC Chorus   21   shall sing the same song./When the leaf is out on the tree, when the elder and may/
LEAGUE (1)
56 Swee Night   26   the cape/Are suspect, thought to be in league;/Therefore the man with heavy eyes/
LEAKAGE (1)
186 FQ: DrySal   66   /In a drifting boat with a slow leakage,/The silent listening to the undeniable/

LEAKS (1)
110 Marina	28	my own./The garboard strake leaks, the seams need caulking./This form, this

LEAN (6)
34 Figlia	2	the highest pavement of the stair —/Lean on a garden urn —/Weave, weave the
74 WL: Thund	408	spider/Or under seals broken by the lean solicitor/In our empty rooms/DA/
177 FQ: ECoker	17	dark in the afternoon,/Where you lean against a bank while a van passes,/And the
210 Old Gumbie	24	and dried peas,/And a *beautiful* fry of lean bacon and cheese./I have a Gumbie Cat in
242 MC Priest2	36	and also the King of France./We can lean on a rock, we can feel a firm foothold/
300 FRDowning	5	was rough,/Didn't like to see her lean over the rail./He was in a rare fright, once

LEANED (2)
52 Whispers	4	breastless creatures under ground/Leaned backward with a lipless grin./Daffodil
64 WL: Chess	106	told upon the walls; staring forms/Leaned out, leaning, hushing the room

LEANING (6)
15 Prufrock	72	pipes/Of lonely men in shirt-sleeves, leaning out of windows?.../I should have been a
57 Swee Night	30	and reappears/Outside the window, leaning in,/Branches of wistaria/Circumscribe a
64 WL: Chess	106	the walls; staring forms/Leaned out, leaning, hushing the room enclosed./Footsteps
83 Hollow Men	3	hollow men/We are the stuffed men/Leaning together/Headpiece filled with straw.
118 SP Dusty	21	the Knave of Hearts *is* Sam!/{Du} (*leaning out of the window*): Hello Sam!/{W}
300 FRDowning	31	I remember, there I saw his Lordship/Leaning over the rail, looking at the water —/

LEAP (5)
13 Prufrock	20	Slipped by the terrace, made a sudden leap,/And seeing that it was a soft October
141 Rannoch	4	/And the soft sky, scarcely room/To leap or soar. Substance crumbles, in the thin air
215 RTTugger	33	doesn't care for a cuddle;/But he'll leap on your lap in the middle of your sewing,/
223 Pekes Pols	58	looked at the sky and he gave a great leap —/And they every last one of them
480 CC Kaghan	9	the moment,/But you'd never take a leap in the dark;/You'd keep me on the rails./

LEAPING (4)
178 FQ: ECoker	35	concorde. Round and round the fire/Leaping through the flames, or joined in circles,
206 To my Wife	1	to my Wife/To whom I owe the leaping delight/That quickens my senses in our
605 Narcissus	5	sand at daybreak, or/Your shadow leaping behind the fire against the red rock:/I
522 ES dedic	1	/TO MY WIFE/*To whom I owe the leaping delight/That quickens my senses in our*

LEARN (37)
20 Portrait	91	back,/You will find so much to learn.'/My smile falls heavily among the
164 Rock 9	15	the way of penitence,/And then let us learn the joyful communion of saints./The soul
182 FQ: ECoker	176	of *l'entre deux guerres* —/Trying to learn to use words, and every attempt/Is a
204 de la Mare	18	the well known is what we have yet to learn,/And two worlds meet, and intersect, and
224 Mr Mistoff	14	greatest magicians have something to learn/From Mr. Mistoffelees' Conjuring Turn./
247 MC Thomas	16	things happen again and again./Men learn little from others' experience./But in the
299 FR Charles	6	voyage from New York —/We didn't learn very much about the circumstances;/We
327 FR Agatha	6	/Is evasion of suffering. We must learn to suffer more./{V} Agatha's remarks are
330 FR Harry	18	as an explanation./{H} I still have to learn exactly what their meaning is./At the
333 FR Agatha	35	flame./Indeed it is possible. You may learn hereafter,/Moving alone through flames of
339 FR Harry	4	are you going?/{H} I shall have to learn. That is still unsettled./I have not yet had
343 FR Mary	18	myself. It takes so many years/To learn that one is dead! So you must help me./I
344 FR Gerald	23	troublesome. But you'll have to learn the language/And several dialects. It
404 CP Reilly	8	with me, Mr. Chamberlayne:/I learn a good deal by merely observing you,/And
411 CP Reilly	29	is not to clear your conscience/But to learn how to bear the burdens on your
417 CP Reilly	28	themselves by the common routine,/Learn to avoid excessive expectation,/Become
428 CP Edward	32	/{E} No indeed: we are anxious to learn the solution./{A} I'm not sure that there *is*
436 CP Edward	4	remember/That some men have to learn much worse things/About themselves, and
436 CP Edward	5	worse things/About themselves, and learn them later/When it's harder to recover,
440 CP Edward	27	only mean the worst./{E} I never shall learn how to pay a compliment./{L} What you
448 CC Claude	22	to him. This afternoon/She will only learn that you have finally retired/And that you
463 CC Colby	19	person. Just as, I suppose,/If you learn to speak a foreign language fluently,/So
467 CC Claude	31	Meanwhile, we must simply wait to learn/What new conditions life will impose on
469 CC Lucasta	3	/You know that. But I'd like to learn about music./I wish you would teach me
469 CC Colby	9	know it well,/Then you will want to learn about its structure/And the various forms,
470 CC Colby	18	I will./But I'm sure that when you learn about music —/And that won't take you
472 CC Lucasta	29	had all collapsed/And that you must learn to do something different./And so you
479 CC Kaghan	3	for a drink./{K} I told Colby, never learn to mix cocktails,/If you don't want women
489 CC Claude	28	had sent me on a business tour/To learn about his overseas investments./{LE} Then
516 CC Claude	20	your feelings/On beginning to learn the ways of business;/The exhilaration of
536 ES Gomez	11	a word of English,/Didn't want to learn English, wasn't interested/In anything that
536 ES Gomez	14	priest told her./I made my children learn English — it's useful;/I always talk to
547 ES Piggott	36	from the motor roads. You must learn the best walks./I won't apologise for the
565 ES Ld Clav	36	I would teach? Come, I'll start to learn again./Michael and I shall go to school

574 ES	Ld Clav	29	Father. I'll explain why./{LC} And I learn that you have discussed your problems/
575 ES	Gomez	20	told him myself./I thought he'd better learn the facts from me/Before he heard your
580 ES	Monica	27	/But perhaps, perhaps, Michael may learn his lesson./I believe he'll come back. If it's

LEARNED (10)

234 Ad-dress		5	their character./You now have learned enough to see/That Cats are much like
327 FR	Agatha	1	the worst./{Ag} Whatever you have learned, Harry, you must remember/That there
337 FR	Agatha	14	have wished to know, what you have learned/Mean the end of a relation, make it
368 CP	Alex	25	/Any scraps you have will do. I learned that in the East./With a handful of rice
436 CP	Julia	14	enough for Celia./{J} You must have learned how to look at people, Peter,/When you
457 CC	Lady E	28	with it. No, I forgot:/You haven't learned yet how to make tea properly./A cup of
506 CC	Eggers	27	days ago,/As I said, Lady Elizabeth learned your name;/And the name struck her as
539 ES	Gomez	15	that you're supposed to be./And I've learned something of other vicissitudes./Dick, I
551 ES	Ld Clav	9	our account./What harm was done? I learned my lesson/And you learned yours, if
551 ES	Ld Clav	10	done? I learned my lesson/And you learned yours, if you needed the lesson./{MC}

LEARNING (7)

164 Rock 9		14	/Let us mourn in a private chamber, learning the way of penitence,/And then let us
258 MC	Thomas	11	and praise./Delight in sense, in learning and in thought,/Music and philosophy,
332 FR	Agatha	18	together,/For three years childless, learning the meaning/Of loneliness. Your
466 CC	Colby	32	At least, I understand *you* better/In learning to understand the conditions/Which
544 ES	Monica	27	to escape;/Now I want to see you learning to enjoy yourself!/{LC} Perhaps I've
569 ES	Monica	15	better./There's nothing I'm afraid of learning about Charles,/There's nothing I'm
569 ES	Monica	16	Charles,/There's nothing I'm afraid of learning about you./{C} I was thinking, Sir —

LEARNT (6)

182 FQ: ECoker		178	kind of failure/Because one has only learnt to get the better of words/For the thing
234 Ad-dress		14	them both at work and games,/And learnt about their proper names,/Their habits
387 CP	Celia	2	at anything, yesterday;/But I've learnt a lot in twenty-four hours./It wasn't a
471 CC	Lucasta	31	Well, there's one thing you haven't learnt yet,/And that is, to know when you're
496 CC	Lady E	8	are!/Not that there isn't a lot to be learnt,/I don't doubt, from the dervish rituals./
533 ES	Gomez	33	I've had to pay pretty heavily;/But I learnt by experience whom to pay;/And a little

LEAST (63)

19 Portrait		35	own,/Capricious monotone/That is at least one definite 'false note.'/— Let us take the
74 WL: Thund		425	the arid plain behind me/Shall I at least set my lands in order?/London Bridge is
225 Mr Mistoff		48	he was about on the roof —/(At least we all *heard* that somebody purred)/Which
242 MC	Mess	7	any illusions,/Or yet to diminish the least of his pretensions./If you ask my opinion, I
245 MC	Priest2	7	like frogs in the treetops:/But frogs at least can be cooked and eaten./Whatever you
245 MC	Priest2	9	apprehension,/Let me ask you at the least to put on pleasant faces,/And give a hearty
277 MC	Knight3	26	at the beginning, please give us/at least the credit for being completely
289 FR	Gerald	3	show themselves./{G} I don't in the least know what you're talking about./You
291 FR	Amy	11	has the shortest way to come./John at least, if not Arthur. Hark, there is someone
296 FR	Harry	12	away, but you explained them/Or at least, made me cease to be afraid of them./I will
299 FRDowning		18	it is those that talk/That are the least likely. To my way of thinking/She only did
303 FR	Agatha	15	.../{Ag} And also Dr. Warburton. At least, Amy has invited him./{M} Dr.
305 FR	Harry	24	journey?/{H} Not very./But, at least, it did not last long. How are you, Mary?/
306 FR	Mary	31	We were rather in awe of you —/At least, I was./{H} Why were we not happy?/{M}
307 FR	Harry	8	night/After being put to bed. But at least they never knew/Where we had been./{M}
310 FR	Mary	6	bud./These are the ones that suffer least:/The aconite under the snow/And the
318 FR	Harry	35	am saying./But if you want to talk, at least you can tell me/Something useful. Do you
334 FR	Harry	32	mother —/More compassionate at least — by understanding./But she would not
340 FR	Amy	13	what I had, you would have left me at least a memory/Of something to live upon. You
341 FR	Agatha	4	that I had, until this evening./But at least I wanted to. Now I must begin./There is
342 FR	Agatha	37	one who knows./No one who has the least suspicion of what is to be found there./But
359 CP	Edward	22	But she always turns up when she's least wanted. {}/[*Opens the door*]/{E} Julia! {}/
366 CP	Peter	22	Of course I don't mind./{P} Well, at least you must let me take you down in the lift./
368 CP	Edward	38	of the minor successes/For a time at least./{P} I wouldn't say that./But Lavinia was
371 CP	Peter	16	a memory./{P} But I must see Celia at least to make her tell me/What has happened, in
389 CP	Lavinia	27	were one of my dearest friends —At least, in so far as a girl *can* be a friend/Of a
394 CP	Edward	17	just as they were leaving./{E} Well, at least, *they* can't have thought I was the butler./
396 CP	Lavinia	18	to you —/Or if that's impossible, at least be horrid to you —/Anything but nothing,
397 CP	Edward	23	Where there are no doctors —At least, not in a professional capacity./{L} One
402 CP	Edward	13	could see that for himself./Or at least that he would enquire about the
405 CP	Edward	18	before he enters the court./{E} I am at least free to leave. And I propose to do so./My
406 CP	Reilly	8	have come to see it in that light —At least, for the moment. But, Mrs. Chamberlayne,
409 CP	Reilly	13	And were not prepared to make the least sacrifice/On her account. This injured your
411 CP	Lavinia	22	/{L} But I wish you would say it./At least, there is something I would like to ask.
413 CP	Celia	8	that someone else is to blame./{C} I at least have no one to blame but myself./{R} And

413 CP	Celia	30	then there's something wrong,/Or at least, very different from what it seemed to be,/
414 CP	Celia	6	they get over it/More or less, or at least they carry on./No. I mean that what has
415 CP	Celia	12	accompanied by a sense of sin:/At least, I have never come across it./I suppose it is
420 CP	Celia	4	at the sanatorium./{C} I don't in the least know what I am doing/Or why I am doing
426 CP	Edward	5	Lavinia/No one will be coming for at least half an hour;/So just stretch out./{L} You
427 CP	Alex	37	a symptom, I am not so sure./At least, the monkeys have become the pretext/For
431 CP	Peter	22	noble mansion in England!/At least, of any that are still inhabited./We've got a
434 CP	Alex	20	And then they found her body,/Or at least, they found the traces of it./{E} But before
452 CC	Lucasta	17	/Which no one ever wanted — at least, not till yesterday./Then, just by bad luck,
455 CC	Colby	35	now, that's different./{C} At least, I don't suppose Lady Elizabeth/Can be
456 CC	Eggers	23	she sometimes remembers when you least expect it./But she does forget things. And
463 CC	Colby	24	/And yet from time to time, when I least expect it,/When my mind is cleared and
466 CC	Colby	31	... make-believe?/{C} I think I do. At least, I understand *you* better/In learning to
472 CC	Colby	6	very badly hurt, at some time./Or at least, there may have been something in your
476 CC	Colby	2	only one thing I can't tell you./At least, not yet. I'm not allowed to tell./And that's
476 CC	Lucasta	7	can tell you all about *my* parents:/At least, I'm going to./{C} Does that matter, either?
479 CC	Kaghan	28	afraid of her as anybody!/{K} Well, at least, I've always managed to escape her./{L}
504 CC	Guzzard	28	/But I didn't mind waiting in the least, Sir Claude./I know that you are always
511 CC	Lady E	15	very good regiment —/For a time, at least./{K} Well, I must get used to that./But I
534 ES	Ld Clav	15	of./{LC} That's something, at least, to be thankful for./I trust you've no need
537 ES	Gomez	27	other way. You stayed the course, at least./I had plenty of time to think things over,
538 ES	Gomez	22	get moved to another post/Where at least you can't make quite the same mistake./At
539 ES	Gomez	8	been good for another five years/At least. Why did they let you retire?/{LC} If you
544 ES	Ld Clav	29	living/As much as most people. At least, as they seem to do/Without knowing that
559 ES	Ld Clav	7	your feet./I have connections, or at least correspondents/Almost everywhere.
567 ES	Monica	16	yet .../{M} We're engaged now./At least *I'm* engaged. I'm engaged to you for ever./
569 ES	Charles	24	/{M} Oh Father, do let him./{C} At least, I think I know the best man to advise you.
572 ES	Ld Clav	5	heard, from time to time,/When I least expected, between waking and sleeping,/A

LEAVE (108)

21 Portrait	105	can hardly understand./We must leave it now to fate./You will write, at any rate./
21 Portrait	116	yellow and rose;/Should die and leave me sitting pen in hand/With the smoke
34 Figlia	8	your hair./So I would have had him leave,/So I would have had her stand and
66 WL: Chess	163	fool, I said./Well, if Albert won't leave you alone, there it is, I said,/What you get
129 Cor2 State	15	shillings at Christmas/And one week's leave a year./A committee has been appointed
142 Cape Ann	4	the dance/Of the goldfinch at noon. Leave to chance/The Blackburnian warbler, the
154 Rock 3	22	to the shore of smoky ships?/Will you leave my people forgetful and forgotten/To
157 Rock 4	8	Jerusalem;/And the King gave him leave to depart/That he might rebuild the city./
181 FQ: ECoker	163	absolute paternal care/That will not leave us, but prevents us everywhere./The chill
191 FQ: Little	29	for,/It would be the same, when you leave the rough road/And turn behind the
192 FQ: Little	57	sleeve/Is all the ash the burnt roses leave./Dust in the air suspended/Marks the
196 FQ: Little	196	from the defeated/What they had to leave us — a symbol:/A symbol perfected in
233 Skimble	49	be bothered by mice —/You can leave all that to the Railway Cat,/The Cat of the
592 Grad 2	4	time shall not restore,/And when they leave they fully understand/That though again
595 Grad 13	4	and a friend to bless/Before they leave thy care for lands unseen;/And let thy
604 Ode	12	away/In the place of the life that we leave./And only the years that efface and
242 MC	Mess	12	said to the King,/My Lord, he said, I leave you as a man/Whom in this life I shall not
243 MC	Chorus	19	to France./Return. Quickly. Quietly. Leave us to perish in quiet./You come with
244 MC	Chorus	25	Archbishop,/O Thomas our Lord, leave us and leave us be, in our humble and
244 MC	Chorus	25	/O Thomas our Lord, leave us and leave us be, in our humble and tarnished frame
244 MC	Chorus	25	and tarnished frame of existence, leave us; do not ask us/To stand to the doom on
244 MC	Chorus	30	of the world?/O Thomas, Archbishop, leave us, leave us, leave sullen Dover, and set
244 MC	Chorus	30	/O Thomas, Archbishop, leave us, leave us, leave sullen Dover, and set sail for
244 MC	Chorus	30	Archbishop, leave us, leave us, leave sullen Dover, and set sail for France.
244 MC	Chorus	30	the grey sky and the bitter sea, leave us, leave us for France./{P2} What a way
244 MC	Chorus	30	grey sky and the bitter sea, leave us, leave us for France./{P2} What a way to talk at
245 MC	Thomas	35	as you left them./{T} And will try to leave them in order as I find them./I am more
247 MC	Tempt1	37	best dinners./Take a friend's advice. Leave well alone,/Or your goose may be cooked
247 MC	Tempt1	40	twenty years too late./{T1} Then I leave you to your fate./I leave you to the
248 MC	Tempt1	1	/{T1} Then I leave you to your fate./I leave you to the pleasures of your higher vices,/
248 MC	Tempt1	4	Lord, I do not wait upon ceremony,/I leave as I came, forgetting all acrimony,/Hoping
250 MC	Tempt2	7	my open office. No! Go./{T2} Then I leave you to your fate./Your sin soars sunward,
260 MC	Thomas	27	He said to His/disciples, 'Peace I leave with you, my peace I give unto you.' Did
266 MC	Thomas	11	with you alone. {}/[*to* PRIESTS]/{T} Leave us then alone./Now what is the matter?/
285 FR	Amy	11	in the dark!/Put on the lights. But leave the curtains undrawn./Make up the fire.
286 FR	Charles	1	and dogs and guns/Ever to want to leave England in the winter./But a single man

287 FR   Amy   25   /If you want to know why I never leave Wishwood/That is the reason. I keep
298 FR   Agatha   11   is all quite irrelevant;/We had better leave Charles to talk to Downing/And pursue
300 FR Downing   15   opinion,/I dare say. She wouldn't leave him alone./And there's my complaint
300 FR Downing   20   can't follow him./She wouldn't leave him out of her sight./{C} During that
309 FR   Harry   10   /{H} No, no, don't go! Please don't leave me/Just at this moment. I feel it is
311 FR   Harry   15   me? — When I remember them/They leave me alone: when I forget them/Only for an
319 FR   Warburt   14   festered/Then, has only left a cautery./Leave it alone. You know that your mother/
323 FR   Warburt   29   /As your doctor, I forbid you to leave the house tonight./There is nothing you
323 FR   Charles   34   I do not believe you./{C} Much better leave it to Warburton, Amy./Extremely
325 FR   Agatha   6   behaviour./{Ag} I think it is as well to leave Harry to establish/If he can, some
336 FR   Harry   17   I know that you are ready,/Ready to leave Wishwood, and I am going with you./You
342 FR   Mary   23   keep him here, you must not let him leave./I do not know what must be done, what
343 FR   Amy   21   get a fellowship?/{A} So you will all leave me!/An old woman alone in a damned
345 FR   Amy   28   Where I can lie down./Then you can leave me./{G} Oh, certainly, Amy./{V} I do not
346 FR   Mary   11   Downing, will you promise never to leave his Lordship/While you are away?/{Do}
346 FR Downing   14   /{Do} Oh, certainly, Miss;/I'll never leave him so long as he requires me./{M} But he
346 FR   Mary   15   But he will need you. You must never leave him./{Do} You may think it laughable,
358 CP   Julia   21   /It's such a nice party, I hate to leave it./It's such a nice party, I'd like to repeat
368 CP   Alex   17   you can have alone. And then we'll leave you./Meanwhile, you and Peter can go on
368 CP   Edward   29   *to kitchen]*/{E} Well, where did you leave off?/{P} You asked me how I came to
371 CP   Edward   9   time. There it is./You can take it or leave it./{P} But what am I to do?/{E} Nothing.
372 CP   Alex   28   toast. I've left it simmering./Don't leave it longer than another ten minutes./Now
374 CP   Celia   28   that Lavinia would never want to leave you./Surely you don't hold to that silly
375 CP   m   36   I must go and investigate. {}/[*Starts to leave the room]*/{E} For heaven's sake, don't
376 CP   Celia   4   lose your head./You see, I really did leave my umbrella;/And I'll say I found you
383 CP   Edward   2   spectacles again ... where did you leave them?/Or have we ... have I got to hunt all
389 CP   Lavinia   15   people who go there never want to leave it./{C} Lavinia, I think I understand about
391 CP   Julia   1   what I'll do .../{J} No, Alex./We must leave them alone, and let Lavinia rest./Now
399 CP   Nurse   16   through/The moment she arrives. I leave her there/Until you ring three times./{R}
405 CP   Edward   18   the court./{E} I am at least free to leave. And I propose to do so./My mind is
411 CP   Lavinia   4   /I could go down with you, and then leave you there/If you want to be alone .../{E}
411 CP   Edward   10   /{E} No, they won't let me./I must leave tomorrow — but how did you know/I was
411 CP   Lavinia   14   sense of responsibility./I was going to leave some shirts there for you./{E} It seems to
414 CP   Celia   18   been in the family so long, they won't leave it./{R} And you live in London?/{C} I
424 CP   Lavinia   3   in the trolley with the glasses/And leave them ready./{CM} Very good, Madam. {}/
434 CP   Alex   13   you./They knew of it, but would not leave the dying natives./Eventually, two of them
436 CP   Lavinia   24   that she died because she would not leave/A few dying natives./{R} Who knows,
439 CP   Edward   24   we see you again, Peter,/Before you leave England?/{L} Do try to come to see us./
440 CP   Julia   14   And I think, Henry,/That we should leave before the party begins./They will get on
445 CC   Claude   22   /But he'll be back, I hope, before you leave./{E} And how's he getting on?
447 CC   Claude   1   find them if anybody./{SC} Well, we'll leave that for the present. As we have a little
447 CC   Claude   26   absence,/You must say you had to leave under medical orders./She's always been
450 CC   Claude   22   should be back by now. And then I'll leave you./I must telephone to Amsterdam, and
450 CC   Claude   31   half an hour, Mr. Simpkins./{SC} I'll leave you now. But when Eggerson comes back/
450 CC   Colby   33   /{C} I'm glad you don't have to leave just yet./I'm rather nervous about this
453 CC   Eggers   19   asked me out to lunch./{E} We will leave Mrs. Eggerson out of this, Miss Angel./{L}
454 CC   Kaghan   6   comes./{K} And I don't propose to leave you with Colby./He's had enough for one
488 CC   Colby   23   to say about it./I must leave that to you./{SC} I should have told you
493 CC   Lady E   24   armchair .../{LE} Not such a low one. Leave that in the corner/For Colby. He won't
497 CC   Lady E   26   to know:/I am perfectly content to leave things as they are,/So that we may regard
504 CC   Claude   37   /{SC} Elizabeth, you know we are to leave that to Eggerson./This is Mr. Eggerson,
506 CC   Claude   7   /{SC} That's not relevant./Leave it to Eggerson./{E} The father died
517 CC   Colby   15   on false pretences:/That's why I must leave you./{SC} Eggerson!/Can't you persuade
518 CC   Guzzard   9   to a taxi./Do you mind if I take my sir Claude?/I'm no longer needed here. {}/
519 CC   Claude   22   *around* SIR CLAUDE]/{SC} Don't leave me, Lucasta./Eggerson! Do *you* really
545 ES   Ld Clav   15   What she said. She said: 'I'm going to leave you alone!'/You want perfect peace: that's
547 ES   Monica   18   considers proper courtesies,/She will leave us alone. {}/[*Re-enter* MRS. PIGGOTT]/
548 ES   Piggott   2   quiet is our *raison d'être.*/Now I'll leave you to enjoy it. {}/[*Exit]*/{M} I hope she
550 ES   Ld Clav   33   have thought we both preferred to leave buried./{MC} There you're wrong,
554 ES   Carghil   7   once, perhaps she'll take the hint/And leave us alone tomorrow./Good morning, Mrs.
556 ES   Monica   29   /Perhaps you'll get to the point if I leave you together. {}/[*Exit]*/{Mi} You know, it's
561 ES   Michael   33   /{Mi} What is there to say?/I want to leave England, and make my own career:/And
565 ES   Carghil   23   it. Perhaps I could advise you./We'll leave you now, Richard. Au revoir, Monica./
569 ES   Charles   33   why should you submit?/Why not leave Badgley and escape from them?/{LC}
579 ES   Charles   6   same Michael./{C} And when do you leave England?/{Mi} When we can get a

579 ES   Gomez   26   end of five years he will get his first leave./{Mi} Well ... there's nothing more to say,
581 ES   Monica   11   one thing I'm convinced of: you must leave Badgley Court./{C} Monica is right. You
581 ES   Charles 12   /{C} Monica is right. You should leave./{LC} This may surprise you: I feel at
582 ES   Ld Clav 12   —/Well, that is something./I shall leave you for a while./This is your first visit to
582 ES   Ld Clav 18   ought to have a little time together./I leave Monica to you. Look after her, Charles,/
582 ES   Charles 30   going for a walk./{C} He wanted to leave us alone together!/{M} Yes, he wanted to
582 ES   Monica   31   alone together!/{M} Yes, he wanted to leave us alone together./And yet, Charles,

LEAVE-WELL-ALONE (1)
248 MC   Thomas   9   at kissing-time below the stairs./{T} Leave-well-alone, the springtime fancy,/So one

LEAVES (17)
22 Preludes   7   wraps/The grimy scraps/Of withered leaves about your feet/And newspapers from
34 Figlia   11   /So he would have left/As the soul leaves the body torn and bruised,/As the mind
57 Swee Night   29   /Declines the gambit, shows fatigue,/Leaves the room and reappears/Outside the
74 WL: Thund   395   rain/Ganga was sunken, and the limp leaves/Waited for rain, while the black clouds/
109 Marina   20   /Whispers and small laughter between leaves and hurrying feet/Under sleep, where all
171 FQ: BurntN   26   without pressure, over the dead leaves,/In the autumn heat, through the vibrant
172 FQ: BurntN   42   was empty./Go, said the bird, for the leaves were full of children,/Hidden excitedly,
187 FQ: DrySal   130   here to regret,/Pressed between yellow leaves of a book that has never been opened./
189 FQ: DrySal   194   release omens/By sortilege, or tea leaves, riddle the inevitable/With playing cards,
193 FQ: Little   85   horizon of his homing/While the dead leaves still rattled on like tin/Over the asphalt
193 FQ: Little   89   As if blown towards me like the metal leaves/Before the urban dawn wind unresisting./
596 When we   2   we came home across the hill/No leaves were fallen from the trees;/The gentle
596 When we   8   in your wreath/Were faded, and the leaves were brown./Before Morning/While all
241 MC   Mess   34   their capes,/Strewing the way with leaves and late flowers of the season./The streets
309 FR   Harry   36   usual noises/In the grass and leaves, of life persisting,/Which ordinarily pass
355 CP   m   16   the wedding cake. {}/[EDWARD *leaves the room*]/{J} No, we'll wait until Edward
418 CP   Celia   5   that/If I might still have it. Yet it leaves me cold./Perhaps that's just a part of my

LEAVING (24)
107 Animula   30   shadows, spectre in its own gloom,/Leaving disordered papers in a dusty room;/
177 FQ: ECoker   15   the light falls/Across the open field, leaving the deep lane/Shuttered with branches,
179 FQ: ECoker   71   study in a worn-out poetical fashion,/Leaving one still with the intolerable wrestle/
180 FQ: ECoker   122   face the mental emptiness deepen/Leaving only the growing terror of nothing to
257 MC   Chorus   25   and the mouth and the eye./God is leaving us, God is leaving us, more pang, more
257 MC   Chorus   25   and the eye./God is leaving us, God is leaving us, more pang, more pain than birth or
340 FR   Amy   16   the walls, the furniture, the acres;/Leaving nothing — but what I could breed for
342 FR   Mary   2   /She came to tell me that Harry is leaving:/Downing told her. He has got the car
344 FR   Violet   6   I cannot understand at all. Why is he leaving?/{A} Ask Agatha./{V} Really, it
355 CP   Julia   22   Lavinia! He's quite impossible!/Leaving it to me to keep things going./What a
360 CP   Edward   6   /She left a note to say that she was leaving me;/But I don't know where she's gone./
379 CP   Edward   19   being fair to *me*!/{E} But for Lavinia leaving, this would never have arisen./What
386 CP   Reilly   9   myself, I shall take the precaution/Of leaving by the service staircase./{E} May I ask
393 CP   Lavinia   14   mean by giving in to *me*:/You mean, leaving all the practical decisions/That you
394 CP   Lavinia   16   didn't arrive until just as they were leaving./{E} Well, at least, *they* can't have
427 CP   Alex   10   party/And, as I thought you might be leaving for the country,/I said, I must not miss
481 CC   Lady E   16   Have you just arrived, or are you just leaving?/{L} We're on the point of leaving, Lady
481 CC   Lucasta 17   leaving?/{L} We're on the point of leaving, Lady Elizabeth./{LE} I've come over to
481 CC   Lady E   23   to see you in it. Did you say you were leaving?/{K} We're going out to dinner.
525 ES   Charles   1   have a grievance./On Monday you're leaving London, with your father:/I arranged to
525 ES   Charles   18   /He's at home every day. And you're leaving London./And because your father
525 ES   Monica   30   in the library/And he won't think of leaving it until he's called for tea./So why not
538 ES   Gomez   27   Dick .../That would account for your leaving politics/And taking a conspicuous job in
554 ES   Piggott   30   your morning tipple myself/Instead of leaving it, as usual, to Nurse)/When I saw that

LECHERY (2)
152 Rock 2   29   of the Word of GOD,/For pride, for lechery, treachery, for every act of sin./And of
163 Rock 8   36   few,/Part faith of many,/Not avarice, lechery, treachery,/Envy, sloth, gluttony,

LECTEUR (1)
63 WL: Burial   76   he'll dig it up again!/'You! hypocrite lecteur! — mon semblable, — mon frère!'/A

LED (18)
104 Journ Magi   35   set down/This set down/This: were we led all that way for/Birth or Death? There was a
148 Rock 1 m   46   is the truth inborn./*Enter the* ROCK, *led by a* BOY:/THE ROCK:/The lot of man is
160 Rock 7   4   light and the shadow, and the light led them forward to light and the shadow led
160 Rock 7   4   them forward to light and the shadow led them to darkness,/Worshipping snakes or
160 Rock 7   10   the Higher Religions were good/And led men from light to light, to knowledge of
288 FR   Agatha   38   plantation, down the corridor/That led to the nursery, round the corner/Of the new
310 FR   Harry   37   had felt sure/That every corridor only led to another,/Or to a blank wall; that I kept

342 FR	Agatha	38	be found there./But Harry has been led across the frontier: he must follow;/For him
354 CP	Julia	17	once upon a time./What a life she led! I used to say to her: 'Greta!/You have too
396 CP	Lavinia	39	not to relapse into the kind of life we led/Until yesterday morning./{E} There was a
415 CP	Celia	24	psychological./And bad form always led to disaster/Because the people one knew
437 CP	Reilly	31	/That way, which she accepted, led to this death./And if that is not a happy
487 CC	Claude	32	right./{SC} But Elizabeth, what has led you to believe/That Colby is your son?/{LE}
527 ES	Monica	23	terror of being alone./In the life he's led, he's never had to be alone./And when he's
537 ES	Gomez	35	what happened to you later./{G} You led me on at Oxford, and left me to it./And so it
538 ES	Gomez	36	you were fifty:/That should have led you to the very top!/And yet you withdrew
545 ES	Piggott	29	in directly after breakfast:/He's led a busy life, too.' But I hope you're happy?/Is
571 ES	Ld Clav	9	What did I make of his admiration?/I led him to acquire tastes beyond his means:/So

LEER (1)

62 WL: Burial	42	the heart of light, the silence./*Oed' und leer das Meer.*/Madame Sosostris, famous

LEEWARD (1)

69 WL: Fire S	272	the turning tide/Red sails/Wide/To leeward, swing on the heavy spar./The barges

LEFT (107)

18 Portrait	7	for all the things to be said, or left unsaid./We have been, let us say, to hear the
24 Rhapsody	31	to the form that the strength has left/Hard and curled and ready to snap./
34 Figlia	10	stand and grieve,/So he would have left/As the soul leaves the body torn and
40 Burb Blei	8	bell/Slowly: the God Hercules/Had left him, that had loved him well./The horses,
67 WL: Fire S	181	of City directors;/Departed, have left no addresses./By the waters of Leman I sat
92 Ash-Wed 3	8	second turning of the second stair/I left them twisting, turning below;/There were no
152 Rock 2	24	of a mission/Performed it, but left much at home unsure./Of all that was done
154 Rock 3	24	and delirious stupor?/There shall be left the broken chimney,/The peeled hull, a pile
161 Rock 7	27	or why, or how, or where./Men have left GOD not for other gods, they say, but for
162 Rock 8	18	were rapacious and lustful./Many left their bodies to the kites of Syria/Or
162 Rock 8	20	Or sea-strewn along the routes;/Many left their souls in Syria,/Living on, sunken in
163 Rock 8	31	or another,/There was something left that was more than the tales/Of old men on
166 Rock 10	8	and moving his head to right and to left prepares for his hour to devour./But the
188 FQ: DrySal	136	/(And those who saw them off have left the platform)/Their faces relax from grief
188 FQ: DrySal	141	/You are not the same people who left that station/Or who will arrive at any
194 FQ: Little	127	never thought I should revisit/When I left my body on a distant shore./Since our
195 FQ: Little	150	breaking. In the disfigured street/He left me, with a kind of valediction,/And faded
197 FQ: Little	246	gate/When the last of earth left to discover/Is that which was the beginning;
209 NamingCats	21	and beyond there's still one name left over,/And that is the name that you never
218 Mung Rump	16	— And most of the time they left it at that./Mungojerrie and Rumpelteazer
219 Mung Rump	29	— And most of the time they left it at that./Mungojerrie and Rumpelteazer
223 Pekes Pols	61	*to his beat,/There wasn't a single one left in the street.*/Mr. Mistoffelees/You ought to
587 Fable	21	times./He stole the fatter cows and left the thinner/To furnish all the milk — upset
588 Fable	38	a rather lengthy story shorter,/He left no wise precaution incomplete;/He doused
594 Grad 10	4	so./That which has made it great, not left behind,/The same school in the future shall
604 Ode	1	ELIOT/For the hour that is left us, Fair Harvard, with thee,/Ere we face the
239 MC Chorus	19	/Seven years since the Archbishop left us,/He who was always kind to his people./
239 MC Chorus	24	oppression,/But mostly we are left to our own devices,/And we are content if
239 MC Chorus	25	devices,/And we are content if we are left alone./We try to keep our households in
240 MC Priest1	27	/Seven years since the Archbishop left us./{P2} What does the Archbishop do, and
245 MC Priest2	34	will find your rooms in order as you left them./{T} And will try to leave them in
255 MC Thomas	4	/{T} But what is there to do? what is left to be done?/Is there no enduring crown to
279 MC Knight4	26	evidence/to the effect that before he left France he clearly prophesied, in the/
287 FR Gerald	4	got to make allowances:/We haven't left them such an easy world to live in./Let the
288 FR Amy	29	/Everything is kept as it was when he left it,/Except the old pony, and the mongrel
288 FR Agatha	35	will have to meet/The boy who left. Round by the stables,/In the coach-house,
297 FR Agatha	6	it will do/But that nothing may be left undone/On the margin of the impossible./
298 FR Agatha	19	I shall return/When Downing has left you. {}/[*Exit*]/{C} Well, I'm very sorry/You
301 FR Violet	11	investigations,/You seem to have left matters much as they were —/Except for
305 FR Mary	32	being kept the same as when you left it./{H} I wish she had not done that. It's
314 FR Warburt	27	I've had forty years' experience/I've left off thinking in terms of the laboratory./
315 FR Warburt	14	all grown up/I haven't a patient left at Wishwood./Wishwood was always a cold
316 FR Charles	7	on my nerves./{C} If the matter were left in my hands, I think I could manage the
319 FR Warburt	13	but what festered/Then, has only left a cautery./Leave it alone. You know that
327 FR Charles	39	I bought a lunch edition/Before I left St. Pancras. If I did, it's in my overcoat./I'll
331 FR Harry	7	I got back to Wishwood, as I had left it,/Everything would fall into place. But
335 FR Harry	16	/Until the chain broke, and I was left/Under the single eye above the desert./{Ag}
340 FR Amy	13	taken what I had, you would have left me at least a memory/Of something to live
341 FR Amy	11	/Because of the misery that he has left behind him,/Because of the waste. I wanted

346 FR	Downing	8	because he remembered/He thinks he left his cigarette-case on the table./Oh, there it
360 CP	Edward	1	know./The fact is, that Lavinia has left me./{UG} Your wife has left you?/{E}
360 CP	Reilly	2	has left me./{UG} Your wife has left you?/{E} Without warning, of course;/Just
360 CP	Edward	6	when I came in, this afternoon./She left a note to say that she was leaving me;/But I
362 CP	Edward	16	understand it./Nobody likes to be left with a mystery:/It's so ... unfinished./{UG}
362 CP	Reilly	19	unfinished;/And nobody likes to be left with a mystery./But there's more to it than
364 CP	Julia	32	find you./Do you know, I must have left my glasses here,/And I simply can't see a
365 CP	Julia	15	in my life./It's very lucky that I left my spectacles:/*This* is what I call an
367 CP	Peter	39	was with you./{P} Julia must have left it open./{E} Never mind;/So long as you
369 CP	Edward	22	finished./{E} Oh no, no, everything is left unfinished./But you haven't told me how
372 CP	Alex	27	coffee/And a little dry toast. I've left it simmering./Don't leave it longer than
374 CP	Celia	16	it was perfectly simple./Lavinia has left you./{E} Yes, that *was* the situation./I
376 CP	Edward	23	thieves was luckier than I:/He was left at an inn./{J} Edward, how ungrateful./
377 CP	Edward	10	with him, when the rest of you had left,/And he said he would bring Lavinia back,
378 CP	Celia	28	laugh at you/Because your wife has left you for another man?/I shall soon put that
379 CP	Celia	30	/And it came to me that Lavinia had left you/And that you would be free — then I
381 CP	Edward	15	can desire;/Before you know what is left to be desired;/And you go on wishing that
381 CP	Edward	17	that you could desire/What desire has left behind. But you cannot understand./How
382 CP	Celia	25	not what you are. It is only what was left/Of what I had thought you were. I see
384 CP	Edward	25	As it was only yesterday that my wife left me./{UG} Ah, but we die to each other
389 CP	Peter	1	And come in to say good-bye before I left./{L} And Celia's going too? Was that what I
391 CP	Edward	10	going./{E} Are you sure you haven't left anything, Julia?/{J} Left anything? Oh, you
391 CP	Julia	11	you haven't left anything, Julia?/{J} Left anything? Oh, you mean my spectacles./
391 CP	Julia	31	me?/Good-bye. I believe ... I haven't left anything. {}/[*Enter* PETER]/{P} I've got a
392 CP	Lavinia	13	it?/I only remembered after I had left./{E} I telephoned to everyone I knew was
398 CP	Edward	6	I had made a decision./What devil left the door on the latch/For these doubts to
399 CP	Nurse	22	others out;/And only after they have left the house..../{R} Quite right, Miss
403 CP	Reilly	22	to explain what has happened since I left you./{E} I see now why I wanted my wife to
403 CP	Edward	32	was vacancy./When I thought she had left me, I began to dissolve,/To cease to exist.
409 CP	Reilly	9	when you thought your wife had left you,/You discovered, to your surprise and
410 CP	Reilly	24	imagining,/For you would have been left with what you brought with you:/The
416 CP	Celia	37	my way out of the forest/I shall be left with the inconsolable memory/Of the
424 CP	Lavinia	13	your clerk told me you had already left./But all I rang up for was to reassure you ...
425 CP	Lavinia	38	it straight now?/{L} Too much to the left./{E} How's that now?/{L} No, I meant the
430 CP	Peter	6	over from New York last night —/I left Los Angeles three days ago./I saw Sheila
446 CC	Claude	19	tell him about myself./But so far, I've left him to his own devices:/I thought he would
460 CC	Lady E	20	/Don't you remember, I said before I left:/'Trust my guidance for once, and engage
462 CC	Claude	29	back to it./You know I've deliberately left you alone,/And so far we've discussed only
472 CC	Colby	2	afraid of what would happen if you left things to themselves./You jump — because
481 CC	Lady E	38	Kaghan,/And ask for the table in the left hand corner:/It has the best waitress. Good
489 CC	Lady E	34	say that. But she had a child/Left on her hands. The father had died/And
501 CC	Eggers	35	come back after Mrs. Guzzard has left?/{SC} That's not a bad idea. If Colby
508 CC	Guzzard	28	him. So they adopted him./Then they left Teddington, and we lost sight of them./{E}
515 CC	Guzzard	10	/My husband also had died. I was left very poor./If I let you continue to think the
517 CC	Colby	14	*my* illusions and ambitions/All that's left is love. But not on false pretences:/That's
530 ES	Ld Clav	14	the slightest longing for the life I've left —/Only fear of the emptiness before me./If I
530 ES	Ld Clav	23	after all the other passengers/Have left, and the booking office is closed/And the
531 ES	Ld Clav	1	do for visiting cards — if people still left cards/And if I was going to have any
532 ES	Ld Clav	5	see him in the library./No, stop. I've left too many papers about there./I'd better see
533 ES	Ld Clav	10	you lived out there ever since ... you left England?/{G} Ever since I finished my
537 ES	Gomez	7	/{G} You led me on at Oxford, and left me to it./And so it came about that I was
543 ES	Gomez	7	/That we can begin just where we left off. {}/[*Exit* GOMEZ]/[LORD
545 ES	Monica	13	she looks rather dominating,/Has left us alone./{LC} Yes, but remember/What she
548 ES	Monica	6	see from her expression when she left/That she thought she'd done her duty by us
550 ES	Ld Clav	25	was very successful .../I mean, that he left you comfortably provided for?/{MC} Well,
564 ES	Gomez	24	/{G} I expect that was after I had left England./{MC} Of course, that explains it.
576 ES	Charles	30	—/{C} A post the nature of which is left very vague/{Mi} It's confidential, I tell you./
578 ES	Monica	40	your father and your family/What is left between you and me?/{Mi} That makes no

LEG (2)

43	Swee Erect	29	in the sun.)/Tests the razor on his leg/Waiting until the shriek subsides./The
116 SP	Doris	18	you like: say I'm ill,/Say I broke my leg on the stairs/Say we've had a fire/{Du} Hello

LEG-PULL (1)

430 CP	Peter	30	London./{P} You always did enjoy a leg-pull, Julia:/But you all know I'm working

LEGACY (1)

593	Grad 7	1	As shall on future centuries bestow/A legacy of benefits — may we/In future years be

LEGAL (4)

278 MC	Knight2	11	for seditious ends, and to reform the legal system./He therefore intended that Becket,
292 FR	Amy	22	— wants to call tomorrow/On some legal business, a question about taxes —/But I
508 CC	Lady E	11	that you, Eggerson, with your legal training,/Should talk about straws! Colby
527 ES	Charles	4	with each other,/And, there being no legal impediment/Isn't that enough to constitute

LEGALITY (1)

268 MC	Knight1	8	the young prince,/Denying the legality of his coronation./{K2} Binding with the

LEGERDEMAIN (1)

224 Mr Mistoff		11	/At prestidigitation/And at legerdemain/He'll defy examination/And

LEGION (2)

129 Cor2	State	4	the Cavaliers,/O Cavaliers! of the Legion of Honour,/The Order of the Black
307 FR	Harry	36	you,/Or to fling it away, to join the legion of the hopeless/Unrecognised by other

LEGS (6)

14 Prufrock		44	(They will say: 'But how his arms and legs are thin!')/Do I dare/Disturb the universe?/
91 Ash-Wed 2		3	the day, having fed to satiety/On my legs my heart my liver and that which had been
107 Animula		4	chilly or warm;/Moving between the legs of tables and of chairs,/Rising or falling,
221 Old Deut		46	... No! .../Ho! hi!/Oh, my eye!/My legs may be tottery, I must go slow/And be
588 Fable		49	/A mighty peacock standing on both legs/With difficulty kept from toppling over,/
382 CP	Celia	16	might have made it by scraping your legs together —/Or however grasshoppers do it.

LEIA (2)

69 WL: Fire S		277	reach/Past the Isle of Dogs./Weialala leia/Wallala leialala/Elizabeth and Leicester/
70 WL: Fire S		290	peal of bells/White towers/Weialala leia/Wallala leialala/'Trams and dusty trees./

LEIALALA (2)

69 WL: Fire S		278	Isle of Dogs./Weialala leia/Wallala leialala/Elizabeth and Leicester/Beating oars/
70 WL: Fire S		291	/White towers/Weialala leia/Wallala leialala/'Trams and dusty trees./Highbury bore

LEICESTER (1)

70 WL: Fire S		279	leia/Wallala leialala/Elizabeth and Leicester/Beating oars/The stern was formed/A

LEICESTERSHIRE (1)

287 FR	Amy	35	and John,/Arthur in London, John in Leicestershire:/They should both be here in

LEMAN (1)

67 WL: Fire S		182	left no addresses./By the waters of Leman I sat down and wept .../Sweet Thames,

LEMON (1)

31 Apollinax		22	Mrs. Cheetah/I remember a slice of lemon, and a bitten macaroon./Hysteria/As she

LEMURS (1)

204 de la Mare		7	of a mango grove,/And shadowy lemurs glide from tree to tree —/The guardians

LEND (2)

253 MC	Tempt4	11	/Your services as long as you have to lend./You would wait for trap to snap/Having
547 ES	Piggott	34	/{MP} There are indeed. I can lend you a map./There are lovely walks, on the

LENDER (1)

557 ES	Michael	24	... from the firm?/{Mi} I went to a lender,/A man whom a friend of mine

LENGTH (1)

42 Swee Erect		21	pillow slip./Sweeney addressed full length to shave/Broadbottomed, pink from

LENGTHEN (1)

263 MC	Chorus	5	not a breath./Do the days begin to lengthen?/Longer and darker the day, shorter

LENGTHENED (1)

43 Swee Erect		25	wipes the suds around his face./(The lengthened shadow of a man/Is history, said

LENGTHY (1)

588 Fable		37	from head to feet./To make a rather lengthy story shorter,/He left no wise precaution

LENS (1)

365 CP	Julia	4	/But I'd know them, because one lens is missing. {}/[*Sings*]./{UG} *As I was*

LENT (1)

109 Marina		19	less strong and stronger —/Given or lent? more distant than stars and nearer than

LEONIDS (1)

178 FQ: ECoker		64	Moon go down/Comets weep and Leonids fly/Hunt the heavens and the plains/

LEOPARD (3)

210 Old Gumbie		2	the tabby kind, with tiger stripes and leopard spots./All day she sits upon the stair or
257 MC	Chorus	29	shape in the dark air:/Puss-purr of leopard, footfall of padding bear,/Palm-pat of
273 MC	Priests	27	bar the door/Against the lion, the leopard, the wolf or the boar,/Why not more/

LEOPARDS (2)

91 Ash-Wed 2		1	hour of our death./Lady, three white leopards sat under a juniper-tree/In the cool of
91 Ash-Wed 2		16	the indigestible portions/Which the leopards reject. The Lady is withdrawn/In a

LEROUX (4)

459 CC	Claude	32	Rebmann? I thought it was a Dr. Leroux./{LE} Dr. Leroux is in Lausanne./I have
459 CC	Lady E	33	it was a Dr. Leroux./{LE} Dr. Leroux is in Lausanne./I have been in Zürich,
459 CC	Claude	35	/{SC} But you were going out to Dr. Leroux/In Lausanne. What made you go to

460 CC   Lady E 19   /No, at your stage, I think, with Dr. Leroux./Don't you remember, I said before I

LES (13)

46 Directeur	7	/Du Spectateur/Empeste la brise./Les actionnaires/Réactionnaires/Du Spectateur/
48 Lune Miel	1	/Lune de Miel/Ils ont vu les Pays-Bas, ils rentrent à Terre Haute;/Mais
48 Lune Miel	2	à Terre Haute;/Mais une nuit d'été, les voici à Ravenne,/A l'aise entre deux draps,
48 Lune Miel	5	chienne./Ils restent sur le dos écartant les genoux/De quatre jambes molles tout
51 Restaurant	2	qui n'a rien à faire/Que de se gratter les doigts et se pencher sur mon épaule:/'Dans
51 Restaurant	8	moins, ne bave pas dans la soupe)./'Les saules trempés, et des bourgeons sur les
51 Restaurant	8	saules trempés, et des bourgeons sur les ronces —/C'est là, dans une averse, qu'on
51 Restaurant	12	je lui ai donné des primevères.'/Les taches de son gilet montent au chiffre de
51 Restaurant	21	tu as ton vautour!/Va t'en te décrotter les rides du visage;/Tiens, ma fourchette,
51 Restaurant	26	pendant quinze jours noyé,/Oubliait les cris des mouettes et la houle de Cornouaille,/
51 Restaurant	27	et la houle de Cornouaille,/Et les profits et les pertes, et la cargaison d'étain:/
51 Restaurant	27	houle de Cornouaille,/Et les profits et les pertes, et la cargaison d'étain:/Un courant de
128 Cor1 March	51	you/Give us a light?/Light/Light/*Et les soldats faisaient la haie? ILS LA*

LESS (31)

109 Marina	17	dissolved in place/What is this face, less clear and clearer/The pulse in the arm, less
109 Marina	18	and clearer/The pulse in the arm, less strong and stronger —/Given or lent? more
151 Rock 2	10	to be flung in the end, on a heap less useful than dung'./You, have you built well,
166 Rock 10	19	Greater Light, we praise Thee for the less;/The eastern light our spires touch at
195 FQ: Little	159	use of memory:/For liberation — not less of love but expanding/Of love beyond
198 FQ: Little	256	of complete simplicity/(Costing not less than everything)/And all shall be well and/
203 Indians	20	a common purpose, action/None the less fruitful if neither you nor we/Know, until
232 Skimble	20	/He will supervise them all, more or less./Down the corridor he paces and examines
594 Grad 13	2	those that follow may'st thou be no less;/A guide to warn them, and a friend to bless
604 Ode	10	to-morrow has lost/We are still the less able to grieve,/With so much that of
256 MC Tempts	16	decoration./All things become less real, man passes/From unreality to
261 MC Thomas	25	Saints are not made by/accident. Still less is a Christian martyrdom the effect of a
282 MC Chorus	9	/Who fear the injustice of men less than the justice of God;/Who fear the hand
282 MC Chorus	11	in the tavern, the push into the canal,/Less than we fear the love of God./We
287 FR Amy	21	let us drop the subject. The less said the better./{G} That reminds me, Amy,/
290 FR Amy	10	painted shadow/In life, she is less than a shadow in death./You might as well
293 FR Harry	19	please do so/In my absence. I shall be less embarrassing to you. Agatha?/{Ag} I think,
293 FR Harry	25	I explain to *you*?/You will understand less after I have explained it./All that I could
318 FR Harry	13	/For punishment made us feel less guilty. Mother/Never punished us, but
363 CP Reilly	17	know any more than I do,/But rather less. You are nothing but a set/Of obsolete
380 CP Celia	27	more acquaintances,/I found him less interesting, and rather conceited./But why
392 CP Lavinia	29	better have told the truth:/Nothing less than the truth could deceive Julia./But how
408 CP Edward	20	could not have chosen/Anyone I was less likely to suspect./And then he came to *me*
414 CP Celia	6	people, and they get over it/More or less, or at least they carry on./No. I mean that
418 CP Reilly	23	all have seen it,/Illustrated, more or less, in lives of those about us./The second is
435 CP Lavinia	39	what I've been saying/Will seem less unkind if I can make you understand/That
438 CP Reilly	12	always at his shoulder/Suffered any less from hunger, damp, exposure,/Bowel
473 CC Colby	38	/What I mean is, my garden's no less unreal to me/Than the world outside it. If
482 CC Lady E	38	far from intellectual;/And — what's less surprising — intellectual people/Are often
538 ES Gomez	25	/Until your own have been more or less forgotten./I dare say you did make some
544 ES Ld Clav	19	has grown to consciousness/It comes less often./I hope this benignant sunshine/And

LESSER (1)

253 MC Tempt4	14	and crushed./As for barons, envy of lesser men/Is still more stubborn than king's

LESSIVE (1)

51 Restaurant	5	pluie;/C'est ce qu'on appelle le jour de lessive des gueux.'/(Bavard, baveux, à la croupe

LESSON (5)

339 FR Harry	12	care over lives of humble people,/The lesson of ignorance, of incurable diseases./Such
551 ES Ld Clav	9	/What harm was done? I learned my lesson/And you learned yours, if you needed the
551 ES Ld Clav	10	you learned yours, if you needed the lesson./{MC} You refuse to believe that I was
565 ES Ld Clav	36	Do I understand the meaning/Of the lesson I would teach? Come, I'll start to learn
580 ES Monica	27	perhaps, Michael may learn his lesson./I believe he'll come back. If it's all a

LESSONS (3)

459 CC Lady E	9	you look rather frail./I must give you lessons in the art of health./Where is your
504 CC Lady E	11	quiet hour./I've been giving her lessons in recollection./But she shouldn't be
518 CC Eggers	1	ways/Of making up an income. Piano lessons? —/As a temporary measure; because,

LET (171)

13 Prufrock	1	/The Love Song of J. Alfred Prufrock/Let us go then, you and I,/When the evening is
13 Prufrock	4	/Like a patient etherised upon a table;/Let us go, through certain half-deserted streets,/
13 Prufrock	12	/Oh, do not ask, 'What is it?'/Let us go and make our visit./In the room the

13 Prufrock	19	upon the pools that stand in drains,/Let fall upon its back the soot that falls from
18 Portrait	8	be said, or left unsaid./We have been, let us say, to hear the latest Pole/Transmit the
19 Portrait	36	is at least one definite 'false note.'/— Let us take the air, in a tobacco trance,/Admire
19 Portrait	47	/(Slowly twisting the lilac stalks)/'You let it flow from you, you let it flow,/And youth
19 Portrait	47	stalks)/'You let it flow from you, you let it flow,/And youth is cruel, and has no more
21 Portrait	113	/Cry like a parrot, chatter like an ape./Let us take the air, in a tobacco trance —/Well!
57 Swee Night	39	/When Agamemnon cried aloud/And let their liquid siftings fall/To stain the stiff
84 Hollow Men	29	and more solemn/Than a fading star./Let me be no nearer/In death's dream kingdom/
84 Hollow Men	31	no nearer/In death's dream kingdom/Let me also wear/Such deliberate disguises/
90 Ash-Wed 1	31	/Because I do not hope to turn again/Let these words answer/For what is done, not
91 Ash-Wed 2	18	to contemplation, in a white gown./Let the whiteness of bones atone to
98 Ash-Wed 6	24	shaken from the yew-tree drift away/Let the other yew be shaken and reply./Blessèd
99 Ash-Wed 6	35	/Suffer me not to be separated/And let my cry come unto Thee./ARIEL POEMS/
105 Song Sime	22	/Now at this birth season of decease,/Let the Infant, the still unspeaking and
106 Song Sime	36	and the deaths of those after me./Let thy servant depart,/Having seen thy
110 Marina	30	to live in a world of time beyond me; let me/Resign my life for this life, my speech for
111 Xmas Trees	10	child wonders at the Christmas Tree:/Let him continue in the spirit of wonder/At the
124 SA Snow	10	/A woman runs a terrible risk./{Sn} Let Mr. Sweeney continue his story./I assure
124 SA Snow	25	A woman runs a terrible risk./{Sn} Let Mr. Sweeney continue his story./{S} This
136 5FingerEx3	8	/I have had the Bread and Wine,/Let the feathered mortals take/That which is
140 Usk	5	lance, do not spell/Old enchantments. Let them sleep./'Gently dip, but not too deep',/
147 Rock 1	23	few chop-houses. There I was told:/Let the vicars retire. Men do not need the
147 Rock 1	26	/In the City, we need no bells:/Let them waken the suburbs./I journeyed to the
149 Rock 1	78	take heart. Make perfect your will./Let me show you the work of the humble.
153 Rock 2	53	much to build, much to restore;/Let the work not delay, time and the arm not
153 Rock 2	54	delay, time and the arm not waste;/Let the clay be dug from the pit, let the saw cut
153 Rock 2	54	/Let the clay be dug from the pit, let the saw cut the stone,/Let the fire not be
153 Rock 2	55	from the pit, let the saw cut the stone,/Let the fire not be quenched in the forge./The
158 Rock 5	6	say, 'This house is a nest of serpents, let us destroy it,/And have done with these
160 Rock 7	16	or the hills where the wind will not let the snow rest./Waste and void. Waste and
163 Rock 8	48	/To men of faith and conviction./Let us therefore make perfect our will./O GOD,
164 Rock 9	14	festivity,/Doing themselves very well./Let us mourn in a private chamber, learning the
164 Rock 9	15	the way of penitence,/And then let us learn the joyful communion of saints./The
179 FQ: ECoker	94	lights,/Risking enchantment. Do not let me hear/Of the wisdom of old men, but
180 FQ: ECoker	113	bury./I said to my soul, be still, and let the dark come upon you/Which shall be the
194 FQ: Little	115	things have served their purpose: let them be./So with your own, and pray they be
194 FQ: Little	131	the mind to aftersight and foresight,/Let me disclose the gifts reserved for age/To set
201 Def Island	1	VERSES/Defence of the Islands/Let these memorials of built stone — music's/
203 Indians	15	one with his destiny, that soil is his./Let his village remember./This was not your
203 Indians	18	Rivers, may have the same graveyard./Let those who go home tell the same story of
211 Old Gumbie	37	Tattoo./So for Old Gumbie Cats let us now give three cheers —/On whom
214 RTTugger	13	Tugger is a terrible bore:/When you let him in, then he wants to be out;/He's always
228 Gus	24	knew how to gag,/And I knew how to let the cat out of the bag./I knew how to act
233 Skimble	44	to remind him./For Skimble won't let anything go wrong./And when you creep
590 Time Space	13	bee flew/To suck the eglantine./So let us haste to pluck anew/Nor mourn to see
590 Time Space	16	though our days of love be few/Yet let them be divine./Song/If space and time, as
590 Space Time	5	day/Has lived as long as we./But let us live while yet we may,/While love and life
590 Space Time	13	bee flew/To suck the eglantine./But let us haste to pluck anew/Nor mourn to see
590 Space Time	16	though the flowers of life be few/Yet let them be divine./Standing upon the shore of
592 Grad 1	6	to warn of rocks which lie below,/But let us yet put forth courageously./As colonists
595 Grad 13	5	leave thy care for lands unseen;/And let thy motto be, proud and serene,/Still as the
239 MC Chorus	1	*December 29th*, 1170/Part I/{C} Here let us stand, close by the cathedral. Here let us
239 MC Chorus	1	us stand, close by the cathedral. Here let us wait./Are we drawn by danger? Is it the
243 MC Priest2	2	/The rock of God is beneath our feet. Let us meet the Archbishop with cordial
243 MC Priest2	4	returns/Our doubts are dispelled. Let us therefore rejoice,/I say rejoice, and show
243 MC Priest2	6	welcome./I am the Archbishop's man. Let us give the Archbishop welcome!/{P3} For
243 MC Priest3	7	welcome!/{P3} For good or ill, let the wheel turn./The wheel has been still,
243 MC Priest3	9	years, and no good./For ill or good, let the wheel turn./For who knows the end of
245 MC Priest2	9	of, in your craven apprehension,/Let me ask you at the least to put on pleasant
245 MC Thomas	11	{}/[*Enter* THOMAS]/{T} Peace. And let them be, in their exaltation./They speak
248 MC Tempt2	18	Now that I have recalled them,/Let us but set these not too pleasant memories/
251 MC Tempt3	25	is a land for Norman/Sovereignty. Let the Angevin/Destroy himself, fighting in
266 MC Knight1	29	in the land./{K1} Saving your order! let your order save you —/As I do not think it is
267 MC Thomas	14	King!/{3K} God bless him!/{T} Then let your new coat of loyalty be worn/Carefully,
268 MC Thomas	24	is laid upon them, or mine to revoke./Let them go to the Pope. It was he who

268 MC	Thomas	32	can loose whom the Pope has bound./Let them go to him, upon whom redounds/
273 MC	Chorus	5	/Dead upon the tree, my Saviour,/Let not be in vain Thy labour;/Help me, Lord,
275 MC	Chorus	26	stay with us, stop sun, hold season, let the day not come, let the spring not come./
275 MC	Chorus	26	hold season, let the day not come, let the spring not come./Can I look again at the
281 MC	Priest3	5	gone before you,/Remember us./{P3} Let our thanks ascend/To God, who has given
287 FR	Gerald	5	them such an easy world to live in./Let the younger generation speak for itself:/It's
287 FR	Amy	21	but life may still go right./Meanwhile, let us drop the subject. The less said the better./
289 FR	Gerald	9	taken his medicine, I've no doubt./Let him marry again and carry on at
291 FR	Amy	18	want the curtains drawn you should let me ring for Denman./{H} How can you sit in
292 FR	Ivy	35	time the old man was pensioned./He's let the rock garden go to rack and ruin,/And
293 FR	Agatha	21	so far —/If you want no pretences, let us have no pretences:/And you must try at
296 FR	Charles	24	are thinking./{C} He has probably let this notion grow in his mind,/Living among
297 FR	Gerald	23	know that we knew it also./Why not let sleeping dogs lie?/{C} All the same, there's a
304 FR	Mary	27	on to me/Because she couldn't bear to let any project go;/And even when *she* died: I
311 FR	Harry	11	Come out!/Come out! Where are you? Let me see you,/Since I know you are there, I
311 FR	Harry	13	do you play with me, why do you let me go,/Only to surround me? — When I
311 FR	Harry	18	the sleepless hunters/That will not let me sleep. At the moment before sleep/I
311 FR	Harry	36	person, if person/You thought I was: let your necrophily/Feed upon that carcase.
313 FR	Ivy	8	/Did you arrange these flowers? Just let me change them./You don't mind, do you? I
318 FR	Harry	28	Very important./You must let me explain, and then you can talk./I don't
320 FR	Warburt	1	your brothers will be here. Won't you let me tell you/What I had to say?/{H} Very
321 FR	Harry	29	shoulders]/{H} He *is* real, Doctor./So let us resume the conversation. You, and I/And
325 FR	Charles	12	worse than Winchell said, then he'll let us know at once./{G} I am really more afraid
325 FR	Ivy	16	the one thing that matters/Is not to let her see that anyone is worried./We must
336 FR	Harry	22	one itinerary/And one destination. Let us lose no time. I will follow. {}/[*The*
339 FR	Harry	14	waits and wants me, and will not let me fall./Let the cricket chirp. John shall be
339 FR	Harry	15	wants me, and will not let me fall./Let the cricket chirp. John shall be the master./
340 FR	Amy	24	if I could not have a husband:/Then I let him go. I abased myself./Did I show any
342 FR	Mary	23	must keep him here, you must not let him leave./I do not know what must be
343 FR	Amy	23	alone in a damned house./I will let the walls crumble. Why should I worry/To
343 FR	Amy	30	tomb/To bother about the upkeep. Let the wind and rain do that. {}/[*While* AMY
357 CP	Julia	38	But let's be sensible:/Now you must let me be *your* maiden aunt —/Living on an
358 CP	Julia	20	crisps were really excellent./Now let me see. Have I got everything?/It's such a
360 CP	Reilly	15	you the same prescription .../Let me prepare it for you, if I may .../Strong ...
361 CP	Reilly	27	an intimate disclosure to a stranger./Let me, therefore, remain the stranger./But let
361 CP	Reilly	28	therefore, remain the stranger./But let me tell you, that to approach the stranger/Is
361 CP	Reilly	30	unexpected, release a new force,/Or let the genie out of the bottle./It is to start a
361 CP	Reilly	32	of events/Beyond your control. So let me continue./I will say then, you experience
366 CP	Peter	22	mind./{P} Well, at least you must let me take you down in the lift./{J} No, you
391 CP	Julia	1	Alex./We must leave them alone, and let Lavinia rest./Now we'll all go back to *my*
392 CP	Lavinia	12	won't believe I forgot all about it!/I let you down badly. What did you do about it?/
399 CP	Nurse	20	into the small room;/And I need not let you know that she has arrived./Then, when
401 CP	Reilly	33	is so, that is so. But all in good time./Let us dismiss that question for the moment./
404 CP	Edward	30	again. And at my club/They won't let you keep a room for more than seven days;/I
407 CP	Reilly	31	them — omitting the important facts./Let me take your husband first. {}/[*To*
407 CP	Lavinia	36	blind/There were plenty of people to let me know about it./I wonder if there was
409 CP	Reilly	25	say, Mrs. Chamberlayne./And now, let us turn to your side of the problem./When
411 CP	Edward	9	stop at your club?/{E} No, they won't let me./I must leave tomorrow — but how did
412 CP	Reilly	4	her here myself./{R} Oh? You didn't let her know you were seeing me first?/{J} Of
419 CP	Reilly	37	on a slip of paper]/{R} You had better let your family know at once./I will send a car
422 CP	Reilly	13	{}/[*They raise their glasses*]/{R} Let them build the hearth/Under the protection
422 CP	Alex	15	Under the protection of the stars./{A} Let them place a chair each side of it./{J} May
438 CP	Reilly	19	for myself. I'm sure that *I* am./{R} Let me free your mind from one impediment:/
447 CC	Claude	36	herself. By the way, don't forget/To let her know that he's very musical./She can
449 CC	Eggers	34	— then what follows?/Will we let her know, then, that Mr. Simpkins/Is
453 CC	Lucasta	15	you're out of the way. Why don't you let him speak?/Eggy's really quite human,
454 CC	Lucasta	15	time, Colby./I'll ring you up, and let you take me out to lunch. {}/[*Exit*
457 CC	Eggers	32	happened?/{E} It's perfectly amazing. Let *me* go down to meet her./{SC} Where ought
466 CC	Claude	26	And perhaps, some time, you will let me hear you play./I shan't mention it again.
471 CC	Colby	3	to *yourself*./{C} And perhaps you'll let me tell you beforehand/About the
479 CC	Kaghan	26	the moment for firmness. Don't let her cross the threshold./{L} As if you weren't
488 CC	Claude	20	Colby,/It seems to me that we must let her know the truth./{C} It seems to me ...
491 CC	Lady E	8	we make any further enquiries?/Let us regard him as being *our* son:/It won't be
492 CC	Claude	13	Eggerson! He knows all about it./Let us say no more tonight. Now, Colby,/Can
497 CC	Lady E	22	it./{LE} Claude, that's not quite right. Let me explain./I am convinced that Sir Claude

499	CC	Claude	6	/{SC} And put the case to her./Don't let her think that *I* have any doubts:/You are
500	CC	Lady E	5	is what Sir Claude believes. Claude, let me explain./{SC} No, I'll explain. There's
501	CC	Eggers	34	pair./It's all in the family. Why not let them wait downstairs/And come back after
504	CC	Lucasta	6	nobody to answer the door./I've just let someone in. It's the Mrs. Guzzard/Whom
504	CC	Eggers	14	singing./{L} Well, what shall I do?/{E} Let me go down and explain to Mrs. Guzzard/
504	CC	Claude	30	are always much engaged./{SC} First, let me introduce you to my wife./Lady Elizabeth
506	CC	Guzzard	21	/That Lady Elizabeth's child was lost./Let us hope that her son may be restored to her.
508	CC	Eggers	15	drop of oil on these troubled waters?/Let us approach the question from another
513	CC	Colby	23	he can afford another relationship./Let my mother rest in peace. As for a father —/
514	CC	Guzzard	14	/{C} And who was my mother?/{MG} Let your mother rest in peace./I *was* your
515	CC	Guzzard	11	had died. I was left very poor./If I let you continue to think the child was yours,/
515	CC	Guzzard	25	than the sacrifice I made/When I let you claim him. Do you think it is a small
515	CC	Claude	37	it./Well, believe it, then. But don't let it make a difference/To our relations. Or,
519	CC	Kaghan	20	to mean something to you ... if you'd let us;/And we'd take the responsibility of
526	ES	Monica	27	/{M} and I shall say, 'Lambert,/Please let his lordship know that tea is waiting'./{L}
532	ES	Monica	11	/{C} I ought to be going./{M} Let *us* go into the library. And then I'll see you
535	ES	Gomez	15	— in this respect or that./*A* won't let me down in this relationship,/*B* won't let me
535	ES	Gomez	16	me down in this relationship,/*B* won't let me down in some other connection./But, as
538	ES	Gomez	24	worst, you go into opposition/And let the other people make mistakes/Until your
539	ES	Gomez	8	five years/At least. Why did they let you retire?/{LC} If you want to know, I had
544	ES	Monica	2	expected,/Isn't it, Father? They've let us alone;/The people in the dining-room
547	ES	Piggott	4	on my hands!/But before I go, just let me tuck you up .../You must be very careful
547	ES	Piggott	7	now you look more comfy. Don't let him stay out late/In the afternoon, Miss
551	ES	Carghil	14	I'd really suffered/I shouldn't want to let you know who I am,/I shouldn't want to
555	ES	Piggott	8	now. If she bothers you again/Just let me know. I'm afraid it's the penalty/Of being
558	ES	Ld Clav	11	here so precipitately —/In order to let me have your version first./I dare say Sir
563	ES	Ld Clav	22	San Marco./That's my name./{LC} So let me introduce you — by that name —/To
569	ES	Monica	23	sure I could help./{M} Oh Father, do let him./{C} At least, I think I know the best
570	ES	Monica	16	/{M} It is time to break the silence! Let us share your ghosts!/{C} But these are only
572	ES	Charles	30	it's their means of self-justification./Let them tell their versions of their miserable
573	ES	Ld Clav	18	of liberation/Are, I think, determined. Let us say no more about it./Meanwhile, I feel
573	ES	Monica	21	me./I see Mrs. Carghill coming./{M} Let us go./{LC} We will stay here. Let her join
573	ES	Ld Clav	22	Let us go./{LC} We will stay here. Let her join us. {}/[*Enter* MRS. CARGHILL]/
573	ES	Carghil	32	approval, Mrs. Carghill./{MC} And let me congratulate *you*, Mr. Hemington./
575	ES	Ld Clav	14	reasons/From what you think. Let me tell you about Gomez./He's unlikely to
580	ES	Monica	1	/{M} Good-bye Michael. Will you let me write to you?/{G} Oh, I'm glad you
580	ES	Michael	10	you a card, now and again,/Just to let you know I'm flourishing./{LC} Yes, write to
583	ES	Charles	13	/I could speak to you now./{C} Let me go and find him./{M} We will go to him

LET'S (17)

315	FR	Warburt	11	/That is something real./{W} Well, let's not talk of such matters./How did we get
321	FR	Warburt	6	very much like you./And now, Harry, let's talk about yourself./{H} I never saw a
357	CP	Julia	37	Lavinia/On my way to Cornwall. But let's be sensible:/Now you must let me be *your*
401	CP	Reilly	26	had seen her./{E} So this *is* a trap!/{R} Let's not call it a trap./But if it is a trap, then
425	CP	Edward	25	to us later, roaring for drink./Well, let's hope that those who come to us early/Will
447	CC	Claude	3	Northolt — the car will be ready —/Let's think what you're to say to Lady
453	CC	Kaghan	28	to protect Colby from you./But first, let's cope with the financial crisis./{L} Yes,
457	CC	Eggers	2	her ticket, or even her passport./But let's not be crossing any bridges/Until we come
461	CC	Eggers	18	Park, at this time of year!'/I said: 'Let's think about it in the Spring/When the
481	CC	Kaghan	12	that *you* like./— For a change, let's talk about Lucasta. {}/[*rising*]./{L} If you
505	CC	Eggers	19	If you please, Eggerson./{E} Then let's make a start./The question has to do, as
533	ES	Gomez	17	now's the time to take a long holiday,/Let's say a rest cure — that's what I've come
538	ES	Gomez	10	I shall tell you why presently./Now let's look for a moment at *your* life history./You
544	ES	Monica	24	of frost on the fruit trees./{M} Oh, let's make the most of this weather while it lasts.
547	ES	Monica	15	worse than Mrs. Piggott./{M} Let's hope this was merely the concoction/
556	ES	Ld Clav	8	be patient./{LC} Well then, fetch him./Let's get this over. {}/[*calls*]/{M} Michael! {}/
574	ES	Carghil	25	/And he was so perplexed, poor lamb. Let's all rejoice together. {}/[*Enter* GOMEZ *and*

LETS (2)

388	CP		m 19	/I am going away too. {}/[LAVINIA *lets herself in with a latch-key*]/{P} You're going
424	CP		m 11	CATERER'S MAN]/[EDWARD *lets himself in at the front door*]/{E} I'm in good

LETTER (4)

446	CC	Eggers	38	Claude. Only the other day/I read a letter in *The Times* about wild birds seen in
452	CC	Lucasta	18	just by bad luck, the boss did want a letter/And I couldn't find it. And then he got
532	ES	Ld Clav	15	Señor Gomez/But he comes with a letter of introduction/From a man I used to
567	ES	Charles	18	/But my darling, since I got your letter this morning/About your father and

LETTERS (12)
180 FQ:	ECoker	104	merchant bankers, eminent men of letters./The generous patrons of art, the
187 FQ:	DrySal	135	/To fruit, periodicals and business letters/(And those who saw them off have left
246 MC	Thomas	3	/Would have intercepted our letters,/Filled the coast with spies and sent to
246 MC	Thomas	7	aware of their prevision/I sent my letters on another day,/Had fair crossing, found
459 CC	Lady E	6	*on her fingers].*/{LE} Thirteen letters. That's very auspicious —/Contrary to
552 ES	Ld Clav	3	your name appeared in very large letters/In Shaftesbury Avenue./{MC} Yes, I had
553 ES	Carghil	19	Do you know what I do?/I read your letters every night./{LC} My letters!/{MC} Have
553 ES	Ld Clav	20	your letters every night./{LC} My letters!/{MC} Have you forgotten that you
553 ES	Carghil	21	you forgotten that you wrote me letters?/Oh, not very many. Only a few worth
553 ES	Ld Clav	34	/{LC} And have you shown these letters/To many people?/{MC} Only a few
553 ES	Carghil	38	be in want, you could have these letters auctioned.'/Yes, I'll bring the photostats
562 ES	Carghil	13	back to have a quiet read of your letters;/But how nice to find a little family party!

LETTING (2)
56 Swee	Night	2	/Apeneck Sweeney spreads his knees/Letting his arms hang down to laugh,/The zebra
404 CP	Reilly	9	deal by merely observing you,/And letting you talk as long as you please,/And

LEURS (1)
48 Lune	Miel	12	le train de huit heures/Prolonger leurs misères de Padoue à Milan/Où se trouve la

LEVEL (3)
27 Morning		9	in the air/And vanishes along the level of the roofs./The Boston Evening
290 FR	Amy	8	only to bring Harry down to her own level./A restless shivering painted shadow/In
480 CC	Colby	13	that you're a gambler./You've got as level a head as anyone,/And you never get

LEVIED (1)
587 Fable		6	founded by some Norman/Who levied on all travelers his tax;/Nearby this

LEVITATION (1)
226 Macavity		7	the law of gravity./His powers of levitation would make a fakir stare,/And when

LEVITY (2)
246 MC	Tempt1	27	/Will find excuse for my humble levity/Remembering all the good time past./
248 MC	Tempt1	6	/Will find excuse for my humble levity./If you will remember me, my Lord, at

LEVY (1)
530 ES	Ld Clav	36	this piece of silver! The inadequate levy/That made the Chairman's Price! And my

LIABLE (2)
186 FQ:	DrySal	73	wastage/Or of a future that is not liable/Like the past, to have no destination./We
450 CC	Claude	4	you understand a person/That you're liable to make the worst mistake about him./As

LIBATION (1)
422 CP	Reilly	11	now we are ready to proceed to the libation./{A} The words for the building of the

LIBEL (1)
576 ES	Charles	37	/{C} I know enough about the law of libel and slander/To know that you are hardly

LIBERAL (2)
501 CC	Lady E	10	/I have always been a person of liberal views —/That's why I never got on with
501 CC	Lucasta	12	family./{L} Well, I'm not a person of liberal views./I'm very conventional. And I'm

LIBERALLY (1)
535 ES		m 21	help yourself? {}/[GOMEZ *does so, liberally*]/{G} And what about you?/{LC} I don't

LIBERATED (1)
331 FR	Harry	30	of you as the completely strong,/The liberated from the human wheel./So I looked to

LIBERATION (4)
195 FQ:	Little	159	nettle. This is the use of memory:/For liberation — not less of love but expanding/Of
195 FQ:	Little	160	/Of love beyond desire, and so liberation/From the future as well as the past.
331 FR	Harry	32	I think it is/A common pursuit of liberation./{Ag} Your father might have lived —
573 ES	Ld Clav	17	To the end. The place and time of liberation/Are, I think, determined. Let us say

LIBERTY (3)
251 MC	Tempt3	39	powerful protection/In the fight for liberty. You, my Lord,/In being with us, would
275 MC	Thomas	8	/That his Church may have peace and liberty./Do with me as you will, to your hurt
334 FR	Harry	39	mind! Now I can live in public./Liberty is a different kind of pain from prison./

LIBIDINOUS (1)
280 MC	Priest3	27	and try to snatch/Forgetfulness in his libidinous courts,/Oblivion in the fountain by

LIBRARIES (1)
285 FR	Violet	19	Go south! to the English circulating libraries,/To the military widows and the

LIBRARY (5)
219 Mung	Rump	36	came a loud crash/Or down from the library came a loud *ping*/From a vase which
317 FR	2m	1	/END OF PART I/PART II/*The library, after dinner.*/Scene I/HARRY,
525 ES	Monica	29	/Father's sure to be buried in the library/And he won't think of leaving it until
532 ES	Ld Clav	4	*the note].*/{LC} I'll see him in the library./No, stop. I've left too many papers
532 ES	Monica	11	to be going./{M} Let *us* go into the library. And then I'll see you off./{LC} I'm sorry

LICENCE (1)
243 MC Chorus 27 luxury,/There have been poverty and licence,/There has been minor injustice./Yet we
LICKED (1)
13 Prufrock   17 rubs its muzzle on the window-panes,/Licked its tongue into the corners of the
LICKS (1)
235 Ad-dress   62 but rabbit,/And when he's finished, licks his paws/So's not to waste the onion
LIDLESS (1)
65 WL: Chess   138 shall play a game of chess,/Pressing lidless eyes and waiting for a knock upon the
LIE (14)
15 Prufrock   67 That makes me so digress?/Arms that lie along a table, or wrap about a shawl./And
44 Cook Egg   15 meet Sir Alfred Mond./We two shall lie together, lapt/In a five per cent. Exchequer
72 WL: Thund   340 spit/Here one can neither stand nor lie nor sit/There is not even silence in the
158 Rock 5   5 use is forgotten: are like snakes that lie on mouldering stairs, content in the sunlight.
214 RTTugger   16 he'd like to get about./He likes to lie in the bureau drawer,/But he makes such a
592 Grad 1   5 show/No light to warn of rocks which lie below,/But let us yet put forth courageously./
257 MC Chorus 32 Hell are here./They curl round you, lie at your feet, swing and wing through the
297 FR   Gerald 23 it also./Why not let sleeping dogs lie?/{C} All the same, there's a question or two
325 FR   Harry   4 {H} I think, mother,/I shall make you lie down. You must be very tired. {}/[*Exeunt*
332 FR   Agatha 32 a whole Thibet of broken stones/That lie, fang up, a lifetime's march. I have believed
345 FR   Amy   27 me to the next room. Where I can lie down./Then you can leave me./{G} Oh,
361 CP   Reilly   6 /It was inconvenient, having to lie about it/Because you can't tell the truth on
407 CP   Reilly   25 /This is the consequence of trying to lie to me./{L} I did not come here to be insulted.
426 CP   Edward   4 some champagne,/Just ourselves. You lie down now, Lavinia/No one will be coming
LIED (1)
266 MC Knights 23 /The man who cheated, swindled, lied; broke his oath and betrayed his King./{T}
LIES (9)
166 Rock 10   7 conquer the World?/The great snake lies ever half awake, at the bottom of the pit of
196 FQ: Little   207 error./The only hope, or else despair/Lies in the choice of pyre or pyre —/To be
221 Old Deut   32 Deuteronomy!'/Old Deuteronomy lies on the floor/Of the Fox and French Horn
598 Circe   11 the garden stairs/The sluggish python lies;/The peacocks walk, stately and slow,/And
278 MC Knight2   5 In/the answer to these questions lies the key to the problem./The King's aim has
280 MC Priest1   11 inherit/Your strength? The Church lies bereft,/Alone, desecrated, desolated, and the
327 FR   Harry   23 mind,/But always the filthiness, that lies a little deeper ... {}/[*Enter* IVY]/{I} Where is
348 FR   Chorus   32 meaning of happening?/What ambush lies beyond the heather/And behind the
411 CP   2m 36 /[REILLY *goes to the couch and lies down. The house-telephone rings. He/gets up*
LIEU (1)
453 CC Kaghan   35 /{K} She's had a week's salary in lieu of notice./{L} B., remember you're only my
LIEUE (1)
48 Lune Miel   8 pour mieux égratigner./Moins d'une lieue d'ici est Saint Apollinaire/En Classe,
LIFE (189)
14 Prufrock   51 afternoons,/I have measured out my life with coffee spoons;/I know the voices dying
18 Portrait   21 how rare and strange it is, to find/In a life composed so much, so much of odds and
18 Portrait   28 you —/Without these friendships — life, what *cauchemar!*/Among the windings of
19 Portrait   45 do not know, you do not know/What life is, you who hold it in your hands';/(Slowly
19 Portrait   53 that somehow recall/My buried life, and Paris in the Spring,/I feel immeasurably
26 Rhapsody   77 shoes at the door, sleep, prepare for life.'/The last twist of the knife./Morning at the
28 Boston ET   4 the street,/Wakening the appetites of life in some/And to others bringing the *Boston*
61 WL: Burial   7 in forgetful snow, feeding/A little life with dried tubers./Summer surprised us,
85 Hollow Men   83 /And the response/Falls the Shadow/*Life is very long*/Between the desire/And the
86 Hollow Men   93 *Thine is the Kingdom*/For Thine is/Life is/For Thine is the/*This is the way the*
91 Ash-Wed 2   19 atone to forgetfulness./There is no life in them. As I am forgotten/And would be
105 Song Sime   4 stubborn season had made stand./My life is light, waiting for the death wind,/Like a
106 Song Sime   34 /Thine also)./I am tired with my own life and the lives of those after me,/I am dying
110 Marina   29 caulking./This form, this face, this life/Living to live in a world of time beyond me;
110 Marina   31 of time beyond me; let me/Resign my life for this life, my speech for that unspoken,/
110 Marina   31 me; let me/Resign my life for this life, my speech for that unspoken,/
121 SA Sweeney   20 this egg/You see this egg/Well that's life on a crocodile isle./There's no telephones/
123 SA   Doris   12 I never liked eggs;/And I don't like life on your crocodile isle. {}/SONG BY
123 SA   Doris   30 /*Noontime/Night/*{Do} That's not life, that's no life/Why I'd just as soon be dead./
123 SA   Doris   30 /*Night/*{Do} That's not life, that's no life/Why I'd just as soon be dead./{S} That's
123 SA Sweeney   32 just as soon be dead./{S} That's what life is. Just is/{Do} What is?/What's that life is?/
123 SA   Doris   34 is. Just is/{Do} What is?/What's that life is?/{S} Life is death./I knew a man once did
124 SA Sweeney   1 /{Do} What is?/What's that life is?/{S} Life is death./I knew a man once did a girl in —
125 SA Sweeney   19 tell you again it don't apply/Death or life or life or death/Death is life and life is death
125 SA Sweeney   19 again it don't apply/Death or life or life or death/Death is life and life is death/I

125	SA	Sweeney	20	Death or life or life or death/Death is life and life is death/I gotta use words when I
125	SA	Sweeney	20	life or life or death/Death is life and life is death/I gotta use words when I talk to
127	Cor1	March	10	Is he coming?/The natural wakeful life of our Ego is a perceiving./We can wait with
134	Wind		3	and broke the bells/Swinging between life and death/Here, in death's dream kingdom/
147	Rock 1		14	no nearer to GOD./Where is the Life we have lost in living?/Where is the wisdom
150	Rock 1		107	*In this land/No man has hired us./Our life is unwelcome, our death/Unmentioned in 'The*
152	Rock 2		36	from without;/For this is the law of life; and you must remember that while there is
152	Rock 2		38	of adversity they will decry it./What life have you if you have not life together?/
152	Rock 2		38	it./What life have you if you have not life together?/There is no life that is not in
152	Rock 2		39	have not life together?/There is no life that is not in community,/And no
156	Rock 3		74	remembers the way to your door:/Life you may evade, but Death you shall not./
159	Rock 6		18	they love her laws?/She tells them of Life and Death, and of all that they would
160	Rock 7		5	devils rather than nothing: crying for life beyond life, for ecstasy not of the flesh./
160	Rock 7		5	than nothing: crying for life beyond life, for ecstasy not of the flesh./Waste and void.
160	Rock 7		13	a dead end stirred with a flicker of life,/And they came to the withered ancient look
161	Rock 7		29	and Power, and what they call Life, or Race, or Dialectic./The Church
164	Rock 9		18	stone,/Spring always new forms of life, from the soul of man that is joined to the
164	Rock 9		20	/Joined with the artist's eye, new life, new form, new colour./Out of the sea of
164	Rock 9		21	colour./Out of the sea of sound the life of music,/Out of the slimy mud of words,
164	Rock 9		27	to Your service all our powers/For life, for dignity, grace and order,/And
167	Rock 10		36	Thee!/In our rhythm of earthly life we tire of light. We are glad when the day
187	FQ: DrySal		100	meaning/Is not the experience of one life only/But of many generations — not
190	FQ: DrySal		237	/(Not too far from the yew-tree)/The life of significant soil./Little Gidding/Midwinter
195	FQ: Little		156	the others as death resembles life,/Being between two lives — unflowering,
202	War Poetry		16	but a poem is not poetry —/That is a life./War is not a life: it is a situation,/One
202	War Poetry		17	poetry —/That is a life./War is not a life: it is a situation,/One which may neither be
211	Old Gumbie		35	helpful boy-scouts,/With a purpose in life and a good deed to do —/And she's even
231	Bust Jones		36	because he's observed/All his life a routine, so he'd say./Or, to put it in
590	Space Time		6	live while yet we may,/While love and life are free,/For time is time, and runs away,/
590	Space Time		15	them pine,/And though the flowers of life be few/Yet let them be divine./Standing
600	Moonflower		8	brighter tropic flowers/With scarlet life, for me?/Nocturne/Romeo, *grand sérieux*, to
603	Spleen		11	/Against this dull conspiracy./And Life, a little bald and gray,/Languid, fastidious,
604	Ode		12	we carry away/In the place of the life that we leave./And only the years that efface
242	MC	Mess	13	I leave you as a man/Whom in this life I shall not see again./I have this, I assure
247	MC	Thomas	17	from others' experience./But in the life of one man, never/The same time returns.
248	MC	Tempt2	28	Lord,/Power obtained grows to glory,/Life lasting, a permanent possession./A templed
254	MC	Tempt4	1	Thomas, wind/The thread of eternal life and death./You hold this power, hold it./{T}
256	MC	Tempts	9	on the back of my hand?/{4T} Man's life is a cheat and a disappointment;/All things
264	MC	Priest1	11	hands have handled/Of the word of life; that which we have seen and heard/Declare
264	MC	Priest1	25	he offereth for sins./He lays down his life for the sheep./{3P} *Rejoice we all, keeping*
269	MC	Knight1	15	you have spoken in peril of your life./{K2} Priest, you have spoken in danger of
271	MC	Thomas	22	To the altar, to the altar./{T} All my life they have been coming, these feet. All my
271	MC	Thomas	22	have been coming, these feet. All my life/I have waited. Death will come only when I
271	MC	Thomas	31	you are, and what is happening;/No life here is sought for but mine,/And I am not in
273	MC	Thomas	34	bad./You defer to the fact. For every life and every act/Consequence of good and evil
274	MC	Thomas	5	being gives entire consent./I give my life/To the Law of God above the Law of Man./
274	MC	Thomas	36	for blood./His blood given to buy my life,/My blood given to pay for His death,/My
276	MC	Chorus	11	/Every sorrow had a kind of end:/In life there is not time to grieve long./But this, this
276	MC	Chorus	12	to grieve long./But this, this is out of life, this is out of time,/An instant eternity of
278	MC	Knight2	23	adopted an ascetic/manner of life, he affirmed immediately that there was a
287	FR	Amy	20	easy for her/At the moment: but life may still go right./Meanwhile, let us drop
290	FR	Amy	10	restless shivering painted shadow/In life, she is less than a shadow in death./You
293	FR	Gerald	32	—/Been in tight corners most of my life/And some pretty nasty messes./{C} And
293	FR	Harry	38	events. You have gone through life in sleep,/Never woken to the nightmare. I
293	FR	Harry	39	woken to the nightmare. I tell you, life would be unendurable/If you were wide
295	FR	Charles	11	my boy,/I understand, your life together made it seem more horrible.
295	FR	Charles	12	horrible./There's a lot in my own past life that presses on my chest/When I wake, as I
306	FR	Harry	14	I thought it was a place/Where life was substantial and simplified —/But the
306	FR	Harry	21	I thought I might escape from one life to another,/And it may be all one life, with
306	FR	Harry	22	life to another,/And it may be all one life, with no escape. Tell me,/Were you ever
309	FR	Harry	36	noises/In the grass and leaves, of life persisting,/Which ordinarily pass unnoticed.
326	FR	Harry	20	/From some imaginary course that life ought to take,/That you call normal. What
326	FR	Harry	24	long as I could think/Even of my own life as an isolated ruin,/A casual bit of waste in
327	FR	Harry	22	I can clean my skin,/Purify my life, void my mind,/But always the filthiness,
330	FR	Harry	4	/Should be in the routine of normal life at Wishwood./John is the only one of us I

500 CC Lucasta 33 either./B. needs me. He's been hurt by life, just as I have,/And we can help each other.
513 CC Colby 30   by documents —/The story of his life, of his success or failure .../Perhaps his
513 CC Colby 36 that image. An ordinary man/Whose life I could in some way perpetuate/By being the
515 CC Guzzard 12 son was assured of a proper start in life —/That I knew. And it would make you so
527 ES Monica 23 First, his terror of being alone./In the life he's led, he's never had to be alone./And
530 ES Ld Clav 11   they tell me to be cautious,/To take life easily. Take life easily!/It's like telling a man
530 ES Ld Clav 11   be cautious,/To take life easily. Take life easily!/It's like telling a man he mustn't run
530 ES Ld Clav 14   I've not the slightest longing for the life I've left —/Only fear of the emptiness before
538 ES Gomez 10 /Now let's look for a moment at *your* life history./You had plenty of money, and you
541 ES Gomez 23 keep me in comfort for the rest of my life./Really, Dick, you owe me an apology./
545 ES Ld Clav 3 within myself/Has impelled me all my life to find justification/Not so much to the
545 ES Monica 10   admit that at the moment you find life pleasant,/That it really does seem quiet here
545 ES Piggott 29   after breakfast:/He's led a busy life, too.' But I hope you're happy?/Is there
549 ES Carghill 8 it —/The turning point of all my life!/Now whatever were the names of those
554 ES Piggott 14   for us./{MP} It's the breath of life to me, Mrs. Carghill,/Attending to my
559 ES Ld Clav 10 there are all in the cities:/An outdoor life would suit you better./How would you like
559 ES Ld Clav 17   do you want to go?/What kind of a life do you think you want?/{Mi} I simply want
559 ES Michael 18 want?/{Mi} I simply want to lead a life of my own,/According to my own ideas of
560 ES Michael 8 very much pleasanter/You will find life become, once I'm out of the country./What
561 ES Monica 35   You know that I would give my life for you./Oh, how silly that phrase sounds!
568 ES Ld Clav 11 /Has there been nothing in your life, Charles Hemington,/Which you wish to
568 ES Ld Clav 23 a man has one person, just one in his life,/To whom he is willing to confess everything
568 ES Ld Clav 37 of fiction about you!/I've spent my life in trying to forget myself,/In trying to
570 ES Ld Clav 14 /Completely without interest in the life that lay behind her/And completely
570 ES Monica 19 and what do they stand for in your life?/{LC} ... And yet they've both done better
571 ES Ld Clav 31   Culverwell,/He re-enters my life to make himself a reminder/Of one occasion
572 ES Ld Clav 4 him. But *I* didn't stop./And all my life I have heard, from time to time,/When I
572 ES Monica 8   /{M} Poor Father! All your life! And no one to share it with;/I never knew
575 ES Carghil 36   indeed./{MC} The romance of my life./Your father was simply *irresistible*/In those
578 ES Ld Clav 6   mistakes I have made/My whole life through, mistake upon mistake,/The
578 ES Michael 33 /That needn't interfere with your life or mine./{M} Oh Michael, you haven't
578 ES Monica 35   I said. You must make your own life/Of course, just as I must make mine./It's not
581 ES Ld Clav 20 /Because I wanted you to give your life to adoring/The man that I pretended to
582 ES Ld Clav 5 is worth while dying, to find out what life is./And I love you, my daughter, the more
LIFE'S (1)
515 CC Guzzard 26   it is a small thing/For me, to see my life's ambition come to nothing?/When I gave
LIFE-GIVING (1)
91 Ash-Wed 2 30 /Rose of forgetfulness/Exhausted and life-giving/Worried reposeful/The single Rose/Is
LIFELESS (1)
164 Rock 9 19 practical shapes of all that is living or lifeless/Joined with the artist's eye, new life, new
LIFELONG (1)
577 ES Charles 14 who aims to gratify, through you,/His lifelong grievance against your father?/
LIFETIME (5)
124 SA Sweeney 15   has to, needs to, wants to/Once in a lifetime, do a girl in/Well he kept her there in a
182 FQ: ECoker 196   with no before and after,/But a lifetime burning in every moment/And not the
182 FQ: ECoker 197 burning in every moment/And not the lifetime of one man only/But of old stones that
333 FR Agatha 11 carried/Death in life, death through lifetime, death in my womb./I felt that you were
518 CC Eggers 4   —/I don't see you spending a lifetime as an organist./I think you'll come to
LIFETIME'S (3)
190 FQ: DrySal 208 but something given/And taken, in a lifetime's death in love,/Ardour and selflessness
194 FQ: Little 132   for age/To set a crown upon your lifetime's effort./First, the cold friction of
332 FR Agatha 32 of broken stones/That lie, fang up, a lifetime's march. I have believed this./{H} I have
LIFT (5)
14 Prufrock 30 all the works and days of hands/That lift and drop a question on your plate;/Time for
140 Usk 7 sleep./'Gently dip, but not too deep',/Lift your eyes/Where the roads dip and where
155 Rock 3 43   build without the LORD./Shall we lift up our feet among perpetual ruins?/I have
366 CP Peter 22 you must let me take you down in the lift./{J} No, you stop and talk to Edward. I'm
366 CP Julia 25 to manage the machine myself —/In a lift I can meditate. Good-bye then./And thank
LIFTED (2)
178 FQ: ECoker 38 in clumsy shoes,/Earth feet, loam feet, lifted in country mirth/Mirth of those long since
540 ES Gomez 27   it, if only for a second?/You never lifted your foot from the accelerator./{LC} We
LIFTING (2)
165 Rock 9 41 visible crucifix,/The dressed altar, the lifting light,/Light/Light/The visible reminder of
178 FQ: ECoker 37   solemn or in rustic laughter/Lifting heavy feet in clumsy shoes,/Earth feet,

175	FQ: BurntN	138	light to light, and is silent, the light is still/At the still point of the turning
177	FQ: ECoker	14	/In my beginning is my end. Now the light falls/Across the open field, leaving the
177	FQ: ECoker	20	In a warm haze the sultry light/Is absorbed, not refracted, by grey stone./
180	FQ: ECoker	129	thought:/So the darkness shall be the light, and the stillness the dancing./Whisper of
197	FQ: Little	237	/Of timeless moments. So, while the light fails/On a winter's afternoon, in a secluded
216	Jellicles	28	powers/To dance by the light of the Jellicle Moon./Jellicle Cats are black
233	Skimble	37	on the floor./There is every sort of light — you can make it dark or bright;/There's
592	Grad 1	5	harbor bar — no chart to show/No light to warn of rocks which lie below,/But let
254	MC Tempt4	33	the gold spent,/The jewels gone for light ladies' ornament,/The sanctuary broken,
256	MC Chorus	8	smell, the vapour? the dark green light from a cloud on a withered tree? The earth
261	MC Thomas	35	seen, not as we/see them, but in the light of the Godhead from which they draw
269	MC Chorus	34	twisting, rat tails twining, in the thick light of dawn. I have eaten/Smooth creatures
270	MC Chorus	2	bowels, and my bowels dissolve in the light of dawn. I have smelt/Death in the rose,
270	MC Chorus	10	ground heaved. I have seen/Rings of light coiling downwards, descending/To the
281	MC Chorus	10	by Thee, all things exist/Only in Thy light, and Thy glory is declared even in that
281	MC Chorus	10	the darkness declares the glory of light./Those who deny Thee could not deny, if
285	FR Amy	1	yet! I will ring for you. It is still quite light./I have nothing to do but watch the days
285	FR Amy	6	/O Sun, that was once so warm, O Light that was taken for granted/When I was
285	FR Amy	7	I was young and strong, and sun and light unsought for/And the night unfeared and
291	FR Harry	19	/{H} How can you sit in this blaze of light for all the world to look at?/If you knew
294	FR Harry	20	of conduct/In flickering intervals of light and darkness;/The partial anthesia of
310	FR Harry	39	so as not to stay still. Singing and light./Stop!/What is that? do you feel it?/{M}
332	FR Agatha	27	/Only a present moment of pointed light/When you want to burn. When you stretch
364	CP Reilly	13	illusion of having ever been in the light./The fact that you can't give a reason for
374	CP Edward	24	difficulties?/{E} It has only brought to light the real difficulties./{C} But surely, these
378	CP Julia	2	Celia!/You must come and have a light supper with me —/Something very light./
378	CP Julia	3	supper with me —/Something very light./{C} Thank you, Julia./I think I will, if I
406	CP Reilly	7	that you have come to see it in that light —/At least, for the moment. But, Mrs.
448	CC Eggers	9	/I did mention her interest in Light from the East./{SC} And the Book of
459	CC Lady E	27	baneful to Mr. Colby./He needs a light mauve. I shall see about that./But not
493	CC Lady E	7	desk?/{LE} On the other side, with the light behind me:/But won't you be sitting at the
493	CC Lady E	21	place her?/{LE} Over there, with the light full on her:/I want to be able to watch her
561	ES Monica	38	in/But not looked at, love within the light of which/All else is seen, the love within

LIGHT-IN-LEAVES (1)

138	New Hamp	8	to-morrow grieves,/Cover me over, light-in-leaves;/Golden head, black wing,/Cling,

LIGHTED (2)

24	Rhapsody	42	in the street/Trying to peer through lighted shutters,/And a crab one afternoon in a
349	FR	3m 13	*carrying a birthday cake with/lighted candles, which she sets on the table. Exit*

LIGHTING (1)

22	Preludes	13	steams and stamps./And then the lighting of the lamps./The morning comes to

LIGHTNING (5)

74	WL: Thund	393	/Co co rico co co rico/In a flash of lightning. Then a damp gust/Bringing rain/
129	Cor2 State	26	/Fireflies flare against the faint sheet lightning/What shall I cry?/Mother mother/
129	Cor2 State	47	with the small flare of the firefly or lightning bug,/'Rising and falling, crowned with
180	FQ: ECoker	130	of running streams, and winter lightning./The wild thyme unseen and the wild
190	FQ: DrySal	213	/The wild thyme unseen, or the winter lightning/Or the waterfall, or music heard so

LIGHTNING-WINGED (1)

592	Grad 3	1	be as citizens no more./We go; as lightning-winged clouds that fly/After a summer

LIGHTS (17)

41	Burb Blei	27	hand/To climb the waterstair. Lights, lights,/She entertains Sir Ferdinand/
41	Burb Blei	27	hand/To climb the waterstair. Lights, lights,/She entertains Sir Ferdinand/Klein. Who
68	WL: Fire S	222	home at teatime, clears her breakfast, lights/Her stove, and lays out food in tins./Out
107	Animula	2	soul'/To a flat world of changing lights and noise,/To light, dark, dry or damp,
149	Rock 1 m	79	the work of the humble. Listen./*The lights fade; in the semi-darkness the voices of*
164	Rock 9	6	/Among a few flickering scattered lights?/They would put upon GOD their own
166	Rock 10	26	worship Thee!/We thank Thee for the lights that we have kindled,/The light of altar
167	Rock 10	28	light of altar and of sanctuary;/Small lights of those who meditate at midnight/And
167	Rock 10	29	those who meditate at midnight/And lights directed through the coloured panes of
167	Rock 10	44	Light, we may set thereon the little lights for which our bodily vision is made./And
179	FQ: ECoker	93	/And menaced by monsters, fancy lights,/Risking enchantment. Do not let me hear
180	FQ: ECoker	115	of God. As, in a theatre,/The lights are extinguished, for the scene to be
588	Fable	63	he ought t' have of grape juice./The lights began to burn distinctly blue,/As in ghost
588	Fable	64	distinctly blue,/As in ghost stories lights most always do./The doors, though
603	Spleen	7	this unwarranted digression./Evening, lights, and tea!/Children and cats in the alley;/
285	FR Amy	11	not stop in the dark!/Put on the lights. But leave the curtains undrawn./Make up

286 FR	m 30	/{C} That's what it comes to. {}/[*Lights a cigarette*]/{I} The younger generation/

LIKE (346)

13 Prufrock		3	evening is spread out against the sky/Like a patient etherised upon a table;/Let us go,
13 Prufrock		8	with oyster-shells:/Streets that follow like a tedious argument/Of insidious intent/To
19 Portrait		56	youthful, after all.'/The voice returns like the insistent out-of-tune/Of a broken violin
21 Portrait		99	not developed into friends.'/I feel like one who smiles, and turning shall remark/
21 Portrait		111	/To find expression ... dance, dance/Like a dancing bear,/Cry like a parrot, chatter
21 Portrait		112	dance/Like a dancing bear,/Cry like a parrot, chatter like an ape./Let us take the
21 Portrait		112	bear,/Cry like a parrot, chatter like an ape./Let us take the air, in a tobacco
23 Preludes		53	and laugh;/The worlds revolve like ancient women/Gathering fuel in vacant
24 Rhapsody		9	/Every street lamp that I pass/Beats like a fatalistic drum,/And through the spaces of
24 Rhapsody		18	light of the door/Which opens on her like a grin./You see the border of her dress/Is
24 Rhapsody		22	you see the corner of her eye/Twists like a crooked pin.'/The memory throws up
28 Boston ET		2	*Evening Transcript*/Sway in the wind like a field of ripe corn./When evening quickens
31 Apollinax		7	Channing-Cheetah's/He laughed like an irresponsible fœtus./His laughter was
31 Apollinax		9	was submarine and profound/Like the old man of the sea's/Hidden under
64 WL: Chess		77	Game of Chess/The Chair she sat in, like a burnished throne,/Glowed on the marble,
66 WL: Chess		153	UP PLEASE ITS TIME/If you don't like it you can get on with it, I said./Others can
68 WL: Fire S		217	desk, when the human engine waits/Like a taxi throbbing waiting,/I Tiresias, though
84 Hollow Men		45	the twinkle of a fading star./Is it like this/In death's other kingdom/Waking
92 Ash-Wed 3		10	the stair was dark,/Damp, jaggèd, like an old man's mouth drivelling, beyond
92 Ash-Wed 3		13	stair/Was a slotted window bellied like the fig's fruit/And beyond the hawthorn
104 Journ Magi		39	was/Hard and bitter agony for us, like Death, our death./We returned to our
105 Song Sime		5	is light, waiting for the death wind,/Like a feather on the back of my hand./Dust in
115 SP	Doris	19	through and through./{Do} I like Sam/{Du} *I* like Sam/Yes and Sam's a nice
115 SP	Dusty	20	and through./{Do} I like Sam/{Du} *I* like Sam/Yes and Sam's a nice boy too./He's a
115 SP	Doris	24	fellow/{Do} He *is* a funny fellow/He's like a fellow once I knew./*He* could make you
116 SP	Doris	17	What'll I say?/{Do} Say what you like: say I'm ill,/Say I broke my leg on the stairs
118 SP	Doris	12	they're no use at all./{Do} I'd like to know about that coffin./{Du} Well I
118 SP	Doris	31	DORIS): Cards are queer./{Do} I'd like to know about that coffin. {}/KNOCK
119 SP	Doris	26	it won't be the last time./{Do} You like London, Mr. Klipstein?/{Kr} Do we like
119 SP	Krum	27	London, Mr. Klipstein?/{Kr} Do we like London? do we like London!/Do we like
119 SP	Krum	27	/{Kr} Do we like London? do we like London!/Do we like London!! Eh what
119 SP	Krum	28	London? do we like London!/Do we like London!! Eh what Klip?/{Kl} Say, Miss —
119 SP	Klip	30	— er — uh — London's swell./We like London fine./{Kr} Perfectly slick./{Du}
120 SP	Krum	8	you got a real live Britisher/A guy like Sam to show you around./Sam of course is
123 SA	Doris	11	*sound of the coral sea.*/{Do} I don't like eggs; I never liked eggs;/And I don't like life
123 SA	Doris	12	eggs; I never liked eggs;/And I don't like life on your crocodile isle. {}/SONG BY
125 SA	Sweeney	16	when you're alone/When you're alone like he was alone/You're either or neither/I tell
125 SA	Chorus	34	the middle of the bed and/you wake like someone hit you in the head/You've had a
129 Cor2 State		30	remarkably Roman,/Remarkably like each other, lit up successively by the flare/
135 5FingerEx2		12	must/Jellicle cats and dogs all must/Like undertakers, come to dust./Here a little
151 Rock 2		7	moved on the face of the waters like a lantern set on the back of a tortoise./And
158 Rock 5		5	of which the use is forgotten: are like snakes that lie on mouldering stairs, content
158 Rock 5		6	sunlight./And the others run about like dogs, full of enterprise, sniffing and
159 Rock 6		19	would be hard, and hard where they like to be soft./She tells them of Evil and Sin,
160 Rock 7		19	of time, a moment in time but not like a moment of time,/A moment in time but
162 Rock 8		14	evil,/And most who were neither./Like all men in all places,/Some went from love
164 Rock 9		9	they walk in the street proudnecked, like thoroughbreds ready for races,/Adorning
182 FQ: ECoker	171	our only food:/In spite of which we like to think/That we are sound, substantial
186 FQ: DrySal	74	/Or of a future that is not liable/Like the past, to have no destination./We have
187 FQ: DrySal	118	the destroyer is time the preserver,/Like the river with its cargo of dead negroes,
191 FQ: Little	27	of the journey,/If you came at night like a broken king,/If you came by day not
193 FQ: Little	85	/While the dead leaves still rattled on like tin/Over the asphalt where no other sound
193 FQ: Little	89	and hurried/As if blown towards me like the metal leaves/Before the urban dawn
194 FQ: Little	124	/Between two worlds become much like each other,/So I find words I never thought
195 FQ: Little	148	/Where you must move in measure, like a dancer.'/The day was breaking. In the
214 RTTugger	15	as soon as he's at home, then he'd like to get about./He likes to lie in the bureau
215 RTTugger	34	sewing,/For there's nothing he enjoys like a horrible muddle./Yes the Rum Tum
216 Jellicles	11	Cats have bright black eyes;/They like to practise their airs and graces/And wait
216 Jellicles	23	are of moderate size;/Jellicles jump like a jumping-jack,/Jellicle Cats have moonlit
218 Mung Rump	8	found ajar/And the basement looked like a field of war,/If a tile or two came loose on
219 Mung Rump	27	the joint has gone from the oven — like that!'/Then the family would say: 'It's that
219 Mung Rump	32	/They would go through the house like a hurricane, and no sober person could take
222 Pekes Pols	5	most people say/That they do not like fighting, yet once in a way,/Or now and

223 Pekes Pols   32   /But a terrible din is what Pollicles like,/For your Pollicle Dog is a dour Yorkshire
223 Pekes Pols   52   RUMPUSCAT./His eyes were like fireballs fearfully blazing,/He gave a great
223 Pekes Pols   59   they every last one of them scattered like sheep./*And when the Police Dog returned*
226 Macavity   5   /Macavity, Macavity, there's no one like Macavity,/He's broken every human law,
226 Macavity   15   from side to side, with movements like a snake;/And when you think he's half
226 Macavity   17   /Macavity, Macavity, there's no one like Macavity,/For he's a fiend in feline shape, a
227 Macavity   35   /Macavity, Macavity, there's no one like Macavity,/There never was a Cat of such
233 Skimble   42   will ask you very brightly/'Do you like your morning tea weak or strong?'/But
234 Ad-dress   6   enough to see/That Cats are much like you and me/And other people whom we
234 Ad-dress   20   A DOG./Now Dogs pretend they like to fight;/They often bark, more seldom bite;
235 Ad-dress   55 Some little token of esteem/Is needed, like a dish of cream;/And you might now and
236 Cat Morgan   12   I guess that's enough;/'You can't but like Morgan, 'e's got a good 'art.'/I got knocked
594 Grad 11   1   which as pupils now we go./We go; like flitting faces in a dream;/Out of thy care
595 Grad 14   3   tale: 'Farewell',/A word that echoes like a funeral bell/And one that we are ever loth
599 On a Port   5   at evening in the room alone./Not like a tranquil carved goddess of stone/But
242 MC   Mess   9   I think that this peace/Is nothing like an end, or like a beginning./It is common
242 MC   Mess   9   this peace/Is nothing like an end, or like a beginning./It is common knowledge that
244 MC Chorus   20   a fear not of one but of many,/A fear like birth and death, when we see birth and
244 MC Chorus   23   torn from us, our brains unskinned like the layers of an onion, our selves are lost
245 MC Priest2   6   and cheering,/You go on croaking like frogs in the treetops:/But frogs at least can
252 MC Thomas   16   /I ruled once as Chancellor/And men like you were glad to wait at my door./Not only
252 MC Thomas   19   I made many yield./Shall I who ruled like an eagle over doves/Now take the shape of
264 MC Priest3   18   blood of thy saints have they shed like water,/And there was no man to bury them.
265 MC Priest3   5   or hope from. One moment/Weighs like another. Only in retrospection, selection,/
265 MC Priest1   26   also./Dinner before business. Do you like roast pork?/{K1} Business before dinner.
266 MC Knights   22   out of the London dirt,/Crawling up like a louse on your shirt,/The man who
266 MC Knight1   30   save you —/As I do not think it is like to do./Saving your ambition is what you
270 MC Chorus   20   in our veins, our brains,/Is woven like a pattern of living worms/In the guts of the
271 MC Thomas   17   forgetfulness sweeten memory/Only like a dream that has often been told/And often
273 MC   Priests   24   these come not as men come, but/Like maddened beasts. They come not like men,
273 MC   Priests   24   maddened beasts. They come not like men, who/Respect the sanctuary, who kneel
273 MC   Priests   26   who kneel to the Body of Christ,/But like beasts. You would bar the door/Against the
274 MC Thomas   29   in the feast./{T} It is the just man who/Like a bold lion, should be without fear./I am
276 MC Knight3   33   /{K3} I am afraid I am not anything like such an experienced/speaker as my old
277 MC Knight3   1   But there is one thing I should like to say, and I might as/well say it at once. It
277 MC Knight2   35   Sir/Hugh de Morville./{K2} I should like first to recur to a point that was very/well
278 MC Knight2   28   /offends the instincts of a people like ours. So far, I know that I have/your
286 FR Charles   2   in the winter./But a single man like me is better off in London:/A man can be
290 FR Chorus   37   fretful, ill at ease,/Assembled like amateur actors who have not been assigned
290 FR Chorus   38   have not been assigned their parts?/Like amateur actors in a dream when the
291 FR   Harry   21 saw you through the window!/Do you like to be stared at by eyes through a window?/
292 FR   Amy   18   forward to your coming:/Would you like to have them in after dinner/Or wait till
294 FR   Harry   38   /That she was unkillable. It was not like that./Everything is true in a different sense./
297 FR Charles   25   or two {}/[*Rings the bell*]/{C} That I'd like to ask Downing./He shan't know why I'm
297 FR Charles   29   his Lordship's car./{C} Tell him I'd like to have a word with him, please. {}/[Exit
298 FR Charles   21   {C} Well, I'm very sorry/You all see it like this: but there simply are times/When
298 FR Charles   29   so abruptly,/But I've a question I'd like to put to you,/I'm sure you won't mind, it's
300 FR Downing   5   when the weather was rough,/Didn't like to see her lean over the rail./He was in a
301 FR Downing   6   /{Do} Nothing wrong, Sir:/Only I like to have her always ready./Would there be
301 FR Chorus   16   /{Ch} Why should we stand here like guilty conspirators, waiting for some
301 FR Chorus   28   /To the universal bondage./We like to appear in the newspapers/So long as we
302 FR Chorus   1 /And the slowly hardening artery./We like to be thought well of by others/So that we
303 FR   Mary   28   /When he thinks he is behaving like a man of the world?/Cousin Agatha, I want
304 FR   Mary   19   moral courage,/Even against a will like hers. I know very well/Why she wanted to
304 FR   Mary   31 Did you ever meet her? What was she like?/{Ag} I am the only one who ever met her,/
305 FR Agatha   6   me capable of such a feeling./I would like to help you: but you must not run away,/
305 FR   Harry   35 normal change of things:/But it's very like her. What I might have expected./It only
306 FR   Harry   38   not for us./{H} No, it didn't seem like that. I was part of the design/As well as
308 FR   Harry   22   had happened,/Isn't that all folly? It's like the hollow tree,/Not there./{M} But surely,
309 FR   Mary   26   misdirected. You deceive yourself/Like the man convinced that he is paralysed/Or
309 FR   Mary   27   convinced that he is paralysed/Or like the man who believes that he is blind/While
309 FR   Harry   31   have staid in England, yet you seem/Like someone who comes from a very long
311 FR   Harry   4   /Deeper than the sense of smell, but like a smell/In that it is indescribable, a sweet
311 FR   Harry   9 me into it. O Mary!/Don't look at me like that! Stop! Try to stop it!/I am going. Oh
314 FR Warburt   13 a time to keep you in bed./You didn't like being ill in the holidays./{I} It *was*

317 FR	Harry	9	difficult./But talk about it, if you like./{W} You don't understand me./I'm sure
318 FR	Harry	4	I remember. That was why/We all felt like failures, before we had begun./When we
320 FR	Warburt	30	Wishwood/Depends on you. I don't like to say this;/But you know that I am a very
321 FR	Harry	2	of course I did./{H} What did he look like then? Did he look at all like me?/{W} Very
321 FR	Harry	2	he look like then? Did he look at all like me?/{W} Very much like you. Of course
321 FR	Warburt	3	he look at all like me?/{W} Very much like you. Of course there are differences:/But,
321 FR	Warburt	5	your being clean-shaven, very much like you./And now, Harry, let's talk about
323 FR	Warburt	14	tonight. I'd trust Owen/On a matter like this. You can trust Owen./We'll bring him
324 FR	Harry	14	can be very serious./A minor trouble like a concussion/Cannot make very much
325 FR	Amy	1	I will not talk yours./{A} You looked like your father/When you said that./{H} I
325 FR	Charles	10	use in any of us going —/On a night like this — it's a good three miles;/There's
326 FR	Harry	11	off to sleep in the middle of calamity/Like children, or like hardened campaigners.
326 FR	Harry	11	middle of calamity/Like children, or like hardened campaigners. She looked/Very
326 FR	Harry	23	unreal and the unimportant./I was like that in a way, so long as I could think/Even
327 FR	Harry	9	now?/That was only what I should like to believe./I was talking in abstractions: and
334 FR	Harry	4	rid of/But in a different vision. This is like an end./{Ag} And a beginning. Harry, my
334 FR	Harry	33	by understanding./But she would not like that. Now I see/I have been wounded in a
336 FR	Harry	11	... but not just as before,/Not quite like, not the same ... {}/[The EUMENIDES
336 FR	Agatha	29	Knowing what is intended./A curse is like a child, formed/In a moment of
336 FR	Agatha	35	/Of the determined moon./A curse is like a child, formed/To grow to maturity:/
337 FR	Agatha	10	nothing to stay for./Think of it as like a children's treasure hunt:/Here you have
346 FR	Charles	4	Arcade./What if every moment were like that, if one were awake?/You both seem to
346 FR	Downing	27	to circumstance,/But with people like him, there's something inside them/That
348 FR	Chorus	6	*and* WARBURTON]/{Ch} We do not like to look out of the same window, and see
348 FR	Chorus	7	a different landscape./We do not like to climb a stair, and find that it takes us
348 FR	Chorus	8	find that it takes us down./We do not like to walk out of a door, and find ourselves
348 FR	Chorus	9	back in the same room./We do not like to take the maze in the garden, because it too
348 FR	Chorus	10	the maze in the brain./We do not like what happens when we are awake, because
353 CP	Peter	16	her mouth out with champagne./I like that story./{C} I love that story./{A} *I'm*
355 CP	Julia	25	party/For a gluttonous old woman like me/Is a really nice tit-bit. I can drink at
357 CP	Julia	19	it's very unselfish of Lavinia/Yet very like her. But really, Edward,/Lavinia may be
358 CP	Julia	10	Yes, alone!/Without Lavinia! You'll like the other people —/But you're to talk to
358 CP	Julia	22	to leave it./It's such a nice party, I'd like to repeat it./Why don't you *all* come to
361 CP	Edward	14	in examining witnesses,/So I don't like them. May I put it to *you*?/I know that I
361 CP	Reilly	39	/Arranging life a little better than you like it,/Preferring not quite the same friends as
362 CP	Reilly	1	as yourself,/Or making your friends like her better than you;/And, turning the past
364 CP	Edward	1	I no longer remember what my wife is like./I am not quite sure that I could describe
366 CP	Julia	24	I'm not helpless yet./And besides, I like to manage the machine myself —/In a lift I
367 CP	Edward	36	you know why *I've* looked in?/{E} I'd like to know first how you *got* in, Alex./{A}
369 CP	Peter	29	I preferred to go alone./But a girl like Celia, it seemed very strange,/Because I
370 CP	Peter	11	/Desire for possession. It was not like that at all./It was something very strange.
370 CP	Peter	21	faded — into some other picture —/Like a film effect. She doesn't want to see me;/
370 CP	Edward	35	might have become an ordinary affair/Like any other. As the fever cooled/You would
374 CP	Celia	10	on the telephone./It did not seem like you. So I felt I must see you./Tell me it's all
375 CP	Edward	3	the grounds .../{E} I see. But it is not like that at all./Lavinia is coming back./{C}
375 CP	Edward	14	/I've never tasted anything like it .../Yes, that's very interesting. But I just
379 CP	Celia	35	reality,/And if this is reality, it is very like a dream./Perhaps it was I who betrayed my
380 CP	Edward	32	you had better have her./{E} It's not like that./It is not that I am in love with
381 CP	Edward	39	may be the *guardian* —/But in men like me, the dull, the implacable,/The
382 CP	Edward	23	is what I am./Tread on me, if you like./{C} No, I won't tread on you./That is not
383 CP	Edward	6	sure? ... Very well, hold on if you like;/We ... I'll look for them./{C} Yes, you look
385 CP	Edward	24	{E} There are certainly things I should like to forget./{UG} And persons also. But you
385 CP	Edward	36	don't know why,/But I think I should like you to bring her yourself./{UG} Yes, I
386 CP	Edward	24	/{E} It seems very odd. And not like Lavinia./I suppose there is nothing to do
386 CP	Celia	32	forgive my laughing./You look like a little boy who's been sent for/To the
389 CP	Celia	24	going away — somewhere —/I should like to say good-bye — as friends./{L} Why,
389 CP	Celia	31	/What I want to say is this: I should like you to remember me/As someone who
391 CP	Lavinia	20	/And I cannot stop it; no, it's not like a machine —/Or if it's a machine, someone
392 CP	Lavinia	2	/{L} Yes, that was a silly thing to say./Like a schoolgirl. Like Celia. I don't know why
392 CP	Lavinia	2	a silly thing to say./Like a schoolgirl. Like Celia. I don't know why I said it./Well,
394 CP	Lavinia	39	could have taught you to answer back like that?/{E} I have had quite enough
396 CP	Lavinia	17	of your own./Oh, Edward, I should like to be good to you —/Or if that's
399 CP	Reilly	2	morning, Miss Barraway:/I should like to run over my instructions again./You
401 CP	Edward	12	But he *is* a blunderer./I should like to know ... but what is the use!/I suppose I
402 CP	Edward	33	I doubt if you have ever had a case like mine:/I have ceased to believe in my own

403 CP	Edward	18	think well of themselves./{E} If I am like that/I must have done a great deal of harm.
403 CP	Reilly	20	/{R} Oh, not so much as you would like to think:/Only, shall we say, within your
404 CP	Reilly	37	journey./But before I treat a patient like yourself/I need to know a great deal more
406 CP	Edward	37	a hotel/In the New Forest .../{E} How like you, Lavinia./You always know of
407 CP	Edward	2	because you've told me so often./I'd like to see *you* filling up an income-tax form./
407 CP	Reilly	23	when you put yourselves into hands like mine/You surrender a great deal more than
408 CP	Lavinia	12	have been./{L} Well, tell him if you like./{R} A young man named Peter./{E} Peter?
411 CP	Lavinia	22	/At least, there is something I would like you to ask./{E} It's about the future of ...
413 CP	Celia	28	I must tell you/That I should really *like* to think there's something wrong with me —/
416 CP	Reilly	29	this man. What does he now seem like, to you?/{C} Like a child who has wandered
416 CP	Celia	30	does he now seem like, to you?/{C} Like a child who has wandered into a forest/
417 CP	Celia	9	/For what happened is remembered like a dream/In which one is exalted by intensity
418 CP	Reilly	1	else,/And the other life will be only like a book/You have read once, and lost. In a
418 CP	Celia	8	—/No, not a surrender — more like a betrayal./You see, I think I really had a
418 CP	Celia	17	to that life./Oh, I'm afraid this sounds like raving!/Or just cantankerousness ... still,/If
418 CP	Celia	30	in the wrong place./{C} That sounds like what I want. But what is my duty?/{R}
419 CP	Celia	22	come back as these did./{C} It sounds like a prison. But they can't *all* stay there!/I
420 CP	Reilly	14	is no fee./{C} But .../{R} For a case like yours/There is no fee. {}/[*Presses button*]/
421 CP	Julia	27	hills,/Through the valley of derision, like a child sent on an errand/In eagerness and
421 CP	Reilly	34	grateful./{R} And when I say to one like her/'Work out your salvation with
424 CP	Edward	25	I'll be glad/When it's all over./{E} I like the dress you're wearing:/I'm glad you put
425 CP	Edward	22	what the Gunnings' parties were like./Their guests will get just enough to make
435 CP	Peter	14	now; but I never thought/Of anything like this. I suppose I didn't know her,/I didn't
436 CP	Edward	3	things about yourself/That you don't like to face: well, just remember/That some men
436 CP	Julia	18	eye. You will come to think of Celia/Like that, one day. And then you'll understand
440 CP	Edward	29	But I've already told you how much I like it./{L} But so much has happened since
445 CC	Claude	3	way from Joshua Park, on an errand like this./But you know my wife wouldn't like
445 CC	Claude	4	this./But you know my wife wouldn't like anyone to meet her/At Northolt, but you.
446 CC	Claude	12	so. I understand his feelings./He's like me, Eggerson. The same disappointment/In
447 CC	Eggers	7	on her arrival./{E} How would you like me to approach the subject?/{SC} Of course,
447 CC	Claude	32	very tempting offer./Something like that. Don't make too much of it./And I
448 CC	Eggers	15	/But there's one thing I should like to know —/If you don't mind — before I
449 CC	Claude	9	what you mean./{SC} She must get to like him first:/And then, Eggerson, I am not
449 CC	Eggers	21	/I have never been able to make her like Miss Angel;/She becomes abstracted,
451 CC	Colby	15	know why it should be so different./I like B. Kaghan. I've found him very helpful/
452 CC	Lucasta	35	comes of being cursed with a name like Angel./I'm thinking of changing it. But,
453 CC	Lucasta	9	take me out to dinner. A working girl like me/Is often very hungry — living on a
455 CC	Eggers	14	for her./In any case, he's behaved like a father —/A very generous man, is Sir
455 CC	Colby	29	joke./{C} Well, I've never met anyone like Miss Angel./{E} You'll get used to her, Mr.
457 CC	Eggers	4	*I* always say./And I'm sure you'll like her. She's *such* a lady!/And what's more,
460 CC	Claude	10	that I can't decipher your writing./I like to have the cards, just to know where you
462 CC	Colby	8	you've had in mind still seems to me/Like building my life upon a deception./Do you
462 CC	Claude	15	*will* become her son, in her eyes. She's like that./Why, it wouldn't surprise me if she
462 CC	Claude	27	a reason for asking —/How do you like your work? You don't find it uncongenial?/
463 CC	Colby	22	talking it./I'm not at all sure that I like the other person/That I feel myself
464 CC	Claude	19	/Never until now. Do you feel at all like that/When you are alone with your music?/
465 CC	Colby	38	to myself,/I hear the music I should like to have written,/As the composer heard it
469 CC	Lucasta	3	for anything:/You know that. But I'd like to learn about music./I wish you would
469 CC	Colby	7	music. And to find out what you like./When you know what you like, and begin
469 CC	Colby	8	you like./When you know what you like, and begin to know it well,/Then you will
469 CC	Lucasta	11	of playing it./{L} But suppose I only like the wrong things?/{C} No, I'm sure you'll
469 CC	Colby	15	very second-rate,/And you didn't like them. You liked the right ones./{L} Colby, I
469 CC	Lucasta	17	things I liked were the right ones to like?/Still, I'm awfully ignorant. Can you believe
470 CC	Lucasta	29	not with me?/{L} Because you don't like them —/American Musicals. Do you think
470 CC	Lucasta	31	a woman to something she would like/When she knows *you* wouldn't like it?
470 CC	Lucasta	32	like/When she knows *you* wouldn't like it? That's not a compliment:/That's just
470 CC	Lucasta	34	if you invite me/To something you like — that *is* a compliment./It shows you want
471 CC	Lucasta	13	suspect./Perhaps that's why I like you./{C} That's not quite the reason./{L}
471 CC	Lucasta	15	reason./{L} Oh, so you believe that I like you?/I didn't know that you were so
472 CC	Lucasta	13	/One finds them in some ways very like oneself,/In unexpected ways. And then you
472 CC	Lucasta	17	—/But your insecurity is nothing like mine./{C} In what way is it different?/{L}
472 CC	Lucasta	32	to go into business/And be someone like Claude ... or B. I was sorry,/Very sorry for
473 CC	Lucasta	9	/In a shabby part of London — like the one where I lived/For a time, with my
474 CC	Lucasta	34	music is a ... symbol./I really would like to understand music,/Not in order to be
474 CC	Lucasta	40	than any *I've* ever lived in./And I'd like to understand *you*./{C} I believe you do

475 CC	Lucasta	19	now that we begin to understand,/I'd like you to know a little more about me./You
477 CC	Lucasta	23	understand./Little you know what it's like to be a bastard/And wanted by nobody. I
477 CC	Lucasta	25	shocked:/Claude has just accepted me like a debit item/Always in his cash account. I
477 CC	Lucasta	26	/Always in his cash account. I don't like myself./I don't like the person I've forced
477 CC	Lucasta	27	account. I don't like myself./I don't like the person I've forced myself to be;/And I
477 CC	Lucasta	28	/And I liked you because you didn't like that person either,/And I thought you'd
477 CC	Lucasta	38	yourself up in that garden/Where you like to be alone with yourself?/Or perhaps you
479 CC	Kaghan	6	between a couple of man-eating tigers/Like you and Lizzie, he's got to have protection.
479 CC	Kaghan	20	Lucasta./{L} You know I don't like sherry./{K} You've got to drink it,/To
479 CC	Kaghan	33	have to live down./— I must say, I like the way you've had the place done up./{C}
479 CC	Kaghan	35	decorations./{K} Then I'm not sure I like them. You must change the colours./It's all
480 CC	Colby	15	get involved in anything risky./You like to pretend to other people/That you're a
480 CC	Kaghan	33	background at all./That's one thing I like about Lucasta:/She doesn't despise me./{L}
481 CC	Kaghan	11	eight;/Not at any restaurant that *you* like./— For a change, let's talk about Lucasta.
482 CC	Colby	29	/I don't know, myself. And I should like to know./{LE} In the first place, you ought
485 CC	Lady E	28	/{LE} Still, you were brought up, like me, in the country./Teddington. I seem to
487 CC	Claude	8	/{C} I'll try./{SC} It's just in ways like this, Elizabeth,/That Colby can be of
488 CC	Claude	28	a silly thought .../What happens is so like what one had planned for,/And yet such a
490 CC	Colby	22	gap that never can be filled. Never./I like you both, I could even come to love you —/
493 CC	Claude	14	On the other hand,/We mustn't look like a couple of barristers/Ready to
494 CC	Lady E	8	/Oh dear, what do I want? I should like him to be mine,/But for you to believe that
494 CC	Claude	23	can't communicate an inspiration,/Like that, by force of will. He was a great
494 CC	Lady E	27	to do./{LE} You've never talked like this to me before!/Why haven't you? I don't
494 CC	Lady E	40	really mean, to make jugs and jars/Like those in your collection?/{SC} That's what
495 CC	Lady E	22	/I know now that poets don't look like poets:/And financiers, it seems, don't look
495 CC	Lady E	23	/And financiers, it seems, don't look like potters —/Is that what I mean? I'm getting
496 CC	Eggers	20	wishes I'd come up oftener!/Isn't that like the ladies! She used to complain/At my
498 CC	Claude	39	the situation:/And I thought I would like you to conduct the proceedings./Will you
502 CC	Lucasta	12	your reaction./It wouldn't have been like you — the way I thought it was./You're
502 CC	Lucasta	17	I got. But I couldn't believe it!/It isn't like you, to despise people:/You don't care
503 CC	Lucasta	14	I'm going to marry B./I know you like B./{C} I'm very fond of him;/And I'm glad
503 CC	Colby	23	in this proposal./{C} Of course I'd like them ... Can't B. come up now?/{E} Better
504 CC	Claude	1	/She ought to be here. It wouldn't be like her/To be late for an appointment. She
506 CC	Eggers	37	/There are other places that sound like Teddington/But not so many names that
506 CC	Eggers	38	/But not so many names that sound like Guzzard —/Or if there are, they are equally
508 CC	Guzzard	31	name?/{MG} Yes, I know their name:/Like mine, a somewhat unusual one./Perhaps a
509 CC	Claude	27	to sign his full name./But he doesn't like the name, for some reason;/So we call him
511 CC	Kaghan	17	I must get used to that./But I should like to know how I ought to address you,/Lady
511 CC	Lucasta	30	/{L} Why is it that you don't like the name of Barnabas?/{K} I don't want
512 CC	Guzzard	21	it is my turn to ask them./I should like to gratify everyone's wishes./{LE} Oh, of
513 CC	Colby	25	/It's only just come to me. I should like a father/Whom I have never known and
516 CC	Claude	31	able to fulfil them./Believe, if you like, that I am not your father:/I'll accept that. I
517 CC	Colby	10	that/I should be guilty towards you. I like you too much./You've become a man
517 CC	Colby	37	*I* am the Vicar's Warden./{C} I'd like to apply./{E} The stipend is small —/Very
519 CC	Kaghan	16	our children./{K} And we should like to understand *you* .../I mean, I'm including
519 CC	Kaghan	20	Claude, both Lucasta and I/Would like to mean something to you ... if you'd let us;
524 ES	Monica	17	/But I know what men are — they like to show off./That's masculine vanity, to
524 ES	Charles	21	with him./{C} Well, tease me if you like. But a man does feel a fool/If he takes you
525 ES	Monica	9	expedition .../{M} If you don't like shopping with me .../{C} Of course I like
525 ES	Charles	10	shopping with me .../{C} Of course I like shopping with you./But how can one *talk*
529 ES	Monica	7	he was your age — when he started like you,/With the same hopes, the same
529 ES	Ld Clav	31	looked at this book — or one just like it —/You know I keep the old ones on a
530 ES	Ld Clav	12	take life easily. Take life easily!/It's like telling a man he mustn't run for trains/
530 ES	Ld Clav	20	and no desire to fill it./It's just like sitting in an empty waiting room/In a
532 ES	Ld Clav	12	I'm sorry to turn you out of the room like this,/But I'll have to see this man by myself,
533 ES	Gomez	14	/Curiosity, restlessness, whatever you like./But I've been a pretty hard worker all these
533 ES	Gomez	18	come for./You see, I'm a widower, like you, Dick./So I'm pretty footloose. Gomez,
534 ES	Gomez	34	don't know what serious politics is like!/I said to my boys: 'Never touch politics./
535 ES	Ld Clav	24	A reformed character!/{LC} I should like to know why you need to trust *me*./{G}
535 ES	Gomez	27	Can you imagine/What it would be like to have been away from home/For
536 ES	Gomez	18	God, Dick, *you* don't know what it's like/To be so cut off! Homesickness!/
536 ES	Gomez	26	—/Everybody knows what that's like./Your loneliness — so cosy, warm and
539 ES	Gomez	35	become the history master/In a school like that from which I went to Oxford./As it is,
543 ES	Monica	20	alone with me tonight,/What will it be like at Badgley Court? {}/CURTAIN/Act Two/
545 ES	Ld Clav	17	that very ominous. When people talk like that/It indicates a latent desire to interfere/

546 ES   Piggott   11 see, we've studied to avoid/Anything like a nursing-home atmosphere./We don't want
546 ES   Piggott   14   well —/Except when they come like you, Miss Claverton./{M} Claverton-Ferry.
546 ES   Piggott   29 They're all convalescents,/Or resting, like you. So you'll remember/Always to call me
547 ES   Piggott   30 /But there are one or two who don't like being beaten,/And that spoils any sport, in
553 ES   Carghil   29 They were very loving. Would you like to read them?/I'm afraid I can't show you
553 ES   Carghil   32 are quite as good, I'm told. And I like to read them/In your own handwriting./
554 ES   Piggott   15 Carghill,/Attending to my guests. I like to feel they *need* me!/{MC} You do look
556 ES   Monica   4 /And you know what Michael is like when he's frightened./He's apt to be sullen
558 ES   Michael   15 say?/{Mi} He took the usual line,/Just like the headmaster. And my tutor at Oxford./
559 ES   Ld Clav   11 suit you better./How would you like to go to Western Canada?/Or what about
560 ES   Michael   9 once I'm out of the country./What I'd like is a chance to go abroad/As a partner in
560 ES   Ld Clav   32 you/To find your feet. But I shouldn't like to think/That what inspired you was no
561 ES   Michael   14 years in dying./{Mi} Very well: if you like, call me a coward./I wonder whether you
561 ES   Monica   22   How can you speak to Father like that?/Father! What has happened? Why do
562 ES   Carghil   20 How did I know? Because you're so like your age. He's the
562 ES   Michael   33 of mine once./{Mi} Did he really look like me?/{MC} You've his voice! and his way of
564 ES   Carghil   19 looks that you were Spanish./I do like Spaniards. They're so aristocratic./But it's
565 ES   Carghil   16 — it's not far away./{MC} Then I'd like to walk a little way with you./{Mi}
567 ES   Charles   21 and that's very much what it looks like,/Do you think I could persuade him to
569 ES   Ld Clav   39 my spectral existence into something like reality./{M} But what did the ghosts mean?
573 ES   Carghil   33 You're a very lucky man, to get a girl like Monica./I take a great interest in her future.
573 ES   Carghil   36 only known her two days!/But I feel like a mother to her already./You may say that
583 ES   Charles   6 that words are so inadequate./Yet, like the asthmatic struggling for breath,/So the

LIKED (17)

123 SA   Doris   11   sea./{Do} I don't like eggs; I never liked eggs;/And I don't like life on your
218 Mung Rump   20   /They were plausible fellows, and liked to engage a friendly policeman in
602 Humoresque   6 /But this deceasèd marionette/I rather liked: a common face,/(The kind of face that we
241 MC   Mess   39 of France,/Who indeed would have liked to detain him in his kingdom:/But as for
242 MC   Priest1   21 as Chancellor, flattered by the King./Liked or feared by courtiers, in their
320 FR   Warburt   25 sorry for you, Harry./I should have liked to spare you this,/Just now. But there were
338 FR   Harry   13 /And to tell you that I would have liked to explain./{A} Why should Agatha know,
409 CP   Reilly   15   This injured your vanity./You liked to think of yourself as a passionate lover./
451 CC   Eggers   24 I was horrified./But she actually liked it. Muriel *is* her name./He has a way with
469 CC   Colby   15 /And you didn't like them. You liked the right ones./{L} Colby, I didn't know
469 CC   Lucasta   17 you were so artful!/So the things I liked were the right ones to like?/Still, I'm
476 CC   Lucasta   34 never could see/How Claude had ever liked her. Oh, that childhood —/Always living
477 CC   Lucasta   28 person I've forced myself to be;/and I liked you because you didn't like that person
485 CC   Lady E   2 me think so./But you know, I actually *liked* to believe/That I was a foundling — or do I
494 CC   Lady E   38 /And now you tell me, you'd have liked to be a potter!/You really mean, to make
513 CC   Colby   37 /By being the person he would have liked to be,/And by doing the things he had
537 ES   Gomez   30 This is how it worked out, Dick. You liked to play the rake,/But you never went too

LIKELY (19)

191 FQ: Little   22 way,/Taking the route you would be likely to take/From the place you would be
191 FQ: Little   23 to take/From the place you would be likely to come from,/If you came this way in
223 Pekes Pols   29   /There were surely a dozen, more likely a score./And together they started to
246 MC   Priest2   4 know that the good Archbishop/Is likely to arrive at any moment?/The crowds in
288 FR   Violet   1   /{V} Harry was always the most likely to be late./{A} This time, it will not be his
297 FR   Charles   17 myself./Nobody knows what he's likely to do/Until there's somebody he wants to
299 FR Downing   12 Sir, if I may say so./Much more likely to have been an accident./I mean,
299 FR Downing   18 it is those that talk/That are the least likely. To my way of thinking/She only did it to
317 FR   Warburt   14 prepared/For something that is very likely to happen./{H} O God, man, the things
323 FR   Winch   1 come round/In the morning, most likely, but he mustn't be moved./But Dr. Owen
325 FR   Charles   23 he's had at Brooklands,/*He*'s not likely to get into trouble./{G} A brilliant driver,
327 FR   Violet   37 this distance from London/Nobody's likely to have this evening's paper./{C} Stop, I
328 FR   Gerald   2 I said that Arthur was every bit as likely/To have an accident as John. And it
343 FR   Agatha   7 Harry. You and I,/My dear, may very likely meet again/In our wanderings in the
408 CP   Edward   20 not have chosen/Anyone I was less likely to suspect./And then he came to *me* to
455 CC   Colby   23 her. If anyone can./{C} But is she likely to be a nuisance?/{E} Not unless you give
528 ES   Monica   28   —/If he's hopeful, he's likely to live a little longer./That's why Selby
550 ES   Carghil   14 mistake in love,/You're more than likely to make another'./How true that is! Algy
576 ES   Charles   38 slander/To know that you are hardly likely to invoke it./And, Michael, here's another

LIKENESS (3)

472 CC   Lucasta   15 /To discover differences inside the likeness./You may *feel* insecure, in some ways
513 CC   Colby   33 /In which I should try to decipher a likeness;/Whose image I could create in my own
516 CC   Claude   33 upon you —/Except the claim of our likeness to each other./We have undergone the

LIKES (10)

210 Old Gumbie	14	/Her equal would be hard to find, she likes the warm and sunny spots./All day she sits
210 Old Gumbie	26	is Jennyanydots;/The curtain-cord she likes to wind, and tie it into sailor-knots./She
214 RTTugger	16	home, then he'd like to get about./He likes to lie in the bureau drawer,/But he makes
214 RTTugger	28	then he sniffs and sneers,/For he only likes what he finds for himself;/So you'll catch
228 Gus	17	Irving, he's acted with Tree./And he likes to relate his success on the Halls,/Where
362 CP Edward	16	well, I can't understand it./Nobody likes to be left with a mystery:/It's so ...
362 CP Reilly	19	Yes, it's unfinished;/And nobody likes to be left with a mystery./But there's more
425 CP Lavinia	32	you can do about it:/And everyone likes to be seen at a party/Where everybody else
440 CP Lavinia	31	then. And besides,/One sometimes likes to hear the same compliment twice./{E}
456 CC Eggers	24	/But she does forget things. And she likes to travel,/Mostly for her health. And when

LIKEWISE (2)

187 FQ: DrySal	109	wrong things,/Is not the question) are likewise permanent/With such permanence as
236 Cat Morgan	5	Square./I'm partial to partridges, likewise grouse,/And I favour that

LIL (1)

66 WL: Chess	145	I was there./You have them all out, Lil, and get a nice set,/He said, I swear, I can't

LIL'S (1)

65 WL: Chess	139	for a knock upon the door./When Lil's husband got demobbed, I said —/I didn't

LILAC (4)

19 Portrait	46	it in your hands';/(Slowly twisting the lilac stalks)/'You let it flow from you, you let it
92 Ash-Wed 3	18	brown hair over the mouth blown,/Lilac and brown hair;/Distraction, music of the
98 Ash-Wed 6	12	heart stiffens and rejoices/In the lost lilac and the lost sea voices/And the weak spirit
258 MC Thomas	13	curiosity,/The purple bullfinch in the lilac tree,/The tiltyard skill, the strategy of

LILACS (3)

19 Portrait	41	hour and drink our bocks./Now that lilacs are in bloom/She has a bowl of lilacs in
19 Portrait	42	lilacs are in bloom/She has a bowl of lilacs in her room/And twists one in her fingers
61 WL: Burial	2	/April is the cruellest month, breeding/Lilacs out of the dead land, mixing/Memory

LILY (1) [*Proper name*]

291 FR Ivy	3	/{I} I might have been visiting Cousin Lily at Sidmouth, if I had not had to come to

LIMB (2)

136 5FingerEx4	7	you faster and faster/And tear you limb from limb./How delightful to meet Mr.
136 5FingerEx4	7	and faster/And tear you limb from limb./How delightful to meet Mr. Hodgson!/

LIMBO'S (1)

602 Humoresque	13	maybe, to the moon./With Limbo's other useless things/Haranguing

LIMBS (4)

52 Whispers	7	knew that thought clings round dead limbs/Tightening its lusts and luxuries./Donne, I
598 Circe	6	and stain;/They sprang from the limbs of the dead. —We shall not come here
605 Narcissus	6	/I will show you his bloody cloth and limbs/And the gray shadow on his lips./He
605 Narcissus	9	the wind made him aware of his limbs smoothly passing each other/And of his

LIME (1)

149 Rock 1	83	*machines/And clay for new brick/And lime for new mortar/Where the bricks are fallen/*

LIMEY (1)

575 ES Michael	1	sneer at the fellow from London,/The limey remittance man for whom a job was

LIMIT (2)

276 MC Chorus	8	fire at daybreak,/These acts marked a limit to our suffering./Every horror had its
483 CC Colby	4	and that's the rarest./{C} That would limit my acquaintance to a very small number,/

LIMITATION (1)

175 FQ: BurntN	170	aspect of time/Caught in the form of limitation/Between un-being and being./Sudden

LIMITATIONS (1)

421 CP Julia	37	am saying./{J} You must accept your limitations./— But how much longer will Alex

LIMITED (3)

179 FQ: ECoker	83	is, it seems to us,/At best, only a limited value/In the knowledge derived from
348 FR Chorus	25	/Is a very restricted area./Except for a limited number/Of strictly practical purposes/
438 CP Reilly	29	beyond the intention/And beyond our limited understanding/Of ourselves and others,

LIMITS (4)

592 Grad 3	4	water's waste,/Some to the western limits of the sky/Which the sun stains with
482 CC Lady E	35	intellectual society./Now, that already limits your acquaintance:/Because, what's
502 CC Lucasta	37	What's so difficult/Is to recognise the limits of one's understanding./It may be that
583 ES Charles	4	/Oh my dear,/I love you to the limits of speech, and beyond./It's strange that

LIMOGES (1)

37 Gerontion	24	Mr. Silvero/With caressing hands, at Limoges/Who walked all night in the next

LIMP (1)

74 WL: Thund	395	rain/Ganga was sunken, and the limp leaves/Waited for rain, while the black

LINE (7)

103 Journ Magi	22	valley,/Wet, below the snow line, smelling of vegetation,/With a running
232 Skimble	1	Cat/There's a whisper down the line at 11.39/When the Night Mail's ready to
254 MC Tempt4	17	shade;/Think of pilgrims, standing in line/Before the glittering jewelled shrine,/From
497 CC Eggers	32	*She* doesn't know that./{E} A natural line for Mr. Simpkins to take,/If I may say so.
530 ES Ld Clav	21	/In a railway station on a branch line,/After the last train, after all the other
558 ES Michael	14	did he say?/{Mi} He took the usual line,/Just like the headmaster. And my tutor at
579 ES Michael	10	you see, he has friends in the shipping line/Who he thinks can be helpful in getting

LINED (2)

| 210 Old Gumbie | 11 | not nice;/So when she has got them lined up on the matting,/She teaches them |
| 226 Macavity | 13 | eyes are sunken in./His brow is deeply lined with thought, his head is highly domed;/ |

LINER (2)

| 188 FQ: DrySal | 144 | /And on the deck of the drumming liner/Watching the furrow that widens behind |
| 289 FR Charles | 27 | 'Well-known Peeress Vanishes from Liner'./{G} Yes, it's odd to think of her as |

LINERS (1)

| 300 FRDowning | 16 | my complaint against these ocean liners/With all their swimming baths and |

LINES (9)

135 5FingerEx1	t	their spears./Five-Finger Exercises/*Lines to a Persian Cat*/The songsters of the air
135 5FingerEx2	t	day delay?/*When* will Time flow away?/*Lines to a Yorkshire Terrier*/In a brown field
135 5FingerEx3	t	prior paws,/Pause, and sleep endlessly./*Lines to a Duck in the Park*/The long light
136 5FingerEx4	t	try/Our well-preserved complacency./*Lines to Ralph Hodgson Esqre.*/How delightful to
136 5FingerEx5	t	/(Everyone wants to know *him*)./*Lines for Cuscuscaraway and Mirza Murad Ali*
143 Lines OM	t	the sea-gull./The palaver is finished./*Lines for an Old Man*/The tiger in the tiger-pit/
263 MC	2m 27	of St. Stephen borne before him./*The lines sung are in italics.*]/{P1} Since Christmas a
279 MC Knight4	13	nothing to add along their particular lines of argument./What I have to say may be
334 FR Harry	27	made ready —/The book laid out, lines underscored, and the costume/Ready to be

LING (8)

116 SP phone	6	what you going to do?/{Tel} Ting a ling ling/Ting a ling ling/{Du} That's Pereira/
116 SP phone	6	you going to do?/{Tel} Ting a ling ling/Ting a ling ling/{Du} That's Pereira/{Do}
116 SP phone	7	to do?/{Tel} Ting a ling ling/Ting a ling ling/{Du} That's Pereira/{Do} That's
116 SP phone	7	do?/{Tel} Ting a ling ling/Ting a ling ling/{Du} That's Pereira/{Do} Yes that's
116 SP phone	11	what you going to do?/{Tel} Ting a ling ling/Ting a ling ling/{Du} That's Pereira/
116 SP phone	11	you going to do?/{Tel} Ting a ling ling/Ting a ling ling/{Du} That's Pereira/{Do}
116 SP phone	12	to do?/{Tel} Ting a ling ling/Ting a ling ling/{Du} That's Pereira/{Do} Well can't
116 SP phone	12	do?/{Tel} Ting a ling ling/Ting a ling ling/{Du} That's Pereira/{Do} Well can't you

LINGER (1)

| 592 Grad 1 | 2 | upon the shore of all we know/We linger for a moment doubtfully,/Then with a |

LINGERED (3)

13 Prufrock	18	into the corners of the evening,/Lingered upon the pools that stand in drains,/
17 Prufrock	129	the water white and black./We have lingered in the chambers of the sea/By sea-girls
269 MC Thomas	1	a mendicant on foreign charity/I lingered abroad: seven years is no brevity./I

LINGERS (1)

| 553 ES Carghil | 13 | /Pawed it, perhaps, and the touch still lingers./And I've touched yours./It's frightening |

LINING (1)

| 241 MC Mess | 33 | with scenes of frenzied enthusiasm,/Lining the road and throwing down their capes, |

LINK (1)

| 369 CP Edward | 19 | once —/But she herself had to be the link between them./That is why, I think, her |

LINTEL (2)

| 103 Journ Magi | 26 | to a tavern with vine-leaves over the lintel,/Six hands at an open door dicing for |
| 129 Cor2 State | 35 | there the clematis droops over the lintel/O mother (not among these busts, all |

LION (3)

212 Growltiger	28	stol'n away —/In the yard behind the Lion he was prowling for his prey./In the
273 MC Priests	27	You would bar the door/Against the lion, the leopard, the wolf or the boar,/Why not
274 MC Thomas	29	{T} It is the just man who/Like a bold lion, should be without fear./I am here./No

LION'S (1)

| 41 Burb Blei | 29 | Sir Ferdinand/Klein. Who clipped the lion's wings/And flea'd his rump and pared his |

LIONS (2)

| 159 Rock 6 | 9 | has conquered the World/And that lions no longer need keepers?/Do you need to |
| 438 CP Reilly | 13 | /Bowel trouble, and the fear of lions,/Cold of the night and heat of the day, |

LIONS' (3)

274 MC Knights	18	priest?/Come down Daniel to the lions' den,/Come down Daniel for the mark of
274 MC Knights	22	the beast?/Come down Daniel to the lions' den,/Come down Daniel and join in the
274 MC Knights	26	priest?/Come down Daniel to the lions' den,/Come down Daniel and join in the

LIPLESS (1)

| 52 Whispers | 4 | ground/Leaned backward with a lipless grin./Daffodil bulbs instead of balls/ |

LIPS (7)

84 Hollow Men	50	we are/Trembling with tenderness/Lips that would kiss/Form prayers to broken
110 Marina	32	for that unspoken,/The awakened, lips parted, the hope, the new ships./What seas
154 Rock 3	9	set up commissions,/I have given you lips, to express friendly sentiments,/I have given
189 FQ: DrySal	184	their voyage on the sand, in the sea's lips/Or in the dark throat which will not reject
592 Grad 1	3	/Then with a song upon our lips, sail we/Across the harbor bar — no chart
599 On a Port	10	glad or ominous/Disturb her lips, or move the slender hands;/Her dark eyes
605 Narcissus	7	limbs/And the gray shadow on his lips./He walked once between the sea and the

LIQUID (2)

57 Swee Night	39	cried aloud/And let their liquid siftings fall/To stain the stiff dishonoured
64 WL: Chess	88	perfumes,/Unguent, powdered, or liquid — troubled, confused/And drowned the

LIQUOR (1)

103 Journ Magi	12	And running away, and wanting their liquor and women,/And the night-fires going

LIST (1)

558 ES Ld Clav	28	does this bring us to the end of the list of your shortcomings?/Or did Sir Alfred

LISTEN (10)

91 Ash-Wed 2	23	the wind only for only/The wind will listen. And the bones sang chirping/With the
149 Rock 1	78	me show you the work of the humble. Listen./*The lights fade; in the semi-darkness the*
224 Mr Mistoff	4	can be no doubt about that)./Please listen to me and don't scoff. All his/Inventions
303 FR Mary	27	of what to say to John,/Or having to listen to Arthur's chatter/When he thinks he is
329 FR Chorus	26	it is nearly time for the news/We must listen to the weather report/And the
372 CP Peter	5	/{P} Yes, I'm sure that she would listen to you/As someone disinterested./{E}
451 CC Eggers	4	hit it off with Lady Elizabeth./Don't listen to him. He understands Sir Claude,/And
499 CC Lucasta	19	I might as well make it now. If you'll listen./{SC} Of course I'll listen. But we haven't
499 CC Claude	20	If you'll listen./{SC} Of course I'll listen. But we haven't much time./{L} It won't
530 ES Monica	31	/And the speeches that you had to listen to! {}/[*pointing to a silver salver, still lying*

LISTENED (4)

312 FR Harry	4	you were so obtuse, I would not have listened/To your nonsense. Can't you help me?/
382 CP Celia	12	as if I had unwrapped a mummy./I listened to your voice, that had always thrilled
382 CP Celia	18	grasshoppers do it. I looked,/And listened for your heart, your blood;/And saw
469 CC Lucasta	23	times,/But I'm afraid I never really listened to the music:/I just enjoyed going — to

LISTENER (1)

353 CP Celia	25	never heard it./{C} Here's one new listener for you, Julia;/And I don't believe that

LISTENING (8)

186 FQ: DrySal	67	boat with a slow leakage,/The silent listening to the undeniable/Clamour of the bell
328 FR Chorus	34	/{Ch} In an old house there is always listening, and more is heard than is spoken./
353 CP Alex	6	perfectly hopeless. You haven't been listening./{P} You'll have to tell us all over
355 CP Peter	19	/{P} But do go on. Edward wasn't listening anyway./{J} No, he wasn't listening,
355 CP Julia	20	listening anyway./{J} No, he wasn't listening, but he's such a strain —/Edward
356 CP Julia	32	you talk. Perhaps she's in the pantry/Listening to all we say!/{E} No, she's not in the
396 CP Edward	2	way of passing the evening/Than listening to the gramophone./{L} We have very
579 ES Carghil	15	—/On my part, I mean. Are you listening to me, Richard?/You look very

LISTENS (1)

457 CC	m 20	that? {}/[*Opens door on to landing and listens*]/{SC} She's here, Eggerson! That's her

LISTLESSNESS (1)

141 Rannoch	6	cold or moon hot. The road winds in/Listlessness of ancient war,/Languor of broken

LIT (3)

129 Cor2 State	30	Roman,/Remarkably like each other, lit up successively by the flare/Of a sweaty
161 Rock 7	24	their march on the way that was lit by the light;/Often halting, loitering, straying,
204 de la Mare	10	nursery tea/And when the lamps are lit and curtains drawn/Demand some poetry,

LITAUEN (1)

61 WL: Burial	12	/Bin gar keine Russin, stamm' aus Litauen, echt deutsch./And when we were

LITERALLY (2)

426 CP Julia	29	Well, my dears, and here I am!/I seem *literally* to have caught you napping!/I know I'm
473 CC Colby	32	/{C} Well, he retires to his garden — literally,/And also in the same sense that I retire

LITERARY (1)

367 CP Edward	28	in Celia./Apart, of course, from its literary merit/Which I don't pretend to judge./

LITHUANIAN (2)

354 CP Celia	8	unless she wants to./{C} Especially the Lithuanian accent./{J} Lithuanian? Lady
354 CP Julia	9	Especially the Lithuanian accent./{J} Lithuanian? Lady Klootz?/{P} I thought she was

LITTER (2)

154 Rock 3	19	roofing,/To be filled with a litter of Sunday newspapers?/1ST MALE
240 MC Chorus	23	the Son of Man be born again in the litter of scorn?/For us, the poor, there is no

LITTERED (1)

186 FQ: DrySal	72	that is oceanless/Or of an ocean not littered with wastage/Or of a future that is not

LITTLE (103)

26 Rhapsody	74	/Memory!/You have the key,/The	little lamp spreads a ring on the stair./Mount./
40 Burb Blei	1	with a Cigar/Burbank crossed a	little bridge/Descending at a small hotel;/
61 WL: Burial	7	/Earth in forgetful snow, feeding/A	little life with dried tubers./Summer surprised
67 WL: Fire S	194	damp ground/And bones cast in a	little low dry garret,/Rattled by the rat's foot
72 WL: Thund	330	who were living are now dying/With a	little patience/Here is no water but only rock/
92 Ash-Wed 2	49	/We are glad to be scattered, we did	little good to each other,/Under a tree in the
119 SP Klip	36	meet you all the same) —/London's a	little too gay for us/Yes I'll say a little too gay./
119 SP Klip	37	a little too gay for us/Yes I'll say a	little too gay./{Kr} Yes London's a little too gay
119 SP Krum	38	a little too gay./{Kr} Yes London's a	little too gay for us/Don't think I mean
121 SA Sweeney	5	be the missionary!/You'll be my	little seven stone missionary!/I'll gobble you up.
121 SA Sweeney	13	I'll convert you!/Into a stew./A nice	little, white little, missionary stew./{Do} You
121 SA Sweeney	13	you!/Into a stew./A nice little, white	little, missionary stew./{Do} You wouldn't eat
121 SA Sweeney	16	eat me!/{S} Yes I'd eat you!/In a nice	little, white little, soft little, tender little,/Juicy
121 SA Sweeney	16	Yes I'd eat you!/In a nice little, white	little, soft little, tender little,/Juicy little, right
121 SA Sweeney	16	you!/In a nice little, white little, soft	little, tender little,/Juicy little, right little,
121 SA Sweeney	16	little, white little, soft little, tender	little,/Juicy little, right little, missionary stew./
121 SA Sweeney	17	little, soft little, tender little,/Juicy	little, right little, missionary stew./You see this
121 SA Sweeney	17	little, tender little,/Juicy little, right	little, missionary stew./You see this egg/You see
123 SA Kl&Kr	13	SWARTS AS BEFORE/{Kl&Kr} *My*	*little island girl/My little island girl/I'm going to*
123 SA Kl&Kr	14	/{Kl&Kr} *My little island girl/My*	*little island girl/I'm going to stay with you/And*
129 Cor2 State	47	night./Come with the sweep of the	little bat's wing, with the small flare of the
133 Eyes	13	/Where, as in this,/The eyes outlast a	little while/A little while outlast the tears/And
133 Eyes	14	this,/The eyes outlast a little while/A	little while outlast the tears/And hold us in
135 5FingerEx2	6	Screamed, rattled, muttered endlessly./Little dog was safe and warm/Under a cretonne
135 5FingerEx2	13	undertakers, come to dust./Here a	little dog I pause/Heaving up my prior paws,/
155 Rock 3	51	with numbered doors/Or a house a	little better than your neighbour's;/When the
167 Rock 10	42	/Therefore we thank Thee for our	little light, this is dappled with shadow./We
167 Rock 10	44	Light, we may set thereon the	little lights for which our bodily vision is made./
173 FQ: BurntN	86	past and time future/Allow but a	little consciousness./To be conscious is not to be
177 FQ: ECoker	27	the music/Of the weak pipe and the	little drum/And see them dancing around the
191 FQ: Little	t	yew-tree)/The life of significant soil./Little Gidding/Midwinter spring is its own
195 FQ: Little	163	/And comes to find that action of	little importance/Though never indifferent.
218 Mung Rump	6	Square —/They had really a	little more reputation than a couple of cats can
228 Gus	29	/I have sat by the bedside of poor	Little Nell;/When the Curfew was rung, then I
233 Skimble	33	pleasant when you have found your	little den/With your name written up on the
233 Skimble	39	to make a breeze./There's a funny	little basin you're supposed to wash your face in
235 Ad-dress	54	treat you as a trusted friend,/Some	little token of esteem/Is needed, like a dish of
603 Spleen	11	this dull conspiracy./And Life, a	little bald and gray,/Languid, fastidious, and
240 MC Chorus	2	shy and cautious, tries to compile a	little fortune,/And the labourer bends to his
245 MC Thomas	37	attentions./These are small matters. Little rest in Canterbury/With eager enemies
246 MC Thomas	16	But do they follow after?/{T} For a	little time the hungry hawk/Will only soar and
247 MC Thomas	16	happen again and again./Men learn	little from others' experience./But in the life of
286 FR Gerald	8	climate/For a man who can exercise a	little common prudence;/And your servants
288 FR Agatha	26	thought to creep back through the	little door./He will find a new Wishwood.
290 FR Gerald	19	the last eight years./{G} That will be a	little difficult./{V} Nonsense, Gerald!/You must
292 FR Charles	32	you;/Your cellar could do with a	little attention./{I} And you'll really have to find
298 FR Charles	37	now that we've seen him,/We're a	little worried about his health./He doesn't seem
303 FR Agatha	19	She only thought of asking him a	little while ago./{M} Well, there's something to
304 FR Mary	24	a tame daughter-in-law with very	little money,/A housekeeper-companion for her
324 FR Amy	27	get older, I am coming to think/How	little I have ever known./But I think your
327 FR Harry	23	/But always the filthiness, that lies a	little deeper ... {}/[Enter IVY]/{I} Where is there
328 FR Charles	27	make capital out of./{C} There's a	little more. 'The Piper family ...' no, we needn't
329 FR Chorus	8	old pony/The stumble and the wail of	little pain/The chopping of wood in autumn/
333 FR Agatha	3	him./I can take no credit for a	little common sense,/He would have bungled it./
334 FR Agatha	17	burden of all the family. And I am a	little frightened./{H} You, frightened! I can
334 FR Agatha	40	/{Ag} I only looked through the	little door/When the sun was shining on the
335 FR Harry	35	my dear, and you walked through the	little door/And I ran to meet you in the
345 FR Harry	1	/Just now? I only want, please,/As	little fuss as possible. You must get used to it;/
361 CP Reilly	39	misunderstander/Arranging life a	little better than you like it,/Preferring not quite
362 CP Reilly	4	/And perhaps at times you will feel a	little jealous/That she saw it first, and had the
363 CP Reilly	14	granted,/As we have to, and live on a	little knowledge/About ourselves as we were.
368 CP Alex	13	what I'll do./I'm going to give you a	little surprise:/You know, I'm rather a famous
368 CP Alex	16	now/And I shall prepare you a nice	little dinner/Which you can have alone. And
368 CP Alex	26	the East./With a handful of rice and a	little dried fish/I can make half a dozen dishes.

370 CP	Edward	33	only know/How lucky you are. In a little while/This might have become an ordinary
372 CP	Alex	27	want is a cup of black coffee/And a little dry toast. I've left it simmering./Don't
375 CP	Edward	29	forgotten./He made his way in, a little while ago,/And insisted on cooking me
383 CP	Edward	13	bottle?/{E} It isn't empty. It may be a little flat —/But why did she say that it was a
386 CP	Celia	32	forgive my laughing./You look like a little boy who's been sent for/To the
395 CP	Lavinia	19	/{L} Oh, Edward, when you were a little boy,/I'm sure you were always getting
395 CP	Lavinia	29	get over it/And find yourself another little part to play,/With another face, to take
418 CP	Reilly	27	be described;/You will know very little until you get there;/You will journey blind.
428 CP	Julia	4	Mallington's monkey,/The horrid little beast — stole my ticket to Mentone/And I
435 CP	Peter	8	to think myself a success/And got a little more self-confidence;/And then I thought
447 CC	Claude	1	that for the present. As we have a little time/Before you start for Northolt — the
448 CC	Claude	2	I asked you to prepare him a little;/There are some things you could say
450 CC	Colby	35	this meeting./You've told me very little about Lady Elizabeth,/And Sir Claude
466 CC	Colby	36	/I was struck by what you said, a little while ago,/When you spoke of never
474 CC	Lucasta	37	what it stands for./You know, I'm a little jealous of your music!/When I see it as a
475 CC	Lucasta	19	to understand,/I'd like you to know a little more about me./You must have wondered.
476 CC	Lucasta	9	either?/{L} In one way, it matters. A little while ago/You said, very cleverly, that
477 CC	Lucasta	23	of me. I thought you'd understand./Little you know what it's like to be a bastard/
479 CC	Kaghan	25	her, Colby;/Assert your right to a little privacy./Now's the moment for firmness.
486 CC	Colby	24	own./That is to say, they had had one little boy/Who died when I was very young
508 CC	Guzzard	20	that./{MG} We parted with it. A dear little boy./I was happy to have him while the
509 CC	Colby	12	/{C} Barnabas Kaghan. Is he the little cousin/Who died? Don't you remember,
509 CC	Colby	15	/And your telling me I had had a little cousin/Who had died?/{MG} Yes, Colby,
510 CC	Kaghan	30	to the country./So I found them a little place near Sevenoaks/Where they keep
518 CC	Eggers	7	every day, you know,/For quite a little time, and I've watched you pretty closely./
522 ES	dedic	9	*to return as best I can/With words a little part of what you have given me./The words*
528 ES	Monica	28	—/If he's hopeful, he's likely to live a little longer./That's why Selby chose the place.
533 ES	Gomez	34	by experience whom to pay;/And a little money laid out in the right manner/In the
549 ES	Carghil	15	we had a tea basket/With some lovely little cakes — I've forgotten what you called
556 ES	Michael	16	two miles from here. Not a bad little place./{LC} Why are you staying there? I
557 ES	Ld Clav	14	/{LC} I dare say you've tried a little private speculation./{Mi} Several of my
562 ES	Carghil	14	of your letters;/But how nice to find a little family party!/I know who you are! You're
565 ES	Carghil	16	away./{MC} Then I'd like to walk a little way with you./{Mi} Delighted, I'm sure./
566 ES	Ld Clav	1	together./We'll sit side by side, at little desks/And suffer the same humiliations/At
569 ES	Ld Clav	10	/But I hope that you'll find a little love in your heart/Still, for your father,
575 ES	Gomez	27	morals:/Though of course you went a little *faster* than I did./{LC} On that point, Fred,
578 ES	Ld Clav	12	childhood,/When I think of the happy little boy who was Michael,/When I think of
580 ES	Carghil	17	We talked it all over./But I've got a little piece of news of my own:/Next autumn,
582 ES	Ld Clav	17	agreeable./You two ought to have a little time together./I leave Monica to you.

LITURGY (1)

531 ES	Ld Clav	11	Upper House .../{LC} The established liturgy/Of the Press on any conspicuous

LIVE (69)

91 Ash-Wed 2		5	skull. And God said/Shall these bones live? shall these/Bones live? And that which had
91 Ash-Wed 2		6	these bones live? shall these/Bones live? And that which had been contained/In the
105 Song Sime		13	shall remember my house, where shall live my children's children/When the time of
110 Marina		30	This form, this face, this life/Living to live in a world of time beyond me; let me/Resign
119 SP	Dusty	32	slick./{Du} Why don't you come and live here then?/{Kl} Well, no, Miss — er — you
120 SP	Krum	7	—/{Kr} Specially when you got a real live Britisher/A guy like Sam to show you
122 SAWa & Ho		18	*bamboo/Under the bamboo tree/Two live as one/One live as two/Two live as three/*
122 SAWa & Ho		19	*the bamboo tree/Two live as one/One live as two/Two live as three/Under the bam/*
122 SAWa & Ho		20	*/Two live as one/One live as two/Two live as three/Under the bam/Under the boo/Under*
124 SA Sweeney		36	did he do?/That don't apply./Talk to live men about what they do./He used to come
150 Rock 1		112	*/If men do not build/How shall they live?/When the field is tilled/And the wheat is*
152 Rock 2		44	of Christ incarnate./And now you live dispersed on ribbon roads,/And no man
159 Rock 6		4	persecution./It is hard for those who live near a Bank/To doubt the security of their
159 Rock 6		6	their money./It is hard for those who live near a Police Station/To believe in the
177 FQ: ECoker		9	and beast, cornstalk and leaf./Houses live and die: there is a time for building/And a
195 FQ: Little		158	lives — unflowering, between/The live and the dead nettle. This is the use of
196 FQ: Little		214	power cannot remove./We only live, only suspire/Consumed by either fire or
590 Time Space		6	why, Love, should we ever pray/To live a century?/The butterfly that lives a day/
590 Space Time		5	/Has lived as long as we./But let us live while yet we may,/While love and life are
605 Narcissus		17	by such knowledge/He could not live men's ways, but became a dancer before
244 MC Chorus		28	the pattern of fate, the small folk who live among small things,/The strain on the brain
270 MC Chorus		2	the whelk and the prawn; and they live and spawn in my bowels, and my bowels
279 MC Knight4		27	witnesses, that he had not long to live, and/that he would be killed in England. He

287	FR	Gerald	4	left them such an easy world to live in./Let the younger generation speak for
287	FR	Amy	28	together,/To keep me alive, and I live to keep them./You none of you understand
295	FR	Harry	24	is diseased, but the world I have to live in./— I lay two days in contented
314	FR	Warburt	38	I never saw a man/More anxious to live./{H} Not at all extraordinary./It is really
318	FR	Warburt	22	in the future,/For the time she has to live: not with the past./{H} Oh, is there any
319	FR	Warburt	17	by mutual consent/And he went to live abroad. You were only a boy/When he
320	FR	Warburt	14	and avoiding all excitement/She may live several years. A sudden shock/Might send
320	FR	Warburt	28	her happy for the time she has to live./The other is yourself: the future of
326	FR	Harry	29	knew the years that I have had to live/Since I came home, a few hours ago, to
334	FR	Harry	38	/Of the insane mind! Now I can live in public./Liberty is a different kind of pain
340	FR	Amy	14	at least a memory/Of something to live upon. You knew that you took everything/
342	FR	Agatha	34	That is his privilege./For those who live in this world, this world only,/Do you think
346	FR	Downing	26	what I mean:/We most of us seem to live according to circumstance,/But with people
357	CP	Julia	30	say Hampstead./{J} But she must live somewhere./{E} She lives in Essex./{J}
363	CP	Reilly	14	for granted,/As we have to, and live on a little knowledge/About ourselves as we
392	CP	Lavinia	30	Julia./But how did the aunt come to live in Essex?/{E} Julia compelled me to make
392	CP	Edward	31	/{E} Julia compelled me to make her live somewhere./{L} I see. So Julia made her live
392	CP	Lavinia	32	/{L} I see. So Julia made her live in Essex;/And made the telegrams come
397	CP	Edward	12	took place. And now I must live with it/Day by day, hour by hour, for ever
403	CP	Edward	34	what she had done to me!/I cannot live with her — that is now intolerable;/I cannot
403	CP	Edward	35	— that is now intolerable;/I cannot live without her, for she has made me incapable/
403	CP	Edward	38	has made the world a place I cannot live in/Except on her terms. I must be alone,/
413	CP	Celia	19	delusions —/Except that the world I live in seems all a delusion!/But oughtn't I first
414	CP	Celia	15	about your parents?/{C} Oh, they live in the country,/Now they can't afford to
414	CP	Reilly	19	long, they won't leave it./{R} And you live in London?/{C} I share a flat/With a cousin:
418	CP	Celia	11	is. I don't want to forget it./I want to live with it. I could do without everything,/Put
437	CP	Reilly	11	*shadows of all forms that think and live/Till death unite them and they part no more!/*
439	CP	Reilly	6	Celia./{R} You will have to live with these memories and make them/Into
462	CC	Colby	22	seem quite honest./If we all have to live in a world of make-believe,/Is that good for
466	CC	Claude	21	it seems to me, who have at best to live/In two worlds — each a kind of
479	CC	Kaghan	32	good impression; which he'll have to live down./— I must say, I like the way you've
480	CC	Kaghan	40	who might chuck it all/And go to live on a desert island./But I hope you won't do
485	CC	Lady E	24	than to anyone./— Where did you live, as a child?/{C} In Teddington./{LE}
491	CC	Colby	24	be. If it was pure fiction —/One can live on a fiction — but not on such a mixture/Of
491	CC	Colby	33	about those others?/I should have to live with those ghosts, one indignant/At being
510	CC	Guzzard	24	/{MG} And did they at one time live in Teddington?/{K} I believe they did. But
512	CC	Kaghan	30	than being a foundling —/If I can live up to it. And ... yes, of course,/If I can
513	CC	Colby	35	I could create in my own mind,/To live with that image. An ordinary man/Whose
517	CC	Eggers	39	Very small, I'm afraid. Not enough to live on./We'll have to think of other ways/Of
528	ES	Monica	28	—/If he's hopeful, he's likely to live a little longer./That's why Selby chose the
533	ES	Gomez	7	in a modest way./You know, where *I* live, people do change their names;/And
551	ES	Carghil	4	memory, a kind of testimonial./Men live by forgetting — women live on memories./
551	ES	Carghil	4	/Men live by forgetting — women live on memories./Besides a woman has nothing
561	ES	Ld Clav	10	to greet you./You're all I have to live for, Michael —/You and Monica. If I lived
561	ES	Michael	19	one in particular,/So you'd nothing to live up to. Those standards of conduct/You've
582	ES	Ld Clav	4	/And in becoming no one, I begin to live./It is worth while dying, to find out what

LIVED (30)

29	Aunt Helen	2	Slingsby was my maiden aunt,/And lived in a small house near a fashionable square/
29	Aunt Helen	13	been so careful while her mistress lived./Cousin Nancy/Miss Nancy Ellicott/
152	Rock 2	40	community,/And no community not lived in praise of GOD./Even the anchorite who
220	Old Deut	1	Deuteronomy/Old Deuteronomy's lived a long time;/He's a Cat who has lived
220	Old Deut	2	lived a long time;/He's a Cat who has lived many lives in succession./He was famous
589	Fable	90	the monks grew most devout,/And lived on milk and breakfast food entirely;/Each
589	Fable	94	that time forth they did without,/And lived the admiration of the shire. We/Got the
590	Time Space	8	/The butterfly that lives a day/Has lived eternity./The flowers I gave thee when the
590	Space Time	4	be,/The fly that lives a single day/Has lived as long as we./But let us live while yet we
243	MC	Chorus	23	to happen./Seven years we have lived quietly,/Succeeded in avoiding notice,/
307	FR	Mary	22	the stupidity of older people —/They lived in another world, which did not touch me.
320	FR	Warburt	17	another woman/She would not have lived until now./Her determination has kept her
320	FR	Warburt	19	has kept her going:/She has only lived for your return to Wishwood,/For you to
331	FR	Agatha	33	/{Ag} Your father might have lived — or so I see him —/An exceptionally
379	CP	Celia	23	before we began,/And after that I lived in a present/Where time was meaningless,
462	CC	Claude	18	instead of being mine./She has always lived in a world of make-believe,/And the best
473	CC	Lucasta	9	of London — like the one where I lived/For a time, with my mother. I've no
474	CC	Lucasta	39	a world/More real than any *I've* ever lived in./And I'd like to understand *you.*/{C} I

481 CC	Lady E	21	/Is *right*, until the place has been lived in/By the person for whom it was
482 CC	Lady E	11	and Miss Angel./I can see you've lived a rather sheltered life,/And I've noticed
490 CC	Colby	20	don't understand/That when one has lived without parents, as a child,/There's a gap
494 CC	Lady E	37	only thinking/How strange to have lived with you, all these years,/And now you tell
533 ES	Ld Clav	10	easier to pronounce./{LC} Have you lived out there ever since ... you left England?/
534 ES	Gomez	11	/Of carrying on such business if I lived in England./I have the same standards of
546 ES	Piggott	4	Nurse,/And of course I've always lived in what you might call/A medical milieu.
555 ES	Ld Clav	24	after that last escapade of his,/I've lived in terror of his running over somebody./
561 ES	Ld Clav	11	for, Michael —/You and Monica. If I lived for twenty years/Knowing that my son
561 ES	Michael	21	/I wonder whether *you* have always lived up to them. {}/[MONICA *has entered*
561 ES	Monica	37	/For love within a family, love that's lived in/But not looked at, love within the light
570 ES	Ld Clav	11	understood each other./And so we lived, with a deep silence between us,/And she

LIVELY (1)

385 CP	Reilly	12	ghosts: the grandmother,/The lively bachelor uncle at the Christmas party,/

LIVER (1)

91 Ash-Wed 2		3	fed to satiety/On my legs my heart my liver and that which had been contained/In the

LIVERPOOL (1)

496 CC	Eggers	27	/Of the papers that I picked up at Liverpool Street./But I've so much to do, in

LIVERYMEN (1)

127 Corl March		27	/And now come the Mayor and the Liverymen. Look/There he is now, look:/There

LIVES (24)

18 Portrait		26	Those qualities upon which friendship lives./How much it means that I say this to you
68 WL: Fire S		218	though blind, throbbing between two lives,/Old man with wrinkled female breasts,
106 Song Sime		34	/I am tired with my own life and the lives of those after me,/I am dying in my own
151 Rock 2		5	many are born to idleness, to frittered lives and squalid deaths, embittered scorn in
159 Rock 6		28	the martyrs not shed once for all,/The lives of the Saints not given once for all:/But the
163 Rock 8		29	/The broken standards, the broken lives,/The broken faith in one place or another,/
188 FQ: DrySal		140	escaping from the past/Into different lives, or into any future;/You are not the same
188 FQ: DrySal		162	moment)/Which shall fructify in the lives of others:/And do not think of the fruit of
195 FQ: Little		157	resembles life,/Being between two lives — unflowering, between/The live and the
213 Growltiger		39	sang their last duet, in danger of their lives —/For the foe was armed with toasting
220 Old Deut		2	time;/He's a Cat who has lived many lives in succession./He was famous in proverb
590 Time Space		7	/To live a century?/The butterfly that lives a day/Has lived eternity./The flowers I
590 Space Time		3	things that cannot be,/The fly that lives a single day/Has lived as long as we./But
247 MC Tempt1		36	friends. Be easy, man!/The easy man lives to eat the best dinners./Take a friend's
258 MC Thomas		8	the venial sin/Is the way in which our lives begin./Thirty years ago, I searched all the
277 MC Knight3		20	we shall have to/spend the rest of our lives abroad. And even when reasonable/people
339 FR	Harry	11	the sun and the icy vigil,/A care over lives of humble people,/The lesson of ignorance,
357 CP	Edward	31	But she must live somewhere./{E} She lives in Essex./{J} Anywhere near Colchester?
384 CP	Reilly	19	motion/Forces in your life and in the lives of others/Which cannot be reversed. That
402 CP	Reilly	4	worse. You might have ruined three lives/By your indecision. Now there are only
418 CP	Reilly	23	seen it,/Illustrated, more or less, in lives of those about us./The second is unknown,
419 CP	Reilly	30	one disappears. They lead very active lives/Very often, in the world./{C} How soon
473 CC	Colby	39	the world outside it. If you have two lives/Which have nothing whatever to do with
505 CC	Claude	4	who recently retired./Now he lives ... in the country. But he knows the whole

LIVING (74)

62 WL: Burial		40	and my eyes failed, I was neither/Living nor dead, and I knew nothing,/Looking
72 WL: Thund		328	over distant mountains/He who was living is now dead/We who were living are now
72 WL: Thund		329	was living is now dead/We who were living are now dying/With a little patience/Here
107 Animula		21	not, desire and control./The pain of living and the drug of dreams/Curl up the small
107 Animula		31	disordered papers in a dusty room;/Living first in the silence after the viaticum./
110 Marina		30	caulking./This form, this face, this life/Living to live in a world of time beyond me; let
139 Virginia		9	/White trees, wait, wait,/Delay, decay. Living, living,/Never moving. Ever moving/Iron
139 Virginia		9	wait, wait,/Delay, decay. Living, living,/Never moving. Ever moving/Iron
147 Rock 1		14	/Where is the Life we have lost in living?/Where is the wisdom we have lost in
162 Rock 8		21	routes;/Many left their souls in Syria,/Living on, sunken in moral corruption;/Many
164 Rock 9		19	practical shapes of all that is living or lifeless/Joined with the artist's eye, new
175 FQ: BurntN		141	/Only in time; but that which is only living/Can only die. Words, after speech, reach/
177 FQ: ECoker		10	is a time for building/And a time for living and for generation/And a time for the
178 FQ: ECoker		42	rhythm in their dancing/As in their living in the living seasons/The time of the
178 FQ: ECoker		42	their dancing/As in their living in the living seasons/The time of the seasons and the
182 FQ: ECoker		194	more complicated/Of dead and living. Not the intense moment/Isolated, with
185 FQ: DrySal		60	to itself the emotionless/Years of living among the breakage/Of what was
191 FQ: Little		13	There is no earth smell/Or smell of living thing. This is the spring time/But not in
192 FQ: Little		51	the dead had no speech for, when living,/They can tell you, being dead: the

192 FQ:	Little	53	with fire beyond the language of the living./Here, the intersection of the timeless
243 MC	Chorus	25	quietly,/Succeeded in avoiding notice,/Living and partly living./There have been
243 MC	Chorus	25	in avoiding notice,/Living and partly living./There have been oppression and luxury,/
243 MC	Chorus	29	minor injustice./Yet we have gone on living,/Living and partly living./Sometimes the
243 MC	Chorus	30	injustice./Yet we have gone on living,/Living and partly living./Sometimes the corn
243 MC	Chorus	30	gone on living,/Living and partly living./Sometimes the corn has failed us,/
244 MC	Chorus	2	are lacking./Yet we have gone on living,/Living and partly living./We have kept
244 MC	Chorus	3	lacking./Yet we have gone on living,/Living and partly living./We have kept the
244 MC	Chorus	3	gone on living,/Living and partly living./We have kept the feasts, heard the
244 MC	Chorus	10	/Talked not always in whispers,/Living and partly living./We have seen births,
244 MC	Chorus	10	always in whispers,/Living and partly living./We have seen births, deaths and
257 MC	Chorus	17	/And meanwhile we have gone on living,/Living and partly living,/Picking together
257 MC	Chorus	18	meanwhile we have gone on living,/Living and partly living,/Picking together the
257 MC	Chorus	18	gone on living,/Living and partly living,/Picking together the pieces,/Gathering
270 MC	Chorus	1	I have eaten/Smooth creatures still living, with the strong salt taste of living things
270 MC	Chorus	1	living, with the strong salt taste of living things under the sea; I have tasted/The
270 MC	Chorus	2	under the sea; I have tasted/The living lobster, the crab, the oyster, the whelk
270 MC	Chorus	20	our brains,/Is woven like a pattern of living worms/In the guts of the women of
276 MC	Chorus	2	The personal loss, the general misery,/Living and partly living;/The terror by night
276 MC	Chorus	2	the general misery,/Living and partly living;/The terror by night that ends in daily
281 MC	Chorus	12	would not exist./They affirm Thee in living; all things affirm Thee in living; the bird
281 MC	Chorus	12	in living; all things affirm Thee in living; the bird in the air, both the hawk and the
285 FR	Charles	25	has been too long used to our ways/Living with horses and dogs and guns/Ever to
293 FR	Ivy	13	Harry's back, is the time to think of living./{H} Time and time and time, and change,
296 FR	Charles	25	let this notion grow in his mind,/Living among strangers, with no one to talk to./
304 FR	Agatha	38	And it could not have been easy,/Living with Harry. It's not what she did to
324 FR	Harry	34	what it is to be awake,/To be living on several planes at once/Though one
330 FR	Harry	9	/Of Wishwood, being unconscious, living in gentle motion/Of horses, and right
334 FR	Agatha	9	at the beginning. It is as if/I had been living all these years upon my capital,/Instead of
334 FR	Agatha	11	I am old, to start again to make my living./{H} But you are not unhappy, just now?/
344 FR	Violet	16	mind .../{V} You can't really think of *living* in a tropical climate!/{G} There's nothing
348 FR	Chorus	11	understand the ordinary business of living,/We know how to work the machine,/We
357 CP	Julia	39	must let me be *your* maiden aunt —/Living on an annuity, of course./I am going to
362 CP	Reilly	24	to the status of an object —/A living object, but no longer a person./It's always
430 CP	Peter	33	/{P} You must have been living a quiet life!/Don't you go to the movies?/
435 CP	Lavinia	33	We none of us did./What you've been living on is an image of Celia/Which you made
446 CC	Eggers	22	No doubt that's best. While he's still living/With his aunt in Teddington, and coming
453 CC	Lucasta	10	girl like me/Is often very hungry — living on a pittance —/Cooking a sausage on a
459 CC	Lady E	14	/{LE} I prefer Colby./Where are you living?/{SC} His home's outside London./But I
464 CC	Claude	10	is, decoration as a background for living;/For me, they are life itself. To be among
464 CC	Claude	12	things,/If it is an escape, is escape into living,/Escape from a sordid world to a pure
473 CC	Lucasta	12	even a person:/Nothing but a bit of living matter/Floating on the surface of the
476 CC	Lucasta	35	her. Oh, that childhood —/Always living in seedy lodgings/And being turned out
484 CC	Lady E	14	your parents .../But was your father living?/{C} I never knew my father./{LE} Then,
490 CC	Colby	37	—/If you are my mother — was a living fact./Now, it is a dead fact, and out of
490 CC	Colby	39	fact, and out of dead facts/Nothing living can spring. Now, it is too late./I never
505 CC	Eggers	28	was struck by your name and your living in Teddington./And now we must go
509 CC	Lady E	18	what I told you./{LE} So my child is living. I was sure of that./But I believe that
510 CC	Eggers	5	/And if Mr. and Mrs. Kaghan are still living/Mrs. Guzzard should be able to identify
510 CC	Eggers	28	Kaghan, are your adoptive parents living?/{K} In Kent. They wanted to retire to the
544 ES	Ld Clav	28	Perhaps I've never really enjoyed living/As much as most people. At least, as they
550 ES	Ld Clav	19	Just what I needed./{LC} Is he still living?/{MC} He had a weak heart./And he
558 ES	Michael	23	superfluous;/They knew I couldn't be living on my pay;/They had a lot of fun with me
569 ES	Ld Clav	36	it was not till lately that I found the living persons/Whose ghosts tormented me, to
583 ES	Charles	22	dead has poured out a blessing on the living./{M} Age and decrepitude can have no

LIZARD (1)

335 FR	Harry	26	the clasping branches/And the giant lizard. To and fro./Until the chain breaks./The

LIZZIE (6)

454 CC	Lucasta	3	Northolt./{L} You're going to meet Lizzie?/{E} I am meeting Lady Elizabeth at
454 CC	Colby	30	/{C} And does she call Lady Elizabeth *Lizzie*?/{E} Well, not in her presence. Not when
454 CC	Eggers	32	think she would. But she does call her Lizzie,/Sometimes, to Sir Claude. And do you
479 CC	Kaghan	6	of man-eating tigers/Like you and Lizzie, he's got to have protection./{L} Colby
479 CC	Lucasta	8	far as I'm concerned, B. And as for Lizzie,/You'd better not get in *her* way when
479 CC	Kaghan	23	depends, of course, on preventing Lizzie/From always interfering. Be firm with

LOAM (1)
178 FQ: ECoker 38   feet in clumsy shoes,/Earth feet, loam feet, lifted in country mirth/Mirth of those
LOATHE (3)
381 CP   Celia 21   that whatever happens/I shall not loathe you. I shall only feel sorry for you./It's
410 CP   Lavinia 11   /Might be just enough to make us loathe one another./{R} See it rather as the
484 CC   Lady E 12   No. By my aunt./{LE} And did you loathe her? No, of course not./Or you wouldn't
LOATHED (4)
464 CC   Claude 33 in awe of him./I was wrong, in both. I loathed this occupation/Until I began to feel my
484 CC   Lady E   9   a governess;/Several, in fact. And I loathed them all./Were you brought up by a
488 CC   Claude 25   have told you one day./I've always loathed keeping such a thing from you./I see
495 CC   Lady E 25   I was escaping from a world that I loathed/In Tony — and then, too late, I
LOATHING (8)
242 MC   Priest1 27   drawing sustenance from generosity,/Loathing power given by temporal devolution,/
309 FR   Mary 23   what you feel. You attach yourself to loathing/As others do to loving: an infatuation/
329 FR   Chorus 12   the corridor/The moment of sudden loathing/And the season of stifled sorrow/The
330 FR   Harry 30   lack of emotion, as before: the same loathing/Diffused, I not a person, in a world not
381 CP   Celia 22   /It's only myself I am in danger of loathing./But what will your life be? I cannot
437 CP   Reilly 37   we should suffer/In fear and pain and loathing — all these together —/And reluctance
484 CC   Lady E 18   parents,/You can't understand what loathing really is./Yet we must have *some*
530 ES Ld Clav 18   waiting,/With no desire to act, yet a loathing of inaction./A fear of the vacuum, and
LOBELIAS (1)
155 Rock 3   31 My Word is unspoken,/In the land of lobelias and tennis flannels/The rabbit shall
LOBSTER (1)
270 MC Chorus   2 under the sea; I have tasted/The living lobster, the crab, the oyster, the whelk and the
LOBSTERPOT (1)
184 FQ: DrySal 23   losses, the torn seine,/The shattered lobsterpot, the broken oar/And the gear of
LOCAL (3)
278 MC Knight2 10 order: to curb the excessive/powers of local government, which were usually exercised
427 CP   Alex 31   been out on a tour of inspection/Of local conditions./{J} What about? Monkey nuts?
434 CP   Alex 23   to tell./But from what we know of local practices/It would seem that she must have
LOCK (5)
126 SA Chorus   4 wait for a knock and the turning of a lock/for you know the hangman's waiting for
212 Growltiger   11   /They would fortify the hen-house, lock up the silly goose,/When the rumour ran
256 MC   Priests 30   made fast, is the door under lock and bolt?/{4T} Is it rain that taps at the
473 CC Lucasta   3   garden; to which you can retire/And lock the gate behind you./{C} And lock the gate
473 CC   Colby   4   lock the gate behind you./{C} And lock the gate behind me?/Are you sure that you
LOCKED (3)
129 Cor2 State 32   Where the dove's foot rested and locked for a moment,/A still moment, repose of
356 CP   Julia 26   Lavinia/Except for the time she got locked in the lavatory/And couldn't get out. I
477 CC Lucasta   2   /When I was sent out. I've been locked in a cupboard!/I was only eight years old
LODGEMENT (1)
160 Rock 7   3 way and that, and finding no place of lodgement and germination./They followed the
LODGINGS (3)
155 Rock 3   48   shelters and institutions,/Precarious lodgings while the rent is paid,/Subsiding
476 CC Lucasta 35   childhood —/Always living in seedy lodgings/And being turned out when the
518 CC   Eggers 17 In Joshua Park, before you settled on lodgings;/We have a spare room. We should be
LOGGERHEADS (1)
527 ES   Monica 37 was too severe — so they're always at loggerheads./{C} But you spoke of several
LOGIC (2)
602 Humoresque 21 'Now in New York' — and so it goes./Logic a marionette's, all wrong/Of premises; yet
534 ES   Gomez   1 /{G} No, Dick, there's a fault in your logic./How can one corrupt those who are
LOGICAL (1)
429 CP   Alex 11   /{A} The native is not, I fear, very logical./{J} I wondered where you were taking
LOGS (1)
69 WL: Fire S 274 heavy spar./The barges wash/Drifting logs/Down Greenwich reach/Past the Isle of
LOIN (1)
51 Restaurant 28   courant de sous-mer l'emporta très loin,/Le repassant aux étapes de sa vie
LOITER (1)
280 MC Knight1   3 your homes./Please be careful not to loiter in groups at street corners, and do/
LOITERING (3)
67 WL: Fire S 180   are departed./And their friends, the loitering heirs of City directors;/Departed, have
161 Rock 7   25   was lit by the light;/Often halting, loitering, straying, delaying, returning, yet
193 FQ: Little 88   the smoke arose/I met one walking, loitering and hurried/As if blown towards me
LOLLING (1)
325 FR   Violet 36   so,/And you feel so conspicuous, lolling back/And so near the street, and

LONDON (57)

37 Gerontion	10	in Brussels, patched and peeled in	London./The goat coughs at night in the field
62 WL: Burial	62	a winter dawn,/A crowd flowed over	London Bridge, so many,/I had not thought
68 WL: Fire S	211	with a pocket full of currants/C.i.f.	London: documents at sight,/Asked me in
73 WL: Thund	375	/Jerusalem Athens Alexandria/Vienna	London/Unreal/A woman drew her long black
74 WL: Thund	426	/Shall I at least set my lands in order?/	London Bridge is falling down falling down
119 SP Dusty	22	in Bordeaux./{Du} Do you know	London well, Mr. Krumpacker?/{Kl} No we
119 SP Doris	26	won't be the last time./{Do} You like	London, Mr. Klipstein?/{Kr} Do we like
119 SP Krum	27	Mr. Klipstein?/{Kr} Do we like	London? do we like London!/Do we like
119 SP Krum	27	/{Kr} Do we like London? do we like	London!/Do we like London!! Eh what Klip?/
119 SP Krum	28	do we like London!/Do we like	London!! Eh what Klip?/{Kl} Say, Miss — er —
119 SP Klip	30	er — uh — London's swell./We like	London fine./{Kr} Perfectly slick./{Du} Why
120 SP Krum	9	around./Sam of course is at *home* in	London,/And he's promised to show us around.
147 Rock 1	19	nearer to the Dust./I journeyed to	London, to the timekept City,/Where the River
174 FQ: BurntN	113	wind that sweeps the gloomy hills of	London./Hampstead and Clerkenwell, Camden
246 MC Thomas	2	about us./Rebellious bishops, York,	London, Salisbury,/Would have intercepted our
246 MC Tempt1	30	/Old Tom, gay Tom, Becket of	London,/Your Lordship won't forget that
266 MC Knights	21	with pride./Creeping out of the	London dirt,/Crawling up like a louse on your
286 FR Charles	2	a single man like me is better off in	London:/A man can be very cosy at his club/
287 FR Amy	35	certain of Arthur and John,/Arthur in	London, John in Leicestershire:/They should
287 FR Amy	38	would come by air to Paris, and so to	London,/And hoped to arrive in the course of
327 FR Ivy	27	/That was Arthur, ringing up from	London:/The connection was so bad, I could
327 FR Violet	36	as well as I do, at this distance from	London/Nobody's likely to have this evening's
345 FR Harry	12	mother,/Will be care of the bank in	London until you hear from me./Good-bye,
349 FR Ivy	8	till after the funeral: will my ticket to	London still be valid?/{G} I do not look forward
352 CP m	11	MEN/*The scene is laid in*	London/Act One. Scene 1/*The drawing-room of*
353 CP 2m	1	*drawing-room of the Chamberlaynes'*	London *flat. Early evening.*/EDWARD
399 CP 2m	1	*consulting room in*	London. *Morning:/several weeks later.* SIR
414 CP Reilly	19	won't leave it./{R} And you live in	London?/{C} I share a flat/With a cousin: but
424 CP 2m	1	*drawing-room of the Chamberlaynes'*	London *flat. Two years later./A late afternoon in*
430 CP Julia	29	/We lead such a quiet life, here in	London,/{P} You always did enjoy a leg-pull,
445 CC 3m	1	*of* SIR CLAUDE MULHAMMER'S/*London house. Early afternoon.* SIR CLAUDE
445 CC Claude	2	/I'm sorry to have to bring you up to	London/All the way from Joshua Park, on an
445 CC Eggers	11	glad of the excuse for coming up to	London:/I've spent the morning shopping!
446 CC Eggers	38	in *The Times* about wild birds seen in	London:/And I'm sure Mr. Simpkins will find
459 CC Claude	15	you living?/{SC} His home's outside	London./But I want to have him closer at hand
460 CC Claude	39	/I seem to have brought you up to	London for nothing./{E} Oh, not for nothing! I
473 CC Lucasta	9	public square/In a shabby part of	London — like the one where I lived/For a
485 CC Colby	27	In what county?/{C} It's very close to	London./{LE} Still, you were brought up, like
496 CC Claude	15	sorry, Eggerson, to bring you up to	London/At such short notice./{E} Don't say
496 CC Eggers	21	used to complain/At my being up in	London five or six days a week:/But now she
496 CC Eggers	24	fact is, she misses the contact with	London,/Though she doesn't admit it. She
496 CC Eggers	30	/And really, now, I'm quite lost in	London./Every time I come, I notice the traffic/
523 ES m	11	*The drawing-room of Lord Claverton's*	London *house. Four o'clock in the afternoon/*
524 ES 2m	1	*of* LORD CLAVERTON'S	London *house. Four o'clock in the afternoon./*
525 ES Charles	1	grievance./On Monday you're leaving	London, with your father:/I arranged to be free
525 ES Charles	18	home every day. And you're leaving	London./And because your father simply can't
556 ES Ld Clav	14	I'm here? Did you drive down from	London?/{Mi} I drove down last night. I'm
563 ES Carghil	28	was a time, once, when everyone in	London/Knew the name of Maisie Montjoy in
563 ES Gomez	36	with things in England./Had I been in	London, and in Dick's position/I should have
565 ES Gomez	19	a holiday?/You're in business in	London, aren't you?/{Mi} Not a holiday, no.
565 ES Michael	20	a holiday, no. I've been in business in	London,/But I think of cutting loose, and going
567 ES Charles	11	that you need me./On that last day in	London, you admitted that you loved me,/But I
574 ES Michael	34	same sort of job/You got me here in	London? With another Sir Alfred/Who'd
574 ES Michael	37	would sneer at the fellow from	London,/The limey remittance man for whom a
575 ES Michael	9	created for me./Señor Gomez came to	London to find a man to fill it,/And he thinks
576 ES Michael	28	—/{Mi} I told you he'd come to	London looking for a man/For an important
579 ES Michael	8	buy my kit. We're just going up to	London./Señor Gomez will attend to my needs

LONDON'S (6)

119 SP Klip	29	Klip?/{Kl} Say, Miss — er — uh —	London's swell./We like London fine./{Kr}
119 SP Klip	36	pleased to meet you all the same) —/	London's a little too gay for us/Yes I'll say a
119 SP Krum	38	/Yes I'll say a little too gay./{Kr} Yes	London's a little too gay for us/Don't think I
120 SP Klip	5	it Klip?/{Kl} You said it, Krum./	London's a slick place, London's a swell place,/
120 SP Klip	5	said it, Krum./London's a slick place,	London's a swell place,/London's a fine place to
120 SP Klip	6	a slick place, London's a swell place,/	London's a fine place to come on a visit —/{Kr}

LONDRES (1)

47 Mél	Adult	6	piste./En Yorkshire, conférencier;/A Londres, un peu banquier,/Vous me paierez

LONELIER (1)

418 CP	Reilly	40	I suppose it is a lonely way?/{R} No lonelier than the other. But those who take the

LONELINESS (8)

282 MC	Chorus	8	/Who fear the blessing of God, the loneliness of the night of God, the surrender
332 FR	Agatha	19	childless, learning the meaning/Of loneliness. Your mother wanted a sister here/
419 CP	Reilly	1	who take the other/Can forget their loneliness. You will not forget yours./Each way
419 CP	Reilly	2	not forget yours./Each way means loneliness — and communion./Both ways avoid
478 CC	Lucasta	20	you're on the point of release/From loneliness, then loneliness swoops down upon
478 CC	Lucasta	20	point of release/From loneliness, then loneliness swoops down upon you;/When you
536 ES	Gomez	25	I do,/I've always been alone./{G} Oh, loneliness —/Everybody knows what that's like.
536 ES	Gomez	27	knows what that's like./Your loneliness — so cosy, warm and padded:/You're

LONELY (10)

15 Prufrock		72	smoke that rises from the pipes/Of lonely men in shirt-sleeves, leaning out of
22 Preludes		12	/And at the corner of the street/A lonely cab-horse steams and stamps./And then
332 FR	Agatha	17	and a woman/Married, alone in a lonely country house together,/For three years
380 CP	Celia	24	he had talent; I saw that he was lonely;/I thought that I could help him. I took
418 CP	Celia	39	frightened/But glad. I suppose it is a lonely way?/{R} No lonelier than the other. But
484 CC	Lady E	26	differences:/You must have been a lonely child, having no relatives —/No brothers
484 CC	Lady E	27	/No brothers or sisters — and I was lonely/Because they were so numerous — and
542 ES	Gomez	8	you a smoke now and then./I'm a lonely man, Dick, with a craving for affection./
572 ES	Monica	9	to share it with;/I never knew how lonely you were/Or why you were lonely./{C}
572 ES	Monica	10	lonely you were/Or why you were lonely./{C} And Mrs. Carghill:/What has she

LONG (106)

15 Prufrock		76	sleeps so peacefully!/Smoothed by long fingers,/Asleep ... tired ... or it malingers,/
66 WL: Chess		158	/I can't help it, she said, pulling a long face,/It's them pills I took, to bring it off,
67 WL: Fire S		184	run softly, for I speak not loud or long./But at my back in a cold blast I hear/The
73 WL: Thund		377	London/Unreal/A woman drew her long black hair out tight/And fiddled whisper
85 Hollow Men		83	response/Falls the Shadow/*Life is very long*/Between the desire/And the spasm/Between
103 Journ Magi		3	of the year/For a journey, and such a long journey:/The ways deep and the weather
104 Journ Magi		32	may say) satisfactory./All this was a long time ago, I remember,/And I would do it
135 5FingerEx3		1	/*Lines to a Duck in the Park*/The long light shakes across the lake,/The forces of
141 Rannoch		11	Pride snapped,/Shadow of pride is long, in the long pass/No concurrence of bone./
141 Rannoch		11	/Shadow of pride is long, in the long pass/No concurrence of bone./Cape Ann/O
149 Rock 1		76	/And some of the things that were long ago done,/That you may take heart. Make
167 Rock 10		37	as the rocket is fired; and the day is long for work or play./We tire of distraction or
172 FQ: BurntN		53	below inveterate scars/Appeasing long forgotten wars./The dance along the artery
173 FQ: BurntN		71	say where./And I cannot say, how long, for that is to place it in time./The inner
178 FQ: ECoker		39	lifted in country mirth/Mirth of those long since under earth/Nourishing the corn.
179 FQ: ECoker		74	/What was to be the value of the long looked forward to,/Long hoped for calm,
179 FQ: ECoker		75	value of the long looked forward to,/Long hoped for calm, the autumnal serenity/
180 FQ: ECoker		119	train, in the tube, stops too long between stations/And the conversation
212 Growltiger		25	/His bucko mate, GRUMBUSKIN, long since had disappeared,/For to the Bell at
220 Old Deut		1	/Old Deuteronomy's lived a long time;/He's a Cat who has lived many lives
220 Old Deut		4	in proverb and famous in rhyme/A long while before Queen Victoria's accession./
222 Pekes Pols		13	for nearly a week/(And that's a long time for a Pol or a Peke)./The big Police
225 Mr Mistoff		54	he was asleep in the hall./And not long ago this phenomenal Cat/Produced *seven*
227 Macavity		34	/Or engaged in doing complicated long division sums./Macavity, Macavity, there's
233 Skimble		63	to get out!/He gives you a wave of his long brown tail/Which says: 'I'll see you again!/
587 Fable		1	/A Fable for Feasters/In England, long before that royal Mormon/King Henry
590 Space Time		4	fly that lives a single day/Has lived as long as we./But let us live while yet we may,/
598 Circe		14	with the eyes/Of men whom we knew long ago./On a Portrait/Among a crowd of
253 MC Tempt4		11	cautiously, employ/Your services as long as you have to lend./You would wait for
254 MC Thomas		8	to tell you what you know./{T} How long shall this be?/{T4} Save what you know
263 MC Chorus		27	and the time is short/But waiting is long. {}/[*Enter the* FIRST PRIEST *with a*
276 MC Chorus		11	end:/In life there is not time to grieve long./But this, this is out of life, this is out of
279 MC Knight4		27	numerous witnesses, that he had not long to live, and/that he would be killed in
279 MC Knight4		34	he/could have kept himself from us long enough to allow our righteous/anger to
280 MC Priest3		16	fortified/By persecution: supreme, so long as men will die for it./Go, weak sad men,
285 FR Charles		24	people./Amy has been too long used to our ways/Living with horses and
299 FRDowning		29	that a very few cocktails/Went a long way with her Ladyship./She wasn't one of
301 FR Chorus		29	like to appear in the newspapers/So long as we are in the right column./We know
305 FR Harry		24	Not very./But, at least, it did not last long. How are you, Mary?/{M} Oh, very well.
309 FR Harry		31	Like someone who comes from a very long distance,/Or the distant waterfall in the

310 FR	Harry	32	were someone who had come from a long distance./Whether I know what I am
313 FR	Violet	4	/{V} Very well, I think, after such a long journey;/You know what a rush he had to
315 FR	Chorus	32	about to happen, and the future was long since settled./And the wings of the future
326 FR	Harry	23	/I was like that in a way, so long as I could think/Even of my own life as an
330 FR	Harry	2	again be sober, though not for very long;/And everything will go on as before.
331 FR	Harry	11	is./Here I have been finding/A misery long forgotten, and a new torture,/The shadow
332 FR	Agatha	22	at Oxford. I came/Once for a long vacation. I remember/A summer day of
336 FR	Agatha	3	and deceived in waking./You have a long journey./{H} Not yet! not yet! this is the
337 FR	Agatha	9	I think I was saying/That you have a long journey. You have nothing to stay for./
340 FR	Amy	2	/But I thought, thirty-five years is long, and death is an end,/And I thought that
346 FRDowning	14		certainly, Miss;/I'll never leave him so long as he requires me./{M} But he will need
346 FRDowning	21		that his Lordship won't need me/Very long now. I can't give you any reasons./But to
346 FRDowning	32		have a feeling/That he won't want me long, and he won't want anybody./{Ag} And,
347 FR	Agatha	13	will be wondering why you've been so long. {}/[Exit DOWNING. Enter IVY]/{I}
347 FR	Warburt	33	to be out in./That's why I've been so long, going and coming./But I'm glad to say
360 CP	Reilly	19	are. Now for a few questions./How long married?/{E} Five years./{UG} Children?/
362 CP	Reilly	3	only that you endured it for so long./And perhaps at times you will feel a little
364 CP	Reilly	12	in remaining in the dark/Except long enough to clear from the mind/The illusion
368 CP	Edward	2	have left it open./{E} Never mind;/So long as you both shut it when you go out./{A}
373 CP	Edward	3	Is Miss Celia Coplestone in? ... How long ago? .../No, it doesn't matter. {}/
381 CP	Edward	29	/I see that my life was determined long ago/And that the struggle to escape from it
390 CP	Julia	36	recovered, Alex —/And after that long journey on the old Great Eastern,/Waiting
404 CP	Reilly	9	you,/And letting you talk as long as you please,/And taking note of what
404 CP	Reilly	36	/Is it far to go?/{R} You might say, a long journey./But before I treat a patient like
409 CP	Reilly	35	to yourself,/I suspect, and for as long as you could,/That he was aiming at a
414 CP	Celia	18	going:/But it's been in the family so long, they won't leave it./{R} And you live in
456 CC	Eggers	29	some rare adventures!/I remember long ago, saying to Mrs. E.,/When we'd bought
462 CC	Claude	3	/So I feel pretty confident that, before long,/We can put matters onto a permanent
464 CC	Claude	40	I am sure,/That I cherished for a long time a secret reproach:/But after his death,
466 CC	Claude	10	I am alone, and look at one thing long enough,/I sometimes have that sense of
470 CC	Colby	19	music —/And that won't take you long — and hear good performers,/You'll very
490 CC	Lady E	28	mother and son,/No matter how long they have lost each other./{C} No, Lady
496 CC	Claude	4	/Health cures. And modern art — so long as it was modern —/And dervish dancing./
505 CC	Eggers	32	future both seem very brief —/But long enough ago for the question to be possible.
507 CC	Guzzard	20	/{MG} Very satisfactory —/So long, that is to say, as the money was
516 CC	Claude	18	remember a talk we had —/So very long ago! — when we shared our ambitions/
516 CC	Colby	38	you. But it is very different./As long as I believed that you were my father/I was
526 ES	Monica	10	and stood behind my back/Quietly, a long time, a long long time/Before I felt its
526 ES	Monica	10	my back/Quietly, a long time, a long long time/Before I felt its presence./{C}
526 ES	Monica	10	my back/Quietly, a long time, a long long time/Before I felt its presence./{C} Your
526 ES	Charles	34	a reminder/That I mustn't stay too long, for you belong to him./He seems so
527 ES	Lambert	14	at the moment. But he won't be very long. {}/[Exit]/{C} Don't you understand that
527 ES	Charles	16	that you're torturing me?/How long will you be imprisoned, alone with your
528 ES	Charles	34	/For this situation may persist for a long time,/And you'll go on postponing and
528 ES	Monica	36	marriage./{M} I'm afraid ... not a very long time, Charles./It's almost certain that the
529 ES	Monica	19	/{M} You've been very long in coming, Father. What have you been
531 ES	Charles	7	/That his sagacious counsel will long continue/To be at the disposal of the
533 ES	Gomez	16	I thought, now's the time to take a long holiday,/Let's say a rest cure — that's what
536 ES	Gomez	9	up/To the fact that Dick Ferry died long ago./I married a girl who didn't know a
536 ES	Gomez	34	Perfectly simple./My father's dead long since — that's a good thing./My mother —
541 ES	Gomez	38	distress./Well, I shan't keep you long, though I dare say your caller/Could hang
542 ES	Gomez	10	want is as much of your company,/So long as I stay here, as I can get./And the more I
550 ES	Carghil	12	ago, the first time. That didn't last long./People sometimes say: 'Make one mistake
553 ES	Ld Clav	1	writes it./{LC} Considering how long ago it was when you knew me/And
556 ES	Ld Clav	23	/Are you staying there long? For the whole of this holiday?/{Mi} Well,
557 ES	Ld Clav	31	on to the capital./{LC} And how long ago was that?/{Mi} Nearly two years./Time
558 ES	Michael	27	to sneer at me./I wonder I stood it as long as I did./{LC} And does this bring us to the
562 ES	Carghil	25	nothing to you, my dears./It's a very long time since the name of Maisie Montjoy/
564 ES	Carghil	12	you've known Lord Claverton/As long as I have, Señor Gomez./{G} My dear lady,
564 ES	Gomez	14	/To have known Dick Ferry as long as I have./We were friends at Oxford./
564 ES	Carghil	23	and I became great friends/Not long afterwards, didn't we, Richard?/{G} I
569 ES	Charles	19	persons who, she says, claim a very long acquaintance —/I was thinking that if
569 ES	Ld Clav	26	heard that word before,/Not so very long ago. When I asked him what he wanted./
573 ES	Charles	15	that./But what do you propose? How long, Lord Claverton,/Will you stay here and
573 ES	Carghil	38	/I've known her father for a very long time,/And there was a moment when I

574 ES   Carghil   1   when I almost married him,/Oh so long ago. So you see, Mr. Hemington,/I've
LONG-ESTABLISHED (1)
276 MC Knight1   25   case. That is in accordance with our long-established/principle of Trial by Jury. I am
LONG-LOST (1)
204 de la Mare   8   tree to tree —/The guardians of some long-lost treasure-trove)/Recount their exploits
LONGDRAWN (1)
164 Rock 9   4 must walk in black and go sadly, with longdrawn faces,/We must go between empty
LONGED (2)
464 CC   Claude   15   this ... remoteness I have always longed for./I want a world where the form is the
489 CC   Claude   13 keeping silent./I came to see how you longed for a son of your own,/And I thought,
LONGER (41)
89 Ash-Wed 1   5   man's gift and that man's scope/I no longer strive to strive towards such things/(Why
90 Ash-Wed 1   34   upon us/Because these wings are no longer wings to fly/But merely vans to beat the
104 Journ Magi   41   our places, these Kingdoms,/But no longer at ease here, in the old dispensation,/
159 Rock 6   9   the World/And that lions no longer need keepers?/Do you need to be told
161 Rock 7   42   the Church?/When the Church is no longer regarded, not even opposed, and men
179 FQ: ECoker   89   /Of that which, deceiving, could no longer harm./In the middle, not only in the
182 FQ: ECoker 179   better of words/For the thing one no longer has to say, or the way in which/One is no
182 FQ: ECoker 180 to say, or the way in which/One is no longer disposed to say it. And so each venture/
187 FQ: DrySal 133   time is no healer: the patient is no longer here./When the train starts, and the
223 Pekes Pols   38   /Then the Pugs and the Poms held no longer aloof,/But some from the balcony, some
228 Gus   8   quite the smartest of Cats —/But no longer a terror to mice and to rats,/For he isn't
258 MC Thomas 18   force is spent/And when we find no longer all things possible./Ambition comes
259 MC Thomas   5   be punished. So must you./I shall no longer act or suffer, to the sword's end./Now
261 MC Thomas 31   will in the will of God, and who no/longer desires anything for himself, not even the
263 MC Chorus   6   /Do the days begin to lengthen?/Longer and darker the day, shorter and colder
265 MC Knight4 34   tell His Lordship./{K4} How much longer will you keep us waiting? {}/[*Enter*
272 MC Thomas   6 of heaven, a whisper,/And I would no longer be denied; all things/Proceed to a joyful
272 MC Chorus   28   /Where those who were men can no longer turn the mind/To distraction, delusion,
272 MC Chorus   30 dream, pretence,/Where the soul is no longer deceived, for there are no objects, no
314 FR   Amy   4   of the family,/And he's known you longer than anybody, Harry./When he heard
314 FR   Warburt   9 doesn't get younger./It takes me back longer than you can remember/To see you
362 CP   Reilly   22   /You thought you were. You no longer feel quite human./You're suddenly
362 CP   Reilly   24 of an object —/A living object, but no longer a person./It's always happening, because
364 CP   Edward   1   morning when we had breakfast/I no longer remember what my wife is like./I am not
366 CP   Peter   35 This evening I felt I could bear it no longer./That awful party! I'm sorry, Edward;/Of
372 CP   Alex   28 I've left it simmering./Don't leave it longer than another ten minutes./Now I'll be
404 CP   Edward   18   what you mean./{E} I can no longer act for myself./Coming to see you —
414 CP   Celia   13   *everybody*. Do you know —/It no longer seems worth while to *speak* to anyone!/
421 CP   Julia   38   your limitations./— But how much longer will Alex keep us waiting?/{R} He should
429 CP   Alex   20 with a European/He is, as a rule, no longer fit to eat./{E} And what has your
453 CC   Eggers   38 I have some money, Eggy?/{E} I'm no longer in charge/And that duty has *not*
500 CC   Claude   14 There were reasons for that/Which no longer exist. But I ought to have told you./{L}
511 CC   Lucasta   2   don't need to talk that language any longer:/Just say you're embarrassed./{K} Well, I
518 CC   Guzzard   36 if I take my leave, Sir Claude?/I'm no longer needed here. {}/[*Exit* COLBY]/{SC}
528 ES   Monica   28   he's hopeful, he's likely to live a little longer./That's why Selby chose the place. A
542 ES   Gomez   11   as I can get./And the more I get, the longer I may stay./{LC} This is preposterous!/
552 ES   Ld Clav   35 you've always looked it./{LC} I've no longer any part to play, Maisie./{MC} There'll
559 ES   Michael   30 politics, not without dignity,/Being no longer wanted. And you wished to be Lord
568 ES   Ld Clav   39   part/I had chosen to play. And the longer we pretend/The harder it becomes to
570 ES   Ld Clav   25 /Who is Fred Culverwell?/{LC} He no longer exists./He's Federico Gomez, the Central
570 ES   Ld Clav   37   is Maisie Batterson?/{LC} She no longer exists./Nor the musical comedy star,
LONGEST (1)
197 FQ: Little   248   the beginning;/At the source of the longest river/The voice of the hidden waterfall/
LONGING (3)
306 FR   Harry   12   know yet./All these years I'd been longing to get back/Because I thought I never
530 ES   Ld Clav   14 anywhere!/No, I've not the slightest longing for the life I've left —/Only fear of the
544 ES   Monica   26 /With anxieties from which you were longing to escape;/Now I want to see you
LOOK (85)
62 WL: Burial   48   /(Those are pearls that were his eyes. Look!)/Here is Belladonna, the Lady of the
66 WL: Chess   146   set,/He said, I swear, I can't bear to look at you./And no more can't I, I said, and
66 WL: Chess   151   she said, and give me a straight look./HURRY UP PLEASE ITS TIME/If you
66 WL: Chess   156 /You ought to be ashamed, I said, to look so antique./(And her only thirty-one.)/I
71 WL: DWater 320 or Jew/O you who turn the wheel and look to windward,/Consider Phlebas, who was
73 WL: Thund   361   only you and I together/But when I look ahead up the white road/There is always

127 Cor1 March	27	come the Mayor and the Liverymen. Look/There he is now, look:/There is no
127 Cor1 March	28	Liverymen. Look/There he is now, look:/There is no interrogation in his eyes/Or in
151 Rock 2	6	turn out the palms of their hands, or look in vain towards foreign lands for alms to
160 Rock 7	14	they came to the withered ancient look of a child that has died of starvation./
167 Rock 10	32	/Our gaze is submarine, our eyes look upward/And see the light that fractures
172 FQ: BurntN	31	crossed, for the roses/Had the look of flowers that are looked at./There they
172 FQ: BurntN	35	empty alley, into the box circle,/To look down into the drained pool./Dry the pool,
187 FQ: DrySal	103	quite ineffable:/The backward look behind the assurance/Of recorded history,
193 FQ: Little	94	the waning dusk/I caught the sudden look of some dead master/Whom I had known,
195 FQ: Little	152	are three conditions which often look alike/Yet differ completely, flourish in the
225 Mr Mistoff	33	a spoon and a bit of fish-paste;/If you look for a knife or a fork/And you think it is
226 Macavity	9	seek him in the basement, you may look up in the air —/But I tell you once and
593 Grad 4	6	that we might know!/Would we might look into the future years./Great duties call —
598 Circe	13	walk, stately and slow,/And they look at us with the eyes/Of men whom we knew
247 MC Thomas	27	/I am your man./{T} Not in this train/Look to your behaviour. You were safer/Think
251 MC Tempt3	13	/With Henry the King. You look only/To blind assertion in isolation./That
275 MC Chorus	27	come, let the spring not come./Can I look again at the day and its common things,
280 MC Priest1	7	find you, from what far place/Do you look down on us? You now in Heaven,/Who
286 FR Gerald	9	prudence;/And your servants look after you very much better./{A} My
291 FR Harry	19	this blaze of light for all the world to look at?/If you knew how you looked, when I
291 FR Harry	26	all want to see you back, Harry./{H} Look there, look there: do you see them?/{G}
291 FR Harry	26	see you back, Harry./{H} Look there, look there: do you see them?/{G} No, I don't see
292 FR Harry	1	anyone about./{H} No, no, not there. Look there!/Can't you see them? *You* don't see
292 FR Harry	26	say that nothing is changed?/You all look so withered and young./{G} We must have
311 FR Harry	9	and me into it. O Mary!/Don't look at me like that! Stop! Try to stop it!/I am
311 FR Mary	8	and thought I might stay there./{M} Look at me. You can depend on me./Harry!
315 FR Violet	18	That I ever see your mother./{V} Yes, look at your mother!/Except that she can't get
321 FR Harry	2	of course I did./{H} What did he look like then? Did he look at all like me?/{W}
321 FR Harry	2	What did he look like then? Did he look at all like me?/{W} Very much like you. Of
321 FR Winch	32	at your jokes, I see. You don't look a year older/Than when I saw you last, my
323 FR Winch	2	was anxious that you should have a look at him./{W} Quite right, quite right. I'll go
323 FR Warburt	3	right, quite right. I'll go and have a look at him./We must explain to your mother ...
327 FR Ivy	26	what's the matter./{I} Somebody, look for Arthur in the evening paper./That was
333 FR Harry	38	under which we suffer./{H} Look, I do not know why,/I feel happy for a
346 FRDowning	17	strange, Miss, when you come to look at it:/After all these years that I've been
347 FR Ivy	15	is Downing going? where is Harry?/Look. Here's a telegram come from Arthur; {}/
347 FR Ivy	28	can't you explain?/Why do you all look so peculiar? I think I might be allowed/To
348 FR Chorus	6	/{Ch} We do not like to look out of the same window, and see quite a
349 FR Gerald	9	to London still be valid?/{G} I do not look forward with pleasure to dealing with
360 CP Reilly	23	/{UG} Children?/{E} No./{UG} Then look at the brighter side./You say you don't
366 CP Julia	2	Why aren't you looking for them?/Look on the mantelpiece. Where was I sitting?/
366 CP Julia	4	bottom of that sofa —/No, this chair. Look under the cushion./{E} Are you quite sure
369 CP Peter	34	she went to concerts alone/And to look at pictures. So we often met/In the same
383 CP Edward	7	well, hold on if you like;/We ... I'll look for them./{C} Yes, you look for them./I
383 CP Celia	8	We ... I'll look for them./{C} Yes, you look for them./I shall never go into your kitchen
386 CP Celia	32	Edward, forgive my laughing./You look like a little boy who's been sent for/To the
398 CP Lavinia	15	do about it./I ought to go and have a look in the kitchen./I know there are some eggs.
431 CP Peter	2	have pictures?/Pan-Am-Eagle must look into this./Perhaps it would be a good place
436 CP Julia	14	/{J} You must have learned how to look at people, Peter,/When you look at them
436 CP Julia	15	to look at people, Peter,/When you look at them with an eye for the films:/That is,
440 CP Edward	22	almost say, your best. But you always look your best./{L} Oh, Edward, that spoils it.
440 CP Lavinia	26	to cheer me up./To say I always look my best can only mean the worst./{E} I
458 CC Claude	4	and pick up some papers./We must look as if we'd been engaged in business. {}/
459 CC Lady E	8	think./You should be artistic. But you look rather frail./I must give you lessons in the
461 CC Eggers	19	the garden will really be a treat to look at.'/Well, I'll be going./{SC} Goodbye, and
466 CC Claude	10	see them!/But when I am alone, and look at one thing long enough,/I sometimes
478 CC Lucasta	29	away. I shall never/Never forget that look on your face/When I told you about
481 CC Lady E	18	/{LE} I've come over to have a look at the flat/Now that you've moved in.
483 CC Lady E	7	can be found./But I came to have a look at the flat/To see if the colour scheme
493 CC Claude	9	desk yourself?/{SC} No, that would look too formal. I thought it would be better/To
493 CC Claude	14	/{SC} On the other hand,/We mustn't look like a couple of barristers/Ready to
495 CC Lady E	22	/I know now that poets don't look like poets:/And financiers, it seems, don't
495 CC Lady E	23	poets:/And financiers, it seems, don't look like potters —/Is that what I mean? I'm
526 ES Monica	21	world —/The meanings are different. Look! We're back in the room/That we entered
529 ES Ld Clav	33	old ones on a shelf together;/I could look in the right book, and find out what I was

532	ES	Charles	24	coat?/{C} I'll say goodbye, sir./And look forward to seeing you both at Badgley
538	ES	Gomez	10	shall tell you why presently./Now let's look for a moment at *your* life history./You had
541	ES	Gomez	3	you'd get! The Press wouldn't look at it./Besides, you can't think I've any
547	ES	Piggott	7	be very treacherous./There, now you look more comfy. Don't let him stay out late/In
548	ES	Monica	8	to prowl about the grounds. Don't look so alarmed!/If you spy any guest who
552	ES	Carghil	33	/Is practically negligible. And you look the part./Whatever part you've played, I
554	ES	Carghil	16	to feel they *need* me!/{MC} You do look after us well, Mrs. Piggott:/You're so
555	ES	Monica	13	/So I hurried to your rescue. You look tired, Father./She ought to know better.
561	ES	Monica	23	What has happened? Why do you look so angry?/I know that Michael must be in
562	ES	Michael	33	of mine once./{Mi} Did he really look like me?/{MC} You've his voice! and his
563	ES	Gomez	30	If Maisie Montjoy was as beautiful to look at/As Mrs. Carghill, I can well understand/
579	ES	Carghil	16	you listening to me, Richard?/You look very *distrait*. You ought to be excited!/
579	ES	Michael	19	/{Mi} Well, that just depends./I could look in again. If there's any point in it./
582	ES	Ld Clav	18	time together./I leave Monica to you. Look after her, Charles,/Now and always. I

LOOKED (29)

31	Apollinax		13	/Dropping from fingers of surf./I looked for the head of Mr. Apollinax rolling
172	FQ: BurntN		31	roses/Had the look of flowers that are looked at./There they were as our guests,
179	FQ: ECoker		74	/What was to be the value of the long looked forward to,/Long hoped for calm, the
198	FQ: Little		251	apple-tree/Not known, because not looked for/But heard, half-heard, in the stillness
218	Mung Rump		8	was found ajar/And the basement looked like a field of war,/If a tile or two came
223	Pekes Pols		54	his jaws were amazing;/And when he looked out through the bars of the area,/You
223	Pekes Pols		58	Pollicles quickly took warning./He looked at the sky and he gave a great leap —/
265	MC	Priest1	25	dine with us./Your men shall be looked after also./Dinner before business. Do
291	FR	Harry	20	to look at?/If you knew how you looked, when I saw you through the window!/
296	FR	Gerald	36	natural/That he should be asked. He looked after all the boys/When they were
298	FR	Charles	31	mind, it's about his Lordship./You've looked after his Lordship for over ten years .../
322	FR	Winch	38	a bit of luck/Dr. Owen was there, and looked him over;/Says there's nothing wrong
325	FR	Amy	1	talking. I will not talk yours./{A} You looked like your father/When you said that./{H}
326	FR	Harry	11	or like hardened campaigners. She looked/Very much as she must have looked
326	FR	Harry	12	looked/Very much as she must have looked when she was a child./You've been
331	FR	Harry	31	liberated from the human wheel./So I looked to you for strength. Now I think it is/A
334	FR	Agatha	40	kind of pain from prison./{Ag} I only looked through the little door/When the sun
367	CP	Alex	35	are, Edward! Do you know why *I've* looked in?/{E} I'd like to know first how you
371	CP	Peter	20	/When we heard certain music? Or looked at certain pictures?/There was something
377	CP	Julia	21	nothing in the place fit to eat:/I've looked high and low. But I found some
382	CP	Celia	9	since I have been looking at you./I looked at your face: and I thought that I knew/
382	CP	Celia	10	/And loved every contour; and as I looked/It withered, as if I had unwrapped a
382	CP	Celia	17	—/Or however grasshoppers do it. I looked,/And listened for your heart, your
383	CP	Edward	4	have I got to hunt all over?/Have you looked in your bag? ... Well, don't snap my
529	ES	Ld Clav	31	after year, over my breakfast,/I have looked at this book — or one just like it —/You
538	ES	Gomez	39	/And chairman of companies. You looked the part —/Cut out to be an impressive
552	ES	Carghil	34	played, I must say you've always looked it./{LC} I've no longer any part to play,
561	ES	Monica	38	a family, love that's lived in/But not looked at, love within the light of which/All else
575	ES	Carghil	38	those days. I melted the first time he looked at me!/Some day, Monica, I'll tell you all

LOOKING (33)

62	WL: Burial		41	Living nor dead, and I knew nothing,/Looking into the heart of light, the silence./*Oed'*
129	Cor2 State		29	of family portraits, dingy busts, all looking remarkably Roman,/Remarkably like
281	MC Chorus		21	sightseers come with guide-books looking over it;/From where the western seas
292	FR	Amy	17	for dinner./The servants have been looking forward to your coming/Would you
300	FR	Downing	31	his Lordship/Leaning over the rail, looking at the water —/There wasn't a moon,
300	FR	Downing	34	half an hour/He stayed there alone, looking over the rail./Her Ladyship must have
305	FR	Mary	25	/{M} Oh, very well. What are you looking for?/{H} I had only just noticed that this
305	FR	Harry	29	sofa ... all in the same positions./I was looking to see if anything was changed,/But if
308	FR	Harry	32	here and there — wherever I am not looking,/Always flickering at the corner of my
311	FR	Harry	33	you./I tell you, it is not me you are looking at,/Not me you are grinning at, not me
313	FR	Violet	2	yet?/How do you think that Harry is looking?/Why, who could have pulled those
335	FR	Agatha	21	/Pervaded by a smell of disinfectant,/Looking straight ahead, passing barred
364	CP	Julia	35	I've been dragging Peter all over town/Looking for them everywhere I've been./Has
366	CP	Julia	1	mystery./Peter! Why aren't you looking for them?/Look on the mantelpiece.
378	CP	Julia	10	And take a taxi./You know, you're looking absolutely famished./Good night,
382	CP	Celia	8	you have changed since I have been looking at you./I looked at your face: and I
386	CP	Celia	31	here in silence./{C} Oh, I could./Just looking at you. Edward, forgive my laughing./
401	CP	m	1	*and stares at* REILLY]/[*without looking up from his papers*]./{R} Good morning,
430	CP	Peter	14	/So I knew you wouldn't mind my looking in so early./It does seem ages since I last
431	CP	Peter	34	we've got the casting director:/He's looking for some typical English faces —/Of

436 CP	Lavinia	22	us what had happened to Celia/I was looking at your face. And it seemed from your
440 CP	Lavinia	20	*and* ALEX]/{L} Edward, how am I looking?/{E} Very well./I might almost say, your
487 CC	m	7	then we'll go over it tomorrow. {}/[*looking at the notes*]./{C} I'll try./{SC} It's just in
492 CC	Colby	22	dinner/Tomorrow night?/{C} I was looking at your notes —/Before you brought me
498 CC	Eggers	13	Guzzard made a profession/Of ... looking after other people's children?/In a
503 CC	m	36	are we expecting Mrs. Guzzard? {}/[*looking at his watch*]./{SC} She ought to be here
517 CC	Eggers	28	/Died two months ago. We've been looking for another./{C} Do you think that they
529 ES	Monica	6	to seeing me about./{M} I've seen him looking at you. He was thinking of himself/
529 ES	Ld Clav	35	hour of the afternoon./If I've been looking at this engagement book, to-day,/Not
530 ES	Monica	27	For nothing./Yet you've been looking forward/To this very time! You know
576 ES	Michael	28	/{Mi} I told you he'd come to London looking for a man/For an important post on his
580 ES	Carghil	25	But you'd better rest now./You're looking rather tired. I'll run and see them off. {}
582 ES	Charles	27	by us/And had turned and was looking back at us/With a glance of farewell./

LOOKS (20)

69 WL:	Fire S	249	the stairs unlit .../She turns and looks a moment in the glass,/Hardly aware of
230 Bust Jones		27	*Siamese* — or at the *Glutton*;/If he looks full of gloom then he's lunched at the
233 Skimble		41	window if you sneeze./Then the guard looks in politely and will ask you very brightly/
601 Nocturne		9	the lady sinks into a swoon./Blood looks effective on the moonlit ground —/The
311 FR	Harry	34	grinning at, not me your confidential looks/Incriminate, but that other person, if
319 FR	Harry	26	to be heard, with the sidewise looks,/That bring death into the heart of a
424 CP	m	4	good, Madam. {}/[*Exit.* LAVINIA looks about the room critically and moves a bowl
432 CP	Julia	8	know, I was afraid of him at first:/He looks so forbidding .../{R} My dear Julia,/You
440 CP	Lavinia	24	woman can believe/That she always looks her best. You're rather transparent,/You
457 CC	m	13	just going. There's plenty of time. {}/[*Looks at his watch*]/{E} I'll arrive at the airport
457 CC	m	23	out again. {}/[*Goes to the window and looks down on the street*]/{SC} She's having a
479 CC	Kaghan	37	something brighter./But otherwise, it looks pretty comfortable./If I was as snug as
504 CC	Lucasta	7	/Whom you are expecting. She looks rather formidable./{SC} It's Parkman's
532 ES	Lambert	2	a person?/{L} A foreign person/By the looks of him. But talks good English./A
540 ES	Gomez	8	/Has to make up his face before he looks in the mirror./{LC} Isn't that the kind of
545 ES	Monica	12	restful./Even the matron, though she looks rather dominating,/Has left us alone./
546 ES	Piggott	24	Nor do we accept/Any guest who *looks* incurable —/We make that stipulation to
546 ES	Piggott	28	around the dining-room:/Nobody looks ill! They're all convalescents,/Or resting,
564 ES	Carghil	18	/Of course, I could tell from your looks that you were Spanish./I do like
567 ES	Charles	21	and that's very much what it looks like,/Do you think I could persuade him

LOOM (1)

| 270 MC | Chorus | 17 | of powers./What is woven on the loom of fate/What is woven in the councils of |

LOON (1)

| 269 MC | Chorus | 33 | of mouse and jerboa; the laugh of the loon, the lunatic bird. I have seen/Grey necks |

LOOP (1)

| 289 FR | Agatha | 1 | not be a very *jolly* corner./When the loop in time comes — and it does not come for |

LOOSE (7)

158 Rock 5		4	trowel in hand, and the gun rather loose in the holster.'/Those who sit in a house of
212 Growltiger		12	shore: GROWLTIGER'S ON THE LOOSE!/Woe to the weak canary, that fluttered
218 Mung Rump		9	a field of war,/If a tile or two came loose on the roof,/Which presently ceased to be
250 MC	Thomas	2	alone in England,/Who bind and loose, with power from the Pope,/Descend to
253 MC	Tempt4	30	heaven and hell./Power to bind and loose: bind, Thomas, bind,/King and bishop
268 MC	Thomas	31	through me. But it is not I/Who can loose whom the Pope has bound./Let them go
565 ES	Michael	21	in London,/But I think of cutting loose, and going abroad./{MC} You must tell

LOOSENED (1)

| 177 FQ: | ECoker | 11 | /And a time for the wind to break the loosened pane/And to shake the wainscot where |

LOOT (2)

| 119 SP | Klip | 11 | acquainted/{Kl} Sam — I should say Loot Sam Wauchope/{Kr} Of the Canadian |
| 119 SP | Klip | 13 | Expeditionary Force —/{Kl} The Loot has told us a lot about you./{Kr} We were |

LOOTED (1)

| 226 Macavity | | 23 | Yard's./And when the larder's looted, or the jewel-case is rifled,/Or when the |

LORD (112)

16 Prufrock		112	was meant to be;/Am an attendant lord, one that will do/To swell a progress, start
54 Mr E Sun		2	/The sapient sutlers of the Lord/Drift across the window-panes./In the
70 WL:	Fire S	309	/Burning burning burning burning/O Lord Thou pluckest me out/O Lord Thou
70 WL:	Fire S	310	/O Lord Thou pluckest me out/O Lord Thou pluckest/burning/Death by Water/
92 Ash-Wed 3		22	and despair/Climbing the third stair./Lord, I am not worthy/Lord, I am not worthy/
92 Ash-Wed 3		23	the third stair./Lord, I am not worthy/but speak the word only.
105 Song Sime		1	of another death./A Song for Simeon/Lord, the Roman hyacinths are blooming in
154 Rock 3		1	in the forge./The Word of the LORD came unto me, saying:/O miserable cities
155 Rock 3		37	/We build in vain unless the LORD build with us./Can you keep the City

155 Rock 3	38	us./Can you keep the City that the LORD keeps not with you?/A thousand
155 Rock 3	42	than they that build without the LORD./Shall we lift up our feet among
158 Rock 5	1	hand and the trowel in the other./O Lord, deliver me from the man of excellent
164 Rock 9	25	and the beauty of incantation./LORD, shall we not bring these gifts to Your
165 Rock 9	29	pleasures of the senses?/The LORD who created must wish us to create/And
589 Fable	84	/St. Peter'd snatcht to heaven their lord renowned,/Though the wicked said (such
240 MC Priest2	28	Archbishop do, and our Sovereign Lord the Pope/With the stubborn King and the
241 MC Priest1	17	/{P1} What, is the exile ended, is our Lord Archbishop/Reunited with the King? what
242 MC Mess	5	/And if you ask me, I think the Lord Archbishop/Is not the man to cherish any
242 MC Mess	12	the King, he said to the King,/My Lord, he said, I leave you as a man/Whom in
242 MC Priest2	31	different for Thomas./{P2} Yet our lord is returned. Our lord has come back to his
242 MC Priest2	31	/{P2} Yet our lord is returned. Our lord has come back to his own again./We have
242 MC Priest2	35	give us our orders, instruct us./Our Lord is at one with the Pope, and also the King
243 MC Priest2	3	with cordial thanksgiving:/Our lord, our Archbishop returns. And when the
244 MC Chorus	25	Thomas Archbishop,/O Thomas our Lord, leave us and leave us be, in our humble
244 MC Chorus	29	doom of the house, the doom of their lord, the doom of the world?/O Thomas,
245 MC Priest2	23	and still/Be forever still./{P2} O my Lord, forgive me, I did not see you coming,/
245 MC Priest2	25	these foolish women./Forgive us, my Lord, you would have had a better welcome/If
246 MC Tempt1	24	TEMPTER]/{T1} You see, my Lord, I do not wait upon ceremony:/Here I
246 MC Tempt1	34	than biting Time can sever./What, my Lord, now that you recover/Favour with the
247 MC Tempt1	22	the wheel on which he turns./{T1} My Lord, a nod is as good as a wink./A man will
248 MC Tempt1	3	for at higher prices./Farewell, my Lord, I do not wait upon ceremony,/I leave as I
248 MC Tempt1	7	levity./If you will remember me, my Lord, at your prayers,/I'll remember you at
248 MC Tempt2	26	— still may be regained. Think, my Lord,/Power obtained grows to glory,/Life
250 MC Tempt3	23	brings surprise./{T3} Well, my Lord,/I am no trifler, and no politician./To idle
250 MC Tempt3	29	estates in order,/A country-keeping lord who minds his own business./It is we
251 MC Tempt3	23	We are in England./You and I, my Lord, are Normans./England is a land for
251 MC Tempt3	39	/In the fight for liberty. You, my Lord,/In being with us, would fight a good
252 MC Tempt3	23	that I betrayed a king./{T3} Then, my Lord, I shall not wait at your door./And I well
256 MC Priests	24	enemy of himself./{3P} O Thomas my Lord do not fight the intractable tide,/Do not
257 MC Chorus	6	/{C} We have not been happy, my Lord, we have not been too happy./We are not
260 MC Thomas	7	the Passion and Death of Our Lord; and/on this Christmas Day we do this in
260 MC Thomas	15	we/celebrate at once the Birth of Our Lord and His Passion and Death upon/the
260 MC Thomas	26	and a cheat?/Reflect now, how Our Lord Himself spoke of Peace. He said to His/
261 MC Thomas	14	in the/Birth and in the Passion of Our Lord; so also, in a smaller figure, we/both
263 MC Chorus	12	/What, at the time of the birth of the Lord, at Christmastide,/Is there not peace upon
263 MC Chorus	15	defiles this world, but death in the Lord renews it,/And the world must be cleaned
264 MC Priest1	5	down and cried with a loud voice:/Lord, lay not this sin to their charge./Princes
264 MC Priest3	19	was no man to bury them. Avenge, O Lord,/The blood of thy saints. In Rama, a voice
270 MC Chorus	26	last humiliation./I have consented, Lord Archbishop, have consented./Am torn
271 MC Chorus	6	final ecstasy of waste and shame,/O Lord Archbishop, O Thomas Archbishop,
271 MC Priests	20	[Enter PRIESTS]/[severally]./{3P} My Lord, you must not stop here. To the minster./
271 MC Priests	22	to make perfect my will./{3P} My Lord, they are coming. They will break through
271 MC Priests	28	Come to the altar./Make haste, my Lord. Don't stop here talking. It is not right./
271 MC Priests	29	right./What shall become of us, my Lord, if you are killed; what shall become of us?
271 MC Priests	33	danger: only near to death./{3P} My Lord, to vespers! You must not be absent from
273 MC Chorus	6	not be in vain Thy labour;/Help me, Lord, in my last fear./Dust I am, to dust am
273 MC Chorus	9	the final doom impending/Help me, Lord, for death is near. {}/[In the cathedral.
273 MC Priests	23	our enemies. Open the door!/{3P} My Lord! these are not men, these come not as men
273 MC Priests	30	would damn themselves to beasts. My Lord! My Lord!/{T} You think me reckless,
273 MC Priests	30	themselves to beasts. My Lord! My Lord!/{T} You think me reckless, desperate and
274 MC Priests	14	slightly tipsy]/{3P} This way, my Lord! Quick. Up the stair. To the roof./To the
275 MC Thomas	7	you have violated./{T} For my Lord I am now ready to die,/That his Church
275 MC Thomas	16	vassal,/Traitor to me as your spiritual lord,/Traitor to God in desecrating His Church.
280 MC Priest1	37	think no further of you./{P1} O my lord/The glory of whose new state is hidden
282 MC Chorus	6	blessing to Canterbury./Forgive us, O Lord, we acknowledge ourselves as type of the
282 MC Chorus	15	of the saints/Is upon our heads./Lord, have mercy upon us./Christ, have mercy
282 MC Chorus	17	upon us./Christ, have mercy upon us./Lord, have mercy upon us./Blessed Thomas,
284 FR	m 6	DENMAN, a parlourmaid/HARRY, LORD MONCHENSEY, Amy's eldest son/
321 FR Denman	9	{D} It's Sergeant Winchell is here, my Lord,/And wants to see your Lordship very
321 FR Winch	24	/{Wi} Good evening, my Lord. Good evening, Doctor./Many happy ...
321 FR Winch	25	/Many happy ... Oh, I'm sorry, my Lord,/I was thinking it was your birthday, not
321 FR Winch	33	older/Than when I saw you last, my Lord. But a country sergeant/Doesn't get
321 FR Winch	34	get younger. Thank you, no, my Lord;/I don't find port agrees with the
322 FR Winch	7	is her Ladyship,/If I may ask, my Lord?/{H} Why do you keep asking/About her

322 FR	Winch	11	of you./{Wi} I should hope not, my Lord./I didn't mean to put myself forward./But
322 FR	Winch	13	put myself forward./But you see, my Lord, I had good reason for asking .../{H} Well,
322 FR	Winch	15	her for you?/{Wi} Oh no indeed, my Lord, I'd much rather not .../{H} You mean you
322 FR	Winch	18	shock enough for one evening, my Lord:/That's what I've come about./{W} For
322 FR	Winch	24	Mr. John./{H} John!/{Wi} Yes, my Lord, I'm sorry./I thought I'd better have a
328 FR	Charles	12	Charles Piper, younger brother of Lord/Monchensey, who ran into and
499 CC	Claude	9	{}/[*A knock on the door*]/{SC} Good Lord, she's here already! Well ... Come in! {}/
523 ES	m	5	HEMINGTON/LAMBERT/LORD CLAVERTON/FEDERICO GOMEZ/
523 ES	m	11	/ACT ONE/*The drawing-room of Lord Claverton's London house. Four o'clock in*
524 ES	2m	1	day/Act One/*The drawing-room of* LORD CLAVERTON'S *London house. Four*
529 ES	m	19	And Oh, Charles dear — {}/[*Enter* LORD CLAVERTON]/{M} You've been very
531 ES	Lambert	32	LAMBERT]/{L} Excuse me, my Lord. There's a gentleman downstairs/Is very
531 ES	Lambert	34	/I told him you never saw anyone, my Lord,/But by previous appointment. He said he
532 ES	Lambert	7	see him here./{L} Very good, my Lord./Shall I take the trolley, Miss Monica?/
532 ES	Lambert	26	LAMBERT]/{L} Mr. Gomez, my Lord./{LC} Goodbye, Charles. And please
533 ES	Gomez	5	Claverton-Ferry;/And finally, Lord Claverton. I've followed your example,/
535 ES	Lambert	7	whisky. And soda./{L} Very good, my Lord./{G} And some ice./{L} Ice? Yes, my Lord.
535 ES	Lambert	9	/{G} And some ice./{L} Ice? Yes, my Lord. {}/[*Exit*]/{G} I began to say: when I say
541 ES	Lambert	31	LAMBERT]/{L} Excuse me, my Lord, but Miss Monica asked me/To remind
543 ES	m	8	where we left off. {}/[*Exit* GOMEZ]/[LORD CLAVERTON *sits for a few minutes*
544 ES	3m	1	*morning, several days later./Enter* LORD CLAVERTON *and* MONICA./{M}
545 ES	Piggott	22	PIGGOTT]/{MP} Good morning, Lord Claverton! Good morning, Miss
545 ES	Piggott	27	these last few days,/And I thought, 'Lord Claverton will understand/My not coming
548 ES	1m	14	the hint. {}/[*Exit*]/*A moment later,* LORD CLAVERTON *spreads his newspaper*
548 ES	Carghil	25	last night./You are the great Lord Claverton, aren't you?/Somebody said you
551 ES	Carghil	38	/And then you wouldn't have become Lord Claverton./So perhaps I laid the
554 ES	Piggott	18	introduce you. You've been talking to Lord Claverton,/The famous Lord Claverton.
554 ES	Piggott	19	to Lord Claverton,/The famous Lord Claverton. This is Mrs. Carghill./Two of
554 ES	Piggott	21	nicest guests!/I just came to see that Lord Claverton was comfortable:/We can't
554 ES	Carghil	24	Mrs. Carghill?/{MC} Oh, I knew that Lord Claverton had come for a rest cure,/And it
554 ES	Piggott	36	/But you and I should remember her, Lord Claverton./That tune she was humming,
559 ES	Michael	13	Zealand?/{Mi} Sheep farming? Good Lord, no./That's not my idea. I want to make
559 ES	Michael	30	longer wanted. And you wished to be Lord Claverton/Also, to hold your own with
559 ES	Michael	32	your own with Mother's family —/To lord it over them, in fact. Oh, I've no doubt/
563 ES	Carghil	27	when we first became friends —/Lord Claverton and I — I was known by my
564 ES	Carghil	11	/{MC} I don't believe you've known Lord Claverton/As long as I have, Señor
571 ES	Ld Clav	6	/From Gomez, Mrs. Carghill and Lord Claverton./Freddy admired me, when we
573 ES	Charles	15	But what do you propose? How long, Lord Claverton,/Will you stay here and endure

LORD'S (1)

| 261 MC | Thomas | 9 | of Christmas celebrate at once Our Lord's/Birth and His Death: but on the next |

LORDS (4)

180 FQ:	ECoker	107	of many committees,/Industrial lords and petty contractors, all go into the dark,
250 MC	Tempt3	30	his own business./It is we country lords who know the country/And we who know
257 MC	Chorus	31	/For laughter, laughter, laughter. The Lords of Hell are here./They curl round you, lie
531 ES	Ld Clav	27	/Walking in the City or sitting in the Lords./And I, who recognise myself as a ghost/

LORDSHIP (32)

245 MC	Priest2	27	prepared for the event./But your Lordship knows that seven years of waiting,/
245 MC	Priest2	33	chill off our English December,/Your Lordship now being used to a better climate./
245 MC	Priest2	1	being used to a better climate./Your Lordship will find your rooms in order as you
246 MC	Tempt1	29	all the good time past./Your Lordship won't despise an old friend out of
246 MC	Tempt1	31	gay Tom, Becket of London,/Your Lordship won't forget that evening on the river/
247 MC	Tempt1	31	go so fast, others may go faster./Your Lordship is too proud!/The safest beast is not
248 MC	Tempt2	15	SECOND TEMPTER]/{T2} Your Lordship has forgotten me, perhaps. I will
251 MC	Tempt3	38	direction —/To gain from you, your Lordship asks./For us, Church favour would be
265 MC	Priest1	33	{}/[*to attendant*]./{P1} Go, tell His Lordship./{K4} How much longer will you keep
297 FR	Charles	27	where is Downing? Is he up with his Lordship?/{D} He's out in the garage, Sir, with
298 FR	Charles	30	sure you won't mind, it's about his Lordship./You've looked after his Lordship for
298 FR	Charles	31	his Lordship./You've looked after his Lordship for over ten years .../{Do} Eleven
299 FR	Charles	10	might have been suicide,/And that his Lordship knew it?/{Do} Unlikely, Sir, if I may
299 FR	Charles	32	for others./{C} And how was his Lordship, during the voyage?/{Do} Well, you
299 FR	Downing	34	say depressed, Sir./But you know his Lordship was always very quiet:/Very
299 FR	Downing	36	judgment's worth, I always said his Lordship/Suffered from what they call a kind of
300 FR	Downing	8	it is just my opinion, Sir,/That his Lordship is rather psychic, as they say./{C}
300 FR	Downing	24	to say that he had any orders —/His Lordship is always most considerate/About
300 FR	Downing	30	/And I remember, there I saw his Lordship/Leaning over the rail, looking at the

96 Ash-Wed 5	1	the yew/And after this our exile/If the lost word is lost, if the spent word is spent/If the
96 Ash-Wed 5	1	after this our exile/If the lost word is lost, if the spent word is spent/If the unheard,
98 Ash-Wed 6	11	flying/Unbroken wings/And the lost heart stiffens and rejoices/In the lost lilac
98 Ash-Wed 6	12	lost heart stiffens and rejoices/In the lost lilac and the lost sea voices/And the weak
98 Ash-Wed 6	12	and rejoices/In the lost lilac and the lost sea voices/And the weak spirit quickens to
98 Ash-Wed 6	14	rebel/For the bent golden-rod and the lost sea smell/Quickens to recover/The cry of
147 Rock 1	14	to GOD./Where is the Life we have lost in living?/Where is the wisdom we have lost
147 Rock 1	15	living?/Where is the wisdom we have lost in knowledge?/Where is the knowledge we
147 Rock 1	16	/Where is the knowledge we have lost in information?/The cycles of Heaven in
155 Rock 3	36	the asphalt road/And a thousand lost golf balls'./CHORUS:/We build in vain
180 FQ: ECoker	110	of Directors,/And cold the sense and lost the motive of action./And we all go with
180 FQ: ECoker	133	in the garden, echoed ecstasy/Not lost, but requiring, pointing to the agony/Of
182 FQ: ECoker	188	the fight to recover what has been lost/And found and lost again and again: and
182 FQ: ECoker	189	what has been lost/And found and lost again and again: and now, under conditions
190 FQ: DrySal	212	in and out of time,/The distraction fit, lost in a shaft of sunlight,/The wild thyme
604 Ode	9	all of these years that to-morrow has lost/We are still the less able to grieve,/With so
244 MC Chorus	23	the layers of an onion, our selves are lost lost/In a final fear which none understands.
244 MC Chorus	23	layers of an onion, our selves are lost lost/In a final fear which none understands. O
256 MC Tempt5	22	grandeur to grandeur to final illusion,/Lost in the wonder of his own greatness,/The
261 MC Thomas	30	the/instrument of God, who has lost his will in the will of God, and who no/
280 MC Priest1	5	/{P1} O father, father, gone from us, lost to us,/How shall we find you, from what far
280 MC Priest3	17	will die for it./Go, weak sad men, lost erring souls, homeless in earth or heaven./
286 FR Charles	28	care what they're eating;/They've lost their sense of taste and smell/Because of
289 FR Charles	13	/{C} I never wrote to him when he lost his wife —/That was just about a year ago,
307 FR Harry	33	know what hope is, until you have lost it./You only know what it is not to hope:/
319 FR Harry	22	day of unusual heat,/The day I lost my butterfly net;/I remember the silence,
337 FR Agatha	12	in the obvious place./Delay, and it is lost. Love compels cruelty/To those who do not
349 FR Chorus	7	more than a personal loss —/We have lost our way in the dark./{I} I shall have to stay
362 CP Reilly	21	loss of personality;/Or rather, you've lost touch with the person/You thought you
364 CP Edward	10	analysis/If I am to remain always lost in the dark?/{UG} There is certainly no
370 CP Edward	25	/{E} Do you think she has simply lost interest in you?/{P} You put it just wrong. I
370 CP Peter	31	/In your terms, perhaps, she's lost interest in me./{E} That is all very normal.
381 CP Edward	12	moment, when you feel that you have lost/The desire for all that was most desirable,/
393 CP Lavinia	8	that the effect upon me was/That I lost all sense of humour myself./That's what
416 CP Celia	33	suddenly discovers he is only a child/Lost in a forest, wanting to go home./{R}
418 CP Reilly	2	like a book/You have read once, and lost. In a world of lunacy,/Violence, stupidity,
448 CC Claude	38	you and your wife, to have had a son/Lost in action, and his grave unknown./{E} And
449 CC Eggers	2	Would be put in mind of the child *she* lost./{SC} In a very different way, yes. You
452 CC Lucasta	11	LUCASTA ANGEL]/{L} Eggy, I've lost my job!/{E} Again, Miss Angel?/{L} Yes,
455 CC Colby	5	ago./Then I'd have been certain I'd lost my reason:/Her influence is perfectly
456 CC Eggers	40	could happen. She sometimes gets lost,/Or loses her ticket, or even her passport./
472 CC Lucasta	39	it's only the outer world that you've lost/You've still got your inner world — a
487 CC Lady E	20	has come out./It's Colby. Colby is my lost child!/{SC} What? Your child, Elizabeth?
488 CC Lady E	4	as you know, in Africa,/And I had lost the name. Mrs. Guzzard./{SC} I'm
489 CC Claude	7	fair enough — though yours had been lost,/And mine I couldn't lose. But if I had
490 CC Lady E	28	son,/No matter how long they have lost each other./{C} No, Lady Elizabeth. The
496 CC Eggers	30	moment./And really, now, I'm quite lost in London./Every time I come, I notice the
506 CC Guzzard	19	I can sympathise./I had a child, and lost him. Not in the way/That Lady Elizabeth's
506 CC Guzzard	20	way/That Lady Elizabeth's child was lost./Let us hope that her son may be restored
508 CC Eggers	6	yourself in her position./If you had lost your son, in a similar way,/Wouldn't you
508 CC Guzzard	28	/Then they left Teddington, and we lost sight of them./{E} But you know their
533 ES Ld Clav	26	out there/By the sort of activity that lost you respect/Here in England?/{G} Not at
536 ES Gomez	29	when you come to see that you have lost *yourself*/That you are quite alone./{LC} I'm
551 ES Carghil	31	political ambitions for him./If he's lost a breach of promise suit/Some people won't
557 ES Michael	7	me what's happened./{Mi} Well, I've lost my job./{LC} The position that Sir Alfred
563 ES Gomez	35	/That's a pity, Señor Gomez./{G} I lost touch with things in England./Had I been in

LOT (21)

41 Burb Blei	23	the piles./The Jew is underneath the lot./Money in furs. The boatman smiles,/
53 Whispers	31	/Circumambulate her charm;/But our lot crawls between dry ribs/To keep our
92 Ash-Wed 2	53	is the land which ye/Shall divide by lot. And neither division nor unity/Matters.
118 SP Doris	4	I draw court cards —/{Do} There's a lot in the way you pick them up/{Du} There's an
118 SP Dusty	5	pick them up/{Du} There's an awful lot in the way you feel/{Do} Sometimes they'll
119 SP Klip	13	Force —/{Kl} The Loot has told us a lot about you./{Kr} We were all in the war
148 Rock 1	46	*led by a* BOY:/THE ROCK:/The lot of man is ceaseless labour,/Or ceaseless
211 Old Gumbie	33	/So she's formed, from that lot of disorderly louts,/A troop of

555	ES	Piggott	1	*It's Not Too Late For You To Love Me,*/Everybody was singing it once. A
561	ES	Monica	37	But there's no vocabulary/For love within a family, love that's lived in/But not
561	ES	Monica	37	vocabulary/For love within a family, love that's lived in/But not looked at, love
561	ES	Monica	38	love that's lived in/But not looked at, love within the light of which/All else is seen,
561	ES	Monica	39	the light of which/All else is seen, the love within which/All other love finds speech./
562	ES	Monica	1	seen, the love within which/All other love finds speech./This love is silent./What can I
562	ES	Monica	2	/All other love finds speech./This love is silent./What can I say to you?/However
562	ES	Monica	6	must forgive each other, you must love each other./{Mi} I could have loved Father,
562	ES	Michael	7	have loved Father, if he'd wanted love,/But he never did, Monica, not from me./
563	ES	Carghil	5	America./{MC} How romantic! I'd love to meet him./He's coming to speak to us.
564	ES	Carghil	1	/{MC} *It's Not Too Late For You To Love Me!* That's the song/That made my
568	ES	Ld Clav	18	/Then all is well with you. You're in love with each other —/I don't need to be told
568	ES	Ld Clav	29	—/Then he loves that person, and his love will save him./I'm afraid that I've never
568	ES	Ld Clav	31	never loved anyone, really./No, I do love my Monica — but there's the impediment:/
569	ES	Ld Clav	5	/How could I be sure that she would love the actor/If she saw him, off the stage,
569	ES	Ld Clav	8	stage words. Monica!/I've had your love under false pretences./Now, I'm tired of
569	ES	Ld Clav	10	/But I hope that you'll find a little love in your heart/Still, for your father, when
569	ES	Monica	13	actor./{M} I think I should only love you the better, Father,/The more I knew
571	ES	Ld Clav	19	and foolish —/But we should respect love always when we meet it;/Even when it's
571	ES	Monica	27	you wish to conceal from those who love you/What is known so well to those who
581	ES	Ld Clav	24	the illumination/Of knowing what love is. We all think we know,/But how few of
581	ES	Ld Clav	29	have found a man/Whom you can love for the man he really is./{M} Oh Father,
581	ES	Monica	31	Father, I've always loved you,/But I love you more since I have come to know you/
581	ES	Monica	32	you/Here, at Badgley Court. And I love you the more/Because I love Charles./{LC}
581	ES	Monica	33	And I love you the more/Because I love Charles./{LC} Yes, my dear./Your love is
581	ES	Ld Clav	35	Charles./{LC} Yes, my dear./Your love is for the real Charles, not a make-believe,/
581	ES	Ld Clav	36	not a make-believe,/As was your love for me./{M} But not now, Father!/It's the
581	ES	Monica	38	not now, Father!/It's the real you I love — the man you are,/Not the man I thought
582	ES	Ld Clav	1	you were./{LC} And Michael —/I love him, even for rejecting me,/For the *me* he
582	ES	Ld Clav	6	dying, to find out what life is./And I love you, my daughter, the more truly for
582	ES	Ld Clav	7	knowing/That there is someone you love more than your father —/That you love
582	ES	Ld Clav	8	more than your father —/That you love and are loved. And now that I love
582	ES	Ld Clav	8	love and are loved. And now that I love Michael,/I think, for the first time —
583	ES	Charles	4	you and me together./Oh my dear,/I love you to the limits of speech, and beyond./
583	ES	Monica	9	/Before you and I were born, the love was always there/That brought us together.
583	ES	Monica	26	or amaze me/Fixed in the certainty of love unchanging./I feel utterly secure/In you; I

LOVED (22)

40	Burb Blei		8	God Hercules/Had left him, that had loved him well./The horses, under the axletree/
155	Rock 3		44	feet among perpetual ruins?/I have loved the beauty of Thy House, the peace of
195	FQ: Little		166	with the self which, as it could, loved them,/To become renewed, transfigured,
319	FR Warburt		31	/I am sure that your mother always loved him;/There was never the slightest
382	CP	Celia	10	face: and I thought that I knew/And loved every contour; and as I looked/It
409	CP	Reilly	40	It was a shock. You had wanted to be loved;/You had come to see that no one had
410	CP	Reilly	1	had come to see that no one had ever loved you./Then you began to fear that no one
417	CP	Celia	14	/When awake. But what, or whom I loved,/Or what in me was loving, I do not
464	CC	Claude	2	/{SC} A potter. When I was a boy/I loved to shape things. I loved form and colour/.
464	CC	Claude	2	I was a boy/I loved to shape things. I loved form and colour/And I loved the material
464	CC	Claude	3	things. I loved form and colour/And I loved the material that the potter handles./Most
464	CC	Claude	29	from nothing./He loved it with the same devotion/That I gave to
495	CC	Lady E	2	what I mean./{LE} But I should have loved you to be a potter!/Why have you never
526	ES	Charles	4	frightened. For I didn't *know* you loved me —/I merely wanted to believe it. And
551	ES	Carghil	1	prefer to forget all the women/He has loved. But a woman doesn't want to forget/A
562	ES	Michael	7	love each other./{Mi} I could have loved Father, if he'd wanted love,/But he never
567	ES	Charles	11	in London, you admitted that you loved me,/But I wondered ... I'm sorry, I
568	ES	Ld Clav	30	save him./I'm afraid that I've never loved anyone, really./No, I do love my Monica
571	ES	Ld Clav	17	that they were born with./And Maisie loved me, with whatever capacity/For loving she
581	ES	Monica	30	really is./{M} Oh Father, I've always loved you,/But I love you more since I have
582	ES	Ld Clav	8	your father —/That you love and are loved. And now that I love Michael,/I think, for
583	ES	Monica	8	must struggle for words./{M} I've loved you from the beginning of the world./

LOVELINESS (2)

91	Ash-Wed 2		9	of this Lady/And because of her loveliness, and because/She honours the Virgin
381	CP	Edward	27	misery does not feed on the ruin of loveliness,/That the tedium is not the residue of

LOVELY (9)

69	WL: Fire S		253	done: and I'm glad it's over.'/When lovely woman stoops to folly and/Paces about
354	CP	Alex	14	in Denmark./There were several very lovely daughters:/I wonder what's become of

354 CP	Julia	16	them now./{J} Lady Klootz was very lovely, once upon a time./What a life she led! I
547 ES	Piggott	35	I can lend you a map./There are lovely walks, on the shore or in the hills,/Quite
549 ES	Carghil	15	and we had a tea basket/With some lovely little cakes — I've forgotten what you
549 ES	Carghil	37	changes in me, Richard./I was very lovely once. So *you* thought,/And others
556 ES	Michael	12	Father. {}/[*A pause*]/{Mi} What a lovely day!/I'm glad you're here, to enjoy such
576 ES	Carghil	3	/About you./{MC} But I was very lovely then./{G} We are sure of that! You're so
576 ES	Gomez	4	/{G} We are sure of that! You're so lovely now/That we can well imagine you at ...

LOVER (8)

69 WL: Fire S		250	glass,/Hardly aware of her departed lover;/Her brain allows one half-formed thought
408 CP	Reilly	6	distress/Was the defection of your lover — who suddenly/For the first time in his
409 CP	Reilly	15	to think of yourself as a passionate lover./Then you realised, what your wife has
409 CP	Reilly	37	the honour conferred by being *your* lover./When you had to face the fact that his
416 CP	Celia	27	one *is* alone, and if one is alone/Then lover and belovèd are equally unreal/And the
551 ES	Carghil	2	of her admirers. Why, even a faithless lover/Is still, in her memory, a kind of
572 ES	Ld Clav	13	she against you?/{LC} I was her first lover./I would have married her — but my
583 ES	Charles	7	struggling for breath,/So the lover must struggle for words./{M} I've loved

LOVERS (4)

206 To my Wife		5	/The breathing in unison/Of lovers whose bodies smell of each other/Who
213 Growltiger		39	there was not heard a sound./The lovers sang their last duet, in danger of their
601 Nocturne		14	—'The perfect climax all true lovers seek!'/Humouresque/(AFTER J.
522 ES	dedic	5	*|The breathing in unison/Of lovers ...|Who think the same thoughts without*

LOVES (6)

92 Ash-Wed 2		34	Rose/Is now the Garden/Where all loves end/Terminate torment/Of love unsatisfied
228 Gus		13	the back of the neighbouring pub)/He loves to regale them, if someone else pays,/With
228 Gus		19	/But his grandest creation, as he loves to tell,/Was Firefrorefiddle, the Fiend of
357 CP	Julia	32	Anywhere near Colchester? Lavinia loves oysters./{E} No. In the *depths* of Essex./{J}
568 ES	Ld Clav	29	the fool (as who has not?) —/Then he loves that person, and his love will save him./
580 ES	Monica	34	self that he's ashamed of./I'm sure he loves us./{LC} Monica my dear,/What you say

LOVING (10)

309 FR	Mary	24	yourself to loathing/As others do to loving: an infatuation/That's wrong, a good
409 CP	Reilly	19	suspect that you were incapable/Of loving. To men of a certain type/The suspicion
409 CP	Reilly	20	suspicion that they are incapable of loving/Is as disturbing to their self-esteem/As, in
410 CP	Reilly	8	A man who finds himself incapable of loving/And a woman who finds that no man
417 CP	Celia	10	In which one is exalted by intensity of loving/In the spirit, a vibration of delight/
417 CP	Celia	13	for desire is fulfilled/In the delight of loving. A state one does not know/When awake.
417 CP	Celia	15	or whom I loved,/Or what in me was loving, I do not know./And if that is all
553 ES	Carghil	29	passionate?/{MC} They were very loving. Would you like to read them?/I'm afraid
571 ES	Ld Clav	18	loved me, with whatever capacity/For loving she had — self-centred and foolish —/
582 ES	Ld Clav	10	am only a beginner in the practice of loving —/Well, that is something./I shall leave

LOW (11)

67 WL: Fire S		193	him./White bodies naked on the low damp ground/And bones cast in a little low
67 WL: Fire S		194	ground/And bones cast in a little low dry garret,/Rattled by the rat's foot only,
68 WL: Fire S		233	clerk, with one bold stare,/One of the low on whom assurance sits/As a silk hat on a
103 Journ Magi		24	the darkness,/And three trees on the low sky./And an old white horse galloped away
232 Skimble		6	/They are searching high and low,/Saying 'Skimble where is Skimble for
243 MC Priest3		13	daughters of music shall be brought low./{C} Here is no continuing city, here is no
261 MC Thomas		34	high, having made themselves most low, and are seen, not as we/see them, but in the
319 FR	Harry	24	and the hushed excitement/And the low conversation of triumphant aunts./It is the
377 CP	Julia	21	place fit to eat:/I've looked high and low. But I found some champagne —/Only a
493 CC	Lady E	24	have an armchair .../{LE} Not such a low one. Leave that in the corner/For Colby.
573 ES	Carghil	23	/{MC} I've been hunting high and low for you, Richard!/I've some very exciting

LOW-SPIRITED (1)

496 CC	Eggers	36	is well?/{E} Pretty well./She's always low-spirited, around this season,/When we're

LOWER (4)

69 WL: Fire S		260	sometimes hear/Beside a public bar in Lower Thames Street,/The pleasant whining of
174 FQ: BurntN		117	in this twittering world./Descend lower, descend only/Into the world of perpetual
246 MC Thomas		17	/Will only soar and hover, circling lower,/Waiting excuse, pretence, opportunity./
400 CP	Reilly	9	to delay his appointment/To lower his resistance. But what I mean is,/Does

LOWERED (1)

149 Rock 1		96	*has hired us|With pocketed hands|And lowered faces|We stand about in open places|And*

LOWERS (1)

186 FQ: DrySal		76	and hauling, while the North East lowers/Over shallow banks unchanging and

LOWEST (2)

69 WL: Fire S		246	the wall/And walked among the lowest of the dead.)/Bestows one final
255 MC Tempt4		12	way of martyrdom, make yourself the lowest/On earth, to be high in heaven./And see

519 CC   m 22   the responsibility of meaning it. {}/[LUCASTA *puts her arms around* SIR
519 CC   Claude 22 SIR CLAUDE]/{SC} Don't leave me, Lucasta./Eggerson! Do *you* really believe her? {}

LUCASTA'S (4)
452 CC   Kaghan   5   How so Mr. Kaghan?/{K} Because Lucasta's with me! The usual catastrophe./She's
480 CC   Kaghan   3   no, not quite the right expression —/Lucasta's the most exciting speculation/I've ever
481 CC   Kaghan 24   /{K} We're going out to dinner. Lucasta's very hungry./{LE} Hungry? At six
503 CC   Claude 38 how the time was passing,/What with Lucasta's unexpected visit./She ought to be

LUCID (2)
173 FQ: BurntN 96   neither daylight/Investing form with lucid stillness/Turning shadow into transient
594 Grad 9   3   rise to thee/From spotless fanes of lucid purity,/O school of ours! The passing

LUCK (9)
117 SP   Doris 37   going to draw any more,/You cut for luck. You cut for luck./It might break the spell.
117 SP   Doris 37   more,/You cut for luck. You cut for luck./It might break the spell. You cut for luck./
117 SP   Doris 38   /It might break the spell. You cut for luck./{Du} The Knave of Spades./{Do} That'll
219 Mung Rump 31 some of the time you would say it was luck, and some of the time you would say it was
322 FR   Winch 37   —/Mr. John, I mean. By a bit of luck/Dr. Owen was there, and looked him over;/
323 FR   Winch 25   yet./Dr. Owen was there, by a bit of luck./{G} I'll go down and see him, Amy, and
452 CC   Lucasta 18   not till yesterday./Then, just by bad luck, the boss did want a letter/And I couldn't
479 CC   Kaghan 14 bachelor quarters,/And to wish Colby luck. I've always been lucky,/And I always
479 CC   Kaghan 15   been lucky,/And I always bring luck to other people./{C} Will you have a glass

LUCKIER (1)
376 CP   Edward 22 The man who fell among thieves was luckier than I:/He was left at an inn./{J}

LUCKY (13)
288 FR   Amy   3   it will not be his fault./We are very lucky to have Harry at all./{I} And when will
359 CP   Julia 24   {}/[*Enter* JULIA]/{J} Edward! How lucky that it's raining!/It made me remember
359 CP   Julia 27 what are you two plotting?/How very lucky it was my umbrella,/And not Alexander's
365 CP   Julia 15   been so insulted in my life./It's very lucky that I left my spectacles:/*This* is what I
370 CP   Edward 33 normal. If you could only know/How lucky you are. In a little while/This might have
372 CP   Alex 15 your refrigerator. But of course/I was lucky to find half-a-dozen eggs./{E} What! You
376 CP   Julia 20   up./Edward! Don't you realise how lucky you are/To have *two* Good Samaritans? I
452 CC   Kaghan   3   Eggers! I'm glad to find you here./It's lucky for Colby./{E} How so Mr. Kaghan?/{K}
477 CC   Lucasta 5 /Then Claude took me over. That was lucky./But I was old enough to remember ... too
479 CC   Kaghan 14 to wish Colby luck. I've always been lucky,/And I always bring luck to other people./
552 ES   Ld Clav 14   at all./I thought, perhaps, what a lucky escape/It had been, for both of us./{MC}
552 ES   Carghil 17   us'/Was an afterthought, Richard. A lucky escape/You thought, for you. You felt no
573 ES   Carghil 33   *you*, Mr. Hemington./You're a very lucky man, to get a girl like Monica./I take a

LUCRETIA (1)
44 Cook Egg   18   /I shall not want Society in Heaven,/Lucretia Borgia shall be my Bride;/Her

LUCY (1)
111 Xmas Trees 26   I remember also with gratitude/St. Lucy, her carol, and her crown of fire):/So that

LUDGATE (1)
174 FQ: BurntN 115   and Putney,/Highgate, Primrose and Ludgate. Not here/Not here the darkness, in

LUDICROUS (3)
315 FR   Chorus 36 mutilated/The family album, rendered ludicrous/The tenants' dinner, the family picnic
386 CP   Celia 35   saw you so before./This is really a ludicrous situation./{E} I'm afraid I can't see the
408 CP   Edward 22 I have never heard anything so utterly ludicrous:/This is the best joke that ever

LUGGAGE (2)
232 Skimble   12   to the rear:/He's been busy in the luggage van!/He gives one flash of his
398 CP   Lavinia 17   go out for dinner./Meanwhile, my luggage is in the hall downstairs:/Will you get

LUI (2)
48 Lune Miel   14   la Cène, et un restaurant pas cher./Lui pense aux pourboires, et rédige son bilan./
51 Restaurant   11   petite./Elle était toute mouillée, je lui ai donné des primevères.'/Les taches de son

LUKE (1)
260 MC Thomas 2   *of the Gospel according to Saint Luke*. In the/Name of the Father, and of the Son,

LUMBAGO (1)
348 FR   Chorus 22   /Specifics against insomnia,/Lumbago, and the loss of money./But the circle

LUMP (1)
315 FR   Harry   2 believe in cancer. Cancer is here:/The lump, the dull pain, the occasional sickness:/

LUNACY (1)
418 CP   Reilly   2   read once, and lost. In a world of lunacy,/Violence, stupidity, greed ... it is a good

LUNAR (2)
24 Rhapsody   3   the reaches of the street/Held in a lunar synthesis,/Whispering lunar incantations/
24 Rhapsody   4   Held in a lunar synthesis,/Whispering lunar incantations/Dissolve the floors of

LUNATIC (4)
258 MC Thomas 35   futility,/Senseless self-slaughter of a lunatic,/Arrogant passion of a fanatic./I know
269 MC Chorus 33   and jerboa; the laugh of the loon, the lunatic bird. I have seen/Grey necks twisting,
406 CP Lavinia 21   /{L} Are you a devil/Or merely a lunatic practical joker?/{E} I incline to the
406 CP Edward 23   /Without the qualification 'lunatic'./Why should *you* go to a sanatorium?/I

LUNCH (14)
327 FR Charles 38   paper./{C} Stop, I think I bought a lunch edition/Before I left St. Pancras. If I did,
427 CP Alex 15   try to get you on the telephone/After lunch, but my secretary couldn't get through to
430 CP Peter 7   three days ago./I saw Sheila Paisley at lunch to-day/And she told me you were giving a
445 CC Eggers 19   they have a restaurant;/An excellent lunch, and cheap, for nowadays./But where's
453 CC Lucasta 18   why he's never asked me out to lunch./{E} We will leave Mrs. Eggerson out of
453 CC Kaghan 31   I'm starving./{K} I've just given her lunch. The problem with Lucasta/Is how to
454 CC Lucasta 15   you up, and let you take me out to lunch. {}/[*Exit* LUCASTA]/{K} Take it easy,
457 CC Lady E 25   {LE} No, Gertrude, I haven't had any lunch,/And I don't want it now. Just bring me
524 ES Charles 15   *you're* with me/It must be a perfect lunch./{M} It was a perfect lunch./But I know
524 ES Monica 16   a perfect lunch./{M} It was a perfect lunch./But I know what men are — they like to
546 ES Piggott 26   send people here. When you go in to lunch/Just take a glance around the
549 ES Carghil 10   /And which one was it invited us to lunch?/I declare, I've utterly forgotten their
549 ES Carghil 12   their names./And you gave us lunch — I've forgotten what hotel —/But such a
549 ES Carghil 13   what hotel —/But such a good lunch — and we all went in a punt/On the river

LUNCHED (2)
230 Bust Jones 27   /If he looks full of gloom then he's lunched at the *Tomb*/On cabbage, rice pudding
445 CC Eggers 18   wanting. So *she*'ll be pleased./Then I lunched at the store — they have a restaurant;/

LUNCHEON (3)
68 WL: Fire S 213   /Asked me in demotic French/To luncheon at the Cannon Street Hotel/Followed
456 CC Eggers 3   —/He'd just come back from a public luncheon —/'Eggerson', he said, 'I wanted a
524 ES Charles 8   say what I wanted to say to you/Over luncheon .../{M} That's your own fault./You

LUNE (2)
24 Rhapsody 51   lamp hummed:/'Regard the moon,/La lune ne garde aucune rancune,/She winks a
48 Lune Miel t   Aux côtes brûlantes de Mozambique./Lune de Miel/Ils ont vu les Pays-Bas, ils

LUNGS (1)
174 FQ: BurntN 109   /Wind in and out of unwholesome lungs/Time before and time after./Eructation of

LURKED (1)
64 WL: Chess 87   and coloured glass/Unstoppered, lurked her strange synthetic perfumes,/Unguent,

LURKS (1)
212 Growltiger 15   /Woe to the bristly Bandicoot, that lurks on foreign ships,/And woe to any Cat with

LUST (3)
161 Rock 7 43   forgotten/All gods except Usury, Lust and Power./O Father we welcome your
241 MC Priest3 5   can manipulate the greed and lust of others,/The feeble is devoured by his
271 MC Chorus 3   powers of spirit,/Dominated by the lust of self-demolition,/By the final utter

LUSTFUL (1)
162 Rock 8 17   curious,/Some were rapacious and lustful./Many left their bodies to the kites of

LUSTRELESS (1)
40 Burb Blei 17   out,/Chicago Semite Viennese./A lustreless protrusive eye/Stares from the

LUSTS (1)
52 Whispers 8   round dead limbs/Tightening its lusts and luxuries./Donne, I suppose, was such

LUXURIES (1)
52 Whispers 8   dead limbs/Tightening its lusts and luxuries./Donne, I suppose, was such another/

LUXURY (2)
243 MC Chorus 26   /There have been oppression and luxury,/There have been poverty and licence,/
361 CP Reilly 25   I knew that all you wanted was the luxury/Of an intimate disclosure to a stranger./

LYING (8)
103 Journ Magi 7   camels galled, sore-footed, refractory,/Lying down in the melting snow./There were
185 FQ: DrySal 42   counted by anxious worried women/Lying awake, calculating the future,/Trying to
225 Mr Mistoff 36   it is *gawn*!/But you'll find it next week lying out on the lawn./And we all say: OH!/Well
309 FR Harry 40   not an evil time, that excites us with lying voices?/{M} The cold spring now is the
392 CP Lavinia 36   /We have wasted such a lot of time in lying./{E} I don't quite know what you mean./
407 CP Reilly 32   first. {}/[*To* EDWARD]/{R} You were lying to me/By concealing your relations with
530 ES m 32   to! {}/[*pointing to a silver salver, still lying in its case*]./{LC} I don't know which
571 ES Ld Clav 36   road./I ran over an old man lying in the road/And I did not stop. Then

LYMPH (1)
172 FQ: BurntN 55   the artery/The circulation of the lymph/Are figured in the drift of stars/Ascend

LYNNE (1)
229 Gus 36   tell how he once played a part in *East Lynne*./At a Shakespeare performance he once

LYSOL (1)
124 SA Sweeney 17   her there in a bath/With a gallon of lysol in a bath/{Sw} These fellows always get

MA (2)
47 Mél Adult	4	et en sueur/Que vous suivrez à peine ma piste./En Yorkshire, conférencier;/A
51 Restaurant	22	te décrotter les rides du visage;/Tiens, ma fourchette, décrasse-toi le crâne./De quel

MACAROON (1)
31 Apollinax	22	a slice of lemon, and a bitten macaroon./Hysteria/As she laughed I was aware

MACAVITY (12)
226 Macavity	t	clever/As Magical Mr. Mistoffelees!/Macavity: the Mystery Cat/Macavity's a
226 Macavity	5	of crime — *Macavity's not there*!/Macavity, Macavity, there's no one like
226 Macavity	5	— *Macavity's not there*!/Macavity, Macavity, there's no one like Macavity,/He's
226 Macavity	5	Macavity, there's no one like Macavity,/He's broken every human law, he
226 Macavity	17	half asleep, he's always wide awake./Macavity, Macavity, there's no one like
226 Macavity	17	he's always wide awake./Macavity, Macavity, there's no one like Macavity,/For
226 Macavity	17	Macavity, there's no one like Macavity,/For he's a fiend in feline shape, a
227 Macavity	32	Secret Service say:/'It *must* have been Macavity!' — but he's a mile away./You'll be
227 Macavity	35	complicated long division sums./Macavity, Macavity, there's no one like
227 Macavity	35	long division sums./Macavity, Macavity, there's no one like Macavity,/There
227 Macavity	35	Macavity, there's no one like Macavity,/There never was a Cat of such
227 Macavity	38	whatever time the deed took place — MACAVITY WASN'T THERE!/And they say

MACAVITY'S (8)
226 Macavity	1	/Macavity: the Mystery Cat/Macavity's a Mystery Cat: he's called the
226 Macavity	4	when they reach the scene of crime — *Macavity's not there*!/Macavity, Macavity,
226 Macavity	8	when you reach the scene of crime — *Macavity's not there*!/You may seek him in the
226 Macavity	10	—/But I tell you once and once again, *Macavity's not there*!/Macavity's a ginger cat,
226 Macavity	11	and once again, *Macavity's not there*!/Macavity's a ginger cat, he's very tall and thin;/
226 Macavity	20	—/But when a crime's discovered, then *Macavity's not there*!/He's outwardly
226 Macavity	26	—/Ay, there's the wonder of the thing! *Macavity's not there*!/And when the Foreign
227 Macavity	30	—/But it's useless to investigate — *Macavity's not there*!/And when the loss has been

MACCOLGIE (3)
352 CP	m 5	COPLESTONE/ALEXANDER MACCOLGIE GIBBS/PETER QUILPE/AN
353 CP	4m 1	PETER QUILPE, ALEXANDER MACCOLGIE GIBBS,/*and an*
432 CP Lavinia	29	—/I don't know why I should. Mr. MacColgie Gibbs./{A} Indeed, yes, we have

MACHINE (9)
127 Cor1 March	14	/5,800,000 rifles and carbines,/102,000 machine guns,/28,000 trench mortars,/53,000
184 FQ: DrySal	10	unpropitiated/By worshippers of the machine, but waiting, watching and waiting./
320 FR Warburt	11	/At the present moment. The whole machine is weak/And running down. Her
348 FR Chorus	12	of living,/We know how to work the machine,/We can usually avoid accidents,/We
366 CP Julia	24	yet./And besides, I like to manage the machine myself —/In a lift I can meditate.
391 CP Lavinia	19	to me that yesterday/I started some machine, that goes on working,/And I cannot
391 CP Lavinia	20	I cannot stop it; no, it's not like a machine —/Or if it's a machine, someone else is
391 CP Lavinia	21	it's not like a machine —/Or if it's a machine, someone else is running it./But who?
530 ES Monica	8	of the power that wears out the machine./{LC} They've dried up, Monica, and

MACHINERY (1)
335 FR Harry	29	/The wheel stops, and the noise of machinery/And the desert is cleared, under the

MACHINES (1)
149 Rock 1	81	*with new bricks/There are hands and machines/And clay for new brick/And lime for*

MACTATIONS (1)
129 Cor2 State	42	time, almost now, together,/If the mactations, immolations, oblations,

MACULATE (1)
56 Swee Night	4	zebra stripes along his jaw/Swelling to maculate giraffe./The circles of the stormy

MAD (9)
33 Conv Gal	17	and imperious/At a stroke our mad poetics to confute —'/And — 'Are we then
75 WL: Thund	431	/Why then Ile fit you. Hieronymo's mad againe./Datta. Dayadhvam. Damyata./
143 Lines OM	13	eye/The dullard knows that he is mad./Tell me if I am not glad!/Choruses from
209 NamingCats	3	games;/You may think at first I'm as mad as a hatter/When I tell you, a cat must
234 Ad-dress	9	/For some are sane and some are mad/And some are good and some are bad/And
273 MC Thomas	31	You think me reckless, desperate and mad./You argue by results, as this world does,/
363 CP Edward	32	answer 'Nothing'. They will think me mad/Or simply contemptible./{UG} All to the
378 CP Celia	36	/Really, Edward, I think you are mad —/I mean, you're on the edge of a nervous
406 CP Edward	27	a ... battleship. That's what drove me mad./I am the one who needs a sanatorium —/

MADAM (4)
33 Conv Gal	13	/'Oh no, it is I who am inane.'/'You, madam, are the eternal humorist,/The eternal
424 CP Caterer	1	Have you any further orders for us, Madam?/{L} You could bring in the trolley with
424 CP Caterer	4	leave them ready./{CM} Very good, Madam. {}/[*Exit*. LAVINIA *looks about the*
424 CP Caterer	8	find in the kitchen?/{CM} Nothing, Madam./Will there be anything more you

MADAME (3)

37 Gerontion	27	bowing among the Titians;/By Madame de Tornquist, in the dark room/
44 Cook Egg	22	/I shall not want Pipit in Heaven:/Madame Blavatsky will instruct me/In the
62 WL: Burial	43	the silence./*Oed' und leer das Meer.*/Madame Sosostris, famous clairvoyante,/Had a

MADDENED (2)

204 de la Mare	20	intersect, and change;/When cats are maddened in the moonlight dance,/Dogs cower,
273 MC Priests	24	come not as men come, but/Like maddened beasts. They come not like men, who

MADDEST (1)

338 FR Harry	40	that is when/One begins to seem the maddest to other people./It is hard for you too,

MADE (165)

13 Prufrock	20	chimneys,/Slipped by the terrace, made a sudden leap,/And seeing that it was a
38 Gerontion	51	rented house. Think at last/I have not made this show purposelessly/And it is not by
70 WL: Fire S	299	wept. He promised "a new start."/I made no comment. What should I resent?'/'On
94 Ash-Wed 4	8	the others as they walked,/Who then made strong the fountains and made fresh the
94 Ash-Wed 4	8	then made strong the fountains and made fresh the springs/Made cool the dry rock
94 Ash-Wed 4	9	fountains and made fresh the springs/Made cool the dry rock and made firm the sand
94 Ash-Wed 4	9	springs/Made cool the dry rock and made firm the sand/In blue of larkspur, blue of
105 Song Sime	3	snow hills;/The stubborn season had made stand./My life is light, waiting for the
108 Animula	34	blown to pieces,/For this one who made a great fortune,/And that one who went
109 Marina	23	ice and paint cracked with heat./I made this, I have forgotten/And remember./The
110 Marina	27	one June and another September./Made this unknowing, half conscious,
151 Rock 2	1	*to his work.*/Thus your fathers were made/Fellow citizens of the saints, of the
151 Rock 2	8	love our neighbour? For love must be made real in act, as desire unites with desired;
160 Rock 7	20	time,/A moment in time but time was made through that moment: for without the
163 Rock 8	38	jealousy, pride:/It was not these that made the Crusades,/But these that unmade
167 Rock 10	44	lights for which our bodily vision is made./And we thank Thee that darkness
173 FQ: BurntN	78	both a new world/And the old made explicit, understood/In the completion of
218 Mung Rump	3	had an extensive reputation. They made their home in Victoria Grove —/That was
218 Mung Rump	19	smart at a smash-and-grab./They made their home in Victoria Grove. They had
218 Mung Rump	22	for Sunday dinner,/With their minds made up that they wouldn't get thinner/On
229 Gus	54	tell,/That moment of mystery/When I made history/As Firefrorefiddle, the Fiend of
588 Fable	41	/So when all preparations had been made,/The jovial epicures sat down to table./
588 Fable	45	able/I'll go through the account: They made a raid/On every bird and beast in Æsop's
588 Fable	51	toppling over,/Next came a viand made of turtle eggs,/And after that a great pie
588 Fable	52	turtle eggs,/And after that a great pie made of plover,/And flagons which perhaps
594 Grad 10	4	t'will be so./That which has made it great, not left behind,/The same school
605 Narcissus	9	sea and the high cliffs/When the wind made him aware of his limbs smoothly passing
246 MC Thomas	13	name, warning against treason,/Made them hold their hands. So for the time/
248 MC Tempt2	25	that you resigned/When you were made Archbishop — that was a mistake/On
252 MC Thomas	18	but in the field/And in the tilt-yard I made many yield./Shall I who ruled like an
256 MC Priests	30	the trees?/{3P} Is the window-bar made fast, is the door under lock and bolt?/{4T}
257 MC Chorus	14	labour taken away from us,/Our sins made heavier upon us./We have seen the young
261 MC Thomas	24	never an accident, for Saints are not made by/accident. Still less is a Christian
261 MC Thomas	34	the Saints are/most high, having made themselves most low, and are seen, not as
266 MC Knights	15	/You are the Archbishop who was made by the King; whom he set in your place to
268 MC Knight2	1	by your friends, offered clemency,/Made a pact of peace, and all dispute ended/
271 MC Thomas	13	/When the figure of God's purpose is made complete./You shall forget these things,
277 MC Knight1	29	de Traci has/spoken well and has made a very important point. The gist of his/
277 MC Knight1	33	call upon Hugh de Morville, who/has made a special study of statecraft and
278 MC Knight2	20	at the King's instance, had been made Archbishop, he/resigned the office of
281 MC Chorus	13	/Therefore man, whom Thou hast made to be conscious of Thee, must consciously
295 FR Harry	2	/Later, I became excited, I think I made enquiries;/The purser and the steward
295 FR Charles	11	boy,/I understand, your life together made it seem more horrible./There's a lot in my
296 FR Harry	12	but you explained them/Or at least, made me cease to be afraid of them./I will go
301 FR Chorus	18	the street?/When the private shall be made public, the common photographer/
305 FR Agatha	11	moment, there is no decision to be made;/The decision will be made by powers
305 FR Agatha	12	to be made;/The decision will be made by powers beyond us/Which now and
307 FR Harry	13	reception/And the family festivities, I made my escape/As soon as I could, and slipped
316 FR Agatha	24	is uncrossed/And the crooked is made straight. {}/[*Exit to dinner*]/END OF
318 FR Harry	1	/What was wrong was whatever made her suffer,/And whatever made her happy
318 FR Harry	2	made her suffer,/And whatever made her happy was what was virtuous —/
318 FR Harry	10	to make her more unhappy, and made us/Feel more guilty, and so we
318 FR Harry	13	to be punished,/For punishment made us feel less guilty. Mother/Never punished
318 FR Harry	14	Mother/Never punished us, but made us feel guilty./I think that the things that
334 FR Harry	26	/And I returned to find another one made ready —/The book laid out, lines

337	FR	Agatha	7	shall be unknotted/And the crooked made straight. {}/[*She moves back into the*
337	FR	Harry	22	each other./{H} I know that I have made a decision/In a moment of clarity, and
337	FR	Harry	24	I feel dull again./I only know that I made a decision/Which your words echo. I am
340	FR	Amy	3	/And I thought that time might have made a change in Agatha —/It has made
340	FR	Amy	4	made a change in Agatha —/It has made enough in *me*. Thirty-five years ago/You
341	FR	Agatha	17	we can make of the mess we have made of things,/It is what he can make, not
343	FR	Agatha	3	have another meaning./*They* have made this clear. And I who have seen them
343	FR	Mary	12	evening?/I knew that I was right: you made me wait for this —/Only for this. I
347	FR	Warburt	35	/It wasn't so serious as Winchell made out,/And we'll have him up here in the
350	FR	Agatha	19	crossed be uncrossed/The crooked be made straight/And the curse be ended/By
355	CP	Julia	37	but not the solution./He only made the situation more difficult./You know
359	CP	Julia	25	How lucky that it's raining!/It made me remember my umbrella,/And there it
360	CP	Reilly	33	/With another man, she might have made a mistake/And want to come back to you.
372	CP	Alex	13	when travelling in Albania,/Have I made such a supper out of so few materials/As I
375	CP	Edward	29	of?/{E} I had quite forgotten./He made his way in, a little while ago,/And insisted
382	CP	Celia	16	inhuman —/You might have made it by scraping your legs together —/Or
384	CP	Reilly	8	have come to remind you — you have made a decision./{E} Are you thinking that I
384	CP	Reilly	11	mind/Until you recover from having made a decision./No. I have come to tell you
384	CP	Reilly	18	of freedom was yesterday./You made a decision. You set in motion/Forces in
390	CP	Julia	5	well, thank you./{J} She must have made a marvellous recovery./I said so to myself,
392	CP	Lavinia	32	her live somewhere./{L} I see. So Julia made her live in Essex;/And made the telegrams
392	CP	Lavinia	33	So Julia made her live in Essex;/And made the telegrams come from Essex./Well, I
393	CP	Lavinia	15	decisions/That you should have made yourself. I remember —/Oh, I ought to
393	CP	Lavinia	33	of yourself./You know it was I who made you work at the Bar .../{E} You nagged
394	CP	Lavinia	18	the butler./{L} Everything I tried only made matters worse,/And the moment you were
397	CP	Edward	36	You don't understand me. Have I not made it clear/That in future you will find me a
398	CP	Edward	5	yesterday./Before I thought that I had made a decision./What devil left the door on the
399	CP	Nurse	5	/To avoid any meeting?/{N} You made that clear, Sir Henry:/The first
403	CP	Edward	24	back./It was because of what she had made me into./We had not been alone again for
403	CP	Edward	35	/I cannot live without her, for she has made me incapable/Of having any existence of
403	CP	Edward	38	to me in five years together!/She has made the world a place I cannot live in/Except
405	CP	Edward	19	And I propose to do so./My mind is made up. I shall go to a hotel./{R} It is just
408	CP	Lavinia	2	completely prostrated;/Even if I have made a partial recovery./{R} Certainly, you
409	CP	Reilly	2	of emotional strain/And so I made enquiries./{E} It was two months ago/
409	CP	Reilly	18	been in love with anybody;/Which made you suspect that you were incapable/Of
411	CP	Lavinia	32	to tell us, themselves, that they had made their decision./{E} Have you anything else
414	CP	Celia	7	I mean that what has happened has made me aware/That I've always been alone.
416	CP	Celia	9	That's clever of you./No, perhaps I made it obvious. You don't need to know/
416	CP	Celia	22	nor taking/But that we had merely made use of each other/Each for his purpose.
420	CP	Celia	8	/{C} But I know it is I who have made the decision:/I must tell you that. Oh, I
422	CP	Alex	9	accept their destiny./{A} And *she* has made the choice?/{R} She will be fetched this
429	CP	Edward	23	up an interim report./{E} Will it be made public?/{A} It cannot be, at present:/There
435	CP	Lavinia	34	on is an image of Celia/Which you made for yourself, to meet your own needs./
436	CP	Reilly	27	Chamberlayne,/The difference that made to the natives who were dying/Or the state
437	CP	Julia	2	you speaking poetry .../{J} She has made a point, Henry./{L} ... if it answers my
438	CP	Reilly	33	to a patient —/And sometimes I have made the wrong decision./As for Miss
451	CC	Eggers	7	out/And gave him his start. And he's made the most of it —/That I will say. An
455	CC	Eggers	13	was a friend of Sir Claude's,/And he's made himself responsible for her./In any case,
458	CC	Eggers	29	orders, Lady Elizabeth:/The doctor made it very imperative .../{SC} Mr. Simpkins
459	CC	Claude	36	to Dr. Leroux/In Lausanne. What made you go to Zürich?/{LE} Why, I'd we
463	CC	Claude	2	you belonged to your aunt,/Or so she made me feel. I never saw you alone./And then
464	CC	Colby	25	how did it happen/That you never made it your profession?/{SC} Family pressure,
465	CC	Claude	23	what the man must have felt when he made it./But nothing *I* made ever gave me that
465	CC	Claude	24	felt when he made it./But nothing *I* made ever gave me that contentment —/That
467	CC	Claude	19	to avoid the mistakes/My father made with me. And yet I seem/To have made a
467	CC	Claude	20	with me. And yet I seem/To have made a greater mistake than he did./{C} I know
470	CC	Colby	27	see it./{L} But not with you!/{C} You made that very clear./But why not with me?/{L}
471	CC	Lucasta	40	your kind of self-defence./{L} What made you think it was self-defence?/{C} Because
472	CC	Lucasta	31	applied for Eggerson's position,/And made up your mind to go into business/And be
479	CC	Kaghan	30	wanted to pursue you./{K} Yes, I made a bad impression at the start:/I saw that it
479	CC	Kaghan	32	was necessary. I'm afraid Colby/Has made a good impression; which he'll have to
481	CC	Lady E	32	great deal of salad./You remember, I made you take a note of the address;/And I
484	CC	Lady E	29	— and so uncongenial./They made me feel an outcast. And yet they were so
485	CC	Lady E	1	feeble-minded: though my family made me think so./But you know, I actually
485	CC	Lady E	15	it now./That was only a phase. But it made it all so simple!/To be able to think that

487 CC	Lady E	17	What is it, Elizabeth?/{LE} I've just made a startling discovery!/All through a name
491 CC	Colby	1	thought about it. Now, you have made me think,/And I wish that I could have
496 CC	Lady E	1	feeling very stupid./You always made me feel that I wasn't worth talking to./
496 CC	Claude	2	talking to./{SC} And you always made me feel that *your* interests/Were much too
498 CC	Eggers	12	/That perhaps Mrs. Guzzard made a profession/Of ... looking after other
499 CC	Lucasta	24	/That was just the trouble. You made it so obvious/That this would be the ideal
499 CC	Lucasta	28	always found me!/And I haven't made it easier. I didn't try to./And knowing that
499 CC	Lucasta	30	that you wanted me to marry B./Made me determined that I wouldn't. Just to
500 CC	Claude	11	my brain reel./{SC} I ought to have made things clear to you/At the time when he
500 CC	Lucasta	24	him for the shock he'd given me./He made me see what I really wanted./B. makes me
501 CC	Claude	1	nevertheless/I'm sure that you have made the right decision./{L} But the reasons
501 CC	Lady E	3	And I'm sure too, Lucasta, you have made a wise decision./{L} And I know very well
507 CC	Guzzard	17	whom the monthly payments were made./{E} The terms were satisfactory?/{MG}
508 CC	Guzzard	21	to have him while the payments were made;/But we could not afford to adopt the
512 CC	Guzzard	38	turn/Against those who have made them. {}/[*To* LADY ELIZABETH *and*
515 CC	Guzzard	24	is even greater than the sacrifice I made/When I let you claim him. Do you think
519 CC	Kaghan	7	{K} You know, Claude, I think we all made the same mistake —/All except Eggers .../
526 ES	Charles	5	merely wanted to believe it. And I've made you say so!/But now that you've said so,
530 ES	Ld Clav	37	of silver! The inadequate levy/That made the Chairman's Price! And my fellow
536 ES	Gomez	14	what the parish priest told her./I made my children learn English — it's useful;/I
537 ES	Gomez	22	/Later, I came to understand: you made friends with me/Because it flattered *you*
538 ES	Gomez	11	/You had plenty of money, and you made a good marriage —/Or so it seemed —
538 ES	Gomez	19	responsibility/Isn't the man who made the mistake./That's your convention. Or if
538 ES	Gomez	20	your convention. Or if it's known you made it/You simply get moved to another post/
538 ES	Gomez	31	didn't have to take your advice .../I've made a point, you see, of following your career.
548 ES	Carghil	18	of you to find it so quickly./What made you choose it? {}/[*throwing down*
549 ES	Carghil	16	what you called them,/And you made me try to punt, and I got soaking wet/
552 ES	Carghil	6	art./Don't you remember what a hit I made/With a number called *It's Not Too Late*
556 ES	Monica	1	garden/Until I had prepared you. I've made him understand/That the doctors want
556 ES	Michael	31	explain things to *you*./You've always made up your mind that I was to blame/Before
557 ES	Ld Clav	8	The position that Sir Alfred Walter made for you./{Mi} I'd stuck it for two years.
558 ES	Michael	21	place, they all knew the job had been made for me/Because I was your son. They
561 ES	Michael	20	standards of conduct/You've always made so much of, for my benefit:/I wonder
561 ES	Ld Clav	27	/And to meet him half way. I have made him an offer/Which he must think over.
564 ES	Carghil	2	*To Love Me!* That's the song/That made my reputation, Señor Gomez./{G} It will
570 ES	Ld Clav	27	the Central American,/A man who's made a fortune by his own peculiar methods,/A
572 ES	Ld Clav	15	her — but my father prevented that:/Made it worth while for her not to marry me —
572 ES	Ld Clav	17	his way of putting it — and of course/Made it worth while for me not to marry her./In
572 ES	Ld Clav	37	I shall at last escape them./— I've made my confession to you, Monica:/That is the
573 ES	Ld Clav	10	is in relation to the sinner./What has made the difference in the last five minutes/Is
575 ES	Michael	1	remittance man for whom a job was made./No! I want to go where I can make my
576 ES	Michael	11	It was his experience/With you, that made him so understanding/Of my predicament.
576 ES	Ld Clav	13	/Of my predicament./{LC} And made him invent/The position which he'd come
576 ES	Michael	17	some pickings in commissions./He's made a fortune there. San Marco for me!/{LC}
578 ES	Ld Clav	5	/The many many mistakes I have made/My whole life through, mistake upon

MADMAN (2)

24 Rhapsody		12	/Midnight shakes the memory/As a madman shakes a dead geranium./Half-past
269 MC	Knight1	7	insult with gross indignity;/Insolent madman, whom nothing deters/From attainting

MADNESS (1)

248 MC	Tempt2	30	of marble./Rule over men reckon no madness./{T} To the man of God what

MAGI (1)

103 Journ Magi		t	/ARIEL POEMS/Journey of the Magi/'A cold coming we had of it,/Just the

MAGIC (1)

16 Prufrock		105	to say just what I mean!/But as if a magic lantern threw the nerves in patterns on a

MAGICAL (4)

224 Mr Mistoff		22	/Was there ever/A Cat so clever/As Magical Mr. Mistoffelees!/He is quiet and small,
225 Mr Mistoff		41	/Was there ever/A Cat so clever/As Magical Mr. Mistoffelees!/His manner is vague
225 Mr Mistoff		50	is incontestable proof/Of his singular magical powers:/And I have known the family
225 Mr Mistoff		60	you ever/Know a Cat so clever/As Magical Mr. Mistoffelees!/Macavity: the

MAGICIANS (1)

224 Mr Mistoff		14	/And deceive you again./The greatest magicians have something to learn/From Mr.

MAGNITUDE (1)

573 ES	Ld Clav	5	hard to make other people realise/The magnitude of things that appear to them petty;/

MAGNUS (1)

69 WL: Fire S		264	lounge at noon: where the walls/Of Magnus Martyr hold/Inexplicable splendour of

MAGUS (1)
437 CP   Reilly   5   /{R} *Ere Babylon was dust/The magus Zoroaster, my dead child,/Met his own*
MAHARAJA (1)
353 CP   Julia   4   you doing, up in a tree:/You and the Maharaja?/{A} My dear Julia!/It's perfectly
MAIDEN (3)
29 Aunt Helen   1   Helen/Miss Helen Slingsby was my maiden aunt,/And lived in a small house near a
204 de la Mare   22   owls range/At witches' sabbath of the maiden aunts;/When the nocturnal traveller can
357 CP   Julia   38   /Now you must let me be *your* maiden aunt —/Living on an annuity, of course.
MAIDENHEAD (2)
147 Rock 1   29   we must motor/To Hindhead, or Maidenhead./If the weather is foul we stay at
213 Growltiger   54   the news flew through the land;/At Maidenhead and Henley there was dancing on
MAIDS (1)
122 SAWa & Ho   30   *the bamboo tree/Where the Gauguin maids/In the banyan shades/Wear palmleaf*
MAIL (4)
232 Skimble   8   he's very nimble/Then the Night Mail just can't go.'/At 11.42 then the signal's
232 Skimble   31   nothing goes wrong on the Northern Mail/When Skimbleshanks is aboard./Oh it's
233 Skimble   65   meet without fail on the Midnight Mail/The Cat of the Railway Train.'/The
580 ES   Gomez   4   some days, you know, even by air mail./{M} Take the card, Charles. If I write to
MAIL'S (1)
232 Skimble   2   the line at 11.39/When the Night Mail's ready to depart,/Saying 'Skimble where
MAINE (1)
248 MC Tempt2   17   /And last at Montmirail, in Maine. Now that I have recalled them,/Let us
MAINLAND (1)
96 Ash-Wed 5   14   the sea or on the islands, not/On the mainland, in the desert or the rain land,/For
MAINTAIN (1)
417 CP   Reilly   27   have had, but they cease to regret it,/Maintain themselves by the common routine,/
MAINTAINING (1)
540 ES   Ld Clav 9   that the kind of pretence that you're maintaining/In trying to persuade me of your ...
MAIS (3)
48 Lune Miel   2   Pays-Bas, ils rentrent à Terre Haute;/Mais une nuit d'été, les voici à Ravenne,/A
51 Restaurant   15   un instant de puissance et de délire.'/Mais alors, vieux lubrique, à cet âge .../
51 Restaurant   20   quittée à mi-chemin./C'est dommage.'/Mais alors, tu as ton vautour!/Va t'en te
MAISIE (18)
550 ES   Ld Clav 2   once more./{LC} Your name was Maisie Batterson./{MC} Oh, Richard, you're
550 ES   Ld Clav 5   which you knew me./{LC} Well, then, Maisie Montjoy./{MC} Yes. Maisie Montjoy./I
550 ES   Carghil 6   then, Maisie Montjoy./{MC} Yes. Maisie Montjoy./I was Maisie Montjoy once.
550 ES   Carghil 7   /{MC} Yes. Maisie Montjoy./I was Maisie Montjoy once. And you didn't recognise
552 ES   Ld Clav 35   /{LC} I've no longer any part to play, Maisie./{MC} There'll always be some sort of
553 ES   Carghil 25   /'They'll be worth a fortune to you, Maisie.'/They would have figured at the trial, I
554 ES   Piggott 33   but you might remember her/As Maisie Montjoy in revue./She was well-known
562 ES   Carghil 23   us,/I'll introduce myself. I'm Maisie Montjoy!/That means nothing to you,
562 ES   Carghil 25   It's a very long time since the name of Maisie Montjoy/Topped the bill in revue. Now
563 ES   Carghil 29   in London/Knew the name of Maisie Montjoy in revue./{G} If Maisie
563 ES   Gomez 30   of Maisie Montjoy in revue./{G} If Maisie Montjoy was as beautiful to look at/As
570 ES   Ld Clav 34   somewhere in the Midlands./As for Maisie Batterson .../{M} Maisie Batterson?/Who
570 ES   Monica 35   /As for Maisie Batterson .../{M} Maisie Batterson?/Who is Maisie Batterson?/
570 ES   Monica 36   .../{M} Maisie Batterson?/Who is Maisie Batterson?/{LC} She no longer exists./
570 ES   Ld Clav 38   exists./Nor the musical comedy star, Maisie Montjoy./There is Mrs. John Carghill,
571 ES   Ld Clav 2   widow./But Freddy Culverwell and Maisie Batterson,/And Dick Ferry too, and
571 ES   Ld Clav 17   faults that they were born with./And Maisie loved me, with whatever capacity/For
572 ES   Ld Clav 22   to the ghost of the woman who was Maisie./We should have been poor, we should
MAISONNETTE (1)
52 Whispers   24   subtle effluence of cat;/Grishkin has a maisonnette;/The sleek Brazilian jaguar/Does
MAÎTRE (1)
524 ES   Monica 11   restaurant/Instead of to one where the *maître d'hôtel*/And the waiters all seem to be
MAJESTY (1)
269 MC Knight1   5   /{K1} The King's justice, the King's majesty,/You insult with gross indignity;/
MAJORITY (1)
428 CP   Alex   11   are a pest?/{A} Unfortunately,/The majority of the natives are heathen:/They hold
MAKE (186)
13 Prufrock   12   not ask, 'What is it?'/Let us go and make our visit./In the room the women come
20 Portrait   69   to friends..../'I take my hat: how can I make a cowardly amends/For what she has said
65 WL: Chess   142   TIME/Now Albert's coming back, make yourself a bit smart./He'll want to know
115 SP   Doris   25   like a fellow once I knew./*He* could make you laugh./{Du} Sam can make you
116 SP   Dusty   1   could make you laugh./{Du} Sam can make you laugh:/Sam's all right/{Do} But

119 SP	Klip	9	do you do/{Kl} I'm very pleased to	make your acquaintance/{Kr} Extremely
148 Rock 1		57	most expect dividends./I say to you:	*Make perfect your will.*/I say: take no thought of
149 Rock 1		77	ago done,/That you may take heart.	Make perfect your will./Let me show you the
155 Rock 3		55	answer? 'We all dwell together/To	make money from each other'? or 'This is a
163 Rock 8		48	faith and conviction./Let us therefore	make perfect our will./O GOD, help us./Son of
197 FQ: Little		217	the beginning is often the end/And to	make an end is to make a beginning./The end is
197 FQ: Little		217	the end/And to make an end is to	make a beginning./The end is where we start
216 Jellicles		18	/Until the Jellicle Moon appears/They	make their toilette and take their repose:/
226 Macavity		7	/His powers of levitation would	make a fakir stare,/And when you reach the
233 Skimble		37	There is every sort of light — you can	make it dark or bright;/There's a button that
233 Skimble		38	/There's a button that you turn to	make a breeze./There's a funny little basin
236 Cat Morgan		20	you'll spare yourself labour/If jist you	make friends with the Cat at the door./
588 Fable		37	the door from head to feet./To	make a rather lengthy story shorter,/He left no
593 Grad 6		2	/Than those before, her sons must	make her so,/And we are of her sons, and we
245 MC	Priest2	30	your coming,/Than seven days could	make ready Canterbury./However, I will have
249 MC	Tempt2	7	of the better cause,/Dispensing justice	make all even,/Is thrive on earth, and perhaps in
250 MC	Thomas	14	ignorance, but arrest disorder,/	Make it fast, breed fatal disease,/Degrade what
252 MC	Thomas	26	his regard for your loyalty./{T} To	make, then break, this thought has come before,
255 MC	Tempt4	12	/Seek the way of martyrdom,	make yourself the lowest/On earth, to be high in
258 MC	Thomas	29	those who serve the greater cause may	make the cause serve them,/Still doing right:
258 MC	Thomas	31	and striving with political men/May	make that cause political, not by what they do/
267 MC	Thomas	23	—/Should be said in public. If you	make charges,/Then in public I will refute them.
267 MC	m	25	them./{K1} No! here and now! {}/[*They*	make *to attack him, but the priests and*
267 MC	Knight1	27	/{K1} Of your earlier misdeeds I shall	make no mention./They are too well known.
269 MC	Thomas	3	back again./Never again, you must	make no doubt,/Shall the sea run between the
269 MC	Chorus	33	/Laughter in the noises of beasts that	make strange noises: jackal, jackass, jackdaw;
271 MC	Thomas	25	is no danger./I have therefore only to	make perfect my will./{3P} My Lord, they are
271 MC	Priests	28	You will be killed. Come to the altar./	Make haste, my Lord. Don't stop here talking.
277 MC	Knight3	6	country first. I dare say that we didn't	make a/very good impression when we came in
280 MC	Priest3	21	the sullen coasts/Where blackamoors	make captive Christian men;/Go to the northern
285 FR	Amy	12	But leave the curtains undrawn./	Make up the fire. Will the spring never come? I
287 FR	Gerald	3	as I remember. Besides, you've got to	make allowances:/We haven't left them such an
287 FR	Amy	19	as I intended./Harry's return does not	make things easy for her/At the moment: but
289 FR	Gerald	6	birthday/Or for Harry's homecoming.	Make him feel at home, I say!/Make him feel
289 FR	Gerald	7	Make him feel at home, I say!/	Make him feel that what has happened doesn't
289 FR	Amy	36	that none of you ever met her./It will	make the situation very much easier/And is why
293 FR	Amy	8	to keep Wishwood going/And to	make no changes before your return./Now it's
293 FR	Agatha	22	/And you must try at once to	make us understand,/And we must try to
293 FR	Harry	26	explained it./All that I could hope to	make you understand/Is only events: not what
299 FR	Downing	27	in a way, irresponsible, Sir./If I may	make so bold, Sir,/I always thought that a very
301 FR	Violet	23	acquaintance./{V} Gerald is certain to	make some blunder, he is useless out of the
301 FR	Chorus	25	will be diminished./{Ch} We all of us	make the pretension/To be the uncommon
302 FR	Chorus	8	the curtains be drawn,/The cellar	make some dreadful disclosure, the roof
309 FR	Harry	2	understand:/Explaining would only	make a worse misunderstanding;/Explaining
313 FR	Gerald	16	him back again, isn't it?/We must	make him feel at home. And most auspicious/
317 FR	Harry	8	going to be useless,/Or if anything,	make matters rather more difficult./But talk
317 FR	Warburt	20	Or do not know, at any moment/May	make an endless difference to the future./It's
318 FR	Harry	7	a time/In which we were supposed to	make up to mother/For all the weeks during
318 FR	Harry	10	and seeing us then/Only seemed to	make her more unhappy, and made us/Feel
318 FR	Harry	16	that are taken for granted/At home,	make a deeper impression upon children/Than
320 FR	Warburt	28	had to know. One is your mother,/To	make her happy for the time she has to live./The
324 FR	Harry	15	trouble like a concussion/Cannot	make very much difference to John./A brief
324 FR	Harry	17	consciousness/That John enjoys, can't	make very much difference/To him or to anyone
325 FR	Harry	4	said that./{H} I think, mother,/I shall	make you lie down. You must be very tired. {}/
326 FR	Violet	31	hours ago, to Wishwood./{V} I will	make no observations on what you say, Harry;/
328 FR	Gerald	26	/{G} This is what the Communists	make capital out of./{C} There's a little more.
330 FR	Harry	6	us I can conceive/As settling down to	make himself at home at Wishwood,/Make a
330 FR	Harry	7	make himself at home at Wishwood,/	Make a dull marriage, marry some woman
334 FR	Agatha	11	daily:/And I am old, to start again to	make my living./{H} But you are not unhappy,
337 FR	Agatha	15	learned/Mean the end of a relation,	make it impossible./You did not intend this, I
341 FR	Agatha	17	Success is relative:/It is what we can	make of the mess we have made of things,/It is
341 FR	Agatha	18	have made of things,/It is what he can	make, not what you would make for him./{A}
341 FR	Agatha	18	he can make, not what you would	make for him./{A} Success is one thing, what
341 FR	Amy	19	Success is one thing, what you would	make for him/Is another. I call it failure. Your
342 FR	Amy	7	how./I have been always trying to	make myself believe/That he was not such a

344 FR	Charles	15	And why in such a hurry? Before you make up your mind .../{V} You can't really
344 FR	Harry	37	What I have seen. Oh why should you make it so ridiculous/Just now? I only want,
356 CP	Peter	6	/{C} Making a film./{P} Trying to make a film./{J} Oh, what film was it? I wonder
356 CP	Julia	31	why she went away —/So that I could make you talk. Perhaps she's in the pantry/
357 CP	Julia	40	an annuity, of course./I am going to make you dine alone with me/On Friday, and
367 CP	Peter	24	a possible profession?/{P} She might make it a profession;/Though she had her
368 CP	Alex	27	of rice and a little dried fish/I can make half a dozen dishes. Don't say a word./I
371 CP	Peter	16	/{P} But I must see Celia at least to make her tell me/What has happened, in her
372 CP	Alex	11	my triumphs/This is the greatest. To make something out of nothing!/Never, even
378 CP	Edward	18	the effect of all his argument/Was to make me see that I wanted her back./{C} That's
380 CP	Celia	26	to concerts./But then, as he came to make more acquaintances,/I found him less
392 CP	Edward	31	in Essex?/{E} Julia compelled me to make her live somewhere./{L} I see. So Julia
393 CP	Lavinia	18	planning our honeymoon,/I couldn't make you say where you wanted to go .../{E}
393 CP	Edward	19	to go .../{E} But I wanted you to make that decision./{L} But how could I tell
394 CP	Edward	29	me:/Then why did you always make me feel insignificant?/I may not have
396 CP	Edward	32	were a child./{E} I don't want you to make yourself responsible for me:/It's only
397 CP	Edward	18	you./{E} If I go to a doctor, I shall make my own choice;/Not take one whom you
398 CP	Edward	11	I become after all what you would make me?/{L} Well, Edward, as I am unable to
398 CP	Lavinia	12	/{L} Well, Edward, as I am unable to make you laugh,/And as I can't persuade you to
401 CP	Edward	39	you realise/That I was in no state to make a decision?/{R} If I had not brought your
403 CP	Reilly	4	dreams, to oblige me./I could make you dream any kind of dream I suggested,
403 CP	Reilly	8	/{R} Precisely. And I could make you feel important,/And you would
407 CP	Reilly	39	you, Mrs. Chamberlayne,/Tried to make me believe that it was this discovery/
409 CP	Reilly	13	/{R} And were not prepared to make the least sacrifice/On her account. This
410 CP	Lavinia	11	in common/Might be just enough to make us loathe one another./{R} See it rather as
410 CP	Edward	33	you have said./{E} Lavinia, we must make the best of a bad job./That is what he
410 CP	Reilly	36	/The best of a bad job is all any of us make of it —/Except of course, the saints —
412 CP	Julia	9	to tell you, I am sure she is ready/To make a decision./{R} Was she reluctant?/Was
414 CP	Celia	27	alone — or so it seems to me./They make noises, and think they are talking to each
414 CP	Celia	28	they are talking to each other;/They make faces, and think they understand each
415 CP	Celia	34	/But I don't see why mistakes should make one feel sinful!/And yet I can't find any
418 CP	Celia	14	be dishonest/For me, now, to try to make a life with anybody!/I couldn't give
418 CP	Reilly	35	are necessary. It is also necessary/To make a choice between them./{C} Then I choose
419 CP	Celia	23	can't all stay there!/I mean, it would make the place so over-crowded./{R} Not very
419 CP	Reilly	35	nine o'clock./{R} Go home then, and make your preparations./Here is the address for
425 CP	Edward	23	/Their guests will get just enough to make them thirsty;/They'll come on to us later,
425 CP	Edward	27	on to the Gunnings afterwards,/To make room for those who come from the
431 CP	Peter	3	/Perhaps it would be a good place to make one./— Alex knows all about
433 CP	Peter	15	films,/And I always thought she could make a success of it/If she only got the chance.
435 CP	Peter	20	in myself./I thought I had ideas to make a revolution/In the cinema, that no one
435 CP	Lavinia	39	saying/Will seem less unkind if I can make you understand/That in fact I've been
436 CP	Edward	6	later/When it's harder to recover, and make a new beginning./It's not so hard for you.
438 CP	Reilly	31	/Mrs. Chamberlayne, I often have to make a decision/Which may mean restoration
439 CP	Reilly	6	have to live with these memories and make them/Into something new. Only by
446 CC	Eggers	30	think of everything./But if I might make a suggestion: window boxes!/He's
447 CC	Claude	30	recommended,/And say that I had to make a quick decision/Because he'd had
447 CC	Claude	32	offer./Something like that. Don't make too much of it./And I rather hope that she
449 CC	Claude	6	/In the circumstances, that might make her jealous./I've explained all this to
449 CC	Eggers	21	influence./I have never been able to make her like Miss Angel;/She becomes
450 CC	Claude	4	a person/That you're liable to make the worst mistake about him./As a matter
451 CC	Eggers	20	says to me: 'Eggerson, why can't you make me laugh/The way B. Kaghan did?' She's
452 CC	Lucasta	21	I'm sure he didn't want —/Just to make trouble! And I couldn't find one of them./
454 CC	Kaghan	12	Come along, Lucasta,/I'm going to make a day of it, and take you out to lunch./{L}
454 CC	Colby	36	perhaps I'll be amused./But it did make my head spin — all those first names/The
457 CC	Lady E	28	/You haven't learned yet how to make tea properly./A cup of black coffee. Is Sir
458 CC	Eggers	32	another tempting offer:/So we had to make a quick decision./{SC} I didn't want to
461 CC	Colby	28	with everyone./{C} I'm sure that will make it easier for both of us./{SC} Her sudden
470 CC	Lucasta	21	playing is./{L} Really, Colby, you do make difficulties!/But what about taking me to
474 CC	Colby	6	walk in my garden/And that would make the world outside it real/And acceptable, I
478 CC	Lucasta	2	boy./Perhaps he'll adopt you, and make you his heir/And you'll marry another
480 CC	Kaghan	8	But I sometimes guess wrong./I make decisions on the spur of the moment,/But
487 CC	Claude	38	I know that. But why should that make him your son?/{LE} It's the name I've
488 CC	Claude	18	Elizabeth. If Mrs. Guzzard comes/To make her confession, it will be very different/
491 CC	Lady E	7	ours than only yours./Why should we make any further enquiries?/Let us regard him
494 CC	Lady E	39	to be a potter!/You really mean, to make jugs and jars/Like those in your

499 CC	Lucasta	18	/In any case, I've an announcement to make,/And I might as well make it now. If
499 CC	Lucasta	19	to make,/And I might as well make it now. If you'll listen./{SC} Of course I'll
500 CC	Lucasta	10	Colby's aunt./{L} Colby's aunt? You make my brain reel./{SC} I ought to have made
501 CC	Eggers	26	at your meeting./{E} Allow me. May I make a suggestion?/Though first of all I must
501 CC	Lucasta	37	/{L} I trust you, Eggy. And I want to make my peace with him./{SC} We'll get him
504 CC	Lucasta	18	you show her up, Lucasta?/{L} I'll make B. do it. {}/[*Exit* LUCASTA]/{SC} I wish
505 CC	Guzzard	10	from Colby./I am very happy to make his acquaintance./{SC} And I thought he
505 CC	Eggers	19	you please, Eggerson./{E} Then let's make a start./The question has to do, as you
508 CC	Eggers	3	Mrs. Guzzard. Far from it. You must make allowances/For a mother who has been
511 CC	Kaghan	34	— it sounds rather flashy:/It wouldn't make the right impression in the City./{L} When
512 CC	Kaghan	31	to it. And ... yes, of course,/If I can make it right with my parents./I'm fond of
515 CC	Guzzard	13	in life —/That I knew. And it would make you so happy!/If I said the child was
515 CC	Claude	37	/Well, believe it, then. But don't let it make a difference/To our relations. Or, perhaps,
516 CC	Claude	1	that./If you will stay with me. It shall make no difference/To my plans for your
516 CC	Claude	35	the same disillusionment:/I want us to make the best of it, together./{C} No, Sir
519 CC	Lady E	14	should ask of other people,/One does make mistakes! But I mean to do better./
527 ES	Monica	29	that can't be interrupted./Someone to make a remark to now and then./And mostly
528 ES	Monica	38	in Jamaica/Will never take place. 'Make the reservations'/Selby said, 'as if you
530 ES	Monica	30	and the speech you had to make/And the speeches that you had to listen
535 ES	Gomez	19	you need to trust someone/You must make it worth his while to be trustworthy. {}/
537 ES	Ld Clav	5	people, how do you propose/To make it worth my while to be trustworthy?/{G}
538 ES	Gomez	22	another post/Where at least you can't make quite the same mistake./At the worst, you
538 ES	Gomez	24	opposition/And let the other people make mistakes/Until your own have been more
538 ES	Gomez	26	or less forgotten./I dare say you did make some mistake, Dick .../That would
540 ES	Gomez	8	the man who in the morning/Has to make up his face before he looks in the mirror./
541 ES	Gomez	19	over. San Marco's a good place/To make money in — though not to *keep* it in./My
542 ES	Gomez	3	that you want?/{G} I've been trying to make clear that I only want your friendship!/
544 ES	Monica	24	frost on the fruit trees./{M} Oh, let's make the most of this weather while it lasts./I
545 ES	Piggott	31	provided?/All you have to do is to make your wants known./Just ring through to
546 ES	Piggott	25	Any guest who *looks* incurable —/We make that stipulation to all the doctors/Who
550 ES	Carghil	13	last long./People sometimes say: 'Make one mistake in love,/You're more than
550 ES	Carghil	14	in love,/You're more than likely to make another'./How true that is! Algy was a
550 ES	Carghil	22	heard/Of Carghill Equipments? They make office furniture./{LC} I've never had to
556 ES	Monica	3	you to be free from worry./He won't make a scene. But I can see he's frightened./And
557 ES	Michael	20	I needed a good deal more capital/To make anything of it. If I could have borrowed
558 ES	Ld Clav	29	your shortcomings?/Or did Sir Alfred make other unflattering criticisms?/{Mi} Well,
559 ES	Michael	14	no./That's not my idea. I want to make money./I want to be somebody on my
560 ES	Ld Clav	16	for you, Michael./I will help you to make a start in any business/You may find for
561 ES	Michael	33	to say?/I want to leave England, and make my own career:/And Father simply calls
564 ES	Carghil	31	I'm going to cross-examine you/And make you tell me all about Richard/In his
567 ES	Charles	17	another shopping expedition we must make!/But my darling, since I got your letter
570 ES	Ld Clav	9	is sure of the wrong response?/How make a confession with no hope of absolution?/
571 ES	Ld Clav	8	when we were at Oxford;/What did I make of his admiration?/I led him to acquire
571 ES	Ld Clav	31	Culverwell,/He re-enters my life to make himself a reminder/Of one occasion the
573 ES	Ld Clav	4	when I'm just recovering!/It's hard to make other people realise/The magnitude of
575 ES	Michael	2	made./No! I want to go where I can make my own way,/Not merely be your son.
577 ES	Carghil	35	all this time for opportunity/To make use of his gifts; and now, opportunity —/
578 ES	Monica	35	single word/Of what I said. You must make your own life/Of course, just as I must
578 ES	Monica	36	own life/Of course, just as I must make mine./It's not a question of your going
581 ES	Ld Clav	3	and Charles will do what you can/To make him feel that he is not estranged from
581 ES	Charles	6	we can. But it's both of you together/Make the force to attract him: you and Monica

MAKE-BELIEVE (10)

280 MC	Priest3	34	weave,/Pacing forever in the hell of make-believe/Which never is belief: this is your
327 FR	Agatha	5	penetrate the other private worlds/Of make-believe and fear. To rest in our own
381 CP	Edward	31	struggle to escape from it/Is only a make-believe, a pretence/That what is, is not, or
462 CC	Claude	18	/She has always lived in a world of make-believe,/And the best one can do is to
462 CC	Colby	22	/If we all have to live in a world of make-believe,/Is that good for us? Or a kindness
464 CC	Claude	36	is changing you:/It begins as a kind of make-believe/And the make-believing makes it
466 CC	Claude	22	live/In two worlds — each a kind of make-believe./That's you and me. Some day,
466 CC	Claude	30	you/Even to the point of accepting ... make-believe?/{C} I think I do. At least, I
467 CC	Colby	30	my position/To be, in any way, a make-believe./{SC} It shan't be. Meanwhile, we
581 ES	Ld Clav	35	love is for the real Charles, not a make-believe,/As was your love for me./{M} But

MAKE-BELIEVING (1)

| 464 CC | Claude | 37 | as a kind of make-believe/And the make-believing makes it real./That's not the |

MAKER (1)
466 CC Claude 12   that sense of identification/With the maker, of which I spoke — an agonising ecstasy
MAKES (37)
 15 Prufrock   66   hair!)/Is it perfume from a dress/That makes me so digress?/Arms that lie along a
 37 Gerontion   13   merds./The woman keeps the kitchen, makes tea,/Sneezes at evening, poking the
 66 WL: Chess   155   and choose if you can't./But if Albert makes off, it won't be for lack of telling./You
 68 WL: Fire S   242   /His vanity requires no response,/And makes a welcome of indifference./(And I
152 Rock 2   46   is his neighbour/Unless his neighbour makes too much disturbance,/But all dash to
210 Old Gumbie   4   and sits and sits — and that's what makes a Gumbie Cat!/But when the day's hustle
210 Old Gumbie   16   and sits and sits — and that's what makes a Gumbie Cat!/But when the day's hustle
210 Old Gumbie   23   work with her baking and frying./She makes them a mouse-cake of bread and dried
211 Old Gumbie   28   and sits and sits — and that's what makes a Gumbie Cat!/But when the day's hustle
214 RTTugger   17   to lie in the bureau drawer,/But he makes such a fuss if he can't get out./Yes the
228 Gus   6   rake,/And he suffers from palsy that makes his paw shake./Yet he was, in his youth,
235 Ad-dress   60   personal taste./(I know a Cat, who makes a habit,/Of eating nothing else but rabbit,
280 MC   Priest3   23   with ice/Where the dead breath makes numb the hand, makes dull the brain;/
280 MC   Priest3   23   dead breath makes numb the hand, makes dull the brain;/Find an oasis in the desert
296 FR   Ivy   22   can be very cunning —/Their malady makes them so. They do not want to be cured/
296 FR   Charles   27   simply that the wish to get rid of her/Makes him believe he did. He cannot trust his
305 FR   Harry   36   What I might have expected./It only makes the changing of people/All the more
338 FR   Harry   7   in which to explain it —/That is what makes it harder. You must just believe me,/
363 CP   Edward   22   /Besides, don't you see that it makes me ridiculous?/{UG} It will do you no
370 CP   Peter   22   effect. She doesn't want to see me;/Makes excuses, not very plausible,/And when I
376 CP   Julia   33   have warned you:/Anything that Alex makes is absolutely deadly./I could tell such
412 CP   Celia   32   of Mrs. Shuttlethwaite./{C} That makes it even more perplexing. However,/I
425 CP   Lavinia   34   they've been invited./That's what makes it a success. Is that picture straight?/{E}
439 CP   Julia   10   time that *I* said something:/Everyone makes a choice, of one kind or another,/And
447 CC   Claude   15   it comes to appointing a successor./Makes it very difficult to replace you./She
451 CC   Eggers   18   Kaghan is very good company./He makes me laugh sometimes. I don't laugh easily.
458 CC   Lady E   23   /And she can't go by air — she says it makes her sea-sick;/So we took the night train,
464 CC   Claude   37   make-believe/And the make-believing makes it real./That's not the whole story. My
466 CC   Claude   13   spoke — an agonising ecstasy/Which makes life bearable. It's all I have./I suppose it
473 CC   Lucasta   31   mine.{L} Eggerson's garden?/What makes you think of Eggerson — of all people?/
474 CC   Colby   11   the fact of being alone there/That makes it unreal./{L} Can no one else enter?/{C}
486 CC   Colby   16   I suppose ...{C} Her sister — which makes Mrs. Guzzard my aunt./{LE} And are
487 CC   Claude   21   Your child, Elizabeth? What on earth makes you think so?/{LE} I must see this Mrs.
500 CC   Lucasta   25   made me see what I really wanted./B. makes me feel safe. And that's what I want./
502 CC   Lucasta   32   told that you're my brother;/Which makes it more difficult to know *what* you are./It
531 ES   Ld Clav   29   ghost/Shan't want to be seen there. It makes me smile/To think that men should be
579 ES   Michael   1   is left between you and me?/{Mi} That makes no difference./You'll be seeing me again./
MAKEUP (1)
569 ES   Ld Clav   6   off the stage, without his costume and makeup/And without his stage words. Monica!/
MAKING (25)
186 FQ: DrySal   79   drying sails at dockage;/Not as making a trip that will be unpayable/For a haul
295 FR   Amy   34   overwrought. Coming so far/And making such haste, the change is too sudden for
303 FR   Mary   23   people/Who meet very seldom, making conversation./I am very glad if Dr.
314 FR   Warburt   24   at Cambridge,/I used to dream of making some great discovery/To do away with
317 FR   Warburt   12   know what is on my mind;/And as for making matters more difficult —/It is much
326 FR   Harry   18   to think of each thing separately,/Making small things important, so that
329 FR   Chorus   16   /The keeping up of appearances/The making the best of a bad job/All twined and
332 FR   Agatha   13   many years/Before she succeeded in making terms with Wishwood,/Until she took
356 CP   Celia   5   you were doing in California./{C} Making a film./{P} Trying to make a film./{J}
362 CP   Reilly   1   quite the same friends as yourself,/Or making your friends like her better than you;/
382 CP   Celia   33   is it?/Edward, I see that I was simply making use of you./And I ask you to forgive
404 CP   Edward   20   the last decision/I was capable of making. I am in your hands./I cannot take any
405 CP   Reilly   15   /To convince me that you have been making up your case/So to speak, as you went
431 CP   Peter   16   /{P} And do him a good turn./We're making a film of English life/And we want to
432 CP   Julia   35   very important in films./He's making a film of English life/And he's going to
435 CP   Peter   22   one could ignore —/And here I am, making a second-rate film!/But I thought it was
447 CC   Claude   25   to be puzzled, or annoyed/At my making the appointment during her absence,/
474 CC   Lucasta   9   religious./Is there no other way of making it real to you?/{C} It's simply the fact of
482 CC   Lady E   24   not intelligent and kind./I'm not making any malicious suggestions:/But they are
491 CC   Lady E   11   better! And prevent us both/From making unreasonable claims upon you, Colby./
504 CC   Lady E   21   beginning./{LE} She's been making progress, under my direction;/But she
507 CC   Guzzard   25   that the father had died/Without making a will./{LE} He was very careless./{MG}

518 CC	Eggers	1	/We'll have to think of other ways/Of making up an income. Piano lessons? —/As a
538 ES	Ld Clav	16	hoped./{LC} I was never accused of making a mistake./{G} No, in England mistakes
574 ES	Carghil	16	what Michael really wanted/For making a new start. He wants to go abroad!/

MALADY (4)

240 MC	Chorus	15	orchards for another October?/Some malady is coming upon us. We wait, we wait,/
296 FR	Ivy	22	They can be very cunning —/Their malady makes them so. They do not want to be
314 FR	Harry	20	health/Is only incubation of another malady./{W} You mustn't take such a
402 CP	Reilly	35	yes; this is serious. A very common malady./Very prevalent indeed./{E} I remember,

MALE (2)

| 154 Rock 3 m | | 20 | a litter of Sunday newspapers?/1ST MALE VOICE:/A Cry from the East:/What |
| 154 Rock 3 m | | 28 | /Where My Word is unspoken./2ND MALE VOICE:/A Cry from the North, from |

MALEVOLENT (1)

| 362 CP | Reilly | 34 | of being an object/At the mercy of a malevolent staircase./Or, take a surgical |

MALFEASANCE (1)

| 269 MC | Knights | 18 | /{3K} Priest! traitor, confirmed in malfeasance./{T} I submit my cause to the |

MALHEUR (1)

| 46 Directeur | | 1 | in a hundred A.B.C.'s./Le Directeur/Malheur à la malheureuse Tamise/Qui coule si |

MALHEUREUSE (1)

| 46 Directeur | | 1 | A.B.C.'s./Le Directeur/Malheur à la malheureuse Tamise/Qui coule si près du |

MALICE (1)

| 327 FR | Agatha | 3 | in being/The impatient spectators of malice or stupidity./We must try to penetrate |

MALICIOUS (3)

345 FR	Amy	25	in this room,/Violet, you are the most malicious in a harmless way;/I prefer your
482 CC	Lady E	24	and kind./I'm not making any malicious suggestions:/But they are rather
569 ES	Ld Clav	38	me, to be only human beings,/Malicious, petty, and I see myself emerging/

MALIGNED (1)

| 344 FR | Gerald | 21 | /Some of them very decent fellows. A maligned profession./They're sometimes very |

MALINGERS (1)

| 15 Prufrock | | 77 | by long fingers,/Asleep ... tired ... or it malingers,/Stretched on the floor, here beside |

MALL (2)

| 231 Bust Jones | | 39 | /It must and it shall be Spring in Pall Mall/While Bustopher Jones wears white spats!/ |
| 345 FR | Charles | 38 | centre, as I was about to cross Pall Mall./I thought that life could bring no further |

MALLINGTON'S (1)

| 428 CP | Julia | 3 | destructive./I shall never forget Mary Mallington's monkey,/The horrid little beast — |

MALVERSATION (1)

| 241 MC | Priest3 | 1 | /But violence, duplicity and frequent malversation./King rules or barons rule:/The |

MAN (228)

31 Apollinax		9	submarine and profound/Like the old man of the sea's/Hidden under coral islands/
31 Apollinax		18	the afternoon./'He is a charming man' — 'But after all what did he mean?' —/
37 Gerontion		1	/Poems/Gerontion/Here I am, an old man in a dry month,/Being read to by a boy,
37 Gerontion		15	poking the peevish gutter./I an old man,/A dull head among windy spaces./Signs
38 Gerontion		31	the wind. I have no ghosts,/An old man in a draughty house/Under a windy knob./
39 Gerontion		72	snow, the Gulf claims,/And an old man driven by the Trades/To a sleepy corner./
43 Swee Erect		25	his face./(The lengthened shadow of a man/Is history, said Emerson/Who had not seen
56 Swee Night		17	and draws a stocking up;/The silent man in mocha brown/Sprawls at the window-sill
57 Swee Night		27	thought to be in league;/Therefore the man with heavy eyes/Declines the gambit,
61 WL: Burial		20	/Out of this stony rubbish? Son of man,/You cannot say, or guess, for you know
62 WL: Burial		51	/The lady of situations./Here is the man with three staves, and here the Wheel,/And
62 WL: Burial		55	to see. I do not find/The Hanged Man. Fear death by water./I see crowds of
62 WL: Burial		65	infrequent, were exhaled,/And each man fixed his eyes before his feet./Flowed up
68 WL: Fire S		219	throbbing between two lives,/Old man with wrinkled female breasts, can see/At
68 WL: Fire S		228	camisoles, and stays./I Tiresias, old man with wrinkled dugs/Perceived the scene,
68 WL: Fire S		231	the expected guest./He, the young man carbuncular, arrives,/A small house agent's
73 WL: Thund		364	hooded/I do not know whether a man or a woman/— But who is that on the
124 SA Sweeney		2	that life is?/{S} Life is death./I knew a man once did a girl in —/{Do} Oh Mr. Sweeney,
124 SA Sweeney		12	we are very interested./{S} I knew a man once did a girl in./Any man might do a girl
124 SA Sweeney		13	I knew a man once did a girl in./Any man might do a girl in/Any man has to, needs
124 SA Sweeney		14	in./Any man might do a girl in/Any man has to, needs to, wants to/Once in a
143 Lines OM		t	palaver is finished./Lines for an Old Man/The tiger in the tiger-pit/Is not more
148 Rock 1		46	*by a* BOY:/THE ROCK:/The lot of man is ceaseless labour,/Or ceaseless idleness,
149 Rock 1		74	the heart of your brother./The good man is the builder, if he build what is good./I
149 Rock 1		93	*for all/And a job for each/Every* man *to his work./Now a group of* WORKMEN *is*
149 Rock 1		94	*by voices of the* UNEMPLOYED./*No* man *has hired us/With pocketed hands/And*
150 Rock 1		106	*half pint of bitter/Ale. In this land/No* man *has hired us./Our life is unwelcome, our*
150 Rock 1		124	*Church for all/And a job for each/Each* man *to his work./Thus your fathers were made/*

152 Rock 2	31	/For good and ill deeds belong to a man alone, when he stands alone on the other
152 Rock 2	45	dispersed on ribbon roads,/And no man knows or cares who is his neighbour/
158 Rock 5	1	other./O Lord, deliver me from the man of excellent intention and impure heart: for
158 Rock 5	10	home, they are not in the City./The man who has builded during the day would
159 Rock 6	24	no one will need to be good./But the man that is will shadow/The man that pretends
159 Rock 6	25	/But the man that is will shadow/The man that pretends to be./And the Son of Man
159 Rock 6	26	that pretends to be./And the Son of Man was not crucified once for all,/The blood
159 Rock 6	29	not given once for all:/But the Son of Man is crucified always/And there shall be
160 Rock 7	3	towards GOD/Blindly and vainly, for man is a vain thing, and man without GOD is a
160 Rock 7	3	vainly, for man is a vain thing, and man without GOD is a seed upon the wind:
161 Rock 7	39	(more faintly):/In this land/No man has hired us..../CHORUS:/Waste and void.
164 Rock 9	1	our will./O GOD, help us./Son of Man, behold with thine eyes, and hear with
164 Rock 9	16	communion of saints./The soul of Man must quicken to creation./Out of the
164 Rock 9	18	new forms of life, from the soul of man that is joined to the soul of stone;/Out of
165 Rock 9	32	is already His service in creating./For Man is joined spirit and body,/And therefore
165 Rock 9	34	and invisible, two worlds meet in Man;/Visible and invisible must meet in His
177 FQ: ECoker	8	already flesh, fur and faeces,/Bone of man and beast, cornstalk and leaf./Houses live
177 FQ: ECoker	29	around the bonfire/The association of man and woman/In daunsinge, signifying
178 FQ: ECoker	45	of harvest/The time of the coupling of man and woman/And that of beasts. Feet rising
182 FQ: ECoker	197	moment/And not the lifetime of one man only/But of old stones that cannot be
188 FQ: DrySal	159	sphere of being/The mind of a man may be intent/At the time of death" —
202 War Poetry	15	poem might happen/To a very young man: but a poem is not poetry —/That is a life./
203 Indians	12	destiny/Every country is home to one man/And exile to another. Where a man dies
203 Indians	13	man/And exile to another. Where a man dies bravely/At one with his destiny, that
232 Skimble	10	/And the passengers are frantic to a man —/Then Skimble will appear and he'll
598 Circe	3	of men in pain,/Are flowers that no man knows./Their petals are fanged and red/
605 Narcissus	29	in the woods by a drunken old man/Knowing at the end the taste of his own
240 MC Chorus	23	shall preserve you?/Shall the Son of Man be born again in the litter of scorn?/For
241 MC Priest3	3	King rules or barons rule:/The strong man strongly and the weak man by caprice./
241 MC Priest3	3	strong man strongly and the weak man by caprice./They have but one law, to seize
242 MC Mess	6	think the Lord Archbishop/Is not the man to cherish any illusions,/Or yet to diminish
242 MC Mess	12	/My Lord, he said, I leave you as a man/Whom in this life I shall not see again./I
243 MC Priest2	6	his welcome./I am the Archbishop's man. Let us give the Archbishop welcome!/{P3}
247 MC Thomas	17	experience./But in the life of one man, never/The same time returns. Sever/The
247 MC Tempt1	23	Lord, a nod is as good as a wink./A man will often love what he spurns./For the
247 MC Tempt1	25	past, that are come again/I am your man./{T} Not in this train/Look to your
247 MC Tempt1	35	they were your friends. Be easy, man!/The easy man lives to eat the best dinners.
247 MC Tempt1	36	your friends. Be easy, man!/The easy man lives to eat the best dinners./Take a friend's
248 MC Thomas	31	men reckon no madness./{T} To the man of God what gladness?/{T2} Sadness/Only
249 MC Tempt2	4	poor,/Beneath the throne of God can man do more?/Disarm the ruffian, strengthen
253 MC Tempt4	9	the King will never trust/Twice, the man who has been his friend./Borrow use
253 MC Tempt4	28	/To general grasp of spiritual power?/Man oppressed by sin, since Adam fell —/You
255 MC Tempt4	3	that there was no mystery/About this man who played a certain part in history./{T}
256 MC Tempts	16	/All things become less real, man passes/From unreality to unreality./This
256 MC Tempts	18	/From unreality to unreality./This man is obstinate, blind, intent/On
257 MC Chorus	3	or a sudden shock on the skull./{C} A man may walk with a lamp at night, and yet be
257 MC Priests	4	and yet be drowned in a ditch./{3P} A man may climb the stair in the day, and slip on
257 MC Tempts	5	and slip on a broken step./{4T} A man may sit at meat, and feel the cold in his
257 MC Chorus	15	upon us./We have seen the young man mutilated,/The torn girl trembling by the
258 MC Thomas	28	of greater sin/And sorrow, than the man who serves a king./For those who serve the
261 MC Thomas	26	a man's will to/become a Saint, as a man by willing and contriving may become a
261 MC Thomas	29	to His ways. It is/never the design of man; for the true martyr is he who has become
264 MC Priest3	19	shed like water,/And there was no man to bury them. Avenge, O Lord,/The blood
266 MC Knights	19	the seal and the ring./This is the man who was the tradesman's son:
266 MC Knights	23	up like a louse on your shirt,/The man who cheated, swindled, lied; broke his oath
269 MC Knight4	23	take, hold, detain,/Restrain this man, in the King's name./{K1} Or answer with
274 MC Thomas	6	To the Law of God above the Law of Man./Unbar the door! unbar the door!/We are
274 MC Thomas	28	and join in the feast./{T} It is the just man who/Like a bold lion, should be without
276 MC Knight1	21	in fair/play: and when you see one man being set upon by four, then your/
276 MC Knight1	27	to/put our case to you. I am a man of action and not of words. For that/
277 MC Knight3	9	a good deal — I am not a drinking man/ordinarily — to brace myself up for it.
278 MC Knight2	18	I/may say that I have never known a man so well qualified for the/highest rank of the
279 MC Knight4	40	upon/one who was, after all, a great man. {K1} Thank you, Brito, I think that there
281 MC Chorus	13	and the worm in the belly./Therefore man, whom Thou hast made to be conscious of
282 MC Chorus	6	ourselves as type of the common man,/Of the men and women who shut the door

286 FR	Charles	2	England in the winter./But a single man like me is better off in London:/A man can
286 FR	Charles	3	like me is better off in London:/A man can be very cosy at his club/Even in an
286 FR	Gerald	8	East. An incomparable climate/For a man who can exercise a little common
288 FR	Agatha	34	he will find another Harry./The man who returns will have to meet/The boy
292 FR	Ivy	34	Hawkins./It's really high time the old man was pensioned./He's let the rock garden go
293 FR	Violet	3	what she is doing./It really needs a man in charge of things at Wishwood./{A} You
300 FR	Downing	12	against my Lady./It's my opinion that man and wife/Shouldn't see too much of each
300 FR	Downing	18	/There's not even a place where a man can go/For a quiet smoke, where the
303 FR	Mary	28	/When he thinks he is behaving like a man of the world?/Cousin Agatha, I want your
309 FR	Mary	26	You deceive yourself/Like the man convinced that he is paralysed/Or like the
309 FR	Mary	27	that he is paralysed/Or like the man who believes that he is blind/While he still
314 FR	Warburt	37	he fought against it! I never saw a man/More anxious to live./{H} Not at all
317 FR	Harry	15	is very likely to happen./{H} O God, man, the things that are going to happen/Have
331 FR	Agatha	39	weakness,/The diffidence of a solitary man:/Where he was weak he recognised your
332 FR	Agatha	7	You tell me nothing./{Ag} The dead man whom you have assumed to be your father,
332 FR	Agatha	16	/At first it was a vacancy. A man and a woman/Married, alone in a lonely
355 CP	Julia	1	sense of hearing —/The only man I ever met who could hear the cry of bats./
360 CP	Reilly	26	I do not./{UG} Do you know who the man is?/{E} There was no other man —/None
360 CP	Edward	27	the man is?/{E} There was no other man —/None that I know of./{UG} Or another
360 CP	Reilly	33	it's all for the best./With another man, she might have made a mistake/And want
360 CP	Reilly	37	there's no other woman/And no other man, then the reason may be deeper/And you've
360 CP	Reilly	39	she won't come back at all./If another man, then you'd want to re-marry/To prove to
365 CP	Julia	13	/{J} Edward, who is that dreadful man?/I've never been so insulted in my life./It's
370 CP	Edward	37	woman/And that you were another man. I congratulate you/On a timely escape./{P}
376 CP	Edward	22	I never heard of that before./{E} The man who fell among thieves was luckier than I:/
377 CP	Edward	6	know?/{E} No, but I believe it. That man who was here —/{C} Yes, who was that
377 CP	Celia	7	was here —/{C} Yes, who was that man? I was rather afraid of him;/He has some
377 CP	Celia	12	tomorrow./{C} But why should that man want to bring her back —/Unless he is the
378 CP	Celia	28	your wife has left you for another man?/I shall soon put that right, Edward,/When
378 CP	Edward	33	reasons were suggested to me/By the man I call Riley —/though his name is not
378 CP	Celia	35	.../{C} He sang you a song about a man named Riley!/Really, Edward, I think you
380 CP	Celia	5	/Would feel degraded to find that a man/With whom they thought they had shared
380 CP	Edward	39	permanent thing:/You should have a man ... nearer your own age./{C} I don't think I
381 CP	Edward	10	/I have met myself as a middle-aged man/Beginning to know what it is to feel old./
382 CP	Celia	19	/And saw only a beetle the size of a man/With nothing more inside it than what
382 CP	Celia	28	person whom I never saw before./The man I saw before, he was only a projection —/
388 CP	Peter	3	happen, overnight?/{P} Why, it's a man Alex put me in touch with/And we settled
393 CP	Lavinia	6	spent five years of your life/With a man who has no sense of humour;/And that the
400 CP	Reilly	5	difficulty/In convincing him I was the man for his case?/{A} Difficulty? No! He was
401 CP	Edward	8	here/On the recommendation of a man who did not know you./Yet Alex is so
408 CP	Reilly	13	tell him if you like./{R} A young man named Peter./{E} Peter? Peter who?/{R}
410 CP	Reilly	8	in common. The same isolation./A man who finds himself incapable of loving/And
410 CP	Reilly	9	/And a woman who finds that no man can love her./{L} It seems to me that what
410 CP	Reilly	15	woman;'/You could always say: 'no man could love her.'/You could accuse each
416 CP	Reilly	7	believed were your relations with this man?/{C} Oh, you'd guessed that, had you?
416 CP	Reilly	29	real than his dreams./{R} And this man. What does he now seem like, to you?/{C}
424 CP	3m	1	afternoon in July. A CATERER'S MAN is arranging a buffet/table. LAVINIA
424 CP	m	5	of flowers.]/[Re-enter CATERER'S MAN with trolley]/{L} There, in that corner.
424 CP	m	10	till half past six. {}/[Exit CATERER'S MAN]/[EDWARD lets himself in at the front
425 CP	Lavinia	29	can't get at the cocktails,/And the man won't be able to take the tray about,/So
446 CC	Claude	4	/{SC} And experience./With a young man, some readjustment is necessary./But I'm
451 CC	Eggers	29	/She'll see at once that you're a man of culture;/And besides, she's very musical.
455 CC	Eggers	15	like a father —/A very generous man, is Sir Claude./To tell the truth, she's
455 CC	Eggers	21	marry Mr. Kaghan/In the end. He's a man who gets his own way,/And I think he can
458 CC	Lady E	25	crossing./But who is this young man? His face is familiar./{SC} This young man
458 CC	Claude	26	His face is familiar./{SC} This young man is Eggerson's successor./You know that
458 CC	Lady E	38	/{LE} Musical?/Isn't this the young man I interviewed/And recommended to Sir
460 CC	Lady E	21	for once, and engage that young man?'/Well, that was Mr. Colby./{SC} Oh, I see.
462 CC	Claude	12	comes to think of you/As the kind of man that her son would have been —/And I
465 CC	Claude	12	it in me. It's strange, isn't it,/That a man should have a consuming passion/To do
465 CC	Claude	14	which he lacks the capacity?/Could a man be said to have a vocation/To be a
465 CC	Claude	23	creation,/And I feel what the man must have felt when he made it./But
471 CC	Lucasta	11	are full of surprises!/I've never met a man so ignorant as you/Yet knowing so much
472 CC	Lucasta	37	now I think I know./It's awful for a man to have to give up,/A career that he's set
500 CC	Lucasta	35	you think of him/Simply as a business man. As you thought of me/Simply as a

506 CC	Eggers	15	/If he is alive, must be a grown man./I believe you have had no children of your
509 CC	Claude	23	young colleague —/In fact, the young man who showed you upstairs —/Whose name
513 CC	Colby	35	/To live with that image. An ordinary man/Whose life I could in some way perpetuate/
514 CC	Guzzard	1	Claude's — or the son of some other man/Obscure and silent? A dead man, Colby./
514 CC	Guzzard	2	man/Obscure and silent? A dead man, Colby./Be careful what you say./{C} A
514 CC	Colby	4	what you say./{C} A dead obscure man./{MG} You shall have your wish. And
516 CC	Colby	4	Sir Claude./You're a very generous man. But now I know who was my father/I
517 CC	Colby	11	like you too much./You've become a man without illusions/About himself, and
517 CC	Eggers	21	I wouldn't venture./Mr. Simpkins is a man who knows his own mind./Is it true, Mr.
524 ES	Charles	21	/{C} Well, tease me if you like. But a man does feel a fool/If he takes you to a place
525 ES	Charles	20	father simply can't bear it/That any man but he should have you to himself,/Before
525 ES	Monica	37	love me./{M} Oh, what a dominating man you are!/Really, you must imagine you're a
528 ES	Monica	10	with authority's costume,/When the man that people see when they meet you/Is not
528 ES	Monica	11	when they meet you/Is not the private man, but the public personage./In politics
530 ES	Ld Clav	12	Take life easily!/It's like telling a man he mustn't run for trains/When the last
531 ES	Charles	19	{C} That's the reward/Of every public man./{LC} Say rather, the exequies/Of the failed
532 ES	Ld Clav	13	like this,/But I'll have to see this man by myself, Monica./I've never heard of this
532 ES	Ld Clav	16	with a letter of introduction/From a man I used to know. I can't refuse to see him./
532 ES	Ld Clav	17	Though from what I remember of the man who introduces him/I expect he wants
535 ES	Gomez	13	What does that mean? One trusts a man/Or a woman — in this respect or that./A
538 ES	Gomez	18	mistakes are anonymous/Because the man who accepts responsibility/Isn't the man
538 ES	Gomez	19	who accepts responsibility/Isn't the man who made the mistake./That's your
539 ES	Gomez	36	I'm somebody — a more important man/In San Marco than I should ever have been
540 ES	Gomez	6	kind of failure, in my opinion,/Is the man who has to keep on pretending to himself/
540 ES	Gomez	7	to himself/That he's a success — the man who in the morning/Has to make up his
540 ES	Gomez	22	—/The night you ran over the old man in the road./{LC} You *said* I ran over an
540 ES	Ld Clav	23	road./{LC} You *said* I ran over an old man in the road./{G} You knew it too. If you
542 ES	Gomez	8	a smoke now and then./I'm a lonely man, Dick, with a craving for affection./All I
542 ES	Ld Clav	14	to impose your company/On a man by threats? Why keep up the pretence?/{G}
543 ES	Ld Clav	9	/{M} Who was it, Father?/{LC} A man I used to know./{M} Oh, so you knew him?
549 ES	Carghil	26	way things happen./I said 'there's a man I could follow round the world!'/But Effie
549 ES	Carghil	29	Effie said, 'if you chose to follow *that* man/He'd give you the slip: he's not to be
549 ES	Carghil	31	the slip: he's not to be trusted./That man is hollow'. That's what she said./Or did she
550 ES	Carghil	37	*him* would soon find that out'./A man may prefer to forget all the women/He has
551 ES	Carghil	6	has nothing to be ashamed of:/A man is always trying to forget/His own shabby
552 ES	Carghil	29	were. You wanted to pose/As a man of the world. And now you're posing/As
553 ES	Carghil	37	/Effie said: 'If he becomes a famous man/And you should be in want, you could
555 ES	Ld Clav	29	{LC} Yes, a tree./It might have been a man. But it can't be that,/Or he wouldn't be at
557 ES	Michael	25	the firm?/{Mi} I went to a lender,/A man whom a friend of mine recommended./He
558 ES	Michael	7	shocked./Said he couldn't retain any man on his staff/Who'd taken to gambling.
558 ES	Michael	19	joke/Being the son of a famous public man./You don't know what I suffered, working
563 ES	Ld Clav	1	you know him, Richard?/{LC} It's a man I used to know./{MC} How interesting!
568 ES	Ld Clav	23	of the world — your soul is safe./If a man has one person, just one in his life,/To
569 ES	Charles	24	/{C} At least, I think I know the best man to advise you./{LC} Blackmail? Yes, I've
569 ES	Ld Clav	29	and your company./He's a very rich man. And she's a rich woman./If people merely
570 ES	Ld Clav	27	Gomez, the Central American,/A man who's made a fortune by his own peculiar
570 ES	Ld Clav	28	by his own peculiar methods,/A man of great importance and the highest
571 ES	Ld Clav	36	A secondary road./I ran over an old man lying in the road/And I did not stop. Then
571 ES	Ld Clav	37	/And I did not stop. Then another man ran over him./A lorry driver. He stopped
571 ES	Ld Clav	40	It was definitely shown/That the old man had died a natural death/And had been
572 ES	Ld Clav	21	/And she knows that the ghost of the man I was/Still clings to the ghost of the woman
572 ES	Charles	26	forgotten or forgiven me./{C} This man, and this woman, who are so vindictive:/
573 ES	Carghil	33	Mr. Hemington./You're a very lucky man, to get a girl like Monica./I take a great
574 ES	Carghil	19	to Señor Gomez?/He's a wealthy man, and very important/In his own country.
575 ES	Michael	1	from London,/The limey remittance man for whom a job was made./No! I want to
575 ES	Michael	9	Gomez came to London to find a man to fill it,/And he thinks I'm just the man./
575 ES	Michael	10	to fill it,/And he thinks I'm just the man./{G} Yes, wasn't it extraordinary./{LC} Of
575 ES	Ld Clav	12	/{LC} Of course you're just the man that Señor Gomez wants,/But in a different
576 ES	Ld Clav	14	position which he'd come to find the man for./{Mi} I don't care about that. He's
576 ES	Michael	28	he'd come to London looking for a man/For an important post on his staff —/{C}
577 ES	Charles	13	really feel confidence,/Michael, in a man who aims to gratify, through you,/His
577 ES	Charles	16	yourself completely in the power/Of a man you don't know, of the nature of whose
577 ES	Carghil	27	husband, Mr. Carghill, was a business man —/I wish you could have known him,
581 ES	Ld Clav	21	you to give your life to adoring/The man that I pretended to myself that I was,/So
581 ES	Ld Clav	28	Monica, that you have found a man/Whom you can love for the man he really

581 ES	Ld Clav	29	a man/Whom you can love for the man he really is./{M} Oh Father, I've always
581 ES	Monica	38	Father!/It's the real you I love — the man you are,/Not the man I thought you were./
581 ES	Monica	39	I love — the man you are,/Not the man I thought you were./{LC} And Michael —/
582 ES	Charles	25	/{C} He's a very different man from the man he used to be./It's as if he
582 ES	Charles	25	He's a very different man from the man he used to be./It's as if he had passed

MAN'S (10)

84 Hollow Men	43	receive/The supplication of a dead man's hand/Under the twinkle of a fading star./
89 Ash-Wed 1	4	I do not hope to turn/Desiring this man's gift and that man's scope/I no longer
89 Ash-Wed 1	4	turn/Desiring this man's gift and that man's scope/I no longer strive to strive towards
92 Ash-Wed 3	10	was dark,/Damp, jaggèd, like an old man's mouth drivelling, beyond repair,/Or the
192 FQ: Little	56	Never and always./Ash on an old man's sleeve/Is all the ash the burnt roses leave./
201 Def Island	11	on the sea floor/and of those who, in man's newest form of gamble/with death, fight
203 Indians	1	/To the Indians who Died in Africa/A man's destination is his own village,/His own
203 Indians	11	places,/Foreign to each other./A man's destination is not his destiny/Every
256 MC Tempts	9	forms on the back of my hand?/{4T} Man's life is a cheat and a disappointment;/All
261 MC Thomas	25	a Christian martyrdom the effect of a man's will to/become a Saint, as a man by

MAN-EATING (1)

| 479 CC Kaghan | 5 | in on you./And between a couple of man-eating tigers/Like you and Lizzie, he's got |

MANAGE (9)

293 FR	Amy	9	your return./Now it's for you to manage. I am an old woman./They can give me
316 FR	Charles	7	were left in my hands, I think I could manage the situation. {}/[*Exeunt*]/[*Enter*
356 CP	Celia	37	some time./{C} And how will you manage while she is away?/{E} I really don't
366 CP	Julia	24	not helpless yet./And besides, I like to manage the machine myself —/In a lift I can
381 CP	Celia	4	I only hope you're competent/To manage your own. But if you are not in love/
389 CP	Lavinia	34	mysterious./I'm sure that we shall manage somehow, thank you,/As we have in the
455 CC	Eggers	22	gets his own way,/And I think he can manage her. If anyone can./{C} But is she likely
458 CC	Eggers	15	your ticket?/{E} Yes, how did you manage to change your ticket?/{LE} I went to
579 ES	Carghil	12	wonderful, Señor Gomez, how you manage *everything*!/— No sooner had I put my

MANAGED (1)

| 479 CC Kaghan | 28 | /{K} Well, at least, I've always managed to escape her./{L} Only because she's |

MANAGING (1)

| 528 ES Charles | 6 | most alive when he's among people/Managing, manœuvring, cajoling or bullying — |

MANDOLINE (1)

| 69 WL: Fire S | 261 | Street,/The pleasant whining of a mandoline/And a clatter and a chatter from |

MANGABEY (1)

| 204 de la Mare | 5 | buffalo may rove,/The kinkajou, the mangabey, abound/In the dark jungle of a |

MANGO (2)

| 49 Hippopot | 14 | /The 'potamus can never reach/The mango on the mango-tree;/But fruits of |
| 204 de la Mare | 6 | abound/In the dark jungle of a mango grove,/And shadowy lemurs glide from |

MANGO-TREE (1)

| 49 Hippopot | 14 | can never reach/The mango on the mango-tree;/But fruits of pomegranate and |

MANGOES (1)

| 370 CP | Alex | 17 | think./I didn't expect to find any mangoes,/But I *did* count upon curry powder. {} |

MANIA (1)

| 279 MC Knight4 | 25 | until it/became at last an undoubted mania. I have unimpeachable evidence/to the |

MANIFEST (1)

| 305 FR | Harry | 37 | the changing of people/All the more manifest./{M} Yes, nothing changes here,/And |

MANIPULATE (1)

| 241 MC Priest3 | 5 | and keep it,/And the steadfast can manipulate the greed and lust of others,/The |

MANKIND (3)

161 Rock 7	41	of the deep./Has the Church failed mankind, or has mankind failed the Church?/
161 Rock 7	41	the Church failed mankind, or has mankind failed the Church?/When the Church
173 FQ: BurntN	83	of the changing body,/Protects mankind from heaven and damnation/Which

MANLY (1)

| 213 Growltiger | 34 | the Lady seemed enraptured by his manly baritone,/Disposed to relaxation, and |

MANNER (9)

195 FQ: Little	170	but/All shall be well, and/All manner of thing shall be well./If I think, again,
196 FQ: Little	199	in death./And all shall be well and/All manner of thing shall be well/By the
198 FQ: Little	258	/And all shall be well and/All manner of thing shall be well/When the tongues
225 Mr Mistoff	42	/As Magical Mr. Mistoffelees!/His manner is vague and aloof,/You would think
278 MC Knight2	23	and offensively adopted an ascetic/manner of life, he affirmed immediately that
347 FRDowning	10	so I could see them cheerful-like,/In a manner of speaking. There's no harm in *them*,/
374 CP	Celia	9	/But I could not understand your manner on the telephone./It did not seem like
498 CC	Eggers	14	after other people's children?/In a manner of speaking, it's perfectly respectable./
533 ES	Gomez	34	a little money laid out in the right manner/In the right places, pays many times

MANNERS (5)

210 Old Gumbie	10	/Their behaviour's not good and their manners not nice;/So when she has got them
212 Growltiger	5	of 'The Terror of the Thames'./His manners and appearance did not calculate to
236 Cat Morgan	9	me patrol./I ain't got much polish, me manners is gruff,/But I've got a good coat, and
258 MC Thomas	24	/The raw nobility, whose manners matched their finger-nails./While I ate
345 FR Harry	2	it;/Meanwhile, I apologise for my bad manners./But if you *could* understand you

MANŒUVRE (1)

249 MC Tempt2	28	hounds./{T} No!/{T2} Yes! men must manœuvre. Monarchs also,/Waging war

MANŒUVRING (1)

528 ES Charles	6	when he's among people/Managing, manœuvring, cajoling or bullying —/At all of

MANSION (1)

431 CP Peter	21	interested./The most decayed noble mansion in England!/At least, of any that are

MANSLAUGHTER (3)

560 ES Ld Clav	21	what you've told me? It isn't ... manslaughter?/{Mi} Manslaughter? Why
560 ES Michael	22	me? It isn't ... manslaughter?/{Mi} Manslaughter? Why manslaughter? Oh, you
560 ES Michael	22	/{Mi} Manslaughter? Why manslaughter? Oh, you mean on the road./

MANTEL (1)

64 WL: Chess	97	dolphin swam./Above the antique mantel was displayed/As though a window gave

MANTELPIECE (3)

29 Aunt Helen	10	clock continued ticking on the mantelpiece,/And the footman sat upon the
44 Cook Egg	7	great great aunts,/Supported on the mantelpiece/An *Invitation to the Dance.*/I shall
366 CP Julia	2	you looking for them?/Look on the mantelpiece. Where was I sitting?/Just turn out

MANTLE (1)

73 WL: Thund	363	beside you/Gliding wrapt in a brown mantle, hooded/I do not know whether a man

MANTUAN (1)

129 Cor2 State	25	dice on the marches/And the frogs (O Mantuan) croak in the marshes./Fireflies flare

MANUSCRIPT (1)

589 Fable	96	record of these doings/From an old manuscript found in the ruins./If Time and

MANY (89)

20 Portrait	63	prevailed/You can say: at this point many a one has failed./But what have I, but
34 Figlia	18	weather/Compelled my imagination many days,/Many days and many hours:/Her
34 Figlia	19	my imagination many days,/Many days and many hours:/Her hair over her
34 Figlia	19	many days,/Many days and many hours:/Her hair over her arms and her
38 Gerontion	34	forgiveness? Think now/History has many cunning passages, contrived corridors/
62 WL: Burial	62	crowd flowed over London Bridge, so many,/I had not thought death had undone so
62 WL: Burial	63	had not thought death had undone so many,/Sighs, short and infrequent, were
105 Song Sime	9	/Grant us thy peace./I have walked many years in this city,/Kept faith and fast,
127 Cor1 March	3	the flags. And the trumpets. And so many eagles./How many? Count them. And
127 Cor1 March	4	trumpets. And so many eagles./How many? Count them. And such a press of people.
127 Cor1 March	6	is the way to the temple, and we so many crowding the way./So many waiting, how
127 Cor1 March	7	we so many crowding the way./So many waiting, how many waiting? what did it
127 Cor1 March	7	the way./So many waiting, how many waiting? what did it matter, on such a
127 Cor1 March	17	and heavy guns,/I cannot tell how many projectiles, mines and fuses,/13,000
128 Cor1 March	42	/That is all we could see. But how many eagles! and how many trumpets!/(And
128 Cor1 March	42	see. But how many eagles! and how many trumpets!/(And Easter Day, we didn't get
147 Rock 1	21	/There I was told: we have too many churches,/And too few chop-houses.
151 Rock 2	5	sit helpless in a ruined house?/Where many are born to idleness, to frittered lives and
154 Rock 3	13	speculation and unconsidered action./Many are engaged in writing books and
154 Rock 3	14	in writing books and printing them,/Many desire to see their names in print,/Many
154 Rock 3	15	desire to see their names in print,/Many read nothing but the race reports./Much
156 Rock 3	68	morality,/Engaged in printing as many books as possible,/Plotting of happiness
162 Rock 8	12	his hearers were a few good men,/Many who were evil,/And most who were
162 Rock 8	18	/Some were rapacious and lustful./Many left their bodies to the kites of Syria/Or
162 Rock 8	20	Syria/Or sea-strewn along the routes;/Many left their souls in Syria/Living on,
162 Rock 8	22	on, sunken in moral corruption;/Many came back well broken,/Diseased and
163 Rock 8	35	it;/Whole faith of a few,/Part faith of many./Not avarice, lechery, treachery,/Envy,
165 Rock 9	38	completed:/After much striving, after many obstacles;/For the work of creation is
180 FQ: ECoker	106	civil servants, chairmen of many committees,/Industrial lords and petty
184 FQ: DrySal	24	gear of foreign dead men. The sea has many voices,/Many gods and many voices./The
184 FQ: DrySal	25	dead men. The sea has many voices,/Many gods and many voices./The salt is on the
184 FQ: DrySal	25	sea has many voices,/Many gods and many voices./The salt is on the briar rose,/The
187 FQ: DrySal	101	the experience of one life only/But of many generations — not forgetting/Something
193 FQ: Little	96	forgotten, half recalled/Both one and many; in the brown baked features/The eyes of
201 Def Island	2	— music's/enduring instrument, of many centuries of/patient cultivation of the
203 Indians	6	together./Scarred but secure, he has many memories/Which return at the hour of

220 Old Deut	2	a long time;/He's a Cat who has lived many lives in succession./He was famous in
592 Grad 3	5	of the sky/Which the sun stains with many a splendid dye,/Until their passing may
244 MC Chorus	19	is upon us, a fear not of one but of many,/A fear like birth and death, when we see
252 MC Thomas	18	the field/And in the tilt-yard I made many yield./Shall I who ruled like an eagle over
264 MC Priest3	16	*of very babes, O God.*/As the voice of many waters, of thunder, of harps,/They sang as
273 MC Thomas	36	be shown./And as in time results of many deeds are blended/So good and evil in the
278 MC Knight2	25	he as the King's servant, had/for so many years striven to establish; and that —
292 FR Harry	13	have met them!/Why here? why here?/Many happy returns of the day, mother./Aunt
294 FR Harry	16	in a crowded desert/In a thick smoke, many creatures moving/Without direction, for
303 FR Agatha	9	as I know them./{Ag} I wonder how many we shall be for dinner./{M} Seven ... nine
309 FR Harry	29	that this is true./{H} I have spent many years in useless travel;/You have staid in
321 FR Winch	25	my Lord. Good evening, Doctor./Many happy ... Oh, I'm sorry, my Lord,/I was
324 FR Warburt	4	/{W} You have trusted me a good many years, Lady Monchensey;/This is not the
331 FR Agatha	21	that much./{Ag} I had to fight for many years to win my dispossession,/And many
331 FR Agatha	22	years to win my dispossession,/And many years to keep it. What people know me
332 FR Agatha	12	—/It was not always so. There were many years/Before she succeeded in making
343 FR Mary	17	/But I deceived myself. It takes so many years/To learn that one is dead! So you
347 FR Ivy	19	/{I} 'Regret delayed business in town many happy returns see you tomorrow many
347 FR Ivy	19	happy returns see you tomorrow many happy returns hurrah love Arthur.'/I
354 CP Julia	31	one who had three brothers?/{J} How many brothers? Two, I think./{A} No, there
355 CP Julia	30	was at the Vincewell wedding. Oh, so many years ago! {}/[*To the* UNIDENTIFIED
356 CP Julia	18	guest/At Lavinia's party. There are so many questions/I want to ask you. It's a golden
393 CP Edward	3	/To have arrived at in ... how many? ... thirty-two hours./{L} Yes, a very
404 CP Reilly	22	take any further responsibility./{R} Many patients come in that belief./{E} And now
419 CP Reilly	24	place so over-crowded./{R} Not very many go. But I said they did not come back/In
425 CP Edward	5	Well, you deserve it. — We asked too many people./{L} It's true, a great many more
425 CP Lavinia	6	too many people./{L} It's true, a great many more accepted/Than we thought would
429 CP Alex	25	It cannot be, at present:/There are too many international complications./Eventually,
476 CC Lucasta	24	of such a thing!/There are not many men who wouldn't have thought it./I
484 CC Colby	20	But you had parents. And no doubt, many relatives./{LE} Oh, swarms of relatives!
489 CC Claude	9	thought you might think — 'and how many more?'/You might have suspected any
505 CC Claude	6	and I may say, my friend — /For very many years. So I asked him to be present./I
505 CC Eggers	29	/And now we must go back, many years:/Well, not so many years — when
505 CC Eggers	30	go back, many years:/Well, not so many years — when you get to my age/The past
506 CC Eggers	13	have instituted enquiries./So, for many years, she has been without a clue/Until
506 CC Eggers	38	sound like Teddington/But not so many names that sound like Guzzard —/Or if
530 ES Ld Clav	4	say it to./I've been wondering ... how many more empty pages?/{M} You would soon
531 ES Ld Clav	23	other men covet./When we go, a good many folk are mildly grieved,/And our closest
532 ES Ld Clav	5	in the library./No, stop. I've left too many papers about there./I'd better see him
533 ES Gomez	35	right manner/In the right places, pays many times over./I assure you it does./{LC} In
537 ES Gomez	6	/{G} It's done already, Dick; done many years ago:/Adoption tried, and grappled
541 ES Gomez	2	/About something that happened so many years ago?/What damages you'd get! The
542 ES Ld Clav	19	when I gave you my friendship/So many years ago, I only gained in return/Your
550 ES Ld Clav	11	/{LC} You married, I suppose, many years ago?/{MC} Many years ago, the
550 ES Carghil	12	I suppose, many years ago?/{MC} Many years ago, the first time. That didn't last
553 ES Carghil	22	you wrote me letters?/Oh, not very many. Only a few worth keeping./Only a few.
553 ES Ld Clav	35	And have you shown these letters/To many people?/{MC} Only a few friends./Effie
562 ES Carghil	30	a good deal/Since I knew him ever so many years ago,/Yet you're the image of what
568 ES Ld Clav	5	said about guilty secrets./There are many things not crimes, Monica,/Beyond
577 ES Gomez	6	pays your passage .../{G} Just as many years ago/His father paid mine./{C} This
577 ES Gomez	25	back/He'll be able to buy you out many times over./{MC} Richard, I think it's
578 ES Ld Clav	5	repudiate me. I see now clearly/The many many mistakes I have made/My whole life
578 ES Ld Clav	5	me. I see now clearly/The many many mistakes I have made/My whole life

MANY'S (2)

| 118 SP Wauch | 23 | Hello Sam!/{W} Hello dear/How many's up there?/{Du} Nobody's up here/How |
| 118 SP Dusty | 25 | there?/{Du} Nobody's up here/How many's down there?/{W} Four of us here./Wait |

MAP (1)

| 547 ES Piggott | 34 | There are indeed. I can lend you a map./There are lovely walks, on the shore or in |

MARBLE (2)

| 64 WL: Chess | 78 | a burnished throne,/Glowed on the marble, where the glass/Held up by standards |
| 248 MC Tempt2 | 29 | /A templed tomb, monument of marble./Rule over men reckon no madness./{T} |

MARCH (6)

127 Corl March	t	/KNOCK/Coriolan/Triumphal March/Stone, bronze, stone, steel, stone,
161 Rock 7	24	reaffirming, always resuming their march on the way that was lit by the light;/
263 MC Chorus	19	done?/The ploughman shall go out in March and turn the same earth/He has turned

285 FR   2m   1   *after tea. An afternoon in late March.*/Scene I/AMY, IVY, VIOLET,
332 FR   Agatha   32   stones/That lie, fang up, a lifetime's march. I have believed this./{H} I have known
400 CP   Alex   20   /Because he thinks he's stolen a march on her./And when you've sent him to a

MARCHES (1)
129 Cor2 State   24   the guards shake dice on the marches/And the frogs (O Mantuan) croak in

MARCO (12)
533 ES   Gomez   21   /Of a central American republic: San Marco./It's as hard to become a respected
539 ES   Ld Clav 26   /In the respected citizen of San Marco/Is that in the midst of the engrossing
539 ES   Gomez   37   — a more important man/In San Marco than I should ever have been in England.
541 ES   Gomez   1   statement/Of Federico Gomez of San Marco/About something that happened so
563 ES   Gomez   20   Gomez,/The prominent citizen of San Marco./That's my name./{LC} So let me
564 ES   Gomez   27   your home?/{G} The republic of San Marco./{MC} Went back to San Marco./Señor
564 ES   Carghil   28   San Marco./{MC} Went back to San Marco./Señor Gomez, if it's true you're staying
576 ES   Michael   17   /He's made a fortune there. San Marco for me!/{LC} And what are your duties
576 ES   Gomez   21   there./The nature of business in San Marco/Is easier explained in San Marco than in
576 ES   Gomez   22   San Marco/Is easier explained in San Marco than in England./{LC} Perhaps you
577 ES   Charles   2   Gomez has offered you a post in San Marco,/Señor Gomez pays your passage .../{Mi}
580 ES   Carghil   20   Gomez has invited me to visit San Marco./I'm so excited! But what pleases me

MARCO'S (1)
541 ES   Gomez   18   buy you out/Several times over. San Marco's a good place/To make money in —

MARE (1)
204 de la Mare   t   is the fruit of action./To Walter de la Mare/The children who explored the brook and

MARGATE (1)
70 WL: Fire S   300 comment. What should I resent?'/'On Margate Sands./I can connect/Nothing with

MARGIN (1)
297 FR   Agatha   7   nothing may be left undone/On the margin of the impossible./{A} Very well./I will

MARIE (2)
61 WL: Burial   15 a sled,/And I was frightened. He said, Marie,/Marie, hold on tight. And down we
61 WL: Burial   16 And I was frightened. He said, Marie,/Marie, hold on tight. And down we went./In the

MARINA (1)
109 Marina   t   us now and at the hour of our birth./Marina/What seas what shores what grey rocks

MARIONETTE (1)
602 Humoresque   5   has such a frame)./But this deceasèd marionette/I rather liked: a common face,/(The

MARIONETTE'S (1)
602 Humoresque   21 New York' — and so it goes./Logic a marionette's, all wrong/Of premises; yet in some

MARIONETTES (1)
602 Humoresque   1 (AFTER J. LAFORGUE)/One of my marionettes is dead,/Though not yet tired of the

MARK (4)
274 MC Knights   19 lions' den,/Come down Daniel for the mark of the beast./Are you washed in the blood
274 MC Knights   21 the Lamb?/Are you marked with the mark of the beast?/Come down Daniel to the
549 ES   Carghil   29   'you'd be throwing yourself away./Mark my words' Effie said, 'if you chose to
581 ES   Ld Clav 17   to dominate my children?/Why did I mark out a narrow path for Michael?/Because I

MARKED (3)
274 MC Knights   21   in the blood of the Lamb?/Are you marked with the mark of the beast?/Come down
276 MC Chorus   8   on the fire at daybreak,/These acts marked a limit to our suffering./Every horror
407 CP   Reilly   7   /Which must occur together, and to a marked degree,/To qualify a patient for *my*

MARKET (2)
164 Rock 9   10 Adorning themselves, and busy in the market, the forum,/And all other secular
220 Old Deut   18   street,/He sits in the High Street on market day;/The bullocks may bellow, the sheep

MARKET-PLACE (2)
270 MC Chorus   13   mews in the barn in the byre in the market-place/In our veins our bowels our skulls
276 MC Chorus   5 that ends in sleep;/But the talk in the market-place, the hand on the broom,/The

MARKS (2)
192 FQ: Little   59 roses leave./Dust in the air suspended/Marks the place where a story ended./Dust
460 CC   Claude   38   has done for her,/I give him full marks. Well, Eggerson,/I seem to have brought

MARMALADE (1)
15 Prufrock   88   worth it, after all,/After the cups, the marmalade, the tea,/Among the porcelain,

MARMOSET (1)
52 Whispers   22   jaguar/Compels the scampering marmoset/With subtle effluence of cat;/Grishkin

MARMOTS (1)
155 Rock 3   41   colony of cavies or a horde of active marmots/Build better than they that build

MARRED (1)
193 FQ: Little   77   denied./Water and fire shall rot/The marred foundations we forgot,/Of sanctuary

MARRIAGE (6)
330 FR   Harry   7   at home at Wishwood,/Make a dull marriage, marry some woman stupider —/
480 CC   Kaghan   1   always free to think again./{K} Marriage is a gamble. But I'm a born gambler/
505 CC   Eggers 33   possible./Lady Elizabeth, before her marriage/Had a child .../{LE} A son./{E} Had a
528 ES   Charles 35   go on postponing and postponing our marriage./{M} I'm afraid ... not a very long
538 ES   Gomez   11   of money, and you made a good marriage —/Or so it seemed — and with your
539 ES   Gomez   17   very sorry when I heard/That your marriage had not been altogether happy./And

MARRIAGES (1)
244 MC   Chorus 11   /We have seen births, deaths and marriages,/We have had various scandals,/We

MARRIED (24)
 66 WL: Chess 164   alone, there it is, I said,/What you get married for if you don't want children?/
287 FR   Charles 17   getting on for thirty?/She ought to be married, that's what it is./{A} So she should
304 FR   Mary   26   for her and Harry./Even when he married, she still held on to me/Because she
332 FR   Agatha 17   was a vacancy. A man and a woman/Married, alone in a lonely country house
360 CP   Reilly 19   Now for a few questions./How long married?/{E} Five years./{UG} Children?/{E}
364 CP   Edward   7   /During the five years that we've been married./I must find out who she is, to find out
396 CP   Edward   7   /{E} I've often wondered why you married me./{L} Well, you really were rather
433 CP   Peter   28   you can't have Celia./{P} Oh ... Is she married?/{A} Not married, but dead./{L} Celia?/
433 CP   Alex   29   /{P} Oh ... Is she married?/{A} Not married, but dead./{L} Celia?/{A} Dead./{P}
449 CC   Claude 29   And Miss Angel/Will soon be getting married, I expect./{E} And so I hope. A most
453 CC   Lucasta 6   mind him, Colby./Colby, are you married?/{C} No, I'm not married./{L} Then I
453 CC   Colby   7   are you married?/{C} No, I'm not married./{L} Then I don't mind being seen with
485 CC   Colby   35   name?/Is it Simpkins?/{C} No, a married aunt./A widow. Her name is Mrs.
495 CC   Lady E 13   /It's a great mistake, I do believe,/For married people to take anything for granted./
509 CC   Guzzard 11   chose the name./We had been married in the church of St. Barnabas./{C}
511 CC   Lucasta 38   your wedding./{L} We'd meant to be married very quietly/In a register office./{LE}
533 ES   Gomez   3   plain Dick Ferry./Then, when you married, you took your wife's name/And
536 ES   Gomez   10   fact that Dick Ferry died long ago./I married a girl who didn't know a word of
536 ES   Gomez   37   must think I'm dead;/And as for my married sisters — I don't suppose their
546 ES   Piggott   2   /No, I don't simply mean that I'm a married woman —/A widow in fact. But I was a
550 ES   Ld Clav 11   Is Mrs. John Carghill./{LC} You married, I suppose, many years ago?/{MC}
550 ES   Carghil 17   he was — not sly and slippery./Then I married Mr. Carghill. Twenty years older/Than
572 ES   Ld Clav 14   I was her first lover./I would have married her — but my father prevented that:/
573 ES   Carghil 39   there was a moment when I almost married him,/Oh so long ago. So you see, Mr.

MARROW (2)
 52 Whispers   13   /He knew the anguish of the marrow/The ague of the skeleton;/No contact
295 FR   Harry   29   /The contamination has reached the marrow/And *they* are always near. Here, nearer

MARROWS (1)
473 CC   Colby   35   there. And when he comes out/He has marrows, or beetroot, or peas ... for Mrs.

MARRY (16)
289 FR   Gerald   9   his medicine, I've no doubt./Let him marry again and carry on at Wishwood./{A}
330 FR   Harry   7   at Wishwood,/Make a dull marriage, marry some woman stupider —/Stupider than
361 CP   Reilly   1   If another woman, you might have to marry her —/You might even imagine that you
361 CP   Reilly   2   even imagine that you wanted to marry her./{E} But I want my wife back./{UG}
455 CC   Eggers 20   /About her, Mr. Simpkins. She'll marry Mr. Kaghan/In the end. He's a man who
478 CC   Lucasta 3   and make you his heir/And you'll marry another Lady Elizabeth./But in that
491 CC   Claude 38   want?/Think of the future. When you marry/You will want parents, for the sake of
491 CC   Colby   40   don't feel, tonight, that I ever want to marry./You may be right. I can't take account
499 CC   Lucasta 21   It won't take much time. I'm going to marry B./{SC} To marry B.! But I thought that
499 CC   Claude 22   time. I'm going to marry B./{SC} To marry B.! But I thought that was all settled./{L}
499 CC   Lucasta 29   /And knowing that you wanted me to marry B./Made me determined that I wouldn't.
503 CC   Lucasta 13   time./I shall be happy. I'm going to marry B./I know you like B./{C} I'm very fond
527 ES   Charles 6   /Aren't you sure that you want to marry me?/{M} Yes, Charles. I'm sure that I
527 ES   Monica   7   Yes, Charles. I'm sure that I want to marry you/When I'm free to do so. But by that
572 ES   Ld Clav 15   /Made it worth while for her not to marry me —/That was his way of putting it —
572 ES   Ld Clav 17   /Made it worth while for me not to marry her./In fact, we were wholly unsuited to

MARRYING (1)
527 ES   Charles 20   with him./{C} Better reasons than for marrying me?/What reasons?/{M} First, his

MARS (1)
189 FQ: DrySal 188   angelus./To communicate with Mars, converse with spirits,/To report the

MARSEILLES (1)
287 FR   Amy   37   dinner./Harry telephoned to me from Marseilles,/He would come by air to Paris, and

MARSH (1)
 37 Gerontion   5   warm rain/Nor knee deep in the salt marsh, heaving a cutlass,/Bitten by flies, fought.

MARSHES (1)
129 Cor2 State   25   the frogs (O Mantuan) croak in the marshes./Fireflies flare against the faint sheet
MARTIN (1)
142 Cape Ann   9   /Of the dancing arrow, the purple martin. Greet/In silence the bullbat. All are
MARTYR (12)
69 WL: Fire S   264   at noon: where the walls/Of Magnus Martyr hold/Inexplicable splendour of Ionian
254 MC Tempt4   14   when another shall come:/Saint and Martyr rule from the tomb./Think, Thomas,
261 MC Thomas   11   celebrate the martyrdom/of His first martyr, the blessed Stephen. Is it an accident,
261 MC Thomas   12   do you think,/that the day of the first martyr follows immediately the day of the Birth
261 MC Thomas   19   of men./Beloved, we do not think of a martyr simply as a good Christian who/has
261 MC Thomas   29   /never the design of man; for the true martyr is he who has become the/instrument of
261 MC Thomas   32   himself, not even the glory of being a/martyr. So thus as on earth the Church mourns
261 MC Thomas   38   you to remember especially our martyr of Canterbury,/the blessed Archbishop
262 MC Thomas   2   short time you may have yet another martyr,/and that one perhaps not the last. I
264 MC   Priest1   1   day: and the day of St. Stephen, First Martyr./*Princes moreover did sit, and did*
275 MC Thomas   20   apostles Peter and Paul, to the blessed martyr Denys, and to all the Saints, I commend
281 MC   Chorus   19   a saint has dwelt, wherever a martyr has given his blood for the blood of
MARTYR'D (1)
50 Hippopot   34   washed as white as snow,/By all the martyr'd virgins kist,/While the True Church
MARTYRDOM (8)
105 Song Sime   29   the saints' stair./Not for me the martyrdom, the ecstasy of thought and prayer,/
255 MC Tempt4   12   heavenly grandeur?/Seek the way of martyrdom, make yourself the lowest/On earth,
261 MC Thomas   4   disappointment, to suffer/death by martyrdom. What then did He mean? If you ask
261 MC Thomas   10   but on the next day we celebrate the martyrdom/of His first martyr, the blessed
261 MC Thomas   24   is as the world's is./A Christian martyrdom is never an accident, for Saints are
261 MC Thomas   25   by/accident. Still less is a Christian martyrdom the effect of a man's will to/become
261 MC Thomas   27   may become a ruler/of men. A martyrdom is always the design of God, for His
279 MC Knight4   30   he had determined upon a death by martyrdom. Even/at the last, he could have
MARTYRED (1)
261 MC Thomas   16   for the sins/of the world that has martyred them; we rejoice, that another soul is/
MARTYRS (12)
151 Rock 2   16   all the inconvenient saints,/Apostles, martyrs, in a kind of Whipsnade,/Then they
159 Rock 6   27   once for all,/The blood of the martyrs not shed once for all,/The lives of the
159 Rock 6   30   is crucified always/And there shall be Martyrs and Saints./And if blood of Martyrs is
159 Rock 6   31   Martyrs and Saints./And if blood of Martyrs is to flow on the steps/We must first
239 MC   Chorus   15   at All Hallows,/Remembered the martyrs and saints who wait? and who shall/
240 MC   Chorus   16   We wait, we wait,/And the saints and martyrs wait, for those who shall be martyrs
240 MC   Chorus   16   martyrs wait, for those who shall be martyrs and saints./Destiny waits in the hand of
261 MC Thomas   15   rejoice and mourn in the death of martyrs. We mourn, for the sins/of the world
261 MC Thomas   37   to-day, dear children of God, of the martyrs of/the past, asking you to remember
281 MC   Priest2   3   /Conjoined with all the saints and martyrs gone before you,/Remember us./{P3}
281 MC   Chorus   17   by blood. For the blood of Thy martyrs and saints/Shall enrich the earth, shall
282 MC   Chorus   13   upon our heads; that the blood of the martyrs and the agony of the saints/Is upon our
MARVELLOUS (5)
375 CP   Edward   13   yes, Alex;/Yes, of course ... it was marvellous./I've never tasted anything like it .../
390 CP   Julia   5   thank you./{J} She must have made a marvellous recovery./I said so to myself, when I
403 CP   Reilly   9   /And you would imagine it a marvellous cure;/And you would go on, doing
465 CC   Claude   22   /Transfigured in the vision of some marvellous creation,/And I feel what the man
562 ES   Carghil   34   his voice! and his way of moving! It's marvellous./And the charm! He's inherited all
MARY (25)
62 WL: Burial   67   King William Street,/To where Saint Mary Woolnoth kept the hours/With a dead
275 MC Thomas   20   Now to Almighty God, to the Blessed Mary ever Virgin, to the blessed John the
284 FR   m   4   *brothers of her deceased husband/*MARY, *daughter of a deceased cousin of Lady*
285 FR   4m   1   AGATHA, GERALD, CHARLES, MARY/[DENMAN *enters to draw the*
303 FR   3m   1   /Scene II/AGATHA/[*Enter* MARY *with flowers*]/{M} The spring is very
305 FR   Agatha   4   can help me./{Ag} I am very sorry, Mary, I am very sorry for you;/Though you
305 FR   Agatha   13   now and then emerge. You and I, Mary,/Are only watchers and waiters: not the
305 FR   Harry   24   it did not last long. How are you, Mary?/{M} Oh, very well. What are you looking
311 FR   Harry   8   /All other worlds, and me into it. O Mary!/Don't look at me like that! Stop! Try to
313 FR   2m   1   {M} Oh, Harry! {}/Scene III/HARRY, MARY, IVY, VIOLET, GERALD,
313 FR   Violet   1   CHARLES/{V} Good evening, Mary: aren't you dressed yet?/How do you
313 FR   Ivy   7   in time/For his mother's birthday./{I} Mary, my dear,/Did you arrange these flowers?
313 FR   Gerald   14   an authority./{G} Good evening, Mary. You've seen Harry, I see./It's good to
316 FR   m   8   the situation. {}/[*Exeunt*]/[*Enter* MARY, *and passes through to dinner. Enter*
342 FR   m   1   from me,/You take him ... {}/[*Enter* MARY]/{M} Excuse me, Cousin Amy. I have

345 FR	Harry	17	/{Ag} Good-bye./{H} Good-bye, Mary./{M} Good-bye, Harry. Take care of
346 FR	Downing	10	Good night, Miss; good night,/Miss Mary; good night, Sir./{M} Downing, will you
346 FR	Agatha	38	/And we have seen them too — Miss Mary and I./{Do} I understand you, Miss. And
347 FR	Amy	30	what has happened./{A} Agatha! Mary! come!/The clock has stopped in the dark!
347 FR	m	32	the dark! {}/[*Exeunt* AGATHA *and* MARY. *Pause. Enter* WARBURTON]/{W}
348 FR	m	4	Why, what's the trouble? {}/[*Enter* MARY]/{M} Dr. Warburton!/{W} Excuse me. {}
348 FR	m	5	/{W} Excuse me. {}/[*Exeunt* MARY *and* WARBURTON]/{Ch} We do not
349 FR	1m	13	*from one door,* AGATHA *and* MARY, *and set a small portable table./From*
349 FR	4m	13	*Exit* DENMAN. AGATHA/*and* MARY *walk slowly in single file round and*
428 CP	Julia	3	are destructive./I shall never forget Mary Mallington's monkey,/The horrid little

MARY'S (3)

94 Ash-Wed 4		4	green/Going in white and blue, in Mary's colour,/Talking of trivial things/In
94 Ash-Wed 4		10	the sand/In blue of larkspur, blue of Mary's colour,/Sovegna vos/Here are the years
287 FR	Gerald	6	generation speak for itself:/It's Mary's generation. What does she think about

MASCULINE (1)

| 524 ES | Monica | 18 | are — they like to show off./That's masculine vanity, to want to have the waiters/ |

MASK (1)

| 602 Humoresque | | 24 | he belong?/But, even at that, what mask *bizarre!*/Spleen/Sunday: this satisfied |

MASKED (1)

| 363 CP | Reilly | 1 | /For those who surround you, the masked actors;/All there is of you is your body/ |

MASQUERADES (1)

| 22 Preludes | | 19 | early coffee-stands./With the other masquerades/That time resumes,/One thinks of |

MASS (1)

| 260 MC | Thomas | 7 | of Christmas Day. For whenever/Mass is said, we re-enact the Passion and Death |

MASSES (2)

| 244 MC | Chorus | 4 | /We have kept the feasts, heard the masses,/We have brewed beer and cider,/ |
| 260 MC | Thomas | 6 | the/deep meaning and mystery of our masses of Christmas Day. For whenever/Mass |

MASTER (14)

136 5FingerEx4		5	/Which, just at a word from his master/Will follow you faster and faster/And
193 FQ: Little		94	caught the sudden look of some dead master/Whom I had known, forgotten, half
226 Macavity		2	the Hidden Paw —/For he's the master criminal who can defy the Law./He's the
239 MC	Chorus	16	out his hand to the fire, and deny his master? who shall be warm/By the fire, and
239 MC	Chorus	17	be warm/By the fire, and deny his master?/Seven years and the summer is over/
247 MC	Thomas	28	/Think of penitence and follow your master./{T1} Not at this gait!/If you go so fast,
247 MC	Tempt1	33	This was not the way of the King our master!/You were not used to be so hard upon
248 MC	Tempt2	21	/See how the late ones rise! You, master of policy/Whom all acknowledged,
253 MC	Tempt4	36	conspiracies, broken pacts;/To be master or servant within an hour,/This is the
339 FR	Harry	15	the cricket chirp. John shall be the master./All I have is his. No harm can come to
343 FR	Harry	33	worry —/The destined and the perfect master of Wishwood,/The satisfactory son. And
528 ES	Charles	7	or bullying —/At all of which he's a master. Strangers!/{M} You don't understand.
539 ES	Gomez	34	/And I might have become the history master/In a school like that from which I went
566 ES	Ld Clav	3	/At the hands of the same master. But have I still time?/There is time for

MASTERED (1)

| 271 MC | Chorus | 2 | United to the spiritual flesh of nature,/Mastered by the animal powers of spirit,/ |

MASTERS (1)

| 55 Mr E Sun | | 31 | /Stirring the water in his bath./The masters of the subtle schools/Are controversial,' |

MASTERY (1)

| 253 MC | Tempt4 | 33 | bishop, baron, king:/Uncertain mastery of melting armies,/War, plague, and |

MASTIFF (1)

| 256 MC | Tempts | 34 | walk by the wall?/{4T} Does the mastiff prowl by the gate?/{C} Death has a |

MAT (1)

| 210 Old Gumbie | | 3 | the stair or on the steps or on the mat:/She sits and sits and sits and sits — and |

MATCHED (2)

| 258 MC | Thomas | 24 | /The raw nobility, whose manners matched their finger-nails./While I ate out of |
| 445 CC | Eggers | 16 | at the end of the winter/And I matched some material for Mrs. E.,/Which she's |

MATCHES (1)

| 247 MC | Tempt1 | 12 | orchard/Send the sap shooting. Mirth matches melancholy./{T} We do not know very |

MATE (1)

| 212 Growltiger | | 25 | show his sentimental side./His bucko mate, GRUMBUSKIN, long since had |

MATERIAL (3)

49 Hippopot		10	feeble steps may err/In compassing material ends,/While the True Church need
445 CC	Eggers	16	of the winter/And I matched some material for Mrs. E.,/Which she's been wanting.
464 CC	Claude	3	form and colour/And I loved the material that the potter handles./Most people

MATERIALISTIC (1)

| 482 CC | Lady E | 25 | /But they are rather worldly and materialistic,/And ... well, rather vulgar. They're |

MATERIALS (1)
372 CP   Alex   13   I made such a supper out of so few materials/As I found in your refrigerator. But of
MATERNAL (3)
 73 WL: Thund 367   that sound high in the air/Murmur of maternal lamentation/Who are those hooded
105 Song Sime   20   desolation,/Before the certain hour of maternal sorrow,/Now at this birth season of
448 CC   Claude   31   Simpkins,/Is, that she has a strong maternal instinct .../{E} I realise that./{SC}
MATERNITY (1)
505 CC   Lady E   22   a problem of paternity./{LE} Or of maternity./{SC} Don't interrupt, Elizabeth./
MATES (1)
589 Fable   92   one took a knout/And flogged his mates 'till they grew good and friarly./Spirits
MATILDA (1)
278 MC Knight2   7   During the reign of/the late Queen Matilda and the irruption of the unhappy
MATING (1)
 49 Hippopot   17 Refresh the Church from over sea./At mating time the hippo's voice/Betrays inflexions
MATRIMONIE (1)
178 FQ: ECoker   30   and woman/In daunsinge, signifying matrimonie —/A dignified and commodious
MATRON (6)
362 CP   Reilly   38 in the nursing home,/In talking to the matron, you are still the subject,/The centre of
545 ES   Monica 12   seem quiet here and restful./Even the matron, though she looks rather dominating,/
545 ES   Monica 37 ought to address you./Do we call you 'Matron'?/{MP} Oh no, not 'Matron'!/Of course,
545 ES   Piggott 38   call you 'Matron'?/{MP} Oh no, not 'Matron'!/Of course, I *am* a matron in a sense —
546 ES   Piggott   1   no, not 'Matron'!/Of course, I *am* a matron in a sense —/No, I don't simply mean
546 ES   Piggott   9   nurse. But you mustn't call me 'Matron'/At Badgley Court. You see, we've
MATTER (58)
 15 Prufrock   83 am no prophet — and here's no great matter;/I have seen the moment of my greatness
 15 Prufrock   91   worth while,/To have bitten off the matter with a smile,/To have squeezed the
127 Cor1 March   7   how many waiting? what did it matter, on such a day?/Are they coming? No,
179 FQ: ECoker   72   and meanings. The poetry does not matter./It was not (to start again) what one had
182 FQ: ECoker 203   itself/When here and now cease to matter./Old men ought to be explorers/Here
183 FQ: ECoker 205 be explorers/Here and there does not matter/We must be still and still moving/Into
209 NamingCats   1   /The Naming of Cats is a difficult matter,/It isn't just one of your holiday games;/
214 RTTugger   24   beast:/His disobliging ways are a matter of habit./If you offer him fish then he
242 MC   Mess   1   /But as for our King, that is another matter./{P1} But again, is it war or peace?/{M}
266 MC Thomas   12 Leave us then alone./Now what is the matter?/{K1} This is the matter./{3K} You are
266 MC Knight1 13   what is the matter?/{K1} This is the matter./{3K} You are the Archbishop in revolt
279 MC Knight2   2   if there is any guilt whatever in the matter, you/must share it with us./{K1} Morville
289 FR   Gerald   7   feel that what has happened doesn't matter./He's taken his medicine, I've no doubt./
289 FR   Amy   18   wants to talk about it, that's another matter;/But I don't believe he will. He will wish
291 FR   Charles 17   to Wishwood!/{C} Why, what's the matter?/{A} Harry, if you want the curtains
310 FR   Harry   34   saying, or why I say it,/That does not matter. You bring me news/Of a door that
316 FR   Charles   7   that gets on my nerves./{C} If the matter were left in my hands, I think I could
317 FR   Warburt 5   with you/On a confidential matter./{H} I can imagine —/Though I think it
323 FR   Warburt 14   moved tonight. I'd trust Owen/On a matter like this. You can trust Owen./We'll
324 FR   Harry   13   what Winchell says/I don't think the matter can be very serious./A minor trouble like
327 FR   Gerald   25   evening paper?/{G} Why, what's the matter./{I} Somebody, look for Arthur in the
342 FR   Mary   4   He has got the car out./What is the matter?/{A} That woman there,/She has
344 FR   Charles   2   Where is Harry going? What is the matter?/{A} Ask Agatha./{G} Why, what's the
344 FR   Gerald   34   {A} Ask Agatha./{G} Why, what's the matter? Where is he going?/{A} Ask Agatha./{V}
356 CP   Peter   8   No, you wouldn't have seen it. As a matter of fact/It was never produced. They did
365 CP   Reilly   12 {UG} *Tooryooly toory-iley,/What's the matter with One Eyed Riley?* {}/[*Exit*]/{J}
367 CP   Edward   8   /But I think she had some other matter on her mind./{P} It's about Celia. Myself
373 CP   Edward   4   ... How long ago? .../No, it doesn't matter. {}/CURTAIN/Act One. Scene 2/*The*
374 CP   Celia   22   better, for Julia;/But it doesn't really matter. They will know soon enough./Doesn't
384 CP   Reilly   13 change your mind,/But that it will not matter. It will be too late./{E} I have half a mind
384 CP   Reilly   21   /And another is this: it is a serious matter/To bring someone back from the dead./
407 CP   Lavinia   4   practical in the things that really matter./{R} May I interrupt this interesting
408 CP   Reilly   30   not ask me to reveal it —/That is a matter of professional etiquette./{L} I have not
413 CP   Reilly   4   /By telling me exactly what is the matter with them,/And what I am to do about
428 CP   Alex   34   does not bring us to the heart of the matter./There are also foreign agitators,/Stirring
446 CC   Claude   15   organist,/Just as I can't forget ... no matter./The great thing was to find something
450 CC   Claude   5   the worst mistake about him./As a matter of fact, there's a lot I don't know/About
460 CC   Lady E   6   control./Mind control is a different matter:/It's more advanced. But I wrote you all
461 CC   Claude   24 Mr. Simpkins/In public, till now, as a matter of prudence./As we arranged. But after
470 CC   Colby   10 a strain, then, playing to me?/{C} As a matter of fact, I think I played better./I can't
471 CC   Colby   26 trying to give?/{C} That doesn't really matter. But, for some reason,/You thought I'd

473 CC	Lucasta	12	a person:/Nothing but a bit of living matter/Floating on the surface of the Regent's
475 CC	Lucasta	30	me before./Of course the facts don't matter, in a sense./But now we've got to this
476 CC	Colby	8	/At least, I'm going to./{C} Does that matter, either?/{L} In one way, it matters. A
481 CC	Kaghan	34	been there yet./{K} Why no, as a matter of fact, I haven't./I've kept meaning to.
490 CC	Colby	18	I've only been thinking: 'What does it matter/Whose son I am?' You don't understand
490 CC	Colby	24	sorry. But that's why I say it doesn't matter/To me, which of you should be my
490 CC	Lady E	28	a bond between mother and son,/No matter how long they have lost each other./{C}
496 CC	Lady E	10	the dervish rituals./But it doesn't matter what Mrs. Guzzard tells us,/If it satisfies
499 CC	Lucasta	16	{L} I came to apologise/To Colby. No matter. It'll do another time./Oh, I'm glad
501 CC	Lady E	19	can understand each other,/No matter how late. And perhaps that will help us/
513 CC	Colby	15	to know the truth./What it is, doesn't matter. All I wanted was relief/From the
514 CC	Eggers	30	your word, Mrs. Guzzard:/But in a matter of such extreme importance/You'll
516 CC	Colby	8	I want to be an organist./It doesn't matter about success —/I aimed too high before
541 ES	Gomez	21	—/Are pretty well spread. For the matter of that,/My current account in
554 ES	Piggott	28	exercises. {}/[*Exit*]/{MP} As a matter of fact, I flew to your rescue/(That's why
555 ES	Ld Clav	16	for you./{LC} Oh, indeed. What's the matter?/{M} I didn't get far./I met Michael in
568 ES	Ld Clav	4	/{LC} I feel drawn to that spot./No matter. I heard what you said about guilty

MATTERED (3)

359 CP	Edward	20	only that dreadful old woman who mattered —/I shouldn't have minded anyone
435 CP	Peter	27	do something for Celia —/But what mattered was, that Celia was alive./And now it's
476 CC	Lucasta	38	allowance;/But it wouldn't have mattered how much he'd given her:/It was

MATTERS (27)

89 Ash-Wed 1		28	/And I pray that I may forget/These matters that with myself I too much discuss/Too
92 Ash-Wed 2		54	by lot. And neither division nor unity/Matters. This is the land. We have our
245 MC	Thomas	37	your kind attentions./These are small matters. Little rest in Canterbury/With eager
265 MC	Knight1	12	ridden far?/{K1} Not far to-day, but matters urgent/Have brought us from France.
266 MC	Thomas	4	It comes when we are/Engrossed with matters of other urgency./On my table you will
278 MC	Knight2	30	/we have had to adopt, in order to set matters to rights, that you/take issue. No one
289 FR	Amy	20	will wish to forget it./I do not mince matters in front of the family:/You can call it
294 FR	Harry	11	what is always present. That is what matters./{Ag} Nevertheless, Harry, best tell us
294 FR	Harry	25	discolouring the bone —/This is what matters, but it is unspeakable,/Untranslatable: I
301 FR	Violet	11	investigations,/You seem to have left matters much as they were —/Except for having
315 FR	Warburt	11	real./{W} Well, let's not talk of such matters./How did we get onto the subject of
317 FR	Harry	8	to be useless,/Or if anything, make matters rather more difficult./But talk about it,
317 FR	Warburt	12	is on my mind;/And as for making matters more difficult —/It is much more
325 FR	Ivy	15	quite right, Gerald, the one thing that matters/Is not to let her see that anyone is
327 FR	Harry	21	— to be alone with the horror./What matters is the filthiness. I can clean my skin,/
379 CP	Celia	9	is all right between us?/That's all that matters. Truly, Edward,/If that is right,
380 CP	Celia	28	should we talk about Peter? All that matters/Is, that you think you want Lavinia./
394 CP	Lavinia	18	/{L} Everything I tried only made matters worse,/And the moment you were
448 CC	Eggers	11	Sir Claude, I only touched on these matters,/They're much too deep for me. And I
449 CC	Claude	17	mustn't overdo it! But your approval matters./You know she thinks the world of your
453 CC	Eggers	40	/Sir Claude intends to deal with these matters himself./You will have to ask Sir
462 CC	Claude	4	that, before long,/We can put matters onto a permanent basis./{C} I must
476 CC	Lucasta	5	Oh, I see./Well, I can't believe that matters./But I can tell you all about *my* parents:
476 CC	Lucasta	9	that matter, either?/{L} In one way, it matters. A little while ago/You said, very
479 CC	Lucasta	10	way when she's hunting./But all that matters now is, that I'm hungry,/And you've
509 CC	Guzzard	1	/My husband was particular in such matters,/So we had it given conditional baptism.
516 CC	Claude	22	of finding you could handle/Matters you would have thought so

MATTHEW (1)

30 Cous	Nancy	12	/Upon the glazen shelves kept watch/Matthew and Waldo, guardians of the faith,/

MATTING (1)

210 Old Gumbie		11	she has got them lined up on the matting,/She teaches them music, crocheting

MATURE (1)

465 CC	Claude	5	/I was too young. And when I was mature enough/To understand him, he was not

MATURITY (1)

336 FR	Agatha	36	is like a child, formed/To grow to maturity:/Accident is design/And design is

MAUD (1)

549 ES	Carghil	22	you over afterwards —/Effie and Maud and I. What a time ago it seems!/It's

MAUDIE (1)

549 ES	Carghil	6	There were the three of us — Effie, Maudie and me./That day we spent on the river

MAULED (1)

212 Growltiger		20	fear —/Because it was a Siamese had mauled his missing ear./Now on a peaceful

MAUVE (1)

459 CC	Lady E	27	to Mr. Colby./He needs a light mauve. I shall see about that./But not today. I

MAY (221)
MAY (3) [*Proper name*]
37 Gerontion	21	/Came Christ the tiger/In depraved May, dogwood and chestnut, flowering judas,/
66 WL: Chess	170	Bill. Goonight Lou. Goonight May. Goonight./Ta ta. Goonight. Goonight./
191 FQ: Little	25	find the hedges/White again, in May, with voluptuary sweetness./It would be

MAY'ST (1)
| 594 Grad 13 | 2 | sons hast been/To those that follow may'st thou be no less;/A guide to warn them, |

MAYBE (2)
| 602 Humoresque | 12 | stare;/Translated, maybe, to the moon./With Limbo's other |
| 481 CC Kaghan | 5 | have a very sound head for business./Maybe you're a better financier than I am!/ |

MAYOR (1)
| 127 Corl March | 27 | *de Poissy*/And now come the Mayor and the Liverymen. Look/There he is |

MAYTIME (1)
| 92 Ash-Wed 3 | 16 | drest in blue and green/Enchanted the maytime with an antique flute./Blown hair is |

MAZE (2)
| 348 FR Chorus | 9 | in the same room./We do not like the maze in the garden, because it too closely |
| 348 FR Chorus | 9 | because it too closely resembles the maze in the brain./We do not like what happens |

MAZES (1)
| 154 Rock 3 | 4 | of enlightened men,/Betrayed in the mazes of your ingenuities,/Sold by the proceeds |

ME (908)
ME (2) [*Foreign word*]
| 47 Mél Adult | 7 | /A Londres, un peu banquier,/Vous me paierez bien la tête./C'est à Paris que je me |
| 47 Mél Adult | 8 | bien la tête./C'est à Paris que je me coiffe/Casque noir de jemenfoutiste./En |

MEADOW (1)
| 103 Journ Magi | 25 | old white horse galloped away in the meadow./Then we came to a tavern with |

MEADOWS (2)
| 605 Narcissus | 11 | his breast./When he walked over the meadows/He was stifled and soothed by his own |
| 246 MC Templ1 | 37 | good time cannot last?/Fluting in the meadows, viols in the hall,/Laughter and |

MEAGRE (2)
| 41 Burb Blei | 26 | smiles,/Princess Volupine extends/A meagre, blue-nailed, phthisic hand/To climb the |
| 331 FR Harry | 12 | The shadow of something behind our meagre childhood,/Some origin of |

MEAL (4)
68 WL: Fire S	236	is now propitious, as he guesses,/The meal is ended, she is bored and tired,/
587 Fable	26	the Abbot vowed/They'd eat their meal from ghosts and phantoms free,/The fiend
368 CP Alex	24	gift —/Concocting a toothsome meal out of nothing./Any scraps you have will
565 ES Monica	2	and have absolute quiet/Before every meal./{LC} But Michael and I/Must continue

MEALS (1)
| 453 CC Kaghan | 32 | /Is how to keep her fed between meals./{L} B., you're a beast. I've a very small |

MEAN (127)
16 Prufrock	104	—/It is impossible to say just what I mean!/But as if a magic lantern threw the nerves
18 Portrait	19	/'You do not know how much they mean to me, my friends,/And how, how rare
31 Apollinax	18	man' — 'But after all what did he mean?' —/'His pointed ears.... He must be
117 SP Doris	8	the four of diamonds, what's that mean?/{Du} (*reading*) 'A small sum of money,
117 SP Doris	12	/{Do} Here's the three. What's that mean?/{Du} 'News of an absent friend'. —
117 SP Dusty	31	/{Du} Well it needn't be yours, it may mean a friend./{Do} No it's mine. I'm sure it's
120 SP Krum	1	a little too gay for us/Don't think I mean anything *coarse* —/But I'm afraid we
250 MC Thomas	18	once exaltation/Would now be only mean descent. { }/[*Enter* THIRD TEMPTER]/
255 MC Thomas	32	/I well know that these temptations/Mean present vanity and future torment./Can
260 MC Thomas	28	my peace I give unto you.' Did He/mean peace as we think of it: the kingdom of
261 MC Thomas	4	by martyrdom. What then did He mean? If you ask that, remember/then that He
266 MC Knight1	31	do./Saving your ambition is what you mean,/Saving your pride, envy and spleen./{K2}
288 FR Agatha	18	you know what Agatha means./{Ag} I mean painful, because everything is irrevocable,
288 FR Agatha	33	I have seen to that./{Ag} Yes. I mean that at Wishwood he will find another
296 FR Harry	8	freedom./{H} I think I see what you mean,/Dimly — as you once explained the
299 FR Downing	13	likely to have been an accident./I mean, knowing her Ladyship,/I don't think she
299 FR Downing	23	always about the same, Sir./What I mean is, always up and down./Down in the
299 FR Downing	39	me ... more nervous than usual;/I mean to say, you could see that he was nervous.
300 FR Downing	23	yes, Sir, I'm sure I saw him./I don't mean to say that he had any orders —/His
300 FR Downing	26	me up. But when I say I saw him,/I mean that I saw him accidental./You see, Sir, I
307 FR Mary	38	by each other./{M} I know what you mean. That is an experience/I have not had.
309 FR Mary	22	/Everything you feel — I don't mean what you think,/But what you feel. You
318 FR Warburt	19	/{W} Stop, Harry, you're mistaken./I mean, you don't know what I want to tell you./
319 FR Harry	29	was the day he died. Of course./I mean, I suppose, the day on which the news
319 FR Warburt	38	strongly, not to ask your aunt —/I mean, there is nothing she could tell you. But,
322 FR Winch	12	I should hope not, my Lord./I didn't mean to put myself forward./But you see, my
322 FR Harry	16	Lord, I'd much rather not .../{H} You mean you think I can't. But I might surprise

322	FR	Winch	37	got him at the Arms —/Mr. John, I mean. By a bit of luck/Dr. Owen was there, and
330	FR	Agatha	13	guess about the past and what you mean about the future;/But a present is missing,
331	FR	Harry	18	told me that, though he did not mean to./What I want to know is something I
334	FR	Agatha	13	just now?/{Ag} What does the word mean?/There's relief from a burden that I
337	FR	Agatha	15	to know, what you have learned/Mean the end of a relation, make it impossible./
343	FR	Mary	13	for this. I suppose I did not really mean it/Then, but I mean it now. Of course it
343	FR	Mary	14	I did not really mean it/Then, but I mean it now. Of course it was much too late/
346	FR	Downing	22	any reasons./But to show you what I mean, though you'd hardly credit it,/I've always
346	FR	Downing	25	of language, but I'm sure of what I mean:/We most of us seem to live according to
347	FR	Downing	4	it,/So I had the car all ready. You mean them ghosts, Miss!/I wondered when his
347	FR	Ivy	20	happy returns hurrah love Arthur.'/I mean, after what we know of what did happen,/
354	CP	Julia	34	kept him rather quiet./{J} Oh, you mean *that* one./{A} He was feeble-minded./{J}
358	CP	Julia	3	Everything?/{J} Oh, you know what I mean./The next election. And the secrets of
364	CP	Edward	18	see her again — here./{E} Do you mean to say that you know where she is?/{UG}
372	CP	Edward	20	A substantial proof./{E} No, no ... I mean, this is another aunt./{A} I understand.
375	CP	Celia	6	/{C} Lavinia coming back!/Do you mean to say that she's laid a trap for us?/{E}
375	CP	Edward	12	answer it./Hello ... oh, hello! ... No. I mean yes, Alex;/Yes, of course ... it was
378	CP	Celia	37	Edward, I think you are mad —/I mean, you're on the edge of a nervous
379	CP	Celia	6	everything is right,/That you do not mean to have Lavinia back/And that you do
379	CP	Celia	7	have Lavinia back/And that you do mean to gain your freedom,/And that
387	CP	Peter	35	/Because I've changed my mind. I mean, I've decided/That it's all no use. I'm
388	CP	Lavinia	28	to Alex./{L} I don't know what you mean./Edward, have you been sending
391	CP	Julia	11	Julia?/{J} Left anything? Oh, you mean my spectacles./No, they're here. Besides,
392	CP	Edward	37	/{E} I don't quite know what you mean./{L} Oh, Edward!/The point is, that since
393	CP	Lavinia	13	given in to *you*./{L} I know what you mean by giving in to *me*:/You mean, leaving all
393	CP	Lavinia	14	you mean by giving in to *me*:/You mean, leaving all the practical decisions/That
395	CP	Edward	8	to take you as you are./{E} You mean, you are prepared to take me/As I was, or
400	CP	Reilly	9	/To lower his resistance. But what I mean is,/Does he trust your judgement?/{A}
402	CP	Reilly	21	is a term I never use:/It can mean almost anything./{E} And since then, I
403	CP	Reilly	1	see, your memories of childhood —/I mean, in your present state of mind —/Would
403	CP	Reilly	14	want to feel important./They don't mean to do harm — but the harm does not
404	CP	Reilly	17	I suffer?/{R} I understand what you mean./{E} I can no longer act for myself./
405	CP	Edward	9	to the other patient./{E} What do you mean? Who is this other patient?/I consider this
406	CP	Edward	1	to what hotel?/{E} I don't know — I mean to say,/That doesn't concern you./{L} In
406	CP	Lavinia	10	my sanatorium./{L} What do you mean? I asked to be sent/And you took me
407	CP	Lavinia	4	silly, Edward. When I say practical,/I mean practical in the things that really matter./
413	CP	Celia	39	/But that sounds so flat. I don't mean simply/That there's been a crash: though
414	CP	Celia	7	less, or at least they carry on./No. I mean that what has happened has made me
415	CP	Reilly	2	term 'abnormal'./Tell me what you mean by a sense of sin./{C} It's much easier to
415	CP	Celia	3	much easier to tell you what I don't mean:/I don't mean sin in the ordinary sense./
415	CP	Celia	4	to tell you what I don't mean:/I don't mean sin in the ordinary sense./{R} And what,
415	CP	Celia	21	taught to disbelieve in sin./Oh, I don't mean that it was ever mentioned!/But anything
419	CP	Celia	15	and come back again —/I don't mean to say they weren't much better for it —/
419	CP	Celia	17	to you. But they returned .../Well ... I mean ... to everyday life./{R} True. But the
419	CP	Celia	23	prison. But they can't *all* stay there!/I mean, it would make the place so over-crowded.
422	CP	Julia	31	They can not be spoken yet./{J} You mean Peter Quilpe./{R} He has not yet come to
433	CP	Lavinia	25	them now, Alex./{L} What does Julia mean?/{A} I was about to speak of her/When
434	CP	Lavinia	32	thing to say!/But you know what I mean./{E} And you know what I'm thinking.
435	CP	Lavinia	30	Peter. You've only just begun./I mean, this only brings you to the point/At
437	CP	Edward	33	what death is happy?/{E} Do you mean that having chosen this form of death/She
437	CP	Reilly	35	people suffer?/{R} Not at all what I mean. Rather the contrary./I'd say that she
438	CP	Lavinia	4	through greater agony beforehand./I mean — I know nothing of her last two years./
438	CP	Reilly	32	have to make a decision/Which may mean restoration or ruin to a patient —/And
439	CP	Peter	15	got to go there .../{P} I see what you mean./I wish I didn't have to. But the car will
440	CP	Lavinia	1	face my guests. I wish it was over./I mean ... I am glad you came ... I am glad Alex
440	CP	Lavinia	26	say I always look my best can only mean the worst./{E} I never shall learn how to
449	CC	Eggers	8	— Mr. Simpkins./{E} I see what you mean./{SC} She must get to like him first:/And
456	CC	Colby	19	absent-minded./{C} I hope you don't mean,/She has lapses of memory?/{E} I didn't
456	CC	Eggers	21	has lapses of memory?/{E} I didn't mean that./No. She hasn't very much memory
458	CC	Claude	14	air. I arrived at Victoria./{SC} Do you mean to say that you changed your ticket?/{E}
463	CC	Colby	16	time/It's rather disturbing. I don't mean the work:/I mean, about myself. As if I
463	CC	Colby	17	disturbing. I don't mean the work:/I mean, about myself. As if I was becoming/A
470	CC	Colby	6	piano./{C} That's not what I meant. I mean that I've not played/To anyone, since I
473	CC	Colby	38	/{C} I'm being very serious./What I mean is, my garden's no less unreal to me/Than
474	CC	Lucasta	23	afterwards./{L} I know what you mean. Then the flowers would fade/And the

475 CC	Colby	24	in which I find myself./But if you mean, wondered about your ... background:/
475 CC	Colby	27	the ordinary sense./Is that what you mean? I've just accepted you./{L} Oh, that's so
483 CC	Colby	31	in reincarnation?/{C} No, I don't. I mean, I've never thought about it./{LE} I can't
485 CC	Lady E	3	/That I was a foundling — or do I mean 'changeling'?/{C} I don't know which you
485 CC	Colby	4	/{C} I don't know which you mean./{LE} However that may be,/I didn't want
494 CC	Lady E	39	have liked to be a potter!/You really mean, to make jugs and jars/Like those in your
495 CC	Claude	1	in your collection?/{SC} That's what I mean./{LE} But I should have loved you to be a
495 CC	Lady E	24	look like potters —/Is that what I mean? I'm getting confused./I thought I was
500 CC	Lucasta	3	Yes, half-brother./{L} What do you mean?/{SC} Colby is my son./{LE} That is what
502 CC	Lucasta	21	/Or else you're insensible — I don't mean insensitive!/But you're terribly cold. Or
503 CC	Lucasta	18	you, both of you, Lucasta!/{L} We'll mean something to you. But you don't *need*
504 CC	Guzzard	35	are aware of./{MG} I suppose you mean Colby?/{LE} Yes. To do with Colby./{SC}
507 CC	Eggers	3	/{MG} None./{E} Whether, I mean, in Teddington or elsewhere?/Now I must
509 CC	Lady E	38	What with Colby being Barnabas —/I mean, not Barnabas. And Mr. Kaghan/Being
511 CC	Kaghan	27	/{K} But, Lady Elizabeth —/I mean, Aunt Elizabeth: if I call you Aunt
514 CC	Claude	8	unknown to you./{SC} What do you mean?/{MG} Colby is not your son, Sir Claude./
516 CC	Claude	6	to know him./{SC} What do you mean?/{C} I want to be an organist./It doesn't
516 CC	Claude	27	own experience, exactly./Does that mean nothing to you, the experience we shared?
519 CC	Lady E	14	/One does make mistakes! But I mean to do better./Claude, we've got to try to
519 CC	Kaghan	17	we should like to understand *you* .../I mean, I'm including both of you,/Claude ... and
519 CC	Kaghan	20	both Lucasta and I/Would like to mean something to you ... if you'd let us;/And
522 ES	dedic	10	*of what you have given me./The words mean what they say, but some have a further*
526 ES	Charles	19	as a moment ago./What do the words mean now — *I* and *you*?/{M} In our private
533 ES	Ld Clav	25	rather different reasons./{LC} Do you mean that you've won respect out there/By the
535 ES	Gomez	13	people/In general. What does that mean? One trusts a man/Or a woman — in this
540 ES	Ld Clav	15	you've come to see me/Or what you mean by saying you can trust me./{G} Dick, do
546 ES	Piggott	2	in a sense —/No, I don't simply mean that I'm a married woman —/A widow in
550 ES	Ld Clav	25	the business was very successful .../I mean, that he left you comfortably provided
551 ES	Carghil	22	been repaired? But I know what you mean./You mean that I would never have
551 ES	Carghil	23	But I know what you mean./You mean that I would never have started an action/
560 ES	Michael	22	Why manslaughter? Oh, you mean on the road./Certainly not. I'm far too
560 ES	Ld Clav	30	England./{LC} I'm sure you don't mean that. But it's natural enough/To want a
570 ES	Monica	1	reality./{M} But what did the ghosts mean? All these years/You've kept them to
579 ES	Carghil	15	was an inspiration —/On my part, I mean. Are you listening to me, Richard?/You
581 ES	Monica	10	it is as well./{M} What do you mean, Father? You'll be here to greet him./But

MEANING (41)

109 Marina		6	who sharpen the tooth of the dog, meaning/Death/Those who glitter with the glory
109 Marina		8	with the glory of the hummingbird, meaning/Death/Those who sit in the sty of
109 Marina		10	who sit in the sty of contentment, meaning/Death/Those who suffer the ecstasy of
109 Marina		12	who suffer the ecstasy of the animals, meaning/Death/Are become unsubstantial,
111 Xmas Trees		28	the eightieth Christmas/(By 'eightieth' meaning whichever is the last)/The accumulated
150 Rock 1		121	*and the end of this street./We build the meaning:/A Church for all/And a job for each/*
155 Rock 3		52	/When the Stranger says: 'What is the meaning of this city?/Do you huddle close
160 Rock 7		20	through that moment: for without the meaning there is no time, and that moment of
160 Rock 7		20	and that moment of time gave the meaning./Then it seemed as if men must
174 FQ: BurntN		105	/Filled with fancies and empty of meaning/Tumid apathy with no concentration/
186 FQ: DrySal		95	We had the experience but missed the meaning,/And approach to the meaning restores
186 FQ: DrySal		96	the meaning,/And approach to the meaning restores the experience/In a different
186 FQ: DrySal		97	/In a different form, beyond any meaning/We can assign to happiness. I have
187 FQ: DrySal		99	the past experience revived in the meaning/Is not the experience of one life only/
192 FQ: Little		32	came for/Is only a shell, a husk of meaning/From which the purpose breaks only
206 To my Wife		7	the same speech without need of meaning./No peevish winter wind shall chill/No
248 MC Thomas		23	guide the state again./{T} Your meaning?/{T2} The Chancellorship that you
251 MC Thomas		9	For a countryman/You wrap your meaning in as dark generality/As any courtier./
258 MC Thomas		3	/{T} Now is my way clear, now is the meaning plain:/Temptation shall not come in
260 MC Thomas		6	meditate in your hearts the/deep meaning and mystery of our masses of
260 MC Thomas		21	/Now think for a moment about the meaning of this word 'peace'. Does/it seem
287 FR	Amy	32	/Only Agatha seems to discover some meaning in death/Which I cannot find./— I am
299 FRDowning		20	it to frighten people./If you take my meaning — just for the effect./{C} I understand,
330 FR	Harry	18	I still have to learn exactly what their meaning is./At the beginning, eight years ago,/I
331 FR	Harry	9	it./I still have to find out what their meaning is./Here I have been finding/A misery
332 FR	Agatha	18	/For three years childless, learning the meaning/Of loneliness. Your mother wanted a
342 FR	Agatha	32	safety and danger have a different meaning,/And he cannot return. That is his
343 FR	Agatha	2	him, danger and safety have another meaning./*They* have made this clear. And I who
347 FRDowning		2	relieved —/If you understand my meaning. I thought that was the reason/We was

348 FR	Chorus	31	outside of the circle?/And what is the meaning of happening?/What ambush lies
379 CP	Celia	25	the word 'happiness' had a different meaning/Or so it seemed./{E} I have heard of
407 CP	Reilly	27	come where the word 'insult' has no meaning;/And you must put up with that. All
410 CP	Reilly	32	/Though you do not know the meaning of what you have said./{E} Lavinia, we
439 CP	Reilly	8	/Of the past will you alter its meaning./{J} Henry, I think it is time that *I* said
458 CC	Claude	27	/You know that Eggerson's been meaning to retire .../{E} Under medical orders,
481 CC	Kaghan	35	a matter of fact, I haven't./I've kept meaning to. Shall we go there, Lucasta?/{L} I'm
512 CC	Guzzard	9	a confusion in your mind/Between the meaning of *confusion* and *imposture*./{SC} I
519 CC	Kaghan	21	/And we'd take the responsibility of meaning it. {}/[LUCASTA *puts her arms*
522 ES	dedic	7	*babble the same speech without need of meaning:/To you I dedicate this book, to return*
522 ES	dedic	10	*what they say, but some have a further meaning/For you and me only./*Characters/
565 ES	Ld Clav	35	from experience. Do I understand the meaning/Of the lesson I would teach? Come, I'll

MEANINGLESS (6)

83 Hollow Men		7	/We whisper together/Are quiet and meaningless/As wind in dry grass/Or rats' feet
164 Rock 9		19	joined to the soul of stone;/Out of the meaningless practical shapes of all that is living
333 FR	Harry	16	/A sense that would have seemed meaningless before./Everything tends towards
379 CP	Celia	24	I lived in a present/Where time was meaningless, a private world of *ours*,/Where the
382 CP	Celia	15	the noise of an insect,/Dry, endless, meaningless, inhuman —/You might have made
417 CP	Celia	16	I do not know./And if that is all meaningless, I want to be cured/Of a craving for

MEANINGS (3)

160 Rock 7		15	affirmation of rites with forgotten meanings/In the restless wind-whipped sand, or
179 FQ: ECoker		72	intolerable wrestle/With words and meanings. The poetry does not matter./It was
526 ES	Monica	21	we have our private world —/The meanings are different. Look! We're back in the

MEANNESS (2)

| 420 CP | Reilly | 28 | /Each unable to disguise his own meanness/From himself, because it is known to |
| 568 ES | Ld Clav | 26 | things criminal,/Not only turpitude, meanness and cowardice,/But also situations |

MEANS (30)

18 Portrait		27	which friendship lives./How much it means that I say this to you —/Without these
186 FQ: DrySal		91	becomes, in the popular mind, a means of disowning the past./The moments of
205 de la Mare		26	empty house;/By whom, and by what means, was this designed?/The whispered
244 MC	Chorus	27	what you ask, do you realise what it means/To the small folk drawn into the pattern
249 MC	Thomas	9	and perhaps in heaven./{T} What means?/{T2} Real power/Is purchased at price
261 MC	Thomas	13	the day of the Birth/of Christ? By no means. Just as we rejoice and mourn at once, in
268 MC	Knight3	10	chains of anathema./{K3} Using every means in your power to evince/The King's
279 MC	Knight4	28	be killed in England. He used every means of provocation;/from his conduct, step
288 FR	Violet	17	/{V} Gerald! you know what Agatha means./{Ag} I mean painful, because everything
289 FR	Amy	10	Thank you, Gerald. Though Agatha means/As a rule, a good deal more than she
297 FR	Violet	34	/Both against your purpose and the means you are employing./{C} My purpose is, to
298 FR	Charles	1	do nothing for him./And as for my means, we can't afford to be squeamish/In
298 FR	Charles	4	Harry/You can hardly object to the means./{V} I do object./{I} And I wish to
305 FR	Mary	18	always waiting./I think this house *means* to keep us waiting. {}/[*Enter* HARRY]/
324 FR	Violet	11	/Of what is going on? and what it means to your mother?/{H} Oh, of course I'm
344 FR	Gerald	24	the language/And several dialects. It means a lot of preparation./{V} And you need
410 CP	Edward	34	the best of a bad job./That is what he means./{R} When you find, Mr. Chamberlayne,/
419 CP	Reilly	2	You will not forget yours./Each way means loneliness — and communion./Both ways
474 CC	Lucasta	38	of your music!/When I see it as a means of contact with a world/More real than
485 CC	Lady E	17	one's earthly parents/Are only the means that we have to employ/To become
485 CC	Lady E	23	... straight from God./That means that we are nearer to God than to
485 CC	Lady E	38	/Guzzard, did you say? The name means something to me./Yes. Guzzard. *That* is
490 CC	Colby	32	/Than to know the fact and know it means nothing./At the time I was born, you
511 CC	Claude	25	the Kaghans to dinner./{SC} By all means, Elizabeth./{K} But, Lady Elizabeth —/I
535 ES	Gomez	33	take another name. Think what that means —/To take another name. {}/[*Gets up*
554 ES	Piggott	35	at one time. I'm afraid her name/Means nothing at all to the younger generation,
562 ES	Carghil	24	myself. I'm Maisie Montjoy!/That means nothing to you, my dears./It's a very long
571 ES	Ld Clav	9	/I led him to acquire tastes beyond his means:/So he became a forger. And so he served
572 ES	Charles	29	are inspired/With revenge — it's their means of self-justification./Let them tell their
578 ES	Monica	21	I didn't know till now/How much it means to me to have a brother./{Mi} Why of

MEANT (22)

16 Prufrock		97	head,/Should say: 'That is not what I meant at all./That is not it, at all.'/And would it
16 Prufrock		110	is not it at all,/That is not what I meant, at all.'/No! I am not Prince Hamlet, nor
16 Prufrock		111	/No! I am not Prince Hamlet, nor was meant to be;/Am an attendant lord, one that
187 FQ: DrySal		126	wonder if that is what Krishna meant —/Among other things — or one way of
242 MC	Mess	15	are several opinions as to what he meant,/But no one considers it a happy
277 MC	Knight3	18	say, for reasons of state, that he never meant this to happen; and/there is going to be
287 FR	Gerald	14	sorry: but why was she upset?/I only meant to draw her into the conversation./{C}

325 FR   Violet   34   him at all —/Though of course he meant well — but I think an open car/Is so
326 FR   Violet   6   trouble in getting home./I am sure he meant well. But I do think he is reckless./{G} I
393 CP   Edward   26   mind'./{E} Of course I didn't mind./I meant it as a compliment./{L} You meant it as a
393 CP   Lavinia 27   /I meant it as a compliment./{L} You meant it as a compliment!/And you were so
407 CP   Reilly   24   surrender a great deal more than you meant to./This is the consequence of trying to
426 CP   Lavinia   1   left./{E} How's that now?/{L} No, I meant the right./That will do. I'm too tired to
466 CC   Claude   28   me./Do you understand now what I meant when I spoke/Of accepting the terms life
470 CC   Colby   6   play *this* piano./{C} That's not what I meant. I mean that I've not played/To anyone,
475 CC   Colby   6   it deliberately?/{C} That's not what I meant./I meant, there's no end to understanding
475 CC   Colby   7   /{C} That's not what I meant./I meant, there's no end to understanding a
488 CC   Claude   35   own child./{SC} That's not what I meant. Elizabeth,/Colby is *my* son./{LE} Quite
511 CC   Lucasta 38   charge of your wedding./{L} We'd meant to be married very quietly/In a register
525 ES   Charles   6   free for the whole afternoon,/That meant you were to give *me* the whole afternoon.
550 ES   Carghil   4   saying that to tease me./You know I meant my stage name. The name by which you
567 ES   Charles 13   wondering/How much your words meant. You didn't seem to need me then./And
MEANWHILE (15)
129 Cor2 State   24   against the reduction of orders./Meanwhile the guards shake dice on the
246 MC   Thomas   20   will be simple, sudden, God-given./Meanwhile the substance of our first act/Will be
257 MC   Chorus   17   trembling by the mill-stream./And meanwhile we have gone on living,/Living and
287 FR   Amy   21   moment: but life may still go right./Meanwhile, let us drop the subject. The less said
297 FR   Charles 10   up the doctor myself. {}/[*Exit*]/{C} Meanwhile, I have an idea. Why not question
344 FR   m   2 go now, I shall never see you again. {}/[*Meanwhile* VIOLET, GERALD *and* CHARLES
345 FR   Harry   2   as possible. You must get used to it;/Meanwhile, I apologise for my bad manners./
368 CP   Alex   18   have alone. And then we'll leave you./Meanwhile, you and Peter can go on talking/
388 CP   Lavinia 35   I shall ask *them* for an explanation./Meanwhile, I suppose we might as well sit
398 CP   Lavinia 17   eggs. But we must go out for dinner./Meanwhile, my luggage is in the hall
429 CP   Edward   29   when?/{A} In a year or two./{E} And meanwhile?/{A} Meanwhile the monkeys
429 CP   Alex   30   year or two./{E} And meanwhile?/{A} Meanwhile the monkeys multiply./{L} And the
453 CC   Lucasta 30   you break the sad news to Claude?/Meanwhile, you'll have to raid the till for me.
467 CC   Claude   31   a make-believe./{SC} It shan't be. Meanwhile, we must simply wait to learn/What
573 ES   Ld Clav 19   Let us say no more about it./Meanwhile, I feel sure they are conspiring
MEASLES (1)
314 FR   Warburt 11   you came back from school with measles/And we had such a time to keep you in
MEASURE (3)
195 FQ: Little   148   refining fire/Where you must move in measure, like a dancer.'/The day was breaking.
205 de la Mare   30   cadences/Wherewith the common measure is refined;/By conscious art practised
518 CC   Eggers   2   Piano lessons? —/As a temporary measure; because, Mr. Simpkins —/I hope you
MEASURED (2)
14 Prufrock   51   mornings, afternoons,/I have measured out my life with coffee spoons;/I
395 CP   Lavinia 20   sure you were always getting yourself measured/To prove how you had grown since
MEASURES (3)
185 FQ: DrySal   38   of the silent fog/The tolling bell/Measures time not our time, rung by the
278 MC   Knight2 29   it in your faces. It is only with the measures/we have had to adopt, in order to set
278 MC   Knight2 37   a later time still, even such temperate/measures as these would become unnecessary.
MEAT (1)
257 MC   Tempts   5   a broken step./{4T} A man may sit at meat, and feel the cold in his groin./{C} We
MECHANICAL (1)
20 Portrait   79   /Except when a street-piano, mechanical and tired/Reiterates some worn-out
MEDDLING (1)
274 MC   Knights 17   to the King?/Where is Becket, the meddling priest?/Come down Daniel to the
MEDICAL (4)
344 FR   Gerald   19 to go in for some sort of training;/The medical knowledge is the first thing./I've met
447 CC   Claude   26   You must say you had to leave under medical orders./She's always been concerned
458 CC   Eggers   28   been meaning to retire .../{E} Under medical orders, Lady Elizabeth:/The doctor
546 ES   Piggott   5 always lived in what you might call/A medical milieu. My father was a specialist/In
MEDICINE (2)
289 FR   Gerald   8   doesn't matter./He's taken his medicine, I've no doubt./Let him marry again
457 CC   Lady E   17   of it./Unwrap that — It's a bottle of medicine./Now, Parkman, will you give it to the
MEDIOCRITY (1)
381 CP   Edward   40   implacable,/The indomitable spirit of mediocrity./The willing self can contrive the
MEDITATE (3)
167 Rock 10   28   sanctuary;/Small lights of those who meditate at midnight/And lights directed
260 MC   Thomas   5 short one. I wish only that you should meditate in your hearts the/deep meaning and
366 CP   Julia   25   the machine myself —/In a lift I can meditate. Good-bye then./And thank you —

MEDITATES (1)
152 Rock 2   41   of GOD./Even the anchorite who meditates alone,/For whom the days and nights
MEDITATING (1)
41 Burb Blei   31   pared his claws?/Thought Burbank, meditating on/Time's ruins, and the seven laws./
MEDITATION (2)
91 Ash-Wed 2   10   because/She honours the Virgin in meditation,/We shine with brightness. And I
209 NamingCats   25   /When you notice a cat in profound meditation,/The reason, I tell you, is always the
MEDITATIONS (1)
599 On a Port   9   immaterial fancy of one's own./No meditations glad or ominous/Disturb her lips,
MEDITERRANEAN (1)
288 FR Agatha   22   /Or against the painted scene of the Mediterranean,/Harry must often have
MEDIUM (2)
294 FR Harry   6   you/Comparisons in a more familiar medium. I am the old house/With the noxious
465 CC Colby   33   you have expressed,/Although the medium is different. I know/I should never have
MEER (1)
62 WL: Burial   42   of light, the silence./*Oed' und leer das Meer.*/Madame Sosostris, famous clairvoyante,/
MEET (66)
14 Prufrock   27   will be time/To prepare a face to meet the faces that you meet;/There will be time
14 Prufrock   27   a face to meet the faces that you meet;/There will be time to murder and create,/
38 Gerontion   54   /Of the backward devils./I would meet you upon this honestly./I that was near
44 Cook Egg   10   want Honour in Heaven/For I shall meet Sir Philip Sidney/And have talk with
44 Cook Egg   14   want Capital in Heaven/For I shall meet Sir Alfred Mond./We two shall lie
61 WL: Burial   29   /Or your shadow at evening rising to meet you;/I will show you fear in a handful of
64 WL: Chess   84   as/The glitter of her jewels rose to meet it,/From satin cases poured in rich
83 Hollow Men   19   men/The stuffed men./Eyes I dare not meet in dreams/In death's dream kingdom/
109 Marina   21   feet/Under sleep, where all the waters meet./Bowsprit cracked with ice and paint
119 SP Wauch   4   Captain Horsfall —/We want you to meet two friends of ours,/American gentlemen
119 SP Wauch   6   gentlemen here on business./Meet Mr. Klipstein. Meet Mr. Krumpacker./
119 SP Wauch   6   here on business./Meet Mr. Klipstein. Meet Mr. Krumpacker./{Kl} How do you do/
119 SP Klip   35   your name —/But I'm very pleased to meet you all the same) —/London's a little too
136 5FingerEx4   1   *Hodgson Esqre.*/How delightful to meet Mr. Hodgson!/(Everyone wants to know
136 5FingerEx4   8   limb from limb./How delightful to meet Mr. Hodgson!/Who is worshipped by all
136 5FingerEx4   13   gooseberry tart./How delightful to meet Mr. Hodgson!/(Everyone wants to know
136 5FingerEx4   18   rapture skim./How delightful to meet Mr. Hodgson!/(Everyone wants to know
137 5FingerEx5   1   *Murad Ali Beg*/How unpleasant to meet Mr. Eliot!/With his features of clerical cut,
137 5FingerEx5   8   Perhaps and But./How unpleasant to meet Mr. Eliot!/With a bobtail cur/In a coat of
137 5FingerEx5   13   a wopsical hat:/How unpleasant to meet Mr. Eliot!/(Whether his mouth be open or
165 Rock 9   34   /Visible and invisible, two worlds meet in Man;/Visible and invisible must meet in
165 Rock 9   35   in Man;/Visible and invisible must meet in His Temple;/You must not deny the
204 de la Mare   19   we have yet to learn,/And two worlds meet, and intersect, and change;/When cats are
222 Pekes Pols   18   a Peke and a Pollicle happened to meet./They did not advance, or exactly retreat,/
226 Macavity   19   a monster of depravity./You may meet him in a by-street, you may see him in the
233 Skimble   65   Which says: 'I'll see you again!/You'll meet without fail on the Midnight Mail/The Cat
599 On a Port   6   stone/But evanescent, as if one should meet/A pensive lamia in some wood-retreat,/An
241 MC Mess   16   possible,/That you may prepare to meet him./{P1} What, is the exile ended, is our
243 MC Priest2   2   of God is beneath our feet. Let us meet the Archbishop with cordial thanksgiving:/
246 MC Thomas   4   Filled the coast with spies and sent to meet me/Some who hold me in bitterest hate./
253 MC Tempt4   2   me, but have never seen my face./To meet before was never time or place./{T} Say
288 FR Agatha   34   /The man who returns will have to meet/The boy who left. Round by the stables,/
303 FR Mary   23   of uncomfortable people/Who meet very seldom, making conversation./I am
304 FR Mary   31   I know that it does./Did you ever meet her? What was she like?/{Ag} I am the only
335 FR Harry   36   through the little door/And I ran to meet you in the rose-garden./{Ag} This is the
337 FR Harry   18   ... You must go./{H} Shall we ever meet again?/{Ag} Shall we ever meet again?/And
337 FR Agatha   19   ever meet again?/{Ag} Shall we ever meet again?/And who will meet again? Meeting
337 FR Agatha   20   we ever meet again?/And who will meet again? Meeting is for strangers./Meeting is
343 FR Agatha   7   You and I,/My dear, may very likely meet again/In our wanderings in the neutral
345 FR Harry   4   it,/So I shall say good-bye, until we meet again./{G} Well, if you are determined,
358 CP Julia   7   already chosen the people you're to meet./{E} But you asked me to dine with you
364 CP Reilly   28   come to you here. You will be here to meet her. {}/[*The doorbell rings*]/{E} I must
385 CP Reilly   26   them./You must face them all, but meet them as strangers./{E} Then I myself must
393 CP Edward   35   work/And said that I ought to meet more people:/But when the briefs began to
394 CP Lavinia   15   /Whom I particularly wanted you to meet,/You didn't arrive until just as they were
405 CP Lavinia   27   /I didn't say I was prepared to meet him./{E} And I did not expect to meet *you*,
405 CP Edward   28   meet him./{E} And I did not expect to meet *you*, Lavinia./I call this a very
432 CP Julia   4   {}/[*Enter* REILLY]/{J} I want you to meet Sir Henry Harcourt-Reilly —/{E} We're

435 CP	Lavinia	34	/Which you made for yourself, to meet your own needs./Peter, please don't think
445 CC	Claude	4	my wife wouldn't like anyone to meet her/At Northolt, but you. And I couldn't
447 CC	Claude	6	give her warning/Of whom she is to meet on her arrival./{E} How would you like me
448 CC	Eggers	16	/If you don't mind — before I go to meet her./How soon do you propose to ...
454 CC	Lucasta	3	from Northolt./{L} You're going to meet Lizzie?/{E} I am meeting Lady Elizabeth at
457 CC	Eggers	32	perfectly amazing. Let *me* go down to meet her./{SC} Where ought we to be? What
458 CC	Eggers	10	{E} I was just starting for Northolt to meet you./{LE} That was very thoughtful of
459 CC	Lady E	38	got to Lausanne/Than whom should I meet but Mildred Deverell./She was going on to
482 CC	Lady E	15	not the sort of person/They ever meet in their kind of society./So naturally, they
511 CC	Lady E	23	certainly./{LE} And I shall wish to meet them./Claude, we must invite the Kaghans
528 ES	Monica	10	the man that people see when they meet you/Is not the private man, but the public
550 ES	Carghil	29	isn't it strange that you and I/Should meet here at last? Here, of all places!/{LC} Why
555 ES	Piggott	4	mine./I suspected that she wanted to meet you, so I thought/That I'd take the first
561 ES	Ld Clav	27	/{LC} I am trying to help him,/And to meet him half way. I have made him an offer/
563 ES	Carghil	5	/{MC} How romantic! I'd love to meet him./He's coming to speak to us. You
571 ES	Ld Clav	19	should respect love always when we meet it;/Even when it's vain and selfish, we must
578 ES	Michael	32	of you, and always shall be./We don't meet often, but if we're fond of each other,/That
579 ES	Ld Clav	24	the sooner the better./We may never meet again, Michael./{Mi} I don't see why not./

MEETING (29)

84	Hollow Men	37	behaves/No nearer —/Not that final meeting/In the twilight kingdom/This is the
85	Hollow Men	57	of our lost kingdoms/In this last of meeting places/We grope together/And avoid
194	FQ: Little	108	concord at this intersection time/Of meeting nowhere, no before and after,/We trod
202	War Poetry	7	a symbol/Out of the impact? This is a meeting/On which we attend/Of forces beyond
326	FR Harry	13	was a child./You've been holding a meeting — the usual family inquest/On the
337	FR Agatha	20	again?/And who will meet again? Meeting is for strangers./Meeting is for those
337	FR Agatha	21	meet again? Meeting is for strangers./Meeting is for those who do not know each
385	CP Reilly	5	must also remember/That at every meeting we are meeting a stranger./{E} So you
385	CP Reilly	5	/That at every meeting we are meeting a stranger./{E} So you want me to greet
399	CP Reilly	4	that it is important/To avoid any meeting?/{N} You made that clear, Sir Henry:/
445	CC Claude	6	not the way to arrange their first meeting,/On her return from Switzerland./{E}
445	CC Eggers	10	/A very delicate situation —/Her first meeting with Mr. Simpkins./But I was glad of
448	CC Claude	30	told her about him,/The reason for meeting him as merely Mr. Simpkins,/Is, that
450	CC Colby	34	just yet./I'm rather nervous about this meeting./You've told me very little about Lady
451	CC Colby	39	I still don't feel very well prepared for meeting her. {}/[*A loud knock. Enter B.*
454	CC Eggers	4	You're going to meet Lizzie?/{E} I am meeting Lady Elizabeth at Northolt./{L} Well, I
461	CC Claude	31	a thing never happened before./So the meeting didn't go quite the way I'd intended;/
467	CC Colby	37	I must remind you:/You have that meeting in the City/Tomorrow morning. You
468	CC Claude	3	with her, Colby./— Oh yes, that meeting. We must run through the figures. {}/
493	CC Claude	3	important, when you have a difficult meeting,/To decide on the seating arrangements
499	CC Lucasta	10	in! {}/[*Enter* LUCASTA]/{L} Is this a meeting? I came to speak to Colby./I'm sorry./
499	CC Claude	13	here./But you're not involved in this meeting, Lucasta./Won't it do another time?/{L}
500	CC Claude	8	is *her* son./That is the reason for this meeting today./We're awaiting Mrs. Guzzard —
501	CC Lucasta	25	/I don't suppose you want *us* at your meeting./{E} Allow me. May I make a
502	CC Lucasta	3	I've not come to interrupt your meeting./I've been told what it's about. But I
505	CC Guzzard	14	you wish./But is the subject of this meeting —I suppose to do with Colby — so
528	ES Monica	8	You don't understand. It's one thing meeting people/When you're in authority, with
549	ES Carghil	24	me, you know, at the very first meeting —I can't think why, but it's the way
572	ES Ld Clav	36	away from *them*./It is through this meeting that I shall at last escape them./— I've

MEETINGS (4)

164	Rock 9	11	the forum,/And all other secular meetings./Thinking good of themselves, ready
240	MC Priest2	31	intrigue, combinations,/In conference, meetings accepted, meetings refused,/Meetings
240	MC Priest2	31	/In conference, meetings accepted, meetings refused,/Meetings unended or endless/
240	MC Priest2	32	meetings accepted, meetings refused,/Meetings unended or endless/At one place or

MEETS (3)

140	Usk	10	/Seek only there/Where the grey light meets the green air/The hermit's chapel, the
338	FR Harry	23	the safe shelter,/That is where one meets them. That is the way of spectres .../{A}
573	ES Charles	31	name!/{C} I'm glad my name meets with your approval, Mrs. Carghill./{MC}

MEIN (1)

62	WL: Burial	33	/*Frisch weht der Wind/Der Heimat zu/Mein Irisch Kind/Wo weilest du?*/'You gave me

MELANCHOLY (1)

247	MC Tempt1	12	Send the sap shooting. Mirth matches melancholy./{T} We do not know very much of

MÉLANGE (1)

47	Mél Adult	t	/Conservateur/Et crève d'amour./Mélange Adultère de Tout/En Amérique,

MELLIFEROUS (1)

236	Cat Morgan	14	Coast,/And me voice it ain't no sich melliferous horgan;/But yet I can state, and I'm

MELODRAMA (1)
| 115 S | m | */Fragments of an Aristophanic Melodrama/*Fragment of a Prologue/DUSTY. |

MELTED (1)
| 575 ES | Carghil | 38 | was simply *irresistible*/In those days. I melted the first time he looked at me!/Some |

MELTING (3)
103 Journ Magi	7	refractory,/Lying down in the melting snow./There were times we regretted/
191 FQ: Little	11	/In the dark time of the year. Between melting and freezing/The soul's sap quivers.
253 MC Tempt4	33	baron, king:/Uncertain mastery of melting armies,/War, plague, and revolution,/

MEMBER (1)
| 276 MC Knight1 | 31 | problem. I/shall call upon our eldest member to speak first, my neighbour in/the |

MEMBERS (2)
| 326 FR | Harry | 14 | /On the characters of all the junior members?/Or engaged in predicting the minor |
| 492 CC | Claude | 30 | /To be a potter. Not that the Members/Of the Potters' Company know |

MEMBRANE (1)
| 38 Gerontion | 63 | of their chilled delirium,/Excite the membrane, when the sense has cooled,/With |

MEMORIALS (1)
| 201 Def Island | 1 | /Defence of the Islands/Let these memorials of built stone — music's/enduring |

MEMORIES (12)
74 WL: Thund	407	to be found in our obituaries/Or in memories draped by the beneficent spider/Or
111 Xmas Trees	29	is the last)/The accumulated memories of annual emotion/May be
203 Indians	6	/Scarred but secure, he has many memories/Which return at the hour of
248 MC Tempt2	18	/Let us but set these not too pleasant memories/In balance against other, earlier/And
306 FR	Harry	18	escape;/And at the same time, other memories,/Earlier, forgotten, begin to return/
385 CP	Reilly	31	strangle each other with knotted memories./Now I shall go./{E} Stop! Will you
402 CP	Reilly	40	far as I find necessary./You see, your memories of childhood —/I mean, in your
419 CP	Reilly	5	world/Of imagination, shuffling memories and desires./{C} That is the hell I have
439 CP	Reilly	6	/{R} You will have to live with these memories and make them/Into something new.
550 ES	Ld Clav	32	/Finding me here, to revive old memories/Which I should have thought we both
551 ES	Carghil	4	live by forgetting — women live on memories./Besides a woman has nothing to be
551 ES	Carghil	18	the past — about you and me./These memories are painful — but I cherish them./

MEMORISE (1)
| 487 CC | Claude | 2 | have my speech written out/And then memorise it. I can't use notes:/It's got to sound |

MEMORY (37)
24 Rhapsody	5	incantations/Dissolve the floors of memory/And all its clear relations,/Its divisions
24 Rhapsody	11	of the dark/Midnight shakes the memory/As a madman shakes a dead geranium.
24 Rhapsody	23	eye/Twists like a crooked pin.'/The memory throws up high and dry/A crowd of
24 Rhapsody	55	of the grass./The moon has lost her memory./A washed-out smallpox cracks her
26 Rhapsody	72	/Here is the number on the door./Memory!/You have the key,/The little lamp
38 Gerontion	41	not believed in, or if still believed,/In memory only, reconsidered passion. Gives too
61 WL: Burial	3	/Lilacs out of the dead land, mixing/Memory and desire, stirring/Dull roots with
91 Ash-Wed 2	28	/Torn and most whole/Rose of memory/Rose of forgetfulness/Exhausted and
105 Song Sime	6	of my hand./Dust in sunlight and memory in corners/Wait for the wind that chills
141 Rannoch	9	of confused wrong, apt/In silence. Memory is strong/Beyond the bone. Pride
171 FQ: BurntN	11	always present./Footfalls echo in the memory/Down the passage which we did not
195 FQ: Little	158	and the dead nettle. This is the use of memory:/For liberation — not less of love but
201 Def Island	5	of English/verse/be joined with the memory of this defence of/the islands/and the
201 Def Island	7	of this defence of/the islands/and the memory of those appointed to the grey/ships —
234 Ad-dress	18	*you ad-dress a Cat?*/So first, your memory I'll jog,/And say: A CAT IS NOT A
594 Grad 9	6	/Shall not have power to quench the memory./We shall return; and it will be to find/
268 MC Knight3	3	you demanded./{K3} And burying the memory of your transgressions/Restored your
271 MC Thomas	16	/When age and forgetfulness sweeten memory/Only like a dream that has often been
306 FR	Harry	15	the simplification took place in my memory,/I think. It seems I shall get rid of
307 FR	Harry	18	children'./It's absurd that one's only memory of freedom/Should be a hollow tree in
340 FR	Amy	13	had, you would have left me at least a memory/Of something to live upon. You knew
371 CP	Edward	15	/Remember! I say it's already a memory./{P} But I must see Celia at least to
371 CP	Peter	18	shan't know the truth about even the memory./Did we really share these interests?
371 CP	Peter	29	people?/If I can only hold to the memory/I can bear any future. But I must find
371 CP	Peter	31	about the past, for the sake of the memory./{E} There's no memory you can wrap
371 CP	Edward	32	sake of the memory./{E} There's no memory you can wrap in camphor/But the
384 CP	Reilly	28	we know of other people/Is only our memory of the moments/During which we knew
390 CP	Julia	12	Don't say you've had a lapse of memory!/Then that accounts for the aunt —
390 CP	Julia	30	inquisitive./Lavinia has had a lapse of memory,/And so, of course, she sent us
416 CP	Celia	37	/I shall be left with the inconsolable memory/Of the treasure I went into the forest to
456 CC	Colby	20	you don't mean,/She has lapses of memory?/{E} I didn't mean that./No. She hasn't
456 CC	Eggers	22	mean that./No. She hasn't very much memory to lose,/Though she sometimes

460 CC	Lady E	17	the first sign that I've noticed/Of your memory failing. I must persuade you/To have a
551 ES	Carghil	3	even a faithless lover/Is still, in her memory, a kind of testimonial./Men live by
553 ES	Carghil	10	/And you needn't think I idolise your memory./It's simply that I feel that we belong
571 ES	Ld Clav	21	it./That is where I failed. And the memory frets me./{C} But all the same, these
571 ES	Ld Clav	32	a reminder/Of one occasion the memory of which/He knows very well, has

MEN (119)

15 Prufrock	72	that rises from the pipes/Of lonely men in shirt-sleeves, leaning out of windows?.../
31 Apollinax	11	/Where worried bodies of drowned men drift down in the green silence,/Dropping
63 WL: Burial	74	the Dog far hence, that's friend to men,/'Or with his nails he'll dig it up again!/
65 WL: Chess	116	we are in rats' alley/Where the dead men lost their bones./'What is that noise?'/The
83 Hollow Men	t	/Shantih shantih shantih/The Hollow Men/We are the hollow men/We are the stuffed
83 Hollow Men	1	/The Hollow Men/We are the hollow men/We are the stuffed men/Leaning together/
83 Hollow Men	2	the hollow men/We are the stuffed men/Leaning together/Headpiece filled with
83 Hollow Men	17	/Violent souls, but only/As the hollow men/The stuffed men./Eyes I dare not meet in
83 Hollow Men	18	only/As the hollow men/The stuffed men./Eyes I dare not meet in dreams/In death's
85 Hollow Men	67	kingdom/The hope only/Of empty men./*Here we go round the prickly pear/Prickly*
103 Journ Magi	11	girls bringing sherbet./Then the camel men cursing and grumbling/And running away,
115 SP	Dusty	7	Yes he pays the rent/{Du} Well some men don't and some men do/Some men don't
115 SP	Dusty	7	/{Du} Well some men don't and some men do/Some men don't and you know who/
115 SP	Dusty	8	men don't and some men do/Some men don't and you know who/{Do} You can
124 SA Sweeney	36	he do?/That don't apply./Talk to live men about what they do./He used to come and
147 Rock 1	23	There I was told:/Let the vicars retire. Men do not need the Church/In the place where
148 Rock 1	51	useful, resigning/The things that men count for happiness, seeking/The good
148 Rock 1	55	of all or the love of none./All men are ready to invest their money/But most
148 Rock 1	66	your shrines and churches;/The men you are in these times deride/What has
150 Rock 1	103	/*There shall be one cigarette to two men,/To two women one half pint of bitter/Ale. In*
150 Rock 1	111	*and starling have no time to waste./If men do not build/How shall they live?/When the*
151 Rock 2	12	/Talking of right relations of men, but not of relations of men to GOD./'Our
151 Rock 2	12	of men, but not of relations of men to GOD./'Our citizenship is in Heaven';
154 Rock 3	2	saying:/O miserable cities of designing men,/O wretched generation of enlightened
154 Rock 3	3	O wretched generation of enlightened men,/Betrayed in the mazes of your ingenuities,/
155 Rock 3	59	how to ask questions./O weariness of men who turn from GOD/To the grandeur of
157 Rock 4	17	self-seekers within,/When he and his men laid their hands to rebuilding the wall./So
157 Rock 4	18	rebuilding the wall./So they built as men must build/With the sword in one hand
158 Rock 5	2	Geshem the Arabian: were doubtless men of public spirit and zeal./Preserve me from
159 Rock 6	14	to which they owe their significance?/Men! polish your teeth on rising and retiring;/
159 Rock 6	17	and the talon of the cat./Why should men love the Church? Why should they love her
160 Rock 7	2	of the deep./And when there were men, in their various ways, they struggled in
160 Rock 7	8	upon the face of the water./And men who turned towards the light and were
160 Rock 7	10	Higher Religions were good/And led men from light to light, to knowledge of Good
161 Rock 7	21	the meaning./Then it seemed as if men must proceed from light to light, in the
161 Rock 7	27	just when, or why, or how, or where./Men have left GOD not for other gods, they
161 Rock 7	28	this has never happened before/That men both deny gods and worship gods,
161 Rock 7	34	/*There shall be one cigarette to two men,/To two women one half pint of bitter/Ale..../*
161 Rock 7	42	regarded, not even opposed, and men have forgotten/All gods except Usury, Lust
162 Rock 8	11	among his hearers were a few good men,/Many who were evil,/And most who were
162 Rock 8	14	/And most who were neither./Like all men in all places,/Some went from love of glory,
163 Rock 8	32	that was more than the tales/Of old men on winter evenings./Only the faith could
163 Rock 8	40	them./Remember the faith that took men from home/At the call of a wandering
163 Rock 8	44	virtue/And of moderate vice/When men will not lay down the Cross/Because they
163 Rock 8	47	nothing is impossible, nothing,/To men of faith and conviction./Let us therefore
174 FQ: BurntN	107	/Tumid apathy with no concentration/Men and bits of paper, whirled by the cold wind
179 FQ: ECoker	95	not let me hear/Of the wisdom of old men, but rather of their folly,/Their fear of fear
180 FQ: ECoker	104	captains, merchant bankers, eminent men of letters./The generous patrons of art, the
182 FQ: ECoker	186	/Once or twice, or several times, by men whom one cannot hope/To emulate — but
182 FQ: ECoker	204	here and now cease to matter./Old men ought to be explorers/Here and there does
184 FQ: DrySal	9	rages, destroyer, reminder/Of what men choose to forget. Unhonoured,
184 FQ: DrySal	24	oar/And the gear of foreign dead men. The sea has many voices,/Many gods and
195 FQ: Little	178	I think of a king at nightfall,/Of three men, and more, on the scaffold/And a few who
196 FQ: Little	183	/Why should we celebrate/These dead men more than the dying?/It is not to ring the
196 FQ: Little	190	/Or follow an antique drum./These men, and those who opposed them/And those
203 Indians	9	according to the climate)/Of foreign men, who fought in foreign places,/Foreign to
221 Old Deut	34	for his afternoon sleep;/And when the men say: 'There's just time for one more,'/Then
587 Fable	3	their lands and money from the poor men,/And brought their abbeys tumbling at
598 Circe	2	which flows/With the voice of men in pain,/Are flowers that no man knows./

598	Circe	14	/And they look at us with the eyes/Of men whom we knew long ago./On a Portrait/
241	MC Priest1	19	what reconciliation/Of two proud men?/{P3} What peace can be found/To grow
247	MC Thomas	16	same things happen again and again./Men learn little from others' experience./But in
248	MC Tempt2	30	monument of marble./Rule over men reckon no madness./{T} To the man of
249	MC Tempt2	28	with hounds./{T} No!/{T2} Yes! men must manœuvre. Monarchs also,/Waging
252	MC Thomas	16	/I ruled once as Chancellor/And men like you were glad to wait at my door./Not
253	MC Tempt4	14	crushed./As for barons, envy of lesser men/Is still more stubborn than king's anger./
253	MC Tempt4	25	is pleasure, kingly rule,/Or rule of men beneath a king,/With craft in corners,
254	MC Tempt4	37	and the faithful desert you./And men shall only do their best to forget you./And
254	MC Tempt4	38	forget you./And later is worse, when men will not hate you/Enough to defame or to
255	MC Tempt4	2	try to find the historical fact./When men shall declare that there was no mystery/
258	MC Thomas	23	own game. I/Could then despise the men who thought me most contemptible,/The
258	MC Thomas	30	doing right: and striving with political men/May make that cause political, not by what
260	MC Thomas	1	in the highest, and on earth peace to men of good will.' *The/fourteenth verse of the*
260	MC Thomas	9	in His coming for the salvation of men, and/offer again to God His Body and
260	MC Thomas	14	in the highest, and on/earth peace to men of good will'; at this same time of all the
261	MC Thomas	1	his wife singing to the children? Those men His disciples/knew no such things: they
261	MC Thomas	18	glory of God and for the/salvation of men./Beloved, we do not think of a martyr
261	MC Thomas	27	and contriving may become a ruler/of men. A martyrdom is always the design of God,
261	MC Thomas	27	the design of God, for His love of men,/to warn them and to lead them, to bring
263	MC Chorus	13	peace upon earth, goodwill among men?/The peace of this world is always
263	MC Chorus	14	this world is always uncertain, unless men keep the peace of God./And war among
263	MC Chorus	15	the peace of God./And war among men defiles this world, but death in the Lord
265	MC Knight1	19	/{K2} By the King's order./{K1} Our men are outside./{P1} You know the
265	MC Priest1	25	business. Please dine with us./Your men shall be looked after also./Dinner before
272	MC Chorus	28	the Void,/Where those who were men can no longer turn the mind/To
273	MC Priests	23	the door!/{3P} My Lord! these are not men, these come not as men come, but/Like
273	MC Priests	23	these are not men, these come not as men come, but/Like maddened beasts. They
273	MC Priests	24	maddened beasts. They come not like men, who/Respect the sanctuary, who kneel to
273	MC Priests	29	beasts with the souls of damned men, against men/Who would damn themselves
273	MC Priests	29	the souls of damned men, against men/Who would damn themselves to beasts.
274	MC Thomas	9	resistance,/Not to fight with beasts as men. We have fought the beast/And have
280	MC Priest3	16	/By persecution: supreme, so long as men will die for it./Go, weak sad men, lost
280	MC Priest3	17	as men will die for it./Go, weak sad men, lost erring souls, homeless in earth or
280	MC Priest3	21	blackamoors make captive Christian men;/Go to the northern seas confined with ice/
282	MC Chorus	7	as type of the common man,/Of the men and women who shut the door and sit by
282	MC Chorus	9	inflicted;/Who fear the injustice of men less than the justice of God;/Who fear the
290	FR Agatha	26	/Of that which is already prepared/Men tighten the knot of confusion/Into perfect
307	FR Harry	37	the hopeless/Unrecognised by other men, though sometimes by each other./{M} I
326	FR Harry	28	mistake and aberration/Of all men, of the world, which I cannot put in order./
352	CP m	10	/TWO CATERER'S MEN/*The scene is laid in London*/Act One.
381	CP Edward	38	who cannot argue;/And who in some men may be the *guardian* —/But in men like
381	CP Edward	39	men may be the *guardian* —/But in men like me, the dull, the implacable,/The
409	CP Reilly	19	you were incapable/Of loving. To men of a certain type/The suspicion that they
409	CP Reilly	22	to their self-esteem/As, in cruder men, the fear of impotence./{L} You *are*
426	CP Julia	36	party;/I recognised one of their men at the door —/An old friend of mine, in
436	CP Edward	4	face: well, just remember/That some men have to learn much worse things/About
437	CP Reilly	7	*in the garden./That apparition, sole of men, he saw./For know there are two worlds of*
466	CC Claude	20	some unity./Then there are also the men of genius./There are others, it seems to me,
476	CC Lucasta	18	me, and he knows/That what some men have thought about me wasn't true./{C}
476	CC Lucasta	24	of such a thing!/There are not many men who wouldn't have thought it./I don't
501	CC Eggers	30	/Is one of the most promising young men in the City,/And he has a heart of gold. So
524	ES Monica	17	was a perfect lunch./But I know what men are — they like to show off./That's
531	ES Ld Clav	22	/Who occupy positions that other men covet./When we go, a good many folk are
531	ES Ld Clav	30	It makes me smile/To think that men should be frightened of ghosts./If they only
531	ES Ld Clav	31	how frightened a ghost can be of men! {}/[*Knock. Enter* LAMBERT]/{L} Excuse
537	ES Gomez	16	as anyone could be/From the sort of men you'd been at school with —/I didn't fit
551	ES Carghil	4	in her memory, a kind of testimonial./Men live by forgetting — women live on
559	ES Ld Clav	9	everywhere. Australia — no./The men I know there are all in the cities:/An
577	ES Gomez	22	over, Hemington .../{G} As two men of the world, we discussed things very

MEN'S (2)

189	FQ: DrySal	203	of Asia, or in the Edgware Road./Men's curiosity searches past and future/And
605	Narcissus	17	by such knowledge/He could not live men's ways, but became a dancer before God/If

MENACE (1)

185	FQ: DrySal	31	heard: the whine in the rigging,/The menace and caress of wave that breaks on

MENACED (1)
179 FQ: ECoker 93   where is no secure foothold,/And menaced by monsters, fancy lights,/Risking
MEND (1)
345 FR   Amy   20   the truth/About things too late to mend: and that is to be old./Nevertheless, I am
MENDED (1)
251 MC Tempt3   4 real friendship, once ended, cannot be mended./Sooner shall enmity turn to alliance./
MENDICANT (1)
268 MC Thomas   39   of misery and pain./Seven years a mendicant on foreign charity/I lingered abroad:
MENSUAL (1)
54 Mr E Sun   7 /Superfetation of τὸ ἕν,/And at the mensual turn of time/Produced enervate Origen.
MENTAL (5)
180 FQ: ECoker 121   /And you see behind every face the mental emptiness deepen/Leaving only the
181 FQ: ECoker 165 from feet to knees,/The fever sings in mental wires./If to be warmed, then I must
603 Spleen   5   /In repetition that displaces/Your mental self-possession/By this unwarranted
406 CP   Edward 26 known anyone in my life/With fewer mental complications than you;/You're stronger
415 CP   Celia   27 /But when everything's bad form, or mental kinks,/You either become bad form, and
MENTION (16)
227 Macavity   40   deeds are widely known/(I might mention Mungojerrie, I might mention
227 Macavity   40 might mention Mungojerrie, I might mention Griddlebone)/Are nothing more than
267 MC Knight1   27 your earlier misdeeds I shall make no mention./They are too well known. But after
289 FR   Charles 15   it?/Do you think that I ought to mention it now?/It seems to me too late./{A}
326 FR   Charles   8 Arthur?/{C} More than she cares to mention, I imagine. {}/[*Enter* HARRY]/{H}
386 CP   Reilly   3 speak of me to her;/And she will not mention me to you./{E} I promise./{UG} And
400 CP   Reilly   18   upon her/That she was not to mention my name to him./{A} With your usual
408 CP   Reilly   5   recovered./But you failed to mention that the cause of your distress/Was the
448 CC   Eggers   9 my best to gain his confidence./I did mention her interest in Light from the East./
449 CC   Eggers   22 /She becomes abstracted, whenever I mention her./{SC} But she knew about Lucasta
451 CC   Eggers   32   /{E} So if you don't mind, I shall mention at once/That you are a musician./{C}
453 CC   Lucasta   21 what he always says, Colby,/When I mention Mrs. Eggerson. He never fails to rise./
466 CC   Claude   27 you will let me hear you play./I shan't mention it again. I'll wait until you ask me./Do
481 CC   Lady E   37 a herbal salad./{LE} That's right. Just mention my name, Mr. Kaghan,/And ask for
547 ES   Piggott   29 /To know whom *not* to play with. I'll mention no names,/But there are one or two
552 ES   Carghil   23 clear./I've very seldom heard people mention their consciences/Except to observe
MENTIONED (9)
319 FR   Harry   6 he went away./We never heard him mentioned, but in some way or another/We felt
415 CP   Celia   21 sin./Oh, I don't mean that it was ever mentioned!/But anything wrong, from our point
446 CC   Eggers   8 disappointment?/Of course, I never mentioned that:/It's only what you told me./
488 CC   Lady E   7 about his family .../{LE} And when he mentioned *Teddington*, there was a faint echo
497 CC   Claude   12   Colby about himself,/And he mentioned the name of his aunt, Mrs. Guzzard./
504 CC   Claude   2 late for an appointment. She always mentioned it/If *I* was late when I went to see
505 CC   Eggers   27   Lady Elizabeth/Heard your name mentioned, by Mr. Simpkins./She was struck by
538 ES   Ld Clav   5 {LC} That's the second time you have mentioned your reflections./But there's just one
548 ES   Ld Clav   21 the advantages/Which you have just mentioned. I am glad you can confirm them./
MENTONE (1)
428 CP   Julia   4 horrid little beast — stole my ticket to Mentone/And I had to travel in a very slow
MENUS (1)
588 Fable   43 jovial epicures sat down to table./The menus of that time I am afraid/I don't know
MERCHANT (5)
62 WL: Burial   52 the Wheel,/And here is the one-eyed merchant, and this card,/Which is blank, is
68 WL: Fire S   209   noon/Mr. Eugenides, the Smyrna merchant/Unshaven, with a pocket full of
180 FQ: ECoker 104 vacant into the vacant,/The captains, merchant bankers, eminent men of letters./The
240 MC Chorus   2 to keep our households in order;/The merchant, shy and cautious, tries to compile a
292 FR   Charles 31 new hunters.../{C} And I've a new wine merchant to recommend you;/Your cellar could
MERCHANTMAN (1)
201 Def Island   8   to the grey/ships — battleship, merchantman, trawler —/contributing their
MERCIES (1)
281 MC Chorus   17 praise Thee./We thank Thee for Thy mercies of blood, for Thy redemption by blood.
MERCY (5)
89 Ash-Wed 1   26   to rejoice/And pray to God to have mercy upon us/And I pray that I may forget/
282 MC Chorus   15 saints/Is upon our heads./Lord, have mercy upon us./Christ, have mercy upon us./
282 MC Chorus   16   have mercy upon us./Christ, have mercy upon us./Lord, have mercy upon us./
282 MC Chorus   17   have mercy upon us./Lord, have mercy upon us./Blessed Thomas, pray for us. {}/
362 CP   Reilly   34 experience of being an object/At the mercy of a malevolent staircase./Or, take a
MERDS (1)
37 Gerontion   12   /Rocks, moss, stonecrop, iron, merds./The woman keeps the kitchen, makes

MERE (1)
186 FQ: DrySal   88   another pattern, and ceases to be a mere sequence —/Or even development: the
MERELY (30)
 49 Hippopot   4 Although he seems so firm to us/He is merely flesh and blood./Flesh and blood is weak
 90 Ash-Wed 1   35   wings are no longer wings to fly/But merely vans to beat the air/The air which is now
175 FQ: BurntN 157   voices/Scolding, mocking, or merely chattering,/Always assail them. The
179 FQ: ECoker   78   quiet-voiced elders,/Bequeathing us merely a receipt for deceit?/The serenity only a
187 FQ: DrySal 122 fogs conceal it;/On a halcyon day it is merely a monument,/In navigable weather it is
202 War Poetry   3   /Where is the point at which the merely individual/Explosion breaks/In the path
202 War Poetry   5   breaks/In the path of an action merely typical/To create the universal, originate
218 Mung Rump   4   home in Victoria Grove —/That was merely their centre of operation, for they were
225 Mr Mistoff   34   a knife or a fork/And you think it is merely misplaced —/You have seen it one
326 FR   Harry 22   normal. What you call the normal/Is merely the unreal and the unimportant./I was
364 CP   Edward 26   I want her./Do I want her? Or is it merely your suggestion?/{UG} We do not know
369 CP   Peter 30   strange,/Because I thought of her merely as a name//In a society column, to find
397 CP   Edward   6   /Hell is alone, the other figures in it/Merely projections. There is nothing to escape
404 CP   Reilly   8 Chamberlayne:/I learn a good deal by merely observing you,/And letting you talk as
406 CP Lavinia 21   deceived./{L} Are you a devil/Or merely a lunatic practical joker?/{E} I incline to
416 CP   Celia 22   giving nor taking/But that we had merely made use of each other/Each for his
427 CP   Alex 36   are the core of the problem/Or merely a symptom, I am not sure./At least,
448 CC   Eggers 25 successor,/A Mr. Colby Simpkins./{E} Merely Mr. Simpkins./{SC} The reasons for
448 CC   Claude 30   him,/The reason for meeting him as merely Mr. Simpkins,/Is, that she has a strong
464 CC   Claude   7 people think of china or porcelain/As merely for use, or for decoration —/In either
490 CC   Colby 31   Suppose I am your son./Then it's merely a fact. Better not know/Than to know
494 CC   Claude 24 He was a great financier —/And I am merely a successful one./I might have been truer
526 ES Charles   5 For I didn't *know* you loved me —/I merely wanted to believe it. And I've made you
536 ES   Gomez   3 — by easy stages,/And each step was merely a step up the ladder,/So you weren't
536 ES   Gomez 28   and padded:/You're not isolated — merely insulated./It's only when you come to
547 ES   Monica 15 Mrs. Piggott./{M} Let's hope this was merely the concoction/Which she decants for
561 ES Ld Clav 13   had played the coward —/I should merely be another twenty years in dying./{Mi}
569 ES Ld Clav 30   And she's a rich woman./If people merely blackmail you to get your company/I'm
569 ES Ld Clav 34   they are not real, Charles. They are merely ghosts/Spectres from my past. They've
575 ES Michael   3   where I can make my own way,/Not merely be your son. That's what Señor Gomez
MERIT (2)
279 MC Knight2   1   We have served your interests; we merit/your applause; and if there is any guilt
367 CP Edward   28   /Apart, of course, from its literary merit/Which I don't pretend to judge./{P} Well,
MERITS (1)
276 MC Knight1   30   will be able/to lay before you the merits of this extremely complex problem. I/
MERMAIDS (1)
 16 Prufrock   124   upon the beach./I have heard the mermaids singing, each to each./I do not think
MERRY (3)
216 Jellicles   7 Cats are rather small;/Jellicle Cats are merry and bright,/And pleasant to hear when
587 Fable   8   /Inhabited by a band of friars merry./They were possessors of rich lands and
587 Fable   20   /Whene'er the monks were having merry times./He stole the fatter cows and left
MESELF (1)
236 Cat Morgan 10   /But I've got a good coat, and I keep meself smart;/And everyone says, and I guess
MESHES (1)
350 FR   Agatha   5   /And in the nether world/Where the meshes we have woven/Bind us to each other/
MESS (2)
182 FQ: ECoker 183   always deteriorating/In the general mess of imprecision of feeling,/Undisciplined
341 FR   Agatha 17 relative:/It is what we can make of the mess we have made of things,/It is what he can
MESSAGE (2)
515 CC Guzzard   4 You were very far away;/I sent you a message, which never reached you./On your
567 ES Charles   1   here I am. I hope you got my message./{M} Oh Charles, Charles, Charles, I'm
MESSENGER (2)
238 MC   m   5   OF THE CATHEDRAL/A MESSENGER/ARCHBISHOP THOMAS
241 MC   m 11   /That they had a friend? {}/[*Enter* MESSENGER]/{M} Servants of God, and
MESSES (1)
293 FR   Gerald 33   of my life/And some pretty nasty messes./{C} And there isn't much would surprise
MET (34)
193 FQ: Little   88   districts whence the smoke arose/I met one walking, loitering and hurried/As if
202 War Poetry   19   nor accepted,/A problem to be met with ambush and stratagem,/Enveloped or
235 Ad-dress   47 Cat next door,/Whom I have often met before/(He comes to see me in my flat)/I
248 MC Tempt2   16 me, perhaps. I will remind you./We met at Clarendon, at Northampton,/And last at
287 FR   Gerald   1   now, myself;/But I must say I've met some very decent specimens/And some

289 FR	Gerald	33	done it in a fit of temper./{G} I never met her./{A} I am very glad you did not./I am
289 FR	Amy	35	/I am very glad that none of you ever met her./It will make the situation very much
292 FR	Harry	11	a thousand places where I might have met them!/Why here? why here?/Many happy
304 FR	Agatha	32	like?/{Ag} I am the only one who ever met her,/The only one Harry asked to his
307 FR	Mary	4	John./{M} It was the cave where we met by moonlight/To raise the evil spirits./{H}
344 FR	Gerald	20	knowledge is the first thing./I've met with missionaries, often enough —/Some of
354 CP	Reilly	20	know Lady Klootz?/{UG} No, I never met her./{C} Go on with the story about the
355 CP	Julia	1	of hearing —/The only man I ever met who could hear the cry of bats./{P} Hear
368 CP	Peter	31	me how I came to know Celia./I met her here, about a year ago./{E} At one of
369 CP	Peter	3	I owe her a great deal. And then I met Celia./She was different from any girl I'd
369 CP	Peter	34	/And to look at pictures. So we often met/In the same way, and sometimes went
381 CP	Edward	10	Is, that only since this morning/I have met myself as a middle-aged man/Beginning to
412 CP	Celia	27	me to come to you. — But I've met you before,/Haven't I, somewhere? ... Oh,
432 CP	Edward	5	delighted to see him. But we *have* met before./{J} Then if you know him already,
432 CP	Alex	30	Gibbs./{A} Indeed, yes, we have met./{R} On several commissions./{J} We've
437 CP	Reilly	6	/*The magus Zoroaster, my dead child,/Met his own image walking in the garden./That*
437 CP	Reilly	13	*and they part no more!*/When I first met Miss Coplestone, in this room,/I saw the
451 CC	Eggers	21	/The way B. Kaghan did?' She's only met him once;/But do you know, he began
453 CC	Kaghan	25	believe in your existence/Until they met you. Colby's still reeling./It's going to be
454 CC	Colby	37	all those first names/The first time I met her. I'm not used to it./{E} You'll soon get
455 CC	Colby	29	That's my joke./{C} Well, I've never met anyone like Miss Angel./{E} You'll get used
471 CC	Lucasta	11	really are full of surprises!/I've never met a man so ignorant as you/Yet knowing so
471 CC	Colby	21	*I* don't know./{C} The first time we met/You were trying very hard to give a false
476 CC	Lucasta	10	said, very cleverly, that when we first met/You saw I was trying to give a false
486 CC	Lady E	4	known my aunt./{LE} No. I never met ... your aunt./But the name is familiar. How
507 CC	Lady E	23	{LE} That must have been when Tony met with his accident./{MG} I was informed
539 ES	Gomez	33	to me, I wonder,/If I had never met you? I should have got my First,/And I
555 ES	Monica	18	the matter?/{M} I didn't get far./I met Michael in the drive. He says he must see
564 ES	Carghil	20	/But it's very strange that we never met before./You were a friend of Richard's at

METAL (1)

193 FQ: Little		89	/As if blown towards me like the metal leaves/Before the urban dawn wind

METALLED (1)

174 FQ: BurntN		128	the world moves/In appetency, on its metalled ways/Of time past and time future./

METAPHYSICS (1)

53 Whispers		32	crawls between dry ribs/To keep our metaphysics warm./Mr. Eliot's Sunday Morning

METHOD (2)

378 CP	Celia	19	her back./{C} That's the Devil's method! So you want Lavinia back!/Lavinia! So
408 CP	Reilly	28	I cannot disclose./I have my own method of collecting information/About my

METHODS (3)

298 FR	Agatha	12	talk to Downing/And pursue his own methods. {}/[*Rises*]/{V} I do not agree./I think
570 ES	Ld Clav	27	made a fortune by his own peculiar methods,/A man of great importance and the
578 ES	Ld Clav	8	attempts to correct mistakes/By methods which proved to be equally mistaken./I

METICULOUS (1)

16 Prufrock		116	to be of use,/Politic, cautious, and meticulous;/Full of high sentence, but a bit

MÉTIER (2)

435 CP	Reilly	16	nothing./{R} You understand your *métier*, Mr. Quilpe —/Which is the most that any
435 CP	Peter	18	any of us can ask for./{P} And what a *métier*! I've tried to believe in it/So that I might

METROPOLE (1)

68 WL: Fire S		214	Hotel/Followed by a weekend at the Metropole./At the violet hour, when the eyes

METROPOLIS (1)

224 Mr Mistoff		6	own bat./There's no such Cat in the metropolis;/He holds all the patent monopolies/

MEWS (5)

270 MC	Chorus	13	in the kitchen, in the passage,/In the mews in the barn in the byre in the market-place
446 CC	Eggers	24	/Just as I used to. And the flat in the mews?/How soon will that be ready for him?/
446 CC	Claude	34	a bird bath!/{SC} A bird bath? In the mews?/{E} He told me
459 CC	Claude	18	—/So I'm having the flat in the mews done over./{LE} But all in the wrong
469 CC		2m 1	{}/CURTAIN/Act Two/*The flat in the mews a few weeks later.* COLBY *is seated at the*

MI-CHEMIN (1)

51 Restaurant		18	/Moi j'avais peur, je l'ai quittée à mi-chemin./C'est dommage.'/Mais alors, tu as

MIASMAL (1)

50 Hippopot		36	remains below/Wrapt in the old miasmal mist./Dans le Restaurant/Le garçon

MICE (5)

210 Old Gumbie		9	deeply concerned with the ways of the mice —/Their behaviour's not good and their
210 Old Gumbie		19	hardly begun./As she finds that the mice will not ever keep quiet,/She is sure it is
224 Mr Mistoff		30	believing/That he's only hunting for mice./He can play any trick with a cork/Or a

| 228 | Gus | 8 | of Cats —/But no longer a terror to mice and to rats./For he isn't the Cat that he |
| 233 | Skimble | 48 | know that you won't be bothered by mice —/You can leave all that to the Railway |

MICHAEL (66)

523	ES	m	9	PIGGOTT/MRS. CARGHILL/MICHAEL CLAVERTON-FERRY/ACT
527	ES	Monica	36	any use to anybody,/I'm afraid. Poor Michael! Mother spoilt him/And Father was
555	ES	Monica	18	the matter?/{M} I didn't get far./I met Michael in the drive. He says he must see you./
556	ES	Monica	4	he's frightened./And you know what Michael is like when he's frightened./He's apt to
556	ES	Monica	9	him./Let's get this over. {}/[calls]/{M} Michael! {}/[Enter MICHAEL]/{LC} Good
556	ES	m	10	over. {}/[calls]/{M} Michael! {}/[Enter MICHAEL]/{LC} Good morning, Michael./
556	ES	Ld Clav	10	MICHAEL]/{LC} Good morning, Michael./{Mi} Good morning, Father. {}/[A
556	ES	Monica	27	stop being so polite to each other./Michael, you know what you've come to ask of
560	ES	Ld Clav	15	/{LC} This is what I will do for you, Michael./I will help you to make a start in any
560	ES	Ld Clav	20	to get out of England./{LC} Michael! Are there reasons for your wanting to
561	ES	Ld Clav	1	—/Only a fugitive from reality./Oh Michael! If you had some aim of high
561	ES	Ld Clav	5	in the northern night. Believe me, Michael:/Those who flee from their past will
561	ES	Ld Clav	10	you./You're all I have to live for, Michael —/You and Monica. If I lived for
561	ES	Monica	22	has entered unobserved]/{M} Michael! How can you speak to Father like
561	ES	Monica	24	do you look so angry?/I know that Michael must be in great trouble,/So can't you
561	ES	Monica	31	he has just been exhibiting./{M} Michael! Say something./{Mi} What is there to
562	ES	Monica	4	/What can I say to you?/However Michael has behaved, Father,/Whatever Father
562	ES	Monica	5	Father,/Whatever Father has said, Michael,/You must forgive each other, you
562	ES	Carghil	16	/And this must be your brother, Michael./I'm right, aren't I?/{Mi} Yes, you're
562	ES	Carghil	29	hardly resembles you at all,/But Michael — your father has changed a good deal
564	ES	Ld Clav	6	this is your son?/{LC} This is my son Michael,/And my daughter Monica./{M} How
564	ES	Monica	9	Monica./{M} How do you do./Michael!/{Mi} How do you do./{MC} I don't
565	ES	Ld Clav	3	quiet/Before every meal./{LC} But Michael and I/Must continue our discussion.
565	ES	Ld Clav	4	our discussion. This afternoon, Michael./{M} No, I think you've had enough
565	ES	Monica	6	you've had enough talk for to-day./Michael, as you're staying so close at hand/Will
565	ES	Carghil	10	you staying in the neighbourhood, Michael?/Your father is such an old friend of
565	ES	Carghil	12	That it seems most natural to call you Michael./You don't mind, do you?/{Mi} No, I
565	ES	m	24	{}/[Exeunt MRS. CARGHILL and MICHAEL]/{G} Well, Dick, we've got to obey
565	ES	Ld Clav	33	few minutes ago I was pleading with Michael/Not to try to escape from his own past
565	ES	Ld Clav	37	teach? Come, I'll start to learn again./Michael and I shall go to school together./We'll
566	ES	Ld Clav	4	But have I still time?/There is time for Michael. Is it too late for me, Monica? {}/
567	ES	Charles	19	this morning/About your father and Michael, and those people from his past,/I've
574	ES	Carghil	8	to impart it?/{MC} It's about dear Michael./{LC} Oh? What about Michael?/{MC}
574	ES	Ld Clav	9	dear Michael./{LC} Oh? What about Michael?/{MC} He's told me all his story./
574	ES	Carghil	15	/And in the end I discovered what Michael really wanted/For making a new start.
574	ES	Carghil	24	which I've come to prepare you./Dear Michael is so happy — all his problems are
574	ES	m	26	together. {}/[Enter GOMEZ and MICHAEL]/{LC} Well, Michael, you know I
574	ES	Ld Clav	26	GOMEZ and MICHAEL]/{LC} Well, Michael, you know I expected you this
575	ES	Gomez	19	your time, rehearsing ancient history./Michael knows it already. I've told him myself./
576	ES	Ld Clav	7	you?/{MC} Just eighteen./{LC} Now, Michael,/Señor Gomez says he has told you his
576	ES	Monica	25	are plenty of other good names./{M} Michael, Michael, you can't abandon your
576	ES	Monica	25	of other good names./{M} Michael, Michael, you can't abandon your family/And
576	ES	Charles	27	very self — it's a kind of suicide./{C} Michael, you think Señor Gomez is inspired by
577	ES	Charles	1	are hardly likely to invoke it./And, Michael, here's another point to think of:/Señor
577	ES	Charles	13	view. Can you really feel confidence,/Michael, in a man who aims to gratify, through
577	ES	Gomez	19	prison sentence for forgery./{G} Well, Michael, what do you say to all this?/{Mi} I'll
577	ES	Carghil	31	Mr. Carghill told me so./Now, Michael has great abilities for business./I saw
578	ES	Ld Clav	3	him. I have something to say to you,/Michael, before you go. I shall never repudiate
578	ES	Ld Clav	12	think of the happy little boy who was Michael,/When I think of your boyhood and
578	ES	Monica	17	sorrow and compunction?/{M} Oh Michael, remember, you're my only brother/
578	ES	Monica	34	with your life or mine./{M} Oh Michael, you haven't understood a single word/
579	ES	Monica	5	always pretend that it is the same Michael./{C} And when do you leave England?/
579	ES	Ld Clav	17	excited!/{LC} Is this good-bye then, Michael?/{Mi} Well, that just depends./I could
579	ES	Ld Clav	24	the better./We may never meet again, Michael./{Mi} I don't see why not./{G} At the
580	ES	Monica	1	It's truly providential!/{M} Good-bye Michael. Will you let me write to you?/{G} Oh,
580	ES	Monica	5	the card, Charles. If I write to you, Michael,/Will you ever answer?/{Mi} Oh of
580	ES	Monica	14	Mr. ... Hemington./{M} Good-bye Michael. {}/[Exeunt MICHAEL and GOMEZ]
580	ES	m	14	/{M} Good-bye Michael. {}/[Exeunt MICHAEL and GOMEZ]/{MC} I'm afraid this
580	ES	Carghil	22	I shall be able to bring you news of Michael./And now that we've found each other
580	ES	Monica	27	I'm so sorry!/But perhaps, perhaps, Michael may learn his lesson./I believe he'll
580	ES	Monica	31	—/It's only self-confidence that Michael is lacking./Oh Father, it's not you and
580	ES	Ld Clav	36	you say comes home to me. I fear for Michael;/Nevertheless, you are right to hope for

581 ES Ld Clav 17   did I mark out a narrow path for Michael?/Because I wanted to perpetuate myself
581 ES Ld Clav 40   man I thought you were./{LC} And Michael —/I love him, even for rejecting me,/
582 ES Ld Clav 8   and are loved. And now that I love Michael,/I think, for the first time — remember,
582 ES Charles 36   some mysterious fashion,/Even with Michael, and despite those people,/Because
MICHAEL'S (5)
574 ES Carghil 20   /In his own country. And a friend of Michael's father!/And I found him only too
575 ES Gomez   23   /About my not being custodian of Michael's morals./That is just what I should be!
577 ES Gomez   23   very frankly;/And I can tell you, Michael's head is well screwed on./He's got
577 ES Ld Clav 39   bar his way, as you know very well./Michael's a free agent. So if he chooses/To
583 ES Monica   18   /He is only my father now, and Michael's./And I am happy. Isn't it strange,
MICHELANGELO (2)
 13 Prufrock   14   the women come and go/Talking of Michelangelo./The yellow fog that rubs its back
 14 Prufrock   36   the women come and go/Talking of Michelangelo./And indeed there will be time/To
MID-ATLANTIC (1)
294 FR Harry   32   wheel/That cloudless night in the mid-Atlantic/When I pushed her over./{V}
MIDDLE (10)
 14 Prufrock   40   the stair,/With a bald spot in the middle of my hair —/(They will say: 'How his
125 SA Chorus   31   /{Ch} When you're alone in the middle of the night and/you wake in a sweat
125 SA Chorus   33   of a fright/When you're alone in the middle of the bed and/you wake like someone
179 FQ: ECoker   90   could no longer harm./In the middle, not only in the middle of the way/But
179 FQ: ECoker   90   harm./In the middle, not only in the middle of the way/But all the way, in a dark
182 FQ: ECoker 174   this Friday good./So here I am, in the middle way, having had twenty years —/Twenty
215 RTTugger   33   /But he'll leap on your lap in the middle of your sewing,/For there's nothing he
289 FR Ivy   25   *that* way —/Swept off the deck in the middle of a storm,/And never even to recover
326 FR Harry   10   the old/Can drop off to sleep in the middle of calamity/Like children, or like
460 CC Claude   32   /{SC} Yes, you go and rest./I'm in the middle of some business with Mr. .../{LE}
MIDDLE-AGED (1)
381 CP Edward   10   this morning/I have met myself as a middle-aged man/Beginning to know what it is
MIDLANDS (2)
203 Indians   16   your land, or ours: but a village in the Midlands,/And one in the Five Rivers, may
570 ES Ld Clav 33   grammar school somewhere in the Midlands./As for Maisie Batterson .../{M}
MIDNIGHT (7)
 24 Rhapsody   11   /And through the spaces of the dark/Midnight shakes the memory/As a madman
 34 Figlia   24   cogitations still amaze/The troubled midnight and the noon's repose./Poems/
111 Xmas Trees   4   /The rowdy (the pubs being open till midnight),/And the childish — which is not that
167 Rock 10   28   /Small lights of those who meditate at midnight/And lights directed through the
177 FQ: ECoker   26   do not come too close,/On a summer midnight, you can hear the music/Of the weak
185 FQ: DrySal   45   the past and the future,/Between midnight and dawn, when the past is all
233 Skimble   65   again!/You'll meet without fail on the Midnight Mail/The Cat of the Railway Train.'/
MIDST (3)
264 MC Priest2   8   the day of St. John the Apostle./*In the midst of the congregation he opened his mouth.*/
264 MC Priest2 13   and heard/Declare we unto you./*In the midst of the congregation.* {}/[*Introit of St. John*
539 ES Ld Clav 27   citizen of San Marco/Is that in the midst of the engrossing business/Of the nature
MIDWINTER (1)
191 FQ: Little   1   life of significant soil./Little Gidding/Midwinter spring is its own season/Sempiternal
MIEL (1)
 48 Lune Miel   t   brûlantes de Mozambique./Lune de Miel/Ils ont vu les Pays-Bas, ils rentrent à Terre
MIEUX (1)
 48 Lune Miel   7   de morsures./On relève le drap pour mieux égratigner./Moins d'une lieue d'ici est
MIGHT (144)
 31 Apollinax   20   /'There was something he said that I might have challenged.'/Of dowager Mrs.
 32 Hysteria   10   of the fragments of the afternoon might be collected, and I concentrated/my
 43 Swee Erect   38   lack of taste/Observing that hysteria/Might easily be misunderstood;/Mrs. Turner
117 SP Doris   4   of Clubs/{Du} That's Pereira/{Do} It might be Sweeney/{Du} It's Pereira/{Do} It
117 SP Doris   6   be Sweeney/{Du} It's Pereira/{Do} It might *just* as well be Sweeney/{Du} Well
117 SP Dusty   15   of Hearts! — Mrs. Porter!/{Du} Or it might be you/{Do} Or it might be you/We're all
117 SP Doris   16   /{Du} Or it might be you/{Do} Or it might be you/We're all hearts. You can't be
117 SP Doris   38   You cut for luck. You cut for luck./It might break the spell. You cut for luck./{Du}
118 SP Dusty   1   /{Do} That'll be Snow/{Du} Or it might be Snow/{Do} Or it might be Snow/{Du}
118 SP Doris   2   {Du} Or it might be Swarts/{Do} Or it might be Snow/{Du} It's a funny thing how I
124 SA Sweeney 13   a man once did a girl in./Any man might do a girl in/Any man has to, needs to,
157 Rock 4   9   gave him leave to depart/That he might rebuild the city./So he went, with a few,
171 FQ: BurntN   6   /All time is unredeemable./What might have been is an abstraction/Remaining a
171 FQ: BurntN   9   /Only in a world of speculation./What might have been and what has been/Point to
172 FQ: BurntN   47   /Time past and time future/What might have been and what has been/Point to

186 FQ: DrySal	65	/The unattached devotion which	might pass for devotionless,/In a drifting boat
202 War Poetry	14	/It seems just possible that a poem	might happen/To a very young man: but a
227 Macavity	40	wicked deeds are widely known/(I	might mention Mungojerrie, I might mention
227 Macavity	40	/(I might mention Mungojerrie, I	might mention Griddlebone)/Are nothing more
235 Ad-dress	56	needed, like a dish of cream;/And you	might now and then supply/Some caviare, or
593 Grad 4	5	/We hope it may be; would that we	might know!/Would we might look into the
593 Grad 4	6	that we might know!/Would we	might look into the future years./Great duties
277 MC Knight3	1	is one thing I should like to say, and I	might as/well say it at once. It is this: in what
280 MC Knight1	4	at street corners, and do/nothing that	might provoke any public outbreak. {}/[Exeunt
287 FR Violet	12	tactless,/And I think that Charles	might have been more considerate./{G} I'm very
290 FR Amy	11	is less than a shadow in death./You	might as well all of you know the truth/For the
291 FR Charles	2	and catcalls in the gallery?/{C} I	might have been in St. James's Street, in a
291 FR Ivy	3	chair rather nearer the fire./{I} I	might have been visiting Cousin Lily at
291 FR Gerald	4	not had to come to this party./{G} I	might have been staying with Compton-Smith,
292 FR Harry	11	There were a thousand places where I	might have met them!/Why here? why here?
297 FR Charles	12	/He was with them on the boat. He	might be of use./{I} Charles! you don't really
297 FR Ivy	14	you don't really suppose/That he	might have pushed her over?/{C} In any case, I
297 FR Charles	16	any case, I shouldn't blame Harry./I	might have done the same thing once, myself./
299 FR Charles	9	/Downing, do you think that it	might have been suicide,/And that his Lordship
299 FR Downing	33	during the voyage?/{Do} Well, you	might say depressed, Sir./But you know his
299 FR Downing	40	behaved as if he thought something	might happen./{C} What sort of thing?/{Do}
302 FR Chorus	7	/Why do we all behave as if the door	might suddenly open, the curtains be drawn,/
303 FR Mary	16	him./{M} Dr. Warburton? I think she	might have told me;/It is very difficult, having
304 FR Mary	1	wanted of that, when at college./{M} I	might have known you'd throw that up against
305 FR Harry	35	things:/But it's very like her. What I	might have expected./It only makes the
306 FR Harry	21	I can't explain./But I thought I	might escape from one life to another,/And it
311 FR Harry	22	I stood in sunlight, and thought I	might stay there./{M} Look at me. You can
315 FR Amy	23	waiting for Arthur and John?/{A} We	might as well go in to dinner./They may come
320 FR Warburt	15	live several years. A sudden shock/Might	send her off at any moment./If she had
322 FR Harry	16	You mean you think I can't. But I	might surprise you;/I think I might be able to
322 FR Harry	17	But I might surprise you;/I think I	might be able to give you a shock./{Wi} There's
324 FR Violet	9	/{V} Well, Harry,/I think that you	might have had something to say./Aren't you
324 FR Violet	24	care what happens to John,/You	might show some consideration to your mother.
327 FR Harry	12	puzzle. Were they simply outside,/I	might escape somewhere, perhaps. Were they
328 FR Charles	1	overcoat./I'll see if it's there. There	might be something in that. {}/[Exit]/{G} Well,
331 FR Agatha	33	of liberation./{Ag} Your father	might have lived — or so I see him —/An
334 FR Harry	31	/Stifled my decision. Now I see/I	might even become fonder of my mother —/
340 FR Amy	3	is an end,/And I thought that time	might have made a change in Agatha —/It has
340 FR Amy	28	visits, after he was gone,/So that there	might be no ugly rumours./You thought I did
347 FR Ivy	28	do you all look so peculiar? I think I	might be allowed/To know what has happened./
349 FR Charles	11	— or was it? — and yet I think that I	might understand./{all} But we must adjust
355 CP Celia	7	how could you believe him?/He	might have imagined it./{J} My darling Celia,
357 CP Edward	1	too?/{E} No, I haven't any aunt. But I	might go away./{C} But, Edward ... what was I
357 CP Julia	36	address, and the telephone number?/I	might run down and see Lavinia/On my way to
360 CP Reilly	33	for the best./With another man, she	might have made a mistake/And want to come
360 CP Reilly	35	back to you. If another woman,/She	might decide to be forgiving/And gain an
361 CP Reilly	1	wanted you;/If another woman, you	might have to marry her —/You might even
361 CP Reilly	2	you might have to marry her —/You	might even imagine that you wanted to marry
362 CP Edward	7	herself a permanent advantage./{E} It	might turn out so, yet .../{UG} Are you going to
367 CP Peter	24	/{E} As a possible profession?/{P} She	might make it a profession;/Though she had her
370 CP Edward	34	lucky you are. In a little while/This	might have become an ordinary affair/Like any
377 CP Julia	29	Come, I give you/Lavinia's aunt! You	might have guessed it./{E&C} Lavinia's aunt./{J}
382 CP Celia	16	meaningless, inhuman —/You	might have made it by scraping your legs
388 CP Lavinia	35	/Meanwhile, I suppose we	might as well sit down./What shall we talk
396 CP Lavinia	25	hard to bear./I thought that there	might be some way out for you/If I went away.
396 CP Lavinia	28	had been only a ghost to you,/You	might be able to find the road back/To a time
401 CP Edward	5	/Before I entered the door, that you	might be the same person:/But I dismissed that
401 CP Edward	13	... but what is the use!/I suppose I	might as well go away at once./{R} No. If you
401 CP Reilly	15	/You are not going away, so you	might as well sit down./You were going to ask a
401 CP Reilly	28	cannot escape from it:/And so ... you	might as well sit down./I think that you will find
402 CP Reilly	4	could hardly be worse./{R} They	might be much worse. You might have ruined
402 CP Reilly	4	/{R} They might be much worse. You	might have ruined three lives/By your
404 CP Reilly	36	where I am./Is it far to go?/{R} You	might say, a long journey./But before I treat a
410 CP Lavinia	11	to me that what we have in common/Might	be just enough to make us loathe one
411 CP Edward	15	for you./{E} It seems to me that I	might as well go home./{L} Then we can share a

413 CP	Celia	27	things I can't understand,/Which you might consider symptoms. But first I must tell
416 CP	Celia	2	of anything I've ever *done*,/Which I might get away from, or of anything in me/I
418 CP	Celia	5	I ought to be able to accept that/If I might still have it. Yet it leaves me cold./
418 CP	Celia	12	everything,/Put up with anything, if I might cherish it./In fact, I think it would really
421 CP	Julia	8	to start from./Oh, of course, they might just murder each other!/But I don't think
427 CP	Alex	10	your party/And, as I thought you might be leaving for the country,/I said, I must
432 CP	Reilly	22	{E} And will you have a cocktail?/{R} Might I have a glass of water?/{E} Anything
435 CP	Peter	19	I've tried to believe in it/So that I might believe in myself./I thought I had ideas to
439 CP	Lavinia	5	that. If I had understood you/Then I might not have misunderstood Celia./{R} You
440 CP	Edward	22	how am I looking?/{E} Very well./I might almost say, your best. But you always
446 CC	Eggers	30	You think of everything./But if I might make a suggestion: window boxes!/He's
449 CC	Claude	3	{SC} In a very different way, yes. You might say *mislaid*,/Since the father is dead, and
449 CC	Claude	6	child:/In the circumstances, that might make her jealous./I've explained all this
462 CC	Claude	31	current business,/Thinking that you might find it easier/To start by a rather formal
475 CC	Lucasta	31	now we've got to this point — you might as well know them./{C} I'd gladly tell you
477 CC	Lucasta	33	someone else sees me/As I really am, I might become myself./{C} Oh Lucasta, I'm not
478 CC	Lucasta	12	you wouldn't mind at all. That you might be sorry for me./But now I don't want
480 CC	Kaghan	39	for Colby,/He's the sort of fellow who might chuck it all/And go to live on a desert
482 CC	Lady E	9	hint./I feared it was possible you might become too friendly/With Mr. Kaghan
488 CC	Claude	26	such a thing from you./I see now I might as well have told you before,/But I'd
488 CC	Claude	31	become fond of Colby,/And that he might come to take the place of your own child,
489 CC	Claude	9	But if I had another/I thought you might think — 'and how many more?'/You
489 CC	Claude	10	think — 'and how many more?'/You might have suspected any number of children!/
490 CC	Colby	33	nothing./At the time I was born, you might have been my mother,/But you chose not
494 CC	Lady E	2	at all./I wish that Colby, somehow, might prove to be *your* son/Instead of mine.
494 CC	Claude	25	/And I am merely a successful one./I might have been truer to my father's inspiration
494 CC	Lady E	32	as if I did understand,/And perhaps I might come to understand better./What did you
497 CC	Eggers	33	to take,/If I may say so. Of course, we might discover/Another Mrs. Guzzard .../{LE}
498 CC	Eggers	19	saw more than one baby./{E} She might have taken in another one/As a
499 CC	Lucasta	19	an announcement to make,/And I might as well make it now. If you'll listen./{SC}
500 CC	Lucasta	30	He has his own world,/And he might vanish into it at any moment —/At just
503 CC	Lucasta	3	necessary to each other/In the way we might have been. But a different way/That
503 CC	Lucasta	5	And perhaps — who knows? —/We might become more necessary to each other,/As
505 CC	Claude	11	acquaintance./{SC} And I thought he might ... conduct the proceedings:/He's the very
506 CC	Guzzard	25	to be present./{MG} You think that I might be able to help you?/{E} It seems just
506 CC	Eggers	34	child was confided./Of course she might be mistaken about Teddington .../{LE} I
508 CC	Claude	1	/And I asked you here so that you might tell her so./{E} Don't take this as a
508 CC	Guzzard	32	a somewhat unusual one./Perhaps it might be possible to trace them./The name was
512 CC	Guzzard	8	— that's all./{MG} I feared there might be a confusion in your mind/Between the
529 ES	Ld Clav	20	/{LC} Good afternoon, Charles. You might have guessed, Monica,/What I've been
532 ES	Gomez	32	/{G} We're as thick as thieves, you might almost say./Don't you know me, Dick?/
534 ES	Ld Clav	8	that, if carried on in England,/It might land you in gaol again?/{G} That's true
539 ES	Ld Clav	10	to know, I had had a stroke./And I might have another./{G} Yes. You might have
539 ES	Gomez	11	I might have another./{G} Yes. You might have another./But I wonder what brought
539 ES	Gomez	34	I should have got my First,/And I might have become the history master/In a
541 ES	Gomez	7	secret's safe with me./Of course, I might give it to a few friends, in confidence./It
541 ES	Gomez	8	it to a few friends, in confidence./It might even reach the ears of some of your
546 ES	Piggott	4	course I've always lived in what you might call/A medical milieu. My father was a
551 ES	Carghil	37	want to ruin you./If I'd carried on, it might have ended your career,/And then you
554 ES	Carghil	25	a rest cure,/And it struck me that he might find it a strain/To have to cope with both
554 ES	Piggott	32	wouldn't know that name, but you might remember her,/As Maisie Montjoy in
555 ES	Ld Clav	29	ran into a tree./{LC} Yes, a tree./It might have been a man. So it might be that,/Or
557 ES	Michael	21	of it. If I could have borrowed more/I might have pulled it off./{LC} Borrowed? From
559 ES	Ld Clav	6	of England/In one of the Dominions, might set you on your feet./I have connections,
559 ES	Michael	22	if I took a different name — and I might choose to —/No one would know or care
560 ES	Michael	11	in some interesting business./But I might be expected to put up some capital./{LC}
560 ES	Ld Clav	31	/To want a few years abroad. It might be very good for you/To find your feet.
563 ES	Carghil	17	lately?/Richard, I think that you might introduce us./{LC} Oh. This is .../{G}
571 ES	Ld Clav	5	with good in them,/People who might all have been very different/From Gomez,
572 ES	Ld Clav	24	/We should have been unhappy, might have come to divorce;/But she hasn't
573 ES	Ld Clav	2	/From brooding over faults I might well have forgotten./You think that I'm
579 ES	Michael	29	/{LC} Nothing at all./{Mi} Then we might as well be going./{G} Yes, we might as
579 ES	Gomez	30	might as well be going./{G} Yes, we might as well be going./You'll be grateful to me
581 ES	Ld Clav	8	You heard me say to him/That this might be a final good-bye./I am sure of it now.

MIGHTN'T (2)

219 Mung Rump	33	or could you have sworn that it mightn't be both?/And when you heard a
375 CP Edward	16	But I just wondered/Whether it mightn't be rather indigestible? .../Oh, no, Alex,

MIGHTY (1)

588 Fable	49	cakes among the good things./A mighty peacock standing on both legs/With

MILAN (1)

48 Lune Miel	12	/Prolonger leurs misères de Padoue à Milan/Où se trouve la Cène, et un restaurant

MILD (2)

287 FR Amy	30	are/And death will come to you as a mild surprise,/A momentary shudder in a
330 FR Harry	3	everything will go on as before. These mild surprises/Should be in the routine of

MILDLY (1)

531 ES Ld Clav	23	/When we go, a good many folk are mildly grieved,/And our closest associates, the

MILDRED (2)

458 CC Lady E	21	change your plans?/{LE} Because of Mildred Deverell./She's been having the
459 CC Lady E	38	/Than whom should I meet but Mildred Deverell./She was going on to Zürich.

MILE (1)

227 Macavity	32	have been Macavity!' — but he's a mile away./You'll be sure to find him resting, or

MILES (5)

325 FR Charles	10	a night like this — it's a good three miles;/There's nothing we could do that
328 FR Charles	23	and was/travelling at the rate of 66 miles an hour. When asked why he/did not stop
535 ES Gomez	30	— when I went away,/Thousands of miles away, to another climate,/To another
536 ES Gomez	12	that happened four thousand miles away,/Only believed what the parish priest
556 ES Michael	16	I'm staying at a pub/About two miles from here. Not a bad little place./{LC}

MILIEU (1)

546 ES Piggott	5	in what you might call/A medical milieu. My father was a specialist/In

MILITARY (2)

285 FR Violet	20	English circulating libraries,/To the military widows and the English chaplains,/To
463 CC Claude	7	/And then your school, and your military service,/And then your absorption in

MILK (5)

124 SA Sweeney	31	/And nobody went/But he took in the milk and he paid the rent./{Sw} What did he do?
226 Macavity	24	the jewel-case is rifled,/Or when the milk is missing, or another Peke's been stifled,/
587 Fable	22	and left the thinner/To furnish all the milk — upset the chimes,/And once he sat the
589 Fable	90	grew most devout,/And lived on milk and breakfast food entirely;/Each morn
257 MC Chorus	12	fire in winter,/The child without milk in summer,/Our labour taken away from

MILKING (1)

178 FQ: ECoker	44	and the constellations/The time of milking and the time of harvest/The time of the

MILKMAN (1)

125 SA Sweeney	10	were dead/If he was alive then the milkman wasn't/and the rent-collector wasn't/

MILL-STREAM (1)

257 MC Chorus	16	/The torn girl trembling by the mill-stream./And meanwhile we have gone on

MILLIONAIRE (2)

68 WL: Fire S	234	sits/As a silk hat on a Bradford millionaire./The time is now propitious, as he
181 FQ: ECoker	160	our hospital/Endowed by the ruined millionaire,/Wherein, if we do well, we shall/Die

MIMIC (3)

354 CP Celia	4	person to tell it./She's such a good mimic./{J} Am I a good mimic?/{P} You *are* a
354 CP Julia	5	such a good mimic./{J} Am I a good mimic?/{P} You *are* a good mimic. You never
354 CP Peter	6	I a good mimic?/{P} You *are* a good mimic. You never miss anything./{A} She never

MINCE (2)

65 WL: Chess	140	got demobbed, I said —/I didn't mince my words, I said to her myself,/HURRY
289 FR Amy	20	will. He will wish to forget it./I do not mince matters in front of the family:/You can

MIND (112)

34 Figlia	12	the body torn and bruised,/As the mind deserts the body it has used./I should find/
92 Ash-Wed 3	19	of the flute, stops and steps of the mind over the third stair,/Fading, fading;
116 SP Dusty	32	be all right on Monday/I say do you mind if I ring off now/She's got her feet in
149 Rock 1	68	satisfy the rational and enlightened mind./Second, you neglect and belittle the
155 Rock 3	60	from GOD/To the grandeur of your mind and the glory of your action,/To arts and
171 FQ: BurntN	15	My words echo/Thus, in your mind./But to what purpose/Disturbing the dust
180 FQ: ECoker	123	about;/Or when, under ether, the mind is conscious but conscious of nothing —/I
186 FQ: DrySal	91	/Which becomes, in the popular mind, a means of disowning the past./The
188 FQ: DrySal	156	the future/And the past with an equal mind./At the moment which is not of action or
188 FQ: DrySal	159	"on whatever sphere of being/The mind of a man may be intent/At the time of
192 FQ: Little	50	conscious occupation/Of the praying mind, or the sound of the voice praying./And
194 FQ: Little	130	the dialect of the tribe/And urge the mind to aftersight and foresight,/Let me disclose
205 de la Mare	28	/Free passage to the phantoms of the mind?/By you; by those deceptive cadences/
209 NamingCats	27	I tell you, is always the same:/His mind is engaged in a rapt contemplation/Of the

210	Old Gumbie	1	Gumbie Cat/I have a Gumbie Cat in mind, her name is Jennyanydots;/Her coat is of
210	Old Gumbie	13	and tatting./I have a Gumbie Cat in mind, her name is Jennyanydots;/Her equal
210	Old Gumbie	25	and cheese./I have a Gumbie Cat in mind, her name is Jennyanydots;/The
220	Old Deut	15	... Yes! .../Ho! hi!/Oh, my eye!/My mind may be wandering, but I confess/I *believe*
234	Ad-dress	8	we find/Possessed of various types of mind./For some are sane and some are mad/
235	Ad-dress	42	ad-dress a Cat./But always keep in mind that he/Resents familiarity./I bow, and
248	MC Thomas	14	waking a dead world,/So that the mind may not be whole in the present. {}/[*Enter*
267	MC Knight1	32	England, not exiled/Or threatened, mind you; but in the hope/Of stirring up trouble
272	MC Chorus	28	who were men can no longer turn the mind/To distraction, delusion, escape into
279	MC Knight4	39	a verdict of Suicide while of/Unsound Mind. It is the only charitable verdict you can
295	FR Harry	24	It is not my conscience,/Not my mind, that is diseased, but the world I have to
296	FR Charles	24	probably let this notion grow in his mind,/Living among strangers, with no one to
296	FR Charles	29	is someone to talk to,/To get it off his mind. I'll have a talk to him tomorrow./{A}
298	FR Charles	30	like to put to you,/I'm sure you won't mind, it's about his Lordship./You've looked
313	FR Ivy	9	Just let me change them./You don't mind, do you? I know so much about flowers;/
317	FR Warburt	11	sure you cannot know what is on my mind;/And as for making matters more difficult
320	FR Warburt	6	mother/Is still so alert, so vigorous of mind,/Although she seems as vital as ever —/It
327	FR Harry	22	clean my skin,/Purify my life, void my mind,/But always the filthiness, that lies a little
330	FR Agatha	12	landlord./{Ag} What is in your mind, Harry?/I can guess about the past and
334	FR Harry	38	O that awful privacy/Of the insane mind! Now I can live in public./Liberty is a
344	FR Charles	15	a hurry? Before you make up your mind .../{V} You can't really think of *living* in a
348	FR Warburt	3	worrying?/I'm anxious to relieve her mind. Why, what's the trouble? {}/[*Enter*
349	FR Charles	11	in the morning./{C} I fear that my mind is not what it was — or was it? — and yet
361	CP Edward	17	expected./I only wanted to relieve my mind/By telling someone what I'd been
364	CP Reilly	12	/Except long enough to clear from the mind/The illusion of having ever been in the
366	CP Peter	14	along, Peter./{P} I hope you won't mind/If I don't come with you, Julia? On the
366	CP Julia	21	could do it now./{J} Of course I don't mind./{P} Well, at least you must let me take
367	CP Edward	8	she had some other matter on her mind./{P} It's about Celia. Myself and Celia./{E}
368	CP Edward	1	must have left it open./{E} Never mind;/So long as you both shut it when you go
372	CP Peter	32	she comes back ... but, if you don't mind,/I'd rather you didn't tell *her* what I've
372	CP Edward	37	night, Alex. Oh, and if you don't mind,/Please *shut the door after you*, so that it
384	CP Edward	9	thinking that I may have changed my mind?/{UG} No. You will not be ready to
384	CP Reilly	10	You will not be ready to change your mind/Until you recover from having made a
384	CP Reilly	12	to tell you that you will change your mind,/But that it will not matter. It will be too
384	CP Edward	14	It will be too late./{E} I have half a mind to change my mind now/To show you that
384	CP Edward	14	/{E} I have half a mind to change my mind now/To show you that I am free to
384	CP Reilly	16	change it./{UG} You will change your mind, but you are not free./Your moment of
387	CP Peter	35	I'm so glad./Because I've changed my mind. I mean, I've decided/That it's all no use.
393	CP Lavinia	24	Peacehaven' —/And you said 'I don't mind'./{E} Of course I didn't mind./I meant it as
393	CP Edward	25	'I don't mind'./{E} Of course I didn't mind./I meant it as a compliment./{L} You
395	CP Edward	4	cease to feel/And then you speak your mind./{L} That will be a novelty/To find that
395	CP Lavinia	6	be a novelty/To find that you have a mind to speak./Anyway, I'm prepared to take
395	CP Lavinia	28	very shattering for you./But never mind, you'll soon get over it/And find yourself
401	CP Edward	4	Chamberlayne?/{E} It came into my mind/Before I entered the door, that you might
403	CP Reilly	1	—/I mean, in your present state of mind —/Would be largely fictitious; and as for
405	CP Edward	19	to leave. And I propose to do so./My mind is made up. I shall go to a hotel./{R} It is
406	CP Lavinia	39	It's only that I have a more practical mind/Than you have, Edward. You do know
407	CP Reilly	9	/And one of them is an honest mind./That is one of the causes of their
407	CP Lavinia	11	can say my husband has an honest mind./{E} And I could not honestly say that of
413	CP Reilly	25	first to describe your present state of mind./{C} Well, there are two things I can't
414	CP Reilly	31	return from./There are other states of mind, which we take to be delusion,/But which
415	CP Celia	17	I may have been a fool:/But I don't mind at all having been a fool./{R} And what is
416	CP Celia	6	you treat a patient for such a state of mind?/{R} What had you believed were your
419	CP Reilly	18	/{R} True. But the friends you have in mind/Cannot have been to this sanatorium./I
421	CP Julia	10	thought of Celia that weighs upon my mind./{R} Of Celia?/{J} Of Celia./{R} But when
425	CP Edward	16	That's true. You have a very practical mind./{L} But you know, I don't think that you
427	CP Alex	16	couldn't get through to you./Never mind, I said — to myself, not to her —/Never
427	CP Alex	17	said — to myself, not to her —/Never mind: the unexpected guest/Is the one to whom
430	CP Peter	14	this evening,/So I knew you wouldn't mind my looking in so early./It does seem ages
436	CP Reilly	28	who were dying/Or the state of mind in which they died?/{L} I'm willing to
436	CP Reilly	40	the position correctly, Julia./Do you mind if I quote poetry, Mrs. Chamberlayne?/{L}
438	CP Reilly	19	sure that *I* am./{R} Let me free your mind from one impediment:/You must try to
448	CC Eggers	16	I should like to know —/If you don't mind — before I go to meet her./How soon do
449	CC Eggers	2	that Lady Elizabeth/Would be put in mind of the child *she* lost./{SC} In a very
451	CC Eggers	32	for the warning!/{E} So if you don't mind, I shall mention at once/That you are a

453 CC	Lucasta	5	L. for Lucasta./Go on, Eggy. Don't mind him, Colby./Colby, are you married?/{C}
453 CC	Lucasta	8	I'm not married./{L} Then I don't mind being seen with you in public./You may
460 CC	Lady E	1	a wonderful doctor who teaches mind control.'/So on I went to Zürich./{SC} So
460 CC	Claude	4	that the doctor in Lausanne taught mind control?/{LE} No, Claude, he only teaches
460 CC	Lady E	6	he only teaches *thought* control./Mind control is a different matter:/It's more
462 CC	Colby	7	very settled./And what you've had in mind still seems to me/Like building my life
463 CC	Colby	25	time, when I least expect it,/When my mind is cleared and empty, walking in the street
471 CC	Colby	30	see what happened./I hope you don't mind: I know it sounds impertinent./{L} Well,
472 CC	Lucasta	31	position,/And made up your mind to go into business/And be someone like
474 CC	Colby	21	It's not the hurting that one would mind/But the sense of desolation afterwards./
478 CC	Lucasta	12	told you all I did,/That you wouldn't mind at all. That you might be sorry for me./
482 CC	Lady E	8	/But, Colby, I hope you won't mind a gentle hint./I feared it was possible you
490 CC	Claude	9	Yes, tell us everything that's in your mind./I know this situation must be more of an
497 CC	Eggers	1	speak of it;/Yet I know what's on her mind, for days beforehand./But here I am,
504 CC	Guzzard	28	I believe I was punctual./But I didn't mind waiting in the least, Sir Claude./I know
505 CC	Claude	7	him to be present./I hope you don't mind?/{MG} Why should I mind?/I have heard
505 CC	Guzzard	8	you don't mind?/{MG} Why should I mind?/I have heard about Mr. Eggerson from
508 CC	Lady E	10	There isn't a shadow of doubt in my mind./I'm surprised that you, Eggerson, with
511 CC	Kaghan	28	I call you Aunt Elizabeth/Would you mind very much calling me ... just 'B'?/{LE}
512 CC	Guzzard	8	there might be a confusion in your mind/Between the meaning of *confusion* and
512 CC	Kaghan	34	that, Barnabas./{K} *B.* — if you don't mind, Aunt Elizabeth./{LE} B. — and I'm sure
513 CC	Colby	34	image I could create in my own mind,/To live with that image. An ordinary man
517 CC	Eggers	21	is a man who knows his own mind./Is it true, Mr. Simpkins, that what you
518 CC	Guzzard	35	/{MG} Home? Only to a taxi./Do you mind if I take my leave, Sir Claude?/I'm no
518 CC	Claude	37	needed here. {}/[*Exit* COLBY]/{SC} Mind? What do I mind?/{MG} Then I will say
518 CC	Claude	37	[*Exit* COLBY]/{SC} Mind? What do I mind?/{MG} Then I will say goodbye. You have
527 ES	Monica	9	time/You may have changed your mind. Such things have happened./{C} That
537 ES	Ld Clav	11	us?/{LC} It has never crossed my mind. Develop the point./{G} Well, consider
556 ES	Michael	31	to *you.*/You've always made up your mind that I was to blame/Before you knew the
560 ES	Ld Clav	12	What sort of business have you in mind?/{Mi} Oh, I don't know. Import and
565 ES	Carghil	13	to call you Michael./You don't mind, do you?/{Mi} No, I don't mind./I'm
565 ES	Michael	14	don't mind, do you?/{Mi} No, I don't mind./I'm staying at the George — it's not far
568 ES	Ld Clav	25	everything —/And that includes, mind you, not only things criminal,/Not only

MINDED (2)

359 CP	Edward	21	who mattered —/I shouldn't have minded anyone else, {}/[*The doorbell rings.*
476 CC	Lucasta	26	very generous./I don't think he'd have minded. But he's very clever too;/And he

MINDS (5)

218 Mung	Rump	22	for Sunday dinner,/With their minds made up that they wouldn't get thinner/
250 MC	Tempt3	29	in order,/A country-keeping lord who minds his own business./It is we country lords
333 FR	Harry	22	a dream/Dreamt through me by the minds of others. Perhaps/I only dreamt I
420 CP	Reilly	27	stale thoughts mouldering in their minds./Each unable to disguise his own
437 CP	Reilly	19	/That a sudden intuition, in certain minds,/May tend to express itself at once in a

MINE (35)

117 SP	Doris	32	it may mean a friend./{Do} No it's mine. I'm sure it's mine./I dreamt of weddings
117 SP	Doris	32	friend./{Do} No it's mine. I'm sure it's mine./I dreamt of weddings all last night./Yes
117 SP	Doris	34	of weddings all last night./Yes it's mine. I know it's mine./Oh good heavens
117 SP	Doris	34	last night./Yes it's mine. I know it's mine./Oh good heavens what'll I do./Well I'm
268 MC	Thomas	23	my yoke/That is laid upon them, or mine to revoke./Let them go to the Pope. It was
271 MC	Thomas	31	/No life here is sought for but mine,/And I am not in danger: only near to
333 FR	Agatha	7	—/Something that should have been *mine*, as I felt then./Most people would not have
333 FR	Agatha	12	/I felt that you were in some way mine!/And that in any case I should have no
355 CP	Alex	14	And is he still there?/Julia is really a mine of information./{C} There isn't much that
365 CP	Julia	1	found them? You can tell if they're mine —/Some kind of a plastic sort of frame —
402 CP	Edward	23	And since then, I have realised/That mine is a very unusual case./{R} All cases are
402 CP	Edward	33	doubt if you have ever had a case like mine:/I have ceased to believe in my own
407 CP	Reilly	23	you put yourselves into hands like mine/You surrender a great deal more than you
426 CP	Julia	37	men at the door —/An old friend of mine, in fact. But I'm forgetting!/I've got a
439 CP	Edward	3	/{E} Your responsibility is nothing to mine, Lavinia./{L} I'm not sure about that. If I
462 CC	Claude	17	really are her son, instead of being mine./She has always lived in a world of
472 CC	Lucasta	17	—/But your insecurity is nothing like mine./{C} In what way is it different?/{L} It's
473 CC	Colby	29	Eggerson's garden/Is more real than mine./{L} Eggerson's garden?/What makes you
473 CC	Colby	33	also in the same sense that I retire to mine./But he doesn't feel alone there. And when
489 CC	Claude	8	— though yours had been lost,/And mine I couldn't lose. But if I had another/I
494 CC	Lady E	3	might prove to be *your* son/Instead of mine. Really, I do!/It would be so much fairer.
494 CC	Lady E	4	/It would be so much fairer. If he is mine —/As I am sure he is — then you never

494 CC Lady E   8   do I want? I should like him to be mine,/But for you to believe that he is yours!/So

508 CC Guzzard 31   /{MG} Yes, I know their name:/Like mine, a somewhat unusual one./Perhaps it

515 CC Guzzard 14   you so happy!/If I said the child was mine, what future could he have?/And then I

517 CC Colby   2   knew your inheritance. Now I know mine./{SC} I shall never ask you to think of me

536 ES Gomez   22   don't understand such isolation/As mine, you think you do .../{LC} I'm sure I do,/

550 ES Ld Clav   8   name, no doubt. And I've changed mine./Your name now and here .../{MC} Is

555 ES Piggott   3   /I dare say, but not quite your sort or mine./I suspected that she wanted to meet you,

557 ES Michael 25   to a lender,/A man whom a friend of mine recommended./He gave me good terms, on

562 ES Carghil   32 /Your father was a very dear friend of mine once./{Mi} Did he really look like me?/

565 ES Carghil   11   /Your father is such an old friend of mine/That it seems most natural to call you

577 ES Gomez   7   as many years ago/His father paid mine./{C} This return of past kindness/No

578 ES Michael 33   needn't interfere with your life or mine./{M} Oh Michael, you haven't understood

578 ES Monica 36   life/Of course, just as I must make mine./It's not a question of your going abroad/

MINES (1)

127 Corl March 17   /I cannot tell how many projectiles, mines and fuses,/13,000 aeroplanes,/24,000

MING (1)

219 Mung Rump 37   vase which was commonly said to be Ming —/Then the family would say: 'Now

MINGLED (1)

18 Portrait   17   /Through attenuated tones of violins/Mingled with remote cornets/And begins./'You

MINIMUM (1)

286 FR   Violet   21   they dance all night/In the absolute *minimum* of clothes./{C} It's the cocktail-drinking

MINISTERS (1)

269 MC Knight1   8   /From attainting his servants and ministers./{T} It is not I who insult the King,/

MINISTRY (1)

538 ES Gomez   35   has puzzled me./You were given a ministry before you were fifty:/That should

MINOR (11)

131   t   /RESIGN RESIGN RESIGN/MINOR POEMS/Eyes that last I saw in tears/

243 MC Chorus 28   poverty and licence,/There has been minor injustice./Yet we have gone on living,/

314 FR   Violet   15 /{V} It was always the same with your minor ailments/And children's epidemics: you

323 FR   Winch   9   the doctor,/It's really nothing but a minor accident./{W} It's John has had the

324 FR   Harry   14   the matter can be very serious./A minor trouble like a concussion/Cannot make

326 FR   Harry   15   /Or engaged in predicting the minor event,/Engaged in foreseeing the minor

326 FR   Harry   16   event,/Engaged in foreseeing the minor disaster?/You go on trying to think of

348 FR   Chorus 19 various spells and enchantments./And minor forms of sorcery,/Divination and

368 CP   Edward 35   a salon,/Where I entertained the minor guests/And dealt with the misfits,

368 CP   Edward 37   mistakes./But you were one of the minor successes/For a time at least./{P} I

431 CP   Peter   35   English faces —/Of course, only for minor parts —/And I'll help him decide what

MINORITY (1)

531 ES Ld Clav 24 /And our closest associates, the small minority/Of those who really understand the

MINOTAUR (1)

438 CP   Reilly   8   it/We talk of darkness, labyrinths, Minotaur terrors./But that world does not take

MINSTER (1)

271 MC Priests 20 Lord, you must not stop here. To the minster./Through the cloister. No time to waste.

MINUTE (4)

14 Prufrock   47 /Do I dare/Disturb the universe?/In a minute there is time/For decisions and revisions

14 Prufrock   48 /For decisions and revisions which a minute will reverse./For I have known them all

387 CP   Peter   18   bring me with him. He'll be here in a minute./Celia! Have you heard from Lavinia

525 ES   Charles 26 /But you know that I shan't have a minute alone with you./{M} You've already had

MINUTES (21)

123 SA Kl & Kr 20 *gather hibiscus flowers/For it won't be minutes but hours/For it won't be hours but years*

317 FR Warburt   1   /{W} I'm glad of a few minutes alone with you, Harry./In fact, I had

372 CP   Alex   28 Don't leave it longer than another ten minutes./Now I'll be going, and I'll take Peter

373 CP   Alex   1   Edward, not more than ten minutes,/Twenty minutes, and my work will be

373 CP   Alex   2   not more than ten minutes,/Twenty minutes, and my work will be ruined. {}/[*Exeunt*

375 CP   Edward 31 /And he said I must eat it within ten minutes./I suppose it's still cooking./{C} You

378 CP   Celia   6 will, if I may follow you/In about ten minutes? Before I go, there's something/I want

385 CP   Reilly   17   or they to you/After the first ten minutes? You would find it difficult/To treat

403 CP   Edward 25 had not been alone again for fifteen minutes/Before I felt, and still more acutely —/

437 CP   Reilly   16   the astonishment/Of the first five minutes after a violent death./If this strains your

439 CP   Lavinia 39 have been thinking, for these last five minutes,/How I could face my guests. I wish it

451 CC   Eggers 23   her as Muriel —/Within the first ten minutes! I was horrified./But she actually liked

457 CC   Eggers 13   /{E} I'll arrive at the airport with minutes to spare,/And besides, there's the

487 CC   Claude   5   phrases. It should last about ten minutes./And then we'll go over it tomorrow. {}/

525 ES   Monica 27 you./{M} You've already had several minutes alone with me/Which you've wasted in

526 ES   Monica 22 the room/That we entered only a few minutes ago./Here's an armchair, there's the

532 ES   Monica   20   you haven't got rid of him in twenty minutes/I'll send Lambert to tell you that you
543 ES   m   8   /[LORD CLAVERTON *sits for a few minutes brooding. A knock. Enter* MONICA.]/
565 ES   Ld Clav   33   And what a hypocrite!/A few minutes ago I was pleading with Michael/Not to
573 ES   Ld Clav   10   made the difference in the last five minutes/Is not the heinousness of my misdeeds/
582 ES   Monica   33   we've been alone to-day/Only a few minutes, I've felt all the time .../{C} I know what

MINUTES' (1)
541 ES   Lambert   33   call coming through for you/In five minutes' time./{LC} I'll be ready to take it. {}/

MIRACLES (2)
254 MC   Tempt4   21   the knee in supplication,/Think of the miracles, by God's grace,/And think of your
254 MC   Tempt4   36   laps of parasites and whores./When miracles cease, and the faithful desert you./And

MIRROR (7)
191 FQ: Little   7   heart's heat,/Reflecting in a watery mirror/A glare that is blindness in the early
247 MC   Tempt1   11   as blossoms. Ice along the ditches/Mirror the sunlight. Love in the orchard/Send
350 FR   Mary   10   side of things/Behind the smiling mirror/And behind the smiling moon/Follow
420 CP   Reilly   32   the other understands the motive —/Mirror to mirror, reflecting vanity./I have taken
420 CP   Reilly   32   understands the motive —/Mirror to mirror, reflecting vanity./I have taken a great
540 ES   Gomez   8   up his face before he looks in the mirror./{LC} Isn't that the kind of pretence that
542 ES   Gomez   33   of whispers,/The reflection in the mirror of the face behind you,/The ambiguous

MIRRORS (1)
38 Gerontion   65   multiply variety/In a wilderness of mirrors. What will the spider do,/Suspend its

MIRTH (6)
178 FQ: ECoker   38   Earth feet, loam feet, lifted in country mirth/Mirth of those long since under earth/
178 FQ: ECoker   39   feet, loam feet, lifted in country mirth/Mirth of those long since under earth/
193 FQ: Little   70   at the vanity of toil,/Laughs without mirth./This is the death of earth./Water and fire
247 MC   Tempt1   5   Clergy and laity may return to gaiety,/Mirth and sportfulness need not walk warily./
247 MC   Tempt1   12   in the orchard/Send the sap shooting. Mirth matches melancholy./{T} We do not
385 CP   Reilly   14   /Your childhood years in comfort, mirth, security —/If they returned, would it not

MIRZA (1)
136 5FingerEx5   t   *him)./Lines for Cuscuscaraway and Mirza Murad Ali Beg*/How unpleasant to meet

MISBEHAVED (1)
318 FR   Harry   11   made us/Feel more guilty, and so we misbehaved/Next day at school, in order to be

MISCHIEF (2)
388 CP   Lavinia   31   telegrams./{L} This is some of Julia's mischief./And is *she* coming?/{P} Yes, and Alex.
403 CP   Reilly   10   would go on, doing such amount of mischief/As lay within your power — until you

MISCONDUCT (1)
317 FR   Harry   26   conduct was simply pleasing mother;/Misconduct was simply being unkind to mother/

MISDEEDS (2)
267 MC   Knight1   27   Now and here!/{K1} Of your earlier misdeeds I shall make no mention./They are too
573 ES   Ld Clav   11   minutes/Is not the heinousness of my misdeeds/But the fact of my confession. And to

MISDIRECTED (1)
309 FR   Mary   25   /That's wrong, a good that's misdirected. You deceive yourself/Like the man

MISERABLE (4)
154 Rock 3   2   the LORD came unto me, saying:/O miserable cities of designing men,/O wretched
491 CC   Colby   30   I should always be haunted/By the miserable ghosts of the other parents!/It's
537 ES   Gomez   38   which you remember:/A miserable clerkship — which your father found
572 ES   Charles   30   /Let them tell their versions of their miserable stories,/Confide them in whispers.

MISÈRES (1)
48 Lune Miel   12   le train de huit heures/Prolonger leurs misères de Padoue à Milan/Où se trouve la

MISERY (7)
593 Grad 5   5   see,/What conquest over pain and misery,/What heroes greater than were e'er of
268 MC   Thomas   38   without/My presence; seven years of misery and pain./Seven years a mendicant on
276 MC   Chorus   1   /The personal loss, the general misery,/Living and partly living;/The terror by
319 FR   Warburt   11   Harry, there's no good probing for misery./There was enough once: but what
331 FR   Harry   11   is./Here I have been finding/A misery long forgotten, and a new torture,/The
341 FR   Amy   11   of his unhappiness,/Because of the misery that he has left behind him,/Because of
381 CP   Edward   27   the happiness of knowing/That the misery does not feed on the ruin of loveliness,/

MISFIT (1)
307 FR   Mary   26   you are wholly conscious/Of being a misfit, of being superfluous./But why should I

MISFITS (1)
368 CP   Edward   36   the minor guests/And dealt with the misfits, Lavinia's mistakes./But you were one of

MISFORTUNE (3)
301 FR   Chorus   20   huddle together/In a horrid amity of misfortune? why should we be implicated,
489 CC   Claude   4   and you told me/About your own ... misfortune. And I almost told you/About
537 ES   Ld Clav   14   /{LC} You cannot attribute your ... misfortune to *my* influence./{G} I was just about

MISLAID (1)

| 449 CC | Claude | 3 | very different way, yes. You might say *mislaid*,/Since the father is dead, and there's no |

MISPLACED (1)

| 225 Mr Mistoff | | 34 | or a fork/And you think it is merely misplaced —/You have seen it one moment, and |

MISS (8)

354 CP	Peter	6	{P} You *are* a good mimic. You never miss anything./{A} She never misses anything
370 CP	Peter	27	/It is not her interest in *me* that I miss —/But those moments in which we seemed
388 CP	Celia	9	sake,/Though of course we ... I shall miss you;/You know how I depended on you
388 CP	Celia	14	to realise your ambitions./I shall miss you./{P} It's nice of you to say so;/But
392 CP	Lavinia	24	going to happen./Trust her not to miss any awkward situation!/And what did you
426 CP	Julia	33	of food and drink!/And I've had to miss my tea, and I'm simply ravenous/And
427 CP	Alex	11	for the country,/I said, I must not miss the opportunity/To see Edward and
450 CC	Colby	29	/Mr. Eggerson. I was afraid I'd miss you./{E} I'm off in half an hour, Mr.

MISS (64) [*Proper name*]

29 Aunt Helen	1	*Evening Transcript.*'/Aunt Helen/Miss Helen Slingsby was my maiden aunt,/And
30 Cous Nancy	1	her mistress lived./Cousin Nancy/Miss Nancy Ellicott/Strode across the hills and
30 Cous Nancy	7	to hounds/Over the cow-pasture./Miss Nancy Ellicott smoked/And danced all the
116 SP	Dusty	21	Hello Hello are you there?/Yes this is Miss Dorrance's *flat* —/Oh Mr. Pereira is that
119 SP	Krum	20	that poker game in Bordeaux?/Yes Miss Dorrance you get Sam/To tell about that
119 SP	Klip	29	London!! Eh what Klip?/{Kl} Say, Miss — er — uh — London's swell./We like
119 SP	Klip	33	and live here then?/{Kl} Well, no, Miss — er — you haven't quite got it/(I'm
326 FR	Denman	33	{}/[*Enter* DENMAN]/{D} Excuse me, Miss Ivy. There's a trunk call for you./{I} A
326 FR	Denman	35	me?/{D} He wouldn't give his name, Miss; but it's Mr. Arthur./{I} Arthur! Oh dear,
346 FR	Downing	6	*costume*]/{Do} Oh, excuse me, Miss, excuse me, Mr. Charles:/His Lordship
346 FR	Downing	9	there it is. Thank you. Good night, Miss; good night,/Miss Mary; good night, Sir./
346 FR	Downing	10	you. Good night, Miss; good night,/Miss Mary; good night, Sir./{M} Downing, will
346 FR	Downing	13	you are away?/{Do} Oh, certainly, Miss;/I'll never leave him so long as he requires
346 FR	Downing	17	to say —/But it's not really strange, Miss, when you come to look at it:/After all
346 FR	Agatha	38	that,/And we have seen them too — Miss Mary and I./{Do} I understand you, Miss.
346 FR	Downing	39	Mary and I./{Do} I understand you, Miss. And if I may say so,/Now that you've
347 FR	Downing	4	car all ready. You mean them ghosts, Miss!/I wondered when his Lordship would get
347 FR	Downing	11	/I'll take my oath. Will that be all, Miss?/{Ag} That will be all, thank you,
373 CP	Edward	3	*telephone, and dials a number*]/{E} Is Miss Celia Coplestone in? ... How long ago? .../
399 CP	Reilly	1	three appointments this morning, Miss Barraway:/I should like to run over my
399 CP	Reilly	23	have left the house..../{R} Quite right, Miss Barraway. That's all for the moment./{N}
407 CP	Reilly	33	me/By concealing your relations with Miss Coplestone./{E} This is monstrous! My
409 CP	Reilly	11	/That you were not really in love with Miss Coplestone .../{L} My husband has never
409 CP	Reilly	31	friend/Had actually fallen in love with Miss Coplestone,/It took you some time, I have
412 CP	Reilly	24	*shows in* CELIA]/{R} Miss Celia Coplestone? ... Won't you sit down?/
413 CP	Reilly	3	again./{R} Most of my patients begin, Miss Coplestone,/By telling me exactly what is
414 CP	Reilly	37	/{R} You suffer from a sense of sin, Miss Coplestone?/This is most unusual./{C} It
419 CP	Reilly	28	becomes of them?/{R} They choose, Miss Coplestone. Nothing is forced on them,
421 CP	Reilly	39	should be here by now. I'll speak to Miss Barraway. {}/[*Takes up house-telephone*]/
422 CP	Reilly	1	{}/[*Takes up house-telephone*]/{R} Miss Barraway, when Mr. Gibbs arrives .../Oh,
422 CP	Reilly	4	/{R} You may bring the tray in now, Miss Barraway. {}/[*Enter* ALEX]/{A} Well!
437 CP	Reilly	13	*they part no more!*/When I first met Miss Coplestone, in this room,/I saw the image,
438 CP	Reilly	34	have made the wrong decision./As for Miss Coplestone, because you think her death
449 CC	Eggers	21	have never been able to make her like Miss Angel;/She becomes abstracted, whenever
449 CC	Claude	23	/{SC} But she knew about Lucasta — Miss Angel, from the start./That was one
449 CC	Claude	27	I don't think she takes much notice of Miss Angel./She just doesn't see her. And Miss
449 CC	Claude	28	Angel./She just doesn't see her. And Miss Angel/Will soon be getting married, I
452 CC	Eggers	12	{L} Eggy, I've lost my job!/{E} Again, Miss Angel?/{L} Yes, again! And serve them
452 CC	Eggers	25	the other of you./{E} Mr. Simpkins, Miss Angel. As you know, Miss Angel,/
452 CC	Eggers	25	Simpkins, Miss Angel. As you know, Miss Angel,/Mr. Simpkins has taken over my
452 CC	Lucasta	30	I'm Lucasta./It's only Eggy calls me Miss Angel,/Just to annoy me. Don't you agree/
453 CC	Eggers	2	do. I always say/That if you give Miss Angel an inch/She'll take an ell./{L} L. for
453 CC	Eggers	19	will leave Mrs. Eggerson out of this, Miss Angel./{L} That's what he always says,
454 CC	Colby	23	/{C} But you never warned me about Miss Angel./What about *her*?/{E} Oh, Miss
454 CC	Eggers	25	Miss Angel./What about *her*?/{E} Oh, Miss Angel./She's rather flighty. But she has a
455 CC	Colby	7	frightening./But tell me about Lu ... Miss Angel/What's her connection with this
455 CC	Colby	29	/{C} Well, I've never met anyone like Miss Angel./{E} You'll get used to her, Mr.
455 CC	Colby	36	Elizabeth/Can be quite so unusual as Miss Angel./{E} O yes, Mr. Simpkins, much
482 CC	Lady E	10	too friendly/With Mr. Kaghan and Miss Angel./I can see you've lived a rather
500 CC	Eggers	1	is your brother./{E} Half-brother, Miss Angel./{SC} Yes, half-brother./{L} What
501 CC	Eggers	28	all I must take the occasion/To wish Miss Angel every happiness./And I'm sure she

501 CC	Eggers	31	he has a heart of gold. So have you, Miss Angel./We have this very important
503 CC	Eggers	19	/{E} And now may I interrupt, Miss Angel?/Why shouldn't you and Mr.
526 ES	Lambert	28	know that tea is waiting'./{L} Yes, Miss Monica./{M} I'm very glad, Charles,/That
527 ES	Lambert	11	*Enter* LAMBERT]/{L} Excuse me, Miss Monica. His Lordship said to tell you/Not
532 ES	Lambert	8	my Lord./Shall I take the trolley, Miss Monica?/{M} Yes, thank you, Lambert. {}/
541 ES	Lambert	31	/{L} Excuse me, my Lord, but Miss Monica asked me/To remind you there's a
545 ES	Piggott	22	Lord Claverton! Good morning, Miss Claverton!/Isn't this a glorious morning!/
545 ES	Piggott	33	I'm not there/My secretary will be — Miss Timmins./She'd be overjoyed to have the
546 ES	Piggott	14	—/Except when they come like you, Miss Claverton./{M} Claverton-Ferry. Or Ferry:
546 ES	Piggott	16	Or Ferry: it's shorter./{MP} So sorry. Miss Claverton-Ferry. I'm Mrs. Piggott./Just
547 ES	Piggott	8	let him stay out late/In the afternoon, Miss Claverton-Ferry./And remember, when
547 ES	Piggott	20	/{MP} I really *am* neglectful!/Miss Claverton-Ferry, I ought to tell you more/
555 ES	Piggott	10	{}/[*Enter* MONICA]/{MP} Oh, Miss Claverton-Ferry!/I didn't see you coming.

MISSED (6)

186 FQ: DrySal		95	—/We had the experience but missed the meaning,/And approach to the
218 Mung Rump		14	after supper one of the girls/Suddenly missed her Woolworth pearls:/Then the family
327 FR	Ivy	32	hasn't got the use of his car,/And he missed the last train, so he's coming up
353 CP	Alex	1	GUEST./{A} You've missed the point completely, Julia:/There *were*
461 CC	Eggers	1	Oh, not for nothing! I wouldn't have missed it./And besides, as I told you, I've done
573 ES	Carghil	37	her already./You may say that I just missed being her mother!/I've known her father

MISSES (3)

354 CP	Alex	7	never miss anything./{A} She never misses anything unless she wants to./{C}
496 CC	Eggers	24	with public affairs.'/The fact is, she misses the contact with London,/Though she
496 CC	Eggers	25	/Though she doesn't admit it. She misses my news/When I came home in the

MISSHAPEN (1)

107 Animula		25	the simple soul/Irresolute and selfish, misshapen, lame,/Unable to fare forward or

MISSING (8)

212 Growltiger		7	at the knees;/One ear was somewhat missing, no need to tell you why,/And he
212 Growltiger		20	it was a Siamese had mauled his missing ear./Now on a peaceful summer night,
226 Macavity		24	is rifled,/Or when the milk is missing, or another Peke's been stifled,/Or the
289 FR	Gerald	28	it's odd to think of her as permanently *missing*./{V} Had she been drinking?/{A} I would
330 FR	Agatha	14	about the future;/But a present is missing, needed to connect them./You may be
365 CP	Julia	4	I'd know them, because one lens is missing. {}/[*Sings*]./{UG} *As I was drinkin' gin*
449 CC	Claude	5	tracing it./Yes, I was thinking of her missing child:/In the circumstances, that might
467 CC	Colby	11	than a father —/The father who was missing in the years of childhood./Those years

MISSION (1)

152 Rock 2		23	GOD:/The British race assured of a mission/Performed it, but left much at home

MISSIONARIES (1)

344 FR	Gerald	20	is the first thing./I've met with missionaries, often enough —/Some of them

MISSIONARY (8)

121 SA	Sweeney	4	be the cannibal!/{S} You'll be the missionary!/You'll be my little seven stone
121 SA	Sweeney	5	/You'll be my little seven stone missionary!/I'll gobble you up. I'll be the
121 SA	Doris	9	I'll be the cannibal./{Do} I'll be the missionary. I'll convert you!/{S} I'll convert *you!*
121 SA	Sweeney	13	/Into a stew./A nice little, white little, missionary stew./{Do} You wouldn't eat me!/{S}
121 SA	Sweeney	17	tender little,/Juicy little, right little, missionary stew./You see this egg/You see this
344 FR	Amy	12	Harry is going away — to become a missionary./{H} But ...!/{C} A missionary! that's
344 FR	Charles	14	a missionary./{H} But ...!/{C} A missionary! that's never happened in our family!
344 FR	Harry	33	I never said that I was going to be a missionary./I would explain, but you would

MIST (3)

50 Hippopot		36	below/Wrapt in the old miasmal mist./Dans le Restaurant/Le garçon délabré qui
600 Moonflower		2	moonflower opens to the moth,/The mist crawls in from sea;/A great white bird, a
600 Moonflower		6	Love, you hold,/Than the white mist on the sea;/Have you no brighter tropic

MISTAKE (21)

248 MC	Tempt2	25	were made Archbishop — that was a mistake/On your part — still may be regained.
251 MC	Tempt3	15	blind assertion in isolation./That is a mistake./{T} O Henry, O my King!/{T3} Other
277 MC	Knight3	25	we have done for ourselves, there's/no mistake about that. So, as I said at the
326 FR	Harry	27	some huge disaster,/Some monstrous mistake and aberration/Of all men, of the
327 FR	Ivy	34	about it in the paper,/But it's all a mistake. And not to tell his mother./{V} What's
360 CP	Reilly	33	another man, she might have made a mistake/And want to come back to you. If
415 CP	Celia	33	and over;/I can see now, it was all a mistake:/But I don't see why mistakes should
435 CP	Peter	1	a waste./Two years! And it was all a mistake./Julia! Why don't *you* say anything?/{J}
450 CC	Claude	4	/That you're liable to make the worst mistake about him./As a matter of fact, there's
463 CC	Claude	4	/In the war — that was perhaps a mistake,/Though it seemed to have such
467 CC	Claude	20	yet I seem/To have made a greater mistake than he did./{C} I know that I'm
495 CC	Lady E	12	me chiefly as a hostess./It's a great mistake, I do believe,/For married people to

500 CC	Lucasta	19	Anyway, I *knew* there had been some mistake./You don't know at all what I'm
519 CC	Kaghan	7	Claude, I think we all made the same mistake —/All except Eggers .../{E} Me, Mr.
538 ES	Ld Clav	16	{LC} I was never accused of making a mistake./{G} No, in England mistakes are
538 ES	Gomez	19	/Isn't the man who made the mistake./That's your convention. Or if it's
538 ES	Gomez	22	at least you can't make quite the same mistake./At the worst, you go into opposition/
538 ES	Gomez	26	/I dare say you did make some mistake, Dick .../That would account for your
550 ES	Carghil	13	/People sometimes say: 'Make one mistake in love,/You're more than likely to
578 ES	Ld Clav	6	I have made/My whole life through, mistake upon mistake,/The mistaken attempts
578 ES	Ld Clav	6	/My whole life through, mistake upon mistake,/The mistaken attempts to correct

MISTAKEN (11)

260 MC	Thomas	24	to you that the angelic voices were mistaken, and/that the promise was a
318 FR	Warburt	18	they are told./{W} Stop, Harry, you're mistaken./I mean, you don't know what I want
413 CP	Reilly	10	/Is to try to show them that they are mistaken/About the nature of their illness, and
472 CC	Lucasta	25	/For all I can tell, you may have been mistaken,/And perhaps you could be a very
497 CC	Claude	18	/{SC} That's what it is,/Unless she is mistaken .../{LE} Now, Claude!/{SC} And she
497 CC	Lady E	23	/I am convinced that Sir Claude is mistaken,/Or has been deceived, and that Colby
506 CC	Eggers	34	was confided./Of course she might be mistaken about Teddington .../{LE} I am *not*
506 CC	Lady E	35	about Teddington .../{LE} I am *not* mistaken about Teddington./{E} I am only
526 ES	Charles	7	assurance! Are you sure you're not mistaken?/{M} How did this come, Charles? It
578 ES	Ld Clav	7	through, mistake upon mistake,/The mistaken attempts to correct mistakes/By
578 ES	Ld Clav	8	methods which proved to be equally mistaken./I see that your mother and I, in our

MISTAKES (10)

341 FR	Amy	10	because of Harry,/Because of his mistakes, because of his unhappiness,/Because
368 CP	Edward	36	/And dealt with the misfits, Lavinia's mistakes./But you were one of the minor
415 CP	Celia	34	was all a mistake:/But I don't see why mistakes should make one feel sinful!/And yet I
467 CC	Claude	18	/I was always anxious to avoid the mistakes/My father made with me. And yet I
519 CC	Lady E	14	ask of other people,/One does make mistakes! But I mean to do better./Claude,
534 ES	Gomez	28	country, Dick,/Politicians can't afford mistakes. The prudent ones/Always have an
538 ES	Gomez	17	a mistake./{G} No, in England mistakes are anonymous/Because the man who
538 ES	Gomez	24	/And let the other people make mistakes/Until your own have been more or less
578 ES	Ld Clav	5	me. I see now clearly/The many many mistakes I have made/My whole life through,
578 ES	Ld Clav	7	/The mistaken attempts to correct mistakes/By methods which proved to be

MISTOFFELEES (5)

224 Mr Mistoff		t	*a single one left in the street.*/Mr. Mistoffelees/You ought to know Mr.
224 Mr Mistoff		1	Mistoffelees/You ought to know Mr. Mistoffelees!/The Original Conjuring Cat —/
224 Mr Mistoff		22	ever/A Cat so clever/As Magical Mr. Mistoffelees!/He is quiet and small, he is black/
225 Mr Mistoff		41	ever/A Cat so clever/As Magical Mr. Mistoffelees!/His manner is vague and aloof,/
225 Mr Mistoff		60	a Cat so clever/As Magical Mr. Mistoffelees!/Macavity: the Mystery Cat/

MISTOFFELEES' (1)

224 Mr Mistoff		15	have something to learn/From Mr. Mistoffelees' Conjuring Turn./Presto!/Away we

MISTRESS (4)

29 Aunt	Helen	13	had always been so careful while her mistress lived./Cousin Nancy/Miss Nancy
476 CC	Lucasta	20	wasn't true?/{L} That I was Claude's mistress —/Or had been his mistress, palmed off
476 CC	Lucasta	21	Claude's mistress —/Or had been his mistress, palmed off on B./{C} I never thought
477 CC	Lucasta	20	/Than if I'd told you I *was* Claude's mistress./Claude has always been ashamed of

MISUNDERSTANDER (1)

361 CP	Reilly	38	the consistent critic, the patient misunderstander/Arranging life a little better

MISUNDERSTANDING (5)

187 FQ: DrySal		107	of agony/(Whether, or not, due to misunderstanding,/Having hopes for the wrong
194 FQ: Little		106	wind,/Too strange to each other for misunderstanding,/In concord at this
290 FR	Agatha	27	the knot of confusion/Into perfect misunderstanding,/Reflecting a pocket-torch of
309 FR	Harry	2	/Explaining would only make a worse misunderstanding;/Explaining would only set
500 CC	Claude	6	No, I'll explain. There's been some misunderstanding./My wife believes that Colby

MISUNDERSTOOD (6)

43 Swee	Erect	38	that hysteria/Might easily be misunderstood;/Mrs. Turner intimates/It does
439 CP	Lavinia	5	you/Then I might not have misunderstood Celia./{R} You will have to live
501 CC	Claude	15	of anything./Perhaps, as you say, I've misunderstood B.,/And I've never thought that
502 CC	Lucasta	11	Oh, because I knew/That I must have misunderstood your reaction./It wouldn't have
574 ES	Carghil	11	told me all his story./You've cruelly misunderstood him, Richard./How he must
578 ES	Ld Clav	10	/To understand each other, both misunderstood you/In our divergent ways.

MIX (2)

479 CC	Kaghan	3	/{K} I told Colby, never learn to mix cocktails,/If you don't want women always
482 CC	Lady E	30	/{LE} In the first place, you ought to mix with people of breeding./I said to myself,

MIXED (2)
| 498 CC | Claude | 26 | she took two babies, and got them mixed./{LE} That seems to be what happened. |
| 529 ES | Monica | 16 | .../And tenderness, Charles! are mixed with envy:/I do believe that he is fond of |

MIXING (1)
| 61 WL: Burial | | 2 | breeding/Lilacs out of the dead land, mixing/Memory and desire, stirring/Dull roots |

MIXTURE (1)
| 491 CC | Colby | 24 | live on a fiction — but not on such a mixture/Of fiction and fact. Already, it's been |

MOBILE (1)
| 270 MC Chorus | | 7 | the beetle, the scale of the viper, the mobile hard insensitive skin of the elephant, the |

MOCHA (1)
| 56 Swee Night | | 17 | a stocking up;/The silent man in mocha brown/Sprawls at the window-sill and |

MOCK (1)
| 98 Ash-Wed 6 | | 26 | spirit of the garden,/Suffer us not to mock ourselves with falsehood/Teach us to care |

MOCKED (1)
| 491 CC | Colby | 36 | imputation/Of false parenthood. Both mocked at./{SC} Then what do you want, |

MOCKING (1)
| 175 FQ: BurntN | 157 | stay still. Shrieking voices/Scolding, mocking, or merely chattering,/Always assail |

MOCKING-BIRD (1)
| 139 Virginia | | 5 | Will heat move/Only through the mocking-bird/Heard once? Still hills/Wait. |

MODE (1)
| 601 Nocturne | | 10 | —/The hero smiles; in my best mode oblique/Rolls toward the moon a frenzied |

MODEL (2)
| 151 Rock 2 | | 13 | is in Heaven'; yes, but that is the model and type for your citizenship upon earth. |
| 517 CC | Colby | 1 | /You had your father before you, as a model;/You knew your inheritance. Now I |

MODERATE (4)
163 Rock 8		42	preacher./Our age is an age of moderate virtue/And of moderate vice/When
163 Rock 8		43	is an age of moderate virtue/And of moderate vice/When men will not lay down the
216 Jellicles		22	white and black,/Jellicle Cats are of moderate size;/Jellicles jump like a
309 FR	Harry	35	/Between two storms, one hears the moderate usual noises/In the grass and leaves,

MODERN (7)
30 Cous Nancy		8	Ellicott smoked/And danced all the modern dances;/And her aunts were not quite
30 Cous Nancy		10	about it,/But they knew that it was modern./Upon the glazen shelves kept watch/
229 Gus		51	certainly not what it was./These modern productions are all very well,/But
286 FR	Charles	26	dry sherry or two before dinner./The modern young people don't know what they're
286 FR	Charles	27	don't know what they're drinking,/Modern young people don't care what they're
496 CC	Claude	4	with *me*:/Health cures. And modern art — so long as it was modern —/And
496 CC	Claude	4	And modern art — so long as it was modern —/And dervish dancing./{LE} Dervish

MODEST (4)
14 Prufrock		43	to the chin,/My necktie rich and modest, but asserted by a simple pin —/(They
159 Rock 6		11	Do you need to be told that even such modest attainments/As you can boast in the
403 CP	Reilly	21	think:/Only, shall we say, within your modest capacity./Try to explain what has
533 ES	Gomez	6	example,/And done the same, in a modest way./You know, where *I* live, people do

MOI (2)
| 51 Restaurant | | 18 | est venu, nous peloter, un gros chien;/Moi j'avais peur, je l'ai quittée à mi-chemin./ |
| 51 Restaurant | | 23 | droit payes-tu des expériences comme moi?/Tiens, voilà dix sous, pour la |

MOINS (2)
| 48 Lune Miel | | 8 | relève le drap pour mieux égratigner./Moins d'une lieue d'ici est Saint Apollinaire/En |
| 51 Restaurant | | 7 | à la croupe arrondie,/Je te prie, au moins, ne bave pas dans la soupe)./'Les saules |

MOLD (1)
| 593 Grad 6 | | 4 | we must go/With eager hearts to help mold well her fate,/And see that she shall gain |

MOLESEY (1)
| 212 Growltiger | | 22 | moon was shining bright, the barge at Molesey lay./All in the balmy moonlight it lay |

MOLLES (1)
| 48 Lune Miel | | 6 | écartant les genoux/De quatre jambes molles tout gonflées de morsures./On relève le |

MOMENT (125)
15 Prufrock		80	ices,/Have the strength to force the moment to its crisis?/But though I have wept
15 Prufrock		84	here's no great matter;/I have seen the moment of my greatness flicker,/And I have
69 WL: Fire S		249	stairs unlit .../She turns and looks a moment in the glass,/Hardly aware of her
74 WL: Thund		416	aethereal rumours/Revive for a moment a broken Coriolanus/DA/*Damyata:*
103 Journ Magi		30	/And arrived at evening, not a moment too soon/Finding the place; it was (you
129 Cor2 State		32	dove's foot rested and locked for a moment,/A still moment, repose of noon, set
129 Cor2 State		33	and locked for a moment,/A still moment, repose of noon, set under the upper
160 Rock 7		18	deep./Then came, at a predetermined moment, a moment in time and of time,/A
160 Rock 7		18	came, at a predetermined moment, a moment in time and of time,/A moment not out
160 Rock 7		19	a moment in time and of time,/A moment not out of time, but in time, in what we

160 Rock 7	19	bisecting the world of time, a	moment in time but not like a moment of time,/
160 Rock 7	19	time, a moment in time but not like a	moment of time,/A moment in time but time
160 Rock 7	20	but not like a moment of time,/A	moment in time but time was made through
160 Rock 7	20	time but time was made through that	moment: for without the meaning there is no
160 Rock 7	20	the meaning there is no time, and that	moment of time gave the meaning./Then it
173 FQ: BurntN	88	to be in time/But only in time can the	moment in the rose-garden,/The moment in the
173 FQ: BurntN	89	the moment in the rose-garden,/The	moment in the arbour where the rain beat,/The
173 FQ: BurntN	90	the arbour where the rain beat,/The	moment in the draughty church at smokefall/Be
179 FQ: ECoker	86	/For the pattern is new in every	moment/And every moment is a new and
179 FQ: ECoker	87	is new in every moment/And every	moment is a new and shocking/Valuation of all
182 FQ: ECoker	194	/Of dead and living. Not the intense	moment/Isolated, with no before and after,/But
182 FQ: ECoker	196	after,/But a lifetime burning in every	moment/And not the lifetime of one man only/
188 FQ: DrySal	157	the past with an equal mind./At the	moment which is not of action or inaction/You
188 FQ: DrySal	161	action/(And the time of death is every	moment)/Which shall fructify in the lives of
190 FQ: DrySal	211	of us, there is only the unattended/Moment, the	moment in and out of time,/The
190 FQ: DrySal	211	is only the unattended/Moment, the	moment in and out of time,/The distraction fit,
192 FQ: Little	54	/Here, the intersection of the timeless	moment/Is England and nowhere. Never and
197 FQ: Little	234	return, and bring us with them./The	moment of the rose and the moment of the
197 FQ: Little	234	/The moment of the rose and the	moment of the yew-tree/Are of equal duration.
225 Mr Mistoff	35	misplaced —/You have seen it one	moment, and then it is *gawn!*/But you'll find it
229 Gus	53	to equal, from what I hear tell,/That	moment of mystery/When I made history/As
230 Bust Jones	23	bones;/And just before noon's not a	moment too soon/To drop in for a drink at the
592 Grad 1	2	shore of all we know/We linger for a	moment doubtfully,/Then with a song upon our
246 MC Priest2	4	Archbishop/Is likely to arrive at any	moment?/The crowds in the streets will be
260 MC Thomas	9	of His Birth. So that at/the same	moment we rejoice in His coming for the
260 MC Thomas	21	for the same reason./Now think for a	moment about the meaning of this word 'peace'.
265 MC Priest3	4	should fear from or hope from. One	moment/Weighs like another. Only in
265 MC Priest3	6	We say, that was the day. The critical	moment/That is always now, and here. Even
266 MC Thomas	2	However certain our expectation/The	moment foreseen may be unexpected/When it
271 MC Thomas	10	/The perpetual glory. This is one	moment,/But know that another/Shall pierce
278 MC Knight2	19	Service. And what happened? The	moment/that Becket, at the King's instance, had
279 MC Knight4	21	that it so badly needed. From the	moment he/became Archbishop, he completely
287 FR Amy	20	not make things easy for her/At the	moment: but life may still go right./Meanwhile,
305 FR Agatha	8	right. Now, the courage is only the	moment/And the moment is only fear and
305 FR Agatha	9	courage is only the moment/And the	moment is only fear and pride. I see more than
305 FR Agatha	11	than there are words for./At this	moment, there is no decision to be made;/The
307 FR Mary	25	you ought to be happy/At the very	moment when you are wholly conscious/Of
309 FR Harry	11	go! Please don't leave me/Just at this	moment. I feel it is important./Something
310 FR Mary	8	snow/And the snowdrop crying for a	moment in the wood./{H} Spring is an issue of
310 FR Mary	19	/But joy is a kind of pain/I believe the	moment of birth/Is when we have knowledge of
311 FR Harry	18	/That will not let me sleep. At the	moment before sleep/I always see their claws
311 FR Harry	21	if they had never stirred./It was only a	moment, it was only one moment/That I stood
311 FR Harry	21	It was only a moment, it was only one	moment/That I stood in sunlight, and thought I
311 FR Harry	30	with me. The accident of a dreaming	moment,/Of a dreaming age, when I was
317 FR Warburt	19	you know/Or do not know, at any	moment/May make an endless difference to the
320 FR Warburt	11	go into technicalities/At the present	moment. The whole machine is weak/And
320 FR Warburt	15	shock/Might send her off at any	moment./If she had been another woman/She
329 FR Chorus	12	the steps at night in the corridor/The	moment of sudden loathing/And the season of
332 FR Agatha	27	be no past or future,/Only a present	moment of pointed light/When you want to
333 FR Harry	39	I do not know why,/I feel happy for a	moment, as if I had come home./It is quite
334 FR Agatha	15	that I carried,/And exhaustion at the	moment of relief./The burden's yours now,
335 FR Agatha	37	the rose-garden./{Ag} This is the next	moment. This is the beginning./We do not pass
336 FR Agatha	30	/A curse is like a child, formed/In a	moment of unconsciousness/In an accidental
337 FR Harry	23	that I have made a decision/In a	moment of clarity, and now I feel dull again./I
341 FR Amy	36	what have you given?/And now at the	moment of success against failure,/When I felt
346 FR Charles	4	the Burlington Arcade./What if every	moment were like that, if one were awake?/You
349 FR All	12	But we must adjust ourselves to the	moment: we must do the right thing. {}/[*Exeunt*]
356 CP Julia	15	cake./{J} Edward, do sit down for a	moment./I know you're always the perfect host,
362 CP Reilly	32	you come down with a jolt. Just for a	moment/You have the experience of being an
371 CP Edward	22	[*The telephone rings*]/{E} Excuse me a	moment. {}/[*Into telephone*]/{E} Hello! ... I can't
374 CP Celia	20	a pure invention/On the spur of the	moment, and not a very good one./You should
378 CP Celia	23	think it's that./I think it is just a	moment of surrender/To fatigue. And panic.
381 CP Edward	12	what it is to feel old./That is the worst	moment, when you feel that you have lost/The
384 CP Reilly	17	mind, but you are not free./Your	moment of freedom was yesterday./You made a
386 CP Edward	17	you come?/I expect Lavinia at any	moment./You must not be here. Why have you

387 CP	Celia	22	to Edward —/I only got here this moment myself —/That she telegraphed to Julia
394 CP	Lavinia	19	only made matters worse,/And the moment you were offered something that you
397 CP	Lavinia	9	to yourself. Could you bear, for a moment,/To think about *me*?/{E} It was only
398 CP	Edward	9	destruction — just as I felt sure./In a moment, at your touch, there is nothing but
399 CP	Nurse	16	/{N} I telephone through/The moment she arrives. I leave her there/Until you
399 CP	Reilly	23	Miss Barraway. That's all for the moment./{N} Mr. Gibbs is here, Sir Henry./{R}
401 CP	Reilly	2	/Please sit down. I won't keep you a moment./— Now, Mr. Chamberlayne?/{E} It
401 CP	Reilly	33	/Let us dismiss that question for the moment./Tell me first, about the difficulties/On
406 CP	Reilly	8	see it in that light —/At least, for the moment. But, Mrs. Chamberlayne,/You have
412 CP	Julia	7	the taxi, round the corner;/Waited a moment, and slipped in by the back way./I only
413 CP	Reilly	24	know quite enough about you for the moment:/Try first to describe your present state
414 CP	Celia	21	With a cousin: but she's abroad at the moment,/And my family want me to come
426 CP	Edward	9	/Then I can relax./{E} This is the best moment/Of the whole party./{L} Oh no,
426 CP	Lavinia	12	party./{L} Oh no, Edward./The best moment is the moment it's over;/And then to
426 CP	Lavinia	12	no, Edward./The best moment is the moment it's over;/And then to remember, it's
439 CP	Lavinia	1	spiteful./I shall go on seeing her at the moment/When she said good-bye to us, two
439 CP	Julia	36	/Their guests may be arriving at any moment./{R} Julia, you are right. It is also right
440 CP	Edward	7	has been saying,/I think, that every moment is a fresh beginning;/And Julia, that life
445 CC	Eggers	14	a garden!/And I thought, now's the moment to buy some new tools/So as not to
445 CC	Eggers	15	some new tools/So as not to lose a moment at the end of the winter/And I matched
455 CC	Colby	4	I shouldn't wonder./I nearly did, a moment ago./Then I'd have been certain I'd lost
456 CC	Eggers	2	about her./He said to me once, in a moment of confidence —/He'd just come back
463 CC	Colby	29	the disappointed organist,/And for a moment the thing I cannot do,/The art that I
476 CC	Lucasta	27	guessed the truth from the very first moment./{C} But what is there to know?/{L}
478 CC	Lucasta	17	him, it will be so wonderful/All in a moment. And now there's nothing,/Nothing at
479 CC	Lucasta	1	/{L} You're *my* guardian angel at the moment, B./You're to take me out to dinner.
479 CC	Kaghan	26	right to a little privacy./Now's the moment for firmness. Don't let her cross the
480 CC	Kaghan	8	/I make decisions on the spur of the moment,/But you'd never take a leap in the
483 CC	Colby	18	already begun to work here. At the moment/I'm working on a company report./
487 CC	Lady E	35	my excitement: you arrived the very moment/When the truth dawned on me. Mrs.
491 CC	Colby	18	/{C} I can only say what I feel at the moment:/And yet I believe I shall always feel
492 CC	Colby	16	the piano would help me:/At the moment, I never want to touch it again./But
496 CC	Eggers	29	the garden — that I've not an idle moment./And really, now, I'm quite lost in
498 CC	Eggers	8	in Teddington./But assuming, for the moment, only one Mrs. Guzzard,/Could there
500 CC	Lucasta	30	/And he might vanish into it at any moment —/At just the moment when you
500 CC	Lucasta	31	into it at any moment —/At just the moment when you needed him most!/And he
509 CC	Colby	40	he's waiting downstairs! Isn't this the moment/For me to bring him up? And Lucasta?
515 CC	Guzzard	8	you were so pleased, I shrank, at the moment,/From undeceiving you. And then I
526 ES	Charles	3	love with you./{C} So I was right! The moment I'd said it/I was badly frightened. For I
526 ES	Charles	18	is you?/I'm not the same person as a moment ago./What do the words mean now —
527 ES	Lambert	14	you, Lambert./{L} He's busy at the moment. But he won't be very long. {}/[*Exit*]/{C}
538 ES	Gomez	10	why presently./Now let's look for a moment at *your* life history./You had plenty of
541 ES	Gomez	29	once/As you pointedly reminded me a moment ago./Now it's my turn, perhaps, to do
545 ES	Monica	10	drove us?/{M} You admit that at the moment you find life pleasant,/That it really
547 ES	Piggott	24	us/We dance in the evening. At the moment there's no dancing,/And it's still too
548 ES	1m	14	have to take the hint. {}/[*Exit*]/*A moment later*, LORD CLAVERTON *spreads his*
568 ES	Ld Clav	9	/Moments we regret in the very next moment,/Episodes we try to conceal from the
573 ES	Carghil	39	for a very long time,/And there was a moment when I almost married him,/Oh so long
579 ES	Gomez	37	/That I came to England at the very moment/When I could be helpful./{MC} It's
583 ES	Monica	20	strange, Charles,/To be happy at this moment?/{C} It is not at all strange./The dead

MOMENT'S (2)

| 74 WL: Thund | 403 | my heart/The awful daring of a moment's surrender/Which an age of prudence |
| 362 CP | Edward | 13 | to each other. So her going away/At a moment's notice, without explanation,/Only a |

MOMENTARY (4)

32 Hysteria	3	in by short gasps, inhaled at each momentary/recovery, lost finally in the dark
594 Grad 11	4	after class,/O queen of schools — a momentary gleam,/A bubble on the surface of
287 FR	Amy	31	will come to you as a mild surprise,/A momentary shudder in a vacant room./Only
294 FR	Harry	31	reversing the senseless direction/For a momentary rest on the burning wheel/That

MOMENTS (10)

186 FQ: DrySal	92	a means of disowning the past./The moments of happiness — not the sense of
187 FQ: DrySal	106	/Now, we come to discover that the moments of agony/(Whether, or not, due to
197 FQ: Little	237	for history is a pattern/Of timeless moments. So, while the light fails/On a winter's
589 Fable	71	/For often they drop in at awkward moments,/As everybody'll know who reads this
976 MC Knight1	2	to give us your attention for a few/moments. We know that you may be disposed
370 CP	Peter	28	interest in *me* that I miss —/But those moments in which we seemed to share some

384 CP	Reilly	28	people/Is only our memory of the moments/During which we knew them. And
417 CP	Celia	7	either hurt or heal./I have thought at moments that the ecstasy is real/Although those
465 CC	Claude	19	I had always known, at the secret moments,/That I didn't have it in me. There are
568 ES	Ld Clav	9	surrenders, unexplainable impulses,/Moments we regret in the very next moment,/

MON (6)

47 Mél	Adult	16	Damas jusqu'à Omaha./Je célébrai mon jour de fête/Dans une oasis d'Afrique/Vêtu
47 Mél	Adult	19	d'une peau de girafe./On montrera mon cénotaphe/Aux côtes brûlantes de
51 Restaurant		2	se gratter les doigts et se pencher sur mon épaule:/'Dans mon pays il fera temps
51 Restaurant		3	et se pencher sur mon épaule:/'Dans mon pays il fera temps pluvieux,/Du vent, du
63 WL: Burial		76	up again!/'You! hypocrite lecteur! — mon semblable, — mon frère!'/A Game of
63 WL: Burial		76	lecteur! — mon semblable, — mon frère!'/A Game of Chess/The Chair she sat

MONARCHS (1)

| 249 MC | Tempt2 | 28 | No!/{T2} Yes! men must manœuvre. Monarchs also,/Waging war abroad, need fast |

MONASTERY (1)

| 587 Fable | | 7 | his tax;/Nearby this hamlet was a monastery/Inhabited by a band of friars merry./ |

MONCHENSEY (10)

284 FR	m	2	/Persons/AMY, DOWAGER LADY MONCHENSEY, IVY, VIOLET, *and*
284 FR	m	4	*daughter of a deceased cousin of Lady Monchensey*/DENMAN, *a parlourmaid*/
284 FR	m	6	*a parlourmaid*/HARRY, LORD MONCHENSEY, *Amy's eldest son*/
315 FR	Warburt	28	in to dinner./{W} With pleasure, Lady Monchensey,/And I hope that next year will
323 FR	Warburt	10	It's John has had the accident, Lady Monchensey;/And Winchell tells me Dr. Owen
323 FR	Warburt	28	the car at once./{W} I forbid it, Lady Monchensey./As your doctor, I forbid you to
323 FR	Warburt	37	orders./{W} I repeat, Lady Monchensey, that you must not go out./If you
324 FR	Warburt	4	trusted me a good many years, Lady Monchensey;/This is not the time to begin to
328 FR	Charles	13	Piper, younger brother of Lord/Monchensey, who ran into and demolished a
348 FR	Warburt	2	up here in the morning./I hope Lady Monchensey hasn't been worrying?/I'm anxious

MOND (1)

| 44 Cook Egg | | 14 | in Heaven/For I shall meet Sir Alfred Mond./We two shall lie together, lapt/In a five |

MONDAY (5)

116 SP	Dusty	30	a doctor/She says will you ring up on Monday/She hopes to be all right on Monday/I
116 SP	Dusty	31	Monday/She hopes to be all right on Monday/I say do you mind if I ring off now/
116 SP	Dusty	35	her mustard and water/All right, Monday you'll phone through./Yes I'll tell her.
411 CP	Edward	7	away!/I have a case coming on next Monday./{L} Then will you stop at your club?/
525 ES	Charles	1	is that I have a grievance./On Monday you're leaving London, with your

MONEY (28)

41 Burb Blei		24	piles./The Jew is underneath the lot./Money in furs. The boatman smiles,/Princess
65 WL: Chess		143	to know what you done with that money he gave you/To get yourself some teeth.
117 SP	Dusty	9	mean?/{Du} *(reading)* 'A small sum of money, or a present/Of wearing apparel, or a
148 Rock 1		55	/All men are ready to invest their money/But most expect dividends./I say to you:
155 Rock 3		55	'We all dwell together/To make money from each other'? or 'This is a
159 Rock 6		5	a Bank/To doubt the security of their money./It is hard for those who live near a
161 Rock 7		29	professing first Reason,/And then Money, and Power, and what they call Life, or
186 FQ: DrySal		78	and erosionless/Or drawing their money, drying sails at dockage;/Not as making
587 Fable		3	quacks,/And took their lands and money from the poor men,/And brought their
275 MC Knight3		5	/{K3} Restore to the King the money you appropriated./{K1} Renew the
286 FR	Violet	18	out of their way at home;/People with money from heaven knows where —/{G}
304 FR	Mary	24	tame daughter-in-law with very little money,/A housekeeper-companion for her and
348 FR	Chorus	22	insomnia,/Lumbago, and the loss of money./But the circle of our understanding/Is a
453 CC	Lucasta	37	fiancé on approval./Can I have some money, Eggy?/{E} I'm no longer in charge/And
455 CC	Eggers	11	that's quite the right term./She's no money of her own, as you may have gathered;/
476 CC	Lucasta	37	/Oh of course Claude gave her money, a regular allowance;/But it wouldn't
489 CC	Lady E	32	was expected./{LE} In order to get money from you, perhaps./No, I shouldn't say
507 CC	Guzzard	20	—/So long, that is to say, as the money was forthcoming./{E} Did the payments
532 ES	Ld Clav	18	who introduces him/I expect he wants money. Or to sell me something worthless./{M}
533 ES	Gomez	34	experience whom to pay;/And a little money laid out in the right manner/In the right
538 ES	Gomez	11	*your* life history./You had plenty of money, and you made a good marriage —/Or
538 ES	Gomez	12	so it seemed — and with your father's money/And your wife's family influence, you
541 ES	Ld Clav	12	do you want then? Do you need money?/{G} My dear chap, you are obtuse!/I
541 ES	Gomez	19	San Marco's a good place/To make money in — though not to *keep* it in./My
543 ES	Monica	1	name./{M} Then I suppose he wanted money?/{LC} No, he didn't want money./{M}
543 ES	Ld Clav	13	money?/{LC} No, he didn't want money./{M} Father, this interview has worn you
555 ES	Monica	33	me to know about./{M} It's probably money./{LC} If it's only debts/Once more, I
559 ES	Michael	14	/That's not my idea. I want to make money./I want to be somebody on my own

MONEY-BOX (1)

| 452 CC | Kaghan | 6 | She's come to pry some cash from the money-box./Bankrupt again! So I thought I'd |

MONGOLIAN (1)
213 Growltiger   41   gave the signal to his fierce Mongolian horde;/With a frightful burst of
MONGREL (1)
288 FR   Amy   30   left it,/Except the old pony, and the mongrel setter/Which I had to have destroyed./
MONICA (46)
523 ES   m   2   /*For you and me only.*/Characters/MONICA CLAVERTON-FERRY/CHARLES
524 ES   m   5   point in my staying to tea. {}/[*Enter* MONICA *and* CHARLES *carrying parcels*]/
526 ES Lambert 28   that tea is waiting'./{L} Yes, Miss Monica./{M} I'm very glad, Charles,/That you
527 ES Lambert 11   LAMBERT]/{L} Excuse me, Miss Monica. His Lordship said to tell you/Not to
529 ES Ld Clav 20   Charles. You might have guessed, Monica,/What I've been doing. Don't you
530 ES Ld Clav   9   the machine./{LC} They've dried up, Monica, and you know it./They talk of rest,
532 ES Lambert   8   Lord./Shall I take the trolley, Miss Monica?/{M} Yes, thank you, Lambert. {}/[*Exit*
532 ES Ld Clav 13   I'll have to see this man by myself, Monica./I've never heard of this Señor Gomez/
532 ES Ld Clav 29   /If you're in the vicinity. Don't we, Monica?/{M} Yes, Father. {}/[*To* CHARLES]/
532 ES   m 30   We *both* want to see you. {}/[*Exeunt* MONICA *and* CHARLES]/[LAMBERT *shows*
541 ES Lambert 31   /{L} Excuse me, my Lord, but Miss Monica asked me/To remind you there's a
543 ES   m   8   *minutes brooding. A knock. Enter* MONICA.]/{M} Who was it, Father?/{LC} A
544 ES   3m   1   /*Enter* LORD CLAVERTON *and* MONICA./{M} Well, so far, it's better than you
555 ES   m 10   penalty/Of being famous. {}/[*Enter* MONICA]/{MP} Oh, Miss Claverton-Ferry!/I
561 ES Ld Clav 11   have to live for, Michael —/You and Monica. If I lived for twenty years/Knowing
561 ES   m 21   *you* have always lived up to them. {}/[MONICA *has entered unobserved*]/{M}
562 ES Michael   8   if he'd wanted love,/But he never did, Monica, not from me./You know I've always
562 ES Carghil 15   party!/I know who you are! You're Monica, of course:/And this must be your
562 ES Carghil 28   It's astonishing about your children:/Monica hardly resembles you at all,/But
564 ES Ld Clav   7   is my son Michael,,/And my daughter Monica./{M} How do you do./Michael!/{Mi}
565 ES Carghil 23   leave you now, Richard. Au revoir, Monica./And Señor Gomez, I shall hold you to
566 ES Ld Clav   4   time for Michael. Is it too late for me, Monica? {}/CURTAIN/Act Three/*Same as Act*
567 ES   2m   1   *Late afternoon of the following day.* MONICA *seated*/*alone. Enter* CHARLES./{C}
567 ES Charles   1   /*alone. Enter* CHARLES./{C} Well, Monica, here I am. I hope you got my message./
568 ES Ld Clav   5   /There are many things not crimes, Monica,/Beyond anything of which the law
568 ES Charles 15   things you don't yet know about me, Monica,/But there's nothing I would ever wish
568 ES Ld Clav 17   truly nothing, that you couldn't tell Monica/Then all is well with you. You're in
568 ES Ld Clav 31   anyone, really./No, I do love my Monica — but there's the impediment:/It's
569 ES Ld Clav   4   ourselves. So I'd become an idol/To Monica. She worshipped the part I played:/How
569 ES Ld Clav   7   makeup/And without his stage words. Monica!/I've had your love under false
569 ES Charles 18   forgive the suspicion —/From what Monica has told me about your fellow guests,/
572 ES Ld Clav 37   /— I've made my confession to you, Monica:/That is the first step taken towards my
573 ES Ld Clav 12   fact of my confession. And to you, Monica,/To you, of all people./{C} I grant you
573 ES Carghil 25   suspect ... Dare I? Yes, I'm sure of it, Monica!/I can tell by the change in your
573 ES Carghil 33   a very lucky man, to get a girl like Monica./I take a great interest in her future./
575 ES Carghil 39   first time he looked at me!/Some day, Monica, I'll tell you all about it./{M} I am
578 ES Michael 22   have a brother./{Mi} Why of course, Monica. You know I'm very fond of you/
580 ES Michael   7   you ever answer?/{Mi} Oh of course, Monica./You know I'm not much of a
580 ES Ld Clav 11   I'm flourishing./{LC} Yes, write to Monica./{G} Well, good-bye Dick. And
580 ES Gomez 12   Well, good-bye Dick. And good-bye Monica./Good-bye, Mr. ... Hemington./{M}
580 ES Ld Clav 35   of./I'm sure he loves us./{LC} Monica my dear,/What you say comes home to
581 ES Charles   6   the force to attract him: you and Monica combined./{LC} I shall not be here.
581 ES Charles 12   you must leave Badgley Court./{C} Monica is right. You should leave./{LC} This
581 ES Ld Clav 19   did I want to keep you to myself, Monica?/Because I wanted you to give your life
581 ES Ld Clav 28   wing of happiness./And I am happy, Monica, that you have found a man/Whom you
582 ES Ld Clav 18   to have a little time together./I leave Monica to you. Look after her, Charles,/Now
MONK (1)
269 MC Knight4 22   God's throne. {}/[*Exit*]/{K4} Priest! monk! and servant! take, hold, detain,/Restrain
MONKEY (4)
427 CP   Julia 32   /Of local conditions./{J} What about? Monkey nuts?/{A} That was a nearer guess than
427 CP   Alex 34   nearer guess than you think./No, not monkey nuts. But it had to do with monkeys —
428 CP   Julia   3   shall never forget Mary Mallington's monkey,/The horrid little beast — stole my
430 CP   Peter 22   dined the other night/At the Saffron Monkey. That's the place to go now./{A} How
MONKEYS (22)
427 CP   Alex 34   monkey nuts. But it had to do with monkeys —/Though whether the monkeys are
427 CP   Alex 35   with monkeys —/Though whether the monkeys are the core of the problem/Or merely
427 CP   Alex 37   I am not so sure./At least, the monkeys have become the pretext/For general
427 CP Edward 39   the natives./{E} But how do the monkeys create unrest?/{A} To begin with, the
428 CP   Alex   1   create unrest?/{A} To begin with, the monkeys are very destructive .../{J} You don't
428 CP   Julia   2   .../{J} You don't need to tell me that monkeys are destructive./I shall never forget

428 CP	Lavinia	8	/{L} But can't they exterminate these monkeys/If they are a pest?/{A} Unfortunately,/
428 CP	Alex	12	natives are heathen:/They hold these monkeys in peculiar veneration/And do not
428 CP	Alex	14	Government/For the damage that the monkeys do./{E} That seems unreasonable./{A}
428 CP	Alex	20	take a different view./They trap the monkeys. And they eat them./The young
428 CP	Alex	21	And they eat them./The young monkeys are extremely palatable:/I've cooked
428 CP	Alex	27	/But you see, what with eating the monkeys/And what with protecting their crops
428 CP	Alex	28	with protecting their crops from the monkeys/The Christian natives prosper
429 CP	Alex	4	the heathen/That the slaughter of monkeys has put a curse on them/Which can
429 CP	Alex	8	heathendom. So, instead of eating monkeys/They are eating Christians./{J} Who
429 CP	Julia	10	eating Christians./{J} Who have eaten monkeys./{A} The native is not, I fear, very
429 CP	Julia	12	where you were taking us, with your monkeys./I thought I was going to dine out on
429 CP	Julia	13	I was going to dine out on those monkeys:/But one can't dine out on eating
429 CP	Alex	30	And meanwhile?/{A} Meanwhile the monkeys multiply./{L} And the Christians?/{A}
430 CP	Alex	23	to go now./{A} How very odd. *My* monkeys are saffron./{P} Your monkeys, Alex?
430 CP	Peter	24	*My* monkeys are saffron./{P} Your monkeys, Alex? I always said/That Alex knew
430 CP	Peter	26	But I didn't know/That he knew any monkeys./{J} But give us your news;/Give us

MONKS (5)

587 Fable		2	/King Henry VIII found out that monks were quacks,/And took their lands and
587 Fable		20	came to dinner,/Whene'er the monks were having merry times./He stole the
588 Fable		57	/Over their Christmas wassail the monks dozed,/A fine old drink, though now
589 Fable		83	shred of Bishop could be found,/The monks, when anyone questioned, would declare
589 Fable		89	all such scandal./But after this the monks grew most devout,/And lived on milk

MONOPOLIES (1)

| 224 Mr Mistoff | | 7 | metropolis;/He holds all the patent monopolies/For performing surprising illusions/ |

MONOTONE (1)

| 19 Portrait | | 34 | a prelude of its own,/Capricious monotone/That is at least one definite 'false |

MONOTONOUS (1)

| 561 ES | Ld Clav | 4 | away from me forever/To suffer the monotonous sun of the tropics/Or shiver in the |

MONSIEUR (1)

| 51 Restaurant | | 16 | alors, vieux lubrique, à cet âge .../'Monsieur, le fait est dur./Il est venu, nous |

MONSTER (3)

189 FQ: DrySal		189	/To report the behaviour of the sea monster,/Describe the horoscope, haruspicate
226 Macavity		18	/For he's a fiend in feline shape, a monster of depravity./You may meet him in a
279 MC Knight4		24	fate of the country, to be, in/fact, a monster of egotism. This egotism grew upon

MONSTERS (1)

| 179 FQ: ECoker | | 93 | no secure foothold,/And menaced by monsters, fancy lights,/Risking enchantment. |

MONSTROUS (3)

291 FR	Chorus	6	to play an unread part in some monstrous farce, ridiculous in some nightmare
326 FR	Harry	27	just part of some huge disaster,/Some monstrous mistake and aberration/Of all men,
407 CP	Edward	34	with Miss Coplestone./{E} This is monstrous! My wife knew nothing about it./{L}

MONTENEGRO (1)

| 372 CP | Alex | 22 | /There are very few peasants in Montenegro/Who can have the dish that you'll |

MONTENT (1)

| 51 Restaurant | | 12 | primevères.'/Les taches de son gilet montent au chiffre de trente-huit./'Je la |

MONTH (4)

37 Gerontion		1	/Here I am, an old man in a dry month,/Being read to by a boy, waiting for rain.
61 WL: Burial		1	of the Dead/April is the cruellest month, breeding/Lilacs out of the dead land,
157 Rock 4		5	rule./In Shushan the palace, in the month Nisan,/He served the wine to the king
249 MC Thomas		16	who will come./{T} What shall be the month?/{T2} The last from the first./{T} What

MONTHLY (1)

| 507 CC Guzzard | | 17 | by a third party,/Through whom the monthly payments were made./{E} The terms |

MONTHS (7)

124 SA	Sweeney	28	too./This went on for a couple of months/Nobody came/And nobody went/But
328 FR	Charles	16	to drive a car for the/next twelve months./While trying to extricate his car from
408 CP	Reilly	39	when you came to me two months ago/I was dissatisfied with your
409 CP	Edward	3	so I made enquiries./{E} It was two months ago/That your breakdown began! and I
452 CC	Lucasta	16	wrong, Eggy. It's rank injustice./Two months I'd gone on filing those papers/Which
461 CC	Claude	25	/As we arranged. But after two months —/And as my wife insists upon your
517 CC	Eggers	28	you. The organist we had/Died two months ago. We've been looking for another./

MONTHS' (2)

| 333 FR | Agatha | 1 | ingenious. You were due in three months' time;/You would not have been born in |
| 371 CP | Edward | 8 | to you with Celia/In another six months' time. There it is./You can take it or |

MONTJOY (9)

| 550 ES | Ld Clav | 5 | knew me./{LC} Well, then, Maisie Montjoy./{MC} Yes. Maisie Montjoy./I was |
| 550 ES | Carghil | 6 | Maisie Montjoy./{MC} Yes. Maisie Montjoy./I was Maisie Montjoy once. And you |

550 ES	Carghil	7	Yes. Maisie Montjoy./I was Maisie Montjoy once. And you didn't recognise me./
554 ES	Piggott	33	you might remember her/As Maisie Montjoy in revue./She was well-known at one
562 ES	Carghil	23	us,/I'll introduce myself. I'm Maisie Montjoy!/That means nothing to you, my dears.
562 ES	Carghil	25	Long time since the name of Maisie Montjoy/Topped the bill in revue. Now I'm
563 ES	Carghil	29	in London/Knew the name of Maisie Montjoy in revue./{G} If Maisie Montjoy was as
563 ES	Gomez	30	Montjoy in revue./{G} If Maisie Montjoy was as beautiful to look at/As Mrs.
570 ES	Ld Clav	38	/Nor the musical comedy star, Maisie Montjoy./There is Mrs. John Carghill, the

MONTMIRAIL (1)

| 248 MC | Tempt2 | 17 | at Northampton,/And last at Montmirail, in Maine. Now that I have recalled |

MONTRERA (1)

| 47 Mél | Adult | 19 | /Vêtu d'une peau de girafe./On montrera mon cénotaphe/Aux côtes brûlantes |

MONUMENT (3)

155 Rock 3		35	decent godless people:/Their only monument the asphalt road/And a thousand
187 FQ: DrySal		122	it;/On a halcyon day it is merely a monument,/In navigable weather it is always a
248 MC Tempt2		29	possession./A templed tomb, monument of marble./Rule over men reckon no

MONUMENTS (1)

| 19 Portrait | | 37 | air, in a tobacco trance,/Admire the monuments,/Discuss the late events,/Correct |

MOOD (3)

492 CC	Colby	25	I couldn't understand./'Reminiscent mood.' I can't develop that/Unless you can tell
492 CC	Claude	28	what?/'Tonight I feel in a reminiscent mood' —/Oh yes. To say something of my early
492 CC	Claude	33	don't think I shall be in a reminiscent mood./Cross that out. It would only remind me/

MOODS (1)

| 33 Conv Gal | | 15 | of the absolute,/Giving our vagrant moods the slightest twist!/With your air |

MOON (26)

24 Rhapsody		50	dark./The lamp hummed:/'Regard the moon,/La lune ne garde aucune rancune,/She
24 Rhapsody		55	smooths the hair of the grass./The moon has lost her memory./A washed-out
33 Conv Gal		1	I observe: 'Our sentimental friend the moon!/Or possibly (fantastic, I confess)/It may
56 Swee Night		5	giraffe./The circles of the stormy moon/Slide westward toward the River Plate,/
67 WL: Fire S		199	to Mrs. Porter in the spring./O the moon shone bright on Mrs. Porter/And on her
141 Rannoch		5	Substance crumbles, in the thin air/Moon cold or moon hot. The road winds in/
141 Rannoch		5	in the thin air/Moon cold or moon hot. The road winds in/Listlessness of
166 Rock 10		23	over stagnant pools at batflight,/Moon light and star light, owl and moth light,/
178 FQ: ECoker		63	against the Sun/Until the Sun and Moon go down/Comets weep and Leonids fly/
180 FQ: ECoker		108	into the dark,/And dark the Sun and Moon, and the Almanach de Gotha/And the
212 Growltiger		22	all nature seemed at play,/The tender moon was shining bright, the barge at Molesey
216 Jellicles		3	*Cats come one come all:/The Jellicle Moon is shining bright* —*/Jellicles come to the*
216 Jellicles		12	and graces/And wait for the Jellicle Moon to rise./Jellicle Cats develop slowly,/
216 Jellicles		17	a gavotte and a jig./Until the Jellicle Moon appears/They make their toilette and
216 Jellicles		28	/To dance by the light of the Jellicle Moon./Jellicle Cats are black and white,/Jellicle
217 Jellicles		36	themselves to be right/For the Jellicle Moon and the Jellicle Ball./Mungojerrie and
601 Nocturne		4	love, beneath a bored but courteous moon;/The conversation failing, strikes some
601 Nocturne		11	best mode oblique/Rolls toward the moon a frenzied eye profound,/(No need of
602 Humoresque		12	stare;/Translated, maybe, to the moon./With Limbo's other useless things/
290 FR Agatha		33	dry holly-tree/The inclination of the moon/The attraction of the dark passage/The
300 FRDowning		32	at the water —/There wasn't a moon, but I was sure it was him./While I took
310 FR Mary		29	into the rain cloud/Harefoot over the moon?/{H} What have we been saying? I think I
336 FR Agatha		34	to the phase/Of the determined moon./A curse is like a child, formed/To grow
349 FR Chorus		1	Layer/And behind the smiling moon?/And what is being done to us?/And what
350 FR Mary		11	mirror/And behind the smiling moon/Follow follow/{Ag} This way the
422 CP Julia		17	ones watch over the roof,/May the moon herself influence the bed. {}/[*They drink*]/

MOONFLOWER (1)

| 600 Moonflower | | 1 | with a patient curious eye./Song/The moonflower opens to the moth,/The mist crawls |

MOONLIGHT (8)

73 WL: Thund		386	among the mountains/In the faint moonlight, the grass is singing/Over the
204 de la Mare		20	/When cats are maddened in the moonlight dance,/Dogs cower, flitter bats, and
212 Growltiger		23	at Molesey lay./All in the balmy moonlight it lay rocking on the tide —/And
213 Growltiger		36	and awaiting no surprise —/But the moonlight shone reflected from a hundred
602 Humoresque		19	of nose),/'Your damned thin moonlight, worse than gas —/'Now in New
307 FR Mary		4	/{M} It was the cave where we met by moonlight/To raise the evil spirits./{H} Arthur
540 ES Gomez		16	me./{G} Dick, do you remember the moonlight night/We drove back to Oxford?
540 ES Gomez		21	I'm referring —/A summer night of moonlight and shadows —/The night you ran

MOONLIT (2)

| 216 Jellicles | | 24 | like a jumping-jack,/Jellicle Cats have moonlit eyes./They're quiet enough in the |
| 601 Nocturne | | 9 | a swoon./Blood looks effective on the moonlit ground —/The hero smiles; in my best |

323 FR	Winch	1	says he'll come round/In the morning, most likely, but he mustn't be moved./
328 FR	Charles	14	/cart in Ebury Street early on the morning of January 1st, was/fined 50 and costs
348 FR	Warburt	1	/And we'll have him up here in the morning./I hope Lady Monchensey hasn't been
349 FR	Gerald	9	dealing with Arthur and John in the morning./{V} We must wait for the will to be
349 FR	Violet	10	to be read. I shall send a wire in the morning./{C} I fear that my mind is not what it
361 CP	Reilly	35	to you slowly:/When you wake in the morning, when you go to bed at night,/That
363 CP	Edward	39	that is not all./Since I saw her this morning when we had breakfast/I no longer
381 CP	Edward	9	certain/Is, that only since this morning/I have met myself as a middle-aged
388 CP	Peter	4	with/And we settled everything this morning./Alex is a wonderful person to know,/
396 CP	Lavinia	40	the kind of life we led/Until yesterday morning./{E} There was a door/And I could not
399 CP	2m	1	*consulting room in London. Morning:/several weeks later.* SIR HENRY
399 CP	Reilly	1	About those three appointments this morning, Miss Barraway:/I should like to run
400 CP	Alex	31	him up./{A} You will have a busy morning!/I will go out by the service staircase/
401 CP	Reilly	1	*up from his papers].*/{R} Good morning, Mr. Chamberlayne./Please sit down. I
417 CP	Reilly	32	do not repine;/Are contented with the morning that separates/And with the evening
427 CP	Julia	1	Alex with me!/He only got back this morning from somewhere —/One of his
427 CP	Alex	9	have heard of/Yet. Got back this morning. I heard about your party/And, as I
445 CC	Eggers	12	coming up to London:/I've spent the morning shopping! Gardening tools./The
445 CC	Claude	21	I had to send him to the City this morning,/But he'll be back, I hope, before you
450 CC	Claude	27	/It was time you were back. Was your morning satisfactory?/{C} I've got what you
467 CC	Colby	38	that meeting in the City/Tomorrow morning. You asked me to prepare/Some
496 CC	Claude	13	*Enter EGGERSON]*/{SC} Good morning, Eggerson./{E} Good morning, Sir
496 CC	Eggers	14	Good morning, Eggerson./{E} Good morning, Sir Claude. And Lady Elizabeth!/{SC}
504 CC	Claude	24	*Exit KAGHAN]*/{SC} Good morning, Mrs. Guzzard. I must apologise:/I'm
504 CC	Lady E	32	Elizabeth Mulhammer./{LE} Good morning, Mrs. Guzzard./You don't know me,
523 ES	m	13	TWO/*The Terrace at Badgley Court. Morning*/ACT THREE/*The Same. Late*
540 ES	Gomez	7	he's a success —the man who in the morning/Has to make up his face before the
544 ES	2m	1	*of Badgley Court. A bright sunny morning, several days later.*/Enter LORD
544 ES	Monica	7	/For when I asked about morning coffee/She said 'I'm not the one for
545 ES	Piggott	22	*[Enter MRS. PIGGOTT]*/{MP} Good morning, Lord Claverton! Good morning, Miss
545 ES	Piggott	22	morning, Lord Claverton! Good morning, Miss Claverton!/Isn't this a glorious
545 ES	Piggott	23	Miss Claverton!/Isn't this a glorious morning!/I'm afraid you'll think I've come
554 ES	Carghil	1	I'll bring the photostats tomorrow morning,/And them to you./— Oh, there's
554 ES	Carghil	8	/And leave us alone tomorrow./Good morning, Mrs. Piggott!/Isn't it a glorious
554 ES	Carghil	9	Mrs. Piggott!/Isn't it a glorious morning! {}/[*Enter* MRS. PIGGOTT]/{MP}
554 ES	Piggott	10	[*Enter* MRS. PIGGOTT]/{MP} Good morning, Mrs. Carghill!/{MC} Dear Mrs.
554 ES	Piggott	29	rescue/(That's why I've brought your morning tipple myself/Instead of leaving it, as
556 ES	Ld Clav	10	{}/[*Enter* MICHAEL]/{LC} Good morning, Michael./{Mi} Good morning, Father.
556 ES	Michael	11	Good morning, Michael./{Mi} Good morning, Father. {}/[*A pause*]/{Mi} What a
563 ES	Gomez	7	him. {}/[*Enter* GOMEZ]/{G} Good morning, Dick./{LC} Good morning, Fred./{G}
563 ES	Ld Clav	8	{G} Good morning, Dick./{LC} Good morning, Fred./{G} You weren't expecting me
565 ES	Monica	7	at hand/Will you come back in the morning? After breakfast?/{LC} Yes, come
565 ES	Ld Clav	8	breakfast?/{LC} Yes, come tomorrow morning./{Mi} Well, I'll come tomorrow
565 ES	Michael	9	/{Mi} Well, I'll come tomorrow morning./{MC} Are you staying in the
567 ES	Monica	5	find me/When you telephoned this morning. That Mrs. Piggott/Should have heard
567 ES	Charles	18	my darling, since I got your letter this morning/About your father and Michael, and
574 ES	Ld Clav	26	you know I expected you this morning,/But you never came./{Mi} No, Father.

MORNING'S (1)

597	Before Mor	5	flowers, flowers of dawn./This morning's flowers and flowers of yesterday/

MORNINGS (2)

14	Prufrock	50	them all —/Have known the evenings, mornings, afternoons,/I have measured out my
493 CC	2m	1	*Business Room, as in Act 1. Several mornings later.* SIR CLAUDE *is/moving chairs*

MORSEL (1)

24	Rhapsody	37	/Slips out its tongue/And devours a morsel of rancid butter.'/So the hand of the

MORSELS (1)

253 MC	Tempt4	5	at last./Hooks have been baited with morsels of the past./Wantonness is weakness.

MORSURES (1)

48	Lune Miel	6	quatre jambes molles tout gonflées de morsures./On relève le drap pour mieux

MORTAL (4)

136	5FingerEx3	4	across the lawn,/Here is no eft or mortal snake/But only sluggish duck and drake/
136	5FingerEx3	9	mortals take/That which is their mortal due,/Pinching bread and finger too,/
166	Rock 10	9	of Iniquity is a pit too deep for mortal eyes to plumb. Come/Ye out from
166	Rock 10	18	we praise Thee!/Too bright for mortal vision./O Greater Light, we praise Thee

MORTALS (1)

136	5FingerEx3	8	Bread and Wine,/Let the feathered mortals take/That which is their mortal due,/

MORTAR (1)

149 Rock 1	83	*clay for new brick/And lime for new mortar/Where the bricks are fallen/We will build*

MORTARS (1)

127 Cor1 March	15	/102,000 machine guns,/28,000 trench mortars,/53,000 field and heavy guns,/I cannot

MORTGAGE (1)

456 CC Eggers	31	our house in Joshua Park/(On a mortgage, of course) 'now we've settled down/

MORVILLE (3)

277 MC Knight1	32	I shall next call upon Hugh de Morville, who/has made a special study of
277 MC Knight1	34	and constitutional law. Sir/Hugh de Morville./{K2} I should like first to recur to a
279 MC Knight1	4	you/must share it with us./{K1} Morville has given us a great deal to think

MOSS (1)

37 Gerontion	12	at night in the field overhead;/Rocks, moss, stonecrop, iron, merds./The woman keeps

MOST (91)

91 Ash-Wed 2	27	/Calm and distressed/Torn and most whole/Rose of memory/Rose of
148 Rock 1	56	are ready to invest their money/But most expect dividends./I say to you: *Make*
162 Rock 8	13	good men,/Many who were evil,/And most who were neither./Like all men in all
175 FQ: BurntN	159	assail them. The Word in the desert/Is most attacked by voices of temptation,/The
182 FQ: ECoker	202	with the photograph album)./Love is most nearly itself/When here and now cease to
185 FQ: DrySal	61	/Of what was believed in as the most reliable —/And therefore the fittest for
190 FQ: DrySal	210	selflessness and self-surrender./For most of us, there is only the unattended/
190 FQ: DrySal	230	/From past and future also./For most of us, this is the aim/Never here to be
212 Growltiger	17	whom Growltiger came to grips!/But most to Cats of foreign race his hatred had been
218 Mung Rump	16	— or Rumpelteazer!' — And most of the time they left it at that./Mungojerrie
219 Mung Rump	29	— or Rumpelteazer!' — And most of the time they left it at that./Mungojerrie
222 Pekes Pols	4	And the Pugs and the Poms, although most people say/That they do not like fighting,
222 Pekes Pols	15	beat —/I don't know the reason, but most people think/He'd slipped into the
229 Gus	41	that he still can, much better than most,/Produce blood-curdling noises to bring
588 Fable	64	blue,/As in ghost stories lights most always do./The doors, though barred and
589 Fable	65	/The doors, though barred and bolted most securely,/Gave way — my statement
589 Fable	89	/But after this the monks grew most devout,/And lived on milk and breakfast
247 MC Templ1	32	safest beast is not the one that roars most loud,/This was not the way of the King
258 MC Thomas	23	then despise the men who thought me most contemptible,/The raw nobility, whose
258 MC Thomas	34	show you of my history/Will seem to most of you at best futility,/Senseless
261 MC Thomas	34	so in Heaven the Saints are/most high, having made themselves most low,
261 MC Thomas	34	/most high, having made themselves most low, and are seen, not as we/see them, but
264 MC Templ1	3	*against me.*/A day that was always most dear to the Archbishop Thomas./And he
266 MC Knight1	9	be./You say, from the King?/{K1} Most surely from the King./We must speak with
266 MC Thomas	28	order, I am at his command,/As his most faithful vassal in the land./{K1} Saving
273 MC Chorus	3	for me,/Who intercede for me, in my most need?/Dead upon the tree, my Saviour,/
288 FR Violet	1	evening./{V} Harry was always the most likely to be late./{A} This time, it will not
290 FR Agatha	22	the only thing to do./{Ag} Thus with most careful devotion/Thus with precise
293 FR Gerald	32	Frontier —/Been in tight corners most of my life/And some pretty nasty messes./
293 FR Harry	37	/To whom nothing has happened, at most a continual impact/Of external events.
296 FR Ivy	20	in his condition/Often betray the most immoderate resentment/At such a
296 FR Amy	30	I'll have a talk to him tomorrow./{A} Most certainly not, Charles, you are not the
300 FRDowning	24	any orders —/His Lordship is always most considerate/About keeping me up. But
308 FR Harry	3	another; if there is nothing else/The most real is what I fear. The bright colour fades
313 FR Gerald	16	We must make him feel at home. And most auspicious/That he could be here for his
313 FR Amy	27	with DR. WARBURTON]/{A} It is most vexing. What can have happened?/I
316 FR Ivy	4	chimney. I am afraid./{I} This is a most undignified terror, and I must struggle
320 FR Warburt	21	Wishwood,/And for that reason, it is most essential/That nothing should disturb or
323 FR Winch	1	says he'll come round/In the morning, most likely, but he mustn't be moved./But Dr.
333 FR Agatha	8	should have been *mine*, as I felt then./Most people would not have felt that
345 FR Amy	25	in this room,/Violet, you are the most malicious in a harmless way;/I prefer your
346 FRDowning	26	but I'm sure of what I mean:/We most of us seem to live according to
347 FRDowning	1	that you've raised the subject, I'm most relieved —/If you understand my meaning.
358 CP Edward	5	And the secrets of your cases./{E} Most of my secrets are quite uninteresting./{J}
363 CP Reilly	13	you really are among other people./Most of the time we take ourselves for granted,/
380 CP Celia	4	/To humiliate me. I suppose that most women/Would feel degraded to find that a
381 CP Edward	13	have lost/The desire for all that was most desirable,/Before you are contented with
395 CP Edward	31	face, to take people in./{E} One of the most infuriating things about you/Has always
395 CP Lavinia	34	I understood myself./{L} And the most infuriating thing about you/Has always
412 CP Reilly	17	to be taken seriously./{R} That is most uncommon./{J} Henry, get up./You can't
412 CP Celia	35	I am wasting it anyway./I suppose most people, when they come to see you,/Are
413 CP Reilly	3	simply tell me to go away again./{R} Most of my patients begin, Miss Coplestone,/By

414 CP	Reilly	38	sense of sin, Miss Coplestone?/This is most unusual./{C} It seemed to *me* abnormal./
424 CP	Lavinia	5	/{L} There, in that corner. That's the most convenient;/You can get in and out. Is
431 CP	Peter	21	And that's why we're interested./The most decayed noble mansion in England!/At
435 CP	Reilly	17	métier, Mr. Quilpe —/Which is the most that any of us can ask for./{P} And what a
449 CC	Eggers	30	I expect./{E} And so I hope. A most suitable arrangement./But will you tell me
451 CC	Eggers	7	gave him his start. And he's made the most of it —/That I will say. An encouraging
456 CC	Eggers	14	Why, yes, indeed, I must admit she is./Most of her oddities are perfectly harmless./
458 CC	Eggers	8	/{E} Lady Elizabeth! This is most surprising./{LE} What's surprising,
459 CC	Lady E	7	very auspicious —/Contrary to what most people think./You should be artistic. But
459 CC	Lady E	31	quiet hour. A quiet hour a day/Is most essential, Dr. Rebmann says./{SC}
464 CC	Claude	4	the material that the potter handles./Most people think that a sculptor or a painter/
464 CC	Claude	6	more excellent to be than a potter./Most people think of china or porcelain/As
475 CC	Colby	33	about myself;/But you know most of what there is to say/Already, either
480 CC	Kaghan	3	the right expression —/Lucasta's the most exciting speculation/I've ever thought of
481 CC	Lady E	28	to you. You can have dinner early:/Most of its patrons dine at half past six./They
481 CC	Lady E	29	dine at half past six./They have the most delicious salads!/And I told you, Mr.
483 CC	Lady E	10	The walls; and the curtains;/And most of the furniture. But, that writing-table!/
497 CC	Eggers	36	Mrs. Guzzards?/{E} I agree, it is a most uncommon name,/But stranger things
498 CC	Eggers	1	/{E} I agree, that would be most surprising./And at the same address?/{LE}
498 CC	Claude	16	that she ran a baby farm./That's most unlikely, nowadays./Besides, I should have
500 CC	Lucasta	31	the moment when you needed him most!/And he doesn't depend upon other
501 CC	Eggers	30	be happy. Mr. Kaghan/Is one of the most promising young men in the City,/And he
504 CC	Claude	20	servants' time-table better./This is a most unfortunate beginning./{LE} She's been
518 CC	Eggers	18	/We have a spare room. We should be most happy/If you cared to stop with us, until
528 ES	Charles	5	exposed to strangers./{C} But he's most alive when he's among people/Managing,
528 ES	Charles	33	/{C} This is your best reason, and the most depressing;/For this situation may persist
529 ES	Monica	13	/Who is without envy? And most people/Are unaware or unashamed of
534 ES	Ld Clav	6	/{LC} It would seem then that most of your business/Has been of such a
542 ES	Gomez	16	How can you speak of threats?/It's most unkind of you. My only aim/Is to renew
544 ES	Monica	24	the fruit trees./{M} Oh, let's make the most of this weather while it lasts./I never
544 ES	Ld Clav	29	really enjoyed living/As much as most people. At least, as they seem to do/
548 ES	Carghil	15	I always sit here./It's the sunniest and most sheltered corner,/And none of the other
563 ES	Gomez	37	position/I should have been your most devoted admirer./{MC} *It's Not Too Late*
565 ES	Carghil	12	an old friend of mine/That it seems most natural to call you Michael./You don't
567 ES	Monica	24	Father?/Father, of all people the most scrupulous,/The most austere. It's quite
567 ES	Monica	25	all people the most scrupulous,/The most austere. It's quite impossible./Father with
572 ES	Ld Clav	39	my freedom,/And perhaps the most important. I know what you think./You
575 ES	Gomez	24	/That is just what I should be! And most appropriate,/Isn't it, Dick, when we recall!/
580 ES	Carghil	21	/I'm so excited! But what pleases me most/Is that I shall be able to bring you news of

MOSTLY (5)

202 War Poetry	10	—/Of Nature and the Spirit. Mostly the individual/Experience is too large, or
239 MC Chorus	24	have suffered various oppression,/But mostly we are left to our own devices,/And we
322 FR Winch	27	/So I slipped along on my bike. Mostly walking,/What with the fog so thick, or
456 CC Eggers	25	forget things. And she likes to travel,/Mostly for her health. And when she's abroad/
527 ES Monica	30	make a remark to now and then./And mostly it's been me./{C} I know it's been you./

MOTH (2)

166 Rock 10	23	/Moon light and star light, owl and moth light,/Glow-worm glowlight on a
600 Moonflower	1	/Song/The moonflower opens to the moth,/The mist crawls in from sea;/A great

MOTHER (93)

92 Ash-Wed 2	45	and/Word of no speech/Grace to the Mother/For the Garden/Where all love ends./
98 Ash-Wed 6	25	shaken and reply./Blessèd sister, holy mother, spirit of the fountain, spirit of the
99 Ash-Wed 6	32	/And even among these rocks/Sister, mother/And spirit of the river, spirit of the sea,/
129 Cor2 State	28	faint sheet lightning/What shall I cry?/Mother mother/Here is the row of family
129 Cor2 State	28	lightning/What shall I cry?/Mother mother/Here is the row of family portraits,
129 Cor2 State	36	the clematis droops over the lintel/O mother (not among these busts, all correctly
129 Cor2 State	40	them/Noses strong to break the wind/Mother/May we not be some time, almost now,
129 Cor2 State	50	the dust, through the night./O mother/What shall I cry?/We demand a
292 FR	Harry	13	here?/Many happy returns of the day, mother./Aunt Ivy, Aunt Violet, Uncle Gerald,
292 FR	Ivy	36	nearly half blind. I've spoken to your mother/Time and time again: she's done
292 FR	Violet	39	and time again I have spoken to your mother/About the waste that goes on in the
295 FR	Charles	8	fancies./It's only doing harm to your mother and yourself./Of course we know what
305 FR	Mary	31	/But if so, I can't find it./{M} Your mother insisted/On everything being kept the
315 FR Warburt	17	to dinner/That I ever see your mother./{V} Yes, look at your mother!/Except
315 FR	Violet	18	your mother./{V} Yes, look at your mother!/Except that she can't get about now in
317 FR Warburt	21	to the future./It's about your mother .../{H} What about my mother?/

317 FR	Harry	22	your mother .../{H} What about my mother?/Everything has always been referred
317 FR	Harry	23	has always been referred back to mother./When we were children, before we went
317 FR	Harry	25	rule of conduct was simply pleasing mother;/Misconduct was simply being unkind
317 FR	Harry	26	was simply being unkind to mother,/What was wrong was whatever made
318 FR	Harry	7	we were supposed to make up to mother/For all the weeks during which she had
318 FR	Harry	13	punishment made us feel less guilty. Mother/Never punished us, but made us feel
319 FR	Warburt	14	/Leave it alone. You know that your mother/And your father were never very happy
319 FR	Warburt	31	overinterpret./I am sure that your mother always loved him;/There was never the
320 FR	Warburt	5	tell you, Harry, that although your mother/Is still so alert, so vigorous of mind,/
320 FR	Warburt	27	/Why you had to know. One is your mother,/To make her happy for the time she has
320 FR	Warburt	34	been a great disappointment to your mother./John's very steady — but he's not
323 FR	Warburt	4	look at him./We must explain to your mother .../{A} Harry! Harry!/Who's there with
324 FR	Violet	11	going on? and what it means to your mother?/{H} Oh, of course I'm sorry. But from
324 FR	Violet	24	show some consideration to your mother./{A} I do not know very much:/And as I
325 FR	Harry	3	/When you said that./{H} I think, mother,/I shall make you lie down. You must
325 FR	Agatha	7	he can, some communication with his mother./{V} I do not seem to be very popular
326 FR	Harry	9	I imagine. {}/[Enter HARRY]/{H} Mother is asleep, I think: it's strange how the
327 FR	Ivy	34	it's all a mistake. And not to tell his mother./{V} What's the use of asking for an
332 FR	Agatha	5	parents?/{Ag} Your father and your mother./{H} You tell me nothing./{Ag} The
332 FR	Agatha	8	sister whom you acknowledge as your mother:/There is no mystery here./{H} What
332 FR	Agatha	11	/{H} What then?/{Ag} You see your mother as identified with this house —/It was
332 FR	Agatha	19	the meaning/Of loneliness. Your mother wanted a sister here/Always. I was the
332 FR	Agatha	37	him thinking/How to get rid of your mother. What simple plots!/He was not suited
334 FR	Harry	31	see/I might even become fonder of my mother —/More compassionate at least — by
337 FR	Harry	37	you intended to happen./{H} Oh, mother,/This is not to do with Agatha, any
339 FR	Harry	1	other people./It is hard for you too, mother, it is indeed harder,/Not to understand./
343 FR	Harry	31	dressed for departure.]/{H} But, mother, you will always have Arthur and John/
343 FR	Harry	38	I cannot account for this/But it is so, mother. Until I come again./{A} If you go now,
345 FR	Harry	11	John:/Take care of them. My address, mother,/Will be care of the bank in London
345 FR	Harry	13	until you hear from me./Good-bye, mother./{A} Good-bye, Harry./{H} Good-bye./
473 CC	Lucasta	10	one where I lived/For a time, with my mother. I've no garden./I hardly feel that I'm
476 CC	Lucasta	33	Oh, it's a sordid story./I hated my mother. I never could see/How Claude had ever
478 CC	Lucasta	9	Oh, I'm sorry:/I suppose it's my mother coming out in me./You know, Colby,
478 CC	Lucasta	30	I told you about Claude and my mother./I may be a bastard, but I have some
483 CC	Lady E	36	previous incarnation. — Is this your mother?/{C} No, that is my aunt. I never knew
483 CC	Colby	37	No, that is my aunt. I never knew my mother./She died when I was born./{LE} She
485 CC	Lady E	8	earl!/And I couldn't believe that my mother was my mother./These were foolish
485 CC	Lady E	8	believe that my mother was my mother./These were foolish fancies. I was a silly
486 CC	Lady E	14	was my aunt./{LE} And as for your mother —/Mrs. Guzzard's sister, I suppose .../
486 CC	Lady E	18	sister —/Who you say was your mother — really was your mother?/{C} Why,
486 CC	Lady E	18	was your mother — really was your mother?/{C} Why, Lady Elizabeth! Why should
489 CC	Lady E	35	she'd never been told the name of the mother;/And the mother had forgotten the
489 CC	Lady E	36	told the name of the mother;/And the mother had forgotten the name of Mrs.
489 CC	Lady E	37	of Mrs. Guzzard,/And I was the mother and the child was Colby;/And Mrs.
490 CC	Lady E	26	you should be my parent./{LE} But a mother, Colby, isn't that different?/There
490 CC	Lady E	27	should always be a bond between mother and son,/No matter how long they have
490 CC	Colby	33	I was born, you might have been my mother,/But you chose not to be. I don't blame
490 CC	Colby	36	time when I was born, your being my mother —/If you are my mother — was a living
490 CC	Colby	37	being my mother —/If you are my mother — was a living fact./Now, it is a dead
491 CC	Colby	2	that I could have had a father and a mother —/{LE} Stop, Colby! Something has come
498 CC	Claude	30	/{SC} What became of my child!/The mother of my child was Mrs. Guzzard's sister./
507 CC	Eggers	12	the name of the father/Or of the mother?/{MG} I was not told either./I
507 CC	Guzzard	28	acknowledged no responsibility./The mother, I suppose, could have got an order/If
508 CC	Eggers	4	it. You must make allowances/For a mother who has been hoping against hope/To
511 CC	Kaghan	5	embarrassed./If Lady Elizabeth is my mother .../{LE} There is no doubt whatever
511 CC	Lady E	7	about it, Barnabas./I am your mother./{K} But who was my father?/{LE} He
511 CC	Kaghan	19	/To regard Mrs. Kaghan as my mother./{LE} Then in order to avoid any danger
512 CC	Claude	12	convinced;/And Mr. Kaghan's ... mother, I am sure, will confirm it./{MG} That is
513 CC	Guzzard	19	no preference? Between a father and a mother?/{C} I've never had a father or a mother
513 CC	Colby	20	/{C} I've never had a father or a mother —/It's different for B. He's had his
513 CC	Colby	23	afford another relationship./Let my mother rest in peace. As for a father —/I have
514 CC	Colby	13	musician./{C} And who was my mother?/{MG} Let your mother rest in peace./I
514 CC	Guzzard	14	who was my mother?/{MG} Let your mother rest in peace./I was your mother; but I
514 CC	Guzzard	15	your mother rest in peace./I was your mother; but I chose to be your aunt./So you
514 CC	Guzzard	16	you may have your wish, and have no mother./{SC} Mrs. Guzzard, this is perfectly

515	CC	Guzzard	27	/When I gave up my place as Colby's mother/I gave up something I could never have
527	ES	Monica	36	anybody,/I'm afraid. Poor Michael! Mother spoilt him/And Father was too severe
536	ES	Gomez	35	long since — that's a good thing./My mother — I dare say she's still alive,/But she
559	ES	Michael	27	title,/I know why you took it. And Mother knew./First, because it gave you the
570	ES	Monica	2	/You've kept them to yourself. Did Mother know of them?/{LC} Your mother knew
570	ES	Ld Clav	3	Mother know of them?/{LC} Your mother knew nothing about them. And I know/
570	ES	Ld Clav	4	And I know/That I never knew your mother, as she never knew me./I thought that
570	ES	Ld Clav	13	nothing to say to me./I think of your mother, when she lay dying:/Completely
573	ES	Carghil	36	known her two days!/But I feel like a mother to her already./You may say that I just
573	ES	Carghil	37	may say that I just missed being her mother!/I've known her father for a very long
578	ES	Ld Clav	9	be equally mistaken./I see that your mother and I, in our failure/To understand each
578	ES	Michael	27	with your nose in a book./And once, Mother snatched a book away from you/And

MOTHER'S (10)

313	FR	Violet	6	rush he had to be here in time/For his mother's birthday./{I} Mary, my dear,/Did you
313	FR	Violet	17	/That he could be here for his mother's birthday./{M} I must go and change. I
317	FR	Warburt	3	/Than simply in honour of your mother's birthday./I wanted a private
318	FR	Warburt	21	we are concerned with/Now, is your mother's happiness in the future,/For the time
320	FR	Warburt	4	well, tell me./{W} It's about your mother's health that I wanted to talk to you./I
320	FR	Warburt	37	been rather irresponsible./Your mother's hopes are all centred on you./{H}
322	FR	Winch	5	pardon, I'm forgetting./If it was my mother's. God rest her soul,/She's been dead
332	FR	Agatha	1	he was weak he recognised your mother's power,/And yielded to it./{H} There
357	CP	Edward	7	aunt/Whom you wouldn't know. Her mother's sister/And rather a recluse./{J} Her
559	ES	Michael	31	/Also, to hold your own with Mother's family —/To lord it over them, in fact.

MOTHS (1)

| 371 | CP | Edward | 33 | you can wrap in camphor/But the moths will get in. So you want to see Celia./I |

MOTION (7)

42	Swee Erect		16	O cropped out with teeth:/The sickle motion from the thighs/Jackknifes upward at
83	Hollow Men		12	/Paralysed force, gesture without motion;/Those who have crossed/With direct
85	Hollow Men		74	the idea/And the reality/Between the motion/And the act/Falls the Shadow/*For*
147	Rock 1		8	experiment,/Brings knowledge of motion, but not of stillness;/Knowledge of
173	FQ: BurntN		76	still and moving,/*Erhebung* without motion, concentration/Without elimination,
330	FR	Harry	9	being unconscious, living in gentle motion/Of horses, and right visits to the right
384	CP	Reilly	18	/You made a decision. You set in motion/Forces in your life and in the lives of

MOTIONLESS (2)

| 185 | FQ: DrySal | | 53 | /Dropping their petals and remaining motionless;/Where is there an end to the drifting |
| 186 | FQ: DrySal | | 83 | movement of pain that is painless and motionless,/To the drift of the sea and the |

MOTIVE (3)

180	FQ: ECoker	110	/And cold the sense and lost the motive of action./And we all go with them, into
196	FQ: Little	200	be well/By the purification of the motive/In the ground of our beseeching./The
420	CP	Reilly	31	that the other understands the motive —/Mirror to mirror, reflecting vanity./I

MOTIVES (1)

| 194 | FQ: Little | 142 | have done, and been; the shame/Of motives late revealed, and the awareness/Of |

MOTOR (6)

121	SA	Sweeney	23	/There's no gramophones/There's no motor cars/No two-seaters, no six-seaters,/No
147	Rock 1		28	for six days, on the seventh we must motor/To Hindhead, or Maidenhead./If the
152	Rock 2		47	/But all dash to and fro in motor cars,/Familiar with the roads and settled
153	Rock 2		50	/But every son would have his motor cycle,/And daughters ride away on casual
328	FR	Charles	11	us. {}/[*reads*]./{C} '*Peer's Brother in Motor Smash*/The Hon. Arthur Gerald Charles
547	ES	Piggott	36	or in the hills,/Quite away from the motor roads. You must learn the best walks./I

MOTORS (1)

| 67 | WL: Fire S | 197 | time I hear/The sound of horns and motors, which shall bring/Sweeney to Mrs. |

MOTTO (2)

| 177 | FQ: ECoker | 13 | the tattered arras woven with a silent motto./In my beginning is my end. Now the |
| 595 | Grad 13 | | 5 | thy care for lands unseen;/And let thy motto be, proud and serene,/Still as the years |

MOUETTES (1)

| 51 | Restaurant | | 26 | jours noyé,/Oubliait les cris des mouettes et la houle de Cornouaille,/Et les |

MOUILLÉE (1)

| 51 | Restaurant | | 11 | elle était plus petite./Elle était toute mouillée, je lui ai donné des primevères.'/Les |

MOULDERING (3)

158	Rock 5		5	is forgotten: are like snakes that lie on mouldering stairs, content in the sunlight./And
420	CP	Reilly	26	they to go back to?/To the stale food mouldering in the larder,/The stale thoughts
420	CP	Reilly	27	in the larder,/The stale thoughts mouldering in their minds./Each unable to

MOUNT (3)

20 Portrait	86	a slight sensation of being ill at ease/I mount the stairs and turn the handle of the door
26 Rhapsody	75	little lamp spreads a ring on the stair./Mount./The bed is open; the tooth-brush hangs
28 Boston ET	6	the *Boston Evening Transcript,*/I mount the steps and ring the bell, turning/

MOUNTAIN (3)

72 WL: Thund	339	only water amongst the rock/Dead mountain mouth of carious teeth that cannot
105 Song Sime	19	thy peace./Before the stations of the mountain of desolation,/Before the certain hour
422 CP Alex	22	in the desert./Watch over her in the mountain./Watch over her in the labyrinth./

MOUNTAINS (9)

61 WL: Burial	17	on tight. And down we went./In the mountains, there you feel free./I read, much of
72 WL: Thund	327	/Of thunder of spring over distant mountains/He who was living is now dead/We
72 WL: Thund	333	/The road winding above among the mountains/Which are mountains of rock
72 WL: Thund	334	among the mountains/Which are mountains of rock without water/If there were
72 WL: Thund	341	nor sit/There is not even silence in the mountains/But dry sterile thunder without rain/
72 WL: Thund	343	rain/There is not even solitude in the mountains/But red sullen faces sneer and snarl/
73 WL: Thund	371	horizon only/What is the city over the mountains/Cracks and reforms and bursts in
73 WL: Thund	385	wells./In this decayed hole among the mountains/In the faint moonlight, the grass is
155 Rock 3	64	the seas and developing the mountains,/Dividing the stars into common and

MOUNTED (1)

| 20 Portrait | 87 | of the door/And feel as if I had mounted on my hands and knees./'And so you |

MOUNTING (2)

| 14 Prufrock | 42 | thin!')/My morning coat, my collar mounting firmly to the chin,/My necktie rich |
| 105 Song Sime | 28 | glory and derision,/Light upon light, mounting the saints' stair./Not for me the |

MOURN (10)

89 Ash-Wed 1	7	eagle stretch its wings?)/Why should I mourn/The vanished power of the usual reign?/ ~
164 Rock 9	14	/Doing themselves very well./Let us mourn in a private chamber, learning the way of
590 Time Space	14	/So let us haste to pluck anew/Nor mourn to see them pine,/And though our days
590 Space Time	14	/But let us haste to pluck anew/Nor mourn to see them pine,/And though the
260 MC Thomas	17	For who in the World will both mourn and rejoice at once and/for the same
260 MC Thomas	20	/mysteries that we can rejoice and mourn at once for the same reason./Now think
261 MC Thomas	13	By no means. Just as we rejoice and mourn at once, in the/Birth and in the Passion
261 MC Thomas	15	a smaller figure, we/both rejoice and mourn in the death of martyrs. We mourn, for
261 MC Thomas	15	mourn in the death of martyrs. We mourn, for the sins/of the world that has
261 MC Thomas	21	Christian: for that would be solely to/mourn. We do not think of him simply as a

MOURNING (3)

260 MC Thomas	18	For either joy will be overborne by mourning, or/mourning will be cast out by joy;
260 MC Thomas	19	will be overborne by mourning, or/mourning will be cast out by joy; so it is only in
261 MC Thomas	23	be simply to/rejoice: and neither our mourning nor our rejoicing is as the world's is./

MOURNS (2)

| 254 MC Tempt4 | 31 | turns,/The nest is rifled, and the bird mourns;/That the shrine shall be pillaged, and |
| 261 MC Thomas | 32 | So thus as on earth the Church mourns and rejoices at once, in/a fashion that |

MOUSE (4)

192 FQ: Little	61	—/The wall, the wainscot and the mouse./The death of hope and despair,/This is
214 RTTugger	5	have a house./If you set him on a mouse then he only wants a rat,/If you set him
214 RTTugger	6	him on a rat then he'd rather chase a mouse./Yes the Rum Tum Tugger is a Curious
269 MC Chorus	33	jackdaw; the scurrying noise of mouse and jerboa; the laugh of the loon, the

MOUSE-CAKE (1)

| 210 Old Gumbie | 23 | baking and frying./She makes them a mouse-cake of bread and dried peas,/And a |

MOUSERS (1)

| 230 Bust Jones | 7 | of fastidious black:/No commonplace mousers have such well-cut trousers/Or such an |

MOUTH (16)

23 Preludes	52	thing./Wipe your hand across your mouth, and laugh;/The worlds revolve like
72 WL: Thund	339	amongst the rock/Dead mountain mouth of carious teeth that cannot spit/Here
92 Ash-Wed 3	10	/Damp, jaggèd, like an old man's mouth drivelling, beyond repair,/Or the toothed
92 Ash-Wed 3	17	hair is sweet, brown hair over the mouth blown,/Lilac and brown hair;/
97 Ash-Wed 5	35	desert/Of drouth, spitting from the mouth the withered apple-seed./O my people./
137 5FingerEx5	4	cut,/And his brow so grim/And his mouth so prim/And his conversation, so nicely/
137 5FingerEx5	14	to meet Mr. Eliot!/(Whether his mouth be open or shut)./Landscapes/New
192 FQ: Little	65	and drouth/Over the eyes and in the mouth,/Dead water and dead sand/Contending
588 Fable	56	to bring in took four pages,/His mouth an apple held, his skull held sausages./
602 Humoresque	10	/Half bullying, half imploring air,/Mouth twisted to the latest tune;/His
606 Narcissus	39	and stained/With the shadow in his mouth./MURDER IN THE CATHEDRAL/
257 MC Chorus	24	flowing in at the ear and the mouth and the eye./God is leaving us, God is
264 MC Priest2	8	*of the congregation he opened his mouth./*That which was from the beginning,
264 MC Priest3	15	day of the Holy Innocents./*Out of the mouth of very babes, O God./*As the voice of

| 264 | MC | Priest3 | 21 | a voice heard, weeping./Out of the mouth of very babes, O God! {}/[THE |
| 353 | CP | Peter | 15 | found her in the pantry, rinsing her mouth out with champagne./I like that story./ |

MOVE (9)

139	Virginia		4	will is still as a river/Still. Will heat move/Only through the mocking-bird/Heard
152	Rock 2		49	nowhere./Nor does the family even move about together,/But every son would have
172	FQ: BurntN		58	/Ascend to summer in the tree/We move above the moving tree/In light upon the
175	FQ: BurntN		140	point of the turning world./Words move, music moves/Only in time; but that
195	FQ: Little		148	by that refining fire/Where you must move in measure, like a dancer.'/The day was
232	Skimble		28	/When Skimble is about and on the move./You can play no pranks with
599	On a Port		10	glad or ominous/Disturb her lips, or move the slender hands;/Her dark eyes keep
297	FR	Agatha	3	think?/{Ag} It seems a necessary move/In an unnecessary action,/Not for the
534	ES	Gomez	22	And then what happens? You have to move on./That wouldn't do for me. I'm too

MOVED (11)

23	Preludes		48	/Impatient to assume the world./I am moved by fancies that are curled/Around these
94	Ash-Wed 4		7	in knowledge of eternal dolour/Who moved among the others as they walked,/Who
151	Rock 2		7	of GOD in the Spirit, the Spirit which moved on the face of the waters like a lantern
160	Rock 7		7	the face of the deep./And the Spirit moved upon the face of the water./And men
167	Rock 10		43	shadow./We thank Thee who hast moved us to building, to finding, to forming at
172	FQ: BurntN		33	guests, accepted and accepting./So we moved, and they, in a formal pattern,/Along the
190	FQ: DrySal		225	movement/Of that which is only moved/And has in it no source of movement —/
323	FR	Winch	1	most likely, but he mustn't be moved./But Dr. Owen was anxious that you
323	FR	Warburt	13	a slight concussion,/But he mustn't be moved tonight. I'd trust Owen/On a matter like
481	CC	Lady E	19	a look at the flat/Now that you've moved in. Because you can't tell/Whether a
538	ES	Gomez	21	known you made it/You simply get moved to another post/Where at least you can't

MOVEMENT (15)

150	Rock 1		117	*In this street/There is no beginning, no movement, no peace and no end/But noise without*
173	FQ: BurntN		66	the dance is,/But neither arrest nor movement. And do not call it fixity,/Where past
173	FQ: BurntN		67	past and future are gathered. Neither movement from nor towards,/Neither ascent
174	FQ: BurntN		126	way, and the other/Is the same, not in movement/But abstention from movement;
174	FQ: BurntN		127	not in movement/But abstention from movement; while the world moves/In appetency,
175	FQ: BurntN		162	chimera./The detail of the pattern is movement,/As in the figure of the ten stairs./
175	FQ: BurntN		164	figure of the ten stairs./Desire itself is movement/Not in itself desirable;/Love is itself
175	FQ: BurntN		167	unmoving,/Only the cause and end of movement,/Timeless, and undesiring/Except in
180	FQ: ECoker		116	a hollow rumble of wings, with a movement of darkness on darkness,/And we
186	FQ: DrySal		83	withering of withered flowers,/To the movement of pain that is painless and
190	FQ: DrySal		224	/Where action were otherwise movement/Of that which is only moved/And
190	FQ: DrySal		226	moved/And has in it no source of movement —/Driven by dmonic, chthonic/
256	MC	Chorus	6	is no rest in the street./I hear restless movement of feet. And the air is heavy and
335	FR	Agatha	11	the feet: the unwinking eye/Fixing the movement. Over and under./{H} In and out, in
335	FR	Harry	15	/On dissolving bone. In and out, the movement/Until the chain broke, and I was left/

MOVEMENTS (1)

| 226 | Macavity | | 15 | sways his head from side to side, with movements like a snake;/And when you think |

MOVES (10)

94	Ash-Wed 4		14	and the flutes, restoring/One who moves in the time between sleep and waking,
149	Rock 1		99	*shiver in unlit rooms./Only the wind moves/Over empty fields, untilled/Where the*
174	FQ: BurntN		127	from movement; while the world moves/In appetency, on its metalled ways/Of
175	FQ: BurntN		140	turning world./Words move, music moves/Only in time; but that which is only
175	FQ: BurntN		146	/The stillness, as a Chinese jar still/Moves perpetually in its stillness./Not the
176	FQ: BurntN		173	shaft of sunlight/Even while the dust moves/There rises the hidden laughter/Of
337	FR	m	8	the crooked made straight. {}/[*She moves back into the room*]/{Ag} What have I
376	CP	m	1	*and inspects his game of Patience. He moves/a card. The doorbell rings repeatedly.*
386	CP	m	14	{}/[*Exit. A pause.* EDWARD *moves about restlessly. The bell rings, and he*
424	CP	m	4	*looks about the room critically and moves a bowl of flowers.*]/[*Re-enter*

MOVIES (1)

| 430 | CP | Peter | 34 | living a quiet life!/Don't you go to the movies?/{L} Occasionally./{P} Alex knows./Did |

MOVING (15)

107	Animula		4	dark, dry or damp, chilly or warm;/Moving between the legs of tables and of chairs,
139	Virginia		10	/Delay, decay. Living, living,/Never moving. Ever moving/Iron thoughts came with
139	Virginia		10	Living, living,/Never moving. Ever moving/Iron thoughts came with me/And go
166	Rock 10		8	until he awakens in hunger and moving his head to right and to left prepares for
171	FQ: BurntN		26	/There they were, dignified, invisible,/Moving without pressure, over the dead leaves,/
172	FQ: BurntN		58	in the tree/We move above the moving tree/In light upon the figured leaf/And
173	FQ: BurntN		75	a grace of sense, a white light still and moving,/*Erhebung* without motion,
183	FQ: ECoker		206	not matter/We must be still and still moving/Into another intensity/For a further
294	FR	Harry	16	/In a thick smoke, many creatures moving/Without direction, for no direction/

310 FR	Mary	2	now is the time/For the ache in the moving root/The agony in the dark/The slow
310 FR	Harry	38	/Or to a blank wall; that I kept moving/Only so as not to stay still. Singing and
333 FR	Agatha	36	is possible. You may learn hereafter,/Moving alone through flames of ice, chosen/To
367 CP	Edward	19	of us./{E} A common interest in the moving pictures/Frequently brings young
493 CC	3m	1	*mornings later.* SIR CLAUDE *is*/*moving chairs about. Enter* LADY
562 ES	Carghil	34	You've his voice! and his way of moving! It's marvellous./And the charm! He's

MOWING (1)

| 329 FR | Chorus | 6 | /The treble voices on the lawn/The mowing of hay in summer/The dogs and the old |

MOZAMBIQUE (1)

| 47 Mél | Adult | 20 | cénotaphe/Aux côtes brûlantes de Mozambique./Lune de Miel/Ils ont vu les |

MR. (150) [*Abbreviation*]

31 Apollinax		t	faith,/The army of unalterable law./Mr. Apollinax/When Mr. Apollinax visited the
31 Apollinax		1	unalterable law./Mr. Apollinax/When Mr. Apollinax visited the United States/His
31 Apollinax		13	of surf./I looked for the head of Mr. Apollinax rolling under a chair/Or grinning
37 Gerontion		23	to be drunk/Among whispers; by Mr. Silvero/With caressing hands, at Limoges/
54 Mr E Sun		t	ribs/To keep our metaphysics warm./Mr. Eliot's Sunday Morning Service/
68 WL: Fire S		209	the brown fog of a winter noon/Mr. Eugenides, the Smyrna merchant/
116 SP	Dusty	22	Yes this is Miss Dorrance's *flat* —/Oh Mr. Pereira is that you? how do you do!/Oh I'm
119 SP	Wauch	6	gentlemen here on business./Meet Mr. Klipstein. Meet Mr. Krumpacker./{Kl}
119 SP	Wauch	6	business./Meet Mr. Klipstein. Meet Mr. Krumpacker./{Kl} How do you do/{Kr}
119 SP	Dusty	22	{Du} Do you know London well, Mr. Krumpacker?/{Kl} No we never been here
119 SP	Doris	26	the last time./{Do} You like London, Mr. Klipstein?/{Kr} Do we like London? do we
124 SA	Doris	3	a man once did a girl in —/{Do} Oh Mr. Sweeney, please don't talk,/I cut the cards
124 SA	Snow	10	woman runs a terrible risk./{Sn} Let Mr. Sweeney continue his story./I assure you,
124 SA	Snow	25	woman runs a terrible risk./{Sn} Let Mr. Sweeney continue his story./{S} This one
136 5FingerEx4		1	*Esqre.*/How delightful to meet Mr. Hodgson!/(Everyone wants to know *him*)/
136 5FingerEx4		8	from limb./How delightful to meet Mr. Hodgson!/Who is worshipped by all
136 5FingerEx4		13	tart./How delightful to meet Mr. Hodgson!/(Everyone wants to know *him*)./
136 5FingerEx4		18	rapture skim./How delightful to meet Mr. Hodgson!/(Everyone wants to know *him*)./
137 5FingerEx5		1	*Ali Beg*/How unpleasant to meet Mr. Eliot!/With his features of clerical cut,/And
137 5FingerEx5		8	and But./How unpleasant to meet Mr. Eliot!/With a bobtail cur/In a coat of fur/
137 5FingerEx5		13	hat:/How unpleasant to meet Mr. Eliot!/(Whether his mouth be open or
224 Mr Mistoff		t	*wasn't a single one left in the street.*/Mr. Mistoffelees/You ought to know Mr.
224 Mr Mistoff		1	/Mr. Mistoffelees/You ought to know Mr. Mistoffelees!/The Original Conjuring Cat
224 Mr Mistoff		15	have something to learn/From Mr. Mistoffelees' Conjuring Turn./Presto!/
224 Mr Mistoff		22	there ever/A Cat so clever/As Magical Mr. Mistoffelees!/He is quiet and small, he is
225 Mr Mistoff		41	there ever/A Cat so clever/As Magical Mr. Mistoffelees!/His manner is vague and
225 Mr Mistoff		60	/Know a Cat so clever/As Magical Mr. Mistoffelees!/Macavity: the Mystery Cat/
292 FR	Amy	21	here, and everything the same./Mr. Bevan — you remember — wants to call
322 FR	Winch	22	/Tell us your business./{Wi} It's about Mr. John./{H} John!/{Wi} Yes, my Lord, I'm
322 FR	Winch	31	he was here, and that you'd arrived./Mr. John's had a bit of an accident/On the West
322 FR	Winch	37	We've got him at the Arms —/Mr. John, I mean. By a bit of luck/Dr. Owen
326 FR	Denman	35	wouldn't give his name, Miss; but it's Mr. Arthur./{I} Arthur! Oh dear, I'm afraid *he's*
328 FR	Charles	17	to extricate his car from the collision, Mr. Piper reversed/into a shop-window. When
328 FR	Charles	18	a shop-window. When challenged, Mr. Piper said:/"I thought it was all open
328 FR	Charles	22	stated that at the time of the/accident Mr. Piper was being pursued by a patrol, and
346 FRDowning		6	{Do} Oh, excuse me, Miss, excuse me, Mr. Charles:/His Lordship sent me back
384 CP	Reilly	2	GUEST]/{UG} Good evening, Mr. Chamberlayne./{E} Well. May I offer you
399 CP	Nurse	24	That's all for the moment./{N} Mr. Gibbs is here, Sir Henry./{R} Ask him to
401 CP	Reilly	1	*from his papers*]./{R} Good morning, Mr. Chamberlayne./Please sit down. I won't
401 CP	Reilly	3	I won't keep you a moment./— Now, Mr. Chamberlayne?/{E} It came into my mind/
401 CP	Reilly	14	once./{R} No. If you please, sit down, Mr. Chamberlayne./You are not going away, so
402 CP	Reilly	1	If I had not brought your wife back, Mr. Chamberlayne,/Do you suppose that things
402 CP	Reilly	27	/{R} You are very impetuous, Mr. Chamberlayne./There are several kinds of
404 CP	Reilly	7	/{R} You must have patience with me, Mr. Chamberlayne:/I learn a good deal by
405 CP	Reilly	20	{R} It is just because you are not free, Mr. Chamberlayne,/That you have come to me.
405 CP	Reilly	30	trick./{R} Honesty before honour, Mr. Chamberlayne./Sit down, please, both of
406 CP	Reilly	30	not going there./{R} You are right, Mr. Chamberlayne./You are no case for my
408 CP	Reilly	15	Peter./{E} Peter? Peter who?/{R} Mr. Peter Quilpe/Was a frequent guest./{E}
409 CP	Reilly	9	well-suited to each other./Mr. Chamberlayne, when you thought your
410 CP	Reilly	35	is what he means./{R} When you find, Mr. Chamberlayne,/The best of a bad job is all
422 CP	Reilly	1	/{R} Miss Barraway, when Mr. Gibbs arrives .../Oh, very good. {}/[*To*
429 CP	Caterer	38	I'm freezing — in July!/{CM} Mr. Quilpe!/{E} Now who ... {}/[*Enter* PETER]/
432 CP	Lavinia	25	thank you./{L} May I introduce Mr. Peter Quilpe?/Sir Henry Harcourt-Reilly.
432 CP	Lavinia	29	other —/I don't know why I should. Mr. MacColgie Gibbs./{A} Indeed, yes, we have

435 CP	Reilly	16	/{R} You understand your *métier*, Mr. Quilpe —/Which is the most that any of us
445 CC	Eggers	10	situation —/Her first meeting with Mr. Simpkins./But I was glad of the excuse for
445 CC	Eggers	20	cheap, for nowadays./But where's Mr. Simpkins? Will he be here?/{SC} I had to
445 CC	Eggers	27	Sir Claude, you shouldn't say that!/Mr. Simpkins is far better qualified than I was/
446 CC	Eggers	39	birds seen in London:/And I'm sure Mr. Simpkins will find them if anybody./{SC}
447 CC	Claude	29	And as for Colby —/Say that Mr. Simpkins was highly recommended,/And
448 CC	Eggers	12	too deep for me. And I thought, Mr. Simpkins,/He's highly educated. He'll soon
448 CC	Eggers	17	soon do you propose to ... *explain* Mr. Simpkins?/Regularize his position in the
448 CC	Claude	24	that you have a young successor,/A Mr. Colby Simpkins./{E} Merely Mr. Simpkins.
448 CC	Eggers	25	/A Mr. Colby Simpkins./{E} Merely Mr. Simpkins./{SC} The reasons for starting
448 CC	Claude	30	The reason for meeting him as merely Mr. Simpkins,/Is, that she has a strong maternal
449 CC	Claude	7	/I've explained all this to Colby — Mr. Simpkins./{E} I see what you mean./{SC}
449 CC	Eggers	34	/Will you let her know, then, that Mr. Simpkins/Is actually your son?/{SC} That's
450 CC	Eggers	20	/That you're not sure you understand Mr. Simpkins, either?/{SC} A timely reminder.
450 CC	Colby	29	wanted, Sir Claude. Good afternoon,/Mr. Eggerson. I was afraid I'd miss you./{E} I'm
450 CC	Eggers	30	miss you./{E} I'm off in half an hour, Mr. Simpkins./{SC} I'll leave you now. But
451 CC	Eggers	2	her,/But that's rather alarming./{E} Mr. Kaghan is prejudiced./He's never hit it off
451 CC	Eggers	9	An encouraging example/For you, Mr. Simpkins. He'll be a power in the City!/And
451 CC	Eggers	13	has never taken to him./But you, Mr. Simpkins, that's very different./{C} I don't
451 CC	Eggers	17	apart from business./{E} Oh yes, Mr. Kaghan is very good company./He makes
452 CC	Eggers	4	here./It's lucky for Colby./{E} How so Mr. Kaghan?/{K} Because Lucasta's with me!
452 CC	Eggers	25	him, one or the other of you./{E} Mr. Simpkins, Miss Angel. As you know, Miss
452 CC	Eggers	26	Angel. As you know, Miss Angel,/Mr. Simpkins has taken over my duties./{L}
452 CC	Eggers	39	/{E} You mustn't give way to her, Mr. Simpkins./I never do. I always say/That if
453 CC	Lucasta	13	mustn't believe a word she says./{L} *Mr.* Simpkins is going to believe all I say,/*Mr.*
453 CC	Lucasta	14	Simpkins is going to believe all I say,/*Mr.* Eggerson. And I know he'll be nice to me/
453 CC	Eggers	39	/And that duty has *not* devolved on Mr. Simpkins:/Sir Claude intends to deal with
454 CC	Colby	17	to her. {}/[*Exit* KAGHAN]/{C} Egg ... Mr. Eggerson!/{E} Yes, Mr. Simpkins?/{C} You
454 CC	Eggers	18	/{C} Egg ... Mr. Eggerson!/{E} Yes, Mr. Simpkins?/{C} You seem to me sane. And I
455 CC	Eggers	20	But you needn't worry/About her, Mr. Simpkins. She'll marry Mr. Kaghan/In the
455 CC	Eggers	20	her, Mr. Simpkins. She'll marry Mr. Kaghan/In the end. He's a man who gets
455 CC	Eggers	30	Angel./{E} You'll get used to her, Mr. Simpkins./Time works wonders, that's what
455 CC	Eggers	35	so unusual as Miss Angel./{E} O yes, Mr. Simpkins, much more unusual./{C} Oh!/{E}
457 CC	Colby	7	/But there's one thing I do believe, Mr. Eggerson:/That *you* have a kind heart. And
458 CC	Claude	30	made it very imperative .../{SC} Mr. Simpkins had very strong recommendations
458 CC	Eggers	34	during your treatment .../{E} And Mr. Simpkins is much more highly qualified/
459 CC	Lady E	10	art of health./Where is your home, Mr. Colby?/{C} Simpkins./{E} Mr. Colby
459 CC	Eggers	12	home, Mr. Colby?/{C} Simpkins./{E} Mr. Colby Simpkins./{LE} I prefer Colby./
459 CC	Lady E	21	of colour/For our spiritual life, Mr. Colby./Neither, I regret to say, does
459 CC	Lady E	26	/Would be absolutely baneful to Mr. Colby./He needs a light mauve. I shall see
460 CC	Lady E	15	advice? About what?/{LE} To engage Mr. Colby. I really am distressed!/This is not
460 CC	Lady E	22	that young man?'/Well, that was Mr. Colby./{SC} Oh, I see./Yes, now I am
460 CC	Lady E	26	guidance./{LE} I must explain to you, Mr. Colby,/That I am to share you with my
460 CC	Claude	32	in the middle of some business with Mr. .../{LE} Colby! {}/[*Exit* LADY
461 CC	Eggers	3	shopping./But I'd better be off now. Mr. Simpkins —/If anything *should* turn up
461 CC	Eggers	22	{E} Good day, Sir Claude. Good day, Mr. Simpkins. {}/[*Exit* EGGERSON]/{SC} Well,
461 CC	Claude	23	Well, Colby! I've been calling you Mr. Simpkins/In public, till now, as a matter of
461 CC	Claude	26	as my wife insists upon your being Mr. Colby —/I shall begin to call you Colby
481 CC	Lady E	15	Oh, good evening./Good evening, Mr. Kaghan. Good evening, Lucasta./Have you
481 CC	Lady E	30	most delicious salads!/And I told you, Mr. Kaghan, you're the type of person/Who
481 CC	Lady E	37	That's right. Just mention my name, Mr. Kaghan,/And ask for the table in the left
482 CC	Lady E	10	you might become too friendly/With Mr. Kaghan and Miss Angel./I can see you've
486 CC	Lady E	22	*is* your aunt. Did Mrs. Guzzard/And Mr. Guzzard — have any children?/{C} They
497 CC	Eggers	32	know that./{E} A natural line for Mr. Simpkins to take,/If I may say so. Of
501 CC	Lady E	22	/And shall be happy to accept Mr. Kaghan as a son-in-law./{L} Thank you.
501 CC	Eggers	29	/And I'm sure she will be happy. Mr. Kaghan/Is one of the most promising
503 CC	Eggers	20	Miss Angel?/Why shouldn't you and Mr. Kaghan wait downstairs/And rejoin us
503 CC	Eggers	22	when this interview is over?/I'm sure Mr. Simpkins will concur in this proposal./{C}
505 CC	Claude	1	are to leave that to Eggerson./This is Mr. Eggerson, Mrs. Guzzard:/My confidential
505 CC	Guzzard	9	should I mind?/I have heard about Mr. Eggerson from Colby./I am very happy to
505 CC	Eggers	20	has to do, as you surmised, with Mr. Simpkins./It also concerns a problem of
505 CC	Eggers	27	/Heard your name mentioned, by Mr. Simpkins./She was struck by your name
509 CC	Lady E	38	—/I mean, not Barnabas. And Mr. Kaghan/Being Barnabas. I suppose I'll get
510 CC	Eggers	2	Lucasta?/{E} An excellent suggestion, Mr. Simpkins. {}/[*Exit* COLBY]/{E} And now, if
510 CC	Eggers	4	agree, Lady Elizabeth,/We can ask Mr. Kaghan about his parents;/And if Mr. and

510 CC Eggers   5   Kaghan about his parents;/And if Mr. and Mrs. Kaghan are still living/Mrs.
510 CC Lady E   7   them./{LE} And will that prove that Mr. Kaghan —/This Mr. Kaghan — is my son?
510 CC Lady E   8   that prove that Mr. Kaghan —/This Mr. Kaghan — is my son?/{E} It creates an
510 CC Claude   19 Mrs. Guzzard who revealed it./This is Mr. Barnabas Kaghan —/Mrs. Guzzard. And
510 CC Guzzard 22 Guzzard know my name?/{MG} Were Mr. and Mrs. Alfred Kaghan your parents?/{K}
510 CC Eggers   28 from your unjust suspicion./{E} Mr. Kaghan, are your adoptive parents living?/
510 CC Eggers   34 /Of this interesting discovery, Mr. Kaghan,/By putting your adoptive parents
512 CC Claude   12 my wife is perfectly convinced;/And Mr. Kaghan's ... mother, I am sure, will confirm
514 CC Guzzard 32 /{MG} I understand that, Mr. Eggerson. Quite well./{SC} I shall not
517 CC Eggers   21 Eggerson./{E} I wouldn't venture./Mr. Simpkins is a man who knows his own
517 CC Eggers   22 who knows his own mind./Is it true, Mr. Simpkins, that what you desire/Is to
517 CC Eggers   33 good organist!/{E} Don't say that, Mr. Simpkins, until you've tried our organ!/{C}
518 CC Eggers   2   —/As a temporary measure; because, Mr. Simpkins —/I hope you won't take this as
518 CC Eggers   8   and I've watched you pretty closely./Mr. Simpkins! You'll be thinking of reading for
518 CC Eggers   9   you'll still have your music. Why, Mr. Simpkins,/Joshua Park may be only a
518 CC Guzzard 23 E.;/Of that I can assure you./{MG} Mr. Eggerson,/I cannot see eye to eye with you,/
519 CC Eggers   9   —/All except Eggers .../{E} Me, Mr. Kaghan?/{K} We wanted Colby to be
532 ES Lambert 26 or two. {}/[*Enter* LAMBERT]/{L} Mr. Gomez, my Lord./{LC} Goodbye, Charles.
532 ES Ld Clav 31 *in* GOMEZ]/{LC} Good evening, Mr. ... Gomez. You're a friend of Mr.
532 ES Ld Clav 31 Mr. ... Gomez. You're a friend of Mr. Culverwell?/{G} We're as thick as thieves,
533 ES Gomez   4   took your wife's name/And became Mr. Richard Claverton-Ferry;/And finally,
550 ES Carghil 17 not sly and slippery./Then I married Mr. Carghill. Twenty years older/Than me, he
551 ES Carghil 29 'I advise you to accept','Because Mr. Ferry will be standing for Parliament:/His
573 ES Monica   28 your fiancé. Do introduce him./{M} Mr. Charles Hemington. Mrs. Carghill./{C}
573 ES Carghil 32 /{MC} And let me congratulate *you*, Mr. Hemington./You're a very lucky man, to
574 ES Carghil 1   him,/Oh so long ago. So you see, Mr. Hemington,/I've come to regard her as my
574 ES Carghil 3   much so, that it seems odd to call you Mr. Hemington:/I'm going to call you Charles!/
576 ES Gomez   34 Highly confidential .../{G} Be careful, Mr. Barrister./You ought to know something
577 ES Carghil 27 the conversation./My late husband, Mr. Carghill, was a business man —/I wish you
577 ES Carghil 30 ways —/So I understand business. Mr. Carghill told me so./Now, Michael has
580 ES Gomez   13 And good-bye Monica./Good-bye, Mr. ... Hemington./{M} Good-bye Michael. {}/

MRS. (166) [*Abbreviation*]
31 Apollinax   6   the lady in the swing./In the palace of Mrs. Phlaccus, at Professor Channing-Cheetah's
31 Apollinax   21   I might have challenged.'/Of dowager Mrs. Phlaccus, and Professor and Mrs. Cheetah
31 Apollinax   21   Mrs. Phlaccus, and Professor and Mrs. Cheetah/I remember a slice of lemon, and
39 Gerontion   67   weevil/Delay? De Bailhache, Fresca, Mrs. Cammel, whirled/Beyond the circuit of the
43 Swee Erect   39   /Might easily be misunderstood;/Mrs. Turner intimates/It does the house no sort
62 WL: Burial   57   in a ring./Thank you. If you see dear Mrs. Equitone,/Tell her I bring the horoscope
67 WL: Fire S   198 motors, which shall bring/Sweeney to Mrs. Porter in the spring./O the moon shone
67 WL: Fire S   199 spring./O the moon shone bright on Mrs. Porter/And on her daughter/They wash
117 SP Doris   14   /{Do} The Queen of Hearts! — Mrs. Porter!/{Du} Or it might be you/{Do} Or it
293 FR Violet   2   the waste that goes on in the kitchen./Mrs. Packell is too old to know what she is
352 CP m   3   CHAMBERLAYNE/JULIA (MRS. SHUTTLETHWAITE)/CELIA
358 CP Julia   24 on Friday?/No, I'm afraid my good Mrs. Batten/Would give me notice. And now I
401 CP Reilly   21 say that I had been invited;/And Mrs. Chamberlayne did not know that I was
405 CP Reilly   31 /Sit down, please, both of you. Mrs. Chamberlayne,/Your husband wishes to
406 CP Reilly   8   —/At least, for the moment. But, Mrs. Chamberlayne,/You have never visited my
407 CP Reilly   38 /{R} There was one, in fact. But you, Mrs. Chamberlayne,/Tried to make me believe
408 CP Reilly   39 all obtained from outside sources./Mrs. Chamberlayne, when you came to me two
409 CP Reilly   24 Edward./{R} So you say, Mrs. Chamberlayne./And now, let us turn to
412 CP Reilly   25 sit down?/I believe you are a friend of Mrs. Shuttlethwaite./{C} Yes, it was Julia ...
412 CP Celia   26 /{C} Yes, it was Julia ... Mrs. Shuttlethwaite/Who advised me to come
412 CP Reilly   31 know./I was there at the instance of Mrs. Shuttlethwaite./{C} That makes it even
426 CP Caterer 26 so early? I simply *can't* get up./{CM} Mrs. Shuttlethwaite!/{L} Oh, it's Julia! {}/[*Enter*
436 CP Reilly   26 A few dying natives./{R} Who knows, Mrs. Chamberlayne,/The difference that made
436 CP Reilly   34 was one of ... satisfaction!/{R} Mrs. Chamberlayne, I must be very transparent/
436 CP Reilly   40 Julia./Do you mind if I quote poetry, Mrs. Chamberlayne?/{L} Oh no, I should love
437 CP Reilly   17 death./If this strains your credulity, Mrs. Chamberlayne,/I ask you only to entertain
438 CP Reilly   5   shows some insight on your part, Mrs. Chamberlayne,/But such experience can
438 CP Reilly   31 others, we should all be condemned./Mrs. Chamberlayne, I often have to make a
444 CC m   8   ELIZABETH MULHAMMER/MRS. GUZZARD/Act One/*The Business*
445 CC Eggers   16 /And I matched some material for Mrs. E.,/Which she's been wanting. So *she*'ll be
451 CC Eggers   19 /Quite a humorist, he is. In fact, Mrs. E./Sometimes says to me: 'Eggerson, why
453 CC Lucasta 17 Colby./It's only that he's terrified of Mrs. Eggerson;/That's why he's never asked me
453 CC Eggers   19 me out to lunch./{E} We will leave Mrs. Eggerson out of this, Miss Angel./{L}

453 CC	Lucasta	21	always says, Colby,/When I mention	Mrs. Eggerson. He never fails to rise./B.! What
455 CC	Colby	26	encouraged her./{C} But you have	Mrs. Eggerson./{E} Yes, she's a great
455 CC	Eggers	28	my garden/To protect me against	Mrs. E. That's my joke./{C} Well, I've never
456 CC	Eggers	29	/I remember long ago, saying to	Mrs. E.,/When we'd bought our house in
461 CC	Eggers	8	any day, if you want me./In fact,	Mrs. E. said: 'I wish he'd ring us up!/I'm sure he
461 CC	Eggers	14	you often./{E} Oh, and I forgot ...	Mrs. E. keeps saying:/'Why don't you ask him
473 CC	Colby	35	marrows, or beetroot, or peas ... for	Mrs. Eggerson./{L} Are you laughing at me?/{C}
485 CC	Colby	36	married aunt./A widow. Her name is	Mrs. Guzzard./{LE} Guzzard? Did you say
486 CC	Lady E	12	that the only relative you knew/Was	Mrs. Guzzard. And you always called her
486 CC	Lady E	15	/{LE} And as for your mother —/Mrs.	Guzzard's sister, I suppose .../{C} Her
486 CC	Colby	16	...{C} Her sister — which makes	Mrs. Guzzard my aunt./{LE} And are you quite
486 CC	Lady E	17	/{LE} And are you quite sure that	Mrs. Guzzard's sister —/Who you say was your
486 CC	Lady E	21	/{LE} Not if she *is* your aunt. Did	Mrs. Guzzard/And Mr. Guzzard — have any
487 CC	Lady E	22	you think so?/{LE} I must see this	Mrs. Guzzard. I must confront her./This
487 CC	Lady E	36	/When the truth dawned on me.	Mrs. Guzzard!/Claude, Colby was brought up
487 CC	Lady E	37	/Claude, Colby was brought up by a	Mrs. Guzzard./{SC} I know that. But why
488 CC	Lady E	2	and the other name, *Teddington*:/Mrs.	Guzzard of Teddington. That was all I
488 CC	Lady E	4	in Africa,/And I had lost the name.	Mrs. Guzzard./{SC} I'm beginning now to piece
488 CC	Lady E	8	there was a faint echo —/And then	Mrs. Guzzard! It must be true./{SC} It is
488 CC	Lady E	16	you be so sceptical!/We must see this	Mrs. Guzzard, and get her to confess it./{SC}
488 CC	Claude	17	it./{SC} I'm sorry, Elizabeth. If	Mrs. Guzzard comes/To make her confession, it
489 CC	Claude	19	is your son?/{SC} Colby is the son of	Mrs. Guzzard's sister,/Who died when he was
489 CC	Claude	20	sister,/Who died when he was born.	Mrs. Guzzard brought him up,/And I provided
489 CC	Claude	22	/I have watched him grow. And	Mrs. Guzzard/Knows he is my son./{LE} But
489 CC	Lady E	30	that the sister had a child?/Perhaps	Mrs. Guzzard invented the story..../{SC} Why
489 CC	Lady E	36	the mother had forgotten the name of	Mrs. Guzzard,/And I was the mother and the
489 CC	Lady E	38	mother and the child was Colby;/And	Mrs. Guzzard thought you would be happy/To
492 CC	Claude	3	Then the first thing is: we must see	Mrs. Guzzard./{LE} Oh Claude! I am terribly
492 CC	Claude	10	Colby to you./But we must see	Mrs. Guzzard. I'll arrange to get her here./{LE}
493 CC	Claude	17	We don't want to start/By offending	Mrs. Guzzard. That's why I thought/That
494 CC	Lady E	10	to believe that he is yours!/So I hope	Mrs. Guzzard will say he is your son/And I
496 CC	Lady E	10	rituals./But it doesn't matter what	Mrs. Guzzard tells us,/If it satisfies Colby.
496 CC	Eggers	19	much nowadays to bring me;/But	Mrs. E. wishes I'd come up oftener!/Isn't that
496 CC	Lady E	34	always getting worse./{LE} — I hope	Mrs. Eggerson is well?/{E} Pretty well./She's
497 CC	Claude	4	/{SC} Eggerson, I'm expecting	Mrs. Guzzard./{E} Indeed! Mrs. Guzzard! And
497 CC	Eggers	5	expecting Mrs. Guzzard./{E} Indeed!	Mrs. Guzzard! And why are we expecting her?/
497 CC	Claude	7	/Is sure that she knows the name of	Mrs. Guzzard./{LE} Mrs. Guzzard, of
497 CC	Lady E	8	the name of Mrs. Guzzard./{LE}	Mrs. Guzzard, of Teddington./{E} Ah, indeed!/I
497 CC	Claude	12	he mentioned the name of his aunt,	Mrs. Guzzard./Now she's convinced that Mrs.
497 CC	Claude	13	Guzzard./Now she's convinced that	Mrs. Guzzard/Of Teddington is the name of the
497 CC	Claude	31	facts. And that is why/I have asked	Mrs. Guzzard here. *She* doesn't know that./{E}
497 CC	Eggers	34	Of course, we might discover/Another	Mrs. Guzzard .../{LE} *Two* Mrs. Guzzards?/{E}
497 CC	Lady E	35	/Another Mrs. Guzzard .../{LE} *Two*	Mrs. Guzzards?/{E} I agree, it is a most
498 CC	Lady E	4	/{LE} I don't know the address./Mrs.	Guzzard of Teddington, that's all I know,/I
498 CC	Eggers	7	unlikely/That there should be two	Mrs. Guzzards in Teddington./But assuming,
498 CC	Eggers	8	assuming, for the moment, only one	Mrs. Guzzard,/Could there not have been two
498 CC	Eggers	12	I was only suggesting/That perhaps	Mrs. Guzzard made a profession/Of ... looking
498 CC	Claude	30	*my* child!/The mother of *my* child was	Mrs. Guzzard's sister./She wouldn't dispose of
498 CC	Eggers	35	/Our first step must be to question	Mrs. Guzzard./{SC} And that's what we are
500 CC	Claude	9	this meeting today./We're awaiting	Mrs. Guzzard — Colby's aunt./{L} Colby's
501 CC	Eggers	35	wait downstairs/And come back after	Mrs. Guzzard has left?/{SC} That's not a bad
503 CC	Eggers	35	And now, how soon are we expecting	Mrs. Guzzard? {}/[*looking at his watch*]./{SC}
504 CC	Lucasta	6	door./I've just let someone in. It's the	Mrs. Guzzard/Whom you are expecting. She
504 CC	Eggers	14	/{E} Let me go down and explain to	Mrs. Guzzard/And then bring her up./{SC} No,
504 CC		m 24	*knock. Enter* KAGHAN, *escorting*	MRS. GUZZARD. *Exit* KAGHAN]/{SC}
504 CC	Claude	24	KAGHAN]/{SC} Good morning,	Mrs. Guzzard. I must apologise:/I'm afraid
504 CC	Lady E	32	Mulhammer./{LE} Good morning,	Mrs. Guzzard./You don't know me, but I know
505 CC	Claude	1	to Eggerson./This is Mr. Eggerson,	Mrs. Guzzard:/My confidential clerk. That is to
505 CC	Eggers	16	/{E} Yes, that is what I should call it,	Mrs. Guzzard./I take it, Sir Claude, I should
505 CC	Eggers	25	understand you./{E} It's this way,	Mrs. Guzzard./It is only recently that Lady
505 CC	Eggers	38	/That happens not infrequently,	Mrs. Guzzard./{MG} So I am aware. I have
506 CC	Eggers	14	a clue/Until the other day. This son,	Mrs. Guzzard,/If he is alive, must be a grown
506 CC	Eggers	30	name./{E} That is what impressed her.	Mrs. Guzzard/Of Teddington! Lady Elizabeth is
506 CC	Eggers	32	Elizabeth is convinced/That it was a	Mrs. Guzzard of Teddington/To whom her
506 CC	Eggers	40	are, they are equally uncommon./But,	Mrs. Guzzard, this is where you can help us —/

507 CC   Eggers   1   help us —/Do you know of any other Mrs. Guzzard?/{MG} None./{E} Whether, I
508 CC   Eggers   3   take this as a personal reflection,/Mrs. Guzzard. Far from it. You must make
508 CC   Eggers   16   from another angle,/And ask Mrs. Guzzard what became of the child/She
509 CC   Claude   21   is Barnabas./I must explain this, Mrs. Guzzard./I have a very promising young
510 CC   Eggers   5   about his parents;/And if Mr. and Mrs. Kaghan are still living/Mrs. Guzzard
510 CC   Eggers   6   Mr. and Mrs. Kaghan are still living/Mrs. Guzzard should be able to identify them./
510 CC   Claude   18   her, Sir Claude?/{SC} No, B. It was Mrs. Guzzard who revealed it./This is Mr.
510 CC   Claude   20   it./This is Mr. Barnabas Kaghan —/Mrs. Guzzard. And ... my daughter Lucasta./
510 CC   Kaghan   21   daughter Lucasta./{K} But how did Mrs. Guzzard know my name?/{MG} Were Mr.
510 CC   Guzzard 22   know my name?/{MG} Were Mr. and Mrs. Alfred Kaghan your parents?/{K} Yes.
510 CC   Eggers   36   your adoptive parents in touch/With Mrs. Guzzard. It's for them to confirm/That
510 CC   Eggers   37   /That they took you, as a child, from Mrs. Guzzard,/To whom, it seems, you had first
511 CC   Kaghan   19   always been accustomed/To regard Mrs. Kaghan as my mother./{LE} Then in order
512 CC   Lady E   6   me were wholly unfounded./{LE} Oh, Mrs. Guzzard, I had no suspicions!/I thought
512 CC   Claude   18   /{SC} That seems a strange question, Mrs. Guzzard./{MG} I have been asked here to
514 CC   Claude   17   your wish, and have no mother./{SC} Mrs. Guzzard, this is perfectly incredible!/You
514 CC   Eggers   20   *should* you have deceived me?/{E} Mrs. Guzzard, can you substantiate this
514 CC   Claude   26   believe it. I simply can't believe it./Mrs. Guzzard, you are inventing this fiction/In
514 CC   Eggers   29   /Not that we doubt your word, Mrs. Guzzard:/But in a matter of such extreme
518 CC   Colby   20   /{C} I'd be very glad indeed — if Mrs. Eggerson approved./{E} There'll be no one
518 CC   Eggers   21   /{E} There'll be no one so pleased as Mrs. E.;/Of that I can assure you./{MG} Mr.
519 CC   Claude   4   /{SC} What's that? Oh. Good-bye, Mrs. Guzzard. {}/[*Exit* MRS. GUZZARD]/{SC}
519 CC   m   4   Oh. Good-bye, Mrs. Guzzard. {}/[*Exit* MRS. GUZZARD]/{SC} What's happened?
523 ES   m   7   /FEDERICO GOMEZ/MRS. PIGGOTT/MRS. CARGHILL/
523 ES   m   8   GOMEZ/MRS. PIGGOTT/MRS. CARGHILL/MICHAEL
545 ES   m   22   and start reading to me. {}/[*Enter* MRS. PIGGOTT]/{MP} Good morning, Lord
546 ES   Piggott 16   So sorry. Miss Claverton-Ferry. I'm Mrs. Piggott./Just call me Mrs. Piggott. It's a
546 ES   Piggott 17   I'm Mrs. Piggott./Just call me Mrs. Piggott. It's a short and simple name/And
546 ES   Piggott 30   So you'll remember/Always to call me Mrs. Piggott, won't you?/{M} Yes, Mrs. Piggott,
546 ES   Monica   31   me Mrs. Piggott, won't you?/{M} Yes, Mrs. Piggott, but please tell me one thing./We
546 ES   Piggott 38   balanced:/For me to be simply 'Mrs. Piggott'/Reassures the guests in one
547 ES   Ld Clav 13   could be worse. Where there's a Mrs. Piggott/There may be, among the guests,
547 ES   Ld Clav 14   the guests, something worse than Mrs. Piggott./{M} Let's hope this was merely
547 ES   m   19   /She will leave us alone. {}/[*Re-enter* MRS. PIGGOTT]/{MP} I really *am* neglectful!/
547 ES   Monica   32   sport, in my opinion./{M} Thank you, Mrs. Piggott. But I'm very fond of walking/And
548 ES   2m   14   *his newspaper over his face./Enter* MRS. CARGHILL. *She sits in a deckchair*
550 ES   Carghill 10   /Your name now and here .../{MC} Is Mrs. John Carghill./{LC} You married, I
554 ES   Carghil   3   And read them to you./— Oh, there's Mrs. Piggott!/She's bearing down on us. Isn't
554 ES   Carghil   8   us alone tomorrow./Good morning, Mrs. Piggott!/Isn't it a glorious morning! {}/
554 ES   m   10   /Isn't it a glorious morning! {}/[*Enter* MRS. PIGGOTT]/{MP} Good morning, Mrs.
554 ES   Piggott 10   PIGGOTT]/{MP} Good morning, Mrs. Carghill!/{MC} Dear Mrs. Piggott!/It
554 ES   Carghil   11   morning, Mrs. Carghill!/{MC} Dear Mrs. Piggott!/It seems to me that you never sit
554 ES   Piggott 14   us./{MP} It's the breath of life to me, Mrs. Carghill,/Attending to my guests. I like to
554 ES   Carghil   16   me!/{MC} You do look after us well, Mrs. Piggott:/You're so considerate — and so
554 ES   Piggott 19   /The famous Lord Claverton. This is Mrs. Carghill./Two of our very nicest guests!/I
554 ES   Piggott 23   he needs *rest*! You're not going, Mrs. Carghill?/{MC} Oh, I knew that Lord
554 ES   Piggott 31   as usual, to Nurse)/When I saw that Mrs. Carghill had caught you./You wouldn't
555 ES   Monica   12   Now I must fly. {}/[*Exit*]/{M} I saw Mrs. Piggott bothering you again/So I hurried
562 ES   m   12   nature, really,/But ... {}/[*Enter* MRS. CARGHILL *with despatch-case*]/{MC}
562 ES   Carghil   26   /Topped the bill in revue. Now I'm Mrs. John Carghill./Richard! It's astonishing
563 ES   Ld Clav 23   introduce you — by that name —/To Mrs. ... Mrs. .../{MC} Mrs. John Carghill./{G}
563 ES   Ld Clav 23   you — by that name —/To Mrs. ... Mrs. .../{MC} Mrs. John Carghill./{G} We seem
563 ES   Carghil   24   name —/To Mrs. ... Mrs. .../{MC} Mrs. John Carghill./{G} We seem a bit weak on
563 ES   Gomez   31   was as beautiful to look at/As Mrs. Carghill, I can well understand/her!
565 ES   m   24   hold you to your promise! {}/[*Exeunt* MRS. CARGHILL *and* MICHAEL]/{G} Well,
567 ES   Monica   5   you telephoned this morning. That Mrs. Piggott/Should have heard my beloved's
571 ES   Ld Clav   1   star, Maisie Montjoy./There is Mrs. John Carghill, the wealthy widow./But
571 ES   Ld Clav   6   been very different/From Gomez, Mrs. Carghill and Lord Claverton./Freddy
572 ES   Charles 11   /Or why you were lonely./{C} And Mrs. Carghill:/What has she against you?/{LC}
573 ES   Ld Clav 20   they are conspiring against me./I see Mrs. Carghill coming./{M} Let us go./{LC} We
573 ES   m   23   stay here. Let her join us. {}/[*Enter* MRS. CARGHILL]/{MC} I've been hunting
573 ES   Monica   28   him./{M} Mr. Charles Hemington. Mrs. Carghill./{C} How do you do./{MC} What
573 ES   Charles 31   my name meets with your approval, Mrs. Carghill!/{MC} And let me congratulate
574 ES   Charles   5   call you Charles!/{C} As you please, Mrs. Carghill,/{LC} You said you had some
574 ES   Ld Clav 30   have discussed your problems/With Mrs. Carghill and then with Señor Gomez./{Mi}

576 ES	Monica	1	satisfied with what I know already, Mrs. Carghill,/About you./{MC} But I was very
576 ES	Gomez	36	about the law of slander./Here's Mrs. Carghill, a reliable witness./{C} I know
580 ES		m 25	I'll run and see them off. {}/[*Exit* MRS. CARGHILL]/{M} Oh Father, Father,

MUCH (200)

MUD (4)

49 Hippopot		2	/Rests on his belly in the mud;/Although he seems so firm to us/He is
164 Rock 9		22	the life of music,/Out of the slimy mud of words, out of the sleet and hail of verbal
172 FQ: BurntN		49	present./Garlic and sapphires in the mud/Clot the bedded axle-tree./The trilling wire
239 MC	Chorus	10	of death in a waste of water and mud,/The New Year waits, breathes, waits,

MUDCRACKED (1)

72 WL: Thund		345	faces sneer and snarl/From doors of mudcracked houses/If there were water/And no

MUDDLE (1)

215 RTTugger		34	nothing he enjoys like a horrible muddle./Yes the Rum Tum Tugger is a Curious

MUDDY (3)

22 Preludes		17	sawdust-trampled street/With all its muddy feet that press/To early coffee-stands./
27 Morning		7	/And tear from a passer-by with muddy skirts/An aimless smile that hovers in
239 MC	Chorus	12	/While the labourer kicks off a muddy boot and stretches his hand to the fire,/

MUG'S (1)

534 ES	Gomez	18	/Forgery, I can tell you, is a mug's game./I say that — with conviction./No,

MULHAMMER (7)

444 CC		m 2	CLERK/Characters/SIR CLAUDE MULHAMMER/EGGERSON/COLBY
444 CC		m 7	ANGEL/LADY ELIZABETH MULHAMMER/MRS. GUZZARD/Act One/
454 CC	Colby	27	/{C} But does she address Sir Claude Mulhammer/As Claude? To his face?/{E} She
458 CC		1m 5	{}/[*Enter* LADY ELIZABETH MULHAMMER]/[*simultaneously*]./{E} Lady
504 CC	Claude	31	you to my wife./Lady Elizabeth Mulhammer./{LE} Good morning, Mrs.
512 CC	Guzzard	28	yourself the son/Of Lady Elizabeth Mulhammer?/{K} It's very much better than
513 CC	Guzzard	6	/And the daughter of Sir Claude Mulhammer./{SC} That is *my* concern — that

MULHAMMER'S (3)

445 CC		2m 1	*on the first floor of* SIR CLAUDE MULHAMMER'S/*London house. Early*
457 CC		m 16	experience. {}/LADY ELIZABETH MULHAMMER'S *voice off.**/* *Lady*
457 CC		m 25	coming in! {}/LADY ELIZABETH MULHAMMER'S *voice off.**/{LE} No,

MULTIFOLIATE (1)

85 Hollow Men		64	eyes reappear/As the perpetual star/Multifoliate rose/Of death's twilight kingdom/

MULTIPLIED (1)

587 Fable		13	he/Had done before — their fortune multiplied,/As if they had been kept by a kind

MULTIPLY (2)

38 Gerontion		64	has cooled,/With pungent sauces, multiply variety/In a wilderness of mirrors.
429 CP	Alex	30	/{A} Meanwhile the monkeys multiply./{L} And the Christians?/{A} Ah, the

MULTITUDE (1)

260 MC	Thomas	12	night that has/just passed, that a multitude of the heavenly host appeared before

MULTITUDES (1)

45 Cook Egg		32	and crumpets/Weeping, weeping multitudes/Droop in a hundred A.B.C.'s./Le

MUMMY (1)

382 CP	Celia	11	/It withered, as if I had unwrapped a mummy./I listened to your voice, that had

MUNGOJERRIE (9)

218 Mung Rump		t	the Jellicle Moon and the Jellicle Ball./Mungojerrie and Rumpelteazer/Mungojerrie
218 Mung Rump		1	Ball./Mungojerrie and Rumpelteazer/Mungojerrie and Rumpelteazer were a very
218 Mung Rump		16	say: 'It's that horrible cat!/It was Mungojerrie — or Rumpelteazer!' — And most
218 Mung Rump		17	most of the time they left it at that./Mungojerrie and Rumpelteazer had a very
219 Mung Rump		29	say: 'It's that horrible cat!/It was Mungojerrie — or Rumpelteazer!' — And most
219 Mung Rump		30	most of the time they left it at that./Mungojerrie and Rumpelteazer had a wonderful
219 Mung Rump		33	person could take his oath/Was it Mungojerrie — or Rumpelteazer? or could you
219 Mung Rump		39	'Now which was which cat?/It was Mungojerrie! AND Rumpelteazer!' — And
227 Macavity		40	are widely known/(I might mention Mungojerrie, I might mention Griddlebone)/

MUNKUSTRAP (1)

209 NamingCats		18	I can give you a quorum,/Such as Munkustrap, Quaxo, or Coricopat,/Such as

MURAD (1)

136 5FingerEx5		t	/*Lines for Cuscuscaraway and Mirza Murad Ali Beg*/How unpleasant to meet Mr.

MURDER (8)

14 Prufrock		28	that you meet;/There will be time to murder and create,/And time for all the works
237 MC		t	/With the shadow in his mouth./MURDER IN THE CATHEDRAL/Characters
276 MC		m 18	KNIGHTS, *having completed the murder, advance to the front of the stage and*
314 FR	Harry	40	/It is really harder to believe in murder/Than to believe in cancer. Cancer is
315 FR	Harry	3	the dull pain, the occasional sickness:/Murder a reversal of sleep and waking./Murder
315 FR	Harry	4	a reversal of sleep and waking./Murder was there. Your ordinary murderer/

332 FR	Harry	39	/{H} In what way did he wish to murder her?/{Ag} Oh, a dozen foolish ways,
421 CP	Julia	8	from./Oh, of course, they might just murder each other!/But I don't think they will

MURDERED (2)

20 Portrait		75	goes upon the stage./A Greek was murdered at a Polish dance,/Another bank
429 CP	Edward	17	have any of the English residents been murdered?/{A} Yes, but they are not usually

MURDERER (4)

278 MC	Knight2	36	to bear the burden of/being called murderer. And at a later time still, even such
314 FR	Warburt	35	wouldn't believe it, ladies — was a murderer,/Who suffered from an incurable
315 FR	Harry	4	/Murder was there. Your ordinary murderer/Regards himself as an innocent
332 FR	Agatha	38	plots!/He was not suited to the role of murderer./{H} In what way did he wish to

MURDEROUS (1)

56 Swee Night		24	Rabinovitch/Tears at the grapes with murderous paws;/She and the lady in the cape/

MURIEL (2)

451 CC	Eggers	22	you know, he began addressing her as Muriel —/Within the first ten minutes! I was
451 CC	Eggers	24	horrified./But she actually liked it. Muriel *is* her name./He has a way with the

MURMUR (1)

73 WL: Thund		367	/What is that sound high in the air/Murmur of maternal lamentation/Who are

MURMURING (1)

188 FQ: DrySal		150	(though not to the ear,/The murmuring shell of time, and not in any

MUSCLE (1)

276 MC	Chorus	17	take the skin from the arm, take the muscle from the bone, and wash them. Wash

MUSCLES (1)

32 Hysteria		5	bruised by/the ripple of unseen muscles. An elderly waiter with trembling hands

MUSIC (43)

14 Prufrock		53	dying with a dying fall/Beneath the music from a farther room./So how should I
21 Portrait		122	have the advantage, after all?/This music is successful with a 'dying fall'/Now that
33 Conv Gal		9	we explain/The night and moonshine; music which we seize/To body forth our own
40 Burb Blei		5	were together, and he fell./Defunctive music under sea/Passed seaward with the
69 WL: Fire S		257	a record on the gramophone./'This music crept by me upon the waters'/And along
73 WL: Thund		378	hair out tight/And fiddled whisper music on those strings/And bats with baby faces
92 Ash-Wed 3		19	/Lilac and brown hair;/Distraction, music of the flute, stops and steps of the mind
164 Rock 9		21	/Out of the sea of sound the life of music,/Out of the slimy mud of words, out of
172 FQ: BurntN		29	called, in response to/The unheard music hidden in the shrubbery,/And the unseen
175 FQ: BurntN		140	of the turning world./Words move, music moves/Only in time; but that which is
175 FQ: BurntN		144	the form, the pattern,/Can words or music reach/The stillness, as a Chinese jar still/
177 FQ: ECoker		26	a summer midnight, you can hear the music/Of the weak pipe and the little drum/And
190 FQ: DrySal		214	winter lightning/Or the waterfall, or music heard so deeply/That it is not heard at all,
190 FQ: DrySal		215	it is not heard at all, but you are the music/While the music lasts. These are only
190 FQ: DrySal		216	all, but you are the music/While the music lasts. These are only hints and guesses,/
210 Old Gumbie		12	up on the matting,/She teaches them music, crocheting and tatting./I have a Gumbie
243 MC	Priest3	13	in the street,/And all the daughters of music shall be brought low./{C} Here is no
258 MC	Thomas	12	in sense, in learning and in thought,/Music and philosophy, curiosity,/The purple
329 FR	Chorus	22	laws/Unalterable, in the nature of music./There is nothing at all to be done about
371 CP	Peter	20	feel the same/When we heard certain music? Or looked at certain pictures?/There was
396 CP	Lavinia	4	suspected that you really hated music/And that the gramophone was only your
446 CC	Claude	10	what you told me./{SC} About his music./Yes, I think so. I understand his feelings.
447 CC	Eggers	38	overdo it!/{E} I'll remember that. Music./{SC} And by the way,/How much have
451 CC	Eggers	35	/{C} I'll be on my guard./{E} Your music will certainly be a great asset/With Lady
463 CC	Claude	8	/And then your absorption in your music .../{C} You started by asking me how I
464 CC	Claude	20	that/When you are alone with your music?/{C} Just the same./All the time you've
464 CC	Colby	23	I've been translating/Into terms of music. But may I ask,/With this passion for ...
465 CC	Colby	38	when I play to myself,/I hear the music I should like to have written,/As the
466 CC	Colby	3	/What I hear is a great musician's music,/What they hear is an inferior rendering./
469 CC	3m	1	*The concluding bars of a piece of music are/heard as the curtain rises.*/{L} *I* think
469 CC	Lucasta	3	know that. But I'd like to learn about music./I wish you would teach me how to
469 CC	Colby	7	All you need at first/Is to hear more music. And to find out what you like./When
469 CC	Lucasta	23	afraid I never really listened to the music:/I just enjoyed going — to see the other
470 CC	Lucasta	16	play to me again/And teach me about music?/{C} Yes, of course I will./But I'm sure
470 CC	Colby	18	I'm sure that when you learn about music —/And that won't take you long — and
472 CC	Lucasta	20	/Perhaps it's something that your music stands for./There's one thing I know.
473 CC	Lucasta	19	garden is a garden/Where you hear a music that no one else could hear,/And the
474 CC	Lucasta	24	Then the flowers would fade/And the music would stop. And the walls would be
474 CC	Lucasta	28	so secure, to me. Not only in your music —/That's just its expression. You don't
474 CC	Lucasta	33	I haven't got:/Something of which the music is a ... symbol./I really would like to
474 CC	Lucasta	34	/I really would like to understand music,/Not in order to be able to talk about it,/

474 CC Lucasta   37 You know, I'm a little jealous of your music!/When I see it as a means of contact with
518 CC Eggers   9 for orders./And you'll still have your music. Why, Mr. Simpkins,/Joshua Park may

MUSIC'S (1)
201 Def Island   1 /Let these memorials of built stone — music's/enduring instrument, of many centuries

MUSICAL (9)
136 5FingerEx4   3   wants to know *him*)/With his musical sound/And his Baskerville Hound/
447 CC Claude   36 forget/To let her know that he's very musical./She can take him to concerts. But
451 CC Eggers   30 of culture;/And besides, she's very musical./{C} Thank you for the warning!/{E} So
451 CC Eggers   38 at the carol service. But I wish I was musical./{C} I still don't feel very well prepared
458 CC Eggers   36 a confidential clerk./Besides, he's very musical./{LE} Musical?/Isn't this the young man
458 CC Lady E   37 clerk./Besides, he's very musical./{LE} Musical?/Isn't this the young man I interviewed/
470 CC Lucasta   24 you .../{L} To go to see that American Musical!/{C} Well, I'd heard you say you
516 CC Claude   29 /In the way of your fulfilling your musical ambitions —/Had you been able to
570 ES Ld Clav   38 /{LC} She no longer exists./Nor the musical comedy star, Maisie Montjoy./There is

MUSICALS (1)
470 CC Lucasta   30   you don't like them —/American Musicals. Do you think it's any compliment/To

MUSICIAN (6)
451 CC Eggers   33 shall mention at once/That you are a musician./{C} I'll be on my guard./{E} Your
470 CC Colby   8   /That I should never become a musician./{L} Did you find it a strain, then,
472 CC Lucasta   23 you found that you'd never be a good musician —/Of course, *I* don't know whether
472 CC Lucasta   26   perhaps you could be a very great musician:/But that's not the point. You'd
495 CC Claude   31 /Colby. But Colby is an artist./{SC} A musician./I am a disappointed craftsman,/And
514 CC Guzzard   12 /You are the son of a disappointed musician./{C} And who was my mother?/{MG}

MUSICIAN'S (1)
466 CC Colby   3 play to myself./What I hear is a great musician's music,/What they hear is an inferior

MUSING (1)
67 WL: Fire S   191   evening round behind the gashouse/Musing upon the king my brother's wreck/And

MUST (352)

MUSTARD (2)
116 SP Dusty   33 if I ring off now/She's got her feet in mustard and water/I said I'm giving her
116 SP Dusty   34   and water/I said I'm giving her mustard and water/All right, Monday you'll

MUSTN'T (23)
221 Old Deut   37 the back door,/For Old Deuteronomy mustn't be woken —/I'll have the police if
295 FR Charles   7 heavily, alone./{A} Harry!/{C} You mustn't indulge such dangerous fancies./It's
300 FRDowning   36   must have been all right then,/Mustn't she, Sir? or else he'd have known it./{C}
314 FR Warburt   21 of another malady./{W} You mustn't take such a pessimistic view/Which is
323 FR Winch   1 · /In the morning, most likely, but he mustn't be moved./But Dr. Owen was anxious
323 FR Warburt   13 but a slight concussion,/But he mustn't be moved tonight. I'd trust Owen/On a
346 FR Agatha   34 seems unaccountable/At times, you mustn't worry about that./He is every bit as
347 FR Agatha   12 will be all, thank you, Downing. We mustn't keep you;/His Lordship will be
376 CP Julia   30 /I forgot all about it./{J} But you mustn't touch it./{E} Of course I shan't touch it.
404 CP Edward   34   I shall need./But of course you mustn't tell her where I am./Is it far to go?/{R}
448 CC Eggers   7 you/Than he is with me./{E} Oh, you mustn't say that!/Though I've done my best to
449 CC Claude   17 happy to commend him./{SC} You mustn't overdo it! But your approval matters./
452 CC Eggers   39 afraid I didn't know that./{E} You mustn't give way to her, Mr. Simpkins./I never
453 CC Eggers   12 a sausage on a gas ring .../{E} You mustn't believe a word she says./{L} *Mr.*
467 CC Claude   23 myself for hurting you./{SC} You mustn't think of that./{C} I'm very grateful for
478 CC Colby   6 Even if I am a guttersnipe .../{C} You mustn't use such words! You don't know how
478 CC Colby   24 escape./Well, I'll be going./{C} You mustn't go yet!/There's something else that I
493 CC Claude   14 idea./{SC} On the other hand,/We mustn't look like a couple of barristers/Ready
526 ES Charles   34 which is always a reminder/That I mustn't stay too long, for you belong to him./
530 ES Ld Clav   12 life easily!/It's like telling a man he mustn't run for trains/When the last thing he
546 ES Piggott   9 /I was a theatre nurse. But you mustn't call me 'Matron'/At Badgley Court.
565 ES Monica   28 /{M} Father, those awful people. We mustn't stay here./I want you to escape from
571 ES Charles   22 {C} But all the same, these two people mustn't persecute you./We can't allow that.

MUTILATED (2)
257 MC Chorus   15   us./We have seen the young man mutilated,/The torn girl trembling by the
315 FR Chorus   35 the bedroom, the noise in the nursery, mutilated/The family album, rendered ludicrous

MUTTERED (3)
24 Rhapsody   15   sputtered,/The street-lamp muttered,/The street-lamp said, 'Regard that
24 Rhapsody   48 three,/The lamp sputtered,/The lamp muttered in the dark./The lamp hummed:/
135 5FingerEx2   5   shriek'd aloud,/Screamed, rattled, muttered endlessly./Little dog was safe and

MUTTERING (1)
13 Prufrock   5   certain half-deserted streets,/The muttering retreats/Of restless nights in one-night

MUTTON (1)
230 Bust Jones   28   *Tomb*/On cabbage, rice pudding and mutton./So, much in this way, passes
MUTUAL (3)
319 FR Warburt   16   happy together:/They separated by mutual consent/And he went to live abroad.
420 CP   Reilly   30   other./It's not the knowledge of the mutual treachery/But the knowledge that the
552 ES Ld Clav   21   in the only way possible/To our mutual satisfaction./{MC} Your conscience was
MUZZLE (1)
13 Prufrock   16   /The yellow smoke that rubs its muzzle on the window-panes,/Licked its tongue
MY (801)
MYLAE (1)
62 WL: Burial   70   who were with me in the ships at Mylae!/'That corpse you planted last year in
MYSELF (109)
21 Portrait   104   our feelings would relate/So closely! I myself can hardly understand./We must leave it
62 WL: Burial   58   /Tell her I bring the horoscope myself:/One must be so careful these days./
65 WL: Chess   140   I didn't mince my words, I said to her myself,HURRY UP PLEASE ITS TIME/Now
89 Ash-Wed 1   28   I may forget/These matters that with myself I too much discuss/Too much explain/
193 FQ: Little   102   not. I was still the same,/Knowing myself yet being someone other —/And he a
235 Ad-dress   40   */Don't speak till you are spoken to.*/Myself, I do not hold with that —/I say, you
252 MC Thomas   29   no more./But if I break, I must break myself alone. {}/[Enter FOURTH TEMPTER]/
276 MC Knight1   26   /principle of Trial by Jury. I am not myself qualified to/put our case to you. I am a
277 MC Knight3   9   a pretty stiff job; I'll only speak for/myself, but I had drunk a good deal — I am not
277 MC Knight3   10   a drinking man/ordinarily — to brace myself up for it. When you come to the/point, it
286 FR   Gerald 37   come across them very much now, myself;/But I must say I've met some very
297 FR   Amy   2   speaks to Dr. Warburton/It should be myself. What does Agatha think?/{Ag} It seems
297 FR   Amy   9   Very well./I will ring up the doctor myself. {}/[Exit]/{C} Meanwhile, I have an idea.
297 FR Charles 16   might have done the same thing once, myself./Nobody knows what he's likely to do/
298 FR   Ivy   6   do object./{I} And I wish to associate myself with my sister/In her objections —/{Ag} I
322 FR   Winch   12   not, my Lord./I didn't mean to put myself forward./But you see, my Lord, I had
323 FR   Amy   27   and report to you./{A} I must see for myself. Order the car at once./{W} I forbid it,
323 FR Warburt   32   for the consequences/I am going myself. I will come back and report to you./{A}
323 FR   Amy   33   and report to you./{A} I must see for myself. I do not believe you./{C} Much better
330 FR   Harry   28   /All this last year, I could not fit myself together:/When I was inside the old
331 FR   Harry   5   /I could associate nothing of it with myself,/Though nothing else was real. I thought
340 FR   Amy   16   nothing — but what I could breed for myself,/What I could plant here. Seven years I
340 FR   Amy   24   husband:/Then I let him go. I abased myself./Did I show any weakness, any self-pity?/
340 FR   Amy   26   any weakness, any self-pity?/I forced myself to the purposes of Wishwood;/I even
342 FR   Amy   7   /I have been always trying to make myself believe/That he was not such a weakling
343 FR   Mary   17   before it began;/But I deceived myself. It takes so many years/To learn that one
356 CP Edward   38   I really don't know. I may go away myself./{C} Go away yourself!/{J} Have you an
357 CP   Julia   23   these tough old women —/I'm one myself. I feel as if I knew/All about that aunt in
366 CP   Julia   24   besides, I like to manage the machine myself —/In a lift I can meditate. Good-bye
367 CP   Peter   9   on her mind./{P} It's about Celia. Myself and Celia./{E} Why, what could there be
368 CP Edward   11   No, I shan't want much, and I'll get it myself./{A} Ah, in that case I know what I'll do.
380 CP   Celia   2   — it's something I've done to myself./I am not sure even that you seem real
381 CP Edward   10   only since this morning/I have met myself as a middle-aged man/Beginning to
381 CP   Celia   22   shall only feel sorry for you./It's only myself I am in danger of loathing./But what will
385 CP Edward   27   meet them as strangers./{E} Then I myself must also be a stranger./{UG} And to
386 CP   Reilly   8   comes. The strangers./As for myself, I shall take the precaution/Of leaving by
387 CP   Celia   22   —/I only got here this moment myself —/That she telegraphed to Julia to come
390 CP   Julia   6   a marvellous recovery./I said so to myself, when I got your telegram./{L} But
393 CP Lavinia   8   was/That I lost all sense of humour myself./That's what came of always giving in to
395 CP Edward   33   me better than I understood myself./{L} And the most infuriating thing
396 CP Edward   34   I do not want you to explain me to myself./You're still trying to invent a
396 CP Edward   36   /Which will only keep me away from myself./{L} You're complicating what is in fact
402 CP Edward   18   breakdown./I didn't know it then myself — but if they saw it/I should have
402 CP Edward   26   to which you send such patients/As myself, under your personal observation?/{R}
404 CP Edward   18   you mean./{E} I can no longer act for myself./Coming to see you — that's the last
407 CP   Reilly   16   I have to say to you./I do not trouble myself with the common cheat,/Or with the
412 CP   Julia   3   know that, Henry. I brought her here myself./{R} Oh? You didn't let her know you
413 CP   Celia   8   I at least have no one to blame but myself./{R} And after that, the prologue to my
413 CP   Celia   23   it for granted that I needn't explain myself./{R} I know quite enough about you for
415 CP   Celia   26   of it./I don't worry much about form, myself —/But when everything's bad form, or
416 CP   Celia   4   someone, or something, outside of myself;/And I feel I must ... *atone* — is that the
421 CP   Reilly   36   I do not understand/What I myself am saying./{J} You must accept your
427 CP   Alex   16   to you./Never mind, I said — to myself, not to her —/Never mind: the

428 CP	Alex	22	extremely palatable:/I've cooked them myself .../{E} And did anybody eat them/When
432 CP	Lavinia	27	an old friend/Of my husband and myself. Oh, I forgot — {}/[*Turning to* ALEX]/
435 CP	Peter	7	about her,/Until I began to think myself a success/And got a little more
435 CP	Peter	19	believe in it/So that I might believe in myself./I thought I had ideas to make a
435 CP	Lavinia	40	/That in fact I've been talking about myself./{E} Lavinia is right. This is where you
436 CP	Peter	12	—/That I've only been interested in myself:/And that isn't good enough for Celia./
438 CP	Edward	18	in the wrong,/I should only speak for myself. I'm sure that *I* am./{R} Let me free your
438 CP	Lavinia	39	/{L} Yet I know I shall go on blaming myself/For being so unkind to her ... so spiteful.
446 CC	Claude	18	it,/Just as I did. I shall tell him about myself./But so far, I've left him to his own
456 CC	Eggers	10	Socialist./I'm a staunch Conservative, myself./{C} But is Lady Elizabeth very unusual/
463 CC	Colby	17	I don't mean the work:/I mean, about myself. As if I was becoming/A different person.
463 CC	Colby	23	that I like the other person/That I feel myself becoming — though he fascinates me./
465 CC	Colby	37	composers./Always, when I play to myself,/I hear the music I should like to have
466 CC	Colby	2	/Was not what I hear when I play to myself./What I hear is a great musician's music,
466 CC	Colby	6	/I am only happy when I play to myself./{SC} You shall play to yourself. And as
467 CC	Colby	22	hurting you and I know/That I hate myself for hurting you./{SC} You mustn't think
470 CC	Colby	11	I think I played better./I can't bring myself to play to other people,/And when I'm
470 CC	Colby	13	I'm alone I can't forget/That it's only myself to whom I'm playing./But with you, it
475 CC	Colby	23	/To me, you know, in which I find myself./But if you mean, wondered about your
475 CC	Colby	32	I'd gladly tell you everything about myself;/But you know most of what there is to
477 CC	Lucasta	26	in his cash account. I don't like myself./I don't like the person I've forced myself
477 CC	Lucasta	27	/I don't like the person I've forced myself to be;/And I liked you because you
477 CC	Lucasta	33	me/As I really am, I might become myself./{C} Oh Lucasta, I'm not shocked. Not
477 CC	Colby	35	by anything you think. It's to do with myself./{L} Yourself, indeed! Your precious self!
482 CC	Colby	29	you think, *is* my sort?/I don't know, myself. And I should like to know./{LE} In the
482 CC	Lady E	31	mix with people of breeding./I said to myself, when I first saw you,/'He is very well
484 CC	Lady E	22	such unpleasant people!/I thought of myself as a dove in an eagle's nest./They were so
485 CC	Lady E	11	it goes to show/How different I felt myself to be/And then I took up the Wisdom of
502 CC	Colby	28	you know me better than I know myself./But now that you know what I am .../
510 CC	Lady E	14	/{LE} And to my being able to adjust myself to it. {}/[*Re-enter* COLBY, *with*
514 CC	Eggers	28	wanted./{E} I'll examine the records myself, Sir Claude./Not that we doubt your
518 CC	Guzzard	25	see eye to eye with you,/Having been, myself, the wife of an organist;/But you too, I
524 ES	Charles	3	But if I'm not going to have you to myself/There's really no point in my staying to
530 ES	Ld Clav	16	me./If I had the energy to work myself to death/How gladly would I face death!
531 ES	Ld Clav	28	in the Lords./And I, who recognise myself as a ghost/Shan't want to be there.
532 ES	Ld Clav	13	this,/But I'll have to see this man by myself, Monica./I've never heard of this Señor
534 ES	Gomez	13	/As the society in which I find myself./I do nothing in England that you would
535 ES	Gomez	32	of behaviour,/To fabricate for myself another personality/And to take another
536 ES	Gomez	7	can't jump back again./I parted from myself by a sudden effort,/You, so slowly and
540 ES	Gomez	12	I know the value of the coinage/I pay myself in./{LC} Indeed! How interesting!/I still
543 ES	Gomez	6	an elixir/To see you again, and assure myself/That we can begin just where we left off.
545 ES	Ld Clav	2	enjoy it. Some dissatisfaction/With myself, I suspect, very deep within myself/Has
545 ES	Ld Clav	2	myself, I suspect, very deep within myself/Has impelled me all my life to find
545 ES	Ld Clav	4	so much to the world — first of all to myself./What is this self inside us, this silent
554 ES	Piggott	29	why I've brought your morning tipple myself/Instead of leaving it, as usual, to Nurse)/
560 ES	Michael	26	/{Mi} I'm not such a fool/As to get myself involved in a breach of promise suit/Or
562 ES	Carghil	23	not to introduce us,/I'll introduce myself. I'm Maisie Montjoy!/That means
565 ES	Ld Clav	31	/{LC} What I want to escape from/Is myself, is the past. But what a coward I am,/To
568 ES	Ld Clav	19	need to be told what I've seen for myself!/And if there is nothing that you conceal
568 ES	Ld Clav	37	/I've spent my life in trying to forget myself,/In trying to identify myself with the part
568 ES	Ld Clav	38	to forget myself,/In trying to identify myself with the part/I had chosen to play. And
569 ES	Ld Clav	38	beings,/Malicious, petty, and I see myself emerging/From my spectral existence
575 ES	Gomez	19	knows it already. I've told him myself./I thought he'd better learn the facts
581 ES	Ld Clav	18	/Because I wanted to perpetuate myself in him./Why did I want to keep you to
581 ES	Ld Clav	19	him./Why did I want to keep you to myself, Monica?/Because I wanted you to give
581 ES	Ld Clav	21	adoring/The man that I pretended to myself that I was,/So that I could believe in my

MYSTERIES (1)

260 MC	Thomas	20	so it is only in these our Christian/mysteries that we can rejoice and mourn at once

MYSTERIOUS (5)

49	Hippopot	23	at night he hunts;/God works in a mysterious way —/The Church can sleep and
389 CP	Lavinia	33	/{L} You are very kind, but very mysterious./I'm sure that we shall manage
390 CP	Julia	27	Dedham./{J} Well, it's all delightfully mysterious./{A} But what is the mystery?/{J}
427 CP	Julia	2	from somewhere —/One of his mysterious expeditions,/And we're going to get
582 ES	Charles	35	say!/We *were* alone together, in some mysterious fashion,/Even with Michael, and

MYSTERY (13)

166 Rock 10	9	for his hour to devour./But the Mystery of Iniquity is a pit too deep for mortal
205 de la Mare	33	web you wove —/The inexplicable mystery of sound./A Dedication to my Wife/To
226 Macavity	t	Mr. Mistoffelees!/Macavity: the Mystery Cat/Macavity's a Mystery Cat: he's
226 Macavity	1	the Mystery Cat/Macavity's a Mystery Cat: he's called the Hidden Paw —/For
229 Gus	53	what I hear tell,/That moment of mystery/When I made history/As
255 MC Tempt4	2	men shall declare that there was no mystery/About this man who played a certain
260 MC Thomas	6	in your hearts the/deep meaning and mystery of our masses of Christmas Day. For
332 FR Agatha	9	as your mother:/There is no mystery here./{H} What then?/{Ag} You see
362 CP Edward	16	it./Nobody likes to be left with a mystery:/It's so ... unfinished./{UG} Yes, it's
362 CP Reilly	19	/And nobody likes to be left with a mystery./But there's more to it than that.
365 CP Julia	33	the time?/There's altogether too much mystery/About this place to-day./{E} I'm very
365 CP Julia	37	/About my glasses. That's the greatest mystery./Peter! Why aren't you looking for
390 CP Alex	28	mysterious./{A} But what is the mystery?/{J} Alex, *don't* be inquisitive./Lavinia

MYTHS (1)

438 CP Reilly	7	experience can only be hinted at/In myths and images. To speak about it/We talk of

N' (1)

51 Restaurant	1	le Restaurant/Le garçon délabré qui	n'a rien à faire/Que de se gratter les doigts et se

NAGGED (1)

393 CP Edward	34	made you work at the Bar .../{E} You	nagged me because I didn't get enough work/

NAGGING (1)

513 CC Colby	16	All I wanted was relief/From the	nagging annoyance of knowing there's a fact/

NAILS (3)

63 WL: Burial	75	that's friend to men,/'Or with his	nails he'll dig it up again!/'You! hypocrite
280 MC Priest3	29	by the date-tree;/Or sit and bite your	nails in Aquitaine./In the small circle of pain
454 CC Kaghan	10	to be tough with her;/She's hard as	nails. Now I'll take her off your hands./I'll show

NAKED (2)

67 WL: Fire S	193	death before him./White bodies	naked on the low damp ground/And bones cast
421 CP Julia	4	/And now, when they are stripped	naked to their souls/And can choose, whether to

NAME (125)

119 SP Klip	34	it/(I'm afraid I didn't quite catch your	name —/But I'm very pleased to meet you all
196 FQ: Little	210	torment? Love./Love is the unfamiliar	Name/Behind the hands that wove/The
209 NamingCats	5	NAMES./First of all, there's the	name that the family use daily,/Such as Peter,
209 NamingCats	13	names./But I tell you, a cat needs a	name that's particular,/A name that's peculiar,
209 NamingCats	14	cat needs a name that's particular,/A	name that's peculiar, and more dignified,/Else
209 NamingCats	21	above and beyond there's still one	name left over,/And that is the name that you
209 NamingCats	22	one name left over,/And that is the	name that you never will guess;/The name that
209 NamingCats	23	name that you never will guess;/The	name that no human research can discover —/
209 NamingCats	28	of the thought, of the thought of his	name:/His ineffable effable/Effanineffable/Deep
209 NamingCats	31	/Deep and inscrutable singular	Name./The Old Gumbie Cat/I have a Gumbie
210 Old Gumbie	1	/I have a Gumbie Cat in mind, her	name is Jennyanydots;/Her coat is of the tabby
210 Old Gumbie	13	/I have a Gumbie Cat in mind, her	name is Jennyanydots;/Her equal would be hard
210 Old Gumbie	25	/I have a Gumbie Cat in mind, her	name is Jennyanydots;/The curtain-cord she
212 Growltiger	10	and Putney people shuddered at his	name./They would fortify the hen-house, lock
212 Growltiger	18	had been avowed;/To Cats of foreign	name and race no quarter was allowed./The
228 Gus	2	is the Cat at the Theatre Door./His	name, as I ought to have told you before,/Is
228 Gus	10	that he was in his prime;/Though his	name was quite famous, he says, in its time./
230 Bust Jones	10	James's the smartest of names is/The	name of this Brummell of Cats;/And we're all of
233 Skimble	34	have found your little den/With your	name written up on the door./And the berth is
235 Ad-dress	67	your aim,/And finally call him by his	NAME./So this is this, and that is that:/And
589 Fable	87	/But the church straightway put to his	name the handle/Of Saint, thereby rebuking all
594 Grad 12	6	from far and near/To spread thy	name o'er distant lands and seas!/As thou to thy
246 MC Thomas	12	of Salisbury,/Fearing for the King's	name, warning against treason,/Made them
252 MC Tempt4	38	you do not know me, I do not need a	name,/And, as you know me, that is why I
260 MC Thomas	3	*according to Saint Luke*. In the/	Name of the Father, and of the Son, and of the
262 MC Thomas	4	think of them at another time. In the	Name of the Father, and of the Son, and of the
269 MC Knight4	23	/Restrain this man, in the King's	name./{K1} Or answer with your bodies./{K2}
275 MC Thomas	10	/But none of my people, in God's	name,/Whether layman or clerk, shall you
326 FR Denman	35	want me?/{D} He wouldn't give his	name, Miss; but it's Mr. Arthur./{I} Arthur! Oh
359 CP Edward	31	sorry. I'm afraid I don't know your	name./{UG} I ought to be going./{E} Don't go
365 CP Julia	25	/{J} *You* don't know! And what's his	name?/Did I hear him say his name was Riley?/
365 CP Julia	26	his name?/Did I hear him say his	name was Riley?/{E} I don't know his name./{J}
365 CP Edward	27	name was Riley?/{E} I don't know his	name./{J} You don't know his *name*?/{E} I tell
365 CP Julia	28	his name./{J} You don't know his	*name*?/{E} I tell you I've no idea who he is/
369 CP Peter	30	/Because I thought of her merely as a	name/In a society column, to find her there
378 CP Edward	33	/By the man I call Riley — though his	name is not Riley;/It was just a name in a song
378 CP Edward	34	his name is not Riley;/It was just a	name in a song he sang .../{C} He sang you a
379 CP Celia	1	/Whom I have heard of — and his	name *is* Reilly!/{E} It would need someone
400 CP Reilly	18	her/That she was not to mention my	name to him./{A} With your usual foresight.
431 CP Peter	8	my boss. I thought everyone knew *his*	name./{J} Is he your connection in California,
451 CC Eggers	24	But she actually liked it. Muriel *is* her	name./He has a way with the ladies, you know./
452 CC Lucasta	35	what comes of being cursed with a	name like Angel./I'm thinking of changing it.
459 CC Lady E	4	than their faces./What did you say his	name was?/{SC} Colby Simpkins. { }/[*counting*
481 CC Lady E	37	/{LE} That's right. Just mention my	name, Mr. Kaghan,/And ask for the table in the
485 CC Lady E	33	/I have no doubt. What is your aunt's	name?/Is it Simpkins?/{C} No, a married aunt./
485 CC Colby	36	No, a married aunt./A widow. Her	name is Mrs. Guzzard./{LE} Guzzard? Did you
485 CC Lady E	37	Did you say Guzzard? An unusual	name./Guzzard, did you say? The name means
485 CC Lady E	38	name./Guzzard, did you say? The	name means something to me./Yes. Guzzard.
485 CC Lady E	39	to me./Yes. Guzzard. *That* is the	name I've been hunting for!/{C} You may have
486 CC Colby	1	/{C} You may have come across the	name before;/Although, as you say, it is an
486 CC Lady E	5	No. I never met ... your aunt./But the	name is familiar. How old are you, Colby?/{C}

487 CC	Lady E	18	a startling discovery!/All through a name — and intuition./But it shall be proved.
487 CC	Lady E	39	that make him your son?/{LE} It's the name I've been hunting for all these years —/
488 CC	Lady E	1	all these years —/That, and the other name, *Teddington:*/Mrs. Guzzard of
488 CC	Lady E	4	know, in Africa,/And I had lost the name. Mrs. Guzzard./{SC} I'm beginning now
488 CC	Claude	14	see him as your son,/And then — any name you heard would have seemed the right
489 CC	Lady E	35	died/And she'd never been told the name of the mother;/And the mother had
489 CC	Lady E	36	/And the mother had forgotten the name of Mrs. Guzzard,/And I was the mother
497 CC	Claude	7	Elizabeth/Is sure that she knows the name of Mrs. Guzzard./{LE} Mrs. Guzzard, of
497 CC	Eggers	10	indeed!/I shouldn't have expected her name to be known to you./{SC} She'd been
497 CC	Claude	12	about himself,/And he mentioned the name of his aunt, Mrs. Guzzard./Now she's
497 CC	Claude	14	Mrs. Guzzard/Of Teddington is the name of the person/To whom her own child was
497 CC	Eggers	36	/{E} I agree, it is a most uncommon name,/But stranger things have happened./{LE}
505 CC	Eggers	27	that Lady Elizabeth/Heard your name mentioned, by Mr. Simpkins./She was
505 CC	Eggers	28	Simpkins./She was struck by your name and your living in Teddington./And now
506 CC	Eggers	9	/Lady Elizabeth did not know the name of the lady/Who had taken the child. Or
506 CC	Eggers	27	I said, Lady Elizabeth learned your name;/And the name struck her as being
506 CC	Eggers	28	learned your name;/And the name struck her as being familiar./{MG}
506 CC	Guzzard	29	Indeed? It is not a very common name./{E} That is what impressed her. Mrs.
507 CC	Eggers	11	/{E} And did you know the name of the father/Or of the mother?/{MG} I
508 CC	Eggers	29	sight of them./{E} But you know their name?/{MG} Yes, I know their name:/Like
508 CC	Guzzard	30	their name?/{MG} Yes, I know their name:/Like mine, a somewhat unusual one./
508 CC	Guzzard	33	might be possible to trace them./The name was Kaghan./{SC} Their name was
508 CC	Claude	34	/The name was Kaghan./{SC} Their name was Kaghan!/{MG} K-A-G-H-A-N. An
508 CC	Guzzard	35	/{MG} K-A-G-H-A-N. An odd name./They were excellent people.
508 CC	Eggers	37	child, I suppose he had a Christian name?/{MG} There was nothing to show that
509 CC	Eggers	3	given conditional baptism./{E} What name did you give him?/{MG} We named the
509 CC	Lady E	5	Barnabas? There's never been such a name/In my family. Or, I'm sure, in his father's.
509 CC	Guzzard	10	it is?/{MG} My husband chose the name./We had been married in the church of St.
509 CC	Claude	24	who showed you upstairs —/Whose name is Barnabas Kaghan./{LE} Barnabas?/
509 CC	Claude	26	He sometimes has to sign his full name./But he doesn't like the name, for some
509 CC	Claude	27	his full name./But he doesn't like the name, for some reason;/So we call him B./{MG}
509 CC	Guzzard	29	/So we call him B./{MG} A very good name./He ought to be proud of it./{LE} How
510 CC	Lady E	16	for a surprise./{LE} Barnabas! Is your name Barnabas?/{K} Why, yes, it is. Did you
510 CC	Kaghan	21	But how did Mrs. Guzzard know my name?/{MG} Were Mr. and Mrs. Alfred
511 CC	Lucasta	30	/{L} Why is it that you don't like the name of Barnabas?/{K} I don't want people
532 ES	Ld Clav	35	/Why do you come back with another name?/{G} You've changed your name too,
533 ES	Gomez	1	name?/{G} You've changed your name too, since I knew you./When we were up
533 ES	Gomez	3	you married, you took your wife's name/And became Mr. Richard
533 ES	Gomez	8	their names;/And besides, my wife's name is a good deal more normal/In my
535 ES	Gomez	33	personality/And to take another name. Think what that means —/To take
535 ES	Gomez	34	what that means —/To take another name. {}/[*Gets up and helps himself to whisky*]/
536 ES	Gomez	2	than you do./You've changed your name twice — by easy stages,/And each step
536 ES	Gomez	5	person:/But where *I* changed my name, there was no social ladder./It was
541 ES	Gomez	20	/My investments — not all in my own name either —/Are pretty well spread. For the
543 ES	Ld Clav	11	him?/{LC} Yes. He'd changed his name./{M} Then I suppose he wanted money?/
546 ES	Piggott	17	Mrs. Piggott. It's a short and simple name/And easy to remember. But, as I was
549 ES	Carghil	39	/Please, Richard, just repeat my name — just once:/The name by which you
549 ES	Carghil	40	just repeat my name — just once:/The name by which you knew me. It would give me
550 ES	Carghil	1	such a thrill/To hear you speak my name once more./{LC} Your name was Maisie
550 ES	Ld Clav	2	my name once more./{LC} Your name was Maisie Batterson./{MC} Oh, Richard,
550 ES	Carghil	4	me./You know I meant my stage name. The name by which you knew me./{LC}
550 ES	Carghil	4	know I meant my stage name. The name by which you knew me./{LC} Well, then,
550 ES	Ld Clav	8	me./{LC} You've changed your name, no doubt. And I've changed mine./Your
550 ES	Ld Clav	9	doubt. And I've changed mine./Your name now and here .../{MC} Is Mrs. John
552 ES	Ld Clav	3	it was only a year or so/Before your name appeared in very large letters/In
554 ES	Piggott	32	caught you./You wouldn't know that name, but you might remember her/As Maisie
554 ES	Piggott	34	at one time. I'm afraid her name/Means nothing at all to the younger
557 ES	Michael	26	me good terms, on the strength of my name:/The only good the name has ever done
557 ES	Michael	27	of my name:/The only good the name has ever done me./{LC} On the strength of
557 ES	Ld Clav	28	me./{LC} On the strength of your name. And what do you call good terms?/{Mi}
558 ES	Michael	3	me into debt./Just because of your name they insist on giving credit./{LC} And
559 ES	Michael	21	country where no one has heard the name of Claverton;/Or where, if I took a
559 ES	Michael	22	/Or where, if I took a different name — and I might choose to —/No one
559 ES	Michael	23	/No one would know or care what my name had been./{LC} So you are ready to
559 ES	Michael	33	/That the thought of passing on your name and title/To a son, was gratifying. But it

562 ES Carghil 25   dears./It's a very long time since the name of Maisie Montjoy/Topped the bill in
563 ES Gomez 21   citizen of San Marco./That's my name./{LC} So let me introduce you — by that
563 ES Ld Clav 22   So let me introduce you — by that name —/To Mrs. ... Mrs. .../{MC} Mrs. John
563 ES Carghil 27   and I — I was known by my stage name./There was a time, once, when everyone in
563 ES Carghil 29   when everyone in London/Knew the name of Maisie Montjoy in revue./{G} If Maisie
573 ES Carghil 30   do you do./{MC} What a charming name!/{C} I'm glad my name meets with your
573 ES Charles 31   a charming name!/{C} I'm glad my name meets with your approval, Mrs. Carghill./
575 ES Ld Clav 16   be custodian of your morals;/His real name is Culverwell .../{G} My dear Dick,/
576 ES Ld Clav 23   Perhaps you intend to change your name to Gomez?/{G} Oh no, Dick, there are

NAMED (3)
378 CP Celia 35   /{C} He sang you a song about a man named Riley!/Really, Edward, I think you are
408 CP Reilly 13   tell him if you like./{R} A young man named Peter./{E} Peter? Peter who?/{R} Mr.
509 CC Guzzard 4   name did you give him?/{MG} We named the child Barnabas./{LE} Barnabas?

NAMES (19)
154 Rock 3 14   them,/Many desire to see their names in print,/Many read nothing but the race
209 NamingCats 4   cat must have THREE DIFFERENT NAMES./First of all, there's the name that the
209 NamingCats 8   —/All of them sensible everyday names./There are fancier names if you think
209 NamingCats 9   everyday names./There are fancier names if you think they sound sweeter,/Some
209 NamingCats 12   —/But all of them sensible everyday names./But I tell you, a cat needs a name that's
209 NamingCats 17   his whiskers, or cherish his pride?/Of names of this kind, I can give you a quorum,/
209 NamingCats 20   as Bombalurina, or else Jellylorum —/Names that never belong to more than one cat./
230 Bust Jones 9   whole of St. James's the smartest of names is/The name of this Brummell of Cats;/
234 Ad-dress 14   games,/And learnt about their proper names,/Their habits and their habitat:/But/*How*
235 Ad-dress 51   James —/But we've not got so far as names./Before a Cat will condescend/To treat
359 CP Edward 18   thought that Lavinia had told me the names/Of all the people she said she'd invited./
454 CC Colby 36   make my head spin — all those first names/The first time I met her. I'm not used to
506 CC Eggers 38   like Teddington/But not so many names that sound like Guzzard —/Or if there
533 ES Gomez 7   where *I* live, people do change their names;/And besides, my wife's name is a good
540 ES Gomez 31   who were with us (what were their names?/I've completely forgotten them) you
547 ES Piggott 29   *not* to play with. I'll mention no names,/But there are one or two who don't like
549 ES Carghil 9   of all my life!/Now whatever were the names of those friends of yours/And which one
549 ES Carghil 11   /I declare, I've utterly forgotten their names./And you gave us lunch — I've forgotten
576 ES Gomez 24   Dick, there are plenty of other good names./{M} Michael, Michael, you can't

NAMING (2)
209 NamingCats t   BOOK OF PRACTICAL CATS/The Naming of Cats/The Naming of Cats is a
209 NamingCats 1   CATS/The Naming of Cats/The Naming of Cats is a difficult matter,/It isn't just

NANCY (3)
30 Cous Nancy t   while her mistress lived./Cousin Nancy/Miss Nancy Ellicott/Strode across the
30 Cous Nancy 1   mistress lived./Cousin Nancy/Miss Nancy Ellicott/Strode across the hills and broke
30 Cous Nancy 7   hounds/Over the cow-pasture./Miss Nancy Ellicott smoked/And danced all the

NAPE (1)
42 Swee Erect 22   to shave/Broadbottomed, pink from nape to base,/Knows the female temperament/

NAPOLEON (1)
227 Macavity 42   /Just controls their operations: the Napoleon of Crime!/Gus: the Theatre Cat/Gus

NAPPING (1)
426 CP Julia 29   /I seem *literally* to have caught you napping!/I know I'm much too early; but the

NARCISSUS (1)
605 Narcissus t   thine and to thee./The Death of Saint Narcissus/Come under the shadow of this gray

NARROW (4)
15 Prufrock 70   I say, I have gone at dusk through narrow streets/And watched the smoke that
70 WL: Fire S 295   my knees/Supine on the floor of a narrow canoe.'/'My feet are at Moorgate, and
150 Rock 1 116   *shall not die in a shortened bed/And a narrow sheet. In this street/There is no beginning,*
581 ES Ld Clav 17   my children?/Why did I mark out a narrow path for Michael?/Because I wanted to

NARROWEST (1)
224 Mr Mistoff 26   the tiniest crack/He can walk on the narrowest rail./He can pick any card from a

NARROWING (1)
188 FQ: DrySal 143   will arrive at any terminus,/While the narrowing rails slide together behind you;/And

NASTY (2)
293 FR Gerald 33   most of my life/And some pretty nasty messes./{C} And there isn't much would
322 FR Winch 39   /Says there's nothing wrong but some nasty cuts/And a bad concussion; says he'll

NATION (3)
156 Rock 3 71   vacancy to fevered enthusiasm/For nation or race or what you call humanity;/
250 MC Tempt3 33   country./We are the backbone of the nation./We, not the plotting parasites/About
268 MC Knight3 12   in his absence, the business of the nation./{K1} These are the facts./Say therefore

NATIONS (1)
189 FQ: DrySal 201   especially/When there is distress of nations and perplexity/Whether on the shores of
NATIVE (1)
429 CP   Alex   11   Who have eaten monkeys./{A} The native is not, I fear, very logical./{J} I wondered
NATIVES (10)
344 FR   Gerald   22   sometimes very useful, knowing the natives,/Though occasionally troublesome. But
427 CP   Alex   38   /For general unrest amongst the natives./{E} But how do the monkeys create
428 CP   Alex   11   Unfortunately,/The majority of the natives are heathen:/They hold these monkeys
428 CP   Alex   26   {A} Oh yes, indeed./I invented for the natives several new recipes./But you see, what
428 CP   Alex   29   from the monkeys/The Christian natives prosper exceedingly:/And that creates
434 CP   Alex   8   in a Christian village;/And half the natives were dying of pestilence./They must
434 CP   Alex   13   of it, but would not leave the dying natives./Eventually, two of them escaped:/One
434 CP   Edward 27   just for a handful of plague-stricken natives/Who would have died anyway./{A} Yes,
436 CP   Lavinia   25   she would not leave/A few dying natives./{R} Who knows, Mrs. Chamberlayne,/
436 CP   Reilly   27   /The difference that made to the natives who were dying/Or the state of mind in
NATURAL (18)
127 Cor1 March   10   /Here they come. Is he coming?/The natural wakeful life of our Ego is a perceiving./
135 5FingerEx2   4   /In a black sky, from a green cloud/Natural forces shriek'd aloud,/Screamed,
205 de la Mare   31   /By conscious art practised with natural ease;/By the delicate, invisible web you
258 MC Thomas   7   right deed for the wrong reason./The natural vigour in the venial sin/Is the way in
296 FR   Gerald   35   old friend of the family, it's perfectly natural/That he should be asked. He looked
299 FRDowning   2   to be ... quite himself./{Do} Quite natural, if I may say so, Sir,/After what
299 FRDowning   31   that are *designed* for drinking:/It's natural for some and unnatural for others./{C}
346 FRDowning   30   going to happen,/And it seems quite natural, being his Lordship./And that's why I
361 CP   Reilly   4   I want my wife back./{UG} That's the natural reaction./It's embarrassing, and
497 CC   Eggers   32   here. *She* doesn't know that./{E} A natural line for Mr. Simpkins to take,/If I may
499 CC   Lucasta   34   Colby!/{L} Why not? That's perfectly natural./But I'm grateful to Colby. But for
535 ES   Gomez   2   me that already!/To see you, Dick. A natural desire!/For you're the only old friend I
551 ES   Carghil   12   was really in love with you!/Well, it's natural that you shouldn't want to believe it./
556 ES   Michael   35   If you always blame a person/It's natural he should end by getting into trouble./
560 ES   Ld Clav   30   I'm sure you don't mean that. But it's natural enough/To want a few years abroad. It
565 ES   Carghil   12   old friend of mine/That it seems most natural to call you Michael./You don't mind,
571 ES   Ld Clav   40   shown/That the old man had died a natural death/And had been run over after he
574 ES   Carghil   17   his own way in the world. That's very natural./So I thought, why not appeal to Señor
NATURALLY (5)
589 Fable   81   had vanisht swiftly up the chimney./Naturally every one searcht everywhere,/But
405 CP   Reilly   33   /And that is a question which naturally concerns you./{E} I am not going to
428 CP   Alex   19   tribes are Christian converts,/And, naturally, take a different view./They trap the
436 CP   Edward   7   /It's not so hard for you. You're naturally good./{P} I'm sorry. I don't believe
482 CC   Lady E   16   ever meet in their kind of society./So naturally, they want to take you up./I can speak
NATURE (14)
202 War Poetry   10   beyond control by experiment —/Of Nature and the Spirit. Mostly the individual/
212 Growltiger   21   /Now on a peaceful summer night, all nature seemed at play,/The tender moon was
271 MC Chorus   1   /United to the spiritual flesh of nature,/Mastered by the animal powers of spirit,
329 FR   Chorus   22   inflexible laws/Unalterable, in the nature of music./There is nothing at all to be
413 CP   Reilly   11   that they are mistaken/About the nature of their illness, and lead them to see/That
499 CC   Eggers   4   when I'm behind a desk:/It's second nature./{SC} And put the case to her./Don't let
534 ES   Ld Clav   7   of your business/Has been of such a nature that, if carried on in England,/It might
534 ES   Gomez   20   washing cheques, or anything of that nature,/Is certain to be found out sooner or
539 ES   Ld Clav   28   of the engrossing business/Of the nature of which dark hints have been given,/
560 ES   Ld Clav   18   investigation,/I am satisfied about the nature of the business./{Mi} Anyway, I'm
562 ES   Michael   10   of you —/I've a very affectionate nature, really,/But ... {}/[*Enter* MRS.
576 ES   Gomez   21   better to wait until we get there./The nature of business in San Marco/Is easier
576 ES   Charles   30   post on his staff —/{C} A post the nature of which is left very vague/{Mi} It's
577 ES   Charles   16   /Of a man you don't know, of the nature of whose business/You know nothing.
NAUGHTY (1)
306 FR   Mary   26   never to be happy was always to be naughty./But there were reasons: I was only a
NAUSICAA (1)
42 Swee Erect   10   /Morning stirs the feet and hands/(Nausicaa and Polypheme)./Gesture of
NAVIGABLE (1)
187 FQ: DrySal   123   day it is merely a monument,/In navigable weather it is always a seamark/To lay
NE (2)
24 Rhapsody   51   hummed:/'Regard the moon,/La lune ne garde aucune rancune,/She winks a feeble
51 Restaurant   7   croupe arrondie,/Je te prie, au moins, ne bave pas dans la soupe)./'Les saules trempés,

NE'ER (2)

587 Fable		12	added to their hoards — a deed which ne'er he/Had done before — their fortune
593 Grad 8		6	have gone,/Through all the years will ne'er have been forgot./For in the sanctuaries of

NEAR (23)

29 Aunt Helen		2	aunt,/And lived in a small house near a fashionable square/Cared for by servants
38 Gerontion		55	you upon this honestly./I that was near your heart was removed therefrom/To lose
57 Swee Night		35	apart,/The nightingales are singing near/The Convent of the Sacred Heart,,/And
159 Rock 6		4	/It is hard for those who live near a Bank/To doubt the security of their
159 Rock 6		6	money./It is hard for those who live near a Police Station/To believe in the triumph
193 FQ: Little		81	uncertain hour before the morning/Near the ending of interminable night/At the
587 Fable		25	the people./When Christmas time was near the Abbot vowed/They'd eat their meal
594 Grad 12		5	worthier sons be thine, from far and near/To spread thy name o'er distant lands and
271 MC Thomas		32	mine,/And I am not in danger: only near to death./{3P} My Lord, to vespers! You
273 MC Chorus		9	/Help me, Lord, for death is near. {}/[*In the cathedral.* THOMAS *and*
295 FR Harry		30	the marrow/And *they* are always near. Here, nearer than ever./They are near
300 FRDowning		33	him./While I took my turn about, for near half an hour/He stayed there alone,
307 FR Harry		2	we called the wilderness/{H} Down near the river. That was the stockade/From
308 FR Harry		31	here, indeed! where I have felt them near me,/Here and here and here — wherever I
325 FR Violet		37	so conspicuous, lolling back/And so near the street, and everyone staring;/And the
357 CP Julia		32	/{E} She lives in Essex./{J} Anywhere near Colchester? Lavinia loves oysters./{E} No.
434 CP Alex		25	she must have been crucified/Very near an ant-hill./{L} But Celia! ... Of all people
484 CC Lady E		2	when you were born./Have you other near relatives? Brothers or sisters?/{C} No
493 CC Claude		5	/I don't think you and I should be near together./Will you sit there, beside the
496 CC Eggers		37	this season,/When we're getting near the anniversary./{SC} The anniversary? Of
510 CC Kaghan		30	/So I found them a little place near Sevenoaks/Where they keep bees. But why
526 ES Charles		13	come/From very far away. Yet very near. You are changing me/And I am changing
529 ES Monica		1	were going'./But Badgley Court's so near your constituency!/You can come down at

NEARBY (2)

587 Fable		7	/Who levied on all travelers his tax;/Nearby this hamlet was a monastery/Inhabited
548 ES	2m	14	CARGHILL. *She sits in a deckchair nearby, composes/herself and takes out her*

NEARER (14)

84 Hollow Men		29	/Than a fading star./Let me be no nearer/In death's dream kingdom/Let me also
84 Hollow Men		36	/Behaving as the wind behaves/No nearer —/Not that final meeting/In the twilight
109 Marina		19	or lent? more distant than stars and nearer than the eye/Whispers and small laughter
147 Rock 1		11	Word./All our knowledge brings us nearer to our ignorance,/All our ignorance
147 Rock 1		12	/All our ignorance brings us nearer to death,/But nearness to death no
147 Rock 1		13	to death,/But nearness to death no nearer to GOD./Where is the Life we have lost
147 Rock 1		18	/Bring us farther from GOD and nearer to the Dust./I journeyed to London, to
589 Fable		86	not rare)/That the Abbot's course lay nearer underground;/But the church
291 FR Charles		2	Street, in a comfortable chair rather nearer the fire./{I} I might have been visiting
295 FR Harry		28	the last time./And also waking. She is nearer than ever./The contamination has
295 FR Harry		30	/And *they* are always near. Here, nearer than ever./They are very close here. I had
380 CP Edward		39	thing:/You should have a man ... nearer your own age./{C} I don't think I care for
427 CP Alex		33	about? Monkey nuts?/{A} That was a nearer guess than you think./No, not monkey
485 CC Lady E		23	from God./That means that we are nearer to God than to anyone./— Where did

NEAREST (1)

192 FQ: Little		39	in a desert or a city —/But this is the nearest, in place and time,/Now and in England.

NEARLY (13)

66 WL: Chess		160	she said./(She's had five already, and nearly died of young George.)/The chemist said
182 FQ: ECoker		202	the photograph album)./Love is most nearly itself/When here and now cease to
187 FQ: DrySal		111	this better/In the agony of others, nearly experienced,/Involving ourselves, than in
222 Pekes Pols		12	/Almost nothing had happened for nearly a week/(And that's a long time for a Pol
291 FR Charles		9	pass the window./What time is it?/{C} Nearly twenty to seven./{A} John should be here
292 FR Ivy		36	garden go to rack and ruin,/And he's nearly half blind. I've spoken to your mother/
298 FR Charles		35	to him, too./*We* haven't seen him for nearly eight years;/And to tell the truth, now
329 FR Chorus		25	to do about anything,/And now it is nearly time for the news/We must listen to the
450 CC Claude		7	although we worked together/For nearly thirty years./{E} Nearly thirty-one./But
450 CC Eggers		8	together/For nearly thirty years./{E} Nearly thirty-one./But now you put it so
455 CC Colby		4	know it!/{C} I shouldn't wonder./I nearly did, a moment ago./Then I'd have been
549 ES Carghil		17	to punt, and I got soaking wet/And nearly dropped the punt pole, and you all
557 ES Michael		32	And how long ago was that?/{Mi} Nearly two years./Time passes pretty quickly,

NEARNESS (1)

147 Rock 1		13	brings us nearer to death,/But nearness to death no nearer to GOD./Where is

NEAT (3)

43 Swee Erect	44	sal volatile/And a glass of brandy neat./A Cooking Egg/Pipit sate upright in her
233 Skimble	35	up on the door./And the berth is very neat with a newly folded sheet/And there's not a
307 FR Harry	16	gone,/The tree had been felled, and a neat summer-house/Had been erected, 'to please

NEATLY (1)

542 ES Gomez	26	welcomed my companionship./{G} Neatly argued, and almost convincing:/Don't

NECESSARY (10)

297 FR Agatha	3	does Agatha think?/{Ag} It seems a necessary move/In an unnecessary action,/Not
400 CP Reilly	8	days for the appointment./{R} It was necessary to delay his appointment/To lower his
402 CP Reilly	39	/And then go back as far as I find necessary./You see, your memories of childhood
418 CP Reilly	34	Neither way is better./Both ways are necessary. It is also necessary/To make a choice
418 CP Reilly	34	/Both ways are necessary. It is also necessary/To make a choice between them./{C}
432 CP Reilly	11	/Supposing that an introduction was necessary./{J} My dear Henry, you are
446 CC Claude	4	a young man, some readjustment is necessary./But I'm satisfied that he's getting the
479 CC Kaghan	31	at the start:/I saw that it was necessary. I'm afraid Colby/Has made a good
503 CC Lucasta	2	And accept the fact/That we're not necessary to each other/In the way we might
503 CC Lucasta	5	knows? —We might become more necessary to each other,/As a brother and a

NECESSARYE (1)

178 FQ: ECoker	32	sacrament./Two and two, necessarye coniunction,/Holding eche other by

NECESSITY (2)

278 MC Knight2	31	you/take issue. No one regrets the necessity for violence more than we/do.
557 ES Ld Clav	5	of blame:/Which will spare you the necessity of blaming someone else./Just tell me

NECK (1)

127 Cor1 March	30	in the hands, quiet over the horse's neck,/And the eyes watchful, waiting,

NECKS (2)

129 Cor2 State	38	/I a tired head among these heads/Necks strong to bear them/Noses strong to
269 MC Chorus	34	the lunatic bird. I have seen/Grey necks twisting, rat tails twining, in the thick

NECKTIE (1)

14 Prufrock	43	mounting firmly to the chin,/My necktie rich and modest, but asserted by a

NECROPHILY (1)

311 FR Harry	36	if person/You thought I was: let your necrophily/Feed upon that carcase. They will

NÉE (1)

56 Swee Night	23	and concentrates, withdraws;/Rachel *née* Rabinovitch/Tears at the grapes with

NEED (93)

38 Gerontion	57	/I have lost my passion: why should I need to keep it/Since what is kept must be
49 Hippopot	11	material ends,/While the True Church need never stir/To gather in its dividends./The
110 Marina	28	/The garboard strake leaks, the seams need caulking./This form, this face, this life/
147 Rock 1	23	told:/Let the vicars retire. Men do not need the Church/In the place where they work,
147 Rock 1	25	spend their Sundays./In the City, we need no bells/Let them waken the suburbs./I
159 Rock 6	9	the World/And that lions no longer need keepers?/Do you need to be told that
159 Rock 6	10	lions no longer need keepers?/Do you need to be told that whatever has been, can still
159 Rock 6	11	has been, can still be?/Do you need to be told that even such modest
159 Rock 6	23	of systems so perfect that no one will need to be good./But the man that is will
206 To my Wife	6	Who think the same thoughts without need of speech/And babble the same speech
206 To my Wife	7	/And babble the same speech without need of meaning./No peevish winter wind shall
211 Old Gumbie	31	/She thinks that the cockroaches just need employment/To prevent them from idle
212 Growltiger	7	/One ear was somewhat missing, no need to tell you why,/And he scowled upon a
215 RTTugger	36	a Curious Cat —/And there isn't any need for me to spout it:/For he will do/As he do
229 Gus	38	pat,/When one actor suggested the need for a cat./He once played a Tiger — could
234 Ad-dress	3	my opinion now is that/You should need no interpreter/To understand their
601 Nocturne	12	moon a frenzied eye profound,/(No need of 'Love forever?' — 'Love next week?')/
247 MC Tempt1	5	to gaiety,/Mirth and sportfulness need not walk warily./{T} You talk of seasons
249 MC Tempt2	29	Monarchs also,/Waging war abroad, need fast friends at home./Private policy is
252 MC Tempt4	38	As you do not know me, I do not need a name,/And, as you know me, that is why
265 MC Knight3	31	Go, tell the Archbishop/We have no need of his hospitality./We will find our own
266 MC Knight3	34	us to pray to God for you, in your need?/{K3} Yes, we'll pray for you!/{K1} Yes,
273 MC Chorus	3	/Who intercede for me, in my most need?/Dead upon the tree, my Saviour,/Let not
279 MC Knight4	37	that the doors/should be opened. Need I say more? I think, with these facts before
295 FR Charles	10	we read it in the papers —/No need to revert to it. Remember, my boy,/I
296 FR Agatha	5	do not understand/That you feel the need to declare what you do./There is more to
296 FR Gerald	38	him./He can talk to Harry, and Harry have no suspicion./I'd trust Warburton's
300 FR Charles	38	you, Downing,/I don't think we need you any more./{G} Oh, Downing,/Is there
304 FR Mary	20	she wanted to keep me. She didn't need me:/She would have done just as well with
308 FR Mary	28	can only do for yourself./What you need to alter is something inside you/Which you
313 FR Charles	21	you'll all be together, Harry;/They need the influence of their elder brother./

318 FR	Harry	30	this evening/I feel an overwhelming need for explanation —/But perhaps I only
331 FR	Harry	19	/What I want to know is something I need to know,/And only you can tell me. I
343 FR	Harry	35	son. And as for me,/I am the last you need to worry about;/I have my course to
344 FR	Violet	25	a lot of preparation./{V} And you need some religious qualification!/I think you
344 FR	Gerald	28	.../{G} And don't forget/That you'll need various inoculations —/That depends on
345 FR	Harry	9	Oh, yes, I'm taking Downing./You need not fear that I am in any danger/Of such
346 FR	Mary	15	as he requires me./{M} But he will need you. You must never leave him./{Do} You
346 FR	Downing	20	of feeling that his Lordship won't need me/Very long now. I can't give you any
377 CP	Julia	24	/And I thought, we are all in need of a stimulant/After this disaster. Now I'll
379 CP	Edward	2	and his name *is* Reilly!/{E} It would need someone greater than the greatest doctor/
397 CP	Edward	21	From *your* point of view? But I don't need a doctor./I am simply in hell. Where there
399 CP	Nurse	20	be shown into the small room;/And I need not let you know that she has arrived./
402 CP	Edward	8	of action:/If I were, I should not need to consult you/Or anyone else. I came here
404 CP	Edward	32	to go to a hotel,/And besides, I need more shirts — you can get my wife/To
404 CP	Edward	33	my things sent on: whatever I shall need./But of course you mustn't tell her where I
404 CP	Reilly	38	before I treat a patient like yourself/I need to know a great deal more about him,/
406 CP	Reilly	14	/For people who imagine that they need a respite/From everyday life. They return
406 CP	Reilly	18	sending them to one./The people who need my sort of sanatorium/Are not easily
412 CP	Reilly	30	know .../{R} There is nothing you need to know./I was there at the instance of
416 CP	Celia	9	perhaps I made it obvious. You don't need to know/About him, do you?/{R} No./{C}
419 CP	Celia	39	you at nine o'clock./{C} What do I need to take with me?/{R} Nothing./Everything
420 CP	Reilly	2	me?/{R} Nothing./Everything you need will be provided for you,/And you will
420 CP	Julia	22	one./{J} Very far, I think./You do not need to tell me. I knew from the beginning./{R}
424 CP	Lavinia	6	get in and out. Is there anything you need/That you can't find in the kitchen?/{CM}
425 CP	Lavinia	17	But you know, I don't think that you need worry:/They won't all come, out of those
426 CP	Edward	23	for not seeing people;/And you do need to rest now. {}/[*The doorbell rings*]/{L} Oh,
428 CP	Julia	2	are very destructive .../{J} You don't need to tell me that monkeys are destructive./I
469 CC	Colby	5	it./{C} I don't think that you'll need much teaching;/Not at this stage, anyway.
469 CC	Colby	6	/Not at this stage, anyway. All you need at first/Is to hear more music. And to find
474 CC	Lucasta	30	expression. You don't seem to me/To need anybody./{C} That's quite untrue./{L} But
479 CC	Lucasta	7	to have protection./{L} Colby doesn't need your protection racket/So far as I'm
479 CC	Kaghan	36	the colours./It's all a bit too dim. You need something brighter./But otherwise, it looks
480 CC	Lucasta	20	a good judge of character./{L} You'd need to be a better judge of character/Yourself,
481 CC	Kaghan	1	/But I hope you won't do that. We need you where you are./{C} I'm beginning to
482 CC	Lady E	33	nothing about you,/But one doesn't need to know, if one knows what breeding is./
482 CC	Lady E	34	what breeding is./And, second, you need intellectual society./Now, that already
483 CC	Lady E	2	often ill-bred. But that's not all./You need intellectual, well-bred people/Of
487 CC	Claude	14	It's much too good for me./{SC} You need a good piano. You'll play all the better./
500 CC	Lucasta	27	that he needs. Colby doesn't need me,/He doesn't need anyone. He's
500 CC	Lucasta	28	Colby doesn't need me,/He doesn't need anyone. He's fascinating,/But he's
503 CC	Colby	17	he'll be my brother-in-law./I shall need you, both of you, Lucasta!/{L} We'll mean
503 CC	Lucasta	18	mean something to you. But you don't *need* anybody./{E} And now may I interrupt, Miss
511 CC	Lucasta	2	emotion to register .../{L} You don't need to talk that language any longer:/Just say
514 CC	Eggers	31	importance/You'll understand the need for exact confirmation./{MG} I understand
522 ES	dedic	6	/*Who think the same thoughts without need of speech*/*And babble the same speech*
522 ES	dedic	7	/*And babble the same speech without need of meaning:*/*To you I dedicate this book*, *to*
526 ES	Charles	7	said so, you must say it again,/For I need so much assurance! Are you sure you're
534 ES	Ld Clav	16	to be thankful for./I trust you've no need to engage in forgery./{G} Forgery, Dick?
535 ES	Gomez	18	you come to the point where you need to trust someone/You must make it worth
535 ES	Ld Clav	24	/{LC} I should like to know why you need to trust *me*./{G} That's perfectly simple.
536 ES	Ld Clav	32	I'm waiting to hear/Why you should need to trust me./{G} Perfectly simple./My
536 ES	Gomez	39	*They* wouldn't want to see me./No, I need one old friend, a friend whom I can trust
537 ES	Gomez	2	as Gomez — Gomez as Culverwell./I need you, Dick, to give me reality!/{LC} But
541 ES	Ld Clav	12	What do you want then? Do you need money?/{G} My dear chap, you are obtuse!
545 ES	Piggott	30	you're happy?/Is there anything you need that hasn't been provided?/All you have to
554 ES	Piggott	15	to my guests. I like to feel they *need* me!/{MC} You do look after us well, Mrs.
557 ES	Michael	11	dull, nine-tenths of the time .../{Mi} I need something much more stimulating./{LC}
563 ES	Gomez	11	I persuaded my doctor/That I was in need of a rest cure too./And when I heard you'd
567 ES	Monica	9	how I've wanted you! And now I *need* you./{C} My darling, what I want is to know
567 ES	Charles	10	what I want is to know that you need me./On that last day in London, you
567 ES	Charles	13	words meant. You didn't seem to need me then./And you said we weren't engaged
568 ES	Ld Clav	19	in love with each other —/I don't need to be told what I've seen for myself!/And if

NEEDED (10)

235 Ad-dress	55	friend,/Some little token of esteem/Is needed, like a dish of cream;/And you might
279 MC	Knight4	21	/and justice that it so badly needed. From the moment he/became

330 FR   Agatha   14   the future;/But a present is missing, needed to connect them./You may be afraid
483 CC   Colby   13 desk. Sir Claude got it for me./I said I needed a desk in my room:/You see, I shall do a
495 CC   Lady E   11   but financial affairs;/And that you needed me chiefly as a hostess./It's a great
500 CC   Lucasta   31   —/At just the moment when you needed him most!/And he doesn't depend upon
518 CC   Guzzard   36   my leave, Sir Claude?/I'm no longer needed here. {}/[*Exit* COLBY]/{SC} Mind?
550 ES   Carghil   18   older/Than me, he was. Just what I needed./{LC} Is he still living?/{MC} He had a
551 ES   Ld Clav   10   lesson/And you learned yours, if you needed the lesson./{MC} You refuse to believe
557 ES   Michael   19 so well, for some reason./The fact is, I needed a good deal more capital/To make

NEEDFUL (1)
278 MC   Knight2   9   Our King saw that/the one thing needful was to restore order: to curb the

NEEDN'T (10)
117 SP   Dusty   31 /Just before a party too!/{Du} Well it needn't be yours, it may mean a friend./{Do}
320 FR   Warburt   10   will, that keeps her alive./I needn't go into technicalities/At the present
328 FR   Charles   27   more. 'The Piper family ...' no, we needn't read that./{V} This is just what I
355 CP   Julia   9   it./{J} My darling Celia,/You needn't be so sceptical. I stayed there once/At
413 CP   Celia   23 /I somehow took it for granted that I needn't explain myself./{R} I know quite enough
455 CC   Eggers   19 Though she's always in debt. But you needn't worry/About her, Mr. Simpkins. She'll
494 CC   Lady E   11 Guzzard will say he is your son/And I needn't believe her. I don't believe in facts./You
553 ES   Carghil   10   I'm still in love with you;/And you needn't think I idolise your memory./It's simply
560 ES   Michael   27 suit/Or somebody's divorce. No, you needn't worry/About that girl — or any other./
578 ES   Michael   33 but if we're fond of each other,/That needn't interfere with your life or mine./{M} Oh

NEEDS (22)
124 SA   Sweeney   14   might do a girl in/Any man has to, needs to, wants to/Once in a lifetime, do a girl
209 NamingCats   13   everyday names./But I tell you, a cat needs a name that's particular,/A name that's
250 MC   Tempt3   31 /And we who know what the country needs./It is our country. We care for the
277 MC   Knight1   31   disinterested. But/our act itself needs more justification than that; and you
286 FR   Charles   24 the young./All that a civilised person needs/Is a glass of dry sherry or two before
293 FR   Violet   3 to know what she is doing./It really needs a man in charge of things at Wishwood./
296 FR   Charles   28 his good fortune./I believe that all he needs is someone to talk to,/To get it off his
296 FR   Amy   32 /Among his own family, is all that he needs./{G} Nevertheless, Amy, there's
323 FR   Warburt   16 rest,/I've no doubt, will be all that he needs./{A} Accident? What sort of an accident?/
406 CP   Lavinia   6   /To which you sent me? Well, he needs it more than I did./{R} I am glad that you
406 CP   Edward   28   drove me mad./I am the one who needs a sanatorium —/But I'm not going there./
425 CP   Lavinia   4 /*Before* a party? And that's when one needs them./{E} Well, you deserve it. — We
435 CP   Lavinia   34 made for yourself, to meet your own needs./Peter, please don't think I'm being
445 CC   Eggers   13   tools./The number of things one needs for a garden!/And I thought, now's the
446 CC   Eggers   2   the time we worked together./All he needs is confidence./{SC} And experience./With
459 CC   Lady E   27 absolutely baneful to Mr. Colby./He needs a light mauve. I shall see about that./But
481 CC   Lady E   31   you're the type of person/Who needs to eat a great deal of salad./You
500 CC   Lucasta   27   to give him —/Something that he needs. Colby doesn't need me,/He doesn't need
500 CC   Lucasta   33 depend upon other people, either./B. needs me. He's been hurt by life, just as I have,/
527 ES   Monica   26 reading, or busy with his papers/He needs to have someone else in the room with
554 ES   Piggott   23 to tire himself with talking./What he needs is *rest*! You're not going, Mrs. Carghill?/
579 ES   Michael   9 /Señor Gomez will attend to my needs for that climate./And you see, he has

NEGATIVE (1)
161 Rock 7   22   and Sacrifice saved in spite of their negative being;/Bestial as always before, carnal,

NEGLECT (6)
148 Rock 1   65 .   of Good and Evil./Forgetful, you neglect your shrines and churches;/The men you
149 Rock 1   69 and enlightened mind./Second, you neglect and belittle the desert./The desert is not
152 Rock 2   28 /For sloth, for avarice, gluttony, neglect of the Word of GOD,/For pride, for
152 Rock 2   37 is time of prosperity/The people will neglect the Temple, and in time of adversity
226 Macavity   14 highly domed;/His coat is dusty from neglect, his whiskers are uncombed./He sways
334 FR   Harry   23 obligation, a duty/Only noticed by its neglect. One had that part to play./After such

NEGLECTFUL (1)
547 ES   Piggott   19   MRS. PIGGOTT]/{MP} I really *am* neglectful!/Miss Claverton-Ferry, I ought to tell

NEGLECTING (3)
290 FR   Agatha   30   /Upon each other's opacity/Neglecting all the admonitions/From the world
331 FR   Agatha   37 to his county neighbours,/But not neglecting public duties./He hid his strength
545 ES   Piggott   24 /I'm afraid you'll think I've been neglecting you;/So I've come to apologise and

NEGLIGIBLE (1)
552 ES   Carghil   33 as an elder statesman/Is practically negligible. And you look the part./Whatever

NEGROES (1)
187 FQ: DrySal   118 /Like the river with its cargo of dead negroes, cows and chicken coops,/The bitter

NEHEMIAH (2)

157	Rock 4	3	should not be built./In the days of Nehemiah the Prophet/There was no exception
158	Rock 5	4	to lose./Remembering the words of Nehemiah the Prophet: 'The trowel in hand,

NEIGHBOUR (4)

151	Rock 2	8	/And some say: 'How can we love our neighbour? For love must be made real in act,
152	Rock 2	45	no man knows or cares who is his neighbour/Unless his neighbour makes too
152	Rock 2	46	cares who is his neighbour/Unless his neighbour makes too much disturbance,/But all
276	MC Knight1	31	our eldest member to speak first, my neighbour in/the country: Baron William de

NEIGHBOUR'S (2)

155	Rock 3	51	/Or a house a little better than your neighbour's;/When the Stranger says: 'What is
203	Indians	4	sunset/And see his grandson, and his neighbour's grandson/Playing in the dust

NEIGHBOURHOOD (2)

547	ES Monica	33	told there are very good walks in this neighbourhood./{MP} There are indeed. I can
565	ES Carghil	10	/{MC} Are you staying in the neighbourhood, Michael?/Your father is such

NEIGHBOURING (2)

228	Gus	12	/(Which takes place at the back of the neighbouring pub)/He loves to regale them, if
428	CP Alex	38	/{A} They are citizens of a friendly neighbouring state/Which we have just

NEIGHBOURS (6)

223	Pekes Pols	48	trembled,/And some of the neighbours were so much afraid/That they
260	MC Thomas	29	kingdom of England at peace with its/neighbours, the barons at peace with the King,
330	FR Harry	10	Of horses, and right visits to the right neighbours/At the right times; and be an
331	FR Agatha	36	/Something of an oddity to his county neighbours,/But not neglecting public duties./
476	CC Lucasta	36	/And being turned out when the neighbours complained./Oh of course Claude
508	CC Guzzard	25	you dispose of him?/{MG} We had neighbours/Who were childless, and eager to

NEITHER (38)

37	Gerontion	3	to by a boy, waiting for rain./I was neither at the hot gates/Nor fought in the warm
38	Gerontion	44	the refusal propagates a fear. Think/Neither fear nor courage saves us. Unnatural
62	WL: Burial	39	not/Speak, and my eyes failed, I was neither/Living nor dead, and I knew nothing,/
72	WL: Thund	340	teeth that cannot spit/Here one can neither stand nor lie nor sit/There is not even
92	Ash-Wed 2	53	which ye/Shall divide by lot. And neither division nor unity/Matters. This is the
125	SA Sweeney	17	like he was alone/You're either or neither/I tell you again it don't apply/Death or
162	Rock 8	13	who were evil,/And most who were neither./Like all men in all places,/Some went
173	FQ: BurntN	64	At the still point of the turning world. Neither flesh nor fleshless;/Neither from nor
173	FQ: BurntN	65	world. Neither flesh nor fleshless;/Neither from nor towards; at the still point,
173	FQ: BurntN	66	the still point, there the dance is,/But neither arrest nor movement. And do not call it
173	FQ: BurntN	67	/Where past and future are gathered. Neither movement from nor towards,/Neither
173	FQ: BurntN	68	Neither movement from nor towards,/Neither ascent nor decline. Except for the point,
173	FQ: BurntN	95	before and time after/In a dim light: neither daylight/Investing form with lucid
174	FQ: BurntN	102	affection from the temporal./Neither plenitude nor vacancy. Only a flicker/
182	FQ: ECoker	190	/That seem unpropitious. But perhaps neither gain nor loss./For us, there is only the
191	FQ: Little	17	more sudden/Than that of summer, neither budding nor fading,/Not in the scheme
197	FQ: Little	221	place to support the others,/The word neither diffident nor ostentatious,/An easy
202	War Poetry	18	a life: it is a situation,/One which may neither be ignored nor accepted,/A problem to
202	War Poetry	22	is not a substitute for the transient,/Neither one for the other. But the abstract
203	Indians	20	action/None the less fruitful if neither you nor we/Know, until the judgment
245	MC Thomas	15	is suffering/And suffering is action. Neither does the agent suffer/Nor the patient
255	MC Thomas	34	out/Only by more sinful? Can I neither act nor suffer/Without perdition?/{T4}
255	MC Tempt4	38	is suffering,/And suffering action. Neither does the agent suffer/Nor the patient
261	MC Thomas	23	that would be simply to/rejoice: and neither our mourning nor our rejoicing is as the
313	FR Violet	26	Has Arthur or John come yet?/{V} Neither of them is here yet, Amy. {}/[*Enter*
332	FR Harry	33	have believed this./{H} I have known neither./{Ag} The autumn came too soon, not
341	FR Agatha	24	{Ag} Why should we quarrel for what neither can have?/If neither has ever had a
341	FR Agatha	25	quarrel for what neither can have?/If neither has ever had a husband or a son/We
410	CP Lavinia	29	what can we do/When we can go neither back nor forward? Edward!/What can
416	CP Celia	21	strangers/And that there had been neither giving nor taking/But that we had
418	CP Reilly	33	duty./{C} Which way is better?/{R} Neither way is better./Both ways are necessary.
459	CC Lady E	22	/For our spiritual life, Mr. Colby./Neither, I regret to say, does Eggerson./What
464	CC Claude	9	case, an inferior art./For me, they are neither 'use' nor 'decoration' —/That is,
470	CC Colby	14	I'm playing./But with you, it was neither solitude nor ... people./{L} I'm glad I'm
470	CC Lucasta	38	/That you wanted to be educated./{L} Neither did I./But I wanted you to want to
490	CC Colby	23	you —/But as friends ... older friends. Neither, as a parent./I am sorry. But that's why
491	CC Colby	23	you both in the place of parents/If neither of you could be. If it was pure fiction —
572	ES Ld Clav	3	a corpse that we had run over/So neither of us killed him. But *I* didn't stop./And

NEL (1)

75	WL: Thund	427	falling down falling down/*Poi s'ascose nel foco che gli affina*/*Quando fiam uti chelidon*

NELL (1)

228 Gus		29	have sat by the bedside of poor Little Nell;/When the Curfew was rung, then I swung

NERVES (5)

16 Prufrock		105	/But as if a magic lantern threw the nerves in patterns on a screen:/Would it have
65 WL:	Chess	111	then would be savagely still./'My nerves are bad to-night. Yes, bad. Stay with me.
316 FR	Violet	6	and that doctor, that gets on my nerves./{C} If the matter were left in my hands, I
555 ES	Monica	26	of that?/This shows how bad your nerves have been./He only ran into a tree./{LC}
578 ES	Michael	25	holidays/How it used to get on my nerves, when I saw you/Always sitting there

NERVOUS (10)

49 Hippopot		6	is weak and frail,/Susceptible to nervous shock;/While the True Church can
299 FRDowning		38	/But what struck me ... more nervous than usual;/I mean to say, you could
299 FRDowning		39	to say, you could see that he was nervous./He behaved as if he thought something
378 CP	Celia	37	—/I mean, you're on the edge of a nervous breakdown./Edward, if I go away now/
397 CP	Lavinia	14	/{L} I think you're on the edge of a nervous breakdown!/{E} Don't say that!/{L} I
402 CP	Edward	17	words —/That I was on the edge of a nervous breakdown./I didn't know it then
402 CP	Reilly	20	that a doctor could see it./{R} 'Nervous breakdown' is a term I never use:/It
407 CP	Reilly	40	/Precipitated what you called your nervous breakdown./{L} But it's true! I was
413 CP	Reilly	6	They are quite sure/They have had a nervous breakdown — that is what they call it
450 CC	Colby	34	have to leave just yet./I'm rather nervous about this meeting./You've told me

NEST (3)

158 Rock 5		6	barking: they say, 'This house is a nest of serpents, let us destroy it,/And have
254 MC Tempt4		31	lasts, but the wheel turns,/The nest is rifled, and the bird mourns;/That the
484 CC	Lady E	22	of myself as a dove in an eagle's nest./They were so carnivorous. Always killing

NET (1)

319 FR	Harry	22	heat,/The day I lost my butterfly net;/I remember the silence, and the hushed

NETHER (1)

350 FR	Agatha	4	/{Ag} But in the night time/And in the nether world/Where the meshes we have woven/

NETTLE (2)

155 Rock 3		33	burrow and the thorn revisit,/The nettle shall flourish on the gravel court,/And the
195 FQ: Little		158	between/The live and the dead nettle. This is the use of memory:/For liberation

NETTLED (1)

575 ES	Gomez	22	distorted version./But, Dick, I was nettled by that insinuation/About my not being

NEUTRAL (1)

343 FR	Agatha	8	meet again/In our wanderings in the neutral territory/Between two worlds./{M} Then

NEVER (309)

NEVERTHELESS (8)

62 WL: Burial		44	famous clairvoyante,/Had a bad cold, nevertheless/Is known to be the wisest woman
276 MC Knight1		23	I respect such feelings, I/share them. Nevertheless, I appeal to your sense of honour.
294 FR	Agatha	12	present. That is what matters./{Ag} Nevertheless, Harry, best tell us as you can:/
296 FR	Gerald	33	own family, is all that he needs./{G} Nevertheless, Amy, there's something in Violet's
307 FR	Mary	39	That is an experience/I have not had. Nevertheless, however real,/However cruel, it
345 FR	Amy	21	late to mend: and that is to be old./Nevertheless, I am glad if I can come to know
500 CC	Claude	39	I don't know what's happened, but nevertheless/I'm sure that you have made the
580 ES	Ld Clav	37	home to me. I fear for Michael;/Nevertheless, you are right to hope for

NEW (70)

30 Cous Nancy		4	hills and broke them —/The barren New England hills —/Riding to hounds/Over
38 Gerontion		48	tree./The tiger springs in the new year. Us he devours. Think at last/We have
70 WL: Fire S		298	the event/He wept. He promised "a new start."/I made no comment. What should I
94 Ash-Wed 4		16	sheathed about her, folded./The new years walk, restoring/Through a bright
94 Ash-Wed 4		18	of tears, the years, restoring/With a new verse the ancient rhyme. Redeem/The time.
110 Marina		32	awakened, lips parted, the hope, the new ships./What seas what shores what granite
111 Xmas Trees		14	Tree,/So that the surprises, delight in new possessions/(Each one with its peculiar and
138 New Hamp		t	mouth be open or shut)./Landscapes/New Hampshire/Children's voices in the
149 Rock 1		80	*In the vacant places/We will build with new bricks/There are hands and machines/And*
149 Rock 1		82	*are hands and machines/And clay for new brick/And lime for new mortar/Where the*
149 Rock 1		83	*/And clay for new brick/And lime for new mortar/Where the bricks are fallen/We will*
149 Rock 1		85	*the bricks are fallen/We will build with new stone/Where the beams are rotten/We will*
149 Rock 1		87	*beams are rotten/We will build with new timbers/Where the word is unspoken/We will*
149 Rock 1		89	*word is unspoken/We will build with new speech/There is work together/A Church for*
164 Rock 9		18	himself with stone,/Spring always new forms of life, from the soul of man that is
164 Rock 9		20	or lifeless/Joined with the artist's eye, new life, new form, new colour./Out of the sea
164 Rock 9		20	/Joined with the artist's eye, new life, new form, new colour./Out of the sea of sound
164 Rock 9		20	the artist's eye, new life, new form, new colour./Out of the sea of sound the life of
173 FQ: BurntN		77	/Without elimination, both a new world/And the old made explicit,
177 FQ: ECoker		5	a factory, or a by-pass./Old stone to new building, old timber to new fires,/Old fires

177 FQ: ECoker	5	stone to new building, old timber to new fires,/Old fires to ashes, and ashes to the
179 FQ: ECoker	86	and falsifies,/For the pattern is new in every moment/And every moment is a
179 FQ: ECoker	87	every moment/And every moment is a new and shocking/Valuation of all we have
182 FQ: ECoker	177	words, and every attempt/Is a wholly new start, and a different kind of failure/
182 FQ: ECoker	181	to say it. And so each venture/Is a new beginning, a raid on the inarticulate/With
197 FQ: Little	222	/An easy commerce of the old and the new,/The common word exact without
602 Humoresque	20	worse than gas —/'Now in New York' — and so it goes./Logic a
605 Narcissus	27	/Caught fast in the pink tips of his new beauty./Then he had been a young girl/
239 MC Chorus	11	in a waste of water and mud,/The New Year waits, breathes, waits, whispers in
239 MC Chorus	13	and stretches his hand to the fire,/The New Year waits, destiny waits for the coming./
247 MC Tempt1	8	worth forgetting./{T1} And of the new season./Spring has come in winter. Snow
252 MC Tempt3	8	forgotten./We expect the rise of a new constellation./{T} And if the Archbishop
253 MC Tempt4	35	armies,/War, plague, and revolution,/New conspiracies, broken pacts;/To be master
257 MC Chorus	23	some reason, some hope; but now a new terror has soiled us, which none can avert,
264 MC Priest3	17	of harps,/They sang as it were a new song./The blood of thy saints have they
267 MC Thomas	14	God bless him!/{T} Then let your new coat of loyalty be worn/Carefully, so it get
280 MC Priest1	38	/{P1} O my lord/The glory of whose new state is hidden from us,/Pray for us of your
288 FR Agatha	27	through the little door./He will find a new Wishwood. Adaptation is hard./{A}
288 FR Agatha	39	the nursery, round the corner/Of the new wing, he will have to face him —/And it
292 FR Gerald	30	you'll have to see about a couple of new hunters./{C} And I've a new wine merchant
292 FR Charles	31	couple of new hunters./{C} And I've a new wine merchant to recommend you;/Your
299 FR Charles	5	were with them on the voyage from New York —/We didn't learn very much about
310 FR Harry	11	season of sacrifice/And the wail of the new full tide/Returning the ghosts of the dead/
331 FR Harry	11	/A misery long forgotten, and a new torture,/The shadow of something behind
353 CP Celia	25	I've never heard it./{C} Here's one new listener for you, Julia;/And I don't believe
361 CP Reilly	29	/Is to invite the unexpected, release a new force,/Or let the genie out of the bottle./It
388 CP Peter	1	going to California!/{P} Yes, I have a new job./{E} And how did that happen,
406 CP Lavinia	36	Now I know of a hotel/In the New Forest .../{E} How like you, Lavinia./You
411 CP Lavinia	1	/{L} Edward, there *is* that hotel in the New Forest/If you want to go there. The
416 CP Celia	18	the persons we had been/But for the new person, *us.* If I could feel/As I did then,
421 CP Julia	6	costumes/Or huddle quickly into new disguises,/They have, for the first time,
428 CP Alex	26	/I invented for the natives several new recipes./But you see, what with eating the
430 CP Peter	5	did you arrive?/{P} I flew over from New York last night —/I left Los Angeles three
430 CP Lavinia	17	Julia!/{L} So you've just come from New York./{P} Yes, from New York./The
430 CP Peter	18	come from New York./{P} Yes, from New York./The Bologolomskys saw me off./
436 CP Edward	6	it's harder to recover, and make a new beginning./It's not so hard for you. You're
439 CP Reilly	7	and make them/Into something new. Only by acceptance/Of the past will you
445 CC Eggers	14	now's the moment to buy some new tools/So as not to lose a moment at the end
462 CC Claude	33	relationship/In adapting yourself to a new situation./{C} I'm very grateful to you, for
462 CC Colby	35	grateful to you, for that:/It is indeed a new and strange situation,/And nothing about it
467 CC Claude	32	we must simply wait to learn/What new conditions life will impose on us./Just when
467 CC Claude	34	settled our account/Life presents a new one, more difficult to pay./— I shall go
477 CC Lucasta	31	to be. That I know I am./That was new to me. I suppose I was flattered./And I
478 CC Kaghan	36	/{K} Enter B. Kaghan./To see the new flat. And here's Lucasta./I knew I should
479 CC Kaghan	13	in good time./I've come to inspect the new bachelor quarters,/And to wish Colby luck.
549 ES Ld Clav	35	you have just repeated./That is new to me. But I do remember you./{MC} Time
559 ES Ld Clav	12	/Or what about sheep farming in New Zealand?/{Mi} Sheep farming? Good Lord,
562 ES Carghil	37	But who's this coming?/It's another new guest here. He's waving to us./Do you
574 ES Carghil	16	Michael really wanted/For making a new start. He wants to go abroad!/And find his
583 ES Charles	1	{C} So that now we are conscious of a new person/Who is you and me together./Oh

NEW-BORN (1)

506 CC Eggers	33	Guzzard of Teddington/To whom her new-born child was confided./Of course she

NEWCOMER (1)

547 ES Monica	16	/Which she decants for every newcomer./Perhaps after what she considers

NEWEST (2)

201 Def Island	11	sea floor/and of those who, in man's newest form of gamble/with death, fight the
602 Humoresque	16	fashion since last spring's,/'The newest style, on Earth, I swear./'Why don't you

NEWLY (1)

233 Skimble	35	/And the berth is very neat with a newly folded sheet/And there's not a speck of

NEWS (19)

117 SP Dusty	13	the three. What's that mean?/{Du} 'News of an absent friend'. — Pereira!/{Do} The
213 Growltiger	53	there was joy in Wapping when the news flew through the land;/At Maidenhead
302 FR Ivy	12	or John come yet?/{I} There is no news of Arthur or John. {}/[*Enter* AMY *and*
310 FR Harry	34	/That does not matter. You bring me news/Of a door that opens at the end of a
319 FR Harry	29	I suppose, the day on which the news arrived./{W} You overinterpret./I am sure

329 FR   Chorus 25   /And now it is nearly time for the news/We must listen to the weather report/And
359 CP   Alex   4   Edward. I do hope/You'll have better news of Lavinia's aunt./{E} Oh ... yes ... thank
430 CP   Julia   27   any monkeys./{J} But give us your news;/Give us your news of the world, Peter./
430 CP   Julia   28   But give us your news;/Give us your news of the world, Peter./We lead such a quiet
433 CP   Julia   35   You had better tell them, Alex,/The news that you bring back from Kinkanja./{L}
453 CC   Lucasta 29   /{L} Yes, Eggy, will you break the sad news to Claude?/Meanwhile, you'll have to raid
496 CC   Eggers 25   she doesn't admit it. She misses my news/When I came home in the evening. And
496 CC   Eggers 39   death?/{E} Of the day we got the news. We don't often speak of it;/Yet I know
515 CC   Guzzard 6   /And I found that I had to break the news to you./You saw the child. You assumed
555 ES   Monica 15   Because I have some ... not very good news for you./{LC} Oh, indeed. What's the
573 ES   Carghil 24   you, Richard!/I've some very exciting news for you!/But I suspect ... Dare I? Yes, I'm
574 ES   Ld Clav 6   {LC} You said you had some exciting news for us./Would you care to impart it?/{MC}
580 ES   Carghil 17   it all over./But I've got a little piece of news of my own:/Next autumn, I'm going out
580 ES   Carghil 22   /Is that I shall be able to bring you news of Michael./And now that we've found

NEWSBOY (1)

301 FR   Chorus 17   the hidden shall be exposed, and the newsboy shall shout in the street?/When the

NEWSPAPER (6)

328 FR   m   7   {}/[*Re-enter* CHARLES, *with a newspaper*]/{C} Yes, there is a paragraph ... I'm
540 ES   Ld Clav 36   not sell your version to a Sunday newspaper?/{G} My dear Dick, what a
545 ES   Monica 21   coming from the house./Take your newspaper and start reading to me. {}/[*Enter*
548 ES   Monica 10   seems to be stalking you/Put your newspaper over your face/And pretend you're
548 ES   1m   14   LORD CLAVERTON *spreads his newspaper over his face.*/*Enter* MRS.
548 ES   m   19   made you choose it? {}/[*throwing down newspaper*]./{LC} My daughter chose it./She

NEWSPAPERS (4)

 22 Preludes   8   withered leaves about your feet/And newspapers from vacant lots;/The showers beat/
 23 Preludes   44   fingers stuffing pipes,/And evening newspapers, and eyes/Assured of certain
154 Rock 3   19   /To be filled with a litter of Sunday newspapers?/1ST MALE VOICE:/A Cry from
301 FR   Chorus 28   bondage./We like to appear in the newspapers/So long as we are in the right

NEXT (31)

 37 Gerontion   25   Limoges/Who walked all night in the next room;/By Hakagawa, bowing among the
117 SP   Doris   18   sure./It just depends on what comes next./You've got to *think* when you read the
117 SP   Dusty   22   a touch with the cards/What comes next?/{Do} What comes next. It's the six./{Du}
117 SP   Doris   23   /What comes next?/{Do} What comes next. It's the six./{Du} 'A quarrel. An
149 Rock 1   72   desert is squeezed in the tube-train next to you,/The desert is in the heart of your
194 FQ: Little 121   belong to last year's language/And next year's words await another voice./But, as
225 Mr Mistoff   36   and then it is *gawn*!/But you'll find it next week lying out on the lawn./And we all
235 Ad-dress   46   this form: O CAT!/But if he is the Cat next door,/Whom I have often met before/(He
588 Fable   51   difficulty kept from toppling over,/Next came a viand made of turtle eggs,/And
601 Nocturne   12   /(No need of 'Love forever?' — 'Love next week?')/While female readers all in tears
261 MC Thomas   10   /Birth and His Death: but on the next day we celebrate the martyrdom/of His
277 MC Knight1   32   must hear/our other speakers. I shall next call upon Hugh de Morville, who/has made
298 FRDowning   32   ten years .../{Do} Eleven years, Sir, next Lady Day./{C} Eleven years, and you know
315 FR Warburt   29   Lady Monchensey,/And I hope that next year will bring me the same honour. {}/
318 FR   Harry   12   more guilty, and so we misbehaved/Next day at school, in order to be punished,/
328 FR   Charles 16   and forbidden to drive a car for the/next twelve months./While trying to extricate
335 FR   Agatha 37   in the rose-garden./{Ag} This is the next moment. This is the beginning./We do not
345 FR   Amy   27   of the others/Just to help me to the next room. Where I can lie down./Then you can
358 CP   Julia   4   /{J} Oh, you know what I mean./The next election. And the secrets of your cases./{E}
366 CP   Julia   10   have found them but for you./The next time I lose *anything*, Edward,/I'll come
377 CP   Julia   31   /{E&C} Lavinia's aunt./{J} Now, the next question/Is, what's to be done. That's very
384 CP   2m   1   3/*The same room: late afternoon of the next day.* EDWARD *alone. He goes to*/*answer
411 CP Edward   7   go away!/I have a case coming on next Monday./{L} Then will you stop at your
412 CP   Julia   19   be as tired as that. I shall wait in the next room,/And come back when she's gone./
426 CP Edward   17   we get away soon?/{E} By the end of next week/I shall be quite free./{L} And we can
439 CP Edward   30   shan't be able to./{E} But on your next visit?/{P} The next time I come to England,
439 CP   Peter   31   /{E} But on your next visit?/{P} The next time I come to England, I promise you./I
471 CC   Colby   1   Well, I'm going to invite you to the next concert .../{L} The next that you want to
471 CC   Lucasta 2   you to the next concert .../{L} The next that you want to go *yourself*./{C} And
568 ES   Ld Clav 9   /Moments we regret in the very next moment,/Episodes we try to conceal from
580 ES   Carghil 18   got a little piece of news of my own:/Next autumn, I'm going out to Australia,/On

NICE (20)

 52 Whispers   17   the fever of the bone./Grishkin is nice: her Russian eye/Is underlined for
 66 WL: Chess   145   /You have them all out, Lil, and get a nice set,/He said, I swear, I can't bear to look at
115 SP   Doris   17   do./{Do} No it wouldn't do to be too nice to Pereira./{Du} Now Sam's a gentleman
115 SP   Dusty   21   Sam/{Du} *I* like Sam/Yes and Sam's a nice boy too./He's a funny fellow/{Do} He *is* a

121 SA Sweeney	13	/{S} I'll convert *you*!/Into a stew./A nice little, white little, missionary stew./{Do}
121 SA Sweeney	16	eat me!/{S} Yes I'd eat you!/In a nice little, white little, soft little, tender little,/
210 Old Gumbie	10	not good and their manners not nice;/So when she has got them lined up on the
233 Skimble	47	/You ought to reflect that it's very nice/To know that you won't be bothered by
287 FR Charles	15	her into the conversation./{C} She's a nice girl; but it's a difficult age for her./I
306 FR Mary	34	to be imposed upon us;/Even the nice things were laid out ready,/And the treats
355 CP Julia	26	old woman like me/Is a really nice tit-bit. I can drink at home. {}/[EDWARD
358 CP Julia	21	see. Have I got everything?/It's such a nice party, I hate to leave it./It's such a nice
358 CP Julia	22	party, I hate to leave it./It's such a nice party, I'd like to repeat it./Why don't you
359 CP Edward	6	... thank you. Good-bye, Alex,/It was nice of you to come. {}/[*Exeunt* ALEX *and*
366 CP Peter	37	/Of course it was really a very nice party/For everyone but me. And that
368 CP Alex	16	now/And I shall prepare you a nice little dinner/Which you can have alone.
388 CP Peter	15	ambitions./I shall miss you./{P} It's nice of you to say so;/But you'll find someone
453 CC Lucasta	14	/*Mr*. Eggerson. And I know he'll be nice to me/When you're out of the way. Why
558 ES Michael	35	she was the only one/Who was at all nice to me. She wasn't exciting,/But it served to
562 ES Carghil	14	a quiet read of your letters;/But how nice to find a little family party!/I know who

NICELY (2)

| 137 5FingerEx5 | 5 | so prim/And his conversation, so nicely/Restricted to What Precisely/And If and |
| 347 FR Warburt | 34 | I'm glad to say that John is getting on nicely;/It wasn't so serious as Winchell made |

NICEST (1)

| 554 ES Piggott | 20 | is Mrs. Carghill./Two of our very nicest guests!/I just came to see that Lord |

NIECE (1)

| 357 CP Edward | 10 | aunt?/{E} Her aunt's favourite niece. And she's rather difficult./When she's ill, |

NIGHT (90)

13 Prufrock	21	/And seeing that it was a soft October night,/Curled once about the house, and fell
20 Portrait	84	ideas right or wrong?/The October night comes down; returning as before/Except
23 Preludes	26	waited;/You dozed, and watched the night revealing/The thousand sordid images/Of
24 Rhapsody	t	in vacant lots./Rhapsody on a Windy Night/Twelve o'clock./Along the reaches of the
33 Conv Gal	9	nocturne, with which we explain/The night and moonshine; music which we seize/To
37 Gerontion	11	peeled in London./The goat coughs at night in the field overhead;/Rocks, moss,
37 Gerontion	25	hands, at Limoges/Who walked all night in the next room;/By Hakagawa, bowing
49 Hippopot	22	day/Is passed in sleep; at night he hunts;/God works in a mysterious way
61 WL: Burial	18	you feel free./I read, much of the night, and go south in the winter./What are the
66 WL: Chess	172	/Ta ta. Goonight. Goonight./Good night, ladies, good night, sweet ladies, good
66 WL: Chess	172	Goonight./Good night, ladies, good night, sweet ladies, good night, good night./The
66 WL: Chess	172	ladies, good night, sweet ladies, good night, good night./The Fire Sermon/The river's
66 WL: Chess	172	night, sweet ladies, good night, good night./The Fire Sermon/The river's tent is
68 WL: Fire S	226	last rays,/On the divan are piled (at night her bed)/Stockings, slippers, camisoles,
96 Ash-Wed 5	16	/Both in the day time and in the night time/The right time and the right place are
103 Journ Magi	17	/At the end we preferred to travel all night,/Sleeping in snatches,/With the voices
117 SP Doris	33	mine./I dreamt of weddings all last night./Yes it's mine. I know it's mine./Oh good
119 SP Krum	24	here before/{Kr} We hit this town last night for the first time/{Kl} And I certainly hope
123 SA Kl & Kr	25	/And the evening/And noontide/And night/Morning/Evening/Noontime/Night/{Do}
123 SA Kl & Kr	29	*And night/Morning/Evening/Noontime/Night/*{Do} That's not life, that's no life/Why I'd
125 SA Chorus	31	you're alone in the middle of the night and/you wake in a sweat and a hell of a
129 Cor2 State	46	of noon, in the silent croaking night./Come with the sweep of the little bat's
129 Cor2 State	49	thinly through the dust, through the night./O mother/What shall I cry?/We demand
166 Rock 10	2	it adorned/By one who came in the night, it is now dedicated to GOD./It is now a
167 Rock 10	37	tired: children who are up in the night and fall asleep as the rocket is fired; and
167 Rock 10	39	rhythm of blood and the day and the night and the seasons./And we must extinguish
191 FQ: Little	27	the end of the journey,/If you came at night like a broken king,/If you came by day
193 FQ: Little	81	/Near the ending of interminable night/At the recurrent end of the unending/
202 War Poetry	13	/In the effort to keep day and night together./It seems just possible that a
212 Growltiger	21	ear./Now on a peaceful summer night, all nature seemed at play,/The tender
217 Jellicles	31	are small;/If it happens to be a stormy night/They will practise a caper or two in the
232 Skimble	2	down the line at 11.39/When the Night Mail's ready to depart,/Saying 'Skimble
232 Skimble	8	for unless he's very nimble/Then the Night Mail just can't go.'/At 11.42 then the
233 Skimble	51	Railway Train!/In the watches of the night he is always fresh and bright;/Every now
256 MC Priests	26	not wait for the sea to subside, in the night/Abide the coming of day, when the
257 MC Chorus	3	/{C} A man may walk with a lamp at night, and yet be drowned in a ditch./{3P} A
260 MC Thomas	11	the whole world. It was in this same night that has/just passed, that a multitude of
263 MC Chorus	6	darker the day, shorter and colder the night./Still and stifling the air: but a wind is
265 MC Priest2	2	{P2} To-day, what is to-day? Another night, and another dawn./{P3} What day is the
265 MC Knight1	14	/Took ship yesterday, landed last night,/Having business with the Archbishop./
275 MC Chorus	26	ever return, to the soft quiet seasons?/Night stay with us, stop sun, hold season, let the

276 MC Chorus   3   and partly living;/The terror by night that ends in daily action,/The terror by
282 MC Chorus   8   blessing of God, the loneliness of the night of God, the surrender required,
285 FR Amy   8   sun and light unsought for/And the night unfeared and the day expected/And clocks
286 FR Violet   20   They bathe all day and they dance all night/In the absolute *minimum* of clothes./{C}
292 FR Harry   5   Sea,/In the sweet sickly tropical night, I knew they were coming./In Italy, from
294 FR Harry   2   the plumbers, that has its hour of the night; you do not know/The unspoken voice of
294 FR Harry   32   on the burning wheel/That cloudless night in the mid-Atlantic/When I pushed her
295 FR Harry   5   /And the doctor very attentive./That night I slept heavily, alone./{A} Harry!/{C} You
307 FR Harry   7   we were punished for being out at night/After being put to bed. But at least they
316 FR Agatha   20   eye of the day time/And the eye of the night time/Be diverted from this house/Till the
319 FR Harry   34   I did not./Yes, I see now. That night, when she kissed me,/I felt the trap close.
323 FR Warburt   31   out in this weather/At this time of night, I would not answer for the consequences/
325 FR Charles   10   sort of use in any of us going —/On a night like this — it's a good three miles;/There's
329 FR Chorus   11   in the kitchen/And the steps at night in the corridor/The moment of sudden
345 FR Gerald   6   we must accept it;/But it's a bad night, and you will have to be careful./You're
346 FR Downing   9   /Oh, there it is. Thank you. Good night, Miss; good night,/Miss Mary; good night,
346 FR Downing   9   Thank you. Good night, Miss; good night,/Miss Mary; good night, Sir./{M}
346 FR Downing   10   Miss; good night,/Miss Mary; good night, Sir./{M} Downing, will you promise never
347 FR Warburt   32   /{W} Well! it's a filthy night to be out in./That's why I've been so long,
350 FR Agatha   3   /Follow follow/{Ag} But in the night time/And in the nether world/Where the
361 CP Reilly   35   the morning, when you go to bed at night,/That you are beginning to enjoy your
372 CP Peter   35   /{P} Thank you, Edward. Good night./{E} Good night, Peter,/And good night,
372 CP Edward   36   you, Edward. Good night./{E} Good night, Peter,/And good night, Alex. Oh, and if
372 CP Edward   37   /{E} Good night, Peter,/And good night, Alex. Oh, and if you don't mind,/Please
375 CP Edward   23   tired. Thanks awfully, Alex./Good night./{C} What on earth was that about?/{E}
378 CP Julia   11   looking absolutely famished./Good night, Edward. {}/[*Exit* JULIA]/{C} Well, how
383 CP Celia   24   Give me the spectacles./Good night, Edward./{E} Good night ... Celia. {}/[*Exit*
383 CP Edward   25   /Good night, Edward./{E} Good night ... Celia. {}/[*Exit* CELIA]/{E} Oh! {}/[*He*
383 CP Edward   30   she's bringing them now ... Good night. {}/CURTAIN/Act One. Scene 3/*The*
430 CP Peter   5   /{P} I flew over from New York last night —/I left Los Angeles three days ago./I saw
430 CP Peter   21   /In the old days? We dined the other night/At the Saffron Monkey. That's the place
438 CP Reilly   14   and the fear of lions,/Cold of the night and heat of the day, than we should?/{E}
458 CC Lady E   24   it makes her sea-sick;/So we took the night train, and did the Channel crossing./But
463 CC Colby   26   walking in the street/Or waking in the night, then the former person,/The person I
481 CC Lady E   39   corner:/It has the best waitress. Good night./{L} Good night./{K} And thank you so
482 CC Lucasta   1   best waitress. Good night./{L} Good night./{K} And thank you so much. You give
486 CC Colby   37   Company./{C} That's tomorrow night, I believe./{SC} Yes it is./But you know
492 CC Colby   19   for the Potters' Company/Tomorrow night. I must get to work on it./{SC} Tomorrow
492 CC Claude   20   get to work on it./{SC} Tomorrow night. Must I go to that dinner/Tomorrow
492 CC Claude   21   Must I go to that dinner/Tomorrow night?/{C} I was looking at your notes —/Before
494 CC Lady E   1   over and over —/All through the night. I hardly slept at all./I wish that Colby,
540 ES Gomez   16   do you remember the moonlight night/We drove back to Oxford? *You*
540 ES Gomez   21   occasion I'm referring —/A summer night of moonlight and shadows —/The night
540 ES Gomez   22   of moonlight and shadows —/The night you ran over the old man in the road./
548 ES Carghil   24   you both in the dining-room last night./You are the great Lord Claverton, aren't
553 ES Carghil   19   what I do?/I read your letters every night./{LC} My letters!/{MC} Have you
556 ES Michael   15   from London?/{Mi} I drove down last night. I'm staying at a pub/About two miles
561 ES Ld Clav   5   the tropics/Or shiver in the northern night. Believe me, Michael:/Those who flee
571 ES Ld Clav   35   had two girls with us./It was late at night. A secondary road./I ran over an old man

NIGHT-FIRES (1)
103 Journ Magi   13   their liquor and women,/And the night-fires going out, and the lack of shelters,/
NIGHT-TIME (2)
269 MC Chorus   29   I have heard/Fluting in the night-time, fluting and owls, have seen at noon/
276 MC Chorus   6   the hand on the broom,/The night-time heaping of the ashes,/The fuel laid on
NIGHTFALL (7)
74 WL: Thund   415   key, each confirms a prison/Only at nightfall, aethereal rumours/Revive for a
158 Rock 5   10   the day would return to his hearth at nightfall: to be blessed with the gift of silence,
188 FQ: DrySal 148   /Or 'the future is before us'./At nightfall, in the rigging and the aerial,/Is a voice
195 FQ: Little 177   divided them;/If I think of a king at nightfall,/Of three men, and more, on the
246 MC Templ1   39   floating on the water,/Singing at nightfall, whispering in chambers,/Fires
257 MC Chorus   20   the pieces,/Gathering faggots at nightfall,/Building a partial shelter,/For
269 MC Chorus   32   I have felt/The heaving of earth at nightfall, restless, absurd. I have heard/
NIGHTINGALE (1)
64 WL: Chess   100   king/So rudely forced; yet there the nightingale/Filled all the desert with inviolable

NIGHTINGALE'S (1)
292 FR   Harry   6   coming./In Italy, from behind the nightingale's thicket,/The eyes stared at me, and
NIGHTINGALES (2)
56 Swee Night   t   polymath./Sweeney Among the Nightingales/Apeneck Sweeney spreads his
57 Swee Night   35   /Converses at the door apart,/The nightingales are singing near/The Convent of
NIGHTLY (1)
308 FR   Harry   35   of earshot —/And inside too, in the nightly panic/Of dreaming dissolution. You do
NIGHTMARE (3)
125 SA   Chorus   35   in the head/You've had a cream of a nightmare dream and/you've got the hoo-ha's
291 FR   Chorus   6   monstrous farce, ridiculous in some nightmare pantomime./{A} What's that? I
293 FR   Harry   39   life in sleep,/Never woken to the nightmare. I tell you, life would be unendurable
NIGHTS (4)
13 Prufrock   6   /The muttering retreats/Of restless nights in one-night cheap hotels/And sawdust
67 WL: Fire S   179   ends/Or other testimony of summer nights. The nymphs are departed./And their
152 Rock 2   42   alone,/For whom the days and nights repeat the praise of GOD,/Prays for the
343 FR   Amy   27   nourish investments/With wakeful nights and patient calculations/With the
NIMBLE (1)
232 Skimble   7   where is Skimble for unless he's very nimble/Then the Night Mail just can't go.'/At
NIMBUS (1)
54 Mr E Sun   11   /Designed upon a gesso ground/The nimbus of the Baptized God./The wilderness is
NINE (6)
62 WL: Burial   68   a dead sound on the final stroke of nine./There I saw one I knew, and stopped him,
220 Old Deut   5   accession./Old Deuteronomy's buried nine wives/And more — I am tempted to say,
230 Bust Jones   3   doesn't haunt pubs — he has eight or nine clubs,/For he's the St. James's Street Cat!/
303 FR   Mary   10   we shall be for dinner./{M} Seven ... nine ... ten surely./I hear that Harry has arrived
419 CP   Celia   34   will you be ready?/{C} Tonight, by nine o'clock./{R} Go home then, and make your
419 CP   Reilly   38   at once./I will send a car for you at nine o'clock./{C} What do I need to take with
NINE-TENTHS (1)
557 ES   Ld Clav   10   dull it was./{LC} Every job is dull, nine-tenths of the time .../{Mi} I need something
NINETY-NINE (1)
220 Old Deut   6   /And more — I am tempted to say, ninety-nine;/And his numerous progeny
NISAN (1)
157 Rock 4   5   /In Shushan the palace, in the month Nisan,/He served the wine to the king
NO (627)
NOBILITY (1)
258 MC Thomas   24   me most contemptible,/The raw nobility, whose manners matched their
NOBLE (1)
431 CP   Peter   21   we're interested./The most decayed noble mansion in England!/At least, of any that
NOBODY (17)
124 SA   Sweeney   29   /This went on for a couple of months/Nobody came/And nobody went/But he took in
124 SA   Sweeney   30   couple of months/Nobody came/And nobody went/But he took in the milk and he
151 Rock 2   9   bring the songs we can sing which nobody wants to hear sung;/Waiting to be flung
225 Mr Mistoff   43   aloof,/You would think there was nobody shyer —/But his voice has been heard
589 Fable   66   securely,/Gave way — my statement nobody can doubt,/Who knows the well known
297 FR   Charles   17   done the same thing once, myself./Nobody knows what he's likely to do/Until
362 CP   Edward   16   back — well, I can't understand it./Nobody likes to be left with a mystery:/It's so ...
362 CP   Reilly   19   /{UG} Yes, it's unfinished;/And nobody likes to be left with a mystery./But
376 CP   Celia   26   /What's in that saucepan?/{C} Nobody knows./{E} It's something that Alex
394 CP   Lavinia   5   It was you who complained/Of seeing nobody but solicitors and clients .../{E} And you
450 CC   Claude   15   rule is to remember that I understand nobody,/But on the other hand never to be sure
469 CC   Lucasta   28   out of it. And can you realise/That nobody has ever played to me before?/{C} And
477 CC   Lucasta   24   like to be a bastard/And wanted by nobody. I know why you're shocked:/Claude
480 CC   Lucasta   35   Lucasta:/She doesn't despise me./{L} Nobody could despise you./And what's more
480 CC   Kaghan   37   important, you don't despise me./{K} Nobody could despise *you*, Lucasta;/And we
504 CC   Lucasta   5   an anti-climax./But there seems to be nobody to answer the door./I've just let
546 ES   Piggott   28   a glance around the dining-room:/Nobody looks ill! They're all convalescents,/Or
NOBODY'D (1)
453 CC   Kaghan   24   It's no use telling anybody about you:/Nobody'd ever believe in your existence/Until
NOBODY'S (3)
118 SP   Dusty   24   dear/How many's up there?/{Du} Nobody's up here/How many's down there?/
180 FQ: ECoker   112   go with them, into the silent funeral,/Nobody's funeral, for there is no one to bury./I
327 FR   Violet   37   as I do, at this distance from London/Nobody's likely to have this evening's paper./
NOCTURNAL (2)
24 Rhapsody   60   Cologne,/She is alone/With all the old nocturnal smells/That cross and cross across her
205 de la Mare   23   of the maiden aunts;/When the nocturnal traveller can arouse/No sleeper by his

NOCTURNE (2)
33 Conv Gal   8   frames upon the keys/That exquisite nocturne, with which we explain/The night and
601 Nocturne   t   flowers/With scarlet life, for me?/Nocturne/Romeo, *grand sérieux*, to importune/

NOD (2)
28 Boston ET   7   turning/Wearily, as one would turn to nod good-bye to La Rochefoucauld,/If the
247 MC Tempt1   22   on which he turns./{T1} My Lord, a nod is as good as a wink./A man will often love

NODDED (1)
230 Bust Jones   11   Cats;/And we're all of us proud to be nodded or bowed to/By Bustopher Jones in

NODDING (1)
257 MC Chorus   30   footfall of padding bear,/Palm-pat of nodding ape, square hyaena waiting/For

NODS (1)
519 CC   1m 23   really believe her? {}/[EGGERSON *nods*]/CURTAIN/THE ELDER STATESMAN

NOIR (1)
47 Mél Adult   9   /C'est à Paris que je me coiffe/Casque noir de jemenfoutiste./En Allemagne,

NOISE (12)
65 WL: Chess   117   men lost their bones./'What is that noise?'/The wind under the door./'What is that
65 WL: Chess   119   wind under the door./'What is that noise now? What is the wind doing?'/Nothing
96 Ash-Wed 5   19   to rejoice for those who walk among noise and deny the voice/Will the veiled sister
107 Animula   2   To a flat world of changing lights and noise,/To light, dark, dry or damp, chilly or
116 SP   Doris   14   {Do} Well can't you stop that horrible noise?/Pick up the receiver/{Du} What'll I say?/
150 Rock 1   118   *no movement, no peace and no end/But noise without speech, food without taste./Without*
269 MC Chorus   33   jackal, jackass, jackdaw; the scurrying noise of mouse and jerboa; the laugh of the
315 FR   Chorus   35   /The first cry in the bedroom, the noise in the nursery, mutilated/The family
335 FR   Agatha   8   scraping. Over and under/Echo and noise of feet./I was only the feet, and the eye/
335 FR   Harry   29   breaks,/The wheel stops, and the noise of machinery,/And the desert is cleared,
377 CP   m 18   you to want her back? {}/[*A popping noise is heard from the kitchen*]/{E} What the
382 CP   Celia   14   a voice:/What I heard was only the noise of an insect,/Dry, endless, meaningless,

NOISES (6)
229 Gus   42   than most,/Produce blood-curdling noises to bring on the Ghost./And he once
269 MC Chorus   33   absurd. I have heard/Laughter in the noises of beasts that make strange noises:
269 MC Chorus   33   the noises of beasts that make strange noises: jackal, jackass, jackdaw; the scurrying
302 FR   Chorus   5   only ask to be reassured/About the noises in the cellar/And the window that should
309 FR   Harry   35   storms, one hears the moderate usual noises/In the grass and leaves, of life persisting,/
414 CP   Celia   27   — or so it seems to me./They make noises, and think they are talking to each other;/

NOMINATE (1)
129 Cor2 State   16   /A committee has been appointed to nominate a commission of engineers/To

NON-PLUSSED (1)
461 CC Eggers   5   up unexpected/And you find yourself non-plussed, you must get me on the phone./If

NONCONFORMISTS (1)
508 CC Guzzard   36   name./They were excellent people. Nonconformists./{E} And the child, I suppose

NONE (22)
148 Rock 1   54   /The applause of all or the love of none./All men are ready to invest their money/
203 Indians   20   with a common purpose, action/None the less fruitful if neither you nor we/
244 MC Chorus   22   know, which we cannot face, which none understands,/And our hearts are torn
244 MC Chorus   24   are lost lost/In a final fear which none understands. O Thomas Archbishop,/O
252 MC Thomas   14   Throne,/He has good cause to trust none but God alone./I ruled once as Chancellor
257 MC Chorus   23   now a new terror has soiled us, which none can avert, none can avoid, flowing under
257 MC Chorus   23   has soiled us, which none can avert, none can avoid, flowing under our feet and over
275 MC Thomas   10   you will, to your hurt and shame;/But none of my people, in God's name,/Whether
287 FR   Amy   29   alive, and I live to keep them./You none of you understand how old you are/And
289 FR   Amy   35   glad you did not./I am very glad that none of you ever met her./It will make the
304 FR   Mary   22   as well with a hired servant/Or with none. She only wanted me for Harry —/Not
306 FR   Harry   17   It seems I shall get rid of nothing./Of none of the shadows that I wanted to escape;/
342 FR   Agatha   15   is going./But that is not my spell, it is none of my doing:/I have only watched and
344 FR   Harry   34   /I would explain, but you would none of you believe it;/If you believed it, still
360 CP   Edward   28   is?/{E} There was no other man —/None that I know of./{UG} Or another woman/
421 CP   Reilly   1   alternative can you imagine?/{R} None./{J} Very well then. We must take the risk.
435 CP   Lavinia   32   now/That you never knew Celia. We none of us did./What you've been living on is an
446 CC   Claude   36   /{SC} But there won't be any birds — none worth watching./{E} I don't know, Sir
454 CC   Eggers   20   /{E} I have no doubt on either point, none at all./{C} And B. Kaghan has always
507 CC Guzzard   2   of any other Mrs. Guzzard?/{MG} None./{E} Whether, I mean, in Teddington or
537 ES   Ld Clav   34   I certainly admit no responsibility,/None whatever, for what happened to you later.
548 ES   Carghil   16   and most sheltered corner,/And none of the other guests have discovered it./It

NONSENSE (6)

290 FR	Violet	20	/{G} That will be a little difficult./{V} Nonsense, Gerald!/You must see for yourself
312 FR	Harry	5	I would not have listened/To your nonsense. Can't you help me?/You're of no use
420 CP	Julia	24	other ones I am worried about./{J} Nonsense, Henry. *I* shall keep an eye on them./
480 CC	Colby	11	keep me on the rails./{C} That's just nonsense./You only pretend that you're a
535 ES	Gomez	12	term as experience has taught me./It's nonsense to talk of trusting people/In general.
551 ES	Carghil	25	cared for you./What sentimental nonsense! One starts an action/Simply because

NOON (8)

68 WL: Fire S		208	City/Under the brown fog of a winter noon/Mr. Eugenides, the Smyrna merchant/
69 WL: Fire S		263	from within/Where fishmen lounge at noon: where the walls/Of Magnus Martyr hold/
128 Cor1 March		33	turtle's breast,/Under the palmtree at noon, under the running water/At the still point
129 Cor2 State		33	a moment,/A still moment, repose of noon, set under the upper branches of noon's
129 Cor2 State		34	feather stirred by the small wind after noon/There the cyclamen spreads its wings,
129 Cor2 State		46	be/O hidden/Hidden in the stillness of noon, in the silent croaking night./Come with
142 Cape Ann		4	Follow the dance/Of the goldfinch at noon. Leave to chance/The Blackburnian
269 MC Chorus		29	fluting and owls, have seen at noon/Scaly wings slanting over, huge and

NOON'S (3)

34 Figlia		24	amaze/The troubled midnight and the noon's repose./Poems/Gerontion/Here I am, an
129 Cor2 State		33	noon, set under the upper branches of noon's widest tree/Under the breast feather
230 Bust Jones		23	succulent bones;/And just before noon's not a moment too soon/To drop in for a

NOONTIDE (1)

123 SA Kl & Kr		24	*And the morning/And the evening/And noontide/And night/Morning/Evening/Noontime/*

NOONTIME (1)

123 SA Kl & Kr		28	*noontide/And night/Morning/Evening/Noontime/Night/*{Do} That's not life, that's no

NOR (36)

16 Prufrock		111	at all.'/No! I am not Prince Hamlet, nor was meant to be;/Am an attendant lord, one
37 Gerontion		4	for rain./I was neither at the hot gates/Nor fought in the warm rain/Nor knee deep in
37 Gerontion		5	gates/Nor fought in the warm rain/Nor knee deep in the salt marsh, heaving a
38 Gerontion		44	propagates a fear. Think/Neither fear nor courage saves us. Unnatural vices/Are
62 WL: Burial		40	my eyes failed, I was neither/Living nor dead, and I knew nothing,/Looking into the
72 WL: Thund		340	spit/Here one can neither stand nor lie nor sit/There is not even silence in the
72 WL: Thund		340	/Here one can neither stand nor lie nor sit/There is not even silence in the
92 Ash-Wed 2		53	divide by lot. And neither division nor unity/Matters. This is the land. We have
152 Rock 2		49	with the roads and settled nowhere./Nor does the family even move about together,/
158 Rock 5		7	And these are not justified, nor the others./And they write innumerable
173 FQ: BurntN		64	of the turning world. Neither flesh nor fleshless;/Neither from nor towards; at the
173 FQ: BurntN		65	flesh nor fleshless;/Neither from nor towards; at the still point, there the dance
173 FQ: BurntN		66	there the dance is,/But neither arrest nor movement. And do not call it fixity,/Where
173 FQ: BurntN		67	are gathered. Neither movement from nor towards,/Neither ascent nor decline. Except
173 FQ: BurntN		68	from nor towards,/Neither ascent nor decline. Except for the point, the still point,/
173 FQ: BurntN		99	slow rotation suggesting permanence/Nor darkness to purify the soul/Emptying the
174 FQ: BurntN		102	from the temporal./Neither plenitude nor vacancy. Only a flicker/Over the strained
182 FQ: ECoker		190	But perhaps neither gain nor loss./For us, there is only the trying. The
191 FQ: Little		17	that of summer, neither budding nor fading,/Not in the scheme of generation./
196 FQ: Little		185	/It is not to ring the bell backward/Nor is it an incantation/To summon the spectre
197 FQ: Little		221	the others,/The word neither diffident nor ostentatious,/An easy commerce of the old
202 War Poetry		18	/One which may neither be ignored nor accepted,/A problem to be met with
203 Indians		20	/None the less fruitful if neither you nor we/Know, until the judgment after death,/
590 Time Space		14	/So let us haste to pluck anew/Nor mourn to see them pine,/And though our
590 Space Time		14	/But let us haste to pluck anew/Nor mourn to see them pine,/And though the
245 MC Thomas		16	action. Neither does the agent suffer/Nor the patient act. But both are fixed/In an
255 MC Thomas		34	by more sinful? Can I neither act nor suffer/Without perdition?/{T4} You know
255 MC Tempt4		39	action. Neither does the agent suffer/Nor the patient act. But both are fixed/In an
261 MC Thomas		23	to/rejoice: and neither our mourning nor our rejoicing is as the world's is./A
410 CP Lavinia		29	we do/When we can go neither back nor forward? Edward!/What can we do?/{R}
416 CP Celia		21	that there had been neither giving nor taking/But that we had merely made use of
464 CC Claude		9	art./For me, they are neither 'use' nor 'decoration' —/That is, decoration as a
470 CC Colby		14	/But with you, it was neither solitude nor ... people./{L} I'm glad I'm not people. Will
513 CC Guzzard		1	with you. {}/[*To* LUCASTA]/{MG} Nor, so far as I can judge, with you./Perhaps
546 ES Piggott		23	here to die!/We never accept them. Nor do we accept/Any guest who *looks*
570 ES Ld Clav		38	Batterson?/{LC} She no longer exists./Nor the musical comedy star, Maisie Montjoy./

NORMAL (9)

305 FR	Harry	34	very unnatural,/This arresting of the normal change of things:/But it's very like her.
326 FR	Harry	21	that life ought to take,/That you call normal. What you call the normal/Is merely the
326 FR	Harry	21	you call normal. What you call the normal/Is merely the unreal and the

330 FR   Harry   4   surprises/Should be in the routine of normal life at Wishwood./John is the only one
343 FR   Harry   36   course to pursue, and I am safe from normal dangers/If I pursue it. I cannot account
370 CP   Edward   32   lost interest in me./{E} That is all very normal. If you could only know/How lucky you
414 CP   Reilly   40   We have yet to find what would be normal/For *you*, before we use the term
434 CP   Alex   16   and the other/Will never be fit for normal life again./But Celia Coplestone, she
533 ES   Gomez   8   my wife's name is a good deal more normal/In my country, than Culverwell — and
NORMALITY (2)
413 CP   Celia   34   anything you told me, to get back to normality./{R} We must find out about you,
413 CP   Reilly   36   about you, before we decide/What *is* normality. You say there are two things:/What
NORMALLY (1)
556 ES   Ld Clav 22   not at all expensive./{LC} You don't normally consider that a recommendation./Are
NORMAN (2)
587 Fable   5   /There was a village founded by some Norman/Who levied on all travelers his tax;/
251 MC   Tempt3   24   are Normans./England is a land for Norman/Sovereignty. Let the Angevin/Destroy
NORMANS (1)
251 MC   Tempt3   23   in England./You and I, my Lord, are Normans./England is a land for Norman/
NORTH (5)
154 Rock 3   28   2ND MALE VOICE:/A Cry from the North, from the West and from the South/
186 FQ: DrySal   76   bailing,/Setting and hauling, while the North East lowers/Over shallow banks
592 Grad 3   3   a summer tempest, when some haste/North, South, and Eastward o'er the water's
284 FR   m 11   *scene is laid in a country house in the North of England*/PART I/*The drawing-room*,
355 CP   Julia   10   there once/At their castle in the North. How he suffered!/They had to find an
NORTH-WEST (1)
293 FR   Gerald   31   to *me*./I started as a youngster on the North-West Frontier —/Been in tight corners
NORTHAMPTON (1)
248 MC   Tempt2   16   remind you./We met at Clarendon, at Northampton,/And last at Montmirail, in
NORTHERN (7)
232 Skimble   15   Clear!'/And we're off at last for the northern part/Of the Northern Hemisphere!/
232 Skimble   16   at last for the northern part/Of the Northern Hemisphere!/You may say that by
232 Skimble   31   /So nothing goes wrong on the Northern Mail/When Skimbleshanks is aboard./
280 MC   Priest3 22   captive Christian men;/Go to the northern seas confined with ice/Where the dead
295 FR   Amy   36   unused to our foggy climate/And the northern country. When you see Wishwood/
303 FR   Mary   1   /{M} The spring is very late in this northern country,/Late and uncertain, clings to
561 ES   Ld Clav 5   sun of the tropics/Or shiver in the northern night. Believe me, Michael:/Those who
NORTHOLT (5)
445 CC   Claude   5   wouldn't like anyone to meet her/At Northolt, but you. And I couldn't send Colby./
447 CC   Claude   2   have a little time/Before you start for Northolt — the car will be ready —/Let's think
454 CC   Eggers   2   I'll speak to him/When I return from Northolt./{L} Well, you're going to meet Lizzie?/{E} I
454 CC   Eggers   4   /{E} I am meeting Lady Elizabeth at Northolt./{L} Well, I don't propose to be on the
458 CC   Eggers   10   that's all./{E} I was just starting for Northolt to meet you./{LE} That was very
NORTON (1)
171 FQ: BurntN   t   glory!/FOUR QUARTETS/Burnt Norton/Time present and time past/Are both
NORWEGIAN (1)
375 CP   Edward   18   /I've got some cheese ... No, not Norwegian;/But I don't really want cheese ...
NOSE (2)
602 Humoresque   18   some class?/(Feebly contemptuous of nose),/'Your damned thin moonlight, worse
578 ES   Michael 26   you/Always sitting there with your nose in a book./And once, Mother snatched a
NOSES (1)
129 Cor2 State   39   heads/Necks strong to bear them/Noses strong to break the wind/Mother/May
NOT (1114)
NOTABLE (1)
223 Pekes Pols   35   biters,/And every dog-jack of them notable fighters;/And so they stepped out, with
NOTE (12)
 19 Portrait   35   /That is at least one definite 'false note.'/— Let us take the air, in a tobacco
142 Cape Ann   6   shy one. Hail!/With shrill whistle the note of the quail, the bob-white/Dodging by
175 FQ: BurntN   147   the stillness of the violin, while the note lasts,/Not that only, but the co-existence,/
202 War Poetry   t   in obedience to instructions./A Note on War Poetry/Not the expression of
263 MC   Chorus 9   wood/The owl rehearses the hollow note of death./What signs of a bitter spring?/
360 CP   Edward 6   I came in, this afternoon./She left a note to say that she was leaving me;/But I don't
362 CP   Edward 14   notice, without explanation,/Only a note to say that she had gone/And was not
404 CP   Reilly 10   as long as you please,/And taking note of what you do not say./{E} I once
481 CC   Lady E 32   /You remember, I made you take a note of the address;/And I don't believe that
492 CC   Colby   24   the conversation —/And I found one note I couldn't understand./'Reminiscent
531 ES   Lambert 36   he knew that,/So he had brought this note. He said that when you read it/You would
532 ES   m 4   gentleman. {}/[*after reading the note*]./{LC} I'll see him in the library./No, stop.

NOTED (1)
277 MC Knight3   23 admiration for him —/you must have noted what a good show he put up at the end —
NOTES (6)
486 CC   Claude 35 of telephoning,/Just to give him these notes. They're notes for my speech/At the
486 CC   Claude 35 /Just to give him these notes. They're notes for my speech/At the dinner of the
487 CC   Claude   2 out/And then memorise it. I can't use notes:/It's got to sound spontaneous. I've jotted
487 CC   m   7 go over it tomorrow. {}/[*looking at the notes*]./{C} I'll try./{SC} It's just in ways like
492 CC   Colby   22 night?/{C} I was looking at your notes —/Before you brought me into the
530 ES   Ld Clav 2 Parliament./I used to jot down notes of what I had to say to people:/Now I've
NOTHING (195)
 24 Rhapsody   40 running along the quay,/I could see nothing behind that child's eye./I have seen eyes
 62 WL: Burial   40 neither/Living nor dead, and I knew nothing,/Looking into the heart of light, the
 65 WL: Chess   120 noise now? What is the wind doing?'/Nothing again nothing./'Do/'You know
 65 WL: Chess   120 is the wind doing?'/Nothing again nothing./'Do/'You know nothing? Do you see
 65 WL: Chess   122 again nothing./'Do/'You know nothing? Do you see nothing? Do you
 65 WL: Chess   122 /'Do/'You know nothing? Do you see nothing? Do you remember/'Nothing?'/I
 65 WL: Chess   123 you see nothing? Do you remember/'Nothing?'/I remember/Those are pearls that
 65 WL: Chess   126 eyes./'Are you alive, or not? Is there nothing in your head?'/But/O O O O that
 70 WL: Fire S   302 /'On Margate Sands./I can connect/Nothing with nothing./The broken fingernails
 70 WL: Fire S   302 Sands./I can connect/Nothing with nothing./The broken fingernails of dirty hands./
 70 WL: Fire S   305 My people humble people who expect/Nothing.'/la la/To Carthage then I came/
 89 Ash-Wed 1   15 flower, and springs flow, for there is nothing again/Because I know that time is
118 SP   Doris   6 feel/{Do} Sometimes they'll tell you nothing at all/{Du} You've got to know what
121 SA Sweeney   26 /No Citroën, no Rolls-Royce./Nothing to eat but the fruit as it grows./
121 SA Sweeney   27 to eat but the fruit as it grows./Nothing to see but the palmtrees one way/And
121 SA Sweeney   29 one way/And the sea the other way,/Nothing to hear but the sound of the surf./
121 SA Sweeney   30 to hear but the sound of the surf./Nothing at all but three things/{Do} What
125 SA Sweeney   23 you understand or if you don't/That's nothing to me and nothing to you/We all gotta
125 SA Sweeney   23 if you don't/That's nothing to me and nothing to you/We all gotta do what we gotta
125 SA Sweeney   30 rent/{Do} I know who/{S} But that's nothing to me and nothing to you. {}/FULL
125 SA Sweeney   30 who/{S} But that's nothing to me and nothing to you. {}/FULL CHORUS:
151 Rock 2   9 required./We wait on corners, with nothing to bring but the songs we can sing
154 Rock 3   15 see their names in print,/Many read nothing but the race reports./Much is your
160 Rock 7   5 trees, worshipping devils rather than nothing: crying for life beyond life, for ecstasy
163 Rock 8   46 Because they will never assume it./Yet nothing is impossible, nothing,/To men of faith
163 Rock 8   46 assume it./Yet nothing is impossible, nothing,/To men of faith and conviction./Let us
180 FQ: ECoker   122 /Leaving only the growing terror of nothing to think about;/Or when, under ether,
180 FQ: ECoker   123 mind is conscious but conscious of nothing —/I said to my soul, be still, and wait
201 Def Island   16 /unalterable in triumph, changing nothing —/of their ancestors' ways but the
210 Old Gumbie   21 to irregular diet/And believing that nothing is done without trying,/She sets to work
215 RTTugger   34 middle of your sewing,/For there's nothing he enjoys like a horrible muddle./Yes
217 Jellicles   34 bright/You would say they had nothing to do at all:/They are resting and saving
219 Mung Rump   39 AND Rumpelteazer!' — And there's nothing at all to be done about that!/Old
220 Old Deut   23 a notice: ROAD CLOSED —/So that nothing untoward may chance to disturb/
222 Pekes Pols   12 of which I shall speak/Almost nothing had happened for nearly a week/(And
227 Macavity   41 I might mention Griddlebone)/Are nothing more than agents for the Cat who all
229 Gus   52 are all very well,/But there's nothing to equal, from what I hear tell,/That
232 Skimble   31 He's a Cat that cannot be ignored;/So nothing goes wrong on the Northern Mail/
235 Ad-dress   61 a Cat, who makes a habit/Of eating nothing else but rabbit,/And when he's finished,
240 MC   Priest3 34 place or another in France?/{P3} I see nothing quite conclusive in the art of temporal
242 MC   Mess   9 my opinion, I think that this peace/Is nothing like an end, or like a beginning./It is
254 MC   Tempt4   9 Save what you know already, ask nothing of me./But think, Thomas, think of
254 MC   Tempt4   30 thought of further scorning./That nothing lasts, but the wheel turns,/The nest is
269 MC   Knight1   7 indignity;/Insolent madman, whom nothing deters/From attainting his servants and
270 MC   Chorus   24 /For action, too soon for contrition:/Nothing is possible but the shamed swoon/Of
272 MC   Chorus   32 seeing itself, foully united forever, nothing with nothing,/Not what we call death,
272 MC   Chorus   32 foully united forever, nothing with nothing,/Not what we call death, but what
279 MC   Knight4 11 who have preceded me, to say nothing/of our leader, Reginald Fitz Urse, have
279 MC   Knight4 13 spoken very much to the/point. I have nothing to add along their particular lines of
280 MC   Knight1   4 in groups at street corners, and do/nothing that might provoke any public
285 FR   Amy   2 for you. It is still quite light./I have nothing to do but watch the days draw out,/
286 FR   Charles 23 does the harm:/There's nothing on earth so bad for the young./All that
288 FR   Amy   28 Wishwood. Adaptation is hard./{A} Nothing is changed, Agatha, at Wishwood./
288 FR   Amy   32 setter/Which I had to have destroyed./Nothing has been changed. I have seen to that./
289 FR   Amy   21 in front of the family:/You can call it nothing but a blessed relief./{V} *I* call it

290 FR	Amy	18	his absence. Please behave only/As if nothing had happened in the last eight years./
292 FR	Amy	24	/Your room is all ready for you. Nothing has been changed./{H} Changed?
292 FR	Harry	25	has been changed./{H} Changed? nothing changed? how can you say that nothing
292 FR	Harry	25	changed? how can you say that nothing is changed?/You all look so withered
292 FR	Ivy	37	/Time and time again: she's done nothing about it/Because she preferred to wait
293 FR	Harry	15	/You all of you try to talk as if nothing had happened,/And yet you are talking
293 FR	Harry	16	happened,/And yet you are talking of nothing else. Why not get to the point/Or if you
293 FR	Harry	28	has happened./And people to whom nothing has ever happened/Cannot understand
293 FR	Gerald	30	of events./{G} Well, you can't say that nothing has happened to *me*./I started as a
293 FR	Harry	37	/{H} You are all people/To whom nothing has happened, at most a continual
297 FR	Agatha	6	for the good that it will do/But that nothing may be left undone/On the margin of
297 FR	Charles	36	/Until we know that, we can do nothing for him./And as for my means, we can't
298 FR	Charles	22	there simply are times/When there's nothing to do but take the bull by the horns,/
301 FR Downing	5	been busy about it tonight./{Do} Nothing wrong, Sir:/Only I like to have her
301 FR	Gerald	9	more, Sir?/{G} Thank you, Downing;/Nothing more. {}/[*Exit* DOWNING]/{V} Well,
305 FR	Mary	38	/All the more manifest./{M} Yes, nothing changes here,/And we just go on ...
306 FR	Harry	16	/I think. It seems I shall get rid of nothing./Of none of the shadows that I wanted
306 FR	Mary	28	a cousin/Kept here because there was nothing else to do with me./I didn't belong here.
308 FR	Harry	2	be one dream or another; if there is nothing else/The most real is what I fear. The
308 FR	Harry	21	of departure/And start again as if nothing had happened,/Isn't that all folly? It's
311 FR	Harry	29	same person./I was not any person. Nothing that I did/Has to do with me. The
319 FR	Warburt	38	to ask your aunt —/I mean, there is nothing she could tell you. But, Harry,/We can't
320 FR	Warburt	22	that reason, it is most essential/That nothing should disturb or excite her./{H} Well!/
321 FR	Warburt	14	/{W} I wonder what he wants. I hope nothing has happened/To either of your
321 FR	Harry	16	/To either of your brothers./{H} Nothing can have happened/To either of my
321 FR	Harry	17	happened/To either of my brothers. Nothing can happen —/If Sergeant Winchell is
322 FR	Winch	39	and looked him over;/Says there's nothing wrong but some nasty cuts/And a bad
323 FR	Winch	9	I've just told the doctor,/It's really nothing but a minor accident./{W} It's John has
323 FR	Warburt	12	Dr. Owen has seen him/And says it's nothing but a slight concussion,/But he mustn't
323 FR	Warburt	30	to leave the house tonight./There is nothing you could do, and out in this weather/
324 FR	Harry	30	Harry's./{H} It's only when they see nothing/That people can always show the
325 FR	Charles	11	this — it's a good three miles;/There's nothing we could do that Warburton can't./If
325 FR	Ivy	17	is worried./We must carry on as if nothing had happened,/And have the cake and
329 FR	Chorus	19	avoiding these things/And we know nothing of exorcism/And whether in Argos or
329 FR	Chorus	23	in the nature of music./There is nothing at all to be done about it,/There is
329 FR	Chorus	24	at all to be done about it,/There is nothing to do about anything,/And now it is
331 FR	Harry	5	When I was outside,/I could associate nothing of it with myself,/Though nothing else
331 FR	Harry	6	nothing of it with myself,/Though nothing else was real. I thought foolishly/That
332 FR	Harry	6	and your mother./{H} You tell me nothing./{Ag} The dead man whom you have
337 FR	Agatha	9	you have a long journey. You have nothing to stay for./Think of it as like a
337 FR	Agatha	35	why you wish him to go./{Ag} I wish nothing. I only say what I know must happen./
340 FR	Agatha	6	take my son./{Ag} What did I take? nothing that you ever had./What did I get?
340 FR	Amy	16	the furniture, the acres;/Leaving nothing — but what I could breed for myself,/
341 FR	Agatha	5	to. Now I must begin./There is nothing more difficult. But you are just the
341 FR	Amy	13	to obliterate/His past life, and have nothing except to remind him/Of the years when
344 FR	Gerald	17	in a tropical climate!/{G} There's nothing wrong with a tropical climate —/But
355 CP	Julia	23	keep things going./What a host! And nothing fit to eat!/The only reason for a cocktail
360 CP	Reilly	13	/{UG} Gin./{E} Anything in it?/{UG} Nothing but water./And I recommend you the
360 CP	Edward	31	had cause to be jealous?/{E} She had nothing to complain of in my behaviour./{UG}
363 CP	Reilly	17	than I do,/But rather less. You are nothing but a set/Of obsolete responses. The
363 CP	Reilly	19	The one thing to do/Is to do nothing. Wait./{E} Wait!/But waiting is the one
363 CP	Edward	32	are you going to do?'/And I answer 'Nothing'. They will think me mad/Or simply
368 CP	Edward	21	you./{E} My dear Alex,/There'll be nothing in the larder worthy of your cooking./I
368 CP	Alex	24	/Concocting a toothsome meal out of nothing./Any scraps you have will do. I learned
370 CP	Peter	5	what happened after that?/{P} Oh, nothing happened./But I thought that she really
371 CP	Edward	11	leave it./{P} But what am I to do?/{E} Nothing. Wait. Go back to California./{P} But I
372 CP	Alex	11	greatest. To make something out of nothing!/Never, even when travelling in
377 CP	Julia	20	/{J} I've had an inspiration!/There's nothing in the place fit to eat:/I've looked high
382 CP	Celia	20	only a beetle the size of a man/With nothing more inside it than what comes out/
385 CP	Reilly	22	five years./{UG} I ask you to forget nothing./To try to forget is to try to conceal./
386 CP	Edward	25	not like Lavinia./I suppose there is nothing to do but wait./Won't you sit down?/
387 CP	Peter	32	{E} Of course./{P} I hope you've done nothing about it./{E} No, I've done nothing./{P}
387 CP	Edward	33	nothing about it./{E} No, I've done nothing./{P} I'm so glad./Because I've changed
389 CP	Peter	22	so you advised him?/{P} She knew nothing about it./{C} But now that I may be
392 CP	Lavinia	29	You had better have told the truth:/Nothing less than the truth could deceive Julia./

396 CP	Lavinia	19	be horrid to you —/Anything but nothing, which is all you seem to want of me./
397 CP	Edward	6	in it/Merely projections. There is nothing to escape from/And nothing to escape
397 CP	Edward	7	There is nothing to escape from/And nothing to escape to. One is always alone./{L}
397 CP	Lavinia	38	/{L} Indeed. And has the difference nothing to do/With Celia going to California?/
398 CP	Edward	9	/In a moment, at your touch, there is nothing but ruin./O God, what have I done?
398 CP	Lavinia	14	persuade you to see a doctor,/There's nothing else at present that I can do about it./I
404 CP	Reilly	24	me to the sanatorium?/{R} You have nothing else to tell me?/{E} What else can I tell
405 CP	Reilly	13	it can be discussed. You have told me nothing./You have had the opportunity, and
407 CP	Edward	34	/{E} This is monstrous! My wife knew nothing about it./{L} Really, Edward! Even if
412 CP	Reilly	30	/But I didn't know .../{R} There is nothing you need to know./I was there at the
413 CP	Celia	21	/I'd forgotten that you know nothing about me;/And with what I've been
417 CP	Celia	6	that I'm afraid of being hurt again:/Nothing again can either hurt or heal./I have
417 CP	Reilly	40	come to the end. But you will want nothing else,/And the other life will be only like
419 CP	Reilly	28	/{R} They choose, Miss Coplestone. Nothing is forced on them./Some of them
420 CP	Reilly	1	What do I need to take with me?/{R} Nothing./Everything you need will be provided
420 CP	Celia	5	doing/Or why I am doing it. There is nothing else to do:/That is the only reason./{R}
421 CP	Julia	24	innocence./She will be afraid of nothing; she will not even know/That there is
424 CP	Caterer	8	you can't find in the kitchen?/{CM} Nothing, Madam./Will there be anything more
424 CP	Lavinia	10	be anything more you require?/{L} Nothing more, I think, till half past six. {}/[Exit
425 CP	Lavinia	31	again. Anyway, at that stage/There's nothing whatever you can do about it:/And
432 CP	Reilly	24	of water?/{E} Anything with it?/{R} Nothing, thank you./{L} May I introduce Mr.
435 CP	Peter	15	/I didn't understand her. I understand nothing./{R} You understand your métier, Mr.
438 CP	Lavinia	4	agony beforehand./I mean — I know nothing of her last two years./{R} That shows
439 CP	Edward	3	years ago./{E} Your responsibility is nothing to mine, Lavinia./{L} I'm not sure
445 CC	Eggers	24	Swimmingly, I'm sure,/As I've heard nothing since the last time I came./{SC} Well, of
456 CC	Eggers	8	/He's not petty-minded — though nothing escapes him./And such a generous
457 CC	Lady E	27	want it now. Just bring me some tea./Nothing with it. No, I forgot:/You haven't
460 CC	Claude	39	have brought you up to London for nothing./{E} Oh, not for nothing! I wouldn't
461 CC	Eggers	1	London for nothing./{E} Oh, not for nothing! I wouldn't have missed it./And besides,
462 CC	Colby	36	a new and strange situation,/And nothing about it is real to me yet./{SC} But now
464 CC	Claude	28	built up this business/Starting from nothing. It was *his* passion./He loved it with the
465 CC	Claude	24	must have felt when he made it./But nothing *I* made ever gave me that contentment
472 CC	Lucasta	17	some ways —/But your insecurity is nothing like mine./{C} In what way is it
473 CC	Lucasta	12	/I hardly feel that I'm even a person/Nothing but a bit of living matter/Floating on
473 CC	Colby	40	it. If you have two lives/Which have nothing whatever to do with each other —/Well,
478 CC	Lucasta	17	/All in a moment. And now there's nothing,/Nothing at all. It's far worse than ever.
478 CC	Lucasta	18	a moment. And now there's nothing,/Nothing at all. It's far worse than ever./Just
481 CC	Colby	3	shrewd insight/Into things that have nothing to do with business./{K} And you have
482 CC	Lady E	32	you,/'He is very well bred'. I knew nothing about you,/But one doesn't need to
486 CC	Colby	28	why you are so interested:/There's nothing very interesting about my background
488 CC	Colby	21	truth./{C} It seems to me ... there is nothing for me —/Absolutely nothing — for me
488 CC	Colby	22	there is nothing for me —/Absolutely nothing — for me to say about it./I must leave
490 CC	Colby	32	to know the fact and know it means nothing./At the time I was born, you might
490 CC	Colby	39	it is a dead fact, and out of dead facts/Nothing living can spring. Now, it is too late./I
508 CC	Guzzard	38	a Christian name?/{MG} There was nothing to show that the child had been
512 CC	Eggers	36	friends./{E} I'm sure we all wish for nothing better./{MG} Wishes, when realised,
515 CC	Guzzard	26	me, to see my life's ambition come to nothing?/When I gave up my place as Colby's
516 CC	Claude	27	experience, exactly./Does that mean nothing to you, the experience we shared?/
528 ES	Monica	31	/With the atmosphere of an hotel —/Nothing about it to suggest the clinic —/
529 ES	Monica	26	relaxation/And to think about nothing. Though I know that won't be easy.
529 ES	Monica	28	what I was doing./{M} Thinking of nothing?/{LC} Contemplating nothingness. Just
530 ES	Ld Clav	26	an empty grate?/For no one. For nothing./{M} Yet you've been looking forward/
534 ES	Gomez	14	society in which I find myself./I do nothing in England that you would disapprove
547 ES	Ld Clav	13	I had feared. But I'm not going to say/Nothing could be worse. Where there's a Mrs.
551 ES	Carghil	5	on memories./Besides a woman has nothing to be ashamed of:/A man is always
552 ES	Ld Clav	12	it./{MC} And what did you feel?/{LC} Nothing at all. I remember my surprise/At
552 ES	Ld Clav	13	my surprise/At finding that I felt nothing at all./I thought, perhaps, what a lucky
554 ES	Piggott	35	one time. I'm afraid her name/Means nothing at all to the younger generation,/But
557 ES	Michael	29	what do you call good terms?/{Mi} I'd nothing at all to pay for two years:/The interest
558 ES	Michael	25	/That I was overworked, when I'd nothing to do./Even the office boys began to
561 ES	Michael	19	was no one in particular,/So you'd nothing to live up to. Those standards of
562 ES	Carghil	24	I'm Maisie Montjoy!/That means nothing to you, my dears./It's a very long time
568 ES	Ld Clav	11	from the world./Has there been nothing in your life, Charles Hemington,/Which
568 ES	Charles	16	know about me, Monica,/But there's nothing I would ever wish to conceal from you./
568 ES	Ld Clav	17	to conceal from you./{LC} If there's nothing, truly nothing, that you couldn't tell

568 ES Ld Clav 17   you./{LC} If there's nothing, truly nothing, that you couldn't tell Monica/Then all
568 ES Ld Clav 20   I've seen for myself!/And if there is nothing that you conceal from *her*/However
569 ES Monica   15   understand you better./There's nothing I'm afraid of learning about Charles,/
569 ES Monica   16   of learning about Charles,/There's nothing I'm afraid of learning about you./{C} I
569 ES Ld Clav 27   he wanted./Oh no, he said, I want nothing from you/Except your friendship and
570 ES Ld Clav   3   of them?/{LC} Your mother knew nothing about them. And I know/That I never
570 ES Ld Clav 12   us,/And she died silently. She had nothing to say to me./I think of your mother,
577 ES Charles 17   nature of whose business/You know nothing. All you can be sure of/Is that he served
579 ES Michael 27   get his first leave./{Mi} Well ... there's nothing more to say, is there?/{LC} Nothing at
579 ES Michael 28   nothing more to say, is there?/{LC} Nothing at all./{Mi} Then we might as well be
NOTHINGNESS (1)
529 ES Ld Clav 29   of nothing?/{LC} Contemplating nothingness. Just remember:/Every day, year
NOTICE (15)
209 NamingCats 25   and will never confess./When you notice a cat in profound meditation,/The
220 Old Deut   22   the kerb,/And the villagers put up a notice: ROAD CLOSED —/So that nothing
241 MC   Mess   15 I was sent before in haste/To give you notice of his coming, as much as was possible,/
243 MC   Chorus 24   lived quietly,/Succeeded in avoiding notice,/Living and partly living./There have
358 CP   Julia   25   my good Mrs. Batten/Would give me notice. And now I must be going./{A} I'm afraid
362 CP   Edward 13   So her going away/At a moment's notice, without explanation,/Only a note to say
367 CP   Peter   3 /{P} Oh, I'm very glad that you didn't notice:/I must have behaved rather better than I
367 CP   Peter   5   better than I thought./If you didn't notice, I don't suppose the others did,/Though
409 CP   Lavinia 5 I never noticed it./{L} You wouldn't notice anything. You never noticed *me*./{R}
449 CC   Claude 27 {SC} But I don't think she takes much notice of Miss Angel./She just doesn't see her.
453 CC   Kaghan 35   She's had a week's salary in lieu of notice./{L} B., remember you're only my fiancé
496 CC   Claude 16   you up to London/At such short notice./{E} Don't say that, Sir Claude./It's true,
496 CC   Eggers 31 lost in London./Every time I come, I notice the traffic/Has got so much worse./{SC}
506 CC   Eggers   2 placed out to be cared for/Till further notice by a foster-mother./Unfortunately, the
578 ES   Monica 18   only sister. You never took much notice of me./When we were growing up we
NOTICED (14)
305 FR   Harry   26   you looking for?/{H} I had only just noticed that this room is quite unchanged:/The
334 FR   Harry   23   of formal obligation, a duty/Only noticed by its neglect. One had that part to play.
366 CP   Peter   39   your fault./I don't suppose you noticed the situation./{E} I did think I noticed
367 CP   Edward   1 noticed the situation./{E} I did think I noticed one or two things;/But I don't pretend I
375 CP   Celia   34   suppose it's still cooking!/I thought I noticed a peculiar smell:/Of course it's still
408 CP   Lavinia 31   professional etiquette./{L} I have not noticed much professional etiquette/About your
409 CP   Edward   4   your breakdown began! and I never noticed it./{L} You wouldn't notice anything.
409 CP   Lavinia 5   wouldn't notice anything. You never noticed *me*./{R} Now, I want to point out to you
415 CP   Celia   10   say have no moral sense?/I've never noticed that immorality/Was accompanied by a
460 CC   Lady E 16   /This is not the first sign that I've noticed/Of your memory failing. I must
482 CC   Lady E 12 lived a rather sheltered life,/And I've noticed them paying you a good deal of
498 CC   Claude 17   nowadays./Besides, I should have noticed it. I visited her house/Often. I never saw
544 ES   Ld Clav 17 /When we are young, but then it's not noticed;/And by the time one has grown to
548 ES   Ld Clav 20   /{LC} My daughter chose it./She noticed that it seemed to offer the advantages/
NOTICING (1)
306 FR   Mary   2   go on ... drying up, I suppose,/Not noticing the change. But to you, I am sure,/We
NOTION (3)
 23 Preludes   50 /Around these images, and cling:/The notion of some infinitely gentle/Infinitely
192 FQ: Little   45   you would have to put off/Sense and notion. You are not here to verify,/Instruct
296 FR   Charles 24   thinking./{C} He has probably let this notion grow in his mind,/Living among
NOTIONS (1)
186 FQ: DrySal   90   fallacy/Encouraged by superficial notions of evolution,/Which becomes, in the
NOTORIOUS (1)
218 Mung Rump   1   and Rumpelteazer were a very notorious couple of cats./As knockabout
NOUGHT (1)
589 Fable   77 in accents hollow./The friars could do nought but gape and stare,/The spirit pulled
NOURISH (3)
190 FQ: DrySal 235   at the last/If our temporal reversion nourish/(Not too far from the yew-tree)/The life
343 FR   Amy   26   taxes/And unpaid rents and tithes? nourish investments/With wakeful nights and
571 ES   Ld Clav 16   did admire us!/And that again may nourish the faults that they were born with./
NOURISHING (1)
178 FQ: ECoker   40 Mirth of those long since under earth/Nourishing the corn. Keeping time,/Keeping the
NOUS (1)
 51 Restaurant   17 /'Monsieur, le fait est dur./Il est venu, nous peloter, un gros chien;/Moi j'avais peur, je
NOVEL (1)
367 CP   Peter   16   practise?/{P} You won't have seen my novel,/Though it had some very good reviews./

NOVELS (1)
16 Prufrock   102   and the sprinkled streets,/After the novels, after the teacups, after the skirts that
NOVELTY (1)
395 CP   Lavinia   5   speak your mind./{L} That will be a novelty/To find that you have a mind to speak./
NOVEMBER (2)
178 FQ: ECoker   52   In my beginning./What is the late November doing/With the disturbance of the
239 MC   Chorus   9   golden October declined into sombre November/And the apples were gathered and
NOW (417)
NOW'S (3)
445 CC   Eggers   14   needs for a garden!/And I thought, now's the moment to buy some new tools/So as
479 CC   Kaghan   26   /Assert your right to a little privacy./Now's the moment for firmness. Don't let her
533 ES   Gomez   16   worker all these years/And I thought, now's the time to take a long holiday,/Let's say
NOWADAYS (6)
328 FR   Charles   33   were kept out of the papers;/But nowadays, there's no such thing as privacy./
372 CP   Alex   23   have the dish that you'll be eating, nowadays./{E} But what about my breakfast?/
445 CC   Eggers   19   /An excellent lunch, and cheap, for nowadays./But where's Mr. Simpkins? Will he
482 CC   Lady E   6   You call her Lucasta? Young people nowadays/Seem to have dropped the use of
496 CC   Eggers   18   Sir Claude./It's true, I haven't much nowadays to bring me;/But Mrs. E. wishes I'd
498 CC   Claude   16   a baby farm./That's most unlikely, nowadays./Besides, I should have noticed it. I
NOWHERE (5)
152 Rock 2   48   /Familiar with the roads and settled nowhere./Nor does the family even move about
192 FQ: Little   55   the timeless moment/Is England and nowhere. Never and always./Ash on an old
194 FQ: Little   108   at this intersection time/Of meeting nowhere, no before and after,/We trod the
297 FR   Violet   31   I am convinced is going to lead us nowhere,/And which I am sure Amy would
480 CC   Kaghan   29   had any parents. Just adopted, from nowhere./That's why I want to be a power in
NOXIOUS (2)
294 FR   Harry   1   wide awake. You do not know/The noxious smell untraceable in the drains,/
294 FR   Harry   7   medium. I am the old house/With the noxious smell and the sorrow before morning,/
NOYÉ (1)
51 Restaurant   25   le Phénicien, pendant quinze jours noyé,/Oubliait les cris des mouettes et la houle
NUISANCE (3)
455 CC   Colby   23   can./{C} But is she likely to be a nuisance?/{E} Not unless you give her
499 CC   Lucasta   27   off your hands./Oh, I know what a nuisance you've always found me!/And I
500 CC   Lucasta   36   As you thought of me/Simply as a nuisance. We're suited to each other:/You
NUIT (1)
48 Lune Miel   2   ils rentrent à Terre Haute;/Mais une nuit d'été, les voici à Ravenne,/A l'aise entre
NUMB (3)
272 MC   Chorus   11   *Latin by a choir in the distance*]./{C} Numb the hand and dry the eyelid,/Still the
280 MC   Priest3   23   ice/Where the dead breath makes numb the hand, makes dull the brain;/Find an
490 CC   Colby   14   this conversation. I only feel ... numb./If there's agony, it's part of a total agony
NUMBER (10)
26 Rhapsody   71   lamp said, 'Four o'clock,/Here is the number on the door./Memory!/You have the
29 Aunt Helen   3   square/Cared for by servants to the number of four./Now when she died there was
348 FR   Chorus   25   restricted area./Except for a limited number/Of strictly practical purposes/We do
357 CP   Julia   35   have the address, and the telephone number?/I might run down and see Lavinia/On
373 CP   m   3   *picks up the telephone, and dials a number*]/{E} Is Miss Celia Coplestone in? ... How
445 CC   Eggers   13   shopping! Gardening tools./The number of things one needs for a garden!/And I
471 CC   Colby   38   afterwards,/When I had seen you a number of times,/I decided that was only your
483 CC   Colby   4   limit my acquaintance to a very small number,/And I don't know where to find them./
489 CC   Claude   10   more?'/You might have suspected any number of children!/That seems grotesque now.
552 ES   Carghil   7   remember what a hit I made/With a number called *It's Not Too Late For You To*
NUMBERED (2)
155 Rock 3   50   rat breeds/Or sanitary dwellings with numbered doors/Or a house a little better than
261 MC   Thomas   17   them; we rejoice, that another soul is/numbered among the Saints in Heaven, for the
NUMBERS (1)
303 FR   Mary   18   having to plan/For uncertain numbers. Why did she ask him?/{Ag} She only
NUMBNESS (1)
330 FR   Harry   24   it lasts. That is one hell./Then the numbness came to cover it — that is another —/
NUMEROUS (3)
220 Old Deut   7   tempted to say, ninety-nine;/And his numerous progeny prospers and thrives/And
279 MC   Knight4   27   clearly prophesied, in the/presence of numerous witnesses, that he had not long to
484 CC   Lady E   28 and I was lonely/Because they were so numerous — and so uncongenial./They made
NURSE (9)
181 FQ: ECoker 155   is the disease/If we obey the dying nurse/Whose constant care is not to please/But
357 CP   Celia   4   /And almost impossible to get a nurse./{J} Is that her Aunt Laura?/{E} No;

546 ES   Piggott   3 /A widow in fact. But I was a Trained Nurse,/And of course I've always lived in what
546 ES   Piggott   9   operation!/I was a theatre nurse. But you mustn't call me 'Matron'/At
546 ES   Monica   33   but the chambermaid/Referred to a nurse. When we see her/Do we address her as
546 ES   Monica   34   we see her/Do we address her as 'Nurse'?/{MP} Oh yes, that's different./She is a
546 ES   Piggott   36   Oh yes, that's different./She is a real nurse, you know, fully qualified./Our system is
546 ES   Piggott   40   one respect;/And calling our nurses 'Nurse' reassures them/In another respect./{LC}
554 ES   Piggott   30   /Instead of leaving it, as usual, to Nurse)/When I saw that Mrs. Carghill had

NURSE'S (1)
544 ES   Monica   9   'I'm not the one for elevens's,/That's Nurse's business'./{LC} So far, so good./I'll feel

NURSE-SECRETARY (8)
352 CP   m   9   /LAVINIA CHAMBERLAYNE/A NURSE-SECRETARY/TWO CATERER'S
399 CP   4m   1   *He presses an/electric button. The* NURSE-SECRETARY *enters, with*
399 CP   1m 25   Ask him to come straight in. {}/[*Exit* NURSE-SECRETARY]/[ALEX *enters almost*
400 CP   1m 35   *side door*]/[EDWARD *is shown in by* NURSE-SECRETARY]/{E} Sir Henry
405 CP   m 23   {}/[LAVINIA *is shown in by the* NURSE-SECRETARY]/{R} But here is the
412 CP   m 24   *side door*]/[REILLY *presses button.* NURSE-SECRETARY *shows in* CELIA]/{R}
420 CP   1m 19   out your salvation with diligence. {}/[NURSE-SECRETARY *appears at door. Exit*
422 CP   1m 11   She will be fetched this evening. {}/[NURSE-SECRETARY *enters with a tray, a*

NURSEMAID (1)
385 CP   Reilly   13   at the Christmas party,/The beloved nursemaid — those who enfolded/Your

NURSERY (5)
184 FQ: DrySal   11   /His rhythm was present in the nursery bedroom,/In the rank ailanthus of the
204 de la Mare   9   /Recount their exploits at the nursery tea/And when the lamps are lit and
288 FR   Agatha   24   have remembered Wishwood —/The nursery tea, the school holiday,/The daring feats
288 FR   Agatha   38   down the corridor/That led to the nursery, round the corner/Of the new wing, he
315 FR   Chorus   35   cry in the bedroom, the noise in the nursery, mutilated/The family album, rendered

NURSES (1)
546 ES   Piggott   40   guests in one respect;/And calling our nurses 'Nurse' reassures them/In another

NURSING (3)
362 CP   Reilly   37   the surgeon,/In going to bed in the nursing home,/In talking to the matron, you are
433 CP   Lavinia   37   /We heard that she had joined some nursing order .../{A} She had joined an order. A
433 CP   Alex   39   /And as she already had experience of nursing .../{L} Yes, she had been a V.A.D. I

NURSING-HOME (1)
546 ES   Piggott   11   studied to avoid/Anything like a nursing-home atmosphere./We don't want our

NUTS (2)
427 CP   Julia   32   conditions./{J} What about? Monkey nuts?/{A} That was a nearer guess than you
427 CP   Alex   34   than you think./No, not monkey nuts. But it had to do with monkeys —/Though

NYMPHS (2)
67 WL: Fire S   175 Crosses the brown land, unheard. The nymphs are departed./Sweet Thames, run softly,
67 WL: Fire S   179   testimony of summer nights. The nymphs are departed./And their friends, the

O (82)

42	Swee Erect	15	and gashed with eyes,/This oval O cropped out with teeth:/The sickle motion
63	WL: Burial	74	the sudden frost disturbed its bed?/'O keep the Dog far hence, that's friend to men,/
65	WL: Chess	128	Is there nothing in your head?'/But/O O O O that Shakespeherian Rag —/It's so
65	WL: Chess	128	Is there nothing in your head?'/But/O O O O that Shakespeherian Rag —/It's so elegant/
65	WL: Chess	128	there nothing in your head?'/But/O O O O that Shakespeherian Rag —/It's so elegant/
65	WL: Chess	128	nothing in your head?'/But/O O O O that Shakespeherian Rag —/It's so elegant/So
67	WL: Fire S	199	Sweeney to Mrs. Porter in the spring./O the moon shone bright on Mrs. Porter/And
67	WL: Fire S	202	They wash their feet in soda water/Et O ces voix d'enfants, chantant dans la coupole!/
69	WL: Fire S	259	the Strand, up Queen Victoria Street./O City city, I can sometimes hear/Beside a
70	WL: Fire S	309	/Burning burning burning burning/O Lord Thou pluckest me out/O Lord Thou
70	WL: Fire S	310	/O Lord Thou pluckest me out/O Lord Thou pluckest/burning/Death by Water
71	WL: DWater	320	the whirlpool./Gentile or Jew/O you who turn the wheel and look to
75	WL: Thund	428	*affina/Quando fiam uti chelidon —* O swallow swallow/*Le Prince d'Aquitaine à la*
96	Ash-Wed 5	10	/About the centre of the silent Word./O my people, what have I done unto thee./
96	Ash-Wed 5	28	Pray for those who chose and oppose/O my people, what have I done unto thee./Will
97	Ash-Wed 5	36	the mouth the withered apple-seed./O my people./Although I do not hope to turn
109	Marina	5	through the fog/What images return/O my daughter./Those who sharpen the tooth
127	Cor1 March	32	waiting, perceiving, indifferent./O hidden under the dove's wing, hidden in the
128	Cor1 March	34	At the still point of the turning world. O hidden./Now they go up to the temple. Then
129	Cor2 State	4	of the British Empire, the Cavaliers,/O Cavaliers! of the Legion of Honour,/The
129	Cor2 State	25	dice on the marches/And the frogs (O Mantuan) croak in the marshes./Fireflies
129	Cor2 State	32	/Of a sweaty torchbearer, yawning./O hidden under the... Hidden under the...
129	Cor2 State	36	the clematis droops over the lintel/O mother (not among these busts, all correctly
129	Cor2 State	45	/Are now observed/May we not be/O hidden/Hidden in the stillness of noon, in the
129	Cor2 State	50	through the dust, through the night./O mother/What shall I cry?/We demand a
135	5FingerEx1	7	Bear./There is no relief but in grief./O when will the creaking heart cease?/When will
142	Cape Ann	1	/No concurrence of bone./Cape Ann/O quick quick quick, quick hear the
147	Rock 1	3	with his dogs pursues his circuit./O perpetual revolution of configured stars,/O
147	Rock 1	4	revolution of configured stars,/O perpetual recurrence of determined seasons,/
147	Rock 1	5	recurrence of determined seasons,/O world of spring and autumn, birth and dying!
154	Rock 3	2	of the LORD came unto me, saying:/O miserable cities of designing men,/O wretched
154	Rock 3	3	/O miserable cities of designing men,/O wretched generation of enlightened men,/
155	Rock 3	57	will depart and return to the desert./O my soul, be prepared for the coming of the
155	Rock 3	59	who knows how to ask questions./O weariness of men who turn from GOD/To
158	Rock 5	1	one hand and the trowel in the other./O Lord, deliver me from the man of excellent
162	Rock 8	1	gods except Usury, Lust and Power./O Father we welcome your words,/And we will
163	Rock 8	49	us therefore make perfect our will./O GOD, help us./Son of Man, behold with
166	Rock 10	17	your step and find your foothold./O Light Invisible, we praise Thee!/Too bright
166	Rock 10	19	Thee!/Too bright for mortal vision./O Greater Light, we praise Thee for the less;/
166	Rock 10	25	glowlight on a grassblade./O Light Invisible, we worship Thee!/We thank
167	Rock 10	35	the light but see not whence it comes./O Light Invisible, we glorify Thee!/In our
167	Rock 10	46	that darkness reminds us of light./O Light Invisible, we give Thee thanks for Thy
180	FQ: ECoker	102	dancers are all gone under the hill./O dark dark dark. They all go into the dark,/
188	FQ: DrySal	165	of the fruit of action./Fare forward./O voyagers, O seamen,/You who come to port,
188	FQ: DrySal	165	of action./Fare forward./O voyagers, O seamen,/You who come to port, and you
235	Ad-dress	45	my hat,/Ad-dress him in this form: O CAT!/But if he is the Cat next door,/Whom I
589	Fable	79	collar,/And before any one could say 'O jiminy!'/The pair had vanisht swiftly up the
594	Grad 9	4	/From spotless fanes of lucid purity,/O school of ours! The passing years that roll/
594	Grad 11	4	unknown world — class after class,/O queen of schools — a momentary gleam,/A
243	MC Chorus	16	the profit, certain the danger./O late late late, late is the time, late too late, and
243	MC Chorus	18	sea, and grey the sky, grey grey grey./O Thomas, return, Archbishop; return, return
244	MC Chorus	24	a final fear which none understands. O Thomas Archbishop,/O Thomas our Lord,
244	MC Chorus	25	understands. O Thomas Archbishop,/O Thomas our Lord, leave us and leave us be,
244	MC Chorus	30	of their lord, the doom of the world?/O Thomas, Archbishop, leave us, leave us, leave
245	MC Priest2	23	turn and still/Be forever still./{P2} O my Lord, forgive me, I did not see you
251	MC Thomas	16	in isolation./That is a mistake./{T} O Henry, O my King!/{T3} Other friends/May
251	MC Thomas	16	/That is a mistake./{T} O Henry, O my King!/{T3} Other friends/May be found in
256	MC Priests	24	of society, enemy of himself./{3P} O Thomas my Lord do not fight the intractable
258	MC Chorus	1	swing and wing through the dark air./O Thomas Archbishop, save us, save us, save
264	MC Priest3	15	*Out of the mouth of very babes, O God./*As the voice of many waters, of thunder,
264	MC Priest3	19	was no man to bury them. Avenge, O Lord,/The blood of thy saints. In Rama, a
264	MC Priest3	21	/*Out of the mouth of very babes, O God!* {}/[THE PRIESTS *stand together with*
271	MC Chorus	6	the final ecstasy of waste and shame,/O Lord Archbishop, O Thomas Archbishop,
271	MC Chorus	6	and shame,/O Lord Archbishop, O Thomas Archbishop, forgive us, forgive us,

275 MC	Chorus	24	where is Kent? where is Canterbury?/O far far far far in the past; and I wander in a
280 MC	Priest1	5	outbreak. {}/[*Exeunt* KNIGHTS]/{P1} O father, father, gone from us, lost to us,/How
280 MC	Priest1	37	we must think no further of you./{P1} O my lord/The glory of whose new state is
281 MC	Chorus	7	*in the distance].*/{C} We praise Thee, O God, for Thy glory displayed in all the
282 MC	Chorus	4	it is forever denied. Therefore, O God, we thank Thee/Who hast given such
282 MC	Chorus	6	blessing to Canterbury./Forgive us, O Lord, we acknowledge ourselves as type of
285 FR	Amy	6	will be gone before I am out again./O Sun, that was once so warm, O Light that
285 FR	Amy	6	again./O Sun, that was once so warm, O Light that was taken for granted/When I was
311 FR	Harry	8	/All other worlds, and me into it. O Mary!/Don't look at me like that! Stop! Try
317 FR	Harry	15	that is very likely to happen./{H} O God, man, the things that are going to
334 FR	Harry	37	what I thought were private shadows. O that awful privacy/Of the insane mind! Now I
335 FR	Harry	35	happen is as true as what did happen/O my dear, and you walked through the little
337 FR	Agatha	4	is accident/In a cloud of unknowing./O my child, my curse,/You shall be fulfilled:/
398 CP	Edward	4	out laughing. But you won't./{E} O God, O God, if I could return to yesterday/
398 CP	Edward	4	laughing. But you won't./{E} O God, O God, if I could return to yesterday/Before I
398 CP	Edward	10	your touch, there is nothing but ruin./O God, what have I done? The python. The
455 CC	Eggers	37	quite so unusual as Miss Angel./{E} O yes, Mr. Simpkins, much more unusual./{C}
536 ES	Gomez	18	their thoughts are Indian thoughts./O God, Dick, *you* don't know what it's like/To

O' (2)

66 WL: Chess		150	said./Oh is there, she said. Something o' that, I said./Then I'll know who to thank, she
236 Cat Morgan		8	with a drink on the 'ouse/And a bit o' cold fish when I done me patrol./I ain't got

O'CLOCK (17)

22 Preludes		3	smell of steaks in passageways./Six o'clock./The burnt-out ends of smoky days./
23 Preludes		42	insistent feet/At four and five and six o'clock;/And short square fingers stuffing pipes,
24 Rhapsody		1	/Rhapsody on a Windy Night/Twelve o'clock./Along the reaches of the street/Held in
26 Rhapsody		70	smells in bars./The lamp said,/'Four o'clock,/Here is the number on the door./
85 Hollow Men		71	*we go round the prickly pear/At five o'clock in the morning.*/Between the idea/And the
126 SA	Chorus	2	/You dreamt you waked up at seven o'clock and it's/foggy and it's damp and it's
134 Wind		t	derision./The wind sprang up at four o'clock/The wind sprang up at four o'clock/The
134 Wind		1	o'clock/The wind sprang up at four o'clock/The wind sprang up and broke the bells/
294 FR	Harry	4	in the ancient bedroom/At three o'clock in the morning. I am not speaking/Of
399 CP	Nurse	6	/The first appointment at eleven o'clock./He is to be shown into the small
400 CP	Reilly	2	appointment?/{R} At eleven o'clock,/The conventional hour. We have not
419 CP	Celia	34	you be ready?/{C} Tonight, by nine o'clock./{R} Go home then, and make your
419 CP	Reilly	38	once./I will send a car for you at nine o'clock./{C} What do I need to take with me?/
481 CC	Kaghan	10	can't want dinner yet./It's only six o'clock. We can't dine till eight;/Not at any
481 CC	Lady E	25	very hungry./{LE} Hungry? At six o'clock? Where will you get dinner?/Oh, I know.
523 ES		m 11	*Lord Claverton's London house. Four o'clock in the afternoon*/ACT TWO/*The Terrace*
524 ES		2m 1	CLAVERTON'S *London house. Four o'clock in the afternoon.*/[*Voices in the hall*]/{C}

O'ER (2)

592 Grad 3		3	haste/North, South, and Eastward o'er the water's waste,/Some to the western
594 Grad 12		6	far and near/To spread thy name o'er distant lands and seas!/As thou to thy

OAK (2)

273 MC	Thomas	20	her own, in her own way, not/As oak and stone; stone and oak decay,/Give no
273 MC	Thomas	20	way, not/As oak and stone; stone and oak decay,/Give no stay, but the Church shall

OAKLEAVES (2)

127 Cor1 March		1	/Stone, bronze, stone, steel, stone, oakleaves, horses' heels/Over the paving./And
128 Cor1 March		40	/Stone, bronze, stone, steel, stone, oakleaves, horses' heels/Over the paving./That

OAR (2)

74 WL: Thund		419	to the hand expert with sail and oar/The sea was calm, your heart would have
184 FQ: DrySal		23	/The shattered lobsterpot, the broken oar/And the gear of foreign dead men. The sea

OARS (1)

70 WL: Fire S		280	/Elizabeth and Leicester/Beating oars/The stern was formed/A gilded shell/Red

OASIS (2)

47 Mél Adult		17	Je célébrai mon jour de fête/Dans une oasis d'Afrique/Vêtu d'une peau de girafe./On
280 MC	Priest3	24	hand, makes dull the brain;/Find an oasis in the desert sun,/Go seek alliance with the

OATH (3)

219 Mung Rump		32	and no sober person could take his oath/Was it Mungojerrie — or Rumpelteazer?
266 MC	Knights	23	who cheated, swindled, lied; broke his oath and betrayed his King./{T} This is not true.
347 FR	Downing	11	There's no harm in *them*,/I'll take my oath. Will that be all, Miss?/{Ag} That will be

OBEDIENCE (3)

201 Def Island		22	that we took up/our positions, in obedience to instructions./A Note on War
275 MC	Knight1	6	you appropriated./{K1} Renew the obedience you have violated./{T} For my Lord I
495 CC	Claude	36	organist./We have both chosen ... obedience to the facts./{LE} I believe that was

OBEDIENT (1)
74 WL: Thund 421   /Gaily, when invited, beating obedient/To controlling hands/I sat upon the
OBEY (2)
181 FQ: ECoker 155   /Our only health is the disease/If we obey the dying nurse/Whose constant care is not
565 ES   Gomez 25   /{G} Well, Dick, we've got to obey our doctors' orders./But while we're here,
OBITUARIES (1)
74 WL: Thund 406   /Which is not to be found in our obituaries/Or in memories draped by the
OBITUARY (2)
531 ES   Ld Clav 13   on any conspicuous retirement./My obituary, if I had died in harness,/Would have
552 ES   Carghil 38   You'll still be playing a part/In your obituary, whoever writes it./{LC} Considering
OBJECT (10)
298 FR   Charles 4   in helping Harry/You can hardly object to the means./{V} I do object./{I} And I
298 FR   Violet 5   hardly object to the means./{V} I do object./{I} And I wish to associate myself with
298 FR   Agatha 9   I have no objection,/Any more than I object to asking Dr. Warburton:/I only see that
308 FR   Harry 5   upon the world, that never found its object;/And the eye adjusts itself to a twilight/
362 CP   Reilly 23   suddenly reduced to the status of an object —/A living object, but no longer a
362 CP   Reilly 24   to the status of an object —/A living object, but no longer a person./It's always
362 CP   Reilly 25   always happening, because one is an object/As well as a person. But we forget about
362 CP   Reilly 33   /You have the experience of being an object/At the mercy of a malevolent staircase./
482 CC   Colby 21   But, Lady Elizabeth, what is it you object to?/They're both intelligent ... and kind./
483 CC   Lady E 15   here./{LE} And what is that shrouded object on it?/Don't tell me it's a typewriter./{C}
OBJECTION (1)
298 FR   Agatha 8   /In her objections —/{Ag} I have no objection,/Any more than I object to asking Dr.
OBJECTIONS (1)
298 FR   Ivy 7   associate myself with my sister/In her objections —/{Ag} I have no objection,/Any
OBJECTS (2)
272 MC   Chorus 30   is no longer deceived, for there are no objects, no tones,/No colours, no forms to
513 CC   Colby 32   failure more than his success —/By objects that belonged to him, and faded
OBLATION (1)
260 MC   Thomas 10   God His Body and Blood in sacrifice, oblation and satisfaction/for the sins of the
OBLATIONS (1)
129 Cor2 State 42   /If the mactations, immolations, oblations, impetrations,/Are now observed/May
OBLIGATION (1)
334 FR   Harry 22   affection/Was a kind of formal obligation, a duty/Only noticed by its neglect.
OBLIGE (1)
403 CP   Reilly 3   would produce amazing dreams, to oblige me./I could make you dream any kind of
OBLIGED (2)
279 MC   Knight4 17   /consider the course of events. I am obliged, very briefly, to go over/the ground
431 CP   Alex 10   Alex?/{A} Yes, we have sometimes obliged each other./{P} Well, it was Bela sent me
OBLIQUE (1)
601 Nocturne 10   —/The hero smiles; in my best mode oblique/Rolls toward the moon a frenzied eye
OBLITERATE (2)
341 FR   Amy 12   /Because of the waste. I wanted to obliterate/His past life, and have nothing except
385 CP   Edward 20   /{E} You can hardly expect me to obliterate/The last five years./{UG} I ask you to
OBLIVION (2)
91 Ash-Wed 2 12   here dissembled/Proffer my deeds to oblivion, and my love/To the posterity of the
280 MC   Priest3 28   Forgetfulness in his libidinous courts,/Oblivion in the fountain by the date-tree;/Or sit
OBSCURE (3)
514 CC   Guzzard 2   — or the son of some other man/Obscure and silent? A dead man, Colby./Be
514 CC   Colby 4   /Be careful what you say./{C} A dead obscure man./{MG} You shall have your wish.
570 ES   Ld Clav 33   me? Only a schoolmaster/In an obscure grammar school somewhere in the
OBSCURITY (1)
148 Rock 1 52   seeking/The good deeds that lead to obscurity, accepting/With equal face those that
OBSERVANCE (1)
190 FQ: DrySal 218   by guesses; and the rest/Is prayer, observance, discipline, thought and action./The
OBSERVANT (2)
367 CP   Edward 7   Shuttlethwaite./{E} Julia is certainly observant,/But I think she had some other
436 CP   Julia 37   /{J} Oh, Henry!/Lavinia is much more observant than you think./I believe that she has
OBSERVATION (4)
290 FR   Agatha 28   /Reflecting a pocket-torch of observation/Upon each other's opacity/
294 FR   Harry 22   suffering without feeling/And partial observation of one's own automatism/While the
309 FR   Mary 18   books, or from thinking, or from observation:/Something which I did not know I
402 CP   Edward 26   /As myself, under your personal observation?/{R} You are very impetuous, Mr.

OBSERVATIONS (2)

11	t	/PRUFROCK and Other Observations/The Love Song of J. Alfred
326 FR Violet	31	ago, to Wishwood./{V} I will make no observations on what you say, Harry;/My

OBSERVE (5)

33 Conv Gal	1	to this end./Conversation Galante/I observe: 'Our sentimental friend the moon!/Or
189 FQ: DrySal	191	the horoscope, haruspicate or scry,/Observe disease in signatures, evoke/Biography
240 MC Chorus	22	/Come, happy December, who shall observe you, who shall preserve you?/Shall the
519 CC Guzzard	2	years ago;/But we failed to observe, when we had our wishes,/That there
552 ES Carghil	24	mention their consciences/Except to observe that their consciences were clear./You

OBSERVED (2)

129 Cor2 State	43	oblations, impetrations,/Are now observed/May we not be/O hidden/Hidden in
231 Bust Jones	35	he's so well preserved because he's observed/All his life a routine, so he'd say./Or,

OBSERVER (1)

545 ES Ld Clav	5	/What is this self inside us, this silent observer,/Severe and speechless critic, who can

OBSERVING (2)

43 Swee Erect	37	/And deprecate the lack of taste/Observing that hysteria/Might easily be
404 CP Reilly	8	/I learn a good deal by merely observing you,/And letting you talk as long as

OBSESSED (1)

403 CP Edward	7	of feeling interesting./{E} But I am obsessed by the thought of my own

OBSESSIONS (2)

484 CC Lady E	31	Colby, when I was a child/I had three obsessions, and I never told anyone./I wonder if
484 CC Lady E	32	anyone./I wonder if *you* had the same obsessions?/{C} What were they?/{LE} The first

OBSOLETE (1)

363 CP Reilly	18	less. You are nothing but a set/Of obsolete responses. The one thing to do/Is to do

OBSTACLES (1)

165 Rock 9	38	/After much striving, after many obstacles;/For the work of creation is never

OBSTINATE (3)

256 MC Tempts	18	unreality to unreality./This man is obstinate, blind, intent/On self-destruction,/
381 CP Edward	36	to come to terms in the end/With the obstinate, the tougher self; who does not speak,/
403 CP Edward	30	always imposed upon me/With the obstinate, unconscious, sub-human strength/

OBSTRUCTION (1)

516 CC Claude	28	knows — and you know — I put no obstruction/In the way of your fulfilling your

OBTAIN (1)

510 CC Eggers	33	you are my son./{E} You will wish to obtain confirmation/Of this interesting

OBTAINED (2)

248 MC Tempt2	27	be regained. Think, my Lord,/Power obtained grows to glory,/Life lasting, a
408 CP Reilly	38	have exchanged between you/Was all obtained from outside sources./Mrs.

OBTUSE (3)

16 Prufrock	117	/Full of high sentence, but a bit obtuse;/At times, indeed, almost ridiculous —/
312 FR Harry	4	If I had realised/That you were so obtuse, I would not have listened/To your
541 ES Gomez	13	money?/{G} My dear chap, you are obtuse!/I said: 'Your secret is safe with me',/

OBTUSENESS (1)

316 FR Violet	6	to what I can understand./{V} It is the obtuseness of Gerald and Charles and that

OBVIOUS (9)

337 FR Agatha	11	you have found a clue, hidden in the obvious place./Delay, and it is lost. Love
374 CP Edward	18	the situation./I suppose it was pretty obvious to everyone./{C} It was obvious that the
374 CP Celia	19	pretty obvious to everyone./{C} It was obvious that the aunt was a pure invention/On
409 CP Reilly	1	with your explanation/Of your obvious symptoms of emotional strain/And so I
416 CP Celia	9	clever of you./No, perhaps I made it obvious. You don't need to know/About him,
437 CP Reilly	21	happens to me, sometimes. So it was obvious/That here was a woman under sentence
461 CC Claude	33	best./It went off very well. It's very obvious/That she took to you at once./{C} Did
463 CC Claude	5	/Though it seemed to have such obvious advantages/That I had no doubts at the
499 CC Lucasta	24	was just the trouble. You made it so obvious/That this would be the ideal solution/

OBVIOUSLY (2)

412 CP Celia	36	when they come to see you,/Are obviously ill, or can give good reasons/For
548 ES Carghil	23	— that very charming girl?/And obviously devoted to her father./I was watching

OCCASION (13)

111 Xmas Trees	31	shall be also a great fear, as on the occasion/When fear came upon every soul:/
222 Pekes Pols	11	them all over the Park./Now on the occasion of which I shall speak/Almost nothing
288 FR Amy	10	at tea./{A} This is a very particular occasion/As you ought to know. It will be the
303 FR Mary	22	than a family dinner?/An official occasion of uncomfortable people/Who meet
318 FR Warburt	38	/What that has to do with the present occasion/Or with what I have to tell you./{H}
360 CP Reilly	8	where she's gone./{UG} This is an occasion./May I take another drink?/{E}
369 CP Peter	5	/And not easy to talk to, on that occasion./{E} Did you see her often?/{A}
384 CP Reilly	4	No, thank you. This is a different occasion./{E} I take it that as you have come

440 CP   Reilly   18 another engagement./{R} And on this occasion I shall not be unexpected./{J} Now,
501 CC   Eggers   27   /Though first of all I must take the occasion/To wish Miss Angel every happiness./
540 ES   Gomez   20   /You know quite well to which occasion I'm referring —/A summer night of
571 ES   Ld Clav   32 to make himself a reminder/Of one occasion the memory of which/He knows very
572 ES   Ld Clav   33   /Each of them remembers an occasion/On which I ran away. Very well./I
OCCASIONAL (3)
199   t fire/And the fire and the rose are one./OCCASIONAL VERSES/Defence of the
230 Bust Jones   13   Jones in white spats!/His visits are occasional to the *Senior Educational*/And it is
315 FR   Harry   2 is here:/The lump, the dull pain, the occasional sickness:/Murder a reversal of sleep
OCCASIONALLY (2)
344 FR   Gerald   23 useful, knowing the natives,/Though occasionally troublesome. But you'll have to
430 CP   Lavinia   35 life!/Don't you go to the movies?/{L} Occasionally./{P} Alex knows./Did you see my
OCCASIONS (3)
164 Rock 9   8 and faults as they go about their daily occasions./Yet they walk in the street
394 CP   Lavinia   14   I *was* the butler./{L} And on several occasions, when somebody was coming/Whom I
465 CC   Claude   20 /That I didn't have it in me. There are occasions/When I am transported — a different
OCCUPATION (5)
190 FQ: DrySal 206   of the timeless/With time, is an occupation for the saint —/No occupation
190 FQ: DrySal 207   is an occupation for the saint —/No occupation either, but something given/And
192 FQ: Little   49   an order of words, the conscious occupation/Of the praying mind, or the sound
218 Mung Rump   19   Victoria Grove. They had no regular occupation./They were plausible fellows, and
464 CC   Claude   33 /I was wrong, in both. I loathed this occupation/Until I began to feel my power in it.
OCCUPIED (4)
336 FR   3m 23 *the place which the* EUMENIDES *had occupied.*]/{Ag} A curse comes to being/As a
527 ES   Monica   28 too — or just sitting — someone/Not occupied with anything that can't be
531 ES   Ld Clav   14 if I had died in harness,/Would have occupied a column and a half/With an inset, a
544 ES   Monica   25 /I never remember you as other than occupied/With anxieties from which you were
OCCUPY (1)
531 ES   Ld Clav   22 successes, the successful failures,/Who occupy positions that other men covet./When
OCCUR (2)
395 CP   Edward   17 a change for the better./But doesn't it occur to you that possibly/I may have changed
407 CP   Reilly   7   are several symptoms/Which must occur together, and to a marked degree,/To
OCCURRED (2)
29 Aunt Helen   7 was aware that this sort of thing had occurred before./The dogs were handsomely
232 Skimble   24 /And he'd know at once if anything occurred./He will watch you without winking
OCEAN (2)
186 FQ: DrySal   72   of a time that is oceanless/Or of an ocean not littered with wastage/Or of a future
300 FRDowning   16   there's my complaint against these ocean liners/With all their swimming baths and
OCEANLESS (1)
186 FQ: DrySal   71   /We cannot think of a time that is oceanless/Or of an ocean not littered with
OCTOBER (6)
13 Prufrock   21   leap,/And seeing that it was a soft October night,/Curled once about the house,
20 Portrait   84 /Are these ideas right or wrong?/The October night comes down; returning as before/
239 MC   Chorus   9 forced to bear witness./Since golden October declined into sombre November/And
240 MC   Chorus   10   poor shall wait for another decaying October./Why should the summer bring
240 MC   Chorus   14   wait in barren orchards for another October?/Some malady is coming upon us. We
285 FR   Amy   3 out,/Now that I sit in the house from October to June,/And the swallow comes too
OCTOPUS (1)
398 CP   Edward   10   what have I done? The python. The octopus./Must I become after all what you
ODD (11)
49 Hippopot   18   voice/Betrays inflexions hoarse and odd,/But every week we hear rejoice/The
270 MC   Chorus   4 /Trunk and horn, tusk and hoof, in odd places;/I have lain on the floor of the sea
289 FR   Gerald   28   Vanishes from Liner'./{G} Yes, it's odd to think of her as permanently *missing.*/{V}
334 FR   Harry   28   /Ready to be put on. But it is very odd:/When other people seemed so strong, their
345 FR   Charles   32   VIOLET, GERALD]/{C} It's very odd,/But I am beginning to feel, just beginning
386 CP   Edward   24   sent me on ahead./{E} It seems very odd. And not like Lavinia./I suppose there is
392 CP   Lavinia   18   were here this evening .../{L} That's odd./{E} ... and one other. I don't know who he
430 CP   Alex   23   the place to go now./{A} How very odd. *My* monkeys are saffron./{P} Your
462 CC   Claude   37 But now I want it to be different. It's odd, Colby./I didn't realise, till you started with
508 CC   Guzzard   35   Kaghan!/{MG} K-A-G-H-A-N. An odd name./They were excellent people.
574 ES   Carghil   3   daughter./So much so, that it seems odd to call you Mr. Hemington:/I'm going to
ODDITIES (1)
456 CC   Eggers   14   I must admit she is./Most of her oddities are perfectly harmless./You'll soon get
ODDITY (1)
331 FR   Agatha   36 playing on the flute,/Something of an oddity to his county neighbours,/But not

ODDS (1)
　18 Portrait　　　　21　a life composed so much, so much of odds and ends,/(For indeed I do not love it ...
ODE (1)
　604 Ode　　　　　　t　/On the doorstep of the Absolute./Ode/THOMAS STEARNS ELIOT/For the
ODEUR (1)
　48 Lune Miel　　　4　/La sueur aestivale, et une forte odeur de chienne./Ils restent sur le dos écartant
ODOURS (1)
　64 WL: Chess　　89　confused/And drowned the sense in odours; stirred by the air/That freshened from
OED' (1)
　62 WL: Burial　　42　into the heart of light, the silence./*Oed' und leer das Meer.*/Madame Sosostris,
OF (3114)
OFF (62)
　15 Prufrock　　　　91　　　　been worth while,/To have bitten off the matter with a smile,/To have squeezed
　16 Prufrock　　　107　/If one, settling a pillow or throwing off a shawl,/And turning toward the window,
　66 WL: Chess　　155　　　if you can't./But if Albert makes off, it won't be for lack of telling./You ought to
　66 WL: Chess　　159　face,/It's them pills I took, to bring it off, she said./(She's had five already, and nearly
　116 SP　　Dusty　32　Monday/I say do you mind if I ring off now/She's got her feet in mustard and water
　121 SA Sweeney　　1　DORIS. DUSTY./{S} I'll carry you off/To a cannibal isle./{Do} You'll be the
　121 SA　　Doris　　7　be the cannibal./{Do} You'll carry me off? To a cannibal isle?/{S} I'll be the cannibal./
　161 Rock 7 m　　33　　　OF THE UNEMPLOYED (*afar off*):/*In this land/There shall be one cigarette to*
　188 FQ: DrySal　136　letters/(And those who saw them off have left the platform)/Their faces relax
　192 FQ: Little　　44　be the same: you would have to put off/Sense and notion. You are not here to
　224 Mr Mistoff　　5　and don't scoff. All his/Inventions are off his own bat./There's no such Cat in the
　232 Skimble　　　15　the signal goes 'All Clear!'/And we're off at last for the northern part/Of the Northern
　235 Ad-dress　　44　Resents familiarity./I bow, and taking off my hat,/Ad-dress him in this form: O CAT!/
　588 Fable　　　　32　course,/I'll be compelled to keep them off by force.'/He drencht the gown he wore with
　239 MC Chorus　12　in darkness./While the labourer kicks off a muddy boot and stretches his hand to the
　245 MC Priest2　32　in all your rooms/To take the chill off our English December,/Your Lordship now
　255 MC Tempt4　14　to be high in heaven./And see far off below you, where the gulf is fixed,/Your
　267 MC Knight2　20　Without delay,/Before the old fox is off and away./{T} What you have to say/By the
　272 MC Thomas　9　him! drag him!/{T} Keep your hands off!/{3P} To vespers! Hurry. {}/[*They drag him*
　272 MC　　　　m 10　To vespers! Hurry. {}/[*They drag him off. While the* CHORUS *speak, the scene is*
　286 FR　Charles　　2　/But a single man like me is better off in London:/A man can be very cosy at his
　289 FR　　　Ivy　25　to lose anybody in *that* way —/Swept off the deck in the middle of a storm,/And never
　296 FR　Charles　29　needs is someone to talk to,/To get it off his mind. I'll have a talk to him tomorrow./
　306 FR　　Harry　40　what was the design?/It never came off. But do you remember/{M} The hollow tree
　314 FR Warburt　27　had forty years' experience/I've left off thinking in terms of the laboratory./We're
　320 FR Warburt　15　A sudden shock/Might send her off at any moment./If she had been another
　325 FR　　　Ivy　29　one./He was always the one to fall off the pony,/Or out of a tree — and always on
　326 FR　　Harry　10　it's strange how the old/Can drop off to sleep in the middle of calamity/Like
　347 FRDowning　　3　I thought that was the reason/We was off tonight. In fact, I half expected it,/So I had
　359 CP　Edward　14　this evening./The fact is, I tried to put off this party:/These were only the people I
　359 CP　Edward　15　were only the people I couldn't put off/Because I couldn't get at them in time;/And
　359 CP　　Julia　30　business./Well, good-bye again. I'm off at last. {}/[*Exit*]/{E} I'm sorry. I'm afraid I
　368 CP　Edward　29　/{E} Well, where did you leave off?/{P} You asked me how I came to know
　383 CP　Edward　　4　bag? ... Well, don't snap my head off .../You're sure, in the kitchen? Beside the
　389 CP　　Celia　30　herself./{C} Lavinia,/Don't put me off. I may not see you again./What I want to
　401 CP　Edward　30　to persuade me/That I was better off without her. But didn't you realise/That I
　430 CP　　Peter　19　York./The Bologolomskys saw me off./You remember Princess Bologolomsky/In
　450 CC　Eggers　30　I was afraid I'd miss you./{E} I'm off in half an hour, Mr. Simpkins./{SC} I'll
　451 CC　Eggers　　3　is prejudiced./He's never hit it off with Lady Elizabeth./Don't listen to him. He
　454 CC　Kaghan　10　/She's hard as nails. Now I'll take her off your hands./I'll show you how it's done.
　457 CC　Claude　11　Hello! Still here? It's time you were off./{E} I'm just going. There's plenty of time. {}
　457 CC　　　m 16　MULHAMMER'S *voice off.*/* Lady Elizabeth's words off stage are not*
　457 CC note 16&　25　*voice off.*/* Lady Elizabeth's words off stage are not intended to be heard distinctly*
　457 CC　　　m 25　MULHAMMER'S *voice off.*/{LE} No, Gertrude, I haven't had any lunch,
　461 CC　Eggers　　3　some shopping./But I'd better be off now. Mr. Simpkins —/If anything *should*
　461 CC　Claude　33　that it's all for the best./It went off very well. It's very obvious/That she took to
　476 CC Lucasta　21　—/Or had been his mistress, palmed off on B./{C} I never thought of such a thing!/
　499 CC Lucasta　26　/From your point of view. To get me off your hands./Oh, I know what a nuisance
　500 CC Lucasta　38　the wrong reasons,/And that put me off. So I'm grateful to Colby./{SC} I don't know
　504 CC　Claude　　8　formidable./{SC} It's Parkman's day off. But where's the parlourmaid?/{L} I thought
　524 ES　Monica　17　what men are — they like to show off./That's masculine vanity, to want to have
　524 ES　Monica　24　avoiding his eye./{M} We're getting off the point .../{C} You've got me off *my* point
　524 ES　Charles　25　off the point .../{C} You've got me off *my* point .../I was trying to explain .../{M}

532 ES	Monica	11	into the library. And then I'll see you off./{LC} I'm sorry to turn you out of the room
536 ES	Gomez	19	don't know what it's like/To be so cut off! Homesickness!/Homesickness is a sickly
543 ES	Gomez	7	/That we can begin just where we left off. {}/[*Exit* GOMEZ]/[LORD CLAVERTON
550 ES	Carghil	27	have sent me *here*/If I wasn't well off. Yes, I'm provided for./But isn't it strange
557 ES	Michael	16	me excellent tips./They always came off — the tips I didn't take./{LC} And the ones
557 ES	Michael	21	borrowed more/I might have pulled it off./{LC} Borrowed? From whom?/Not ... from
569 ES	Ld Clav	2	becomes to drop the pretence,/Walk off the stage, change into our own clothes/And
569 ES	Ld Clav	6	would love the actor/If she saw him, off the stage, without his costume and makeup/
580 ES	Carghil	25	rather tired. I'll run and see them off. {}/[*Exit* MRS. CARGHILL]/{M} Oh

OFFENCE (1)

556 ES	Monica	5	apt to be sullen and quick to take offence./So I hope you'll be patient./{LC} Well

OFFEND (1)

97 Ash-Wed 5		30	slender/Yew trees pray for those who offend her/And are terrified and cannot

OFFENDED (2)

413 CP	Celia	1	came in desperation. And I shan't be offended/If you simply tell me to go away again.
425 CP	Lavinia	9	/But all the same would be bitterly offended/To hear we'd given a party without

OFFENDING (1)

493 CC	Claude	17	awkward. We don't want to start/By offending Mrs. Guzzard. That's why I thought/

OFFENDS (3)

107 Animula		17	of the growing soul/Perplexes and offends more, day by day;/Week by week,
107 Animula		18	more, day by day;/Week by week, offends and perplexes more/With the
278 MC Knight2		28	such interference by an Archbishop/offends the instincts of a people like ours. So

OFFENSIVE (1)

361 CP	Edward	23	—/I think your speculations rather offensive./{UG} I know you as well as I know

OFFENSIVELY (1)

278 MC Knight2		22	than the/priests, he ostentatiously and offensively adopted an ascetic/manner of life, he

OFFER (15)

214 RTTugger		2	Tum Tugger is a Curious Cat:/If you offer him pheasant he would rather have grouse.
214 RTTugger		25	ways are a matter of habit./If you offer him fish then he always wants a feast;/
214 RTTugger		27	fish then he won't eat rabbit./If you offer him cream then he sniffs and sneers,/For
255 MC Thomas		21	power at palpable price./What do you offer? what do you ask?/{T4} I offer what you
255 MC Tempt4		22	do you offer? what do you ask?/{T4} I offer what you desire. I ask/What you have to
255 MC Thomas		26	goods, worthless/But real. You only offer/Dreams to damnation./{T4} You have
260 MC Thomas		10	coming for the salvation of men, and/offer again to God His Body and Blood in
265 MC Priest1		23	would be vexed/If we did not offer you entertainment/Before your business.
384 CP	Edward	3	Mr. Chamberlayne./{E} Well. May I offer you some gin and water?/{UG} No, thank
426 CP	Julia	32	party —/And you know what *they* offer in the way of food and drink!/And I've
447 CC	Claude	31	he'd had another very tempting offer./Something like that. Don't make too
458 CC	Eggers	31	same time, he had another tempting offer:/So we had to make a quick decision./{SC}
547 ES	Piggott	22	amenities which Badgley Court/Can offer to guests of the younger generation./When
548 ES	Ld Clav	20	chose it./She noticed that it seemed to offer the advantages/Which you have just
561 ES	Ld Clav	27	him half way. I have made him an offer/Which he must think over. But if he goes

OFFERED (9)

107 Animula		27	retreat,/Fearing the warm reality, the offered good,/Denying the importunity of the
255 MC Thomas		25	vision of eternal grandeur?/{T} Others offered real goods, worthless/But real. You only
267 MC Knight2		38	charity,/And urged by your friends, offered clemency,/Made a pact of peace, and all
394 CP	Lavinia	19	worse,/And the moment you were offered something that you wanted/You wanted
507 CC Guzzard		10	... at the time,/And very poor. It offered two advantages./{E} And did you know
508 CC	Eggers	8	you grasp at any straw/That offered hope of finding him?/{MG} Perhaps
575 ES	Michael	5	point of view, if *you* don't./And he's offered me a job which is just what I wanted./
576 ES	Michael	15	for./{Mi} I don't care about that. He's offered me the job/With a jolly good screw, and
577 ES	Charles	2	point to think of:/Señor Gomez has offered you a post in San Marco,/Señor Gomez

OFFERETH (1)

264 MC Priest1		24	for the people, so also for himself, he offereth for sins./He lays down his life for the

OFFERING (3)

194 FQ: Little		134	expiring sense/Without enchantment, offering no promise/But bitter tastelessness of
544 ES	Ld Clav	13	days of people not staring/Or offering picture papers, or wanting a fourth at
551 ES	Carghil	33	/He said: 'What his lawyers are offering in settlement/Is twice as much as I

OFFERS (3)

184 FQ: DrySal		20	whale's backbone;/The pools where it offers to our curiosity/The more delicate algae
400 CP	Reilly	24	He's enjoying his illness./{R} Illness offers him a double advantage:/To escape from
462 CC	Claude	25	life, you must accept the terms it offers you./But tell me first — I've a reason for

OFFICE (12)

55 Mr E Sun		28	/The staminate and pistillate,/Blest office of the epicene./Sweeney shifts from ham
226 Macavity		27	*not there*!/And when the Foreign Office find a Treaty's gone astray,/Or the

250 MC	Thomas	6	among their servants,/Is my open office. No! Go./{T2} Then I leave you to your
272 MC	Priests	1	must not be absent from the divine office. To vespers./Into the Cathedral!/{T} Go
278 MC	Knight2	21	made Archbishop, he/resigned the office of Chancellor, he became more priestly
483 CC	Colby	12	writing-table come from?/{C} It's an office desk. Sir Claude got it for me./I said I
511 CC	Lucasta	39	be married very quietly/In a register office./{LE} You must have a church wedding./
530 ES	Ld Clav	23	/Have left, and the booking office is closed/And the porters have gone.
545 ES	Piggott	32	known./Just ring through to my office. If I'm not there/My secretary will be —
550 ES	Carghil	22	/Of Carghill Equipments? They make office furniture./{LC} I've never had to deal
558 ES	Michael	20	know what I suffered, working in that office./In the first place, they all knew the job
558 ES	Michael	26	when I'd nothing to do./Even the office boys began to sneer at me./I wonder I

OFFICES (1)

278 MC	Knight2	14	no one denies that — should unite/the offices of Chancellor and Archbishop. Had

OFFICIAL (4)

278 MC	Knight2	17	I knew Becket well, in various official relations; and I/may say that I have
303 FR	Mary	22	formal than a family dinner?/An official occasion of uncomfortable people/Who
429 CP	Alex	26	/Eventually, there may be an official publication./{E} But when?/{A} In a year
534 ES	Gomez	4	/In fact, I've never come across an official/Innocent enough to be corruptible./{LC}

OFTEN (37)

161 Rock 7		25	on the way that was lit by the light;/Often halting, loitering, straying, delaying,
185 FQ:	DrySal	30	/And the sea yelp, are different voices/Often together heard: the whine in the rigging,/
195 FQ:	Little	152	/There are three conditions which often look alike/Yet differ completely, flourish
197 FQ:	Little	216	or fire./What we call the beginning is often the end/And to make an end is to make a
234 Ad-dress		21	Dogs pretend they like to fight;/They often bark, more seldom bite;/But yet a Dog is,
235 Ad-dress		47	he is the Cat next door,/Whom I have often met before/(He comes to see me in my
589 Fable		71	folk should be allowed about,/For often they drop in at awkward moments,/As
247 MC	Templ1	23	nod is as good as a wink./A man will often love what he spurns./For the good times
255 MC	Templ4	28	Dreams to damnation./{T4} You have often dreamt them./{T} Is there no way, in my
271 MC	Thomas	17	memory/Only like a dream that has often been told/And often been changed in the
271 MC	Thomas	18	a dream that has often been told/And often been changed in the telling. They will
278 MC	Knight2	11	were usually exercised for/selfish and often for seditious ends, and to reform the legal
288 FR	Agatha	21	of the Mediterranean,/Harry must often have remembered Wishwood —/The
296 FR	Ivy	20	before — that people in his condition/Often betray the most immoderate resentment/
344 FR	Gerald	20	first thing./I've met with missionaries, often enough —Some of them very decent
361 CP	Edward	13	/{E} And please don't suggest./I have often used these terms in examining witnesses,/
369 CP	Edward	6	on that occasion./{E} Did you see her often?/{A} Edward, have you a double boiler?/
369 CP	Peter	12	I must think of another./{P} Not very often./And when I did, I got no chance to talk
369 CP	Peter	34	alone/And to look at pictures. So we often met/In the same way, and sometimes went
396 CP	Edward	7	me when we had to be alone./{E} I've often wondered why you married me./{L} Well,
405 CP	Reilly	1	can always tell me./Indeed, it is often the case that my patients/Are only pieces
407 CP	Edward	1	/{E} Only because you've told me so often./I'd like to see *you* filling up an
419 CP	Reilly	31	They lead very active lives/Very often, in the world./{C} How soon will you send
438 CP	Reilly	31	be condemned./Mrs. Chamberlayne, I often have to make a decision/Which may mean
453 CC	Lucasta	10	to dinner. A working girl like me/Is often very hungry — living on a pittance —/
461 CC	Colby	13	/That I shan't have to call upon you often./{E} Oh, and I forgot ... Mrs. E. keeps
467 CC	Colby	1	/Of father and son. It must often happen./And the reconcilement, after his
483 CC	Lady E	1	surprising — intellectual people/Are often ill-bred. But that's not all./You need
496 CC	Eggers	39	Of the day we got the news. We don't often speak of it;/Yet I know what's on her
498 CC	Claude	18	have noticed it. I visited her house/Often. I never saw more than one baby./{E} She
529 ES	Monica	18	he is fond of you./So you must come often. And Oh, Charles dear — {}/[*Enter* LORD
544 ES	Ld Clav	16	last —/The sense of wellbeing! It's often with us/When we are young, but then it's
544 ES	Ld Clav	19	grown to consciousness/It comes less often./I hope this benignant sunshine/And
544 ES	Ld Clav	23	that's hardly seasonable,/Is so often a harbinger of frost on the fruit trees./{M}
544 ES	Ld Clav	30	that they enjoy it. Whereas I've often known/That I didn't enjoy it. Some
549 ES	Carghil	1	all seen your portrait in the papers/So often. And everybody knows *you*. But still,/I
578 ES	Michael	32	and always shall be./We don't meet often, but if we're fond of each other,/That

OFTENER (1)

496 CC	Eggers	19	me;/But Mrs. E. wishes I'd come up oftener!/Isn't that like the ladies! She used to

OH (222)

OIL (2)

69 WL:	Fire S	267	white and gold./The river sweats/Oil and tar/The barges drift/With the turning
508 CC	Eggers	14	remark./{E} May I pour a drop of oil on these troubled waters?/Let us approach

OLD (118)

16 Prufrock		120	—/Almost, at times, the Fool./I grow old ... I grow old .../I shall wear the bottoms of
16 Prufrock		120	times, the Fool./I grow old ... I grow old .../I shall wear the bottoms of my trousers
24 Rhapsody		44	a crab one afternoon in a pool,/An old crab with barnacles on his back,/Gripped

24 Rhapsody	60	de Cologne,/She is alone/With all the old nocturnal smells/That cross and cross across
31 Apollinax	9	submarine and profound/Like the old man of the sea's/Hidden under coral islands
33 Conv Gal	4	may be Prester John's balloon/Or an old battered lantern hung aloft/To light poor
37 Gerontion	1	/Poems/Gerontion/Here I am, an old man in a dry month,/Being read to by a
37 Gerontion	15	poking the peevish gutter./I an old man,/A dull head among windy spaces./
38 Gerontion	31	Weave the wind. I have no ghosts,/An old man in a draughty house/Under a windy
39 Gerontion	72	in the snow, the Gulf claims,/And an old man driven by the Trades/To a sleepy
50 Hippopot	36	Church remains below/Wrapt in the old miasmal mist./Dans le Restaurant/Le
68 WL: Fire S	219	blind, throbbing between two lives,/Old man with wrinkled female breasts, can see/
68 WL: Fire S	228	camisoles, and stays./I Tiresias, old man with wrinkled dugs/Perceived the
92 Ash-Wed 3	10	stair was dark,/Damp, jaggèd, like an old man's mouth drivelling, beyond repair,/Or
103 Journ Magi	25	three trees on the low sky./And an old white horse galloped away in the meadow./
104 Journ Magi	41	/But no longer at ease here, in the old dispensation,/With an alien people clutching
123 SAWa & Ho	5	/Or under the bamboo tree?/Any old tree will do for me/Any old wood is just as
123 SAWa & Ho	6	tree?/Any old tree will do for me/Any old wood is just as good/Any old isle is just my
123 SAWa & Ho	7	me/Any old wood is just as good/Any old isle is just my style/Any fresh egg/Any fresh
140 Usk	5	aside, not for lance, do not spell/Old enchantments. Let them sleep./'Gently dip,
143 Lines OM	t	/The palaver is finished./Lines for an Old Man/The tiger in the tiger-pit/Is not more
163 Rock 8	32	left that was more than the tales/Of old men on winter evenings./Only the faith
173 FQ: BurntN	78	both a new world/And the old made explicit, understood/In the completion
177 FQ: ECoker	5	open field, or a factory, or a by-pass./Old stone to new building, old timber to new
177 FQ: ECoker	5	a by-pass./Old stone to new building, old timber to new fires,/Old fires to ashes, and
177 FQ: ECoker	6	new building, old timber to new fires,/Old fires to ashes, and ashes to the earth/Which
179 FQ: ECoker	95	Do not let me hear/Of the wisdom of old men, but rather of their folly,/Their fear of
182 FQ: ECoker	198	the lifetime of one man only/But of old stones that cannot be deciphered./There is a
182 FQ: ECoker	204	/When here and now cease to matter./Old men ought to be explorers/Here and there
192 FQ: Little	56	Never and always./Ash on an old man's sleeve/Is all the ash the burnt roses
196 FQ: Little	187	spectre of a Rose./We cannot revive old factions/We cannot restore old policies/Or
196 FQ: Little	188	revive old factions/We cannot restore old policies/Or follow an antique drum./These
197 FQ: Little	222	/An easy commerce of the old and the new,/The common word exact
207	t	words addressed to you in public./OLD POSSUM'S BOOK OF PRACTICAL
210 Old Gumbie	t	and inscrutable singular Name./The Old Gumbie Cat/I have a Gumbie Cat in mind,
211 Old Gumbie	37	even created a Beetles' Tattoo./So for Old Gumbie Cats let us now give three cheers
220 Old Deut	t	nothing at all to be done about that!/Old Deuteronomy/Old Deuteronomy's lived a
220 Old Deut	1	done about that!/Old Deuteronomy/Old Deuteronomy's lived a long time;/He's a
220 Old Deut	5	before Queen Victoria's accession./Old Deuteronomy's buried nine wives/And
220 Old Deut	16	wandering, but I confess/I believe it is Old Deuteronomy!'/Old Deuteronomy sits in
220 Old Deut	17	/I believe it is Old Deuteronomy!'/Old Deuteronomy sits in the street,/He sits in
220 Old Deut	31	guess/That the cause of the trouble is Old Deuteronomy!'/Old Deuteronomy lies on
221 Old Deut	32	of the trouble is Old Deuteronomy!'/Old Deuteronomy lies on the floor/Of the Fox
221 Old Deut	37	out you go, by the back door,/For Old Deuteronomy mustn't be woken —/I'll
221 Old Deut	47	I must go slow/And be careful of Old Deuteronomy!/Of the Awefull Battle of
236 Cat Morgan	16	That some of the gals is dead keen on old Morgan./So if you 'ave business with Faber
587 Fable	11	and a dairy;/Whenever some old villainous baron died,/He added to their
587 Fable	17	a ghost./Some wicked and heretical old sinner/Perhaps, who had been walled up for
588 Fable	58	wassail the monks dozed,/A fine old drink, though now gone out of use —/His
589 Fable	96	record of these doings/From an old manuscript found in the ruins./If Time and
593 Grad 8	2	when we are grown/Gray-haired and old, whatever be our lot,/We shall desire to see
605 Narcissus	29	/Caught in the woods by a drunken old man/Knowing at the end the taste of his
606 Narcissus	32	smoothness,/And he felt drunken and old./So he became a dancer to God./Because his
241 MC Priest2	23	and the anvil?/{P2} Tell us,/Are the old disputes at an end, is the wall of pride cast
246 MC Tempt1	29	past./Your Lordship won't despise an old friend out of favour?/Old Tom, gay Tom,
246 MC Tempt1	30	despise an old friend out of favour?/Old Tom, gay Tom, Becket of London,/Your
249 MC Tempt2	26	servant of a powerless Pope,/The old stag, circled with hounds./{T} No!/{T2} Yes!
253 MC Tempt4	38	is the course of temporal power./The Old King shall know it, when at last breath,/No
257 MC Chorus	11	violence,/Destitution, disease,/The old without fire in winter,/The child without
263 MC Chorus	4	of the year?/Only the death of the old: not a stir, not a shoot, not a breath./Do the
267 MC Knight2	20	now?/{K2} Without delay,/Before the old fox is off and away./{T} What you have to
276 MC Knight3	34	such an experienced/speaker as my old friend Reginald Fitz Urse would lead you to
287 FR Amy	29	/You none of you understand how old you are/And death will come to you as a
288 FR Agatha	25	holiday,/The daring feats on the old pony,/And thought to creep back through
288 FR Amy	30	as it was when he left it,/Except the old pony, and the mongrel setter/Which I had
290 FR Amy	6	wanted/Harry's relations or Harry's old friends;/She never wanted to fit herself to
292 FR Ivy	33	really have to find a successor to old Hawkins./It's really high time the old man
292 FR Ivy	34	old Hawkins./It's really high time the old man was pensioned./He's let the rock

293 FR	Violet	2	on in the kitchen./Mrs. Packell is too old to know what she is doing./It really needs a
293 FR	Amy	9	/Now it's for you to manage. I am an old woman./They can give me no further advice
294 FR	Harry	6	in a more familiar medium. I am the old house/With the noxious smell and the
296 FR	Gerald	35	and ask him to join us?/He's an old friend of the family, it's perfectly natural/
307 FR	Harry	15	slipped down to the river/To find the old hiding place. The wilderness was gone,/The
320 FR	Warburt	31	this;/But you know that I am a very old friend,/And have always been a party to the
326 FR	Harry	9	is asleep, I think: it's strange how the old/Can drop off to sleep in the middle of
328 FR	Chorus	34	no such thing as privacy./{Ch} In an old house there is always listening, and more is
329 FR	Chorus	7	of hay in summer/The dogs and the old pony/The stumble and the wail of little pain
330 FR	Harry	29	together:/When I was inside the old dream, I felt all the same emotion/Or lack
334 FR	Agatha	6	my dear,/I feel very tired, as only the old feel./The young feel tired at the end of an
334 FR	Agatha	8	tired at the end of an action —/The old, at the beginning. It is as if/I had been living
334 FR	Agatha	11	my spiritual income daily:/And I am old, to start again to make my living./{H} But
343 FR	Amy	22	/{A} So you will all leave me!/An old woman alone in a damned house./I will let
345 FR	Amy	20	too late to mend: and that is to be old./Nevertheless, I am glad if I can come to
345 FR	Charles	35	I want to know. I suppose I'm getting old:/Old age came softly up to now. I felt safe
345 FR	Charles	36	to know. I suppose I'm getting old:/Old age came softly up to now. I felt safe
355 CP	Julia	25	for a cocktail party/For a gluttonous old woman like me/Is a really nice tit-bit. I can
356 CP	Julia	28	thinking!/I know you think I'm a silly old woman/But I'm really very serious. Lavinia
357 CP	Celia	3	was I going to say?/It's dreadful for old ladies alone in the country,/And almost
357 CP	Julia	22	away again./I understand these tough old women —/I'm one myself. I feel as if I knew
359 CP	Edward	20	invited./But it's only that dreadful old woman who mattered —/I shouldn't have
381 CP	Edward	11	/Beginning to know what it is to feel old./That is the worst moment, when you feel
381 CP	Edward	18	*you* understand what it is to feel old?/{C} But I want to understand you. I could
390 CP	Julia	36	—/And after that long journey on the old Great Eastern,/Waiting at junctions. And I
397 CP	Lavinia	35	your sort of compromise will be the old one./{E} You don't understand me. Have I
426 CP	Julia	37	one of their men at the door —/An old friend of mine, in fact. But I'm forgetting!/
430 CP	Peter	16	/And how are you, Alex? And dear old Julia!/{L} So you've just come from New
430 CP	Peter	21	Princess Bologolomsky/In the old days? We dined the other night/At the
432 CP	Lavinia	26	Sir Henry Harcourt-Reilly. Peter's an old friend/Of my husband and myself. Oh, I
477 CC	Lucasta	3	in a cupboard!/I was only eight years old/When she died of an 'accidental overdose'./
477 CC	Lucasta	6	me over. That was lucky./But I was old enough to remember ... too much./{C} You
486 CC	Lady E	5	aunt./But the name is familiar. How old are you, Colby?/{C} I'm twenty-five./{LE}
509 CC	Lady E	31	ought to be proud of it./{LE} How old is this Barnabas?/{SC} About twenty-eight, I
529 ES	Ld Clav	32	just like it —/You know I keep the old ones on a shelf together;/I could look in the
535 ES	Gomez	3	A natural desire!/For you're the only old friend I can trust./{LC} You really trust me?
536 ES	Gomez	36	she's still alive,/But she must be very old. And she must think I'm dead;/And as for
536 ES	Gomez	39	want to see me./No, I need one old friend, a friend whom I can trust —/And
540 ES	Gomez	22	—/The night you ran over the old man in the road./{LC} You *said* I ran over
540 ES	Ld Clav	23	the road./{LC} You *said* I ran over an old man in the road./{G} You knew it too. If
541 ES	Gomez	16	believed/That you would accuse an old friend of ... blackmail!/On the contrary, I
542 ES	Gomez	4	friendship!/Just as it used to be in the old days/When you taught me expensive tastes.
550 ES	Ld Clav	32	/Finding me here, to revive old memories/Which I should have thought we
563 ES	Gomez	19	us./{LC} Oh. This is ...{G} Your old friend Federico Gomez,/The prominent
564 ES	Gomez	13	Gomez./{G} My dear lady, you're not old enough/To have known Dick Ferry as long
565 ES	Carghil	11	Michael?/Your father is such an old friend of mine/That it seems most natural to
565 ES	Gomez	27	we must have some good talks/About old times. Bye bye for the present. {}/[*Exit*]/{M}
571 ES	Ld Clav	36	A secondary road./I ran over an old man lying in the road/And I did not stop.
571 ES	Ld Clav	40	It was definitely shown/That the old man had died a natural death/And had been
577 ES	Gomez	11	Yes, it's always pleasant/To repay an old debt. And better late than never./{C} I see

OLDER (16)

182 FQ:	ECoker	192	is where one starts from. As we grow older/The world becomes stranger, the pattern
185 FQ:	DrySal	40	the unhurried/Ground swell, a time/Older than the time of chronometers, older/
185 FQ:	DrySal	40	/Older than the time of chronometers, older/Than time counted by anxious worried
186 FQ:	DrySal	87	/It seems, as one becomes older,/That the past has another pattern, and
306 FR	Mary	30	for you./And you seemed so much older. We were rather in awe of you —/At least,
307 FR	Mary	21	for granted,/Including the stupidity of older people —/They lived in another world,
315 FR	Violet	20	wouldn't think that she was a day older/Than on her birthday ten years ago./{G}
321 FR	Winch	32	jokes, I see. You don't look a year older/Than when I saw you last, my Lord. But a
324 FR	Amy	26	do not know very much:/And as I get older, I am coming to think/How little I have
372 CP	Peter	3	way from me/And you are so much older./{E} So much older?/{P} Yes, I'm sure that
372 CP	Edward	4	you are so much older./{E} So much older?/{P} Yes, I'm sure that she would listen to
389 CP	Lavinia	28	*can* be a friend/Of a woman so much older than herself./{C} Lavinia,/Don't put me
482 CC	Lady E	19	{C} But, Lady Elizabeth ...{LE} Well, older than you are,/And a good deal wiser in
490 CC	Colby	23	come to love you —/But as friends ... older friends. Neither, as a parent./I am sorry.

550 ES	Carghil	17	I married Mr. Carghill. Twenty years older/Than me, he was. Just what I needed./
568 ES	Ld Clav	33	you've never been honest with anyone older,/On terms of equality. To one's child one

OLDEST (7)

220 Old Deut		11	in the sun on the vicarage wall,/The Oldest Inhabitant croaks: 'Well, of all .../Things
220 Old Deut		26	in domestic economy:/And the Oldest Inhabitant croaks: 'Well, of all .../Things
221 Old Deut		42	be broken, whatever befall:/And the Oldest Inhabitant croaks: 'Well, of all .../Things
314 FR	Amy	3	Dr. Warburton?/You know he's the oldest friend of the family,/And he's known you
315 FR	Amy	25	Doctor?/I think we are very much the oldest present —/In fact we are the oldest
315 FR	Amy	26	oldest present —/In fact we are the oldest inhabitants./As we came first, we will go
354 CP	Alex	12	to a Baltic family —/One of the *oldest* Baltic families/With a branch in Sweden

OLIVES (1)

355 CP	Julia	27	give me another of those delicious olives./What's that? Potato crisps? No, I can't

OMAHA (1)

47 Mél Adult		15	coups de tra là là/De Damas jusqu'à Omaha./Je célébrai mon jour de fête/Dans une

OMENS (1)

189 FQ: DrySal		193	/And tragedy from fingers; release omens/By sortilege, or tea leaves, riddle the

OMINOUS (2)

599 On a Port		9	of one's own./No meditations glad or ominous/Disturb her lips, or move the slender
545 ES	Ld Clav	17	Court is for.'/I thought that very ominous. When people talk like that/It indicates

OMITTING (1)

407 CP	Reilly	30	your feelings —/Or some of them — omitting the important facts./Let me take your

OMNES (1)

595 Grad 14		6	'tis a call we cannot disobey,/*Exeunt omnes*, with a last 'farewell'./Song/When we

ON (563)

ON (4) [*Foreign word*]

47 Mél Adult		19	d'Afrique/Vêtu d'une peau de girafe./On montrera mon cénotaphe/Aux côtes
48 Lune Miel		7	molles tout gonflées de morsures./On relève le drap pour mieux égratigner./Moins
51 Restaurant		5	grand soleil, et de la pluie;/C'est ce qu'on appelle le jour de lessive des gueux.'/(Bavard,
51 Restaurant		9	—'C'est là, dans une averse, qu'on s'abrite./J'avais sept ans, elle était plus

ONCE (107)

13 Prufrock		22	it was a soft October night,/Curled once about the house, and fell asleep./And
41 Burb Blei		21	end of time/Declines. On the Rialto once./The rats are underneath the piles./The
49 Hippopot		24	—/The Church can sleep and feed at once./I saw the 'potamus take wing/Ascending
68 WL: Fire S		239	/Flushed and decided, he assaults at once;/Exploring hands encounter no defence;/
71 WL: DWater		321	/Consider Phlebas, who was once handsome and tall as you./What the
74 WL: Thund		412	I have heard the key/Turn in the door once and turn once only/We think of the key,
74 WL: Thund		412	key/Turn in the door once and turn once only/We think of the key, each in his
115 SP	Doris	24	He *is* a funny fellow/He's like a fellow once I knew./*He* could make you laugh./{Du}
118 SP	Doris	10	/{Do} It's no use asking more than once/{Du} Sometimes they're no use at all./{Do}
122 SA	Sweeney	12	and death./I've been born, and once is enough./You don't remember, but I
122 SA	Sweeney	14	don't remember, but I remember,/Once is enough. {}/SONG BY WAUCHOPE
124 SA	Sweeney	2	life is?/{S} Life is death./I knew a man once did a girl in —/{Do} Oh Mr. Sweeney,
124 SA	Sweeney	12	are very interested./{S} I knew a man once did a girl in./Any man might do a girl in/
124 SA	Sweeney	15	/Any man has to, needs to, wants to/Once in a lifetime, do a girl in/Well he kept her
139 Virginia		6	through the mocking-bird/Heard once? Still hills/Wait. Gates wait. Purple trees,/
159 Rock 6		26	the Son of Man was not crucified once for all,/The blood of the martyrs not shed
159 Rock 6		27	all,/The blood of the martyrs not shed once for all,/The lives of the Saints not given
159 Rock 6		28	all,/The lives of the Saints not given once for all:/But the Son of Man is crucified
182 FQ: ECoker		186	has already been discovered/Once or twice, or several times, by men whom
184 FQ: DrySal		6	the builder of bridges./The problem once solved, the brown god is almost forgotten/
195 FQ: Little		144	and done to others' harm/Which once you took for exercise of virtue./Then fools'
222 Pekes Pols		5	say/That they do not like fighting, yet once in a way,/Or now and again, they join in to
226 Macavity		10	look up in the air —/But I tell you once and once again, *Macavity's not there!*/
226 Macavity		10	in the air —/But I tell you once and once again, *Macavity's not there!*/Macavity's a
228 Gus		15	drawn from his palmiest days./For he once was a Star of the highest degree —/He has
228 Gus		18	on the Halls,/Where the Gallery once gave him seven cat-calls./But his grandest
228 Gus		32	season I never fell flat,/And I once understudied Dick Whittington's Cat./But
229 Gus		36	a toothful of gin,/He will tell how he once played a part in *East Lynne*./At a
229 Gus		37	/At a Shakespeare performance he once walked on pat,/When some actor
229 Gus		39	actor suggested the need for a cat./He once played a Tiger — could do it again —/
229 Gus		43	noises to bring on the Ghost./And he once crossed the stage on a telegraph wire,/To
232 Skimble		24	by a regular patrol/And he'd know at once if anything occurred./He will watch you
236 Cat Morgan		1	/Cat Morgan Introduces Himself/I once was a Pirate what sailed the 'igh seas —/
587 Fable		23	all the milk — upset the chimes,/And once he sat the prior on the steeple,/To the
605 Narcissus		8	gray shadow on his lips./He walked once between the sea and the high cliffs/When

250	MC	Thomas	17	arm, his better reason./But what was once exaltation/Would now be only mean
251	MC	Tempt3	4	may turn to real/But real friendship, once ended, cannot be mended./Sooner shall
252	MC	Tempt3	1	with us, would fight a good stroke/At once, for England and for Rome,/Ending the
252	MC	Thomas	15	to trust none but God alone./I ruled once as Chancellor/And men like you were glad
260	MC	Thomas	15	of all the year that we/celebrate at once the Birth of Our Lord and His Passion and
260	MC	Thomas	17	World will both mourn and rejoice at once and/for the same reason? For either joy
260	MC	Thomas	20	that we can rejoice and mourn at once for the same reason./Now think for a
261	MC	Thomas	9	at the feast of Christmas celebrate at once Our Lord's/Birth and His Death: but on
261	MC	Thomas	13	Just as we rejoice and mourn at once, in the/Birth and in the Passion of Our
261	MC	Thomas	32	the Church mourns and rejoices at once, in/a fashion that the world cannot
277	MC	Knight3	2	to say, and I might as/well say it at once. It is this: in what we have done, and
285	FR	Amy	6	I am out again./O Sun, that was once so warm, O Light that was taken for
293	FR	Agatha	22	no pretences:/And you must try at once to make us understand,/And we must try
296	FR	Harry	9	see what you mean,/Dimly — as you once explained the sobbing in the chimney/The
297	FR	Charles	16	/I might have done the same thing once, myself./Nobody knows what he's likely to
298	FR	Violet	16	Downing says./I want to know at once, not be told about it later./{I} And I shall
300	FR	Downing	6	over the rail./He was in a rare fright, once or twice./But you know, it is just my
313	FR	Ivy	11	/You know I had my own garden once, in Cornwall,/When I could afford a
319	FR	Warburt	12	for misery./There was enough once: but what festered/Then, has only left a
323	FR	Amy	27	I must see for myself. Order the car at once./{W} I forbid it, Lady Monchensey./As
324	FR	Warburt	2	are only delaying me. I shall return at once./{A} Well, I suppose you are right. But can
324	FR	Harry	34	/To be living on several planes at once/Though one cannot speak with several
324	FR	Harry	35	cannot speak with several voices at once./I have all of the rightminded feeling about
325	FR	Charles	12	said, then he'll let us know at once./{G} I am really more afraid of the shock
332	FR	Agatha	22	/An undergraduate at Oxford. I came/Once for a long vacation. I remember/A
332	FR	Agatha	29	hand/To the flames. They only come once,/Thank God, that kind. Perhaps there is
338	FR	Harry	30	way, had there been any other!/It is at once the hardest thing, and the only thing
354	CP	Julia	16	/{J} Lady Klootz was very lovely, once upon a time./What a life she led! I used to
355	CP	Julia	9	needn't be so sceptical. I stayed there once/At their castle in the North. How he
368	CP	Alex	28	Don't say a word./I shall begin at once. {}/[Exit to kitchen]/{E} Well, where did
369	CP	Edward	18	/To establish herself in two worlds at once —/But she herself had to be the link
369	CP	Peter	38	And we sometimes had tea/And once or twice dined together./{E} And after that
370	CP	Peter	2	/Or to any of her friends?/{P} No, but once or twice she spoke of them/And about
383	CP	Edward	10	and a bottle]/{E} She was right for once./{C} She is always right./But why bring an
399	CP	Nurse	8	/And you will see him almost at once./{R} I shall see him at once. And the
399	CP	Reilly	9	almost at once./{R} I shall see him at once. And the second?/{N} The second to be
401	CP	Edward	13	/I suppose I might as well go away at once./{R} No. If you please, sit down, Mr.
404	CP	Edward	11	note of what you do not say./{E} I once experienced the extreme of physical pain,/
418	CP	Reilly	2	be only like a book/You have read once, and lost. In a world of lunacy,/Violence,
419	CP	Reilly	37	had better let your family know at once./I will send a car for you at nine o'clock./
437	CP	Reilly	20	minds,/May tend to express itself at once in a picture./That happens to me,
447	CC	Claude	33	hope that she will take to him at once:/If so, she is certain to come to believe/
449	CC	Eggers	19	your opinion./{E} Well, I believe that once or twice, perhaps ...But I'm afraid you
451	CC	Eggers	21	B. Kaghan did?' She's only met him once;/But do you know, he began addressing
451	CC	Eggers	27	Elizabeth he wasn't so successful./She once referred to him as 'undistinguished';/But
451	CC	Eggers	29	it will be very different./She'll see at once that you're a man of culture;/And besides,
451	CC	Eggers	32	if you don't mind, I shall mention at once/That you are a musician./{C} I'll be on my
456	CC	Eggers	2	admires about her./He said to me once, in a moment of confidence —/He'd just
456	CC	Eggers	34	to Joshua Park in the evening,/And once a year our holiday at Dawlish'./And to
460	CC	Lady E	21	before I left:/'Trust my guidance for once, and engage that young man?'/Well, that
461	CC	Claude	34	very obvious/That she took to you at once./{C} Did she really think/That she had seen
471	CC	Lucasta	8	them./We'll begin my education at once./{C} I suspect that it's you who are
513	CC	Colby	18	But the fact itself/Is unimportant, once one knows it./{MG} You had no
515	CC	Guzzard	5	you./On your return, you came at once to see me;/And I found that I had to break
525	ES	Charles	34	You think I'm going to tell you/Once more, that I'm in love with you. Well,
541	ES	Gomez	28	/You were a generous friend to me once/As you pointedly reminded me a moment
549	ES	Carghil	37	in me, Richard./I was very lovely once. So you thought,/And others thought so
549	ES	Carghil	39	Richard, just repeat my name — just once:/The name by which you knew me. It
550	ES	Carghil	1	a thrill/To hear you speak my name once more./{LC} Your name was Maisie
550	ES	Carghil	7	Montjoy./I was Maisie Montjoy once. And you didn't recognise me./{LC}
551	ES	Carghil	22	say whether a heart's been broken/Once it's been repaired? But I know what you
554	ES	Carghil	6	talking. Can you bear it?/If I go at once, perhaps she'll take the hint/And leave us
554	ES	Carghil	26	/To have to cope with both of us at once./Besides, I ought to do my breathing
555	ES	Piggott	2	Love Me,/Everybody was singing it once. A charming person,/I dare say, but not
555	ES	Ld Clav	35	money./{LC} If it's only debts/Once more, I expect I can put up with it./But

560 ES	Michael	8	pleasanter/You will find life become, once I'm out of the country./What I'd like is a
562 ES	Carghil	22	picture of you, Richard,/As you were once. You're not to introduce us,/I'll introduce
562 ES	Carghil	32	father was a very dear friend of mine once./{Mi} Did he really look like me?/{MC}
563 ES	Carghil	28	by my stage name./There was a time, once, when everyone in London/Knew the name
575 ES	Gomez	26	Dick, when we recall/That you were once custodian of *my* morals:/Though of course
578 ES	Michael	27	there with your nose in a book./And once, Mother snatched a book away from you/
579 ES	Michael	21	/It's as well to say good-bye at once and be done with it./{LC} Yes, if you're

ONE (431)
ONE'S (16)

599 On a Port		8	wood-retreat,/An immaterial fancy of one's own./No meditations glad or ominous/
294 FR	Harry	22	feeling/And partial observation of one's own automatism/While the slow stain
307 FR	Harry	18	please the children'./It's absurd that one's only memory of freedom/Should be a
449 CC	Claude	39	my wife./There's always something one's ignorant of/About anyone, however well
459 CC	Lady E	30	it is quite impossible/To get one's quiet hour. A quiet hour a day/Is most
485 CC	Lady E	16	all so simple!/To be able to think that one's earthly parents/Are only the means that
485 CC	Lady E	18	/To become reincarnate. And that one's real ancestry/Is one's previous existences.
485 CC	Lady E	19	And that one's real ancestry/Is one's previous existences. Of course, there's
488 CC	Claude	29	for,/And yet such a travesty of all one's plans —/I'd hoped that you would
488 CC	Lady E	34	want to adopt him, Claude!/That is, if one's allowed to adopt one's own child./{SC}
488 CC	Lady E	34	/That is, if one's allowed to adopt one's own child./{SC} That's not what I meant.
502 CC	Lucasta	34	no one so hard to understand/As one's brother .../{C} Or sister .../{L} What's so
502 CC	Lucasta	37	difficult/Is to recognise the limits of one's understanding./It may be that
568 ES	Ld Clav	34	older,/On terms of equality. To one's child one can't reveal oneself/While she is
570 ES	Ld Clav	7	I'm still of that opinion. How open one's heart/When one is sure of the wrong
579 ES	Michael	20	in it./Personally, I think that when one's come to a decision,/It's as well to say

ONE-EYED (1)

| 62 WL: Burial | | 52 | and here the Wheel,/And here is the one-eyed merchant, and this card,/Which is |

ONE-NIGHT (1)

| 13 Prufrock | | 6 | retreats/Of restless nights in one-night cheap hotels/And sawdust restaurants |

ONES (12)

248 MC	Tempt2	20	against other, earlier/And weightier ones: those of the Chancellorship./See how the
248 MC	Tempt2	21	the Chancellorship./See how the late ones rise! You, master of policy/Whom all
310 FR	Mary	6	of the breaking bud./These are the ones that suffer least:/The aconite under the
420 CP	Reilly	23	from the beginning./{R} It's the other ones I am worried about./{J} Nonsense, Henry.
422 CP	Julia	16	chair each side of it./{J} May the holy ones watch over the roof,/May the moon herself
469 CC	Colby	15	didn't like them. You liked the right ones./{L} Colby, I didn't know you were so
469 CC	Lucasta	17	/So the things I liked were the right ones to like?/Still, I'm awfully ignorant. Can
501 CC	Lucasta	2	why you think so are the wrong ones./{LE} And I'm sure too, Lucasta, you have
529 ES	Ld Clav	32	like it —/You know I keep the old ones on a shelf together;/I could look in the
534 ES	Gomez	28	can't afford mistakes. The prudent ones/Always have an aeroplane ready:/And
534 ES	Gomez	31	account in a bank in Switzerland./The ones who don't get out in time/Find themselves
557 ES	Ld Clav	17	the tips I didn't take./{LC} And the ones you did take?/{Mi} Not so well, for some

ONESELF (4)

395 CP	Edward	26	The change that comes/From seeing oneself through the eyes of other people./{L}
397 CP	Edward	4	of my prison?/What is hell? Hell is oneself,/Hell is alone, the other figures in it/
472 CC	Lucasta	13	finds them in some ways very like oneself,/In unexpected ways. And then you
568 ES	Ld Clav	34	To one's child one can't reveal oneself/While she is a child. And by the time

ONION (2)

| 235 Ad-dress | | 63 | licks his paws/So's not to waste the onion sauce.)/A Cat's entitled to expect/These |
| 244 MC | Chorus | 23 | brains unskinned like the layers of an onion, our selves are lost lost/In a final fear |

ONLY (417)
ONT (1)

| 48 Lune Miel | | 1 | de Mozambique./Lune de Miel/Ils ont vu les Pays-Bas, ils rentrent à Terre Haute;/ |

ONTO (2)

| 315 FR | Warburt | 12 | talk of such matters./How did we get onto the subject of cancer?/I really don't know. |
| 462 CC | Claude | 4 | that, before long,/We can put matters onto a permanent basis./{C} I must confess, that |

ONWARD (1)

| 594 Grad 9 | | 5 | years that roll/Between, as we press onward to the goal,/Shall not have power to |

OOPSA (1)

| 235 Ad-dress | | 49 | see me in my flat)/I greet him with an OOPSA CAT!/I think I've heard them call him |

OPACITY (1)

| 290 FR | Agatha | 29 | of observation/Upon each other's opacity/Neglecting all the admonitions/From |

OPEN (27)

| 26 Rhapsody | | 76 | a ring on the stair./Mount./The bed is open; the tooth-brush hangs on the wall,/Put |
| 103 Journ Magi | | 27 | over the lintel,/Six hands at an open door dicing for pieces of silver,/And feet |

111 Xmas Trees   4   /The rowdy (the pubs being open till midnight),/And the childish — which is
137 5FingerEx5   14   Mr. Eliot!/(Whether his mouth be open or shut)./Landscapes/New Hampshire/
149 Rock 1   97   /And lowered faces/We stand about in open places/And shiver in unlit rooms./Only the
177 FQ: ECoker   4   restored, or in their place/Is an open field, or a factory, or a by-pass./Old stone
177 FQ: ECoker   15   end. Now the light falls/Across the open field, leaving the deep lane/Shuttered with
177 FQ: ECoker   24   /Wait for the early owl./In that open field/If you do not come too close, if you
250 MC Thomas   6 not serve among their servants,/Is my open office. No! Go./{T2} Then I leave you to
273 MC Thomas   16   are safe./{T} Unbar the doors! throw open the doors!/I will not have the house of
273 MC Thomas   22   shall endure./The Church shall be open, even to our enemies. Open the door!/{3P}
273 MC Thomas   22   shall be open, even to our enemies. Open the door!/{3P} My Lord! these are not
274 MC Thomas   13 Now is the triumph of the Cross, now/Open the door! I command it. OPEN THE
274 MC Thomas   13   now/Open the door! I command it. OPEN THE DOOR! {}/[*The door is opened.*
288 FR   Ivy   5 have your birthday cake, Amy,/And open your presents?/{A} After dinner:/That is
302 FR   Chorus   6   window that should not have been open./Why do we all behave as if the door
302 FR   Chorus   7 behave as if the door might suddenly open, the curtains be drawn,/The cellar make
325 FR   Violet   34   he meant well — but I think an open car/Is so undignified: you're blown about
328 FR   Charles   19   Mr. Piper said:/"I thought it was all open country about here"—'/{G} Where?/{C} In
345 FR   Charles   37 don't feel safe. As if the earth should open/Right to the centre, as I was about to
367 CP   Alex   37   I came and found that the door was open/And so I thought I'd slip in and see if
367 CP   Peter   39   with you./{P} Julia must have left it open./{E} Never mind;/So long as you both shut
397 CP   Edward   2 {E} There was a door/And I could not open it. I could not touch the handle./Why
457 CC   Lady E   16   *an audience in the theatre.*/{LE} Just open that case, I want something out of it./
458 CC   m   2 What ought we to be doing? {}/[*at the open door*]./{E} She's speaking to the
505 CC   Eggers   17   /I take it, Sir Claude, I should open the discussion?/{SC} If you please,
570 ES Ld Clav   7 /And I'm still of that opinion. How open one's heart/When one is sure of the wrong

OPENED (5)
171 FQ: BurntN   13 not take/Towards the door we never opened/Into the rose-garden. My words echo/
187 FQ: DrySal   130 leaves of a book that has never been opened./And the way up is the way down, the
264 MC Priest2   8   /In the midst of the congregation he opened his mouth./That which was from the
274 MC   m   14 OPEN THE DOOR! {}/[*The door is opened. The* KNIGHTS *enter, slightly tipsy*]/
279 MC Knight4   37 with wrath, that the doors/should be opened. Need I say more? I think, with these

OPENING (1)
474 CC   Colby   15 them coming./I should not hear the opening of the gate./They would simply ... be

OPENS (6)
24 Rhapsody   18 you in the light of the door/Which opens on her like a grin./You see the border of
600 Moonflower   1 curious eye./Song/The moonflower opens to the moth,/The mist crawls in from sea;
310 FR   Harry   35 You bring me news/Of a door that opens at the end of a corridor,/Sunlight and
336 FR   2m   23   *in a somnambular fashion,/and opens the curtains, disclosing the empty*
359 CP   m   23 turns up when she's least wanted. {}/[*Opens the door*]/{E} Julia! {}/[*Enter* JULIA]/{J}
457 CC   m   20 catarrh./{SC} Hello! What's that? {}/[*Opens door on to landing and listens*]/{SC} She's

OPERA (2)
469 CC Lucasta   22   me to a concert./I've been to the Opera, of course, several times,/But I'm afraid I
469 CC Lucasta   26 feel out of it/If you never go to the Opera, in the season./Though I've always felt

OPERATION (4)
218 Mung Rump   4   —/That was merely their centre of operation, for they were incurably given to rove.
350 FR   Mary   1 what we are doing/There is not its operation/Follow follow/{Ag} But in the night
362 CP   Reilly   35   staircase./Or, take a surgical operation./In consultation with the doctor and
546 ES Piggott   8 love with him/During an appendicitis operation!/I was a theatre nurse. But you

OPERATIONS (2)
39 Gerontion   66 What will the spider do,/Suspend its operations, will the weevil/Delay? De Bailhache,
227 Macavity   42 who all the time/Just controls their operations: the Napoleon of Crime!/Gus: the

OPERATOR (1)
129 Cor2 State   12 Cyril Parker is appointed telephone operator/At a salary of one pound ten a week

OPHIDIAN (1)
308 FR   Harry   8 be batrachian,/The aphyllous branch ophidian./{M} You bring your own landscape/

OPINION (16)
234 Ad-dress   2 read of several kinds of Cat,/And my opinion now is that/You should need no
242 MC   Mess   4   /A patched up affair, if you ask my opinion./And if you ask me, I think the Lord
242 MC   Mess   8 least of his pretensions./If you ask my opinion, I think that this peace/Is nothing like
296 FR   Gerald   39 no suspicion./I'd trust Warburton's opinion./{A} If anyone speaks to Dr.
299 FRDowning   17 did, every now and again./But in my opinion, it is those that talk/That are the least
300 FRDowning   7 or twice./But you know, it is just my opinion, Sir,/That his Lordship is rather
300 FRDowning   12 complaint against my Lady./It's my opinion that man and wife/Shouldn't see too
300 FRDowning   14 Sir./Quite the contrary of the usual opinion,/I dare say. She wouldn't leave him
396 CP   Lavinia   16 were./{L} It's a pity that you had no opinion of your own./Oh, Edward, I should like

401 CP   Reilly   35   /On which you want my professional opinion./{E} It's not for me to blame you for
415 CP   Reilly   5   sense./{R} And what, in your opinion, is the ordinary sense?/{C} Well ... I
449 CC   Claude   18   know she thinks the world of your opinion./{E} Well, I believe that once or twice,
469 CC   Lucasta   2   awfully well, Colby —/Not that *my* opinion counts for anything:/You know that.
540 ES   Gomez   5   /The worst kind of failure, in my opinion,/Is the man who has to keep on
547 ES   Piggott   31   /And that spoils any sport, in my opinion./{M} Thank you, Mrs. Piggott. But I'm
570 ES   Ld Clav   7 who haunted me./And I'm still of that opinion. How open one's heart/When one is

OPINIONS (2)
242 MC   Mess   15   highest authority;/There are several opinions as to what he meant,/But no one
267 MC   Knight1   36   Pope,/Raising up against him false opinions./{K2} Yet the King, out of his charity,/

OPPORTUNITY (15)
246 MC   Thomas   18   lower,/Waiting excuse, pretence, opportunity./End will be simple, sudden,
356 CP   Julia   19   /I want to ask you. It's a golden opportunity/Now Lavinia's away. I've always
366 CP   Peter   33   to see you later;/But this seemed an opportunity./{E} And what's your trouble?/{P}
391 CP   Edward   35 me./{E} I can't say that I've had much opportunity/To seem anything. But of course
394 CP   Edward   11 would have given me about as much opportunity/If you had hired me as your butler:
405 CP   Reilly   14   told me nothing./You have had the opportunity, and you have said enough/To
427 CP   Alex   11   country,/I said, I must not miss the opportunity/To see Edward and Lavinia./{L}
462 CC   Colby   40   /{C} I suppose there hasn't been the opportunity./{SC} When you were a child, you
550 ES   Ld Clav   31   /Is why you should take the first opportunity,/Finding me here, to revive old
555 ES   Piggott   5   so I thought/That I'd take the first opportunity of hinting —/Tactfully, of course
559 ES   Michael   28 knew./First, because it gave you the opportunity/Of retiring from politics, not
560 ES   Michael   14 know. Import and export,/With an opportunity of profits both ways./{LC} This is
577 ES   Carghil   34 /He's been waiting all this time for opportunity/To make use of his gifts; and now,
577 ES   Carghil   35   /To make use of his gifts; and now, opportunity —/Opportunity has come knocking
577 ES   Carghil   36 of his gifts; and now, opportunity —/Opportunity has come knocking at the door./

OPPOSE (2)
96 Ash-Wed 5   21 walk in darkness, who chose thee and oppose thee,/Those who are torn on the horn
96 Ash-Wed 5   27 pray:/Pray for those who chose and oppose/O my people, what have I done unto

OPPOSED (3)
161 Rock 7   42   is no longer regarded, not even opposed, and men have forgotten/All gods
196 FQ: Little   190   drum./These men, and those who opposed them/And those whom they opposed/
196 FQ: Little   191 opposed them/And those whom they opposed/Accept the constitution of silence/And

OPPOSITE (3)
310 FR   Mary   17   dead want to return?/{M} Pain is the opposite of joy/But joy is a kind of pain/I
338 FR   Agatha   35   of fugitives/The person taking the opposite direction/Will appear to run away./{A}
528 ES   Monica   3 /{M} The second reason is exactly the opposite:/It's his fear of being exposed to

OPPOSITION (1)
538 ES   Gomez   23   mistake./At the worst, you go into opposition/And let the other people make

OPPRESSED (1)
253 MC   Tempt4   28   grasp of spiritual power?/Man oppressed by sin, since Adam fell —/You hold

OPPRESSION (6)
185 FQ: DrySal   36   and the seagull:/And under the oppression of the silent fog/The tolling bell/
239 MC   Chorus   23 barons rule;/We have suffered various oppression,/But mostly we are left to our own
243 MC   Chorus   26   and partly living./There have been oppression and luxury,/There have been poverty
257 MC   Chorus   8   expect and not expect./We know of oppression and torture,/We know of extortion
259 MC   Thomas   2   evil, every sacrilege,/Crime, wrong, oppression and the axe's edge,/Indifference,
403 CP   Edward   28 perhaps, for the first time,/The whole oppression, the unreality/Of the role she had

OR (540)

ORANG-OUTANG (1)
42 Swee Erect   11   and Polypheme)./Gesture of orang-outang/Rises from the sheets in steam./

ORANGE (1)
64 WL: Chess   95   fed with copper/Burned green and orange, framed by the coloured stone,/In which

ORANGES (1)
56 Swee Night   19   and gapes;/The waiter brings in oranges/Bananas figs and hothouse grapes;/The

ORCHARD (4)
138 New Hamp   1   Hampshire/Children's voices in the orchard/Between the blossom- and the
587 Fable   10 possessors of rich lands and wide,/An orchard, and a vineyard, and a dairy;/Whenever
247 MC   Tempt1   11   /Mirror the sunlight. Love in the orchard/Send the sap shooting. Mirth matches
288 FR   Agatha   36 the stables,/In the coach-house, in the orchard,/In the plantation, down the corridor/

ORCHARDS (1)
240 MC   Chorus   14 heat of summer/But wait in barren orchards for another October?/Some malady is

ORDER (40)
74 WL: Thund   425   me/Shall I at least set my lands in order?/London Bridge is falling down falling
129 Cor2 State   5   of the Legion of Honour,/The Order of the Black Eagle (1st and 2nd class),/

129 Cor2	State	6	Eagle (1st and 2nd class),/And the Order of the Rising Sun./Cry cry what shall I
164 Rock	9	24	and feelings,/There spring the perfect order of speech, and the beauty of incantation./
164 Rock	9	27	powers/For life, for dignity, grace and order,/And intellectual pleasures of the senses?/
181 FQ: ECoker		137	say it again./Shall I say it again? In order to arrive there,/To arrive where you are,
181 FQ: ECoker		140	a way wherein there is no ecstasy./In order to arrive at what you do not know/You
181 FQ: ECoker		142	way which is the way of ignorance./In order to possess what you do not possess/You
181 FQ: ECoker		144	go by the way of dispossession./In order to arrive at what you are not/You must
192 FQ: Little		49	valid. And prayer is more/Than an order of words, the conscious occupation/Of the
223 Pekes Pols		36	they stepped out, with their pipers in order,/Playing *When the Blue Bonnets Came*
240 MC	Chorus	1	/We try to keep our households in order;/The merchant, shy and cautious, tries to
245 MC	Priest2	34	Lordship will find your rooms in order as you left them./{T} And will try to leave
245 MC	Thomas	35	/{T} And will try to leave them in order as I find them./I am more than grateful
250 MC	Thomas	10	to build a good world,/To keep order, as the world knows order./Those who put
250 MC	Thomas	10	/To keep order, as the world knows order./Those who put their faith in worldly
250 MC	Thomas	11	/Those who put their faith in worldly order/Not controlled by the order of God,/In
250 MC	Thomas	12	worldly order/Not controlled by the order of God,/In confident ignorance, but arrest
250 MC	Tempt3	28	/I know how to hold my estates in order,/A country-keeping lord who minds his
265 MC	Knight2	18	From the King./{K2} By the King's order./{K1} Our men are outside./{P1} You
266 MC	Thomas	6	my table you will find/The papers in order, and the documents signed. {}/[*To*
266 MC	Thomas	27	loyal subject to the King./Saving my order, I am at his command,/As his most
266 MC	Knight1	29	vassal in the land./{K1} Saving your order! let your order save you —/As I do not
266 MC	Knight1	29	/{K1} Saving your order! let your order save you —/As I do not think it is like to
278 MC	Knight2	9	/the one thing needful was to restore order: to curb the excessive/powers of local
278 MC	Knight2	24	immediately that there was a higher/order than that which our King, and he as the
278 MC	Knight2	30	measures/we have had to adopt, in order to set matters to rights, that you/take
279 MC	Knight4	20	to give it the unity, the stability, order, tranquillity,/and justice that it so badly
301 FRDowning		1	Oh no, Sir, she's in good running order:/I see to that./{G} I only wondered/Why
318 FR	Harry	12	we misbehaved/Next day at school, in order to be punished,/For punishment made us
323 FR	Amy	27	to you./{A} I must see for myself. Order the car at once./{W} I forbid it, Lady
326 FR	Harry	28	of the world, which I cannot put in order./If you only knew the years that I have
422 CP	Julia	6	have we got on?/{J} Everything is in order./{A} The Chamberlaynes have chosen?/
433 CP	Lavinia	37	that she had joined some nursing order .../{A} She had joined an order. A very
433 CP	Alex	38	order .../{A} She had joined an order. A very austere one./And as she already
474 CC	Lucasta	35	like to understand music,/Not in order to be able to talk about it,/But ... partly,
489 CC	Lady E	32	it? The child was expected./{LE} In order to get money from you, perhaps./No, I
507 CC	Guzzard	28	mother, I suppose, could have got an order/If she could have established the
511 CC	Lady E	20	Kaghan as my mother./{LE} Then in order to avoid any danger of confusion/You
558 ES	Ld Clav	11	down here so precipitately —/In order to let me have your version first./I dare

ORDERLY (1)

| 326 FR | Harry | 25 | ruin,/A casual bit of waste in an orderly universe./But it begins to seem just part |

ORDERS (10)

129 Cor2	State	23	to protest against the reduction of orders./Meanwhile the guards shake dice on the
242 MC	Priest2	34	what we are to do, he will give us our orders, instruct us./Our Lord is at one with the
278 MC	Knight2	26	that — God knows/why — the two orders were incompatible./You will agree with
300 FRDowning		23	/I don't mean to say that he had any orders —/His Lordship is always most
323 FR	Charles	36	put ourselves under Warburton's orders./{W} I repeat, Lady Monchensey, that
424 CP	Caterer	1	*door.*/{CM} Have you any further orders for us, Madam?/{L} You could bring in
447 CP	Claude	26	say you had to leave under medical orders./She's always been concerned about your
458 CC	Eggers	28	to retire .../{E} Under medical orders, Lady Elizabeth:/The doctor made it very
518 CC	Eggers	8	You'll be thinking of reading for orders./And you'll still have your music. Why,
565 ES	Gomez	25	Dick, we've got to obey our doctors' orders./But while we're here, we must have

ORDINARILY (2)

| 277 MC | Knight3 | 10 | deal — I am not a drinking man/ordinarily — to brace myself up for it. When |
| 309 FR | Harry | 37 | and leaves, of life persisting,/Which ordinarily pass unnoticed./Perhaps you are |

ORDINARY (14)

307 FR	Mary	29	very trivial indeed to you./It's just ordinary hopelessness./{H} One thing you
309 FR	Mary	14	I am not a wise person,/And in the ordinary sense I don't know you very well,/
315 FR	Harry	4	and waking./Murder was there. Your ordinary murderer/Regards himself as an
324 FR	Harry	20	to have a breathing spell:/But John's ordinary day isn't much more than breathing./
348 FR	Chorus	11	we are asleep./We understand the ordinary business of living,/We know how to
370 CP	Edward	34	while/This might have become an ordinary affair/Like any other. As the fever
414 CP	Celia	3	simply the end of an illusion/In the ordinary way, or being ditched./Of course that's
415 CP	Celia	4	I don't mean:/I don't mean sin in the ordinary sense./{R} And what, in your opinion,
415 CP	Reilly	5	/{R} And what, in your opinion, is the ordinary sense?/{C} Well ... I suppose it's being
437 CP	Edward	34	form of death/She did not suffer as ordinary people suffer?/{R} Not at all what I

475 CC   Colby   26   you *are*,/But not who you are, in the ordinary sense./Is that what you mean? I've just
485 CC   Lady E   7   /That my father could have been an ordinary earl!/And I couldn't believe that my
513 CC   Colby   35   mind,/To live with that image. An ordinary man/Whose life I could in some way
557 ES   Michael 35   And have you other debts?/{Mi} Oh, ordinary debts:/My tailor's bill, for instance./
ORGAN (1)
517 CC   Eggers   33   Mr. Simpkins, until you've tried our organ!/{C} Well, if you could induce them to try
ORGANISATION (1)
331 FR   Agatha   25   /That is the surface. There is a deeper/Organisation, which your question disturbs./{H}
ORGANIST (13)
446 CC   Claude   14   /That his great ambition was to be an organist,/Just as I can't forget ... no matter./The
463 CC   Colby   28   /And I am again the disappointed organist,/And for a moment the thing I cannot
465 CC   Colby   34   /I should never have become a great organist,/As I aspired to be. I'm not an
495 CC   Claude   35   he would have been a second-rate organist./We have both chosen ... obedience to
516 CC   Colby   7   do you mean?/{C} I want to be an organist./It doesn't matter about success —/I
516 CC   Colby   10   /I thought I didn't want to be an organist/When I found I had no chance of
516 CC   Colby   12   to the top —/That is, to become the organist of a cathedral./But my father was an
516 CC   Colby   13   /But my father was an unsuccessful organist./{MG} You should say, Colby, not
517 CC   Eggers   23   that what you desire/Is to become the organist of some parish church?/{C} That is
517 CC   Eggers   27   —/If it should appeal to you. The organist we had/Died two months ago. We've
517 CC   Colby   32   But I've told you, I'm not a very good organist!/{E} Don't say that, Mr. Simpkins,
518 CC   Eggers   4   see you spending a lifetime as an organist./I think you'll come to find you've
518 CC Guzzard   25   /Having been, myself, the wife of an organist;/But you too, I think, have had a wish
ORGANISTS (1)
517 CC   Eggers   31   Give you a trial? I'm certain./Good organists don't seem to want to come to Joshua
ORIGEN (1)
54 Mr E Sun   8   turn of time/Produced enervate Origen./A painter of the Umbrian school/
ORIGIN (1)
331 FR   Harry   13   behind our meagre childhood,/Some origin of wretchedness. Is that what they would
ORIGINAL (2)
224 Mr Mistoff   2   ought to know Mr. Mistoffelees!/The Original Conjuring Cat —/(There can be no
431 CP   Peter   30   with it./He thought I should see the original Boltwell;/And besides, he thought that
ORIGINALS (1)
553 ES   Carghil   30   them?/I'm afraid I can't show you the originals;/They're in my lawyer's safe. But I
ORIGINATE (1)
202 War Poetry   6   typical/To create the universal, originate a symbol/Out of the impact? This is a
ORION (1)
56 Swee Night   9   guards the hornèd gate./Gloomy Orion and the Dog/Are veiled; and hushed the
ORNAMENT (1)
254 MC Tempt4   33   /The jewels gone for light ladies' ornament,/The sanctuary broken, and its stores/
ORPHAN (1)
449 CC   Claude   11   under the impression that he is an orphan,/She will want us to adopt him./{E}
OSTENTATIOUS (1)
197 FQ: Little   221   others,/The word neither diffident nor ostentatious,/An easy commerce of the old and
OSTENTATIOUSLY (1)
278 MC Knight2   22   more priestly than the/priests, he ostentatiously and offensively adopted an
OTHER (209)
OTHER'S (1)
290 FR   Agatha   29   of observation/Upon each other's opacity/Neglecting all the admonitions/
OTHERS (42)
28 Boston ET   5   the appetites of life in some/And to others bringing the *Boston Evening Transcript*,/
66 WL: Chess   149   /And if you don't give it him, there's others will, I said./Oh is there, she said.
66 WL: Chess   154   like it you can get on with it, I said./Others can pick and choose if you can't./But if
94 Ash-Wed 4   7   dolour/Who moved among the others as they walked,/Who then made strong
158 Rock 5   6   content in the sunlight./And the others run about like dogs, full of enterprise,
158 Rock 5   7   And these are not justified, nor the others./And they write innumerable books;
158 Rock 5   11   therefore some must labour, and others must hold the spears./It is hard for those
179 FQ: ECoker   97   /Of belonging to another, or to others, or to God./The only wisdom we can
187 FQ: DrySal 111   appreciate this better/In the agony of others, nearly experienced,/Involving ourselves,
187 FQ: DrySal 114   currents of action,/But the torment of others remains an experience/Unqualified,
188 FQ: DrySal 162   /Which shall fructify in the lives of others:/And do not think of the fruit of action./
194 FQ: Little 117   own, and pray they be forgiven/By others, as I pray you to forgive/Both bad and
195 FQ: Little 156   indifference/Which resembles the others as death resembles life,/Being between
197 FQ: Little 220   home,/Taking its place to support the others,/The word neither diffident nor
206 To my Wife 11   ours only/But this dedication is for others to read:/These are private words
241 MC Priest3   5   can manipulate the greed and lust of others,/The feeble is devoured by his own./{P1}

247 MC	Temptl	30	Not at this gait!/If you go so fast, others may go faster./Your Lordship is too
255 MC	Thomas	19	you, tempting with my own desires?/Others have come, temporal tempters,/With
255 MC	Thomas	25	such a vision of eternal grandeur?/{T} Others offered real goods, worthless/But real.
299 FR	Downing	31	natural for some and unnatural for others./{C} And how was his Lordship, during
302 FR	Chorus	1	/We like to be thought well of by others/So that we may think well of ourselves./
309 FR	Mary	24	You attach yourself to loathing/As others do to loving: an infatuation/That's
318 FR	Harry	33	/Or talked to the stone deaf: and the others/Seem to hear something else than what I
333 FR	Harry	22	/Dreamt through me by the minds of others. Perhaps/I only dreamt I pushed her./
345 FR	Amy	26	your company to that of any of the others/Just to help me to the next room. Where
349 FR	Mary	19	attempt to divert it/Only implicates others/At the day of consummation/{Ag} A
367 CP	Peter	5	you didn't notice, I don't suppose the others did,/Though I'm rather afraid of Julia
384 CP	Reilly	19	/Forces in your life and in the lives of others/Which cannot be reversed. That is one
399 CP	Nurse	21	/Then, when you ring, I show the others out;/And only after they have left the
402 CP	Reilly	24	cases are unique, and very similar to others./{E} Is there a sanatorium to which you
411 CP	Edward	23	ask./{E} It's about the future of ... the others./I don't want to build on other people's
411 CP	Reilly	30	conscience./With the future of the others you are not concerned./{L} I think you
416 CP	Reilly	13	different types. Some are rarer than others./{C} Oh, I thought that I was giving him
417 CP	Reilly	29	/Become tolerant of themselves and others,/Giving and taking, in the usual actions/
423 CP	Alex	2	/{J} Shall we ever speak them?/{A} Others, perhaps, will speak them./You know, I
428 CP	Alex	30	creates friction between them and the others./And that's the real problem. I hope I'm
438 CP	Reilly	30	understanding/Of ourselves and others, we should all be condemned./Mrs.
449 CC	Claude	24	That was one difficulty. And there are others./For one, they're both of them women./
466 CC	Claude	21	are also the men of genius./There are others, it seems to me, who have at best to live/
491 CC	Colby	32	I should have four! What about those others?/I should have to live with those ghosts,
545 ES	Ld Clav	19	desire to interfere/With the privacy of others, which is certain to explode./{M} Hush,
549 ES	Carghil	38	lovely once. So *you* thought,/And others thought so too. But as you remember,/

OTHERS' (2)

194 FQ:	Little	143	/Of things ill done and done to others' harm/Which once you took for exercise
247 MC	Thomas	16	and again./Men learn little from others' experience./But in the life of one man,

OTHERWISE (4)

190 FQ:	DrySal	224	and reconciled,/Where action were otherwise movement/Of that which is only
479 CC	Kaghan	37	You need something brighter./But otherwise, it looks pretty comfortable./If I was
507 CC	Guzzard	15	the child was very well connected:/Otherwise, I should not have taken him./But he
515 CC	Guzzard	31	very much rather that the facts were otherwise./{C} I believe you. I must believe you:

OTTER (1)

316 FR	Agatha	17	straightened/May the weasel and the otter/Be about their proper business/The eye of

OÙ (1)

48 Lune	Miel	13	leurs misères de Padoue à Milan/Où se trouve la Cène, et un restaurant pas cher./

OUBLIAIT (1)

51 Restaurant		26	Phénicien, pendant quinze jours noyé,/Oubliait les cris des mouettes et la houle de

OUGHT (63)

66 WL:	Chess	156	it won't be for lack of telling./You ought to be ashamed, I said, to look so antique.
182 FQ:	ECoker	204	and now cease to matter./Old men ought to be explorers/Here and there does not
224 Mr	Mistoff	1	*in the street./*Mr. Mistoffelees/You ought to know Mr. Mistoffelees!/The Original
228 Gus		2	at the Theatre Door./His name, as I ought to have told you before,/Is really
233 Skimble		47	/And pull up the counterpane,/You ought to reflect that it's very nice/To know that
233 Skimble		60	the police/If there's anything they ought to know about:/When you get to
588 Fable		62	every toast/Had drank more than he ought t' have of grape juice./The lights began to
287 FR	Charles	17	she must be getting on for thirty?/She ought to be married, that's what it is./{A} So she
288 FR	Amy	11	is a very particular occasion/As you ought to know. It will be the first time/For eight
289 FR	Charles	15	ago, wasn't it?/Do you think that I ought to mention it now?/It seems to me too
307 FR	Mary	24	/They are always assured that you ought to be happy/At the very moment when
326 FR	Harry	20	From some imaginary course that life ought to take,/That you call normal. What you
328 FR	Violet	6	reckless./{V} I think these racing cars ought to be prohibited. {}/[*Re-enter* CHARLES,
347 FR	Ivy	21	what did happen,/Do you think Amy ought to see it?/{V} No, certainly not./You do
358 CP	Alex	26	now I must be going./{A} I'm afraid *I* ought to be going./{P} Celia —/May I walk
359 CP	Reilly	32	I don't know your name./{UG} I ought to be going./{E} Don't go yet./I very
378 CP	Edward	16	best/That Lavinia had gone; that I ought to be thankful./And yet, the effect of all
392 CP	Lavinia	9	to talk about?/{L} There is one thing I ought to know, because of other people/And
392 CP	Edward	20	I don't know who he was,/But *you* ought to know./{L} Yes, I think I know./But
393 CP	Lavinia	16	made yourself. I remember —/Oh, I ought to have realised what was coming —/
393 CP	Edward	35	get enough work/And said that I ought to meet more people:/But when the briefs
397 CP	Edward	26	more practical than you are./{E} I ought to know by now what you consider
398 CP	Lavinia	15	at present that I can do about it./I ought to go and have a look in the kitchen./I
402 CP	Edward	15	/Almost in the same words, that I ought to see a doctor./They said — again, in

405 CP	Reilly	17	speak, as you went along. A barrister/Ought to know his brief before he enters the
418 CP	Celia	4	greed ... it is a good life./{C} I know I ought to be able to accept that/If I might still
421 CP	Julia	33	in which I am so useful to you./You ought to be grateful./{R} And when I say to one
425 CP	Edward	11	without asking them./{E} Perhaps we ought to have arranged to have two parties/
428 CP	Julia	7	angry/When I told her the creature ought to be destroyed./{L} But can't they
429 CP	Alex	32	{A} Ah, the Christians! Now, I think I ought to tell you/About someone you know —
431 CP	Peter	32	he thought that as I'm English/I ought to know the best way to handle a duke./
446 CC	Eggers	32	interest in my garden/That I think he ought to have window boxes./Some day, he'll
447 CC	Claude	5	the airport, about Colby./I think, you ought to give her warning/Of whom she is to
447 CC	Claude	16	to replace you./She thinks she ought to have a hand in the choosing;/And
450 CC	Colby	37	me very much:/So I've no idea how I ought to behave./B. Kaghan has told me
451 CC	Eggers	6	very grateful to Sir Claude,/As he ought to be. Sir Claude picked him out/And
458 CC	Claude	1	*me* go down to meet her./{SC} Where ought we to be? What ought we to be doing? {}/
458 CC	Claude	1	/{SC} Where ought we to be? What ought we to be doing? {}/[*at the open door*]./{E}
477 CC	Lucasta	18	well enough you *are* shocked./You ought to see your face! I'm disappointed./I
480 CC	Kaghan	6	You know, Colby,/You and I ought to be in business together./I'm a good
481 CC	Kaghan	6	financier than I am!/That's why we ought to be in business together./{L} You're
482 CC	Lady E	30	to know./{LE} In the first place, you ought to mix with people of breeding./I said to
487 CC	Lady E	27	it were only a coincidence./Perhaps I ought not to believe it yet,/Perhaps it is wrong
489 CC	Claude	2	you have a son. But it isn't Colby./I ought to have told you, years ago./I told you
489 CC	Claude	17	now I regret the decision bitterly./I ought to have told you that I had a son./{LE}
492 CC	Lady E	11	to get her here./{LE} And I think you ought to get Eggerson as well. {}/[*rising*]./{SC}
500 CC	Claude	11	aunt? You make my brain reel./{SC} I ought to have made things clear to you/At the
500 CC	Claude	14	for that/Which no longer exist. But I ought to have told you./{L} Well, I don't
501 CC	Lady E	9	can play them./{LE} I don't think you ought to say that, Lucasta;/I have always been a
503 CC	Claude	36	{}/[*looking at his watch*]./{SC} She ought to be here now! It's surprising,/I hadn't
504 CC	Claude	1	with Lucasta's unexpected visit./She ought to be here. It wouldn't be like her/To be
509 CC	Guzzard	30	him B./{MG} A very good name./He ought to be proud of it./{LE} How old is this
511 CC	Kaghan	17	that./But I should like to know how I ought to address you,/Lady Elizabeth. I've
532 ES	Charles	10	Lambert. {}/[*Exit LAMBERT*]/{C} I ought to be going./{M} Let *us* go into the
532 ES	Monica	19	sell me something worthless./{M} You ought not to bother with such people now,
545 ES	Monica	36	I'm sorry,/We don't know how we ought to address you./Do we call you 'Matron'?
547 ES	Piggott	20	neglectful!/Miss Claverton-Ferry, I ought to tell you more/About the amenities
554 ES	Piggott	18	— and so understanding./{MP} But I ought to introduce you. You've been talking to
554 ES	Carghil	27	with both of us at once./Besides, I ought to do my breathing exercises. {}/[*Exit*]/
555 ES	Monica	14	rescue. You look tired, Father./She ought to know better. But I'm all the more
576 ES	Gomez	35	.../{G} Be careful, Mr. Barrister./You ought to know something about the law of
579 ES	Carghil	16	Richard?/You look very *distrait*. You ought to be excited!/{LC} Is this good-bye then,
582 ES	Ld Clav	17	not very agreeable./You two ought to have a little time together./I leave

OUGHTN'T (1)

413 CP	Celia	20	I live in seems all a delusion!/But oughtn't I first to tell you the circumstances?/I'd

OUR (261)

OURS (8)

119 SP	Wauch	4	/We want you to meet two friends of ours,/American gentlemen here on business./
203 Indians		16	remember./This was not your land, or ours: but a village in the Midlands,/And one in
206 To my Wife		10	/The roses in the rose-garden which is ours and ours only/But this dedication is for
206 To my Wife		10	in the rose-garden which is ours and ours only/But this dedication is for others to
594 Grad 9		4	fanes of lucid purity,/O school of ours! The passing years that roll/Between, as we
278 MC	Knight2	28	/offends the instincts of a people like ours. So far, I know that I have/your approval:
379 CP	Celia	24	was meaningless, a private world of *ours*,/Where the word 'happiness' had a different
491 CC	Lady E	6	said,/That you would rather he was *ours* than only *yours*./Why should we make any

OURSELVES (22)

98 Ash-Wed 6		26	of the garden,/Suffer us not to mock ourselves with falsehood/Teach us to care and
127 Cor1 March		5	a press of people./We hardly knew ourselves that day, or knew the City./This is the
187 FQ: DrySal		112	others, nearly experienced,/Involving ourselves, than in our own./For our own past is
251 MC	Tempt3	1	of friendship does not depend/Upon ourselves, but upon circumstance./But
275 MC	Chorus	22	foul, the water is foul, our beasts and ourselves defiled with blood./A rain of blood
277 MC	Knight3	15	duty,/but all the same we had to work ourselves up to it. And, as I said,/*we* are not
277 MC	Knight3	24	us any glory. No, we have done for ourselves, there's/no mistake about that. So, as
282 MC	Chorus	6	/Forgive us, O Lord, we acknowledge ourselves as type of the common man,/Of the
302 FR	Chorus	2	others/So that we may think well of ourselves./And any explanation will satisfy:/We
323 FR	Charles	36	for us that he's here./We must put ourselves under Warburton's orders./{W} I
348 FR	Chorus	8	like to walk out of a door, and find ourselves back in the same room./We do not
349 FR	All	12	understand./{all} But we must adjust ourselves to the moment: we must do the right
363 CP	Reilly	13	people./Most of the time we take ourselves for granted,/As we have to, and live

73 WL: Thund	369	are those hooded hordes swarming/Over endless plains, stumbling in cracked earth/
73 WL: Thund	371	the flat horizon only/What is the city over the mountains/Cracks and reforms and
73 WL: Thund	387	faint moonlight, the grass is singing/Over the tumbled graves, about the chapel/
74 WL: Thund	397	the black clouds/Gathered far distant, over Himavant./The jungle crouched, humped
83 Hollow Men	9	/As wind in dry grass/Or rats' feet over broken glass/In our dry cellar/Shape
92 Ash-Wed 3	17	flute./Blown hair is sweet, brown hair over the mouth blown,/Lilac and brown hair;/
92 Ash-Wed 3	19	the flute, stops and steps of the mind over the third stair,/Fading, fading; strength
103 Journ Magi	26	we came to a tavern with vine-leaves over the lintel,/Six hands at an open door dicing
127 Cor1 March	2	steel, stone, oakleaves, horses' heels/Over the paving./And the flags. And the
127 Cor1 March	30	in his eyes/Or in the hands, quiet over the horse's neck,/And the eyes watchful,
128 Cor1 March	41	steel, stone, oakleaves, horses' heels/Over the paving./That is all we could see. But
129 Cor2 State	35	its wings, there the clematis droops over the lintel/O mother (not among these
138 New Hamp	5	root./Black wing, brown wing, hover over/Twenty years and the spring is over;/
138 New Hamp	6	over/Twenty years and the spring is over;/To-day grieves, to-morrow grieves,/Cover
138 New Hamp	8	grieves, to-morrow grieves,/Cover me over, light-in-leaves;/Golden head, black wing,/
143 Lines OM	8	I lay bare the tooth of wit/The hissing over the archèd tongue/Is more affectionate
149 Rock 1	100	*in unlit rooms./Only the wind moves/Over empty fields, untilled/Where the plough*
166 Rock 10	22	doors at evening,/The twilight over stagnant pools at batflight,/Moon light
171 FQ: BurntN	26	invisible,/Moving without pressure, over the dead leaves,/In the autumn heat,
174 FQ: BurntN	103	plenitude nor vacancy. Only a flicker/Over the strained time-ridden faces/Distracted
186 FQ: DrySal	77	hauling, while the North East lowers/Over shallow banks unchanging and erosionless
187 FQ: DrySal	105	history, the backward half-look/Over the shoulder, towards the primitive terror./
187 FQ: DrySal	121	in the restless waters,/Waves wash over it, fogs conceal it;/On a halcyon day it is
192 FQ: Little	38	world's end, some at the sea jaws,/Or over a dark lake, in a desert or a city —/But this
192 FQ: Little	65	of air./There are flood and drouth/Over the eyes and in the mouth,/Dead water
193 FQ: Little	86	the dead leaves still rattled on like tin/Over the asphalt where no other sound was/
209 NamingCats	21	and beyond there's still one name left over,/And that is the name that you never will
220 Old Deut	21	away./The cars and the lorries run over the kerb,/And the villagers put up a notice:
222 Pekes Pols	10	BARK/Until you can hear them all over the Park./Now on the occasion of which I
222 Pekes Pols	24	BARK/Until you could hear them all over the Park./Now the Peke, although people
223 Pekes Pols	37	/Playing *When the Blue Bonnets Came Over the Border.*/Then the Pugs and the Poms
223 Pekes Pols	45	BARK/Until you could hear them all over the Park./Now when these bold heroes
587 Fable	28	allowed/At this exclusive feast. From over sea/He purchased at his own expense a
588 Fable	50	/With difficulty kept from toppling over,/Next came a viand made of turtle eggs,/
588 Fable	57	an apple held, his skull held sausages./Over their Christmas wassail the monks dozed,/
593 Grad 5	5	distant years may see,/What conquest over pain and misery,/What heroes greater than
605 Narcissus	4	from either/Your shadow sprawling over the sand at daybreak, or/Your shadow
605 Narcissus	10	each other/And of his arms crossed over his breast./When he walked over the
605 Narcissus	11	over his breast./When he walked over the meadows/He was stifled and soothed
239 MC Chorus	18	/Seven years and the summer is over/Seven years since the Archbishop left us,/
240 MC Priest1	26	/{P1} Seven years and the summer is over./Seven years since the Archbishop left us./
246 MC Tempt1	35	the King, shall we say that summer's over/Or that the good time cannot last?/Fluting
248 MC Tempt2	30	tomb, monument of marble./Rule over men reckon no madness./{T} To the man
252 MC Tempt3	3	tyrannous jurisdiction/Of king's court over bishop's court,/Of king's court over
252 MC Tempt3	4	over bishop's court,/Of king's court over baron's court./{T} Which I helped to
252 MC Thomas	19	yield./Shall I who ruled like an eagle over doves/Now take the shape of a wolf among
257 MC Chorus	23	can avoid, flowing under our feet and over the sky;/Under doors and down chimneys,
259 MC Thomas	7	appoints,/To be my guardian, hover over the swords' points. {}/Interlude/THE
260 MC Thomas	30	the King, the householder counting/over his peaceful gains, the swept hearth, his
263 MC Chorus	22	tree, when the elder and may/Burst over the stream, and the air is clear and high,/
269 MC Chorus	30	seen at noon/Scaly wings slanting over, huge and ridiculous. I have tasted/The
279 MC Knight4	17	I am obliged, very briefly, to go over/the ground traversed by the last speaker.
281 MC Chorus	21	from it/Though armies trample over it, though sightseers come with
281 MC Chorus	21	come with guide-books looking over it;/From where the western seas gnaw at
285 FR Amy	4	comes too soon and the spring will be over/And the cuckoo will be gone before I am
290 FR Amy	3	That's why she dragged him/All over Europe and half round the world/To
294 FR Harry	33	the mid-Atlantic/When I pushed her over./{V} Pushed her?/{H} You would never
297 FR Ivy	14	/That he might have pushed her over?/{C} In any case, I shouldn't blame Harry./
298 FR Charles	31	/You've looked after his Lordship for over ten years .../{Do} Eleven years, Sir, next
300 FRDowning	5	was rough,/Didn't like to see her lean over the rail./He was in a rare fright, once or
300 FRDowning	31	there I saw his Lordship/Leaning over the rail, looking at the water —/There
300 FRDowning	34	hour/He stayed there alone, looking over the rail./Her Ladyship must have been all
310 FR Mary	29	wings into the rain cloud/Harefoot over the moon?/{H} What have we been saying?
322 FR Winch	38	/Dr. Owen was there, and looked him over;/Says there's nothing wrong but some
331 FR Harry	4	action,/I only felt the repetition of it/Over and over. When I was outside,/I could

331 FR	Harry	4	only felt the repetition of it/Over and over. When I was outside,/I could associate
335 FR	Agatha	3	voices/And then a black raven flew over./And then I was only my own feet walking/
335 FR	Agatha	7	walking/And sharp heels scraping. Over and under/Echo and noise of feet./I was
335 FR	Agatha	11	unwinking eye/Fixing the movement. Over and under./{H} In and out, in an endless
339 FR	Harry	11	of the sun and the icy vigil,/A care over lives of humble people,/The lesson of
342 FR	Amy	10	woman./*I* have no influence over him; *you* can try,/But you will not succeed:
342 FR	Agatha	36	the responsibility/Of tempting them over the border? No one could, no one who
343 FR	Mary	16	me: I should have known it;/It was all over, I believe, before it began;/But I deceived
353 CP	Peter	7	listening./{P} You'll have to tell us all over again, Alex./{A} I never tell the same story
362 CP	Reilly	2	than you;/And, turning the past over over,/You'll wonder only that you
362 CP	Reilly	2	you;/And, turning the past over and over,/You'll wonder only that you endured it
364 CP	Julia	34	them./I've been dragging Peter all over town/Looking for them everywhere I've
376 CP	m	1	you in the kitchen? {}/[EDWARD *goes over to the table and inspects his game of*
383 CP	Edward	3	/Or have we ... have I got to hunt all over?/Have you looked in your bag? ... Well,
395 CP	Lavinia	28	you./But never mind, you'll soon get over it/And find yourself another little part to
399 CP	Reilly	2	Miss Barraway:/I should like to run over my instructions again./You understand, of
411 CP	Lavinia	3	The proprietor/Who has just taken over, is a friend of Alex's./I could go down with
414 CP	Celia	5	/To all sorts of people, and they get over it/More or less, or at least they carry on./
415 CP	Celia	32	the time!/I've been thinking about it, over and over;/I can see now, it was all a
415 CP	Celia	32	/I've been thinking about it, over and over;/I can see now, it was all a mistake:/But I
422 CP	Julia	16	of it./{J} May the holy ones watch over the roof,/May the moon herself influence
422 CP	Alex	21	travellers/Bless the road./{A} Watch over her in the desert./Watch over her in the
422 CP	Alex	22	Watch over her in the desert./Watch over her in the mountain./Watch over her in the
422 CP	Alex	23	over her in the mountain./Watch over her in the labyrinth./Watch over her by the
422 CP	Alex	24	over her in the labyrinth./Watch over her by the quicksand./{J} Protect her from
424 CP	Lavinia	24	I know that I'll be glad/When it's all over./{E} I like the dress you're wearing:/I'm
426 CP	Lavinia	12	/The best moment is the moment it's over;/And then to remember, it's the end of the
429 CP	Julia	35	/Somebody must have walked over my grave:/I'm feeling so chilly. Give me
430 CP	Peter	5	/{L} When did you arrive?/{P} I flew over from New York last night —/I left Los
430 CP	Peter	12	to see Edward and Lavinia./I'm only over for a week, you see,/And I'm driving down
431 CP	Peter	11	other./{P} Well, it was Bela sent me over/Just for a week. And I have my hands full/
431 CP	Peter	23	/We've got a team of experts over/To study the decay, so as to reproduce it./
431 CP	Julia	40	your casting director/To take us all over? We're all very typical./{P} No, I'm afraid
432 CP	Julia	33	interesting conversation./Peter's just over from California/Where he's something very
439 CP	Lavinia	40	I could face my guests. I wish it was over./I mean ... I am glad you came ... I am glad
440 CP	Edward	34	Now for the party./{E} It will soon be over./{L} I wish it would begin./{E} There's the
446 CC	Eggers	7	take a keen interest./{E} And getting over his disappointment?/Of course, I never
452 CC	Eggers	26	Miss Angel/Mr. Simpkins has taken over my duties./{L} And does he know that *I'm*
452 CC	Lucasta	28	Have you prepared him for taking *me* over?/Did you know that, Colby? I'm Lucasta./
459 CC	Claude	18	I'm having the flat in the mews done over./{LE} But all in the wrong colours, I'm
463 CC	Claude	3	alone./And then when I sent you both over to Canada/In the war — that was perhaps
477 CC	Lucasta	5	overdose'./Then Claude took me over. That was lucky./But I was old enough to
481 CC	Lady E	18	Lady Elizabeth./{LE} I've come over to have a look at the flat/Now that you've
486 CC	Claude	34	you were here with Colby./So I came over instead of telephoning,/Just to give him
487 CC	Claude	6	about ten minutes./And then we'll go over it tomorrow. {}/[*looking at the notes*]./{C}
493 CC	Lady E	21	But where shall we place her?/{LE} Over there, with the light full on her:/I want to
493 CC	Lady E	29	Claude, I've been thinking things over and over —/All through the night. I hardly
493 CC	Lady E	29	I've been thinking things over and over —/All through the night. I hardly slept at
503 CC	Eggers	21	/And rejoin us when this interview is over?/I'm sure Mr. Simpkins will concur in this
506 CC	Lady E	4	died suddenly .../{LE} He was run over. By a rhinoceros/In Tanganyika./{SC}
514 CC	Claude	19	have carried out such a deception/Over all these years. And why *should* you have
524 ES	Charles	8	say what I wanted to say to you/Over luncheon .../{M} That's your own fault./
529 ES	Ld Clav	23	book./{LC} Yes, I've been brooding over it./{M} But what a time for your
529 ES	Ld Clav	30	remember:/Every day, year after year, over my breakfast,/I have looked at this book
529 ES	Ld Clav	36	at this engagement book, to-day,/Not over breakfast, but before tea,/It's the empty
533 ES	Gomez	35	/In the right places, pays many times over./I assure you it does./{LC} In other words/
537 ES	Gomez	28	/I had plenty of time to think things over, later./{LC} And what is the conclusion
540 ES	Gomez	22	and shadows —/The night you ran over the old man in the road./{LC} You *said* I
540 ES	Ld Clav	23	man in the road./{LC} You *said* I ran over an old man in the road./{G} You knew it
540 ES	Gomez	25	/When I said 'Dick, you've run over somebody'/Wouldn't you have shown it, if
541 ES	Gomez	18	say I could buy you out/Several times over. San Marco's a good place/To make
548 ES	Monica	10	be stalking you/Put your newspaper over your face/And pretend you're pretending
548 ES	1m	14	CLAVERTON *spreads his newspaper over his face./Enter* MRS. CARGHILL. *She sits*
549 ES	Carghil	21	/{MC} And the three of us talked you over afterwards —/Effie and Maud and I. What
555 ES	Ld Clav	24	his,/I've lived in terror of his running over somebody./{M} Why, Father, should you

556 ES   Ld Clav   8   Well then, fetch him./Let's get this over. {}/[*calls*]/{M} Michael! {}/[*Enter*
556 ES   Michael   34   something I hadn't done./I never got over that. If you always blame a person/It's
559 ES   Michael   32   with Mother's family —/To lord it over them, in fact. Oh, I've no doubt/That the
561 ES   Ld Clav   28   him an offer/Which he must think over. But if he goes abroad/I want him to go in
571 ES   Ld Clav   36   late at night. A secondary road./I ran over an old man lying in the road/And I did not
571 ES   Ld Clav   37   I did not stop. Then another man ran over him./A lorry driver. He stopped and was
572 ES   Ld Clav   1   a natural death/And had been run over after he was dead./It was only a corpse
572 ES   Ld Clav   2   /It was only a corpse that we had run over/So neither of us killed him. But *I* didn't
573 ES   Ld Clav   2   a morbid conscience,/From brooding over faults I might well have forgotten./You
577 ES   Michael   21   Gomez and I have talked things over, Hemington .../{G} As two men of the
577 ES   Gomez   25   be able to buy you out many times over./{MC} Richard, I think it's time *I* joined
580 ES   Carghil   16   /It isn't so sudden. We talked it all over./But I've got a little piece of news of my

OVER-CROWDED (2)
294 FR   Harry   29   violence, but one is still alone/In an over-crowded desert, jostled by ghosts./It was
419 CP   Celia   23   /I mean, it would make the place so over-crowded./{R} Not very many go. But I said

OVERBEARING (1)
242 MC   Priest1   21   /Liked or feared by courtiers, in their overbearing fashion,/Despised and despising,

OVERBORNE (1)
260 MC   Thomas   18   same reason? For either joy will be overborne by mourning, or/mourning will be

OVERCOAT (1)
327 FR   Charles   39   I left St. Pancras. If I did, it's in my overcoat./I'll see if it's there. There might be

OVERDO (2)
447 CC   Claude   37   can take him to concerts. But don't overdo it!/{E} I'll remember that. Music./{SC}
449 CC   Claude   17   to commend him./{SC} You mustn't overdo it! But your approval matters./You

OVERDOSE (1)
477 ES   Lucasta   4   old/When she died of an 'accidental overdose'./Then Claude took me over. That was

OVERDUE (1)
232 Skimble   9   can't go.'/At 11.42 then the signal's overdue/And the passengers are frantic to a

OVERHEAD (2)
 18 Portrait   5   /Four rings of light upon the ceiling overhead,/An atmosphere of Juliet's tomb/
 37 Gerontion   11   /The goat coughs at night in the field overhead;/Rocks, moss, stonecrop, iron, merds./

OVERHEARD (1)
319 FR   Harry   25   aunts./It is the conversations not overheard,/Not intended to be heard, with the

OVERINTERPRET (1)
319 FR   Warburt   30   on which the news arrived./{W} You overinterpret./I am sure that your mother

OVERJOYED (1)
545 ES   Piggott   34   will be — Miss Timmins./She'd be overjoyed to have the privilege of helping you!/

OVERNIGHT (1)
388 CP   Edward   2   job./{E} And how did that happen, overnight?/{P} Why, it's a man Alex put me in

OVERRATE (1)
449 CC   Eggers   20   twice, perhaps .../But I'm afraid you overrate my influence./I have never been able to

OVERSEAS (1)
489 CC   Claude   28   on a business tour/To learn about his overseas investments./{LE} Then how do you

OVERTHROWN (1)
161 Rock 7   30   /The Church disowned, the tower overthrown, the bells upturned, what have we to

OVERTURNS (1)
 56 Swee Night   14   knees/Slips and pulls the table cloth/Overturns a coffee-cup,/Reorganised upon the

OVERWHELMING (3)
 13 Prufrock   10   /Of insidious intent/To lead you to an overwhelming question.../Oh, do not ask, 'What
 15 Prufrock   93   into a ball/To roll it towards some overwhelming question,/To say: 'I am Lazarus,
318 FR   Harry   30   why, but just this evening/I feel an overwhelming need for explanation —/But

OVERWORKED (2)
434 CP   Alex   9   of pestilence./They must have been overworked for weeks./{E} And then?/{A} And
558 ES   Michael   25   sometimes they'd pretend/That I was overworked, when I'd nothing to do./Even the

OVERWROUGHT (1)
295 FR   Amy   33   Harry, Harry, you are very tired/And overwrought. Coming so far/And making such

OWE (8)
159 Rock 6   13   survive the Faith to which they owe their significance?/Men! polish your teeth
206 To my Wife   1   /A Dedication to my Wife/To whom I owe the leaping delight/That quickens my senses
604 Ode   15   us also the vision to see/What we owe for the future, the present, and past,/Fair
275 MC   Knight1   18   His Church./{K1} No faith do I owe to a renegade,/And what I owe shall now
275 MC   Knight1   19   do I owe to a renegade,/And what I owe shall now be paid./{T} Now to Almighty
369 CP   Peter   3   was awfully kind to me/And I owe her a great deal. And then I met Celia./She
522 ES   dedic   1   /TO MY WIFE/*To whom I owe the leaping delight/That quickens my senses*
541 ES   Gomez   24   the rest of my life./Really, Dick, you owe me an apology./Blackmail! On the contrary

OWEN (6)

322 FR	Winch	38	John, I mean. By a bit of luck/Dr. Owen was there, and looked him over;/Says
323 FR	Winch	2	but he mustn't be moved./But Dr. Owen was anxious that you should have a look
323 FR	Warburt	11	/And Winchell tells me Dr. Owen has seen him/And says it's nothing but a
323 FR	Warburt	13	he mustn't be moved tonight. I'd trust Owen/On a matter like this. You can trust
323 FR	Warburt	14	/On a matter like this. You can trust Owen./We'll bring him up tomorrow; and a few
323 FR	Winch	25	course, he hasn't come round yet./Dr. Owen was there, by a bit of luck./{G} I'll go

OWL (5)

166 Rock 10		23	batflight,/Moon light and star light, owl and moth light,/Glow-worm glowlight on a
177 FQ: ECoker		23	the empty silence./Wait for the early owl./In that open field/If you do not come too
600 Moonflower		3	from sea;/A great white bird, a snowy owl,/Slips from the alder tree./Whiter the
256 MC	Chorus	29	TEMPTERS *alternately.*/{C} Is it the owl that calls, or a signal between the trees?/
263 MC	Chorus	9	field, attentive; and in the wood/The owl rehearses the hollow note of death./What

OWLS (2)

204 de la Mare		21	dance,/Dogs cower, flitter bats, and owls range/At witches' sabbath of the maiden
269 MC	Chorus	29	/Fluting in the night-time, fluting and owls, have seen at noon/Scaly wings slanting

OWN (131)

19 Portrait		33	/Absurdly hammering a prelude of its own,/Capricious monotone/That is at least one
33 Conv Gal		10	which we seize/To body forth our own vacuity.'/She then: 'Does this refer to me?'/
106 Song Sime		34	heart,/Thine also)./I am tired with my own life and the lives of those after me,/I am
106 Song Sime		35	of those after me,/I am dying in my own death and the deaths of those after me./Let
107 Animula		29	of the blood,/Shadow of its own shadows, spectre in its own gloom,/Leaving
107 Animula		29	of its own shadows, spectre in its own gloom,/Leaving disordered papers in a
108 Animula		35	fortune,/And that one who went his own way./Pray for Floret, by the boarhound
110 Marina		27	half conscious, unknown, my own./The garboard strake leaks, the seams need
158 Rock 5		8	for silence: seeking every one after his own elevation, and dodging his emptiness./If
164 Rock 9		7	/They would put upon GOD their own sorrow, the grief they should feel/For their
181 FQ: ECoker		147	only thing you know/And what you own is what you do not own/And where you are
181 FQ: ECoker		147	what you own is what you do not own/And where you are is where you are not./
187 FQ: DrySal		112	/Involving ourselves, than in our own./For our own past is covered by the
187 FQ: DrySal		113	ourselves, than in our own./For our own past is covered by the currents of action,/
191 FQ: Little		1	Little Gidding/Midwinter spring is its own season/Sempiternal though sodden towards
194 FQ: Little		116	purpose: let them be./So with your own, and pray they be forgiven/By others, as I
195 FQ: Little		162	country/Begins as attachment to our own field of action/And comes to find that
203 Indians		1	in Africa/A man's destination is his own village,/His own fire, and his wife's
203 Indians		2	destination is his own village,/His own fire, and his wife's cooking;/To sit in front
203 Indians		3	wife's cooking;/To sit in front of his own door at sunset/And see his grandson, and
224 Mr Mistoff		5	scoff. All his/Inventions are off his own bat./There's no such Cat in the metropolis;
587 Fable		29	From over sea/He purchased at his own expense a crowd/Of relics from a Spanish
599 On a Port		8	/An immaterial fancy of one's own./No meditations glad or ominous/Disturb
605 Narcissus		12	/He was stifled and soothed by his own rhythm./By the river/His eyes were aware
605 Narcissus		25	slippery white belly held tight in his own fingers,/Writhing in his own clutch, his
605 Narcissus		26	in his own fingers,/Writhing in his own clutch, his ancient beauty/Caught fast in
606 Narcissus		30	/Knowing at the end the taste of his own whiteness/The horror of his own
606 Narcissus		31	his own whiteness/The horror of his own smoothness,/And he felt drunken and old./
239 MC	Chorus	24	/But mostly we are left to our own devices,/And we are content if we are left
240 MC	Chorus	3	to his piece of earth, earth-colour, his own colour,/Preferring to pass unobserved./
241 MC	Priest3	6	others,/The feeble is devoured by his own./{P1} Shall these things not end/Until the
242 MC	Priest1	24	/His pride always feeding upon his own virtues,/Pride drawing sustenance from
242 MC	Priest2	31	Our lord has come back to his own again./We have had enough of waiting,
250 MC	Tempt3	29	country-keeping lord who minds his own business./It is we country lords who know
252 MC	Tempt3	11	Kings will allow no power but their own;/Church and people have good cause
255 MC	Thomas	18	No!/Who are you, tempting with my own desires?/Others have come, temporal
256 MC	Tempts	22	illusion,/Lost in the wonder of his own greatness,/The enemy of society, enemy of
258 MC	Thomas	22	Toulouse,/I beat the barons at their own game. I/Could then despise the men who
265 MC	Knight3	32	of his hospitality./We will find our own dinner. {}/[*to attendant*]./{P1} Go, tell His
268 MC	Thomas	19	people of me and keep me from my own/And bid me sit in Canterbury, alone?/I
273 MC	Thomas	19	fortress./The Church shall protect her own, in her own way, not/As oak and stone;
273 MC	Thomas	19	Church shall protect her own, in her own way, not/As oak and stone; stone and oak
290 FR	Amy	8	/But only to bring Harry down to her own level./A restless shivering painted shadow/
294 FR	Harry	5	morning. I am not speaking/Of my own experience, but trying to give you/
294 FR	Agatha	13	best tell us as you can:/Talk in your own language, without stopping to debate/
294 FR	Harry	22	/And partial observation of one's own automatism/While the slow stain sinks
295 FR	Charles	12	more horrible./There's a lot in my own past life that presses on my chest/When I
296 FR	Amy	32	a few days at Wishwood/Among his own family, is all that he needs./{G}

298 FR	Agatha	12	to talk to Downing/And pursue his own methods. {}/[*Rises*]/{V} I do not agree./I
306 FR	Mary	25	/It always seemed that it must be my own fault,/And never to be happy was always to
306 FR	Mary	36	was never any time to invent our own enjoyments./But perhaps it was all
308 FR	Mary	9	branch ophidian./{M} You bring your own landscape/No more real than the other.
313 FR	Ivy	11	been my passion./You know I had my own garden once, in Cornwall,/When I could
326 FR	Harry	24	so long as I could think/Even of my own life as an isolated ruin,/A casual bit of
327 FR	Agatha	5	make-believe and fear. To rest in our own suffering/Is evasion of suffering. We must
335 FR	Agatha	4	flew over./And then I was only my own feet walking/Away, down a concrete
340 FR	Amy	19	future, a discontented ghost,/In his own house. What of the humiliation,/Of the
343 FR	Agatha	5	too!/{Ag} We must all go, each in his own direction,/You, and I, and Harry. You and
349 FR	Agatha	24	reason/Each curse has its course/Its own way of expiation/Follow follow/{M} Not in
350 FR	Agatha	25	depart/In several directions/For their own redemption/And that of the departed —/
379 CP	Celia	36	/Perhaps it was I who betrayed my own dream/All the while; and to find I wanted/
380 CP	Edward	39	should have a man ... nearer your own age./{C} I don't think I care for advice
381 CP	Celia	4	you're competent/To manage your own./Oh, Edward, I should like to be good to
396 CP	Lavinia	16	pity that you had no opinion of your own./Oh, Edward, I should like to be good to
397 CP	Edward	18	If I go to a doctor, I shall make my own choice;/Not take one whom you choose.
402 CP	Edward	34	mine:/I have ceased to believe in my own personality./{R} Oh, dear yes; this is
403 CP	Edward	7	I am obsessed by the thought of my own insignificance./{R} Precisely. And I could
403 CP	Edward	36	/Of having any existence of my own./That is what she has done to me in
405 CP	Reilly	6	situation is much the same as your own. {}/[*Presses the bell on his desk three times*]/
407 CP	Reilly	22	both, tried to impose upon me/Your own diagnosis, and prescribe your own cure./
407 CP	Reilly	22	own diagnosis, and prescribe your own cure./But when you put yourselves into
408 CP	Reilly	28	{R} That I cannot disclose./I have my own method of collecting information/About
410 CP	Reilly	16	/You could accuse each other of your own faults,/And so could avoid understanding
410 CP	Reilly	31	we do?/{R} You have answered your own question,/Though you do not know the
416 CP	Celia	24	only love/Something created by our own imagination?/Are we all in fact unloving
416 CP	Reilly	35	already a clue/Towards finding your own way out of the forest./{C} But even if I find
417 CP	Reilly	21	the form of treatment must be your own choice:/I cannot choose for you. If that is
418 CP	Reilly	31	way you choose will prescribe its own duty./{C} Which way is better?/{R} Neither
420 CP	Reilly	28	minds./Each unable to disguise his own meanness/From himself, because it is
435 CP	Lavinia	34	you made for yourself, to meet your own needs./Peter, please don't think I'm being
437 CP	Reilly	6	*Zoroaster, my dead child,/Met his own image walking in the garden./That*
446 CC	Claude	19	myself./But so far, I've left him to his own devices:/I thought he would fall into this
446 CC	Eggers	33	/Some day, he'll want a garden of his own. And yes, a bird bath!/{SC} A bird bath? In
455 CC	Eggers	11	the right term./She's no money of her own, as you may have gathered;/But I think her
455 CC	Eggers	21	/In the end. He's a man who gets his own way,/And I think he can manage her. If
460 CC	Claude	34	She actually went and changed her own ticket./It's something unheard of./{E}
462 CC	Claude	24	haven't the strength to impose your own terms/Upon life, you must accept the terms
463 CC	Claude	34	/Much better than you think. It's my own experience/That you are repeating./{C}
463 CC	Colby	36	/That you are repeating./{C} Your own experience?/{SC} Yes, I did not want to be
465 CC	Colby	32	you've been talking,/That it's my own feelings you have expressed,/Although the
467 CC	Claude	17	/That life has imposed./{SC} It's my own fault./I was always anxious to avoid the
471 CC	Colby	28	/You preferred it to be one of your own creation/Rather than wait to see what
473 CC	Colby	5	/Are you sure that you haven't your own secret garden/Somewhere, if you could find
486 CC	Colby	23	/{C} They had no children of their own./That is to say, they had had one little boy/
488 CC	Claude	31	might come to take the place of your own child,/If you got to know him first — and
488 CC	Lady E	34	is, if one's allowed to adopt one's own child./{SC} That's not what I meant.
489 CC	Claude	4	Lucasta, and you told me/About your own ... misfortune. And I almost told you/
489 CC	Claude	13	see how you longed for a son of your own,/And I thought, I'll wait for children of *our*
489 CC	Claude	14	I thought, I'll wait for children of *our* own,/And tell her then. And they never came./
497 CC	Claude	15	the name of the person/To whom her own child was entrusted./{E} What an amazing
500 CC	Lucasta	29	/But he's undependable. He has his own world,/And he might vanish into it at any
506 CC	Eggers	16	you have had no children of your own;/But I'm sure you can sympathise./{MG} I
513 CC	Colby	34	/Whose image I could create in my own mind,/To live with that image. An ordinary
516 CC	Claude	26	my son,/Because you described my own experience, exactly./Does that mean
517 CC	Eggers	21	Simpkins is a man who knows his own mind./Is it true, Mr. Simpkins, that what
517 CC	Eggers	26	I happen to know of a vacancy/In my own parish, in Joshua Park —/If it should
524 ES	Monica	9	/Over luncheon .../{M} That's your own fault./You should have taken me to some
530 ES	Monica	7	know I'm to protect you/From your own restless energy — the inexhaustible/Sources
538 ES	Gomez	25	people make mistakes/Until your own have been more or less forgotten./I dare
539 ES	Gomez	31	to give you a detailed account/Of my own career. I've been very successful./What
541 ES	Gomez	20	it in./My investments — not all in my own name either —/Are pretty well spread. For
545 ES	Ld Clav	9	severely/For the errors into which his own reproaches drove us?/{M} You admit that
551 ES	Carghil	7	/A man is always trying to forget/His own shabby behaviour./{LC} But we'd settled

552 ES	Ld Clav	1	And perhaps at the same time of your own?/I seem to remember, it was only a year or
553 ES	Carghil	33	told. And I like to read them/In your own handwriting./{LC} And have you shown
557 ES	Michael	39	the same at Oxford./{Mi} It's their own fault./They won't send in their bills, and
559 ES	Michael	15	money./I want to be somebody on my own account./{LC} But what do you want to
559 ES	Michael	18	I simply want to lead a life of my own,/According to my own ideas of good and
559 ES	Michael	19	a life of my own,/According to my own ideas of good and bad,/Of right and
559 ES	Michael	31	be Lord Claverton/Also, to hold your own with Mother's family —/To lord it over
561 ES	Michael	33	want to leave England, and make my own career:/And Father simply calls me a
565 ES	Ld Clav	34	Michael/Not to try to escape from his own past failures:/I said I knew from
569 ES	Ld Clav	2	/Walk off the stage, change into our own clothes/And speak as ourselves. So I'd
570 ES	Ld Clav	27	/A man who's made a fortune by his own peculiar methods,/A man of great
574 ES	Carghil	17	He wants to go abroad!/And find his own way in the world. That's very natural./So I
574 ES	Carghil	20	man, and very important/In his own country. And a friend of Michael's father!/
575 ES	Michael	2	I want to go where I can make my own way,/Not merely be your son. That's what
578 ES	Ld Clav	1	your power, Fred Culverwell,/Of his own volition to contract his enslavement,/I
578 ES	Monica	35	/Of what I said. You must make your own life/Of course, just as I must make mine./
580 ES	Carghil	17	I've got a little piece of news of my own:/Next autumn, I'm going out to Australia,/
581 ES	Ld Clav	22	I was,/So that I could believe in my own pretences./I've only just now had the

OWNER (2)

37 Gerontion		8	the Jew squats on the window sill, the owner,/Spawned in some estaminet of Antwerp,
142 Cape Ann		12	land at the end, resign it/To its true owner, the tough one, the sea-gull./The palaver

OXFORD (21)

44 Cook Egg		3	from where I was sitting;/*Views of Oxford Colleges*/Lay on the table, with the
212 Growltiger		3	at large./From Gravesend up to Oxford he pursued his evil aims,/Rejoicing in
306 FR	Harry	5	seen you since you came down from Oxford./{M} Well, I must go and change for
332 FR	Agatha	21	I was then/An undergraduate at Oxford. I came/Once for a long vacation. I
355 CP	Julia	38	Tony Vincewell? You knew him at Oxford?/{P} No, I never knew him at Oxford:/I
356 CP	Peter	1	Oxford?/{P} No, I never knew him at Oxford:/I came across him last year in
533 ES	Gomez	2	I knew you./When we were up at Oxford, you were plain Dick Ferry./Then, when
537 ES	Gomez	12	what we were when we went up to Oxford/And then what I became under your
537 ES	Gomez	18	it./When you started to take me up at Oxford/I've no doubt your friends wondered
537 ES	Gomez	35	to you later./{G} You led me on at Oxford, and left me to it./And so it came about
539 ES	Gomez	35	school like that from which I went to Oxford./As it is, I'm somebody — a more
540 ES	Gomez	17	moonlight night/We drove back to Oxford? *You* were driving./{LC} That happened
557 ES	Ld Clav	38	expected that./It was just the same at Oxford./{Mi} It's their own fault./They won't
558 ES	Michael	15	like the headmaster. And my tutor at Oxford./'Not what we expected from the son of
564 ES	Gomez	15	as long as I have./We were friends at Oxford./{MC} Oh, so you were at Oxford!/Is
564 ES	Carghil	16	at Oxford./{MC} Oh, so you were at Oxford!/Is that how you come to speak such
564 ES	Carghil	21	/You were a friend of Richard's at Oxford/And Richard and I became great friends
564 ES	Carghil	25	Of course, that explains it. After Oxford/I suppose you went back to ... where is
564 ES	Carghil	32	you tell me all about Richard/In his Oxford days./{G} On one condition:/That you
571 ES	Ld Clav	7	Freddy admired me, when we were at Oxford;/What did I make of his admiration?/I
571 ES	Ld Clav	34	haunted me./I was driving back to Oxford. We had two girls with us./It was late at

OYSTER (1)

270 MC Chorus		2	tasted/The living lobster, the crab, the oyster, the whelk and the prawn; and they live

OYSTER-SHELLS (1)

13 Prufrock		7	hotels/And sawdust restaurants with oyster-shells:/Streets that follow like a tedious

OYSTERS (1)

357 CP	Julia	32	near Colchester? Lavinia loves oysters./{E} No. In the *depths* of Essex./{J}

PACE (3)

120 SP	Krum	2	/But I'm afraid we couldn't stand the pace./What about it Klip?/{Kl} You said it,
322 FR	Winch	33	fog, coming along/At a pretty smart pace, I fancy, ran into a lorry/Drawn up round
325 FR	Violet	38	street, and everyone staring;/And the pace he went at was simply terrifying./I said I

PACES (2)

| 69 WL: Fire S | 254 | lovely woman stoops to folly and/Paces about her room again, alone,/She |
| 232 Skimble | 21 | more or less./Down the corridor he paces and examines all the faces/Of the |

PACING (1)

| 280 MC Priest3 | 34 | fiction which unravels as you weave,/Pacing forever in the hell of make-believe/ |

PACK (2)

| 62 WL: Burial | 46 | woman in Europe,/With a wicked pack of cards. Here, said she,/Is your card, the |
| 224 Mr Mistoff | 27 | rail./He can pick any card from a pack,/He is equally cunning with dice;/He is |

PACKED (1)

| 241 MC Mess | 35 | season./The streets of the city will be packed to suffocation,/And I think that his |

PACKELL (1)

| 293 FR Violet | 2 | that goes on in the kitchen./Mrs. Packell is too old to know what she is doing./It |

PACT (1)

| 268 MC Knight2 | 1 | friends, offered clemency,/Made a pact of peace, and all dispute ended/Sent you |

PACTS (1)

| 253 MC Tempt4 | 35 | revolution,/New conspiracies, broken pacts;/To be master or servant within an hour,/ |

PADDED (1)

| 536 ES Gomez | 27 | Your loneliness — so cosy, warm and padded:/You're not isolated — merely |

PADDING (2)

| 43 Swee Erect | 42 | Doris, towelled from the bath,/Enters padding on broad feet,/Bringing sal volatile/ |
| 257 MC Chorus | 29 | air:/Puss-purr of leopard, footfall of padding bear,/Palm-pat of nodding ape, square |

PADOUE (1)

| 48 Lune Miel | 12 | huit heures/Prolonger leurs misères de Padoue à Milan/Où se trouve la Cène, et un |

PAGANS (1)

| 429 CP Julia | 15 | on eating Christians —/Even among pagans!/{A} Not on the *whole* story./{E} And |

PAGE (1)

| 20 Portrait | 72 | /Reading the comics and the sporting page./Particularly I remark./An English |

PAGES (4)

588 Fable	55	head, which to bring in took four pages,/His mouth an apple held, his skull held
529 ES Ld Clav	37	but before tea,/It's the empty pages that I've been fingering —/The first
530 ES Ld Clav	1	I've been fingering —/The first empty pages since I entered Parliament./I used to jot
530 ES Ld Clav	4	wondering ... how many more empty pages?/{M} You would soon fill them up if we

PAID (9)

124 SA Sweeney	31	went/But he took in the milk and he paid the rent./{Sw} What did he do?/All that
155 Rock 3	48	/Precarious lodgings while the rent is paid,/Subsiding basements where the rat breeds/
248 MC Tempt1	2	higher vices,/Which will have to be paid for at higher prices./Farewell, my Lord, I
275 MC Knight1	19	/And what I owe shall now be paid./{T} Now to Almighty God, to the Blessed
425 CP Lavinia	3	Do you know it's the first time you've paid me a compliment/*Before* a party? And
438 CP Reilly	1	conscious/Than the rest of us. She paid the highest price/In suffering. That is part
538 ES Gomez	8	when you were released./{G} Yes, and paid my passage out. I know the reason:/You
549 ES Carghil	2	*you.* But still,/I wish you could have paid *me* that compliment, Richard./{LC} What!/
577 ES Gomez	7	{G} Just as many years ago/His father paid mine./{C} This return of past kindness/No

PAIEREZ (1)

| 47 Mél Adult | 7 | Londres, un peu banquier,/Vous me paierez bien la tête./C'est à Paris que je me |

PAIL (1)

| 194 FQ: Little | 119 | the fullfed beast shall kick the empty pail./For last year's words belong to last year's |

PAIN (18)

107 Animula	21	and may not, desire and control./The pain of living and the drug of dreams/Curl up
167 Rock 10	36	the play ends; and ecstasy is too much pain./We are children quickly tired: children
186 FQ: DrySal	83	flowers,/To the movement of pain that is painless and motionless,/To the drift
194 FQ: Little	140	to amuse./And last, the rending pain of re-enactment/Of all that you have done,
593 Grad 5	5	years may see,/What conquest over pain and misery,/What heroes greater than were
598 Circe	2	which flows/With the voice of men in pain,/Are flowers that no man knows./Their
257 MC Chorus	25	God is leaving us, more pang, more pain than birth or death./Sweet and cloying
268 MC Thomas	38	presence; seven years of misery and pain./Seven years a mendicant on foreign
280 MC Priest3	30	in Aquitaine./In the small circle of pain within the skull/You still shall tramp and
310 FR Mary	5	slow flow throbbing the trunk/The pain of the breaking bud./These are the ones
310 FR Mary	17	/Do the dead want to return?/{M} Pain is the opposite of joy/But joy is a kind of
310 FR Mary	18	opposite of joy/But joy is a kind of pain/I believe the moment of birth/Is when we
315 FR Harry	2	Cancer is here:/The lump, the dull pain, the occasional sickness:/Murder a reversal
329 FR Chorus	8	/The stumble and the wail of little pain/The chopping of wood in autumn/And the

334 FR   Harry   39   public./Liberty is a different kind of pain from prison./{Ag} I only looked through
404 CP   Edward   11   experienced the extreme of physical pain,/And now I know there is suffering worse
437 CP   Reilly   37   all that we should suffer/In fear and pain and loathing — all these together —/And
551 ES   Carghil 16   /You're wrong, you know. It's both pain and pleasure/To talk about the past —

PAINED (1)
34 Figlia   4   —/Clasp your flowers to you with a pained surprise —/Fling them to the ground

PAINFUL (6)
271 MC Thomas   12   /Shall pierce you with a sudden painful joy/When the figure of God's purpose is
288 FR Agatha   13   together./{Ag} It is going to be rather painful for Harry/After eight years and all that
288 FR Gerald   16   come back to Wishwood./{G} Why, painful?/{V} Gerald! you know what Agatha
288 FR Agatha   18   what Agatha means./{Ag} I mean painful, because everything is irrevocable,/
512 CC Guzzard   25   wish that is granted. That can be a painful process,/As I know. And you, Barnabas
551 ES   Carghil 18   you and me./These memories are painful — but I cherish them./{LC} If you had

PAINLESS (1)
186 FQ: DrySal   83   /To the movement of pain that is painless and motionless,/To the drift of the sea

PAINS (1)
407 CP   Reilly   19   are the self-deceivers/Taking infinite pains, exhausting their energy,/Yet never quite

PAINT (3)
42 Swee Erect   1   and the seven laws./Sweeney Erect/Paint me a cavernous waste shore/Cast in the
42 Swee Erect   3   shore/Cast in the unstilled Cyclades,/Paint me the bold anfractuous rocks/Faced by
109 Marina   22   meet./Bowsprit cracked with ice and paint cracked with heat./I made this, I have

PAINTED (2)
288 FR Agatha   22   in the tropics/Or against the painted scene of the Mediterranean,/Harry must
290 FR   Amy   9   to her own level./A restless shivering painted shadow/In life, she is less than a shadow

PAINTER (3)
54 Mr E Sun   9   of time/Produced enervate Origen./A painter of the Umbrian school/Designed upon a
54 Mr E Sun   15   unoffending feet/And there above the painter set/The Father and the Paraclete./The
464 CC   Claude   4   people think that a sculptor or a painter/Is something more excellent to be than a

PAINTING (1)
464 CC   Claude 14   world to a pure one./Sculpture and painting — I have some good things —/But

PAIR (3)
15 Prufrock   73   of windows?.../I should have been a pair of ragged claws/Scuttling across the floors
589 Fable   80   any one could say 'O jiminy!'/The pair had vanisht swiftly up the chimney./
501 CC   Eggers 33   sure that we want to greet the happy pair./It's all in the family. Why not let them

PAISLEY (1)
430 CP   Peter   7   Angeles three days ago./I saw Sheila Paisley at lunch to-day/And she told me you

PAL (1)
542 ES   Gomez   39   my welcome?/Your telephone pal may be getting impatient./I'll see you soon

PALACE (4)
31 Apollinax   6   at the lady in the swing./In the palace of Mrs. Phlaccus, at Professor
72 WL: Thund   326   shouting and the crying/Prison and palace and reverberation/Of thunder of spring
157 Rock 4   5   to the general rule./In Shushan the palace, in the month Nisan,/He served the wine
598 Circe   t   flowers, flowers of dawn./Circe's Palace/Around her fountain which flows/With

PALACES (1)
103 Journ Magi   9   were times we regretted/The summer palaces on slopes, the terraces,/And the silken

PALATABLE (1)
428 CP   Alex   21   /The young monkeys are extremely palatable:/I've cooked them myself .../{E} And

PALATE (1)
136 5FingerEx4   11   him as something apart)/While on his palate fine he presses/The juice of the

PALAVER (2)
142 Cape Ann   13   the tough one, the sea-gull./The palaver is finished./Lines for an Old Man/The
154 Rock 3   7   /I have given you speech, for endless palaver,/I have given you my Law, and you set

PALE (1)
54 Mr E Sun   13   and browned/But through the water pale and thin/Still shine the unoffending feet/

PALL (2)
231 Bust Jones   39   Cats./It must and it shall be Spring in Pall Mall/While Bustopher Jones wears white
345 FR Charles   38   to the centre, as I was about to cross Pall Mall./I thought that life could bring no

PALM (2)
189 FQ: DrySal   192   /Biography from the wrinkles of the palm/And tragedy from fingers; release omens/
292 FR   Harry   8   and corrupted that song./Behind the palm trees in the Grand Hotel/They were

PALM-PAT (1)
257 MC Chorus   30   of leopard, footfall of padding bear,/Palm-pat of nodding ape, square hyaena

PALMED (1)
476 CC Lucasta   21   mistress —/Or had been his mistress, palmed off on B./{C} I never thought of such a

PALMIEST (1)
228 Gus   14 pays,/With anecdotes drawn from his palmiest days./For he once was a Star of the
PALMLEAF (2)
122 SAWa & Ho   32   *maids/In the banyan shades/Wear palmleaf drapery/Under the bam/Under the boo/*
123 SAWa & Ho   3   *me?/Under the breadfruit, banyan, palmleaf/Or under the bamboo tree?/Any old tree*
PALMS (4)
 23 Preludes   38 clasped the yellow soles of feet/In the palms of both soiled hands./His soul stretched
 40 Burb Blei   15   of the knees/And elbows, with the palms turned out,/Chicago Semite Viennese./A
151 Rock 2   6 would build and restore turn out the palms of their hands, or look in vain towards
161 Rock 7   31 do/But stand with empty hands and palms turned upwards/In an age which
PALMTREE (1)
128 Cor1 March   33   in the turtle's breast,/Under the palmtree at noon, under the running water/At
PALMTREES (1)
121 SA Sweeney   27   as it grows./Nothing to see but the palmtrees one way/And the sea the other way,/
PALPABLE (1)
255 MC Thomas   20 tempters,/With pleasure and power at palpable price./What do you offer? what do you
PALSY (1)
228 Gus   6   thin as a rake,/And he suffers from palsy that makes his paw shake./Yet he was, in
PAMPERED (1)
212 Growltiger   14   fluttered from its cage;/Woe to the pampered Pekinese, that faced Growltiger's
PAN-AM-EAGLE (4)
430 CP   Peter   31   /But you all know I'm working for Pan-Am-Eagle?/{E} No. Tell us, what is
430 CP   Edward 32   /{E} No. Tell us, what is Pan-Am-Eagle?/{P} You must have been living
431 CP   Peter   2   that? They don't have pictures?/Pan-Am-Eagle must look into this./Perhaps it
431 CP   Peter   4 to make one./— Alex knows all about Pan-Am-Eagle:/It was he who introduced me to
PANCRAS (1)
327 FR   Charles   39   a lunch edition/Before I left St. Pancras. If I did, it's in my overcoat./I'll see if
PANE (1)
177 FQ: ECoker   11   for the wind to break the loosened pane/And to shake the wainscot where the
PANES (1)
167 Rock 10   29   lights directed through the coloured panes of windows/And light reflected from the
PANG (1)
257 MC Chorus   25 is leaving us, God is leaving us, more pang, more pain than birth or death./Sweet and
PANIC (3)
308 FR   Harry   35   —/And inside too, in the nightly panic/Of dreaming dissolution. You do not
357 CP   Edward 14   why when she's ill/She gets into a panic./{J} And sends for Lavinia./I quite
378 CP   Celia   24 moment of surrender/To fatigue. And panic. You can't face the trouble./{E} No, it is
PANORAMA (1)
180 FQ: ECoker   117 that the hills and the trees, the distant panorama/And the bold imposing façade are all
PANTHERS (1)
598 Circe   8   —/We shall not come here again./Panthers rise from their lairs/In the forest which
PANTOMIME (3)
228 Gus   31 rung, then I swung on the bell./In the Pantomime season I never fell flat,/And I once
256 MC Tempts   12   /The Catherine wheel, the pantomime cat,/The prizes given at the
291 FR   Chorus   6 farce, ridiculous in some nightmare pantomime./{A} What's that? I thought I saw
PANTRY (5)
219 Mung Rump   35 a dining-room smash/Or up from the pantry there came a loud crash/Or down from
353 CP   Peter   15 And how the butler found her in the pantry, rinsing her mouth out with champagne./
356 CP   Julia   31 make you talk. Perhaps she's in the pantry/Listening to all we say!/{E} No, she's not
356 CP   Edward   33 to all we say!/{E} No, she's not in the pantry./{C} Will she be away for some time,
504 CC Lucasta   9   I heard someone singing in the pantry./{LE} Oh, I forgot. It's Gertrude's quiet
PAPER (10)
 24 Rhapsody   57   cracks her face,/Her hand twists a paper rose,/That smells of dust and eau de
174 FQ: BurntN   107   no concentration/Men and bits of paper, whirled by the cold wind/That blows
227 Macavity   29 by the way,/There may be a scrap of paper in the hall or on the stair —/But it's
327 FR   Ivy   24   IVY]/{I} Where is there an evening paper?/{G} Why, what's the matter./{I}
327 FR   Ivy   26   look for Arthur in the evening paper./That was Arthur, ringing up from
327 FR   Ivy   33 there was something about it in the paper,/But it's all a mistake. And not to tell his
327 FR   Violet   35   the use of asking for an evening paper?/You know as well as I do, at this
327 FR   Violet   37 Nobody's likely to have this evening's paper./{C} Stop, I think I bought a lunch
397 CP   Edward   28   always wrapping things up in tissue paper/And then had to unwrap everything again
419 CP   m 36   your friends; {}/[*Writes on a slip of paper*]/{R} You had better let your family know
PAPERS (22)
 23 Preludes   36 the bed's edge, where/You curled the papers from your hair,/Or clasped the yellow
 67 WL: Fire S   177   bears no empty bottles, sandwich papers,/Silk handkerchiefs, cardboard boxes,

107 Animula	30	in its own gloom,/Leaving disordered	papers in a dusty room;/Living first in the
124 SA	Snow	21	on Epsom Heath?/I seen that in the papers/You seen it in the papers/They *don't* all
124 SA	Snow	22	that in the papers/You seen it in the papers/They *don't* all get pinched in the end./
147 Rock 1	30	is foul we stay at home and read the	papers./In industrial districts, there I was told/
202 War Poetry	2	/Imperfectly reflected in the daily	papers./Where is the point at which the merely
266 MC Thomas	6	/On my table you will find/The	papers in order, and the documents signed. {}/
295 FR	Charles	9	really happened, we read it in the papers —/No need to revert to it. Remember,
299 FR	Charles	7	/We only knew what we read in the papers —/Of course, there was a great deal too
299 FR	Charles	8	there was a great deal too much in the papers./Downing, do you think that it might
301 FR	Chorus	19	/Flashlight for the picture papers: why do we huddle together/In a horrid
328 FR	Charles	32	these affairs were kept out of the papers;/But nowadays, there's no such thing as
401 CP	m	1	/[*without looking up from his papers*]./{R} Good morning, Mr. Chamberlayne./
452 CC	Lucasta	16	/Two months I'd gone on filing those papers/Which no one ever wanted — at least,
458 CC	Claude	3	sit at the desk, and pick up some papers./We must look as if we'd been engaged
496 CC	Eggers	27	evening. And the late editions/Of the papers that I picked up at Liverpool Street./But
527 ES	Monica	25	when he's reading, or busy with his papers/He needs to have someone else in the
531 ES	Monica	5	read every word about you in the papers./{C} And the leading articles saying 'we
532 ES	Ld Clav	5	library./No, stop. I've left too many papers about there./I'd better see him here./{L}
544 ES	Ld Clav	13	people not staring/Or offering picture papers, or wanting a fourth at bridge;/Still, I'll
548 ES	Carghil	32	we've all seen your portrait in the papers/So often. And everybody knows *you*.

PAR (1)

47 Mél Adult	11	/En Allemagne, philosophe/Surexcité par Emporheben/Au grand air de

PARACLETE (1)

54 Mr E Sun	16	the painter set/The Father and the Paraclete./The sable presbyters approach/The

PARADISE (1)

561 ES Ld Clav	8	you reach your goal,/Your imagined paradise of success and grandeur,/You will find

PARAGRAPH (2)

328 FR Charles	7	*with a newspaper*]/{C} Yes, there is a paragraph ... I'm glad to say/It's not very
531 ES Ld Clav	17	the half of that;/In ten years' time, a paragraph./{C} That's the reward/Of every

PARALYSED (2)

83 Hollow Men	12	without form, shade without colour,/Paralysed force, gesture without motion;/Those
309 FR Mary	26	/Like the man convinced that he is paralysed/Or like the man who believes that he

PARASITES (2)

250 MC Tempt3	34	of the nation./We, not the plotting parasites/About the King. Excuse my bluntness:
254 MC Tempt4	35	and its stores/Swept into the laps of parasites and whores./When miracles cease, and

PARCELS (1)

524 ES	m	5	MONICA *and* CHARLES *carrying parcels*]/{M} But you *must* stay to tea. That was

PARCHED (3)

193 FQ: Little	68	/Contending for the upper hand./The parched eviscerate soil/Gapes at the vanity of
255 MC Tempt4	16	persecutors, in timeless torment,/Parched passion, beyond expiation./{T} No!/
263 MC Chorus	17	or we shall have only/A sour spring, a parched summer, an empty harvest./Between

PARDON (2)

322 FR Winch	4	same if it was my birthday —/I beg pardon, I'm forgetting./If it was my mother's.
401 CP Edward	11	always been satisfactory./I beg your pardon. But he *is* a blunderer./I should like to

PARED (1)

41 Burb Blei	30	lion's wings/And flea'd his rump and pared his claws?/Thought Burbank, meditating

PARENT (4)

490 CC	Colby	23	friends ... older friends. Neither, as a parent./I am sorry. But that's why I say it
490 CC	Colby	25	/To me, which of you should be my parent./{LE} But a mother, Colby, isn't that
490 CC	Colby	40	Now, it is too late./I never wanted a parent till now —/I never thought about it.
579 ES	Carghil	32	to me in the end, Dick./{MC} A parent isn't always the right person, Richard,/

PARENTHOOD (2)

491 CC	Colby	34	/At being cheated of his — or her — parenthood,/The other indignant at the
491 CC	Colby	36	indignant at the imputation/Of false parenthood. Both mocked at./{SC} Then what

PARENTS (24)

332 FR	Harry	4	ecstasy./Tell me now, who were my parents?/{Ag} Your father and your mother./
355 CP	Peter	35	tell the story./{P} Were they the parents of Tony Vincewell?/{J} Yes. Tony was
414 CP	Reilly	14	to anyone!/{R} And what about your parents?/{C} Oh, they live in the country,/Now
476 CC	Colby	3	allowed to tell./And that's about my parents./{L} Oh, I see./Well, I can't believe that
476 CC	Lucasta	6	/But I can tell you all about *my* parents:/At least, I'm going to./{C} Does that
480 CC	Kaghan	29	You didn't know that!/Never had any parents. Just adopted, from nowhere./That's
484 CC	Lady E	8	how you felt./How I disliked my parents! I had a governess;/Several, in fact. And
484 CC	Lady E	13	her portrait. If you never knew your parents .../But was your father living?/{C} I
484 CC	Lady E	17	/And if you never knew either of your parents,/You can't understand what loathing
484 CC	Colby	20	of background./{C} But you had parents. And no doubt, many relatives./{LE}

485 CC Lady E 16 /To be able to think that one's earthly parents/Are only the means that we have to
490 CC Colby 20 /That when one has lived without parents, as a child,/There's a gap that never can
491 CC Colby 22 /To accept you both in the place of parents/If neither of you could be. If it was pure
491 CC Colby 27 of a son,/To be disputed between two parents./But, if we followed your suggestion,/I
491 CC Colby 30 /By the miserable ghosts of the other parents!/It's strange enough to have two parents
491 CC Colby 31 /It's strange enough to have two parents —But I should have four! What about
491 CC Claude 39 When you marry/You will want parents, for the sake of your children./{C} I
507 CC Eggers 6 take in a child —/A child, that is, of parents unknown to you —/Under such
510 CC Eggers 4 /We can ask Mr. Kaghan about his parents;/And if Mr. and Mrs. Kaghan are still
510 CC Guzzard 22 Mr. and Mrs. Alfred Kaghan your parents?/{K} Yes. They are. My adoptive
510 CC Kaghan 23 /{K} Yes. They are. My adoptive parents./{MG} And did they at one time live in
510 CC Eggers 28 /{E} Mr. Kaghan, are your adoptive parents living?/{K} In Kent. They wanted to
510 CC Eggers 35 Kaghan,/By putting your adoptive parents in touch/With Mrs. Guzzard. It's for
512 CC Kaghan 31 course,/If I can make it right with my parents./I'm fond of them, you know./{LE} I

PARIS (4)

19 Portrait 53 somehow recall/My buried life, and Paris in the Spring,/I feel immeasurably at
47 Mél Adult 8 /Vous me paierez bien la tête./C'est à Paris que je me coiffe/Casque noir de
287 FR Amy 38 Marseilles,/He would come by air to Paris, and so to London,/And hoped to arrive
450 CC Claude 23 to Amsterdam, and possibly to Paris./But when you return with Lady Elizabeth

PARISH (3)

517 CC Eggers 23 /Is to become the organist of some parish church?/{C} That is what I want. If
517 CC Eggers 26 to know of a vacancy/In my own parish, in Joshua Park —If it should appeal to
536 ES Gomez 13 miles away,/Only believed what the parish priest told her./I made my children learn

PARK (14)

20 Portrait 71 /You will see me any morning in the park/Reading the comics and the sporting page.
135 5FingerEx3 t sleep endlessly./*Lines to a Duck in the Park*/The long light shakes across the lake,/The
222 Pekes Pols 10 /Until you can hear them all over the Park./Now on the occasion of which I shall
222 Pekes Pols 24 you could hear them all over the Park./Now the Peke, although people may say
223 Pekes Pols 45 you could hear them all over the Park./Now when these bold heroes together
445 CC Claude 3 to London/All the way from Joshua Park, on an errand like this./But you know my
456 CC Eggers 30 we'd bought our house in Joshua Park/(On a mortgage, of course) 'now we've
456 CC Eggers 33 is up to the City/And back to Joshua Park in the evening,/And once a year our
461 CC Eggers 17 him to come/All the way to Joshua Park, at this time of year!'/I said: 'Let's think
496 CC Eggers 28 /But I've so much to do, in Joshua Park —/Apart from the garden — that I've not
517 CC Eggers 26 vacancy/In my own parish, in Joshua Park —If it should appeal to you. The organist
517 CC Eggers 31 don't seem to want to come to Joshua Park./{C} But I've told you, I'm not a very good
518 CC Eggers 10 music. Why, Mr. Simpkins,/Joshua Park may be only a stepping-stone/To a
518 CC Eggers 17 want to find your feet/In Joshua Park, before you settled on lodgings;/We have a

PARKER (1)

129 Cor2 State 12 shall I cry?/Arthur Edward Cyril Parker is appointed telephone operator/At a

PARKINSON (1)

426 CP Julia 35 do for me?/Oh yes, I know this is a Parkinson party;/I recognised one of their men

PARKINSON'S (1)

426 CP Julia 34 /And dying of thirst. What can Parkinson's do for me?/Oh yes, I know this is a

PARKMAN (1)

457 CC Lady E 18 — It's a bottle of medicine./Now, Parkman, will you give it to the driver?/He tells

PARKMAN'S (1)

504 CC Claude 8 She looks rather formidable./{SC} It's Parkman's day off. But where's the

PARLIAMENT (3)

278 MC Knight2 34 /condemn an Archbishop by vote of Parliament and execute him/formally as a
530 ES Ld Clav 1 /The first empty pages since I entered Parliament./I used to jot down notes of what I
551 ES Carghil 29 Mr. Ferry will be standing for Parliament:/His father has political ambitions

PARLOUR (1)

221 Old Deut 35 /Then the landlady from her back parlour will peep/And say: 'Now then, out you

PARLOURMAID (3)

284 FR m 5 *of Lady Monchensey/*DENMAN, *a parlourmaid/*HARRY, LORD MONCHENSEY,
458 CC Eggers 2 *open door]./*{E} She's speaking to the parlourmaid. She's coming up./{SC} Colby, sit
504 CC Claude 8 Parkman's day off. But where's the parlourmaid?/{L} I thought I heard someone

PAROCHIAL (1)

517 CC Eggers 35 induce them to try me .../{E} The Parochial Church Council will be only too

PARROT (3)

21 Portrait 112 dance/Like a dancing bear,/Cry like a parrot, chatter like an ape./Let us take the air,
29 Aunt Helen 9 for,/But shortly afterwards the parrot died too./The Dresden clock continued
599 On a Port 13 circle of our thought she stands./The parrot on his bar, a silent spy,/Regards her with

PART (46)

16	Prufrock		122	bottoms of my trousers rolled./Shall I part my hair behind? Do I dare to eat a peach?/I
32	Hysteria		2	involved in her laughter and/being part of it, until her teeth were only accidental
123	SAWa & Ho		1	*the bamboo tree./Tell me in what part of the wood/Do you want to flirt with me?/*
163	Rock 8		35	was good of it;/Whole faith of a few,/Part faith of many./Not avarice, lechery,
181	FQ: ECoker		150	steel/That questions the distempered part;/Beneath the bleeding hands we feel/The
193	FQ: Little		99	unidentifiable./So I assumed a double part, and cried/And heard another's voice cry:
228	Gus		21	played', so he says, 'every possible part,/And I used to know seventy speeches by
229	Gus		36	gin,/He will tell how he once played a part in *East Lynne.*/At a Shakespeare
232	Skimble		15	/And we're off at last for the northern part/Of the Northern Hemisphere!/You may say
238	MC	m	2	IN THE CATHEDRAL/Characters/PART I/A CHORUS OF WOMEN OF
238	MC	m	10	*Hall, on December 2nd,* 1170/PART II/THREE PRIESTS/FOUR
239	MC	m	1	*Cathedral, on December 29th,* 1170/Part I/{C} Here let us stand, close by the
248	MC Tempt2		26	— that was a mistake/On your part — still may be regained. Think, my Lord,/
255	MC Tempt4		3	/About this man who played a certain part in history./{T} But what is there to do?
263	MC	m	1	Son, and of the Holy Ghost. Amen./Part II/{C} Does the bird sing in the South?/
277	MC Knight3		14	understand why it was; and for/my part I am awfully sorry about it. We realised
285	FR	1m	1	*house in the North of England/PART I/The drawing-room, after tea. An*
291	FR	Chorus	6	Amy's command, to play an unread part in some monstrous farce, ridiculous in
306	FR	Harry	38	{H} No, it didn't seem like that. I was part of the design/As well as you. But what was
309	FR	Harry	7	no better./They have seen to that: it is part of the torment./{M} If you think I am
311	FR	m	27	right./{H} Come out! {}/[*The curtains part, revealing the Eumenides in the window*
316	FR	2m	24	straight. {}/[*Exit to dinner*]/END OF PART I/PART II/*The library, after dinner.*/
317	FR	1m	1	{}/[*Exit to dinner*]/END OF PART I/PART II/*The library, after dinner.*/Scene I/
322	FR	Winch	35	up for this:/Says he doesn't know this part of the country/And stopped to take his
326	FR	Harry	26	universe./But it begins to seem just part of some huge disaster,/Some monstrous
334	FR	Harry	23	noticed by its neglect. One had that part to play./After such training, I could
334	FR	Harry	25	endure, these ten years,/Playing a part that had been imposed upon me;/And I
395	CP	Lavinia	29	it/And find yourself another little part to play,/With another face, to take people
418	CP	Celia	6	it leaves me cold./Perhaps that's just a part of my illness,/But I feel it would be a kind
437	CP	Reilly	12	*and live/Till death unite them and they part no more!*/When I first met Miss Coplestone,
438	CP	Reilly	2	the highest price/In suffering. That is part of the design./{L} Perhaps she had been
438	CP	Reilly	5	/{R} That shows some insight on your part, Mrs. Chamberlayne;/But such experience
473	CC	Lucasta	9	is ... a dirty public square/In a shabby part of London — like the one where I lived/
474	CC	Colby	2	But for Eggerson/His garden is a part of one single world./{L} But what do you
490	CC	Colby	15	feel ... numb./If there's agony, it's part of a total agony/Which I can't begin to feel
522	ES	dedic	9	*return as best I can/With words a little part of what you have given me./The words mean*
538	ES	Gomez	39	of companies. You looked the part —/Cut out to be an impressive figurehead./
552	ES	Carghil	33	negligible. And you look the part./Whatever part you've played, I must say
552	ES	Carghil	34	And you look the part./Whatever part you've played, I must say you've always
552	ES	Ld Clav	35	looked it./{LC} I've no longer any part to play, Maisie./{MC} There'll always be
552	ES	Carghil	36	/{MC} There'll always be some sort of part for you/Right to the end. You'll still be
552	ES	Carghil	37	to the end. You'll still be playing a part/In your obituary, whoever writes it./{LC}
568	ES	Ld Clav	38	/In trying to identify myself with the part/I had chosen to play. And the longer we
569	ES	Ld Clav	4	idol/To Monica. She worshipped the part I played:/How could I be sure that she
579	ES	Carghil	15	It really was an inspiration —/On my part, I mean. Are you listening to me, Richard?/
583	ES	Monica	28	/I feel utterly secure/In you; I am a part of you. Now take me to my father. {}/

PARTED (5)

110	Marina		32	that unspoken,/The awakened, lips parted, the hope, the new ships./What seas what
242	MC	Mess	11	knowledge that when the Archbishop/Parted from the King, he said to the King,/My
330	FR	Harry	26	being there,/The degradation of being parted from my self,/From the self which
508	CC Guzzard		20	sanity. Thank you for that./{MG} We parted with it. A dear little boy./I was happy to
536	ES	Gomez	7	— and you can't jump back again./I parted from myself by a sudden effort,/You, so

PARTIAL (8)

173	FQ: BurntN		79	understood/In the completion of its partial ecstasy,/The resolution of its partial
173	FQ: BurntN		80	partial ecstasy,/The resolution of its partial horror./Yet the enchainment of past and
186	FQ: DrySal		89	—/Or even development: the latter a partial fallacy/Encouraged by superficial
236	Cat Morgan		5	door in a Bloomsbury Square./I'm partial to partridges, likewise to grouse,/And I
257	MC	Chorus	21	faggots at nightfall,/Building a partial shelter,/For sleeping, and eating and
294	FR	Harry	21	intervals of light and darkness;/The partial ansthesia of suffering without feeling/
294	FR	Harry	22	of suffering without feeling/And partial observation of one's own automatism/
408	CP	Lavinia	2	prostrated;/Even if I have made a partial recovery./{R} Certainly, you were

PARTICIPATION (1)

222	Pekes Pols		m1	*/Together with some Account of the Participation/of the Pugs and the Poms, and the*

PARTICULAR (8)

209 NamingCats	13	I tell you, a cat needs a name that's particular,/A name that's peculiar, and more
244 MC	Chorus	18	have all had our private terrors,/Our particular shadows, our secret fears./But now a
279 MC	Knight4	13	I have nothing to add along their particular lines of argument./What I have to say
288 FR	Amy	10	presents at tea./{A} This is a very particular occasion/As you ought to know. It
294 FR	Harry	27	I talk in general terms/Because the particular has no language. One thinks to
509 CC	Guzzard	1	could not be sure./My husband was particular in such matters,/So we had it given
540 ES	Gomez	19	several times./{G} One time in particular./You know quite well to which
561 ES	Michael	18	father was rich, but was no one in particular,/So you'd nothing to live up to.

PARTICULARLY (2)

20 Portrait	73	the comics and the sporting page./Particularly I remark./An English countess goes
394 CP	Lavinia	15	when somebody was coming/Whom I particularly wanted you to meet,/You didn't

PARTICULARS (1)

265 MC	Priest3	7	now, and here. Even now, in sordid particulars/The eternal design may appear. {}/

PARTIES (5)

424 CP	Lavinia	17	/You know that we've given *several* parties/In the last two years. And I've attended
425 CP	Edward	11	ought to have arranged to have two parties/Instead of one./{L} That's never
425 CP	Edward	22	But I'd forgotten what the Gunnings' parties were like./Their guests will get just
426 CP	Lavinia	14	the end of the season/And no more parties./{E} And no more committees./{L} Can
534 ES	Gomez	36	/Stay out of politics, and play both parties:/What you don't get from one you may

PARTLY (8)

243 MC	Chorus	25	in avoiding notice,/Living and partly living./There have been oppression and
243 MC	Chorus	30	we have gone on living,/Living and partly living./Sometimes the corn has failed us,/
244 MC	Chorus	3	we have gone on living,/Living and partly living./We have kept the feasts, heard the
244 MC	Chorus	10	not always in whispers,/Living and partly living./We have seen births, deaths and
257 MC	Chorus	18	we have gone on living,/Living and partly living./Picking together the pieces,/
276 MC	Chorus	2	loss, the general misery,/Living and partly living;/The terror by night that ends in
474 CC	Lucasta	36	to be able to talk about it,/But ... partly, to enjoy it ... and because of what it
558 ES	Michael	5	of your being discharged?/{Mi} Well, partly. Sir Alfred did come to hear about it,/

PARTNER (2)

382 CP	Edward	3	submission to the rule of the stronger partner./{C} I am not sure, Edward, that I
560 ES	Michael	10	I'd like is a chance to go abroad/As a partner in some interesting business./But I

PARTNERSHIP (1)

382 CP	Edward	2	contrive the disaster/Of this unwilling partnership — but can only flourish/In

PARTRIDGES (1)

236 Cat Morgan	5	a Bloomsbury Square./I'm partial to partridges, likewise to grouse,/And I favour that

PARTS (7)

228 Gus	28	I took the lead, or in character parts./I have sat by the bedside of poor Little
290 FR	Chorus	37	who have not been assigned their parts?/Like amateur actors in a dream when the
290 FR	Chorus	38	play, or having rehearsed the wrong parts,/Waiting for the rustling in the stalls, the
431 CP	Peter	35	faces —/Of course, only for minor parts —/And I'll help him decide what faces are
432 CP	Julia	36	of English life/And he's going to find parts for all of us. Think of it!/{P} But, Julia, I
432 CP	Peter	38	to explain —/I'm afraid I can't find parts for anybody/In *this* film — it's not my
501 CC	Lucasta	8	knows you think so./*You* gave us our parts. And we've shown that we can play them./

PARTURITION (1)

256 MC	Chorus	8	withered tree? The earth is heaving to parturition of issue of hell. What is the sticky

PARTY (39)

117 SP	Dusty	10	or a present/Of wearing apparel, or a party'./That's queer too./{Do} Here's the three.
117 SP	Doris	30	heavens what'll I do?/Just before a party too!/{Du} Well it needn't be yours, it may
196 FQ: Little	193	of silence/And are folded in a single party./Whatever we inherit from the fortunate/
251 MC	Tempt3	34	for barons —/{T3} For a powerful party/Which has turned its eyes in your
256 MC	Tempts	13	cat,/The prizes given at the children's party,/The prize awarded for the English Essay,
291 FR	Ivy	3	if I had not had to come to this party./{G} I might have been staying with
320 FR	Warburt	32	old friend,/And have always been a party to the family secrets —/You know as well
351 CP		t	rest in peace. {}/THE COCKTAIL PARTY/Persons/EDWARD
355 CP	Julia	24	to eat!/The only reason for a cocktail party/For a gluttonous old woman like me/Is a
356 CP	Julia	18	you're another guest/At Lavinia's party. There are so many questions/I want to
358 CP	Julia	21	I got everything?/It's such a nice party, I hate to leave it./It's such a nice party,
358 CP	Julia	22	I hate to leave it./It's such a nice party, I'd like to repeat it./Why don't you *all*
359 CP	Edward	14	/The fact is, I tried to put off this party:/These were only the people I couldn't put
360 CP	Edward	4	/Just when she'd arranged a cocktail party./She'd gone when I came in, this
362 CP	Reilly	27	as we can. When you've dressed for a party/And are going downstairs, with
366 CP	Peter	36	I could bear it no longer./That awful party! I'm sorry, Edward;/Of course it was
366 CP	Peter	37	/Of course it was really a very nice party/For everyone but me. And that wasn't
385 CP	Reilly	12	lively bachelor uncle at the Christmas party,/The beloved nursemaid — those who

387 CP	Peter	26	intended/To have yesterday's cocktail	party to-day./So I don't suppose her aunt can
391 CP	Julia	3	PETER]/{J} We'll have a cocktail	party at *my* house to-day./{C} Well, I'll go now.
392 CP	Lavinia	10	to do about them. It's about that	party./I suppose you won't believe I forgot all
425 CP	Lavinia	4	paid me a compliment/*Before* a	party? And that's when one needs them./{E}
425 CP	Lavinia	10	offended/To hear we'd given a	party without asking them./{E} Perhaps we
425 CP	Lavinia	14	/Everyone who's asked to either	party/Suspects that the other one was more
425 CP	Lavinia	32	it:/And everyone likes to be seen at a	party/Where everybody else is, to show they've
426 CP	Edward	10	This is the best moment/Of the whole	party./{L} Oh no, Edward./The best moment is
426 CP	Julia	31	I have to go on to the Gunnings'	party —/And you know what *they* offer in the
426 CP	Julia	35	/Oh yes, I know this is a Parkinson	party;/I recognised one of their men at the door
427 CP	Alex	9	this morning. I heard about your	party/And, as I thought you might be leaving
430 CP	Peter	8	/And she told me you were giving a	party —/She's coming on later, after the
439 CP	Julia	35	Chamberlaynes' choice/Is a cocktail	party. They must be ready for it./Their guests
439 CP	Reilly	38	should now be giving a	party./{L} And I have been thinking, for these
440 CP	Reilly	11	appointed burden. And as for the	party,/I am sure it will be a success./{J} And I
440 CP	Julia	14	/That we should leave before the	party begins./They will get on better without us.
440 CP	Edward	32	twice./{E} And now for the	party./{L} Now for the party./{E} It will soon be
440 CP	Lavinia	33	now for the party./{L} Now for the	party./{E} It will soon be over./{L} I wish it
507 CC	Guzzard	16	/But he was brought to me by a third	party,/Through whom the monthly payments
543 ES	Ld Clav	17	us./I wish we were having a dinner	party./{M} Father, can't you bear to be alone
562 ES	Carghill	14	/But how nice to find a little family	party!/I know who you are! You're Monica, of

PAS (4)

46 Directeur		13	dessus bras dessous/Font des tours/A	pas de loup./Dans un égout/Une petite fille/En
47 Mél Adult		3	Angleterre, journaliste;/C'est à grands	pas et en sueur/Que vous suivrez à peine ma
48 Lune Miel		13	Où se trouve la Cène, et un restaurant	pas cher./Lui pense aux pourboires, et rédige
51 Restaurant		7	/Je te prie, au moins, ne bave	pas dans la soupe)./'Les saules trempés, et des

PASS (16)

24 Rhapsody		8	precisions./Every street lamp that I	pass/Beats like a fatalistic drum,/And through
54 Mr E Sun		26	the bees/With hairy bellies	pass between/The staminate and pistillate,/Blest
69 WL: Fire S		251	allows one half-formed thought to	pass:/'Well now that's done: and I'm glad it's
141 Rannoch		11	/Shadow of pride is long, in the long	pass/No concurrence of bone./Cape Ann/O
157 Rock 4		14	with fire;/No place for a beast to	pass./There were enemies without to destroy
186 FQ: DrySal		65	The unattached devotion which might	pass for devotionless,/In a drifting boat with a
594 Grad 11		2	/Out of thy care and tutelage we	pass/Into the unknown world — class after
595 Grad 13		6	proud and serene,/Still as the years	pass by, the word 'Progress!'/So we are done;
240 MC	Chorus	4	his own colour,/Preferring to	pass unobserved./Now I fear disturbance of the
257 MC	Priests	1	may come in the sight of all, he may	pass unseen unheard./{4T} Come whispering
291 FR	Amy	7	What's that? I thought I saw someone	pass the window./What time is it?/{C} Nearly
309 FR	Harry	37	of life persisting,/Which ordinarily	pass unnoticed./Perhaps you are right, though I
335 FR	Agatha	38	This is the beginning./We do not	pass twice through the same door/Or return to
335 FR	Agatha	39	to the door through which we did not	pass./I have seen the first stage: relief from what
421 CP	Julia	26	afraid of./She is too humble. She will	pass between the scolding hills,/Through the
558 ES	Michael	36	She wasn't exciting,/But it served to	pass the time. It would never have happened/If

PASSAGE (11)

171 FQ: BurntN		12	echo in the memory/Down the	passage which we did not take/Towards the
194 FQ: Little		122	await another voice./But, as the	passage now presents no hindrance/To the spirit
205 de la Mare		28	incantation which allows/Free	passage to the phantoms of the mind?/By you;
270 MC	Chorus	6	the worm. In the air/Flirted with the	passage of the kite, I have plunged with the kite
270 MC	Chorus	12	be? It was here, in the kitchen, in the	passage,/In the mews in the barn in the byre in the
272 MC	Chorus	17	in the skull./More than footfall in the	passage,/More than shadow in the doorway,/
290 FR	Agatha	34	the moon/The attraction of the dark	passage/The paw under the door. {}/CHORUS
538 ES	Gomez	8	were released./{G} Yes, and paid my	passage out. I know the reason:/You wanted to
577 ES	Charles	3	San Marco,/Señor Gomez pays your	passage .../{Mi} And an advance of salary./{C}
577 ES	Charles	5	of salary./{C} Señor Gomez pays your	passage .../{G} Just as many years ago/His
579 ES	Michael	7	England?/{Mi} When we can get a	passage./And I must buy my kit. We're just

PASSAGES (2)

38 Gerontion		34	now/History has many cunning	passages, contrived corridors/And issues,
335 FR	Agatha	18	{Ag} Up and down, through the stone	passages/Of an immense and empty hospital/

PASSAGEWAYS (1)

22 Preludes		2	settles down/With smell of steaks in	passageways./Six o'clock./The burnt-out ends of

PASSED (7)

40 Burb Blei		6	he fell./Defunctive music under sea/	Passed seaward with the passing bell/Slowly: the
49 Hippopot		22	God./The hippopotamus's day/Is	passed in sleep; at night he hunts;/God works in
71 WL: DWater		317	in whispers. As he rose and fell/He	passed the stages of his age and youth/Entering
172 FQ: BurntN		41	us, reflected in the pool./Then a cloud	passed, and the pool was empty./Go, said the

186 FQ: DrySal	74	of a future that is not liable/Like the past, to have no destination./We have to think
186 FQ: DrySal	88	as one becomes older,/That the past has another pattern, and ceases to be a
186 FQ: DrySal	91	mind, a means of disowning the past./The moments of happiness — not the
187 FQ: DrySal	99	I have said before/That the past experience revived in the meaning/Is not
187 FQ: DrySal	113	than in our own./For our own past is covered by the currents of action,/But
188 FQ: DrySal	139	travellers! not escaping from the past/Into different lives, or into any future;/You
188 FQ: DrySal	146	behind you,/You shall not think 'the past is finished'/Or 'the future is before us'./At
188 FQ: DrySal	156	consider the future/And the past with an equal mind./At the moment which
189 FQ: DrySal	203	Road./Men's curiosity searches past and future/And clings to that dimension.
190 FQ: DrySal	222	of existence is actual,/Here the past and future/Are conquered, and reconciled,/
190 FQ: DrySal	229	And right action is freedom/From past and future also./For most of us, this is the
195 FQ: Little	161	/From the future as well as the past. Thus, love of a country/Begins as
201 Def Island	20	the streets of Britain:/to say, to the past and the future generations/of our kin and
226 Macavity	25	glass is broken, and the trellis past repair —/Ay, there's the wonder of the
604 Ode	8	at thy feet/To the thoughts of the past as we go./Yet for all of these years that
604 Ode	15	owe for the future, the present, and past,/Fair Harvard, to thine and to thee./The
246 MC Templ	28	levity/Remembering all the good time past./Your Lordship won't despise an old friend
247 MC Thomas	6	/{T} You talk of seasons that are past. I remember/Not worth forgetting./{T1}
247 MC Templ	24	what he spurns./For the good times past, that are come again/I am your man./{T}
252 MC Templ3	7	Which you helped to found./But time past is time forgotten./We expect the rise of a
253 MC Templ4	5	have been baited with morsels of the past./Wantonness is weakness. As for the King,/
261 MC Thomas	38	children of God, of the martyrs of/the past, asking you to remember especially our
275 MC Chorus	24	is Canterbury?/O far far far far in the past; and I wander in a land of barren boughs:
288 FR Agatha	19	everything is irrevocable,/Because the past is irremediable,/Because the future can only
288 FR Agatha	21	future can only be built/Upon the real past. Wandering in the tropics/Or against the
294 FR Harry	8	sorrow before morning,/In which all past is present, all degradation/Is unredeemable.
294 FR Harry	10	As for what happens —/Of the past you can only see what is past,/Not what is
294 FR Harry	10	/Of the past you can only see what is past,/Not what is always present. That is what
295 FR Charles	12	horrible./There's a lot in my own past life that presses on my chest/When I wake,
315 FR Harry	9	/That everything is irrevocable,/The past unredeemable. But cancer, now,/That is
315 FR Chorus	32	they had been there always./And the past is about to happen, and the future was long
315 FR Chorus	33	the wings of the future darken the past, the beak and claws have desecrated/
318 FR Warburt	22	the time she has to live: not with the past./{H} Oh, is there any difference!/How can
318 FR Harry	24	/How can we be concerned with the past/And not with the future? or with the future
318 FR Harry	26	or with the future/And not with the past? What I'm telling you/Is very important.
329 FR Chorus	2	/And whatever happens began in the past, and presses hard on the future./The agony
329 FR Chorus	4	in to itself all the voices of the past, and projects them into the future./The
330 FR Agatha	13	mind, Harry?/I can guess about the past and what you mean about the future;/But a
332 FR Agatha	26	are hours when there seems to be no past or future,/Only a present moment of
341 FR Amy	13	the waste. I wanted to obliterate/His past life, and have nothing except to remind him
362 CP Reilly	2	her better than you;/And, turning the past over and over,/You'll wonder only that
371 CP Peter	31	I must find out/The truth about the past, for the sake of the memory./{E} There's no
389 CP Lavinia	35	thank you,/As we have in the past./{C} Oh, not as in the past! {}/[*The doorbell*
389 CP Celia	36	have in the past./{C} Oh, not as in the past! {}/[*The doorbell rings, and* EDWARD
399 CP Nurse	11	/Just as usual. She arrives at a quarter past;/But you may keep her waiting./{R} Or she
424 CP Lavinia	10	/{L} Nothing more, I think, till half past six. {}/[*Exit* CATERER'S MAN]/
439 CP Reilly	8	new. Only by acceptance/Of the past will you alter its meaning./{J} Henry, I
481 CC Lady E	28	early:/Most of its patrons dine at half past six./They have the most delicious salads!/
488 CC Claude	11	has happened is that, brooding on the past,/You began to think of Colby as what your
505 CC Eggers	31	years — when you get to my age/The past and the future both seem very brief —/But
551 ES Carghil	15	want to come and talk about the past./You're wrong, you know. It's both pain
551 ES Carghil	17	pain and pleasure/To talk about the past — about you and me./These memories are
561 ES Ld Clav	6	Michael:/Those who flee from their past will always lose the race./I know this from
561 ES Ld Clav	9	and grandeur,/You will find your past failures waiting there to greet you./You're
565 ES Ld Clav	31	I want to escape from/Is myself, is the past. But what a coward I am,/To talk of
565 ES Ld Clav	34	/Not to try to escape from his own past failures:/I said I knew from experience. Do
567 ES Charles	19	Michael, and those people from his past,/I've been trying to think what I could do
567 ES Monica	26	/Father with a guilty secret in his past!/I just can't imagine it. {}/[CLAVERTON
569 ES Ld Clav	35	are merely ghosts:/Spectres from my past. They've always been with me/Though it
577 ES Charles	8	father paid mine./{C} This return of past kindness/No doubt gives you pleasure?/{G}

PASTE (1)

| 235 Ad-dress | 58 | Pie,/Some potted grouse, or salmon paste —/He's sure to have his personal taste./(I |

PASTED (1)

| 589 Fable | 73 | reads this romance./The Abbot sat as pasted to his chair,/His eye became the size of |

PASTIES (1)
588 Fable   48   and pies and puddings,/And jellies, pasties, cakes among the good things./A mighty
PASTIMES (1)
189 FQ: DrySal 199   tomb, or dreams; all these are usual/Pastimes and drugs, and features of the press:/
PASTURE (2)
92 Ash-Wed 3   14   beyond the hawthorn blossom and a pasture scene/The broadbacked figure drest in
193 FQ: Little   73   Water and fire succeed/The town, the pasture and the weed./Water and fire deride/
PAT (1)
229 Gus   37   performance he once walked on pat,/When some actor suggested the need for a
PATCHED (2)
37 Gerontion   10   of Antwerp,/Blistered in Brussels, patched and peeled in London./The goat coughs
242 MC   Mess   4   Peace, but not the kiss of peace./A patched up affair, if you ask my opinion./And if
PATENT (1)
224 Mr Mistoff   7   in the metropolis;/He holds all the patent monopolies/For performing surprising
PATENTLY (1)
111 Xmas Trees   3   disregard:/The social, the torpid, the patently commercial,/The rowdy (the pubs
PATERNAL (1)
181 FQ: ECoker 162   do well, we shall/Die of the absolute paternal care/That will not leave us, but
PATERNITY (2)
505 CC   Eggers   21   /It also concerns a problem of paternity./{LE} Or of maternity./{SC} Don't
507 CC   Guzzard 29   /If she could have established the paternity;/But I didn't know who she was! What
PATH (4)
105 Song Sime   15   is come?/They will take to the goat's path, and the fox's home,/Fleeing from the
202 War Poetry   5   individual/Explosion breaks/In the path of an action merely typical/To create the
592 Grad 4   1   may no more be traced./Although the path be tortuous and slow,/Although it bristle
581 ES Ld Clav 17   /Why did I mark out a narrow path for Michael?/Because I wanted to
PATHS (1)
201 Def Island   18   /and those again for whom the paths of glory are/the lanes and the streets of
PATIENCE (7)
72 WL: Thund 330   living are now dying/With a little patience/Here is no water but only rock/Rock
245 MC Thomas 17   fixed/In an eternal action, an eternal patience/To which all must consent that it may
255 MC Tempt4 40   fixed/In an eternal action, an eternal patience/To which all must consent that it may
374 CP   3m   1   *later. EDWARD is alone, playing/Patience. The doorbell rings, and he goes to*
376 CP   m   1   *to the table and inspects his game of Patience. He moves/a card. The doorbell rings*
404 CP   Reilly   7   have been saying./{R} You must have patience with me, Mr. Chamberlayne:/I learn a
421 CP   Julia   28   sent on an errand/In eagerness and patience. Yet she must suffer./{R} When I
PATIENT (29)
13 Prufrock   3   is spread out against the sky/Like a patient etherised upon a table;/Let us go,
141 Rannoch   1   /Here the crow starves, here the patient stag/Breeds for the rifle. Between the
184 FQ: DrySal   3   — sullen, untamed and intractable,/Patient to some degree, at first recognised as a
187 FQ: DrySal 133   is sure,/That time is no healer: the patient is no longer here./When the train starts,
201 Def Island   3   instrument, of many centuries of/patient cultivation of the earth, of English/verse
599 On a Port   14   bar, a silent spy,/Regards her with a patient curious eye./Song/The moonflower
245 MC Thomas 16   Neither does the agent suffer/Nor the patient act. But both are fixed/In an eternal
255 MC Tempt4 39   Neither does the agent suffer/Nor the patient act. But both are fixed/In an eternal
308 FR   Mary 38   understand, but you would have to be patient/With me, and with people who have not
314 FR Warburt   34   /Even in a country practice. My first patient, now —/You wouldn't believe it, ladies
315 FR Warburt   14   now you're all grown up/I haven't a patient left at Wishwood./Wishwood was
343 FR   Amy   27   investments/With wakeful nights and patient calculations/With the solicitor, the
361 CP   Reilly   38   /Without the consistent critic, the patient misunderstander/Arranging life a little
399 CP   Reilly   18   ring three times./{R} And the third patient?/{N} The third one to be shown into the
402 CP Edward   9   you/Or anyone else. I came here as a patient./If you take no interest in my case, I can
402 CP   Reilly   29   of sanatoria/For several kinds of patient. And there are also patients/For whom a
404 CP   Reilly   37   a long journey./But before I treat a patient like yourself/I need to know a great deal
404 CP   Reilly   39   great deal more about him,/Than the patient himself can always tell me./Indeed, it is
405 CP   Reilly   3   /Which I have to explore. The single patient/Who is ill by himself, is rather the
405 CP   Reilly   5   /I have recently had another patient/Whose situation is much the same as
405 CP   Reilly   8   propose to introduce you to the other patient./{E} What do you mean? Who is this
405 CP Edward   9   What do you mean? Who is this other patient?/I consider this very unprofessional
405 CP Edward   11   not discuss my case before another patient./{R} On the contrary. That is the only
405 CP   Reilly   23   /{R} But here is the other patient./{E} Lavinia!/{L} Well, Sir Henry!/I said
407 CP   Reilly   8   and to a marked degree,/To qualify a patient for *my* sanatorium:/And one of them is
416 CP   Celia   6   — is that the word?/Can you treat a patient for such a state of mind?/{R} What had
438 CP   Reilly   32   may mean restoration or ruin to a patient —/And sometimes I have made the
468 CC   Claude   2   /{SC} Much depends on my wife. Be patient with her, Colby./— Oh yes, that

556 ES   Monica   6   to take offence./So I hope you'll be patient./{LC} Well then, fetch him./Let's get this
PATIENTS (8)
402 CP   Edward   25   a sanatorium to which you send such patients/As myself, under your personal
402 CP   Reilly   29   kinds of patient. And there are also patients/For whom a sanatorium is the worst
404 CP   Reilly   22   any further responsibility./{R} Many patients come in that belief./{E} And now will
405 CP   Reilly   1   /Indeed, it is often the case that my patients/Are only pieces of a total situation/
407 CP   Reilly   18   the insuperably, innocently dull:/My patients such as you are the self-deceivers/
408 CP   Reilly   29   of collecting information/About my patients. You must not ask me to reveal it —/
413 CP   Reilly   3   me to go away again./{R} Most of my patients begin, Miss Coplestone,/By telling me
434 CP   Alex   29   have died anyway./{A} Yes, the patients died anyway;/Being tainted with the
PATROL (4)
194 FQ: Little   109 after,/We trod the pavement in a dead patrol./I said: 'The wonder that I feel is easy,/
232 Skimble   23   /He establishes control by a regular patrol/And he'd know at once if anything
236 Cat Morgan 8   And a bit o' cold fish when I done me patrol./I ain't got much polish, me manners is
328 FR   Charles   22   Mr. Piper was being pursued by a patrol, and was/travelling at the rate of 66 miles
PATRON (1)
467 CC   Colby   10   a generous provider:/Rather as a patron than a father —/The father who was
PATRONISING (2)
69 WL: Fire S   247 lowest of the dead.)/Bestows one final patronising kiss,/And gropes his way, finding
470 CC   Lucasta   33   a compliment:/That's just being ... patronising. But if you invite me/To something
PATRONS (2)
180 FQ: ECoker 105 eminent men of letters./The generous patrons of art, the statesmen and the rulers,/
481 CC   Lady E   28   can have dinner early:/Most of its patrons dine at half past six./They have the
PATS (1)
564 ES   m 35 all about Dick when you knew him. {}/[*pats her despatch-case*]./{MC} Secret for secret,
PATTERN (18)
64 WL: Chess   93   smoke into the laquearia,/Stirring the pattern on the coffered ceiling./Huge sea-wood
107 Animula   11   and the sea;/Studies the sunlit pattern on the floor/And running stags around
172 FQ: BurntN 33   /So we moved, and they, in a formal pattern,/Along the empty alley, into the box
172 FQ: BurntN 62   boarhound and the boar/Pursue their pattern as before/But reconciled among the
175 FQ: BurntN 143 Into the silence. Only by the form, the pattern,/Can words or music reach/The stillness,
175 FQ: BurntN 162 chimera./The detail of the pattern is movement,/As in the figure of the ten
179 FQ: ECoker 85   experience./The knowledge imposes a pattern, and falsifies,/For the pattern is new in
179 FQ: ECoker 86   a pattern, and falsifies,/For the pattern is new in every moment/And every
182 FQ: ECoker 193 /The world becomes stranger, the pattern more complicated/Of dead and living.
186 FQ: DrySal   88   older,/That the past has another pattern, and ceases to be a mere sequence —/Or
195 FQ: Little   167 renewed, transfigured, in another pattern./Sin is Behovely, but/All shall be well,
197 FQ: Little   236 redeemed from time, for history is a pattern/Of timeless moments. So, while the light
240 MC Chorus   21   aims which turn in their hands in the pattern of time./Come, happy December, who
244 MC Chorus   28   /To the small folk drawn into the pattern of fate, the small folk who live among
245 MC Thomas   20   suffer that they may will it,/That the pattern may subsist, for the pattern is the action
245 MC Thomas   20   /That the pattern may subsist, for the pattern is the action/And the suffering, that the
256 MC Tempt4   3   suffer that they may will it,/That the pattern may subsist, that the wheel may turn
270 MC Chorus   20   our veins, our brains,/Is woven like a pattern of living worms/In the guts of the
PATTERNS (1)
16 Prufrock   105 if a magic lantern threw the nerves in patterns on a screen:/Would it have been worth
PAUL (1)
275 MC Thomas   20   Baptist, the holy apostles Peter and Paul, to the blessed martyr Denys, and to all the
PAUSE (8)
135 5FingerEx2 13   come to dust./Here a little dog I pause/Heaving up my prior paws,/Pause, and
135 5FingerEx2 15   I pause/Heaving up my prior paws,/Pause, and sleep endlessly./*Lines to a Duck in*
347 FR   m 32 {}/[*Exeunt* AGATHA *and* MARY. *Pause. Enter* WARBURTON]/{W} Well! it's a
386 CP   m 14 /{UG} I also am a stranger. {}/[*Exit. A pause.* EDWARD *moves about restlessly. The*
386 CP   m 27   you sit down?/{C} Thank you. {}/[*Pause*]/{E} Oh, my God, what shall we talk
477 CC   m 11   he would prefer to forget. {}/[*A pause*]/{L} But why don't you say something? Are
548 ES   4m 14   *and takes out her knitting.*/[*after a pause*]./{MC} I hope I'm not disturbing you. I
556 ES   m 12 /{Mi} Good morning, Father. {}/[*A pause*]/{Mi} What a lovely day!/I'm glad you're
PAVEMENT (3)
34 Figlia   1   Che Piange/Stand on the highest pavement of the stair —/Lean on a garden urn
194 FQ: Little   109 no before and after,/We trod the pavement in a dead patrol./I said: 'The wonder
201 Def Island 9   /contributing their share to the ages' pavement/of British bone on the sea floor/and
PAVING (2)
127 Cor1 March 2   oakleaves, horses' heels/Over the paving./And the flags. And the trumpets. And
128 Cor1 March 41   oakleaves, horses' heels/Over the paving./That is all we could see. But how many

PAW (4)

226 Macavity	1	a Mystery Cat: he's called the Hidden Paw —/For he's the master criminal who can
228 Gus	6	he suffers from palsy that makes his paw shake./Yet he was, in his youth, quite the
235 Ad-dress	32	the chin/Or slap his back or shake his paw,/And he will gambol and guffaw./He's such
290 FR Agatha	35	attraction of the dark passage/The paw under the door. {}/CHORUS (IVY,

PAWED (1)

553 ES Carghil	13	alarmed. But you touched my soul —/Pawed it, perhaps, and the touch still lingers./

PAWS (3)

56 Swee Night	24	/Tears at the grapes with murderous paws;/She and the lady in the cape/Are suspect,
135 5FingerEx2	14	dog I pause/Heaving up my prior paws,/Pause, and sleep endlessly./*Lines to a*
235 Ad-dress	62	/And when he's finished, licks his paws/So's not to waste the onion sauce.)/A

PAY (9)

125 SA Sweeney	28	we're gona go/And somebody's gotta pay the rent/{Do} I know who/{S} But that's
275 MC Thomas	1	to buy my life,/My blood given to pay for His death,/My death for His death./
440 CP Edward	27	worst./{E} I never shall learn how to pay a compliment./{L} What you should have
467 CC Claude	34	presents a new one, more difficult to pay./— I shall go now, and sit for a while with
533 ES Gomez	32	side to *me*./Sometimes I've had to pay pretty heavily;/But I learnt by experience
533 ES Gomez	33	/But I learnt by experience whom to pay;/And a little money laid out in the right
540 ES Gomez	12	I know the value of the coinage/I pay myself in./{LC} Indeed! How interesting!/I
557 ES Michael	29	good terms?/{Mi} I'd nothing at all to pay for two years:/The interest was just added
558 ES Michael	23	They knew I couldn't be living on my pay;/They had a lot of fun with me —

PAYES (1)

51 Restaurant	23	décrasse-toi le crâne./De quel droit payes-tu des expériences comme moi?/Tiens,

PAYING (3)

471 CC Lucasta	32	yet,/And that is, to know when you're paying a compliment./*That* was a compliment.
481 CC Lucasta	7	/{L} You're both very good at paying compliments;/But I remarked that I was
482 CC Lady E	12	sheltered life,/And I've noticed them paying you a good deal of attention./You see,

PAYMENT (1)

552 ES Carghil	25	got out of a tangle for a large cash payment/And no publicity. So your conscience

PAYMENTS (4)

507 CC Guzzard	17	party,/Through whom the monthly payments were made./{E} The terms were
507 CC Eggers	21	money was forthcoming./{E} Did the payments come to an end?/{MG} Very
508 CC Guzzard	21	/I was happy to have him while the payments were made;/But we could not afford
508 CC Guzzard	23	/Or continue to keep him, when the payments ended./{E} And how did you dispose

PAYS (7)

51 Restaurant	3	pencher sur mon épaule:/'Dans mon pays il fera temps pluvieux,/Du vent, du grand
115 SP Dusty	5	care./{Du} You don't care!/Who pays the rent?/{Do} Yes he pays the rent/{Du}
115 SP Doris	6	care!/Who pays the rent?/{Do} Yes he pays the rent/{Du} Well some men don't and
228 Gus	13	loves to regale them, if someone else pays,/With anecdotes drawn from his palmiest
533 ES Gomez	35	the right manner/In the right places, pays many times over./I assure you it does./
577 ES Charles	3	a post in San Marco,/Señor Gomez pays your passage .../{Mi} And an advance of
577 ES Charles	5	advance of salary./{C} Señor Gomez pays your passage .../{G} Just as many years

PAYS-BAS (1)

48 Lune Miel	1	/Lune de Miel/Ils ont vu les Pays-Bas, ils rentrent à Terre Haute;/Mais une

PEA (1)

270 MC Chorus	3	rose, death in the hollyhock, sweet pea, hyacinth, primrose and cowslip. I have seen

PEACE (49)

19 Portrait	54	in the Spring,/I feel immeasurably at peace, and find the world/To be wonderful and
98 Ash-Wed 6	30	sit still/Even among these rocks,/Our peace in His will/And even among these rocks/
105 Song Sime	8	towards the dead land./Grant us thy peace./I have walked many years in this city,/
105 Song Sime	18	and lamentation/Grant us thy peace./Before the stations of the mountain of
106 Song Sime	31	me the ultimate vision./Grant me thy peace./(And a sword shall pierce thy heart,/
129 Cor2 State	22	commission/About perpetual peace: the fletchers and javelin-makers and
150 Rock 1	117	*is no beginning, no movement, no peace and no end/But noise without speech, food*
155 Rock 3	44	loved the beauty of Thy House, the peace of Thy sanctuary,/I have swept the floors
241 MC Priest3	20	/Of two proud men?/{P3} What peace can be found/To grow between the
241 MC Priest2	24	cast down/That divided them? Is it peace or war?/{P1} Does he come/In full
242 MC Priest1	2	matter./{P1} But again, is it war or peace?/{M} Peace, but not the kiss of peace./A
242 MC Mess	3	But again, is it war or peace?/{M} Peace, but not the kiss of peace./A patched up
242 MC Mess	3	peace?/{M} Peace, but not the kiss of peace./A patched up affair, if you ask my
242 MC Mess	8	you ask my opinion, I think that this peace/Is nothing like an end, or like a
245 MC Thomas	11	Archbishop. {}/[*Enter* THOMAS]/{T} Peace. And let them be, in their exaltation./
260 MC Thomas	1	to God in the highest, and on earth peace to men of good will.' *The/fourteenth verse*
260 MC Thomas	14	to God in the highest, and on/earth peace to men of good will'; at this same time of
260 MC Thomas	21	about the meaning of this word 'peace'. Does/it seem strange to you that the

260	MC	Thomas	22	the angels should have announced Peace,/when ceaselessly the world has been
260	MC	Thomas	26	now, how Our Lord Himself spoke of Peace. He said to His/disciples, 'Peace I leave
260	MC	Thomas	27	of Peace. He said to His/disciples, 'Peace I leave with you, my peace I give unto
260	MC	Thomas	27	/disciples, 'Peace I leave with you, my peace I give unto you.' Did He/mean peace as
260	MC	Thomas	28	peace I give unto you.' Did He/mean peace as we think of it: the kingdom of England
260	MC	Thomas	28	of it: the kingdom of England at peace with its/neighbours, the barons at peace
260	MC	Thomas	29	with its/neighbours, the barons at peace with the King, the householder counting/
261	MC	Thomas	6	/So then, He gave to His disciples peace, but not peace as the world/gives./
261	MC	Thomas	6	gave to His disciples peace, but not peace as the world/gives./Consider also one
261	MC	Thomas	40	birth/day, to remember what is that Peace which He brought; and because,/dear
263	MC	Chorus	13	Lord, at Christmastide,/Is there not peace upon earth, goodwill among men?/The
263	MC	Chorus	14	earth, goodwill among men?/The peace of this world is always uncertain, unless
263	MC	Chorus	14	always uncertain, unless men keep the peace of God./And war among men defiles this
268	MC	Knight2	1	offered clemency,/Made a pact of peace, and all dispute ended/Sent you back to
271	MC	Thomas	7	our shame. {}/[*Enter* THOMAS]/{T} Peace, and be at peace with your thoughts and
271	MC	Thomas	7	THOMAS]/{T} Peace, and be at peace with your thoughts and visions./These
271	MC	Thomas	30	killed; what shall become of us?/{T} Peace! be quiet! remember where you are, and
275	MC	Thomas	8	to die,/That his Church may have peace and liberty./Do with me as you will, to
350	FR	Agatha	27	of the departed —/May they rest in peace. {}/THE COCKTAIL PARTY/Persons/
370	CP	Peter	8	together —/So ... contented, so ... at peace: I can't express it;/I had never imagined
411	CP	Reilly	36	will send you my account./Go in peace. And work out your salvation with
420	CP	Reilly	17	You have been very kind./{R} Go in peace, my daughter./Work out your salvation
465	CC	Claude	25	—/That state of utter exhaustion and peace/Which comes in dying to give something
501	CC	Lucasta	37	you, Eggy. And I want to make my peace with him./{SC} We'll get him now. {}/
513	CC	Colby	23	relationship./Let my mother rest in peace. As for a father —/I have the idea of a
514	CC	Guzzard	14	/{MG} Let your mother rest in peace./I *was* your mother; but I chose to be
545	ES	Ld Clav	16	to leave you alone!/You want perfect peace: that's what Badgley Court is for.'/I
548	ES	Piggott	1	for the lack of excitement:/After all, peace and quiet is our *raison d'être.*/Now I'll
548	ES	Ld Clav	4	come back to tell us more about the peace and quiet./{M} I don't believe she'll be
581	ES	Ld Clav	13	/{LC} This may surprise you: I feel at peace now./It is the peace that ensues upon
581	ES	Ld Clav	14	you: I feel at peace now./It is the peace that ensues upon contrition/When

PEACEFUL (2)

212		Growltiger	21	mauled his missing ear./Now on a peaceful summer night, all nature seemed at
260	MC	Thomas	30	the householder counting/over his peaceful gains, the swept hearth, his best wine

PEACEFULLY (1)

15		Prufrock	75	the afternoon, the evening, sleeps so peacefully!/Smoothed by long fingers,/Asleep ...

PEACEHAVEN (1)

393	CP	Lavinia	23	/I said: 'I suppose you'd as soon go to Peacehaven' —/And you said 'I don't mind'./{E}

PEACH (2)

16		Prufrock	122	my hair behind? Do I dare to eat a peach?/I shall wear white flannel trousers, and
49		Hippopot	15	/But fruits of pomegranate and peach/Refresh the Church from over sea./At

PEACOCK (1)

588		Fable	49	among the good things./A mighty peacock standing on both legs/With difficulty

PEACOCKS (1)

598		Circe	12	stairs/The sluggish python lies;/The peacocks walk, stately and slow,/And they look

PEAL (1)

70	WL: Fire S		288	wind/Carried down stream/The peal of bells/White towers/Weialala leia/Wallala

PEAR (4)

85		Hollow Men	68	men./*Here we go round the prickly pear/Prickly pear prickly pear/Here we go round*
85		Hollow Men	69	*we go round the prickly pear/Prickly pear prickly pear/Here we go round the prickly*
85		Hollow Men	69	*the prickly pear/Prickly pear prickly pear/Here we go round the prickly pear/At five*
85		Hollow Men	70	*pear/Here we go round the prickly pear/At five o'clock in the morning./Between the*

PEARLS (3)

62	WL: Burial		48	Phoenician Sailor,/(Those are pearls that were his eyes. Look!)/Here is
65	WL: Chess		125	/'Nothing?'/I remember/Those are pearls that were his eyes.'Are you alive, or not?
218	Mung Rump		14	girls/Suddenly missed her Woolworth pearls:/Then the family would say: 'It's that

PEAS (2)

210		Old Gumbie	23	a mouse-cake of bread and dried peas,/And a *beautiful* fry of lean bacon and
473	CC	Colby	35	out/He has marrows, or beetroot, or peas ... for Mrs. Eggerson./{L} Are you laughing

PEASANTS (1)

372	CP	Alex	22	you'll be grateful./There are very few peasants in Montenegro/Who can have the dish

PEAU (1)

47	Mél Adult		18	/Dans une oasis d'Afrique/Vêtu d'une peau de girafe./On montrera mon cénotaphe/

PECULIAR (8)

111 Xmas Trees	15	in new possessions/(Each one with its peculiar and exciting smell),/The expectation of
195 FQ: Little	174	kin or kindness,/But some of peculiar genius,/All touched by a common
209 NamingCats	14	name that's particular,/A name that's peculiar, and more dignified,/Else how can he
347 FR Ivy	28	you explain?/Why do you all look so peculiar? I think I might be allowed/To know
375 CP Celia	34	it's still cooking!/I thought I noticed a peculiar smell:/Of course it's still cooking — or
428 CP Alex	12	heathen:/They hold these monkeys in peculiar veneration/And do not want them
570 ES Ld Clav	27	man who's made a fortune by his own peculiar methods,/A man of great importance
572 ES Ld Clav	19	unsuited to each other,/Yet she had a peculiar physical attraction/Which no other

PEDANTIC (1)

197 FQ: Little	224	/The formal word precise but not pedantic,/The complete consort dancing

PEELED (2)

37 Gerontion	10	/Blistered in Brussels, patched and peeled in London./The goat coughs at night in
154 Rock 3	25	shall be left the broken chimney,/The peeled hull, a pile of rusty iron,/In a street of

PEEP (1)

221 Old Deut	35	landlady from her back parlour will peep/And say: 'Now then, out you go, by the

PEEPED (1)

64 WL: Chess	80	vines/From which a golden Cupidon peeped out/(Another hid his eyes behind his

PEER (1)

24 Rhapsody	42	have seen eyes in the street/Trying to peer through lighted shutters,/And a crab one

PEER'S (1)

328 FR Charles	11	better read it to us. {}/[*reads*]./{C} '*Peer's Brother in Motor Smash*/The Hon. Arthur

PEERAGE (1)

543 ES Gomez	4	friends in the press — if not in the peerage./Goodbye for the present. It's been an

PEERED (1)

179 FQ: ECoker	81	in the darkness into which they peered/Or from which they turned their eyes.

PEERESS (1)

289 FR Charles	27	to recover the body./{C} 'Well-known Peeress Vanishes from Liner'./{G} Yes, it's odd

PEERS (1)

205 de la Mare	25	or when by chance/An empty face peers from an empty house;/By whom, and by

PEEVISH (2)

37 Gerontion	14	tea,/Sneezes at evening, poking the peevish gutter./I an old man,/A dull head
206 To my Wife	8	speech without need of meaning./No peevish winter wind shall chill/No sullen tropic

PEINE (1)

47 Mél Adult	4	pas et en sueur/Que vous suivrez à peine ma piste./En Yorkshire, conférencier;/A

PEKE (3)

222 Pekes Pols	13	/(And that's a long time for a Pol or a Peke)./The big Police Dog was away from his
222 Pekes Pols	18	at all was about on the street/When a Peke and a Pollicle happened to meet./They did
222 Pekes Pols	25	hear them all over the Park./Now the Peke, although people may say what they

PEKE'S (1)

226 Macavity	24	when the milk is missing, or another Peke's been stifled,/Or the greenhouse glass is

PEKES (5)

222 Pekes Pols	t	/Of the Awefull Battle of the Pekes and the Pollicles/*Together with some*
222 Pekes Pols	1	/*of the Great Rumpuscat*/The Pekes and the Pollicles, everyone knows,/Are
223 Pekes Pols	27	a Heathen Chinese./And so all the Pekes, when they heard the uproar,/Some came
223 Pekes Pols	57	glare of his eyes and his yawning,/The Pekes and the Pollicles quickly took warning./
234 Ad-dress	24	soul./Of course I'm not including Pekes,/And such fantastic canine freaks./The

PEKINESE (1)

212 Growltiger	14	from its cage;/Woe to the pampered Pekinese, that faced Growltiger's rage;/Woe to

PELOTER (1)

51 Restaurant	17	le fait est dur./Il est venu, nous peloter, un gros chien;/Moi j'avais peur, je l'ai

PEN (1)

21 Portrait	116	rose;/Should die and leave me sitting pen in hand/With the smoke coming down

PENALTY (1)

555 ES Piggott	8	/Just let me know. I'm afraid it's the penalty/Of being famous. {}/[*Enter* MONICA]/

PENANCE (1)

254 MC Tempt4	16	of enemies dismayed,/Creeping in penance, frightened of a shade;/Think of

PENCE (1)

54 Mr E Sun	20	and pustular/Clutching piaculative pence./Under the penitential gates/Sustained by

PENCHER (1)

51 Restaurant	2	faire/Que de se gratter les doigts et se pencher sur mon épaule:/'Dans mon pays il fera

PENDANT (1)

51 Restaurant	25	salle-de-bains./Phlébas, le Phénicien, pendant quinze jours noyé,/Oubliait les cris des

PENETRATE (2)
52 Whispers   11   for sense,/To seize and clutch and penetrate;/Expert beyond experience,/He knew
327 FR   Agatha   4 of malice or stupidity./We must try to penetrate the other private worlds/Of
PENGUIN (1)
122 SAWa & Ho   25 *tree./Where the breadfruit fall/And the penguin call/And the sound is the sound of the sea*
PÉNIBLE (1)
51 Restaurant   30   /Figurez-vous donc, c'était un sort pénible;/Cependant, ce fut jadis un bel homme,
PENITENCE (3)
54 Mr E Sun   18   presbyters approach/The avenue of penitence;/The young are red and pustular/
164 Rock 9   14   private chamber, learning the way of penitence,/And then let us learn the joyful
247 MC Thomas   28   behaviour. You were safer/Think of penitence and follow your master./{T1} Not at
PENITENT (1)
400 CP   Alex 23   — then, he believes,/She will be very penitent. He's enjoying his illness./{R} Illness
PENITENTIAL (1)
54 Mr E Sun   21   piaculative pence./Under the penitential gates/Sustained by staring Seraphim/
PENMANSHIP (1)
538 ES   Gomez   1 And, equally unfortunate, a talent for penmanship./Hence, as you have just reminded
PENNILESS (1)
453 CC Lucasta   34   appetite./But the point is, that I'm penniless./{K} She's had a week's salary in lieu
PENNY (2)
45 Cook Egg   25   will conduct me./But where is the penny world I bought/To eat with Pipit behind
277 MC Knight3 16 it. And, as I said,/*we* are not getting a penny out of this. We know perfectly well how/
PENSE (1)
48 Lune Miel   14   Cène, et un restaurant pas cher./Lui pense aux pourboires, et rédige son bilan./Ils
PENSIONED (1)
292 FR   Ivy   34 /It's really high time the old man was pensioned./He's let the rock garden go to rack
PENSIVE (1)
599 On a Port   7   evanescent, as if one should meet/A pensive lamia in some wood-retreat,/An
PENTAGRAMS (1)
189 FQ: DrySal 195   /With playing cards, fiddle with pentagrams/Or barbituric acids, or dissect/The
PENTECOSTAL (1)
191 FQ: Little   10   /Stirs the dumb spirit: no wind, but pentecostal fire/In the dark time of the year.
PEOPLE (159)
20 Portrait   82 the garden/Recalling things that other people have desired./Are these ideas right or
62 WL: Burial   56   Fear death by water./I see crowds of people, walking round in a ring./Thank you. If
70 WL: Fire S   304   broken fingernails of dirty hands./My people humble people who expect/Nothing.'/la
70 WL: Fire S   304   of dirty hands./My people humble people who expect/Nothing.'/la la/To Carthage
96 Ash-Wed 5   10   the centre of the silent Word./O my people, what have I done unto thee./Where shall
96 Ash-Wed 5   28   those who chose and oppose/O my people, what have I done unto thee./Will the
97 Ash-Wed 5   36 mouth the withered apple-seed./O my people./Although I do not hope to turn again/
104 Journ Magi   42 in the old dispensation,/With an alien people clutching their gods./I should be glad of
127 Cor l March   4   Count them. And such a press of people./We hardly knew ourselves that day, or
152 Rock 2   37   while there is time of prosperity/The people will neglect the Temple, and in time of
154 Rock 3   22   of smoky ships?/Will you leave my people forgetful and forgotten/To idleness,
155 Rock 3   34   shall say: 'Here were decent godless people:/Their only monument the asphalt road/
187 FQ: DrySal 116   unworn by subsequent attrition./People change, and smile: but the agony abides.
188 FQ: DrySal 141   into any future;/You are not the same people who left that station/Or who will arrive
195 FQ: Little   172 If I think, again, of this place,/And of people, not wholly commendable,/Of no
197 FQ: Little   235 the yew-tree/Are of equal duration. A people without history/Is not redeemed from
212 Growltiger   10   fame;/At Hammersmith and Putney people shuddered at his name./They would
222 Pekes Pols   4   Pugs and the Poms, although most people say/That they do not like fighting, yet
222 Pekes Pols   15 —/I don't know the reason, but most people think/He'd slipped into the Wellington
222 Pekes Pols   25   the Park./Now the Peke, although people may say what they please,/Is no British
234 Ad-dress   7   are much like you and me/And other people whom we find/Possessed of various types
587 Fable   24 steeple,/To the astonishment of all the people./When Christmas time was near the
602 Humoresque 17   on Earth, I swear./'Why don't you people get some class?/(Feebly contemptuous of
239 MC Chorus   20   us,/He who was always kind to his people./But it would not be well if he should
241 MC Priest1 28 assurance of right, and the love of the people?/{M} You are right to express a certain
241 MC   Mess   31   beyond doubt, of the devotion of the people,/Who receive him with scenes of frenzied
251 MC Tempt3 28   us, the English barons./We are the people./{T} To what does this lead?/{T3} To a
252 MC Tempt3 12   no power but their own;/Church and people have good cause against the throne./{T}
264 MC Priest1 24   *all, keeping holy day./*{P1} As for the people, so also for himself, he offereth for sins./
268 MC Thomas 19   Why should he wish/To deprive my people of me and keep me from my own/And
268 MC Thomas 37   be bold/To say: seven years were my people without/My presence; seven years of
275 MC Thomas 10 your hurt and shame;/But none of my people, in God's name,/Whether layman or

464 CC Claude 4   that the potter handles./Most people think that a sculptor or a painter/Is
464 CC Claude 6 excellent to be than a potter./Most people think of china or porcelain/As merely for
465 CC Colby 40 him;/But when I played before other people/I was always conscious that what *they*
466 CC Colby 5 I've given up trying to play to other people:/I am only happy when I play to myself./
466 CC Claude 18 for religion./I dare say truly religious people —/I've never known any — can find
469 CC Lucasta 24 just enjoyed going — to see the other people,/And to be seen there! And because you
470 CC Colby 11 /I can't bring myself to play to other people,/And when I'm alone I can't forget/That
470 CC Colby 14 you, it was neither solitude nor ... people./{L} I'm glad I'm not people. Will you
470 CC Lucasta 15 nor ... people./{L} I'm glad I'm not people. Will you play to me again/And teach me
473 CC Lucasta 31 makes you think of Eggerson — of all people?/{C} Well, he retires to his garden —
475 CC Colby 2 you do already,/Better than ... other people. And I want to understand *you*./Does
476 CC Lucasta 13 that./And it's always succeeded with people before:/I got into the habit of giving that
479 CC Kaghan 15 /And I always bring luck to other people./{C} Will you have a glass of sherry?/{K}
480 CC Colby 15 risky./You like to pretend to other people/That you're a gambler. I don't believe
482 CC Lady E 3 LUCASTA]/{LE} Were those young people here by appointment?/Or did they come
482 CC Lady E 6 /{LE} You call her Lucasta? Young people nowadays/Seem to have dropped the use
482 CC Lady E 30 the first place, you ought to mix with people of breeding./I said to myself, when I first
482 CC Lady E 36 /Because, what's surprising, well-bred people/Are sometimes far from intellectual;/
482 CC Lady E 38 what's less surprising — intellectual people/Are often ill-bred. But that's not all./
483 CC Lady E 2 all./You need intellectual, well-bred people/Of spirituality — and that's the rarest./
484 CC Lady E 21 of relatives! And such unpleasant people!/I thought of myself as a dove in an
495 CC Lady E 13 mistake, I do believe,/For married people to take anything for granted./{SC} That
500 CC Lucasta 32 /And he doesn't depend upon other people, either./B. needs me. He's been hurt by
501 CC Lady E 20 that will help us/To understand other people. I hope so./Lucasta, I regard you as a ...
502 CC Lucasta 17 believe it!/It isn't like you, to despise people:/You don't care enough./{C} I don't care
502 CC Lucasta 24 same kind of fire/That warms other people. You're either an egotist/Or something
508 CC Guzzard 36 An odd name./They were excellent people. Nonconformists./{E} And the child, I
511 CC Kaghan 31 name of Barnabas?/{K} I don't want people calling me 'Barney' —/Barney Kaghan!
519 CC Lady E 12 /Between not knowing what other people want of one,/And not knowing what one
519 CC Lady E 13 what one should ask of other people,/One does make mistakes! But I mean to
528 ES Charles 5 But he's most alive when he's among people/Managing, manœuvring, cajoling or
528 ES Monica 8 understand. It's one thing meeting people/When you're in authority, with
528 ES Monica 10 costume,/When the man that people see when they meet you/Is not the
529 ES Monica 13 /Who is without envy? And most people/Are unaware or unashamed of being
530 ES Ld Clav 2 down notes of what I had to say to people:/Now I've no more to say, and no one to
531 ES Ld Clav 1 /This would do for visiting cards — if people still left cards/And if I was going to have
532 ES Monica 19 You ought not to bother with such people now, Father./If you haven't got rid of
533 ES Gomez 7 modest way./You know, where *I* live, people do change their names;/And besides, my
535 ES Gomez 12 me./It's nonsense to talk of trusting people/In general. What does that mean? One
537 ES Ld Clav 4 you have given/Of trusting people, how do you propose/To make it worth
538 ES Gomez 24 go into opposition/And let the other people make mistakes/Until your own have
544 ES Monica 3 it, Father? They've let us alone;/The people in the dining-room show no curiosity;/
544 ES Ld Clav 12 a fortnight —/After fourteen days of people not staring/Or offering picture papers, or
544 ES Ld Clav 29 really enjoyed living/As much as most people. At least, as they seem to do/Without
545 ES Ld Clav 17 /I thought that very ominous. When people talk like that/It indicates a latent desire
546 ES Piggott 22 been deluged with applications/From people who want to come here to die!/We never
546 ES Piggott 26 to all the doctors/Who send people here. When you go in to lunch/Just take
547 ES Piggott 23 /When there are enough young people among us/We dance in the evening. At
550 ES Carghil 13 the first time. That didn't last long./People sometimes say: 'Make one mistake in
551 ES Carghil 32 lost a breach of promise suit/Some people won't want to appear as his supporters.'/
552 ES Carghil 23 was clear./I've very seldom heard people mention their consciences/Except to
553 ES Ld Clav 35 you shown these letters/To many people?/{MC} Only a few friends./Effie said: 'If
565 ES Monica 28 {}/[*Exit*]/{M} Father, those awful people. We mustn't stay here./I want you to
567 ES Charles 19 your father and Michael, and those people from his past,/I've been trying to think
567 ES Monica 24 blackmail Father?/Father, of all people the most scrupulous,/The most austere.
569 ES Ld Clav 30 rich man. And she's a rich woman./If people merely blackmail you to get your
571 ES Ld Clav 4 —/These are my ghosts. They were people with good in them,/People who might all
571 ES Ld Clav 5 They were people with good in them,/People who might all have been very different/
571 ES Charles 22 me./{C} But all the same, these two people mustn't persecute you./We can't allow
573 ES Ld Clav 4 recovering!/It's hard to make other people realise/The magnitude of things that
573 ES Ld Clav 13 And to you, Monica,/To you, of all people./{C} I grant you all that./But what do
582 ES Charles 36 /Even with Michael, and despite those people,/Because somehow we'd begun to belong

PEOPLE'S (4)

359 CP Julia 29   /But *I* never poke into other people's business./Well, good-bye again. I'm off
411 CP Edward 24 others./I don't want to build on other people's ruins./{L} Exactly. And I have a

| 459 CC | Lady E | 3 | 'He has a good aura.'/I remember people's auras almost better than their faces./ |
| 498 CC | Eggers | 13 | a profession/Of ... looking after other people's children?/In a manner of speaking, it's |

PER (1)

| 44 Cook Egg | 16 | two shall lie together, lapt/In a five per cent. Exchequer Bond./I shall not want |

PERCEIVE (1)

| 148 Rock 1 | 39 | preserve respectful distance./For I perceive approaching/The Rock. Who will |

PERCEIVED (1)

| 68 WL: Fire S | 229 | Tiresias, old man with wrinkled dugs/Perceived the scene, and foretold the rest —/I |

PERCEIVING (2)

| 127 Cor1 March | 10 | natural wakeful life of our Ego is a perceiving./We can wait with our stools and our |
| 127 Cor1 March | 31 | neck,/And the eyes watchful, waiting, perceiving, indifferent./O hidden under the |

PERCEPTION (1)

| 370 CP | Peter | 28 | in which we seemed to share some perception,/Some feeling, some indefinable |

PERCEPTIVE (1)

| 436 CP | Reilly | 35 | very transparent/Or else you are very perceptive./{J} Oh, Henry!/Lavinia is much |

PERDITION (2)

| 249 MC Tempt2 | 12 | /Your spiritual power is earthly perdition./Power is present, for him who will |
| 255 MC Thomas | 35 | Can I neither act nor suffer/Without perdition?/{T4} You know and do not know, |

PEREGRINE (1)

| 194 FQ: Little | 123 | /To the spirit unappeased and peregrine/Between two worlds become much |

PEREIRA (15)

115 SP	Dusty	1	/DUSTY. DORIS./{Du} How about Pereira?/{Do} What about Pereira?/I don't care.
115 SP	Doris	2	about Pereira?/{Do} What about Pereira?/I don't care./{Du} You don't care!/
115 SP	Doris	9	you know who/{Do} You can have Pereira/{Du} What about Pereira?/{Do} He's no
115 SP	Dusty	10	can have Pereira/{Du} What about Pereira?/{Do} He's no gentleman, Pereira:/You
115 SP	Doris	11	Pereira?/{Do} He's no gentleman, Pereira:/You can't trust him!/{Du} Well that's
115 SP	Doris	17	No it wouldn't do to be too nice to Pereira./{Du} Now Sam's a gentleman through
116 SP	Doris	3	you laugh:/Sam's all right/{Do} But Pereira won't do./We can't have Pereira/{Du}
116 SP	Doris	4	But Pereira won't do./We can't have Pereira/{Du} Well what you going to do?/{Tel}
116 SP	Dusty	8	ling ling/Ting a ling ling/{Du} That's Pereira/{Do} Yes that's Pereira/{Du} Well what
116 SP	Doris	9	/{Du} That's Pereira/{Do} Yes that's Pereira/{Du} Well what you going to do?/{Tel}
116 SP	Dusty	13	ling ling/Ting a ling ling/{Du} That's Pereira/{Do} Well can't you stop that horrible
116 SP	Dusty	22	is Miss Dorrance's *flat* —/Oh Mr. Pereira is that you? how do you do!/Oh I'm *so*
117 SP	Dusty	3	/{Do} The King of Clubs/{Du} That's Pereira/{Do} It might be Sweeney/{Du} It's
117 SP	Dusty	5	/{Do} It might be Sweeney/{Du} It's Pereira/{Do} It might *just* as well be Sweeney/
117 SP	Dusty	13	/{Du} 'News of an absent friend'. — Pereira!/{Do} The Queen of Hearts! — Mrs.

PERFECT (18)

148 Rock 1	57	expect dividends./I say to you: *Make perfect your will.*/I say: take no thought of the
149 Rock 1	77	/That you may take heart. Make perfect your will./Let me show you the work of
155 Rock 3	66	preferred,/Engaged in devising the perfect refrigerator,/Engaged in working out a
159 Rock 6	23	and within/By dreaming of systems so perfect that no one will need to be good./But
163 Rock 8	48	and conviction./Let us therefore make perfect our will./O GOD, help us./Son of Man,
164 Rock 9	24	and feelings,/There spring the perfect order of speech, and the beauty of
601 Nocturne	14	all in tears are drowned: —/'The perfect climax all true lovers seek!'/
271 MC Thomas	25	danger./I have therefore only to make perfect my will./{3P} My Lord, they are coming.
290 FR Agatha	27	tighten the knot of confusion/Into perfect misunderstanding,/Reflecting a
343 FR Harry	33	is any worry —/The destined and the perfect master of Wishwood,/The satisfactory
356 CP Julia	16	a moment./I know you're always the perfect host,/But just try to pretend you're
395 CP Edward	32	about you/Has always been your perfect assurance/That you understood me
432 CP Lavinia	14	Julia, Sir Henry,/You are the perfect guest we've been waiting for./{R} I
524 ES Charles	15	when *you're* with me/It must be a perfect lunch./{M} It was a perfect lunch./But I
524 ES Monica	16	must be a perfect lunch./{M} It was a perfect lunch./But I know what men are — they
545 ES Ld Clav	16	going to leave you alone!/You want perfect peace: that's what Badgley Court is for.'/
546 ES Piggott	19	But, as I was saying,/Guests in perfect health are exceptional/Though we never
564 ES Carghil	17	/Is that how you come to speak such perfect English?/Of course, I could tell from

PERFECTED (1)

| 196 FQ: Little | 197 | to leave us — a symbol:/A symbol perfected in death./And all shall be well and/All |

PERFECTLY (27)

119 SP	Krum	31	swell./We like London fine./{Kr} Perfectly slick./{Du} Why don't you come and
277 MC Knight3	3	/you may think of it, we have been perfectly disinterested. [*The other*/KNIGHTS:
277 MC Knight3	16	getting a penny out of this. We know perfectly well how/things will turn out. King
278 MC Knight2	6	problem./The King's aim has been perfectly consistent. During the reign of/the late
286 FR Amy	10	much better./{A} My servants are perfectly competent, Gerald./I can still see to
296 FR Gerald	35	/He's an old friend of the family, it's perfectly natural/That he should be asked. He
304 FR Mary	14	/Whether I understand. You know perfectly well,/What Cousin Amy wants, she

353 CP   Alex   6 the Maharaja?/{A} My dear Julia!/It's perfectly hopeless. You haven't been listening./
374 CP   Celia   15   /{C} I should have thought it was perfectly simple./Lavinia has left you./{E} Yes,
394 CP   Edward   2 *never* complained./{E} No; and it was perfectly infuriating,/The way you *didn't*
413 CP   Celia   15   /But I shan't begin that way. I feel perfectly well./I could lead an active life — if
448 CC   Claude   27 starting him during her absence/Are perfectly clear. But beyond that point/I haven't
455 CC   Colby   6   I'd lost my reason:/Her influence is perfectly frightening./But tell me about Lu ...
456 CC   Eggers   5   he said, 'I wanted a lady,/And I'm perfectly satisfied with the bargain.'/Of course
456 CC   Eggers   14 admit she is./Most of her oddities are perfectly harmless./You'll soon get used to
457 CC   Eggers   32   what *can* have happened?/{E} It's perfectly amazing. Let *me* go down to meet her.
462 CC   Claude   13 —/And I believe she will: though I'm perfectly convinced/That her son would have
497 CC   Lady E   26 he is. But I don't want to know:/I am perfectly content to leave things as they are,/So
497 CC   Claude   28   regard him as *our* son./{SC} That is perfectly correct. It is Colby/Who is not
498 CC   Eggers   14   /In a manner of speaking, it's perfectly respectable./{SC} You're suggesting
499 CC   Lucasta 34 /{SC} In Colby!/{L} Why not? That's perfectly natural./But I'm grateful to Colby. But
512 CC   Claude   11   now:/I'm sure that my wife is perfectly convinced;/And Mr. Kaghan's ...
514 CC   Claude   17 no mother./{SC} Mrs. Guzzard, this is perfectly incredible!/You couldn't have carried
535 ES   Gomez   25 why you need to trust *me*./{G} That's perfectly simple. I come back to England/After
536 ES   Gomez   33   you should need to trust me./{G} Perfectly simple./My father's dead long since —
546 ES   Piggott 13 Though we never have guests who are perfectly well —/Except when they come like
547 ES   Ld Clav 2 /In another respect./{LC} I follow you perfectly./{MP} And now I must fly. I've so
PERFECTS (1)
467 CC   Colby   3   reconcilement, after his death,/That perfects the relation. You have always been his
PERFORMANCE (1)
229 Gus   37 part in *East Lynne*./At a Shakespeare performance he once walked on pat,/When
PERFORMED (1)
152 Rock 2   24 /The British race assured of a mission/Performed it, but left much at home unsure./Of
PERFORMERS (1)
470 CC   Colby   19 won't take you long — and hear good performers,/You'll very quickly realise how bad
PERFORMING (2)
50 Hippopot   32 /Among the saints he shall be seen/Performing on a harp of gold./He shall be
224 Mr Mistoff   8   holds all the patent monopolies/For performing surprising illusions/And creating
PERFUME (1)
15 Prufrock   65 downed with light brown hair!)/Is it perfume from a dress/That makes me so
PERFUMES (1)
64 WL: Chess   87   lurked her strange synthetic perfumes,/Unguent, powdered, or liquid —
PERHAPS (112)
20 Portrait   93 falls heavily among the bric-à-brac./'Perhaps you can write to me.'/My
21 Portrait   107 to fate./You will write, at any rate./Perhaps it is not too late./I shall sit here, serving
126 SA   Chorus   6   the hangman's waiting for you./And perhaps you're alive/And perhaps you're dead/
126 SA   Chorus   7   you./And perhaps you're alive/And perhaps you're dead/Hoo ha ha/Hoo ha ha/
137 5FingerEx5   7   to What Precisely/And If and Perhaps and But./How unpleasant to meet Mr.
148 Rock 1   40 approaching/The Rock. Who will perhaps answer our doubtings./The Rock. The
171 FQ: BurntN   2 /Time present and time past/Are both perhaps present in time future/And time future
182 FQ: ECoker   190   /That seem unpropitious. But perhaps neither gain nor loss./For us, there is
233 Skimble   53 and then he has a cup of tea/With perhaps a drop of Scotch while he's keeping on
587 Fable   18 /Some wicked and heretical old sinner/Perhaps, who had been walled up for his crimes;
588 Fable   53 made of plover,/And flagons which perhaps held several kegs/Of ale, and cheese
242 MC   Priest1 30 or had he been weaker/Things had perhaps been different for Thomas./{P2} Yet
248 MC   Tempt2   15   Your Lordship has forgotten me, perhaps. I will remind you./We met at
249 MC   Tempt2   8 make all even,/Is thrive on earth, and perhaps in heaven./{T} What means?/{T2} Real
262 MC   Thomas   3   yet another martyr,/and that one perhaps not the last. I would have you keep in
306 FR   Mary   37 to invent our own enjoyments./But perhaps it was all designed for you, not for us./
309 FR   Harry   38 /Which ordinarily pass unnoticed./Perhaps you are right, though I do not know/
316 FR   Chorus   2   torn/The roof from the house, or perhaps it was never there./And the bird sits on
318 FR   Harry   31   need for explanation —/But perhaps I only dream that I am talking/And
322 FR   Winch   26 you quiet,/Rather than phone and perhaps disturb her Ladyship./So I slipped
327 FR   Harry   12 outside,/I might escape somewhere, perhaps. Were they simply inside/I could cheat
327 FR   Harry   13 they simply inside/I could cheat them perhaps with the aid of Dr. Warburton —/Or
332 FR   Agatha   30 come once,/Thank God, that kind. Perhaps there is another kind,/I believe, across a
333 FR   Harry   21   /Would have seemed the ruin./Perhaps my life has only been a dream/Dreamt
333 FR   Harry   22 through me by the minds of others. Perhaps/I only dreamt I pushed her./{Ag} So I
341 FR   Agatha   2 /That you have never changed. And perhaps I have not./I thought that I had, until
356 CP   Julia   31 —/So that I could make you talk. Perhaps she's in the pantry/Listening to all we
358 CP   Edward   39 Edward./Shall I see you soon?/{E} Perhaps. I don't know./{C} Perhaps you don't
359 CP   Celia   1 soon?/{E} Perhaps. I don't know./{C} Perhaps you don't know? Very well, good-bye./

362 CP	Reilly	4	that you endured it for so long./And perhaps at times you will feel a little jealous/
370 CP	Peter	31	unaware of ourselves./In your terms, perhaps, she's lost interest in me./{E} That is all
371 CP	Peter	5	—/My first experience of reality/And perhaps it is the last. And you don't understand.
379 CP	Celia	34	waited, and wanted to run to tell you./Perhaps the dream was better. It seemed the real
379 CP	Celia	36	this is reality, it is very like a dream./Perhaps it was I who betrayed my own dream/
380 CP	Edward	37	in love with anyone but you,/And perhaps I still am. But this can't go on./It never
382 CP	Edward	22	out/When you tread on a beetle./{E} Perhaps that is what I am./Tread on me, if you
383 CP	Celia	23	may be that even Julia is a guardian./Perhaps she is *my* guardian. Give me the
385 CP	Reilly	9	/{UG} It is very difficult./But it is perhaps still more difficult/To keep up the
388 CP	Celia	20	going abroad?/{C} I don't know. Perhaps./{E} You're both going away! {}/[*Enter*
390 CP	Lavinia	14	aunt — and the telegram./{L} Well, perhaps I was in Essex. I really don't know./{J}
395 CP	Edward	38	in the trap,/With only one difference, perhaps — we can fight each other,/Instead of
396 CP	Lavinia	31	or other, before you ever knew me:/Perhaps only when you were a child./{E} I don't
403 CP	Edward	27	still more acutely —/Indeed, acutely, perhaps, for the first time,/The whole
409 CP	Reilly	33	/Before you would admit it. Though perhaps you knew it/Before he did. You
416 CP	Celia	9	had you? That's clever of you./No, perhaps I made it obvious. You don't need to
416 CP	Celia	12	/About him, do you?/{R} No./{C} Perhaps I'm only typical./{R} There are
416 CP	Celia	40	found, and which was not there/And perhaps is not anywhere? But if not anywhere,/
418 CP	Celia	6	still have it. Yet it leaves me cold./Perhaps that's just a part of my illness,/But I
423 CP	Alex	2	Shall we ever speak them?/{A} Others, perhaps, will speak them./You know, I have
425 CP	Edward	11	a party without asking them./{E} Perhaps we ought to have arranged to have two
431 CP	Peter	3	/Pan-Am-Eagle must look into this./Perhaps it would be a good place to make one./
435 CP	Lavinia	38	I know that you're right./{L} And perhaps what I've been saying/Will seem less
438 CP	Lavinia	3	That is part of the design./{L} Perhaps she had been through greater agony
449 CC	Eggers	19	/{E} Well, I believe that once or twice, perhaps .../But I'm afraid you overrate my
450 CC	Claude	18	better/Than I should care to think, perhaps./{E} And do I infer/That you're not
454 CC	Colby	35	—/I think it amuses him./{C} Well, perhaps I'll be amused./But it did make my
456 CC	Colby	39	Elizabeth out of her difficulties./{C} Perhaps she won't even arrive by this plane./{E}
463 CC	Claude	4	to Canada/In the war — that was perhaps a mistake,/Though it seemed to have
466 CC	Claude	23	/That's you and me. Some day, perhaps,/I will show you my collection./{C}
466 CC	Claude	26	collection./{C} Thank you./{SC} And perhaps, some time, you will let me hear you
471 CC	Colby	3	you want to go to *yourself*./{C} And perhaps you'll let me tell you beforehand/About
471 CC	Lucasta	13	so much that one wouldn't suspect./Perhaps that's why I like you./{C} That's not
472 CC	Colby	5	— and I think that you're frightened./Perhaps you've been very badly hurt, at some
472 CC	Lucasta	20	is it different?/{L} It's hard to explain./Perhaps it's something that your music stands
472 CC	Lucasta	26	you may have been mistaken,/And perhaps you could be a very great musician:/But
475 CC	Colby	14	And I think I'm changing too. But perhaps what we call change .../{L} Is
475 CC	Lucasta	16	the reason why that comes about, perhaps .../{C} Is, beginning to understand
477 CC	Lucasta	32	I was flattered./And I thought, now, perhaps, if someone else sees me/As I really am,
477 CC	Lucasta	39	you like to be alone with yourself?/Or perhaps you think it would be bad for your
478 CC	Lucasta	2	you're Claude's white-headed boy./Perhaps he'll adopt you, and make you his heir/
482 CC	Colby	27	all./{C} I shouldn't call them vulgar. Perhaps I'm vulgar too./But what, do you
487 CC	Lady E	27	/If it were only a coincidence./Perhaps I ought not to believe it yet,/Perhaps I
487 CC	Lady E	28	/Perhaps I ought not to believe it yet,/Perhaps it is wrong of me to feel so sure,/But it
489 CC	Claude	1	to take your son away from you./Perhaps you have a son. But it isn't Colby./I
489 CC	Lady E	30	you know that the sister had a child?/Perhaps Mrs. Guzzard invented the story..../
489 CC	Lady E	32	{LE} In order to get money from you, perhaps./No, I shouldn't say that. But she had a
493 CC	Claude	28	insisted/On this ... investigation. But perhaps you're right./{LE} Claude, I've been
494 CC	Lady E	30	think I understand anything,/And perhaps I don't. But I wish you would talk/
494 CC	Lady E	32	to me as if I did understand,/And perhaps I might come to understand better./
495 CC	Claude	15	That was a very intelligent remark./Perhaps I have taken too much for granted/
498 CC	Eggers	12	/{E} I was only suggesting/That perhaps Mrs. Guzzard made a profession/Of ...
500 CC	Lucasta	18	knew it./{L} Why didn't he tell me? Perhaps he was about to./Anyway, I *knew* there
501 CC	Claude	14	And I'm not ashamed of it./{SC} Perhaps you are right. I'm not sure of anything.
501 CC	Claude	15	are right. I'm not sure of anything./Perhaps, as you say, I've misunderstood B.,/
501 CC	Lady E	19	each other,/No matter how late. And perhaps that will help us/To understand other
502 CC	Colby	28	That's me, is it? I simply don't know./Perhaps you know me better than I know
502 CC	Lucasta	39	and a sister,/Will come, in time. Perhaps, one day/We may understand each
503 CC	Lucasta	4	way/That reveals itself in time. And perhaps — who knows? —/We might become
508 CC	Guzzard	9	offered hope of finding him?/{MG} Perhaps I should./{LE} There isn't a shadow of
508 CC	Guzzard	32	/Like mine, a somewhat unusual one./Perhaps it might be possible to trace them./The
513 CC	Guzzard	2	Nor, so far as I can judge, with you./Perhaps you are the wisest wisher here:/I shall
513 CC	Colby	31	of his life, of his success or failure .../Perhaps his failure more than his success —/By
515 CC	Claude	38	a difference/To our relations. Or, perhaps, for the better?/Perhaps we'll be happier
515 CC	Claude	39	relations. Or, perhaps, for the better?/Perhaps we'll be happier together if you think/I

541 ES   Gomez   30   me a moment ago./Now it's my turn, perhaps, to do you a kindness. {}/[*Enter*
544 ES   Ld Clav 28   you learning to enjoy yourself!/{LC} Perhaps I've never really enjoyed living/As
547 ES   Monica   17   she decants for every newcomer./Perhaps after what she considers proper
551 ES   Carghil 27   one must do *something*./Well, perhaps I shouldn't have settled out of court./
551 ES   Carghil 39   have become Lord Claverton./So perhaps I laid the foundation of your fortunes!/
552 ES   Ld Clav   1   of your fortunes!/{LC} And perhaps at the same time of your own?/I seem
552 ES   Ld Clav 14   that I felt nothing at all./I thought, perhaps, what a lucky escape/It had been, for
553 ES   Carghil 13   you touched my soul —/Pawed it, perhaps, and the touch still lingers./And I've
554 ES   Carghil   6   Can you bear it?/If I go at once, perhaps she'll take the hint/And leave us alone
555 ES   Ld Clav 30   be that,/Or he wouldn't be at large. Perhaps he's in trouble/With some woman or
556 ES   Monica   29   that you want something from him./Perhaps you'll get to the point if I leave you
558 ES   Ld Clav 33   a good deal further than it had./{LC} Perhaps it had gone further than you're willing
565 ES   Carghil 22   /{MC} You must tell me all about it. Perhaps I could advise you./We'll leave you
572 ES   Ld Clav 39   step taken towards my freedom,/And perhaps the most important. I know what you
576 ES   Ld Clav 23   in San Marco than in England./{LC} Perhaps you intend to change your name to
580 ES   Monica   27   Oh Father, Father, I'm so sorry!/But perhaps, perhaps, Michael may learn his lesson.
580 ES   Monica   27   Father, I'm so sorry!/But perhaps, perhaps, Michael may learn his lesson./I believe
581 ES   Ld Clav   9   a final good-bye./I am sure of it now. Perhaps it is as well./{M} What do you mean,

PERIL (1)
269 MC   Knight1   15   /{K1} Priest, you have spoken in peril of your life./{K2} Priest, you have spoken

PERILOUSLY (1)
 68 WL: Fire S 224   out food in tins./Out of the window perilously spread/Her drying combinations

PERIODICALS (1)
187 FQ: DrySal 135   the passengers are settled/To fruit, periodicals and business letters/(And those who

PERIPHRASTIC (1)
179 FQ: ECoker 70   putting it — not very satisfactory:/A periphrastic study in a worn-out poetical

PERISH (2)
175 FQ: BurntN 154   burden,/Under the tension, slip, slide, perish,/Decay with imprecision, will not stay in
243 MC   Chorus   19   Return. Quickly. Quietly. Leave us to perish in quiet./You come with applause, you

PERJURED (1)
 42 Swee Erect   8   hair/And swell with haste the perjured sails./Morning stirs the feet and hands/

PERMANENCE (2)
173 FQ: BurntN   98   beauty/With slow rotation suggesting permanence/Nor darkness to purify the soul/
187 FQ: DrySal 110   are likewise permanent/With such permanence as time has. We appreciate this

PERMANENT (5)
187 FQ: DrySal 109   /Is not the question) are likewise permanent/With such permanence as time has.
248 MC   Tempt2   28   grows to glory,/Life lasting, a permanent possession./A templed tomb,
362 CP   Reilly   6   to break it —/Thus giving herself a permanent advantage./{E} It might turn out so,
380 CP   Edward   38   go on./It never could have been ... a permanent thing:/You should have a man ...
462 CC   Claude   4   long,/We can put matters onto a permanent basis./{C} I must confess, that up to

PERMANENTLY (1)
289 FR   Gerald   28   /{G} Yes, it's odd to think of her as permanently *missing*./{V} Had she been

PERMIT (2)
119 SP   Wauch   2   do!/How come? how come? will you permit me —/I think you girls both know
408 CP   Reilly   34   to-day./{R} A point well taken./But permit me to remark that my revelations/About

PERPENDICULAR (1)
209 NamingCats 15   /Else how can he keep up his tail perpendicular,/Or spread out his whiskers, or

PERPETUAL (11)
 85 Hollow Men   63   unless/The eyes reappear/As the perpetual star/Multifoliate rose/Of death's
129 Cor2 State   22   with a Volscian commission/About perpetual peace: the fletchers and
147 Rock 1   3   with his dogs pursues his circuit./O perpetual revolution of configured stars,/O
147 Rock 1   4   revolution of configured stars,/O perpetual recurrence of determined seasons,/O
148 Rock 1   64   it, this thing does not change:/The perpetual struggle of Good and Evil./Forgetful,
155 Rock 3   43   /Shall we lift up our feet among perpetual ruins?/I have loved the beauty of Thy
171 FQ: BurntN   7   been is an abstraction/Remaining a perpetual possibility/Only in a world of
174 FQ: BurntN 118   lower, descend only/Into the world of perpetual solitude,/World not world, but that
189 FQ: DrySal 187   reach them the sound of the sea bell's/Perpetual angelus./To communicate with Mars,
243 MC   Priest2   1   can feel a firm foothold/Against the perpetual wash of tides of balance of forces of
271 MC   Thomas   10   your share of the eternal burden,/The perpetual glory. This is one moment,/But know

PERPETUALLY (1)
175 FQ: BurntN 146   stillness, as a Chinese jar still/Moves perpetually in its stillness./Not the stillness of

PERPETUATE (2)
513 CC   Colby   36   man/Whose life I could in some way perpetuate/By being the person he would have
581 ES   Ld Clav 18   for Michael?/Because I wanted to perpetuate myself in him./Why did I want to

PERPLEXED (1)
574 ES   Carghil   25   problems are solved;/And he was so perplexed, poor lamb. Let's all rejoice together.
PERPLEXES (2)
107 Animula   17   heavy burden of the growing soul/Perplexes and offends more, day by day;/Week
107 Animula   18   by day;/Week by week, offends and perplexes more/With the imperatives of 'is and
PERPLEXING (1)
412 CP   Celia   32   /{C} That makes it even more perplexing. However,/I don't want to waste
PERPLEXITY (1)
189 FQ: DrySal   201   /When there is distress of nations and perplexity/Whether on the shores of Asia, or in
PERSECUTE (1)
571 ES   Charles 22   all the same, these two people mustn't persecute you./We can't allow that. What hold
PERSECUTED (1)
413 CP   Celia   17   for;/I don't imagine that I am being persecuted;/I don't hear any voices, I have no
PERSECUTION (4)
159 Rock 6   1   hard for those who have never known persecution,/And who have never known a
159 Rock 6   3   /To believe these tales of Christian persecution./It is hard for those who live near a
280 MC   Priest3   16   in adversity. It is fortified/By persecution: supreme, so long as men will die
573 ES   Charles 16   /Will you stay here and endure this persecution?/{LC} To the end. The place and
PERSECUTORS (1)
255 MC   Tempt4   15   you, where the gulf is fixed,/Your persecutors, in timeless torment,/Parched
PERSIAN (2)
135 5FingerEx1   t   /Five-Finger Exercises/*Lines to a Persian Cat*/The songsters of the air repair/To
212 Growltiger   19   and race no quarter was allowed./The Persian and the Siamese regarded him with fear
PERSIST (1)
528 ES   Charles 34   depressing;/For this situation may persist for a long time,/And you'll go on
PERSISTED (1)
330 FR   Harry   27   from my self,/From the self which persisted only as an eye, seeing./All this last
PERSISTENTLY (1)
452 CC   Eggers 14   right!/{E} You have been, I presume, persistently unpunctual./{L} You're wrong,
PERSISTING (1)
309 FR   Harry   36   noises/In the grass and leaves, of life persisting,/Which ordinarily pass unnoticed./
PERSON (66)
 56 Swee Night   11   and hushed the shrunken seas;/The person in the Spanish cape/Tries to sit on
219 Mung Rump   32   house like a hurricane, and no sober person could take his oath/Was it Mungojerrie
286 FR   Charles 24   bad for the young./All that a civilised person needs/Is a glass of dry sherry or two
293 FR   Harry   17   want to pretend that I am another person —/A person that you have conspired to
293 FR   Harry   18   that I am another person —/A person that you have conspired to invent, please
296 FR   Amy   30   not, Charles, you are not the right person./I prefer to believe that a few days at
309 FR   Mary   13   conversation./{M} I am not a wise person,/And in the ordinary sense I don't know
311 FR   Harry   28   /When I knew her, I was not the same person./I was not any person. Nothing that I
311 FR   Harry   29   not the same person./I was not any person. Nothing that I did/Has to do with me.
311 FR   Harry   35   looks/Incriminate, but that other person, if person/You thought I was: let your
311 FR   Harry   35   /Incriminate, but that other person, if person/You thought I was: let your necrophily/
330 FR   Harry   31   the same loathing,/Diffused, I not a person, in a world not of persons/But only of
338 FR   Agatha 35   /{Ag} In a world of fugitives/The person taking the opposite direction/Will
344 FR   Violet   9   seems to me/That I am the only sane person in this house./Your behaviour all seems
345 FR   Amy   24   for it./Gerald! you are the stupidest person in this room,/Violet, you are the most
354 CP   Celia   3   remember it./{C} And Julia's the only person to tell it./She's such a good mimic./{J}
359 CP   Edward 35   somebody;/And it's easier to talk to a person you don't know./The fact is, that
362 CP   Edward 11   I should be any happier/With another person. Why speak of love?/We were used to
362 CP   Reilly   21   /Or rather, you've lost touch with the person/You thought you were. You no longer
362 CP   Reilly   24   —/A living object, but no longer a person./It's always happening, because one is an
362 CP   Reilly   26   because one is an object/As well as a person. But we forget about it/As quickly as we
379 CP   Edward 14   /And I think you are a very rare person./But it was too late. And I should have
380 CP   Celia   30   Lavinia./And if that is the sort of person you are —/Well, you had better have
382 CP   Celia   26   I had thought you were. I see another person,/I see you as a person whom I never saw
382 CP   Celia   27   I see another person,/I see you as a person whom I never saw before./The man I
388 CP   Peter   5   this morning./Alex is a wonderful person to know,/Because, you see, he knows
395 CP   Lavinia 12   /As for me, I'm rather a different person/Whom you must get to know./{E} This
397 CP   Edward 37   in future you will find me a different person?/{L} Indeed. And has the difference
400 CP   Alex   13   thinks I'm well informed: the sort of person/Who would know the right doctor, as
401 CP   Edward   5   the door, that you might be the same person:/But I dismissed that as just another
416 CP   Celia   18   persons we had been/But for the new person, us. If I could feel/As I did then, even
450 CC   Claude   3   when you're sure you understand a person/That you're liable to make the worst
462 CC   Claude 14   would have been a different type of person —/Then you *will* become her son, in her

463 CC	Colby	18	As if I was becoming/A different	person. Just as, I suppose,/If you learn to speak
463 CC	Colby	21	feel yourself to be/Rather a different	person when you're talking it./I'm not at all
463 CC	Colby	22	I'm not at all sure that I like the other	person/That I feel myself becoming — though
463 CC	Colby	26	waking in the night, then the former	person,/The person I used to be, returns to take
463 CC	Colby	27	night, then the former person,/The	person I used to be, returns to take possession:/
463 CC	Colby	32	That I want to do. I have to fight that	person./{SC} I understand what you are saying/
465 CC	Claude	21	When I am transported — a different	person,/Transfigured in the vision of some
472 CC	Lucasta	12	isn't it,/That as one gets to know a	person better/One finds them in some ways very
473 CC	Lucasta	11	garden./I hardly feel that I'm even a	person:/Nothing but a bit of living matter/
473 CC	Colby	15	that's it./{C} You're very much a	person./I'm sure that there is a garden
475 CC	Colby	7	there's no end to understanding a	person./All one can do is to understand them
475 CC	Colby	17	Is, beginning to understand another	person./{L} Oh Colby, now that we begin to
477 CC	Lucasta	27	I don't like myself./I don't like the	person I've forced myself to be;/And I liked you
477 CC	Lucasta	28	liked you because you didn't like that	person either,/And I thought you'd come to see
477 CC	Lucasta	29	come to see me as the real kind of	person/That I want to be. That I know I am./
481 CC	Lady E	22	the place has been lived in/By the	person for whom it was designed./So I have to
481 CC	Lady E	30	you, Mr. Kaghan, you're the type of	person/Who needs to eat a great deal of salad./
482 CC	Lady E	14	both of them — you're not the sort of	person/They ever meet in their kind of society./
482 CC	Lady E	17	/I can speak more freely, as an elderly	person./{C} But, Lady Elizabeth .../{LE} Well,
497 CC	Claude	14	/Of Teddington is the name of the	person/To whom her own child was entrusted./
501 CC	Lady E	10	that, Lucasta;/I have always been a	person of liberal views./That's why I never
501 CC	Lucasta	12	with my family./{L} Well, I'm not a	person of liberal views./I'm very conventional.
513 CC	Colby	37	in some way perpetuate/By being the	person he would have liked to be,/And by doing
526 ES	Charles	18	much of me is you?/I'm not the same	person as a moment ago./What do the words
531 ES	Ld Clav	39	your seeing him./{LC} What sort of a	person?/{L} A foreign person/By the looks of
532 ES	Lambert	1	What sort of a person?/{L} A foreign	person/By the looks of him. But talks good
536 ES	Gomez	4	weren't aware of becoming a different	person:/But where *I* changed my name, there
555 ES	Piggott	2	was singing it once. A charming	person,/I dare say, but not quite your sort or
556 ES	Michael	34	got over that. If you always blame a	person/It's natural he should end by getting into
568 ES	Ld Clav	23	— your soul is safe./If a man has one	person, just one in his life,/To whom he is
568 ES	Ld Clav	29	who has not?) —/Then he loves that	person, and his love will save him./I'm afraid
579 ES	Carghil	32	/{MC} A parent isn't always the right	person, Richard,/To solve a son's problems.
583 ES	Charles	1	that now we are conscious of a new	person/Who is you and me together./Oh my

PERSONAGE (1)

528 ES	Monica	11	/Is not the private man, but the public	personage./In politics Father wore a public

PERSONAL (5)

235 Ad-dress		59	salmon paste —/He's sure to have his	personal taste./(I know a Cat, who makes a
276 MC	Chorus	1	the private catastrophe,/The	personal loss, the general misery,/Living and
349 FR	Chorus	6	/We have suffered far more than a	personal loss —/We have lost our way in the
402 CP	Edward	26	such patients/As myself, under your	personal observation?/{R} You are very
508 CC	Eggers	2	tell her so./{E} Don't take this as a	personal reflection,/Mrs. Guzzard. Far from it.

PERSONALITY (5)

320 FR	Warburt	8	as ever —/It is only the force of her	personality,/Her indomitable will, that keeps
362 CP	Reilly	20	more to it than that. There's a loss of	personality;/Or rather, you've lost touch with
396 CP	Edward	35	myself./You're still trying to invent a	personality for me/Which will only keep me
402 CP	Edward	34	/I have ceased to believe in my own	personality./{R} Oh, dear yes; this is serious. A
535 ES	Gomez	32	/To fabricate for myself another	personality/And to take another name. Think

PERSONALLY (2)

277 MC	Knight3	22	*had* to be put out of the/way — and	personally I had a tremendous admiration for
579 ES	Michael	20	in again. If there's any point in it./	Personally, I think that when one's come to a

PERSONS (10)

195 FQ:	Little	154	to self and to things and to	persons, detachment/From self and from things
195 FQ:	Little	155	/From self and from things and from	persons; and, growing between them,
284 FR		m 1	for us. {}/THE FAMILY REUNION/	Persons/AMY, DOWAGER LADY
330 FR	Harry	31	I not a person, in a world not of	persons/But only of contaminating presences./
352 CP		m 1	peace. {}/THE COCKTAIL PARTY/	Persons/EDWARD CHAMBERLAYNE/
385 CP	Reilly	25	I should like to forget./{UG} And	persons also. But you must not forget them./
416 CP	Celia	17	calculation/Of what was good for the	persons we had been/But for the new person, *us*.
569 ES	Charles	19	me about your fellow guests,/Two	persons who, she says, claim a very long
569 ES	Ld Clav	36	not till lately that I found the living	persons/Whose ghosts tormented me, to be only
582 ES	Ld Clav	15	sorry you have had to see so much of	persons/And situations not very agreeable./You

PERSPECTIVE (1)

40 Burb	Blei	19	/Stares from the protozoic slime/At a	perspective of Canaletto./The smoky candle end

PERSPICACITY (1)

407 CP	Reilly	13	/{R} I congratulate you both on your	perspicacity./Your sympathetic understanding

388 CP	Celia	8	come for is to say good-bye./{C} Well, Peter, I'm awfully glad, for your sake,/Though
388 CP	Lavinia	22	Who's going away? Well, Celia. Well, Peter./I didn't expect to find either of you here./
389 CP	Celia	16	Lavinia, I think I understand about Peter .../{L} I have no doubt you do./{C} And
391 CP	Julia	2	/Now we'll all go back to *my* house. Peter, call a taxi. {}/[*Exit* PETER]/{J} We'll have
391 CP	m	2	to *my* house. Peter, call a taxi. {}/[*Exit* PETER]/{J} We'll have a cocktail party at *my*
391 CP	m	32	... I haven't left anything. {}/[*Enter* PETER]/{P} I've got a taxi, Julia./{J} Splendid!
391 CP	m	33	{}/[*Exeunt* JULIA, ALEX *and* PETER]/{L} I must say, you don't seem very
398 CP	Lavinia	1	Going to California?/{L} Yes, with Peter./Really, Edward, if you were human/You
408 CP	Reilly	13	if you like./{R} A young man named Peter./{E} Peter? Peter who?/{R} Mr. Peter
408 CP	Edward	14	/{R} A young man named Peter./{E} Peter? Peter who?/{R} Mr. Peter Quilpe/Was a
408 CP	Edward	14	A young man named Peter./{E} Peter? Peter who?/{R} Mr. Peter Quilpe/Was a
408 CP	Reilly	15	Peter./{E} Peter? Peter who?/{R} Mr. Peter Quilpe/Was a frequent guest./{E} Peter
408 CP	Edward	17	Quilpe/Was a frequent guest./{E} Peter Quilpe./Peter Quilpe! Really Lavinia!/I
408 CP	Edward	18	a frequent guest./{E} Peter Quilpe./Peter Quilpe! Really Lavinia!/I congratulate
422 CP	Julia	31	can not be spoken yet./{J} You mean Peter./{R} He has not yet come to where
430 CP	m	1	Mr. Quilpe!/{E} Now who ... {}/[*Enter* PETER]/{E} Why, it's Peter!/{L} Peter!/{P}
430 CP	Edward	1	... {}/[*Enter* PETER]/{E} Why, it's Peter!/{L} Peter!/{P} Hullo, everybody!/{L}
430 CP	Lavinia	2	PETER]/{E} Why, it's Peter!/{L} Peter!/{P} Hullo, everybody!/{L} When did you
430 CP	Julia	28	/Give us your news of the world, Peter./We lead such a quiet life, here in London.
431 CP	Julia	26	/{J} But what is your position, Peter?/Have you become an expert on decaying
431 CP	Julia	37	him decide what faces are typical./{J} Peter, I've thought of a wonderful idea!/I've
432 CP	Lavinia	25	thank you./{L} May I introduce Mr. Peter Quilpe?/Sir Henry Harcourt-Reilly.
433 CP	Julia	3	that's not the way we do it./{J} But, Peter;/If you're taking Boltwell to California/
433 CP	Alex	27	to speak of her/When you came in, Peter. I'm afraid you can't have Celia./{P} Oh ...
435 CP	Lavinia	29	alive./{L} No, it's not all worthless, Peter. You've only just begun./I mean, this only
435 CP	Lavinia	35	for yourself, to meet your own needs./Peter, please don't think I'm being unkind .../
436 CP	Edward	2	you start from./If you find out now, Peter, things about yourself/That you don't like
436 CP	Julia	14	have learned how to look at people, Peter,/When you look at them with an eye for
439 CP	Julia	13	which the consequence was Kinkanja./Peter chose a way that leads him to Boltwell:/
439 CP	Edward	23	be going./{E} Shall we see you again, Peter,/Before you leave England?/{L} Do try to
440 CP	Lavinia	2	... I am glad Alex told us .../And Peter had to know .../{E} Now I think I

PETER'D (1)

589 Fable		84	anyone questioned, would declare/St. Peter'd snatcht to heaven their lord renowned,/

PETER'S (3)

388 CP	Edward	37	down./What shall we talk about?/{E} Peter's going to America./{P} Yes, and I would
432 CP	Lavinia	26	Quilpe?/Sir Henry Harcourt-Reilly. Peter's an old friend/Of my husband and
432 CP	Julia	33	such an interesting conversation./Peter's just over from California/Where he's

PETITE (2)

46 Directeur		15	/A pas de loup./Dans un égout/Une petite fille/En guenilles/Camarde/Regarde/Le
51 Restaurant		10	/J'avais sept ans, elle était plus petite./Elle était toute mouillée, je lui ai donné

PETREL (1)

183 FQ: ECoker		211	the wind cry, the vast waters/Of the petrel and the porpoise. In my end is my

PETTY (4)

180 FQ: ECoker		107	committees,/Industrial lords and petty contractors, all go into the dark,/And
249 MC	Thomas	37	will not forget/Constant curbing of petty privilege./{T2} Against the barons/Is
569 ES	Ld Clav	38	to be only human beings,/Malicious, petty, and I see myself emerging/From my
573 ES	Ld Clav	5	of things that appear to them petty;/It's harder to confess the sin that no one

PETTY-MINDED (1)

456 CC	Eggers	8	But he didn't think of that:/He's not petty-minded — though nothing escapes him./

PEU (1)

47 Mél	Adult	6	conférencier;/A Londres, un peu banquier,/Vous me paierez bien la tête./

PEUR (1)

51 Restaurant		18	peloter, un gros chien;/Moi j'avais peur, je l'ai quittée à mi-chemin./C'est

PHANTASMAL (1)

419 CP	Reilly	4	the final desolation/Of solitude in the phantasmal world/Of imagination, shuffling

PHANTASMS (1)

335 FR	Harry	33	there, you were not there, only our phantasms/And what did not happen is as true

PHANTOMS (4)

205 de la Mare		28	which allows/Free passage to the phantoms of the mind?/By you; by those
587 Fable		26	They'd eat their meal from ghosts and phantoms free,/The fiend must stay at home —
334 FR	Harry	34	I see/I have been wounded in a war of phantoms,/Not by human beings — they have
338 FR	Harry	21	that all my life has been a flight/And phantoms fed upon me while I fled. Now I

PHARMACOLOGY (1)

546 ES	Piggott	6	milieu. My father was a specialist/In pharmacology. And my husband/Was a

PHASE (2)
336 FR   Agatha   33   under an elder tree/According to the phase/Of the determined moon./A curse is like a
485 CC   Lady E   15   don't believe it now./That was only a phase. But it made it all so simple!/To be able to
PHEASANT (1)
214 RTTugger   2   is a Curious Cat:/If you offer him pheasant he would rather have grouse./If you
PHÉNICIEN (1)
51 Restaurant   25   pour la salle-de-bains./Phlébas, le Phénicien, pendant quinze jours noyé,/Oubliait
PHENOMENAL (1)
225 Mr Mistoff   54   in the hall./And not long ago this phenomenal Cat/Produced *seven kittens* right
PHILIP (1)
44 Cook Egg   10   in Heaven/For I shall meet Sir Philip Sidney/And have talk with Coriolanus/
PHILOMEL (1)
64 WL: Chess   99   upon the sylvan scene/The change of Philomel, by the barbarous king/So rudely
PHILOSOPHE (1)
47 Mél Adult   10   noir de jemenfoutiste./En Allemagne, philosophe/Surexcité par Emporheben/Au
PHILOSOPHY (1)
258 MC Thomas   12   in learning and in thought,/Music and philosophy, curiosity,/The purple bullfinch in
PHLACCUS (2)
31 Apollinax   6   in the swing./In the palace of Mrs. Phlaccus, at Professor Channing-Cheetah's/He
31 Apollinax   21   have challenged.'/Of dowager Mrs. Phlaccus, and Professor and Mrs. Cheetah/I
PHLEBAS (2)
71 WL: DWater 312   pluckest/burning/Death by Water/Phlebas the Phoenician, a fortnight dead,/
71 WL: DWater 321   and look to windward,/Consider Phlebas, who was once handsome and tall as
PHLÉBAS (1)
51 Restaurant   25   voilà dix sous, pour la salle-de-bains./Phlébas, le Phénicien, pendant quinze jours
PHOENICIAN (2)
62 WL: Burial   47   said she,/Is your card, the drowned Phoenician Sailor,/(Those are pearls that were
71 WL: DWater 312   /burning/Death by Water/Phlebas the Phoenician, a fortnight dead,/Forgot the cry of
PHONE (3)
116 SP   Dusty   35   and water/All right, Monday you'll phone through./Yes I'll tell her. Good bye.
322 FR   Winch   26   a word with you quiet,/Rather than phone and perhaps disturb her Ladyship./So I
461 CC   Eggers   5   non-plussed, you must get me on the phone./If I'm not in the house, I'll be out in the
PHOTOGRAPH (3)
182 FQ: ECoker 201   lamplight/(The evening with the photograph album)./Love is most nearly itself/
321 FR   Harry   7   talk about yourself./{H} I never saw a photograph. There is no portrait./{W} What I
483 CC   Lady E   23   I wanted. {}/[*rising*]./{LE} And I see a photograph in a silver frame./I'm afraid I shall
PHOTOGRAPHER (1)
301 FR   Chorus   18   shall be made public, the common photographer/Flashlight for the picture papers:
PHOTOGRAPHIC (2)
483 CC   Lady E   25   I shall have to instruct you, Colby./Photographic portraits — even in silver frames
483 CC   Lady E   28   your bedroom/Is the proper place for photographic souvenirs. {}/[*She sits down,*
PHOTOGRAPHS (1)
513 CC   Colby   32   that belonged to him, and faded photographs/In which I should try to decipher a
PHOTOSTATS (2)
553 ES   Carghil   31   in my lawyer's safe. But I have photostats/Which are quite as good, I'm told.
554 ES   Carghil   1   letters auctioned.'/Yes, I'll bring the photostats tomorrow morning,/And read them
PHRASE (6)
14 Prufrock   56   /The eyes that fix you in a formulated phrase,/And when I am formulated, sprawling
197 FQ: Little   218   end is where we start from. And every phrase/And sentence that is right (where every
197 FQ: Little   226   consort dancing together)/Every phrase and every sentence is an end and a
410 CP   Reilly   38   the sanatorium — you will forget this phrase,/And in forgetting it will alter the
553 ES   Carghil   17   we may *always* be together./There's a phrase I seem to remember reading somewhere:/
561 ES   Monica   36   my life for you./Oh, how silly that phrase sounds! But there's no vocabulary/For
PHRASES (1)
487 CC   Claude   5   them for me/With a few striking phrases. It should last about ten minutes./And
PHTHISIC (1)
41 Burb Blei   26   extends/A meagre, blue-nailed, phthisic hand/To climb the waterstair. Lights,
PHYSICAL (3)
404 CP   Edward   11   /{E} I once experienced the extreme of physical pain,/And now I know there is
419 CP   Reilly   29   on them./Some of them return, in a physical sense;/No one disappears. They lead
572 ES   Ld Clav   19   to each other,/Yet she had a peculiar physical attraction/Which no other woman has
PHYSIOGNOMY (1)
220 Old Deut   9   /At the sight of that placid and bland physiognomy,/When he sits in the sun on the
PIACULATIVE (1)
54 Mr E Sun   20   young are red and pustular/Clutching piaculative pence./Under the penitential gates/

PIANGE (1)

34 Figlia		t	we then so serious?'/La Figlia Che Piange/Stand on the highest pavement of the

PIANO (14)

446 CC	Claude	27	/I'm trying to find him a really good piano./{E} A piano? Yes, I'm sure he'll feel at
446 CC	Eggers	28	to find him a really good piano./{E} A piano? Yes, I'm sure he'll feel at home/When he
446 CC	Eggers	29	sure he'll feel at home/When he has a piano. You think of everything./But if I might
465 CC	Claude	27	.../I intend that you shall have a good piano. The best./And when you are alone at
465 CC	Claude	28	best./And when you are alone at your piano, in the evening,/I believe you will go
469 CC	2m	1	*weeks later.* COLBY *is seated at the piano;*/LUCASTA *in an armchair. The*
470 CC	Lucasta	2	a fraud. You know you told me/The piano was only delivered this week/And you
470 CC	Lucasta	5	to be the first to hear you play *this* piano./{C} That's not what I meant. I mean that
487 CC	Claude	11	me./Oh, by the way, Colby, how's the piano?/{C} It's a wonderful piano. I've never
487 CC	Colby	12	how's the piano?/{C} It's a wonderful piano. I've never played/On such an instrument.
487 CC	Claude	14	good for me./{SC} You need a good piano. You'll play all the better./{LE} Claude!/
492 CC	Claude	14	Can you find some consolation at the piano?/{C} I don't think, tonight, the piano
492 CC	Colby	15	piano?/{C} I don't think, tonight, the piano would help me:/At the moment, I never
518 CC	Eggers	1	other ways/Of making up an income. Piano lessons? —As a temporary measure;

PICCARDA (1)

44 Cook	Egg	24	me/In the Seven Sacred Trances;/Piccarda de Donati will conduct me./But where

PICK (5)

66 WL:	Chess	154	can get on with it, I said./Others can pick and choose if you can't./But if Albert
116 SP	Doris	15	can't you stop that horrible noise?/Pick up the receiver/{Du} What'll I say?/{Do}
118 SP	Doris	4	—/{Do} There's a lot in the way you pick them up/{Du} There's an awful lot in the
224 Mr Mistoff		27	walk on the narrowest rail./He can pick any card from a pack,/He is equally
458 CC	Claude	3	up./{SC} Colby, sit at the desk, and pick up some papers./We must look as if we'd

PICKED (3)

71 WL:	DWater	316	profit and loss./A current under sea/Picked his bones in whispers. As he rose and fell
451 CC	Eggers	6	Claude,/As he ought to be. Sir Claude picked him out/And gave him his start. And
496 CC	Eggers	27	the late editions/Of the papers that I picked up at Liverpool Street./But I've so much

PICKING (1)

257 MC	Chorus	19	on living,/Living and partly living,/Picking together the pieces,/Gathering faggots

PICKINGS (1)

576 ES	Michael	16	/With a jolly good screw, and some pickings in commissions./He's made a fortune

PICKS (1)

373 CP	m	3	ALEX *and* PETER]/[EDWARD *picks up the telephone, and dials a number*]/{E}

PICNIC (1)

316 FR	Chorus	1	/The tenants' dinner, the family picnic on the moors. Have torn/The roof from

PICNICS (1)

148 Rock 1		34	/That the country now is only fit for picnics./And the Church does not seem to be

PICTURE (9)

301 FR	Chorus	19	photographer/Flashlight for the picture papers: why do we huddle together/In a
370 CP	Peter	20	has simply faded — into some other picture —/Like a film effect. She doesn't want
388 CP	Celia	11	I depended on you for concerts,/And picture exhibitions — more than you realised./It
425 CP	Lavinia	34	That's what makes it a success. Is that picture straight?/{E} Yes, it is./{L} No, it isn't.
430 CP	Peter	37	/{P} Alex knows./Did you see my last picture, Alex?/{A} I knew about it, but I didn't
437 CP	Reilly	20	May tend to express itself at once in a picture./That happens to me, sometimes. So it
454 CC	Eggers	22	sane./{E} I should call him the very picture of sanity./{C} But you never warned me
544 ES	Ld Clav	13	days of people not staring/Or offering picture papers, or wanting a fourth at bridge;/
562 ES	Carghil	21	/When he was your age. He's the picture of you, Richard,/As you were once.

PICTURES (5)

305 FR	Harry	27	/The same hangings ... the same pictures ... even the table,/The chairs, the sofa ...
367 CP	Edward	19	/{E} A common interest in the moving pictures/Frequently brings young people
369 CP	Peter	34	went to concerts alone/And to look at pictures. So we often met/In the same way, and
371 CP	Peter	20	certain music? Or looked at certain pictures?/There was something real. But what is
431 CP	Peter	1	Where's that? They don't have pictures?/Pan-Am-Eagle must look into this./

PIE (2)

235 Ad-dress		57	supply/Some caviare, or Strassburg Pie,/Some potted grouse, or salmon paste —/
588 Fable		52	of turtle eggs,/And after that a great pie made of plover,/And flagons which perhaps

PIECE (7)

185 FQ:	DrySal	44	to unweave, unwind, unravel/And piece together the past and the future,/Between
240 MC	Chorus	3	/And the labourer bends to his piece of earth, earth-colour, his own colour,/
362 CP	Reilly	40	But, stretched on the table,/You are a piece of furniture in a repair shop/For those
469 CC	3m	1	*an armchair. The concluding bars of a piece of music are/heard as the curtain rises.*/{L} I
488 CC	Claude	5	Guzzard./{SC} I'm beginning now to piece it together./You've been asking Colby
530 ES	Ld Clav	36	contributions/That bought this piece of silver! The inadequate levy/That made

580 ES	Carghil	17	talked it all over./But I've got a little piece of news of my own:/Next autumn, I'm

PIECES (6)

103 Journ Magi		27	/Six hands at an open door dicing for pieces of silver,/And feet kicking the empty
108 Animula		33	and power,/For Boudin, blown to pieces,/For this one who made a great fortune,/
257 MC Chorus		19	and partly living,/Picking together the pieces,/Gathering faggots at nightfall,/Building
405 CP	Reilly	2	the case that my patients/Are only pieces of a total situation/Which I have to
466 CC	Claude	8	to yourself. And as for me,/I keep my pieces in a private room./It isn't that I don't
469 CC	Colby	13	/I've given you a test. Several of the pieces/That I've just played you were very

PIERCE (2)

106 Song Sime		32	me thy peace./(And a sword shall pierce thy heart,/Thine also)./I am tired with my
271 MC Thomas		12	/But know that another/Shall pierce you with a sudden painful joy/When the

PIERCED (1)

160 Rock 7		12	/As the air of temperate seas is pierced by the still dead breath of the Arctic

PIERRES (1)

48 Lune Miel		18	de Dieu, tient encore/Dans ses pierres écroulantes la forme précise de Byzance./

PIES (1)

588 Fable		47	fable/To fill out their repast, and pies and puddings,/And jellies, pasties, cakes

PIETY (1)

111 Xmas Trees		22	the consciousness of failure,/Or in the piety of the convert/Which may be tainted with

PIG-STY (1)

191 FQ: Little		30	the rough road/And turn behind the pig-sty to the dull façade/And the tombstone.

PIGGOTT (18)

523 ES	m	7	/FEDERICO GOMEZ/MRS. PIGGOTT/MRS. CARGHILL/MICHAEL
545 ES	m	22	start reading to me. {}/[*Enter* MRS. PIGGOTT]/{MP} Good morning, Lord
546 ES	Piggott	16	Miss Claverton-Ferry. I'm Mrs. Piggott./Just call me Mrs. Piggott. It's a short
546 ES	Piggott	17	I'm Mrs. Piggott./Just call me Mrs. Piggott. It's a short and simple name/And easy
546 ES	Piggott	30	remember/Always to call me Mrs. Piggott, won't you?/{M} Yes, Mrs. Piggott, but
546 ES	Monica	31	Piggott, won't you?/{M} Yes, Mrs. Piggott, but please tell me one thing./We
546 ES	Piggott	38	balanced:/For me to be simply 'Mrs. Piggott'/Reassures the guests in one respect;/
547 ES	Ld Clav	13	could be worse. Where there's a Mrs. Piggott/There may be, among the guests,
547 ES	Ld Clav	14	guests, something worse than Mrs. Piggott./{M} Let's hope this was merely the
547 ES	m	19	will leave us alone. {}/[*Re-enter* MRS. PIGGOTT]/{MP} I really *am* neglectful!/Miss
547 ES	Monica	32	in my opinion./{M} Thank you, Mrs. Piggott. But I'm very fond of walking/And I'm
554 ES	Carghil	3	read them to you./— Oh, there's Mrs. Piggott!/She's bearing down on us. Isn't she
554 ES	Carghil	8	tomorrow./Good morning, Mrs. Piggott!/Isn't it a glorious morning! {}/[*Enter*
554 ES	m	10	it a glorious morning! {}/[*Enter* MRS. PIGGOTT]/{MP} Good morning, Mrs.
554 ES	Carghil	11	Mrs. Carghill!/{MC} Dear Mrs. Piggott!/It seems to me that you never sit still:/
554 ES	Carghil	16	{MC} You do look after us well, Mrs. Piggott:/You're so considerate — and so
555 ES	Monica	12	I must fly. {}/[*Exit*]/{M} I saw Mrs. Piggott bothering you again/So I hurried to
567 ES	Monica	5	telephoned this morning. That Mrs. Piggott/Should have heard my beloved's voice/

PILE (1)

154 Rock 3		25	broken chimney,/The peeled hull, a pile of rusty iron,/In a street of scattered brick

PILED (1)

68 WL: Fire S		226	the sun's last rays,/On the divan are piled (at night her bed)/Stockings, slippers,

PILES (1)

41 Burb Blei		22	once./The rats are underneath the piles./The Jew is underneath the lot./Money in

PILGRIM'S (1)

140 Usk		11	the green air/The hermit's chapel, the pilgrim's prayer./Rannoch, by Glencoe/Here the

PILGRIMAGE (2)

350 FR	Agatha	13	/Follow follow/{Ag} This way the pilgrimage/Of expiation/Round and round the
350 FR	Agatha	22	the curse be ended/By intercession/By pilgrimage/By those who depart/In several

PILGRIMS (1)

254 MC Tempt4		17	frightened of a shade;/Think of pilgrims, standing in line/Before the glittering

PILLAGED (1)

254 MC Tempt4		32	bird mourns;/That the shrine shall be pillaged, and the gold spent,/The jewels gone for

PILLIONS (1)

153 Rock 2		51	/And daughters ride away on casual pillions./Much to cast down, much to build,

PILLOW (3)

16 Prufrock		96	I shall tell you all' —/If one, settling a pillow by her head,/Should say: 'That is not
16 Prufrock		107	been worth while/If one, settling a pillow or throwing off a shawl,/And turning
42 Swee Erect		20	of the bed/And clawing at the pillow slip./Sweeney addressed full length to

PILLS (1)

66 WL: Chess		159	she said, pulling a long face,/It's them pills I took, to bring it off, she said./(She's had

PIN (3)

14 Prufrock	43	and modest, but asserted by a simple pin —/(They will say: 'But how his arms and
14 Prufrock	57	I am formulated, sprawling on a pin,/When I am pinned and wriggling on the
24 Rhapsody	22	of her eye/Twists like a crooked pin.'/The memory throws up high and dry/A

PINCHED (5)

124 SA Swarts	18	a bath/{Sw} These fellows always get pinched in the end./{Sn} Excuse me, they don't
124 SA Snow	19	/{Sn} Excuse me, they don't all get pinched in the end./What about them bones on
124 SA Snow	23	it in the papers/They *don't* all get pinched in the end./{Do} A woman runs a
124 SA Sweeney	26	his story./{S} This one didn't get pinched in the end/But that's another story too.
602 Humoresque	8	face,/(The kind of face that we forget)/Pinched in a comic, dull grimace;/Half bullying,

PINCHING (1)

136 5FingerEx3	10	take/That which is their mortal due,/Pinching bread and finger too,/Easier had than

PINE (5)

73 WL: Thund	356	/Where the hermit-thrush sings in the pine trees/Drip drop drip drop drop drop drop/
109 Marina	3	water lapping the bow/And scent of pine and the woodthrush singing through the
109 Marina	15	reduced by a wind,/A breath of pine, and the woodsong fog/By this grace
590 Time Space	14	pluck anew/Nor mourn to see them pine,/And though our days of love be few/Yet
590 Space Time	14	pluck anew/Nor mourn to see them pine,/And though the flowers of life be few/Yet

PING (1)

219 Mung Rump	36	/Or down from the library came a loud *ping*/From a vase which was commonly said to be

PINK (3)

32 Hysteria	6	hands/was hurriedly spreading a pink and white checked cloth over the rusty/
42 Swee Erect	22	full length to shave/Broadbottomed, pink from nape to base,/Knows the female
605 Narcissus	27	his ancient beauty/Caught fast in the pink tips of his new beauty./Then he had been a

PINNED (1)

14 Prufrock	58	sprawling on a pin,/When I am pinned and wriggling on the wall,/Then how

PINT (2)

150 Rock 1	104	*to two men,/To two women one half pint of bitter/Ale. In this land/No man has hired*
161 Rock 7	35	*to two men,/To two women one half pint of bitter/Ale..../CHORUS:/What does the*

PIPE (1)

177 FQ: ECoker	27	you can hear the music/Of the weak pipe and the little drum/And see them dancing

PIPER (7)

284 FR m	3	*sisters/COL. THE HON. GERALD PIPER, and THE HON. CHARLES PIPER,*
284 FR m	3	PIPER, *and* THE HON. CHARLES PIPER, *brothers of her deceased husband/*
328 FR Charles	12	/The Hon. Arthur Gerald Charles Piper, younger brother of Lord/Monchensey,
328 FR Charles	17	his car from the collision, Mr. Piper reversed/into a shop-window. When
328 FR Charles	18	shop-window. When challenged, Mr. Piper said:/"I thought it was all open country
328 FR Charles	22	that at the time of the/accident Mr. Piper was being pursued by a patrol, and was/
328 FR Charles	27	out of./{C} There's a little more. 'The Piper family ...' no, we needn't read that./{V}

PIPERS (1)

223 Pekes Pols	36	/And so they stepped out, with their pipers in order,/Playing *When the Blue Bonnets*

PIPES (2)

15 Prufrock	71	watched the smoke that rises from the pipes/Of lonely men in shirt-sleeves, leaning out
23 Preludes	43	/And short square fingers stuffing pipes,/And evening newspapers, and eyes/

PIPIT (3)

44 Cook Egg	1	glass of brandy neat./A Cooking Egg/Pipit sate upright in her chair/Some distance
44 Cook Egg	21	could provide./I shall not want Pipit in Heaven:/Madame Blavatsky will
45 Cook Egg	26	the penny world I bought/To eat with Pipit behind the screen?/The red-eyed

PIPIT'S (1)

44 Cook Egg	20	anecdotes will be more amusing/Than Pipit's experience could provide./I shall not

PIRATE (1)

236 Cat Morgan	1	Introduces Himself/I once was a Pirate what sailed the 'igh seas —/But now I've

PISTE (1)

47 Mél Adult	4	en sueur/Que vous suivrez à peine ma piste./En Yorkshire, conférencier;/A Londres,

PISTILLATE (1)

55 Mr E Sun	27	pass between/The staminate and pistillate./Blest office of the epicene./Sweeney

PIT (3)

153 Rock 2	54	waste;/Let the clay be dug from the pit, let the saw cut the stone,/Let the fire not be
166 Rock 10	7	ever half awake, at the bottom of the pit of the world, curled/In folds of himself until
166 Rock 10	9	/But the Mystery of Iniquity is a pit too deep for mortal eyes to plumb. Come/Ye

PITTANCE (1)

453 CC Lucasta	10	/Is often very hungry — living on a pittance —/Cooking a sausage on a gas ring .../

PITY (4)

601 Nocturne		6	strikes some tune/Banal, and out of pity for their fate/Behind the wall I have some
396 CP	Lavinia	16	me how well suited we were./{L} It's a pity that you had no opinion of your own./Oh,
527 ES	Charles	32	me./{C} I know it's been you./It's a pity that you haven't had brothers and sisters/
563 ES	Carghil	34	Oh, did you never see me?/That's a pity, Señor Gomez./{G} I lost touch with things

PLACE (92)

89 Ash-Wed 1		17	I know that time is always time/And place is always and only place/And what is
89 Ash-Wed 1		17	time/And place is always and only place/And what is actual is actual only for one
89 Ash-Wed 1		19	only for one time/And only for one place/I rejoice that things are as they are and/I
96 Ash-Wed 5		17	time/The right time and the right place are not here/No place of grace for those
96 Ash-Wed 5		18	and the right place are not here/No place of grace for those who avoid the face/No
98 Ash-Wed 6		21	tension between dying and birth/The place of solitude where three dreams cross/
103 Journ Magi		31	not a moment too soon/Finding the place; it was (you may say) satisfactory./All this
109 Marina		16	fog/By this grace dissolved in place/What is this face, less clear and clearer/
120 SP	Klip	5	You said it, Krum./London's a slick place, London's a swell place,/London's a fine
120 SP	Klip	5	a slick place, London's a swell place,/London's a fine place to come on a visit
120 SP	Klip	6	a swell place,/London's a fine place to come on a visit —/{Kr} Specially when
147 Rock 1		24	Men do not need the Church/In the place where they work, but where they spend
151 Rock 2		14	earth./When your fathers fixed the place of GOD,/And settled all the inconvenient
157 Rock 4		14	lay waste, consumed with fire;/No place for a beast to pass./There were enemies
160 Rock 7		3	this way and that, and finding no place of lodgement and germination./They
163 Rock 8		30	broken lives,/The broken faith in one place or another,/There was something left that
164 Rock 9		23	feelings, words that have taken the place of thoughts and feelings,/There spring the
173 FQ: BurntN		71	I cannot say, how long, for that is to place it in time./The inner freedom from the
173 FQ: BurntN		93	time time is conquered./Here is a place of disaffection/Time before and time after/
175 FQ: BurntN	155		with imprecision, will not stay in place,/Will not stay still. Shrieking voices/
177 FQ: ECoker		3	destroyed, restored, or in their place/Is an open field, or a factory, or a by-pass.
191 FQ: Little		23	you would be likely to take/From the place you would be likely to come from,/If you
192 FQ: Little		39	or a city —/But this is the nearest, in place and time,/Now and in England./If you
192 FQ: Little		59	/Dust in the air suspended/Marks the place where a story ended./Dust inbreathed was
195 FQ: Little	171		shall be well./If I think, again, of this place,/And of people, not wholly commendable,
197 FQ: Little	220		every word is at home,/Taking its place to support the others,/The word neither
197 FQ: Little	244		where we started/And know the place for the first time./Through the unknown,
204 de la Mare		3	island with a sandy cove/(A hiding place, but very dangerous ground,/For here the
218 Mung Rump		5	in Cornwall Gardens, in Launceston Place and in Kensington Square —/They had
227 Macavity		38	/At whatever time the deed took place — MACAVITY WASN'T THERE!/And
228 Gus		12	his friends at their club/(Which takes place at the back of the neighbouring pub)/He
604 Ode		12	that of Harvard we carry away/In the place of the life that we leave./And only the
240 MC Priest2		33	/Meetings unended or endless/At one place or another in France?/{P3} I see nothing
253 MC Tempt4		2	/To meet before was never time or place./{T} Say what you come to say./{T4} It
254 MC Tempt4		22	think of your enemies, in another place./{T} I have thought of these things./{T4}
266 MC Knights		15	by the King; whom he set in your place to carry out his command./You are his
280 MC Priest1		6	How shall we find you, from what far place?/Do you look down on us? You now in
285 FR Agatha		13	/{Ag} Wishwood was always a cold place, Amy./{I} I have always told Amy she
291 FR Gerald		4	with Compton-Smith, down at his place in Dorset./{V} I should have been helping
300 FR Downing		18	and gymnasiums/There's not even a place where a man can go/For a quiet smoke,
306 FR Harry	13		I never should. I thought it was a place/Where life was substantial and simplified
306 FR Harry	15		—/But the simplification took place in my memory,/I think. It seems I shall get
307 FR Harry	15		to the river/To find the old hiding place. The wilderness was gone,/The tree had
308 FR Mary	15		keeps springing/In an unexpected place, while we are unconscious of it./You
315 FR Warburt	15		/Wishwood was always a cold place, but healthy./It's only when I get an
331 FR Harry	8		had left it,/Everything would fall into place. But *they* prevent it./I still have to find out
332 FR Agatha	14		/Until she took your father's place, and reached the point where/Wishwood
336 FR Harry	3		the pursuers,/And come into a quiet place./Why is it so quiet?/Do you feel a kind of
336 FR	3m 23		*empty embrasure. She steps into/the place which the EUMENIDES had occupied.*]/
337 FR Agatha	11		found a clue, hidden in the obvious place./Delay, and it is lost. Love compels
365 CP	Julia	34	too much mystery/About this place to-day./{E} I'm very sorry./{J} No, I love
377 CP	Julia	20	an inspiration!/There's nothing in the place fit to eat:/I've looked high and low. But I
393 CP	Lavinia	21	go/Unless you suggested some other place first?/And I remember that finally in
397 CP	Edward	12	only yesterday/That damnation took place. And now I must live with it/Day by day,
402 CP	Reilly	30	/For whom a sanatorium is the worst place possible./We must first find out what is
403 CP	Edward	38	together!/She has made the world a place I cannot live in/Except on her terms. I
414 CP	Celia	16	/Now they can't afford to have a place in town./It's all they can do to keep the
418 CP	Reilly	29	you have sought for in the wrong place./{C} That sounds like what I want. But
419 CP	Celia	23	stay there!/I mean, it would make the place so over-crowded./{R} Not very many go.

422 CP	Alex	15	protection of the stars./{A} Let them place a chair each side of it./{J} May the holy
427 CP	Julia	21	/What were you doing in this strange place —/What's it called?/{A} Kinkanja./{J}
430 CP	Peter	22	/At the Saffron Monkey. That's the place to go now./{A} How very odd. *My*
431 CP	Peter	3	into this./Perhaps it would be a good place to make one./— Alex knows all about
438 CP	Reilly	9	/But that world does not take the place of this one./Do you imagine that the Saint
464 CC	Claude	26	/{SC} Family pressure, in the first place./My father — your grandfather — built
466 CC	Claude	14	It's all I have./I suppose it takes the place of religion:/Just as my wife's
479 CC	Kaghan	33	say, I like the way you've had the place done up./{C} It was Lady Elizabeth chose
481 CC	Lady E	21	of decoration/Is *right*, until the place has been lived in/By the person for whom
482 CC	Lady E	30	should like to know./{LE} In the first place, you ought to mix with people of
483 CC	Lady E	28	it? Surely your bedroom/Is the proper place for photographic souvenirs. {}/[*She sits*
488 CC	Claude	31	/And that he might come to take the place of your own child,/If you got to know him
491 CC	Colby	22	I think,/To accept you both in the place of parents/If neither of you could be. If it
493 CC	Claude	20	roundabout way. But where shall we place her?/{LE} Over there, with the light full on
494 CC	Lady E	6	were yours ... he could still take the place/Of my son: and so he could be *our* son./
510 CC	Kaghan	30	the country./So I found them a little place near Sevenoaks/Where they keep bees.
515 CC	Guzzard	27	come to nothing?/When I gave up my place as Colby's mother/I gave up something I
524 ES	Charles	13	intimate friends./{C} It's the only place where I'm really well known/And get well
524 ES	Charles	22	does feel a fool/If he takes you to a place where he's utterly unknown/And the
527 ES	Monica	1	right to criticise my father./In the first place, you don't understand him;/In the second
527 ES	Monica	2	don't understand him;/In the second place, we're not engaged yet./{C} Aren't we?
528 ES	Monica	29	longer./That's why Selby chose the place. A *convalescent* home/With the
528 ES	Monica	38	the winter in Jamaica/Will never take place. 'Make the reservations'/Selby said, 'as if
531 ES	Ld Clav	25	/Of those who really understand the place we filled/Are inwardly delighted. They
541 ES	Gomez	18	times over. San Marco's a good place/To make money in — though not to *keep*
556 ES	Michael	16	two miles from here. Not a bad little place./{LC} Why are you staying there? I
556 ES	Ld Clav	18	have thought/It would be the sort of place that you'd choose for a holiday./{Mi}
558 ES	Michael	21	working in that office./In the first place, they all knew the job had been made for
561 ES	Michael	16	play the hero/If you were in my place. I don't believe you would./*You* didn't
563 ES	Ld Clav	4	foreigner?/{LC} He comes from some place in Central America./{MC} How romantic!
573 ES	Ld Clav	17	persecution?/{LC} To the end. The place and time of liberation/Are, I think,
574 ES	Michael	36	send you back reports. Some sort of place/Where everyone would sneer at the fellow
577 ES	Ld Clav	40	a free agent. So if he chooses/To place himself in your power, Fred Culverwell,/

PLACED (1)

506 CC	Eggers	1	of by the father./That is to say, placed out to be cared for/Till further notice by

PLACES (20)

72 WL: Thund	324	the gardens/After the agony in stony places/The shouting and the crying/Prison and
85 Hollow Men	57	lost kingdoms/In this last of meeting places/We grope together/And avoid speech/
104 Journ Magi	40	Death, our death./We returned to our places, these Kingdoms,/But no longer at ease
149 Rock 1	79	*are heard chanting./In the vacant places/We will build with new bricks/There are*
149 Rock 1	97	*lowered faces/We stand about in open places/And shiver in unlit rooms./Only the wind*
162 Rock 8	9	the shame of Jerusalem/And the holy places defiled;/Peter the Hermit, scourging with
162 Rock 8	14	who were neither./Like all men in all places,/Some went from love of glory,/Some
192 FQ: Little	36	altered in fulfilment. There are other places/Which also are the world's end, some at
195 FQ: Little	166	See, now they vanish,/The faces and places, with the self which, as it could, loved
196 FQ: Little	180	a few who died forgotten/In other places, here and abroad,/And of one who died
203 Indians	9	foreign men, who fought in foreign places,/Foreign to each other./A man's
270 MC Chorus	4	and horn, tusk and hoof, in odd places;/I have lain on the floor of the sea and
281 MC Chorus	18	enrich the earth, shall create the holy places./For wherever a saint has dwelt, wherever
282 MC Chorus	2	in the desert, the prayer in forgotten places by the broken imperial column,/From
292 FR	Harry	11	to Wishwood?/There were a thousand places where I might have met them!/Why here?
493 CC	Claude	2	what are you doing?/{SC} Settling the places./It's important, when you have a difficult
506 CC	Eggers	37	Lady Elizabeth,/There are other places that sound like Teddington/But not so
533 ES	Gomez	35	out in the right manner/In the right places, pays many times over./I assure you it
550 ES	Carghil	29	/Should meet here at last? Here, of all places!/{LC} Why not, of all places? What I
550 ES	Ld Clav	30	of all places!/{LC} Why not, of all places? What I don't understand/Is why you

PLACID (2)

220 Old Deut	9	him in his decline./At the sight of that placid and bland physiognomy,/When he sits in
395 CP	Lavinia	35	about you/Has always been your placid assumption/That I wasn't worth the

PLACIDLY (1)

526 ES	Charles	35	for you belong to him./He seems so placidly to take it for granted/That you don't

PLAGUE (3)

253 MC Tempt4	34	mastery of melting armies,/War, plague, and revolution,/New conspiracies,
434 CP	Alex	4	the conditions are favourable to plague./{E} Go on./{A} It seems that there were
434 CP	Alex	30	died anyway;/Being tainted with the plague, they were not eaten./{L} Oh, Edward,

PLAGUE-STRICKEN (1)
434 CP Edward 27 .../{E} And just for a handful of plague-stricken natives/Who would have died
PLAIN (6)
74 WL: Thund 424 upon the shore/Fishing, with the arid plain behind me/Shall I at least set my lands in
250 MC Tempt3 38 straight forward./{T3} Purpose is plain./Endurance of friendship does not depend/
258 MC Thomas 3 is my way clear, now is the meaning plain:/Temptation shall not come in this kind
277 MC Knight3 5 to lose than to gain. We are four plain Englishmen/who put our country first. I
525 ES Charles 3 free for the whole afternoon/On the plain understanding .../{M} That you should
533 ES Gomez 2 we were up at Oxford, you were plain Dick Ferry./Then, when you married, you
PLAINS (2)
73 WL: Thund 369 hordes swarming/Over endless plains, stumbling in cracked earth/Ringed by
178 FQ: ECoker 65 Leonids fly/Hunt the heavens and the plains/Whirled in a vortex that shall bring/The
PLAN (1)
303 FR Mary 17 told me;/It is very difficult, having to plan/For uncertain numbers. Why did she ask
PLANE (1)
456 CC Colby 39 Perhaps she won't even arrive by this plane./{E} Oh, that could happen. She
PLANES (1)
324 FR Harry 34 to be awake,/To be living on several planes at once/Though one cannot speak with
PLANK (1)
213 Growltiger 50 vast surprise was forced to walk the plank./He who a hundred victims had driven to
PLANNED (3)
341 FR Amy 31 family and his happiness?/Who has planned his good? is it you or I?/Thirty-five
488 CC Claude 28 What happens is so like what one had planned for,/And yet such a travesty of all one's
579 ES Carghil 14 before him/Than he had it all planned out! It really was an inspiration —/On
PLANNING (2)
240 MC Chorus 20 /Who do, some well, some ill, planning and guessing,/Having their aims which
393 CP Lavinia 17 what was coming —/When we were planning our honeymoon,/I couldn't make you
PLANS (5)
226 Macavity 28 astray,/Or the Admiralty lose some plans and drawings by the way,/There may be a
448 CC Claude 28 that point/I haven't yet explained my plans to you./Why I've never told her about
458 CC Claude 20 /But why did you change your plans?/{LE} Because of Mildred Deverell./She's
488 CC Claude 29 /And yet such a travesty of all one's plans —/I'd hoped that you would become fond
516 CC Claude 2 It shall make no difference/To my plans for your future./{C} Thank you, Sir
PLANT (1)
340 FR Amy 17 could breed for myself,/What I could plant here. Seven years I kept him,/For the sake
PLANTATION (1)
288 FR Agatha 37 coach-house, in the orchard,/In the plantation, down the corridor/That led to the
PLANTED (1)
63 WL: Burial 71 the ships at Mylae!/'That corpse you planted last year in your garden,/'Has it begun
PLASTER (1)
154 Rock 3 18 GOD./Will you build me a house of plaster, with corrugated roofing,/To be filled
PLASTIC (1)
365 CP Julia 2 tell if they're mine —/Some kind of a plastic sort of frame —/I'm afraid I don't
PLATE (2)
14 Prufrock 30 That lift and drop a question on your plate;/Time for you and time for me,/And time
56 Swee Night 6 /Slide westward toward the River Plate,/Death and the Raven drift above/And
PLATES (1)
27 Morning 1 Window/They are rattling breakfast plates in basement kitchens,/And along the
PLATFORM (1)
188 FQ: DrySal 136 those who saw them off have left the platform)/Their faces relax from grief into relief,
PLATO (1)
209 NamingCats 11 some for the dames:/Such as Plato, Admetus, Electra, Demeter —/But all of
PLATTER (1)
15 Prufrock 82 slightly bald) brought in upon a platter,/I am no prophet — and here's no great
PLAUSIBLE (4)
218 Mung Rump 20 no regular occupation./They were plausible fellows, and liked to engage a friendly
370 CP Peter 22 to see me;/Makes excuses, not very plausible,/And when I do see her, she seems
401 CP Edward 9 who did not know you./Yet Alex is so plausible. And his recommendations/Of shops,
515 CC Claude 19 so it went on./{SC} This is horribly plausible. But it can't be true./{MG} Consider,
PLAY (35)
65 WL: Chess 137 a closed car at four./And we shall play a game of chess,/Pressing lidless eyes and
167 Rock 10 36 are glad when the day ends, when the play ends; and ecstasy is too much pain./We are
167 Rock 10 37 fired; and the day is long for work or play./We tire of distraction or concentration, we
212 Growltiger 21 summer night, all nature seemed at play,/The tender moon was shining bright,/the
224 Mr Mistoff 31 he's only hunting for mice./He can play any trick with a cork/Or a spoon and a bit

PLEAD (1)
273 MC Chorus   2   /We fear, we fear. Who shall then plead for me,/Who intercede for me, in my most
PLEADING (1)
565 ES Ld Clav   33   a hypocrite!/A few minutes ago I was pleading with Michael/Not to try to escape
PLEASANT (10)
 69 WL: Fire S 261   bar in Lower Thames Street,/The pleasant whining of a mandoline/And a clatter
148 Rock 1   33   I was told/Of economic laws./In the pleasant countryside, there it seemed/That the
148 Rock 1   48   /Or irregular labour, which is not pleasant./I have trodden the winepress alone,
216 Jellicles   8   Cats are merry and bright,/And pleasant to hear when they caterwaul./Jellicle
233 Skimble   33   Skimbleshanks is aboard./Oh it's very pleasant when you have found your little den/
245 MC Priest2   9   /Let me ask you at the least to put on pleasant faces,/And give a hearty welcome to
248 MC Tempt2   18   them,/Let us but set these not too pleasant memories/In balance against other,
387 CP Celia   3   in twenty-four hours./It wasn't a very pleasant experience./Oh, I'm glad I came!/I can
545 ES Monica   10   that at the moment you find life pleasant,/That it really does seem quiet here and
577 ES Gomez   10   you pleasure?/{G} Yes, it's always pleasant/To repay an old debt. And better late
PLEASANT-SPOKEN (1)
532 ES Lambert   3   of him. But talks good English./A pleasant-spoken gentleman. {}/[*after reading the*
PLEASANTER (1)
560 ES Michael   7   simply don't know how very much pleasanter/You will find life become, once I'm
PLEASE (38)
 65 WL: Chess   141   I said to her myself,/HURRY UP PLEASE ITS TIME/Now Albert's coming
 66 WL: Chess   152   give me a straight look./HURRY UP PLEASE ITS TIME/If you don't like it you can
 66 WL: Chess   165   don't want children?/HURRY UP PLEASE ITS TIME/Well, that Sunday Albert
 66 WL: Chess   168   the beauty of it hot —/HURRY UP PLEASE ITS TIME/HURRY UP PLEASE
 66 WL: Chess   169   PLEASE ITS TIME/HURRY UP PLEASE ITS TIME/Goonight Bill. Goonight
124 SA Doris   3   did a girl in —/{Do} Oh Mr. Sweeney, please don't talk,/I cut the cards before you
128 Cor1 March   47   /It'll come in handy. He's artful. Please, will you/Give us a light?/Light/Light/*Et*
181 FQ: ECoker 156   nurse/Whose constant care is not to please/But to remind of our, and Adam's curse,/
204 de la Mare   11   curtains drawn/Demand some poetry, please. Whose shall it be,/At not quite time for
212 Growltiger   5   and appearance did not calculate to please;/His coat was torn and seedy, he was
222 Pekes Pols   25   although people may say what they please,/Is no British Dog, but a Heathen
224 Mr Mistoff   4   /(There can be no doubt about that)./Please listen to me and don't scoff. All his/
265 MC Priest1 24   entertainment/Before your business. Please dine with us./Your men shall be looked
277 MC Knight3 25   that. So, as I said at the beginning, please give us/at least the credit for being
280 MC Knight1   3   now disperse quietly to your homes./Please be careful not to loiter in groups at street
290 FR Amy   17   /Do not discuss his absence. Please behave only/As if nothing had happened
293 FR Harry   18   that you have conspired to invent, please do so/In my absence. I shall be less
297 FR Charles 29   him I'd like to have a word with him, please. {}/[Exit DENMAN]/{V} Charles, if you
307 FR Harry   17   summer-house/Had been erected, 'to please the children'./It's absurd that one's only
309 FR Harry   10   for dinner./{H} No, no, don't go! Please don't leave me/Just at this moment. I feel
341 FR Amy   27   Who set you up to judge? what, if you please,/Gives *you* the power to know what is
344 FR Harry   38   it so ridiculous/Just now? I only want, please,/As little fuss as possible. You must get
361 CP Edward 12   me./{UG} Then I suggest .../{E} And please don't suggest./I have often used these
372 CP Edward 38   Alex. Oh, and if you don't mind,/Please *shut the door after you*, so that it latches.
381 CP Celia   20   I could understand./And, Edward, please believe that whatever happens/I shall not
401 CP Reilly   2   Good morning, Mr. Chamberlayne./Please sit down. I won't keep you a moment./—
401 CP Reilly   14   well go away at once./{R} No. If you please, sit down, Mr. Chamberlayne./You are
404 CP Reilly   9   /And letting you talk as long as you please,/And taking note of what you do not say.
405 CP Reilly   31   Mr. Chamberlayne./Sit down, both of you. Mrs. Chamberlayne,/Your
425 CP Lavinia 36   /{E} Yes, it is./{L} No, it isn't. Do please straighten it./{E} Is it straight now?/{L}
435 CP Lavinia 35   to meet your own needs./Peter, please don't think I'm being unkind .../{P} No, I
505 CC Claude   18   open the discussion?/{SC} If you please, Eggerson./{E} Then let's make a start./
526 ES Monica   27   *trolley*]/{M} and I shall say, 'Lambert,/Please let his lordship know that tea is waiting'./
532 ES Ld Clav 27   Lord./{LC} Goodbye, Charles. And please remember/That we both want to see you,
546 ES Monica   31   you?/{M} Yes, Mrs. Piggott, but please tell me one thing./We haven't seen her
549 ES Carghil 39   so too. But as you remember,/Please, Richard, just repeat my name — just
557 ES Ld Clav   4   in trouble again./We'll ignore, if you please, the question of blame:/Which will spare
574 ES Charles   5   going to call you Charles!/{C} As you please, Mrs. Carghill,/{LC} You said you had
PLEASED (10)
119 SP Klip   9   do/{Kr} How do you do/{Kl} I'm very pleased to make your acquaintance/{Kr}
119 SP Krum   10   your acquaintance/{Kr} Extremely pleased to become acquainted/{Kl} Sam — I
119 SP Klip   35   catch your name —/But I'm very pleased to meet you all the same) —/London's a
374 CP Celia   7   .../I must say you don't seem very pleased to see me./Edward, I understand what
391 CP Lavinia 34   /{L} I must say, you don't seem very pleased to see me./{E} I can't say that I've had
431 CP Peter   29   script of this film,/And Bela is very pleased with it./He thought I should see the

445 CC   Eggers   17   she's been wanting. So *she*'ll be pleased./Then I lunched at the store — they
515 CC   Guzzard   8   that it was yours;/And you were so pleased, I shrank, at the moment,/From
517 CC   Eggers   35   Church Council will be only too pleased,/And I have some influence. *I* am the
518 CC   Eggers   21   approved./{E} There'll be no one so pleased as Mrs. E.;/Of that I can assure you./

PLEASES (1)
580 ES   Carghil   21   San Marco./I'm so excited! But what pleases me most/Is that I shall be able to bring

PLEASING (1)
317 FR   Harry   25   /The rule of conduct was simply pleasing mother;/Misconduct was simply being

PLEASURE (10)
107 Animula   8   knee,/Eager to be reassured, taking pleasure/In the fragrant brilliance of the
107 Animula   10   brilliance of the Christmas tree,/Pleasure in the wind, the sunlight and the sea;/
253 MC   Tempt4   24   the way already chosen./But what is pleasure, kingly rule,/Or rule of men beneath a
255 MC   Thomas   20   have come, temporal tempters,/With pleasure and power at palpable price./What do
258 MC   Thomas   10   I searched all the ways/That lead to pleasure, advancement and praise./Delight in
315 FR   Warburt   28   will go first, in to dinner./{W} With pleasure, Lady Monchensey,/And I hope that
349 FR   Gerald   9   valid?/{G} I do not look forward with pleasure to dealing with Arthur and John in the
542 ES   Ld Clav   29   And what if I decline/To give you the pleasure of my company?/{G} Oh, I can wait,
551 ES   Carghil   16   wrong, you know. It's both pain and pleasure/To talk about the past — about you
577 ES   Charles   9   of past kindness/No doubt gives you pleasure?/{G} Yes, it's always pleasant/To repay

PLEASURES (2)
164 Rock 9   28   grace and order,/And intellectual pleasures of the senses?/The LORD who created
248 MC   Tempt1   1   you to your fate./I leave you to the pleasures of your higher vices,/Which will have

PLENITUDE (2)
174 FQ: BurntN   102   affection from the temporal./Neither plenitude nor vacancy. Only a flicker/Over the
410 CP   Reilly   26   prey/To the devils who arrive at their plenitude of power/When they have you to

PLENTY (6)
407 CP   Lavinia   36   Even if I'd been blind/There were plenty of people to let me know about it./I
457 CC   Eggers   12   were off./{E} I'm just going. There's plenty of time. {}/[*Looks at his watch*]/{E} I'll
537 ES   Gomez   28   You stayed the course, at least./I had plenty of time to think things over, later./{LC}
538 ES   Gomez   11   moment at *your* life history./You had plenty of money, and you made a good
576 ES   Gomez   24   Gomez?/{G} Oh no, Dick, there are plenty of other good names./{M} Michael,
577 ES   Michael   20   this?/{Mi} I'll say that Hemington has plenty of cheek./Señor Gomez and I have talked

PLIES (1)
181 FQ: ECoker   149   you are not./The wounded surgeon plies the steel/That questions the distempered

PLOTS (1)
332 FR   Agatha   37   get rid of your mother. What simple plots!/He was not suited to the role of murderer.

PLOTTING (3)
156 Rock 3   69   printing as many books as possible,/Plotting of happiness and flinging empty
250 MC   Tempt3   34   backbone of the nation./We, not the plotting parasites/About the King. Excuse my
359 CP   Julia   26   there it is! Now what are you two plotting?/How very lucky it was my umbrella,/

PLOTTINGS (1)
270 MC   Chorus   15   our skulls as well/As well as in the plottings of potentates/As well as in the

PLOUGH (1)
150 Rock 1   101   /*Over empty fields, untilled*/*Where the plough rests, at an angle*/*To the furrow. In this*

PLOUGHMAN (1)
263 MC   Chorus   19   Easter what work shall be done?/The ploughman shall go out in March and turn the

PLOVER (2)
98 Ash-Wed 6   16   /The cry of quail and the whirling plover/And the blind eye creates/The empty
588 Fable   52   /And after that a great pie made of plover,/And flagons which perhaps held several

PLUCK (2)
590 Time Space   13   suck the eglantine./So let us haste to pluck anew/Nor mourn to see them pine,/And
590 Space Time   13   suck the eglantine./But let us haste to pluck anew/Nor mourn to see them pine,/And

PLUCKEST (2)
70 WL: Fire S   309   burning burning/O Lord Thou pluckest me out/O Lord Thou pluckest/burning
70 WL: Fire S   310   Thou pluckest me out/O Lord Thou pluckest/burning/Death by Water/Phlebas the

PLUIE (1)
51 Restaurant   4   /Du vent, du grand soleil, et de la pluie;/C'est ce qu'on appelle le jour de lessive

PLUMB (1)
166 Rock 10   9   is a pit too deep for mortal eyes to plumb. Come/Ye out from among those who

PLUMBERS (1)
294 FR   Harry   2   in the drains,/Inaccessible to the plumbers, that has its hour of the night; you do

PLUMBING (1)
348 FR   Chorus   16   larceny and illness,/Against defective plumbing,/But not against the act of God./We

PLUMS (1)
244 MC   Chorus   1   are abundant,/Another year the plums are lacking./Yet we have gone on living,/

PLUNGED (1)
270 MC Chorus 6   with the passage of the kite, I have plunged with the kite and cowered with the
PLUS (1)
51 Restaurant 10   s'abrite./J'avais sept ans, elle était plus petite./Elle était toute mouillée, je lui ai
PLUVIEUX (1)
51 Restaurant 3   épaule:/'Dans mon pays il fera temps pluvieux,/Du vent, du grand soleil, et de la
PNEUMATIC (1)
52 Whispers 20   her friendly bust/Gives promise of pneumatic bliss./The couched Brazilian jaguar/
POCKET (1)
68 WL: Fire S 210   Smyrna merchant/Unshaven, with a pocket full of currants/C.i.f. London:
POCKET-TORCH (1)
290 FR Agatha 28   misunderstanding,/Reflecting a pocket-torch of observation/Upon each other's
POCKETED (2)
24 Rhapsody 39 the child, automatic,/Slipped out and pocketed a toy that was running along the quay,
149 Rock 1 95   */No man has hired us/With pocketed hands/And lowered faces/We stand*
POCKETS (1)
530 ES Ld Clav 38 Saying 'we must put our hands in our pockets/To double this collection — it must be
POEM (3)
197 FQ: Little 227   is an end and a beginning,/Every poem an epitaph. And any action/Is a step to
202 War Poetry 14 together./It seems just possible that a poem might happen/To a very young man: but
202 War Poetry 15 happen/To a very young man: but a poem is not poetry —/That is a life./War is not
POEMS (6)
35   t   midnight and the noon's repose./Poems/Gerontion/Here I am, an old man in a
101   t   let my cry come unto Thee./ARIEL POEMS/Journey of the Magi/'A cold coming
113   t   the second coming./UNFINISHED POEMS/Sweeney Agonistes/*Fragments of an*
131   t   RESIGN RESIGN/MINOR POEMS/Eyes that last I saw in tears/Eyes that
585   t with the Cat at the door./MORGAN./POEMS WRITTEN IN EARLY YOUTH/A
495 CC Lady E 21   was a poet./Because he wrote me poems. And he was so beautiful./I know now
POET (2)
495 CC Lady E 20 inspire an artist!/{LE} Or to inspire a poet. I thought Tony was a poet./Because he
495 CC Lady E 20 inspire a poet. I thought Tony was a poet./Because he wrote me poems. And he was
POETICAL (1)
179 FQ: ECoker 70   /A periphrastic study in a worn-out poetical fashion,/Leaving one still with the
POETICS (1)
33 Conv Gal 17   and imperious/At a stroke our mad poetics to confute —'/And — 'Are we then so
POETRY (9)
179 FQ: ECoker 72   /With words and meanings. The poetry does not matter./It was not (to start
202 War Poetry t   to instructions./A Note on War Poetry/Not the expression of collective emotion/
202 War Poetry 15 a very young man: but a poem is not poetry —/That is a life./War is not a life: it is a
202 War Poetry 24 /Becoming universal, which we call 'poetry',/May be affirmed in verse./To the
204 de la Mare 11 lit and curtains drawn/Demand some poetry, please. Whose shall it be,/At not quite
367 CP Peter 25 it a profession;/Though she had her poetry./{P} Yes, I've seen her poetry —/
367 CP Edward 26 had her poetry./{E} Yes, I've seen her poetry —/Interesting if one is interested in
436 CP Reilly 40 Julia./Do you mind if I quote poetry, Mrs. Chamberlayne?/{L} Oh no, I
437 CP Lavinia 1 I should love to hear you speaking poetry .../{J} She has made a point, Henry./{L}
POETS (2)
495 CC Lady E 22 he was so beautiful./I know now that poets don't look like poets:/And financiers, it
495 CC Lady E 22 I know now that poets don't look like poets:/And financiers, it seems, don't look like
POI (1)
75 WL: Thund 427 falling down falling down falling down/*Poi s'ascose nel foco che gli affina/Quando fiam*
POINT (65)
20 Portrait 63   have prevailed/You can say: at this point many a one has failed./But what have I,
128 Cor1 March 34 under the running water/At the still point of the turning world. O hidden./Now they
171 FQ: BurntN 10 might have been and what has been/Point to one end, which is always present./
172 FQ: BurntN 48 might have been and what has been/Point to one end, which is always present./
173 FQ: BurntN 64   among the stars./At the still point of the turning world. Neither flesh nor
173 FQ: BurntN 65 /Neither from nor towards; at the still point, there the dance is,/But neither arrest nor
173 FQ: BurntN 68 ascent nor decline. Except for the point, the still point,/There would be no dance,
173 FQ: BurntN 68 decline. Except for the point, the still point,/There would be no dance, and there is
175 FQ: BurntN 139 is silent, the light is still/At the still point of the turning world./Words move, music
189 FQ: DrySal 205 dimension. But to apprehend/The point of intersection of the timeless/With time,
202 War Poetry 3 in the daily papers./Where is the point at which the merely individual/Explosion
277 MC Knight3 11 up for it. When you come to the/point, it does go against the grain to kill an
277 MC Knight1 29 well and has made a very important point. The gist of his/argument is this: that we
277 MC Knight2 35 /{K2} I should like first to recur to a point that was very/well put by our leader,

279 MC Knight1 7 speaker, who has I think another point of view/to express. If there are any who
279 MC Knight4 13 have all spoken very much to the/point. I have nothing to add along their
293 FR Harry 16 of nothing else. Why not get to the point/Or if you want to pretend that I am
308 FR Harry 20 find it./The instinct to return to the point of departure/And start again as if nothing
332 FR Agatha 14 your father's place, and reached the point where/Wishwood supported her, and she
353 CP Alex 1 GUEST./{A} You've missed the point completely, Julia:/There *were* no tigers.
353 CP Alex 2 /There *were* no tigers. *That* was the point./{J} Then what were you doing, up in a
367 CP Peter 31 it's very good. But that's not the point./The point is, I thought we had a great
367 CP Peter 32 good. But that's not the point./The point is, I thought we had a great deal in
392 CP Lavinia 39 what you mean./{L} Oh, Edward!/The point is, that since I've been away/I see that I've
395 CP Edward 1 humiliation/Lately, to bring me to the point/At which humiliation ceases to humiliate./
395 CP Edward 3 ceases to humiliate./You get to the point at which you cease to feel/And then you
396 CP Lavinia 38 is in fact very simple./But there is one point which I see clearly:/We are not to relapse
397 CP Edward 21 and tell him all about me/From *your* point of view? But I don't need a doctor./I am
408 CP Reilly 33 /About your behaviour to-day./{R} A point well taken./But permit me to remark that
409 CP Reilly 6 never noticed *me*./{R} Now, I want to point out to both of you/How much you have
415 CP Reilly 18 been a fool./{R} And what is the point of view of your family?/{C} Well, my
415 CP Celia 22 /But anything wrong, from our point of view,/Was either bad form, or was
435 CP Lavinia 30 /I mean, this only brings you to the point/At which you *must* begin. You were
437 CP Julia 2 speaking poetry .../{J} She has made a point, Henry./{L} ... if it answers my question./
446 CC Claude 34 A bird bath? In the mews? What's the point of that?/{E} He told me he was very fond
448 CC Claude 27 /Are perfectly clear. But beyond that point/I haven't yet explained my plans to you./
449 CC Eggers 31 will you tell me this: if it comes to the point/At which Lady Elizabeth wants to adopt
453 CC Lucasta 34 I've a very small appetite./But the point is, that I'm penniless./{K} She's had a
454 CC Eggers 20 I am./{E} I have no doubt on either point, none at all./{C} And B. Kaghan has
461 CC Claude 38 before?/{SC} Impossible to tell./The point is that she's taken a fancy to you/And so
462 CC Colby 5 /{C} I must confess, that up to this point/I haven't been able to feel very settled./
466 CC Claude 30 life imposes upon you/Even to the point of accepting ... make-believe?/{C} I think I
472 CC Lucasta 27 great musician:/But that's not the point. You'd convinced yourself;/And you felt
473 CC Colby 21 smell./{C} You may be right, up to a point./And yet, you know, it's not quite real to
475 CC Lucasta 31 in a sense./But now we've got to this point — you might as well know them./{C} I'd
478 CC Lucasta 19 /Just when you think you're on the point of release/From loneliness, then loneliness
481 CC Lucasta 17 are you just leaving?/{L} We're on the point of leaving, Lady Elizabeth./{LE} I've
499 CC Lucasta 26 be the ideal solution/From your point of view. To get me off your hands./Oh, I
507 CC Claude 38 it was his?/{SC} That is just the point. My wife has convinced herself/That
518 CC Eggers 15 delighted./And by the way, a practical point:/If you took the position, you'd want to
524 ES Charles 4 have you to myself/There's really no point in my staying to tea. {}/[Enter MONICA
524 ES Monica 24 his eye./{M} We're getting off the point .../{C} You've got me off *my* point .../I
524 ES Charles 25 the point .../{C} You've got me off *my* point .../I was trying to explain .../{M} It's
535 ES Gomez 18 to my boys:/'When you come to the point where you need to trust someone/You
537 ES Ld Clav 11 never crossed my mind. Develop the point./{G} Well, consider what we were when
538 ES Gomez 31 to take your advice .../I've made a point, you see, of following your career./{LC} I
549 ES Carghil 8 I've never forgotten it —/The turning point of all my life!/Now whatever were the
556 ES Monica 29 from him./Perhaps you'll get to the point if I leave you together. {}/[Exit]/{Mi} You
557 ES Ld Clav 3 school for stealing./But come to the point. You're in trouble again./We'll ignore, if
574 ES Michael 32 to get abroad,/You couldn't see my point of view. What's the use of chasing/Half
575 ES Michael 4 Gomez sees./*He* understands my point of view, if *you* don't./And he's offered me
575 ES Ld Clav 28 a little *faster* than I did./{LC} On that point, Fred, you're wasting *your* time:/My
577 ES Charles 1 it./And, Michael, here's another point to think of:/Señor Gomez has offered you
577 ES Charles 12 better late than never./{C} I see your point of view. Can you really feel confidence,/
579 ES Michael 19 /I could look in again. If there's any point in it./Personally, I think that when one's

POINTED (6)

31 Apollinax 19 after all what did he mean?' —'His pointed ears.... He must be unbalanced.' —/
193 FQ: Little 92 upon the down-turned face/That pointed scrutiny with which we challenge/The
605 Narcissus 14 the river/His eyes were aware of the pointed corners of his eyes/And his hands aware
605 Narcissus 15 his eyes/And his hands aware of the pointed tips of his fingers./Struck down by such
327 FR Violet 7 /{V} Agatha's remarks are invariably pointed./{H} Do you think that I believe what I
332 FR Agatha 27 or future,/Only a present moment of pointed light/When you want to burn. When

POINTEDLY (1)

541 ES Gomez 29 a generous friend to me once/As you pointedly reminded me a moment ago./Now it's

POINTING (2)

180 FQ: ECoker 133 ecstasy/Not lost, but requiring, pointing to the agony/Of death and birth./You
530 ES m 32 speeches that you had to listen to! {}/[*pointing to a silver salver, still lying in its case*]./

POINTS (6)

65	WL: Chess	109	the brush, her hair/Spread out in fiery points/Glowed into words, then would be
178	FQ: ECoker	48	and drinking. Dung and death./Dawn points, and another day/Prepares for heat and
239	MC Chorus	10	and the land became brown sharp points of death in a waste of water and mud,/
259	MC Thomas	7	my guardian, hover over the swords' points. {}/Interlude/THE ARCHBISHOP/
276	MC Knight1	29	their various abilities, and different points of view, will be able/to lay before you the
296	FR Agatha	1	will feel better./{Ag} There are certain points I do not yet understand:/They will be

POISONING (1)

376	CP Julia	34	deadly./I could tell such tales of his poisoning people./Now, my dear, you give me

POISSY (1)

127	Cor1 March	26	/And now the *société gymnastique de Poissy*/And now come the Mayor and the

POKE (1)

359	CP Julia	29	— *he's* so inquisitive!/But *I* never poke into other people's business./Well,

POKER (3)

119	SP Krum	18	Hun on the run/{Kr} What about that poker game? eh what Sam?/What about that
119	SP Krum	19	game? eh what Sam?/What about that poker game in Bordeaux?/Yes Miss Dorrance
119	SP Krum	21	you get Sam/To tell about that poker game in Bordeaux./{Du} Do you know

POKES (1)

256	MC Tempts	31	taps at the window, is it wind that pokes at the door?/{C} Does the torch flame in

POKING (1)

37	Gerontion	14	makes tea,/Sneezes at evening, poking the peevish gutter./I an old man,/A dull

POL (1)

222	Pekes Pols	13	a week/(And that's a long time for a Pol or a Peke)./The big Police Dog was away

POLE (3)

18	Portrait	8	been, let us say, to hear the latest Pole/Transmit the Preludes, through his hair
191	FQ: Little	3	sundown,/Suspended in time, between pole and tropic./When the short day is
549	ES Carghil	17	wet/And nearly dropped the punt pole, and you all laughed at me./Don't you

POLICE (8)

159	Rock 6	6	/It is hard for those who live near a Police Station/To believe in the triumph of
221	Old Deut	38	mustn't be woken —/I'll have the police if there's any uproar' —/And out they all
222	Pekes Pols	14	time for a Pol or a Peke)./The big Police Dog was away from his beat —/I don't
223	Pekes Pols	60	scattered like sheep./*And when the Police Dog returned to his beat,/There wasn't a*
233	Skimble	59	at Dumfries, where he summons the police/If there's anything they ought to know
328	FR Charles	21	{G} Where?/{C} In Ebury Street. 'The police stated that at the time of the/accident Mr.
328	FR Charles	24	he/did not stop when signalled by the police car, he said: "I/thought you were having
364	CP Edward	3	could describe her/If I had to ask the police to search for her./I'm sure I don't know

POLICEMAN (1)

218	Mung Rump	20	fellows, and liked to engage a friendly policeman in conversation./When the family

POLICEMEN (1)

155	Rock 3	39	keeps not with you?/A thousand policemen directing the traffic/Cannot tell you

POLICIES (1)

196	FQ: Little	188	old factions/We cannot restore old policies/Or follow an antique drum./These men,

POLICY (4)

248	MC Tempt2	21	how the late ones rise! You, master of policy/Whom all acknowledged, should guide
249	MC Tempt2	30	need fast friends at home./Private policy is public profit;/Dignity still shall be
253	MC Tempt4	16	than king's anger./Kings have public policy, barons private profit,/Jealousy raging
279	MC Knight4	22	he completely reversed his policy; he showed/himself to be utterly

POLISH (4)

159	Rock 6	14	they owe their significance?/Men! polish your teeth on rising and retiring;/
159	Rock 6	15	teeth on rising and retiring;/Women! polish your fingernails:/You polish the tooth of
159	Rock 6	16	/Women! polish your fingernails:/You polish the tooth of the dog and the talon of the
236	Cat Morgan	9	I done me patrol./I ain't got much polish, me manners is gruff,/But I've got a good

POLISH (1) [*Proper name*]

20	Portrait	75	the stage./A Greek was murdered at a Polish dance,/Another bank defaulter has

POLISHED (2)

24	Rhapsody	26	upon the beach/Eaten smooth, and polished/As if the world gave up/The secret of
167	Rock 10	30	windows/And light reflected from the polished stone,/The gilded carven wood, the

POLITE (2)

159	Rock 6	12	/As you can boast in the way of polite society/Will hardly survive the Faith to
556	ES Monica	26	I?/{M} I wish you'd stop being so polite to each other./Michael, you know what

POLITELY (1)

233	Skimble	41	if you sneeze./Then the guard looks in politely and will ask you very brightly/'Do you

POLITIC (1)

16	Prufrock	116	tool,/Deferential, glad to be of use,/Politic, cautious, and meticulous;/Full of high

POLITICAL (3)
258 MC Thomas	30		/Still doing right: and striving with political men/May make that cause political,
258 MC Thomas	31		political men/May make that cause political, not by what they do/But by what they
551 ES Carghil	30		for Parliament:/His father has political ambitions for him./If he's lost a breach

POLITICIAN (1)
250 MC Tempt3	24	my Lord,/I am no trifler, and no politician./To idle or intrigue at court/I have no

POLITICIANS (1)
534 ES Gomez	28	go into politics. In my country, Dick,/Politicians can't afford mistakes. The prudent

POLITICS (9)
528 ES Monica	12	man, but the public personage./In politics Father wore a public label./And later, as
534 ES Gomez	27	allow either of my sons/To go into politics. In my country, Dick,/Politicians can't
534 ES Gomez	34	squad./You don't know what serious politics is like!/I said to my boys: 'Never touch
534 ES Gomez	35	like!/I said to my boys: 'Never touch politics./Stay out of politics, and play both
534 ES Gomez	36	'Never touch politics./Stay out of politics, and play both parties:/What you don't
538 ES Gomez	13	wife's family influence, you got on in politics./Shall we say that you did very well by
538 ES Gomez	27	/That would account for your leaving politics/And taking a conspicuous job in the
538 ES Gomez	37	yet you withdrew from the world of politics/And went into the City. Director of a
559 ES Michael	29	you the opportunity/Of retiring from politics, not without dignity,/Being no longer

POLLICLE (3)
135 5FingerEx2	10	/And the tree was cramped and dry./Pollicle dogs and cats all must/Jellicle cats and
222 Pekes Pols	18	on the street/When a Peke and a Pollicle happened to meet./They did not
223 Pekes Pols	33	din is what Pollicles like,/For your Pollicle Dog is a dour Yorkshire tyke,/And his

POLLICLES (4)
222 Pekes Pols	t	Awefull Battle of the Pekes and the Pollicles/*Together with some Account of the*
222 Pekes Pols	l	*Great Rumpuscat*/The Pekes and the Pollicles, everyone knows,/Are proud and
223 Pekes Pols	32	Chinese./But a terrible din is what Pollicles like,/For your Pollicle Dog is a dour
223 Pekes Pols	57	and his yawning,/The Pekes and the Pollicles quickly took warning./He looked at the

POLYMATH (1)
55 Mr E Sun	32	the subtle schools/Are controversial, polymath./Sweeney Among the Nightingales/

POLYPHEME (1)
42 Swee Erect	10	the feet and hands/(Nausicaa and Polypheme)./Gesture of orang-outang/Rises

POLYPHILOPROGENITIVE (1)
54 Mr E Sun	1	/Mr. Eliot's Sunday Morning Service/Polyphiloprogenitive/The sapient sutlers of the

POMEGRANATE (1)
49 Hippopot	15	on the mango-tree;/But fruits of pomegranate and peach/Refresh the Church

POMS (3)
222 Pekes Pols	m2	*the Participation/of the Pugs and the Poms, and the Intervention/of the Great*
222 Pekes Pols	4	one goes./And the Pugs and the Poms, although most people say/That they do
223 Pekes Pols	38	*the Border.*/Then the Pugs and the Poms held no longer aloof,/But some from the

POND (1)
191 FQ: Little	5	fire,/The brief sun flames the ice, on pond and ditches,/In windless cold that is the

PONDERING (1)
254 MC Tempt4	40	to defame or to execrate you,/But pondering the qualities that you lacked/Will

PONY (4)
288 FR Agatha	25	holiday,/The daring feats on the old pony,/And thought to creep back through the
288 FR Amy	30	it was when he left it,/Except the old pony, and the mongrel setter/Which I had to
325 FR Ivy	29	/He was always the one to fall off the pony,/Or out of a tree — and always on his
329 FR Chorus	7	hay in summer/The dogs and the old pony/The stumble and the wail of little pain/

POOL (9)
24 Rhapsody	43	/And a crab one afternoon in a pool,/An old crab with barnacles on his back,/
72 WL: Thund	351	also water/And water/A spring/A pool among the rock/If there were the sound of
157 Rock 4	12	/By the fountain gate, by the king's pool,/Jerusalem lay waste, consumed with fire;/
172 FQ: BurntN	35	circle,/To look down into the drained pool./Dry the pool, dry concrete, brown edged,/
172 FQ: BurntN	36	down into the drained pool./Dry the pool, dry concrete, brown edged,/And the pool
172 FQ: BurntN	37	dry concrete, brown edged,/And the pool was filled with water out of sunlight,/And
172 FQ: BurntN	40	they were behind us, reflected in the pool./Then a cloud passed, and the pool was
172 FQ: BurntN	41	pool./Then a cloud passed, and the pool was empty./Go, said the bird, for the
547 ES Piggott	25	/And it's still too early for the bathing pool./But several of our guests are keen on

POOLS (3)
13 Prufrock	18	of the evening,/Lingered upon the pools that stand in drains,/Let fall upon its back
166 Rock 10	22	at evening,/The twilight over stagnant pools at batflight,/Moon light and star light,
184 FQ: DrySal	20	crab, the whale's backbone;/The pools where it offers to our curiosity/The more

POOR (24)
33 Conv Gal	5	battered lantern hung aloft/To light poor travellers to their distress.'/She then: 'How
66 WL: Chess	147	no more can't I, I said, and think of poor Albert,/He's been in the army four years,

PORTERS (2)
232 Skimble		5	can't start.'/All the guards and all the porters and the stationmaster's daughters/They
530 ES Ld Clav		24	the booking office is closed/And the porters have gone. What am I waiting for/In a

PORTIONS (1)
91 Ash-Wed 2		15	strings of my eyes and the indigestible portions/Which the leopards reject. The Lady is

PORTRAIT (7)
18 Portrait		t	voices wake us, and we drown./Portrait of a Lady/Among the smoke and fog of
599 On a Port		t	men whom we knew long ago./On a Portrait/Among a crowd of tenuous dreams,
321 FR Harry		7	I never saw a photograph. There is no portrait./{W} What I want to know is, whether
483 CC	m	29	{}/[*She sits down, holding the portrait*]/{LE} What was I going to say? Oh, I
484 CC Lady E		13	course not./Or you wouldn't have her portrait. If you never knew your parents .../But
531 ES Ld Clav		15	a column and a half/With an inset, a portrait taken twenty years ago./In five years'
548 ES Carghil		32	/But then, we've all seen your portrait in the papers/So often. And everybody

PORTRAITS (2)
129 Cor2 State		29	mother/Here is the row of family portraits, dingy busts, all looking remarkably
483 CC Lady E		25	to instruct you, Colby./Photographic portraits — even in silver frames —/Are much

POSE (2)
34 Figlia		22	/I should have lost a gesture and a pose./Sometimes these cogitations still amaze/
552 ES Carghil		28	/You always were. You wanted to pose/As a man of the world. And now you're

POSING (2)
552 ES Carghil		29	a man of the world. And now you're posing/As what? I presume, as an elder
552 ES Carghil		32	being an elder statesman/And posing successfully as an elder statesman/Is

POSITION (15)
285 FR Ivy		15	south in the winter./Were I in Amy's position, I would go south in the winter./I
360 CP Reilly		17	/Breathe deeply, and adopt a relaxed position./There we are. Now for a few
409 CP Reilly		29	/That you had forced him into this position) —/When, I say, you discovered that
431 CP Julia		26	in California./{J} But what is your position, Peter?/Have you become an expert on
436 CP Reilly		39	to a show-down./{R} You state the position correctly, Julia./Do you mind if I quote
448 CC Eggers		18	*explain* Mr. Simpkins?/Regularize his position in the household?/You told me that
467 CC Colby		29	/And eager for more. I don't want my position/To be, in any way, a make-believe./
472 CC Lucasta		30	/And so you applied for Eggerson's position,/And made up your mind to go into
490 CC Colby		29	other./{C} No, Lady Elizabeth. The position is the same/Or crueller. Suppose I am
506 CC Eggers		11	it./She was not, in any case, in a position/In which she could have instituted
508 CC Eggers		5	/To find her son. Put yourself in her position./If you had lost your son, in a similar
518 CC Eggers		16	a practical point:/If you took the position, you'd want to find your feet/In Joshua
557 ES Ld Clav		8	/{Mi} Well, I've lost my job./{LC} The position that Sir Alfred Walter made for you./
563 ES Gomez		36	/Had I been in London, and in Dick's position/I should have been your most devoted
576 ES Ld Clav		14	/{LC} And made him invent/The position which he'd come to find the man for./

POSITIONS (3)
201 Def Island		22	of our speech, that we took up/our positions, in obedience to instructions./A Note
305 FR Harry		28	/The chairs, the sofa ... all in the same positions./I was looking to see if anything was
531 ES Ld Clav		22	the successful failures,/Who occupy positions that other men covet./When we go, a

POSITIVE (2)
89 Ash-Wed 1		10	to know again/The infirm glory of the positive hour/Because I do not think/Because I
560 ES Ld Clav		33	think/That what inspired you was no positive ambition/But only the desire to escape./

POSSESS (2)
181 FQ: ECoker	142		is the way of ignorance./In order to possess what you do not possess/You must go
181 FQ: ECoker	142		/In order to possess what you do not possess/You must go by the way of

POSSESSED (3)
52 Whispers		1	of Immortality/Webster was much possessed by death/And saw the skull beneath
234 Ad-dress		8	me/And other people whom we find/Possessed of various types of mind./For some
465 CC Claude		16	To be, at best,/A competent copier, possessed by the craving/To create, when one is

POSSESSION (9)
162 Rock 8		24	finding/A stranger at the door in possession:/Came home cracked by the sun of
179 FQ: ECoker	96		fear of fear and frenzy, their fear of possession,/Of belonging to another, or to
248 MC Tempt2		28	to glory,/Life lasting, a permanent possession./A templed tomb, monument of
253 MC Tempt4		17	barons private profit,/Jealousy raging possession of the fiend./Barons are employable
338 FR Harry		39	sanity,/And not yet assured in possession, that is when/One begins to seem the
341 FR Amy		20	another. I call it failure. Your fury for possession/Is only the stronger for all these
370 CP Peter		11	excitement, delirium,/Desire for possession. It was not like that at all./It was
418 CP Reilly		28	blind. But the way leads towards possession/Of what you have sought for in the
463 CC Colby		27	person I used to be, returns to take possession:/And I am again the disappointed

POSSESSIONS (2)
111 Xmas Trees		14	/So that the surprises, delight in new possessions/(Each one with its peculiar and
268 MC Knight3		4	/Restored your honours and your possessions./All was granted for which you

POSSESSIVE (1)
526 ES   Charles   32   your father will come. With his calm possessive air/And his kindly welcome, which is
POSSESSORS (1)
587 Fable   9   by a band of friars merry./They were possessors of rich lands and wide,/An orchard,
POSSIBILITY (1)
171 FQ: BurntN   7   an abstraction/Remaining a perpetual possibility/Only in a world of speculation./What
POSSIBLE (25)
52 Whispers   15   /The ague of the skeleton;/No contact possible to flesh/Allayed the fever of the bone./
156 Rock 3   68   in printing as many books as possible,/Plotting of happiness and flinging
202 War Poetry   14   day and night together./It seems just possible that a poem might happen/To a very
228 Gus   21   /'I have played', so he says, 'every possible part,/And I used to know seventy
241 MC   Mess   15   notice of his coming, as much as was possible,/That you may prepare to meet him./
258 MC   Thomas   18   when we find no longer all things possible./Ambition comes behind and
262 MC   Thomas   2   preach to you again; and because/it is possible that in a short time you may have yet
270 MC   Chorus   24   too soon for contrition./Nothing is possible but the shamed swoon/Of those
333 FR   Agatha   27   but of sin and expiation./It is possible that you have not known what sin/You
333 FR   Agatha   30   of it must precede the expiation./It is possible that sin may strain and struggle/In its
333 FR   Agatha   32   /And so find expurgation. It is possible/You are the consciousness of your
333 FR   Agatha   35   the purgatorial flame./Indeed it is possible. You may learn hereafter,/Moving
338 FR   Harry   30   the hardest thing, and the only thing possible./Now they will lead me. I shall be safe
339 FR   Harry   13   of incurable diseases./Such things are possible. It is love and terror/Of what waits and
345 FR   Harry   1   I only want, please,/As little fuss as possible. You must get used to it;/Meanwhile, I
367 CP   Edward   23   in the art of the film./{E} As a possible profession?/{P} She might make it a
402 CP   Reilly   30   whom a sanatorium is the worst place possible./We must first find out what is wrong
410 CP Lavinia   20   /And put them together./{L} Is that possible?/{R} If I had sent either of you to the
420 CP   Julia   36   Since you question the decision/What possible alternative can you imagine?/{R} None.
435 CP   Peter   24   to something better,/And that seemed possible, while Celia was alive./I wanted it,
482 CC   Lady E   9   mind a gentle hint./I feared it was possible you might become too friendly/With
505 CC   Eggers   32   enough ago for the question to be possible./Lady Elizabeth, before her marriage/
506 CC   Eggers   26   be able to help you?/{E} It seems just possible. A few days ago,/As I said, Lady
508 CC Guzzard   32   unusual one./Perhaps it might be possible to trace them./The name was Kaghan./
552 ES   Ld Clav   20   infatuation, ended in the only way possible/To our mutual satisfaction./{MC} Your
POSSIBLY (4)
33 Conv Gal   2   'Our sentimental friend the moon!/Or possibly (fantastic, I confess)/It may be Prester
395 CP   Edward   17   /But doesn't it occur to you that possibly/I may have changed too?/{L} Oh,
450 CC   Claude   23   /I must telephone to Amsterdam, and possibly to Paris./But when you return with
487 CC   Lady E   23   I must confront her./This couldn't possibly be a coincidence./It seems incredible,
POSSUM'S (1)
207   t   addressed to you in public./OLD POSSUM'S BOOK OF PRACTICAL CATS/
POST (4)
538 ES   Gomez   21   it/You simply get moved to another post/Where at least you can't make quite the
576 ES Michael   29   looking for a man/For an important post on his staff —/{C} A post the nature of
576 ES Charles   30   important post on his staff —/{C} A post the nature of which is left very vague/{Mi}
577 ES Charles   2   of:/Señor Gomez has offered you a post in San Marco,/Señor Gomez pays your
POSTCARDS (1)
460 CC   Claude   8   it./{SC} It's true, you did send me postcards from Zürich;/But you know that I
POSTERITY (1)
91 Ash-Wed 2   13   deeds to oblivion, and my love/To the posterity of the desert and the fruit of the
POSTMARK (1)
460 CC   Claude   11   know where you are/By reading the postmark./{LE} But Claude, I'm glad to find/
POSTPONED (1)
478 CC Lucasta   15   thought of telling you before,/And I postponed telling you, just for the fun of it:/I
POSTPONING (2)
528 ES Charles   35   for a long time,/And you'll go on postponing and postponing our marriage./{M}
528 ES Charles   35   /And you'll go on postponing and postponing our marriage./{M} I'm afraid ... not
POTATO (2)
355 CP   Julia   28   of those delicious olives./What's that? Potato crisps? No, I can't endure them./Well, I
358 CP   Julia   19   it's been a delightful evening:/The potato crisps were really excellent./Now let me
POTATOES (1)
219 Mung Rump   23   get thinner/On Argentine joint, potatoes and greens,/And the cook would
POTENCY (1)
85 Hollow Men   86   the desire/And the spasm/Between the potency/And the existence/Between the essence/
POTENT (1)
311 FR   Harry   7   world. I know it, I know it!/More potent than ever before, a vapour dissolving/All

POTENTATES (1)
270 MC Chorus 15 as well/As well as in the plottings of potentates/As well as in the consultations of
POTHUNTER'S (1)
230 Bust Jones 22 of venison he gives his ben'son/To the *Pothunter's* succulent bones;/And just before
POTTED (1)
235 Ad-dress 58 caviare, or Strassburg Pie,/Some potted grouse, or salmon paste —/He's sure to
POTTER (12)
463 CC Claude 39 want to do?/{SC} I wanted to be a potter./{C} A potter!/{SC} A potter. When I was
463 CC Colby 40 /{SC} I wanted to be a potter./{C} A potter!/{SC} A potter. When I was a boy/I loved
464 CC Claude 1 to be a potter./{C} A potter!/{SC} A potter. When I was a boy/I loved to shape
464 CC Claude 3 /And I loved the material that the potter handles./Most people think that a
464 CC Claude 5 something more excellent to be than a potter./Most people think of china or porcelain/
465 CC Claude 10 should never have become a first-rate potter./I didn't have it in me. It's strange, isn't
465 CC Claude 15 have a vocation/To be a second-rate potter? To be, at best,/A competent copier,
492 CC Claude 30 of my early ambitions/To be a potter. Not that the Members/Of the Potters'
494 CC Claude 34 did you want to do?/{SC} To be a potter./Don't laugh./{LE} I'm not laughing. I
494 CC Lady E 38 you tell me, you'd have liked to be a potter!/You really mean, to make jugs and jars/
495 CC Lady E 2 But I should have loved you to be a potter!/Why have you never told me?/{SC} I
495 CC Claude 34 /I should have been a second-rate potter,/And he would have been a second-rate
POTTERS (1)
495 CC Lady E 23 financiers, it seems, don't look like potters —/Is that what I mean? I'm getting
POTTERS' (4)
486 CC Claude 36 for my speech/At the dinner of the Potters' Company./{C} That's tomorrow night,
492 CC Colby 18 you/About your speech for the Potters' Company/Tomorrow night. I must get
492 CC Claude 31 potter. Not that the Members/Of the Potters' Company know anything at all/About
492 CC Claude 35 me/Of things that would surprise the Potters' Company/If I told them what I was
POUND (1)
129 Cor2 State 13 telephone operator/At a salary of one pound ten a week rising by annual increments
POUNDER (1)
231 Bust Jones 33 round./He's a twenty-five pounder, or I am a bounder,/And he's putting
POUNDS (1)
129 Cor2 State 14 increments of five shillings/To two pounds ten a week; with a bonus of thirty
POUR (1)
508 CC Eggers 14 I ignore that remark./{E} May I pour a drop of oil on these troubled waters?/Let
POUR (3) [*Foreign word*]
48 Lune Miel 7 de morsures./On relève le drap pour mieux égratigner./Moins d'une lieue d'ici
51 Restaurant 13 de trente-huit./'Je la chatouillais, pour la faire rire./J'éprouvais un instant de
51 Restaurant 24 comme moi?/Tiens, voilà dix sous, pour la salle-de-bains./Phlébas, le Phénicien,
POURBOIRES (1)
48 Lune Miel 14 un restaurant pas cher./Lui pense aux pourboires, et rédige son bilan./Ils auront vu la
POURED (2)
64 WL: Chess 85 rose to meet it,/From satin cases poured in rich profusion./In vials of ivory and
583 ES Charles 22 It is not at all strange./The dead has poured out a blessing on the living./{M} Age
POURS (2)
422 CP 2m 11 *and three glasses, and/exit.* REILLY *pours drinks.*]/{R} And now we are ready to
539 ES m 22 I'm beginning to be thirsty again. { }/[*Pours himself whisky*]/{LC} An interesting
POVERTY (2)
243 MC Chorus 27 and luxury,/There have been poverty and licence,/There has been minor
255 MC Tempt4 10 /What earthly pride, that is not poverty/Compared with richness of heavenly
POWDER (3)
370 CP Alex 14 /{A} Edward, I can't find any curry powder./{E} There isn't any curry powder.
370 CP Edward 15 powder./{E} There isn't any curry powder. Lavinia hates curry./{A} There goes
370 CP Alex 18 mangoes,/But I *did* count upon curry powder. { }/[*Exit*]/{P} That is exactly what I want
POWDERED (1)
64 WL: Chess 88 strange synthetic perfumes,/Unguent, powdered, or liquid — troubled, confused/And
POWER (52)
89 Ash-Wed 1 8 /Why should I mourn/The vanished power of the usual reign?/Because I do not hope
89 Ash-Wed 1 13 know/The one veritable transitory power/Because I cannot drink/There, where
96 Ash-Wed 5 23 /Hour and hour, word and word, power and power, those who wait/In darkness?
96 Ash-Wed 5 23 and hour, word and word, power and power, those who wait/In darkness? Will the
108 Animula 32 Pray for Guiterriez, avid of speed and power,/For Boudin, blown to pieces,/For this
154 Rock 3 11 reciprocal distrust./I have given you power of choice, and you only alternate/
161 Rock 7 29 first Reason,/And then Money, and Power, and what they call Life, or Race, or
161 Rock 7 43 /All gods except Usury, Lust and Power./O Father we welcome your words,/And
196 FQ: Little 213 shirt of flame/Which human power cannot remove./We only live, only

201 Def Island	12	form of gamble/with death, fight the power of darkness in air/and fire/and of those
594 Grad 9	6	onward to the goal,/Shall not have power to quench the memory./We shall return;
241 MC Priest3	4	/They have but one law, to seize the power and keep it,/And the steadfast can
241 MC Priest1	27	full assurance, or only secure/In the power of Rome, the spiritual rule,/The
242 MC Priest1	27	sustenance from generosity,/Loathing power given by temporal devolution,/Wishing
248 MC Tempt2	27	may be regained. Think, my Lord,/Power obtained grows to glory,/Life lasting, a
248 MC Tempt2	36	waking with deceitful shadows?/Power is present. Holiness hereafter./{T} Who
249 MC Tempt2	10	heaven./{T} What means?/{T2} Real power/Is purchased at price of a certain
249 MC Tempt2	12	a certain submission./Your spiritual power is earthly perdition./Power is present, for
249 MC Tempt2	13	spiritual power is earthly perdition./Power is present, for him who will wield./{T}
249 MC Tempt2	19	give for it?/{T2} Pretence of priestly power./{T} Why should we give it?/{T2} For the
249 MC Tempt2	21	Why should we give it?/{T2} For the power and the glory./{T} No!/{T2} Yes! Or
250 MC Thomas	2	England,/Who bind and loose, with power from the Pope,/Descend to desire a
250 MC Thomas	3	the Pope,/Descend to desire a punier power?/Delegate to deal the doom of
250 MC Thomas	9	covering kings' falcons./{T} Temporal power, to build a good world,/To keep order, as
250 MC Thomas	15	disease,/Degrade what they exalt. Power with the King —/I *was* the King, his
252 MC Tempt3	11	undoing?/{T3} Kings will allow no power but their own;/Church and people have
252 MC Thomas	27	/The desperate exercise of failing power./Samson in Gaza did no more./But if I
253 MC Tempt4	27	/To general grasp of spiritual power?/Man oppressed by sin, since Adam fell
253 MC Tempt4	30	You hold the keys of heaven and hell./Power to bind and loose: bind, Thomas, bind,/
253 MC Tempt4	37	hour,/This is the course of temporal power./The Old King shall know it, when at last
254 MC Tempt4	2	eternal life and death./You hold this power, hold it./{T} Supreme, in this land?/{T4}
254 MC Tempt4	25	I tell you./Your thoughts have more power than kings to compel you./You have also
255 MC Thomas	20	temporal tempters,/With pleasure and power at palpable price./What do you offer?
266 MC Knights	18	from his hand; from him you had the power, the seal and the ring./This is the man
268 MC Knight3	10	/{K3} Using every means in your power to evince/The King's faithful servants,
268 MC Thomas	18	son, or to diminish/His honour and power. Why should he wish/To deprive my
332 FR Agatha	1	weak he recognised your mother's power,/And yielded to it./{H} There was no
334 FR Harry	35	human beings — they have no more power than I./The things I thought were real are
341 FR Amy	28	what, if you please,/Gives *you* the power to know what is best for Harry?/What
349 FR Agatha	21	of consummation/{Ag} A curse is a power/Not subject to reason/Each curse has its
377 CP Celia	8	afraid of him;/He has some sort of power./{E} I don't know who he is./But I had
403 CP Reilly	11	of mischief/As lay within your power — until you came to grief./Half of the
410 CP Reilly	26	devils who arrive at their plenitude of power/When they have you to themselves./{L}
451 CC Eggers	9	/For you, Mr. Simpkins. He'll be a power in the City!/And he has a heart of gold.
464 CC Claude	34	occupation/Until I began to feel my power in it./The life changed me, as it is
480 CC Kaghan	30	nowhere./That's why I want to be a power in the City,/On the boards of all the
494 CC Claude	16	/I thought that what he cared for was power and wealth;/And I came to see that what
530 ES Monica	8	— the inexhaustible/Sources of the power that wears out the machine./{LC}
531 ES Charles	8	at the disposal of the Government in power'./And the expectation that your voice will
537 ES Gomez	23	it flattered *you* — tickled your love of power/To see that I was flattered, and that I
577 ES Charles	15	you put yourself completely in the power/Of a man you don't know, of the nature
577 ES Ld Clav	40	if he chooses/To place himself in your power, Fred Culverwell,/Of his own volition to

POWERFUL (2)

251 MC Tempt3	34	do speak for barons —/{T3} For a powerful party/Which has turned its eyes in
251 MC Tempt3	38	be an advantage,/Blessing of Pope powerful protection/In the fight for liberty.

POWERLESS (1)

249 MC Tempt2	25	ruler,/Self-bound servant of a powerless Pope,/The old stag, circled with

POWERS (11)

164 Rock 9	26	we not bring to Your service all our powers/For life, for dignity, grace and order,/
186 FQ: DrySal	64	failing/Pride or resentment at failing powers,/The unattached devotion which might
190 FQ: DrySal	228	—/Driven by dmonic, chthonic/Powers. And right action is freedom/From past
216 Jellicles	27	/Reserving their terpsichorean powers/To dance by the light of the Jellicle
225 Mr Mistoff	50	proof/Of his singular magical powers:/And I have known the family to call/
226 Macavity	7	law, he breaks the law of gravity./His powers of levitation would make a fakir stare,/
270 MC Chorus	16	/As well as in the consultations of powers./What is woven on the loom of fate/
271 MC Chorus	2	of nature,/Mastered by the animal powers of spirit,/Dominated by the lust of
275 MC Knight2	4	excommunicated./{K2} Resign the powers you have arrogated./{K3} Restore to the
278 MC Knight2	10	to restore order: to curb the excessive/powers of local government, which were usually
305 FR Agatha	12	made;/The decision will be made by powers beyond us/Which now and then emerge.

PRACTICAL (15)

164 Rock 9	19	soul of stone;/Out of the meaningless practical shapes of all that is living or lifeless/
173 FQ: BurntN	72	in time./The inner freedom from the practical desire,/The release from action and
207	t	public./OLD POSSUM'S BOOK OF PRACTICAL CATS/The Naming of Cats/The
348 FR Chorus	26	for a limited number/Of strictly practical purposes/We do not know what we are

393 CP	Lavinia	14	in to *me*:/You mean, leaving all the	practical decisions/That you should have made
397 CP	Lavinia	24	professional capacity./{L} One can be	practical, even in hell:/And you know I am
397 CP	Lavinia	25	hell!/And you know I am much more	practical than you are./{E} I ought to know by
397 CP	Edward	26	to know by now what you consider	practical./Practical! I remember, on our
397 CP	Edward	27	by now what you consider practical./	Practical! I remember, on our honeymoon,/You
406 CP	Lavinia	21	Are you a devil/Or merely a lunatic	practical joker?/{E} I incline to the second
406 CP	Lavinia	39	/{L} It's only that I have a more	practical mind/Than you have, Edward. You do
407 CP	Lavinia	3	Don't be silly, Edward. When I say	practical,/I mean practical in the things that
407 CP	Lavinia	4	Edward. When I say practical,/I mean	practical in the things that really matter./{R}
425 CP	Edward	16	/{E} That's true. You have a very	practical mind./{L} But you know, I don't think
518 CC	Eggers	15	I'm delighted./And by the way, a	practical point:/If you took the position, you'd

PRACTICALLY (2)

| 524 ES | Monica | 28 | /Of your staying to tea. As you | practically promised./{C} What you don't |
| 552 ES | Carghil | 33 | successfully as an elder statesman/Is | practically negligible. And you look the part./ |

PRACTICE (3)

314 FR	Warburt	34	/{W} Indeed, yes./Even in a country	practice. My first patient, now —/You wouldn't
569 ES	Charles	21	/I've seen something of it in my	practice at the bar./I'm sure I could help./{M}
582 ES	Ld Clav	10	my dear,/I am only a beginner in the	practice of loving —/Well, that is something./I

PRACTICES (1)

| 434 CP | Alex | 23 | tell./But from what we know of local | practices/It would seem that she must have been |

PRACTISE (3)

216 Jellicles		11	have bright black eyes;/They like to	practise their airs and graces/And wait for the
217 Jellicles		32	to be a stormy night/They will	practise a caper or two in the hall./If it happens
367 CP	Edward	15	thought of that./What arts do you	practise?/{P} You won't have seen my novel,/

PRACTISED (1)

| 205 de la Mare | | 31 | measure is refined;/By conscious art | practised with natural ease;/By the delicate, |

PRACTITIONER (1)

| 314 FR | Warburt | 8 | a good deal, Harry./A country | practitioner doesn't get younger./It takes me |

PRAISE (10)

50 Hippopot		28	quiring angels round him sing/The	praise of God, in loud hosannas./Blood of the
105 Song Sime		26	/According to thy word./They shall	praise Thee and suffer in every generation/With
152 Rock 2		40	/And no community not lived in	praise of GOD./Even the anchorite who
152 Rock 2		42	whom the days and nights repeat the	praise of GOD,/Prays for the Church, the Body
166 Rock 10		17	your foothold./O Light Invisible, we	praise Thee!/Too bright for mortal vision./O
166 Rock 10		19	mortal vision./O Greater Light, we	praise Thee for the less;/The eastern light our
258 MC Thomas		10	lead to pleasure, advancement and	praise./Delight in sense, in learning and in
281 MC Chorus		7	*by a choir in the distance*]./{C} We	praise Thee, O God, for Thy glory displayed in
281 MC Chorus		13	conscious of Thee, must consciously	praise Thee, in thought and in word and in
281 MC Chorus		16	the voices of beasts and of birds,	praise Thee./We thank Thee for Thy mercies of

PRANKS (1)

| 232 Skimble | | 29 | and on the move./You can play no | pranks with Skimbleshanks!/He's a Cat that |

PRAWN (1)

| 270 MC Chorus | | 2 | crab, the oyster, the whelk and the | prawn; and they live and spawn in my bowels, |

PRAY (26)

89 Ash-Wed 1		26	/Upon which to rejoice/And	pray to God to have mercy upon us/And I pray
89 Ash-Wed 1		27	to God to have mercy upon us/And I	pray that I may forget/These matters that with
90 Ash-Wed 1		40	and not to care/Teach us to sit still./	Pray for us sinners now and at the hour of our
90 Ash-Wed 1		41	now and at the hour of our death/	Pray for us now and at the hour of our death./
96 Ash-Wed 5		20	deny the voice/Will the veiled sister	pray for/Those who walk in darkness, who
96 Ash-Wed 5		24	/In darkness? Will the veiled sister	pray/For children at the gate/Who will not go
96 Ash-Wed 5		26	/Who will not go away and cannot	pray:/Pray for those who chose and oppose/O
96 Ash-Wed 5		27	will not go away and cannot pray:/	Pray for those who chose and oppose/O my
97 Ash-Wed 5		30	sister between the slender/Yew trees	pray for those who offend her/And are terrified
108 Animula		32	first in the silence after the viaticum./	Pray for Guiterriez, avid of speed and power,/
108 Animula		36	And that one who went his own way./	Pray for Floret, by the boarhound slain between
108 Animula		37	slain between the yew trees,/	Pray for us now and at the hour of our birth./
189 FQ: DrySal		174	shrine stands on the promontory,/	Pray for all those who are in ships, those/Whose
189 FQ: DrySal		183	del tuo figlio,/Queen of Heaven./Also	pray for those who were in ships, and/Ended
194 FQ: Little		116	let them be./So with your own, and	pray they be forgiven/By others, as I pray you
194 FQ: Little		117	pray they be forgiven/By others, as I	pray you to forgive/Both bad and good. Last
590 Time Space		5	we./So why, Love, should we ever	pray/To live a century?/The butterfly that lives
266 MC Knight2		34	and greed./Won't you ask us to	pray to God for you, in your need?/{K3} Yes,
267 MC Knight3		1	for you, in your need?/{K3} Yes, we'll	pray for you!/{K1} Yes, we'll pray for you!/{3K}
267 MC Knight1		2	we'll pray for you!/{K1} Yes, we'll	pray for you!/{3K} Yes, we'll pray that God
267 MC Knights		3	we'll pray for you!/{3K} Yes, we'll	pray that God may help you!/{T} But,

271 MC Chorus   6   Archbishop, forgive us, forgive us, pray for us that we may pray for you, out of
271 MC Chorus   6   forgive us, pray for us that we may pray for you, out of our shame. {}/[*Enter*
281 MC Priest1   1   of whose new state is hidden from us,/Pray for us of your charity./{P2} Now in the
282 MC Chorus   18   have mercy upon us./Blessed Thomas, pray for us. {}/THE FAMILY REUNION/
549 ES Ld Clav 19   at me./Don't you remember?/{LC} Pray continue./The more you remind me of, the

PRAYABLE (1)
186 FQ: DrySal   85   its God. Only the hardly, barely prayable/Prayer of the one Annunciation./It

PRAYED (1)
15 Prufrock   81   I have wept and fasted, wept and prayed,/Though I have seen my head (grown

PRAYER (14)
105 Song Sime   29   the ecstasy of thought and prayer,/Not for me the ultimate vision./Grant
140 Usk   11   air/The hermit's chapel, the pilgrim's prayer./Rannoch, by Glencoe/Here the crow
160 Rock 7   15   of a child that has died of starvation./Prayer wheels, worship of the dead, denial of
185 FQ: DrySal   55   an end to the drifting wreckage,/The prayer of the bone on the beach, the unprayable
185 FQ: DrySal   56   bone on the beach, the unprayable/Prayer at the calamitous annunciation?/There is
186 FQ: DrySal   85   and the drifting wreckage,/The bone's prayer to Death its God. Only the hardly,
186 FQ: DrySal   86   Only the hardly, barely prayable/Prayer of the one Annunciation./It seems, as
189 FQ: DrySal 178   those who conduct them./Repeat a prayer also on behalf of/Women who have seen
190 FQ: DrySal 218   followed by guesses; and the rest/Is prayer, observance, discipline, thought and
192 FQ: Little   48   report. You are here to kneel/Where prayer has been valid. And prayer is more/Than
192 FQ: Little   48   /Where prayer has been valid. And prayer is more/Than an order of words, the
245 MC Priest2 28   seven years of waiting,/Seven years of prayer, seven years of emptiness,/Have better
273 MC Thomas   17   the doors!/I will not have the house of prayer, the church of Christ,/The sanctuary,
282 MC Chorus   2   Iona,/To the death in the desert, the prayer in forgotten places by the broken

PRAYERS (4)
84 Hollow Men   51   tenderness/Lips that would kiss/Form prayers to broken stone./The eyes are not here/
248 MC Tempt1   7   will remember me, my Lord, at your prayers,/I'll remember you at kissing-time below
254 MC Tempt4   26   have also thought, sometimes at your prayers,/Sometimes hesitating at the angles of
272 MC Thomas   3   Go to vespers, remember me at your prayers./They shall find the shepherd here; the

PRAYING (2)
192 FQ: Little   50   the conscious occupation/Of the praying mind, or the sound of the voice praying.
192 FQ: Little   50   mind, or the sound of the voice praying./And what the dead had no speech for,

PRAYS (1)
152 Rock 2   43   and nights repeat the praise of GOD,/Prays for the Church, the Body of Christ

PRE-ARRANGED (1)
541 ES Gomez   35   it. {}/[*Exit* LAMBERT]/{G} Ah, the pre-arranged interruption/To terminate the

PRE-CONSCIOUS (1)
189 FQ: DrySal 197   or dissect/The recurrent image into pre-conscious terrors —/To explore the womb,

PREACH (1)
262 MC Thomas   1   children, I do not think I shall ever preach to you again; and because/it is possible

PREACHER (1)
163 Rock 8   41   from home/At the call of a wandering preacher./Our age is an age of moderate virtue/

PREACHES (1)
260 MC   3m 1   {}/Interlude/THE ARCHBISHOP/*preaches in the Cathedral on Christmas Morning,*

PRECARIOUS (1)
155 Rock 3   48   you have shelters and institutions,/Precarious lodgings while the rent is paid,/

PRECAUTION (2)
588 Fable   38   lengthy story shorter,/He left no wise precaution incomplete;/He doused the room in
386 CP Reilly   8   /As for myself, I shall take the precaution/Of leaving by the service staircase./

PRECEDE (2)
252 MC Tempt4   36   I had been here before./I always precede expectation./{T} Who are you?/{T4} As
333 FR Agatha   29   certain/That the knowledge of it must precede the expiation./It is possible that sin may

PRECEDED (2)
194 FQ: Little 104   /To compel the recognition they preceded./And so, compliant to the common
279 MC Knight4   11   Brito./{K4} The speakers who have preceded me, to say nothing/of our leader,

PRECEDES (1)
175 FQ: BurntN 149   the co-existence,/Or say that the end precedes the beginning,/And the end and the

PRECENTORSHIP (1)
518 CC Eggers   11   may be only a stepping-stone/To a precentorship! And a canonry!/{C} We'll cross

PRECIOUS (2)
241 MC Mess   37   tail,/A single hair of which becomes a precious relic./He is at one with the Pope, and
477 CC Lucasta 36   myself./{L} Yourself, indeed! Your precious self!/Why don't you shut yourself up in

PRECIPITATED (1)
407 CP Reilly   40   me believe that it was this discovery/Precipitated what you called your nervous

PRECIPITATELY (1)
558 ES Ld Clav 10   for your coming down here so precipitately —/In order to let me have your
PRECISE (3)
197 FQ: Little 224   without vulgarity,/The formal word precise but not pedantic,/The complete consort
290 FR Agatha 23 with most careful devotion/Thus with precise attention/To detail, interfering
339 FR Harry 5 still unsettled./I have not yet had the precise directions./Where does one go from a
PRÉCISE (1)
48 Lune Miel 18 /Dans ses pierres écroulantes la forme précise de Byzance./The Hippopotamus/The
PRECISELY (2)
137 5FingerEx5 6   so nicely/Restricted to What Precisely/And If and Perhaps and But./How
403 CP Reilly 8   of my own insignificance./{R} Precisely. And I could make you feel important,
PRECISIONS (1)
24 Rhapsody 7 all its clear relations,/Its divisions and precisions./Every street lamp that I pass/Beats
PREDECESSOR (1)
505 CC Claude 3   clerk. That is to say,/Colby's predecessor, who recently retired./Now he lives
PREDETERMINED (1)
160 Rock 7 18 the face of the deep./Then came, at a predetermined moment, a moment in time and
PREDICAMENT (1)
576 ES Michael 12   made him so understanding/Of my predicament./{LC} And made him invent/The
PREDICTED (1)
475 CC Colby 11 happens,/Though you couldn't have predicted it./{L} I think I'm changing./I've
PREDICTING (1)
326 FR Harry 15   the junior members?/Or engaged in predicting the minor event,/Engaged in
PREFER (11)
157 Rock 4 2   build the Temple,/And those who prefer that the Temple should not be built./In
214 RTTugger 3   put him in a house he would much prefer a flat,/If you put him in a flat then he'd
296 FR Amy 31   you are not the right person./I prefer to believe that a few days at Wishwood/
345 FR Amy 26 most malicious in a harmless way;/I prefer your company to that of any of the
371 CP Peter 1 you/On a timely escape./{P} I should prefer to be spared/Your congratulations. I had
429 CP Alex 7   of the converts —/Who, after all, prefer not to be slaughtered —/To relapse into
459 CC Lady E 13   /{E} Mr. Colby Simpkins./{LE} I prefer Colby./Where are you living?/{SC} His
469 CC Colby 12 wrong things?/{C} No, I'm sure you'll prefer the right things, when you hear them./
477 CC Lucasta 11   to him/Of something he would prefer to forget. {}/[*A pause*]/{L} But why don't
511 CC Lady E 29 me ... just 'B'?/{LE} Certainly, if you prefer that, Barnabas./{L} Why is it that you
550 ES Carghil 37   soon find that out'./A man may prefer to forget all the women/He has loved.
PREFERENCE (1)
513 CC Guzzard 19 once one knows it./{MG} You had no preference? Between a father and a mother?/{C}
PREFERRED (6)
103 Journ Magi 17 hard time we had of it./At the end we preferred to travel all night,/Sleeping in
155 Rock 3 65 /Dividing the stars into common and preferred,/Engaged in devising the perfect
292 FR Ivy 38   done nothing about it/Because she preferred to wait for your coming./{V} And time
369 CP Peter 28 one to go with,/And later, I found I preferred to go alone./But a girl like Celia, it
471 CC Colby 28 get a false impression anyway./You preferred it to be one of your own creation/
550 ES Ld Clav 33 Which I should have thought we both preferred to leave buried./{MC} There you're
PREFERRING (2)
240 MC Chorus 4 earth, earth-colour, his own colour,/Preferring to pass unobserved./Now I fear
361 CP Reilly 40   life a little better than you like it,/Preferring not quite the same friends as
PREJUDICED (1)
451 CC Eggers 2 rather alarming./{E} Mr. Kaghan is prejudiced./He's never hit it off with Lady
PRELUDE (1)
19 Portrait 33   begins/Absurdly hammering a prelude of its own,/Capricious monotone/That
PRELUDES (2)
18 Portrait 9 to hear the latest Pole/Transmit the Preludes, through his hair and finger-tips./'So
22 Preludes t /And should I have the right to smile?/Preludes/The winter evening settles down/With
PREMISES (1)
602 Humoresque 22 /Logic a marionette's, all wrong/Of premises; yet in some star/A hero! — Where
PRENDRE (1)
48 Lune Miel 11   que tournoie le vent./Ils vont prendre le train de huit heures/Prolonger leurs
PREOCCUPIED (1)
370 CP Peter 23 /And when I do see her, she seems preoccupied/With some secret excitement which
PREP (1)
557 ES Ld Clav 2 /When you were expelled from your prep school for stealing./But come to the point.
PREPARATION (4)
290 FR Agatha 24 precise attention/To detail, interfering preparation/Of that which is already prepared/
344 FR Gerald 24 And several dialects. It means a lot of preparation./{V} And you need some religious

346 FRDowning   24   to his Lordship/Was just a kind of preparation for something else./I've no gift of
437 CP   Reilly   30   do/Was to direct her in the way of preparation./That way, which she accepted, led
PREPARATIONS (2)
588 Fable   41   except the wine./So when all preparations had been made,/The jovial
419 CP   Reilly   35   /{R} Go home then, and make your preparations./Here is the address for you to give
PREPARE (10)
 14 Prufrock   27   will be time, there will be time/To prepare a face to meet the faces that you meet;/
 26 Rhapsody   77   /Put your shoes at the door, sleep, prepare for life.'/The last twist of the knife./
241 MC   Mess   16   much as was possible,/That you may prepare to meet him./{P1} What, is the exile
246 MC Thomas   23   than the consummation./All things prepare the event. Watch. {}/[*Enter* FIRST
360 CP   Reilly   15   you the same prescription .../Let me prepare it for you, if I may .../Strong ... but sip
368 CP   Alex   16   to your kitchen now/And I shall prepare you a nice little dinner/Which you can
407 CP   Reilly   15   understanding of each other/Will prepare you to appreciate what I have to say to
448 CC   Claude   2   her?/You remember, I asked you to prepare him a little;/There are some things you
467 CC   Colby   38   morning. You asked me to prepare/Some figures for you. I've got them
574 ES Carghil   23   the surprise for which I've come to prepare you./Dear Michael is so happy — all
PREPARED (21)
 18 Portrait   7   /An atmosphere of Juliet's tomb/Prepared for all the things to be said, or left
155 Rock 3   57   return to the desert./O my soul, be prepared for the coming of the Stranger,/Be
155 Rock 3   58   for the coming of the Stranger,/Be prepared for him who knows how to ask
245 MC Priest2   26   better welcome/If we had been sooner prepared for the event./But your Lordship
245 MC Priest2   29   seven years of emptiness,/Have better prepared our hearts for your coming,/Than
290 FR   Agatha   25   preparation/Of that which is already prepared/Men tighten the knot of confusion/
306 FR   Mary   35   the treats were always so carefully prepared;/There was never any time to invent
317 FR Warburt   13   —/It is much more difficult not to be prepared/For something that is very likely to
341 FR   Amy   8   have/Because you repel it./{A} I prepared the situation/For us to be reconciled,
372 CP   Alex   9   *his jacket on*]/{A} Oh, Edward! I've prepared you such a treat!/I really think that of
374 CP   Celia   21   very good one./You should have been prepared with something better, for Julia;/But it
376 CP   Edward   27   {E} It's something that Alex came and prepared for me./He *would* do it. Three Good
386 CP   Reilly   1   for definite reasons/Which I am not prepared to explain to you/I must ask you not
395 CP Lavinia   7   have a mind to speak./Anyway, I'm prepared to take you as you are./{E} You mean,
395 CP   Edward   8   as you are./{E} You mean, you are prepared to take me/As I was, or as you think I
405 CP Lavinia   27   about my husband:/I didn't say I was prepared to meet him./{E} And I did not expect
409 CP   Reilly   13   love with anybody./{R} And were not prepared to make the least sacrifice/On her
451 CC   Colby   39   musical./{C} I still don't feel very well prepared for meeting her. {}/[*A loud knock.*
452 CC Lucasta   28   that I'm one of his duties?/Have you prepared him for taking *me* over?/Did you
510 CC   Colby   15   /{C} I have told them to be prepared for a surprise./{LE} Barnabas! Is your
556 ES Monica   1   must wait in the garden/Until I had prepared you. I've made him understand/That
PREPARES (2)
166 Rock 10   8   moving his head to right and to left prepares for his hour to devour./But the
178 FQ: ECoker   49   death./Dawn points, and another day/Prepares for heat and silence. Out at sea the
PREPARING (1)
339 FR   Harry   19   do not understand. It must have been preparing always,/And I see it was what I
PREPOSTEROUS (2)
540 ES   Gomez   37   /{G} My dear Dick, what a preposterous suggestion!/Who's going to accept
542 ES Ld Clav 12   the longer I may stay./{LC} This is preposterous!/Do you call it friendship to
PRÈS (1)
 46 Directeur   2   à la malheureuse Tamise/Qui coule si près du Spectateur./Le directeur/Conservateur/
PRESAGE (1)
239 MC Chorus   6   is no safety in the cathedral. Some presage of an act/Which our eyes are compelled
PRESBYTERS (1)
 54 Mr E Sun   17   Father and the Paraclete./The sable presbyters approach/The avenue of penitence;/
PRESCRIBE (2)
407 CP   Reilly   22   upon me/Your own diagnosis, and prescribe your own cure./But when you put
418 CP   Reilly   31   /{R} Whichever way you choose will prescribe its own duty./{C} Which way is better?
PRESCRIPTION (1)
360 CP   Reilly   14   /And I recommend you the same prescription .../Let me prepare it for you, if I
PRESENCE (8)
604 Ode   3   /In thy shadow we wait, while thy presence dispels/Our vain hesitations and fears./
255 MC Tempt4   8   glory of Saints/Dwelling forever in presence of God?/What earthly glory, of king or
268 MC Knight1   15   be content/To answer in the King's presence. Therefore were we sent./{T} Never was
268 MC Thomas   38   years were my people without/My presence; seven years of misery and pain./Seven
279 MC Knight4   27   France he clearly prophesied, in the/presence of numerous witnesses, that he had not
280 MC Priest1 10   further dread/Shall we recover your presence? when inherit/Your strength? The
454 CC Eggers   31   Elizabeth *Lizzie*?/{E} Well, not in her presence. Not when I've been there./No, I don't

526 ES Monica 11 time, a long long time/Before I felt its presence./{C} Your words seem to come/From
PRESENCES (1)
331 FR Harry   1 of persons/But only of contaminating presences./And then I had no horror of my
PRESENT (36)
117 SP Dusty   9 (*reading*) 'A small sum of money, or a present/Of wearing apparel, or a party'./That's
171 FQ: BurntN   1   QUARTETS/Burnt Norton/Time present and time past/Are both perhaps present
171 FQ: BurntN   2   and time past/Are both perhaps present in time future/And time future
171 FQ: BurntN   4   in time past./If all time is eternally present/All time is unredeemable./What might
171 FQ: BurntN 10   /Point to one end, which is always present./Footfalls echo in the memory/Down
172 FQ: BurntN 48   /Point to one end, which is always present./Garlic and sapphires in the mud/Clot
184 FQ: DrySal 11   and waiting./His rhythm was present in the nursery bedroom,/In the rank
604 Ode   15   see/What we owe for the future, the present, and past,/Fair Harvard, to thine and to
246 MC Templ1 26   all acrimony,/Hoping that your present gravity/Will find excuse for my humble
248 MC Templ1   5   all acrimony,/Hoping that your present gravity/Will find excuse for my humble
248 MC Thomas 14   the mind may not be whole in the present. {}/[*Enter* SECOND TEMPTER]/{T2}
248 MC Tempt2 36   with deceitful shadows?/Power is present. Holiness hereafter./{T} Who then?/{T2}
249 MC Tempt2 13   power is earthly perdition./Power is present, for him who will wield./{T} Who shall
250 MC Tempt3 21   /{T3} But not in this guise, or for my present purpose./{T} No purpose brings
251 MC Tempt3 18   Other friends/May be found in the present situation./King in England is not
255 MC Thomas 32   know that these temptations/Mean present vanity and future torment./Can sinful
294 FR Harry   8   before morning,/In which all past is present, all degradation/Is unredeemable. As for
294 FR Harry   11   see what is past,/Not what is always present. That is what matters./{Ag}
298 FR Violet 15   I intend to remain./And I wish to be present to hear what Downing says./I want to
315 FR Amy   25   /I think we are very much the oldest present —In fact we are the oldest inhabitants./
318 FR Warburt 38   see/What that has to do with the present occasion/Or with what I have to tell
320 FR Warburt 11   /I needn't go into technicalities/At the present moment. The whole machine is weak/
320 FR Harry   39   Did you know my father at about my present age?/{W} Why, yes, Harry, of course I
330 FR Agatha 14   you mean about the future;/But a present is missing, needed to connect them./You
332 FR Agatha 27   seems to be no past or future,/Only a present moment of pointed light/When you
338 FR Harry   5   is the best thing for everybody./But at present, I cannot explain it to anyone:/I do not
379 CP Celia   23   we began,/And after that I lived in a present/Where time was meaningless, a private
398 CP Lavinia 14   see a doctor,/There's nothing else at present that I can do about it./I ought to go and
403 CP Reilly   1   of childhood —/I mean, in your present state of mind —/Would be largely
413 CP Reilly 25   moment:/Try first to describe your present state of mind./{C} Well, there are two
429 CP Alex   24   be made public?/{A} It cannot be, at present:/There are too many international
447 CC Claude   1   /{SC} Well, we'll leave that for the present. As we have a little time/Before you
505 CC Claude   6   very many years. So I asked him to be present./I hope you don't mind?/{MG} Why
506 CC Eggers 24   is why Sir Claude has asked you to be present./{MG} You think that I might be able to
543 ES Gomez   5   if not in the peerage./Goodbye for the present. It's been an elixir/To see you again, and
565 ES Gomez   27   /About old times. Bye bye for the present. {}/[*Exit*]/{M} Father, those awful
PRESENTATION (1)
530 ES Monica 30   with the tributes from the staff,/The presentation, and the speech you had to make/
PRESENTED (1)
277 MC Knight2 40   much admired, has throughout been/presented as the under dog. But is this really the
PRESENTLY (3)
218 Mung Rump   10   or two came loose on the roof,/Which presently ceased to be waterproof,/If the
271 MC Priests 26   are coming. They will break through presently./You will be killed. Come to the altar.
538 ES Gomez   9   to get rid of me. I shall tell you why presently./Now let's look for a moment at *your*
PRESENTS (5)
194 FQ: Little 122   voice./But, as the passage now presents no hindrance/To the spirit unappeased
288 FR Ivy   5   birthday cake, Amy,/And open your presents?/{A} After dinner:/That is the best
288 FR Ivy   9   have not had your cake and your presents at tea./{A} This is a very particular
325 FR Ivy   18   happened,/And have the cake and presents./{G} But I'm worried about Arthur:/
467 CC Claude 34   we have settled our account/Life presents a new one, more difficult to pay./— I
PRESERVE (5)
148 Rock 1   38   /CHORUS LEADER:/Silence! and preserve respectful distance./For I perceive
158 Rock 5   3   `men of public spirit and zeal./Preserve me from the enemy who has something
240 MC Chorus 22   who shall observe you, who shall preserve you?/Shall the Son of Man be born
296 FR Gerald 14   and have my bath. {}/[*Exit*]/{G} God preserve us!/I never thought it would be as bad
528 ES Charles 17   there was any .../Private self to preserve./{M} There *is* a private self, Charles./
PRESERVED (3)
231 Bust Jones 35   on weight every day:/But he's so well preserved because he's observed/All his life a
528 ES Monica 14   /Always his privacy has been preserved./{C} His privacy has been so well
528 ES Charles 15   /{C} His privacy has been so well preserved/That I've sometimes wondered

PRESERVER (1)
187 FQ: DrySal   117   abides./Time the destroyer is time the preserver,/Like the river with its cargo of dead
PRESS (8)
22 Preludes   17   street/With all its muddy feet that press/To early coffee-stands./With the other
127 Cor1 March   4   /How many? Count them. And such a press of people./We hardly knew ourselves that
189 FQ: DrySal   199   and drugs, and features of the press:/And always will be, some of them
594 Grad 9   5   passing years that roll/Between, as we press onward to the goal,/Shall not have power
397 CP   Lavinia 32   /{L} Very well, then, I shall not try to press you./You're much too divided to know
531 ES   Ld Clav 12   .../{LC} The established liturgy/Of the Press on any conspicuous retirement./My
541 ES   Gomez   3   ago?/What damages you'd get! The Press wouldn't look at it./Besides, you can't
543 ES   Gomez   4   been informed./I have friends in the press — if not in the peerage./Goodbye for the
PRESSED (3)
187 FQ: DrySal   130   those who are not yet here to regret,/Pressed between yellow leaves of a book that
204 de la Mare   14   time for bed? .../Or when the lawn/Is pressed by unseen feet, and ghosts return/
213 Growltiger   49   did surround./The ruthless foe pressed forward, in stubborn rank on rank;/
PRESSES (9)
136 5FingerEx4   11   apart)/While on his palate fine he presses/The juice of the gooseberry tart./How
256 MC Chorus   7   and heavy the sky. And the earth presses up against our feet./What is the sickly
295 FR Charles 12   /There's a lot in my own past life that presses on my chest/When I wake, as I do now,
329 FR Chorus   2   happens began in the past, and presses hard on the future./The agony in the
399 CP   3m   1   SIR HENRY *alone at his desk. He presses an/electric button. The*
405 CP   m   7   is much the same as your own. {}/[*Presses the bell on his desk three times*]/{R} You
412 CP   m 24   [*Exit* JULIA *by side door*]/[REILLY *presses button.* NURSE-SECRETARY *shows in*
420 CP   m 15   a case like yours/There is no fee. {}/[*Presses button*]/{C} You have been very kind./{R}
534 ES   m 39   house?/{LC} I can provide whisky. {}/[*Presses the bell*]/{LC} But why have you come?/
PRESSING (1)
65 WL: Chess   138   /And we shall play a game of chess,/Pressing lidless eyes and waiting for a knock
PRESSURE (2)
171 FQ: BurntN   26   dignified, invisible,/Moving without pressure, over the dead leaves,/In the autumn
464 CC   Claude   26   made it your profession?/{SC} Family pressure, in the first place./My father — your
PRESTER (1)
33 Conv Gal   3   (fantastic, I confess)/It may be Prester John's balloon/Or an old battered
PRESTIDIGITATION (1)
224 Mr Mistoff   10   And creating eccentric confusions./At prestidigitation/And at legerdemain/He'll defy
PRESTO (1)
224 Mr Mistoff   16   Mr. Mistoffelees' Conjuring Turn./Presto!/Away we go!/And we all say: OH!/Well
PRESUME (6)
14 Prufrock   54   from a farther room./So how should I presume?/And I have known the eyes already,
15 Prufrock   61   my days and ways?/And how should I presume?/And I have known the arms already,
15 Prufrock   68   about a shawl./And should I then presume?/And how should I begin?/Shall I say,
406 CP   Lavinia   5   me either. {}/[*To* REILLY]/{L} I presume you will send him to the same
452 CC   Eggers   14   them right!/{E} You have been, I presume, persistently unpunctual./{L} You're
552 ES   Carghil 30   And now you're posing/As what? I presume, as an elder statesman;/And the
PRETENCE (8)
246 MC Thomas   18   hover, circling lower,/Waiting excuse, pretence, opportunity./End will be simple,
249 MC Tempt2   19   /{T} What shall we give for it?/{T2} Pretence of priestly power./{T} Why should we
272 MC Chorus   29   delusion, escape into dream, pretence,/Where the soul is no longer deceived,
381 CP   Edward   31   from it/Is only a make-believe, a pretence/That what is, is not, or could be
385 CP   Reilly   10   still more difficult/To keep up the pretence that you are not strangers./The
540 ES   Ld Clav   9   the mirror./{LC} Isn't that the kind of pretence that you're maintaining/In trying to
542 ES   Ld Clav 14   a man by threats? Why keep up the pretence?/{G} Threats, Dick! How can you
569 ES   Ld Clav   1   /The harder it becomes to drop the pretence,/Walk off the stage, change into our
PRETENCES (7)
293 FR Agatha   21   having got so far —/If you want no pretences, let us have no pretences:/And you
293 FR Agatha   21   you want no pretences, let us have no pretences:/And you must try at once to make us
340 FR Amy   20   What of the humiliation,/Of the chilly pretences in the silent bedroom,/Forcing sons
517 CC   Colby   14   /All that's left is love. But not on false pretences:/That's why I must leave you./{SC}
569 ES   Ld Clav   8   /I've had your love under false pretences./Now, I'm tired of keeping up those
569 ES   Ld Clav   9   /Now, I'm tired of keeping up those pretences,/But I hope that you'll find a little
581 ES   Ld Clav 22   /So that I could believe in my own pretences./I've only just now had the
PRETEND (16)
234 Ad-dress   20   A CAT IS NOT A DOG./Now Dogs pretend they like to fight;/They often bark,
293 FR Harry   17   not get to the point/Or if you want to pretend that I am another person —/A person
356 CP   Julia   17   the perfect host,/But just try to pretend you're another guest/At Lavinia's
367 CP   Edward   2   noticed one or two things;/But I don't pretend I was aware of everything./{P} Oh, I'm

367 CP	Edward	29	from its literary merit/Which I don't	pretend to judge./{P} Well, I can judge it,/And I
385 CP	Reilly	2	they have changed since then./To	pretend that they and we are the same/Is a
385 CP	Reilly	19	strangers, but still more difficult/To	pretend that you were not strange to each other.
413 CP	Celia	14	to be done./{C} Well, I can't	pretend that my trouble is interesting;/But I
480 CC	Colby	12	/{C} That's just nonsense./You only	pretend that you're a gambler./You've got as
480 CC	Colby	15	in anything risky./You like to	pretend to other people/That you're a gambler.
514 CC	Claude	34	it. I'll not believe those records./You	pretend to have carried out a deception/For
542 ES	Ld Clav	23	You were a free moral agent./You	pretend that I taught you expensive tastes:/If
548 ES	Monica	11	your newspaper over your face/And	pretend you're pretending to be asleep./If they
558 ES	Michael	24	of fun with me — sometimes they'd	pretend/That I was overworked, when I'd
568 ES	Ld Clav	39	chosen to play. And the longer we	pretend/The harder it becomes to drop the
579 ES	Monica	5	Whoever you are then/I shall always	pretend that it is the same Michael./{C} And

PRETENDED (4)

407 CP	Reilly	20	successful. You have both of you	pretended/To be consulting me; both, tried to
409 CP	Reilly	34	you knew it/Before he did. You	pretended to yourself,/I suspect, and for as long
558 ES	Michael	6	did come to hear about it,/And so he	pretended to be very shocked./Said he couldn't
581 ES	Ld Clav	21	your life to adoring/The man that I	pretended to myself that I was,/So that I could

PRETENDING (3)

507 CC	Guzzard	37	of yours/And deceived Sir Claude by	pretending it was his?/{SC} That is just the
540 ES	Gomez	6	/Is the man who has to keep on	pretending to himself/That he's a success — the
548 ES	Monica	11	over your face/And pretend you're	pretending to be asleep./If they think you *are*

PRETENDS (3)

159 Rock	6	25	man that is will shadow/The man that	pretends to be./And the Son of Man was not
501 CC	Lucasta	6	you think him common. And so he	pretends/To be very common, because he knows
582 ES	Ld Clav	3	also./I've been freed from the self that	pretends to be someone;/And in becoming no

PRETENSION (1)

301 FR	Chorus	25	/{Ch} We all of us make the	pretension/To be the uncommon exception/To

PRETENSIONS (2)

242 MC	Mess	7	/Or yet to diminish the least of his	pretensions./If you ask my opinion, I think that
278 MC	Knight2	38	/arrived at a just subordination of the	pretensions of the Church to/the welfare of the

PRETEXT (2)

111 Xmas Trees	11		Feast as an event not accepted as a	pretext;/So that the glittering rapture, the
427 CP	Alex	37	least, the monkeys have become the	pretext/For general unrest amongst the natives./

PRETTY (17)

277 MC	Knight3	8	is that/we knew we had taken on a	pretty stiff job; I'll only speak for/myself, but I
293 FR	Gerald	33	corners most of my life/And some	pretty nasty messes./{C} And there isn't much
298 FR	Charles	33	/{C} Eleven years, and you know him	pretty well./And I'm sure that you've been a
322 FR	Winch	33	Road, in the fog, coming along/At a	pretty smart pace, I fancy, ran into a lorry/
374 CP	Edward	18	*was* the situation./I suppose it was	pretty obvious to everyone./{C} It was obvious
415 CP	Celia	19	family?/{C} Well, my bringing up was	pretty conventional —/I had always been taught
462 CC	Claude	3	it was she who proposed it./So I feel	pretty confident that, before long,/We can put
479 CC	Kaghan	37	brighter./But otherwise, it looks	pretty comfortable./If I was as snug as Colby is,
481 CC	Colby	2	/{C} I'm beginning to believe you've a	pretty shrewd insight/Into things that have
496 CC	Eggers	35	— I hope Mrs. Eggerson is well?/{E}	Pretty well./She's always low-spirited, around
518 CC	Eggers	7	a little time, and I've watched you	pretty closely./Mr. Simpkins! You'll be thinking
533 ES	Gomez	15	whatever you like./But I've been a	pretty hard worker all these years/And I
533 ES	Gomez	19	I'm a widower, like you, Dick./So I'm	pretty footloose. Gomez, you see,/Is now a
533 ES	Gomez	32	side to *me*./Sometimes I've had to pay	pretty heavily;/But I learnt by experience whom
541 ES	Gomez	21	not all in my own name either —/Are	pretty well spread. For the matter of that,/My
557 ES	Ld Clav	1	getting into trouble./{LC} You started	pretty early getting into trouble,/When you were
557 ES	Michael	33	/{Mi} Nearly two years./Time passes	pretty quickly, when you're in debt./{LC} And

PREVAILED (1)

19 Portrait	62		/You will go on, and when you have	prevailed/You can say: at this point many a one

PREVALENT (1)

402 CP	Reilly	36	A very common malady./Very	prevalent indeed./{E} I remember, in my

PREVENT (5)

211 Old Gumbie	32		just need employment/To	prevent them from idle and wanton
331 FR	Harry	8	would fall into place. But *they*	prevent it./I still have to find out what their
491 CC	Lady E	10	—/But in some ways better! And	prevent us both/From making unreasonable
530 ES	Monica	6	allowed you to!/That's my business to	prevent. You know I'm to protect you/From
578 ES	Ld Clav	2	to contract his enslavement,/I cannot	prevent him. I have something to say to you,/

PREVENTED (2)

290 FR	Amy	14	regret and no remorse./I would have	prevented it if I could. For the sake of the
572 ES	Ld Clav	14	have married her — but my father	prevented that:/Made it worth while for her not

PREVENTING (1)
479 CC Kaghan   23   life!/Which depends, of course, on preventing Lizzie/From always interfering. Be
PREVENTS (1)
181 FQ: ECoker 163   care/That will not leave us, but prevents us everywhere./The chill ascends from
PREVIOUS (5)
463 CC   Colby 13   that I can do/So remote from my previous interests./It gives me, in a way, a kind
483 CC   Lady E 36   we had known each other/In some previous incarnation. — Is this your mother?/
485 CC   Lady E 19   And that one's real ancestry/Is one's previous existences. Of course, there's
515 CC Guzzard 23   for Colby./I am sacrificing also my previous sacrifice./This is even greater than the
531 ES Lambert 35   never saw anyone, my Lord,/But by previous appointment. He said he knew that,/So
PREVISION (1)
246 MC Thomas   6   hate./By God's grace aware of their prevision/I sent my letters on another day,/Had
PREY (2)
212 Growltiger   28   the Lion he was prowling for his prey./In the forepeak of the vessel Growltiger
410 CP   Reilly 25   /The shadow of desires of desires. A prey/To the devils who arrive at their plenitude
PRIAPUS (1)
31 Apollinax   4   figure among the birch-trees,/And of Priapus in the shrubbery/Gaping at the lady in
PRICE (4)
249 MC Tempt2   11   /{T2} Real power/Is purchased at price of a certain submission./Your spiritual
255 MC Thomas   20   /With pleasure and power at palpable price./What do you offer? what do you ask?/
438 CP   Reilly   1   the rest of us. She paid the highest price/In suffering. That is part of the design./{L}
530 ES Ld Clav 37   levy/That made the Chairman's Price! And my fellow directors/Saying 'we must
PRICES (2)
103 Journ Magi   15   the villages dirty and charging high prices:/A hard time we had of it./At the end we
248 MC Tempt1   2   will have to be paid for at higher prices./Farewell, my Lord, I do not wait upon
PRICKLY (4)
85 Hollow Men   68   /Of empty men./*Here we go round the prickly pear/Prickly pear prickly pear/Here we*
85 Hollow Men   69   /*Here we go round the prickly pear/Prickly pear prickly pear/Here we go round the*
85 Hollow Men   69   *go round the prickly pear/Prickly pear prickly pear/Here we go round the prickly pear/*
85 Hollow Men   70   *prickly pear/Here we go round the prickly pear/At five o'clock in the morning./*
PRIDE (19)
141 Rannoch   10   Memory is strong/Beyond the bone. Pride snapped,/Shadow of pride is long, in the
141 Rannoch   11   the bone. Pride snapped,/Shadow of pride is long, in the long pass/No concurrence
152 Rock 2   29   neglect of the Word of GOD,/For pride, for lechery, treachery, for every act of sin.
163 Rock 8   37   /Envy, sloth, gluttony, jealousy, pride:/It was not these that made the Crusades,/
186 FQ: DrySal   64   /There is the final addition, the failing/Pride or resentment at failing powers,/The
209 NamingCats   16   spread out his whiskers, or cherish his pride?/Of names of this kind, I can give you a
234 Ad-dress   28   /And far from showing too much pride/Is frequently undignified./He's very easily
241 MC   Priest2 23   old disputes at an end, is the wall of pride cast down/That divided them? Is it peace
241 MC   Mess   30   a certain incredulity./He comes in pride and sorrow, affirming all his claims,/
242 MC   Priest1 18   I fear for the Church,/I know that the pride bred of sudden prosperity/Was but
242 MC   Priest1 24   among them, always insecure;/His pride always feeding upon his own virtues,/
242 MC   Priest1 25   always feeding upon his own virtues,/Pride drawing sustenance from impartiality,/
242 MC   Priest1 26   sustenance from impartiality,/Pride drawing sustenance from generosity,/
255 MC   Tempt4   10   of king or emperor,/What earthly pride, that is not poverty/Compared with
255 MC Thomas   30   /Does not lead to damnation in pride?/I well know that these temptations/Mean
255 MC Thomas   33   vanity and future torment./Can sinful pride be driven out/Only by more sinful? Can I
266 MC Knights   20   swollen with blood and swollen with pride./Creeping out of the London dirt,/
266 MC Knight1   32   is what you mean,/Saving your pride, envy and spleen./{K2} Saving your
305 FR   Agatha   9   /And the moment is only fear and pride. I see more than this,/More than I can tell
PRIE (1)
51 Restaurant   7   baveux, à la croupe arrondie,/Je te prie, au moins, ne bave pas dans la soupe)./'Les
PRIEST (12)
263 MC   1m 27   waiting is long. {}/[*Enter the* FIRST PRIEST *with a banner of St. Stephen borne*
264 MC   m   7   *is heard*]/[*Enter the* SECOND PRIEST, *with a banner of St. John the Apostle*
264 MC   m 14   *St. John is heard*]/[*Enter the* THIRD PRIEST, *with a banner of the Holy Innocents*
269 MC Knight1 15   the judgement of Rome./{K1} Priest, you have spoken in peril of your life./
269 MC Knight2 16   have spoken in peril of your life./{K2} Priest, you have spoken in danger of the knife./
269 MC Knight3 17   spoken in danger of the knife./{K3} Priest, you have spoken treachery and treason./
269 MC Knights 18   spoken treachery and treason./{3K} Priest! traitor, confirmed in malfeasance./{T} I
269 MC Knight4 22   before God's throne. {}/[*Exit*]/{K4} Priest! monk! and servant! take, hold, detain,/
274 MC Knights 17   King?/Where is Becket, the meddling priest?/Come down Daniel to the lions' den,/
274 MC Knights 25   brat?/Where is Becket the faithless priest?/Come down Daniel to the lions' den,/
274 MC Thomas   31   here./No traitor to the King. I am a priest,/A Christian, saved by the blood of
536 ES   Gomez   13   away,/Only believed what the parish priest told her./I made my children learn

PRIESTLY (2)
249 MC Tempt2 19   shall we give for it?/{T2} Pretence of priestly power./{T} Why should we give it?/{T2}
278 MC Knight2 21   office of Chancellor, he became more priestly than the/priests, he ostentatiously and
PRIESTS (11)
238 MC   m 4   OF CANTERBURY/THREE PRIESTS OF THE CATHEDRAL/A
238 MC   m 11   *2nd*, 1170/PART II/THREE PRIESTS/FOUR KNIGHTS/ARCHBISHOP
240 MC   m 26   only to wait and to witness. {}/[*Enter* PRIESTS]/{P1} Seven years and the summer is
256 MC   m 29   lay course by the sun? {}/CHORUS, PRIESTS *and* TEMPTERS *alternately*./{C} Is it
264 MC   m 22 mouth of very babes, O God! {}/[THE PRIESTS *stand together with the banners*
266 MC   m 1   us waiting? {}/[*Enter* THOMAS]/[*to* PRIESTS]./{T} However certain our expectation
266 MC   m 11 /We must speak with you alone. {}/[*to* PRIESTS]/{T} Leave us then alone./Now what
267 MC   m 25   {}/[*They make to attack him, but the priests and attendants return and quietly*
271 MC   m 20   bear very much reality. {}/[*Enter* PRIESTS]/[*severally*]./{3P} My Lord, you must
273 MC   m 10   {}/[*In the cathedral.* THOMAS *and* PRIESTS]/{3P} Bar the door. Bar the door/The
278 MC Knight2 22   he became more priestly than the/priests, he ostentatiously and offensively
PRIM (1)
137 5FingerEx5   4   his brow so grim/And his mouth so prim/And his conversation, so nicely/Restricted
PRIME (1)
228 Gus   9 For he isn't the Cat that he was in his prime;/Though his name was quite famous, he
PRIMEVÈRES (1)
51 Restaurant   11   toute mouillée, je lui ai donné des primevères.'/Les taches de son gilet montent au
PRIMITIVE (2)
187 FQ: DrySal 105   /Over the shoulder, towards the primitive terror./Now, we come to discover that
339 FR   Harry 9 deprivation,/A stony sanctuary and a primitive altar,/The heat of the sun and the icy
PRIMROSE (4)
174 FQ: BurntN 115   Camden and Putney,/Highgate, Primrose and Ludgate. Not here/Not here the
270 MC Chorus   3 in the hollyhock, sweet pea, hyacinth, primrose and cowslip. I have seen/Trunk and
459 CC   Claude 24   between you?/{SC} I thought a primrose yellow would be cheerful./{LE} Just
459 CC   Lady E 25 cheerful./{LE} Just what I expected. A primrose yellow/Would be absolutely baneful to
PRINCE (3)
16 Prufrock   111   what I meant, at all.'/No! I am not Prince Hamlet, nor was meant to be;/Am an
16 Prufrock   114   start a scene or two,/Advise the prince; no doubt, an easy tool,/Deferential, glad
268 MC Knight1   7   those who had crowned the young prince,/Denying the legality of his coronation./
PRINCE (1) [*Proper name*]
75 WL: Thund 429 *uti chelidon* — O swallow swallow/*Le Prince d'Aquitaine à la tour abolie*/These
PRINCES (3)
264 MC Priest1   2   the day of St. Stephen, First Martyr./*Princes moreover did sit, and did witness falsely*
264 MC Priest1   6 /Lord, lay not this sin to their charge./*Princes moreover did sit.* {}/[*Introit of St.*
270 MC Chorus   18   fate/What is woven in the councils of princes/Is woven also in our veins, our brains,/
PRINCESS (3)
40 Burb Blei   3   bridge/Descending at a small hotel;/Princess Volupine arrived,/They were together,
41 Burb Blei   25 /Money in furs. The boatman smiles,/Princess Volupine extends/A meagre,
430 CP   Peter 20   saw me off./You remember Princess Bologolomsky/In the old days? We
PRINCIPAL (1)
331 FR   Agatha 23   people know me as,/The efficient principal of a women's college —/That is the
PRINCIPLE (2)
276 MC Knight1 26 accordance with our long-established/principle of Trial by Jury. I am not myself
294 FR   Harry 19   —/Without purpose, and without principle of conduct/In flickering intervals of
PRINCIPLES (1)
43 Swee Erect   35   disgraced,/Call witness to their principles/And deprecate the lack of taste/
PRINT (1)
154 Rock 3   14   /Many desire to see their names in print,/Many read nothing but the race reports./
PRINTING (2)
154 Rock 3   13   are engaged in writing books and printing them,/Many desire to see their names
156 Rock 3   68   out a rational morality,/Engaged in printing as many books as possible,/Plotting of
PRIOR (2)
135 5FingerEx2 14   a little dog I pause/Heaving up my prior paws,/Pause, and sleep endlessly./*Lines to*
587 Fable   23 upset the chimes,/And once he sat the prior on the steeple,/To the astonishment of all
PRISON (8)
72 WL: Thund   326   places/The shouting and the crying/Prison and palace and reverberation/Of thunder
74 WL: Thund   413   only/We think of the key, each in his prison/Thinking of the key, each confirms a
74 WL: Thund   414 /Thinking of the key, each confirms a prison/Only at nightfall, aethereal rumours/
334 FR   Harry 39   is a different kind of pain from prison./{Ag} I only looked through the little
397 CP   Edward 3   /Why could I not walk out of my prison?/What is hell? Hell is oneself,/Hell is
419 CP   Celia 22 back as these did./{C} It sounds like a prison. But they can't *all* stay there!/I mean, it

| 576 ES | Ld Clav | 9 | the fact that he served a term in prison?/{Mi} He told me everything. It was his |
| 577 ES | Charles | 18 | you can be sure of/Is that he served a prison sentence for forgery./{G} Well, Michael, |

PRIVACY (6)

328 FR	Charles	33	nowadays, there's no such thing as privacy./{Ch} In an old house there is always
334 FR	Harry	37	were private shadows. O that awful privacy/Of the insane mind! Now I can live in
479 CC	Kaghan	25	Colby;/Assert your right to a little privacy./Now's the moment for firmness. Don't
528 ES	Monica	14	of public companies,/Always his privacy has been preserved./{C} His privacy has
528 ES	Charles	15	privacy has been preserved./{C} His privacy has been so well preserved/That I've
545 ES	Ld Clav	19	a latent desire to interfere/With the privacy of others, which is certain to explode./

PRIVATE (21)

164 Rock 9		14	very well./Let us mourn in a private chamber, learning the way of penitence,/
202 War Poetry		23	other. But the abstract conception/Of private experience at its greatest intensity/
206 To my Wife		12	is for others to read:/These are private words addressed to you in public./OLD
244 MC	Chorus	17	not able to./We have all had our private terrors,/Our particular shadows, our
249 MC	Tempt2	30	abroad, need fast friends at home./Private policy is public profit;/Dignity still shall
253 MC	Tempt4	16	/Kings have public policy, barons private profit,/Jealousy raging possession of the
275 MC	Chorus	29	to happen./We understood the private catastrophe,/The personal loss, the
301 FR	Chorus	18	shall shout in the street?/When the private shall be made public, the common
317 FR	Warburt	4	of your mother's birthday./I wanted a private conversation with you/On a confidential
327 FR	Agatha	4	/We must try to penetrate the other private worlds/Of make-believe and fear. To
327 FR	Harry	11	answered in abstractions./I have a private puzzle. Were they simply outside,/I
334 FR	Harry	37	and the real/Are what I thought were private shadows. O that awful privacy/Of the
379 CP	Celia	24	/Where time was meaningless, a private world of *ours*,/Where the word
465 CC	Claude	29	/I believe you will go through the private door/Into the real world, as I do,
466 CC	Claude	8	And as for me,/I keep my pieces in a private room./It isn't that I don't want anyone
526 ES	Monica	20	mean now — *I* and *you*?/{M} In our private world — now we have our private world
526 ES	Monica	20	private world — now we have our private world —/The meanings are different.
528 ES	Monica	11	see when they meet you/Is not the private man, but the public personage./In
528 ES	Charles	17	wondered whether there was any .../Private self to preserve./{M} There *is* a private
528 ES	Monica	18	self to preserve./{M} There *is* a private self, Charles./I'm sure of that./{C}
557 ES	Ld Clav	14	/{LC} I dare say you've tried a little private speculation./{Mi} Several of my friends

PRIVILEGE (5)

249 MC	Thomas	37	not forget/Constant curbing of petty privilege./{T2} Against the barons/Is King's
267 MC	Knight1	30	you were endued/With your former privilege, how did you show your gratitude?/
342 FR	Agatha	33	/And he cannot return. That is his privilege./For those who live in this world, this
456 CC	Eggers	36	of my travels!/It's been a very unusual privilege/To see as much of Europe as I have,/
545 ES	Piggott	34	/She'd be overjoyed to have the privilege of helping you!/{M} You're very kind

PRIZE (2)

| 166 Rock 10 | | 10 | Come/Ye out from among those who prize the serpent's golden eyes,/The |
| 256 MC | Tempts | 14 | given at the children's party,/The prize awarded for the English Essay,/The |

PRIZES (2)

| 256 MC | Tempts | 13 | wheel, the pantomime cat,/The prizes given at the children's party,/The prize |
| 313 FR | Ivy | 12 | afford a garden; and I took several prizes/With my delphiniums. I was rather an |

PROBABILITY (1)

| 510 CC | Eggers | 9 | is my son?/{E} It creates an inherent probability —/If that's the right expression./ |

PROBABLY (7)

187 FQ: DrySal		102	— not forgetting/Something that is probably quite ineffable:/The backward look
213 Growltiger		47	it, but she quickly disappeared./She probably escaped with ease, I'm sure she was
230 Bust Jones		25	/When he's seen in a hurry there's probably curry/At the *Siamese* — or at the
261 MC	Thomas	8	also one thing of which you have probably never thought./Not only do we at the
296 FR	Charles	24	what you are thinking./{C} He has probably let this notion grow in his mind,/
317 FR	Harry	7	I can imagine —/Though I think it is probably going to be useless,/Or if anything,
555 ES	Monica	33	you or me to know about./{M} It's probably money./{LC} If it's only debts/Once

PROBE (1)

| 357 CP | Julia | 34 | *depths* of Essex./{J} Well, we won't probe into it./You have the address, and the |

PROBING (1)

| 319 FR | Warburt | 11 | father?/{W} Harry, there's no good probing for misery./There was enough once: but |

PROBLEM (11)

184 FQ: DrySal		5	a conveyor of commerce;/Then only a problem confronting the builder of bridges./The
184 FQ: DrySal		6	the builder of bridges./The problem once solved, the brown god is almost
202 War Poetry		19	neither be ignored nor accepted,/A problem to be met with ambush and stratagem,/
276 MC	Knight1	30	the merits of this extremely complex problem. I/shall call upon our eldest member to
278 MC	Knight2	5	to these questions lies the key to the problem./The King's aim has been perfectly
409 CP	Reilly	25	now, let us turn to your side of the problem./When you discovered that your young
411 CP	Reilly	27	think I will dispose of your husband's problem. {}/[*To* EDWARD]/{R} Your business

243 MC	Chorus	15	Ill the wind, ill the time, uncertain the profit, certain the danger./O late late late, late is
249 MC	Tempt2	30	at home./Private policy is public profit;/Dignity still shall be dressed with
253 MC	Tempt4	16	have public policy, barons private profit,/Jealousy raging possession of the fiend./
560 ES	Michael	3	/Poor ghost! reckoning up its profit and loss/And wondering why it bothered

PROFITS (1)

560 ES	Michael	14	and export,/With an opportunity of profits both ways./{LC} This is what I will do

PROFITS (1) [*Foreign word*]

51 Restaurant		27	et la houle de Cornouaille,/Et les profits et les pertes, et la cargaison d'étain:/Un

PROFOUND (3)

31 Apollinax		8	/His laughter was submarine and profound/Like the old man of the sea's/Hidden
209 NamingCats		25	confess./When you notice a cat in profound meditation,/The reason, I tell you, is
601 Nocturne		11	Rolls toward the moon a frenzied eye profound,/(No need of 'Love forever?' — 'Love

PROFUSION (1)

64 WL: Chess		85	it,/From satin cases poured in rich profusion./In vials of ivory and coloured glass/

PROGENY (1)

220 Old Deut		7	say, ninety-nine;/And his numerous progeny prospers and thrives/And the village is

PROGNOSTIC (1)

242 MC	Mess	16	/But no one considers it a happy prognostic. {}/[*Exit*]/{P1} I fear for the

PROGRAMME (1)

471 CC	Colby	4	let me tell you beforehand/About the programme — or the things I want to hear./I'll

PROGRESS (4)

16 Prufrock		113	lord, one that will do/To swell a progress, start a scene or two,/Advise the
595 Grad 13		6	/Still as the years pass by, the word 'Progress!'/So we are done; we may no more
504 CC	Lady E	21	beginning./{LE} She's been making progress, under my direction;/But she shouldn't
553 ES	Carghil	5	character./{MC} I've followed your progress year by year, Richard./And although

PROGRESSIVELY (1)

161 Rock 7		32	upwards/In an age which advances progressively backwards?/VOICE OF THE

PROHIBITED (1)

328 FR	Violet	6	I think these racing cars ought to be prohibited. {}/[*Re-enter* CHARLES, *with a*

PROJECT (1)

304 FR	Mary	27	/Because she couldn't bear to let any project go;/And even when *she* died: I believed

PROJECTED (1)

421 CP	Reilly	22	frightened/By the first appearance of projected spirits?/{J} Henry, you simply do not

PROJECTILES (1)

127 Cor1 March		17	heavy guns,/I cannot tell how many projectiles, mines and fuses,/13,000 aeroplanes,/

PROJECTION (1)

382 CP	Celia	28	/The man I saw before, he was only a projection —/I see that now — of something

PROJECTIONS (1)

397 CP	Edward	6	is alone, the other figures in it/Merely projections. There is nothing to escape from/

PROJECTS (1)

329 FR	Chorus	4	to itself all the voices of the past, and projects them into the future./The treble voices

PROLOGUE (2)

115 SP		t	*Melodrama*/Fragment of a Prologue/DUSTY. DORIS./{Du} How about
413 CP	Reilly	9	but myself./{R} And after that, the prologue to my treatment/Is to try to show

PROLONGATION (1)

559 ES	Michael	36	your son — that is to say,/A kind of prolongation of your existence,/A representative

PROLONGED (1)

64 WL: Chess		91	these ascended/In fattening the prolonged candle-flames,/Flung their smoke

PROLONGER (1)

48 Lune Miel		12	vont prendre le train de huit heures/Prolonger leurs misères de Padoue à Milan/Où

PROMINENT (1)

563 ES	Gomez	20	old friend Federico Gomez,/The prominent citizen of San Marco./That's my

PROMISE (15)

52 Whispers		20	/Uncorseted, her friendly bust/Gives promise of pneumatic bliss./The couched
194 FQ: Little		134	/Without enchantment, offering no promise/But bitter tastelessness of shadow fruit/
260 MC Thomas		25	voices were mistaken, and/that the promise was a disappointment and a cheat?/
346 FR	Mary	11	night, Sir./{M} Downing, will you promise never to leave his Lordship/While you
364 CP	Reilly	21	it must be on one condition:/That you promise to ask her no questions/Of where she
378 CP	Celia	39	/Edward, if I go away now/Will you promise me to speak to a very great doctor/Whom I
379 CP	Celia	11	that is right, everything else will be,/I promise you./{E} No, Celia./It has been very
386 CP	Edward	4	she will not mention me to you./{E} I promise./{UG} And now you must await your
439 CP	Peter	31	The next time I come to England, I promise you./I really do want to see you both,
478 CC	Colby	26	now I'm going to. I'm breaking a promise. But .../{L} I don't believe there's
541 ES	Gomez	10	who knew the story and who didn't. I promise you./Rely upon me as the soul of
551 ES	Carghil	24	have started an action/For breach of promise, if I'd really cared for you./What

551 ES	Carghil	31		for him./If he's lost a breach of promise suit/Some people won't want to appear
560 ES	Michael	26		to get myself involved in a breach of promise suit/Or somebody's divorce. No, you
565 ES	Carghil	24		Gomez, I shall hold you to your promise! {}/[*Exeunt* MRS. CARGHILL *and*

PROMISED (4)

70 WL: Fire S		298		my feet. After the event/He wept. He promised "a new start."/I made no comment.
120 SP	Krum	10		is at *home* in London,/And he's promised to show us around. {}/Fragment of an
302 FR	Amy	13		/{A} It is very annoying. They both promised to be here/In good time for dinner. It
524 ES	Monica	28		staying to tea. As you practically promised./{C} What you don't understand is

PROMISING (2)

501 CC	Eggers	30		Mr. Kaghan/Is one of the most promising young men in the City,/And he has a
509 CC	Claude	22		this, Mrs. Guzzard./I have a very promising young colleague —/In fact, the young

PROMONTORY (1)

189 FQ: DrySal		173		/Lady, whose shrine stands on the promontory,/Pray for all those who are in ships,

PRONOUNCE (2)

228 Gus			4	Asparagus. That's such a fuss/To pronounce, that we usually call him just Gus./
533 ES	Gomez	9		than Culverwell — and easier to pronounce./{LC} Have you lived out there ever

PRONOUNCES (1)

269 MC Thomas		13		that you strive./It is not Becket who pronounces doom,/But the Law of Christ's

PROOF (2)

225 Mr Mistoff		49		purred)/Which is incontestable proof/Of his singular magical powers:/And I
372 CP	Alex	19		the aunt/Really exists. A substantial proof./{E} No, no ... I mean, this is another

PROPAGATES (1)

38 Gerontion			43	can be dispensed with/Till the refusal propagates a fear. Think/Neither fear nor

PROPER (9)

66 WL: Chess		162		I've never been the same./You *are* a proper fool, I said./Well, if Albert won't leave
148 Rock 1			59	thought of the harvest,/But only of proper sowing./The world turns and the world
154 Rock 3			5	/Sold by the proceeds of your proper inventions:/I have given you hands
234 Ad-dress			14	and games,/And learnt about their proper names,/Their habits and their habitat:/
316 FR	Agatha	18		weasel and the otter/Be about their proper business/The eye of the day time/And
421 CP	Julia	5		/And can choose, whether to put on proper costumes/Or huddle quickly into new
483 CC	Lady E	28		it? Surely your bedroom/Is the proper place for photographic souvenirs. {}/[*She*
515 CC	Guzzard	12		was yours,/My son was assured of a proper start in life —/That I knew. And it
547 ES	Monica	17		/Perhaps after what she considers proper courtesies,/She will leave us alone. {}/

PROPERLY (1)

457 CC	Lady E	28		haven't learned yet how to make tea properly./A cup of black coffee. Is Sir Claude at

PROPERTY (1)

174 FQ: BurntN		121		deprivation/And destitution of all property,/Desiccation of the world of sense,/

PROPHESIED (1)

279 MC Knight4		26		that before he left France he clearly prophesied, in the/presence of numerous

PROPHESY (1)

91 Ash-Wed 2		22		in purpose. And God said/Prophesy to the wind, to the wind only for only/

PROPHET (3)

15 Prufrock			83	brought in upon a platter,/I am no prophet — and here's no great matter;/I have
157 Rock 4			3	be built./In the days of Nehemiah the Prophet/There was no exception to the general
158 Rock 5			4	the words of Nehemiah the Prophet: 'The trowel in hand, and the gun

PROPHETS (1)

151 Rock 2			3	upon the foundation/Of apostles and prophets, Christ Jesus Himself the chief

PROPITIOUS (1)

68 WL: Fire S		235		Bradford millionaire./The time is now propitious, as he guesses,/The meal is ended, she

PROPOSAL (2)

503 CC	Eggers	22		sure Mr. Simpkins will concur in this proposal./{C} Of course I'd like them ... Can't
579 ES	Carghil	13		/— No sooner had I put my proposal before him/Than he had it all planned

PROPOSE (11)

377 CP	Julia	25		stimulant/After this disaster. Now I'll propose a health./Can you guess whose health
377 CP	Julia	26		you guess whose health I'm going to propose?/{E} No, I can't. But I won't drink to
405 CP	Reilly	8		accept a rather unusual procedure:/I propose to introduce you to the other patient./
405 CP	Edward	18		/{E} I am at least free to leave. And I propose to do so./My mind is made up. I shall
448 CC	Eggers	17		I go to meet her./How soon do you propose to ... *explain* Mr. Simpkins?/Regularize
454 CC	Lucasta	5		at Northolt./{L} Well, I don't propose to be on the scene when *she* comes./{K}
454 CC	Kaghan	6		when *she* comes./{K} And I don't propose to leave you with Colby./He's had
537 ES	Ld Clav	4		given/Of trusting people, how do you propose/To make it worth my while to be
539 ES	Gomez	30		carefully about my career./{G} I don't propose to give you a detailed account/Of my
559 ES	Ld Clav	2		work!/{LC} And what do you now propose to do with yourself?/{Mi} I want to go
573 ES	Charles	15		I grant you all that./But what do you propose? How long, Lord Claverton,/Will you

PROPOSED (1)
462 CC Claude 2   she'll be sure it was she who proposed it./So I feel pretty confident that,
PROPOSING (1)
588 Fable 61 eaten so much goose./The Abbot with proposing every toast/Had drank more than he
PROPOSITIONS (1)
410 CP Reilly 18 /Now, you have only to reverse the propositions/And put them together./{L} Is that
PROPRIETOR (1)
411 CP Lavinia 2 Forest/If you want to go there. The proprietor/Who has just taken over, is a friend
PROSPECTS (2)
357 CP Julia 16 /I quite understand. Are there any prospects?/{E} No, I think she put it all into an
477 CC Lucasta 39 you think it would be bad for your prospects/Now that you're Claude's
PROSPER (1)
428 CP Alex 29 the monkeys/The Christian natives prosper exceedingly:/And that creates friction
PROSPERITY (2)
152 Rock 2 36 remember that while there is time of prosperity/The people will neglect the Temple,
242 MC Priest1 18 /I know that the pride bred of sudden prosperity/Was but confirmed by bitter
PROSPERS (2)
220 Old Deut 7   /And his numerous progeny prospers and thrives/And the village is proud of
580 ES Monica 30 sure, will bring him back to us;/If he prospers, that will give him confidence —/It's
PROSTRATED (2)
408 CP Lavinia 1 /{L} But it's true! I was completely prostrated;/Even if I have made a partial
408 CP Reilly 3 /{R} Certainly, you were completely prostrated,/And certainly, you have somewhat
PROTECT (12)
249 MC Tempt2 3 in the schools./To set down the great, protect the poor,/Beneath the throne of God
273 MC Thomas 19   into a fortress./The Church shall protect her own, in her own way, not/As oak
280 MC Priest1 8 in Heaven,/Who shall now guide us, protect us, direct us?/After what journey
371 CP Edward 35 I should be taking all this trouble/To protect you from the fool you are./What do you
422 CP Julia 25 /Watch over her by the quicksand./{J} Protect her from the Voices/Protect her from
422 CP Julia 26   /{J} Protect her from the Voices/Protect her from the Visions/Protect her in the
422 CP Julia 27 Voices/Protect her from the Visions/Protect her in the tumult/Protect her in the
422 CP Julia 28 the Visions/Protect her in the tumult/Protect her in the silence. {}/[*They drink*]/{R}
453 CC Kaghan 27 my responsibility,/As your fiancé, to protect Colby from you./But first, let's cope
455 CC Eggers 28 protection. And I have my garden/To protect me against Mrs. E. That's my joke./{C}
478 CC Kaghan 39 I'm your guardian angel,/Colby, to protect you from Lucasta./{L} You're *my*
530 ES Monica 6 business to prevent. You know I'm to protect you/From your own restless energy —
PROTECTING (2)
428 CP Alex 28 eating the monkeys/And what with protecting their crops from the monkeys/The
582 ES Monica 39 that awareness .../{M} Was a shield protecting both of us .../{C} So that now we are
PROTECTION (6)
251 MC Tempt3 38 advantage,/Blessing of Pope powerful protection/In the fight for liberty. You, my
422 CP Reilly 14 Let them build the hearth/Under the protection of the stars./{A} Let them place a
455 CC Eggers 27 Mrs. Eggerson./{E} Yes, she's a great protection. And I have my garden/To protect
479 CC Kaghan 6 /Like you and Lizzie, he's got to have protection./{L} Colby doesn't need your
479 CC Lucasta 7   /{L} Colby doesn't need your protection racket/So far as I'm concerned, B.
539 ES Gomez 20 undergraduate career/Without the protection of that prudent devil/Of yours, to tell
PROTECTOR (2)
422 CP Reilly 19 for those who go upon a journey./{R} Protector of travellers/Bless the road./{A}
467 CC Colby 9   thought of you —/As a kind of protector, a generous provider:/Rather as a
PROTECTS (1)
173 FQ: BurntN 83 the weakness of the changing body,/Protects mankind from heaven and damnation/
PROTEST (2)
129 Cor2 State 23 /Have appointed a joint committee to protest against the reduction of orders./
297 FR Violet 33 /I only wish to express my emphatic protest/Both against your purpose and the
PROTOZOIC (1)
40 Burb Blei 18   protrusive eye/Stares from the protozoic slime/At a perspective of Canaletto./
PROTRACT (1)
38 Gerontion 62 with a thousand small deliberations/Protract the profit of their chilled delirium,/
PROTRUSIVE (1)
40 Burb Blei 17 Chicago Semite Viennese./A lustreless protrusive eye/Stares from the protozoic slime/
PROUD (8)
220 Old Deut 8   and thrives/And the village is proud of him in his decline./At the sight of that
222 Pekes Pols 2 the Pollicles, everyone knows,/Are proud and implacable passionate foes;/It is
230 Bust Jones 11 Brummell of Cats;/And we're all of us proud to be nodded or bowed to/By Bustopher
593 Grad 6 5 fate,/And see that she shall gain such proud estate/As shall on future centuries bestow
595 Grad 13 5 lands unseen;/And let thy motto be, proud and serene,/Still as the years pass by, the

241 MC Priest1   19 the King? what reconciliation/Of two proud men?/{P3} What peace can be found/To
247 MC Tempt1   31 may go faster./Your Lordship is too proud!/The safest beast is not the one that roars
509 CC Guzzard 30   A very good name./He ought to be proud of it./{LE} How old is this Barnabas?/

PROUDNECKED (1)
164 Rock 9   9 occasions./Yet they walk in the street proudnecked, like thoroughbreds ready for

PROVE (4)
360 CP Reilly   40 man, then you'd want to re-marry/To prove to the world that somebody wanted you;/
395 CP Lavinia 21 always getting yourself measured/To prove how you had grown since the last
494 CC Lady E   2 /I wish that Colby, somehow, might prove to be *your* son/Instead of mine. Really, I
510 CC Lady E   7 to identify them./{LE} And will that prove that Mr. Kaghan —/This Mr. Kaghan —

PROVED (3)
278 MC Knight2 12   intended that Becket, who had proved himself an extremely/able administrator
487 CC Lady E   19 name — and intuition./But it shall be proved. The truth has come out./It's Colby.
578 ES Ld Clav   8 to correct mistakes/By methods which proved to be equally mistaken./I see that your

PROVERB (1)
220 Old Deut   3 lives in succession./He was famous in proverb and famous in rhyme/A long while

PROVES (1)
308 FR Mary   25 /{M} But surely, what you say/Only proves that you expected Wishwood/To be your

PROVIDE (3)
 44 Cook Egg   20   /Than Pipit's experience could provide./I shall not want Pipit in Heaven:/
369 CP Edward 16   of Lavinia's discoveries;/Celia's, to provide society and fashion./Lavinia always had
534 ES Ld Clav 39 any whisky in the house?/{LC} I can provide whisky. {}/[*Presses the bell*]/{LC} But

PROVIDED (7)
 29 Aunt Helen   8   before./The dogs were handsomely provided for,/But shortly afterwards the parrot
105 Song Sime   10 years in this city,/Kept faith and fast, provided for the poor,/Have given and taken
420 CP Reilly   2 Nothing./Everything you need will be provided for you,/And you will have no
489 CC Claude   21 Mrs. Guzzard brought him up,/And I provided for his education./I have watched him
545 ES Piggott   30   anything you need that hasn't been provided?/All you have to do is to make your
550 ES Ld Clav   25 /I mean, that he left you comfortably provided for?/{MC} Well, Richard, my doctor
550 ES Carghil   27 me *here*/If I wasn't well off. Yes, I'm provided for./But isn't it strange that you and I/

PROVIDENCE (1)
487 CC Lady E   29 me to feel so sure,/But it seems that Providence has brought you back to me,/And

PROVIDENTIAL (2)
289 FR Violet   22   but a blessed relief./{V} *I* call it providential./{I} Yet it must have been
579 ES Carghil 39   I could be helpful./{MC} It's truly providential!/{M} Good-bye Michael. Will you

PROVIDER (1)
467 CC Colby   9 —/As a kind of protector, a generous provider:/Rather as a patron than a father —/

PROVOCATION (1)
279 MC Knight4 28 in England. He used every means of provocation;/from his conduct, step by step,

PROVOKE (1)
280 MC Knight1   4 corners, and do/nothing that might provoke any public outbreak. {}/[*Exeunt*

PROWL (2)
256 MC Tempts   34 by the wall?/{4T} Does the mastiff prowl by the gate?/{C} Death has a hundred
548 ES Monica   8 duty by us for to-day./I'm going to prowl about the grounds. Don't look so

PROWLING (1)
212 Growltiger   28 /In the yard behind the Lion he was prowling for his prey./In the forepeak of the

PRUDENCE (3)
 74 WL: Thund   404 moment's surrender/Which an age of prudence can never retract/By this, and this
286 FR Gerald   8 man who can exercise a little common prudence;/And your servants look after you
461 CC Claude   24 /In public, till now, as a matter of prudence./As we arranged. But after two

PRUDENT (3)
534 ES Gomez   28 /Politicians can't afford mistakes. The prudent ones/Always have an aeroplane ready:/
537 ES Gomez   31 But you never went too far. There's a prudent devil/Inside you, Dick. He never came
539 ES Gomez   20 career/Without the protection of that prudent devil/Of yours, to tell him not to go too

PRUFROCK (2)
 11   t   /PRUFROCK and Other Observations/The
 13 Prufrock   t /The Love Song of J. Alfred Prufrock/Let us go then, you and I,/When the

PRUNES (1)
375 CP Edward 20   what? .../Oh, from Jugoslavia ... prunes and alcohol?/No, really, Alex, I don't

PRY (1)
452 CC Kaghan   6 The usual catastrophe./She's come to pry some cash from the money-box./Bankrupt

PSYCHIC (1)
300 FRDowning   8   Sir,/That his Lordship is rather psychic, as they say./{C} Were they always

PSYCHOLOGICAL (1)
415 CP Celia   23 of view,/Was either bad form, or was psychological./And bad form always led to

PUB (2)

228 Gus	12	place at the back of the neighbouring pub)/He loves to regale them, if someone else
556 ES Michael	15	down last night. I'm staying at a pub/About two miles from here. Not a bad little

PUBLIC (30)

19 Portrait	39	events,/Correct our watches by the public clocks./Then sit for half an hour and
69 WL: Fire S	260	city, I can sometimes hear/Beside a public bar in Lower Thames Street,/The
129 Cor2 State	19	/A commission is appointed/For Public Works, chiefly the question of rebuilding
158 Rock 5	2	the Arabian: were doubtless men of public spirit and zeal./Preserve me from the
206 To my Wife	12	are private words addressed to you in public./OLD POSSUM'S BOOK OF
249 MC Tempt2	30	fast friends at home./Private policy is public profit;/Dignity still shall be dressed with
253 MC Tempt4	16	than king's anger./Kings have public policy, barons private profit,/Jealousy
267 MC Thomas	23	King's command —/Should be said in public. If you make charges,/Then in public I
267 MC Thomas	24	public. If you make charges,/Then in public I will refute them./{K1} No! here and
280 MC Knight1	4	do/nothing that might provoke any public outbreak. {}/[*Exeunt* KNIGHTS]/{P1} O
301 FR Chorus	18	/When the private shall be made public, the common photographer/Flashlight
331 FR Agatha	37	neighbours,/But not neglecting public duties./He hid his strength beneath
334 FR Harry	38	Of the insane mind! Now I can live in public./Liberty is a different kind of pain from
394 CP Edward	33	/You wanted me to supply a public background/For your kind of public life.
394 CP Edward	34	public background/For your kind of public life. You wished to be a hostess/For
429 CP Edward	23	an interim report./{E} Will it be made public?/{A} It cannot be, at present:/There are
453 CC Lucasta	8	I don't mind being seen with you in public./You may take me out to dinner. A
456 CC Eggers	3	—/He'd just come back from a public luncheon —/'Eggerson', he said, 'I
461 CC Claude	24	I've been calling you Mr. Simpkins/In public, till now, as a matter of prudence./As we
473 CC Lucasta	8	it!/No, my only garden is ... a dirty public square/In a shabby part of London —
474 CC Lucasta	26	/A bomb-site ... willow-herb ... a dirty public square./But I can't imagine that
496 CC Eggers	23	/You're losing touch with public affairs.'/The fact is, she misses the
526 ES Monica	31	/{M} — Now we're in the public world./{C} And your father will come.
528 ES Monica	11	you/Is not the private man, but the public personage./In politics Father wore a
528 ES Monica	12	personage./In politics Father wore a public label./And later, as chairman of public
528 ES Monica	13	label./And later, as chairman of public companies,/Always his privacy has been
531 ES Charles	19	/{C} That's the reward/Of every public man./{LC} Say rather, the exequies/Of
540 ES Ld Clav	35	that this story would interest the public/Why not sell your version to a Sunday
541 ES Gomez	5	think I've any desire/To appear in public as Frederick Culverwell?/No, Dick, your
558 ES Michael	19	it's no joke/Being the son of a famous public man./You don't know what I suffered,

PUBLICATION (1)

429 CP Alex	26	/Eventually, there may be an official publication./{E} But when?/{A} In a year or

PUBLICITY (1)

552 ES Carghil	26	for a large cash payment/And no publicity. So your conscience was clear./At

PUBS (2)

111 Xmas Trees	4	patently commercial,/The rowdy (the pubs being open till midnight),/And the childish
230 Bust Jones	3	he's remarkably fat./He doesn't haunt pubs — he has eight or nine clubs,/For he's the

PUDDING (1)

230 Bust Jones	28	at the *Tomb*/On cabbage, rice pudding and mutton./So, much in this way,

PUDDINGS (1)

588 Fable	47	/To fill out their repast, and pies and puddings,/And jellies, pasties, cakes among the

PUGS (3)

222 Pekes Pols	m2	*Account of the Participation/of the Pugs and the Poms, and the Intervention/of the*
222 Pekes Pols	4	the same, wherever one goes./And the Pugs and the Poms, although most people say/
223 Pekes Pols	38	*Came Over the Border.*/Then the Pugs and the Poms held no longer aloof,/But

PUISSANCE (1)

51 Restaurant	14	la faire rire./J'éprouvais un instant de puissance et de délire.'/Mais alors, vieux

PULL (2)

233 Skimble	46	you creep into your cosy berth/And pull up the counterpane,/You ought to reflect
321 FR Warburt	22	if *you* saw him, and .../{W} Harry! Pull yourself together./Something may have

PULLAWAYS (1)

213 Growltiger	43	Abandoning their sampans, and their pullaways and junks,/They battened down the

PULLED (4)

218 Mung Rump	11	to be waterproof,/If the drawers were pulled out from the bedroom chests,/And you
589 Fable	78	nought but gape and stare,/The spirit pulled him rudely by the collar,/And before any
313 FR Violet	3	is looking?/Why, who could have pulled those curtains apart? {}/[*Pulls them*
557 ES Michael	21	have borrowed more/I might have pulled it off./{LC} Borrowed? From whom?/Not

PULLING (1)

66 WL: Chess	158	thirty-one.)/I can't help it, she said, pulling a long face,/It's them pills I took, to

PULLS (3)

56 Swee Night		13	to sit on Sweeney's knees/Slips and pulls the table cloth/Overturns a coffee-cup,/
311 FR	m	38	here. {}/[*She goes to the window and pulls the curtains across*]/{H} They were here, I
313 FR	m	3	have pulled those curtains apart? {}/[*Pulls them together*]/{V} Very well, I think, after

PULSE (1)

109 Marina	18	is this face, less clear and clearer/The pulse in the arm, less strong and stronger —/

PUNAISES (1)

48 Lune Miel	3	deux draps, chez deux centaines de punaises;/La sueur aestivale, et une forte odeur

PUNCTILIOUS (1)

603 Spleen	14	bland,/Waits, hat and gloves in hand,/Punctilious of tie and suit/(Somewhat impatient

PUNCTUAL (3)

399 CP	Reilly	14	me waiting;/But I think she will be punctual./{N} I telephone through/The moment
445 CC	Claude	1	/{SC} Ah, there you are, Eggerson! Punctual as always./I'm sorry to have to bring
504 CC	Guzzard	27	announced./{MG} I believe I was punctual./But I didn't mind waiting in the least,

PUNGENT (1)

38 Gerontion	64	when the sense has cooled,/With pungent sauces, multiply variety/In a wilderness

PUNIER (1)

250 MC Thomas	3	from the Pope,/Descend to desire a punier power?/Delegate to deal the doom of

PUNISHED (5)

259 MC	Thomas	4	you, and you,/And you, must all be punished. So must you./I shall no longer act or
307 FR	Harry	7	Arthur and John./Of course we were punished for being out at night/After being put
318 FR	Harry	12	/Next day at school, in order to be punished,/For punishment made us feel less
318 FR	Harry	14	us feel less guilty. Mother/Never punished us, but made us feel guilty./I think
345 FR	Amy	23	than life can give. And now I am punished for it./Gerald! you are the stupidest

PUNISHMENT (2)

318 FR	Harry	13	school, in order to be punished,/For punishment made us feel less guilty. Mother/
333 FR	Agatha	26	not a story of detection,/Of crime and punishment, but of sin and expiation./It is

PUNT (3)

549 ES	Carghil	13	a good lunch — and we all went in a punt/On the river — and we had a tea basket/
549 ES	Carghil	16	called them,/And you made me try to punt, and I got soaking wet/And nearly
549 ES	Carghil	17	soaking wet/And nearly dropped the punt pole, and you all laughed at me./Don't you

PUPILS (1)

594 Grad 10	6	shall we find/As this from which as pupils now we go./We go; like flitting faces in a

PURBLIND (1)

161 Rock 7	23	as always before, selfish and purblind as ever before,/Yet always struggling,

PURCHASED (2)

587 Fable	29	this exclusive feast. From over sea/He purchased at his own expense a crowd/Of relics
249 MC Tempt2	11	/{T} What means?/{T2} Real power/Is purchased at price of a certain submission./

PURE (3)

374 CP	Celia	19	It was obvious that the aunt was a pure invention/On the spur of the moment, and
464 CC	Claude	13	/Escape from a sordid world to a pure one./Sculpture and painting — I have
491 CC	Colby	23	/If neither of you could be. If it was pure fiction —/One can live on a fiction — but

PURELY (1)

446 CC	Claude	21	of life more quickly/If we started on a purely business basis./{E} No doubt that's best.

PURGATORIAL (2)

181 FQ: ECoker	167	I must freeze/And quake in frigid purgatorial fires/Of which the flame is roses,
333 FR	Agatha	34	/Its bird sent flying through the purgatorial flame./Indeed it is possible. You

PURIFICATION (1)

196 FQ: Little	200	manner of thing shall be well/By the purification of the motive/In the ground of our

PURIFY (3)

173 FQ: BurntN	99	permaneecy/Nor darkness to purify the soul/Emptying the sensual with
194 FQ: Little	129	speech, and speech impelled us/To purify the dialect of the tribe/And urge the mind
327 FR	Harry	22	is the filthiness. I can clean my skin,/Purify my life, void my mind,/But always the

PURITY (2)

158 Rock 5	9	his emptiness./If humility and purity be not in the heart, they are not in the
594 Grad 9	3	to thee/From spotless fanes of lucid purity,/O school of ours! The passing years that

PURPLE (3)

139 Virginia	7	once? Still hills/Wait. Gates wait. Purple trees,/White trees, wait, wait,/Delay,
142 Cape Ann	9	the flight/Of the dancing arrow, the purple martin. Greet/In silence the bullbat. All
258 MC Thomas	13	Music and philosophy, curiosity,/The purple bullfinch in the lilac tree,/The tiltyard

PURPOSE (17)

91 Ash-Wed 2	21	forget/Thus devoted, concentrated in purpose. And God said/Prophesy to the wind,
171 FQ: BurntN	16	echo/Thus, in your mind./But to what purpose/Disturbing the dust on a bowl of
192 FQ: Little	33	a husk of meaning/From which the purpose breaks only when it is fulfilled/If at all.
192 FQ: Little	34	is fulfilled/If at all. Either you had no purpose/Or the purpose is beyond the end you

192 FQ: Little	35	all. Either you had no purpose/Or the	purpose is beyond the end you figured/And is
194 FQ: Little	115	/These things have served their	purpose: let them be./So with your own, and
203 Indians	19	of you:/Of action with a common	purpose, action/None the less fruitful if neither
211 Old Gumbie	35	helpful boy-scouts,/With a	purpose in life and a good deed to do —/And
250 MC Tempt3	21	not in this guise, or for my present	purpose./{T} No purpose brings surprise./{T3}
250 MC Thomas	22	or for my present purpose./{T} No	purpose brings surprise./{T3} Well, my Lord,/I
250 MC Tempt3	38	/{T} Proceed straight forward./{T3}	Purpose is plain./Endurance of friendship does
271 MC Thomas	13	painful joy/When the figure of God's	purpose is made complete./You shall forget
294 FR Harry	19	and round in that vapour —/Without	purpose, and without principle of conduct/In
297 FR Violet	34	emphatic protest/Both against your	purpose and the means you are employing./{C}
297 FR Charles	35	the means you are employing./{C} My	purpose is, to find out what's wrong with
364 CP Reilly	11	the dark?/{UG} There is certainly no	purpose in remaining in the dark/Except long
416 CP Celia	23	made use of each other/Each for his	purpose. That's horrible. Can we only love/

PURPOSELESSLY (1)

38 Gerontion	51	at last/I have not made this show	purposelessly/And it is not by any concitation/

PURPOSES (3)

340 FR Amy	26	any self-pity?/I forced myself to the	purposes of Wishwood;/I even asked you back,
348 FR Chorus	26	a limited number/Of strictly practical	purposes/We do not know what we are doing;/
369 CP Edward	14	and Celia were asked for different	purposes./Your role was to be one of Lavinia's

PURRED (1)

225 Mr Mistoff	48	/(At least we all *heard* that somebody	purred)/Which is incontestable proof/Of his

PURSER (1)

295 FR Harry	3	excited, I think I made enquiries;/The	purser and the steward were extremely

PURSUE (7)

172 FQ: BurntN	62	/Below, the boarhound and the boar/	Pursue their pattern as before/But reconciled
252 MC Thomas	21	the shape of a wolf among wolves?/	Pursue your treacheries as you have done
298 FR Agatha	12	Charles to talk to Downing/And	pursue his own methods. {}/[*Rises*]/{V} I do not
338 FR Harry	27	my business is not to run away, but to	pursue,/Not to avoid being found, but to seek./I
343 FR Harry	36	to worry about;/I have my course to	pursue, and I am safe from normal dangers/If I
343 FR Harry	37	I am safe from normal dangers/If I	pursue it. I cannot account for this/But it is so,
479 CC Lucasta	29	Only because she's never wanted to	pursue you./{K} Yes, I made a bad impression

PURSUED (3)

212 Growltiger	3	/From Gravesend up to Oxford he	pursued his evil aims,/Rejoicing in his title of
229 Gus	40	it again —/Which an Indian Colonel	pursued down a drain./And he thinks that he
328 FR Charles	22	of the/accident Mr. Piper was being	pursued by a patrol, and was/travelling at the

PURSUERS (2)

336 FR Harry	5	of ghosts with joined hands, from the	pursuers,/And come into a quiet place./Why is
338 FR Harry	19	/But always in ignorance of invisible	pursuers./Now I know that all my life has been

PURSUES (2)

64 WL: Chess	102	And still she cried, and still the world	pursues,/'Jug Jug' to dirty ears./And other
147 Rock 1	2	of Heaven,/The Hunter with his dogs	pursues his circuit./O perpetual revolution of

PURSUIT (1)

331 FR Harry	32	strength. Now I think it is/A common	pursuit of liberation./{Ag} Your father might

PUSH (1)

282 MC Chorus	10	the thatch, the fist in the tavern, the	push into the canal,/Less than we fear the love

PUSHED (5)

294 FR Harry	33	night in the mid-Atlantic/When I	pushed her over./{V} Pushed her?/{H} You
294 FR Violet	34	/When I pushed her over./{V}	Pushed her?/{H} You would never imagine
297 FR Ivy	14	really suppose/That he might have	pushed her over?/{C} In any case, I shouldn't
333 FR Harry	23	of others. Perhaps/I only dreamt I	pushed her./{Ag} So I had supposed. What of it?
472 CC Colby	3	— because you're afraid of being	pushed./I think that you're brave — and I think

PUSHING (1)

42 Swee Erect	19	Then straightens out from heel to hip/	Pushing the framework of the bed/And clawing

PUSS-PURR (1)

257 MC Chorus	29	/The forms take shape in the dark air:/	Puss-purr of leopard, footfall of padding bear,/

PUSTULAR (1)

54 Mr E Sun	19	of penitence;/The young are red and	pustular/Clutching piaculative pence./Under the

PUT (68)

26 Rhapsody	77	the tooth-brush hangs on the wall,/	Put your shoes at the door, sleep, prepare for
118 SP Wauch	27	there?/{W} Four of us here./Wait till I	put the car round the corner/We'll be right up/
164 Rock 9	7	scattered lights?/They would	put upon GOD their own sorrow, the grief they
167 Rock 10	40	/And we must extinguish the candle,	put out the light and relight it;/Forever must
192 FQ: Little	44	be the same: you would have to	put off/Sense and notion. You are not here to
214 RTTugger	3	he would rather have grouse./If you	put him in a house he would much prefer a flat,/
214 RTTugger	4	he would much prefer a flat,/If you	put him in a flat then he'd rather have a house./

214 RT	Tugger	30	him in it right up to the ears,/If you put it away on the larder shelf./The Rum Tum
220 Old Deut		22	run over the kerb,/And the villagers put up a notice: ROAD CLOSED —/So that
231 Bust Jones		37	his life a routine, so he'd say./Or, to put it in rhyme: 'I shall last out my time'/Is the
589 Fable		87	/But the church straightway put to his name the handle/Of Saint, thereby
592 Grad 1		6	rocks which lie below,/But let us yet put forth courageously./As colonists embarking
245 MC	Priest2	9	/Let me ask you at the least to put on pleasant faces,/And give a hearty
250 MC	Thomas	11	as the world knows order./Those who put their faith in worldly order/Not controlled
276 MC	Knight1	27	by Jury. I am not myself qualified to/put our case to you. I am a man of action and
277 MC	Knight3	6	We are four plain Englishmen/who put our country first. I dare say that we didn't
277 MC	Knight3	21	to see that the Archbishop *had* to be put out of the/way — and personally I had a
277 MC	Knight3	23	have noted what a good show he put up at the end —/they won't give *us* any
277 MC	Knight2	36	to recur to a point that was very/well put by our leader, Reginald Fitz Urse: that you
279 MC	Knight4	14	argument./What I have to say may be put in the form of a question: *Who killed/the*
285 FR	Amy	11	And time would not stop in the dark!/Put on the lights. But leave the curtains
298 FR	Charles	29	/But I've a question I'd like to put to you,/I'm sure you won't mind, it's about
307 FR	Harry	8	for being out at night/After being put to bed. But at least they never knew/Where
322 FR	Winch	12	hope not, my Lord./I didn't mean to put myself forward./But you see, my Lord, I
323 FR	Charles	36	for us that he's here./We must put ourselves under Warburton's orders./{W} I
324 FR	Warburt	6	doubt me./Come, Winchell. We can put your bicycle/On the back of my car. {}/
326 FR	Harry	28	all men, of the world, which I cannot put in order./If you only knew the years that I
334 FR	Harry	28	and the costume/Ready to be put on. But it is very odd:/When other people
357 CP	Edward	17	any prospects?/{E} No, I think she put it all into an annuity./{J} So it's very
359 CP	Edward	14	for this evening./The fact is, I tried to put off this party:/These were only the people I
359 CP	Edward	15	These were only the people I couldn't put off/Because I couldn't get at them in time;/
361 CP	Reilly	9	time that you can't well spare;/But I put it to you .../{E} Don't put it to me./{UG}
361 CP	Edward	10	spare;/But I put it to you .../{E} Don't put it to me./{UG} Then I suggest .../{E} And
361 CP	Edward	14	witnesses,/So I don't like them. May I put it to *you*?/I know that I invited this
370 CP	Peter	26	simply lost interest in you?/{P} You put it just wrong. I think of it differently./It is
378 CP	Celia	29	left you for another man?/I shall soon put that right, Edward,/When you are free./{E}
388 CP	Peter	3	overnight?/{P} Why, it's a man Alex put me in touch with/And we settled everything
389 CP	Celia	30	older than herself./{C} Lavinia,/Don't put me off. I may not see you again./What I
397 CP	Edward	31	And I never could teach you/How to put the cap on a tube of tooth-paste./{L} Very
404 CP	Edward	1	in the same world. So I want you to put me/Into your sanatorium. I could be alone
407 CP	Reilly	23	your own cure./But when you put yourselves into hands like mine/You
407 CP	Reilly	28	has no meaning;/And you must put up with that. All that you have told me —/
410 CP	Reilly	19	only to reverse the propositions/And put them together./{L} Is that possible?/{R} If I
413 CP	Celia	33	wrong with me, that could be put right./I'd do anything you told me, to get
418 CP	Celia	12	it. I could do without everything,/Put up with anything, if I might cherish it./In
421 CP	Julia	5	souls/And can choose, whether to put on proper costumes/Or huddle quickly into
425 CP	Edward	1	dress you're wearing:/I'm glad you put on that one./{L} Well, Edward!/Do you
429 CP	Alex	4	/That the slaughter of monkeys has put a curse on them/Which can result in
449 CC	Eggers	2	doubt that Lady Elizabeth/Would be put in mind of the child *she* lost./{SC} In a very
450 CC	Eggers	9	/{E} Nearly thirty-one./But now you put it so convincingly,/I must admit there's a lot
462 CC	Claude	4	confident that, before long,/We can put matters onto a permanent basis./{C} I must
480 CC	Kaghan	2	But I'm a born gambler/And I've put my shirt ... no, not quite the right
493 CC	Claude	10	I thought it would be better/To put Eggerson there, behind the desk./You see, I
493 CC	Claude	18	why I thought/That Eggerson should put the first questions./He's very good at
499 CC	Claude	5	a desk:/It's second nature./{SC} And put the case to her./Don't let her think that *I*
500 CC	Lucasta	38	but for the wrong reasons,/And that put me off. So I'm grateful to Colby./{SC} I
508 CC	Eggers	5	hoping against hope/To find her son. Put yourself in her position./If you had lost
516 CC	Claude	28	/Heaven knows — and you know — I put no obstruction/In the way of your fulfilling
516 CC	Claude	32	am not your father:/I'll accept that. I put no claim upon you —/Except the claim of
530 ES	Ld Clav	38	my fellow directors/Saying 'we must put our hands in our pockets/To double this
548 ES	Monica	10	guest who seems to be stalking you/Put your newspaper over your face/And pretend
552 ES	Carghil	8	*You To Love Me*?/I couldn't have put the feeling into it I did/But for what I'd
555 ES	Ld Clav	35	only debts/Once more, I expect I can put up with it./But where is he?/{M} I told him
560 ES	Michael	11	business./But I might be expected to put up some capital./{LC} What sort of business
564 ES	Carghil	36	Gomez!/You've got to be the first to put your cards on the table!/{M} Father, I think
574 ES	Carghil	12	/How he must have suffered! So I put on my thinking cap./I know you've always
577 ES	Charles	15	against your father?/Remember, you put yourself completely in the power/Of a man
579 ES	Carghil	13	*everything*!/— No sooner had I put my proposal before him/Than he had it all

PUTNEY (2)

174 FQ: BurntN	114	and Clerkenwell, Camden and Putney,/Highgate, Primrose and Ludgate. Not
212 Growltiger	10	of his fame;/At Hammersmith and Putney people shuddered at his name./They

PUTRESCENT (1)
335 FR   Harry   14   desert/Weaving with contagion of putrescent embraces/On dissolving bone. In and
PUTRID (1)
269 MC Chorus   31   I have tasted/The savour of putrid flesh in the spoon. I have felt/The
PUTS (3)
 69 WL: Fire S   256   her hair with automatic hand,/And puts a record on the gramophone./'This music
311 FR   Harry   32   else/Thinking of something else, puts me among you./I tell you, it is not me you
519 CC   m 22   of meaning it. {}/[LUCASTA *puts her arms around* SIR CLAUDE]/{SC}
PUTTING (8)
179 FQ: ECoker   69 the ice-cap reigns./That was a way of putting it — not very satisfactory:/A
187 FQ: DrySal 127 Among other things — or one way of putting the same thing:/That the future is a
231 Bust Jones   34   or I am a bounder,/And he's putting on weight every day:/But he's so well
279 MC Knight4 16   you may feel some surprise at my putting it in this way. But/consider the course of
474 CC   Colby 19   /That's the only way I can think of putting it./{L} How afraid one is of ... being
499 CC   Claude   7 think that *I* have any doubts:/You are putting the questions on behalf of my wife./{E} I
510 CC   Eggers 35   discovery, Mr. Kaghan,/By putting your adoptive parents in touch/With
572 ES   Ld Clav 16 to marry me —/That was his way of putting it — and of course/Made it worth while
PUZZLE (1)
327 FR   Harry   11   in abstractions./I have a private puzzle. Were they simply outside,/I might
PUZZLED (3)
392 CP   Lavinia 22   /{L} Yes, I think I know./But I'm puzzled by Julia. That woman is the devil./She
447 CC   Claude 24   guidance./But if she appears to be puzzled, or annoyed/At my making the
538 ES   Gomez 34   in your success. But one thing has puzzled me./You were given a ministry before
PUZZLING (1)
575 ES   Ld Clav 32 of our ... intimacy/Which they found puzzling./{MC} Oh, Richard!/Have you
PYRE (2)
196 FQ: Little   207   or else despair/Lies in the choice of pyre or pyre —/To be redeemed from fire by
196 FQ: Little   207   despair/Lies in the choice of pyre or pyre —/To be redeemed from fire by fire./Who
PYTHON (2)
598 Circe   11 /Along the garden stairs/The sluggish python lies;/The peacocks walk, stately and
398 CP   Edward 10 ruin./O God, what have I done? The python. The octopus./Must I become after all

QU' (2)

51 Restaurant	5	du grand soleil, et de la pluie;/C'est ce qu'on appelle le jour de lessive des gueux.'/
51 Restaurant	9	ronces —/C'est là, dans une averse, qu'on s'abrite./J'avais sept ans, elle était plus

QUACKS (1)

587 Fable	2	VIII found out that monks were quacks,/And took their lands and money from

QUAIL (2)

98 Ash-Wed 6	16	smell/Quickens to recover/The cry of quail and the whirling plover/And the blind eye
142 Cape Ann	6	/With shrill whistle the note of the quail, the bob-white/Dodging by bay-bush.

QUAKE (2)

135 5FingerEx3	2	the lake,/The forces of the morning quake,/The dawn is slant across the lawn,/Here
181 FQ: ECoker	167	to be warmed, then I must freeze/And quake in frigid purgatorial fires/Of which the

QUALIFICATION (3)

344 FR	Violet	25	/{V} And you need some religious qualification!/I think you should consult the
406 CP	Edward	23	the second explanation/Without the qualification 'lunatic'./Why should *you* go to a
533 ES	Gomez	23	/Out there, as it is here. With this qualification:/Out there they respect you for

QUALIFIED (5)

276 MC	Knight1	26	of Trial by Jury. I am not myself qualified to/put our case to you. I am a man of
278 MC	Knight2	18	I have never known a man so well qualified for the/highest rank of the Civil
445 CC	Eggers	27	say that!/Mr. Simpkins is far better qualified than I was/To be your confidential
458 CC	Eggers	34	Mr. Simpkins is much more highly qualified/Than I am, to be a confidential clerk./
546 ES	Piggott	36	/She is a real nurse, you know, fully qualified./Our system is very delicately

QUALIFY (1)

407 CP	Reilly	8	together, and to a marked degree,/To qualify a patient for *my* sanatorium:/And one

QUALITIES (5)

18 Portrait	24	are!)/To find a friend who has these qualities,/Who has, and gives/Those qualities
18 Portrait	26	qualities,/Who has, and gives/Those qualities upon which friendship lives./How
254 MC Tempt4	40	or to execrate you,/But pondering the qualities that you lacked/Will only try to find
277 MC Knight2	39	the worthy Archbishop,/whose good qualities I very much admired, has throughout
571 ES Ld Clav	15	well as our virtues —/Or whatever the qualities for which they did admire us!/And that

QUANDO (1)

75 WL: Thund	428	/*Poi s'ascose nel foco che gli affina*/*Quando fiam uti chelidon* — O swallow swallow/

QUARREL (2)

117 SP	Dusty	24	What comes next. It's the six./{Du} 'A quarrel. An estrangement. Separation of
341 FR	Agatha	24	take my son./{Ag} Why should we quarrel for what neither can have?/If neither has

QUARRELLED (1)

572 ES	Ld Clav	23	been poor, we should certainly have quarrelled,/We should have been unhappy,

QUARTER (6)

212 Growltiger	18	/To Cats of foreign name and race no quarter was allowed./The Persian and the
338 FR	Harry	1	has come from quite a different quarter,/But I cannot explain that to you now.
374 CP	2m	1	/Act One. Scene 2/*The same room: a quarter of an hour later.* EDWARD *is alone,*
399 CP	Nurse	11	room/Just as usual. She arrives at a quarter past;/But you may keep her waiting./{R}
476 CC	Lucasta	39	always spent before the end of the quarter/On gin and betting, I should guess./And
542 ES	Gomez	1	caller/Could hang on for another quarter of an hour./{LC} Before you go — what

QUARTERS (1)

479 CC	Kaghan	13	I've come to inspect the new bachelor quarters,/And to wish Colby luck. I've always

QUARTETS (1)

169 4 Quartets	t	thanks for Thy great glory!/FOUR QUARTETS/Burnt Norton/Time present and

QUATRE (1)

48 Lune Miel	6	sur le dos écartant les genoux/De quatre jambes molles tout gonflées de morsures.

QUAVERING (1)

164 Rock 9	5	/We must go between empty walls, quavering lowly, whispering faintly,/Among a

QUAXO (1)

209 NamingCats	18	you a quorum,/Such as Munkustrap, Quaxo, or Coricopat,/Such as Bombalurina, or

QUAY (1)

24 Rhapsody	39	a toy that was running along the quay,/I could see nothing behind that child's

QUE (4)

47 Mél Adult	4	/C'est à grands pas et en sueur/Que vous suivrez à peine ma piste./En
47 Mél Adult	8	me paierez bien la tête./C'est à Paris que je me coiffe/Casque noir de jemenfoutiste./
48 Lune Miel	10	des amateurs/De chapiteaux d'acanthe que tournoie le vent./Ils vont prendre le train de
51 Restaurant	2	/Le garçon délabré qui n'a rien à faire/Que de se gratter les doigts et se pencher sur

QUEEN (6)

69 WL: Fire S	258	the waters'/And along the Strand, up Queen Victoria Street./O City city, I can
117 SP	Doris	14	absent friend'. — Pereira!/{Do} The Queen of Hearts! — Mrs. Porter!/{Du} Or it
189 FQ: DrySal	182	not returning:/Figlia del tuo figlio,/Queen of Heaven./Also pray for those who were
220 Old Deut	4	famous in rhyme/A long while before Queen Victoria's accession./Old Deuteronomy's

594 Grad 11   4 unknown world — class after class,/O queen of schools — a momentary gleam,/A
278 MC Knight2   7   During the reign of/the late Queen Matilda and the irruption of the
QUEENS (1)
107 Animula   14   with playing-cards and kings and queens,/What the fairies do and what the
QUEER (5)
117 SP   Dusty   7 Sweeney/{Du} Well anyway it's very queer./{Do} Here's the four of diamonds, what's
117 SP   Dusty   11 wearing apparel, or a party'./That's queer too./{Do} Here's the three. What's that
118 SP   Dusty   17 *never*/What a coincidence! Cards are queer! {}/(*Whistle again*.)/{Do} Is that Sam?/
118 SP   Dusty   30 come up./(*to* DORIS): Cards are queer./{Do} I'd like to know about that coffin.
327 FR   Ivy   29 hear him,/And his voice was very queer. It seems that Arthur too/Has had an
QUEL (1)
 51 Restaurant   23 fourchette, décrasse-toi le crâne./De quel droit payes-tu des expériences comme moi?
QUENCH (2)
167 Rock 10   41 the light and relight it;/Forever must quench, forever relight the flame./Therefore we
594 Grad 9   6 to the goal,/Shall not have power to quench the memory./We shall return; and it will
QUENCHED (2)
153 Rock 2   55 saw cut the stone,/Let the fire not be quenched in the forge./The Word of the LORD
553 ES   Carghil 18 somewhere:/*Where their fires are not quenched.* Do you know what I do?/I read your
QUESTION (37)
 13 Prufrock   10 /To lead you to an overwhelming question.../Oh, do not ask, 'What is it?'/Let us
 14 Prufrock   30 days of hands/That lift and drop a question on your plate;/Time for you and time
 15 Prufrock   93 To roll it towards some overwhelming question,/To say: 'I am Lazarus, come from the
 20 Portrait   89 do you return?/But that's a useless question./You hardly know when you are
129 Cor2 State   19   /For Public Works, chiefly the question of rebuilding the fortifications./A
187 FQ: DrySal   109 dreaded the wrong things,/Is not the question) are likewise permanent/With such
279 MC Knight4   14 to say may be put in the form of a question: *Who killed/the Archbishop?* As you
292 FR   Amy   22 tomorrow/On some legal business, a question about taxes —/But I think you would
297 FR   Charles 10 Meanwhile, I have an idea. Why not question Downing?/He's been with Harry ten
297 FR   Charles 24 dogs lie?/{C} All the same, there's a question or two {}/[*Rings the bell*]/{C} That I'd
298 FR   Charles 29 send for you so abruptly,/But I've a question I'd like to put to you,/I'm sure you
331 FR   Agatha 25 is a deeper/Organisation, which your question disturbs./{H} When I know, I know
364 CP   Reilly 19 you know where she is?/{UG} That question is not worth the trouble of an answer./
377 CP   Julia   31 Lavinia's aunt./{J} Now, the next question/Is, what's to be done. That's very
378 CP   Celia   26 only that./{C} It cannot be simply a question of vanity:/That you think the world
386 CP   Edward 10 service staircase./{E} May I ask one question?/{UG} You may ask it./{E} Who are
401 CP   Reilly 16 sit down./You were going to ask a question./{E} When you came to my flat/Had
401 CP   Reilly 33 all in good time./Let us dismiss that question for the moment./Tell me first, about
405 CP   Reilly 33 to enter a sanatorium,/And that is a question which naturally concerns you./{E} I am
410 CP   Reilly 31 do?/{R} You have answered your own question,/Though you do not know the
411 CP   Lavinia 25 ruins./{L} Exactly. And I have a question too./Sir Henry, was it you who sent
411 CP   Lavinia 31 /{L} I think you have answered my question too./They had to tell us, themselves,
420 CP   Julia   35 risks./That is our destiny. Since you question the decision/What possible alternative
437 CP   Lavinia 3 a point, Henry./{L} ... if it answers my question./{R} *Ere Babylon was dust*/*The magus*
437 CP   Reilly 23 death./That was her destiny. The only question/Then was, what sort of death? *I* could
498 CC   Eggers 35 Sir Claude:/Our first step must be to question Mrs. Guzzard./{SC} And that's what
505 CC   Eggers 20 /{E} Then let's make a start./The question has to do, as you surmised, with Mr.
505 CC   Eggers 32 brief —/But long enough ago for the question to be possible./Lady Elizabeth, before
507 CC   Eggers   4 /Now I must ask a more delicate question:/Did you, at any time, take in a child
508 CC   Eggers 15 troubled waters?/Let us approach the question from another angle,/And ask Mrs.
512 CC   Claude 18 your son?/{SC} That seems a strange question, Mrs. Guzzard./{MG} I have been
513 CC   Colby   12 the truth./{C} That is a very strange question, Aunt Sarah:/To which I can only give
524 ES   Monica 27 to explain .../{M} It's simply the question/Of your staying to tea. As you
557 ES   Ld Clav 4 again./We'll ignore, if you please, the question of blame:/Which will spare you the
569 ES   Charles 20 —/I was thinking that if there's any question of blackmail,/I've seen something of it
578 ES   Monica 37 just as I must make mine./It's not a question of your going abroad/But a question
578 ES   Monica 38 question of your going abroad/But a question of the spirit which inspired your
QUESTIONED (3)
 18 Portrait   13 touch the bloom/That is rubbed and questioned in the concert room.'/— And so the
589 Fable   83 be found,/The monks, when anyone questioned, would declare/St. Peter'd snatch to
434 CP   Alex   18 /When our people got there, they questioned the villagers —/Those who survived.
QUESTIONING (1)
497 CC   Claude 11 to be known to you./{SC} She'd been questioning Colby about himself,/And he
QUESTIONS (15)
155 Rock 3   58   for him who knows how to ask questions./O weariness of men who turn from
181 FQ: ECoker 150 wounded surgeon plies the steel/That questions the distempered part;/Beneath the

278 MC Knight2   5   Henry's aims? In/the answer to these questions lies the key to the problem./The
279 MC Knight4   32   you have seen how he/evaded our questions. And when he had deliberately
349 FR Chorus   4   we doing?/To each and all of these questions/There is no conceivable answer./We
356 CP Julia   18   Lavinia's party. There are so many questions/I want to ask you. It's a golden
360 CP Reilly   18 position./There we are. Now for a few questions./How long married?/{E} Five years./
364 CP Reilly   21   /That you promise to ask her no questions/Of where she has been./{E} I will not
385 CP Reilly   29   you see your wife, you must ask no questions/And give no explanations. I have said
392 CP Edward   4 it./Well, here I am./{E} I am to ask no questions./{L} And I know I am to give no
392 CP Lavinia   7 explanations./{L} And I am to ask no questions. And yet ... why not?/{E} I don't know
493 CC Claude   18   /That Eggerson should put the first questions./He's very good at approaching a
499 CC Claude   7 have any doubts:/You are putting the questions on behalf of my wife./{E} I
512 CC Guzzard 19   been asked here to answer strange questions —/And now it is my turn to ask them.
550 ES Ld Clav 23   /{LC} I've never had to deal with questions of equipment./I trust that the business

QUI (2)
 46 Directeur   2   /Malheur à la malheureuse Tamise/Qui coule si près du Spectateur./Le directeur/
 51 Restaurant   1   le Restaurant/Le garçon délabré qui n'a rien à faire/Que de se gratter les doigts

QUICK (13)
135 5FingerEx1   5   dull brain, the sharp desires/And the quick eyes of Woolly Bear./There is no relief
142 Cape Ann   1   concurrence of bone./Cape Ann/O quick quick quick, quick hear the song-sparrow,
142 Cape Ann   1   of bone./Cape Ann/O quick quick quick, quick hear the song-sparrow,/
142 Cape Ann   1   of bone./Cape Ann/O quick quick quick, quick hear the song-sparrow,/
142 Cape Ann   1   /Cape Ann/O quick quick quick, quick hear the song-sparrow,/Swamp-sparrow,
171 FQ: BurntN   21 /Inhabit the garden. Shall we follow?/Quick, said the bird, find them, find them,/
176 FQ: BurntN   176   laughter/Of children in the foliage/Quick now, here, now, always —/Ridiculous the
198 FQ: Little   254   /Between two waves of the sea./Quick now, here, now, always —/A condition of
274 MC Priests   14   *tipsy*]/{3P} This way, my Lord! Quick. Up the stair. To the roof./To the crypt.
274 MC Priests   15   the stair. To the roof./To the crypt. Quick. Come. Force him./{4K} Where is Becket.
447 CC Claude   30   /And say that I had to make a quick decision/Because he'd had another very
458 CC Eggers   32 tempting offer:/So we had to make a quick decision./{SC} I didn't want to bother
556 ES Monica   5 frightened./He's apt to be sullen and quick to take offence./So I hope you'll be

QUICK-CHANGE (1)
218 Mung Rump   2   of cats./As knockabout clowns, quick-change comedians, tight-rope walkers and

QUICKEN (1)
164 Rock 9   16   of saints./The soul of Man must quicken to creation./Out of the formless stone,

QUICKENED (1)
269 MC Chorus   27   them, the death-bringers, senses are quickened/By subtile forebodings; I have heard/

QUICKENS (5)
 28 Boston ET   3   a field of ripe corn./When evening quickens faintly in the street,/Wakening the
 98 Ash-Wed 6   13   lost sea voices/And the weak spirit quickens to rebel/For the bent golden-rod and
 98 Ash-Wed 6   15 bent golden-rod and the lost sea smell/Quickens to recover/The cry of quail and the
206 To my Wife   2 whom I owe the leaping delight/That quickens my senses in our wakingtime/And the
522 ES dedic   2 *whom I owe the leaping delight/That quickens my senses in our wakingtime/And the*

QUICKLY (13)
167 Rock 10   37   is too much pain./We are children quickly tired: children who are up in the night
213 Growltiger   46   /I am sorry to admit it, but she quickly disappeared./She probably escaped with
223 Pekes Pols   57   yawning,/The Pekes and the Pollicles quickly took warning./He looked at the sky and
243 MC Chorus   19   return, return to France./Return. Quickly. Quietly. Leave us to perish in quiet./
294 FR Harry   35   never imagine anyone could sink so quickly./I had always supposed, wherever I
362 CP Reilly   27 as a person. But we forget about it/As quickly as we can. When you've dressed for a
378 CP Julia   9   /{J} About Lavinia?/Well, come on quickly. And take a taxi./You know, you're
421 CP Julia   6 to put on proper costumes/Or huddle quickly into new disguises,/They have, for the
445 CC Eggers   29   clerk./He was finding his feet, very quickly,/During the time we worked together./
446 CC Claude   20   would fall into this way of life more quickly/If we started on a purely business basis./
470 CC Colby   20   hear good performers,/You'll very quickly realise how bad my playing is./{L}
548 ES Carghil   17   it./It was clever of you to find it so quickly./What made you choose it? {}/[*throwing*
557 ES Michael   33 Nearly two years./Time passes pretty quickly, when you're in debt./{LC} And have

QUICKSAND (1)
422 CP Alex   24   the labyrinth./Watch over her by the quicksand./{J} Protect her from the Voices/

QUIET (35)
 83 Hollow Men   7   when/We whisper together/Are quiet and meaningless/As wind in dry grass/Or
 92 Ash-Wed 2   52   and each other, united/In the quiet of the desert. This is the land which ye/
127 Cor1 March   30   in his eyes/Or in the hands, quiet over the horse's neck,/And the eyes
196 FQ: Little   181   /And of one who died blind and quiet,/Why should we celebrate/These dead men
210 Old Gumbie   19 finds that the mice will not ever keep quiet,/She is sure it is due to irregular diet/And
216 Jellicles   25   Cats have moonlit eyes./They're quiet enough in the morning hours,/They're

216 Jellicles   26 enough in the morning hours,/They're quiet enough in the afternoon,/Reserving their
224 Mr Mistoff   23   /As Magical Mr. Mistoffelees!/He is quiet and small, he is black/From his ears to the
232 Skimble   27 hilarity and riot, so the folk are very quiet/When Skimble is about and on the move./
240 MC Chorus   5   /Now I fear disturbance of the quiet seasons:/Winter shall come bringing death
243 MC Chorus   19   Quietly. Leave us to perish in quiet./You come with applause, you come with
271 MC Thomas   30   shall become of us?/{T} Peace! be quiet! remember where you are, and what is
275 MC Chorus   25   how can I ever return, to the soft quiet seasons?/Night stay with us, stop sun,
299 FRDowning   34   know his Lordship was always very quiet:/Very uncommon that I saw him in high
300 FRDowning   19   a place where a man can go/For a quiet smoke, where the women can't follow
322 FR   Winch   25   I'd better have a word with you quiet,/Rather than phone and perhaps disturb
336 FR   Harry   6   from the pursuers,/And come into a quiet place./Why is it so quiet?/Do you feel a
336 FR   Harry   7   come into a quiet place./Why is it so quiet?/Do you feel a kind of stirring underneath
354 CP   Alex   33   the third one:/They kept him rather quiet./{J} Oh, you mean *that* one./{A} He was
370 CP   Peter   9   express it;/I had never imagined such quiet happiness./I had only experienced
424 CP   Edward   20   you're not too tired?/{E} Oh no, a quiet day./Two consultations with solicitors/On
430 CP   Julia   29   of the world, Peter./We lead such a quiet life, here in London./{P} You always did
430 CP   Peter   33   /{P} You must have been living a quiet life!/Don't you go to the movies?/{L}
459 CC   Lady E   30   it is quite impossible/To get one's quiet hour. A quiet hour a day/Is most essential,
459 CC   Lady E   30   impossible/To get one's quiet hour. A quiet hour a day/Is most essential, Dr.
504 CC   Lady E   10   /{LE} Oh, I forgot. It's Gertrude's quiet hour./I've been giving her lessons in
504 CC   m   24   /{SC} Well, are we ready? {}/[A *quiet knock. Enter* KAGHAN, *escorting* MRS.
545 ES   Monica   11   life pleasant,/That it really does seem quiet here and restful./Even the matron, though
547 ES   Piggott   9   remember, when you want to be *very* quiet/There's the Silence Room. With a
548 ES   Piggott   1   of excitement:/After all, peace and quiet is our *raison d'être.*/Now I'll leave you to
548 ES   Ld Clav   4   to tell us more about the peace and quiet./{M} I don't believe she'll be bothering us
558 ES   Michael   18   he says,/That he wants to keep things quiet. I can tell you, it's no joke/Being the son
562 ES   Carghil   13   still be here./I came back to have a quiet read of your letters;/But how nice to find a
565 ES   Monica   1   father should rest and have absolute quiet/Before every meal./{LC} But Michael and
583 ES   Monica   16   to us./He is under the beech tree. It is quiet and cold there./In becoming no one, he

QUIET-VOICED (1)
179 FQ: ECoker   77   us,/Or deceived themselves, the quiet-voiced elders,/Bequeathing us merely a

QUIETLY (9)
172 FQ: BurntN   38   out of sunlight,/And the lotos rose, quietly, quietly,/The surface glittered out of
172 FQ: BurntN   38   sunlight,/And the lotos rose, quietly, quietly,/The surface glittered out of heart of
243 MC Chorus   19   return to France./Return. Quickly. Quietly. Leave us to perish in quiet./You come
243 MC Chorus   19   to happen./Seven years we have lived quietly,/Succeeded in avoiding notice,/Living
267 MC   m   25   *the priests and attendants return and quietly interpose themselves.*]/{T} Now and here!/
280 MC Knight1   2   and I suggest that you now disperse quietly to your homes./Please be careful not to
311 FR   Harry   20   /I always see their claws distended/Quietly, as if they had never stirred./It was only
511 CC   Lucasta   38   /{L} We'd meant to be married very quietly/In a register office./{LE} You must have
526 ES   Monica   10   silent feet, and stood behind my back/Quietly, a long time, a long long time/Before I

QUILPE (10)
352 CP   m   6   MACCOLGIE GIBBS/PETER QUILPE/AN UNIDENTIFIED GUEST, *later*
353 CP   4m   1   CELIA/COPLESTONE, PETER QUILPE, ALEXANDER MACCOLGIE
380 CP   Edward   14   Peter?/{C} Peter? Peter who?/{E} Peter Quilpe, who was here this evening. *He* was in a
408 CP   Reilly   15   /{E} Peter? Peter who?/{R} Mr. Peter Quilpe/Was a frequent guest./{E} Peter Quilpe./
408 CP   Edward   17   /Was a frequent guest./{E} Peter Quilpe./Peter Quilpe! Really Lavinia!/I
408 CP   Edward   18   guest./{E} Peter Quilpe./Peter Quilpe! Really Lavinia! I congratulate you. You
422 CP   Julia   31   be spoken yet./{J} You mean Peter Quilpe./{R} He has not yet come to where the
429 CP   Caterer   38   I'm freezing — in July!/{CM} Mr. Quilpe!/{E} Now who ... {}/[*Enter* PETER]/{E}
432 CP   Lavinia   25   you./{L} May I introduce Mr. Peter Quilpe?/Sir Henry Harcourt-Reilly. Peter's an
435 CP   Reilly   16   {R} You understand your *métier*, Mr. Quilpe —/Which is the most that any of us can

QUINZE (1)
 51 Restaurant   25   /Phlébas, le Phénicien, pendant quinze jours noyé,/Oubliait les cris des mouettes

QUIRING (1)
 50 Hippopot   27   from the damp savannas,/And quiring angels round him sing/The praise of

QUITE (84)
 30 Cous Nancy   9   dances;/And her aunts were not quite sure how they felt about it,/But they knew
119 SP   Klip   33   Well, no, Miss — er — you haven't quite got it/(I'm afraid I didn't quite catch your
119 SP   Klip   34   quite got it/(I'm afraid I didn't quite catch your name —/But I'm very pleased
187 FQ: DrySal   102 forgetting/Something that is probably quite ineffable:/The backward look behind the
204 de la Mare   12   please. Whose shall it be,/At not quite time for bed? .../Or when the lawn/Is
228 Gus   7   paw shake./Yet he was, in his youth, quite the smartest of Cats —/But no longer a
228 Gus   10   in his prime;/Though his name was quite famous, he says, in its time./And whenever
240 MC Priest3   34   another in France?/{P3} I see nothing quite conclusive in the art of temporal

285	FR	Amy	1	Not yet! I will ring for you. It is still quite light./I have nothing to do but watch the
298	FR	Agatha	10	Warburton:/I only see that this is all quite irrelevant;/We had better leave Charles to
299	FR	Charles	1	his health./He doesn't seem to be ... quite himself./{Do} Quite natural, if I may say
299	FR	Downing	2	seem to be ... quite himself./{Do} Quite natural, if I may say so, Sir,/After what
299	FR	Charles	4	say so, Sir,/After what happened./{C} Quite so, quite./Downing, you were with them
299	FR	Charles	4	/After what happened./{C} Quite so, quite./Downing, you were with them on the
300	FR	Downing	14	see too much of each other, Sir./Quite the contrary of the usual opinion,/I dare
300	FR	Charles	37	else he'd have known it./{C} Oh yes ... quite so. Thank you, Downing,/I don't think we
305	FR	Harry	26	had only just noticed that this room is quite unchanged:/The same hangings ... the
318	FR	Warburt	20	what I want to tell you./You may be quite right, but what we are concerned with/
323	FR	Warburt	3	you should have a look at him./{W} Quite right, quite right. I'll go and have a look
323	FR	Warburt	3	have a look at him./{W} Quite right, quite right. I'll go and have a look at him./We
325	FR	Ivy	15	understands *that*./{I} You are quite right, Gerald, the one thing that matters/Is
333	FR	Harry	40	moment, as if I had come home./It is quite irrational, but now/I feel quite happy, as if
334	FR	Harry	1	/It is quite irrational, but now/I feel quite happy, as if happiness/Did not consist in
336	FR	Harry	11	brain ... but not just as before,/Not quite like, not the same ... {}/[*The*
338	FR	Harry	1	rest of you./My advice has come from quite a different quarter,/But I cannot explain
344	FR	Violet	10	/Your behaviour all seems to me quite unaccountable./What *has* happened,
345	FR	Harry	3	if you *could* understand you would be quite happy about it,/So I shall say good-bye,
346	FR	Downing	30	going to happen,/And it seems quite natural, being his Lordship./And that's
348	FR	Chorus	6	look out of the same window, and see quite a different landscape./We do not like to
355	CP	Julia	21	—/Edward without Lavinia! He's quite impossible!/Leaving it to me to keep
357	CP	Julia	16	a panic./{J} And sends for Lavinia./I quite understand. Are there any prospects?/{E}
358	CP	Edward	5	your cases./{E} Most of my secrets are quite uninteresting./{J} Well, you shan't escape.
361	CP	Reilly	40	better than you like it,/Preferring not quite the same friends as yourself,/Or making
362	CP	Reilly	22	thought you were. You no longer feel quite human./You're suddenly reduced to
364	CP	Edward	2	what my wife is like./I am not quite sure that I could describe her/If I had to
366	CP	Edward	5	Look under the cushion./{E} Are you quite sure they're not in your bag?/{J} Why no,
375	CP	Edward	28	But what was he talking of?/{E} I had quite forgotten./He made his way in, a little
383	CP	Edward	6	Beside the champagne bottle?/You're quite sure? ... Very well, hold on if you like;/We
386	CP	Celia	33	To the headmaster's study;/and is not quite sure/What he's been found out in. I never
390	CP	Julia	33	really wants us./I can see that she is quite worn out/After her anxiety about her aunt
390	CP	Julia	35	—/Who, you'll be glad to hear, has quite recovered, Alex —/And after that long
392	CP	Edward	37	such a lot of time in lying./{E} I don't quite know what you mean./{L} Oh, Edward!/
394	CP	Edward	40	answer back like that?/{E} I have had quite enough humiliation/Lately, to bring me to
399	CP	Reilly	23	after they have left the house..../{R} Quite right, Miss Barraway. That's all for the
400	CP	Alex	19	With your usual foresight. Now, he's quite triumphant/Because he thinks he's stolen a
407	CP	Reilly	20	exhausting their energy,/Yet never quite successful. You have both of you
410	CP	Edward	5	exceptionally unlovable,/And I never quite knew why. I thought it was *my* fault./{R}
413	CP	Reilly	5	what I am to do about it. They are quite sure/They have had a nervous breakdown
413	CP	Reilly	24	I needn't explain myself./{R} I know quite enough about you for the moment:/Try
419	CP	Reilly	9	of anything else./Now — do you feel quite sure?/{C} I want your second way./So
424	CP	Edward	22	/Two consultations with solicitors/On quite straightforward cases. It's you who should
426	CP	Edward	18	{E} By the end of next week/I shall be quite free./{L} And we can be alone./I love that
449	CC	Eggers	14	/That would be the solution. Yes, quite ideal./{SC} I'm glad you agree. Your
451	CC	Eggers	19	laugh sometimes. I don't laugh easily./Quite a humorist, he is. In fact, Mrs. E./
453	CC	Lucasta	16	don't you let him speak?/Eggy's really quite human, Colby./It's only that he's terrified
455	CC	Eggers	10	relationship./No, I don't think that's quite the right term./She's no money of her
455	CC	Colby	36	don't suppose Lady Elizabeth/Can be quite so unusual as Miss Angel./{E} O yes, Mr.
458	CC	Lady E	12	thoughtful of you, Eggerson,/But quite unnecessary. And besides,/I didn't come
459	CC	Lady E	29	go and rest now./In a sleeping-car it is quite impossible/To get one's quiet hour. A
461	CC	Claude	31	before./So the meeting didn't go quite the way I'd intended;/And yet I believe
462	CC	Colby	21	right direction./{C} It doesn't seem quite honest./If we all have to live in a world of
471	CC	Colby	14	that's why I like you./{C} That's not quite the reason./{L} Oh, so you believe that I
471	CC	Colby	18	that I'm thinking of./It's something quite simple./{L} Then I wish you'd tell me./
473	CC	Colby	22	a point./And yet, you know, it's not quite real to me —/Although it's as real to me
474	CC	Colby	31	to me/To need anybody./{C} That's quite untrue./{L} But you've something else,
475	CC	Lucasta	13	I think I'm changing./I've changed quite a lot in the last two hours./{C} And I think
480	CC	Kaghan	2	/And I've put my shirt ... no, not quite the right expression —/Lucasta's the most
486	CC	Lady E	17	Guzzard my aunt./{LE} And are you quite sure that Mrs. Guzzard's sister —/Who
488	CC	Lady E	37	Elizabeth,/Colby is *my* son./{LE} Quite impossible, Claude!/You have a daughter.
496	CC	Eggers	30	an idle moment./And really, now, I'm quite lost in London./Every time I come, I
497	CC	Lady E	22	believe it./{LE} Claude, that's not quite right. Let me explain./I am convinced that
503	CC	Claude	25	/{E} Better wait till afterwards./{SC} Quite right, Eggerson./{L} Good-bye, Colby./
514	CC	Guzzard	32	I understand that, Mr. Eggerson. Quite well./{SC} I shall not believe it. I'll not

514 CC	Claude	35	deception/For twenty-five years? It's quite impossible./{MG} I had no intention of
518 CC	Eggers	7	together every day, you know,/For quite a little time, and I've watched you pretty
536 ES	Gomez	30	you have lost *yourself*/That you are quite alone./{LC} I'm waiting to hear/Why you
538 ES	Gomez	22	post/Where at least you can't make quite the same mistake./At the worst, you go
540 ES	Gomez	20	One time in particular./You know quite well to which occasion I'm referring —/A
547 ES	Piggott	36	walks, on the shore or in the hills,/Quite away from the motor roads. You must
549 ES	Carghil	32	said./Or did she say 'yellow'? I'm not quite sure./You do remember now, don't you,
553 ES	Carghil	32	safe. But I have photostats/Which are quite as good, I'm told. And I like to read them/
555 ES	Piggott	3	charming person,/I dare say, but not quite your sort or mine./I suspected that she
567 ES	Monica	25	scrupulous,/The most austere. It's quite impossible./Father with a guilty secret in
568 ES	Ld Clav	32	the impediment:/It's impossible to be quite honest with your child/If you've never

QUITTÉE (1)

| 51 Restaurant | | 18 | un gros chien;/Moi j'avais peur, je l'ai quittée à mi-chemin./C'est dommage.'/Mais |

QUIVERING (1)

| 596 When we | | 4 | fingers of the breeze/Had torn no quivering cobweb down./The hedgerow |

QUIVERS (1)

| 191 FQ: Little | | 12 | melting and freezing/The soul's sap quivers. There is no earth smell/Or smell of |

QUORUM (1)

| 209 NamingCats | | 17 | names of this kind, I can give you a quorum,/Such as Munkustrap, Quaxo, or |

QUOTE (1)

| 436 CP | Reilly | 40 | correctly, Julia./Do you mind if I quote poetry, Mrs. Chamberlayne?/{L} Oh no, I |

RABBIT (3)
155 Rock 3	32	of lobelias and tennis flannels/The	rabbit shall burrow and the thorn revisit,/The
214 RTTugger	26	there isn't any fish then he won't eat	rabbit./If you offer him cream then he sniffs and
235 Ad-dress	61	a habit/Of eating nothing else but	rabbit,/And when he's finished, licks his paws/

RABINOVITCH (1)
56 Swee Night	23	concentrates, withdraws;/Rachel *née*	Rabinovitch/Tears at the grapes with

RACE (7)
152 Rock 2	23	of the Word of GOD:/The British	race assured of a mission/Performed it, but left
154 Rock 3	15	in print,/Many read nothing but the	race reports./Much is your reading, but not the
156 Rock 3	71	to fevered enthusiasm/For nation or	race or what you call humanity;/Though you
161 Rock 7	29	Power, and what they call Life, or	Race, or Dialectic./The Church disowned, the
212 Growltiger	17	to grips!/But most to Cats of foreign	race his hatred had been vowed;/To Cats of
212 Growltiger	18	vowed;/To Cats of foreign name and	race no quarter was allowed./The Persian and
561 ES Ld Clav	6	from their past will always lose the	race./I know this from experience. When you

RACES (1)
164 Rock 9	9	like thoroughbreds ready for	races,/Adorning themselves, and busy in the

RACHEL (1)
56 Swee Night	23	and concentrates, withdraws;/	Rachel *née* Rabinovitch/Tears at the grapes

RACING (1)
328 FR Violet	6	is definitely reckless./{V} I think these	racing cars ought to be prohibited. {}/[*Re-enter*

RACK (1)
292 FR Ivy	35	/He's let the rock garden go to	rack and ruin,/And he's nearly half blind. I've

RACKET (1)
479 CC Lucasta	7	Colby doesn't need your protection	racket/So far as I'm concerned, B. And as for

RAFFISH (1)
213 Growltiger	31	the Lady GRIDDLEBONE./And his	raffish crew were sleeping in their barrels and

RAG (1)
65 WL: Chess	128	/But/O O O O that Shakespeherian	Rag —/It's so elegant/So intelligent/'What shall

RAGE (2)
194 FQ: Little	137	/Second, the conscious impotence of	rage/At human folly, and the laceration/Of
212 Growltiger	14	Pekinese, that faced Growltiger's	rage;/Woe to the bristly Bandicoot, that lurks

RAGES (1)
184 FQ: DrySal	8	implacable,/Keeping his seasons and	rages, destroyer, reminder/Of what men choose

RAGGED (2)
15 Prufrock	73	/I should have been a pair of	ragged claws/Scuttling across the floors of silent
187 FQ: DrySal	120	and the bite in the apple./And the	ragged rock in the restless waters,/Waves wash

RAGING (1)
253 MC Tempt4	17	policy, barons private profit,/Jealousy	raging possession of the fiend./Barons are

RAID (3)
182 FQ: ECoker	181	so each venture/Is a new beginning, a	raid on the inarticulate/With shabby equipment
588 Fable	45	go through the account: They made a	raid/On every bird and beast in Æsop's fable/To
453 CC Lucasta	30	to Claude?/Meanwhile, you'll have to	raid the till for me. I'm starving./{K} I've just

RAIDE (1)
48 Lune Miel	16	la France./Et Saint Apollinaire,	raide et ascétique,/Vieille usine désaffectée de

RAIL (4)
224 Mr Mistoff	26	crack/He can walk on the narrowest	rail./He can pick any card from a pack,/He is
300 FRDowning	5	/Didn't like to see her lean over the	rail./He was in a rare fright, once or twice./But
300 FRDowning	31	I saw his Lordship/Leaning over the	rail, looking at the water —/There wasn't a
300 FRDowning	34	stayed there alone, looking over the	rail./Her Ladyship must have been all right

RAILS (2)
188 FQ: DrySal	143	at any terminus,/While the narrowing	rails slide together behind you;/And on the deck
480 CC Kaghan	10	in the dark;/You'd keep me on the	rails./{C} That's just nonsense./You only

RAILWAY (6)
232 Skimble		t wears white spats!/Skimbleshanks: the	Railway Cat/There's a whisper down the line at
233 Skimble	49	mice —/You can leave all that to the	Railway Cat,/The Cat of the Railway Train!/In
233 Skimble	50	to the Railway Cat,/The Cat of the	Railway Train!/In the watches of the night he is
233 Skimble	66	on the Midnight Mail/The Cat of the	Railway Train.'/The Ad-dressing of Cats/
301 FR Chorus	30	the right column./We know about the	railway accident/We know about the sudden
530 ES Ld Clav	21	sitting in an empty waiting room/In a	railway station on a branch line,/After the last

RAIN (17)
37 Gerontion	2	/Being read to by a boy, waiting for	rain./I was neither at the hot gates/Nor fought
37 Gerontion	4	the hot gates/Nor fought in the warm	rain/Nor knee deep in the salt marsh, heaving a
61 WL: Burial	4	desire, stirring/Dull roots with spring	rain./Winter kept us warm, covering/Earth in
61 WL: Burial	9	the Starnbergersee/With a shower of	rain; we stopped in the colonnade,/And went on
72 WL: Thund	342	/But dry sterile thunder without	rain/There is not even solitude in the mountains

74 WL: Thund 394 lightning. Then a damp gust/Bringing rain/Ganga was sunken, and the limp leaves/
74 WL: Thund 396 and the limp leaves/Waited for rain, while the black clouds/Gathered far
96 Ash-Wed 5 14 /On the mainland, in the desert or the rain land,/For those who walk in darkness/Both
173 FQ: BurntN 89 /The moment in the arbour where the rain beat,/The moment in the draughty church
243 MC Chorus 33 harvest is good,/One year is a year of rain,/Another a year of dryness,/One year the
256 MC Tempts 31 door under lock and bolt?/{4T} Is it rain that taps at the window, is it wind that
275 MC Chorus 23 and ourselves defiled with blood./A rain of blood has blinded my eyes. Where is
281 MC Chorus 8 of the earth,/In the snow, in the rain, in the wind, in the storm; in all of Thy
303 FR Mary 8 which do not know/The wind and rain, as I know them./{Ag} I wonder how many
310 FR Mary 28 the violent sun/Wet wings into the rain cloud/Harefoot over the moon?/{H} What
332 FR Agatha 35 came too soon, not soon enough./The rain and wind had not shaken your father/
343 FR Amy 30 about the upkeep. Let the wind and rain do that. {}/[*While* AMY *has been speaking,*
RAINING (1)
359 CP Julia 24 /{J} Edward! How lucky that it's raining!/It made me remember my umbrella,/
RAINS (2)
65 WL: Chess 136 do?'/'The hot water at ten./And if it rains, a closed car at four./And we shall play a
123 SA Kl & Kr 18 *trains/And we won't go home when it rains/We'll gather hibiscus flowers/For it won't*
RAISE (3)
307 FR Mary 5 cave where we met by moonlight/To raise the evil spirits./{H} Arthur and John./Of
421 CP Reilly 30 confidence in anything/You always raise doubts; when I am apprehensive/Then you
422 CP m 13 for the building of the hearth. {}/[*They raise their glasses*]/{R} Let them build the hearth/
RAISED (4)
70 WL: Fire S 294 and Kew/Undid me. By Richmond I raised my knees/Supine on the floor of a narrow
84 Hollow Men 42 land/Here the stone images/Are raised, here they receive/The supplication of a
593 Grad 7 6 victory,/That with their aid the flag is raised on high./Sometime in distant years when
347 FRDowning 1 And if I may say so,/Now that you've raised the subject, I'm most relieved —/If you
RAISES (1)
411 CP m 35 *takes out his cheque-book.* REILLY *raises his hand*]/{R} My secretary will send you
RAISING (2)
22 Preludes 22 /One thinks of all the hands/That are raising dingy shades/In a thousand furnished
267 MC Knight1 36 to the King of France, to the Pope,/Raising up against him false opinions./{K2} Yet
RAISON (1)
548 ES Piggott 1 /After all, peace and quiet is our *raison d'être.*/Now I'll leave you to enjoy it. {}/
RAKE (2)
228 Gus 5 /His coat's very shabby, he's thin as a rake,/And he suffers from palsy that makes his
537 ES Gomez 30 out, Dick. You liked to play the rake,/But you never went too far. There's a
RALLY (1)
603 Spleen 9 cats in the alley;/Dejection unable to rally/Against this dull conspiracy./And Life, a
RALPH (1)
136 5FingerEx4 t well-preserved complacency./*Lines to Ralph Hodgson Esqre.*/How delightful to meet
RAMA (1)
264 MC Priest3 20 O Lord,/The blood of thy saints. In Rama, a voice heard, weeping./Out of the
RAN (11)
212 Growltiger 12 up the silly goose,/When the rumour ran along the shore: GROWLTIGER'S ON
322 FR Winch 33 along/At a pretty smart pace, I fancy, ran into a lorry/Drawn up round the bend.
328 FR Charles 13 brother of Lord/Monchensey, who ran into and demolished a roundsman's/cart in
335 FR Harry 36 walked through the little door/And I ran to meet you in the rose-garden./{Ag} This is
498 CC Claude 15 /{SC} You're suggesting that she ran a baby farm./That's most unlikely,
540 ES Gomez 22 and shadows —/The night you ran over the old man in the road./{LC} You *said*
540 ES Ld Clav 23 old man in the road./{LC} You *said* I ran over an old man in the road./{G} You knew
555 ES Monica 27 bad your nerves have been./He only ran into a tree./{LC} Yes, a tree./It might have
571 ES Ld Clav 36 was late at night. A secondary road./I ran over an old man lying in the road/And I did
571 ES Ld Clav 37 I did not stop. Then another man ran over him./A lorry driver. He stopped and
572 ES Ld Clav 34 remembers an occasion/On which I ran away. Very well./I shan't run away now —
RANCID (1)
24 Rhapsody 37 its tongue/And devours a morsel of rancid butter.'/So the hand of the child,
RANCUNE (1)
24 Rhapsody 51 the moon,/La lune ne garde aucune rancune,/She winks a feeble eye,/She smiles into
RANG (2)
128 Cor1 March 44 took young Cyril to church. And they rang a bell/And he said right out loud,
424 CP Lavinia 14 told me you had already left./But all I rang up for was to reassure you ... {}/[*smiling*]./
RANGE (1)
204 de la Mare 21 /Dogs cower, flitter bats, and owls range/At witches' sabbath of the maiden aunts;/

RANK (6)

53 Whispers	27	not in its arboreal gloom/Distil so rank a feline smell/As Grishkin in a
184 FQ: DrySal	12	in the nursery bedroom,/In the rank ailanthus of the April dooryard,/In the
213 Growltiger	49	foe pressed forward, in stubborn rank on rank;/Growltiger to his vast surprise
213 Growltiger	49	pressed forward, in stubborn rank on rank;/Growltiger to his vast surprise was forced
278 MC Knight2	19	man so well qualified for the/highest rank of the Civil Service. And what happened?
452 CC Lucasta	15	/{L} You're wrong, Eggy. It's rank injustice./Two months I'd gone on filing

RANKS (1)

94 Ash-Wed 4	3	/Who walked between/The various ranks of varied green/Going in white and blue,

RANNOCH (1)

141 Rannoch	t	hermit's chapel, the pilgrim's prayer./Rannoch, by Glencoe/Here the crow starves,

RAPACIOUS (2)

162 Rock 8	17	were restless and curious,/Some were rapacious and lustful./Many left their bodies to
340 FR Amy	11	return to Wishwood?/{A} The more rapacious, to take what I never had;/The more

RAPT (1)

209 NamingCats	27	the same:/His mind is engaged in a rapt contemplation/Of the thought, of the

RAPTURE (2)

111 Xmas Trees	12	as a pretext;/So that the glittering rapture, the amazement/Of the
136 5FingerEx4	17	head finches and fairies/In jubilant rapture skim./How delightful to meet Mr.

RARE (5)

18 Portrait	20	to me, my friends,/And how, how rare and strange it is, to find/In a life composed
589 Fable	85	the wicked said (such rascals are not rare)/That the Abbot's course lay nearer
300 FRDowning	6	see her lean over the rail./He was in a rare fright, once or twice./But you know, it is
379 CP Edward	14	grateful,/And I think you are a very rare person./But it was too late. And I should
456 CC Eggers	28	/And very costly. I've had some rare adventures!/I remember long ago, saying to

RARER (1)

416 CP Reilly	13	There are different types. Some are rarer than others./{C} Oh, I thought that I was

RAREST (1)

483 CC Lady E	3	/Of spirituality — and that's the rarest./{C} That would limit my acquaintance to

RASCALS (1)

589 Fable	85	/Though the wicked said (such rascals are not rare)/That the Abbot's course

RAT (5)

67 WL: Fire S	187	and chuckle spread from ear to ear./A rat crept softly through the vegetation/Dragging
155 Rock 3	49	paid,/Subsiding basements where the rat breeds/Or sanitary dwellings with numbered
214 RTTugger	5	him on a mouse then he only wants a rat,/If you set him on a rat then he'd rather
214 RTTugger	6	only wants a rat,/If you set him on a rat then he'd rather chase a mouse./Yes the
269 MC Chorus	34	bird. I have seen/Grey necks twisting, rat tails twining, in the thick light of dawn. I

RAT'S (2)

67 WL: Fire S	195	a little low dry garret,/Rattled by the rat's foot only, year to year./But at my back
84 Hollow Men	33	also wear/Such deliberate disguises/Rat's coat, crowskin, crossed staves/In a field/

RATE (3)

21 Portrait	106	it now to fate./You will write, at any rate./Perhaps it is not too late./I shall sit here,
587 Fable	19	been walled up for his crimes;/At any rate, he sometimes came to dinner,/Whene'er
328 FR Charles	23	by a patrol, and was/travelling at the rate of 66 miles an hour. When asked why he/

RATHER (86)

158 Rock 5	4	'The trowel in hand, and the gun rather loose in the holster.'/Those who sit in a
160 Rock 7	5	snakes or trees, worshipping devils rather than nothing: crying for life beyond life,
179 FQ: ECoker	95	hear/Of the wisdom of old men, but rather of their folly,/Their fear of fear and
214 RTTugger	2	/If you offer him pheasant he would rather have grouse./If you put him in a house he
214 RTTugger	4	flat,/If you put him in a flat then he'd rather have a house./If you set him on a mouse
214 RTTugger	6	rat,/If you set him on a rat then he'd rather chase a mouse./Yes the Rum Tum
216 Jellicles	6	are black and white,/Jellicle Cats are rather small;/Jellicle Cats are merry and bright,/
588 Fable	37	door from head to feet./To make a rather lengthy story shorter,/He left no wise
602 Humoresque	6	/But this deceasèd marionette/I rather liked: a common face,/(The kind of face
268 MC Thomas	21	alone?/I would wish him three crowns rather than one,/And as for the bishops, it is not
288 FR Agatha	13	been together./{Ag} It is going to be rather painful for Harry/After eight years and
291 FR Charles	2	James's Street, in a comfortable chair rather nearer the fire./{I} I might have been
292 FR Amy	23	about taxes —/But I think you would rather wait till you are rested./Your room is all
299 FRDowning	25	the evening,/And *then* she used to get rather excited,/And, in a way, irresponsible, Sir.
300 FRDowning	8	my opinion, Sir,/That his Lordship is rather psychic, as they say./{C} Were they
303 FR Mary	5	how late the spring is, here./{M} I had rather wait for our windblown blossoms,/Such
306 FR Mary	30	you seemed so much older. We were rather in awe of you —/At least, I was./{H}
313 FR Ivy	13	prizes/With my delphiniums. I was rather an authority./{G} Good evening, Mary.
317 FR Harry	8	useless,/Or if anything, make matters rather more difficult./But talk about it, if you
320 FR Warburt	36	brilliant;/And Arthur has always been rather irresponsible./Your mother's hopes are

322 FR	Winch	15	Oh no indeed, my Lord, I'd much rather not .../{H} You mean you think I can't.
322 FR	Winch	26	I'd better have a word with you quiet,/Rather than phone and perhaps disturb her
323 FR	Winch	19	my Lady,/And he must have been in rather a hurry./There was a lorry drawn up
325 FR	Violet	39	was simply terrifying./I said I would rather walk: and I did./{G} Walk? where to?/{V}
354 CP	Alex	33	know the third one:/They kept him rather quiet./{J} Oh, you mean *that* one./{A} He
357 CP	Edward	8	know. Her mother's sister/And rather a recluse./{J} Her favourite aunt?/{E} Her
357 CP	Edward	10	Her aunt's favourite niece. And she's rather difficult./When she's ill, she insists on
359 CP	Edward	9	finish the cocktails./Or would you rather have whisky?/{UG} Gin./{E} Anything in
361 CP	Edward	23	appears —/I think your speculations rather offensive./{UG} I know you as well as I
362 CP	Reilly	21	that. There's a loss of personality;/Or rather, you've lost touch with the person/You
363 CP	Reilly	17	don't know any more than I do,/But rather less. You are nothing but a set/Of
366 CP	Edward	29	been disturbed already;/And I did rather want to be alone./But what's it all about?
367 CP	Peter	4	didn't notice:/I must have behaved rather better than I thought./If you didn't
367 CP	Peter	6	suppose the others did,/Though I'm rather afraid of Julia Shuttlethwaite./{E} Julia is
368 CP	Edward	8	of you, Alex, I'm sure;/But I rather *want* to be alone, this evening./{A} But
368 CP	Alex	14	you a little surprise:/You know, I'm rather a famous cook./I'm going straight to
372 CP	Peter	33	back ... but, if you don't mind,/I'd rather you didn't tell *her* what I've told you./{E}
375 CP	Edward	16	just wondered/Whether it mightn't be rather indigestible? .../Oh, no, Alex, don't bring
377 CP	Celia	7	—/{C} Yes, who was that man? I was rather afraid of him;/He has some sort of
380 CP	Celia	27	I found him less interesting, and rather conceited./But why should we talk about
389 CP	Celia	37	{C} Oh, I'm afraid that all this sounds rather silly!/But ... {}/[EDWARD *re-enters with*
395 CP	Lavinia	12	what you always were./As for me, I'm rather a different person/Whom you must get to
396 CP	Lavinia	8	married me./{L} Well, you really were rather attractive, you know;/And you kept on
405 CP	Reilly	4	single patient/Who is ill by himself, is rather the exception./I have recently had
405 CP	Reilly	7	*three times]*/{R} You must accept a rather unusual procedure:/I propose to
410 CP	Reilly	12	us loathe one another./{R} See it rather as the bond which holds you together./
413 CP	Celia	32	/That would be terrible. So I'd rather believe/There is something wrong with
432 CP	Lavinia	28	forgot — {}/[*Turning to* ALEX]/{L} I rather assumed that you knew each other —/I
437 CP	Reilly	35	suffer?/{R} Not at all what I mean. Rather the contrary./I'd say that she suffered all
440 CP	Lavinia	24	she always looks her best. You're rather transparent,/You know, when you're
447 CC	Claude	13	/{SC} And well deserved; but rather inconvenient/When it comes to
447 CC	Claude	33	Don't make too much of it./And I rather hope that she will take to him at once:/If
450 CC	Colby	34	you don't have to leave just yet./I'm rather nervous about this meeting./You've told
451 CC	Colby	1	me something about her,/But that's rather alarming./{E} Mr. Kaghan is prejudiced./
451 CC	Eggers	11	But not to beat about the bush,/He's rather a rough diamond. Very free and easy
454 CC	Eggers	26	about *her*?/{E} Oh, Miss Angel./She's rather flighty. But she has a good heart./{C} But
455 CC	Eggers	40	as I told you, she really is a lady,/Rather a *grande dame*, as the French say./
456 CC	Eggers	9	him./And such a generous heart! He's rather a Socialist./I'm a staunch Conservative,
459 CC	Lady E	8	/You should be artistic. But you look rather frail./I must give you lessons in the art of
462 CC	Claude	32	you might find it easier/To start by a rather formal relationship/In adapting yourself
463 CC	Colby	16	had before. Yet at the same time/It's rather disturbing. I don't mean the work:/I
463 CC	Colby	21	think in it — you feel yourself to be/Rather a different person when you're talking it.
467 CC	Colby	10	of protector, a generous provider:/Rather as a patron than a father —/The father
471 CC	Lucasta	7	you the gramophone records./{L} I'd rather you played me bits yourself, and
471 CC	Colby	29	it to be one of your own creation/Rather than wait to see what happened./I hope
475 CC	Lucasta	38	me much. And as for B. —/I'd much rather hear it from yourself./{C} There's only
482 CC	Lady E	11	Miss Angel./I can see you've lived a rather sheltered life,/And I've noticed them
482 CC	Lady E	13	deal of attention./You see, you're rather a curiosity/To both of them — you're not
482 CC	Lady E	25	malicious suggestions:/But they are rather worldly and materialistic,/And ... well,
482 CC	Lady E	26	and materialistic,/And ... well, rather vulgar. They're not your sort at all./{C}
490 CC	Lady E	5	happened./Oh, Claude, you know I'm rather weak in the head/Though I try to be
491 CC	Lady E	6	from what you said,/That you would rather he was *ours* than only *yours*./Why should
504 CC	Lucasta	7	/Whom you are expecting. She looks rather formidable./{SC} It's Parkman's day off.
506 CC	Eggers	10	the lady/Who had taken the child. Or rather, had forgotten it./She was not, in any
511 CC	Kaghan	33	/But Barney Kaghan — it sounds rather flashy:/It wouldn't make the right
515 CC	Guzzard	31	it in the wound?/I had very much rather that the facts were otherwise./{C} I
531 ES	Ld Clav	20	/Of every public man./{LC} Say rather, the exequies/Of the failed successes, the
533 ES	Gomez	24	/Out there they respect you for rather different reasons./{LC} Do you mean
533 ES	Gomez	29	Not at all, not at all./I think that was rather an unkind suggestion./I've always kept
540 ES	Gomez	2	both of us failures. But even so,/I'd rather be my kind of failure than yours./{LC}
545 ES	Monica	12	/Even the matron, though she looks rather dominating,/Has left us alone./{LC} Yes,
558 ES	Ld Clav	12	first./I dare say Sir Alfred's will be rather different./And what else did he say?/{Mi}
563 ES	Carghil	3	He's a very good figure/And he's rather exotic-looking. Is he a foreigner?/{LC}
567 ES	Monica	3	come!/I've been so worried, and rather frightened./It was exasperating that they
568 ES	Charles	14	things I would gladly forget, Sir,/Or rather, which I wish had never happened./I can

580 ES   Carghil   25 you'd better rest now./You're looking rather tired. I'll run and see them off. {}/[*Exit*
RATIONAL (2)
149 Rock 1   68 you find explanations/To satisfy the rational and enlightened mind./Second, you
156 Rock 3   67   /Engaged in working out a rational morality,/Engaged in printing as many
RATS (3)
 41 Burb Blei   22 /Declines. On the Rialto once./The rats are underneath the piles./The Jew is
213 Growltiger   55 there was dancing on the strand./Rats were roasted whole at Brentford, and at
228 Gus   8 /But no longer a terror to mice and to rats./For he isn't the Cat that he was in his
RATS' (2)
 65 WL: Chess   115 are thinking. Think.'/I think we are in rats' alley/Where the dead men lost their bones./
 83 Hollow Men   9 meaningless/As wind in dry grass/Or rats' feet over broken glass/In our dry cellar/
RATTLE (2)
 67 WL: Fire S   186 at my back in a cold blast I hear/The rattle of the bones, and chuckle spread from ear
509 CC   Colby   14 remember, Aunt Sarah,/My finding a rattle and a jingle-bell,/And your telling me I
RATTLED (3)
 67 WL: Fire S   195 bones cast in a little low dry garret,/Rattled by the rat's foot only, year to year./But
135 5FingerEx2   5 forces shriek'd aloud,/Screamed, rattled, muttered endlessly./Little dog was safe
193 FQ: Little   85 his homing/While the dead leaves still rattled on like tin/Over the asphalt where no
RATTLING (1)
 27 Morning   1 /Morning at the Window/They are rattling breakfast plates in basement kitchens,/
RAVEN (2)
 56 Swee Night   7   the River Plate,/Death and the Raven drift above/And Sweeney guards the
335 FR   Agatha   3 distance tiny voices/And then a black raven flew over./And then I was only my own
RAVENNE (1)
 48 Lune Miel   2 Haute;/Mais une nuit d'été, les voici à Ravenne,/A l'aise entre deux draps, chez deux
RAVENOUS (1)
426 CP   Julia   33 had to miss my tea, and I'm simply ravenous/And dying of thirst. What can
RAVING (1)
418 CP   Celia   17 life./Oh, I'm afraid this sounds like raving!/Or just cantankerousness ... still,/If
RAW (1)
258 MC Thomas   24 thought me most contemptible,/The raw nobility, whose manners matched their
RAYS (1)
 68 WL: Fire S   225   touched by the sun's last rays,/On the divan are piled (at night her bed)/
RAZOR (1)
 43 Swee Erect   29   straddled in the sun.)/Tests the razor on his leg/Waiting until the shriek
RE-ENACT (1)
260 MC Thomas   7 Day. For whenever/Mass is said, we re-enact the Passion and Death of Our Lord;
RE-ENACTMENT (1)
194 FQ: Little   140 amuse./And last, the rending pain of re-enactment/Of all that you have done, and
RE-ENTER (6)
328 FR   m 7 racing cars ought to be prohibited. {}/[*Re-enter* CHARLES, *with a newspaper*]/{C}
376 CP   m 2 /*a card. The doorbell rings repeatedly. Re-enter* CELIA, *in an apron.*]/{C} You'd better
377 CP   m 19 *kitchen*]/{E} What the devil's that? {}/[*Re-enter* JULIA, *in apron, with a tray and three*
424 CP   m 5 *and moves a bowl of flowers.*]/[*Re-enter* CATERER'S MAN *with trolley*]/{L}
510 CC   m 15 being able to adjust myself to it. {}/[*Re-enter* COLBY, *with* KAGHAN *and*
547 ES   m 19 courtesies,/She will leave us alone. {}/[*Re-enter* MRS. PIGGOTT]/{MP} I really *am*
RE-ENTERS (2)
389 CP   m 38 rather silly!/But ... {}/[EDWARD *re-enters with* JULIA]/{J} There you are,
571 ES   Ld Clav 31   As for Frederick Culverwell,/He re-enters my life to make himself a reminder/Of
RE-MARRY (1)
360 CP   Reilly   39 /If another man, then you'd want to re-marry/To prove to the world that somebody
REACH (13)
 19 Portrait   60 you feel,/Sure that across the gulf you reach your hand./You are invulnerable, you
 20 Portrait   67 and the sympathy/Of one about to reach her journey's end./I shall sit here, serving
 49 Hippopot   13 its dividends./The 'potamus can never reach/The mango on the mango-tree;/But fruits
 69 WL: Fire S   275 wash/Drifting logs/Down Greenwich reach/Past the Isle of Dogs./Weialala leia/
175 FQ: BurntN   142 /Can only die. Words, after speech, reach/Into the silence. Only by the form, the
175 FQ: BurntN   144 the pattern,/Can words or music reach/The stillness, as a Chinese jar still/Moves
189 FQ: DrySal   186 not reject them/Or wherever cannot reach them the sound of the sea bell's/Perpetual
226 Macavity   4 Squad's despair:/For when they reach the scene of crime — *Macavity's not*
226 Macavity   8 make a fakir stare,/And when you reach the scene of crime — *Macavity's not*
235 Ad-dress   66 of respect./And so in time you reach your aim,/And finally call him by his
541 ES   Gomez   8 friends, in confidence./It might even reach the ears of some of your acquaintance —/
561 ES   Ld Clav 7 know this from experience. When you reach your goal,/Your imagined paradise of
580 ES   Gomez   3 With the full address. You can always reach him there./But it takes some days, you

REACHED (4)

38 Gerontion	49	devours. Think at last/We have not reached conclusion, when I/Stiffen in a rented
295 FR Harry	29	than ever./The contamination has reached the marrow/And *they* are always near.
332 FR Agatha	14	she took your father's place, and reached the point where/Wishwood supported
515 CC Guzzard	4	/I sent you a message, which never reached you./On your return, you came at once

REACHES (3)

24 Rhapsody	2	Night/Twelve o'clock./Along the reaches of the street/Held in a lunar synthesis,/
184 FQ: DrySal	17	edge also, the granite/Into which it reaches, the beaches where it tosses/Its hints of
501 CC m	38	with him./{SC} We'll get him now. {}/[*Reaches for the telephone*]/[*A knock. Enter*

REACTION (3)

361 CP Reilly	4	wife back./{UG} That's the natural reaction./It's embarrassing, and inconvenient./It
449 CC Claude	37	dark./I simply can't guess what her reaction would be./There's a lot I don't
502 CC Lucasta	11	That I must have misunderstood your reaction./It wouldn't have been like you — the

RÉACTIONNAIRES (1)

46 Directeur	8	/Empeste la brise./Les actionnaires/Réactionnaires/Du Spectateur/Conservateur/

READ (24)

37 Gerontion	2	an old man in a dry month,/Being read to by a boy, waiting for rain./I was neither
61 WL: Burial	18	the mountains, there you feel free./I read, much of the night, and go south in the
117 SP Doris	19	next./You've got to *think* when you read the cards,/It's not a thing that anyone can
147 Rock 1	30	weather is foul we stay at home and read the papers./In industrial districts, there I
154 Rock 3	15	to see their names in print,/Many read nothing but the race reports./Much is your
206 To my Wife	11	/But this dedication is for others to read:/These are private words addressed to you
234 Ad-dress	1	/The Ad-dressing of Cats/You've read of several kinds of Cat,/And my opinion
278 MC Knight2	29	I know that I have/your approval: I read it in your faces. It is only with the
295 FR Charles	9	we know what really happened, we read it in the papers —/No need to revert to it.
299 FR Charles	7	/We only knew what we read in the papers —/Of course, there was a
328 FR Gerald	10	in the later editions./You'd better read it to us. {}/[*reads*]./{C} 'Peer's Brother in
328 FR Charles	27	'The Piper family ...' no, we needn't read that./{V} This is just what I expected. But if
347 FR Ivy	17	he sent it, after telephoning./Shall I read it to you? I was wondering/Whether to
349 FR Violet	10	/{V} We must wait for the will to be read. I shall send a wire in the morning./{C} I
418 CP Reilly	2	life will be only like a book/You have read once, and lost. In a world of lunacy,/
446 CC Eggers	38	Sir Claude. Only the other day/I read a letter in *The Times* about wild birds seen
531 ES Monica	5	retired in a blaze of glory —/You've read every word about you in the papers./{C}
531 ES Lambert	36	this one. He said that when you read it/You would want to see him. Said you'd
539 ES Ld Clav	4	about me as you do/You must have read that I retired at the insistence of my
553 ES Carghil	19	*quenched.* Do you know what I do?/I read your letters every night./{LC} My letters!/
553 ES Carghil	29	were very loving. Would you like to read them?/I'm afraid I can't show you the
553 ES Carghil	32	quite as good, I'm told. And I like to read them/In your own handwriting./{LC} And
554 ES Carghil	2	photostats tomorrow morning,/And read them to you./— Oh, there's Mrs. Piggott!/
562 ES Carghil	13	be here./I came back to have a quiet read of your letters;/But how nice to find a little

READERS (2)

28 Boston ET	1	/The Boston Evening Transcript/The readers of the *Boston Evening Transcript*/Sway
601 Nocturne	13	— 'Love next week?')/While female readers all in tears are drowned: —/'The perfect

READING (11)

20 Portrait	72	will see me any morning in the park/Reading the comics and the sporting page./
117 SP Dusty	9	of diamonds, what's that mean?/{Du} (*reading*) 'A small sum of money, or a present/Of
154 Rock 3	16	but the race reports./Much is your reading, but not the Word of GOD,/Much is
331 FR Agatha	35	cultivated country squire,/Reading, sketching, playing on the flute,/
460 CC Claude	11	cards, just to know where you are/By reading the postmark./{LE} But Claude, I'm
518 CC Eggers	8	/Mr. Simpkins! You'll be thinking of reading for orders./And you'll still have your
527 ES Monica	25	home in the evening,/Even when he's reading, or busy with his papers/He needs to
527 ES Monica	27	someone else in the room with him,/Reading too — or just sitting — someone/Not
532 ES m	4	A pleasant-spoken gentleman. {}/[*after reading the note*]./{LC} I'll see him in the library.
545 ES Monica	21	/Take your newspaper and start reading to me. {}/[*Enter* MRS. PIGGOTT]/
553 ES Carghil	17	/There's a phrase I seem to remember reading somewhere:/*Where their fires are not*

READJUSTMENT (1)

446 CC Claude	4	experience./With a young man, some readjustment is necessary./But I'm satisfied that

READS (3)

589 Fable	72	moments,/As everybody'll know who reads this romance./The Abbot sat as pasted to
328 FR m	11	editions./You'd better read it to us. {}/[*reads*]./{C} *Peer's Brother in Motor Smash*/The
347 FR m	19	/Whether to show it to Amy or not. {}/[*Reads*]/{I} 'Regret delayed business in town many

READY (36)

24 Rhapsody	32	strength has left/Hard and curled and ready to snap./Half-past two,/The street-lamp
148 Rock 1	55	of all or the love of none./All men are ready to invest their money/But most expect
164 Rock 9	9	proudnecked, like thoroughbreds ready for races,/Adorning themselves, and busy

164 Rock 9		12	/Thinking good of themselves, ready for any festivity,/Doing themselves very
180 FQ: ECoker		128	without thought, for you are not ready for thought:/So the darkness shall be the
232 Skimble		2	line at 11.39/When the Night Mail's ready to depart,/Saying 'Skimble where is
233 Skimble		43	Skimble's just behind him and was ready to remind him./For Skimble won't let
245 MC	Priest2	30	coming,/Than seven days could make ready Canterbury./However, I will have fires
274 MC	Thomas	33	saved by the blood of Christ,/Ready to suffer with my blood./This is the sign
275 MC	Thomas	7	violated./{T} For my Lord I am now ready to die,/That his Church may have peace
292 FR	Amy	24	till you are rested./Your room is all ready for you. Nothing has been changed./{H}
301 FR	Downing	6	Sir:/Only I like to have her always ready./Would there be anything more, Sir?/{G}
306 FR	Mary	34	us;/Even the nice things were laid out ready,/And the treats were always so carefully
309 FR	Mary	9	you —/But in any case, I must get ready for dinner./{H} No, no, don't go! Please
334 FR	Harry	26	I returned to find another one made ready —/The book laid out, lines underscored,
334 FR	Harry	28	lines underscored, and the costume/Ready to be put on. But it is very odd:/When
336 FR	Harry	16	just endurable. I know that you are ready,/Ready to leave Wishwood, and I am
336 FR	Harry	17	endurable. I know that you are ready,/Ready to leave Wishwood, and I am going with
347 FR	Downing	4	I half expected it,/So I had the car all ready. You mean them ghosts, Miss!/I
384 CP	Reilly	10	my mind?/{UG} No. You will not be ready to change your mind/Until you recover
400 CP	Alex	15	as the right shops./Besides, he was ready to consult any doctor/Recommended by
412 CP	Julia	8	only came to tell you, I am sure she is ready/To make a decision./{R} Was she
419 CP	Reilly	33	me there?/{R} How soon will you be ready?/{C} Tonight, by nine o'clock./{R} Go
422 CP	Reilly	11	*pours drinks.*]/{R} And now we are ready to proceed to the libation./{A} The words
424 CP	Lavinia	3	with the glasses/And leave them ready./{CM} Very good, Madam. {}/[*Exit.*
439 CP	Julia	35	/Is a cocktail party. They must be ready for it./Their guests may be arriving at any
446 CC	Eggers	25	in the mews?/How soon shall that be ready for him?/{SC} They have still to do the
447 CC	Claude	2	start for Northolt — the car will be ready —/Let's think what you're to say to Lady
450 CC	Claude	25	you return with Lady Elizabeth/I'll be ready waiting to introduce him. {}/[*Enter*
493 CC	Claude	15	look like a couple of barristers/Ready to cross-examine a witness./It's very
504 CC	Claude	23	have been singing./{SC} Well, are we ready? {}/[*A quiet knock. Enter* KAGHAN,
534 ES	Gomez	29	ones/Always have an aeroplane ready:/And keep an account in a bank in
541 ES	Ld Clav	34	you/In five minutes' time./{LC} I'll be ready to take it. {}/[*Exit* LAMBERT]/{G} Ah,
559 ES	Ld Clav	24	my name had been./{LC} So you are ready to repudiate your family,/To throw away
574 ES	Carghil	21	father!/And I found him only too ready to help./{LC} And what was Señor
581 ES	Charles	4	you./{C} We will indeed. We shall be ready to welcome him/And give all the aid we

REAFFIRMING (1)

161 Rock 7		24	before,/Yet always struggling, always reaffirming, always resuming their march on the

REAL (56)

120 SP	Krum	7	visit —/{Kr} Specially when you got a real live Britisher/A guy like Sam to show you
151 Rock 2		8	neighbour? For love must be made real in act, as desire unites with desired; we have
188 FQ: DrySal		168	sea,/Or whatever event, this is your real destination.'/So Krishna, as when he
249 MC	Tempt2	10	in heaven./{T} What means?/{T2} Real power/Is purchased at price of a certain
251 MC	Tempt3	3	/Unreal friendship may turn to real/But real friendship, once ended, cannot be
251 MC	Tempt3	4	friendship may turn to real/But real friendship, once ended, cannot be mended./
255 MC	Thomas	25	eternal grandeur?/{T} Others offered real goods, worthless/But real. You only offer/
255 MC	Thomas	26	offered real goods, worthless/But real. You only offer/Dreams to damnation./{T4}
256 MC	Tempts	16	decoration./All things become less real, man passes/From unreality to unreality./
288 FR	Agatha	21	the future can only be built/Upon the real past. Wandering in the tropics/Or against
302 FR	Chorus	9	we should cease to be sure of what is real or unreal?/Hold tight, hold tight, we must
307 FR	Mary	39	I have not had. Nevertheless, however real,/However cruel, it may be a deception./{H}
308 FR	Harry	3	if there is nothing else/The most real is what I fear. The bright colour fades/
308 FR	Mary	10	bring your own landscape/No more real than the other. And in a way you contradict
308 FR	Mary	26	you expected Wishwood/To be your real self, to do something for you/That you can
309 FR	Mary	16	than you think,/And what is the real you. I haven't much experience,/But I see
315 FR	Harry	10	But cancer, now,/That is something real./{W} Well, let's not talk of such matters./
321 FR	Harry	18	can happen —/If Sergeant Winchell is real. But Denman saw him./But what if
321 FR	Harry	19	Denman saw him, and yet he was not real?/That would be worse than anything that
321 FR	Harry	28	*seizes him by the shoulders*]/{H} He *is* real, Doctor./So let us resume the conversation.
327 FR	Harry	16	another doctor on me./But this is too real for your words to alter./Oh, there *must* be
331 FR	Harry	6	with myself,/Though nothing else was real. I thought foolishly/That when I got back
334 FR	Harry	36	than I./The things I thought were real are shadows, and the real/Are what I
334 FR	Harry	36	were real are shadows, and the real/Are what I thought were private shadows.
336 FR	Harry	15	afraid to see you./This time, you are real, this time, you are outside me,/And just
371 CP	Peter	3	I have been telling you of something real —/My first experience of reality/And
371 CP	Peter	21	certain pictures?/There was something real. But what is the reality ... {}/[*The telephone*
372 CP	Alex	21	another aunt./{A} I understand. The real aunt. But you'll be grateful./There are very
374 CP	Edward	24	/{E} It has only brought to light the real difficulties./{C} But surely, these are only

379 CP	Celia	34	the dream was better. It seemed the real reality,/And if this is reality, it is very like a
380 CP	Celia	3	/I am not sure even that you seem real enough/To humiliate me. I suppose that
396 CP	Lavinia	29	road back/To a time when you were real — for you must have been real/At some
396 CP	Lavinia	29	were real — for you must have been real/At some time or other, before you ever
415 CP	Celia	38	frightened by the fear/That it is more real than anything I believed in./{R} What is
415 CP	Reilly	39	I believed in./{R} What is more real than anything you believed in?/{C} It's not
416 CP	Celia	28	unreal/And the dreamer is no more real than his dreams./{R} And this man. What
417 CP	Celia	7	at moments that the ecstasy is real/Although those who experience it may have
428 CP	Alex	31	them and the others./And that's the real problem. I hope I'm not boring you?/{E}
462 CC	Colby	36	situation,/And nothing about it is real to me yet./{SC} But now I want it to be
464 CC	Claude	37	/And the make-believing makes it real./That's not the whole story. My father
465 CC	Claude	30	go through the private door/Into the real world, as I do, sometimes./{C} Indeed, I
472 CC	Lucasta	40	inner world — a world that's more real./That's why you're different from the rest
473 CC	Colby	22	/And yet, you know, it's not quite real to me —/Although it's as real to me as ...
473 CC	Colby	23	quite real to me —/Although it's as real to me as ... this world./But that's just the
473 CC	Colby	27	that's the thing. That's why it's not real./You know, I think that Eggerson's garden/
473 CC	Colby	29	think that Eggerson's garden/Is more real than mine./{L} Eggerson's garden?/What
474 CC	Colby	6	that would make the world outside it real/And acceptable, I think./{L} You sound
474 CC	Lucasta	9	/Is there no other way of making it real to you?/{C} It's simply the fact of being
474 CC	Lucasta	39	means of contact with a world/More real than any *I've* ever lived in./And I'd like to
477 CC	Lucasta	29	I thought you'd come to see me as the real kind of person/That I want to be. That I
485 CC	Lady E	18	become reincarnate. And that one's real ancestry/Is one's previous existences. Of
546 ES	Piggott	36	{MP} Oh yes, that's different./She is a real nurse, you know, fully qualified./Our
569 ES	Ld Clav	34	them?/{LC} Because they are not real, Charles. They are merely ghosts:/Spectres
575 ES	Ld Clav	16	to be custodian of your morals;/His real name is Culverwell .../{G} My dear Dick,/
581 ES	Ld Clav	35	Yes, my dear./Your love is for the real Charles, not a make-believe,/As was your
581 ES	Monica	38	me./{M} But not now, Father!/It's the real you I love — the man you are,/Not the man

REALISE (13)

244 MC	Chorus	27	unaffrayed among the shades, do you realise what you ask, do you realise what it
244 MC	Chorus	27	do you realise what you ask, do you realise what it means/To the small folk drawn
315 FR	Harry	7	be/Or what he would be. He cannot realise/That everything is irrevocable,/The past
376 CP	Julia	20	his strength up./Edward! Don't you realise how lucky you are/To have *two* Good
388 CP	Celia	13	now you'll have a chance,/I hope, to realise your ambitions./I shall miss you./{P} It's
389 CP	Lavinia	5	Now you'll have a chance/At last, to realise your ambitions./You're going together?/
401 CP	Edward	38	better off without her. But didn't you realise/That I was in no state to make a
439 CP	Peter	18	— I'd almost forgotten them./I realise that I can't get out of it —/And what else
448 CC	Eggers	32	has a strong maternal instinct .../{E} I realise that./{SC} Which has always been
462 CC	Claude	38	be different. It's odd, Colby./I didn't realise, till you started with me here,/That we
469 CC	Lucasta	27	I've always felt out of it. And can you realise/That nobody has ever played to me
470 CC	Colby	20	good performers,/You'll very quickly realise how bad my playing is./{L} Really,

REALISED (9)

190 FQ: DrySal		231	of us, this is the aim/Never here to be realised;/Who are only undefeated/Because we
277 MC	Knight3	14	part I am awfully sorry about it. We realised this was our duty,/but all the same we
312 FR	Harry	3	That you could not see them? If I had realised/That you were so obtuse, I would not
388 CP	Celia	11	picture exhibitions — more than you realised./It *was* fun, wasn't it! But now you'll
393 CP	Lavinia	16	I remember —/Oh, I ought to have realised what was coming —/When we were
402 CP	Edward	22	anything./{E} And since then, I have realised/That mine is a very unusual case./{R}
409 CP	Reilly	16	as a passionate lover./Then you realised, what your wife has justly remarked,/
512 CC	Guzzard	37	nothing better./{MG} Wishes, when realised, sometimes turn/Against those who
518 CC	Guzzard	26	But you too, I think, have had a wish realised./— I believe that this interview can now

REALITY (15)

85 Hollow Men		73	*morning.*/Between the idea/And the reality/Between the motion/And the act/Falls
107 Animula		27	forward or retreat,/Fearing the warm reality, the offered good,/Denying the
172 FQ: BurntN		45	human kind/Cannot bear very much reality./Time past and time future/What might
271 MC	Thomas	19	/Human kind cannot bear very much reality. {}/[*Enter* PRIESTS]/[*severally*]./{3P} My
362 CP	Reilly	39	you are still the subject,/The centre of reality. But, stretched on the table,/You are a
371 CP	Peter	4	real —/My first experience of reality/And perhaps it is the last. And you don't
371 CP	Peter	21	was something real. But what is the reality ... {}/[*The telephone rings*]/{E} Excuse me
371 CP	Peter	27	saying?/{P} I was saying, what is the reality/Of experience between two unreal
379 CP	Celia	34	dream was better. It seemed the real reality,/And if this is reality, it is very like a
379 CP	Celia	35	seemed the real reality,/And if this is reality, it is very like a dream./Perhaps it was I
417 CP	Celia	8	those who experience it may have no reality./For what happened is remembered like
464 CC	Claude	16	/I want a world where the form is the reality,/Of which the substantial is only a
537 ES	Gomez	2	/I need you, Dick, to give me reality!/{LC} But according to the description

560 ES   Ld Clav 37 from justice —/Only a fugitive from reality./Oh Michael! If you had some aim of
569 ES   Ld Clav 39 spectral existence into something like reality./{M} But what did the ghosts mean? All

REALLY (134)

21 Portrait   101 /My self-possession gutters; we are really in the dark./'For everybody said so, all
148 Rock 1   50 and I know/That it is hard to be really useful, resigning/The things that men
218 Mung Rump   6 in Kensington Square —/They had really a little more reputation than a couple of
220 Old Deut   12 'Well, of all .../Things ... Can it be ... really! ... No! ... Yes! .../Ho! hi!/Oh, my eye!/My
220 Old Deut   27 'Well, of all .../Things ... Can it be ... really! ... No! ... Yes! .../Ho! hi!/Oh, my eye!/My
221 Old Deut   43 'Well, of all .../Things ... Can it be ... really! ... Yes! ... No! .../Ho! hi!/Oh, my eye!/My
228 Gus   3 as I ought to have told you before,/Is really Asparagus. That's such a fuss/To
277 MC Knight2   40 presented as the under dog. But is this really the case? I am going/to appeal not to your
287 FR   Mary   7 What does she think about it?/{M} Really, Cousin Gerald, if you want information/
287 FR   Violet   11 belong to any generation. {}/[*Exit*]/{V} Really, Gerald, I must say you're very tactless,/
292 FR   Ivy   33 with a little attention./{I} And you'll really have to find a successor to old Hawkins./
292 FR   Ivy   34 find a successor to old Hawkins./It's really high time the old man was pensioned./
293 FR   Violet   3 too old to know what she is doing./It really needs a man in charge of things at
295 FR   Charles   9 yourself./Of course we know what really happened, we read it in the papers —/No
297 FR   Ivy   13 be of use./{I} Charles! you don't really suppose/That he might have pushed her
304 FR   Mary   6 see you any differently now;/But I really wish that I'd taken your advice/And tried
306 FR   Mary   24 child at Wishwood?/{M} Happy? not really, though I never knew why:/It always
314 FR   Harry   40 /{H} Not at all extraordinary./It is really harder to believe in murder/Than to
315 FR Warburt   13 we get onto the subject of cancer?/I really don't know. — But now you're all grown
318 FR Warburt   37 {W} Why, yes, of course, Harry, but I really don't see/What that has to do with the
323 FR   Winch   9 but I've just told the doctor,/It's really nothing but a minor accident./{W} It's
324 FR   Harry   18 him or to anyone else. If he was ever really conscious,/I should be glad for him to
324 FR   Ivy   21 isn't much more than breathing./{I} Really, Harry! how can you be so callous?/I
325 FR   Violet   5 {}/[*Exeunt* HARRY *and* AMY]/{V} I really do not understand Harry's behaviour./
325 FR   Gerald   13 he'll let us know at once./{G} I am really more afraid of the shock for Amy;/But I
342 FR   Mary   13 to generation./{M} Is Harry really going?/{Ag} He is going./But that is not
343 FR   Mary   13 —/Only for this. I suppose I did not really mean it/Then, but I mean it now. Of
344 FR   Violet   8 is he leaving?/{A} Ask Agatha./{V} Really, it sometimes seems to me/That I am the
344 FR   Violet   16 make up your mind .../{V} You can't really think of *living* in a tropical climate!/{G}
346 FR Downing   17 what I'm going to say —/But it's not really strange, Miss, when you come to look at
354 CP   Julia   22 the wedding cake./{J} Well, but it really isn't my story./I heard it first from Delia
355 CP   Alex   14 bats./{A} And is he still there?/Julia is really a mine of information./{C} There isn't
355 CP   Julia   26 a gluttonous old woman like me/Is a really nice tit-bit. I can drink at home. {}/
356 CP   Julia   22 only get Edward alone/And have a really *serious* conversation!'/I said so to
356 CP   Julia   29 think I'm a silly old woman/But I'm really very serious. Lavinia takes me seriously./I
356 CP   Edward   35 be away for some time, Edward?/{E} I really don't know until I hear from her./If her
356 CP   Edward   38 you manage while she is away?/{E} I really don't know. I may go away myself./{C}
357 CP   Julia   19 of Lavinia/Yet very like her. But really, Edward,/Lavinia may be away for weeks,
358 CP   Julia   19 evening:/The potato crisps were really excellent./Now let me see. Have I got
363 CP   Reilly   11 lead?/{UG} To finding out/What you really are. What you really feel/What you really
363 CP   Reilly   11 out/What you really are. What you really feel./What you really are among other
363 CP   Reilly   12 are. What you really feel./What you really are among other people./Most of the time
366 CP   Julia   8 they are! Thank you, Edward;/That really was very clever of you;/I'd never have
366 CP   Peter   37 I'm sorry, Edward;/Of course it was really a very nice party/For everyone but me.
370 CP   Peter   6 happened./But I thought that she really cared about me./And I was so happy
371 CP   Peter   19 truth about even the memory./Did we really share these interests? Did we really feel
371 CP   Peter   19 we really share these interests? Did we really feel the same/When we heard certain
372 CP   Alex   10 I've prepared you such a treat!/I really think that of all my triumphs/This is the
372 CP   Alex   19 from the country./{A} Ah, so the aunt/Really exists. A substantial proof./{E} No, no ...
374 CP   Celia   22 better, for Julia;/But it doesn't really matter. They will know soon enough./
375 CP   Edward   19 ... No, not Norwegian;/But I don't really want cheese ... Slipper what? .../Oh, from
375 CP   Edward   21 ... prunes and alcohol?/No, really, Alex, I don't want anything./I'm very
376 CP   Celia   4 do. Don't lose your head./You see, I really did leave my umbrella;/And I'll say I
378 CP   Celia   36 a song about a man named Riley!/Really, Edward, I think you are mad —/I mean,
380 CP   Celia   17 you are talking about./Edward, this is really too crude a subterfuge/To justify yourself.
380 CP   Edward   34 with Lavinia./I don't think I was ever really in love with her./If I have ever been in
386 CP   Celia   35 in. I never saw you so before./This is really a ludicrous situation./{E} I'm afraid I
386 CP   Celia   37 the humorous side of it./{C} I'm not really laughing at *you*, Edward./I couldn't have
388 CP   Peter   7 everybody, everywhere./So what I've really come for is to say good-bye./{C} Well,
390 CP   Lavinia   14 /{L} Well, perhaps I was in Essex. I really don't know./{J} You don't know where
390 CP   Julia   32 /And now I don't believe she really wants us./I can see that she is quite worn
392 CP   Lavinia   28 the country, and had sent for you./{L} Really, Edward! You had better have told the

396 CP	Lavinia	4	/But I always suspected that you really hated music/And that the gramophone
396 CP	Lavinia	8	why you married me./{L} Well, you really were rather attractive, you know;/And
398 CP	Lavinia	2	to California?/{L} Yes, with Peter./Really, Edward, if you were human/You would
407 CP	Lavinia	4	/I mean practical in the things that really matter./{R} May I interrupt this
407 CP	Lavinia	35	My wife knew nothing about it./{L} Really, Edward! Even if I'd been blind/There
408 CP	Edward	9	you had reason to be jealous./{E} Really, Lavinia! This is very interesting./You
408 CP	Edward	18	guest./{E} Peter Quilpe./Peter Quilpe! Really Lavinia!/I congratulate you. You could
409 CP	Reilly	11	and consternation,/That you were not really in love with Miss Coplestone .../{L} My
410 CP	Edward	4	for you, Lavinia./You know, you really are exceptionally unlovable,/And I never
411 CP	Lavinia	12	know/I was staying at the club?/{L} Really, Edward!/I have *some* sense of
413 CP	Celia	28	But first I must tell you/That I should really *like* to think there's something wrong
418 CP	Celia	9	like a betrayal./You see, I think I really had a vision of something/Though I don't
418 CP	Celia	13	cherish it./In fact, I think it would really be dishonest/For me, now, to try to make
426 CP	Edward	21	/{E} That's why we took it. And I'm really thankful/To have that excuse for not
430 CP	Peter	10	after the Gunnings —/So I said, I really must crash in:/It's my only chance to see
432 CP	Julia	19	interrupt my interruptions:/That's really worse than interrupting./Now my head's
433 CP	Peter	14	I wanted to ask about,/Who did really want to get into films,/And I always
439 CP	Peter	32	I come to England, I promise you./I really do want to see you both, very much./
446 CC	Claude	27	be furnished./I'm trying to find him a really good piano./{E} A piano? Yes, I'm sure
453 CC	Lucasta	16	Why don't you let him speak?/Eggy's really quite human, Colby./It's only that he's
455 CC	Eggers	39	/{C} Oh!/{E} Well, as I told you, she really is a lady,/Rather a *grande dame*, as the
460 CC	Lady E	15	what?/{LE} To engage Mr. Colby. I really am distressed!/This is not the first sign
461 CC	Eggers	19	it in the Spring/When the garden will really be a treat to look at.'/Well, I'll be going./
461 CC	Colby	35	she took to you at once./{C} Did she really think/That she had seen me before?/{SC}
462 CC	Colby	9	my life upon a deception./Do you really believe that Lady Elizabeth/Can ever
462 CC	Claude	17	me if she came to believe/That you really are her son, instead of being mine./She
467 CC	Colby	28	As my confidential clerk./{C} I'm really interested by the work I'm doing/And
469 CC	Lucasta	23	several times,/But I'm afraid I never really listened to the music:/I just enjoyed going
470 CC	Lucasta	21	realise how bad my playing is./{L} Really, Colby, you do make difficulties!/But
471 CC	Lucasta	10	are educating *me*./{L} Colby, you really are full of surprises!/I've never met a man
471 CC	Colby	26	was I trying to give?/{C} That doesn't really matter. But, for some reason,/You
474 CC	Lucasta	34	of which the music is a ... symbol./I really would like to understand music,/Not in
475 CC	Lucasta	15	/{L} Is understanding better what one really is./And the reason why that comes about,
477 CC	Lucasta	33	perhaps, if someone else sees me/As I really am, I might become myself./{C} Oh
480 CC	Kaghan	26	respectability! Now Colby/Doesn't really care about being respectable —/He was
483 CC	Lady E	8	at the flat/To see if the colour scheme really suited you./I believe it does. The walls;
484 CC	Lady E	18	/You can't understand what loathing really is./Yet we must have *some* similarity of
486 CC	Lady E	18	—/Who you say was your mother — really was your mother?/{C} Why, Lady
492 CC	Claude	36	Company/If I told them what I was really remembering./Come, Elizabeth./{LE} My
494 CC	Lady E	3	prove to be *your* son/Instead of mine. Really, I do!/It would be so much fairer. If he is
494 CC	Lady E	39	you'd have liked to be a potter!/You really mean, to make jugs and jars/Like those in
495 CC	Claude	8	despise me/If you knew what I'd really wanted to be./{LE} And I took it for
496 CC	Lady E	7	dancing./{LE} Dervish dancing!/Really, Claude, how absurd you are!/Not that
496 CC	Eggers	30	— that I've not an idle moment./And really, now, I'm quite lost in London./Every
498 CC	Claude	25	it was Colby./{SC} But Eggerson, you really can't ask me to believe/That she took two
500 CC	Lucasta	24	given me./He made me see what I really wanted./B. makes me feel safe. And that's
511 CC	Kaghan	1	you had first been entrusted./{K} I really don't know what emotion to register .../
519 CC	Claude	23	leave me, Lucasta./Eggerson! Do *you* really believe her? {}/[EGGERSON *nods*]
524 ES	Charles	4	going to have you to myself/There's really no point in my staying to tea. {}/[*Enter*
524 ES	Charles	13	/{C} It's the only place where I'm really well known/And get well served. And
525 ES	Monica	38	Oh, what a dominating man you are!/Really, you must imagine you're a hypnotist./
526 ES	Charles	36	to take it for granted/That you don't really care for any company but his!/{M} You're
531 ES	Ld Clav	25	the small minority/Of those who really understand the place we filled/Are
535 ES	Ld Clav	4	only old friend I can trust./{LC} You really trust me? I appreciate the compliment./
541 ES	Gomez	24	me in comfort for the rest of my life./Really, Dick, you owe me an apology./
544 ES	Monica	6	breakfast;/And the chambermaid really *is* a chambermaid:/For when I asked
544 ES	Ld Clav	28	yourself!/{LC} Perhaps I've never really enjoyed living/As much as most people.
545 ES	Monica	11	moment you find life pleasant,/That it really does seem quiet here and restful./Even the
547 ES	Piggott	19	/[*Re-enter* MRS. PIGGOTT]/{MP} I really *am* neglectful!/Miss Claverton-Ferry, I
548 ES	Carghil	28	/But I couldn't believe that it would really happen!/And now I'm sitting here talking
551 ES	Carghil	11	{MC} You refuse to believe that I was really in love with you!/Well, it's natural that
551 ES	Carghil	13	you think, or try to think, that if I'd really suffered/I shouldn't want to let you know
551 ES	Ld Clav	19	but I cherish them./{LC} If you had really been broken-hearted/I can't see how you
551 ES	Carghil	24	action/For breach of promise, if I'd really cared for you./What sentimental
562 ES	Michael	10	you —/I've a very affectionate nature, really,/But ... {}/[*Enter* MRS. CARGHILL *with*

562 ES	Michael	33	dear friend of mine once./{Mi} Did he really look like me?/{MC} You've his voice! and
568 ES	Ld Clav	30	afraid that I've never loved anyone, really./No, I do love my Monica — but there's
574 ES	Carghil	15	in the end I discovered what Michael really wanted/For making a new start. He wants
577 ES	Charles	12	/{C} I see your point of view. Can you really feel confidence,/Michael, in a man who
578 ES	Michael	23	very fond of you/Though we never really seemed to have much in common./I
579 ES	Carghil	14	him/Than he had it all planned out! It really was an inspiration —/On my part, I
581 ES	Ld Clav	29	/Whom you can love for the man he really is./{M} Oh Father, I've always loved you,/

REALMLESS (1)

| 249 MC | Tempt2 | 24 | be broken,/Cabined in Canterbury, realmless ruler,/Self-bound servant of a |

REAPPEAR (1)

| 85 Hollow Men | | 62 | tumid river/Sightless, unless/The eyes reappear/As the perpetual star/Multifoliate rose |

REAPPEARS (2)

| 57 Swee Night | | 29 | shows fatigue,/Leaves the room and reappears/Outside the window, leaning in,/ |
| 133 Eyes | | 4 | dream kingdom/The golden vision reappears/I see the eyes but not the tears/This is |

REAR (1)

| 232 Skimble | | 11 | will appear and he'll saunter to the rear:/He's been busy in the luggage van!/He |

REASON (51)

161 Rock 7		28	and worship gods, professing first Reason,/And then Money, and Power, and
209 NamingCats		26	a cat in profound meditation,/The reason, I tell you, is always the same:/His mind
222 Pekes Pols		15	from his beat —/I don't know the reason, but most people think/He'd slipped into
230 Bust Jones		17	*Joint Superior Schools.*/For a similar reason, when game is in season/He is found, not
250 MC Thomas		16	—/I *was* the King, his arm, his better reason./But what was once exaltation/Would
257 MC Chorus		23	laughter./God gave us always some reason, some hope; but now a new terror has
258 MC Thomas		6	/To do the right deed for the wrong reason./The natural vigour in the venial sin/Is
260 MC Thomas		18	and rejoice at once and/for the same reason? For either joy will be overborne by
260 MC Thomas		20	and mourn at once for the same reason./Now think for a moment about the
276 MC Knight1		28	of action and not of words. For that/reason I shall do no more than introduce the
278 MC Knight2		1	not to your emotions but to your reason. You are hard-headed/sensible people, as
279 MC Knight4		31	/at the last, he could have given us reason: you have seen how he/evaded our
287 FR Amy		26	I never leave Wishwood/That is the reason. I keep Wishwood alive/To keep the
295 FR Charles		15	than you know —/But *you* have no reason to reproach yourself./Your conscience
317 FR Warburt		2	you, Harry./In fact, I had another reason for coming this evening/Than simply in
320 FR Warburt		21	command at Wishwood,/And for that reason, it is most essential/That nothing should
322 FR Winch		13	/But you see, my Lord, I had good reason for asking .../{H} Well, do you want me
347 FR Downing		2	my meaning. I thought that was the reason/We was off tonight. In fact, I half
349 FR Agatha		22	A curse is a power/Not subject to reason/Each curse has its course/Its own way of
355 CP Julia		24	host! And nothing fit to eat!/The only reason for a cocktail party/For a gluttonous old
356 CP Julia		30	takes me seriously./I believe that's the reason why she went away —/So that I could
360 CP Reilly		37	woman/And no other man, then the reason may be deeper/And you've ground for
364 CP Reilly		14	light./The fact that you can't give a reason for wanting her/Is the best reason for
364 CP Reilly		15	a reason for wanting her/Is the best reason for believing that you want her./{E} I
379 CP Edward		39	well, it's humiliating./{E} There is no reason why you should feel humiliated .../{C}
380 CP Celia		23	is ridiculous! I never gave Peter/Any reason to suppose I cared for him./I thought he
402 CP Reilly		11	I can go elsewhere./{R} You have reason to believe that you are very ill?/{E} I
406 CP Reilly		17	it to be a sanatorium/That is good reason for not sending them to one./The people
408 CP Reilly		8	/And with someone of whom you had reason to be jealous./{E} Really, Lavinia! This is
420 CP Celia		6	is nothing else to do:/That is the only reason./{R} It is the best reason./{C} But I know
420 CP Reilly		7	is the only reason./{R} It is the best reason./{C} But I know it is I who have made
421 CP Reilly		31	I am apprehensive/Then you see no reason for anything but confidence./{J} That's
448 CC Claude		30	I've never told her about him,/The reason for meeting him as merely Mr. Simpkins,
455 CC Colby		5	Then I'd have been certain I'd lost my reason:/Her influence is perfectly frightening./
462 CC Claude		26	offers you./But tell me first — I've a reason for asking —/How do you like your
471 CC Colby		14	I like you./{C} That's not quite the reason./{L} Oh, so you believe that I like you?/I
471 CC Colby		17	/{C} No, it's not conceit — the reason that I'm thinking of./It's something quite
471 CC Colby		26	doesn't really matter. But, for some reason,/You thought I'd get a false impression
475 CC Lucasta		16	better what one really is./And the reason why that comes about, perhaps .../{C} Is,
489 CC Claude		5	Colby. I didn't. For such a foolish reason./Absurd it sounds now. One child each
489 CC Claude		12	it influenced me./And I found a better reason for keeping silent./I came to see how you
492 CC Colby		17	to touch it again./But there's another reason. I must remind you/About your speech
500 CC Claude		8	that Colby is *her* son./That is the reason for this meeting today./We're awaiting
509 CC Claude		27	he doesn't like the name, for some reason;/So we call him B./{MG} A very good
528 ES Charles		2	with your father./Is there any better reason than his fear of solitude?/{M} The second
528 ES Monica		3	his fear of solitude?/{M} The second reason is exactly the opposite:/It's his fear of
528 ES Monica		23	/Can there be a third?/{M} The third reason is this:/I've only just been given it by Dr.
528 ES Charles		33	recovery./{C} This is your best reason, and the most depressing;/For this

538 ES   Gomez   8   and paid my passage out. I know the reason:/You wanted to get rid of me. I shall tell
557 ES   Michael   18 did take?/{Mi} Not so well, for some reason./The fact is, I needed a good deal more
581 ES   Ld Clav   26 /In spite of everything, in defiance of reason,/I have been brushed by the wing of

REASONABLE (1)
277 MC Knight3   20 of our lives abroad. And even when reasonable/people come to see that the

REASONING (1)
279 MC Knight1   6   been able to follow his very subtle reasoning. We have,/however, one more

REASONING'S (1)
572 ES   Ld Clav   32 They cannot harm you./{LC} Your reasoning's sound enough. But it's irrelevant./

REASONS (19)
277 MC Knight3   18 God bless him — will have to/say, for reasons of state, that he never meant this to
306 FR   Mary   27 always to be naughty./But there were reasons: I was only a cousin/Kept here because
320 FR   Warburt   26 this,/Just now. But there were two reasons/Why you had to know. One is your
346 FR Downing   21 /Very long now. I can't give you any reasons./But to show you what I mean, though
378 CP   Edward   32 /{E} No, it is not that./And all these reasons were suggested to me/By the man I call
385 CP   Reilly   37 I know you would. And for definite reasons/Which I am not prepared to explain to
412 CP   Celia   36 /Are obviously ill, or can give good reasons/For wanting to see you. Well, I can't./I
448 CC   Claude   26 /{E} Merely Mr. Simpkins./{SC} The reasons for starting him during her absence/Are
500 CC   Claude   13 you/To keep a secret. There were reasons for that/Which no longer exist. But I
500 CC   Lucasta   37 so too, Claude, but for the wrong reasons,/And that put me off. So I'm grateful to
501 CC   Lucasta   2 made the right decision./{L} But the reasons why you think so are the wrong ones./
527 ES   Monica   19 that?/{M} There are several good reasons why I should go with him./{C} Better
527 ES   Charles   20 why I should go with him./{C} Better reasons than for marrying me?/What reasons?/
527 ES   Charles   21 reasons than for marrying me?/What reasons?/{M} First, his terror of being alone./
528 ES   Charles   1 /{C} But you spoke of several reasons for your going with your father./Is there
528 ES   Charles   20 sure of that./{C} You've given two reasons,/One the contradiction of the other./
533 ES   Gomez   24 they respect you for rather different reasons./{LC} Do you mean that that you've won
560 ES   Ld Clav   20 of England./{LC} Michael! Are there reasons for your wanting to go/Beyond what
575 ES   Ld Clav   13 in a different sense, and for different reasons/From what you think. Let me tell you

REASSURE (2)
424 CP   Lavinia   14 left./But all I rang up for was to reassure you ... {}/[*smiling*]./{E} That you hadn't
448 CC   Claude   4 I could,/And ways in which you could reassure him/Better than I. He's more at ease

REASSURED (2)
107 Animula   8   corner of arm and knee,/Eager to be reassured, taking pleasure/In the fragrant
302 FR   Chorus   4   will satisfy:/We only ask to be reassured/About the noises in the cellar/And the

REASSURES (2)
546 ES   Piggott   39 /For me to be simply 'Mrs. Piggott'/Reassures the guests in one respect;/And calling
546 ES   Piggott   40 /And calling our nurses 'Nurse' reassures them/In another respect./{LC} I follow

REASSURING (1)
461 CC   Colby   10 /{C} Thank you very much, I will. It's reassuring/To know that I have you always at

REBEL (1)
98 Ash-Wed 6   13 /And the weak spirit quickens to rebel/For the bent golden-rod and the lost sea

REBELLING (1)
467 CC   Colby   15 to explain what I said just now/About rebelling against the terms/That life has

REBELLION (1)
266 MC Knights   14 in revolt against the King; in rebellion to the King and the law of the land;/

REBELLIOUS (1)
246 MC Thomas   2 /With eager enemies restless about us./Rebellious bishops, York, London, Salisbury,/

REBELS (1)
466 CC   Colby   34 upon you. But ... something in me/Rebels against accepting such conditions./It

REBMANN (4)
459 CC   Lady E   31 hour a day/Is most essential, Dr. Rebmann says./{SC} Rebmann? I thought it was
459 CC   Claude   32 essential, Dr. Rebmann says./{SC} Rebmann? I thought it was a Dr. Leroux./{LE}
459 CC   Lady E   34 /I have been in Zürich, under Dr. Rebmann./{SC} But you were going out to Dr.
460 CC   Lady E   18 have a course of treatment with Dr. Rebmann —/No, at your stage, I think, with

REBORN (1)
310 FR   Mary   26 of the terrified spirit/Compelled to be reborn/To rise toward the violent sun/Wet

REBUILD (1)
157 Rock 4   9   him leave to depart/That he might rebuild the city./So he went, with a few, to

REBUILDING (2)
129 Cor2 State   19 Public Works, chiefly the question of rebuilding the fortifications./A commission is
157 Rock 4   17 he and his men laid their hands to rebuilding the wall./So they built as men must

REBUKING (1)
589 Fable   88 his name the handle/Of Saint, thereby rebuking all such scandal./But after this the

RECALL (2)
| 19 Portrait | 52 | these April sunsets, that somehow recall/My buried life, and Paris in the Spring,/I |
| 575 ES Gomez | 25 | appropriate,/Isn't it, Dick, when we recall/That you were once custodian of *my* |

RECALLED (2)
| 193 FQ: Little | 95 | /Whom I had known, forgotten, half recalled/Both one and many; in the brown |
| 248 MC Tempt2 | 17 | in Maine. Now that I have recalled them,/Let us but set these not too |

RECALLING (1)
| 20 Portrait | 82 | smell of hyacinths across the garden/Recalling things that other people have desired./ |

RECEDING (1)
| 188 FQ: DrySal | 153 | are not those who saw the harbour/Receding, or those who will disembark./Here |

RECEIPT (1)
| 179 FQ: ECoker | 78 | elders,/Bequeathing us merely a receipt for deceit?/The serenity only a deliberate |

RECEIVE (5)
20 Portrait	65	my friend,/To give you, what can you receive from me?/Only the friendship and the
84 Hollow Men	42	the stone images/Are raised, here they receive/The supplication of a dead man's hand/
188 FQ: DrySal	158	is not of action or inaction/You can receive this: "on whatever sphere of being/The
241 MC Mess	32	of the devotion of the people,/Who receive him with scenes of frenzied enthusiasm,/
252 MC Tempt4	34	not four./{T4} Do not be surprised to receive one more./Had I been expected, I had

RECEIVED (1)
| 266 MC Thomas | 25 | is not true./Both before and after I received the ring/I have been a loyal subject to |

RECEIVER (2)
| 116 SP Doris | 15 | stop that horrible noise?/Pick up the receiver/{Du} What'll I say?/{Do} Say what you |
| 383 CP m | 27 | /{E} Oh! {}/[*He snatches up the receiver*]/{E} Hello, Julia! are you there? .../Well, |

RECENTLY (4)
402 CP Edward	14	symptoms./Two people advised me recently,/Almost in the same words, that I
405 CP Reilly	5	is rather the exception./I have recently had another patient/Whose situation is
505 CC Claude	3	is to say,/Colby's predecessor, who recently retired./Now he lives ... in the country.
505 CC Eggers	26	It's this way, Mrs. Guzzard./It is only recently that Lady Elizabeth/Heard your name

RECEPTION (1)
| 307 FR Harry | 12 | /For the holidays, after the formal reception/And the family festivities, I made my |

RECIPES (1)
| 428 CP Alex | 26 | /I invented for the natives several new recipes./But you see, what with eating the |

RECIPROCAL (1)
| 154 Rock 3 | 10 | /I have given you hearts, for reciprocal distrust./I have given you power of |

RECKLESS (5)
273 MC Thomas	31	Lord! My Lord!/{T} You think me reckless, desperate and mad./You argue by
325 FR Gerald	24	/{G} A brilliant driver, but more reckless./{I} Yet I remember, when they were
326 FR Violet	6	he meant well. But I do think he is reckless./{G} I wonder how much Amy knows
328 FR Gerald	5	is unlucky,/But Arthur is definitely reckless./{V} I think these racing cars ought to
568 ES Ld Clav	8	failures, irreflective aberrations,/Reckless surrenders, unexplainable impulses,/

RECKON (1)
| 248 MC Tempt2 | 30 | monument of marble./Rule over men reckon no madness./{T} To the man of God |

RECKONED (2)
| 20 Portrait | 95 | flares up for a second;/*This* is as I had reckoned./'I have been wondering frequently of |
| 483 CC Lady E | 20 | on a company report./{LE} I hadn't reckoned on reports and typewriters/When I |

RECKONING (1)
| 560 ES Michael | 3 | state of consciousness./Poor ghost! reckoning up its profit and loss/And wondering |

RECLUSE (1)
| 357 CP Edward | 8 | Her mother's sister/And rather a recluse./{J} Her favourite aunt?/{E} Her aunt's |

RECOGNISE (7)
471 CC Colby	5	/I'll play you the themes, so you'll recognise them./Better still, I'll play you the
502 CC Lucasta	37	sister .../{L} What's so difficult/Is to recognise the limits of one's understanding./It
512 CC Guzzard	16	evidence the Kaghans will supply,/To recognise Barnabas Kaghan as her son? {}/[*To*
529 ES Ld Clav	21	/What I've been doing. Don't you recognise this book?/{M} It's your engagement
531 ES Ld Clav	28	or sitting in the Lords./And I, who recognise myself as a ghost/Shan't want to be
548 ES Carghil	31	all these years;/And you don't even recognise me! I'd know you anywhere./But then,
550 ES Carghil	7	Maisie Montjoy once. And you didn't recognise me./{LC} You've changed your name,

RECOGNISED (4)
184 FQ: DrySal	3	/Patient to some degree, at first recognised as a frontier;/Useful, untrustworthy,
332 FR Agatha	1	solitary man:/Where he was weak he recognised your mother's power,/And yielded to
426 CP Julia	36	I know this is a Parkinson party;/I recognised one of their men at the door —/An
428 CP Alex	39	state/Which we have just recognised. You see, Lavinia,/These are very

RECOGNITION (1)
| 194 FQ: Little | 104 | yet the words sufficed/To compel the recognition they preceded./And so, compliant to |

RECOLLECTION (1)
504 CC   Lady E   11   hour./I've been giving her lessons in recollection./But she shouldn't be singing./{L}
RECOMMEND (2)
292 FR   Charles   31   /{C} And I've a new wine merchant to recommend you;/Your cellar could do with a
360 CP   Reilly   14   in it?/{UG} Nothing but water./And I recommend you the same prescription .../Let me
RECOMMENDATION (3)
401 CP   Edward   8   better than to come here/On the recommendation of a man who did not know
556 ES   Ld Clav   22   You don't normally consider that a recommendation./Are you staying there long?
563 ES   Gomez   14   'Well, what about it?/What better recommendation could I have?'/So he sent me
RECOMMENDATIONS (2)
401 CP   Edward   9   you./Yet Alex is so plausible. And his recommendations/Of shops, have always been
458 CC   Claude   30   .../{SC} Mr. Simpkins had very strong recommendations .../{E} And at the same time,
RECOMMENDED (6)
400 CP   Alex   16   he was ready to consult any doctor/Recommended by anyone except his wife./{R} I
447 CC   Claude   29   —/Say that Mr. Simpkins was highly recommended,/And say that I had to make a
459 CC   Lady E   1   this the young man I interviewed/And recommended to Sir Claude? Of course it is./I
481 CC   Lady E   27   to try that Herbal Restaurant/I recommended to you. You can have dinner
556 ES   Michael   20   exactly./But this hotel was very well recommended./Good cooking, for a country
557 ES   Michael   25   lender,/A man whom a friend of mine recommended./He gave me good terms, on the
RECONCILE (1)
417 CP   Reilly   23   you. If that is what you wish,/I can reconcile you to the human condition,/The
RECONCILED (4)
172 FQ: BurntN   63   /Pursue their pattern as before/But reconciled among the stars./At the still point of
190 FQ: DrySal   223   past and future/Are conquered, and reconciled,/Where action were otherwise
341 FR   Amy   9   I prepared the situation/For us to be reconciled, because of Harry,/Because of his
436 CP   Julia   19   then you'll understand her/And be reconciled, and be happy in the thought of her./
RECONCILEMENT (1)
467 CC   Colby   2   son. It must often happen./And the reconcilement, after his death,/That perfects the
RECONCILIATION (4)
241 MC   Priest1   18   /Reunited with the King? what reconciliation/Of two proud men?/{P3} What
251 MC   Tempt3   12   the simple fact!/You have no hope of reconciliation/With Henry the King. You look
333 FR   Harry   17   before./Everything tends towards reconciliation/As the stone falls, as the tree falls.
337 FR   Harry   27   —/Which leads in the end to reconciliation./And I know that I must go./{Ag}
RECONSIDERED (1)
38 Gerontion   41   or if still believed,/In memory only, reconsidered passion. Gives too soon/Into weak
RECONSTRUCT (2)
433 CP   Peter   7   /{P} We're not taking Boltwell./We reconstruct a Boltwell./{J} Very well, then:/Why
433 CP   Julia   9   Boltwell./{J} Very well, then:/Why not reconstruct *me*? It's very much cheaper./Oh,
RECORD (2)
69 WL: Fire S   256   hair with automatic hand,/And puts a record on the gramophone./'This music crept by
589 Fable   95   of the shire. We/Got the veracious record of these doings/From an old manuscript
RECORDED (2)
187 FQ: DrySal   104   look behind the assurance/Of recorded history, the backward half-look/Over
329 FR   Chorus   17   twined and tangled together, all are recorded./There is no avoiding these things/And
RECORDS (4)
396 CP   Lavinia   3   gramophone./{L} We have very good records;/But I always suspected that you really
471 CC   Colby   6   still, I'll play you the gramophone records./{L} I'd rather you played me bits
514 CC   Eggers   28   said he wanted./{E} I'll examine the records myself, Sir Claude./Not that we doubt
514 CC   Claude   33   not believe it. I'll not believe those records./You pretend to have carried out a
RECOUNT (1)
204 de la Mare   9   of some long-lost treasure-trove)/Recount their exploits at the nursery tea/And
RECOVER (8)
98 Ash-Wed 6   15   and the lost sea smell/Quickens to recover/The cry of quail and the whirling plover
182 FQ: ECoker   188   —/There is only the fight to recover what has been lost/And found and lost
246 MC   Tempt1   34   sever./What, my Lord, now that you recover/Favour with the King, shall we say that
280 MC   Priest1   10   through what further dread/Shall we recover your presence? when inherit/Your
289 FR   Ivy   26   middle of a storm,/And never even to recover the body./{C} 'Well-known Peeress
330 FR   Harry   1   II/HARRY, AGATHA/{H} John will recover, be what he always was;/Arthur again
384 CP   Reilly   11   ready to change your mind/Until you recover from having made a decision./No. I
436 CP   Edward   6   learn them later/When it's harder to recover, and make a new beginning./It's not so
RECOVERED (4)
295 FR   Harry   26   days in contented drowsiness;/Then I recovered. I am afraid of sleep:/A condition in
338 FR   Harry   38   /{H} It is very hard, when one has just recovered sanity,/And not yet assured in
390 CP   Julia   35   Who, you'll be glad to hear, has quite recovered, Alex —/And after that long journey
408 CP   Reilly   4   /And certainly, you have somewhat recovered./But you failed to mention that the

RECOVERING (1)
573 ES Ld Clav   3   that I'm sickening, when I'm just recovering!/It's hard to make other people
RECOVERS (1)
91 Ash-Wed 2   14 the fruit of the gourd./It is this which recovers/My guts the strings of my eyes and the
RECOVERY (4)
32 Hysteria   4   gasps, inhaled at each momentary/recovery, lost finally in the dark caverns of her
390 CP   Julia   5 /{J} She must have made a marvellous recovery./I said so to myself, when I got your
408 CP   Lavinia   2   /Even if I have made a partial recovery./{R} Certainly, you were completely
528 ES   Monica 32   —/Everything about it to suggest recovery./{C} This is your best reason, and the
RECUR (1)
277 MC Knight2 35 de Morville./{K2} I should like first to recur to a point that was very/well put by our
RECURRENCE (1)
147 Rock 1   4   of configured stars,/O perpetual recurrence of determined seasons,/O world of
RECURRENT (2)
189 FQ: DrySal 197 /Or barbituric acids, or dissect/The recurrent image into pre-conscious terrors —/
193 FQ: Little   82 ending of interminable night/At the recurrent end of the unending/After the dark
RED (15)
17 Prufrock   130 /By sea-girls wreathed with seaweed red and brown/Till human voices wake us, and
54 Mr E Sun   19 avenue of penitence;/The young are red and pustular/Clutching piaculative pence./
61 WL: Burial   25   Only/There is shadow under this red rock,/(Come in under the shadow of this red
61 WL: Burial   26 /(Come in under the shadow of this red rock),/And I will show you something
69 WL: Fire S   270 The barges drift/With the turning tide/Red sails/Wide/To leeward, swing on the heavy
70 WL: Fire S   283 /The stern was formed/A gilded shell/Red and gold/The brisk swell/Rippled both
72 WL: Thund   322 the Thunder said/After the torchlight red on sweaty faces/After the frosty silence in
72 WL: Thund   344   even solitude in the mountains/But red sullen faces sneer and snarl/From doors of
139 Virginia   1 Swing up into the apple-tree./Virginia/Red river, red river,/Slow flow heat is silence/
139 Virginia   1   the apple-tree./Virginia/Red river, red river,/Slow flow heat is silence/No will is
139 Virginia   13   came with me/And go with me:/Red river, river, river./Usk/Do not suddenly
178 FQ: ECoker 57 /And hollyhocks that aim too high/Red into grey and tumble down/Late roses filled
597 Before Mor   1   /While all the East was weaving red with gray,/The flowers at the window
598 Circe   4 knows./Their petals are fanged and red/With hideous streak and stain;/They sprang
605 Narcissus   5 leaping behind the fire against the red rock:/I will show you his bloody cloth and
RED-EYED (1)
45 Cook Egg   27 eat with Pipit behind the screen?/The red-eyed scavengers are creeping/From Kentish
REDDENS (1)
280 MC   Priest3 18 earth or heaven./Go where the sunset reddens the last grey rock/Of Brittany, or the
REDEEM (4)
94 Ash-Wed 4   18 /With a new verse the ancient rhyme. Redeem/The time. Redeem/The unread vision
94 Ash-Wed 4   19 the ancient rhyme. Redeem/The time. Redeem/The unread vision in the higher dream/
95 Ash-Wed 4   26   sprang up and the bird sang down/Redeem the time, redeem the dream/The token
95 Ash-Wed 4   26 the bird sang down/Redeem the time, redeem the dream/The token of the word
REDEEMED (2)
196 FQ: Little   208 in the choice of pyre or pyre —/To be redeemed from fire by fire./Who then devised
197 FQ: Little   236   A people without history/Is not redeemed from time, for history is a pattern/Of
REDEEMING (1)
402 CP   Reilly   6 —/Which you still have the chance of redeeming from ruin./{E} You talk as if I was
REDEMPTION (2)
281 MC Chorus 17   for Thy mercies of blood, for Thy redemption by blood. For the blood of Thy
350 FR   Agatha 25 /In several directions/For their own redemption/And that of the departed —/May
RÉDIGE (1)
48 Lune Miel   14 pas cher./Lui pense aux pourboires, et rédige son bilan./Ils auront vu la Suisse et
REDNESS (1)
606 Narcissus   37 his white skin surrendered itself to the redness of blood, and satisfied him./Now he is
REDOUNDS (1)
268 MC Thomas 32 /Let them go to him, upon whom redounds/Their contempt towards me, their
REDUCED (2)
109 Marina   14 /Death/Are become unsubstantial, reduced by a wind,/A breath of pine, and the
362 CP   Reilly 23 feel quite human./You're suddenly reduced to the status of an object —/A living
REDUCTION (1)
129 Cor2 State   23 joint committee to protest against the reduction of orders./Meanwhile the guards
REEL (1)
500 CC Lucasta 10 Colby's aunt? You make my brain reel./{SC} I ought to have made things clear to
REELING (1)
453 CC Kaghan 25 /Until they met you. Colby's still reeling./It's going to be my responsibility,/As

REFER (1)
33 Conv Gal   11   own vacuity.'/She then: 'Does this refer to me?'/'Oh no, it is I who am inane.'/

REFERRED (3)
317 FR   Harry 23   mother?/Everything has always been referred back to mother./When we were
451 CC   Eggers 27   he wasn't so successful./She once referred to him as 'undistinguished';/But with
546 ES   Monica 33   seen her yet, but the chambermaid/Referred to a nurse. When we see her/Do we

REFERRING (1)
540 ES   Gomez 20   quite well to which occasion I'm referring —/A summer night of moonlight and

REFINED (1)
205 de la Mare   30   /Wherewith the common measure is refined;/By conscious art practised with natural

REFINING (1)
195 FQ: Little   147   /Proceeds, unless restored by that refining fire/Where you must move in measure,

REFLECT (2)
233 Skimble   47   up the counterpane,/You ought to reflect that it's very nice/To know that you
260 MC Thomas 26   was a disappointment and a cheat?/Reflect now, how Our Lord Himself spoke of

REFLECTED (5)
143 Lines OM   12   /And inaccessible by the young./Reflected from my golden eye/The dullard
167 Rock 10   30 coloured panes of windows/And light reflected from the polished stone,/The gilded
172 FQ: BurntN 40   of light,/And they were behind us, reflected in the pool./Then a cloud passed, and
202 War Poetry   2   of collective emotion/Imperfectly reflected in the daily papers./Where is the point
213 Growltiger   36 surprise —/But the moonlight shone reflected from a hundred bright blue eyes./And

REFLECTING (4)
64 WL: Chess   83   flames of sevenbranched candelabra/Reflecting light upon the table as/The glitter of
191 FQ: Little   7   windless cold that is the heart's heat,/Reflecting in a watery mirror/A glare that is
290 FR   Agatha 28   /Into perfect misunderstanding,/Reflecting a pocket-torch of observation/Upon
420 CP   Reilly 32   the motive —/Mirror to mirror, reflecting vanity./I have taken a great risk./{J}

REFLECTION (2)
508 CC   Eggers 2   so./{E} Don't take this as a personal reflection,/Mrs. Guzzard. Far from it. You
542 ES   Gomez 33   You'll be afraid of whispers,/The reflection in the mirror of the face behind you,/

REFLECTIONS (1)
538 ES Ld Clav 5 second time you have mentioned your reflections./But there's just one thing you seem

REFORM (1)
278 MC Knight2 11   and often for seditious ends, and to reform the legal system./He therefore intended

REFORMED (1)
535 ES   Gomez 23 {LC} I don't take it, thank you./{G} A reformed character!/{LC} I should like to know

REFORMS (1)
73 WL: Thund 372   city over the mountains/Cracks and reforms and bursts in the violet air/Falling

REFRACTED (1)
177 FQ: ECoker 21   haze the sultry light/Is absorbed, not refracted, by grey stone./The dahlias sleep in the

REFRACTORY (1)
103 Journ Magi 6   /And the camels galled, sore-footed, refractory,/Lying down in the melting snow./

REFRESH (1)
49 Hippopot 16 /But fruits of pomegranate and peach/Refresh the Church from over sea./At mating

REFRESHED (1)
406 CP   Reilly 15   /From everyday life. They return refreshed;/And if they believe it to be a

REFRESHING (1)
377 CP   Julia 23   of course it isn't chilled. But it's so refreshing;/And I thought, we are all in need of

REFRIGERATOR (2)
155 Rock 3   66   /Engaged in devising the perfect refrigerator,/Engaged in working out a rational
372 CP   Alex 14   so few materials/As I found in your refrigerator. But of course/I was lucky to find

REFUGE (1)
338 FR   Harry 22   Now I know/That the last apparent refuge, the safe shelter,/That is where one meets

REFUSAL (1)
38 Gerontion   43   can be dispensed with/Till the refusal propagates a fear. Think/Neither fear

REFUSE (2)
532 ES Ld Clav 16 /From a man I used to know. I can't refuse to see him./Though from what I
551 ES Carghil 11 if you needed the lesson./{MC} You refuse to believe that I was really in love with

REFUSED (2)
240 MC Priest2 31   meetings accepted, meetings refused,/Meetings unended or endless/At one
485 CC Lady E 6   be,/I didn't want to belong there. I refused to believe/That my father could have

REFUTE (1)
267 MC Thomas 24   make charges,/Then in public I will refute them./{K1} No! here and now! {}/[*They*

REGAINED (1)
248 MC Tempt2 26   mistake/On your part — still may be regained. Think, my Lord,/Power obtained

REGALE (1)
228 Gus   13 of the neighbouring pub)/He loves to regale them, if someone else pays,/With
REGARD (13)
 24 Rhapsody   16   muttered,/The street-lamp said, 'Regard that woman/Who hesitates towards you
 24 Rhapsody   50   in the dark./The lamp hummed:/'Regard the moon,/La lune ne garde aucune
136 5FingerEx4   10 is worshipped by all waitresses/(They regard him as something apart)/While on his
252 MC Tempt3   25   spring/The King will show his regard for your loyalty./{T} To make, then
330 FR Agatha   17   of being understood,/Try not to regard it as an explanation./{H} I still have to
491 CC Lady E   8 we make any further enquiries?/Let us regard him as being *our* son:/It won't be the
497 CC Lady E   27   things as they are,/So that we may regard him as *our* son./{SC} That is perfectly
501 CC Lady E   21   other people. I hope so./Lucasta, I regard you as a ... step-daughter;/And shall be
511 CC Kaghan   19   I've always been accustomed/To regard Mrs. Kaghan as my mother./{LE} Then
517 CC Claude   4 me as a father;/All I ask you is — to regard me as a friend./{C} But you would still
517 CC Colby   7   it works both ways. For you to regard me —/As you would — as your son,
574 ES Carghil   2   see, Mr. Hemington,/I've come to regard her as my adopted daughter./So much
579 ES Gomez   36 deserve any credit for it./We can only regard it as a stroke of good fortune/That I
REGARDE (1)
 46 Directeur   18 Une petite fille/En guenilles/Camarde/Regarde/Le directeur/Du Spectateur/
REGARDED (2)
161 Rock 7   42   /When the Church is no longer regarded, not even opposed, and men have
212 Growltiger   19 allowed./The Persian and the Siamese regarded him with fear —/Because it was a
REGARDS (4)
599 On a Port   14   /The parrot on his bar, a silent spy,/Regards her with a patient curious eye./Song/
315 FR   Harry   5   was there. Your ordinary murderer/Regards himself as an innocent victim./To
400 CP   Alex   12 /{A} Yes, implicitly./It's not that he regards me as very intelligent,/But he thinks I'm
447 CC Claude   10   replacing you./But you know she regards you — well, completely/As one of the
REGENT'S (1)
473 CC Lucasta   13 matter/Floating on the surface of the Regent's Canal./Floating, that's it./{C} You're
REGIMENT (1)
511 CC Lady E   14 the family./But he was in a very good regiment —/For a time, at least./{K} Well, I
REGINALD (4)
275 MC Thomas   14   Traitor! traitor! traitor!/{T} You, Reginald, three times traitor you:/Traitor to me
276 MC Knight3   34 experienced/speaker as my old friend Reginald Fitz Urse would lead you to/believe.
277 MC Knight2   36 that was very/well put by our leader, Reginald Fitz Urse: that you are Englishmen,/
279 MC Knight4   12   me, to say nothing/of our leader, Reginald Fitz Urse, have all spoken very much
REGISTER (2)
511 CC Kaghan   1 I really don't know what emotion to register .../{L} You don't need to talk that
511 CC Lucasta   39 meant to be married very quietly/In a register office./{LE} You must have a church
REGISTRATION (2)
514 CC Guzzard   21   substantiate this statement?/{MG} Registration of birth. To Herbert and Sarah
514 CC Guzzard   24 about your sister and her child?/{MG} Registration of death. The child was never born.
REGRET (8)
187 FQ: DrySal   129   Rose or a lavender spray/Of wistful regret for those who are not yet here to regret,/
187 FQ: DrySal   129   for those who are not yet here to regret,/Pressed between yellow leaves of a book
290 FR   Amy   13 future. There can be no grief/And no regret and no remorse./I would have prevented
347 FR   Ivy   19 show it to Amy or not. {}/[*Reads*]/{I} 'Regret delayed business in town many happy
417 CP   Reilly   26   they have had, but they cease to regret it,/Maintain themselves by the common
459 CC Lady E   22 spiritual life, Mr. Colby./Neither, I regret to say, does Eggerson./What colour have
489 CC Claude   16   And they never came./And now I regret the decision bitterly./I ought to have told
568 ES Ld Clav   9 unexplainable impulses,/Moments we regret in the very next moment,/Episodes we try
REGRETS (2)
 18 Portrait   15 Among velleities and carefully caught regrets/Through attenuated tones of violins/
278 MC Knight2   31 to rights, that you/take issue. No one regrets the necessity for violence more than we/
REGRETTED (1)
103 Journ Magi   8   melting snow./There were times we regretted/The summer palaces on slopes, the
REGULAR (4)
218 Mung Rump   19 home in Victoria Grove. They had no regular occupation./They were plausible fellows,
229 Gus   47   reigned./They never get drilled in a regular troupe,/And they think they are smart,
232 Skimble   23 the Third;/He establishes control by a regular patrol/And he'd know at once if
476 CC Lucasta   37   of course Claude gave her money, a regular allowance;/But it wouldn't have
REGULARIZE (1)
448 CC Eggers   18   propose to ... *explain* Mr. Simpkins?/Regularize his position in the household?/You
REHEARSAL (1)
228 Gus   26 my back and my tail;/With an hour of rehearsal, I never could fail./I'd a voice that

REHEARSE (1)
194 FQ: Little   113   /And he: 'I am not eager to rehearse/My thoughts and theory which you
REHEARSED (1)
290 FR   Chorus 38 dressed for a different play, or having rehearsed the wrong parts,/Waiting for the
REHEARSES (1)
263 MC Chorus   9   attentive; and in the wood/The owl rehearses the hollow note of death./What signs
REHEARSING (1)
575 ES   Gomez 18 dear Dick,/You're wasting your time, rehearsing ancient history./Michael knows it
REIGN (3)
 89 Ash-Wed 1   8   /The vanished power of the usual reign?/Because I do not hope to know again/
254 MC Tempt4 12 king,/And one more king is another reign./King is forgotten, when another shall
278 MC Knight2   6 been perfectly consistent. During the reign of/the late Queen Matilda and the
REIGNED (1)
229 Gus   46 /As we did in the days when Victoria reigned./They never get drilled in a regular
REIGNS (1)
179 FQ: ECoker 68 fire/Which burns before the ice-cap reigns./That was a way of putting it — not very
REILLY (11)
379 CP   Celia   1   I have heard of — and his name *is* Reilly!/{E} It would need someone greater than
400 CP   2m 35   — {}/[*Stops and stares at* REILLY]/[*without looking up from his papers*].
406 CP   m 5 your clothes concern me either. {}/[*To* REILLY]/{L} I presume you will send him to
411 CP   m 35   *takes out his cheque-book.* REILLY *raises his hand*]/{R} My secretary will
411 CP   2m 36 /[*Exeunt* EDWARD *and* LAVINIA]/[REILLY *goes to the couch and lies down. The*
412 CP   m 24 be here. {}/[*Exit* JULIA *by side door*]/[REILLY *presses button.*
420 CP   1m 19   *appears at door. Exit* CELIA. REILLY *dials on/house-telephone.*]/[*into*
422 CP   2m 11 *a decanter and three glasses, and/exit.* REILLY *pours drinks.*]/{R} And now we are
432 CP   m 4 I'd another surprise for you. {}/[*Enter* REILLY]/{J} I want you to meet Sir Henry
432 CP   m 21   I must have a cocktail. {}/[*To* REILLY]./{E} And will you have a cocktail?/
440 CP   m 19 to the Gunnings. {}/[*Exeunt* JULIA, REILLY *and* ALEX]/{L} Edward, how am I
REINCARNATE (1)
485 CC Lady E 18   that we have to employ/To become reincarnate. And that one's real ancestry/Is
REINCARNATION (2)
483 CC Lady E 30 to say? Oh, I know./Do you believe in reincarnation?/{C} No, I don't. I mean, I've
485 CC Lady E 13 the East/And believed, for a while, in reincarnation./That seemed to explain it all. I
REITERATES (1)
 20 Portrait   80 a street-piano, mechanical and tired/Reiterates some worn-out common song/With
REJECT (3)
 91 Ash-Wed 2 16   portions/Which the leopards reject. The Lady is withdrawn/In a white gown,
189 FQ: DrySal 185 /Or in the dark throat which will not reject them/Or wherever cannot reach them the
582 ES Ld Clav 2 rejecting me,/For the *me* he rejected, I reject also./I've been freed from the self that
REJECTED (2)
105 Song Sime 12   and ease./There went never any rejected from my door./Who shall remember my
582 ES Ld Clav 2 even for rejecting me,/For the *me* he rejected, I reject also./I've been freed from the
REJECTING (1)
582 ES Ld Clav 1   And Michael —/I love him, even for rejecting me,/For the *me* he rejected, I reject
REJECTS (1)
580 ES Monica 32 /Oh Father, it's not you and me he rejects,/But himself, the unhappy self that he's
REJOICE (17)
 49 Hippopot   19   and odd,/But every week we hear rejoice/The Church, at being one with God./The
 89 Ash-Wed 1 20 for one time/And only for one place/I rejoice that things are as they are and/I
 89 Ash-Wed 1 24   hope to turn again/Consequently I rejoice, having to construct something/Upon
 89 Ash-Wed 1 25 construct something/Upon which to rejoice/And pray to God to have mercy upon us
 96 Ash-Wed 5 19 those who avoid the face/No time to rejoice for those who walk among noise and
243 MC Priest2   4 doubts are dispelled. Let us therefore rejoice,/I say rejoice, and show a glad face for
243 MC Priest2   5   Let us therefore rejoice,/I say rejoice, and show a glad face for his welcome./I
260 MC Thomas   9 Birth. So that at/the same moment we rejoice in His coming for the salvation of men,
260 MC Thomas 17   in the World will both mourn and rejoice at once and/for the same reason? For
260 MC Thomas 20 our Christian/mysteries that we can rejoice and mourn at once for the same reason./
261 MC Thomas 13 /of Christ? By no means. Just as we rejoice and mourn at once, in the/Birth and in
261 MC Thomas 15 so also, in a smaller figure, we/both rejoice and mourn in the death of martyrs. We
261 MC Thomas 16 the world that has martyred them; we rejoice, that another soul is/numbered among
261 MC Thomas 23   Saints: for that would be simply to/rejoice: and neither our mourning nor our
264 MC Priests 23 the fourth day from Christmas./{3P} *Rejoice we all, keeping holy day.*/{P1} As for the
264 MC Priests 26 lays down his life for the sheep./{3P} *Rejoice we all, keeping holy day.*/{P1} To-day?/
574 ES Carghil 25 was so perplexed, poor lamb. Let's all rejoice together. {}/[*Enter* GOMEZ *and*

REJOICED (1)
538 ES   Gomez   34   /{G} I have a gift for friendship./I rejoiced in your success. But one thing has
REJOICES (2)
 98 Ash-Wed 6   11   wings/And the lost heart stiffens and rejoices/In the lost lilac and the lost sea voices/
261 MC Thomas   32   as on earth the Church mourns and rejoices at once, in/a fashion that the world
REJOICING (3)
212 Growltiger   4   to Oxford he pursued his evil aims,/Rejoicing in his title of 'The Terror of the
243 MC Chorus   20   come with applause, you come with rejoicing, but you come bringing death into
261 MC Thomas   23   and neither our mourning nor our rejoicing is as the world's is./A Christian
REJOIN (2)
450 CC   Claude   32   back/With Lady Elizabeth, I will rejoin you. {}/[*Exit* SIR CLAUDE]/{C} I'm glad
503 CC   Eggers   21   Mr. Kaghan wait downstairs/And rejoin us when this interview is over?/I'm sure
RELAPSE (2)
396 CP   Lavinia   39   which I see clearly:/We are not to relapse into the kind of life we led/Until
429 CP   Alex   8   all, prefer not to be slaughtered —/To relapse into heathendom. So, instead of eating
RELATE (2)
 21 Portrait   103   /They all were sure our feelings would relate/So closely! I myself can hardly
228 Gus   17   he's acted with Tree./And he likes to relate his success on the Halls,/Where the
RELATION (5)
337 FR   Agatha   15   you have learned/Mean the end of a relation, make it impossible./You did not intend
467 CC   Colby   3   after his death,/That perfects the relation. You have always been his son/And he
517 CC   Colby   6   of me as your son./There can be no relation of father and son/Unless it works both
573 ES   Ld Clav   8   can appreciate./For the crime is in relation to the law/And the sin is in relation to
573 ES   Ld Clav   9   in relation to the law/And the sin is in relation to the sinner./What has made the
RELATIONS (9)
 24 Rhapsody   6   the floors of memory/And all its clear relations,/Its divisions and precisions./Every
151 Rock 2   12   the cornerstone?/Talking of right relations of men, but not of relations of men to
151 Rock 2   12   of right relations of men, but not of relations of men to GOD./'Our citizenship is in
278 MC Knight2   17   I knew Becket well, in various official relations; and I/may say that I have never
290 FR   Amy   6   herself. She never wanted/Harry's relations or Harry's old friends;/She never
407 CP   Reilly   33   were lying to me/By concealing your relations with Miss Coplestone./{E} This is
416 CP   Reilly   7   {R} What had you believed were your relations with this man?/{C} Oh, you'd guessed
515 CC   Claude   38   don't let it make a difference/To our relations. Or, perhaps, for the better?/Perhaps
553 ES   Carghil   7   that our acquaintance was brief,/Our relations were intense enough, I think,/To have
RELATIONSHIP (9)
414 CP   Celia   9   alone./Not simply the ending of one relationship,/Not even simply finding that it
414 CP   Celia   11   existed —/But a revelation about my relationship/With *everybody*. Do you know —/
455 CC   Eggers   9   /{E} Well. A kind of fiduciary relationship./No, I don't think that's quite the
462 CC   Claude   32   it easier/To start by a rather formal relationship/In adapting yourself to a new
466 CC   Colby   40   /Of which you spoke — that was a relationship/Of father and son. It must often
503 CC   Lucasta   7   could have been/In any other form of relationship./{C} I want you to be happy./{L} I
503 CC   Lucasta   11   me as a sister/For the happiness that relationship may bring us/In twenty or thirty or
513 CC   Colby   22   /So he can afford another relationship./Let my mother rest in peace. As
535 ES   Gomez   15   or that./*A* won't let me down in this relationship,/*B* won't let me down in some other
RELATIVE (3)
314 FR   Warburt   30   no symptom/Of illness. Health is a relative term./{I} You must have had a very rich
341 FR   Agatha   16   For his future success./{Ag} Success is relative:/It is what we can make of the mess we
486 CC   Lady E   11   An illegitimate child./So that the only relative you knew/Was Mrs. Guzzard. And you
RELATIVELY (1)
381 CP   Edward   8   not sure./The one thing of which I am relatively certain/Is, that only since this morning
RELATIVES (7)
484 CC   Lady E   2   you were born./Have you other near relatives? Brothers or sisters?/{C} No brothers
484 CC   Colby   3   brothers or sisters. No. As for other relatives,/I never knew any, when I was a child./
484 CC   Colby   5   I've never been interested ... in relatives./{LE} You did not want to know your
484 CC   Lady E   6   /{LE} You did not want to know your relatives!/I understand exactly how you felt./
484 CC   Colby   20   had parents. And no doubt, many relatives./{LE} Oh, swarms of relatives! And
484 CC   Lady E   21   many relatives./{LE} Oh, swarms of relatives! And such unpleasant people!/I
484 CC   Lady E   26   have been a lonely child, having no relatives —/No brothers or sisters — and I was
RELAX (4)
188 FQ: DrySal   137   off have left the platform)/Their faces relax from grief into relief,/To the sleepy
355 CP   Julia   18   back into the room./Now I want to relax, Are there any more cocktails?/{P} But do
426 CP   Lavinia   8   You must sit beside me,/Then I can relax./{E} This is the best moment/Of the whole
452 CC   Kaghan   9   /But as you're here, Eggers, I can just relax./I'm going to enjoy the game from the

RELAXATION (2)
213 Growltiger 35 by his manly baritone,/Disposed to relaxation, and awaiting no surprise —/But the
529 ES Monica 25 know what the doctors said: complete relaxation/And to think about nothing. Though
RELAXED (1)
360 CP Reilly 17 down./Breathe deeply, and adopt a relaxed position./There we are. Now for a few
RELEASE (5)
173 FQ: BurntN 73 from the practical desire,/The release from action and suffering, release from
173 FQ: BurntN 73 The release from action and suffering, release from the inner/And the outer
189 FQ: DrySal 193 the palm/And tragedy from fingers; release omens/By sortilege, or tea leaves, riddle
361 CP Reilly 29 stranger/Is to invite the unexpected, release a new force,/Or let the genie out of the
478 CC Lucasta 19 when you think you're on the point of release/From loneliness, then loneliness swoops
RELEASED (1)
538 ES Ld Clav 7 to your assistance when you were released./{G} Yes, and paid my passage out. I
RELENT (1)
542 ES Gomez 30 /{G} Oh, I can wait, Dick. You'll relent at last./You'll come to feel easier when
RELEVANT (1)
506 CC Claude 6 /In Tanganyika./{SC} That's not relevant./Leave it to Eggerson./{E} The father
RELÈVE (1)
48 Lune Miel 7 molles tout gonflées de morsures./On relève le drap pour mieux égratigner./Moins
RELIABLE (2)
185 FQ: DrySal 61 /Of what was believed in as the most reliable —/And therefore the fittest for
576 ES Gomez 36 of slander./Here's Mrs. Carghill, a reliable witness./{C} I know enough about the
RELIC (1)
241 MC Mess 37 hair of which becomes a precious relic./He is at one with the Pope, and with the
RELICS (1)
587 Fable 30 at his own expense a crowd/Of relics from a Spanish saint — said he:/'If ghosts
RELIEF (10)
61 WL: Burial 23 tree gives no shelter, the cricket no relief,/And the dry stone no sound of water.
135 5FingerEx1 6 eyes of Woolly Bear./There is no relief but in grief./O when will the creaking
188 FQ: DrySal 137 /Their faces relax from grief into relief,/To the sleepy rhythm of a hundred hours.
289 FR Amy 21 /You can call it nothing but a blessed relief./{V} *I* call it providential./{I} Yet it must
334 FR Agatha 14 What does the word mean?/There's relief from a burden that I carried,/And
334 FR Agatha 15 /And exhaustion at the moment of relief./The burden's yours now, yours/The
335 FR Agatha 40 not pass./I have seen the first stage: relief from what happened/Is also relief from
336 FR Agatha 1 relief from what happened/Is also relief from that unfulfilled craving/Flattered in
361 CP Reilly 33 /I will say then, you experience some relief/Of which you're not aware. It will come to
513 CC Colby 15 it is, doesn't matter. All I wanted was relief/From the nagging annoyance of knowing
RELIEVE (2)
348 FR Warburt 3 hasn't been worrying?/I'm anxious to relieve her mind. Why, what's the trouble? {}/
361 CP Edward 17 not what I expected./I only wanted to relieve my mind/By telling someone what I'd
RELIEVED (1)
347 FRDowning 1 you've raised the subject, I'm most relieved —/If you understand my meaning. I
RELIGHT (2)
167 Rock 10 40 the candle, put out the light and relight it;/Forever must quench, forever relight
167 Rock 10 41 it;/Forever must quench, forever relight the flame./Therefore we thank Thee for
RELIGION (2)
466 CC Claude 14 I have./I suppose it takes the place of religion:/Just as my wife's investigations/Into
466 CC Claude 17 the spirit/Are a kind of substitute for religion./I dare say truly religious people —/I've
RELIGIONS (2)
160 Rock 7 9 of the light/Invented the Higher Religions; and the Higher Religions were good/
160 Rock 7 9 the Higher Religions; and the Higher Religions were good/And led men from light to
RELIGIOUS (4)
344 FR Violet 25 preparation./{V} And you need some religious qualification!/I think you should
466 CC Claude 18 substitute for religion./I dare say truly religious people —/I've never known any — can
474 CC Colby 5 /{C} Not to be alone there./If I were religious, God would walk in my garden/And
474 CC Lucasta 8 I think./{L} You sound awfully religious./Is there no other way of making it real
RELUCTANCE (1)
437 CP Reilly 38 loathing — all these together —/And reluctance of the body to become a *thing*./I'd
RELUCTANT (2)
412 CP Reilly 10 /To make a decision./{R} Was she reluctant?/Was that why you brought her?/{J}
412 CP Julia 12 why you brought her?/{J} Oh no, not reluctant:/Only diffident. She cannot believe/
RELY (1)
541 ES Gomez 11 story and who didn't. I promise you./Rely upon me as the soul of discretion./{LC}

REMAIN (4)
20 Portrait	78	confessed./I keep my countenance,/I remain self-possessed/Except when a
298 FR Violet	14	there should be witnesses. I intend to remain./And I wish to be present to hear what
361 CP Reilly	27	to a stranger./Let me, therefore, remain the stranger./But let me tell you, that to
364 CP Edward	10	the use of all your analysis/If I am to remain always lost in the dark?/{UG} There is

REMAINING (3)
171 FQ: BurntN	7	might have been is an abstraction/Remaining a perpetual possibility/Only in a
185 FQ: DrySal	53	flowers/Dropping their petals and remaining motionless;/Where is there an end to
364 CP Reilly	11	{UG} There is certainly no purpose in remaining in the dark/Except long enough to

REMAINS (4)
50 Hippopot	35	virgins kist,/While the True Church remains below/Wrapt in the old miasmal mist./
187 FQ: DrySal	114	of action,/But the torment of others remains an experience/Unqualified, unworn by
258 MC Thomas	33	by what they are. I know/What yet remains to show you of my history/Will seem to
329 FR Chorus	1	than is spoken./And what is spoken remains in the room, waiting for the future to

REMARK (7)
20 Portrait	73	and the sporting page./Particularly I remark./An English countess goes upon the
21 Portrait	99	like one who smiles, and turning shall remark/Suddenly, his expression in a glass./My
24 Rhapsody	35	/Half-past two,/The street-lamp said,/'Remark the cat which flattens itself in the
408 CP Reilly	34	A point well taken./But permit me to remark that my revelations/About each of you,
495 CC Claude	14	/{SC} That was a very intelligent remark./Perhaps I have taken too much for
508 CC Guzzard	13	In the circumstances, I ignore that remark./{E} May I pour a drop of oil on these
527 ES Monica	29	be interrupted./Someone to make a remark to now and then./And mostly it's been

REMARKABLE (2)
354 CP Julia	40	at repairing clocks;/And he had a remarkable sense of hearing —/The only man I
488 CC Claude	9	It must be true./{SC} It is certainly a remarkable coincidence —/If it is a coincidence.

REMARKABLY (4)
129 Cor2 State	29	portraits, dingy busts, all looking remarkably Roman,/Remarkably like each
129 Cor2 State	30	busts, all looking remarkably Roman,/Remarkably like each other, lit up successively
218 Mung Rump	18	efficient cat-burglars as well, and remarkably smart at a smash-and-grab./They
230 Bust Jones	2	is *not* skin and bones —/In fact, he's remarkably fat./He doesn't haunt pubs — he

REMARKED (2)
409 CP Reilly	16	realised, what your wife has justly remarked,/That you had never been in love with
481 CC Lucasta	8	good at paying compliments;/But I remarked that I was hungry./{K} You can't

REMARKS (2)
324 FR Amy	28	I have ever known./But I think your remarks are much more inappropriate/Than
327 FR Violet	7	learn to suffer more./{V} Agatha's remarks are invariably pointed./{H} Do you

REMEMBER (110)
31 Apollinax	22	and Professor and Mrs. Cheetah/I remember a slice of lemon, and a bitten
65 WL: Chess	122	nothing? Do you see nothing? Do you remember/'Nothing?'/I remember/Those are
65 WL: Chess	124	Do you remember/'Nothing?'/I remember/Those are pearls that were his eyes./
83 Hollow Men	15	direct eyes, to death's other Kingdom/Remember us — if at all — not as lost/Violent
104 Journ Magi	32	/All this was a long time ago, I remember,/And I would do it again, but set
105 Song Sime	13	rejected from my door./Who shall remember my house, where shall live my
109 Marina	24	/I made this, I have forgotten/And remember./The rigging weak and the canvas
111 Xmas Trees	25	to the children/(And here I remember also with gratitude/St. Lucy, her
122 SA Sweeney	13	born, and once is enough./You don't remember, but I remember,/Once is enough. {}/
122 SA Sweeney	13	is enough./You don't remember, but I remember,/Once is enough. {}/SONG BY
152 Rock 2	36	this is the law of life; and you must remember that while there is time of prosperity/
163 Rock 8	40	/But these that unmade them./Remember the faith that took men from home/
194 FQ: Little	112	/I may not comprehend, may not remember.'/And he: 'I am not eager to rehearse/
203 Indians	15	destiny, that soil is his./Let his village remember./This was not your land, or ours: but
247 MC Thomas	6	You talk of seasons that are past. I remember/Not worth forgetting./{T1} And of
248 MC Tempt1	7	for my humble levity./If you will remember me, my Lord, at your prayers,/I'll
248 MC Tempt1	8	me, my Lord, at your prayers,/I'll remember you at kissing-time below the stairs./
261 MC Thomas	4	then did He mean? If you ask that, remember/then that He said also, 'Not as the
261 MC Thomas	38	the martyrs of/the past, asking you to remember especially our martyr of Canterbury,/
261 MC Thomas	40	it is fitting, on Christ's birth/day, to remember what is that Peace which He brought;
271 MC Thomas	15	toiling in the household,/You shall remember them, droning by the fire,/When age
271 MC Thomas	30	become of us?/{T} Peace! be quiet! remember where you are, and what is
272 MC Thomas	3	the Cathedral!/{T} Go to vespers, remember me at your prayers./They shall find
278 MC Knight2	39	Church to/the welfare of the State, remember that it is we who took the first/step.
281 MC Priest2	4	saints and martyrs gone before you,/Remember us./{P3} Let our thanks ascend/To
287 FR Gerald	3	— better than you were,/Charles, as I remember. Besides, you've got to make
292 FR Amy	21	the same./Mr. Bevan — you remember — wants to call tomorrow/On some
295 FR Charles	10	the papers —/No need to revert to it. Remember, my boy,/I understand, your life

300 FR Downing 30   the corner of the upper deck./And I remember, there I saw his Lordship/Leaning
306 FR Harry 40   design?/It never came off. But do you remember/{M} The hollow tree in what we
309 FR Mary 15   don't know you very well,/Although I remember you better than you think,/And what
311 FR Harry 14   go,/Only to surround me? — When I remember them/They leave me alone: when I
314 FR Warburt 9   /It takes me back longer than you can remember/To see you again. But you can't have
314 FR Warburt 23   to my profession./But I remember, when I was a student at Cambridge,/
318 FR Harry 3   —/Though never very happy, I remember. That was why/We all felt like
318 FR Harry 36   can tell me/Something useful. Do you remember my father?/{W} Why, yes, of course,
319 FR Harry 4   know more about my father./I hardly remember him, and I know very well/That I was
319 FR Warburt 18   a boy/When he died. You would not remember./{H} But now I do remember. Not
319 FR Harry 19   not remember./{H} But now I do remember. Not Arthur or John,/They were too
319 FR Harry 20   /They were too young. But now I remember/A summer day of unusual heat,/The
319 FR Harry 23   /The day I lost my butterfly net;/I remember the silence, and the hushed
325 FR Ivy 25   driver, but more reckless./{I} Yet I remember, when they were boys,/Arthur was
327 FR Agatha 1   you have learned, Harry, you must remember/That there is always more: we cannot
332 FR Agatha 22   I came/Once for a long vacation. I remember/A summer day of unusual heat/For
343 FR Mary 11   /{M} Then you *will* help me!/You remember what I said to you this evening?/I
346 FR Charles 2   bring no further surprises;/But I remember now, that I am always surprised/By
354 CP Edward 2   it./{E} I may have heard it, but I don't remember it./{C} And Julia's the only person to
359 CP Julia 25   lucky that it's raining!/It made me remember my umbrella,/And there it is! Now
364 CP Edward 1   when we had breakfast/I no longer remember what my wife is like./I am not quite
365 CP Julia 3   sort of frame —/I'm afraid I don't remember the colour,/But I'd know them,
371 CP Edward 14   /Better be content with the Celia you remember./Remember! I say it's already a
371 CP Edward 15   content with the Celia you remember./Remember! I say it's already a memory./{P} But
373 CP Alex 1   *door after you*, so that it latches./{A} Remember, Edward, not more than ten
385 CP Reilly 4   sometimes be broken. We must also remember/That at every meeting we are meeting
385 CP Reilly 28   /{UG} And to yourself as well. But remember,/When you see your wife, you must
387 CP Peter 30   told us about./But Edward — you remember our conversation yesterday?/{E} Of
389 CP Celia 31   to say is this: I should like you to remember me/As someone who wants you and
393 CP Lavinia 15   you should have made yourself. I remember —/Oh, I ought to have realised what
393 CP Lavinia 22   some other place first?/And I remember that finally in desperation/I said: 'I
397 CP Edward 27   you consider practical./Practical! I remember, on our honeymoon,/You were
402 CP Edward 37   malady./Very prevalent indeed./{E} I remember, in my childhood .../{R} I always
417 CP Reilly 25   succeeded in returning. They may remember/The vision they have had, but they
426 CP Lavinia 13   is the moment it's over;/And then to remember, it's the end of the season/And no
430 CP Peter 20   /The Bologolomskys saw me off./You remember Princess Bologolomsky/In the old
433 CP Lavinia 40   .../{L} Yes, she had been a V.A.D. I remember./{A} She was directed to Kinkanja,/
436 CP Edward 3   /That you don't like to face: well, just remember/That some men have to learn much
447 CC Eggers 38   concerts. But don't overdo it!/{E} I'll remember that. Music./{SC} And by the way,/
448 CC Claude 2   you actually told him about her?/You remember, I asked you to prepare him a little;/
450 CC Claude 15   I'm not so sure of that!/My rule is to remember that I understand nobody,/But on the
453 CC Lucasta 36   week's salary in lieu of notice./{L} B., remember you're only my fiancé on approval./
456 CC Eggers 29   I've had some rare adventures!/I remember long ago, saying to Mrs. E.,/When
459 CC Lady E 2   to Sir Claude? Of course it is./I remember saying: 'He has a good aura.'/I
459 CC Lady E 3   saying: 'He has a good aura.'/I remember people's auras almost better than
460 CC Lady E 20   I think, with Dr. Leroux./Don't you remember, I said before I left:/'Trust my
460 CC Claude 24   Oh, I see./Yes, now I am beginning to remember./I must have acted on your guidance.
477 CC Lucasta 6   was lucky./But I was old enough to remember ... too much./{C} You are Claude's
481 CC Lady E 32   to eat a great deal of salad./You remember, I made you take a note of the
486 CC Colby 26   I was very young indeed./I don't remember him. I was told about him./But I
509 CC Colby 13   the little cousin/Who died? Don't you remember, Aunt Sarah,/My finding a rattle and
513 CC Colby 28   before I was born/Or before I could remember; whom I could get to know/Only by
516 CC Claude 17   father./{SC} But, Colby:/Don't you remember a talk we had —/So very long ago! —
529 ES Ld Clav 29   Contemplating nothingness. Just remember:/Every day, year after year, over my
532 ES Ld Clav 17   to see him./Though from what I remember of the man who introduces him/I
532 ES Ld Clav 27   /{LC} Goodbye, Charles. And please remember/That we both want to see you,
537 ES Gomez 37   /With the consequences which you remember:/A miserable clerkship — which your
540 ES Gomez 16   you can trust me./{G} Dick, do you remember the moonlight night/We drove back
544 ES Monica 25   of this weather while it lasts./I never remember you as other than occupied/With
545 ES Ld Clav 14   /Has left us alone./{LC} Yes, but remember/What she said. She said: 'I'm going
546 ES Piggott 18   a short and simple name/And easy to remember. But, as I was saying,/Guests in
546 ES Piggott 29   /Or resting, like you. So you'll remember/Always to call me Mrs. Piggott,
547 ES Piggott 9   Miss Claverton-Ferry./And remember, when you want to be *very* quiet/
548 ES Monica 3   it. {}/[*Exit*]/{M} I hope she won't remember anything else./{LC} She'll come back
549 ES Carghil 18   and you all laughed at me./Don't you remember?/{LC} Pray continue./The more you

549 ES Ld Clav   20 more you remind me of, the better I'll remember./{MC} And the three of us talked you
549 ES Carghil   23 a time ago it seems!/It's surprising I remember it all so clearly./You attracted me,
549 ES Carghil   33 'yellow'? I'm not quite sure./You do remember now, don't you, Richard?/{LC} Not
549 ES Ld Clav   35 repeated./That is new to me. But I do remember you./{MC} Time has wrought sad
549 ES Carghil   38 others thought so too. But as you remember,/Please, Richard, just repeat my
552 ES Ld Clav   2 the same time of your own?/I seem to remember, it was only a year or so/Before your
552 ES Carghil   6 /{MC} Yes, I had my art./Don't you remember what a hit I made/With a number
552 ES Ld Clav   12 did you feel?/{LC} Nothing at all. I remember my surprise/At finding that I felt
553 ES Carghil   17 together./There's a phrase I seem to remember reading somewhere:/*Where their fires*
553 ES Carghil   27 /If there had been a trial. Don't you remember them?/{LC} Vaguely. Were they very
554 ES Piggott   32 know that name, but you might remember her/As Maisie Montjoy in revue./She
554 ES Piggott   36 generation,/But you and I should remember her, Lord Claverton./That tune she
556 ES Michael   32 you knew the facts. The first thing I remember/Is being blamed for something I
577 ES Charles   15 grievance against your father?/Remember, you put yourself completely in the
578 ES Monica   17 and compunction?/{M} Oh Michael, you're my only brother/And I'm
578 ES Michael   24 seemed to have much in common./I remember, when I came home for the holidays/
582 ES Ld Clav   9 Michael,/I think, for the first time — remember, my dear,/I am only a beginner in the

REMEMBERED (9)

173 FQ: BurntN   91 the draughty church at smokefall/Be remembered; involved with past and future./
197 FQ: Little   245 the first time./Through the unknown, remembered gate/When the last of earth left to
239 MC Chorus   14 stretched out his hand to the fire and remembered the Saints at All Hallows,/
239 MC Chorus   15 the Saints at All Hallows,/Remembered the martyrs and saints who wait?
288 FR Agatha   23 /Harry must often have remembered Wishwood —/The nursery tea, the
346 FRDowning   7 Lordship sent me back because he remembered/He thinks he left his cigarette-case
366 CP   Peter   16 with you, Julia? On the way back/I remembered something I had to say to Edward
392 CP Lavinia 13 What did you do about it?/I only remembered after I had left./{E} I telephoned to
417 CP   Celia   9 have no reality./For what happened is remembered like a dream/In which one is

REMEMBERING (4)

158 Rock 5   4 the friend who has something to lose./Remembering the words of Nehemiah the
162 Rock 8   3 And we will take heart for the future,/Remembering the past./The heathen are come
246 MC Temptl 28 Will find excuse for my humble levity/Remembering all the good time past./Your
492 CC Claude 36 /If I told them what I was really remembering./Come, Elizabeth./{LE} My poor

REMEMBERS (3)

156 Rock 3   73 way to the Temple,/There is one who remembers the way to your door:/Life you may
456 CC Eggers 23 to lose,/Though she sometimes remembers when you least expect it./But she
572 ES Ld Clav 33 But it's irrelevant./Each of them remembers an occasion/On which I ran away.

REMIND (12)

111 Xmas Trees 33 soul:/Because the beginning shall remind us of the end/And the first coming of
181 FQ: ECoker 157 constant care is not to please/But to remind of our, and Adam's curse,/And that, to
233 Skimble   43 just behind him and was ready to remind him./For Skimble won't let anything go
235 Ad-dress   36 any hail or shout./Again I must remind you that/A Dog's a Dog — A CAT'S A
248 MC Tempt2   15 has forgotten me, perhaps. I will remind you./We met at Clarendon, in
341 FR   Amy   13 past life, and have nothing except to remind him/Of the years when he had been a
384 CP Reilly   8 /{UG} Not at all./I have come to remind you — you have made a decision./{E}
467 CC Colby   36 my china./{C} Excuse me, but I must remind you:/You have that meeting in the City/
492 CC Colby   17 /But there's another reason. I must remind you/About your speech for the Potters'
492 CC Claude   34 mood./Cross that out. It would only remind me/Of things that would surprise me
541 ES Lambert   32 Lord, but Miss Monica asked me/To remind you there's a trunk call coming through
549 ES Ld Clav 20 /{LC} Pray continue./The more you remind me of, the better I'll remember./{MC}

REMINDED (3)

538 ES Gomez   2 penmanship./Hence, as you have just reminded me/Defalcation and forgery. And then
541 ES Gomez   29 friend to me once/As you pointedly reminded me a moment ago./Now it's my turn,
580 ES Gomez   2 write to you?/{G} Oh, I'm glad you reminded me. Here's my business card/With the

REMINDER (6)

165 Rock 9   44 lifting light,/Light/Light/The visible reminder of Invisible Light./You have seen the
184 FQ: DrySal   8 his seasons and rages, destroyer, reminder/Of what men choose to forget.
450 CC Claude 21 Mr. Simpkins, either?/{SC} A timely reminder. You may have to repeat it./But he
477 CC Lucasta 10 to me/In his way. But I'm always a reminder to him/Of something he would prefer
526 ES Charles 33 his kindly welcome, which is always a reminder/That I mustn't stay too long, for you
571 ES Ld Clav 31 He re-enters my life to make himself a reminder/Of one occasion the memory of which

REMINDS (5)

167 Rock 10   45 /And we thank Thee that darkness reminds us of light./O Light Invisible, we give
287 FR Gerald 22 The less said the better./{G} That reminds me, Amy,/When are the boys all due to
365 CP   Julia 36 very sorry./{J} No, I love it. But that reminds me/About my glasses. That's the
501 CC Lucasta 24 sure he'll appreciate *that*./But that reminds me. He's waiting downstairs./I don't

524 ES   Monica   19   waiters/All buzzing round you: and it reminds the girl/That she's not the only one
REMINISCENCE (1)
24 Rhapsody   62   cross and cross across her brain.'/The reminiscence comes/Of sunless dry geraniums/
REMINISCENT (7)
73 WL: Thund   383   down in air were towers/Tolling reminiscent bells, that kept the hours/And
492 CC   Colby   25   one note I couldn't understand.'Reminiscent mood.' I can't develop that/Unless
492 CC   Colby   26   that/Unless you can tell me — reminiscent of what?/{SC} Reminiscent of what?
492 CC   Claude 27   tell me — reminiscent of what?/{SC} Reminiscent of what? Reminiscent of what?/
492 CC   Claude 27   of what?/{SC} Reminiscent of what? Reminiscent of what?/'Tonight I feel in a
492 CC   Claude 28   of what?/'Tonight I feel in a reminiscent mood' —/Oh yes. To say something
492 CC   Claude 33   art./No, I don't think I shall be in a reminiscent mood./Cross that out. It would only
REMITTANCE (1)
575 ES   Michael   1   at the fellow from London,/The limey remittance man for whom a job was made./No!
REMORSE (2)
19 Portrait   48   /And youth is cruel, and has no more remorse/And smiles at situations which it
290 FR   Amy   13   can be no grief/And no regret and no remorse./I would have prevented it if I could.
REMOTE (4)
18 Portrait   17   tones of violins/Mingled with remote cornets/And begins.'You do not know
149 Rock 1   70   belittle the desert./The desert is not remote in southern tropics,/The desert is not
426 CC   Lavinia 20   be alone./I love that house being so remote./{E} That's why we took it. And I'm
463 CC   Colby   13   there is something that I can do/So remote from my previous interests./It gives me,
REMOTENESS (1)
464 CC   Claude   15   things —/But they haven't this ... remoteness I have always longed for./I want a
REMOTEST (1)
258 MC Thomas   38   /The strangest consequence from remotest cause./But for every evil, every
REMOVE (2)
196 FQ: Little   213   of flame/Which human power cannot remove./We only live, only suspire/Consumed
483 CC   Lady E   27   intimate for the sitting-room./May I remove it? Surely your bedroom/Is the proper
REMOVED (3)
38 Gerontion   55   /I that was near your heart was removed therefrom/To lose beauty in terror,
177 FQ: ECoker   3   and fall, crumble, are extended,/Are removed, destroyed, restored, or in their place/
429 CP   Alex   5   a curse on them/Which can only be removed by slaughtering the Christians./They
RENDER (1)
279 MC Knight4   38   before/you, you will unhesitatingly render a verdict of Suicide while of/Unsound
RENDERED (1)
315 FR   Chorus   36   nursery, mutilated/The family album, rendered ludicrous/The tenants' dinner, the
RENDERING (1)
466 CC   Colby   4   music,/What they hear is an inferior rendering./So I've given up trying to play to
RENDING (1)
194 FQ: Little   140   at what ceases to amuse./And last, the rending pain of re-enactment/Of all that you
RENEGADE (1)
275 MC Knight1   18   Church./{K1} No faith do I owe to a renegade,/And what I owe shall now be paid./
RENEW (2)
275 MC Knight1   6   the money you appropriated./{K1} Renew the obedience you have violated./{T} For
542 ES   Gomez   17   unkind of you. My only aim/Is to renew our friendship. Don't you understand?/
RENEWED (1)
195 FQ: Little   167   as it could, loved them,/To become renewed, transfigured, in another pattern./Sin is
RENEWS (3)
98 Ash-Wed 6   19   between the ivory gates/And smell renews the salt savour of the sandy earth/This is
263 MC Chorus   15   this world, but death in the Lord renews it,/And the world must be cleaned in the
282 MC Chorus   3   ground springs that which forever renews the earth/Though it is forever denied.
RENOUNCE (3)
89 Ash-Wed 1   21   that things are as they are and/I renounce the blessèd face/And renounce the
89 Ash-Wed 1   22   and/I renounce the blessèd face/And renounce the voice/Because I cannot hope to
578 ES   Monica   39   inspired your decision:/If you wish to renounce your father and your family/What is
RENOWNED (1)
589 Fable   84   Peter'd snatcht to heaven their lord renowned,/Though the wicked said (such rascals
RENT (5)
115 SP   Dusty   5   /{Du} You don't care!/Who pays the rent?/{Do} Yes he pays the rent/{Du} Well some
115 SP   Doris   6   pays the rent?/{Do} Yes he pays the rent/{Du} Well some men don't and some men
124 SA Sweeney   31   he took in the milk and he paid the rent./{Sw} What did he do?/All that time, what
125 SA Sweeney   28   go/And somebody's gotta pay the rent/{Do} I know who/{S} But that's nothing to
155 Rock 3   48   /Precarious lodgings while the rent is paid,/Subsiding basements where the rat
RENT-COLLECTOR (1)
125 SA Sweeney   11   then the milkman wasn't/and the rent-collector wasn't/And if they were alive then

RENTED (1)
38 Gerontion   50   conclusion, when I/Stiffen in a rented house. Think at last/I have not made this
RENTRENT (1)
48 Lune Miel   1   de Miel/Ils ont vu les Pays-Bas, ils rentrent à Terre Haute;/Mais une nuit d'été, les
RENTS (1)
343 FR   Amy   26   with increasing taxes/And unpaid rents and tithes? nourish investments/With
RENUNCIATION (2)
185 FQ: DrySal   62   —/And therefore the fittest for renunciation./There is the final addition, the
342 FR   Agatha   30   /Elsewhere no doubt is agony, renunciation,/But birth and life. Harry has
REORGANISED (1)
56 Swee Night   15   table cloth/Overturns a coffee-cup,/Reorganised upon the floor/She yawns and
REPAIR (5)
92 Ash-Wed 3   10   old man's mouth drivelling, beyond repair,/Or the toothed gullet of an agèd shark./
135 5FingerEx1   1   *a Persian Cat*/The songsters of the air repair/To the green fields of Russell Square./
152 Rock 2   33   you./And all that is ill you may repair if you walk together in humble
226 Macavity   25   glass is broken, and the trellis past repair —/Ay, there's the wonder of the thing!
362 CP   Reilly 40   /You are a piece of furniture in a repair shop/For those who surround you, the
REPAIRED (1)
551 ES   Carghil   22   a heart's been broken/Once it's been repaired? But I know what you mean./You
REPAIRING (1)
354 CP   Julia   39   harmless./{J} He was very clever at repairing clocks;/And he had a remarkable
REPASSANT (1)
51 Restaurant   29   de sous-mer l'emporta très loin,/Le repassant aux étapes de sa vie antérieure./
REPAST (1)
588 Fable   47   beast in Æsop's fable/To fill out their repast, and pies and puddings,/And jellies,
REPAY (1)
577 ES   Gomez   11   /{G} Yes, it's always pleasant/To repay an old debt. And better late than never./
REPEAT (7)
152 Rock 2   42   alone,/For whom the days and nights repeat the praise of GOD,/Prays for the
189 FQ: DrySal   178   traffic/And those who conduct them./Repeat a prayer also on behalf of/Women who
268 MC Knight3   6   for which you sued:/Yet how, I repeat, did you show your gratitude?/{K1}
323 FR Warburt   37   under Warburton's orders./{W} I repeat, Lady Monchensey, that you must not go
358 CP   Julia   22   it./It's such a nice party, I'd like to repeat it./Why don't you *all* come to dinner on
450 CC   Claude   21   A timely reminder. You may have to repeat it./But he should be back by now. And
549 ES   Carghil   39   you remember,/Please, Richard, just repeat my name — just once:/The name by
REPEATED (1)
549 ES   Ld Clav   34   Not the conversation you have just repeated./That is new to me. But I do remember
REPEATEDLY (1)
376 CP   m   2   *He moves/a card. The doorbell rings repeatedly. Re-enter* CELIA, *in an apron.*]/{C}
REPEATING (2)
181 FQ: ECoker   135   /Of death and birth./You say I am repeating/Something I have said before. I shall
463 CC   Claude   35   It's my own experience/That you are repeating./{C} Your own experience?/{SC} Yes,
REPEL (1)
341 FR   Agatha   7   what you cannot have/Because you repel it./{A} I prepared the situation/For us to
REPENTANCE (1)
152 Rock 2   33   repair if you walk together in humble repentance, expiating the sins of your fathers;/
REPETITION (2)
603 Spleen   4   silk hats, and conscious graces/In repetition that displaces/Your mental
331 FR   Harry   3   no horror of my action,/I only felt the repetition of it/Over and over. When I was
REPINE (1)
417 CP   Reilly 31   there is to give and take. They do not repine;/Are contented with the morning that
REPLACE (1)
447 CC   Claude   15   a successor./Makes it very difficult to replace you./She thinks she ought to have a
REPLACING (1)
447 CC   Claude   9   /As we had some discussion about replacing you./But you know she regards you —
REPLENISH (1)
363 CP   Reilly   3   /And the 'you' is withdrawn. May I replenish?/{E} Oh, I'm sorry. What were you
REPLY (3)
98 Ash-Wed 6   24   /Let the other yew be shaken and reply./Blessèd sister, holy mother, spirit of the
363 CP   Edward   30   'But when will she be back?'/And I reply 'I don't know that she *is* coming back'./
530 ES   Ld Clav   33   /Of what was said about me, or of my reply —/All to thank them for that./Oh the
REPORT (8)
189 FQ: DrySal   189   with Mars, converse with spirits,/To report the behaviour of the sea monster,/
192 FQ: Little   47   yourself, or inform curiosity/Or carry report. You are here to kneel/Where prayer has
323 FR   Gerald   26   see him, Amy, and come back and report to you./{A} I must see for myself. Order

323 FR Warburt 32   going myself. I will come back and report to you./{A} I must see for myself. I do
329 FR Chorus 26   news/We must listen to the weather report/And the international catastrophes. {}/
429 CP Alex 22 {A} We have just drawn up an interim report./{E} Will it be made public?/{A} It cannot
483 CC Colby 19   moment/I'm working on a company report./{LE} I hadn't reckoned on reports and
513 CC Colby 29   whom I could get to know/Only by report, by documents —/The story of his life, of
REPORTS (3)
154 Rock 3 15   /Many read nothing but the race reports./Much is your reading, but not the
483 CC Lady E 20   report./{LE} I hadn't reckoned on reports and typewriters/When I designed this
574 ES Michael 36   of my morals/And send you back reports. Some sort of place/Where everyone
REPOSE (6)
 34 Figlia 24 The troubled midnight and the noon's repose./Poems/Gerontion/Here I am, an old
129 Cor2 State 33 locked for a moment,/A still moment, repose of noon, set under the upper branches of
206 To my Wife 3   /And the rhythm that governs the repose of our sleepingtime,/The breathing in
216 Jellicles 18   make their toilette and take their repose:/Jellicles wash behind their ears,/Jellicles
221 Old Deut 40 without a word spoken./The digestive repose of that feline's gastronomy/Must never
522 ES dedic 3   *|And the rhythm that governs the repose of our sleepingtime,/The breathing in*
REPOSEFUL (1)
 91 Ash-Wed 2 31   /Exhausted and life-giving/Worried reposeful/The single Rose/Is now the Garden/
REPRESENTATIVE (2)
129 Cor2 State 52   I cry?/We demand a committee, a representative committee, a committee of
559 ES Michael 37 of prolongation of your existence,/A representative carrying on business in your
REPRESSION (1)
299 FRDowning 37 Suffered from what they call a kind of repression./But what struck me ... more nervous
REPROACH (2)
295 FR Charles 15   know —/But *you* have no reason to reproach yourself./Your conscience can be
464 CC Claude 40   I cherished for a long time a secret reproach:/But after his death, and then it was
REPROACHES (1)
545 ES Ld Clav 9   /For the errors into which his own reproaches drove us?/{M} You admit that at the
REPRODUCE (1)
431 CP Peter 24   over/To study the decay, so as to reproduce it./Then we build another Boltwell in
REPUBLIC (2)
533 ES Gomez 21   citizen/Of a central American republic: San Marco./It's as hard to become a
564 ES Gomez 27   to ... where is your home?/{G} The republic of San Marco./{MC} Went back to San
REPUDIATE (3)
559 ES Ld Clav 24   had been./{LC} So you are ready to repudiate your family,/To throw away the
578 ES Ld Clav 3   /Michael, before you go. I shall never repudiate you/Though you repudiate me. I see
578 ES Ld Clav 4   never repudiate you/Though you repudiate me. I see now clearly/The many many
REPUTATION (3)
218 Mung Rump 3   and acrobats/They had an extensive reputation. They made their home in Victoria
218 Mung Rump 6   —/They had really a little more reputation than a couple of cats can very well
564 ES Carghil 2   *Me!* That's the song/That made my reputation, Señor Gomez./{G} It will never be
REQUIRE (1)
424 CP Caterer 9   /Will there be anything more you require?/{L} Nothing more, I think, till half past
REQUIRED (2)
151 Rock 2 8   labour to give and our labour is not required./We wait on corners, with nothing to
282 MC Chorus 8   of the night of God, the surrender required, the deprivation inflicted;/Who fear the
REQUIRES (3)
 68 WL: Fire S 241   encounter no defence;/His vanity requires no response,/And makes a welcome of
346 FRDowning 14   /I'll never leave him so long as he requires me./{M} But he will need you. You
418 CP Reilly 24   us./The second is unknown, and so requires faith —/The kind of faith that issues
REQUIRING (1)
180 FQ: ECoker 133 garden, echoed ecstasy/Not lost, but requiring, pointing to the agony/Of death and
RESCUE (3)
229 Gus 44   the stage on a telegraph wire,/To rescue a child when a house was on fire./And he
554 ES Piggott 28   As a matter of fact, I flew to your rescue/(That's why I've brought your morning
555 ES Monica 13   you again/So I hurried to your rescue. You look tired, Father./She ought to
RESEARCH (1)
209 NamingCats 23 will guess;/The name that no human research can discover —/But THE CAT
RESEMBLES (5)
195 FQ: Little 156   between them, indifference/Which resembles the others as death resembles life,/
195 FQ: Little 156   /Which resembles the others as death resembles life,/Being between two lives —
348 FR Chorus 9   in the garden, because it too closely resembles the maze in the brain./We do not like
348 FR Chorus 10   we are awake, because it too closely resembles what happens when we are asleep./
562 ES Carghil 28   about your children:/Monica hardly resembles you at all,/But Michael — your father

RESENT (2)
70 WL: Fire S   299   /I made no comment. What should I resent?'/'On Margate Sands./I can connect/
434 CP   Edward   38   about Celia./{E} It's the waste that I resent./{P} You know more than I do:/For *me*,
RESENTMENT (3)
34 Figlia   6   the ground and turn/With a fugitive resentment in your eyes:/But weave, weave the
186 FQ: DrySal   64   the final addition, the failing/Pride or resentment at failing powers,/The unattached
296 FR   Ivy   20   /Often betray the most immoderate resentment/At such a suggestion. They can be
RESENTS (1)
235 Ad-dress   43   Cat./But always keep in mind that he/Resents familiarity./I bow, and taking off my
RESERVATIONS (2)
528 ES   Monica   38   /Will never take place. 'Make the reservations'/Selby said, 'as if you were going'./
579 ES   Michael   11   he thinks can be helpful in getting reservations./{MC} It's wonderful, Señor
RESERVED (1)
194 FQ: Little   131   foresight,/Let me disclose the gifts reserved for age/To set a crown upon your
RESERVING (1)
216 Jellicles   27   quiet enough in the afternoon,/Reserving their terpsichorean powers/To dance
RESIDENTS (1)
429 CP   Edward   17   /{E} And have any of the English residents been murdered?/{A} Yes, but they are
RESIDUE (1)
381 CP   Edward   28   loveliness,/That the tedium is not the residue of ecstasy./I see that my life was
RESIGN (8)
110 Marina   31   in a world of time beyond me; let me/Resign my life for this life, my speech for that
129 Cor2 State   53   a committee of investigation/RESIGN RESIGN RESIGN/MINOR POEMS
129 Cor2 State   53   committee of investigation/RESIGN RESIGN RESIGN/MINOR POEMS/Eyes that
129 Cor2 State   53   of investigation/RESIGN RESIGN RESIGN/MINOR POEMS/Eyes that last I saw
142 Cape Ann   11   are delectable. Sweet sweet sweet/But resign this land at the end, resign it/To its true
142 Cape Ann   11   sweet/But resign this land at the end, resign it/To its true owner, the tough one, the
275 MC Knight2   4   you have excommunicated./{K2} Resign the powers you have arrogated./{K3}
363 CP   Reilly   24   no harm to find yourself ridiculous./Resign yourself to be the fool you are./That's
RESIGNED (2)
248 MC Tempt2   24   /{T2} The Chancellorship that you resigned/When you were made Archbishop —
278 MC Knight2   21   had been made Archbishop, he/resigned the office of Chancellor, he became
RESIGNING (1)
148 Rock 1   50   /That it is hard to be really useful, resigning/The things that men count for
RESIST (2)
330 FR   Harry   8   —/Stupider than himself. He can resist the influence/Of Wishwood, being
343 FR   Amy   25   the roof, combat the endless weather,/Resist the wind? fight with increasing taxes/And
RESISTANCE (2)
274 MC Thomas   8   by fighting, by stratagem, or by resistance,/Not to fight with beasts as men. We
400 CP   Reilly   9   to delay his appointment/To lower his resistance. But what I mean is,/Does he trust
RESOLUTION (2)
173 FQ: BurntN   80   completion of its partial ecstasy,/The resolution of its partial horror./Yet the
342 FR   Agatha   17   In this world/It is inexplicable, the resolution is in another./{M} Oh, but it is the
RESOLVE (1)
333 FR   Agatha   37   through flames of ice, chosen/To resolve the enchantment under which we suffer./
RESOLVING (1)
181 FQ: ECoker 153   sharp compassion of the healer's art/Resolving the enigma of the fever chart./Our
RESOUND (1)
96 Ash-Wed 5   12   word be found, where will the word/Resound? Not here, there is not enough silence/
RESOURCES (1)
541 ES   Gomez   27   you're in a tight corner/My entire resources are at your disposal./You were a
RESPECT (11)
235 Ad-dress   65   entitled to expect/These evidences of respect./And so in time you reach your aim,/
273 MC   Priests   25   beasts. They come not like men, who/Respect the sanctuary, who kneel to the Body of
276 MC Knight1   22   are all with the under dog. I respect such feelings, I/share them.
447 CC   Eggers   20   that, Sir Claude!/She has too much respect for your business genius./But it's true
533 ES   Gomez   24   this qualification:/Out there they respect you for rather different reasons./{LC}
533 ES   Ld Clav   25   /{LC} Do you mean that you've won respect out there/By the sort of activity that lost
533 ES   Ld Clav   26   /By the sort of activity that lost you respect/Here in England?/{G} Not at all, not at
535 ES   Gomez   14   trusts a man/Or a woman — in this respect or that./*A* won't let me down in this
546 ES   Piggott   39   Piggott'/Reassures the guests in one respect;/And calling our nurses 'Nurse'
547 ES   Piggott   1   'Nurse' reassures them/In another respect./{LC} I follow you perfectly./{MP} And
571 ES   Ld Clav   19   and foolish —/But we should respect love always when we meet it;/Even when
RESPECTABILITY (1)
480 CC   Kaghan   25   one thing *we* want is security/And respectability! Now Colby/Doesn't really care

RESPECTABLE (3)
226 Macavity 21 *Macavity's not there!*/He's outwardly respectable. (They say he cheats at cards.)/And
480 CC Kaghan 26 Colby/Doesn't really care about being respectable —/He was born and bred to it. I
498 CC Eggers 14 In a manner of speaking, it's perfectly respectable./{SC} You're suggesting that she ran
RESPECTED (3)
533 ES Gomez 20 Gomez, you see,/Is now a highly respected citizen/Of a central American
533 ES Gomez 22 San Marco./It's as hard to become a respected citizen/Out there, as it is here. With
539 ES Ld Clav 26 The only thing I find surprising/In the respected citizen of San Marco/Is that in the
RESPECTFUL (3)
148 Rock 1 38 LEADER:/Silence! and preserve respectful distance./For I perceive approaching/
525 ES Monica 24 doesn't amble./You're not at all respectful./{C} I try to be respectful;/But you
525 ES Charles 25 not at all respectful./{C} I try to be respectful;/But you know that I shan't have a
RESPITE (1)
406 CP Reilly 14 people who imagine that they need a respite/From everyday life. They return
RESPONDED (2)
74 WL: Thund 418 Coriolanus/DA/*Damyata:* The boat responded/Gaily, to the hand expert with sail
74 WL: Thund 420 sea was calm, your heart would have responded/Gaily, when invited, beating
RESPONSE (5)
68 WL: Fire S 241 no defence;/His vanity requires no response,/And makes a welcome of indifference.
85 Hollow Men 81 /Between the emotion/And the response/Falls the Shadow/*Life is very long*/
172 FQ: BurntN 28 vibrant air,/And the bird called, in response to/The unheard music hidden in the
514 CC Claude 27 you are inventing this fiction/In response to what Colby said he wanted./{E} I'll
570 ES Ld Clav 8 heart/When one is sure of the wrong response?/How make a confession with no hope
RESPONSES (1)
363 CP Reilly 18 You are nothing but a set/Of obsolete responses. The one thing to do/Is to do nothing.
RESPONSIBILITIES (1)
452 CC Lucasta 37 /Do you know that I'm one of your responsibilities?/{C} No, I'm afraid I didn't
RESPONSIBILITY (12)
286 FR Charles 35 the stamina,/Haven't the sense of responsibility./{G} You're being very hard on
342 FR Agatha 35 /Do you think that I would take the responsibility/Of tempting them over the
404 CP Edward 21 your hands./I cannot take any further responsibility./{R} Many patients come in that
411 CP Lavinia 13 Really, Edward!/I have *some* sense of responsibility./I was going to leave some shirts
438 CP Reilly 21 from what you still feel/As your responsibility./{E} I cannot help the feeling/
438 CP Edward 23 the feeling/That, in some way, my responsibility/Is greater than that of a band of
439 CP Edward 3 to us, two years ago./{E} Your responsibility is nothing to mine, Lavinia./{L}
453 CC Kaghan 26 still reeling./It's going to be my responsibility,/As your fiancé, to protect Colby
507 CC Guzzard 27 And that the heirs acknowledged no responsibility./The mother, I suppose, could
519 CC Kaghan 21 ... if you'd let us;/And we'd take the responsibility of meaning it. {}/[LUCASTA *puts*
537 ES Ld Clav 33 to *my* help./{LC} I certainly admit no responsibility,/None whatever, for what
538 ES Gomez 18 /Because the man who accepts responsibility/Isn't the man who made the
RESPONSIBILITY'S (1)
455 CC Eggers 33 you'll have to see much of her:/That responsibility's not on your shoulders./Lady
RESPONSIBLE (7)
339 FR Harry 18 destroy me will be life for John,/I am responsible for him. Why I have this election/I
396 CP Edward 32 {E} I don't want you to make yourself responsible for me:/It's only another kind of
438 CP Reilly 37 It was triumphant./But I am no more responsible for the triumph —/And just as
438 CP Reilly 38 for the triumph —/And just as responsible for her death as you are./{L} Yet I
455 CC Eggers 13 Sir Claude's,/And he's made himself responsible for her./In any case, he's behaved
542 ES Ld Clav 21 /Your downfall to me. But how was I responsible?/We were the same age. You were a
571 ES Ld Clav 11 And so he served his term./Was I responsible for that weakness in him?/Yes, I
REST (44)
68 WL: Fire S 229 /Perceived the scene, and foretold the rest —/I too awaited the expected guest./He, the
160 Rock 7 16 where the wind will not let the snow rest./Waste and void. Waste and void. And
182 FQ: ECoker 191 /For us, there is only the trying. The rest is not our business./Home is where one
190 FQ: DrySal 217 /Hints followed by guesses; and the rest/Is prayer, observance, discipline, thought
220 Old Deut 24 chance to disturb/Deuteronomy's rest when he feels so disposed/Or when he's
245 MC Thomas 37 /These are small matters. Little rest in Canterbury/With eager enemies restless
256 MC Chorus 5 still/Be forever still./{C} There is no rest in the house. There is no rest in the street./I
256 MC Chorus 5 is no rest in the house. There is no rest in the street./I hear restless movement of
277 MC Knight3 20 at the best we shall have to/spend the rest of our lives abroad. And even when
294 FR Harry 31 senseless direction/For a momentary rest on the burning wheel/That cloudless night
295 FR Amy 38 same again./I beg you to go now and rest before dinner./Get Downing to draw you a
302 FR Amy 19 I hope Harry will feel better/After his rest upstairs. {}/[*Exeunt, except* AGATHA]/
322 FR Winch 5 /If it was my mother's. God rest her soul,/She's been dead these ten years.
323 FR Warburt 15 him up tomorrow; and a few days' rest,/I've no doubt, will be all that he needs./{A}

327 FR	Agatha	2	/That there is always more: we cannot	rest	in being/The impatient spectators of malice
327 FR	Agatha	5	worlds/Of make-believe and fear. To	rest	in our own suffering/Is evasion of suffering.
337 FR	Harry	38	with Agatha, any more than with the	rest	of you./My advice has come from quite a
350 FR	Agatha	27	that of the departed —/May they	rest	in peace. {}/THE COCKTAIL PARTY/
377 CP	Edward	10	I had some talk with him, when the	rest	of you had left,/And he said he would bring
391 CP	Julia	1	leave them alone, and let Lavinia	rest	./Now we'll all go back to *my* house. Peter,
417 CP	Reilly	3	can become itself an illusion/If we	rest	in it./{C} I cannot argue./It's not that I'm
426 CP	Edward	23	seeing people;/And you do need to	rest	now. {}/[*The doorbell rings*]/{L} Oh, bother!
438 CP	Reilly	1	because more conscious/Than the	rest	of us. She paid the highest price/In
438 CP	Edward	17	else that is terribly wrong,/And the	rest	of us are somehow involved in the wrong,/I
459 CC	Lady E	28	that./But not today. I shall go and	rest	now./In a sleeping-car it is quite impossible/
460 CC	Lady E	30	about my committees./I must go and	rest	now./{SC} Yes, you go and rest./I'm in the
460 CC	Claude	31	and rest now./{SC} Yes, you go and	rest	./I'm in the middle of some business with
473 CC	Lucasta	1	/That's why you're different from the	rest	of us:/You have your secret garden; to
502 CC	Lucasta	25	/Or something so different from the	rest	of us/That we can't judge you. That's you,
513 CC	Colby	23	another relationship./Let my mother	rest	in peace. As for a father —/I have the idea
514 CC	Guzzard	14	my mother?/{MG} Let your mother	rest	in peace./I *was* your mother; but I chose to
530 ES	Ld Clav	10	and you know it./They talk of	rest	, these doctors, Charles; they tell me to be
533 ES	Gomez	17	to take a long holiday,/Let's say a	rest	cure — that's what I've come for./You see,
541 ES	Gomez	23	/Would keep me in comfort for the	rest	of my life./Really, Dick, you owe me an
543 ES	Monica	15	has worn you out./You must go and	rest	now, before dinner./{LC} Yes, I'll go and
543 ES	Ld Clav	16	before dinner./{LC} Yes, I'll go and	rest	now. I wish Charles was dining with us./I
554 ES	Piggott	23	himself with talking./What he needs is	*rest*!	You're not going, Mrs. Carghill?/{MC} Oh,
554 ES	Carghil	24	that Lord Claverton had come for a	rest	cure,/And it struck me that he might find it
563 ES	Gomez	10	you here, were you?/You're here for a	rest	cure. I persuaded my doctor/That I was in
563 ES	Gomez	11	my doctor/That I was in need of a	rest	cure too./And when I heard you'd chosen
564 ES	Monica	37	Father, I think you should take your	rest	now./— I must explain that the doctors
565 ES	Monica	1	very insistent/That my father should	rest	and have absolute quiet/Before every meal./
568 ES	Ld Clav	22	may consider it/To conceal from the	rest	of the world — your soul is safe./If a man
580 ES	Carghil	24	keep in touch. But you'd better	rest	now./You're looking rather tired. I'll run

RESTAURANT (8)

48 Lune Miel	13	à Milan/Où se trouve la Cène, et un	restaurant	pas cher./Lui pense aux pourboires,
51 Restaurant	t	in the old miasmal mist./Dans le	Restaurant	/Le garçon délabré qui n'a rien à
377 CP Julia	33	/It's too late, or too early, to go to a	restaurant	./You must both come home with me.
445 CC Eggers	18	I lunched at the store — they have a	restaurant	;/An excellent lunch, and cheap, for
481 CC Kaghan	11	We can't dine till eight;/Not at any	restaurant	that *you* like./— For a change, let's
481 CC Lady E	26	know. It's a chance to try that Herbal	Restaurant	/I recommended to you. You can
524 ES Monica	10	should have taken me to some other	restaurant	/Instead of to one where the *maître*
525 ES Charles	7	/I couldn't say what I wanted to, in a	restaurant	/And then you took me on a

RESTAURANTS (1)

13 Prufrock	7	one-night cheap hotels/And sawdust	restaurants	with oyster-shells:/Streets that

RESTED (2)

129 Cor2 State	32	under the... Where the dove's foot	rested	and locked for a moment,/A still
292 FR Amy	23	you would rather wait till you are	rested	./Your room is all ready for you. Nothing

RESTENT (1)

48 Lune Miel	5	et une forte odeur de chienne./Ils	restent	sur le dos écartant les genoux/De quatre

RESTFUL (1)

545 ES Monica	11	it really does seem quiet here and	restful	./Even the matron, though she looks

RESTING (4)

217 Jellicles	35	had nothing to do at all:/They are	resting	and saving themselves to be right/For
227 Macavity	33	mile away./You'll be sure to find him	resting	, or a-licking of his thumbs,/Or engaged
347 FR Violet	26	you? Amy is not well;/And she is	resting	./{I} Oh, I'm sorry. But can't you explain?
546 ES Piggott	29	ill! They're all convalescents,/Or	resting	, like you. So you'll remember/Always to

RESTLESS (10)

13 Prufrock	6	streets,/The muttering retreats/Of	restless	nights in one-night cheap hotels/And
160 Rock 7	16	rites with forgotten meanings/In the	restless	wind-whipped sand, or the hills where
162 Rock 8	16	love of glory,/Some went who were	restless	and curious,/Some were rapacious and
187 FQ: DrySal	120	the apple./And the ragged rock in the	restless	waters,/Waves wash over it, fogs conceal
599 On a Port	2	tenuous dreams, unknown/To us of	restless	brain and weary feet,/Forever hurrying,
246 MC Thomas	1	in Canterbury/With eager enemies	restless	about us./Rebellious bishops, York,
256 MC Chorus	6	There is no rest in the street./I hear	restless	movement of feet. And the air is heavy
269 MC Chorus	32	felt/The heaving of earth at nightfall,	restless	, absurd. I have heard/Laughter in the
290 FR Amy	9	bring Harry down to her own level./A	restless	shivering painted shadow/In life, she is
530 ES Monica	7	I'm to protect you/From your own	restless	energy — the inexhaustible/Sources of

RESTLESSLY (1)
386 CP   m 14   *A pause.* EDWARD *moves about restlessly. The bell rings, and he goes to the front*
RESTLESSNESS (1)
533 ES   Gomez 14   /{G} Call it homesickness,/Curiosity, restlessness, whatever you like./But I've been a
RESTORATION (2)
314 FR   Harry 19   some justification:/For what you call restoration to health/Is only incubation of
438 CP   Reilly 32   to make a decision/Which may mean restoration or ruin to a patient —/And
RESTORE (6)
151 Rock 2   6   /And those who would build and restore turn out the palms of their hands, or
153 Rock 2   52   to cast down, much to build, much to restore;/Let the work not delay, time and the
196 FQ: Little   188   cannot revive old factions/We cannot restore old policies/Or follow an antique drum./
592 Grad 2   3   know they lose what time shall not restore,/And when they leave they fully
275 MC Knight3   5   the powers you have arrogated./{K3} Restore to the King the money you
278 MC Knight2   9   saw that/the one thing needful was to restore order: to curb the excessive/powers of
RESTORED (6)
152 Rock 2   26   always decaying, and always being restored./For every ill deed in the past we suffer
177 FQ: ECoker   3   extended,/Are removed, destroyed, restored, or in their place/Is an open field, or a
181 FQ: ECoker   158   and Adam's curse,/And that, to be restored, our sickness must grow worse./The
195 FQ: Little   147   exasperated spirit/Proceeds, unless restored by that refining fire/Where you must
268 MC Knight3   4   the memory of your transgressions/Restored your honours and your possessions./
506 CC Guzzard   21   lost./Let us hope that her son may be restored to her./{E} That is exactly what we are
RESTORES (1)
186 FQ: DrySal   96   /And approach to the meaning restores the experience/In a different form,
RESTORING (3)
94 Ash-Wed 4   13   /Away the fiddles and the flutes, restoring/One who moves in the time between
94 Ash-Wed 4   16   her, folded./The new years walk, restoring/Through a bright cloud of tears, the
94 Ash-Wed 4   17   a bright cloud of tears, the years, restoring/With a new verse the ancient rhyme.
RESTRAIN (1)
269 MC Knight4   23   and servant! take, hold, detain,/Restrain this man, in the King's name./{K1} Or
RESTRICTED (2)
137 5FingerEx5   6   prim/And his conversation, so nicely/Restricted to What Precisely/And If and
348 FR   Chorus 24   circle of our understanding/Is a very restricted area./Except for a limited number/Of
RESTS (2)
49 Hippopot   2   /The broad-backed hippopotamus/Rests on his belly in the mud;/Although he
150 Rock 1   101   *fields, untilled/Where the plough rests, at an angle/To the furrow. In this land/*
RESULTS (2)
273 MC Thomas   32   desperate and mad./You argue by results, as this world does,/To settle if an act be
273 MC Thomas   36   and evil can be shown./And as in time results of many deeds are blended/So good and
RESUME (1)
321 FR   Harry   29   /{H} He *is* real, Doctor./So let us resume the conversation. You, and I/And
RESUMES (1)
22 Preludes   20   the other masquerades/That time resumes,/One thinks of all the hands/That are
RESUMING (1)
161 Rock 7   24   struggling, always reaffirming, always resuming their march on the way that was lit by
RESURRECTED (1)
18 Portrait   11   that I think his soul/Should be resurrected only among friends/Some two or
RETAIN (1)
558 ES   Michael 7   to be very shocked./Said he couldn't retain any man on his staff/Who'd taken to
RETIRE (7)
147 Rock 1   23   There I was told:/Let the vicars retire. Men do not need the Church/In the place
447 CC   Claude   8   she knows you were wanting to retire,/As we had some discussion about
458 CC   Claude 27   that Eggerson's been meaning to retire .../{E} Under medical orders, Lady
473 CC   Lucasta 2   your secret garden; to which you can retire/And lock the gate behind you./{C} And
473 CC   Colby   33   /And also in the same sense that I retire to mine./But he doesn't feel alone there.
510 CC   Kaghan 29   living?/{K} In Kent. They wanted to retire to the country./So I found them a little
539 ES   Gomez   8   years/At least. Why did they let you retire?/{LC} If you want to know, I had had a
RETIRED (7)
236 Cat Morgan   2   sailed the 'igh seas —/But now I've retired as a com-mission-aire:/And that's how
448 CC   Claude 22   will only learn that you have finally retired/And that you have a young successor,/A
505 CC   Claude   3   /Colby's predecessor, who recently retired./Now he lives ... in the country. But he
525 ES   Charles 17   know that. Now that your father's retired/He's at home every day. And you're
531 ES   Monica   4   to revel in gloom!/You know you've retired in a blaze of glory —/You've read every
539 ES   Gomez   2   figurehead./But again, you've retired at sixty. Why at sixty?/{LC} Knowing as
539 ES   Ld Clav 4   as you do/You must have read that I retired at the insistence of my doctors./{G} Oh

RETIREMENT (1)
531 ES   Ld Clav   12   /Of the Press on any conspicuous retirement./My obituary, if I had died in
RETIRES (1)
473 CC   Colby   32   — of all people?/{C} Well, he retires to his garden — literally,/And also in the
RETIRING (2)
159 Rock 6   14   /Men! polish your teeth on rising and retiring;/Women! polish your fingernails:/You
559 ES   Michael   29   it gave you the opportunity/Of retiring from politics, not without dignity,/Being
RETRACT (1)
74 WL: Thund   404   /Which an age of prudence can never retract/By this, and this only, we have existed/
RETREAT (3)
107 Animula   26   lame,/Unable to fare forward or retreat,/Fearing the warm reality, the offered
222 Pekes Pols   19   /They did not advance, or exactly retreat,/But they glared at each other, and
406 CP   Reilly   13   /What was it?/{R} A kind of hotel. A retreat/For people who imagine that they need a
RETREATING (1)
107 Animula   7   boldly, sudden to take alarm,/Retreating to the corner of arm and knee,/Eager
RETREATS (1)
13 Prufrock   5   half-deserted streets,/The muttering retreats/Of restless nights in one-night cheap
RETROSPECTION (1)
265 MC   Priest3   5   moment/Weighs like another. Only in retrospection, selection,/We say, that was the
RETURN (42)
20 Portrait   88   are going abroad; and when do you return?/But that's a useless question./You
109 Marina   4   singing through the fog/What images return/O my daughter./Those who sharpen the
155 Rock 3   56   /And the Stranger will depart and return to the desert./O my soul, be prepared for
158 Rock 5   10   has builded during the day would return to his hearth at nightfall: to be blessed
197 FQ: Little   233   /We are born with the dead:/See, they return, and bring us with them./The moment of
203 Indians   7   secure, he has many memories/Which return at the hour of conversation,/(The warm
204 de la Mare   14   /Is pressed by unseen feet, and ghosts return/Gently at twilight, gently go at dawn,/
594 Grad 10   1   to quench the memory./We shall return; and it will be to find/A different school
239 MC Chorus   21   /But it would not be well if he should return./King rules or barons rule;/We have
243 MC Chorus   18   the sky, grey grey grey./O Thomas, return, Archbishop; return, return to France./
243 MC Chorus   18   grey./O Thomas, return, Archbishop; return, return to France./Return. Quickly.
243 MC Chorus   18   Thomas, return, Archbishop; return, return to France./Return. Quickly. Quietly.
243 MC Chorus   19   Archbishop; return, return to France./Return. Quickly. Quietly. Leave us to perish in
247 MC Tempt1   4   are in amity,/Clergy and laity may return to gaiety,/Mirth and sportfulness need
267 MC   m 25   *him, but the priests and attendants return and quietly interpose themselves.*]/{T}
275 MC Chorus   25   them they bleed./How how can I ever return, to the soft quiet seasons?/Night stay
287 FR   Amy   19   had gone as I intended./Harry's return does not make things easy for her/At the
293 FR   Amy   8   /And to make no changes before your return./Now it's for you to manage. I am an old
298 FR   Agatha   18   I shall stay with Violet./{Ag} I shall return/When Downing has left you. {}/[*Exit*]/{C}
306 FR   Harry   19   memories,/Earlier, forgotten, begin to return/Out of my childhood. I can't explain./
308 FR   Harry   20   I shall not find it./The instinct to return to the point of departure/And start again
310 FR   Harry   15   /Do not the ghosts of the drowned/Return to land in the spring?/Do the dead want
310 FR   Harry   16   in the spring?/Do the dead want to return?/{M} Pain is the opposite of joy/But joy
320 FR Warburt   19   her going:/She has only lived for your return to Wishwood,/For you to take command
324 FR Warburt   2   /You are only delaying me. I shall return at once./{A} Well, I suppose you are
335 FR   Agatha   39   pass twice through the same door/Or return to the door through which we did not
340 FR   Agatha   10   /Do you suppose that I wanted to return to Wishwood?/{A} The more rapacious,
342 FR   Agatha   33   a different meaning,/And he cannot return. That is his privilege./For those who live
398 CP   Edward   4   won't./{E} O God, O God, if I could return to yesterday/Before I thought that I had
406 CP   Reilly   15   a respite/From everyday life. They return refreshed;/And if they believe it to be a
414 CP   Reilly   30   /{R} A delusion is something we must return from./There are other states of mind,
419 CP   Reilly   29   is forced on them./Some of them return, in a physical sense;/No one disappears.
445 CC   Claude   7   to arrange their first meeting,/On her return from Switzerland./{E} Impossible, Sir
450 CC   Claude   24   and possibly to Paris./But when you return with Lady Elizabeth/I'll be ready waiting
454 CC   Eggers   2   Claude. But I'll speak to him/When I return from Northolt./{L} You're going to meet
515 CC Guzzard   5   which never reached you./On your return, you came at once to see me;/And I
518 CC Guzzard   30   /{SC} Excuse you? Yes./{MG} I shall return to Teddington. Colby,/Will you get me a
522 ES   dedic   8   /*To you I dedicate this book, to return as best I can*/*With words a little part of*
528 ES   Monica   26   is aware of:/It may be, he will never return from Badgley Court./But Selby wants
542 ES   Ld Clav   19   /So many years ago, I only gained in return/Your envy, spite and hatred. That is why
577 ES   Charles   8   ago/His father paid mine./{C} This return of past kindness/No doubt gives you
583 ES   Monica   15   hand,/Though he has gone too far to return to us./He is under the beech tree. It is
RETURNED (7)
104 Journ Magi   40   for us, like Death, our death./We returned to our places, these Kingdoms,/But no
223 Pekes Pols   60   like sheep./*And when the Police Dog returned to his beat,*/*There wasn't a single one*

242 MC	Priest2	31	for Thomas./{P2} Yet our lord is returned. Our lord has come back to his own
305 FR	Mary	1	it wasn't till I knew that Harry had returned/That I felt the strength to go. I know I
334 FR	Harry	26	had been imposed upon me;/And I returned to find another one made ready —/The
385 CP	Reilly	15	in comfort, mirth, security —/If they returned, would it not be embarrassing?/What
419 CP	Celia	16	/That's why I came to you. But they returned .../Well ... I mean ... to everyday life./

RETURNING (5)

20 Portrait		84	/The October night comes down; returning as before/Except for a slight sensation
161 Rock 7		25	halting, loitering, straying, delaying, returning, yet following no other way./But it
189 FQ: DrySal		180	or husbands/Setting forth, and not returning:/Figlia del tuo figlio,/Queen of
310 FR	Harry	12	/And the wail of the new full tide/Returning the ghosts of the dead/Those whom
417 CP	Reilly	25	gone as far as you/Have succeeded in returning. They may remember/The vision they

RETURNS (13)

19 Portrait		56	and youthful, after all.'/The voice returns like the insistent out-of-tune/Of a
243 MC	Priest2	3	/Our lord, our Archbishop returns. And when the Archbishop returns/Our
243 MC	Priest2	3	returns. And when the Archbishop returns/Our doubts are dispelled. Let us
247 MC	Thomas	18	life of one man, never/The same time returns. Sever/The cord, shed the scale. Only/
288 FR	Agatha	34	find another Harry./The man who returns will have to meet/The boy who left.
292 FR	Harry	13	/Why here? why here?/Many happy returns of the day, mother./Aunt Ivy, Aunt
347 FR	Ivy	19	delayed business in town many happy returns see you tomorrow many happy returns
347 FR	Ivy	19	see you tomorrow many happy returns hurrah love Arthur.'/I mean, after what
355 CP	m	27	I can drink at home. {}/[EDWARD *returns with a tray*]/{J} Edward, give me another
374 CP	m	2	it./{C} Are you alone? {}/[EDWARD *returns with* CELIA]/{E} Celia! Why have you
376 CP	m	7	*staying*/And I'm not going to hide. {}/[*Returns to kitchen. The bell rings again.*
383 CP	m	10	kitchen again. {}/[*Exit* EDWARD. *He returns with the spectacles and a bottle*]/{E} She
463 CC	Colby	27	person,/The person I used to be, returns to take possession:/And I am again the

REUNION (1)

283 FR		t	pray for us. {}/THE FAMILY REUNION/Persons/AMY, DOWAGER

REUNITED (1)

241 MC	Priest1	18	exile ended, is our Lord Archbishop/Reunited with the King? what reconciliation/Of

REVEAL (3)

408 CP	Reilly	29	my patients. You must not ask me to reveal it —/That is a matter of professional
448 CC	Claude	20	/{SC} When — or indeed whether — I reveal his identity/Depends on how she takes to
568 ES	Ld Clav	34	of equality. To one's child one can't reveal oneself/While she is a child. And by the

REVEALED (3)

194 FQ: Little		142	and been; the shame/Of motives late revealed, and the awareness/Of things ill done
289 FR	Agatha	2	come for everybody —/The hidden is revealed, and the spectres show themselves./{G}
510 CC	Claude	18	{SC} No, B. It was Mrs. Guzzard who revealed it./This is Mr. Barnabas Kaghan —/

REVEALING (2)

23 Preludes		26	/You dozed, and watched the night revealing/The thousand sordid images/Of which
311 FR	m	27	/{H} Come out! {}/[*The curtains part, revealing the Eumenides in the window*

REVEALS (1)

503 CC	Lucasta	4	have been. But a different way/That reveals itself in time. And perhaps — who

REVEL (1)

531 ES	Monica	3	/{M} Father, you simply want to revel in gloom!/You know you've retired in a

REVELATION (4)

301 FR	Chorus	16	guilty conspirators, waiting for some revelation/When the hidden shall be exposed,
414 CP	Celia	11	finding that it never existed —/But a revelation about my relationship/With
448 CC	Claude	10	from the East./{SC} And the Book of Revelation? And the Wisdom of Atlantis?/{E}
515 CC	Guzzard	29	back./Don't you understand that this revelation/Drives the knife deeper and twists it

REVELATIONS (1)

408 CP	Reilly	34	/But permit me to remark that my revelations/About each of you, to one another,/

REVENGE (1)

572 ES	Charles	29	it? That's why they are inspired/With revenge — it's their means of self-justification./

REVERBERATION (1)

72 WL: Thund		326	and the crying/Prison and palace and reverberation/Of thunder of spring over distant

REVERENCE (1)

111 Xmas Trees		18	awe on its appearance,/So that the reverence and the gaiety/May not be forgotten

REVERSAL (1)

315 FR	Harry	3	the occasional sickness:/Murder a reversal of sleep and waking./Murder was there.

REVERSE (2)

14 Prufrock		48	and revisions which a minute will reverse./For I have known them all already,
410 CP	Reilly	18	each other./Now, you have only to reverse the propositions/And put them together.

REVERSED (3)
279 MC Knight4 22 he/became Archbishop, he completely reversed his policy; he showed/himself to be
328 FR Charles 17   his car from the collision, Mr. Piper reversed/into a shop-window. When challenged,
384 CP   Reilly 20 in the lives of others/Which cannot be reversed. That is one consideration./And
REVERSING (1)
294 FR   Harry 30   desert, jostled by ghosts./It was only reversing the senseless direction/For a
REVERSION (1)
190 FQ: DrySal 235   content at the last/If our temporal reversion nourish/(Not too far from the
REVERT (1)
295 FR Charles 10   read it in the papers —/No need to revert to it. Remember, my boy,/I understand,
REVIEWING (1)
 42 Swee Erect   6   seas./Display me Aeolus above/Reviewing the insurgent gales/Which tangle
REVIEWS (1)
367 CP   Peter 17 novel,/Though it had some very good reviews./But it's more the cinema that interests
REVILED (1)
267 MC Knight1 34   /You sowed strife abroad, you reviled/The King to the King of France, to the
REVISIONS (2)
 14 Prufrock   33   /And for a hundred visions and revisions,/Before the taking of a toast and tea./
 14 Prufrock   48   there is time/For decisions and revisions which a minute will reverse./For I
REVISIT (2)
155 Rock 3   32   rabbit shall burrow and the thorn revisit,/The nettle shall flourish on the gravel
194 FQ: Little 126   /In streets I never thought I should revisit/When I left my body on a distant shore./
REVIVE (3)
 74 WL: Thund 416 /Only at nightfall, aethereal rumours/Revive for a moment a broken Coriolanus/DA/
196 FQ: Little 187   the spectre of a Rose./We cannot revive old factions/We cannot restore old
550 ES   Ld Clav 32 first opportunity,/Finding me here, to revive old memories/Which I should have
REVIVED (1)
187 FQ: DrySal   99 said before/That the past experience revived in the meaning/Is not the experience of
REVOIR (1)
565 ES   Carghil 23 /We'll leave you now, Richard. Au revoir, Monica./And Señor Gomez, I shall hold
REVOKE (1)
268 MC Thomas 23 /That is laid upon them, or mine to revoke./Let them go to the Pope. It was he who
REVOLT (1)
266 MC Knights 14 /{3K} You are the Archbishop in revolt against the King; in rebellion to the King
REVOLUTION (4)
147 Rock 1   3 dogs pursues his circuit./O perpetual revolution of configured stars,/O perpetual
253 MC Tempt4 34 of melting armies,/War, plague, and revolution,/New conspiracies, broken pacts;/To
349 FR   5m 13 *round the table, clockwise./At each revolution they blow out a few candles, so that*
435 CP   Peter 20 /I thought I had ideas to make a revolution/In the cinema, that no one could
REVOLVE (1)
 23 Preludes   53 your mouth, and laugh;/The worlds revolve like ancient women/Gathering fuel in
REVUE (3)
554 ES   Piggott 33 remember her/As Maisie Montjoy in revue./She was well-known at one time. I'm
562 ES   Carghil 26 of Maisie Montjoy/Topped the bill in revue. Now I'm Mrs. John Carghill./Richard!
563 ES   Carghil 29 Knew the name of Maisie Montjoy in revue./{G} If Maisie Montjoy was as beautiful
REWARD (2)
152 Rock 2   32 /But here upon earth you have the reward of the good and ill that was done by
531 ES Charles 18   time, a paragraph./{C} That's the reward/Of every public man./{LC} Say rather,
RHAPSODY (1)
 24 Rhapsody   t women/Gathering fuel in vacant lots./Rhapsody on a Windy Night/Twelve o'clock./
RHEUMATISM (1)
321 FR   Winch 35   /I don't find port agrees with the rheumatism./{W} For God's sake, Winchell, tell
RHINOCEROS (1)
506 CC Lady E   4   .../{LE} He was run over. By a rhinoceros/In Tanganyika./{SC} That's not
RHYME (3)
 94 Ash-Wed 4   18   /With a new verse the ancient rhyme. Redeem/The time. Redeem/The unread
220 Old Deut   3 was famous in proverb and famous in rhyme/A long while before Queen Victoria's
231 Bust Jones   37 a routine, so he'd say./Or, to put it in rhyme: 'I shall last out my time'/Is the word for
RHYTHM (8)
167 Rock 10   36   Invisible, we glorify Thee!/In our rhythm of earthly life we tire of light. We are
167 Rock 10   39 are glad to sleep,/Controlled by the rhythm of blood and the day and the night and
178 FQ: ECoker 41 the corn. Keeping time,/Keeping the rhythm in their dancing/As in their living in the
184 FQ: DrySal 11 waiting, watching and waiting./His rhythm was present in the nursery bedroom,/In
188 FQ: DrySal 138 from grief into relief,/To the sleepy rhythm of a hundred hours./Fare forward,
206 To my Wife   3 my senses in our wakingtime/And the rhythm that governs the repose of our

605 Narcissus		12	was stifled and soothed by his own rhythm./By the river/His eyes were aware of the
522 ES	dedic	3	*my senses in our wakingtime/And the rhythm that governs the repose of our*

RIALTO (1)

41 Burb Blei		21	candle end of time/Declines. On the Rialto once./The rats are underneath the piles./

RIBBON (1)

152 Rock 2		44	/And now you live dispersed on ribbon roads,/And no man knows or cares who

RIBS (1)

53 Whispers		31	/But our lot crawls between dry ribs/To keep our metaphysics warm./Mr. Eliot's

RICE (2)

230 Bust Jones		28	lunched at the *Tomb*/On cabbage, rice pudding and mutton./So, much in this way,
368 CP	Alex	26	that in the East./With a handful of rice and a little dried fish/I can make half a

RICH (7)

14 Prufrock		43	firmly to the chin,/My necktie rich and modest, but asserted by a simple pin —
64 WL: Chess		85	to meet it,/From satin cases poured in rich profusion./In vials of ivory and coloured
587 Fable		9	friars merry./They were possessors of rich lands and wide,/An orchard, and a
314 FR	Ivy	31	term./{I} You must have had a very rich experience, Doctor,/In forty years./{W}
561 ES	Michael	18	that I've had./Your father was rich, but was no one in particular,/So you'd
569 ES	Ld Clav	29	and your company./He's a very rich man. And she's a rich woman./If people
569 ES	Ld Clav	29	/He's a very rich man. And she's a rich woman./If people merely blackmail you to

RICHARD (33)

279 MC	Knight1	9	are still unconvinced, I think that/Richard Brito, coming as he does of a family
279 MC	Knight1	10	will be able to convince them. Richard Brito./{K4} The speakers who have
533 ES	Gomez	4	your wife's name/And became Mr. Richard Claverton-Ferry;/And finally, Lord
549 ES	Carghil	2	could have paid *me* that compliment, Richard./{LC} What!/{MC} Don't you know me
549 ES	Carghil	33	/You do remember now, don't you, Richard?/{LC} Not the conversation you have
549 ES	Carghil	36	Time has wrought sad changes in me, Richard./I was very lovely once. So *you*
549 ES	Carghil	39	so too. But as you remember,/Please, Richard, just repeat my name — just once:/The
550 ES	Carghil	3	was Maisie Batterson./{MC} Oh, Richard, you're only saying that to tease me./
550 ES	Carghil	26	provided for?/{MC} Well, Richard, my doctor could hardly have sent me
550 ES	Carghil	34	buried./{MC} There you're wrong, Richard. Effie always said —/What a clever girl
552 ES	Carghil	17	'both of us'/Was an afterthought, Richard. A lucky escape/You thought, for you.
552 ES	Carghil	27	I believe you're still the same silly Richard/You always were. You wanted to pose/
553 ES	Carghil	5	followed your progress year by year, Richard./And although it's true that our
553 ES	Carghil	9	me one or two insights into you./No, Richard, don't imagine that I'm still in love
562 ES	Carghil	12	*with despatch-case]*/{MC} Richard! I didn't think you'd still be here./I
562 ES	Carghil	21	was your age. He's the picture of you, Richard,/As you were once. You're not to
562 ES	Carghil	27	revue. Now I'm Mrs. John Carghill./Richard! It's astonishing about your children:/
562 ES	Carghil	35	He's inherited all of your charm, Richard./There's no denying it. But who's this
562 ES	Carghil	38	He's waving to us./Do you know him, Richard?/{LC} It's a man I used to know./{MC}
563 ES	Carghil	17	Oh, you've seen each other lately?/Richard, I think that you might introduce us./
564 ES	Carghil	22	a friend of Richard's at Oxford/And Richard and I became great friends/Not long
564 ES	Carghil	23	/Not long afterwards, didn't we, Richard?/{G} I expect that was after I had left
564 ES	Carghil	31	you/And make you tell me all about Richard/In his Oxford days./{G} On one
565 ES	Carghil	23	advise you./We'll leave you now, Richard. Au revoir, Monica./And Señor
571 ES	Ld Clav	3	Batterson,/And Dick Ferry too, and Richard Ferry —/These are my ghosts. They
573 ES	Carghil	23	been hunting high and low for you, Richard!/I've some very exciting news for you!/
574 ES	Carghil	11	/You've cruelly misunderstood him, Richard./How he must have suffered! So I put
575 ES	Carghil	33	they found puzzling./{MC} Oh, Richard!/Have you explained to them our
577 ES	Carghil	26	buy you out many times over./{MC} Richard, I think it's time *I* joined the
577 ES	Carghil	37	has come knocking at the door./Richard, you must not bar his way. That would
579 ES	Carghil	15	part, I mean. Are you listening to me, Richard?/You look very *distrait*. You ought to
579 ES	Carghil	32	parent isn't always the right person, Richard,/To solve a son's problems. Sometimes
580 ES	Carghil	15	this seems awfully sudden to you, Richard;/It isn't so sudden. We talked it all

RICHARD'S (1)

564 ES	Carghil	21	met before./You were a friend of Richard's at Oxford/And Richard and I became

RICHLY (1)

249 MC	Tempt2	1	/King commands. Chancellor richly rules./This is a sentence not taught in the

RICHMOND (2)

70 WL: Fire S		293	and dusty trees./Highbury bore me. Richmond and Kew/Undid me. By Richmond I
70 WL: Fire S		294	Richmond and Kew/Undid me. By Richmond I raised my knees/Supine on the

RICHNESS (1)

255 MC	Tempt4	11	that is not poverty/Compared with richness of heavenly grandeur?/Seek the way of

RID (10)

296 FR	Charles	26	it is simply that the wish to get rid of her/Makes him believe he did. He cannot
297 FR	Charles	18	there's somebody he wants to get rid of./{G} Even so, we don't want Downing to

306 FR	Harry	16	memory,/I think. It seems I shall get rid of nothing./Of none of the shadows that I
332 FR	Agatha	37	yet. I found him thinking/How to get rid of your mother. What simple plots!/He was
334 FR	Harry	3	getting what one wanted/Or in getting rid of what can't be got rid of/But in a different
334 FR	Harry	3	/Or in getting rid of what can't be got rid of/But in a different vision. This is like an
416 CP	Celia	3	from, or of anything in me/I could get rid of — but of emptiness, of failure/Towards
532 ES	Monica	20	now, Father./If you haven't got rid of him in twenty minutes/I'll send Lambert
538 ES	Gomez	9	I know the reason:/You wanted to get rid of me. I shall tell you why presently./Now
560 ES	Michael	6	/{Mi} And to help my father to be rid of *me.*/You simply don't know how very

RIDDEN (1)

265 MC	Priest1	11	to us./You are welcome. Have you ridden far?/{K1} Not far to-day, but matters

RIDDLE (1)

189 FQ: DrySal	194	omens/By sortilege, or tea leaves, riddle the inevitable/With playing cards, fiddle

RIDE (2)

153 Rock 2	51	have his motor cycle,/And daughters ride away on casual pillions./Much to cast
292 FR	Gerald	27	and young./{G} We must have a ride tomorrow./You'll find you know the

RIDES (1)

51 Restaurant	21	ton vautour!/Va t'en te décrotter les rides du visage;/Tiens, ma fourchette,

RIDICULOUS (10)

16 Prufrock	118	a bit obtuse;/At times, indeed, almost ridiculous —/Almost, at times, the Fool./I grow
176 FQ: BurntN	177	/Quick now, here, now, always —/Ridiculous the waste sad time/Stretching before
269 MC	Chorus	30	/Scaly wings slanting over, huge and ridiculous. I have tasted/The savour of putrid
291 FR	Chorus	6	unread part in some monstrous farce, ridiculous in some nightmare pantomime./{A}
344 FR	Harry	37	seen. Oh why should you make it so ridiculous/Just now? I only want, please,/As
363 CP	Edward	22	don't you see that it makes me ridiculous?/{UG} It will do you no harm to find
363 CP	Reilly	23	will do you no harm to find yourself ridiculous./Resign yourself to be the fool you
380 CP	Celia	22	to talk to me about it./{C} But this is ridiculous! I never gave Peter/Any reason to
414 CP	Celia	35	/{C} That's stranger still./It sounds ridiculous — but the only word for it/That I can
568 ES	Ld Clav	27	/But also situations which are simply ridiculous,/When he has played the fool (as who

RIDING (2)

17 Prufrock	126	they will sing to me./I have seen them riding seaward on the waves/Combing the white
30 Cous Nancy	5	—/The barren New England hills —/Riding to hounds/Over the cow-pasture./Miss

RIEN (1)

51 Restaurant	1	Restaurant/Le garçon délabré qui n'a rien à faire/Que de se gratter les doigts et se

RIFLE (1)

141 Rannoch	2	here the patient stag/Breeds for the rifle. Between the soft moor/And the soft sky,

RIFLED (2)

226 Macavity	23	the larder's looted, or the jewel-case is rifled,/Or when the milk is missing, or another
254 MC	Tempt4	31	lasts, but the wheel turns,/The nest is rifled, and the bird mourns;/That the shrine

RIFLES (1)

127 Cor1 March	13	Can you see? Tell us. It is/5,800,000 rifles and carbines,/102,000 machine guns,/

RIGGING (3)

109 Marina	25	I have forgotten/And remember./The rigging weak and the canvas rotten/Between one
185 FQ: DrySal	30	Often together heard: the whine in the rigging,/The menace and caress of wave that
188 FQ: DrySal	148	is before us'./At nightfall, in the rigging and the aerial,/Is a voice descanting

RIGHT (113)

20 Portrait	83	people have desired./Are these ideas right or wrong?/The October night comes down;
21 Portrait	124	of dying —/And should I have the right to smile?/Preludes/The winter evening
66 WL: Chess	161	/The chemist said it would be all right, but I've never been the same./You *are* a
96 Ash-Wed 5	17	day time and in the night time/The right time and the right place are not here/No
96 Ash-Wed 5	17	the night time/The right time and the right place are not here/No place of grace for
116 SP	Dusty	2	Sam can make you laugh:/Sam's all right/{Do} But Pereira won't do./We can't have
116 SP	Dusty	31	up on Monday/She hopes to be all right on Monday/I say do you mind if I ring off
116 SP	Dusty	35	I'm giving her mustard and water/All right, Monday you'll phone through./Yes I'll
118 SP	Wauch	28	put the car round the corner/We'll be right up/{Du} All right, come up./(*to* DORIS):
118 SP	Dusty	29	the corner/We'll be right up/{Du} All right, come up./(*to* DORIS): Cards are queer./
121 SA Sweeney	17	soft little, tender little,/Juicy little, right little, missionary stew./You see this egg/
128 Cor1 March	45	And they rang a bell/And he said right out loud, *crumpets.*)/Don't throw away
151 Rock 2	12	forgotten the cornerstone?/Talking of right relations of men, but not of relations of
166 Rock 10	8	in hunger and moving his head to right and to left prepares for his hour to devour.
190 FQ: DrySal	228	by dmonic, chthonic/Powers. And right action is freedom/From past and future
197 FQ: Little	219	every phrase/And sentence that is right (where every word is at home,/Taking its
214 RTTugger	29	for himself;/So you'll catch him in it right up to the ears,/If you put it away on the
217 Jellicles	35	resting and saving themselves to be right/For the Jellicle Moon and the Jellicle Ball.
225 Mr Mistoff	55	Cat/Produced *seven kittens* right out of a hat!/And we all said: OH!/Well I
241 MC	Priest1	28	the spiritual rule,/The assurance of right, and the love of the people?/{M} You are

241 MC	Mess	29	the love of the people?/{M} You are	right	to express a certain incredulity./He comes
258 MC	Thomas	6	is the greatest treason:/To do the	right	deed for the wrong reason./The natural
258 MC	Thomas	30	the cause serve them,/Still doing	right	: and striving with political men/May make
271 MC	Priests	28	Don't stop here talking. It is not	right	./What shall become of us, my Lord, if you
287 FR	Amy	20	/At the moment: but life may still go	right	./Meanwhile, let us drop the subject. The
296 FR	Amy	30	certainly not, Charles, you are not the	right	person./I prefer to believe that a few days
300 FR	Downing	35	rail./Her Ladyship must have been all	right	then,/Mustn't she, Sir? or else he'd have
301 FR	Chorus	29	newspapers/So long as we are in the	right	column./We know about the railway
305 FR	Agatha	8	shown courage/And would have been	right	. Now, the courage is only the moment/
309 FR	Harry	38	pass unnoticed./Perhaps you are	right	, though I do not know/How you should
311 FR	Mary	24	depend on me./Harry! Harry! It's all	right	, I tell you./If you will depend on me, it will
311 FR	Mary	25	If you will depend on me, it will be all	right	./{H} Come out! {}/[The curtains part,
318 FR	Warburt	20	I want to tell you./You may be quite	right	, but what we are concerned with/Now, is
323 FR	Warburt	3	should have a look at him./{W} Quite	right	, quite right. I'll go and have a look at him.
323 FR	Warburt	3	a look at him./{W} Quite right, quite	right	. I'll go and have a look at him./We must
324 FR	Amy	3	at once./{A} Well, I suppose you are	right	. But can I trust you?/{W} You have
325 FR	Ivy	15	understands that./{I} You are quite	right	, Gerald, the one thing that matters/Is not
330 FR	Harry	10	living in gentle motion/Of horses, and	right	visits to the right neighbours/At the right
330 FR	Harry	10	/Of horses, and right visits to the	right	neighbours/At the right times; and be an
330 FR	Harry	11	visits to the right neighbours/At the	right	times; and be an excellent landlord./{Ag}
343 FR	Mary	12	to you this evening?/I knew that I was	right	: you made me wait for this —/Only for
345 FR	Charles	38	feel safe. As if the earth should open/	Right	to the centre, as I was about to cross Pall
349 FR	All	12	to the moment: we must do the	right	thing. {}/[Exeunt]/[Enter, from one door,
374 CP	Celia	11	I felt I must see you./Tell me it's all	right	, and then I'll go./{E} But how can you say
378 CP	Celia	29	another man?/I shall soon put that	right	, Edward,/When you are free./{E} No, it is
379 CP	Celia	5	/Will you assure me that everything is	right	,/That you do not mean to have Lavinia
379 CP	Celia	8	freedom,/And that everything is all	right	between us?/That's all that matters. Truly,
379 CP	Celia	10	that matters. Truly, Edward,/If that is	right	, everything else will be,/I promise you./{E}
383 CP	Edward	10	spectacles and a bottle]/{E} She was	right	for once./{C} She is always right./But why
383 CP	Celia	11	was right for once./{C} She is always	right	./But why bring an empty champagne
389 CP	Celia	20	that either./{C} And I believe he is	right	to go./{L} Oh, so you advised him?/{P} She
391 CP	Julia	27	herself:/That's the only way./{J} How	right	you are!/Well, my dears, I shall see you
399 CP	Reilly	23	they have left the house..../{R} Quite	right	, Miss Barraway. That's all for the
400 CP	Alex	14	sort of person/Who would know the	right	doctor, as well as the right shops./Besides,
400 CP	Alex	14	know the right doctor, as well as the	right	shops./Besides, he was ready to consult
406 CP	Reilly	30	/But I'm not going there./{R} You are	right	, Mr. Chamberlayne./You are no case for
413 CP	Celia	33	wrong with me, that could be put	right	./I'd do anything you told me, to get back
415 CP	Celia	31	'kink'?/{C} But everything seemed so	right	, at the time!/I've been thinking about it,
416 CP	Celia	16	the giving and the taking/Seemed so	right	: not in terms of calculation/Of what was
416 CP	Celia	19	I did then, even now it would seem	right	./And then I found we were only strangers/
426 CP	Lavinia	1	How's that now?/{L} No, I meant the	right	./That will do. I'm too tired to bother./{E}
435 CP	Peter	37	Lavinia;/And I know that you're	right	./{L} And perhaps what I've been saying/
436 CP	Edward	1	talking about myself./{E} Lavinia is	right	. This is where you start from./If you find
438 CP	Edward	15	than we should?/{E} But if this was	right	— if this was right for Celia —/There must
438 CP	Edward	15	/{E} But if this was right — if this was	right	for Celia —/There must be something else
439 CP	Reilly	37	at any moment./{R} Julia, you are	right	. It is also right/That the Chamberlaynes
439 CP	Reilly	37	/{R} Julia, you are right. It is also	right	/That the Chamberlaynes should now be
452 CC	Lucasta	13	/{L} Yes, again! And serve them	right	!/{E} You have been, I presume,
455 CC	Eggers	10	/No, I don't think that's quite the	right	term./She's no money of her own, as you
457 CC	Eggers	10	/{E} You'll come to find that I'm	right	, I assure you. {}/[Enter SIR CLAUDE]/
462 CC	Claude	20	can do is to guide her delusions/In the	right	direction./{C} It doesn't seem quite honest.
465 CC	Claude	2	it was too late,/I knew that he was	right	. And all my life/I have been atoning. To a
465 CC	Claude	4	a dead father,/Who had always been	right	. I never understood him./I was too young.
465 CC	Colby	8	to think/That your father had been	right	./{SC} Because I came to see/That I should
469 CC	Colby	12	/{C} No, I'm sure you'll prefer the	right	things, when you hear them./I've given
469 CC	Colby	15	you didn't like them. You liked the	right	ones./{L} Colby, I didn't know you were
469 CC	Lucasta	17	artful!/So the things I liked were the	right	ones to like?/Still, I'm awfully ignorant.
472 CC	Lucasta	24	I don't know whether you were	right	./For all I can tell, you may have been
473 CC	Colby	21	one else could smell./{C} You may be	right	, up to a point./And yet, you know, it's not
479 CC	Kaghan	25	Be firm with her, Colby;/Assert your	right	to a little privacy./Now's the moment for
480 CC	Kaghan	2	I've put my shirt ... no, not quite the	right	expression —/Lucasta's the most exciting
481 CC	Lady E	21	tell/Whether a scheme of decoration/Is	right	, until the place has been lived in/By the
481 CC	Lady E	37	even eat a herbal salad./{LE} That's	right	. Just mention my name, Mr. Kaghan,/And
487 CC	Lady E	31	have been the instruments./I must be	right	. Claude, tell me I am right./{SC} But
487 CC	Lady E	31	/I must be right. Claude, tell me I am	right	./{SC} But Elizabeth, what has led you to

488 CC	Claude	14	you heard would have seemed the right one./{LE} Oh Claude, how can you be so
492 CC	Colby	1	I ever want to marry./You may be right. I can't take account of that./But now I
493 CC	Claude	28	... investigation. But perhaps you're right./{LE} Claude, I've been thinking things
497 CC	Lady E	22	it./{LE} Claude, that's not quite right. Let me explain./I am convinced that Sir
501 CC	Claude	1	/I'm sure that you have made the right decision./{L} But the reasons why you
501 CC	Claude	14	ashamed of it./{SC} Perhaps you are right. I'm not sure of anything./Perhaps, as you
503 CC	Claude	25	Better wait till afterwards./{SC} Quite right, Eggerson./{L} Good-bye, Colby./{C} Why
510 CC	Eggers	10	inherent probability —/If that's the right expression./{SC} I believe, Elizabeth,/That
511 CC	Kaghan	32	—/Barney Kaghan! Kaghan's all right./But Barney Kaghan — it sounds rather
511 CC	Kaghan	34	rather flashy:/It wouldn't make the right impression in the City./{L} When you're
512 CC	Kaghan	31	And ... yes, of course,/If I can make it right with my parents./I'm fond of them, you
513 CC	Colby	14	give a strange answer./Sir Claude is right: I wished to know the truth./What it is,
525 ES	Charles	34	I'm in love with you. Well, you're right./But I've something else to say that I
526 ES	Monica	2	yourself as well./{M} You're right. I am. Because *I am* in love with you./{C}
526 ES	Charles	3	*I am* in love with you./{C} So I was right! The moment I'd said it/I was badly
526 ES	Monica	38	I've said to you/Has given you the right to criticise my father./In the first place,
529 ES	Ld Clav	33	a shelf together;/I could look in the right book, and find out what I was doing/
533 ES	Gomez	30	suggestion./I've always kept on the right side of the law —/And seen that the law
533 ES	Gomez	31	—/And seen that the law turned its right side to *me*./Sometimes I've had to pay
533 ES	Gomez	34	/And a little money laid out in the right manner/In the right places, pays many
533 ES	Gomez	35	laid out in the right manner/In the right places, pays many times over./I assure you
552 ES	Carghil	37	always be some sort of part for you/Right to the end. You'll still be playing a part/
559 ES	Michael	20	to my own ideas of good and bad,/Of right and wrong. I want to go far away/To some
562 ES	Carghil	17	must be your brother, Michael./I'm right, aren't I?/{Mi} Yes, you're right./But .../
562 ES	Michael	18	/I'm right, aren't I?/{Mi} Yes, you're right./But .../{MC} How did I know? Because
579 ES	Carghil	32	Dick./{MC} A parent isn't always the right person, Richard,/To solve a son's
580 ES	Ld Clav	37	for Michael;/Nevertheless, you are right to hope for something better./And when
581 ES	Charles	12	leave Badgley Court./{C} Monica is right. You should leave./{LC} This may surprise

RIGHTEOUS (1)

279 MC	Knight4	34	from us long enough to allow our righteous/anger to cool. That was just what he

RIGHTMINDED (1)

324 FR	Harry	36	voices at once./I have all of the rightminded feeling about John/That you

RIGHTS (1)

278 MC	Knight2	30	to adopt, in order to set matters to rights, that you/take issue. No one regrets the

RILEY (6)

365 CP	Reilly	6	*and water,/And me bein' the One Eyed Riley,/Who came in but the landlord's daughter/*
365 CP	Reilly	12	*/What's the matter with One Eyed Riley?* {}/[*Exit*]/{J} Edward, who *is* that dreadful
365 CP	Julia	26	/Did I hear him say his name was Riley?/{E} I don't know his name./{J} You don't
378 CP	Edward	33	suggested to me/By the man I call Riley — though his name is not Riley;/It was
378 CP	Edward	33	I call Riley — though his name is not Riley;/It was just a name in a song he sang .../
378 CP	Celia	35	sang you a song about a man named Riley!/Really, Edward, I think you are mad —/I

RING (23)

26 Rhapsody		74	the key,/The little lamp spreads a ring on the stair./Mount./The bed is open; the
28 Boston ET		6	*Transcript,*/I mount the steps and ring the bell, turning/Wearily, as one would
62 WL: Burial		56	crowds of people, walking round in a ring./Thank you. If you see dear Mrs. Equitone,
116 SP	Dusty	30	having a doctor/She says will you ring up on Monday/She hopes to be all right on
116 SP	Dusty	32	on Monday/I say do you mind if I ring off now/She's got her feet in mustard and
196 FQ: Little		184	men more than the dying?/It is not to ring the bell backward/Nor is it an incantation/
213 Growltiger		48	she was not drowned —/But a serried ring of flashing steel Growltiger did surround./
223 Pekes Pols		49	so much afraid/That they started to ring up the Fire Brigade./When suddenly, up
266 MC	Knights	18	you had the power, the seal and the ring./This is the man who was the tradesman's
266 MC	Thomas	20	/Both before and after I received the ring/I have been a loyal subject to the King./
285 FR	Amy	1	*draw the curtains*]/{A} Not yet! I will ring for you. It is still quite light./I have nothing
291 FR	Amy	18	the curtains drawn you should let me ring for Denman./{H} How can you sit in this
296 FR	Gerald	34	in Violet's suggestion./Why not ring up Warburton, and ask him to join us?/
297 FR	Amy	9	the impossible./{A} Very well./I will ring up the doctor myself. {}/[*Exit*]/{C}
336 FR	Harry	5	time that I have been free/From the ring of ghosts with joined hands, from the
371 CP	Edward	24	now .../Yes, there is ... Well then, I'll ring you/As soon as I can. {}/[*To* PETER]/{E}
399 CP	Nurse	17	arrives. I leave her there/Until you ring three times./{R} And the third patient?/{N}
399 CP	Nurse	21	that she has arrived./Then, when you ring, I show the others out;/And only after they
424 CP	Lavinia	12	worrying./{L} Oh no. I did in fact ring up your chambers,/And your clerk told me
453 CC	Lucasta	11	—/Cooking a sausage on a gas ring .../{E} You mustn't believe a word she says.
454 CC	Lucasta	15	for me. Another time, Colby./I'll ring you up, and let you take me out to lunch. {}
461 CC	Eggers	8	me./In fact, Mrs. E. said: 'I wish he'd ring us up!'/I'm sure he has a very cultivated
545 ES	Piggott	32	is to make your wants known./Just ring through to my office. If I'm not there/My

RINGED (1)
73 WL: Thund 370   plains, stumbling in cracked earth/Ringed by the flat horizon only/What is the city
RINGING (1)
327 FR   Ivy   27   the evening paper./That was Arthur, ringing up from London:/The connection was
RINGS (19)
18 Portrait   5   candles in the darkened room,/Four rings of light upon the ceiling overhead,/An
270 MC Chorus   10   while the ground heaved. I have seen/Rings of light coiling downwards, descending/
297 FR   m 25   the same, there's a question or two {}/[*Rings the bell*]/{C} That I'd like to ask Downing.
359 CP   m 22   minded anyone else, {}/[*The doorbell rings. EDWARD goes to the door, saying:*]/{E}
364 CP   m 29   be here to meet her. {}/[*The doorbell rings*]/{E} I must answer the door. {}/[EDWARD
371 CP   m 22   what is the reality ... {}/[*The telephone rings*]/{E} Excuse me a moment. {}/[*Into*
374 CP   3m   1   *alone, playing/Patience. The doorbell rings, and he goes to answer it.*]/{C} Are you
375 CP   m 11   what has happened? {}/[*The doorbell rings*]/{E} Damn the telephone. I suppose I must
376 CP   m   2   *He moves/a card. The doorbell rings repeatedly. Re-enter CELIA, in an apron.*]/
376 CP   m   7   hide. {}/[*Returns to kitchen. The bell rings again. EDWARD goes to front door, and is*
382 CP   m 37   two things. First ... {}/[*The telephone rings*]/{E} Damn the telephone./I suppose I had
386 CP   m 14   *moves about restlessly. The bell rings, and he goes to the front door.*]/{E} Celia!
387 CP   m 11   /Can't you see that ... {}/[*The doorbell rings*]/{E} There's Lavinia. {}/[*Goes to front*
389 CP   m 37   Oh, not as in the past! {}/[*The doorbell rings, and EDWARD goes to answer it*]/{C} Oh,
390 CP   m 17   Tell us/I'm thrilled ... {}/[*The doorbell rings. EDWARD goes to answer it. Enter*
400 CP   m 30   he wrote from. {}/[*The house-telephone rings*]/{R} Hello! Yes, show him up./{A} You will
404 CP   1m   3   be alone there? {}/[*House-telephone rings*]/[*into telephone*]/{R} Yes. {}/[*To*
411 CP   2m 36   *and lies down. The house-telephone rings. He/gets up and answers it.*]/{R} Yes? ...
426 CP   m 24   do need to rest now. {}/[*The doorbell rings*]/{L} Oh, bother!/Now who would come so
RINSING (1)
353 CP   Peter 15   the butler found her in the pantry, rinsing her mouth out with champagne./I like
RIOT (1)
232 Skimble   27   he doesn't approve/Of hilarity and riot, so the folk are very quiet/When Skimble is
RIPE (2)
28 Boston ET   2   /Sway in the wind like a field of ripe corn./When evening quickens faintly in the
152 Rock 2   25   past, you eat the fruit, either rotten or ripe./And the Church must be forever building,
RIPPLE (1)
32 Hysteria   5   caverns of her throat, bruised by/the ripple of unseen muscles. An elderly waiter with
RIPPLED (1)
70 WL: Fire S   285   shell/Red and gold/The brisk swell/Rippled both shores/Southwest wind/Carried
RIRE (1)
51 Restaurant   13   /'Je la chatouillais, pour la faire rire./J'éprouvais un instant de puissance et de
RISE (10)
140 Usk   8   the roads dip and where the roads rise/Seek only there/Where the grey light meets
177 FQ: ECoker   2   is my end. In succession/Houses rise and fall, crumble, are extended,/Are
216 Jellicles   12   /And wait for the Jellicle Moon to rise./Jellicle Cats develop slowly,/Jellicle Cats
594 Grad 9   2   the soul/Incense of altar-smoke shall rise to thee/From spotless fanes of lucid purity,/
598 Circe   8   shall not come here again./Panthers rise from their lairs/In the forest which thickens
248 MC Tempt2   21   Chancellorship./See how the late ones rise! You, master of policy/Whom all
252 MC Tempt3   8   past is time forgotten./We expect the rise of a new constellation./{T} And if the
269 MC Thomas   20   of Rome./But if you kill me, I shall rise from my tomb/To submit my cause before
310 FR   Mary   27   spirit/Compelled to be reborn/To rise toward the violent sun/Wet wings into the
453 CC Lucasta   21   Mrs. Eggerson. He never fails to rise./B.! What have you told Colby about me?/
RISES (7)
15 Prufrock   71   streets/And watched the smoke that rises from the pipes/Of lonely men in
42 Swee Erect   12   /Gesture of orang-outang/Rises from the sheets in steam./This withered
176 FQ: BurntN 174   /Even while the dust moves/There rises the hidden laughter/Of children in the
180 FQ: ECoker 120   stations/And the conversation rises and slowly fades into silence/And you see
290 FR Chorus 38   actors in a dream when the curtain rises, to find themselves dressed for a different
298 FR   m 12   /And pursue his own methods. {}/[*Rises*]/{V} I do not agree./I think there should be
469 CC   4m   1   *piece of music are/heard as the curtain rises.*]/{L} *I* think you play awfully well, Colby —/
RISING (10)
61 WL: Burial   29   you/Or your shadow at evening rising to meet you;/I will show you fear in a
107 Animula   5   the legs of tables and of chairs,/Rising or falling, grasping at kisses and toys,/
129 Cor2 State   6   and 2nd class),/and the Order of the Rising Sun./Cry cry what shall I cry?/The first
129 Cor2 State   13   /At a salary of one pound ten a week rising by annual increments of five shillings/To
129 Cor2 State   48   flare of the firefly or lightning bug,/'Rising and falling, crowned with dust', the small
159 Rock 6   14   /Men! polish your teeth on rising and retiring;/Women! polish your
178 FQ: ECoker   46   and woman/And that of beasts. Feet rising and falling./Eating and drinking. Dung
481 CC   m 13   a change, let's talk about Lucasta. {}/[*rising*]./{L} If you want to discuss *me* ... {}/[*A*

483 CC		m 23	/{C} It's the sort of room I wanted. {}/[*rising*]./{LE} And I see a photograph in a silver
492 CC		m 12	you ought to get Eggerson as well. {}/[*rising*]./{SC} Oh, of course, Eggerson! He knows

RISK (4)

124 SA	Doris	9	conversation/A woman runs a terrible risk./{Sn} Let Mr. Sweeney continue his story./I
124 SA	Doris	24	end./{Do} A woman runs a terrible risk./{Sn} Let Mr. Sweeney continue his story./
420 CP	Reilly	33	reflecting vanity./I have taken a great risk./{J} We must always take risks./That is our
421 CP	Julia	2	/{J} Very well then. We must take the risk./All we could do was to give them the

RISKING (1)

179 FQ: ECoker		94	menaced by monsters, fancy lights,/Risking enchantment. Do not let me hear/Of

RISKS (1)

420 CP	Julia	34	a great risk./{J} We must always take risks./That is our destiny. Since you question

RISKY (1)

480 CC	Colby	14	you never get involved in anything risky./You like to pretend to other people/That

RITES (2)

160 Rock 7		15	denial of this world, affirmation of rites with forgotten meanings/In the restless
280 MC	Priest3	26	heathen Saracen,/To share his filthy rites, and try to snatch/Forgetfulness in his

RITUALS (1)

496 CC	Lady E	9	/I don't doubt, from the dervish rituals./But it doesn't matter what Mrs.

RIVER (27)

56 Swee Night		6	moon/Slide westward toward the River Plate,/Death and the Raven drift above/
67 WL: Fire S		177	run softly, till I end my song./The river bears no empty bottles, sandwich papers,/
69 WL: Fire S		266	of Ionian white and gold./The river sweats/Oil and tar/The barges drift/With
85 Hollow Men		60	/Gathered on this beach of the tumid river/Sightless, unless/The eyes reappear/As the
99 Ash-Wed 6		33	rocks/Sister, mother/And spirit of the river, spirit of the sea,/Suffer me not to be
134 Wind		7	/When the surface of the blackened river/Is a face that sweats with tears?/I saw
134 Wind		9	with tears?/I saw across the blackened river/The camp fire shake with alien spears./
134 Wind		11	spears./Here, across death's other river/The Tartar horsemen shake their spears./
139 Virginia		1	up into the apple-tree./Virginia/Red river, red river,/Slow flow heat is silence/No will
139 Virginia		1	the apple-tree./Virginia/Red river, red river,/Slow flow heat is silence/No will is still as
139 Virginia		3	flow heat is silence/No will is still as a river/Still. Will heat move/Only through the
139 Virginia		13	came with me/And go with me:/Red river, river, river./Usk/Do not suddenly break
139 Virginia		13	with me/And go with me:/Red river, river, river./Usk/Do not suddenly break the
139 Virginia		13	me/And go with me:/Red river, river, river./Usk/Do not suddenly break the branch,
147 Rock 1		20	to the timekept City,/Where the River flows, with foreign flotations./There I was
150 Rock 1		109	/*Chant of* WORKMEN *again.*/*The river flows, the seasons turn/The sparrow and*
184 FQ: DrySal		1	much about gods; but I think that the river/Is a strong brown god — sullen, untamed
184 FQ: DrySal		15	circle in the winter gaslight./The river is within us, the sea is all about us;/The sea
187 FQ: DrySal		118	is time the preserver,/Like the river with its cargo of dead negroes, cows and
197 FQ: Little		248	/At the source of the longest river/The voice of the hidden waterfall/And the
605 Narcissus		13	soothed by his own rhythm./By the river/His eyes were aware of the pointed corners
246 MC Tempt1		31	won't forget that evening on the river/When the King, and you and I were all
307 FR	Harry	2	the wilderness/{H} Down near the river. That was the stockade/From which we
307 FR	Harry	14	as I could, and slipped down to the river/To find the old hiding place. The
307 FR	Harry	19	be a hollow tree in a wood by the river./{M} But when I was a child I took
549 ES	Carghil	7	and me./That day we spent on the river — I've never forgotten it —/The turning
549 ES	Carghil	14	— and we all went in a punt/On the river — and we had a tea basket/With some

RIVER'S (1)

67 WL: Fire S		173	good night./The Fire Sermon/The river's tent is broken; the last fingers of leaf/

RIVERS (1)

203 Indians		17	in the Midlands,/And one in the Five Rivers, may have the same graveyard./Let those

ROAD (18)

72 WL: Thund		332	/Rock and no water and the sandy road/The road winding above among the
72 WL: Thund		333	and no water and the sandy road/The road winding above among the mountains/
73 WL: Thund		361	/But when I look ahead up the white road/There is always another one walking
141 Rannoch		5	thin air/Moon cold or moon hot. The road winds in/Listlessness of ancient war,/
155 Rock 3		35	/Their only monument the asphalt road/And a thousand lost golf balls'./
189 FQ: DrySal		202	the shores of Asia, or in the Edgware Road./Men's curiosity searches past and future/
191 FQ: Little		29	the same, when you leave the rough road/And turn behind the pig-sty to the dull
220 Old Deut		22	/And the villagers put up a notice: ROAD CLOSED —/So that nothing untoward
241 MC	Mess	33	of frenzied enthusiasm,/Lining the road and throwing down their capes,/Strewing
322 FR	Winch	32	had a bit of an accident/On the West Road, in the fog, coming along/At a pretty
323 FR	Winch	21	/Outside of the village, on the West Road./{A} Where is he?/{Wi} At the Arms, my
396 CP	Lavinia	28	to you,/You might be able to find the road back/To a time when you were real — for
422 CP	Reilly	20	/{R} Protector of travellers/Bless the road./{A} Watch over her in the desert./Watch
540 ES	Gomez	22	night you ran over the old man in the road./{LC} You *said* I ran over an old man in

540 ES	Ld Clav	23	You *said* I ran over an old man in the road./{G} You knew it too. If you had been
560 ES	Michael	22	manslaughter? Oh, you mean on the road./Certainly not. I'm far too good a driver./
571 ES	Ld Clav	35	us./It was late at night. A secondary road./I ran over an old man lying in the road/
571 ES	Ld Clav	36	/I ran over an old man lying in the road/And I did not stop. Then another man ran

ROADS (5)

140 Usk		8	too deep',/Lift your eyes/Where the roads dip and where the roads rise/Seek only
140 Usk		8	/Where the roads dip and where the roads rise/Seek only there/Where the grey light
152 Rock 2		44	now you live dispersed on ribbon roads,/And no man knows or cares who is his
152 Rock 2		48	fro in motor cars,/Familiar with the roads and settled nowhere./Nor does the family
547 ES	Piggott	36	the hills,/Quite away from the motor roads. You must learn the best walks./I won't

ROAMED (1)

212 Growltiger		2	fact he was the roughest cat that ever roamed at large./From Gravesend up to Oxford

ROARING (1)

425 CP	Edward	24	thirsty;/They'll come on to us later, roaring for drink./Well, let's hope that those

ROARS (1)

247 MC	Tempt1	32	/The safest beast is not the one that roars most loud,/This was not the way of the

ROAST (2)

265 MC	Priest1	26	/Dinner before business. Do you like roast pork?/{K1} Business before dinner. We
265 MC	Knight1	27	/{K1} Business before dinner. We will roast your pork/First, and dine upon it after./

ROASTED (1)

213 Growltiger		55	was dancing on the strand./Rats were roasted whole at Brentford, and at Victoria

ROB (1)

472 CC	Colby	7	have been something in your life/To rob you of any sense of security./{L} And I'm

ROCHEFOUCAULD (1)

28 Boston ET		7	would turn to nod good-bye to La Rochefoucauld,/If the street were time and he at

ROCK (27)

49 Hippopot		8	can never fail/For it is based upon a rock./The hippo's feeble steps may err/In
61 WL: Burial		25	Only/There is shadow under this red rock,/(Come in under the shadow of this red
61 WL: Burial		26	in under the shadow of this red rock),/And I will show you something different
72 WL: Thund		331	patience/Here is no water but only rock/Rock and no water and the sandy road/
72 WL: Thund		332	/Here is no water but only rock/Rock and no water and the sandy road/The
72 WL: Thund		334	mountains/Which are mountains of rock without water/If there were water we
72 WL: Thund		336	should stop and drink/Amongst the rock one cannot stop or think/Sweat is dry and
72 WL: Thund		338	/If there were only water amongst the rock/Dead mountain mouth of carious teeth
72 WL: Thund		346	houses/If there were water/And no rock/If there were rock/And also water/And
72 WL: Thund		347	were water/And no rock/If there were rock/And also water/And water/A spring/A
72 WL: Thund		351	water/A spring/A pool among the rock/If there were the sound of water only/Not
73 WL: Thund		355	singing/But sound of water over a rock/Where the hermit-thrush sings in the pine
94 Ash-Wed 4		9	fresh the springs/Made cool the dry rock and made firm the sand/In blue of
145 Rock		t	if I am not glad!/Choruses from 'The Rock'/The Eagle soars in the summit of
148 Rock 1		40	/For I perceive approaching/The Rock. Who will perhaps answer our doubtings./
148 Rock 1		41	perhaps answer our doubtings./The Rock. The Watcher. The Stranger./He who has
148 Rock 1 m		46	whom is the truth inborn./*Enter the* ROCK, *led by a* BOY:/THE ROCK:/The lot of
148 Rock 1 m		46	*the* ROCK, *led by a* BOY:/THE ROCK:/The lot of man is ceaseless labour,/Or
187 FQ: DrySal		120	the bite in the apple./And the ragged rock in the restless waters,/Waves wash over it,
605 Narcissus		1	/Come under the shadow of this gray rock —/Come in under the shadow of this gray
605 Narcissus		2	in under the shadow of this gray rock,/And I will show you something different
605 Narcissus		5	leaping behind the fire against the red rock:/I will show you his bloody cloth and limbs
605 Narcissus		20	and knees./So he came out under the rock./First he was sure that he had been a tree,/
242 MC	Priest2	36	the King of France./We can lean on a rock, we can feel a firm foothold/Against the
243 MC	Priest2	2	of barons and landholders./The rock of God is beneath our feet. Let us meet the
280 MC	Priest3	18	where the sunset reddens the last grey rock/Of Brittany, or the Gates of Hercules./Go
292 FR	Ivy	35	old man was pensioned./He's let the rock garden go to rack and ruin,/And he's

ROCKET (1)

167 Rock 10		37	up in the night and fall asleep as the rocket is fired; and the day is long for work or

ROCKING (1)

212 Growltiger		23	lay./All in the balmy moonlight it lay rocking on the tide —/And Growltiger was

ROCKS (10)

37 Gerontion		12	coughs at night in the field overhead;/Rocks, moss, stonecrop, iron, merds./The
42 Swee Erect		3	/Paint me the bold anfractuous rocks/Faced by the snarled and yelping seas./
62 WL: Burial		49	/Here is Belladonna, the Lady of the Rocks,/The lady of situations./Here is the man
97 Ash-Wed 5		32	the world and deny between the rocks/In the last desert between the last blue
97 Ash-Wed 5		33	In the last desert between the last blue rocks/The desert in the garden the garden in the
98 Ash-Wed 6		22	three dreams cross/Between blue rocks/But when the voices shaken from the
98 Ash-Wed 6		29	Teach us to sit still/Even among these rocks,/Our peace in His will/And even among

99 Ash-Wed 6	31	in His will/And even among these rocks/Sister, mother/And spirit of the river,
109 Marina	1	/What seas what shores what grey rocks and what islands/What water lapping the
592 Grad 1	5	no chart to show/No light to warn of rocks which lie below,/But let us yet put forth

RODE (2)

30 Cous Nancy	3	across the hills and broke them,/Rode across the hills and broke them —/The
265 MC Knight1	13	/Have brought us from France. We rode hard,/Took ship yesterday, landed last

ROLE (4)

332 FR Agatha	38	simple plots!/He was not suited to the role of murderer./{H} In what way did he wish
362 CP Reilly	29	you/Arranged to support you in the role you have chosen,/Then sometimes, when
369 CP Edward	15	asked for different purposes./Your role was to be one of Lavinia's discoveries;/
403 CP Edward	29	oppression, the unreality/Of the role she had always imposed upon me/With the

RÔLE (1)

305 FR Agatha	14	watchers and waiters: not the easiest rôle./I must go and change for dinner. {}/[*Exit*]/

ROLL (2)

15 Prufrock	93	squeezed the universe into a ball/To roll it towards some overwhelming question,/To
594 Grad 9	4	school of ours! The passing years that roll/Between, as we press onward to the goal,/

ROLLED (3)

16 Prufrock	121	shall wear the bottoms of my trousers rolled./Shall I part my hair behind? Do I dare to
178 FQ: ECoker	59	roses filled with early snow?/Thunder rolled by the rolling stars/Simulates triumphal
180 FQ: ECoker	118	the bold imposing façade are all being rolled away —/Or as, when an underground

ROLLING (2)

31 Apollinax	13	looked for the head of Mr. Apollinax rolling under a chair/Or grinning over a screen/
178 FQ: ECoker	59	early snow?/Thunder rolled by the rolling stars/Simulates triumphal cars/Deployed

ROLLS (1)

601 Nocturne	11	hero smiles; in my best mode oblique/Rolls toward the moon a frenzied eye profound,

ROLLS-ROYCE (1)

121 SA Sweeney	25	no six-seaters,/No Citroën, no Rolls-Royce./Nothing to eat but the fruit as it

ROLY-POLY (1)

216 Jellicles	15	Cats are not too big;/Jellicle Cats are roly-poly,/They know how to dance a gavotte

ROMAN (2)

105 Song Sime	1	death./A Song for Simeon/Lord, the Roman hyacinths are blooming in bowls and/
129 Cor2 State	29	dingy busts, all looking remarkably Roman,/Remarkably like each other, lit up

ROMANCE (2)

589 Fable	72	/As everybody'll know who reads this romance./The Abbot sat as pasted to his chair,/
575 ES Carghil	36	too?/{LC} I have indeed./{MC} The romance of my life./Your father was simply

ROMANTIC (2)

485 CC Lady E	10	fancies. I was a silly girl,/And very romantic. But it goes to show/How different I
563 ES Carghil	5	place in Central America./{MC} How romantic! I'd love to meet him./He's coming to

ROME (4)

241 MC Priest1	27	or only secure/In the power of Rome, the spiritual rule,/The assurance of right,
252 MC Tempt3	1	stroke/At once, for England and for Rome,/Ending the tyrannous jurisdiction/Of
269 MC Thomas	14	of Christ's Church, the judgement of Rome./{K1} Priest, you have spoken in peril of
269 MC Thomas	19	submit my cause to the judgement of Rome./But if you kill me, I shall rise from my

ROMEO (1)

601 Nocturne	1	/With scarlet life, for me?/Nocturne/Romeo, *grand sérieux*, to importune/Guitar and

RONCES (1)

51 Restaurant	8	trempés, et des bourgeois sur les ronces —/C'est là, dans une averse, qu'on

ROOF (9)

218 Mung Rump	9	war,/If a tile or two came loose on the roof,/Which presently ceased to be waterproof,/
223 Pekes Pols	39	from the balcony, some from the roof,/Joined in/To the din/With a/Bark bark
225 Mr Mistoff	44	/But his voice has been heard on the roof/When he was curled up by the fire./And
225 Mr Mistoff	47	by the fire/When he was about on the roof —/(At least we all *heard* that somebody
274 MC Priests	14	my Lord! Quick. Up the stair. To the roof./To the crypt. Quick. Come. Force him./
302 FR Chorus	8	make some dreadful disclosure, the roof disappear,/And we should cease to be sure
316 FR Chorus	2	picnic on the moors. Have torn/The roof from the house, or perhaps it was never
343 FR Amy	24	I worry/To keep the tiles on the roof, combat the endless weather,/Resist the
422 CP Julia	16	/{J} May the holy ones watch over the roof,/May the moon herself influence the bed. {}

ROOFING (1)

154 Rock 3	18	a house of plaster, with corrugated roofing,/To be filled with a litter of Sunday

ROOFS (1)

27 Morning	9	/And vanishes along the level of the roofs./The Boston Evening Transcript/The

ROOFTREE (1)

74 WL: Thund	391	no one./Only a cock stood on the rooftree/Co co rico co co rico/In a flash of

ROOM (52)

13	Prufrock	13	/Let us go and make our visit./In the room the women come and go/Talking of
14	Prufrock	35	the taking of a toast and tea./In the room the women come and go/Talking of
14	Prufrock	53	fall/Beneath the music from a farther room./So how should I presume?/And I have
18	Portrait	4	And four wax candles in the darkened room,/Four rings of light upon the ceiling
18	Portrait	13	rubbed and questioned in the concert room.'/— And so the conversation slips/Among
19	Portrait	42	bloom/She has a bowl of lilacs in her room/And twists one in her fingers while she
37	Gerontion	25	/Who walked all night in the next room;/By Hakagawa, bowing among the
37	Gerontion	27	By Madame de Tornquist, in the dark room/Shifting the candles; Fräulein von Kulp/
57	Swee Night	29	the gambit, shows fatigue,/Leaves the room and reappears/Outside the window,
64	WL: Chess	106	/Leaned out, leaning, hushing the room enclosed./Footsteps shuffled on the stair./
69	WL: Fire S	254	stoops to folly and/Paces about her room again, alone,/She smoothes her hair with
107	Animula	30	/Leaving disordered papers in a dusty room;/Living first in the silence after the
141	Rannoch	3	soft moor/And the soft sky, scarcely room/To leap or soar. Substance crumbles, in
588	Fable	39	precaution incomplete;/He doused the room in which they were to dine,/And watered
597	Before Mor	6	/Their fragrance drifts across the room at dawn,/Fragrance of bloom and
599	On a Port	4	street,/She stands at evening in the room alone./Not like a tranquil carved goddess
256	MC Chorus	32	flame in the hall, the candle in the room?/{3P} Does the watchman walk by the
287	FR Amy	31	/A momentary shudder in a vacant room./Only Agatha seems to discover some
292	FR Amy	24	rather wait till you are rested./Your room is all ready for you. Nothing has been
305	FR Harry	26	/{H} I had only just noticed that this room is quite unchanged:/The same hangings ...
329	FR Chorus	1	/And what is spoken remains in the room, waiting for the future to hear it./And
337	FR m	8	straight. {}/[*She moves back into the room*]/{Ag} What have I been saying? I think I
345	FR Amy	24	you are the stupidest person in this room,/Violet, you are the most malicious in a
345	FR Amy	27	the others/Just to help me to the next room. Where I can lie down./Then you can
348	FR Chorus	8	and find ourselves back in the same room./We do not like the maze in the garden,
355	CP m	16	cake. {}/[EDWARD *leaves the room*]/{J} No, we'll wait until Edward comes
355	CP Julia	17	until Edward comes back into the room./Now I want to relax, Are there any more
374	CP 2m	1	/Act One. Scene 2/*The same room: a quarter of an hour later.* EDWARD *is*
375	CP m	36	and investigate. {}/[*Starts to leave the room*]/{E} For heaven's sake, don't bother! {}/
384	CP 2m	1	/Act One. Scene 3/*The same room: late afternoon of the next day.* EDWARD
399	CP 2m	1	HARCOURT-REILLY'S *consulting room in London. Morning:*/*several weeks later.*
399	CP Nurse	10	second to be shown into the other room/Just as usual. She arrives at a quarter
399	CP Nurse	19	third one to be shown into the small room;/And I need not let you know that she has
404	CP Edward	30	at my club/They won't let you keep a room for more than seven days;/I haven't the
412	CP Julia	19	tired as that. I shall wait in the next room,/And come back when she's gone./{R}
424	CP m	4	{}/[*Exit.* LAVINIA *looks about the room critically and moves a bowl of flowers.*]/
425	CP Edward	27	to the Gunnings afterwards,/To make room for those who come from the Gunnings./
437	CP Reilly	13	I first met Miss Coplestone, in this room,/I saw the image, standing behind her
445	CC 2m	1	GUZZARD/Act One/*The Business Room on the first floor of* SIR CLAUDE
466	CC Claude	8	for me,/I keep my pieces in a private room./It isn't that I don't want anyone to see
483	CC Colby	13	it for me./I said I needed a desk in my room:/You see, I shall do a good deal of my
483	CC Lady E	21	and typewriters/When I designed this room./{C} It's the sort of room I wanted. {}/
483	CC Colby	22	this room./{C} It's the sort of room I wanted. {}/[*rising*]./{LE} And I see a
493	CC 2m	1	/CURTAIN/Act Three/*The Business Room, as in Act 1. Several mornings later.* SIR
518	CC Eggers	18	settled on lodgings;/We have a spare room. We should be most happy/If you cared to
526	ES Monica	21	are different. Look! We're back in the room/That we entered only a few minutes ago./
527	ES Monica	26	/He needs to have someone else in the room with him,/Reading too — or just sitting
530	ES Ld Clav	20	just like sitting in an empty waiting room/In a railway station on a branch line,/
530	ES Ld Clav	25	am I waiting for/In a cold and empty room before an empty grate?/For no one. For
532	ES Ld Clav	12	/{LC} I'm sorry to turn you out of the room like this,/But I'll have to see this man by
542	ES Gomez	35	silence when you enter the smoking room./Don't forget, Dick:/You *didn't stop*!
547	ES Piggott	10	to be *very* quiet/There's the Silence Room. With a television set./It's popular in the

ROOMS (6)

22	Preludes	23	dingy shades/In a thousand furnished rooms./You tossed a blanket from the bed,/You
24	Rhapsody	66	/And female smells in shuttered rooms,/And cigarettes in corridors/And cocktail
74	WL: Thund	409	by the lean solicitor/In our empty rooms/DA/*Dayadhvam:* I have heard the key/
149	Rock 1	98	*in open places/And shiver in unlit rooms./Only the wind moves/Over empty fields,*
245	MC Priest2	31	I will have fires laid in all your rooms/To take the chill off our English
245	MC Priest2	34	climate./Your Lordship will find your rooms in order as you left them./{T} And will

ROOT (4)

42	Swee Erect	13	the sheets in steam./This withered root of knots of hair/Slitted below and gashed
138	New Hamp	4	head,/Between the green tip and the root./Black wing, brown wing, hover over;/
240	MC Chorus	8	spring shall beat at our doors,/Root and shoot shall eat our eyes and our ears,/
310	FR Mary	2	is the time/For the ache in the moving root/The agony in the dark/The slow flow

ROOTS (3)

61 WL: Burial	4	/Memory and desire, stirring/Dull roots with spring rain./Winter kept us warm,
61 WL: Burial	19	go south in the winter./What are the roots that clutch, what branches grow/Out of
605 Narcissus	23	among each other/And tangling its roots among each other./Then he knew that he

ROSE (16)

21 Portrait	115	grey and smoky, evening yellow and rose;/Should die and leave me sitting pen in
24 Rhapsody	57	her face,/Her hand twists a paper rose,/That smells of dust and eau de Cologne,/
64 WL: Chess	84	the table as/The glitter of her jewels rose to meet it,/From satin cases poured in rich
71 WL: DWater	316	/Picked his bones in whispers. As he rose and fell/He passed the stages of his age and
85 Hollow Men	64	/As the perpetual star/Multifoliate rose/Of death's twilight kingdom/The hope only
91 Ash-Wed 2	28	and distressed/Torn and most whole/Rose of memory/Rose of forgetfulness/
91 Ash-Wed 2	29	and most whole/Rose of memory/Rose of forgetfulness/Exhausted and life-giving/
91 Ash-Wed 2	32	/Worried reposeful/The single Rose/Is now the Garden/Where all loves end/
172 FQ: BurntN	38	water out of sunlight,/And the lotos rose, quietly, quietly,/The surface glittered out
184 FQ: DrySal	26	many voices./The salt is on the briar rose,/The fog is in the fir trees./The sea howl/
187 FQ: DrySal	128	the future is a faded song, a Royal Rose or a lavender spray/Of wistful regret for
196 FQ: Little	186	/To summon the spectre of a Rose./We cannot revive old factions/We cannot
197 FQ: Little	234	us with them./The moment of the rose and the moment of the yew-tree/Are of
198 FQ: Little	261	knot of fire/And the fire and the rose are one./OCCASIONAL VERSES/
592 Grad 4	4	it still appears/A lane by which the rose and hawthorn grow./We hope it may be;
270 MC Chorus	3	of dawn. I have smelt/Death in the rose, death in the hollyhock, sweet pea,

ROSE-GARDEN (5)

171 FQ: BurntN	14	the door we never opened/Into the rose-garden. My words echo/Thus, in your
173 FQ: BurntN	88	only in time can the moment in the rose-garden,/The moment in the arbour where
206 To my Wife	10	sun shall wither/The roses in the rose-garden which is ours and ours only/But
335 FR Agatha	1	/When the sun was shining on the rose-garden;/And heard in the distance tiny
335 FR Harry	36	door/And I ran to meet you in the rose-garden./{Ag} This is the next moment. This

ROSE-LEAVES (1)

171 FQ: BurntN	17	/Disturbing the dust on a bowl of rose-leaves/I do not know./Other echoes/

ROSES (6)

172 FQ: BurntN	30	the unseen eyebeam crossed, for the roses/Had the look of flowers that are looked
178 FQ: ECoker	58	/Red into grey and tumble down/Late roses filled with early snow?/Thunder rolled by
181 FQ: ECoker	168	purgatorial fires/Of which the flame is roses, and the smoke is briars./The dripping
192 FQ: Little	57	man's sleeve/Is all the ash the burnt roses leave./Dust in the air suspended/Marks
206 To my Wife	10	/No sullen tropic sun shall wither/The roses in the rose-garden which is ours and ours
596 When we	7	petals lay beneath;/But the wild roses in your wreath/Were faded, and the leaves

ROT (1)

193 FQ: Little	76	that we denied./Water and fire shall rot/The marred foundations we forgot,/Of

ROTATION (1)

173 FQ: BurntN	98	into transient beauty/With slow rotation suggesting permanence/Nor darkness

ROTE (1)

185 FQ: DrySal	32	that breaks on water,/The distant rote in the granite teeth,/And the wailing

ROTHERHITHE (1)

212 Growltiger	9	one forbidding eye./The cottagers of Rotherhithe knew something of his fame;/At

ROTTEN (4)

109 Marina	25	/The rigging weak and the canvas rotten/Between one June and another
149 Rock 1	86	*with new stone/Where the beams are rotten/We will build with new timbers/Where the*
152 Rock 2	25	in the past, you eat the fruit, either rotten or ripe./And the Church must be forever
243 MC Chorus	16	late, late is the time, late too late, and rotten the year;/Evil the wind, and bitter the

ROUGH (4)

191 FQ: Little	29	be the same, when you leave the rough road/And turn behind the pig-sty to the
250 MC Tempt3	36	King. Excuse my bluntness:/I am a rough straightforward Englishman./{T} Proceed
300 FRDowning	4	to keep her in when the weather was rough,/Didn't like to see her lean over the rail./
451 CC Eggers	11	to beat about the bush,/He's rather a rough diamond. Very free and easy ways;/And

ROUGHEST (1)

212 Growltiger	2	on a barge:/In fact he was the roughest cat that ever roamed at large./From

ROUGHLY (1)

589 Fable	75	any dollar,/The ghost then took him roughly by the hair/And bade him come with

ROUND (36)

50 Hippopot	27	damp savannas,/And quiring angels round him sing/The praise of God, in loud
52 Whispers	7	the eyes!/He knew that thought clings round dead limbs/Tightening its lusts and
62 WL: Burial	56	/I see crowds of people, walking round in a ring./Thank you. If you see dear
67 WL: Fire S	190	in the dull canal/On a winter evening round behind the gashouse/Musing upon the
85 Hollow Men	68	hope only/Of empty men./*Here we go round the prickly pear/Prickly pear prickly pear/*
85 Hollow Men	70	/*Prickly pear prickly pear/Here we go round the prickly pear/At five o'clock in the*

91 Ash-Wed 2	4	had been contained/In the hollow round of my skull. And God said/Shall these
118 SP Wauch	27	Four of us here./Wait till I put the car round the corner/We'll be right up/{Du} All
136 5FingerEx4	16	know *him*)./He has 999 canaries/And round his head finches and fairies/In jubilant
171 FQ: BurntN	22	said the bird, find them, find them,/Round the corner. Through the first gate,/Into
178 FQ: ECoker	34	arm/Whiche betokeneth concorde. Round and round the fire/Leaping through the
178 FQ: ECoker	34	betokeneth concorde. Round and round the fire/Leaping through the flames, or
213 Growltiger	37	still and closer the sampans circled round,/And yet from all the enemy there was
231 Bust Jones	32	our eyes/He has grown unmistakably round./He's a twenty-five pounder, or I am a
251 MC Tempt3	21	is in France, squabbling in Anjou;/Round him waiting hungry sons./We are for
257 MC Chorus	32	The Lords of Hell are here./They curl round you, lie at your feet, swing and wing
280 MC Priest3	31	still shall tramp and tread one endless round/Of thought, to justify your action to
288 FR Agatha	35	will have to meet/The boy who left. Round by the stables,/In the coach-house, in the
288 FR Agatha	38	the corridor/That led to the nursery, round the corner/Of the new wing, he will have
290 FR Amy	3	him/All over Europe and half round the world/To expensive hotels and
294 FR Harry	18	for no direction/Leads anywhere but round and round in that vapour —/Without
294 FR Harry	18	/Leads anywhere but round and round in that vapour —/Without purpose, and
322 FR Winch	34	I fancy, ran into a lorry/Drawn up round the bend. We'll have the driver up for
322 FR Winch	40	a bad concussion; says he'll come round/In the morning, most likely, but he
323 FR Winch	24	my Lady;/Of course, he hasn't come round yet./Dr. Owen was there, by a bit of luck.
347 FRDowning	5	when his Lordship would get round to seeing them —/And so you've seen
349 FR 4m	13	/and MARY *walk slowly in single file round and round the table, clockwise./At each*
349 FR 4m	13	*walk slowly in single file round and round the table, clockwise./At each revolution*
350 FR Agatha	15	This way the pilgrimage/Of expiation/Round and round the circle/Completing the
350 FR Agatha	15	pilgrimage/Of expiation/Round and round the circle/Completing the charm/So the
412 CP Julia	6	at the door/And went on in the taxi, round the corner;/Waited a moment, and
436 CP Peter	11	talking,/One thought has been going round and round in my head —/That I've only
436 CP Peter	11	thought has been going round and round in my head —/That I've only been
524 ES Monica	19	want to have the waiters/All buzzing round you: and it reminds the girl/That she's
549 ES Carghil	26	/I said 'there's a man I could follow round the world!'/But Effie it was — you know,
574 ES Michael	33	view. What's the use of chasing/Half round the world, for the same sort of job/You
ROUNDABOUT (1)		
493 CC Claude	20	good at approaching a subject/In a roundabout way. But where shall we place her?/
ROUNDED (1)		
185 FQ: DrySal	35	sea voices, and the heaving groaner/Rounded homewards, and the seagull:/And
ROUNDSMAN'S (1)		
328 FR Charles	13	who ran into and demolished a roundsman's/cart in Ebury Street early on the
ROUSED (1)		
311 FR Harry	17	for an instant of inattention/They are roused again, the sleepless hunters/That will not
ROUTE (2)		
191 FQ: Little	22	/If you came this way,/Taking the route you would be likely to take/From the
192 FQ: Little	42	/If you came this way,/Taking any route, starting from anywhere,/At any time or
ROUTES (1)		
162 Rock 8	19	kites of Syria/Or sea-strewn along the routes;/Many left their souls in Syria,/Living on,
ROUTINE (3)		
231 Bust Jones	36	because he's observed/All his life a routine, so he'd say./Or, to put it in rhyme: 'I
330 FR Harry	4	These mild surprises/Should be in the routine of normal life at Wishwood./John is the
417 CP Reilly	27	/Maintain themselves by the common routine,/Learn to avoid excessive expectation,/
ROVE (2)		
204 de la Mare	4	/For here the water buffalo may rove,/The kinkajou, the mangabey, abound/In
218 Mung Rump	4	for they were incurably given to rove./They were very well known in Cornwall
ROW (2)		
129 Cor2 State	29	I cry?/Mother mother/Here is the row of family portraits, dingy busts, all looking
277 MC Knight3	19	and/there is going to be an awful row; and at the best we shall have to/spend the
ROWDY (2)		
111 Xmas Trees	4	torpid, the patently commercial,/The rowdy (the pubs being open till midnight),/And
277 MC Knight3	13	traditions. So if/we seemed a bit rowdy, you will understand why it was; and for/
ROYAL (2)		
187 FQ: DrySal	128	/That the future is a faded song, a Royal Rose or a lavender spray/Of wistful
587 Fable	1	Feasters/In England, long before that royal Mormon/King Henry VIII found out that
RUBBED (1)		
18 Portrait	13	who will not touch the bloom/That is rubbed and questioned in the concert room.'/
RUBBING (1)		
14 Prufrock	25	smoke that slides along the street/Rubbing its back upon the window-panes;/
RUBBISH (1)		
61 WL: Burial	20	what branches grow/Out of this stony rubbish? Son of man,/You cannot say, or guess,

RUBS (2)

| 13 Prufrock | 15 | of Michelangelo./The yellow fog that rubs its back upon the window-panes,/The |
| 13 Prufrock | 16 | /The yellow smoke that rubs its muzzle on the window-panes,/Licked its |

RUDELY (3)

64 WL: Chess	100	Philomel, by the barbarous king/So rudely forced; yet there the nightingale/Filled all
68 WL: Fire S	205	twit twit/Jug jug jug jug jug jug/So rudely forc'd./Tereu/Unreal City/Under the
589 Fable	78	gape and stare,/The spirit pulled him rudely by the collar,/And before any one could

RUFFIAN (1)

| 249 MC Tempt2 | 5 | God can man do more?/Disarm the ruffian, strengthen the laws,/Rule for the good |

RUIN (9)

292 FR	Ivy	35	let the rock garden go to rack and ruin,/And he's nearly half blind. I've spoken to
326 FR	Harry	24	/Even of my own life as an isolated ruin,/A casual bit of waste in an orderly
333 FR	Harry	20	the beginning/Would have seemed the ruin./Perhaps my life has only been a dream/
374 CP	Celia	27	the situation/Because a divorce would ruin your career;/And we thought that Lavinia
381 CP	Edward	27	/That the misery does not feed on the ruin of loveliness,/That the tedium is not the
398 CP	Edward	9	at your touch, there is nothing but ruin./O God, what have I done? The python.
402 CP	Reilly	6	have the chance of redeeming from ruin./{E} You talk as if I was capable of action:/
438 CP	Reilly	32	/Which may mean restoration or ruin to a patient —/And sometimes I have made
551 ES	Carghil	36	/But I gave way. I didn't want to ruin you./If I'd carried on, it might have ended

RUINED (6)

151 Rock 2	4	well, that you now sit helpless in a ruined house?/Where many are born to idleness,
181 FQ: ECoker	160	earth is our hospital/Endowed by the ruined millionaire,/Wherein, if we do well, we
373 CP	Alex	2	Twenty minutes, and my work will be ruined. {}/[*Exeunt* ALEX *and* PETER]/
376 CP	Celia	11	*with saucepan*]/{C} Edward, it's ruined!/{E} What a good thing./{C} But it's
376 CP	Celia	13	/{E} What a good thing./{C} But it's ruined the saucepan too./{E} *And* half a dozen
402 CP	Reilly	4	be much worse. You might have ruined three lives/By your indecision. Now there

RUINOUS (1)

| 240 MC Chorus | 7 | come bringing death from the sea,/Ruinous spring shall beat at our doors,/Root |

RUINS (6)

41 Burb Blei	32	Burbank, meditating on/Time's ruins, and the seven laws./Sweeney Erect/Paint
75 WL: Thund	430	fragments I have shored against my ruins/Why then Ile fit you. Hieronymo's mad
155 Rock 3	43	we lift up our feet among perpetual ruins?/I have loved the beauty of Thy House,
589 Fable	96	/From an old manuscript found in the ruins./If Time and Space, as Sages say,/Are
280 MC Priest1	12	and the heathen shall build on the ruins,/Their world without God. I see it. I see it.
411 CP Edward	24	don't want to build on other people's ruins./{L} Exactly. And I have a question too./

RULE (15)

157 Rock 4	4	There was no exception to the general rule./In Shushan the palace, in the month
235 Ad-dress	38	A CAT./With Cats, some say, one rule is true:/*Don't speak till you are spoken to.*/
229 MC Chorus	22	should return./King rules or barons rule;/We have suffered various oppression,/But
241 MC Priest3	2	malversation./King rules or barons rule:/The strong man strongly and the weak
241 MC Priest1	27	/In the power of Rome, the spiritual rule,/The assurance of right, and the love of the
248 MC Tempt2	30	templed tomb, monument of marble./Rule over men reckon no madness./{T} To the
249 MC Tempt2	6	the ruffian, strengthen the laws,/Rule for the good of the better cause,/
253 MC Tempt4	24	chosen./But what is pleasure, kingly rule,/Or rule of men beneath a king,/With craft
253 MC Tempt4	25	/But what is pleasure, kingly rule,/Or rule of men beneath a king,/With craft in
254 MC Tempt4	14	another shall come:/Saint and Martyr rule from the tomb./Think, Thomas, think of
289 FR	Amy	11	Gerald. Though Agatha means/As a rule, a good deal more than she cares to betray,/
317 FR	Harry	25	before we went to school,/The rule of conduct was simply pleasing mother;/
382 CP	Edward	3	can only flourish/In submission to the rule of the stronger partner./{C} I am not sure,
429 CP	Alex	20	done with a European/He is, as a rule, no longer fit to eat./{E} And what has your
450 CC	Claude	15	me — I'm not so sure of that!/My rule is to remember that I understand nobody,/

RULED (2)

| 252 MC Thomas | 15 | cause to trust none but God alone./I ruled once as Chancellor/And men like you |
| 252 MC Thomas | 19 | I made many yield./Shall I who ruled like an eagle over doves/Now take the |

RULER (2)

| 249 MC Tempt2 | 24 | /Cabined in Canterbury, realmless ruler,/Self-bound servant of a powerless Pope,/ |
| 261 MC Thomas | 26 | willing and contriving may become a ruler/of men. A martyrdom is always the design |

RULERS (1)

| 180 FQ: ECoker | 105 | patrons of art, the statesmen and the rulers,/Distinguished civil servants, chairmen of |

RULES (4)

230 Bust Jones	14	*Educational*/And it is against the rules/For any one Cat to belong both to that/
229 MC Chorus	22	not be well if he should return./King rules or barons rule;/We have suffered various
241 MC Priest3	2	and frequent malversation./King rules or barons rule:/The strong man strongly
249 MC Tempt2	1	/King commands. Chancellor richly rules./This is a sentence not taught in the

RUM (9)

214 RTTugger	t	was commanded in Bangkok./The Rum Tum Tugger/The Rum Tum Tugger is a
214 RTTugger	1	Bangkok./The Rum Tum Tugger/The Rum Tum Tugger is a Curious Cat:/If you offer
214 RTTugger	7	he'd rather chase a mouse./Yes the Rum Tum Tugger is a Curious Cat —/And
214 RTTugger	12	no doing anything about it!/The Rum Tum Tugger is a terrible bore:/When you
214 RTTugger	18	such a fuss if he can't get out./Yes the Rum Tum Tugger is a Curious Cat —/And it
214 RTTugger	23	no doing anything about it!/The Rum Tum Tugger is a curious beast:/His
214 RTTugger	31	put it away on the larder shelf./The Rum Tum Tugger is artful and knowing,/The
215 RTTugger	32	Tugger is artful and knowing,/The Rum Tum Tugger doesn't care for a cuddle;/But
215 RTTugger	35	enjoys like a horrible muddle./Yes the Rum Tum Tugger is a Curious Cat —/And

RUMBLE (1)

| 180 FQ: ECoker | 116 | scene to be changed/With a hollow rumble of wings, with a movement of darkness |

RUMOUR (1)

| 212 Growltiger | 12 | lock up the silly goose,/When the rumour ran along the shore: GROWLTIGER'S |

RUMOURS (2)

| 74 WL: Thund | 415 | a prison/Only at nightfall, aethereal rumours/Revive for a moment a broken |
| 340 FR | Amy | 28 | gone,/So that there might be no ugly rumours./You thought I did not know!/You |

RUMP (1)

| 41 Burb Blei | 30 | clipped the lion's wings/And flea'd his rump and pared his claws?/Thought Burbank, |

RUMPELTEAZER (8)

218 Mung Rump	t	and the Jellicle Ball./Mungojerrie and Rumpelteazer/Mungojerrie and Rumpelteazer
218 Mung Rump	1	and Rumpelteazer/Mungojerrie and Rumpelteazer were a very notorious couple of
218 Mung Rump	16	horrible cat!/It was Mungojerrie — or Rumpelteazer!' — And most of the time they
218 Mung Rump	17	they left it at that./Mungojerrie and Rumpelteazer had a very unusual gift of the
219 Mung Rump	29	horrible cat!/It was Mungojerrie — or Rumpelteazer!' — And most of the time they
219 Mung Rump	30	they left it at that./Mungojerrie and Rumpelteazer had a wonderful way of working
219 Mung Rump	33	his oath/Was it Mungojerrie — or Rumpelteazer? or could you have sworn that it
219 Mung Rump	39	which cat?/It was Mungojerrie! AND Rumpelteazer!' — And there's nothing at all to

RUMPUSCAT (2)

| 222 Pekes Pols | m3 | *and the Intervention/of the Great Rumpuscat*/The Pekes and the Pollicles, everyone |
| 223 Pekes Pols | 51 | who should stalk out but the GREAT RUMPUSCAT./His eyes were like fireballs |

RUN (24)

67 WL: Fire S	176	nymphs are departed./Sweet Thames, run softly, till I end my song./The river bears no
67 WL: Fire S	183	sat down and wept .../Sweet Thames, run softly till I end my song,/Sweet Thames, run
67 WL: Fire S	184	till I end my song,/Sweet Thames, run softly, for I speak not loud or long./But at
119 SP	Klip	17	tell the world we got the Hun on the run/{Kr} What about that poker game? eh what
158 Rock 5	6	in the sunlight./And the others run about like dogs, full of enterprise, sniffing
220 Old Deut	21	them away./The cars and the lorries run over the kerb,/And the villagers put up a
269 MC Thomas	4	must make no doubt,/Shall the sea run between the shepherd and his fold./{K1}
305 FR	Agatha	6	like to help you: but you must not run away./Any time before now, it would have
338 FR	Harry	27	I know/That my business is not to run away, but to pursue,/Not to avoid being
338 FR	Amy	33	I am not safe here./{A} So you *will* run away./{Ag} In a world of fugitives/The
338 FR	Agatha	36	the opposite direction/Will appear to run away./{A} I was speaking to Harry./{H} It is
357 CP	Julia	36	and the telephone number?/I might run down and see Lavinia/On my way to
379 CP	Celia	33	more/And I waited, and wanted to run to tell you./Perhaps the dream was better. It
399 CP	Reilly	2	Miss Barraway:/I should like to run over my instructions again./You
424 CP	Edward	15	... {}/[*smiling*]./{E} That you hadn't run away?/{L} Now Edward, that's unfair!/You
468 CC	Claude	3	/— Oh yes, that meeting. We must run through the figures. {}/CURTAIN/Act Two
506 CC	Lady E	4	father died suddenly .../{LE} He was run over. By a rhinoceros/In Tanganyika./{SC}
530 ES	Ld Clav	12	/It's like telling a man he mustn't run for trains/When the last thing he wants is to
540 ES	Gomez	25	surprised/When I said 'Dick, you've run over somebody'/Wouldn't you have shown
572 ES	Ld Clav	1	died a natural death/And had been run over after he was dead./It was only a corpse
572 ES	Ld Clav	2	/It was only a corpse that we had run over/So neither of us killed him. But *I*
572 ES	Ld Clav	35	which I ran away. Very well./I shan't run away now — run away from *them*./It is
572 ES	Ld Clav	35	Very well./I shan't run away now — run away from *them*./It is through this meeting
580 ES	Carghil	25	now./You're looking rather tired. I'll run and see them off. {}/[*Exit* MRS.

RUNG (3)

185 FQ: DrySal	38	bell/Measures time not our time, rung by the unhurried/Ground swell, a time/
228 Gus	30	Little Nell;/When the Curfew was rung, then I swung on the bell./In the
388 CP	Peter	38	America./{P} Yes, and I would have rung you up tomorrow/And come in to say

RUNNING (11)

24 Rhapsody	39	out and pocketed a toy that was running along the quay,/I could see nothing
39 Gerontion	70	in the windy straits/Of Belle Isle, or running on the Horn./White feathers in the
103 Journ Magi	12	men cursing and grumbling/And running away, and wanting their liquor and
103 Journ Magi	23	line, smelling of vegetation,/With a running stream and a water-mill beating the

107 Animula   12   the sunlit pattern on the floor/And running stags around a silver tray;/Confounds
128 Corl March   33   the palmtree at noon, under the running water/At the still point of the turning
180 FQ: ECoker   130   the stillness the dancing./Whisper of running streams, and winter lightning./The wild
301 FRDowning   1   car?/{Do} Oh no, Sir, she's in good running order:/I see to that./{G} I only
320 FR Warburt   12   The whole machine is weak/And running down. Her heart's very feeble./With
391 CP Lavinia   21   /Or if it's a machine, someone else is running it./But who? Somebody is always
555 ES Ld Clav   24   of his,/I've lived in terror of his running over somebody./{M} Why, Father,

RUNS (3)
124 SA   Doris   9   care for such conversation/A woman runs a terrible risk./{Sn} Let Mr. Sweeney
124 SA   Doris   24   pinched in the end./{Do} A woman runs a terrible risk./{Sn} Let Mr. Sweeney
590 Space Time   7 and life are free,/For time is time, and runs away,/Though sages disagree./The flowers

RUSH (3)
65 WL: Chess   132   I do now? What shall I do?/'I shall rush out as I am, and walk the street/'With my
313 FR   Violet   5   a long journey;/You know what a rush he had to be here in time/For his mother's
545 ES   Piggott   26   and explain./I've been in such a rush, these last few days,/And I thought, 'Lord

RUSHES (1)
312 FR   m   9   /Yet I must speak to them. {}/[*He rushes forward and tears apart the curtains: but*

RUSSELL (1)
135 5FingerEx1   2 of the air repair/To the green fields of Russell Square./Beneath the trees there is no

RUSSIAN (1)
52 Whispers   17   of the bone./Grishkin is nice: her Russian eye/Is underlined for emphasis;/

RUSSIN (1)
61 WL: Burial   12 and talked for an hour./Bin gar keine Russin, stamm' aus Litauen, echt deutsch./And

RUST (1)
24 Rhapsody   31   /A broken spring in a factory yard,/Rust that clings to the form that the strength

RUSTIC (1)
178 FQ: ECoker   36   in circles,/Rustically solemn or in rustic laughter/Lifting heavy feet in clumsy

RUSTICALLY (1)
178 FQ: ECoker   36   the flames, or joined in circles,/Rustically solemn or in rustic laughter/Lifting

RUSTLING (1)
291 FR Chorus   1   the wrong parts,/Waiting for the rustling in the stalls, the titter in the dress circle,

RUSTY (2)
32 Hysteria   6 pink and white checked cloth over the rusty/green iron table, saying: 'If the lady and
154 Rock 3   25   chimney,/The peeled hull, a pile of rusty iron,/In a street of scattered brick where

RUTHLESS (1)
213 Growltiger   49   steel Growltiger did surround./The ruthless foe pressed forward, in stubborn rank

S' (2)
51 Restaurant   9   —/C'est là, dans une averse, qu'on s'abrite./J'avais sept ans, elle était plus petite./
75 WL: Thund   427   down falling down falling down/*Poi s'ascose nel foco che gli affina*/*Quando fiam uti*
SA (1)
51 Restaurant   29   très loin,/Le repassant aux étapes de sa vie antérieure./Figurez-vous donc, c'était un
SABBATH (1)
204 de la Mare   22   bats, and owls range/At witches' sabbath of the maiden aunts;/When the
SABLE (1)
54 Mr E Sun   17 set/The Father and the Paraclete./The sable presbyters approach/The avenue of
SACRAMENT (1)
178 FQ: ECoker   31   —/A dignified and commodious sacrament./Two and two, necessarye
SACRED (2)
44 Cook Egg   23   will instruct me/In the Seven Sacred Trances;/Piccarda de Donati will
57 Swee Night   36 are singing near/The Convent of the Sacred Heart,/And sang within the bloody
SACRIFICE (11)
128 Cor1 March   35   they go up to the temple. Then the sacrifice./Now come the virgins bearing urns,
161 Rock 7   22   the Word,/Through the Passion and Sacrifice saved in spite of their negative being;/
166 Rock 10   11   eyes,/The worshippers, self-given sacrifice of the snake. Take/Your way and be ye
193 FQ: Little   75   the weed./Water and fire deride/The sacrifice that we denied./Water and fire shall rot
260 MC Thomas   10 again to God His Body and Blood in sacrifice, oblation and satisfaction/for the sins
310 FR   Harry 10   is an issue of blood/A season of sacrifice/And the wail of the new full tide/
310 FR   Mary   22   the season of birth/Is the season of sacrifice/For the tree and the beast, and the fish/
409 CP   Reilly 13   were not prepared to make the least sacrifice/On her account. This injured your
515 CC Guzzard   23   /I am sacrificing also my previous sacrifice./This is even greater than the sacrifice I
515 CC Guzzard   24 sacrifice./This is even greater than the sacrifice I made/When I let you claim him. Do
554 ES   Carghil 13   that you never sit still:/You simply sacrifice yourself for us./{MP} It's the breath of
SACRIFICING (2)
515 CC Guzzard   22 was true? In telling you the truth/I am sacrificing my ambitions for Colby./I am
515 CC Guzzard   23   my ambitions for Colby./I am sacrificing also my previous sacrifice./This is
SACRILEGE (1)
259 MC Thomas   1   cause./But for every evil, every sacrilege,/Crime, wrong, oppression and the
SAD (6)
64 WL: Chess   96   by the coloured stone,/In which sad light a carvèd dolphin swam./Above the
176 FQ: BurntN 177 now, always —/Ridiculous the waste sad time/Stretching before and after./East
204 de la Mare   16   at twilight, gently go at dawn,/The sad intangible who grieve and yearn;/When the
280 MC Priest3 17 long as men will die for it./Go, weak sad men, lost erring souls, homeless in earth or
453 CC Lucasta   29 /{L} Yes, Eggy, will you break the sad news to Claude?/Meanwhile, you'll have to
549 ES   Carghil 36   you./{MC} Time has wrought sad changes in me, Richard./I was very lovely
SADLY (1)
164 Rock 9   4   /We must walk in black and go sadly, with longdrawn faces,/We must go
SADNESS (1)
248 MC Tempt2   32 the man of God what gladness?/{T2} Sadness/Only to those giving love to God alone.
SAFE (16)
135 5FingerEx2   6   muttered endlessly./Little dog was safe and warm/Under a cretonne eiderdown,/
273 MC   Priests 12   the door/The door is barred./We are safe. We are safe./They dare not break in./They
273 MC   Priests 12   door is barred./We are safe. We are safe./They dare not break in./They cannot
273 MC   Priests 15   in. They have not the force./We are safe. We are safe./{T} Unbar the doors! throw
273 MC   Priests 15   not the force./We are safe. We are safe./{T} Unbar the doors! throw open the
338 FR   Harry 22   /That the last apparent refuge, the safe shelter,/That is where one meets them. That
338 FR   Harry 31   /Now they will lead me. I shall be safe with them;/I am not safe here./{A} So you
338 FR   Harry 32   I shall be safe with them;/I am not safe here./{A} So you *will* run away./{Ag} In a
343 FR   Harry 36 /I have my course to pursue, and I am safe from normal dangers/If I pursue it. I
345 FR   Charles 36 /Old age came softly up to now. I felt safe enough;/And now I don't feel safe. As if the
345 FR   Charles 37 felt safe enough;/And now I don't feel safe. As if the earth should open/Right to the
500 CC Lucasta   25   I really wanted./B. makes me feel safe. And that's what I want./And somehow or
541 ES   Gomez   6   Culverwell?/No, Dick, your secret's safe with me./Of course, I might give it to a few
541 ES   Gomez   14 you are obtuse!/I said: 'Your secret is safe with me',/And then you ... well, I'd never
553 ES   Carghil 31   the originals;/They're in my lawyer's safe. But I have photostats/Which are quite as
568 ES   Ld Clav 22   the rest of the world — your soul is safe./If a man has one person, just one in his
SAFER (1)
247 MC Thomas   27 /Look to your behaviour. You were safer/Think of penitence and follow your
SAFEST (1)
247 MC Tempt1   32   /Your Lordship is too proud!/The safest beast is not the one that roars most loud,/

SAFETY (4)
239 MC	Chorus	2	by danger? Is it the knowledge of safety, that draws our feet/Towards the
239 MC	Chorus	6	is no danger/For us, and there is no safety in the cathedral. Some presage of an act/
342 FR	Agatha	32	crossed the frontier/Beyond which safety and danger have a different meaning,/
343 FR	Agatha	2	on this side,/For him, danger and safety have another meaning./*They* have made

SAFFRON (2)
430 CP	Peter	22	days? We dined the other night/At the Saffron Monkey. That's the place to go now./
430 CP	Alex	23	/{A} How very odd. *My* monkeys are saffron./{P} Your monkeys, Alex? I always said/

SAGACIOUS (1)
531 ES	Charles	7	saying 'we are confident/That his sagacious counsel will long continue/To be at

SAGES (3)
590 Time Space		1	in the ruins./If Time and Space, as Sages say,/Are things which cannot be,/The sun
590 Space Time		1	be divine./Song/If space and time, as sages say,/Are things that cannot be,/The fly
590 Space Time		8	time is time, and runs away,/Though sages disagree./The flowers I sent thee when the

SAGGY (1)
40 Burb Blei		14	this or such was Bleistein's way:/A saggy bending of the knees/And elbows, with

SAID (174)
18 Portrait	7	tomb/Prepared for all the things to be said, or left unsaid./We have been, let us say, to
20 Portrait	70	a cowardly amends/For what she has said to me?/You will see me any morning in the
21 Portrait	102	are really in the dark./'For everybody said so, all our friends,/They all were sure our
24 Rhapsody	16	street-lamp muttered,/The street-lamp said, 'Regard that woman/Who hesitates
24 Rhapsody	34	snap./Half-past two,/The street-lamp said,/'Remark the cat which flattens itself in the
26 Rhapsody	69	And cocktail smells in bars./The lamp said,/'Four o'clock,/Here is the number on the
31 Apollinax	20	—/'There was something he said that I might have challenged.'/Of dowager
43 Swee Erect	26	shadow of a man/Is history, said Emerson/Who had not seen the silhouette/
61 WL: Burial	15	on a sled,/And I was frightened. He said, Marie,/Marie, hold on tight. And down we
62 WL: Burial	46	/With a wicked pack of cards. Here, said she,/Is your card, the drowned Phoenician
65 WL: Chess	139	/When Lil's husband got demobbed, I said —/I didn't mince my words, I said to her
65 WL: Chess	140	I said —/I didn't mince my words, I said to her myself,/HURRY UP PLEASE ITS
66 WL: Chess	146	all out, Lil, and get a nice set,/He said, I swear, I can't bear to look at you./And
66 WL: Chess	147	look at you./And no more can't I, I said, and think of poor Albert,/He's been in the
66 WL: Chess	149	don't give it him, there's others will, I said./Oh is there, she said. Something o' that, I
66 WL: Chess	150	others will, I said./Oh is there, she said. Something o' that, I said./Then I'll know
66 WL: Chess	150	is there, she said. Something o' that, I said./Then I'll know who to thank, she said, and
66 WL: Chess	151	/Then I'll know who to thank, she said, and give me a straight look./HURRY UP
66 WL: Chess	153	don't like it you can get on with it, I said./Others can pick and choose if you can't./
66 WL: Chess	156	telling./You ought to be ashamed, I said, to look so antique./(And her only
66 WL: Chess	158	only thirty-one.)/I can't help it, she said, pulling a long face,/It's them pills I took,
66 WL: Chess	159	them pills I took, to bring it off, she said./(She's had five already, and nearly died of
66 WL: Chess	161	died of young George.)/The chemist said it would be all right, but I've never been the
66 WL: Chess	162	the same./You *are* a proper fool, I said./Well, if Albert won't leave you alone,
66 WL: Chess	163	won't leave you alone, there it is, I said,/What you get married for if you don't
72 WL: Thund	t	and tall as you./What the Thunder said/After the torchlight red on sweaty faces/
91 Ash-Wed 2	4	hollow round of my skull. And God said/Shall these bones live? shall these/Bones
91 Ash-Wed 2	7	In the bones (which were already dry) said chirping:/Because of the goodness of this
91 Ash-Wed 2	21	concentrated in purpose. And God said/Prophesy to the wind, to the wind only for
116 SP	Dusty	34	got her feet in mustard and water/I said I'm giving her mustard and water/All right,
120 SP	Klip	4	pace./What about it Klip?/{Kl} You said it, Krum./London's a slick place, London's
128 Corl March	45	church. And they rang a bell/And he said right out loud, *crumpets.*)/Don't throw
164 Rock 9	3	that I show thee./Who is this that has said: the House of GOD is a House of Sorrow;/
171 FQ: BurntN	21	the garden. Shall we follow?/Quick, said the bird, find them, find them,/Round the
172 FQ: BurntN	42	passed, and the pool was empty./Go, said the bird, for the leaves were full of children,
172 FQ: BurntN	44	containing laughter./Go, go, go, said the bird: human kind/Cannot bear very
180 FQ: ECoker	113	funeral, for there is no one to bury./I said to my soul, be still, and let the dark come
180 FQ: ECoker	124	but conscious of nothing —/I said to my soul, be still, and wait without hope/
181 FQ: ECoker	136	say I am repeating/Something I have said before. I shall say it again./Shall I say it
186 FQ: DrySal	98	/We can assign to happiness. I have said before/That the past experience revived in
194 FQ: Little	110	trod the pavement in a dead patrol./I said: 'The wonder that I feel is easy,/Yet ease is
216 Jellicles	30	are black and white,/Jellicle Cats (as I said) are small;/If it happens to be a stormy
219 Mung Rump	37	/From a vase which was commonly said to be Ming —/Then the family would say:
225 Mr Mistoff	56	*kittens* right out of a hat!/And we all said: OH!/Well I never!/Did you ever/Know a
587 Fable	30	/Of relics from a Spanish saint — said he:/'If ghosts come uninvited, then, of
589 Fable	85	lord renowned,/Though the wicked said (such rascals are not rare)/That the Abbot's
242 MC	Mess	11	Archbishop/Parted from the King, he said to the King,/My Lord, he said, I leave you
242 MC	Mess	12	he said to the King,/My Lord, he said, I leave you as a man/Whom in this life I

253 MC	Tempt4	4	what you come to say./{T4} It shall be said at last./Hooks have been baited with
260 MC	Thomas	7	Day. For whenever/Mass is said, we re-enact the Passion and Death of Our
260 MC	Thomas	26	Our Lord Himself spoke of Peace. He said to His/disciples, 'Peace I leave with you, my
261 MC	Thomas	5	you ask that, remember/then that He said also, 'Not as the world gives, give I unto
267 MC	Thomas	5	gentlemen, your business/Which you said so urgent, is it only/Scolding and
267 MC	Thomas	23	be the King's command —/Should we said in public. If you make charges,/Then in
277 MC	Knight3	15	to work ourselves up to it. And, as I said,/we are not getting a penny out of this. We
277 MC	Knight3	25	there's/no mistake about that. So, as I said at the beginning, please give us/at least the
279 MC	Knight1	5	about. It/seems to me that he has said almost the last word, for those who/have
280 MC	Knight1	2	I think that there is no more to be/said; and I suggest that you now disperse quietly
287 FR	Amy	21	let us drop the subject. The less she said the better./{G} That reminds me, Amy,/
296 FR	Harry	10	The evil in the dark closet, which they said was not there,/Which they explained away,
299 FR	Downing	36	what my judgment's worth, I always said his Lordship/Suffered from what they call a
303 FR	Mary	20	/{M} Well, there's something to be said for having an outsider;/For what is more
319 FR	Harry	33	of scandal./{H} Scandal? who said scandal? I did not./Yes, I see now. That
325 FR	Amy	2	looked like your father/When you said that./{H} I think, mother,/I shall make you
325 FR	Charles	12	can't./If he's worse than Winchell said, then he'll let us know at once./{G} I am
325 FR	Violet	39	he went at was simply terrifying./I said I would rather walk: and I did./{G} Walk?
327 FR	Harry	8	Do you think that I believe what I said just now?/That was only what I should like
327 FR	Ivy	33	so he's coming up tomorrow;/And he said there was something about it in the paper,/
328 FR	Gerald	2	in that. {}/[Exit]/{G} Well, I said that Arthur was every bit as likely/To have
328 FR	Charles	18	When challenged, Mr. Piper said:/"I thought it was all open country about
328 FR	Charles	24	when signalled by the police car, he said: "I/thought you were having a game with
343 FR	Mary	11	will help me!/You remember what I said to you this evening?/I knew that I was
344 FR	Harry	33	I cannot understand it./{H} I never said that I was going to be a missionary./I
346 FR	Downing	23	you'd hardly credit it,/I've always said, whatever happened to his Lordship/Was
353 CP	Alex	11	it started as a story about tigers./{A} I said there were no tigers./{C} Oh do stop
355 CP	Julia	5	hear the cry of bats?/{J} Because he said so. And I believed him./{C} But if he was so
356 CP	Julia	20	/Now Lavinia's away. I've always said:/'If I could only get Edward alone/And
356 CP	Julia	23	have a really serious conversation!'/I said so to Lavinia. She agreed with me./She
356 CP	Julia	24	to Lavinia. She agreed with me./She said: 'I wish you'd try.' And this is the first time
359 CP	Edward	19	me the names/Of all the people she said she'd invited./But it's only that dreadful old
363 CP	Edward	37	I agree that much of what you've said/Is true enough. But that is not all./Since I
374 CP	Edward	3	Celia! Why have you come back?/I said I would telephone as soon as I could:/And
375 CP	Edward	31	me something for supper;/And he said I must eat it within ten minutes./I suppose
377 CP	Edward	11	when the rest of you had left,/And he said he would bring Lavinia back, tomorrow./
385 CP	Reilly	30	/And give no explanations. I have said the same to her./Don't strangle each other
390 CP	Julia	6	have made a marvellous recovery./I said so to myself, when I got your telegram./{L}
392 CP	Lavinia	2	Like Celia. I don't know why I said it./Well, here I am./{E} I am to ask no
393 CP	Lavinia	23	remember that finally in desperation/I said: 'I suppose you'd as soon go to
393 CP	Lavinia	24	soon go to Peacehaven' —/And you said 'I don't mind'./{E} Of course I didn't mind.
393 CP	Lavinia	28	/And you were so considerate, people said;/And you thought you were unselfish. It
393 CP	Edward	35	I didn't get enough work/And he said that I ought to meet more people:/But
402 CP	Edward	16	that I ought to see a doctor./They said — again, in almost the same words —/That
405 CP	Reilly	14	had the opportunity, and you have said enough/To convince me that you have been
405 CP	Lavinia	26	/{E} Lavinia!/{L} Well, Sir Henry!/I said I would come to talk about my husband:/I
410 CP	Reilly	32	know the meaning of what you have said./{E} Lavinia, we must make the best of a
419 CP	Reilly	24	/{R} Not very many go. But I said they did not come back/In the sense in
421 CP	Reilly	13	Of Celia?/{J} Of Celia./{R} But when I said just now/That she would go so far, you agreed
425 CP	Lavinia	19	of those who accepted./You know we said, 'we can ask twenty more/Because they will
425 CP	Edward	21	instead'./{E} I know, that's what we said at the time;/But I'd forgotten what the
427 CP	Alex	11	might be leaving for the country,/I said, I must not miss the opportunity/To see
427 CP	Alex	16	get through to you./Never mind, I said — to myself, not to her —/Never mind: the
430 CP	Peter	10	on later, after the Gunnings —/So I said, I really must crash in:/It's my only chance
430 CP	Peter	24	/{P} Your monkeys, Alex? I always said/That Alex knew everybody. But I didn't
439 CP	Lavinia	2	seeing her at the moment/When she said good-bye to us, two years ago./{E} Your
439 CP	Julia	9	/{J} Henry, I think it is time that I said something:/Everyone makes a choice, of
451 CC	Eggers	28	'undistinguished';/But with you, as I said, it will be very different./She'll see at once
456 CC	Eggers	2	Sir Claude admires about her./He said to me once, in a moment of confidence —/
456 CC	Eggers	4	a public luncheon —/'Eggerson', he said, 'I wanted a lady,/And I'm perfectly
456 CC	Eggers	15	used to them. That's what Sir Claude said:/'Humour her, Eggerson,' he said, 'humour
456 CC	Eggers	16	said:/'Humour her, Eggerson,' he said, 'humour her.'/But she has one trait that I
459 CC	Lady E	39	/She was going on to Zürich. So she said: 'Come to Zürich!/There's a wonderful
460 CC	Lady E	20	Dr. Leroux./Don't you remember, I said before I left:/'Trust my guidance for once,
461 CC	Eggers	8	day, if you want me./In fact, Mrs. E. said: 'I wish he'd ring us up!'/I'm sure he has a

461 CC	Eggers	18	to Joshua Park, at this time of year!'/I said: 'Let's think about it in the Spring/When
465 CC	Claude	14	lacks the capacity?/Could a man be said to have a vocation/To be a second-rate
466 CC	Colby	36	my father!/I was struck by what you said, a little while ago,/When you spoke of
467 CC	Colby	14	this;/But it goes to explain what I said just now/About rebelling against the terms/
476 CC	Lucasta	10	it matters. A little while ago/You said, very cleverly, that when we first met/You
480 CC	Lucasta	21	of character/Yourself, before you said that of Colby./{K} Oh, I'm a good judge.
482 CC	Lady E	31	to mix with people of breeding./I said to myself, when I first saw you,/'He is very
483 CC	Colby	13	office desk. Sir Claude got it for me./I said I needed a desk in my room:/You see, I
483 CC	Lady E	35	to say, *if* I believed in it/I should have said that we had known each other/In some
491 CC	Lady E	5	yours. And I know from what you said,/That you would rather he was *ours* than
500 CC	Lucasta	22	/He must have been staggered when I said I was your daughter!/I came to thank him
503 CC	Lucasta	30	/We've changed since then: as you said, we're always changing./When I come back,
506 CC	Eggers	27	just possible. A few days ago,/As I said, Lady Elizabeth learned your name;/And
514 CC	Claude	27	this fiction/In response to what Colby said he wanted./{E} I'll examine the records
515 CC	Guzzard	2	It did not concern you./As I have just said, my sister died/Before the child could be
515 CC	Guzzard	14	And it would make you so happy!/If I said the child was mine, what future could he
515 CC	Guzzard	16	what I had done./Though I had never said 'this child is yours',/I feared you would ask
524 ES	Monica	6	tea. That was understood/When you said you could give me the whole afternoon./{C}
525 ES	Charles	5	you should stop to tea./{C} When I said that I was free for the whole afternoon,/
525 ES	Charles	21	have you to himself,/Before I've said two words he'll come ambling in .../{M}
525 ES	Monica	22	he'll come ambling in .../{M} You've said a good deal more than two words already./
525 ES	Charles	35	something else to say that I haven't said before,/That will give you a shock. I believe
526 ES	Charles	3	/{C} So I was right! The moment I'd said it/I was badly frightened. For I didn't *know*
526 ES	Charles	6	you say so!/But now that you've said so, you must say it again,/For I need so
526 ES	Monica	37	not to assume that anything I've said to you/Has given you the right to criticise
527 ES	Lambert	11	me, Miss Monica. His Lordship said to tell you/Not to wait tea for him./{M}
528 ES	Monica	39	place. 'Make the reservations'/Selby said, 'as if you were going'./But Badgley Court's
529 ES	Monica	25	book!/You know what the doctors said: complete relaxation/And to think about
530 ES	Ld Clav	33	me more, the insincerity/Of what was said about me, or of my reply —/All to thank
531 ES	Lambert	35	/But by previous appointment. He said he knew that,/So he had brought this note.
531 ES	Lambert	36	that,/So he had brought this note. He said that when you read it/You would want to
531 ES	Lambert	37	read it/You would want to see him. Said you'd be very angry/If you heard that he'd
534 ES	Gomez	35	know what serious politics is like!/I said to my boys: 'Never touch politics./Stay out
535 ES	Gomez	17	other connection./But, as I've always said to my boys:/'When you come to the point
540 ES	Ld Clav	23	over the old man in the road./{LC} You *said* I ran over an old man in the road./{G} You
540 ES	Gomez	25	If you had been surprised/When I said 'Dick, you've run over somebody'/
541 ES	Gomez	14	/{G} My dear chap, you are obtuse!/I said: 'Your secret is safe with me',/And then
544 ES	Monica	8	I asked about morning coffee/She said 'I'm not the one for elevens's,/That's
545 ES	Ld Clav	15	/{LC} Yes, but remember/What she said. She said: 'I'm going to leave you alone!/
545 ES	Ld Clav	15	but remember/What she said. She said: 'I'm going to leave you alone!/You want
548 ES	Carghil	26	Claverton, aren't you?/Somebody said you were coming here —/It's been the topic
549 ES	Carghil	26	why, but it's the way things happen./I said 'there's a man I could follow round the
549 ES	Carghil	28	Effie was very shrewd —/Effie it was said 'you'd be throwing yourself away./Mark
549 ES	Carghil	29	yourself away./Mark my words' Effie said, 'if you chose to follow *that* man/He'd give
549 ES	Carghil	31	/That man is hollow'. That's what she said./Or did she say 'yellow'? I'm not quite sure.
550 ES	Carghil	34	you're wrong, Richard. Effie always said —/What a clever girl she was! — 'he
551 ES	Carghil	28	have settled out of court./My lawyer said: 'I advise you to accept','/Because Mr.
551 ES	Carghil	33	want to appear as his supporters./He said: 'What his lawyers are offering in
553 ES	Carghil	24	a few. But very beautiful!/It was Effie said, when the break came,/'They'll be worth a
553 ES	Carghil	37	/{MC} Only a few friends./Effie said: 'If he becomes a famous man/And you
556 ES	Michael	25	this isn't a holiday, exactly./Oh. I said that before, didn't I?/{M} I wish you'd stop
558 ES	Michael	7	so he pretended to be very shocked./Said he couldn't retain any man on his staff/
558 ES	Michael	9	to gambling. Called me a gambler!/Said he'd communicate with you about it./{LC}
562 ES	Monica	5	Father,/Whatever Father has said, Michael,/You must forgive each other, you
563 ES	Gomez	13	chosen to come to Badgley Court/I said to my doctor, 'Well, what about it?/What
565 ES	Ld Clav	35	to escape from his own past failures:/I said I knew from experience. Do I understand
567 ES	Charles	14	seem to need me then./And you said we weren't engaged yet .../{M} We're
568 ES	Ld Clav	4	spot./No matter. I heard what you said about guilty secrets./There are many things
569 ES	Ld Clav	27	asked him what he wanted./Oh no, he said, I want nothing from you/Except your
574 ES	Ld Clav	6	you please, Mrs. Carghill,/{LC} You said you had some exciting news for us./Would
578 ES	Monica	35	understood a single word/Of what I said. You must make your own life/Of course,

SAIL (5)

74 WL: Thund	419		/Gaily, to the hand expert with sail and oar/The sea was calm, your heart would
592 Grad 1	3		/Then with a song upon our lips, sail we/Across the harbor bar — no chart to
244 MC	Chorus	30	leave us, leave sullen Dover, and set sail for France. Thomas our Archbishop still

244 MC	Chorus	30	Thomas Archbishop, set the white sail between the grey sky and the bitter sea,
256 MC	Priests	25	not fight the intractable tide,/Do not sail the irresistible wind; in the storm,/Should

SAILED (1)

236 Cat	Morgan	1	Himself/I once was a Pirate what sailed the 'igh seas —/But now I've retired as a

SAILING (1)

186 FQ:	DrySal	69	is the end of them, the fishermen sailing/Into the wind's tail, where the fog

SAILOR (3)

62 WL:	Burial	47	Is your card, the drowned Phoenician Sailor,/(Those are pearls that were his eyes.
68 WL:	Fire S	221	strives/Homeward, and brings the sailor home from sea,/The typist home at
256 MC	Priests	28	the traveller may find his way,/The sailor lay course by the sun? {}/CHORUS,

SAILOR-KNOTS (1)

210 Old	Gumbie	26	she likes to wind, and tie it into sailor-knots./She sits upon the window-sill, or

SAILS (4)

42 Swee	Erect	8	/And swell with haste the perjured sails./Morning stirs the feet and hands/
69 WL:	Fire S	270	drift/With the turning tide/Red sails/Wide/To leeward, swing on the heavy spar.
98 Ash-Wed	6	9	towards the granite shore/The white sails still fly seaward, seaward flying/Unbroken
186 FQ:	DrySal	78	/Or drawing their money, drying sails at dockage;/Not as making a trip that will

SAINT (13)

48 Lune	Miel	8	égratigner./Moins d'une lieue d'ici est Saint Apollinaire/En Classe, basilique connue
48 Lune	Miel	16	vu la Suisse et traversé la France./Et Saint Apollinaire, raide et ascétique,/Vieille
62 WL:	Burial	67	down King William Street,/To where Saint Mary Woolnoth kept the hours/With a
190 FQ:	DrySal	206	/With time, is an occupation for the saint —/No occupation either, but something
587 Fable		30	a crowd/Of relics from a Spanish saint — said he:/'If ghosts come uninvited, then,
589 Fable		88	put to his name the handle/Of Saint, thereby rebuking all such scandal./But
605 Narcissus		t	to thine and to thee./The Death of Saint Narcissus/Come under the shadow of this
254 MC	Tempt4	14	forgotten, when another shall come:/Saint and Martyr rule from the tomb./Think,
260 MC	Thomas	2	*chapter of the Gospel according to Saint Luke.* In the/Name of the Father, and of
261 MC	Thomas	26	the effect of a man's will to/become a Saint, as a man by willing and contriving may
281 MC	Priest3	6	/To God, who has given us another Saint in Canterbury. {}/[*while a* Te Deum *is*
281 MC	Chorus	19	create the holy places./For wherever a saint has dwelt, wherever a martyr has given his
438 CP	Reilly	10	of this one./Do you imagine that the Saint in the desert/With spiritual evil always at

SAINTS (22)

50 Hippopot		31	heavenly arms enfold,/Among the saints he shall be seen/Performing on a harp of
151 Rock 2		2	were made/Fellow citizens of the saints, of the household of GOD, being built
151 Rock 2		15	/And settled all the inconvenient saints,/Apostles, martyrs, in a kind of
159 Rock 6		28	not shed once for all,/The lives of the Saints not given once for all:/But the Son of
159 Rock 6		30	/And there shall be Martyrs and Saints./And if blood of Martyrs is to flow on
164 Rock 9		15	let us learn the joyful communion of saints./The soul of Man must quicken to
239 MC	Chorus	14	hand to the fire and remembered the Saints at All Hallows,/Remembered the martyrs
239 MC	Chorus	15	/Remembered the martyrs and saints who wait? and who shall/Stretch out his
240 MC	Chorus	16	upon us. We wait, we wait,/And the saints and martyrs wait, for those who shall be
240 MC	Chorus	16	for those who shall be martyrs and saints./Destiny waits in the hand of God,
255 MC	Tempt4	7	too./What can compare with glory of Saints/Dwelling forever in presence of God?/
261 MC	Thomas	17	another soul is/numbered among the Saints in Heaven, for the glory of God and for
261 MC	Thomas	22	been/elevated to the company of the Saints: for that would be simply to/rejoice: and
261 MC	Thomas	24	martyrdom is never an accident, for Saints are not made by/accident. Still less is a
261 MC	Thomas	33	cannot understand; so in Heaven the Saints are/most high, having made themselves
264 MC	Priest3	18	it were a new song./The blood of thy saints have they shed like water,/And there was
264 MC	Priest3	20	Avenge, O Lord,/The blood of thy saints. In Rama, a voice heard, weeping./Out of
275 MC	Thomas	20	blessed martyr Denys, and to all the Saints, I commend my cause and that of the
281 MC	Priest2	3	sight of God/Conjoined with all the saints and martyrs gone before you,/Remember
281 MC	Chorus	17	For the blood of Thy martyrs and saints/Shall enrich the earth, shall create the
282 MC	Chorus	13	of the martyrs and the agony of the saints/Is upon our heads./Lord, have mercy
410 CP	Reilly	37	us make of it —/Except of course, the saints — such as those who go/To the

SAINTS' (1)

105 Song	Sime	28	/Light upon light, mounting the saints' stair./Not for me the martyrdom, the

SAKE (11)

290 FR	Amy	12	well all of you know the truth/For the sake of the future. There can be no grief/And no
290 FR	Amy	14	have prevented it if I could. For the sake of the future:/Harry is to take command at
321 FR	Warburt	36	with the rheumatism./{W} For God's sake, Winchell, tell us your business./His
322 FR	Warburt	20	I've come about./{W} For Heaven's sake, Winchell,/Tell us your business./{Wi} It's
340 FR	Amy	18	here. Seven years I kept him,/For the sake of the future, a discontented ghost,/In his
371 CP	Peter	31	out/The truth about the past, for the sake of the memory./{E} There's no memory
375 CP	Edward	37	*to leave the room*]/{E} For heaven's sake, don't bother! {}/[*Exit* CELIA]/{E} Suppose
388 CP	Celia	8	Peter, I'm awfully glad, for your sake,/Though of course we ... I shall miss you;/

491 CC   Claude   39   marry/You will want parents, for the sake of your children./{C} I don't feel, tonight,
558 ES   Michael 17   /And that sort of thing. It's for your sake, he says,/That he wants to keep things
559 ES   Michael 34   was gratifying. But it wasn't for *my* sake!/I was just your son — that is to say,/A

SAL (1)
43 Swee Erect   43   padding on broad feet,/Bringing sal volatile/And a glass of brandy neat./A

SALAD (2)
481 CC   Lady E   31   /Who needs to eat a great deal of salad./You remember, I made you take a note
481 CC   Lucasta 36   so hungry, I could even eat a herbal salad./{LE} That's right. Just mention my name,

SALADS (1)
481 CC   Lady E   29   past six./They have the most delicious salads!/And I told you, Mr. Kaghan, you're the

SALARY (3)
129 Cor2 State   13   is appointed telephone operator/At a salary of one pound ten a week rising by annual
453 CC   Kaghan   35   I'm penniless./{K} She's had a week's salary in lieu of notice./{L} B., remember you're
577 ES   Michael 4   passage .../{Mi} And an advance of salary./{C} Señor Gomez pays your passage .../

SALISBURY (2)
246 MC Thomas   2   /Rebellious bishops, York, London, Salisbury,/Would have intercepted our letters,/
246 MC Thomas   11   from me/Only John, the Dean of Salisbury,/Fearing for the King's name, warning

SALLE-DE-BAINS (1)
51 Restaurant   24   moi?/Tiens, voilà dix sous, pour la salle-de-bains./Phlébas, le Phénicien, pendant

SALMON (1)
235 Ad-dress   58   Pie,/Some potted grouse, or salmon paste —/He's sure to have his personal

SALON (1)
368 CP   Edward   34   /{E} Lavinia's attempts at starting a salon,/Where I entertained the minor guests/

SALT (4)
37 Gerontion   5   the warm rain/Nor knee deep in the salt marsh, heaving a cutlass,/Bitten by flies,
98 Ash-Wed 6   19   the ivory gates/And smell renews the salt savour of the sandy earth/This is the time of
184 FQ: DrySal   26   /Many gods and many voices./The salt is on the briar rose,/The fog is in the fir
270 MC Chorus   1   creatures still living, with the strong salt taste of living things under the sea; I have

SALUTATION (1)
542 ES   Gomez   34   /The ambiguous smile, the distant salutation,/The sudden silence when you enter

SALVAGES (1)
184 FQ: DrySal   t   In my end is my beginning./The Dry Salvages/I do not know about gods; but I

SALVATION (6)
106 Song Sime   37   thy servant depart,/Having seen thy salvation./Animula/'Issues from the hand of
260 MC Thomas   9   we rejoice in His coming for the salvation of men, and/offer again to God His
261 MC Thomas   18   for the glory of God and for the/salvation of men./Beloved, we do not think of a
411 CP   Reilly   36   /Go in peace. And work out your salvation with diligence. {}/[*Exeunt* EDWARD
420 CP   Reilly   18   peace, my daughter./Work out your salvation with diligence. {}/
421 CP   Reilly   35   I say to one like her/'Work out your salvation with diligence', I do not understand/

SALVER (1)
530 ES   m 32   had to listen to! {}/[*pointing to a silver salver, still lying in its case*]./{LC} I don't know

SAM (14)
115 SP   Doris   19   through and through./{Do} I like Sam/{Du} *I* like Sam/Yes and Sam's a nice boy
115 SP   Dusty   20   through./{Do} I like Sam/{Du} *I* like Sam/Yes and Sam's a nice boy too./He's a
116 SP   Dusty   1   /He could make you laugh./{Du} Sam can make you laugh:/Sam's all right/{Do}
118 SP   Doris   18   queer! {}/(*Whistle again*.)/{Do} Is that Sam?/{Du} Of course it's Sam!/{Do} Of course,
118 SP   Dusty   19   /{Do} Is that Sam?/{Du} Of course it's Sam!/{Do} Of course, the Knave of Hearts *is*
118 SP   Doris   20   Of course, the Knave of Hearts *is* Sam!/{Du} (*leaning out of the window*): Hello
118 SP   Dusty   21   (*leaning out of the window*): Hello Sam!/{W} Hello dear/How many's up there?/
119 SP   Klip   11   pleased to become acquainted/{Kl} Sam — I should say Loot Sam Wauchope/{Kr}
119 SP   Klip   11   /{Kl} Sam — I should say Loot Sam Wauchope/{Kr} Of the Canadian
119 SP   Krum   15   /Klip and me and the Cap and Sam./{Kl} Yes we did our bit, as you folks say,/
119 SP   Krum   18   about that poker game? eh what Sam?/What about that poker game in
119 SP   Krum   20   /Yes Miss Dorrance you get Sam/To tell about that poker game in
120 SP   Krum   8   got a real live Britisher/A guy like Sam to show you around./Sam of course is at
120 SP   Krum   9   /A guy like Sam to show you around./Sam of course is at *home* in London,/And he's

SAM'S (3)
115 SP   Dusty   18   to be too nice to Pereira./{Du} Now Sam's a gentleman through and through./{Do} I
115 SP   Dusty   21   I like Sam/{Du} *I* like Sam/Yes and Sam's a nice boy too./He's a funny fellow/{Do}
116 SP   Dusty   2   /{Du} Sam can make you laugh:/Sam's all right/{Do} But Pereira won't do./We

SAMARITANS (2)
376 CP   Julia   21   lucky you are/To have *two* Good Samaritans? I never heard of that before./{E}
376 CP   Edward   28   for me./He *would* do it. Three Good Samaritans./I forgot all about it./{J} But you

SAME (113)

66	WL: Chess		161
69	WL: Fire S		244
92	Ash-Wed 3		3
119	SP	Klip	35
174	FQ: BurntN		126
187	FQ: DrySal		127
188	FQ: DrySal		141
191	FQ: Little		26
191	FQ: Little		29
192	FQ: Little		44
193	FQ: Little		101
195	FQ: Little		153
203	Indians		17
203	Indians		18
206	To my Wife		6
206	To my Wife		7
209	NamingCats		26
222	Pekes Pols		3
594	Grad 10		5
247	MC	Thomas	15
247	MC	Thomas	18
260	MC	Thomas	9
260	MC	Thomas	11
260	MC	Thomas	14
260	MC	Thomas	18
260	MC	Thomas	20
263	MC	Chorus	19
263	MC	Chorus	20
277	MC	Knight3	15
292	FR	Amy	20
295	FR	Amy	37
297	FR	Charles	16
297	FR	Charles	24
299	FR Downing		22
305	FR	Harry	27
305	FR	Harry	27
305	FR	Harry	28
305	FR	Mary	32
306	FR	Harry	18
311	FR	Harry	28
314	FR	Violet	15
315	FR	Warburt	29
322	FR	Winch	3
330	FR	Harry	29
330	FR	Harry	30
335	FR	Agatha	38
336	FR	Harry	11
341	FR	Agatha	5
348	FR	Chorus	6
348	FR	Chorus	8
353	CP	Alex	8
360	CP	Reilly	14
361	CP	Edward	20
361	CP	Reilly	40
369	CP	Peter	35
371	CP	Edward	13
371	CP	Peter	19
374	CP	2m	1
376	CP	Julia	17
384	CP	2m	1
385	CP	Reilly	2
385	CP	Reilly	30
401	CP	Edward	5
402	CP	Edward	15

be all right, but I've never been the same./You *are* a proper fool, I said./Well, if
have foresuffered all/Enacted on this same divan or bed;/I who have sat by Thebes
stair/I turned and saw below/The same shape twisted on the banister/Under the
I'm very pleased to meet you all the same) —/London's a little too gay for us/Yes
is the one way, and the other/Is the same, not in movement/But abstention from
things — or one way of putting the same thing:/That the future is a faded song, a
or into any future;/You are not the same people who left that station/Or who will
voluptuary sweetness./It would be the same at the end of the journey,/If you came at
what you came for,/It would be the same, when you leave the rough road/And turn
at any season,/It would always be the same: you would have to put off/Sense and
/Although we were not. I was still the same,/Knowing myself yet being someone other
/Yet differ completely, flourish in the same hedgerow:/Attachment to self and to
one in the Five Rivers, may have the same graveyard./Let those who go home tell the
/Let those who go home tell the same story of you:/Of action with a common
smell of each other/Who think the same thoughts without need of speech/And
need of speech/And babble the same speech without need of meaning./No
/The reason, I tell you, is always the same:/His mind is engaged in a rapt
passionate foes;/It is always the same, wherever one goes./And the Pugs and the
made it great, not left behind,/The same school in the future shall we find/As this
from generation to generation/The same things happen again and again./Men learn
/But in the life of one man, never/The same time returns. Sever/The cord, shed the
of His Birth. So that at/the same moment we rejoice in His coming for the
sins of the whole world. It was in this same night that has/just passed, that a
peace to men of good will'; at this same time of all the year that we/celebrate at
mourn and rejoice at once and/for the same reason? For either joy will be overborne
can rejoice and mourn at once for the same reason./Now think for a moment about
shall go out in March and turn same earth/He has turned before, the bird shall
turned before, the bird shall sing the same song./When the leaf is out on the tree,
realised this was our duty,/but all the same we had to work ourselves up to it. And, as
everybody here, and everything same./Mr. Bevan — you remember — wants to
/Again by day, all will be the same again./I beg you to go now and rest before
blame Harry./I might have done the same thing once, myself./Nobody knows what
not let sleeping dogs lie?/{C} All the same, there's a question or two { }/[*Rings the
spirits?/{Do} Well, always about the same, Sir./What I mean is, always up and down.
this room is quite unchanged:/The same hangings ... the same pictures ... even the
unchanged:/The same hangings ... the same pictures ... even the table,/The chairs, the
table,/The chairs, the sofa ... all in the same positions./I was looking to see if anything
insisted/On everything being kept the same as when you left it./{H} I wish she had not
that I wanted to escape;/And at the same time, other memories,/Earlier, forgotten,
time?/When I knew her, I was not the same person./I was not any person. Nothing
have an illness./{V} It was always the same with your minor ailments/And children's
hope that next year will bring me the same honour. { }/[*Exeunt* AMY, DR.
/{Wi} I understand, Sir./It'd be the same if it was my birthday —/I beg pardon, I'm
was inside the old dream, I felt all the same emotion/Or lack of emotion, as before: the
/Or lack of emotion, as before: the same loathing/Diffused, I not a person, in a
/We do not pass twice through the same door/Or return to the door through which
just as before,/Not quite like, not the same ... { }/[*The* EUMENIDES *appear*]/{H} and
more difficult. But you are just the same:/Just as voracious for what you cannot
We do not like to look out of the same window, and see quite a different
a door, and find ourselves back in the same room./We do not like the maze in the
over again, Alex./{A} I never tell the same story twice./{J} But I'm still waiting to
but water./And I recommend you the same prescription .../Let me prepare it for you,
to know who you are;/But, at the same time, unless you know my wife/A good
you like it,/Preferring not quite the same friends as yourself,/Or making your
at pictures. So we often met/In the same way, and sometimes went together./And
I must see Celia./{E} Will it be the same Celia?/Better be content with the Celia
these interests? Did we really feel the same/When we heard certain music? Or looked
{ }/CURTAIN/Act One. Scene 2/*The same room: a quarter of an hour later.*
cook./{J} Celia! I see you've had the same inspiration/That I had. Edward must be
{ }/CURTAIN/Act One. Scene 3/*The same room: late afternoon of the next day.*
/To pretend that they and we are the same/Is a useful and convenient social
give no explanations. I have said the same to her./Don't strangle each other with
the door, that you might be the same person:/But I dismissed that as just
advised me recently,/Almost in the same words, that I ought to see a doctor./They

402 CP	Edward	16	/They said — again, in almost the same words —/That I was on the edge of a
404 CP	Edward	1	terms. I must be alone,/But not in the same world. So I want you to put me/Into your
405 CP	Reilly	6	patient/Whose situation is much the same as your own. {}/[*Presses the bell on his*
406 CP	Lavinia	5	I presume you will send him to the same sanatorium/To which you sent me? Well,
410 CP	Reilly	7	How much you have in common. The same isolation./A man who finds himself
415 CP	Celia	37	kind of hallucination;/Yet, at the same time, I'm frightened by the fear/That it is
425 CP	Lavinia	9	who don't want to come/But all the same would be bitterly offended/To hear we'd
436 CP	Peter	9	been saying. But I'm grateful all the same./You know, all the time that you've been
440 CP	Lavinia	10	seem to fit together./{L} But all the same ... I don't want to see these people./{R} It
440 CP	Lavinia	31	/One sometimes likes to hear the same compliment twice./{E} And now for the
446 CC	Claude	12	feelings./He's like me, Eggerson. The same disappointment/In a different form. He
458 CC	Eggers	31	recommendations .../{E} And at the same time, he had another tempting offer:/So
463 CC	Colby	15	/I've never had before. Yet at the same time/It's rather disturbing. I don't mean
464 CC	Colby	21	alone with your music?/{C} Just the same./All the time you've been speaking, I've
464 CC	Claude	29	was *his* passion./He loved it with the same devotion/That I gave to clay, and what
473 CC	Colby	33	garden — literally,/And also in the same sense that I retire to mine./But he doesn't
480 CC	Kaghan	38	*you*, Lucasta;/And we want the same things. But as for Colby,/He's the sort of
484 CC	Lady E	32	told anyone./I wonder if *you* had the same obsessions?/{C} What were they?/{LE} The
490 CC	Colby	29	Lady Elizabeth. The position is the same/Or crueller. Suppose I am your son./Then
491 CC	Lady E	9	him as being *our* son:/It won't be the same as what he had wanted —/But in some
491 CC	Colby	19	yet I believe I shall always feel the same./{SC} Well?/{C} It would be easier, I think,
498 CC	Eggers	2	would be most surprising./And at the same address?/{LE} I don't know the address./
502 CC	Lucasta	23	some fire/To warm you, that isn't the same kind of fire/That warms other people.
516 CC	Claude	34	to each other./We have undergone the same disillusionment:/I want us to make the
516 CC	Colby	39	father/I was content to have had the same ambitions/And in the same way to accept
516 CC	Colby	40	had the same ambitions/And in the same way to accept their failure./You had your
519 CC	Kaghan	7	Claude, I think we all made the same mistake —/All except Eggers .../{E} Me,
522 ES •	dedic	6	*in unison/Of lovers .../Who think the same thoughts without need of speech/And babble*
522 ES	dedic	7	*without need of speech/And babble the same speech without need of meaning:/To you I*
523 ES	m	15	Court. Morning/ACT THREE/*The Same. Late afternoon of the following day*/Act
526 ES	Charles	18	how much of me is you?/I'm not the same person as a moment ago./What do the
529 ES	Monica	8	— when he started like you,/With the same hopes, the same ambitions —/And of his
529 ES	Monica	8	like you,/With the same hopes, the same ambitions —/And of his disappointments./
533 ES	Gomez	6	followed your example,/And done the same, in a modest way./You know, where *I* live,
534 ES	Gomez	12	if I lived in England./I have the same standards of morality/As the society in
535 ES	Gomez	29	years? I was twenty-five —/The same age as you — when I went away,/
538 ES	Gomez	22	at least you can't make quite the same mistake./At the worst, you go into
542 ES	Ld Clav	22	how was I responsible?/We were the same age. You were a free moral agent./You
552 ES	Ld Clav	1	fortunes!/{LC} And perhaps at the same time of your own?/I seem to remember, it
552 ES	Carghil	27	/At bottom, I believe you're still the same silly Richard/You always were. You
557 ES	Ld Clav	38	/{LC} I expected that./It was just the same at Oxford./{Mi} It's their own fault./They
566 ES	Ld Clav	2	by side, at little desks/And suffer the same humiliations/At the hands of the same
566 ES	Ld Clav	3	humiliations/At the hands of the same master. But have I still time?/There is time
567 ES	2m	1	me, Monica? {}/CURTAIN/Act Three/*Same as Act Two. Late afternoon of the*
571 ES	Charles	22	the memory frets me./{C} But all the same, these two people mustn't persecute you./
574 ES	Michael	33	chasing/Half round the world, for the same sort of job/You got me here in London?
578 ES	Monica	19	were growing up we seldom had the same friends./I took all that for granted. So I
578 ES	Michael	31	about my highbrow sister./But all the same, I was fond of you, and always shall be./
579 ES	Monica	5	/I shall always pretend that it is the same Michael./{C} And when do you leave

SAMPANS (3)

213 Growltiger		32	As the Siamese came creeping in their sampans and their junks./Growltiger had no eye
213 Growltiger		37	eyes./And closer still and closer the sampans circled round,/And yet from all the
213 Growltiger		43	swarmed aboard./Abandoning their sampans, and their pullaways and junks,/They

SAMSON (1)

| 252 MC | Thomas | 28 | desperate exercise of failing power./Samson in Gaza did no more./But if I break, I |

SAN (13)

533 ES	Gomez	21	/Of a central American republic: San Marco./It's as hard to become a respected
539 ES	Ld Clav	26	surprising/In the respected citizen of San Marco/Is that in the midst of the engrossing
539 ES	Gomez	37	— a more important man/In San Marco than I should ever have been in
541 ES	Gomez	1	statement/Of Federico Gomez of San Marco/About something that happened so
541 ES	Gomez	18	could buy you out/Several times over. San Marco's a good place/To make money in —
563 ES	Gomez	20	Gomez,/The prominent citizen of San Marco./That's my name./{LC} So let me
564 ES	Gomez	27	is your home?/{G} The republic of San Marco./{MC} Went back to San Marco./
564 ES	Carghil	28	of San Marco./{MC} Went back to San Marco./Señor Gomez, if it's true you're
576 ES	Michael	17	/He's made a fortune there. San Marco for me!/{LC} And what are your

576 ES	Gomez	21	get there./The nature of business in San Marco/Is easier explained in San Marco
576 ES	Gomez	22	in San Marco/Is easier explained in San Marco than in England./{LC} Perhaps you
577 ES	Charles	2	Gomez has offered you a post in San Marco,/Señor Gomez pays your passage .../
580 ES	Carghil	20	/Señor Gomez has invited me to visit San Marco./I'm so excited! But what pleases me

SANATORIA (1)

402 CP	Reilly	28	/There are several kinds of sanatoria/For several kinds of patient. And

SANATORIUM (23)

400 CP	Alex	21	her./And when you've sent him to a sanatorium/Where she can't get at him — then,
402 CP	Edward	25	very similar to others./{E} Is there a sanatorium to which you send such patients/As
402 CP	Reilly	30	there are also patients/For whom a sanatorium is the worst place possible./We must
404 CP	Edward	2	So I want you to put me/Into your sanatorium. I could be alone there? {}/
404 CP	Edward	23	/{E} And now will you send me to the sanatorium?/{R} You have nothing else to tell
404 CP	Edward	28	/{E} And so will you send me to the sanatorium?/I can't go home again. And at my
405 CP	Reilly	32	/Your husband wishes to enter a sanatorium,/And that is a question which
405 CP	Edward	34	you./{E} I am not going to any sanatorium./I am going to a hotel. And I shall
406 CP	Lavinia	5	you will send him to the same sanatorium/To which you sent me? Well, he
406 CP	Reilly	9	/You have never visited my sanatorium./{L} What do you mean? I asked to
406 CP	Lavinia	11	you took me there. If that was not a sanatorium/What was it?/{R} A kind of hotel. A
406 CP	Reilly	16	/And if they believe it to be a sanatorium/That is good reason for not sending
406 CP	Reilly	18	one./The people who need my sort of sanatorium/Are not easily deceived./{L} Are you
406 CP	Edward	24	'lunatic'./Why should *you* go to a sanatorium?/I have never known anyone in my
406 CP	Edward	28	me mad./I am the one who needs a sanatorium —/But I'm not going there./{R}
406 CP	Reilly	31	/You are no case for my sanatorium:/You are much too ill./{E} Much
407 CP	Reilly	8	degree,/To qualify a patient for *my* sanatorium:/And one of them is an honest
410 CP	Reilly	21	/{R} If I had sent either of you to the sanatorium/In the state in which you came to
410 CP	Reilly	38	saints — such as those who go/To the sanatorium — you will forget this phrase,/And
419 CP	Reilly	12	am I to do?/{R} You will go to the sanatorium./{C} Oh, what an anti-climax! I have
419 CP	Celia	14	people/Who have been to your sanatorium, and come back again —/I don't
419 CP	Reilly	19	in mind/Cannot have been to this sanatorium./I am very careful whom I send
420 CP	Reilly	3	/And you will have no expenses at the sanatorium./{C} I don't in the least know what I

SANBALLAT (1)

158 Rock 5		2	all things, and desperately wicked./Sanballat the Horonite and Tobiah the

SANCTITY (1)

281 MC	Chorus	20	Christ,/There is holy ground, and the sanctity shall not depart from it/Though armies

SANCTUARIES (1)

594 Grad 9		1	will ne'er have been forgot./For in the sanctuaries of the soul/Incense of altar-smoke

SANCTUARY (7)

155 Rock 3		44	of Thy House, the peace of Thy sanctuary,/I have swept the floors and
166 Rock 10		27	kindled,/The light of altar and of sanctuary;/Small lights of those who meditate at
193 FQ: Little		78	marred foundations we forgot,/Of sanctuary and choir./This is the death of water
254 MC	Tempt4	34	gone for light ladies' ornament,/The sanctuary broken, and its stores/Swept into the
273 MC	Thomas	18	of prayer, the church of Christ,/The sanctuary, turned into a fortress./The Church
273 MC	Priests	25	come not like men, who/Respect the sanctuary, who kneel to the Body of Christ,/But
339 FR	Harry	9	the thirst and deprivation,/A stony sanctuary and a primitive altar,/The heat of the

SAND (9)

24 Rhapsody		20	of her dress/Is torn and stained with sand,/And you see the corner of her eye/Twists
72 WL: Thund		337	think/Sweat is dry and feet are in the sand/If there were only water amongst the rock/
92 Ash-Wed 2		50	cool of the day, with the blessing of sand,/Forgetting themselves and each other,
94 Ash-Wed 4		9	cool the dry rock and made firm the sand/In blue of larkspur, blue of Mary's colour,
160 Rock 7		16	/In the restless wind-whipped sand, or the hills where the wind will not let the
189 FQ: DrySal		184	ships, and/Ended their voyage on the sand, in the sea's lips/Or in the dark throat
193 FQ: Little		66	in the mouth,/Dead water and dead sand/Contending for the upper hand./The
605 Narcissus		4	/Your shadow sprawling over the sand at daybreak, or/Your shadow leaping
606 Narcissus		35	burning arrows/He danced on the hot sand/Until the arrows came./As he embraced

SANDS (1)

70 WL: Fire S		300	What should I resent?'/'On Margate Sands./I can connect/Nothing with nothing./

SANDWICH (2)

67 WL: Fire S		177	/The river bears no empty bottles, sandwich papers,/Silk handkerchiefs, cardboard
246 MC	Thomas	8	day,/Had fair crossing, found at Sandwich/Broc, Warenne, and the Sheriff of

SANDY (3)

72 WL: Thund		332	only rock/Rock and no water and the sandy road/The road winding above among the
98 Ash-Wed 6		19	smell renews the salt savour of the sandy earth/This is the time of tension between
204 de la Mare		2	and found/A desert island with a sandy cove/(A hiding place, but very dangerous

SANE (5)

234 Ad-dress		9	various types of mind./For some are sane and some are mad/And some are good and
344 FR	Violet	9	seems to me/That I am the only sane person in this house./Your behaviour all
346 FR	Agatha	35	worry about that./He is every bit as sane as you or I,/He sees the world as clearly as
454 CC	Colby	19	Mr. Simpkins?/{C} You seem to me sane. And I think I am./{E} I have no doubt on
454 CC	Colby	21	B. Kaghan has always seemed to me sane./{E} I should call him the very picture of

SANG (8)

57 Swee Night		37	Convent of the Sacred Heart,/And sang within the bloody wood/When
91 Ash-Wed 2		23	/The wind will listen. And the bones sang chirping/With the burden of the
92 Ash-Wed 2		48	ends./Under a juniper-tree the bones sang, scattered and shining/We are glad to be
95 Ash-Wed 4		25	the fountain sprang up and the bird sang down/Redeem the time, redeem the dream/
213 Growltiger		39	was not heard a sound./The lovers sang their last duet, in danger of their lives —/
264 MC	Priest3	17	waters, of thunder, of harps,/They sang as it were a new song./The blood of thy
378 CP	Edward	34	Riley;/It was just a name in a song he sang .../{C} He sang you a song about a man
378 CP	Celia	35	a name in a song he sang .../{C} He sang you a song about a man named Riley!/

SANITARY (1)

155 Rock 3		50	basements where the rat breeds/Or sanitary dwellings with numbered doors/Or a

SANITY (3)

338 FR	Harry	38	hard, when one has just recovered sanity,/And not yet assured in possession, that
454 CC	Eggers	22	I should call him the very picture of sanity./{C} But you never warned me about
508 CC	Claude	19	suggestion, Eggerson./A breath of sanity. Thank you for that./{MG} We parted

SAP (2)

191 FQ: Little		12	melting and freezing/The soul's sap quivers. There is no earth smell/Or smell of
247 MC Tempt1		12	Love in the orchard/Send the sap shooting. Mirth matches melancholy./{T}

SAPIENT (1)

54 Mr E Sun		2	Service/Polyphiloprogenitive/The sapient sutlers of the Lord/Drift across the

SAPPHIRES (1)

172 FQ: BurntN		49	which is always present./Garlic and sapphires in the mud/Clot the bedded axle-tree./

SARACEN (1)

280 MC Priest3		25	/Go seek alliance with the heathen Saracen,/To share his filthy rites, and try to

SARAH (4)

509 CC	Colby	13	died? Don't you remember, Aunt Sarah,/My finding a rattle and a jingle-bell,/
513 CC	Colby	12	That is a very strange question, Aunt Sarah:/To which I can only give a strange
514 CC Guzzard		21	Registration of birth. To Herbert and Sarah Guzzard/A son./{E} And what about
518 CC	Colby	32	/{C} Get you a taxi? Yes, Aunt Sarah;/But I should see you home./{MG}

SARCASTIC (1)

367 CP	Peter	21	together./{P} Now you're only being sarcastic:/Celia was interested in the art of the

SAT (10)

29 Aunt Helen		11	on the mantelpiece,/And the footman sat upon the dining-table/Holding the second
64 WL: Chess		77	/A Game of Chess/The Chair she sat in, like a burnished throne,/Glowed on the
67 WL: Fire S		182	addresses./By the waters of Leman I sat down and wept .../Sweet Thames, run softly
69 WL: Fire S		245	this same divan or bed;/I who have sat by Thebes below the wall/And walked
74 WL: Thund		423	obedient/To controlling hands/I sat upon the shore/Fishing, with the arid plain
91 Ash-Wed 2		1	our death./Lady, three white leopards sat under a juniper-tree/In the cool of the day,
228 Gus		29	the lead, or in character parts./I have sat by the bedside of poor Little Nell;/When the
587 Fable		23	— upset the chimes,/And once he sat the prior on the steeple,/To the astonishment
588 Fable		42	had been made,/The jovial epicures sat down to table./The menus of that time I am
589 Fable		73	who reads this romance./The Abbot sat as pasted to his chair,/His eye became the

SATE (2)

44 Cook Egg		1	of brandy neat./A Cooking Egg/Pipit sate upright in her chair/Some distance from
213 Growltiger		29	the forepeak of the vessel Growltiger sate alone,/Concentrating his attention on the

SATIETY (1)

91 Ash-Wed 2		2	/In the cool of the day, having fed to satiety/On my legs my heart my liver and that

SATIN (1)

64 WL: Chess		85	of her jewels rose to meet it,/From satin cases poured in rich profusion./In vials of

SATISFACTION (4)

260 MC Thomas		10	and Blood in sacrifice, oblation and satisfaction/for the sins of the whole world. It
436 CP	Lavinia	33	thought your expression was one of ... satisfaction!/{R} Mrs. Chamberlayne, I must be
552 ES	Ld Clav	21	the only way possible/To our mutual satisfaction./{MC} Your conscience was clear./
559 ES	Michael	39	for imposing this upon me?/And what satisfaction, I wonder, will it give you/In the

SATISFACTORY (9)

103 Journ Magi		31	the place; it was (you may say) satisfactory./All this was a long time ago, I
179 FQ: ECoker		69	was a way of putting it — not very satisfactory:/A periphrastic study in a worn-out
343 FR	Harry	34	the perfect master of Wishwood,/The satisfactory son. And as for me,/I am the last
401 CP	Edward	10	/Of shops, have always been satisfactory./I beg your pardon. But he *is* a

SAVES (1)

  38 Gerontion   44 fear. Think/Neither fear nor courage saves us. Unnatural vices/Are fathered by our

SAVING (6)

217 Jellicles   35   to do at all:/They are resting and saving themselves to be right/For the Jellicle

266 MC Thomas   27 have been a loyal subject to the King./Saving my order, I am at his command,/As his

266 MC Knight1   29 most faithful vassal in the land./{K1} Saving your order! let your order save you —/

266 MC Knight1   31 —/As I do not think it is like to do./Saving your ambition is what you mean,/Saving

266 MC Knight1   32   your ambition is what you mean,/Saving your pride, envy and spleen./{K2} Saving

266 MC Knight2   33   your pride, envy and spleen./{K2} Saving your insolence and greed./Won't you ask

SAVIOUR (1)

273 MC Chorus   4   most need?/Dead upon the tree, my Saviour,/Let not be in vain Thy labour;/Help

SAVOUR (2)

  98 Ash-Wed 6   19 ivory gates/And smell renews the salt savour of the sandy earth/This is the time of

269 MC Chorus   31   and ridiculous. I have tasted/The savour of putrid flesh in the spoon. I have felt/

SAW (59)

  50 Hippopot   25 Church can sleep and feed at once./I saw the 'potamus take wing/Ascending from the

  52 Whispers   2 was much possessed by death/And saw the skull beneath the skin;/And breastless

  62 WL: Burial   69 on the final stroke of nine./There I saw one I knew, and stopped him, crying:

  92 Ash-Wed 3   2   of the second stair/I turned and saw below/The same shape twisted on the

133 Eyes   t /MINOR POEMS/Eyes that last I saw in tears/Eyes that last I saw in tears/

133 Eyes   1 that last I saw in tears/Eyes that last I saw in tears/Through division/Here in death's

134 Wind   9 /Is a face that sweats with tears?/I saw across the blackened river/The camp fire

153 Rock 2   54 the clay be dug from the pit, let the saw cut the stone,/Let the fire not be quenched

188 FQ: DrySal 136 and business letters/(And those who saw them off have left the platform)/Their faces

188 FQ: DrySal 152 are voyaging;/You are not those who saw the harbour/Receding, or those who will

223 Pekes Pols   55 the bars of the area,/You never saw anything fiercer or hairier./And what with

226 Macavity   12 and thin;/You would know him if you saw him, for his eyes are sunken in./His brow is

233 Skimble   59 stationmaster with elation./But you saw him at Dumfries, where he summons the

242 MC Priest1   20 but confirmed by bitter adversity./I saw him as Chancellor, flattered by the King./

278 MC Knight2   8 was very much divided. Our King saw that/the one thing needful was to restore

291 FR   Amy   7   /{A} What's that? I thought I saw someone pass the window./What time is it?/

291 FR   Harry 20 /If you knew how you looked, when I saw you through the window!/Do you like to be

299 FR Downing   35 very quiet;/Very uncommon that I saw him in high spirits./For what my

300 FR Downing   22 see him?/{Do} Oh yes, Sir, I'm sure I saw him./I don't mean to say that he had any

300 FR Downing   25 keeping me up. But when I say I saw him,/I mean that I saw him accidental./You

300 FR Downing   26 when I say I saw him,/I mean that I saw him accidental./You see, Sir, I was down in

300 FR Downing   30 upper deck./And I remember, there I saw his Lordship/Leaning over the rail, looking

304 FR   Mary   3 one of your favourite students:/I only saw you as a hard headmistress/Who knew the

314 FR Warburt   37 /How he fought against it! I never saw a man/More anxious to live./{H} Not at all

321 FR   Harry   7 let's talk about yourself./{H} I never saw a photograph. There is no portrait./{W}

321 FR   Harry   18   Winchell is real. But Denman saw him./But what if Denman saw him, and yet

321 FR   Harry   19 saw him./But what if Denman saw him, and yet he was not real?/That would

321 FR   Harry   21 that has happened./What if *you* saw him, and .../{W} Harry! Pull yourself

321 FR   Winch 33 don't look a year older/Than when I saw you last, my Lord. But a country sergeant/

340 FR   Amy   30 /You may be close, but I always saw through *him*./And now it is my son./{Ag} I

362 CP   Reilly   5 you will feel a little jealous/That she saw it first, and had the courage to break it —/

363 CP Edward 39 enough. But that is not all./Since I saw her this morning when we had breakfast/I

364 CP Edward   5 know what she was wearing/When I saw her last. And yet I want her back./And I

365 CP Edward 22 /{J} *You* don't know?/{E} I never saw him before in my life./{J} But how did he

369 CP   Peter 24 how you came to know Celia./{P} I saw her again a few days later/Alone at a

380 CP   Celia 24 for him./I thought he had talent; I saw that he was lonely;/I thought that I could

382 CP   Celia 19 for your heart, your blood;/And saw only a beetle the size of a man/With

382 CP   Celia 27 /I see you as a person whom I never saw before./The man I saw before, he was only

382 CP   Celia 28 whom I never saw before./The man I saw before, he was only a projection —/I see

386 CP   Celia 34 /What he's been found out in. I never saw you so before./This is really a ludicrous

402 CP Edward 18 know it then myself — but if they saw it/I should have thought that a doctor

430 CP   Peter   7 /I left Los Angeles three days ago./I saw Sheila Paisley at lunch to-day/And she told

430 CP   Peter 15 so early./It does seem ages since I last saw any of you!/And how are you, Alex? And

430 CP   Peter 19 from New York./The Bologolomskys saw me off./You remember Princess

437 CP   Reilly   7   */That apparition, sole of men, he saw./For know there are two worlds of life and*

437 CP   Reilly 14 met Miss Coplestone, in this room,/I saw the image, standing behind her chair,/Of a

463 CC Claude   2 aunt,/Or so she made me feel. I never saw you alone./And then when I sent you both

472 CC Lucasta 34 /In facing facts — or the facts as you saw them./And yet, all the time, I found I

476 CC Lucasta 11 cleverly, that when we first met/You saw I was trying to give a false impression./I

479 CC Kaghan 31 made a bad impression at the start:/I saw that it was necessary. I'm afraid Colby/Has

482 CC	Lady E	31	breeding./I said to myself, when I first saw you,/'He is very well bred'. I knew nothing
498 CC	Claude	18	it. I visited her house/Often. I never saw more than one baby./{E} She might have
515 CC	Guzzard	7	I had to break the news to you./You saw the child. You assumed that it was yours;/
531 ES	Lambert	34	he must see you./I told him you never saw anyone, my Lord,/But by previous
554 ES	Piggott	31	leaving it, as usual, to Nurse)/When I saw that Mrs. Carghill had caught you./You
555 ES	Monica	12	Now I must fly. {}/[*Exit*]/{M} I saw Mrs. Piggott bothering you again/So I
569 ES	Ld Clav	6	that she would love the actor/If she saw him, off the stage, without his costume and
577 ES	Carghil	32	has great abilities for business./I saw that, and so does Señor Gomez./He's
578 ES	Michael	25	it used to get on my nerves, when I saw you/Always sitting there with your nose in

SAWDUST (1)

13 Prufrock		7	nights in one-night cheap hotels/And sawdust restaurants with oyster-shells:/Streets

SAWDUST-TRAMPLED (1)

22 Preludes		16	Of faint stale smells of beer/From the sawdust-trampled street/With all its muddy feet

SAY (314)

14 Prufrock		41	in the middle of my hair —/(They will say: 'How his hair is growing thin!')/My
14 Prufrock		44	asserted by a simple pin —/(They will say: 'But how his arms and legs are thin!')/Do I
15 Prufrock		70	/And how should I begin?/Shall I say, I have gone at dusk through narrow streets/
16 Prufrock		94	some overwhelming question,/To say: 'I am Lazarus, come from the dead,/Come
16 Prufrock		97	settling a pillow by her head,/Should say: 'That is not what I meant at all./That is not
16 Prufrock		104	so much more? —It is impossible to say just what I mean!/But as if a magic lantern
16 Prufrock		108	turning toward the window, should say:/'That is not it at all,/That is not what I
18 Portrait		8	or left unsaid./We have been, let us say, to hear the latest Pole/Transmit the
18 Portrait		27	lives./How much it means that I say this to you —/Without these friendships —
20 Portrait		63	when you have prevailed/You can say: at this point many a one has failed./But
28 Boston ET		9	and he at the end of the street,/And I say, 'Cousin Harriet, here is the *Boston Evening*
61 WL: Burial		21	rubbish? Son of man,/You cannot say, or guess, for you know only/A heap of
103 Journ Magi		31	/Finding the place; it was (you may say) satisfactory./All this was a long time ago, I
107 Animula		15	the fairies do and what the servants say./The heavy burden of the growing soul/
116 SP	Dusty	16	/Pick up the receiver/{Du} What'll I say?/{Do} Say what you like: say I'm ill,/Say
116 SP	Doris	17	the receiver/{Du} What'll I say?/{Do} Say what you like: say I'm ill,/Say I broke my
116 SP	Doris	17	I say?/{Do} Say what you like: say I'm ill,/Say I broke my leg on the stairs/Say
116 SP	Doris	18	/{Do} Say what you like: say I'm ill,/Say I broke my leg on the stairs/Say we've had a
116 SP	Doris	18	ill,/Say I broke my leg on the stairs/Say we've had a fire/{Du} Hello Hello are you
116 SP	Dusty	32	hopes to be all right on Monday/I say do you mind if I ring off now/She's got her
119 SP	Klip	11	acquainted/{Kl} Sam — I should say Loot Sam Wauchope/{Kr} Of the Canadian
119 SP	Klip	16	/{Kl} Yes we did our bit, as you folks say,/I'll tell the world we got the Hun on the
119 SP	Klip	29	we like London!! Eh what Klip?/{Kl} Say, Miss — er — uh — London's swell./We
119 SP	Klip	37	A little too gay for us/Yes I'll say a little too gay./{Kr} Yes London's a little
125 SA Sweeney		3	you./But here's what I was going to say./He didn't know if he was alive/and the girl
148 Rock 1		57	money/But most expect dividends./I say to you: *Make perfect your will.*/I say: take
148 Rock 1		58	say to you: *Make perfect your will.*/I say: take no thought of the harvest,/But only of
151 Rock 2		8	on the back of a tortoise./And some say: 'How can we love our neighbour? For love
155 Rock 3		34	the gravel court,/And the wind shall say: 'Here were decent godless people:/Their
158 Rock 5		6	enterprise, sniffing and barking: they say, 'This house is a nest of serpents, let us
161 Rock 7		27	left GOD not for other gods, they say, but for no god; and this has never
161 Rock 7		37	/CHORUS:/What does the world say, does the whole world stray in high-powered
166 Rock 10		5	portents of fear./And what shall we say of the future? Is one church all we can
173 FQ: BurntN		70	there is only the dance./I can only say, *there* we have been: but I cannot say where.
173 FQ: BurntN		70	say, *there* we have been: but I cannot say where./And I cannot say, how long, for that
173 FQ: BurntN		71	but I cannot say where./And I cannot say, how long, for that is to place it in time./The
175 FQ: BurntN	149	that only, but the co-existence,/Or say that the end precedes the beginning,/And
181 FQ: ECoker	135	to the agony/Of death and birth./You say I am repeating/Something I have said
181 FQ: ECoker	136	/Something I have said before. I shall say it again./Shall I say it again? In order to
181 FQ: ECoker	137	before. I shall say it again./Shall I say it again? In order to arrive there,/To arrive
182 FQ: ECoker	179	/For the thing one no longer has to say, or the way in which/One is no longer
182 FQ: ECoker	180	in which/One is no longer disposed to say it. And so each venture/Is a new beginning,
201 Def Island		20	the lanes and the streets of Britain:/to say, to the past and the future generations/of
217 Jellicles		34	the sun is shining bright/You would say they had nothing to do at all:/They are
218 Mung Rump	15	pearls:/Then the family would say: 'It's that horrible cat!/It was Mungojerrie
219 Mung Rump	25	appear from behind the scenes/And say in a voice that was broken with sorrow:/'I'm
219 Mung Rump	28	— like that!'/Then the family would say: 'It's that horrible cat!/It was Mungojerrie
219 Mung Rump	31	/And some of the time you would say it was luck, and some of the time you would
219 Mung Rump	31	luck, and some of the time you would say it was weather./They would go through the
219 Mung Rump	38	to be Ming —/Then the family would say: 'Now which was which cat?/It was
220 Old Deut		6	wives/And more — I am tempted to say, ninety-nine;/And his numerous progeny

221 Old Deut   34   afternoon sleep;/And when the men say: 'There's just time for one more,'/Then the
221 Old Deut   36   from her back parlour will peep/And say: 'Now then, out you go, by the back door,/
222 Pekes Pols   4   and the Poms, although most people say/That they do not like fighting, yet once in a
222 Pekes Pols   25   /Now the Peke, although people may say what they please,/Is no British Dog, but a
224 Mr Mistoff   18   /Presto!/Away we go!/And we all say: OH!/Well I never!/Was there ever/A Cat so
225 Mr Mistoff   37   lying out on the lawn./And we all say: OH!/Well I never!/Was there ever/A Cat so
226 Macavity   21   /He's outwardly respectable. (They say he cheats at cards.)/And his footprints are
227 Macavity   31   has been disclosed, the Secret Service say:/'It *must* have been Macavity!' — but he's a
227 Macavity   39   WASN'T THERE!/And they say that all the Cats whose wicked deeds are
229 Gus   49   to jump through a hoop.'/And he'll say, as he scratches himself with his claws,/
231 Bust Jones   36   observed/All his life a routine, so he'd say./Or, to put it in rhyme: 'I shall last out my
232 Skimble   17   the Northern Hemisphere!/You may say that by and large it is Skimble who's in
234 Ad-dress   19   /So first, your memory I'll jog,/And say: A CAT IS NOT A DOG./Now Dogs
235 Ad-dress   38   A CAT'S A CAT./With Cats, some say, one rule is true:/*Don't speak till you are*
235 Ad-dress   41   /Myself, I do not hold with that —/I say, you should ad-dress a Cat./But always keep
589 Fable   79   the collar,/And before any one could say 'O jiminy!'/The pair had vanisht swiftly up
590 Time Space   1   the ruins./If Time and Space, as Sages say,/Are things which cannot be,/The sun which
590 Space Time   1   /Song/If space and time, as sages say,/Are things that cannot be,/The fly that lives
595 Grad 14   4   bell/And one that we are ever loth to say./But 'tis a call we cannot disobey,/*Exeunt*
243 MC Priest2   5   dispelled. Let us therefore rejoice,/I say rejoice, and show a glad face for his
246 MC Tempt1   35   /Favour with the King, shall we say that summer's over/Or that the good time
252 MC Thomas   22   you have done before:/No one shall say that I betrayed a king./{T3} Then, my Lord,
253 MC Thomas   3   before was never time or place./{T} Say what you come to say./{T4} It shall be said
253 MC Thomas   3   or place./{T} Say what you come to say./{T4} It shall be said at last./Hooks have
262 MC Thomas   4   keep in your hearts/these words that I say, and think of them at another time. In the
265 MC Priest3   6   Only in retrospection, selection,/We say, that was the day. The critical moment/That
266 MC Thomas   8   whatever your business may be./You say, from the King?/{K1} Most surely from the
267 MC Thomas   16   or torn./Have you something to say?/{K1} By the King's command./Shall we say
267 MC Knight1   18   By the King's command./Shall we say it now?/{K2} Without delay,/Before the old
267 MC Thomas   21   off and away./{T} What you have to say/By the King's command — if it be the
268 MC Knight1   14   the nation./{K1} These are the facts./Say therefore if you will be content/To answer
268 MC Thomas   37   King's command, I will be bold/To say: seven years were my people without/My
277 MC Knight3   1   But there is one thing I should like to say, and I might as/well say it at once. It is this:
277 MC Knight3   2   should like to say, and I might as/well say it at once. It is this: in what we have done,
277 MC Knight3   6   /who put our country first. I dare say that we didn't make a/very good impression
277 MC Knight3   18   — God bless him — will have to/say, for reasons of state, that he never meant
277 MC Knight3   27   /I think that is about all I have to say./{K1} I think we will all agree that William
278 MC Knight2   18   various official relations; and I/may say that I have never known a man so well
279 MC Knight4   11   speakers who have preceded me, to say nothing/of our leader, Reginald Fitz Urse,
279 MC Knight4   14   lines of argument./What I have to say may be put in the form of a question: *Who*
279 MC Knight4   37   the doors/should be opened. Need I say more? I think, with these facts before/you,
287 FR   Gerald   1   very much now, myself;/But I must say I've met some very decent specimens/And
287 FR   Violet   11   {}/[*Exit*]/{V} Really, Gerald, I must say you're very tactless,/And I think that
289 FR   Gerald   5   to give us all the hump./I must say, this isn't cheerful for Amy's birthday/Or
289 FR   Gerald   6   Make him feel at home, I say!/Make him feel that what has happened
289 FR   Amy   12   she cares to betray,/I am bound to say that I agree with you./{C} I never wrote to
292 FR   Harry   25   nothing changed? how can you say that nothing is changed?/You all look so
293 FR   Gerald   30   of events./{G} Well, you can't say that nothing has happened to *me*./I started
299 FR Downing   2   himself./{Do} Quite natural, if I may say so, Sir,/After what happened./{C} Quite so,
299 FR Downing   11   knew it?/{Do} Unlikely, Sir, if I may say so./Much more likely to have been an
299 FR Downing   33   the voyage?/{Do} Well, you might say depressed, Sir./But you know his Lordship
299 FR Downing   39   more nervous than usual;/I mean to say, you could see that he was nervous./He
300 FR Downing   8   his Lordship is rather psychic, as they say./{C} Were they always together?/{Do}
300 FR Downing   15   contrary of the usual opinion,/I dare say. She wouldn't leave him alone./And there's
300 FR Downing   23   I'm sure I saw him./I don't mean to say that he had any orders —/His Lordship is
300 FR Downing   25   /About keeping me up. But when I say I saw him,/I mean that I saw him accidental.
301 FR   Violet   10   /{V} Well, Charles, I must say, with your investigations,/You seem to have
303 FR   Mary   26   /Which is worse, thinking of what to say to John,/Or having to listen to Arthur's
308 FR   Mary   24   /Not there./{M} But surely, what you say/Only proves that you expected Wishwood/
309 FR   Mary   20   did not know I knew./Even if, as you say, Wishwood is a cheat,/Your family a
310 FR   Harry   33   I know what I am saying, or why I say it,/That does not matter. You bring me
314 FR Warburt   7   engagement to come./{W} I dare say we've both changed a good deal, Harry./A
320 FR Warburt   2   you let me tell you/What I had to say?/{H} Very well, tell me./{W} It's about your
320 FR Warburt   30   /Depends on you. I don't like to say this;/But you know that I am a very old
324 FR   Violet   9   you might have had something to say./Aren't you sorry for your brother? Aren't

326	FR	Violet	31	make no observations on what you say, Harry;/My comments are not always
328	FR	Charles	7	there is a paragraph ... I'm glad to say/It's not very conspicuous .../{G} There'll
337	FR	Amy	33	/{A} He shall go? and who are you to say he shall go?/I think I know well enough why
337	FR	Agatha	35	him to go./{Ag} I wish nothing. I only say what I know must happen./{A} You only
337	FR	Amy	36	I know must happen./{A} You only say what you intended to happen./{H} Oh,
345	FR	Harry	4	be quite happy about it,/So I shall say good-bye, until we meet again./{G} Well, if
346	FR	Downing	16	think it laughable, what I'm going to say —/But it's not really strange, Miss, when
346	FR	Downing	31	being his Lordship./And that's why I say now, I have a feeling/That he won't want
346	FR	Downing	39	I understand you, Miss. And if I may say so,/Now that you've raised the subject, I'm
347	FR	Warburt	34	going and coming./But I'm glad to say that John is getting on nicely;/It wasn't so
354	CP	Julia	17	a time./What a life she led! I used to say to her: 'Greta!/You have too much vitality.'
356	CP	Julia	32	she's in the pantry/Listening to all we say!/{E} No, she's not in the pantry./{C} Will
357	CP	Celia	2	But, Edward ... what was I going to say?/It's dreadful for old ladies alone in the
357	CP	Julia	26	/{E} Hampshire?/{J} Didn't you say Hampshire?/{E} No, I didn't say
357	CP	Edward	27	you say Hampshire?/{E} No, I didn't say Hampshire./{J} Did you say Hampstead?/
357	CP	Julia	28	I didn't say Hampshire./{J} Did you say Hampstead?/{E} No, I didn't say
357	CP	Edward	29	you say Hampstead?/{E} No, I didn't say Hampstead./{J} But she must live
360	CP	Edward	6	in, this afternoon./She left a note to say that she was leaving me;/But I don't know
360	CP	Reilly	24	Then look at the brighter side./You say you don't know where she's gone?/{E} No, I
361	CP	Reilly	33	control. So let me continue./I will say then, you experience some relief/Of which
362	CP	Reilly	8	out so, yet .../{UG} Are you going to say, you love her?/{E} Why, I thought we took
362	CP	Edward	14	without explanation,/Only a note to say that she had gone/And was not coming
363	CP	Edward	27	what I'm waiting for?/Shall I say to my friends, 'My wife has gone away'?/
363	CP	Edward	28	/And they answer 'Where?' and I say 'I don't know';/And they say, 'But when will
363	CP	Edward	29	and I say 'I don't know';/And they say, 'But when will she be back?'/And I reply 'I
364	CP	Edward	18	again — here./{E} Do you mean to say that you know where she is?/{UG} That
365	CP	Julia	26	And what's her name?/Did I hear him say his name was Riley?/{E} I don't know his
366	CP	Peter	16	/I remembered something I had to say to Edward .../{J} Oh, about Lavinia?/{P}
368	CP	Alex	27	I can make half a dozen dishes. Don't say a word./I shall begin at once. {}/[*Exit to*
368	CP	Peter	33	/{P} A Thursday. Why do you say amateur?/{E} Lavinia's attempts at starting
369	CP	Peter	1	/For a time at least./{P} I wouldn't say that./But Lavinia was awfully kind to me/
371	CP	Edward	15	Celia you remember./Remember! I say it's already a memory./{P} But I must see
372	CP	Edward	34	*her* what I've told you./{E} I shall not say anything about it to Lavinia./{P} Thank
374	CP	Celia	6	to be anyone with you/I was going to say I'd come back for my umbrella ... ./I must
374	CP	Celia	7	back for my umbrella ... ./I must say you don't seem very pleased to see me./
374	CP	Edward	12	and then I'll go./{E} But how can you say you understand what has happened?/*I* don't
375	CP	Celia	6	coming back!/Do you mean to say that she's laid a trap for us?/{E} No. If there
376	CP	Celia	5	really did leave my umbrella,/And I'll say I found you here starving and helpless/And
376	CP	m	8	*goes to front door, and is/heard to say:*]/{E} Julia!/What have you come back for? {}
378	CP	Celia	7	I go, there's something/I want to say to Edward./{J} About Lavinia?/Well, come
380	CP	Celia	8	as a passing diversion./Oh, I dare say that you deceived yourself:/But that's what
381	CP	Edward	33	could be changed./The self that can say 'I want this — or want that' —/The self that
383	CP	Edward	14	may be a little flat —/But why did she say that it was a half-bottle?/It's one of my best:
385	CP	Reilly	16	be embarrassing?/What would you say to them, or they to you/After the first ten
388	CP	Peter	7	/So what I've really come for is to say good-bye./{C} Well, Peter, I'm awfully glad,
388	CP	Peter	15	shall miss you./{P} It's nice of you to say so;/But you'll find someone better, to go
389	CP	Peter	1	you up tomorrow/And come in to say good-bye before I left./{L} And Celia's
389	CP	Celia	24	— somewhere —/I should like to say good-bye — as friends./{L} Why, Celia, but
389	CP	Celia	31	not see you again./What I want to say is this: I should like you to remember me/As
390	CP	Julia	12	I've been in Essex!/{J} Lavinia! Don't say you've had a lapse of memory!/Then that
391	CP	Julia	30	/{E} *When* shall we see you?/{J} Did I say you'd see me?/Good-bye. I believe ... I
391	CP	Lavinia	34	ALEX *and* PETER]/{L} I must say, you don't seem very pleased to see me./{E}
391	CP	Edward	35	very pleased to see me./{E} I can't say that I've had much opportunity/To seem
392	CP	Lavinia	1	you./{L} Yes, that was a silly thing to say./Like a schoolgirl. Like Celia. I don't know
393	CP	Lavinia	18	our honeymoon,/I couldn't make you say where you wanted to go .../{E} But I wanted
394	CP	Edward	28	me?/{E} I don't know either./You say you were trying to 'encourage' me:/Then
396	CP	Edward	21	/But I'm sorry for you .../{E} Don't say you are sorry for me!/I have had enough of
397	CP	Edward	15	of a nervous breakdown!/{E} Don't say that!/{L} I must say it./I know ... of a doctor
397	CP	Lavinia	16	/{E} Don't say that!/{L} I must say it./I know ... of a doctor who I think could
401	CP	Reilly	20	... Or did she *send* you?/{R} I cannot say that I had been invited;/And Mrs.
403	CP	Reilly	21	would like to think:/Only, shall we say, within your modest capacity./Try to
404	CP	Reilly	10	/And taking note of what you do not say./{E} I once experienced the extreme of
404	CP	Reilly	36	I am./Is it far to go?/{R} You might say, a long journey./But before I treat a patient
405	CP	Lavinia	27	to talk about my husband:/I didn't say I was prepared to meet him./{E} And I did
406	CP	Edward	1	hotel?/{E} I don't know — I mean to say,/That doesn't concern you./{L} In that case,

407 CP	Lavinia	3	/{L} Don't be silly, Edward. When I say practical,/I mean practical in the things that
407 CP	Reilly	6	interrupt this interesting discussion?/I say you are both too ill. There are several
407 CP	Lavinia	11	of their suffering./{L} No one can say my husband has an honest mind./{E} And I
407 CP	Edward	12	mind./{E} And I could not honestly say that of *you*, Lavinia./{R} I congratulate you
407 CP	Reilly	15	you to appreciate what I have to say to you./I do not trouble myself with the
409 CP	Reilly	24	*are* cold-hearted, Edward./{R} So you say, Mrs. Chamberlayne./And now, let us turn
409 CP	Reilly	30	him into this position) —/When, I say, you discovered that your young friend/Had
410 CP	Reilly	14	unenlightenment,/*You* could always say: 'he could not love any woman;'/*You* could
410 CP	Reilly	15	love any woman;'/*You* could always say: 'no man could love her.'/You could accuse
411 CP	Edward	20	/{E} Yes, I have./But it's difficult to say./{L} But I wish you would say it./At least,
411 CP	Lavinia	21	to say./{L} But I wish you would say it./At least, there is something I would like
411 CP	Edward	33	/{E} Have you anything else to say to us, Sir Henry?/{R} No. Not in this
413 CP	Reilly	36	we decide/What *is* normality. You say there are two things:/What is the first?/{C}
415 CP	Celia	9	of as immoral/Just the people who we say have no moral sense?/I've never noticed that
419 CP	Celia	15	come back again —/I don't mean to say they weren't much better for it —/That's
419 CP	Reilly	26	your friends came back./I did not say they stayed there./{C} What becomes of
421 CP	Reilly	34	ought to be grateful./{R} And when I say to one like her/'Work out your salvation
434 CP	Lavinia	31	I'm so sorry — what a feeble thing to say!/But you know what I mean./{E} And you
435 CP	Peter	2	all a mistake./Julia! Why don't *you* say anything?/{J} You gave her those two years,
436 CP	Lavinia	20	Henry, there is something I want to say to you./While Alex was telling us what had
437 CP	Reilly	36	what I mean. Rather the contrary./I'd say that she suffered all that we should suffer/In
437 CP	Reilly	39	of the body to become a *thing*./I'd say she suffered more, because more conscious/
440 CP	Edward	22	/{E} Very well./I might almost say, your best. But you always look your best./
440 CP	Lavinia	26	you're trying to cheer me up./To say I always look my best can only mean the
445 CC	Eggers	26	.../{E} Oh, Sir Claude, you shouldn't say that!/Mr. Simpkins is far better qualified
447 CC	Claude	3	ready —/Let's think what you're to say to Lady Elizabeth,/Coming back from the
447 CC	Eggers	19	than I am./{E} Oh, I wouldn't say that, Sir Claude!/She has too much respect
447 CC	Claude	26	during her absence,/You must say you had to leave under medical orders./
447 CC	Claude	29	be sympathetic. And as for Colby —/Say that Mr. Simpkins was highly
447 CC	Claude	30	was highly recommended,/And say that I had to make a quick decision/Because
448 CC	Claude	3	/There are some things you could say better than I could,/And ways in which you
448 CC	Eggers	7	he is with me./{E} Oh, you mustn't say that!/Though I've done my best to gain his
449 CC	Claude	3	a very different way, yes. You might say *mislaid*,/Since the father is dead, and there's
451 CC	Eggers	8	made the most of it —/That I will say. An encouraging example/For you, Mr.
453 CC	Eggers	1	Mr. Simpkins./I never do. I always say/That if you give Miss Angel an inch/She'll
453 CC	Lucasta	13	*Mr.* Simpkins is going to believe all I say,/*Mr.* Eggerson. And I know he'll be nice to
455 CC	Eggers	31	works wonders, that's what I always say./But I don't expect you'll have to see much
455 CC	Eggers	40	/Rather a *grande dame*, as the French say./That's what Sir Claude admires about her./
457 CC	Eggers	3	come to them. That's what *I* always say./And I'm sure you'll like her. She's *such* a
458 CC	Claude	14	at Victoria./{SC} Do you mean to say that you changed your ticket?/{E} Yes, how
459 CC	Lady E	4	better than their faces./What did you say his name was?/{SC} Colby Simpkins. {}/
459 CC	Lady E	22	life, Mr. Colby./Neither, I regret to say, does Eggerson./What colour have you
461 CC	Eggers	16	him out to dinner one Sunday?'/But I say: 'We couldn't ask him to come/All the way
466 CC	Claude	18	kind of substitute for religion./I dare say truly religious people —/I've never known
470 CC	Colby	25	Musical!/{C} Well, I'd heard you say you wanted to see it./{L} But not with you!/
475 CC	Colby	33	you know most of what there is to say/Already, either from what I've told you/Or
477 CC	Lucasta	12	{}/[*A pause*]/{L} But why don't you say something? Are you shocked?/{C} Shocked?
479 CC	Kaghan	33	he'll have to live down./— I must say, I like the way you've had the place done
481 CC	Lady E	23	/So I have to see you in it. Did you say you were leaving?/{K} We're going out to
482 CC	Lady E	23	... and kind./{LE} Oh, I don't say they're not intelligent and kind./I'm not
483 CC	Lady E	29	*portrait*]/{LE} What was I going to say? Oh, I know./Do you believe in
483 CC	Lady E	32	never thought about it./{LE} I can't say that *I* believe in it./I did, for a time. I
483 CC	Lady E	34	the doctrine./But I was going to say, *if* I believed in it/I should have said that we
485 CC	Lady E	37	Guzzard./{LE} Guzzard? Did you say Guzzard? An unusual name./Guzzard, did
485 CC	Lady E	38	An unusual name./Guzzard, did you say? The name means something to me./Yes.
486 CC	Colby	2	the name before;/Although, as you say, it is an uncommon one./You couldn't have
486 CC	Lady E	18	Mrs. Guzzard's sister —/Who you say was your mother — really was your mother?
486 CC	Colby	24	no children of their own./That is to say, they had had one little boy/Who died when
488 CC	Colby	22	—/Absolutely nothing — for me to say about it./I must leave that to you./{SC} I
489 CC	Lady E	33	from you, perhaps./No, I shouldn't say that. But she had a child/Left on her hands.
490 CC	Colby	24	a parent./I am sorry. But that's why I say it doesn't matter/To me, which of you
491 CC	Colby	18	in that way, Colby?/{C} I can only say what I feel at the moment:/And yet I believe
492 CC	Claude	13	He knows all about it./Let us say no more tonight. Now, Colby,/Can you find
492 CC	Claude	29	in a reminiscent mood' —/Oh yes. To say something of my early ambitions/To be a
494 CC	Lady E	10	is yours!/So I hope Mrs. Guzzard will say he is your son/And I needn't believe her. I

496 CC	Eggers	17	/At such short notice./{E} Don't say that, Sir Claude./It's true, I haven't much
497 CC	Eggers	33	for Mr. Simpkins to take,/If I may say so. Of course, we might discover/Another
499 CC	Lucasta	31	I wouldn't. Just to spite you,/I dare say. That was why I took an interest/In Colby.
501 CC	Lady E	9	them./{LE} I don't think you ought to say that, Lucasta;/I have always been a person
501 CC	Claude	15	not sure of anything./Perhaps, as you say, I've misunderstood B.,/And I've never
503 CC	Colby	27	Good-bye, Colby./{C} Why do you say good-bye?/{L} Good-bye to Colby as
505 CC	Claude	2	/My confidential clerk. That is to say,/Colby's predecessor, who recently retired./
505 CC	Claude	5	been in my confidence — and I may say, my friend —/For very many years. So I
506 CC	Eggers	1	charge of by the father./That is to say, placed out to be cared for/Till further
507 CC	Guzzard	20	satisfactory —/So long, that is to say, as the money was forthcoming./{E} Did the
511 CC	Lucasta	3	to talk that language any longer:/Just say you're embarrassed./{K} Well, I am
512 CC	Guzzard	2	wedding./{MG} I am glad to hear you say so, Lady Elizabeth./But are you satisfied?/
514 CC	Guzzard	3	man, Colby./Be careful what you say./{C} A dead obscure man./{MG} You shall
516 CC	Guzzard	14	organist./{MG} You should say, Colby, not very successful./{C} And I wish
517 CC	Eggers	33	not a very good organist!/{E} Don't say that, Mr. Simpkins, until you've tried our
518 CC	Guzzard	38	What do I mind?/{MG} Then I will say goodbye. You have all had your wish/In
522 ES	dedic	10	given me./*The words mean what they say, but some have a further meaning/For you*
524 ES	Charles	7	whole afternoon./{C} But I couldn't say what I wanted to say to you/Over luncheon
524 ES	Charles	7	But I couldn't say what I wanted to say to you/Over luncheon .../{M} That's your
525 ES	Charles	7	*me* the whole afternoon./I couldn't say what I wanted to, in a restaurant;/And then
525 ES	Monica	32	very well/What it is you want to say. I've heard it all before./{C} And you'll hear
525 ES	Charles	35	right./But I've something else to say that I haven't said before,/That will give
526 ES	Charles	5	to believe it. And I've made you say so!/But now that you've said so, you must
526 ES	Charles	6	now that you've said so, you must say it again,/For I need so much assurance! Are
526 ES	Monica	26	*with trolley*]/{M} and I shall say, 'Lambert,/Please let his lordship know that
527 ES	Charles	33	To share the burden. Sisters, I should say,/For your brother's never been of any use to
530 ES	Ld Clav	2	to jot down notes of what I had to say to people:/Now I've no more to say, and no
530 ES	Ld Clav	3	say to people:/Now I've no more to say, and no one to say it to./I've been
530 ES	Ld Clav	3	I've no more to say, and no one to say it to./I've been wondering ... how many
531 ES	Ld Clav	20	the reward/Of every public man./{LC} Say rather, the exequies/Of the failed successes,
532 ES	Charles	23	Will you bring my coat?/{C} I'll say goodbye, sir./And look forward to seeing
532 ES	Gomez	32	as thick as thieves, you might almost say./Don't you know me, Dick?/{LC} Fred
533 ES	Gomez	17	the time to take a long holiday,/Let's say a rest cure — that's what I've come for./
534 ES	Gomez	19	I can tell you, is a mug's game./I say that — with conviction./No, forgery, or
535 ES	Gomez	5	you're sure you deserve. But when I say 'trust' ... {}/[*Knock. Enter* LAMBERT]/
535 ES	Gomez	10	Yes, my Lord. {}/[*Exit*]/{G} I began to say: when I say 'trust'/I use the term as
535 ES	Gomez	10	{}/[*Exit*]/{G} I began to say: when I say 'trust'/I use the term as experience has
536 ES	Gomez	35	a good thing./My mother — I dare say she's still alive,/But she must be very old.
538 ES	Gomez	14	you got on in politics./Shall we say that you did very well by yourself?/Though
538 ES	Gomez	26	been more or less forgotten./I dare say you did make some mistake, Dick .../That
540 ES	Gomez	34	face it./Do you see now, Dick, why I say I can trust you?/{LC} If you think that this
541 ES	Gomez	17	... blackmail!/On the contrary, I dare say I could buy you out/Several times over. San
541 ES	Gomez	38	I shan't keep you long, though I dare say your caller/Could hang on for another
547 ES	Ld Clav	12	as I had feared. But I'm not going to say/Nothing could be worse. Where there's a
549 ES	Carghil	32	That's what she said./Or did she say 'yellow'? I'm not quite sure./You do
550 ES	Carghil	13	didn't last long./People sometimes say: 'Make one mistake in love,/You're more
551 ES	Carghil	21	acted as you did./{MC} Who can say whether a heart's been broken/Once it's
552 ES	Carghil	34	/Whatever part you've played, I must say you've always looked it./{LC} I've no longer
553 ES	Ld Clav	3	/You're surprisingly confident, I must say,/About your understanding of my character.
555 ES	Piggott	3	it once. A charming person,/I dare say, but not quite your sort or mine./I suspected
557 ES	Ld Clav	14	speculative business./{LC} I dare say you've tried a little private speculation./{Mi}
558 ES	Ld Clav	12	let me have your version first./I dare say Sir Alfred's will be rather different./And
558 ES	Ld Clav	13	rather different./And what else did he say?/{Mi} He took the usual line,/Just like the
559 ES	Michael	35	sake!/I was just your son — that is to say,/A kind of prolongation of your existence,/
561 ES	Monica	31	has just been exhibiting./{M} Michael! Say something./{Mi} What is there to say?/I
561 ES	Michael	32	Say something./{Mi} What is there to say?/I want to leave England, and make my
562 ES	Monica	3	speech./This love is silent./What can I say to you?/However Michael has behaved,
570 ES	Ld Clav	12	she died silently. She had nothing to say to me./I think of your mother, when she lay
573 ES	Ld Clav	18	/Are, I think, determined. Let us say no more about it./Meanwhile, I feel sure
573 ES	Carghil	37	a mother to her already./You may say that I just missed being her mother!/I've
577 ES	Gomez	19	/{G} Well, Michael, what do you say to all this?/{Mi} I'll say that Hemington has
577 ES	Michael	20	what do you say to all this?/{Mi} I'll say that Hemington has plenty of cheek./Señor
578 ES	Ld Clav	2	prevent him. I have something to say to you,/Michael, before you go. I shall never
579 ES	Michael	21	come to a decision,/It's as well to say good-bye at once and be done with it./{LC}
579 ES	Michael	27	/{Mi} Well ... there's nothing more to say, is there?/{LC} Nothing at all./{Mi} Then we

580 ES	Ld Clav	36	us./{LC} Monica my dear,/What you say comes home to me. I fear for Michael;/
581 ES	Ld Clav	7	I shall not be here. You heard me say to him/That this might be a final good-bye./
582 ES	Charles	34	.../{C} I know what you're going to say!/We *were* alone together, in some

SAYING (37)

32 Hysteria	7	cloth over the rusty/green iron table, saying: 'If the lady and gentleman wish to take
91 Ash-Wed 2	24	/With the burden of the grasshopper, saying/Lady of silences/Calm and distressed/
103 Journ Magi	19	/With the voices singing in our ears, saying/That this was all folly./Then at dawn we
118 SP Dusty	14	I never! What did I tell you?/Wasn't I saying I always draw court cards?/The Knave of
154 Rock 3	1	Word of the LORD came unto me, saying:/O miserable cities of designing men,/O
232 Skimble	3	the Night Mail's ready to depart,/Saying 'Skimble where is Skimble has he gone
232 Skimble	7	/They are searching high and low,/Saying 'Skimble where is Skimble for unless he's
260 MC Thomas	13	before the/shepherds at Bethlehem, saying 'Glory to God in the highest, and on/
310 FR Harry	30	the moon?/{H} What have we been saying? I think I was saying/That it seemed as if
310 FR Harry	30	have we been saying? I think I was saying/That it seemed as if I had been always
310 FR Harry	33	distance./Whether I know what I am saying, or why I say it,/That does not matter.
318 FR Harry	34	hear something else than what I am saying./But if you want to talk, at least you can
337 FR Agatha	8	*into the room*]/{Ag} What have I been saying? I think I was saying/That you have a
337 FR Agatha	8	have I been saying? I think I was saying/That you have a long journey. You have
337 FR Amy	30	go. {}/[*Enter* AMY]/{A} What are you saying to Harry? He has only arrived,/And you
359 CP m	22	rings. EDWARD *goes to the door, saying*:]/{E} But she always turns up when she's
371 CP Edward	26	[*To* PETER]/{E} I'm sorry. You were saying?/{P} I was saying, what is the reality/Of
371 CP Peter	27	I'm sorry. You were saying?/{P} I was saying, what is the reality/Of experience
396 CP Lavinia	9	attractive, you know;/And you kept on *saying* that you were in love with me —/I believe
404 CP Edward	6	a word of what I have been saying./{R} You must have patience with me,
421 CP Reilly	36	do not understand/What I myself am saying./{J} You must accept your limitations./—
435 CP Lavinia	31	/At which you *must* begin. You were saying just now/That you never knew Celia. We
435 CP Lavinia	38	right./{L} And perhaps what I've been saying/Will seem less unkind if I can make you
436 CP Peter	9	I've taken in/All that you've been saying. But I'm grateful all the same./You
440 CP Edward	6	yet! But Sir Henry has been saying,/I think, that every moment is a fresh
450 CC Claude	26	*briefcase*]/{SC} Ah, Colby, I was just saying to Eggerson/It was time you were back.
456 CC Eggers	29	adventures!/I remember long ago, saying to Mrs. E.,/When we'd bought our house
459 CC Lady E	2	Claude? Of course it is./I remember saying: 'He has a good aura.'/I remember
461 CC Eggers	14	/{E} Oh, and I forgot ... Mrs. E. keeps saying:/'Why don't you ask him out to dinner
463 CC Claude	33	/{SC} I understand what you are saying/Much better than you think. It's my own
467 CC Colby	13	years./Oh, I'm terribly sorry to be saying this;/But it goes to explain what I said
525 ES Charles	40	to torment me? But I'm selfish/In saying that, because I think —/I think you're
530 ES Ld Clav	38	Price! And my fellow directors/Saying 'we must put our hands in our pockets/
531 ES Charles	6	papers./{C} And the leading articles saying 'we are confident/That his sagacious
540 ES Ld Clav	15	come to see me/Or what you mean by saying you can trust me./{G} Dick, do you
546 ES Piggott	18	/And easy to remember. But, as I was saying,/Guests in perfect health are exceptional/
550 ES Carghil	3	/{MC} Oh, Richard, you're only saying that to tease me./You know I meant my

SAYS (26)

116 SP Dusty	30	/Doris just hates having a doctor/She says will you ring up on Monday/She hopes to
155 Rock 3	52	your neighbour's;/When the Stranger says: 'What is the meaning of this city?/Do you
228 Gus	10	his name was quite famous, he says, in its time./And whenever he joins his
228 Gus	21	of the Fell./'I have played', so he says, 'every possible part,/And I used to know
229 Gus	45	when a house was on fire./And he says: 'Now, these kittens, they do not get
233 Skimble	64	a wave of his long brown tail/Which says: 'I'll see you again!/You'll meet without fail
236 Cat Morgan	11	I keep meself smart;/And everyone says, and I guess that's enough;/'You can't but
298 FR Violet	15	to be present to hear what Downing says./I want to know at once, not be told about
321 FR Denman	11	very urgent,/And Dr. Warburton. He says it's very urgent/Or he wouldn't have
322 FR Winch	35	We'll have the driver up for this:/Says he doesn't know this part of the country/
322 FR Winch	39	was there, and looked him over;/Says there's nothing wrong but some nasty cuts/
322 FR Winch	40	nasty cuts/And a bad concussion; says he'll come round/In the morning, most
323 FR Warburt	12	tells me Dr. Owen has seen him/And says it's nothing but a slight concussion,/But he
324 FR Harry	12	I'm sorry. But from what Winchell says/I don't think the matter can be very
327 FR Ivy	31	I don't think he's hurt,/But he says that he hasn't got the use of his car,/And
389 CP Lavinia	14	don't you go to California?/Everyone says it's a wonderful climate:/The people who
451 CC Eggers	20	he is. In fact, Mrs. E./Sometimes says to me: 'Eggerson, why can't you make me
453 CC Eggers	12	.../{E} You mustn't believe a word she says./{L} *Mr.* Simpkins is going to believe all I
453 CC Lucasta	20	Angel./{L} That's what he always says, Colby,/When I mention Mrs. Eggerson.
458 CC Lady E	23	me,/And she can't go by air — she says it makes her sea-sick;/So we took the night
459 CC Lady E	31	a day/Is most essential, Dr. Rebmann says./{SC} Rebmann? I thought it was a Dr.
496 CC Eggers	22	five or six days a week:/But now she says: 'You're becoming such a countryman!'/
555 ES Monica	18	get far./I met Michael in the drive. He says he must see you./I'm afraid that something

558 ES   Michael   17   sort of thing. It's for your sake, he says,/That he wants to keep things quiet. I can
569 ES   Charles   19   fellow guests,/Two persons who, she says, claim a very long acquaintance —/I was
576 ES   Ld Clav   8   /{LC} Now, Michael,/Señor Gomez says he has told you his story./Did he include

SCAFFOLD (1)
195 FQ: Little   178   /Of three men, and more, on the scaffold/And a few who died forgotten/In other

SCALE (2)
247 MC Thomas   19   time returns. Sever/The cord, shed the scale. Only/The fool, fixed in his folly, may
270 MC Chorus   7   I have felt/The horn of the beetle, the scale of the viper, the mobile hard insensitive

SCALY (1)
269 MC Chorus   30   fluting and owls, have seen at noon/Scaly wings slanting over, huge and ridiculous. I

SCAMPERING (1)
 52 Whispers   22   couched Brazilian jaguar/Compels the scampering marmoset/With subtle effluence of

SCANDAL (4)
589 Fable   88   /Of Saint, thereby rebuking all such scandal./But after this the monks grew most
319 FR Warburt   32   was never the slightest suspicion of scandal./{H} Scandal? who said scandal? I did
319 FR   Harry   33   the slightest suspicion of scandal./{H} Scandal? who said scandal? I did not./Yes, I see
319 FR   Harry   33   of scandal./{H} Scandal? who said scandal? I did not./Yes, I see now. That night,

SCANDALS (1)
244 MC Chorus   12   and marriages,/We have had various scandals,/We have been afflicted with taxes,/We

SCARCELY (1)
141 Rannoch   3   the soft moor/And the soft sky, scarcely room/To leap or soar. Substance

SCARLET (1)
600 Moonflower   8   you no brighter tropic flowers/With scarlet life, for me?/Nocturne/Romeo, *grand*

SCARRED (1)
203 Indians   6   /Playing in the dust together./Scarred but secure, he has many memories/

SCARS (1)
172 FQ: BurntN   52   in the blood/Sings below inveterate scars/Appeasing long forgotten wars./The dance

SCATTERED (6)
 92 Ash-Wed 2   48   /Under a juniper-tree the bones sang, scattered and shining/We are glad to be
 92 Ash-Wed 2   49   and shining/We are glad to be scattered, we did little good to each other,/
154 Rock 3   26   hull, a pile of rusty iron,/In a street of scattered brick where the goat climbs,/Where
164 Rock 9   6   faintly,/Among a few flickering scattered lights?/They would put upon GOD
202 War Poetry   20   ambush and stratagem,/Enveloped or scattered./The enduring is not a substitute for
223 Pekes Pols   59   —/And they every last one of them scattered like sheep./*And when the Police Dog*

SCAVENGERS (1)
 45 Cook Egg   27   Pipit behind the screen?/The red-eyed scavengers are creeping/From Kentish Town

SCENARIO (1)
356 CP   Peter   10   did a film/But they used a different scenario./{J} Not the one you wrote?/{P} Not

SCENE (28)
 16 Prufrock   113   will do/To swell a progress, start a scene or two,/Advise the prince; no doubt, an
 18 Portrait   2   a December afternoon/You have the scene arrange itself — as it will seem to do —/
 64 WL: Chess   98   a window gave upon the sylvan scene/The change of Philomel, by the barbarous
 68 WL: Fire S   229   man with wrinkled dugs/Perceived the scene, and foretold the rest —/I too awaited the
 92 Ash-Wed 3   14   the hawthorn blossom and a pasture scene/The broadbacked figure drest in blue and
180 FQ: ECoker   115   /The lights are extinguished, for the scene to be changed/With a hollow rumble of
204 de la Mare   17   grieve and yearn;/When the familiar scene is suddenly strange/Or the well known is .
226 Macavity   4   despair:/For when they reach the scene of crime — *Macavity's not there!*/
226 Macavity   8   a fakir stare,/And when you reach the scene of crime — *Macavity's not there!*/You
238 MC   m 9   TEMPTERS/ATTENDANTS/*The scene is the Archbishop's Hall, on December 2nd,*
238 MC   m 16   /ATTENDANTS/*The first scene is in the Archbishop's Hall,/the second*
238 MC   m 17   *is in the Archbishop's Hall,/the second scene is in the Cathedral, on December 29th,*
272 MC   m 10   *off. While the* CHORUS *speak, the scene is changed to the cathedral.*]/[*while a* Dies
279 MC Knight4   16   been eye-witnesses of this lamentable/scene, you may feel some surprise at my putting
284 FR   m 11   /THE EUMENIDES/*The scene is laid in a country house in the North of*
285 FR   3m 1   *after tea. An afternoon in late March.*/Scene I/AMY, IVY, VIOLET, AGATHA,
288 FR   Agatha   22   in the tropics/Or against the painted scene of the Mediterranean,/Harry must often
303 FR   1m 1   {}/[*Exeunt, except* AGATHA]/Scene II/AGATHA/[*Enter* MARY *with*
313 FR   1m 1   *is empty.*]/{M} Oh, Harry! {}/Scene III/HARRY, MARY, IVY, VIOLET,
317 FR   3m 1   I/PART II/*The library, after dinner.*/Scene I/HARRY, WARBURTON,/{W} I'm
330 FR   1m 1   catastrophes. {}/[*Exeunt* CHORUS]/Scene II/HARRY, AGATHA/{H} John will
340 FR   1m 1   follow the bright angels. {}/[*Exit*]/Scene III/AMY, AGATHA/{A} I was a fool, to
352 CP   m 11   /TWO CATERER'S MEN/*The scene is laid in London*/Act One. Scene 1/*The*
353 CP   1m 1   /*The scene is laid in London*/Act One. Scene 1/*The drawing-room of the*
374 CP   1m 1   matter. {}/CURTAIN/Act One. Scene 2/*The same room: a quarter of an hour*
384 CP   1m 1   Good night. {}/CURTAIN/Act One. Scene 3/*The same room: late afternoon of the*

| 454 CC | Lucasta | 5 | {L} Well, I don't propose to be on the scene when *she* comes./{K} And I don't propose |
| 556 ES | Monica | 3 | be free from worry./He won't make a scene. But I can see he's frightened./And you |

SCENES (2)

| 219 Mung Rump | | 24 | cook would appear from behind the scenes/And say in a voice that was broken with |
| 241 MC | Mess | 32 | of the people,/Who receive him with scenes of frenzied enthusiasm,/Lining the road |

SCENT (5)

109 Marina		3	/What water lapping the bow/And scent of pine and the woodthrush singing
257 MC	Chorus	27	through the dark air/Falls the stifling scent of despair;/The forms take shape in the
270 MC	Chorus	9	soap in the woodpath, a hellish sweet scent in the woodpath, while the ground heaved.
336 FR	Harry	9	you? don't you? a communication, a scent/Direct to the brain ... but not just as
473 CC	Lucasta	20	could hear,/And the flowers have a scent that no one else could smell./{C} You may

SCEPTICAL (2)

| 355 CP | Julia | 9 | My darling Celia,/You needn't be so sceptical. I stayed there once/At their castle in |
| 488 CC | Lady E | 15 | /{LE} Oh Claude, how can you be so sceptical!/We must see this Mrs. Guzzard, and |

SCHEME (3)

191 FQ: Little		18	budding nor fading,/Not in the scheme of generation./Where is the summer, the
481 CC	Lady E	20	in. Because you can't tell/Whether a scheme of decoration/Is *right*, until the place
483 CC	Lady E	8	a look at the flat/To see if the colour scheme really suited you./I believe it does. The

SCHEMES (1)

| 155 Rock 3 | | 62 | inventions and daring enterprises,/To schemes of human greatness thoroughly |

SCHOLAR'S (1)

| 256 MC | Tempts | 15 | awarded for the English Essay,/The scholar's degree, the statesman's decoration./All |

SCHOLARSHIP (1)

| 537 ES | Gomez | 20 | wondered what you found in me —/A scholarship boy from an unknown grammar |

SCHOOL (17)

54 Mr E Sun		9	Origen./A painter of the Umbrian school/Designed upon a gesso ground/The
594 Grad 9		4	From spotless fanes of lucid purity,/O school of ours! The passing years that roll/
594 Grad 10		2	and it will be to find/A different school from that which now we know;/But only
594 Grad 10		5	it great, not left behind,/The same school in the future shall we find/As this from
288 FR	Agatha	24	Wishwood —/The nursery tea, the school holiday,/The daring feats on the old
307 FR	Harry	11	then. But later, coming back from school/For the holidays, after the formal
314 FR	Warburt	11	/The day when you came back from school with measles/And we had such a time to
317 FR	Harry	24	we were children, before we went to school,/The rule of conduct was simply pleasing
318 FR	Harry	5	begun./When we came back, for the school holidays,/They were not holidays, but
318 FR	Harry	12	and so we misbehaved/Next day at school, in order to be punished,/For
463 CC	Claude	7	— that's five years;/And then your school, and your military service,/And then
537 ES	Gomez	16	/From the sort of men you'd been at school with —/I didn't fit into your set, and I
537 ES	Gomez	20	boy from an unknown grammar school./I didn't know either, but I was flattered.
539 ES	Gomez	35	have become the history master/In a school like that from which I went to Oxford./
557 ES	Ld Clav	2	you were expelled from your prep school for stealing./But come to the point.
565 ES	Ld Clav	37	learn again./Michael and I shall go to school together./We'll sit side by side, at little
570 ES	Ld Clav	33	schoolmaster/In an obscure grammar school somewhere in the Midlands./As for

SCHOOLGIRL (1)

| 392 CP | Lavinia | 2 | that was a silly thing to say./Like a schoolgirl. Like Celia. I don't know why I said |

SCHOOLMASTER (1)

| 570 ES | Ld Clav | 32 | been/If he hadn't known me? Only a schoolmaster/In an obscure grammar school |

SCHOOLS (4)

55 Mr E Sun		31	in his bath./The masters of the subtle schools/Are controversial, polymath./Sweeney
230 Bust Jones		16	both to that/And the *Joint Superior Schools.*/For a similar reason, when game is in
594 Grad 11		4	world — class after class,/O queen of schools — a momentary gleam,/A bubble on the
249 MC	Tempt2	2	/This is a sentence not taught in the schools./To set down the great, protect the

SCOFF (1)

| 224 Mr Mistoff | | 4 | that)./Please listen to me and don't scoff. All his/Inventions are off his own bat./ |

SCOLDING (3)

175 FQ: BurntN		157	/Will not stay still. Shrieking voices/Scolding, mocking, or merely chattering,/
267 MC	Thomas	6	/Which you said so urgent, is it only/Scolding and blaspheming?/{K1} That was only/
421 CP	Julia	26	too humble. She will pass between the scolding hills,/Through the valley of derision,

SCONES (1)

| 45 Cook Egg | | 31 | some snow-deep Alps./Over buttered scones and crumpets/Weeping, weeping |

SCOPE (1)

| 89 Ash-Wed 1 | | 4 | this man's gift and that man's scope/I no longer strive to strive towards such |

SCORE (1)

| 223 Pekes Pols | | 29 | were surely a dozen, more likely a score./And together they started to grumble and |

SCORN (2)
151 Rock 2   5   lives and squalid deaths, embittered scorn in honeyless hives,/And those who would
240 MC Chorus 23 of Man be born again in the litter of scorn?/For us, the poor, there is no action,/But
SCORNING (1)
254 MC Tempt4 29 the bird cries, have thought of further scorning./That nothing lasts, but the wheel
SCORPION (1)
178 FQ: ECoker 62 cars/Deployed in constellated wars/Scorpion fights against the Sun/Until the Sun
SCOTCH (1)
233 Skimble   53 a cup of tea/With perhaps a drop of Scotch while he's keeping on the watch,/Only
SCOTLAND (2)
226 Macavity   3 defy the Law./He's the bafflement of Scotland Yard, the Flying Squad's despair:/For
226 Macavity 22 footprints are not found in any file of Scotland Yard's./And when the larder's looted,
SCOTTISH (1)
223 Pekes Pols 34 a dour Yorkshire tyke,/And his braw Scottish cousins are snappers and biters,/And
SCOURGES (1)
105 Song Sime 17 swords./Before the time of cords and scourges and lamentation/Grant us thy peace./
SCOURGING (1)
162 Rock 8   10 holy places defiled;/Peter the Hermit, scourging with words./And among his hearers
SCOUTS (1)
127 Cor1 March 25 are the golf club Captains, these the Scouts,/And now the *société gymnastique de*
SCOWLED (1)
212 Growltiger 8 no need to tell you why,/And he scowled upon a hostile world from one
SCRAP (1)
227 Macavity 29 drawings by the way,/There may be a scrap of paper in the hall or on the stair —/But
SCRAPED (1)
222 Pekes Pols 20 /But they glared at each other, and scraped their hind feet,/And started to/Bark
SCRAPING (2)
335 FR Agatha 7 Only feet walking/And sharp heels scraping. Over and under/Echo and noise of
382 CP Celia 16 —/You might have made it by scraping your legs together —/Or however
SCRAPS (2)
22 Preludes   6 now a gusty shower wraps/The grimy scraps/Of withered leaves about your feet/And
368 CP Alex 25 toothsome meal out of nothing./Any scraps you have will do. I learned that in the
SCRATCHES (1)
229 Gus   49 through a hoop.'/And he'll say, as he scratches himself with his claws,/'Well, the
SCREAM (1)
328 FR Violet 29 /Is going to moralise about it, I shall scream./{G} It's going to be awkward,
SCREAMED (1)
135 5FingerEx2 5 cloud/Natural forces shriek'd aloud,/Screamed, rattled, muttered endlessly./Little
SCREECH (1)
213 Growltiger 45 bunks./Then Griddlebone she gave a screech, for she was badly skeered;/I am sorry
SCREEN (4)
16 Prufrock   105 threw the nerves in patterns on a screen:/Would it have been worth while/If one,
31 Apollinax 14 under a chair/Or grinning over a screen/With seaweed in its hair./I heard the beat
45 Cook Egg 26 I bought/To eat with Pipit behind the screen?/The red-eyed scavengers are creeping/
230 Bust Jones 19 frequently seen at the gay *Stage and Screen*/Which is famous for winkles and shrimps.
SCREW (1)
576 ES Michael 16 offered me the job/With a jolly good screw, and some pickings in commissions./He's
SCREWED (1)
577 ES Gomez 23 I can tell you, Michael's head is well screwed on./He's got brains, he's got flair.
SCRIPT (1)
431 CP Peter 28 /{P} Oh dear no! I've written the script of this film,/And Bela is very pleased with
SCRUBBERS (1)
281 MC Chorus 14 bent in cleaning the hearth, we, the scrubbers and sweepers of Canterbury,/The
SCRUPULOUS (1)
567 ES Monica 24 Father?/Father, of all people the most scrupulous,/The most austere. It's quite
SCRUTINY (1)
193 FQ: Little 92 the down-turned face/That pointed scrutiny with which we challenge/The first-met
SCRY (1)
189 FQ: DrySal 190 the horoscope, haruspicate or scry,/Observe disease in signatures, evoke/
SCULPTOR (1)
464 CC Claude 4 handles./Most people think that a sculptor or a painter/Is something more
SCULPTURE (1)
464 CC Claude 14 from a sordid world to a pure one./Sculpture and painting — I have some good
SCURRYING (1)
269 MC Chorus 33 noises: jackal, jackass, jackdaw; the scurrying noise of mouse and jerboa; the laugh

SEA-SICK (1)
458 CC Lady E 23   go by air — she says it makes her sea-sick;/So we took the night train, and did the
SEA-STREWN (1)
162 Rock 8   19   their bodies to the kites of Syria/Or sea-strewn along the routes;/Many left their
SEA-WOOD (1)
 64 WL: Chess   94   pattern on the coffered ceiling./Huge sea-wood fed with copper/Burned green and
SEAGULL (1)
185 FQ: DrySal   35   /Rounded homewards, and the seagull:/And under the oppression of the silent
SEAL (1)
266 MC Knights   18   from him you had the power, the seal and the ring./This is the man who was the
SEALS (1)
 74 WL: Thund 408   by the beneficent spider/Or under seals broken by the lean solicitor/In our empty
SEAMARK (1)
187 FQ: DrySal 123   /In navigable weather it is always a seamark/To lay a course by: but in the sombre
SEAMEN (1)
188 FQ: DrySal 165   action./Fare forward./O voyagers, O seamen,/You who come to port, and you whose
SEAMS (1)
110 Marina   28   own./The garboard strake leaks, the seams need caulking./This form, this face, this
SEARCH (1)
364 CP Edward   3   her/If I had to ask the police to search for her./I'm sure I don't know what she
SEARCHED (1)
258 MC Thomas   9   our lives begin./Thirty years ago, I searched all the ways/That lead to pleasure,
SEARCHES (1)
189 FQ: DrySal 203 in the Edgware Road./Men's curiosity searches past and future/And clings to that
SEARCHING (1)
232 Skimble   6   stationmaster's daughters/They are searching high and low,/Saying 'Skimble where
SEARCHT (1)
589 Fable   81   up the chimney./Naturally every one searcht everywhere,/But not a shred of Bishop
SEAS (11)
 15 Prufrock   74   /Scuttling across the floors of silent seas./And the afternoon, the evening, sleeps so
 42 Swee Erect   4   /Faced by the snarled and yelping seas./Display me Aeolus above/Reviewing the
 56 Swee Night   10 /Are veiled; and hushed the shrunken seas;/The person in the Spanish cape/Tries to sit
109 Marina   1   the hour of our birth./Marina/What seas what shores what grey rocks and what
110 Marina   33   parted, the hope, the new ships./What seas what shores what granite islands towards
155 Rock 3   64   water to your service,/Exploiting the seas and developing the mountains,/Dividing
160 Rock 7   12   with darkness/As the air of temperate seas is pierced by the still dead breath of the
236 Cat Morgan   1   once was a Pirate what sailed the 'igh seas —/But now I've retired as a
594 Grad 12   6   thy name o'er distant lands and seas!/As thou to thy departing sons hast been/
280 MC Priest3 22   Christian men;/Go to the northern seas confined with ice/Where the dead breath
282 MC Chorus   1   over it;/From where the western seas gnaw at the coast of Iona,/To the death in
SEASON (23)
 39 Gerontion   75   /Thoughts of a dry brain in a dry season./Burbank with a Baedeker: Bleistein with
 96 Ash-Wed 5   22   who are torn on the horn between season and season, time and time, between/
 96 Ash-Wed 5   22 torn on the horn between season and season, time and time, between/Hour and hour,
105 Song Sime   3   by the snow hills;/The stubborn season had made stand./My life is light, waiting
105 Song Sime   21 of maternal sorrow,/Now at this birth season of decease,/Let the Infant, the still
187 FQ: DrySal 124 /To lay a course by: but in the sombre season/Or the sudden fury, is what it always
191 FQ: Little   1   Gidding/Midwinter spring is its own season/Sempiternal though sodden towards
192 FQ: Little   43 from anywhere,/At any time or at any season,/It would always be the same: you would
228 Gus   31   swung on the bell./In the Pantomime season I never fell flat,/And I once understudied
230 Bust Jones   17 For a similar reason, when game is in season/He is found, not at *Fox's*, but *Blimp's*;/
230 Bust Jones   21   for winkles and shrimps./In the season of venison he gives his ben'son/To the
241 MC   Mess   34   with leaves and late flowers of the season./The streets of the city will be packed to
247 MC Tempt1   1   chambers,/Fires devouring the winter season,/Eating up the darkness, with wit and
247 MC Tempt1   8   forgetting./{T1} And of the new season./Spring has come in winter. Snow in the
275 MC Chorus   26 /Night stay with us, stop sun, hold season, let the day not come, let the spring not
310 FR Harry   10 /{H} Spring is an issue of blood/A season of sacrifice/And the wail of the new full
310 FR Mary   21 have knowledge of death/I believe the season of birth/Is the season of sacrifice/For the
310 FR Mary   22 /I believe the season of birth/Is the season of sacrifice/For the tree and the beast,
329 FR Chorus   13   moment of sudden loathing/And the season of stifled sorrow/The whisper, the
426 CP Lavinia   13   then to remember, it's the end of the season/And no more parties./{E} And no more
469 CC Lucasta   26 it/If you never go to the Opera, in the season./Though I've always felt out of it. And
496 CC Eggers   36 She's always low-spirited, around this season,/When we're getting near the
582 ES Monica   22   not allowed to stop out late/At this season. It's chilly at dusk./{LC} Yes, it's chilly

SEASON'S (1)
194 FQ: Little   118   to forgive/Both bad and good. Last season's fruit is eaten/And the fullfed beast shall
SEASONABLE (1)
544 ES Ld Clav   22   /But this early summer, that's hardly seasonable,/Is so often a harbinger of frost on
SEASONS (10)
147 Rock 1   4 O perpetual recurrence of determined seasons,/O world of spring and autumn, birth
150 Rock 1   109   *again./The river flows, the seasons turn/The sparrow and starling have no*
167 Rock 10   39   and the day and the night and the seasons./And we must extinguish the candle, put
178 FQ: ECoker   42 dancing/As in their living in the living seasons/The time of the seasons and the
178 FQ: ECoker   43 in the living seasons/The time of the seasons and the constellations/The time of
184 FQ: DrySal   8   however, implacable,/Keeping his seasons and rages, destroyer, reminder/Of what
240 MC Chorus   5 /Now I fear disturbance of the quiet seasons:/Winter shall come bringing death from
247 MC Thomas   6 need not walk warily./{T} You talk of seasons that are past. I remember/Not worth
275 MC Chorus   25   can I ever return, to the soft quiet seasons?/Night stay with us, stop sun, hold
281 MC Chorus   16   under grief,/Even in us the voices of seasons, the snuffle of winter, the song of
SEAT (1)
107 Animula   22 /Curl up the small soul in the window seat/Behind the *Encyclopaedia Britannica./*
SEATED (2)
469 CC   2m   1 *the mews a few weeks later.* COLBY *is seated at the piano;/*LUCASTA *in an armchair.*
567 ES   2m   1   *of the following day.* MONICA *seated/alone. Enter* CHARLES./{C} Well,
SEATING (1)
493 CC Claude   4 a difficult meeting,/To decide on the seating arrangements beforehand./I don't think
SEAWARD (4)
17 Prufrock   126 sing to me./I have seen them riding seaward on the waves/Combing the white hair
40 Burb Blei   6 /Defunctive music under sea/Passed seaward with the passing bell/Slowly: the God
98 Ash-Wed 6   9 granite shore/The white sails still fly seaward, seaward flying/Unbroken wings/And
98 Ash-Wed 6   9 shore/The white sails still fly seaward, seaward flying/Unbroken wings/And the lost
SEAWEED (2)
17 Prufrock   130 of the sea/By sea-girls wreathed with seaweed red and brown/Till human voices wake
31 Apollinax   15 chair/Or grinning over a screen/With seaweed in its hair./I heard the beat of centaur's
SECLUDED (1)
197 FQ: Little   238 fails/On a winter's afternoon, in a secluded chapel/History is now and England./
SECOND (26)
20 Portrait   94 /My self-possession flares up for a second;/*This* is as I had reckoned./'I have been
29 Aunt Helen   12 sat upon the dining-table/Holding the second housemaid on his knees —/Who had
92 Ash-Wed 3   1 inheritance./At the first turning of the second stair/I turned and saw below/The same
92 Ash-Wed 3   7 face of hope and of despair./At the second turning of the second stair/I left them
92 Ash-Wed 3   7 despair./At the second turning of the second stair/I left them twisting, turning below;/
111 Xmas Trees   34 of the end/And the first coming of the second coming./UNFINISHED POEMS/
149 Rock 1   69   the rational and enlightened mind./Second, you neglect and belittle the desert./The
194 FQ: Little   137 body and soul begin to fall asunder./Second, the conscious impotence of rage/At
238 MC   m 17 *scene is in the Archbishop's Hall,/the second scene is in the Cathedral, on December*
248 MC   m 15 not be whole in the present. {}/[*Enter* SECOND TEMPTER]/{T2} Your Lordship has
260 MC Thomas   2 good will.' The/*fourteenth verse of the second chapter of the Gospel according to Saint*
264 MC   m 7   *of St. Stephen is heard*]/[*Enter the* SECOND PRIEST, *with a banner of St. John*
330 FR Harry   25 it — that is another —/That was the second hell of not being there,/The degradation
399 CP Reilly   9 /{R} I shall see him at once. And the second?/{N} The second to be shown into the
399 CP Nurse   10 at once. And the second?/{N} The second to be shown into the other room/Just as
406 CP Edward   22 practical joker?/{E} I incline to the second explanation/Without the qualification
414 CP Reilly   33 to accept and go on from./And the second symptom?/{C} That's stranger still./It
418 CP Reilly   24 or less, in lives of those about us./The second is unknown, and so requires faith —/The
418 CP Celia   36 between them./{C} Then I choose the second./{R} It is a terrifying journey./{C} I am
419 CP Celia   10 you feel quite sure?/{C} I want your second way./So what am I to do?/{R} You will
482 CC Lady E   34 if one knows what breeding is./And, second, you need intellectual society./Now, that
499 CC Eggers   4 at ease when I'm behind a desk:/It's second nature./{SC} And put the case to her./
527 ES Monica   2 you don't understand him;/In the second place, we're not engaged yet./{C} Aren't
528 ES Monica   3 than his fear of solitude?/{M} The second reason is exactly the opposite:/It's his
538 ES Ld Clav   5 to think it all out./{LC} That's the second time you have mentioned your
540 ES Gomez   26   you have shown it, if only for a second?/You never lifted your foot from the
SECOND-RATE (5)
435 CP Peter   22 ignore —/And here I am, making a second-rate film!/But I thought it was going to
465 CC Claude   15 be said to have a vocation/To be a second-rate potter? To be, at best,/A competent
469 CC Colby   14 /That I've just played you were very second-rate,/And you didn't like them. You
495 CC Claude   34 composer./I should have been a second-rate potter,/And he would have been a
495 CC Claude   35 potter,/And he would have been a second-rate organist./We have both chosen ...

SECONDARY (1)
571 ES Ld Clav 35 girls with us./It was late at night. A secondary road./I ran over an old man lying in
SECRET (14)
24 Rhapsody 28 polished/As if the world gave up/The secret of its skeleton,/Stiff and white./A broken
227 Macavity 31 when the loss has been disclosed, the Secret Service say:/'It *must* have been
244 MC Chorus 18 terrors,/Our particular shadows, our secret fears./But now a great fear is upon us, a
307 FR Mary 10 had been./{M} They never found the secret./{H} Not then. But later, coming back
370 CP Peter 24 she seems preoccupied/With some secret excitement which I cannot share./{E} Do
464 CC Claude 40 /That I cherished for a long time a secret reproach:/But after his death, and then it
465 CC Claude 19 see/That I had always known, at the secret moments,/That I didn't have it in me.
473 CC Lucasta 2 from the rest of us:/You have your secret garden; to which you can retire/And lock
473 CC Colby 5 you sure that you haven't your own secret garden/Somewhere, if you could find it?/
500 CC Claude 13 here. But I didn't trust you/To keep a secret. There were reasons for that/Which no
541 ES Gomez 14 chap, you are obtuse!/I said: 'Your secret is safe with me',/And then you ... well, I'd
564 ES Carghil 35 him. {}/[*pats her despatch-case*]./{MC} Secret for secret, Señor Gomez!/You've got to
564 ES Carghil 35 *her despatch-case*]./{MC} Secret for secret, Señor Gomez!/You've got to be the first
567 ES Monica 26 quite impossible./Father with a guilty secret in his past!/I just can't imagine it. {}/
SECRET'S (1)
541 ES Gomez 6 Frederick Culverwell?/No, Dick, your secret's safe with me./Of course, I might give it
SECRETARY (5)
129 Cor2 State 10 committees and sub-committees./One secretary will do for several committees./What
411 CP Reilly 35 REILLY *raises his hand*]/{R} My secretary will send you my account./Go in
420 CP Reilly 11 what your fee is?/{R} I have told my secretary/That there is no fee./{C} But .../{R}
427 CP Alex 15 on the telephone/After lunch, but my secretary couldn't get through to you./Never
545 ES Piggott 33 to my office. If I'm not there/My secretary will be — Miss Timmins./She'd be
SECRETS (6)
179 FQ: ECoker 80 wisdom only the knowledge of dead secrets/Useless in the darkness into which they
599 On a Port 11 hands;/Her dark eyes keep their secrets hid from us,/Beyond the circle of our
320 FR Warburt 32 always been a party to the family secrets —/You know as well as I do that Arthur
358 CP Julia 4 I mean./The next election. And the secrets of your cases./{E} Most of my secrets are
358 CP Edward 5 secrets of your cases./{E} Most of my secrets are quite uninteresting./{J} Well, you
568 ES Ld Clav 4 I heard what you said about guilty secrets./There are many things not crimes,
SECULAR (1)
164 Rock 9 11 the market, the forum,/And all other secular meetings./Thinking good of themselves,
SECURE (6)
179 FQ: ECoker 92 On the edge of a grimpen, where is no secure foothold,/And menaced by monsters,
203 Indians 6 in the dust together./Scarred but secure, he has many memories/Which return at
241 MC Priest1 26 he come/In full assurance, or only secure/In the power of Rome, the spiritual rule,/
244 MC Chorus 27 the doom on the world./Archbishop, secure and assured of your fate, unaffrayed
474 CC Lucasta 28 that happening to you./You seem so secure, to me. Not only in your music —/That's
583 ES Monica 27 of love unchanging./I feel utterly secure/In you; I am a part of you. Now take me
SECURED (1)
278 MC Knight2 33 way in/which social justice can be secured. At another time, you would/condemn
SECURELY (1)
589 Fable 65 though barred and bolted most securely,/Gave way — my statement nobody
SECURITY (6)
159 Rock 6 5 who live near a Bank/To doubt the security of their money./It is hard for those who
186 FQ: DrySal 93 of well-being,/Fruition, fulfilment, security or affection,/Or even a very good
385 CP Reilly 14 childhood years in comfort, mirth, security —/If they returned, would it not be
472 CC Colby 7 your life/To rob you of any sense of security./{L} And I'm sure you have *that* — the
472 CC Lucasta 8 I'm sure you have *that* — the sense of security./{C} No, I haven't either./{L} There, I
480 CC Kaghan 24 and me —/The one thing *we* want is security/And respectability! Now Colby/Doesn't
SEDITIOUS (1)
278 MC Knight2 11 exercised for/selfish and often for seditious ends, and to reform the legal system./
SEE (321)
19 Portrait 49 smiles at situations which it cannot see.'/I smile, of course,/And go on drinking tea./
20 Portrait 71 what she has said to me?/You will see me any morning in the park/Reading the
24 Rhapsody 19 /Which opens on her like a grin./You see the border of her dress/Is torn and stained
24 Rhapsody 21 torn and stained with sand,/And you see the corner of her eye/Twists like a crooked
24 Rhapsody 40 was running along the quay,/I could see nothing behind that child's eye./I have seen
37 Gerontion 17 are taken for wonders. 'We would see a sign!'/The word within a word, unable to
62 WL: Burial 54 on his back,/Which I am forbidden to see. I do not find/The Hanged Man. Fear death
62 WL: Burial 56 Hanged Man. Fear death by water./I see crowds of people, walking round in a ring./
62 WL: Burial 57 round in a ring./Thank you. If you see dear Mrs. Equitone,/Tell her I bring the
65 WL: Chess 122 /'Do'/You know nothing? Do you see nothing? Do you remember/'Nothing?'/I

68	WL: Fire S	219	with wrinkled female breasts, can	see/At the violet hour, the evening hour that
121	SA Sweeney	18	right little, missionary stew./You	see this egg/You see this egg/Well that's life on
121	SA Sweeney	19	stew./You see this egg/You	see this egg/Well that's life on a crocodile isle./
121	SA Sweeney	27	but the fruit as it grows./Nothing to	see but the palmtrees one way/And the sea the
124	SA Sweeney	37	what they do./He used to come and	see me sometimes/I'd give him a drink and cheer
127	Cor1 March	8	they coming? No, not yet. You can	see some eagles. And hear the trumpets./Here
127	Cor1 March	12	sausages./What comes first? Can you	see? Tell us. It is/5,800,000 rifles and carbines,/
128	Cor1 March	42	/Over the paving./That is all we could	see. But how many eagles! and how many
133	Eyes	5	/The golden vision reappears/I	see the eyes but not the tears/This is my
133	Eyes	8	/This is my affliction/Eyes I shall not	see again/Eyes of decision/Eyes I shall not see
133	Eyes	10	/Eyes of decision/Eyes I shall not	see unless/At the door of death's other kingdom
154	Rock 3	14	and printing them,/Many desire to	see their names in print,/Many read nothing but
165	Rock 9	37	not deny the body./Now you shall	see the Temple completed:/After much striving,
167	Rock 10	33	our eyes look upward/And	see the light that fractures through unquiet
167	Rock 10	34	fractures through unquiet water./We	see the light but see not whence it comes./O
167	Rock 10	34	unquiet water./We see the light but	see not whence it comes./O Light Invisible, we
177	FQ: ECoker	28	weak pipe and the little drum/And	see them dancing around the bonfire/The
180	FQ: ECoker	121	and slowly fades into silence/And you	see behind every face the mental emptiness
195	FQ: Little	165	servitude,/History may be freedom. See,	now they vanish,/The faces and places, with
197	FQ: Little	231	we start./We die with the dying:/See,	they depart, and we go with them./We are
197	FQ: Little	233	them./We are born with the dead:/See,	they return, and bring us with them./The
203	Indians	4	front of his own door at sunset/And	see his grandson, and his neighbour's grandson/
226	Macavity	19	may meet him in a by-street, you may	see him in the square —/But when a crime's
233	Skimble	64	his long brown tail/Which says: 'I'll	see you again!/You'll meet without fail on the
234	Ad-dress	5	/You now have learned enough to	see/That Cats are much like you and me/And
235	Ad-dress	48	I have often met before/(He comes to	see me in my flat)/I greet him with an OOPSA
590	Time Space	14	us haste to pluck anew/Nor mourn to	see them pine,/And though our days of love be
590	Space Time	14	us haste to pluck anew/Nor mourn to	see them pine,/And though the flowers of life be
592	Grad 2	5	understand/That though again they	see their fatherland/They there shall be as
593	Grad 5	4	great deeds the distant years may	see,/What conquest over pain and misery,/What
593	Grad 6	5	hearts to help mold well her fate,/And	see that she shall gain such proud estate/As
593	Grad 8	3	be our lot,/We shall desire to	see again the spot/Which, whatsoever we have
604	Ode	14	and destroy/Give us also the vision to	see/What we owe for the future, the present,
240	MC Priest3	34	one place or another in France?/{P3} I	see nothing quite conclusive in the art of
242	MC Mess	13	as a man/Whom in this life I shall not	see again./I have this, I assure you, on the
244	MC Chorus	20	/A fear like birth and death, when we	see birth and death alone/In a void apart. We/
245	MC Priest2	23	{P2} O my Lord, forgive me, I did not	see you coming,/Engrossed by the chatter of
246	MC Tempt1	24	/[Enter FIRST TEMPTER]/{T1} You	see, my Lord, I do not wait upon ceremony:/
248	MC Tempt2	21	ones: those of the Chancellorship./See	how the late ones rise! You, master of
255	MC Tempt4	14	/On earth, to be high in heaven./And	see far off below you, where the gulf is fixed,/
261	MC Thomas	35	most low, and are seen, not as we/see	them, but in the light of the Godhead from
265	MC Knight2	29	and dine upon it after./{K2} We must	see the Archbishop./{K3} Go, tell the
275	MC Chorus	27	the day and its common things, and	see them all smeared with blood, through a
276	MC Knight1	21	believe in fair/play: and when you	see one man being set upon by four, then your/
277	MC Knight3	21	even when reasonable/people come to	see that the Archbishop had to be put out of the
278	MC Knight2	2	hard-headed/sensible people, as I can	see, and not to be taken in by/emotional
280	MC Priest1	13	the ruins,/Their world without God. I	see it. I see it./{P3} No. For the Church is
280	MC Priest1	13	/Their world without God. I see it. I	see it./{P3} No. For the Church is stronger for
286	FR Amy	11	competent, Gerald./I can still	see to that./{V} Well, as for me,/I would never
286	FR Violet	16	I would never go south,/Simply to	see the vulgarest people —/You can keep out of
290	FR Violet	21	/{V} Nonsense, Gerald!/You must	see for yourself it's the only thing to do./{Ag}
291	FR Amy	24	to close the blinds./There is no one to	see you but our servants who belong here,/And
291	FR Amy	25	belong here,/And who all want to	see you back, Harry./{H} Look there, look
291	FR Harry	26	/{H} Look there, look there: do you	see them?/{G} No, I don't see anyone about./
291	FR Gerald	27	do you see them?/{G} No, I don't	see anyone about./{H} No, no, not there. Look
292	FR Harry	2	no, not there. Look there!/Can't you	see them? You don't see them, but I see them,/
292	FR Harry	2	there!/Can't you see them? You don't	see them, but I see them,/And they see me. This
292	FR Harry	2	see them? You don't see them, but I	see them,/And they see me. This is the first time
292	FR Harry	3	see them, but I see them,/And they	see me. This is the first time that I have seen
292	FR Harry	9	/They were always there. But I did not	see them./Why should they wait until I came back
292	FR Gerald	30	it you didn't know./But you'll have to	see about a couple of new hunters./{C} And I've
293	FR Amy	4	of things at Wishwood./{A} You	see your aunts and uncles are very helpful,
294	FR Harry	10	happens —/Of the past you can only	see what is past,/Not what is always present.
295	FR Amy	36	And the northern country. When you	see Wishwood/Again by day, all will be the
296	FR Harry	8	/As the way to freedom./{H} I think I	see what you mean,/Dimly — as you once

372 CP	Peter	1	are./What do you want me to do?/{P} See Celia for me./You know her in a different
372 CP	Edward	7	someone disinterested./{E} Well, I will see Celia./{P} Thank you, Edward. It's very
374 CP	Celia	7	say you don't seem very pleased to see me./Edward, I understand what has
374 CP	Celia	10	did not seem like you. So I felt I must see me./Tell me it's all right, and then I'll go./
375 CP	Edward	3	to give *you* the grounds .../{E} I see. But it is not like that at all./Lavinia is
376 CP	Celia	4	to do. Don't lose your head./You see, I really did leave my umbrella;/And I'll say
376 CP	Julia	17	thing I know how to cook./{J} Celia! I see you've had the same inspiration/That I had.
377 CP	Julia	2	you give me that apron/And we'll see what I can do. You stay and talk to
378 CP	Edward	18	of all his argument/Was to make me see that I wanted her back./{C} That's the
378 CP	Celia	39	go away now/Will you promise me to see a very great doctor/Whom I have heard of
381 CP	Edward	29	tedium is not the residue of ecstasy./I see that my life was determined long ago/And
382 CP	Celia	26	/Of what I had thought you were. I see another person,/I see you as a person whom
382 CP	Celia	27	you were. I see another person,/I see you as a person whom I never saw before./
382 CP	Celia	29	before, he was only a projection —/I see that now — of something that I wanted —/
382 CP	Celia	33	but what, and where is it?/Edward, I see that I was simply making use of you./And I
385 CP	Reilly	29	as well. But remember,/When you see your wife, you must ask no questions/And
386 CP	Edward	36	situation./{E} I'm afraid I can't see the humorous side of it./{C} I'm not really
387 CP	Celia	5	/Oh, I'm glad I came!/I can see you at last as a human being./Can't you see
387 CP	Celia	6	at last as a human being./Can't you see me that way too, and laugh about it?/{E} I
387 CP	Celia	10	/{C} But it's all so simple./Can't you see that ... {}/[*The doorbell rings*]/{E} There's
388 CP	Peter	6	person to know,/Because, you see, he knows everybody, everywhere./So what
389 CP	Celia	30	Lavinia,/Don't put me off. I may not see you again./What I want to say is this: I
390 CP	Julia	33	believe she really wants us./I can see that she is quite worn out/After her anxiety
391 CP	Julia	28	right you are!/Well, my dears, I shall see you very soon./{E} *When* shall we see you?/
391 CP	Edward	29	see you very soon./{E} *When* shall we see you?/{J} Did I say you'd see me?/Good-bye.
391 CP	Julia	30	shall we see you?/{J} Did I say you'd see me?/Good-bye. I believe ... I haven't left
391 CP	Lavinia	34	say, you don't seem very pleased to see me./{E} I can't say that I've had much
391 CP	Edward	36	anything. But of course I'm glad to see you./{L} Yes, that was a silly thing to say./
392 CP	Lavinia	32	me to make her live somewhere./{L} I see. So Julia made her live in Essex;/And made
392 CP	Lavinia	40	point is, that since I've been away/I see that I've taken you much too seriously./And
393 CP	Lavinia	1	much too seriously./And now I can see how absurd you are./{E} That is a very
394 CP	Edward	23	But tell me,/Since this is how you see me, why did you come back?/{L} Frankly, I
396 CP	Lavinia	38	simple./But there is one point which I see clearly:/We are not to relapse into the kind
397 CP	Edward	20	How do I know/That you wouldn't see him first, and tell him all about me/From
398 CP	Lavinia	13	laugh,/And as I can't persuade you to see a doctor,/There's nothing else at present that
399 CP	Nurse	8	the small waiting-room;/And you will see him almost at once./{R} I shall see him at
399 CP	Reilly	9	see him almost at once./{R} I shall see him at once. And the second?/{N} The
402 CP	Edward	12	I should have thought a doctor could see that for himself./Or at least that he would
402 CP	Edward	15	in the same words, that I ought to see a doctor./They said — again, in almost the
402 CP	Edward	19	have thought that a doctor could see it./{R} 'Nervous breakdown' is a term I
402 CP	Reilly	40	back as far as I find necessary./You see, your memories of childhood —/I mean, in
403 CP	Reilly	15	not interest them./Or they do not see it, or they justify it/Because they are
403 CP	Edward	23	has happened since I left you./{E} I see now why I wanted my wife to come back./It
404 CP	Edward	19	no longer act for myself./Coming to see you — that's the last decision/I was capable
406 CP	Reilly	7	/{R} I am glad that you have come to see it in that light —/At least, for the moment.
407 CP	Edward	2	you've told me so often./I'd like to see *you* filling up an income-tax form./{L} Don't
410 CP	Reilly	1	wanted to be loved;/{R} And you have come to see that no one had ever loved you./Then you
410 CP	Reilly	6	*my* fault./{R} And now you begin to see, I hope,/How much you have in common.
410 CP	Reilly	12	to make us loathe one another./{R} See it rather as the bond which holds you
412 CP	Celia	35	most people, when they come to see you,/Are obviously ill, or can give good
412 CP	Celia	37	can give good reasons/For wanting to see you. Well, I can't./I just came in
413 CP	Reilly	11	of their illness, and lead them to see/That it's not so interesting as they had
414 CP	Reilly	24	I just can't face it./{R} So you want to see no one?/{C} No ... it isn't that I *want* to be
415 CP	Celia	33	about it, over and over;/I can see now, it was all a mistake:/But I don't see
415 CP	Celia	34	now, it was all a mistake:/But I don't see why mistakes should make one feel sinful!/
418 CP	Celia	9	— more like a betrayal./You see, I think I really had a vision of something/
421 CP	Julia	9	don't think they will do that. We shall see./It's the thought of Celia that weighs upon
421 CP	Reilly	31	when I am apprehensive/Then you see no reason for anything but confidence./{J}
427 CP	Alex	12	I must not miss the opportunity/To see Edward and Lavinia./{L} How are you,
428 CP	Alex	27	natives several new recipes./But you see, what with eating the monkeys/And what
428 CP	Alex	39	/Which we have just recognised. You see, Lavinia,/These are very deep waters./{E}
430 CP	Peter	11	must crash in:/It's my only chance to see Edward and Lavinia./I'm only over for a
430 CP	Peter	12	/I'm only over for a week, you see,/And I'm driving down to the country this
430 CP	Peter	37	/{P} Alex knows./Did you see my last picture, Alex?/{A} I knew about it,
430 CP	Alex	38	/{A} I knew about it, but I didn't see it./There is no cinema in Kinkanja./{P}

431 CP	Peter	30	pleased with it./He thought I should see the original Boltwell;/And besides, he
432 CP	Edward	5	—/{E} We're delighted to see him. But we *have* met before./{J} Then if
433 CP	Julia	10	very much cheaper./Oh, dear, I can see you're determined not to have me:/So
439 CP	Peter	15	/And he's got to go there .../{P} I see what you mean./I wish I didn't have to. But
439 CP	Edward	23	/{P} So now I'll be going./{E} Shall we see you again, Peter,/Before you leave England?
439 CP	Lavinia	25	leave England?/{L} Do try to come to see us./You know, I think it would do us all
439 CP	Peter	32	I promise you./I really do want to see you both, very much./Good-bye, Julia.
440 CP	Lavinia	10	{L} But all the same ... I don't want to see these people./{R} It is your appointed
449 CC	Eggers	8	this to Colby — Mr. Simpkins./{E} I see what you mean./{SC} She must get to like
449 CC	Claude	28	notice of Miss Angel./She just doesn't see her. And Miss Angel/Will soon be getting
451 CC	Eggers	29	I said, it will be very different./She'll see at once that you're a man of culture;/And
455 CC	Eggers	32	say./But I don't expect you'll have to see much of her:/That responsibility's not on
456 CC	Eggers	37	/It's been a very unusual privilege/To see as much of Europe as I have,/Getting Lady
459 CC	Lady E	27	/He needs a light mauve. I shall see about that./But not today. I shall go and
460 CC	Claude	23	/Well, that was Mr. Colby./{SC} Oh, I see./Yes, now I am beginning to remember./I
465 CC	Claude	9	been right./{SC} Because I came to see/That I should never have become a first-rate
465 CC	Claude	18	/I don't think so. For I came to see/That I had always known, at the secret
466 CC	Claude	9	/It isn't that I don't want anyone to see them!/But when I am alone, and look at one
467 CC	Colby	8	will have, with your father./I begin to see how I have always thought of you —/As a
469 CC	Lucasta	24	the music:/I just enjoyed going — to see the other people,/And to be seen there! And
470 CC	Lucasta	24	day, I invited you .../{L} To go to see that American Musical!/{C} Well, I'd heard
470 CC	Colby	25	I'd heard you say you wanted to see it./{L} But not with you!/{C} You made that
471 CC	Colby	23	impression./And then you came to see that you hadn't succeeded./{L} Oh, so I was
471 CC	Colby	29	own creation/Rather than wait to see what happened./I hope you don't mind: I
472 CC	Colby	1	/{C} Because you couldn't wait to see what happened./You're afraid of what
474 CC	Colby	14	just have to come. And I should not see them coming./I should not hear the opening
474 CC	Lucasta	38	a little jealous of your music!/When I see it as a means of contact with a world/More
476 CC	Lucasta	4	that's about my parents./{L} Oh, I see./Well, I can't believe that matters./But I can
476 CC	Lucasta	33	/I hated my mother. I never could see/How Claude had ever liked her. Oh, that
477 CC	Lucasta	17	into this house!/Lucasta .../{L} I can see well enough you *are* shocked./You ought to
477 CC	Lucasta	18	you *are* shocked./You ought to see your face! I'm disappointed./I suppose that's
477 CC	Lucasta	29	either,/And I thought you'd come to see me as the real kind of person/That I want to
478 CC	Kaghan	36	/{K} Enter B. Kaghan./To see the new flat. And here's Lucasta./I knew I
481 CC	Lady E	23	whom it was designed./So I have to see you in it. Did you say you were leaving?/{K}
482 CC	Lady E	11	Mr. Kaghan and Miss Angel./I can see you've lived a rather sheltered life,/And I've
482 CC	Lady E	13	you a good deal of attention./You see, you're rather a curiosity/To both of them
483 CC	Lady E	8	I came to have a look at the flat/To see if the colour scheme really suited you./I
483 CC	Colby	14	I needed a desk in my room:/You see, I shall do a good deal of my work here./
483 CC	Lady E	23	room I wanted. {}/[*rising*]./{LE} And I see a photograph in a silver frame./I'm afraid I
486 CC	Colby	9	Well ... I didn't have a father./You see ... I was an illegitimate child./{LE} Oh yes.
487 CC	Claude	4	I've jotted down some headings./Just see if you can develop them for me/With a few
487 CC	Lady E	22	makes you think so?/{LE} I must see this Mrs. Guzzard. I must confront her.
488 CC	Claude	13	son would be,/And then you began to see him as your son,/And then — any name you
488 CC	Lady E	16	how can you be so sceptical!/We must see this Mrs. Guzzard, and get her to confess it./
488 CC	Claude	26	keeping such a thing from you./I see now I might as well have told you before,/
489 CC	Claude	13	reason for keeping silent./I came to see how you longed for a son of your own,/And
492 CC	Claude	3	/{SC} Then the first thing is: we must see Mrs. Guzzard./{LE} Oh Claude! I am
492 CC	Claude	10	Colby to you./But we must see Mrs. Guzzard. I'll arrange to get her here./
493 CC	Claude	11	Eggerson there, behind the desk./You see, I want him to be a sort of chairman./{LE}
494 CC	Claude	17	was power and wealth;/And I came to see that what I had interpreted/In this way, was
500 CC	Lucasta	24	the shock he'd given me./He made me see what I really wanted./B. makes me feel safe.
502 CC	Lucasta	4	what it's about. But I did come to see you./I came to apologise for my behaviour/
504 CC	Claude	3	it/If *I* was late when I went to see her. {}/[*Enter* LUCASTA]/{L} I'm sorry to
507 CC	Lady E	31	could I be?/{LE} Oh, Claude, you see? You understand, Colby?/{SC} Don't be
509 CC	Claude	9	Elizabeth, it isn't Colby!/Don't you see who it is?/{MG} My husband chose the
512 CC	Lady E	33	fond of them, you know./{LE} I shall see to that, Barnabas./{K} B. — if you don't
515 CC	Guzzard	5	/On your return, you came at once to see me;/And I found that I had to break the
515 CC	Guzzard	26	think it is a small thing/For me, to see my life's ambition come to nothing?/When I
515 CC	Claude	36	— of course it can't be true! —/But I see you believe it. You want to believe it./Well,
518 CC	Eggers	4	this as an impertinence —/I don't see you spending a lifetime as an organist./
518 CC	Guzzard	24	you./{MG} Mr. Eggerson,/I cannot see eye to eye with you,/Having been, myself,
518 CC	Colby	33	a taxi? Yes, Aunt Sarah;/But I should see you home./{MG} Home? Only to a taxi./Do
524 ES	Monica	2	father at home to-day?/{M} You'll see him at tea./{C} But if I'm not going to have
528 ES	Monica	10	costume,/When the man that people see when they meet you/Is not the private man,
531 ES	Lambert	33	/Is very insistent that he must see you./I told him you never saw anyone, my

531 ES	Lambert	37	when you read it/You would want to see him. Said you'd be very angry/If you heard
532 ES	Ld Clav	4	{}/[*after reading the note*]./{LC} I'll see him in the library./No, stop. I've left too
532 ES	Ld Clav	6	many papers about there./I'd better see him here./{L} Very good, my Lord./Shall I
532 ES	Monica	11	us go into the library. And then I'll see you off./{LC} I'm sorry to turn you out of
532 ES	Ld Clav	13	of the room like this,/But I'll have to see this man by myself, Monica./I've never
532 ES	Ld Clav	16	man I used to know. I can't refuse to see him./Though from what I remember of the
532 ES	Ld Clav	28	remember/That we both want to see you, whenever you can come/If you're in the
532 ES	Monica	30	CHARLES]/{M} We *both* want to see you. {}/[*Exeunt* MONICA *and* CHARLES]/
533 ES	Gomez	18	— that's what I've come for./You see, I'm a widower, like you, Dick./So I'm
533 ES	Gomez	19	/So I'm pretty footloose. Gomez, you see,/Is now a highly respected citizen/Of a
535 ES	Gomez	2	You've asked me that already!/To see you, Dick. A natural desire!/For you're the
536 ES	Gomez	29	insulated./It's only when you come to see that you have lost *yourself*/That you are
536 ES	Gomez	38	told the story. *They* wouldn't want to see me./No, I need one old friend, a friend
537 ES	Gomez	1	both Culverwell and Gomez —/See Culverwell as Gomez — Gomez as
537 ES	Gomez	24	*you* — tickled your love of power/To see that I was flattered, and that I admired you./
538 ES	Gomez	31	your advice .../I've made a point, you see, of following your career./{LC} I am touched
540 ES	Ld Clav	14	I still don't know why you've come to see me/Or what you mean by saying you can
540 ES	Gomez	34	You just couldn't face it./Do you see now, Dick, why I say I can trust you?/{LC}
542 ES	Ld Clav	18	Don't you understand?/{LC} I see that when I gave you my friendship/So
542 ES	Gomez	40	pal may be getting impatient./I'll see you soon again./{LC} Not very soon, I
543 ES	Gomez	6	for the present. It's been an elixir/To see you again, and assure myself/That we can
544 ES	Monica	27	longing to escape;/Now I want to see you learning to enjoy yourself!/{LC} Perhaps
545 ES	Monica	20	to explode./{M} Hush, Father. I see her coming from the house./Take your
546 ES	Piggott	10	me 'Matron'/At Badgley Court. You see, we've studied to avoid/Anything like a
546 ES	Monica	33	/Referred to a nurse. When we see her/Do we address her as 'Nurse'?/{MP} Oh
548 ES	Monica	6	she'll be bothering us again:/I could see from her expression when she left/That she
548 ES	Monica	13	something to wake you,/But if they see you're shamming they'll have to take the
551 ES	Ld Clav	20	really been broken-hearted/I can't see how you could have acted as you did./{MC}
554 ES	Piggott	21	our very nicest guests!/I just came to see that Lord Claverton was comfortable:/We
555 ES	Piggott	11	Oh, Miss Claverton-Ferry!/I didn't see you coming. Now I must fly. {}/[*Exit*]/{M} I
555 ES	Monica	18	Michael in the drive. He says he must see you./I'm afraid that something unpleasant
556 ES	Monica	3	/He won't make a scene. But I can see he's frightened./And you know what
563 ES	Carghil	26	the surnames, Dick!/{MC} Well, you see, Señor Gomez, when we first became friends
563 ES	Carghil	33	on the stage./{MC} Oh, did you never see me?/That's a pity, Señor Gomez./{G} I lost
569 ES	Ld Clav	38	human beings,/Malicious, petty, and I see myself emerging/From my spectral existence
572 ES	Charles	27	who are so vindictive:/Don't you see that they were as much at fault as you/And
573 ES	Ld Clav	20	sure they are conspiring against me./I see Mrs. Carghill coming./{M} Let us go./{LC}
574 ES	Carghil	1	married him,/Oh so long ago. So you see, Mr. Hemington,/I've come to regard her as
574 ES	Michael	32	my wish to get abroad,/You couldn't see my point of view. What's the use of chasing/
575 ES	Ld Clav	6	is just what I wanted./{LC} Yes, I see the advantage of a job created for you/By
577 ES	Charles	12	debt. And better late than never./{C} I see your point of view. Can you really feel
578 ES	Ld Clav	4	you/Though you repudiate me. I see now clearly/The many many mistakes I have
578 ES	Ld Clav	9	proved to be equally mistaken./I see that your mother and I, in our failure/To
578 ES	Ld Clav	14	your boyhood and adolescence,/And see how all the efforts aimed at your good/Only
579 ES	Monica	4	/{M} But who will you be/When I see you again? Whoever you are then/I shall
579 ES	Michael	10	my needs for that climate./And you see, he has friends in the shipping line/Who he
579 ES	Ld Clav	22	it./{LC} Yes, if you're going, and I see no way to stop you,/Then I agree with you,
579 ES	Michael	25	meet again, Michael./{Mi} I don't see why not./{G} At the end of five years he will
579 ES	Carghil	34	outsider,/A friend of the family, can see more clearly./{G} Not that I deserve any
580 ES	Carghil	25	looking rather tired. I'll run and see them off. {}/[*Exit* MRS. CARGHILL]/{M}
582 ES	Ld Clav	15	expecting./I am sorry you have had to see so much of persons/And situations not very

SEE (1) [*Proper name*]

268 MC	Knight2	2	dispute ended/Sent you back to your See as you demanded./{K3} And burying the

SEED (1)

160 Rock	7	3	thing, and man without GOD is a seed upon the wind: driven this way and that,

SEEDY (2)

212 Growltiger		6	to please;/His coat was torn and seedy, he was baggy at the knees;/One ear was
476 CC	Lucasta	35	that childhood —/Always living in seedy lodgings/And being turned out when the

SEEING (17)

13 Prufrock		21	the terrace, made a sudden leap,/And seeing that it was a soft October night,/Curled
272 MC	Chorus	32	to distract, to divert the soul/From seeing itself, foully united forever, nothing with
309 FR	Harry	5	for you to understand/And that is by seeing. They are much too clever/To admit you
318 FR	Harry	9	not seen us/Except at half-term, and seeing us then/Only seemed to make her more
330 FR	Harry	27	self which persisted only as an eye, seeing./All this last year, I could not fit myself
335 FR	Agatha	10	feet./I was only the feet, and the eye/Seeing the feet: the unwinking eye/Fixing the

347 FR	Downing	5	his Lordship would get round to seeing them —/And so you've seen them too!
394 CP	Lavinia	5	.../{L} It was you who complained/Of seeing nobody but solicitors and clients .../{E}
395 CP	Edward	26	/{E} The change that comes/From seeing oneself through the eyes of other people./
412 CP	Reilly	4	You didn't let her know you were seeing me first?/{J} Of course not. I dropped her
426 CP	Edward	22	thankful/To have that excuse for not seeing people;/And you do need to rest now. {}/
433 CP	Julia	11	have me:/So good-bye to my hopes of seeing California./{P} You know you'd never
439 CP	Lavinia	1	to her ... so spiteful./I shall go on seeing her at the moment/When she said
529 ES	Charles	5	to talk to!/{C} I know he's used to seeing me about./{M} I've seen him looking at
531 ES	Lambert	38	that he'd gone away without your seeing him./{LC} What sort of a person?/{L} A
532 ES	Charles	24	goodbye, sir./And look forward to seeing you both at Badgley Court/In a week or
579 ES	Michael	2	That makes no difference./You'll be seeing me again./{M} But who will you be/When

SEEK (8)

140 Usk		9	roads dip and where the roads rise/Seek only there/Where the grey light meets the
166 Rock 10		14	Be not too curious of Good and Evil;/Seek not to count the future waves of Time;/But
226 Macavity		9	— *Macavity's not there*!/You may seek him in the basement, you may look up in
592 Grad 2		2	embarking from the strand/To seek their fortunes on some foreign shore/Well
601 Nocturne		14	—/'The perfect climax all true lovers seek!'/Humouresque/(AFTER J. LAFORGUE)
255 MC Tempt4		12	with richness of heavenly grandeur?/Seek the way of martyrdom, make yourself the
280 MC Priest3		25	/Find an oasis in the desert sun,/Go seek alliance with the heathen Saracen,/To share
338 FR	Harry	28	/Not to avoid being found, but to seek./I would not have chosen this way, had

SEEKING (2)

148 Rock 1		51	things that men count for happiness, seeking/The good deeds that lead to obscurity,
158 Rock 5		8	too vain and distracted for silence: seeking every one after his own elevation, and

SEEM (61)

18 Portrait		2	the scene arrange itself — as it will seem to do —/With 'I have saved this afternoon
148 Rock 1		35	for picnics./And the Church does not seem to be wanted/In country or in suburb; and
182 FQ: ECoker		190	and now, under conditions/That seem unpropitious. But perhaps neither gain nor
258 MC Thomas		34	to show you of my history/Will seem to most of you at best futility,/Senseless
260 MC Thomas		22	meaning of this word 'peace'. Does/it seem strange to you that the angels should have
260 MC Thomas		24	War and the fear of/War? Does it seem to you that the angelic voices were
271 MC Thomas		18	been changed in the telling. They will seem unreal./Human kind cannot bear very
289 FR	Gerald	4	know what you're talking about./You seem to be wanting to give us all the hump./I
295 FR	Charles	11	understand, your life together made it seem more horrible./There's a lot in my own
299 FR	Charles	1	worried about his health./He doesn't seem to be ... quite himself./{Do} Quite natural,
301 FR	Violet	11	say, with your investigations,/You seem to have left matters much as they were —/
306 FR	Mary	3	But to you, I am sure,/We must seem very altered./{H} You have hardly changed
306 FR	Harry	38	for you, not for us./{H} No, it didn't seem like that. I was part of the design/As well
307 FR	Mary	28	commonplace troubles?/They must seem very trivial indeed to you./It's just
309 FR	Harry	30	/You have staid in England, yet you seem/Like someone who comes from a very
318 FR	Harry	34	to the stone deaf: and the others/Seem to hear something else than what I am
325 FR	Violet	8	with his mother./{V} I do not seem to be very popular tonight./{C} Well,
326 FR	Harry	26	an orderly universe./But it begins to seem just part of some huge disaster,/Some
338 FR	Harry	40	that is when/One begins to seem the maddest to other people./It is hard for
346 FR	Charles	5	that, if one were awake?/You both seem to know more about this than I do. {}/
346 FR	Downing	26	sure of what I mean:/We most of us seem to live according to circumstance,/But
346 FR	Downing	29	to them. You get a feeling of it./So I seem to know beforehand, when something's
353 CP	Julia	19	of hearing that story./{J} Well, you all seem to know it./{C} Do we all know it?/But
366 CP	Edward	28	I'm not disturbing you, Edward./{E} I seem to have been disturbed already;/And I did
374 CP	Celia	7	my umbrella ... ./I must say you don't seem very pleased to see me./Edward, I
374 CP	Celia	10	manner on the telephone./It did not seem like you. So I felt I must see you./Tell me
380 CP	Celia	3	to myself./I am not sure even that you seem real enough/To humiliate me. I suppose
391 CP	Lavinia	34	PETER]/{L} I must say, you don't seem very pleased to see me./{E} I can't say that
391 CP	Edward	36	that I've had much opportunity/To seem anything. But of course I'm glad to see
395 CP	Edward	15	/{E} This is very interesting:/But you seem to assume that you've done all the
396 CP	Lavinia	19	but nothing, which is all you seem to want of me./But I'm sorry for you .../
408 CP	Edward	10	Lavinia! This is very interesting./You seem to have been much more successful at
416 CP	Celia	19	feel/As I did then, even now it would seem right./And then I found we were only
416 CP	Reilly	29	{R} And this man. What does he now seem like, to you?/{C} Like a child who has
426 CP	Julia	29	/{J} Well, my dears, and here I am!/I seem *literally* to have caught you napping!/I
430 CP	Peter	15	mind my looking in so early./It does seem ages since I last saw any of you!/And how
434 CP	Alex	24	we know of local practices/It would seem that she must have been crucified/Very
435 CP	Lavinia	39	perhaps what I've been saying/Will seem less unkind if I can make you understand/
440 CP	Edward	9	on;/And somehow, the two ideas seem to fit together./{L} But all the same ... I
454 CC	Colby	19	/{E} Yes, Mr. Simpkins?/{C} You seem to me sane. And I think I am./{E} I have
460 CC	Claude	39	give him full marks. Well, Eggerson,/I seem to have brought you up to London for

462 CC	Colby	21	/In the right direction./{C} It doesn't seem quite honest./If we all have to live in a
467 CC	Claude	19	/My father made with me. And yet I seem/To have made a greater mistake than he
473 CC	Colby	24	/But that's just the trouble. They seem so unrelated./I turn the key, and walk
474 CC	Lucasta	28	imagine that happening to you./You seem so secure, to me. Not only in your music
474 CC	Lucasta	29	/That's just its expression. You don't seem to me/To need anybody./{C} That's quite
482 CC	Lady E	7	her Lucasta? Young people nowadays/Seem to have dropped the use of surnames
485 CC	Lady E	29	like me, in the country./Teddington. I seem to have heard of it./Was it a large house?/
498 CC	Eggers	6	And that I could swear to./{E} It does seem unlikely/That there should be two Mrs.
505 CC	Eggers	31	my age/The past and the future both seem very brief —/But long enough ago for the
517 CC	Eggers	31	I'm certain./Good organists don't seem to want to come to Joshua Park./{C} But
524 ES	Monica	12	the *maître d'hôtel*/And the waiters all seem to be your intimate friends./{C} It's the
526 ES	Charles	12	I felt its presence./{C} Your words seem to come/From very far away. Yet very
534 ES	Ld Clav	6	to be corruptible./{LC} It would seem then that most of your business/Has been
538 ES	Ld Clav	6	/But there's just one thing you seem to have forgotten:/I came to your
544 ES	Ld Clav	29	as most people. At least, as they seem to do/Without knowing that they enjoy it.
545 ES	Monica	11	find life pleasant,/That it really does seem quiet here and restful./Even the matron,
552 ES	Ld Clav	2	at the same time of your own?/I seem to remember, it was only a year or so/
553 ES	Carghil	17	*always* be together./There's a phrase I seem to remember reading somewhere:/*Where*
563 ES	Gomez	25	.../{MC} Mrs. John Carghill./{G} We seem a bit weak on the surnames, Dick!/{MC}
567 ES	Charles	13	much your words meant. You didn't seem to need me then./And you said we weren't

SEEMED (38)

148 Rock	1	33	/In the pleasant countryside, there it seemed/That the country now is only fit for
161 Rock	7	21	of time gave the meaning./Then it seemed as if men must proceed from light to
212 Growltiger		21	a peaceful summer night, all nature seemed at play,/The tender moon was shining
213 Growltiger		34	but Griddlebone,/And the Lady seemed enraptured by his manly baritone,/
605 Narcissus		19	God/If he walked in city streets/He seemed to tread on faces, convulsive thighs and
277 MC Knight3		13	in good Church traditions. So if/we seemed a bit rowdy, you will understand why it
300 FR Downing		3	/{Do} Well, I don't know, Sir./But he seemed very anxious about my Lady./Tried to
306 FR	Mary	25	though I never knew why:/It always seemed that it must be my own fault,/And never
306 FR	Mary	30	It was different for you./And you seemed so much older. We were rather in awe of
306 FR	Mary	33	were we not happy?/{M} Well, it all seemed to be imposed upon us;/Even the nice
310 FR	Harry	31	saying? I think I was saying/That it seemed as if I had been always here/And you
318 FR	Harry	10	at half-term, and seeing us then/Only seemed to make her more unhappy, and made
333 FR	Harry	16	sense,/A sense that would have seemed meaningless before./Everything tends
333 FR	Harry	20	which at the beginning/Would have seemed the ruin./Perhaps my life has only been
334 FR	Harry	29	But it is very odd:/When other people seemed so strong, their apparent strength/Stifled
366 CP	Peter	33	and try to see you later;/But this seemed an opportunity./{E} And what's your
367 CP	Peter	12	in common, do you think?/{P} It seemed to me we had a great deal in common./
369 CP	Peter	29	to go alone./But a girl like Celia, it seemed very strange,/Because I thought of her
370 CP	Peter	28	—/But those moments in which we seemed to share some perception,/Some feeling,
379 CP	Celia	26	had a different meaning/Or so it seemed./{E} I have heard of that experience./{C}
379 CP	Celia	34	you./Perhaps the dream was better. It seemed the real reality,/And if this is reality, it is
396 CP	Lavinia	11	to persuade yourself you were./I seemed always on the verge of some wonderful
401 CP	Edward	37	my wife back,/I suppose. You seemed to be trying to persuade me/That I was
413 CP	Celia	30	at least, very different from what it seemed to be,/With the world itself — and that's
414 CP	Celia	39	/This is most unusual./{C} It seemed to *me* abnormal./{R} We have yet to
415 CP	Celia	31	you call a 'kink'?/{C} But everything seemed so right, at the time!/I've been thinking
416 CP	Celia	16	me — and the giving and the taking/Seemed so right: not in terms of calculation/Of
435 CP	Peter	24	to lead to something better,/And that seemed possible, while Celia was alive./I wanted
436 CP	Lavinia	22	I was looking at your face. And it seemed from your expression/That the way in
454 CC	Colby	21	at all./{C} And B. Kaghan has always seemed to me sane./{E} I should call him the
463 CC	Claude	5	was perhaps a mistake,/Though it seemed to have such obvious advantages/That I
485 CC	Lady E	14	for a while, in reincarnation./That seemed to explain it all. I don't believe it now./
488 CC	Claude	14	— any name you heard would have seemed the right one./{LE} Oh Claude, how can
489 CC	Claude	7	sounds now. One child each —/That seemed fair enough — though yours had been
538 ES	Gomez	12	made a good marriage —/Or so it seemed — and with your father's money/And
548 ES	Ld Clav	20	daughter chose it./She noticed that it seemed to offer the advantages/Which you have
578 ES	Michael	23	fond of you/Though we never really seemed to have much in common./I remember,
578 ES	Michael	29	the fire. How I laughed!/You never seemed even to want a flirtation,/And my

SEEMS (54)

49 Hippopot		3	on his belly in the mud;/Although he seems so firm to us/He is merely flesh and
107 Animula		19	more/With the imperatives of 'is and seems'/And may and may not, desire and
161 Rock	7	26	yet following no other way./But it seems that something has happened that has
179 FQ: ECoker		82	they turned their eyes. There is, it seems to us,/At best, only a limited value/In the
186 FQ: DrySal		87	/Prayer of the one Annunciation./It seems, as one becomes older,/That the past has

202 War Poetry	14	to keep day and night together./It seems just possible that a poem might happen/
279 MC Knight1	5	us a great deal to think about. It/seems to me that he has said almost the last
287 FR Amy	32	in a vacant room./Only Agatha seems to discover some meaning in death/Which
289 FR Charles	16	that I ought to mention it now?/It seems to me too late./{A} Much too late./If he
297 CP Agatha	3	What does Agatha think?/{Ag} It seems a necessary move/In an unnecessary
306 FR Harry	16	took place in my memory,/I think. It seems I shall get rid of nothing./Of none of the
320 FR Warburt	7	so vigorous of mind,/Although she seems as vital as ever —/It is only the force of
327 FR Ivy	29	him,/And his voice was very queer. It seems that Arthur too/Has had an accident. I
332 FR Agatha	26	/{Ag} There are hours when there seems to be no past or future,/Only a present
339 FR Harry	21	wanted. Strength demanded/That seems too much, is just strength enough given./I
344 FR Violet	8	Ask Agatha./{V} Really, it sometimes seems to me/That I am the only sane person in
344 FR Violet	10	in this house./Your behaviour all seems to me quite unaccountable./What *has*
346 FRDowning	30	something's going to happen,/And it seems quite natural, being his Lordship./And
346 FR Agatha	33	/{Ag} And, Downing, if his behaviour seems unaccountable/At times, you mustn't
364 CP Edward	24	/{E} I will not ask them./And yet — it seems to me — when we began to talk/I was not
370 CP Peter	23	plausible,/And when I do see her, she seems preoccupied/With some secret excitement
386 CP Edward	24	delayed, and sent me on ahead./{E} It seems very odd. And not like Lavinia./I suppose
391 CP Lavinia	18	telegram./I don't know why. But it seems to me that yesterday/I started some
410 CP Lavinia	10	finds that no man can love her./{L} It seems to me that what we have in common/
411 CP Edward	15	leave some shirts there for you./{E} It seems to me that I might as well go home./{L}
413 CP Celia	19	—/Except that the world I live in seems all a delusion!/But oughtn't I first to tell
414 CP Celia	13	Do you know —/It no longer seems worth while to *speak* to anyone!/{R} And
414 CP Celia	26	/But that everyone's alone — or so it seems to me./They make noises, and think they
428 CP Edward	15	that the monkeys do./{E} That seems unreasonable./{A} It is unreasonable,/But
434 CP Alex	6	to plague./{E} Go on./{A} It seems that there were three of them —/Three
457 CC Colby	6	she has a good heart./{C} Everybody seems to be kind-hearted./But there's one thing
462 CC Colby	7	/And what you've had in mind still seems to me/Like building my life upon a
463 CC Colby	31	/The art that I could never excel in,/Seems the one thing worth doing, the one thing/
466 CC Claude	21	the men of genius./There are others, it seems to me, who have at best to live/In two
487 CC Lady E	24	couldn't possibly be a coincidence./It seems incredible, doesn't it, Claude?/And yet it
487 CC Lady E	29	is wrong of me to feel so sure,/But it seems that Providence has brought you back to
488 CC Claude	20	what you expect. I'm afraid, Colby,/It seems to me that we must let her know the
488 CC Colby	21	we must let her know the truth./{C} It seems to me ... there is nothing for me —/
488 CC Claude	27	before,/But I'd hoped — and now it seems a silly thought .../What happens is so like
489 CC Claude	11	any number of children!/That seems grotesque now. But it influenced me./And
495 CC Lady E	23	look like poets:/And financiers, it seems, don't look like potters —/Is that what I
498 CC Lady E	27	and got them mixed./{LE} That seems to be what happened. And now we must
504 CC Lucasta	5	back. It's an anti-climax./But there seems to be nobody to answer the door./I've
506 CC Eggers	26	I might be able to help you?/{E} It seems just possible. A few days ago,/As I said,
510 CC Lady E	32	asking?/{LE} Because, Barnabas, it seems you are my son./{E} You will wish to
510 CC Eggers	38	from Mrs. Guzzard,/To whom, it seems, you had first been entrusted./{K} I really
512 CC Claude	18	to have him as your son?/{SC} That seems a strange question, Mrs. Guzzard./{MG}
526 ES Charles	35	too long, for you belong to him./He seems so placidly to take it for granted/That
548 ES Monica	9	so alarmed!/If you spy any guest who seems to be stalking you/Put your newspaper
549 ES Carghil	22	and Maud and I. What a time ago it seems!/It's surprising I remember it all so
554 ES Carghil	12	Carghill!/{MC} Dear Mrs. Piggott!/It seems to me that you never sit still:/You simply
565 ES Carghil	12	is such an old friend of mine/That it seems most natural to call you Michael./You
574 ES Carghil	3	adopted daughter./So much so, that it seems odd to call you Mr. Hemington:/I'm
580 ES Carghil	15	*and* GOMEZ]/{MC} I'm afraid this seems awfully sudden to you, Richard;/It isn't

SEEN (78)

15 Prufrock	82	wept and prayed,/Though I have seen my head (grown slightly bald) brought in
15 Prufrock	84	— and here's no great matter;/I have seen the moment of my greatness flicker,/And I
15 Prufrock	85	of my greatness flicker,/And I have seen the eternal Footman hold my coat, and
17 Prufrock	126	think that they will sing to me./I have seen them riding seaward on the waves/
24 Rhapsody	41	behind that child's eye./I have seen eyes in the street/Trying to peer through
43 Swee Erect	27	history, said Emerson/Who had not seen the silhouette/Of Sweeney straddled in the
50 Hippopot	31	enfold,/Among the saints he shall be seen/Performing on a harp of gold./He shall be
104 Journ Magi	37	We had evidence and no doubt. I had seen birth and death,/But had thought they
106 Song Sime	37	me./Let thy servant depart,/Having seen thy salvation./Animula/'Issues from the
124 SA Snow	21	them bones on Epsom Heath?/I seen that in the papers/You seen it in the papers
124 SA Snow	22	Heath?/I seen that in the papers/They seen it in the papers/They *don't* all get pinched
136 5FingerEx3	6	only sluggish duck and drake./I have seen the morning shine,/I have had the Bread
148 Rock 1	42	Watcher. The Stranger./He who has seen what has happened/And who sees what is
166 Rock 10	1	reminder of Invisible Light./You have seen the house built, you have seen it adorned/
166 Rock 10	1	have seen the house built, you have seen it adorned/By one who came in the night, it

189 FQ: DrySal	179	also on behalf of/Women who have	seen their sons or husbands/Setting forth, and
225 Mr Mistoff	35	it is merely misplaced —/You have	seen it one moment, and then it is *gawn!*/But
230 Bust Jones	19	but *Blimp's*;/But he's frequently	seen at the gay *Stage and Screen*/Which is
230 Bust Jones	25	for a drink at the *Drones.*/When he's	seen in a hurry there's probably curry/At the
234 Ad-dress	13	all may be described in verse./You've	seen them both at work and games,/And learnt
240 MC Chorus	18	shaping the still unshapen:/I have	seen these things in a shaft of sunlight,/Destiny
244 MC Chorus	11	/Living and partly living./We have	seen births, deaths and marriages,/We have had
253 MC Tempt4	1	come./You know me, but have never	seen my face./To meet before was never time or
257 MC Chorus	15	sins made heavier upon us./We have	seen the young man mutilated,/The torn girl
261 MC Thomas	34	made themselves most low, and are	seen, not as we/see them, but in the light of the
264 MC Priest2	10	which we have heard,/Which we have	seen with our eyes, and our hands have handled
264 MC Priest2	11	the word of life; that which we have	seen and heard/Declare we unto you./*In the*
269 MC Chorus	29	the night-time, fluting and owls, have	seen at noon/Scaly wings slanting over, huge
269 MC Chorus	33	of the loon, the lunatic bird. I have	seen/Grey necks twisting, rat tails twining, in
270 MC Chorus	3	primrose and cowslip. I have	seen/Trunk and horn, tusk and hoof, in odd
270 MC Chorus	9	while the ground heaved. I have	seen/Rings of light coiling downwards,
279 MC Knight4	31	could have given us reason: you have	seen how he/evaded our questions. And when
281 MC Chorus	9	hunted./For all things exist only as	seen by Thee, only as known by Thee, all things
288 FR Amy	32	/Nothing has been changed. I have	seen to that./{Ag} Yes. I mean that at
292 FR Harry	3	me. This is the first time that I have	seen them./In the Java Straits, in the Sunda Sea,
298 FR Charles	35	a good friend to him, too./*We* haven't	seen him for nearly eight years;/And to tell the
298 FR Charles	36	/And to tell the truth, now that we've	seen him,/We're a little worried about his
306 FR Harry	5	changed at all —/And I haven't	seen you since you came down from Oxford./
308 FR Harry	7	to a twilight/Where the dead stone is	seen to be batrachian,/The aphyllous branch
309 FR Harry	7	world. Yours is no better./They have	seen to that: it is part of the torment./{M} If you
313 FR Gerald	14	/{G} Good evening, Mary. You've	seen Harry, I see./It's good to have him back
314 FR Amy	2	anywhere. Harry!/Haven't you	seen Dr. Warburton?/You know he's the oldest
318 FR Harry	8	the weeks during which she had not	seen us/Except at half-term, and seeing us then/
323 FR Warburt	11	/And Winchell tells me Dr. Owen has	seen him/And says it's nothing but a slight
335 FR Agatha	40	which we did not pass./I have	seen the first stage: relief from what happened/
342 FR Mary	1	Excuse me, Cousin Amy. I have just	seen Denman./She came to tell me that Harry is
342 FR Mary	20	him!/You do not know what I have	seen and what I know!/He is in great danger, I
343 FR Agatha	3	have made this clear. And I who have	seen them must believe them./{M} Oh! ... so ...
343 FR Mary	4	them./{M} Oh! ... so ... *you* have	seen them too!/{Ag} We must all go, each in his
344 FR Harry	36	know why I am going. You have not	seen/What I have seen. Oh why should you
344 FR Harry	37	You have not seen/What I have	seen. Oh why should you make it so ridiculous/
346 FR Agatha	37	you or I see it,/It is only that he has	seen a great deal more than that,/And we have
346 FR Agatha	38	deal more than that,/And we have	seen them too — Miss Mary and I./{Do} I
347 FRDowning	6	to seeing them —/And so you've	seen them too! They must have given you a
356 CP Julia	7	Oh, what film was it? I wonder if I've	seen it./{P} No, you wouldn't have seen it. As a
356 CP Peter	8	seen it./{P} No, you wouldn't have	seen it. As a matter of fact/It was never
356 CP Julia	25	And this is the first time/I've ever	seen you without Lavinia/Except for the time
367 CP Peter	16	do you practise?/{P} You won't have	seen my novel,/Though it had some very good
367 CP Edward	26	she had her poetry./{E} Yes, I've	seen her poetry —/Interesting if one is interested
401 CP Edward	23	find with you./{E} But you had	seen my wife?/{R} Oh yes, I had seen her./{E} So
401 CP Reilly	24	had seen my wife?/{R} Oh yes, I had	seen her./{E} So this *is* a trap!/{R} Let's not call
418 CP Reilly	22	in familiar terms/Because you have	seen it, as we all have seen it,/Illustrated, more
418 CP Reilly	22	you have seen it, as we all have	seen it,/Illustrated, more or less, in lives of those
425 CP Lavinia	32	do about it:/And everyone likes to be	seen at a party/Where everybody else is, to show
446 CC Eggers	38	a letter in *The Times* about wild birds	seen in London:/And I'm sure Mr. Simpkins
453 CC Lucasta	8	married./{L} Then I don't mind being	seen with you in public./You may take me out
461 CC Colby	36	{C} Did she really think/That she had	seen me before?/{SC} Impossible to tell./The
469 CC Lucasta	25	— to see the other people,/And to be	seen there! And because you feel out of it/If you
471 CC Colby	38	B./{C} Only afterwards,/When I had	seen you a number of times,/I decided that was
529 ES Monica	6	he's used to seeing me about./{M} I've	seen him looking at you. He was thinking of
531 ES Ld Clav	29	myself as a ghost/Shan't want to be	seen there. It makes me smile/To think that men
533 ES Gomez	31	on the right side of the law —/And	seen that the law turned its right side to *me.*/
546 ES Monica	32	please tell me one thing./We haven't	seen her yet, but the chambermaid/Referred to a
548 ES Carghil	32	you anywhere./But then, we've all	seen your portrait in the papers/So often. And
561 ES Monica	39	within the light of which/All else is	seen, the love within which/All other love finds
563 ES Carghil	16	/So he sent me here./{MC} Oh, you've	seen each other lately?/Richard, I think that you
568 ES Ld Clav	19	—/I don't need to be told what I've	seen for myself!/And if there is nothing that you
569 ES Charles	21	any question of blackmail,/I've	seen something of it in my practice at the bar./

SEES (7)
148 Rock 1		43	seen what has happened/And who sees what is to happen./The Witness. The Critic.
232 Skimble		25	watch you without winking and he sees what you are thinking/And it's certain that
260 MC	Thomas	16	/the Cross. Beloved, as the World sees, this is to behave in a strange/fashion. For
309 FR	Mary	28	believes that he is blind/While he still sees the sunlight. I know that this is true./{H} I
346 FR	Agatha	36	He is every bit as sane as you or I,/He sees the world as clearly as you or I see it,/It is
477 CC	Lucasta	32	now, perhaps, if someone else sees me/As I really am, I might become myself./
575 ES	Michael	3	your son. That's what Señor Gomez sees./*He* understands my point of view, if *you*

SEINE (1)
184 FQ: DrySal		22	/It tosses up our losses, the torn seine,/The shattered lobsterpot, the broken oar/

SEIZE (4)
33 Conv Gal		9	night and moonshine; music which we seize/To body forth our own vacuity.'/She then:
52 Whispers		11	found no substitute for sense,/To seize and clutch and penetrate;/Expert beyond
241 MC	Priest3	4	by caprice./They have but one law, to seize the power and keep it,/And the steadfast
272 MC	Priests	8	to a joyful consummation./{3P} Seize him! force him! drag him!/{T} Keep your

SEIZES (1)
321 FR	m	28	{}/[*He darts at* WINCHELL *and seizes him by the shoulders*]/{H} He *is* real,

SELBY (4)
528 ES	Monica	24	/I've only just been given it by Dr. Selby —/Father is much iller than he is aware
528 ES	Monica	27	never return from Badgley Court./But Selby wants him to have every encouragement
528 ES	Monica	29	to live a little longer./That's why Selby chose the place. A *convalescent* home/
528 ES	Monica	39	take place. 'Make the reservations'/Selby said, 'as if you were going'./But Badgley

SELDOM (5)
234 Ad-dress		21	like to fight;/They often bark, more seldom bite;/But yet a Dog is, on the whole,/
303 FR	Mary	23	uncomfortable people/Who meet very seldom, making conversation./I am very glad if
304 FR	Mary	16	she usually gets./Why do *you* so seldom come here? *You*'re not afraid of her,/
552 ES	Carghil	23	Your conscience was clear./I've very seldom heard people mention their consciences/
578 ES	Monica	19	of me./When we were growing up we seldom had the same friends./I took all that for

SELECT (1)
129 Cor2 State		9	councils, the standing committees, select committees and sub-committees./One

SELECTION (1)
265 MC	Priest3	5	like another. Only in retrospection, selection,/We say, that was the day. The critical

SELF (18)
195 FQ: Little		154	in the same hedgerow:/Attachment to self and to things and to persons, detachment/
195 FQ: Little		155	and to persons, detachment/From self and from things and from persons; and,
195 FQ: Little		166	vanish,/The faces and places, with the self which, as it could, loved them,/To become
295 FR	Harry	19	is just the cancer/That eats away the self. I knew how you would take it./First of all,
308 FR	Mary	26	expected Wishwood/To be your real self, to do something for you/That you can only
330 FR	Harry	26	degradation of being parted from my self,/From the self which persisted only as an
330 FR	Harry	27	being parted from my self,/From the self which persisted only as an eye, seeing./All
381 CP	Edward	33	is, is not, or could be changed./The self that can say 'I want this — or want that' —/
381 CP	Edward	34	'I want this — or want that' —/The self that wills — he is a feeble creature;/He has
381 CP	Edward	36	end/With the obstinate, the tougher self; who does not speak,/Who never talks, who
382 CP	Edward	1	spirit of mediocrity./The willing self can contrive the disaster/Of this unwilling
477 CC	Lucasta	36	/{L} Yourself, indeed! Your precious self!/Why don't you shut yourself up in that
528 ES	Charles	17	whether there was any .../Private self to preserve./{M} There *is* a private self,
528 ES	Monica	18	to preserve./{M} There *is* a private self, Charles./I'm sure of that./{C} You've given
545 ES	Ld Clav	5	— first of all to myself./What is this self inside us, this silent observer,/Severe and
576 ES	Monica	26	abandon your family/And your very self — it's a kind of suicide./{C} Michael, you
580 ES	Monica	33	he rejects,/But himself, the unhappy self that he's ashamed of./I'm sure he loves us.
582 ES	Ld Clav	3	I reject also./I've been freed from the self that pretends to be someone;/And in

SELF-BOUND (1)
249 MC	Tempt2	25	in Canterbury, realmless ruler,/Self-bound servant of a powerless Pope,/The old

SELF-CENTRED (1)
571 ES	Ld Clav	18	capacity/For loving she had — self-centred and foolish —/But we should

SELF-CONCEIT (1)
111 Xmas Trees		23	convert/Which may be tainted with a self-conceit/Displeasing to God and

SELF-CONFIDENCE (3)
435 CP	Peter	8	myself a success/And got a little more self-confidence;/And then I thought about her
463 CC	Colby	14	/It gives me, in a way, a kind of self-confidence/I've never had before. Yet at the
580 ES	Monica	31	will give him confidence —/It's only self-confidence that Michael is lacking./Oh

SELF-DECEIVERS (1)
407 CP	Reilly	18	dull:/My patients such as you are the self-deceivers/Taking infinite pains, exhausting

SELF-DEFENCE (2)
471 CC   Colby   39 /I decided that was only your kind of self-defence./{L} What made you think it was
471 CC Lucasta   40   /{L} What made you think it was self-defence?/{C} Because you couldn't wait to
SELF-DEMOLITION (1)
271 MC Chorus   3   of spirit,/Dominated by the lust of self-demolition,/By the final utter uttermost
SELF-DESTRUCTION (1)
256 MC Tempts   19   man is obstinate, blind, intent/On self-destruction,/Passing from deception to
SELF-ESTEEM (1)
409 CP   Reilly   21   of loving/Is as disturbing to their self-esteem/As, in cruder men, the fear of
SELF-GIVEN (1)
166 Rock 10   11   golden eyes,/The worshippers, self-given sacrifice of the snake. Take/Your way
SELF-INTEREST (1)
249 MC Tempt2   35   /Will not strive against intelligent self-interest./{T} You forget the barons. Who
SELF-JUSTIFICATION (1)
572 ES   Charles 29   /With revenge — it's their means of self-justification./Let them tell their versions of
SELF-PITY (1)
340 FR   Amy   25 myself./Did I show any weakness, any self-pity?/I forced myself to the purposes of
SELF-POSSESSED (1)
 20 Portrait   78   /I keep my countenance,/I remain self-possessed/Except when a street-piano,
SELF-POSSESSION (3)
 20 Portrait   94   /'Perhaps you can write to me.'/My self-possession flares up for a second;/*This* is as
 21 Portrait   101   his expression in a glass./My self-possession gutters; we are really in the dark.
603 Spleen   5 repetition that displaces/Your mental self-possession/By this unwarranted digression./
SELF-RESPECT (1)
478 CC Lucasta   31 /I may be a bastard, but I have some self-respect./Well, there's always B. I think that
SELF-SEEKERS (1)
157 Rock 4   16   to destroy him,/And spies and self-seekers within,/When he and his men laid
SELF-SEEKING (1)
161 Rock 7   23   /Bestial as always before, carnal, self-seeking as always before, selfish and
SELF-SLAUGHTER (1)
258 MC Thomas   35 most of you at best futility,/Senseless self-slaughter of a lunatic,/Arrogant passion of
SELF-SURRENDER (1)
190 FQ: DrySal 209 in love,/Ardour and selflessness and self-surrender./For most of us, there is only the
SELFISH (5)
107 Animula   25 of time the simple soul/Irresolute and selfish, misshapen, lame,/Unable to fare
161 Rock 7   23 carnal, self-seeking as always before, selfish and purblind as ever before,/Yet always
278 MC Knight2   11   which were usually exercised for/selfish and often for seditious ends, and to
525 ES   Charles 39 Is this a time to torment me? But I'm selfish/In saying that, because I think —/I think
571 ES   Ld Clav 20   we meet it;/Even when it's vain and selfish, we must not abuse it./That is where I
SELFLESSNESS (1)
190 FQ: DrySal 209 a lifetime's death in love,/Ardour and selflessness and self-surrender./For most of us,
SELL (2)
532 ES   Ld Clav 18   him/I expect he wants money. Or to sell me something worthless./{M} You ought
540 ES   Ld Clav 36   would interest the public/Why not sell your version to a Sunday newspaper?/{G}
SELVES (1)
244 MC Chorus   23   like the layers of an onion, our selves are lost lost/In a final fear which none
SEMBLABLE (1)
 63 WL: Burial   76   /'You! hypocrite lecteur! — mon semblable, — mon frère!'/A Game of Chess/The
SEMI-DARKNESS (1)
149 Rock 1 m   79 humble. Listen./*The lights fade; in the semi-darkness the voices of* WORKMEN *are*
SEMITE (1)
 40 Burb Blei   16   with the palms turned out,/Chicago Semite Viennese./A lustreless protrusive eye/
SEMPITERNAL (1)
191 FQ: Little   2 /Midwinter spring is its own season/Sempiternal though sodden towards sundown,/
SEND (23)
247 MC Tempt1   12   the sunlight. Love in the orchard/Send the sap shooting. Mirth matches
298 FR Charles   28 very well indeed, Sir./{C} I'm sorry to send for you so abruptly,/But I've a question I'd
320 FR Warburt   15 several years. A sudden shock/Might send her off at any moment./If she had been
349 FR   Violet 10   wait for the will to be read. I shall send a wire in the morning./{C} I fear that my
401 CP Edward   19 as a guest/As I supposed? ... Or did she *send* you?/{R} I cannot say that I had been
402 CP Edward   25   Is there a sanatorium to which you send such patients/As myself, under your
404 CP Edward   23   in that belief./{E} And now will you send me to the sanatorium?/{R} You have
404 CP Edward   28   *early* history./{E} And so will you send me to the sanatorium?/I can't go home
405 CP Edward   36 ask you, Lavinia,/To be so good as to send me on some clothes./{L} Oh, to what hotel?
406 CP Lavinia   5 /[*To* REILLY]/{L} I presume you will send him to the same sanatorium/To which you

411 CP	Reilly	35	*raises his hand*]/{R} My secretary will send you my account./Go in peace. And work
419 CP	Reilly	20	sanatorium./I am very careful whom I send there:/Those who go do not come back as
419 CP	Celia	32	in the world./{C} How soon will you send me there?/{R} How soon will you be ready?
419 CP	Reilly	38	let your family know at once./I will send a car for you at nine o'clock./{C} What do
420 CP	Reilly	25	*I* shall keep an eye on them./{R} To send them back: what have they to go back to?/
445 CC	Claude	5	/At Northolt, but you. And I couldn't send Colby./That's not the way to arrange their
445 CC	Claude	21	Will he be here?/{SC} I had to send him to the City this morning,/But he'll be
460 CC	Claude	8	all about it./{SC} It's true, you did send me postcards from Zürich;/But you know
532 ES	Monica	21	got rid of him in twenty minutes/I'll send Lambert to tell you that you have to take a
546 ES	Piggott	26	stipulation to all the doctors/Who send people here. When you go in to lunch/Just
558 ES	Michael	1	/{Mi} It's their own fault./They won't send in their bills, and then I forget them./It's
574 ES	Michael	36	himself custodian of my morals/And send you back reports. Some sort of place/
580 ES	Michael	9	not much of a correspondent;/But I'll send you a card, now and again,/Just to let you

SENDING (2)

388 CP	Lavinia	29	you mean./Edward, have you been sending telegrams?/{E} Of course I haven't sent
406 CP	Reilly	17	/That is good reason for not sending them to one./The people who need my

SENDS (1)

357 CP	Julia	15	she's ill/She gets into a panic./{J} And sends for Lavinia./I quite understand. Are there

SENIOR (1)

230 Bust	Jones	13	spats!/His visits are occasional to the *Senior Educational*/And it is against the rules/For

SEÑOR (26)

532 ES	Ld Clav	14	Monica./I've never heard of this Señor Gomez/But he comes with a letter of
563 ES	Carghil	26	surnames, Dick!/{MC} Well, you see, Señor Gomez, when we first became friends —/
563 ES	Carghil	34	did you never see me?/That's a pity, Señor Gomez./{G} I lost touch with things in
564 ES	Carghil	2	the song/That made my reputation, Señor Gomez./{G} It will never be too late.
564 ES	Carghil	12	Lord Claverton/As long as I have, Señor Gomez./{G} My dear lady, you're not old
564 ES	Carghil	29	/{MC} Went back to San Marco./Señor Gomez, if it's true you're staying at
564 ES	Carghil	35	/{MC} Secret for secret, Señor Gomez!/You've got to be the first to put
565 ES	Carghil	24	Richard. Au revoir, Monica./And Señor Gomez, I shall hold you to your promise!
574 ES	Carghil	18	/So I thought, why not appeal to Señor Gomez?/He's a wealthy man, and very
574 ES	Ld Clav	22	ready to help./{LC} And what was Señor Gomez able to suggest?/{MC} Ah! That's
574 ES	Ld Clav	30	/With Mrs. Carghill and then with Señor Gomez./{Mi} When I spoke, Father, of
575 ES	Michael	3	/Not merely be your son. That's what Señor Gomez sees./*He* understands my point of
575 ES	Ld Clav	7	advantage of a job created for you/By Señor Gomez .../{Mi} It's not created for me./
575 ES	Michael	9	.../{Mi} It's not created for me./Señor Gomez came to London to find a man to
575 ES	Ld Clav	12	Of course you're just the man that Señor Gomez wants,/But in a different sense,
576 ES	Ld Clav	8	Just eighteen./{LC} Now, Michael,/Señor Gomez says he has told you his story./
576 ES	Charles	27	of suicide./{C} Michael, you think Señor Gomez is inspired by benevolence —/
577 ES	Charles	2	here's another point to think of:/Señor Gomez has offered you a post in San
577 ES	Charles	3	has offered you a post in San Marco,/Señor Gomez pays your passage .../{Mi} And an
577 ES	Charles	5	.../{Mi} And an advance of salary./{C} Señor Gomez pays your passage .../{G} Just as
577 ES	Michael	21	that Hemington has plenty of cheek./Señor Gomez and I have talked things over,
577 ES	Carghil	28	—/I wish you could have known him, Señor Gomez!/You're very much alike in some
577 ES	Carghil	32	for business./I saw that, and so does Señor Gomez./He's simply been suffering, poor
579 ES	Michael	9	kit. We're just going up to London./Señor Gomez will attend to my needs for that
579 ES	Carghil	12	reservations./{MC} It's wonderful, Señor Gomez, how you manage *everything*!/—
580 ES	Carghil	20	doctor's advice. And on my way back/Señor Gomez has invited me to visit San

SENSATION (1)

20 Portrait		85	returning as before/Except for a slight sensation of being ill at ease/I mount the stairs

SENSE (48)

38 Gerontion		63	/Excite the membrane, when the sense has cooled,/With pungent sauces, multiply
52 Whispers		10	another/Who found no substitute for sense,/To seize and clutch and penetrate;/Expert
64 WL: Chess		89	troubled, confused/And drowned the sense in odours; stirred by the air/That
173 FQ: BurntN		75	yet surrounded/By a grace of sense, a white light still and moving,/*Erhebung*
174 FQ: BurntN		122	property,/Desiccation of the world of sense,/Evacuation of the world of fancy,/
180 FQ: ECoker		110	Directory of Directors,/And cold the sense and lost the motive of action./And we all
186 FQ: DrySal		92	The moments of happiness — not the sense of well-being,/Fruition, fulfilment,
192 FQ: Little		45	the same: you would have to put off/Sense and notion. You are not here to verify,/
194 FQ: Little		133	/First, the cold friction of expiring sense/Without enchantment, offering no
258 MC Thomas		11	advancement and praise./Delight in sense, in learning and in thought,/Music and
276 MC Knight1		23	them. Nevertheless, I appeal to your sense of honour. You/are Englishmen, and
286 FR Charles		28	what they're eating;/They've lost their sense of taste and smell/Because of their
286 FR Charles		35	Haven't the stamina,/Haven't the sense of responsibility./{G} You're being very
294 FR Harry		39	that./Everything is true in a different sense./I expected to find her when I went back
309 FR Mary		14	a wise person,/And in the ordinary sense I don't know you very well,/Although I

311 FR	Harry	3	That apprehension deeper than all sense,/Deeper than the sense of smell, but like a
311 FR	Harry	4	deeper than all sense,/Deeper than the sense of smell, but like a smell/In that it is
317 FR	Warburt	17	already happened./{W} That is in a sense true,/But without your knowing it, and
330 FR	Harry	20	eight years ago,/I felt, at first, that sense of separation,/Of isolation unredeemable,
333 FR	Agatha	3	can take no credit for a little common sense,/He would have bungled it./I did not want
333 FR	Harry	15	/Everything is true in a different sense,/A sense that would have seemed
333 FR	Harry	16	is true in a different sense,/A sense that would have seemed meaningless
354 CP	Julia	40	clocks;/And he had a remarkable sense of hearing —/The only man I ever met
393 CP	Lavinia	6	of your life/With a man who has no sense of humour;/And that the effect upon me
393 CP	Lavinia	8	the effect upon me was/That I lost all sense of humour myself./That's what came of
408 CP	Lavinia	24	/{L} I never knew you had such a sense of humour./{R} It is the first more hopeful
411 CP	Lavinia	13	/{L} Really, Edward!/I have *some* sense of responsibility./I was going to leave
414 CP	Celia	36	only word for it/That I can find, is a sense of sin./{R} You suffer from a sense of sin,
414 CP	Reilly	37	a sense of sin./{R} You suffer from a sense of sin, Miss Coplestone?/This is most
415 CP	Reilly	2	/Tell me what you mean by a sense of sin./{C} It's much easier to tell you
415 CP	Celia	4	/I don't mean sin in the ordinary sense./{R} And what, in your opinion, is the
415 CP	Reilly	5	what, in your opinion, is the ordinary sense?/{C} Well ... I suppose it's being immoral
415 CP	Celia	9	the people who we say have no moral sense?/I've never noticed that immorality/Was
415 CP	Celia	11	immorality/Was accompanied by a sense of sin:/At least, I have never come across
419 CP	Reilly	25	I said they did not come back/In the sense in which your friends came back./I did not
419 CP	Reilly	29	/Some of them return, in a physical sense;/No one disappears. They lead very active
466 CC	Claude	11	long enough,/I sometimes have that sense of identification/With the maker, of which
472 CC	Colby	7	in your life/To rob you of any sense of security./{L} And I'm sure you have
472 CC	Lucasta	8	{L} And I'm sure you have *that* — the sense of security./{C} No, I haven't either./{L}
473 CC	Colby	33	— literally,/And also in the same sense that I retire to mine./But he doesn't feel
474 CC	Colby	22	hurting that one would mind/But the sense of desolation afterwards./{L} I know what
475 CC	Colby	26	/But not who you are, in the ordinary sense./Is that what you mean? I've just accepted
475 CC	Lucasta	30	/Of course the facts don't matter, in a sense./But now we've got to this point — you
502 CC	Lucasta	31	what I am .../{L} *Who* you are,/In the sense I've been told that you're my brother;/
539 ES	Gomez	39	A worldly success, Dick. In another sense/We're both of us failures. But even so,/I'd
544 ES	Ld Clav	16	I only hope that it will last —/The sense of wellbeing! It's often with us/When we
546 ES	Piggott	1	/Of course, I *am* a matron in a sense —/No, I don't simply mean that I'm a
575 ES	Ld Clav	13	Gomez wants,/But in a different sense, and for different reasons/From what you

SENSELESS (2)

| 258 MC | Thomas | 35 | seem to most of you at best futility,/Senseless self-slaughter of a lunatic,/Arrogant |
| 294 FR | Harry | 30 | by ghosts./It was only reversing the senseless direction/For a momentary rest on the |

SENSES (5)

164 Rock 9		28	/And intellectual pleasures of the senses?/The LORD who created must wish us to
206 To my Wife		2	the leaping delight/That quickens my senses in our wakingtime/And the rhythm that
269 MC	Chorus	27	I have smelt them, the death-bringers, senses are quickened/By subtle forebodings; I
312 FR	Harry	2	so imperceptive, have you such dull senses/That you could not see them? If I had
522 ES	dedic	2	*the leaping delight/That quickens my senses in our wakingtime/And the rhythm that*

SENSIBLE (5)

209 NamingCats		8	George or Bill Bailey —/All of them sensible everyday names./There are fancier
209 NamingCats		12	Electra, Demeter —/But all of them sensible everyday names./But I tell you, a cat
278 MC	Knight2	2	to your reason. You are hard-headed/sensible people, as I can see, and not to be taken
357 CP	Julia	37	/On my way to Cornwall. But let's be sensible:/Now you must let me be *your* maiden
508 CC	Claude	18	Lady Elizabeth's./{SC} That's a very sensible suggestion, Eggerson./A breath of

SENSUAL (1)

| 174 FQ: BurntN | | 100 | to purify the soul/Emptying the sensual with deprivation/Cleansing affection |

SENT (36)

590 Space Time		9	/Though sages disagree./The flowers I sent thee when the dew/Was trembling on the
241 MC	Mess	14	and is close outside the city./I was sent before in haste/To give you notice of his
246 MC	Thomas	4	letters,/Filled the coast with spies and sent to meet me/Some who hold me in bitterest
246 MC	Thomas	7	God's grace aware of their prevision/I sent my letters on another day,/Had fair
268 MC	Knight2	2	a pact of peace, and all dispute ended/Sent you back to your See as you demanded./
268 MC	Knight1	15	King's presence. Therefore were we sent./{T} Never was it my wish/To uncrown the
333 FR	Agatha	34	of your unhappy family,/Its bird sent flying through the purgatorial flame./
346 FR	Downing	7	excuse me, Mr. Charles:/His Lordship sent me back because he remembered/He thinks
347 FR	Ivy	16	*and* VIOLET]/{I} I wonder why he sent it, after telephoning./Shall I read it to you?
372 CP	Edward	17	all those eggs! Lavinia's aunt/Has just sent them from the country./{A} Ah, so the aunt
386 CP	Celia	23	me with her./Julia was delayed, and sent me on ahead./{E} It seems very odd. And
386 CP	Celia	32	/You look like a little boy who's been sent for/To the headmaster's study; and is not
387 CP	Edward	15	/{E} Don't tell me that Lavinia/Sent you a telegram .../{P} No, not to me,/But
388 CP	Celia	26	/{L} What telegram?/{C} The one you sent to Julia./{P} And the one you sent to Alex./

388 CP	Peter	27	sent to Julia./{P} And the one you sent to Alex./{L} I don't know what you mean./
388 CP	Edward	30	telegrams?/{E} Of course I haven't sent any telegrams./{L} This is some of Julia's
390 CP	Lavinia	7	where, may I ask, was this telegram sent from?/{J} Why, from Essex, of course./{L}
390 CP	Julia	31	of memory,/And so, of course, she sent us telegrams:/And now I don't believe she
392 CP	Edward	27	/Who was ill in the country, and had sent for you./{L} Really, Edward! You had
400 CP	Alex	21	a march on her./And when you've sent him to a sanatorium/Where she can't get at
404 CP	Edward	33	can get my wife/To have my things sent on: whatever I shall need./But of course
406 CP	Lavinia	6	to the same sanatorium/To which you sent me? Well, he needs it more than I did./{R} I
406 CP	Lavinia	10	{L} What do you mean? I asked to be sent/And you took me there. If that was not a
410 CP	Reilly	21	/{L} Is that possible?/{R} If I had sent either of you to the sanatorium/In the state
411 CP	Lavinia	26	too./Sir Henry, was it you who sent those telegrams?/{R} I think I will dispose
421 CP	Julia	27	the valley of derision, like a child sent on an errand/In eagerness and patience.
431 CP	Peter	11	each other./{P} Well, it was Bela sent me over/Just for a week. And I have my
463 CC	Claude	3	saw you alone./And then when I sent you both over to Canada/In the war —
477 CC	Lucasta	2	supplemented her income/When I was sent out. I've been locked in a cupboard!/I was
489 CC	Claude	27	was I? In Canada./My father had sent me on a business tour/To learn about his
515 CC	Guzzard	4	be born. You were very far away;/I sent you a message, which never reached you./
537 ES	Gomez	26	suppose your tutor thought you'd be sent down./It went the other way. You stayed
537 ES	Gomez	36	to it./And so it came about that I was sent down/With the consequences which you
542 ES	Gomez	6	Now it's my turn./I can have cigars sent direct to you from Cuba/If your doctors
550 ES	Carghil	26	my doctor could hardly have sent me *here*/If I wasn't well off. Yes, I'm
563 ES	Gomez	15	recommendation could I have?'/So he sent me here./{MC} Oh, you've seen each other

SENTENCE (7)

16 Prufrock	117	cautious, and meticulous;/Full of high sentence, but a bit obtuse;/At times, indeed,
197 FQ: Little	219	we start from. And every phrase/And sentence that is right (where every word is at
197 FQ: Little	226	together)/Every phrase and every sentence is an end and a beginning,/Every poem
249 MC Tempt2	2	Chancellor richly rules./This is a sentence not taught in the schools./To set down
437 ER Reilly	22	/That here was a woman under sentence of death./That was her destiny. The
533 ES Gomez	11	England?/{G} Ever since I finished my sentence./{LC} What has brought you to
577 ES Charles	18	be sure of/Is that he served a prison sentence for forgery./{G} Well, Michael, what

SENTIMENTAL (3)

33 Conv Gal	1	Conversation Galante/I observe: 'Our sentimental friend the moon!/Or possibly
212 Growltiger	24	Growltiger was disposed to show his sentimental side./His bucko mate,
551 ES Carghil	25	if I'd really cared for you./What sentimental nonsense! One starts an action/

SENTIMENTS (1)

154 Rock 3	9	given you lips, to express friendly sentiments,/I have given you hearts, for

SEPARATE (1)

166 Rock 10	12	the snake. Take/Your way and be ye separate./Be not too curious of Good and Evil;/

SEPARATED (3)

99 Ash-Wed 6	34	spirit of the sea,/Suffer me not to be separated/And let my cry come unto Thee./
316 FR Agatha	11	are three together/May the three be separated/May the knot that was tied/Become
319 FR Warburt	16	were never very happy together:/They separated by mutual consent/And he went to

SEPARATELY (1)

326 FR Harry	17	go on trying to think of each thing separately,/Making small things important, so

SEPARATES (1)

417 CP Reilly	32	/Are contented with the morning that separates/And with the evening that brings

SEPARATION (3)

117 SP Dusty	24	/{Du} 'A quarrel. An estrangement. Separation of friends'./{Do} Here's the two of
272 MC Chorus	25	shapes of hell;/Emptiness, absence, separation from God;/The horror of the
330 FR Harry	20	years ago,/I felt, at first, that sense of separation,/Of isolation unredeemable,

SEPT (1)

51 Restaurant	10	une averse, qu'on s'abrite./J'avais sept ans, elle était plus petite./Elle était toute

SEPTEMBER (1)

109 Marina	26	rotten/Between one June and another September./Made this unknowing, half

SEQUENCE (1)

186 FQ: DrySal	88	pattern, and ceases to be a mere sequence —/Or even development: the latter a

SERAPHIM (1)

54 Mr E Sun	22	penitential gates/Sustained by staring Seraphim/Where the souls of the devout/Burn

SERENE (1)

595 Grad 13	5	/And let thy motto be, proud and serene,/Still as the years pass by, the word

SERENITY (2)

179 FQ: ECoker	75	/Long hoped for calm, the autumnal serenity/And the wisdom of age? Had they
179 FQ: ECoker	79	us merely a receipt for deceit?/The serenity only a deliberate hebetude,/The wisdom

SERGEANT (4)

284 FR		m	9	*and chauffeur*/DR. WARBURTON/SERGEANT WINCHELL/THE
321 FR	Denman		9	... {}/[*Enter* DENMAN]/{D} It's Sergeant Winchell is here, my Lord,/And wants
321 FR	Harry		18	brothers. Nothing can happen —/If Sergeant Winchell is real. But Denman saw him.
321 FR	Winch		33	saw you last, my Lord. But a country sergeant/Doesn't get younger. Thank you, no,

SÉRIEUX (1)

601 Nocturne		1	life, for me?/Nocturne/Romeo, *grand sérieux*, to importune/Guitar and hat in hand,

SERIOUS (10)

33 Conv Gal		18	to confute —'/And — 'Are we then so serious?'/La Figlia Che Piange/Stand on the
324 FR	Harry	13	/I don't think the matter can be very serious./A minor trouble like a concussion/
347 FR	Warburt	35	John is getting on nicely;/It wasn't so serious as Winchell made out,/And we'll have
356 CP	Julia	22	get Edward alone/And have a really *serious* conversation!'/I said so to Lavinia. She
356 CP	Julia	29	a silly old woman/But I'm really very serious. Lavinia takes me seriously./I believe
384 CP	Reilly	21	/And another is this: it is a serious matter/To bring someone back from the
393 CP	Edward	2	absurd you are./{E} That is a very serious conclusion/To have arrived at in ... how
402 CP	Reilly	35	personality./{R} Oh, dear yes; this is serious. A very common malady./Very prevalent
473 CC	Colby	37	laughing at me?/{C} I'm being very serious./What I mean is, my garden's no less
534 ES	Gomez	34	a firing squad./You don't know what serious politics is like!/I said to my boys: 'Never

SERIOUSLY (5)

356 CP	Julia	29	really very serious. Lavinia takes me seriously./I believe that's the reason why she
392 CP	Lavinia	40	/I see that I've taken you much too seriously./And now I can see how absurd you
412 CP	Julia	14	cannot believe/That you will take her seriously./{R} That is not uncommon./{J} Or
412 CP	Julia	16	/{J} Or that she deserves to be taken seriously./{R} That is most uncommon./{J}
525 ES	Monica	28	you've wasted in wrangling. But seriously, Charles,/Father's sure to be buried in

SERMON (2)

67 WL: Fire S		t	good night, good night./The Fire Sermon/The river's tent is broken; the last
260 MC Thomas		4	Amen./Dear children of God, my sermon this Christmas morning will be a/very

SERPENT'S (1)

166 Rock 10	10	out from among those who prize the serpent's golden eyes,/The worshippers,

SERPENTS (1)

158 Rock 5	6	they say, 'This house is a nest of serpents, let us destroy it,/And have done with

SERRIED (1)

213 Growltiger	48	sure she was not drowned —/But a serried ring of flashing steel Growltiger did

SERVANT (12)

106 Song Sime		36	the deaths of those after me./Let thy servant depart,/Having seen thy salvation./
601 Nocturne		7	their fate/Behind the wall I have some servant wait,/Stab, and the lady sinks into a
249 MC Tempt2		25	realmless ruler,/Self-bound servant of a powerless Pope,/The old stag,
253 MC Tempt4		36	broken pacts;/To be master or servant within an hour,/This is the course of
258 MC Thomas		26	ate out of the King's dish/To become servant of God was never my wish./Servant of
258 MC Thomas		27	servant of God was never my wish./Servant of God has chance of greater sin/And
266 MC Knights		16	carry out his command./You are his servant, his tool, and his jack,/You wore his
269 MC Knight4		22	{}/[*Exit*]/{K4} Priest! monk! and servant! take, hold, detain,/Restrain this man, in
272 MC Chorus		22	white flat face of Death, God's silent servant,/And behind the face of Death the
278 MC Knight2		24	which our King, and he as the King's servant, had/for so many years striven to
284 FR		m	7	*Amy's eldest son*/DOWNING, *his servant and chauffeur*/DR. WARBURTON/
304 FR	Mary		21	have done just as well with a hired servant/Or with none. She only wanted me for

SERVANTS (13)

29 Aunt Helen		3	a fashionable square/Cared for by servants to the number of four./Now when she
107 Animula		15	/What the fairies do and what the servants say./The heavy burden of the growing
180 FQ: ECoker		106	and the rulers,/Distinguished civil servants, chairmen of many committees,/
241 MC	Mess	11	friend? {}/[*Enter* MESSENGER]/{M} Servants of God, and watchers of the temple,/I
250 MC Thomas		5	condemn kings, not serve among their servants,/Is my open office. No! Go./{T2} Then
265 MC Knight1		9	*The banners disappear*/{K1} Servants of the King./{P1} And known to us./
268 MC Knight3		11	power to evince/The King's faithful servants, every one who transacts/His business
268 MC Knight1		35	King's command:/That you and your servants depart from this land./{T} If that *is* the
269 MC Knight1		8	nothing deters/From attainting his servants and ministers./{T} It is not I who insult
286 FR	Gerald	9	a little common prudence;/And your servants look after you very much better./{A}
286 FR	Amy	10	after you very much better./{A} My servants are perfectly competent, Gerald./I can
291 FR	Amy	24	/There is no one to see you but our servants who belong here,/And who all want to
292 FR	Amy	17	shall all be together for dinner./The servants have been looking forward to your

SERVANTS' (1)

504 CC	Claude	19	/{SC} I wish you could arrange the servants' time-table better./This is a most

SERVE (5)

165 Rock 9		33	spirit and body,/And therefore must serve as spirit and body./Visible and invisible,
250 MC Thomas		5	damnation,/To condemn kings, not serve among their servants,/Is my open office.

258 MC Thomas   29   who serves a king./For those who serve the greater cause may make the cause
258 MC Thomas   29   the greater cause may make the cause serve them,/Still doing right: and striving with
452 CC Lucasta 13   Miss Angel?/{L} Yes, again! And serve them right!/{E} You have been, I presume,

SERVED (9)
157 MC   6   the palace, in the month Nisan,/He served the wine to the king Artaxerxes,/And he
194 FQ: Little 115   have forgotten./These things have served their purpose: let them be./So with your
253 MC Tempt4   13   would wait for trap to snap/Having served your turn, broken and crushed./As for
279 MC Knight2 1   of/affairs that you approve. We have served your interests; we merit/your applause;
524 ES Charles 14   I'm really well known/And get well served. And when *you're* with me/It must be a
558 ES Michael 36   nice to me. She wasn't exciting,/But it served to pass the time. It would never have
571 ES Ld Clav 10   /So he became a forger. And so he served his term./Was I responsible for that
576 ES Ld Clav 9   story./Did he include the fact that he served a term in prison?/{Mi} He told me
577 ES Charles 18   All you can be sure of/Is that he served a prison sentence for forgery./{G} Well,

SERVES (1)
258 MC Thomas   28   sin/And sorrow, than the man who serves a king./For those who serve the greater

SERVICE (12)
54 Mr E Sun   t   warm./Mr. Eliot's Sunday Morning Service/Polyphiloprogenitive/The sapient sutlers
155 Rock 3   63   the earth and the water to your service,/Exploiting the seas and developing the
164 Rock 9   25   shall we not bring these gifts to Your service?/Shall we not bring to Your service all
164 Rock 9   26   service?/Shall we not bring to Your service all our powers/For life, for dignity, grace
165 Rock 9   30   And employ our creation again in His service/Which is already His service in creating./
165 Rock 9   31   in His service/Which is already His service in creating./For Man is joined spirit and
227 Macavity   31   the loss has been disclosed, the Secret Service say:/'It *must* have been Macavity!' —
278 MC Knight2 19   for the/highest rank of the Civil Service. And what happened? The moment/that
386 CP Reilly 9   take the precaution/Of leaving by the service staircase./{E} May I ask one question?/
400 CP Alex   32   a busy morning!/I will go out by the service staircase/And come back when they've
451 CC Eggers 38   our voluntary choir/And at the carol service. But I wish I was musical./{C} I still
463 CC Claude 7   then your school, and your military service,/And then your absorption in your

SERVICES (1)
253 MC Tempt4   11   /Borrow use cautiously, employ/Your services as long as you have to lend./You would

SERVING (2)
20 Portrait   68   her journey's end./I shall sit here, serving tea to friends..../'I take my hat: how can
21 Portrait   108   it is not too late./I shall sit here, serving tea to friends.'/And I must borrow every

SERVITUDE (1)
195 FQ: Little 164   never indifferent. History may be servitude,/History may be freedom. See, now

SES (1)
48 Lune Miel   18   de Dieu, tient encore/Dans ses pierres écroulantes la forme précise de

SET (34)
54 Mr E Sun   15   feet/And there above the painter set/The Father and the Paraclete./The sable
66 WL: Chess   145   have them all out, Lil, and get a nice set,/He said, I swear, I can't bear to look at you.
74 WL: Thund   425   arid plain behind me/Shall I at least set my lands in order?/London Bridge is falling
104 Journ Magi 33   /And I would do it again, but set down/This set down/This: were we led all
104 Journ Magi 34   would do it again, but set down/This set down/This: were we led all that way for/
129 Cor2 State 33   /A still moment, repose of noon, set under the upper branches of noon's widest
151 Rock 2   7   the face of the waters like a lantern set on the back of a tortoise./And some say:
151 Rock 2   17   kind of Whipsnade,/Then they could set about imperial expansion/Accompanied by
154 Rock 3   8   /I have given you my Law, and you set up commissions,/I have given you lips, to
164 Rock 9   2   eyes, and hear with thine ears/And set up commissions,/I have given you lips, to
166 Rock 10   3   now a visible church, one more light set on a hill/In a world confused and dark and
167 Rock 10   44   altar to the Invisible Light, we may set thereon the little lights for which our bodily
194 FQ: Little 132   disclose the gifts reserved for age/To set a crown upon your lifetime's effort./First,
214 RTTugger   5   then he'd rather have a house./If you set him on a mouse then he only wants a rat,/If
214 RTTugger   6   then he only wants a rat,/If you set him on a rat then he'd rather chase a mouse.
602 Humoresque 14   useless things/Haranguing spectres, set him there;/'The snappiest fashion since last
244 MC Chorus   30   us, leave us, leave sullen Dover, and set sail for France. Thomas our Archbishop still
244 MC Chorus   30   even in France. Thomas Archbishop, set the white sail between the grey sky and the
248 MC Tempt2   18   that I have recalled them,/Let us but set these not too pleasant memories/In balance
249 MC Tempt2   3   sentence not taught in the schools./To set down the great, protect the poor,/Beneath
266 MC Knights 15   who was made by the King; whom he set in your place to carry out his command./
276 MC Knight1 21   and when you see one man being set upon by four, then your/sympathies are all
278 MC Knight2 30   /we have had to adopt, in order to set matters to rights, that you/take issue. No
309 FR Harry   3   /Explaining would only set me farther away from you./There is only one
327 FR Harry   15   another Warburton,/If you decided to set another doctor on me./But this is too real
341 FR Amy   27   no ground for argument./{A} Who set you up to judge? what, if you please,/Gives
349 FR   1m 13   one door, AGATHA *and* MARY, *and* set *a small portable table./From another door,*

363 CP   Reilly   17 But rather less. You are nothing but a set/Of obsolete responses. The one thing to do/
375 CP   Edward   8 a trap, we are all in the trap,/We have set it for ourselves. But I do not know/What
384 CP   Reilly   18 yesterday./You made a decision. You set in motion/Forces in your life and in the lives
472 CC   Lucasta 38 to have to give up,/A career that he's set his heart on, I'm sure:/But it's only the outer
537 ES   Gomez   17 at school with —/I didn't fit into your set, and I knew it./When you started to take me
547 ES   Piggott 10 the Silence Room. With a television set./It's popular in the evenings. But not *too*
559 ES   Ld Clav   6 /In one of the Dominions, might set you on your feet./I have connections, or at

SETS (2)
210 Old Gumbie   22 nothing is done without trying,/She sets to work with her baking and frying./She
349 FR   3m   13 *cake with/lighted candles, which she sets on the table. Exit* DENMAN. AGATHA/

SETTER (1)
288 FR   Amy   30 Except the old pony, and the mongrel setter/Which I had to have destroyed./Nothing

SETTING (2)
186 FQ: DrySal   76 to think of them as forever bailing,/Setting and hauling, while the North East
189 FQ: DrySal   180 who have seen their sons or husbands/Setting forth, and not returning:/Figlia del tuo

SETTLE (2)
273 MC   Thomas   33 by results, as this world does,/To settle if an act be good or bad./You defer to the
374 CP   Celia   23 will know soon enough./Doesn't that settle all our difficulties?/{E} It has only brought

SETTLED (15)
151 Rock 2   15 fathers fixed the place of GOD,/And settled all the inconvenient saints,/Apostles,
152 Rock 2   48 cars,/Familiar with the roads and settled nowhere./Nor does the family even move
187 FQ: DrySal   134 train starts, and the passengers are settled/To fruit, periodicals and business letters/
315 FR   Chorus   32 happen, and the future was long since settled./And the wings of the future darken the
358 CP   Julia   11 /But you're to talk to me. So that's all settled./And now I must be going./{E} Must you
388 CP   Peter   4 Alex put me in touch with/And we settled everything this morning./Alex is a
456 CC   Eggers   31 a mortgage, of course) 'now we've settled down/All the travel *I* want is up to the
462 CC   Colby   6 point/I haven't been able to feel very settled./And what you've had in mind still seems
467 CC   Claude   33 on us./Just when we think we have settled our account/Life presents a new one,
499 CC   Claude   22 marry B.! But I thought that was all settled./{L} Yes, of course, Claude. You thought
499 CC   Lucasta 23 Claude. You thought everything settled./That was just the trouble. You made it
518 CC   Eggers   17 your feet/In Joshua Park, before you settled on lodgings;/We have a spare room. We
518 CC   Eggers   19 cared to stop with us, until you were settled./{C} I'd be very glad indeed — if Mrs.
551 ES   Ld Clav   8 shabby behaviour./{LC} But we'd settled our account./What harm was done? I
551 ES   Carghil 27 /Well, perhaps I shouldn't have settled out of court./My lawyer said: 'I advise

SETTLEMENT (2)
341 FR   Amy   37 failure,/When I felt assured of his settlement and happiness,/You who took my
551 ES   Carghil 33 said: 'What his lawyers are offering in settlement/Is twice as much as I think you'd be

SETTLES (1)
22 Preludes   1 to smile?/Preludes/The winter evening settles down/With smell of steaks in

SETTLING (4)
16 Prufrock   96 you all, I shall tell you all' —/If one, settling a pillow by her head,/Should say: 'That
16 Prufrock   107 it have been worth while/If one, settling a pillow or throwing off a shawl,/And
330 FR   Harry   6 the only one of us I can conceive/As settling down to make himself at home at
493 CC   Claude   2 Claude, what are you doing?/{SC} Settling the places./It's important, when you

SEVEN (28)
41 Burb Blei   32 meditating on/Time's ruins, and the seven laws./Sweeney Erect/Paint me a cavernous
44 Cook Egg   23 Blavatsky will instruct me/In the Seven Sacred Trances;/Piccarda de Donati with
121 SA Sweeney   5 be the missionary!/You'll be my little seven stone missionary!/I'll gobble you up. I'll
126 SA Chorus   2 hoo/You dreamt you waked up at seven o'clock and it's/foggy and it's damp and
162 Rock 8   26 by the sun of the East/And the seven deadly sins in Syria./But our King did
225 Mr Mistoff   55 ago this phenomenal Cat/Produced *seven kittens* right out of a hat!/And we all said:
228 Gus   18 /Where the Gallery once gave him seven cat-calls./But his grandest creation, as he
239 MC   Chorus   18 /By the fire, and deny his master?/Seven years and the summer is over/Seven years
239 MC   Chorus   19 /Seven years and the summer is over/Seven years since the Archbishop left us,/He
240 MC   Priest1 26 to witness. {}/[*Enter* PRIESTS]/{P1} Seven years and the summer is over./Seven
240 MC   Priest1 27 Seven years and the summer is over./Seven years since the Archbishop left us./{P2}
243 MC   Priest3   8 turn./The wheel has been still, these seven years, and no good./For ill or good, let
243 MC   Chorus   23 /We do not wish anything to happen./Seven years we have lived quietly,/Succeeded in
245 MC   Priest2 27 event./But your Lordship knows that seven years of waiting,/Seven years of prayer,
245 MC   Priest2 28 knows that seven years of waiting,/Seven years of prayer, seven years of emptiness,
245 MC   Priest2 28 of waiting,/Seven years of prayer, seven years of emptiness,/Have better prepared
245 MC   Priest2 30 our hearts for your coming,/Than seven days could make ready Canterbury./
268 MC   Thomas   37 command, I will be bold/To say: seven years were my people without/My
268 MC   Thomas   38 were my people without/My presence; seven years of misery and pain./Seven years a
268 MC   Thomas   39 seven years of misery and pain./Seven years a mendicant on foreign charity/I

269	MC	Thomas	1	on foreign charity/I lingered abroad: seven years is no brevity./I shall not get those
269	MC	Thomas	2	is no brevity./I shall not get those seven years back again./Never again, you must
291	FR	Charles	9	/What time is it?/{C} Nearly twenty to seven./{A} John should be here now, he has the
303	FR	Mary	10	how many we shall be for dinner./{M} Seven ... nine ... ten surely./I hear that Harry
304	FR	Mary	7	advice/And tried for a fellowship, seven years ago./Now I want your advice,
304	FR	Agatha	11	I do. I want to get away./{Ag} After seven years?/{M} Oh, you don't understand!/But
340	FR	Amy	17	for myself,/What I could plant here. Seven years I kept him,/For the sake of the
404	CP	Edward	30	let you keep a room for more than seven days;/I haven't the courage to go to a

SEVENBRANCHED (1)

| 64 | WL: Chess | 82 | his wing)/Doubled the flames of sevenbranched candelabra/Reflecting light upon |

SEVENOAKS (1)

| 510 | CC | Kaghan | 30 | /So I found them a little place near Sevenoaks/Where they keep bees. But why are |

SEVENTH (1)

| 147 | Rock 1 | | 28 | was told:/We toil for six days, on the seventh we must motor/To Hindhead, or |

SEVENTY (1)

| 228 | Gus | | 22 | possible part,/And I used to know seventy speeches by heart./I'd extemporize |

SEVER (2)

| 246 | MC | Templl | 33 | should be more than biting Time can sever./What, my Lord, now that you recover/ |
| 247 | MC | Thomas | 18 | man, never/The same time returns. Sever/The cord, shed the scale. Only/The fool, |

SEVERAL (36)

111	Xmas Trees		1	of Christmas Trees/There are several attitudes towards Christmas,/Some of
129	Cor2 State		10	/One secretary will do for several committees./What shall I cry?/Arthur
152	Rock 2		22	everything, including capital/And several versions of the Word of GOD:/The
182	FQ: ECoker		186	been discovered/Once or twice, or several times, by men whom one cannot hope/
234	Ad-dress		1	Ad-dressing of Cats/You've read of several kinds of Cat,/And my opinion now is
588	Fable		53	/And flagons which perhaps held several kegs/Of ale, and cheese which they kept
242	MC	Mess	15	on the highest authority;/There are several opinions as to what he meant,/But no
244	MC	Chorus	15	/We have had laughter and gossip,/Several girls have disappeared/Unaccountably,
313	FR	Ivy	12	I could afford a garden; and I took several prizes/With my delphiniums. I was
320	FR	Warburt	14	avoiding all excitement/She may live several years. A sudden shock/Might send her
324	FR	Harry	34	it is to be awake,/To be living on several planes at once/Though one cannot speak
324	FR	Harry	35	once/Though one cannot speak with several voices at once./I have all of the
344	FR	Gerald	24	you'll have to learn the language/And several dialects. It means a lot of preparation./
350	FR	Agatha	24	pilgrimage/By those who depart/In several directions/For their own redemption/
354	CP	Alex	14	and one in Denmark./There were several very lovely daughters:/I wonder what's
394	CP	Lavinia	14	thought I *was* the butler./{L} And on several occasions, when somebody was coming/
399	CP	3m	1	consulting room in London. Morning:/several weeks later. SIR HENRY *alone at his*
402	CP	Reilly	28	Mr. Chamberlayne./There are several kinds of sanatoria/For several kinds of
402	CP	Reilly	29	are several kinds of sanatoria/For several kinds of patient. And there are also
407	CP	Reilly	6	/I say you are both too ill. There are several symptoms/Which must occur together,
424	CP	Lavinia	17	unfair!/You know that we've given *several* parties/In the last two years. And I've
428	CP	Alex	26	yes, indeed./I invented for the natives several new recipes./But you see, what with
432	CP	Reilly	31	/{A} Indeed, yes, we have met./{R} On several commissions./{J} We've been having
469	CC	Colby	13	you hear them./I've given you a test. Several of the pieces/That I've just played you
469	CC	Lucasta	22	/I've been to the Opera, of course, several times,/But I'm afraid I never really
484	CC	Lady E	9	my parents! I had a governess;/Several, in fact. And I loathed them all./Were
493	CC	2m	1	Three/*The Business Room, as in Act* 1. *Several mornings later.* SIR CLAUDE *is/moving*
525	ES	Monica	27	with you./{M} You've already had several minutes alone with me/Which you've
527	ES	Monica	19	And what after that?/{M} There are several good reasons why I should go with him./
528	ES	Charles	1	at loggerheads./{C} But you spoke of several reasons for your going with your father./
534	ES	Gomez	24	too domestic./And by the way, I've several children,/All grown up, doing well for
540	ES	Ld Clav	18	were driving./{LC} That happened several times./{G} One time in particular./You
541	ES	Gomez	18	I dare say I could buy you out/Several times over. San Marco's a good place/
544	ES	2m	1	Court. A bright sunny morning, *several days later./Enter* LORD CLAVERTON
547	ES	Piggott	26	too early for the bathing pool./But several of our guests are keen on tennis,/And of
557	ES	Michael	15	tried a little private speculation./{Mi} Several of my friends gave me excellent tips./

SEVERALLY (2)

| 271 | MC | m | 20 | much reality. {}/[*Enter* PRIESTS]/[*severally*]./{3P} My Lord, you must not stop |
| 323 | FR | m | 7 | or John? {}/[*Enter* AMY, *followed severally by* VIOLET, IVY, AGATHA, |

SEVERE (2)

| 527 | ES | Monica | 37 | spoilt him/And Father was too severe — so they're always at loggerheads./{C} |
| 545 | ES | Ld Clav | 6 | this self inside us, this silent observer,/Severe and speechless critic, who can terrorise |

SEVERELY (1)

| 545 | ES | Ld Clav | 8 | /And in the end, judge us still more severely/For the errors into which his own |

SEWER (1)
270 MC Chorus   9   in the dish, incense in the latrine, the sewer in the incense, the smell of sweet soap in
SEWING (1)
215 RT Tugger   33   leap on your lap in the middle of your sewing,/For there's nothing he enjoys like a
SHABBY (5)
182 FQ: ECoker   182   a raid on the inarticulate/With shabby equipment always deteriorating/In the
228 Gus   5   call him just Gus./His coat's very shabby, he's thin as a rake,/And he suffers from
301 FR   Gerald   22   for herself, and her credit among her shabby genteel acquaintance./{V} Gerald is
473 CC   Lucasta   9   garden is ... a dirty public square/In a shabby part of London — like the one where I
551 ES   Carghil   7   is always trying to forget/His own shabby behaviour./{LC} But we'd settled our
SHADE (2)
 83 Hollow Men   11   In our dry cellar/Shape without form, shade without colour,/Paralysed force, gesture
254 MC Tempt4   16   /Creeping in penance, frightened of a shade;/Think of pilgrims, standing in line/
SHADES (3)
 22 Preludes   22   all the hands/That are raising dingy shades/In a thousand furnished rooms./You
122 SAWa & Ho   31   *the Gauguin maids/In the banyan shades/Wear palmleaf drapery/Under the bam/*
244 MC Chorus   27   of your fate, unaffrayed among the shades, do you realise what you ask, do you
SHADOW (32)
 43 Swee Erect   25   suds around his face./(The lengthened shadow of a man/Is history, said Emerson/Who
 61 WL: Burial   25   no sound of water. Only/There is shadow under this red rock,/(Come in under the
 61 WL: Burial   26   this red rock,/(Come in under the shadow of this red rock),/And I will show you
 61 WL: Burial   28   something different from either/Your shadow at morning striding behind you/Or your
 61 WL: Burial   29   morning striding behind you/Or your shadow at evening rising to meet you;/I will
 85 Hollow Men   76   the motion/And the act/Falls the Shadow/*For Thine is the Kingdom*/Between the
 85 Hollow Men   82   emotion/And the response/Falls the Shadow/*Life is very long*/Between the desire/
 85 Hollow Men   90   the essence/And the descent/Falls the Shadow/*For Thine is the Kingdom*/For Thine is
107 Animula   29   the importunity of the blood,/Shadow of its own shadows, spectre in its own
141 Rannoch   11   /Beyond the bone. Pride snapped,/Shadow of pride is long, in the long pass/No
159 Rock 6   24   to be good./But the man that is will shadow/The man that pretends to be./And the
160 Rock 7   4   /They followed the light and the shadow, and the light led them forward to light
160 Rock 7   4   led them forward to light and the shadow led them to darkness,/Worshipping
167 Rock 10   42   for our little light, this is dappled with shadow./We thank Thee who hast moved us to
173 FQ: BurntN   97   form with lucid stillness/Turning shadow into transient beauty/With slow
175 FQ: BurntN   160   by voices of temptation,/The crying shadow in the funeral dance,/The loud lament
194 FQ: Little   135   no promise/But bitter tastelessness of shadow fruit/As body and soul begin to fall
604 Ode   3   we face the importunate years,/In thy shadow we wait, while thy presence dispels/Our
605 Narcissus   1   of Saint Narcissus/Come under the shadow of this gray rock —/Come in under the
605 Narcissus   2   this gray rock —/Come in under the shadow of this gray rock,/And I will show you
605 Narcissus   4   something different from either/Your shadow sprawling over the sand at daybreak, or
605 Narcissus   5   over the sand at daybreak, or/Your shadow leaping behind the fire against the red
605 Narcissus   7   bloody cloth and limbs/And the gray shadow on his lips./He walked once between the
606 Narcissus   39   he is green, dry and stained/With the shadow in his mouth./MURDER IN THE
272 MC Chorus   18   footfall in the passage,/More than shadow in the doorway,/More than fury in the
290 FR   Amy   9   own level./A restless shivering painted shadow/In life, she is less than a shadow in
290 FR   Amy   10   shadow/In life, she is less than a shadow in death./You might as well all of you
331 FR   Harry   12   forgotten, and a new torture,/The shadow of something behind our meagre
410 CP   Reilly   25   with what you brought with you:/The shadow of desires of desires. A prey/To the
464 CC   Claude   17   /Of which the substantial is only a shadow./It's strange. I have never talked of this
465 CC   Colby   36   be. I'm not an executant;/I'm only a shadow of the great composers./Always, when I
508 CC   Lady E   10   Perhaps I should./{LE} There isn't a shadow of a doubt in my mind./I'm surprised that
SHADOWS (11)
107 Animula   29   of the blood,/Shadow of its own shadows, spectre in its own gloom,/Leaving
244 MC Chorus   18   our private terrors,/Our particular shadows, our secret fears./But now a great fear
246 MC Thomas   21   the substance of our first act/Will be shadows, and the strife with shadows./Heavier
246 MC Thomas   21   /Will be shadows, and the strife with shadows./Heavier the interval than the
248 MC Tempt2   35   /Wander waking with deceitful shadows?/Power is present. Holiness hereafter./
306 FR   Harry   17   get rid of nothing./Of none of the shadows that I wanted to escape;/And at the
334 FR   Harry   36   I./The things I thought were real are shadows, and the real/Are what I thought were
334 FR   Harry   37   real/Are what I thought were private shadows. O that awful privacy/Of the insane
335 FR   Harry   24   fro, dragging my feet/Among inner shadows in the smoky wilderness,/Trying to
437 CP   Reilly   11   *the grave, where do inhabit/The shadows of all forms that think and live/Till death*
540 ES   Gomez   21   —/A summer night of moonlight and shadows —/The night you ran over the old man
SHADOWY (1)
204 de la Mare   7   dark jungle of a mango grove,/And shadowy lemurs glide from tree to tree —/The

SHAFT (3)

176 FQ: BurntN	172	un-being and being./Sudden in a shaft of sunlight/Even while the dust moves/
190 FQ: DrySal	212	of time,/The distraction fit, lost in a shaft of sunlight,/The wild thyme unseen, or the
240 MC Chorus	18	/I have seen these things in a shaft of sunlight./Destiny waits in the hand of

SHAFTESBURY (1)

552 ES Ld Clav	4	name appeared in very large letters/In Shaftesbury Avenue./{MC} Yes, I had my art./

SHAKE (9)

34 Figlia	16	/Simple and faithless as a smile and shake of the hand./She turned away, but with
95 Ash-Wed 4	28	unheard, unspoken/Till the wind shake a thousand whispers from the yew/And
129 Cor2 State	24	of orders./Meanwhile the guards shake dice on the marches/And the frogs (O
134 Wind	10	the blackened river/The camp fire shake with alien spears./Here, across death's
134 Wind	12	other river/The Tartar horsemen shake their spears./Five-Finger Exercises/*Lines*
177 FQ: ECoker	12	to break the loosened pane/And to shake the wainscot where the field-mouse trots/
177 FQ: ECoker	13	where the field-mouse trots/And to shake the tattered arras woven with a silent
228 Gus	6	suffers from palsy that makes his paw shake./Yet he was, in his youth, quite the
235 Ad-dress	32	the chin/Or slap his back or shake his paw,/And he will gambol and guffaw./

SHAKEN (4)

38 Gerontion	47	our impudent crimes./These tears are shaken from the wrath-bearing tree./The tiger
98 Ash-Wed 6	23	blue rocks/But when the voices shaken from the yew-tree drift away/Let the
98 Ash-Wed 6	24	drift away/Let the other yew be shaken and reply./Blessèd sister, holy mother,
332 FR Agatha	35	enough./The rain and wind had not shaken your father/Awake yet. I found him

SHAKES (3)

24 Rhapsody	11	the spaces of the dark/Midnight shakes the memory/As a madman shakes a dead
24 Rhapsody	12	shakes the memory/As a madman shakes a dead geranium./Half-past one,/The
135 5FingerEx3	1	*to a Duck in the Park*/The long light shakes across the lake,/The forces of the

SHAKESPEARE (1)

229 Gus	37	played a part in *East Lynne*./At a Shakespeare performance he once walked on

SHAKESPEHERIAN (1)

65 WL: Chess	128	in your head?'/But/O O O O that Shakespeherian Rag —/It's so elegant/So

SHAKING (2)

32 Hysteria	9	in the/garden ...' I decided that if the shaking of her breasts could be stopped,/some
74 WL: Thund	402	have we given?/My friend, blood shaking my heart/The awful daring of a

SHALL (317)

SHALLOW (1)

186 FQ: DrySal	77	while the North East lowers/Over shallow banks unchanging and erosionless/Or

SHAME (6)

162 Rock 8	8	/There came one who spoke of the shame of Jerusalem/And the holy places defiled;
194 FQ: Little	141	all that you have done, and been; the shame/Of motives late revealed, and the
271 MC Chorus	5	/By the final ecstasy of waste and shame,/O Lord Archbishop, O Thomas
271 MC Chorus	6	that we may pray for you, out of our shame. {}/[*Enter* THOMAS]/{T} Peace, and be
275 MC Thomas	9	with me as you will, to your hurt and shame;/But none of my people, in God's name,/
417 CP Celia	18	something I cannot find/And of the shame of never finding it./Can you cure me?/{R}

SHAMED (2)

270 MC Chorus	24	/Nothing is possible but the shamed swoon/Of those consenting to the last
315 FR Chorus	34	and claws have desecrated/History. Shamed/The first cry in the bedroom, the noise

SHAMEFUL (1)

577 ES Carghil	37	must not bar his way. That would be shameful./{LC} I cannot bar his way, as you

SHAMMING (1)

548 ES Monica	13	to wake you,/But if they see you're shamming they'll have to take the hint. {}/[*Exit*]/

SHAN'T (17)

116 SP Dusty	28	I hope so too —/Well I *hope* we shan't have to call a doctor/Doris just hates
297 FR Charles	26	/{C} That I'd like to ask Downing./He shan't know why I'm asking. {}/[*Enter*
358 CP Julia	6	are quite uninteresting./{J} Well, you shan't escape. You dine with me on Friday./I've
368 CP Edward	11	here to get dinner for you?/{E} No, I shan't want much, and I'll get it myself./{A} Ah,
368 CP Alex	19	and Peter can go on talking/And I shan't disturb you./{E} My dear Alex,/There'll
371 CP Peter	18	in her terms. Until I know that/I shan't know the truth about even the memory./
376 CP Edward	31	you mustn't touch it./{E} Of course I shan't touch it./{J} My dear, I should have
413 CP Celia	1	/I just came in desperation. And I shan't be offended/If you simply tell me to go
413 CP Celia	15	that my trouble is interesting;/But I shan't begin that way. I feel perfectly well./I
439 CP Peter	29	much. But not this time —/I simply shan't be able to./{E} But on your next visit?/{P}
461 CC Colby	13	I get into trouble. But I hope/That I shan't have to call upon you often./{E} Oh, you
466 CC Claude	27	time, you will let me hear you play./I shan't mention it again. I'll wait until you ask
467 CC Claude	31	in any way, a make-believe./{SC} It shan't be. Meanwhile, we must simply wait to
525 ES Charles	26	to be respectful;/But you know that I shan't have a minute alone with you./{M}
531 ES Ld Clav	29	I, who recognise myself as a ghost/Shan't want to be seen there. It makes me smile/

541 ES   Gomez   38 the visitor in financial distress./Well, I shan't keep you long, though I dare say your
572 ES   Ld Clav 35 /On which I ran away. Very well./I shan't run away now — run away from *them.*/It

SHANTIH (3)
75 WL: Thund   433   /Datta. Dayadhvam. Damyata./Shantih shantih shantih/The Hollow Men/We
75 WL: Thund   433   Dayadhvam. Damyata./Shantih shantih shantih/The Hollow Men/We are the
75 WL: Thund   433   Damyata./Shantih shantih shantih/The Hollow Men/We are the hollow

SHAPE (7)
21 Portrait   109 /And I must borrow every changing shape/To find expression ... dance, dance/Like a
83 Hollow Men   11 over broken glass/In our dry cellar/Shape without form, shade without colour,/
92 Ash-Wed 3   3 /I turned and saw below/The same shape twisted on the banister/Under the vapour
226 Macavity   18 Macavity,/For he's a fiend in feline shape, a monster of depravity./You may meet
252 MC Thomas   20 like an eagle over doves/Now take the shape of a wolf among wolves?/Pursue your
257 MC Chorus   28 scent of despair;/The forms take shape in the dark air:/Puss-purr of leopard,
464 CC   Claude   2 potter. When I was a boy/I loved to shape things. I loved form and colour/And I

SHAPES (2)
164 Rock 9   19   /Out of the meaningless practical shapes of all that is living or lifeless/Joined with
272 MC Chorus   24   the Void, more horrid than active shapes of hell;/Emptiness, absence, separation

SHAPING (1)
240 MC Chorus   17 /Destiny waits in the hand of God, shaping the still unshapen:/I have seen these

SHARE (15)
201 Def Island   9   trawler —/contributing their share to the ages' pavement/of British bone on
271 MC Thomas   9 and you to accept them,/This is your share of the eternal burden,/The perpetual
276 MC Knight1   23 under dog. I respect such feelings, I/share them. Nevertheless, I appeal to your sense
279 MC Knight2   3 whatever in the matter, you/must share it with us./{K1} Morville has given us a
280 MC   Priest3   26 alliance with the heathen Saracen,/To share his filthy rites, and try to snatch/
341 FR   Amy   35 bitterness and disappointment./What share had you in this? what have you given?/
370 CP   Peter   24 secret excitement which I cannot share./{E} Do you think she has simply lost
370 CP   Peter   28 those moments in which we seemed to share some perception,/Some feeling, some
371 CP   Peter   19   even the memory./Did we really share these interests? Did we really feel the same
411 CP   Lavinia   16 as well go home./{L} Then we can share a taxi, and be economical./Edward, have
414 CP   Celia   20 it./{R} And you live in London?/{C} I share a flat/With a cousin: but she's abroad at
460 CC   Lady E   27 to you, Mr. Colby,/That I am to share you with my husband./You shall have tea
527 ES   Charles   33 haven't had brothers and sisters/To share the burden. Sisters, I should say,/For your
570 ES   Monica   16 It is time to break the silence! Let us share your ghosts!/{C} But these are only
572 ES   Monica   8 Father! All your life! And no one to share it with;/I never knew how lonely you were

SHARED (4)
380 CP   Celia   6 /With whom they thought they had shared something wonderful/Had taken them
516 CC   Claude   18 had —/So very long ago! — when we shared our ambitions/And shared our
516 CC   Claude   19 when we shared our ambitions/And shared our disappointment. And you described
516 CC   Claude   27 nothing to you, the experience we shared?/Heaven knows — and you know — I

SHARES (1)
286 FR   Gerald   19   —/{G} Dividends from aeroplane shares./{V} They bathe all day and they dance

SHARK (1)
92 Ash-Wed 3   11 /Or the toothed gullet of an agèd shark./At the first turning of the third stair/Was

SHARP (5)
103 Journ Magi   4 /The ways deep and the weather sharp,/The very dead of winter.'/And the camels
135 5FingerEx1   4 is no ease/For the dull brain, the sharp desires/And the quick eyes of Woolly
181 FQ: ECoker   152 the bleeding hands we feel/The sharp compassion of the healer's art/Resolving
239 MC Chorus   10 stored, and the land became brown sharp points of death in a waste of water and
335 FR   Agatha   7 /In a dead air. Only feet walking/And sharp heels scraping. Over and under/Echo and

SHARPEN (1)
109 Marina   6   return/O my daughter./Those who sharpen the tooth of the dog, meaning/Death/

SHATTERED (1)
184 FQ: DrySal   23   up our losses, the torn seine,/The shattered lobsterpot, the broken oar/And the

SHATTERING (1)
395 CP   Lavinia   27 people./{L} That must have been very shattering for you./But never mind, you'll soon

SHAVE (1)
42 Swee Erect   21 slip./Sweeney addressed full length to shave/Broadbottomed, pink from nape to base,/

SHAWL (2)
15 Prufrock   67 that lie along a table, or wrap about a shawl./And should I then presume?/And how
16 Prufrock   107 settling a pillow or throwing off a shawl,/And turning toward the window, should

SHE (446)

SHE'D (8)
359 CP   Edward   19 the names/Of all the people she said she'd invited./But it's only that dreadful old
360 CP   Edward   4 warning, of course;/Just when she'd arranged a cocktail party./She'd gone

360 CP	Edward	5	when she'd arranged a cocktail party./She'd gone when I came in, this afternoon./She
478 CC	Kaghan	37	here's Lucasta./I knew I should find she'd got in first!/Trust Kaghan's intuitions! I'm
489 CC	Lady E	35	her hands. The father had died/And she'd never been told the name of the mother;/
497 CC	Claude	11	her name to be known to you./{SC} She'd been questioning Colby about himself,/
545 ES	Piggott	34	secretary will be — Miss Timmins./She'd be overjoyed to have the privilege of
548 ES	Monica	7	when she left/That she thought she'd done her duty by us for to-day./I'm going

SHE'LL (9)

447 CC	Claude	28	about your state of health,/So she'll be sympathetic. And as for Colby —/Say
451 CC	Eggers	29	you, as I said, it will be very different./She'll see at once that you're a man of culture;/
453 CC	Eggers	3	/That if you give Miss Angel an inch/She'll take an ell./{L} L. for Lucasta./Go on,
454 CC	Kaghan	9	Lucasta the slightest advantage/Or she'll exploit it. You have to be tough with her;/
455 CC	Eggers	20	worry/About her, Mr. Simpkins. She'll marry Mr. Kaghan/In the end. He's a
462 CC	Claude	2	should have the flat —/By tomorrow she'll be sure it was she who proposed it./So I
548 ES	Ld Clav	4	won't remember anything else./{LC} She'll come back to tell us more about the peace
548 ES	Monica	5	peace and quiet./{M} I don't believe she'll be bothering us again:/I could see from
554 ES	Carghil	6	you bear it?/If I go at once, perhaps she'll take the hint/And leave us alone

SHE'S (64)

66 WL:	Chess	160	pills I took, to bring it off, she said./(She's had five already, and nearly died of young
116 SP	Dusty	33	/I say do you mind if I ring off now/She's got her feet in mustard and water/I said
211 Old	Gumbie	33	idle and wanton destroyment./So she's formed, from that lot of disorderly louts,/
211 Old	Gumbie	36	in life and a good deed to do —/And she's even created a Beetles' Tattoo./So for Old
287 FR	Charles	15	to draw her into the conversation./{C} She's a nice girl; but it's a difficult age for her./I
292 FR	Ivy	37	to your mother/Time and time again: she's done nothing about it/Because she
301 FR	Downing	1	his Lordship's car?/{Do} Oh no, Sir, she's in good running order:/I see to that./{G} I
322 FR	Winch	6	was my mother's. God rest her soul,/She's been dead these ten years. How is her
354 CP	Celia	4	And Julia's the only person to tell it./She's such a good mimic./{J} Am I a good
356 CP	Julia	31	that I could make you talk. Perhaps she's in the pantry/Listening to all we say!/{E}
356 CP	Edward	33	/Listening to all we say!/{E} No, she's not in the pantry./{C} Will she be away for
357 CP	Edward	10	/{E} Her aunt's favourite niece. And she's rather difficult./When she's ill, she insists
357 CP	Edward	11	And she's rather difficult./When she's ill, she insists on having Lavinia./{J} I
357 CP	Edward	13	heard of her being ill before./{E} No, she's always very strong. That's why when she's
357 CP	Edward	13	always very strong. That's why when she's ill/She gets into a panic./{J} And sends for
359 CP	Edward	22	/{E} But she always turns up when she's least wanted. {}/[*Opens the door*]/{E} Julia!
360 CP	Edward	7	leaving me;/But I don't know where she's gone./{UG} This is an occasion./May I
360 CP	Reilly	24	side./You say you don't know where she's gone?/{E} No, I do not./{UG} Do you
370 CP	Peter	31	of ourselves./In your terms, perhaps, she's lost interest in me./{E} That is all very
375 CP	Celia	6	back!/Do you mean to say that she's laid a trap for us?/{E} No. If there is a
383 CP	Edward	30	for them ... No, I found them./... Yes, she's bringing them now ... Good night. {}/
390 CP	Julia	37	/Waiting at junctions. And I suppose she's famished./{A} Ah, in that case I know
412 CP	Reilly	2	in. {}/[*Enter* JULIA *by side door*]/{R} She's waiting downstairs./{J} I know that,
412 CP	Julia	20	the next room,/And come back when she's gone./{R} Yes, when she's gone./{J} Will
412 CP	Reilly	21	back when she's gone./{R} Yes, when she's gone./{J} Will Alex be here?/{R} Yes, he'll
414 CP	Celia	21	/{C} I share a flat/With a cousin: but she's abroad at the moment,/And my family
430 CP	Peter	9	told me you were giving a party —/She's coming on later, after the Gunnings —/So
445 CC	Eggers	17	some material for Mrs. E.,/Which she's been wanting. So *she*'ll be pleased./Then I
447 CC	Claude	27	had to leave under medical orders./She's always been concerned about your state of
451 CC	Eggers	21	me laugh/The way B. Kaghan did?' She's only met him once;/But do you know, he
451 CC	Eggers	30	you're a man of culture;/And besides, she's very musical./{C} Thank you for the
452 CC	Kaghan	6	with me! The usual catastrophe./She's come to pry some cash from the
453 CC	Kaghan	35	the point is, that I'm penniless./{K} She's had a week's salary in lieu of notice./{L}
454 CC	Kaghan	10	it. You have to be tough with her;/She's hard as nails. Now I'll take her off your
454 CC	Eggers	26	What about *her*?/{E} Oh, Miss Angel./She's rather flighty. But she has a good heart./
455 CC	Eggers	11	think that's quite the right term./She's no money of her own, as you may have
455 CC	Eggers	16	man, is Sir Claude./To tell the truth, she's something of a thorn in his flesh,/Always
455 CC	Eggers	19	— very adequate indeed,/Though she's always in debt. But you needn't worry/
455 CC	Eggers	27	you have Mrs. Eggerson./{E} Yes, she's a great protection. And I have my garden/
456 CC	Eggers	18	one trait that I think I did touch on:/She's very absent-minded./{C} I hope you don't
456 CC	Eggers	25	/Mostly for her health. And when she's abroad/She is apt to buy a house. And
457 CC	Eggers	4	say./And I'm sure you'll like her. She's *such* a lady!/And what's more, she has a
457 CC	Claude	21	*door on to landing and listens*]/{SC} She's here, Eggerson! That's her voice./Where is
457 CC	Claude	22	That's her voice./Where is she? Oh, she's gone out again. {}/[*Goes to the window*
457 CC	Claude	23	*and looks down on the street*]/{SC} She's having a conversation with the cabman./
457 CC	Claude	24	/What can they be talking about? She's coming in! {}/LADY ELIZABETH
458 CC	Eggers	2	to be doing? {}/[*at the open door*]./{E} She's speaking to the parlourmaid. She's
458 CC	Eggers	2	She's speaking to the parlourmaid. She's coming up./{SC} Colby, sit at the desk,

458 CC Lady E   22   /{LE} Because of Mildred Deverell./She's been having the treatment with me,/And
461 CC Claude   38   Impossible to tell./The point is that she's taken a fancy to you/And so she lays claim
462 CC Claude   1   claim to you. That's very satisfactory./She's taken it for granted that you should have
462 CC Claude   15   you *will* become her son, in her eyes. She's like that./Why, it wouldn't surprise me if
479 CC Lucasta   9   /You'd better not get in *her* way when she's hunting./But all that matters now is, that
479 CC Lucasta 29   to escape her./{L} Only because she's never wanted to pursue you./{K} Yes, I
496 CC Eggers   36   Eggerson is well?/{E} Pretty well./She's always low-spirited, around this season,/
497 CC Claude   13   of his aunt, Mrs. Guzzard./Now she's convinced that Mrs. Guzzard/Of
499 CC Claude   9   *knock on the door]*/{SC} Good Lord, she's here already! Well ... Come in! {}/[*Enter*
504 CC Lady E   21   is a most unfortunate beginning./{LE} She's been making progress, under my
524 ES Monica   20   you: and it reminds the girl/That she's not the only one who's been there with
536 ES Gomez   35   good thing./My mother — I dare say she's still alive,/But she must be very old. And
554 ES Carghil   4   to you./— Oh, there's Mrs. Piggott!/She's bearing down on us. Isn't she frightful!/
555 ES Piggott   7   you should not be disturbed./Well, she's gone now. If she bothers you again/Just let
568 ES Ld Clav 35   /While she is a child. And by the time she's grown/You've woven such a web of fiction
569 ES Ld Clav 29   company./He's a very rich man. And she's a rich woman./If people merely blackmail

SHEATHED (1)
 94 Ash-Wed 4   15   waking, wearing/White light folded, sheathed about her, folded./The new years walk,

SHED (3)
159 Rock 6   27   for all,/The blood of the martyrs not shed once for all,/The lives of the Saints not
247 MC Thomas 19   same time returns. Sever/The cord, shed the scale. Only/The fool, fixed in his folly,
264 MC Priest3 18   /The blood of thy saints have they shed like water,/And there was no man to bury

SHEEP (5)
220 Old Deut   19   day;/The bullocks may bellow, the sheep they may bleat,/But the dogs and the
223 Pekes Pols 59   every last one of them scattered like sheep./*And when the Police Dog returned to his*
264 MC Priest1 25   for sins./He lays down his life for the sheep./{3P} *Rejoice we all, keeping holy day.*/
559 ES Ld Clav 12   to Western Canada?/Or what about sheep farming in New Zealand?/{Mi} Sheep
559 ES Michael 13   sheep farming in New Zealand?/{Mi} Sheep farming? Good Lord, no./That's not my

SHEET (3)
129 Cor2 State 26   /Fireflies flare against the faint sheet lightning/What shall I cry?/Mother
150 Rock 1   116   *die in a shortened bed/And a narrow sheet. In this street/There is no beginning, no*
233 Skimble   35   berth is very neat with a newly folded sheet/And there's not a speck of dust on the

SHEETS (1)
 42 Swee Erect 12   of orang-outang/Rises from the sheets in steam./This withered root of knots of

SHEILA (1)
430 CP Peter   7   left Los Angeles three days ago./I saw Sheila Paisley at lunch to-day/And she told me

SHELF (2)
214 RTTugger   30   ears,/If you put it away on the larder shelf./The Rum Tum Tugger is artful and
529 ES Ld Clav 32   /You know I keep the old ones on a shelf together;/I could look in the right book,

SHELL (3)
 70 WL: Fire S 282 oars/The stern was formed/A gilded shell/Red and gold/The brisk swell/Rippled
188 FQ: DrySal 150 not to the ear,/The murmuring shell of time, and not in any language)/'Fare
192 FQ: Little   32   you thought you came for/Is only a shell, a husk of meaning/From which the

SHELTER (3)
 61 WL: Burial 23   sun beats,/And the dead tree gives no shelter, the cricket no relief,/And the dry stone
257 MC Chorus 21   faggots at nightfall,/Building a partial shelter,/For sleeping, and eating and drinking
338 FR Harry   22   That the last apparent refuge, the safe shelter,/That is where one meets them. That is

SHELTERED (2)
482 CC Lady E 11   Angel./I can see you've lived a rather sheltered life,/And I've noticed them paying you
548 ES Carghil 15   sit here./It's the sunniest and most sheltered corner,/And none of the other guests

SHELTERS (2)
103 Journ Magi 13   night-fires going out, and the lack of shelters,/And the cities hostile and the towns
155 Rock 3   47   shall be no homes,/Though you have shelters and institutions,/Precarious lodgings

SHELVES (1)
 30 Cous Nancy 11   that it was modern./Upon the glazen shelves kept watch/Matthew and Waldo,

SHEPHERD (2)
269 MC Thomas   4   doubt,/Shall the sea run between the shepherd and his fold./{K1} The King's justice,
272 MC Thomas   4   at your prayers./They shall find the shepherd here; the flock shall be spared./I have

SHEPHERDS (1)
260 MC Thomas 13   the heavenly host appeared before the/shepherds at Bethlehem, saying 'Glory to God

SHERBET (1)
103 Journ Magi 10   terraces,/And the silken girls bringing sherbet./Then the camel men cursing and

SHERIFF (1)
246 MC Thomas   9   at Sandwich/Broc, Warenne, and the Sheriff of Kent,/Those who had sworn to have

SHERRY (6)

286 FR   Charles 25 civilised person needs/Is a glass of dry sherry or two before dinner./The modern young
286 FR   m 29 cigarettes. {}/[*Enter* DENMAN *with sherry and whisky.* CHARLES *takes sherry and*
286 FR   m 29 *sherry and whisky.* CHARLES *takes sherry and* GERALD *whisky.*]/{C} That's what it
479 CC   Colby 16 people./{C} Will you have a glass of sherry?/{K} Yes, I'll have a glass of sherry,/To
479 CC   Kaghan 17 of sherry?/{K} Yes, I'll have a glass of sherry,/To drink success to the flat. Lucasta too:
479 CC   Lucasta 20 Lucasta./{L} You know I don't like sherry./{K} You've got to drink it,/To Colby,

SHIELD (1)

582 ES   Monica 39 /And that awareness .../{M} Was a shield protecting both of us .../{C} So that now

SHIFTING (1)

37 Gerontion   28 de Tornquist, in the dark room/Shifting the candles; Fräulein von Kulp/Who

SHIFTS (1)

55 Mr E Sun   29 /Blest office of the epicene./Sweeney shifts from ham to ham/Stirring the water in his

SHILLINGS (3)

129 Cor2 State 13 rising by annual increments of five shillings/To two pounds ten a week; with a
129 Cor2 State 14 ten a week; with a bonus of thirty shillings at Christmas/And one week's leave a
285 FR   Ivy 18 in Bayswater, by a gas-fire counting shillings./{V} Go south! to the English

SHINE (3)

54 Mr E Sun   14 through the water pale and thin/Still shine the unoffending feet/And there above the
91 Ash-Wed 2 11 honours the Virgin in meditation,/We shine with brightness. And I who am here
136 5FingerEx3 6 and drake./I have seen the morning shine,/I have had the Bread and Wine,/Let the

SHINING (5)

92 Ash-Wed 2 48 the bones sang, scattered and shining/We are glad to be scattered, we did little
212 Growltiger 22 seemed at play,/The tender moon was shining bright, the barge at Molesey lay./All in
216 Jellicles   3 *one come all:/The Jellicle Moon is shining bright* —/*Jellicles come to the Jellicle*
217 Jellicles 33 in the hall./If it happens the sun is shining bright/You would say they had nothing
335 FR   Agatha 1 the little door/When the sun was shining on the rose-garden:/And heard in the

SHIP (1)

265 MC Knight1 14 us from France. We rode hard,/Took ship yesterday, landed last night,/Having

SHIPPING (1)

579 ES   Michael 10 /And you see, he has friends in the shipping line/Who he thinks can be helpful in

SHIPS (7)

62 WL: Burial 70 /'You who were with me in the ships at Mylae!'/'That corpse you planted last
110 Marina   32 lips parted, the hope, the new ships./What seas what shores what granite
154 Rock 3   21 shall be done to the shore of smoky ships?/Will you leave my people forgetful and
189 FQ: DrySal 174 /Pray for all those who are in ships, those/Whose business has to do with fish,
189 FQ: DrySal 183 /Also pray for those who were in ships, and/Ended their voyage on the sand, in
201 Def Island   8 of those appointed to the grey/ships — battleship, merchantman, trawler —/
212 Growltiger 15 Bandicoot, that lurks on foreign ships,/And woe to any Cat with whom

SHIPWRECK (1)

280 MC Priest3 20 or the Gates of Hercules./Go venture shipwreck on the sullen coasts/Where

SHIRE (1)

589 Fable   94 /And lived the admiration of the shire. We/Got the veracious record of these

SHIRT (3)

196 FQ: Little 212 the hands that wove/The intolerable shirt of flame/Which human power cannot
266 MC Knights 22 dirt,/Crawling up like a louse on your shirt,/The man who cheated, swindled, lied;
480 CC Kaghan   2 I'm a born gambler/And I've put my shirt ... no, not quite the right expression —/

SHIRT-SLEEVES (1)

15 Prufrock   72 rises from the pipes/Of lonely men in shirt-sleeves, leaning out of windows?.../I should

SHIRTS (2)

404 CP Edward 32 to a hotel,/And besides, I need more shirts — you can get my wife/To have my things
411 CP Lavinia 14 /I was going to leave some shirts there for you./{E} It seems to me that I

SHIRTSLEEVES (1)

370 CP   m 14 interesting affair? {}/[*Enter* ALEX *in shirtsleeves and an apron*]/{A} Edward, I can't

SHIVER (2)

149 Rock 1   98 /*We stand about in open places/And shiver in unlit rooms./Only the wind moves/Over*
561 ES Ld Clav   5 the monotonous sun of the tropics/Or shiver in the northern night. Believe me,

SHIVERING (1)

290 FR   Amy   9 down to her own level./A restless shivering painted shadow/In life, she is less than

SHOCK (11)

49 Hippopot   6 weak and frail,/Susceptible to nervous shock;/While the True Church can never fail/
257 MC Tempts   2 through the ear, or a sudden shock on the skull./{C} A man may walk with a
293 FR   Charles 35 much would surprise me, Harry;/Or shock me, either./{H} You are all people/To
320 FR Warburt 14 /She may live several years. A sudden shock/Might send her off at any moment./If she
322 FR   Harry 17 /I think I might be able to give you a shock./{Wi} There's been shock enough for one

322 FR	Winch	18	give you a shock./{Wi} There's been	shock enough for one evening, my Lord:/That's
325 FR	Gerald	13	/{G} I am really more afraid of the	shock for Amy;/But I think that Warburton
409 CP	Reilly	40	you had aroused in him —/It was a	shock. You had wanted to be loved;/You had
452 CC	Kaghan	8	/And come upstairs ahead, to ease the	shock for Colby./But as you're here, Eggers, I
500 CC	Lucasta	23	daughter!/I came to thank him for the	shock he'd given me./He made me see what I
525 ES	Charles	36	said before,/That will give you a	shock. I believe *you* love *me*./{M} Oh, what a

SHOCKED (8)

477 CC	Lucasta	12	don't you say something? Are you	shocked?/{C} Shocked? No. Yes. You don't
477 CC	Colby	13	say something? Are you shocked?/{C}	Shocked? No. Yes. You don't understand./I
477 CC	Lucasta	17	.../{L} I can see well enough you are	shocked./You ought to see your face! I'm
477 CC	Lucasta	19	that's all. I believe you're more	shocked/Than if I'd told you I *was* Claude's
477 CC	Lucasta	24	by nobody. I know why you're	shocked:/Claude has just accepted me like a
477 CC	Colby	34	myself./{C} Oh Lucasta, I'm not	shocked. Not by you,/Not by anything you
502 CC	Lucasta	13	much too ... detached, ever to be	shocked/In the way I thought you were. I was
558 ES	Michael	6	it,/And so he pretended to be very	shocked./Said he couldn't retain any man on his

SHOCKING (2)

179 FQ: ECoker		87	/And every moment is a new and	shocking/Valuation of all we have been. We are
289 FR	Ivy	23	/{I} Yet it must have been	shocking,/Especially to lose anybody in *that*

SHOES (2)

26 Rhapsody		77	hangs on the wall,/Put your	shoes at the door, sleep, prepare for life.'/The
178 FQ: ECoker		37	laughter/Lifting heavy feet in clumsy	shoes,/Earth feet, loam feet, lifted in country

SHONE (3)

67 WL: Fire S		199	Porter in the spring./O the moon	shone bright on Mrs. Porter/And on her
96 Ash-Wed 5		7	and for the world;/And the light	shone in darkness and/Against the Word the
213 Growltiger		36	no surprise —/But the moonlight	shone reflected from a hundred bright blue eyes.

SHOOT (2)

240 MC	Chorus	8	shall beat at our doors,/Root and	shoot shall eat our eyes and our ears,/
263 MC	Chorus	4	the death of the old: not a stir, not a	shoot, not a breath./Do the days begin to

SHOOTING (2)

247 MC	Tempt1	12	Love in the orchard/Send the sap	shooting. Mirth matches melancholy./{T} We do
427 CP	Julia	26	Visiting some Sultan?/You were	shooting tigers?/{A} There are no tigers, Julia,/

SHOP (1)

362 CP	Reilly	40	are a piece of furniture in a repair	shop/For those who surround you, the masked

SHOP-WINDOW (1)

328 FR	Charles	18	collision, Mr. Piper reversed/into a	shop-window. When challenged, Mr. Piper said:

SHOPPING (7)

445 CC	Eggers	12	up to London:/I've spent the morning	shopping! Gardening tools./The number of
461 CC	Eggers	2	besides, as I told you, I've done some	shopping./But I'd better be off now. Mr.
525 ES	Charles	8	/And then you took me on a	shopping expedition .../{M} If you don't like
525 ES	Monica	9	expedition .../{M} If you don't like	shopping with me .../{C} Of course I like
525 ES	Charles	10	with me .../{C} Of course I like	shopping with you./But how can one *talk* on a
525 ES	Charles	11	with you./But how can one *talk* on a	shopping expedition —/Except to guess what
567 ES	Charles	17	to you for ever./{C} There's another	shopping expedition we must make!/But my

SHOPS (2)

400 CP	Alex	14	the right doctor, as well as the right	shops./Besides, he was ready to consult any
401 CP	Edward	10	And his recommendations/Of	shops, have always been satisfactory./I beg your

SHORE (10)

42 Swee Erect		1	Erect/Paint me a cavernous waste	shore/Cast in the unstilled Cyclades,/Paint me
74 WL: Thund		423	/To controlling hands/I sat upon the	shore/Fishing, with the arid plain behind me/
98 Ash-Wed 6		8	the wide window towards the granite	shore/The white sails still fly seaward, seaward
154 Rock 3		21	the East:/What shall be done to the	shore of smoky ships?/Will you leave my people
188 FQ: DrySal		154	between the hither and the farther	shore/While time is withdrawn, consider the
194 FQ: Little		127	/When I left my body on a distant	shore./Since our concern was speech, and
212 Growltiger		12	/When the rumour ran along the	shore: GROWLTIGER'S ON THE LOOSE!/
592 Grad 1		1	let them be divine./Standing upon the	shore of all we know/We linger for a moment
592 Grad 2		2	seek their fortunes on some foreign	shore/Well know they lose what time shall not
547 ES	Piggott	35	a map./There are lovely walks, on the	shore or in the hills,/Quite away from the motor

SHORED (1)

75 WL: Thund		430	*la tour abolie*/These fragments I have	shored against my ruins/Why then Ile fit you.

SHORES (4)

70 WL: Fire S		285	gold/The brisk swell/Rippled both	shores/Southwest wind/Carried down stream/
109 Marina		1	of our birth./Marina/What seas what	shores what grey rocks and what islands/What
110 Marina		33	hope, the new ships./What seas what	shores what granite islands towards my timbers/
189 FQ: DrySal		202	and perplexity/Whether on the	shores of Asia, or in the Edgware Road./Men's

SHORT (11)

15 Prufrock	86	hold my coat, and snicker,/And in short, I was afraid./And would it have been
23 Preludes	43	At four and five and six o'clock;/And short square fingers stuffing pipes,/And evening
32 Hysteria	3	/for squad-drill. I was drawn in by short gasps, inhaled at each momentary/
62 WL: Burial	64	death had undone so many./Sighs, short and infrequent, were exhaled,/And each
191 FQ: Little	4	between pole and tropic./When the short day is brightest, with frost and fire,/The
260 MC Thomas	5	this Christmas morning will be a/very short one. I wish only that you should meditate
262 MC Thomas	2	and because/it is possible that in a short time you may have yet another martyr,/
263 MC Chorus	26	earth cover? We wait, and the time is short/But waiting is long. {}/[*Enter the* FIRST
374 CP Edward	4	as I could:/And I tried to get you a short while ago./{C} If there had happened to be
496 CC Claude	16	to bring you up to London/At such short notice./{E} Don't say that, Sir Claude./It's
546 ES Piggott	17	/Just call me Mrs. Piggott. It's a short and simple name/And easy to remember.

SHORTCOMINGS (1)

558 ES Ld Clav	28	bring us to the end of the list of your shortcomings?/Or did Sir Alfred make other

SHORTENED (1)

150 Rock 1	115	*wheat is bread/They shall not die in a shortened bed/And a narrow sheet. In this street/*

SHORTER (3)

588 Fable	37	feet./To make a rather lengthy story shorter,/He left no wise precaution incomplete;/
263 MC Chorus	6	lengthen?/Longer and darker the day, shorter and colder the night./Still and stifling
546 ES Monica	15	/{M} Claverton-Ferry. Or Ferry: it's shorter./{MP} So sorry. Miss Claverton-Ferry.

SHORTEST (1)

291 FR Amy	10	John should be here now, he has the shortest way to come./John at least, if not

SHORTLY (2)

29 Aunt Helen	9	were handsomely provided for,/But shortly afterwards the parrot died too./The
498 CC Claude	36	what we are here for. She will be here shortly./And when she arrives I will summon

SHOT (1)

160 Rock 7	11	their light was ever surrounded and shot with darkness/As the air of temperate seas

SHOTS (1)

287 FR Gerald	2	decent specimens/And some first-class shots — better than you were,/Charles, as I

SHOULD (245)

SHOULDER (2)

187 FQ: DrySal	105	the backward half-look/Over the shoulder, towards the primitive terror./Now, we
438 CP Reilly	11	desert/With spiritual evil always at his shoulder/Suffered any less from hunger, damp,

SHOULDERS (2)

321 FR	m 28	*at* WINCHELL *and seizes him by the shoulders*]/{H} He *is* real, Doctor./So let us
455 CC Eggers	33	her:/That responsibility's not on your shoulders./Lady Elizabeth, now, that's different.

SHOULDN'T (20)

297 FR Charles	15	pushed her over?/{C} In any case, I shouldn't blame Harry./I might have done the
297 FR Gerald	22	knew, it's very much better/That he shouldn't know that we knew it also./Why not
300 FRDowning	13	/It's my opinion that man and wife/Shouldn't see too much of each other, Sir./Quite
323 FR Winch	20	/There was a lorry drawn up where it shouldn't be,/Outside of the village, on the West
359 CP Edward	21	old woman who mattered —/I shouldn't have minded anyone else, {}/[*The
432 CP Julia	18	is interrupting now?/{J} Well, you shouldn't interrupt my interruptions:/That's
445 CC Eggers	26	.../{E} Oh, Sir Claude, you shouldn't say that!/Mr. Simpkins is far better
455 CC Colby	3	me Eggers/Before you know it!/{C} I shouldn't wonder./I nearly did, a moment ago./
482 CC Colby	27	They're not your sort at all./{C} I shouldn't call them vulgar. Perhaps I'm vulgar
489 CC Lady E	33	get money from you, perhaps./No, I shouldn't say that. But she had a child/Left on
497 CC Eggers	10	of Teddington./{E} Ah, indeed!/I shouldn't have expected her name to be known
503 CC Eggers	20	may I interrupt, Miss Angel?/Why shouldn't you and Mr. Kaghan wait downstairs
504 CC Lady E	12	her lessons in recollection./But she shouldn't be singing./{L} Well, what shall I do?/
504 CC Lady E	22	progress, under my direction;/But she shouldn't have been singing./{SC} Well, are we
551 ES Carghil	12	with you!/Well, it's natural that you shouldn't want to believe it./But you think, or
551 ES Carghil	14	to think, that if I'd really suffered/I shouldn't want to let you know who I am,/I
551 ES Carghil	15	want to let you know who I am,/I shouldn't want to come and talk about the past.
551 ES Carghil	27	must do *something*./Well, perhaps I shouldn't have settled out of court./My lawyer
556 ES Ld Clav	17	/{LC} Why are you staying there? I shouldn't have thought/It would be the sort of
560 ES Ld Clav	32	good for you/To find your feet. But I shouldn't like to think/That what inspired you

SHOUT (3)

214 RTTugger	8	—/And there isn't any call for me to shout it:/For he will do/As he do do/And there's
235 Ad-dress	35	lout,/He'll answer any hail or shout./Again I must remind you that/A Dog's a
301 FR Chorus	17	be exposed, and the newsboy shall shout in the street?/When the private shall be

SHOUTING (1)

72 WL: Thund	325	/After the agony in stony places/The shouting and the crying/Prison and palace and

SHOW (39)

38 Gerontion	51	Think at last/I have not made this	show purposelessly/And it is not by any
61 WL: Burial	27	shadow of this red rock),/And I will	show you something different from either/Your
61 WL: Burial	30	at evening rising to meet you;/I will	show you fear in a handful of dust./*Frisch weht*
120 SP Krum	8	a real live Britisher/A guy like Sam to	show you around./Sam of course is at *home* in
120 SP Krum	10	in London,/And he's promised to	show us around. {}/Fragment of an Agon/
149 Rock 1	75	if he build what is good./I will	show you the things that are now being done,/
149 Rock 1	78	heart. Make perfect your will./Let me	show you the work of the humble. Listen./*The*
164 Rock 9	2	/And set thine heart upon all that I	show thee./Who is this that has said: the House
212 Growltiger	24	—/And Growltiger was disposed to	show his sentimental side./His bucko mate,
592 Grad 1	4	/Across the harbor bar — no chart to	show/No light to warn of rocks which lie below,
605 Narcissus	3	shadow of this gray rock,/And I will	show you something different from either/Your
605 Narcissus	6	the fire against the red rock:/I will	show you his bloody cloth and limbs/And the
243 MC Priest2	5	us therefore rejoice,/I say rejoice, and	show a glad face for his welcome./I am the
252 MC Tempt3	25	before another spring/The King will	show his regard for your loyalty./{T} To make,
258 MC Thomas	33	they are. I know/What yet remains to	show you of my history/Will seem to most of
267 MC Knight1	30	your former privilege, how did you	show your gratitude?/You had fled from
268 MC Knight3	6	you sued:/Yet how, I repeat, did you	show your gratitude?/{K1} Suspending those
277 MC Knight3	23	—/you must have noted what a good	show he put up at the end —/they won't give *us*
289 FR Agatha	2	hidden is revealed, and the spectres	show themselves./{G} I don't in the least know
311 FR Harry	27	*window embrasure*.]/{H} Why do you	show yourselves now for the first time?/When I
324 FR Violet	24	what happens to John,/You might	show some consideration to your mother./{A} I
324 FR Harry	31	see nothing/That people can always	show the suitable emotions —/And so far as
331 FR Harry	13	Is that what they would	show me?/And now I want you to tell me about
340 FR Amy	25	I let him go. I abased myself./Did I	show any weakness, any self-pity?/I forced
346 FRDowning	22	I can't give you any reasons./But to	show you what I mean, though you'd hardly
347 FR Ivy	18	to you? I was wondering/Whether to	show it to Amy or not. {}/[*Reads*]/{I} 'Regret
384 CP Edward	15	a mind to change my mind now/To	show you that I am free to change it./{UG} You
399 CP Nurse	21	has arrived./Then, when you ring, I	show the others out;/And only after they have
400 CP Reilly	30	*rings*]/{R} Hello! Yes,	show him up./{A} You will have a busy
413 CP Reilly	10	prologue to my treatment/Is to try to	show them that they are mistaken/About the
425 CP Lavinia	33	at a party/Where everybody else is, to	show they've been invited./That's what makes it
454 CC Kaghan	11	Now I'll take her off your hands./I'll	show you how it's done. Come along, Lucasta,/
466 CC Claude	24	and me. Some day, perhaps,/I will	show you my collection./{C} Thank you./{SC}
485 CC Lady E	10	/And very romantic. But it goes to	show/How different I felt myself to be/And then
504 CC Claude	17	I want you here, Eggerson./Will you	show her up, Lucasta?/{L} I'll make B. do it. {}/
508 CC Guzzard	38	name?/{MG} There was nothing to	show that the child had been baptised/When it
524 ES Monica	17	I know what men are — they like to	show off./That's masculine vanity, to want to
544 ES Monica	3	alone;/The people in the dining-room	show no curiosity;/The beds are comfortable,
553 ES Carghil	30	like to read them?/I'm afraid I can't	show you the originals;/They're in my lawyer's

SHOW-DOWN (1)

436 CP Julia	38	/I believe that she has forced you to a	show-down./{R} You state the position

SHOWED (4)

279 MC Knight4	22	he completely reversed his policy; he	showed/himself to be utterly indifferent to the
436 CP Lavinia	30	me, though,/Was that your face	showed no surprise or horror/At the way in
437 CP Reilly	15	/Of a Celia Coplestone whose face	showed the astonishment/Of the first five
509 CC Claude	23	—/In fact, the young man who	showed you upstairs —/Whose name is

SHOWER (2)

22 Preludes	5	ends of smoky days./And now a gusty	shower wraps/The grimy scraps/Of withered
61 WL: Burial	9	over the Starnbergersee/With a	shower of rain; we stopped in the colonnade,/

SHOWERS (1)

22 Preludes	9	newspapers from vacant lots;/The	showers beat/On broken blinds and

SHOWING (1)

234 Ad-dress	28	to play the clown,/And far from	showing too much pride/Is frequently

SHOWN (12)

268 MC Thomas	33	their contempt towards the Church	shown./{K1} Be that as it may, here is the
273 MC Thomas	35	/Consequence of good and evil can be	shown./And as in time results of many deeds are
305 FR Agatha	7	/Any time before now, it would have	shown courage/And would have been right.
399 CP Nurse	7	at eleven o'clock./He is to be	shown into the small waiting-room;/And you
399 CP Nurse	10	the second?/{N} The second to be	shown into the other room/Just as usual. She
399 CP Nurse	19	third patient?/{N} The third one to be	shown into the small room;/And I need not let
400 CP 1m	35	ALEX *by side door*]/[EDWARD *is*	shown *in by* NURSE-SECRETARY]/{E} Sir
405 CP m	23	That is my affair. {}/[LAVINIA *is*	shown *in by the* NURSE-SECRETARY]/{R}
501 CC Lucasta	8	so./*You* gave us our parts. And we've	shown that we can play them./{LE} I don't
540 ES Gomez	26	over somebody'/Wouldn't you have	shown it, if only for a second?/You never lifted

553 ES   Ld Clav   34   own handwriting./{LC} And have you shown these letters/To many people?/{MC}
571 ES   Ld Clav   39   was later discharged. It was definitely shown/That the old man had died a natural
SHOWS (7)
 57 Swee Night   28   with heavy eyes/Declines the gambit, shows fatigue,/Leaves the room and reappears/
412 CP   m 24   *button.* NURSE-SECRETARY *shows in* CELIA]/{R} Miss Celia Coplestone? ...
438 CP   Reilly   5   of her last two years./{R} That shows some insight on your part, Mrs.
469 CC   Lucasta 20   to a concert in my life?/I only go to shows when somebody invites me,/And no one
470 CC   Lucasta 35   you like — that *is* a compliment./It shows you want to educate me./{C} But I didn't
532 ES   m 31   *and* CHARLES]/[LAMBERT *shows in* GOMEZ]/{LC} Good evening, Mr. ...
555 ES   Monica   26   should you be afraid of that?/This shows how bad your nerves have been./He only
SHOWY (1)
530 ES   Ld Clav   39   collection — it must be something showy'./This would do for visiting cards — if
SHRANK (1)
515 CC   Guzzard   8   yours;/And you were so pleased, I shrank, at the moment,/From undeceiving you.
SHRED (1)
589 Fable   82   one searcht everywhere,/But not a shred of Bishop could be found,/The monks,
SHREWD (2)
481 CC   Colby   2   beginning to believe you've a pretty shrewd insight/Into things that have nothing to
549 ES   Carghil   27   it was — you know, Effie was very shrewd —/Effie it was said 'you'd be throwing
SHRIEK (1)
 43 Swee Erect   30   the razor on his leg/Waiting until the shriek subsides./The epileptic on the bed/Curves
SHRIEK'D (1)
135 5FingerEx2   4   from a green cloud/Natural forces shriek'd aloud,/Screamed, rattled, muttered
SHRIEKING (2)
175 FQ: BurntN 156   not stay in place,/Will not stay still. Shrieking voices/Scolding, mocking, or merely
335 FR   Harry   13 /{H} In and out, in an endless drift/Of shrieking forms in a circular desert/Weaving
SHRILL (1)
142 Cape Ann   6   warbler, the shy one. Hail/With shrill whistle the note of the quail,
SHRIMPS (1)
230 Bust Jones   20   /Which is famous for winkles and shrimps./In the season of venison he gives his
SHRINE (3)
189 FQ: DrySal 173   fare forward, voyagers./Lady, whose shrine stands on the promontory,/Pray for all
254 MC Tempt4   18   in line/Before the glittering jewelled shrine,/From generation to generation/Bending
254 MC Tempt4   32   rifled, and the bird mourns;/That the shrine shall be pillaged, and the gold spent,/The
SHRINES (1)
148 Rock 1   65   and Evil./Forgetful, you neglect your shrines and churches;/The men you are in these
SHRINK (1)
272 MC Chorus   20   of hell disappear, the human, they shrink and dissolve/Into dust on the wind,
SHROUD (1)
 57 Swee Night   40   fall/To stain the stiff dishonoured shroud./The Waste Land/The Burial of the
SHROUDED (1)
483 CC   Lady E   15   my work here./{LE} And what is that shrouded object on it?/Don't tell me it's a
SHRUBBERY (2)
 31 Apollinax   4   the birch-trees,/And of Priapus in the shrubbery/Gaping at the lady in the swing./In
172 FQ: BurntN   29   to/The unheard music hidden in the shrubbery,/And the unseen eyebeam crossed,
SHRUNKEN (1)
 56 Swee Night   10   the Dog/Are veiled; and hushed the shrunken seas;/The person in the Spanish cape/
SHUDDER (1)
287 FR   Amy   31   you as a mild surprise,/A momentary shudder in a vacant room./Only Agatha seems
SHUDDERED (1)
212 Growltiger   10   /At Hammersmith and Putney people shuddered at his name./They would fortify the
SHUDDERING (1)
 39 Gerontion   68   whirled/Beyond the circuit of the shuddering Bear/In fractured atoms. Gull
SHUFFLE (1)
221 Old Deut   39   any uproar' —/And out they all shuffle, without a word spoken./The digestive
SHUFFLED (1)
 64 WL: Chess 107 hushing the room enclosed./Footsteps shuffled on the stair./Under the firelight, under
SHUFFLING (1)
419 CP   Reilly   5   phantasmal world/Of imagination, shuffling memories and desires./{C} That is the
SHUSHAN (1)
157 Rock 4   5   no exception to the general rule./In Shushan the palace, in the month Nisan,/He
SHUT (7)
137 5FingerEx5   14 Eliot!/(Whether his mouth be open or shut)./Landscapes/New Hampshire/Children's
233 Skimble   40   to wash your face in/And a crank to shut the window if you sneeze./Then the guard
243 MC Priest3   12   grinders cease/And the door shall be shut in the street,/And all the daughters of

282 MC	Chorus	7	man,/Of the men and women who shut the door and sit by the fire;/Who fear the
368 CP	Edward	2	/{E} Never mind;/So long as you both shut it when you go out./{A} Ah, but you're
372 CP	Edward	38	Oh, and if you don't mind,/Please *shut the door after you*, so that it latches./{A}
477 CC	Lucasta	37	Your precious self!/Why don't you shut yourself up in that garden/Where you like

SHUTTERED (3)

24 Rhapsody		66	in the streets,/And female smells in shuttered rooms,/And cigarettes in corridors/
40 Burb Blei		11	dawn from Istria/With even feet. Her shuttered barge/Burned on the water all the
177 FQ: ECoker		16	the open field, leaving the deep lane/Shuttered with branches, dark in the afternoon,/

SHUTTERS (3)

23 Preludes		31	/And the light crept up between the shutters/And you heard the sparrows in the
24 Rhapsody		42	street/Trying to peer through lighted shutters,/And a crab one afternoon in a pool,/
29 Aunt Helen		6	silence at her end of the street./The shutters were drawn and the undertaker wiped

SHUTTLES (1)

38 Gerontion		29	hall, one hand on the door. Vacant shuttles/Weave the wind. I have no ghosts,/An

SHUTTLETHWAITE (7)

352 CP	m	3	CHAMBERLAYNE/JULIA (MRS. SHUTTLETHWAITE)/CELIA
353 CP	3m	1	CHAMBERLAYNE, JULIA SHUTTLETHWAITE, CELIA/
367 CP	Peter	6	did,/Though I'm rather afraid of Julia Shuttlethwaite./{E} Julia is certainly observant,/
412 CP	Reilly	25	/I believe you are a friend of Mrs. Shuttlethwaite./{C} Yes, it was Julia ... Mrs.
412 CP	Celia	26	/{C} Yes, it was Julia ... Mrs. Shuttlethwaite/Who advised me to come to you.
412 CP	Reilly	31	/I was there at the instance of Mrs. Shuttlethwaite./{C} That makes it even more
426 CP	Caterer	26	I simply *can't* get up./{CM} Mrs. Shuttlethwaite!/{L} Oh, it's Julia! {}/[*Enter*

SHY (3)

31 Apollinax		3	teacups./I thought of Fragilion, that shy figure among the birch-trees,/And of
142 Cape Ann		5	/The Blackburnian warbler, the shy one. Hail/With shrill whistle the note of the
240 MC	Chorus	2	households in order;/The merchant, shy and cautious, tries to compile a little

SHYER (1)

225 Mr Mistoff		43	/You would think there was nobody shyer —/But his voice has been heard on the

SI (1)

46 Directeur		2	à la malheureuse Tamise/Qui coule si près du Spectateur./Le directeur/Conservateur

SIAMESE (4)

212 Growltiger		19	was allowed./The Persian and the Siamese regarded him with fear —/Because it
212 Growltiger		20	him with fear —/Because it was a Siamese had mauled his missing ear./Now on a
213 Growltiger		32	barrels and their bunks —/As the Siamese came creeping in their sampans and
230 Bust Jones		26	a hurry there's probably curry/At the *Siamese* — or at the *Glutton*;/If he looks full of

SICH (1)

236 Cat Morgan		14	Coast,/And me voice it ain't no sich melliferous horgan;/But yet I can state, and

SICKENING (1)

573 ES	Ld Clav	3	have forgotten./You think that I'm sickening, when I'm just recovering!/It's hard to

SICKLE (1)

42 Swee Erect		16	oval O cropped out with teeth:/The sickle motion from the thighs/Jackknifes

SICKLY (3)

256 MC	Chorus	8	up against our feet./What is the sickly smell, the vapour? the dark green light
292 FR	Harry	5	Straits, in the Sunda Sea,/In the sweet sickly tropical night, I knew they were coming./
536 ES	Gomez	20	off! Homesickness!/Homesickness is a sickly word./You don't understand such

SICKNESS (3)

181 FQ: ECoker		158	curse,/And that, to be restored, our sickness must grow worse./The whole earth is
255 MC	Thomas	29	/{T} Is there no way, in my soul's sickness,/Does not lead to damnation in pride?/I
315 FR	Harry	2	lump, the dull pain, the occasional sickness:/Murder a reversal of sleep and waking.

SIDE (24)

73 WL: Thund		365	/— But who is that on the other side of you?/What is that sound high in the air/
152 Rock 2		31	when he stands alone on the other side of death,/But here upon earth you have the
212 Growltiger		24	was disposed to show his sentimental side./His bucko mate, GRUMBUSKIN, long
214 RTTugger		14	to be out;/He's always on the wrong side of every door,/And as soon as he's at home,
226 Macavity		15	uncombed./He sways his head from side to side, with movements like a snake;/And
226 Macavity		15	/He sways his head from side to side, with movements like a snake;/And when
339 FR	Harry	7	of insanity?/Somewhere on the other side of despair./To the worship in the desert, the
343 FR	Agatha	1	For him the death is now only on this side,/For him, danger and safety have another
350 FR	Mary	9	/{M} A curse is written/On the under side of things/Behind the smiling mirror/And
360 CP	Reilly	23	No./{UG} Then look at the brighter side./You say you don't know where she's gone?
386 CP	Edward	36	I'm afraid I can't see the humorous side of it./{C} I'm not really laughing at *you*,
400 CP	m	34	when they've gone. {}/[*Exit* ALEX *by side door*]/[EDWARD *is shown in by*
409 CP	Reilly	25	/And now, let us turn to your side of the problem./When you discovered that
412 CP	m	2	... Yes. Come in. {}/[*Enter* JULIA *by side door*]/{R} She's waiting downstairs./{J} I
412 CP	m	23	Yes, he'll be here. {}/[*Exit* JULIA *by side door*]/[REILLY *presses button.*

420 CP   m   20   can come in now. {}/[*Enter* JULIA *by side door*]/{R} She will go far, that one./{J} Very
422 CP   Alex   15   stars./{A} Let them place a chair each side of it./{J} May the holy ones watch over the
424 CP   4m   1   *a buffet/table.* LAVINIA *enters from side door.*/{CM} Have you any further orders for
493 CC   Lady E   7   beside the desk?/{LE} On the other side, with the light behind me:/But won't you be
511 CC   Lady E   13   ability/Comes, I suppose, from my side of the family./But he was in a very good
533 ES   Gomez   30   /I've always kept on the right side of the law —/And seen that the law turned
533 ES   Gomez   31   /And seen that the law turned its right side to *me.*/Sometimes I've had to pay pretty
566 ES   Ld Clav   1   I shall go to school together./We'll sit side by side, at little desks/And suffer the same
566 ES   Ld Clav   1   to school together./We'll sit side by side, at little desks/And suffer the same

SIDELINES (1)
452 CC   Kaghan   10   /I'm going to enjoy the game from the sidelines. {}/[*Enter* LUCASTA ANGEL]/{L}

SIDES (2)
43 Swee Erect   32   /Curves backward, clutching at her sides./The ladies of the corridor/Find
276 MC Knight1   25   judge anybody without/hearing both sides of the case. That is in accordance with our

SIDEWISE (1)
319 FR   Harry   26   /Not intended to be heard, with the sidewise looks,/That bring death into the heart

SIDMOUTH (1)
291 FR   Ivy   3   have been visiting Cousin Lily at Sidmouth, if I had not had to come to this

SIDNEY (1)
44 Cook Egg   10   in Heaven/For I shall meet Sir Philip Sidney/And have talk with Coriolanus/And

SIFTINGS (1)
57 Swee Night   39   cried aloud/And let their liquid siftings fall/To stain the stiff dishonoured

SIGHS (1)
62 WL: Burial   64   thought death had undone so many./Sighs, short and infrequent, were exhaled,/And

SIGHT (8)
38 Gerontion   59   must be adulterated?/I have lost my sight, smell, hearing, taste and touch:/How
68 WL: Fire S   211   currants/C.i.f. London: documents at sight,/Asked me in demotic French/To luncheon
220 Old Deut   9   is proud of him in his decline./At the sight of that placid and bland physiognomy,/
257 MC   Priests   1   ways./{3P} He may come in the sight of all, he may pass unseen unheard./{4T}
281 MC   Priest2   2   us of your charity./{P2} Now in the sight of God/Conjoined with all the saints and
300 FRDowning   20   /She wouldn't leave him out of her sight./{C} During that evening, did you see him?
508 CC   Guzzard   28   they left Teddington, and we lost sight of them./{E} But you know their name?/
542 ES   Gomez   32   I'm with you/Than when I'm out of sight. You'll be afraid of whispers,/The

SIGHT'S (1)
220 Old Deut   30   ... Yes! .../Ho! hi!/Oh, my eye!/My sight's unreliable, but I can guess/That the cause

SIGHTLESS (1)
85 Hollow Men   61   on this beach of the tumid river/Sightless, unless/The eyes reappear/As the

SIGHTSEERS (1)
281 MC   Chorus   21   armies trample over it, though sightseers come with guide-books looking over

SIGN (6)
37 Gerontion   17   taken for wonders. 'We would see a sign!'/The word within a word, unable to speak
263 MC   Chorus   3   driven inland by the storm./What sign of the spring of the year?/Only the death of
274 MC   Thomas   34   to suffer with my blood./This is the sign of the Church always,/The sign of blood.
274 MC   Thomas   35   is the sign of the Church always,/The sign of blood. Blood for blood./His blood given
460 CC   Lady E   16   am distressed!/This is not the first sign that I've noticed/Of your memory failing. I
509 CC   Claude   26   Yes, Elizabeth. He sometimes has to sign his full name./But he doesn't like the name,

SIGNAL (3)
213 Growltiger   41   knives./Then GILBERT gave the signal to his fierce Mongolian horde;/With a
232 Skimble   14   flash of his glass-green eyes/And the signal goes 'All Clear!'/And we're off at last for
256 MC   Chorus   29   /{C} Is it the owl that calls, or a signal between the trees?/{3P} Is the window-bar

SIGNAL'S (1)
232 Skimble   9   Mail just can't go.'/At 11.42 then the signal's overdue/And the passengers are frantic

SIGNALLED (1)
328 FR   Charles   24   asked why he/did not stop when signalled by the police car, he said: "I/thought

SIGNATURES (1)
189 FQ: DrySal   191   or scry,/Observe disease in signatures, evoke/Biography from the wrinkles

SIGNED (2)
94 Ash-Wed 4   24   flute is breathless, bent her head and signed but spoke no word/But the fountain
266 MC   Thomas   6   papers in order, and the documents signed. {}/[*To* KNIGHTS]./{T} You are

SIGNIFICANCE (1)
159 Rock 6   13   the Faith to which they owe their significance?/Men! polish your teeth on rising

SIGNIFICANT (1)
190 FQ: DrySal   237   too far from the yew-tree)/The life of significant soil./Little Gidding/Midwinter spring

SIGNIFYING (1)
178 FQ: ECoker   30   of man and woman/In daunsinge, signifying matrimonie —/A dignified and

453 CC	Eggers	39	that duty has *not* devolved on Mr. Simpkins:/Sir Claude intends to deal with these
454 CC	Eggers	18	Egg ... Mr. Eggerson!/{E} Yes, Mr. Simpkins?/{C} You seem to me sane. And I
455 CC	Eggers	20	you needn't worry/About her, Mr. Simpkins. She'll marry Mr. Kaghan/In the end.
455 CC	Eggers	30	Angel./{E} You'll get used to her, Mr. Simpkins./Time works wonders, that's what I
455 CC	Eggers	37	as Miss Angel./{E} O yes, Mr. Simpkins, much more unusual./{C} Oh!/{E}
458 CC	Claude	30	made it very imperative .../{SC} Mr. Simpkins had very strong recommendations .../
458 CC	Eggers	34	during your treatment .../{E} And Mr. Simpkins is much more highly qualified/Than I
459 CC	Claude	5	you say his name was?/{SC} Colby Simpkins. {}/[*counting on her fingers*]./{LE}
459 CC	Colby	11	/Where is your home, Mr. Colby?/{C} Simpkins./{E} Mr. Colby Simpkins./{LE} I
459 CC	Eggers	12	Colby?/{C} Simpkins./{E} Mr. Colby Simpkins./{LE} I prefer Colby./Where are you
461 CC	Eggers	3	/But I'd better be off now. Mr. Simpkins —/If anything *should* turn up
461 CC	Eggers	22	day, Sir Claude. Good day, Mr. Simpkins. {}/[*Exit* EGGERSON]/{SC} Well,
461 CC	Claude	23	Colby! I've been calling you Mr. Simpkins./Is it true, now, as a matter of
485 CC	Lady E	34	What is your aunt's name?/Is it Simpkins?/{C} No, a married aunt./A widow.
497 CC	Eggers	32	know that./{E} A natural line for Mr. Simpkins to take,/If I may say so. Of course, we
503 CC	Eggers	22	this interview is over?/I'm sure Mr. Simpkins will concur in this proposal./{C} Of
505 CC	Eggers	20	has to do, as you surmised, with Mr. Simpkins./It also concerns a problem of
505 CC	Eggers	27	/Heard your name mentioned, by Mr. Simpkins./She was struck by your name and
510 CC	Eggers	2	/{E} An excellent suggestion, Mr. Simpkins. {}/[*Exit* COLBY]/{E} And now, if you
517 CC	Eggers	21	/{E} I wouldn't venture./Mr. Simpkins is a man who knows his own mind./Is
517 CC	Eggers	22	knows his own mind./Is it true, Mr. Simpkins, that what you desire/Is to become the
517 CC	Eggers	33	organist!/{E} Don't say that, Mr. Simpkins, until you've tried our organ!/{C}
518 CC	Eggers	2	a temporary measure; because, Mr. Simpkins —/I hope you won't take this as an
518 CC	Eggers	8	I've watched you pretty closely./Mr. Simpkins! You'll be thinking of reading for
518 CC	Eggers	9	you'll still have your music. Why, Mr. Simpkins,/Joshua Park may be only a

SIMPLE (18)

14 Prufrock		43	rich and modest, but asserted by a simple pin —/(They will say: 'But how his arms
34 Figlia		16	way we both should understand,/Simple and faithless as a smile and shake of the
107 Animula		1	/'Issues from the hand of God, the simple soul'/To a flat world of changing lights
107 Animula		24	/Issues from the hand of time the simple soul/Irresolute and selfish, misshapen,
234 Ad-dress		23	on the whole,/What you would call a simple soul./Of course I'm not including Pekes,/
246 MC	Thomas	19	pretence, opportunity./End will be simple, sudden, God-given./Meanwhile the
251 MC	Tempt3	11	/As any courtier./{T3} This is the simple fact!/You have no hope of reconciliation/
332 FR	Agatha	37	/How to get rid of your mother. What simple plots!/He was not suited to the role of
374 CP	Celia	15	I should have thought it was perfectly simple./Lavinia has left you./{E} Yes, that *was*
377 CP	Julia	32	/Is, what's to be done. That's very simple./It's too late, or too early, to go to a
387 CP	Celia	9	in the dark./{C} But it's all so simple./Can't you see that ... {}/[*The doorbell*
396 CP	Lavinia	37	complicating what is in fact very simple./But there is one point which I see
471 CC	Colby	18	I'm thinking of./It's something quite simple./{L} Then I wish you'd tell me./Because *I*
485 CC	Lady E	15	was only a phase. But it made it all so simple!/To be able to think that one's earthly
535 ES	Gomez	25	need to trust *me*./{G} That's perfectly simple. I come back to England/After thirty-five
536 ES	Gomez	33	should need to trust me./{G} Perfectly simple./My father's dead long since — that's a
546 ES	Piggott	17	call me Mrs. Piggott. It's a short and simple name/And easy to remember. But, as I
550 ES	Carghil	16	true that is! Algy was a weakling,/But simple he was — not sly and slippery./Then I

SIMPLER (1)

466 CC	Colby	35	such conditions./It would be so much simpler if you *weren't* my father!/I was struck

SIMPLICITY (1)

198 FQ: Little		255	always —/A condition of complete simplicity/(Costing not less than everything)/

SIMPLIFICATION (1)

306 FR	Harry	15	substantial and simplified —/But the simplification took place in my memory,/I

SIMPLIFIED (1)

306 FR	Harry	14	place/Where life was substantial and simplified —/But the simplification took place

SIMPLY (58)

261 MC	Thomas	19	/Beloved, we do not think of a martyr simply as a good Christian who/has been killed
261 MC	Thomas	21	to/mourn. We do not think of him simply as a good Christian who has been/
261 MC	Thomas	22	of the Saints: for that would be simply to/rejoice: and neither our mourning nor
286 FR	Violet	16	bad enough, I would never go south,/Simply to see the vulgarest people —/You can
296 FR	Charles	26	with no one to talk to./I suspect it is simply that the wish to get rid of her/Makes him
298 FR	Charles	21	sorry/You all see it like this: but there simply are times/When there's nothing to do but
317 FR	Warburt	3	reason for coming this evening/Than simply in honour of your mother's birthday./I
317 FR	Harry	25	to school,/The rule of conduct was simply pleasing mother;/Misconduct was simply
317 FR	Harry	26	pleasing mother;/Misconduct was simply being unkind to mother;/What was
318 FR	Harry	6	holidays,/They were not holidays, but simply a time/In which we were supposed to
325 FR	Violet	38	staring;/And the pace he went at was simply terrifying./I said I would rather walk:
327 FR	Harry	11	/I have a private puzzle. Were they simply outside,/I might escape somewhere,

333 FR	Agatha	30	the expiation./It is possible that sin may strain and struggle/In its dark
414 CP	Celia	36	for it/That I can find, is a sense of sin./{R} You suffer from a sense of sin, Miss
414 CP	Reilly	37	of sin./{R} You suffer from a sense of sin, Miss Coplestone?/This is most unusual./{C}
415 CP	Reilly	2	/Tell me what you mean by a sense of sin./{C} It's much easier to tell you what I don't
415 CP	Celia	4	you what I don't mean:/I don't mean sin in the ordinary sense./{R} And what, in your
415 CP	Celia	11	/Was accompanied by a sense of sin:/At least, I have never come across it./I
415 CP	Celia	20	always been taught to disbelieve in sin./Oh, I don't mean that it was ever
573 ES	Ld Clav	6	them petty;/It's harder to confess the sin that no one believes in/Than the crime that
573 ES	Ld Clav	9	crime is in relation to the law/And the sin is in relation to the sinner./What has made

SINCE (42)

38 Gerontion		58	passion: why should I need to keep it/Since what is kept must be adulterated?/I have
178 FQ: ECoker		39	in country mirth/Mirth of those long since under earth/Nourishing the corn. Keeping
194 FQ: Little		128	I left my body on a distant shore./Since our concern was speech, and speech
212 Growltiger		25	bucko mate, GRUMBUSKIN, long since had disappeared,/For to the Bell at
602 Humoresque		15	set him there;/'The snappiest fashion since last spring's,'The newest style, on Earth, I
239 MC	Chorus	9	We are forced to bear witness./Since golden October declined into sombre
239 MC	Chorus	19	and the summer is over/Seven years since the Archbishop left us,/He who was
240 MC	Priest1	27	and the summer is over./Seven years since the Archbishop left us./{P2} What does the
253 MC	Tempt4	28	power?/Man oppressed by sin, since Adam fell —/You hold the keys of heaven
264 MC	Priest1	1	/*The lines sung are in italics.*]/{P1} Since Christmas a day: and the day of St.
264 MC	Priest2	7	*the Apostle borne before him.*]/{P2} Since St. Stephen a day: and the day of St. John
264 MC	Priest3	14	*Innocents borne before him.*]/{P3} Since St. John the Apostle a day: and the day of
264 MC	Priest1	22	*with the banners behind them*]/{P1} Since the Holy Innocents a day: the fourth day
306 FR	Harry	5	at all —/And I haven't seen you since you came down from Oxford./{M} Well, I
311 FR	Harry	12	out! Where are you? Let me see you,/Since I know you are there, I know you are
315 FR	Chorus	32	to happen, and the future was long since settled./And the wings of the future
326 FR	Harry	30	knew the years that I have had to live/Since I came home, a few hours ago, to
363 CP	Edward	39	/Is true enough. But that is not all./Since I saw her this morning when we had
381 CP	Edward	9	I am relatively certain/Is, that only since this morning/I have met myself as a
382 CP	Celia	8	with me./Twice you have changed since I have been looking at you./I looked at
385 CP	Reilly	1	knew them. And they have changed since then./To pretend that they and we are the
392 CP	Lavinia	39	/{L} Oh, Edward!/The point is, that since I've been away/I see that I've taken you
394 CP	Edward	23	you for the warning. But tell me,/Since this is how you see me, why did you come
395 CP	Lavinia	21	/To prove how you had grown since the last holidays./You were always
402 CP	Edward	22	can mean almost anything./{E} And since then, I have realised/That mine is a very
403 CP	Reilly	22	/Try to explain what has happened since I left you./{E} I see now why I wanted my
420 CP	Julia	35	always take risks./That is our destiny. Since you question the decision/What possible
430 CP	Peter	15	looking in so early./It does seem ages since I last saw any of you!/And how are you,
440 CP	Lavinia	30	like it./{L} But so much has happened since then. And besides,/One sometimes likes to
445 CC	Eggers	24	I'm sure,/As I've heard nothing since the last time I came./{SC} Well, of course,
449 CC	Claude	4	way, yes. You might say *mislaid*,/Since the father is dead, and there's no way of
470 CC	Colby	7	mean that I've not played/To anyone, since I came to the conclusion/That I should
503 CC	Lucasta	30	whom Colby knew./We've changed since then: as you said, we're always changing./
530 ES	Ld Clav	1	fingering —/The first empty pages since I entered Parliament./I used to jot down
533 ES	Gomez	1	/{G} You've changed your name too, since I knew you./When we were up at Oxford,
533 ES	Ld Clav	10	/{LC} Have you lived out there ever since ... you left England?/{G} Ever since I
533 ES	Gomez	11	since ... you left England?/{G} Ever since I finished my sentence./{LC} What has
536 ES	Gomez	34	simple./My father's dead long since — that's a good thing./My mother — I
562 ES	Carghil	25	to you, my dears./It's a very long time since the name of Maisie Montjoy/Topped the
562 ES	Carghil	30	your father has changed a good deal/Since I knew him ever so many years ago,/Yet
567 ES	Charles	18	we must make!/But my darling, since I got your letter this morning/About your
581 ES	Monica	31	loved you,/But I love you more since I have come to know you/Here, at Badgley

SINFUL (3)

255 MC	Thomas	33	vanity and future torment./Can sinful pride be driven out/Only by more sinful?
255 MC	Thomas	34	pride be driven out/Only by more sinful? Can I neither act nor suffer/Without
415 CP	Celia	34	why mistakes should make one feel sinful!/And yet I can't find any other word for

SING (8)

16 Prufrock		125	to each./I do not think that they will sing to me./I have seen them riding seaward on
50 Hippopot		27	/And quiring angels round him sing/The praise of God, in loud hosannas./
138 New Hamp		11	black wing,/Cling, swing,/Spring, sing,/Swing up into the apple-tree./Virginia/Red
151 Rock 2		9	nothing to bring but the songs we can sing which nobody wants to hear sung;/Waiting
263 MC	Chorus	1	Amen./Part II/{C} Does the bird sing in the South?/Only the sea-bird cries,
263 MC	Chorus	20	/He has turned before, the bird shall sing the same song./When the leaf is out on the
552 ES	Carghil	9	I'd gone through. Did you hear me sing it?/{LC} Yes, I heard you sing it./{MC} And
552 ES	Ld Clav	10	me sing it?/{LC} Yes, I heard you sing it./{MC} And what did you feel?/{LC}

SINGING (19)

16	Prufrock	124	the beach./I have heard the mermaids singing, each to each./I do not think that they
57	Swee Night	35	the door apart,/The nightingales are singing near/The Convent of the Sacred Heart,/
73	WL: Thund	354	only/Not the cicada/And dry grass singing/But sound of water over a rock/Where
73	WL: Thund	384	bells, that kept the hours/And voices singing out of empty cisterns and exhausted
73	WL: Thund	386	/In the faint moonlight, the grass is singing/Over the tumbled graves, about the
84	Hollow Men	26	swinging/And voices are/In the wind's singing/More distant and more solemn/Than a
103	Journ Magi	19	/Sleeping in snatches,/With the voices singing in our ears, saying/That this was all
109	Marina	3	scent of pine and the woodthrush singing through the fog/What images return/O
246	MC Temptl	39	apple-blossom floating on the water,/Singing at nightfall, whispering in chambers,/
258	MC Thomas	15	strategy of chess,/Love in the garden, singing to the instrument,/Were all things
261	MC Thomas	1	wine for a friend/at the table, his wife singing to the children? Those men His disciples
310	FR Harry	36	at the end of a corridor,/Sunlight and singing; when I had felt sure/That every
310	FR Harry	39	moving/Only so as not to stay still. Singing and light./Stop!/What is that? do you
329	FR Chorus	10	chopping of wood in autumn/And the singing in the kitchen/And the steps at night in
365	CP Julia	32	what did you talk about/Or were you singing songs all the time?/There's altogether
504	CC Lucasta	9	/{L} I thought I heard someone singing in the pantry./{LE} Oh, I forgot. It's
504	CC Lady E	12	in recollection./But she shouldn't be singing./{L} Well, what shall I do?/{E} Let me
504	CC Lady E	22	/But she shouldn't have been singing./{SC} Well, are we ready? {}/[*A quiet*
555	ES Piggott	2	*You To Love Me,*/Everybody was singing it once. A charming person,/I dare say,

SINGLE (14)

91	Ash-Wed 2	32	and life-giving/Worried reposeful/The single Rose/Is now the Garden/Where all loves
196	FQ: Little	193	of silence/And are folded in a single party./Whatever we inherit from the
223	Pekes Pols	61	*returned to his beat,/There wasn't a single one left in the street./*Mr. Mistoffelees/You
590	Space Time	3	that cannot be,/The fly that lives a single day/Has lived as long as we./But let us
241	MC Mess	37	his horse will be deprived of its tail,/A single hair of which becomes a precious relic./
286	FR Charles	2	to leave England in the winter./But a single man like me is better off in London:/A
295	FR Harry	20	take it./First of all, you isolate the single event/As something so dreadful that it
335	FR Harry	17	chain broke, and I was left/Under the single eye above the desert./{Ag} Up and down,
345	FR Violet	31	Amy./{V} I do not understand/A single thing that's happened. {}/[*Exeunt* AMY,
349	FR	4m	AGATHA/*and* MARY *walk slowly in single file round and round the table, clockwise.*/
405	CP Reilly	3	/Which I have to explore. The single patient/Who is ill by himself, is rather the
474	CC Colby	2	Eggerson/His garden is a part of one single world./{L} But what do you want?/{C}
551	ES Carghil	2	a woman doesn't want to forget/A single one of her admirers. Why, even a faithless
578	ES Monica	34	Michael, you haven't understood a single word/Of what I said. You must make

SINGS (5)

73	WL: Thund	356	over a rock/Where the hermit-thrush sings in the pine trees/Drip drop drip drop drop
172	FQ: BurntN	52	/The trilling wire in the blood/Sings below inveterate scars/Appeasing long
181	FQ: ECoker	165	ascends from feet to knees,/The fever sings in mental wires./If to be warmed, then I
365	CP	m 5	them, because one lens is missing. {}/[*Sings*]./{UG} *As I was drinkin' gin and water,/*
365	CP	m 11	appointment?/{E} I shall keep it. {}/[*Sings*]./{UG} *Tooryooly toory-iley,/What's the*

SINGULAR (2)

209	NamingCats	31	/Effanineffable/Deep and inscrutable singular Name./The Old Gumbie Cat/I have a
225	Mr Mistoff	50	/Which is incontestable proof/Of his singular magical powers:/And I have known the

SINK (2)

67	WL: Fire S	174	the last fingers of leaf/Clutch and sink into the wet bank. The wind/Crosses the
294	FR Harry	35	would never imagine anyone could sink so quickly./I had always supposed,

SINKS (2)

601	Nocturne	8	some servant wait,/Stab, and the lady sinks into a swoon./Blood looks effective on the
294	FR Harry	23	own automatism/While the slow stain sinks deeper through the skin/Tainting the flesh

SINNER (2)

587	Fable	17	ghost./Some wicked and heretical old sinner/Perhaps, who had been walled up for his
573	ES Ld Clav	9	law/And the sin is in relation to the sinner./What has made the difference in the last

SINNERS (2)

90	Ash-Wed 1	40	care/Teach us to sit still./Pray for us sinners now and at the hour of our death/Pray
247	MC Temptl	34	were not used to be so hard upon sinners/When they were your friends. Be easy,

SINS (7)

152	Rock 2	33	in humble repentance, expiating the sins of your fathers;/And all that was good you
162	Rock 8	26	sun of the East/And the seven deadly sins in Syria./But our King did well at Acre./
164	Rock 9	8	the grief they should feel/For their sins and faults as they go about their daily
257	MC Chorus	14	/Our labour taken away from us,/Our sins made heavier upon us./We have seen the
260	MC Thomas	11	oblation and satisfaction/for the sins of the whole world. It was in this same
261	MC Thomas	15	death of martyrs. We mourn, for the sins/of the world that has martyred them; we
264	MC Priestl	24	so also for himself, he offereth for sins./He lays down his life for the sheep./{3P}

SIP (1)

360 CP	Reilly	16	it for you, if I may .../Strong ... but sip it slowly ... and drink it sitting down./

SIR (109)

41 Burb Blei		28	Lights, lights,/She entertains Sir Ferdinand/Klein. Who clipped the lion's
44 Cook Egg		10	Honour in Heaven/For I shall meet Sir Philip Sidney/And have talk with Coriolanus
44 Cook Egg		14	Capital in Heaven/For I shall meet Sir Alfred Mond./We two shall lie together, lapt
124 SA	Snow	11	continue his story./I assure you, Sir, we are very interested./{S} I knew a man
277 MC	Knight1	33	of statecraft and constitutional law. Sir/Hugh de Morville./{K2} I should like first to
297 FR	Denman	28	Lordship?/{D} He's out in the garage, Sir, with his Lordship's car./{C} Tell him I'd like
298 FR	Downing	27	/{Do} Thank you, very well indeed, Sir./{C} I'm sorry to send for you so abruptly,/
298 FR	Downing	32	over ten years .../{Do} Eleven years, Sir, next Lady Day./{C} Eleven years, and you
299 FR	Downing	2	/{Do} Quite natural, if I may say so, Sir,/After what happened./{C} Quite so, quite./
299 FR	Downing	11	his Lordship knew it?/{Do} Unlikely, Sir, if I may say so./Much more likely to have
299 FR	Downing	22	/{Do} Well, always about the same, Sir./What I mean is, always up and down./
299 FR	Downing	26	excited,/And, in a way, irresponsible, Sir./If I may make so bold, Sir,/I always
299 FR	Downing	27	Sir./If I may make so bold, Sir,/I always thought that a very few cocktails/
299 FR	Downing	33	/{Do} Well, you might say depressed, Sir./But you know his Lordship was always very
300 FR	Downing	2	of thing?/{Do} Well, I don't know, Sir./But he seemed very anxious about my
300 FR	Downing	7	/But you know, it is just my opinion, Sir,/That his Lordship is rather psychic, as they
300 FR	Downing	10	they always together?/{Do} Always, Sir./That was just my complaint against my
300 FR	Downing	13	Shouldn't see too much of each other, Sir./Quite the contrary of the usual opinion,/I
300 FR	Downing	22	did you see him?/{Do} Oh yes, Sir, I'm sure I saw him./I don't mean to say that
300 FR	Downing	27	that I saw him accidental./You see, Sir, I was down in the Tourist,/And I took a bit
300 FR	Downing	36	have been all right then,/Mustn't she, Sir? or else he'd have known it./{C} Oh yes ...
301 FR	Downing	1	with his Lordship's car?/{Do} Oh no, Sir, she's in good running order:/I see to that./
301 FR	Downing	5	it tonight./{Do} Nothing wrong, Sir:/Only I like to have her always ready./
301 FR	Downing	7	/Would there be anything more, Sir?/{G} Thank you, Downing;/Nothing more.
322 FR	Winch	2	well this evening./{Wi} I understand, Sir./It'd be the same if it was my birthday —/I
346 FR	Downing	10	good night,/Miss Mary; good night, Sir./{M} Downing, will you promise never to
352 CP	m	7	GUEST, *later identified as* SIR HENRY HARCOURT-REILLY/
399 CP	2m	1	it up for me? {}/CURTAIN/Act Two/SIR HENRY HARCOURT-REILLY'S
399 CP	3m	1	*Morning:*/*several weeks later.* SIR HENRY *alone at his desk. He presses an*/
399 CP	Nurse	5	meeting?/{N} You made that clear, Sir Henry:/The first appointment at eleven
399 CP	Nurse	24	the moment./{N} Mr. Gibbs is here, Sir Henry./{R} Ask him to come straight in. {}/
400 CP	Edward	35	*in by* NURSE-SECRETARY]/{E} Sir Henry Harcourt-Reilly — {}/[*Stops and*
405 CP	Lavinia	25	other patient./{E} Lavinia!/{L} Well, Sir Henry!/I said I would come to talk about my
411 CP	Lavinia	26	Exactly. And I have a question too./Sir Henry, was it you who sent those telegrams?
411 CP	Edward	33	Have you anything else to say to us, Sir Henry?/{R} No. Not in this capacity. {}/
432 CP	Caterer	2	typical./{P} No, I'm afraid .../{CM} Sir Henry Harcourt-Reilly!/{J} Oh, I forgot! I'd
432 CP	Julia	4	REILLY]/{J} I want you to meet Sir Henry Harcourt-Reilly —/{E} We're
432 CP	Lavinia	13	me./{L} If you can interrupt Julia, Sir Henry,/You are the perfect guest we've been
432 CP	Lavinia	26	May I introduce Mr. Peter Quilpe?/Sir Henry Harcourt-Reilly. Peter's an old friend
436 CP	Lavinia	20	be happy in the thought of her./{L} Sir Henry, there is something I want to say to
439 CP	Peter	33	Julia. Good-bye, Alex. Good-bye, Sir Henry. {}/[*Exit*]/{J} ... And now the
440 CP	Edward	6	isn't much/That I understand yet! But Sir Henry has been saying,/I think, that every
444 CC	m	2	CLERK/Characters/SIR CLAUDE MULHAMMER/EGGERSON
445 CC	2m	1	*Business Room on the first floor of* SIR CLAUDE MULHAMMER'S/*London*
445 CC	3m	1	/*London house. Early afternoon.* SIR CLAUDE *writing at desk. Enter*/
445 CC	Eggers	8	from Switzerland./{E} Impossible, Sir Claude!/A very delicate situation —/Her
445 CC	Eggers	26	you're irreplaceable .../{E} Oh, Sir Claude, you shouldn't say that!/Mr.
446 CC	Eggers	37	worth watching./{E} I don't know, Sir Claude. Only the other day/I read a letter in
447 CC	Eggers	19	I am./{E} Oh, I wouldn't say that, Sir Claude!/She has too much respect for your
448 CC	Eggers	11	of Atlantis?/{E} Well, to tell the truth, Sir Claude, I only touched on these matters,/
450 CC	Colby	28	/{C} I've got what you wanted, Sir Claude. Good afternoon,/Mr. Eggerson. I
450 CC	m	32	Elizabeth, I will rejoin you. {}/[*Exit* SIR CLAUDE]/{C} I'm glad you don't have to
450 CC	Colby	36	very little about Lady Elizabeth,/And Sir Claude himself hasn't told me very much:/So
451 CC	Eggers	4	/Don't listen to him. He understands Sir Claude,/And he's always been very grateful
451 CC	Eggers	5	And he's always been very grateful to Sir Claude,/As he ought to be. Sir Claude
451 CC	Eggers	6	to Sir Claude,/As he ought to be. Sir Claude picked him out/And gave him his
453 CC	Eggers	40	has *not* devolved on Mr. Simpkins:/Sir Claude intends to deal with these matters
454 CC	Eggers	1	matters himself./You will have to ask Sir Claude. But I'll speak to him/When I return
454 CC	Colby	27	good heart./{C} But does she address Sir Claude Mulhammer/As Claude? To his face?
454 CC	Eggers	33	does call her Lizzie,/Sometimes, to Sir Claude. And do you know —/I think it
455 CC	Eggers	12	/But I think her father was a friend of Sir Claude's,/And he's made himself responsible
455 CC	Eggers	15	a father —/A very generous man, is Sir Claude./To tell the truth, she's something of

456 CC	Eggers	1	*dame*, as the French say./That's what Sir Claude admires about her./He said to me
456 CC	Eggers	15	soon get used to them. That's what Sir Claude said:/'Humour her, Eggerson,' he
457 CC	m	11	that I'm right, I assure you. {}/[*Enter* SIR CLAUDE]/{SC} Hello! Still here? It's time
457 CC	Lady E	29	tea properly./A cup of black coffee. Is Sir Claude at home?/I'll speak to him first./{SC}
459 CC	Lady E	1	I interviewed/And recommended to Sir Claude? Of course it is./I remember saying:
461 CC	Eggers	22	thank you, Eggerson./{E} Good day, Sir Claude. Good day, Mr. Simpkins. {}/[*Exit*
475 CC	Colby	35	/Or from what I've told B.; or from Sir Claude./{L} Claude hasn't told me anything
483 CC	Colby	12	come from?/{C} It's an office desk. Sir Claude got it for me./I said I needed a desk
486 CC	m	33	*the door*]/{LE} Who's that? {}/[*Enter* SIR CLAUDE]/{SC} Elizabeth! I was told that
492 CC	1m	38	/{LE} My poor Claude! {}/[*Exeunt* SIR CLAUDE *and* LADY ELIZABETH]/
493 CC	2m	1	*as in Act* 1. *Several mornings later.* SIR CLAUDE *is/moving chairs about. Enter*
496 CC	Eggers	14	Eggerson./{E} Good morning, Sir Claude. And Lady Elizabeth!/{SC} I'm
496 CC	Eggers	17	such short notice./{E} Don't say that, Sir Claude./It's true, I haven't much nowadays
497 CC	Lady E	23	Let me explain./I am convinced that Sir Claude is mistaken,/Or has been deceived,
498 CC	Eggers	34	we must try to trace it. Certainly, Sir Claude:/Our first step must be to question
499 CC	Eggers	2	you sit at the desk?/{E} If you wish, Sir Claude./I do feel more at ease when I'm
499 CC	Eggers	8	behalf of my wife./{E} I understand, Sir Claude: I understand completely. {}/[*A*
500 CC	Lady E	5	Colby is my son./{LE} That is what Sir Claude believes. Claude, let me explain./{SC}
504 CC	Guzzard	28	But I didn't mind waiting in the least, Sir Claude./I know that you are always much
505 CC	Guzzard	13	tact and discretion./{MG} Certainly, Sir Claude, if that is what you wish./But is the
505 CC	Eggers	17	should call it, Mrs. Guzzard./I take it, Sir Claude, I should open the discussion?/{SC}
506 CC	Eggers	24	appears to be a clue./That is why Sir Claude has asked you to be present./{MG}
507 CC	Guzzard	37	I kept a child of yours/And deceived Sir Claude by pretending it was his?/{SC} That
510 CC	Kaghan	17	/{K} Why, yes, it is. Did you tell her, Sir Claude?/{SC} No, B. It was Mrs. Guzzard
511 CC	Lucasta	35	When you're an alderman, you'll be Sir Barney Kaghan!/{LE} And I'm very glad
513 CC	Guzzard	6	Lady Elizabeth,/And the daughter of Sir Claude Mulhammer./{SC} That is *my*
513 CC	Colby	14	I can only give a strange answer./Sir Claude is right: I wished to know the truth./
514 CC	Guzzard	1	son would you wish to be, Colby:/Sir Claude's — or the son of some other man/
514 CC	Guzzard	9	mean?/{MG} Colby is not your son, Sir Claude./{C} Who was my father, then?/
514 CC	Eggers	28	/{E} I'll examine the records myself, Sir Claude./Not that we doubt your word, Mrs.
514 CC	Guzzard	36	I had no intention of deceiving you, Sir Claude,/Till you deceived yourself. When
515 CC	Guzzard	20	But it can't be true./{MG} Consider, Sir Claude. Would I tell you all this/Unless it
516 CC	Colby	3	plans for your future./{C} Thank you, Sir Claude./You're a very generous man. But
516 CC	Colby	36	make the best of it, together./{C} No, Sir Claude. I hate to hurt you/As I am hurting
518 CC	Guzzard	28	be terminated./If you will excuse me, Sir Claude .../{SC} Excuse you? Yes./{MG} I
518 CC	Guzzard	35	taxi./Do you mind if I take my leave, Sir Claude?/I'm no longer needed here. {}/[*Exit*
518 CC	Guzzard	39	/In one form or another. You and I, Sir Claude,/Had our wishes twenty-five years
519 CC	m	7	Claude! {}/[LUCASTA *crosses to* SIR CLAUDE *and kneels beside him*]/{K} You
519 CC	m	22	{}/[LUCASTA *puts her arms around* SIR CLAUDE]/{SC} Don't leave me, Lucasta./
532 ES	Charles	23	bring my coat?/{C} I'll say goodbye, sir./And look forward to seeing you both at
557 ES	Ld Clav	8	lost my job./{LC} The position that Sir Alfred Walter made for you./{Mi} I'd stuck
558 ES	Michael	5	being discharged?/{Mi} Well, partly. Sir Alfred did come to hear about it,/And so he
558 ES	Ld Clav	12	me have your version first./I dare say Sir Alfred's will be rather different./And what
558 ES	Ld Clav	29	the list of your shortcomings?/Or did Sir Alfred make other unflattering criticisms?/
568 ES	Charles	13	certainly things I would gladly forget, Sir,/Or rather, which I wish had never
569 ES	Charles	17	about you./{C} I was thinking, Sir — forgive the suspicion —/From what
574 ES	Michael	34	got me here in London? With another Sir Alfred/Who'd constitute himself custodian

SISTER (28)

94 Ash-Wed 4	22	draw by the gilded hearse./The silent sister veiled in white and blue/Between the yews,
96 Ash-Wed 5	20	and deny the voice/Will the veiled sister pray for/Those who walk in darkness,
96 Ash-Wed 5	24	who wait/In darkness? Will the veiled sister pray/For children at the gate/Who will
97 Ash-Wed 5	29	have I done unto thee./Will the veiled sister between the slender/Yew trees pray for
98 Ash-Wed 6	25	yew be shaken and reply./Blessèd sister, holy mother, spirit of the fountain, spirit
99 Ash-Wed 6	32	His will/And even among these rocks/Sister, mother/And spirit of the river, spirit of
298 FR	Ivy	6	I wish to associate myself with my sister/In her objections —/{Ag} I have no
301 FR	Charles	24	is afraid that her status as Amy's sister will be diminished./{Ch} We all of us make
332 FR	Agatha	8	assumed to be your father,/And my sister whom you acknowledge as your mother:/
332 FR	Agatha	19	/Of loneliness. Your mother wanted a sister here/Always. I was the youngest: I was
357 CP	Edward	7	you wouldn't know. Her mother's sister/And rather a recluse./{J} Her favourite
478 CC	Lucasta	5	you'll have to accept me/As your sister! Even if I am a guttersnipe .../{C} You
486 CC	Lady E	15	as for your mother —/Mrs. Guzzard's sister, I suppose .../{C} Her sister — which
486 CC	Colby	16	Guzzard's sister, I suppose .../{C} Her sister — which makes Mrs. Guzzard my aunt./
486 CC	Lady E	17	you quite sure that Mrs. Guzzard's sister —/Who you say was your mother —
489 CC	Claude	19	Colby is the son of Mrs. Guzzard's sister,/Who died when he was born. Mrs.
489 CC	Lady E	29	{LE} Then how do you know that the sister had a child?/Perhaps Mrs. Guzzard

498 CC	Claude	30	of *my* child was Mrs. Guzzard's sister./She wouldn't dispose of *him*. It's your
502 CC	Colby	35	/As one's brother .../{C} Or sister .../{L} What's so difficult/Is to recognise
502 CC	Lucasta	38	understanding, as a brother and a sister,/Will come, in time. Perhaps, one day/We
503 CC	Lucasta	6	to each other,/As a brother and a sister, than we could have been/In any other
503 CC	Lucasta	10	be happy,/If you will accept me as a sister/For the happiness that relationship may
503 CC	Lucasta	31	I come back, we'll be brother and sister —/Or so I hope. Yes, in any event,/
514 CC	Eggers	23	/A son./{E} And what about your sister and her child?/{MG} Registration of
514 CC	Guzzard	38	When you went to Canada/My sister found that she was to have a child:/That
515 CC	Guzzard	2	concern you./As I have just said, my sister died/Before the child could be born. You
578 ES	Monica	18	my only brother/And I'm your only sister. You never took much notice of me./
578 ES	Michael	30	used to chaff me about my highbrow sister./But all the same, I was fond of you, and

SISTERS (8)

284 FR		m 2	VIOLET, *and* AGATHA, *her younger sisters*/COL. THE HON. GERALD PIPER, *and*
434 CP	Alex	7	there were three of them —/Three sisters at this station, in a Christian village;/And
484 CC	Lady E	2	you other near relatives? Brothers or sisters?/{C} No brothers or sisters. No. As for
484 CC	Colby	3	or sisters?/{C} No brothers or sisters. No. As for other relatives,/I never knew
484 CC	Lady E	27	having no relatives —/No brothers or sisters — and I was lonely/Because they were so
527 ES	Charles	32	that you haven't had brothers and sisters/To share the burden. Sisters, I should
527 ES	Charles	33	and sisters/To share the burden. Sisters, I should say,/For your brother's never
536 ES	Gomez	37	I'm dead;/And as for my married sisters — I don't suppose their husbands/Were

SIT (44)

19 Portrait		40	watches by the public clocks./Then sit for half an hour and drink our bocks./Now
20 Portrait		68	to reach her journey's end./I shall sit here, serving tea to friends....'/I take my hat:
21 Portrait		108	rate./Perhaps it is not too late./I shall sit here, serving tea to friends.'/And I must
56 Swee Night		12	person in the Spanish cape/Tries to sit on Sweeney's knees/Slips and pulls the table
72 WL: Thund		340	Here one can neither stand nor lie nor sit/There is not even silence in the mountains/
90 Ash-Wed 1		39	us to care and not to care/Teach us to sit still./Pray for us sinners now and at the hour
98 Ash-Wed 6		28	us to care and not to care/Teach us to sit still/Even among these rocks,/Our peace in
109 Marina		10	meaning/Death/Those who sit in the sty of contentment, meaning/Death/
125 SA Sweeney		25	do what we gotta do/We're gona sit here and drink this booze/We're gona sit
125 SA Sweeney		26	here and drink this booze/We're gona sit here and have a tune/We're gona stay and
151 Rock 2		4	have you built well, that you now sit helpless in a ruined house?/Where many are
151 Rock 2		7	not fitly framed together, you sit ashamed and wonder whether and how you
158 Rock 5		5	loose in the holster.'/Those who sit in a house of which the use is forgotten: are
203 Indians		3	own fire, and his wife's cooking;/To sit in front of his own door at sunset/And see
257 MC Tempts		5	on a broken step./{4T} A man may sit at meat, and feel the cold in his groin./{C}
264 MC Priest1		2	First Martyr./*Princes moreover did sit, and did witness falsely against me.*/A day that
264 MC Priest1		6	to their charge./*Princes moreover did sit.* {}/[*Introit of St. Stephen is heard*]/[*Enter the*
268 MC Thomas		20	keep me from my own/And bid me sit in Canterbury, alone?/I would wish him three
280 MC Priest3		29	in the fountain by the date-tree;/Or sit and bite your nails in Aquitaine./In the small
282 MC Chorus		7	and women who shut the door and sit by the fire;/Who fear the blessing of God, the
285 FR Amy		3	watch the days draw out,/Now that I sit in the house from October to June,/And the
291 FR Harry		19	ring for Denman./{H} How can you sit in this blaze of light for all the world to look
303 FR Mary		25	Warburton is coming./I shall have to sit between Arthur and John./Which is worse,
315 FR Chorus		31	is to come;/Of the things to come that sit at the door, as if they had been there always./
319 FR Warburt		39	could tell you. But, Harry,/We can't sit here all the evening, you know;/You will
321 FR Harry		30	You, and I/And Winchell. Sit down, Winchell,/And have a glass of port.
356 CP Julia		15	the wedding cake./{J} Edward, do sit down for a moment./I know you're always
386 CP Edward		26	is nothing to do but wait./Won't you sit down?/{C} Thank you. {}/[*Pause*]/{E} Oh, my
386 CP Edward		29	what shall we talk about?/We can't sit here in silence./{C} Oh, I could./Just looking
388 CP Lavinia		35	I suppose we might as well sit down./What shall we talk about?/{E} Peter's
401 CP Reilly		2	morning, Mr. Chamberlayne./Please sit down. I won't keep you a moment./— Now,
401 CP Reilly		14	away at once./{R} No. If you please, sit down, Mr. Chamberlayne./You are not
401 CP Reilly		15	not going away, so you might as well sit down./You were going to ask a question./{E}
401 CP Reilly		28	from it:/And so ... you might as well sit down./I think that you will find that chair
405 CP Reilly		31	before honour, Mr. Chamberlayne./Sit down, please, both of you. Mrs.
412 CP Reilly		24	Miss Celia Coplestone? ... Won't you sit down?/I believe you are a friend of Mrs.
426 CP Lavinia		7	/So just stretch out./{L} You must sit beside me,/Then I can relax./{E} This is the
458 CC Claude		3	She's coming up./{SC} Colby, sit at the desk, and pick up some papers./We
467 CC Claude		35	to pay./— I shall go now, and sit for a while with my china./{C} Excuse me,
493 CC Claude		6	I should be near together./Will you sit there, beside the desk?/{LE} On the other
499 CC Claude		1	to conduct the proceedings./Will you sit at the desk?/{E} If you wish, Sir Claude./I do
548 ES Carghil		14	hope I'm not disturbing you. I always sit here./It's the sunniest and most sheltered
554 ES Carghil		12	Piggott!/It seems to me that you never sit still:/You simply sacrifice yourself for us./
566 ES Ld Clav		1	I shall go to school together./We'll sit side by side, at little desks/And suffer the

SITS (24)

68 WL: Fire S	233	/One of the low on whom assurance sits/As a silk hat on a Bradford millionaire./The
210 Old Gumbie	3	stripes and leopard spots./All day she sits upon the stair or on the steps or on the mat:
210 Old Gumbie	4	or on the steps or on the mat:/She sits and sits and sits and sits — and that's what
210 Old Gumbie	4	the steps or on the mat:/She sits and sits and sits and sits — and that's what makes a
210 Old Gumbie	4	or on the mat:/She sits and sits and sits and sits — and that's what makes a Gumbie
210 Old Gumbie	4	the mat:/She sits and sits and sits and sits — and that's what makes a Gumbie Cat!/
210 Old Gumbie	15	warm and sunny spots./All day she sits beside the hearth or in the sun or on my hat:
210 Old Gumbie	16	or in the sun or on my hat:/She sits and sits and sits and sits — and that's what
210 Old Gumbie	16	in the sun or on my hat:/She sits and sits and sits and sits — and that's what makes a
210 Old Gumbie	16	or on my hat:/She sits and sits and sits and sits — and that's what makes a Gumbie
210 Old Gumbie	16	my hat:/She sits and sits and sits and sits — and that's what makes a Gumbie Cat!/
211 Old Gumbie	27	wind, and tie it into sailor-knots./She sits upon the window-sill, or anything that's
211 Old Gumbie	28	anything that's smooth and flat:/She sits and sits and sits and sits — and that's what
211 Old Gumbie	28	that's smooth and flat:/She sits and sits and sits and sits — and that's what makes a
211 Old Gumbie	28	smooth and flat:/She sits and sits and sits and sits — and that's what makes a Gumbie
211 Old Gumbie	28	and flat:/She sits and sits and sits and sits — and that's what makes a Gumbie Cat!/
220 Old Deut	10	and bland physiognomy,/When he sits in the sun on the vicarage wall,/The Oldest
220 Old Deut	17	Deuteronomy!'/Old Deuteronomy sits in the street,/He sits in the High Street on
220 Old Deut	18	Deuteronomy sits in the street,/He sits in the High Street on market day;/The
263 MC Chorus	8	up in the East./The starved crow sits in the field, attentive; and in the wood/The
316 FR Chorus	3	it was never there./And the bird sits on the broken chimney. I am afraid./{I} This
483 CC	m 29	for photographic souvenirs. {}/[*She sits down, holding the portrait*]/{LE} What was I
543 ES	m 8	GOMEZ]/[LORD CLAVERTON *sits for a few minutes brooding. A knock. Enter*
548 ES	2m 14	*face./Enter* MRS. CARGHILL. *She sits in a deckchair nearby, composes/herself and*

SITTING (12)

21 Portrait	116	and rose;/Should die and leave me sitting pen in hand/With the smoke coming
23 Preludes	35	/As the street hardly understands;/Sitting along the bed's edge, where/You curled
44 Cook Egg	2	chair/Some distance from where I was sitting;/*Views of Oxford Colleges*/Lay on the
360 CP Reilly	16	... but sip it slowly ... and drink it sitting down./Breathe deeply, and adopt a
366 CP Julia	2	on the mantelpiece. Where was I sitting?/Just turn out the bottom of that sofa —/
493 CC Lady E	8	the light behind me:/But won't you be sitting at the desk yourself?/{SC} No, that
527 ES Monica	27	with him,/Reading too — or just sitting — someone/Not occupied with anything
529 ES Monica	2	at weekends, even when the House is sitting./And you can take me out, if Father can
530 ES Ld Clav	20	and no desire to fill it./It's just like sitting in an empty waiting room/In a railway
531 ES Ld Clav	27	want my ghost/Walking in the City or sitting in the Lords./And I, who recognise
548 ES Carghil	29	it would really happen!/And now I'm sitting here talking to you./Dear me, it's
578 ES Michael	26	my nerves, when I saw you/Always sitting there with your nose in a book./And

SITTING-ROOM (1)

483 CC Lady E	26	—/Are much too intimate for the sitting-room./May I remove it? Surely your

SITUATION (20)

202 War Poetry	17	/That is a life./War is not a life: it is a situation,/One which may neither be ignored
251 MC Tempt3	18	friends/May be found in the present situation./King in England is not all-powerful;/
289 FR Amy	36	of you ever met her./It will make the situation very much easier/And is why I was so
316 FR Charles	7	my hands, I think I could manage the situation. {}/[*Exeunt*]/[*Enter* MARY, *and passes*
341 FR Amy	8	you repel it./{A} I prepared the situation/For us to be reconciled, because of
355 CP Julia	37	not the solution./He only made the situation more difficult./You know Tony
366 CP Peter	39	fault./I don't suppose you noticed the situation./{E} I did think I noticed one or two
374 CP Edward	17	has left you./{E} Yes, that *was* the situation./I suppose it was pretty obvious to
374 CP Celia	26	temporary./You know I accepted the situation/Because a divorce would ruin your
386 CP Celia	35	so before./This is really a ludicrous situation./{E} I'm afraid I can't see the
392 CP Lavinia	24	/Trust her not to miss any awkward situation!/And what did you tell them?/{E} I
402 CP Reilly	38	I always begin from the immediate situation/And then go back as far as I find
405 CP Reilly	2	my patients/Are only pieces of a total situation/Which I have to explore. The single
405 CP Reilly	6	recently had another patient/Whose situation is much the same as your own. {}/
445 CC Eggers	9	Sir Claude!/A very delicate situation —/Her first meeting with Mr.
462 CC Claude	33	/In adapting yourself to a new situation./{C} I'm very grateful to you, for that:/
462 CC Colby	35	that:/It is indeed a new and strange situation,/And nothing about it is real to me
490 CC Claude	10	that's in your mind./I know this situation must be more of an agony/To you,
498 CC Claude	38	I wanted you here first, to explain the situation:/And I thought I would like you to
528 ES Charles	34	and the most depressing;/For this situation may persist for a long time,/And you'll

SITUATIONS (4)

19 Portrait	49	has no more remorse/And smiles at situations which it cannot see.'/I smile, of
62 WL: Burial	50	the Lady of the Rocks,/The lady of situations./Here is the man with three staves,
568 ES Ld Clav	27	meanness and cowardice,/But also situations which are simply ridiculous,/When he

582 ES Ld Clav 16   had to see so much of persons/And situations not very agreeable./You two ought to
SIX (11)
  22 Preludes   3   /With smell of steaks in passageways./Six o'clock./The burnt-out ends of smoky days./
  23 Preludes   42   by insistent feet/At four and five and six o'clock;/And short square fingers stuffing
 103 Journ Magi   27   tavern with vine-leaves over the lintel,/Six hands at an open door dicing for pieces of
 117 SP   Doris 23   next?/{Do} What comes next. It's the six./{Du} 'A quarrel. An estrangement.
 147 Rock 1   28   and there I was told:/We toil for six days, on the seventh we must motor/To
 371 CP Edward   8   to you with Celia/In another six months' time. There it is./You can take it or
 424 CP Lavinia 10   Nothing more, I think, till half past six. {}/[*Exit* CATERER'S MAN]/[EDWARD
 481 CC Kaghan   10   You can't want dinner yet./It's only six o'clock. We can't dine till eight;/Not at any
 481 CC Lady E   25   very hungry./{LE} Hungry? At six o'clock? Where will you get dinner?/Oh, I
 481 CC Lady E   28   /Most of its patrons dine at half past six./They have the most delicious salads!/And I
 496 CC Eggers   21   /At my being up in London five or six days a week:/But now she says: 'You're
SIX-SEATERS (1)
 121 SA Sweeney 24   no motor cars/No two-seaters, no six-seaters,/No Citroën, no Rolls-Royce./
SIXTY (2)
 539 ES   Gomez   2   /But again, you've retired at sixty. Why at sixty?/{LC} Knowing as much
 539 ES   Gomez   2   again, you've retired at sixty. Why at sixty?/{LC} Knowing as much about me as you
SIZE (3)
 216 Jellicles   22   black,/Jellicle Cats are of moderate size;/Jellicles jump like a jumping-jack,/Jellicle
 589 Fable   74   to his chair,/His eye became the size of any dollar,/The ghost then took him
 382 CP   Celia 19   blood;/And saw only a beetle the size of a man/With nothing more inside it than
SKEERED (1)
 213 Growltiger   45   she gave a screech, for she was badly skeered;/I am sorry to admit it, but she quickly
SKEIN (1)
 253 MC Tempt4   40   he bites broken teeth./You hold the skein: wind, Thomas, wind/The thread of
SKELETON (2)
  24 Rhapsody   28   if the world gave up/The secret of its skeleton,/Stiff and white./A broken spring in a
  52 Whispers   14   of the marrow/The ague of the skeleton;/No contact possible to flesh/Allayed
SKETCHING (1)
 331 FR Agatha   35   cultivated country squire,/Reading, sketching, playing on the flute,/Something of an
SKIES (1)
  23 Preludes   39   /His soul stretched tight across the skies/That fade behind a city block,/Or
SKILL (2)
 250 MC Tempt3   26   /To idle or intrigue at court/I have no skill. I am no courtier./I know a horse, a dog, a
 258 MC Thomas   14   bullfinch in the lilac tree,/The tiltyard skill, the strategy of chess,/Love in the garden,
SKIM (1)
 136 5FingerEx4   17   finches and fairies/In jubilant rapture skim./How delightful to meet Mr. Hodgson!/
SKIMBLE (8)
 232 Skimble   3   Night Mail's ready to depart,/Saying 'Skimble where is Skimble has he gone to hunt
 232 Skimble   3   to depart,/Saying 'Skimble where is Skimble has he gone to hunt the thimble?/We
 232 Skimble   7   are searching high and low,/Saying 'Skimble where is Skimble for unless he's very
 232 Skimble   7   and low,/Saying 'Skimble where is Skimble for unless he's very nimble/Then the
 232 Skimble   11   are frantic to a man —/Then Skimble will appear and he'll saunter to the
 232 Skimble   17   /You may say that by and large it is Skimble who's in charge/Of the Sleeping Car
 232 Skimble   28   riot, so the folk are very quiet/When Skimble is about and on the move./You can
 233 Skimble   44   and was ready to remind him./For Skimble won't let anything go wrong./And
SKIMBLE'S (1)
 233 Skimble   43   morning tea weak or strong?'/But Skimble's just behind him and was ready to
SKIMBLESHANKS (4)
 232 Skimble   t   Bustopher Jones wears white spats!/Skimbleshanks: the Railway Cat/There's a
 232 Skimble   29   move./You can play no pranks with Skimbleshanks!/He's a Cat that cannot be
 232 Skimble   32   wrong on the Northern Mail/When Skimbleshanks is aboard./Oh it's very pleasant
 233 Skimble   62   there you do not have to wait —/For Skimbleshanks will help you to get out!/He
SKIN (7)
  52 Whispers   2   death/And saw the skull beneath the skin;/And breastless creatures under ground/
 230 Bust Jones   1   About Town/Bustopher Jones is *not* skin and bones —/In fact, he's remarkably fat./
 606 Narcissus   37   came./As he embraced them his white skin surrendered itself to the redness of blood,
 270 MC Chorus   7   the viper, the mobile hard insensitive skin of the elephant, the evasive flank of the
 276 MC Chorus   17   the stone from the stone, take the skin from the arm, take the muscle from the
 294 FR   Harry   23   slow stain sinks deeper through the skin/Tainting the flesh and discolouring the
 327 FR   Harry   21   is the filthiness. I can clean my skin,/Purify my life, void my mind,/But always

SKIRTS (3)

16 Prufrock	102	the novels, after the teacups, after the skirts that trail along the floor —/And this, and
27 Morning	7	tear from a passer-by with muddy skirts/An aimless smile that hovers in the air/
210 Old Gumbie	8	in bed and asleep,/She tucks up her skirts to the basement to creep./She is deeply

SKULL (6)

52 Whispers	2	possessed by death/And saw the skull beneath the skin;/And breastless creatures
91 Ash-Wed 2	4	contained/In the hollow round of my skull. And God said/Shall these bones live? shall
588 Fable	56	pages,/His mouth an apple held, his skull held sausages./Over their Christmas
257 MC Tempts	2	the ear, or a sudden shock on the skull./{C} A man may walk with a lamp at
272 MC Chorus	16	the fingers,/Than when splitting in the skull./More than footfall in the passage,/More
280 MC Priest3	30	/In the small circle of pain within the skull/You still shall tramp and tread one endless

SKULLS (1)

270 MC Chorus	14	/In our veins our bowels our skulls as well/As well as in the plottings of

SKY (13)

13 Prufrock	2	the evening is spread out against the sky/Like a patient etherised upon a table;/Let us
103 Journ Magi	24	darkness,/And three trees on the low sky./And an old white horse galloped away in
135 5FingerEx2	3	tree was crookt and dry./In a black sky, from a green cloud/Natural forces shriek'd
141 Rannoch	3	Between the soft moor/And the soft sky, scarcely room/To leap or soar. Substance
149 Rock 1 m	94	*is silhouetted against the dim sky. From farther/away, they are answered by*
223 Pekes Pols	58	took warning./He looked at the sky and he gave a great leap —/And they every
592 Grad 3	4	/Some to the western limits of the sky/Which the sun stains with many a splendid
243 MC Chorus	17	wind, and bitter the sea, and grey the sky, grey grey grey./O Thomas, return,
244 MC Chorus	30	set the white sail between the grey sky and the bitter sea, leave us, leave us for
256 MC Chorus	7	heavy and thick./Thick and heavy the sky. And the earth presses up against our feet./
257 MC Chorus	23	flowing under our feet and over the sky;/Under doors and down chimneys, flowing
275 MC Chorus	21	/{C} Clear the air! clean the sky! wash the wind! take stone from stone and
276 MC Chorus	17	is wholly foul./Clear the air! clean the sky! wash the wind! take the stone from the

SLAIN (1)

108 Animula	36	/Pray for Floret, by the boarhound slain between the yew trees,/Pray for us now

SLANDER (2)

576 ES Gomez	35	to know something about the law of slander./Here's Mrs. Carghill, a reliable witness.
576 ES Charles	37	enough about the law of libel and slander./To know that you are hardly likely to

SLANT (1)

136 5FingerEx3	3	of the morning quake,/The dawn is slant across the lawn,/Here is no eft or mortal

SLANTING (1)

269 MC Chorus	30	owls, have seen at noon/Scaly wings slanting over, huge and ridiculous. I have tasted

SLANTS (1)

166 Rock 10	21	touch at morning,/The light that slants upon our western doors at evening,/The

SLAP (1)

235 Ad-dress	32	chuck him underneath the chin/Or slap his back or shake his paw,/And he will

SLAUGHTER (1)

429 CP Alex	4	By convincing the heathen/That the slaughter of monkeys has put a curse on them/

SLAUGHTERED (1)

429 CP Alex	7	—/Who, after all, prefer not to be slaughtered —/To relapse into heathendom. So,

SLAUGHTERING (1)

429 CP Alex	5	them/Which can only be removed by slaughtering the Christians./They have even

SLED (1)

61 WL: Burial	14	/My cousin's, he took me out on a sled,/And I was frightened. He said, Marie,/

SLEEK (1)

52 Whispers	25	cat;/Grishkin has a maisonnette;/The sleek Brazilian jaguar/Does not in its arboreal

SLEEP (21)

26 Rhapsody	77	the wall,/Put your shoes at the door, sleep, prepare for life.'/The last twist of the
49 Hippopot	22	/The hippopotamus's day/Is passed in sleep; at night he hunts;/God works in a
49 Hippopot	24	a mysterious way —/The Church can sleep and feed at once./I saw the 'potamus take
94 Ash-Wed 4	14	/One who moves in the time between sleep and waking, wearing/White light folded,
109 Marina	21	leaves and hurrying feet/Under sleep, where all the waters meet./Bowsprit
135 5FingerEx2	15	up my prior paws,/Pause, and sleep endlessly./*Lines to a Duck in the Park*/The
140 Usk	5	not spell/Old enchantments. Let them sleep./'Gently dip, but not too deep',/Lift your
167 Rock 10	38	of distraction or concentration, we sleep and are glad to sleep,/Controlled by the
167 Rock 10	38	we sleep and are glad to sleep,/Controlled by the rhythm of blood and
177 FQ: ECoker	22	refracted, by grey stone./The dahlias sleep in the empty silence./Wait for the early
221 Old Deut	33	and French Horn for his afternoon sleep;/And when the men say: 'There's just time
248 MC Thomas	13	the undesirable,/Voices under sleep, waking a dead world,/So that the mind
254 MC Tempt4	28	at the angles of stairs,/And between sleep and waking, early in the morning,/When
276 MC Chorus	4	action,/The terror by day that ends in sleep;/But the talk in the market-place, the hand

293 FR	Harry	38	events. You have gone through life in sleep,/Never woken to the nightmare. I tell you,
295 FR	Harry	26	/Then I recovered. I am afraid of sleep:/A condition in which one can be caught
311 FR	Harry	18	sleepless hunters/That will not let me sleep. At the moment before sleep/I always see
311 FR	Harry	18	let me sleep. At the moment before sleep/I always see their claws distended/Quietly,
315 FR	Harry	3	sickness:/Murder a reversal of sleep and waking./Murder was there. Your
326 FR	Harry	10	strange how the old/Can drop off to sleep in the middle of calamity/Like children, or
336 FR	Agatha	2	that unfulfilled craving/Flattered in sleep, and deceived in waking./You have a long

SLEEPER (1)

| 205 de la Mare | | 24 | the nocturnal traveller can arouse/No sleeper by his call; or when by chance/An empty |

SLEEPING (8)

103 Journ Magi		18	end we preferred to travel all night,/Sleeping in snatches,/With the voices singing in
213 Growltiger		31	/And his raffish crew were sleeping in their barrels and their bunks —/As
232 Skimble		18	it is Skimble who's in charge/Of the Sleeping Car Express./From the driver and the
233 Skimble		57	up and down the station;/You were sleeping all the while he was busy at Carlisle,/
257 MC Chorus		22	/Building a partial shelter,/For sleeping, and eating and drinking and laughter./
297 FR Gerald		23	that we knew it also./Why not let sleeping dogs lie?/{C} All the same, there's a
321 FR Warburt		8	want to know is, whether you've been sleeping ... {}/[*Enter* DENMAN]/{D} It's
572 ES Ld Clav		5	I least expected, between waking and sleeping,/A voice that whispered, 'you didn't

SLEEPING-CAR (1)

| 459 CC Lady E | | 29 | today. I shall go and rest now./In a sleeping-car it is quite impossible/To get one's |

SLEEPINGTIME (2)

| 206 To my Wife | | 3 | rhythm that governs the repose of our sleepingtime,/The breathing in unison/Of lovers |
| 522 ES dedic | | 3 | *rhythm that governs the repose of our sleepingtime,/The breathing in unison/Of lovers ...* |

SLEEPLESS (1)

| 311 FR Harry | | 17 | /They are roused again, the sleepless hunters/That will not let me sleep. At |

SLEEPS (2)

| 15 Prufrock | | 75 | seas./And the afternoon, the evening, sleeps so peacefully!/Smoothed by long fingers,/ |
| 158 Rock 5 | | 10 | the gift of silence, and doze before he sleeps./But we are encompassed with snakes and |

SLEEPY (2)

| 39 Gerontion | | 73 | an old man driven by the Trades/To a sleepy corner./Tenants of the house,/Thoughts |
| 188 FQ: DrySal | | 138 | relax from grief into relief,/To the sleepy rhythm of a hundred hours./Fare |

SLEET (1)

| 164 Rock 9 | | 22 | of the slimy mud of words, out of the sleet and hail of verbal imprecisions,/ |

SLEEVE (1)

| 192 FQ: Little | | 56 | and always./Ash on an old man's sleeve/Is all the ash the burnt roses leave./Dust |

SLENDER (2)

| 97 Ash-Wed 5 | | 29 | /Will the veiled sister between the slender/Yew trees pray for those who offend her |
| 599 On a Port | | 10 | /Disturb her lips, or move the slender hands;/Her dark eyes keep their secrets |

SLEPT (2)

| 295 FR Harry | | 5 | the doctor very attentive./That night I slept heavily, alone./{A} Harry!/{C} You mustn't |
| 494 CC Lady E | | 1 | —/All through the night. I hardly slept at all./I wish that Colby, somehow, might |

SLICE (1)

| 31 Apollinax | | 22 | and Mrs. Cheetah/I remember a slice of lemon, and a bitten macaroon./Hysteria/ |

SLICK (2)

| 119 SP | Krum | 31 | /We like London fine./{Kr} Perfectly slick./{Du} Why don't you come and live here |
| 120 SP | Klip | 5 | /{Kl} You said it, Krum./London's a slick place, London's a swell place,/London's a |

SLIDE (3)

56 Swee Night		6	/The circles of the stormy moon/Slide westward toward the River Plate,/Death
175 FQ: BurntN		154	the burden,/Under the tension, slip, slide, perish,/Decay with imprecision, will not
188 FQ: DrySal		143	terminus,/While the narrowing rails slide together behind you;/And on the deck of

SLIDES (2)

| 13 Prufrock | | 24 | be time/For the yellow smoke that slides along the street/Rubbing its back upon |
| 178 FQ: ECoker | | 50 | at sea the dawn wind/Wrinkles and slides. I am here/Or there, or elsewhere. In my |

SLIGHT (3)

20 Portrait		85	returning as before/Except for a slight sensation of being ill at ease/I mount the
323 FR Warburt		12	seen him/And says it's nothing but a slight concussion,/But he mustn't be moved
326 FR Harry		19	everything/May be unimportant, a slight deviation/From some imaginary course

SLIGHTEST (4)

33 Conv Gal		15	/Giving our vagrant moods the slightest twist!/With your air indifferent and
319 FR Warburt		32	loved him;/There was never the slightest suspicion of scandal./{H} Scandal? who
454 CC Kaghan		8	Colby./Never allow Lucasta the slightest advantage/Or she'll exploit it. You
530 ES Ld Clav		14	a train for anywhere!/No, I've not the slightest longing for the life I've left —/Only

SLIGHTLY (2)

| 15 Prufrock | | 82 | /Though I have seen my head (grown slightly bald) brought in upon a platter,/I am no |
| 274 MC | | m 14 | *door is opened. The* KNIGHTS *enter, slightly tipsy*]/{3P} This way, my Lord! Quick. |

SLIME (1)
40 Burb Blei | 18 | eye/Stares from the protozoic slime/At a perspective of Canaletto./The smoky
SLIMY (2)
67 WL: Fire S | 188 | through the vegetation/Dragging its slimy belly on the bank/While I was fishing in
164 Rock 9 | 22 | of sound the life of music,/Out of the slimy mud of words, out of the sleet and hail of
SLINGSBY (1)
29 Aunt Helen | 1 | *Transcript.*'/Aunt Helen/Miss Helen Slingsby was my maiden aunt,/And lived in a
SLIP (7)
42 Swee Erect | 20 | of the bed/And clawing at the pillow slip./Sweeney addressed full length to shave/
175 FQ: BurntN | 154 | under the burden,/Under the tension, slip, slide, perish,/Decay with imprecision, will
257 MC Priests | 4 | may climb the stair in the day, and slip on a broken step./{4T} A man may sit at
367 CP Alex | 38 | door was open/And so I thought I'd slip in and see if anyone was with you./{P} Julia
419 CP m | 36 | to give your friends; {}/[*Writes on a slip of paper*]/{R} You had better let your family
461 CC Eggers | 7 | I'll be out in the garden./And I'll slip up to town any day, if you want me./In fact,
549 ES Carghil | 30 | to follow *that* man/He'd give you the slip: he's not to be trusted./That man is hollow'.
SLIPPED (6)
13 Prufrock | 20 | the soot that falls from chimneys,/Slipped by the terrace, made a sudden leap,/
24 Rhapsody | 39 | /So the hand of the child, automatic,/Slipped out and pocketed a toy that was
222 Pekes Pols | 16 | reason, but most people think/He'd slipped into the Wellington Arms for a drink —
307 FR Harry | 14 | my escape/As soon as I could, and slipped down to the river/To find the old hiding
322 FR Winch | 27 | perhaps disturb her Ladyship./So I slipped along on my bike. Mostly walking,/
412 CP Julia | 7 | the corner;/Waited a moment, and slipped in by the back way./I only came to tell
SLIPPER (1)
375 CP Edward | 19 | /But I don't really want cheese ... Slipper what? .../Oh, from Jugoslavia ... prunes
SLIPPERS (1)
68 WL: Fire S | 227 | are piled (at night her bed)/Stockings, slippers, camisoles, and stays./I Tiresias, old
SLIPPERY (3)
589 Fable | 70 | is a thing to be lamented sorely/Such slippery folk should be allowed about,/For
605 Narcissus | 25 | he knew that he had been a fish/With slippery white belly held tight in his own fingers,
550 ES Carghil | 16 | /But simple he was — not sly and slippery./Then I married Mr. Carghill. Twenty
SLIPS (4)
18 Portrait | 14 | room.'/— And so the conversation slips/Among velleities and carefully caught
24 Rhapsody | 36 | cat which flattens itself in the gutter,/Slips out its tongue/And devours a morsel of
56 Swee Night | 13 | cape/Tries to sit on Sweeney's knees/Slips and pulls the table cloth/Overturns a
600 Moonflower | 4 | sea;/A great white bird, a snowy owl,/Slips from the alder tree./Whiter the flowers,
SLITTED (1)
42 Swee Erect | 14 | /This withered root of knots of hair/Slitted below and gashed with eyes,/This oval O
SLOPES (1)
103 Journ Magi | 9 | we regretted/The summer palaces on slopes, the terraces,/And the silken girls
SLOTH (2)
152 Rock 2 | 28 | past we suffer the consequence:/For sloth, for avarice, gluttony, neglect of the Word
163 Rock 8 | 37 | Not avarice, lechery, treachery,/Envy, sloth, gluttony, jealousy, pride:/It was not these
SLOTTED (1)
92 Ash-Wed 3 | 13 | first turning of the third stair/Was a slotted window bellied like the fig's fruit/And
SLOW (11)
139 Virginia | 2 | /Virginia/Red river, red river,/Slow flow heat is silence/No will is still as a
173 FQ: BurntN | 98 | shadow into transient beauty/With slow rotation suggesting permanence/Nor
186 FQ: DrySal | 66 | devotionless,/In a drifting boat with a slow leakage,/The silent listening to the
221 Old Deut | 46 | /My legs may be tottery, I must go slow/And be careful of Old Deuteronomy!'/Of
592 Grad 4 | 1 | /Although the path be tortuous and slow,/Although it bristle with a thousand fears,/
598 Circe | 12 | lies;/The peacocks walk, stately and slow,/And they look at us with the eyes/Of men
294 FR Harry | 23 | of one's own automatism/While the slow stain sinks deeper through the skin/
310 FR Mary | 4 | root/The agony in the dark/The slow flow throbbing the trunk/The pain of the
325 FR Ivy | 28 | /Somehow, just because he *was* the slow one./He was always the one to fall off the
349 FR Agatha | 13 | *spoken in the dark*.]/{Ag} A curse is slow in coming/To complete fruition/It cannot
428 CP Julia | 5 | /And I had to travel in a very slow train/And in a *couchette*. She was very
SLOWLY (9)
19 Portrait | 46 | is, you who hold it in your hands';/(Slowly twisting the lilac stalks)/'You let it flow
40 Burb Blei | 7 | /Passed seaward with the passing bell/Slowly: the God Hercules/Had left him, that
180 FQ: ECoker | 120 | /And the conversation rises and slowly fades into silence/And you see behind
216 Jellicles | 13 | Moon to rise./Jellicle Cats develop slowly,/Jellicle Cats are not too big;/Jellicle Cats
301 FR Chorus | 32 | about the sudden thrombosis/And the slowly hardening artery./We like to be thought
349 FR 4m | 13 | AGATHA/*and* MARY *walk slowly in single file round and round the table*,
360 CP Reilly | 16 | you, if I may .../Strong ... but sip it slowly ... and drink it sitting down./Breathe
361 CP Reilly | 34 | you're not aware. It will come to you slowly:/When you wake in the morning, when

536 ES   Gomez   8   myself by a sudden effort,/You, so slowly and sweetly, that you've never woken up/
SLUGGISH (2)
136 5FingerEx3   5   is no eft or mortal snake/But only sluggish duck and drake./I have seen the
598 Circe   11   below,/Along the garden stairs/The sluggish python lies;/The peacocks walk, stately
SLY (1)
550 ES   Carghil   16   a weakling,/But simple he was — not sly and slippery./Then I married Mr. Carghill.
SMALL (35)
29 Aunt Helen   2   was my maiden aunt,/And lived in a small house near a fashionable square/Cared for
38 Gerontion   61   closer contact?/These with a thousand small deliberations/Protract the profit of their
40 Burb Blei   2   crossed a little bridge/Descending at a small hotel;/Princess Volupine arrived,/They
68 WL: Fire S   232   young man carbuncular, arrives,/A small house agent's clerk, with one bold stare,/
90 Ash-Wed 1   36   air/The air which is now thoroughly small and dry/Smaller and dryer than the will/
107 Animula   22   and the drug of dreams/Curl up the small soul in the window seat/Behind the
109 Marina   20   and nearer than the eye/Whispers and small laughter between leaves and hurrying feet/
117 SP   Dusty   9   what's that mean?/{Du} (*reading*) 'A small sum of money, or a present/Of wearing
129 Cor2 State   34   the breast feather stirred by the small wind after noon/There the cyclamen
129 Cor2 State   47   sweep of the little bat's wing, with the small flare of the firefly or lightning bug,/
129 Cor2 State   48   and falling, crowned with dust', the small creatures,/The small creatures chirp thinly
129 Cor2 State   49   with dust', the small creatures,/The small creatures chirp thinly through the dust,
167 Rock 10   28   /The light of altar and of sanctuary;/Small lights of those who meditate at midnight/
202 War Poetry   11   /Experience is too large, or too small. Our emotions/Are only 'incidents'/In the
216 Jellicles   6   and white,/Jellicle Cats are rather small;/Jellicle Cats are merry and bright,/And
216 Jellicles   30   and white,/Jellicle Cats (as I said) are small;/If it happens to be a stormy night/They
223 Pekes Pols   50   Brigade./When suddenly, up from a small basement flat,/Why who should stalk out
224 Mr Mistoff   23   Mr. Mistoffelees!/He is quiet and small, he is black/From his ears to the tip of his
244 MC Chorus   28   do you realise what it means/To the small folk drawn into the pattern of fate,
244 MC Chorus   28   drawn into the pattern of fate, the small folk who live among small things,/The
244 MC Chorus   28   of fate, the small folk who live among small things,/The strain on the brain of the
244 MC Chorus   29   things,/The strain on the brain of the small folk who stand to the doom of the house,
245 MC Thomas   37   for all your kind attentions./These are small matters. Little rest in Canterbury/With
280 MC   Priest3   30   bite your nails in Aquitaine./In the small circle of pain within the skull/You still
326 FR   Harry   18   of each thing separately,/Making small things important, so that everything/May
349 FR   1m 13   *door, AGATHA and MARY, and set a small portable table./From another door, enter*
399 CP   Nurse   7   o'clock./He is to be shown into the small waiting-room;/And you will see him
399 CP   Nurse   19   The third one to be shown into the small room;/And I need not let you know that
453 CC Lucasta   33   /{L} B., you're a beast. I've a very small appetite./But the point is, that I'm
483 CC   Colby   4   limit my acquaintance to a very small number,/And I don't know where to find
485 CC   Colby   31   /Was it a large house?/{C} No, a very small one./{LE} But you had your aunt. And
515 CC Guzzard   25   you claim him. Do you think it is a small thing/For me, to see my life's ambition
517 CC   Eggers   38   I'd like to apply./{E} The stipend is small —/Very small, I'm afraid. Not enough to
517 CC   Eggers   39   /{E} The stipend is small —/Very small, I'm afraid. Not enough to live on./We'll
531 ES   Ld Clav   24   /And our closest associates, the small minority/Of those who really understand
SMALLER (2)
90 Ash-Wed 1   37   is now thoroughly small and dry/Smaller and dryer than the will/Teach us to care
261 MC Thomas   14   the Passion of Our Lord; so also, in a smaller figure, we/both rejoice and mourn in the
SMALLPOX (1)
24 Rhapsody   56   has lost her memory./A washed-out smallpox cracks her face,/Her hand twists a
SMART (5)
65 WL: Chess   142   coming back, make yourself a bit smart./He'll want to know what you done with
218 Mung Rump   18   cat-burglars as well, and remarkably smart at a smash-and-grab./They made their
229 Gus   48   troupe,/And they think they are smart, just to jump through a hoop.'/And he'll
236 Cat Morgan   10   got a good coat, and I keep meself smart;/And everyone says, and I guess that's
322 FR   Winch   33   in the fog, coming along/At a pretty smart pace, I fancy, ran into a lorry/Drawn up
SMARTEST (2)
228 Gus   7   /Yet he was, in his youth, quite the smartest of Cats —/But no longer a terror to
230 Bust Jones   9   back./In the whole of St. James's the smartest of names is/The name of this Brummell
SMASH (2)
219 Mung Rump   34   /And when you heard a dining-room smash/Or up from the pantry there came a loud
328 FR Charles   11   /[*reads*]./{C} '*Peer's Brother in Motor Smash*/The Hon. Arthur Gerald Charles Piper,
SMASH-AND-GRAB (1)
218 Mung Rump   18   as well, and remarkably smart at a smash-and-grab./They made their home in
SMEARED (1)
275 MC Chorus   27   its common things, and see them all smeared with blood, through a curtain of falling

18 Portrait   1 drown./Portrait of a Lady/Among the smoke and fog of a December afternoon/You
21 Portrait   117 leave me sitting pen in hand/With the smoke coming down above the housetops;/
64 WL: Chess   92 prolonged candle-flames,/Flung their smoke into the laquearia,/Stirring the pattern
181 FQ: ECoker   168 /Of which the flame is roses, and the smoke is briars./The dripping blood our only
193 FQ: Little   87 /Between three districts whence the smoke arose/I met one walking, loitering and
294 FR   Harry   16   in a crowded desert/In a thick smoke, many creatures moving/Without
300 FRDowning   19 place where a man can go/For a quiet smoke, where the women can't follow him./She
542 ES   Gomez   7 Cuba/If your doctors allow you a smoke now and then./I'm a lonely man, Dick,
SMOKED (1)
30 Cous Nancy   7 the cow-pasture./Miss Nancy Ellicott smoked/And danced all the modern dances;/
SMOKEFALL (1)
173 FQ: BurntN   90   moment in the draughty church at smokefall/Be remembered; involved with past
SMOKING (1)
542 ES   Gomez   35   sudden silence when you enter the smoking room./Don't forget, Dick:/You *didn't*
SMOKY (5)
21 Portrait   115 some afternoon,/Afternoon grey and smoky, evening yellow and rose;/Should die and
22 Preludes   4 /Six o'clock./The burnt-out ends of smoky days./And now a gusty shower wraps/
40 Burb Blei   20 /At a perspective of Canaletto./The smoky candle end of time/Declines. On the
154 Rock 3   21 /What shall be done to the shore of smoky ships?/Will you leave my people forgetful
335 FR   Harry   24 my feet/Among inner shadows in the smoky wilderness,/Trying to avoid the clasping
SMOOTH (3)
24 Rhapsody   26 twisted branch upon the beach/Eaten smooth, and polished/As if the world gave up/
211 Old Gumbie   27   the window-sill, or anything that's smooth and flat:/She sits and sits and sits and
270 MC Chorus   1 the thick light of dawn. I have eaten/Smooth creatures still living, with the strong salt
SMOOTHED (1)
15 Prufrock   76   the evening, sleeps so peacefully!/Smoothed by long fingers,/Asleep ... tired ... or
SMOOTHES (1)
69 WL: Fire S   255   about her room again, alone,/She smoothes her hair with automatic hand,/And
SMOOTHLY (1)
605 Narcissus   9 the wind made him aware of his limbs smoothly passing each other/And of his arms
SMOOTHNESS (1)
606 Narcissus   31 own whiteness/The horror of his own smoothness,/And he felt drunken and old./So he
SMOOTHS (1)
24 Rhapsody   54   eye,/She smiles into corners./She smooths the hair of the grass./The moon has
SMYRNA (1)
68 WL: Fire S   209 of a winter noon/Mr. Eugenides, the Smyrna merchant/Unshaven, with a pocket full
SNAKE (4)
136 5FingerEx3   4   the lawn,/Here is no eft or mortal snake/But only sluggish duck and drake./I have
166 Rock 10   7 on to conquer the World?/The great snake lies ever half awake, at the bottom of the
166 Rock 10   11 worshippers, self-given sacrifice of the snake. Take/Your way and be ye separate./Be
226 Macavity   15 side to side, with movements like a snake;/And when you think he's half asleep,
SNAKES (3)
158 Rock 5   5 of which the use is forgotten: are like snakes that lie on mouldering stairs, content in
158 Rock 5   11 sleeps./But we are encompassed with snakes and dogs: therefore some must labour,
160 Rock 7   5 led them to darkness,/Worshipping snakes or trees, worshipping devils rather than
SNAP (3)
24 Rhapsody   32 has left/Hard and curled and ready to snap./Half-past two,/The street-lamp said,/
253 MC Tempt4   12 to lend./You would wait for trap to snap/Having served your turn, broken and
383 CP   Edward   4 looked in your bag? ... Well, don't snap my head off .../You're sure, in the kitchen?
SNAPPED (1)
141 Rannoch   10   is strong/Beyond the bone. Pride snapped,/Shadow of pride is long, in the long
SNAPPERS (1)
223 Pekes Pols   34 /And his braw Scottish cousins are snappers and biters,/And every dog-jack of
SNAPPIEST (1)
602 Humoresque   15   spectres, set him there;/'The snappiest fashion since last spring's,/'The
SNARL (1)
72 WL: Thund   344   /But red sullen faces sneer and snarl/From doors of mudcracked houses/If
SNARLED (1)
42 Swee Erect   4 bold anfractuous rocks/Faced by the snarled and yelping seas./Display me Aeolus
SNATCH (1)
280 MC Priest3   26 /To share his filthy rites, and try to snatch/Forgetfulness in his libidinous courts,/
SNATCHED (1)
578 ES   Michael   27   nose in a book./And once, Mother snatched a book away from you/And tossed it

SOAR (2)
141 Rannoch   4 the soft sky, scarcely room/To leap or soar. Substance crumbles, in the thin air/Moon
246 MC Thomas   17 little time the hungry hawk/Will only soar and hover, circling lower,/Waiting excuse,
SOARS (2)
147 Rock 1   1 Choruses from 'The Rock'/The Eagle soars in the summit of Heaven,/The Hunter
250 MC Tempt2   8 I leave you to your fate./Your sin soars sunward, covering kings' falcons./{T}
SOBBING (1)
296 FR   Harry   9 /Dimly — as you once explained the sobbing in the chimney/The evil in the dark
SOBER (2)
219 Mung Rump   32 the house like a hurricane, and no sober person could take his oath/Was it
330 FR   Harry   2 what he always was;/Arthur again be sober, though not for very long;/And everything
SOBERING (1)
313 FR   Charles 23 you know;/You should have a sobering effect upon him./After all, you're the
SOBERLY (1)
278 MC Knight2   3 I therefore ask you to consider soberly: what/were the Archbishop's aims? and
SOCIAL (5)
111 Xmas Trees   3 of which we may disregard:/The social, the torpid, the patently commercial,/The
278 MC Knight2   33 violence is the only way in/which social justice can be secured. At another time,
385 CP   Reilly   3 the same/Is a useful and convenient social convention/Which must sometimes be
409 CP   Reilly   36 could,/That he was aiming at a higher social distinction/Than the honour conferred by
536 ES   Gomez   5 *I* changed my name, there was no social ladder./It was jumping a gap — and you
SOCIALIST (1)
456 CC   Eggers   9 such a generous heart! He's rather a Socialist./I'm a staunch Conservative, myself./
SOCIALLY (1)
393 CP   Edward   40 busy or too tired/To be of use to you socially .../{L} I *never* complained./{E} No; and
SOCIÉTÉ (1)
127 Cor1 March   26 these the Scouts,/And now the *société gymnastique de Poissy*/And now come the
SOCIETY (9)
 44 Cook Egg   17 Exchequer Bond./I shall not want Society in Heaven,/Lucretia Borgia shall be my
159 Rock 6   12 /As you can boast in the way of polite society/Will hardly survive the Faith to which
256 MC Tempts   23 of his own greatness,/The enemy of society, enemy of himself./{3P} O Thomas my
290 FR   Amy   4 /To expensive hotels and undesirable society/Which she could choose herself. She
369 CP   Edward   16 discoveries;/Celia's, to provide society and fashion./Lavinia always had the
369 CP   Peter   31 thought of her merely as a name/In a society column, to find her there alone./
482 CC   Lady E   15 /They ever meet in their kind of society./So naturally, they want to take you up./
482 CC   Lady E   34 is./And, second, you need intellectual society./Now, that already limits your
534 ES   Gomez   13 same standards of morality/As the society in which I find myself./I do nothing in
SOCKETS (1)
 52 Whispers   6 bulbs instead of balls/Stared from the sockets of the eyes!/He knew that thought clings
SODA (2)
 67 WL: Fire S   201 her daughter/They wash their feet in soda water/Et O ces voix d'enfants, chantant
535 ES   Ld Clav   6 will you bring in the whisky. And soda./{L} Very good, my Lord./{G} And some
SODDEN (2)
172 FQ: BurntN   60 the figured leaf/And hear upon the sodden floor/Below, the boarhound and the
191 FQ: Little   2 is its own season/Sempiternal though sodden towards sundown,/Suspended in time,
SOFA (2)
305 FR   Harry   28 ... even the table,/The chairs, the sofa ... all in the same positions./I was looking
366 CP   Julia   3 /Just turn out the bottom of that sofa —/No, this chair. Look under the cushion./
SOFT (6)
 13 Prufrock   21 sudden leap,/And seeing that it was a soft October night,/Curled once about the
121 SA Sweeney   16 eat you!/In a nice little, white little, soft little, tender little,/Juicy little, right little,
141 Rannoch   2 stag/Breeds for the rifle. Between the soft moor/And the soft sky, scarcely room/To
141 Rannoch   3 rifle. Between the soft moor/And the soft sky, scarcely room/To leap or soar.
159 Rock 6   19 hard, and hard where they like to be soft./She tells them of Evil and Sin, and other
275 MC Chorus   25 /How how can I ever return, to the soft quiet seasons?/Night stay with us, stop sun,
SOFTEN (1)
228 Gus   27 could fail./I'd a voice that would soften the hardest of hearts,/Whether I took the
SOFTLY (6)
 67 WL: Fire S   176 are departed./Sweet Thames, run softly, till I end my song./The river bears no
 67 WL: Fire S   183 down and wept .../Sweet Thames, run softly till I end my song,/Sweet Thames, run
 67 WL: Fire S   184 till I end my song,/Sweet Thames, run softly, for I speak not loud or long./But at my
 67 WL: Fire S   187 spread from ear to ear./A rat crept softly through the vegetation/Dragging its slimy
345 FR   Charles 36 I'm getting old:/Old age came softly up to now. I felt safe enough;/And now I
526 ES   Monica   8 did this come, Charles? It crept so softly/On silent feet, and stood behind my back/

SOIL (5)
190 FQ: DrySal 237   the yew-tree)/The life of significant soil./Little Gidding/Midwinter spring is its own
193 FQ: Little   68   upper hand./The parched eviscerate soil/Gapes at the vanity of toil,/Laughs without
203 Indians   14   bravely/At one with his destiny, that soil is his./Let his village remember./This was
270 MC Chorus   5   of the sponge. I have lain in the soil and criticised the worm. In the air/Flirted
281 MC Chorus   12   wolf and the lamb; the worm in the soil and the worm in the belly./Therefore man,

SOILED (4)
 23 Preludes   38   soles of feet/In the palms of both soiled hands./His soul stretched tight across the
257 MC Chorus   23   some hope; but now a new terror has soiled us, which none can avert, none can avoid,
267 MC Thomas   15   be worn/Carefully, so it get not soiled or torn./Have you something to say?/
276 MC Chorus   14   eternity of evil and wrong./We are soiled by a filth that we cannot clean, united to

SOLD (1)
154 Rock 3   5   in the mazes of your ingenuities,/Sold by the proceeds of your proper inventions:/

SOLDATS (1)
128 Cor1 March   51   you/Give us a light?/Light/Light/*Et les soldats faisaient la haie? ILS LA FAISAIENT.*/

SOLE (1)
437 CP   Reilly 7   *in the garden./That apparition, sole of men, he saw./For know there are two*

SOLEIL (1)
 51 Restaurant   4   temps pluvieux,/Du vent, du grand soleil, et de la pluie;/C'est ce qu'on appelle le

SOLELY (1)
261 MC Thomas   20   he is a Christian: for that would be solely to/mourn. We do not think of him simply

SOLEMN (2)
 84 Hollow Men   27   wind's singing/More distant and more solemn/Than a fading star./Let me be no nearer
178 FQ: ECoker   36   flames, or joined in circles,/Rustically solemn or in rustic laughter/Lifting heavy feet in

SOLES (1)
 23 Preludes   37   from your hair,/Or clasped the yellow soles of feet/In the palms of both soiled hands./

SOLICITOR (2)
 74 WL: Thund   408   /Or under seals broken by the lean solicitor/In our empty rooms/DA/*Dayadhvam:*
343 FR   Amy   28   and patient calculations/With the solicitor, the broker, agent? Why should I?/It is

SOLICITORS (2)
394 CP Lavinia   5   complained/Of seeing nobody but solicitors and clients .../{E} And you were never
424 CP Edward   21   a quiet day./Two consultations with solicitors/On quite straightforward cases. It's

SOLID (1)
248 MC Tempt2   34   to God alone./Shall he who held the solid substance/Wander waking with deceitful

SOLIDEST (1)
480 CC Kaghan   31   in the City,/On the boards of all the solidest companies:/Because I've no background

SOLITARY (1)
331 FR Agatha   39   unusual weakness,/The diffidence of a solitary man:/Where he was weak he recognised

SOLITUDE (10)
 72 WL: Thund   343   without rain/There is not even solitude in the mountains/But red sullen faces
 98 Ash-Wed 6   21   between dying and birth/The place of solitude where three dreams cross/Between blue
174 FQ: BurntN   118   only/Into the world of perpetual solitude,/World not world, but that which is not
294 FR   Harry   15   our understanding./{H} The sudden solitude in a crowded desert/In a thick smoke,
340 FR   Agatha   7   had./What did I get? thirty years of solitude,/Alone, among women, in a women's
379 CP   Peter   36   different/From company or solitude. And we sometimes had tea/And once
413 CP   Celia   38   is the first?/{C} An awareness of solitude./But that sounds so flat. I don't mean
419 CP   Reilly   4   ways avoid the final desolation/Of solitude in the phantasmal world/Of
470 CC   Colby   14   playing./But with you, it was neither solitude nor ... people./{L} I'm glad I'm not
528 ES Charles   2   any better reason than his fear of solitude?/{M} The second reason is exactly the

SOLUTION (7)
355 CP   Julia   36   Tony was the product, but not the solution./He only made the situation more
428 CP   Edward   32   indeed: we are anxious to learn the solution./{A} I'm not sure that there *is* any
428 CP   Alex   33   /{A} I'm not sure that there *is* any solution./But even this does not bring us to the
449 CC   Eggers   14   him! Yes, indeed,/That would be the solution. Yes, quite ideal./{SC} I'm glad you
449 CC   Eggers   33   wants to adopt him —/An admirable solution — then what follows?/Will you let her
497 CC   Claude   29   Colby/Who is not satisfied with that solution./He insists upon the facts. And that is
499 CC Lucasta   25   obvious/That this would be the ideal solution/From your point of view. To get me off

SOLVE (1)
579 ES Carghil   33   always the right person, Richard,/To solve a son's problems. Sometimes an outsider,/

SOLVED (2)
184 FQ: DrySal   6   builder of bridges./The problem once solved, the brown god is almost forgotten/By
574 ES Carghil   24   is so happy — all his problems are solved;/And he was so perplexed, poor lamb.

SOMBRE (2)
187 FQ: DrySal   124   /To lay a course by: but in the sombre season/Or the sudden fury, is what it
239 MC Chorus   9   /Since golden October declined into sombre November/And the apples were

SOME (221)
SOMEBODY (15)

225	Mr Mistoff	48	the roof —/(At least we all *heard* that somebody purred)/Which is incontestable proof
297 FR	Charles	18	what he's likely to do/Until there's somebody he wants to get rid of./{G} Even so,
327 FR	Ivy	26	/{G} Why, what's the matter./{I} Somebody, look for Arthur in the evening
359 CP	Edward	34	go yet./I very much want to talk to somebody;/And it's easier to talk to a person
360 CP	Reilly	40	re-marry/To prove to the world that somebody wanted you;/If another woman, you
391 CP	Lavinia	22	someone else is running it./But who? Somebody is always interfering .../I don't feel
394 CP	Lavinia	14	/{L} And on several occasions, when somebody was coming/Whom I particularly
394 CP	Lavinia	25	of the danger,/Yet something, or somebody, compelled me to come./And why did
429 CP	Julia	35	you know — or knew .../{J} Edward!/Somebody must have walked over my grave:/
469 CC	Lucasta	20	in my life?/I only go to shows when somebody invites me,/And no one has ever
539 ES	Gomez	36	which I went to Oxford./As it is, I'm somebody — a more important man/In San
540 ES	Gomez	25	/When I said 'Dick, you've run over somebody'/Wouldn't you have shown it, if only
548 ES	Carghil	26	the great Lord Claverton, aren't you?/Somebody said you were coming here —/It's
555 ES	Ld Clav	24	I've lived in terror of his running over somebody./{M} Why, Father, should you not
559 ES	Michael	15	I want to make money./I want to be somebody on my own account./{LC} But what

SOMEBODY'S (2)

125 SA	Sweeney	28	gona stay and we're gona go/And somebody's gotta pay the rent/{Do} I know who
560 ES	Michael	27	in a breach of promise suit/Or somebody's divorce. No, you needn't worry/

SOMEHOW (9)

19 Portrait		52	/'Yet with these April sunsets, that somehow recall/My buried life, and Paris in the
325 FR	Ivy	28	was the one that had the accidents,/Somehow, just because he *was* the slow one./He
389 CP	Lavinia	34	/I'm sure that we shall manage somehow, thank you,/As we have in the past./
413 CP	Celia	23	going through, these last weeks,/I somehow took it for granted that I needn't
438 CP	Edward	17	terribly wrong,/And the rest of us are somehow involved in the wrong,/I should only
440 CP	Edward	9	that life is only keeping on;/And somehow, the two ideas seem to fit together./{L}
494 CC	Lady E	2	hardly slept at all./I wish that Colby, somehow, might prove to be *your* son/Instead
500 CC	Lucasta	26	safe. And that's what I want./And somehow or other, I've something to give him
582 ES	Charles	37	and despite those people,/Because somehow we'd begun to belong together,/And

SOMEONE (41)

33 Conv Gal		7	then: 'How you digress!'/And I then: 'Someone frames upon the keys/That exquisite
57 Swee Night		33	a golden grin;/The host with someone indistinct/Converses at the door apart,
125 SA	Chorus	34	middle of the bed and/you wake like someone hit you in the head/You've had a
193 FQ: Little		102	the same,/Knowing myself yet being someone other —/And he a face still forming;
228 Gus		13	pub)/He loves to regale them, if someone else pays,/With anecdotes drawn from
229 Gus		35	the Fiend of the Fell.'/Then, if someone will give him a toothful of gin,/He will
287 FR	Mary	8	the younger generation, you must ask someone else./I'm afraid that I don't deserve the
291 FR	Amy	7	/{A} What's that? I thought I saw someone pass the window./What time is it?/{C}
291 FR	Amy	11	at least, if not Arthur. Hark, there is someone coming:/Yes, it must be John. {}/[*Enter*
296 FR	Charles	28	fortune./I believe that all he needs is someone to talk to,/To get it off his mind. I'll
309 FR	Harry	31	staid in England, yet you seem/Like someone who comes from a very long distance,/
310 FR	Harry	32	I had been always here/And you were someone who had come from a long distance./
311 FR	Harry	31	/Of a dreaming age, when I was someone else/Thinking of something else, puts
361 CP	Edward	18	wanted to relieve my mind/By telling someone what I'd been concealing./I don't think
371 CP	Peter	2	Your congratulations. I had to talk to someone./And I have been telling you of
372 CP	Peter	6	sure that she would listen to you/As someone disinterested./{E} Well, I will see Celia.
376 CP	Edward	1	bother! {}/[*Exit* CELIA]/{E} Suppose someone came and found you in the kitchen? {}/
379 CP	Edward	2	his name *is* Reilly!/{E} It would need someone greater than the greatest doctor/To
384 CP	Reilly	22	is this: it is a serious matter/To bring someone back from the dead./{E} From the
388 CP	Peter	16	nice of you to say so;/But you'll find someone better, to go about with./{C} I don't
389 CP	Celia	32	I should like you to remember me/As someone who wants you and Edward to be
391 CP	Lavinia	21	like a machine —/Or if it's a machine, someone else is running it./But who? Somebody
408 CP	Reilly	7	first time in his life, fell in love with someone,/And with someone of whom you had
408 CP	Reilly	8	fell in love with someone,/And with someone of whom you had reason to be jealous.
413 CP	Reilly	7	call it —/And usually they think that someone else is to blame./{C} I at least have no
416 CP	Celia	4	but of emptiness, of failure/Towards someone, or something, outside of myself;/And
429 CP	Alex	33	I think I ought to tell you/About someone you know — or knew .../{J} Edward!/
433 CP	Peter	13	come if we invited you./But there's someone I wanted to ask about,/Who did really
472 CC	Lucasta	32	your mind to go into business/And be someone like Claude ... or B. I was sorry,/Very
474 CC	Colby	18	an alley/I should become aware of someone walking with me./That's the only way
477 CC	Lucasta	32	/And I thought, now, perhaps, if someone else sees me/As I really am, I might
504 CC	Lucasta	6	to answer the door./I've just let someone in. It's the Mrs. Guzzard/Whom you
504 CC	Lucasta	9	parlourmaid?/{L} I thought I heard someone singing in the pantry./{LE} Oh, I
526 ES	Monica	24	table;/There's the door ... and I hear someone coming:/It's Lambert with the tea ... {}

527 ES	Monica	26	with his papers/He needs to have someone else in the room with him,/Reading
527 ES	Monica	27	him,/Reading too — or just sitting — someone/Not occupied with anything that can't
527 ES	Monica	29	anything that can't be interrupted./Someone to make a remark to now and then./
535 ES	Gomez	18	to the point where you need to trust someone/You must make it worth his while to
557 ES	Ld Clav	5	spare you the necessity of blaming someone else./Just tell me what's happened./
582 ES	Ld Clav	3	freed from the self that pretends to be someone;/And in becoming no one, I begin to
582 ES	Ld Clav	7	more truly for knowing/That there is someone you love more than your father —/

SOMETHING (156)

31 Apollinax	20	must be unbalanced.' —/'There was something he said that I might have challenged.'
61 WL: Burial	27	of this red rock),/And I will show you something different from either/Your shadow at
62 WL: Burial	53	and this card,/Which is blank, is something he carries on his back,/Which I am
66 WL: Chess	150	will, I said./Oh is there, she said. Something o' that, I said./Then I'll know who
89 Ash-Wed 1	24	I rejoice, having to construct something/Upon which to rejoice/And pray to
134 Wind	6	of confusing strife/Is it a dream or something else/When the surface of the
136 5FingerEx4	10	by all waitresses/(They regard him as something apart)/While on his palate fine he
158 Rock 5	3	/Preserve me from the enemy who has something to gain: and from the friend who has
158 Rock 5	3	to gain: and from the friend who has something to lose./Remembering the words of
161 Rock 7	26	no other way./But it seems that something has happened that has never
163 Rock 8	31	in one place or another,/There was something left that was more than the tales/Of
181 FQ: ECoker	136	and birth./You say I am repeating/Something I have said before. I shall say it
187 FQ: DrySal	102	of many generations — not forgetting/Something that is probably quite ineffable:/The
190 FQ: DrySal	207	the saint —/No occupation either, but something given/And taken, in a lifetime's death
212 Growltiger	9	/The cottagers of Rotherhithe knew something of his fame;/At Hammersmith and
224 Mr Mistoff	14	again./The greatest magicians have something to learn/From Mr. Mistoffelees'
605 Narcissus	3	this gray rock,/And I will show you something different from either/Your shadow
267 MC Thomas	16	so it get not soiled or torn./Have you something to say?/{K1} By the King's
295 FR Harry	21	of all, you isolate the single event/As something so dreadful that it couldn't have
296 FR Gerald	33	needs./{G} Nevertheless, Amy, there's something in Violet's suggestion./Why not ring
299 FRDowning	40	nervous./He behaved as if he thought something might happen./{C} What sort of
303 FR Mary	20	a little while ago./{M} Well, there's something to be said for having an outsider;/
306 FR Harry	10	glad to be at home?/{H} There was something/I wanted to ask you. I don't know
308 FR Mary	16	are unconscious of it./You hoped for something, in coming back to Wishwood,/Or
308 FR Mary	26	Wishwood/To be your real self, to do something for you/That you can only do for
308 FR Mary	28	yourself./What you need to alter is something inside you/Which you can change
308 FR Harry	30	— here, as well as elsewhere./{H} Something inside me, you think, that can be
309 FR Harry	12	at this moment. I feel it is important./Something should have come of this
309 FR Mary	17	I haven't much experience,/But I see something now which doesn't come from tutors/
309 FR Mary	19	from thinking, or from observation:/Something which I did not know I knew./Even
311 FR Harry	32	when I was someone else/Thinking of something else, puts me among you./I tell you,
315 FR Harry	10	But cancer, now,/That is something real./{W} Well, let's not talk of such
317 FR Warburt	14	more difficult not to be prepared/For something that is very likely to happen./{H} O
318 FR Harry	34	deaf: and the others/Seem to hear something else than what I am saying./But if
318 FR Harry	36	want to talk, at least you can tell me/Something useful. Do you remember my father?
319 FR Harry	1	What you have to tell me/Is either something that I know already/Or unimportant,
321 FR Warburt	23	.../{W} Harry! Pull yourself together./Something may have happened to one of your
324 FR Violet	9	/I think that you might have had something to say./Aren't you sorry for your
327 FR Ivy	33	up tomorrow;/And he said there was something about it in the paper,/But it's all a
328 FR Charles	1	/I'll see if it's there. There might be something in that. {}/[*Exit*]/{G} Well, I said that
331 FR Harry	12	and a new torture,/The shadow of something behind our meagre childhood,/Some
331 FR Harry	19	not mean to./What I want to know is something I need to know,/And only you can
331 FR Agatha	36	sketching, playing on the flute,/Something of an oddity to his county
333 FR Agatha	1	ways, each one abandoned/For something more ingenious. You were due in
333 FR Agatha	7	you then? only a thing called 'life' —/Something that should have been *mine*, as I felt
340 FR Amy	14	have left me at least a memory/Of something to live upon. You knew that you
345 FR Charles	34	just beginning to feel/That there is something I *could* understand, if I were told it./
346 FRDowning	24	/Was just a kind of preparation for something else./I've no gift of language, but I'm
346 FRDowning	27	/But with people like him, there's something inside them/That accounts for what
366 CP Peter	16	Julia? On the way back/I remembered something I had to say to Edward .../{J} Oh,
366 CP Peter	19	/{P} No, not about Lavinia./It's something I want to consult him about,/And I
369 CP Peter	36	/And to be with Celia, that was something different/From company or solitude.
370 CP Peter	12	It was not like that at all./It was something very strange. There was such ...
371 CP Peter	3	/And I have been telling you of something real —/My first experience of reality/
371 CP Peter	21	looked at certain pictures?/There was something real. But what is the reality ... {}/[*The*
372 CP Alex	11	/This is the greatest. To make something out of nothing!/Never, even when
374 CP Celia	21	/You should have been prepared with something better, for Julia;/But it doesn't really

375 CP	Edward	30	ago,/And insisted on cooking me something for supper;/And he said I must eat it
375 CP	Celia	35	/Of course it's still cooking — or doing *something*./I must go and investigate. {}/[*Starts*
376 CP	Celia	6	starving and helpless/And had to do something. Anyway, I'm *staying*/And I'm not
376 CP	Edward	27	/{C} Nobody knows./{E} It's something that Alex came and prepared for me.
378 CP	Julia	3	and have a light supper with me —/Something very light./{C} Thank you, Julia./I
378 CP	Celia	6	ten minutes? Before I go, there's something/I want to say to Edward./{J} About
379 CP	Celia	32	dream was not enough; that I wanted something more/And I waited, and wanted to
380 CP	Celia	2	can humiliate me!/Humiliation — it's something I've done to myself./I am not sure
380 CP	Celia	6	whom they thought they had shared something wonderful/Had taken them only as a
382 CP	Celia	29	a projection —/I see that now — of something that I wanted —/No, not *wanted* —
382 CP	Celia	30	that I wanted —/No, not *wanted* — something I aspired to —/Something that I
382 CP	Celia	31	*wanted* — something I aspired to —/Something that I desperately wanted to exist./It
394 CP	Lavinia	7	/{L} Well, but I tried to do something about it./That was why I took so
394 CP	Lavinia	19	/And the moment you were offered something that you wanted/You wanted
394 CP	Lavinia	20	that you wanted/You wanted something else. I shall treat you very differently/
394 CP	Lavinia	25	I was warned of the danger,/Yet something, or somebody, compelled me to
406 CP	Edward	38	you, Lavinia./You always know of something better./{L} It's only that I have a
411 CP	Lavinia	22	you would say it./At least, there is something I would like you to ask./{E} It's
413 CP	Reilly	13	/When I get as far as that, there is something to be done./{C} Well, I can't pretend
413 CP	Celia	28	I should really *like* to think there's something wrong with me —/Because, if there
413 CP	Celia	29	—/Because, if there isn't, then there's something wrong,/Or at least, very different
413 CP	Celia	33	terrible. So I'd rather believe/There is something wrong with me, that could be put
414 CP	Celia	4	or being ditched./Of course that's something that's always happening/To all sorts
414 CP	Reilly	30	Is that a delusion?/{R} A delusion is something we must return from./There are other
416 CP	Celia	4	of failure;/Towards someone, or something, outside of myself;/And I feel I must
416 CP	Celia	24	That's horrible. Can we only love/Something created by our own imagination?/
417 CP	Celia	17	I want to be cured/Of a craving for something I cannot find/And of the shame of
418 CP	Celia	9	see, I think I really had a vision of something/Though I don't know what it is. I
432 CP	Julia	34	just over from California/Where he's something very important in films./He's making
435 CP	Peter	23	/But I thought it was going to lead to something better,/And that seemed possible,
435 CP	Peter	26	Celia./And, of course, I wanted to do something for Celia —/But what mattered was,
436 CP	Lavinia	20	thought of her./{L} Sir Henry, there is something I want to say to you./While Alex was
438 CP	Edward	16	was right for Celia —/There must be something else that is terribly wrong,/And the
439 CP	Reilly	7	these memories and make them/Into something new. Only by acceptance/Of the past
439 CP	Julia	9	{J} Henry, I think it is time that *I* said something:/Everyone makes a choice, of one
446 CC	Claude	16	matter./The great thing was to find something else/He could do, and do well. And I
447 CC	Claude	32	he'd had another very tempting offer./Something like that. Don't make too much of it.
449 CC	Claude	39	about my wife./There's always something one's ignorant of/About anyone,
450 CC	Claude	2	one knows them;/And that may be something of the greatest importance./It's when
450 CC	Colby	38	to behave./B. Kaghan has told me something about her,/But that's rather
455 CC	Eggers	16	is Sir Claude./To tell the truth, she's something of a thorn in his flesh,/Always losing
457 CC	Lady E	16	/{LE} Just open that case, I want something out of it./Unwrap that — It's a
460 CC	Claude	35	went and changed her own ticket./It's something unheard of./{E} Amazing, isn't it!/
463 CC	Colby	12	a way, exhilarating./To find there is something that I can do/So remote from my
464 CC	Claude	5	think that a sculptor or a painter/Is something more excellent to be than a potter./
465 CC	Claude	13	have a consuming passion/To do something for which he lacks the capacity?/
465 CC	Claude	26	peace/Which comes in dying to give something life .../I intend that you shall have a
466 CC	Colby	33	life has imposed upon you. But ... something in me/Rebels against accepting such
467 CC	Colby	5	your father. I only wish/That I had something to atone for!/There's something
467 CC	Colby	6	I had something to atone for!/There's something lacking, between you and me,/That
470 CC	Lucasta	31	compliment/To invite a woman to something she would like/When she knows *you*
470 CC	Lucasta	34	patronising. But if you invite me/To something you like — that *is* a compliment./It
471 CC	Colby	18	the reason that I'm thinking of./It's something quite simple./{L} Then I wish you'd
472 CC	Colby	6	time./Or at least, there may have been something in your life/To rob you of any sense
472 CC	Lucasta	20	/{L} It's hard to explain./Perhaps it's something that your music stands for./There's
472 CC	Lucasta	29	/And that you must learn to do something different./And so you applied for
474 CC	Lucasta	32	That's quite untrue./{L} But you've something else, that I haven't got:/Something of
474 CC	Lucasta	33	something else, that I haven't got:/Something of which the music is a ... symbol./I
477 CC	Lucasta	11	But I'm always a reminder to him/Of something he would prefer to forget. {}/[A
477 CC	Lucasta	12	/[*A pause*]/{L} But why don't you say something? Are you shocked?/{C} Shocked? No.
478 CC	Colby	25	/{C} You mustn't go yet!/There's something else that I want to explain,/And now
479 CC	Kaghan	36	/It's all a bit too dim. You need something brighter./But otherwise, it looks
480 CC	Kaghan	18	that isn't a certainty./{K} Well, there's something in that. You know, Lucasta,/Colby is
485 CC	Lady E	19	previous existences. Of course, there's something in us,/In all of us, which isn't just
485 CC	Lady E	21	all of us, which isn't just heredity,/But something unique. Something we have been/

485 CC	Lady E	21	just heredity,/But something unique. Something we have been/From eternity.
485 CC	Lady E	22	we have been/From eternity. Something ... straight from God./That means
485 CC	Lady E	38	did you say? The name means something to me./Yes. Guzzard. *That* is the
491 CC	Lady E	3	and a mother./{LE} Stop, Colby! Something has come to me./Claude! I don't
492 CC	Claude	29	reminiscent mood' —Oh yes. To say something of my early ambitions/To be a
494 CC	Claude	18	I had interpreted/In this way, was something else to *him* —An idea, an
500 CC	Lucasta	26	I want./And somehow or other, I've something to give him —Something that he
500 CC	Lucasta	27	other, I've something to give him —Something that he needs. Colby doesn't need
502 CC	Lucasta	25	people. You're either an egotist/Or something so different from the rest of us/That
503 CC	Lucasta	18	both of you, Lucasta!/{L} We'll mean something to you. But you don't *need* anybody.
515 CC	Guzzard	28	my place as Colby's mother/I gave up something I could never have back./Don't you
519 CC	Kaghan	10	Kaghan?/{K} We wanted Colby to be something he wasn't./{LE} I suppose that's true
519 CC	Kaghan	20	Lucasta and I/Would like to mean something to you ... if you'd let us;/And we'd
525 ES	Charles	35	with you. Well, you're right./But I've something else to say that I haven't said before,/
530 ES	Ld Clav	39	double this collection — it must be something showy'./This would do for visiting
532 ES	Ld Clav	18	expect he wants money. Or to sell me something worthless./{M} You ought not to
534 ES	Ld Clav	15	you would disapprove of./{LC} That's something, at least, to be thankful for./I trust
539 ES	Gomez	15	supposed to be./And I've learned something of other vicissitudes./Dick, I was
541 ES	Gomez	2	Gomez of San Marco/About something that happened so many years ago?/
547 ES	Ld Clav	14	/There may be, among the guests, something worse than Mrs. Piggott./{M} Let's
548 ES	Monica	12	/If they think you *are* asleep they'll do something to wake you,/But if they see you're
551 ES	Carghil	26	an action/Simply because one must do *something*./Well, perhaps I shouldn't have settled
555 ES	Monica	19	says he must see you./I'm afraid that something unpleasant has happened./{LC} Was
556 ES	Monica	28	/And Father knows that you want something from him./Perhaps you'll get to the
556 ES	Michael	33	thing I remember/Is being blamed for something I hadn't done./I never got over that.
557 ES	Michael	11	nine-tenths of the time .../{Mi} I need something much more stimulating./{LC} Well?/
561 ES	Monica	31	been exhibiting./{M} Michael! Say something./{Mi} What is there to say?/I want to
569 ES	Charles	21	any question of blackmail,/I've seen something of it in my practice at the bar./I'm
569 ES	Ld Clav	39	/From my spectral existence into something like reality./{M} But what did the
571 ES	Ld Clav	25	Only the hold of those who know/Something discreditable, dishonourable .../{M}
576 ES	Gomez	35	Mr. Barrister./You ought to know something about the law of slander./Here's Mrs.
578 ES	Ld Clav	2	/I cannot prevent him. I have something to say to you,/Michael, before you
580 ES	Ld Clav	37	you are right to hope for something better./And when he comes back, if
582 ES	Ld Clav	11	the practice of loving —/Well, that is something./I shall leave you for a while./This is

SOMETHING'S (2)

346 FRDowning	29	/So I seem to know beforehand, when something's going to happen,/And it seems
392 CP	Lavinia	23	the devil./She knows by instinct when something's going to happen./Trust her not to

SOMETIME (1)

593 Grad 8	1	their aid the flag is raised on high./Sometime in distant years when we are grown/

SOMETIMES (42)

34 Figlia		23	should have lost a gesture and a pose./Sometimes these cogitations still amaze/The
69 WL: Fire S		259	Victoria Street./O City city, I can sometimes hear/Beside a public bar in Lower
118 SP	Doris	6	an awful lot in the way you feel/{Do} Sometimes they'll tell you nothing at all/{Du}
118 SP	Dusty	11	no use asking more than once/{Du} Sometimes they're no use at all./{Do} I'd like to
124 SA	Sweeney	37	they do./He used to come and see me sometimes/I'd give him a drink and cheer him
175 FQ: BurntN		153	always now. Words strain,/Crack and sometimes break, under the burden,/Under the
187 FQ: DrySal		126	sudden fury, is what it always was./I sometimes wonder if that is what Krishna
225 Mr Mistoff		46	he was curled up by the fire./And he's sometimes been heard by the fire/When he was
587 Fable		19	up for his crimes;/At any rate, he sometimes came to dinner,/Whene'er the monks
243 MC	Chorus	31	on living,/Living and partly living./Sometimes the corn has failed us,/Sometimes
243 MC	Chorus	32	/Sometimes the corn has failed us,/Sometimes the harvest is good,/One year is a
254 MC	Tempt4	26	compel you./You have also thought, sometimes at your prayers,/Sometimes
254 MC	Tempt4	27	thought, sometimes at your prayers,/Sometimes hesitating at the angles of stairs,/
307 FR	Harry	37	/Unrecognised by other men, though sometimes by each other./{M} I know what you
344 FR	Violet	8	/{A} Ask Agatha./{V} Really, it sometimes seems to me/That I am the only sane
344 FR	Gerald	22	A maligned profession./They're sometimes very useful, knowing the natives,/
362 CP	Reilly	30	in the role you have chosen,/Then sometimes, when you come to the bottom step/
369 CP	Peter	35	So we often met/In the same way, and sometimes went together./And to be with Celia,
379 CP	Peter	36	/From company or solitude. And we sometimes had tea/And once or twice dined
385 CP	Reilly	4	social convention/Which must sometimes be broken. We must also remember/
431 CP	Alex	10	in California, Alex?/{A} Yes, we have sometimes obliged each other./{P} Well, it was
437 CP	Reilly	21	in a picture./That happens to me, sometimes. So it was obvious/That here was a
438 CP	Reilly	33	or ruin to a patient —/And sometimes I have made the wrong decision./As
440 CP	Lavinia	31	since then. And besides,/One sometimes likes to hear the same compliment
451 CC	Eggers	18	good company./He makes me laugh sometimes. I don't laugh easily./Quite a

451 CC   Eggers   20   a humorist, he is. In fact, Mrs. E./Sometimes says to me: 'Eggerson, why can't you
454 CC   Eggers   33   would. But she does call her Lizzie,/Sometimes, to Sir Claude. And do you know —
456 CC   Eggers   7   true that her family connections/Have sometimes been useful. But he didn't think of
456 CC   Eggers   23   much memory to lose,/Though she sometimes remembers when you least expect it./
456 CC   Eggers   40   plane./{E} Oh, that could happen. She sometimes gets lost,/Or loses her ticket, or even
465 CC   Claude   30   door/Into the real world, as I do, sometimes./{C} Indeed, I have felt, while you've
466 CC   Claude   11   and look at one thing long enough,/I sometimes have that sense of identification/
480 CC   Kaghan   7   together./I'm a good guesser. But I sometimes guess wrong./I make decisions on the
482 CC   Lady E   37   surprising, well-bred people/Are sometimes far from intellectual;/And — what's
494 CC   Lady E   31   I don't. But I wish you would talk/Sometimes to me as if I did understand,/And
509 CC   Claude   26   Barnabas?/{SC} Yes, Elizabeth. He sometimes has to sign his full name./But he
512 CC   Guzzard   37   better./{MG} Wishes, when realised, sometimes turn/Against those who have made
528 ES   Charles   16   has been so well preserved/That I've sometimes wondered whether there was any .../
533 ES   Gomez   32   the law turned its right side to *me.*/Sometimes I've had to pay pretty heavily;/But I
550 ES   Carghil   13   time. That didn't last long./People sometimes say: 'Make one mistake in love,/
558 ES   Michael   24   pay;/They had a lot of fun with me — sometimes they'd pretend/That I was
579 ES   Carghil   33   Richard,/To solve a son's problems. Sometimes an outsider,/A friend of the family,

SOMEWHAT (5)
212 Growltiger   7   was baggy at the knees;/One ear was somewhat missing, no need to tell you why,/
603 Spleen   15   in hand,/Punctilious of tie and suit/(Somewhat impatient of delay)/On the doorstep
384 CP   Edward   24   the dead?/That figure of speech is somewhat ... dramatic,/As it was only yesterday
408 CP   Reilly   4   prostrated,/And certainly, you have somewhat recovered./But you failed to mention
508 CC   Guzzard   31   Yes, I know their name:/Like mine, a somewhat unusual one./Perhaps it might be

SOMEWHERE (16)
326 FR   Violet   3   me to Cheltenham;/But I stopped him somewhere in Chiswick, I think./Anyway, the
327 FR   Harry   12   they simply outside,/I might escape somewhere, perhaps. Were they simply inside/I
327 FR   Harry   18   way of talking/That would get us somewhere. You don't understand me./You
339 FR   Harry   7   does one go from a world of insanity?/Somewhere on the other side of despair./To the
357 CP   Julia   30   say Hampstead./{J} But she must live somewhere./{E} She lives in Essex./{J} Anywhere
382 CP   Celia   32   wanted to exist./It must happen somewhere — but what, and where is it?/
389 CP   Celia   23   But now that I may be going away — somewhere —/I should like to say good-bye —
392 CP   Edward   31   Julia compelled me to make her live somewhere./{L} I see. So Julia made her live in
412 CP   Celia   28   But I've met you before,/Haven't I, somewhere? ... Oh, of course./But I didn't know
421 CP   Julia   7   /They have, for the first time, somewhere to start from./Oh, of course, they
427 CP   Julia   1   /He only got back this morning from somewhere —/One of his mysterious
452 CC   Lucasta   22   find one of them./But they're all filed somewhere, I'm sure, so why bother?/But who's
473 CC   Colby   6   you haven't your own secret garden/Somewhere, if you could find it?/{L} If I could
473 CC   Colby   16   person./I'm sure that there is a garden somewhere for you —/For anyone who wants
553 ES   Carghil   17   a phrase I seem to remember reading somewhere:/*Where their fires are not quenched.*
570 ES   Ld Clav   33   /In an obscure grammar school somewhere in the Midlands./As for Maisie

SOMNAMBULAR (1)
336 FR   1m 23   AGATHA *goes to the window, in a somnambular fashion,/and opens the curtains,*

SON (100)
61 WL: Burial   20   grow/Out of this stony rubbish? Son of man,/You cannot say, or guess, for you
153 Rock 2   50   even move about together,/But every son would have his motor cycle,/And daughters
159 Rock 6   26   The man that pretends to be./And the Son of Man was not crucified once for all,/The
159 Rock 6   29   Saints not once for all:/But the Son of Man is crucified always/And there shall
164 Rock 9   1   perfect our will./O GOD, help us./Son of Man, behold with thine eyes, and hear
240 MC   Chorus   23   who shall preserve you?/Shall the Son of Man be born again in the litter of scorn?
260 MC   Thomas   3   In the/Name of the Father, and of the Son, and of the Holy Ghost. Amen./Dear
262 MC   Thomas   5   In the Name/of the Father, and of the Son, and of the Holy Ghost. Amen./Part II/{C}
266 MC   Knights 19   is the man who was the tradesman's son: the backstairs brat who was born in
268 MC   Thomas   22   it my wish/To uncrown the King's son, or to diminish/His honour and power. Why
284 FR   m 6   MONCHENSEY, *Amy's eldest son*/DOWNING, *his servant and chauffeur*/DR.
340 FR   Amy   5   husband from me. Now you take my son./{Ag} What did I take? nothing that you
340 FR   Amy   31   saw through *him.*/And now it is my son./{Ag} I know one thing, Amy:/That you
341 FR   Amy   23   from me/And now you take my son./{Ag} Why should we quarrel for what
341 FR   Agatha   25   If neither has ever had a husband or a son/We have no ground for argument./{A} Who
341 FR   Amy   38   took my husband, now you take my son./You take him from Wishwood, you take
343 FR   Harry   34   of Wishwood,/The satisfactory son. And as for me,/I am the last you need to
448 CC   Claude   37   for you and your wife, to have had a son/Lost in action, and his grave unknown./{E}
449 CC   Eggers   35   that Mr. Simpkins/Is actually your son?/{SC} That's where I'm in the dark./I simply
462 CC   Colby   10   /Can ever accept me as if I was her son?/{SC} As if you were her son? If she comes
462 CC   Claude   11   was her son?/{SC} As if you were her son? If she comes to think of you/As the kind of
462 CC   Claude   12   of you/As the kind of man that her son would have been —/And I believe she will:

462 CC	Claude	14	I'm perfectly convinced/That *her* son would have been a different type of person
462 CC	Claude	15	person —/Then you *will* become her son, in her eyes. She's like that./Why, it
462 CC	Claude	17	to believe/That you really are her son, instead of being mine./She has always lived
467 CC	Colby	1	that was a relationship/Of father and son. It must often happen./And the
467 CC	Colby	3	relation. You have always been his son/And he is still your father. I only wish/That
487 CC	Claude	33	led you to believe/That Colby is your son?/{LE} Oh, I forgot/In my excitement: you
487 CC	Claude	38	But why should that make him your son?/{LE} It's the name I've been hunting for all
488 CC	Claude	12	began to think of Colby as what your son would be,/And then you began to see him
488 CC	Claude	13	then you began to see him as your son,/And then — any name you heard would
488 CC	Claude	36	what I meant. Elizabeth,/Colby is *my* son./{LE} Quite impossible, Claude!/You have a
488 CC	Lady E	38	have a daughter. Now you want a son./{SC} I'd never want to take your son away
488 CC	Claude	39	son./{SC} I'd never want to take your son away from you./Perhaps you have a son.
489 CC	Claude	1	away from you./Perhaps you have a son. But it isn't Colby./I ought to have told you,
489 CC	Claude	13	/I came to see how you longed for a son of your own,/And I thought, I'll wait for
489 CC	Claude	17	/I ought to have told you that I had a son./{LE} But why do you think that Colby is
489 CC	Lady E	18	why do you think that Colby is your son?/{SC} Colby is the son of Mrs. Guzzard's
489 CC	Claude	19	Colby is your son?/{SC} Colby is the son of Mrs. Guzzard's sister,/Who died when he
489 CC	Claude	23	And Mrs. Guzzard/Knows he is my son./{LE} But where were you, Claude,/When
489 CC	Lady E	39	would be happy/To think you had a son, and would do well by him —/Because you
490 CC	Colby	19	thinking: 'What does it matter/Whose son I am?' You don't understand/That when
490 CC	Lady E	27	be a bond between mother and son,/No matter how long they have lost each
490 CC	Colby	30	same/Or crueller. Suppose I am your son./Then it's merely a fact. Better not know/
491 CC	Lady E	5	want to take away from you/The son you thought was yours. And I know from
491 CC	Lady E	8	/Let us regard him as being *our* son:/It won't be the same as what we had
491 CC	Colby	26	have never known the feelings of a son,/To be disputed between two parents./But,
492 CC	Colby	2	that./But now I want to know whose son I am./{SC} Then the first thing is: we must
494 CC	Lady E	2	somehow, might prove to be *your* son/Instead of mine. Really, I do!/It would be
494 CC	Lady E	5	am sure he is — then you never had a son;/While, if he were yours ... he could still
494 CC	Lady E	7	... he could still take the place/Of my son: and so he could be *our* son./Oh dear, what
494 CC	Lady E	7	/Of my son: and so he could be *our* son./Oh dear, what do I want? I should like him
494 CC	Lady E	10	hope Mrs. Guzzard will say he is your son/And I needn't believe her. I don't believe in
496 CC	Lady E	12	Whatever happens/He shall be *our* son. {}/[*A knock on the door. Enter*
497 CC	Lady E	24	been deceived, and that Colby is my son./I feel sure he is. But I don't want to know:/
497 CC	Lady E	27	/So that we may regard him as *our* son./{SC} That is perfectly correct. It is Colby/
500 CC	Claude	4	What do you mean?/{SC} Colby is my son./{LE} That is what Sir Claude believes.
500 CC	Claude	7	/My wife believes that Colby is *her* son./That is the reason for this meeting today./
500 CC	Lucasta	21	/But if he knew that he was your son/He must have been staggered when I said I
505 CC	Lady E	35	her marriage/Had a child .../{LE} A son./{E} Had a son/Whom she could not, in the
505 CC	Eggers	36	Had a child .../{LE} A son./{E} Had a son/Whom she could not, in the circumstances,
506 CC	Eggers	14	a clue/Until the other day. This son, Mrs. Guzzard,/If he is alive, must be a
506 CC	Guzzard	21	child was lost./Let us hope that her son may be restored to her./{E} That is exactly
507 CC	Lady E	34	is no doubt about it./Colby is my son./{MG} Your son, Lady Elizabeth?/Are you
507 CC	Guzzard	35	it./Colby is my son./{MG} Your son, Lady Elizabeth?/Are you suggesting that I
507 CC	Claude	39	convinced herself/That Colby is her son. I know he is *my* son./And I asked you here
507 CC	Claude	39	Colby is her son. I know he is *my* son./And I asked you here so that you might tell
508 CC	Eggers	5	been hoping against hope/To find her son. Put yourself in her position./If you had lost
508 CC	Eggers	6	in her position./If you had lost your son, in a similar way,/Wouldn't you grasp at
508 CC	Lady E	12	talk about straws! Colby is my son./{MG} In the circumstances, I ignore that
510 CC	Lady E	8	—This Mr. Kaghan — is my son?/{E} It creates an inherent probability —/If
510 CC	Claude	12	Elizabeth,/That you have found your son./{E} Subject to confirmation./{LE} And to
510 CC	Guzzard	26	Elizabeth, I believe that this is your son./If so, I am cleared from your unjust
510 CC	Lady E	32	Barnabas, it seems you are my son./{E} You will wish to obtain confirmation/
512 CC	Guzzard	16	To recognise Barnabas Kaghan as her son? {}/[*To* LADY ELIZABETH]/{MG} Are
512 CC	Guzzard	17	you contented to have him as your son?/{SC} That seems a strange question, Mrs.
512 CC	Guzzard	23	happy./{MG} You wished for your son, and now you have your son./We all of us
512 CC	Guzzard	23	for your son, and now you have your son./We all of us have to adapt ourselves/To the
512 CC	Guzzard	27	/Are you satisfied to find yourself the son/Of Lady Elizabeth Mulhammer?/{K} It's
513 CC	Guzzard	39	he had wanted to do./{MG} Whose son would you wish to be, Colby:/Sir Claude's
514 CC	Guzzard	1	to be, Colby:/Sir Claude's — or the son of some other man/Obscure and silent? A
514 CC	Guzzard	9	you mean?/{MG} Colby is not your son, Sir Claude./{C} Who was my father, then?/
514 CC	Guzzard	12	/{MG} Herbert Guzzard./You are the son of a disappointed musician./{C} And who
514 CC	Guzzard	22	To Herbert and Sarah Guzzard/A son./{E} And what about your sister and her
515 CC	Guzzard	12	to think the child was yours,/My son was assured of a proper start in life —/That
516 CC	Claude	25	no other evidence, that you were my son,/Because you described my own experience,
517 CC	Colby	5	you would still think of me as your son./There can be no relation of father and son/

517 CC   Colby   6 There can be no relation of father and son/Unless it works both ways. For you to
517 CC   Colby   8   me —/As you would — as your son, when I could not think of you/As my
539 ES   Gomez   18 altogether happy./And as for your son — from what I've heard about *him*,/He's
558 ES   Michael   2   then I forget them./It's being your son that gets me into debt./Just because of your
558 ES   Michael   16   /'Not what we expected from the son of your father'/And that sort of thing. It's
558 ES   Michael   19 I can tell you, it's no joke/Being the son of a famous public man./You don't know
558 ES   Michael   22 been made for me/Because I was your son. They considered me superfluous;/They
559 ES   Michael   34   passing on your name and title/To a son, was gratifying. But it wasn't for *my* sake!/I
559 ES   Michael   35 it wasn't for *my* sake!/I was just your son — that is to say,/A kind of prolongation of
561 ES   Ld Clav   12   for twenty years/Knowing that my son had played the coward —/I should merely
564 ES   Gomez   5 to be your daughter?/And this is your son?/{LC} This is my son Michael,/And my
564 ES   Ld Clav   6 And this is your son?/{LC} This is my son Michael,/And my daughter Monica./{M}
575 ES   Michael   3   my own way,/Not merely be your son. That's what Señor Gomez sees./*He*
SON (2) [*Foreign word*]
 48 Lune Miel   14 /Lui pense aux pourboires, et rédige son bilan./Ils auront vu la Suisse et traversé la
 51 Restaurant   12 donné des primevères.'/Les taches de son gilet montent au chiffre de trente-huit./'Je la
SON'S (2)
496 CC   Claude   38   /{SC} The anniversary? Of your son's death?/{E} Of the day we got the news. We
579 ES   Carghil   33 the right person, Richard,/To solve a son's problems. Sometimes an outsider,/A
SON-IN-LAW (2)
501 CC   Lady E   22 be happy to accept Mr. Kaghan as a son-in-law./{L} Thank you. I'm sure he'll
575 ES   Ld Clav   29   time:/My daughter and my future son-in-law/Understand that allusion. I have told
SONG (21)
 13 Prufrock   t   and Other Observations/The Love Song of J. Alfred Prufrock/Let us go then, you
 20 Portrait   80 /Reiterates some worn-out common song/With the smell of hyacinths across the
 67 WL: Fire S   176   Thames, run softly, till I end my song./The river bears no empty bottles,
 67 WL: Fire S   183 Sweet Thames, run softly till I end my song,/Sweet Thames, run softly, for I speak not
105 Song Sime   t /I should be glad of another death./A Song for Simeon/Lord, the Roman hyacinths
122 SA   1m 15   but I remember,/Once is enough. {}/SONG BY WAUCHOPE AND HORSFALL/
123 SA   1m 13   like life on your crocodile isle. {}/SONG BY KLIPSTEIN AND
187 FQ: DrySal   128 same thing:/That the future is a faded song, a Royal Rose or a lavender spray/Of
216 Jellicles   t   no doing anything about it!/The Song of the Jellicles/*Jellicle Cats come out*
590 Space Time   t of love be few/Yet let them be divine./Song/If space and time, as sages say,/Are things
592 Grad 1   3   a moment doubtfully,/Then with a song upon our lips, sail we/Across the harbor
596 When we   t /*Exeunt omnes*, with a last 'farewell'./Song/When we came home across the hill/No
600 Moonflower   t   her with a patient curious eye./Song/The moonflower opens to the moth,/The
263 MC   Chorus   20 before, the bird shall sing the same song./When the leaf is out on the tree, when the
263 MC   Chorus   25   done, what wrong/Shall the bird's song cover, the green tree cover, what wrong/
264 MC   Priest3   17 of harps,/They sang as it were a new song./The blood of thy saints have they shed
281 MC   Chorus   16 of seasons, the snuffle of winter, the song of spring, the drone of summer, the voices
292 FR   Harry   7 eyes stared at me, and corrupted that song./Behind the palm trees in the Grand Hotel/
378 CP   Edward   34 is not Riley;/It was just a name in a song he sang .../{C} He sang you a song about a
378 CP   Celia   35 a song he sang .../{C} He sang you a song about a man named Riley!/Really,
564 ES   Carghil   1   *For You To Love Me!* That's the song/That made my reputation, Señor Gomez./
SONG-SPARROW (1)
142 Cape Ann   1 /O quick quick quick, quick hear the song-sparrow,/Swamp-sparrow, fox-sparrow,
SONGS (2)
151 Rock 2   9 corners, with nothing to bring but the songs we can sing which nobody wants to hear
365 CP   Julia   32 you talk about/Or were you singing songs all the time?/There's altogether too much
SONGSTERS (1)
135 5FingerEx1   1 Exercises/*Lines to a Persian Cat*/The songsters of the air repair/To the green fields of
SONS (12)
189 FQ: DrySal   179 behalf of/Women who have seen their sons or husbands/Setting forth, and not
593 Grad 6   2 be more great/Than those before, her sons must make her so,/And we are of her sons,
593 Grad 6   3 must make her so,/And we are of her sons, and we must go/With eager hearts to help
594 Grad 12   5 so that all may hear;/May worthier sons be thine, from far and near/To spread thy
594 Grad 13   1 and seas!/As thou to thy departing sons hast been/To those that follow may'st thou
604 Ode   5   and fears./And we turn as thy sons ever turn, in the strength/Of the hopes that
251 MC   Tempt3   21 in Anjou;/Round him waiting hungry sons./We are for England. We are in England./
253 MC   Tempt4   39 shall know it, when at last breath,/No sons, no empire, he bites broken teeth./You
340 FR   Amy   21   in the silent bedroom,/Forcing sons upon an unwilling father?/Dare you think
340 FR   Amy   23 one? Try to think of it./*I would* have sons, if I could not have a husband:/Then I let
534 ES   Gomez   26 /I wouldn't allow either of my sons/To go into politics. In my country, Dick,/
570 ES   Ld Clav   29 /In his adopted country. He even has sons/Following in their father's footsteps/Who

SOON (41)

21 Portrait	120	whether wise or foolish, tardy or too soon .../Would she not have the advantage,
38 Gerontion	41	only, reconsidered passion. Gives too soon/Into weak hands, what's thought can be
103 Journ Magi	30	arrived at evening, not a moment too soon/Finding the place; it was (you may say)
123 SA Doris	31	not life, that's no life/Why I'd just as soon be dead./{S} That's what life is. Just is/
136 5FingerEx3	13	/For I know, and so should you/That soon the enquiring worm shall try/Our
214 RTTugger	15	the wrong side of every door,/And as soon as he's at home, then he'd like to get
230 Bust Jones	23	just before noon's not a moment too soon/To drop in for a drink at the *Drones*./
270 MC Chorus	23	now is too late/For action, too soon for contrition./Nothing is possible but the
285 FR Amy	4	to June,/And the swallow comes too soon and the spring will be over/And the
286 FR Gerald	6	/{G} Well, as for me,/I'd just as soon be a subaltern again/To be back in the
307 FR Harry	14	festivities, I made my escape/As soon as I could, and slipped down to the river/
332 FR Agatha	34	neither./{Ag} The autumn came too soon, not soon enough./The rain and wind had
332 FR Agatha	34	/{Ag} The autumn came too soon, not soon enough./The rain and wind had not
347 FRDowning	7	you a turn!/They did me, at first. You soon get used to them./Of course, I knew they
358 CP Julia	34	And Celia —/I must see you very soon. Now don't all go/Just because I'm going.
358 CP Celia	38	Good-bye, Edward./Shall I see you soon?/{E} Perhaps. I don't know./{C} Perhaps
371 CP Edward	25	there is ... Well then, I'll ring you/As soon as I can. {}/[*To* PETER]/{E} I'm sorry.
374 CP Edward	3	back?/I said I would telephone as soon as I could:/And I tried to get you a short
374 CP Celia	22	doesn't really matter. They will know soon enough./Doesn't that settle all our
378 CP Celia	29	has left you for another man?/I shall soon put that right, Edward,/When you are
391 CP Julia	28	/Well, my dears, I shall see you very soon./{E} *When* shall we see you?/{J} Did I say
393 CP Lavinia	23	/I said: 'I suppose you'd as soon go to Peacehaven' —/And you said 'I
395 CP Lavinia	28	for you./But never mind, you'll soon get over it/And find yourself another little
419 CP Celia	32	/Very often, in the world./{C} How soon will you send me there?/{R} How soon will
419 CP Reilly	33	will you send me there?/{R} How soon will you be ready?/{C} Tonight, by nine
426 CP Lavinia	16	committees./{L} Can we get away soon?/{E} By the end of next week/I shall be
440 CP Edward	34	/{L} Now for the party./{E} It will soon be over./{L} I wish it would begin./{E}
446 CC Eggers	25	to. And the flat in the mews?/How soon will that be ready for him?/{SC} They have
448 CC Eggers	13	Simpkins,/He's highly educated. He'll soon begin to grasp them./No, I haven't told
448 CC Eggers	17	mind — before I go to meet her./How soon do you propose to ... *explain* Mr.
449 CC Claude	29	doesn't see her. And Miss Angel/Will soon be getting married, I expect./{E} And so I
455 CC Eggers	1	met her. I'm not used to it./{E} You'll soon get used to it. You'll be calling me Eggers/
456 CC Eggers	15	oddities are perfectly harmless./You'll soon get used to them. That's what Sir Claude
475 CC Colby	10	/You can understand the change as soon as it happens,/Though you couldn't have
502 CC Colby	1	*Enter* COLBY]/{C} Have I come too soon?/I'm afraid I got impatient of waiting./{L}
503 CC Eggers	35	then, Lucasta./{E} And now, how soon are we expecting Mrs. Guzzard? {}/
530 ES Monica	5	more empty pages?/{M} You would soon fill them up if we allowed you to!/That's
537 ES Gomez	9	sort of thing./We'll come to that, very soon. Isn't it strange/That there should always
542 ES Gomez	40	may be getting impatient./I'll see you soon again./{LC} Not very soon, I think./I am
543 ES Ld Clav	1	I'll see you soon again./{LC} Not very soon, I think./I am going away./{G} So I've
550 ES Carghill	36	/Any woman who trusted *him* would soon find that out'./A man may prefer to forget

SOONER (8)

245 MC Priest2	26	had a better welcome/If we had been sooner prepared for the event./But your
251 MC Tempt3	5	once ended, cannot be mended./Sooner shall enmity turn to alliance./The enmity
251 MC Tempt3	7	that never knew friendship/Can sooner know accord./{T} For a countryman/
322 FR Winch	28	the fog so thick, or I'd have been here sooner./I'd telephoned to Dr. Warburton's,/
459 CC Lady E	37	you go to Zürich?/{LE} Why, I'd no sooner got to Lausanne/Than whom should I
534 ES Gomez	21	that nature,/Is certain to be found out sooner or later./And then what happens? You
579 ES Carghill	13	how you manage *everything*!/— No sooner had I put my proposal before him/Than
579 ES Ld Clav	23	stop you,/Then I agree with you, the sooner the better./We may never meet again,

SOOT (1)

13 Prufrock	19	in drains,/Let fall upon its back the soot that falls from chimneys,/Slipped by the

SOOTHED (1)

605 Narcissus	12	over the meadows/He was stifled and soothed by his own rhythm./By the river/His

SORCERY (1)

348 FR Chorus	19	enchantments./And minor forms of sorcery,/Divination and chiromancy,/Specifics

SORDID (4)

23 Preludes	27	the night revealing/The thousand sordid images/Of which your soul was
265 MC Priest3	7	is always now, and here. Even now, in sordid particulars/The eternal design may
464 CC Claude	13	is escape into living,/Escape from a sordid world to a pure one./Sculpture and
476 CC Lucasta	32	daughter!/{L} His daughter. Oh, it's a sordid story./I hated my mother. I never could

SORE-FOOTED (1)

103 Journ Magi	6	of winter.'/And the camels galled, sore-footed, refractory,/Lying down in the

SORELY (1)
589 Fable   69 keep out;/It is a thing to be lamented sorely/Such slippery folk should be allowed

SORROW (12)
105 Song Sime   14 children's children/When the time of sorrow is come?/They will take to the goat's
105 Song Sime   20 /Before the certain hour of maternal sorrow,/Now at this birth season of decease,/Let
164 Rock 9   3   the House of GOD is a House of Sorrow;/We must walk in black and go sadly,
164 Rock 9   7 They would put upon GOD their own sorrow, the grief they should feel/For their sins
219 Mung Rump   25 say in a voice that was broken with sorrow:/'I'm afraid you must wait and have
241 MC   Mess   30 incredulity./He comes in pride and sorrow, affirming all his claims,/Assured,
258 MC Thomas   28 of God has chance of greater sin/And sorrow, than the man who serves a king./For
276 MC Chorus   10 Every horror had its definition,/Every sorrow had a kind of end:/In life there is not
294 FR   Harry   3 do not know/The unspoken voice of sorrow in the ancient bedroom/At three o'clock
294 FR   Harry   7 house/With the noxious smell and the sorrow before morning,/In which all past is
329 FR Chorus   13 loathing/And the season of stifled sorrow/The whisper, the transparent deception/
578 ES Ld Clav   16 other,/How can I feel anything but sorrow and compunction?/{M} Oh Michael,

SORRY (56)
116 SP   Dusty   23 that you? how do you do!/Oh I'm *so* sorry. I *am* so sorry/But Doris came home with
116 SP   Dusty   23 do you do!/Oh I'm *so* sorry. I *am* so sorry/But Doris came home with a terrible chill/
213 Growltiger   46   for she was badly skeered;/I am sorry to admit it, but she quickly disappeared./
277 MC Knight3   14 it was; and for/my part I am awfully sorry about it. We realised this was our duty,/
287 FR   Gerald   13 been more considerate./{G} I'm very sorry: but why was she upset?/I only meant to
298 FR   Charles   20 left you. {}/[*Exit*]/{C} Well, I'm very sorry/You all see it like this: but there simply
298 FR   Charles   28   you, very well indeed, Sir./{C} I'm sorry to send for you so abruptly,/But I've a
304 FR   Agatha   34   /Amy did not know that. I was sorry for her;/I could see that she distrusted me
305 FR   Agatha   4 and you can help me./{Ag} I am very sorry, Mary, I am very sorry for you;/Though
305 FR   Agatha   4 {Ag} I am very sorry, Mary, I am very sorry for you;/Though you may not think me
320 FR Warburt   24 or excite her./{H} Well!/{W} I'm very sorry for you, Harry./I should have liked to
321 FR   Winch   25   Doctor./Many happy ... Oh, I'm sorry, my Lord,/I was thinking it was your
322 FR   Winch   24 /{H} John!/{Wi} Yes, my Lord, I'm sorry./I thought I'd better have a word with you
323 FR   Winch   8 what are you here for?/{Wi} I'm sorry, my Lady, but I've just told the doctor,/
324 FR   Violet   10 had something to say./Aren't you sorry for your brother? Aren't you aware/Of
324 FR   Harry   12 your mother?/{H} Oh, of course I'm sorry. But from what Winchell says/I don't
347 FR   Ivy   27 well;/And she is resting./{I} Oh, I'm sorry. But can't you explain?/Why do you all
358 CP   Celia   29 I walk along with you?/{C} No, I'm sorry, Peter;/I've got to take a taxi./{J} You
359 CP   Edward   31 again. I'm off at last. {}/[*Exit*]/{E} I'm sorry. I'm afraid I don't know your name./{UG}
363 CP   Edward   4   May I replenish?/{E} Oh, I'm sorry. What were you drinking?/Whisky?/{UG}
365 CP   Edward   35 /About this place to-day./{E} I'm very sorry./{J} No, I love it. But that reminds me/
366 CP   Peter   36 it no longer./That awful party! I'm sorry, Edward;/Of course it was really a very
371 CP   Edward   26 soon as I can. {}/[*To* PETER]/{E} I'm sorry. You were saying?/{P} I was saying, what
377 CP   Edward   35 come home with me./{E} No, I'm sorry, Julia./I'm too tired to go out, and I'm not
381 CP   Celia   21 I shall not loathe you. I shall only feel sorry for you./It's only myself I am in danger of
383 CP   Edward   28 are you there? .../Well, I'm awfully sorry to have kept you waiting;/But we ... I had
390 CP   Julia   1 /{J} There you are, Lavinia! I'm sorry to be late./But your telegram was a bit
396 CP   Lavinia   20 all you seem to want of me./But I'm sorry for you .../{E} Don't say you are sorry for
396 CP   Edward   21 for you .../{E} Don't say you are sorry for me!/I have had enough of people being
396 CP   Edward   22 /I have had enough of people being sorry for me./{L} Yes, because they can never be
396 CP   Lavinia   23 /{L} Yes, because they can never be sorry for you/As you are for yourself. And
410 CP   Edward   3 you./{E} I'm beginning to feel very sorry for you, Lavinia./You know, you really
434 CP   Lavinia   31 not eaten./{L} Oh, Edward, I'm so sorry — what a feeble thing to say!/But you
436 CP   Peter   8 you. You're naturally good./{P} I'm sorry. I don't believe I've taken in/All that
445 CC   Claude   2 Eggerson! Punctual as always./I'm sorry to have to bring you up to London/All the
467 CC   Colby   13 The empty years./Oh, I'm terribly sorry to be saying this;/But it goes to explain
472 CC   Lucasta   32 be someone like Claude ... or B. I was sorry,/Very sorry for you. I admired your
472 CC   Lucasta   33 like Claude ... or B. I was sorry,/Very sorry for you. I admired your courage/In facing
478 CC   Lucasta   8 that,/And I will, if I choose. Oh, I'm sorry:/I suppose it's my mother coming out in
478 CC   Lucasta   12 mind at all. That you might be sorry for me./But now I don't want you to be
478 CC   Lucasta   13 me./But now I don't want you to be sorry, thank you./Why, I'd actually thought of
488 CC   Claude   17 and get her to confess it./{SC} I'm sorry, Elizabeth. If Mrs. Guzzard comes/To
490 CC   Colby   24 friends. Neither, as a parent./I am sorry. But that's why I say it doesn't matter/To
492 CC   Lady E   4 /{LE} Oh Claude! I am terribly sorry for you./I believe that if I had known of
496 CC   Claude   15   And Lady Elizabeth!/{SC} I'm sorry, Eggerson, to bring you up to London/At
499 CC   Lucasta   11   I came to speak to Colby./I'm sorry./{SC} Colby will be here./But you're not
504 CC   Lucasta   4 see her. {}/[*Enter* LUCASTA]/{L} I'm sorry to come back. It's an anti-climax./But
518 CC   Colby   13 when we come to it, Eggers./Oh, I'm sorry .../{E} Don't be sorry: I'm delighted./And
518 CC   Eggers   14 Eggers./Oh, I'm sorry .../{E} Don't be sorry: I'm delighted./And by the way, a

532 ES	Ld Clav	12	And then I'll see you off./{LC} I'm sorry to turn you out of the room like this,/But
539 ES	Gomez	16	vicissitudes./Dick, I was very very sorry when I heard/That your marriage had not
545 ES	Monica	35	you!/{M} You're very kind ... Oh, I'm sorry,/We don't know how we ought to address
546 ES	Piggott	16	Or Ferry: it's shorter./{MP} So sorry. Miss Claverton-Ferry. I'm Mrs. Piggott./
567 ES	Charles	12	you loved me,/But I wondered ... I'm sorry, I couldn't help wondering/How much
580 ES	Monica	26	/{M} Oh Father, Father, I'm so sorry!/But perhaps, perhaps, Michael may learn
582 ES	Ld Clav	15	at all what you were expecting./I am sorry you have had to see so much of persons/

SORT (32)

29	Aunt Helen	7	his feet —/He was aware that this sort of thing had occurred before./The dogs
43	Swee Erect	40	Turner intimates/It does the house no sort of good./But Doris, towelled from the bath,
233	Skimble	37	of dust on the floor./There is every sort of light — you can make it dark or bright;/
300 FR	Charles	1	something might happen./{C} What sort of thing?/{Do} Well, I don't know, Sir./But
323 FR	Amy	17	all that he needs./{A} Accident? What sort of an accident?/{Wi} Coming along in the
325 FR	Charles	9	popular tonight./{C} Well, there's no sort of use in any of us going —/On a night like
344 FR	Gerald	18	—/But you have to go in for some sort of training;/The medical knowledge is the
365 CP	Julia	2	mine —/Some kind of a plastic sort of frame —/I'm afraid I don't remember
377 CP	Celia	8	rather afraid of him;/He has some sort of power./{E} I don't know who he is./But I
380 CP	Celia	30	you want Lavinia./And if that is the sort of person you are —/Well, you had better
397 CP	Lavinia	35	will tend to compromise,/And your sort of compromise will be the old one./{E} You
400 CP	Alex	13	/But he thinks I'm well informed: the sort of person/Who would know the right
406 CP	Reilly	18	to one./The people who need my sort of sanatorium/Are not easily deceived./{L}
437 CP	Reilly	24	The only question/Then was, what sort of death? *I* could not know;/Because it was
471 CC	Lucasta	25	to give a false impression?/What sort of impression was I trying to give?/{C} That
480 CC	Kaghan	39	things. But as for Colby,/He's the sort of fellow who might chuck it all/And go to
482 CC	Lady E	14	/To both of them — you're not the sort of person/They ever meet in their kind of
482 CC	Lady E	26	well, rather vulgar. They're not your sort at all./{C} I shouldn't call them vulgar.
482 CC	Colby	28	too./But what, do you think, *is* my sort?/I don't know, myself. And I should like to
483 CC	Colby	22	I designed this room./{C} It's the sort of room I wanted. {}/[*rising*]./{LE} And I
493 CC	Claude	11	the desk./You see, I want him to be a sort of chairman./{LE} That's a good idea./{SC}
531 ES	Ld Clav	39	without your seeing him./{LC} What sort of a person?/{L} A foreign person/By the
533 ES	Ld Clav	26	you've won respect out there/By the sort of activity that lost you respect/Here in
537 ES	Gomez	8	soul/With hoops of steel, and all that sort of thing./We'll come to that, very soon.
537 ES	Gomez	16	as anyone could be/From the sort of men you'd been at school with —/I
552 ES	Carghil	36	Maisie./{MC} There'll always be some sort of part for you/Right to the end. You'll still
555 ES	Piggott	3	person,/I dare say, but not quite your sort or mine./I suspected that she wanted to
556 ES	Ld Clav	18	have thought/It would be the sort of place that you'd choose for a holiday./
558 ES	Michael	17	from the son of your father'/And that sort of thing. It's for your sake, he says,/That he
560 ES	Ld Clav	12	to put up some capital./{LC} What sort of business have you in mind?/{Mi} Oh, I
574 ES	Michael	33	/Half round the world, for the same sort of job/You got me here in London? With
574 ES	Michael	36	/And send you back reports. Some sort of place/Where everyone would sneer at the

SORT (1) [*Foreign word*]

51	Restaurant	30	/Figurez-vous donc, c'était un sort pénible;/Cependant, ce fut jadis un bel

SORTILEGE (1)

189 FQ: DrySal		194	from fingers; release omens/By sortilege, or tea leaves, riddle the inevitable/

SORTS (1)

414 CP	Celia	5	that's always happening/To all sorts of people, and they get over it/More or

SOSOSTRIS (1)

62 WL: Burial		43	/*Oed' und leer das Meer.*/Madame Sosostris, famous clairvoyante,/Had a bad cold,

SOUGHT (2)

271 MC	Thomas	31	and what is happening;/No life here is sought for but mine,/And I am not in danger:
418 CP	Reilly	29	towards possession/Of what you have sought for in the wrong place./{C} That sounds

SOUL (29)

18	Portrait	10	intimate, this Chopin, that I think his soul/Should be resurrected only among friends/
23	Preludes	28	sordid images/Of which your soul was constituted;/They flickered against the
23	Preludes	39	the palms of both soiled hands./His soul stretched tight across the skies/That fade
34	Figlia	11	grieve,/So he would have left/As the soul leaves the body torn and bruised,/As the
107	Animula	1	from the hand of God, the simple soul'/To a flat world of changing lights and
107	Animula	16	say./The heavy burden of the growing soul/Perplexes and offends more, day by day;/
107	Animula	22	the drug of dreams/Curl up the small soul in the window seat/Behind the
107	Animula	24	from the hand of time the simple soul/Irresolute and selfish, misshapen, lame,/
111	Xmas Trees	32	occasion/When fear came upon every soul:/Because the beginning shall remind us of
155	Rock 3	57	depart and return to the desert./O my soul, be prepared for the coming of the
164	Rock 9	16	the joyful communion of saints./The soul of Man must quicken to creation./Out of
164	Rock 9	18	always new forms of life, from the soul of man that is joined to the soul of stone;/
164	Rock 9	18	the soul of man that is joined to the soul of stone;/Out of the meaningless practical

173 FQ: BurntN   99   /Nor darkness to purify the soul/Emptying the sensual with deprivation/
180 FQ: ECoker   113   there is no one to bury./I said to my soul, be still, and let the dark come upon you/
180 FQ: ECoker   124   conscious of nothing —/I said to my soul, be still, and wait without hope/For hope
194 FQ: Little   136   of shadow fruit/As body and soul begin to fall asunder./Second, the
234 Ad-dress   23   whole,/What you would call a simple soul./Of course I'm not including Pekes,/And
594 Grad 9   1   forgot./For in the sanctuaries of the soul/Incense of altar-smoke shall rise to thee/
261 MC Thomas   16   them; we rejoice, that another soul is/numbered among the Saints in Heaven,
272 MC Chorus   30   into dream, pretence,/Where the soul is no longer deceived, for there are no
272 MC Chorus   31   no forms to distract, to divert the soul/From seeing itself, foully united forever,
276 MC Chorus   17   the bone, wash the brain, wash the soul, wash them wash them! {}/[*The* KNIGHTS,
322 FR Winch   5   /If it was my mother's. God rest her soul,/She's been dead these ten years. How is
505 CC Claude   12   the proceedings:/He's the very soul of tact and discretion./{MG} Certainly, Sir
537 ES Gomez   7   /Adoption tried, and grappled to my soul/With hoops of steel, and all that sort of
541 ES Gomez   11   I promise you./Rely upon me as the soul of discretion./{LC} What do you want
553 ES Carghil   12   get alarmed. But you touched my soul —/Pawed it, perhaps, and the touch still
568 ES Ld Clav   22   from the rest of the world — your soul is safe./If a man has one person, just one in
SOUL'S (2)
191 FQ: Little   12   Between melting and freezing/The soul's sap quivers. There is no earth smell/Or
255 MC Thomas   29   them./{T} Is there no way, in my soul's sickness,/Does not lead to damnation in
SOULS (8)
 27 Morning   3   of the street/I am aware of the damp souls of housemaids/Sprouting despondently at
 54 Mr E Sun   23   by staring Seraphim/Where the souls of the devout/Burn invisible and dim./
 83 Hollow Men   16   us — if at all — not as lost/Violent souls, but only/As the hollow men/The stuffed
162 Rock 8   20   along the routes;/Many left their souls in Syria,/Living on, sunken in moral
174 FQ: BurntN   111   time after./Eructation of unhealthy souls/Into the faded air, the torpid/Driven on
273 MC Priests   29   not more/Against beasts with the souls of damned men, against men/Who would
280 MC Priest3   17   for it./Go, weak sad men, lost erring souls, homeless in earth or heaven./Go where
421 CP Julia   4   when they are stripped naked to their souls/And can choose, whether to put on proper
SOUND (27)
 61 WL: Burial   24   no relief,/And the dry stone no sound of water. Only/There is shadow under
 62 WL: Burial   68   kept the hours/With a dead sound on the final stroke of nine./There I saw
 67 WL: Fire S   197 my back from time to time I hear/The sound of horns and motors, which shall bring/
 72 WL: Thund   352 pool among the rock/If there were the sound of water only/Not the cicada/And dry
 73 WL: Thund   355 the cicada/And dry grass singing/But sound of water over a rock/Where the
 73 WL: Thund   366 on the other side of you?/What is that sound high in the air/Murmur of maternal
121 SA Sweeney   29   other way,/Nothing to hear but the sound of the surf./Nothing at all but three
122 SAWa & Ho   26   *fall/And the penguin call/And the sound is the sound of the sea/Under the bam/*
122 SAWa & Ho   26   *the penguin call/And the sound is the sound of the sea/Under the bam/Under the boo/*
123 SAWa & Ho   10   */Any fresh egg/Any fresh egg/And the sound of the coral sea./*{Do} I don't like eggs; I
136 5FingerEx4   3   wants to know *him*)/With his musical sound/And his Baskerville Hound/Which, just
164 Rock 9   21   form, new colour./Out of the sea of sound the life of music,/Out of the slimy mud of
182 FQ: ECoker   172 of which we like to think/That we are sound, substantial flesh and blood —/Again, in
189 FQ: DrySal   186 /Or wherever cannot reach them the sound of the sea bell's/Perpetual angelus./To
192 FQ: Little   50   /Of the praying mind, or the sound of the voice praying./And what the dead
193 FQ: Little   86   tin/Over the asphalt where no other sound was/Between three districts whence the
205 de la Mare   33   wove —/The inexplicable mystery of sound./A Dedication to my Wife/To whom I
209 NamingCats   9   are fancier names if you think they sound sweeter,/Some for the gentlemen, some
213 Growltiger   38   all the enemy there was not heard a sound./The lovers sang their last duet, in danger
304 FR Mary   30   had killed her by willing./Doesn't that sound awful? I know that it does./Did you ever
474 CC Lucasta   8   real/And acceptable, I think./{L} You sound awfully religious./Is there no other way
481 CC Kaghan   4   business./{K} And you have a very sound head for business./Maybe you're a better
487 CC Claude   3   it. I can't use notes:/It's got to sound spontaneous. I've jotted down some
506 CC Eggers   37 Elizabeth,/There are other places that sound like Teddington/But not so many names
506 CC Eggers   38   /But not so many names that sound like Guzzard —/Or if there are, they are
567 ES Monica   8   when I had been yearning/For the sound of it, for the caress that is in it!/Oh
572 ES Ld Clav   32   harm you./{LC} Your reasoning's sound enough. But it's irrelevant./Each of them
SOUNDLESS (1)
185 FQ: DrySal   51   bell./Where is there an end of it, the soundless wailing,/The silent withering of
SOUNDS (10)
389 CP Celia   37   *it*]/{C} Oh, I'm afraid that all this sounds rather silly!/But ... {}/[EDWARD
413 CP Celia   39   An awareness of solitude./But that sounds so flat. I don't mean simply/That there's
414 CP Celia   35 symptom?/{C} That's stranger still./It sounds ridiculous — but the only word for it/
418 CP Celia   17   to that life./Oh, I'm afraid this sounds like raving!/Or just cantankerousness ...
418 CP Celia   30   for in the wrong place./{C} That sounds like what I want. But what is my duty?/
419 CP Celia   22 do not come back as these did./{C} It sounds like a prison. But they can't *all* stay

471 CC   Colby   30   /I hope you don't mind: I know it sounds impertinent./{L} Well, there's one thing
489 CC   Claude   6   For such a foolish reason./Absurd it sounds now. One child each —/That seemed fair
511 CC   Kaghan   33   all right./But Barney Kaghan — it sounds rather flashy:/It wouldn't make the right
561 ES   Monica   36   life for you./Oh, how silly that phrase sounds! But there's no vocabulary/For love
SOUPE (1)
 51 Restaurant   7   te prie, au moins, ne bave pas dans la soupe)./'Les saules trempés, et des bourgeons
SOUR (1)
263 MC   Chorus   17   in the winter, or we shall have only/A sour spring, a parched summer, an empty
SOURCE (2)
190 FQ: DrySal   226   which is only moved/And has in it no source of movement —/Driven by dmonic,
197 FQ: Little   248   that which was the beginning;/At the source of the longest river/The voice of the
SOURCES (2)
408 CP   Reilly   38   you/Was all obtained from outside sources./Mrs. Chamberlayne, when you came to
530 ES   Monica   8   restless energy — the inexhaustible/Sources of the power that wears out the
SOUS (1)
 51 Restaurant   24   comme moi?/Tiens, voilà dix sous, pour la salle-de-bains./Phlébas, le
SOUS-MER (1)
 51 Restaurant   28   et la cargaison d'étain:/Un courant de sous-mer l'emporta très loin,/Le repassant aux
SOUTH (11)
 61 WL: Burial   18   /I read, much of the night, and go south in the winter./What are the roots that
154 Rock 3   28   North, from the West and from the South/Whence thousands travel daily to the
592 Grad 3   3   tempest, when some haste/North, South, and Eastward o'er the water's waste,/
263 MC   Chorus   1   /Part II/{C} Does the bird sing in the South?/Only the sea-bird cries, driven inland by
285 FR   Ivy   14   I have always told Amy she should go south in the winter./Were I in Amy's position, I
285 FR   Ivy   15   /Were I in Amy's position, I would go south in the winter./I would follow the sun, not
285 FR   Ivy   17   for the sun to come here./I would go south in the winter, if I could afford it,/Not
285 FR   Violet   19   a gas-fire counting shillings./{V} Go south! to the English circulating libraries,/To
286 FR   Violet   13   /{V} Well, as for me,/I would never go south, no, definitely never,/Even could I do it as
286 FR   Violet   15   bad enough, I would never go south,/Simply to see the vulgarest people —/
303 FR   Mary   2   /Late and uncertain, clings to the south wall./The gardener had no garden-flowers
SOUTHERN (1)
149 Rock 1   70   the desert./The desert is not remote in southern tropics,/The desert is not only around
SOUTHWEST (1)
 70 WL: Fire S   286   /The brisk swell/Rippled both shores/Southwest wind/Carried down stream/The peal
SOUVENIRS (1)
483 CC   Lady E   28   /Is the proper place for photographic souvenirs. {}/[*She sits down, holding the*
SOVEGNA (1)
 94 Ash-Wed 4   11   of larkspur, blue of Mary's colour,/Sovegna vos/Here are the years that walk
SOVEREIGN (1)
240 MC   Priest2   28   does the Archbishop do, and our Sovereign Lord the Pope/With the stubborn
SOVEREIGNTY (1)
251 MC   Tempt3   25   /England is a land for Norman/Sovereignty. Let the Angevin/Destroy himself,
SOWED (1)
267 MC   Knight1   34   in the French dominions./You sowed strife abroad, you reviled/The King to
SOWING (1)
148 Rock 1   59   of the harvest,/But only of proper sowing./The world turns and the world changes,
SPACE (2)
590 Time Space   1   found in the ruins./If Time and Space, as Sages say,/Are things which cannot
590 Space Time   1   be few/Yet let them be divine./Song/If space and time, as sages say,/Are things that
SPACES (3)
 24 Rhapsody   10   a fatalistic drum,/And through the spaces of the dark/Midnight shakes the memory
 37 Gerontion   16   old man,/A dull head among windy spaces./Signs are taken for wonders. 'We would
180 FQ: ECoker   103   into the dark,/The vacant interstellar spaces, the vacant into the vacant,/The captains,
SPADES (3)
117 SP   Doris   25   of friends'./{Do} Here's the two of spades./{Du} The *two of spades*!/THAT'S THE
117 SP   Dusty   26   the two of spades./{Du} The *two of spades*!/THAT'S THE COFFIN!!/{Do} THAT'S
117 SP   Dusty   39   You cut for luck./{Du} The Knave of Spades./{Do} That'll be Snow/{Du} Or it might
SPANIARDS (1)
564 ES   Carghil   19   looks that you were Spanish./I do like Spaniards. They're so aristocratic./But it's very
SPANISH (4)
 56 Swee Night   11   the shrunken seas;/The person in the Spanish cape/Tries to sit on Sweeney's knees/
587 Fable   30   own expense a crowd/Of relics from a Spanish saint — said he:/'If ghosts come
536 ES   Gomez   17   No, they do not./They think in Spanish, but their thoughts are Indian thoughts.
564 ES   Carghil   18   tell from your looks that you were Spanish./I do like Spaniards. They're so

SPAR (1)
69 WL: Fire S   272 Wide/To leeward, swing on the heavy spar./The barges wash/Drifting logs/Down
SPARE (8)
227 Macavity   37 always has an alibi, and one or two to spare:/At whatever time the deed took place —
236 Cat Morgan   19 /You'll save yourself time, and you'll spare yourself labour/If jist you make friends
320 FR Warburt   25 for you, Harry./I should have liked to spare you this,/Just now. But there were two
361 CP   Reilly 8 It will all take time that you can't well spare;/But I put it to you .../{E} Don't put it in
457 CC   Eggers 13 arrive at the airport with minutes to spare,/And besides, there's the Customs. That'll
518 CC   Eggers 18 you settled on lodgings;/We have a spare room. We should be most happy/If you
529 ES   Monica   3 you can take me out, if Father can spare me./But he'll simply love having you to
557 ES Ld Clav   5 the question of blame:/Which will spare you the necessity of blaming someone
SPARED (2)
272 MC Thomas   4 the shepherd here; the flock shall be spared./I have had a tremor of bliss, a wink of
371 CP   Peter   1 escape./{P} I should prefer to be spared/Your congratulations. I had to talk to
SPARROW (1)
150 Rock 1   110 /The river flows, the seasons turn/The sparrow and starling have no time to waste./If
SPARROWS (1)
23 Preludes   32   the shutters/And you heard the sparrows in the gutters,/You had such a vision
SPASM (1)
85 Hollow Men   85 very long/Between the desire/And the spasm/Between the potency/And the existence/
SPATS (2)
230 Bust Jones   12   to/By Bustopher Jones in white spats!/His visits are occasional to the *Senior*
231 Bust Jones   40 /While Bustopher Jones wears white spats!/Skimbleshanks: the Railway Cat/There's
SPAWN (1)
270 MC Chorus   2 and the prawn; and they live and spawn in my bowels, and my bowels dissolve in
SPAWNED (1)
37 Gerontion   9 squats on the window sill, the owner,/Spawned in some estaminet of Antwerp,/
SPEAK (52)
37 Gerontion   18 /The word within a word, unable to speak a word,/Swaddled with darkness. In the
62 WL: Burial   39 full, and your hair wet, I could not/Speak, and my eyes failed, I was neither/Living
65 WL: Chess   112 bad to-night. Yes, bad. Stay with me./'Speak to me. Why do you never speak. Speak./
65 WL: Chess   112 me./'Speak to me. Why do you never speak. Speak./'What are you thinking of? What
65 WL: Chess   112 to me. Why do you never speak. Speak./'What are you thinking of? What
67 WL: Fire S   184 song;/Sweet Thames, run softly, for I speak not loud or long./But at my back in a
92 Ash-Wed 3   24 worthy/Lord, I am not worthy/but speak the word only./Who walked between the
194 FQ: Little   111 ease is cause of wonder. Therefore speak:/I may not comprehend, may not
194 FQ: Little   125 /So I find words I never thought to speak/In streets I never thought I should revisit/
222 Pekes Pols   11 /Now on the occasion of which I shall speak/Almost nothing had happened for nearly
235 Ad-dress   39 Cats, some say, one rule is true:/*Don't speak till you are spoken to.*/Myself, I do not
245 MC Thomas   12 let them be, in their exaltation./They speak better than they know, and beyond your
251 MC Thomas   33 /{T} But what have you —/If you do speak for barons —/{T3} For a powerful party/
266 MC Knight1   10 Most surely from the King./We must speak with you alone. {}/[*to* PRIESTS]/{T}
272 MC   m   10 *drag him off. While the* CHORUS *speak, the scene is changed to the cathedral.*]/
276 MC Knight1   31 I/shall call upon our eldest member to speak first, my neighbour in/the country: Baron
277 MC Knight3   8 taken on a pretty stiff job; I'll only speak for/myself, but I had drunk a good deal
287 FR Gerald   5 to live in./Let the younger generation speak for itself:/It's Mary's generation. What
308 FR   Mary   12 of the death of hope/Of which you speak, I know you have experienced it,/And I
312 FR Harry   9 one fight with stupidity?/Yet I must speak to them. {}/[*He rushes forward and tears*
324 FR Harry   35 planes at once/Though one cannot speak with several voices at once./I have all of
338 FR Harry   10 why are you going?/{H} I can only speak/And you cannot hear me. I can only
338 FR Harry   11 /And you cannot hear me. I can only speak/So you may not think I conceal an
362 CP Edward   11 happier/With another person. Why speak of love?/We were used to each other. So
369 CP   Peter   21 her Thursdays were a failure./{P} You speak as if everything was finished./{E} Oh no,
380 CP Edward   11 as a passing diversion!/If you want to speak of passing diversions/How did you take
381 CP Edward   36   the tougher self; who does not speak,/Who never talks, who cannot argue;/
386 CP   Reilly   2 explain to you/I must ask you not to speak of me to her;/And she will not mention
395 CP Edward   4 which you cease to feel/And then you speak your mind./{L} That will be a novelty/To
395 CP Lavinia   6 /To find that you have a mind to speak./Anyway, I'm prepared to take you as
405 CP   Reilly   16 have been making up your case/So to speak, as you went along. A barrister/Ought to
414 CP   Celia   13 —/It no longer seems worth while to *speak* to anyone!/{R} And what about your
421 CP   Reilly   39 /{R} He should be here by now. I'll speak to Miss Barraway. {}/[*Takes up*
423 CP   Julia   1 the words are valid./{J} Shall we ever speak them?/{A} Others, perhaps, will speak
423 CP   Alex   2 speak them?/{A} Others, perhaps, will speak them./You know, I have connections —
433 CP   Alex   26 does Julia mean?/{A} I was about to speak of her/When you came in, Peter. I'm
438 CP   Reilly   7 be hinted at/In myths and images. To speak about it/We talk of darkness, labyrinths,

438 CP	Edward	18	involved in the wrong,/I should only speak for myself. I'm sure that *I* am./{R} Let me
453 CC	Lucasta	15	of the way. Why don't you let him speak?/Eggy's really quite human, Colby./It's
454 CC	Eggers	1	will have to ask Sir Claude. But I'll speak to him/When I return from Northolt./{L}
457 CC	Lady E	30	coffee. Is Sir Claude at home?/I'll speak to him first./{SC} Good heavens,
463 CC	Colby	19	Just as, I suppose,/If you learn to speak a foreign language fluently,/So that you
482 CC	Lady E	17	they want to take you up./I can speak more freely, as an elderly person./{C} But,
496 CC	Eggers	39	day we got the news. We don't often speak of it;/Yet I know what's on her mind, for
499 CC	Lucasta	10	/{L} Is this a meeting? I came to speak to Colby./I'm sorry./{SC} Colby will be
542 ES	Gomez	15	/{G} Threats, Dick! How can you speak of threats?/It's most unkind of you. My
550 ES	Carghil	1	give me such a thrill/To hear you speak my name once more./{LC} Your name
561 ES	Monica	22	/{M} Michael! How can you speak to Father like that?/Father! What has
563 ES	Carghil	6	I'd love to meet him./He's coming to speak to us. You must introduce him. {}/[*Enter*
564 ES	Carghil	17	at Oxford!/Is that how you come to speak such perfect English!/Of course, I could
569 ES	Ld Clav	3	change into our own clothes/And speak as ourselves. So I'd become an idol/To
583 ES	Monica	12	together./Oh Father, Father!/I could speak to you now./{C} Let me go and find him./

SPEAKER (3)

276 MC	Knight3	34	not anything like such an experienced/speaker as my old friend Reginald Fitz Urse
279 MC	Knight1	7	We have,/however, one more speaker, who has I think another point of view/
279 MC	Knight4	18	over/the ground traversed by the last speaker. While the late Archbishop/was

SPEAKERS (3)

276 MC	Knight1	28	do no more than introduce the other speakers, who,/with their various abilities, and
277 MC	Knight1	32	that; and you must hear/our other speakers. I shall next call upon Hugh de
279 MC	Knight4	11	them. Richard Brito./{K4} The speakers who have preceded me, to say nothing/

SPEAKING (8)

294 FR	Harry	4	o'clock in the morning. I am not speaking/Of my own experience, but trying to
338 FR	Amy	37	/Will appear to run away./{A} I was speaking to Harry./{H} It is very hard, when
343 FR		m 31	rain do that. {}/[*While* AMY *has been speaking,* HARRY *has entered, dressed for*
347 FR	Downing	10	see them cheerful-like,/In a manner of speaking. There's no harm in *them*,/I'll take my
437 CP	Lavinia	1	/{L} Oh no, I should love to hear you speaking poetry .../{J} She has made a point,
458 CC	Eggers	2	doing? {}/[*at the open door*]./{E} She's speaking to the parlourmaid. She's coming up./
464 CC	Colby	22	the same./All the time you've been speaking, I've been translating/Into terms of
498 CC	Eggers	14	people's children?/In a manner of speaking, it's perfectly respectable./{SC} You're

SPEAKS (1)

| 297 FR | Amy | 1 | Warburton's opinion./{A} If anyone speaks to Dr. Warburton/It should be myself. |

SPEARS (3)

134 Wind		10	river/The camp fire shake with alien spears./Here, across death's other river/The
134 Wind		12	/The Tartar horsemen shake their spears./Five-Finger Exercises/*Lines to a Persian*
158 Rock 5		11	labour, and others must hold the spears./It is hard for those who have never

SPECIAL (2)

| 277 MC | Knight1 | 33 | Hugh de Morville, who/has made a special study of statecraft and constitutional |
| 368 CP | Alex | 23 | think of it./{A} Ah, but that's my special gift —/Concocting a toothsome meal out |

SPECIALIST (1)

| 546 ES | Piggott | 5 | /A medical milieu. My father was a specialist/In pharmacology. And my husband/ |

SPECIALLY (1)

| 120 SP | Krum | 7 | a fine place to come on a visit —/{Kr} Specially when you got a real live Britisher/A |

SPECIFICS (1)

| 348 FR | Chorus | 21 | sorcery,/Divination and chiromancy,/Specifics against insomnia,/Lumbago, and the |

SPECIMENS (1)

| 287 FR | Gerald | 1 | I must say I've met some very decent specimens/And some first-class shots — better |

SPECK (1)

| 233 Skimble | | 36 | newly folded sheet/And there's not a speck of dust on the floor./There is every sort of |

SPECTACLES (5)

365 CP	Julia	15	my life./It's very lucky that I left my spectacles:/*This* is what I call an adventure!/Tell
383 CP	Edward	2	... Oh, Julia: what is it now?/Your spectacles again ... where did you leave them?/
383 CP		m 10	/[*Exit* EDWARD. *He returns with the spectacles and a bottle*]/{E} She was right for
383 CP	Celia	23	she is *my* guardian. Give me the spectacles./Good night, Edward./{E} Good
391 CP	Julia	11	/{J} Left anything? Oh, you mean my spectacles./No, they're here. Besides, they're no

SPECTATEUR (4)

46 Directeur		2	Tamise/Qui coule si près du Spectateur./Le directeur/Conservateur/Du
46 Directeur		5	/Le directeur/Conservateur/Du Spectateur/Empeste la brise./Les actionnaires/
46 Directeur		9	/Les actionnaires/Réactionnaires/Du Spectateur/Conservateur/Bras dessus bras
46 Directeur		20	/Camarde/Regarde/Le directeur/Du Spectateur/Conservateur/Et crève d'amour./

SPECTATORS (1)

| 327 FR | Agatha | 3 | we cannot rest in being/The impatient spectators of malice or stupidity./We must try |

SPECTRAL (1)
569 ES Ld Clav 39 and I see myself emerging/From my spectral existence into something like reality./
SPECTRE (2)
107 Animula   29 blood,/Shadow of its own shadows, spectre in its own gloom,/Leaving disordered
196 FQ: Little   186 is it an incantation/To summon the spectre of a Rose./We cannot revive old factions
SPECTRES (4)
602 Humoresque   14   other useless things/Haranguing spectres, set him there;/'The snappiest fashion
289 FR Agatha   2 —/The hidden is revealed, and the spectres show themselves./{G} I don't in the
338 FR Harry   23 one meets them. That is the way of spectres .../{A} There is no one here!/No one,
569 ES Ld Clav   35 real, Charles. They are merely ghosts:/Spectres from my past. They've always been
SPECULATION (4)
154 Rock 3   12 and you only alternate/Between futile speculation and unconsidered action./Many are
171 FQ: BurntN   8   possibility/Only in a world of speculation./What might have been and what
480 CC Kaghan   3 —/Lucasta's the most exciting speculation/I've ever thought of investing in./
557 ES Ld Clav   14 I dare say you've tried a little private speculation./{Mi} Several of my friends gave me
SPECULATIONS (1)
361 CP Edward   23 about us than appears —/I think your speculations rather offensive./{UG} I know you
SPECULATIVE (1)
557 ES Michael   13 Well?/{Mi} I want to find some more speculative business./{LC} I dare say you've
SPEECH (26)
 85 Hollow Men   59 places/We grope together/And avoid speech/Gathered on this beach of the tumid
 92 Ash-Wed 2   43 Conclusion of all that/Is inconclusible/Speech without word and/Word of no speech/
 92 Ash-Wed 2   44 Speech without word and/Word of no speech/Grace to the Mother/For the Garden/
110 Marina   31 let me/Resign my life for this life, my speech for that unspoken,/The awakened, lips
147 Rock 1   9   but not of stillness;/Knowledge of speech, but not of silence;/Knowledge of words,
149 Rock 1   89 *is unspoken/We will build with new speech/There is work together/A Church for all/*
150 Rock 1   118 *no peace and no end/But noise without speech, food without taste./Without delay,*
154 Rock 3   7 turn from worship,/I have given you speech, for endless palaver,/I have given you my
164 Rock 9   24 /There spring the perfect order of speech, and the beauty of incantation./LORD,
175 FQ: BurntN   142 only living/Can only die. Words, after speech, reach/Into the silence. Only by the form,
192 FQ: Little   51 praying./And what the dead had no speech for, when living,/They can tell you, being
194 FQ: Little   128 distant shore./Since our concern was speech, and speech impelled us/To purify the
194 FQ: Little   128 /Since our concern was speech, and speech impelled us/To purify the dialect of the
201 Def Island   21 generations/of our kin and of our speech, that we took up/our positions, in
206 To my Wife   6 the same thoughts without need of speech/And babble the same speech without
206 To my Wife   7 need of speech/And babble the same speech without need of meaning./No peevish
384 CP Edward   24 /{E} From the dead?/That figure of speech is somewhat ... dramatic,/As it was only
486 CC Claude   35 him these notes. They're notes for my speech/At the dinner of the Potters' Company./
487 CC Claude   1 you know that I'll have to have my speech written out/And then memorise it. I
487 CC Claude   10 have asked Eggerson to write a speech for me./Oh, by the way, Colby, how's
492 CC Colby   18 I must remind you/About your speech for the Potters' Company/Tomorrow
522 ES dedic   6 *the same thoughts without need of speech/And babble the same speech without need*
522 ES dedic   7 *need of speech/And babble the same speech without need of meaning:/To you I*
530 ES Monica   30 the staff,/The presentation, and the speech you had to make/And the speeches that
562 ES Monica   1 love within which/All other love finds speech./This love is silent./What can I say to
583 ES Charles   4 my dear,/I love you to the limits of speech, and beyond./It's strange that words are
SPEECHES (2)
228 Gus   22   part,/And I used to know seventy speeches by heart./I'd extemporize back-chat, I
530 ES Monica   31 the speech you had to make/And the speeches that you had to listen to! {}/[*pointing*
SPEECHLESS (1)
545 ES Ld Clav   6 us, this silent observer,/Severe and speechless critic, who can terrorise us/And urge
SPEED (1)
108 Animula   32 viaticum./Pray for Guiterriez, avid of speed and power,/For Boudin, blown to pieces,/
SPELL (5)
117 SP Doris   38 You cut for luck./It might break the spell. You cut for luck./{Du} The Knave of
140 Usk   4 /Glance aside, not for lance, do not spell/Old enchantments. Let them sleep./'Gently
324 FR Harry   19 be glad for him to have a breathing spell:/But John's ordinary day isn't much more
342 FR Amy   11 you will not succeed: she has some spell/That works from generation to generation.
342 FR Agatha   15 /{Ag} He is going./But that is not my spell, it is none of my doing:/I have only
SPELLS (1)
348 FR Chorus   18 the act of God./We know various spells and enchantments./And minor forms of
SPEND (3)
147 Rock 1   24 where they work, but where they spend their Sundays./In the City, we need no
277 MC Knight3   20 row; and at the best we shall have to/spend the rest of our lives abroad. And even
368 CP Alex   5 evening,/And I know that he hates to spend an evening alone,/So you're going to

SPENDING (1)
518 CC   Eggers   4   as an impertinence —/I don't see you spending a lifetime as an organist./I think you'll
SPENT (10)
96 Ash-Wed 5   1   our exile/If the lost word is lost, if the spent word is spent/If the unheard, unspoken/
96 Ash-Wed 5   1   lost word is lost, if the spent word is spent/If the unheard, unspoken/Word is
254 MC Tempt4   32   shrine shall be pillaged, and the gold spent,/The jewels gone for light ladies'
258 MC Thomas   17   /Ambition comes when early force is spent/And when we find no longer all things
309 FR   Harry   29   I know that this is true./{H} I have spent many years in useless travel;/You have
393 CP   Lavinia   5   discovery,/Finding that you've spent five years of your life/With a man who
445 CC   Eggers   12   excuse for coming up to London:/I've spent the morning shopping! Gardening tools./
476 CC   Lucasta   39   much he'd given her:/It was always spent before the end of the quarter/On gin and
549 ES   Carghil   7   Effie, Maudie and me./That day we spent on the river — I've never forgotten it —/
568 ES   Ld Clav   37   such a web of fiction about you!/I've spent my life in trying to forget myself,/In trying
SPHERE (1)
188 FQ: DrySal   158   /You can receive this: "on whatever sphere of being/The mind of a man may be
SPHERES (1)
190 FQ: DrySal   221   /Here the impossible union/Of spheres of existence is actual,/Here the past and
SPIDER (2)
38 Gerontion   65   a wilderness of mirrors. What will the spider do,/Suspend its operations, will the
74 WL: Thund   407   in memories draped by the beneficent spider/Or under seals broken by the lean
SPIES (2)
157 Rock 4   16   enemies without to destroy him,/And spies and self-seekers within,/When he and his
246 MC Thomas   4   our letters,/Filled the coast with spies and sent to meet me/Some who hold me in
SPIN (1)
454 CC   Colby   36   be amused./But it did make my head spin — all those first names/The first time I met
SPINNING (1)
432 CP   Julia   20   interrupting./Now my head's fairly spinning. I must have a cocktail. {}/[*To*
SPIRES (1)
166 Rock 10   20   for the less;/The eastern light our spires touch at morning,/The light that slants
SPIRIT (28)
98 Ash-Wed 6   13   and the lost sea voices/And the weak spirit quickens to rebel/For the bent golden-rod
98 Ash-Wed 6   25   and reply./Blessèd sister, holy mother, spirit of the fountain, spirit of the garden,/
98 Ash-Wed 6   25   holy mother, spirit of the fountain, spirit of the garden,/Suffer us not to mock
99 Ash-Wed 6   33   these rocks/Sister, mother/And spirit of the river, spirit of the sea,/Suffer me
99 Ash-Wed 6   33   /Sister, mother/And spirit of the river, spirit of the sea,/Suffer me not to be separated/
111 Xmas Trees   10   Tree:/Let him continue in the spirit of wonder/At the Feast as an event not
151 Rock 2   7   for a habitation of GOD in the Spirit, the Spirit which moved on the face of the
151 Rock 2   7   a habitation of GOD in the Spirit, the Spirit which moved on the face of the waters
158 Rock 5   2   were doubtless men of public spirit and zeal./Preserve me from the enemy
160 Rock 7   7   on the face of the deep./And the Spirit moved upon the face of the water./And
165 Rock 9   32   service in creating./For Man is joined spirit and body,/And therefore must serve as
165 Rock 9   33   body,/And therefore must serve as spirit and body./Visible and invisible, two
174 FQ: BurntN   124   of fancy,/Inoperancy of the world of spirit;/This is the one way, and the other/Is the
191 FQ: Little   10   of branch, or brazier,/Stirs the dumb spirit: no wind, but pentecostal fire/In the dark
194 FQ: Little   123   now presents no hindrance/To the spirit unappeased and peregrine/Between two
195 FQ: Little   146   wrong to wrong the exasperated spirit/Proceeds, unless restored by that refining
202 War Poetry   10   by experiment —/Of Nature and the Spirit. Mostly the individual/Experience is too
589 Fable   78   do nought but gape and stare,/The spirit pulled him rudely by the collar,/And
271 MC Chorus   2   /Mastered by the animal powers of spirit,/Dominated by the lust of self-demolition,
271 MC Chorus   4   /By the final utter uttermost death of spirit,/By the final ecstasy of waste and shame,/
277 MC Knight2   38   with the under dog./It is the English spirit of fair play. Now the worthy Archbishop,/
310 FR   Mary   25   upstream:/And what of the terrified spirit/Compelled to be reborn/To rise toward
381 CP   Edward 40   dull, the implacable,/The indomitable spirit of mediocrity./The willing self can
404 CP   Edward 15   death is terrifying. The death of the spirit —/Can you understand what I suffer?/{R}
417 CP   Celia   11   is exalted by intensity of loving/In the spirit, a vibration of delight/Without desire, for
466 CC   Claude 16   /Into what she calls the life of the spirit/Are a kind of substitute for religion./I
561 ES   Ld Clav 29   /I want him to go in a very different spirit/From that which he has just been
578 ES   Monica 38   going abroad/But a question of the spirit which inspired your decision:/If you wish
SPIRITS (6)
189 FQ: DrySal   188   with Mars, converse with spirits,/To report the behaviour of the sea
589 Fable   93   mates 'till they grew good and friarly./Spirits from that time forth they did without,/
299 FR   Charles 21   Downing. Was she in good spirits?/{Do} Well, always about the same, Sir./
299 FRDowning   35   uncommon that I saw him in high spirits./For what my judgment's worth, I always
307 FR   Mary   5   we met by moonlight/To raise the evil spirits./{H} Arthur and John./Of course we were
421 CP   Reilly   22   /By the first appearance of projected spirits?/{J} Henry, you simply do not

SPIRITUAL (9)

241 MC	Priest1	27	secure/In the power of Rome, the spiritual rule,/The assurance of right, and the
249 MC	Tempt2	12	at price of a certain submission./Your spiritual power is earthly perdition./Power is
253 MC	Tempt4	27	stratagem,/To general grasp of spiritual power?/Man oppressed by sin, since
271 MC	Chorus	1	subdued, violated,/United to the spiritual flesh of nature,/Mastered by the animal
275 MC	Thomas	16	vassal,/Traitor to me as your spiritual lord,/Traitor to God in desecrating His
278 MC	Knight2	16	had an almost ideal State:/a union of spiritual and temporal administration, under the
334 FR	Agatha	10	my capital,/Instead of earning my spiritual income daily:/And I am old, to start
438 CP	Reilly	11	that the Saint in the desert/With spiritual evil always at his shoulder/Suffered any
459 CC	Lady E	21	the importance of colour/For our spiritual life, Mr. Colby./Neither, I regret to

SPIRITUALITY (1)

483 CC	Lady E	3	need intellectual, well-bred people/Of spirituality — and that's the rarest./{C} That

SPIT (2)

15 Prufrock		60	the wall,/Then how should I begin/To spit out all the butt-ends of my days and ways?/
72 WL: Thund		339	mouth of carious teeth that cannot spit/Here one can neither stand nor lie nor sit/

SPITE (7)

161 Rock 7		22	the Passion and Sacrifice saved in spite of their negative being;/Bestial as always
162 Rock 8		28	our King did well at Acre./And in spite of all the dishonour,/The broken
182 FQ: ECoker		171	/The bloody flesh our only food:/In spite of which we like to think/That we are
182 FQ: ECoker		173	flesh and blood —/Again, in spite of that, we call this Friday good./So here I
499 CC	Lucasta	30	determined that I wouldn't. Just to spite you,/I dare say. That was why I took an
542 ES	Ld Clav	20	I only gained in return/Your envy, spite and hatred. That is why you attribute/
581 ES	Ld Clav	26	of us do! And now I feel happy —/In spite of everything, in defiance of reason,/I have

SPITEFUL (1)

438 CP	Lavinia	40	/For being so unkind to her ... so spiteful./I shall go on seeing her at the moment/

SPITTING (1)

97 Ash-Wed 5		35	the garden in the desert/Of drouth, spitting from the mouth the withered

SPLEEN (2)

603 Spleen		t	/But, even at that, what mask *bizarre!*/Spleen/Sunday: this satisfied procession/Of
266 MC	Knight1	32	mean,/Saving your pride, envy and spleen./{K2} Saving your insolence and greed./

SPLENDID (2)

592 Grad 3		5	sky/Which the sun stains with many a splendid dye,/Until their passing may no more
391 CP	Julia	33	PETER]/{P} I've got a taxi, Julia./{J} Splendid! Good-bye! {}/[*Exeunt* JULIA, ALEX

SPLENDOUR (1)

69 WL: Fire S		265	/Of Magnus Martyr hold/Inexplicable splendour of Ionian white and gold./The river

SPLITTING (1)

272 MC	Chorus	16	twisting in the fingers,/Than when splitting in the skull./More than footfall in the

SPOILS (2)

440 CP	Lavinia	23	look your best./{L} Oh, Edward, that spoils it. No woman can believe/That she
547 ES	Piggott	31	who don't like being beaten,/And that spoils any sport, in my opinion./{M} Thank

SPOILT (1)

527 ES	Monica	36	/I'm afraid. Poor Michael! Mother spoilt him/And Father was too severe — so

SPOKE (13)

74 WL: Thund		399	crouched, humped in silence./Then spoke the thunder/DA/*Datta:* what have we
94 Ash-Wed 4		24	bent her head and signed but spoke no word/But the fountain sprang up and
162 Rock 8		8	alone./There came one who spoke of the shame of Jerusalem/And the holy
260 MC	Thomas	26	/Reflect now, how Our Lord Himself spoke of Peace. He said to His/disciples, 'Peace
370 CP	Peter	2	friends?/{P} No, but once or twice she spoke of them/And about their lack of
383 CP	Celia	21	To the Guardians. It was you who spoke of guardians. {}/[*They drink*]/{C} It may
466 CC	Claude	12	/With the maker, of which I spoke — an agonising ecstasy/Which makes life
466 CC	Claude	28	understand now what I meant when I spoke/Of accepting the terms life imposes upon
466 CC	Colby	37	you said, a little while ago,/When you spoke of never having understood your father/
466 CC	Colby	38	father/Until it was too late. And you spoke of atonement./Even your failure to
466 CC	Colby	40	to understand him,/Of which you spoke — that was a relationship/Of father and
528 ES	Charles	1	always at loggerheads./{C} But you spoke of several reasons for your going with
574 ES	Michael	31	then with Señor Gomez./{Mi} When I spoke, Father, of my wish to get abroad,/You

SPOKEN (16)

221 Old Deut		39	out they all shuffle, without a word spoken./The digestive repose of that feline's
235 Ad-dress		39	rule is true:/*Don't speak till you are spoken to.*/Myself, I do not hold with that —/I
261 MC	Thomas	37	which they draw their/being./I have spoken to you to-day, dear children of God, of
269 MC	Knight1	15	of Rome./{K1} Priest, you have spoken in peril of your life./{K2} Priest, you
269 MC	Knight2	16	of your life./{K2} Priest, you have spoken in danger of the knife./{K3} Priest, you
269 MC	Knight3	17	of the knife./{K3} Priest, you have spoken treachery and treason./{3K} Priest!
277 MC	Knight1	29	all agree that William de Traci has/spoken well and has made a very important
279 MC	Knight4	12	leader, Reginald Fitz Urse, have all spoken very much to the/point. I have nothing

292 FR	Ivy	36	ruin,/And he's nearly half blind. I've spoken to your mother/Time and time again:
292 FR	Violet	39	/{V} And time and time again I have spoken to your mother/About the waste that
328 FR	Chorus	34	listening, and more is heard than is spoken./And what is spoken remains in the
329 FR	Chorus	1	is heard than is spoken./And what is spoken remains in the room, waiting for the
349 FR	6m	13	*candles, so that their last/words are spoken in the dark.*]/{Ag} A curse is slow in
422 CP	Reilly	29	is one for whom the words cannot be spoken./{A} They can not be spoken yet./{J}
422 CP	Alex	30	be spoken./{A} They can not be spoken yet./{J} You mean Peter Quilpe./{R} He
433 CP	Peter	18	now I could help her./I've already spoken to Bela about her,/And I want to

SPONGE (1)

| 270 MC | Chorus | 5 | swallowed with ingurgitation of the sponge. I have lain in the soil and criticised the |

SPONTANEOUS (1)

| 487 CC | Claude | 3 | it. I can't use notes:/It's got to sound spontaneous. I've jotted down some headings./ |

SPOON (2)

| 224 Mr Mistoff | | 32 | can play any trick with a cork/Or a spoon and a bit of fish-paste;/If you look for a |
| 269 MC | Chorus | 31 | /The savour of putrid flesh in the spoon. I have felt/The heaving of earth at |

SPOONS (1)

| 14 Prufrock | | 51 | have measured out my life with coffee spoons;/I know the voices dying with a dying |

SPORT (1)

| 547 ES | Piggott | 31 | like being beaten,/And that spoils any sport, in my opinion./{M} Thank you, Mrs. |

SPORTFULNESS (1)

| 247 MC | Tempt1 | 5 | laity may return to gaiety,/Mirth and sportfulness need not walk warily./{T} You talk |

SPORTING (1)

| 20 Portrait | | 72 | the park/Reading the comics and the sporting page./Particularly I remark./An |

SPOT (3)

14 Prufrock		40	and descend the stair,/With a bald spot in the middle of my hair —/(They will say:
593 Grad 8		3	lot,/We shall desire to see again the spot/Which, whatsoever we have been or done/
568 ES Ld Clav		3	beech tree?/{LC} I feel drawn to that spot./No matter. I heard what you said about

SPOTLESS (1)

| 594 Grad 9 | | 3 | of altar-smoke shall rise to thee/From spotless fanes of lucid purity,/O school of ours! |

SPOTS (2)

| 210 Old Gumbie | | 2 | kind, with tiger stripes and leopard spots./All day she sits upon the stair or on the |
| 210 Old Gumbie | | 14 | to find, she likes the warm and sunny spots./All day she sits beside the hearth or in the |

SPOUT (1)

| 215 RTTugger | | 36 | —/And there isn't any need for me to spout it:/For he will do/As he do do/And there's |

SPRANG (6)

95 Ash-Wed 4		25	but spoke no word/But the fountain sprang up and the bird sang down/Redeem the
134 Wind		t	/And hold us in derision./The wind sprang up at four o'clock/The wind sprang up
134 Wind		1	sprang up at four o'clock/The wind sprang up at four o'clock/The wind sprang up
134 Wind		2	sprang up at four o'clock/The wind sprang up and broke the bells/Swinging between
598 Circe		6	/With hideous streak and stain;/They sprang from the limbs of the dead. —/We shall
604 Ode		7	/From the hopes and ambitions that sprang at thy feet/To the thoughts of the past as

SPRAWLING (2)

| 14 Prufrock | | 57 | phrase,/And when I am formulated, sprawling on a pin,/When I am pinned and |
| 605 Narcissus | | 4 | different from either/Your shadow sprawling over the sand at daybreak, or/Your |

SPRAWLS (1)

| 56 Swee Night | | 18 | up;/The silent man in mocha brown/Sprawls at the window-sill and gapes;/The |

SPRAY (2)

| 174 FQ: BurntN | | 133 | /Stray down, bend to us; tendril and spray/Clutch and cling?/Chill/Fingers of yew be |
| 187 FQ: DrySal | | 128 | song, a Royal Rose or a lavender spray/Of wistful regret for those who are not yet |

SPREAD (7)

13 Prufrock		2	then, you and I,/When the evening is spread out against the sky/Like a patient
65 WL: Chess		109	the firelight, under the brush, her hair/Spread out in fiery points/Glowed into words,
67 WL: Fire S		186	/The rattle of the bones, and chuckle spread from ear to ear./A rat crept softly
68 WL: Fire S		224	in tins./Out of the window perilously spread/Her drying combinations touched by the
209 NamingCats		16	he keep up his tail perpendicular,/Or spread out his whiskers, or cherish his pride?/Of
594 Grad 12		6	sons be thine, from far and near/To spread thy name o'er distant lands and seas!/As
541 ES Gomez		21	own name either —/Are pretty well spread. For the matter of that,/My current

SPREADING (2)

| 32 Hysteria | | 6 | with trembling hands/was hurriedly spreading a pink and white checked cloth over |
| 111 Xmas Trees | | 7 | candle is a star, and the gilded angel/Spreading its wings at the summit of the tree/Is |

SPREADS (4)

26 Rhapsody		74	/You have the key,/The little lamp spreads a ring on the stair./Mount./The bed is
56 Swee Night		1	the Nightingales/Apeneck Sweeney spreads his knees/Letting his arms hang down
129 Cor2 State		35	wind after noon/There the cyclamen spreads its wings, there the clematis droops over
548 ES	1m	14	*moment later,* LORD CLAVERTON *spreads his newspaper over his face./Enter* MRS.

SPRING (34)

19 Portrait	53	recall/My buried life, and Paris in the Spring,/I feel immeasurably at peace, and find
24 Rhapsody	30	skeleton,/Stiff and white./A broken spring in a factory yard,/Rust that clings to the
61 WL: Burial	4	and desire, stirring/Dull roots with spring rain./Winter kept us warm, covering/
67 WL: Fire S	198	bring/Sweeney to Mrs. Porter in the spring./O the moon shone bright on Mrs. Porter
72 WL: Thund	327	and reverberation/Of thunder of spring over distant mountains/He who was
72 WL: Thund	350	rock/And also water/And water/A spring/A pool among the rock/If there were the
138 New Hamp	6	hover over;/Twenty years and the spring is over;/To-day grieves, to-morrow
138 New Hamp	11	head, black wing,/Cling, swing,/Spring, sing,/Swing up into the apple-tree./
147 Rock 1	5	of determined seasons,/O world of spring and autumn, birth and dying!/The
164 Rock 9	18	the artist unites himself with stone,/Spring always new forms of life, from the soul
164 Rock 9	24	place of thoughts and feelings,/There spring the perfect order of speech, and the
178 FQ: ECoker	53	doing/With the disturbance of the spring/And creatures of the summer heat,/And
191 FQ: Little	1	soil./Little Gidding/Midwinter spring is its own season/Sempiternal though
191 FQ: Little	13	/Or smell of living thing. This is the spring time/But not in time's covenant. Now the
231 Bust Jones	39	of Cats./It must and it shall be Spring in Pall Mall/While Bustopher Jones
240 MC Chorus	7	bringing death from the sea,/Ruinous spring shall beat at our doors,/Root and shoot
247 MC Tempt1	9	/{T1} And of the new season./Spring has come in winter. Snow in the
252 MC Tempt3	24	/And I well hope, before another spring/The King will show his regard for your
263 MC Chorus	3	inland by the storm./What sign of the spring of the year?/Only the death of the old:
263 MC Chorus	10	note of death./What signs of a bitter spring?/The wind stored up in the East./What,
263 MC Chorus	17	winter, or we shall have only/A sour spring, a parched summer, an empty harvest./
275 MC Chorus	26	season, let the day not come, let the spring not come./Can I look again at the day
281 MC Chorus	16	the snuffle of winter, the song of spring, the drone of summer, the voices of
285 FR Amy	4	the swallow comes too soon and the spring will be over/And the cuckoo will be gone
285 FR Amy	12	undrawn./Make up the fire. Will the spring never come? I am cold./{Ag} Wishwood
303 FR Mary	1	/[*Enter* MARY *with flowers*]/{M} The spring is very late in this northern country,/Late
303 FR Agatha	4	/{Ag} I always forget how late the spring is, here./{M} I had rather wait for our
309 FR Harry	39	/How you should know it. Is the cold spring/Is the spring not an evil time, that excites
309 FR Harry	40	know it. Is the cold spring/Is the spring not an evil time, that excites us with lying
310 FR Mary	1	us with lying voices?/{M} The cold spring now is the time/For the ache in the
310 FR Harry	9	crying for a moment in the wood./{H} Spring is an issue of blood/A season of sacrifice/
310 FR Harry	15	of the drowned/Return to land in the spring?/Do the dead want to return?/{M} Pain is
461 CC Eggers	18	/I said: 'Let's think about it in the Spring/When the garden will really be a treat to
490 CC Colby	39	out of dead facts/Nothing living can spring. Now, it is too late./I never wanted a

SPRING'S (1)

| 602 Humoresque | 15 | /'The snappiest fashion since last spring's,/'The newest style, on Earth, I swear./ |

SPRINGING (1)

| 308 FR Mary | 14 | /But in this world another hope keeps springing/In an unexpected place, while we are |

SPRINGS (4)

38 Gerontion	48	the wrath-bearing tree./The tiger springs in the new year. Us he devours. Think at
89 Ash-Wed 4	15	drink/There, where trees flower, and springs flow, for there is nothing again/Because
94 Ash-Wed 4	8	the fountains and made fresh the springs/Made cool the dry rock and made firm
282 MC Chorus	3	imperial column,/From such ground springs that which forever renews the earth/

SPRINGTIME (1)

| 248 MC Thomas | 9 | the stairs./{T} Leave-well-alone, the springtime fancy,/So one thought goes whistling |

SPRINKLED (1)

| 16 Prufrock | 101 | the sunsets and the dooryards and the sprinkled streets,/After the novels, after the |

SPROUT (1)

| 63 WL: Burial | 72 | year in your garden,/'Has it begun to sprout? Will it bloom this year?/'Or has the |

SPROUTING (1)

| 27 Morning | 4 | of the damp souls of housemaids/Sprouting despondently at area gates./The |

SPUR (2)

| 374 CP Celia | 20 | the aunt was a pure invention/On the spur of the moment, and not a very good one./ |
| 480 CC Kaghan | 8 | guess wrong./I make decisions on the spur of the moment,/But you'd never take a |

SPURNS (1)

| 247 MC Tempt1 | 23 | wink./A man will often love what he spurns./For the good times past, that are come |

SPUTTERED (2)

| 24 Rhapsody | 14 | /Half-past one,/The street-lamp sputtered,/The street-lamp muttered,/The |
| 24 Rhapsody | 47 | I held him./Half-past three,/The lamp sputtered,/The lamp muttered in the dark./The |

SPY (2)

| 599 On a Port | 13 | stands./The parrot on his bar, a silent spy,/Regards her with a patient curious eye./ |
| 548 ES Monica | 9 | Don't look so alarmed!/If you spy any guest who seems to be stalking you/Put |

SPYING (1)

| 311 FR Harry | 12 | I know you are there, I know you are spying on me./Why do you play with me, why |

SQUABBLING (1)
251 MC Tempt3   20   is not all-powerful;/King is in France, squabbling in Anjou;/Round him waiting
SQUAD (1)
534 ES   Gomez   33   very comfortable,/Or before a firing squad./You don't know what serious politics is
SQUAD'S (1)
226 Macavity   3   of Scotland Yard, the Flying Squad's despair:/For when they reach the scene
SQUAD-DRILL (1)
32 Hysteria   3   only accidental stars with a talent/for squad-drill. I was drawn in by short gasps,
SQUADS (1)
182 FQ: ECoker 184   imprecision of feeling,/Undisciplined squads of emotion. And what there is to
SQUALID (1)
151 Rock 2   5   born to idleness, to frittered lives and squalid deaths, embittered scorn in honeyless
SQUARE (9)
23 Preludes   43   and five and six o'clock;/And short square fingers stuffing pipes,/And evening
29 Aunt Helen   2   in a small house near a fashionable square/Cared for by servants to the number of
135 5FingerEx1   2   repair/To the green fields of Russell Square./Beneath the trees there is no ease/For
218 Mung Rump   5   Launceston Place and in Kensington Square —/They had really a little more
226 Macavity   19   in a by-street, you may see him in the square —/But when a crime's discovered, then
236 Cat Morgan   4   keepin' the door in a Bloomsbury Square./I'm partial to partridges, likewise to
257 MC Chorus   30   bear,/Palm-pat of nodding ape, square hyaena waiting/For laughter, laughter,
473 CC Lucasta   8   my only garden is ... a dirty public square/In a shabby part of London — like the
474 CC Lucasta   26   ... willow-herb ... a dirty public square./But I can't imagine that happening to
SQUATS (1)
37 Gerontion   8   is a decayed house,/And the Jew squats on the window sill, the owner,/Spawned
SQUEAMISH (1)
298 FR Charles   1   for my means, we can't afford to be squeamish/In taking hold of anything that
SQUEEZED (2)
15 Prufrock   92   off the matter with a smile,/To have squeezed the universe into a ball/To roll it
149 Rock 1   72   only around the corner,/The desert is squeezed in the tube-train next to you,/The
SQUIRE (1)
331 FR Agatha   34   /An exceptionally cultivated country squire,/Reading, sketching, playing on the flute,
SQUIRMING (1)
136 5FingerEx3   11   bread and finger too,/Easier had than squirming worm;/For I know, and so should
ST. (16) [*Abbreviation*]
111 Xmas Trees   26   here I remember also with gratitude/St. Lucy, her carol, and her crown of fire):/So
230 Bust Jones   4   has eight or nine clubs,/For he's the St. James's Street Cat!/He's the Cat we all greet
230 Bust Jones   9   an impeccable back./In the whole of St. James's the smartest of names is/The name
589 Fable   84   anyone questioned, would declare/St. Peter'd snatcht to heaven their lord
263 MC   1m 27   *the* FIRST PRIEST *with a banner of St. Stephen borne before him./The lines sung are*
264 MC Priest1   1   Since Christmas a day: and the day of St. Stephen, First Martyr./*Princes moreover did*
264 MC   m   6   /*Princes moreover did sit.* {}/[*Introit of St. Stephen is heard*]/[*Enter the* SECOND
264 MC   m   7   SECOND PRIEST, *with a banner of St. John the Apostle borne before him.*]/{P2}
264 MC Priest2   7   *Apostle borne before him.*]/{P2} Since St. Stephen a day: and the day of St. John the
264 MC Priest2   7   St. Stephen a day: and the day of St. John the Apostle./*In the midst of the*
264 MC   m   13   *of the congregation.* {}/[*Introit of St. John is heard*]/[*Enter the* THIRD PRIEST,
264 MC Priest3 14   *borne before him.*]/{P3} Since St. John the Apostle a day: and the day of the
291 FR Charles   2   the gallery?/{C} I might have been in St. James's Street, in a comfortable chair rather
327 FR Charles 39   I bought a lunch edition/Before I left St. Pancras. If I did, it's in my overcoat./I'll see
366 CP   Julia 11   I'll come straight to you, instead of to St. Anthony./And now I must fly. I've kept the
509 CC Guzzard 11   We had been married in the church of St. Barnabas./{C} Barnabas Kaghan. Is he the
STAB (1)
601 Nocturne   8   the wall I have some servant wait,/Stab, and the lady sinks into a swoon./Blood
STABILITY (1)
279 MC Knight4   20   together, to give it the unity, the stability, order, tranquillity,/and justice that it
STABLES (1)
288 FR Agatha   35   meet/The boy who left. Round by the stables,/In the coach-house, in the orchard,/In
STAFF (3)
530 ES Monica   29   banquet, with the tributes from the staff,/The presentation, and the speech you had
558 ES Michael   7   he couldn't retain any man on his staff/Who'd taken to gambling. Called me a
576 ES Michael 29   a man/For an important post on his staff —/{C} A post the nature of which is left
STAG (2)
141 Rannoch   1   the crow starves, here the patient stag/Breeds for the rifle. Between the soft moor/
249 MC Tempt2   26   servant of a powerless Pope,/The old stag, circled with hounds./{T} No!/{T2} Yes!

STAGE (15)

20 Portrait	74	/An English countess goes upon the stage./A Greek was murdered at a Polish dance,
229 Gus	43	the Ghost./And he once crossed the stage on a telegraph wire,/To rescue a child
230 Bust Jones	19	/But he's frequently seen at the gay *Stage and Screen*/Which is famous for winkles
276 MC	m 18	*the murder, advance to the front of the stage and address the audience.*]/{K1} We beg
335 FR Agatha	40	we did not pass./I have seen the first stage: relief from what happened/Is also relief
425 CP Lavinia	30	go away again. Anyway, at that stage/There's nothing whatever you can do
457 CC note 16&	25	*off.*/* Lady Elizabeth's words off stage are not intended to be heard distinctly by an*
460 CC Lady E	19	with Dr. Rebmann —/No, at your stage, I think, with Dr. Leroux./Don't you
469 CC Colby	6	need much teaching;/Not at this stage, anyway. All you need at first/Is to hear
550 ES Carghil	4	to tease me./You know I meant my stage name. The name by which you knew me./
563 ES Carghil	27	and I — I was known by my stage name./There was a time, once, when
563 ES Gomez	32	well understand/Her success on the stage./{MC} Oh, did you never see me?/That's a
569 ES Ld Clav	2	to drop the pretence,/Walk off the stage, change into our own clothes/And speak
569 ES Ld Clav	6	love the actor/If she saw him, off the stage, without his costume and makeup/And
569 ES Ld Clav	7	and makeup/And without his stage words. Monica!/I've had your love under

STAGES (2)

71 WL: DWater	317	As he rose and fell/He passed the stages of his age and youth/Entering the
536 ES Gomez	2	changed your name twice — by easy stages,/And each step was merely a step up the

STAGGERED (1)

500 CC Lucasta	22	he was your son/He must have been staggered when I said I was your daughter!/I

STAGNANT (1)

166 Rock 10	22	doors at evening,/The twilight over stagnant pools at batflight,/Moon light and star

STAGS (1)

107 Animula	12	pattern on the floor/And running stags around a silver tray;/Confounds the actual

STAID (1)

309 FR Harry	30	years in useless travel;/You have staid in England, yet you seem/Like someone

STAIN (3)

57 Swee Night	40	/And let their liquid siftings fall/To stain the stiff dishonoured shroud./The Waste
598 Circe	5	and red/With hideous streak and stain;/They sprang from the limbs of the dead.
294 FR Harry	23	one's own automatism/While the slow stain sinks deeper through the skin/Tainting the

STAINED (2)

24 Rhapsody	20	see the border of her dress/Is torn and stained with sand,/And you see the corner of
606 Narcissus	38	him./Now he is green, dry and stained/With the shadow in his mouth./

STAINS (2)

195 FQ: Little	145	fools' approval stings, and honour stains./From wrong to wrong the exasperated
592 Grad 3	5	limits of the sky/Which the sun stains with many a splendid dye,/Until their

STAIR (16)

14 Prufrock	39	/Time to turn back and descend the stair,/With a bald spot in the middle of my hair
26 Rhapsody	74	/The little lamp spreads a ring on the stair./Mount./The bed is open; the tooth-brush
34 Figlia	1	/Stand on the highest pavement of the stair —/Lean on a garden urn —/Weave, weave
64 WL: Chess	107	enclosed./Footsteps shuffled on the stair./Under the firelight, under the brush, her
92 Ash-Wed 3	1	/At the first turning of the second stair/I turned and saw below/The same shape
92 Ash-Wed 3	7	/At the second turning of the second stair/I left them twisting, turning below;/There
92 Ash-Wed 3	9	/There were no more faces and the stair was dark,/Damp, jaggèd, like an old man's
92 Ash-Wed 3	12	shark./At the first turning of the third stair/Was a slotted window bellied like the fig's
92 Ash-Wed 3	19	and steps of the mind over the third stair,/Fading, fading; strength beyond hope and
92 Ash-Wed 3	21	hope and despair/Climbing the third stair./Lord, I am not worthy/Lord, I am not
105 Song Sime	28	Light upon light, mounting the saints' stair./Not for me the martyrdom, the ecstasy of
210 Old Gumbie	3	spots./All day she sits upon the stair or on the steps or on the mat:/She sits and
227 Macavity	29	a scrap of paper in the hall or on the stair —/But it's useless to investigate —
257 MC Priests	4	in a ditch./{3P} A man may climb the stair in the day, and slip on a broken step./{4T}
274 MC Priests	14	This way, my Lord! Quick. Up the stair. To the roof./To the crypt. Quick. Come.
348 FR Chorus	7	landscape./We do not like to climb a stair, and find that it takes us down./We do not

STAIRCASE (3)

362 CP Reilly	34	object/At the mercy of a malevolent staircase./Or, take a surgical operation./In
386 CP Reilly	9	precaution/Of leaving by the service staircase./{E} May I ask one question?/{UG}
400 CP Alex	32	morning!/I will go out by the service staircase/And come back when they've gone./

STAIRS (9)

20 Portrait	86	of being ill at ease/I mount the stairs and turn the handle of the door/And feel
69 WL: Fire S	248	kiss,/And gropes his way, finding the stairs unlit .../She turns and looks a moment in
92 Ash-Wed 3	5	air/Struggling with the devil of the stairs who wears/The deceitful face of hope and
116 SP Doris	18	say I'm ill,/Say I broke my leg on the stairs/Say we've had a fire/{Du} Hello Hello are
158 Rock 5	5	are like snakes that lie on mouldering stairs, content in the sunlight./And the others
175 FQ: BurntN	163	movement,/As in the figure of the ten stairs./Desire itself is movement/Not in itself

598 Circe	10	thickens below,/Along the garden stairs/The sluggish python lies;/The peacocks
248 MC Temptl	8	you at kissing-time below the stairs./{T} Leave-well-alone, the springtime
254 MC Tempt4	27	/Sometimes hesitating at the angles of stairs,/And between sleep and waking, early in

STALE (3)

22 Preludes	15	comes to consciousness/Of faint stale smells of beer/From the sawdust-trampled
420 CP Reilly	26	what have they to go back to?/To the stale food mouldering in the larder,/The stale
420 CP Reilly	27	food mouldering in the larder,/The stale thoughts mouldering in their minds./Each

STALK (1)

223 Pekes Pols	51	small basement flat,/Why who should stalk out but the GREAT RUMPUSCAT./His

STALKING (1)

548 ES Monica	9	/If you spy any guest who seems to be stalking you/Put your newspaper over your face

STALKS (1)

19 Portrait	46	your hands';/(Slowly twisting the lilac stalks)/'You let it flow from you, you let it flow,

STALLS (1)

291 FR Chorus	1	parts,/Waiting for the rustling in the stalls, the titter in the dress circle, the laughter

STAMINA (1)

286 FR Charles	34	/Are not what we were. Haven't the stamina,/Haven't the sense of responsibility./{G}

STAMINATE (1)

55 Mr E Sun	27	/With hairy bellies pass between/The staminate and pistillate,/Blest office of the

STAMM' (1)

61 WL: Burial	12	for an hour./Bin gar keine Russin, stamm' aus Litauen, echt deutsch./And when we

STAMPS (1)

22 Preludes	12	street/A lonely cab-horse steams and stamps./And then the lighting of the lamps./The

STAND (16)

13 Prufrock	18	/Lingered upon the pools that stand in drains,/Let fall upon its back the soot
34 Figlia	1	so serious?'/La Figlia Che Piange/Stand on the highest pavement of the stair —/
34 Figlia	9	him leave,/So I would have had her stand and grieve,/So he would have left/As the
72 WL: Thund	340	that cannot spit/Here one can neither stand nor lie nor sit/There is not even silence in
105 Song Sime	3	hills;/The stubborn season had made stand./My life is light, waiting for the death
120 SP Krum	2	*coarse* —/But I'm afraid we couldn't stand the pace./What about it Klip?/{Kl} You
149 Rock 1	97	*pocketed hands/And lowered faces/We stand about in open places/And shiver in unlit*
161 Rock 7	31	upturned, what have we to do/But stand with empty hands and palms turned
212 Growltiger	t	depend, it appears./Growltiger's Last Stand/GROWLTIGER was a Bravo Cat, who
239 MC Chorus	1	*29th*, 1170/Part I/{C} Here let us stand, close by the cathedral. Here let us wait./
244 MC Chorus	26	existence, leave us; do not ask us/To stand to the doom on the house, the doom on
244 MC Chorus	29	on the brain of the small folk who stand to the doom of the house, the doom of
264 MC m	22	babes, O God! {}/[THE PRIESTS *stand together with the banners behind them*]/
301 FR Chorus	16	is desirable./{Ch} Why should we stand here like guilty conspirators, waiting for
379 CP Celia	18	/{C} It wasn't fair to *me*!/You can stand there and talk about being fair to *me*!/{E}
570 ES Monica	19	/Who are they, and what do they stand for in your life?/{LC} ... And yet they've

STANDARDS (5)

64 WL: Chess	79	marble, where the glass/Held up by standards wrought with fruited vines/From
163 Rock 8	29	spite of all the dishonour,/The broken standards, the broken lives,/The broken faith in
534 ES Gomez	12	if I lived in England./I have the same standards of morality/As the society in which.I
535 ES Gomez	31	climate,/To another language, other standards of behaviour,/To fabricate for myself
561 ES Michael	19	/So you'd nothing to live up to. Those standards of conduct/You've always made so

STANDING (9)

129 Cor2 State	9	/The consultative councils, the standing committees, select committees and
588 Fable	49	the good things./A mighty peacock standing on both legs/With difficulty kept from
592 Grad 1	1	of life be few/Yet let them be divine./Standing upon the shore of all we know/We
254 MC Tempt4	17	of a shade;/Think of pilgrims, standing in line/Before the glittering jewelled
348 FR Chorus	33	beyond the heather/And behind the Standing Stones?/Beyond the Heaviside Layer/
437 CP Reilly	14	in this room,/I saw the image, standing behind her chair,/Of a Celia
551 ES Carghil	29	to accept',/'Because Mr. Ferry will be standing for Parliament:/His father has political
568 ES Ld Clav	1	have you been?/{LC} Not far away. Standing under the great beech tree./{M} Why
570 ES Ld Clav	28	of great importance and the highest standing/In his adopted country. He even has

STANDS (6)

152 Rock 2	31	deeds belong to a man alone, when he stands alone on the other side of death,/But
189 FQ: DrySal	173	voyagers./Lady, whose shrine stands on the promontory,/Pray for all those
599 On a Port	4	hurrying, up and down the street,/She stands at evening in the room alone./Not like a
599 On a Port	12	/Beyond the circle of our thought she stands./The parrot on his bar, a silent spy,/
472 CC Lucasta	20	it's something that your music stands for./There's one thing I know. When you
474 CC Lucasta	36	to enjoy it ... and because of what it stands for./You know, I'm a little jealous of

STAR (8)

84 Hollow Men	28	and more solemn/Than a fading star./Let me be no nearer/In death's dream
84 Hollow Men	44	hand/Under the twinkle of a fading star./Is it like this/In death's other kingdom/
85 Hollow Men	63	/The eyes reappear/As the perpetual star/Multifoliate rose/Of death's twilight
111 Xmas Trees	6	of the child/For whom the candle is a star, and the gilded angel/Spreading its wings at
166 Rock 10	23	pools at batflight,/Moon light and star light, owl and moth light,/Glow-worm
228 Gus	15	his palmiest days./For he once was a Star of the highest degree —/He has acted with
602 Humoresque	22	all wrong/Of premises; yet in some star/A hero! — Where would he belong?/But,
570 ES Ld Clav	38	exists./Nor the musical comedy star, Maisie Montjoy./There is Mrs. John

STARE (4)

68 WL: Fire S	232	house agent's clerk, with one bold stare,/One of the low on whom assurance sits/
226 Macavity	7	of levitation would make a fakir stare,/And when you reach the scene of crime —
589 Fable	77	friars could do nought but gape and stare,/The spirit pulled him rudely by the collar,
602 Humoresque	11	latest tune;/His who-the-devil-are-you stare;/Translated, maybe, to the moon./With

STARED (3)

52 Whispers	6	grin./Daffodil bulbs instead of balls/Stared from the sockets of the eyes!/He knew
291 FR Harry	21	the window!/Do you like to be stared at by eyes through a window?/{A} You
292 FR Harry	7	the nightingale's thicket,/The eyes stared at me, and corrupted that song./Behind

STARES (3)

40 Burb Blei	18	Viennese./A lustreless protrusive eye/Stares from the protozoic slime/At a perspective
291 FR	m 14	*stops suddenly at the door and stares at the window]*/{I} Welcome, Harry!/{G}
400 CP	2m 35	Harcourt-Reilly — {}/[*Stops and stares at* REILLY]/[*without looking up from his*

STARFISH (1)

184 FQ: DrySal	19	of earlier and other creation:/The starfish, the horseshoe crab, the whale's

STARING (4)

54 Mr E Sun	22	the penitential gates/Sustained by staring Seraphim/Where the souls of the devout/
64 WL: Chess	105	of time/Were told upon the walls; staring forms/Leaned out, leaning, hushing the
325 FR Violet	37	/And so near the street, and everyone staring;/And the pace he went at was simply
544 ES Ld Clav	12	—/After fourteen days of people not staring/Or offering picture papers, or wanting a

STARLIGHT (1)

182 FQ: ECoker	199	/There is a time for the evening under starlight,/A time for the evening under

STARLING (1)

150 Rock 1	110	*the seasons turn/The sparrow and starling have no time to waste./If men do not*

STARNBERGERSEE (1)

61 WL: Burial	8	surprised us, coming over the Starnbergersee/With a shower of rain; we

STARS (9)

32 Hysteria	2	it, until her teeth were only accidental stars with a talent/for squad-drill. I was drawn
84 Hollow Men	54	no eyes here/In this valley of dying stars/In this hollow valley/This broken jaw of
109 Marina	19	—/Given or lent? more distant than stars and nearer than the eye/Whispers and
147 Rock 1	3	/O perpetual revolution of configured stars,/O perpetual recurrence of determined
155 Rock 3	65	the mountains,/Dividing the stars into common and preferred,/Engaged in
172 FQ: BurntN	56	the lymph/Are figured in the drift of stars/Ascend to summer in the tree/We move
172 FQ: BurntN	63	as before/But reconciled among the stars./At the still point of the turning world.
178 FQ: ECoker	59	snow?/Thunder rolled by the rolling stars/Simulates triumphal cars/Deployed in
422 CP Reilly	14	hearth/Under the protection of the stars./{A} Let them place a chair each side of it./

START (24)

16 Prufrock	113	one that will do/To swell a progress, start a scene or two,/Advise the prince; no
70 WL: Fire S	298	event/He wept. He promised "a new start."/I made no comment. What should I
179 FQ: ECoker	73	poetry does not matter./It was not (to start again) what one had expected./What was
182 FQ: ECoker	177	and every attempt/Is a wholly new start, and a different kind of failure/Because one
197 FQ: Little	218	a beginning./The end is where we start from. And every phrase/And sentence that
197 FQ: Little	229	illegible stone: and that is where we start./We die with the dying:/See, they depart,
232 Skimble	4	/We must find him or the train can't start.'/All the guards and all the porters and the
308 FR Harry	21	return to the point of departure/And start again as if nothing had happened,/Isn't
334 FR Agatha	11	income daily:/And I am old, to start again to make my living./{H} But you are
361 CP Reilly	31	let the genie out of the bottle./It is to start a train of events/Beyond your control. So
421 CP Julia	7	have, for the first time, somewhere to start from./Oh, of course, they might just
436 CP Edward	1	{E} Lavinia is right. This is where you start from./If you find out now, Peter, things
447 CC Claude	2	As we have a little time/Before you start for Northolt — the car will be ready —/
449 CC Claude	23	Lucasta — Miss Angel, from the start./That was one difficulty. And there are
451 CC Eggers	7	picked him out/And gave him his start. And he's made the most of it —/That I
462 CC Claude	32	that you might find it easier/To start by a rather formal relationship/In adapting
479 CC Kaghan	30	Yes, I made a bad impression at the start:/I saw that it was necessary. I'm afraid
493 CC Claude	16	/It's very awkward. We don't want to start/By offending Mrs. Guzzard. That's why I
505 CC Eggers	19	Eggerson./{E} Then let's make a start./The question has to do, as you surmised,

515 CC Guzzard 12   /My son was assured of a proper start in life —/That I knew. And it would make
545 ES Monica   21   the house./Take your newspaper and start reading to me. {}/[*Enter* MRS. PIGGOTT]
560 ES Ld Clav 16   Michael./I will help you to make a start in any business/You may find for yourself
565 ES Ld Clav 36   the lesson I would teach? Come, I'll start to learn again./Michael and I shall go to
574 ES Carghil 16   really wanted/For making a new start. He wants to go abroad!/And find his own

STARTED (17)

197 FQ: Little   243   exploring/Will be to arrive where we started/And know the place for the first time./
222 Pekes Pols   21   and scraped their hind feet,/And started to/Bark bark bark bark/Bark bark
223 Pekes Pols   30   likely a score./And together they started to grumble and wheeze/In their
223 Pekes Pols   49   were so much afraid/That they started to ring up the Fire Brigade./When
293 FR Gerald   31   that nothing has happened to *me*./I started as a youngster on the North-West
326 FR Violet   2   I did./{G} Walk? where to?/{V} He started out to take me to Cheltenham;/But I
353 CP Julia   10   to know what happened./I know it started as a story about tigers./{A} I said there
355 CP Julia   29   No, I can't endure them./Well, I started to tell you about Lady Klootz./It was at
391 CP Lavinia 19   But it seems to me that yesterday/I started some machine, that goes on working,/
391 CP Lavinia 23   .../I don't feel free ... and yet I started it .../{J} Alex, do you think we could
446 CC Claude   21   this way of life more quickly/If we started on a purely business basis./{E} No doubt
462 CC Claude   38   odd, Colby./I didn't realise, till you started with me here,/That we hardly know each
463 CC Colby   9   absorption in your music .../{C} You started by asking me how I found this work./
529 ES Monica   7   /When he was your age — when he started like you,/With the same hopes, the same
537 ES Gomez   18   your set, and I knew it./When you started to take me up at Oxford/I've no doubt
551 ES Carghil 23   /You mean that I would never have started an action/For breach of promise, if I'd
557 ES Ld Clav 1   end by getting into trouble./{LC} You started pretty early getting into trouble,/When

STARTING (5)

192 FQ: Little   42   you came this way,/Taking any route, starting from anywhere,/At any time or at any
368 CP Edward   34   amateur?/{E} Lavinia's attempts at starting a salon,/Where I entertained the minor
448 CC Claude   26   Mr. Simpkins./{SC} The reasons for starting him during her absence/Are perfectly
458 CC Eggers   10   I've arrived, that's all./{E} I was just starting for Northolt to meet you./{LE} That
464 CC Claude   28   grandfather — built up this business/Starting from nothing. It was *his* passion./He

STARTLING (1)

487 CC Lady E   17   is it, Elizabeth?/{LE} I've just made a startling discovery!/All through a name — and

STARTS (4)

182 FQ: ECoker   192   not our business./Home is where one starts from. As we grow older/The world
187 FQ: DrySal   134   is no longer here./When the train starts, and the passengers are settled/To fruit,
375 CP m   36   /I must go and investigate. {}/[*Starts to leave the room*]/{E} For heaven's sake,
551 ES Carghil 25   you./What sentimental nonsense! One starts an action/Simply because one must do

STARVATION (1)

160 Rock 7   14   look of a child that has died of starvation./Prayer wheels, worship of the dead,

STARVED (1)

263 MC Chorus   8   a wind is stored up in the East./The starved crow sits in the field, attentive; and in

STARVES (1)

141 Rannoch   1   /Rannoch, by Glencoe/Here the crow starves, here the patient stag/Breeds for the rifle.

STARVING (2)

376 CP Celia   5   /And I'll say I found you here starving and helpless/And had to do something.
453 CC Lucasta 30   you'll have to raid the till for me. I'm starving./{K} I've just given her lunch. The

STATE (20)

236 Cat Morgan 15   sich melliferous horgan;/But yet I can state, and I'm not one to boast,/That some of
248 MC Tempt2   22   all acknowledged, should guide the state again./{T} Your meaning?/{T2} The
277 MC Knight3 18   him — will have to/say, for reasons of state, that he never meant this to happen; and/
278 MC Knight2 15   we should have had an almost ideal State:/a union of spiritual and temporal
278 MC Knight2 39   of the Church to/the welfare of the State, remember that it is we who took the first/
278 MC Knight2 40   instrumental in bringing about the state of/affairs that you approve. We have
280 MC Priest1 38   O my lord/The glory of whose new state is hidden from us,/Pray for us of your
401 CP Edward   39   didn't you realise/That I was in no state to make a decision?/{R} If I had not
403 CP Reilly   1   childhood —/I mean, in your present state of mind —/Would be largely fictitious; and
410 CP Reilly   13   holds you together./While still in a state of unenlightenment,/*You* could always
410 CP Reilly   22   either of you to the sanatorium/In the state in which you came to me — I tell you this:
413 CP Reilly   25   /Try first to describe your present state of mind./{C} Well, there are two things I
416 CP Celia   6   /Can you treat a patient for such a state of mind?/{R} What had you believed were
417 CP Celia   13   is fulfilled/In the delight of loving. A state one does not know/When awake. The
428 CP Alex   38   are citizens of a friendly neighbouring state/Which we have just recognised. You see,
436 CP Reilly   28   to the natives who were dying/Or the state of mind in which they died?/{L} I'm willing
436 CP Reilly   39   forced you to a show-down./{R} You state the position correctly, Julia./Do you mind
447 CC Claude   27   always been concerned about your state of health,/So she'll be sympathetic. And as
465 CC Claude   25   gave me that contentment —/That state of utter exhaustion and peace/Which

560 ES   Michael   2   after death,/I bet it will be a surprised state of consciousness./Poor ghost! reckoning
STATECRAFT (1)
277 MC Knight1   33   who/has made a special study of statecraft and constitutional law. Sir/Hugh de
STATED (1)
328 FR   Charles   21   /{C} In Ebury Street. 'The police stated that at the time of the/accident Mr. Piper
STATELY (1)
598 Circe   12   python lies;/The peacocks walk, stately and slow,/And they look at us with the
STATEMENT (3)
589 Fable   66   most securely,/Gave way — my statement nobody can doubt,/Who knows the
514 CC   Eggers   20   Guzzard, can you substantiate this statement?/{MG} Registration of birth. To
540 ES   Gomez   38   going to accept the unsupported statement/Of Federico Gomez of San Marco/
STATES (2)
 31 Apollinax   1   Mr. Apollinax visited the United States/His laughter tinkled among the teacups./I
414 CP   Reilly   31   we must return from./There are other states of mind, which we take to be delusion,/
STATESMAN (5)
129 Cor2 State   t   *LA FAISAIENT.*/Difficulties of a Statesman/CRY what shall I cry?/All flesh is
521 ES   t   *nods]*/CURTAIN/THE ELDER STATESMAN/TO MY WIFE/*To whom I owe*
552 ES   Carghil   30   /As what? I presume, as an elder statesman;/And the difference between being an
552 ES   Carghil   31   the difference between being an elder statesman/And posing successfully as an elder
552 ES   Carghil   32   /And posing successfully as an elder statesman/Is practically negligible. And you
STATESMAN'S (1)
256 MC Tempts   15   Essay,/The scholar's degree, the statesman's decoration./All things become less
STATESMEN (2)
180 FQ: ECoker 105   /The generous patrons of art, the statesmen and the rulers,/Distinguished civil
240 MC Chorus   19   the hand of God, not in the hands of statesmen/Who do, some well, some ill,
STATION (5)
159 Rock 6   6   hard for those who live near a Police Station/To believe in the triumph of violence./
188 FQ: DrySal 141   are not the same people who left that station/Or who will arrive at any terminus,/
233 Skimble   56   he was walking up and down the station;/You were sleeping all the while he was
434 CP   Alex   7   three of them —/Three sisters at this station, in a Christian village;/And half the
530 ES   Ld Clav 21   an empty waiting room/In a railway station on a branch line,/After the last train,
STATIONMASTER (1)
233 Skimble   58   busy at Carlisle,/Where he greets the stationmaster with elation./But you saw him at
STATIONMASTER'S (1)
232 Skimble   5   the guards and all the porters and the stationmaster's daughters/They are searching
STATIONS (2)
105 Song Sime   19   /Grant us thy peace./Before the stations of the mountain of desolation,/Before
180 FQ: ECoker 119   in the tube, stops too long between stations/And the conversation rises and slowly
STATUS (2)
301 FR   Charles   24   the army./{C} Violet is afraid that her status as Amy's sister will be diminished./{Ch}
362 CP   Reilly   23   /You're suddenly reduced to the status of an object —/A living object, but no
STAUNCH (1)
456 CC   Eggers   10   heart! He's rather a Socialist./I'm a staunch Conservative, myself./{C} But is Lady
STAVES (2)
 62 WL: Burial   51   situations./Here is the man with three staves, and here the Wheel,/And here is the
 84 Hollow Men   33   /Rat's coat, crowskin, crossed staves/In a field/Behaving as the wind behaves/
STAY (32)
 65 WL: Chess   111   nerves are bad to-night. Yes, bad. Stay with me./'Speak to me. Why do you never
123 SA Kl & Kr   15   *girl/My little island girl/I'm going to stay with you/And we won't worry what to do/We*
125 SA Sweeney   27   sit here and have a tune/We're gona stay and we're gona go/And somebody's gotta
147 Rock 1   30   Maidenhead./If the weather is foul we stay at home and read the papers./In industrial
175 FQ: BurntN 155   /Decay with imprecision, will not stay in place,/Will not stay still. Shrieking voices
175 FQ: BurntN 156   will not stay in place,/Will not stay still. Shrieking voices/Scolding, mocking,
587 Fable   27   and phantoms free,/The fiend must stay at home — no ghosts allowed/At this
243 MC Chorus   14   no continuing city, here is no abiding stay./Ill the wind, ill the time, uncertain the
273 MC Thomas   21   stone; stone and oak decay,/Give no stay, but the Church shall endure./The Church
275 MC Chorus   26   to the soft quiet seasons?/Night stay with us, stop sun, hold season, let the day
298 FR   Ivy   17   be told about it later./{I} And I shall stay with Violet./{Ag} I shall return/When
310 FR   Harry   39   that I kept moving/Only so as not to stay still. Singing and light./Stop!/What is that?
311 FR   Harry   22   in sunlight, and thought I might stay there./{M} Look at me. You can depend on
314 FR   Violet   16   children's epidemics: you would never stay in bed/Because you were convinced that
337 FR   Agatha   9   a long journey. You have nothing to stay for./Think of it as like a children's treasure
342 FR   Mary   26   everywhere, he is in danger./I will stay or I will go, whichever is better;/I do not
349 FR   Ivy   8   way in the dark./{I} I shall have to stay till after the funeral: will my ticket to
377 CP   Julia   2   /And we'll see what I can do. You stay and talk to Edward. {}/[*Exit* JULIA]/{C}

414 CP	Celia	22	family want me to come down and stay with them./But I just can't face it./{R} So
419 CP	Celia	22	like a prison. But they can't *all* stay there!/I mean, it would make the place so
431 CP	Julia	14	down tonight, to Boltwell./{J} To stay with the Duke?/{P} And do him a good
516 CC	Claude	1	father. I'll accept that./If you will stay with me. It shall make no difference/To my
524 ES	Monica	5	*carrying parcels*]/{M} But you *must* stay to tea. That was understood/When you
526 ES	Monica	30	I'm very glad, Charles,/That you *can* stay to tea. { }/[*Exit* LAMBERT]/{M} — Now
526 ES	Charles	34	is always a reminder/That I mustn't stay too long, for you belong to him./He seems
534 ES	Gomez	36	to my boys: 'Never touch politics./Stay out of politics, and play both parties:/
542 ES	Gomez	10	much of your company,/So long as I stay here, as I can get./And the more I get, the
542 ES	Gomez	11	/And the more I get, the longer I may stay./{LC} This is preposterous!/Do you call it
547 ES	Piggott	7	you look more comfy. Don't let him stay out late/In the afternoon, Miss
565 ES	Monica	28	those awful people. We mustn't stay here./I want you to escape from them./{LC}
573 ES	Charles	16	How long, Lord Claverton,/Will you stay here and endure this persecution?/{LC} To
573 ES	Ld Clav	22	coming./{M} Let us go./{LC} We will stay here. Let her join us. { }/[*Enter* MRS.
STAYED (4)			
300 FR	Downing	34	turn about, for near half an hour/He stayed there alone, looking over the rail./Her
355 CP	Julia	9	Celia,/You needn't be so sceptical. I stayed there once/At their castle in the North.
419 CP	Reilly	26	friends came back./I did not say they stayed there./{C} What becomes of them?/{R}
537 ES	Gomez	27	down./It went the other way. You stayed the course, at least./I had plenty of time
STAYING (15)			
61 WL:	Burial	13	deutsch./And when we were children, staying at the arch-duke's,/My cousin's, he took
291 FR	Gerald	4	to this party./{G} I might have been staying with Compton-Smith, down at his place
376 CP	Celia	6	had to do something. Anyway, I'm *staying*/And I'm not going to hide. { }/[*Returns to*
400 CP	Alex	28	want to escape from her./{A} He is staying at his club./{R} Yes, that is where he
411 CP	Edward	11	— but how did you know/I was staying at the club?/{L} Really, Edward!/I have
427 CP	Alex	29	And there are no sultans./I have been staying with the Governor./Three of us have
524 ES	Charles	4	myself/There's really no point in my staying to tea. { }/[*Enter* MONICA *and*
524 ES	Monica	28	/{M} It's simply the question/Of your staying to tea. As you practically promised./{C}
556 ES	Michael	15	/{Mi} I drove down last night. I'm staying at a pub/About two miles from here.
556 ES	Ld Clav	17	a bad little place./{LC} Why are you staying there? I shouldn't have thought/It would
556 ES	Ld Clav	23	that a recommendation./Are you staying there long? For the whole of this
564 ES	Carghil	29	/Señor Gomez, if it's true you're staying at Badgley Court,/I warn you — I'm
565 ES	Monica	6	talk for to-day./Michael, as you're staying so close at hand/Will you come back in
565 ES	Carghil	10	tomorrow morning./{MC} Are you staying in the neighbourhood, Michael?/Your
565 ES	Michael	15	do you?/{Mi} No, I don't mind./I'm staying at the George — it's not far away./{MC}
STAYS (1)			
68 WL:	Fire S	227	/Stockings, slippers, camisoles, and stays./I Tiresias, old man with wrinkled dugs/
STEADFAST (1)			
241 MC	Priest3	5	seize the power and keep it,/And the steadfast can manipulate the greed and lust of
STEADILY (1)			
187 FQ:	DrySal	132	is the way back./You cannot face it steadily, but this thing is sure,/That time is no
STEADY (1)			
320 FR	Warburt	35	to your mother./John's very steady — but he's not exactly brilliant;/And
STEAKS (1)			
22 Preludes		2	evening settles down/With smell of steaks in passageways./Six o'clock./The
STEALING (1)			
557 ES	Ld Clav	2	expelled from your prep school for stealing./But come to the point. You're in
STEALTHY (1)			
253 MC	Tempt4	26	beneath a king,/With craft in corners, stealthy stratagem,/To general grasp of spiritual
STEAM (1)			
42 Swee Erect		12	orang-outang/Rises from the sheets in steam./This withered root of knots of hair/
STEAMS (1)			
22 Preludes		12	of the street/A lonely cab-horse steams and stamps./And then the lighting of the
STEARNS (1)			
604 Ode		m	of the Absolute./Ode/THOMAS STEARNS ELIOT/For the hour that is left us,
STEEL (6)			
127 Cor1	March	1	March/Stone, bronze, stone, steel, stone, oakleaves, horses' heels/Over the
128 Cor1	March	40	dust, and now/Stone, bronze, stone, steel, stone, oakleaves, horses' heels/Over the
141 Rannoch		7	of ancient war,/Languor of broken steel./Clamour of confused wrong, apt/In
181 FQ:	ECoker	149	not./The wounded surgeon plies the steel/That questions the distempered part;/
213 Growltiger		48	—/But a serried ring of flashing steel Growltiger did surround./The ruthless foe
537 ES	Gomez	8	grappled to my soul/With hoops of steel, and all that sort of thing./We'll come to
STEEPLE (1)			
587 Fable		23	/And once he sat the prior on the steeple,/To the astonishment of all the people./

STEP (12)

166 Rock 10	16	you have light/Enough to take your step and find your foothold./O Light Invisible,
197 FQ: Little	228	poem an epitaph. And any action/Is a step to the block, to the fire, down the sea's
257 MC Priests	4	stair in the day, and slip on a broken step./{4T} A man may sit at meat, and feel the
278 MC Knight2	40	that it is we who took the first/step. We have been instrumental in bringing
279 MC Knight4	29	of provocation;/from his conduct, step by step, there can be no inference/except
279 MC Knight4	29	/from his conduct, step by step, there can be no inference/except that he
362 CP Reilly	30	when you come to the bottom step/There is one step more than your feet
362 CP Reilly	31	come to the bottom step/There is one step more than your feet expected/And you
498 CC Eggers	35	it. Certainly, Sir Claude:/Our first step must be to question Mrs. Guzzard./{SC}
536 ES Gomez	3	twice — by easy stages,/And each step was merely a step up the ladder,/So you
536 ES Gomez	3	stages,/And each step was merely a step up the ladder,/So you weren't aware of
572 ES Ld Clav	38	to you, Monica:/That is the first step taken towards my freedom,/And perhaps

STEP-DAUGHTER (1)

501 CC Lady E	21	hope so./Lucasta, I regard you as a ... step-daughter;/And shall be happy to accept

STEPHEN (6)

261 MC Thomas	11	/of His first martyr, the blessed Stephen. Is it an accident, do you think,/that the
263 MC 1m	27	FIRST PRIEST *with a banner of St. Stephen borne before him.*/*The lines sung are in*
264 MC Priest1	1	Christmas a day: and the day of St. Stephen, First Martyr./*Princes moreover did sit,*
264 MC m	6	*moreover did sit.* {}/[*Introit of St. Stephen is heard*]/[*Enter the* SECOND
264 MC Priest2	7	*borne before him.*]/{P2} Since St. Stephen a day: and the day of St. John the
278 MC Knight2	8	the irruption of the unhappy usurper/Stephen, the kingdom was very much divided.

STEPPED (1)

223 Pekes Pols	36	of them notable fighters;/And so they stepped out, with their pipers in order,/Playing

STEPPING-STONE (1)

518 CC Eggers	10	Simpkins,/Joshua Park may be only a stepping-stone/To a precentorship! And a

STEPS (8)

28 Boston ET	6	*Evening Transcript,*/I mount the steps and ring the bell, turning/Wearily, as one
49 Hippopot	9	based upon a rock./The hippo's feeble steps may err/In compassing material ends,/
92 Ash-Wed 3	19	music of the flute, stops and steps of the mind over the third stair,/Fading,
159 Rock 6	31	if blood of Martyrs is to flow on the steps/We must first build the steps;/And if the
159 Rock 6	32	on the steps/We must first build the steps;/And if the Temple is to be cast down/We
210 Old Gumbie	3	day she sits upon the stair or on the steps or on the mat:/She sits and sits and sits
329 FR Chorus	11	the singing in the kitchen/And the steps at night in the corridor/The moment of
336 FR 2m	23	*disclosing the empty embrasure. She steps into*/*the place which the* EUMENIDES *had*

STERILE (1)

72 WL: Thund	342	even silence in the mountains/But dry sterile thunder without rain/There is not even

STERN (1)

70 WL: Fire S	281	and Leicester/Beating oars/The stern was formed/A gilded shell/Red and gold/

STETSON (1)

62 WL: Burial	69	one I knew, and stopped him, crying: 'Stetson!/'You who were with me in the ships at

STEW (3)

121 SA Sweeney	12	you!/{S} I'll convert *you*!/Into a stew./A nice little, white little, missionary stew./
121 SA Sweeney	13	/A nice little, white little, missionary stew./{Do} You wouldn't eat me!/{S} Yes I'd eat
121 SA Sweeney	17	/Juicy little, right little, missionary stew./You see this egg/You see this egg/Well

STEWARD (1)

295 FR Harry	3	I made enquiries;/The purser and the steward were extremely sympathetic/And the

STEWED (1)

285 FR Violet	22	the strong cold tea —/The strong cold stewed bad Indian tea./{C} That's not Amy's

STICK (2)

24 Rhapsody	45	on his back,/Gripped the end of a stick which I held him./Half-past three,/The
455 CC Eggers	17	losing her jobs, because she won't stick to them./He gives her an allowance — very

STICKY (1)

256 MC Chorus	8	of issue of hell. What is the sticky dew that forms on the back of my hand?/

STIFF (3)

24 Rhapsody	29	gave up/The secret of its skeleton,/Stiff and white./A broken spring in a factory
57 Swee Night	40	their liquid siftings fall/To stain the stiff dishonoured shroud./The Waste Land/The
277 MC Knight3	8	/we knew we had taken on a pretty stiff job; I'll only speak for/myself, but I had

STIFFEN (1)

38 Gerontion	50	have not reached conclusion, when I/Stiffen in a rented house. Think at last/I have

STIFFENS (1)

98 Ash-Wed 6	11	/Unbroken wings/And the lost heart stiffens and rejoices/In the lost lilac and the lost

STIFLED (4)

226 Macavity	24	is missing, or another Peke's been stifled,/Or the greenhouse glass is broken, and
605 Narcissus	12	he walked over the meadows/He was stifled and soothed by his own rhythm./By the

329 FR	Chorus	13	of sudden loathing/And the season of stifled sorrow/The whisper, the transparent
334 FR	Harry	30	so strong, their apparent strength/Stifled my decision. Now I see/I might even

STIFLING (2)

257 MC	Chorus	27	cloying through the dark air/Falls the stifling scent of despair;/The forms take shape
263 MC	Chorus	7	shorter and colder the night./Still and stifling the air: but a wind is stored up in the

STILL (140)

34 Figlia		23	a pose./Sometimes these cogitations still amaze/The troubled midnight and the
38 Gerontion		40	too late/What's not believed in, or if still believed,/In memory only, reconsidered
54 Mr E Sun		14	/But through the water pale and thin/Still shine the unoffending feet/And there above
64 WL: Chess		102	the desert with inviolable voice/And still she cried, and still the world pursues,/'Jug
64 WL: Chess		102	voice/And still she cried, and still the world pursues,/'Jug Jug' to dirty ears./
65 WL: Chess		110	into words, then would be savagely still./'My nerves are bad to-night. Yes, bad.
68 WL: Fire S		238	to engage her in caresses/Which still are unreproved, if undesired./Flushed and
90 Ash-Wed 1		39	to care and not to care/Teach us to sit still./Pray for us sinners now and at the hour of
96 Ash-Wed 5		4	/Word is unspoken, unheard;/Still is the unspoken word, the Word unheard,/
96 Ash-Wed 5		8	/Against the Word the unstilled world still whirled/About the centre of the silent
98 Ash-Wed 6		9	the granite shore/The white sails still fly seaward, seaward flying/Unbroken
98 Ash-Wed 6		28	to care and not to care/Teach us to sit still/Even among these rocks,/Our peace in His
105 Song Sime		22	season of decease,/Let the Infant, the still unspeaking and unspoken Word,/Grant
128 Cor1 March		34	noon, under the running water/At the still point of the turning world. O hidden./Now
129 Cor2 State		33	rested and locked for a moment,/A still moment, repose of noon, set under the
139 Virginia		3	/Slow flow heat is silence/No will is still as a river/Still. Will heat move/Only
139 Virginia		4	heat is silence/No will is still as a river/Still. Will heat move/Only through the
139 Virginia		6	the mocking-bird/Heard once? Still hills/Wait. Gates wait. Purple trees,/White
143 Lines OM		3	than I./The whipping tail is not more still/Than when I smell the enemy/Writhing in
148 Rock 1		47	labour,/Or ceaseless idleness, which is still harder,/Or irregular labour, which is not
159 Rock 6		10	to be told that whatever has been, can still be?/Do you need to be told that even such
160 Rock 7		12	air of temperate seas is pierced by the still dead breath of the Arctic Current;/And
173 FQ: BurntN		64	reconciled among the stars./At the still point of the turning world. Neither flesh
173 FQ: BurntN		65	/Neither from nor towards; at the still point, there the dance is,/But neither arrest
173 FQ: BurntN		68	nor decline. Except for the point, the still point,/There would be no dance, and there
173 FQ: BurntN		75	/By a grace of sense, a white light still and moving,/*Erhebung* without motion,
175 FQ: BurntN		138	light to light, and is silent, the light is still/At the still point of the turning world./
175 FQ: BurntN		139	and is silent, the light is still/At the still point of the turning world./Words move,
175 FQ: BurntN		145	reach/The stillness, as a Chinese jar still/Moves perpetually in its stillness./Not the
175 FQ: BurntN		156	will not stay in place,/Will not stay still. Shrieking voices/Scolding, mocking, or
179 FQ: ECoker		71	poetical fashion,/Leaving one still with the intolerable wrestle/With words and
180 FQ: ECoker		113	no one to bury./I said to my soul, be still, and let the dark come upon you/Which
180 FQ: ECoker		124	of nothing —/I said to my soul, be still, and wait without hope/For hope would be
183 FQ: ECoker		206	there does not matter/We must be still and still moving/Into another intensity/For
183 FQ: ECoker		206	does not matter/We must be still and still moving/Into another intensity/For a further
193 FQ: Little		85	of his homing/While the dead leaves still rattled on like tin/Over the asphalt where
193 FQ: Little		101	here?'/Although we were not. I was still the same,/Knowing myself yet being
193 FQ: Little		103	someone other —/And he a face still forming; yet the words sufficed/To compel
209 NamingCats		21	cat./But above and beyond there's still one name left over,/And that is the name
213 Growltiger		37	hundred bright blue eyes./And closer still and closer the sampans circled round,/And
229 Gus		41	down a drain./And he thinks that he still can, much better than most,/Produce
592 Grad 4		3	fears,/To hopeful eye of youth it still appears/A lane by which the rose and
595 Grad 13		6	let thy motto be, proud and serene,/Still as the years pass by, the word 'Progress!'/
596 When we		5	/The hedgerow bloomed with flowers still,/No withered petals lay beneath;/But the
604 Ode		10	years that to-morrow has lost/We are still the less able to grieve,/With so much that of
240 MC	Chorus	17	waits in the hand of God, shaping the still unshapen:/I have seen these things in a
243 MC	Priest3	8	the wheel turn./The wheel has been still, these seven years, and no good./For ill or
244 MC	Chorus	30	for France. Thomas our Archbishop still our Archbishop even in France. Thomas
245 MC	Thomas	21	that the wheel may turn and still/Be forever still./{P2} O my Lord, forgive
245 MC	Thomas	22	wheel may turn and still/Be forever still./{P2} O my Lord, forgive me, I did not see
248 MC	Thomas	11	down the wind./The impossible is still temptation./The impossible, the
248 MC	Tempt2	26	that was a mistake/On your part — still may be regained. Think, my Lord,/Power
249 MC	Tempt2	31	Private policy is public profit;/Dignity still shall be dressed with decorum./{T} You
253 MC	Tempt4	15	/As for barons, envy of lesser men/Is still more stubborn than king's anger./Kings
256 MC	Tempt4	3	subsist, that the wheel may turn and still/Be forever still./{C} There is no rest in the
256 MC	Tempt4	4	wheel may turn and still/Be forever still./{C} There is no rest in the house. There is
258 MC	Thomas	30	may make the cause serve them,/Still doing right: and striving with political men/
261 MC	Thomas	25	for Saints are not made by/accident. Still less is a Christian martyrdom the effect of a
263 MC	Chorus	7	the day, shorter and colder the night./Still and stifling the air: but a wind is stored up

270 MC	Chorus	1	dawn. I have eaten/Smooth creatures still living, with the strong salt taste of living
272 MC	Chorus	12	Numb the hand and dry the eyelid,/Still the horror, but more horror/Than when
272 MC	Chorus	14	/Than when tearing in the belly./Still the horror, but more horror/Than when
278 MC	Knight2	36	called murderer. And at a later time still, even such temperate/measures as these
279 MC	Knight1	8	/to express. If there are any who are still unconvinced, I think that/Richard Brito,
279 MC	Knight4	33	beyond human endurance, he could still have easily escaped; he/could have kept
279 MC	Knight4	36	to happen; he/insisted, while we were still inflamed with wrath, that the doors/should
280 MC	Priest3	31	circle of pain within the skull/You still shall tramp and tread one endless round/Of
285 FR	Amy	1	/{A} Not yet! I will ring for you. It is still quite light./I have nothing to do but watch
286 FR	Amy	11	are perfectly competent, Gerald./I can still see to that./{V} Well, as for me,/I would
287 FR	Amy	20	for her/At the moment: but life may still go right./Meanwhile, let us drop the
294 FR	Harry	28	to escape/By violence, but one is still alone/In an over-crowded desert, jostled by
304 FR	Mary	26	Harry./Even when he married, she still held on to me/Because she couldn't bear to
309 FR	Mary	28	who believes that he is blind/While he still sees the sunlight. I know that this is true./
310 FR	Harry	39	I kept moving/Only so as not to stay still. Singing and light./Stop!/What is that? do
315 FR	Harry	6	an innocent victim./To himself he is still what he used to be/Or what he would be.
320 FR	Warburt	6	Harry, that although your mother/Is still so alert, so vigorous of mind,/Although she
330 FR	Harry	18	to regard it as an explanation./{H} I still have to learn exactly what their meaning is./
331 FR	Harry	9	fall into place. But *they* prevent it./I still have to find out what their meaning is./
337 FR	Harry	25	/Which your words echo. I am still befouled,/But I know there is only one way
339 FR	Harry	4	/{H} I shall have to learn. That is still unsettled./I have not yet had the precise
344 FR	Harry	35	of you believe it;/If you believed it, still you would not understand./You can't know
349 FR	Ivy	8	the funeral: will my ticket to London still be valid?/{G} I do not look forward with
353 CP	Julia	9	tell the same story twice./{J} But I'm still waiting to know what happened./I know it
355 CP	Alex	13	there were no bats./{A} And is he still there?/Julia is really a mine of information./
362 CP	Reilly	38	/In talking to the matron, you are still the subject,/The centre of reality. But,
375 CP	Edward	32	it within ten minutes./I suppose it's still cooking./{C} You suppose it's still cooking!/
375 CP	Celia	33	it's still cooking./{C} You suppose it's still cooking!/I thought I noticed a peculiar
375 CP	Celia	35	a peculiar smell:/Of course it's still cooking — or doing *something*./I must go
380 CP	Edward	37	with anyone but you,/And perhaps I still am. But this can't go on./It never could
385 CP	Reilly	9	It is very difficult./But it is perhaps still more difficult/To keep up the pretence that
385 CP	Reilly	18	/To treat them as strangers, but still more difficult/To pretend that you were not
396 CP	Edward	35	you to explain me to myself./You're still trying to invent a personality for me/Which
402 CP	Reilly	6	there are only two —/Which you still have the chance of redeeming from ruin./
403 CP	Edward	26	for fifteen minutes/Before I felt, and still more acutely —/Indeed, acutely, perhaps,
410 CP	Reilly	13	which holds you together./While still in a state of unenlightenment,/*You* could
414 CP	Celia	34	second symptom?/{C} That's stranger still./It sounds ridiculous — but the only word
418 CP	Celia	5	to be able to accept that/If I might still have it. Yet it leaves me cold./Perhaps
418 CP	Celia	18	raving!/Or just cantankerousness ... still,/If there's no other way ... then I feel just
431 CP	Peter	22	in England!/At least, of any that are still inhabited./We've got a team of experts over
438 CP	Reilly	20	try to detach yourself from what you still feel/As your responsibility./{E} I cannot
446 CC	Eggers	22	/{E} No doubt that's best. While he's still living/With his aunt in Teddington, and
446 CC	Claude	26	be ready for him?/{SC} They have still to do the walls. And then it must be
451 CC	Colby	39	But I wish I was musical./{C} I still don't feel very well prepared for meeting
453 CC	Kaghan	25	existence/Until they met you. Colby's still reeling./It's going to be my responsibility,/
457 CC	Claude	11	{}/[*Enter* SIR CLAUDE]/{SC} Hello! Still here? It's time you were off./{E} I'm just
462 CC	Colby	7	settled./And what you've had in mind still seems to me/Like building my life upon a
465 CC	Colby	7	him, he was not there./{C} You've still not explained why you came to think/That
467 CC	Colby	4	have always been his son/And he is still your father. I only wish/That I had
469 CC	Lucasta	18	I liked were the right ones to like?/Still, I'm awfully ignorant. Can you believe/
470 CC	Lucasta	3	week/And you had it tuned yesterday. Still, I'm flattered/To be your first visitor in this
471 CC	Colby	6	so you'll recognise them./Better still, I'll play you the gramophone records./{L}
472 CC	Lucasta	40	outer world that you've lost:/You've still got your inner world — a world that's more
485 CC	Lady E	28	/{C} It's very close to London./{LE} Still, you were brought up, like me, in a
487 CC	Lady E	25	it, Claude?/And yet it would be still more incredible/If it were only a
494 CC	Lady E	6	/While, if he were yours ... he could still take the place/Of my son: and so he could
510 CC	Eggers	5	/And if Mr. and Mrs. Kaghan are still living/Mrs. Guzzard should be able to
517 CC	Colby	5	me as a friend./{C} But you would still think of me as your son./There can be no
518 CC	Eggers	9	of reading for orders./And you'll still have your music. Why, Mr. Simpkins,/
530 ES		m 32	listen to! {}/[*pointing to a silver salver, still lying in its case*]./{LC} I don't know which
531 ES	Ld Clav	1	do for visiting cards — if people still left cards/And if I was going to have any
536 ES	Gomez	35	thing./My mother — I dare say she's still alive,/But she must be very old. And she
540 ES	Ld Clav	14	in./{LC} Indeed! How interesting!/I still don't know why you've come to see me/Or
544 ES	Ld Clav	14	papers, or wanting a fourth at bridge;/Still, I'll admit to a feeling of contentment/
545 ES	Ld Clav	8	activity,/And in the end, judge us still more severely/For the errors into which his

547 ES   Piggott   25   moment there's no dancing,/And it's still too early for the bathing pool./But several
549 ES   Carghil   1   And everybody knows *you*. But still,/I wish you could have paid *me* that
550 ES   Ld Clav   19   was. Just what I needed./{LC} Is he still living?/{MC} He had a weak heart./And he
551 ES   Carghil   3   Why, even a faithless lover/Is still, in her memory, a kind of testimonial./Men
552 ES   Carghil   27   was clear./At bottom, I believe you're still the same silly Richard/You always were.
552 ES   Carghil   37   part for you/Right to the end. You'll still be playing a part/In your obituary, whoever
553 ES   Carghil   9   /No, Richard, don't imagine that I'm still in love with you;/And you needn't think I
553 ES   Carghil   13   —/Pawed it, perhaps, and the touch still lingers./And I've touched yours./It's
553 ES   Carghil   15   /It's frightening to think that we're still together/And more frightening to think that
554 ES   Carghil   12   /It seems to me that you never sit still:/You simply sacrifice yourself for us./{MP}
560 ES   Michael   1   will it give you/In the grave? If you're still conscious after death,/I bet it will be a
562 ES   Carghil   12   /{MC} Richard! I didn't think you'd still be here./I came back to have a quiet read of
566 ES   Ld Clav   3   hands of the same master. But have I still time?/There is time for Michael. Is it too
569 ES   Ld Clav   11   you'll find a little love in your heart/Still, for your father, when you know him/For
570 ES   Ld Clav   7   the ghosts who haunted me./And I'm still of that opinion. How open one's heart/
572 ES   Ld Clav   22   that the ghost of the man I was/Still clings to the ghost of the woman who was

STILLNESS (8)
129 Cor2 State   46   we not be/O hidden/Hidden in the stillness of noon, in the silent croaking night./
147 Rock 1   8   knowledge of motion, but not of stillness;/Knowledge of speech, but not of
173 FQ: BurntN   96   daylight/Investing form with lucid stillness/Turning shadow into transient beauty/
175 FQ: BurntN   145   /Can words or music reach/The stillness, as a Chinese jar still/Moves perpetually
175 FQ: BurntN   146   jar still/Moves perpetually in its stillness./Not the stillness of the violin, while the
175 FQ: BurntN   147   perpetually in its stillness./Not the stillness of the violin, while the note lasts,/Not
180 FQ: ECoker   129   darkness shall be the light, and the stillness the dancing./Whisper of running
198 FQ: Little   252   for/But heard, half-heard, in the stillness/Between two waves of the sea./Quick

STIMULANT (1)
377 CP   Julia   24   And I thought, we are all in need of a stimulant/After this disaster. Now I'll propose a

STIMULATING (1)
557 ES   Michael   11   .../{Mi} I need something much more stimulating./{LC} Well?/{Mi} I want to find

STIMULUS (1)
403 CP   Reilly   6   your vanity/With the temporary stimulus of feeling interesting./{E} But I am

STINGS (1)
195 FQ: Little   145   of virtue./Then fools' approval stings, and honour stains./From wrong to

STIPEND (1)
517 CC   Eggers   38   /{C} I'd like to apply./{E} The stipend is small —/Very small, I'm afraid. Not

STIPULATION (1)
546 ES   Piggott   25   who *looks* incurable —/We make that stipulation to all the doctors/Who send people

STIR (2)
49 Hippopot   11   /While the True Church need never stir/To gather in its dividends./The 'potamus
263 MC Chorus   4   year?/Only the death of the old: not a stir, not a shoot, not a breath./Do the days

STIRRED (4)
64 WL: Chess   89   /And drowned the sense in odours; stirred by the air/That freshened from the
129 Cor2 State   34   widest tree/Under the breast feather stirred by the small wind after noon/There the
160 Rock 7   13   /And they came to an end, a dead end stirred with a flicker of life,/And they came to
311 FR   Harry   20   /Quietly, as if they had never stirred./It was only a moment, it was only one

STIRRING (6)
55 Mr E Sun   30   /Sweeney shifts from ham to ham/Stirring the water in his bath./The masters of
61 WL: Burial   3   land, mixing/Memory and desire, stirring/Dull roots with spring rain./Winter kept
64 WL: Chess   93   /Flung their smoke into the laquearia,/Stirring the pattern on the coffered ceiling./
267 MC Knight1   33   mind you; but in the hope/Of stirring up trouble in the French dominions./
336 FR   Harry   8   is it so quiet?/Do you feel a kind of stirring underneath the air?/Do you? don't you?
428 CP   Alex   36   /There are also foreign agitators,/Stirring up trouble .../{L} Why don't you expel

STIRS (2)
42 Swee Erect   9   with haste the perjured sails./Morning stirs the feet and hands/(Nausicaa and
191 FQ: Little   10   than blaze of branch, or brazier,/Stirs the dumb spirit: no wind, but pentecostal

STOCK (1)
180 FQ: ECoker   109   and the Almanach de Gotha/And the Stock Exchange Gazette, the Directory of

STOCKADE (1)
307 FR   Harry   2   Down near the river. That was the stockade/From which we fought the Indians,

STOCKHOLM (1)
541 ES   Gomez   22   matter of that,/My current account in Stockholm or Zürich/Would keep me in

STOCKING (1)
56 Swee Night   16   the floor/She yawns and draws a stocking up;/The silent man in mocha brown/

STOCKINGS (1)
68 WL: Fire S   227   the divan are piled (at night her bed)/Stockings, slippers, camisoles, and stays./I

STOL'N (1)

212 Growltiger   27   TUMBLEBRUTUS, he too had stol'n away —/In the yard behind the Lion he

STOLE (2)

587 Fable   21   monks were having merry times./He stole the fatter cows and left the thinner/To

428 CP   Julia   4   monkey,/The horrid little beast — stole my ticket to Mentone/And I had to travel

STOLEN (1)

400 CP   Alex 20   triumphant/Because he thinks he's stolen a march on her./And when you've sent

STONE (34)

  61 WL: Burial   24   the cricket no relief,/And the dry stone no sound of water. Only/There is shadow

  64 WL: Chess   95   and orange, framed by the coloured stone,/In which sad light a carvèd dolphin

  84 Hollow Men 41   land/This is cactus land/Here the stone images/Are raised, here they receive/The

  84 Hollow Men 51   would kiss/Form prayers to broken stone./The eyes are not here/There are no eyes

121 SA Sweeney   5   missionary!/You'll be my little seven stone missionary!/I'll gobble you up. I'll be the

127 Cor1 March   1   KNOCK/Coriolan/Triumphal March/Stone, bronze, stone, steel, stone, oakleaves,

127 Cor1 March   1   /Triumphal March/Stone, bronze, stone, steel, stone, oakleaves, horses' heels/Over

127 Cor1 March   1   March/Stone, bronze, stone, steel, stone, oakleaves, horses' heels/Over the paving./

128 Cor1 March   40   /Dust/Dust/Dust of dust, and now/Stone, bronze, stone, steel, stone, oakleaves,

128 Cor1 March   40   Dust of dust, and now/Stone, bronze, stone, steel, stone, oakleaves, horses' heels/Over

128 Cor1 March   40   and now/Stone, bronze, stone, steel, stone, oakleaves, horses' heels/Over the paving./

149 Rock 1   85   *are fallen/We will build with new stone/Where the beams are rotten/We will build*

153 Rock 2   54   dug from the pit, let the saw cut the stone,/Let the fire not be quenched in the forge./

164 Rock 9   17   to creation./Out of the formless stone, when the artist unites himself with stone,/

164 Rock 9   17   when the artist unites himself with stone,/Spring always new forms of life, from the

164 Rock 9   18   of man that is joined to the soul of stone;/Out of the meaningless practical shapes

165 Rock 9   40   is never without travail;/The formed stone, the visible crucifix,/The dressed altar, the

167 Rock 10   30   /And light reflected from the polished stone,/The gilded carven wood, the coloured

177 FQ: ECoker   5   field, or a factory, or a by-pass./Old stone to new building, old timber to new fires,/

177 FQ: ECoker 21   /Is absorbed, not refracted, by grey stone./The dahlias sleep in the empty silence./

197 FQ: Little   229   the sea's throat/Or to an illegible stone: and that is where we start./We die with

201 Def Island   1   Islands/Let these memorials of built stone — music's/enduring instrument, of many

599 On a Port   5   /Not like a tranquil carved goddess of stone/But evanescent, as if one should meet/A

273 MC Thomas 20   own, in her own way, not/As oak and stone; stone and oak decay,/Give no stay, but

273 MC Thomas 20   her own way, not/As oak and stone; stone and oak decay,/Give no stay, but

275 MC Chorus 21   air! clean the sky! wash the wind! take stone from stone and wash them./The land is

275 MC Chorus 21   sky! wash the wind! take stone from stone and wash them./The land is foul, the

276 MC Chorus 17   clean the sky! wash the wind! take stone from the stone, take the skin from the

276 MC Chorus 17   the wind! take the stone from the stone, take the skin from the arm, take the

276 MC Chorus 17   the bone, and wash them. Wash the stone, wash the bone, wash the brain, wash the

308 FR   Harry   7   itself to a twilight/Where the dead stone is seen to be batrachian,/The aphyllous

318 FR   Harry 33   I have been silent/Or talked to the stone deaf: and the others/Seem to hear

333 FR   Harry 18   tends towards reconciliation/As the stone falls, as the tree falls. And in the end/That

335 FR   Agatha 18   /{Ag} Up and down, through the stone passages/Of an immense and empty

STONECROP (1)

  37 Gerontion   12   in the field overhead;/Rocks, moss, stonecrop, iron, merds./The woman keeps the

STONES (4)

182 FQ: ECoker 198   lifetime of one man only/But of old stones that cannot be deciphered./There is a

275 MC Chorus 24   they bleed; I wander in a land of dry stones: if I touch them they bleed./How how

332 FR   Agatha 31   across a whole Thibet of broken stones/That lie, fang up, a lifetime's march. I

348 FR   Chorus 33   the heather/And behind the Standing Stones?/Beyond the Heaviside Layer/And

STONY (3)

  61 WL: Burial   20   what branches grow/Out of this stony rubbish? Son of man,/You cannot say, or

  72 WL: Thund 324   in the gardens/After the agony in stony places/The shouting and the crying/Prison

339 FR   Harry   9   desert, the thirst and deprivation,/A stony sanctuary and a primitive altar,/The heat

STOOD (6)

  74 WL: Thund 391   bones can harm no one./Only a cock stood on the rooftree/Co co rico co co rico/In a

135 5FingerEx2   1   *a Yorkshire Terrier*/In a brown field stood a tree/And the tree was crookt and dry./

588 Fable   36   soakt the uncomplaining porter/Who stood outside the door from head to feet./To

311 FR   Harry 22   it was only one moment/That I stood in sunlight, and thought I might stay

526 ES Monica 9   It crept so softly/On silent feet, and stood behind my back/Quietly, a long time, a

558 ES Michael 27   boys began to sneer at me./I wonder I stood it as long as I did./{LC} And does this

STOOLS (1)

127 Cor1 March 11   is a perceiving./We can wait with our stools and our sausages./What comes first? Can

STOOPS (1)

  69 WL: Fire S 253   glad it's over.'/When lovely woman stoops to folly and/Paces about her room again,

STOP (37)

72 WL: Thund	335	water/If there were water we should stop and drink/Amongst the rock one cannot
72 WL: Thund	336	drink/Amongst the rock one cannot stop or think/Sweat is dry and feet are in the
116 SP	Doris	14	That's Pereira/{Do} Well can't you stop that horrible noise?/Pick up the receiver/
271 MC	Priests	20	/{3P} My Lord, you must not stop here. To the minster./Through the cloister.
271 MC	Priests	28	altar./Make haste, my Lord. Don't stop here talking. It is not right./What shall
275 MC	Chorus	26	quiet seasons?/Night stay with us, stop sun, hold season, let the day not come, let
285 FR	Amy	10	assured/And time would not stop in the dark!/Put on the lights. But leave the
287 FR	Amy	24	arrive?/{A} I do not want the clock to stop in the dark./If you want to know why I
310 FR	Harry	40	as not to stay still. Singing and light./Stop!/What is that? do you feel it?/{M} What,
311 FR	Harry	9	O Mary!/Don't look at me like that! Stop! Try to stop it!/I am going. Oh why, now?
311 FR	Harry	9	look at me like that! Stop! Try to stop it!/I am going. Oh why, now? Come out!/
318 FR Warburt	18	/Than what they are told./{W} Stop, Harry, you're mistaken./I mean, you
327 FR	Charles	37	to have this evening's paper./{C} Stop, I think I bought a lunch edition/Before I
328 FR	Charles	24	an hour. When asked why he/did not stop when signalled by the police car, he said: "I
342 FR	Mary	19	comes from another!/Can you not stop him? Cousin Agatha, stop him!/You do not
342 FR	Mary	19	you not stop him? Cousin Agatha, stop him!/You do not know what I have seen
353 CP	Celia	12	I said there were no tigers./{C} Oh do stop wrangling,/Both of you. It's your turn,
363 CP	Edward	37	experience of incalculable value./{E} Stop! I agree that much of what you've said/Is
366 CP	Julia	23	take you down in the lift./{J} No, you stop and talk to Edward. I'm not helpless yet./
385 CP	Edward	33	memories./Now I shall go./{E} Stop! Will you come back with her?/{UG} No, I
391 CP	Lavinia	14	coming back again *this* evening./{L} Stop! I want you to explain the telegram./{J}
391 CP	Lavinia	20	that goes on working,/And I cannot stop it; no, it's not like a machine —/Or if it's a
411 CP	Lavinia	8	on next Monday./{L} Then will you stop at your club?/{E} No, they won't let me./
474 CC	Lucasta	24	would fade/And the music would stop. And the walls would be broken./And you
491 CC	Lady E	3	have had a father and a mother./{LE} Stop, Colby! Something has come to me./
518 CC	Eggers	19	should be most happy/If you cared to stop with us, until you were settled./{C} I'd be
525 ES	Monica	4	.../{M} That you should stop to tea./{C} When I said that I was free for
525 ES	Monica	14	advise you to buy it./{M} But why not stop to tea?/{C} Very well then, I will stop to
525 ES	Charles	15	stop to tea?/{C} Very well then, I will stop to tea,/But you know I won't get a chance
532 ES	Ld Clav	5	/{LC} I'll see him in the library./No, stop. I've left too many papers about there./I'd
542 ES	Gomez	37	room./Don't forget, Dick:/You *didn't stop*! Well, I'd better be going./I hope I haven't
556 ES	Monica	26	before, didn't I?/{M} I wish you'd stop being so polite to each other./Michael, you
571 ES	Ld Clav	37	man lying in the road/And I did not stop. Then another man ran over him./A lorry
572 ES	Ld Clav	3	neither of us killed him. But *I* didn't stop./And all my life I have heard, from time to
572 ES	Ld Clav	6	/A voice that whispered, 'you didn't stop!'/I knew the voice: it was Fred
579 ES	Ld Clav	22	if you're going, and I see no way to stop you,/Then I agree with you, the sooner the
582 ES	Monica	21	you?/You know you're not allowed to stop out late/At this season. It's chilly at dusk./

STOPPED (9)

32 Hysteria	9	if the shaking of her breasts could be stopped,/some of the fragments of the afternoon
61 WL: Burial	9	/With a shower of rain; we stopped in the colonnade,/And went on in
62 WL: Burial	69	of nine./There I saw one I knew, and stopped him, crying: 'Stetson!/'You who were
223 Pekes Pols	47	together assembled,/The traffic all stopped, and the Underground trembled,/And
322 FR	Winch	36	know this part of the country/And stopped to take his bearings. We've got him at
326 FR	Violet	3	out to take me to Cheltenham;/But I stopped him somewhere in Chiswick, I think./
333 FR	Agatha	2	not have been born in that event:/I stopped him./I can take no credit for a little
347 FR	Amy	31	Agatha! Mary! come!/The clock has stopped in the dark! {}/[*Exeunt* AGATHA *and*
571 ES	Ld Clav	38	man ran over him./A lorry driver. He stopped and was arrested,/But was later

STOPPING (2)

233 Skimble	54	while he's keeping on the watch,/Only stopping here and there to catch a flea./You
294 FR	Agatha	13	/Talk in your own language, without stopping to debate/Whether it may be too far

STOPS (7)

92 Ash-Wed 3	19	hair;/Distraction, music of the flute, stops and steps of the mind over the third stair,/
180 FQ: ECoker	119	an underground train, in the tube, stops too long between stations/And the
185 FQ: DrySal	47	before the morning watch/When time stops and time is never ending;/And the ground
291 FR	m	14	HARRY]/{A} Harry! {}/[HARRY *stops suddenly at the door and stares at the*
335 FR	Harry	29	breaks./The chain breaks,/The wheel stops, and the noise of machinery,/And the
400 CP	2m	35	/{E} Sir Henry Harcourt-Reilly — {}/[*Stops and stares at* REILLY]/[*without looking*
554 ES	Carghil	5	on us. Isn't she frightful!/She never stops talking. Can you bear it?/If I go at once,

STORE (2)

593 Grad 5	3	— who knows what time may hold in store,/Or what great deeds the distant years may
445 CC	Eggers	18	be pleased./Then I lunched at the store — they have a restaurant;/An excellent

STORED (3)

239 MC	Chorus	10	/And the apples were gathered and stored, and the land became brown sharp points
263 MC	Chorus	7	/Still and stifling the air: but a wind is stored up in the East./The starved crow sits in
263 MC	Chorus	11	signs of a bitter spring?/The wind stored up in the East./What, at the time of the

STORES (1)

254 MC	Tempt4	34	/The sanctuary broken, and its stores/Swept into the laps of parasites and

STORIES (2)

588 Fable		64	to burn distinctly blue,/As in ghost stories lights most always do./The doors,
572 ES	Charles	30	tell their versions of their miserable stories,/Confide them in whispers. They cannot

STORM (4)

256 MC	Priests	25	not sail the irresistible wind; in the storm,/Should we not wait for the sea to
263 MC	Chorus	2	sea-bird cries, driven inland by the storm./What sign of the spring of the year?/
281 MC	Chorus	8	snow, in the rain, in the wind, in the storm; in all of Thy creatures, both the hunters
289 FR	Ivy	25	/Swept off the deck in the middle of a storm,/And never even to recover the body./{C}

STORMS (1)

309 FR	Harry	35	voice as in the silence/Between two storms, one hears the moderate usual noises/In

STORMY (2)

56 Swee	Night	5	to maculate giraffe./The circles of the stormy moon/Slide westward toward the River
217 Jellicles		31	I said) are small;/If it happens to be a stormy night/They will practise a caper or two

STORY (33)

124 SA	Snow	10	/{Sn} Let Mr. Sweeney continue his story./I assure you, Sir, we are very interested./
124 SA	Snow	25	/{Sn} Let Mr. Sweeney continue his story./{S} This one didn't get pinched in the end/
124 SA	Sweeney	27	pinched in the end/But that's another story too./This went on for a couple of months/
192 FQ:	Little	59	suspended/Marks the place where a story ended./Dust inbreathed was a house —/
203 Indians		18	/Let those who go home tell the same story of you:/Of action with a common purpose,
588 Fable		37	to feet./To make a rather lengthy story shorter,/He left no wise precaution
333 FR	Agatha	25	of it?/What we have written is not a story of detection,/Of crime and punishment,
353 CP	Alex	8	again, Alex./{A} I never tell the same story twice./{J} But I'm still waiting to know
353 CP	Julia	10	what happened./I know it started as a story about tigers./{A} I said there were no
353 CP	Celia	14	It's your turn, Julia./Do tell us that story you told the other day, about Lady
353 CP	Peter	16	out with champagne./I like that story./{C} I love that story./{A} *I'm* never tired
353 CP	Celia	17	/I like that story./{C} I love that story./{A} *I'm* never tired of hearing that story./
353 CP	Alex	18	/{A} *I'm* never tired of hearing that story./{J} Well, you all seem to know it./{C} Do
354 CP	Celia	21	I never met her./{C} Go on with the story about the wedding cake./{J} Well, but it
354 CP	Julia	22	cake./{J} Well, but it really isn't my story./I heard it first from Delia Verinder/Who
354 CP	Julia	28	can't be too careful/Before one tells a story./{A} Delia Verinder?/Was she the one who
355 CP	Peter	16	doesn't know./{P} Go on with the story about the wedding cake. {}/[EDWARD
355 CP	Julia	34	friends of yours, I couldn't tell the story./{P} Were they the parents of Tony
356 CP	Celia	14	enjoyable time./{C} Go on with the story about the wedding cake./{J} Edward, do
358 CP	Peter	14	be going?/{P} But won't you tell the story about Lady Klootz?/{J} What Lady
429 CP	Alex	16	among pagans!/{A} Not on the *whole* story./{E} And have any of the English residents
464 CC	Claude	38	makes it real./That's not the whole story. My father knew I hated it:/That was a
476 CC	Lucasta	32	/{L} His daughter. Oh, it's a sordid story./I hated my mother. I never could see/
486 CC	Colby	20	I doubt it?/That is not the kind of story my aunt would invent./{LE} Not if she *is*
489 CC	Lady E	30	/Perhaps Mrs. Guzzard invented the story..../{SC} Why should she invent it? The
505 CC	Claude	4	the country. But he knows the whole story:/He's been in my confidence — and I may
513 CC	Colby	30	Only by report, by documents —/The story of his life, of his success or failure .../
536 ES	Gomez	38	their husbands/Were ever told the story. *They* wouldn't want to see me./No, I need
540 ES	Ld Clav	35	trust you?/{LC} If you think that this story would interest the public/Why not sell
541 ES	Gomez	10	to whom I'd told it,/Or who knew the story and who didn't. I promise you./Rely upon
574 ES	Carghil	10	Michael?/{MC} He's told me all his story./You've cruelly misunderstood him,
575 ES	Ld Clav	30	that allusion. I have told them the story/In explanation of our ... intimacy/Which
576 ES	Ld Clav	8	Señor Gomez says he has told you his story./Did he include the fact that he served a

STOUTEST (1)

231 Bust Jones		38	last out my time'/Is the word for this stoutest of Cats./It must and it shall be Spring

STOVE (1)

68 WL:	Fire S	223	clears her breakfast, lights/Her stove, and lays out food in tins./Out of the

STRADDLED (1)

43 Swee	Erect	28	not seen the silhouette/Of Sweeney straddled in the sun.)/Tests the razor on his leg/

STRAIGHT (12)

66 WL:	Chess	151	who to thank, she said, and give me a straight look./HURRY UP PLEASE ITS
250 MC	Thomas	37	Englishman./{T} Proceed straight forward./{T3} Purpose is plain./
316 FR	Agatha	24	is uncrossed/And the crooked is made straight. {}/[*Exit to dinner*]/END OF PART I/
335 FR	Agatha	21	by a smell of disinfectant,/Looking straight ahead, passing barred windows./Up
337 FR	Agatha	7	be unknotted/And the crooked made straight. {}/[*She moves back into the room*]/{Ag}

350 FR	Agatha	19	be uncrossed/The crooked be made straight/And the curse be ended/By intercession/
366 CP	Julia	11	I lose *anything*, Edward,/I'll come straight to you, instead of to St. Anthony./And
368 CP	Alex	15	I'm rather a famous cook./I'm going straight to your kitchen now/And I shall
399 CP	Reilly	25	here, Sir Henry./{R} Ask him to come straight in. {}/[*Exit* NURSE-SECRETARY]/
425 CP	Lavinia	34	makes it a success. Is that picture straight?/{E} Yes, it is./{L} No, it isn't. Do
425 CP	Edward	37	isn't. Do please straighten it./{E} Is it straight now?/{L} Too much to the left./{E}
485 CC	Lady E	22	been/From eternity. Something ... straight from God./That means that we are

STRAIGHTEN (1)

425 CP	Lavinia	36	Yes, it is./{L} No, it isn't. Do please straighten it./{E} Is it straight now?/{L} Too

STRAIGHTENED (1)

316 FR	Agatha	16	bones/In the filled-up well/Be at last straightened/May the weasel and the otter/Be

STRAIGHTENS (1)

42 Swee Erect		18	/Jackknifes upward at the knees/Then straightens out from heel to hip/Pushing the

STRAIGHTFORWARD (2)

250 MC	Tempt3	36	Excuse my bluntness:/I am a rough straightforward Englishman./{T} Proceed
424 CP	Edward	22	consultations with solicitors/On quite straightforward cases. It's you who should be

STRAIGHTWAY (1)

589 Fable		87	nearer underground;/But the church straightway put to his name the handle/Of

STRAIN (9)

175 FQ: BurntN		152	end./And all is always now. Words strain,/Crack and sometimes break, under the
244 MC	Chorus	29	who live among small things,/The strain on the brain of the small folk who stand
333 FR	Agatha	30	expiation./It is possible that sin may strain and struggle/In its dark instinctive birth,
355 CP	Julia	20	he wasn't listening, but he's such a strain —/Edward without Lavinia! He's quite
376 CP	Julia	19	must be fed./He's under such a strain. We must keep his strength up./Edward!
409 CP	Reilly	1	your obvious symptoms of emotional strain/And so I made enquiries./{E} It was two
454 CC	Lucasta	13	to tea./{L} I'm dying for my tea. The strain of this crisis/Has been too much for me.
470 CC	Lucasta	9	a musician./{L} Did you find it a strain, then, playing to me?/{C} As a matter of
554 ES	Carghil	25	it struck me that he might find it a strain/To have to cope with both of us at once./

STRAINED (1)

174 FQ: BurntN		103	nor vacancy. Only a flicker/Over the strained time-ridden faces/Distracted from

STRAINS (1)

437 CP	Reilly	17	minutes after a violent death./If this strains your credulity, Mrs. Chamberlayne,/I

STRAITS (2)

39 Gerontion		69	Gull against the wind, in the windy straits/Of Belle Isle, or running on the Horn./
292 FR	Harry	4	that I have seen them./In the Java Straits, in the Sunda Sea,/In the sweet sickly

STRAKE (1)

110 Marina		28	unknown, my own./The garboard strake leaks, the seams need caulking./This

STRAND (3)

69 WL: Fire S		258	me upon the waters'/And along the Strand, up Queen Victoria Street./O City city, I
213 Growltiger		54	and Henley there was dancing on the strand./Rats were roasted whole at Brentford,
592 Grad 2		1	/As colonists embarking from the strand/To seek their fortunes on some foreign

STRANGE (31)

18 Portrait		20	my friends,/And how, how rare and strange it is, to find/In a life composed so much,
64 WL: Chess		87	glass/Unstoppered, lurked her strange synthetic perfumes,/Unguent, powdered,
194 FQ: Little		106	compliant to the common wind,/Too strange to each other for misunderstanding,/In
204 de la Mare		17	/When the familiar scene is suddenly strange/Or the well known is what we have·yet
260 MC Thomas		16	the World sees, this is to behave in a strange/fashion. For who in the World will both
260 MC Thomas		22	of this word 'peace'. Does/it seem strange to you that the angels should have
269 MC Chorus		33	in the noises of beasts that make strange noises: jackal, jackass, jackdaw; the
326 FR	Harry	9	/{H} Mother is asleep, I think: it's strange how the old/Can drop off to sleep in the
346 FR Downing		17	I'm going to say —/But it's not really strange, Miss, when you come to look at it:/
369 CP	Peter	29	/But a girl like Celia, it seemed very strange,/Because I thought of her merely as a
370 CP	Peter	12	like that at all./It was something very strange. There was such ... tranquillity .../{E}
385 CP	Reilly	19	difficult/To pretend that you were not strange to each other./{E} You can hardly
427 CP	Julia	21	us, Alex./What were you doing in this strange place —/What's it called?/{A} Kinkanja.
462 CC	Colby	35	you, for that:/It is indeed a new and strange situation,/And nothing about it is real
464 CC	Claude	18	the substantial is only a shadow./It's strange. I have never talked of this to anyone./
465 CC	Claude	11	potter./I didn't have it in me. It's strange, isn't it,/That a man should have a
472 CC	Lucasta	11	/What did I think till now? Oh, it's strange, isn't it,/That as one gets to know a
475 CC	Colby	22	/No, I haven't wondered. It's all a strange world/To me, you know, in which I find
491 CC	Colby	31	ghosts of the other parents!/It's strange enough to have two parents —/But I
494 CC	Lady E	37	laughing. I was only thinking/How strange to have lived with you, all these years,/
495 CC	Lady E	38	was what *I* was trying to do./It's very strange, Claude, but this is the first time/I have
512 CC	Claude	18	him as your son?/{SC} That seems a strange question, Mrs. Guzzard./{MG} I have
512 CC	Guzzard	19	I have been asked here to answer strange questions —/And now it is my turn to

513 CC   Colby   12   sure of the truth./{C} That is a very strange question, Aunt Sarah:/To which I can
513 CC   Colby   13   Sarah:/To which I can only give a strange answer./Sir Claude is right: I wished to
537 ES   Gomez   9   /We'll come to that, very soon. Isn't it strange/That there should always have been this
550 ES   Carghil 28   off. Yes, I'm provided for./But isn't it strange that you and I/Should meet here at last?
564 ES   Carghil 20   They're so aristocratic./But it's very strange that we never met before./You were a
583 ES   Charles 5   the limits of speech, and beyond./It's strange that words are so inadequate./Yet, like
583 ES   Monica   19   Michael's./And I am happy. Isn't it strange, Charles,/To be happy at this moment?/
583 ES   Charles 21   at this moment?/{C} It is not at all strange./The dead has poured out a blessing on

STRANGER (18)
148 Rock 1   41   /The Rock. The Watcher. The Stranger./He who has seen what has happened/
148 Rock 1   44   happen./The Witness. The Critic. The Stranger./The God-shaken, in whom is the truth
155 Rock 3   52   than your neighbour's;/When the Stranger says: 'What is the meaning of this city?
155 Rock 3   56   or 'This is a community'?/And the Stranger will depart and return to the desert./O
155 Rock 3   57   be prepared for the coming of the Stranger,/Be prepared for him who knows how
156 Rock 3   75   you shall not./You shall not deny the Stranger./There are those who would build the
162 Rock 8   24   /Diseased and beggared, finding/A stranger at the door in possession:/Came home
182 FQ: ECoker   193   As we grow older/The world becomes stranger, the pattern more complicated/Of dead
193 FQ: Little   93   with which we challenge/The first-met stranger in the waning dusk/I caught the sudden
361 CP   Reilly   26   luxury/Of an intimate disclosure to a stranger./Let me, therefore, remain the stranger.
361 CP   Reilly   27   /Let me, therefore, remain the stranger./But let me tell you, that to approach
361 CP   Reilly   28   let me tell you, that to approach the stranger/Is to invite the unexpected, release a
385 CP   Reilly   5   at every meeting we are meeting a stranger./{E} So you want me to greet my wife
385 CP   Edward   6   So you want me to greet my wife as a stranger?/That will not be easy./{UG} It is very
385 CP   Edward   27   /{E} Then I myself must also be a stranger./{UG} And to yourself as well. But
386 CP   Reilly   13   /{E} Who are you?/{UG} I also am a stranger. {}/[*Exit. A pause.* EDWARD *moves*
414 CP   Celia   34   And the second symptom?/{C} That's stranger still./It sounds ridiculous — but the
497 CC   Eggers   37   it is a most uncommon name,/But stranger things have happened./{LE} And both

STRANGERS (9)
296 FR   Charles 25   grow in his mind,/Living among strangers, with no one to talk to./I suspect it is
337 FR   Agatha   20   who will meet again? Meeting is for strangers./Meeting is for those who do not
385 CP   Reilly   10   keep up the pretence that you are not strangers./The affectionate ghosts: the
385 CP   Reilly   18   find it difficult/To treat them as strangers, but still more difficult/To pretend
385 CP   Reilly   26   must face them all, but meet them as strangers./{E} Then I myself must also be a
386 CP   Reilly   7   visitors?/{UG} Whoever comes. The strangers./As for myself, I shall take the
416 CP   Celia   20   right./And then I found we were only strangers/And that there had been neither
528 ES   Monica   4   /It's his fear of being exposed to strangers./{C} But he's most alive when he's
528 ES   Charles 7   —/At all of which he's a master. Strangers!/{M} You don't understand. It's one

STRANGEST (1)
258 MC Thomas   38   that history at all times draws/The strangest consequence from remotest cause./But

STRANGLE (1)
385 CP   Reilly   31   I have said the same to her./Don't strangle each other with knotted memories./

STRASSBURG (1)
235 Ad-dress   57   and then supply/Some caviare, or Strassburg Pie,/Some potted grouse, or salmon

STRATAGEM (3)
202 War Poetry   19   problem to be met with ambush and stratagem,/Enveloped or scattered./The
253 MC Tempt4   26   a king,/With craft in corners, stealthy stratagem,/To general grasp of spiritual power?/
274 MC Thomas   8   not here to triumph by fighting, by stratagem, or by resistance,/Not to fight with

STRATEGY (1)
258 MC Thomas   14   in the lilac tree,/The tiltyard skill, the strategy of chess,/Love in the garden, singing to

STRAW (2)
 83 Hollow Men   4   together/Headpiece filled with straw. Alas!/Our dried voices, when/We whisper
508 CC   Eggers   7   way,/Wouldn't you grasp at any straw/That offered hope of finding him?/{MG}

STRAWBERRY (1)
180 FQ: ECoker   131   /The wild thyme unseen and the wild strawberry,/The laughter in the garden, echoed

STRAWS (1)
508 CC   Lady E 12   your legal training,/Should talk about straws! Colby is my son./{MG} In the

STRAY (2)
161 Rock 7   37   the world say, does the whole world stray in high-powered cars on a by-pass way?/
174 FQ: BurntN   133   sunflower turn to us, will the clematis/Stray down, bend to us; tendril and spray/

STRAYING (1)
161 Rock 7   25   by the light;/Often halting, loitering, straying, delaying, returning, yet following no

STREAK (1)
598 Circe   5   are fanged and red/With hideous streak and stain;/They sprang from the limbs of

STREAM (4)

70 WL: Fire S	287	shores/Southwest wind/Carried down	stream/The peal of bells/White towers/Weialala
103 Journ Magi	23	of vegetation,/With a running	stream and a water-mill beating the darkness,/
594 Grad 11	5	gleam,/A bubble on the surface of the	stream,/A drop of dew upon the morning grass;/
263 MC Chorus	22	the elder and may/Burst over the	stream, and the air is clear and high,/And voices

STREAMS (2)

180 FQ: ECoker	130	the dancing./Whisper of running	streams, and winter lightning./The wild thyme
240 MC Chorus	9	summer burn up the beds of our	streams/And the poor shall wait for another

STREET (43)

13 Prufrock	24	the yellow smoke that slides along the	street/Rubbing its back upon the
22 Preludes	11	/And at the corner of the	street/A lonely cab-horse steams and stamps./
22 Preludes	16	of beer/From the sawdust-trampled	street/With all its muddy feet that press/To
23 Preludes	33	gutters,/You had such a vision of the	street/As the street hardly understands;/Sitting
23 Preludes	34	had such a vision of the	street/As the street hardly understands;/Sitting along the
23 Preludes	46	/The conscience of a blackened	street/Impatient to assume the world./I am
24 Rhapsody	2	o'clock./Along the reaches of the	street/Held in a lunar synthesis,/Whispering
24 Rhapsody	8	/Its divisions and precisions./Every	street lamp that I pass/Beats like a fatalistic
24 Rhapsody	41	child's eye./I have seen eyes in the	street/Trying to peer through lighted shutters,/
27 Morning	2	/And along the trampled edges of the	street/I am aware of the damp souls of
27 Morning	6	/Twisted faces from the bottom of the	street,/And tear from a passer-by with muddy
28 Boston ET	3	/When evening quickens faintly in the	street,/Wakening the appetites of life in some/
28 Boston ET	8	good-bye to La Rochefoucauld,/If the	street were time and he at the end of the/
28 Boston ET	8	were time and he at the end of the	street,/And I say, 'Cousin Harriet, here is the
29 Aunt Helen	5	heaven/And silence at her end of the	street./The shutters were drawn and the
62 WL: Burial	66	up the hill and down King William	Street,/To where Saint Mary Woolnoth kept the
65 WL: Chess	132	'I shall rush out as I am, and walk the	street/'With my hair down, so. What shall we
68 WL: Fire S	213	French/To luncheon at the Cannon	Street Hotel/Followed by a weekend at the
69 WL: Fire S	258	along the Strand, up Queen Victoria	Street./O City city, I can sometimes hear/Beside
69 WL: Fire S	260	/Beside a public bar in Lower Thames	Street,/The pleasant whining of a mandoline/
150 Rock 1	116	*bed/And a narrow sheet. In this*	*street/There is no beginning, no movement, no*
150 Rock 1	120	*build the beginning and the end of this*	*street./We build the meaning:/A Church for all/*
154 Rock 3	26	peeled hull, a pile of rusty iron,/In a	street of scattered brick where the goat climbs,/
164 Rock 9	9	daily occasions./Yet they walk in the	street proudnecked, like thoroughbreds ready
195 FQ: Little	149	day was breaking. In the disfigured	street/He left me, with a kind of valediction,/
220 Old Deut	17	/Old Deuteronomy sits in the	street,/He sits in the High Street on market day;
220 Old Deut	18	sits in the street,/He sits in the High	Street on market day;/The bullocks may bellow,
222 Pekes Pols	17	/And no one at all was about on the	street/When a Peke and a Pollicle happened to
223 Pekes Pols	61	*/There wasn't a single one left in the*	*street./Mr. Mistoffelees/You ought to know Mr.*
230 Bust Jones	4	or nine clubs,/For he's the St. James's	Street Cat!/He's the Cat we all greet as he walks
230 Bust Jones	5	Cat we all greet as he walks down the	street/In his coat of fastidious black:/No
599 On a Port	3	/Forever hurrying, up and down the	street,/She stands at evening in the room alone./
243 MC Priest3	12	/And the door shall be shut in the	street,/And all the daughters of music shall be
256 MC Chorus	5	in the house. There is no rest in the	street./I hear restless movement of feet. And the
280 MC Knight1	3	be careful not to loiter in groups at	street corners, and do/nothing that might
291 FR Charles	2	/{C} I might have been in St. James's	Street, in a comfortable chair rather nearer the
301 FR Chorus	17	and the newsboy shall shout in the	street?/When the private shall be made public,
325 FR Violet	37	lolling back/And so near the	street, and everyone staring;/And the pace he
328 FR Charles	14	a roundsman's/cart in Ebury	Street early on the morning of January 1st, was/
328 FR Charles	21	here"—'/{G} Where?/{C} In Ebury	Street]. 'The police stated that at the time of the/
457 CC	m 23	*to the window and looks down on the*	*street]/*{SC} She's having a conversation with the
463 CC Colby	25	is cleared and empty, walking in the	street/Or waking in the night, then the former
496 CC Eggers	27	papers that I picked up at Liverpool	Street./But I've so much to do, in Joshua Park

STREET-LAMP (4)

24 Rhapsody	14	a dead geranium./Half-past one,/The	street-lamp sputtered,/The street-lamp
24 Rhapsody	15	one,/The street-lamp sputtered,/The	street-lamp muttered,/The street-lamp said,
24 Rhapsody	16	/The street-lamp muttered,/The	street-lamp said, 'Regard that woman/Who
24 Rhapsody	34	ready to snap./Half-past two,/The	street-lamp said,/'Remark the cat which flattens

STREET-PIANO (1)

20 Portrait	79	I remain self-possessed/Except when a	street-piano, mechanical and tired/Reiterates

STREETS (11)

13 Prufrock	4	us go, through certain half-deserted	streets,/The muttering retreats/Of restless nights
13 Prufrock	8	restaurants with oyster-shells:/	Streets that follow like a tedious argument/Of
15 Prufrock	70	I have gone at dusk through narrow	streets/And watched the smoke that rises from
16 Prufrock	101	and the dooryards and the sprinkled	streets,/After the novels, after the teacups, after
24 Rhapsody	65	in crevices,/Smells of chestnuts in the	streets,/And female smells in shuttered rooms,/

194 FQ: Little	126	words I never thought to speak/In streets I never thought I should revisit/When I
201 Def Island	19	paths of glory are/the lanes and the streets of Britain:/to say, to the past and the
605 Narcissus	18	before God/If he walked in city streets/He seemed to tread on faces, convulsive
241 MC Mess	35	and late flowers of the season./The streets of the city will be packed to suffocation,/
244 MC Chorus	8	of the fire,/Talked at the corners of streets,/Talked not always in whispers,/Living
245 MC Priest2	5	at any moment?/The crowds in the streets will be cheering and cheering,/You go on

STRENGTH (18)

15 Prufrock	80	after tea and cakes and ices,/Have the strength to force the moment to its crisis?/But
24 Rhapsody	31	/Rust that clings to the form that the strength has left/Hard and curled and ready to
92 Ash-Wed 3	20	over the third stair,/Fading, fading; strength beyond hope and despair/Climbing the
182 FQ: ECoker	185	And what there is to conquer/By strength and submission, has already been
604 Ode	5	we turn as thy sons ever turn, in the strength/Of the hopes that thy blessings bestow,
280 MC Priest1	11	your presence? when inherit/Your strength? The Church lies bereft,/Alone,
305 FR Mary	2	Harry had returned/That I felt the strength to go. I know I must go./But where? I
331 FR Agatha	28	I will try to tell you. I hope I have the strength./{H} I have thought of you as the
331 FR Harry	31	human wheel./So I looked to you for strength. Now I think it is/A common pursuit of
331 FR Agatha	38	neglecting public duties./He hid his strength beneath unusual weakness,/The
334 FR Harry	29	seemed so strong, their apparent strength/Stifled my decision. Now I see/I might
339 FR Harry	20	I see it was what I always wanted. Strength demanded/That seems too much, is
339 FR Harry	21	/That seems too much, is just strength enough given./I must follow the bright
376 CP Julia	19	under such a strain. We must keep his strength up./Edward! Don't you realise how
403 CP Edward	30	obstinate, unconscious, sub-human strength/That some women have. Without her,
462 CC Claude	24	to her?/{SC} If you haven't the strength to impose your own terms/Upon life,
557 ES Michael	26	/He gave me good terms, on the strength of my name:/The only good the name
557 ES Ld Clav	28	name has ever done me./{LC} On the strength of your name. And what do you call

STRENGTHEN (1)

| 249 MC Tempt2 | 5 | man do more?/Disarm the ruffian, strengthen the laws,/Rule for the good of the |

STRETCH (5)

89 Ash-Wed 1	6	things/(Why should the agèd eagle stretch its wings?)/Why should I mourn/The
239 MC Chorus	16	and saints who wait? and who shall/Stretch out his hand to the fire, and deny his
332 FR Agatha	28	/When you want to burn. When you stretch out your hand/To the flames. They only
426 CP Edward	6	for at least half an hour;/So just stretch out./{L} You must sit beside me,/Then I
538 ES Gomez	3	and forgery. And then my stretch/Which gave me time to think it all out./

STRETCHED (4)

15 Prufrock	78	/Asleep ... tired ... or it malingers,/Stretched on the floor, here beside you and me./
23 Preludes	39	palms of both soiled hands./His soul stretched tight across the skies/That fade behind
239 MC Chorus	14	waits for the coming./Who has stretched out his hand to the fire and
362 CP Reilly	39	the subject,/The centre of reality. But, stretched on the table,/You are a piece of

STRETCHES (1)

| 239 MC Chorus | 12 | labourer kicks off a muddy boot and stretches his hand to the fire,/The New Year |

STRETCHING (1)

| 176 FQ: BurntN | 178 | —/Ridiculous the waste sad time/Stretching before and after./East Coker/In my |

STREWING (1)

| 241 MC   Mess | 34 | road and throwing down their capes,/Strewing the way with leaves and late flowers of |

STRICKEN (1)

| 260 MC Thomas | 23 | /when ceaselessly the world has been stricken with War and the fear of/War? Does it |

STRICTLY (1)

| 348 FR Chorus | 26 | area./Except for a limited number/Of strictly practical purposes/We do not know |

STRIDING (1)

| 61 WL: Burial | 28 | from either/Your shadow at morning striding behind you/Or your shadow at evening |

STRIFE (4)

134 Wind	5	/The waking echo of confusing strife/Is it a dream or something else/When the
195 FQ: Little	176	by a common genius,/United in the strife which divided them;/If I think of a king at
246 MC Thomas	21	our first act/Will be shadows, and the strife with shadows./Heavier the interval than
267 MC Knight1	34	in the French dominions./You sowed strife abroad, you reviled/The King to the King

STRIKES (1)

| 601 Nocturne | 5 | moon;/The conversation failing, strikes some tune/Banal, and out of pity for |

STRIKING (1)

| 487 CC Claude | 5 | can develop them for me/With a few striking phrases. It should last about ten |

STRINGS (2)

| 73 WL: Thund | 378 | /And fiddled whisper music on those strings/And bats with baby faces in the violet |
| 91 Ash-Wed 2 | 15 | /It is this which recovers/My guts the strings of my eyes and the indigestible portions/ |

STRIPES (2)

| 56 Swee Night | 3 | arms hang down to laugh,/The zebra stripes along his jaw/Swelling to maculate |
| 210 Old Gumbie | 2 | coat is of the tabby kind, with tiger stripes and leopard spots./All day she sits upon |

STRIPPED (1)
421 CP   Julia   4   the chance./And now, when they are stripped naked to their souls/And can choose,
STRIVE (4)
89 Ash-Wed 1   5   gift and that man's scope/I no longer strive to strive towards such things/(Why should
89 Ash-Wed 1   5   that man's scope/I no longer strive to strive towards such things/(Why should the
249 MC Tempt2   35   /{T2} Hungry hatred/Will not strive against intelligent self-interest./{T} You
269 MC Thomas   12 /It is not against me, Becket, that you strive./It is not Becket who pronounces doom,/
STRIVEN (1)
278 MC Knight2   25 King's servant, had/for so many years striven to establish; and that — God knows/
STRIVES (1)
68 WL: Fire S   220 the violet hour, the evening hour that strives/Homeward, and brings the sailor home
STRIVING (2)
165 Rock 9   38   the Temple completed:/After much striving, after many obstacles;/For the work of
258 MC Thomas   30   serve them,/Still doing right: and striving with political men/May make that cause
STRODE (1)
30 Cous Nancy   2   /Cousin Nancy/Miss Nancy Ellicott/Strode across the hills and broke them,/Rode
STROKE (6)
33 Conv Gal   17   air indifferent and imperious/At a stroke our mad poetics to confute —'/And —
62 WL: Burial   68 hours/With a dead sound on the final stroke of nine./There I saw one I knew, and
251 MC Tempt3   40 /In being with us, would fight a good stroke/At once, for England and for Rome,/
539 ES   Ld Clav   9   If you want to know, I had had a stroke./And I might have another./{G} Yes.
539 ES   Gomez   12 I wonder what brought about this ... stroke;/And I wonder whether you're the great
579 ES   Gomez   36   for it./We can only regard it as a stroke of good fortune/That I came to England
STROLL (1)
582 ES   Ld Clav 19   /Now and always. I shall take a stroll./{M} At this time of day? You'll not go
STRONG (19)
94 Ash-Wed 4   8   as they walked,/Who then made strong the fountains and made fresh the springs/
109 Marina   18 and clearer/The pulse in the arm, less strong and stronger —/Given or lent? more
129 Cor2 State   38 tired head among these heads/Necks strong to bear them/Noses strong to break the
129 Cor2 State   39   /Necks strong to bear them/Noses strong to break the wind/Mother/May we not
141 Rannoch   9   wrong, apt/In silence. Memory is strong/Beyond the bone. Pride snapped,/
184 FQ: DrySal   2   gods; but I think that the river/Is a strong brown god — sullen, untamed and
233 Skimble   42 you like your morning tea weak or strong?'/But Skimble's just behind him and was
241 MC Priest3   3   /King rules or barons rule:/The strong man strongly and the weak man by
270 MC Chorus   1 /Smooth creatures still living, with the strong salt taste of living things under the sea; I
285 FR   Amy   7   for granted/When I was young and strong, and sun and light unsought for/And the
285 FR   Violet   21   /To the chilly deck-chair and the strong cold tea —/The strong cold stewed bad
285 FR   Violet   22   and the strong cold tea —/The strong cold stewed bad Indian tea./{C} That's
304 FR   Mary   9 one else to ask,/And because you are strong, and because you don't belong here/Any
331 FR   Harry   29   thought of you as the completely strong,/The liberated from the human wheel./So
334 FR   Harry   29   odd:/When other people seemed so strong, their apparent strength/Stifled my
357 CP Edward   13   ill before./{E} No, she's always very strong. That's why when she's ill/She gets into a
360 CP   Reilly   16 /Let me prepare it for you, if I may .../Strong ... but sip it slowly ... and drink it sitting
448 CC Claude   31   Mr. Simpkins/Is, that she has a strong maternal instinct .../{E} I realise that./
458 CC Claude   30   .../{SC} Mr. Simpkins had very strong recommendations .../{E} And at the same
STRONGER (7)
109 Marina   18 /The pulse in the arm, less strong and stronger —/Given or lent? more distant than
594 Grad 12   3   shall but increase/Forever, and may stronger words than these/Proclaim the glory so
280 MC Priest3   14 it. I see it./{P3} No. For the Church is stronger for this action,/Triumphant in
341 FR   Amy   21 Your fury for possession/Is only the stronger for all these years of abstinence./
382 CP Edward   3   /In submission to the rule of the stronger partner./{C} I am not sure, Edward,
406 CP Edward   27   complications than you;/You're stronger than a ... battleship. That's what drove
478 CC Lucasta   7   hurting./{L} I could use words much stronger than that,/And I will, if I choose. Oh,
STRONGLY (2)
241 MC Priest3   3 rules or barons rule:/The strong man strongly and the weak man by caprice./They
319 FR Warburt   37 never dared before./{W} I advise you strongly, not to ask your aunt —/I mean, there
STRUCK (8)
605 Narcissus   16   of the pointed tips of his fingers./Struck down by such knowledge/He could not
299 FR Downing   38   call a kind of repression./But what struck me ... more nervous than usual;/I mean
393 CP Edward   11   that you'd always given in to me./It struck me very differently. As we're on the
436 CP Lavinia   29   /{L} I'm willing to grant that. What struck me, though,/Was that your face showed
466 CC   Colby   36   if you *weren't* my father!/I was struck by what you said, a little while ago,/
505 CC Eggers   28 mentioned, by Mr. Simpkins./She was struck by your name and your living in
506 CC Eggers   28   learned your name;/And the name struck her as being familiar./{MG} Indeed? It is
554 ES   Carghil   25   had come for a rest cure,/And it struck me that he might find it a strain/To have

STRUCTURE (1)
469 CC   Colby   9 /Then you will want to learn about its structure/And the various forms, and the
STRUGGLE (6)
148 Rock 1   64 thing does not change:/The perpetual struggle of Good and Evil./Forgetful, you
316 FR   Ivy   4 a most undignified terror, and I must struggle against it./{G} I am used to tangible
333 FR   Agatha 30 /It is possible that sin may strain and struggle/In its dark instinctive birth, to come to
381 CP Edward 30 determined long ago/And that the struggle to escape from it/Is only a
403 CP   Reilly 16 they are absorbed in the endless struggle/To think well of themselves./{E} If I am
583 ES Charles   7 for breath,/So the lover must struggle for words./{M} I've loved you from the
STRUGGLED (2)
160 Rock 7   2 were men, in their various ways, they struggled in torment towards GOD/Blindly and
293 FR   Amy   7 Now it is your business./I have only struggled to keep Wishwood going/And to
STRUGGLING (3)
 92 Ash-Wed 3   5 /Under the vapour in the fetid air/Struggling with the devil of the stairs who wears
161 Rock 7   24 purblind as ever before,/Yet always struggling, always reaffirming, always resuming
583 ES Charles   6 so inadequate./Yet, like the asthmatic struggling for breath,/So the lover must struggle
STUBBORN (4)
105 Song Sime   3 sun creeps by the snow hills;/The stubborn season had made stand./My life is
213 Growltiger   49 /The ruthless foe pressed forward, in stubborn rank on rank;/Growltiger to his vast
240 MC Priest2 29 Sovereign Lord the Pope/With the stubborn King and the French King/In ceaseless
253 MC Tempt4 15 envy of lesser men/Is still more stubborn than king's anger./Kings have public
STUCK (1)
557 ES Michael   9 Alfred Walter made for you./{Mi} I'd stuck it for two years. And deadly dull it was./
STUDENT (1)
314 FR Warburt 23 /But I remember, when I was a student at Cambridge,/I used to dream of
STUDENTS (1)
304 FR   Mary   2 I know I wasn't one of your favourite students:/I only saw you as a hard headmistress/
STUDIED (2)
483 CC Lady E   33 that *I* believe in it./I did, for a time. I studied the doctrine./But I was going to say, *if* I
546 ES Piggott 10 /At Badgley Court. You see, we've studied to avoid/Anything like a nursing-home
STUDIES (1)
107 Animula   11 in the wind, the sunlight and the sea;/Studies the sunlit pattern on the floor/And
STUDY (4)
179 FQ: ECoker 70 not very satisfactory:/A periphrastic study in a worn-out poetical fashion,/Leaving
277 MC Knight1 33 de Morville, who/has made a special study of statecraft and constitutional law. Sir/
386 CP   Celia   33 been sent for/To the headmaster's study; and is not quite sure/What he's been
431 CP   Peter   24 /We've got a team of experts over/To study the decay, so as to reproduce it./Then we
STUFFED (2)
 83 Hollow Men   2 /We are the hollow men/We are the stuffed men/Leaning together/Headpiece filled
 83 Hollow Men   18 but only/As the hollow men/The stuffed men./Eyes I dare not meet in dreams/In
STUFFING (1)
 23 Preludes   43 six o'clock;/And short square fingers stuffing pipes,/And evening newspapers, and
STUMBLE (1)
329 FR Chorus   8 /The dogs and the old pony/The stumble and the wail of little pain/The chopping
STUMBLING (1)
 73 WL: Thund 369 hordes swarming/Over endless plains, stumbling in cracked earth/Ringed by the flat
STUMPS (1)
 64 WL: Chess   104 Jug' to dirty ears./And other withered stumps of time/Were told upon the walls;
STUPID (2)
312 FR   Harry   7 them./I must fight them. But they are stupid./How can one fight with stupidity?/Yet I
495 CC Lady E   39 talked to you, without feeling very stupid./You always made me feel that I wasn't
STUPIDER (2)
330 FR   Harry   7 a dull marriage, marry some woman stupider —/Stupider than himself. He can resist
330 FR   Harry   8 marry some woman stupider —/Stupider than himself. He can resist the
STUPIDEST (1)
345 FR   Amy   24 punished for it./Gerald! you are the stupidest person in this room,/Violet, you are
STUPIDITY (4)
307 FR   Mary   21 everything for granted,/Including the stupidity of older people —/They lived in
312 FR   Harry   8 are stupid./How can one fight with stupidity?/Yet I must speak to them. {}/[*He*
327 FR   Agatha   3 /The impatient spectators of malice or stupidity./We must try to penetrate the other
418 CP   Reilly   3 lost. In a world of lunacy,/Violence, stupidity, greed ... it is a good life./{C} I know I
STUPOR (1)
154 Rock 3   23 /To idleness, labour, and delirious stupor?/There shall be left the broken chimney,/
STY (1)
109 Marina   10 meaning/Death/Those who sit in the sty of contentment, meaning/Death/Those who

STYLE (3)

123 SAWa & Ho	7	*is just as good/Any old isle is just my style/Any fresh egg/Any fresh egg/And the sound*
602 Humoresque	16	since last spring's,/'The newest style, on Earth, I swear./'Why don't you people
285 FR Charles	23	bad Indian tea./{C} That's not Amy's style at all. We are country-bred people./Amy

SUAVITY (1)

| 227 Macavity | 36 | was a Cat of such deceitfulness and suavity./He always has an alibi, and one or two |

SUB-COMMITTEES (1)

| 129 Cor2 State | 9 | committees, select committees and sub-committees./One secretary will do for |

SUB-HUMAN (1)

| 403 CP Edward | 30 | me/With the obstinate, unconscious, sub-human strength/That some women have. |

SUBALTERN (1)

| 286 FR Gerald | 6 | Well, as for me,/I'd just as soon be a subaltern again/To be back in the East. An |

SUBDUED (1)

| 270 MC Chorus | 27 | have consented./Am torn away, subdued, violated,/United to the spiritual flesh |

SUBJECT (12)

266 MC Thomas	26	I received the ring/I have been a loyal subject to the King./Saving my order, I am at
287 FR Amy	21	go right./Meanwhile, let us drop the subject. The less said the better./{G} That
315 FR Warburt	12	matters./How did we get onto the subject of cancer?/I really don't know. — But
347 FRDowning	1	say so,/Now that you've raised the subject, I'm most relieved —/If you understand
349 FR Agatha	22	/{Ag} A curse is a power/Not subject to reason/Each curse has its course/Its
362 CP Reilly	38	talking to the matron, you are still the subject,/The centre of reality. But, stretched on
393 CP Edward	11	me very differently. As we're on the subject,/I thought that it was I who had given in
447 CC Eggers	7	would you like me to approach the subject?/{SC} Of course, she knows you were
462 CC Claude	28	it uncongenial?/I'm not changing the subject: I'm coming back to it./You know I've
493 CC Claude	19	/He's very good at approaching a subject/In a roundabout way. But where shall
505 CC Guzzard	14	if that is what you wish./But is the subject of this meeting —/I suppose to do with
510 CC Eggers	13	/That you have found your son./{E} Subject to confirmation./{LE} And to my being

SUBJECTION (1)

| 242 MC Priest1 | 28 | by temporal devolution,/Wishing subjection to God alone./Had the King been |

SUBJECTS (1)

| 267 MC Knight1 | 8 | was only/Our indignation, as loyal subjects./{T} Loyal? to whom?/{K1} To the |

SUBMARINE (2)

| 31 Apollinax | 8 | irresponsible fœtus./His laughter was submarine and profound/Like the old man of |
| 167 Rock 10 | 32 | the coloured fresco./Our gaze is submarine, our eyes look upward/And see the |

SUBMISSION (3)

182 FQ: ECoker	185	there is to conquer/By strength and submission, has already been discovered/Once
249 MC Tempt2	11	/Is purchased at price of a certain submission./Your spiritual power is earthly
382 CP Edward	3	— but can only flourish/In submission to the rule of the stronger partner./

SUBMIT (3)

269 MC Thomas	19	confirmed in malfeasance./{T} I submit my cause to the judgement of Rome./
269 MC Thomas	21	kill me, I shall rise from my tomb/To submit my cause before God's throne. {}/[*Exit*]/
569 ES Charles	32	them./{C} Then why should you submit?/Why not leave Badgley and escape

SUBORDINATION (1)

| 278 MC Knight2 | 38 | But, if you have now/arrived at a just subordination of the pretensions of the Church |

SUBSEQUENT (1)

| 187 FQ: DrySal | 115 | experience/Unqualified, unworn by subsequent attrition./People change, and smile: |

SUBSIDE (1)

| 256 MC Priests | 26 | /Should we not wait for the sea to subside, in the night/Abide the coming of day, |

SUBSIDES (1)

| 43 Swee Erect | 30 | on his leg/Waiting until the shriek subsides./The epileptic on the bed/Curves |

SUBSIDING (1)

| 155 Rock 3 | 49 | lodgings while the rent is paid,/Subsiding basements where the rat breeds/Or |

SUBSIST (2)

| 245 MC Thomas | 20 | may will it,/That the pattern may subsist, for the pattern is the action/And the |
| 256 MC Tempt4 | 3 | may will it,/That the pattern may subsist, that the wheel may turn and still/Be |

SUBSTANCE (3)

141 Rannoch	4	sky, scarcely room/To leap or soar. Substance crumbles, in the thin air/Moon cold
246 MC Thomas	20	sudden, God-given./Meanwhile the substance of our first act/Will be shadows, and
248 MC Tempt2	34	alone./Shall he who held the solid substance/Wander waking with deceitful

SUBSTANTIAL (4)

182 FQ: ECoker	172	we like to think/That we are sound, substantial flesh and blood —/Again, in spite of
306 FR Harry	14	thought it was a place/Where life was substantial and simplified —/But the
372 CP Alex	19	/{A} Ah, so the aunt/Really exists. A substantial proof./{E} No, no ... I mean, this is
464 CC Claude	17	the form is the reality,/Of which the substantial is only a shadow./It's strange. I have

SUBSTANTIATE (1)
514 CC Eggers   20   me?/{E} Mrs. Guzzard, can you substantiate this statement?/{MG} Registration
SUBSTITUTE (3)
52 Whispers   10   was such another/Who found no substitute for sense,/To seize and clutch and
202 War Poetry   21   or scattered./The enduring is not a substitute for the transient,/Neither one for the
466 CC Claude   17   the life of the spirit/Are a kind of substitute for religion./I dare say truly religious
SUBTERFUGE (1)
380 CP Celia   17   /Edward, this is really too crude a subterfuge/To justify yourself. There was never
SUBTILE (1)
269 MC Chorus   28   senses are quickened/By subtile forebodings; I have heard/Fluting in the
SUBTLE (3)
52 Whispers   23   the scampering marmoset/With subtle effluence of cat;/Grishkin has a
55 Mr E Sun   31   water in his bath./The masters of the subtle schools/Are controversial, polymath./
279 MC Knight1   6   who/have been able to follow his very subtle reasoning. We have,/however, one more
SUBTLETY (1)
32 Hysteria   11   /my attention with careful subtlety to this end./Conversation Galante/I
SUBURB (1)
148 Rock 1   36   seem to be wanted/In country or in suburb; and in the town/Only for important
SUBURBAN (1)
406 CP Edward   34   too ill?/Then I'll go and be ill in a suburban boarding-house./{L} That would
SUBURBS (2)
147 Rock 1   26   we need no bells:/Let them waken the suburbs./I journeyed to the suburbs, and there I
147 Rock 1   27   waken the suburbs./I journeyed to the suburbs, and there I was told:/We toil for six
SUCCEED (2)
193 FQ: Little   72   is the death of earth./Water and fire succeed/The town, the pasture and the weed./
342 FR Amy   11   him; *you* can try,/But you will not succeed: she has some spell/That works from
SUCCEEDED (6)
243 MC Chorus   24   /Seven years we have lived quietly,/Succeeded in avoiding notice,/Living and partly
332 FR Agatha   13   so. There were many years/Before she succeeded in making terms with Wishwood,/
417 CP Reilly   25   who have gone as far as you/Have succeeded in returning. They may remember/
471 CC Colby   23   then you came to see that you hadn't succeeded./{L} Oh, so I was trying to give a false
476 CC Lucasta 13   I tried to do that./And it's always succeeded with people before:/I got into the
578 ES Ld Clav 15   the efforts aimed at your good/Only succeeded in defeating each other,/How can I
SUCCEEDING (1)
594 Grad 12   1   grass;/Thou dost not die — for each succeeding year/Thy honor and thy fame shall
SUCCESS (20)
228 Gus   17   with Tree./And he likes to relate his success on the Halls,/Where the Gallery once
341 FR Amy   15   boy at Wishwood;/For his future success./{Ag} Success is relative:/It is what we
341 FR Agatha   16   /For his future success./{Ag} Success is relative:/It is what we can make of the
341 FR Amy   19   what you would make for him./{A} Success is one thing, what you would make for
341 FR Amy   36   given?/And now at the moment of success against failure,/When I felt assured of
425 CP Lavinia 34   been invited./That's what makes it a success. Is that picture straight?/{E} Yes, it is./
433 CP Peter   15   I always thought she could make a success of it/If she only got the chance. It's
435 CP Peter   7   her,/Until I began to think myself a success/And got a little more self-confidence;/
440 CP Reilly   12   as for the party,/I am sure it will be a success./{J} And I think, Henry,/That we should
479 CC Kaghan   18   I'll have a glass of sherry,/To drink success to the flat. Lucasta too:/Much better for
513 CC Colby   30   —/The story of his life, of his success or failure .../Perhaps his failure more
513 CC Colby   31   .../Perhaps his failure more than his success —/By objects that belonged to him, and
516 CC Colby   8   an organist./It doesn't matter about success —/I aimed too high before — beyond
538 ES Gomez   34   a gift for friendship./I rejoiced in your success. But one thing has puzzled me./You
539 ES Ld Clav 38   /{LC} So, as you consider yourself a success .../{G} A worldly success, Dick. In
539 ES Gomez   39   yourself a success .../{G} A worldly success, Dick. In another sense/We're both of us
540 ES Gomez   7   on pretending to himself/That he's a success — the man who in the morning/Has to
540 ES Ld Clav 10   to persuade me of your ... worldly success?/{G} No, because I know the value of
561 ES Ld Clav   8   your goal,/Your imagined paradise of success and grandeur,/You will find your past
563 ES Gomez   32   Carghill, I can well understand/Her success on the stage./{MC} Oh, did you never
SUCCESSES (2)
368 CP Edward   37   /But you were one of the minor successes/For a time at least./{P} I wouldn't say
531 ES Ld Clav 21   Say rather, the exequies/Of the failed successes, the successful failures,/Who occupy
SUCCESSFUL (11)
21 Portrait   122   the advantage, after all?/This music is successful with a 'dying fall'/Now that we talk
394 CP Edward   32   me./You wanted your husband to be *successful*,/You wanted me to supply a public
407 CP Reilly   20   their energy,/Yet never quite successful. You have both of you pretended/To
408 CP Edward   10   /You seem to have been much more successful at concealment/Than I was. Now I
451 CC Eggers   26   But with Lady Elizabeth he wasn't so successful./She once referred to him as

494	CC Claude	24	great financier —/And I am merely a successful one./I might have been truer to my
516	CC Guzzard	14	You should say, Colby, not very successful./{C} And I wish to follow my father./
531	ES Ld Clav	21	exequies/Of the failed successes, the successful failures,/Who occupy positions that
539	ES Gomez	31	/Of my own career. I've been very successful./What would have happened to me, I
550	ES Ld Clav	24	/I trust that the business was very successful .../I mean, that he left you
570	ES Ld Clav	31	their father's footsteps/Who are also successful. What would *he* have been/If he

SUCCESSFULLY (1)

| 552 | ES Carghil | 32 | being an elder statesman/And posing successfully as an elder statesman/Is practically |

SUCCESSION (2)

| 177 | FQ: EColer | 1 | Coker/In my beginning is my end. In succession/Houses rise and fall, crumble, are |
| 220 | Old Deut | 2 | a Cat who has lived many lives in succession./He was famous in proverb and |

SUCCESSIVELY (1)

| 129 | Cor2 State | 30 | /Remarkably like each other, lit up successively by the flare/Of a sweaty |

SUCCESSOR (4)

292	FR Ivy	33	/{I} And you'll really have to find a successor to old Hawkins./It's really high time
447	CC Claude	14	/When it comes to appointing a successor./Makes it very difficult to replace you.
448	CC Claude	23	retired/And that you have a young successor,/A Mr. Colby Simpkins./{E} Merely
458	CC Claude	26	/{SC} This young man is Eggerson's successor./You know that Eggerson's been

SUCCULENT (1)

| 230 | Bust Jones | 22 | gives his ben'son/To the *Pothunter's* succulent bones;/And just before noon's not a |

SUCH (124)

23	Preludes	33	the sparrows in the gutters,/You had such a vision of the street/As the street hardly
38	Gerontion	33	house/Under a windy knob./After such knowledge, what forgiveness? Think now/
38	Gerontion	38	/And what she gives, gives with such supple confusions/That the giving famishes
40	Burb Blei	13	on the water all the day./But this or such was Bleistein's way:/A saggy bending of
52	Whispers	9	and luxuries./Donne, I suppose, was such another/Who found no substitute for
84	Hollow Men	32	dream kingdom/Let me also wear/Such deliberate disguises/Rat's coat, crowskin,
89	Ash-Wed 1	5	/I no longer strive to strive towards such things/(Why should the agèd eagle stretch
103	Journ Magi	3	time of the year/For a journey, and such a long journey:/The ways deep and the
124	SA Doris	8	very last card./I don't care for such conversation/A woman runs a terrible risk.
127	Cor1 March	4	eagles./How many? Count them. And such a press of people./We hardly knew
127	Cor1 March	7	many waiting? what did it matter, on such a day?/Are they coming? No, not yet. You
159	Rock 6	11	be?/Do you need to be told that even such modest attainments/As you can boast in
187	FQ: DrySal	110	are likewise permanent/With such permanence as time has. We appreciate
209	NamingCats	6	the name that the family use daily,/Such as Peter, Augustus, Alonzo or James,/
209	NamingCats	7	as Peter, Augustus, Alonzo or James,/Such as Victor or Jonathan, George or Bill
209	NamingCats	11	the gentlemen, some for the dames:/Such as Plato, Admetus, Electra, Demeter —/
209	NamingCats	18	of this kind, I can give you a quorum,/Such as Munkustrap, Quaxo, or Coricopat,/
209	NamingCats	19	Munkustrap, Quaxo, or Coricopat,/Such as Bombalurina, or else Jellylorum —/
214	RTTugger	17	in the bureau drawer,/But he makes such a fuss if he can't get out./Yes the Rum
224	Mr Mistoff	6	are off his own bat./There's no such Cat in the metropolis;/He holds all the
227	Macavity	36	Macavity,/There never was a Cat of such deceitfulness and suavity./He always has
228	Gus	3	before,/Is really Asparagus. That's such a fuss/To pronounce, that we usually call
230	Bust Jones	7	/No commonplace mousers have such well-cut trousers/Or such an impeccable
230	Bust Jones	8	have such well-cut trousers/Or such an impeccable back./In the whole of St.
234	Ad-dress	25	course I'm not including Pekes,/And such fantastic canine freaks./The usual Dog
235	Ad-dress	34	And he will gambol and guffaw./He's such an easy-going lout,/He'll answer any hail
589	Fable	70	/It is a thing to be lamented sorely/Such slippery folk should be allowed about,/For
589	Fable	85	renowned,/Though the wicked said (such rascals are not rare)/That the Abbot's
589	Fable	88	handle/Of Saint, thereby rebuking all such scandal./But after this the monks grew
593	Grad 6	5	her fate,/And see that she shall gain such proud estate/As shall on future centuries
602	Humoresque	4	body as in head,/(A jumping-jack has such a frame)./But this deceasèd marionette/I
605	Narcissus	16	tips of his fingers./Struck down by such knowledge/He could not live men's ways,
245	MC Priest2	1	France./{P2} What a way to talk at such a juncture!/You are foolish, immodest and
255	MC Tempt4	24	you have to give. Is it too much?/For such a vision of eternal grandeur?/{T} Others
261	MC Thomas	2	Those men His disciples/knew no such things: they went forth to journey afar, to
276	MC Knight1	22	are all with the under dog. I respect such feelings, I/share them. Nevertheless, I
276	MC Knight3	33	I am afraid I am not anything like such an experienced/speaker as my old friend
278	MC Knight2	27	/You will agree with me that such interference by an Archbishop/offends the
278	MC Knight2	36	And at a later time still, even such temperate/measures as these would become
282	MC Chorus	3	by the broken imperial column,/From such ground springs that which forever renews
282	MC Chorus	5	God, we thank Thee/Who hast given such blessing to Canterbury./Forgive us, O
287	FR Gerald	4	allowances:/We haven't left them such an easy world to live in./Let the younger
295	FR Charles	7	/{A} Harry!/{C} You mustn't indulge such dangerous fancies./It's only doing harm to
295	FR Amy	34	Coming so far/And making such haste, the change is too sudden for you./

296 FR	Ivy	19	But I understand —/I have heard of such cases before — that people in his condition
296 FR	Ivy	21	the most immoderate resentment/At such a suggestion. They can be very cunning —/
303 FR	Mary	6	wait for our windblown blossoms,/Such as they are, than have these greenhouse
304 FR	Mary	23	only wanted me for Harry —/Not such a compliment: she only wanted/To have a
305 FR	Agatha	5	you may not think me capable of such a feeling./I would like to help you: but you
312 FR	Harry	2	/Are you so imperceptive, have you such dull senses/That you could not see them? If
313 FR	Violet	4	together]/{V} Very well, I think, after such a long journey;/You know what a rush he
314 FR Warburt		12	from school with measles/And we had such a time to keep you in bed./You didn't like
314 FR Warburt		21	malady./{W} You mustn't take such a pessimistic view/Which is hardly
315 FR Warburt		11	real./{W} Well, let's not talk of such matters./How did we get onto the subject
328 FR	Charles	33	the papers;/But nowadays, there's no such thing as privacy./{Ch} In an old house
334 FR	Harry	24	One had that part to play./After such training, I could endure, these ten years,/
339 FR	Harry	13	of ignorance, of incurable diseases./Such things are possible. It is love and terror/Of
342 FR	Amy	8	make myself believe/That he was not such a weakling as his father/In the hands of
344 FR	Charles	15	happened in our family!/And why in such a hurry? Before you make up your mind ...
344 FR	Charles	30	depends on where you're going./{C} Such a thing/Has never happened in our family.
345 FR	Harry	10	not fear that I am in any danger/Of such accidents as happen to Arthur and John:/
354 CP	Celia	4	Julia's the only person to tell it./She's such a good mimic./{J} Am I a good mimic?/{P}
355 CP	Julia	20	/{J} No, he wasn't listening, but he's such a strain —/Edward without Lavinia! He's
358 CP	Julia	21	let me see. Have I got everything?/It's such a nice party, I hate to leave it./It's such a
358 CP	Julia	22	a nice party, I hate to leave it./It's such a nice party, I'd like to repeat it./Why
370 CP	Peter	9	can't express it;/I had never imagined such quiet happiness./I had only experienced
370 CP	Peter	12	something very strange. There was such ... tranquillity .../{E} And what interrupted
372 CP	Alex	9	/{A} Oh, Edward! I've prepared you such a treat!/I really think that of all my
372 CP	Alex	13	travelling in Albania,/Have I made such a supper out of so few materials/As I
376 CP	Julia	19	had. Edward must be fed./He's under such a strain. We must keep his strength up./
376 CP	Julia	34	is absolutely deadly./I could tell such tales of his poisoning people./Now, my
392 CP	Lavinia	36	tell the truth now./We have wasted such a lot of time in lying./{E} I don't quite
402 CP	Edward	25	there a sanatorium to which you send such patients/As myself, under your personal
403 CP	Reilly	10	cure;/And you would go on, doing such amount of mischief/As lay within your
407 CP	Reilly	18	innocently dull:/My patients such as you are the self-deceivers/Taking infinite
408 CP	Lavinia	24	happened./{L} I never knew you had such a sense of humour./{R} It is the first more
410 CP	Reilly	37	it —/Except of course, the saints — such as those who go/To the sanatorium — you
416 CP	Celia	6	the word?/Can you treat a patient for such a state of mind?/{R} What had you
430 CP	Julia	29	news of the world, Peter./We lead such a quiet life, here in London./{P} You
432 CP	Julia	32	commissions./{J} We've been having such an interesting conversation./Peter's just
438 CP	Reilly	6	your part, Mrs. Chamberlayne;/But such experience can only be hinted at/In myths
446 CC	Eggers	31	window boxes!/He's expressed such an interest in my garden/That I think he
456 CC	Eggers	9	— though nothing escapes him./And such a generous heart! He's rather a Socialist./
457 CC	Eggers	4	say./And I'm sure you'll like her. She's such a lady!/And what's more, she has a good
461 CC	Claude	30	very disconcerting:/As you gather, such a thing never happened before./So the
463 CC	Claude	5	a mistake,/Though it seemed to have such obvious advantages/That I had no doubts
464 CC	Claude	11	me, they are life itself. To be among such things,/If it is an escape, is escape into
466 CC	Colby	34	in me/Rebels against accepting such conditions./It would be so much simpler if
470 CC	Lucasta	1	I've played to anyone .../{L} Don't be such a fraud. You know you told me/The piano
476 CC	Lucasta	15	impression./That's where B. has been such a help to me —/He fosters the impression.
476 CC	Colby	22	off on B./{C} I never thought of such a thing!/{L} You never thought of such a
476 CC	Lucasta	23	a thing!/{L} You never thought of such a thing!/There are not many men who
478 CC	Colby	6	a guttersnipe .../{C} You mustn't use such words! You don't know how it's hurting./
482 CC	Kaghan	2	And thank you so much. You give such good advice. {}/[Exeunt KAGHAN and
484 CC	Lady E	21	/{LE} Oh, swarms of relatives! And such unpleasant people!/I thought of myself as a
487 CC	Colby	13	piano. I've never played/On such an instrument. It's much too good for me./
488 CC	Claude	25	one day./I've always loathed keeping such a thing from you./I see now I might as well
488 CC	Claude	29	what one had planned for,/And yet such a travesty of all one's plans —/I'd hoped
489 CC	Claude	5	told you/About Colby. I didn't. For such a foolish reason./Absurd it sounds now.
491 CC	Claude	15	/{SC} I should be contented with such an understanding;/And indeed, it's not so
491 CC	Colby	24	can live on a fiction — but not on such a mixture/Of fiction and fact. Already, it's
493 CC	Lady E	24	must have an armchair .../{LE} Not such a low one. Leave that in the corner/For
496 CC	Claude	16	to bring you up to London/At such short notice./{E} Don't say that, Sir
496 CC	Eggers	22	/But now she says: 'You're becoming such a countryman!/You're losing touch with
499 CC	Lucasta	17	I'm glad you're here, Eggy! You're such a support./In any case, I've an
507 CC	Eggers	7	of parents unknown to you —/Under such conditions?/{MG} Yes, I did take in a
509 CC	Guzzard	1	sure./My husband was particular in such matters,/So we had it given conditional
509 CC	Lady E	5	/{LE} Barnabas? There's never been such a name/In my family. Or, I'm sure, in his
514 CC	Claude	18	/You couldn't have carried out such a deception/Over all these years. And why

514 CC	Eggers	30	Mrs. Guzzard:/But in a matter of such extreme importance/You'll understand the
527 ES	Monica	9	/You may have changed your mind. Such things have happened./{C} That won't
532 ES	Monica	19	/{M} You ought not to bother with such people now, Father./If you haven't got rid
534 ES	Ld Clav	7	most of your business/Has been of such a nature that, if carried on in England,/It
534 ES	Gomez	11	I wouldn't dream/Of carrying on such business if I lived in England./I have the
536 ES	Gomez	21	a sickly word./You don't understand such isolation/As mine, you think you do .../
545 ES	Piggott	26	to apologise and explain./I've been in such a rush, these last few days,/And I thought,
549 ES	Carghil	13	— I've forgotten what hotel —/But such a good lunch — and we all went in a punt/
549 ES	Carghil	40	which you knew me. It would give me such a thrill/To hear you speak my name once
556 ES	Michael	13	day!/I'm glad you're here, to enjoy such weather./{LC} You're glad I'm here? Did
560 ES	Michael	4	wondering why it bothered about such trifles./{LC} So you want me to help you to
560 ES	Michael	25	That young woman?/{Mi} I'm not such a fool/As to get myself involved in a
564 ES	Carghil	17	/Is that how you come to speak such perfect English?/Of course, I could tell
565 ES	Carghil	11	Michael?/Your father is such an old friend of mine/That it seems most
568 ES	Ld Clav	36	the time she's grown/You've woven such a web of fiction about you!/I've spent my

SUCK (2)

590 Time Space	12	withered ere the wild bee flew/To suck the eglantine./So let us haste to pluck anew
590 Space Time	12	withered ere the wild bee flew/To suck the eglantine./But let us haste to pluck

SUDDEN (25)

13 Prufrock	20	/Slipped by the terrace, made a sudden leap,/And seeing that it was a soft
63 WL: Burial	73	Will it bloom this year?/'Or has the sudden frost disturbed its bed?/'O keep the Dog
107 Animula	6	at kisses and toys,/Advancing boldly, sudden to take alarm,/Retreating to the corner
176 FQ: BurntN	172	/Between un-being and being./Sudden in a shaft of sunlight/Even while the
186 FQ: DrySal	94	/Or even a very good dinner, but the sudden illumination —/We had the experience
187 FQ: DrySal	125	by: but in the sombre season/Or the sudden fury, is what it always was./I sometimes
191 FQ: Little	16	blossom/Of snow, a bloom more sudden/Than that of summer, neither budding
193 FQ: Little	94	in the waning dusk/I caught the sudden look of some dead master/Whom I had
242 MC Priest1	18	Church,/I know that the pride bred of sudden prosperity/Was but confirmed by bitter
246 MC Thomas	19	opportunity./End will be simple, sudden, God-given./Meanwhile the substance of
257 MC Tempts	2	whispering through the ear, or a sudden shock on the skull./{C} A man may walk
271 MC Thomas	12	that another/Shall pierce you with a sudden painful joy/When the figure of God's
294 FR Harry	15	beyond our understanding./{H} The sudden solitude in a crowded desert/In a thick
295 FR Amy	34	making such haste, the change is too sudden for you./You are unused to our foggy
301 FR Chorus	31	railway accident/We know about the sudden thrombosis/And the slowly hardening
307 FR Harry	31	{H} One thing you cannot know:/The sudden extinction of every alternative,/The
308 FR Mary	11	a way you contradict yourself:/That sudden comprehension of the death of hope/Of
320 FR Warburt	14	/She may live several years. A sudden shock/Might send her off at any
329 FR Chorus	12	night in the corridor/The moment of sudden loathing/And the season of stifled
437 CP Reilly	19	to entertain the suggestion/That a sudden intuition, in certain minds,/May tend to
461 CC Claude	29	it easier for both of us./{SC} Her sudden arrival was very disconcerting:/As you
536 ES Gomez	7	back again./I parted from myself by a sudden effort,/You, so slowly and sweetly, that
542 ES Gomez	35	smile, the distant salutation,/The sudden silence when you enter the smoking
580 ES Carghil	15	/{MC} I'm afraid this seems awfully sudden to you, Richard;/It isn't so sudden. We
580 ES Carghil	16	sudden to you, Richard;/It isn't so sudden. We talked it all over./But I've got a

SUDDENLY (16)

21 Portrait	100	who smiles, and turning shall remark/Suddenly, his expression in a glass./My
140 Usk	1	/Red river, river, river./Usk/Do not suddenly break the branch, or/Hope to find/The
204 de la Mare	17	and yearn;/When the familiar scene is suddenly strange/Or the well known is what we
218 Mung Rump	14	vests,/Or after supper one of the girls/Suddenly missed her Woolworth pearls:/Then
223 Pekes Pols	50	to ring up the Fire Brigade./When suddenly, up from a small basement flat,/Why
291 FR m	14	/{A} Harry! {}/[HARRY *stops suddenly at the door and stares at the window*]/
302 FR Chorus	7	do we all behave as if the door might suddenly open, the curtains be drawn,/The
362 CP Reilly	23	no longer feel quite human./You're suddenly reduced to the status of an object —/A
379 CP Celia	31	/And that you would be free — then I suddenly discovered/That the dream was not
393 CP Edward	38	through any of *your* friends —/You suddenly found it inconvenient/That I should be
408 CP Reilly	6	the defection of your lover — who suddenly/For the first time in his life, fell in love
416 CP Celia	32	with an imaginary playmate/And suddenly discovers he is only a child/Lost in a
474 CC Colby	16	gate./They would simply ... be there suddenly,/Unexpectedly. Walking down an alley
506 CC Eggers	3	/Unfortunately, the father died suddenly .../{LE} He was run over. By a
507 CC Guzzard	22	come to an end?/{MG} Very suddenly./{LE} That must have been when Tony
511 CC Lady E	9	was my father?/{LE} He died very suddenly. Of a fatal accident/When you were

SUDS (1)

42 Swee Erect	24	female temperament/And wipes the suds around his face./(The lengthened shadow

SUED (1)

268 MC Knight3	5	/All was granted for which you sued:/Yet how, I repeat, did you show your

SUEUR (2)

47 Mél Adult	3	journaliste;/C'est à grands pas et en sueur/Que vous suivrez à peine ma piste./En
48 Lune Miel	4	chez deux centaines de punaises;/La sueur aestivale, et une forte odeur de chienne./

SUFFER (32)

98 Ash-Wed 6	26	of the fountain, spirit of the garden,/Suffer us not to mock ourselves with falsehood/
99 Ash-Wed 6	34	spirit of the river, spirit of the sea,/Suffer me not to be separated/And let my cry
105 Song Sime	26	thy word./They shall praise Thee and suffer in every generation/With glory and
109 Marina	12	meaning/Death/Those who suffer the ecstasy of the animals, meaning/
152 Rock 2	27	/For every ill deed in the past we suffer the consequence:/For sloth, for avarice,
188 FQ: DrySal	167	to port, and you whose bodies/Will suffer the trial and judgement of the sea,/Or
245 MC Thomas	13	and do not know, what it is to act or suffer./They know and do not know, that action
245 MC Thomas	15	is action. Neither does the agent suffer/Nor the patient act. But both are fixed/In
245 MC Thomas	19	it may be willed/And which all must suffer that they may will it,/That the pattern
255 MC Thomas	34	by more sinful? Can I neither act nor suffer/Without perdition?/{T4} You know and
255 MC Tempt4	36	and do not know, what it is to act or suffer./You know and do not know, that action
255 MC Tempt4	38	action. Neither does the agent suffer/Nor the patient act. But both are fixed/In
256 MC Tempt4	2	it may be willed/And which all must suffer that they may will it,/That the pattern
259 MC Thomas	5	So must you./I shall no longer act or suffer, to the sword's end./Now my good Angel,
261 MC Thomas	2	they went forth to journey afar, to suffer by land/and sea, to know torture,
261 MC Thomas	3	imprisonment, disappointment, to suffer/death by martyrdom. What then did He
274 MC Thomas	33	by the blood of Christ,/Ready to suffer with my blood./This is the sign of the
295 FR Harry	23	bear it. So you must believe/That I suffer from delusions. It is not my conscience,/
310 FR Mary	6	breaking bud./These are the ones that suffer least:/The aconite under the snow/And
318 FR Harry	1	was wrong was whatever made her suffer,/And whatever made her happy was what
327 FR Agatha	6	evasion of suffering. We must learn to suffer more./{V} Agatha's remarks are
333 FR Agatha	37	the enchantment under which we suffer./{H} Look, I do not know why,/I feel
404 CP Edward	16	spirit —/Can you understand what I suffer?/{R} I understand what you mean./{E} I
414 CP Reilly	37	I can find, is a sense of sin./{R} You suffer from a sense of sin, Miss Coplestone?/
421 CP Julia	28	eagerness and patience. Yet she must suffer./{R} When I express confidence in
437 CP Edward	34	chosen this form of death/She did not suffer as ordinary people suffer?/{R} Not at all
437 CP Edward	34	/She did not suffer as ordinary people suffer?/{R} Not at all what I mean. Rather the
437 CP Reilly	36	that she suffered all that we should suffer/In fear and pain and loathing — all these
561 ES Ld Clav	4	carried you away from me forever/To suffer the monotonous sun of the tropics/Or
561 ES Michael	17	I don't believe you would./*You* didn't suffer from the handicap that I've had./Your
566 ES Ld Clav	2	sit side by side, at little desks/And suffer the same humiliations/At the hands of the
573 ES Ld Clav	1	what you think./You think that I suffer from a morbid conscience,/From

SUFFERED (11)

239 MC Chorus	23	/King rules or barons rule;/We have suffered various oppression,/But mostly we are
299 FRDowning	37	worth, I always said his Lordship/Suffered from what they call a kind of
314 FR Warburt	36	it, ladies — was a murderer,/Who suffered from an incurable cancer./How he
349 FR Chorus	6	is no conceivable answer./We have suffered far more than a personal loss —/We
355 CP Julia	10	/At their castle in the North. How he suffered!/They had to find an island for him/
437 CP Reilly	36	Rather the contrary./I'd say that she suffered all that we should suffer/In fear and
437 CP Reilly	39	body to become a *thing*./I'd say she suffered more, because more conscious/Than
438 CP Reilly	12	spiritual evil always at his shoulder/Suffered any less from hunger, damp, exposure,/
551 ES Carghil	13	think, or try to think, that if I'd really suffered/I shouldn't want to let you know who I
558 ES Michael	20	public man./You don't know what I suffered, working in that office./In the first
574 ES Carghil	12	him, Richard./How he must have suffered! So I put on my thinking cap./I know

SUFFERING (18)

23 Preludes	51	of some infinitely gentle/Infinitely suffering thing./Wipe your hand across your
173 FQ: BurntN	73	desire,/The release from action and suffering, release from the inner/And the outer
245 MC Thomas	14	know and do not know, that action is suffering/And suffering is action. Neither does
245 MC Thomas	15	know, that action is suffering/And suffering is action. Neither does the agent suffer
245 MC Thomas	21	for the pattern is the action/And the suffering, that the wheel may turn and still/Be
255 MC Tempt4	37	know and do not know, that action is suffering,/And suffering action. Neither does
255 MC Tempt4	38	know, that action is suffering,/And suffering action. Neither does the agent suffer/
274 MC Thomas	11	We have only to conquer/Now, by suffering. This is the easier victory./Now is the
276 MC Chorus	8	/These acts marked a limit to our suffering./Every horror had its definition,/Every
294 FR Harry	21	darkness;/The partial anesthesia of suffering without feeling/And partial
327 FR Agatha	5	and fear. To rest in our own suffering/Is evasion of suffering. We must learn
327 FR Agatha	6	rest in our own suffering/Is evasion of suffering. We must learn to suffer more./{V}
404 CP Edward	12	pain,/And now I know there is suffering worse than that./It is surprising, if one
407 CP Reilly	10	/That is one of the causes of their suffering./{L} No one can say my husband has
421 CP Julia	19	what do we know/Of the kind of suffering they must undergo/On the way of
438 CP Reilly	2	of us. She paid the highest price/In suffering. That is part of the design./{L} Perhaps

490 CC   Colby   13   /I don't know whether I've been suffering or not/During this conversation. I only
577 ES   Carghil 33   does Señor Gomez./He's simply been suffering, poor boy, from frustration./He's been

SUFFERS (2)

228 Gus   6   shabby, he's thin as a rake,/And he suffers from palsy that makes his paw shake./
457 CC   Lady E 19   it to the driver?/He tells me that he suffers from chronic catarrh./{SC} Hello!

SUFFICED (1)

193 FQ: Little   103   he a face still forming; yet the words sufficed/To compel the recognition they

SUFFOCATION (1)

241 MC   Mess   35   streets of the city will be packed to suffocation,/And I think that his horse will be

SUGGEST (6)

280 MC Knight1 2 that there is no more to be/said; and I suggest that you now disperse quietly to your
361 CP   Reilly   11 /{E} Don't put it to me./{UG} Then I suggest .../{E} And please don't suggest./I have
361 CP   Edward 12   I suggest .../{E} And please don't suggest./I have often used these terms in
528 ES   Monica 31   of an hotel —/Nothing about it to suggest the clinic —/Everything about it to
528 ES   Monica 32   the clinic —/Everything about it to suggest recovery./{C} This is your best reason,
574 ES   Ld Clav 22   And what was Señor Gomez able to suggest?/{MC} Ah! That's the surprise for which

SUGGESTED (4)

229 Gus   38   walked on pat,/When some actor suggested the need for a cat./He once played a
378 CP   Edward 32 is not that./And all these reasons were suggested to me/By the man I call Riley —
393 CP   Lavinia 21 tell where I wanted to go/Unless you suggested some other place first?/And I
403 CP   Reilly   4 make you dream any kind of dream I suggested,/And it would only go to flatter your

SUGGESTING (5)

173 FQ: BurntN 98 transient beauty/With slow rotation suggesting permanence/Nor darkness to purify
498 CC   Eggers   11 *Two* babies, Eggerson?/{E} I was only suggesting/That perhaps Mrs. Guzzard made a
498 CC   Claude   15 it's perfectly respectable./{SC} You're suggesting that she ran a baby farm./That's
506 CC   Eggers   36 about Teddington./{E} I am only suggesting, Lady Elizabeth,/There are other
507 CC   Guzzard 36 Your son, Lady Elizabeth?/Are you suggesting that I kept a child of yours/And

SUGGESTION (12)

296 FR   Ivy   21   immoderate resentment/At such a suggestion. They can be very cunning —/Their
296 FR   Gerald   33 Amy, there's something in Violet's suggestion./Why not ring up Warburton, and
364 CP   Edward 26 /Do I want her? Or is it merely your suggestion?/{UG} We do not know yet. In
437 CP   Reilly   18   /I ask you only to entertain the suggestion/That a sudden intuition, in certain
446 CC   Eggers   30 of everything./But if I might make a suggestion: window boxes!/He's expressed such
491 CC   Colby   28 two parents./But, if we followed your suggestion,/I know, I know I should always be
501 CC   Eggers   26 meeting./{E} Allow me. May I make a suggestion?/Though first of all I must take the
508 CC   Claude   18   /{SC} That's a very sensible suggestion, Eggerson,/A breath of sanity.
510 CC   Eggers   2   up? And Lucasta?/{E} An excellent suggestion, Mr. Simpkins. {}/[*Exit* COLBY]/{E}
533 ES   Gomez   29   all./I think that was rather an unkind suggestion./I've always kept on the right side of
534 ES   Gomez   17   /{G} Forgery, Dick? An absurd suggestion!/Forgery, I can tell you, is a mug's
540 ES   Gomez   37   My dear Dick, what a preposterous suggestion!/Who's going to accept the

SUGGESTIONS (1)

482 CC   Lady E 24   kind./I'm not making any malicious suggestions:/But they are rather worldly and

SUICIDE (4)

279 MC Knight4 38 will unhesitatingly render a verdict of Suicide while of/Unsound Mind. It is the only
299 FR   Charles   9 do you think that it might have been suicide,/And that his Lordship knew it?/{Do}
299 FR   Charles 15 the courage./{C} Did she ever talk of suicide?/{Do} Oh yes, she did, every now and
576 ES   Monica 26   /And your very self — it's a kind of suicide./{C} Michael, you think Señor Gomez is

SUISSE (1)

48 Lune Miel   15   et rédige son bilan./Ils auront vu la Suisse et traversé la France./Et Saint

SUIT (6)

603 Spleen   14 gloves in hand,/Punctilious of tie and suit/(Somewhat impatient of delay)/On the
406 CP   Lavinia 35   /{L} That would never suit you, Edward. Now I know of a hotel/In the
452 CC   Colby   33 me better?/{C} I'm sure they both suit you./{L} Snubbed again! I suppose I asked
551 ES   Carghil 31 him./If he's lost a breach of promise suit/Some people won't want to appear as his
559 ES   Ld Clav 10   in the cities:/An outdoor life would suit you better./How would you like to go to
560 ES   Michael 26   involved in a breach of promise suit/Or somebody's divorce. No, you needn't

SUITABLE (4)

324 FR   Harry   31   /That people can always show the suitable emotions —/And so far as they feel at
324 FR   Harry   32 as they feel at all, their emotions are suitable./They don't understand what it is to be
449 CC   Eggers   30 I expect./{E} And so I hope. A most suitable arrangement./But will you tell me this:
498 CC   Eggers   21 a temporary accommodation —/On suitable terms. But if she did that,/We must

SUITED (5)

332 FR   Agatha 38   What simple plots!/He was not suited to the role of murderer./{H} In what way
396 CP   Edward 15   I was;/And they told me how well suited we were./{L} It's a pity that you had no
483 CC   Lady E   8 flat/To see if the colour scheme really suited you./I believe it does. The walls; and the

500 CC Lucasta 36 of me/Simply as a nuisance. We're suited to each other:/You thought so too,
501 CC Lucasta 5 why *you* think so:/*You* think we're suited because we're both common./B. knows

SUITS (1)
452 CC Lucasta 32 me. Don't you agree/That Lucasta suits me better?/{C} I'm sure they both suit you.

SUIVREZ (1)
47 Mél Adult 4 à grands pas et en sueur/Que vous suivrez à peine ma piste./En Yorkshire,

SULLEN (6)
72 WL: Thund 344 solitude in the mountains/But red sullen faces sneer and snarl/From doors of
184 FQ: DrySal 2 the river/Is a strong brown god — sullen, untamed and intractable,/Patient to
206 To my Wife 9 No peevish winter wind shall chill/No sullen tropic sun shall wither/The roses in the
244 MC Chorus 30 Archbishop, leave us, leave us, leave sullen Dover, and set sail for France. Thomas
280 ES Priest3 20 /Go venture shipwreck on the sullen coasts/Where blackamoors make captive
556 ES Monica 5 when he's frightened./He's apt to be sullen and quick to take offence./So I hope

SULTAN (1)
427 CP Julia 25 you doing/In Kinkanja? Visiting some Sultan?/You were shooting tigers?/{A} There are

SULTANS (1)
427 CP Alex 28 Julia,/In Kinkanja. And there are no sultans./I have been staying with the Governor./

SULTRY (1)
177 FQ: ECoker 20 heat/Hypnotised. In a warm haze the sultry light/Is absorbed, not refracted, by grey

SUM (1)
117 SP Dusty 9 that mean?/{Du} (*reading*) 'A small sum of money, or a present/Of wearing apparel,

SUMMER (25)
61 WL: Burial 8 feeding/A little life with dried tubers./Summer surprised us, coming over the
67 WL: Fire S 179 cigarette ends/Or other testimony of summer nights. The nymphs are departed./And
103 Journ Magi 9 /There were times we regretted/The summer palaces on slopes, the terraces,/And the
135 5FingerEx1 9 broken chair give ease?/Why will the summer day delay?/*When* will Time flow away?/
172 FQ: BurntN 57 figured in the drift of stars/Ascend to summer in the tree/We move above the moving
177 FQ: ECoker 26 if you do not come too close,/On a summer midnight, you can hear the music/Of
178 FQ: ECoker 54 of the spring/And creatures of the summer heat,/And snowdrops writhing under
191 FQ: Little 17 a bloom more sudden/Than that of summer, neither budding nor fading,/Not in the
191 FQ: Little 19 scheme of generation./Where is the summer, the unimaginable/Zero summer?/If you
191 FQ: Little 20 is the summer, the unimaginable/Zero summer?/If you came this way,/Taking the
212 Growltiger 21 his missing ear./Now on a peaceful summer night, all nature seemed at play,/The
592 Grad 3 2 clouds that fly/After a summer tempest, when some haste/North,
239 MC Chorus 18 deny his master?/Seven years and the summer is over/Seven years since the
240 MC Chorus 9 eat our eyes and our ears,/Disastrous summer burn up the beds of our streams/And
240 MC Chorus 11 decaying October./Why should the summer bring consolation/For autumn fires and
240 MC Chorus 13 fogs?/What shall we do in the heat of summer/But wait in barren orchards for
240 MC Priest1 26 PRIESTS]/{P1} Seven years and the summer is over./Seven years since the
257 MC Chorus 12 in winter,/The child without milk in summer,/Our labour taken away from us,/Our
263 MC Chorus 17 have only/A sour spring, a parched summer, an empty harvest./Between Christmas
281 MC Chorus 16 the song of spring, the drone of summer, the voices of beasts and of birds, praise
319 FR Harry 21 too young. But now I remember/A summer day of unusual heat,/The day I lost my
329 FR Chorus 6 on the lawn/The mowing of hay in summer/The dogs and the old pony/The
332 ES Agatha 23 for a long vacation. I remember/A summer day of unusual heat/For this cold
540 ES Gomez 21 to which occasion I'm referring —/A summer night of moonlight and shadows —/
544 ES Ld Clav 22 for a few days more./But this early summer, that's hardly seasonable,/Is so often a

SUMMER'S (1)
246 MC Tempt1 35 with the King, shall we say that summer's over/Or that the good time cannot

SUMMER-HOUSE (1)
307 FR Harry 16 /The tree had been felled, and a neat summer-house/Had been erected, 'to please the

SUMMIT (2)
111 Xmas Trees 7 angel/Spreading its wings at the summit of the tree/Is not only a decoration, but
147 Rock 1 1 'The Rock'/The Eagle soars in the summit of Heaven,/The Hunter with his dogs

SUMMON (2)
196 FQ: Little 186 backward/Nor is it an incantation/To summon the spectre of a Rose./We cannot
498 CC Claude 37 shortly./And when she arrives I will summon Colby./I wanted you here first, to

SUMMONS (2)
233 Skimble 59 you saw him at Dumfries, where he summons the police/If there's anything they
593 Grad 5 3 than those which came before,/Summons — who knows what time may hold in

SUMS (1)
227 Macavity 34 in doing complicated long division sums./Macavity, Macavity, there's no one like

SUN (28)
43 Swee Erect 28 /Of Sweeney straddled in the sun.)/Tests the razor on his leg/Waiting until the
61 WL: Burial 22 /A heap of broken images, where the sun beats,/And the dead tree gives no shelter,

105 Song Sime	2	blooming in bowls and/The winter	sun	creeps by the snow hills;/The stubborn
129 Cor2 State	6	class),/And the Order of the Rising	Sun.	/Cry cry what shall I cry?/The first thing to
162 Rock 8	25	/Came home cracked by the	sun	of the East/And the seven deadly sins in
174 FQ: BurntN	131	the day,/The black cloud carries the	sun	away./Will the sunflower turn to us, will the
178 FQ: ECoker	62	wars/Scorpion fights against the	Sun	/Until the Sun and Moon go down/Comets
178 FQ: ECoker	63	fights against the Sun/Until the	Sun	and Moon go down/Comets weep and
180 FQ: ECoker	108	all go into the dark,/And dark the	Sun	and Moon, and the Almanach de Gotha/
191 FQ: Little	5	with frost and fire,/The brief	sun	flames the ice, on pond and ditches,/In
206 To my Wife	9	wind shall chill/No sullen tropic	sun	shall wither/The roses in the rose-garden
210 Old Gumbie	15	day she sits beside the hearth or in the	sun	or on my hat:/She sits and sits and sits and
217 Jellicles	33	or two in the hall./If it happens the	sun	is shining bright/You would say they had
220 Old Deut	10	physiognomy,/When he sits in the	sun	on the vicarage wall,/The Oldest Inhabitant
590 Time Space	3	say,/Are things which cannot be,/The	sun	which does not feel decay/No greater is
592 Grad 3	5	western limits of the sky/Which the	sun	stains with many a splendid dye,/Until their
256 MC Priests	28	his way,/The sailor lay course by the	sun?	{ }/CHORUS, PRIESTS *and* TEMPTERS
275 MC Chorus	26	seasons?/Night stay with us, stop	sun,	hold season, let the day not come, let the
280 MC Priest3	24	the brain;/Find an oasis in the desert	sun,	/Go seek alliance with the heathen Saracen,/
285 FR Amy	6	will be gone before I am out again./O	Sun,	that was once so warm, O Light that was
285 FR Amy	7	/When I was young and strong, and	sun	and light unsought for/And the night
285 FR Ivy	16	in the winter./I would follow the	sun,	not wait for the sun to come here./I would
285 FR Ivy	16	would follow the sun, not wait for the	sun	to come here./I would go south in the
310 FR Mary	27	be reborn/To rise toward the violent	sun	/Wet wings into the rain cloud/Harefoot
335 FR Agatha	1	through the little door/When the	sun	was shining on the rose-garden:/And heard
335 FR Harry	30	desert is cleared, under the judicial	sun	/Of the final eye, and the awful evacuation/
339 FR Harry	10	and a primitive altar,/The heat of the	sun	and the icy vigil,/A care over lives of
561 ES Ld Clav	4	me forever/To suffer the monotonous	sun	of the tropics/Or shiver in the northern

SUN'S (1)

68 WL: Fire S	225	drying combinations touched by the	sun's	last rays,/On the divan are piled (at night

SUNDA (1)

292 FR Harry	4	seen them./In the Java Straits, in the	Sunda	Sea,/In the sweet sickly tropical night, I

SUNDAY (8)

54 Mr E Sun	t	our metaphysics warm./Mr. Eliot's	Sunday	Morning Service/Polyphiloprogenitive/
66 WL: Chess	166	UP PLEASE ITS TIME/Well, that	Sunday	Albert was home, they had a hot
154 Rock 3	19	roofing,/To be filled with a litter of	Sunday	newspapers?/1ST MALE VOICE:/A
218 Mung Rump	21	/When the family assembled for	Sunday	dinner,/With their minds made up that
603 Spleen	1	at that, what mask *bizarre!*/Spleen/	Sunday:	this satisfied procession/Of definite
603 Spleen	2	this satisfied procession/Of definite	Sunday	faces;/Bonnets, silk hats, and conscious
461 CC Eggers	15	don't you ask him out to dinner one	Sunday?'	/But I say: 'We couldn't ask him to
540 ES Ld Clav	36	public/Why not sell your version to a	Sunday	newspaper?/{G} My dear Dick, what a

SUNDAYS (1)

147 Rock 1	24	they work, but where they spend their	Sundays.	/In the City, we need no bells:/Let

SUNDOWN (1)

191 FQ: Little	2	/Sempiternal though sodden towards	sundown,	/Suspended in time, between pole and

SUNFLOWER (1)

174 FQ: BurntN	132	cloud carries the sun away./Will the	sunflower	turn to us, will the clematis/Stray

SUNG (5)

151 Rock 2	9	can sing which nobody wants to hear	sung;	/Waiting to be flung in the end, on a heap
263 MC 2m	27	*Stephen borne before him./The lines*	*sung*	*are in italics*.]/{P1} Since Christmas a day:
272 MC m	11	*to the cathedral.*]/[*while a* Dies Iræ *is*	*sung*	*in Latin by a choir in the distance*]./{C}
281 MC m	7	in Canterbury. { }/[*while a* Te Deum *is*	*sung*	*in Latin by a choir in the distance*]./{C} We
451 CC Eggers	37	I envy you that./I've always	sung	in our voluntary choir/And at the carol

SUNKEN (3)

74 WL: Thund	395	damp gust/Bringing rain/Ganga was	sunken,	and the limp leaves/Waited for rain,
162 Rock 8	21	left their souls in Syria,/Living on,	sunken	in moral corruption;/Many came back
226 Macavity	12	him if you saw him, for his eyes are	sunken	in./His brow is deeply lined with

SUNLESS (1)

24 Rhapsody	63	brain.'/The reminiscence comes/Of	sunless	dry geraniums/And dust in crevices,/

SUNLIGHT (15)

34 Figlia	3	on a garden urn —/Weave, weave the	sunlight	in your hair —/Clasp your flowers to
34 Figlia	7	in your eyes:/But weave, weave the	sunlight	in your hair./So I would have had him
61 WL: Burial	10	in the colonnade,/And went on in	sunlight,	into the Hofgarten,/And drank coffee,
83 Hollow Men	23	do not appear:/There, the eyes are/	Sunlight	on a broken column/There, is a tree
105 Song Sime	6	on the back of my hand./Dust in	sunlight	and memory in corners/Wait for the
107 Animula	10	tree,/Pleasure in the wind, the	sunlight	and the sea;/Studies the sunlit pattern
158 Rock 5	5	on mouldering stairs, content in the	sunlight.	/And the others run about like dogs,

172 FQ: BurntN	37	the pool was filled with water out of sunlight,/And the lotos rose, quietly, quietly,/
176 FQ: BurntN	172	and being./Sudden in a shaft of sunlight/Even while the dust moves/There rises
190 FQ: DrySal	212	/The distraction fit, lost in a shaft of sunlight,/The wild thyme unseen, or the winter
240 MC Chorus	18	/I have seen these things in a shaft of sunlight./Destiny waits in the hand of God, not
247 MC Tempt1	11	Ice along the ditches/Mirror the sunlight. Love in the orchard/Send the sap
309 FR Mary	28	that he is blind/While he still sees the sunlight. I know that this is true./{H} I have
310 FR Harry	36	that opens at the end of a corridor,/Sunlight and singing; when I had felt sure/That
311 FR Harry	22	was only one moment/That I stood in sunlight, and thought I might stay there./{M}

SUNLIT (1)

107 Animula	11	the sunlight and the sea;/Studies the sunlit pattern on the floor/And running stags

SUNNIEST (1)

548 ES Carghil	15	you. I always sit here./It's the sunniest and most sheltered corner,/And none

SUNNY (2)

210 Old Gumbie	14	hard to find, she likes the warm and sunny spots./All day she sits beside the hearth
544 ES 2m	1	*The terrace of Badgley Court. A bright sunny morning, several days later./Enter* LORD

SUNSET (2)

203 Indians	3	/To sit in front of his own door at sunset/And see his grandson, and his
280 MC Priest3	18	in earth or heaven./Go where the sunset reddens the last grey rock/Of Brittany, or

SUNSETS (2)

16 Prufrock	101	it have been worth while,/After the sunsets and the dooryards and the sprinkled
19 Portrait	52	on drinking tea./'Yet with these April sunsets, that somehow recall/My buried life,

SUNSHINE (1)

544 ES Ld Clav	20	less often./I hope this benignant sunshine/And warmth will last for a few days

SUNWARD (1)

250 MC Tempt2	8	leave you to your fate./Your sin soars sunward, covering kings' falcons./{T} Temporal

SUPERFETATION (1)

54 Mr E Sun	6	/In the beginning was the Word./Superfetation of τὸ ἕν,/And at the mensual turn

SUPERFICIAL (2)

186 FQ: DrySal	90	latter a partial fallacy/Encouraged by superficial notions of evolution,/Which
484 CC Lady E	25	have been similar./These are only superficial differences:/You must have been a

SUPERFLUOUS (2)

307 FR Mary	26	conscious/Of being a misfit, of being superfluous./But why should I talk about my
558 ES Michael	22	I was your son. They considered me superfluous;/They knew I couldn't be living on

SUPERIOR (1)

230 Bust Jones	16	to belong both to that/And the *Joint Superior Schools./For a similar reason, when

SUPERNATURAL (1)

276 MC Chorus	14	a filth that we cannot clean, united to supernatural vermin,/It is not we alone, it is not

SUPERPOSED (1)

588 Fable	59	out of use —/His feet upon the table superposed/Each wisht he had not eaten so

SUPERVISE (1)

232 Skimble	20	to the bagmen playing cards/He will supervise them all, more or less./Down the

SUPINE (1)

70 WL: Fire S	295	me. By Richmond I raised my knees/Supine on the floor of a narrow canoe.'/'My

SUPPER (4)

218 Mung Rump	13	find one of your winter vests,/Or after supper one of the girls/Suddenly missed her
372 CP Alex	13	in Albania,/Have I made such a supper out of so few materials/As I found in
375 CP Edward	30	insisted on cooking me something for supper;/And he said I must eat it within ten
378 CP Julia	2	/You must come and have a light supper with me —/Something very light./{C}

SUPPLE (1)

38 Gerontion	38	/And what she gives, gives with such supple confusions/That the giving famishes the

SUPPLEMENTED (1)

477 CC Lucasta	1	I should guess./And I knew how she supplemented her income/When I was sent out.

SUPPLICATION (2)

84 Hollow Men	43	/Are raised, here they receive/The supplication of a dead man's hand/Under the
254 MC Tempt4	20	to generation/Bending the knee in supplication,/Think of the miracles, by God's

SUPPLY (4)

129 Cor2 State	17	of engineers/To consider the Water Supply./A commission is appointed/For Public
235 Ad-dress	56	cream;/And you might now and then supply/Some caviare, or Strassburg Pie,/Some
394 CP Edward	33	to be *successful,*/You wanted me to supply a public background/For your kind of
512 CC Guzzard	15	she has the evidence the Kaghans will supply,/To recognise Barnabas Kaghan as her

SUPPORT (5)

197 FQ: Little	220	word is at home,/Taking its place to support the others,/The word neither diffident
362 CP Reilly	29	everything about you/Arranged to support you in the role you have chosen,/Then
394 CP Edward	35	/For whom my career would be a support./Well, I tried to be accommodating.
449 CC Claude	15	ideal./{SC} I'm glad you agree. Your support will be helpful./{E} I'm sure I shall be

| 499 CC | Lucasta | 17 | glad you're here, Eggy! You're such a support./In any case, I've an announcement to |

SUPPORTED (3)

44	Cook	Egg	7	grandfather and great great aunts,/Supported on the mantelpiece/An *Invitation to*
332	FR	Agatha	15	reached the point where/Wishwood supported her, and she supported Wishwood./
332	FR	Agatha	15	/Wishwood supported her, and she supported Wishwood./At first it was a vacancy.

SUPPORTERS (1)

| 551 | ES | Carghil | 32 | people won't want to appear as his supporters.'/He said: 'What his lawyers are |

SUPPOSE (67)

52	Whispers	9	its lusts and luxuries./Donne, I suppose, was such another/Who found no
287	FR	Charles	16	girl; but it's a difficult age for her./I suppose she must be getting on for thirty?/She
297	FR	Ivy	13	be of use./{I} Charles! you don't really suppose/That he might have pushed her over?/
302	FR	Amy	18	/Well, we must go and dress, I suppose. I hope Harry will feel better/After his
304	FR	Mary	18	have wanted to avoid collision./I suppose I could have gone, if I'd had the moral
306	FR	Mary	1	/And we just go on ... drying up, I suppose,/Not noticing the change. But to you, I
313	FR	Amy	28	vexing. What can have happened?/I suppose it's the fog that is holding them up,/So
319	FR	Harry	29	the day he died. Of course./I mean, I suppose, the day on which the news arrived./
324	FR	Amy	3	me. I shall return at once./{A} Well, I suppose you are right. But can I trust you?/{W}
340	FR	Agatha	10	years in which to think./Do you suppose that I wanted to return to Wishwood?/
343	FR	Mary	13	me wait for this —/Only for this. I suppose I did not really mean it/Then, but I
343	FR	Mary	19	So you must help me./I will go. But I suppose it is much too late/Now, to try to get a
345	FR	Charles	35	I'm not sure that I want to know. I suppose I'm getting old:/Old age came softly up
366	CP	Peter	39	And that wasn't your fault./I don't suppose you noticed the situation./{E} I did
367	CP	Peter	5	thought./If you didn't notice, I don't suppose the others did,/Though I'm rather
369	CP	Edward	8	have you a double boiler?/{E} I suppose there must be a double boiler:/Isn't
374	CP	Edward	18	you./{E} Yes, that *was* the situation./I suppose it was pretty obvious to everyone./{C}
375	CP	Edward	11	rings]/{E} Damn the telephone./I suppose I must answer it./Hello ... oh, hello! ...
375	CP	Edward	32	I must eat it within ten minutes./I suppose it's still cooking./{C} You suppose it's
375	CP	Celia	33	/I suppose it's still cooking./{C} You suppose it's still cooking!/I thought I noticed a
376	CP	Edward	1	don't bother! {}/[*Exit* CELIA]/{E} Suppose someone came and found you in the
380	CP	Celia	4	seem real enough/To humiliate me. I suppose that most women/Would feel degraded
380	CP	Celia	23	I never gave Peter/Any reason to suppose I cared for him./I thought he had
382	CP	Edward	38	rings]/{E} Damn the telephone./I suppose I had better answer it./{C} Yes, better
386	CP	Edward	25	very odd. And not like Lavinia./I suppose there is nothing to do but wait./Won't
387	CP	Peter	27	cocktail party to-day./So I don't suppose her aunt can have died./{E} What aunt?
388	CP	Lavinia	35	for an explanation./Meanwhile, I suppose we might as well sit down./What shall
390	CP	Julia	37	Eastern,/Waiting at junctions. And I suppose she's famished./{A} Ah, in that case I
392	CP	Lavinia	11	about them. It's about that party./I suppose you won't believe I forgot all about it!/
393	CP	Lavinia	23	that finally in desperation/I said: 'I suppose you'd as soon go to Peacehaven' —/
401	CP	Edward	13	like to know ... but what is the use!/I suppose I might as well go away at once./{R}
401	CP	Edward	37	you for bringing my wife back,/I suppose. You seemed to be trying to persuade
402	CP	Reilly	2	back, Mr. Chamberlayne,/Do you suppose that things would be any better —
412	CP	Celia	35	think that I am wasting it anyway./I suppose most people, when they come to see
415	CP	Celia	6	is the ordinary sense?/{C} Well ... I suppose it's being immoral —/And I don't feel
415	CP	Celia	13	least, I have never come across it./I suppose it is wicked to hurt other people/If you
415	CP	Reilly	30	you must be kinky./{R} And so you suppose you have what you call a 'kink'?/{C}
418	CP	Celia	39	/{C} I am not frightened/But glad. I suppose it is a lonely way?/{R} No lonelier than
435	CP	Peter	14	never thought/Of anything like this. I suppose I didn't know her,/I didn't understand
452	CC	Lucasta	34	both suit you./{L} Snubbed again! I suppose I asked for it./That's what comes of
455	CC	Colby	35	that's different./{C} At least, I don't suppose Lady Elizabeth/Can be quite so
462	CC	Colby	40	hardly know each other at all./{C} I suppose there hasn't been the opportunity./{SC}
463	CC	Colby	18	/A different person. Just as, I suppose,/If you learn to speak a foreign
466	CC	Claude	14	makes life bearable. It's all I have./I suppose it takes the place of religion:/Just as my
469	CC	Lucasta	11	different ways of playing it./{L} But I only like the wrong things?/{C} No,
477	CC	Lucasta	19	to see your face! I'm disappointed./I suppose that's all. I believe you're more shocked
477	CC	Lucasta	31	I know I am./That was new to me. I suppose I was flattered./And I thought, now,
478	CC	Lucasta	9	I will, if I choose. Oh, I'm sorry:/I suppose it's my mother coming out in me./You
484	CC	Colby	5	never knew any, when I was a child./I suppose I've never been interested ... in
486	CC	Lady E	15	mother —/Mrs. Guzzard's sister, I suppose .../{C} Her sister — which makes Mrs.
490	CC	Colby	30	The position is the same/Or crueller. Suppose I am your son./Then it's merely a fact.
494	CC	Lady E	28	me before!/Why haven't you? I don't suppose I understand/And I know you don't
495	CC	Lady E	29	I wanted to forget him,/And so, I suppose, I wanted to forget/Colby. But Colby is
501	CC	Lucasta	25	me. He's waiting downstairs./I don't suppose you want *us* at your meeting./{E} Allow
504	CC	Guzzard	35	than you are aware of./{MG} I suppose you mean Colby?/{LE} Yes. To do with
505	CC	Guzzard	15	/But is the subject of this meeting —/I suppose to do with Colby — so very
507	CC	Guzzard	28	no responsibility./The mother, I suppose, could have got an order/If she could

508 CC	Eggers	37	Nonconformists./{E} And the child, I suppose he had a Christian name?/{MG} There
509 CC	Lady E	39	And Mr. Kaghan/Being Barnabas. I suppose I'll get used to it./{C} But he's waiting
511 CC	Lady E	13	Your business ability/Comes, I suppose, from my side of the family./But he was
519 CC	Lady E	11	to be something he wasn't./{LE} I suppose that's true of you and me, Claude./
536 ES	Gomez	37	as for my married sisters — I don't suppose their husbands/Were ever told the
537 ES	Gomez	26	expected that I should get a First./I suppose your tutor thought you'd be sent down.
543 ES	Monica	12	He'd changed his name./{M} Then I suppose he wanted money?/{LC} No, he didn't
550 ES	Ld Clav	11	John Carghill./{LC} You married, I suppose, many years ago?/{MC} Many years
553 ES	Carghil	26	They would have figured at the trial, I suppose,/If there had been a trial. Don't you
564 ES	Carghil	26	that explains it. After Oxford/I suppose you went back to ... where is your

SUPPOSED (6)

233 Skimble		39	/There's a funny little basin you're supposed to wash your face in/And a crank to
294 FR	Harry	36	could sink so quickly./I had always supposed, wherever I went/That she would be
318 FR	Harry	7	but simply a time/In which we were supposed to make up to mother/For all the
333 FR	Agatha	24	dreamt I pushed her./{Ag} So I had supposed. What of it?/What we have written is
401 CP	Edward	19	invited by my wife as a guest/As I supposed? ... Or did she *send* you?/{R} I cannot
539 ES	Gomez	14	/And financial wizard that you're supposed to be./And I've learned something of

SUPPOSING (1)

432 CP	Reilly	11	giving me a very bad introduction —/Supposing that an introduction was necessary./

SUPREME (4)

250 MC	Thomas	1	keep the keys/Of heaven and hell, supreme alone in England,/Who bind and loose,
254 MC	Thomas	3	/You hold this power, hold it./{T} Supreme, in this land?/{T4} Supreme, but for
254 MC	Tempt4	4	it./{T} Supreme, in this land?/{T4} Supreme, but for one./{T} That I do not
280 MC	Priest3	16	It is fortified/By persecution: supreme, so long as men will die for it./Go,

SUR (3)

48 Lune	Miel	5	une forte odeur de chienne./Ils restent sur le dos écartant les genoux/De quatre jambes
51 Restaurant		2	de se gratter les doigts et se pencher sur mon épaule:/'Dans mon pays il fera temps
51 Restaurant		8	/'Les saules trempés, et des bourgeons sur les ronces —/C'est là, dans une averse,

SURE (132)

19 Portrait		58	on an August afternoon:/'I am always sure that you understand/My feelings, always
19 Portrait		59	you understand/My feelings, always sure that you feel,/Sure that across the gulf you
19 Portrait		60	feelings, always sure that you feel,/Sure that across the gulf you reach your hand./
21 Portrait		103	said so, all our friends,/They all were sure our feelings would relate/So closely! I
30 Cous	Nancy	9	dances;/And her aunts were not quite sure how they felt about it,/But they knew that
116 SP	Dusty	37	tell her. Good bye. Goooood bye./I'm sure, that's very kind of *you*./Ah-h-h/{Do} Now
117 SP	Doris	17	be you/We're all hearts. You can't be sure./It just depends on what comes next./
117 SP	Doris	32	mean a friend./{Do} No it's mine. I'm sure it's mine./I dreamt of weddings all last
187 FQ:	DrySal	132	face it steadily, but this thing is sure,/That time is no healer: the patient is no
210 Old	Gumbie	20	mice will not ever keep quiet,/She is sure it is due to irregular diet/And believing that
213 Growltiger		47	/She probably escaped with ease, I'm sure she was not drowned —/But a serried ring
227 Macavity		33	— but he's a mile away./You'll be sure to find him resting, or a-licking of his
235 Ad-dress		59	grouse, or salmon paste —/He's sure to have his personal taste./I know a Cat,
605 Narcissus		21	came out under the rock./First he was sure that he had been a tree,/Twisting its
292 FR	Amy	19	dinner/Or wait till tomorrow? I am sure you must be tired./You will find everybody
293 FR	Ivy	12	Amy!/No one wants you to die, I'm sure!/Now that Harry's back, is the time to
297 FR	Violet	32	to lead us nowhere,/And which I am sure Amy would disapprove of —/I only wish to
298 FR	Charles	30	a question I'd like to put to you,/I'm sure you won't mind, it's about his Lordship./
298 FR	Charles	34	you know him pretty well./And I am sure that you've been a good friend to him, too.
300 FR	Downing	22	you see him?/{Do} Oh yes, Sir, I'm sure I saw him./I don't mean to say that he had
300 FR	Downing	32	—/There wasn't a moon, but I was sure it was him./While I took my turn about,
302 FR	Chorus	9	disappear,/And we should cease to be sure of what is real or unreal?/Hold tight, hold
306 FR	Mary	2	noticing the change. But to you, I am sure,/We must seem very altered./{H} You have
310 FR	Harry	36	/Sunlight and singing; when I had felt sure/That every corridor only led to another,/Or
317 FR	Warburt	11	/{W} You don't understand me./I'm sure you cannot know what is on my mind;/And
319 FR	Warburt	31	arrived./{W} You overinterpret. I am sure that your mother always loved him;/There
326 FR	Violet	6	greatest trouble in getting home./I am sure he meant well. But I do think he is reckless.
328 FR	Ivy	31	this to Amy./{I} Poor Arthur! I'm sure that you're being much too hard on him./
338 FR	Harry	2	explain that to you now. Only be sure/That I know what I am doing, and what I
345 FR	Charles	35	if I were told it./But I'm not sure that I want to know. I suppose I'm getting
346 FR	Downing	25	else./I've no gift of language, but I'm sure of what I mean:/We most of us seem to live
364 CP	Edward	2	what my wife is like./I am not quite sure that I could describe her/If I had to ask the
364 CP	Edward	4	ask the police to search for her./I'm sure I don't know what she was wearing/When I
364 CP	Edward	25	— when we began to talk/I was not sure I wanted her; and now I want her./Do I
366 CP	Edward	5	under the cushion./{E} Are you quite sure they're not in your bag?/{J} Why no, of
368 CP	Edward	7	very thoughtful of you, Alex, I'm sure;/But I rather *want* to be alone, this evening.

372 CP	Peter	5	/{E} So much older?/{P} Yes, I'm sure that she would listen to you/As someone
377 CP	Julia	22	—/Only a half-bottle, to be sure,/And of course it isn't chilled. But it's so
380 CP	Celia	3	I've done to myself./I am not sure even that you seem real enough/To
381 CP	Edward	7	is it that you want?/{E} I am not sure./The one thing of which I am relatively
382 CP	Celia	4	of the stronger partner./{C} I am not sure, Edward, that I understand you;/And yet I
383 CP	Edward	5	don't snap my head off .../You're sure, in the kitchen? Beside the champagne
383 CP	Edward	6	the champagne bottle?/You're quite sure? ... Very well, hold on if you like;/We ... I'll
386 CP	Celia	33	headmaster's study; and is not quite sure/What he's been found out in. I never saw
389 CP	Lavinia	34	very kind, but very mysterious./I'm sure that we shall manage somehow, thank you,
391 CP	Edward	10	and I should be going./{E} Are you sure you haven't left anything, Julia?/{J} Left
391 CP	Lavinia	17	can't explain the telegram./{L} I am sure that you could explain the telegram./I don't
395 CP	Lavinia	20	when you were a little boy,/I'm sure you were always getting yourself measured/
398 CP	Edward	8	angel of destruction — just as I felt sure./In a moment, at your touch, there is
402 CP	Edward	3	better — now?/{E} I don't know. They could hardly be worse./{R} They
412 CP	Julia	8	way./I only came to tell you, I am sure she is ready/To make a decision./{R} Was
413 CP	Reilly	5	I am to do about it. They are quite sure/They have had a nervous breakdown —
414 CP	Celia	29	they understand each other./And I'm sure that they don't. Is that a delusion?/{R} A
419 CP	Reilly	9	else./Now — do you feel quite sure?/{C} I want your second way./So what am I
427 CP	Alex	36	/Or merely a symptom, I am not so sure./At least, the monkeys have become the
428 CP	Alex	33	to learn the solution./{A} I'm not sure that there *is* any solution./But even this
438 CP	Edward	18	/I should only speak for myself. I'm sure that *I* am./{R} Let me free your mind from
439 CP	Lavinia	4	nothing to mine, Lavinia./{L} I'm not sure about that. If I had understood you/Then I
440 CP	Reilly	12	burden. And as for the party,/I am sure it will be a success./{J} And I think, Henry,/
445 CC	Eggers	23	how's he getting on? Swimmingly, I'm sure,/As I've heard nothing since the last time I
446 CC	Eggers	28	good piano./{E} A piano? Yes, I'm sure he'll feel at home/When he has a piano.
446 CC	Eggers	39	wild birds seen in London:/And I'm sure Mr. Simpkins will find them if anybody./
448 CC	Eggers	34	has always been thwarted./{E} I'm sure it's been a grief to both of you/That you've
449 CC	Eggers	16	Your support will be helpful./{E} I'm sure I shall be very happy to commend him./
450 CC	Claude	3	greatest importance./It's when you're sure you understand a person/That you're liable
450 CC	Claude	14	don't know about me — I'm not so sure of that!/My rule is to remember that I
450 CC	Claude	16	/But on the other hand never to be sure/That they don't understand me — a good
450 CC	Eggers	20	/{E} And do I infer/That you're not sure you understand Mr. Simpkins, either?/{SC}
452 CC	Lucasta	20	suspicious/And asked for things I'm sure he didn't want —/Just to make trouble!
452 CC	Lucasta	22	/But they're all filed somewhere, I'm sure, so why bother?/But who's this, Eggy? Is it
452 CC	Colby	33	That Lucasta suits me better?/{C} I'm sure they both suit you./{L} Snubbed again! I
457 CC	Colby	4	That's what *I* always say./And I'm sure you'll like her. She's *such* a lady!/And
459 CC	Lady E	19	{LE} But all in the wrong colours, I'm sure. My husband/Does not understand the
461 CC	Eggers	9	E. said: 'I wish he'd ring us up!'/I'm sure he has a very cultivated voice.'/{C} Thank
461 CC	Colby	28	call you Colby with everyone./{C} I'm sure that will make it easier for both of us./{SC}
462 CC	Claude	2	the flat —/By tomorrow she'll be sure it was she who proposed it./So I feel pretty
463 CC	Colby	22	when you're talking it./I'm not at all sure that I like the other person/That I feel
464 CC	Claude	39	was a grief to him. He knew, I am sure,/That I cherished for a long time a secret
469 CC	Colby	12	like the wrong things?/{C} No, I'm sure you'll prefer the right things, when you
470 CC	Colby	18	/{C} Yes, of course I will./But I'm sure that when you learn about music —/And
472 CC	Lucasta	8	of any sense of security./{L} And I'm sure you have *that* — the sense of security./{C}
472 CC	Lucasta	38	career that he's set his heart on, I'm sure:/But it's only the outer world that you've
473 CC	Colby	5	lock the gate behind me?/Are you sure that you haven't your own secret garden/
473 CC	Colby	16	/{C} You're very much a person./I'm sure that there is a garden somewhere for you
477 CC	Lucasta	9	/{L} Oh, there's no doubt of that./I'm sure he wished there had been. He's been good
478 CC	Lucasta	11	Colby, I'm truly disappointed./I was sure, when I told you all I did,/That you
479 CC	Kaghan	35	the decorations./{K} Then I'm not sure I like them. You must change the colours./
486 CC	Lady E	17	my aunt./{LE} And are you quite sure that Mrs. Guzzard's sister —/Who you say
487 CC	Lady E	28	/Perhaps it is wrong of me to feel so sure,/But it seems that Providence has brought
490 CC	Claude	7	{SC} It could have happened. But I'm sure it didn't./{LE} Oh, Colby, doesn't your
494 CC	Lady E	5	much fairer. If he is mine —/As I am sure he is — then you never had a son;/While, if
494 CC	Claude	13	between us./{SC} I'm not so sure of that. I've tried to believe in facts;/And
497 CC	Claude	7	asked her to come. Lady Elizabeth/Is sure that she knows the name of Mrs. Guzzard./
497 CC	Lady E	25	and that Colby is my son./I feel sure he is. But I don't want to know:/I am
501 CC	Claude	1	happened, but nevertheless/I'm sure that you have made the right decision./{L}
501 CC	Lady E	3	so are the wrong ones./{LE} And I'm sure too, Lucasta, you have made a wise
501 CC	Claude	14	/{SC} Perhaps you are right. I'm not sure of anything./Perhaps, as you say, I've
501 CC	Lucasta	23	as a son-in-law./{L} Thank you. I'm sure he'll appreciate *that*./But that reminds me.
501 CC	Eggers	29	Miss Angel every happiness./And I'm sure she will be happy. Mr. Kaghan/Is one of
501 CC	Eggers	33	this very important interview,/But I'm sure that we want to greet the happy pair./It's
503 CC	Eggers	22	us when this interview is over?/I'm sure Mr. Simpkins will concur in this proposal./

506 CC	Eggers	17	had no children of your own;/But I'm sure you can sympathise./{MG} I can
508 CC	Guzzard	39	it came to us; but we could not be sure./My husband was particular in such
509 CC	Lady E	6	such a name/In my family. Or, I'm sure, in his father's./But how did he come to be
509 CC	Lady E	18	you./{LE} So my child is living. I was sure of that./But I believe that Colby is
512 CC	Claude	11	think there is any confusion now:/I'm sure that my wife is perfectly convinced;/And
512 CC	Claude	12	/And Mr. Kaghan's ... mother, I am sure, will confirm it./{MG} That is as much to
512 CC	Lady E	22	/{LE} Oh, of course ... Yes, I'm sure ... I shall be very happy./{MG} You wished
512 CC	Lady E	35	Aunt Elizabeth./{LE} B. — and I'm sure we shall become great friends./{E} I'm sure
512 CC	Eggers	36	we shall become great friends./{E} I'm sure we all wish for nothing better./{MG}
513 CC	Claude	11	wish?/{SC} Colby only wanted to be sure of the truth./{C} That is a very strange
525 ES	Monica	29	But seriously, Charles,/Father's sure to be buried in the library/And he won't
526 ES	Charles	7	I need so much assurance! Are you sure you're not mistaken?/{M} How did this
527 ES	Charles	6	constitute an engagement?/Aren't you sure that you want to marry me?/{M} Yes,
527 ES	Monica	7	to marry me?/{M} Yes, Charles. I'm sure that I want to marry you/When I'm free to
528 ES	Monica	19	There *is* a private self, Charles./I'm sure of that./{C} You've given two reasons,/So
535 ES	Gomez	5	the compliment./{G} Which you're sure you deserve. But when I say 'trust' ... {}/
536 ES	Ld Clav	23	mine, you think you do .../{LC} I'm sure I do,/I've always been alone./{G} Oh,
549 ES	Carghil	32	/Or did she say 'yellow'? I'm not quite sure./You do remember now, don't you,
555 ES	Ld Clav	31	/With some woman or other. I'm sure he has friends/Whom he wouldn't care for
560 ES	Ld Clav	30	I'm fed up with England./{LC} I'm sure you don't mean that. But it's natural
565 ES	Michael	17	way with you./{Mi} Delighted, I'm sure./{G} Taking a holiday?/You're in business
569 ES	Ld Clav	5	the part I played:/How could I be sure that she would love the actor/If she saw
569 ES	Charles	22	of it in my practice at the bar./I'm sure I could help./{M} Oh Father, do let him./
570 ES	Ld Clav	8	How open one's heart/When one is sure of the wrong response?/How make a
573 ES	Ld Clav	19	no more about it./Meanwhile, I feel sure they are conspiring against me./I see Mrs.
573 ES	Carghil	25	you!/But I suspect ... Dare I? Yes, I'm sure of it, Monica./I can tell by the change in
576 ES	Gomez	4	I was very lovely then./{G} We are sure of that! You're so lovely now/That we can
577 ES	Charles	17	/You know nothing. All you can be sure of/Is that he served a prison sentence for
580 ES	Monica	29	If it's all a failure/Homesickness, I'm sure, will bring him back to us;/If he prospers,
580 ES	Monica	34	self that he's ashamed of./I'm sure he loves us./{LC} Monica my dear,/What
581 ES	Ld Clav	9	this might be a final good-bye./I am sure of it now. Perhaps it is as well./{M} What

SURELY (8)

223 Pekes Pols	29	some came to the door;/There were surely a dozen, more likely a score./And
589 Fable	67	knows the well known fact, as you do surely —/That ghosts are fellows whom you
266 MC Knight1	9	/You say, from the King?/{K1} Most surely from the King./We must speak with you
303 FR Mary	10	for dinner./{M} Seven ... nine ... ten surely./I hear that Harry has arrived already/
308 FR Mary	24	the hollow tree,/Not there./{M} That sure,/what you say/Only proves that you
374 CP Celia	25	to light the real difficulties./{C} But surely, these are only temporary./You know I
374 CP Celia	29	would never want to leave you./Surely you don't hold to that silly convention/
483 CC Lady E	27	the sitting-room./May I remove it? Surely your bedroom/Is the proper place for

SUREXCITÉ (1)

47 Mél Adult	11	/En Allemagne, philosophe/Surexcité par Emporheben/Au grand air de

SURF (2)

31 Apollinax	12	silence,/Dropping from fingers of surf./I looked for the head of Mr. Apollinax
121 SA Sweeney	29	/Nothing to hear but the sound of the surf./Nothing at all but three things/{Do} What

SURFACE (5)

134 Wind	7	a dream or something else/When the surface of the blackened river/Is a face that
172 FQ: BurntN	39	the lotos rose, quietly, quietly,/The surface glittered out of heart of light,/And they
594 Grad 11	5	a momentary gleam,/A bubble on the surface of the stream,/A drop of dew upon the
331 FR Agatha	24	of a women's college —/That is the surface. There is a deeper/Organisation, which
473 CC Lucasta	13	a bit of living matter/Floating on the surface of the Regent's Canal./Floating, that's

SURGEON (3)

181 FQ: ECoker	149	is where you are not./The wounded surgeon plies the steel/That questions the
362 CP Reilly	36	consultation with the doctor and the surgeon,/In going to bed in the nursing home,/
546 ES Piggott	7	And my husband/Was a distinguished surgeon. Do you know, I fell in love with him/

SURGICAL (1)

362 CP Reilly	35	of a malevolent staircase./Or, take a surgical operation./In consultation with the

SURMISED (1)

505 CC Eggers	20	start./The question has to do, as you surmised, with Mr. Simpkins./It also concerns a

SURNAMES (2)

482 CC Lady E	7	/Seem to have dropped the use of surnames altogether./But, Colby, I hope you
563 ES Gomez	25	/{G} We seem a bit weak on the surnames, Dick!/{MC} Well, you see, Señor

SURPRISE (23)

34 Figlia	4	your flowers to you with a pained surprise —/Fling them to the ground and turn/
213 Growltiger	35	to relaxation, and awaiting no surprise —/But the moonlight shone reflected

213	Growltiger	50	rank on rank;/Growltiger to his vast surprise was forced to walk the plank./He who a
231	Bust Jones	31	or another he's found./It can be no surprise that under our eyes/He has grown
250	MC Thomas	22	purpose./{T} No purpose brings surprise./{T3} Well, my Lord,/I am no trifler,
279	MC Knight4	16	lamentable/scene, you may feel some surprise at my putting it in this way. But/
287	FR Amy	30	And death will come to you as a mild surprise,/A momentary shudder in a vacant
293	FR Charles	34	/{C} And there isn't much would surprise me, Harry;/Or shock me, either./{H}
322	FR Harry	16	mean you think I can't. But I might surprise you;/I think I might be able to give you
368	CP Alex	13	I'll do./I'm going to give you a little surprise:/You know, I'm rather a famous cook./
369	CP Alex	11	/{A} I can't find it./There goes *that* surprise. I must think of another./{P} Not very
370	CP Alex	16	hates curry./{A} There goes another surprise, then. I must think./I didn't expect to
409	CP Reilly	10	had left you,/You discovered, to your surprise and consternation,/That you were not
426	CP Julia	38	in fact. But I'm forgetting!/I've got a surprise: I've brought Alex with me!/He only
432	CP Julia	3	/{J} Oh, I forgot! I'd another surprise for you. {}/[*Enter* REILLY]/{J} I want
436	CP Lavinia	30	/Was that your face showed no surprise or horror/At the way in which she died.
462	CC Claude	16	eyes. She's like that./Why, it wouldn't surprise me if she came to believe/That you
492	CC Claude	35	only remind me/Of things that would surprise the Potters' Company/If I told them
509	CC Claude	35	my calculations./{SC} That wouldn't surprise me./{LE} Yes, what year was it?/I'm
510	CC Colby	15	I have told them to be prepared for a surprise./{LE} Barnabas! Is your name
552	ES Ld Clav	12	/{LC} Nothing at all. I remember my surprise/At finding that I felt nothing at all./I
574	ES Carghil	23	able to suggest?/{MC} Ah! That's the surprise for which I've come to prepare you./
581	ES Ld Clav	13	You should leave./{LC} This may surprise you: I feel at peace now./It is the peace

SURPRISED (9)

61	WL: Burial	8	A little life with dried tubers./Summer surprised us, coming over the Starnbergersee/
252	MC Tempt4	34	visitors, not four./{T4} Do not be surprised to receive one more./Had I been
336	FR Harry	13	this time/You cannot think that I am surprised to see you./And you shall not think
346	FR Charles	2	I remember now, that I am always surprised/By the bull-dog in the Burlington
404	CP Edward	13	/It is surprising, if one had time to be surprised:/I am not afraid of the death of the
458	CC Lady E	17	can't understand why you're both so surprised./You know I'm a very experienced
508	CC Lady E	11	a shadow of doubt in my mind./I'm surprised that you, Eggerson, with your legal
540	ES Gomez	24	{G} You knew it too. If you had been surprised/When I said 'Dick, you've run over
560	ES Michael	2	after death,/I bet it will be a surprised state of consciousness./Poor ghost!

SURPRISES (4)

111	Xmas Trees	14	Christmas Tree,/So that the surprises, delight in new possessions/(Each one
330	FR Harry	3	will go on as before. These mild surprises/Should be in the routine of normal life
346	FR Charles	1	that life could bring no further surprises;/But I remember now, that I am
471	CC Lucasta	10	me./{L} Colby, you really are full of surprises!/I've never met a man so ignorant as

SURPRISING (12)

224	Mr Mistoff	8	patent monopolies/For performing surprising illusions/And creating eccentric
394	CP Lavinia	38	/{L} Bravo! Edward. This is surprising./Now who could have taught you to
404	CP Edward	13	there is suffering worse than that./It is surprising, if one had time to be surprised:/I am
458	CC Eggers	8	/{E} Lady Elizabeth! This is most surprising./{LE} What's surprising, Eggerson?
458	CC Lady E	9	This is most surprising./{LE} What's surprising, Eggerson? I've arrived, that's all./{E}
482	CC Lady E	36	your acquaintance:/Because, what's surprising, well-bred people/Are sometimes far
482	CC Lady E	38	from intellectual;/And — what's less surprising — intellectual people/Are often
498	CC Eggers	1	/{E} I agree, that would be most surprising./And at the same address?/{LE} I
503	CC Claude	36	/{SC} She ought to be here now! It's surprising,/I hadn't been aware how the time
539	ES Gomez	6	euphemism./And yet I wonder. It *is* surprising:/You should have been good for
539	ES Ld Clav	25	accurate./The only thing I find surprising/In the respected citizen of San Marco
549	ES Carghil	23	and I. What a time ago it seems!/It's surprising I remember it all so clearly./You

SURPRISINGLY (1)

| 553 | ES Ld Clav | 3 | brevity of our acquaintance,/You're surprisingly confident, I must say,/About your |

SURRENDER (7)

74	WL: Thund	403	heart/The awful daring of a moment's surrender/Which an age of prudence can never
97	Ash-Wed 5	31	her/And are terrified and cannot surrender/And affirm before the world and deny
282	MC Chorus	8	the loneliness of the night of God, the surrender required, the deprivation inflicted;/
378	CP Celia	23	it's that./I think it is just a moment of surrender/To fatigue. And panic. You can't face
407	CP Reilly	24	yourselves into hands like mine/You surrender a great deal more than you meant to./
418	CP Celia	7	/But I feel it would be a kind of surrender —/No, not a surrender — more like a
418	CP Celia	8	be a kind of surrender —/No, not a surrender — more like a betrayal./You see, I

SURRENDERED (2)

| 606 | Narcissus | 37 | /As he embraced them his white skin surrendered itself to the redness of blood, and |
| 492 | CC Claude | 9 | going to happen,/I would gladly have surrendered Colby to you./But we must see |

SURRENDERS (1)

| 568 | ES Ld Clav | 8 | irreflective aberrations,/Reckless surrenders, unexplainable impulses,/Moments |

SURROUND (3)

213 Growltiger		48	ring of flashing steel Growltiger did surround./The ruthless foe pressed forward, in
311 FR	Harry	14	me, why do you let me go,/Only to surround me? — When I remember them/They
363 CP	Reilly	1	in a repair shop/For those who surround you, the masked actors;/All there is of

SURROUNDED (3)

160 Rock 7		11	and Evil./But their light was ever surrounded and shot with darkness/As the air
173 FQ: BurntN		74	inner/And the outer compulsion, yet surrounded/By a grace of sense, a white light
319 FR	Harry	9	for him, there was only a vacuum/Surrounded by whispering aunts: Ivy and Violet

SURVIVE (2)

159 Rock 6		13	the way of polite society/Will hardly survive the Faith to which they owe their
363 CP	Reilly	35	to the good./You will find that you survive humiliation./And that's an experience of

SURVIVED (1)

434 CP	Alex	19	the villagers —/Those who survived. And then they found her body,/Or at

SUSCEPTIBLE (1)

49 Hippopot		6	/Flesh and blood is weak and frail,/Susceptible to nervous shock;/While the True

SUSPECT (11)

56 Swee Night		26	/She and the lady in the cape/Are suspect, thought to be in league;/Therefore the
296 FR	Charles	26	strangers, with no one to talk to./I suspect it is simply that the wish to get rid of
408 CP	Edward	20	chosen/Anyone I was less likely to suspect./And then he came to *me* to confide
409 CP	Reilly	18	love with anybody;/Which made you suspect that you were incapable/Of loving. To
409 CP	Reilly	35	he did. You pretended to yourself,/I suspect, and for as long as you could,/That he
436 CP	Lavinia	32	died. I don't know if you knew her./I suspect that you did. In any case you knew
471 CC	Colby	9	begin my education at once./{C} I suspect that it's you who are educating *me*./{L}
471 CC	Lucasta	12	knowing so much that one wouldn't suspect./Perhaps that's why I like you./{C}
538 ES	Gomez	15	very well by yourself?/Though not, I suspect, as well as you had hoped./{LC} I was
545 ES	Ld Clav	2	it. Some dissatisfaction/With myself, I suspect, very deep within myself/Has impelled
573 ES	Carghil	25	very exciting news for you!/But I suspect ... Dare I? Yes, I'm sure of it, Monica!/I

SUSPECTED (4)

396 CP	Lavinia	4	have very good records;/But I always suspected that you really hated music/And that
489 CC	Claude	10	how many more?'/You might have suspected any number of children!/That seems
499 CC	Claude	37	B./{SC} But Colby! Lucasta, if I'd suspected this/I would have explained. Colby is
555 ES	Piggott	4	say, but not quite your sort or mine./I suspected that she wanted to meet you, so I

SUSPECTS (1)

425 CP	Lavinia	15	/Everyone who's asked to either party/Suspects that the other one was more

SUSPEND (1)

39 Gerontion		66	of mirrors. What will the spider do,/Suspend its operations, will the weevil/Delay?

SUSPENDED (3)

191 FQ: Little		3	though sodden towards sundown,/Suspended in time, between pole and tropic./
192 FQ: Little		58	the burnt roses leave./Dust in the air suspended/Marks the place where a story ended.
268 MC Knight1		25	them./{K1} Through you they were suspended./{K2} By you be this amended./{K3}

SUSPENDING (1)

268 MC Knight1		7	did you show your gratitude?/{K1} Suspending those who had crowned the young

SUSPICION (6)

296 FR	Gerald	38	to Harry, and Harry need have no suspicion./I'd trust Warburton's opinion./{A} If
319 FR	Warburt	32	him;/There was never the slightest suspicion of scandal./{H} Scandal? who said
342 FR	Agatha	37	who knows./No one who has the least suspicion of what is to be found there./But
409 CP	Reilly	20	loving. To men of a certain type/The suspicion that they are incapable of loving/Is as
510 CC	Guzzard	27	/If so, I am cleared from your unjust suspicion./{E} Mr. Kaghan, are your adoptive
569 ES	Charles	17	/{C} I was thinking, Sir — forgive the suspicion —/From what Monica has told me

SUSPICIONS (2)

512 CC	Guzzard	5	What about?/{MG} That your suspicions of me were wholly unfounded./{LE}
512 CC	Lady E	6	/{LE} Oh, Mrs. Guzzard, I had no suspicions!/I thought there had been a

SUSPICIOUS (1)

452 CC	Lucasta	19	I couldn't find it. And then he got suspicious/And asked for things I'm sure he

SUSPIRE (1)

196 FQ: Little		214	cannot remove./We only live, only suspire/Consumed by either fire or fire./What

SUSTAINED (1)

54 Mr E Sun		22	pence./Under the penitential gates/Sustained by staring Seraphim/Where the souls

SUSTENANCE (2)

242 MC	Priest1	25	upon his own virtues,/Pride drawing sustenance from impartiality,/Pride drawing
242 MC	Priest1	26	from impartiality,/Pride drawing sustenance from generosity,/Loathing power

SUTLERS (1)

54 Mr E Sun		2	/Polyphiloprogenitive/The sapient sutlers of the Lord/Drift across the

SWADDLED (1)

37 Gerontion		19	a word, unable to speak a word,/Swaddled with darkness. In the juvescence of

SWALLOW (3)

75 WL: Thund	428	*affina*/*Quando fiam uti chelidon* — O swallow swallow/*Le Prince d'Aquitaine à la*
75 WL: Thund	428	*fiam uti chelidon* — O swallow swallow/*Le Prince d'Aquitaine à la tour abolie*/
285 FR Amy	4	house from October to June,/And the swallow comes too soon and the spring will be

SWALLOWED (1)

270 MC Chorus	5	the breathing of the sea-anemone, swallowed with ingurgitation of the sponge. I

SWAM (1)

64 WL: Chess	96	/In which sad light a carvèd dolphin swam./Above the antique mantel was displayed/

SWAMP-SPARROW (1)

142 Cape Ann	2	quick, quick hear the song-sparrow,/Swamp-sparrow, fox-sparrow, vesper-sparrow/

SWARMED (1)

213 Growltiger	42	burst of fireworks the Chinks they swarmed aboard./Abandoning their sampans,

SWARMING (1)

73 WL: Thund	368	/Who are those hooded hordes swarming/Over endless plains, stumbling in

SWARMS (1)

484 CC Lady E	21	no doubt, many relatives./{LE} Oh, swarms of relatives! And such unpleasant

SWARTS (4)

118 SP Dusty	1	That'll be Snow/{Du} Or it might be Swarts/{Do} Or it might be Snow/{Du} It's a
121 SA m	1	KLIPSTEIN. KRUMPACKER. SWARTS. SNOW. DORIS. DUSTY./{S} I'll
122 SA 2m	15	WAUCHOPE AND HORSFALL/SWARTS AS TAMBO. SNOW AS BONES/
123 SA 2m	13	KRUMPACKER/SNOW AND SWARTS AS BEFORE/{Kl&Kr} *My little*

SWAY (1)

28 Boston ET	2	of the *Boston Evening Transcript*/Sway in the wind like a field of ripe corn./When

SWAYS (1)

226 Macavity	15	his whiskers are uncombed./He sways his head from side to side, with

SWEAR (4)

66 WL: Chess	146	out, Lil, and get a nice set,/He said, I swear, I can't bear to look at you./And no more
602 Humoresque	16	/'The newest style, on Earth, I swear.'Why don't you people get some class?/
498 CC Lady E	5	that's all I know,/And that I could swear to./{E} It does seem unlikely/That there
534 ES Gomez	3	who are already corrupted?/I can swear that I've never corrupted anybody./In

SWEAT (2)

72 WL: Thund	337	the rock one cannot stop or think/Sweat is dry and feet are in the sand/If there
125 SA Chorus	32	middle of the night and/you wake in a sweat and a hell of a fright/When you're alone

SWEATS (2)

69 WL: Fire S	266	of Ionian white and gold./The river sweats/Oil and tar/The barges drift/With the
134 Wind	8	of the blackened river/Is a face that sweats with tears?/I saw across the blackened

SWEATY (2)

72 WL: Thund	322	said/After the torchlight red on sweaty faces/After the frosty silence in the
129 Cor2 State	31	lit up successively by the flare/Of a sweaty torchbearer, yawning./O hidden under

SWEDEN (1)

354 CP Alex	13	Baltic families/With a branch in Sweden and one in Denmark./There were

SWEENEY (15)

42 Swee Erect	t	on/Time's ruins, and the seven laws./Sweeney Erect/Paint me a cavernous waste
42 Swee Erect	21	bed/And clawing at the pillow slip./Sweeney addressed full length to shave/
43 Swee Erect	28	/Who had not seen the silhouette/Of Sweeney straddled in the sun.)/Tests the razor
55 Mr E Sun	29	pistillate,/Blest office of the epicene./Sweeney shifts from ham to ham/Stirring the
56 Swee Night	t	schools/Are controversial, polymath./Sweeney Among the Nightingales/Apeneck
56 Swee Night	1	Among the Nightingales/Apeneck Sweeney spreads his knees/Letting his arms
56 Swee Night	8	and the Raven drift above/And Sweeney guards the hornèd gate./Gloomy Orion
67 WL: Fire S	198	horns and motors, which shall bring/Sweeney to Mrs. Porter in the spring./O
115 S	t	coming./UNFINISHED POEMS/Sweeney Agonistes/*Fragments of an*
117 SP Doris	4	/{Du} That's Pereira/{Do} It might be Sweeney/{Du} It's Pereira/{Do} It might *just* as
117 SP Doris	6	Pereira/{Do} It might *just* as well be Sweeney/{Du} Well anyway it's very queer./{Do}
121 SA m	1	us around. {}/Fragment of an Agon/SWEENEY. WAUCHOPE. HORSFALL.
124 SA Doris	3	once did a girl in —/{Do} Oh Mr. Sweeney, please don't talk,/I cut the cards
124 SA Snow	10	runs a terrible risk./{Sn} Let Mr. Sweeney continue his story./I assure you, Sir,
124 SA Snow	25	runs a terrible risk./{Sn} Let Mr. Sweeney continue his story./{S} This one didn't

SWEENEY'S (1)

56 Swee Night	12	in the Spanish cape/Tries to sit on Sweeney's knees/Slips and pulls the table cloth/

SWEEP (1)

129 Cor2 State	47	silent croaking night./Come with the sweep of the little bat's wing, with the small

SWEEPERS (1)

281 MC Chorus	14	the hearth, we, the scrubbers and sweepers of Canterbury,/The back bent under

SWEEPS (1)

174 FQ: BurntN	113	the torpid/Driven on the wind that sweeps the gloomy hills of London./Hampstead

SWEET (15)

66 WL: Chess	172		/Good night, ladies, good night, sweet ladies, good night, good night./The Fire
67 WL: Fire S	176		unheard. The nymphs are departed./Sweet Thames, run softly, till I end my song./
67 WL: Fire S	183		of Leman I sat down and wept .../Sweet Thames, run softly till I end my song./
67 WL: Fire S	184		Thames, run softly till I end my song,/Sweet Thames, run softly, for I speak not loud
92 Ash-Wed 3	17		with an antique flute./Blown hair is sweet, brown hair over the mouth blown,/Lilac
142 Cape Ann	10		silence the bullbat. All are delectable. Sweet sweet sweet/But resign this land at the
142 Cape Ann	10		the bullbat. All are delectable. Sweet sweet sweet/But resign this land at the end,
142 Cape Ann	10		All are delectable. Sweet sweet sweet/But resign this land at the end, resign it/
247 MC Tempt1	10		Snow in the branches/Shall float as sweet as blossoms. Ice along the ditches/Mirror
257 MC Chorus	26		pang, more pain than birth or death./Sweet and cloying through the dark air/Falls
270 MC Chorus	3		in the rose, death in the hollyhock, sweet pea, hyacinth, primrose and cowslip. I
270 MC Chorus	9		the sewer in the incense, the smell of sweet soap in the woodpath, a hellish sweet
270 MC Chorus	9		sweet soap in the woodpath, a hellish sweet scent in the woodpath, while the ground
292 FR Harry	5		Java Straits, in the Sunda Sea,/In the sweet sickly tropical night, I knew they were
311 FR Harry	5		a smell/In that it is indescribable, a sweet and bitter smell/From another world. I

SWEETEN (1)

271 MC Thomas	16		the fire,/When age and forgetfulness sweeten memory/Only like a dream that has

SWEETER (1)

209 NamingCats	9		fancier names if you think they sound sweeter,/Some for the gentlemen, some for the

SWEETLY (1)

536 ES Gomez	8		a sudden effort,/You, so slowly and sweetly, that you've never woken up/To the fact

SWEETNESS (1)

191 FQ: Little	25		White again, in May, with voluptuary sweetness./It would be the same at the end of

SWELL (8)

16 Prufrock	113		an attendant lord, one that will do/To swell a progress, start a scene or two,/Advise the
42 Swee Erect	8		/Which tangle Ariadne's hair/And swell with haste the perjured sails./Morning stirs
70 WL: Fire S	284		gilded shell/Red and gold/The brisk swell/Rippled both shores/Southwest wind/
71 WL: DWater	313		the cry of gulls, and the deep sea swell/And the profit and loss./A current under
119 SP Klip	29		Say, Miss — er — uh — London's swell./We like London fine./{Kr} Perfectly slick.
120 SP Klip	5		/London's a slick place, London's a swell place,/London's a fine place to come on a
185 FQ: DrySal	39		time, rung by the unhurried/Ground swell, a time/Older than the time of
185 FQ: DrySal	48		time is never ending;/And the ground swell, that is and was from the beginning,/

SWELLING (1)

56 Swee Night	4		laugh,/The zebra stripes along his jaw/Swelling to maculate giraffe./The circles of the

SWEPT (4)

155 Rock 3	45		the peace of Thy sanctuary,/I have swept the floors and garnished the altars./Where
254 MC Tempt4	35		/The sanctuary broken, and its stores/Swept into the laps of parasites and whores./
260 MC Thomas	30		counting/over his peaceful gains, the swept hearth, his best wine for a friend/at the
289 FR Ivy	25		to lose anybody in *that* way —/Swept off the deck in the middle of a storm,/

SWIFTLY (1)

589 Fable	80		say 'O jiminy!'/The pair had vanisht swiftly up the chimney./Naturally every one

SWIMMING (1)

300 FRDowning	17		these ocean liners/With all their swimming baths and gymnasiums/There's not

SWIMMINGLY (1)

445 CC Eggers	23		leave./{E} And how's he getting on? Swimmingly, I'm sure,/As I've heard nothing

SWINDLED (1)

266 MC Knights	23		on your shirt,/The man who cheated, swindled, lied; broke his oath and betrayed his

SWING (5)

31 Apollinax	5		shrubbery/Gaping at the lady in the swing./In the palace of Mrs. Phlaccus, at
69 WL: Fire S	272		tide/Red sails/Wide/To leeward, swing on the heavy spar./The barges wash/
138 New Hamp	10		/Golden head, black wing,/Cling, swing,/Spring, sing,/Swing up into the
138 New Hamp	12		wing,/Cling, swing,/Spring, sing,/Swing up into the apple-tree./Virginia/Red
257 MC Chorus	32		/They curl round you, lie at your feet, swing and wing through the dark air./O

SWINGING (2)

83 Hollow Men	24		on a broken column/There, is a tree swinging/And voices are/In the wind's singing/
134 Wind	3		wind sprang up and broke the bells/Swinging between life and death/Here, in

SWINGS (1)

74 WL: Thund	389		/It has no windows, and the door swings,/Dry bones can harm no one./Only a

SWITZERLAND (2)

445 CC Claude	7		first meeting,/On her return from Switzerland./{E} Impossible, Sir Claude!/A very
534 ES Gomez	30		/And keep an account in a bank in Switzerland./The ones who don't get out in time

SWOLLEN (2)

266 MC Knights	20		creature that crawled upon the King; swollen with blood and swollen with pride./
266 MC Knights	20		the King; swollen with blood and swollen with pride./Creeping out of the London

SWOON (2)

| 601 Nocturne | 8 | wait,/Stab, and the lady sinks into a swoon./Blood looks effective on the moonlit |
| 270 MC Chorus | 24 | /Nothing is possible but the shamed swoon/Of those consenting to the last |

SWOOPS (1)

| 478 CC Lucasta | 20 | /From loneliness, then loneliness swoops down upon you;/When you think you're |

SWORD (2)

| 106 Song Sime | 32 | vision./Grant me thy peace./(And a sword shall pierce thy heart,/Thine also)./I am |
| 157 Rock 4 | 19 | they built as men must build/With the sword in one hand and the trowel in the other./ |

SWORD'S (1)

| 259 MC Thomas | 5 | /I shall no longer act or suffer, to the sword's end./Now my good Angel, whom God |

SWORDS (2)

| 105 Song Sime | 16 | from the foreign faces and the foreign swords./Before the time of cords and scourges |
| 269 MC Knights | 26 | for the King's justice, we come with swords. {}/[*Exeunt*]/{C} I have smelt them, the |

SWORDS' (1)

| 259 MC Thomas | 7 | /To be my guardian, hover over the swords' points. {}/Interlude/THE |

SWORN (2)

| 219 Mung Rump | 33 | or Rumpelteazer? or could you have sworn that it mightn't be both?/And when you |
| 246 MC Thomas | 10 | the Sheriff of Kent,/Those who had sworn to have my head from me/Only John, the |

SWUNG (1)

| 228 Gus | 30 | /When the Curfew was rung, then I swung on the bell./In the Pantomime season I |

SYLVAN (1)

| 64 WL: Chess | 98 | /As though a window gave upon the sylvan scene/The change of Philomel, by the |

SYMBOL (4)

196 FQ: Little	196	/What they had to leave us — a symbol:/A symbol perfected in death./And all
196 FQ: Little	197	they had to leave us — a symbol:/A symbol perfected in death./And all shall be well
202 War Poetry	6	/To create the universal, originate a symbol/Out of the impact? This is a meeting/On
474 CC Lucasta	33	/Something of which the music is a ... symbol./I really would like to understand music,

SYMPATHETIC (4)

295 FR Harry	3	and the steward were extremely sympathetic/And the doctor very attentive./
394 CP Edward	6	.../{E} And you were never very sympathetic./{L} Well, but I tried to do
407 CP Reilly	14	you both on your perspicacity./Your sympathetic understanding of each other/Will
447 CC Claude	28	your state of health,/So she'll be sympathetic. And as for Colby —/Say that Mr.

SYMPATHIES (2)

| 276 MC Knight1 | 22 | being set upon by four, then your/sympathies are all with the under dog. I respect |
| 277 MC Knight2 | 37 | are Englishmen,/and therefore your sympathies are always with the under dog./It is |

SYMPATHISE (2)

| 506 CC Eggers | 17 | of your own;/But I'm sure you can sympathise./{MG} I can sympathise./I had a |
| 506 CC Guzzard | 18 | sure you can sympathise./{MG} I can sympathise./I had a child, and lost him. Not in |

SYMPATHY (1)

| 20 Portrait | 66 | from me?/Only the friendship and the sympathy/Of one about to reach her journey's |

SYMPTOM (5)

314 FR Warburt	29	/We call it health when we find no symptom/Of illness. Health is a relative term./
401 CP Edward	6	/But I dismissed that as just another symptom./Well, I should have known better
408 CP Reilly	25	/{R} It is the first more hopeful symptom./{L} How did you know all this?/{R}
414 CP Reilly	33	and go on from./And the second symptom?/{C} That's stranger still./It sounds
427 CP Alex	36	the core of the problem/Or merely a symptom, I am not so sure./At least, the ·

SYMPTOMS (4)

402 CP Edward	13	least that he would enquire about the symptoms./Two people advised me recently,/
407 CP Reilly	6	you are both too ill. There are several symptoms/Which must occur together, and to a
409 CP Reilly	1	your explanation/Of your obvious symptoms of emotional strain/And so I made
413 CP Celia	27	/Which you might consider symptoms. But first I must tell you/That I

SYNTHESIS (1)

| 24 Rhapsody | 3 | reaches of the street/Held in a lunar synthesis,/Whispering lunar incantations/ |

SYNTHETIC (1)

| 64 WL: Chess | 87 | glass/Unstoppered, lurked her strange synthetic perfumes,/Unguent, powdered, or |

SYRIA (3)

162 Rock 8	18	/Many left their bodies to the kites of Syria/Or sea-strewn along the routes;/Many left
162 Rock 8	20	the routes;/Many left their souls in Syria,/Living on, sunken in moral corruption;/
162 Rock 8	26	the East/And the seven deadly sins in Syria./But our King did well at Acre./And in

SYSTEM (2)

| 278 MC Knight2 | 11 | seditious ends, and to reform the legal system./He therefore intended that Becket, who |
| 546 ES Piggott | 37 | nurse, you know, fully qualified./Our system is very delicately balanced:/For me to be |

SYSTEMATIC (1)

| 533 ES Ld Clav | 38 | words/You have been engaged in systematic corruption./{G} No, Dick, there's a |

SYSTEMS (1)
159 Rock 6   23   outside and within/By dreaming of systems so perfect that no one will need to be
SZOGODY (1)
431 CP   Peter   7   who is the great Bela?/{P} Why, Bela Szogody —/He's my boss. I thought everyone

T' (1)
588 Fable 62 toast/Had drank more than he ought t' have of grape juice./The lights began to burn

T' (1) [*Foreign word*]
51 Restaurant 21 /Mais alors, tu as ton vautour!/Va t'en te décrotter les rides du visage;/Tiens, ma

T'WILL (1)
594 Grad 10 3 we know;/But only in appearance t'will be so./That which has made it great, not

TA (2)
66 WL: Chess 171 Lou. Goonight May. Goonight./Ta ta. Goonight. Goonight./Good night, ladies,
66 WL: Chess 171 Lou. Goonight May. Goonight./Ta ta. Goonight. Goonight./Good night, ladies,

TABBY (1)
210 Old Gumbie 2 is Jennyanydots;/Her coat is of the tabby kind, with tiger stripes and leopard spots.

TABLE (22)
13 Prufrock 3 sky/Like a patient etherised upon a table;/Let us go, through certain half-deserted
15 Prufrock 67 me so digress?/Arms that lie along a table, or wrap about a shawl./And should I then
32 Hysteria 7 cloth over the rusty/green iron table, saying: 'If the lady and gentleman wish to
44 Cook Egg 4 /*Views of Oxford Colleges*/Lay on the table, with the knitting./Daguerreotypes and
56 Swee Night 13 Sweeney's knees/Slips and pulls the table cloth/Overturns a coffee-cup,/Reorganised
64 WL: Chess 83 candelabra/Reflecting light upon the table as/The glitter of her jewels rose to meet it,/
184 FQ: DrySal 13 /In the smell of grapes on the autumn table,/And the evening circle in the winter
588 Fable 42 made,/The jovial epicures sat down to table./The menus of that time I am afraid/I
588 Fable 59 gone out of use —/His feet upon the table superposed/Each wisht he had not eaten
261 MC Thomas 1 his best wine for a friend/at the table, his wife singing to the children? Those
266 MC Thomas 5 with matters of other urgency./On my table you will find/The papers in order, and the
305 FR Harry 27 ... the same pictures ... even the table,/The chairs, the sofa ... all in the same
346 FRDowning 8 thinks he left his cigarette-case on the table./Oh, there it is. Thank you. Good night,
349 FR 1m 13 *and MARY, and set a small portable table./From another door, enter DENMAN*
349 FR 3m 13 /*lighted candles, which she sets on the table. Exit DENMAN. AGATHA/and MARY*
349 FR 4m 13 *in single file round and round the table, clockwise./At each revolution they blow out*
362 CP Reilly 39 centre of reality. But, stretched on the table,/You are a piece of furniture in a repair
376 CP m 1 {}/[EDWARD *goes over to the table and inspects his game of Patience. He*
424 CP 4m 1 MAN *is arranging a buffet/table.* LAVINIA *enters from side door.*/{CM}
481 CC Lady E 38 name, Mr. Kaghan,/And ask for the table in the left hand corner:/It has the best
526 ES Monica 23 ago./Here's an armchair, there's the table;/There's the door ... and I hear someone
564 ES Carghil 36 be the first to put your cards on the table!/{M} Father, I think you should take your

TABLES (1)
107 Animula 4 or warm;/Moving between the legs of tables and of chairs,/Rising or falling, grasping

TACHES (1)
51 Restaurant 12 je lui ai donné des primevères.'/Les taches de son gilet montent au chiffre de

TACKS (1)
122 SA Sweeney 10 all the facts when you come to brass tacks:/Birth, and copulation, and death./I've

TACT (1)
505 CC Claude 12 the proceedings:/He's the very soul of tact and discretion./{MG} Certainly, Sir Claude,

TACTFULLY (1)
555 ES Piggott 6 the first opportunity of hinting —/Tactfully, of course — that you should not be

TACTLESS (1)
287 FR Violet 11 Really, Gerald, I must say you're very tactless,/And I think that Charles might have

TAIL (7)
143 Lines OM 3 more irritable than I./The whipping tail is not more still/Than when I smell the
186 FQ: DrySal 70 the fishermen sailing/Into the wind's tail, where the fog cowers?/We cannot think of a
209 NamingCats 15 /Else how can he keep up his tail perpendicular,/Or spread out his whiskers,
224 Mr Mistoff 24 is black/From his ears to the tip of his tail;/He can creep through the tiniest crack/He
228 Gus 25 how to act with my back and my tail;/With an hour of rehearsal, I never could
233 Skimble 63 gives you a wave of his long brown tail/Which says: 'I'll see you again!/You'll meet
241 MC Mess 36 that his horse will be deprived of its tail,/A single hair of which becomes a precious

TAILLE (1)
51 Restaurant 31 ce fut jadis un bel homme, de haute taille./Whispers of Immortality/Webster was

TAILOR'S (1)
557 ES Michael 36 debts?/{Mi} Oh, ordinary debts:/My tailor's bill, for instance./{LC} I expected that./

TAILS (1)
269 MC Chorus 34 I have seen/Grey necks twisting, rat tails twining, in the thick light of dawn. I have

TAINTED (2)
111 Xmas Trees 23 piety of the convert/Which may be tainted with a self-conceit/Displeasing to God
434 CP Alex 30 Yes, the patients died anyway;/Being tainted with the plague, they were not eaten./{L}

TAINTING (1)
294 FR Harry 24 stain sinks deeper through the skin/Tainting the flesh and discolouring the bone —/

TAKE (152)

19 Portrait	36	one definite 'false note.'/— Let us take the air, in a tobacco trance,/Admire the
20 Portrait	69	sit here, serving tea to friends....'/I take my hat: how can I make a cowardly
21 Portrait	113	a parrot, chatter like an ape./Let us take the air, in a tobacco trance —/Well! and
32 Hysteria	7	'If the lady and gentleman wish to take their/tea in the garden, if the lady and
32 Hysteria	8	if the lady and gentleman wish to take their tea in the/garden ...' I decided that if
50 Hippopot	25	and feed at once./I saw the 'potamus take wing/Ascending from the damp savannas,/
105 Song Sime	15	the time of sorrow is come?/They will take to the goat's path, and the fox's home,/
107 Animula	6	toys,/Advancing boldly, sudden to take alarm,/Retreating to the corner of arm and
136 5FingerEx3	8	and Wine,/Let the feathered mortals take/That which is their mortal due,/Pinching
148 Rock 1	58	to you: *Make perfect your will.*/I say: take no thought of the harvest,/But only of
149 Rock 1	77	were long ago done,/That you may take heart. Make perfect your will./Let me show
162 Rock 8	2	we welcome your words,/And we will take heart for the future,/Remembering the
166 Rock 10	11	self-given sacrifice of the snake. Take/Your way and be ye separate./Be not too
166 Rock 10	16	that you have light/Enough to take your step and find your foothold./O Light
171 FQ: BurntN	12	/Down the passage which we did not take/Towards the door we never opened/Into
191 FQ: Little	22	the route you would be likely to take/From the place you would be likely to
216 Jellicles	18	appears/They make their toilette and take their repose:/Jellicles wash behind their
219 Mung Rump	32	hurricane, and no sober person could take his oath/Was it Mungojerrie — or
245 MC Priest2	32	have fires laid in all your rooms/To take the chill off our English December,/Your
247 MC Tempt1	37	easy man lives to eat the best dinners./Take a friend's advice. Leave well alone,/Or
252 MC Thomas	20	ruled like an eagle over doves/Now take the shape of a wolf among wolves?/Pursue
257 MC Chorus	28	stifling scent of despair;/The forms take shape in the dark air:/Puss-purr of leopard,
269 MC Knight4	22	[*Exit*]/{K4} Priest! monk! and servant! take, hold, detain,/Restrain this man, in the
275 MC Chorus	21	the air! clean the sky! wash the wind! take stone from stone and wash them./The land
276 MC Chorus	17	the air! clean the sky! wash the wind! take the stone from the stone, take the skin
276 MC Chorus	17	wind! take the stone from the stone, take the skin from the arm, take the muscle
276 MC Chorus	17	the stone, take the skin from the arm, take the muscle from the bone, and wash them.
278 MC Knight2	31	to set matters to rights, that you/take issue. No one regrets the necessity for
290 FR Amy	15	For the sake of the future:/Harry is to take command at Wishwood/And I hope we can
295 FR Harry	19	away the self. I knew how you would take it./First of all, you isolate the single event/
298 FR Charles	22	times/When there's nothing to do but take the bull by the horns,/And this is one. {}/
299 FR Downing	20	only did it to frighten people./If you take my meaning — just for the effect./{C} I
314 FR Warburt	21	of another malady./{W} You mustn't take such a pessimistic view/Which is hardly
315 FR Amy	24	may come before we finish. Will you take me in, Doctor?/I think we are very much
320 FR Warburt	20	your return to Wishwood,/For you to take command at Wishwood,/And for that
322 FR Winch	36	part of the country/And stopped to take his bearings. We've got him at the Arms —
326 FR Violet	2	where to?/{V} He started out to take me to Cheltenham;/But I stopped him
326 FR Harry	20	imaginary course that life ought to take,/That you call normal. What you call the
333 FR Agatha	3	in that event: I stopped him./I can take no credit for a little common sense,/He
340 FR Amy	5	took my husband from me. Now you take my son./{Ag} What did I take? nothing
340 FR Agatha	6	you take my son./{Ag} What did I take? nothing that you ever had./What did I
340 FR Amy	11	/{A} The more rapacious, to take what I never had;/The more unpardonable,
341 FR Amy	23	my husband from me/And now you take my son./{Ag} Why should we quarrel for
341 FR Amy	38	You who took my husband, now you take my son./You take him from Wishwood,
341 FR Amy	39	husband, now you take my son./You take him from Wishwood, you take him from
341 FR Amy	39	/You take him from Wishwood, you take him from me,/You take him ... {}/[*Enter*
341 FR Amy	40	you take him from me,/You take him ... {}/[*Enter* MARY]/{M} Excuse me,
342 FR Agatha	35	only,/Do you think that I would take the responsibility/Of tempting them over
345 FR Harry	11	as happen to Arthur and John:/Take care of *them*. My address, mother,/Will be
345 FR Mary	18	Mary./{M} Good-bye, Harry. Take care of yourself. {}/[*Exit* HARRY]/{A} At
347 FR Downing	11	There's no harm in *them*,/I'll take my oath. Will that be all, Miss?/{Ag} That
358 CP Celia	30	/{C} No, I'm sorry, Peter;/I've got to take a taxi./{J} You come with me, Peter:/You
360 CP Reilly	9	/{UG} This is an occasion./May I take another drink?/{E} Whisky?/{UG} Gin./{E}
361 CP Reilly	8	the truth on the telephone./It will all take time that you can't well spare;/But I put it
362 CP Reilly	35	mercy of a malevolent staircase./Or, take a surgical operation./In consultation with
363 CP Reilly	13	other people./Most of the time we take ourselves for granted,/As we have to, and
366 CP Peter	22	/{P} Well, at least you must let me take you down in the lift./{J} No, you stop and
371 CP Edward	9	six months' time. There it is./You can take it or leave it./{P} But what am I to do?/{E}
372 CP Alex	29	minutes./Now I'll be going, and I'll take Peter with me./{P} Edward, I've taken too
378 CP Julia	9	Lavinia?/Well, come on quickly. And take a taxi./You know, you're looking
380 CP Edward	10	what it was, no doubt./{E} I *didn't* take you as a passing diversion!/If you want to
380 CP Edward	12	of passing diversions/How did you take Peter?/{C} Peter? Peter who?/{E} Peter
381 CP Celia	2	you, Edward:/You are not entitled to take any interest/Now, in *my* future. I only
384 CP Edward	5	you. This is a different occasion./{E} I take it that as you have come alone/You have

386 CP	Reilly	8	The strangers./As for myself, I shall take the precaution/Of leaving by the service
395 CP	Lavinia	7	to speak./Anyway, I'm prepared to take you as you are./{E} You mean, you are
395 CP	Edward	8	/{E} You mean, you are prepared to take me/As I was, or as you think I am./But
395 CP	Lavinia	30	part to play,/With another face, to take people in./{E} One of the most infuriating
397 CP	Edward	19	I shall make my own choice;/Not take one whom you choose. How do I know/
402 CP	Edward	10	else. I came here as a patient./If you take no interest in my case, I can go elsewhere./
404 CP	Edward	21	making. I am in your hands./I cannot take any further responsibility./{R} Many
407 CP	Reilly	31	omitting the important facts./Let me take your husband first. {}/[To EDWARD]/{R}
412 CP	Julia	14	She cannot believe/That you will take her seriously./{R} That is not uncommon./
414 CP	Reilly	31	are other states of mind, which we take to be delusion,/But which we have to
417 CP	Reilly	31	actions/What there is to give and take. They do not repine;/Are contented with
418 CP	Reilly	40	lonelier than the other. But those who take the other/Can forget their loneliness. You
419 CP	Celia	39	nine o'clock./{C} What do I need to take with me?/{R} Nothing./Everything you
420 CP	Julia	34	a great risk./{J} We must always take risks./That is our destiny. Since you
421 CP	Julia	2	None./{J} Very well then. We must take the risk./All we could do was to give them
425 CP	Lavinia	29	/And the man won't be able to take the tray about,/So they'll go away again.
428 CP	Alex	19	Christian converts,/And, naturally, take a different view./They trap the monkeys.
431 CP	Julia	40	persuade your casting director/To take us all over? We're all very typical./{P} No,
433 CP	Julia	5	Boltwell to California/Why can't you take me?/{P} We're not taking Boltwell./I
435 CP	Peter	4	best you could./{P} When did she ... take up this career?/{J} Two years ago./{P} Two
438 CP	Reilly	9	terrors./But that world does not take the place of this one./Do you imagine that
439 CP	Julia	11	one kind or another,/And then must take the consequences. Celia chose/A way of
446 CC	Claude	6	things,/And I think he's beginning to take a keen interest./{E} And getting over his
447 CC	Claude	33	of it./And I rather hope that she will take to him at once:/If so, she is certain to come
447 CC	Claude	37	know that he's very musical./She can take him to concerts. But don't overdo it!/{E}
453 CC	Eggers	3	if you give Miss Angel an inch/She'll take an ell./{L} L. for Lucasta./Go on, Eggy.
453 CC	Lucasta	9	seen with you in public./You may take me out to dinner. A working girl like me/Is
454 CC	Kaghan	7	Colby./He's had enough for one day. Take my advice, Colby./Never allow Lucasta
454 CC	Kaghan	10	with her;/She's hard as nails. Now I'll take her off your hands./I'll show you how it's
454 CC	Kaghan	12	/I'm going to make a day of it, and take you out to tea./{L} I'm dying for my tea.
454 CC	Lucasta	15	Colby./I'll ring you up, and let you take me out to lunch. {}/[Exit LUCASTA]/{K}
454 CC	Kaghan	16	out to lunch. {}/[Exit LUCASTA]/{K} Take it easy, Colby. You'll get used to her. {}/
457 CC	Eggers	14	besides, there's the Customs. That'll take her a time,/From my experience. {}/LADY
463 CC	Colby	27	/The person I used to be, returns to take possession:/And I am again the
470 CC	Colby	19	learn about music —/And that won't take you long — and hear good performers,/
479 CC	Lucasta	2	angel at the moment, B./You're to take me out to dinner. And I'm dying for a
480 CC	Kaghan	9	spur of the moment,/But you'd never take a leap in the dark;/You'd keep me on the
481 CC	Lady E	32	of salad./You remember, I made you take a note of the address;/And I don't believe
482 CC	Lady E	16	of society./So naturally, they want to take you up./I can speak more freely, as an
488 CC	Claude	31	of Colby,/And that he might come to take the place of your own child,/If you got to
488 CC	Claude	39	want a son./{SC} I'd never want to take your son away from you./Perhaps you
490 CC	Colby	35	for that:/God forbid! but we must take the consequences./At the time when I was
491 CC	Lady E	4	come to me./Claude! I don't want to take away from you/The son you thought was
492 CC	Colby	1	to marry./You may be right. I can't take account of that./But now I want to know
494 CC	Lady E	6	if he were yours ... he could still take the place/Of my son: and so he could be
495 CC	Lady E	13	I do believe,/For married people to take anything for granted./{SC} That was a very
497 CC	Eggers	32	A natural line for Mr. Simpkins to take,/If I may say so. Of course, we might
499 CC	Lucasta	21	we haven't much time./{L} It won't take much time. I'm going to marry B./{SC} To
501 CC	Eggers	27	suggestion?/Though first of all I must take the occasion/To wish Miss Angel every
505 CC	Eggers	17	what I should call it, Mrs. Guzzard./I take it, Sir Claude, I should open the
507 CC	Eggers	5	question:/Did you, at any time, take in a child —/A child, that is, of parents
507 CC	Guzzard	8	such conditions?/{MG} Yes, I did take in a child./My husband and I were childless
508 CC	Eggers	2	that you might tell her so./{E} Don't take this as a personal reflection,/Mrs. Guzzard.
511 CC	Lady E	37	your engagement./Lucasta, I shall take charge of your wedding./{L} We'd meant
517 CC	Colby	24	That is what I want. If anyone will take me./{E} If so, I happen to know of a
518 CC	Eggers	3	Mr. Simpkins —/I hope you won't take this as an impertinence —/I don't see you
518 CC	Guzzard	35	Only to a taxi./Do you mind if I take my leave, Sir Claude?/I'm no longer needed
519 CC	Kaghan	21	to you ... if you'd let us;/And we'd take the responsibility of meaning it. {}/
526 ES	Charles	35	to him./He seems so placidly to take it for granted/That you don't really care
528 ES	Monica	38	that the winter in Jamaica/Will never take place. 'Make the reservations'/Selby said,
529 ES	Monica	3	the House is sitting./And you can take me out, if Father can spare me./But he'll
530 ES	Ld Clav	11	they tell me to be cautious,/To take life easily. Take life easily!/It's like telling a
530 ES	Ld Clav	11	me to be cautious,/To take life easily. Take life easily!/It's like telling a man he
530 ES	Ld Clav	13	/When the last thing he wants is to take a train for anywhere!/No, I've not the
532 ES	Lambert	8	here./{L} Very good, my Lord./Shall I take the trolley, Miss Monica?/{M} Yes, thank

532 ES	Monica	21	Lambert to tell you that you have to	take a trunk call./Come, Charles. Will you bring
533 ES	Gomez	16	/And I thought, now's the time to	take a long holiday,/Let's say a rest cure —
535 ES	Ld Clav	22	And what about you?/{LC} I don't	take it, thank you./{G} A reformed character!/
535 ES	Gomez	33	for myself another personality/And to	take another name. Think what that means —/
535 ES	Gomez	34	name. Think what that means —/To	take another name. {}/[*Gets up and helps*
537 ES	Gomez	18	and I knew it./When you started to	take me up at Oxford/I've no doubt your
538 ES	Gomez	30	you/But of course didn't have to	take your advice .../I've made a point, you see,
541 ES	Ld Clav	34	minutes' time./{LC} I'll be ready to	take it. {}/[*Exit* LAMBERT]/{G} Ah, the
545 ES	Monica	21	I see her coming from the house./Take your newspaper and start reading to me. {}
546 ES	Piggott	27	here. When you go in to lunch/Just	take a glance around the dining-room:/Nobody
548 ES	Monica	13	see you're shamming they'll have to	take the hint. {}/[*Exit*]/*A moment later*, LORD
550 ES	Ld Clav	31	I don't understand/Is why you should	take the first opportunity,/Finding me here, to
554 ES	Carghil	6	bear it?/If I go at once, perhaps she'll	take the hint/And leave us alone tomorrow./
555 ES	Piggott	5	to meet you, so I thought/That I'd	take the first opportunity of hinting —/
556 ES	Monica	5	/He's apt to be sullen and quick to	take offence./So I hope you'll be patient./{LC}
557 ES	Michael	16	always came off — the tips I didn't	take./{LC} And the ones you did take?/{Mi} Not
557 ES	Ld Clav	17	take./{LC} And the ones you did	take?/{Mi} Not so well, for some reason./The
564 ES	Gomez	4	agree, Dick?/— This young lady I	take to be your daughter?/And this is your son?/
564 ES	Monica	37	table!/{M} Father, I think you should	take your rest now./— I must explain that the
573 ES	Carghil	34	lucky man, to get a girl like Monica./I	take a great interest in her future./Fancy! I've
580 ES	Monica	5	you know, even by air mail./{M}	Take the card, Charles. If I write to you,
582 ES	Ld Clav	19	her, Charles,/Now and always. I shall	take a stroll./{M} At this time of day? You'll not
583 ES	Monica	28	/In you; I am a part of you. Now	take me to my father. {}/CURTAIN

TAKEN (42)

37 Gerontion		17	head among windy spaces./Signs are	taken for wonders. 'We would see a sign!'/The
105 Song Sime		11	for the poor,/Have given and	taken honour and ease./There went never any
164 Rock 9		23	and feelings, words that have	taken the place of thoughts and feelings,/There
190 FQ: DrySal		208	either, but something given/And	taken, in a lifetime's death in love,/Ardour and
196 FQ: Little		195	inherit from the fortunate/We have	taken from the defeated/What they had to leave
234 Ad-dress		30	undignified./He's very easily	taken in —/Just chuck him underneath the chin/
257 MC Chorus		13	without milk in summer,/Our labour	taken away from us,/Our sins made heavier
274 MC Thomas		2	/It is out of time that my decision is	taken/If you call that decision/To which my
277 MC Knight3		8	now. The fact is that/we knew we had	taken on a pretty stiff job; I'll only speak for/
278 MC Knight2		2	people, as I can see, and not to be	taken in by/emotional clap-trap. I therefore ask
285 FR	Amy	6	was once so warm, O Light that was	taken for granted/When I was young and
289 FR	Gerald	8	has happened doesn't matter./He's	taken his medicine, I've no doubt./Let him
293 FR	Amy	6	with advice/Which I have never	taken. Now it is your business./I have only
302 FR	Chorus	10	that the world is what we have always	taken it to be./{A} Ivy! Violet! has Arthur or
304 FR	Mary	6	now;/But I really wish that I'd	taken your advice/And tried for a fellowship,
307 FR	Harry	35	do not know what it is to have hope	taken from you,/Or to fling it away, to join the
318 FR	Harry	15	guilty./I think that the things that are	taken for granted/At home, make a deeper
340 FR	Amy	13	taunt me with not having it./Had you	taken what I had, you would have left me at
372 CP	Peter	30	take Peter with me./{P} Edward, I've	taken too much of your time,/And you want to
380 CP	Celia	7	had shared something wonderful/Had	taken them only as a passing diversion./Oh, I
392 CP	Lavinia	40	since I've been away/I see that I've	taken you much too seriously./And now I can
408 CP	Reilly	33	behaviour to-day./{R} A point well	taken./But permit me to remark that my
411 CP	Lavinia	3	go there. The proprietor/Who has just	taken over, is a friend of Alex's./I could go
412 CP	Julia	16	/{J} Or that she deserves to be	taken seriously./{R} That is most uncommon./
420 CP	Reilly	33	to mirror, reflecting vanity./I have	taken a great risk./{J} We must always take
434 CP	Alex	17	again./But Celia Coplestone, she was	taken./When our people got there, they
436 CP	Peter	8	/{P} I'm sorry. I don't believe I've	taken in/All that you've been saying. But I'm
451 CC	Eggers	12	ways;/And Lady Elizabeth has never	taken to him./But you, Mr. Simpkins, that's
452 CC	Eggers	26	know, Miss Angel,/Mr. Simpkins has	taken over my duties./{L} And does he know
460 CC	Lady E	13	Claude, I'm glad to find/That you've	taken my advice./{SC} Your advice? About
461 CC	Claude	38	to tell./The point is that she's	taken a fancy to you/And so she lays claim to
462 CC	Claude	1	to you. That's very satisfactory./She's	taken it for granted that you should have the
495 CC	Claude	15	intelligent remark./Perhaps I have	taken too much for granted/About you,
498 CC	Eggers	19	than one baby./{E} She might have	taken in another one/As a temporary
505 CC	Eggers	40	known it to happen./{E} — Who was	taken charge of by the father./That is to say,
506 CC	Eggers	10	know the name of the lady/Who had	taken the child. Or rather, had forgotten it./She
507 CC	Guzzard	15	/Otherwise, I should not have	taken him./But he was brought to me by a third
508 CC	Guzzard	27	and eager to adopt a child./They had	taken a fancy to him. So they adopted him./
524 ES	Monica	10	your own fault./You should have	taken me to some other restaurant/Instead of to
531 ES	Ld Clav	15	and a half/With an inset, a portrait	taken twenty years ago./In five years' time, it
558 ES	Michael	8	retain any man on his staff/Who'd	taken to gambling. Called me a gambler!/Said

572 ES Ld Clav 38   to you, Monica:/That is the first step taken towards my freedom,/And perhaps the

TAKES (16)
185 FQ: DrySal   59   days and hours,/While emotion takes to itself the emotionless/Years of living
228 Gus   12   joins his friends at their club/(Which takes place at the back of the neighbouring pub)
286 FR   m 29   *with sherry and whisky.* CHARLES *takes sherry and* GERALD *whisky.*]/{C} That's
314 FR Warburt   9   practitioner doesn't get younger./It takes me back longer than you can remember/
343 FR   Mary   17   it began;/But I deceived myself. It takes so many years/To learn that one is dead!
348 FR Chorus   7   like to climb a stair, and find that it takes us down./We do not like to walk out of a
356 CP   Julia 29   /But I'm really very serious. Lavinia takes me seriously./I believe that's the reason
411 CP   m 35   Not in this capacity. {}/[EDWARD *takes out his cheque-book.* REILLY *raises his*
421 CP   m 39   now. I'll speak to Miss Barraway. {}/[*Takes up house-telephone*]/{R} Miss Barraway,
448 CC Claude   21   his identity/Depends on how she takes to him. This afternoon/She will only learn
449 CC Claude   27   /{E} True./{SC} But I don't think she takes much notice of Miss Angel./She just
466 CC Claude   14   bearable. It's all I have./I suppose it takes the place of religion:/Just as my wife's
524 ES Charles   22   like. But a man does feel a fool/If he takes you to a place where he's utterly unknown
548 ES   3m 14   *nearby, composes/herself and takes out her knitting.*/[*after a pause*]./{MC} I
568 ES Ld Clav 6   /Beyond anything of which the law takes cognisance:/Temporary failures,
580 ES   Gomez   4   can always reach him there./But it takes some days, you know, even by air mail./

TAKING (26)
14 Prufrock   34   visions and revisions,/Before the taking of a toast and tea./In the room the
107 Animula   8   arm and knee,/Eager to be reassured, taking pleasure/In the fragrant brilliance of the
191 FQ: Little   22   /Zero summer?/If you came this way,/Taking the route you would be likely to take/
192 FQ: Little   42   in England./If you came this way,/Taking any route, starting from anywhere,/At
197 FQ: Little   220   is right (where every word is at home,/Taking its place to support the others,/The
235 Ad-dress   44   he/Resents familiarity./I bow, and taking off my hat,/Ad-dress him in this form: O
298 FR Charles 2   we can't afford to be squeamish/In taking hold of anything that comes to hand./If
338 FR Agatha   35   In a world of fugitives/The person taking the opposite direction/Will appear to run
345 FR Gerald   7   you will have to be careful./You're taking Downing with you?/{H} Oh, yes, I'm
345 FR   Harry   8   Downing with you?/{H} Oh, yes, I'm taking Downing./You need not fear that I am in
371 CP Edward   34   Celia./I don't know why I should be taking all this trouble/To protect you from the
395 CP Edward   39   can fight each other,/Instead of each taking his corner of the cage./Well, it's a better
404 CP   Reilly 10   you talk as long as you please,/And taking note of what you do not say./{E} I once
407 CP   Reilly 19   such as you are the self-deceivers/Taking infinite pains, exhausting their energy,/
415 CP   Celia   15   them. I haven't hurt *her*./I wasn't taking anything away from her —/Anything she
416 CP   Celia   15   he to me — and the giving and the taking/Seemed so right: not in terms of
416 CP   Celia   21   that there had been neither giving nor taking/But that we had merely made use of each
417 CP   Reilly 30   of themselves and others,/Giving and taking, in the usual actions/What there is to give
429 CP   Julia   12   /{J} I wondered where you were taking us, with your monkeys./I thought I was
433 CP   Julia   4   way we do it./{J} But, Peter;/If you're taking Boltwell to California/Why can't you
433 CP   Peter   6   can't you take me?/{P} We're not taking Boltwell./We reconstruct a Boltwell./{J}
452 CC Lucasta 28   duties?/Have you prepared him for taking *me* over?/Did you know that, Colby? I'm
470 CC Lucasta 22   do make difficulties!/But what about taking me to a concert?/{C} Only the other day,
527 ES Charles   18   for convalescents/To which you're taking him? And what after that?/{M} There are
538 ES Gomez   28   account for your leaving politics/And taking a conspicuous job in the City/Where the
565 ES Gomez   18   you./{Mi} Delighted, I'm sure./{G} Taking a holiday?/You're in business in

TALE (1)
595 Grad 14   2   more delay;/Thus is the end of every tale: 'Farewell',/A word that echoes like a

TALENT (3)
32 Hysteria   2   teeth were only accidental stars with a talent/for squad-drill. I was drawn in by short
380 CP   Celia 24   I cared for him./I thought he had talent; I saw that he was lonely;/I thought that I
538 ES   Gomez 1   in me,/And, equally unfortunate, a talent for penmanship./Hence, as you have just

TALES (3)
159 Rock 6   3   known a Christian,/To believe these tales of Christian persecution./It is hard for
163 Rock 8   31   something left that was more than the tales/Of old men on winter evenings./Only the
376 CP   Julia 34   is absolutely deadly./I could tell such tales of his poisoning people./Now, my dear,

TALK (75)
15 Prufrock   89   /Among the porcelain, among some talk of you and me,/Would it have been worth
21 Portrait   123   with a 'dying fall'/Now that we talk of dying —/And should I have the right to
31 Apollinax   17   hard turf/As his dry and passionate talk devoured the afternoon./'He is a charming
44 Cook Egg   11   shall meet Sir Philip Sidney/And have talk with Coriolanus/And other heroes of that
124 SA   Doris   3   /{Do} Oh Mr. Sweeney, please don't talk,/I cut the cards before you came/And I
124 SA Sweeney   36   what did he do?/That don't apply./Talk to live men about what they do./He used
125 SA Sweeney   2   /But I've gotta use words when I talk to you./But here's what I was going to say./
125 SA Sweeney   21   life is death/I gotta use words when I talk to you/But if you understand or if you
245 MC Priest2 1   us for France./{P2} What a way to talk at such a juncture!/You are foolish,

247 MC	Thomas	6	need not walk warily./{T} You talk of seasons that are past. I remember/Not
276 MC	Chorus	5	by day that ends in sleep;/But the talk in the market-place, the hand on the
289 FR	Amy	18	/{A} Much too late./If he wants to talk about it, that's another matter;/But I don't
290 FR	Agatha	32	world around the corner/The wind's talk in the dry holly-tree/The inclination of the
293 FR	Harry	15	no change!/You all of you try to talk as if nothing had happened,/And yet you
294 FR	Agatha	13	Harry, best tell us as you can:/Talk in your own language, without stopping to
294 FR	Harry	26	it is unspeakable,/Untranslatable: I talk in general terms/Because the particular has
296 FR	Charles	25	among strangers, with no one to talk to./I suspect it is simply that the wish to get
296 FR	Charles	28	believe that all he needs is someone to talk to,/To get it off his mind. I'll have a talk to
296 FR	Charles	29	to,/To get it off his mind. I'll have a talk to him tomorrow./{A} Most certainly not,
296 FR	Gerald	38	I'll have a word with him./He can talk to Harry, and Harry need have no
298 FR	Agatha	11	/We had better leave Charles to talk to Downing/And pursue his own methods.
299 FR	Charles	15	she had the courage./{C} Did she ever talk of suicide?/{Do} Oh yes, she did, every now
299 FR	Downing	17	/But in my opinion, it is those that talk/That are the least likely. To my way of
307 FR	Mary	27	being superfluous./But why should I talk about my commonplace troubles?/They
315 FR	Warburt	11	is something real./{W} Well, let's not talk of such matters./How did we get onto the
317 FR	Harry	9	matters rather more difficult./But talk about it, if you like./{W} You don't
318 FR	Harry	28	must let me explain, and then you can talk./I don't know why, but just this evening/I
318 FR	Harry	35	what I am saying./But if you want to talk, at least you can tell me/Something useful.
320 FR	Harry	4	your mother's health that I wanted to talk to you./I must tell you, Harry, that
321 FR	Warburt	6	much like you./And now, Harry, let's talk about yourself./{H} I never saw a
324 FR	Harry	38	That I choose to be talking. I will not talk yours./{A} You looked like your father/
356 CP	Julia	31	away —So that I could make you talk. Perhaps she's in the pantry/Listening to all
358 CP	Julia	1	dine alone with me/On Friday, and talk to me about everything./{E} Everything?/{J}
358 CP	Julia	11	like the other people —/But you're to talk to me. So that's all settled./And now I must
359 CP	Edward	34	{E} Don't go yet./I very much want to talk to somebody;/And it's easier to talk to a
359 CP	Edward	35	talk to somebody;/And it's easier to talk to a person you don't know./The fact is,
364 CP	Edward	24	it seems to me — when we began to talk/I was not sure I wanted her; and now I
365 CP	Julia	31	how he got here./{J} But what did you talk about/Or were you singing songs all the
366 CP	Julia	23	down in the lift./{J} No, you stop and talk to Edward. I'm not helpless yet./And
369 CP	Peter	5	girl I'd ever known/And not easy to talk to, on that occasion./{E} Did you see her
369 CP	Peter	13	/And when I did, I got no chance to talk to her./{E} You and Celia were asked for
371 CP	Peter	2	/Your congratulations. I had to talk to someone./And I have been telling you of
371 CP	Edward	23	/[*Into telephone*]/{E} Hello! ... I can't talk now .../Yes, there is ... Well then, I'll ring
377 CP	Julia	2	we'll see what I can do. You stay and talk to Edward. {}/[*Exit* JULIA]/{C} But what
377 CP	Edward	10	know who he is./But I had some talk with him, when the rest of you had left,/
379 CP	Celia	18	fair to *me*!/You can stand there and talk about being fair to *me*!/{E} But for Lavinia
380 CP	Edward	21	so./He came back this evening to talk to me about it./{C} But this is ridiculous! I
380 CP	Celia	28	rather conceited./But why should we talk about Peter? All that matters/Is, that you
386 CP	Edward	28	/{E} Oh, my God, what shall we talk about?/We can't sit here in silence./{C} Oh,
388 CP	Lavinia	36	might as well sit down./What shall we talk about?/{E} Peter's going to America./{P}
392 CP	Edward	8	know why not. So what are we to talk about?/{L} There is one thing I ought to
402 CP	Edward	7	of redeeming from ruin./{E} You talk as if I was capable of action:/If I were,
404 CP	Reilly	9	observing you,/And letting you talk as long as you please,/And taking note of
405 CP	Lavinia	26	Sir Henry!/I said I would come to talk about my husband:/I didn't say I was
417 CP	Reilly	34	that brings together/For casual talk before the fire/Two people who know they
438 CP	Reilly	8	and images. To speak about it/We talk of darkness, labyrinths, Minotaur terrors./
439 CP	Lavinia	27	—/You and me and Edward ... to talk about Celia./{P} Thanks very much. But
474 CC	Lucasta	35	music,/Not in order to be able to talk about it,/But ... partly, to enjoy it ... and
481 CC	Kaghan	12	that *you* like./— For a change, let's talk about Lucasta. {}/[*rising*]./{L} If you want
494 CC	Lady E	30	perhaps I don't. But I wish you would talk/Sometimes to me as if I did understand,/
508 CC	Lady E	12	with your legal training,/Should talk about straws! Colby is my son./{MG} In the
511 CC	Lucasta	2	to register .../{L} You don't need to talk that language any longer:/Just say you're
516 CC	Claude	17	But, Colby/Don't you remember a talk we had —/So very long ago! — when we
525 ES	Charles	11	shopping with you./But how can one *talk* on a shopping expedition —/Except to guess
525 ES	Charles	16	But you know I won't get a chance to talk to you./You know that. Now that your
525 ES	Monica	31	it until he's called for tea./So why not talk now? Though I know very well/What it is
529 ES	Monica	4	/But he'll simply love having you to talk to!/{C} I know he's used to seeing me
530 ES	Ld Clav	10	up, Monica, and you know it./They talk of rest, these doctors, Charles; they tell me
535 ES	Gomez	12	has taught me./It's nonsense to talk of trusting people/In general. What does
536 ES	Gomez	15	learn English — it's useful;/I always talk to them in English./But do they think in
545 ES	Ld Clav	17	that very ominous. When people talk like that/It indicates a latent desire to
551 ES	Carghil	15	I am,/I shouldn't want to come and talk about the past./You're wrong, you know.
551 ES	Carghil	17	know. It's both pain and pleasure/To talk about the past — about you and me./These
565 ES	Monica	5	/{M} No, I think you've had enough talk for to-day./Michael, as you're staying so

TANGANYIKA (1)
506 CC   Lady E   5   He was run over. By a rhinoceros/In Tanganyika./{SC} That's not relevant./Leave it
TANGIBLE (1)
316 FR   Gerald   5   struggle against it./{G} I am used to tangible danger, but only to what I can
TANGLE (2)
 42 Swee Erect   7   /Reviewing the insurgent gales/Which tangle Ariadne's hair/And swell with haste the
552 ES   Carghil   25   were clear./You got out of a tangle for a large cash payment/And no
TANGLED (1)
329 FR   Chorus   17   the best of a bad job/All twined and tangled together, all are recorded./There is no
TANGLING (1)
605 Narcissus   23   its branches among each other/And tangling its roots among each other./Then he
TAPS (1)
256 MC   Tempts   31   lock and bolt?/{4T} Is it rain that taps at the window, is it wind that pokes at the
TAR (1)
 69 WL: Fire S   267   and gold./The river sweats/Oil and tar/The barges drift/With the turning tide/Red
TARDY (1)
 21 Portrait   120   /Or whether wise or foolish, tardy or too soon .../Would she not have the
TARNISHED (1)
244 MC   Chorus   25 us and leave us be, in our humble and tarnished frame of existence, leave us; do not
TART (1)
136 5FingerEx4   12 he presses/The juice of the gooseberry tart./How delightful to meet Mr. Hodgson!/
TARTAR (1)
134 Wind   12   /Here, across death's other river/The Tartar horsemen shake their spears./Five-Finger
TASTE (7)
 38 Gerontion   59   /I have lost my sight, smell, hearing, taste and touch:/How should I use them for
 43 Swee Erect   36   principles/And deprecate the lack of taste/Observing that hysteria/Might easily be
150 Rock 1   118 /But noise without speech, food without taste./Without delay, without haste/We would
235 Ad-dress   59   —/He's sure to have his personal taste./(I know a Cat, who makes a habit/Of
606 Narcissus   30   old man/Knowing at the end the taste of his own whiteness/The horror of his
270 MC   Chorus   1   still living, with the strong salt taste of living things under the sea; I have tasted
286 FR   Charles   28   eating;/They've lost their sense of taste and smell/Because of their cocktails and
TASTED (3)
269 MC   Chorus   30   over, huge and ridiculous. I have tasted/The savour of putrid flesh in the spoon. I
270 MC   Chorus   1   of living things under the sea; I have tasted/The living lobster, the crab, the oyster,
375 CP   Edward   14   ... it was marvellous./I've never tasted anything like it .../Yes, that's very
TASTELESSNESS (1)
194 FQ: Little   135   offering no promise/But bitter tastelessness of shadow fruit/As body and soul
TASTES (5)
537 ES   Gomez   39   father found for me,/And expensive tastes — which you had fostered in me,/And,
542 ES   Gomez   5   days/When you taught me expensive tastes. Now it's my turn./I can have cigars sent
542 ES   Ld Clav   23   pretend that I taught you expensive tastes:/If you had not had those tastes already/
542 ES   Ld Clav   24   tastes:/If you had not had those tastes already/You would hardly have
571 ES   Ld Clav   9   his admiration?/I led him to acquire tastes beyond his means:/So he became a forger.
TATTERED (1)
177 FQ: ECoker   13   field-mouse trots/And to shake the tattered arras woven with a silent motto./In my
TATTING (1)
210 Old Gumbie   12   teaches them music, crocheting and tatting./I have a Gumbie Cat in mind, her name
TATTOO (1)
211 Old Gumbie   36   —/And she's even created a Beetles' Tattoo./So for Old Gumbie Cats let us now give
TAUGHT (7)
249 MC   Tempt2   2   richly rules./This is a sentence not taught in the schools./To set down the great,
394 CP   Lavinia   39   is surprising./Now who could have taught you to answer back like that?/{E} I have
415 CP   Celia   20   conventional —/I had always been taught to disbelieve in sin./Oh, I don't mean
460 CC   Claude   4 I thought that the doctor in Lausanne taught mind control?/{LE} No, Claude, he only
535 ES   Gomez   11   /I use the term as experience has taught me./It's nonsense to talk of trusting
542 ES   Gomez   5   used to be in the old days/When you taught me expensive tastes. Now it's my turn./I
542 ES   Ld Clav   23   free moral agent./You pretend that I taught you expensive tastes:/If you had not had
TAUNT (1)
340 FR   Amy   12   had;/The more unpardonable, to taunt me with not having it./Had you taken
TAVERN (2)
103 Journ Magi   26   in the meadow./Then we came to a tavern with vine-leaves over the lintel,/Six hands
282 MC   Chorus   10   the fire in the thatch, the fist in the tavern, the push into the canal,/Less than we
TAX (1)
587 Fable   6   /Who levied on all travelers his tax;/Nearby this hamlet was a monastery/

TAXES (3)

244 MC	Chorus	13	scandals,/We have been afflicted with taxes,/We have had laughter and gossip,/Several
292 FR	Amy	22	some legal business, a question about taxes —/But I think you would rather wait till
343 FR	Amy	25	/Resist the wind? fight with increasing taxes/And unpaid rents and tithes? nourish

TAXI (12)

68 WL: Fire S		217	when the human engine waits/Like a taxi throbbing waiting,/I Tiresias, though blind,
358 CP	Celia	30	I'm sorry, Peter;/I've got to take a taxi./{J} You come with me, Peter:/You can get
358 CP	Julia	32	with me, Peter:/You can get *me* a taxi, and then I can drop you./I expect you on
366 CP	Julia	12	/And now I must fly. I've kept the taxi waiting./Come along, Peter./{P} I hope you
378 CP	Julia	9	/Well, come on quickly. And take a taxi./You know, you're looking absolutely
391 CP	Julia	2	all go back to *my* house. Peter, call a taxi. {}/[*Exit* PETER]/{J} We'll have a cocktail
391 CP	Peter	32	{}/[*Enter* PETER]/{P} I've got a taxi, Julia./{J} Splendid! Good-bye! {}/[*Exeunt*
411 CP	Lavinia	16	go home./{L} Then we can share a taxi, and be economical./Edward, have you
412 CP	Julia	6	her at the door/And went on in the taxi, round the corner;/Waited a moment, and
518 CC	Guzzard	31	Teddington. Colby,/Will you get me a taxi to go to Waterloo?/{C} Get you a taxi? Yes,
518 CC	Colby	32	taxi to go to Waterloo?/{C} Get you a taxi? Yes, Aunt Sarah;/But I should see you
518 CC	Guzzard	34	you home./{MG} Home? Only to a taxi./Do you mind if I take my leave, Sir

TE (3)

51 Restaurant		7	baveux, à la croupe arrondie,/Je te prie, au moins, ne bave pas dans la soupe)./
51 Restaurant		21	Mais alors, tu as ton vautour!/Va t'en te décrotter les rides du visage;/Tiens, ma
281 MC	m	7	Saint in Canterbury. {}/[*while a* Te Deum *is sung in Latin by a choir in the*

TEA (41)

14 Prufrock		34	/Before the taking of a toast and tea./In the room the women come and go/
15 Prufrock		79	beside you and me./Should I, after tea and cakes and ices,/Have the strength to
15 Prufrock		88	/After the cups, the marmalade, the tea,/Among the porcelain, among some talk of
19 Portrait		51	smile, of course,/And go on drinking tea./'Yet with these April sunsets, that somehow
20 Portrait		68	journey's end./I shall sit here, serving tea to friends..../'I take my hat: how can I make
21 Portrait		108	is not too late./I shall sit here, serving tea to friends.'/And I must borrow every
32 Hysteria		8	lady and gentleman wish to take their/tea in the garden, if the lady and gentleman
32 Hysteria		8	lady and gentleman wish to take their tea in the/garden ...' I decided that if the
37 Gerontion		13	/The woman keeps the kitchen, makes tea,/Sneezes at evening, poking the peevish
189 FQ: DrySal		194	fingers; release omens/By sortilege, or tea leaves, riddle the inevitable/With playing
204 de la Mare		9	/Recount their exploits at the nursery tea/And when the lamps are lit and curtains
233 Skimble		42	brightly/'Do you like your morning tea weak or strong?'/But Skimble's just behind
233 Skimble		52	/Every now and then he has a cup of tea/With perhaps a drop of Scotch while he's
603 Spleen		7	digression./Evening, lights, and tea!/Children and cats in the alley;/Dejection
285 FR	2m	1	/PART I/*The drawing-room, after tea. An afternoon in late March.*/Scene I/AMY,
285 FR	Violet	21	chilly deck-chair and the strong cold tea —/The strong cold stewed bad Indian tea./
285 FR	Violet	22	—/The strong cold stewed bad Indian tea./{C} That's not Amy's style at all. We are
288 FR	Ivy	9	had your cake and your presents at tea./{A} This is a very particular occasion/As
288 FR	Agatha	24	Wishwood —/The nursery tea, the school holiday,/The daring feats on the
291 FR	Violet	5	Bumpus, at the Vicar's American Tea./{Ch} Yet we are here at Amy's command,
379 CP	Peter	36	or solitude. And we sometimes had tea/And once or twice dined together./{E} And
426 CP	Julia	33	and drink!/And I've had to miss my tea, and I'm simply ravenous/And dying of
454 CC	Kaghan	12	make a day of it, and take you out to tea./{L} I'm dying for my tea. The strain of this
454 CC	Lucasta	13	you out to tea./{L} I'm dying for my tea. The strain of this crisis/Has been too much
457 CC	Lady E	26	want it now. Just bring me some tea./Nothing with it. No, I forgot:/You haven't
457 CC	Lady E	28	You haven't learned yet how to make tea properly./A cup of black coffee. Is Sir
460 CC	Lady E	28	you with my husband./You shall have tea with me tomorrow,/And then I shall tell you
524 ES	Monica	2	home to-day?/{M} You'll see him at tea./{C} But if I'm not going to have you to
524 ES	Charles	4	really no point in my staying to tea. {}/[*Enter* MONICA *and* CHARLES
524 ES	Monica	5	*parcels*]/{M} But you *must* stay to tea. That was understood/When you said you
524 ES	Monica	28	the question/Of your staying to tea. As you practically promised./{C} What you
525 ES	Monica	4	.../{M} That you should stop to tea./{C} When I said that I was free for the
525 ES	Monica	14	to buy it./{M} But why not stop to tea?/{C} Very well then, I will stop to tea,/But
525 ES	Charles	15	tea?/{C} Very well then, I will stop to tea,/But you know I won't get a chance to talk
525 ES	Monica	30	think of leaving it until he's called for tea./So why not talk now? Though I know very
526 ES	Monica	25	coming:/It's Lambert with the tea ... {}/[*Enter* LAMBERT *with trolley*]/{M} I
526 ES	Monica	27	/Please let his lordship know that tea is waiting'./{L} Yes, Miss Monica./{M} I'm
526 ES	Monica	30	glad, Charles,/That you *can* stay to tea. {}/[*Exit* LAMBERT]/{M} — Now we're in
527 ES	Lambert	12	Lordship said to tell you/Not to wait tea for him./{M} Thank you, Lambert./{L} He's
529 ES	Ld Clav	36	/Not over breakfast, but before tea,/It's the empty pages that I've been fingering
549 ES	Carghil	14	a punt/On the river — and we had a tea basket/With some lovely little cakes — I've

TEACH (8)

90 Ash-Wed 1	38	dry/Smaller and dryer than the will/Teach us to care and not to care/Teach us to sit
90 Ash-Wed 1	39	will/Teach us to care and not to care/Teach us to sit still./Pray for us sinners now and
98 Ash-Wed 6	27	not to mock ourselves with falsehood/Teach us to care and not to care/Teach us to sit
98 Ash-Wed 6	28	/Teach us to care and not to care/Teach us to sit still/Even among these rocks,/
397 CP Edward	30	what you wanted. And I never could teach you/How to put the cap on a tube of
469 CC Lucasta	4	learn about music./I wish you would teach me how to appreciate it./{C} I don't think
470 CC Lucasta	16	Will you play to me again/And teach me about music?/{C} Yes, of course I will.
565 ES Ld Clav	36	the meaning/Of the lesson I would teach? Come, I'll start to learn again./Michael

TEACHES (3)

210 Old Gumbie	12	got them lined up on the matting,/She teaches them music, crocheting and tatting./I
460 CC Lady E	1	/There's a wonderful doctor who teaches mind control.'/So on I went to Zürich./
460 CC Lady E	5	control?/{LE} No, Claude, he only teaches *thought* control./Mind control is a

TEACHING (1)

469 CC Colby	5	I don't think that you'll need much teaching;/Not at this stage, anyway. All you

TEACUPS (2)

16 Prufrock	102	streets,/After the novels, after the teacups, after the skirts that trail along the floor
31 Apollinax	2	States/His laughter tinkled among the teacups./I thought of Fragilion, that shy figure

TEAM (1)

431 CP Peter	23	that are still inhabited./We've got a team of experts over/To study the decay, so as

TEAR (2)

27 Morning	7	from the bottom of the street,/And tear from a passer-by with muddy skirts/An
136 5FingerEx4	7	Will follow you faster and faster/And tear you limb from limb./How delightful to

TEARING (1)

272 MC Chorus	13	horror, but more horror/Than when tearing in the belly./Still the horror, but more

TEARS (10)

38 Gerontion	47	us by our impudent crimes./These tears are shaken from the wrath-bearing tree./
56 Swee Night	24	withdraws;/Rachel *née* Rabinovitch/Tears at the grapes with murderous paws;/She
94 Ash-Wed 4	17	restoring/Through a bright cloud of tears, the years, restoring/With a new verse the
133 Eyes	t	POEMS/Eyes that last I saw in tears/Eyes that last I saw in tears/Through
133 Eyes	1	I saw in tears/Eyes that last I saw in tears/Through division/Here in death's dream
133 Eyes	5	reappears/I see the eyes but not the tears/This is my affliction./This is my affliction/
133 Eyes	14	a little while/A little while outlast the tears/And hold us in derision./The wind sprang
134 Wind	8	river/Is a face that sweats with tears?/I saw across the blackened river/The
601 Nocturne	13	week?')/While female readers all in tears are drowned: —/'The perfect climax all
312 FR m	9	to them. {}/[*He rushes forward and tears apart the curtains: but the embrasure is*

TEASE (2)

524 ES Charles	21	who's been there with him./{C} Well, tease me if you like. But a man does feel a fool/
550 ES Carghil	3	Richard, you're only saying that to tease me./You know I meant my stage name.

TEATIME (1)

68 WL: Fire S	222	home from sea,/The typist home at teatime, clears her breakfast, lights/Her stove,

TECHNICALITIES (1)

320 FR Warburt	10	that keeps her alive./I needn't go into technicalities/At the present moment. The whole

TEDDINGTON (22)

446 CC Eggers	23	While he's still living/With his aunt in Teddington, and coming up daily/Just as I used
485 CC Colby	25	Where did you live, as a child?/{C} In Teddington./{LE} Teddington? In what county?/
485 CC Lady E	26	as a child?/{C} In Teddington./{LE} Teddington? In what county?/{C} It's very close
485 CC Lady E	29	brought up, like me, in the country./Teddington. I seem to have heard of it./Was it a
488 CC Lady E	1	years —/That, and the other name, *Teddington*:/Mrs. Guzzard of Teddington. That
488 CC Lady E	2	name, *Teddington*:/Mrs. Guzzard of Teddington. That was all I knew./Then Tony
488 CC Lady E	7	.../{LE} And when he mentioned *Teddington*, there was a faint echo —/And then
497 CC Lady E	8	Mrs. Guzzard./{LE} Mrs. Guzzard, of Teddington./{E} Ah, indeed!/I shouldn't have
497 CC Claude	14	she's convinced that Mrs. Guzzard/Of Teddington is the name of the person/To whom
497 CC Lady E	38	have happened./{LE} And both in Teddington?/{E} I agree, that would be most
498 CC Lady E	4	know the address./Mrs. Guzzard of Teddington, that's all I know,/And that I could
498 CC Eggers	7	there should be two Mrs. Guzzards in Teddington./But assuming, for the moment,
505 CC Eggers	28	by your name and your living in Teddington./And now we must go back, many
506 CC Eggers	31	what impressed her. Mrs. Guzzard/Of Teddington! Lady Elizabeth is convinced/That
506 CC Eggers	32	/That it was a Mrs. Guzzard of Teddington/To whom her new-born child was
506 CC Eggers	34	course she might be mistaken about Teddington .../{LE} I am *not* mistaken about
506 CC Lady E	35	.../{LE} I am *not* mistaken about Teddington./{E} I am only suggesting, Lady
506 CC Eggers	37	There are other places that sound like Teddington/But not so many names that sound
507 CC Eggers	3	/{MG} None./{E} Whether, I mean, in Teddington or elsewhere?/Now I must ask a
508 CC Guzzard	28	So they adopted him./Then they left Teddington, and we lost sight of them./{E} But
510 CC Guzzard	24	{MG} And did they at one time live in Teddington?/{K} I believe they did. But why are

518 CC Guzzard 30   you? Yes./{MG} I shall return to Teddington. Colby,/Will you get me a taxi to go

TEDIOUS (1)
13 Prufrock   8 oyster-shells:/Streets that follow like a tedious argument/Of insidious intent/To lead

TEDIUM (2)
111 Xmas Trees   20 the bored habituation, the fatigue, the tedium,/The awareness of death, the
381 CP Edward 28   on the ruin of loveliness,/That the tedium is not the residue of ecstasy./I see that

TEETH (7)
32 Hysteria   2 laughter and/being part of it, until her teeth were only accidental stars with a talent/for
42 Swee Erect 15   eyes,/This oval O cropped out with teeth:/The sickle motion from the thighs/
66 WL: Chess 144   he gave you/To get yourself some teeth. He did, I was there./You have them all
72 WL: Thund 339   /Dead mountain mouth of carious teeth that cannot spit/Here one can neither
159 Rock 6   14   their significance?/Men! polish your teeth on rising and retiring;/Women! polish
185 FQ: DrySal   32   water,/The distant rote in the granite teeth,/And the wailing warning from the
253 MC Tempt4 39   /No sons, no empire, he bites broken teeth./You hold the skein: wind, Thomas, wind/

TELEGRAM (14)
347 FR   Ivy 15   where is Harry?/Look. Here's a telegram come from Arthur; {}/[*Enter*
386 CP   Celia 21   /{C} Well, not directly. Julia had a telegram/Asking her to come, and to bring me
387 CP Edward 15 Don't tell me that Lavinia/Sent you a telegram .../{P} No, not to me,/But to Alex. She
388 CP Pe & Ce 24 find either of you here./{P&C} But the telegram!/{L} What telegram?/{C} The one you
388 CP Lavinia 25   /{P&C} But the telegram!/{L} What telegram?/{C} The one you sent to Julia./{P}
390 CP   Julia   2   I'm sorry to be late./But your telegram was a bit unexpected./I dropped
390 CP   Julia   6 /I said so to myself, when I got your telegram./{L} But where, may I ask, was this
390 CP Lavinia   7   /{L} But where, may I ask, was this telegram sent from?/{J} Why, from Essex, of
390 CP   Julia 13 that accounts for the aunt — and the telegram./{L} Well, perhaps I was in Essex. I
390 CP   Alex 21   back, Lavinia!/When I got your telegram .../{L} Where from?/{A} Dedham./{L}
391 CP Lavinia 14   /{L} Stop! I want you to explain the telegram./{J} Explain the telegram? What do
391 CP   Julia 15 explain the telegram./{J} Explain the telegram? What do you think, Alex?/{A} No,
391 CP   Alex 16   /{A} No, Julia, *we* can't explain the telegram./{L} I am sure that you could explain
391 CP Lavinia 17 I am sure that you could explain the telegram./I don't know why. But it seems to me

TELEGRAMS (5)
388 CP Lavinia 29   /Edward, have you been sending telegrams?/{E} Of course I haven't sent any
388 CP Edward 30   /{E} Of course I haven't sent any telegrams./{L} This is some of Julia's mischief./
390 CP   Julia 31   /And so, of course, she sent us telegrams:/And now I don't believe she really
392 CP Lavinia 33 made her live in Essex;/And made the telegrams come from Essex./Well, I shall have
411 CP Lavinia 26 /Sir Henry, was it you who sent those telegrams?/{R} I think I will dispose of your

TELEGRAPH (1)
229 Gus   43   /And he once crossed the stage on a telegraph wire,/To rescue a child when a house

TELEGRAPHED (1)
387 CP   Celia 23 here this moment myself —/That she telegraphed to Julia to come and bring me with

TELEPHONE (23)
129 Cor2 State 12   Edward Cyril Parker is appointed telephone operator/At a salary of one pound
314 FR   Amy   1   is holding them up,/So it's no use to telephone anywhere. Harry!/Haven't you seen
357 CP   Julia 35 into it./You have the address, and the telephone number?/I might run down and see
361 CP   Reilly   7 Because you can't tell the truth on the telephone./It will all take time that you can't
366 CP   Peter 32 /{P} I want your help./I was going to telephone and try to see you later;/But this
371 CP   m 22   real. But what is the reality ... {}/[*The telephone rings*]/{E} Excuse me a moment. {}/
371 CP   m 23   /{E} Excuse me a moment. {}/[*Into telephone*]/{E} Hello! ... I can't talk now .../Yes,
373 CP   m   3   PETER]/[EDWARD *picks up the telephone, and dials a number*]/{E} Is Miss Celia
374 CP Edward   3 have you come back?/I said I would telephone as soon as I could;/And I tried to get
374 CP   Celia   9 not understand your manner on the telephone./It did not seem like you. So I felt I
375 CP   m 11 /{C} Then what has happened? {}/[*The telephone rings*]/{E} Damn the telephone. I
375 CP Edward 11 {}/[*The telephone rings*]/{E} Damn the telephone. I suppose I must answer it./Hello ...
382 CP   m 37   Yes, for two things. First ... {}/[*The telephone rings*]/{E} Damn the telephone./I
382 CP Edward 37 {}/[*The telephone rings*]/{E} Damn the telephone./I suppose I had better answer it./{C}
399 CP   Nurse 15 But I think she will be punctual./{N} I telephone through/The moment she arrives./
404 CP   2m   3   {}/[*House-telephone rings*]/[*into telephone*]/{R} Yes. {}/[*To* EDWARD]/{R} Yes,
420 CP   3m 19   dials on/house-telephone.]/[*into telephone*]./{R} It is finished. You can come in
422 CP   m   4   /{R} He's on his way up. {}/[*Into telephone*]/{R} You may bring the tray in now,
427 CP   Alex 14   Alex?/{A} I did try to get you on the telephone/After lunch, but my secretary
433 CP   Peter 22   she is? I couldn't find her/In the telephone directory./{J} Not in the directory,/Or
450 CC   Claude 23   now. And then I'll leave you./I must telephone to Amsterdam, and possibly to Paris./
501 CC   m 38 We'll get him now. {}/[*Reaches for the telephone*]/[*A knock. Enter* COLBY]/{C} Have
542 ES   Gomez 39 haven't outstayed my welcome?/Your telephone pal may be getting impatient./I'll see

TELEPHONED (4)

287 FR	Amy	37	here in good time for dinner./Harry telephoned to me from Marseilles,/He would
322 FR	Winch	29	or I'd have been here sooner./I'd telephoned to Dr. Warburton's,/And they told
392 CP	Edward	14	remembered after I had left./{E} I telephoned to everyone I knew was coming/But
567 ES	Monica	5	that they couldn't find me/When you telephoned this morning. That Mrs. Piggott/

TELEPHONES (1)

121 SA	Sweeney	21	life on a crocodile isle./There's no telephones/There's no gramophones/There's no

TELEPHONING (2)

347 FR	Ivy	16	/{I} I wonder why he sent it, after telephoning./Shall I read it to you? I was
486 CC	Claude	34	with Colby./So I came over instead of telephoning,/Just to give him these notes.

TELEVISION (1)

547 ES	Piggott	10	/There's the Silence Room. With a television set./It's popular in the evenings. But

TELL (177)

16 Prufrock		95	come from the dead,/Come back to tell you all, I shall tell you all' —/If one, settling
16 Prufrock		95	/Come back to tell you all, I shall tell you all' —/If one, settling a pillow by her
62 WL: Burial		58	you. If you see dear Mrs. Equitone,/Tell her I bring the horoscope myself:/One must
116 SP	Dusty	36	you'll phone through./Yes I'll tell her. Good bye. Goooood bye./I'm sure,
118 SP	Doris	6	way you feel/{Do} Sometimes they'll tell you nothing at all/{Du} You've got to know
118 SP	Dusty	13	coffin./{Du} Well I never! What did I tell you?/Wasn't I saying I always draw court
119 SP	Klip	17	we did our bit, as you folks say,/I'll tell the world we got the Hun on the run/{Kr}
119 SP	Krum	21	/Yes Miss Dorrance you get Sam/To tell about that poker game in Bordeaux./{Du}
123 SAWa & Ho		1	*Under the boo/Under the bamboo tree./Tell me in what part of the wood/Do you want to*
125 SA	Sweeney	18	was alone/You're either or neither/I tell you again it don't apply/Death or life or life
127 Cor1 March		12	/What comes first? Can you see? Tell us. It is/5,800,000 rifles and carbines,/
127 Cor1 March		17	53,000 field and heavy guns,/I cannot tell how many projectiles, mines and fuses,/
143 Lines OM		14	/The dullard knows that he is mad./Tell me if I am not glad!/Choruses from 'The
155 Rock 3		40	directing the traffic/Cannot tell you why you come or where you go./A
192 FQ: Little		52	no speech for, when living,/They can tell you, being dead: the communication/Of the
203 Indians		18	graveyard./Let those who go home tell the same story of you:/Of action with a
209 NamingCats		4	at first I'm as mad as a hatter/When I tell you, a cat must have THREE DIFFERENT
209 NamingCats		13	them sensible everyday names./But I tell you, a cat needs a name that's particular,/A
209 NamingCats		26	in profound meditation,/The reason, I tell you, is always the same:/His mind is
212 Growltiger		7	ear was somewhat missing, no need to tell you why,/And he scowled upon a hostile
226 Macavity		10	you may look up in the air —/But I tell you once and once again, *Macavity's not*
228 Gus		19	his grandest creation, as he loves to tell,/Was Firefrorefiddle, the Fiend of the Fell./
229 Gus		33	my grandest creation, as history will tell,/Was Firefrorefiddle, the Fiend of the Fell.'/
229 Gus		36	give him a toothful of gin,/He will tell how he once played a part in *East Lynne./*
229 Gus		52	nothing to equal, from what I hear tell,/That moment of mystery/When I made
241 MC Priest2		22	the hammer and the anvil?/{P2} Tell us,/Are the old disputes at an end, is the
242 MC Priest2		34	dispelling dismay and doubt./He will tell us what we are to do, he will give us our
254 MC Tempt4		6	understand./{T4} It is not for me to tell you how this may be so;/I am only here,
254 MC Tempt4		7	be so;/I am only here, Thomas, to tell you what you know./{T} How long shall this
254 MC Tempt4		24	of these things./{T4} That is why I tell you./Your thoughts have more power than
265 MC Knight3		30	must see the Archbishop./{K3} Go, tell the Archbishop/We have no need of his
265 MC Priest1		33	dinner. {}/[*to attendant*]./{P1} Go, tell His Lordship./{K4} How much longer will
293 FR	Harry	39	/Never woken to the nightmare. I tell you, life would be unendurable/If you were
294 FR	Agatha	12	/{Ag} Nevertheless, Harry, best tell us as you can:/Talk in your own language,
297 FR	Charles	29	Sir, with his Lordship's car./{C} Tell him I'd like to have a word with him,
298 FR	Charles	36	him for nearly eight years;/And to tell the truth, now that we've seen him,/We're a
305 FR	Agatha	10	I see more than this,/More than I can tell you, more than there are words for./At this
306 FR	Harry	22	it may be all one life, with no escape. Tell me,/Were you ever happy here, as a child at
311 FR	Mary	24	on me./Harry! Harry! It's all *right*, I tell you./If you will depend on me, it will be all
311 FR	Harry	33	something else, puts me among you./I tell you, it is not me you are looking at,/Not me
312 FR	Harry	1	*curtains across*]/{H} They were here, I tell you. They are here./Are you so
318 FR Warburt		19	mean, you don't know what I want to tell you./You may be quite right, but what we
318 FR	Harry	35	if you want to talk, at least you can tell me/Something useful. Do you remember my
318 FR Warburt		39	occasion/Or with what I have to tell you./{H} What you have to tell me/Is either
318 FR Warburt		40	to tell you./{H} What you have to tell me/Is either something that I know already/
319 FR	Harry	35	me,/I felt the trap close. If you won't tell me,/I must ask Agatha. I never dared
319 FR Warburt		38	—/I mean, there is nothing she could tell you. But, Harry,/We can't sit here all the
320 FR Warburt		1	will be here. Won't you let me tell you/What I had to say?/{H} Very well, tell
320 FR	Harry	3	/What I had to say?/{H} Very well, tell me./{W} It's about your mother's health that
320 FR Warburt		5	that I wanted to talk to you./I must tell you, Harry, that although your mother/Is
320 FR	Harry	38	are all centred on you./{H} Hopes? ... Tell me/Did you know my father at about my
321 FR Warburt		36	/{W} For God's sake, Winchell, tell us your business./His Lordship isn't very

322 FR	Warburt	21	/{W} For Heaven's sake, Winchell,/Tell us your business./{Wi} It's about Mr. John.
327 FR	Ivy	34	/But it's all a mistake. And not to tell his mother./{V} What's the use of asking for
331 FR	Harry	14	show me?/And now I want you to tell me about my father./{Ag} What do you
331 FR	Harry	20	I need to know,/And only you can tell me. I know that much./{Ag} I had to fight
331 FR	Agatha	28	that will be better./{Ag} I will try to tell you. I hope I have the strength./{H} Am I a
332 FR	Harry	4	to it./{H} There was no ecstasy./Tell me now, who were my parents?/{Ag} Your
332 FR	Harry	6	father and your mother./{H} You tell me nothing./{Ag} The dead man whom you
337 FR	Amy	31	Harry? He has only arrived,/And you tell him to go?/{Ag} He shall go./{A} He shall
338 FR	Harry	13	I conceal an explanation,/And to tell you that I would have liked to explain./{A}
342 FR	Mary	2	I have just seen Denman./She came to tell me that Harry is leaving:/Downing told her.
342 FR	Mary	22	me,/You would not believe me, but I tell you I know./You must keep him here, you
353 CP	Peter	7	been listening./{P} You'll have to tell us all over again, Alex./{A} I never tell the
353 CP	Alex	8	us all over again, Alex./{A} I never tell the same story twice./{J} But I'm still
353 CP	Celia	14	/Both of you. It's your turn, Julia./Do tell us that story you told the other day, about
353 CP	Celia	21	/But we're never tired of hearing you tell it./I don't believe everyone here knows it. {}/
354 CP	Celia	3	it./{C} And Julia's the only person to tell it./She's such a good mimic./{J} Am I a
355 CP	Julia	29	I can't endure them./Well, I started to tell you about Lady Klootz./It was at the
355 CP	Julia	34	been friends of yours, I couldn't tell the story./{P} Were they the parents of Tony
356 CP	Julia	4	wanted to go to California./Do tell us what you were doing in California./{C}
358 CP	Peter	14	you be going?/{P} But won't you tell the story about Lady Klootz?/{J} What
361 CP	Reilly	7	to lie about it/Because you can't tell the truth on the telephone./It will all take
361 CP	Reilly	28	remain the stranger./But let me tell you, that to approach the stranger/Is to
365 CP	Julia	1	/Has anybody found them? You can tell if they're mine —/Some kind of a plastic
365 CP	Julia	17	/This is what I call an adventure!/Tell me about him. You've been drinking
365 CP	Edward	29	/{J} You don't know his name?/{E} I tell you I've no idea who he is/Or how he got
371 CP	Peter	16	I must see Celia at least to make her tell me/What has happened, in her terms. Until
372 CP	Peter	33	you don't mind,/I'd rather you didn't tell her what I've told you./{E} I shall not say
374 CP	Celia	11	like you. So I felt I must see you./Tell me it's all right, and then I'll go./{E} But
376 CP	Julia	34	makes is absolutely deadly./I could tell such tales of his poisoning people./Now, my
379 CP	Celia	33	/And I waited, and wanted to run to tell you./Perhaps the dream was better. It
384 CP	Reilly	12	made a decision./No. I have come to tell you that you will change your mind,/But
387 CP	Edward	14	/{P} Where's Lavinia?/{E} Don't tell me that Lavinia/Sent you a telegram .../{P}
390 CP	Julia	16	where you were? Lavinia!/Don't tell me you were abducted! Tell us/I'm thrilled
390 CP	Julia	16	/Don't tell me you were abducted! Tell us/I'm thrilled ... {}/[The doorbell rings.
392 CP	Lavinia	25	situation!/And what did you tell them?/{E} I invented an aunt/Who was ill in
392 CP	Lavinia	34	from Essex./Well, I shall have to tell Julia the truth./I shall always tell the truth
392 CP	Lavinia	35	to tell Julia the truth./I shall always tell the truth now./We have wasted such a lot of
393 CP	Lavinia	20	that decision./{L} But how could I tell where I wanted to go/Unless you suggested
394 CP	Edward	22	/{E} Thank you for the warning. But tell me,/Since this is how you see me, why did
397 CP	Edward	20	/That you wouldn't see him first, and tell him all about me/From your point of view?
400 CP	Reilly	4	hour. We have not much time./Tell me now, did you have any difficulty/In
401 CP	Edward	31	/{E} You knew,/Before I began to tell you, what had happened?/{R} That is so,
401 CP	Reilly	34	dismiss that question for the moment./Tell me first, about the difficulties/On which
404 CP	Reilly	24	/{R} You have nothing else to tell me?/{E} What else can I tell you?/You didn't
404 CP	Edward	25	else to tell me?/{E} What else can I tell you?/You didn't want to hear about my
404 CP	Edward	34	shall need./But of course you mustn't tell her where I am./Is it far to go?/{R} You
404 CP	Reilly	39	/Than the patient himself can always tell me./Indeed, it is often the case that my
408 CP	Lavinia	12	who it could have been./{L} Well, tell him if you like./{R} A young man named
410 CP	Reilly	22	state in which you came to me — I tell you this:/It would have been a horror
411 CP	Lavinia	32	my question too./They had to tell us, themselves, that they had made their
412 CP	Julia	8	in by the back way./I only came to tell you, I am sure she is ready/To make a
413 CP	Celia	2	I shan't be offended/If you simply tell me to go away again./{R} Most of my
413 CP	Celia	20	all a delusion!/But oughtn't I first to tell you the circumstances?/I'd forgotten that
413 CP	Celia	27	consider symptoms. But first I must tell you/That I should really like to think there's
415 CP	Reilly	2	before we use the term 'abnormal'./Tell me what you mean by a sense of sin./{C}
415 CP	Celia	3	a sense of sin./{C} It's much easier to tell you what I don't mean:/I don't mean sin in
420 CP	Celia	9	I who have made the decision:/I must tell you that. Oh, I almost forgot —/May I ask
420 CP	Julia	22	Very far, I think./You do not need to tell me. I knew from the beginning./{R} It's the
427 CP	Julia	3	/And we're going to get him to tell us all about it./But what's become of him? {}
427 CP	Julia	20	them well enough for that./{J} But tell us, Alex./What were you doing in this
428 CP	Julia	2	destructive .../{J} You don't need to tell me that monkeys are destructive./I shall
429 CP	Alex	32	Christians! Now, I think I ought to tell you/About someone you know — or knew
430 CP	Edward	32	working for Pan-Am-Eagle?/{E} No. Tell us, what is Pan-Am-Eagle?/{P} You must
433 CP	Peter	21	got an idea for another film./Can you tell me where she is? I couldn't find her/In the
433 CP	Julia	24	/Or in any directory. You can tell them now, Alex./{L} What does Julia mean?

433 CP   Julia   34 it./{E} Celia dead./{J} You had better tell them, Alex,/The news that you bring back
434 CP   Alex   22 before that .../{A} It was difficult to tell./But from what we know of local practices/
446 CC   Claude   18 he's found it,/Just as I did. I shall tell him about myself./But so far, I've left him
448 CC   Eggers   11 the Wisdom of Atlantis?/{E} Well, to tell the truth, Sir Claude, I only touched on
449 CC   Eggers   31 suitable arrangement./But will you tell me this: if it comes to the point/At which
455 CC   Colby   7 influence is perfectly frightening./But tell me about Lu ... Miss Angel:/What's her
455 CC   Eggers   16 very generous man, is Sir Claude./To tell the truth, she's something of a thorn in his
460 CC   Lady E   29 with me tomorrow,/And then I shall tell you about my committees./I must go and
461 CC   Claude   37 seen me before?/{SC} Impossible to tell./The point is that she's taken a fancy to you/
462 CC   Claude   26 accept the terms it offers you./But tell me first — I've a reason for asking —/How
471 CC   Colby   3 /{C} And perhaps you'll let me tell you beforehand/About the programme —
471 CC   Lucasta   19 quite simple./{L} Then I wish you'd tell me./Because *I* don't know./{C} The first
472 CC   Lucasta   25 whether you were right./For all I can tell, you may have been mistaken,/And perhaps
475 CC   Colby   32 as well know them./{C} I'd gladly tell you everything about myself;/But you know
475 CC   Lucasta   37 me anything about you;/He doesn't tell me much. And as for B. —/I'd much rather
476 CC   Colby   1 /{C} There's only one thing I can't tell you./At least, not yet. I'm not allowed to
476 CC   Colby   2 /At least, not yet. I'm not allowed to tell./And that's about my parents./{L} Oh, I see.
476 CC   Lucasta   6 I can't believe that matters./But I can tell you all about *my* parents:/At least, I'm
476 CC   Lucasta   12 to give a false impression./I want to tell you now, why I tried to do that./And it's
476 CC   Lucasta   29 to know?/{L} You'll laugh when I tell you:/I'm only Claude's daughter./{C} His
478 CC   Lucasta   16 for the fun of it:/I thought, when I tell him, it will be so wonderful/All in a
480 CC   Kaghan   22 /{K} Oh, I'm a good judge. Now, I'll tell you the difference/Between ourselves and
481 CC   Lady E   19 you've moved in. Because you can't tell/Whether a scheme of decoration/Is *right*,
483 CC   Lady E   16 is that shrouded object on it?/Don't tell me it's a typewriter./{C} It is a typewriter./
487 CC   Lady E   31 instruments./I must be right. Claude, tell me I am right./{SC} But Elizabeth, what has
489 CC   Claude   15 I'll wait for children of *our* own,/And tell her then. And they never came./And now I
490 CC   Lady E   8 {LE} Oh, Colby, doesn't your instinct tell you?/{SC} Yes, tell us everything that's in
490 CC   Claude   9 your instinct tell you?/{SC} Yes, tell us everything that's in your mind./I know
492 CC   Colby   26 I can't develop that/Unless you can tell me — reminiscent of what?/{SC}
494 CC   Lady E   38 you, all these years,/And now you tell me, you'd have liked to be a potter!/You
500 CC   Lucasta   18 /{SC} He knew it./{L} Why didn't he tell me? Perhaps he was about to./Anyway, I
508 CC   Claude   1 I asked you here so that you might tell her so./{E} Don't take this as a personal
510 CC   Kaghan   17 /{K} Why, yes, it is. Did you tell her, Sir Claude?/{SC} No, B. It was Mrs.
515 CC   Guzzard   20 /{MG} Consider, Sir Claude. Would I tell you all this/Unless it was true? In telling you
525 ES   Charles   33 hear it again. You think I'm going to tell you/Once more, that I'm in love with you.
527 ES   Lambert   11 Miss Monica. His Lordship said to tell you/Not to wait tea for him./{M} Thank
530 ES   Ld Clav   10 of rest, these doctors, Charles; they tell me to be cautious,/To take life easily. Take
532 ES   Monica   21 twenty minutes/I'll send Lambert to tell you that you have to take a trunk call./
534 ES   Gomez   18 An absurd suggestion!/Forgery, I can tell you, is a mug's game./I say that — with
534 ES   Gomez   38 may get from the other'./Dick, don't tell me that there isn't any whisky in the house?/
538 ES   Gomez   9 /You wanted to get rid of me. I shall tell you why presently./Now let's look for a
539 ES   Gomez   21 of that prudent devil/Of yours, to tell him not to go too far./Well, now, I'm
546 ES   Monica   31 /{M} Yes, Mrs. Piggott, but please tell me one thing./We haven't seen her yet, but
547 ES   Piggott   20 /Miss Claverton-Ferry, I ought to tell you more/About the amenities which
548 ES   Ld Clav   4 else./{LC} She'll come back to tell us more about the peace and quiet./{M} I
557 ES   Ld Clav   6 of blaming someone else./Just tell me what's happened./{Mi} Well, I've lost my
558 ES   Michael   18 he wants to keep things quiet. I can tell you, it's no joke/Being the son of a famous
564 ES   Carghil   18 perfect English?/Of course, I could tell from your looks that you were Spanish./I do
564 ES   Carghil   31 to cross-examine you/And make you tell me all about Richard/In his Oxford days./
564 ES   Gomez   34 /{G} On one condition:/That you tell me all about Dick when you knew him. {}/
565 ES   Carghil   22 and going abroad./{MC} You must tell me all about it. Perhaps I could advise you./
568 ES   Ld Clav   17 truly nothing, that you couldn't tell Monica/Then all is well with you. You're in
571 ES   Monica   26 .../{M} Then, Father, you should tell *us* what they already know./Why should
571 ES   Ld Clav   29 to those who hate you?/{LC} I will tell you very briefly/And simply. As for
572 ES   Charles   30 means of self-justification./Let them tell their versions of their miserable stories,/
573 ES   Carghil   26 I? Yes, I'm sure of it, Monica!/I can tell by the change in your expression to-day;/
575 ES   Ld Clav   14 reasons/From what you think. Let me tell you about Gomez./He's unlikely to try to be
575 ES   Carghil   39 looked at me!/Some day, Monica, I'll tell you all about it./{M} I am satisfied with
576 ES   Michael   31 very vague/{Mi} It's confidential, I tell you./{C} So I can imagine:/Highly
577 ES   Gomez   23 things very frankly;/And I can tell you, Michael's head is well screwed on./He's

TELLING (16)

66 WL: Chess   155 makes off, it won't be for lack of telling./You ought to be ashamed, I said, to
271 MC   Thomas   18 told/And often been changed in the telling. They will seem unreal./Human kind
318 FR   Harry   26 /And not with the past? What I'm telling you/Is very important. Very important./
361 CP   Edward   18 /I only wanted to relieve my mind/By telling someone what I'd been concealing./I

371 CP	Peter	3	to talk to someone./And I have been telling you of something real —/My first
371 CP	Edward	6	/{E} My dear Peter, I have only been telling you/What would have happened to you
413 CP	Reilly	4	patients begin, Miss Coplestone,/By telling me exactly what is the matter with them,/
434 CP	Alex	12	/Among the heathen, of which I was telling you./They knew of it, but would not
436 CP	Lavinia	21	I want to say to you./While Alex was telling us what had happened to Celia/I was
453 CC	Kaghan	23	told Colby about me?/{K} It's no use telling anybody about you:/Nobody'd ever
478 CC	Lucasta	14	you./Why, I'd actually thought of telling you before,/And I postponed telling you,
478 CC	Lucasta	15	telling you before,/And I postponed telling you, just for the fun of it:/I thought,
502 CC	Lucasta	15	were. I was ashamed/Of what I was telling you, and so I was expecting/What I
509 CC	Colby	15	a rattle and a jingle-bell,/And your telling me I had had a little cousin/Who had
515 CC	Guzzard	21	tell you all this/Unless it was true? In telling you the truth/I am sacrificing my
530 ES	Ld Clav	12	life easily. Take life easily!/It's like telling a man he mustn't run for trains/When

TELLS (6)

159 Rock 6		18	Why should they love her laws?/She tells them of Life and Death, and of all that
159 Rock 6		20	hard where they like to be soft./She tells them of Evil and Sin, and other unpleasant
323 FR	Warburt	11	Lady Monchensey;/And Winchell tells me Dr. Owen has seen him/And says it's
354 CP	Julia	28	one can't be too careful/Before one tells a story./{A} Delia Verinder?/Was she the
457 CC	Lady E	19	will you give it to the driver?/He tells me that he suffers from chronic catarrh./
496 CC	Lady E	10	it doesn't matter what Mrs. Guzzard tells us,/If it satisfies Colby. Whatever happens/

TEMPER (1)

289 FR	Ivy	32	into./She may have done it in a fit of temper./{G} I never met her./{A} I am very glad

TEMPERAMENT (1)

42 Swee Erect		23	from nape to base,/Knows the female temperament/And wipes the suds around his

TEMPERATE (3)

103 Journ Magi		21	/Then at dawn we came down to a temperate valley,/Wet, below the snow line,
160 Rock 7		12	and shot with darkness/As the air of temperate seas is pierced by the still dead breath
278 MC Knight2		36	And at a later time still, even such temperate/measures as these would become

TEMPEST (1)

592 Grad 3		2	clouds that fly/After a summer tempest, when some haste/North, South, and

TEMPLE (13)

127 Cor1 March		6	knew the City./This is the way to the temple, and we so many crowding the way./So
128 Cor1 March		35	O hidden./Now they go up to the temple. Then the sacrifice./Now come the
152 Rock 2		37	prosperity/The people will neglect the Temple, and in time of adversity they will decry
155 Rock 3		46	the altars./Where there is no temple there shall be no homes,/Though you
156 Rock 3		72	/Though you forget the way to the Temple,/There is one who remembers the way
157 Rock 4		1	/There are those who would build the Temple,/And those who prefer that the Temple
157 Rock 4		2	/And those who prefer that the Temple should not be built./In the days of
159 Rock 6		33	must first build the steps;/And if the Temple is to be cast down/We must first build
159 Rock 6		34	be cast down/We must first build the Temple./In the beginning GOD created the
162 Rock 8		5	come into thine inheritance,/And thy temple have they defiled./Who is this that
165 Rock 9		35	Visible and invisible must meet in His Temple;/You must not deny the body./Now you
165 Rock 9		37	deny the body./Now you shall see the Temple completed:/After much striving, after
241 MC	Mess	11	Servants of God, and watchers of the temple,/I am here to inform you, without

TEMPLED (1)

248 MC Tempt2		29	lasting, a permanent possession./A templed tomb, monument of marble./Rule over

TEMPORAL (9)

174 FQ: BurntN		101	/Cleansing affection from the temporal./Neither plenitude nor vacancy. Only
190 FQ: DrySal		235	trying;/We, content at the last/If our temporal reversion nourish/(Not too far from
240 MC Priest3		34	nothing quite conclusive in the art of temporal government,/But violence, duplicity
242 MC Priest1		27	generosity,/Loathing power given by temporal devolution,/Wishing subjection to
250 MC Thomas		9	sunward, covering kings' falcons./{T} Temporal power, to build a good world,/To
253 MC Tempt4		37	within an hour,/This is the course of temporal power./The Old King shall know it,
255 MC Thomas		19	my own desires?/Others have come, temporal tempters,/With pleasure and power at
275 MC Thomas		15	times traitor you:/Traitor to me as my temporal vassal,/Traitor to me as your spiritual
278 MC Knight2		16	ideal State:/a union of spiritual and temporal administration, under the central/

TEMPORARY (5)

374 CP	Celia	25	/{C} But surely, these are only temporary./You know I accepted the situation/
403 CP	Reilly	6	go to flatter your vanity/With the temporary stimulus of feeling interesting./{E}
498 CC	Eggers	20	might have taken in another one/As a temporary accommodation —/On suitable
518 CC	Eggers	2	up an income. Piano lessons? —/As a temporary measure; because, Mr. Simpkins —/I
568 ES	Ld Clav	7	of which the law takes cognisance:/Temporary failures, irreflective aberrations,/

TEMPS (1)

51 Restaurant		3	mon épaule:/'Dans mon pays il fera temps pluvieux,/Du vent, du grand soleil, et de

TENSION (2)
98 Ash-Wed 6   20   of the sandy earth/This is the time of tension between dying and birth/The place of
175 FQ: BurntN 154   break, under the burden,/Under the tension, slip, slide, perish,/Decay with
TENT (1)
67 WL: Fire S   173   night./The Fire Sermon/The river's tent is broken; the last fingers of leaf/Clutch and
TENUOUS (1)
599 On a Port   1   ago./On a Portrait/Among a crowd of tenuous dreams, unknown/To us of restless
TEREU (1)
68 WL: Fire S   206   jug jug jug jug jug/So rudely forc'd./Tereu/Unreal City/Under the brown fog of a
TERM (7)
314 FR Warburt   30   /Of illness. Health is a relative term./{I} You must have had a very rich
402 CP   Reilly   20   see it./{R} 'Nervous breakdown' is a term I never use:/It can mean almost anything./
415 CP   Reilly   1   be normal/For *you*, before we use the term 'abnormal'./Tell me what you mean by a
455 CC   Eggers   10   I don't think that's quite the right term./She's no money of her own, as you may
535 ES   Gomez   11   to say: when I say 'trust'/I use the term as experience has taught me./It's nonsense
571 ES   Ld Clav 10   became a forger. And so he served his term./Was I responsible for that weakness in
576 ES   Ld Clav   9   he include the fact that he served a term in prison?/{Mi} He told me everything. It
TERMINATE (2)
92 Ash-Wed 2   35   now the Garden/Where all loves end/Terminate torment/Of love unsatisfied/The
541 ES   Gomez   36   Ah, the pre-arranged interruption/To terminate the unwelcome intrusion/Of the
TERMINATED (1)
518 CC Guzzard   27   believe that this interview can now be terminated./If you will excuse me, Sir Claude .../
TERMINUS (1)
188 FQ: DrySal   142   that station/Or who will arrive at any terminus,/While the narrowing rails slide
TERMS (21)
294 FR   Harry   26   /Untranslatable: I talk in general terms/Because the particular has no language.
314 FR Warburt   27   experience/I've left off thinking in terms of the laboratory./We're all of us ill in
332 FR Agatha   13   years/Before she succeeded in making terms with Wishwood,/Until she took your
361 CP Edward   13   don't suggest./I have often used these terms in examining witnesses,/So I don't like
370 CP   Peter   31   both unaware of ourselves./In your terms, perhaps, she's lost interest in me./{E}
371 CP   Peter   17   tell me/What has happened, in her terms. Until I know that/I shan't know the truth
381 CP Edward   35   a feeble creature;/He has to come to terms in the end/With the obstinate, the tougher
403 CP Edward   39   a place I cannot live in/Except on her terms. I must be alone,/But not in the same
416 CP   Celia   16   the taking/Seemed so right: not in terms of calculation/Of what was good for the
418 CP   Reilly   21   /The first I could describe in familiar terms/Because you have seen it, as we all have
462 CC   Claude   24   the strength to impose your own terms/Upon life, you must accept the terms it
462 CC   Claude   25   terms/Upon life, you must accept the terms it offers you./But tell me first — I've a
464 CC   Colby   23   speaking, I've been translating/Into terms of music. But may I ask,/With this
466 CC   Claude   29   meant when I spoke/Of accepting the terms life imposes upon you/Even to the point
467 CC   Colby   15   just now/About rebelling against the terms/That life has imposed./{SC} It's my own
498 CC   Eggers   21   accommodation —/On suitable terms. But if she did that,/We must enquire
507 CC   Eggers   18   payments were made./{E} The terms were satisfactory?/{MG} Very satisfactory
514 CC Guzzard   6   your wish/You will have to come to terms with it. You shall have a father/Dead, and
557 ES Michael   26   recommended./He gave me good terms, on the strength of my name:/The only
557 ES Ld Clav   28   name. And what do you call good terms?/{Mi} I'd nothing at all to pay for two
568 ES Ld Clav   34   been honest with anyone older,/On terms of equality. To one's child one can't
TERPSICHOREAN (1)
216 Jellicles   27   in the afternoon,/Reserving their terpsichorean powers/To dance by the light of
TERRACE (3)
13 Prufrock   20   falls from chimneys,/Slipped by the terrace, made a sudden leap,/And seeing that it
523 ES   m 13   *in the afternoon*/ACT TWO/*The Terrace at Badgley Court. Morning*/ACT
544 ES   2m 1   Court? {}/CURTAIN/Act Two/*The terrace of Badgley Court. A bright sunny*
TERRACES (1)
103 Journ Magi   9   /The summer palaces on slopes, the terraces,/And the silken girls bringing sherbet./
TERRE (1)
48 Lune Miel   1   /Ils ont vu les Pays-Bas, ils rentrent à Terre Haute;/Mais une nuit d'été, les voici à
TERRIBLE (6)
116 SP   Dusty   24   so sorry/But Doris came home with a terrible chill/No, just a chill/Oh I *think* it's only
124 SA   Doris   9   such conversation/A woman runs a terrible risk./{Sn} Let Mr. Sweeney continue his
124 SA   Doris   24   in the end./{Do} A woman runs a terrible risk./{Sn} Let Mr. Sweeney continue his
214 RTTugger   12   about it!/The Rum Tum Tugger is a terrible bore:/When you let him in, then he
223 Pekes Pols   32   Heathen Chinese./But a terrible din is what Pollicles like,/For your
413 CP   Celia   32   more frightening!/That would be terrible. So I'd rather believe/There is something

TERRIBLY (4)

438 CP	Edward	16	/There must be something else that is terribly wrong,/And the rest of us are somehow
467 CC	Colby	13	forever. The empty years./Oh, I'm terribly sorry to be saying this;/But it goes to
492 CC	Lady E	4	Mrs. Guzzard./{LE} Oh Claude! I am terribly sorry for you./I believe that if I had
502 CC	Lucasta	22	I don't mean insensitive!/But you're terribly cold. Or else you've some fire/To warm

TERRIER (1)

135 5FingerEx2		t	Time flow away?/*Lines to a Yorkshire Terrier*/In a brown field stood a tree/And the tree

TERRIFIED (4)

97 Ash-Wed 5		31	for those who offend her/And are terrified and cannot surrender/And affirm
310 FR	Mary	25	itself upstream:/And what of the terrified spirit/Compelled to be reborn/To rise
453 CC	Lucasta	17	human, Colby./It's only that he's terrified of Mrs. Eggerson;/That's why he's
484 CC	Lady E	38	and didn't know it./Of course, I was terrified of being ugly,/And of being

TERRIFYING (3)

325 FR	Violet	38	/And the pace he went at was simply terrifying./I said I would rather walk: and I did.
404 CP	Edward	15	death of the body,/But this death is terrifying. The death of the spirit —/Can you
418 CP	Reilly	37	Then I choose the second./{R} It is a terrifying journey./{C} I am not frightened/But

TERRITORY (1)

343 FR	Agatha	8	/In our wanderings in the neutral territory/Between two worlds./{M} Then you

TERROR (14)

38 Gerontion		56	removed therefrom/To lose beauty in terror, terror in inquisition./I have lost my
38 Gerontion		56	therefrom/To lose beauty in terror, terror in inquisition./I have lost my passion:
180 FQ: ECoker		122	deepen/Leaving only the growing terror of nothing to think about;/Or when,
187 FQ: DrySal		105	the shoulder, towards the primitive terror./Now, we come to discover that the
196 FQ: Little		203	the air/With flame of incandescent terror/Of which the tongues declare/The one
212 Growltiger		4	evil aims,/Rejoicing in his title of 'The Terror of the Thames'./His manners and
228 Gus		8	smartest of Cats —/But no longer a terror to mice and to rats./For he isn't the Cat
257 MC	Chorus	23	reason, some hope; but now a new terror has soiled us, which none can avert, none
276 MC	Chorus	3	misery,/Living and partly living;/The terror by night that ends in daily action,/The
276 MC	Chorus	4	night that ends in daily action,/The terror by day that ends in sleep;/But the talk in
316 FR	Ivy	4	afraid./{I} This is a most undignified terror, and I must struggle against it./{G} I am
339 FR	Harry	13	things are possible. It is love and terror/Of what waits and wants me, and will not
527 ES	Monica	22	me?/What reasons?/{M} First, his terror of being alone./In the life he's led, he's
555 ES	Ld Clav	24	that last escapade of his,/I've lived in terror of his running over somebody./{M} Why,

TERRORISE (1)

545 ES	Ld Clav	6	/Severe and speechless critic, who can terrorise us/And urge us on to futile activity,/

TERRORS (5)

189 FQ: DrySal		197	recurrent image into pre-conscious terrors —/To explore the womb, or tomb, or
244 MC	Chorus	17	able to./We have all had our private terrors,/Our particular shadows, our secret
421 CP	Julia	16	is going./But what do we know of the terrors of the journey?/You and I don't know
438 CP	Reilly	8	of darkness, labyrinths, Minotaur terrors./But that world does not take the place
583 ES	Monica	23	{M} Age and decrepitude can have no terrors for me,/Loss and vicissitude cannot

TEST (1)

469 CC	Colby	13	when you hear them./I've given you a test. Several of the pieces/That I've just played

TESTIMONIAL (1)

551 ES	Carghil	3	lover/Is still, in her memory, a kind of testimonial./Men live by forgetting — women

TESTIMONY (1)

67 WL: Fire S		179	boxes, cigarette ends/Or other testimony of summer nights. The nymphs are

TESTS (1)

43 Swee Erect		29	/Of Sweeney straddled in the sun.)/Tests the razor on his leg/Waiting until the

TÊTE (1)

47 Mél Adult		7	banquier,/Vous me paierez bien la tête./C'est à Paris que je me coiffe/Casque noir

THAMES (5)

67 WL: Fire S		176	The nymphs are departed./Sweet Thames, run softly, till I end my song./The river
67 WL: Fire S		183	Leman I sat down and wept .../Sweet Thames, run softly till I end my song,/Sweet
67 WL: Fire S		184	run softly till I end my song,/Sweet Thames, run softly, for I speak not loud or
69 WL: Fire S		260	hear/Beside a public bar in Lower Thames Street,/The pleasant whining of a
212 Growltiger		4	in his title of 'The Terror of the Thames'./His manners and appearance did not

THAN (216)

THANK (45)

62 WL: Burial		57	of people, walking round in a ring./Thank you. If you see dear Mrs. Equitone,/Tell
66 WL: Chess		151	o' that, I said./Then I'll know who to thank, she said, and give me a straight look./
166 Rock 10		26	Light Invisible, we worship Thee!/We thank Thee for the lights that we have kindled,/
167 Rock 10		42	relight the flame./Therefore we thank Thee for our little light, this is dappled
167 Rock 10		43	this is dappled with shadow./We thank Thee who hast moved us to building, to
167 Rock 10		45	our bodily vision is made./And we thank Thee that darkness reminds us of light./O

280 MC Knight1   1   who was, after all, a great man./{K1} Thank you, Brito, I think that there is no more
281 MC Chorus   17   beasts and of birds, praise Thee./We thank Thee for Thy mercies of blood, for Thy
282 MC Chorus   4   forever denied. Therefore, O God, we thank Thee/Who hast given such blessing to
289 FR   Amy   10   again and carry on at Wishwood./{A} Thank you, Gerald. Though Agatha means/As
298 FR Downing 27   these years./You're well, I hope?/{Do} Thank you, very well indeed, Sir./{C} I'm sorry
300 FR   Charles 37   have known it./{C} Oh yes ... quite so. Thank you, Downing,/I don't think we need
301 FR   Gerald   8   there be anything more, Sir?/{G} Thank you, Downing;/Nothing more. {}/[*Exit*
321 FR   Winch   34   sergeant/Doesn't get younger. Thank you, no, my Lord;/I don't find port
332 FR   Agatha 30   /To the flames. They only come once,/Thank God, that kind. Perhaps there is another
346 FR Downing   9   on the table./Oh, there it is. Thank you. Good night, Miss; good night,/Miss
347 FR   Agatha 12   be all, Miss?/{Ag} That will be all, thank you, Downing. We mustn't keep you;/His
359 CP   Edward   5   of Lavinia's aunt./{E} Oh ... yes ... thank you. Good-bye, Alex,/It was nice of you
366 CP   Julia   7   where I keep them./Oh, here they are! Thank you, Edward;/That really was very clever
366 CP   Julia   26   I can meditate. Good-bye then./And thank you — both of you — very much. {}/
372 CP   Peter   8   /{E} Well, I will see Celia./{P} Thank you, Edward. It's very good of you. {}/
372 CP   Peter   35   say anything about it to Lavinia./{P} Thank you, Edward. Good night./{E} Good
378 CP   Celia   4   with me —/Something very light./{C} Thank you, Julia./I think I will, if I may follow
384 CP   Reilly   4   you some gin and water?/{UG} No, thank you. This is a different occasion./{E} I
386 CP   Celia   27   do but wait./Won't you sit down?/{C} Thank you. {}/[*Pause*]/{E} Oh, my God, what
389 CP   Lavinia 34   sure that we shall manage somehow, thank you,/As we have in the past./{C} Oh, not
390 CP   Lavinia   4   /{L} So far as I know, she is very well, thank you./{J} She must have made a
394 CP   Edward 22   you very differently/In future./{E} Thank you for the warning. But tell me,/Since
432 CP   Reilly   24   /{E} Anything with it?/{R} Nothing, thank you./{L} May I introduce Mr. Peter
451 CC   Colby   31   /And besides, she's very musical./{C} Thank you for the warning!/{E} So if you don't
461 CC   Colby   10   he has a very cultivated voice./{C} Thank you very much, I will. It's reassuring/To
461 CC   Claude 21   I'll be going./{SC} Goodbye, and thank you, Eggerson./{E} Good day, Sir
466 CC   Colby   25   /I will show you my collection./{C} Thank you./{SC} And perhaps, some time, you
478 CC   Lucasta 13   But now I don't want you to be sorry, thank you./Why, I'd actually thought of telling
482 CC   Kaghan   2   night./{L} Good night./{K} And thank you so much. You give such good advice.
500 CC   Lucasta 23   I said I was your daughter!/I came to thank him for the shock he'd given me./He
501 CC   Lucasta 23   Mr. Kaghan as a son-in-law./{L} Thank you. I'm sure he'll appreciate *that*./But
508 CC   Claude 19   Eggerson./A breath of sanity. Thank you for that./{MG} We parted with it. A
516 CC   Colby   3   /To my plans for your future./{C} Thank you, Sir Claude./You're a very generous
527 ES   Monica 13   tell you/Not to wait tea for him./{M} Thank you, Lambert./{L} He's busy at the
530 ES   Ld Clav 34   about me, or of my reply —/All to thank them for that./Oh the grudging
532 ES   Monica   9   the trolley, Miss Monica?/{M} Yes, thank you, Lambert. {}/[*Exit* LAMBERT]/{C} I
535 ES   Ld Clav 22   what about you?/{LC} I don't take it, thank you./{G} A reformed character!/{LC} I
547 ES   Monica 32   spoils any sport, in my opinion./{M} Thank you, Mrs. Piggott. But I'm very fond of
559 ES   Michael 38   in your absence./Why should I thank you for imposing this upon me?/And

THANKFUL (3)
378 CP   Edward 16   Lavinia had gone; that I ought to be thankful./And yet, the effect of all his argument
426 CP   Edward 21   That's why we took it. And I'm really thankful/To have that excuse for not seeing
534 ES   Ld Clav 15   {LC} That's something, at least, to be thankful for./I trust you've no need to engage in

THANKS (4)
167 Rock 10   46   light./O Light Invisible, we give Thee thanks for Thy great glory!/FOUR
281 MC Priest3   5   you,/Remember us./{P3} Let our thanks ascend/To God, who has given us
375 CP   Edward 22   I don't want anything./I'm very tired. Thanks awfully, Alex./Good night./{C} What
439 CP   Peter   28   Edward ... to talk about Celia./{P} Thanks very much. But not this time —/I

THANKSGIVING (1)
243 MC Priest2   2   us meet the Archbishop with cordial thanksgiving:/Our lord, our Archbishop returns.

THAT (2085)

THAT'LL (2)
117 SP   Doris   40   /{Du} The Knave of Spades./{Do} That'll be Snow/{Du} Or it might be Swarts/
457 CC   Eggers 14   /And besides, there's the Customs. That'll take her a time,/From my experience. {}/

THAT'S (203)

THATCH (1)
282 MC Chorus   10   hand at the window, the fire in the thatch, the fist in the tavern, the push into the

THE (6940)

THEATRE (5)
180 FQ: ECoker 114 shall be the darkness of God. As, in a theatre,/The lights are extinguished, for the
228 Gus   t   the Napoleon of Crime!/Gus: the Theatre Cat/Gus is the Cat at the Theatre
228 Gus   1   the Theatre Cat/Gus is the Cat at the Theatre Door./His name, as I ought to have
457 CC note 16& 25   *heard distinctly by an audience in the theatre.*/{LE} Just open that case, I want
546 ES   Piggott   9   an appendicitis operation!/I was a theatre nurse. But you mustn't call me 'Matron'

THEATRE'S (1)

229 Gus   50   himself with his claws,/'Well, the Theatre's certainly not what it was./These

THEBES (1)

69 WL: Fire S 245   same divan or bed;/I who have sat by Thebes below the wall/And walked among the

THEE (33)

96 Ash-Wed 5   10 /O my people, what have I done unto thee./Where shall the word be found, where will
96 Ash-Wed 5   21   who walk in darkness, who chose thee and oppose thee,/Those who are torn on
96 Ash-Wed 5   21   darkness, who chose thee and oppose thee,/Those who are torn on the horn between
96 Ash-Wed 5   28 /O my people, what have I done unto thee./Will the veiled sister between the slender/
99 Ash-Wed 6   35   separated/And let my cry come unto Thee./ARIEL POEMS/Journey of the Magi/'A
105 Song Sime   26   to thy word./They shall praise Thee and suffer in every generation/With glory
164 Rock 9   2   set thine heart upon all that I show thee./Who is this that has said: the House of
166 Rock 10   17   foothold./O Light Invisible, we praise Thee!/Too bright for mortal vision./O Greater
166 Rock 10   19   vision./O Greater Light, we praise Thee for the less;/The eastern light our spires
166 Rock 10   25 /O Light Invisible, we worship Thee!/We thank Thee for the lights that we have
166 Rock 10   26   Invisible, we worship Thee!/We thank Thee for the lights that we have kindled,/The
167 Rock 10   35   it comes./O Light Invisible, we glorify Thee!/In our rhythm of earthly life we tire of
167 Rock 10   42   relight the flame./Therefore we thank Thee for our little light, this is dappled with
167 Rock 10   43   is dappled with shadow./We thank Thee who hast moved us to building, to finding,
167 Rock 10   45   bodily vision is made./And we thank Thee that darkness reminds us of light./O Light
167 Rock 10   46   us of light./O Light Invisible, we give Thee thanks for Thy great glory!/FOUR
590 Time Space   9   Has lived eternity./The flowers I gave thee when the dew/Was trembling on the vine,/
590 Space Time   9   sages disagree./The flowers I sent thee when the dew/Was trembling on the vine/
594 Grad 9   2 /Incense of altar-smoke shall rise to thee/From spotless fanes of lucid purity,/O
604 Ode   1   that is left us, Fair Harvard, with thee,/Ere we face the importunate years,/In thy
604 Ode   16   past,/Fair Harvard, to thine and to thee./The Death of Saint Narcissus/Come under
281 MC Chorus   7 *a choir in the distance]./{C}* We praise Thee, O God, for Thy glory displayed in all the
281 MC Chorus   9 /For all things exist only as seen by Thee, only as known by Thee, all things exist/
281 MC Chorus   9   as seen by Thee, only as known by Thee, all things exist/Only in Thy light, and Thy
281 MC Chorus   10   is declared even in that which denies Thee; the darkness declares the glory of light./
281 MC Chorus   11   the glory of light./Those who deny Thee could not deny, if Thou didst not exist;
281 MC Chorus   12   so, they would not exist./They affirm Thee in living; all things affirm Thee in living;
281 MC Chorus   12   affirm Thee in living; all things affirm Thee in living; the bird in the air, both the hawk
281 MC Chorus   13   Thou hast made to be conscious of Thee, must consciously praise Thee, in thought
281 MC Chorus   13   of Thee, must consciously praise Thee, in thought and in word and in deed./Even
281 MC Chorus   16   voices of beasts and of birds, praise Thee./We thank Thee for Thy mercies of blood,
281 MC Chorus   17   and of birds, praise Thee./We thank Thee for Thy mercies of blood, for Thy
282 MC Chorus   4   denied. Therefore, O God, we thank Thee/Who hast given such blessing to

THEIR (179)

32 Hysteria   7   the lady and gentleman wish to take their/tea in the garden, if the lady and
32 Hysteria   8 if the lady and gentleman wish to take their tea in the/garden ...' I decided that if the
33 Conv Gal   5   hung aloft/To light poor travellers to their distress.'/She then: 'How you digress!'/And
38 Gerontion   62   deliberations/Protract the profit of their chilled delirium,/Excite the membrane,
43 Swee Erect   35   involved, disgraced,/Call witness to their principles/And deprecate the lack of taste/
57 Swee Night   39   Agamemnon cried aloud/And let their liquid siftings fall/To stain the stiff
64 WL: Chess   92   the prolonged candle-flames,/Flung their smoke into the laquearia,/Stirring the
65 WL: Chess   116 in rats' alley/Where the dead men lost their bones./'What is that noise?'/The wind
67 WL: Fire S 180   The nymphs are departed./And their friends, the loitering heirs of City
67 WL: Fire S 201 /And on her daughter/They wash their feet in soda water/Et O ces voix d'enfants,
73 WL: Thund 380 in the violet light/Whistled, and beat their wings/And crawled head downward down
103 Journ Magi 12 /And running away, and wanting their liquor and women,/And the night-fires
104 Journ Magi 42 /With an alien people clutching their gods./I should be glad of another death./A
134 Wind   12   river/The Tartar horsemen shake their spears./Five-Finger Exercises/*Lines to a*
136 5FingerEx3   9   feathered mortals take/That which is their mortal due,/Pinching bread and finger too,
147 Rock 1   24   they work, but where they spend their Sundays./In the City, we need no bells:/Let
148 Rock 1   55   of none./All men are ready to invest their money/But most expect dividends./I say to
151 Rock 2   6   and restore turn out the palms of their hands, or look in vain towards foreign
154 Rock 3   14 and printing them,/Many desire to see their names in print,/Many read nothing but the
155 Rock 3   35   'Here were decent godless people:/Their only monument the asphalt road/And a
157 Rock 4   17   within,/When he and his men laid their hands to rebuilding the wall./So they built
159 Rock 6   5 near a Bank/To doubt the security of their money./It is hard for those who live near a
159 Rock 6   13   survive the Faith to which they owe their significance?/Men! polish your teeth on
160 Rock 7   2   deep./And when there were men, in their various ways, they struggled in torment
160 Rock 7   11   to knowledge of Good and Evil./But their light was ever surrounded and shot with
161 Rock 7   22 Passion and Sacrifice saved in spite of their negative being;/Bestial as always before,

161 Rock 7	24	always reaffirming, always resuming their march on the way that was lit by the light;/
162 Rock 8	18	were rapacious and lustful./Many left their bodies to the kites of Syria/Or sea-strewn
162 Rock 8	20	along the routes;/Many left their souls in Syria,/Living on, sunken in moral
164 Rock 9	7	lights?/They would put upon GOD their own sorrow, the grief they should feel/For
164 Rock 9	8	sorrow, the grief they should feel/For their sins and faults as they go about their daily
164 Rock 9	8	their sins and faults as they go about their daily occasions./Yet they walk in the street
172 FQ: BurntN	62	the boarhound and the boar/Pursue their pattern as before/But reconciled among
177 FQ: ECoker	3	removed, destroyed, restored, or in their place/Is an open field, or a factory, or a
178 FQ: ECoker	41	Keeping time,/Keeping the rhythm in their dancing/As in their living in the living
178 FQ: ECoker	42	the rhythm in their dancing/As in their living in the living seasons/The time of the
179 FQ: ECoker	82	peered/Or from which they turned their eyes. There is, it seems to us,/At best, only
179 FQ: ECoker	95	the wisdom of old men, but rather of their folly,/Their fear of fear and frenzy, their
179 FQ: ECoker	96	of old men, but rather of their folly,/Their fear of fear and frenzy, their fear of
179 FQ: ECoker	96	folly,/Their fear of fear and frenzy, their fear of possession,/Of belonging to
185 FQ: DrySal	53	of autumn flowers/Dropping their petals and remaining motionless;/Where is
186 FQ: DrySal	78	and erosionless/Or drawing their money, drying sails at dockage;/Not as
188 FQ: DrySal	137	saw them off have left the platform)/Their faces relax from grief into relief,/To the
189 FQ: DrySal	179	on behalf of/Women who have seen their sons or husbands/Setting forth, and not
189 FQ: DrySal	184	those who were in ships, and/Ended their voyage on the sand, in the sea's lips/Or in
194 FQ: Little	115	forgotten./These things have served their purpose: let them be./So with your own,
201 Def Island	9	trawler —/contributing their share to the ages' pavement/of British
201 Def Island	14	fire/and of those who have followed their forebears/to Flanders and France, those
201 Def Island	17	in triumph, changing nothing/of their ancestors' ways but the weapons/and those
204 de la Mare	9	long-lost treasure-trove)/Recount their exploits at the nursery tea/And when the
210 Old Gumbie	10	with the ways of the mice —/Their behaviour's not good and their manners
210 Old Gumbie	10	—/Their behaviour's not good and their manners not nice;/So when she has got
213 Growltiger	31	/And his raffish crew were sleeping in their barrels and their bunks —/As the Siamese
213 Growltiger	31	were sleeping in their barrels and their bunks —/As the Siamese came creeping in
213 Growltiger	32	—/As the Siamese came creeping in their sampans and their junks./Growltiger had
213 Growltiger	32	came creeping in their sampans and their junks./Growltiger had no eye or ear for
213 Growltiger	39	not heard a sound./The lovers sang their last duet, in danger of their lives —/For
213 Growltiger	39	sang their last duet, in danger of their lives —/For the foe was armed with
213 Growltiger	43	they swarmed aboard./Abandoning their sampans, and their pullaways and junks,/
213 Growltiger	43	/Abandoning their sampans, and their pullaways and junks,/They battened down
213 Growltiger	44	down the hatches on the crew within their bunks./Then Griddlebone she gave a
216 Jellicles	11	black eyes;/They like to practise their airs and graces/And wait for the Jellicle
216 Jellicles	18	the Jellicle Moon appears/They make their toilette and take their repose:/Jellicles
216 Jellicles	18	/They make their toilette and take their repose:/Jellicles wash behind their ears,/
216 Jellicles	19	their repose:/Jellicles wash behind their ears,/Jellicles dry between their toes./
216 Jellicles	20	their ears,/Jellicles dry between their toes./Jellicle Cats are white and black,/
216 Jellicles	27	enough in the afternoon,/Reserving their terpsichorean powers/To dance by the
218 Mung Rump	3	an extensive reputation. They made their home in Victoria Grove —/That was
218 Mung Rump	4	in Victoria Grove —/That was merely their centre of operation, for they were
218 Mung Rump	19	at a smash-and-grab./They made their home in Victoria Grove. They had no
218 Mung Rump	22	assembled for Sunday dinner,/With their minds made up that they wouldn't get
222 Pekes Pols	20	they glared at each other, and scraped their hind feet,/And started to/Bark bark bark
223 Pekes Pols	31	started to grumble and wheeze/In their huffery-snuffery Heathen Chinese./But a
223 Pekes Pols	36	/And so they stepped out, with their pipers in order,/Playing *When the Blue*
227 Macavity	42	the Cat who all the time/Just controls their operations: the Napoleon of Crime!/Gus:
228 Gus	11	/And whenever he joins his friends at their club/(Which takes place at the back of the
234 Ad-dress	4	need no interpreter/To understand their character./You now have learned enough
234 Ad-dress	14	at work and games,/And learnt about their proper names,/Their habits and their
234 Ad-dress	15	And learnt about their proper names,/Their habits and their habitat:/But/*How would*
234 Ad-dress	15	their proper names,/Their habits and their habitat:/But/*How would you ad-dress a*
587 Fable	3	that monks were quacks,/And took their lands and money from the poor men,/And
587 Fable	4	from the poor men,/And brought their abbeys tumbling at their backs,/There was
587 Fable	4	And brought their abbeys tumbling at their backs,/There was a village founded by
587 Fable	12	villainous baron died,/He added to their hoards — a deed which ne'er he/Had done
587 Fable	13	which ne'er he/Had done before — their fortune multiplied,/As if they had been
587 Fable	15	by a kind fairy./Alas! no fairy visited their host,/Oh, no; much worse than that, they
587 Fable	26	was near the Abbot vowed/They'd eat their meal from ghosts and phantoms free,/The
588 Fable	47	and beast in Æsop's fable/To fill out their repast, and pies and puddings,/And jellies,
588 Fable	57	held, his skull held sausages./Over their Christmas wassail the monks dozed,/A fine
589 Fable	84	declare:/St. Peter'd snatcht to heaven their lord renowned,/Though the wicked said
592 Grad 2	2	embarking from the strand/To seek their fortunes on some foreign shore/Well know

592	Grad 2		5	/That though again they see their fatherland/They there shall be as citizens
592	Grad 3		6	with many a splendid dye,/Until their passing may no more be traced./Although
593	Grad 7		6	helpt the cause to victory,/That with their aid the flag is raised on high./Sometime in
597	Before Mor		6	flowers and flowers of yesterday/Their fragrance drifts across the room at dawn,/
598	Circe		4	/Are flowers that no man knows./Their petals are fanged and red/With hideous
598	Circe		8	come here again./Panthers rise from their lairs/In the forest which thickens below,/
599	On a Port		11	the slender hands;/Her dark eyes keep their secrets hid from us,/Beyond the circle of
601	Nocturne		6	some tune/Banal, and out of pity for their fate/Behind the wall I have some servant
240	MC Chorus		21	ill, planning and guessing,/Having their aims which turn in their hands in the
240	MC Chorus		21	/Having their aims which turn in their hands in the pattern of time./Come, happy
241	MC Priest1		9	the poor at the gate/Have forgotten their friend, their Father in God, have forgotten
241	MC Priest1		9	the gate/Have forgotten their friend, their Father in God, have forgotten/That they
241	MC Mess		33	/Lining the road and throwing down their capes,/Strewing the way with leaves and
242	MC Priest1		21	King./Liked or feared by courtiers, in their overbearing fashion,/Despised and
244	MC Chorus		29	the doom of the house, the doom of their lord, the doom of the world?/O Thomas,
245	MC Thomas		11	/{T} Peace. And let them be, in their exaltation./They speak better than they
246	MC Thomas		6	hate./By God's grace aware of their prevision/I sent my letters on another day,/
246	MC Thomas		13	against treason,/Made them hold their hands. So for the time/We are unmolested.
250	MC Thomas		5	/To condemn kings, not serve among their servants,/Is my open office. No! Go./{T2}
250	MC Thomas		11	world knows order./Those who put their faith in worldly order/Not controlled by
252	MC Tempt3		11	/{T3} Kings will allow no power but their own;/Church and people have good cause
254	MC Tempt4		37	desert you./And men shall only do their best to forget you./And later is worse,
258	MC Thomas		22	against Toulouse,/I beat the barons at their own game. I/Could then despise the men
258	MC Thomas		24	raw nobility, whose manners matched their finger-nails./While I ate out of the King's
261	MC Thomas		35	the Godhead from which they draw their/being./I have spoken to you to-day, dear
264	MC Priest1		5	a loud voice;/Lord, lay not this sin to their charge./*Princes moreover did sit.* {}/[*Introit*
268	MC Thomas		33	go to him, upon whom redounds/Their contempt towards me, their contempt
268	MC Thomas		33	/Their contempt towards me, their contempt towards the Church shown./{K1}
276	MC Knight1		29	the other speakers, who,/with their various abilities, and different points of
279	MC Knight4		13	/point. I have nothing to add along their particular lines of argument./What I have
280	MC Priest1		13	the heathen shall build on the ruins,/Their world without God. I see it. I see it./{P3}
281	MC Chorus		11	not deny, if Thou didst not exist; and their denial is never complete, for if it were so,
286	FR Violet		17	people —/You can keep out of their way at home;/People with money from
286	FR Charles		28	care what they're eating;/They've lost their sense of taste and smell/Because of their
286	FR Charles		29	sense of taste and smell/Because of their cocktails and cigarettes. {}/[*Enter*
290	FR Chorus		37	actors who have not been assigned their parts?/Like amateur actors in a dream
295	FR Harry		18	deal deeper/Than what people call their conscience; it is just the cancer/That eats
296	FR Ivy		22	They can be very cunning —/Their malady makes them so. They do not want
300	FR Downing		17	against these ocean liners/With all their swimming baths and gymnasiums/There's
311	FR Harry		19	the moment before sleep/I always see their claws distended/Quietly, as if they had
313	FR Charles		21	Harry;/They need the influence of their elder brother./Arthur's a bit irresponsible,
316	FR Agatha		18	the weasel and the otter/Be about their proper business/The eye of the day time/
324	FR Harry		32	—/And so far as they feel at all, their emotions are suitable./They don't
330	FR Harry		18	/{H} I still have to learn exactly what their meaning is./At the beginning, eight years
331	FR Harry		9	it./I still have to find out what their meaning is./Here I have been finding/A
334	FR Harry		29	/When other people seemed so strong, their apparent strength/Stifled my decision.
349	FR	5m	13	*they blow out a few candles, so that their last/words are spoken in the dark.*]/{Ag} A
350	FR Agatha		25	who depart/In several directions/For their own redemption/And that of the departed
355	CP Julia		10	be so sceptical. I stayed there once/At their castle in the North. How he suffered!/They
370	CP Peter		3	twice she spoke of them/And about their lack of intellectual interests./{E} And what
407	CP Reilly		10	mind./That is one of the causes of their suffering./{L} No one can say my husband
407	CP Reilly		19	/Taking infinite pains, exhausting their energy,/Yet never quite successful. You
409	CP Reilly		21	incapable of loving/Is as disturbing to their self-esteem/As, in cruder men, the fear of
410	CP Reilly		26	A prey/To the devils who arrive at their plenitude of power/When they have you to
411	CP Lavinia		32	us, themselves, that they had made their decision./{E} Have you anything else to say
413	CP Reilly		11	are mistaken/About the nature of their illness, and lead them to see/That it's not
419	CP Reilly		1	those who take the other/Can forget their loneliness. You will not forget yours./Each
420	CP Reilly		27	/The stale thoughts mouldering in their minds./Each unable to disguise his own
421	CP Julia		4	now, when they are stripped naked to their souls/And can choose, whether to put on
422	CP Reilly		8	have chosen?/{R} They accept their destiny./{A} And *she* has made the choice?/
422	CP	m	13	building of the hearth. {}/[*They raise their glasses*]/{R} Let them build the hearth/
425	CP Edward		23	what the Gunnings' parties were like./Their guests will get just enough to make them
426	CP Julia		36	Parkinson party;/I recognised one of their men at the door —/An old friend of mine,
428	CP Alex		28	monkeys/And what with protecting their crops from the monkeys/The Christian
439	CP Julia		36	party. They must be ready for it./Their guests may be arriving at any moment./

445 CC	Claude	6	Colby./That's not the way to arrange their first meeting,/On her return from
459 CC	Lady E	3	people's auras almost better than their faces./What did you say his name was?/
482 CC	Lady E	15	the sort of person/They ever meet in their kind of society./So naturally, they want to
486 CC	Colby	23	children?/{C} They had no children of their own./That is to say, they had had one little
508 CC	Eggers	29	lost sight of them./{E} But you know their name?/{MG} Yes, I know their name:/Like
508 CC	Guzzard	30	know their name?/{MG} Yes, I know their name:/Like mine, a somewhat unusual
508 CC	Claude	34	them./The name was Kaghan./{SC} Their name was Kaghan!/{MG} K-A-G-H-A-N.
516 CC	Colby	40	/And in the same way to accept their failure./You had your father before you, as
533 ES	Gomez	7	know, where *I* live, people do change their names;/And besides, my wife's name is a
536 ES	Gomez	17	do not./They think in Spanish, but their thoughts are Indian thoughts./O God,
536 ES	Gomez	37	my married sisters — I don't suppose their husbands/Were ever told the story. *They*
540 ES	Gomez	31	girls who were with us (what were their names?/I've completely forgotten them)
549 ES	Carghil	11	lunch?/I declare, I've utterly forgotten their names./And you gave us lunch — I've
552 ES	Carghil	23	very seldom heard people mention their consciences/Except to observe that their
552 ES	Carghil	24	consciences/Except to observe that their consciences were clear./You got out of a
553 ES	Carghil	18	remember reading somewhere:/*Where their fires are not quenched.* Do you know what I
557 ES	Michael	39	was just the same at Oxford./{Mi} It's their own fault./They won't send in their bills,
558 ES	Michael	1	their own fault./They won't send in their bills, and then I forget them./It's being
561 ES	Ld Clav	6	me, Michael:/Those who flee from their past will always lose the race./I know this
570 ES	Ld Clav	30	He even has sons/Following in their father's footsteps/Who are also successful.
572 ES	Charles	29	they are inspired/With revenge — it's their means of self-justification./Let them tell
572 ES	Charles	30	of self-justification./Let them tell their versions of their miserable stories,/Confide
572 ES	Charles	30	/Let them tell their versions of their miserable stories,/Confide them in

THEM (320)
THEMES (1)

| 471 CC | Colby | 5 | things I want to hear./I'll play you the themes, so you'll recognise them./Better still, I'll |

THEMSELVES (23)

43 Swee Erect		34	sides./The ladies of the corridor/Find themselves involved, disgraced,/Call witness to
92 Ash-Wed 2		51	with the blessing of sand,/Forgetting themselves and each other, united/In the quiet
164 Rock 9		10	ready for races,/Adorning themselves, and busy in the market, the forum,/
164 Rock 9		12	secular meetings./Thinking good of themselves, ready for any festivity,/Doing
164 Rock 9		13	ready for any festivity,/Doing themselves very well./Let us mourn in a private
179 FQ: ECoker		77	Had they deceived us,/Or deceived themselves, the quiet-voiced elders,/Bequeathing
217 Jellicles		35	do at all:/They are resting and saving themselves to be right/For the Jellicle Moon
261 MC Thomas		34	Saints are/most high, having made themselves most low, and are seen, not as we/
267 MC	m	25	*attendants return and quietly interpose themselves.*]/{T} Now and here!/{K1} Of your
273 MC Priests		30	men, against men/Who would damn themselves to beasts. My Lord! My Lord!/{T}
289 FR Agatha		2	is revealed, and the spectres show themselves./{G} I don't in the least know what
290 FR Chorus		38	dream when the curtain rises, to find themselves dressed for a different play, or
403 CP Reilly		17	the endless struggle/To think well of themselves./{E} If I am like that/I must have
410 CP Reilly		27	of power/When they have you to themselves./{L} Then what can we do/When we
411 CP Lavinia		32	my question too./They had to tell us, themselves, that they had made their decision./
417 CP Reilly		27	but they cease to regret it,/Maintain themselves by the common routine,/Learn to
417 CP Reilly		29	expectation,/Become tolerant of themselves and others,/Giving and taking, in the
436 CP Edward		5	to learn much worse things/About themselves, and learn them later/When it's
472 CC Colby		2	would happen if you left things to themselves./You jump — because you're afraid
534 ES Gomez		25	children,/All grown up, doing well for themselves./I wouldn't allow either of my sons/
534 ES Gomez		32	ones who don't get out in time/Find themselves in gaol and not very comfortable,/Or
546 ES Piggott		12	/We don't want our guests to think of themselves as ill,/Though we never have guests
570 ES Ld Clav		20	And yet they've both done better for themselves/In consequence of it all. He admitted

THEN (277)
THEORY (1)

| 194 FQ: Little | 114 | eager to rehearse/My thoughts and theory which you have forgotten./These things |

THERE (478)
THERE'LL (4)

328 FR	Gerald	9	say/It's not very conspicuous .../{G} There'll have been more in the later editions./
368 CP	Edward	21	shan't disturb you./{E} My dear Alex,/There'll be nothing in the larder worthy of your
518 CC	Eggers	21	— if Mrs. Eggerson approved./{E} There'll be no one so pleased as Mrs. E.;/Of
552 ES	Carghil	36	longer any part to play, Maisie./{MC} There'll always be some sort of part for you/

THERE'S (128)

66 WL: Chess	149	time,/And if you don't give it him, there's others will, I said./Oh is there, she said.
118 SP	Doris	4	thing how I draw court cards —/{Do} There's a lot in the way you pick them up/{Du}
118 SP	Dusty	5	lot in the way you pick them up/{Du} There's an awful lot in the way you feel/{Do}
121 SA	Sweeney	21	egg/Well that's life on a crocodile isle./There's no telephones/There's no gramophones/
121 SA	Sweeney	22	a crocodile isle./There's no telephones/There's no gramophones/There's no motor cars/

121 SA Sweeney	23	telephones/There's no gramophones/There's no motor cars/No two-seaters, no
209 NamingCats	5	DIFFERENT NAMES./First of all, there's the name that the family use daily,/Such
209 NamingCats	21	than one cat./But above and beyond there's still one name left over,/And that is the
214 RTTugger	11	it:/For he will do/As he do do/And there's no doing anything about it!/The Rum
214 RTTugger	22	it:/For he will do/As he do do/And there's no doing anything about it!/The Rum
215 RTTugger	34	lap in the middle of your sewing,/For there's nothing he enjoys like a horrible muddle.
215 RTTugger	39	it:/For he will do/As he do do/And there's no doing anything about it!/The Song of
219 Mung Rump	39	AND Rumpelteazer!' — And there's nothing at all to be done about that!/Old
221 Old Deut	34	sleep;/And when the men say: 'There's just time for one more,'/Then the
221 Old Deut	38	be woken —/I'll have the police if there's any uproar' —/And out they all shuffle,
224 Mr Mistoff	6	All his/Inventions are off his own bat./There's no such Cat in the metropolis;/He holds
226 Macavity	5	*not there*!/Macavity, Macavity, there's no one like Macavity,/He's broken every
226 Macavity	17	wide awake./Macavity, Macavity, there's no one like Macavity,/For he's a fiend in
226 Macavity	26	and the trellis past repair —/Ay, there's the wonder of the thing! *Macavity's not*
227 Macavity	35	division sums./Macavity, Macavity, there's no one like Macavity,/There never was a
229 Gus	52	productions are all very well,/But there's nothing to equal, from what I hear tell,/
230 Bust Jones	25	*Drones.*/When he's seen in a hurry there's probably curry/At the *Siamese* — or at
232 Skimble	1	/Skimbleshanks: the Railway Cat/There's a whisper down the line at 11.39/When
233 Skimble	36	neat with a newly folded sheet/And there's not a speck of dust on the floor./There is
233 Skimble	38	— you can make it dark or bright;/There's a button that you turn to make a
233 Skimble	39	that you turn to make a breeze./There's a funny little basin you're supposed to
233 Skimble	60	where he summons the police/If there's anything they ought to know about:/
235 Ad-dress	69	/So this is this, and that is that:/And there's how you AD-DRESS A CAT./Cat
254 MC Tempt4	11	glory after death./When king is dead, there's another king,/And one more king is
277 MC Knight3	24	No, we have done for ourselves, there's/no mistake about that. So, as I said at
286 FR Charles	23	the cocktail-drinking does the harm:/There's nothing on earth so bad for the young./
295 FR Charles	12	together made it seem more horrible./There's a lot in my own past life that presses on
296 FR Gerald	33	that he needs./{G} Nevertheless, Amy, there's something in Violet's suggestion./Why
297 FR Charles	18	knows what he's likely to do/Until there's somebody he wants to get rid of./{G}
297 FR Charles	24	let sleeping dogs lie?/{C} All the same, there's a question or two {}/[*Rings the bell*]/{C}
298 FR Charles	22	this: but there simply are times/When there's nothing to do but take the bull by the
300 FRDowning	16	She wouldn't leave him alone./And there's my complaint against these ocean liners/
300 FRDowning	18	swimming baths and gymnasiums/There's not even a place where a man can go/
303 FR Mary	20	him a little while ago./{M} Well, there's something to be said for having an
304 FR Mary	8	/Now I want your advice, because there's no one else to ask,/And because you are
319 FR Warburt	11	Where was my father?/{W} Harry, there's no good probing for misery./There was
322 FR Winch	18	be able to give you a shock./{Wi} There's been shock enough for one evening, my
322 FR Winch	39	was there, and looked him over;/Says there's nothing wrong but some nasty cuts/And
325 FR Charles	9	to be very popular tonight./{C} Well, there's no sort of use in any of us going —/On a
325 FR Charles	11	like this — it's a good three miles;/There's nothing we could do that Warburton
326 FR Denman	33	DENMAN]/{D} Excuse me, Miss Ivy. There's a trunk call for you./{I} A trunk call?
328 FR Charles	27	Communists make capital out of./{C} There's a little more. 'The Piper family ...' no,
328 FR Charles	33	out of the papers;/But nowadays, there's no such thing as privacy./{Ch} In an old
334 FR Agatha	14	/{Ag} What does the word mean?/There's relief from a burden that I carried,/And
344 FR Gerald	17	of *living* in a tropical climate!/{G} There's nothing wrong with a tropical climate
346 FRDowning	27	/But with people like him, there's something inside them/That accounts for
347 FRDowning	10	/In a manner of speaking. There's no harm in *them*,/I'll take my oath. Will
360 CP Reilly	36	forgiving/And gain an advantage. If there's no other woman/And no other man,
362 CP Reilly	20	likes to be left with a mystery./But there's more to it than that. There's a loss of
362 CP Reilly	20	/But there's more to it than that. There's a loss of personality;/Or rather, you've
365 CP Julia	33	were you singing songs all the time?/There's altogether too much mystery/About this
371 CP Edward	32	past, for the sake of the memory./{E} There's no memory you can wrap in camphor/
377 CP Julia	20	*glasses*]/{J} I've had an inspiration!/There's nothing in the place fit to eat:/I've
378 CP Celia	6	/In about ten minutes? Before I go, there's something/I want to speak to Edward./{J}
387 CP Edward	11	see that ... {}/[*The doorbell rings*]/{E} There's Lavinia. {}/[*Goes to front door*]/{E}
398 CP Lavinia	14	I can't persuade you to see a doctor,/There's nothing else at present that I can do
413 CP Celia	16	well./I could lead an active life — if there's anything to work for;/I don't imagine
413 CP Celia	28	you/That I should really *like* to think there's something wrong with me —/Because, if
413 CP Celia	29	me —/Because, if there isn't, then there's something wrong,/Or at least, very
414 CP Celia	1	so flat. I don't mean simply/That there's been a crash: though indeed there has
418 CP Celia	19	/Or just cantankerousness ... still,/If there's no other way ... then I feel just hopeless./
425 CP Lavinia	8	want to come. But what can you do?/There's usually a lot who don't want to come/
425 CP Lavinia	31	go away again. Anyway, at that stage/There's nothing whatever you can do about it:/
433 CP Peter	13	never come if we invited you./But there's someone I wanted to ask about,/Who
440 CP Edward	36	be over./{L} I wish it would begin./{E} There's the doorbell./{L} Oh, I'm glad. It's

448 CC	Eggers	15	him much about Lady Elizabeth./But there's one thing I should like to know —/If you
449 CC	Claude	4	*mislaid*,/Since the father is dead, and there's no way of tracing it./Yes, I was thinking
449 CC	Claude	38	guess what her reaction would be./There's a lot I don't understand about my wife./
449 CC	Claude	39	lot I don't understand about my wife./There's always something one's ignorant of/
450 CC	Claude	5	about him./As a matter of fact, there's a lot I don't know/About you, Eggerson,
450 CC	Eggers	10	put it so convincingly,/I must admit there's a lot that *I* don't understand/About my
457 CC	Colby	7	seems to be kind-hearted./But there's one thing I do believe, Mr. Eggerson:/
457 CC	Eggers	12	time you were off./{E} I'm just going. There's plenty of time. {}/[*Looks at his watch*]/
457 CC	Eggers	14	with minutes to spare,/And besides, there's the Customs. That'll take her a time,/
460 CC	Lady E	1	Zürich. So she said: 'Come to Zürich!/There's a wonderful doctor who teaches mind
467 CC	Colby	6	/That I had something to atone for!/There's something lacking, between you and
471 CC	Lucasta	31	know it sounds impertinent./{L} Well, there's one thing you haven't learnt yet,/And
472 CC	Lucasta	21	something that your music stands for./There's one thing I know. When you first told
475 CC	Colby	7	{C} That's not what I meant./I meant, there's no end to understanding a person./All
476 CC	Colby	1	much rather hear it from yourself./{C} There's only one thing I can't tell you./At least,
477 CC	Lucasta	8	You are Claude's daughter!/{L} Oh, there's no doubt of that./I'm sure he wished
478 CC	Lucasta	17	wonderful/All in a moment. And now there's nothing,/Nothing at all. It's far worse
478 CC	Lucasta	22	further in,/And you know at last that there's no escape./Well, I'll be going./{C} You
478 CC	Colby	25	I'll be going./{C} You mustn't go yet!/There's something else that I want to explain,/
478 CC	Lucasta	27	a promise. But .../{L} I don't believe there's anything to explain/That could explain
478 CC	Lucasta	32	but I have some self-respect./Well, there's always B. I think that now/I'm just
480 CC	Kaghan	18	that isn't a certainty./{K} Well, there's something in that. You know, Lucasta,/
485 CC	Lady E	19	one's previous existences. Of course, there's something in us,/In all of us, which isn't
486 CC	Colby	28	wondering why you are so interested:/There's nothing very interesting about my
490 CC	Colby	15	conversation. I only feel ... numb./If there's agony, it's part of a total agony/Which I
490 CC	Colby	21	has lived without parents, as a child,/There's a gap that never can be filled. Never./I
492 CC	Colby	17	I never want to touch it again./But there's another reason. I must remind you/
500 CC	Claude	6	let me explain./{SC} No, I'll explain. There's been some misunderstanding./My wife
502 CC	Lucasta	33	to know *what* you are./It may be there's no one so hard to understand/As one's
509 CC	Lady E	5	the child Barnabas./{LE} Barnabas? There's never been such a name/In my family.
513 CC	Colby	16	the nagging annoyance of knowing there's a fact/That one doesn't know. But the
524 ES	Charles	4	if I'm not going to have you to myself/There's really no point in my staying to tea. {}/
526 ES	Monica	23	few minutes ago./Here's an armchair, there's the table;/There's the door ... and I hear
526 ES	Monica	24	/Here's an armchair, there's the table;/There's the door ... and I hear someone coming:
531 ES	Lambert	32	/{L} Excuse me, my Lord. There's a gentleman downstairs/Is very insistent
534 ES	Gomez	1	systematic corruption./{G} No, Dick, there's a fault in your logic./How can one
537 ES	Gomez	31	the rake,/But you never went too far. There's a prudent devil/Inside you, Dick. He
538 ES	Ld Clav	6	have mentioned your reflections./But there's just one thing you seem to have
541 ES	Lambert	32	Monica asked me/To remind you there's a trunk call coming through for you/In
547 ES	Piggott	10	when you want to be *very* quiet/There's the Silence Room. With a television set./
547 ES	Ld Clav	13	say/Nothing could be worse. Where there's a Mrs. Piggott/There may be, among the
547 ES	Piggott	24	dance in the evening. At the moment there's no dancing,/And it's still too early for
547 ES	Piggott	27	are keen on tennis,/And of course there's always croquet. But I don't advise
549 ES	Carghil	26	but it's the way things happen./I said 'there's a man I could follow round the world!'/
553 ES	Carghil	17	that we may *always* be together./There's a phrase I seem to remember reading
554 ES	Carghil	3	/And read them to you./— Oh, there's Mrs. Piggott!/She's bearing down on us.
561 ES	Monica	36	Oh, how silly that phrase sounds! But there's no vocabulary/For love within a family,
562 ES	Carghil	36	inherited all of your charm, Richard./There's no denying it. But who's this coming?/
567 ES	Charles	17	I'm engaged to you for ever./{C} There's another shopping expedition we must
568 ES	Charles	16	yet know about me, Monica,/But there's nothing I would ever wish to conceal
568 ES	Ld Clav	17	wish to conceal from you./{LC} If there's nothing, truly nothing, that you couldn't
568 ES	Ld Clav	31	/No, I do love my Monica — but there's the impediment:/It's impossible to be
569 ES	Monica	15	you. I should understand you better./There's nothing I'm afraid of learning about
569 ES	Monica	16	I'm afraid of learning about Charles,/There's nothing I'm afraid of learning about
569 ES	Charles	20	acquaintance —/I was thinking that if there's any question of blackmail,/I've seen
576 ES	Michael	19	know?/{Mi} We didn't go into details. There's time for that later./{G} Much better to
579 ES	Michael	19	just depends./I could look in again. If there's any point in it./Personally, I think that
579 ES	Michael	27	he will get his first leave./{Mi} Well ... there's nothing more to say, is there?/{LC}

THEREBY (1)

| 589 Fable | | 88 | put to his name the handle/Of Saint, thereby rebuking all such scandal./But after this |

THEREFORE (19)

57 Swee Night		27	/Are suspect, thought to be in league;/Therefore the man with heavy eyes/Declines the
158 Rock 5		11	encompassed with snakes and dogs: therefore some must labour, and others must
163 Rock 8		48	men of faith and conviction./Let us therefore make perfect our will./O GOD, help
165 Rock 9		33	Man is joined spirit and body,/And therefore must serve as spirit and body./Visible

167 Rock 10	42	quench, forever relight the flame./Therefore we thank Thee for our little light, this
185 FQ: DrySal	62	in as the most reliable —/And therefore the fittest for renunciation./There is
194 FQ: Little	111	is easy,/Yet ease is cause of wonder. Therefore speak:/I may not comprehend, may
243 MC Priest2	4	/Our doubts are dispelled. Let us therefore rejoice,/I say rejoice, and show a glad
268 MC Knight1	14	nation./{K1} These are the facts./Say therefore if you will be content/To answer in the
268 MC Knight1	15	/To answer in the King's presence. Therefore were we sent./{T} Never was it my
271 MC Thomas	25	am worthy, there is no danger./I have therefore only to make perfect my will./{3P} My
276 MC Knight1	20	our action. You are Englishmen, and therefore you believe in fair/play: and when you
276 MC Knight1	24	of honour. You/are Englishmen, and therefore will not judge anybody without/
277 MC Knight2	37	Urse: that you are Englishmen,/and therefore your sympathies are always with the
278 MC Knight2	3	be taken in by/emotional clap-trap. I therefore ask you to consider soberly: what/
278 MC Knight2	12	and to reform the legal system./He therefore intended that Becket, who had proved
281 MC Chorus	13	in the soil and the worm in the belly./Therefore man, whom Thou hast made to be
282 MC Chorus	4	the earth/Though it is forever denied. Therefore, O God, we thank Thee/Who hast
361 CP Reilly	27	disclosure to a stranger./Let me, therefore, remain the stranger./But let me tell

THEREFROM (1)

38 Gerontion	55	was near your heart was removed therefrom/To lose beauty in terror, terror in

THEREON (1)

167 Rock 10	44	to the Invisible Light, we may set thereon the little lights for which our bodily

THESE (121)

18 Portrait	24	you are!)/To find a friend who has these qualities,/Who has, and gives/Those
18 Portrait	28	that I say this to you —/Without these friendships — life, what *cauchemar!*/
19 Portrait	52	/And go on drinking tea./'Yet with these April sunsets, that somehow recall/My
20 Portrait	83	that other people have desired./Are these ideas right or wrong?/The October night
23 Preludes	49	by fancies that are curled/Around these images, and cling:/The notion of some
34 Figlia	23	lost a gesture and a pose./Sometimes these cogitations still amaze/The troubled
38 Gerontion	47	upon us by our impudent crimes./These tears are shaken from the wrath-bearing
38 Gerontion	61	I use them for your closer contact?/These with a thousand small deliberations/
62 WL: Burial	59	myself:/One must be so careful these days./Unreal City,/Under the brown fog
64 WL: Chess	90	air/That freshened from the window, these ascended/In fattening the prolonged
75 WL: Thund	430	*Le Prince d'Aquitaine à la tour abolie*/These fragments I have shored against my ruins
83 Hollow Men	21	in dreams/In death's dream kingdom/These do not appear:/There, the eyes are/
89 Ash-Wed 1	28	upon us/And I pray that I may forget/These matters that with myself I too much
90 Ash-Wed 1	31	I do not hope to turn again/Let these words answer/For what is done, not to be
90 Ash-Wed 1	34	not be too heavy upon us/Because these wings are no longer wings to fly/But
91 Ash-Wed 2	5	of my skull. And God said/Shall these bones live? shall these/Bones live? And
91 Ash-Wed 2	5	God said/Shall these bones live? shall these/Bones live? And that which had been
98 Ash-Wed 6	7	father) though I do not wish to wish these things/From the wide window towards the
98 Ash-Wed 6	29	care/Teach us to sit still/Even among these rocks,/Our peace in His will/And even
99 Ash-Wed 6	31	peace in His will/And even among these rocks/Sister, mother/And spirit of the
104 Journ Magi	40	our death./We returned to our places, these Kingdoms,/But no longer at ease here, in
124 SA Swarts	18	/With a gallon of lysol in a bath/{Sw} These fellows always get pinched in the end./
127 Cor1 March	25	No,/Those are the golf club Captains, these the Scouts,/And now the *société*
129 Cor2 State	36	over the lintel/O mother (not among these busts, all correctly inscribed)/I a tired
129 Cor2 State	37	inscribed)/I a tired head among these heads/Necks strong to bear them/Noses
148 Rock 1	66	and churches;/The men you are in these times deride/What has been done of good,
158 Rock 5	7	let us destroy it,/And have done with these abominations, the turpitudes of the
158 Rock 5	7	the turpitudes of the Christians.' And these are not justified, nor the others./And they
159 Rock 6	3	never known a Christian,/To believe these tales of Christian persecution./It is hard
163 Rock 8	38	gluttony, jealousy, pride:/It was not these that made the Crusades,/But these that
163 Rock 8	39	these that made the Crusades,/But these that unmade them./Remember the faith
164 Rock 9	25	/LORD, shall we not bring these gifts to Your service?/Shall we not bring
189 FQ: DrySal	198	the womb, or tomb, or dreams; all these are usual/Pastimes and drugs, and features
190 FQ: DrySal	216	are the music/While the music lasts. These are only hints and guesses,/Hints
194 FQ: Little	115	and theory which you have forgotten./These things have served their purpose: let them
196 FQ: Little	183	and quiet,/Why should we celebrate/These dead men more than the dying?/It is not
196 FQ: Little	190	policies/Or follow an antique drum./These men, and those who opposed them/And
201 Def Island	1	VERSES/Defence of the Islands/Let these memorials of built stone — music's/
206 To my Wife	12	this dedication is for others to read:/These are private words addressed to you in
223 Pekes Pols	46	them all over the Park./Now when these bold heroes together assembled,/The
229 Gus	45	was on fire./And he says: 'Now, these kittens, they do not get trained/As we did
229 Gus	51	Theatre's certainly not what it was./These modern productions are all very well,/But
235 Ad-dress	65	sauce.)/A Cat's entitled to expect/These evidences of respect./And so in time you
589 Fable	95	shire. We/Got the veracious record of these doings/From an old manuscript found in
594 Grad 12	3	and may stronger words than these/Proclaim the glory so that all may hear;/

604		Ode	9	of the past as we go./Yet for all of these years that to-morrow has lost/We are still
240	MC	Chorus	18	the still unshapen:/I have seen these things in a shaft of sunlight./Destiny waits
241	MC	Priest1	7	is devoured by his own./{P1} Shall these things not end/Until the poor at the gate/
243	MC	Priest3	8	wheel turn./The wheel has been still, these seven years, and no good./For ill or good,
245	MC	Priest2	24	coming,/Engrossed by the chatter of these foolish women./Forgive us, my Lord, you
245	MC	Thomas	37	grateful for all your kind attentions./These are small matters. Little rest in
248	MC	Tempt2	18	I have recalled them,/Let us but set these not too pleasant memories/In balance
254	MC	Thomas	23	another place./{T} I have thought of these things./{T4} That is why I tell you./Your
255	MC	Thomas	31	damnation in pride?/I well know that these temptations/Mean present vanity and
260	MC	Thomas	19	will be cast out by joy; so it is only in these our Christian/mysteries that we can rejoice
262	MC	Thomas	4	I would have you keep in your hearts/these words that I say, and think of them at
268	MC	Knight1	13	the business of the nation./{K1} These are the facts./Say therefore if you will be
271	MC	Thomas	8	peace with your thoughts and visions./These things had to come to you and you to
271	MC	Thomas	14	is made complete./You shall forget these things, toiling in the household,/You shall
271	MC	Thomas	22	All my life they have been coming, these feet. All my life/I have waited. Death will
273	MC	Priests	23	Open the door!/{3P} My Lord! these are not men, these come not as men come,
273	MC	Priests	23	/{3P} My Lord! these are not men, these come not as men come, but/Like
276	MC	Chorus	8	/The fuel laid on the fire at daybreak,/These acts marked a limit to our suffering./
278	MC	Knight2	5	King Henry's aims? In/the answer to these questions lies the key to the problem./The
278	MC	Knight2	37	still, even such temperate/measures as these would become unnecessary. But, if you
279	MC	Knight4	37	Need I say more? I think, with these facts before/you, you will unhesitatingly
289	FR	Ivy	31	/{A} I would never ask him./{I} These things are much better not enquired into./
295	FR	Charles	14	early before morning./I understand these feelings better than you know —/But *you*
298	FR	Charles	25	/It's good to see you again, after all these years./You're well, I hope?/{Do} Thank
300	FR	Downing	16	/And there's my complaint against these ocean liners/With all their swimming
303	FR	Mary	6	blossoms,/Such as they are, than have these greenhouse flowers/Which do not belong
306	FR	Harry	12	to ask you. I don't know yet./All these years I'd been longing to get back/Because
310	FR	Mary	6	trunk/The pain of the breaking bud./These are the ones that suffer least:/The aconite
313	FR	Ivy	8	/{I} Mary, my dear,/Did you arrange these flowers? Just let me change them./You
322	FR	Winch	6	God rest her soul,/She's been dead these ten years. How is her Ladyship,/If I may
328	FR	Violet	6	is definitely reckless./{V} I think these racing cars ought to be prohibited. {}/
328	FR	Charles	32	too hard on him./{C} In my time, these affairs were kept out of the papers;/But
329	FR	Chorus	18	all are recorded./There is no avoiding these things/And we know nothing of exorcism/
330	FR	Harry	3	/And everything will go on as before. These mild surprises/Should be in the routine of
334	FR	Agatha	9	It is as if/I had been living all these years upon my capital,/Instead of earning
334	FR	Harry	24	/After such training, I could endure, these ten years,/Playing a part that had been
341	FR	Amy	21	possession/Is only the stronger for all these years of abstinence./Thirty-five years ago
346	FR	Downing	18	when you come to look at it:/After all these years that I've been with him/I think I
349	FR	Chorus	4	are we doing?/To each and all of these questions/There is no conceivable answer./
357	CP	Julia	22	be called away again./I understand these tough old women —/I'm one myself. I feel
359	CP	Edward	15	fact is, I tried to put off this party:/These were only the people I couldn't put off/
361	CP	Edward	13	don't suggest./I have often used these terms in examining witnesses,/So I don't
371	CP	Peter	19	even the memory./Did we really share these interests? Did we really feel the same/
374	CP	Celia	25	the real difficulties./{C} But surely, these are only temporary./You know I accepted
378	CP	Edward	32	free./{E} No, it is not that./And all these reasons were suggested to me/By the man
398	CP	Edward	7	devil left the door on the latch/For these doubts to enter? And then you came back,
413	CP	Celia	22	with what I've been going through, these last weeks,/I somehow took it for granted
419	CP	Reilly	21	/Those who go do not come back as these./{C} It sounds like a prison. But they
428	CP	Lavinia	8	/{L} But can't they exterminate these monkeys/If they are a pest?/{A}
428	CP	Alex	12	of the natives are heathen:/They hold these monkeys in peculiar veneration/And do
428	CP	Alex	40	just recognised. You see, Lavinia,/These are very deep waters./{E} And the
429	CP	Alex	19	but they are not usually eaten./When these people have done with a European/He is,
437	CP	Reilly	37	/In fear and anger and loathing — all these together —/And reluctance of the body to
439	CP	Reilly	6	Celia./{R} You will have to live with these memories and make them/Into something
439	CP	Lavinia	39	/{L} And I have been thinking, for these last five minutes,/How I could face my
440	CP	Lavinia	10	But all the same ... I don't want to see these people./{R} It is your appointed burden.
448	CC	Eggers	11	truth, Sir Claude, I only touched on these matters,/They're much too deep for me.
453	CC	Eggers	40	/Sir Claude intends to deal with these matters himself./You will have to ask Sir
484	CC	Lady E	25	childhood must have been similar./These are only superficial differences:/You must
485	CC	Lady E	9	that my mother *was* my mother./These were foolish fancies. I was a silly girl,/
486	CC	Claude	35	of telephoning,/Just to give him these notes. They're notes for my speech/At the
487	CC	Lady E	39	It's the name I've been hunting for all these years —/That, and the other name,
494	CC	Lady E	37	strange to have lived with you, all these years,/And now you tell me, you'd have
508	CC	Eggers	14	/{E} May I pour a drop of oil on these troubled waters?/Let us approach the
514	CC	Claude	19	carried out such a deception/Over all these years. And why *should* you have deceived

530 ES Ld Clav   10   and you know it./They talk of rest, these doctors, Charles; they tell me to be
533 ES Gomez   15 But I've been a pretty hard worker all these years/And I thought, now's the time to
545 ES Piggott   26 and explain./I've been in such a rush, these last few days,/And I thought, 'Lord
548 ES Carghil   30   /Dear me, it's astonishing, after all these years;/And you don't even recognise me!
551 ES Carghil   18 about the past — about you and me./These memories are painful — but I cherish
553 ES Ld Clav   34   /{LC} And have you shown these letters/To many people?/{MC} Only a few
553 ES Carghil   38 should be in want, you could have these letters auctioned.'/Yes, I'll bring the
570 ES Monica   1 But what did the ghosts mean? All these years/You've kept them to yourself. Did
570 ES Charles   17   Let us share your ghosts!/{C} But these are only human beings, who can be dealt
571 ES Ld Clav   4 Ferry too, and Richard Ferry —/These are my ghosts. They were people with
571 ES Charles   22 frets me./{C} But all the same, these two people mustn't persecute you./We

THEY (451)
THEY'D (3)
587 Fable   26   time was near the Abbot vowed/They'd eat their meal from ghosts and
355 CP Julia   34 dead now. But I wanted to know./If they'd been friends of yours, I couldn't tell the
558 ES Michael   24 a lot of fun with me — sometimes they'd pretend/That I was overworked, when

THEY'LL (6)
118 SP Doris   6 in the way you feel/{Do} Sometimes they'll tell you nothing at all/{Du} You've got to
425 CP Edward   24 get just enough to make them thirsty;/They'll come on to us later, roaring for drink./
425 CP Lavinia   30   be able to take the tray about,/So they'll go away again. Anyway, at that stage/
548 ES Monica   12 be asleep./If they think you *are* asleep they'll do something to wake you,/But if they
548 ES Monica   13 you,/But if they see you're shamming they'll have to take the hint. {}/[*Exit*]/*A moment*
553 ES Carghil   25 was Effie said, when the break came,/'They'll be worth a fortune to you, Maisie.'/They

THEY'RE (24)
118 SP Dusty   11   more than once/{Du} Sometimes they're no use at all./{Do} I'd like to know
216 Jellicles   25   /Jellicle Cats have moonlit eyes./They're quiet enough in the morning hours,/
216 Jellicles   26 quiet enough in the morning hours,/They're quiet enough in the afternoon,/
286 FR Charles   26   young people don't know what they're drinking,/Modern young people don't
286 FR Charles   27   young people don't care what they're eating;/They've lost their sense of taste
344 FR Gerald   22   fellows. A maligned profession./They're sometimes very useful, knowing the
355 CP Julia   33 I don't know the Vincewells./{J} Oh, they're both dead now. But I wanted to know./
365 CP Julia   1 anybody found them? You can tell if they're mine —/Some kind of a plastic sort of
366 CP Edward   5 the cushion./{E} Are you quite sure they're not in your bag?/{J} Why no, of course
391 CP Julia   12 Oh, you mean my spectacles./No, they're here. Besides, they're no use to me./I'm
391 CP Julia   12 spectacles./No, they're here. Besides, they're no use to me./I'm not coming back
426 CP Edward   3 do. I'm too tired to bother./{E} After they're all gone, we will have some champagne,/
448 CC Eggers   12 I only touched on these matters,/They're much too deep for me. And I thought,
449 CC Claude   25   And there are others./For one, they're both of them women./{E} True./{SC}
452 CC Lucasta   22 And I couldn't find one of them./But they're all filed somewhere, I'm sure, so why
474 CC Colby   1   to do with each other —/Well, they're both unreal. But for Eggerson/His
482 CC Colby   22 Elizabeth, what is it you object to?/They're both intelligent ... and kind./{LE} Oh, I
482 CC Lady E   23 ... and kind./{LE} Oh, I don't say they're not intelligent and kind./I'm not making
482 CC Lady E   26   /And ... well, rather vulgar. They're not your sort at all./{C} I shouldn't call
486 CC Claude   35   /Just to give him these notes. They're notes for my speech/At the dinner of
527 ES Monica   37 him/And Father was too severe — so they're always at loggerheads./{C} But you
546 ES Piggott   28 the dining-room:/Nobody looks ill! They're all convalescents,/Or resting, like you.
553 ES Carghil   31 afraid I can't show you the originals;/They're in my lawyer's safe. But I have
564 ES Carghil   19 were Spanish./I do like Spaniards. They're so aristocratic./But it's very strange that

THEY'VE (8)
286 FR Charles   28 people don't care what they're eating;/They've lost their sense of taste and smell/
400 CP Alex   33   staircase/And come back when they've gone./{R} Yes, when they've gone. {}/
400 CP Reilly   34 when they've gone./{R} Yes, when they've gone. {}/[*Exit* ALEX *by side door*]/
425 CP Lavinia   33   /Where everybody else is, to show they've been invited./That's what makes it a
530 ES Ld Clav   9 that wears out the machine./{LC} They've dried up, Monica, and you know it./
544 ES Monica   2 than you expected,/Isn't it, Father? They've let us alone;/The people in the
569 ES Ld Clav   35 merely ghosts:/Spectres from my past. They've always been with me/Though it was not
570 ES Ld Clav   20 for in your life?/{LC} ... And yet they've both done better for themselves/In

THIBET (1)
332 FR Agatha   31   kind,/I believe, across a whole Thibet of broken stones/That lie, fang up, a

THICK (6)
256 MC Chorus   6   of feet. And the air is heavy and thick./Thick and heavy the sky. And the earth
256 MC Chorus   7 feet. And the air is heavy and thick./Thick and heavy the sky. And the earth presses
269 MC Chorus   34 necks twisting, rat tails twining, in the thick light of dawn. I have eaten/Smooth
294 FR Harry   16   solitude in a crowded desert/In a thick smoke, many creatures moving/Without
322 FR Winch   28 Mostly walking,/What with the fog so thick, or I'd have been here sooner./I'd

532 ES	Gomez	32	of Mr. Culverwell?/{G} We're as thick as thieves, you might almost say./Don't

THICKENS (1)

598 Circe	9	from their lairs/In the forest which thickens below,/Along the garden stairs/The

THICKET (1)

292 FR	Harry	6	In Italy, from behind the nightingale's thicket,/The eyes stared at me, and corrupted

THIEVES (2)

376 CP	Edward	22	before./{E} The man who fell among thieves was luckier than I:/He was left at an inn.
532 ES	Gomez	32	Mr. Culverwell?/{G} We're as thick as thieves, you might almost say./Don't you know

THIGHS (2)

42 Swee Erect	16	teeth:/The sickle motion from the thighs/Jackknifes upward at the knees/Then
605 Narcissus	19	seemed to tread on faces, convulsive thighs and knees./So he came out under the

THIMBLE (1)

232 Skimble	3	is Skimble has he gone to hunt the thimble?/We must find him or the train can't

THIN (7)

14 Prufrock	41	will say: 'How his hair is growing thin!')/My morning coat, my collar mounting
14 Prufrock	44	say: 'But how his arms and legs are thin!')/Do I dare/Disturb the universe?/In a
54 Mr E Sun	13	/But through the water pale and thin/Still shine the unoffending feet/And there
141 Rannoch	4	or soar. Substance crumbles, in the thin air/Moon cold or moon hot. The road
226 Macavity	11	a ginger cat, he's very tall and thin;/You would know him if you saw him, for
228 Gus	5	just Gus./His coat's very shabby, he's thin as a rake,/And he suffers from palsy that
602 Humoresque	19	of nose),/'Your damned thin moonlight, worse than gas —/'Now in New

THINE (11)

85 Hollow Men	77	/And the act/Falls the Shadow/*For Thine is the Kingdom*/Between the conception/
85 Hollow Men	91	the descent/Falls the Shadow/*For Thine is the Kingdom*/For Thine is/Life is/For
86 Hollow Men	92	/*For Thine is the Kingdom*/For Thine is/Life is/For Thine is the/*This is the way*
86 Hollow Men	94	*the Kingdom*/For Thine is/Life is/For Thine is the/*This is the way the world ends*/This
106 Song Sime	33	/(And a sword shall pierce thy heart,/Thine also)./I am tired with my own life and the
162 Rock 8	4	the past./The heathen are come into thine inheritance,/And thy temple have they
164 Rock 9	1	help us./Son of Man, behold with thine eyes, and hear with thine ears/And set
164 Rock 9	1	behold with thine eyes, and hear with thine ears/And set thine heart upon all that I
164 Rock 9	2	eyes, and hear with thine ears/And set thine heart upon all that I show thee./Who is
594 Grad 12	5	all may hear;/May worthier sons be thine, from far and near/To spread thy name
604 Ode	16	present, and past,/Fair Harvard, to thine and to thee./The Death of Saint Narcissus

THING (87)

23 Preludes	51	infinitely gentle/Infinitely suffering thing./Wipe your hand across your mouth, and
29 Aunt Helen	7	feet —/He was aware that this sort of thing had occurred before./The dogs were
117 SP	Doris	20	when you read the cards,/It's not a thing that anyone can do./{Du} Yes I know
118 SP	Dusty	3	Or it might be Snow/{Du} It's a funny thing how I draw court cards —/{Do} There's a
129 Cor2 State	8	/Cry cry what shall I cry?/The first thing to do is to form the committees:/The
148 Rock 1	61	turns and the world changes,/But one thing does not change./In all of my years, one
148 Rock 1	62	not change./In all of my years, one thing does not change./However you disguise it,
148 Rock 1	63	change./However you disguise it, this thing does not change:/The perpetual struggle
160 Rock 7	3	/Blindly and vainly, for man is a vain thing, and man without GOD is a seed upon the
180 FQ: ECoker	125	hope would be hope for the wrong thing; wait without love/For love would be love
180 FQ: ECoker	126	/For love would be love of the wrong thing; there is yet faith/But the faith and the
181 FQ: ECoker	146	what you do not know is the only thing you know/And what you own is what you
182 FQ: ECoker	179	to get the better of words/For the thing one no longer has to say, or the way in
187 FQ: DrySal	127	— or one way of putting the same thing:/That the future is a faded song, a Royal
187 FQ: DrySal	132	/You cannot face it steadily, but this thing is sure,/That time is no healer: the patient
191 FQ: Little	13	is no earth smell/Or smell of living thing. This is the spring time/But not in time's
195 FQ: Little	170	/All shall be well, and/All manner of thing shall be well./If I think, again, of this
196 FQ: Little	199	all shall be well and/All manner of thing shall be well/By the purification of the
198 FQ: Little	258	all shall be well and/All manner of thing shall be well/When the tongues of flame
226 Macavity	26	—/Ay, there's the wonder of the thing! *Macavity's not there*!/And when the
589 Fable	69	whom you *can't* keep out;/It is a thing to be lamented sorely/Such slippery folk
261 MC Thomas	8	as the world/gives./Consider also one thing of which you have probably never
277 MC Knight3	1	lead you to/believe. But there is one thing I should like to say, and I might as/well
278 MC Knight2	9	divided. Our King saw that/the one thing needful was to restore order: to curb the
290 FR	Violet	21	You must see for yourself it's the only thing to do./{Ag} Thus with most careful
296 FR	Violet	16	as bad as this./{V} There is only one thing to be done:/Harry must see a doctor./{I}
297 FR	Charles	16	Harry./I might have done the same thing once, myself./Nobody knows what he's
300 FR	Charles	1	might happen./{C} What sort of thing?/{Do} Well, I don't know, Sir./But he
307 FR	Harry	30	just ordinary hopelessness./{H} One thing you cannot know:/The sudden extinction
325 FR	Ivy	15	You are quite right, Gerald, the one thing that matters/Is not to let her see that
326 FR	Harry	17	/You go on trying to think of each thing separately,/Making small things

328 FR	Charles	33	/But nowadays, there's no such	thing as privacy./{Ch} In an old house there is
333 FR	Agatha	6	be killed! What were you then? only a	thing called 'life' —/Something that should have
338 FR	Harry	4	I must do,/And that it is the best	thing for everybody./But at present, I cannot
338 FR	Harry	30	any other!/It is at once the hardest	thing, and the only thing possible./Now they
338 FR	Harry	30	once the hardest thing, and the only	thing possible./Now they will lead me. I shall be
341 FR	Agatha	1	now it is my son./{Ag} I know one	thing, Amy:/That you have never changed. And
341 FR	Amy	19	make for him./{A} Success is one	thing, what you would make for him/Is another.
344 FR	Gerald	19	/The medical knowledge is the first	thing./I've met with missionaries, often enough
344 FR	Charles	30	on where you're going./{C} Such a	thing/Has never happened in our family./{V} I
345 FR	Violet	31	/{V} I do not understand/A single	thing that's happened. {}/[*Exeunt* AMY,
349 FR	All	12	to the moment: we must do the right	thing. {}/[*Exeunt*]/[*Enter, from one door,*
363 CP	Reilly	18	a set/Of obsolete responses. The one	thing to do/Is to do nothing. Wait./{E} Wait!/
363 CP	Edward	21	/{E} Wait!/But waiting is the one	thing impossible./Besides, don't you see that it
364 CP	Julia	33	glasses here,/And I simply can't see a	thing without them./I've been dragging Peter all
376 CP	Celia	3	the door, Edward./It's the best	thing to do. Don't lose your head./You see, I
376 CP	Edward	12	Edward, it's ruined!/{E} What a good	thing./{C} But it's ruined the saucepan too./{E}
376 CP	Edward	16	breakfast. A boiled egg./It's the only	thing I know how to cook./{J} Celia! I see
378 CP	Celia	20	Lavinia back!/Lavinia! So the one	thing you care about/Is to avoid a break —
380 CP	Edward	38	never could have been ... a permanent	thing:/You should have a man ... nearer your
381 CP	Edward	8	you want?/{E} I am not sure./The one	thing of which I am relatively certain/Is, that
392 CP	Lavinia	1	to see you./{L} Yes, that was a silly	thing to say./Like a schoolgirl. Like Celia. I
392 CP	Lavinia	9	are we to talk about?/{L} There is one	thing I ought to know, because of other people/
395 CP	Lavinia	34	myself./{L} And the most infuriating	thing about you/Has always been your placid
434 CP	Lavinia	31	Edward, I'm so sorry — what a feeble	thing to say!/But you know what I mean./{E}
437 CP	Reilly	38	reluctance of the body to become a	*thing*./I'd say she suffered more, because more
446 CC	Claude	16	I can't forget ... no matter./The great	thing was to find something else/He could do,
448 CC	Eggers	15	Lady Elizabeth./But there's one	thing I should like to know —/If you don't
457 CC	Colby	7	to be kind-hearted./But there's one	thing I do believe, Mr. Eggerson:/That *you* have
461 CC	Claude	30	disconcerting:/As you gather, such a	thing never happened before./So the meeting
463 CC	Colby	29	organist,/And for a moment the	thing I cannot do,/The art that I could never
463 CC	Colby	31	I could never excel in,/Seems the one	thing worth doing, the one thing/That I want to
463 CC	Colby	31	the one thing worth doing, the one	thing/That I want to do. I have to fight that
466 CC	Claude	10	But when I am alone, and look at one	thing long enough,/I sometimes have that sense
471 CC	Lucasta	31	impertinent./{L} Well, there's one	thing you haven't learnt yet,/And that is, to
472 CC	Lucasta	21	your music stands for./There's one	thing I know. When you first told me/What a
473 CC	Colby	27	in my 'garden'./Alone, that's the	thing. That's why it's not real./You know, I
476 CC	Colby	1	it from yourself./{C} There's only one	thing I can't tell you./At least, not yet. I'm not
476 CC	Colby	22	on B./{C} I never thought of such a	thing!/{L} You never thought of such a thing!/
476 CC	Lucasta	23	/{L} You never thought of such a	thing!/There are not many men who wouldn't
480 CC	Kaghan	24	and Colby. You and me —/The one	thing *we* want is security/And respectability!
480 CC	Kaghan	33	— no background at all./That's one	thing I like about Lucasta:/She doesn't despise
488 CC	Claude	25	/I've always loathed keeping such a	thing from you./I see now I might as well have
492 CC	Claude	3	whose son I am./{SC} Then the first	thing is: we must see Mrs. Guzzard./{LE} Oh
515 CC	Guzzard	25	claim him. Do you think it is a small	thing/For me, to see my life's ambition come to
528 ES	Monica	8	/{M} You don't understand. It's one	thing meeting people/When you're in authority,
530 ES	Ld Clav	13	mustn't run for trains/When the last	thing he wants is to take a train for anywhere!/
536 ES	Gomez	34	dead long since — that's a good	thing./My mother — I dare say she's still alive,/
537 ES	Gomez	8	hoops of steel, and all that sort of	thing./We'll come to that, very soon. Isn't it
538 ES	Ld Clav	6	your reflections./But there's just one	thing you seem to have forgotten:/I came to
538 ES	Gomez	34	/I rejoiced in your success. But one	thing has puzzled me./You were given a
539 ES	Ld Clav	25	it as altogether accurate./The only	thing I find surprising/In the respected citizen of
546 ES	Monica	31	Mrs. Piggott, but please tell me one	thing./We haven't seen her yet, but the
556 ES	Michael	32	/Before you knew the facts. The first	thing I remember/Is being blamed for
558 ES	Michael	17	son of your father'/And that sort of	thing. It's for your sake, he says,/That he wants
558 ES	Michael	30	criticisms?/{Mi} Well, there was one	thing he brought up against me,/That I'd been
581 ES	Monica	11	You'll be here to greet him./But one	thing I'm convinced of: you must leave Badgley

THINGS (114)

18 Portrait		7	of Juliet's tomb/Prepared for all the	things to be said, or left unsaid./We have been,
20 Portrait		82	hyacinths across the garden/Recalling	things that other people have desired./Are these
24 Rhapsody		24	up high and dry/A crowd of twisted	things;/A twisted branch upon the beach/Eaten
89 Ash-Wed 1		5	no longer strive to strive towards such	things/(Why should the agèd eagle stretch its
89 Ash-Wed 1		20	/And only for one place/I rejoice that	things are as they are and/I renounce the blessèd
94 Ash-Wed 4		5	in Mary's colour,/Talking of trivial	things/In ignorance and in knowledge of eternal
98 Ash-Wed 6		7	though I do not wish to wish these	things/From the wide window towards the
121 SA Sweeney		30	of the surf./Nothing at all but three	things/{Do} What things?/{S} Birth, and

407 CP	Lavinia	4	I say practical,/I mean practical in the things that really matter./{R} May I interrupt
413 CP	Celia	26	state of mind./{C} Well, there are two things I can't understand,/Which you might
413 CP	Reilly	36	*is* normality. You say there are two things:/What is the first?/{C} An awareness of
436 CP	Edward	2	start from./If you find out now, Peter, things about yourself/That you don't like to
436 CP	Edward	4	some men have to learn much worse things/About themselves, and learn them later/
439 CP	Alex	21	/And I know that Bela expects great things of it./{P} So now I'll be going./{E} Shall
445 CC	Eggers	13	Gardening tools./The number of things one needs for a garden!/And I thought,
446 CC	Claude	5	satisfied that he's getting the hang of things,/And I think he's beginning to take a
448 CC	Claude	3	prepare him a little;/There are some things you could say better than I could,/And
452 CC	Lucasta	20	then he got suspicious/And asked for things I'm sure he didn't want —/Just to make
456 CC	Eggers	24	least expect it./But she does forget things. And she likes to travel,/Mostly for her
464 CC	Claude	2	When I was a boy/I loved to shape things. I loved form and colour/And I loved the
464 CC	Claude	11	they are life itself. To be among such things,/If it is an escape, is escape into living,/
464 CC	Claude	14	and painting — I have some good things —/But they haven't this ... remoteness I
469 CC	Lucasta	11	{L} But suppose I only like the wrong things?/{C} No, I'm sure you'll prefer the right
469 CC	Colby	12	No, I'm sure you'll prefer the right things, when you hear them./I've given you a
469 CC	Lucasta	17	know you were so artful!/So the things I liked were the right ones to like?/Still,
471 CC	Colby	4	/About the programme — or the things I want to hear./I'll play you the themes,
472 CC	Colby	2	of what would happen if you left things to themselves./You jump — because
480 CC	Kaghan	38	*you*, Lucasta;/And we want the same things. But as for Colby,/He's the sort of fellow
481 CC	Colby	3	you've a pretty shrewd insight/Into things that have nothing to do with business./
484 CC	Lady E	23	were so carnivorous. Always killing things and eating them./And yet our childhood
492 CC	Claude	35	that out. It would only remind me/Of things that would surprise the Potters'
493 CC	Lady E	29	right./{LE} Claude, I've been thinking things over and over —/All through the night. I
497 CC	Lady E	26	know:/I am perfectly content to leave things as they are,/So that we may regard him
497 CC	Eggers	37	most uncommon name,/But stranger things have happened./{LE} And both in
500 CC	Claude	11	brain reel./{SC} I ought to have made things clear to you/At the time when he came
513 CC	Colby	38	have liked to be,/And by doing the things he had wanted to do./{MG} Whose son
527 ES	Monica	9	may have changed your mind. Such things have happened./{C} That won't happen
537 ES	Gomez	28	at least./I had plenty of time to think things over, later./{LC} And what is the
549 ES	Carghil	25	—/I can't think why, but it's the way things happen./I said 'there's a man I could
556 ES	Michael	30	know, it's awfully hard to explain things to *you*./You've always made up your
558 ES	Michael	18	sake, he says,/That he wants to keep things quiet. I can tell you, it's no joke/Being
563 ES	Gomez	35	Señor Gomez./{G} I lost touch with things in England./Had I been in London, and
568 ES	Ld Clav	5	about guilty secrets./There are many things not crimes, Monica,/Beyond anything of
568 ES	Charles	13	unknown?/{C} There are certainly things I would gladly forget, Sir,/Or rather,
568 ES	Charles	15	had never happened./I can think of things you don't yet know about me, Monica,/
568 ES	Ld Clav	25	that includes, mind you, not only things criminal,/Not only turpitude, meanness
573 ES	Ld Clav	5	other people realise/The magnitude of things that appear to them petty;/It's harder to
577 ES	Michael	21	/Señor Gomez and I have talked things over, Hemington .../{G} As two men of
577 ES	Gomez	22	two men of the world, we discussed things very frankly;/And I can tell you,

THINK (378)

16 Prufrock	125	singing, each to each./I do not think that they will sing to me./I have seen them
18 Portrait	10	/'So intimate, this Chopin, that I think his soul/Should be resurrected only
38 Gerontion	33	such knowledge, what forgiveness? Think now/History has many cunning passages,
38 Gerontion	36	ambitions,/Guides us by vanities. Think now/She gives when our attention is
38 Gerontion	43	/Till the refusal propagates a fear. Think/Neither fear nor courage saves us.
38 Gerontion	48	in the new year. Us he devours. Think at last/We have not reached conclusion,
38 Gerontion	50	when I/Stiffen in a rented house. Think at last/I have not made this show
65 WL: Chess	114	/'I never know what you are thinking. Think.'/I think we are in rats' alley/Where the
65 WL: Chess	115	what you are thinking. Think.'/I think we are in rats' alley/Where the dead men
66 WL: Chess	147	you./And no more can't I, I said, and think of poor Albert,/He's been in the army
72 WL: Thund	336	Amongst the rock one cannot stop or think/Sweat is dry and feet are in the sand/If
74 WL: Thund	413	the door once and turn once only/We think of the key, each in his prison/Thinking of
89 Ash-Wed 1	11	of the positive hour/Because I do not think/Because I know I shall not know/The one
116 SP	Dusty	26	a terrible chill/No, just a chill/Oh I *think* it's only a chill/Yes indeed I hope so too —/
117 SP	Doris	19	on what comes next./You've got to *think* when you read the cards,/It's not a thing
119 SP	Wauch	3	how come? will you permit me —/I think you girls both know Captain Horsfall —/
120 SP	Krum	1	London's a little too gay for us/Don't think I mean anything *coarse* —/But I'm afraid
159 Rock 6	8	in the triumph of violence./Do you think that the Faith has conquered the World/
180 FQ: ECoker	122	only the growing terror of nothing to think about;/Or when, under ether, the mind is
182 FQ: ECoker	171	only food:/In spite of which we like to think/That we are sound, substantial flesh and
184 FQ: DrySal	1	do not know much about gods; but I think that the river/Is a strong brown god —
186 FQ: DrySal	71	tail, where the fog cowers?/We cannot think of a time that is oceanless/Or of an ocean
186 FQ: DrySal	75	to have no destination./We have to think of them as forever bailing,/Setting and

188 FQ: DrySal	146	widens behind you,/You shall not	think 'the past is finished'/Or 'the future is
188 FQ: DrySal	151	language)/'Fare forward, you who	think that you are voyaging;/You are not those
188 FQ: DrySal	163	in the lives of others:/And do not	think of the fruit of action./Fare forward./O
195 FQ: Little	171	/All manner of thing shall be well./If I	think, again, of this place,/And of people, not
195 FQ: Little	177	in the strife which divided them;/If I	think of a king at nightfall,/Of three men, and
206 To my Wife	6	bodies smell of each other/Who	think the same thoughts without need of speech/
209 NamingCats	3	one of your holiday games;/You may	think at first I'm as mad as a hatter/When I tell
209 NamingCats	9	names./There are fancier names if you	think they sound sweeter,/Some for the
222 Pekes Pols	15	know the reason, but most people	think/He'd slipped into the Wellington Arms
225 Mr Mistoff	34	look for a knife or a fork/And you	think it is merely misplaced —/You have seen it
225 Mr Mistoff	43	is vague and aloof,/You would	think there was nobody shyer —/But his voice
226 Macavity	16	like a snake;/And when you	think he's half asleep, he's always wide awake./
229 Gus	48	drilled in a regular troupe,/And they	think they are smart, just to jump through a
235 Ad-dress	50	/I greet him with an OOPSA CAT!/I	think I've heard them call him James —/But
241 MC Mess	36	will be packed to suffocation,/And I	think that his horse will be deprived of its tail,/
242 MC Mess	5	ask my opinion./And if you ask me, I	think the Lord Archbishop/Is not the man to
242 MC Mess	8	pretensions./If you ask my opinion, I	think that this peace/Is nothing like an end, or
247 MC Thomas	20	Only/The fool, fixed in his folly, may	think/He can turn the wheel on which he turns.
247 MC Thomas	28	to your behaviour. You were safer/	Think of penitence and follow your master.
248 MC Tempt2	26	On your part — still may be regained.	Think, my Lord,/Power obtained grows to
254 MC Tempt4	10	know already, ask nothing of me./But	think, Thomas, think of glory after death./
254 MC Tempt4	10	nothing of me./But think, Thomas,	think of glory after death./When king is dead,
254 MC Tempt4	15	Saint and Martyr rule from the tomb./	Think, Thomas, think of enemies dismayed,/
254 MC Tempt4	15	rule from the tomb./Think, Thomas,	think of enemies dismayed,/Creeping in
254 MC Tempt4	17	in penance, frightened of a shade;/	Think of pilgrims, standing in line/Before the
254 MC Tempt4	21	/Bending the knee in supplication,/	Think of the miracles, by God's grace,/And
254 MC Tempt4	22	of the miracles, by God's grace,/And	think of your enemies, in another place./{T} I
260 MC Thomas	21	at once for the same reason./Now	think for a moment about the meaning of this
260 MC Thomas	28	unto you.' Did He/mean peace as we	think of it: the kingdom of England at peace
261 MC Thomas	11	Stephen. Is it an accident, do you	think,/that the day of the first martyr follows
261 MC Thomas	19	/salvation of men./Beloved, we do not	think of a martyr simply as a good Christian
261 MC Thomas	21	would be solely to/mourn. We do not	think of him simply as a good Christian who
262 MC Thomas	1	and because,/dear children, I do not	think I shall ever preach to you again; and
262 MC Thomas	4	hearts/these words that I say, and	think of them at another time. In the Name/of
266 MC Knight1	30	your order save you —/As I do not	think it is like to do./Saving your ambition is
273 MC Thomas	31	beasts. My Lord! My Lord!/{T} You	think me reckless, desperate and mad./You
277 MC Knight3	3	we have done, and whatever/you may	think of it, we have been perfectly disinterested.
277 MC Knight3	27	disinterested in this business./I	think that is about all I have to say./{K1} I
277 MC Knight1	28	that is about all I have to say./{K1} I	think we will all agree that William de Traci has
279 MC Knight1	4	Morville has given us a great deal to	think about. It/seems to me that he has said
279 MC Knight1	7	one more speaker, who has I	think another point of view/to express. If there
279 MC Knight1	8	are any who are still unconvinced, I	think that/Richard Brito, coming as he does of
279 MC Knight4	37	should be opened. Need I say more? I	think, with these facts before/you, you will
280 MC Knight1	1	great man./{K1} Thank you, Brito, I	think that there is no more to be/said; and I
280 MC Priest3	36	is your fate on earth/And we must	think no further of you./{P1} O my lord/The
287 FR Gerald	6	It's Mary's generation. What does she	think about it?/{M} Really, Cousin Gerald, if
287 FR Violet	12	I must say you're very tactless,/And I	think that Charles might have been more
289 FR Charles	15	about a year ago, wasn't it?/Do you	think that I ought to mention it now?/It seems
289 FR Gerald	28	from Liner'./{G} Yes, it's odd to	think of her as permanently *missing*./{V} Had
292 FR Amy	23	a question about taxes —/But I	think you would rather wait till you are rested./
293 FR Ivy	13	Now that Harry's back, is the time to	think of living./{H} Time and time and time,
293 FR Agatha	20	embarrassing to you. Agatha?/{Ag} I	think, Harry, that having got so far —/If you
295 FR Harry	2	the cabin./Later, I became excited, I	think I made enquiries;/The purser and the
296 FR Harry	8	to that/As the way to freedom./{H} I	think I see what you mean,/Dimly — as you
297 FR Amy	2	should be myself. What does Agatha	think?/{Ag} It seems a necessary move/In an
298 FR Violet	14	{}/[*Rises*]/{V} I do not agree./I	think there should be witnesses. I intend to
299 FR Charles	9	much in the papers./Downing, do you	think that it might have been suicide,/And that
299 FR Downing	14	mean, knowing her Ladyship,/I don't	think she had the courage./{C} Did she ever talk
300 FR Charles	38	so. Thank you, Downing,/I don't	think we need you any more./{G} Oh, Downing,
302 FR Chorus	2	well of by others/So that we may	think well of ourselves./And any explanation
303 FR Mary	16	invited him./{M} Dr. Warburton? I	think she might have told me;/It is very difficult,
304 FR Mary	17	here? *You*'re not afraid of her,/But I	think you must have wanted to avoid collision./
304 FR Agatha	39	she did to Harry,/That's important, I	think, but what he did to himself./{M} But it
305 FR Agatha	5	sorry for you;/Though you may not	think me capable of such a feeling./I would like
305 FR Mary	18	/Waiting, waiting, always waiting./I	think this house *means* to keep us waiting. {}/

306 FR	Harry	16	took place in my memory,/I think. It seems I shall get rid of nothing./Of
308 FR	Harry	30	/{H} Something inside me, you think, that can be altered!/And here, indeed!
308 FR	Mary	38	know, you cannot understand./{M} I think I could understand, but you would have
309 FR	Mary	8	it is part of the torment./{M} If you think I am incapable of understanding you —/
309 FR	Mary	15	I remember you better than you think,/And what is the real you. I haven't much
309 FR	Mary	22	you feel — I don't mean what you think,/But what you feel. You attach yourself to
310 FR	Harry	30	/{H} What have we been saying? I think I was saying/That it seemed as if I had
313 FR	Violet	2	aren't you dressed yet?/How do you think that Harry is looking?/Why, who could
313 FR	Violet	4	/[Pulls them together]/{V} Very well, I think, after such a long journey;/You know
314 FR	Harry	18	you would never get well./{H} Not, I think, without some justification:/For what you
315 FR	Violet	20	about now in winter/You wouldn't think that she was a day older/Than on her
315 FR	Amy	25	finish. Will you take me in, Doctor?/I think we are very much the oldest present —/In
316 FR	Charles	7	If the matter were left in my hands, I think I could manage the situation. {}/[Exeunt]/
317 FR	Harry	7	/{H} I can imagine —/Though I think it is probably going to be useless,/Or if
318 FR	Harry	15	punished us, but made us feel guilty./I think that the things that are taken for granted/
322 FR	Harry	16	rather not .../{H} You mean you think I can't. But I might surprise you;/I think I
322 FR	Harry	17	I can't. But I might surprise you;/I think I might be able to give you a shock./{Wi}
324 FR	Violet	9	and WINCHELL]/{V} Well, Harry,/I think that you might have had something to
324 FR	Harry	13	But from what Winchell says/I don't think the matter can be very serious./A minor
324 FR	Amy	26	/And as I get older, I am coming to think/How little I have ever known./But I think
324 FR	Amy	28	/How little I have ever known./But I think your remarks are much more
325 FR	Harry	3	your father/When you said that./{H} I think, mother,/I shall make you lie down. You
325 FR	Agatha	6	understand Harry's behaviour./{Ag} I think it is as well to leave Harry to establish/If
325 FR	Gerald	14	afraid of the shock for Amy;/But I think that Warburton understands that./{I} You
325 FR	Violet	34	of course he meant well — but I think an open car/Is so undignified: you're
326 FR	Violet	3	him somewhere in Chiswick./Anyway, the district was unfamiliar/And
326 FR	Violet	6	/I am sure he meant well. But I do think he is reckless./{G} I wonder how much
326 FR	Harry	9	HARRY]/{H} Mother is asleep, I think: it's strange how the old/Can drop off to
326 FR	Harry	17	minor disaster?/You go on trying to think of each thing separately,/Making small
326 FR	Harry	23	like that in a way, so long as I could think/Even of my own life as an isolated ruin,/A
327 FR	Harry	8	are invariably pointed./{H} Do you think that I believe what I said just now?/That
327 FR	Ivy	30	too/Has had an accident. I don't think he's hurt,/But he says that he hasn't got
327 FR	Charles	38	have this evening's paper./{C} Stop, I think I bought a lunch edition/Before I left St.
328 FR	Violet	6	But Arthur is definitely reckless./{V} I think these racing cars ought to be prohibited. {}
331 FR	Harry	31	I looked to you for strength. Now I think it is/A common pursuit of liberation./{Ag}
336 FR	Harry	13	appear]/{H} and this time/You cannot think that I am surprised to see you./And you
336 FR	Harry	14	to see you./And you shall not think that I am afraid to see you./This time, you
337 FR	Agatha	8	/{Ag} What have I been saying? I think I was saying/That you have a long
337 FR	Agatha	10	You have nothing to stay for./Think of it as like a children's treasure hunt:/
337 FR	Amy	34	and who are you to say he shall go?/I think I know well enough why you wish him to
338 FR	Harry	12	me. I can only speak/So you may not think I conceal an explanation,/And to tell you
340 FR	Agatha	9	women. Thirty years in which to think./Do you suppose that I wanted to return
340 FR	Amy	22	upon an unwilling father?/Dare you think what that does to one? Try to think of it./
340 FR	Amy	22	think what that does to one? Try to think of it./I would have sons, if I could not
342 FR	Agatha	35	in this world, this world only,/Do you think that I would take the responsibility/Of
344 FR	Violet	16	up your mind .../{V} You can't really think of living in a tropical climate!/{G} There's
344 FR	Violet	26	need some religious qualification!/I think you should consult the vicar .../{G} And
346 FR	Downing	16	must never leave him./{Do} You may think it laughable, what I'm going to say —/But
346 FR	Downing	19	these years that I've been with him/I think I understand his Lordship better than
347 FR	Ivy	21	we know of what did happen,/Do you think Amy ought to see it?/{V} No, certainly
347 FR	Ivy	28	/Why do you all look so peculiar? I think I might be allowed/To know what has
348 FR	Chorus	28	we are doing;/And even, when you think of it,/We do not know much about
349 FR	Charles	11	what it was — or was it? — and yet I think that I might understand./{all} But we must
354 CP	Julia	31	/{J} How many brothers? Two, I think./{A} No, there were three, but you
356 CP	Julia	28	what you're thinking!/I know you think I'm a silly old woman/But I'm really very
357 CP	Edward	17	Are there any prospects?/{E} No, I think she put it all into an annuity./{J} So it's
361 CP	Edward	19	what I'd been concealing./I don't think I want to know who you are;/But, at the
361 CP	Edward	23	deal more about us than appears —/I think your speculations rather offensive./{UG} I
363 CP	Edward	32	/And I answer 'Nothing'. They will think me mad/Or simply contemptible./{UG}
367 CP	Edward	1	you noticed the situation./{E} I did think I noticed one or two things;/But I don't
367 CP	Edward	8	/{E} Julia is certainly observant,/But I think she had some other matter on her mind./
367 CP	Edward	11	you anything in common, do you think?/{P} It seemed to me we had a great deal
367 CP	Peter	31	judge./{P} Well, I can judge it,/And I think it's very good. But that's not the point./
367 CP	Peter	33	we had a great deal in common/And I think she thought so too./{E} How did you
368 CP	Edward	22	worthy of your cooking./I couldn't think of it./{A} Ah, but that's my special gift —/

369 CP	Alex	11	it./There goes *that* surprise. I must think of another./{P} Not very often./And when
369 CP	Edward	20	the link between them./That is why, I think, her Thursdays were a failure./{P} You
370 CP	Alex	16	goes another surprise, then. I must think./I didn't expect to find any mangoes,/But
370 CP	Edward	25	which I cannot share./{E} Do you think she has simply lost interest in you?/{P}
370 CP	Peter	26	in you?/{P} You put it just wrong. I think of it differently./It is not her interest in *me*
372 CP	Alex	10	prepared you such a treat!/I really think that of all my triumphs/This is the
377 CP	Edward	4	/{E} Lavinia is coming back, I think./{C} You think! Don't you know?/{E} No,
377 CP	Celia	5	is coming back, I think./{C} You think! Don't you know?/{E} No, but I believe it.
378 CP	Celia	5	very light./{C} Thank you, Julia./I think I will, if I may follow you/In about ten
378 CP	Celia	22	/No, it can't be that. I won't think it's that./I think it is just a moment of
378 CP	Celia	23	can't be that. I won't think it's that./I think it is just a moment of surrender/To
378 CP	Celia	27	simply a question of vanity:/That you think the world will laugh at you/Because your
378 CP	Celia	36	man named Riley!/Really, Edward, I think you are mad —/I mean, you're on the
379 CP	Edward	14	and I'm very grateful,/And I think you are a very rare person./But it was too
380 CP	Celia	1	feel humiliated .../{C} Oh, don't think that you can humiliate me!/Humiliation
380 CP	Celia	29	Peter? All that matters/Is, that you think that you want Lavinia./And if that is the sort
380 CP	Edward	34	that I am in love with Lavinia./I don't think I was ever really in love with her./If I have
380 CP	Edward	35	/If I have ever been in love — and I think that I have —/I have never been in love
381 CP	Celia	1	... nearer your own age./{C} I don't think I care for advice from you, Edward:/You
381 CP	Celia	23	will your life be? I cannot bear to think of it./Oh, Edward! Can you be happy with
382 CP	Celia	6	I understand as I never did before./I think — I believe — you are being yourself/As
385 CP	Edward	36	with her./{E} I don't know why,/But I think I should like you to bring her yourself./
388 CP	Celia	17	better, to go about with./{C} I don't think that I shall be going to concerts./I am
389 CP	Celia	16	never want to leave it./{C} Lavinia, I think I understand about Peter .../{L} I have no
391 CP	Julia	15	Explain the telegram? What do you think, Alex?/{A} No, Julia, *we* can't explain the
391 CP	Julia	24	and yet I started it .../{J} Alex, do you think we could explain *anything*?/{A} I think
391 CP	Alex	25	we could explain *anything*?/{A} I think not, Julia. She must find out for herself:/
392 CP	Lavinia	21	/But *you* ought to know./{L} Yes, I think I know./But I'm puzzled by Julia. That
393 CP	Lavinia	32	/{E} Encouraged? To what?/{L} To think well of yourself./You know it was I who
395 CP	Edward	9	to take me/As I was, or as you think I am./But what do you think I am?/{L}
395 CP	Edward	10	as you think I am./But what do you think I am?/{L} Oh, what you always were./As
397 CP	Lavinia	10	Could you bear, for a moment,/To think about *me*?/{E} It was only yesterday/That
397 CP	Lavinia	14	hour by hour, for ever and ever./{L} I think you're on the edge of a nervous
397 CP	Lavinia	17	say it./I know ... of a doctor who I think could help you./{E} If I go to a doctor, I
399 CP	Reilly	14	Or she may keep me waiting;/But I think she will be punctual./{N} I telephone
401 CP	Reilly	29	so ... you might as well sit down./I think that you will find that chair comfortable./
403 CP	Reilly	17	absorbed in the endless struggle/To think well of themselves./{E} If I am like that/
403 CP	Reilly	20	Oh, not so much as you would like to think:/Only, shall we say, within your modest
406 CP	Lavinia	4	you./{L} In that case, Edward,/I don't think your clothes concern me either. {}/[*To*
409 CP	Reilly	15	injured your vanity./You liked to think of yourself as a passionate lover./Then
411 CP	Reilly	27	it you who sent those telegrams?/{R} I think I will dispose of your husband's problem.
411 CP	Lavinia	31	others you are not concerned./{L} I think you have answered my question too./They
412 CP	Celia	34	And I'm awfully afraid/That you'll think that I am wasting it anyway./I suppose
413 CP	Reilly	7	what they call it —/And usually they think that someone else is to blame./{C} I at
413 CP	Celia	28	tell you/That I should really *like* to think there's something wrong with me —/
414 CP	Celia	27	seems to me./They make noises, and think they are talking to each other;/They make
414 CP	Celia	28	to each other;/They make faces, and think they understand each other./And I'm sure
418 CP	Celia	9	— more like a betrayal./You see, I think I really had a vision of something/Though
418 CP	Celia	13	if I might cherish it./In fact, I think it would really be dishonest/For me, now,
420 CP	Julia	21	will go far, that one./{J} Very far, I think./You do not need to tell me. I knew from
421 CP	Julia	9	just murder each other!/But I don't think they will do that. We shall see./It's the
424 CP	Lavinia	10	you require?/{L} Nothing more, I think, till half past six. {}/[*Exit* CATERER'S
424 CP	Edward	11	*front door*]/{E} I'm in good time, I think. I hope you've not been worrying./{L} Oh
425 CP	Lavinia	17	mind./{L} But you know, I don't think that you need worry:/They won't all
427 CP	Alex	33	{A} That was a nearer guess than you think./No, not monkey nuts. But it had to do
429 CP	Alex	32	/{A} Ah, the Christians! Now, I think I ought to tell you/About someone you
432 CP	Julia	36	he's going to find parts for all of us. Think of it!/{P} But, Julia, I was just about to
435 CP	Peter	7	to forget about her,/Until I began to think myself a success/And got a little more
435 CP	Lavinia	35	your own needs./Peter, please don't think I'm being unkind .../{P} No, I don't think
435 CP	Peter	36	I'm being unkind .../{P} No, I don't think you're being unkind, Lavinia;/And I know
436 CP	Julia	17	just being an eye. You will come to think of Celia/Like that, one day. And then
436 CP	Julia	37	is much more observant than you think./I believe that she has forced you to a
437 CP	Reilly	11	*inhabit/The shadows of all forms that think and live/Till death unite them and they part*
438 CP	Reilly	34	/As for Miss Coplestone, because you think her death was waste/You blame
438 CP	Reilly	36	because you blame yourselves/You think her life was wasted. It was triumphant./

439	CP	Julia	9	you alter its meaning./{J} Henry, I	think	it is time that *I* said something:/Everyone
439	CP	Lavinia	26	try to come to see us./You know, I	think	it would do us all good —/You and me
440	CP	Edward	3	/And Peter had to know .../{E} Now I	think	I understand .../{L} Then I hope you will
440	CP	Edward	7	yet! But Sir Henry has been saying,/I	think	, that every moment is a fresh beginning;/
440	CP	Julia	13	am sure it will be a success./{J} And I	think	, Henry,/That we should leave before the
446	CC	Claude	6	he's getting the hang of things,/And I	think	he's beginning to take a keen interest./{E}
446	CC	Claude	11	told me./{SC} About his music./Yes, I	think	so. I understand his feelings./He's like me,
446	CC	Claude	17	else/He could do, and do well. And I	think	he's found it,/Just as I did. I shall tell him
446	CC	Eggers	29	at home/When he has a piano. You	think	of everything./But if I might make a
446	CC	Eggers	32	such an interest in my garden/That I	think	he ought to have window boxes./Some
447	CC	Claude	3	— the car will be ready —/Let's	think	what you're to say to Lady Elizabeth,/
447	CC	Claude	5	back from the airport, about Colby./I	think	, you ought to give her warning/Of whom
449	CC	Claude	27	women./{E} True./{SC} But I don't	think	she takes much notice of Miss Angel./She
450	CC	Claude	18	deal better/Than I should care to	think	, perhaps./{E} And do I infer/That you're
454	CC	Colby	19	/{C} You seem to me sane. And I	think	I am./{E} I have no doubt on either point,
454	CC	Eggers	32	Not when I've been there./No, I don't	think	she would. But she does call her Lizzie,/
454	CC	Eggers	34	to Sir Claude. And do you know —/I	think	it amuses him./{C} Well, perhaps I'll be
455	CC	Eggers	10	of fiduciary relationship./No, I don't	think	that's quite the right term./She's no
455	CC	Eggers	12	own, as you may have gathered;/But I	think	her father was a friend of Sir Claude's,/
455	CC	Eggers	22	a man who gets his own way,/And I	think	he can manage her. If anyone can./{C}
456	CC	Eggers	7	sometimes been useful. But he didn't	think	of that:/He's not petty-minded — though
456	CC	Eggers	17	her.'/But she has one trait that I	think	I did touch on:/She's very absent-minded./
456	CC	Eggers	35	year our holiday at Dawlish'./And to	think	that was only the beginning of my travels!
457	CC	Colby	9	/That you always contrive to	think	the best of everyone./{E} You'll come to
459	CC	Lady E	7	—/Contrary to what most people	think	./You should be artistic. But you look
460	CC	Lady E	19	Dr. Rebmann —/No, at your stage, I	think	, with Dr. Leroux./Don't you remember, I
461	CC	Eggers	18	at this time of year!'/I said: 'Let's	think	about it in the Spring/When the garden
461	CC	Colby	35	to you at once./{C} Did she really	think	/That she had seen me before?/{SC}
462	CC	Claude	11	if you were her son? If she comes to	think	of you/As the kind of man that her son
463	CC	Colby	20	language fluently,/So that you can	think	in it — you feel yourself to be/Rather a
463	CC	Claude	34	you are saying,/Much better than you	think	. It's my own experience/That you are
464	CC	Claude	4	that the potter handles./Most people	think	that a sculptor or a painter/Is something
464	CC	Claude	6	to be than a potter./Most people	think	of china or porcelain/As merely for use,
465	CC	Colby	7	still not explained why you came to	think	/That your father had been right./{SC}
465	CC	Claude	18	one is wholly uncreative?/I don't	think	so. For I came to see/That I had always
466	CC	Colby	31	of accepting ... make-believe?/{C} I	think	I do. At least, I understand *you* better/In
467	CC	Claude	23	for hurting you./{SC} You mustn't	think	of that./{C} I'm very grateful for all
467	CC	Claude	33	life will impose on us./Just when we	think	we have settled our account/Life presents
469	CC	Lucasta	1	*are/heard as the curtain rises.*/{L} *I*	think	you play awfully well, Colby —/Not that
469	CC	Colby	5	me how to appreciate it./{C} I don't	think	that you'll need much teaching;/Not at
470	CC	Colby	10	to me?/{C} As a matter of fact, I	think	I played better./I can't bring myself to
470	CC	Lucasta	30	them —/American Musicals. Do you	think	it's any compliment/To invite a woman to
471	CC	Lucasta	40	of self-defence./{L} What made you	think	it was self-defence?/{C} Because you
472	CC	Colby	4	you're afraid of being pushed./I	think	that you're brave — and I think that
472	CC	Colby	4	/I think that you're brave — and I	think	that you're frightened./Perhaps you've
472	CC	Lucasta	11	There, I don't believe you./What did I	think	till now? Oh, it's strange, isn't it,/That as
472	CC	Lucasta	36	/And I didn't know why! And now I	think	I know./It's awful for a man to have to
473	CC	Colby	28	That's why it's not real./You know, I	think	that Eggerson's garden —/Is more real than
473	CC	Lucasta	31	Eggerson's garden?/What makes you	think	of Eggerson — of all people?/{C} Well, he
474	CC	Colby	7	outside it real/And acceptable, I	think	./{L} You sound awfully religious./Is there
474	CC	Colby	19	with me./That's the only way I can	think	of putting it./{L} How afraid one is of ...
475	CC	Lucasta	4	come to understand anyone?/{L} I	think	you're being very discouraging:/Are you
475	CC	Lucasta	12	you couldn't have predicted it./{L} I	think	I'm changing./I've changed quite a lot in
475	CC	Colby	14	a lot in the last two hours./{C} And I	think	I'm changing too. But perhaps what we
476	CC	Lucasta	26	about B. He's very generous./I don't	think	he'd have minded. But he's very clever
477	CC	Colby	35	Not by you,/Not by anything you	think	. It's to do with myself./{L} Yourself,
477	CC	Lucasta	39	alone with yourself?/Or perhaps you	think	it would be bad for your prospects/Now
478	CC	Lucasta	19	far worse than ever./Just when you	think	you're on the point of release/From
478	CC	Lucasta	21	swoops down upon you;/When you	think	you're getting out, you're getting further
478	CC	Lucasta	32	self-respect./Well, there's always B. I	think	that now/I'm just beginning to appreciate
479	CC	Lucasta	40	condition./{L} You're always free to	think	again./{K} Marriage is a gamble. But I'm
482	CC	Colby	28	I'm vulgar too./But what, do you	think	, *is* my sort?/I don't know, myself. And I
485	CC	Lady E	1	though my family made me	think	so./But you know, I actually *liked* to
485	CC	Lady E	16	it made it all so simple!/To be able to	think	that one's earthly parents/Are only the
487	CC	Claude	21	Elizabeth? What on earth makes you	think	so?/{LE} I must see this Mrs. Guzzard. I

488 CC	Claude	12	brooding on the past,/You began to think of Colby as what your son would be,/And
489 CC	Claude	9	if I had another/I thought you might think — 'and how many more?'/You might
489 CC	Lady E	18	I had a son./{LE} But why do you think that Colby is your son?/{SC} Colby is the
489 CC	Lady E	39	thought you would be happy/To think you had a son, and would do well by him
491 CC	Colby	1	about it. Now, you have made me think,/And I wish that I could have had a father
491 CC	Colby	21	/{SC} Well?/{C} It would be easier, I think,/To accept you both in the place of
491 CC	Claude	38	you want, Colby? What do you want?/Think of the future. When you marry/You will
492 CC	Lady E	11	arrange to get her here./{LE} And I think you ought to get Eggerson as well. {}/
492 CC	Colby	15	consolation at the piano?/{C} I don't think, tonight, the piano would help me:/At the
492 CC	Claude	33	... or any other art./No, I don't think I shall be in a reminiscent mood./Cross
493 CC	Claude	5	arrangements beforehand./I don't think you and I should be near together./Will
494 CC	Lady E	29	I understand/And I know you don't think I understand anything,/And perhaps I
495 CC	Claude	4	have you never told me?/{SC} I didn't think/That you would be interested. More than
499 CC	Claude	6	And put the case to her./Don't let her think that *I* have any doubts:/You are putting
500 CC	Lucasta	34	can help each other. Oh, I know you think of him/Simply as a business man. As you
501 CC	Lucasta	2	decision./{L} But the reasons why you think so are the wrong ones./{LE} And I'm sure
501 CC	Lucasta	4	/{L} And I know very well why *you* think so:/*You* think we're suited because we're
501 CC	Lucasta	5	very well why *you* think so:/*You* think we're suited because we're both common./
501 CC	Lucasta	6	we're both common./B. knows you think him common. And so he pretends/To be
501 CC	Lucasta	7	very common, because he knows you think so./*You* gave us our parts. And we've
501 CC	Lady E	9	that we can play them./{LE} I don't think you ought to say that, Lucasta;/I have
503 CC	Colby	16	very fond of him;/And I'm glad to think he'll be my brother-in-law./I shall feel
506 CC	Guzzard	25	asked you to be present./{MG} You think that I might be able to help you?/{E} It
509 CC	Claude	32	Barnabas?/{SC} About twenty-eight, I think./{MG} He should be twenty-eight./{LE}
512 CC	Claude	10	and *imposture*./{SC} I don't think there is any confusion now:/I'm sure that
512 CC	Guzzard	39	*and KAGHAN*]/{MG} Not, I think, with you. {}/[*To* LUCASTA]/{MG} Nor,
515 CC	Guzzard	11	left very poor./If I let you continue to think the child was yours,/My son was assured
515 CC	Guzzard	25	/When I let you claim him. Do you think it is a small thing/For me, to see my life's
515 CC	Claude	39	we'll be happier together if you think/I am not your father. I'll accept that./If
517 CC	Claude	3	mine./{SC} I shall never ask you to think of me as a father;/All I ask you is — to
517 CC	Colby	5	as a friend./{C} But you would still think of me as your son./There can be no
517 CC	Colby	8	— as your son, when I could not think of you/As my father: if I accepted that/I
517 CC	Colby	29	been looking for another./{C} Do you think that they would give me a trial?/{E} Give
517 CC	Eggers	40	Not enough to live on./We'll have to think of other ways/Of making up an income.
518 CC	Eggers	5	spending a lifetime as an organist./I think you'll come to find you've another
518 CC	Guzzard	26	the wife of an organist;/But you too, I think, have had a wish realised./— I believe that
519 CC	Kaghan	7	*beside him*]/{K} You know, Claude, I think we all made the same mistake —/All
522 ES	dedic	6	*breathing in unison/Of lovers .../Who think the same thoughts without need of speech/*
525 ES	Monica	30	be buried in the library/And he won't think of leaving it until he's called for tea./So
525 ES	Charles	33	/{C} And you'll hear it again. You think I'm going to tell you/Once more, that I'm
525 ES	Charles	40	I'm selfish/In saying that, because I think —/I think you're tormenting yourself as
526 ES	Charles	1	/In saying that, because I think —/I think you're tormenting yourself as well./{M}
529 ES	Monica	26	said: complete relaxation/And to think about nothing. Though I know that won't
531 ES	Ld Clav	30	be seen there. It makes me smile/To think that men should be frightened of ghosts./
533 ES	Gomez	29	England?/{G} Not at all, not at all./I think that was rather an unkind suggestion./I've
535 ES	Gomez	33	/And to take another name. Think what that means —/To take another
536 ES	Gomez	1	of course you know!/Just enough to think you know more than you do./You've
536 ES	Gomez	16	talk to them in English./But do they think in English? No, they do not./They think in
536 ES	Gomez	17	in English? No, they do not./They think in Spanish, but their thoughts are Indian
536 ES	Gomez	22	such isolation/As mine, you think you do .../{LC} I'm sure I do,/I've always
536 ES	Gomez	36	she must be very old. And she must think I'm dead;/And as for my married sisters
537 ES	Gomez	28	at least./I had plenty of time to think things over, later./{LC} And what is the
538 ES	Gomez	4	my stretch/Which gave me time to think it all out./{LC} That's the second time you
540 ES	Ld Clav	35	why I say I can trust you?/{LC} If you think that this story would interest the public/
541 ES	Gomez	4	wouldn't look at it./Besides, you can't think I've any desire/To appear in public as
543 ES	Ld Clav	1	soon again./{LC} Not very soon, I think./I am going away./{G} So I've come to
545 ES	Piggott	24	a glorious morning!/I'm afraid you'll think I've been neglecting you;/So I've come to
546 ES	Piggott	12	/We don't want our guests to think of themselves as ill,/Though we never
548 ES	Monica	12	you're pretending to be asleep./If they think you *are* asleep they'll do something to
549 ES	Carghil	25	at the very first meeting —/I can't think why, but it's the way things happen./I said
551 ES	Carghil	13	shouldn't want to believe it./But you think, or try to think, that if I'd really suffered/I
551 ES	Carghil	13	to believe it./But you think, or try to think, that if I'd really suffered/I shouldn't want
551 ES	Carghil	34	in settlement/Is twice as much as I think you'd be awarded.'/Effie was against it —
553 ES	Carghil	7	/Our relations were intense enough, I think,/To have given me one or two insights
553 ES	Carghil	10	in love with you;/And you needn't think I idolise your memory./It's simply that I

553 ES   Carghil   15 I've touched yours./It's frightening to think that we're still together/And more
553 ES   Carghil   16 still together/And more frightening to think that we may *always* be together./There's a
559 ES   Ld Clav   17   to go?/What kind of a life do you think you want?/{Mi} I simply want to lead a
560 ES   Ld Clav   32 find your feet. But I shouldn't like to think/That what inspired you was no positive
561 ES   Ld Clav   28   made him an offer/Which he must think over. But if he goes abroad/I want him to
562 ES   Carghil   12 *despatch-case*]/{MC} Richard! I didn't think you'd still be here./I came back to have a
563 ES   Carghil   17   seen each other lately?/Richard, I think that you might introduce us./{LC} Oh.
564 ES   Monica   37 your cards on the table!/{M} Father, I think you should take your rest now./— I must
565 ES   Monica   5   This afternoon, Michael./{M} No, I think you've had enough talk for to-day./
565 ES   Michael   21   been in business in London,/But I think of cutting loose, and going abroad./{MC}
567 ES   Charles   20   from his past,/I've been trying to think what I could do to help him./If it's
567 ES   Charles   22 very much what it looks like,/Do you think I could persuade him to confide in me?/
568 ES   Charles   15   I wish had never happened./I can think of things you don't yet know about me,
569 ES   Monica   13 he is, the broken-down actor./{M} I think I should only love you the better, Father,/
569 ES   Charles   24 Oh Father, do let him./{C} At least, I think I know the best man to advise you./{LC}
570 ES   Ld Clav   13   She had nothing to say to me./I think of your mother, when she lay dying:/
572 ES   Ld Clav   39 the most important. I know what you think./You think that I suffer from a morbid
573 ES   Ld Clav   1   I know what you think./You think that I suffer from a morbid conscience,/
573 ES   Ld Clav   3   I might well have forgotten./You think that I'm sickening, when I'm just
573 ES   Ld Clav   18 place and time of liberation/Are, I think, determined. Let us say no more about it./
575 ES   Ld Clav   14 for different reasons/From what you think. Let me tell you about Gomez./He's
576 ES   Charles   27   a kind of suicide./{C} Michael, you think Señor Gomez is inspired by benevolence
577 ES   Charles   1 And, Michael, here's another point to think of:/Señor Gomez has offered you a post in
577 ES   Carghil   26   many times over./{MC} Richard, I think it's time *I* joined the conversation./My
578 ES   Ld Clav   11 you/In our divergent ways. When I think of your childhood,/When I think of the
578 ES   Ld Clav   12 I think of your childhood,/When I think of the happy little boy who was Michael,/
578 ES   Ld Clav   13 little boy who was Michael,/When I think of your boyhood and adolescence,/And
579 ES   Michael   20 If there's any point in it./Personally, I think that when one's come to a decision,/It's as
581 ES   Ld Clav   24 /Of knowing what love is. We all think we know,/But how few of us do! And now
582 ES   Ld Clav   9 loved. And now that I love Michael,/I think, for the first time — remember, my dear,/I

THINKING (36)

65 WL: Chess   113   never speak. Speak./'What are you thinking of? What thinking? What?/'I never
65 WL: Chess   113   /'What are you thinking of? What thinking? What?/'I never know what you are
65 WL: Chess   114 What?/'I never know what you are thinking. Think.'/I think we are in rats' alley/
74 WL: Thund   414 think of the key, each in his prison/Thinking of the key, each confirms a prison/
164 Rock 9   12   /And all other secular meetings./Thinking good of themselves, ready for any
232 Skimble   25   winking and he sees what you are thinking/And it's certain that he doesn't
296 FR   Ivy   23 cured/And they know what you are thinking./{C} He has probably let this notion
299 FRDowning   18 are the least likely. To my way of thinking/She only did it to frighten people./If
303 FR   Mary   26 Arthur and John./Which is worse, thinking of what to say to John,/Or having to
309 FR   Mary   18 from tutors/Or from books, or from thinking, or from observation:/Something which
311 FR   Harry   32 age, when I was someone else/Thinking of something else, puts me among
314 FR Warburt   27 forty years' experience/I've left off thinking in terms of the laboratory./We're all of
321 FR   Winch   26 ... Oh, I'm sorry, my Lord,/I was thinking it was your birthday, not her
332 FR Agatha   36 your father/Awake yet. I found him thinking/How to get rid of your mother. What
348 FR Chorus   29 of it,/We do not know much about thinking./What is happening outside of the
356 CP   Julia   27 couldn't get out. I know what you're thinking!/I know you think I'm a silly old
384 CP Edward   9 have made a decision./{E} Are you thinking that I may have changed my mind?/
415 CP   Celia   32 seemed so right, at the time!/I've been thinking about it, over and over;/I can see now,
434 CP Edward   33 I mean./{E} And you know what I'm thinking./{P} I don't understand at all. But then
434 CP   Peter   37 during those two years./Two years! Thinking about Celia./{E} It's the waste that I
438 CP Lavinia   25   I knew! I knew what you were thinking!/Doesn't it help you, that I feel guilty
439 CP Lavinia   39 giving a party./{L} And I have been thinking, for these last five minutes,/How I
449 CC   Eggers   1 his grave unknown./{E} And you're thinking no doubt that Lady Elizabeth/Would
449 CC   Claude   5 no way of tracing it./Yes, I was thinking of her missing child:/In the
452 CC Lucasta   36 cursed with a name like Angel./I'm thinking of changing it. But, Colby,/Do you
462 CC   Claude   31 we've discussed only current business,/Thinking that you might find it easier/To start
471 CC   Colby   17 it's not conceit — the reason that I'm thinking of./It's something quite simple./{L}
490 CC   Colby   18 you've been talking/I've only been thinking: 'What does it matter/Whose son I
493 CC   Lady E   29 you're right./{LE} Claude, I've been thinking things over and over —/All through
494 CC   Lady E   36 /{LE} I'm not laughing. I was only thinking/How strange to have lived with you, all
518 CC   Eggers   8 closely./Mr. Simpkins! You'll be thinking of reading for orders:/And you'll still
529 ES   Monica   6 I've seen him looking at you. He was thinking of himself/When he was your age —
529 ES   Monica   28 That is just what I was doing./{M} Thinking of nothing?/{LC} Contemplating
569 ES   Charles   17   of learning about you./{C} I was thinking, Sir — forgive the suspicion —/From

569 ES	Charles	20	a very long acquaintance —/I was thinking that if there's any question of
574 ES	Carghil	12	he must have suffered! So I put on my thinking cap./I know you've always thought me

THINKS (13)

22 Preludes		21	masquerades/That time resumes,/One thinks of all the hands/That are raising dingy
211 Old Gumbie		31	Cat's work is but hardly begun./She thinks that the cockroaches just need
229 Gus		41	pursued down a drain./And he thinks that he still can, much better than most,/
294 FR	Harry	27	the particular has no language. One thinks to escape/By violence, but one is still
303 FR	Mary	28	to listen to Arthur's chatter/When he thinks he is behaving like a man of the world?/
346 FR	Downing	8	me back because he remembered/He thinks he left his cigarette-case on the table./Oh,
400 CP	Alex	13	regards me as very intelligent,/But he thinks I'm well informed: the sort of person/
400 CP	Alex	20	he's quite triumphant/Because he thinks he's stolen a march on her./And when
415 CP	Celia	8	/In fact, aren't the people one thinks of as immoral/Just the people who we
447 CC	Claude	16	it very difficult to replace you./She thinks she ought to have a hand in the choosing;
449 CC	Claude	18	approval matters./You know she thinks the world of your opinion./{E} Well, I
575 ES	Michael	10	to find a man to fill it,/And he thinks I'm just the man./{G} Yes, wasn't it
579 ES	Michael	11	friends in the shipping line/Who he thinks can be helpful in getting reservations./

THINLY (1)

129 Cor2 State		49	creatures,/The small creatures chirp thinly through the dust, through the night./O

THINNER (2)

218 Mung Rump		22	minds made up that they wouldn't get thinner/On Argentine joint, potatoes and
587 Fable		21	/He stole the fatter cows and left the thinner/To furnish all the milk — upset the

THIRD (13)

73 WL: Thund		359	drop/But there is no water/Who is the third who walks always beside you?/When I
92 Ash-Wed 3		12	agèd shark./At the first turning of the third stair/Was a slotted window bellied like the
92 Ash-Wed 3		19	stops and steps of the mind over the third stair,/Fading, fading; strength beyond
92 Ash-Wed 3		21	hope and despair/Climbing the third stair./Lord, I am not worthy/Lord, I am
232 Skimble		22	the travellers in the First and in the Third;/He establishes control by a regular patrol
250 MC	m	19	now be only mean descent. {}/[*Enter* THIRD TEMPTER]/{T3} I am an unexpected
264 MC	m	14	*of St. John is heard*]/[*Enter the* THIRD PRIEST, *with a banner of the Holy*
354 CP	Alex	32	three, but you wouldn't know the third one:/They kept him rather quiet./{J} Oh,
399 CP	Reilly	18	you ring three times./{R} And the third patient?/{N} The third one to be shown
399 CP	Nurse	19	/{R} And the third patient?/{N} The third one to be shown into the small room;/And
507 CC	Guzzard	16	him./But he was brought to me by a third party,/Through whom the monthly
528 ES	Charles	22	of the other./Can there be a third?/{M} The third reason is this:/I've only
528 ES	Monica	23	other./Can there be a third?/{M} The third reason is this:/I've only just been given it

THIRST (2)

339 FR	Harry	8	/To the worship in the desert, the thirst and deprivation,/A stony sanctuary and a
426 CP	Julia	34	I'm simply ravenous/And dying of thirst. What can Parkinson's do for me?/Oh yes,

THIRSTY (2)

425 CP	Edward	23	will get just enough to make them thirsty;/They'll come on to us later, roaring for
539 ES	Gomez	22	far./Well, now, I'm beginning to be thirsty again. {}/[*Pours himself whisky*]/{LC} An

THIRTEEN (1)

459 CC	Lady E	6	{}/[*counting on her fingers*]./{LE} Thirteen letters. That's very auspicious —/

THIRTY (7)

129 Cor2 State		14	pounds ten a week; with a bonus of thirty shillings at Christmas/And one week's
258 MC Thomas		9	/Is the way in which our lives begin./Thirty years ago, I searched all the ways/That
287 FR	Charles	16	/I suppose she must be getting on for thirty?/She ought to be married, that's what it
340 FR	Agatha	7	that you ever had./What did I get? thirty years of solitude,/Alone, among women,
340 FR	Agatha	9	college,/Trying not to dislike women. Thirty years in which to think./Do you suppose
450 CC	Claude	7	we worked together/For nearly thirty years./{E} Nearly thirty-one./But now you
503 CC	Lucasta	12	may bring us/In twenty or thirty or forty years' time./I shall be happy. I'm

THIRTY-FIVE (6)

340 FR	Amy	2	again to Wishwood;/But I thought, thirty-five years is long, and death is an end,/
340 FR	Amy	4	Agatha —/It has made enough in *me*. Thirty-five years ago/You took my husband
341 FR	Amy	22	for all these years of abstinence./Thirty-five years ago you took my husband
341 FR	Amy	32	has planned his good? is it you or I?/Thirty-five years designing his life,/Eight years
535 ES	Gomez	26	simple. I come back to England/After thirty-five years. Can you imagine/What it
535 ES	Gomez	26	to have been away from home/For thirty-five years? I was twenty-five —/The same

THIRTY-ONE (2)

66 WL: Chess		157	to look so antique./(And her only thirty-one.)/I can't help it, she said, pulling a
450 CC	Eggers	8	/For nearly thirty years./{E} Nearly thirty-one./But now you put it so convincingly,/

THIRTY-TWO (1)

393 CP	Edward	3	To have arrived at in ... how many? ... thirty-two hours./{L} Yes, a very important

THIS (538)
THOMAS (26)
604 Ode   m On the doorstep of the Absolute./Ode/THOMAS STEARNS ELIOT/For the hour
238 MC   m 6   /A MESSENGER/ARCHBISHOP THOMAS BECKET/FOUR TEMPTERS/
238 MC   m 13   /FOUR KNIGHTS/ARCHBISHOP THOMAS BECKET/CHORUS OF WOMEN
242 MC Priest1   30 Things had perhaps been different for Thomas./{P2} Yet our lord is returned. Our lord
243 MC Chorus   18   and grey the sky, grey grey grey./O Thomas, return, Archbishop; return, return to
244 MC Chorus   24   final fear which none understands. O Thomas Archbishop,/O Thomas our Lord,
244 MC Chorus   25   O Thomas Archbishop,/O Thomas our Lord, leave us and leave us be, in
244 MC Chorus   30   their lord, the doom of the world?/O Thomas, Archbishop, leave us, leave us, leave
244 MC Chorus   30   sullen Dover, and set sail for France. Thomas our Archbishop still our Archbishop
244 MC Chorus   30   still our Archbishop even in France. Thomas Archbishop, set the white sail between
245 MC   m 11   to our good Archbishop. {}/[*Enter* THOMAS]/{T} Peace. And let them be, in their
252 MC Tempt4   30   TEMPTER]/{T4} Well done, Thomas, your will is hard to bend./And with me
253 MC Tempt4   30   hell./Power to bind and loose: bind, Thomas, bind,/King and bishop under your
253 MC Tempt4   40   teeth./You hold the skein: wind, Thomas, wind/The thread of eternal life and
254 MC Tempt4   7   how this may be so;/I am only here, Thomas, to tell you what you know./{T} How
254 MC Tempt4   10   ask nothing of me./But think, Thomas, think of glory after death./When king
254 MC Tempt4   15   Martyr rule from the tomb./Think, Thomas, think of enemies dismayed,/Creeping
255 MC Tempt4   6   enduring crown to be won?/{T4} Yes, Thomas, yes; you have thought of that too./
256 MC Priests   24 of society, enemy of himself./{3P} O Thomas my Lord do not fight the intractable
258 MC Chorus   1   and wing through the dark air./O Thomas Archbishop, save us, save us, save
264 MC Priest1   3 always most dear to the Archbishop Thomas./And he kneeled down and cried with a
265 MC   m 34   will you keep us waiting? {}/[*Enter* THOMAS]/[*to* PRIESTS]./{T} However certain
271 MC Chorus   6   and shame,/O Lord Archbishop, O Thomas Archbishop, forgive us, forgive us, pray
271 MC   m 7   for you, out of our shame. {}/[*Enter* THOMAS]/{T} Peace, and be at peace with
273 MC   m 10 for death is near. {}/[*In the cathedral*. THOMAS *and* PRIESTS]/{3P} Bar the door.
282 MC Chorus   18   /Lord, have mercy upon us./Blessed Thomas, pray for us. {}/THE FAMILY
THORN (2)
155 Rock 3   32   /The rabbit shall burrow and the thorn revisit,/The nettle shall flourish on the
455 CC Eggers 16 To tell the truth, she's something of a thorn in his flesh,/Always losing her jobs,
THOROUGHBREDS (1)
164 Rock 9   9   walk in the street proudnecked, like thoroughbreds ready for races,/Adorning
THOROUGHLY (2)
 90 Ash-Wed 1   36   to beat the air/The air which is now thoroughly small and dry/Smaller and dryer
155 Rock 3   62   /To schemes of human greatness thoroughly discredited,/Binding the earth and
THOSE (126)
 18 Portrait   26   these qualities,/Who has, and gives/Those qualities upon which friendship lives./
 62 WL: Burial   48 card, the drowned Phoenician Sailor,/(Those are pearls that were his eyes. Look!)/Here
 65 WL: Chess   125 remember/'Nothing?'/I remember/Those are pearls that were his eyes./'Are you
 73 WL: Thund   368 of maternal lamentation/Who are those hooded hordes swarming/Over endless
 73 WL: Thund   378 tight/And fiddled whisper music on those strings/And bats with baby faces in the
 83 Hollow Men   13   force, gesture without motion;/Those who have crossed/With direct eyes,
 96 Ash-Wed 5   15   in the desert or the rain land,/For those who walk in darkness/Both in the day
 96 Ash-Wed 5   18   are not here/No place of grace for those who avoid the face/No time to rejoice for
 96 Ash-Wed 5   19   avoid the face/No time to rejoice for those who walk among noise and deny the voice
 96 Ash-Wed 5   21   voice/Will the veiled sister pray for/Those who walk in darkness, who chose thee
 96 Ash-Wed 5   22   who chose thee and oppose thee,/Those who are torn on the horn between season
 96 Ash-Wed 5   23   word and word, power and power, those who wait/In darkness? Will the veiled
 96 Ash-Wed 5   27   go away and cannot pray:/Pray for those who chose and oppose/O my people, what
 97 Ash-Wed 5   30   the slender/Yew trees pray for those who offend her/And are terrified and
106 Song Sime   34 tired with my own life and the lives of those after me,/I am dying in my own death and
106 Song Sime   35   in my own death and the deaths of those after me./Let thy servant depart,/Having
109 Marina   6   /What images return/O my daughter./Those who sharpen the tooth of the dog,
109 Marina   8   the tooth of the dog, meaning/Death/Those who glitter with the glory of the
109 Marina   10   of the hummingbird, meaning/Death/Those who sit in the sty of contentment,
109 Marina   12   sty of contentment, meaning/Death/Those who suffer the ecstasy of the animals,
127 Cor1 March   25   that took. Will it be he now? No,/Those are the golf club Captains, these the
148 Rock 1   53   obscurity, accepting/With equal face those that bring ignominy,/The applause of all
151 Rock 2   6   scorn in honeyless hives,/And those who would build and restore turn out the
152 Rock 2   32   of the good and ill that was done by those who have gone before you./And all that is
152 Rock 2   34   to keep with hearts as devoted as those of your fathers who fought to gain it./The
157 Rock 4   1 shall not deny the Stranger./There are those who would build the Temple,/And those
157 Rock 4   2   who would build the Temple,/And those who prefer that the Temple should not be
158 Rock 5   5   the gun rather loose in the holster.'/Those who sit in a house of which the use is

422 CP	Alex	18	{}/[*They drink*]/{A} The words for those who go upon a journey./{R} Protector of
425 CP	Lavinia	18	worry:/They won't all come, out of those who accepted./You know we said, 'we can
425 CP	Edward	25	for drink./Well, let's hope that those who come to us early/Will be going on to
425 CP	Edward	27	afterwards,/To make room for those who come from the Gunnings./{L} And if
429 CP	Julia	13	/I thought I was going to dine out on those monkeys:/But one can't dine out on eating
434 CP	Alex	3	endemic diseases/Besides, of course, those brought by Europeans,/And where the
434 CP	Alex	19	there, they questioned the villagers —/Those who survived. And then they found her
434 CP	Peter	36	what happened/To Celia, during those two years./Two years! Thinking about
435 CP	Julia	3	*you* say anything?/{J} You gave her those two years, as best you could./{P} When
452 CC	Lucasta	16	/Two months I'd gone on filing those papers/Which no one ever wanted — at
454 CC	Colby	36	/But it did make my head spin — all those first names/The first time I met her. I'm
467 CC	Colby	12	was missing in the years of childhood./Those years have gone forever. The empty
482 CC	Lady E	3	*and* LUCASTA]/{LE} Were those young people here by appointment?/Or
491 CC	Colby	32	/But I should have four! What about those others?/I should have to live with those
491 CC	Colby	33	others?/I should have to live with those ghosts, one indignant/At being cheated of
494 CC	Lady E	40	mean, to make jugs and jars/Like those in your collection?/{SC} That's what I
512 CC	Guzzard	38	realised, sometimes turn/Against those who have made them. {}/[*To* LADY
514 CC	Claude	33	I shall not believe it. I'll not believe those records./You pretend to have carried out
531 ES	Ld Clav	25	associates, the small minority/Of those who really understand the place we filled/
534 ES	Gomez	2	in your logic./How can one corrupt those who are already corrupted?/I can swear
542 ES	Ld Clav	24	expensive tastes:/If you had not had those tastes already/You would hardly have
549 ES	Carghil	9	life!/Now whatever were the names of those friends of yours/And which one was it
561 ES	Ld Clav	6	northern night. Believe me, Michael:/Those who flee from their past will always lose
561 ES	Michael	19	/So you'd nothing to live up to. Those standards of conduct/You've always
565 ES	Monica	28	for the present. {}/[*Exit*]/{M} Father, those awful people. We mustn't stay here./I
567 ES	Charles	19	/About your father and Michael, and those people from his past,/I've been trying to
569 ES	Ld Clav	9	/Now, I'm tired of keeping up those pretences,/But I hope that you'll find a
571 ES	Ld Clav	13	/How easily we ignore the fact that those who admire us/Will imitate our vices as
571 ES	Ld Clav	24	they upon you?/{LC} Only the hold of those who know/Something discreditable,
571 ES	Monica	27	Why should you wish to conceal from those who love you/What is known so well to
571 ES	Monica	28	love you/What is known so well to those who hate you?/{LC} I will tell you very
575 ES	Carghil	38	/Your father was simply *irresistible*/In those days. I melted the first time he looked at
582 ES	Charles	36	/Even with Michael, and despite those people,/Because somehow we'd begun to

THOU (8)

70 WL: Fire S		309	burning burning burning/O Lord Thou pluckest me out/O Lord Thou pluckest/
70 WL: Fire S		310	Lord Thou pluckest me out/O Lord Thou pluckest/burning/Death by Water/Phlebas
594 Grad 12		1	drop of dew upon the morning grass;/Thou dost not die — for each succeeding year/
594 Grad 13		1	name o'er distant lands and seas!/As thou to thy departing sons hast been/To those
594 Grad 13		2	hast been/To those that follow may'st thou be no less;/A guide to warn them, and a
281 MC	Chorus	11	who deny Thee could not deny, if Thou didst not exist; and their denial is never
281 MC	Chorus	13	in the belly./Therefore man, whom Thou hast made to be conscious of Thee, must
437 CP	Reilly	9	*of life and death:/One that which thou beholdest; but the other/Is underneath the*

THOUGH (83)

15 Prufrock		81	to force the moment to its crisis?/But though I have wept and fasted, wept and
15 Prufrock		82	wept and fasted, wept and prayed,/Though I have seen my head (grown slightly
64 WL: Chess		98	the antique mantel was displayed/As though a window gave upon the sylvan scene/
68 WL: Fire S		218	a taxi throbbing waiting,/I Tiresias, though blind, throbbing between two lives,/Old
98 Ash-Wed 6		7	birth and dying/(Bless me father) though I do not wish to wish these things/From
155 Rock 3		47	is no temple there shall be no homes,/Though you have shelters and institutions,/
156 Rock 3		72	or race or what you call humanity;/Though you forget the way to the Temple,/
161 Rock 7		26	that has never happened before: though we know not just when, or why, or how,
188 FQ: DrySal		149	and the aerial,/Is a voice descanting (though not to the ear,/The murmuring shell of
191 FQ: Little		2	spring is its own season/Sempiternal though sodden towards sundown,/Suspended in
195 FQ: Little		164	to find that action of little importance/Though never indifferent. History may be
228 Gus		10	isn't the Cat that he was in his prime;/Though his name was quite famous, he says, in
588 Fable		58	the monks dozed,/A fine old drink, though now gone out of use —/His feet upon
589 Fable		65	lights most always do./The doors, though barred and bolted most securely,/Gave
589 Fable		85	to heaven their lord renowned,/Though the wicked said (such rascals are not
590 Time Space		15	/Nor mourn to see them pine,/And though our days of love be few/Yet let them be
590 Space Time		8	free,/For time is time, and runs away,/Though sages disagree./The flowers I sent thee
590 Space Time		15	/Nor mourn to see them pine,/And though the flowers of life be few/Yet let them be
592 Grad 2		5	they leave they fully understand/That though again they see their fatherland/They
602 Humoresque		2	/One of my marionettes is dead,/Though not yet tired of the game —/But weak
281 MC	Chorus	21	the sanctity shall not depart from it/Though armies trample over it, though
281 MC	Chorus	21	it/Though armies trample over it, though sightseers come with guide-books

282	MC	Chorus	4	that which forever renews the earth/Though it is forever denied. Therefore, O God,
289	FR	Amy	10	Wishwood./{A} Thank you, Gerald. Though Agatha means/As a rule, a good deal
305	FR	Agatha	5	sorry, Mary, I am very sorry for you;/Though you may not think me capable of such
306	FR	Mary	24	at Wishwood?/{M} Happy? not really, though I never knew why:/It always seemed that
307	FR	Harry	37	hopeless/Unrecognised by other men, though sometimes by each other./{M} I know
309	FR	Harry	38	unnoticed./Perhaps you are right, though I do not know/How you should know it.
317	FR	Harry	7	matter./{H} I can imagine —/Though I think it is probably going to be
318	FR	Harry	3	her happy was what was virtuous —/Though never very happy, I remember. That
324	FR	Harry	35	To be living on several planes at once/Though one cannot speak with several voices at
325	FR	Violet	34	that I wanted to go with him at all —/Though of course he meant well — but I think
330	FR	Harry	2	always was;/Arthur again be sober, though not for very long;/And everything will
331	FR	Harry	6	associate nothing of it with myself,/Though nothing else was real. I thought
331	FR	Harry	18	is enough:/Warburton told me that, though he did not mean to./What I want to
344	FR	Gerald	23	very useful, knowing the natives,/Though occasionally troublesome. But you'll
346	FR	Downing	22	/But to show you what I mean, though you'd hardly credit it,/I've always said,
367	CP	Peter	6	notice, I don't suppose the others did,/Though I'm rather afraid of Julia
367	CP	Peter	17	/{P} You won't have seen my novel,/Though it had some very good reviews./But it's
367	CP	Peter	25	/{P} She might make it a profession;/Though she had her poetry./{E} Yes, I've seen
378	CP	Edward	33	to me/By the man I call Riley — though his name is not Riley;/It was just a name
388	CP	Celia	9	Peter, I'm awfully glad, for your sake,/Though of course we ... I shall miss you;/You
395	CP	Edward	16	that you've done all the changing —/Though I haven't yet found it a change for the
409	CP	Reilly	27	discovered that your young friend/(Though you knew, in your heart, that he was
409	CP	Reilly	33	no doubt,/Before you would admit it. Though perhaps you knew it/Before he did.
410	CP	Reilly	32	have answered your own question,/Though you do not know the meaning of what
414	CP	Celia	1	simply/That there's been a crash: though indeed there has been./It isn't simply the
417	CP	Reilly	39	that the best life?/{R} It is a good life. Though you will not know how good/Till you
418	CP	Celia	10	I really had a vision of something/Though I don't know what it is. I don't want to
427	CP	Alex	35	But it had to do with monkeys —/Though whether the monkeys are the core of
436	CP	Lavinia	29	willing to grant that. What struck me, though,/Was that your face showed no surprise
448	CC	Eggers	8	me./{E} Oh, you mustn't say that!/Though I've done my best to gain his
455	CC	Eggers	19	allowance — very adequate indeed,/Though she's always in debt. But you needn't
456	CC	Eggers	8	of that:/He's not petty-minded — though nothing escapes him./And such a
456	CC	Eggers	23	hasn't very much memory to lose,/Though she sometimes remembers when you
462	CC	Claude	13	have been —/And I believe she will: though I'm perfectly convinced/That *her* son
463	CC	Claude	5	war — that was perhaps a mistake,/Though it seemed to have such obvious
463	CC	Colby	23	/That I feel myself becoming — though he fascinates me./And yet from time to
469	CC	Lucasta	27	never go to the Opera, in the season./Though I've always felt out of it. And can you
475	CC	Colby	11	the change as soon as it happens,/Though you couldn't have predicted it./{L} I
485	CC	Lady E	1	ugly,/And of being feeble-minded: though my family made me think so./But you
489	CC	Claude	7	each —/That seemed fair enough — though yours had been lost,/And mine I
490	CC	Lady E	6	know I'm rather weak in the head/Though I try to be clever. Do try to help me./
496	CC	Eggers	25	she misses the contact with London,/Though she doesn't admit it. She misses my
501	CC	Eggers	27	Allow me. May I make a suggestion?/Though first of all I must take the occasion/To
515	CC	Guzzard	16	I was frightened by what I had done./Though I had never said 'this child is yours',/I
525	ES	Monica	31	called for tea./So why not talk now? Though I know very well/What it is you want to
529	ES	Monica	26	/And to think about nothing. Though I know that won't be easy./{LC} That is
532	ES	Ld Clav	17	to know. I can't refuse to see him./Though from what I remember of the man who
538	ES	Gomez	15	that you did very well by yourself?/Though not, I suspect, as well as you had
539	ES	Ld Clav	24	An interesting historical epitome./Though I cannot accept it as altogether
541	ES	Gomez	19	a good place/To make money in — though not to *keep* it in./My investments — not
541	ES	Gomez	38	distress./Well, I shan't keep you long, though I dare say your caller/Could hang on for
545	ES	Monica	12	here and restful./Even the matron, though she looks rather dominating,/Has left us
546	ES	Piggott	13	guests to think of themselves as ill,/Though we never have guests who are perfectly
546	ES	Piggott	20	in perfect health are exceptional/Though we never accept any guest who's
561	ES	Ld Clav	3	how gladly would I help you!/Even though it carried you away from me forever/To
569	ES	Ld Clav	36	past. They've always been with me/Though it was not till lately that I found the
575	ES	Gomez	27	were once custodian of *my* morals:/Though of course you went a little *faster* than I
578	ES	Ld Clav	4	you go. I shall never repudiate you/Though you repudiate me. I see now clearly/The
578	ES	Michael	23	You know I'm very fond of you/Though we never really seemed to have much in
582	ES	Monica	32	us alone together./And yet, Charles, though we've been alone to-day/Only a few
583	ES	Monica	15	to him together. He is close at hand,/Though he has gone too far to return to us./He

THOUGHT (193)

31	Apollinax	3	laughter tinkled among the teacups./I thought of Fragilion, that shy figure among the
38	Gerontion	42	too soon/Into weak hands, what's thought can be dispensed with/Till the refusal
41	Burb Blei	31	flea'd his rump and pared his claws?/Thought Burbank, meditating on/Time's ruins,

52	Whispers	7	the sockets of the eyes!/He knew that thought clings round dead limbs/Tightening its
56	Swee Night	26	and the lady in the cape/Are suspect, thought to be in league;/Therefore the man with
62	WL: Burial	63	London Bridge, so many,/I had not thought death had undone so many./Sighs,
69	WL: Fire S	251	/Her brain allows one half-formed thought to pass:/'Well now that's done: and I'm
104	Journ Magi	38	I had seen birth and death,/But had thought they were different; this Birth was/Hard
105	Song Sime	29	for me the martyrdom, the ecstasy of thought and prayer,/Not for me the ultimate
148	Rock 1	58	*Make perfect your will.*/I say: take no thought of the harvest,/But only of proper
180	FQ: ECoker	128	are all in the waiting./Wait without thought, for you are not ready for thought:/So
180	FQ: ECoker	128	thought, for you are not ready for thought:/So the darkness shall be the light, and
190	FQ: DrySal	218	rest/Is prayer, observance, discipline, thought and action./The hint half guessed, the
192	FQ: Little	31	/And the tombstone. And what you thought you came for/Is only a shell, a husk of
194	FQ: Little	125	each other,/So I find words I never thought to speak/In streets I never thought I
194	FQ: Little	126	thought to speak/In streets I never thought I should revisit/When I left my body on
209	NamingCats	28	in a rapt contemplation/Of the thought, of the thought, of the thought of his
209	NamingCats	28	contemplation/Of the thought, of the thought, of the thought of his name:/His
209	NamingCats	28	Of the thought, of the thought, of the thought of his name:/His ineffable effable/
226	Macavity	13	in./His brow is deeply lined with thought, his head is highly domed;/His coat is
599	On a Port	12	hid from us,/Beyond the circle of our thought she stands./The parrot on his bar, a
248	MC Thomas	10	the springtime fancy,/So one thought goes whistling down the wind./The
252	MC Thomas	26	loyalty./{T} To make, then break, this thought has come before,/The desperate exercise
254	MC Thomas	23	enemies, in another place./{T} I have thought of these things./{T4} That is why I tell
254	MC Tempt4	26	kings to compel you./You have also thought, sometimes at your prayers,/Sometimes
254	MC Tempt4	29	morning,/When the bird cries, have thought of further scorning./That nothing lasts,
255	MC Tempt4	6	/{T4} Yes, Thomas, yes; you have thought of that too./What can compare with
258	MC Thomas	11	/Delight in sense, in learning and in thought,/Music and philosophy, curiosity,/The
258	MC Thomas	23	I/Could then despise the men who thought me most contemptible,/The raw
261	MC Thomas	8	of which you have probably never thought./Not only do we at the feast of
280	MC Priest3	32	and tread one endless round/Of thought, to justify your action to yourselves,/
281	MC Chorus	13	must consciously praise Thee, in thought and in word and in deed./Even with the
288	FR Agatha	26	daring feats on the old pony,/And thought to creep back through the little door./
291	FR Amy	7	pantomime./{A} What's that? I thought I saw someone pass the window./What
296	FR Gerald	15	{}/[*Exit*]/{G} God preserve us!/I never thought it would be as bad as this./{V} There is
299	FRDowning	28	/If I may make so bold, Sir,/I always thought that a very few cocktails/Went a long
299	FRDowning	40	he was nervous./He behaved as if he thought something might happen./{C} What
302	FR Chorus	1	hardening artery./We like to be thought well of by others/So that we may think
303	FR Agatha	19	Why did she ask him?/{Ag} She only thought of asking him a little while ago./{M}
303	FR Agatha	30	want your advice./{Ag} I should have thought/You had more than you wanted of
305	FR Mary	21	Harry./You are down very early. I thought/you had just arrived./Did you have a
306	FR Harry	13	been longing to get back/Because I thought I never should. I thought it was a place/
306	FR Harry	13	/Because I thought I never should. I thought it was a place/Where life was
306	FR Harry	21	my childhood. I can't explain./But I thought I might escape from one life to another,
311	FR Harry	22	moment/That I stood in sunlight, and thought I might stay there./{M} Look at me.
311	FR Harry	36	but that other person, if person/You thought I was: let your necrophily/Feed upon
322	FR Winch	25	John!/{Wi} Yes, my Lord, I'm sorry./I thought I'd better have a word with you quiet,/
324	FR Ivy	22	how can you be so callous?/I always thought you were so fond of John./{V} And if
328	FR Charles	19	When challenged, Mr. Piper said:/"I thought it was all open country about here"—'/
328	FR Charles	25	signalled by the police car, he said: "I/thought you were having a game with me.'"/{G}
331	FR Harry	6	/Though nothing else was real. I thought foolishly/That when I got back to
331	FR Harry	29	I hope I have the strength./{H} I have thought of you as the completely strong,/The
334	FR Harry	36	no more power than I./The things I thought were real are shadows, and the real/Are
334	FR Harry	37	are shadows, and the real/Are what I thought were private shadows. O that awful
336	FR Harry	18	you./You followed me here, where I thought I should escape you —No! you were
340	FR Amy	2	to ask you again to Wishwood;/But I thought, thirty-five years is long, and death is
340	FR Amy	3	is long, and death is an end,/And I thought that time might have made a change in
340	FR Amy	29	there might be no ugly rumours./You thought I did not know!/You may be close, but
341	FR Agatha	3	changed. And perhaps I have not./I thought that I had, until this evening./But at
346	FR Charles	1	as I was about to cross Pall Mall./I thought that life could bring no further
347	FRDowning	2	—/If you understand my meaning. I thought that was the reason/We was off tonight.
354	CP Peter	10	/{J} Lithuanian? Lady Klootz?/{P} I thought she was Belgian./{A} Her father
359	CP Edward	18	didn't know that *you* were coming./I thought that Lavinia had told me the names/Of
360	CP Reilly	30	Or another woman/Of whom she thought she had cause to be jealous?/{E} She
361	CP Edward	21	my wife/A good deal better than I thought, or unless you know/A good deal more
362	CP Edward	9	to say, you love her?/{E} Why, I thought we took each other for granted./I never
362	CP Edward	10	took each other for granted./I never thought I should be any happier/With another
362	CP Reilly	22	lost touch with the person/You thought you were. You no longer feel quite

367 CP	Peter	4	have behaved rather better than I thought./If you didn't notice, I don't suppose
367 CP	Edward	14	/We're both of us artists./{E} I never thought of that./What arts do you practise?/{P}
367 CP	Peter	32	that's not the point./The point is, I thought we had a great deal in common/And I
367 CP	Peter	33	deal in common/And I think she thought so too./{E} How did you come to know
367 CP	Alex	38	that the door was open/And so I thought I'd slip in and see if anyone was with
368 CP	Alex	4	you're coming with me, Edward./I thought, Edward may be all alone this evening,/
369 CP	Peter	30	it seemed very strange,/Because I thought of her merely as a name/In a society
370 CP	Peter	6	/{P} Oh, nothing happened./But I thought that she really cared about me./And I
374 CP	Celia	15	I want to be alone./{C} I should have thought it was perfectly simple./Lavinia has left
374 CP	Celia	28	would ruin your career;/And we thought that Lavinia would never want to leave
375 CP	Celia	34	/{C} You suppose it's still cooking!/I thought I noticed a peculiar smell:/Of course it's
377 CP	Julia	24	chilled. But it's so refreshing;/And I thought, we are all in need of a stimulant/After
379 CP	Edward	20	arisen./What future had you ever thought there could be?/{C} What had I thought
379 CP	Celia	21	there could be?/{C} What had I thought that the future could be?/I abandoned
380 CP	Celia	6	to find that a man/With whom they thought they had shared something wonderful/
380 CP	Edward	20	me and Peter./{E} Wasn't there? He thought so./He came back this evening to talk
380 CP	Celia	24	reason to suppose I cared for him./I thought he had talent; I saw that he was lonely;/
380 CP	Celia	25	had talent; I saw that he was lonely;/I thought that I could help him. I took him to
382 CP	Celia	9	at you./I looked at your face: and I thought that I knew/And loved every contour;
382 CP	Celia	26	It is only what was left/Of what I had thought you were. I see another person,/I see
389 CP	Lavinia	26	but haven't we always been friends?/I thought you were one of my dearest friends —/
393 CP	Edward	12	differently. As we're on the subject,/I thought that it was I who had given in to *you.*/
393 CP	Lavinia	29	so considerate, people said;/And you thought you were unselfish. It was only
394 CP	Edward	13	butler:/Some of your guests may have thought I *was* the butler./{L} And on several
394 CP	Edward	17	/{E} Well, at least, *they* can't have thought I was the butler./{L} Everything I tried
396 CP	Lavinia	13	I wonder now/How you could have thought you were in love with me./{E}
396 CP	Lavinia	25	yourself. And that's hard to bear./I thought that there might be some way out for
396 CP	Lavinia	26	way out for you/If I went away. I thought that if I died/To you, I who had been
398 CP	Edward	5	if I could return to yesterday/Before I thought that I had made a decision./What devil
402 CP	Edward	12	you are very ill?/{E} I should have thought a doctor could see that for himself./Or
402 CP	Edward	19	— but if they saw it/I should have thought that a doctor could see it./{R} 'Nervous
403 CP	Edward	7	/{E} But I am obsessed by the thought of my own insignificance./{R} Precisely.
403 CP	Edward	32	Without her, it was vacancy./When I thought she had left me, I began to dissolve,/To
409 CP	Reilly	9	other./Mr. Chamberlayne, when you thought your wife had left you,/You discovered,
410 CP	Edward	5	/And I never quite knew why. I thought it was *my* fault./{R} And now you
416 CP	Celia	14	Some are rarer than others./{C} Oh, I thought that I was giving him so much!/And he
417 CP	Celia	7	again can either hurt or heal./I have thought at moments that the ecstasy is real/
421 CP	Julia	10	will do that. We shall see./It's the thought of Celia that weighs upon my mind./
425 CP	Lavinia	7	a great many more accepted/Than we thought would want to come. But what can you
427 CP	Alex	10	I heard about your party/And, as I thought you might be leaving for the country,/I
429 CP	Julia	13	were taking us, with your monkeys./I thought I was going to dine out on those
431 CP	Peter	8	Bela Szogody —/He's my boss. I thought everyone knew *his* name./{J} Is he your
431 CP	Peter	30	/And Bela is very pleased with it./He thought I should see the original Boltwell;/And
431 CP	Peter	31	the original Boltwell;/And besides, he thought that as I'm English/I ought to know the
431 CP	Julia	37	what faces are typical./{J} Peter, I've thought of a wonderful idea!/I've always wanted
433 CP	Peter	15	want to get into films,/And I always thought she could make a success of it/If she
435 CP	Peter	9	little more self-confidence;/And then I thought about her again. More and more./At
435 CP	Peter	13	you about her just now; but I never thought/Of anything like this. I suppose I didn't
435 CP	Peter	20	it/So that I might believe in myself./I thought I had ideas to make a revolution/In the
435 CP	Peter	23	am, making a second-rate film!/But I thought it was going to lead to something
436 CP	Peter	11	time that you've been talking,/One thought has been going round and round in my
436 CP	Julia	19	be reconciled, and be happy in the thought of her./{L} Sir Henry, there is
436 CP	Lavinia	33	any case you knew *about* her./Yet I thought your expression was one of ...
445 CC	Eggers	14	things one needs for a garden!/And I thought, now's the moment to buy some new
446 CC	Claude	20	far, I've left him to his own devices:/I thought he would fall into this way of life more
448 CC	Eggers	12	They're much too deep for me. And I thought, Mr. Simpkins,/He's highly educated.
452 CC	Kaghan	7	the money-box./Bankrupt again! So I thought I'd better bring her/And come upstairs
459 CC	Claude	24	have you chosen, between you?/{SC} I thought a primrose yellow would be cheerful./
459 CC	Claude	32	Dr. Rebmann says./{SC} Rebmann? I thought it was a Dr. Leroux./{LE} Dr. Leroux is
460 CC	Claude	4	{SC} So on you went to Zürich./But I thought that the doctor in Lausanne taught
460 CC	Lady E	5	/{LE} No, Claude, he only teaches *thought* control./Mind control is a different
464 CC	Claude	31	—/What I hoped I could do with it. I thought I despised him/When I was young. And
467 CC	Colby	8	/I begin to see how I have always thought of you —/As a kind of protector, a
471 CC	Colby	27	matter. But, for some reason,/You thought I'd get a false impression anyway./You
476 CC	Lucasta	18	he knows/That what some men have thought about me wasn't true./{C} What wasn't

476 CC	Colby	22	mistress, palmed off on B./{C} I never thought of such a thing!/{L} You never thought
476 CC	Lucasta	23	of such a thing!/{L} You never thought of such a thing!/There are not many
476 CC	Lucasta	24	are not many men who wouldn't have thought it./I don't know about B. He's very
477 CC	Lucasta	22	of me:/Now *you're* ashamed of me. I thought you'd understand./Little you know
477 CC	Lucasta	29	didn't like that person either,/And I thought you'd come to see me as the real kind
477 CC	Lucasta	32	me. I suppose I was flattered./And I thought, now, perhaps, if someone else sees me/
478 CC	Lucasta	14	sorry, thank you./Why, I'd actually thought of telling you before,/And I postponed
478 CC	Lucasta	16	telling you, just for the fun of it:/I thought, when I tell him, it will be so wonderful
479 CC	Kaghan	39	as Colby is, Lucasta,/I'd never have thought of changing my condition./{L} You're
480 CC	Kaghan	4	most exciting speculation/I've ever thought of investing in./Colby's more cautious.
483 CC	Colby	31	/{C} No, I don't. I mean, I've never thought about it./{LE} I can't say that *I* believe
484 CC	Lady E	22	And such unpleasant people!/I thought of myself as a dove in an eagle's nest./
488 CC	Claude	27	I'd hoped — and now it seems a silly thought .../What happens is so like what one
489 CC	Claude	9	I couldn't lose. But if I had another/I thought you might think — 'and now how many
489 CC	Claude	14	longed for a son of your own,/And I thought, I'll wait for children of *our* own,/And
489 CC	Lady E	38	child was Colby;/And Mrs. Guzzard thought you would be happy/To think you had
491 CC	Colby	1	wanted a parent till now —/I never thought about it. Now, you have made me
491 CC	Lady E	5	to take away from you/The son you thought was yours. And I know from what you
493 CC	Claude	9	No, that would look too formal. I thought it would be better/To put Eggerson
493 CC	Claude	17	offending Mrs. Guzzard. That's why I thought/That Eggerson should put the first
494 CC	Claude	15	acted as if I believed in them./I thought/it was facts that my father believed in;/I
494 CC	Claude	16	was facts that my father believed in;/I thought that what he cared for was power and
495 CC	Claude	7	/Was a husband of importance. I thought you would despise me/If you knew
495 CC	Lady E	20	an artist!/{LE} Or to inspire a poet. I thought Tony was a poet./Because he wrote me
495 CC	Lady E	25	what I mean? I'm getting confused./I thought I was escaping from a world that I
498 CC	Claude	39	first, to explain the situation:/And I thought I would like you to conduct the
499 CC	Claude	22	to marry B./{SC} To marry B.! But I thought that was all settled./{L} Yes, of course,
499 CC	Lucasta	23	/{L} Yes, of course, Claude. You thought everything settled./That was just the
499 CC	Lucasta	32	an interest/In Colby. Because you thought he was too good for me./{SC} In Colby!
500 CC	Lucasta	35	/Simply as a business man. As you thought of me/Simply as a nuisance. We're
500 CC	Lucasta	37	We're suited to each other:/You thought so too, Claude, but for the wrong
501 CC	Claude	16	misunderstood B.,/And I've never thought that I understood *you*;/And I certainly
502 CC	Lucasta	12	have been like you — the way I thought it was./You're much too ... detached,
502 CC	Lucasta	14	ever to be shocked/In the way I thought you were. I was ashamed/Of what I was
502 CC	Lucasta	16	you, and so I was expecting/What I thought I got. But I couldn't believe it!/It isn't
504 CC	Lucasta	9	But where's the parlourmaid?/{L} I thought I heard someone singing in the pantry./
505 CC	Claude	11	to make his acquaintance./{SC} And I thought he might ... conduct the proceedings:/
512 CC	Lady E	7	Mrs. Guzzard, I had no suspicions!/I thought there had been a confusion — that's all.
515 CC	Guzzard	9	/From undeceiving you. And then I thought — why not?/My husband also had
516 CC	Colby	10	high before — beyond my capacity./I thought I didn't want to be an organist/When I
516 CC	Claude	22	could handle/Matters you would have thought so uncongenial;/And the way in which
533 ES	Gomez	16	hard worker all these years/And I thought, now's the time to take a long holiday,/
537 ES	Gomez	26	get a First./I suppose your tutor thought you'd be sent down./It went the other
545 ES	Ld Clav	17	that's what Badgley Court is for.'/I thought that very ominous. When people talk
545 ES	Piggott	27	a rush, these last few days,/And I thought, 'Lord Claverton will understand/My
548 ES	Monica	7	her expression when she left/That she thought she'd done her duty by us for to-day./
549 ES	Carghil	37	/I was very lovely once. So *you* thought,/And others thought so too. But as you
549 ES	Carghil	38	once. So *you* thought,/And others thought so too. But as you remember,/Please,
550 ES	Ld Clav	33	old memories/Which I should have thought we both preferred to leave buried./
552 ES	Ld Clav	14	/At finding that I felt nothing at all./I thought, perhaps, what a lucky escape/It had
552 ES	Carghil	18	Richard. A lucky escape/You thought, for you. You felt no embarrassment?/
555 ES	Piggott	4	that she wanted to meet you, so I thought/That I'd take the first opportunity of
556 ES	Ld Clav	17	you staying there? I shouldn't have thought/It would be the sort of place that you'd
559 ES	Michael	33	in fact. Oh, I've no doubt/That the thought of passing on your name and title/To a
567 ES	Monica	29	you from *that* direction, Father!/I thought you were indoors. Where have you
570 ES	Ld Clav	5	your mother, as she never knew me./I thought that she would never understand/Or
574 ES	Carghil	13	thinking cap./I know you've always thought me utterly brainless,/But I have an idea
574 ES	Carghil	18	in the world. That's very natural./So I thought, why not appeal to Señor Gomez?/He's
575 ES	Gomez	20	it already. I've told him myself./I thought he'd better learn the facts from me/
581 ES	Monica	39	— the man you are,/Not the man I thought you were./{LC} And Michael —/I love

THOUGHTFUL (2)

| 368 CP | Edward | 7 | have dinner with me./{E} That's very thoughtful of you, Alex, I'm sure;/But I rather |
| 458 CC | Lady E | 11 | to meet you./{LE} That was very thoughtful of you, Eggerson,/But quite |

354 CP	Alex	32	Two, I think./{A} No, there were three, but you wouldn't know the third one:/
376 CP	Edward	28	and prepared for me./He *would* do it. Three Good Samaritans./I forgot all about it./
377 CP	m	19	JULIA, *in apron, with a tray and three glasses*]/{J} I've had an inspiration!/There's
399 CP	Reilly	1	*Appointment/Book.*/{R} About those three appointments this morning, Miss
399 CP	Nurse	17	I leave her there/Until you ring three times./{R} And the third patient?/{N} The
402 CP	Reilly	4	much worse. You might have ruined three lives/By your indecision. Now there are
405 CP	m	7	own. {}/[*Presses the bell on his desk three times*]/{R} You must accept a rather
422 CP	1m	11	*enters with a tray, a decanter and three glasses, and/exit.* REILLY *pours drinks.*]/
424 CP	1m	1	even in California. {}/CURTAIN/Act Three/*The drawing-room of the*
427 CP	Alex	30	have been staying with the Governor./Three of us have been out on a tour of
430 CP	Peter	6	York last night —/I left Los Angeles three days ago./I saw Sheila Paisley at lunch
434 CP	Alex	6	Go on./{A} It seems that there were three of them —/Three sisters at this station, in
434 CP	Alex	7	that there were three of them —/Three sisters at this station, in a Christian
484 CC	Lady E	31	Colby, when I was a child/I had three obsessions, and I never told anyone./I
493 CC	1m	1	ELIZABETH]/CURTAIN/Act Three/*The Business Room, as in Act* 1. *Several*
523 ES	m	14	*at Badgley Court. Morning*/ACT THREE/*The Same. Late afternoon of the*
549 ES	Carghil	6	I'm afraid not./{MC} There were the three of us — Effie, Maudie and me./That day
549 ES	Carghil	21	better I'll remember./{MC} And the three of us talked you over afterwards —/Effie
567 ES	1m	1	for me, Monica? {}/CURTAIN/Act Three/*Same as Act Two. Late afternoon of the*

THRESHOLD (1)

479 CC	Kaghan	26	for firmness. Don't let her cross the threshold./{L} As if you weren't as afraid of her

THREW (1)

16 Prufrock		105	I mean!/But as if a magic lantern threw the nerves in patterns on a screen:/Would

THRILL (1)

549 ES	Carghil	40	knew me. It would give me such a thrill/To hear you speak my name once more./

THRILLED (2)

382 CP	Celia	12	to your voice, that had always thrilled me,/And it became another voice — no,
390 CP	Julia	17	me you were abducted! Tell us/I'm thrilled ... {}/[*The doorbell rings.* EDWARD

THRIVE (1)

249 MC	Tempt2	8	/Dispensing justice make all even,/Is thrive on earth, and perhaps in heaven./{T}

THRIVES (1)

220 Old Deut		7	his numerous progeny prospers and thrives/And the village is proud of him in his

THROAT (3)

32 Hysteria		4	lost finally in the dark caverns of her throat, bruised by/the ripple of unseen muscles.
189 FQ: DrySal		185	sand, in the sea's lips/Or in the dark throat which will not reject them/Or wherever
197 FQ: Little		228	the block, to the fire, down the sea's throat/Or to an illegible stone: and that is where

THROBBING (3)

68 WL: Fire S		217	the human engine waits/Like a taxi throbbing waiting,/I Tiresias, though blind,
68 WL: Fire S		218	waiting,/I Tiresias, though blind, throbbing between two lives,/Old man with
310 FR	Mary	4	/The agony in the dark/The slow flow throbbing the trunk/The pain of the breaking

THROMBOSIS (1)

301 FR	Chorus	31	accident/We know about the sudden thrombosis/And the slowly hardening artery./

THRONE (5)

64 WL: Chess		77	/The Chair she sat in, like a burnished throne,/Glowed on the marble, where the glass/
249 MC	Tempt2	4	great, protect the poor,/Beneath the throne of God can man do more?/Disarm the
252 MC	Tempt3	12	people have good cause against the throne./{T} If the Archbishop cannot trust the
252 MC	Thomas	13	{T} If the Archbishop cannot trust the Throne,/He has good cause to trust none but
269 MC	Thomas	21	/To submit my cause before God's throne. {}/[*Exit*]/{K4} Priest! monk! and servant!

THROUGH (81)

13 Prufrock		4	etherised upon a table;/Let us go, through certain half-deserted streets,/The
15 Prufrock		70	/Shall I say, I have gone at dusk through narrow streets/And watched the smoke
18 Portrait		9	the latest Pole/Transmit the Preludes, through his hair and finger-tips.'So intimate,
18 Portrait		16	velleities and carefully caught regrets/Through attenuated tones of violins/Mingled
24 Rhapsody		10	pass/Beats like a fatalistic drum,/And through the spaces of the dark/Midnight shakes
24 Rhapsody		42	seen eyes in the street/Trying to peer through lighted shutters,/And a crab one
54 Mr E Sun		13	is cracked and browned/But through the water pale and thin/Still shine the
67 WL: Fire S		187	from ear to ear./A rat crept softly through the vegetation/Dragging its slimy belly
94 Ash-Wed 4		17	folded./The new years walk, restoring/Through a bright cloud of tears, the years,
109 Marina		3	of pine and the woodthrush singing through the fog/What images return/O my
110 Marina		34	my timbers/And woodthrush calling through the fog/My daughter./The Cultivation
115 SP	Dusty	18	Pereira./{Du} Now Sam's a gentleman through and through./{Do} I like Sam/{Du} *I*
115 SP	Dusty	18	Now Sam's a gentleman through and through./{Do} I like Sam/{Du} *I* like Sam/Yes
116 SP	Dusty	35	water/All right, Monday you'll phone through./Yes I'll tell her. Good bye. Gooooood
129 Cor2 State		49	/The small creatures chirp thinly through the dust, through the night./O mother/
129 Cor2 State		49	chirp thinly through the dust, through the night./O mother/What shall I cry?/

133 Eyes	2	in tears/Eyes that last I saw in tears/Through division/Here in death's dream
139 Virginia	5	as a river/Still. Will heat move/Only through the mocking-bird/Heard once? Still
160 Rock 7	20	A moment in time but time was made through that moment: for without the meaning
161 Rock 7	22	light to light, in the light of the Word,/Through the Passion and Sacrifice saved in spite
167 Rock 10	29	at midnight/And lights directed through the coloured panes of windows/And
167 Rock 10	33	/And see the light that fractures through unquiet water./We see the light but see
171 FQ: BurntN	22	them, find them,/Round the corner. Through the first gate,/Into our first world,
172 FQ: BurntN	27	the dead leaves,/In the autumn heat, through the vibrant air,/And the bird called, in
173 FQ: BurntN	92	involved with past and future./Only through time time is conquered./Here is a place
178 FQ: ECoker	35	Round and round the fire/Leaping through the flames, or joined in circles,/
181 FQ: ECoker	145	at what you are not/You must go through the way in which you are not./And
183 FQ: ECoker	209	a further union, a deeper communion/Through the dark cold and the empty
197 FQ: Little	245	And know the place for the first time./Through the unknown, remembered gate/When
213 Growltiger	53	joy in Wapping when the news flew through the land;/At Maidenhead and Henley
219 Mung Rump	32	say it was weather./They would go through the house like a hurricane, and no
223 Pekes Pols	54	amazing;/And when he looked out through the bars of the area,/You never saw
224 Mr Mistoff	25	to the tip of his tail;/He can creep through the tiniest crack/He can walk on the
229 Gus	48	think they are smart, just to jump through a hoop.'/And he'll say, as he scratches
588 Fable	45	about — as well's I'm able/I'll go through the account: They made a raid/On
593 Grad 8	6	what distant lands we may have gone,/Through all the years will ne'er have been
257 MC Tempts	2	unheard./{4T} Come whispering through the ear, or a sudden shock on the skull.
257 MC Chorus	26	birth or death./Sweet and cloying through the dark air/Falls the stifling scent of
257 MC Chorus	32	you, lie at your feet, swing and wing through the dark air./O Thomas Archbishop,
268 MC Knight1	25	It was he who condemned them./{K1} Through you they were suspended./{K2} By you
268 MC Thomas	30	/{T} I do not deny/That this was done through me. But it is not I/Who can loose
271 MC Priests	21	must not stop here. To the minster./Through the cloister. No time to waste. They
271 MC Priests	26	they are coming. They will break through presently./You will be killed. Come to
275 MC Chorus	27	and see them all smeared with blood, through a curtain of falling blood?/We did not
280 MC Priest1	9	us, direct us?/After what journey through what further dread/Shall we recover
288 FR Agatha	26	old pony,/And thought to creep back through the little door./He will find a new
291 FR Harry	20	how you looked, when I saw you through the window!/Do you like to be stared at
291 FR Harry	21	/Do you like to be stared at by eyes through a window?/{A} You forget, Harry, that
293 FR Harry	38	/Of external events. You have gone through life in sleep,/Never woken to the
294 FR Harry	23	/While the slow stain sinks deeper through the skin/Tainting the flesh and
316 FR m	8	/[Exeunt]/[Enter MARY, and passes through to dinner. Enter AGATHA]/{Ag} The
333 FR Agatha	11	have carried/Death in life, death through lifetime, death in my womb./I felt that
333 FR Harry	22	life has only been a dream/Dreamt through me by the minds of others. Perhaps/I
333 FR Agatha	34	unhappy family,/Its bird sent flying through the purgatorial flame./Indeed it is
333 FR Agatha	36	may learn hereafter,/Moving alone through flames of ice, chosen/To resolve the
334 FR Agatha	40	pain from prison./{Ag} I only looked through the little door/When the sun was
335 FR Agatha	18	above the desert./{Ag} Up and down, through the stone passages/Of an immense and
335 FR Harry	35	happen/O my dear, and you walked through the little door/And I ran to meet you in
335 FR Agatha	38	the beginning./We do not pass twice through the same door/Or return to the door
335 FR Agatha	39	the same door/Or return to the door through which we did not pass./I have seen the
340 FR Amy	30	/You may be close, but I always saw through *him*./And now it is my son./{Ag} I
393 CP Edward	37	to come in —/And they didn't come through any of *your* friends —/You suddenly
395 CP Edward	26	that comes/From seeing oneself through the eyes of other people./{L} That must
399 CP Nurse	15	she will be punctual./{N} I telephone through/The moment she arrives. I leave her
413 CP Celia	22	me;/And with what I've been going through, these last weeks,/I somehow took it for
421 CP Julia	27	will pass between the scolding hills,/Through the valley of derision, like a child sent
427 CP Alex	15	lunch, but my secretary couldn't get through to you./Never mind, I said — to
438 CP Lavinia	3	the design./{L} Perhaps she had been through greater agony beforehand./I mean — I
465 CC Claude	29	in the evening, I believe you will go through the private door/Into the real world, as
468 CC Claude	3	— Oh yes, that meeting. We must run through the figures. {}/CURTAIN/Act Two/
473 CC Colby	25	so unrelated./I turn the key, and walk through the gate,/And there I am ... alone, in
487 CC Lady E	18	just made a startling discovery!/All through a name — and intuition./But it shall be
494 CC Lady E	1	thinking things over and over —/All through the night. I hardly slept at all./I wish
507 CC Guzzard	17	was brought to me by a third party,/Through whom the monthly payments were
541 ES Lambert	32	you there's a trunk call coming through for you/In five minutes' time./{LC} I'll
545 ES Piggott	32	to make your wants known./Just ring through to my office. If I'm not there/My
552 ES Carghil	9	into it I did/But for what I'd gone through. Did you hear me sing it?/{LC} Yes, I
572 ES Ld Clav	36	now — run away from *them*./It is through this meeting that I shall at last escape
577 ES Charles	13	in a man who aims to gratify, through you,/His lifelong grievance against
578 ES Ld Clav	6	mistakes I have made/My whole life through, mistake upon mistake,/The mistaken
582 ES Charles	26	he used to be./It's as if he had passed through some door unseen by us/And had

THROUGHOUT (1)

277 MC Knight2	39	qualities I very much admired, has throughout been/presented as the under dog.

THROW (4)

128 Cor1 March	46	said right out loud, *crumpets*.)/Don't throw away that sausage,/It'll come in handy.
273 MC Thomas	16	We are safe./{T} Unbar the doors! throw open the doors!/I will not have the house
304 FR Mary	1	/{M} I might have known you'd throw that up against me./I know I wasn't one
559 ES Ld Clav	25	ready to repudiate your family,/To throw away the whole of your inheritance?/{Mi}

THROWING (4)

16 Prufrock	107	while/If one, settling a pillow or throwing off a shawl,/And turning toward the
241 MC Mess	33	enthusiasm,/Lining the road and throwing down their capes,/Strewing the way
548 ES m	19	quickly./What made you choose it? {}/[*throwing down newspaper*]./{LC} My daughter
549 ES Carghil	28	shrewd —/Effie it was said 'you'd be throwing yourself away./Mark my words' Effie

THROWS (1)

24 Rhapsody	23	like a crooked pin.'/The memory throws up high and dry/A crowd of twisted

THRUSH (1)

171 FQ: BurntN	24	shall we follow/The deception of the thrush? Into our first world./There they were,

THUMBS (1)

227 Macavity	33	to find him resting, or a-licking of his thumbs,/Or engaged in doing complicated long

THUNDER (6)

72 WL: Thund	t	handsome and tall as you./What the Thunder said/After the torchlight red on sweaty
72 WL: Thund	327	and palace and reverberation/Of thunder of spring over distant mountains/He
72 WL: Thund	342	in the mountains/But dry sterile thunder without rain/There is not even solitude
74 WL: Thund	399	humped in silence./Then spoke the thunder/DA/*Datta:* what have we given?/My
178 FQ: ECoker	59	/Late roses filled with early snow?/Thunder rolled by the rolling stars/Simulates
264 MC Priest3	16	*God.*/As the voice of many waters, of thunder, of harps,/They sang as it were a new

THURSDAY (1)

368 CP Peter	33	Lavinia's amateur Thursdays?/{P} A Thursday. Why do you say amateur?/{E}

THURSDAYS (3)

368 CP Edward	32	ago./{E} At one of Lavinia's amateur Thursdays?/{P} A Thursday. Why do you say
369 CP Edward	20	them./That is why, I think, her Thursdays were a failure./{P} You speak as if
394 CP Lavinia	9	I took so much trouble/To have those Thursdays, to give you the chance/Of talking to

THUS (9)

91 Ash-Wed 2	21	would be forgotten, so I would forget/Thus devoted, concentrated in purpose. And
151 Rock 2	1	*a job for each/Each man to his work.*/Thus your fathers were made/Fellow citizens of
171 FQ: BurntN	15	/Into the rose-garden. My words echo/Thus, in your mind./But to what purpose/
195 FQ: Little	161	/From the future as well as the past. Thus, love of a country/Begins as attachment to
595 Grad 14	2	we are done; we may no more delay;/Thus is the end of every tale: 'Farewell',/A word
261 MC Thomas	32	even the glory of being a/martyr. So thus as on earth the Church mourns and
290 FR Agatha	22	yourself it's the only thing to do./{Ag} Thus with most careful devotion/Thus with
290 FR Agatha	23	{Ag} Thus with most careful devotion/Thus with precise attention/To detail,
362 CP Reilly	6	and had the courage to break it —/Thus giving herself a permanent advantage./{E}

THWARTED (1)

448 CC Claude	33	that./{SC} Which has always been thwarted./{E} I'm sure it's been a grief to both

THY (33)

105 Song Sime	8	towards the dead land./Grant us thy peace./I have walked many years in this city,
105 Song Sime	18	scourges and lamentation/Grant us thy peace./Before the stations of the mountain
105 Song Sime	25	and no to-morrow./According to thy word./They shall praise Thee and suffer in
106 Song Sime	31	for me the ultimate vision./Grant me thy peace./(And a sword shall pierce thy heart,/
106 Song Sime	32	thy peace./(And a sword shall pierce thy heart,/Thine also)./I am tired with my own
106 Song Sime	36	and the deaths of those after me./Let thy servant depart,/Having seen thy salvation./
106 Song Sime	37	/Let thy servant depart,/Having seen thy salvation./Animula/'Issues from the hand of
155 Rock 3	44	ruins?/I have loved the beauty of Thy House, the peace of Thy sanctuary,/I have
155 Rock 3	44	the beauty of Thy House, the peace of Thy sanctuary,/I have swept the floors and
162 Rock 8	5	are come into thine inheritance,/And thy temple have they defiled./Who is this that
167 Rock 10	46	Invisible, we give Thee thanks for Thy great glory!/FOUR QUARTETS/Burnt
594 Grad 11	2	like flitting faces in a dream;/Out of thy care and tutelage we pass/Into the unknown
594 Grad 12	2	not die — for each succeeding year/Thy honor and thy fame shall but increase/
594 Grad 12	2	each succeeding year/Thy honor and thy fame shall but increase/Forever, and may
594 Grad 12	6	be thine, from far and near/To spread thy name o'er distant lands and seas!/As thou to
594 Grad 13	1	distant lands and seas!/As thou to thy departing sons hast been/To those that
595 Grad 13	4	and a friend to bless/Before they leave thy care for lands unseen;/And let thy motto be,
595 Grad 13	5	thy care for lands unseen;/And let thy motto be, proud and serene,/Still as the
604 Ode	3	Ere we face the importunate years,/In thy shadow we wait, while thy presence dispels/
604 Ode	3	years,/In thy shadow we wait, while thy presence dispels/Our vain hesitations and
604 Ode	5	hesitations and fears./And we turn as thy sons ever turn, in the strength/Of the hopes

604 Ode		6	in the strength/Of the hopes that thy blessings bestow,/From the hopes and
604 Ode		7	hopes and ambitions that sprang at thy feet/To the thoughts of the past as we go./
264 MC	Priest3	18	as it were a new song./The blood of thy saints have they shed like water,/And there
264 MC	Priest3	20	them. Avenge, O Lord,/The blood of thy saints. In Rama, a voice heard, weeping./
273 MC	Chorus	5	tree, my Saviour,/Let not be in vain Thy labour;/Help me, Lord, in my last fear./
281 MC	Chorus	7	/{C} We praise Thee, O God, for Thy glory displayed in all the creatures of the
281 MC	Chorus	8	in the wind, in the storm; in all of Thy creatures, both the hunters and the hunted.
281 MC	Chorus	10	by Thee, all things exist/Only in Thy light, and Thy glory is declared even in that
281 MC	Chorus	10	all things exist/Only in Thy light, and Thy glory is declared even in that which denies
281 MC	Chorus	17	birds, praise Thee./We thank Thee for Thy mercies of blood, for Thy redemption by
281 MC	Chorus	17	Thee for Thy mercies of blood, for Thy redemption by blood. For the blood of Thy
281 MC	Chorus	17	by blood. For the blood of Thy martyrs and saints/Shall enrich the earth,

THYME (2)

180 FQ: ECoker	131	and winter lightning./The wild thyme unseen and the wild strawberry,/The
190 FQ: DrySal	213	lost in a shaft of sunlight,/The wild thyme unseen, or the winter lightning/Or the

TICKET (6)

349 FR	Ivy	8	to stay till after the funeral: will my ticket to London still be valid?/{G} I do not
428 CP	Julia	4	/The horrid little beast — stole my ticket to Mentone/And I had to travel in a very
457 CC	Eggers	1	She sometimes gets lost,/Or loses her ticket, or even her passport./But let's not be
458 CC	Claude	14	mean to say that you changed your ticket?/{E} Yes, how did you manage to change
458 CC	Eggers	15	how did you manage to change your ticket?/{LE} I went to the agency and got them
460 CC	Claude	34	actually went and changed her own ticket./It's something unheard of./{E} Amazing,

TICKING (1)

29 Aunt Helen	10	too./The Dresden clock continued ticking on the mantelpiece,/And the footman sat

TICKLED (1)

537 ES	Gomez	23	with me/Because it flattered *you* — tickled your love of power/To see that I was

TIDE (4)

69 WL: Fire S	269	tar/The barges drift/With the turning tide/Red sails/Wide/To leeward, swing on the
212 Growltiger	23	balmy moonlight it lay rocking on the tide —/And Growltiger was disposed to show
256 MC	Priests	24	my Lord do not fight the intractable tide,/Do not sail the irresistible wind; in the
310 FR	Harry	11	sacrifice/And the wail of the new full tide/Returning the ghosts of the dead/Those

TIDES (1)

243 MC	Priest2	1	/Against the perpetual wash of tides of balance of forces of barons and

TIE (2)

210 Old Gumbie	26	curtain-cord she likes to wind, and tie it into sailor-knots./She sits upon the
603 Spleen	14	hat and gloves in hand,/Punctilious of tie and suit/(Somewhat impatient of delay)/On

TIED (1)

316 FR	Agatha	12	be separated/May the knot that was tied/Become unknotted/May the crossed bones/

TIENS (2)

51 Restaurant	22	t'en te décrotter les rides du visage;/Tiens, ma fourchette, décrasse-toi le crâne./De
51 Restaurant	24	payes-tu des expériences comme moi?/Tiens, voilà dix sous, pour la salle-de-bains./

TIENT (1)

48 Lune Miel	17	/Vieille usine désaffectée de Dieu, tient encore/Dans ses pierres écroulantes la

TIGER (5)

37 Gerontion	20	of the year/Came Christ the tiger/In depraved May, dogwood and chestnut,
38 Gerontion	48	from the wrath-bearing tree./The tiger springs in the new year. Us he devours.
143 Lines OM	1	is finished./Lines for an Old Man/The tiger in the tiger-pit/Is not more irritable than I.
210 Old Gumbie	2	/Her coat is of the tabby kind, with tiger stripes and leopard spots./All day she sits
229 Gus	39	the need for a cat./He once played a Tiger — could do it again —/Which an Indian

TIGER-PIT (1)

143 Lines OM	1	Lines for an Old Man/The tiger in the tiger-pit/Is not more irritable than I./The

TIGERS (6)

353 CP	Alex	2	completely, Julia:/There *were* no tigers. *That* was the point./{J} Then what were
353 CP	Julia	10	/I know it started as a story about tigers./{A} I said there were no tigers./{C} Oh do
353 CP	Alex	11	about tigers./{A} I said there were no tigers./{C} Oh do stop wrangling,/Both of you.
427 CP	Julia	26	some Sultan?/You were shooting tigers?/{A} There are no tigers, Julia,/In
427 CP	Alex	27	shooting tigers?/{A} There are no tigers, Julia,/In Kinkanja. And there are no
479 CC	Kaghan	5	/And between a couple of man-eating tigers/Like you and Lizzie, he's got to have

TIGHT (8)

23 Preludes	39	both soiled hands./His soul stretched tight across the skies/That fade behind a city
61 WL: Burial	16	He said, Marie,/Marie, hold on tight. And down we went./In the mountains,
73 WL: Thund	377	woman drew her long black hair out tight/And fiddled whisper music on those
605 Narcissus	25	a fish/With slippery white belly held tight in his own fingers,/Writhing in his own
293 FR	Gerald	32	the North-West Frontier —/Been in tight corners most of my life/And some pretty
302 FR	Chorus	10	sure of what is real or unreal?/Hold tight, hold tight, we must insist that the world is

14 Prufrock	39	'Do I dare?' and, 'Do I dare?'/Time to turn back and descend the stair,/With a
14 Prufrock	47	the universe?/In a minute there is time/For decisions and revisions which a minute
22 Preludes	20	/With the other masquerades/That time resumes,/One thinks of all the hands/
28 Boston ET	8	La Rochefoucauld,/If the street were time and he at the end of the street,/And I say,
40 Burb Blei	20	Canaletto./The smoky candle end of time/Declines. On the Rialto once./The rats are
49 Hippopot	17	the Church from over sea./At mating time the hippo's voice/Betrays inflexions hoarse
54 Mr E Sun	7	of τὸ ἕν,/And at the mensual turn of time/Produced enervate Origen./A painter of
64 WL: Chess	104	ears./And other withered stumps of time/Were told upon the walls; staring forms/
65 WL: Chess	141	myself,/HURRY UP PLEASE ITS TIME/Now Albert's coming back, make
66 WL: Chess	148	the army four years, he wants a good time,/And if you don't give it him, there's others
66 WL: Chess	152	look./HURRY UP PLEASE ITS TIME/If you don't like it you can get on with it,
66 WL: Chess	165	children?/HURRY UP PLEASE ITS TIME/Well, that Sunday Albert was home, they
66 WL: Chess	168	it hot —/HURRY UP PLEASE ITS TIME/HURRY UP PLEASE ITS TIME/
66 WL: Chess	169	TIME/HURRY UP PLEASE ITS TIME/Goonight Bill. Goonight Lou. Goonight
67 WL: Fire S	196	year to year./But at my back from time to time I hear/The sound of horns and
67 WL: Fire S	196	to year./But at my back from time to time I hear/The sound of horns and motors,
68 WL: Fire S	235	hat on a Bradford millionaire./The time is now propitious, as he guesses,/The meal
89 Ash-Wed 1	16	is nothing again/Because I know that time is always time/And place is always and
89 Ash-Wed 1	16	/Because I know that time is always time/And place is always and only place/And
89 Ash-Wed 1	18	what is actual is actual only for one time/And only for one place/I rejoice that things
94 Ash-Wed 4	14	restoring/One who moves in the time between sleep and waking, wearing/White
94 Ash-Wed 4	19	verse the ancient rhyme. Redeem/The time. Redeem/The unread vision in the higher
95 Ash-Wed 4	26	and the bird sang down/Redeem the time, redeem the dream/The token of the word
96 Ash-Wed 5	16	who walk in darkness/Both in the day time and in the night time/The right time and
96 Ash-Wed 5	16	/Both in the day time and in the night time/The right time and the right place are not
96 Ash-Wed 5	17	time and in the night time/The right time and the right place are not here/No place
96 Ash-Wed 5	19	for those who avoid the face/No time to rejoice for those who walk among noise
96 Ash-Wed 5	22	the horn between season and season, time and time, between/Hour and hour, word
96 Ash-Wed 5	22	between season and season, time and time, between/Hour and hour, word and word,
98 Ash-Wed 6	20	savour of the sandy earth/This is the time of tension between dying and birth/The
103 Journ Magi	2	coming we had of it,/Just the worst time of the year/For a journey, and such a long
103 Journ Magi	16	and charging high prices:/A hard time we had of it./At the end we preferred to
104 Journ Magi	32	say) satisfactory./All this was a long time ago, I remember,/And I would do it again,
105 Song Sime	14	live my children's children/When the time of sorrow is come?/They will take to the
105 Song Sime	17	and the foreign swords./Before the time of cords and scourges and lamentation/
107 Animula	24	*Britannica.*/Issues from the hand of time the simple soul/Irresolute and selfish,
110 Marina	30	this life/Living to live in a world of time beyond me; let me/Resign my life for this
119 SP Krum	24	hit this town last night for the first time/{Kl} And I certainly hope it won't be the
119 SP Klip	25	I certainly hope it won't be the last time./{Do} You like London, Mr. Klipstein?/
124 SA Swarts	33	rent./{Sw} What did he do?/All that time, what did he do?/{S} What did he do! what
127 Cor1 March	24	kitchens,/1,150 field bakeries./What a time that took. Will it be he now? No,/Those
129 Cor2 State	41	wind/Mother/May we not be some time, almost now, together,/If the mactations,
135 5FingerEx1	10	will the summer day delay?/*When* will Time flow away?/*Lines to a Yorkshire Terrier*/
150 Rock 1	110	*turn/The sparrow and starling have no time to waste./If men do not build/How shall they*
152 Rock 2	36	must remember that while there is time of prosperity/The people will neglect the
152 Rock 2	37	people will neglect the Temple, and in time of adversity they will decry it./What life
153 Rock 2	53	to restore;/Let the work not delay, time and the arm not waste;/Let the clay be dug
160 Rock 7	18	predetermined moment, a moment in time and of time,/A moment not out of time,
160 Rock 7	18	moment, a moment in time and of time,/A moment not out of time, but in time, in
160 Rock 7	19	and of time,/A moment not out of time, but in time, in what we call history:
160 Rock 7	19	/A moment not out of time, but in time, in what we call history: transecting,
160 Rock 7	19	transecting, bisecting the world of time, a moment in time but not like a moment
160 Rock 7	19	the world of time, a moment in time but not like a moment of time,/A moment
160 Rock 7	19	in time but not like a moment of time,/A moment in time but time was made
160 Rock 7	20	like a moment of time,/A moment in time but time was made through that moment:
160 Rock 7	20	of time,/A moment in time but time was made through that moment: for
160 Rock 7	20	for without the meaning there is no time, and that moment of time gave the
160 Rock 7	20	there is no time, and that moment of time gave the meaning./Then it seemed as if
166 Rock 10	14	Seek not to count the future waves of Time;/But be ye satisfied that you have light/
171 FQ: BurntN	1	/FOUR QUARTETS/Burnt Norton/Time present and time past/Are both perhaps
171 FQ: BurntN	1	/Burnt Norton/Time present and time past/Are both perhaps present in time
171 FQ: BurntN	2	time past/Are both perhaps present in time future/And time future contained in time
171 FQ: BurntN	3	perhaps present in time future/And time future contained in time past./If all time is
171 FQ: BurntN	3	future/And time future contained in time past./If all time is eternally present/All time
171 FQ: BurntN	4	future contained in time past./If all time is eternally present/All time is

222 Pekes Pols	13	for nearly a week/(And that's a long time for a Pol or a Peke)./The big Police Dog
227 Macavity	38	and one or two to spare:/At whatever time the deed took place — MACAVITY
227 Macavity	41	than agents for the Cat who all the time/Just controls their operations: the
228 Gus	10	name was quite famous, he says, in its time./And whenever he joins his friends at their
231 Bust Jones	37	to put it in rhyme: 'I shall last out my time'/Is the word for this stoutest of Cats./It
235 Ad-dress	66	/These evidences of respect./And so in time you reach your aim,/And finally call him
236 Cat Morgan	19	worth a lot more:/You'll save yourself time, and you'll spare yourself labour/If jist you
587 Fable	25	of all the people./When Christmas time was near the Abbot vowed/They'd eat their
588 Fable	43	sat down to table./The menus of that time I am afraid/I don't know much about — as
589 Fable	93	good and friarly./Spirits from that time forth they did without,/And lived the
590 Time Space	1	old manuscript found in the ruins./If Time and Space, as Sages say,/Are things which
590 Space Time	1	let them be divine./Song/If space and time, as sages say,/Are things that cannot be,/
590 Space Time	7	may,/While love and life are free,/For time is time, and runs away,/Though sages
590 Space Time	7	love and life are free,/For time is time, and runs away,/Though sages disagree./
592 Grad 2	3	shore/Well know they lose what time shall not restore,/And when they leave they
593 Grad 5	3	/Summons — who knows what time may hold in store,/Or what great deeds the
240 MC Chorus	21	turn in their hands in the pattern of time./Come, happy December, who shall
243 MC Chorus	15	is no abiding stay./Ill the wind, ill the time, uncertain the profit, certain the danger./O
243 MC Chorus	16	the danger./O late late late, late is the time, late too late, and rotten the year;/Evil the
246 MC Thomas	13	them hold their hands. So for the time/We are unmolested./{P1} But do they
246 MC Thomas	16	do they follow after?/{T} For a little time the hungry hawk/Will only soar and hover,
246 MC Tempt1	28	levity/Remembering all the good time past./Your Lordship won't despise an old
246 MC Tempt1	33	should be more than biting Time can sever./What, my Lord, now that you
246 MC Tempt1	36	that summer's over/Or that the good time cannot last?/Fluting in the meadows, viols
247 MC Thomas	18	the life of one man, never/The same time returns. Sever/The cord, shed the scale.
252 MC Tempt3	7	{T3} Which you helped to found./But time past is time forgotten./We expect the rise
252 MC Tempt3	7	you helped to found./But time past is time forgotten./We expect the rise of a new
253 MC Tempt4	2	my face./To meet before was never time or place./{T} Say what you come to say./
260 MC Thomas	14	to men of good will'; at this same time of all the year that we/celebrate at once the
262 MC Thomas	2	because/it is possible that in a short time you may have yet another martyr,/and that
262 MC Thomas	4	I say, and think of them at another time. In the Name/of the Father, and of
263 MC Chorus	12	stored up in the East./What, at the time of the birth of Our Lord, at Christmastide,
263 MC Chorus	26	fresh earth cover? We wait, and the time is short/But waiting is long. {}/[Enter the
271 MC Priests	21	the minster./Through the cloister. No time to waste. They are coming back, armed. To
273 MC Thomas	36	and evil can be shown./And as in time results of many deeds are blended/So good
274 MC Thomas	1	end become confounded./It is not in time that my death shall be known;/It is out of
274 MC Thomas	2	my death shall be known;/It is out of time that my decision is taken/If you call that
276 MC Chorus	11	had a kind of end:/In life there is not time to grieve long./But this, this is out of life,
276 MC Chorus	12	this, this is out of life, this is out of time,/An instant eternity of evil and wrong./We
278 MC Knight2	33	justice can be secured. At another time, you would/condemn an Archbishop by
278 MC Knight2	36	/being called murderer. And at a later time still, even such temperate/measures as these
285 FR Amy	10	be trusted, tomorrow assured/And time would not stop in the dark!/Put on the
287 FR Amy	36	/They should both be here in good time for dinner./Harry telephoned to me from
288 FR Amy	2	the most likely to be late./{A} This time, it will not be his fault./We are very lucky
288 FR Amy	7	/{A} After dinner:/That is the best time./{I} It is the first time/You have not had
288 FR Ivy	8	/That is the best time./{I} It is the first time/You have not had your cake and your
288 FR Amy	11	you ought to know. It will be the first time/For eight years that we have all been
289 FR Agatha	1	a very jolly corner./When the loop in time comes — and it does not come for
291 FR Amy	8	saw someone pass the window./What time is it?/{C} Nearly twenty to seven./{A} John
292 FR Harry	3	/And they see me. This is the first time that I have seen them./In the Java Straits,
292 FR Ivy	34	to old Hawkins./It's really high time the old man was pensioned./He's let the
292 FR Ivy	37	blind. I've spoken to your mother/Time and time again: she's done nothing about
292 FR Ivy	37	I've spoken to your mother/Time and time again: she's done nothing about it/Because
292 FR Violet	39	to wait for your coming./{V} And time and time again I have spoken to your
292 FR Violet	39	for your coming./{V} And time and time again I have spoken to your mother/About
293 FR Ivy	13	sure!/Now that Harry's back, is the time to think of living./{H} Time and time and
293 FR Harry	14	is the time to think of living./{H} Time and time and time, and change, no
293 FR Harry	14	time to think of living./{H} Time and time and time, and change, no change!/You all
293 FR Harry	14	of living./{H} Time and time and time, and change, no change!/You all of you try
295 FR Harry	27	which one can be caught for the last time./And also waking. She is nearer than ever./
302 FR Amy	14	both promised to be here/In good time for dinner. It is very annoying./Now they
302 FR Amy	15	/Now they can hardly arrive in time to dress./I do not understand what could
305 FR Agatha	7	you: but you must not run away./Any time before now, it would have shown courage/
306 FR Harry	18	I wanted to escape;/And at the same time, other memories,/Earlier, forgotten, begin
306 FR Mary	36	prepared;/There was never any time to invent our own enjoyments./But perhaps

309 FR	Harry	40	cold spring/Is the spring not an evil time, that excites us with lying voices?/{M} The
310 FR	Mary	1	/{M} The cold spring now is the time/For the ache in the moving root/The
311 FR	Harry	27	you show yourselves now for the first time?/When I knew her, I was not the same
313 FR	Violet	5	what a rush he had to be here in time/For his mother's birthday./{I} Mary, my
314 FR Warburt		12	with measles/And we had such a time to keep you in bed./You didn't like being
316 FR	Agatha	19	proper business/The eye of the day time/And the eye of the night time/Be diverted
316 FR	Agatha	20	the day time/And the eye of the night time/Be diverted from this house/Till the knot is
318 FR	Harry	6	/They were not holidays, but simply a time/In which we were supposed to make up to
318 FR Warburt		22	happiness in the future,/For the time she has to live: not with the past./{H} Oh,
320 FR Warburt		28	mother,/To make her happy for the time she has to live./The other is yourself: the
323 FR Warburt		31	do, and out in this weather/At this time of night, I would not answer for the
324 FR Warburt		5	Lady Monchensey;/This is not the time to begin to doubt me./Come, Winchell. We
328 FR	Charles	21	Street. 'The police stated that at the time of the/accident Mr. Piper was being
328 FR	Charles	32	much too hard on him./{C} In my time, these affairs were kept out of the papers;/
329 FR	Chorus	25	about anything,/And now it is nearly time for the news/We must listen to the weather
333 FR	Agatha	1	You were due in three months' time;/You would not have been born in that
336 FR	Harry	4	/{H} Not yet! not yet! this is the first time that I have been free/From the ring of
336 FR	Harry	12	EUMENIDES *appear*]/{H} and this time/You cannot think that I am surprised to
336 FR	Harry	15	that I am afraid to see you./This time, you are real, this time, you are outside me,
336 FR	Harry	15	see you./This time, you are real, this time, you are outside me,/And just endurable. I
336 FR	Harry	22	/And one destination. Let us lose no time. I will follow. {}/[*The curtains close.*
340 FR	Amy	3	death is an end,/And I thought that time might have made a change in Agatha —/It
349 FR	Mary	26	/Follow follow/{M} Not in the day time/And in the hither world/Where we know
350 FR	Agatha	3	/Follow follow/{Ag} But in the night time/And in the nether world/Where the meshes
354 CP	Julia	16	Klootz was very lovely, once upon a time./What a life she led! I used to say to her:
356 CP	Peter	13	I wrote:/But I had a very enjoyable time./{C} Go on with the story about the
356 CP	Julia	24	'I wish you'd try.' And this is the first time/I've ever seen you without Lavinia/Except
356 CP	Julia	26	you without Lavinia/Except for the time she got locked in the lavatory/And
356 CP	Celia	34	pantry./{C} Will she be away for some time, Edward?/{E} I really don't know until I
356 CP	Edward	36	aunt is very ill, she may be gone some time./{C} And how will you manage while she is
359 CP	Edward	16	off/Because I couldn't get at them in time;/And I didn't know that *you* were coming./
361 CP	Reilly	8	truth on the telephone./It will all take time that you can't well spare;/But I put it to
361 CP	Edward	20	know who you are;/But, at the same time, unless you know my wife/A good deal
363 CP	Reilly	13	are among other people./Most of the time we take ourselves for granted,/As we have
365 CP	Julia	32	/Or were you singing songs all the time?/There's altogether too much mystery/
366 CP	Julia	10	found them but for you./The next time I lose *anything*, Edward,/I'll come straight
368 CP	Edward	38	were one of the minor successes/For a time at least./{P} I wouldn't say that./But
371 CP	Edward	8	you with Celia/In another six months' time. There it is./You can take it or leave it./{P}
372 CP	Peter	30	Edward, I've taken too much of your time,/And you want to be alone. Give my love
379 CP	Celia	24	after that I lived in a present/Where time was meaningless, a private world of *ours*,/
392 CP	Lavinia	36	now./We have wasted such a lot of time in lying./{E} I don't quite know what you
396 CP	Lavinia	29	be able to find the road back/To a time when you were real — for you must have
396 CP	Lavinia	30	for you must have been real/At some time or other, before you ever knew me:/
400 CP	Reilly	3	hour. We have not much time./Tell me now, did you have any difficulty/
401 CP	Reilly	32	That is so, that is so. But all in good time./Let us dismiss that question for the
403 CP	Edward	27	/Indeed, acutely, perhaps, for the first time,/The whole oppression, the unreality/Of
404 CP	Edward	13	than that./It is surprising, if one had time to be surprised:/I am not afraid of the
408 CP	Reilly	7	lover — who suddenly/For the first time in his life, fell in love with someone,/And
409 CP	Reilly	32	Miss Coplestone,/It took you some time, I have no doubt,/Before you would admit
412 CP	Celia	33	However,/I don't want to waste your time. And I'm awfully afraid/That you'll think
415 CP	Celia	31	But everything seemed so right, at the time!/I've been thinking about it, over and over;
415 CP	Celia	37	of hallucination;/Yet, at the same time, I'm frightened by the fear/That it is more
421 CP	Julia	7	new disguises,/They have, for the first time, somewhere to start from./Oh, of course,
424 CP	Edward	11	*in at the front door*]/{E} I'm in good time, I think. I hope you've not been worrying./
425 CP	Lavinia	3	Edward!/Do you know it's the first time you've paid me a compliment/*Before* a
425 CP	Edward	21	{E} I know, that's what we said at the time;/But I'd forgotten what the Gunnings'
436 CP	Peter	10	all the same./You know, all the time that you've been talking,/One thought has
439 CP	Julia	9	its meaning./{J} Henry, I think it is time that *I* said something:/Everyone makes a
439 CP	Peter	28	/{P} Thanks very much. But not this time —/I simply shan't be able to./{E} But on
439 CP	Peter	31	But on your next visit?/{P} The next time I come to England, I promise you./I really
445 CC	Eggers	24	/As I've heard nothing since the last time I came./{SC} Well, of course, Eggerson,
446 CC	Eggers	1	his feet, very quickly,/During the time we worked together./All he needs is
447 CC	Claude	1	for the present. As we have a little time/Before you start for Northolt — the car
450 CC	Claude	27	I was just saying to Eggerson/It was time you were back. Was your morning
454 CC	Lucasta	14	/Has been too much for me. Another time, Colby./I'll ring you up, and let you take

454 CC	Colby	37	spin — all those first names/The first time I met her. I'm not used to it./{E} You'll
455 CC	Eggers	31	You'll get used to her, Mr. Simpkins./Time works wonders, that's what I always say./
457 CC	Claude	11	CLAUDE]/{SC} Hello! Still here? It's time you were off./{E} I'm just going. There's
457 CC	Eggers	12	/{E} I'm just going. There's plenty of time. {}/[*Looks at his watch*]/{E} I'll arrive at the
457 CC	Eggers	14	the Customs. That'll take her a time,/From my experience. {}/LADY
458 CC	Eggers	31	.../{E} And at the same time, he had another tempting offer:/So we had
461 CC	Eggers	17	/All the way to Joshua Park, at this time of year!'/I said: 'Let's think about it in the
463 CC	Claude	6	/That I had no doubts at the time — that's five years;/And then your school,
463 CC	Colby	15	I've never had before. Yet at the same time/It's rather disturbing. I don't mean the
463 CC	Colby	24	he fascinates me./And yet from time to time, when I least expect it,/When my
463 CC	Colby	24	fascinates me./And yet from time to time, when I least expect it,/When my mind is
464 CC	Colby	22	music?/{C} Just the same./All the time you've been speaking, I've been translating
464 CC	Claude	40	I am sure,/That I cherished for a long time a secret reproach:/But after his death, and
466 CC	Claude	26	Thank you./{SC} And perhaps, some time, you will let me hear you play./I shan't
469 CC	Colby	29	to me before?/{C} And this is the first time I've played to anyone .../{L} Don't be such
471 CC	Colby	21	/Because *I* don't know./{C} The first time we met/You were trying very hard to give a
472 CC	Colby	5	you've been very badly hurt, at some time./Or at least, there may have been
472 CC	Lucasta	35	as you saw them./And yet, all the time, I found I *envied* you/And I didn't know
473 CC	Lucasta	10	— like the one where I lived/For a time, with my mother. I've no garden./I hardly
479 CC	Kaghan	12	/{K} You shall be fed. All in good time./I've come to inspect the new bachelor
483 CC	Lady E	33	say that *I* believe in it./I did, for a time. I studied the doctrine./But I was going to
490 CC	Colby	17	I'm simply indifferent./And all the time that you've been talking/I've only been
490 CC	Colby	33	and know it means nothing./At the time I was born, you might have been my
490 CC	Colby	36	must take the consequences./At the time when I was born, your being my mother —
495 CC	Lady E	38	strange, Claude, but this is the first time/I have talked to you, without feeling very
496 CC	Eggers	31	now, I'm quite lost in London./Every time I come, I notice the traffic/Has got so
499 CC	Claude	14	Lucasta./Won't it do another time?/{L} I came to apologise/To Colby. No
499 CC	Lucasta	16	To Colby. No matter. It'll do another time./Oh, I'm glad you're here, Eggy! You're
499 CC	Claude	20	I'll listen. But we haven't much time./{L} It won't take much time. I'm going to
499 CC	Lucasta	21	much time./{L} It won't take much time. I'm going to marry B./{SC} To marry B.!
500 CC	Claude	12	have made things clear to you/At the time when he came here. But I didn't trust you/
502 CC	Lucasta	39	a brother and a sister,/Will come, in time. Perhaps, one day/We may understand
503 CC	Lucasta	4	a different way/That reveals itself in time. And perhaps — who knows? —/We might
503 CC	Lucasta	12	us/In twenty or thirty or forty years' time./I shall be happy. I'm going to marry B./I
503 CC	Claude	37	/I hadn't been aware how the time was passing,/What with Lucasta's
507 CC	Eggers	5	delicate question:/Did you, at any time, take in a child —/A child, that is, of
507 CC	Guzzard	9	husband and I were childless ... at the time,/And very poor. It offered two advantages.
510 CC	Guzzard	24	parents./{MG} And did they at one time live in Teddington?/{K} I believe they did.
511 CC	Lady E	15	was in a very good regiment —/For a time, at least./{K} Well, I must get used to that./
518 CC	Eggers	7	day, you know,/For quite a little time, and I've watched you pretty closely./Mr.
525 ES	Charles	39	you're a hypnotist./{C} Is this a time to torment me? But I'm selfish/In saying
526 ES	Monica	10	stood behind my back/Quietly, a long time, a long long time/Before I felt its presence./
526 ES	Monica	10	back/Quietly, a long time, a long long time/Before I felt its presence./{C} Your words
527 ES	Monica	8	/When I'm free to do so. But by that time/You may have changed your mind. Such
528 ES	Charles	34	this situation may persist for a long time,/And you'll go on postponing and
528 ES	Monica	36	/{M} I'm afraid ... not a very long time, Charles./It's almost certain that the winter
529 ES	Monica	24	brooding over it./{M} But what a time for your engagement book!/You know
530 ES	Monica	28	been looking forward/To this very time! You know how you grumbled/At the
531 ES	Ld Clav	16	taken twenty years ago./In five years' time, it will be the half of that;/In ten years'
531 ES	Ld Clav	17	it will be the half of that;/In ten years' time, a paragraph./{C} That's the reward/Of
533 ES	Gomez	16	these years/And I thought, now's the time to take a long holiday,/Let's say a rest cure
534 ES	Gomez	31	/The ones who don't get out in time/Find themselves in gaol and not very
537 ES	Gomez	28	the course, at least./I had plenty of time to think things over, later./{LC} And what
538 ES	Gomez	4	And then my stretch/Which gave me time to think it all out./{LC} That's the second
538 ES	Ld Clav	5	it all out./{LC} That's the second time you have mentioned your reflections./But
540 ES	Gomez	19	That happened several times./{G} One time in particular./You know quite well to
541 ES	Gomez	26	/Blackmail! On the contrary/Any time you're in a tight corner/My entire
541 ES	Lambert	33	through for you/In five minutes' time./{LC} I'll be ready to take it. {}/[*Exit*
544 ES	Ld Clav	18	but then it's not noticed;/And by the time one has grown to consciousness/It comes
547 ES	Piggott	5	up .../You must be very careful at this time of year;/This early warm weather can be
549 ES	Carghil	22	—/Effie and Maud and I. What a time ago it seems!/It's surprising I remember it
549 ES	Carghil	36	to me. But I do remember you./{MC} Time has wrought sad changes in me, Richard./
550 ES	Carghil	12	ago?/{MC} Many years ago, the first time. That didn't last long./People sometimes
552 ES	Ld Clav	1	/{LC} And perhaps at the same time of your own?/I seem to remember, it was
554 ES	Piggott	34	in revue./She was well-known at one time. I'm afraid her name/Means nothing at all

557 ES	Ld Clav	10	Every job is dull, nine-tenths of the time .../{Mi} I need something much more
557 ES	Michael	33	ago was that?/{Mi} Nearly two years./Time passes pretty quickly, when you're in debt.
558 ES	Michael	36	exciting,/But it served to pass the time. It would never have happened/If only I'd
562 ES	Carghil	25	to you, my dears./It's a very long time since the name of Maisie Montjoy/Topped
563 ES	Carghil	28	by my stage name./There was a time, once, when everyone in London/Knew the
566 ES	Ld Clav	3	of the same master. But have I still time?/There is time for Michael. Is it too late for
566 ES	Ld Clav	4	master. But have I still time?/There is time for Michael. Is it too late for me, Monica?
568 ES	Ld Clav	35	/While she is a child. And by the time she's grown/You've woven such a web of
570 ES	Monica	16	whatever lay ahead of her./{M} It is time to break the silence! Let us share your
572 ES	Ld Clav	4	/And all my life I have heard, from time to time,/When I least expected, between
572 ES	Ld Clav	4	all my life I have heard, from time to time,/When I least expected, between waking
573 ES	Ld Clav	17	/{LC} To the end. The place and time of liberation/Are, I think, determined. Let
573 ES	Carghil	38	/I've known her father for a very long time,/And there was a moment when I almost
575 ES	Gomez	18	My dear Dick,/You're wasting your time, rehearsing ancient history./Michael knows
575 ES	Ld Clav	28	that point, Fred, you're wasting *your* time:/My daughter and my future son-in-law/
575 ES	Carghil	38	/In those days. I melted the first time he looked at me!/Some day, Monica, I'll
576 ES	Michael	19	We didn't go into details. There's time for that later./{G} Much better to wait
577 ES	Carghil	26	times over./{MC} Richard, I think it's time *I* joined the conversation./My late
577 ES	Carghil	34	frustration./He's been waiting all this time for opportunity/To make use of his gifts;
582 ES	Ld Clav	9	I love Michael,/I think, for the first time — remember, my dear,/I am only a
582 ES	Ld Clav	17	/You two ought to have a little time together./I leave Monica to you. Look
582 ES	Monica	20	I shall take a stroll./{M} At this time of day? You'll not go far, will you?/You
582 ES	Monica	33	/Only a few minutes, I've felt all the time .../{C} I know what you're going to say!/

TIME'S (2)

41 Burb Blei		32	/Thought Burbank, meditating on/Time's ruins, and the seven laws./Sweeney Erect
191 FQ: Little		14	This is the spring time/But not in time's covenant. Now the hedgerow/Is blanched

TIME-LIMIT (1)

519 CC Guzzard		3	we had our wishes,/That there was a time-limit clause in the contract./{SC} What's

TIME-RIDDEN (1)

174 FQ: BurntN		103	Only a flicker/Over the strained time-ridden faces/Distracted from distraction by

TIME-TABLE (1)

504 CC Claude		19	I wish you could arrange the servants' time-table better./This is a most unfortunate

TIMEKEPT (2)

147 Rock 1		19	Dust./I journeyed to London, to the timekept City,/Where the River flows, with
154 Rock 3		29	/Whence thousands travel daily to the timekept City;/Where My Word is unspoken,/In

TIMELESS (5)

175 FQ: BurntN		168	Only the cause and end of movement,/Timeless, and undesiring/Except in the aspect of
189 FQ: DrySal		205	/The point of intersection of the timeless/With time, is an occupation for the
192 FQ: Little		54	living./Here, the intersection of the timeless moment/Is England and nowhere.
197 FQ: Little		237	from time, for history is a pattern/Of timeless moments. So, while the light fails/On a
255 MC Tempt4		15	the gulf is fixed,/Your persecutors, in timeless torment,/Parched passion, beyond

TIMELY (2)

370 CP	Edward	38	man. I congratulate you/On a timely escape./{P} I should prefer to be spared/
450 CC	Claude	21	Mr. Simpkins, either?/{SC} A timely reminder. You may have to repeat it./But

TIMES (25)

16 Prufrock		118	of high sentence, but a bit obtuse;/At times, indeed, almost ridiculous —/Almost, at
16 Prufrock		119	almost ridiculous —/Almost, at times, the Fool./I grow old ... I grow old .../I
103 Journ Magi		8	in the melting snow./There were times we regretted/The summer palaces on
148 Rock 1		66	churches;/The men you are in these times deride/What has been done of good, you
150 Rock 1		108	our death/*Unmentioned in 'The Times'./Chant of* WORKMEN *again./The river*
182 FQ: ECoker		186	discovered/Once or twice, or several times, by men whom one cannot hope/To
587 Fable		20	the monks were having merry times./He stole the fatter cows and left the
247 MC Tempt1		24	love what he spurns./For the good times past, that are come again/I am your man./
258 MC Thomas		37	of a fanatic./I know that history at all times draws/The strangest consequence from
275 MC Thomas		14	traitor!/{T} You, Reginald, three times traitor you:/Traitor to me as my temporal
278 MC Knight2		32	than we/do. Unhappily, there are times when violence is the only way in/which
298 FR Charles		21	all see it like this: but there simply are times/When there's nothing to do but take the
330 FR Harry		11	to the right neighbours/At the right times; and be an excellent landlord./{Ag} What
346 FR Agatha		34	behaviour seems unaccountable/At times, you mustn't worry about that./He is
362 CP Reilly		4	it for so long./And perhaps at times you will feel a little jealous/That she saw it
399 CP Nurse		17	I leave her there/Until you ring three times./{R} And the third patient?/{N} The third
405 CP m		7	{}/[*Presses the bell on his desk three times*]/{R} You must accept a rather unusual
446 CC Eggers		38	the other day/I read a letter in *The Times* about wild birds seen in London:/And I'm
469 CC Lucasta		22	been to the Opera, of course, several times,/But I'm afraid I never really listened to
471 CC Colby		38	/When I had seen you a number of times,/I decided that was only your kind of

533 ES	Gomez	35	/In the right places, pays many times over./I assure you it does./{LC} In other
540 ES	Ld Clav	18	driving./{LC} That happened several times./{G} One time in particular./You know
541 ES	Gomez	18	dare say I could buy you out/Several times over. San Marco's a good place/To make
565 ES	Gomez	27	have some good talks/About old times. Bye bye for the present. {}/[*Exit*]/{M}
577 ES	Gomez	25	/He'll be able to buy you out many times over./{MC} Richard, I think it's time *I*

TIMID (1)

304 FR	Mary	4	/Who knew the way of dominating timid girls./I don't see you any differently now;/

TIMMINS (1)

545 ES	Piggott	33	there/My secretary will be — Miss Timmins./She'd be overjoyed to have the

TIN (1)

193 FQ: Little		85	the dead leaves still rattled on like tin/Over the asphalt where no other sound was/

TING (4)

116 SP	phone	6	Well what you going to do?/{Tel} Ting a ling ling/Ting a ling ling/{Du} That's
116 SP	phone	7	going to do?/{Tel} Ting a ling ling/Ting a ling ling/{Du} That's Pereira/{Do} Yes
116 SP	phone	11	Well what you going to do?/{Tel} Ting a ling ling/Ting a ling ling/{Du} That's
116 SP	phone	12	going to do?/{Tel} Ting a ling ling/Ting a ling ling/{Du} That's Pereira/{Do} Well

TINIEST (1)

224 Mr Mistoff		25	of his tail;/He can creep through the tiniest crack/He can walk on the narrowest rail./

TINKLED (1)

31 Apollinax		2	visited the United States/His laughter tinkled among the teacups./I thought of

TINS (1)

68 WL: Fire S		223	lights/Her stove, and lays out food in tins./Out of the window perilously spread/Her

TINY (1)

335 FR	Agatha	2	/And heard in the distance tiny voices/And then a black raven flew over./

TIP (3)

138 New Hamp		4	crimson head,/Between the green tip and the root./Black wing, brown wing, hover
224 Mr Mistoff		24	small, he is black/From his ears to the tip of his tail;/He can creep through the tiniest
236 Cat Morgan		18	— or Faber —/I'll give you this tip, and it's worth a lot more:/You'll save

TIPPLE (1)

554 ES	Piggott	29	why I've brought your morning tipple myself/Instead of leaving it, as usual, to

TIPS (4)

605 Narcissus		15	/And his hands aware of the pointed tips of his fingers./Struck down by such
605 Narcissus		27	beauty/Caught fast in the pink tips of his new beauty./Then he had been a
557 ES	Michael	15	of my friends gave me excellent tips./They always came off — the tips I didn't
557 ES	Michael	16	tips./They always came off — the tips I didn't take./{LC} And the ones you did

TIPSY (1)

274 MC		m 14	*opened. The* KNIGHTS *enter, slightly tipsy*]/{3P} This way, my Lord! Quick. Up the

TIRE (3)

167 Rock 10		36	Thee!/In our rhythm of earthly life we tire of light. We are glad when the day ends,
167 Rock 10		38	the day is long for work or play./We tire of distraction or concentration, we sleep
554 ES	Piggott	22	comfortable:/We can't allow him to tire himself with talking./What he needs is *rest*!

TIRED (25)

15 Prufrock		77	/Smoothed by long fingers,/Asleep ... tired ... or it malingers,/Stretched on the floor,
20 Portrait		79	when a street-piano, mechanical and tired/Reiterates some worn-out common song/
68 WL: Fire S		236	/The meal is ended, she is bored and tired,/Endeavours to engage her in caresses/
106 Song Sime		34	pierce thy heart,/Thine also)./I am tired with my own life and the lives of those
129 Cor2 State		37	these busts, all correctly inscribed)/I a tired head among these heads/Necks strong to
167 Rock 10		37	much pain./We are children quickly tired: children who are up in the night and fall
602 Humoresque		2	marionettes is dead,/Though not yet tired of the game —/But weak in body as in
292 FR	Amy	19	till tomorrow? I am sure you must be tired./You will find everybody here, and
295 FR	Amy	32	that./{A} Harry, Harry, you are very tired/And overwrought. Coming so far/And
325 FR	Harry	4	make you lie down. You must be very tired. {}/[*Exeunt* HARRY *and* AMY]/{V} I
334 FR	Agatha	6	beginning. Harry, my dear,/I feel very tired, as only the old feel./The young feel tired
334 FR	Agatha	7	as only the old feel./The young feel tired at the end of an action —/The old, at the
353 CP	Alex	18	/{C} I love that story./{A} *I'm* never tired of hearing that story./{J} Well, you all
353 CP	Celia	21	Do we all know it?/But we're never tired of hearing *you* tell it./I don't believe
375 CP	Edward	22	Alex, I don't want anything./I'm very tired. Thanks awfully, Alex./Good night./{C}
377 CP	Edward	36	me./{E} No, I'm sorry, Julia./I'm too tired to go out, and I'm not at all hungry./I
393 CP	Edward	39	I should be always too busy or too tired/To be of use to you socially .../{L} I *never*
412 CP	Julia	19	/{J} Henry, get up./You can't be as tired as that. I shall wait in the next room,/And
424 CP	Lavinia	19	*all* of them./I hope you're not too tired?/{E} Oh no, a quiet day./Two
424 CP	Edward	22	cases. It's you who should be tired./{L} I'm not tired yet. But I know that I'll
424 CP	Lavinia	23	you who should be tired./{L} I'm not tired yet. But I know that I'll be glad/When it's
426 CP	Lavinia	2	meant the right./That will do. I'm too tired to bother./{E} After they're all gone, we
555 ES	Monica	13	So I hurried to your rescue. You look tired, Father./She ought to know better. But I'm

569 ES	Ld Clav	9	love under false pretences./Now, I'm tired of keeping up those pretences,/But I hope
580 ES	Carghil	25	rest now./You're looking rather tired. I'll run and see them off. {}/[*Exit* MRS.

TIRESIAS (3)

68 WL: Fire S		218	waits/Like a taxi throbbing waiting,/I Tiresias, though blind, throbbing between two
68 WL: Fire S		228	slippers, camisoles, and stays./I Tiresias, old man with wrinkled dugs/Perceived
69 WL: Fire S		243	a welcome of indifference./(And I Tiresias have foresuffered all/Enacted on this

TISSUE (1)

397 CP	Edward	28	were always wrapping things up in tissue paper/And then had to unwrap

TIT-BIT (1)

355 CP	Julia	26	old woman like me/Is a really nice tit-bit. I can drink at home. {}/[EDWARD

TITHES (1)

343 FR	Amy	26	taxes/And unpaid rents and tithes? nourish investments/With wakeful nights

TITIANS (1)

37 Gerontion		26	/By Hakagawa, bowing among the Titians;/By Madame de Tornquist, in the dark

TITLE (3)

212 Growltiger		4	pursued his evil aims,/Rejoicing in his title of 'The Terror of the Thames'./His
559 ES	Michael	26	What is my inheritance? As for your title,/I know why you took it. And Mother
559 ES	Michael	33	thought of passing on your name and title/To a son, was gratifying. But it wasn't for

TITTER (1)

291 FR	Chorus	1	for the rustling in the stalls, the titter in the dress circle, the laughter and catcalls

TO (3838)

τὸ ἔν (1) [*Foreign word*]

54 Mr E Sun		6	was the Word./Superfetation of τὸ ἔν,/And at the mensual turn of time/

TO-DAY (24)

138 New Hamp		7	/Twenty years and the spring is over;/To-day grieves, to-morrow grieves,/Cover me
261 MC	Thomas	37	their/being./I have spoken to you to-day, dear children of God, of the martyrs of/
264 MC	Priest1	27	*Rejoice we all, keeping holy day.*/{P1} To-day?/{P2} To-day, what is to-day? For the
264 MC	Priest2	28	*keeping holy day.*/{P1} To-day?/{P2} To-day, what is to-day? For the day is half
264 MC	Priest2	28	/{P1} To-day?/{P2} To-day, what is to-day? For the day is half gone./{P1} To-day,
265 MC	Priest1	1	to-day? For the day is half gone./{P1} To-day, what is to-day? but another day, the
265 MC	Priest1	1	day is half gone./{P1} To-day, what is to-day? but another day, the dusk of the year./
265 MC	Priest2	2	day, the dusk of the year./{P2} To-day, what is to-day? Another night, and
265 MC	Priest2	2	dusk of the year./{P2} To-day, what is to-day? Another night, and another dawn./{P3}
265 MC	Knight1	12	Have you ridden far?/{K1} Not far to-day, but matters urgent/Have brought us
328 FR	Charles	15	January 1st, was/fined 50 and costs to-day, and forbidden to drive a car for the/next
365 CP	Julia	34	too much mystery/About this place to-day./{E} I'm very sorry./{J} No, I love it. But
379 CP	Celia	28	/{C} A dream. I was happy in it till to-day,/And then, when Julia asked about
387 CP	Peter	26	/To have yesterday's cocktail party to-day./So I don't suppose her aunt can have
391 CP	Julia	3	have a cocktail party at *my* house to-day./{C} Well, I'll go now. Good-bye,
408 CP	Lavinia	32	etiquette/About your behaviour to-day./{R} A point well taken./But permit me
430 CP	Peter	7	ago./I saw Sheila Paisley at lunch to-day/And she told me you were giving a party
524 ES	Charles	1	*in the hall*]/{C} Is your father at home to-day?/{M} You'll see him at tea./{C} But if I'm
529 ES	Ld Clav	34	what I was doing/Twenty years ago, to-day, at this hour of the afternoon./If I've
529 ES	Ld Clav	35	looking at this engagement book, to-day,/Not over breakfast, but before tea,/It's
548 ES	Monica	7	thought she'd done her duty by us for to-day./I'm going to prowl about the grounds.
565 ES	Monica	5	I think you've had enough talk for to-day./Michael, as you're staying so close at
573 ES	Carghil	26	tell by the change in your expression to-day;/This must be your fiancé. Do introduce
582 ES	Monica	32	yet, Charles, though we've been alone to-day/Only a few minutes, I've felt all the time

TO-MORROW (3)

105 Song Sime		24	/To one who has eighty years and no to-morrow./According to thy word./They shall
138 New Hamp		7	the spring is over;/To-day grieves, to-morrow grieves,/Cover me over,
604 Ode		9	we go./Yet for all of these years that to-morrow has lost/We are still the less able to

TO-NIGHT (3)

65 WL: Chess		111	be savagely still./'My nerves are bad to-night. Yes, bad. Stay with me.'/'Speak to me.
116 SP	Doris	39	Now I'm going to cut the cards for to-night./Oh guess what the first is/{Du} First is.
216 Jellicles		1	of the Jellicles/*Jellicle Cats come out to-night,*/*Jellicle Cats come one come all:*/The

TOAST (3)

14 Prufrock		34	and revisions,/Before the taking of a toast and tea./In the room the women come and
588 Fable		61	/The Abbot with proposing every toast/Had drank more than he ought t' have of
372 CP	Alex	27	a cup of black coffee/And a little dry toast. I've left it simmering./Don't leave it

TOASTING (1)

213 Growltiger		40	lives —/For the foe was armed with toasting forks and cruel carving knives./Then

TOBACCO (2)

19 Portrait		36	note.'/— Let us take the air, in a tobacco trance,/Admire the monuments,/
21 Portrait		113	like an ape./Let us take the air, in a tobacco trance —/Well! and what if she should

TOBIAH (1)
158 Rock 5   2   wicked./Sanballat the Horonite and Tobiah the Ammonite and Geshem the
TODAY (2)
459 CC   Lady E   28   mauve. I shall see about that./But not today. I shall go and rest now./In a sleeping-car
500 CC   Claude   8   /That is the reason for this meeting today./We're awaiting Mrs. Guzzard — Colby's
TOES (1)
216 Jellicles   20   their ears,/Jellicles dry between their toes./Jellicle Cats are white and black,/Jellicle
TOGETHER (88)
34 Figlia   21   I wonder how they should have been together!/I should have lost a gesture and a
40 Burb Blei   4   /Princess Volupine arrived,/They were together, and he fell./Defunctive music under
44 Cook Egg   15   Sir Alfred Mond./We two shall lie together, lapt/In a five per cent. Exchequer
73 WL: Thund   360   I count, there are only you and I together/But when I look ahead up the white
83 Hollow Men   3   men/We are the stuffed men/Leaning together/Headpiece filled with straw. Alas!/Our
83 Hollow Men   6   /Our dried voices, when/We whisper together/Are quiet and meaningless/As wind in
85 Hollow Men   58   this last of meeting places/We grope together/And avoid speech/Gathered on this
119 SP   Krum   14   you./{Kr} We were all in the war together/Klip and me and the Cap and Sam./
129 Cor2 State   41   we not be some time, almost now, together,/If the mactations, immolations,
149 Rock 1   90   *build with new speech/There is work together/A Church for all/And a job for each/*
151 Rock 2   7   filled./Your building not fitly framed together, you sit ashamed and wonder whether
151 Rock 2   7   whether and how you may be builded together for a habitation of GOD in the Spirit,
152 Rock 2   33   that is ill you may repair if you walk together in humble repentance, expiating the
152 Rock 2   38   life have you if you have not life together?/There is no life that is not in
152 Rock 2   49   Nor does the family even move about together,/But every son would have his motor
155 Rock 3   53   of this city?/Do you huddle close together because you love each other?'/What
155 Rock 3   54   /What will you answer? 'We all dwell together/To make money from each other'? or
185 FQ: DrySal   30   sea yelp, are different voices/Often together heard: the whine in the rigging,/The
185 FQ: DrySal   44   unweave, unwind, unravel/And piece together the past and the future,/Between
188 FQ: DrySal   143   /While the narrowing rails slide together behind you;/And on the deck of the
197 FQ: Little   225   /The complete consort dancing together)/Every phrase and every sentence is an
202 War Poetry   13   /In the effort to keep day and night together./It seems just possible that a poem
203 Indians   5   grandson/Playing in the dust together./Scarred but secure, he has many
219 Mung Rump   30   had a wonderful way of working together./And some of the time you would say it
222 Pekes Pols   m1   Battle of the Pekes and the Pollicles/*Together with some Account of the Participation/*
223 Pekes Pols   30   a dozen, more likely a score./And together they started to grumble and wheeze/In
223 Pekes Pols   46   Park./Now when these bold heroes together assembled,/The traffic all stopped, and
246 MC Templ1   32   King, and you and I were all friends together?/Friendship should be more than biting
257 MC Chorus   19   /Living and partly living,/Picking together the pieces,/Gathering faggots at
264 MC   m 22   O God! {}/[THE PRIESTS *stand together with the banners behind them*]/{P1}
279 MC Knight4   20   King, did more to weld the/country together, to give it the unity, the stability, order,
287 FR   Amy   27   keep the family alive, to keep them together,/To keep me alive, and I live to keep
288 FR   Amy   12   /For eight years that we have all been together./{Ag} It is going to be rather painful
292 FR   Amy   16   you back, Harry./Now we shall all be together for dinner./The servants have been
295 FR   Charles   11   my boy,/I understand, your life together made it seem more horrible./There's a
300 FR   Charles   9   as they say./{C} Were they always together?/{Do} Always, Sir./That was just my
301 FR   Chorus   19   the picture papers: why do we huddle together/In a horrid amity of misfortune? why
301 FR   Chorus   20   implicated, brought in and brought together?/{I} I do not trust Charles with his
308 FR   Harry   4   is what I fear. The bright colour fades/Together with the unrecapturable emotion,/The
313 FR   m 3   those curtains apart? {}/[*Pulls them together*]/{V} Very well, I think, after such a long
313 FR   Charles   20   and John/I'm glad that you'll all be together, Harry;/They need the influence of
316 FR   Agatha   10   /The eye covers it/There are three together/May the three be separated/May the
319 FR Warburt   15   your father were never very happy together:/They separated by mutual consent/
321 FR Warburt   22   him, and .../{W} Harry! Pull yourself together./Something may have happened to one
329 FR   Chorus   17   of a bad job/All twined and tangled together, all are recorded./There is no avoiding
330 FR   Harry   28   this last year, I could not fit myself together:/When I was inside the old dream, I
332 FR   Agatha   17   alone in a lonely country house together,/For three years childless, learning the
365 CP   Julia   17   me about him. You've been *drinking* together!/So this is the kind of friend you have/
367 CP   Edward   20   /Frequently brings young people together./{P} Now you're only being sarcastic:/
369 CP   Peter   35   In the same way, and sometimes went together./And to be with Celia, that was
369 CP   Peter   38   had tea/And once or twice dined together./{E} And after that/Did she ever
370 CP   Peter   7   /And I was so happy when we were together —/So ... contented, so ... at peace: I
382 CP   Celia   16   have made it by scraping your legs together —/Or however grasshoppers do it. I
389 CP   Lavinia   6   realise your ambitions./You're going together?/{P} We're not going together./Celia
389 CP   Peter   7   going together?/{P} We're not going together./Celia told us she was going away,/But
403 CP   Edward   37   what she has done to me in five years together!/She has made the world a place I
407 CP   Reilly   7   several symptoms/Which must occur together, and to a marked degree,/To qualify a

410 CP	Reilly	12	it rather as the bond which holds you together./While still in a state of
410 CP	Reilly	19	the propositions/And put them together./{L} Is that possible?/{R} If I had sent
417 CP	Reilly	33	/And with the evening that brings together/For casual talk before the fire/Two
437 CP	Reilly	37	and pain and loathing — all these together —/And reluctance of the body to
440 CP	Edward	9	somehow, the two ideas seem to fit together./{L} But all the same ... I don't want to
446 CC	Eggers	1	quickly,/During the time we worked together./All he needs is confidence./{SC} And
450 CC	Claude	6	you, Eggerson, although we worked together/For nearly thirty years./{E} Nearly
480 CC	Kaghan	6	/You and I ought to be in business together./I'm a good guesser. But I sometimes
481 CC	Kaghan	6	That's why we ought to be in business together./{L} You're both very good at paying
488 CC	Claude	5	/{SC} I'm beginning now to piece it together./You've been asking Colby about his
491 CC	Lady E	14	/I feel as if this brought us closer together./{SC} I should be contented with such
493 CC	Claude	5	don't think you and I should be near together./Will you sit there, beside the desk?/
515 CC	Claude	39	the better?/Perhaps we'll be happier together if you think/I am not your father. I'll
516 CC	Claude	35	/I want us to make the best of it, together./{C} No, Sir Claude. I hate to hurt you/
518 CC	Eggers	6	you've another vocation./We worked together every day, you know,/For quite a little
529 ES	Ld Clav	32	know I keep the old ones on a shelf together;/I could look in the right book, and
553 ES	Carghil	11	/It's simply that I feel that we belong together .../Now, don't get alarmed. But you
553 ES	Carghil	15	frightening to think that we're still together/And more frightening to think that we
553 ES	Carghil	16	to think that we may *always* be together./There's a phrase I seem to remember
556 ES	Monica	29	you'll get to the point if I leave you together. {}/[*Exit*]/{Mi} You know, it's awfully
565 ES	Ld Clav	37	/Michael and I shall go to school together./We'll sit side by side, at little desks/
574 ES	Carghil	25	perplexed, poor lamb. Let's all rejoice together. {}/[*Enter* GOMEZ *and* MICHAEL]/
581 ES	Charles	5	the aid we can. But it's both of you together/Make the force to attract him: you and
582 ES	Ld Clav	17	/You two ought to have a little time together./I leave Monica to you. Look after her,
582 ES	Charles	30	walk./{C} He wanted to leave us alone together!/{M} Yes, he wanted to leave us alone
582 ES	Monica	31	/{M} Yes, he wanted to leave us alone together./And yet, Charles, though we've been
582 ES	Charles	35	you're going to say!/We *were* alone together, in some mysterious fashion,/Even with
582 ES	Charles	37	somehow we'd begun to belong together,/And that awareness .../{M} Was a
583 ES	Charles	2	of a new person/Who is you and me together./Oh my dear,/I love you to the limits of
583 ES	Monica	10	was always there/That brought us together./Oh Father, Father!/I could speak to
583 ES	Monica	14	and find him./{M} We will go to him together. He is close at hand,/Though he has

TOI (1)

| 51 Restaurant | 22 | visage;/Tiens, ma fourchette, décrasse-toi le crâne./De quel droit payes-tu des |

TOIL (3)

147 Rock 1	28	the suburbs, and there I was told:/We toil for six days, on the seventh we must motor/
193 FQ: Little	69	eviscerate soil/Gapes at the vanity of toil,/Laughs without mirth./This is the death of
281 MC Chorus	15	of Canterbury,/The back bent under toil, the knee bent under sin, the hands to the

TOILETTE (1)

| 216 Jellicles | 18 | Moon appears/They make their toilette and take their repose:/Jellicles wash |

TOILING (1)

| 271 MC Thomas | 14 | /You shall forget these things, toiling in the household,/You shall remember |

TOKEN (2)

| 95 Ash-Wed 4 | 27 | the time, redeem the dream/The token of the word unheard, unspoken/Till the |
| 235 Ad-dress | 54 | you as a trusted friend,/Some little token of esteem/Is needed, like a dish of cream;/ |

TOLD (102)

64 WL: Chess	105	other withered stumps of time/Were told upon the walls; staring forms/Leaned out,
119 SP	Klip	13	Force —/{Kl} The Loot has told us a lot about you./{Kr} We were all in the
147 Rock 1	21	with foreign flotations./There I was told: we have too many churches,/And too few
147 Rock 1	22	too few chop-houses. There I was told:/Let the vicars retire. Men do not need the
147 Rock 1	27	to the suburbs, and there I was told:/We toil for six days, on the seventh we
147 Rock 1	31	/In industrial districts, there I was told/Of economic laws./In the pleasant
159 Rock 6	10	need keepers?/Do you need to be told that whatever has been, can still be?/Do
159 Rock 6	11	been, can still be?/Do you need to be told that even such modest attainments/As you
228 Gus	2	Door./His name, as I ought to have told you before,/Is really Asparagus. That's
271 MC Thomas	17	Only like a dream that has often been told/And often been changed in the telling.
285 FR	Ivy	14	a cold place, Amy./{I} I have always told Amy she should go south in the winter./
298 FR	Violet	16	says./I want to know at once, not be told about it later./{I} And I shall stay with
303 FR	Mary	16	Warburton? I think she might have told me;/It is very difficult, having to plan/For
318 FR	Harry	17	upon children/Than what they are told./{W} Stop, Harry, you're mistaken./I mean,
322 FR	Winch	30	to Dr. Warburton's,/And they told me he was here, and that you'd arrived./
323 FR	Winch	8	{Wi} I'm sorry, my Lady, but I've just told the doctor,/It's really nothing but a minor
325 FR	Violet	32	Arthur took me out in his car,/And I told him I would never go out with him again./
331 FR	Harry	18	know, and that is enough:/Warburton told me that, though he did not mean to./What
338 FR	Harry	17	she may have —/It was not I who told her ... All this year,/This last year, I have
342 FR	Mary	3	me that Harry is leaving:/Downing told her. He has got the car out./What is the

345 FR	Charles	34	I *could* understand, if I were told it./But I'm not sure that I want to know. I
353 CP	Celia	14	turn, Julia./Do tell us that story you told the other day, about Lady Klootz and the
359 CP	Edward	18	coming./I thought that Lavinia had told me the names/Of all the people she said
369 CP	Edward	23	is left unfinished./But you haven't told me how you came to know Celia./{P} I saw
372 CP	Peter	33	I'd rather you didn't tell *her* what I've told you./{E} I shall not say anything about it to
387 CP	Peter	17	/{P} No, not to me,/But to Alex. She told him to come here/And to bring me with
387 CP	Peter	29	/{E} What aunt?/{P} The aunt you told us about./But Edward — you remember
389 CP	Peter	8	/{P} We're not going together./Celia told us she was going away,/But I don't know
392 CP	Lavinia	28	Really, Edward! You had better have told the truth:/Nothing less than the truth could
396 CP	Edward	14	were in love with me./{E} Everybody told me that I was;/And they told me how well
396 CP	Edward	15	told me that I was;/And they told me how well suited we were./{L} It's a pity
405 CP	Reilly	13	which it can be discussed. You have told me nothing./You have had the
407 CP	Edward	1	know that./{E} Only because you've told me so often./I'd like to see *you* filling up an
407 CP	Reilly	28	put up with that. All that you have told me —/Both of you — was true enough: you
413 CP	Celia	34	be put right./I'd do anything you told me, to get back to normality./{R} We must
420 CP	Reilly	11	I ask what your fee is?/{R} I have told my secretary/That there is no fee./{C} But
424 CP	Lavinia	13	up your chambers,/And your clerk told me you had already left./But all I rang up
428 CP	Julia	7	She was very angry/When I told her the creature ought to be destroyed./{L}
430 CP	Peter	8	Paisley at lunch to-day/And she told me you were giving a party —/She's
440 CP	Lavinia	1	I am glad you came ... I am glad Alex told us .../And Peter had to know .../{E} Now I
440 CP	Edward	29	admire my dress./{E} But I've already told you how much I like it./{L} But so much
446 CC	Eggers	9	mentioned that:/It's only what you told me./{SC} About his music./Yes, I think so.
446 CC	Eggers	35	What's the point of that?/{E} He told me he was very fond of bird watching./{SC}
448 CC	Claude	1	way,/How much have you actually told him about her?/You remember, I asked you
448 CC	Eggers	14	begin to grasp them./No, I haven't told him much about Lady Elizabeth./But
448 CC	Eggers	19	his position in the household?/You told me that was your eventual intention./{SC}
448 CC	Claude	29	my plans to you./Why I've never told her about him,/The reason for meeting him
450 CC	Colby	35	nervous about this meeting./You've told me very little about Lady Elizabeth,/And
450 CC	Colby	36	/And Sir Claude himself hasn't told me very much:/So I've no idea how I ought
450 CC	Colby	38	I ought to behave./B. Kaghan has told me something about her,/But that's rather
453 CC	Lucasta	22	never fails to rise./B.! What have you told Colby about me?/{K} It's no use telling
455 CC	Eggers	39	more unusual./{C} Oh!/{E} Well, as I told you, she really is a lady,/Rather a *grande*
461 CC	Eggers	2	have missed it./And besides, as I told you, I've done some shopping./But I
470 CC	Lucasta	1	Don't be such a fraud. You know you told me/The piano was only delivered this week/
472 CC	Lucasta	21	one thing I know. When you first told me/What a disaster it was in your life/
475 CC	Colby	34	to say/Already, either from what I've told you/Or from what I've told B.; or from Sir
475 CC	Colby	35	what I've told you/Or from what I've told B.; or from Sir Claude./{L} Claude hasn't
475 CC	Lucasta	36	or from Sir Claude./{L} Claude hasn't told me anything about you;/He doesn't tell me
477 CC	Lucasta	20	you're more shocked/Than if I'd told you I *was* Claude's mistress./Claude has
478 CC	Lucasta	11	truly disappointed./I was sure, when I told you all I did,/That you wouldn't mind at
478 CC	Lucasta	30	forget that look on your face/When I told you about Claude and my mother./I may
479 CC	Kaghan	3	And I'm dying for a drink./{K} I told Colby, never learn to mix cocktails,/If you
481 CC	Lady E	30	have the most delicious salads!/And I told you, Mr. Kaghan, you're the type of person
484 CC	Lady E	31	/I had three obsessions, and I never told anyone./I wonder if *you* had the same
486 CC	Colby	26	indeed./I don't remember him. I was told about him./But I can't help wondering why
486 CC	Claude	33	SIR CLAUDE]/{SC} Elizabeth! I was told that you were here with Colby./So I came
488 CC	Claude	24	leave that to you./{SC} I should have told you one day./I've always loathed keeping
488 CC	Claude	26	you./I see now I might as well have told you before,/But I'd hoped — and now it
489 CC	Claude	2	But it isn't Colby./I ought to have told you, years ago./I told you about Lucasta,
489 CC	Claude	3	I ought to have told you, years ago./I told you about Lucasta, and you told me/About
489 CC	Claude	3	/I told you about Lucasta, and you told me/About your own ... misfortune. And I
489 CC	Claude	4	your own ... misfortune. And I almost told you/About Colby. I didn't. For such a
489 CC	Claude	17	the decision bitterly./I ought to have told you that I had a son./{LE} But why do you
489 CC	Lady E	35	father had died/And she'd never been told the name of the mother;/And the mother
492 CC	Claude	36	surprise the Potters' Company/If I told them what I was really remembering./
495 CC	Lady E	3	to be a potter!/Why have you never told me?/{SC} I didn't think/That you would be
497 CC	Claude	21	that her child must be Colby,/So I told her the truth. But she cannot believe it./
500 CC	Claude	14	no longer exist. But I ought to have told you./{L} Well, I don't understand. What I
502 CC	Lucasta	4	to interrupt your meeting./I've been told what it's about. But I did come to see you./
502 CC	Claude	8	afternoon./{C} Apologise?/{SC} I've told her./{C} But why should you apologise?/{L}
502 CC	Lucasta	31	*Who* you are,/In the sense I've been told that you're my brother;/Which makes it
507 CC	Guzzard	13	/Or of the mother?/{MG} I was not told either./I understood the child was very well
509 CC	Guzzard	17	died?/{MG} Yes, Colby, that is what I told you./{LE} So my child is living. I was sure
510 CC	Colby	15	*and* LUCASTA]/{C} I have told them to be prepared for a surprise./{LE}
517 CC	Colby	32	to come to Joshua Park./{C} But I've told you, I'm not a very good organist!/{E}

531 ES	Lambert	34	very insistent that he must see you./I told him you never saw anyone, my Lord,/But
536 ES	Gomez	13	/Only believed what the parish priest told her./I made my children learn English —
536 ES	Gomez	38	suppose their husbands/Were ever told the story. *They* wouldn't want to see me./
541 ES	Gomez	9	/But you'd never know to whom I'd told it,/Or who knew the story and who didn't. I
547 ES	Monica	33	I'm very fond of walking/And I'm told there are very good walks in this
553 ES	Carghil	32	/Which are quite as good, I'm told. And I like to read them/In your own
555 ES	Monica	37	put up with it./But where is he?/{M} I told him he must wait in the garden/Until I had
560 ES	Ld Clav	21	wanting to go/Beyond what you've told me? It isn't ... manslaughter?/{Mi}
568 ES	Ld Clav	19	with each other —/I don't need to be told what I've seen for myself!/And if there is
569 ES	Charles	18	suspicion —/From what Monica has told me about your fellow guests,/Two persons
574 ES	Carghil	10	Oh? What about Michael?/{MC} He's told me all his story./You've cruelly
575 ES	Gomez	19	/Michael knows it already. I've told him myself./I thought he'd better learn the
575 ES	Ld Clav	30	/Understand that allusion. I have told them the story/In explanation of our ...
576 ES	Ld Clav	8	Michael,/Señor Gomez says he has told you his story./Did he include the fact that
576 ES	Michael	10	he served a term in prison?/{Mi} He told me everything. It was his experience/With
576 ES	Michael	28	is inspired by benevolence —/{Mi} I told you he'd come to London looking for a
577 ES	Carghil	30	I understand business. Mr. Carghill told me so./Now, Michael has great abilities for

TOLERABLE (1)

544 ES	Monica	5	hot water is hot,/They give us a very tolerable breakfast;/And the chambermaid

TOLERANT (1)

417 CP	Reilly	29	avoid excessive expectation,/Become tolerant of themselves and others,/Giving and

TOLLING (2)

73 WL: Thund	383	/And upside down in air were towers/Tolling reminiscent bells, that kept the hours/
185 FQ: DrySal	37	the oppression of the silent fog/The tolling bell/Measures time not our time, rung by

TOM (2)

246 MC	Templ1	30	an old friend out of favour?/Old Tom, gay Tom, Becket of London,/Your
246 MC	Templ1	30	friend out of favour?/Old Tom, gay Tom, Becket of London,/Your Lordship won't

TOM-TOM (1)

19 Portrait	32	cornets/Inside my brain a dull tom-tom begins/Absurdly hammering a prelude

TOMB (7)

18 Portrait	6	overhead,/An atmosphere of Juliet's tomb/Prepared for all the things to be said, or
189 FQ: DrySal	198	terrors —/To explore the womb, or tomb, or dreams; all these are usual/Pastimes
230 Bust Jones	27	full of gloom then he's lunched at the *Tomb*/On cabbage, rice pudding and mutton./So,
248 MC	Templ2	29	a permanent possession./A templed tomb, monument of marble./Rule over men
254 MC	Templ4	14	come:/Saint and Martyr rule from the tomb./Think, Thomas, think of enemies
269 MC	Thomas	20	if you kill me, I shall rise from my tomb/To submit my cause before God's throne.
343 FR	Amy	29	I?/It is no concern of the body in the tomb/To bother about the upkeep. Let the wind

TOMBSTONE (1)

192 FQ: Little	31	the pig-sty to the dull façade/And the tombstone. And what you thought you came

TOMORROW (25)

65 WL: Chess	133	my hair down, so. What shall we do tomorrow?/'What shall we ever do?'/'The hot
219 Mung Rump	26	afraid you must wait and have dinner *tomorrow*!/For the joint has gone from the oven
285 FR	Amy	9	expected/And clocks could be trusted, tomorrow assured/And time would not stop in
292 FR	Amy	19	have them in after dinner/Or wait till tomorrow? I am sure you must be tired./You
292 FR	Amy	21	— you remember — wants to call tomorrow/On some legal business, a question
292 FR	Gerald	27	and young./{G} We must have a ride tomorrow./You'll find you know the country as
296 FR	Charles	29	it off his mind. I'll have a talk to him tomorrow./{A} Most certainly not, Charles, you
323 FR Warburt	15	can trust Owen./We'll bring him up tomorrow; and a few days' rest,/I've no doubt,
327 FR	Ivy	32	the last train, so he's coming up tomorrow;/And he said there was something
347 FR	Ivy	19	in town many happy returns see you tomorrow many happy returns hurrah love
377 CP	Edward	11	he said he would bring Lavinia back, tomorrow./{C} But why should that man want
388 CP	Peter	38	Yes, and I would have rung you up tomorrow/And come in to say good-bye before
411 CP	Edward	10	No, they won't let me./I must leave tomorrow — but how did you know/I was
460 CC	Lady E	28	husband./You shall have tea with me tomorrow,/And then I shall tell you about my
462 CC	Claude	2	that you should have the flat —/By tomorrow she'll be sure it was she who
467 CC	Colby	38	/You have that meeting in the City/Tomorrow morning. You asked me to prepare/
486 CC	Colby	37	of the Potters' Company./{C} That's tomorrow night, I believe./{SC} Yes it is./But
487 CC	Claude	6	ten minutes./And then we'll go over it tomorrow. {}/[*looking at the notes*]./{C} I'll try./
492 CC	Colby	19	speech for the Potters' Company/Tomorrow night. I must get to work on it./{SC}
492 CC	Claude	20	night. I must get to work on it./{SC} Tomorrow night. Must I go to that dinner/
492 CC	Claude	21	night. Must I go to that dinner/Tomorrow night?/{C} I was looking at your
554 ES	Carghil	1	/Yes, I'll bring the photostats tomorrow morning,,/And read them to you./—
554 ES	Carghil	7	she'll take the hint/And leave us alone tomorrow./Good morning, Mrs. Piggott!/Isn't he
565 ES	Ld Clav	8	After breakfast?/{LC} Yes, come tomorrow morning./{Mi} Well, I'll come
565 ES	Michael	9	morning./{Mi} Well, I'll come tomorrow morning./{MC} Are you staying in

TON (1)

51 Restaurant	20	/C'est dommage.'/Mais alors, tu as ton vautour!/Va t'en te décrotter les rides du

TONES (2)

18 Portrait	16	caught regrets/Through attenuated tones of violins/Mingled with remote cornets/
272 MC Chorus	30	deceived, for there are no objects, no tones,/No colours, no forms to distract, to

TONGUE (4)

13 Prufrock	17	on the window-panes,/Licked its tongue into the corners of the evening,/Lingered
24 Rhapsody	36	itself in the gutter,/Slips out its tongue/And devours a morsel of rancid butter.'/
143 Lines OM	8	of wit/The hissing over the archèd tongue/Is more affectionate than hate,/More
193 FQ: Little	83	the dark dove with the flickering tongue/Had passed below the horizon of his

TONGUED (1)

192 FQ: Little	53	the communication/Of the dead is tongued with fire beyond the language of the

TONGUES (2)

196 FQ: Little	204	of incandescent terror/Of which the tongues declare/The one discharge from sin and
198 FQ: Little	259	of thing shall be well/When the tongues of flame are in-folded/Into the crowned

TONIGHT (12)

301 FR	Gerald	4	/Why you've been busy about it tonight./{Do} Nothing wrong, Sir:/Only I like to
323 FR	Warburt	13	concussion,/But he mustn't be moved tonight. I'd trust Owen/On a matter like this.
323 FR	Warburt	29	I forbid you to leave the house tonight./There is nothing you could do, and out
325 FR	Violet	8	/{V} I do not seem to be very popular tonight./{C} Well, there's no sort of use in any
347 FRDowning		3	that was the reason/We was off tonight. In fact, I half expected it,/So I had the
419 CP	Celia	34	/{R} How soon will you be ready?/{C} Tonight, by nine o'clock./{R} Go home then,
431 CP	Peter	13	I have my hands full/I'm going down tonight, to Boltwell./{J} To stay with the Duke?/
491 CC	Colby	40	sake of your children./{C} I don't feel, tonight, that I ever want to marry./You may be
492 CC	Claude	13	all about it./Let us say no more tonight. Now, Colby,/Can you find some
492 CC	Colby	15	at the piano?/{C} I don't think, tonight, the piano would help me:/At the
492 CC	Claude	28	of what? Reminiscent of what?/'Tonight I feel in a reminiscent mood' —/Oh yes.
543 ES	Monica	19	you can't bear to dine alone with me tonight,/What will it be like at Badgley Court?

TONY (7)

355 CP	Peter	35	story./{P} Were they the parents of Tony Vincewell?/{J} Yes. Tony was the product,
355 CP	Julia	36	parents of Tony Vincewell?/{J} Yes. Tony was the product, but not the solution./He
355 CP	Julia	38	situation more difficult./You know Tony Vincewell? You knew him at Oxford?/{P}
488 CC	Lady E	3	That was all I knew./Then Tony was killed, as you know, in Africa,/And I
495 CC	Lady E	20	/{LE} Or to inspire a poet. I thought Tony was a poet./Because he wrote me poems.
495 CC	Lady E	26	from a world that I loathed/In Tony — and then, too late, I discovered/He
507 CC	Lady E	23	/{LE} That must have been when Tony met with his accident./{MG} I was

TOO (174)

21 Portrait	107	write, at any rate./Perhaps it is not too late./I shall sit here, serving tea to friends.'/
21 Portrait	120	/Or whether wise or foolish, tardy or too soon .../Would she not have the advantage,
29 Aunt Helen	9	But shortly afterwards the parrot died too./The Dresden clock continued ticking on
38 Gerontion	39	the giving famishes the craving. Gives too late/What's not believed in, or if still
38 Gerontion	41	only, reconsidered passion. Gives too soon/Into weak hands, what's thought can
68 WL: Fire S	230	the scene, and foretold the rest —/I too awaited the expected guest./He, the young
89 Ash-Wed 1	28	/These matters that with myself I too much discuss/Too much explain/Because I
89 Ash-Wed 1	29	that with myself I too much discuss/Too much explain/Because I do not hope to
90 Ash-Wed 1	33	again/May the judgement not be too heavy upon us/Because these wings are no
103 Journ Magi	30	arrived at evening, not a moment too soon/Finding the place; it was (you may
115 SP	Doris	17	to do./{Do} No it wouldn't do to be too nice to Pereira./{Du} Now Sam's a
115 SP	Dusty	21	*I* like Sam/Yes and Sam's a nice boy too./He's a funny fellow/{Do} He *is* a funny
116 SP	Dusty	27	it's only a chill/Yes indeed I hope so too —/Well I *hope* we shan't have to call a
117 SP	Dusty	11	apparel, or a party'./That's queer too/{Do} Here's the three. What's that mean?/
117 SP	Doris	30	what'll I do?/Just before a party too!/{Du} Well it needn't be yours, it may mean
118 SP	Dusty	9	to know/{Du} It's no use asking them too much/{Do} It's no use asking more than
119 SP	Klip	36	you all the same) —/London's a little too gay for us/Yes I'll say a little too gay./{Kr}
119 SP	Klip	37	little too gay for us/Yes I'll say a little too gay./{Kr} Yes London's a little too gay for
119 SP	Krum	38	too gay./{Kr} Yes London's a little too gay for us/Don't think I mean anything
124 SA Sweeney	27	in the end/But that's another story too./This went on for a couple of months/
136 5FingerEx3	10	due,/Pinching bread and finger too,/Easier had than squirming worm;/For I
140 Usk	6	Let them sleep.'Gently dip, but not too deep',/Lift your eyes/Where the roads dip
147 Rock 1	21	flotations./There I was told: we have too many churches,/And too few chop-houses.
147 Rock 1	22	we have too many churches,/And too few chop-houses. There I was told:/Let the
152 Rock 2	46	/Unless his neighbour makes too much disturbance,/But all dash to and fro in
158 Rock 5	8	they write innumerable books; being too vain and distracted for silence: seeking every
166 Rock 10	9	/But the Mystery of Iniquity is a pit too deep for mortal eyes to plumb. Come/Ye
166 Rock 10	13	/Your way and be ye separate./Be not too curious of Good and Evil;/Seek not to

166 Rock 10		18	/O Light Invisible, we praise Thee!/Too bright for mortal vision./O Greater Light,
167 Rock 10		36	when the play ends; and ecstasy is too much pain./We are children quickly tired:
177 FQ: ECoker		25	/In that open field/If you do not come too close, if you do not come too close,/On a
177 FQ: ECoker		25	come too close, if you do not come too close,/On a summer midnight, you can hear
178 FQ: ECoker		56	under feet/And hollyhocks that aim too high/Red into grey and tumble down/Late
180 FQ: ECoker		119	underground train, in the tube, stops too long between stations/And the conversation
190 FQ: DrySal		236	our temporal reversion nourish/(Not too far from the yew-tree)/The life of significant
194 FQ: Little		106	so, compliant to the common wind,/Too strange to each other for
202 War Poetry		11	Mostly the individual/Experience is too large, or too small. Our emotions/Are only
202 War Poetry		11	individual/Experience is too large, or too small. Our emotions/Are only 'incidents'/In
212 Growltiger		27	his bosun, TUMBLEBRUTUS, he too had stol'n away —/In the yard behind the
216 Jellicles		14	develop slowly,/Jellicle Cats are not too big;/Jellicle Cats are roly-poly,/They know
230 Bust Jones		23	And just before noon's not a moment too soon/To drop in for a drink at the *Drones*./
234 Ad-dress		28	the clown,/And far from showing too much pride/Is frequently undignified./He's
243 MC Chorus		16	/O late late late, late is the time, late too late, and rotten the year;/Evil the wind, and
247 MC Templ1		31	may go faster./Your Lordship is too proud!/The safest beast is not the one that
247 MC Thomas		39	the bone./{T} You come twenty years too late./{T1} Then I leave you to your fate./I
248 MC Tempt2		18	recalled them,/Let us but set these not too pleasant memories/In balance against other,
255 MC Tempt4		6	yes; you have thought of that too./What can compare with glory of Saints/
255 MC Tempt4		23	I ask/What you have to give. Is it too much/For such a vision of eternal grandeur?
257 MC Chorus		6	happy, my Lord, we have not been too happy./We are not ignorant women, we
267 MC Knight1		28	I shall make no mention./They are too well known. But after dissension/Had
270 MC Chorus		22	smelt them, the death-bringers; now is too late/For action, too soon for contrition./
270 MC Chorus		23	now is too late/For action, too soon for contrition./Nothing is possible but
285 FR	Amy	4	to June,/And the swallow comes too soon and the spring will be over/And the
285 FR	Charles	24	country-bred people./Amy has been too long used to our ways/Living with horses
289 FR	Charles	16	to mention it now?/It seems to me too late./{A} Much too late./If he wants to talk
289 FR	Amy	17	/It seems to me too late./{A} Much too late./If he wants to talk about it, that's
293 FR	Violet	2	goes on in the kitchen./Mrs. Packell is too old to know what she is doing./It really
294 FR	Agatha	14	stopping to debate/Whether it may be too far beyond our understanding./{H} The
295 FR	Amy	34	And making such haste, the change is too sudden for you./You are unused to our
298 FR	Charles	34	you've been a good friend to him, too./*We* haven't seen him for nearly eight years;
299 FR	Charles	8	—/Of course, there was a great deal too much in the papers./Downing, do you think
300 FR Downing		13	that man and wife/Shouldn't see too much of each other, Sir./Quite the contrary
304 FR	Agatha	37	the weapons of the weak,/Which are too violent. And it could not have been easy,/
308 FR	Harry	35	just out of earshot —/And inside too, in the nightly panic/Of dreaming
309 FR	Harry	5	/And that is by seeing. They are much too clever/To admit you into *our* world. Yours
319 FR	Harry	20	Not Arthur or John,/They were too young. But now I remember/A summer day
327 FR	Harry	16	set another doctor on me./But this is too real for your words to alter./Oh, there *must*
327 FR	Ivy	29	was very queer. It seems that Arthur too/Has had an accident. I don't think he's
328 FR	Ivy	31	I'm sure that you're being much too hard on him./{C} In my time, these affairs
332 FR	Agatha	34	neither./{Ag} The autumn came too soon, not soon enough./The rain and wind
339 FR	Harry	1	to other people./It is hard for you too, mother, it is indeed harder,/Not to
339 FR	Harry	21	Strength demanded/That seems too much, is just strength enough given./I must
343 FR	Mary	4	/{M} Oh! ... so ... *you* have seen them too!/{Ag} We must all go, each in his own
343 FR	Mary	14	I mean it now. Of course it was much too late/Then, for anything to come for me: I
343 FR	Mary	19	me./I will go. But I suppose it is much too late/Now, to try to get a fellowship?/{A} So
345 FR	Amy	20	to apprehend the truth/About things too late to mend: and that is to be old./
345 FR	Amy	22	come to know them./I always wanted too much for my children/More than life can
346 FR	Agatha	38	than that,/And we have seen them too — Miss Mary and I./{Do} I understand
347 FR Downing		6	them —/And so you've seen them too! They must have given you a turn!/They did
348 FR	Chorus	9	like the maze in the garden, because it too closely resembles the maze in the brain./We
348 FR	Chorus	10	when we are awake, because it too closely resembles what happens when we are
354 CP	Julia	18	I used to say to her: 'Greta!/You have too much vitality.' But she enjoyed herself. {}/
354 CP	Julia	27	don't know her./{J} Well, one can't be too careful/Before one tells a story./{A} Delia
356 CP	Julia	40	away yourself!/{J} Have you an aunt too?/{E} No, I haven't any aunt. But I might go
365 CP	Julia	33	songs all the time?/There's altogether too much mystery/About this place to-day./{E}
367 CP	Peter	33	common/And I think she thought so too./{E} How did you come to know her? {}/
372 CP	Peter	30	Peter with me./{P} Edward, I've taken too much of your time,/And you want to be
376 CP	Celia	13	/{C} But it's ruined the saucepan too./{E} *And* half a dozen eggs:/I wanted one
377 CP	Julia	33	to be done. That's very simple./It's too late, or too early, to go to a restaurant./You
377 CP	Julia	33	That's very simple./It's too late, or too early, to go to a restaurant./You must both
377 CP	Edward	36	with me./{E} No, I'm sorry, Julia./I'm too tired to go out, and I'm not at all hungry./I
379 CP	Edward	15	you are a very rare person./But it was too late. And I should have known/That it
380 CP	Celia	17	talking about./Edward, this is really too crude a subterfuge/To justify yourself.

384 CP	Reilly	13	/But that it will not matter. It will be too late./{E} I have half a mind to change my
387 CP	Celia	6	being./Can't you see me that way too, and laugh about it?/{E} I wish I could. I
387 CP	Peter	19	/Celia! Have you heard from Lavinia too?/Or am I interrupting?/{C} I've just
388 CP	Celia	18	going to concerts./I am going away too. {}/[LAVINIA *lets herself in with a*
389 CP	Lavinia	2	before I left./{L} And Celia's going too? Was that what I heard?/I congratulate you
392 CP	Lavinia	40	away/I see that I've taken you much too seriously./And now I can see how absurd
393 CP	Edward	39	inconvenient/That I should be always too busy or too tired/To be of use to you
393 CP	Edward	39	/That I should be always too busy or too tired/To be of use to you socially .../{L} I
395 CP	Edward	18	you that possibly/I may have changed too?/{L} Oh, Edward, when you were a little
395 CP	Lavinia	23	people grow, well, you want to grow too./In what way have you changed?/{E} The
397 CP	Lavinia	33	not try to press you./You're much too divided to know what you want./But, being
406 CP	Reilly	32	for my sanatorium:/You are much too ill./{E} Much too ill?/Then I'll go and be ill
406 CP	Edward	33	/You are much too ill./{E} Much too ill?/Then I'll go and be ill in a suburban
407 CP	Reilly	6	discussion?/I say you are both too ill. There are several symptoms/Which must
411 CP	Lavinia	25	/{L} Exactly. And I have a question too./Sir Henry, was it you who sent those
411 CP	Lavinia	31	think you have answered my question too./They had to tell us, themselves, that they
421 CP	Julia	26	anything there to be afraid of./She is too humble. She will pass between the scolding
424 CP	Lavinia	19	*all* of them./I hope you're not too tired?/{E} Oh no, a quiet day./Two
425 CP	Edward	5	/{E} Well, you deserve it. — We asked too many people./{L} It's true, a great many
425 CP	Lavinia	38	it./{E} Is it straight now?/{L} Too much to the left./{E} How's that now?/{L}
426 CP	Lavinia	2	I meant the right./That will do. I'm too tired to bother./{E} After they're all gone,
426 CP	Julia	30	you napping!/I know I'm much too early; but the fact is, my dears,/That I have
429 CP	Alex	25	{A} It cannot be, at present:/There are too many international complications./
438 CP	Lavinia	26	/Doesn't it help you, that I feel guilty too?/{R} If we all were judged according to the
440 CP	Julia	15	will get on better without us. You too, Alex./{L} We don't *want* you to go!/{A} We
447 CC	Eggers	20	say that, Sir Claude!/She has too much respect for your business genius./But
447 CC	Claude	32	/Something like that. Don't make too much of it./And I rather hope that she will
448 CC	Eggers	12	on these matters,/They're much too deep for me. And I thought, Mr. Simpkins,/
454 CC	Lucasta	14	tea. The strain of this crisis/Has been too much for me. Another time, Colby./I'll ring
465 CC	Claude	1	/But after his death, and then it was too late,/I knew that he was right. And all my
465 CC	Claude	5	right. I never understood him./I was too young. And when I was mature enough/To
466 CC	Colby	38	understood your father/Until it was too late. And you spoke of atonement./Even
475 CC	Colby	14	hours./{C} And I think I'm changing too. But perhaps what we call change .../{L} Is
476 CC	Lucasta	26	have minded. But he's very clever too;/And he guessed the truth from the very
477 CC	Lucasta	6	/But I was old enough to remember ... too much./{C} You are Claude's daughter!/{L}
479 CC	Kaghan	18	/To drink success to the flat. Lucasta too:/Much better for you than cocktails,
479 CC	Kaghan	36	must change the colours./It's all a bit too dim. You need something brighter./But
482 CC	Lady E	9	it was possible you might become too friendly/With Mr. Kaghan and Miss Angel.
482 CC	Colby	27	call them vulgar. Perhaps I'm vulgar too./But what, do you think, *is* my sort?/I don't
483 CC	Lady E	26	— even in silver frames —/Are much too intimate for the sitting-room./May I remove
487 CC	Colby	13	/On such an instrument. It's much too good for me./{SC} You need a good piano.
490 CC	Colby	39	/Nothing living can spring. Now, it is too late./I never wanted a parent till now —/I
493 CC	Claude	9	yourself?/{SC} No, that would look too formal. I thought it would be better/To put
495 CC	Claude	15	remark./Perhaps I have taken too much for granted/About you, Elizabeth.
495 CC	Lady E	26	that I loathed/In Tony — and then, too late, I discovered/He belonged to the world
496 CC	Claude	3	me feel that *your* interests/Were much too deep for discussion with *me*:/Health cures.
499 CC	Lucasta	32	Colby. Because you thought he was too good for me./{SC} In Colby!/{L} Why not?
500 CC	Lucasta	37	suited to each other:/You thought so too, Claude, but for the wrong reasons,/And
501 CC	Lady E	3	the wrong ones./{LE} And I'm sure too, Lucasta, you have made a wise decision./
502 CC	Colby	1	*Enter* COLBY]/{C} Have I come too soon?/I'm afraid I got impatient of waiting./
502 CC	Lucasta	13	way I thought it was./You're much too ... detached, ever to be shocked/In the way I
516 CC	Colby	9	matter about success —/I aimed too high before — beyond my capacity./I
517 CC	Colby	10	be guilty towards you. I like you too much./You've become a man without
517 CC	Eggers	35	Church Council will be only too pleased,/And I have some influence. *I* am
518 CC	Guzzard	26	the wife of an organist;/But you too, I think, have had a wish realised./— I
526 ES	Charles	34	a reminder/That I mustn't stay too long, for you belong to him./He seems so
527 ES	Monica	27	else in the room with him,/Reading too — or just sitting — someone/Not occupied
527 ES	Monica	37	Mother spoilt him/And Father was too severe — so they're always at loggerheads./
532 ES	Ld Clav	5	him in the library./No, stop. I've left too many papers about there./I'd better see him
533 ES	Gomez	1	/{G} You've changed your name too, since I knew you./When we were up at
534 ES	Gomez	23	on./That wouldn't do for me. I'm too domestic./And by the way, I've several
537 ES	Gomez	31	to play the rake,/But you never went too far. There's a prudent devil/Inside you,
539 ES	Gomez	21	devil/Of yours, to tell him not to go too far./Well, now, I'm beginning to be thirsty
540 ES	Gomez	24	old man in the road./{G} You knew it too. If you had been surprised/When I said
545 ES	Piggott	29	after breakfast:/He's led a busy life, too.' But I hope you're happy?/Is there anything

547 ES   Piggott   11   /It's popular in the evenings. But not *too* crowded. {}/[*Exit*]/{LC} Much as I had
547 ES   Piggott   25   there's no dancing,/And it's still too early for the bathing pool./But several of
549 ES   Carghil   38   *you* thought,/And others thought so too. But as you remember,/Please, Richard, just
550 ES   Carghil   21   He had a weak heart./And he worked too hard. Have you never heard/Of Carghill
552 ES   Carghil   7   I made/With a number called *It's Not Too Late For You To Love Me?*/I couldn't have
555 ES   Piggott   1   /That tune she was humming, *It's Not Too Late For You To Love Me,*/Everybody was
558 ES   Michael   31   brought up against me,/That I'd been too familiar with one of the girls./He assumed it
560 ES   Michael   23   on the road./Certainly not. I'm far too good a driver./{LC} What then? That young
563 ES   Gomez   11   /That I was in need of a rest cure too./And when I heard you'd chosen to come to
564 ES   Carghil   1   most devoted admirer./{MC} *It's Not Too Late For You To Love Me!* That's the song/
564 ES   Gomez   3   Señor Gomez./{G} It will never be too late. Don't you agree, Dick?/— This young
566 ES   Ld Clav   4   time?/There is time for Michael. Is it too late for me, Monica? {}/CURTAIN/Act
571 ES   Ld Clav   3   Maisie Batterson,/And Dick Ferry too, and Richard Ferry —/These are my ghosts.
574 ES   Carghil   21   father!/And I found him only too ready to help./{LC} And what was Señor
575 ES   Carghil   34   you explained to them our intimacy too?/{LC} I have indeed./{MC} The romance of
583 ES   Monica   15   is close at hand,/Though he has gone too far to return to us./He is under the beech

TOOK (56)

61 WL: Burial   14   at the arch-duke's,/My cousin's, he took me out on a sled,/And I was frightened.
66 WL: Chess   159   pulling a long face,/It's them pills I took, to bring it off, she said./(She's had five
124 SA Sweeney   31   came/And nobody went/But he took in the milk and he paid the rent./{Sw}
127 Cor1 March   24   1,150 field bakeries./What a time that took. Will it be he now? No,/Those are the golf
128 Cor1 March   44   we didn't get to the country,/So we took young Cyril to church. And they rang a
163 Rock 8   40   them./Remember the faith that took men from home/At the call of a wandering
195 FQ: Little 144   done to others' harm/Which once you took for exercise of virtue./Then fools' approval
201 Def Island   21   /of our kin and of our speech, that we took up/our positions, in obedience to
223 Pekes Pols   57   /The Pekes and the Pollicles quickly took warning./He looked at the sky and he gave
227 Macavity   38   to spare:/At whatever time the deed took place — MACAVITY WASN'T THERE!/
228 Gus   28   the hardest of hearts,/Whether I took the lead, or in character parts./I have sat
587 Fable   3   out that monks were quacks,/And took their lands and money from the poor men,
588 Fable   55   Last, a boar's head, which to bring in took four pages,/His mouth an apple held, his
589 Fable   75   the size of any dollar,/The ghost then took him roughly by the hair/And bade him
589 Fable   91   /Each morn from four to five one took a knout/And flogged his mates 'till they
265 MC Knight1   14   us from France. We rode hard,/Took ship yesterday, landed last night,/Having
278 MC Knight2   39   the State, remember that it is we who took the first/step. We have been instrumental
300 FRDowning   28   Sir, I was down in the Tourist,/And I took a bit of air before I went to bed,/And you
300 FRDowning   33   but I was sure it was him./While I took my turn about, for near half an hour/He
306 FR Harry   15   simplified —/But the simplification took place in my memory, I think. It seems I
307 FR Mary   20   river./{M} But when I was a child I took everything for granted,/Including the
313 FR Ivy   12   /When I could afford a garden; and I took several prizes/With my delphiniums. I was
325 FR Violet   31   his head./{V} But a year ago, Arthur took me out in his car,/And I told him I would
332 FR Agatha   14   terms with Wishwood,/Until she took your father's place, and reached the point
340 FR Amy   5   in *me*. Thirty-five years ago/You took my husband from me. Now you take my
340 FR Amy   14   to live upon. You knew that you took everything/Except the walls, the furniture,
341 FR Amy   22   abstinence./Thirty-five years ago you took my husband from me/And now you take
341 FR Amy   38   settlement and happiness,/You who took my husband, now you take my son./You
362 CP Edward   9   you love her?/{E} Why, I thought we took each other for granted./I never thought I
365 CP Reilly   8   *in but the landlord's daughter/And she took my heart entirely.*/You will keep our
380 CP Celia   25   /I thought that I could help him. I took him to concerts./But then, as he came to
394 CP Lavinia 8   something about it./That was why I took so much trouble/To have those Thursdays,
397 CP Edward   12   was only yesterday/That damnation took place. And now I must live with it/Day by
406 CP Lavinia 11   mean? I asked to be sent/And you took me there. If that was not a sanatorium/
409 CP Reilly   32   in love with Miss Coplestone,/It took you some time, I have no doubt,/Before
413 CP Celia   23   through, these last weeks,/I somehow took it for granted that I needn't explain myself.
426 CP Edward   1   being so remote./{E} That's why we took it. And I'm really thankful/To have that
435 CP Peter   12   to know/And did not dare to ask. It took all my courage/To ask you about her just
458 CC Lady E   24   she says it makes her sea-sick;/So we took the night train, and did the Channel
461 CC Claude   34   very well. It's very obvious/That she took to you at once./{C} Did she really think/
477 CC Lucasta 5   'accidental overdose'./Then Claude took me over. That was lucky./But I was old
485 CC Lady E   12   I felt myself to be/And then I took up the Wisdom of the East/And believed,
495 CC Claude   6   be interested. More than that./I took it for granted that what you wanted/Was a
495 CC Lady E   9   I'd really wanted to be./{LE} And I took it for granted that you were not interested/
498 CC Claude   26   can't ask me to believe/That she took two babies, and got them mixed./{LE}
499 CC Lucasta 31   spite you,/I dare say. That was why I took an interest/In Colby. Because you thought
508 CC Eggers   17   what became of the child/She took in, which may have been Lady Elizabeth's.
510 CC Eggers   37   It's for them to confirm/That they took you, as a child, from Mrs. Guzzard,/To

518 CC	Eggers	16	by the way, a practical point:/If you took the position, you'd want to find your feet/
525 ES	Charles	8	to, in a restaurant;/And then you took me on a shopping expedition .../{M} If you
533 ES	Gomez	3	Ferry./Then, when you married, you took your wife's name/And became Mr.
558 ES	Michael	14	/And what else did he say?/{Mi} He took the usual line,/Just like the headmaster.
559 ES	Michael	22	the name of Claverton;/Or where, if I took a different name — and I might choose to
559 ES	Michael	27	As for your title,/I know why you took it. And Mother knew./First, because it
578 ES	Monica	18	/And I'm your only sister. You never took much notice of me./When we were
578 ES	Monica	20	up we seldom had the same friends./I took all that for granted. So I didn't know till

TOOL (2)

| 16 Prufrock | | 114 | /Advise the prince; no doubt, an easy tool,/Deferential, glad to be of use,/Politic, |
| 266 MC | Knights | 16 | command./You are his servant, his tool, and his jack,/You wore his favours on |

TOOLS (2)

| 445 CC | Eggers | 12 | the morning shopping! Gardening tools./The number of things one needs for a |
| 445 CC | Eggers | 14 | now's the moment to buy some new tools/So as not to lose a moment at the end of |

TOORY-ILEY (1)

| 365 CP | Reilly | 11 | keep it. {}/[*Sings*]./{UG} *Tooryooly toory-iley,/What's the matter with One Eyed* |

TOORYOOLY (1)

| 365 CP | Reilly | 11 | /{E} I shall keep it. {}/[*Sings*]./{UG} *Tooryooly toory-iley,/What's the matter with* |

TOOTH (3)

109 Marina		6	my daughter./Those who sharpen the tooth of the dog, meaning/Death/Those who
143 Lines OM		7	the friendly tree./When I lay bare the tooth of wit/The hissing over the archèd tongue/
159 Rock 6		16	your fingernails:/You polish the tooth of the dog and the talon of the cat./Why

TOOTH-BRUSH (1)

| 26 Rhapsody | | 76 | the stair./Mount./The bed is open; the tooth-brush hangs on the wall,/Put your shoes |

TOOTH-PASTE (1)

| 397 CP | Edward | 31 | you/How to put the cap on a tube of tooth-paste./{L} Very well, then, I shall not try |

TOOTHED (1)

| 92 Ash-Wed 3 | | 11 | drivelling, beyond repair,/Or the toothed gullet of an agèd shark./At the first |

TOOTHFUL (1)

| 229 Gus | | 35 | /Then, if someone will give him a toothful of gin,/He will tell how he once played |

TOOTHSOME (1)

| 368 CP | Alex | 24 | that's my special gift —/Concocting a toothsome meal out of nothing./Any scraps you |

TOP (2)

| 516 CC | Colby | 11 | I had no chance of getting to the top —/That is, to become the organist of a |
| 538 ES | Gomez | 36 | /That should have led you to the very top!/And yet you withdrew from the world of |

TOPIC (1)

| 548 ES | Carghil | 27 | you were coming here —/It's been the topic of conversation./But I couldn't believe |

TOPPED (1)

| 562 ES | Carghil | 26 | since the name of Maisie Montjoy/Topped the bill in revue. Now I'm Mrs. John |

TOPPLING (1)

| 588 Fable | | 50 | both legs/With difficulty kept from toppling over,/Next came a viand made of turtle |

TORCH (1)

| 256 MC | Chorus | 32 | that pokes at the door?/{C} Does the torch flame in the hall, the candle in the room?/ |

TORCHBEARER (1)

| 129 Cor2 State | | 31 | successively by the flare/Of a sweaty torchbearer, yawning./O hidden under the... |

TORCHLIGHT (1)

| 72 WL: Thund | | 322 | /What the Thunder said/After the torchlight red on sweaty faces/After the frosty |

TORMENT (9)

92 Ash-Wed 2		35	/Where all loves end/Terminate torment/Of love unsatisfied/The greater torment
92 Ash-Wed 2		37	/Of love unsatisfied/The greater torment/Of love satisfied/End of the endless/
160 Rock 7		2	their various ways, they struggled in torment towards GOD/Blindly and vainly, for
187 FQ: DrySal		114	by the currents of action,/But the torment of others remains an experience/
196 FQ: Little		209	fire by fire./Who then devised the torment? Love./Love is the unfamiliar Name/
255 MC	Tempt4	15	is fixed,/Your persecutors, in timeless torment,/Parched passion, beyond expiation./
255 MC	Thomas	32	/Mean present vanity and future torment./Can sinful pride be driven out/Only by
309 FR	Harry	7	have seen to that: it is part of the torment./{M} If you think I am incapable of
525 ES	Charles	39	a hypnotist./{C} Is this a time to torment me? But I'm selfish/In saying that,

TORMENTED (1)

| 569 ES | Ld Clav | 37 | the living persons/Whose ghosts tormented me, to be only human beings,/ |

TORMENTING (1)

| 526 ES | Charles | 1 | that, because I think —/I think you're tormenting yourself as well./{M} You're right. I |

TORN (12)

24 Rhapsody		20	/You see the border of her dress/Is torn and stained with sand,/And you see the
34 Figlia		11	have left/As the soul leaves the body torn and bruised,/As the mind deserts the body
91 Ash-Wed 2		27	/Lady of silences/Calm and distressed/Torn and most whole/Rose of memory/Rose of

96	Ash-Wed 5	22	thee and oppose thee,/Those who are torn on the horn between season and season,
184	FQ: DrySal	22	anemone./It tosses up our losses, the torn seine,/The shattered lobsterpot, the broken
212	Growltiger	6	not calculate to please;/His coat was torn and seedy, he was baggy at the knees;/One
596	When we	4	/The gentle fingers of the breeze/Had torn no quivering cobweb down./The hedgerow
244	MC Chorus	23	none understands,/And our hearts are torn from us, our brains unskinned like the
257	MC Chorus	16	seen the young man mutilated,/The torn girl trembling by the mill-stream./And
267	MC Thomas	15	worn/Carefully, so it get not soiled or torn./Have you something to say?/{K1} By the
270	MC Chorus	27	Archbishop, have consented./Am torn away, subdued, violated,/United to the
316	FR Chorus	1	the family picnic on the moors. Have torn/The roof from the house, or perhaps it was

TORNQUIST (1)
| 37 | Gerontion | 27 | among the Titians;/By Madame de Tornquist, in the dark room/Shifting the |

TORPID (2)
| 111 | Xmas Trees | 3 | we may disregard:/The social, the torpid, the patently commercial,/The rowdy (the |
| 174 | FQ: BurntN | 112 | souls/Into the faded air, the torpid/Driven on the wind that sweeps the |

TORTOISE (1)
| 151 | Rock 2 | 7 | like a lantern set on the back of a tortoise./And some say: 'How can we love our |

TORTUOUS (1)
| 592 | Grad 4 | 1 | more be traced./Although the path be tortuous and slow,/Although it bristle with a |

TORTURE (3)
257	MC Chorus	8	expect./We know of oppression and torture,/We know of extortion and violence,/
261	MC Thomas	3	to suffer by land/and sea, to know torture, imprisonment, disappointment, to
331	FR Harry	11	/A misery long forgotten, and a new torture,/The shadow of something behind our

TORTURING (1)
| 527 | ES Charles | 15 | {C} Don't you understand that you're torturing me?/How long will you be imprisoned, |

TOSS (1)
| 27 | Morning | 5 | at area gates./The brown waves of fog toss up to me/Twisted faces from the bottom of |

TOSSED (2)
| 22 | Preludes | 24 | /In a thousand furnished rooms./You tossed a blanket from the bed,/You lay upon |
| 578 | ES Michael | 28 | snatched a book away from you/And tossed it into the fire. How I laughed!/You |

TOSSES (2)
| 184 | FQ: DrySal | 17 | which it reaches, the beaches where it tosses/Its hints of earlier and other creation:/ |
| 184 | FQ: DrySal | 22 | delicate algae and the sea anemone./It tosses up our losses, the torn seine,/The |

TOTAL (2)
| 405 | CP Reilly | 2 | that my patients/Are only pieces of a total situation/Which I have to explore. The |
| 490 | CC Colby | 15 | numb./If there's agony, it's part of a total agony/Which I can't begin to feel yet. I'm |

TOTTERY (1)
| 221 | Old Deut | 46 | /Ho! hi!/Oh, my eye!/My legs may be tottery, I must go slow/And be careful of Old |

TOUCH (22)
18	Portrait	12	/Some two or three, who will not touch the bloom/That is rubbed and questioned
38	Gerontion	59	my sight, smell, hearing, taste and touch:/How should I use them for your closer
117	SP Dusty	21	can do./{Du} Yes I know you've a touch with the cards/What comes next?/{Do}
166	Rock 10	20	the less;/The eastern light our spires touch at morning,/The light that slants upon
275	MC Thomas	11	/Whether layman or clerk, shall you touch./This I forbid./{4K} Traitor! traitor!
275	MC Chorus	24	I wander in a land of dry stones: if I touch them they bleed./How how can I ever
307	FR Mary	22	lived in another world, which did not touch me./Just now, I find them very difficult to
362	CP Reilly	21	of personality;/Or rather, you've lost touch with the person/You thought you were.
376	CP Julia	30	all about it./{J} But you mustn't touch it./{E} Of course I shan't touch it./{J} My
376	CP Edward	31	touch it./{E} Of course I shan't touch it./{J} My dear, I should have warned
388	CP Peter	3	/{P} Why, it's a man Alex put me in touch with/And we settled everything this
397	CP Edward	2	/And I could not open it. I could not touch the handle./Why could I not walk out of
398	CP Edward	9	as I felt sure./In a moment, at your touch, there is nothing but ruin./O God, what
456	CC Eggers	17	But she has one trait that I think I did touch on:/She's very absent-minded./{C} I hope
492	CC Colby	16	me:/At the moment, I never want to touch it again./But there's another reason. I
496	CC Eggers	23	such a countryman!/You're losing touch with public affairs.'/The fact is, she misses
510	CC Eggers	35	/By putting your adoptive parents in touch/With Mrs. Guzzard. It's for them to
534	ES Gomez	35	is like!/I said to my boys: 'Never touch politics./Stay out of politics, and play
553	ES Carghil	13	my soul —/Pawed it, perhaps, and the touch still lingers./And I've touched yours./It's
563	ES Gomez	35	a pity, Señor Gomez./{G} I lost touch with things in England./Had I been in
569	ES Ld Clav	31	company/I'm afraid the law can't touch them./{C} Then why should you submit?/
580	ES Carghil	24	other again,/We must always keep in touch. But you'd better rest now./You're

TOUCHED (6)
68	WL: Fire S	225	spread/Her drying combinations touched by the sun's last rays,/On the divan are
195	FQ: Little	175	/But some of peculiar genius,/All touched by a common genius,/United in the
448	CC Eggers	11	to tell the truth, Sir Claude, I only touched on these matters,/They're much too
538	ES Ld Clav	32	of following your career./{LC} I am touched by your interest./{G} I have a gift for

553 ES	Carghil	12	.../Now, don't get alarmed. But you touched my soul —/Pawed it, perhaps, and the
553 ES	Carghil	14	and the touch still lingers./And I've touched yours./It's frightening to think that

TOUGH (3)

142 Cape Ann		12	end, resign it/To its true owner, the tough one, the sea-gull./The palaver is finished./
357 CP	Julia	22	called away again./I understand these tough old women —/I'm one myself. I feel as if
454 CC	Kaghan	9	/Or she'll exploit it. You have to be tough with her;/She's hard as nails. Now I'll

TOUGHER (1)

381 CP	Edward	36	in the end/With the obstinate, the tougher self; who does not speak,/Who never

TOUJOURS (1)

47 Mél Adult		13	Au grand air de Bergsteigleben;/J'erre toujours de-ci de-là/A divers coups de tra là là/

TOULOUSE (1)

258 MC Thomas		21	and waged war with him against Toulouse,/I beat the barons at their own game.

TOUR (2)

427 CP	Alex	30	/Three of us have been out on a tour of inspection/Of local conditions./{J} What
489 CC	Claude	27	/My father had sent me on a business tour/To learn about his overseas investments./

TOUR (1) [*Foreign word*]

75 WL: Thund		429	swallow/*Le Prince d'Aquitaine à la tour abolie*/These fragments I have shored against

TOURIST (1)

300 FRDowning		27	/You see, Sir, I was down in the Tourist,/And I took a bit of air before I went to

TOURNOIE (1)

48 Lune Miel		10	amateurs/De chapitaux d'acanthe que tournoie le vent./Ils vont prendre le train de huit

TOURS (1)

46 Directeur		12	/Bras dessus bras dessous/Font des tours/A pas de loup./Dans un égout/Une petite

TOUT (2)

47 Mél Adult		t	crève d'amour./Mélange Adultère de Tout/En Amérique, professeur;/En Angleterre,
48 Lune Miel		6	les genoux/De quatre jambes molles tout gonflées de morsures./On relève le drap

TOUTE (1)

51 Restaurant		11	ans, elle était plus petite./Elle était toute mouillée, je lui ai donné des primevères.'/

TOWARD (5)

16 Prufrock		108	or throwing off a shawl,/And turning toward the window, should say:/'That is not it
56 Swee Night		6	of the stormy moon/Slide westward toward the River Plate,/Death and the Raven
597 Before Mor		2	/The flowers at the window turned toward dawn,/Petal on petal, waiting for the
601 Nocturne		11	smiles; in my best mode oblique/Rolls toward the moon a frenzied eye profound,/(No
310 FR	Mary	27	spirit/Compelled to be reborn/To rise toward the violent sun/Wet wings into the rain

TOWARDS (27)

15 Prufrock		93	the universe into a ball/To roll it towards some overwhelming question,/To say:
24 Rhapsody		17	'Regard that woman/Who hesitates towards you in the light of the door/Which
89 Ash-Wed 1		5	scope/I no longer strive to strive towards such things/(Why should the agèd eagle
98 Ash-Wed 6		8	these things/From the wide window towards the granite shore/The white sails still fly
105 Song Sime		7	corners/Wait for the wind that chills towards the dead land./Grant us thy peace./I
110 Marina		33	seas what shores what granite islands towards my timbers/And woodthrush calling
111 Xmas Trees		1	Trees/There are several attitudes towards Christmas,/Some of which we may
151 Rock 2		6	palms of their hands, or look in vain towards foreign lands for alms to be more or
160 Rock 7		2	ways, they struggled in torment towards GOD/Blindly and vainly, for man is a
160 Rock 7		8	of the water./And men who turned towards the light and were known of the light/
171 FQ: BurntN		13	the passage which we did not take/Towards the door we never opened/Into the
173 FQ: BurntN		65	flesh nor fleshless;/Neither from nor towards; at the still point, there the dance is,/
173 FQ: BurntN		67	Neither movement from nor towards,/Neither ascent nor decline. Except for
187 FQ: DrySal		105	half-look/Over the shoulder, towards the primitive terror./Now, we come to
191 FQ: Little		2	season/Sempiternal though sodden towards sundown,/Suspended in time, between
193 FQ: Little		89	loitering and hurried/As if blown towards me like the metal leaves/Before the
239 MC Chorus		3	of safety, that draws our feet/Towards the cathedral? What danger can be/
239 MC Chorus		8	to witness, has forced our feet/Towards the cathedral. We are forced to bear
268 MC Thomas		33	whom redounds/Their contempt towards me, their contempt towards the Church
268 MC Thomas		33	contempt towards me, their contempt towards the Church shown./{K1} Be that as it
333 FR	Harry	17	meaningless before./Everything tends towards reconciliation/As the stone falls, as the
409 CP	Reilly	38	had to face the fact that his feelings towards her/Were different from any you had
416 CP	Celia	4	rid of — but of emptiness, of failure/Towards someone, or something, outside of
416 CP	Reilly	35	Compassion may be already a clue/Towards finding your own way out of the
418 CP	Reilly	28	will journey blind. But the way leads towards possession/Of what you have sought
517 CC	Colby	10	if I accepted that/I should be guilty towards you. I like you too much./You've
572 ES	Ld Clav	38	Monica:/That is the first step taken towards my freedom,/And perhaps the most

TOWELLED (1)

43 Swee Erect		41	the house no sort of good./But Doris, towelled from the bath,/Enters padding on

TOWER (1)
161 Rock 7	30	Dialectic./The Church disowned, the tower overthrown, the bells upturned, what

TOWERS (3)
70 WL: Fire S	289	down stream/The peal of bells/White towers/Weialala leia/Wallala leialala,/'Trams
73 WL: Thund	373	and bursts in the violet air/Falling towers/Jerusalem Athens Alexandria/Vienna
73 WL: Thund	382	wall/And upside down in air were towers/Tolling reminiscent bells, that kept the

TOWN (11)
45 Cook Egg	28	are creeping/From Kentish Town and Golder's Green;/Where are the eagles
119 SP Krum	24	been here before/{Kr} We hit this town last night for the first time/{Kl} And I
148 Rock 1	36	/In country or in suburb; and in the town/Only for important weddings./CHORUS
193 FQ: Little	73	of earth./Water and fire succeed/The town, the pasture and the weed./Water and fire
230 Bust Jones	t	Fell.'/Bustopher Jones: the Cat About Town/Bustopher Jones is *not* skin and bones —
234 Ad-dress	26	freaks./The usual Dog about the Town/Is much inclined to play the clown,/And
291 FR Amy	23	that you are at Wishwood,/Not in town, where you have to close the blinds./There
347 FR Ivy	19	/{I} 'Regret delayed business in town many happy returns see you tomorrow
364 CP Julia	34	/I've been dragging Peter all over town/Looking for them everywhere I've been./
414 CP Celia	16	they can't afford to have a place in town./It's all they can do to keep the country
461 CC Eggers	7	out in the garden./And I'll slip up to town any day, if you want me./In fact, Mrs. E.

TOWNS (1)
103 Journ Magi	14	shelters,/And the cities hostile and the towns unfriendly/And the villages dirty and

TOY (1)
24 Rhapsody	39	/Slipped out and pocketed a toy that was running along the quay,/I could see

TOYS (1)
107 Animula	5	or falling, grasping at kisses and toys,/Advancing boldly, sudden to take alarm,/

TRA (1)
47 Mél Adult	14	toujours de-ci de-là/A divers coups de tra là là/De Damas jusqu'à Omaha./Je célébrai

TRACE (3)
498 CC Claude	32	Elizabeth,/Whom we must try to trace./{E} If there was another child/Then we
498 CC Eggers	34	another child/Then we must try to trace it. Certainly, Sir Claude:/Our first step
508 CC Guzzard	32	one./Perhaps it might be possible to trace them./The name was Kaghan./{SC} Their

TRACED (1)
592 Grad 3	6	/Until their passing may no more be traced./Although the path be tortuous and slow,

TRACES (1)
434 CP Alex	20	her body,/Or at least, they found the traces of it./{E} But before that .../{A} It was

TRACI (2)
276 MC Knight1	32	in/the country: Baron William de Traci./{K3} I am afraid I am not anything like
277 MC Knight1	28	think we will all agree that William de Traci has/spoken well and has made a very

TRACING (1)
449 CC Claude	4	father is dead, and there's no way of tracing it./Yes, I was thinking of her missing

TRADES (1)
39 Gerontion	72	claims,/And an old man driven by the Trades/To a sleepy corner./Tenants of the

TRADESMAN'S (1)
266 MC Knights	19	the ring./This is the man who was the tradesman's son: the backstairs brat who was

TRADITIONS (1)
277 MC Knight3	12	been brought up in good Church traditions. So if/we seemed a bit rowdy, you will

TRAFFIC (4)
155 Rock 3	39	/A thousand policemen directing the traffic/Cannot tell you why you come or where
189 FQ: DrySal	176	/Those concerned with every lawful traffic/And those who conduct them./Repeat a
223 Pekes Pols	47	bold heroes together assembled,/The traffic all stopped, and the Underground
496 CC Eggers	31	/Every time I come, I notice the traffic/Has got so much worse./{SC} Yes, it's

TRAGEDY (1)
189 FQ: DrySal	193	from the wrinkles of the palm/And tragedy from fingers; release omens/By

TRAIL (1)
16 Prufrock	102	after the teacups, after the skirts that trail along the floor —/And this, and so much

TRAILING (1)
185 FQ: DrySal	57	/There is no end, but addition: the trailing/Consequence of further days and hours,

TRAIN (13)
48 Lune Miel	11	tournoie le vent./Ils vont prendre le train de huit heures/Prolonger leurs misères de
180 FQ: ECoker	119	away —/Or as, when an underground train, in the tube, stops too long between
187 FQ: DrySal	134	patient is no longer here./When the train starts, and the passengers are settled/To
232 Skimble	4	the thimble?/We must find him or the train can't start.'/All the guards and all the
233 Skimble	50	Railway Cat,/The Cat of the Railway Train!/In the watches of the night he is always
233 Skimble	66	Mail/The Cat of the Railway Train.'/The Ad-dressing of Cats/You've read of
247 MC Thomas	26	again/I am your man./{T} Not in this train/Look to your behaviour. You were safer/
327 FR Ivy	32	use of his car,/And he missed the last train, so he's coming up tomorrow;/And he said

361 CP	Reilly	31	genie out of the bottle./It is to start a train of events/Beyond your control. So let me
428 CP	Julia	5	/And I had to travel in a very slow train/And in a *couchette*. She was very angry/
458 CC	Lady E	24	her sea-sick;/So we took the night train, and did the Channel crossing./But who is
530 ES	Ld Clav	13	the last thing he wants is to take a train for anywhere!/No, I've not the slightest
530 ES	Ld Clav	22	on a branch line,/After the last train, after all the other passengers/Have left,

TRAINED (2)

229 Gus		45	'Now, these kittens, they do not get trained/As we did in the days when Victoria
546 ES	Piggott	3	—/A widow in fact. But I was a Trained Nurse,/And of course I've always lived

TRAINING (3)

334 FR	Harry	24	One had that part to play./After such training, I could endure, these ten years,/Playing
344 FR	Gerald	18	you have to go in for some sort of training;/The medical knowledge is the first
508 CC	Lady E	11	that you, Eggerson, with your legal training,/Should talk about straws! Colby is my

TRAINS (2)

123 SA	Kl & Kr	17	*what to do/We won't have to catch any trains/And we won't go home when it rains/We'll*
530 ES	Ld Clav	12	like telling a man he mustn't run for trains/When the last thing he wants is to take a

TRAIT (1)

456 CC	Eggers	17	said, 'humour her.'/But she has one trait that I think I did touch on:/She's very

TRAITOR (11)

269 MC	Knights	18	treachery and treason./{3K} Priest! traitor, confirmed in malfeasance./{T} I submit
274 MC	Knights	16	Force him./{4K} Where is Becket, the traitor to the King?/Where is Becket, the
274 MC	Thomas	31	should be without fear./I am here./No traitor to the King. I am a priest,/A Christian,
275 MC	Knights	13	shall you touch./This I forbid./{4K} Traitor! traitor! traitor!/{T} You, Reginald,
275 MC	Knights	13	touch./This I forbid./{4K} Traitor! traitor! traitor!/{T} You, Reginald, three times
275 MC	Knights	13	/This I forbid./{4K} Traitor! traitor! traitor!/{T} You, Reginald, three times traitor
275 MC	Thomas	14	/{T} You, Reginald, three times traitor you:/Traitor to me as my temporal
275 MC	Thomas	15	Reginald, three times traitor you:/Traitor to me as my temporal vassal,/Traitor to
275 MC	Thomas	16	/Traitor to me as my temporal vassal,/Traitor to me as your spiritual lord,/Traitor to
275 MC	Thomas	17	/Traitor to me as your spiritual lord,/Traitor to God in desecrating His Church./{K1}
278 MC	Knight2	35	and execute him/formally as a traitor, and no one would have to bear the

TRAMP (1)

280 MC	Priest3	31	of pain within the skull/You still shall tramp and tread one endless round/Of thought,

TRAMPLE (1)

281 MC	Chorus	21	not depart from it/Though armies trample over it, though sightseers come with

TRAMPLED (2)

23 Preludes		41	/That fade behind a city block,/Or trampled by insistent feet/At four and five and
27 Morning		2	in basement kitchens,/And along the trampled edges of the street/I am aware of the

TRAMS (1)

70 WL: Fire S		292	towers/Weialala leia/Wallala leialala/'Trams and dusty trees./Highbury bore me.

TRANCE (2)

19 Portrait		36	/— Let us take the air, in a tobacco trance,/Admire the monuments,/Discuss the late
21 Portrait		113	ape./Let us take the air, in a tobacco trance —/Well! and what if she should die some

TRANCES (1)

44 Cook Egg		23	will instruct me/In the Seven Sacred Trances;/Piccarda de Donati will conduct me./

TRANQUIL (1)

599 On a Port		5	evening in the room alone./Not like a tranquil carved goddess of stone/But

TRANQUILLITY (2)

279 MC	Knight4	20	give it the unity, the stability, order, tranquillity,/and justice that it so badly needed.
370 CP	Peter	12	very strange. There was such ... tranquillity .../{E} And what interrupted this

TRANSACTS (1)

268 MC	Knight3	11	faithful servants, every one who transacts/His business in his absence, the

TRANSCRIPT (4)

28 Boston ET		t	of the roofs./The Boston Evening Transcript/The readers of the *Boston Evening*
28 Boston ET		1	/The readers of the *Boston Evening Transcript*/Sway in the wind like a field of ripe
28 Boston ET		5	to others bringing the *Boston Evening Transcript,*/I mount the steps and ring the bell,
28 Boston ET		9	Harriet, here is the *Boston Evening Transcript.*'/Aunt Helen/Miss Helen Slingsby

TRANSECTING (1)

160 Rock 7		19	but in time, in what we call history: transecting, bisecting the world of time, a

TRANSFIGURED (2)

195 FQ: Little		167	loved them,/To become renewed, transfigured, in another pattern./Sin is
465 CC	Claude	22	am transported — a different person,/Transfigured in the vision of some marvellous

TRANSGRESSIONS (1)

268 MC	Knight3	3	And burying the memory of your transgressions/Restored your honours and your

TRANSHUMANISED (1)

421 CP	Julia	18	the process by which the human is/Transhumanised: what do we know/Of the kind

TRANSIENT (2)
173 FQ: BurntN   97   lucid stillness/Turning shadow into transient beauty/With slow rotation suggesting
202 War Poetry   21   enduring is not a substitute for the transient,/Neither one for the other. But the
TRANSIT (1)
98 Ash-Wed 6   5   the profit and the loss/In this brief transit where the dreams cross/The
TRANSITORY (2)
89 Ash-Wed 1   13   I shall not know/The one veritable transitory power/Because I cannot drink/There,
191 FQ: Little   15   /Is blanched for an hour with transitory blossom/Of snow, a bloom more
TRANSLATED (1)
602 Humoresque   12   /His who-the-devil-are-you stare;/Translated, maybe, to the moon./With Limbo's
TRANSLATING (1)
464 CC   Colby   22   time you've been speaking, I've been translating/Into terms of music. But may I ask,/
TRANSMIT (2)
18 Portrait   9   let us say, to hear the latest Pole/Transmit the Preludes, through his hair and
494 CC   Claude 19   an inspiration. What he wanted to transmit to me/Was that idea, that inspiration,/
TRANSPARENT (3)
329 FR   Chorus 14   of stifled sorrow/The whisper, the transparent deception/The keeping up of
436 CP   Reilly 34   Mrs. Chamberlayne, I must be very transparent/Or else you are very perceptive./{J}
440 CP   Lavinia 24   always looks her best. You're rather transparent,/You know, when you're trying to
TRANSPORTED (1)
465 CC   Claude 21   me. There are occasions/When I am transported — a different person,/Transfigured
TRAP (11)
253 MC   Tempt4 12   you have to lend./You would wait for trap to snap/Having served your turn, broken
319 FR   Harry   35   night, when she kissed me,/I felt the trap close. If you won't tell me,/I must ask
375 CP   Celia   6   /Do you mean to say that she's laid a trap for us?/{E} No. If there is a trap, we are all
375 CP   Edward   7   laid a trap for us?/{E} No. If there is a trap, we are all in the trap,/We have set it for
375 CP   Edward   7   No. If there is a trap, we are all in the trap,/We have set it for ourselves. But I do not
375 CP   Edward   9   But I do not know/What kind of a trap it is./{C} Then what has happened? {}/[*The*
395 CP   Edward 37   /{E} So here we are again. Back in the trap,/With only one difference, perhaps — we
401 CP   Edward 25   Oh yes, I had seen her./{E} So this *is* a trap!/{R} Let's not call it a trap./But if it is a
401 CP   Reilly 26   So this *is* a trap!/{R} Let's not call it a trap./But if it is a trap, then you cannot escape
401 CP   Reilly 27   Let's not call it a trap./But if it is a trap, then you cannot escape from it:/And so ...
428 CP   Alex   20   naturally, take a different view./They trap the monkeys. And they eat them./The
TRAVAIL (1)
165 Rock 9   39   the work of creation is never without travail;/The formed stone, the visible crucifix,/
TRAVEL (6)
103 Journ Magi   17   had of it./At the end we preferred to travel all night,/Sleeping in snatches,/With the
154 Rock 3   29   from the South/Whence thousands travel daily to the timekept City;/Where My
309 FR   Harry 29   {H} I have spent many years in useless travel;/You have staid in England, yet you seem
428 CP   Julia   5   my ticket to Mentone/And I had to travel in a very slow train/And in a *couchette.*
456 CC   Eggers 24   does forget things. And she likes to travel,/Mostly for her health. And when she's
456 CC   Eggers 32   'now we've settled down/All the travel *I* want is up to the City/And back to
TRAVELERS (1)
587 Fable   6   by some Norman/Who levied on all travelers his tax;/Nearby this hamlet was a
TRAVELLED (1)
212 Growltiger   1   was a Bravo Cat, who travelled on a barge:/In fact he was the roughest
TRAVELLER (3)
205 de la Mare   23   maiden aunts;/When the nocturnal traveller can arouse/No sleeper by his call; or
256 MC   Priests 27   /Abide the coming of day, when the traveller may find his way,/The sailor lay course
458 CC   Lady E 18   /You know I'm a very experienced traveller./{SC} Oh yes, of course we know that,
TRAVELLERS (4)
33 Conv Gal   5   lantern hung aloft/To light poor travellers to their distress.'/She then: 'How you
188 FQ: DrySal   139   of a hundred hours./Fare forward, travellers! not escaping from the past/Into
232 Skimble   22   and examines all the faces/Of the travellers in the First and in the Third;/He
422 CP   Reilly 19   go upon a journey./{R} Protector of travellers/Bless the road./{A} Watch over her in
TRAVELLING (2)
328 FR   Charles 23   being pursued by a patrol, and was/travelling at the rate of 66 miles an hour. When
372 CP   Alex   12   out of nothing!/Never, even when travelling in Albania,/Have I made such a
TRAVELS (1)
456 CC   Eggers 35   that was only the beginning of my travels!/It's been a very unusual privilege/To see
TRAVERSÉ (1)
48 Lune Miel   15   son bilan./Ils auront vu la Suisse et traversé la France./Et Saint Apollinaire, raide et
TRAVERSED (1)
279 MC   Knight4 18   very briefly, to go over/the ground traversed by the last speaker. While the late

TRAVESTY (1)
488 CC   Claude   29   one had planned for,/And yet such a travesty of all one's plans —/I'd hoped that you
TRAWLER (1)
201 Def Island   8   /ships — battleship, merchantman, trawler —/contributing their share to the ages'
TRAY (7)
107 Animula   12   /And running stags around a silver tray;/Confounds the actual and the fanciful,/
355 CP   m 27   at home. {}/[EDWARD *returns with a tray*]/{J} Edward, give me another of those
377 CP   m 19   {}/[*Re-enter* JULIA, *in apron, with a tray and three glasses*]/{J} I've had an
422 CP   Reilly   *telephone*]/{R} You may bring the tray in now, Miss Barraway. {}/[*Enter* ALEX]/
422 CP   1m 11 [NURSE-SECRETARY *enters with a tray, a decanter and three glasses, and*/*exit*.
425 CP   Lavinia   29   the man won't be able to take the tray about,/So they'll go away again. Anyway,
535 ES   m 19   LAMBERT *enters silently, deposits tray and exit*]/{LC} Won't you help yourself? {}/
TREACHERIES (1)
252 MC   Thomas   21   of a wolf among wolves?/Pursue your treacheries as you have done before:/No one
TREACHEROUS (1)
547 ES   Piggott   6   /This early warm weather can be very treacherous./There, now you look more comfy.
TREACHERY (4)
152 Rock 2   29   of GOD,/For pride, for lechery, treachery, for every act of sin./And of all that
163 Rock 8   36   faith of many./Not avarice, lechery, treachery,/Envy, sloth, gluttony, jealousy, pride:
269 MC Knight3   17   knife./{K3} Priest, you have spoken treachery and treason./{3K} Priest! traitor,
420 CP   Reilly   30   /It's not the knowledge of the mutual treachery/But the knowledge that the other
TREAD (5)
605 Narcissus   19   he walked in city streets/He seemed to tread on faces, convulsive thighs and knees./So
280 MC   Priest3   31   the skull/You still shall tramp and tread one endless round/Of thought, to justify
382 CP   Celia   21   it than what comes out/When you tread on a beetle./{E} Perhaps that is what I am.
382 CP   Edward   23   beetle./{E} Perhaps that is what I am./Tread on me, if you like./{C} No, I won't tread
382 CP   Celia   24   on me, if you like./{C} No, I won't tread on you./That is not what you are. It is
TREASON (3)
246 MC   Thomas   12   for the King's name, warning against treason,/Made them hold their hands. So for the
258 MC   Thomas   5   /The last temptation is the greatest treason:/To do the right deed for the wrong
269 MC Knight3   17   Priest, you have spoken treachery and treason./{3K} Priest! traitor, confirmed in
TREASURE (2)
337 FR   Agatha   10   for./Think of it as like a children's treasure hunt:/Here you have found a clue,
416 CP   Celia   38   with the inconsolable memory/Of the treasure I went into the forest to find/And never
TREASURE-TROVE (1)
204 de la Mare   8   —/The guardians of some long-lost treasure-trove)/Recount their exploits at the
TREAT (8)
235 Ad-dress   53   /Before a Cat will condescend/To treat you as a trusted friend,/Some little token
324 FR Warburt   1   you do, I must decline to continue to treat you./You are only delaying me. I shall
372 CP   Alex   9 Oh, Edward! I've prepared you such a treat!/I really think that of all my triumphs/This
385 CP   Reilly   18   You would find it difficult/To treat them as strangers, but still more difficult/
394 CP   Lavinia   20   /You wanted something else. I shall treat you very differently/In future./{E} Thank
404 CP   Reilly   37   say, a long journey./But before I treat a patient like yourself/I need to know a
416 CP   Celia   6   ... *atone* — is that the word?/Can you treat a patient for such a state of mind?/{R}
461 CC   Eggers   19   /When the garden will really be a treat to look at.'/Well, I'll be going./{SC}
TREATMENT (5)
413 CP   Reilly   9   And after that, the prologue to my treatment/Is to try to show them that they are
417 CP   Reilly   21   condition is curable./But the form of treatment must be your own choice:/I cannot
458 CC   Lady E   22   Deverell./She's been having the treatment with me,/And she can't go by air —
458 CC   Claude   33   want to bother you, during your treatment .../{E} And Mr. Simpkins is much
460 CC   Lady E   18   persuade you/To have a course of treatment with Dr. Rebmann —/No, at your
TREATS (1)
306 FR   Mary   35   things were laid out ready,/And the treats were always so carefully prepared;/There
TREATY'S (1)
226 Macavity   27   /And when the Foreign Office find a Treaty's gone astray,/Or the Admiralty lose
TREBLE (1)
329 FR   Chorus   5   projects them into the future./The treble voices on the lawn/The mowing of hay in
TREE (44)
38 Gerontion   47   are shaken from the wrath-bearing tree./The tiger springs in the new year. Us he
61 WL: Burial   23   where the sun beats,/And the dead tree gives no shelter, the cricket no relief,/And
83 Hollow Men   24   on a broken column/There, is a tree swinging/And voices are/In the wind's
92 Ash-Wed 2   50   did little good to each other,/Under a tree in the cool of the day, with the blessing of
107 Animula   9   fragrant brilliance of the Christmas tree,/Pleasure in the wind, the sunlight and the
111 Xmas Trees   7   its wings at the summit of the tree/Is not only a decoration, but an angel./The
111 Xmas Trees   9   /The child wonders at the Christmas Tree:/Let him continue in the spirit of wonder/

111 Xmas Trees	13	/Of the first-remembered Christmas Tree,/So that the surprises, delight in new
122 SAWa & Ho	17	/*Bamboo bamboo/Under the bamboo tree/Two live as one/One live as two/Two live as*
122 SAWa & Ho	23	*bam/Under the boo/Under the bamboo tree./Where the breadfruit fall/And the penguin*
122 SAWa & Ho	29	*bam/Under the boo/Under the bamboo tree/Where the Gauguin maids/In the banyan*
122 SAWa & Ho	35	*bam/Under the boo/Under the bamboo tree./Tell me in what part of the wood/Do you*
123 SAWa & Ho	4	*banyan, palmleaf/Or under the bamboo tree?/Any old tree will do for me/Any old wood is*
123 SAWa & Ho	5	*/Or under the bamboo tree?/Any old tree will do for me/Any old wood is just as good/*
129 Cor2 State	33	the upper branches of noon's widest tree/Under the breast feather stirred by the
135 5FingerEx2	1	*Terrier*/In a brown field stood a tree/And the tree was crookt and dry./In a black
135 5FingerEx2	2	/In a brown field stood a tree/And the tree was crookt and dry./In a black sky, from a
135 5FingerEx2	9	field was cracked and brown/And the tree was cramped and dry./Pollicle dogs and
143 Lines OM	6	blood/Or dangling from the friendly tree./When I lay bare the tooth of wit/The
172 FQ: BurntN	57	drift of stars/Ascend to summer in the tree/We move above the moving tree/In light
172 FQ: BurntN	58	the tree/We move above the moving tree/In light upon the figured leaf/And hear
204 de la Mare	7	/And shadowy lemurs glide from tree to tree —/The guardians of some long-lost
204 de la Mare	7	shadowy lemurs glide from tree to tree —/The guardians of some long-lost
600 Moonflower	4	a snowy owl,/Slips from the alder tree./Whiter the flowers, Love, you hold,/Than
605 Narcissus	21	/First he was sure that he had been a tree,/Twisting its branches among each other/
256 MC Chorus	8	light from a cloud on a withered tree? The earth is heaving to parturition of issue
258 MC Thomas	13	/The purple bullfinch in the lilac tree,/The tiltyard skill, the strategy of chess,/
263 MC Chorus	21	song./When the leaf is out on the tree, when the elder and may/Burst over the
263 MC Chorus	25	/Shall the bird's song cover, the green tree cover, what wrong/Shall the fresh earth
273 MC Chorus	4	me, in my most need?/Dead upon the tree, my Saviour,/Let not be in vain Thy labour;
307 FR Mary	1	do you remember/{M} The hollow tree in what we called the wilderness/{H} Down
307 FR Harry	16	place. The wilderness was gone,/The tree had been felled, and a neat summer-house/
307 FR Harry	19	of freedom/Should be a hollow tree in a wood by the river./{M} But when I was
308 FR Harry	22	Isn't that all folly? It's like the hollow tree,/Not there./{M} But surely, what you say/
310 FR Mary	23	birth/Is the season of sacrifice/For the tree and the beast, and the fish/Thrashing itself
325 FR Ivy	30	one to fall off the pony,/Or out of a tree — and always on his head./{V} But a year
333 FR Harry	18	/As the stone falls, as the tree falls. And in the end/That is the completion
336 FR Agatha	32	an accidental bed/Or under an elder tree/According to the phase/Of the determined
353 CP Julia	3	{J} Then what were you doing, up in a tree:/You and the Maharaja?/{A} My dear Julia!
555 ES Monica	27	nerves have been./He only ran into a tree./{LC} Yes, a tree./It might have been a
555 ES Ld Clav	28	/He only ran into a tree./{LC} Yes, a tree./It might have been a man. But it can't be
568 ES Ld Clav	1	away. Standing under the great beech tree./{M} Why under the beech tree?/{LC} I feel
568 ES Monica	2	beech tree./{M} Why under the beech tree?/{LC} I feel drawn to that spot./No matter.
583 ES Monica	16	to return to us./He is under the beech tree. It is quiet and cold there./In becoming no

TREE (1) [*Proper name*]

228 Gus	16	has acted with Irving, he's acted with Tree./And he likes to relate his success on the

TREES (17)

70 WL: Fire S	292	leia/Wallala leialala/'Trams and dusty trees./Highbury bore me. Richmond and Kew/
73 WL: Thund	356	the hermit-thrush sings in the pine trees/Drip drop drip drop drop drop drop/But
89 Ash-Wed 1	15	/Because I cannot drink/There, where trees flower, and springs flow, for there is
97 Ash-Wed 5	30	veiled sister between the slender/Yew trees pray for those who offend her/And are
103 Journ Magi	24	beating the darkness,/And three trees on the low sky./And an old white horse
108 Animula	36	the boarhound slain between the yew trees,/Pray for us now and at the hour of our
111 Xmas Trees	t	/The Cultivation of Christmas Trees/There are several attitudes towards
135 5FingerEx1	3	fields of Russell Square./Beneath the trees there is no ease/For the dull brain, the
139 Virginia	7	Still hills/Wait. Gates wait. Purple trees,/White trees, wait, wait,/Delay, decay.
139 Virginia	8	Wait. Gates wait. Purple trees./White trees, wait, wait,/Delay, decay. Living, living,/
160 Rock 7	5	to darkness,/Worshipping snakes or trees, worshipping devils rather than nothing:
180 FQ: ECoker	117	/And we know that the hills and the trees, the distant panorama/And the bold
185 FQ: DrySal	27	on the briar rose,/The fog is in the fir trees./The sea howl/And the sea yelp, are
596 When we	2	hill/No leaves were fallen from the trees;/The gentle fingers of the breeze/Had torn
256 MC Chorus	29	owl that calls, or a signal between the trees?/{3P} Is the window-bar made fast, is the
292 FR Harry	8	corrupted that song./Behind the palm trees in the Grand Hotel/They were always
544 ES Ld Clav	23	often a harbinger of frost on the fruit trees./{M} Oh, let's make the most of this

TREETOPS (1)

245 MC Priest2	6	/You go on croaking like frogs in the treetops:/But frogs at least can be cooked and

TRELLIS (1)

226 Macavity	25	greenhouse glass is broken, and the trellis past repair —/Ay, there's the wonder of

TREMBLED (1)

223 Pekes Pols	47	all stopped, and the Underground trembled,/And some of the neighbours were so

TREMBLING (5)

32	Hysteria	5	muscles. An elderly waiter with trembling hands/was hurriedly spreading a pink
84	Hollow Men	49	alone/At the hour when we are/Trembling with tenderness/Lips that would kiss/
590	Time Space	10	flowers I gave thee when the dew/Was trembling on the vine,/Were withered ere the
590	Space Time	10	flowers I sent thee when the dew/Was trembling on the vine/Were withered ere the
257	MC Chorus	16	young man mutilated,/The torn girl trembling by the mill-stream./And meanwhile

TREMENDOUS (1)

277	MC Knight3	22	of the/way — and personally I had a tremendous admiration for him —/you must

TREMOR (1)

272	MC Thomas	5	the flock shall be spared./I have had a tremor of bliss, a wink of heaven, a whisper,/

TREMPÉS (1)

51	Restaurant	8	bave pas dans la soupe)./'Les saules trempés, et des bourgeons sur les ronces —/

TRENCH (1)

127	Cor1 March	15	/102,000 machine guns,/28,000 trench mortars,/53,000 field and heavy guns,/I

TRENTE-HUIT (1)

51	Restaurant	12	de son gilet montent au chiffre de trente-huit./'Je la chatouillais, pour la faire rire./

TRÈS (1)

51	Restaurant	28	/Un courant de sous-mer l'emporta très loin,/Le repassant aux étapes de sa vie

TRESPASS (1)

282	MC Chorus	12	the love of God./We acknowledge our trespass, our weakness, our fault; we

TRIAL (6)

188	FQ: DrySal	167	and you whose bodies/Will suffer the trial and judgement of the sea,/Or whatever
276	MC Knight1	26	with our long-established/principle of Trial by Jury. I am not myself qualified to/put
517	CC Colby	29	you think that they would give me a trial?/{E} Give you a trial? I'm certain./Good
517	CC Eggers	30	would give me a trial?/{E} Give you a trial? I'm certain./Good organists don't seem to
553	ES Carghil	26	/They would have figured at the trial, I suppose,/If there had been a trial. Don't
553	ES Carghil	27	trial, I suppose,/If there had been a trial. Don't you remember them?/{LC} Vaguely.

TRIBE (1)

194	FQ: Little	129	us/To purify the dialect of the tribe/And urge the mind to aftersight and

TRIBES (1)

428	CP Alex	18	that's not the worst of it./Some of the tribes are Christian converts,/And, naturally,

TRIBULATION (1)

239	MC Chorus	4	the poor women of Canterbury? what tribulation/With which we are not already

TRIBUTES (1)

530	ES Monica	29	/At the farewell banquet, with the tributes from the staff,/The presentation, and

TRICK (2)

224	Mr Mistoff	31	hunting for mice./He can play any trick with a cork/Or a spoon and a bit of
405	CP Edward	29	/I call this a very dishonourable trick./{R} Honesty before honour, Mr.

TRIED (18)

300	FRDowning	4	seemed very anxious about my Lady./Tried to keep her in when the weather was
304	FR Mary	7	wish that I'd taken your advice/And tried for a fellowship, seven years ago./Now I
309	FR Harry	1	have not had your experience./{H} If I tried to explain, you could never understand:/
359	CP Edward	14	for this evening./The fact is, I tried to put off this party:/These were only the
374	CP Edward	4	telephone as soon as I could:/And I tried to get you a short while ago./{C} If there
378	CP Edward	15	have a very clear impression/That he tried to persuade me it was all for the best/That
394	CP Lavinia	7	very sympathetic./{L} Well, but I tried to do something about it./That was why I
394	CP Lavinia	18	I was the butler./{L} Everything I tried only made matters worse,/And the
394	CP Edward	36	my career would be a support./Well, I tried to be accommodating. But, in future,/I
407	CP Reilly	21	pretended/To be consulting me; both, tried to impose upon me/Your own diagnosis,
407	CP Reilly	39	in fact. But you, Mrs. Chamberlayne,/Tried to make me believe that it was this
435	CP Peter	6	Two years ago./{P} Two years ago! I tried to forget about her,/Until I began to think
435	CP Peter	18	ask for./{P} And what a *métier*! I've tried to believe in it/So that I might believe in
476	CC Lucasta	12	/I want to tell you now, why I tried to do that./And it's always succeeded with
494	CC Claude	13	us./{SC} I'm not so sure of that. I've tried to believe in facts;/And I've always acted
517	CC Eggers	33	say that, Mr. Simpkins, until you've tried our organ!/{C} Well, if you could induce
537	ES Gomez	7	done many years ago:/Adoption tried, and grappled to my soul/With hoops of
557	ES Ld Clav	14	business./{LC} I dare say you've tried a little private speculation./{Mi} Several of

TRIES (2)

56	Swee Night	12	seas;/The person in the Spanish cape/Tries to sit on Sweeney's knees/Slips and pulls
240	MC Chorus	2	/The merchant, shy and cautious, tries to compile a little fortune,/And the

TRIFLER (1)

250	MC Tempt3	24	surprise./{T3} Well, my Lord,/I am no trifler, and no politician./To idle or intrigue at

TRIFLES (1)

560	ES Michael	4	why it bothered about such trifles./{LC} So you want me to help you to

TRILL (1)
263 MC Chorus 23 the air is clear and high,/And voices trill at windows, and children tumble in front of
TRILLING (1)
172 FQ: BurntN 51 mud/Clot the bedded axle-tree./The trilling wire in the blood/Sings below inveterate
TRIP (1)
186 FQ: DrySal 79 sails at dockage;/Not as making a trip that will be unpayable/For a haul that will
TRIUMPH (5)
159 Rock 6 7 near a Police Station/To believe in the triumph of violence./Do you think that the
201 Def Island 16 undefeated in defeat,/unalterable in triumph, changing nothing/of their ancestors'
274 MC Thomas 8 unbar the door!/We are not here to triumph by fighting, by stratagem, or by
274 MC Thomas 12 This is the easier victory./Now is the triumph of the Cross, now/Open the door! I
438 CP Reilly 37 /But I am no more responsible for the triumph —/And just as responsible for her
TRIUMPHAL (2)
127 Cor1 March t /KNOCK/KNOCK/Coriolan/Triumphal March/Stone, bronze, stone, steel,
178 FQ: ECoker 60 rolled by the rolling stars/Simulates triumphal cars/Deployed in constellated wars/
TRIUMPHANT (4)
280 MC Priest3 15 the Church is stronger for this action,/Triumphant in adversity. It is fortified/By
319 FR Harry 24 /And the low conversation of triumphant aunts./It is the conversations not
400 CP Alex 19 your usual foresight. Now, he's quite triumphant/Because he thinks he's stolen a
438 CP Reilly 36 /You think her life was wasted. It was triumphant./But I am no more responsible for
TRIUMPHS (1)
372 CP Alex 10 a treat!/I really think that of all my triumphs/This is the greatest. To make
TRIVIAL (2)
94 Ash-Wed 4 5 blue, in Mary's colour,/Talking of trivial things/In ignorance and in knowledge of
307 FR Mary 28 troubles?/They must seem very trivial indeed to you./It's just ordinary
TROD (1)
194 FQ: Little 109 nowhere, no before and after,/We trod the pavement in a dead patrol./I said: 'The
TRODDEN (2)
148 Rock 1 49 labour, which is not pleasant./I have trodden the winepress alone, and I know/That it
162 Rock 8 7 this that cometh from Edom?/He has trodden the wine-press alone./There came one
TROLLEY (4)
424 CP Lavinia 2 Madam?/{L} You could bring in the trolley with the glasses/And leave them ready./
424 CP m 5 /[*Re-enter* CATERER'S MAN *with trolley*]/{L} There, in that corner. That's the
526 ES m 26 the tea ... {}/[*Enter* LAMBERT *with trolley*]/{M} and I shall say, 'Lambert,/Please let
532 ES Lambert 8 Very good, my Lord./Shall I take the trolley, Miss Monica?/{M} Yes, thank you,
TROOP (1)
211 Old Gumbie 34 from that lot of disorderly louts,/A troop of well-disciplined helpful boy-scouts,/
TROPIC (3)
191 FQ: Little 3 /Suspended in time, between pole and tropic./When the short day is brightest, with
206 To my Wife 9 winter wind shall chill/No sullen tropic sun shall wither/The roses in the
600 Moonflower 7 mist on the sea;/Have you no brighter tropic flowers/With scarlet life, for me?/
TROPICAL (3)
292 FR Harry 5 in the Sunda Sea,/In the sweet sickly tropical night, I knew they were coming./In
344 FR Violet 16 You can't really think of *living* in a tropical climate!/{G} There's nothing wrong
344 FR Gerald 17 /{G} There's nothing wrong with a tropical climate —/But you have to go in for
TROPICS (3)
149 Rock 1 70 /The desert is not remote in southern tropics,/The desert is not only around the
288 FR Agatha 21 /Upon the real past. Wandering in the tropics/Or against the painted scene of the
561 ES Ld Clav 4 /To suffer the monotonous sun of the tropics/Or shiver in the northern night. Believe
TROTS (1)
177 FQ: ECoker 12 the wainscot where the field-mouse trots/And to shake the tattered arras woven
TROUBLE (26)
220 Old Deut 31 but I can guess/That the cause of the trouble is Old Deuteronomy!'/Old
267 MC Knight1 33 you; but in the hope/Of stirring up trouble in the French dominions./You sowed
324 FR Harry 14 matter can be very serious./A minor trouble like a concussion/Cannot make very
325 FR Gerald 20 much more apt than John to get into trouble./{C} Oh, but Arthur's a brilliant driver./
325 FR Charles 23 /*He*'s not likely to get into trouble./{G} A brilliant driver, but more
326 FR Violet 5 was unfamiliar/And I had the greatest trouble in getting home./I am sure he meant
348 FR Warburt 3 to relieve her mind. Why, what's the trouble? {}/[*Enter* MARY]/{M} Dr. Warburton!/
364 CP Reilly 19 /{UG} That question is not worth the trouble of an answer./But if I bring her back it
366 CP Edward 34 an opportunity./{E} And what's your trouble?/{P} This evening I felt I could bear it
371 CP Edward 34 know why I should be taking all this trouble/To protect you from the fool you are./
378 CP Celia 24 fatigue. And panic. You can't face the trouble./{E} No, it is not that. It is not only
394 CP Lavinia 8 it./That was why I took so much trouble/To have those Thursdays, to give you
395 CP Lavinia 36 assumption/That I wasn't worth the trouble of understanding./{E} So here we are

407 CP	Reilly	16	what I have to say to you./I do not trouble myself with the common cheat,/Or with
413 CP	Celia	14	/{C} Well, I can't pretend that my trouble is interesting;/But I shan't begin that
428 CP	Alex	36	are also foreign agitators,/Stirring up trouble .../{L} Why don't you expel them?/{A}
438 CP	Reilly	13	from hunger, damp, exposure,/Bowel trouble, and the fear of lions,/Cold of the night
452 CC	Lucasta	21	sure he didn't want —/Just to make trouble! And I couldn't find one of them./But
461 CC	Colby	12	you always at my back/If I get into trouble. But I hope/That I shan't have to call
473 CC	Colby	24	me as ... this world./But that's just the trouble. They seem so unrelated./I turn the key,
499 CC	Lucasta	24	everything settled./That was just the trouble. You made it so obvious/That this
555 ES	Ld Clav	30	wouldn't be at large. Perhaps he's in trouble/With some woman or other. I'm sure he
556 ES	Michael	35	natural he should end by getting into trouble./{LC} You started pretty early getting
557 ES	Ld Clav	1	You started pretty early getting into trouble,/When you were expelled from your
557 ES	Ld Clav	3	/But come to the point. You're in trouble again./We'll ignore, if you please, the
561 ES	Monica	24	/I know that Michael must be in great trouble,/So can't you help him?/{LC} I am

TROUBLED (4)

34 Figlia		24	these cogitations still amaze/The troubled midnight and the noon's repose./
64 WL: Chess		88	/Unguent, powdered, or liquid — troubled, confused/And drowned the sense in
321 FR	Denman	12	it's very urgent/Or he wouldn't have troubled you./{H} I'll see him. {}/[*Exit*
508 CC	Eggers	14	/{E} May I pour a drop of oil on these troubled waters?/Let us approach the question

TROUBLES (1)

| 307 FR | Mary | 27 | should I talk about my commonplace troubles?/They must seem very trivial indeed to |

TROUBLESOME (1)

| 344 FR | Gerald | 23 | the natives,/Though occasionally troublesome. But you'll have to learn the |

TROUPE (1)

| 229 Gus | | 47 | /They never get drilled in a regular troupe,/And they think they are smart, just to |

TROUSERS (3)

16 Prufrock		121	old .../I shall wear the bottoms of my trousers rolled./Shall I part my hair behind? Do
16 Prufrock		123	eat a peach?/I shall wear white flannel trousers, and walk upon the beach./I have heard
230 Bust Jones		7	mousers have such well-cut trousers/Or such an impeccable back./In the

TROUVE (1)

| 48 Lune Miel | | 13 | misères de Padoue à Milan/Où se trouve la Cène, et un restaurant pas cher./Lui |

TROWEL (2)

| 157 Rock 4 | | 19 | /With the sword in one hand and the trowel in the other./O Lord, deliver me from the |
| 158 Rock 5 | | 4 | words of Nehemiah the Prophet: 'The trowel in hand, and the gun rather loose in the |

TRUE (39)

49 Hippopot		7	to nervous shock;/While the True Church can never fail/For it is based upon
49 Hippopot		11	compassing material ends,/While the True Church need never stir/To gather in its
50 Hippopot		35	the martyr'd virgins kist,/While the True Church remains below/Wrapt in the old
115 SP	Dusty	13	/You can't trust him!/{Du} Well that's true./He's no gentleman if you can't trust him/
142 Cape Ann		12	this land at the end, resign it/To its true owner, the tough one, the sea-gull./The
235 Ad-dress		38	/With Cats, some say, one rule is true:/*Don't speak till you are spoken to.*/Myself,
601 Nocturne		14	drowned: —/'The perfect climax all true lovers seek!'/Humouresque/(AFTER J.
261 MC Thomas		29	It is/never the design of man; for the true martyr is he who has become the/
266 MC Thomas		24	and betrayed his King./{T} This is not true./Both before and after I received the ring/I
294 FR	Harry	39	It was not like that./Everything is true in a different sense./I expected to find her
309 FR	Mary	28	sees the sunlight. I know that this is true./{H} I have spent many years in useless
317 FR Warburt		17	happened./{W} That is in a sense true,/But without your knowing it, and what
333 FR	Harry	15	the way things happen./Everything is true in a different sense,/A sense that would
335 FR	Harry	34	/And what did not happen is as true as what did happen/O my dear, and you
363 CP	Edward	38	that much of what you've said/Is true enough. But that is not all./Since I saw her
407 CP	Reilly	29	have told me —/Both of you — was true enough: you described your feelings —/Or
408 CP	Lavinia	1	your nervous breakdown./{L} But it's true! I was completely prostrated;/Even if I have
419 CP	Reilly	18	Well ... I mean ... to everyday life./{R} True. But the friends you have in mind/Cannot
425 CP	Lavinia	6	We asked two more people./{L} It's true, a great many more accepted/Than we
425 CP	Edward	16	one was more important./{E} That's true. You have a very practical mind./{L} But
447 CC	Eggers	21	for your business genius./But it's true she believes she has what she calls
449 CC	Eggers	26	one, they're both of them women./{E} True./{SC} But I don't think she takes much
456 CC	Eggers	6	with the bargain.'/Of course it's true that her family connections/Have
460 CC	Claude	8	But I wrote you all about it./{SC} It's true, you did send me postcards from Zürich;/
476 CC	Lucasta	18	men have thought about me wasn't true./{C} What wasn't true?/{L} That I was
476 CC	Colby	19	me wasn't true./{C} What wasn't true?/{L} That I was Claude's mistress —/Or
488 CC	Lady E	8	/And then Mrs. Guzzard! It must be true./{SC} It is certainly a remarkable
496 CC	Eggers	18	/{E} Don't say that, Sir Claude./It's true, I haven't much nowadays to bring me;/But
514 CC Guzzard		39	she was to have a child:/That much is true. I also was expecting one./That you did not
515 CC	Claude	19	is horribly plausible. But it can't be true./{MG} Consider, Sir Claude. Would I tell
515 CC Guzzard		21	Would I tell you all this/Unless it was true? In telling you the truth/I am sacrificing my

515 CC	Claude	35	/{SC} But, Colby —/If this should be true — of course it can't be true! —/But I see
515 CC	Claude	35	should be true — of course it can't be true! —/But I see you believe it. You want to
517 CC	Eggers	22	a man who knows his own mind./Is it true, Mr. Simpkins, that what you desire/Is to
519 CC	Lady E	11	he wasn't./{LE} I suppose that's true of you and me, Claude./Between not
534 ES	Gomez	9	land you in gaol again?/{G} That's true enough,/Except for a false inference. I
550 ES	Carghil	15	than likely to make another'./How true that is! Algy was a weakling,/But simple he
553 ES	Carghil	6	by year, Richard./And although it's true that our acquaintance was brief,/Our
564 ES	Carghil	29	to San Marco./Señor Gomez, if it's true you're staying at Badgley Court,/I warn

TRUER (1)

494 CC	Claude	25	a successful one./I might have been truer to my father's inspiration/If I had done

TRULY (7)

253 MC	Tempt4	8	hatred shall have no end./You know truly, the King will never trust/Twice, the man
379 CP	Celia	9	between us?/That's all that matters. Truly, Edward,/If that is right, everything else
466 CC	Claude	18	of substitute for religion./I dare say truly religious people —/I've never known any
478 CC	Lucasta	10	out in me./You know, Colby, I'm truly disappointed./I was sure, when I told you
568 ES	Ld Clav	17	from you./{LC} If there's nothing, truly nothing, that you couldn't tell Monica/
579 ES	Carghil	39	/When I could be helpful./{MC} It's truly providential!/{M} Good-bye Michael. Will
582 ES	Ld Clav	6	I love you, my daughter, the more truly for knowing/That there is someone you

TRUMPETS (4)

45 Cook	Egg	29	Green;/Where are the eagles and the trumpets?/Buried beneath some snow-deep
127 Corl	March	3	the paving./And the flags. And the trumpets. And so many eagles./How many?
127 Corl	March	8	can see some eagles. And hear the trumpets./Here they come. Is he coming?/The
128 Corl	March	42	But how many eagles! and how many trumpets!/(And Easter Day, we didn't get to the

TRUNK (6)

270 MC	Chorus	4	primrose and cowslip. I have seen/Trunk and horn, tusk and hoof, in odd places;/I
310 FR	Mary	4	the dark/The slow flow throbbing the trunk/The pain of the breaking bud./These are
326 FR	Denman	33	/{D} Excuse me, Miss Ivy. There's a trunk call for you./{I} A trunk call? for me?
326 FR	Ivy	34	There's a trunk call for you./{I} A trunk call? for me? why, who can want me?/{D}
532 ES	Monica	21	to tell you that you have to take a trunk call./Come, Charles. Will you bring my
541 ES	Lambert	32	asked me/To remind you there's a trunk call coming through for you/In five

TRUST (32)

115 SP	Doris	12	no gentleman, Pereira:/You can't trust him!/{Du} Well that's true./He's no
115 SP	Dusty	14	true./He's no gentleman if you can't trust him/And *if* you can't trust him —/Then
115 SP	Dusty	15	you can't trust him/And *if* you can't trust him —/Then you never know what he's
252 MC	Thomas	9	/{T} And if the Archbishop cannot trust the King,/How can he trust those who
252 MC	Thomas	10	cannot trust the King,/How can he trust those who work for King's undoing?/{T3}
252 MC	Thomas	13	throne./{T} If the Archbishop cannot trust the Throne,/He has good cause to trust
252 MC	Thomas	14	the Throne,/He has good cause to trust none but God alone./I ruled once as
253 MC	Tempt4	8	/You know truly, the King will never trust/Twice, the man who has been his friend./
296 FR	Charles	27	/Makes him believe he did. He cannot trust his good fortune./I believe that all he needs
296 FR	Gerald	39	Harry need have no suspicion./I'd trust Warburton's opinion./{A} If anyone
301 FR	Ivy	21	in and brought together?/{I} I do not trust Charles with his confident vulgarity,
323 FR	Warburt	13	/But he mustn't be moved tonight. I'd trust Owen/On a matter like this. You can trust
323 FR	Warburt	14	Owen/On a matter like this. You can trust Owen./We'll bring him up tomorrow; and
324 FR	Amy	3	I suppose you are right. But can I trust you?/{W} You have trusted me a good
392 CP	Lavinia	24	when something's going to happen./Trust her not to miss any awkward situation!/
400 CP	Reilly	10	But what I mean is,/Does he trust your judgement?/{A} Yes, implicitly./It's
460 CC	Lady E	21	you remember, I said before I left:/'Trust my guidance for once, and engage that
478 CC	Kaghan	38	I knew I should find she'd got in first!/Trust Kaghan's intuitions! I'm your guardian
500 CC	Claude	12	time when he came here. But I didn't trust you/To keep a secret. There were reasons
501 CC	Lucasta	37	not a bad idea. If Colby agrees./{L} I trust you, Eggy. And I want to make my peace
534 ES	Ld Clav	16	at least, to be thankful for./I trust you've no need to engage in forgery./{G}
535 ES	Gomez	3	/For you're the only old friend I can trust./{LC} You really trust me? I appreciate the
535 ES	Ld Clav	4	old friend I can trust./{LC} You really trust me? I appreciate the compliment./{G}
535 ES	Gomez	5	sure you deserve. But when I say 'trust' ... {}/[*Knock. Enter* LAMBERT]/{LC}
535 ES	Gomez	10	/[*Exit*]/{G} I began to say: when I say 'trust'/I use the term as experience has taught
535 ES	Gomez	18	come to the point where you need to trust someone/You must make it worth his
535 ES	Ld Clav	24	should like to know why you need to trust *me*./{G} That's perfectly simple. I come
536 ES	Ld Clav	32	to hear/Why you should need to trust me./{G} Perfectly simple./My father's dead
536 ES	Gomez	39	one old friend, a friend whom I can trust —/And one who will accept both
540 ES	Ld Clav	15	/Or what you mean by saying you can trust me./{G} Dick, do you remember the
540 ES	Gomez	34	you see now, Dick, why I say I can trust you?/{LC} If you think that this story
550 ES	Ld Clav	24	to deal with questions of equipment./I trust that the business was very successful .../I

TRUSTED (5)

235 Ad-dress	53	Cat will condescend/To treat you as a	trusted friend,/Some little token of esteem/Is
285 FR	Amy	9	the day expected/And clocks could be	trusted, tomorrow assured/And time would not
324 FR	Warburt	4	But can I trust you?/{W} You have	trusted me a good many years, Lady
549 ES	Carghil	30	/He'd give you the slip: he's not to be	trusted./That man is hollow'. That's what she
550 ES	Carghil	36	understand women./Any woman who	trusted *him* would soon find that out'./A man

TRUSTING (2)

535 ES	Gomez	12	taught me./It's nonsense to talk of	trusting people/In general. What does that
537 ES	Ld Clav	4	to the description you have given/Of	trusting people, how do you propose/To make it

TRUSTS (1)

535 ES	Gomez	13	general. What does that mean? One	trusts a man/Or a woman — in this respect or

TRUSTWORTHY (2)

535 ES	Gomez	19	must make it worth his while to be	trustworthy'. { }/[*During this* LAMBERT *enters*
537 ES	Ld Clav	5	/To make it worth my while to be	trustworthy?/{G} It's done already, Dick; done

TRUTH (22)

148 Rock 1		45	/The God-shaken, in whom is the	truth inborn./*Enter the* ROCK, *led by a* BOY/
290 FR	Amy	11	might as well all of you know the	truth/For the sake of the future. There can be
298 FR	Charles	36	for nearly eight years;/And to tell the	truth, now that we've seen him,/We're a little
345 FR	Amy	19	I only just begin to apprehend the	truth/About things too late to mend: and that is
361 FR	Reilly	7	lie about it/Because you can't tell the	truth on the telephone./It will all take time that
371 CP	Peter	18	Until I know that/I shan't know the	truth about even the memory./Did we really
371 CP	Peter	31	any future. But I must find out/The	truth about the past, for the sake of the
392 CP	Lavinia	28	Edward! You had better have told the	truth:/Nothing less than the truth could deceive
392 CP	Lavinia	29	told the truth:/Nothing less than the	truth could deceive Julia./But how did the aunt
392 CP	Lavinia	34	/Well, I shall have to tell Julia the	truth./I shall always tell the truth now./We have
392 CP	Lavinia	35	Julia the truth./I shall always tell the	truth now./We have wasted such a lot of time in
448 CC	Eggers	11	of Atlantis?/{E} Well, to tell the	truth, Sir Claude, I only touched on these
455 CC	Eggers	16	man, is Sir Claude./To tell the	truth, she's something of a thorn in his flesh,/
476 CC	Lucasta	27	very clever too;/And he guessed the	truth from the very first moment./{C} But what
487 CC	Lady E	19	intuition./But it shall be proved. The	truth has come out./It's Colby. Colby is my lost
487 CC	Lady E	36	arrived the very moment/When the	truth dawned on me. Mrs. Guzzard!/Claude,
488 CC	Claude	20	to me that we must let her know the	truth./{C} It seems to me ... there is nothing for
497 CC	Claude	21	child must be Colby,/So I told her the	truth. But she cannot believe it./{LE} Claude,
513 CC	Claude	11	Colby only wanted to be sure of the	truth./{C} That is a very strange question, Aunt
513 CC	Colby	14	Claude is right: I wished to know the	truth./What it is, doesn't matter. All I wanted
515 CC	Guzzard	21	/Unless it was true? In telling you the	truth/I am sacrificing my ambitions for Colby./I
581 ES	Ld Clav	15	ensues upon knowledge of the	truth./Why did I always want to dominate my

TRY (48)

136 5FingerEx3		13	/That soon the enquiring worm shall	try/Our well-preserved complacency./*Lines to*
159 Rock 6		21	unpleasant facts./They constantly	try to escape/From the darkness outside and
593 Grad 7		2	future years be found with those who	try/To labor for the good until they die,/And
240 MC	Chorus	1	are content if we are left alone./We	try to keep our households in order;/The
245 MC	Thomas	35	order as you left them./{T} And will	try to leave them in order as I find them./I am
255 MC	Tempt4	1	qualities that you lacked/Will only	try to find the historical fact./When men shall
280 MC	Priest3	26	Saracen,/To share his filthy rites, and	try to snatch/Forgetfulness in his libidinous
293 FR	Harry	15	change, no change!/You all of you	try to talk as if nothing had happened,/And yet
293 FR	Agatha	22	us have no pretences:/And you must	try at once to make us understand,/And we
293 FR	Agatha	23	to make us understand,/And we must	try to understand you./{H} But how can I
311 FR	Harry	9	/Don't look at me like that! Stop!	Try to stop it!/I am going. Oh why, now? Come
327 FR	Agatha	4	of malice or stupidity./We must	try to penetrate the other private worlds/Of
330 FR	Agatha	17	also be afraid of being understood,/Try	not to regard it as an explanation./{H} I still
331 FR	Agatha	28	it. And that will be better./{Ag} I will	try to tell you. I hope I have the strength./{H} I
340 FR	Amy	22	you think what that does to one? Try	to think of it./I *would* have sons, if I could
342 FR	Amy	10	*I* have no influence over him; *you* can	try,/But you will not succeed: she has some spell
343 FR	Mary	20	I suppose it is much too late/Now, to	try to get a fellowship?/{A} So you will all leave
356 CP	Julia	17	always the perfect host,/But just	try to pretend you're another guest/At Lavinia's
356 CP	Julia	24	with me./She said: 'I wish you'd	try.' And this is the first time/I've ever seen you
366 CP	Peter	32	help./I was going to telephone and	try to see you later;/But this seemed an
374 CP	Edward	14	or what is going to happen;/And to	try to understand it, I want to be alone./{C} I
385 CP	Reilly	23	/{UG} I ask you to forget nothing./To	try to forget is to try to conceal./{E} There are
385 CP	Reilly	23	forget nothing./To try to forget is to	try to conceal./{E} There are certainly things I
397 CP	Lavinia	32	/{L} Very well, then, I shall not	try to press you./You're much too divided to
403 CP	Reilly	22	we say, within your modest capacity./Try	to explain what has happened since I left
413 CP	Reilly	10	the prologue to my treatment/Is to	try to show them that they are mistaken/About
413 CP	Reilly	25	enough about you for the moment:/Try	first to describe your present state of mind./

418 CP	Celia	14	really be dishonest/For me, now, to try to make a life with *anybody*!/I couldn't give
427 CP	Alex	14	/{L} How are you, Alex?/{A} I did try to get you on the telephone/After lunch, but
438 CP	Reilly	20	from one impediment:/You must try to detach yourself from what you still feel/
439 CP	Lavinia	25	/Before you leave England?/{L} Do try to come to see us./You know, I think it
481 CC	Lady E	26	dinner?/Oh, I know. It's a chance to try that Herbal Restaurant/I recommended to
487 CC	Colby	7	{ }/[*looking at the notes*]./{C} I'll try./{SC} It's just in ways like this, Elizabeth,/
490 CC	Lady E	6	I'm rather weak in the head/Though I try to be clever. Do try to help me./{SC} It
490 CC	Lady E	6	head/Though I try to be clever. Do try to help me./{SC} It could have happened.
498 CC	Claude	32	your child, Elizabeth,/Whom we must try to trace./{E} If there was another child/Then
498 CC	Eggers	34	there was another child/Then we must try to trace it. Certainly, Sir Claude:/Our first
499 CC	Lucasta	28	/And I haven't made it easier. I didn't try to./And knowing that you wanted me to
513 CC	Colby	33	faded photographs/In which I should try to decipher a likeness;/Whose image I could
517 CC	Lady E	19	him?/{LE} Yes. My poor Claude!/Do try to help him, Eggerson./{E} I wouldn't
517 CC	Colby	34	/{C} Well, if you could induce them to try me .../{E} The Parochial Church Council will
519 CC	Lady E	15	to do better./Claude, we've got to try to understand our children./{K} And we
525 ES	Charles	25	/You're not at all respectful./{C} I try to be respectful;/But you know that I shan't
549 ES	Carghil	16	you called them,/And you made me try to punt, and I got soaking wet/And nearly
551 ES	Carghil	13	want to believe it./But you think, or try to think, that if I'd really suffered/I
565 ES	Ld Clav	34	I was pleading with Michael/Not to try to escape from his own past failures:/I said I
568 ES	Ld Clav	10	in the very next moment,/Episodes we try to conceal from the world./Has there been
575 ES	Ld Clav	15	you about Gomez./He's unlikely to try to be custodian of your morals;/His real

TRYING (35)

24 Rhapsody		42	eye./I have seen eyes in the street/Trying to peer through lighted shutters,/And a
182 FQ: ECoker		176	the years of *l'entre deux guerres* —/Trying to learn to use words, and every attempt
182 FQ: ECoker		191	gain nor loss./For us, there is only the trying. The rest is not our business./Home is
185 FQ: DrySal		43	/Lying awake, calculating the future,/Trying to unweave, unwind, unravel/And piece
190 FQ: DrySal		233	undefeated/Because we have gone on trying;/We, content at the last/If our temporal
210 Old Gumbie		21	believing that nothing is done without trying,/She sets to work with her baking and
294 FR	Harry	5	speaking/Of my own experience, but trying to give you/Comparisons in a more
326 FR	Harry	17	the minor disaster?/You go on trying to think of each thing separately,/Making
328 FR	Charles	17	car for the/next twelve months./While trying to extricate his car from the collision, Mr.
335 FR	Harry	25	shadows in the smoky wilderness,/Trying to avoid the clasping branches/And the
340 FR	Agatha	9	among women, in a women's college,/Trying not to dislike women. Thirty years in
342 FR	Amy	7	do not know how./I have been always trying to make myself believe/That he was not
356 CP	Peter	6	in California./{C} Making a film./{P} Trying to make a film./{J} Oh, what film was it?
394 CP	Edward	28	don't know either./You say you were trying to 'encourage' me:/Then why did you
396 CP	Lavinia	10	in love with me —/I believe you were trying to persuade yourself you were./I seemed
396 CP	Edward	35	to explain me to myself./You're still trying to invent a personality for me/Which will
401 CP	Edward	37	back,/I suppose. You seemed to be trying to persuade me/That I was better off
407 CP	Reilly	25	meant to./This is the consequence of trying to lie to me./{L} I did not come here to be
432 CP	Reilly	15	for./{R} I should not dream of trying to interrupt Julia .../{J} But you're both
440 CP	Lavinia	25	transparent,/You know, when you're trying to cheer me up./To say I always look my
446 CC	Claude	27	And then it must be furnished./I'm trying to find him a really good piano./{E} A
466 CC	Colby	5	inferior rendering./So I've given up trying to play to other people:/I am only happy
471 CC	Colby	22	/{C} The first time we met/You were trying very hard to give a false impression./And
471 CC	Lucasta	24	hadn't succeeded./{L} Oh, so I was trying to give a false impression?/What sort of
471 CC	Lucasta	25	/What sort of impression was I trying to give?/{C} That doesn't really matter.
476 CC	Lucasta	11	that when we first met/You saw I was trying to give a false impression./I want to tell
495 CC	Lady E	37	/{LE} I believe that was what *I* was trying to do./It's very strange, Claude, but this
524 ES	Charles	26	You've got me off *my* point .../I was trying to explain .../{M} It's simply the question/
540 ES	Ld Clav	10	pretence that you're maintaining/In trying to persuade me of your ... worldly
542 ES	Gomez	3	is it that you want?/{G} I've been trying to make clear that I only want your
551 ES	Carghil	6	to be ashamed of:/A man is always trying to forget/His own shabby behaviour./
561 ES	Ld Clav	26	/So can't you help him?/{LC} I am trying to help him,/And to meet him half way. I
567 ES	Charles	20	those people from his past,/I've been trying to think what I could do to help him./If
568 ES	Ld Clav	37	about you!/I've spent my life in trying to forget myself,/In trying to identify
568 ES	Ld Clav	38	my life in trying to forget myself,/In trying to identify myself with the part/I had

TU (2)

51 Restaurant		20	/C'est dommage.'/Mais alors, tu as ton vautour!/Va t'en te décrotter les rides
51 Restaurant		23	le crâne./De quel droit payes-tu des expériences comme moi?/Tiens, voilà dix

TUBE (2)

180 FQ: ECoker		119	as, when an underground train, in the tube, stops too long between stations/And the
397 CP	Edward	31	teach you/How to put the cap on a tube of tooth-paste./{L} Very well, then, I shall

TUBE-TRAIN (1)

149 Rock 1		72	corner,/The desert is squeezed in the tube-train next to you,/The desert is in the heart

TUBERS (1)
61 WL: Burial   7   snow, feeding/A little life with dried tubers./Summer surprised us, coming over the
TUCK (1)
547 ES   Piggott   4   my hands!/But before I go, just let me tuck you up .../You must be very careful at this
TUCKS (1)
210 Old Gumbie   8   all the family's in bed and asleep,/She tucks up her skirts to the basement to creep./
TUGGER (9)
214 RTTugger   t   in Bangkok./The Rum Tum Tugger/The Rum Tum Tugger is a Curious Cat:
214 RTTugger   1   Rum Tum Tugger/The Rum Tum Tugger is a Curious Cat:/If you offer him
214 RTTugger   7   chase a mouse./Yes the Rum Tum Tugger is a Curious Cat —/And there isn't any
214 RTTugger   12   anything about it!/The Rum Tum Tugger is a terrible bore:/When you let him in,
214 RTTugger   18   if he can't get out./Yes the Rum Tum Tugger is a Curious Cat —/And it isn't any use
214 RTTugger   23   anything about it!/The Rum Tum Tugger is a curious beast:/His disobliging ways
214 RTTugger   31   on the larder shelf./The Rum Tum Tugger is artful and knowing,/The Rum Tum
215 RTTugger   32   is artful and knowing,/The Rum Tum Tugger doesn't care for a cuddle;/But he'll leap
215 RTTugger   35   a horrible muddle./Yes the Rum Tum Tugger is a Curious Cat —/And there isn't any
TUM (9)
214 RTTugger   t   commanded in Bangkok./The Rum Tum Tugger/The Rum Tum Tugger is a
214 RTTugger   1   /The Rum Tum Tugger/The Rum Tum Tugger is a Curious Cat:/If you offer him
214 RTTugger   7   rather chase a mouse./Yes the Rum Tum Tugger is a Curious Cat —/And there isn't
214 RTTugger   12   no doing anything about it!/The Rum Tum Tugger is a terrible bore:/When you let
214 RTTugger   18   fuss if he can't get out./The Rum Tum Tugger is a Curious Cat —/And it isn't
214 RTTugger   23   no doing anything about it!/The Rum Tum Tugger is a curious beast:/His disobliging
214 RTTugger   31   it away on the larder shelf./The Rum Tum Tugger is artful and knowing,/The Rum
215 RTTugger   32   is artful and knowing,/The Rum Tum Tugger doesn't care for a cuddle;/But he'll
215 RTTugger   35   like a horrible muddle./Yes the Rum Tum Tugger is a Curious Cat —/And there isn't
TUMBLE (2)
178 FQ: ECoker   57   that aim too high/Red into grey and tumble down/Late roses filled with early snow?/
263 MC   Chorus   23   voices trill at windows, and children tumble in front of the door,/What work shall
TUMBLEBRUTUS (1)
212 Growltiger   27   gone to wet his beard;/And his bosun, TUMBLEBRUTUS, he too had stol'n away —/
TUMBLED (1)
73 WL: Thund   387   the grass is singing/Over the tumbled graves, about the chapel/There is the
TUMBLING (1)
587 Fable   4   poor men,/And brought their abbeys tumbling at their backs,/There was a village
TUMID (2)
85 Hollow Men   60   speech/Gathered on this beach of the tumid river/Sightless, unless/The eyes reappear/
174 FQ: BurntN   106   with fancies and empty of meaning/Tumid apathy with no concentration/Men and
TUMULT (1)
422 CP   Julia   27   from the Visions/Protect her in the tumult/Protect her in the silence. { }/[*They drink*]
TUNE (4)
125 SA Sweeney   26   booze/We're gona sit here and have a tune/We're gona stay and we're gona go/And
601 Nocturne   5   The conversation failing, strikes some tune/Banal, and out of pity for their fate/Behind
602 Humoresque   10   air,/Mouth twisted to the latest tune;/His who-the-devil-are-you stare;/
555 ES   Piggott   1   remember her, Lord Claverton./That tune she was humming, *It's Not Too Late For*
TUNED (1)
470 CC   Lucasta   3   delivered this week/And you had it tuned yesterday. Still, I'm flattered/To be your
TUO (1)
189 FQ: DrySal   181   forth, and not returning:/Figlia del tuo figlio,/Queen of Heaven./Also pray for
TURF (1)
31 Apollinax   16   beat of centaur's hoofs over the hard turf/As his dry and passionate talk devoured the
TURKEY (1)
111 Xmas Trees   16   /The expectation of the goose or turkey/And the expected awe on its appearance,
TURKEYS (1)
588 Fable   34   gown he wore with holy water,/The turkeys, capons, boars, they were to eat,/He
TURN (53)
14 Prufrock   39   I dare?' and, 'Do I dare?'/Time to turn back and descend the stair,/With a bald
20 Portrait   86   ill at ease/I mount the stairs and turn the handle of the door/And feel as if I had
28 Boston ET   7   bell, turning/Wearily, as one would turn to nod good-bye to La Rochefoucauld,/If
34 Figlia   5   —/Fling them to the ground and turn/With a fugitive resentment in your eyes:/
54 Mr E Sun   7   of τò ἕν,/And at the mensual turn of time/Produced enervate Origen./A
68 WL: Fire S   216   violet hour, when the eyes and back/Turn upward from the desk, when the human
71 WL: DWater   320   whirlpool./Gentile or Jew/O you who turn the wheel and look to windward,/Consider
74 WL: Thund   412   /*Dayadhvam:* I have heard the key/Turn in the door once and turn once only/We
74 WL: Thund   412   the key/Turn in the door once and turn once only/We think of the key, each in his

89 Ash-Wed 1	1	/Because I do not hope to	turn	again/Because I do not hope/Because I do
89 Ash-Wed 1	3	do not hope/Because I do not hope to	turn	/Desiring this man's gift and that man's
89 Ash-Wed 1	23	the voice/Because I cannot hope to	turn	again/Consequently I rejoice, having to
90 Ash-Wed 1	30	explain/Because I do not hope to	turn	again/Let these words answer/For what is
98 Ash-Wed 6	1	people./Although I do not hope to	turn	again/Although I do not hope/Although I
98 Ash-Wed 6	3	not hope/Although I do not hope to	turn	/Wavering between the profit and the loss/
150 Rock 1	109	*again./The river flows, the seasons*	*turn*	*/The sparrow and starling have no time to*
151 Rock 2	6	those who would build and restore	turn	out the palms of their hands, or look in
154 Rock 3	6	/I have given you hands which you	turn	from worship/I have given you speech, for
155 Rock 3	59	questions./O weariness of men who	turn	from GOD/To the grandeur of your mind
174 FQ: BurntN	132	the sun away./Will the sunflower	turn	to us, will the clematis/Stray down, bend to
191 FQ: Little	30	when you leave the rough road/And	turn	behind the pig-sty to the dull façade/And
220 Old Deut	20	/But the dogs and the herdsmen will	turn	them away./The cars and the lorries run
224 Mr Mistoff	15	/From Mr. Mistoffelees' Conjuring	Turn	./Presto!/Away we go!/And we all say: OH!
233 Skimble	38	or bright;/There's a button that you	turn	to make a breeze./There's a funny little
604 Ode	5	vain hesitations and fears./And we	turn	as thy sons ever turn, in the strength/Of the
604 Ode	5	fears./And we turn as thy sons ever	turn	, in the strength/Of the hopes that thy
240 MC Chorus	21	guessing,/Having their aims which	turn	in their hands in the pattern of time./
243 MC Priest3	7	/{P3} For good or ill, let the wheel	turn	./The wheel has been still, these seven years,
243 MC Priest3	9	good./For ill or good, let the wheel	turn	./For who knows the end of good or evil?/
245 MC Thomas	21	And the suffering, that the wheel may	turn	and still/Be forever still./{P2} O my Lord,
247 MC Thomas	21	fixed in his folly, may think/He can	turn	the wheel on which he turns./{T1} My
251 MC Tempt3	3	undetermined./Unreal friendship may	turn	to real/But real friendship, once ended,
251 MC Tempt3	5	be mended./Sooner shall enmity	turn	to alliance./The enmity that never knew
253 MC Tempt4	13	for trap to snap/Having served your	turn	, broken and crushed./As for barons, envy
256 MC Tempt4	3	may subsist, that the wheel may	turn	and still/Be forever still./{C} There is no
263 MC Chorus	19	ploughman shall go out in March and	turn	the same earth/He has turned before, the
272 MC Chorus	28	those who were men can no longer	turn	the mind/To distraction, delusion, escape
277 MC Knight3	17	know perfectly well how/things will	turn	out. King Henry — God bless him — will
300 FR Downing	33	was sure it was him./While I took my	turn	about, for near half an hour/He stayed
347 FR Downing	6	too! They must have given you a	turn	!/They did me, at first. You soon get used
353 CP Celia	13	stop wrangling,/Both of you. It's your	turn	, Julia./Do tell us that story you told the
362 CP Edward	7	a permanent advantage./{E} It might	turn	out so, yet .../{UG} Are you going to say,
366 CP Julia	3	mantelpiece. Where was I sitting?/Just	turn	out the bottom of that sofa —/No, this
409 CP Reilly	25	Mrs. Chamberlayne./And now, let us	turn	to your side of the problem./When you
427 CP Edward	6	Well, Alex!/On earth do you	turn	up from?/{A} Where on earth? From the
431 CP Peter	15	the Duke?/{P} And do him a good	turn	./We're making a film of English life/And
461 CC Eggers	4	Mr. Simpkins —/If anything *should*	turn	up unexpected/And you find yourself
473 CC Colby	25	the trouble. They seem so unrelated./I	turn	the key, and walk through the gate,/And
512 CC Guzzard	20	questions —/And now it is my	turn	to ask them./I should like to gratify
512 CC Guzzard	37	Wishes, when realised, sometimes	turn	/Against those who have made them. { }/[*To*
532 ES Ld Clav	12	then I'll see you off./{LC} I'm sorry to	turn	you out of the room like this,/But I'll have
541 ES Gomez	30	me a moment ago./Now it's my	turn	, perhaps, to do you a kindness. { }/[*Enter*
542 ES Gomez	5	me expensive tastes. Now it's my	turn	./I can have cigars sent direct to you from

TURNED (14)

34 Figlia	17	as a smile and shake of the hand./She	turned	away, but with the autumn weather/
38 Gerontion	29	the candles; Fräulein von Kulp/Who	turned	in the hall, one hand on the door.
40 Burb Blei	15	the knees/And elbows, with the palms	turned	out,/Chicago Semite Viennese./A
92 Ash-Wed 3	2	the first turning of the second stair/I	turned	and saw below/The same shape twisted
160 Rock 7	8	the face of the water./And men who	turned	towards the light and were known of the
161 Rock 7	31	stand with empty hands and palms	turned	upwards/In an age which advances
179 FQ: ECoker	82	they peered/Or from which they	turned	their eyes. There is, it seems to us,/At
597 Before Mor	2	with gray,/The flowers at the window	turned	toward dawn,/Petal on petal, waiting for
251 MC Tempt3	35	/{T3} For a powerful party/Which has	turned	its eyes in your direction —/To gain
263 MC Chorus	20	and turn the same earth/He has	turned	before, the bird shall sing the same song.
273 MC Thomas	18	the church of Christ,/The sanctuary,	turned	into a fortress./The Church shall protect
476 CC Lucasta	36	living in seedy lodgings/And being	turned	out when the neighbours complained./
533 ES Gomez	31	of the law —/And seen that the law	turned	its right side to *me*./Sometimes I've had
582 ES Charles	27	some door unseen by us/And had	turned	and was looking back at us/With a

TURNER (1)

| 43 Swee Erect | 39 | /Might easily be misunderstood;/Mrs. | Turner | intimates/It does the house no sort of |

TURNING (17)

16 Prufrock	108	a pillow or throwing off a shawl,/And	turning	toward the window, should say:/'That is
21 Portrait	99	/I feel like one who smiles, and	turning	shall remark/Suddenly, his expression in
28 Boston ET	6	/I mount the steps and ring the bell,	turning	/Wearily, as one would turn to nod

514 CC	Claude	35	to have carried out a deception/For twenty-five years? It's quite impossible./{MG} I
519 CC	Guzzard	1	and I, Sir Claude,/Had *our* wishes twenty-five years ago;/But we failed to observe,
535 ES	Gomez	28	home/For thirty-five years? I was twenty-five —/The same age as you — when I

TWENTY-FOUR (2)

364 CP	Reilly	27	/{UG} We do not know yet. In twenty-four hours/She will come to you here.
387 CP	Celia	2	yesterday;/But I've learnt a lot in twenty-four hours./It wasn't a very pleasant

TWICE (12)

182 FQ: ECoker	186	has already been discovered/Once or twice, or several times, by men whom one
253 MC	Tempt4	9	know truly, the King will never trust/Twice, the man who has been his friend./
300 FR	Downing	6	rail./He was in a rare fright, once or twice./But you know, it is just my opinion, Sir,/
335 FR	Agatha	38	This is the beginning./We do not pass twice through the same door/Or return to the
353 CP	Alex	8	Alex./{A} I never tell the same story twice./{J} But I'm still waiting to know what
369 CP	Peter	38	we sometimes had tea/And once or twice dined together./{E} And after that/Did she
370 CP	Peter	2	of her friends?/{P} No, but once or twice she spoke of them/And about their lack of
382 CP	Celia	8	/As you never were before, with me./Twice you have changed since I have been
440 CP	Lavinia	31	likes to hear the same compliment twice./{E} And now for the party./{L} Now for
449 CC	Eggers	19	/{E} Well, I believe that once or twice, perhaps .../But I'm afraid you overrate
536 ES	Gomez	2	you do./You've changed your name twice — by easy stages,/And each step was
551 ES	Carghil	34	lawyers are offering in settlement/Is twice as much as I think you'd be awarded.'/

TWILIGHT (6)

84 Hollow Men	38	—/Not that final meeting/In the twilight kingdom/This is the dead land/This is
85 Hollow Men	65	star/Multifoliate rose/Of death's twilight kingdom/The hope only/Of empty men.
98 Ash-Wed 6	6	the dreams cross/The dreamcrossed twilight between birth and dying/(Bless me
166 Rock 10	22	our western doors at evening,/The twilight over stagnant pools at batflight,/Moon
204 de la Mare	15	feet, and ghosts return/Gently at twilight, gently go at dawn,/The sad intangible
308 FR	Harry	6	object;/And the eye adjusts itself to a twilight/Where the dead stone is seen to be

TWINED (1)

329 FR	Chorus	17	/The making the best of a bad job/All twined and tangled together, all are recorded./

TWINING (1)

269 MC	Chorus	34	seen/Grey necks twisting, rat tails twining, in the thick light of dawn. I have eaten/

TWINKLE (1)

84 Hollow Men	44	of a dead man's hand/Under the twinkle of a fading star./Is it like this/In death's

TWIST (2)

26 Rhapsody	78	door, sleep, prepare for life.'/The last twist of the knife./Morning at the Window/
33 Conv Gal	15	our vagrant moods the slightest twist!/With your air indifferent and imperious/

TWISTED (5)

24 Rhapsody	24	throws up high and dry/A crowd of twisted things;/A twisted branch upon the beach
24 Rhapsody	25	and dry/A crowd of twisted things;/A twisted branch upon the beach/Eaten smooth,
27 Morning	6	brown waves of fog toss up to me/Twisted faces from the bottom of the street,/
92 Ash-Wed 3	3	and saw below/The same shape twisted on the banister/Under the vapour in the
602 Humoresque	10	bullying, half imploring air,/Mouth twisted to the latest tune;/His

TWISTING (5)

19 Portrait	46	who hold it in your hands';/(Slowly twisting the lilac stalks)/'You let it flow from
92 Ash-Wed 3	8	turning of the second stair/I left them twisting, turning below;/There were no more
605 Narcissus	22	he was sure that he had been a tree,/Twisting its branches among each other/And
269 MC	Chorus	34	lunatic bird. I have seen/Grey necks twisting, rat tails twining, in the thick light of
272 MC	Chorus	15	horror, but more horror/Than when twisting in the fingers,/Than when splitting in

TWISTS (4)

19 Portrait	43	has a bowl of lilacs in her room/And twists one in her fingers while she talks./'Ah, my
24 Rhapsody	22	/And you see the corner of her eye/Twists like a crooked pin.'/The memory throws
24 Rhapsody	57	smallpox cracks her face,/Her hand twists a paper rose,/That smells of dust and eau
515 CC	Guzzard	30	/Drives the knife deeper and twists it in the wound?/I had very much rather

TWIT (3)

67 WL: Fire S	203	d'enfants, chantant dans la coupole!/Twit twit twit/Jug jug jug jug jug jug/So rudely
67 WL: Fire S	203	chantant dans la coupole!/Twit twit twit/Jug jug jug jug jug jug/So rudely
67 WL: Fire S	203	chantant dans la coupole!/Twit twit twit/Jug jug jug jug jug jug/So rudely forc'd./

TWITTERING (1)

174 FQ: BurntN	116	here/Not here the darkness, in this twittering world./Descend lower, descend only/

TWO (103)

16 Prufrock	113	/To swell a progress, start a scene or two,/Advise the prince; no doubt, an easy tool,/
18 Portrait	12	resurrected only among friends/Some two or three, who will not touch the bloom/
24 Rhapsody	33	curled and ready to snap./Half-past two,/The street-lamp said,/'Remark the cat
44 Cook Egg	15	For I shall meet Sir Alfred Mond./We two shall lie together, lapt/In a five per cent.
68 WL: Fire S	218	though blind, throbbing between two lives,/Old man with wrinkled female
117 SP	Doris	25	of friends'./{Do} Here's the two of spades./{Du} The *two of spades*!/

117 SP	Dusty	26	Here's the two of spades./{Du} The *two of spades*!/THAT'S THE COFFIN!!/{Do}
119 SP	Wauch	4	Horsfall —/We want you to meet two friends of ours,/American gentlemen here
122 SA	Wa&Ho	18	*bamboo/Under the bamboo tree/Two live as one/One live as two/Two live as three*
122 SA	Wa&Ho	19	*tree/Two live as one/One live as two/Two live as three/Under the bam/Under the*
122 SA	Wa&Ho	20	*tree/Two live as one/One live as two/Two live as three/Under the bam/Under the boo!*
129 Cor2	State	14	annual increments of five shillings/To two pounds ten a week; with a bonus of thirty
150 Rock 1		103	*land/There shall be one cigarette to two men,/To two women one half pint of bitter/*
150 Rock 1		104	*shall be one cigarette to two men,/To two women one half pint of bitter/Ale. In this*
161 Rock 7		34	*land/There shall be one cigarette to two men,/To two women one half pint of bitter/*
161 Rock 7		35	*shall be one cigarette to two men,/To two women one half pint of bitter/Ale..../*
165 Rock 9		34	spirit and body./Visible and invisible, two worlds meet in Man;/Visible and invisible
178 FQ: ECoker		32	and commodious sacrament./Two and two, necessarye coniunction,/Holding
178 FQ: ECoker		32	commodious sacrament./Two and two, necessarye coniunction,/Holding eche
194 FQ: Little		124	unappeased and peregrine/Between two worlds become much like each other,/So I
195 FQ: Little		157	as death resembles life,/Being between two lives — unflowering, between/The live and
198 FQ: Little		253	half-heard, in the stillness/Between two waves of the sea./Quick now, here, now,
204 de la Mare		19	is what we have yet to learn,/And two worlds meet, and intersect, and change;/
217 Jellicles		32	night/They will practise a caper or two in the hall./If it happens the sun is shining
218 Mung Rump		9	looked like a field of war,/If a tile or two came loose on the roof,/Which presently
227 Macavity		37	/He always has an alibi, and one or two to spare:/At whatever time the deed took
241 MC	Priest1	19	with the King? what reconciliation/Of two proud men?/{P3} What peace can be found/
278 MC	Knight2	26	and that — God knows/why — the two orders were incompatible./You will agree
286 FR	Charles	25	needs/Is a glass of dry sherry or two before dinner./The modern young people
295 FR	Harry	25	the world I have to live in./— I lay two days in contented drowsiness;/Then I
297 FR	Charles	24	{C} All the same, there's a question or two { }/[*Rings the bell*]/{C} That I'd like to ask
309 FR	Harry	35	your voice as in the silence/Between two storms, one hears the moderate usual noises
320 FR	Warburt	26	you this,/Just now. But there were two reasons/Why you had to know. One is your
343 FR	Agatha	9	in the neutral territory/Between two worlds./{M} Then you *will* help me!/You
352 CP	m	10	/A NURSE-SECRETARY/TWO CATERER'S MEN/*The scene is laid in*
354 CP	Julia	31	brothers?/{J} How many brothers? Two, I think./{A} No, there were three, but you
359 CP	Julia	26	/And there it is! Now what are you two plotting?/How very lucky it was my
367 CP	Edward	1	/{E} I did think I noticed one or two things;/But I don't pretend I was aware of
369 CP	Edward	18	the ambition/To establish herself in two worlds at once —/But she herself had to be
371 CP	Peter	28	is the reality/Of experience between two unreal people?/If I can only hold to the
376 CP	Julia	21	you realise how lucky you are/To have *two* Good Samaritans? I never heard of that
382 CP	Celia	36	... ask me to forgive *you*!/{C} Yes, for two things. First ... { }/[*The telephone rings*]/{E}
399 CP	1m	1	fetch it up for me? { }/CURTAIN/Act Two/SIR HENRY HARCOURT-REILLY'S
402 CP	Reilly	5	your indecision. Now there are only two —/Which you still have the chance of
402 CP	Edward	14	would enquire about the symptoms./Two people advised me recently,/Almost in the
408 CP	Reilly	39	Chamberlayne, when you came to me two months ago/I was dissatisfied with your
409 CP	Edward	3	/And so I made enquiries./{E} It was two months ago/That your breakdown began!
413 CP	Celia	26	state of mind./{C} Well, there are two things I can't understand,/Which you might
413 CP	Reilly	36	/What *is* normality. You say there are two things:/What is the first?/{C} An awareness
417 CP	Reilly	35	/For casual talk before the fire/Two people who know they do not understand
424 CP	2m	1	*of the Chamberlaynes' London flat. Two years later./A late afternoon in July.* A
424 CP	Lavinia	18	we've given *several* parties/In the last two years. And I've attended *all* of them./I hope
424 CP	Edward	21	not too tired?/{E} Oh no, a quiet day./Two consultations with solicitors/On quite
425 CP	Edward	11	we ought to have arranged to have two parties/Instead of one./{L} That's never
429 CP	Alex	28	/{E} But when?/{A} In a year or two./{E} And meanwhile?/{A} Meanwhile
434 CP	Alex	14	leave the dying natives./Eventually, two of them escaped:/One died in the jungle,
434 CP	Peter	35	at all. But then I've been away/For two years, and I don't know what happened/To
434 CP	Peter	36	happened/To Celia, during those two years./Two years! Thinking about Celia./
434 CP	Peter	37	/To Celia, during those two years./Two years! Thinking about Celia./{E} It's the
435 CP	Peter	1	*me*, it's everything else that's a waste./Two years! And it was all a mistake./Julia! Why
435 CP	Julia	3	say anything?/{J} You gave her those two years, as best you could./{P} When did she
435 CP	Julia	5	did she ... take up this career?/{J} Two years ago./{P} Two years ago! I tried to
435 CP	Peter	6	up this career?/{J} Two years ago./{P} Two years ago! I tried to forget about her,/Until
437 CP	Reilly	8	*of men, he saw./For know there are two worlds of life and death:/One that which thou*
438 CP	Lavinia	4	/I mean — I know nothing of her last two years./{E} That shows some insight on your
439 CP	Lavinia	2	/When she said good-bye to us, two years ago./{E} Your responsibility is
440 CP	Edward	9	only keeping on;/And somehow, the two ideas seem to fit together./{L} But all the
452 CC	Lucasta	16	wrong, Eggy. It's rank injustice./Two months I'd gone on filing those papers/
461 CC	Claude	25	prudence./As we arranged. But after two months —/And as my wife insists upon
466 CC	Claude	22	to me, who have at best to live/In two worlds — each a kind of make-believe./
469 CC	1m	1	the figures. { }/CURTAIN/Act Two/*The flat in the mews a few weeks later.*

473 CC	Colby	39	Than the world outside it. If you have	two lives/Which have nothing whatever to do
475 CC	Lucasta	13	/I've changed quite a lot in the last	two hours./{C} And I think I'm changing too.
491 CC	Colby	27	of a son,/To be disputed between	two parents./But, if we followed your
491 CC	Colby	31	parents!/It's strange enough to have	two parents —/But I should have four! What
497 CC	Lady E	35	/Another Mrs. Guzzard .../{LE}	*Two* Mrs. Guzzards?/{E} I agree, it is a most
498 CC	Eggers	7	seem unlikely/That there should be	two Mrs. Guzzards in Teddington./But
498 CC	Eggers	9	Guzzard,/Could there not have been	two babies?/{LE} *Two* babies, Eggerson?/{E} I
498 CC	Lady E	10	there not have been two babies?/{LE}	*Two* babies, Eggerson?/{E} I was only suggesting/
498 CC	Claude	26	can't ask me to believe/That she took	two babies, and got them mixed./{LE} That
507 CC	Guzzard	10	at the time,/And very poor. It offered	two advantages./{E} And did you know the
517 CC	Eggers	28	to you. The organist we had/Died	two months ago. We've been looking for
523 ES		m 12	*Four o'clock in the afternoon*/ACT	TWO/*The Terrace at Badgley Court. Morning*/
525 ES	Charles	21	have you to himself,/Before I've said	two words he'll come ambling in .../{M} You've
525 ES	Monica	22	You've said a good deal more than	two words already./And besides, my father
528 ES	Charles	20	/I'm sure of that./{C} You've given	two reasons,/One the contradiction of the other.
532 ES	Charles	25	both at Badgley Court/In a week or	two. { }/[*Enter* LAMBERT]/{L} Mr. Gomez, my
544 ES	1m	1	at Badgley Court? { }/CURTAIN/Act	Two/*The terrace of Badgley Court. A bright*
547 ES	Piggott	30	no names,/But there are one or	two who don't like being beaten,/And that
553 ES	Carghil	8	I think,/To have given me one or	two insights into you./No, Richard, don't
554 ES	Piggott	20	Claverton. This is Mrs. Carghill./	Two of our very nicest guests!/I just came to see
556 ES	Michael	16	last night. I'm staying at a pub/About	two miles from here. Not a bad little place./
557 ES	Michael	9	made for you./{Mi} I'd stuck it for	two years. And deadly dull it was./{LC} Every
557 ES	Michael	29	/{Mi} I'd nothing at all to pay for	two years:/The interest was just added on to the
557 ES	Michael	32	how long ago was that?/{Mi} Nearly	two years./Time passes pretty quickly, when
567 ES	2m	1	{ }/CURTAIN/Act Three/*Same as Act*	Two. *Late afternoon of the following day.*
569 ES	Charles	19	has told me about your fellow guests,/	Two persons who, she says, claim a very long
571 ES	Charles	22	frets me./{C} But all the same, these	two people mustn't persecute you./We can't
571 ES	Ld Clav	34	I was driving back to Oxford. We had	two girls with us./It was late at night. A
573 ES	Carghil	35	future./Fancy! I've only known her	two days!/But I feel like a mother to her
574 ES	Carghil	14	brainless,/But I have an idea or	two, now and then./And in the end I discovered
577 ES	Gomez	22	things over, Hemington .../{G} As	two men of the world, we discussed things very
582 ES	Ld Clav	17	situations not very agreeable./You	two ought to have a little time together./I leave

TWO-SEATERS (1)

121 SA	Sweeney	24	/There's no motor cars/No	two-seaters, no six-seaters,/No Citroën, no

TYKE (1)

223 Pekes Pols		33	your Pollicle Dog is a dour Yorkshire	tyke,/And his braw Scottish cousins are

TYPE (5)

151 Rock 2		13	yes, but that is the model and	type for your citizenship upon earth./When
282 MC	Chorus	6	O Lord, we acknowledge ourselves as	type of the common man,/Of the men and
409 CP	Reilly	19	/Of loving. To men of a certain	type/The suspicion that they are incapable of
462 CC	Claude	14	*her* son would have been a different	type of person —/Then you *will* become her
481 CC	Lady E	30	I told you, Mr. Kaghan, you're the	type of person/Who needs to eat a great deal of

TYPES (2)

234 Ad-dress		8	whom we find/Possessed of various	types of mind./For some are sane and some are
416 CP	Reilly	13	only typical./{R} There are different	types. Some are rarer than others./{C} Oh, I

TYPEWRITER (2)

483 CC	Lady E	16	object on it?/Don't tell me it's a	typewriter./{C} It is a typewriter./I've already
483 CC	Colby	17	tell me it's a typewriter./{C} It is a	typewriter./I've already begun to work here. At

TYPEWRITERS (1)

483 CC	Lady E	20	I hadn't reckoned on reports and	typewriters/When I designed this room./{C} It's

TYPICAL (5)

202 War Poetry		5	/In the path of an action merely	typical/To create the universal, originate a
416 CP	Celia	12	you?/{R} No./{C} Perhaps I'm only	typical./{R} There are different types. Some are
431 CP	Peter	34	director:/He's looking for some	typical English faces —/Of course, only for
431 CP	Peter	36	I'll help him decide what faces are	typical./{J} Peter, I've thought of a wonderful
431 CP	Julia	40	/To take us all over? We're all very	typical./{P} No, I'm afraid .../{CM} Sir Henry

TYPIST (1)

68 WL: Fire S		222	brings the sailor home from sea,/The	typist home at teatime, clears her breakfast,

TYRANNOUS (1)

252 MC	Tempt3	2	England and for Rome,/Ending the	tyrannous jurisdiction/Of king's court over

UGLY (3)
340 FR   Amy   28   was gone,/So that there might be no ugly rumours./You thought I did not know!/
484 CC   Lady E   34   /{LE} The first was, that I was very ugly/And didn't know it. Then, that I was
484 CC   Lady E   38   it./Of course, I was terrified of being ugly,/And of being feeble-minded: though my
UH (1)
119 SP   Klip   29   Eh what Klip?/{Kl} Say, Miss — er — uh — London's swell./We like London fine./
ULTIMATE (1)
105 Song Sime   30   thought and prayer,/Not for me the ultimate vision./Grant me thy peace./(And a
UMBRELLA (4)
359 CP   Julia   25   it's raining!/It made me remember my umbrella,/And there it is! Now what are you
359 CP   Julia   27   plotting?/How very lucky it was my umbrella,/And not Alexander's — *he's* so
374 CP   Celia   6   going to say I'd come back for my umbrella ... ./I must say you don't seem very
376 CP   Celia   4   head./You see, I really did leave my umbrella;/And I'll say I found you here starving
UMBRIAN (1)
  54 Mr E Sun   9   enervate Origen./A painter of the Umbrian school/Designed upon a gesso ground/
UN (8)
  46 Directeur   14   /Font des tours/A pas de loup./Dans un égout/Une petite fille/En guenilles/Camarde/
  47 Mél Adult   6   Yorkshire, conférencier;/A Londres, un peu banquier,/Vous me paierez bien la tête./
  48 Lune Miel   13   à Milan/Où se trouve la Cène, et un restaurant pas cher./Lui pense aux
  51 Restaurant   14   pour la faire rire./J'éprouvais un instant de puissance et de délire.'/Mais alors,
  51 Restaurant   17   fait est dur./Il est venu, nous peloter, un gros chien;/Moi j'avais peur, je l'ai quittée à
  51 Restaurant   28   et les pertes, et la cargaison d'étain:/Un courant de sous-mer l'emporta très loin,/Le
  51 Restaurant   30   antérieure./Figurez-vous donc, c'était un sort pénible;/Cependant, ce fut jadis un bel
  51 Restaurant   31   sort pénible;/Cependant, ce fut jadis un bel homme, de haute taille./Whispers of
UN-BEING (1)
175 FQ: BurntN 171   in the form of limitation/Between un-being and being./Sudden in a shaft of
UNABLE (5)
  37 Gerontion   18   see a sign!'/The word within a word, unable to speak a word,/Swaddled with
107 Animula   26   and selfish, misshapen, lame,/Unable to fare forward or retreat,/Fearing the
603 Spleen   9   and cats in the alley;/Dejection unable to rally/Against this dull conspiracy./
398 CP   Lavinia   12   make me?/{L} Well, Edward, as I am unable to make you laugh,/And as I can't
420 CP   Reilly   28   mouldering in their minds./Each unable to disguise his own meanness/From
UNACCOUNTABLE (2)
344 FR   Violet   10   Your behaviour all seems to me quite unaccountable./What *has* happened, Amy?/{A}
346 FR   Agatha   33   Downing, if his behaviour seems unaccountable/At times, you mustn't worry
UNACCOUNTABLY (1)
244 MC   Chorus   16   gossip,/Several girls have disappeared/Unaccountably, and some not able to./We have
UNAFFRAYED (1)
244 MC   Chorus   27   secure and assured of your fate, unaffrayed among the shades, do you realise
UNALTERABLE (3)
  30 Cous Nancy   13   guardians of the faith,/The army of unalterable law./Mr. Apollinax/When Mr.
201 Def Island   16   France, those undefeated in defeat,/unalterable in triumph, changing nothing/of
329 FR   Chorus   22   /There are certain inflexible laws/Unalterable, in the nature of music./There is
UNAPPEASED (1)
194 FQ: Little   123   presents no hindrance/To the spirit unappeased and peregrine/Between two worlds
UNASHAMED (1)
529 ES   Monica   14   And most people/Are unaware or unashamed of being envious./It's all we can ask
UNATTACHED (1)
186 FQ: DrySal   65   or resentment at failing powers,/The unattached devotion which might pass for
UNATTENDED (1)
190 FQ: DrySal   210   /For most of us, there is only the unattended/Moment, the moment in and out of
UNAWARE (3)
370 CP   Peter   30   experience/In which we were both unaware of ourselves./In your terms, perhaps,
393 CP   Edward   10   of always giving in to you./{E} I was unaware that you'd always given in to me./It
529 ES   Monica   14   without envy? And most people/Are unaware or unashamed of being envious./It's all
UNBALANCED (1)
  31 Apollinax   19   —'His pointed ears.... He must be unbalanced.' —'There was something he said
UNBAR (3)
273 MC   Thomas   16   force./We are safe. We are safe./{T} Unbar the doors! throw open the doors!/I will
274 MC   Thomas   7   Law of God above the Law of Man./Unbar the door! unbar the door!/We are not
274 MC   Thomas   7   the Law of Man./Unbar the door! unbar the door!/We are not here to triumph by
UNBROKEN (1)
  98 Ash-Wed 6   10   sails still fly seaward, seaward flying/Unbroken wings/And the lost heart stiffens and

UNCERTAIN (7)
193 FQ: Little   80   is the death of water and fire./In the uncertain hour before the morning/Near the
243 MC Chorus   15   abiding stay./Ill the wind, ill the time, uncertain the profit, certain the danger./O late
253 MC Tempt4   33   /King, emperor, bishop, baron, king:/Uncertain mastery of melting armies,/War,
263 MC Chorus   14   /The peace of this world is always uncertain, unless men keep the peace of God./
303 FR   Mary   2   in this northern country,/Late and uncertain, clings to the south wall./The gardener
303 FR   Mary   12   /And he was the only one that was uncertain./Arthur or John may be late, of
303 FR   Mary   18   It is very difficult, having to plan/For uncertain numbers. Why did she ask him?/{Ag}
UNCHANGED (1)
305 FR   Harry   26   just noticed that this room is quite unchanged:/The same hangings ... the same
UNCHANGING (2)
186 FQ: DrySal   77   East lowers/Over shallow banks unchanging and erosionless/Or drawing their
583 ES   Monica   26   me/Fixed in the certainty of love unchanging./I feel utterly secure/In you; I am a
UNCLE (3)
292 FR   Harry   14   day, mother./Aunt Ivy, Aunt Violet, Uncle Gerald, Uncle Charles. Agatha./{A} We
292 FR   Harry   14   Aunt Ivy, Aunt Violet, Uncle Gerald, Uncle Charles. Agatha./{A} We are very glad to
385 CP   Reilly   12   the grandmother,/The lively bachelor uncle at the Christmas party,/The beloved
UNCLES (1)
293 FR   Amy   4   /{A} You see your aunts and uncles are very helpful, Harry./I have always
UNCOMBED (1)
226 Macavity   14   is dusty from neglect, his whiskers are uncombed./He sways his head from side to side,
UNCOMFORTABLE (1)
303 FR   Mary   22   family dinner?/An official occasion of uncomfortable people/Who meet very seldom,
UNCOMMON (7)
299 FRDowning   35   Lordship was always very quiet:/Very uncommon that I saw him in high spirits./For
301 FR   Chorus   26   of us make the pretension/To be the uncommon exception/To the universal bondage.
412 CP   Reilly   15   will take her seriously./{R} That is not uncommon./{J} Or that she deserves to be taken
412 CP   Reilly   17   be taken seriously./{R} That is most uncommon./{J} Henry, get up./You can't be as
486 CC   Colby   2   before;/Although, as you say, it is an uncommon one./You couldn't have known my
497 CC   Eggers   36   Guzzards?/{E} I agree, it is a most uncommon name,/But stranger things have
506 CC   Eggers   39   —/Or if there are, they are equally uncommon./But, Mrs. Guzzard, this is where
UNCOMPLAINING (1)
588 Fable   35   they were to eat,/He even soakt the uncomplaining porter/Who stood outside the
UNCONGENIAL (3)
462 CC   Claude   27   you like your work? You don't find it uncongenial?/I'm not changing the subject: I'm
484 CC   Lady E   28   they were so numerous — and so uncongenial./They made me feel an outcast.
516 CC   Claude   22   /Matters you would have thought so uncongenial;/And the way in which you felt that
UNCONSCIOUS (4)
301 FR   Charles   15   you disapprove./But I believe that an unconscious accomplice is desirable./{Ch} Why
308 FR   Mary   15   /In an unexpected place, while we are unconscious of it./You hoped for something, in
330 FR   Harry   9   the influence/Of Wishwood, being unconscious, living in gentle motion/Of horses,
403 CP   Edward   30   imposed upon me/With the obstinate, unconscious, sub-human strength/That some
UNCONSCIOUSNESS (1)
336 FR   Agatha   30   is like a child, formed/In a moment of unconsciousness/In an accidental bed/Or under
UNCONSIDERED (1)
154 Rock 3   12   /Between futile speculation and unconsidered action./Many are engaged in
UNCONVINCED (1)
279 MC Knight1   8   express. If there are any who are still unconvinced, I think that/Richard Brito,
UNCORSETED (1)
 52 Whispers   19   eye/Is underlined for emphasis;/Uncorseted, her friendly bust/Gives promise of
UNCREATIVE (1)
465 CC   Claude   17   craving/To create, when one is wholly uncreative?/I don't think so. For I came to see/
UNCROSSED (2)
316 FR   Agatha   23   the knot is unknotted/The crossed is uncrossed/And the crooked is made straight. {}/
350 FR   Agatha   18   the knot be unknotted/The crossed be uncrossed/The crooked be made straight/And
UNCROWN (1)
268 MC Thomas   17   we sent./{T} Never was it my wish/To uncrown the King's son, or to diminish/His
UND (1)
 62 WL: Burial   42   into the heart of light, the silence./*Oed' und leer das Meer.*/Madame Sosostris, famous
UNDECEIVED (2)
179 FQ: ECoker   88   of all we have been. We are only undeceived/Of that which, deceiving, could no
492 CC   Lady E   6   your ... delusion/I would never have undeceived you./{SC} And as for me,/If I could
UNDECEIVING (1)
515 CC   Guzzard   9   I shrank, at the moment,/From undeceiving you. And then I thought — why

UNDEFEATED (2)

190 FQ: DrySal	232	here to be realised;/Who are only undefeated/Because we have gone on trying;/
201 Def Island	15	/to Flanders and France, those undefeated in defeat,/unalterable in triumph,

UNDENIABLE (1)

186 FQ: DrySal	67	leakage,/The silent listening to the undeniable/Clamour of the bell of the last

UNDEPENDABLE (1)

500 CC Lucasta	29	anyone. He's fascinating,/But he's undependable. He has his own world,/And he

UNDER (102)

31 Apollinax	10	/Like the old man of the sea's/Hidden under coral islands/Where worried bodies of
31 Apollinax	13	for the head of Mr. Apollinax rolling under a chair/Or grinning over a screen/With
38 Gerontion	32	/An old man in a draughty house/Under a windy knob./After such knowledge,
40 Burb Blei	5	and he fell./Defunctive music under sea/Passed seaward with the passing bell/
40 Burb Blei	9	that had loved him well./The horses, under the axletree/Beat up the dawn from Istria
52 Whispers	3	the skin;/And breastless creatures under ground/Leaned backward with a lipless
54 Mr E Sun	21	pustular/Clutching piaculative pence./Under the penitential gates/Sustained by staring
61 WL: Burial	25	of water. Only/There is shadow under this red rock,/(Come in under the shadow
61 WL: Burial	26	shadow under this red rock,/(Come in under the shadow of this red rock),/And I will
62 WL: Burial	61	be so careful these days./Unreal City,/Under the brown fog of a winter dawn,,/A
64 WL: Chess	108	/Footsteps shuffled on the stair./Under the firelight, under the brush, her hair/
64 WL: Chess	108	on the stair./Under the firelight, under the brush, her hair/Spread out in fiery
65 WL: Chess	118	bones./'What is that noise?'/The wind under the door./'What is that noise now? What
68 WL: Fire S	208	/So rudely forc'd./Tereu/Unreal City/Under the brown fog of a winter noon/Mr.
70 WL: Fire S	297	feet are at Moorgate, and my heart/Under my feet. After the event/He wept. He
71 WL: DWater	315	/And the profit and loss./A current under sea/Picked his bones in whispers. As he
74 WL: Thund	408	draped by the beneficent spider/Or under seals broken by the lean solicitor/In our
84 Hollow Men	44	supplication of a dead man's hand/Under the twinkle of a fading star./Is it like this
91 Ash-Wed 2	1	death./Lady, three white leopards sat under a juniper-tree/In the cool of the day,
92 Ash-Wed 2	48	/For the Garden/Where all love ends./Under a juniper-tree the bones sang, scattered
92 Ash-Wed 2	50	we did little good to each other,/Under a tree in the cool of the day, with the
92 Ash-Wed 3	4	same shape twisted on the banister/Under the vapour in the fetid air/Struggling
109 Marina	21	between leaves and hurrying feet/Under sleep, where all the waters meet./
122 SAWa & Ho	15	SNOW AS BONES/{W&H} *Under the bamboo/Bamboo bamboo/Under the*
122 SAWa & Ho	17	*Under the bamboo/Bamboo bamboo/Under the bamboo tree/Two live as one/One live*
122 SAWa & Ho	21	*one/One live as two/Two live as three/Under the bam/Under the boo/Under the bamboo*
122 SAWa & Ho	22	*two/Two live as three/Under the bam/Under the boo/Under the bamboo tree./Where the*
122 SAWa & Ho	23	*as three/Under the bam/Under the boo/Under the bamboo tree./Where the breadfruit fall*
122 SAWa & Ho	27	*/And the sound is the sound of the sea/Under the bam/Under the boo/Under the bamboo*
122 SAWa & Ho	28	*is the sound of the sea/Under the bam/Under the boo/Under the bamboo tree/Where the*
122 SAWa & Ho	29	*the sea/Under the bam/Under the boo/Under the bamboo tree/Where the Gauguin maids*
122 SAWa & Ho	33	*banyan shades/Wear palmleaf drapery/Under the bam/Under the boo/Under the bamboo*
122 SAWa & Ho	34	*Wear palmleaf drapery/Under the bam/Under the boo/Under the bamboo tree./Tell me in*
122 SAWa & Ho	35	*drapery/Under the bam/Under the boo/Under the bamboo tree/Tell me in what part of*
123 SAWa & Ho	3	*the wood/Do you want to flirt with me?/Under the breadfruit, banyan, palmleaf/Or under*
123 SAWa & Ho	4	*the breadfruit, banyan, palmleaf/Or under the bamboo tree?/Any old tree will do for*
127 Cor1 March	32	perceiving, indifferent./O hidden under the dove's wing, hidden in the turtle's
128 Cor1 March	33	wing, hidden in the turtle's breast,/Under the palmtree at noon, under the running
128 Cor1 March	33	breast,/Under the palmtree at noon, under the running water/At the still point of the
129 Cor2 State	32	torchbearer, yawning./O hidden under the... Hidden under the... Where the
129 Cor2 State	32	/O hidden under the... Hidden under the... Where the dove's foot rested and
129 Cor2 State	33	/A still moment, repose of noon, set under the upper branches of noon's widest tree/
129 Cor2 State	34	upper branches of noon's widest tree/Under the breast feather stirred by the small
135 5FingerEx2	7	/Little dog was safe and warm/Under a cretonne eiderdown,/Yet the field was
175 FQ: BurntN	153	strain,/Crack and sometimes break, under the burden,/Under the tension, slip, slide,
175 FQ: BurntN	154	sometimes break, under the burden,/Under the tension, slip, slide, perish,/Decay
178 FQ: ECoker	39	mirth/Mirth of those long since under earth/Nourishing the corn. Keeping time,
178 FQ: ECoker	55	heat,/And snowdrops writhing under feet/And hollyhocks that aim too high/
179 FQ: ECoker	100	is endless./The houses are all gone under the sea./The dancers are all gone under
179 FQ: ECoker	101	the sea./The dancers are all gone under the hill./O dark dark dark. They all go
180 FQ: ECoker	123	of nothing to think about;/Or when, under ether, the mind is conscious but conscious
182 FQ: ECoker	189	and lost again and again: and now, under conditions/That seem unpropitious. But
182 FQ: ECoker	199	/There is a time for the evening under starlight,/A time for the evening under
182 FQ: ECoker	200	starlight,/A time for the evening under lamplight/(The evening with the
185 FQ: DrySal	36	homewards, and the seagull:/And under the oppression of the silent fog/The
231 Bust Jones	31	he's found./It can be no surprise that under our eyes/He has grown unmistakably
588 Fable	54	/Of ale, and cheese which they kept under cover./Last, a boar's head, which to bring

605 Narcissus	1	/The Death of Saint Narcissus/Come under the shadow of this gray rock —/Come in
605 Narcissus	2	shadow of this gray rock —/Come in under the shadow of this gray rock,/And I will
605 Narcissus	20	thighs and knees./So he came out under the rock./First he was sure that he had
248 MC Thomas	13	impossible, the undesirable,/Voices under sleep, waking a dead world,/So that the
249 MC Thomas	33	forget the bishops/Whom I have laid under excommunication./{T2} Hungry hatred/
253 MC Tempt4	31	bind, Thomas, bind,/King and bishop under your heel./King, emperor, bishop, baron,
256 MC Priests	30	the window-bar made fast, is the door under lock and bolt?/{4T} Is it rain that taps at
257 MC Chorus	23	can avert, none can avoid, flowing under our feet and over the sky;/Under doors
257 MC Chorus	24	under our feet and over the sky;/Under doors and down chimneys, flowing in at
270 MC Chorus	1	the strong salt taste of living things under the sea; I have tasted/The living lobster,
276 MC Knight1	22	then your/sympathies are all with the under dog. I respect such feelings, I/share them.
277 MC Knight2	37	your sympathies are always with the under dog./It is the English spirit of fair play.
277 MC Knight2	40	has throughout been/presented as the under dog. But is this really the case? I am
278 MC Knight2	16	and temporal administration, under the central/government. I knew Becket
279 MC Knight2	19	Archbishop/was Chancellor, no one, under the King, did more to weld the/country
281 MC Chorus	15	of Canterbury,/The back bent under toil, the knee bent under sin, the hands to
281 MC Chorus	15	back bent under toil, the knee bent under sin, the hands to the face under fear, the
281 MC Chorus	15	bent under sin, the hands to the face under fear, the head bent under grief,/Even in
281 MC Chorus	15	to the face under fear, the head bent under grief,/Even in us the voices of seasons, the
290 FR Agatha	35	of the dark passage/The paw under the door. {}/CHORUS (IVY, VIOLET,
310 FR Mary	7	the ones that suffer least:/The aconite under the snow/And the snowdrop crying for a
323 FR Charles	36	that he's here./We must put ourselves under Warburton's orders./{W} I repeat, Lady
333 FR Agatha	37	chosen/To resolve the enchantment under which we suffer./{H} Look, I do not
335 FR Agatha	7	/And sharp heels scraping. Over and under/Echo and noise of feet./I was only the
335 FR Agatha	11	eye/Fixing the movement. Over and under./{H} In and out, in an endless drift/Of
335 FR Harry	17	/Until the chain broke, and I was left/Under the single eye above the desert./{Ag} Up
335 FR Harry	30	machinery,/And the desert is cleared, under the judicial sun/Of the final eye, and the
336 FR Agatha	32	/In an accidental bed/Or under an elder tree/According to the phase/Of
350 FR Mary	9	follow/{M} A curse is written/On the under side of things/Behind the smiling mirror/
366 CP Julia	4	of that sofa —/No, this chair. Look under the cushion./{E} Are you quite sure
376 CP Julia	19	That I had. Edward must be fed./He's under such a strain. We must keep his strength
402 CP Edward	26	you send such patients/As myself, under your personal observation?/{R} You are
422 CP Reilly	14	*glasses*]/{R} Let them build the hearth/Under the protection of the stars./{A} Let them
437 CP Reilly	22	was obvious/That here was a woman under sentence of death./That was her destiny.
447 CC Claude	26	/You must say you had to leave under medical orders./She's always been
449 CC Claude	11	Eggerson, I am not unhopeful/That, under the impression that he is an orphan,/She
458 CC Eggers	28	been meaning to retire .../{E} Under medical orders, Lady Elizabeth:/The
459 CC Lady E	34	is in Lausanne./I have been in Zürich, under Dr. Rebmann./{SC} But you were going
504 CC Lady E	21	/{LE} She's been making progress, under my direction;/But she shouldn't have
507 CC Eggers	7	that is, of parents unknown to you —/Under such conditions?/{MG} Yes, I did take in
537 ES Gomez	13	to Oxford/And then what I became under your influence./{LC} You cannot
568 ES Ld Clav	1	been?/{LC} Not far away. Standing under the great beech tree./{M} Why under the
568 ES Monica	2	under the great beech tree./{M} Why under the beech tree?/{LC} I feel drawn to the
569 ES Ld Clav	8	words. Monica!/I've had your love under false pretences./Now, I'm tired of keeping
583 ES Monica	16	has gone too far to return to us./He is under the beech tree. It is quiet and cold there./

UNDERGO (1)

| 421 CP Julia | 19 | /Of the kind of suffering they must undergo/On the way of illumination?/{R} Will |

UNDERGONE (1)

| 516 CC Claude | 34 | our likeness to each other./We have undergone the same disillusionment:/I want us |

UNDERGRADUATE (2)

| 332 FR Agatha | 21 | I was the youngest: I was then/An undergraduate at Oxford. I came/Once for a |
| 539 ES Gomez | 19 | heard about *him*,/He's followed your undergraduate career/Without the protection of |

UNDERGROUND (3)

180 FQ: ECoker	119	being rolled away —/Or as, when an underground train, in the tube, stops too long
223 Pekes Pols	47	/The traffic all stopped, and the Underground trembled,/And some of the
589 Fable	86	/That the Abbot's course lay nearer underground;/But the church straightway put to

UNDERLINED (1)

| 52 Whispers | 18 | /Grishkin is nice: her Russian eye/Is underlined for emphasis;/Uncorseted, her |

UNDERNEATH (5)

41 Burb Blei	22	On the Rialto once./The rats are underneath the piles./The Jew is underneath the
41 Burb Blei	23	are underneath the piles./The Jew is underneath the lot./Money in furs. The
234 Ad-dress	31	very easily taken in —/Just chuck him underneath the chin/Or slap his back or shake
336 FR Harry	8	quiet?/Do you feel a kind of stirring underneath the air?/Do you? don't you? a
437 CP Reilly	10	*which thou beholdest; but the other/Is underneath the grave, where do inhabit/The*

UNDERSCORED (1)
334 FR   Harry   27   ready —/The book laid out, lines underscored, and the costume/Ready to be put

UNDERSTAND (160)

19 Portrait		58	afternoon:/'I am always sure that you understand/My feelings, always sure that you
21 Portrait		104	relate/So closely! I myself can hardly understand./We must leave it now to fate./You
21 Portrait		119	while/Not knowing what to feel or if I understand/Or whether wise or foolish, tardy or
34 Figlia		15	and deft,/Some way we both should understand,/Simple and faithless as a smile and
125 SA	Sweeney	22	words when I talk to you/But if you understand or if you don't/That's nothing to me
234 Ad-dress		4	/You should need no interpreter/To understand their character./You now have
592 Grad 2		4	/And when they leave they fully understand/That though again they see their
251 MC	Tempt3	27	fighting in Anjou./He does not understand us, the English barons./We are the
254 MC	Thomas	5	but for one./{T} That I do not understand./{T4} It is not for me to tell you how
261 MC	Thomas	33	in/a fashion that the world cannot understand; so in Heaven the Saints are/most
277 MC	Knight3	13	So if/we seemed a bit rowdy, you will understand why it was; and for/my part I am
287 FR	Amy	29	I live to keep them./You none of you understand how old you are/And death will
293 FR	Agatha	22	/And you must try at once to make us understand,/And we must try to understand
293 FR	Agatha	23	us understand,/And we must try to understand you./{H} But how can I explain,
293 FR	Harry	25	how can I explain to *you*?/You will understand less after I have explained it./All
293 FR	Harry	26	it./All that I could hope to make you understand/Is only events: not what has
293 FR	Harry	29	nothing has ever happened/Cannot understand the unimportance of events./{G}
295 FR	Charles	11	to revert to it. Remember, my boy,/I understand, your life together made it seem
295 FR	Charles	14	as I do now, early before morning./I understand these feelings better than you know
296 FR	Agatha	1	There are certain points I do not yet understand:/They will be clear later. I am also
296 FR	Agatha	4	/It is only because of what you do not understand/That you feel the need to declare
296 FR	Agatha	6	declare what you do./There is more to understand: hold fast to that/As the way to
296 FR	Ivy	18	/Harry must see a doctor./{I} But I understand —/I have heard of such cases before
299 FR	Charles	21	meaning — just for the effect./{C} I understand, Downing. Was she in good spirits?/
302 FR	Amy	16	arrive in time to dress./I do not understand what could have gone wrong/With
304 FR	Mary	12	After seven years?/{M} Oh, you don't understand!/But you do understand. You only
304 FR	Mary	13	you don't understand!/But you do understand. You only want to know/Whether I
304 FR	Mary	14	You only want to know/Whether I understand. You know perfectly well,/What
308 FR	Harry	37	know,/You cannot know, you cannot understand./{M} I think I could understand, but
308 FR	Mary	38	understand./{M} I think I could understand, but you would have to be patient/
309 FR	Harry	1	If I tried to explain, you could never understand:/Explaining would only make a
309 FR	Harry	4	you./There is only one way for you to understand/And that is by seeing. They are
316 FR	Gerald	5	danger, but only to what I can understand./{V} It is the obtuseness of Gerald
317 FR	Warburt	10	about it, if you like./{W} You don't understand me./I'm sure you cannot know what
322 FR	Winch	2	isn't very well this evening./{Wi} I understand, Sir./It'd be the same if it was my
324 FR	Harry	33	emotions are suitable./They don't understand what it is to be awake,/To be living
325 FR	Violet	5	*and* AMY]/{V} I really do not understand Harry's behaviour./{Ag} I think it is
327 FR	Harry	18	would get us somewhere. You don't understand me./You can't understand me. It's
327 FR	Harry	19	You don't understand me./You can't understand me. It's not being alone/That is the
330 FR	Agatha	15	/You may be afraid that I would not understand you,/You may also be afraid of
337 FR	Agatha	13	compels cruelty/To those who do not understand love./What you have wished to
339 FR	Harry	2	mother, it is indeed harder,/Not to understand./{A} Where are you going?/{H} I
339 FR	Harry	19	Why I have this election/I do not understand. It must have been preparing
344 FR	Violet	6	going?/{A} Ask Agatha./{V} I cannot understand at all. Why is he leaving?/{A} Ask
344 FR	Violet	32	happened in our family./{V} I cannot understand it./{H} I never said that I was going
344 FR	Harry	35	/If you believed it, still you would not understand./You can't know why I am going.
345 FR	Harry	3	for my bad manners./But if you *could* understand you would be quite happy about it,/
345 FR	Violet	30	/{G} Oh, certainly, Amy./{V} I do not understand/A single thing that's happened. {}/
345 FR	Charles	34	feel/That there is something I *could* understand, if I were told it./But I'm not sure
346 FR	Downing	19	years that I've been with him/I think I understand his Lordship better than anybody;/
346 FR	Downing	39	them too — Miss Mary and I./{Do} I understand you, Miss. And if I may say so,/
347 FR	Downing	2	subject, I'm most relieved —/If you understand my meaning. I thought that was the
347 FR	Violet	24	Ivy./And if you did, you would not understand it./I do not understand, so how
347 FR	Violet	25	you would not understand it./I do not understand, so how could you? Amy is not well;
348 FR	Chorus	11	happens when we are asleep./We understand the ordinary business of living,/We
349 FR	Charles	11	was it? — and yet I think that I might understand./{all} But we must adjust ourselves
357 CP	Julia	16	/{J} And sends for Lavinia./I quite understand. Are there any prospects?/{E} No, I
357 CP	Julia	22	back and be called away again./I understand these tough old women —/I'm one
362 CP	Edward	15	was not coming back — well, I can't understand it./Nobody likes to be left with a
371 CP	Peter	5	perhaps it is the last. And you don't understand./{E} My dear Peter, I have only been
372 CP	Alex	21	... I mean, this is another aunt./{A} I understand. The real aunt. But you'll be
374 CP	Celia	8	very pleased to see me./Edward, I understand what has happened/But I could not

374 CP	Celia	9	what has happened/But I could not understand your manner on the telephone./It
374 CP	Edward	12	I'll go./{E} But how can you say you understand what has happened?/*I* don't know
374 CP	Edward	14	is going to happen;/And to try to understand it, I want to be alone./{C} I should
381 CP	Edward	17	desire has left behind. But you cannot understand./How could *you* understand what it
381 CP	Edward	18	cannot understand./How could *you* understand what it is to feel old?/{C} But I want
381 CP	Celia	19	it is to feel old?/{C} But I want to understand you. I could understand./And,
381 CP	Celia	19	But I want to understand you. I could understand./And, Edward, please believe that
382 CP	Celia	4	/{C} I am not sure, Edward, that I understand you;/And yet I understand as I
382 CP	Celia	5	that I understand you;/And yet I understand as I never did before./I think — I
389 CP	Celia	16	want to leave it./{C} Lavinia, I think I understand about Peter .../{L} I have no doubt
397 CP	Edward	36	will be the old one./{E} You don't understand me. Have I not made it clear/That
399 CP	Reilly	3	run over my instructions again./You understand, of course, that it is important/To
404 CP	Edward	16	The death of the spirit —/Can you understand what I suffer?/{R} I understand
404 CP	Reilly	17	you understand what I suffer?/{R} I understand what you mean./{E} I can no longer
413 CP	Celia	26	/{C} Well, there are two things I can't understand,/Which you might consider
414 CP	Celia	28	/They make faces, and think they understand each other./And I'm sure that they
417 CP	Reilly	35	/Two people who know they do not understand each other,/Breeding children whom
417 CP	Reilly	36	/Breeding children whom they do not understand/And who will never understand
417 CP	Reilly	37	not understand/And who will never understand them./{C} Is that the best life?/{R} It
421 CP	Julia	23	spirits?/{J} Henry, you simply do not understand innocence./She will be afraid of
421 CP	Reilly	35	salvation with diligence', I do not understand/What I myself am saying./{J} You
434 CP	Peter	34	know what I'm thinking./{P} I don't understand at all. But then I've been away/For
435 CP	Peter	15	I suppose I didn't know her,/I didn't understand her. I understand nothing./{R} You
435 CP	Peter	15	know her,/I didn't understand her. I understand nothing./{R} You understand your
435 CP	Reilly	16	her. I understand nothing./{R} You understand your *métier*, Mr. Quilpe —/Which is
435 CP	Lavinia	39	seem less unkind if I can make you understand/That in fact I've been talking about
436 CP	Julia	18	/Like that, one day. And then you'll understand her/And be reconciled, and be
440 CP	Edward	3	had to know .../{E} Now I think I understand .../{L} Then I hope you will explain
440 CP	Edward	6	it to me!/{E} Oh, it isn't much/That I understand yet! But Sir Henry has been saying,/
446 CC	Claude	11	About his music./Yes, I think so. I understand his feelings./He's like me, Eggerson.
449 CC	Claude	38	would be./There's a lot I don't understand about my wife./There's always
450 CC	Claude	3	importance./It's when you're sure you understand a person/That you're liable to make
450 CC	Eggers	10	/I must admit there's a lot that *I* don't understand/About my wife./{SC} And just as
450 CC	Claude	15	of that!/My rule is to remember that I understand nobody,/But on the other hand
450 CC	Claude	17	hand never to be sure/That they don't understand me — a good deal better/Than I
450 CC	Eggers	20	do I infer/That you're not sure you understand Mr. Simpkins, either?/{SC} A timely
458 CC	Lady E	17	and got them to change it./I can't understand why you're both so surprised./You
459 CC	Lady E	20	I'm sure. My husband/Does not understand the importance of colour/For our
463 CC	Claude	33	do. I have to fight that person./{SC} I understand what you are saying/Much better
465 CC	Claude	6	And when I was mature enough/To understand him, he was not there./{C} You've
466 CC	Claude	28	I'll wait until you ask me./Do you understand now what I meant when I spoke/Of
466 CC	Colby	31	/{C} I think I do. At least, I understand *you* better/In learning to understand
466 CC	Colby	32	I understand *you* better/In learning to understand the conditions/Which life has
466 CC	Colby	39	of atonement./Even your failure to understand him,/Of which you spoke — that
474 CC	Lucasta	34	is a ... symbol./I really would like to understand music,/Not in order to be able to
474 CC	Lucasta	40	any *I've* ever lived in./And I'd like to understand *you*./{C} I believe you do already,/
475 CC	Colby	2	than ... other people. And I want to understand *you*./Does one ever come to
475 CC	Colby	3	*you*./Does one ever come to understand anyone?/{L} I think you're being
475 CC	Colby	8	a person./All one can do is to understand them better,/To keep up with them;
475 CC	Colby	10	so that as the other changes/You can understand the change as soon as it happens,/
475 CC	Colby	17	about, perhaps .../{C} Is, beginning to understand another person./{L} Oh Colby, now
475 CC	Lucasta	18	/{L} Oh Colby, now that we begin to understand,/I'd like you to know a little more
477 CC	Colby	13	/{C} Shocked? No. Yes. You don't understand./I want to explain. But I can't, just
477 CC	Lucasta	22	ashamed of me. I thought you'd understand./Little you know what it's like to be
484 CC	Lady E	7	not want to know your relatives!/I understand exactly how you felt./How I disliked
484 CC	Lady E	18	either of your parents,/You can't understand what loathing really is./Yet we must
490 CC	Colby	19	it matter/Whose son I am?' You don't understand/That when one has lived without
492 CC	Colby	24	—/And I found one note I couldn't understand./'Reminiscent mood.' I can't
494 CC	Lady E	28	/Why haven't you? I don't suppose I understand/And I know you don't think I
494 CC	Lady E	29	/And I know you don't think I understand anything,/And perhaps I don't. But
494 CC	Lady E	31	talk/Sometimes to me as if I did understand,/And perhaps I might come to
494 CC	Lady E	32	/And perhaps I might come to understand better./What did you want to do?/
499 CC	Eggers	8	questions on behalf of my wife./{E} I understand, Sir Claude: I understand
499 CC	Eggers	8	wife./{E} I understand, Sir Claude: I understand completely. {}/[*A knock on the*
500 CC	Lucasta	15	to have told you./{L} Well, I don't understand. What I do understand/Is Colby's

500 CC	Lucasta	15	Well, I don't understand. What I do understand/Is Colby's behaviour. If he knew it./
501 CC	Claude	17	*you*;/And I certainly fail to understand Colby./{LE} But you and I, Claude,
501 CC	Lady E	18	/{LE} But you and I, Claude, can understand each other,/No matter how late.
501 CC	Lady E	20	late. And perhaps that will help us/To understand other people. I hope so./Lucasta, I
502 CC	Lucasta	33	/It may be there's no one so hard to understand/As one's brother .../{C} Or sister .../
503 CC	Lucasta	1	in time. Perhaps, one day/We may understand each other. And accept the fact/
505 CC	Guzzard	24	interrupt, Elizabeth./{MG} I don't understand you./{E} It's this way, Mrs.
507 CC	Lady E	31	I do?/{LE} Oh, Claude, you see? You understand, Colby?/{SC} Don't be certain yet,
514 CC	Eggers	31	of such extreme importance/You'll understand the need for exact confirmation./
514 CC	Guzzard	32	need for exact confirmation./{MG} I understand that, Mr. Eggerson. Quite well./{SC}
515 CC	Guzzard	29	I could never have back./Don't you understand that this revelation/Drives the knife
519 CC	Lady E	15	do better./Claude, we've got to try to understand our children./{K} And we should
519 CC	Kaghan	16	children./{K} And we should like to understand *you* .../I mean, I'm including both
524 ES	Charles	29	promised./{C} What you don't understand is that I have a grievance./On
527 ES	Monica	1	father./In the first place, you don't understand him;/In the second place, we're not
527 ES	Charles	15	be very long. {}/[*Exit*]/{C} Don't you understand that you're torturing me?/How long
528 ES	Monica	8	a master. Strangers!/{M} You don't understand. It's one thing meeting people/When
531 ES	Ld Clav	25	small minority/Of those who really understand the place we filled/Are inwardly
536 ES	Gomez	21	is a sickly word./You don't understand such isolation/As mine, you think
537 ES	Gomez	22	but I was flattered./Later, I came to understand: you made friends with me/Because
542 ES	Gomez	17	Is to renew our friendship. Don't you understand?/{LC} I see that when I gave you my
545 ES	Piggott	27	/And I thought, 'Lord Claverton will understand/My not coming in directly after
550 ES	Ld Clav	30	Why not, of all places? What I don't understand/Is why you should take the first
550 ES	Carghil	35	a clever girl she was! — 'he doesn't understand women./Any woman who trusted
556 ES	Monica	1	I had prepared you. I've made him understand/That the doctors want you to be
563 ES	Gomez	31	look at/As Mrs. Carghill, I can well understand/Her success on the stage./{MC} Oh,
565 ES	Ld Clav	35	/I said I knew from experience. Do I understand the meaning/Of the lesson I would
569 ES	Monica	14	The more I knew about you. I should understand you better./There's nothing I'm
570 ES	Ld Clav	5	me./I thought that she would never understand/Or that she would be jealous of the
575 ES	Ld Clav	30	daughter and my future son-in-law/Understand that allusion. I have told them the
577 ES	Carghil	30	very much alike in some ways —/So I understand business. Mr. Carghill told me so./
578 ES	Ld Clav	10	your mother and I, in our failure/To understand each other, both misunderstood you
582 ES	Monica	29	/With a glance of farewell./{M} I can't understand his going for a walk./{C} He wanted

UNDERSTANDING (19)

245 MC	Thomas	12	than they know, and beyond your understanding./They know and do not know,
294 FR	Agatha	14	Whether it may be too far beyond our understanding./{H} The sudden solitude in a
309 FR	Mary	8	/{M} If you think I am incapable of understanding you —/But in any case, I must
334 FR	Harry	20	/I only now begin to have some understanding/Of you, and of all of us. Family
334 FR	Harry	32	—/More compassionate at least — by understanding./But she would not like that.
348 FR	Chorus	23	loss of money./But the circle of our understanding/Is a very restricted area./Except
395 CP	Lavinia	36	/That I wasn't worth the trouble of understanding./{E} So here we are again. Back
407 CP	Reilly	14	your perspicacity./Your sympathetic understanding of each other/Will prepare you to
410 CP	Reilly	17	your own faults,/And so could avoid understanding each other./Now, you have only
438 CP	Reilly	29	the intention/And beyond our limited understanding/Of ourselves and others, we
475 CC	Colby	7	I meant./I meant, there's no end to understanding a person./All one can do is to
475 CC	Lucasta	15	perhaps what we call change .../{L} Is understanding better what one really is./And the
491 CC	Claude	15	I should be contented with such an understanding;/And indeed, it's not so far from
502 CC	Lucasta	37	/Is to recognise the limits of one's understanding./It may be that understanding, as
502 CC	Lucasta	38	one's understanding./It may be that understanding, as a brother and a sister,/Will
525 ES	Charles	3	for the whole afternoon/On the plain understanding .../{M} That you should stop to
553 ES	Ld Clav	4	confident, I must say,/About your understanding of my character./{MC} I've
554 ES	Carghil	17	/You're so considerate — and so understanding./{MP} But I ought to introduce
576 ES	Michael	11	/With you, that made him so understanding/Of my predicament./{LC} And

UNDERSTANDS (7)

23	Preludes	34	of the street/As the street hardly understands;/Sitting along the bed's edge, where
244 MC	Chorus	22	which we cannot face, which none understands,/And our hearts are torn from us,
244 MC	Chorus	24	are lost lost/In a final fear which none understands. O Thomas Archbishop,/O Thomas
325 FR	Gerald	14	for Amy;/But I think that Warburton understands *that*./{I} You are quite right,
420 CP	Reilly	31	/But the knowledge that the other understands the motive —/Mirror to mirror,
451 CC	Eggers	4	Elizabeth./Don't listen to him. He understands Sir Claude,/And he's always been
575 ES	Michael	4	That's what Señor Gomez sees./*He* understands my point of view, if *you* don't./And

UNDERSTOOD (17)

173 FQ:	BurntN	78	new world/And the old made explicit, understood/In the completion of its partial
190 FQ:	DrySal	219	/The hint half guessed, the gift half understood, is Incarnation./Here the impossible
275 MC	Chorus	29	did not wish anything to happen./We understood the private catastrophe,/The

330 FR	Agatha	16	you,/You may also be afraid of being understood,/Try not to regard it as an
387 CP	Edward	7	about it?/{E} I wish I could. I wish I understood anything./I'm completely in the
395 CP	Edward	33	been your perfect assurance/That you understood me better than I understood myself.
395 CP	Edward	33	That you understood me better than I understood myself./{L} And the most
404 CP	Edward	6	alone there./{E} I wonder/If you have understood a word of what I have been saying./
431 CP	Julia	18	we want to use Boltwell./{J} But I understood that Boltwell/Is in a very decayed
439 CP	Lavinia	4	/{L} I'm not sure about that. If I had understood you/Then I might not have
465 CC	Claude	4	/Who had always been right. I never understood him./I was too young. And when I
466 CC	Colby	37	ago,/When you spoke of never having understood your father/Until it was too late.
501 CC	Claude	16	B.,/And I've never thought that I understood *you*;/And I certainly fail to
507 CC	Guzzard	14	mother?/{MG} I was not told either./I understood the child was very well connected:/
524 ES	Monica	5	But you *must* stay to tea. That was understood/When you said you could give me
570 ES	Ld Clav	10	/It was not her fault. We never understood each other./And so we lived, with a
578 ES	Monica	34	mine./{M} Oh Michael, you haven't understood a single word/Of what I said. You

UNDERSTUDIED (1)

228 Gus		32	season I never fell flat,/And I once understudied Dick Whittington's Cat./But my

UNDERTAKER (1)

29 Aunt Helen		6	/The shutters were drawn and the undertaker wiped his feet —/He was aware that

UNDERTAKERS (1)

135 5FingerEx2		12	/Jellicle cats and dogs all must/Like undertakers, come to dust./Here a little dog I

UNDESIRABLE (2)

248 MC Thomas		12	still temptation./The impossible, the undesirable,/Voices under sleep, waking a dead
290 FR	Amy	4	the world/To expensive hotels and undesirable society/Which she could choose

UNDESIRED (1)

68 WL: Fire S		238	caresses/Which still are unreproved, if undesired./Flushed and decided, he assaults at

UNDESIRING (1)

175 FQ: BurntN		168	and end of movement,/Timeless, and undesiring/Except in the aspect of time/Caught

UNDETERMINED (1)

251 MC Tempt3		2	circumstance./But circumstance is not undetermined./Unreal friendship may turn to

UNDID (1)

70 WL: Fire S		294	bore me. Richmond and Kew/Undid me. By Richmond I raised my knees/

UNDIGNIFIED (3)

234 Ad-dress		29	showing too much pride/Is frequently undignified./He's very easily taken in —/Just
316 FR	Ivy	4	I am afraid./{I} This is a most undignified terror, and I must struggle against
325 FR	Violet	35	well — but I think an open car/Is so undignified: you're blown about so,/And you

UNDISCIPLINED (1)

182 FQ: ECoker		184	mess of imprecision of feeling,/Undisciplined squads of emotion. And what

UNDISTINGUISHED (1)

451 CC	Eggers	27	/She once referred to him as 'undistinguished';/But with you, as I said, it will

UNDOING (1)

252 MC Thomas		10	he trust those who work for King's undoing?/{T3} Kings will allow no power but

UNDONE (2)

62 WL: Burial		63	many,/I had not thought death had undone so many./Sighs, short and infrequent,
297 FR	Agatha	6	it will do/But that nothing may be left undone/On the margin of the impossible./{A}

UNDOUBTED (1)

279 MC Knight4		25	upon him, until it/became at last an undoubted mania. I have unimpeachable

UNDOUBTEDLY (1)

286 FR	Ivy	32	/{I} The younger generation/Are undoubtedly decadent./{C} The younger

UNDRAWN (1)

285 FR	Amy	11	on the lights. But leave the curtains undrawn./Make up the fire. Will the spring

UNE (7)

46 Directeur		15	tours/A pas de loup./Dans un égout/Une petite fille/En guenilles/Camarde/Regarde/
47 Mél Adult		17	/Je célébrai mon jour de fête/Dans une oasis d'Afrique/Vêtu d'une peau de girafe./
47 Mél Adult		18	fête/Dans une oasis d'Afrique/Vêtu d'une peau de girafe./On montrera mon
48 Lune Miel		2	ils rentrent à Terre Haute;/Mais une nuit d'été, les voici à Ravenne,/A l'aise
48 Lune Miel		4	de punaises;/La sueur aestivale, et une forte odeur de chienne./Ils restent sur le dos
48 Lune Miel		8	drap pour mieux égratigner./Moins d'une lieue d'ici est Saint Apollinaire/En Classe,
51 Restaurant		9	sur les ronces —/C'est là, dans une averse, qu'on s'abrite./J'avais sept ans, elle

UNEMPLOYED (3)

149 Rock 1 m		94	*they are answered by voices of the* UNEMPLOYED./*No man has hired us*/*With*
161 Rock 7 m		33	backwards?/VOICE OF THE UNEMPLOYED (*afar off*):/*In this land*/*There*
161 Rock 7 m		38	on a by-pass way?/VOICE OF THE UNEMPLOYED (*more faintly*):/*In this land*/

UNENDED (1)

240 MC Priest2		32	accepted, meetings refused,/Meetings unended or endless/At one place or another in

UNENDING (1)
193 FQ: Little   82   night/At the recurrent end of the unending/After the dark dove with the
UNENDURABLE (1)
293 FR   Harry   39   nightmare. I tell you, life would be unendurable/If you were wide awake. You do
UNENLIGHTENMENT (1)
410 CP   Reilly   13   you together./While still in a state of unenlightenment,/*You* could always say: 'he
UNEXPECTED (11)
250 MC Tempt3   19   THIRD TEMPTER]/{T3} I am an unexpected visitor./{T} I expected you./{T3} But
266 MC Thomas   2   /The moment foreseen may be unexpected/When it arrives. It comes when we
307 FR   Harry   32   extinction of every alternative,/The unexpected crash of the iron cataract./You do
308 FR   Mary   15   another hope keeps springing/In an unexpected place, while we are unconscious of
361 CP   Reilly   29   approach the stranger/Is to invite the unexpected, release a new force,/Or let the genie
390 CP   Julia   2   be late./But your telegram was a bit unexpected./I dropped everything to come. And
427 CP   Alex   17   myself, not to her —/Never mind: the unexpected guest/Is the one to whom they give
440 CP   Reilly   18   And on this occasion I shall not be unexpected./{J} Now, Henry. Now, Alex. We're
461 CC   Eggers   4   —/If anything *should* turn up unexpected/And you find yourself non-plussed,
472 CC   Lucasta   14   in some ways very like oneself,/In unexpected ways. And then you begin/To
503 CC   Claude   38   was passing,/What with Lucasta's unexpected visit./She ought to be here. It
UNEXPECTEDLY (2)
474 CC   Colby   17   would simply ... be there suddenly,/Unexpectedly. Walking down an alley/I should
482 CC   Lady E   4   by appointment?/Or did they come in unexpectedly?/{C} I'd invited Lucasta. She had
UNEXPLAINABLE (1)
568 ES   Ld Clav   8   aberrations,/Reckless surrenders, unexplainable impulses,/Moments we regret in
UNFAIR (1)
424 CP   Lavinia   16   run away?/{L} Now Edward, that's unfair!/You know that we've given *several*
UNFAMILIAR (2)
196 FQ: Little   210   the torment? Love./Love is the unfamiliar Name/Behind the hands that wove/
326 FR   Violet   4   I think./Anyway, the district was unfamiliar/And I had the greatest trouble in
UNFAVOURABLY (1)
976 MC Knight1   2   that you may be disposed to judge unfavourably/of our action. You are
UNFEARED (1)
285 FR   Amy   8   and light unsought for/And the night unfeared and the day expected/And clocks
UNFINISHED (4)
113   t   first coming of the second coming./UNFINISHED POEMS/Sweeney Agonistes/
362 CP   Edward   17   to be left with a mystery:/It's so ... unfinished./{UG} Yes, it's unfinished;/And
362 CP   Reilly   18   /It's so ... unfinished./{UG} Yes, it's unfinished;/And nobody likes to be left with a
369 CP   Edward   22   /{E} Oh no, no, everything is left unfinished./But you haven't told me how you
UNFLATTERING (1)
558 ES   Ld Clav   29   /Or did Sir Alfred make other unflattering criticisms?/{Mi} Well, there was one
UNFLOWERING (1)
195 FQ: Little   157   life,/Being between two lives — unflowering, between/The live and the dead
UNFORTUNATE (2)
504 CC   Claude   20   time-table better./This is a most unfortunate beginning./{LE} She's been making
538 ES   Gomez   1   you had fostered in me,/And, equally unfortunate, a talent for penmanship./Hence, as
UNFORTUNATELY (2)
428 CP   Alex   10   these monkeys/If they are a pest?/{A} Unfortunately,/The majority of the natives are
506 CC   Eggers   3   Till further notice by a foster-mother./Unfortunately, the father died suddenly .../{LE}
UNFOUNDED (1)
512 CC Guzzard   5   your suspicions of me were wholly unfounded./{LE} Oh, Mrs. Guzzard, I had no
UNFRIENDLY (1)
103 Journ Magi   14   /And the cities hostile and the towns unfriendly/And the villages dirty and charging
UNFULFILLED (1)
336 FR   Agatha   1   happened/Is also relief from that unfulfilled craving/Flattered in sleep, and
UNGRATEFUL (1)
376 CP   Julia   24   was left at an inn./{J} Edward, how ungrateful./What's in that saucepan?/{C}
UNGUENT (1)
64 WL: Chess   88   her strange synthetic perfumes,/Unguent, powdered, or liquid — troubled,
UNHAPPILY (1)
278 MC Knight2   32   for violence more than we/do. Unhappily, there are times when violence is the
UNHAPPINESS (1)
341 FR   Amy   10   of his mistakes, because of his unhappiness,/Because of the misery that he has
UNHAPPY (7)
278 MC Knight2   7   Matilda and the irruption of the unhappy usurper/Stephen, the kingdom was
318 FR   Harry   10   then/Only seemed to make her more unhappy, and made us/Feel more guilty, and so
333 FR   Agatha   33   /You are the consciousness of your unhappy family,/Its bird sent flying through the

334 FR   Harry   12   make my living./{H} But you are not unhappy, just now?/{Ag} What does the word
380 CP   Edward 15   was in a dream/And now he is simply unhappy and bewildered./{C} I simply don't
572 ES   Ld Clav 24   have quarrelled,/We should have been unhappy, might have come to divorce;/But she
580 ES   Monica 33   and me he rejects,/But himself, the unhappy self that he's ashamed of./I'm sure he

UNHEALTHY (1)
174 FQ: BurntN 111   before and time after./Eructation of unhealthy souls/Into the faded air, the torpid/

UNHEARD (8)
67 WL: Fire S   175   The wind/Crosses the brown land, unheard. The nymphs are departed./Sweet
95 Ash-Wed 4   27   the dream/The token of the word unheard, unspoken/Till the wind shake a
96 Ash-Wed 5   2   lost, if the spent word is spent/If the unheard, unspoken/Word is unspoken, unheard;
96 Ash-Wed 5   3   unspoken/Word is unspoken, unheard;/Still is the unspoken word, the Word
96 Ash-Wed 5   4   /Still is the unspoken word, the Word unheard,/The Word without a word, the Word
172 FQ: BurntN   29   the bird called, in response to/The unheard music hidden in the shrubbery,/And
257 MC   Priests 1   in the sight of all, he may pass unseen unheard./{4T} Come whispering through the
460 CC   Claude 35   her own ticket./It's something unheard of./{E} Amazing, isn't it!/{SC} If this is

UNHESITATINGLY (1)
279 MC Knight4 38   with these facts before/you, you will unhesitatingly render a verdict of Suicide while

UNHONOURED (1)
184 FQ: DrySal   9   /Of what men choose to forget. Unhonoured, unpropitiated/By worshippers of

UNHOPEFUL (1)
449 CC   Claude 10   first:/And then, Eggerson, I am not unhopeful/That, under the impression that he is

UNHURRIED (1)
185 FQ: DrySal   38   time not our time, rung by the unhurried/Ground swell, a time/Older than the

UNICORNS (1)
94 Ash-Wed 4   21   in the higher dream/While jewelled unicorns draw by the gilded hearse./The silent

UNIDENTIFIABLE (1)
193 FQ: Little   98   compound ghost/Both intimate and unidentifiable./So I assumed a double part, and

UNIDENTIFIED (8)
352 CP   m   7   GIBBS/PETER QUILPE/AN UNIDENTIFIED GUEST, *later identified as*
353 CP   5m   1   MACCOLGIE GIBBS,/*and an* UNIDENTIFIED GUEST./{A} You've missed
353 CP   m   23   everyone here knows it. {}/[*To the* UNIDENTIFIED GUEST]/{C} You don't
354 CP   m   19   But she enjoyed herself. {}/[*To the* UNIDENTIFIED GUEST]/{J} Did *you* know
354 CP   m   25   there when it happened. {}/[*To the* UNIDENTIFIED GUEST]/{J} Do *you* know
355 CP   m   31   Oh, so many years ago! {}/[*To the* UNIDENTIFIED GUEST]/{J} Did *you* know
359 CP   m   7   /[*Exeunt* ALEX *and* CELIA]/[*To the* UNIDENTIFIED GUEST]/{E} Don't go yet./
384 CP   m   2   /{E} Oh ... good evening. {}/[*Enter the* UNIDENTIFIED GUEST]/{UG} Good

UNIMAGINABLE (1)
191 FQ: Little   19   generation./Where is the summer, the unimaginable/Zero summer?/If you came this

UNIMPEACHABLE (1)
279 MC Knight4 25   at last an undoubted mania. I have unimpeachable evidence/to the effect that before

UNIMPORTANCE (1)
293 FR   Harry   29   happened/Cannot understand the unimportance of events./{G} Well, you can't say

UNIMPORTANT (4)
319 FR   Harry   2   something that I know already/Or unimportant, or else untrue./But I want to
326 FR   Harry   19   important, so that everything/May be unimportant, a slight deviation/From some
326 FR   Harry   22   normal/Is merely the unreal and the unimportant./I was like that in a way, so long as
513 CC   Colby   18   doesn't know. But the fact itself/Is unimportant, once one knows it./{MG} You

UNINTERESTING (1)
358 CP   Edward   5   /{E} Most of my secrets are quite uninteresting./{J} Well, you shan't escape. You

UNINVITED (1)
588 Fable   31   saint — said he:/'If ghosts come uninvited, then, of course,/I'll be compelled to

UNION (3)
183 FQ: ECoker 208   /Into another intensity/For a further union, a deeper communion/Through the dark
190 FQ: DrySal 220   is Incarnation./Here the impossible union/Of spheres of existence is actual,/Here the
278 MC Knight2   16   have had an almost ideal State:/a union of spiritual and temporal administration,

UNIQUE (2)
402 CP   Reilly   24   a very unusual case./{R} All cases are unique, and very similar to others./{E} Is there a
485 CC   Lady E   21   isn't just heredity,/But something unique. Something we have been/From eternity.

UNISON (2)
206 To my Wife   4   of our sleepingtime,/The breathing in unison/Of lovers whose bodies smell of each
522 ES   dedic   4   *of our sleepingtime,/The breathing in unison/Of lovers .../Who think the same thoughts*

UNITE (2)
278 MC Knight2   13   — no one denies that — should unite/the offices of Chancellor and Archbishop.
437 CP   Reilly   12   *all forms that think and live/Till death unite them and they part no more!/*When I first

UNITED (6)

31 Apollinax	1	/When Mr. Apollinax visited the United States/His laughter tinkled among the
92 Ash-Wed 2	51	Forgetting themselves and each other, united/In the quiet of the desert. This is the land
195 FQ: Little	176	/All touched by a common genius,/United in the strife which divided them;/If I
271 MC Chorus	1	/Am torn away, subdued, violated,/United to the spiritual flesh of nature,/Mastered
272 MC Chorus	32	the soul/From seeing itself, foully united forever, nothing with nothing,/Not what
276 MC Chorus	14	soiled by a filth that we cannot clean, united to supernatural vermin,/It is not we

UNITES (2)

| 151 Rock 2 | 8 | must be made real in act, as desire unites with desired; we have only our labour to |
| 164 Rock 9 | 17 | of the formless stone, when the artist unites himself with stone,/Spring always new |

UNITY (3)

92 Ash-Wed 2	53	by lot. And neither division nor unity/Matters. This is the land. We have our
279 MC Knight4	20	the/country together, to give it the unity, the stability, order, tranquillity,/and
466 CC Claude	19	never known any — can find some unity./Then there are also the men of genius./

UNIVERSAL (3)

202 War Poetry	6	an action merely typical/To create the universal, originate a symbol/Out of the impact?
202 War Poetry	24	at its greatest intensity/Becoming universal, which we call 'poetry',/May be
301 FR Chorus	27	be the uncommon exception/To the universal bondage./We like to appear in the

UNIVERSE (3)

14 Prufrock	46	legs are thin!')/Do I dare/Disturb the universe?/In a minute there is time/For
15 Prufrock	92	with a smile,/To have squeezed the universe into a ball/To roll it towards some
326 FR Harry	25	/A casual bit of waste in an orderly universe./But it begins to seem just part of some

UNJUST (1)

| 510 CC Guzzard | 27 | son./If so, I am cleared from your unjust suspicion./{E} Mr. Kaghan, are your |

UNKILLABLE (1)

| 294 FR Harry | 38 | with me; whatever I did/That she was unkillable. It was not like that./Everything is |

UNKIND (7)

317 FR Harry	26	mother;/Misconduct was simply being unkind to mother;/What was wrong was
435 CP Lavinia	35	/Peter, please don't think I'm being unkind .../{P} No, I don't think you're being
435 CP Peter	36	.../{P} No, I don't think you're being unkind, Lavinia;/And I know that you're right./
435 CP Lavinia	39	what I've been saying/Will seem less unkind if I can make you understand/That in
438 CP Lavinia	40	go on blaming myself/For being so unkind to her ... so spiteful./I shall go on seeing
533 ES Gomez	29	not at all./I think that was rather an unkind suggestion./I've always kept on the right
542 ES Gomez	16	can you speak of threats?/It's most unkind of you. My only aim/Is to renew our

UNKNOTTED (4)

316 FR Agatha	13	/May the knot that was tied/Become unknotted/May the crossed bones/In the
316 FR Agatha	22	from this house/Till the knot is unknotted/The crossed is uncrossed/And the
337 FR Agatha	6	shall be fulfilled:/The knot shall be unknotted/And the crooked made straight. {}/
350 FR Agatha	17	Completing the charm/So the knot be unknotted/The crossed be uncrossed/The

UNKNOWING (2)

| 110 Marina | 27 | and another September./Made this unknowing, half conscious, unknown, my own./ |
| 337 FR Agatha | 3 | /And design is accident/In a cloud of unknowing./O my child, my curse,/You shall be |

UNKNOWN (11)

110 Marina	27	Made this unknowing, half conscious, unknown, my own./The garboard strake leaks,
197 FQ: Little	245	place for the first time./Through the unknown, remembered gate/When the last of
594 Grad 11	3	thy care and tutelage we pass/Into the unknown world — class after class,/O queen of
599 On a Port	1	/Among a crowd of tenuous dreams, unknown/To us of restless brain and weary feet,
418 CP Reilly	24	lives of those about us./The second is unknown, and so requires faith —/The kind of
448 CC Claude	38	a son/Lost in action, and his grave unknown./{E} And you're thinking no doubt
507 CC Eggers	6	a child —/A child, that is, of parents unknown to you —/Under such conditions?/
514 CC Guzzard	7	it. You shall have a father/Dead, and unknown to you./{SC} What do you mean?/
524 ES Charles	22	takes you to a place where he's utterly unknown/And the waiters all appear to be
537 ES Gomez	20	in me —/A scholarship boy from an unknown grammar school./I didn't know either,
568 ES Ld Clav	12	to forget? Which you wish to keep unknown?/{C} There are certainly things I

UNLESS (17)

85 Hollow Men	61	beach of the tumid river/Sightless, unless/The eyes reappear/As the perpetual star/
133 Eyes	10	/Eyes of decision/Eyes I shall not see unless/At the door of death's other kingdom/
152 Rock 2	46	knows or cares who is his neighbour/Unless his neighbour makes too much
155 Rock 3	37	balls'./CHORUS:/We build in vain unless the LORD build with us./Can you keep
195 FQ: Little	147	the exasperated spirit/Proceeds, unless restored by that refining fire/Where you
232 Skimble	7	/Saying 'Skimble where is Skimble for unless he's very nimble/Then the Night Mail
263 MC Chorus	14	of this world is always uncertain, unless men keep the peace of God./And war
354 CP Alex	7	/{A} She never misses anything unless she wants to./{C} Especially the
361 CP Edward	20	who you are;/But, at the same time, unless you know my wife/A good deal better
361 CP Edward	21	A good deal better than I thought, or unless you know/A good deal more about us

377 CP	Celia	13	that man want to bring her back —/Unless he is the Devil! I could believe he was./
393 CP	Lavinia	21	how could I tell where I wanted to go/Unless you suggested some other place first?/
455 CC	Eggers	24	is she likely to be a nuisance?/{E} Not unless you give her encouragement./I have never
492 CC	Colby	26	mood.' I can't develop that/Unless you can tell me — reminiscent of what?/
497 CC	Claude	18	coincidence!/{SC} That's what it is,/Unless she is mistaken .../{LE} Now, Claude!/
515 CC	Guzzard	21	Sir Claude. Would I tell you all this/Unless it was true? In telling you the truth/I am
517 CC	Colby	7	can be no relation of father and son/Unless it works both ways. For you to regard

UNLIKELY (4)

299 FR	Downing	11	/And that his Lordship knew it?/{Do} Unlikely, Sir, if I may say so./Much more likely
498 CC	Eggers	6	I could swear to./{E} It does seem unlikely/That there should be two Mrs.
498 CC	Claude	16	that she ran a baby farm./That's most unlikely, nowadays./Besides, I should have
575 ES	Ld Clav	15	Let me tell you about Gomez./He's unlikely to try to be custodian of your morals;/

UNLIT (2)

| 69 WL: Fire S | | 248 | And gropes his way, finding the stairs unlit .../She turns and looks a moment in the |
| 149 Rock 1 | | 98 | *about in open places/And shiver in unlit rooms./Only the wind moves/Over empty* |

UNLOVABLE (2)

| 410 CP | Edward | 4 | know, you really are exceptionally unlovable,/And I never quite knew why. I |
| 416 CP | Celia | 25 | /Are we all in fact unloving and unlovable?/Then one *is* alone, and if one is |

UNLOVING (1)

| 416 CP | Celia | 25 | own imagination?/Are we all in fact unloving and unlovable?/Then one *is* alone, and |

UNLUCKY (1)

| 328 FR | Gerald | 4 | John's fault,/I don't believe. John is unlucky,/But Arthur is definitely reckless./{V} I |

UNMADE (1)

| 163 Rock 8 | | 39 | made the Crusades,/But these that unmade them./Remember the faith that took |

UNMEMORABLE (1)

| 272 MC | Chorus | 21 | /Into dust on the wind, forgotten, unmemorable; only is here/The white flat face |

UNMENTIONED (1)

| 150 Rock 1 | | 108 | *us./Our life is unwelcome, our death/Unmentioned in 'The Times'./Chant of* |

UNMISTAKABLY (1)

| 231 Bust | Jones | 32 | that under our eyes/He has grown unmistakably round./He's a twenty-five |

UNMOLESTED (1)

| 246 MC | Thomas | 14 | their hands. So for the time/We are unmolested./{P1} But do they follow after?/{T} |

UNMOVING (1)

| 175 FQ: BurntN | | 166 | /Not in itself desirable;/Love is itself unmoving,/Only the cause and end of |

UNNATURAL (3)

38 Gerontion		44	/Neither fear nor courage saves us. Unnatural vices/Are fathered by our heroism.
299 FR	Downing	31	drinking:/It's natural for some and unnatural for others./{C} And how was his
305 FR	Harry	33	I wish she had not done that. It's very unnatural,/This arresting of the normal change

UNNECESSARY (3)

278 MC	Knight2	37	/measures as these would become unnecessary. But, if you have now/arrived at a
297 FR	Agatha	4	/{Ag} It seems a necessary move/In an unnecessary action,/Not for the good that it will
458 CC	Lady E	12	of you, Eggerson,/But quite unnecessary. And besides,/I didn't come by air.

UNNOTICED (1)

| 309 FR | Harry | 37 | life persisting,/Which ordinarily pass unnoticed./Perhaps you are right, though I do |

UNOBSERVABLE (1)

| 258 MC | Thomas | 19 | possible./Ambition comes behind and unobservable./Sin grows with doing good. |

UNOBSERVED (3)

240 MC	Chorus	4	his own colour,/Preferring to pass unobserved./Now I fear disturbance of the quiet
561 ES		m 21	up to them. {}/[MONICA *has entered unobserved*]/{M} Michael! How can you speak to
567 ES		m 27	it. {}/[CLAVERTON *has entered unobserved*]/{M} I never expected you from *that*

UNOFFENDING (1)

| 54 Mr E Sun | | 14 | the water pale and thin/Still shine the unoffending feet/And there above the painter |

UNPAID (1)

| 343 FR | Amy | 26 | wind? fight with increasing taxes/And unpaid rents and tithes? nourish investments/ |

UNPARDONABLE (1)

| 340 FR | Amy | 12 | to take what I never had;/The more unpardonable, to taunt me with not having it./ |

UNPAYABLE (1)

| 186 FQ: DrySal | | 79 | /Not as making a trip that will be unpayable/For a haul that will not bear |

UNPLEASANT (8)

136 5FingerEx5		1	*and Mirza Murad Ali Beg/How* unpleasant to meet Mr. Eliot!/With his features
137 5FingerEx5		8	/And If and Perhaps and But./How unpleasant to meet Mr. Eliot!/With a bobtail
137 5FingerEx5		13	cat/And a wopsical hat:/How unpleasant to meet Mr. Eliot!/(Whether his
159 Rock 6		20	tells them of Evil and Sin, and other unpleasant facts./They constantly try to escape/
314 FR	Ivy	14	like being ill in the holidays./{I} It *was* unpleasant, coming home to have an illness./{V}
378 CP	Celia	21	about/Is to avoid a break — anything unpleasant!/No, it can't be that. I won't think

484 CC   Lady E   21   Oh, swarms of relatives! And such unpleasant people!/I thought of myself as a
555 ES   Monica   19   see you./I'm afraid that something unpleasant has happened./{LC} Was he driving
UNPRAYABLE (1)
185 FQ: DrySal   55   prayer of the bone on the beach, the unprayable/Prayer at the calamitous
UNPROFESSIONAL (1)
405 CP   Edward   10   this other patient?/I consider this very unprofessional conduct —/I will not discuss my
UNPROPITIATED (1)
184 FQ: DrySal   9   men choose to forget. Unhonoured, unpropitiated/By worshippers of the machine,
UNPROPITIOUS (1)
182 FQ: EColker 190   and now, under conditions/That seem unpropitious. But perhaps neither gain nor loss.
UNPUNCTUAL (1)
452 CC   Eggers   14   have been, I presume, persistently unpunctual./{L} You're wrong, Eggy. It's rank
UNQUALIFIED (1)   ✎
187 FQ: DrySal   115   of others remains an experience/Unqualified, unworn by subsequent attrition./
UNQUIET (1)
167 Rock 10   33   see the light that fractures through unquiet water./We see the light but see not
UNRAVEL (1)
185 FQ: DrySal   43   future,/Trying to unweave, unwind, unravel/And piece together the past and the
UNRAVELS (1)
280 MC   Priest3 33   yourselves,/Weaving a fiction which unravels as you weave,/Pacing forever in the
UNREAD (2)
 94 Ash-Wed 4   20   Redeem/The time. Redeem/The unread vision in the higher dream/While
291 FR   Chorus   6   here at Amy's command, to play an unread part in some monstrous farce, ridiculous
UNREAL (14)
 62 WL: Burial   60   /One must be so careful these days./Unreal City,/Under the brown fog of a winter
 68 WL: Fire S   207   jug jug jug/So rudely forc'd./Tereu/Unreal City/Under the brown fog of a winter
 73 WL: Thund   376   Athens Alexandria/Vienna London/Unreal/A woman drew her long black hair out
251 MC   Tempt3   3   circumstance is not undetermined./Unreal friendship may turn to real/But real
256 MC   Tempts   10   and a disappointment;/All things are unreal,/Unreal or disappointing:/The Catherine
256 MC   Tempts   11   /All things are unreal,/Unreal or disappointing:/The Catherine wheel,
271 MC   Thomas   18   changed in the telling. They will seem unreal./Human kind cannot bear very much
302 FR   Chorus   9   cease to be sure of what is real or unreal?/Hold tight, hold tight, we must insist
326 FR   Harry   22   you call the normal/Is merely the unreal and the unimportant./I was like that in a
371 CP   Peter   28   the reality/Of experience between two unreal people?/If I can only hold to the memory
416 CP   Celia   27   /Then lover and belovèd are equally unreal/And the dreamer is no more real than his
473 CC   Colby   38   /What I mean is, my garden's no less unreal to me/Than the world outside it. If you
474 CC   Colby   1   with each other —/Well, they're both unreal. But for Eggerson/His garden is a part of
474 CC   Colby   11   of being alone there/That makes it unreal./{L} Can no one else enter?/{C} It can't
UNREALITY (3)
256 MC   Tempts   17   become less real, man passes/From unreality to unreality./This man is obstinate,
256 MC   Tempts   17   real, man passes/From unreality to unreality./This man is obstinate, blind, intent/
403 CP   Edward   28   first time,/The whole oppression, the unreality/Of the role she had always imposed
UNREASONABLE (3)
428 CP   Edward   15   that the monkeys do./{E} That seems unreasonable./{A} It is unreasonable,/But
428 CP   Alex   16   That seems unreasonable./{A} It is unreasonable,/But characteristic. And that's not
491 CC   Lady E   11   And prevent us both/From making unreasonable claims upon you, Colby./It's a
UNRECAPTURABLE (1)
308 FR   Harry   4   bright colour fades/Together with the unrecapturable emotion,/The glow upon the
UNRECOGNISED (1)
307 FR   Harry   37   to join the legion of the hopeless/Unrecognised by other men, though sometimes
UNREDEEMABLE (4)
171 FQ: BurntN   5   all time is eternally present/All time is unredeemable./What might have been is an
294 FR   Harry   9   all past is present, all degradation/Is unredeemable. As for what happens —/Of the
315 FR   Harry   9   everything is irrevocable,/The past unredeemable. But cancer, now,/That is
330 FR   Harry   21   that sense of separation,/Of isolation unredeemable, irrevocable —/It's eternal, or
UNRELATED (1)
473 CC   Colby   24   that's just the trouble. They seem so unrelated./I turn the key, and walk through the
UNRELIABLE (1)
220 Old Deut   30   .../Ho! hi!/Oh, my eye!/My sight's unreliable, but I can guess/That the cause of the
UNREPROVED (1)
 68 WL: Fire S   238   engage her in caresses/Which still are unreproved, if undesired./Flushed and decided,
UNRESISTING (1)
193 FQ: Little   90   leaves/Before the urban dawn wind unresisting./And as I fixed upon the

UNREST (2)
427 CP   Alex   38   have become the pretext/For general unrest amongst the natives./{E} But how do the
427 CP   Edward 39   /{E} But how do the monkeys create unrest?/{A} To begin with, the monkeys are very
UNSAID (1)
 18 Portrait   7   for all the things to be said, or left unsaid./We have been, let us say, to hear the
UNSATISFIED (1)
 92 Ash-Wed 2   36   loves end/Terminate torment/Of love unsatisfied/The greater torment/Of love
UNSCRUPULOUS (1)
342 FR   Amy   9   as his father/In the hands of any unscrupulous woman./*I* have no influence over
UNSEEN (8)
 32 Hysteria   5   of her throat, bruised by/the ripple of unseen muscles. An elderly waiter with
172 FQ: BurntN   30   hidden in the shrubbery,/And the unseen eyebeam crossed, for the roses/Had the
180 FQ: ECoker   131   and winter lightning./The wild thyme unseen and the wild strawberry,/The laughter in
190 FQ: DrySal   213   in a shaft of sunlight,/The wild thyme unseen, or the winter lightning/Or the waterfall,
204 de la Mare   14   .../Or when the lawn/Is pressed by unseen feet, and ghosts return/Gently at
595 Grad 13   4   /Before they leave thy care for lands unseen/And let thy motto be, proud and serene,
257 MC   Priests   1   come in the sight of all, he may pass unseen unheard./{4T} Come whispering through
582 ES   Charles 26   if he had passed through some door unseen by us/And had turned and was looking
UNSELFISH (2)
357 CP   Julia   18   it all into an annuity./{J} So it's very unselfish of Lavinia/Yet very like her. But
393 CP   Lavinia 29   said;/And you thought you were unselfish. It was only passivity;/You only
UNSETTLED (1)
339 FR   Harry   4   /{H} I shall have to learn. That is still unsettled./I have not yet had the precise
UNSHAPEN (1)
240 MC   Chorus   17   in the hand of God, shaping the still unshapen:/I have seen these things in a shaft of
UNSHAVEN (1)
 68 WL: Fire S   210   Mr. Eugenides, the Smyrna merchant/Unshaven, with a pocket full of currants/C.i.f.
UNSKINNED (1)
244 MC   Chorus   23   hearts are torn from us, our brains unskinned like the layers of an onion, our selves
UNSOUGHT (1)
285 FR   Amy   7   young and strong, and sun and light unsought for/And the night unfeared and the
UNSOUND (1)
279 MC Knight4   39   render a verdict of Suicide while of/Unsound Mind. It is the only charitable verdict
UNSPEAKABLE (1)
294 FR   Harry   25   bone —/This is what matters, but it is unspeakable,/Untranslatable: I talk in general
UNSPEAKING (1)
105 Song Sime   22   of decease,/Let the Infant, the still unspeaking and unspoken Word,/Grant Israel's
UNSPOKEN (10)
 95 Ash-Wed 4   27   /The token of the word unheard, unspoken/Till the wind shake a thousand
 96 Ash-Wed 5   2   spent word is spent/If the unheard, unspoken/Word is unspoken, unheard;/Still is
 96 Ash-Wed 5   3   /If the unheard, unspoken/Word is unspoken, unheard;/Still is the unspoken word,
 96 Ash-Wed 5   4   is unspoken, unheard;/Still is the unspoken word, the Word unspoken,/The Word
105 Song Sime   22   the Infant, the still unspeaking and unspoken Word,/Grant Israel's consolation/To
110 Marina   31   life for this life, my speech for that unspoken,/The awakened, lips parted, the hope,
149 Rock 1   88   *with new timbers/Where the word is unspoken/We will build with new speech/There is*
154 Rock 3   27   the goat climbs,/Where My Word is unspoken./2ND MALE VOICE:/A Cry from
155 Rock 3   30   the timekept City;/Where My Word is unspoken,/In the land of lobelias and tennis
294 FR   Harry   3   of the night; you do not know/The unspoken voice of sorrow in the ancient
UNSTILLED (2)
 42 Swee Erect   2   a cavernous waste shore/Cast in the unstilled Cyclades,/Paint me the bold
 96 Ash-Wed 5   8   darkness and/Against the Word the unstilled world still whirled/About the centre of
UNSTOPPERED (1)
 64 WL: Chess   87   /In vials of ivory and coloured glass/Unstoppered, lurked her strange synthetic
UNSUBSTANTIAL (1)
109 Marina   14   animals, meaning/Death/Are become unsubstantial, reduced by a wind,/A breath of
UNSUCCESSFUL (2)
384 CP   Edward   6   you have come alone/You have been unsuccessful./{UG} Not at all./I have come to
516 CC   Colby   13   of a cathedral./But my father was an unsuccessful organist./{MG} You should say,
UNSUITED (1)
572 ES   Ld Clav 18   to marry her./In fact, we were wholly unsuited to each other,/Yet she had a peculiar
UNSUPPORTED (1)
540 ES   Gomez   38   suggestion!/Who's going to accept the unsupported statement/Of Federico Gomez of
UNSURE (1)
152 Rock 2   24   /Performed it, but left much at home unsure./Of all that was done in the past, you eat

UNTAMED (1)
184 FQ: DrySal   2   river/Is a strong brown god — sullen, untamed and intractable,/Patient to some
UNTIL (54)
32 Hysteria   2   in her laughter and/being part of it, until her teeth were only accidental stars with a
43 Swee Erect   30   /Tests the razor on his leg/Waiting until the shriek subsides./The epileptic on the
166 Rock 10   8   the world, curled/In folds of himself until he awakens in hunger and moving his head
178 FQ: ECoker   63   wars/Scorpion fights against the Sun/Until the Sun and Moon go down/Comets weep
203 Indians   21   fruitful if neither you nor we/Know, until the judgment after death,/What is the fruit
216 Jellicles   17   how to dance a gavotte and a jig./Until the Jellicle Moon appears/They make
222 Pekes Pols   10   bark bark/Bark bark BARK BARK/Until you can hear them all over the Park./Now
222 Pekes Pols   24   bark bark/Bark bark BARK BARK/Until you could hear them all over the Park./
223 Pekes Pols   45   bark bark/Bark bark BARK BARK/Until you could hear them all over the Park./
592 Grad 3   6   sun stains with many a splendid dye,/Until their passing may no more be traced./
593 Grad 7   3   those who try/To labor for the good until they die,/And ask no other guerdon than
606 Narcissus   36   arrows/He danced on the hot sand/Until the arrows came./As he embraced them
241 MC   Priest1   8   own./{P1} Shall these things not end/Until the poor at the gate/Have forgotten their
243 MC   Priest3   11   who knows the end of good or evil?/Until the grinders cease/And the door shall be
279 MC Knight4   24   egotism. This egotism grew upon him, until it/became at last an undoubted mania. I
292 FR   Harry   10   not *see* them./Why should they wait until I came back to Wishwood?/There were a
297 FR   Charles   18   Nobody knows what he's likely to do/Until there's somebody he wants to get rid of./
297 FR   Charles   36   to find out what's wrong with Harry:/Until we know that, we can do nothing for him.
307 FR   Harry   33   /You do not know what hope is, until you have lost it./You only know what it is
320 FR Warburt   17   woman/She would not have lived until now./Her determination has kept her
332 FR   Agatha   14   in making terms with Wishwood,/Until she took your father's place, and reached
335 FR   Harry   16   bone. In and out, the movement/Until the chain broke, and I was left/Under the
335 FR   Agatha   22   barred windows./Up and down. Until the chain breaks./{H} To and fro,
335 FR   Harry   27   /And the giant lizard. To and fro./Until the chain breaks./The chain breaks,/The
338 FR   Harry   8   it harder. You must just believe me,/Until I come again./{A} But why are you going?
341 FR   Agatha   3   I have not./I thought that I had, until this evening./But at least I wanted to. Now
343 FR   Harry   38   account for this/But it is so, mother. Until I come again./{A} If you go now, I shall
345 FR   Harry   4   about it,/So I shall say good-bye, until we meet again./{G} Well, if you are
345 FR   Harry   12   /Will be care of the bank in London until you hear from me./Good-bye, mother./{A}
355 CP   Julia   17   *leaves the room*/{J} No, we'll wait until Edward comes back into the room./Now I
356 CP   Edward   35   Edward?/{E} I really don't know until I hear from her./If her aunt is very ill, she
371 CP   Peter   17   me/What has happened, in her terms. Until I know that/I shan't know the truth about
384 CP   Reilly   11   not be ready to change your mind/Until you recover from having made a decision.
394 CP   Lavinia   16   you to meet,/You didn't arrive until just as they were leaving./{E} Well, at least,
396 CP   Lavinia   40   to relapse into the kind of life we led/Until yesterday morning./{E} There was a door/
399 CP   Nurse   17   moment she arrives. I leave her there/Until you ring three times./{R} And the third
403 CP   Reilly   11   mischief/As lay within your power — until you came to grief./Half of the harm that is
418 CP   Reilly   27   described;/You will know very little until you get there;/You will journey blind. But
435 CP   Peter   7   years ago! I tried to forget about her,/Until I began to think myself a success/And got
453 CC   Kaghan   25   ever believe in your existence/Until they met you. Colby's still reeling./It's
457 CC   Eggers   3   /But let's not be crossing any bridges/Until we come to them. That's what *I* always
464 CC   Claude   19   never talked of this to anyone./Never until now. Do you feel at all like that/When you
464 CC   Claude   34   in both. I loathed this occupation/Until I began to feel my power in it./The life
466 CC   Claude   27   /I shan't mention it again. I'll wait until you ask me./Do you understand now what
466 CC   Colby   38   never having understood your father/Until it was too late. And you spoke of
481 CC   Lady E   21   a scheme of decoration/Is *right*, until the place has been lived in/By the person
506 CC   Eggers   14   years, she has been without a clue/Until the other day. This son, Mrs. Guzzard,/If
517 CC   Eggers   33   /{E} Don't say that, Mr. Simpkins, until you've tried our organ!/{C} Well, if you
518 CC   Eggers   19   happy/If you cared to stop with us, until you were settled./{C} I'd be very glad
525 ES   Monica   30   /And he won't think of leaving it until he's called for tea./So why not talk now?
538 ES   Gomez   25   let the other people make mistakes/Until your own have been more or less
547 ES   Piggott   28   croquet. But I don't advise croquet/Until you know enough about the other guests/
556 ES   Monica   1   I told him he must wait in the garden/Until I had prepared you. I've made him
576 ES   Gomez   20   that later./{G} Much better to wait until we get there./The nature of business in San
UNTILLED (1)
149 Rock 1   100   *the wind moves/Over empty fields, untilled/Where the plough rests, at an angle/To*
UNTO (7)
96 Ash-Wed 5   10   /O my people, what have I done unto thee./Where shall the word be found,
96 Ash-Wed 5   28   /O my people, what have I done unto thee./Will the veiled sister between the
99 Ash-Wed 6   35   to be separated/And let my cry come unto Thee./ARIEL POEMS/Journey of the
154 Rock 3   1   forge./The Word of the LORD came unto me, saying:/O miserable cities of designing
260 MC Thomas   27   I leave with you, my peace I give unto you.' Did He/mean peace as we think of it:

261 MC Thomas   5   also, 'Not as the world gives, give I unto you.'/So then, He gave to His disciples
264 MC Priest2   12   we have seen and heard/Declare we unto you./*In the midst of the congregation.* {}/
UNTOWARD (1)
220 Old Deut   23   ROAD CLOSED —/So that nothing untoward may chance to disturb/
UNTRACEABLE (1)
294 FR   Harry   1   You do not know/The noxious smell untraceable in the drains,/Inaccessible to the
UNTRANSLATABLE (1)
294 FR   Harry   26   is what matters, but it is unspeakable,/Untranslatable: I talk in general terms/Because
UNTRUE (2)
319 FR   Harry   2 know already/Or unimportant, or else untrue./But I want to know more about my
474 CC   Colby   31   /To need anybody./{C} That's quite untrue./{L} But you've something else, that I
UNTRUSTWORTHY (1)
184 FQ: DrySal   4   first recognised as a frontier;/Useful, untrustworthy, as a conveyor of commerce;/
UNUSED (1)
295 FR   Amy   35   is too sudden for you./You are unused to our foggy climate/And the northern
UNUSUAL (13)
218 Mung Rump   17   and Rumpelteazer had a very unusual gift of the gab./They were highly
319 FR   Harry   21   now I remember/A summer day of unusual heat,/The day I lost my butterfly net;/I
331 FR   Agatha   38   duties./He hid his strength beneath unusual weakness,/The diffidence of a solitary
332 FR   Agatha   23   I remember/A summer day of unusual heat/For this cold country./{H} And
402 CP   Edward   23   I have realised/That mine is a very unusual case./{R} All cases are unique, and very
405 CP   Reilly   7   *times*]/{R} You must accept a rather unusual procedure:/I propose to introduce you
414 CP   Reilly   38   of sin, Miss Coplestone?/This is most unusual./{C} It seemed to *me* abnormal./{R} We
455 CC   Colby   36   Lady Elizabeth/Can be quite so unusual as Miss Angel./{E} O yes, Mr.
455 CC   Eggers   37   /{E} O yes, Mr. Simpkins, much more unusual./{C} Oh!/{E} Well, as I told you, she
456 CC   Colby   11   /{C} But is Lady Elizabeth very unusual/In any other way, besides being a lady?
456 CC   Eggers   36   of my travels!/It's been a very unusual privilege/To see as much of Europe as I
485 CC   Lady E   37   Guzzard? Did you say Guzzard? An unusual name./Guzzard, did you say? The name
508 CC Guzzard   31   their name:/Like mine, a somewhat unusual one./Perhaps it might be possible to
UNWARRANTED (1)
603 Spleen   6   /Your mental self-possession/By this unwarranted digression./Evening, lights, and
UNWEAVE (1)
185 FQ: DrySal   43   calculating the future,/Trying to unweave, unwind, unravel/And piece together
UNWELCOME (2)
150 Rock 1   107   *land/No man has hired us./Our life is unwelcome, our death/Unmentioned in 'The*
541 ES   Gomez   36   interruption/To terminate the unwelcome intrusion/Of the visitor in financial
UNWHOLESOME (1)
174 FQ: BurntN   109   and after time,/Wind in and out of unwholesome lungs/Time before and time after.
UNWILLING (2)
340 FR   Amy   21   silent bedroom,/Forcing sons upon an unwilling father?/Dare you think what that does
382 CP   Edward   2   self can contrive the disaster/Of this unwilling partnership — but can only flourish/
UNWIND (1)
185 FQ: DrySal   43   the future,/Trying to unweave, unwind, unravel/And piece together the past
UNWINKING (1)
335 FR   Agatha   10   feet, and the eye/Seeing the feet: the unwinking eye/Fixing the movement. Over and
UNWORN (1)
187 FQ: DrySal   115   remains an experience/Unqualified, unworn by subsequent attrition./People change,
UNWRAP (2)
397 CP   Edward   29   up in tissue paper/And then had to unwrap everything again/To find what you
457 CC   Lady E   17   that case, I want something out of it./Unwrap that — It's a bottle of medicine./Now,
UNWRAPPED (1)
382 CP   Celia   11   as I looked/It withered, as if I had unwrapped a mummy./I listened to your voice,
UP (193)
20 Portrait   94   write to me.'/My self-possession flares up for a second;/*This* is as I had reckoned./'I
23 Preludes   31   world came back/And the light crept up between the shutters/And you heard the
24 Rhapsody   23   a crooked pin.'/The memory throws up high and dry/A crowd of twisted things;/A
24 Rhapsody   27   and polished/As if the world gave up/The secret of its skeleton,/Stiff and white./A
27 Morning   5   gates./The brown waves of fog toss up to me/Twisted faces from the bottom of the
40 Burb Blei   10   /The horses, under the axletree/Beat up the dawn from Istria/With even feet. Her
56 Swee Night   16 floor/She yawns and draws a stocking up;/The silent man in mocha brown/Sprawls at
62 WL: Burial   66   fixed his eyes before his feet./Flowed up the hill and down King William Street,/To
63 WL: Burial   75   to men,/'Or with his nails he'll dig it up again!/'You! hypocrite lecteur! — mon
64 WL: Chess   79   on the marble, where the glass/Held up by standards wrought with fruited vines/
65 WL: Chess   141   words, I said to her myself,/HURRY UP PLEASE ITS TIME/Now Albert's coming
66 WL: Chess   152   and give me a straight look./HURRY UP PLEASE ITS TIME/If you don't like it you

285	FR	Amy	12	leave the curtains undrawn./Make up the fire. Will the spring never come? I am
296	FR	Gerald	34	in Violet's suggestion./Why not ring up Warburton, and ask him to join us?/He's an
297	FR	Amy	9	impossible./{A} Very well./I will ring up the doctor myself. {}/[Exit]/{C} Meanwhile, I
297	FR	Charles	27	{C} Denman, where is Downing? Is he up with his Lordship?/{D} He's out in the
299	FR	Downing	23	the same, Sir./What I mean is, always up and down./Down in the morning, and up in
299	FR	Downing	24	and down./Down in the morning, and up in the evening,/And then she used to get
300	FR	Downing	25	most considerate/About keeping me up. But when I say I saw him,/I mean that I saw
304	FR	Mary	1	I might have known you'd throw that up against me./I know I wasn't one of your
306	FR	Mary	1	here,/And we just go on ... drying up, I suppose,/Not noticing the change. But to
313	FR	Amy	28	it's the fog that is holding them up,/So it's no use to telephone anywhere. Harry!
315	FR	Warburt	13	know. — But now you're all grown up/I haven't a patient left at Wishwood./I
318	FR	Harry	7	/In which we were supposed to make up to mother/For all the weeks during which
322	FR	Winch	34	pace, I fancy, ran into a lorry/Drawn up round the bend. We'll have the driver up for
322	FR	Winch	34	round the bend. We'll have the driver up for this:/Says he doesn't know this part of
323	FR	Warburt	15	You can trust Owen./We'll bring him up tomorrow; and a few days' rest,/I've no
323	FR	Winch	20	a hurry./There was a lorry drawn up where it shouldn't be,/Outside of the village,
327	FR	Ivy	27	paper./That was Arthur, ringing up from London:/The connection was so bad, I
327	FR	Ivy	32	missed the last train, so he's coming up tomorrow;/And he said there was something
329	FR	Chorus	15	transparent deception/The keeping up of appearances/The making the best of a bad
332	FR	Agatha	32	Thibet of broken stones/That lie, fang up, a lifetime's march. I have believed this./{H} I
335	FR	Agatha	18	the single eye above the desert./{Ag} Up and down, through the stone passages/Of an
335	FR	Agatha	22	ahead, passing barred windows./Up and down. Until the chain breaks./{H} To
341	FR	Amy	27	for argument./{A} Who set you up to judge? what, if you please,/Gives you the
344	FR	Charles	15	in such a hurry? Before you make up your mind .../{V} You can't really think of
345	FR	Charles	36	I'm getting old:/Old age came softly up to now. I felt safe enough;/And now I don't
348	FR	Warburt	1	made out,/And we'll have him up here in the morning./I hope Lady
353	CP	Julia	3	point./{J} Then what were you doing, up in a tree:/You and the Maharaja?/{A} My
359	CP	Edward	22	saying:]/{E} But she always turns up when she's least wanted. {}/[Opens the door]/
373	CP	m	3	and PETER]/[EDWARD picks up the telephone, and dials a number]/{E} Is Miss
376	CP	Julia	19	a strain. We must keep his strength up./Edward! Don't you realise how lucky you
383	CP	m	27	CELIA]/{E} Oh! {}/[He snatches up the receiver]/{E} Hello, Julia! are you there?
385	CP	Reilly	10	is perhaps still more difficult/To keep up the pretence that you are not strangers./The
388	CP	Peter	38	/{P} Yes, and I would have rung you up tomorrow/And come in to say good-bye
397	CP	Edward	28	/You were always wrapping things up in tissue paper/And then had to unwrap
398	CP	Lavinia	18	/Will you get the porter to fetch it up for me? {}/CURTAIN/Act Two/SIR
400	CP	Reilly	30	rings]/{R} Hello! Yes, show him up./{A} You will have a busy morning!/I will go
401	CP	m	1	stares at REILLY]/[without looking up from his papers]./{R} Good morning, Mr.
405	CP	Reilly	15	me that you have been making up your case/So to speak, as you went along. A
405	CP	Edward	19	I propose to do so./My mind is made up. I shall go to a hotel./{R} It is just because
407	CP	Edward	2	me so often./I'd like to see you filling up an income-tax form./{L} Don't be silly,
407	CP	Reilly	28	has no meaning;/And you must put up with that. All that you have told me —/Both
411	CP	3m	36	The house-telephone rings. He/gets up and answers it.]/{R} Yes? ... Yes. Come in. {}/
412	CP	Julia	18	is most uncommon./{J} Henry, get up./You can't be as tired as that. I shall wait in
415	CP	Celia	19	of your family?/{C} Well, my bringing up was pretty conventional —/I had always
418	CP	Celia	12	it. I could do without everything,/Put up with anything, if I might cherish it./In fact, I
421	CP	m	39	I'll speak to Miss Barraway. {}/[Takes up house-telephone]/{R} Miss Barraway, when
422	CP	Reilly	3	{}/[To JULIA]/{R} He's on his way up. {}/[Into telephone]/{R} You may bring the
424	CP	Lavinia	12	worrying./{L} Oh no. I did in fact ring up your chambers,/And your clerk told me you
424	CP	Lavinia	14	you had already left./But all I rang up for was to reassure you ... {}/[smiling]./{E}
426	CP	Lavinia	25	come so early? I simply can't get up./{CM} Mrs. Shuttlethwaite!/{L} Oh, it's
427	CP	Edward	6	Alex!/Where on earth do you turn up from?/{A} Where on earth? From the East.
428	CP	Alex	36	are also foreign agitators,/Stirring up trouble .../{L} Why don't you expel them?/
429	CP	Alex	22	/{A} We have just drawn up an interim report./{E} Will it be made
435	CP	Peter	4	you could./{P} When did she ... take up this career?/{J} Two years ago./{P} Two years
440	CP	Lavinia	25	know, when you're trying to cheer me up./To say I always look my best can only mean
445	CC	Claude	2	/I'm sorry to have to bring you up to London/All the way from Joshua Park,
445	CC	Eggers	11	I was glad of the excuse for coming up to London:/I've spent the morning shopping!
446	CC	Eggers	23	his aunt in Teddington, and coming up daily/Just as I used to. And the flat in the
454	CC	Lucasta	15	Another time, Colby./I'll ring you up, and let you take me out to lunch. {}/[Exit
456	CC	Eggers	32	settled down/All the travel I want is up to the City/And back to Joshua Park in the
458	CC	Eggers	2	to the parlourmaid. She's coming up./{SC} Colby, sit at the desk, and pick up
458	CC	Claude	3	/{SC} Colby, sit at the desk, and pick up some papers./We must look as if we'd been
460	CC	Claude	39	/I seem to have brought you up to London for nothing./{E} Oh, not for
461	CC	Eggers	4	Simpkins —/If anything should turn up unexpected/And you find yourself
461	CC	Eggers	7	I'll be out in the garden./And I'll slip up to town any day, if you want me./In fact,

461 CC	Eggers	8	fact, Mrs. E. said: 'I wish he'd ring us	up!/I'm sure he has a very cultivated voice.'/{C}
462 CC	Colby	5	basis./{C} I must confess, that	up to this point/I haven't been able to feel very
464 CC	Claude	27	father — your grandfather — built	up this business/Starting from nothing. It was
466 CC	Colby	5	is an inferior rendering./So I've given	up trying to play to other people:/I am only
472 CC	Lucasta	31	for Eggerson's position,/And made	up your mind to go into business/And be
472 CC	Lucasta	37	/It's awful for a man to have to give	up,/A career that he's set his heart on, I'm sure:/
473 CC	Colby	21	could smell./{C} You may be right,	up to a point./And yet, you know, it's not quite
475 CC	Colby	9	is to understand them better,/To keep	up with them; so that as the other changes/You
477 CC	Lucasta	37	self!/Why don't you shut yourself	up in that garden/Where you like to be alone
479 CC	Kaghan	33	the way you've had the place done	up./{C} It was Lady Elizabeth chose the
482 CC	Lady E	16	/So naturally, they want to take you	up./I can speak more freely, as an elderly
484 CC	Lady E	10	I loathed them all./Were you brought	up by a governess?/{C} No. By my aunt./{LE}
485 CC	Lady E	12	I felt myself to be/And then I took	up the Wisdom of the East/And believed, for a
485 CC	Lady E	28	London./{LE} Still, you were brought	up, like me, in the country./Teddington. I seem
487 CC	Lady E	37	Guzzard!/Claude, Colby was brought	up by a Mrs. Guzzard./{SC} I know that. But
489 CC	Claude	20	was born. Mrs. Guzzard brought him	up,/And I provided for his education./I have
496 CC	Claude	15	I'm sorry, Eggerson, to bring you	up to London/At such short notice./{E} Don't
496 CC	Eggers	19	me;/But Mrs. E. wishes I'd come	up oftener!/Isn't that like the ladies! She used to
496 CC	Eggers	21	She used to complain/At my being	up in London five or six days a week:/But now
496 CC	Eggers	27	editions/Of the papers that I picked	up at Liverpool Street./But I've so much to do,
503 CC	Colby	23	course I'd like them ... Can't B. come	up now?/{E} Better wait till afterwards./{SC}
504 CC	Eggers	15	to Mrs. Guzzard/And then bring her	up./{SC} No, I want you here, Eggerson./Will
504 CC	Claude	17	here, Eggerson./Will you show her	up, Lucasta?/{L} I'll make B. do it. {}/[*Exit*
510 CC	Colby	1	this the moment/For me to bring him	up? And Lucasta?/{E} An excellent suggestion,
512 CC	Kaghan	30	than being a foundling —/If I can live	up to it. And ... yes, of course,/If I can make it
515 CC	Guzzard	27	come to nothing?/When I gave	up my place as Colby's mother/I gave up
515 CC	Guzzard	28	up my place as Colby's mother/I gave	up something I could never have back./Don't
518 CC	Eggers	1	to think of other ways/Of making	up an income. Piano lessons? —/As a temporary
530 ES	Monica	5	pages?/{M} You would soon fill them	up if we allowed you to!/That's my business to
530 ES	Ld Clav	9	out the machine./{LC} They've dried	up, Monica, and you know it./They talk of rest,
533 ES	Gomez	2	too, since I knew you./When we were	up at Oxford, you were plain Dick Ferry./Then,
534 ES	Gomez	25	way, I've several children,/All grown	up, doing well for themselves./I wouldn't allow
535 ES	m	34	—/To take another name. {}/[*Gets	up and helps himself to whisky*]/{G} But of course
536 ES	Gomez	3	/And each step was merely a step	up the ladder,/So you weren't aware of
536 ES	Gomez	8	and sweetly, that you've never woken	up/To the fact that Dick Ferry died long ago./I
537 ES	Gomez	12	consider what we were when we went	up to Oxford/And then what I became under
537 ES	Gomez	18	knew it./When you started to take me	up at Oxford/I've no doubt your friends
540 ES	Gomez	8	who in the morning/Has to make	up his face before he looks in the mirror./{LC}
542 ES	Ld Clav	14	/On a man by threats? Why keep	up the pretence?/{G} Threats, Dick! How can
547 ES	Piggott	4	/But before I go, just let me tuck you	up .../You must be very careful at this time of
555 ES	Ld Clav	35	debts/Once more, I expect I can put	up with it./But where is he?/{M} I told him he
556 ES	Michael	31	things to *you*./You've always made	up your mind that I was to blame/Before you
558 ES	Michael	30	Well, there was one thing he brought	up against me,/That I'd been too familiar with
560 ES	Michael	3	consciousness./Poor ghost! reckoning	up its profit and loss/And wondering why it
560 ES	Michael	11	/But I might be expected to put	up some capital./{LC} What sort of business
560 ES	Michael	29	other./But I want to get out. I'm fed	up with England./{LC} I'm sure you don't mean
561 ES	Michael	19	in particular,/So you'd nothing to live	up to. Those standards of conduct/You've
561 ES	Michael	21	whether *you* have always lived	up to them. {}/[MONICA *has entered*
569 ES	Ld Clav	9	pretences./Now, I'm tired of keeping	up those pretences,/But I hope that you'll find a
578 ES	Monica	19	notice of me./When we were growing	up we seldom had the same friends./I took all
579 ES	Michael	8	I must buy my kit. We're just going	up to London./Señor Gomez will attend to my

UPKEEP (1)

| 343 FR | Amy | 30 | in the tomb/To bother about the | upkeep. Let the wind and rain do that. {}/[*While* |

UPON (118)

13 Prufrock		3	the sky/Like a patient etherised	upon a table;/Let us go, through certain
13 Prufrock		15	/The yellow fog that rubs its back	upon the window-panes,/The yellow smoke that
13 Prufrock		18	the corners of the evening,/Lingered	upon the pools that stand in drains,/Let fall
13 Prufrock		19	the pools that stand in drains,/Let fall	upon its back the soot that falls from chimneys,/
14 Prufrock		25	along the street/Rubbing its back	upon the window-panes;/There will be time,
15 Prufrock		82	head (grown slightly bald) brought in	upon a platter,/I am no prophet — and here's
16 Prufrock		123	wear white flannel trousers, and walk	upon the beach./I have heard the mermaids
18 Portrait		5	darkened room,/Four rings of light	upon the ceiling overhead,/An atmosphere of
18 Portrait		26	/Who has, and gives/Those qualities	upon which friendship lives./How much it
20 Portrait		74	I remark./An English countess goes	upon the stage./A Greek was murdered at a
22 Preludes		25	a blanket from the bed,/You lay	upon your back, and waited;/You dozed, and

24 Rhapsody	25	of twisted things;/A twisted branch	upon the beach/Eaten smooth, and polished/As
29 Aunt Helen	11	the mantelpiece,/And the footman sat	upon the dining-table/Holding the second
30 Cous Nancy	11	it,/But they knew that it was modern./	Upon the glazen shelves kept watch/Matthew
33 Conv Gal	7	/And I then: 'Someone frames	upon the keys/That exquisite nocturne, with
38 Gerontion	46	by our heroism. Virtues/Are forced	upon us by our impudent crimes./These tears
38 Gerontion	54	backward devils./I would meet you	upon this honestly./I that was near your heart
49 Hippopot	8	Church can never fail/For it is based	upon a rock./The hippo's feeble steps may err/
54 Mr E Sun	10	of the Umbrian school/Designed	upon a gesso ground/The nimbus of the
56 Swee Night	15	/Overturns a coffee-cup,/Reorganised	upon the floor/She yawns and draws a stocking
64 WL: Chess	83	candelabra/Reflecting light	upon the table as/The glitter of her jewels rose
64 WL: Chess	98	displayed/As though a window gave	upon the sylvan scene/The change of Philomel,
64 WL: Chess	105	withered stumps of time/Were told	upon the walls; staring forms/Leaned out,
65 WL: Chess	138	lidless eyes and waiting for a knock	upon the door./When Lil's husband got
67 WL: Fire S	191	round behind the gashouse/Musing	upon the king my brother's wreck/And on the
69 WL: Fire S	257	gramophone./'This music crept by me	upon the waters'/And along the Strand, up
74 WL: Thund	423	obedient/To controlling hands/I sat	upon the shore/Fishing, with the arid plain
89 Ash-Wed 1	25	having to construct something/	Upon which to rejoice/And pray to God to have
89 Ash-Wed 1	26	/And pray to God to have mercy	upon us/And I pray that I may forget/These
90 Ash-Wed 1	33	/May the judgement not be too heavy	upon us/Because these wings are no longer
105 Song Sime	28	/With glory and derision,/Light	upon light, mounting the saints' stair./Not for
111 Xmas Trees	32	as on the occasion/When fear came	upon every soul:/Because the beginning shall
151 Rock 2	2	of the household of GOD, being built	upon the foundation/Of apostles and prophets,
151 Rock 2	13	model and type for your citizenship	upon earth./When your fathers fixed the place
152 Rock 2	32	on the other side of death,/But here	upon earth you have the reward of the good
160 Rock 7	1	Waste and void. And darkness was	upon the face of the deep./And when there were
160 Rock 7	3	and man without GOD is a seed	upon the wind: driven this way and that, and
160 Rock 7	7	of the deep./And the Spirit moved	upon the face of the water./And men who
164 Rock 9	2	with thine ears/And set thine heart	upon all that I show thee./Who is this that has
164 Rock 9	7	scattered lights?/They would put	upon GOD their own sorrow, the grief they
166 Rock 10	21	at morning,/The light that slants	upon our western doors at evening,/The twilight
172 FQ: BurntN	59	move above the moving tree/In light	upon the figured leaf/And hear upon the sodden
172 FQ: BurntN	60	light upon the figured leaf/And hear	upon the sodden floor/Below, the boarhound
180 FQ: ECoker	113	soul, be still, and let the dark come	upon you/Which shall be the darkness of God.
193 FQ: Little	91	dawn wind unresisting./And as I fixed	upon the down-turned face/That pointed
194 FQ: Little	132	gifts reserved for age/To set a crown	upon your lifetime's effort./First, the cold
210 Old Gumbie	3	and leopard spots./All day she sits	upon the stair or on the steps or on the mat:/
211 Old Gumbie	27	and tie it into sailor-knots./She sits	upon the window-sill, or anything that's smooth
212 Growltiger	8	need to tell you why,/And he scowled	upon a hostile world from one forbidding eye./
588 Fable	59	now gone out of use —/His feet	upon the table superposed/Each wisht he had
592 Grad 1	1	few/Yet let them be divine./Standing	upon the shore of all we know/We linger for a
592 Grad 1	3	moment doubtfully,/Then with a song	upon our lips, sail we/Across the harbor bar —
594 Grad 11	6	surface of the stream,/A drop of dew	upon the morning grass;/Thou dost not die —
240 MC Chorus	15	October?/Some malady is coming	upon us. We wait, we wait,/And the saints and
242 MC Priest1	24	insecure;/His pride always feeding	upon his own virtues,/Pride drawing sustenance
244 MC Chorus	19	secret fears./But now a great fear is	upon us, a fear not of one but of many,/A fear
246 MC Tempt1	24	/{T1} You see, my Lord, I do not wait	upon ceremony:/Here I have come, forgetting
247 MC Tempt1	34	/You were not used to be so hard	upon sinners/When they were your friends. Be
248 MC Tempt1	3	/Farewell, my Lord, I do not wait	upon ceremony,/I leave as I came, forgetting all
251 MC Tempt3	1	of friendship does not depend/	Upon ourselves, but upon circumstance./But
251 MC Tempt3	1	does not depend/Upon ourselves, but	upon circumstance./But circumstance is not
257 MC Chorus	14	away from us,/Our sins made heavier	upon us./We have seen the young man
260 MC Thomas	15	Our Lord and His Passion and Death	upon/the Cross. Beloved, as the World sees, this
263 MC Chorus	13	at Christmastide,/Is there not peace	upon earth, goodwill among men?/The peace of
265 MC Knight1	28	will roast your pork/First, and dine	upon it after./{K2} We must see the Archbishop.
266 MC Knights	20	/This is the creature that crawled	upon the King; swollen with blood and swollen
268 MC Thomas	23	bishops, it is not my yoke/That is laid	upon them, or mine to revoke./Let them go to
268 MC Thomas	32	Pope has bound./Let them go to him,	upon whom redounds/Their contempt towards
273 MC Chorus	4	for me, in my most need?/Dead	upon the tree, my Saviour,/Let not be in vain
276 MC Knight1	21	and when you see one man being set	upon by four, then your/sympathies are all with
276 MC Knight1	31	complex problem. I/shall call	upon our eldest member to speak first, my
277 MC Knight1	32	/our other speakers. I shall next call	upon Hugh de Morville, who/has made a
279 MC Knight4	24	of egotism. This egotism grew	upon him, until it/became at last an undoubted
279 MC Knight4	30	/except that he had determined	upon a death by martyrdom. Even/at the last,
279 MC Knight4	39	only charitable verdict you can give,	upon/one who was, after all, a great man./{K1}
282 MC Chorus	13	/That the sin of the world is	upon our heads; that the blood of the martyrs

282 MC Chorus 14 martyrs and the agony of the saints/Is upon our heads./Lord, have mercy upon us./
282 MC Chorus 15 /Is upon our heads./Lord, have mercy upon us./Christ, have mercy upon us./Lord,
282 MC Chorus 16   mercy upon us./Christ, have mercy upon us./Lord, have mercy upon us./Blessed
282 MC Chorus 17   mercy upon us./Lord, have mercy upon us./Blessed Thomas, pray for us. {}/THE
288 FR Agatha 21 /Because the future can only be built/Upon the real past. Wandering in the tropics/Or
290 FR Agatha 29   a pocket-torch of observation/Upon each other's opacity/Neglecting all the
297 FR Violet 30 /{V} Charles, if you are determined upon this investigation,/Which I am convinced
306 FR Mary 33 /{M} Well, it all seemed to be imposed upon us;/Even the nice things were laid out
308 FR Harry 5   unrecapturable emotion,/The glow upon the world, that never found its object;/
311 FR Harry 37   I was: let your necrophily/Feed upon that carcase. They will not go./{M} Harry!
313 FR Charles 23 /You should have a sobering effect upon him./After all, you're the head of the
318 FR Harry 16 /At home, make a deeper impression upon children/Than what they are told./{W}
334 FR Agatha 9 as if/I had been living all these years upon my capital,/Instead of earning my spiritual
334 FR Harry 25 Playing a part that had been imposed upon me;/And I returned to find another one
338 FR Harry 21 has been a flight/And phantoms fed upon me while I fled. Now I know/That the last
340 FR Amy 14 least a memory/Of something to live upon. You knew that you took everything/
340 FR Amy 21 in the silent bedroom,/Forcing sons upon an unwilling father?/Dare you think what
354 CP Julia 16 {J} Lady Klootz was very lovely, once upon a time./What a life she led! I used to say
370 CP Alex 18 to find any mangoes,/But I *did* count upon curry powder. {}/[*Exit*]/{P} That is exactly
393 CP Lavinia 7   sense of humour;/And that the effect upon me was/That I lost all sense of humour
400 CP Reilly 17 his wife./{R} I had already impressed upon her/That she was not to mention my name
403 CP Edward 29 /Of the role she had always imposed upon me/With the obstinate, unconscious,
407 CP Reilly 21   consulting me; both, tried to impose upon me/Your own diagnosis, and prescribe
421 CP Julia 10 /It's the thought of Celia that weighs upon my mind./{R} Of Celia?/{J} Of Celia./{R}
422 CP Alex 18   /{A} The words for those who go upon a journey./{R} Protector of travellers/Bless
461 CC Colby 13 But I hope/That I shan't have to call upon you often./{E} Oh, and I forgot ... Mrs. E.
461 CC Claude 26 two months —/And as my wife insists upon your being Mr. Colby —/I shall begin to
462 CC Colby 8 still seems to me/Like building my life upon a deception./Do you really believe that
462 CC Claude 25   strength to impose your own terms/Upon life, you must accept the terms it offers
466 CC Claude 29 /Of accepting the terms life imposes upon you/Even to the point of accepting ...
466 CC Colby 33   conditions/Which life has imposed upon you. But ... something in me/Rebels
478 CC Lucasta 20   then loneliness swoops down upon you;/When you think you're getting out,
491 CC Lady E 11 /From making unreasonable claims upon you, Colby./It's a good idea! Why should
497 CC Claude 30 satisfied with that solution./He insists upon the facts. And that is why/I have asked
500 CC Lucasta 32   him most!/And he doesn't depend upon other people, either./B. needs me. He's
516 CC Claude 32 father:/I'll accept that. I put no claim upon you —/Except the claim of our likeness to
541 ES Gomez 11 and who didn't. I promise you./Rely upon me as the soul of discretion./{LC} What
559 ES Michael 38 should I thank you for imposing this upon me?/And what satisfaction, I wonder, will
571 ES Charles 23 can't allow that. What hold have they upon you?/{LC} Only the hold of those who
578 ES Ld Clav 6 made/My whole life through, mistake upon mistake,/The mistaken attempts to correct
581 ES Ld Clav 14 peace now./It is the peace that ensues upon contrition/When contrition ensues upon
581 ES Ld Clav 15   contrition/When contrition ensues upon knowledge of the truth./Why did I always

UPPER (4)
129 Cor2 State 33   repose of noon, set under the upper branches of noon's widest tree/Under the
193 FQ: Little 67 and dead sand/Contending for the upper hand./The parched eviscerate soil/Gapes
300 FRDowning 29 /And you could see the corner of the upper deck./And I remember, there I saw his
531 ES Charles 10   voice will be heard/In debate in the Upper House .../{LC} The established liturgy/Of

UPRIGHT (1)
44 Cook Egg 1   neat./A Cooking Egg/Pipit sate upright in her chair/Some distance from where I

UPROAR (2)
221 Old Deut 38 —/I'll have the police if there's any uproar' —/And out they all shuffle, without a
223 Pekes Pols 27 so all the Pekes, when they heard the uproar,/Some came to the window, some came

UPSET (2)
587 Fable 22 the thinner/To furnish all the milk — upset the chimes,/And once he sat the prior on
287 FR Gerald 13 /{G} I'm very sorry: but why was she upset?/I only meant to draw her into the

UPSIDE (1)
73 WL: Thund 382   down a blackened wall/And upside down in air were towers/Tolling

UPSTAIRS (3)
302 FR Amy 19 Harry will feel better/After his rest upstairs. {}/[*Exeunt, except* AGATHA]/Scene II
452 CC Kaghan 8   I'd better bring her/And come upstairs ahead, to ease the shock for Colby./But
509 CC Claude 23 fact, the young man who showed you upstairs —/Whose name is Barnabas Kaghan./

UPSTREAM (1)
310 FR Mary 24 beast, and the fish/Thrashing itself upstream:/And what of the terrified spirit/

UPTURNED (1)
161 Rock 7 30   the tower overthrown, the bells upturned, what have we to do/But stand with

UPWARD (3)

42 Swee Erect	17	motion from the thighs/Jackknifes upward at the knees/Then straightens out from
68 WL: Fire S	216	hour, when the eyes and back/Turn upward from the desk, when the human engine
167 Rock 10	32	/Our gaze is submarine, our eyes look upward/And see the light that fractures through

UPWARDS (1)

| 161 Rock 7 | 31 | with empty hands and palms turned upwards/In an age which advances |

URBAN (1)

| 193 FQ: Little | 90 | me like the metal leaves/Before the urban dawn wind unresisting./And as I fixed |

URGE (2)

| 194 FQ: Little | 130 | /To purify the dialect of the tribe/And urge the mind to aftersight and foresight,/Let |
| 545 ES Ld Clav | 7 | critic, who can terrorise us/And urge us on to futile activity,/And in the end, |

URGED (1)

| 267 MC Knight2 | 38 | Yet the King, out of his charity,/And urged by your friends, offered clemency,/Made |

URGENCY (1)

| 266 MC Thomas | 4 | are/Engrossed with matters of other urgency./On my table you will find/The papers |

URGENT (5)

265 MC Knight1	12	far?/{K1} Not far to-day, but matters urgent/Have brought us from France. We rode
265 MC Knight2	16	business with the Archbishop./{K2} Urgent business./{K3} From the King./{K2} By
267 MC Thomas	5	your business/Which you said so urgent, is it only/Scolding and blaspheming?/
321 FR Denman	10	/And wants to see your Lordship very urgent,/And Dr. Warburton. He says it's very
321 FR Denman	11	And Dr. Warburton. He says it's very urgent/Or he wouldn't have troubled you./{H}

URN (2)

| 34 Figlia | 2 | of the stair —/Lean on a garden urn —/Weave, weave the sunlight in your hair |
| 151 Rock 2 | 6 | lands for alms to be more or the urn to be filled./Your building not fitly framed |

URNS (2)

| 128 Cor1 March | 36 | /Now come the virgins bearing urns, urns containing/Dust/Dust/Dust of dust, |
| 128 Cor1 March | 36 | /Now come the virgins bearing urns, urns containing/Dust/Dust/Dust of dust, and |

URSE (3)

276 MC Knight3	34	as my old friend Reginald Fitz Urse would lead you to/believe. But there is one
277 MC Knight2	36	/well put by our leader, Reginald Fitz Urse: that you are Englishmen,/and therefore
279 MC Knight4	12	nothing/of our leader, Reginald Fitz Urse, have all spoken very much to the/point. I

US (329)

USE (43)

16 Prufrock	115	easy tool,/Deferential, glad to be of use,/Politic, cautious, and meticulous;/Full of
38 Gerontion	60	taste and touch:/How should I use them for your closer contact?/These with a
118 SP Dusty	9	what you want to know/{Du} It's no use asking them too much/{Do} It's no use
118 SP Doris	10	asking them too much/{Do} It's no use asking more than once/{Du} Sometimes
118 SP Dusty	11	than once/{Du} Sometimes they're no use at all./{Do} I'd like to know about that
125 SA Sweeney	2	again that don't apply/But I've gotta use words when I talk to you./But here's what I
125 SA Sweeney	21	/Death is life and life is death/I gotta use words when I talk to you/But if you
158 Rock 5	5	Those who sit in a house of which the use is forgotten: are like snakes that lie on
182 FQ: ECoker	176	*deux guerres* —/Trying to learn to use words, and every attempt/Is a wholly new
195 FQ: Little	158	live and the dead nettle. This is the use of memory:/For liberation — not less of
209 NamingCats	5	of all, there's the name that the family use daily,/Such as Peter, Augustus, Alonzo or
214 RTTugger	19	is a Curious Cat —/And it isn't any use for you to doubt it:/For he will do/As he do
588 Fable	58	old drink, though now gone out of use —/His feet upon the table superposed/Each
253 MC Tempt4	10	man who has been his friend./Borrow use cautiously, employ/Your services as long as
297 FR Charles	12	them on the boat. He might be of use./{I} Charles! you don't really suppose/That
312 FR Harry	6	Can't you help me?/You're of no use to me. I must face them./I must fight them.
314 FR Amy	1	fog that is holding them up,/So it's no use to telephone anywhere. Harry!/Haven't you
315 FR Gerald	22	ten years ago./{G} Is there any use in waiting for Arthur and John?/{A} We
325 FR Charles	9	tonight./{C} Well, there's no sort of use in any of us going —/On a night like this —
327 FR Ivy	31	/But he says that he hasn't got the use of his car,/And he missed the last train, so
327 FR Violet	35	not to tell his mother./{V} What's the use of asking for an evening paper?/You know
364 CP Edward	9	to find out who I am./And what is the use of all your analysis/If I am to remain always
382 CP Celia	33	I see that I was simply making use of you./And I ask you to forgive me./{E}
387 CP Peter	36	I mean, I've decided/That it's all no use. I'm going to California./{C} You're going
391 CP Julia	12	/No, they're here. Besides, they're no use to me./I'm not coming back again *this*
393 CP Edward	40	always too busy or too tired/To be of use to you socially .../{L} I *never* complained./
401 CP Edward	12	should like to know ... but what is the use!/I suppose I might as well go away at once./
402 CP Reilly	20	breakdown' is a term I never use:/It can mean almost anything./{E} And since
415 CP Reilly	1	would be normal/For *you*, before we use the term 'abnormal'./Tell me what you
416 CP Celia	22	taking/But that we had merely made use of each other/Each for his purpose. That's
431 CP Peter	17	a film of English life/And we want to use Boltwell./{J} But I understood that Boltwell/
453 CC Kaghan	23	you told Colby about me?/{K} It's no use telling anybody about you:/Nobody'd ever

464 CC	Claude	7	of china or porcelain/As merely for use, or for decoration —/In either case, an
464 CC	Claude	9	inferior art./For me, they are neither 'use' nor 'decoration' —/That is, decoration as a
478 CC	Colby	6	I am a guttersnipe .../{C} You mustn't use such words! You don't know how it's
478 CC	Lucasta	7	know how it's hurting./{L} I could use words much stronger than that,/And I will,
482 CC	Lady E	7	nowadays/Seem to have dropped the use of surnames altogether./But, Colby, I hope
487 CC	Claude	2	out/And then memorise it. I can't use notes:/It's got to sound spontaneous. I've
527 ES	Charles	34	/For your brother's never been of any use to you./{M} And never will be of any use to
527 ES	Monica	35	to you./{M} And never will be of any use to anybody,/I'm afraid. Poor Michael!
535 ES	Gomez	11	I began to say: when I say 'trust'/I use the term as experience has taught me./It's
574 ES	Michael	32	see my point of view. What's the use of chasing/Half round the world, for the
577 ES	Carghil	35	all this time for opportunity/To make use of his gifts; and now, opportunity —/

USED (37)

34 Figlia		12	/As the mind deserts the body it has used./I should find/Some way incomparably
124 SA	Sweeney	37	to live men about what they do./He used to come and see me sometimes/I'd give him
228 Gus		22	so he says, 'every possible part,/And I used to know seventy speeches by heart./I'd
245 MC	Priest2	33	December,/Your Lordship now being used to a better climate./Your Lordship will
247 MC	Templ1	34	of the King our master!/You were not used to be so hard upon sinners/When they
279 MC	Knight4	28	he would be killed in England. He used every means of provocation;/from his
285 FR	Charles	24	people./Amy has been too long used to our ways/Living with horses and dogs
299 FR	Downing	25	and up in the evening,/And *then* she used to get rather excited,/And, in a way,
314 FR	Warburt	24	when I was a student at Cambridge,/I used to dream of making some great discovery/
315 FR	Harry	6	victim./To himself he is still what he used to be/Or what he would be. He cannot
316 FR	Gerald	5	I must struggle against it./{G} I am used to tangible danger, but only to what I can
345 FR	Harry	1	little fuss as possible. You must get used to it;/Meanwhile, I apologise for my bad
347 FR	Downing	7	/They did me, at first. You soon get used to them./Of course, I knew they was to do
354 CP	Julia	17	upon a time./What a life she led! I used to say to her: 'Greta!/You have too much
356 CP	Peter	10	produced. They did a film/But they used a different scenario./{J} Not the one you
361 CP	Edward	13	please don't suggest./I have often used these terms in examining witnesses,/So I
362 CP	Edward	12	person. Why speak of love?/We were used to each other. So her going away/At a
372 CP	Edward	16	half-a-dozen eggs./{E} What! You used all those eggs! Lavinia's aunt/Has just sent
446 CC	Eggers	24	and coming up daily/Just as I used to. And the flat in the mews?/How soon
454 CC	Kaghan	16	/{K} Take it easy, Colby. You'll get used to her. {}/[*Exit* KAGHAN]/{C} Egg ... Mr.
454 CC	Colby	37	/The first time I met her. I'm not used to it./{E} You'll soon get used to it. You'll
455 CC	Eggers	1	I'm not used to it./{E} You'll soon get used to it. You'll be calling me Eggers/Before
455 CC	Eggers	30	like Miss Angel./{E} You'll get used to her, Mr. Simpkins./Time works
456 CC	Eggers	15	perfectly harmless./You'll soon get used to them. That's what Sir Claude said:/
463 CC	Colby	27	then the former person,/The person I used to be, returns to take possession:/And I am
496 CC	Eggers	20	oftener!/Isn't that like the ladies! She used to complain/At my being up in London
509 CC	Lady E	39	/Being Barnabas. I suppose I'll get used to it./{C} But he's waiting downstairs! Isn't
511 CC	Kaghan	16	a time, at least./{K} Well, I must get used to that./But I should like to know how I
529 ES	Charles	5	having you to talk to!/{C} I know he's used to seeing me about./{M} I've seen him
530 ES	Ld Clav	2	pages since I entered Parliament./I used to jot down notes of what I had to say to
532 ES	Ld Clav	16	a letter of introduction/From a man I used to know. I can't refuse to see him./Though
542 ES	Gomez	4	I only want your friendship!/Just as it used to be in the old days/When you taught me
543 ES	Ld Clav	9	Who was it, Father?/{LC} A man I used to know./{M} Oh, so you knew him?/{LC}
563 ES	Ld Clav	1	know him, Richard?/{LC} It's a man I used to know./{MC} How interesting! He's a
578 ES	Michael	25	I came home for the holidays/How it used to get on my nerves, when I saw you/
578 ES	Michael	30	to want a flirtation,/And my friends used to chaff me about my highbrow sister./But
582 ES	Charles	25	a very different man from the man he used to be./It's as if he had passed through

USEFUL (9)

148 Rock 1		50	I know/That it is hard to be really useful, resigning/The things that men count for
151 Rock 2		10	to be flung in the end, on a heap less useful than dung'./You, have you built well,
184 FQ: DrySal		4	at first recognised as a frontier;/Useful, untrustworthy, as a conveyor of
318 FR	Harry	36	at least you can tell me/Something useful. Do you remember my father?/{W} Why,
344 FR	Gerald	22	profession./They're sometimes very useful, knowing the natives,/Though
385 CP	Reilly	3	that they and we are the same/Is a useful and convenient social convention/Which
421 CP	Julia	32	/{J} That's one way in which I am so useful to you./You ought to be grateful./{R}
456 CC	Eggers	7	connections/Have sometimes been useful. But he didn't think of that:/He's not
536 ES	Gomez	14	my children learn English — it's useful;/I always talk to them in English./But do

USELESS (7)

20 Portrait		89	and when do you return?/But that's a useless question./You hardly know when you
179 FQ: ECoker		81	only the knowledge of dead secrets/Useless in the darkness into which they peered/
227 Macavity		30	in the hall or on the stair —/But it's useless to investigate — *Macavity's not there*!/
602 Humoresque		13	to the moon./With Limbo's other useless things/Haranguing spectres, set him
301 FR	Violet	23	is certain to make some blunder, he is useless out of the army./{C} Violet is afraid that

309 FR   Harry   29   true./{H} I have spent many years in useless travel;/You have staid in England, yet
317 FR   Harry   7   I think it is probably going to be useless,/Or if anything, make matters rather
USINE (1)
48 Lune Miel   17 Apollinaire, raide et ascétique,/Vieille usine désaffectée de Dieu, tient encore/Dans ses
USING (1)
268 MC Knight3   10   with the chains of anathema./{K3} Using every means in your power to evince/The
USK (1)
140 Usk   t   go with me:/Red river, river, river./Usk/Do not suddenly break the branch, or/
USUAL (15)
89 Ash-Wed 1   8   I mourn/The vanished power of the usual reign?/Because I do not hope to know
189 FQ: DrySal   198   or tomb, or dreams; all these are usual/Pastimes and drugs, and features of the
234 Ad-dress   26 And such fantastic canine freaks./The usual Dog about the Town/Is much inclined to
601 Nocturne   3   beside the gate/With Juliet, in the usual debate/Of love, beneath a bored but
299 FRDowning   38 what struck me ... more nervous than usual;/I mean to say, you could see that he was
300 FRDowning   14   other, Sir./Quite the contrary of the usual opinion,/I dare say. She wouldn't leave
309 FR   Harry   35   two storms, one hears the moderate usual noises/In the grass and leaves, of life
326 FR   Harry   13 You've been holding a meeting — the usual family inquest/On the characters of all the
399 CP   Nurse   11   be shown into the other room/Just as usual. She arrives at a quarter past;/But you
400 CP   Alex   19   my name to him./{A} With your usual foresight. Now, he's quite triumphant/
417 CP   Reilly   30 and others,/Giving and taking, in the usual actions/What there is to give and take.
452 CC   Kaghan   5   /{K} Because Lucasta's with me! The usual catastrophe./She's come to pry some cash
539 ES   Gomez   5   of my doctors./{G} Oh yes, the usual euphemism./And yet I wonder. It *is*
554 ES   Piggott 30 tipple myself/Instead of leaving it, as usual, to Nurse)/When I saw that Mrs. Carghill
558 ES   Michael 14   else did he say?/{Mi} He took the usual line,/Just like the headmaster. And my
USUALLY (7)
228 Gus   4   such a fuss/To pronounce, that we usually call him just Gus./His coat's very
278 MC Knight2   10   of local government, which were usually exercised for/selfish and often for
304 FR   Mary   15   well,/What Cousin Amy wants, she usually gets./Why do *you* so seldom come here?
348 FR   Chorus   13   how to work the machine,/We can usually avoid accidents,/We are insured against
413 CP   Reilly   7   — that is what they call it —/And usually they think that someone else is to blame.
425 CP   Lavinia 8   come. But what can you do?/There's usually a lot who don't want to come/But all the
429 CP   Alex   18   murdered?/{A} Yes, but they are not usually eaten./When these people have done
USURPER (1)
278 MC Knight2   7   and the irruption of the unhappy usurper/Stephen, the kingdom was very much
USURY (1)
161 Rock 7   43   men have forgotten/All gods except Usury, Lust and Power./O Father we welcome
UTI (1)
75 WL: Thund   428   *nel foco che gli affina/Quando fiam uti chelidon* — O swallow swallow/*Le Prince*
UTTER (2)
271 MC Chorus   4   lust of self-demolition,/By the final utter uttermost death of spirit,/By the final
465 CC   Claude   25 me that contentment —/That state of utter exhaustion and peace/Which comes in
UTTERLY (6)
279 MC Knight4   23   his policy; he showed/himself to be utterly indifferent to the fate of the country, to
408 CP   Edward   22   Celia!/I have never heard anything so utterly ludicrous:/This is the best joke that ever
524 ES   Charles 22 /If he takes you to a place where he's utterly unknown/And the waiters all appear to
549 ES   Carghil 11   it invited us to lunch?/I declare, I've utterly forgotten their names./And you gave us
574 ES   Carghil 13   /I know you've always thought me utterly brainless,/But I have an idea or two, now
583 ES   Monica   27 certainty of love unchanging./I feel utterly secure/In you; I am a part of you. Now
UTTERMOST (1)
271 MC Chorus   4   of self-demolition,/By the final utter uttermost death of spirit,/By the final ecstasy of

V.A.D. (1)
433 CP   Lavinia   40   of nursing .../{L} Yes, she had been a V.A.D. I remember./{A} She was directed to
VA (1)
51 Restaurant   21   /Mais alors, tu as ton vautour!/Va t'en te décrotter les rides du visage;/Tiens,
VACANCY (5)
156 Rock 3   70   empty bottles,/Turning from your vacancy to fevered enthusiasm/For nation or
174 FQ: BurntN 102   the temporal./Neither plenitude nor vacancy. Only a flicker/Over the strained
332 FR   Agatha   16   Wishwood./At first it was a vacancy. A man and a woman/Married, alone
403 CP   Edward   31   women have. Without her, it was vacancy./When I thought she had left me, I
517 CC   Eggers   25   me./{E} If so, I happen to know of a vacancy/In my own parish, in Joshua Park —/If
VACANT (8)
22 Preludes   8   your feet/And newspapers from vacant lots;/The showers beat/On broken blinds
23 Preludes   54   like ancient women/Gathering fuel in vacant lots./Rhapsody on a Windy Night/
38 Gerontion   29   in the hall, one hand on the door. Vacant shuttles/Weave the wind. I have no
149 Rock 1   79   *are heard chanting./In the vacant places/We will build with new bricks/*
180 FQ: ECoker 103   dark. They all go into the dark,/The vacant interstellar spaces, the vacant into the
180 FQ: ECoker 103   /The vacant interstellar spaces, the vacant into the vacant,/The captains, merchant
180 FQ: ECoker 103   interstellar spaces, the vacant into the vacant,/The captains, merchant bankers,
287 FR   Amy   31   surprise,/A momentary shudder in a vacant room./Only Agatha seems to discover
VACATION (2)
324 FR   Harry   16   very much difference to John./A brief vacation from the kind of consciousness/That
332 FR   Agatha   22   at Oxford. I came/Once for a long vacation. I remember/A summer day of unusual
VACUITY (1)
33 Conv Gal   10   we seize/To body forth our own vacuity.'/She then: 'Does this refer to me?'/'Oh
VACUUM (2)
319 FR   Harry   8   grasped for him, there was only a vacuum/Surrounded by whispering aunts: Ivy
530 ES   Ld Clav   19   a loathing of inaction./A fear of the vacuum, and no desire to fill it./It's just like
VAGRANT (1)
33 Conv Gal   15   enemy of the absolute,/Giving our vagrant moods the slightest twist!/With your air
VAGUE (2)
225 Mr Mistoff   42   Mr. Mistoffelees!/His manner is vague and aloof,/You would think there was
576 ES   Charles   30   A post the nature of which is left very vague/{Mi} It's confidential, I tell you./{C} So I
VAGUELY (1)
553 ES   Ld Clav   28   Don't you remember them?/{LC} Vaguely. Were they very passionate?/{MC}
VAIN (7)
151 Rock 2   6   the palms of their hands, or look in vain towards foreign lands for alms to be more
155 Rock 3   37   golf balls'./CHORUS:/We build in vain unless the LORD build with us./Can you
158 Rock 5   8   write innumerable books; being too vain and distracted for silence: seeking every
160 Rock 7   3   GOD/Blindly and vainly, for man is a vain thing, and man without GOD is a seed
604 Ode   4   wait, while thy presence dispels/Our vain hesitations and fears./And we turn as thy
273 MC Chorus   5   the tree, my Saviour,/Let not be in vain Thy labour;/Help me, Lord, in my last
571 ES   Ld Clav   20   when we meet it;/Even when it's vain and selfish, we must not abuse it./That is
VAINLY (1)
160 Rock 7   3   in torment towards GOD/Blindly and vainly, for man is a vain thing, and man without
VALEDICTION (1)
195 FQ: Little   150   street/He left me, with a kind of valediction,/And faded on the blowing of the
VALID (3)
192 FQ: Little   48   here to kneel/Where prayer has been valid. And prayer is more/Than an order of
349 FR   Ivy   8   will my ticket to London still be valid?/{G} I do not look forward with pleasure
422 CP   Reilly   32   not yet come to where the words are valid./{J} Shall we ever speak them?/{A} Others,
VALLEY (4)
84 Hollow Men   54   here/There are no eyes here/In this valley of dying stars/In this hollow valley/This
84 Hollow Men   55   valley of dying stars/In this hollow valley/This broken jaw of our lost kingdoms/In
103 Journ Magi   21   dawn we came down to a temperate valley,/Wet, below the snow line, smelling of
421 CP   Julia   27   the scolding hills,/Through the valley of derision, like a child sent on an errand/
VALUATION (1)
179 FQ: ECoker   88   every moment is a new and shocking/Valuation of all we have been. We are only
VALUE (4)
179 FQ: ECoker   74   one had expected./What was to be the value of the long looked forward to,/Long
179 FQ: ECoker   83   it seems to us,/At best, only a limited value/In the knowledge derived from
363 CP   Reilly   36   that's an experience of incalculable value./{E} Stop! I agree that much of what
540 ES   Gomez   11   success?/{G} No, because I know the value of the coinage/I pay myself in./{LC}
VAN (2)
177 FQ: ECoker   17   you lean against a bank while a van passes,/And the deep lane insists on the
232 Skimble   12   rear:/He's been busy in the luggage van!/He gives one flash of his glass-green eyes/

VANISH (2)

| 195 | FQ: Little | 165 | may be freedom. See, now they vanish,/The faces and places, with the self |
| 500 | CC Lucasta | 30 | He has his own world,/And he might vanish into it at any moment —/At just the |

VANISHED (1)

| 89 | Ash-Wed 1 | 8 | its wings?)/Why should I mourn/The vanished power of the usual reign?/Because I do |

VANISHES (2)

| 27 | Morning | 9 | smile that hovers in the air/And vanishes along the level of the roofs./The |
| 289 | FR Charles | 27 | the body./{C} 'Well-known Peeress Vanishes from Liner'./{G} Yes, it's odd to think |

VANISHT (1)

| 589 | Fable | 80 | could say 'O jiminy!'/The pair had vanisht swiftly up the chimney./Naturally every |

VANITIES (1)

| 38 | Gerontion | 36 | whispering ambitions,/Guides us by vanities. Think now/She gives when our |

VANITY (9)

68	WL: Fire S	241	hands encounter no defence;/His vanity requires no response,/And makes a
193	FQ: Little	69	parched eviscerate soil/Gapes at the vanity of toil,/Laughs without mirth./This is the
255	MC Thomas	32	that these temptations/Mean present vanity and future torment./Can sinful pride be
290	FR Amy	2	to keep him to herself/To satisfy her vanity. That's why she dragged him/All over
378	CP Celia	26	/{C} It cannot be simply a question of vanity:/That you think the world will laugh at
403	CP Reilly	5	/And it would only go to flatter your vanity/With the temporary stimulus of feeling
409	CP Reilly	14	/On her account. This injured your vanity./You liked to think of yourself as a
420	CP Reilly	32	motive —/Mirror to mirror, reflecting vanity./I have taken a great risk./{J} We must
524	ES Monica	18	like to show off./That's masculine vanity, to want to have the waiters/All buzzing

VANS (1)

| 90 | Ash-Wed 1 | 35 | are no longer wings to fly/But merely vans to beat the air/The air which is now |

VAPOUR (4)

92	Ash-Wed 3	4	twisted on the banister/Under the vapour in the fetid air/Struggling with the devil
256	MC Chorus	8	our feet./What is the sickly smell, the vapour? the dark green light from a cloud on a
294	FR Harry	18	but round and round in that vapour —/Without purpose, and without
311	FR Harry	7	it!/More potent than ever before, a vapour dissolving/All other worlds, and me into

VARIED (1)

| 94 | Ash-Wed 4 | 3 | walked between/The various ranks of varied green/Going in white and blue, in Mary's |

VARIETY (1)

| 38 | Gerontion | 64 | /With pungent sauces, multiply variety/In a wilderness of mirrors. What will the |

VARIOUS (11)

94	Ash-Wed 4	3	the violet/Who walked between/The various ranks of varied green/Going in white
160	Rock 7	2	/And when there were men, in their various ways, they struggled in torment towards
234	Ad-dress	8	people whom we find/Possessed of various types of mind./For some are sane and
239	MC Chorus	23	or barons rule;/We have suffered various oppression,/But mostly we are left to
244	MC Chorus	12	deaths and marriages,/We have had various scandals,/We have been afflicted with
276	MC Knight1	29	the other speakers, who,/with their various abilities, and different points of view,
278	MC Knight2	17	/government. I knew Becket well, in various official relations; and I/may say that I
344	FR Gerald	28	And don't forget/That you'll need various inoculations —/That depends on where
348	FR Chorus	18	not against the act of God./We know various spells and enchantments./And minor
434	CP Alex	2	directed to Kinkanja,/Where there are various endemic diseases/Besides, of course,
469	CC Colby	10	to learn about its structure/And the various forms, and the different ways of playing

VASE (1)

| 219 | Mung Rump | 37 | the library came a loud *ping*/From a vase which was commonly said to be Ming —/ |

VASSAL (2)

| 266 | MC Thomas | 28 | at his command,/As his most faithful vassal in the land./{K1} Saving your order! let |
| 275 | MC Thomas | 15 | you:/Traitor to me as my temporal vassal,/Traitor to me as your spiritual lord,/ |

VAST (2)

| 183 | FQ: ECoker | 210 | /The wave cry, the wind cry, the vast waters/Of the petrel and the porpoise. In |
| 213 | Growltiger | 50 | rank on rank;/Growltiger to his vast surprise was forced to walk the plank./He |

VAUTOUR (1)

| 51 | Restaurant | 20 | C'est dommage.'/Mais alors, tu as ton vautour!/Va t'en te décrotter les rides du visage; |

VEGETATION (2)

| 67 | WL: Fire S | 187 | to ear./A rat crept softly through the vegetation/Dragging its slimy belly on the bank/ |
| 103 | Journ Magi | 22 | /Wet, below the snow line, smelling of vegetation,/With a running stream and a |

VEILED (5)

56	Swee Night	10	gate./Gloomy Orion and the Dog/Are veiled; and hushed the shrunken seas;/The
94	Ash-Wed 4	22	by the gilded hearse./The silent sister veiled in white and blue/Between the yews,
96	Ash-Wed 5	20	noise and deny the voice/Will the veiled sister pray for/Those who walk in
96	Ash-Wed 5	24	those who wait/In darkness? Will the veiled sister pray/For children at the gate/Who
97	Ash-Wed 5	29	what have I done unto thee./Will the veiled sister between the slender/Yew trees pray

VEINS (2)
270 MC Chorus 14 in the byre in the market-place/In our veins our bowels our skulls as well/As well as in
270 MC Chorus 19   of princes/Is woven also in our veins, our brains,/Is woven like a pattern of
VELLEITIES (1)
 18 Portrait   15 And so the conversation slips/Among velleities and carefully caught regrets/Through
VENERATION (1)
428 CP   Alex 12 /They hold these monkeys in peculiar veneration/And do not want them killed. So
VENIAL (1)
258 MC Thomas   7   reason./The natural vigour in the venial sin/Is the way in which our lives begin./
VENISON (1)
230 Bust Jones   21 winkles and shrimps./In the season of venison he gives his ben'son/To the *Pothunter's*
VENT (2)
 48 Lune Miel   10   chapitaux d'acanthe que tournoie le vent./Ils vont prendre le train de huit heures/
 51 Restaurant   4   mon pays il fera temps pluvieux,/Du vent, du grand soleil, et de la pluie;/C'est ce
VENTURE (3)
182 FQ: ECoker 180 longer disposed to say it. And so each venture/Is a new beginning, a raid on the
280 MC   Priest3 20   or the Gates of Hercules./Go venture shipwreck on the sullen coasts/Where
517 CC   Eggers 20 to help him, Eggerson./{E} I wouldn't venture./Mr. Simpkins is a man who knows his
VENU (1)
 51 Restaurant   17 âge .../'Monsieur, le fait est dur./Il est venu, nous peloter, un gros chien;/Moi j'avais
VERACIOUS (1)
589 Fable   95   admiration of the shire. We/Got the veracious record of these doings/From an old
VERBAL (1)
164 Rock 9   22   of words, out of the sleet and hail of verbal imprecisions,/Approximate thoughts and
VERDICT (2)
279 MC Knight4   38 /you, you will unhesitatingly render a verdict of Suicide while of/Unsound Mind. It is
279 MC Knight4   39   Mind. It is the only charitable verdict you can give, upon/one who was, after
VERGE (1)
396 CP   Lavinia 11   you were./I seemed always on the verge of some wonderful experience/And then it
VERIFY (1)
192 FQ: Little   45 Sense and notion. You are not here to verify,/Instruct yourself, or inform curiosity/Or
VERINDER (3)
354 CP   Julia 23   my story./I heard it first from Delia Verinder/Who was there when it happened. {}/
354 CP   Julia 25   GUEST]/{J} Do *you* know Delia Verinder?/{UG} No, I don't know her./{J} Well,
354 CP   Alex 29 /Before one tells a story./{A} Delia Verinder?/Was she the one who had three
VERITABLE (1)
 89 Ash-Wed 1   13   I know I shall not know/The one veritable transitory power/Because I cannot
VERMIN (1)
276 MC Chorus   14 cannot clean, united to supernatural vermin,/It is not we alone, it is not the house, it
VERSE (5)
 94 Ash-Wed 4   18 tears, the years, restoring/With a new verse the ancient rhyme. Redeem/The time.
201 Def Island   4   cultivation of the earth, of English/verse/be joined with the memory of this defence
202 War Poetry   25 we call 'poetry',/May be affirmed in verse./To the Indians who Died in Africa/A
234 Ad-dress   12 worse —But all may be described in verse./You've seen them both at work and
260 MC Thomas   2 to men of good will.' *The/fourteenth verse of the second chapter of the Gospel*
VERSES (1)
199   t and the rose are one./OCCASIONAL VERSES/Defence of the Islands/Let these
VERSION (3)
540 ES Ld Clav 36 interest the public/Why not sell your version to a Sunday newspaper?/{G} My dear
558 ES Ld Clav 11   —/In order to let me have your version first./I dare say Sir Alfred's will be
575 ES Gomez   21 me/Before he heard your distorted version./But, Dick, I was nettled by that
VERSIONS (2)
152 Rock 2   22   including capital/And several versions of the Word of GOD:/The British race
572 ES Charles 30 of self-justification./Let them tell their versions of their miserable stories,/Confide them
VERTEBRATE (1)
 56 Swee Night   21 figs and hothouse grapes;/The silent vertebrate in brown/Contracts and
VERY (439)
VESPER-SPARROW (1)
142 Cape Ann   2   /Swamp-sparrow, fox-sparrow, vesper-sparrow/At dawn and dusk. Follow the
VESPERS (5)
271 MC Priests 33 only near to death./{3P} My Lord, to vespers! You must not be absent from vespers./
271 MC Priests 33 vespers! You must not be absent from vespers./You must not be absent from the
272 MC Priests   1   be absent from the divine office. To vespers./Into the Cathedral!/{T} Go to vespers,
272 MC Thomas   3   /Into the Cathedral!/{T} Go to vespers, remember me at your prayers./They
272 MC Priests 10 /{T} Keep your hands off!/{3P} To vespers! Hurry. {}/[*They drag him off. While the*

VESSEL (1)
213 Growltiger   29   for his prey./In the forepeak of the vessel Growltiger sate alone,/Concentrating his
VESTS (1)
218 Mung Rump   12   you couldn't find one of your winter vests,/Or after supper one of the girls/Suddenly
VÊTU (1)
47 Mél Adult   18   jour de fête/Dans une oasis d'Afrique/Vêtu d'une peau de girafe./On montrera mon
VEXED (1)
265 MC Priest1   22   /The good Archbishop would be vexed/If we did not offer you entertainment/
VEXING (1)
313 FR   Amy   27   DR. WARBURTON]/{A} It is most vexing. What can have happened?/I suppose it's
VIALS (1)
64 WL: Chess   86   cases poured in rich profusion./In vials of ivory and coloured glass/Unstoppered,
VIAND (1)
588 Fable   51   kept from toppling over,/Next came a viand made of turtle eggs,/And after that a
VIATICUM (1)
107 Animula   31   /Living first in the silence after the viaticum./Pray for Guiterriez, avid of speed and
VIBRANT (1)
172 FQ: BurntN   27   /In the autumn heat, through the vibrant air,/And the bird called, in response to/
VIBRATION (1)
417 CP   Celia   11   by intensity of loving/In the spirit, a vibration of delight/Without desire, for desire is
VICAR (1)
344 FR   Violet   26   /I think you should consult the vicar .../{G} And don't forget/That you'll need
VICAR'S (2)
291 FR   Violet   5   been helping Lady Bumpus, at the Vicar's American Tea./{Ch} Yet we are here at
517 CC   Eggers   36   /And I have some influence. *I* am the Vicar's Warden./{C} I'd like to apply./{E} The
VICARAGE (1)
220 Old Deut   10   /When he sits in the sun on the vicarage wall,/The Oldest Inhabitant croaks:
VICARS (1)
147 Rock 1   23   There I was told:/Let the vicars retire. Men do not need the Church/In
VICE (1)
163 Rock 8   43   of moderate virtue/And of moderate vice/When men will not lay down the Cross/
VICES (3)
38 Gerontion   44   fear nor courage saves us. Unnatural vices/Are fathered by our heroism. Virtues/Are
248 MC Tempt1   1   you to the pleasures of your higher vices,/Which will have to be paid for at higher
571 ES Ld Clav   14   those who admire us/Will imitate our vices as well as our virtues —/Or whatever the
VICINITY (1)
532 ES Ld Clav   29   you to come/If you're in the vicinity. Don't we, Monica?/{M} Yes, Father. {}/
VICISSITUDE (1)
583 ES Monica   24   can have no terrors for me,/Loss and vicissitude cannot appal me,/Not even death can
VICISSITUDES (1)
539 ES Gomez   15   /And I've learned something of other vicissitudes./Dick, I was very very sorry when I
VICTIM (1)
315 FR   Harry   5   /Regards himself as an innocent victim./To himself he is still what he used to be/
VICTIMS (1)
213 Growltiger   51   to walk the plank./He who a hundred victims had driven to that drop,/At the end of
VICTOR (1)
209 NamingCats   7   Augustus, Alonzo or James,/Such as Victor or Jonathan, George or Bill Bailey —/All
VICTORIA (6)
69 WL: Fire S   258   /And along the Strand, up Queen Victoria Street./O City city, I can sometimes
213 Growltiger   55   roasted whole at Brentford, and at Victoria Dock,/And a day of celebration was
218 Mung Rump   3   reputation. They made their home in Victoria Grove —/That was merely their centre
218 Mung Rump   19   /They made their home in Victoria Grove. They had no regular
229 Gus   46   trained/As we did in the days when Victoria reigned./They never get drilled in a
458 CC Lady E   13   /I didn't come by air. I arrived at Victoria./{SC} Do you mean to say that you
VICTORIA'S (1)
220 Old Deut   4   in rhyme/A long while before Queen Victoria's accession./Old Deuteronomy's buried
VICTORY (2)
593 Grad 7   5   /That they have helpt the cause to victory,/That with their aid the flag is raised on
274 MC Thomas   11   /Now, by suffering. This is the easier victory./Now is the triumph of the Cross, now/
VIE (1)
51 Restaurant   29   loin,/Le repassant aux étapes de sa vie antérieure./Figurez-vous donc, c'était un
VIEILLE (1)
48 Lune Miel   17   Saint Apollinaire, raide et ascétique,/Vieille usine désaffectée de Dieu, tient encore/
VIENNA (1)
73 WL: Thund   375   towers/Jerusalem Athens Alexandria/Vienna London/Unreal/A woman drew her

VIENNESE (1)
40 Burb Blei   16   the palms turned out,/Chicago Semite Viennese./A lustreless protrusive eye/Stares
VIEUX (1)
51 Restaurant   15   de puissance et de délire.'/Mais alors, vieux lubrique, à cet âge .../'Monsieur, le fait est
VIEW (11)
276 MC Knight1   29   abilities, and different points of view, will be able/to lay before you the merits of
279 MC Knight1   7   who has I think another point of view/to express. If there are any who are still
314 FR Warburt   21   You mustn't take such a pessimistic view/Which is hardly complimentary to my
397 CP Edward   21   him all about me/From *your* point of view? But I don't need a doctor./I am simply in
415 CP   Reilly   18   a fool./{R} And what is the point of view of your family?/{C} Well, my bringing up
415 CP   Celia   22   anything wrong, from our point of view,/Was either bad form, or was
428 CP   Alex   19   /And, naturally, take a different view./They trap the monkeys. And they eat
499 CC Lucasta 26   the ideal solution/From your point of view. To get me off your hands./Oh, I know
574 ES Michael   32   abroad,/You couldn't see my point of view. What's the use of chasing/Half round the
575 ES Michael   4   sees./*He* understands my point of view, if *you* don't./And he's offered me a job
577 ES Charles   12   than never./{C} I see your point of view. Can you really feel confidence,/Michael,
VIEWS (3)
 44 Cook Egg   3   distance from where I was sitting;/*Views of Oxford Colleges*/Lay on the table, with
501 CC Lady E   10   I have always been a person of liberal views —/That's why I never got on with my
501 CC Lucasta 12   /{L} Well, I'm not a person of liberal views./I'm very conventional. And I'm not
VIGIL (1)
339 FR   Harry   10   altar,/The heat of the sun and the icy vigil,/A care over lives of humble people,/The
VIGOROUS (1)
320 FR Warburt   6   your mother/Is still so alert, so vigorous of mind,/Although she seems as vital
VIGOUR (1)
258 MC Thomas   7   for the wrong reason./The natural vigour in the venial sin/Is the way in which our
VIII (1)
587 Fable   2   that royal Mormon/King Henry VIII found out that monks were quacks,/And
VILLAGE (8)
177 FQ: ECoker   19   lane insists on the direction/Into the village, in the electric heat/Hypnotised. In a
203 Indians   1   Africa/A man's destination is his own village,/His own fire, and his wife's cooking;/To
203 Indians   15   his destiny, that soil is his./Let his village remember./This was not your land, or
203 Indians   16   This was not your land, or ours: but a village in the Midlands,/And one in the Five
220 Old Deut   8   progeny prospers and thrives/And the village is proud of him in his decline./At the
587 Fable   5   tumbling at their backs,/There was a village founded by some Norman/Who levied
323 FR   Winch   21   where it shouldn't be,/Outside of the village, on the West Road./{A} Where is he?/
434 CP   Alex   7   sisters at this station, in a Christian village;/And half the natives were dying of
VILLAGERS (2)
220 Old Deut   22   the lorries run over the kerb,/And the villagers put up a notice: ROAD CLOSED —/
434 CP   Alex   18   people got there, they questioned the villagers —/Those who survived. And then they
VILLAGES (1)
103 Journ Magi   15   and the towns unfriendly/And the villages dirty and charging high prices:/A hard
VILLAINOUS (1)
587 Fable   11   and a dairy;/Whenever some old villainous baron died,/He added to their hoards
VINCEWELL (3)
355 CP   Julia   30   you about Lady Klootz./It was at the Vincewell wedding. Oh, so many years ago! {}/
355 CP   Peter   35   /{P} Were they the parents of Tony Vincewell?/{J} Yes. Tony was the product, but
355 CP   Julia   38   more difficult./You know Tony Vincewell? You knew him at Oxford?/{P} No, I
VINCEWELLS (2)
355 CP   Julia   31   GUEST]/{J} Did *you* know the Vincewells?/{UG} No, I don't know the
355 CP   Reilly   32   /{UG} No, I don't know the Vincewells./{J} Oh, they're both dead now. But I
VINDICTIVE (1)
572 ES Charles   26   man, and this woman, who are so vindictive:/Don't you see that they were as
VINE (2)
590 Time Space   10   when the dew/Was trembling on the vine,/Were withered ere the wild bee flew/To
590 Space Time   10   when the dew/Was trembling on the vine/Were withered ere the wild bee flew/To
VINE-LEAVES (1)
103 Journ Magi   26   /Then we came to a tavern with vine-leaves over the lintel,/Six hands at an open
VINES (1)
 64 WL: Chess   79   up by standards wrought with fruited vines/From which a golden Cupidon peeped out
VINEYARD (1)
587 Fable   10   lands and wide,/An orchard, and a vineyard, and a dairy;/Whenever some old
VIOLATED (2)
270 MC Chorus   27   consented./Am torn away, subdued, violated,/United to the spiritual flesh of nature,/
275 MC Knight1   6   /{K1} Renew the obedience you have violated./{T} For my Lord I am now ready to

VISAGE (1)
51 Restaurant	21	/Va t'en te décrotter les rides du visage;/Tiens, ma fourchette, décrasse-toi le

VISIBLE (6)
165 Rock 9	34	must serve as spirit and body./Visible and invisible, two worlds meet in Man;/
165 Rock 9	35	invisible, two worlds meet in Man;/Visible and invisible must meet in His Temple;/
165 Rock 9	40	travail;/The formed stone, the visible crucifix,/The dressed altar, the lifting
165 Rock 9	44	the lifting light,/Light/Light/The visible reminder of Invisible Light./You have
166 Rock 10	3	is now dedicated to GOD./It is now a visible church, one more light set on a hill/In a
166 Rock 10	6	church all we can build?/Or shall the Visible Church go on to conquer the World?/

VISION (12)
23 Preludes	33	in the gutters,/You had such a vision of the street/As the street hardly
94 Ash-Wed 4	20	/The time. Redeem/The unread vision in the higher dream/While jewelled
105 Song Sime	30	and prayer,/Not for me the ultimate vision./Grant me thy peace./(And a sword shall
133 Eyes	4	in death's dream kingdom/The golden vision reappears/I see the eyes but not the tears/
166 Rock 10	18	we praise Thee!/Too bright for mortal vision./O Greater Light, we praise Thee for the
167 Rock 10	44	the little lights for which our bodily vision is made./And we thank Thee that
604 Ode	14	efface and destroy/Give us also the vision to see/What we owe for the future, the
255 MC Tempt4	24	to give. Is it too much/For such a vision of eternal grandeur?/{T} Others offered
334 FR Harry	4	can't be got rid of/But in a different vision. This is like an end./{Ag} And a
417 CP Reilly	26	returning. They may remember/The vision they have had, but they cease to regret it,/
418 CP Celia	9	/You see, I think I really had a vision of something/Though I don't know what
465 CC Claude	22	different person,/Transfigured in the vision of some marvellous creation,/And I feel

VISIONS (3)
14 Prufrock	33	indecisions,/And for a hundred visions and revisions,/Before the taking of a
271 MC Thomas	7	be at peace with your thoughts and visions./These things had to come to you and
422 CP Julia	26	from the Voices/Protect her from the Visions/Protect her in the tumult/Protect her in

VISIT (6)
13 Prufrock	12	'What is it?'/Let us go and make our visit./In the room the women come and go/
120 SP Klip	6	/London's a fine place to come on a visit —/{Kr} Specially when you got a real live
439 CP Edward	30	be able to./{E} But on your next visit?/{P} The next time I come to England, I
503 CC Claude	38	/What with Lucasta's unexpected visit./She ought to be here. It wouldn't be like
580 ES Carghil	20	back/Señor Gomez has invited me to visit San Marco./I'm so excited! But what
582 ES Ld Clav	13	you for a while./This is your first visit to us at Badgley Court,/Charles, and not at

VISITED (4)
31 Apollinax	1	/Mr. Apollinax/When Mr. Apollinax visited the United States/His laughter tinkled
587 Fable	15	kept by a kind fairy./Alas! no fairy visited their host,/Oh, no; much worse than
406 CP Reilly	9	Mrs. Chamberlayne,/You have never visited my sanatorium./{L} What do you mean?
498 CC Claude	17	/Besides, I should have noticed it. I visited her house/Often. I never saw more than

VISITING (3)
291 FR Ivy	3	nearer the fire./{I} I might have been visiting Cousin Lily at Sidmouth, if I had not
427 CP Julia	25	What were you doing/In Kinkanja? Visiting some Sultan?/You were shooting tigers?
531 ES Ld Clav	1	something showy'./This would do for visiting cards — if people still left cards/And if I

VISITOR (3)
250 MC Tempt3	19	TEMPTER]/{T3} I am an unexpected visitor./{T} I expected you./{T3} But not in this
470 CC Lucasta	4	Still, I'm flattered/To be your first visitor in this flat/And to be the first to hear you
541 ES Gomez	37	the unwelcome intrusion/Of the visitor in financial distress./Well, I shan't keep

VISITORS (5)
252 MC Thomas	33	/{T} Who are you? I expected/Three visitors, not four./{T4} Do not be surprised to
386 CP Reilly	5	/{UG} And now you must await your visitors./{E} Visitors? What visitors?/{UG}
386 CP Edward	6	now you must await your visitors./{E} Visitors? What visitors?/{UG} Whoever comes.
386 CP Edward	6	your visitors./{E} Visitors? What visitors?/{UG} Whoever comes. The strangers./
531 ES Ld Clav	2	cards/And if I was going to have any visitors./{M} Father, you simply want to revel in

VISITS (3)
230 Bust Jones	13	Bustopher Jones in white spats!/His visits are occasional to the *Senior Educational*/
330 FR Harry	10	in gentle motion/Of horses, and right visits to the right neighbours/At the right times;/
340 FR Amy	27	/I even asked you back, for visits, after he was gone,/So that there might be

VITAL (1)
320 FR Warburt	7	of mind,/Although she seems as vital as ever —/It is only the force of her

VITALITY (1)
354 CP Julia	18	to her: 'Greta!/You have too much vitality.' But she enjoyed herself. {}/[*To the*

VOCABULARY (1)
561 ES Monica	36	that phrase sounds! But there's no vocabulary/For love within a family, love that's

VOCATION (2)
465 CC Claude	14	/Could a man be said to have a vocation/To be a second-rate potter? To be, at
518 CC Eggers	5	you'll come to find you've another vocation./We worked together every day, you

VOICE (38)

19 Portrait	56	and youthful, after all.'/The voice returns like the insistent out-of-tune/Of a
49 Hippopot	17	over sea./At mating time the hippo's voice/Betrays inflexions hoarse and odd,/But
64 WL: Chess	101	/Filled all the desert with inviolable voice/And still she cried, and still the world
89 Ash-Wed 1	22	the blessèd face/And renounce the voice/Because I cannot hope to turn again/
96 Ash-Wed 5	19	who walk among noise and deny the voice/Will the veiled sister pray for/Those who
154 Rock 3 m	20	of Sunday newspapers?/1ST MALE VOICE:/A Cry from the East:/What shall be
154 Rock 3 m	28	My Word is unspoken./2ND MALE VOICE:/A Cry from the North, from the West
161 Rock 7 m	33	advances progressively backwards?/VOICE OF THE UNEMPLOYED (*afar off*):/
161 Rock 7 m	38	high-powered cars on a by-pass way?/VOICE OF THE UNEMPLOYED (*more*
188 FQ: DrySal	149	in the rigging and the aerial,/Is a voice descanting (though not to the ear,/The
192 FQ: Little	50	the praying mind, or the sound of the voice praying./And what the dead had no
193 FQ: Little	100	part, and cried/And heard another's voice cry: 'What! are *you* here?'/Although we
194 FQ: Little	121	/And next year's words await another voice./But, as the passage now presents no
197 FQ: Little	240	the drawing of this Love and the voice of this Calling/We shall not cease from
197 FQ: Little	249	At the source of the longest river/The voice of the hidden waterfall/And the children
219 Mung Rump	25	from behind the scenes/And say in a voice that was broken with sorrow:/'I'm afraid
225 Mr Mistoff	44	there was nobody shyer —/But his voice has been heard on the roof/When he was
228 Gus	27	of rehearsal, I never could fail./I'd a voice that would soften the hardest of hearts,/
236 Cat Morgan	14	about on the Barbary Coast,/And me voice it ain't no sich melliferous horgan;/But yet
598 Circe	2	her fountain which flows/With the voice of men in pain,/Are flowers that no man
264 MC Priest1	4	kneeled down and cried with a loud voice:/Lord, lay not this sin to their charge./
264 MC Priest3	16	*mouth of very babes, O God.*/As the voice of many waters, of thunder, of harps,/
264 MC Priest3	20	/The blood of thy saints. In Rama, a voice heard, weeping./Out of the mouth of very
294 FR Harry	3	you do not know/The unspoken voice of sorrow in the ancient bedroom/At three
309 FR Harry	34	half-heard./And I hear your voice as in the silence/Between two storms, one
327 FR Ivy	29	bad, I could hardly hear him,/And his voice was very queer. It seems that Arthur too/
382 CP Celia	12	a mummy./I listened to your voice, that had always thrilled me,/And it
382 CP Celia	13	thrilled me,/And it became another voice — no, not a voice:/What I heard was only
382 CP Celia	13	it became another voice — no, not a voice:/What I heard was only the noise of an
457 CC m	16	ELIZABETH MULHAMMER'S *voice off.*/* *Lady Elizabeth's words off stage are*
457 CC Claude	21	/{SC} She's here, Eggerson! That's her voice./Where is she? Oh, she's gone out again. {}
457 CC m	25	ELIZABETH MULHAMMER'S *voice off.*/{LE} No, Gertrude, I haven't had any
461 CC Eggers	9	up!/I'm sure he has a very cultivated voice.'/{C} Thank you very much, I will. It's
531 ES Charles	9	/And the expectation that your voice will be heard/In debate in the Upper
562 ES Carghil	34	really look like me?/{MC} You've his voice! and his way of moving! It's marvellous./
567 ES Monica	6	/Should have heard my beloved's voice/And I couldn't, just when I had been
572 ES Ld Clav	6	between waking and sleeping,/A voice that whispered, 'you didn't stop!'/I knew
572 ES Ld Clav	7	'you didn't stop!'/I knew the voice: it was Fred Culverwell's./{M} Poor

VOICELESS (1)

| 186 FQ: DrySal | 81 | /There is no end of it, the voiceless wailing,/No end to the withering of |

VOICES (30)

14 Prufrock	52	life with coffee spoons;/I know the voices dying with a dying fall/Beneath the music
17 Prufrock	131	seaweed red and brown/Till human voices wake us, and we drown./Portrait of a
73 WL: Thund	384	bells, that kept the hours/And voices singing out of empty cisterns and
83 Hollow Men	5	filled with straw. Alas!/Our dried voices, when/We whisper together/Are quiet
84 Hollow Men	25	column/There, is a tree swinging/And voices are/In the wind's singing/More distant
98 Ash-Wed 6	12	/In the lost lilac and the lost sea voices/And the weak spirit quickens to rebel/
98 Ash-Wed 6	23	/Between blue rocks/But when the voices shaken from the yew-tree drift away/Let
103 Journ Magi	19	night,/Sleeping in snatches,/With the voices singing in our ears, saying/That this was
138 New Hamp	1	/New Hampshire/Children's voices in the orchard/Between the blossom- and
149 Rock 1 m	79	*lights fade; in the semi-darkness the voices of* WORKMEN *are heard chanting.*/*In the*
149 Rock 1 m	94	*farther/away, they are answered by voices of the* UNEMPLOYED.*/No man has*
175 FQ: BurntN	156	in place,/Will not stay still. Shrieking voices/Scolding, mocking, or merely chattering,/
175 FQ: BurntN	159	in the desert/Is most attacked by voices of temptation,/The crying shadow in the
184 FQ: DrySal	24	foreign dead men. The sea has many voices,/Many gods and many voices./The salt is
184 FQ: DrySal	25	many voices,/Many gods and many voices./The salt is on the briar rose,/The fog is
185 FQ: DrySal	29	howl/And the sea yelp, are different voices/Often together heard: the whine in the
185 FQ: DrySal	34	the approaching headland/Are all sea voices, and the heaving groaner/Rounded
248 MC Thomas	13	/The impossible, the undesirable,/Voices under sleep, waking a dead world,/So
260 MC Thomas	24	Does it seem to you that the angelic voices were mistaken, and/that the promise was
263 MC Chorus	23	and the air is clear and high,/And voices trill at windows, and children tumble in
281 MC Chorus	16	head bent under grief,/Even in us the voices of seasons, the snuffle of winter, the song
281 MC Chorus	16	of spring, the drone of summer, the voices of beasts and of birds, praise Thee./We
309 FR Harry	40	an evil time, that excites us with lying voices?/{M} The cold spring now is the time/For

324 FR	Harry	35	one cannot speak with several voices at once./I have all of the rightminded
329 FR	Chorus	4	or of dying,/Gathers in to itself all the voices of the past, and projects them into the
329 FR	Chorus	5	them into the future./The treble voices on the lawn/The mowing of hay in
335 FR	Agatha	2	/And heard in the distance tiny voices/And then a black raven flew over./And
413 CP	Celia	18	am being persecuted;/I don't hear any voices, I have no delusions —/Except that the
422 CP	Julia	25	quicksand./{J} Protect her from the Voices/Protect her from the Visions/Protect her
524 ES		3m 1	*house. Four o'clock in the afternoon.*/[*Voices in the hall*]/{C} Is your father at home

VOICI (1)

48 Lune Miel		2	Terre Haute;/Mais une nuit d'été, les voici à Ravenne,/A l'aise entre deux draps, chez

VOID (12)

160 Rock 7		1	GOD created the world. Waste and void. Waste and void. And darkness was upon
160 Rock 7		1	world. Waste and void. Waste and void. And darkness was upon the face of the
160 Rock 7		6	ecstasy not of the flesh./Waste and void. Waste and void. And darkness on the face
160 Rock 7		6	the flesh./Waste and void. Waste and void. And darkness on the face of the deep./
160 Rock 7		17	will not let the snow rest./Waste and void. Waste and void. And darkness on the face
160 Rock 7		17	rest./Waste and void. Waste and void. And darkness on the face of the deep./
161 Rock 7		40	*has hired us*..../CHORUS:/Waste and void. Waste and void. And darkness on the face
161 Rock 7		40	/Waste and void. Waste and void. And darkness on the face of the deep./Has
244 MC	Chorus	21	we see birth and death alone/In a void apart. We/Are afraid in a fear which we
272 MC	Chorus	24	/And behind the Judgement the Void, more horrid than active shapes of hell;/
272 MC	Chorus	27	no land, only emptiness, absence, the Void,/Where those who were men can no longer
327 FR	Harry	22	I can clean my skin,/Purify my life, void my mind,/But always the filthiness, that

VOILÀ (1)

51 Restaurant		24	des expériences comme moi?/Tiens, voilà dix sous, pour la salle-de-bains./Phlébas, le

VOIX (1)

67 WL: Fire S		202	wash their feet in soda water/Et O ces voix d'enfants, chantant dans la coupole!/Twit

VOLATILE (1)

43 Swee Erect		43	padding on broad feet,/Bringing sal volatile/And a glass of brandy neat./A Cooking

VOLITION (1)

578 ES	Ld Clav	1	power, Fred Culverwell,/Of his own volition to contract his enslavement,/I cannot

VOLSCIAN (1)

129 Cor2 State		21	is appointed/To confer with a Volscian commission/About perpetual peace:

VOLUNTARY (1)

451 CC	Eggers	37	you that./I've always sung in our voluntary choir/And at the carol service. But I

VOLUPINE (2)

40 Burb Blei		3	/Descending at a small hotel;/Princess Volupine arrived,/They were together, and he
41 Burb Blei		25	in furs. The boatman smiles,/Princess Volupine extends/A meagre, blue-nailed,

VOLUPTUARY (1)

191 FQ: Little		25	the hedges/White again, in May, with voluptuary sweetness./It would be the same at

VON (1)

37 Gerontion		28	room/Shifting the candles; Fräulein von Kulp/Who turned in the hall, one hand on

VONT (1)

48 Lune Miel		11	d'acanthe que tournoie le vent./Ils vont prendre le train de huit heures/Prolonger

VORACIOUS (1)

341 FR	Agatha	6	But you are just the same:/Just as voracious for what you cannot have/Because

VORTEX (1)

179 FQ: ECoker		66	heavens and the plains/Whirled in a vortex that shall bring/The world to that

VOS (1)

94 Ash-Wed 4		11	blue of Mary's colour,/Sovegna vos/Here are the years that walk between,

VOTE (1)

278 MC Knight2		34	would/condemn an Archbishop by vote of Parliament and execute him/formally as

VOUS (3)

47 Mél Adult		4	/C'est à grands pas et en sueur/Que vous suivrez à peine ma piste./En Yorkshire,
47 Mél Adult		7	/A Londres, un peu banquier,/Vous me paierez bien la tête./C'est à Paris que je
51 Restaurant		30	étapes de sa vie antérieure./Figurez-vous donc, c'était un sort pénible;/Cependant,

VOWED (2)

212 Growltiger		17	of foreign race his hatred had been vowed;/To Cats of foreign name and race no
587 Fable		25	Christmas time was near the Abbot vowed/They'd eat their meal from ghosts and

VOYAGE (3)

189 FQ: DrySal		184	who were in ships, and/Ended their voyage on the sand, in the sea's lips/Or in the
299 FR	Charles	5	/Downing, you were with them on the voyage from New York —/We didn't learn very
299 FR	Charles	32	how was his Lordship, during the voyage?/{Do} Well, you might say depressed,

VOYAGERS (2)

188 FQ: DrySal		165	the fruit of action./Fare forward./O voyagers, O seamen,/You who come to port,
188 FQ: DrySal		172	/Not fare well,/But fare forward, voyagers./Lady, whose shrine stands on the

VOYAGING (1)
188 FQ: DrySal 151   forward, you who think that you are voyaging;/You are not those who saw the
VU (2)
 48 Lune Miel   1   Mozambique./Lune de Miel/Ils ont vu les Pays-Bas, ils rentrent à Terre Haute;/
 48 Lune Miel   15   et rédige son bilan./Ils auront vu la Suisse et traversé la France./Et Saint
VULGAR (3)
482 CC   Lady E 26   and materialistic,/And ... well, rather vulgar. They're not your sort at all./{C} I
482 CC   Colby   27   sort at all./{C} I shouldn't call them vulgar. Perhaps I'm vulgar too./But what, do
482 CC   Colby   27   call them vulgar. Perhaps I'm vulgar too./But what, do you think, *is* my sort?/
VULGAREST (1)
286 FR   Violet 16   never go south,/Simply to see the vulgarest people —/You can keep out of their
VULGARITY (2)
197 FQ: Little   223   /The common word exact without vulgarity,/The formal word precise but not
301 FR   Ivy   21   not trust Charles with his confident vulgarity, acquired from worldly associates./{G}

386 CP   Edward   25   /I suppose there is nothing to do but wait./Won't you sit down?/{C} Thank you. {}/
400 CP   Alex   7   He was only impatient/At having to wait four days for the appointment./{R} It was
412 CP   Julia   19   /You can't be as tired as that. I shall wait in the next room,/And come back when
466 CC   Claude   27   play./I shan't mention it again. I'll wait until you ask me./Do you understand now
467 CC   Claude   31   shan't be. Meanwhile, we must simply wait to learn/What new conditions life will
471 CC   Colby   29   of your own creation/Rather than wait to see what happened./I hope you don't
472 CC   Colby   1   /{C} Because you couldn't wait to see what happened./You're afraid of
478 CC   Colby   34   to appreciate B./{C} Lucasta, wait! {}/[*Enter* B. KAGHAN]/{K} Enter B.
489 CC   Claude   14   a son of your own,/And I thought, I'll wait for children of *our* own,/And tell her then.
501 CC   Eggers   34   all in the family. Why not let them wait downstairs/And come back after Mrs.
503 CC   Eggers   20   /Why shouldn't you and Mr. Kaghan wait downstairs/And rejoin us when this
503 CC   Eggers   24   ... Can't B. come up now?/{E} Better wait till afterwards./{SC} Quite right, Eggerson./
527 ES   Lambert   12   His Lordship said to tell you/Not to wait tea for him./{M} Thank you, Lambert./{L}
542 ES   Gomez   30   of my company?/{G} Oh, I can wait, Dick. You'll relent at last./You'll come to
555 ES   Monica   37   where is he?/{M} I told him he must wait in the garden/Until I had prepared you.
576 ES   Gomez   20   for that later./{G} Much better to wait until we get there./The nature of business
WAITED (6)
 22 Preludes   25   bed,/You lay upon your back, and waited;/You dozed, and watched the night
 74 WL: Thund   396   was sunken, and the limp leaves/Waited for rain, while the black clouds/
271 MC Thomas   23   coming, these feet. All my life/I have waited. Death will come only when I am
342 FR   Agatha   16   of my doing:/I have only watched and waited. In this world/It is inexplicable, the
379 CP   Celia   33   that I wanted something more/And I waited, and wanted to run to tell you./Perhaps
412 CP   Julia   7   went on in the taxi, round the corner;/Waited a moment, and slipped in by the back
WAITER (2)
 32 Hysteria   5   ripple of unseen muscles. An elderly waiter with trembling hands/was hurriedly
 56 Swee Night   19   at the window-sill and gapes;/The waiter brings in oranges/Bananas figs and
WAITERS (4)
305 FR   Agatha   14   and I, Mary,/Are only watchers and waiters: not the easiest rôle./I must go and
524 ES   Monica   12   one where the *maître d'hôtel*/And the waiters all seem to be your intimate friends./{C}
524 ES   Monica   18   masculine vanity, to want to have the waiters/All buzzing round you: and it reminds
524 ES   Charles 23   where he's utterly unknown/And the waiters all appear to be avoiding his eye./{M}
WAITING (55)
 37 Gerontion   2   a dry month,/Being read to by a boy, waiting for rain./I was neither at the hot gates/
 43 Swee Erect   30   in the sun.)/Tests the razor on his leg/Waiting until the shriek subsides./The epileptic
 65 WL: Chess   138   of chess,/Pressing lidless eyes and waiting for a knock upon the door./When Lil's
 68 WL: Fire S   217   engine waits/Like a taxi throbbing waiting,/I Tiresias, though blind, throbbing
105 Song Sime   4   had made stand./My life is light, waiting for the death wind,/Like a feather on
126 SA Chorus   5   a lock/for you know the hangman's waiting for you./And perhaps you're alive/And
127 Cor1 March   7   so many crowding the way./So many waiting, how many waiting? what did it matter,
127 Cor1 March   7   the way./So many waiting, how many waiting? what did it matter, on such a day?/Are
127 Cor1 March   31   horse's neck,/And the eyes watchful, waiting, perceiving, indifferent./O hidden under
151 Rock 2   10   which nobody wants to hear sung;/Waiting to be flung in the end, on a heap less
180 FQ: ECoker   127   the love and the hope are all in the waiting./Wait without thought, for you are not
184 FQ: DrySal   10   /By worshippers of the machine, but waiting, watching and waiting./His rhythm was
184 FQ: DrySal   10   machine, but waiting, watching and waiting./His rhythm was present in the nursery
597 Before Mor   3   turned toward dawn,/Petal on petal, waiting for the day,/Fresh flowers, withered
242 MC Priest2   32   own again./We have had enough of waiting, from December to dismal December./
245 MC Priest2   27   Lordship knows that seven years of waiting,/Seven years of prayer, seven years of
246 MC Thomas   18   only soar and hover, circling lower,/Waiting excuse, pretence, opportunity./End will
251 MC Tempt3   21   squabbling in Anjou;/Round him waiting hungry sons./We are for England. We
257 MC Chorus   30   of nodding ape, square hyaena waiting/For laughter, laughter, laughter. The
263 MC Chorus   27   We wait, and the time is short/But waiting is long. {}/[*Enter the* FIRST PRIEST
265 MC Knight4   34   How much longer will you keep us waiting? {}/[*Enter* THOMAS]/[*to* PRIESTS]./
291 FR   Chorus   1   or having rehearsed the wrong parts,/Waiting for the rustling in the stalls, the titter in
301 FR   Chorus   16   we stand here like guilty conspirators, waiting for some revelation/When the hidden
305 FR   Mary   17   {}/[*Exit*]/{M} So you will not help me!/Waiting, waiting, always waiting./I think this
305 FR   Mary   17   So you will not help me!/Waiting, waiting, always waiting./I think this house
305 FR   Mary   17   not help me!/Waiting, waiting, always waiting./I think this house *means* to keep us
305 FR   Mary   18   /I think this house *means* to keep us waiting. {}/[*Enter* HARRY]/{H} Waiting? For
305 FR   Harry   19   us waiting. {}/[*Enter* HARRY]/{H} Waiting? For what?/{M} How do you do,
315 FR   Gerald   22   ten years ago./{G} Is there any use in waiting for Arthur and John?/{A} We might as
329 FR   Chorus   1   what is spoken remains in the room, waiting for the future to hear it./And whatever
353 CP   Julia   9   the same story twice./{J} But I'm still waiting to know what happened./I know it
363 CP   Edward   21   Is to do nothing. Wait./{E} Wait!/But waiting is the one thing impossible./Besides,
363 CP   Edward   26   can I wait, not knowing what I'm waiting for?/Shall I say to my friends, 'My wife

366 CP	Julia	12	And now I must fly. I've kept the taxi waiting./Come along, Peter./{P} I hope you
383 CP	Edward	28	I'm awfully sorry to have kept you waiting;/But we ... I had to hunt for them ...
390 CP	Julia	37	journey on the old Great Eastern,/Waiting at junctions. And I suppose she's
399 CP	Nurse	12	a quarter past;/But you may keep her waiting./{R} Or she may keep me waiting;/But I
399 CP	Reilly	13	her waiting./{R} Or she may keep me waiting;/But I think she will be punctual./{N} I
412 CP	Reilly	2	[*Enter* JULIA *by side door*]/{R} She's waiting downstairs./{J} I know that, Henry. I
421 CP	Julia	38	how much longer will Alex keep us waiting?/{R} He should be here by now. I'll
432 CP	Lavinia	14	/You are the perfect guest we've been waiting for./{R} I should not dream of trying to
439 CP	Peter	16	I didn't have to. But the car will be waiting,/And the experts — I'd almost forgotten
450 CC	Claude	25	with Lady Elizabeth/I'll be ready waiting to introduce him. {}/[*Enter* COLBY
501 CC	Lucasta	24	*that.*/But that reminds me. He's waiting downstairs./I don't suppose you need
502 CC	Colby	2	soon?/I'm afraid I got impatient of waiting./{L} Colby! I've not come to interrupt
504 CC	Guzzard	28	I was punctual./But I didn't mind waiting in the least, Sir Claude./I know that you
509 CC	Colby	40	I'll get used to it./{C} But he's waiting downstairs! Isn't this the moment/For
526 ES	Monica	27	let his lordship know that tea is waiting'./{L} Yes, Miss Monica./{M} I'm very
530 ES	Ld Clav	17	/How gladly would I face death! But waiting, simply waiting,/With no desire to act,
530 ES	Ld Clav	17	I face death! But waiting, simply waiting,/With no desire to act, yet a loathing of
530 ES	Ld Clav	20	fill it./It's just like sitting in an empty waiting room/In a railway station on a branch
530 ES	Ld Clav	24	the porters have gone. What am I waiting for/In a cold and empty room before an
536 ES	Ld Clav	31	/That you are quite alone./{LC} I'm waiting to hear/Why you should need to trust
561 ES	Ld Clav	9	/You will find your past failures waiting there to greet you./You're all I have to
577 ES	Carghil	34	poor boy, from frustration./He's been waiting all this time for opportunity/To make

WAITING-ROOM (1)

399 CP	Nurse	7	/He is to be shown into the small waiting-room;/And you will see him almost at

WAITRESS (1)

481 CC	Lady E	39	in the left hand corner:/It has the best waitress. Good night./{L} Good night./{K} And

WAITRESSES (1)

136 5FingerEx4		9	Hodgson!/Who is worshipped by all waitresses/(They regard him as something

WAITS (9)

68 WL: Fire S		216	the desk, when the human engine waits/Like a taxi throbbing waiting,/I Tiresias,
603 Spleen		13	gray,/Languid, fastidious, and bland,/Waits, hat and gloves in hand,/Punctilious of tie
239 MC	Chorus	11	of water and mud,/The New Year waits, breathes, waits, whispers in darkness./
239 MC	Chorus	11	mud,/The New Year waits, breathes, whispers in darkness./While the labourer
239 MC	Chorus	13	his hand to the fire,/The New Year waits, destiny waits for the coming./Who has
239 MC	Chorus	13	the fire,/The New Year waits, destiny waits for the coming./Who has stretched out his
240 MC	Chorus	17	shall be martyrs and saints./Destiny waits in the hand of God, shaping the still
240 MC	Chorus	19	things in a shaft of sunlight./Destiny waits in the hand of God, not in the hands of
339 FR	Harry	14	possible. It is love and terror/Of what waits and wants me, and will not let me fall./Let

WAKE (7)

17 Prufrock		131	red and brown/Till human voices wake us, and we drown./Portrait of a Lady/
125 SA	Chorus	32	in the middle of the night and/you wake in a sweat and a hell of a fright/When
125 SA	Chorus	34	in the middle of the bed and/you wake like someone hit you in the head/You've
295 FR	Charles	13	life that presses on my chest/When I wake, as I do now, early before morning./I
318 FR	Harry	32	dream that I am talking/And shall wake to find that I have been silent/Or talked to
361 CP	Reilly	35	It will come to you slowly:/When you wake in the morning, when you go to bed at
548 ES	Monica	12	you *are* asleep they'll do something to wake you,/But if they see you're shamming

WAKED (1)

126 SA	Chorus	2	you./Hoo hoo hoo/You dreamt you waked up at seven o'clock and it's/foggy and it's

WAKEFUL (2)

127 Cor1 March		10	they come. Is he coming?/The natural wakeful life of our Ego is a perceiving./We can
343 FR	Amy	27	and tithes? nourish investments/With wakeful nights and patient calculations/With

WAKEN (1)

147 Rock 1		26	the City, we need no bells:/Let them waken the suburbs./I journeyed to the suburbs,

WAKENING (1)

28 Boston ET		4	evening quickens faintly in the street,/Wakening the appetites of life in some/And to

WAKING (11)

84 Hollow Men		47	it like this/In death's other kingdom/Waking alone/At the hour when we are/
94 Ash-Wed 4		14	moves in the time between sleep and waking, wearing/White light folded, sheathed
134 Wind		5	/Here, in death's dream kingdom/The waking echo of confusing strife/Is it a dream or
248 MC	Thomas	13	the undesirable,/Voices under sleep, waking a dead world,/So that the mind may not
248 MC	Tempt2	35	who held the solid substance/Wander waking with deceitful shadows?/Power is
254 MC	Tempt4	28	of stairs,/And between sleep and waking, early in the morning,/When the bird
295 FR	Harry	28	be caught for the last time./And also waking. She is nearer than ever./The
315 FR	Harry	3	/Murder a reversal of sleep and waking./Murder was there. Your ordinary
336 FR	Agatha	2	/Flattered in sleep, and deceived in waking./You have a long journey./{H} Not yet!

| 463 CC | Colby | 26 | and empty, walking in the street/Or waking in the night, then the former person,/ |
| 572 ES | Ld Clav | 5 | time,/When I least expected, between waking and sleeping,/A voice that whispered, |

WAKINGTIME (2)

| 206 To my Wife | | 2 | /That quickens my senses in our wakingtime/And the rhythm that governs the |
| 522 ES | dedic | 2 | *delight/That quickens my senses in our wakingtime/And the rhythm that governs the* |

WALDO (1)

| 30 Cous Nancy | | 12 | shelves kept watch/Matthew and Waldo, guardians of the faith,/The army of |

WALK (27)

16 Prufrock		123	shall wear white flannel trousers, and walk upon the beach./I have heard the
65 WL: Chess		132	I do?/'I shall rush out as I am, and walk the street/'With my hair down, so. What
94 Ash-Wed 4		12	/Sovegna vos/Here are the years that walk between, bearing/Away the fiddles and the
94 Ash-Wed 4		16	about her, folded./The new years walk, restoring/Through a bright cloud of tears,
96 Ash-Wed 5		15	desert or the rain land,/For those who walk in darkness/Both in the day time and in
96 Ash-Wed 5		19	face/No time to rejoice for those who walk among noise and deny the voice/Will the
96 Ash-Wed 5		21	the veiled sister pray for/Those who walk in darkness, who chose thee and oppose
152 Rock 2		33	all that is ill you may repair if you walk together in humble repentance, expiating
164 Rock 9		4	GOD is a House of Sorrow;/We must walk in black and go sadly, with longdrawn
164 Rock 9		9	about their daily occasions./Yet they walk in the street proudnecked, like
213 Growltiger		50	to his vast surprise was forced to walk the plank./He who a hundred victims had
224 Mr Mistoff		26	through the tiniest crack/He can walk on the narrowest rail./He can pick any
598 Circe		12	sluggish python lies;/The peacocks walk, stately and slow,/And they look at us with
247 MC Templ1		5	/Mirth and sportfulness need not walk warily./{T} You talk of seasons that are
256 MC Priests		33	in the room?/{3P} Does the watchman walk by the wall?/{4T} Does the mastiff prowl
257 MC Chorus		3	shock on the skull./{C} A man may walk with a lamp at night, and yet be drowned
325 FR	Violet	39	terrifying./I said I would rather walk: and I did./{G} Walk? where to?/{V} He
326 FR	Gerald	1	I would rather walk: and I did./{G} Walk? where to?/{V} He started out to take me
348 FR	Chorus	8	it takes us down./We do not like to walk out of a door, and find ourselves back in
349 FR	4m	13	DENMAN. AGATHA/*and* MARY *walk slowly in single file round and round the*
358 CP	Peter	28	ought to be going./{P} Celia —/May I walk along with you?/{C} No, I'm sorry, Peter;/
397 CP	Edward	3	touch the handle./Why could I not walk out of my prison?/What is hell? Hell is
473 CC	Colby	25	seem so unrelated./I turn the key, and walk through the gate,/And there I am ... alone,
474 CC	Colby	5	there./If I were religious, God would walk in my garden/And that would make the
565 ES	Carghil	16	not far away./{MC} Then I'd like to walk a little way with you./{Mi} Delighted, I'm
569 ES	Ld Clav	2	it becomes to drop the pretence,/Walk off the stage, change into our own clothes
582 ES	Monica	29	{M} I can't understand his going for a walk./{C} He wanted to leave us alone together!/

WALKED (12)

37 Gerontion		25	caressing hands, at Limoges/Who walked all night in the next room;/By
69 WL: Fire S		246	sat by Thebes below the wall/And walked among the lowest of the dead.)/Bestows
94 Ash-Wed 4		1	/but speak the word only./Who walked between the violet and the violet/Who
94 Ash-Wed 4		2	between the violet and the violet/Who walked between/The various ranks of varied
94 Ash-Wed 4		7	Who moved among the others as they walked,/Who then made strong the fountains
105 Song Sime		9	dead land./Grant us thy peace./I have walked many years in this city,/Kept faith and
229 Gus		37	a Shakespeare performance he once walked on pat,/When some actor suggested the
605 Narcissus		8	/And the gray shadow on his lips./He walked once between the sea and the high cliffs/
605 Narcissus		11	crossed over his breast./When he walked over the meadows/He was stifled and
605 Narcissus		18	but became a dancer before God/If he walked in city streets/He seemed to tread on
335 FR	Harry	35	what did happen/O my dear, and you walked through the little door/And I ran to
429 CP	Julia	35	.../{J} Edward!/Somebody must have walked over my grave:/I'm feeling so chilly.

WALKER (1)

| 142 Cape Ann | | 8 | by bay-bush. Follow the feet/Of the walker, the water-thrush. Follow the flight/Of |

WALKERS (1)

| 218 Mung Rump | | 2 | quick-change comedians, tight-rope walkers and acrobats/They had an extensive |

WALKING (14)

62 WL: Burial		56	by water./I see crowds of people, walking round in a ring./Thank you. If you see
73 WL: Thund		362	road/There is always another one walking beside you/Gliding wrapt in a brown
193 FQ: Little		88	whence the smoke arose/I met one walking, loitering and hurried/As if blown
233 Skimble		56	and so you never knew/That he was walking up and down the station;/You were
322 FR	Winch	27	I slipped along on my bike. Mostly walking,/What with the fog so thick, or I'd have
335 FR	Agatha	4	/And then I was only my own feet walking/Away, down a concrete corridor/In a
335 FR	Agatha	6	corridor/In a dead air. Only feet walking/And sharp heels scraping. Over and
437 CP	Reilly	6	*my dead child,/Met his own image walking in the garden./That apparition, sole of*
463 CC	Colby	25	/When my mind is cleared and empty, walking in the street/Or waking in the night,
474 CC	Colby	17	... be there suddenly,/Unexpectedly. Walking down an alley/I should become aware
474 CC	Colby	18	/I should become aware of someone walking with me./That's the only way I can
531 ES	Ld Clav	27	delighted. They won't want my ghost/Walking in the City or sitting in the Lords./And

547 ES	Monica	32	Mrs. Piggott. But I'm very fond of walking/And I'm told there are very good walks
555 ES	Monica	21	he driving his car?/{M} No, he was walking./{LC} I hope he's not had another

WALKS (6)

73 WL: Thund		359	is no water/Who is the third who walks always beside you?/When I count, there
230 Bust Jones		5	Cat!/He's the Cat we all greet as he walks down the street/In his coat of fastidious
256 MC	Chorus	35	/{C} Death has a hundred hands and walks by a thousand ways./{3P} He may come
547 ES	Monica	33	/And I'm told there are very good walks in this neighbourhood./{MP} There are
547 ES	Piggott	35	can lend you a map./There are lovely walks, on the shore or in the hills,/Quite away
547 ES	Piggott	36	motor roads. You must learn the best walks./I won't apologise for the lack of

WALL (12)

14 Prufrock		58	I am pinned and wriggling on the wall,/Then how should I begin/To spit out all
26 Rhapsody		76	is open; the tooth-brush hangs on the wall,/Put your shoes at the door, sleep, prepare
69 WL: Fire S		245	/I who have sat by Thebes below the wall/And walked among the lowest of the dead.)
73 WL: Thund		381	head downward down a blackened wall/And upside down in air were towers/
157 Rock 4		17	men laid their hands to rebuilding the wall./So they built as men must build/With the
192 FQ: Little		61	/Dust inbreathed was a house —/The wall, the wainscot and the mouse./The death of
220 Old Deut		10	he sits in the sun on the vicarage wall,/The Oldest Inhabitant croaks: 'Well, of all
601 Nocturne		7	out of pity for their fate/Behind the wall I have some servant wait,/Stab, and the
241 MC	Priest2	23	/Are the old disputes at an end, is the wall of pride cast down/That divided them? Is it
256 MC	Priests	33	/{3P} Does the watchman walk by the wall?/{4T} Does the mastiff prowl by the gate?/
303 FR	Mary	2	and uncertain, clings to the south wall./The gardener had no garden-flowers to
310 FR	Harry	38	only led to another,/Or to a blank wall; that I kept moving/Only so as not to stay

WALLALA (2)

69 WL: Fire S		278	/Past the Isle of Dogs./Weialala leia/Wallala leialala/Elizabeth and Leicester/Beating
70 WL: Fire S		291	of bells/White towers/Weialala leia/Wallala leialala/'Trams and dusty trees./

WALLED (1)

587 Fable		18	old sinner/Perhaps, who had been walled up for his crimes;/At any rate, he

WALLS (8)

64 WL: Chess		105	stumps of time/Were told upon the walls; staring forms/Leaned out, leaning,
69 WL: Fire S		263	fishmen lounge at noon: where the walls/Of Magnus Martyr hold/Inexplicable
164 Rock 9		5	faces,/We must go between empty walls, quavering lowly, whispering faintly,/
340 FR	Amy	15	that you took everything/Except the walls, the furniture, the acres;/Leaving nothing
343 FR	Amy	23	in a damned house./I will let the walls crumble. Why should I worry/To keep the
446 CC	Claude	26	him?/{SC} They have still to do the walls. And then it must be furnished./I'm trying
474 CC	Lucasta	24	/And the music would stop. And the walls would be broken./And you would find
483 CC	Lady E	9	suited you./I believe it does. The walls; and the curtains;/And most of the

WALTER (2)

204 de la Mare		t	death,/What is the fruit of action./To Walter de la Mare/The children who explored
557 ES	Ld Clav	8	job./{LC} The position that Sir Alfred Walter made for you./{Mi} I'd stuck it for two

WANDER (3)

248 MC	Tempt2	35	/Shall he who held the solid substance/Wander waking with deceitful shadows?/Power
275 MC	Chorus	24	/O far far far far in the past; and I wander in a land of barren boughs: if I break
275 MC	Chorus	24	boughs: if I break them, they bleed; I wander in a land of dry stones: if I touch them

WANDERED (1)

416 CP	Celia	30	like, to you?/{C} Like a child who has wandered into a forest/Playing with an

WANDERING (3)

163 Rock 8		41	took men from home/At the call of a wandering preacher./Our age is an age of
220 Old Deut		15	Ho! hi!/Oh, my eye!/My mind may be wandering, but I confess/I *believe* it is Old
288 FR	Agatha	21	can only be built/Upon the real past. Wandering in the tropics/Or against the painted

WANDERINGS (1)

343 FR	Agatha	8	may very likely meet again/In our wanderings in the neutral territory/Between two

WANING (1)

193 FQ: Little		93	challenge/The first-met stranger in the waning dusk/I caught the sudden look of some

WANT (256)

44 Cook Egg		9	*Invitation to the Dance./*I shall not want Honour in Heaven/For I shall meet Sir
44 Cook Egg		13	heroes of that kidney./I shall not want Capital in Heaven/For I shall meet Sir
44 Cook Egg		17	per cent. Exchequer Bond./I shall not want Society in Heaven,/Lucretia Borgia shall
44 Cook Egg		21	experience could provide./I shall not want Pipit in Heaven:/Madame Blavatsky will
65 WL: Chess		143	back, make yourself a bit smart./He'll want to know what you done with that money
66 WL: Chess		164	What you get married for if you don't want children?/HURRY UP PLEASE ITS
118 SP	Dusty	7	/{Du} You've got to know what you want to ask them/{Do} You've got to know
118 SP	Doris	8	/{Do} You've got to know what you want to know/{Du} It's no use asking them too
119 SP	Wauch	4	both know Captain Horsfall —/We want you to meet two friends of ours,/American
123 SAWa & Ho		2	*me in what part of the wood/Do you want to flirt with me?/Under the breadfruit,*
286 FR	Charles	1	horses and dogs and guns/Ever to want to leave England in the winter./But a

287 FR	Mary	7	it?/{M} Really, Cousin Gerald, if you want information/About the younger
287 FR	Amy	24	boys all due to arrive?/{A} I do not want the clock to stop in the dark./If you want
287 FR	Amy	25	the clock to stop in the dark./If you want to know why I never leave Wishwood/
291 FR	Amy	18	what's the matter?/{A} Harry, if you want the curtains drawn you should let me ring
291 FR	Amy	25	who belong here,/And who all want to see you back, Harry./{H} Look there,
293 FR	Harry	17	Why not get to the point/Or if you want to pretend that I am another person —/A
293 FR	Agatha	21	that having got so far —/If you want no pretences, let us have no pretences:/
296 FR	Ivy	22	malady makes them so. They do not want to be cured/And they know what you are
297 FR	Gerald	19	to get rid of./{G} Even so, we don't want Downing to know/Any more than he
298 FR	Violet	16	present to hear what Downing says./I want to know at once, not be told about it later.
303 FR	Mary	29	a man of the world?/Cousin Agatha, I want your advice./{Ag} I should have thought/
304 FR	Mary	8	a fellowship, seven years ago./Now I want your advice, because there's no one else to
304 FR	Mary	10	belong here/Any more than I do. I want to get away./{Ag} After seven years?/{M}
304 FR	Mary	13	/But you do understand. You only want to know/Whether I understand. You
305 FR	Mary	3	to go. I know I must go./But where? I want a job: and you can help me./{Ag} I am
310 FR	Harry	16	to land in the spring?/Do the dead want to return?/{M} Pain is the opposite of joy/
313 FR	Charles	19	in very late. {}/[Exit]/{C} Now we only want Arthur and John/I'm glad that you'll all
318 FR	Warburt	19	/I mean, you don't know what I want to tell you./You may be quite right, but
318 FR	Harry	35	else than what I am saying./But if you want to talk, at least you can tell me/Something
319 FR	Harry	3	Or unimportant, or else untrue./But I want to know more about my father./I hardly
321 FR	Warburt	8	There is no portrait./{W} What I want to know is, whether you've been sleeping
322 FR	Harry	14	reason for asking .../{H} Well, do you want me to produce her for you?/{Wi} Oh no
326 FR	Ivy	34	A trunk call? for me? why, who can want me?/{D} He wouldn't give his name, Miss;
331 FR	Harry	14	they would show me?/And now I want you to tell me about my father./{Ag} What
331 FR	Agatha	15	about my father./{Ag} What do you want to know about your father?/{H} If I knew,
331 FR	Harry	17	not have to ask./You know what I want to know, and that is enough:/Warburton
331 FR	Harry	19	though he did not mean to./What I want to know is something I need to know,/And
332 FR	Agatha	28	moment of pointed light/When you want to burn. When you stretch out your hand/
333 FR	Agatha	5	/He would have bungled it./I did not want to kill you!/You to be killed! What were
344 FR	Harry	38	make it so ridiculous/Just now? I only want, please,/As little fuss as possible. You
345 FR	Charles	35	I were told it./But I'm not sure that I want to know. I suppose I'm getting old:/Old
346 FR	Downing	32	now, I have a feeling/That he won't want me long, and he won't want anybody./
346 FR	Downing	32	he won't want me long, and he won't want anybody./{Ag} And, Downing, if his
355 CP	Julia	18	comes back into the room./Now I want to relax, Are there any more cocktails?/{P}
356 CP	Julia	19	party. There are so many questions/I want to ask you. It's a golden opportunity/Now
359 CP	Edward	13	in it?/{UG} A drop of water./{E} I want to apologise for this evening./The fact is, I
359 CP	Edward	34	going./{E} Don't go yet./I very much want to talk to somebody;/And it's easier to
360 CP	Reilly	34	she might have made a mistake/And want to come back to you. If another woman,/
360 CP	Reilly	39	at all./If another man, then you'd want to re-marry/To prove to the world that
361 CP	Edward	3	you wanted to marry her./{E} But I want my wife back./{UG} That's the natural
361 CP	Edward	19	I'd been concealing./I don't think I want to know who you are;/But, at the same
364 CP	Edward	5	/When I saw her last. And yet I want her back./And I must get her back, to find
364 CP	Reilly	15	the best reason for believing that you want her./{E} I want to see her again — here./
364 CP	Edward	16	for believing that you want her./{E} I want to see her again — here./{UG} You shall
364 CP	Edward	25	was not sure I wanted her; and now I want her./Do I want her? Or is it merely your
364 CP	Edward	26	wanted her; and now I want her./Do I want her? Or is it merely your suggestion?/{UG}
366 CP	Peter	19	not about Lavinia./It's something I want to consult him about,/And I could do it
366 CP	Edward	29	disturbed already;/And I did rather want to be alone./But what's it all about?/{P} I
366 CP	Peter	31	alone./But what's it all about?/{P} I want your help./I was going to telephone and
368 CP	Edward	8	of you, Alex, I'm sure;/But I rather want to be alone, this evening./{A} But you've got
368 CP	Edward	11	get dinner for you?/{E} No, I shan't want much, and I'll get it myself./{A} Ah, in
370 CP	Peter	19	{}/[Exit]/{P} That is exactly what I want to know./She has simply faded — into
370 CP	Peter	21	—/Like a film effect. She doesn't want to see me;/Makes excuses, not very
371 CP	Edward	33	/But the moths will get in. So you want to see Celia./I don't know why I should be
371 CP	Edward	36	from the fool you are./What do you want me to do?/{P} See Celia for me./You know
372 CP	Alex	26	about breakfast./All you should want is a cup of black coffee/And a little dry
372 CP	Peter	31	too much of your time,/And you want to be alone. Give my love to Lavinia/
374 CP	Edward	14	/And to try to understand it, I want to be alone./{C} I should have thought it
374 CP	Celia	28	we thought that Lavinia would never want to leave you./Surely you don't hold to that
375 CP	Edward	19	not Norwegian/But I don't really want cheese ... Slipper what? .../Oh, from
375 CP	Edward	21	and alcohol?/No, really, Alex, I don't want anything./I'm very tired. Thanks awfully,
377 CP	Celia	12	/{C} But why should that man want to bring her back —/Unless he is the
377 CP	Celia	17	you./How did he persuade you to want her back? {}/[A popping noise is heard
378 CP	Celia	7	Before I go, there's something/I want to say to Edward./{J} About Lavinia?/
378 CP	Celia	19	{C} That's the Devil's method! So you want Lavinia back!/Lavinia! So the one thing

380 CP	Edward	11	you as a passing diversion!/If you want to speak of passing diversions/How did
380 CP	Celia	29	that matters/Is, that you think you want Lavinia./And if that is the sort of person
381 CP	Celia	6	love with Lavinia,/What is it that you want?/{E} I am not sure./The one thing of which
381 CP	Celia	19	what it is to feel old?/{C} But I want to understand you. I could understand./
381 CP	Edward	33	be changed./The self that can say 'I want this — or want that' —/The self that wills
381 CP	Edward	33	self that can say 'I want this — or want that' —/The self that wills — he is a feeble
385 CP	Edward	6	we are meeting a stranger./{E} So you want me to greet my wife as a stranger?/That
389 CP	Lavinia	15	/The people who go there never want to leave it./{C} Lavinia, I think I
389 CP	Celia	31	off. I may not see you again./What I want to say is this: I should like you to
391 CP	Lavinia	14	back again *this* evening./{L} Stop! I want you to explain the telegram./{J} Explain
394 CP	Lavinia	26	me to come./And why did you want me?/{E} I don't know either./You say you
395 CP	Lavinia	23	/And if other people grow, well, you want too./In what way have you
396 CP	Lavinia	19	but nothing, which is all you seem to want of me./But I'm sorry for you .../{E} Don't
396 CP	Edward	32	when you were a child./{E} I don't want you to make yourself responsible for me:/
396 CP	Edward	34	kind of contempt./And I do not want you to explain me to myself./You're still
397 CP	Lavinia	33	much too divided to know what you want./But, being divided, you will tend to
400 CP	Reilly	27	to escape from her?/{R} He doesn't want to escape from her./{A} He is staying at his
401 CP	Reilly	35	about the difficulties/On which you want my professional opinion./{E} It's not for
403 CP	Reilly	13	in this world/Is due to people who want to feel important./They don't mean to do
404 CP	Edward	1	/But not in the same world. So I want you to put me/Into your sanatorium. I
404 CP	Edward	26	What else can I tell you?/You didn't want to hear about my early history./{R} No, I
404 CP	Reilly	27	my early history./{R} No, I did not want to hear about your *early* history./{E} And
409 CP	Reilly	6	You never noticed *me*./{R} Now, I want to point out to both of you/How much
411 CP	Lavinia	2	*is* that hotel in the New Forest/If you want to go there. The proprietor/Who has just
411 CP	Lavinia	5	you, and then leave you there/If you want to be alone .../{E} But I can't go away!/I
411 CP	Edward	24	the future of ... the others./I don't want to build on other people's ruins./{L}
412 CP	Celia	33	more perplexing. However,/I don't want to waste your time. And I'm awfully afraid
414 CP	Celia	22	at the moment,/And my family want me to come down and stay with them./But
414 CP	Reilly	24	/But I just can't face it./{R} So you want to see no one?/{C} No ... it isn't that I
414 CP	Celia	25	to see no one?/{C} No ... it isn't that I *want* to be alone,/But that everyone's alone — or
417 CP	Celia	16	know./And if that is all meaningless, I want to be cured/Of a craving for something I
417 CP	Reilly	40	Till you come to the end. But you will want nothing else,/And the other life will be
418 CP	Celia	10	I don't know what it is. I don't want to forget it./I want to live with it. I could
418 CP	Celia	11	what it is. I don't want to forget it./I want to live with it. I could do without
418 CP	Celia	30	place./{C} That sounds like what I want. But what is my duty?/{R} Whichever way
419 CP	Celia	10	/Now — do you feel quite sure?/{C} I want your second way./So what am I to do?/{R}
425 CP	Lavinia	7	accepted/Than we thought would want to come. But what can you do?/There's
425 CP	Lavinia	8	do?/There's usually a lot who don't want to come/But all the same would be bitterly
428 CP	Alex	13	in peculiar veneration/And do not want them killed. So they blame the
431 CP	Peter	17	making a film of English life/And we want to use Boltwell./{J} But I understood that
432 CP	Julia	4	for you. {}/[*Enter* REILLY]/{J} I want you to meet Sir Henry Harcourt-Reilly —/
433 CP	Peter	14	wanted to ask about,/Who did really want to get into films,/And I always thought
433 CP	Peter	19	spoken to Bela about her,/And I want to introduce her to our casting director./
435 CP	Peter	10	More and more./At first I did not want to know about Celia/And so I never
436 CP	Lavinia	20	/{L} Sir Henry, there is something I want to say to you./While Alex was telling us
439 CP	Peter	32	to England, I promise you./I really do want to see you both, very much./Good-bye,
440 CP	Lavinia	10	/{L} But all the same ... I don't want to see these people./{R} It is your
440 CP	Lavinia	16	us. You too, Alex./{L} We don't *want* you to go!/{A} We have another
446 CC	Eggers	33	have window boxes./Some day, he'll want a garden of his own. And yes, a bird bath!/
449 CC	Claude	12	that he is an orphan,/She will want us to adopt him./{E} Adopt him! Yes,
452 CC	Lucasta	18	/Then, just by bad luck, the boss did want a letter/And I couldn't find it. And then he
452 CC	Lucasta	20	asked for things I'm sure he didn't want —/Just to make trouble! And I couldn't
456 CC	Eggers	32	we've settled down/All the travel *I* want is up to the City/And back to Joshua Park
457 CC	Lady E	16	*theatre.*/{LE} Just open that case, I want something out of it./Unwrap that — It's a
457 CC	Lady E	26	I haven't had any lunch,/And I don't want it now. Just bring me some tea./Nothing
458 CC	Claude	33	make a quick decision./{SC} I didn't want to bother you, during your treatment .../
459 CC	Claude	16	His home's outside London./But I want to have him closer at hand —/You know
461 CC	Eggers	7	I'll slip up to town any day, if you want me./In fact, Mrs. E. said: 'I wish he'd ring
462 CC	Claude	37	it is real to me yet./{SC} But now I want it to be different. It's odd, Colby./I didn't
463 CC	Colby	32	worth doing, the one thing/That I want to do. I have to fight that person./{SC}
463 CC	Claude	37	own experience?/{SC} Yes, I did not want to be a financier.../{C} What did you want
463 CC	Colby	38	to be a financier./{C} What did you want to do?/{SC} I wanted to be a potter./{C} A
464 CC	Claude	16	I have always longed for./I want a world where the form is the reality,/Of
466 CC	Claude	9	in a private room./It isn't that I don't want anyone to see them!/But when I am alone,
467 CC	Colby	25	for all you've done for me;/And I want to do my best to justify your kindness/By

467 CC Colby 29 doing/And eager for more. I don't want my position/To be, in any way, a
469 CC Colby 9 begin to know it well,/Then you will want to learn about its structure/And the
470 CC Lucasta 35 — that *is* a compliment./It shows you want to educate me./{C} But I didn't know/That
470 CC Lucasta 39 Neither did I./But I wanted you to want to educate me;/And now I'm beginning to
470 CC Lucasta 40 now I'm beginning to believe that I want it./{C} Well, I'm going to invite you to the
471 CC Lucasta 2 next concert .../{L} The next that you want to go to *yourself*./{C} And perhaps you'll
471 CC Colby 4 the programme — or the things I want to hear./I'll play you the themes, so you'll
474 CC Lucasta 3 single world./{L} But what do you want?/{C} Not to be alone there./If I were
475 CC Colby 2 /Better than ... other people. And I want to understand *you*./Does one ever come to
476 CC Lucasta 12 trying to give a false impression./I want to tell you now, why I tried to do that./
477 CC Colby 14 No. Yes. You don't understand./I want to explain. But I can't, just yet./Oh, why
477 CC Lucasta 30 me as the real kind of person/That I want to be. That I know I am./That was new to
478 CC Lucasta 13 be sorry for me./But now I don't want you to be sorry, thank you./Why, I'd
478 CC Colby 25 go yet!/There's something else that I want to explain,/And now I'm going to. I'm
479 CC Kaghan 4 learn to mix cocktails,/If you don't want women always dropping in on you./And
480 CC Kaghan 24 You and me —/The one thing *we* want is security/And respectability! Now Colby/
480 CC Kaghan 30 adopted, from nowhere./That's why I want to be a power in the City,/On the boards
480 CC Kaghan 38 could despise *you*, Lucasta;/And we want the same things. But as for Colby,/He's
481 CC Kaghan 9 that I was hungry./{K} You can't want dinner yet./It's only six o'clock. We can't
481 CC Lucasta 13 about Lucasta. {}/[*rising*]./{L} If you want to discuss *me* ... {}/[*A knock at the door.*
482 CC Lady E 16 kind of society./So naturally, they want to take you up./I can speak more freely, as
484 CC Lady E 6 ... in relatives./{LE} You did not want to know your relatives!/I understand
485 CC Lady E 6 /{LE} However that may be,/I didn't want to belong there. I refused to believe/That
488 CC Claude 32 to know him first — and that you'd want to adopt him./{LE} But of course I want
488 CC Lady E 33 to adopt him./{LE} But of course I want to adopt him, Claude!/That is, if one's
488 CC Lady E 38 /You have a daughter. Now you want a son./{SC} I'd never want to take your
488 CC Claude 39 Now you want a son./{SC} I'd never want to take your son away from you./Perhaps
491 CC Lady E 4 has come to me./Claude! I don't want to take away from you/The son you
491 CC Claude 37 mocked at./{SC} Then what do you want, Colby? What do you want?/Think of the
491 CC Claude 37 do you want, Colby? What do you want?/Think of the future. When you marry/
491 CC Claude 39 the future. When you marry/You will want parents, for the sake of your children./{C}
491 CC Colby 40 /{C} I don't feel, tonight, that I ever want to marry./You may be right. I can't take
492 CC Colby 2 can't take account of that./But now I want to know whose son I am./{SC} Then the
492 CC Colby 16 help me:/At the moment, I never want to touch it again./But there's another
493 CC Claude 11 there, behind the desk./You see, I want him to be a sort of chairman./{LE} That's
493 CC Claude 16 witness./It's very awkward. We don't want to start/By offending Mrs. Guzzard.
493 CC Lady E 22 there, with the light full on her:/I want to be able to watch her expression./{SC}
493 CC Lady E 25 in the corner/For Colby. He won't want to be conspicuous,/Poor boy!/{SC} After
494 CC Lady E 8 could be *our* son./Oh dear, what do I want? I should like him to be mine,/But for you
494 CC Lady E 33 to understand better./What did you want to do?/{SC} To be a potter./Don't laugh./
495 CC Claude 16 /About you, Elizabeth. What did *you* want?/{LE} To inspire an artist. Don't laugh./
497 CC Lady E 25 is my son./I feel sure he is. But I don't want to know:/I am perfectly content to leave
500 CC Lucasta 25 makes me feel safe. And that's what I want./And somehow or other, I've something to
501 CC Lucasta 25 downstairs./I don't suppose you want *us* at your meeting./{E} Allow me. May I
501 CC Eggers 33 interview,/But I'm sure that we want to greet the happy pair./It's all in the
501 CC Lucasta 37 agrees./{L} I trust you, Eggy. And I want to make my peace with him./{SC} We'll
503 CC Colby 8 any other form of relationship./{C} I want you to be happy./{L} I shall be happy,/If
504 CC Claude 16 /And then bring her up./{SC} No, I want you here, Eggerson./Will you show her up,
511 CC Kaghan 31 the name of Barnabas?/{K} I don't want people calling me 'Barney' —Barney
515 CC Claude 36 true! —But I see you believe it. You want to believe it./Well, believe it, then. But
516 CC Colby 7 him./{SC} What do you mean?/{C} I want to be an organist./It doesn't matter about
516 CC Colby 10 my capacity./I thought I didn't want to be an organist/When I found I had no
516 CC Claude 35 undergone the same disillusionment:/I want us to make the best of it, together./{C} No,
517 CC Colby 24 parish church?/{C} That is what I want. If anyone will take me./{E} If so, I happen
517 CC Eggers 31 certain./Good organists don't seem to want to come to Joshua Park./{C} But I've told
518 CC Eggers 16 point:/If you took the position, you'd want to find your feet/In Joshua Park, before
519 CC Lady E 12 not knowing what other people want of one,/And not knowing what one should
524 ES Monica 18 show off./That's masculine vanity, to want to have the waiters/All buzzing round you:
525 ES Charles 12 —/Except to guess what you want to buy/And advise you to buy it./{M} But
525 ES Monica 32 I know very well/What it is that you want to say. I've heard it all before./{C} And
527 ES Charles 6 /Aren't you sure that you want to marry me?/{M} Yes, Charles. I'm sure
527 ES Monica 7 me?/{M} Yes, Charles. I'm sure that I want to marry you/When I'm free to do so. But
531 ES Monica 3 any visitors./{M} Father, you simply want to revel in gloom!/You know you've
531 ES Ld Clav 26 /Are inwardly delighted. They won't want my ghost/Walking in the City or sitting in
531 ES Ld Clav 29 recognise myself as a ghost/Shan't want to be seen there. It makes me smile/To

531 ES	Lambert	37	said that when you read it/You would want to see him. Said you'd be very angry/If
532 ES	Ld Clav	28	And please remember/That we both want to see you, whenever you can come/If
532 ES	Monica	30	{}/[*To* CHARLES]/{M} We *both* want to see you. {}/[*Exeunt* MONICA *and*
536 ES	Gomez	11	know a word of English,/Didn't want to learn English, wasn't interested/In
536 ES	Gomez	38	ever told the story. *They* wouldn't want to see me./No, I need one old friend, a
539 ES	Ld Clav	9	did they let you retire?/{LC} If you want to know, I had had a stroke./And I might
540 ES	Gomez	30	{G} More than in a hurry./You didn't want it to be known where we'd been./The girls
540 ES	Gomez	32	completely forgotten them) you didn't want *them*/To be called to give evidence. You
541 ES	Ld Clav	12	soul of discretion./{LC} What do you want then? Do you need money?/{G} My dear
542 ES	Ld Clav	2	Before you go — what is it that you want?/{G} I've been trying to make clear that I
542 ES	Gomez	3	been trying to make clear that I only want your friendship!/Just as it used to be in the
542 ES	Gomez	9	with a craving for affection./All I want is as much of your company,/So long as I
543 ES	Ld Clav	13	he wanted money?/{LC} No, he didn't want money./{M} Father, this interview has
544 ES	Monica	27	you were longing to escape;/Now I want to see you learning to enjoy yourself!/{LC}
545 ES	Ld Clav	16	'I'm going to leave you alone!/You want perfect peace: that's what Badgley Court is
546 ES	Piggott	12	nursing-home atmosphere./We don't want our guests to think of themselves as ill,/
546 ES	Piggott	22	with applications/From people who want to come here to die!/We never accept
547 ES	Piggott	9	/And remember, when you want to be *very* quiet/There's the Silence Room.
551 ES	Carghil	1	/He has loved. But a woman doesn't want to forget/A single one of her admirers.
551 ES	Carghil	12	/Well, it's natural that you shouldn't want to believe it./But you think, or try to
551 ES	Carghil	14	that if I'd really suffered/I shouldn't want to let you know who I am,/I shouldn't
551 ES	Carghil	15	let you know who I am,/I shouldn't want to come and talk about the past./You're
551 ES	Carghil	32	of promise suit/Some people won't want to appear as his supporters.'/He said:
551 ES	Carghil	36	you exposed./But I gave way. I didn't want to ruin you./If I'd carried on, it might
553 ES	Carghil	38	a famous man/And you should be in want, you could have these letters auctioned.'/
556 ES	Monica	2	him understand/That the doctors want you to be free from worry./He won't make
556 ES	Monica	28	of Father/And Father knows that you want something from him./Perhaps you'll get to
557 ES	Michael	13	more stimulating./{LC} Well?/{Mi} I want to find some more speculative business./
559 ES	Michael	3	propose to do with yourself?/{Mi} I want to go abroad./{LC} You want to go
559 ES	Ld Clav	4	/{Mi} I want to go abroad./{LC} You want to go abroad?/Well, that's not a bad idea.
559 ES	Michael	14	Good Lord, no./That's not my idea. I want to make money./I want to be somebody
559 ES	Michael	15	not my idea. I want to make money./I want to be somebody on my own account./{LC}
559 ES	Ld Clav	16	own account./{LC} But what do you want to do? Where do you want to go?/What
559 ES	Ld Clav	16	do you want to do? Where do you want to go?/What kind of a life do you think
559 ES	Ld Clav	17	/What kind of a life do you think you want?/{Mi} I simply want to lead a life of my
559 ES	Michael	18	do you think you want?/{Mi} I simply want to lead a life of my own,/According to my
559 ES	Michael	20	good and bad,/Of right and wrong. I want to go far away/To some country where no
560 ES	Ld Clav	5	about such trifles./{LC} So you want me to help you to escape from your father!
560 ES	Michael	29	About that girl — or any other./But I want to get out. I'm fed up with England./{LC}
560 ES	Ld Clav	31	mean that. But it's natural enough/To want a few years abroad. It might be very good
561 ES	Ld Clav	29	think over. But if he goes abroad/I want him to go in a very different spirit/From
561 ES	Michael	33	/{Mi} What is there to say?/I want to leave England, and make my own
565 ES	Monica	29	awful people. We mustn't stay here./I want you to escape from them./{LC} What I
565 ES	Ld Clav	30	to escape from them./{LC} What I want to escape from/Is myself, is the past. But
567 ES	Charles	10	I *need* you./{C} My darling, what I want is to know that you need me./On that last
569 ES	Ld Clav	27	what he wanted./Oh no, he said, I want nothing from you/Except your friendship
575 ES	Michael	2	man for whom a job was made./No! I want to go where I can make my own way,/Not
578 ES	Michael	29	I laughed!/You never seemed even to want a flirtation,/And my friends used to chaff
581 ES	Ld Clav	16	of the truth./Why did I always want to dominate my children?/Why did I mark
581 ES	Ld Clav	19	perpetuate myself in him./Why did I want to keep you to myself, Monica?/Because I

WANTED (106)

148 Rock 1		35	/And the Church does not seem to be wanted/In country or in suburb; and in the
290 FR	Amy	1	to be one of the family,/She only wanted to keep him to herself/To satisfy her
290 FR	Amy	5	she could choose herself. She never wanted/Harry's relations or Harry's old friends;
290 FR	Amy	7	or Harry's old friends;/She never wanted to fit herself to Harry,/But only to bring
303 FR	Agatha	31	have thought/You had more than you wanted of that, when at college./{M} I might
304 FR	Mary	17	of her,/But I think you must have wanted to avoid collision./I suppose I could
304 FR	Mary	20	like hers. I know very well/Why she wanted to keep me. She didn't need me:/She
304 FR	Mary	22	hired servant/Or with none. She only wanted me for Harry —/Not such a
304 FR	Mary	23	—/Not such a compliment: she only wanted/To have a tame daughter-in-law with
304 FR	Agatha	36	she was frightened of the family,/She wanted to fight them — with the weapons of the
306 FR	Harry	11	at home?/{H} There was something/I wanted to ask you. I don't know yet./All these
306 FR	Harry	17	/Of none of the shadows that I wanted to escape;/And at the same time, other
317 FR	Warburt	4	honour of your mother's birthday./I wanted a private conversation with you/On a
320 FR	Warburt	4	It's about your mother's health that I wanted to talk to you./I must tell you, Harry,

325 FR	Violet	33	go out with him again./Not that I wanted to go with him at all —/Though of
332 FR	Agatha	19	meaning/Of loneliness. Your mother wanted a sister here/Always. I was the youngest:
333 FR	Agatha	9	/If they felt no other. But I wanted you!/If that had happened, I knew I
334 FR	Harry	2	/Did not consist in getting what one wanted/Or in getting rid of what can't be got rid
339 FR	Harry	20	/And I see it was what I always wanted. Strength demanded/That seems too
340 FR	Agatha	10	to think./Do you suppose that I wanted to return to Wishwood?/{A} The more
341 FR	Agatha	4	I had, until this evening./But at least I wanted to. Now I must begin./There is nothing
341 FR	Amy	12	behind him,/Because of the waste. I wanted to obliterate/His past life, and have
345 FR	Amy	22	if I can come to know them./I always wanted too much for my children/More than
355 CP	Julia	33	/{J} Oh, they're both dead now. But I wanted to know./If they'd been friends of yours,
356 CP	Julia	3	last year in California./{J} I've always wanted to go to California./Do tell us what you
359 CP	Edward	22	she always turns up when she's least wanted. {}/[*Opens the door*]/{E} Julia! {}/[*Enter*
360 CP	Reilly	40	To prove to the world that somebody wanted you;/If another woman, you might have
361 CP	Reilly	2	—/You might even imagine that you wanted to marry her./{E} But I want my wife
361 CP	Edward	17	This is not what I expected./I only wanted to relieve my mind/By telling someone
361 CP	Reilly	25	your wife;/And I knew that all you wanted was the luxury/Of an intimate disclosure
364 CP	Edward	25	we began to talk/I was not sure I wanted her; and now I want her./Do I want her?
376 CP	Edward	15	too./{E} *And* half a dozen eggs:/I wanted one for breakfast. A boiled egg./It's the
378 CP	Edward	18	argument/Was to make me see that I wanted her back./{C} That's the Devil's method!
379 CP	Celia	32	the dream was not enough; that I wanted something more/And I waited, and
379 CP	Celia	33	something more/And I waited, and wanted to run to tell you./Perhaps the dream
379 CP	Celia	37	dream/All the while; and to find I wanted/This world as well as that ... well, it's
382 CP	Celia	29	/I see that now — of something that I wanted —/No, not *wanted* — something I
382 CP	Celia	30	of something that I wanted —/No, not *wanted* — something I aspired to —/Something
382 CP	Celia	31	to —/Something that I desperately wanted to exist./It must happen somewhere —
393 CP	Lavinia	18	/I couldn't make you say where you wanted to go .../{E} But I wanted *you* to make
393 CP	Edward	19	where you wanted to go .../{E} But I wanted *you* to make that decision./{L} But how
393 CP	Lavinia	20	/{L} But how could I tell where I wanted to go/Unless you suggested some other
393 CP	Lavinia	30	It was only passivity;/You only wanted to be bolstered, encouraged..../{E}
394 CP	Lavinia	15	was coming/Whom I particularly wanted you to meet,/You didn't arrive until just
394 CP	Lavinia	19	you were offered something that you wanted/You wanted something else. I shall treat
394 CP	Lavinia	20	something that you wanted/You wanted something else. I shall treat you very
394 CP	Edward	30	/I may not have known what life I wanted,/But it wasn't the life you chose for me./
394 CP	Edward	32	wasn't the life you chose for me./You wanted your husband to be *successful*,/You
394 CP	Edward	33	your husband to be *successful*,/You wanted me to supply a public background/For
397 CP	Edward	30	everything again?/To find what you wanted. And I never could teach you/How to
403 CP	Edward	23	since I left you./{E} I see now why I wanted my wife to come back./It was because of
409 CP	Reilly	40	in him —/It was a shock. You had wanted to be loved;/You had come to see that
415 CP	Celia	16	away from her —/Anything she wanted. I may have been a fool:/But I don't
431 CP	Julia	38	of a wonderful idea!/I've always wanted to go to California:/Couldn't you
433 CP	Peter	13	we invited you./But there's someone I wanted to ask about,/Who did really want to
433 CP	Peter	17	It's Celia Coplestone./She always wanted to. And now I could help her./I've
435 CP	Peter	11	Celia/And so I never asked. Then I wanted to know/And did not dare to ask. It
435 CP	Peter	25	possible, while Celia was alive./I wanted it, believed in it, for Celia./And, of
435 CP	Peter	26	in it, for Celia./And, of course, I wanted to do something for Celia —/But what
450 CC	Colby	28	satisfactory?/{C} I've got what you wanted, Sir Claude. Good afternoon,/Mr.
452 CC	Lucasta	17	filing those papers/Which no one ever wanted — at least, not till yesterday./Then, just
456 CC	Eggers	4	luncheon —/'Eggerson', he said, 'I wanted a lady,/And I'm perfectly satisfied with
463 CC	Claude	39	/{C} What did you want to do?/{SC} I wanted to be a potter./{C} A potter!/{SC} A
470 CC	Colby	25	/{C} Well, I'd heard you say you wanted to see it./{L} But not with you!/{C} You
470 CC	Colby	37	me./{C} But I didn't know/That you wanted to be educated./{L} Neither did I./But I
470 CC	Lucasta	39	be educated./{L} Neither did I./But I wanted you to want to educate me;/And now
477 CC	Lucasta	24	what it's like to be a bastard/And wanted by nobody. I know why you're shocked:
479 CC	Lucasta	29	her./{L} Only because she's never wanted to pursue you./{K} Yes, I made a bad
483 CC	Colby	22	this room./{C} It's the sort of room I wanted. {}/[*rising*]./{LE} And I see a photograph
490 CC	Colby	40	can spring. Now, it is too late./I never wanted a parent till now —/I never thought
491 CC	Lady E	9	/It won't be the same as what we had wanted —/But in some ways better! And
494 CC	Claude	19	—/An idea, an inspiration. What he wanted to transmit to me/Was that idea, that
494 CC	Claude	26	inspiration/If I had done what I wanted to do./{LE} You've never talked like this
495 CC	Claude	6	/I took it for granted that what you wanted/Was a husband of importance. I
495 CC	Claude	8	me/If you knew what I'd really wanted to be./{LE} And I took it for granted
495 CC	Claude	19	/{SC} I'm not laughing./So what you wanted was to inspire an artist!/{LE} Or to
495 CC	Lady E	27	/He belonged to the world I wanted to escape from./He was so
495 CC	Lady E	28	from./He was so commonplace! I wanted to forget him,/And so, I suppose,
495 CC	Lady E	29	to forget him,/And so, I suppose, I wanted to forget/Colby. But Colby is an artist./

498	CC	Claude	38	she arrives I will summon Colby./I wanted you here first, to explain the situation:/
499	CC	Lucasta	29	I didn't try to./And knowing that you wanted me to marry B./Made me determined
500	CC	Lucasta	24	me./He made me see what I really wanted./B. makes me feel safe. And that's what
510	CC	Kaghan	29	parents living?/{K} In Kent. They wanted to retire to the country./So I found them
513	CC	Claude	11	you had your wish?/{SC} Colby only wanted to be sure of the truth./{C} That is a
513	CC	Colby	15	truth./What it is, doesn't matter. All I wanted was relief/From the nagging annoyance
513	CC	Colby	38	to be,/And by doing the things he had wanted to do./{MG} Whose son would you wish
514	CC	Claude	27	/In response to what Colby said he wanted./{E} I'll examine the records myself, Sir
519	CC	Kaghan	10	.../{E} Me, Mr. Kaghan?/{K} We wanted Colby to be something he wasn't./{LE} I
524	ES	Charles	7	/{C} But I couldn't say what I wanted to say to you/Over luncheon .../{M}
525	ES	Charles	7	afternoon./I couldn't say what I wanted to, in a restaurant;/And then you took
526	ES	Charles	5	didn't *know* you loved me —I merely wanted to believe it. And I've made you say so!/
538	ES	Gomez	9	passage out. I know the reason:/You wanted to get rid of me. I shall tell you why
543	ES	Monica	12	his name./{M} Then I suppose he wanted money?/{LC} No, he didn't want
551	ES	Carghil	35	awarded.'/Effie was against it — she wanted you exposed./But I gave way. I didn't
552	ES	Carghil	28	silly Richard/You always were. You wanted to pose/As a man of the world. And
555	ES	Piggott	4	sort or mine./I suspected that she wanted to meet you, so I thought/That I'd take
559	ES	Michael	30	not without dignity,/Being no longer wanted. And you wished to be Lord Claverton/
562	ES	Michael	7	I could have loved Father, if he'd wanted love,/But he never did, Monica, not
567	ES	Monica	9	that is in it!/Oh Charles, how I've wanted you! And now I *need* you./{C} My
569	ES	Ld Clav	26	long ago. When I asked him what he wanted./Oh no, he said, I want nothing from
574	ES	Carghil	15	end I discovered what Michael really wanted/For making a new start. He wants to go
575	ES	Michael	5	offered me a job which is just what I wanted./{LC} Yes, I see the advantage of a job
581	ES	Ld Clav	18	a narrow path for Michael?/Because I wanted to perpetuate myself in him./Why did I
581	ES	Ld Clav	20	you to myself, Monica?/Because I wanted you to give your life to adoring/The
582	ES	Charles	30	his going for a walk./{C} He wanted to leave us alone together!/{M} Yes, he
582	ES	Monica	31	leave us alone together!/{M} Yes, he wanted to leave us alone together./And yet,

WANTING (9)

103	Journ Magi	12	grumbling/And running away, and wanting their liquor and women,/And the
289	FR	Gerald	4	you're talking about./You seem to be wanting to give us all the hump./I must say, this
364	CP	Reilly	14	fact that you can't give a reason for wanting her/Is the best reason for believing that
412	CP	Celia	37	ill, or can give good reasons/For wanting to see you. Well, I can't./I just came in
416	CP	Celia	33	he is only a child/Lost in a forest, wanting to go home./{R} Compassion may be
445	CC	Eggers	17	for Mrs. E.,/Which she's been wanting. So *she'll* be pleased./Then I lunched at
447	CC	Claude	8	/{SC} Of course, she knows you were wanting to retire,/As we had some discussion
544	ES	Ld Clav	13	staring/Or offering picture papers, or wanting a fourth at bridge;/Still, I'll admit to a
560	ES	Ld Clav	20	Michael! Are there reasons for your wanting to go/Beyond what you've told me? It

WANTON (1)

| 211 | Old Gumbie | 32 | /To prevent them from idle and wanton destroyment./So she's formed, from |

WANTONNESS (1)

| 253 | MC Tempt4 | 6 | been baited with morsels of the past./Wantonness is weakness. As for the King,/His |

WANTS (29)

66	WL: Chess	148	/He's been in the army four years, he wants a good time,/And if you don't give it him,
124	SA Sweeney	14	do a girl in/Any man has to, needs to, wants to/Once in a lifetime, do a girl in/Well I
136	5FingerEx4	2	to meet Mr. Hodgson!/(Everyone wants to know *him*)/With his musical sound/
136	5FingerEx4	14	to meet Mr. Hodgson!/(Everyone wants to know *him*)./He has 999 canaries/And
136	5FingerEx4	19	to meet Mr. Hodgson!/(Everyone wants to know *him*)./*Lines for Cuscuscaraway*
151	Rock 2	9	the songs we can sing which nobody wants to hear sung;/Waiting to be flung in the
214	RTTugger	5	you set him on a mouse then he only wants a rat,/If you set him on a rat then he'd
214	RTTugger	13	bore:/When you let him in, then he wants to be out;/He's always on the wrong side
214	RTTugger	25	/If you offer him fish then he always wants a feast;/When there isn't any fish then he
289	FR	Amy	18	me too late./{A} Much too late./If he wants to talk about it, that's another matter;/
292	FR	Amy	21	same./Mr. Bevan — you remember — wants to call tomorrow/On some legal business,
293	FR	Ivy	12	I'm dead./{I} Oh, dear Amy!/No one wants you to die, I'm sure!/Now that Harry's
297	FR	Charles	18	to do/Until there's somebody he wants to get rid of./{G} Even so, we don't want
304	FR	Mary	15	perfectly well,/What Cousin Amy wants, she usually gets./Why do *you* so seldom
321	FR	Denman	10	Winchell is here, my Lord,/And wants to see your Lordship very urgent,/And
321	FR	Warburt	14	DENMAN]/{W} I wonder what he wants. I hope nothing has happened/To either
339	FR	Harry	14	is love and terror/Of what waits and wants me, and will not let me fall./Let the
354	CP	Alex	7	She never misses anything unless she wants to./{C} Especially the Lithuanian accent./
389	CP	Celia	32	to remember me/As someone who wants you and Edward to be happy./{L} You
390	CP	Julia	32	/And now I don't believe she really wants us./I can see that she is quite worn out/
449	CC	Eggers	32	to the point/At which Lady Elizabeth wants to adopt him —An admirable solution
473	CC	Colby	17	for you —/For anyone who wants one as much as you do./{L} And *your*
528	ES	Monica	27	return from Badgley Court./But Selby wants him to have every encouragement —/If

530 ES Ld Clav   13   run for trains/When the last thing he wants is to take a train for anywhere!/No, I've
532 ES Ld Clav   18   man who introduces him/I expect he wants money. Or to sell me something
545 ES Piggott   31   /All you have to do is to make your wants known./Just ring through to my office. If
558 ES Michael   18   It's for your sake, he says,/That he wants to keep things quiet. I can tell you, it's no
574 ES Carghil   16   wanted/For making a new start. He wants to go abroad!/And find his own way in
575 ES Ld Clav   12   just the man that Señor Gomez wants,/But in a different sense, and for different

WAPPING (1)
213 Growltiger   53   ker-flip, ker-flop./Oh there was joy in Wapping when the news flew through the land;/

WAR (15)
119 SP   Krum   14   lot about you./{Kr} We were all in the war together/Klip and me and the Cap and
141 Rannoch   6   road winds in/Listlessness of ancient war,/Languor of broken steel,/Clamour of
202 War Poetry   t   obedience to instructions./A Note on War Poetry/Not the expression of collective
202 War Poetry   17   a poem is not poetry —/That is a life./War is not a life: it is a situation,/One which
218 Mung Rump   8   the basement looked like a field of war,/If a tile or two came loose on the roof,/
241 MC Priest2   24   /That divided them? Is it peace or war?/{P1} Does he come/In full assurance, or
242 MC Priest1   2   is another matter./{P1} But again, is it war or peace?/{M} Peace, but not the kiss of
249 MC Tempt2   29   manœuvre. Monarchs also,/Waging war abroad, need fast friends at home./Private
253 MC Tempt4   34   /Uncertain mastery of melting armies,/War, plague, and revolution,/New conspiracies,
258 MC Thomas   21   King's law/In England, and waged war with him against Toulouse,/I beat the
260 MC Thomas   23   the world has been stricken with War and the fear of/War? Does it seem to you
260 MC Thomas   24   stricken with War and the fear of/War? Does it seem to you that the angelic voices
263 MC Chorus   15   men keep the peace of God./And war among men defiles this world, but death in
334 FR   Harry   34   Now I see/I have been wounded in a war of phantoms,/Not by human beings — they
463 CC   Claude   4   I sent you both over to Canada/In the war — that was perhaps a mistake,/Though it

WARBLER (1)
142 Cape Ann   5   Leave to chance/The Blackburnian warbler, the shy one. Hail/With shrill whistle

WARBURTON (22)
284 FR   m 8   *his servant and chauffeur*/DR. WARBURTON/SERGEANT WINCHELL/
296 FR Gerald   34   Violet's suggestion./Why not ring up Warburton, and ask him to join us?/He's an old
297 FR Amy   1   opinion./{A} If anyone speaks to Dr. Warburton/It should be myself. What does
298 FR Agatha   9   /Any more than I object to asking Dr. Warburton:/I only see that this is all quite
303 FR Agatha   15   the dinner back .../{Ag} And also Dr. Warburton. At least, Amy has invited him./{M}
303 FR Mary   16   least, Amy has invited him./{M} Dr. Warburton? I think she might have told me;/It
303 FR Mary   24   conversation./I am very glad if Dr. Warburton is coming./I shall have to sit
313 FR   m 27   yet, Amy. {}/[*Enter* AMY, *with* DR. WARBURTON]/{A} It is most vexing. What
314 FR Amy   2   Harry!/Haven't you seen Dr. Warburton?/You know he's the oldest friend of
315 FR   m 29   same honour. {}/[*Exeunt* AMY, DR. WARBURTON, HARRY]/{Ch} I am afraid of
317 FR   4m 1   *after dinner.*/Scene I/HARRY, WARBURTON/{W} I'm glad of a few minutes
321 FR Denman   11   your Lordship very urgent,/And Dr. Warburton. He says it's very urgent/Or he
323 FR Charles   34   you./{C} Much better leave it to Warburton, Amy./Extremely fortunate for us
324 FR   m 7   /On the back of my car. {}/[*Exeunt* WARBURTON *and* WINCHELL]/{V} Well,
325 FR Charles   11   /There's nothing we could do that Warburton can't./If he's worse than Winchell
325 FR Gerald   14   the shock for Amy;/But I think that Warburton understands *that*./{I} You are quite
327 FR Harry   13   them perhaps with the aid of Dr. Warburton —/Or any other doctor, who would
327 FR Harry   14   other doctor, who would be another Warburton,/If you decided to set another
331 FR Harry   18   I want to know, and that is enough:/Warburton told me that, though he did not
347 FR   m 32   AGATHA *and* MARY. *Pause. Enter* WARBURTON]/{W} Well! it's a filthy night to
348 FR Mary   4   trouble? {}/[*Enter* MARY]/{M} Dr. Warburton!/{W} Excuse me. {}/[*Exeunt* MARY
348 FR   m 5   Excuse me. {}/[*Exeunt* MARY *and* WARBURTON]/{Ch} We do not like to look

WARBURTON'S (3)
296 FR Gerald   39   need have no suspicion./I'd trust Warburton's opinion./{A} If anyone speaks to
322 FR Winch   29   here sooner./I'd telephoned to Dr. Warburton's,/And they told me he was here,
323 FR Charles   36   here./We must put ourselves under Warburton's orders./{W} I repeat, Lady

WARDEN (1)
517 CC Eggers   36   have some influence. *I* am the Vicar's Warden./{C} I'd like to apply./{E} The stipend is

WARENNE (1)
246 MC Thomas   9   crossing, found at Sandwich/Broc, Warenne, and the Sheriff of Kent,/Those who

WARILY (1)
247 MC Tempt1   5 Mirth and sportfulness need not walk warily./{T} You talk of seasons that are past. I

WARM (15)
37 Gerontion   4   at the hot gates/Nor fought in the warm rain/Nor knee deep in the salt marsh,
53 Whispers   32   dry ribs/To keep our metaphysics warm./Mr. Eliot's Sunday Morning Service/
61 WL: Burial   5   roots with spring rain./Winter kept us warm, covering/Earth in forgetful snow, feeding
107 Animula   3   /To light, dark, dry or damp, chilly or warm;/Moving between the legs of tables and of
107 Animula   27   fare forward or retreat,/Fearing the warm reality, the offered good,/Denying the

135	5FingerEx2	6	endlessly./Little dog was safe and warm/Under a cretonne eiderdown,/Yet the
177	FQ: ECoker	20	in the electric heat/Hypnotised. In a warm haze the sultry light/Is absorbed, not
203	Indians	8	at the hour of conversation,/(The warm or the cool hour, according to the
210	Old Gumbie	14	would be hard to find, she likes the warm and sunny spots./All day she sits beside
239	MC Chorus	16	and deny his master? who shall be warm/By the fire, and deny his master?/Seven
285	FR Amy	6	out again./O Sun, that was once so warm, O Light that was taken for granted/
502	CC Lucasta	23	cold. Or else you've some fire/To warm you, that isn't the same kind of fire/That
536	ES Gomez	27	like./Your loneliness — so cosy, warm and padded:/You're not isolated —
547	ES Piggott	6	careful at this time of year;/This early warm weather can be very treacherous./There,
582	ES Ld Clav	23	Yes, it's chilly at dusk. But I'll be warm enough./I shall not go far. {}/[*Exit*

WARMED (1)

| 181 | FQ: ECoker | 166 | fever sings in mental wires./If to be warmed, then I must freeze/And quake in frigid |

WARMEST (1)

| 427 | CP Alex | 18 | /Is the one to whom they give the warmest welcome./I know them well enough for |

WARMS (1)

| 502 | CC Lucasta | 24 | that isn't the same kind of fire/That warms other people. You're either an egotist/Or |

WARMTH (1)

| 544 | ES Ld Clav | 21 | /I hope this benignant sunshine/And warmth will last for a few days more./But this |

WARN (4)

592	Grad 1	5	bar — no chart to show/No light to warn of rocks which lie below,/But let us yet put
594	Grad 13	3	may'st thou be no less;/A guide to warn them, and a friend to bless/Before they
261	MC Thomas	28	of God, for His love of men,/to warn them and to lead them, to bring them
564	ES Carghill	30	you're staying at Badgley Court,/I warn you — I'm going to cross-examine you/

WARNED (3)

376	CP Julia	32	touch it./{J} My dear, I should have warned you:/Anything that Alex makes is
394	CP Lavinia	24	/{L} Frankly, I don't know. I was warned of the danger,/Yet something, or
454	CC Colby	23	picture of sanity./{C} But you never warned me about Miss Angel./What about *her*?/

WARNING (7)

185	FQ: DrySal	33	in the granite teeth,/And the wailing warning from the approaching headland/Are all
223	Pekes Pols	57	Pekes and the Pollicles quickly took warning./He looked at the sky and he gave a
246	MC Thomas	12	/Fearing for the King's name, warning against treason,/Made them hold their
360	CP Edward	3	Your wife has left you?/{E} Without warning, of course;/Just when she'd arranged a
394	CP Edward	22	/In future./{E} Thank you for the warning. But tell me,/Since this is how you see
447	CC Claude	5	Colby./I think, you ought to give her warning/Of whom she is to meet on her arrival./
451	CC Colby	31	very musical./{C} Thank you for the warning!/{E} So if you don't mind, I shall

WARS (2)

| 172 | FQ: BurntN | 53 | scars/Appeasing long forgotten wars./The dance along the artery/The |
| 178 | FQ: ECoker | 61 | cars/Deployed in constellated wars/Scorpion fights against the Sun/Until the |

WAS (883)

WASH (17)

50	Hippopot	29	hosannas./Blood of the Lamb shall wash him clean/And him shall heavenly arms
67	WL: Fire S	201	Porter/And on her daughter/They wash their feet in soda water/Et O ces voix
69	WL: Fire S	273	swing on the heavy spar./The barges wash/Drifting logs/Down Greenwich reach/Past
187	FQ: DrySal	121	rock in the restless waters,/Waves wash over it, fogs conceal it;/On a halcyon day
216	Jellicles	19	toilette and take their repose:/Jellicles wash behind their ears,/Jellicles dry between
233	Skimble	39	funny little basin you're supposed to wash your face in/And a crank to shut the
243	MC Priest2	1	a firm foothold/Against the perpetual wash of tides of balance of forces of barons and
275	MC Chorus	21	/{C} Clear the air! clean the sky! wash the wind! take stone from stone and wash
275	MC Chorus	21	the wind! take stone from stone and wash them./The land is foul, the water is foul,
276	MC Chorus	17	foul./Clear the air! clean the sky! wash the wind! take the stone from the stone,
276	MC Chorus	17	take the muscle from the bone, and wash them. Wash the stone, wash the bone,
276	MC Chorus	17	from the bone, and wash them. Wash the stone, wash the bone, wash the brain,
276	MC Chorus	17	and wash them. Wash the stone, wash the bone, wash the brain, wash the soul,
276	MC Chorus	17	them. Wash the stone, wash the bone, wash the brain, wash the soul, wash them wash
276	MC Chorus	17	stone, wash the bone, wash the brain, wash the soul, wash them wash them! {}/[*The*
276	MC Chorus	17	bone, wash the brain, wash the soul, wash them wash them! {}/[*The* KNIGHTS,
276	MC Chorus	17	the brain, wash the soul, wash them wash them! {}/[*The* KNIGHTS, *having*

WASHED (2)

| 50 | Hippopot | 33 | on a harp of gold./He shall be washed as white as snow,/By all the martyr'd |
| 274 | MC Knights | 20 | for the mark of the beast./Are you washed in the blood of the Lamb?/Are you |

WASHED-OUT (1)

| 24 | Rhapsody | 56 | /The moon has lost her memory./A washed-out smallpox cracks her face,/Her hand |

WASHING (1)

| 534 | ES Gomez | 20 | — with conviction./No, forgery, or washing cheques, or anything of that nature,/Is |

WASN'T (38)

118 SP	Dusty	14	Well I never! What did I tell you?/Wasn't I saying I always draw court cards?/The
125 SA	Sweeney	10	dead/If he was alive then the milkman wasn't/and the rent-collector wasn't/And if they
125 SA	Sweeney	11	wasn't/and the rent-collector wasn't/And if they were alive then he was dead./
125 SA	Sweeney	13	were alive then he was dead./There wasn't any joint/There wasn't any joint/For
125 SA	Sweeney	14	dead./There wasn't any joint/There wasn't any joint/For when you're alone/When
223 Pekes Pols		61	*Police Dog returned to his beat,/There wasn't a single one left in the street./*Mr.
227 Macavity		38	the deed took place — MACAVITY WASN'T THERE!/And they say that all the
289 FR	Charles	14	—/That was just about a year ago, wasn't it?/Do you think that I ought to mention
292 FR	Gerald	29	the country as well as ever./There wasn't an inch of it you didn't know./But you'll
299 FRDowning		30	a long way with her Ladyship./She wasn't one of those that are *designed* for
300 FRDowning		32	the rail, looking at the water —/There wasn't a moon, but I was sure it was him./While
304 FR	Mary	2	throw that up against me./I know I wasn't one of your favourite students:/I only
305 FR	Mary	1	but what he did to himself./{M} But it wasn't till I knew that Harry had returned/That
328 FR	Gerald	3	/To have an accident as John. And it wasn't John's fault,/I don't believe. John is
347 FR	Warburt	35	say that John is getting on nicely;/It wasn't so serious as Winchell made out,/And
355 CP	Peter	19	cocktails?/{P} But do go on. Edward wasn't listening anyway./{J} No, he wasn't
355 CP	Julia	20	wasn't listening anyway./{J} No, he wasn't listening, but he's such a strain —/
358 CP	Julia	17	wedding cake./{J} Wedding cake? I wasn't at her wedding./Edward, it's been a
366 CP	Peter	38	party/For everyone but me. And that wasn't your fault./I don't suppose you noticed
379 CP	Edward	16	And I should have known/That it wasn't fair to you./{C} It wasn't fair to *me*!/You
379 CP	Celia	17	/That it wasn't fair to you./{C} It wasn't fair to *me*!/You can stand there and talk
380 CP	Edward	20	anything/Between me and Peter./{E} Wasn't there? He thought so./He came back this
387 CP	Celia	3	learnt a lot in twenty-four hours./It wasn't a very pleasant experience./Oh, I'm glad
388 CP	Celia	12	— more than you realised./It *was* fun, wasn't it! But now you'll have a chance,/I hope,
394 CP	Edward	31	have known what life I wanted,/But it wasn't the life you chose for me./You wanted
395 CP	Lavinia	36	been your placid assumption/That I wasn't worth the trouble of understanding./{E}
415 CP	Celia	15	hurting them. I haven't hurt *her*./I wasn't taking anything away from her —/
451 CC	Eggers	26	know./But with Lady Elizabeth he wasn't so successful./She once referred to him as
476 CC	Lucasta	18	some men have thought about me wasn't true./{C} What wasn't true?/{L} That I
476 CC	Colby	19	about me wasn't true./{C} What wasn't true?/{L} That I was Claude's mistress —
480 CC	Kaghan	27	—/He was born and bred to it. I wasn't, Colby./Do you know, I was a
496 CC	Lady E	1	/You always made me feel that I wasn't worth talking to./{SC} And you always
519 CC	Kaghan	10	We wanted Colby to be something he wasn't./{LE} I suppose that's true of you and
536 ES	Gomez	11	English,/Didn't want to learn English, wasn't interested/In anything that happened
550 ES	Carghil	27	could hardly have sent me *here*/If I wasn't well off. Yes, I'm provided for./But isn't
558 ES	Michael	35	one/Who was at all nice to me. She wasn't exciting,/But it served to pass the time. It
559 ES	Michael	34	title/To a son, was gratifying. But it wasn't for *my* sake!/I was just your son — that
575 ES	Gomez	11	he thinks I'm just the man./{G} Yes, wasn't it extraordinary./{LC} Of course you're

WASSAIL (1)

588 Fable		57	held sausages./Over their Christmas wassail the monks dozed,/A fine old drink,

WASTAGE (1)

186 FQ: DrySal		72	/Or of an ocean not littered with wastage/Or of a future that is not liable/Like

WASTE (26)

42 Swee Erect		1	/Sweeney Erect/Paint me a cavernous waste shore/Cast in the unstilled Cyclades,/
59 Waste Land		t	the stiff dishonoured shroud./The Waste Land/The Burial of the Dead/April is the
150 Rock 1		110	*sparrow and starling have no time to waste./If men do not build/How shall they live?/*
153 Rock 2		53	work not delay, time and the arm not waste;/Let the clay be dug from the pit, let the
157 Rock 4		13	by the king's pool,/Jerusalem lay waste, consumed with fire;/No place for a beast
160 Rock 7		1	beginning GOD created the world. Waste and void. Waste and void. And darkness
160 Rock 7		1	created the world. Waste and void. Waste and void. And darkness was upon the
160 Rock 7		6	life, for ecstasy not of the flesh./Waste and void. Waste and void. And darkness
160 Rock 7		6	not of the flesh./Waste and void. Waste and void. And darkness on the face of
160 Rock 7		17	the wind will not let the snow rest./Waste and void. Waste and void. And darkness
160 Rock 7		17	not let the snow rest./Waste and void. Waste and void. And darkness on the face of
161 Rock 7		40	/No man has hired us..../CHORUS:/Waste and void. Waste and void. And darkness
161 Rock 7		40	us..../CHORUS:/Waste and void. Waste and void. And darkness on the face of
176 FQ: BurntN		177	here, now, always —/Ridiculous the waste sad time/Stretching before and after./East
235 Ad-dress		63	finished, licks his paws/So's not to waste the onion sauce.)/A Cat's entitled to
592 Grad 3		3	South, and Eastward o'er the water's waste,/Some to the western limits of the sky/
239 MC Chorus		10	brown sharp points of death in a waste of water and mud,/The New Year waits,
271 MC Chorus		5	death of spirit,/By the final ecstasy of waste and shame,/O Lord Archbishop, O
271 MC Priests		21	/Through the cloister. No time to waste. They are coming back, armed. To the
293 FR	Violet	1	spoken to your mother/About the waste that goes on in the kitchen./Mrs. Packell
326 FR	Harry	25	life as an isolated ruin,/A casual bit of waste in an orderly universe./But it begins to

341 FR	Amy	12	he has left behind him,/Because of the waste. I wanted to obliterate/His past life, and
412 CP	Celia	33	perplexing. However,/I don't want to waste your time. And I'm awfully afraid/That
434 CP	Edward	38	Thinking about Celia./{E} It's the waste that I resent./{P} You know more than I
434 CP	Peter	40	/For *me*, it's everything else that's a waste./Two years! And it was all a mistake./
438 CP	Reilly	34	because you think her death was waste/You blame yourselves, and because you

WASTED (4)

182 FQ: ECoker	175	twenty years —/Twenty years largely wasted, the years of *l'entre deux guerres* —/
392 CP	Lavinia	36	always tell the truth now./We have wasted such a lot of time in lying./{E} I don't
438 CP	Reilly	36	yourselves/You think her life was wasted. It was triumphant./But I am no more
525 ES	Monica	28	minutes alone with me/Which you've wasted in wrangling. But seriously, Charles,/

WASTING (3)

412 CP	Celia	34	afraid/That you'll think that I am wasting it anyway./I suppose most people, when
575 ES	Gomez	18	.../{G} My dear Dick,/You're wasting your time, rehearsing ancient history./
575 ES	Ld Clav	28	did./{LC} On that point, Fred, you're wasting *your* time:/My daughter and my future

WATCH (14)

30 Cous Nancy	11	/Upon the glazen shelves kept watch/Matthew and Waldo, guardians of the
185 FQ: DrySal	46	future futureless, before the morning watch/When time stops and time is never
232 Skimble	25	at once if anything occurred./He will watch you without winking and he sees what
233 Skimble	53	of Scotch while he's keeping on the watch,/Only stopping here and there to catch a
246 MC Thomas	23	/All things prepare the event. Watch. {}/[*Enter* FIRST TEMPTER]/{T1} You
285 FR	Amy	2	quite light./I have nothing to do but watch the days draw out,/Now that I sit in the
422 CP	Julia	16	each side of it./{J} May the holy ones watch over the roof,/May the moon herself
422 CP	Alex	21	of travellers/Bless the road./{A} Watch over her in the desert./Watch over her in
422 CP	Alex	22	/{A} Watch over her in the desert./Watch over her in the mountain./Watch over
422 CP	Alex	23	/Watch over her in the mountain./Watch over her in the labyrinth./Watch over her
422 CP	Alex	24	/Watch over her in the labyrinth./Watch over her by the quicksand./{J} Protect
457 CC	m	13	There's plenty of time. {}/[*Looks at his watch*]/{E} I'll arrive at the airport with minutes
493 CC	Lady E	22	light full on her:/I want to be able to watch her expression./{SC} But not in this chair!
503 CC	m	36	Mrs. Guzzard? {}/[*looking at his watch*]./{SC} She ought to be here now! It's

WATCHED (5)

15 Prufrock	71	at dusk through narrow streets/And watched the smoke that rises from the pipes/Of
23 Preludes	26	back, and waited;/You dozed, and watched the night revealing/The thousand
342 FR	Agatha	16	it is none of my doing:/I have only watched and waited. In this world/It is
489 CC	Claude	22	I provided for his education./I have watched him grow. And Mrs. Guzzard/Knows
518 CC	Eggers	7	know,/For quite a little time, and I've watched you pretty closely./Mr. Simpkins!

WATCHER (1)

| 148 Rock 1 | 41 | our doubtings./The Rock. The Watcher. The Stranger./He who has seen what |

WATCHERS (2)

| 241 MC | Mess | 11 | /{M} Servants of God, and watchers of the temple,/I am here to inform |
| 305 FR | Agatha | 14 | emerge. You and I, Mary,/Are only watchers and waiters: not the easiest rôle./I |

WATCHES (2)

| 19 Portrait | 39 | /Discuss the late events,/Correct our watches by the public clocks./Then sit for half |
| 233 Skimble | 51 | /The Cat of the Railway Train!/In the watches of the night he is always fresh and |

WATCHFUL (1)

| 127 Cor1 March | 31 | over the horse's neck,/And the eyes watchful, waiting, perceiving, indifferent./O |

WATCHING (6)

184 FQ: DrySal	10	of the machine, but waiting, watching and waiting./His rhythm was present
188 FQ: DrySal	145	on the deck of the drumming liner/Watching the furrow that widens behind you,/
341 FR	Amy	33	years designing his life,/Eight years watching, without him, at Wishwood,/Years of
446 CC	Eggers	35	He told me he was very fond of bird watching./{SC} But there won't be any birds —
446 CC	Claude	36	won't be any birds — none worth watching./{E} I don't know, Sir Claude. Only
548 ES	Carghil	24	obviously devoted to her father./I was watching you both in the dining-room last

WATCHMAN (1)

| 256 MC | Priests | 33 | the candle in the room?/{3P} Does the watchman walk by the wall?/{4T} Does the |

WATER (49)

17 Prufrock	128	blown back/When the wind blows the water white and black./We have lingered in the
40 Burb Blei	12	Her shuttered barge/Burned on the water all the day./But this or such was
54 Mr E Sun	13	and browned/But through the water pale and thin/Still shine the unoffending
55 Mr E Sun	30	shifts from ham to ham/Stirring the water in his bath./The masters of the subtle
61 WL: Burial	24	relief,/And the dry stone no sound of water. Only/There is shadow under this red
62 WL: Burial	55	find/The Hanged Man. Fear death by water./I see crowds of people, walking round in
65 WL: Chess	135	/'What shall we ever do?'/'The hot water at ten./And if it rains, a closed car at four.
67 WL: Fire S	201	daughter/They wash their feet in soda water/Et O ces voix d'enfants, chantant dans la
71 WL: DWater	t	Thou pluckest/burning/Death by Water/Phlebas the Phoenician, a fortnight dead,
72 WL: Thund	331	/With a little patience/Here is no water but only rock/Rock and no water and the

72 WL: Thund	332	no water but only rock/Rock and no water and the sandy road/The road winding
72 WL: Thund	334	Which are mountains of rock without water/If there were water we should stop and
72 WL: Thund	335	of rock without water/If there were water we should stop and drink/Amongst the
72 WL: Thund	338	feet are in the sand/If there were only water amongst the rock/Dead mountain mouth
72 WL: Thund	345	of mudcracked houses/If there were water/And no rock/If there were rock/And also
72 WL: Thund	348	no rock/If there were rock/And also water/And water/A spring/A pool among the
72 WL: Thund	349	there were rock/And also water/And water/A spring/A pool among the rock/If there
72 WL: Thund	352	the rock/If there were the sound of water only/Not the cicada/And dry grass
73 WL: Thund	355	/And dry grass singing/But sound of water over a rock/Where the hermit-thrush
73 WL: Thund	358	drop drop drop drop/But there is no water/Who is the third who walks always beside
109 Marina	2	grey rocks and what islands/What water lapping the bow/And scent of pine and
116 SP Dusty	33	now/She's got her feet in mustard and water/I said I'm giving her mustard and water/
116 SP Dusty	34	/I said I'm giving her mustard and water/All right, Monday you'll phone through./
128 Cor1 March	33	palmtree at noon, under the running water/At the still point of the turning world. O
129 Cor2 State	17	of engineers/To consider the Water Supply./A commission is appointed/For
155 Rock 3	63	discredited,/Binding the earth and the water to your service,/Exploiting the seas and
160 Rock 7	7	the Spirit moved upon the face of the water./And men who turned towards the light
167 Rock 10	33	light that fractures through unquiet water./We see the light but see not whence it
172 FQ: BurntN	37	edged,/And the pool was filled with water out of sunlight,/And the lotos rose,
185 FQ: DrySal	31	and caress of wave that breaks on water,/The distant rote in the granite teeth,/And
193 FQ: Little	66	Over the eyes and in the mouth,/Dead water and dead sand/Contending for the upper
193 FQ: Little	72	mirth./This is the death of earth./Water and fire succeed/The town, the pasture
193 FQ: Little	74	/The town, the pasture and the weed./Water and fire deride/The sacrifice that we
193 FQ: Little	76	deride/The sacrifice that we denied./Water and fire shall rot/The marred
193 FQ: Little	79	and choir./This is the death of water and fire./In the uncertain hour before the
204 de la Mare	4	very dangerous ground,/For here the water buffalo may rove,/The kinkajou, the
588 Fable	33	drencht the gown he wore with holy water,/The turkeys, capons, boars, they were to
239 MC Chorus	10	sharp points of death in a waste of water and mud,/The New Year waits, breathes,
246 MC Tempt1	38	and apple-blossom floating on the water,/Singing at nightfall, whispering in
264 MC Priest3	18	of thy saints have they shed like water,/And there was no man to bury them.
275 MC Chorus	22	and wash them./The land is foul, the water is foul, our beasts and ourselves defiled
300 FRDowning	31	/Leaning over the rail, looking at the water —/There wasn't a moon, but I was sure it
359 CP Reilly	12	/{E} Anything in it?/{UG} A drop of water./{E} I want to apologise for this evening./
360 CP Reilly	13	{E} Anything in it?/{UG} Nothing but water./And I recommend you the same
363 CP Reilly	8	Gin./{E} Anything with it?/{UG} Water./{E} To what does this lead?/{UG} To
365 CP Reilly	5	/{UG} *As I was drinkin' gin and water,/And me bein' the One Eyed Riley,/Who*
384 CP Edward	3	Well. May I offer you some gin and water?/{UG} No, thank you. This is a different
432 CP Reilly	22	cocktail?/{R} Might I have a glass of water?/{E} Anything with it?/{R} Nothing,
544 ES Monica	4	/The beds are comfortable, the hot water is hot,/They give us a very tolerable

WATER'S (1)

592 Grad 3	3	/North, South, and Eastward o'er the water's waste,/Some to the western limits of the

WATER-MILL (1)

103 Journ Magi	23	/With a running stream and a water-mill beating the darkness,/And three trees

WATER-THRUSH (1)

142 Cape Ann	8	Follow the feet/Of the walker, the water-thrush. Follow the flight/Of the dancing

WATERED (1)

588 Fable	40	room in which they were to dine,/And watered everything except the wine./So when all

WATERFALL (3)

190 FQ: DrySal	214	unseen, or the winter lightning/Or the waterfall, or music heard so deeply/That it is
197 FQ: Little	249	longest river/The voice of the hidden waterfall/And the children in the apple-tree/Not
309 FR Harry	32	a very long distance,/Or the distant waterfall in the forest,/Inaccessible, half-heard./

WATERLOO (1)

518 CC Guzzard	31	Colby,/Will you get me a taxi to go to Waterloo?/{C} Get you a taxi? Yes, Aunt Sarah;

WATERPROOF (1)

218 Mung Rump	10	roof,/Which presently ceased to be waterproof,/If the drawers were pulled out from

WATERS (9)

67 WL: Fire S	182	have left no addresses./By the waters of Leman I sat down and wept .../Sweet
69 WL: Fire S	257	/'This music crept by me upon the waters'/And along the Strand, up Queen
109 Marina	21	feet/Under sleep, where all the waters meet./Bowsprit cracked with ice and
151 Rock 2	7	Spirit which moved on the face of the waters like a lantern set on the back of a
183 FQ: ECoker	210	/The wave cry, the wind cry, the vast waters/Of the petrel and the porpoise. In my
187 FQ: DrySal	120	/And the ragged rock in the restless waters,/Waves wash over it, fogs conceal it;/On
264 MC Priest3	16	*babes, O God.*/As the voice of many waters, of thunder, of harps,/They sang as it
428 CP Alex	40	You see, Lavinia,/These are very deep waters./{E} And the agitators;/How do they
508 CC Eggers	14	I pour a drop of oil on these troubled waters?/Let us approach the question from

WATERSTAIR (1)
41 Burb Blei   27   phthisic hand/To climb the waterstair. Lights, lights,/She entertains Sir
WATERY (1)
191 FQ: Little   7 that is the heart's heat,/Reflecting in a watery mirror/A glare that is blindness in the
WAUCHOPE (5)
119 SP   m 1   /KNOCK/DORIS. DUSTY. WAUCHOPE. HORSFALL. KLIPSTEIN.
119 SP   Klip 11 /{Kl} Sam — I should say Loot Sam Wauchope/{Kr} Of the Canadian Expeditionary
121 SA   m 1 {}/Fragment of an Agon/SWEENEY. WAUCHOPE. HORSFALL. KLIPSTEIN.
122 SA   1m 15   /Once is enough. {}/SONG BY WAUCHOPE AND HORSFALL/SWARTS
125 SA   m 31 nothing to you. {}/FULL CHORUS: WAUCHOPE, HORSFALL, KLIPSTEIN,
WAVE (3)
183 FQ: ECoker 210   cold and the empty desolation,/The wave cry, the wind cry, the vast waters/Of the
185 FQ: DrySal 31 the rigging,/The menace and caress of wave that breaks on water,/The distant rote in
233 Skimble   63   help you to get out!/He gives you a wave of his long brown tail/Which says: 'I'll
WAVERING (1)
98 Ash-Wed 6   4   hope/Although I do not hope to turn/Wavering between the profit and the loss/In this
WAVES (6)
17 Prufrock   126 have seen them riding seaward on the waves/Combing the white hair of the waves
17 Prufrock   127 waves/Combing the white hair of the waves blown back/When the wind blows the
27 Morning   5   at area gates./The brown waves of fog toss up to me/Twisted faces from
166 Rock 10   14 and Evil;/Seek not to count the future waves of Time;/But be ye satisfied that you have
187 FQ: DrySal 121 the ragged rock in the restless waters,/Waves wash over it, fogs conceal it;/On a
198 FQ: Little   253   in the stillness/Between two waves of the sea./Quick now, here, now, always
WAVING (1)
562 ES   Carghil 37   /It's another new guest here. He's waving to us./Do you know him, Richard?/{LC}
WAX (1)
18 Portrait   4   this afternoon for you';/And four wax candles in the darkened room,/Four rings
WAY (188)
34 Figlia   14   body it has used./I should find/Some way incomparably light and deft,/Some way we
34 Figlia   15   incomparably light and deft,/Some way we both should understand,/Simple and
40 Burb Blei   13   day./But this or such was Bleistein's way:/A saggy bending of the knees/And elbows,
49 Hippopot   23 he hunts;/God works in a mysterious way —/The Church can sleep and feed at once./
69 WL: Fire S 248 final patronising kiss,/And gropes his way, finding the stairs unlit .../She turns and
86 Hollow Men 95 is/Life is/For Thine is the/*This is the way the world ends*/*This is the way the world ends*
86 Hollow Men 96 *is the way the world ends*/*This is the way the world ends*/*This is the way the world ends*
86 Hollow Men 97 *is the way the world ends*/*This is the way the world ends*/*Not with a bang but a*
104 Journ Magi 35 set down/This: were we led all that way for/Birth or Death? There was a Birth,
108 Animula   35   /And that one who went his own way./Pray for Floret, by the boarhound slain
118 SP   Doris 4   cards —/{Do} There's a lot in the way you pick them up/{Du} There's an awful lot
118 SP   Dusty 5   up/{Du} There's an awful lot in the way you feel/{Do} Sometimes they'll tell you
121 SA Sweeney 27 /Nothing to see but the palmtrees one way/And the sea the other way,/Nothing to
121 SA Sweeney 28   one way/And the sea the other way,/Nothing to hear but the sound of the surf./
127 Corl March 6 that day, or knew the City./This is the way to the temple, and we so many crowding
127 Corl March 6 temple, and we so many crowding the way./So many waiting, how many waiting? what
156 Rock 3   72 call humanity;/Though you forget the way to the Temple,/There is one who
156 Rock 3   73   /There is one who remembers the way to your door:/Life you may evade, but
159 Rock 6   12   attainments/As you can boast in the way of polite society/Will hardly survive the
160 Rock 7   3   is a seed upon the wind: driven this way and that, and finding no place of
161 Rock 7   24   always resuming their march on the way that was lit by the light;/Often halting,
161 Rock 7   25   returning, yet following no other way./But it seems that something has happened
161 Rock 7   37   in high-powered cars on a by-pass way?/VOICE OF THE UNEMPLOYED (*more*
164 Rock 9   14   in a private chamber, learning the way of penitence,/And then let us learn the
166 Rock 10   12   sacrifice of the snake. Take/Your way and be ye separate./Be not too curious of
174 FQ: BurntN 125 of the world of spirit;/This is the one way, and the other/Is the same, not in
179 FQ: ECoker 69 before the ice-cap reigns./That was a way of putting it — not very satisfactory:/A
179 FQ: ECoker 90 middle, not only in the middle of the way/But all the way, in a dark wood, in a
179 FQ: ECoker 91 in the middle of the way/But all the way, in a dark wood, in a bramble,/On the edge
181 FQ: ECoker 139 where you are not,/You must go by a way wherein there is no ecstasy./In order to
181 FQ: ECoker 141 you do not know/You must go by a way which is the way of ignorance./In order to
181 FQ: ECoker 141 /You must go by a way which is the way of ignorance./In order to possess what you
181 FQ: ECoker 143 do not possess/You must go by the way of dispossession./In order to arrive at what
181 FQ: ECoker 145 you are not/You must go through the way in which you are not./And what you do not
182 FQ: ECoker 174 good./So here I am, in the middle way, having had twenty years —/Twenty years
182 FQ: ECoker 179 thing one no longer has to say, or the way in which/One is no longer disposed to say
187 FQ: DrySal 127 —/Among other things — or one way of putting the same thing:/That the future

187 FQ: DrySal	131	that has never been opened./And the way up is the way down, the way forward is the
187 FQ: DrySal	131	been opened./And the way up is the way down, the way forward is the way back./
187 FQ: DrySal	131	/And the way up is the way down, the way forward is the way back./You cannot face
187 FQ: DrySal	131	the way down, the way forward is the way back./You cannot face it steadily, but this
191 FQ: Little	21	/Zero summer?/If you came this way,/Taking the route you would be likely to
191 FQ: Little	24	likely to come from,/If you came in may time, you would find the hedges/
192 FQ: Little	41	and in England./If you came this way,/Taking any route, starting from anywhere,
219 Mung Rump	30	and Rumpelteazer had a wonderful way of working together./And some of the time
222 Pekes Pols	5	they do not like fighting, yet once in a way,/Or now and again, they join in to the fray/
226 Macavity	28	lose some plans and drawings by the way,/There may be a scrap of paper in the hall
230 Bust Jones	29	and mutton./So, much in this way, passes Bustopher's day —/At one club or
589 Fable	66	and bolted most securely,/Gave way — my statement nobody can doubt,/Who
241 MC Mess	34	down their capes,/Strewing the way with leaves and late flowers of the season./
245 MC Priest2	1	us, leave us for France./{P2} What a way to talk at such a juncture!/You are foolish,
247 MC Tempt1	33	roars most loud,/This was not the way of the King our master!/You were not used
253 MC Tempt4	23	ways are closed to you/Except the way already chosen./But what is pleasure,
255 MC Tempt4	12	of heavenly grandeur?/Seek the way of martyrdom, make yourself the lowest/
255 MC Thomas	29	often dreamt them./{T} Is there no way, in my soul's sickness,/Does not lead to
256 MC Priests	27	day, when the traveller may find his way,/The sailor lay course by the sun? {}/
258 MC Thomas	3	and we are destroyed./{T} Now is my way clear, now is the meaning plain:/
258 MC Thomas	8	natural vigour in the venial sin/Is the way in which our lives begin./Thirty years ago, I
273 MC Thomas	19	shall protect her own, in her own way, not/As oak and stone; stone and oak
274 MC Priests	14	*enter, slightly tipsy*]/{3P} This way, my Lord! Quick. Up the stair. To the roof.
277 MC Knight3	22	Archbishop *had* to be put out of the/way — and personally I had a tremendous
278 MC Knight2	32	are times when violence is the only way in/which social justice can be secured. At
279 MC Knight4	16	some surprise at my putting it in this way. But/consider the course of events. I am
286 FR Violet	17	people —/You can keep out of their way at home;/People with money from heaven
289 FR Ivy	24	/Especially to lose anybody in *that* way —/Swept off the deck in the middle of a
291 FR Amy	10	be here now, he has the shortest way to come./John at least, if not Arthur. Hark,
296 FR Agatha	7	understand: hold fast to that/As the way to freedom./{H} I think I see what you
299 FR Downing	18	talk/That are the least likely. To my way of thinking/She only did it to frighten
299 FR Downing	26	used to get rather excited,/And, in a way, irresponsible, Sir./If I may make so bold,
299 FR Downing	29	that a very few cocktails/Went a long way with her Ladyship./She wasn't one of those
304 FR Mary	4	as a hard headmistress/Who knew the way of dominating timid girls./I don't see you
308 FR Mary	10	more real than the other. And in a way you contradict yourself:/That sudden
309 FR Harry	4	away from you./There is only one way for you to understand/And that is by
314 FR Warburt	28	laboratory./We're all of us ill in one way or another:/We call it health when we find
319 FR Harry	6	heard him mentioned, but in some way or another/We felt that he was always here.
326 FR Harry	23	the unimportant./I was like that in a way, so long as I could think/Even of my own
327 FR Harry	17	to alter./Oh, there *must* be another way of talking/That would get us somewhere.
331 FR Harry	26	When I know, I know that in some way I shall find/That I have always known it.
332 FR Harry	39	to the role of murderer./{H} In what way did he wish to murder her?/{Ag} Oh, a
333 FR Agatha	12	womb./I felt that you were in some way mine!/And that in any case I should have
333 FR Harry	14	child./{H} And have me. That is the way things happen./Everything is true in a
337 FR Harry	26	/But I know there is only one way out of defilement —/Which leads in the end
338 FR Harry	23	is where one meets them. That is the way of spectres .../{A} There is no one here!/No
338 FR Harry	29	to seek./I would not have chosen this way, had there been any other!/It is at once the
345 FR Amy	25	are the most malicious in a harmless way;/I prefer your company to that of any of
349 FR Chorus	7	a personal loss —/We have lost our way in the dark./{I} I shall have to stay till after
349 FR Agatha	24	/Each curse has its course/Its own way of expiation/Follow follow/{M} Not in the
350 FR Agatha	13	moon/Follow follow/{Ag} This way the pilgrimage/Of expiation/Round and
357 CP Julia	37	run down and see Lavinia/On my way to Cornwall. But let's be sensible:/Now you
365 CP Julia	19	you have/When Lavinia is out of the way! Who is he?/{E} *I* don't know./{J} *You*
366 CP Peter	15	I don't come with you, Julia? On the way back/I remembered something I had to say
369 CP Peter	35	pictures. So we often met/In the same way, and sometimes went together./And to be
372 CP Peter	2	for me./You know her in a different way from me/And you are so much older./{E}
375 CP Edward	29	I had quite forgotten./He made his way in, a little while ago,/And insisted on
387 CP Celia	6	a human being./Can't you see me that way too, and laugh about it?/{E} I wish I could.
391 CP Alex	26	find out for herself:/That's the only way./{J} How right you are!/Well, my dears, I
394 CP Edward	3	and it was perfectly infuriating,/The way you *didn't* complain .../{L} It was you who
395 CP Lavinia	24	well, you want to grow too./In what way have you changed?/{E} The change that
396 CP Edward	1	corner of the cage./Well, it's a better way of passing the evening/Than listening to the
396 CP Lavinia	25	/I thought that there might be some way out for you/If I went away. I thought that
405 CP Reilly	12	/{R} On the contrary. That is the only way/In which it can be discussed. You have told
412 CP Julia	7	a moment, and slipped in by the back way./I only came to tell you, I am sure she is

413 CP	Celia	15	is interesting;/But I shan't begin that way. I feel perfectly well./I could lead an active
414 CP	Celia	3	the end of an illusion/In the ordinary way, or being ditched./Of course that's
416 CP	Reilly	35	a clue/Towards finding your own way out of the forest./{C} But even if I find my
416 CP	Celia	36	of the forest./{C} But even if I find my way out of the forest/I shall be left with the
418 CP	Celia	19	... still,/If there's no other way ... then I feel just hopeless./{R} There *is*
418 CP	Reilly	20	just hopeless./{R} There *is* another way, if you have the courage./The first I could
418 CP	Reilly	28	there;/You will journey blind. But the way leads towards possession/Of what you have
418 CP	Reilly	31	But what is my duty?/{R} Whichever way you choose will prescribe its own duty./{C}
418 CP	Celia	32	will prescribe its own duty./{C} Which way is better?/{R} Neither way is better./Both
418 CP	Reilly	33	/{C} Which way is better?/{R} Neither way is better./Both ways are necessary. It is also
418 CP	Celia	39	/But glad. I suppose it is a lonely way?/{R} No lonelier than the other. But those
419 CP	Reilly	2	You will not forget yours./Each way means loneliness — and communion./Both
419 CP	Celia	10	quite sure?/{C} I want your second way./So what am I to do?/{R} You will go to
421 CP	Julia	20	suffering they must undergo/On the way of illumination?/{R} Will she be frightened/
421 CP	Julia	32	but confidence./{J} That's one way in which I am so useful to you./You ought
422 CP	Reilly	3	good. {}/[*To* JULIA]/{R} He's on his way up. {}/[*Into telephone*]/{R} You may bring
426 CP	Julia	32	/And you know what *they* offer in the way of food and drink!/And I've had to miss my
431 CP	Peter	32	I'm English/I ought to know the best way to handle a duke./Besides that, we've got
433 CP	Peter	2	not my business;/And that's not the way we do it./{J} But, Peter;/If you're taking
436 CP	Lavinia	23	from your expression/That the way in which she died did not disturb you/Or
436 CP	Lavinia	31	showed no surprise or horror/At the way in which she died. I don't know if you
437 CP	Reilly	25	/Because it was for her to choose the way of life/To lead to death, and, without
437 CP	Reilly	28	not know that she would die in this way;/*She* did not know. So all that I could do/
437 CP	Reilly	30	I could do/Was to direct her in the way of preparation./That way, which she
437 CP	Reilly	31	her in the way of preparation./That way, which she accepted, led to this death./And
438 CP	Edward	23	cannot help the feeling/That, in some way, my responsibility/Is greater than that of a
439 CP	Julia	12	take the consequences. Celia chose/A way of which the consequence was Kinkanja./
439 CP	Julia	13	was Kinkanja./Peter chose a way that leads him to Boltwell/And he's got to
445 CC	Claude	3	to bring you up to London/All the way from Joshua Park, on an errand like this./
445 CC	Claude	6	I couldn't send Colby./That's not the way to arrange their first meeting,/On her
446 CC	Claude	20	/I thought he would fall into this way of life more quickly/If we started on a
447 CC	Claude	35	/That she chose him herself. By the way, don't forget/To let her know that he's very
447 CC	Claude	39	that. Music./{SC} And by the way,/How much have you actually told him
449 CC	Claude	3	child *she* lost./{SC} In a very different way, yes. You might say *mislaid*,/Since the
449 CC	Claude	4	the father is dead, and there's no way of tracing it./Yes, I was thinking of her
451 CC	Eggers	21	why can't you make me laugh/The way B. Kaghan did?' She's only met him once;/
451 CC	Eggers	25	liked it. Muriel *is* her name./He has a way with the ladies, you know./But with Lady
452 CC	Eggers	39	know that./{E} You mustn't give way to her, Mr. Simpkins./I never do. I always
453 CC	Lucasta	15	be nice to me/When you're out of the way. Why don't you let him speak?/Eggy's
455 CC	Eggers	21	the end. He's a man who gets his own way,/And I think he can manage her. If anyone
456 CC	Colby	12	Elizabeth very unusual/In any other way, besides being a lady?/{E} Why, yes, indeed,
461 CC	Eggers	17	'We couldn't ask him to come/All the way to Joshua Park, at this time of year!'/I said:
461 CC	Claude	31	/So the meeting didn't go quite the way I'd intended;/And yet I believe that it's all
463 CC	Colby	11	Yes, how do you find it?/{C} In a way, exhilarating./To find there is something
463 CC	Colby	14	previous interests./It gives me, in a way, a kind of self-confidence/I've never had
467 CC	Colby	30	don't want my position/To be, in any way, a make-believe./{SC} It shan't be.
472 CC	Colby	18	is nothing like mine./{C} In what way is it different?/{L} It's hard to explain./
474 CC	Lucasta	9	awfully religious./Is there no other way of making it real to you?/{C} It's simply the
474 CC	Colby	19	walking with me./That's the only way I can think of putting it./{L} How afraid
476 CC	Lucasta	9	Does that matter, either?/{L} In one way, it matters. A little while ago/You said,
477 CC	Lucasta	10	been. He's been good to me/In his way. But I'm always a reminder to him/Of
479 CC	Lucasta	9	for Lizzie,/You'd better not get in *her* way when she's hunting./But all that matters
479 CC	Kaghan	33	to live down./— I must say, I like the way you've had the place done up./{C} It was
487 CC	Claude	11	to write a speech for me./Oh, by the way, Colby, how's the piano?/{C} It's a
490 CC	Lady E	4	/{LE} Very well then./That is the way it must have happened./Oh, Claude, you
491 CC	Claude	17	/Could you accept us both in that way, Colby?/{C} I can only say what I feel at the
493 CC	Claude	20	a subject/In a roundabout way. But where shall we place her?/{LE} Over
494 CC	Claude	18	see that what I had interpreted/In this way, was something else to *him* —/An idea, an
502 CC	Lucasta	12	/It wouldn't have been like you — the way I thought it was./You're much too ...
502 CC	Lucasta	14	... detached, ever to be shocked/In the way I thought you were. I was ashamed/Of
503 CC	Lucasta	3	not necessary to each other/In the way we might have been. But a different way/
503 CC	Lucasta	3	we might have been. But a different way/That reveals itself in time. And perhaps —
505 CC	Eggers	25	I don't understand you./{E} It's this way, Mrs. Guzzard./It is only recently that
506 CC	Guzzard	19	I had a child, and lost him. Not in the way/That Lady Elizabeth's child was lost./Let
508 CC	Eggers	6	/If you had lost your son, in a similar way,/Wouldn't you grasp at any straw/That

WE'LL (27)

118 SP	Wauch	28	till I put the car round the corner/We'll be right up/{Du} All right, come up./(to
123 SA	Kl & Kr	19	/And we won't go home when it rains/We'll gather hibiscus flowers/For it won't be
267 MC	Knight3	1	God for you, in your need?/{K3} Yes, we'll pray for you!/{K1} Yes, we'll pray for you!
267 MC	Knight1	2	Yes, we'll pray for you!/{K1} Yes, we'll pray for you!/{3K} Yes, we'll pray that
267 MC	Knights	3	Yes, we'll pray for you!/{3K} Yes, we'll pray that God may help you!/{T} But,
322 FR	Winch	34	a lorry/Drawn up round the bend. We'll have the driver up for this:/Says he
323 FR	Warburt	15	matter like this. You can trust Owen./We'll bring him up tomorrow; and a few days'
348 FR	Warburt	1	so serious as Winchell made out,/And we'll have him up here in the morning./I hope
355 CP	Julia	17	/[EDWARD *leaves the room*]/{J} No, we'll wait until Edward comes back into the
359 CP	Edward	8	/{E} Don't go yet./Don't go yet. We'll finish the cocktails./Or would you rather
368 CP	Alex	17	/Which you can have alone. And then we'll leave you./Meanwhile, you and Peter can
377 CP	Julia	2	my dear, you give me that apron/And we'll see what I can do. You stay and talk to
391 CP	Julia	2	them alone, and let Lavinia rest./Now we'll all go back to *my* house. Peter, call a taxi.
391 CP	Julia	3	Peter, call a taxi. {}/[*Exit* PETER]/{J} We'll have a cocktail party at *my* house to-day./
447 CC	Claude	1	will find them if anybody./{SC} Well, we'll leave that for the present. As we have a
471 CC	Lucasta	8	me bits yourself, and explained them./We'll begin my education at once./{C} I suspect
487 CC	Claude	6	last about ten minutes./And then we'll go over it tomorrow. {}/[*looking at the*
501 CC	Claude	38	to make my peace with him./{SC} We'll get him now. {}/[*Reaches for the*
503 CC	Lucasta	18	need you, both of you, Lucasta!/{L} We'll mean something to you. But you don't
503 CC	Lucasta	31	always changing./When I come back, we'll be brother and sister —/Or so I hope. Yes,
515 CC	Claude	39	Or, perhaps, for the better?/Perhaps we'll be happier together if you think/I am not
517 CC	Eggers	40	I'm afraid. Not enough to live on./We'll have to think of other ways/Of making up
518 CC	Colby	12	a precentorship! And a canonry!/{C} We'll cross that bridge when we come to it,
537 ES	Gomez	9	of steel, and all that sort of thing./We'll come to that, very soon. Isn't it strange/
557 ES	Ld Clav	4	to the point. You're in trouble again./We'll ignore, if you please, the question of
565 ES	Carghil	23	about it. Perhaps I could advise you./We'll leave you now, Richard. Au revoir,
566 ES	Ld Clav	1	and I shall go to school together./We'll sit side by side, at little desks/And suffer

WE'RE (42)

117 SP	Doris	17	might be you/{Do} Or it might be you/We're all hearts. You can't be sure./It just
125 SA	Sweeney	25	you/We all gotta do what we gotta do/We're gona sit here and drink this booze/We're
125 SA	Sweeney	26	gona sit here and drink this booze/We're gona sit here and have a tune/We're gona
125 SA	Sweeney	27	/We're gona sit here and have a tune/We're gona stay and we're gona go/And
125 SA	Sweeney	27	and have a tune/We're gona stay and we're gona go/And somebody's gotta pay the
230 Bust	Jones	11	name of this Brummell of Cats;/And we're all of us proud to be nodded or bowed to/
232 Skimble		15	/And the signal goes 'All Clear!'/And we're off at last for the northern part/Of the
298 FR	Charles	37	the truth, now that we've seen him,/We're a little worried about his health./He
314 FR	Warburt	28	thinking in terms of the laboratory./We're all of us ill in one way or another:/We
353 CP	Celia	21	know it./{C} Do we all know it?/But we're never tired of hearing *you* tell it./I don't
367 CP	Peter	13	me we had a great deal in common./We're both of us artists./{E} I never thought of
389 CP	Peter	7	ambitions./You're going together?/{P} We're not going together./Celia told us she was
393 CP	Edward	11	me./It struck me very differently. As we're on the subject,/I thought that it was I who
427 CP	Julia	3	of his mysterious expeditions,/And we're going to get him to tell us all about it./But
431 CP	Peter	16	Duke?/{P} And do him a good turn./We're making a film of English life/And we
431 CP	Peter	20	/{P} Exactly. It is. And that's why we're interested./The most decayed noble
431 CP	Julia	40	casting director/To take us all over? We're all very typical./{P} No, I'm afraid .../
432 CP	Edward	5	Sir Henry Harcourt-Reilly —/{E} We're delighted to see him. But we *have* met
433 CP	Peter	6	/Why can't you take me?/{P} We're not taking Boltwell./We reconstruct a
440 CP	Julia	19	/{J} Now, Henry. Now, Alex. We're going to the Gunnings. {}/[*Exeunt*
481 CC	Lucasta	17	arrived, or are you just leaving?/{L} We're on the point of leaving, Lady Elizabeth./
481 CC	Kaghan	24	it. Did you say you were leaving?/{K} We're going out to dinner. Lucasta's very
496 CC	Eggers	37	around this season,/When we're getting near the anniversary./{SC} The
500 CC	Claude	9	is the reason for this meeting today./We're awaiting Mrs. Guzzard — Colby's aunt./
500 CC	Lucasta	36	thought of me/Simply as a nuisance. We're suited to each other/You thought so too,
501 CC	Lucasta	5	well why *you* think so:/*You* think we're suited because we're both common./B.
501 CC	Lucasta	5	so:/*You* think we're suited because we're both common./B. knows you think him
503 CC	Lucasta	2	each other. And accept the fact/That we're not necessary to each other/In the way we
503 CC	Lucasta	30	changed since then: as you said, we're always changing./When I come back, we'll
524 ES	Monica	24	all appear to be avoiding his eye./{M} We're getting off the point .../{C} You've got me
526 ES	Monica	21	—/The meanings are different. Look! We're back in The room/That we entered only a
526 ES	Monica	31	tea. {}/[*Exit* LAMBERT]/{M} — Now we're in the public world./{C} And your father
527 ES	Monica	2	understand him;/In the second place, we're not engaged yet./{C} Aren't we? We're
527 ES	Charles	3	we're not engaged yet./{C} Aren't we? We're agreed that we're in love with each other,
527 ES	Charles	3	yet./{C} Aren't we? We're agreed that we're in love with each other,/And, there being
532 ES	Gomez	32	a friend of Mr. Culverwell?/{G} We're as thick as thieves, you might almost say.

540 ES   Gomez   1   success, Dick. In another sense/We're both of us failures. But even so,/I'd
553 ES   Carghil 15   yours./It's frightening to think that we're still together/And more frightening to
565 ES   Gomez   26   obey our doctors' orders./But while we're here, we must have some good talks/
567 ES   Monica   15   said we weren't engaged yet .../{M} We're engaged now./At least *I'm* engaged. I'm
578 ES   Michael 32   shall be./We don't meet often, but if we're fond of each other,/That needn't interfere
579 ES   Michael 8   get a passage./And I must buy my kit. We're just going up to London./Señor Gomez

WE'VE (25)
116 SP   Doris   19   /Say I broke my leg on the stairs/Say we've had a fire/{Du} Hello Hello are you there?
235 Ad-dress   51   heard them call him James —/But we've not got so far as names./Before a Cat will
298 FR   Charles 36   years;/And to tell the truth, now that we've seen him,/We're a little worried about his
314 FR   Warburt 7   engagement to come./{W} I dare say we've both changed a good deal, Harry./A
322 FR   Winch   36   /And stopped to take his bearings. We've got him at the Arms —/Mr. John, I
364 CP   Edward   7   happened/During the five years that we've been married./I must find out who she is,
424 CP   Lavinia 17   Edward, that's unfair!/You know that we've given *several* parties/In the last two years.
431 CP   Peter   23   least, of any that are still inhabited./We've got a team of experts over/To study the
431 CP   Peter   33   way to handle a duke./Besides that, we've got the casting director/He's looking for
432 CP   Lavinia 14   Sir Henry,/You are the perfect guest we've been waiting for./{R} I should not dream
432 CP   Julia   32   met./{R} On several commissions./{J} We've been having such an interesting
456 CC   Eggers   31   Park/(On a mortgage, of course) 'now we've settled down/All the travel *I* want is up to
462 CC   Claude   30   deliberately left you alone,/And so far we've discussed only current business,/Thinking
475 CC   Lucasta 31   don't matter, in a sense./But now we've got to this point — you might as well
497 CC   Eggers   3   I am, talking about ourselves!/And we've more important business, I imagine./{SC}
501 CC   Lucasta 8   think so./*You* gave us our parts. And we've shown that we can play them./{LE} I
503 CC   Lucasta 30   to the Lucasta whom Colby knew./We've changed since then: as you said, we're
517 CC   Eggers   28   we had/Died two months ago. We've been looking for another./{C} Do you
519 CC   Lady E   15   But I mean to do better./Claude, we've got to try to understand our children./{K}
546 ES   Piggott 10   'Matron'/At Badgley Court. You see, we've studied to avoid/Anything like a
546 ES   Piggott 21   guest who's incurable./You know, we've been deluged with applications/From
548 ES   Carghil 32   I'd know you anywhere./But then, we've all seen your portrait in the papers/So
565 ES   Gomez   25   *and* MICHAEL]/{G} Well, Dick, we've got to obey our doctors' orders./But while
580 ES   Carghil 23   you news of Michael./And now that we've found each other again,/We must always
582 ES   Monica   32   together./And yet, Charles, though we've been alone to-day/Only a few minutes,

WEAK (16)
38 Gerontion   42   passion. Gives too soon/Into weak hands, what's thought can be dispensed
49 Hippopot   5   flesh and blood./Flesh and blood is weak and frail,/Susceptible to nervous shock;/
98 Ash-Wed 6   13   lilac and the lost sea voices/And the weak spirit quickens to rebel/For the bent
109 Marina   25   forgotten/And remember./The rigging weak and the canvas rotten/Between one June
177 FQ: ECoker   27   you can hear the music/Of the weak pipe and the little drum/And see them
212 Growltiger   13   ON THE LOOSE!/Woe to the weak canary, that fluttered from its cage;/Woe
233 Skimble   42   /'Do you like your morning tea weak or strong?'/But Skimble's just behind him
602 Humoresque   3   not yet tired of the game —/But weak in body as in head,/(A jumping-jack has
241 MC   Priest3   3   rule:/The strong man strongly and the weak man by caprice./They have but one law, to
280 MC   Priest3   17   so long as men will die for it./Go, weak sad men, lost erring souls, homeless in
304 FR   Agatha   36   fight them — with the weapons of the weak,/Which are too violent. And it could not
320 FR   Warburt   11   moment. The whole machine is weak/And running down. Her heart's very
332 FR   Agatha   1   of a solitary man:/Where he was weak he recognised your mother's power,/And
490 CC   Lady E   5   /Oh, Claude, you know I'm rather weak in the head/Though I try to be clever. Do
550 ES   Carghil   20   {LC} Is he still living?/{MC} He had a weak heart./And he worked too hard. Have you
563 ES   Gomez   25   John Carghill./{G} We seem a bit weak on the surnames, Dick!/{MC} Well, you

WEAKER (1)
242 MC   Priest1   29   the King been greater, or had he been weaker/Things had perhaps been different for

WEAKLING (2)
342 FR   Amy   8   myself believe/That he was not such a weakling as his father/In the hands of any
550 ES   Carghil   15   /How true that is! Algy was a weakling,/But simple he was — not sly and

WEAKNESS (6)
173 FQ: BurntN   82   of past and future/Woven in the weakness of the changing body,/Protects
253 MC   Tempt4   6   morsels of the past./Wantonness is weakness. As for the King,/His hardened hatred
282 MC   Chorus   12   /We acknowledge our trespass, our weakness, our fault; we acknowledge/That the
331 FR   Agatha   38   /He hid his strength beneath unusual weakness,/The diffidence of a solitary man:/
340 FR   Amy   25   go. I abased myself./Did I show any weakness, any self-pity?/I forced myself to the
571 ES   Ld Clav   11   his term./Was I responsible for that weakness in him?/Yes, I was./How easily we

WEALTH (1)
494 CC   Claude   16   that what he cared for was power and wealth;/And I came to see that what I had

WEALTHY (2)
571 ES Ld Clav   1   /There is Mrs. John Carghill, the wealthy widow./But Freddy Culverwell and
574 ES Carghil 19   not appeal to Señor Gomez?/He's a wealthy man, and very important/In his own
WEAPONS (2)
201 Def Island   17   /of their ancestors' ways but the weapons/and those again for whom the paths of
304 FR Agatha 36 /She wanted to fight them — with the weapons of the weak,/Which are too violent.
WEAR (4)
 16 Prufrock   121   /I grow old ... I grow old .../I shall wear the bottoms of my trousers rolled./Shall I
 16 Prufrock   123   Do I dare to eat a peach?/I shall wear white flannel trousers, and walk upon the
 84 Hollow Men   31   death's dream kingdom/Let me also wear/Such deliberate disguises/Rat's coat,
122 SAWa & Ho   32 *Gauguin maids/In the banyan shades/Wear palmleaf drapery/Under the bam/Under the*
WEARILY (1)
 28 Boston ET   7   the steps and ring the bell, turning/Wearily, as one would turn to nod good-bye to
WEARINESS (1)
155 Rock 3   59   who knows how to ask questions./O weariness of men who turn from GOD/To the
WEARING (4)
 94 Ash-Wed 4   14 in the time between sleep and waking, wearing/White light folded, sheathed about her,
117 SP   Dusty 10 small sum of money, or a present/Of wearing apparel, or a party'./That's queer too./
364 CP Edward   4 /I'm sure I don't know what she was wearing/When I saw her last. And yet I want
424 CP Edward   25 it's all over./{E} I like the dress you're wearing:/I'm glad you put on that one./{L}
WEARS (3)
 92 Ash-Wed 3   5   with the devil of the stairs who wears/The deceitful face of hope and of despair.
231 Bust Jones   40 in Pall Mall/While Bustopher Jones wears white spats!/Skimbleshanks: the Railway
530 ES Monica   8   /Sources of the power that wears out the machine./{LC} They've dried up,
WEARY (1)
599 On a Port   2 unknown/To us of restless brain and weary feet,/Forever hurrying, up and down the
WEASEL (1)
316 FR Agatha   17 well/Be at last straightened/May the weasel and the otter/Be about their proper
WEATHER (12)
 34 Figlia   17   turned away, but with the autumn weather/Compelled my imagination many days,
103 Journ Magi   4 long journey:/The ways deep and the weather sharp,/The very dead of winter.'/And
147 Rock 1   30 /To Hindhead, or Maidenhead./If the weather is foul we stay at home and read the
187 FQ: DrySal 123 it is merely a monument,/In navigable weather it is always a seamark/To lay a course
219 Mung Rump   31 some of the time you would say it was weather./They would go through the house like
300 FRDowning   4 Lady./Tried to keep her in when the weather was rough,/Didn't like to see her lean
323 FR Warburt 30 nothing you could do, and out in this weather/At this time of night, I would not
329 FR Chorus 26   for the news/We must listen to the weather report/And the international
343 FR   Amy   24 tiles on the roof, combat the endless weather,/Resist the wind? fight with increasing
544 ES Monica   24 /{M} Oh, let's make the most of this weather while it lasts./I never remember you as
547 ES Piggott   6 at this time of year;/This early warm weather can be very treacherous./There, now
556 ES Michael 13 /I'm glad you're here, to enjoy such weather./{LC} You're glad I'm here? Did you
WEAVE (6)
 34 Figlia   3   the stair —/Lean on a garden urn —/Weave, weave the sunlight in your hair —/Clasp
 34 Figlia   3   —/Lean on a garden urn —/Weave, weave the sunlight in your hair —/Clasp your
 34 Figlia   7 fugitive resentment in your eyes:/But weave, weave the sunlight in your hair./So I
 34 Figlia   7 resentment in your eyes:/But weave, weave the sunlight in your hair./So I would
 38 Gerontion   30   hand on the door. Vacant shuttles/Weave the wind. I have no ghosts,/An old man
280 MC Priest3 33   a fiction which unravels as you weave,/Pacing forever in the hell of
WEAVING (3)
597 Before Mor   1   Morning/While all the East was weaving red with gray,/The flowers at the
280 MC Priest3 33 to justify your action to yourselves,/Weaving a fiction which unravels as you weave,/
335 FR Harry   14 Of shrieking forms in a circular desert/Weaving with contagion of putrescent embraces
WEB (2)
205 de la Mare   32 natural ease;/By the delicate, invisible web you wove —/The inexplicable mystery of
568 ES Ld Clav 36 she's grown/You've woven such a web of fiction about you!/I've spent my life in
WEBSTER (1)
 52 Whispers   1 haute taille./Whispers of Immortality/Webster was much possessed by death/And saw
WEDDING (11)
304 FR Agatha   33 her,/The only one Harry asked to his wedding:/Amy did not know that. I was sorry
353 CP Celia   14   day, about Lady Klootz and the wedding cake./{P} And how the butler found
354 CP Celia   21 /{C} Go on with the story about the wedding cake./{J} Well, but it really isn't my
355 CP Peter   16 /{P} Go on with the story about the wedding cake. {}/[EDWARD *leaves the room*]/
355 CP Julia   30 Lady Klootz./It was at the Vincewell wedding. Oh, so many years ago! {}/[*To the*
356 CP Celia   14 /{C} Go on with the story about the wedding cake./{J} Edward, do sit down for a
358 CP Celia   16 /{J} What Lady Klootz?/{C} And the wedding cake./{J} Wedding cake? I wasn't at her

358 CP   Julia   17   /{C} And the wedding cake./{J} Wedding cake? I wasn't at her wedding./
358 CP   Julia   17   /{J} Wedding cake? I wasn't at her wedding./Edward, it's been a delightful evening:
511 CC   Lady E 37   /Lucasta, I shall take charge of your wedding./{L} We'd meant to be married very
512 CC   Lady E 1   office./{LE} You must have a church wedding./{MG} I am glad to hear you say so,
WEDDINGS (2)
117 SP   Doris   33   mine. I'm sure it's mine./I dreamt of weddings all last night./Yes it's mine. I know
148 Rock 1   37   and in the town/Only for important weddings./CHORUS LEADER:/Silence! and
WEED (1)
193 FQ: Little   73   /The town, the pasture and the weed./Water and fire deride/The sacrifice that
WEEK (14)
 49 Hippopot   19   inflexions hoarse and odd,/But every week we hear rejoice/The Church, at being one
107 Animula   18   and offends more, day by day;/Week by week, offends and perplexes more/
107 Animula   18   offends more, day by day;/Week by week, offends and perplexes more/With the
129 Cor2 State   13   /At a salary of one pound ten a week rising by annual increments of five
129 Cor2 State   14   of five shillings/To two pounds ten a week; with a bonus of thirty shillings a
222 Pekes Pols   12   nothing had happened for nearly a week/(And that's a long time for a Pol or a
225 Mr Mistoff   36   then it is *gawn*!/But you'll find it next week lying out on the lawn./And we all say:
601 Nocturne   12   need of 'Love forever?' — 'Love next week?')/While female readers all in tears are
426 CP   Edward 17   get away soon?/{E} By the end of next week/I shall be quite free./{L} And we can be
430 CP   Peter   12   and Lavinia./I'm only over for a week, you see,/And I'm driving down to the
431 CP   Peter   12   it was Bela sent me over/Just for a week. And I have my hands full/I'm going down
470 CC   Lucasta 2   me/The piano was only delivered this week/And you had it tuned yesterday. Still, I'm
496 CC   Eggers 21   being up in London five or six days a week:/But now she says: 'You're becoming such
532 ES   Charles 25   you both at Badgley Court/In a week or two. {}/[*Enter* LAMBERT]/{L} Mr.
WEEK'S (2)
129 Cor2 State   15   thirty shillings at Christmas/And one week's leave a year./A committee has been
453 CC   Kaghan 35   is, that I'm penniless./{K} She's had a week's salary in lieu of notice./{L} B., remember
WEEKEND (1)
 68 WL: Fire S 214   Cannon Street Hotel/Followed by a weekend at the Metropole./At the violet hour,
WEEKENDS (1)
529 ES   Monica 2   constituency!/You can come down at weekends, even when the House is sitting./And
WEEKS (6)
318 FR   Harry   8   to make up to mother/For all the weeks during which she had not seen us/Except
357 CP   Julia   20   Edward,/Lavinia may be away for weeks,/Or she may come back and be called
399 CP   3m   1   *room in London. Morning:/several weeks later.* SIR HENRY *alone at his desk. He*
413 CP   Celia   22   I've been going through, these last weeks,/I somehow took it for granted that I
434 CP   Alex   9   /They must have been overworked for weeks./{E} And then?/{A} And then, the
469 CC   2m   1   /*Act Two/The flat in the mews a few weeks later.* COLBY *is seated at the piano;/*
WEEP (1)
178 FQ: ECoker 64   the Sun and Moon go down/Comets weep and Leonids fly/Hunt the heavens and the
WEEPING (3)
 45 Cook Egg   32   /Over buttered scones and crumpets/Weeping, weeping multitudes/Droop in a
 45 Cook Egg   32   scones and crumpets/Weeping, weeping multitudes/Droop in a hundred
264 MC   Priest3 20   of thy saints. In Rama, a voice heard, weeping./Out of the mouth of very babes, O
WEEVIL (1)
 39 Gerontion   66   do,/Suspend its operations, will the weevil/Delay? De Bailhache, Fresca, Mrs.
WEHT (1)
 61 WL: Burial   31   you fear in a handful of dust./*Frisch weht der Wind/Der Heimat zu/Mein Irisch Kind/*
WEIALALA (2)
 69 WL: Fire S 277   reach/Past the Isle of Dogs./Weialala leia/Wallala leialala/Elizabeth and
 70 WL: Fire S 290   stream/The peal of bells/White towers/Weialala leia/Wallala leialala/'Trams and dusty
WEIGHS (2)
265 MC   Priest3 5   fear from or hope from. One moment/Weighs like another. Only in retrospection,
421 CP   Julia   10   see./It's the thought of Celia that weighs upon my mind./{R} Of Celia?/{J} Of
WEIGHT (1)
231 Bust Jones   34   I am a bounder,/And he's putting on weight every day:/But he's so well preserved
WEIGHTIER (1)
248 MC   Tempt2 20   /In balance against other, earlier/And weightier ones: those of the Chancellorship./See
WEILEST (1)
 62 WL: Burial   34   /*Der Heimat zu/Mein Irisch Kind/Wo weilest du?/*'You gave me hyacinths first a year
WELCOME (16)
 68 WL: Fire S 242   requires no response,/And makes a welcome of indifference./(And I Tiresias have
162 Rock 8   1   Usury, Lust and Power./O Father we welcome your words,/And we will take heart for
243 MC   Priest2 5   rejoice, and show a glad face for his welcome./I am the Archbishop's man. Let us
243 MC   Priest2 6   man. Let us give the Archbishop welcome!/{P3} For good or ill, let the wheel

245 MC	Priest2	10	on pleasant faces,/And give a hearty welcome to our good Archbishop. {}/[*Enter*
245 MC	Priest2	25	Lord, you would have had a better welcome/If we had been sooner prepared for the
265 MC	Priest1	11	/{P1} And known to us./You are welcome. Have you ridden far?/{K1} Not far
266 MC	Thomas	7	{}/[*To* KNIGHTS]./{T} You are welcome, whatever your business may be./You
291 FR	Ivy	14	*the door and stares at the window*]/{I} Welcome, Harry!/{G} Well done!/{V} Welcome
291 FR	Violet	16	Welcome, Harry!/{G} Well done!/{V} Welcome home to Wishwood!/{C} Why, what's
326 FR	Violet	32	Harry;/My comments are not always welcome in this family. {}/[*Enter* DENMAN]/
390 CP	Alex	20	{A} Has Lavinia arrived?/{E} Yes./{A} Welcome back, Lavinia!/When I got your
427 CP	Alex	18	one to whom they give the warmest welcome./I know them well enough for that./{J}
526 ES	Charles	33	his calm possessive air/And his kindly welcome, which is always a reminder/That I
542 ES	Gomez	38	going./I hope I haven't outstayed my welcome?/Your telephone pal may be getting
581 ES	Charles	4	We will indeed. We shall be ready to welcome him/And give all the aid we can. But

WELCOMED (1)

| 542 ES | Ld Clav | 25 | tastes already/You would hardly have welcomed my companionship./{G} Neatly |

WELD (1)

| 279 MC | Knight4 | 19 | no one, under the King, did more to weld the/country together, to give it the unity, |

WELFARE (1)

| 278 MC | Knight2 | 39 | the pretensions of the Church to/the welfare of the State, remember that it is we who |

WELL (332)

WELL'S (1)

| 588 Fable | | 44 | afraid/I don't know much about — as well's I'm able/I'll go through the account: They |

WELL-BEING (1)

| 186 FQ: DrySal | | 92 | of happiness — not the sense of well-being,/Fruition, fulfilment, security or |

WELL-BRED (2)

| 482 CC | Lady E | 36 | /Because, what's surprising, well-bred people/Are sometimes far from |
| 483 CC | Lady E | 2 | that's not all./You need intellectual, well-bred people/Of spirituality — and that's |

WELL-CUT (1)

| 230 Bust Jones | | 7 | /No commonplace mousers have such well-cut trousers/Or such an impeccable back./ |

WELL-DISCIPLINED (1)

| 211 Old Gumbie | | 34 | lot of disorderly louts,/A troop of well-disciplined helpful boy-scouts,/With a |

WELL-KNOWN (2)

| 289 FR | Charles | 27 | never even to recover the body./{C} 'Well-known Peeress Vanishes from Liner'./{G} |
| 554 ES | Piggott | 34 | As Maisie Montjoy in revue./She was well-known at one time. I'm afraid her name/ |

WELL-ORDERED (1)

| 211 Old Gumbie | | 38 | us now give three cheers —/On whom well-ordered households depend, it appears./ |

WELL-PRESERVED (1)

| 136 5FingerEx3 | | 14 | the enquiring worm shall try/Our well-preserved complacency./*Lines to Ralph* |

WELL-SUITED (1)

| 409 CP | Reilly | 8 | I consider/That you are exceptionally well-suited to each other./Mr. Chamberlayne, |

WELLBEING (1)

| 544 ES | Ld Clav | 16 | hope that it will last —/The sense of wellbeing! It's often with us/When we are |

WELLINGTON (1)

| 222 Pekes Pols | | 16 | people think/He'd slipped into the Wellington Arms for a drink —/And no one at |

WELLS (1)

| 73 WL: Thund | | 384 | out of empty cisterns and exhausted wells./In this decayed hole among the |

WENCH (1)

| 250 MC | Tempt3 | 27 | no courtier./I know a horse, a dog, a wench;/I know how to hold my estates in order, |

WENT (44)

61 WL: Burial		10	we stopped in the colonnade,/And went on in sunlight, into the Hofgarten,/And
61 WL: Burial		16	/Marie, hold on tight. And down we went./In the mountains, there you feel free./I
105 Song Sime		12	and taken honour and ease./There went never any rejected from my door./Who
108 Animula		35	a great fortune,/And that one who went his own way./Pray for Floret, by the
124 SA Sweeney		28	end/But that's another story too./This went on for a couple of months/Nobody came/
124 SA Sweeney		30	months/Nobody came/And nobody went/But he took in the milk and he paid the
157 Rock 4		10	/That he might rebuild the city./So he went, with a few, to Jerusalem,/And there, by
162 Rock 8		15	/Like all men in all places,/Some went from love of glory,/Some went who were
162 Rock 8		16	/Some went from love of glory,/Some went who were restless and curious,/Some were
261 MC	Thomas	2	disciples/knew no such things: they went forth to journey afar, to suffer by land/and
294 FR	Harry	36	/I had always supposed, wherever I went/That she would be with me; whatever I did
295 FR	Harry	1	sense./I expected to find her when I went back to the cabin./Later, I became excited,
299 FRDowning		29	thought that a very few cocktails/Went a long way with her Ladyship./She wasn't
300 FRDowning		28	/And I took a bit of air before I went to bed,/And you could see the corner of
317 FR	Harry	24	/When we were children, before we went to school,/The rule of conduct was simply
319 FR	Harry	5	I was kept apart from him, till he went away./We never heard him mentioned, but
319 FR	Warburt	17	separated by mutual consent/And he went to live abroad. You were only a boy/When

325 FR	Violet	38	everyone staring;/And the pace he went at was simply terrifying./I said I would
356 CP	Julia	30	/I believe that's the reason why she went away —/So that I could make you talk.
369 CP	Peter	33	conversation/And I found that she went to concerts alone/And to look at pictures.
369 CP	Peter	35	met/In the same way, and sometimes went together./And to be with Celia, that was
396 CP	Lavinia	26	might be some way out for you/If I went away. I thought that if I died/To you, I
405 CP	Reilly	16	up your case/So to speak, as you went along. A barrister/Ought to know his brief
412 CP	Julia	6	not. I dropped her at the door/And went on in the taxi, round the corner;/Waited a
416 CP	Celia	38	memory/Of the treasure I went into the forest to find/And never found,
458 CC	Lady E	16	manage to change your ticket?/{LE} I went to the agency and got them to change it./I
460 CC	Lady E	2	who teaches mind control.'/So on I went to Zürich./{SC} So on you went to Zürich.
460 CC	Claude	3	on I went to Zürich./{SC} So on you went to Zürich./But I thought that the doctor in
460 CC	Claude	34	ELIZABETH]/{SC} She actually went and changed her own ticket./It's
461 CC	Claude	33	I believe that it's all for the best./It went off very well. It's very obvious/That she
504 CC	Claude	3	mentioned it/If *I* was late when I went to see her. {}/[*Enter* LUCASTA]/{L} I'm
514 CC	Guzzard	37	/Till you deceived yourself. When you went to Canada/My sister found that she was to
515 CC	Guzzard	18	certificate./You never did. And so it went on./{SC} This is horribly plausible. But it
535 ES	Gomez	29	—/The same age as you — when I went away,/Thousands of miles away, to
537 ES	Gomez	12	Well, consider what we were when we went up to Oxford/And then what I became
537 ES	Gomez	27	tutor thought you'd be sent down./It went the other way. You stayed the course, at
537 ES	Gomez	31	liked to play the rake,/But you never went too far. There's a prudent devil/Inside you,
538 ES	Gomez	38	from the world of politics/And went into the City. Director of a bank/And
539 ES	Gomez	35	/In a school like that from which I went to Oxford./As it is, I'm somebody — a
549 ES	Carghil	13	/But such a good lunch — and we all went in a punt/On the river — and we had a tea
557 ES	Michael	24	whom?/Not ... from the firm?/{Mi} I went to a lender,/A man whom a friend of mine
564 ES	Carghil	26	it. After Oxford/I suppose you went back to ... where is your home?/{G} The
564 ES	Carghil	28	{G} The republic of San Marco./{MC} Went back to San Marco./Señor Gomez, if it's
575 ES	Gomez	27	of *my* morals:/Though of course you went a little *faster* than I did./{LC} On that

WEPT (4)

15 Prufrock		81	to its crisis?/But though I have wept and fasted, wept and prayed,/Though I
15 Prufrock		81	/But though I have wept and fasted, wept and prayed,/Though I have seen my head
67 WL: Fire S		182	the waters of Leman I sat down and wept .../Sweet Thames, run softly till I end my
70 WL: Fire S		298	/Under my feet. After the event/He wept. He promised "a new start."/I made no

WERE (323)

WEREN'T (6)

419 CP	Celia	15	again —/I don't mean to say they weren't much better for it —/That's why I came
466 CC	Colby	35	/It would be so much simpler if you *weren't* my father!/I was struck by what you said,
479 CC	Lucasta	27	her cross the threshold./{L} As if you weren't as afraid of her as anybody!/{K} Well,
536 ES	Gomez	4	merely a step up the ladder,/So you weren't aware of becoming a different person:/
563 ES	Gomez	9	/{LC} Good morning, Fred./{G} You weren't expecting me to join you here, were
567 ES	Charles	14	to need me then./And you said we weren't engaged yet .../{M} We're engaged now.

WEST (3)

154 Rock 3		28	/A Cry from the North, from the West and from the South/Whence thousands
322 FR	Winch	32	had a bit of an accident/On the West Road, in the fog, coming along/At a
323 FR	Winch	21	be,/Outside of the village, on the West Road./{A} Where is he?/{Wi} At the Arms,

WESTERN (4)

166 Rock 10		21	/The light that slants upon our western doors at evening,/The twilight over
592 Grad 3		4	o'er the water's waste,/Some to the western limits of the sky/Which the sun stains
282 MC	Chorus	1	looking over it;/From where the western seas gnaw at the coast of Iona,/To the
559 ES	Ld Clav	11	better./How would you like to go to Western Canada?/Or what about sheep farming

WESTWARD (1)

56 Swee Night		6	/The circles of the stormy moon/Slide westward toward the River Plate,/Death and

WET (6)

62 WL: Burial		38	garden,/Your arms full, and your hair wet, I could not/Speak, and my eyes failed, I
67 WL: Fire S		174	of leaf/Clutch and sink into the wet bank. The wind/Crosses the brown land,
103 Journ Magi		22	we came down to a temperate valley,/Wet, below the snow line, smelling of
212 Growltiger		26	the Bell at Hampton he had gone to wet his beard;/And his bosun,
310 FR	Mary	28	reborn/To rise toward the violent sun/Wet wings into the rain cloud/Harefoot over the
549 ES	Carghil	16	me try to punt, and I got soaking wet/And nearly dropped the punt pole, and you

WHALE'S (1)

184 FQ: DrySal		19	/The starfish, the horseshoe crab, the whale's backbone;/The pools where it offers to

WHAT (967)

WHAT'LL (3)

116 SP	Dusty	16	noise?/Pick up the receiver/{Du} What'll I say?/{Do} Say what you like: say I'm
117 SP	Doris	29	THE COFFIN?/Oh good heavens what'll I do?/Just before a party too!/{Du} Well
117 SP	Doris	35	I know it's mine./Oh good heavens what'll I do./Well I'm not going to draw any

WHAT'S (38)

38	Gerontion		40	famishes the craving. Gives too late/What's not believed in, or if still believed,/In
38	Gerontion		42	Gives too soon/Into weak hands, what's thought can be dispensed with/Till the
117	SP	Doris	8	/{Do} Here's the four of diamonds, what's that mean?/{Du} (*reading*) 'A small sum
117	SP	Doris	12	queer too./{Do} Here's the three. What's that mean?/{Du} 'News of an absent
123	SA	Doris	34	what life is. Just is/{Do} What is?/What's that life is?/{S} Life is death./I knew a
291	FR	Amy	7	in some nightmare pantomime./{A} What's that? I thought I saw someone pass the
291	FR	Charles	17	home to Wishwood!/{C} Why, what's the matter?/{A} Harry, if you want the
297	FR	Charles	35	/{C} My purpose is, to find out what's wrong with Harry:/Until we know that,
327	FR	Gerald	25	is there an evening paper?/{G} Why, what's the matter./{I} Somebody, look for
327	FR	Violet	35	And not to tell his mother./{V} What's the use of asking for an evening paper?/
344	FR	Gerald	4	matter?/{A} Ask Agatha./{G} Why, what's the matter? Where is he going?/{A} Ask
348	FR	Warburt	3	I'm anxious to relieve her mind. Why, what's the trouble? {}/[*Enter* MARY]/{M} Dr.
354	CP	Alex	15	very lovely daughters:/I wonder what's become of them now./{J} Lady Klootz
355	CP	Julia	28	me another of those delicious olives./What's that? Potato crisps? No, I can't endure
365	CP	Reilly	12	{}/[*Sings*]./{UG} *Tooryooly toory-iley,/What's the matter with One Eyed Riley?* {}/
365	CP	Julia	25	know./{J} *You* don't know! And what's his name?/Did I hear him say his name
366	CP	Edward	30	I did rather want to be alone./But what's it all about?/{P} I want your help./I was
366	CP	Edward	34	this seemed an opportunity./{E} And what's your trouble?/{P} This evening I felt I
376	CP	Julia	25	an inn./{J} Edward, how ungrateful./What's in that saucepan?/{C} Nobody knows./
377	CP	Julia	32	aunt./{J} Now, the next question/Is, what's to be done. That's very simple./It's too
427	CP	Julia	4	to get him to tell us all about it./But what's become of him? {}/[*Enter* ALEX]/{E}
427	CP	Julia	22	you doing in this strange place —/What's it called?/{A} Kinkanja./{J} What were
446	CC	Claude	34	bath!/{SC} A bird bath? In the mews? What's the point of that?/{E} He told me he was
455	CC	Colby	8	/But tell me about Lu ... Miss Angel:/What's her connection with this household?/{E}
457	CC	Eggers	5	you'll like her. She's *such* a lady!/And what's more, she has a good heart./{C}
457	CC	Claude	20	from chronic catarrh./{SC} Hello! What's that? {}/[*Opens door on to landing and*
458	CC	Lady E	9	This is most surprising./{LE} What's surprising, Eggerson? I've arrived, that's
480	CC	Lucasta	36	/{L} Nobody could despise you./And what's more important, you don't despise *me*./
482	CC	Lady E	36	limits your acquaintance:/Because, what's surprising, well-bred people/Are
482	CC	Lady E	38	far from intellectual;/And — what's less surprising — intellectual people/Are
497	CC	Eggers	1	don't often speak of it;/Yet I know what's on her mind, for days beforehand./But
500	CC	Claude	39	grateful to Colby./{SC} I don't know what's happened, but nevertheless/I'm sure that
502	CC	Lucasta	36	one's brother .../{C} Or sister .../{L} What's so difficult/Is to recognise the limits of
519	CC	Claude	4	time-limit clause in the contract./{SC} What's that? Oh. Good-bye, Mrs. Guzzard. {}/
519	CC	Claude	5	{}/[*Exit* MRS. GUZZARD]/{SC} What's happened? Have they gone? Is Colby
555	ES	Ld Clav	16	good news for you./{LC} Oh, indeed. What's the matter?/{M} I didn't get far./I met
557	ES	Ld Clav	6	of blaming someone else./Just tell me what's happened./{Mi} Well, I've lost my job./
574	ES	Michael	32	/You couldn't see my point of view. What's the use of chasing/Half round the world,

WHATEVER (32)

159	Rock 6		10	keepers?/Do you need to be told that whatever has been, can still be?/Do you need to
188	FQ: DrySal		158	or inaction/You can receive this: "on whatever sphere of being/The mind of a man
188	FQ: DrySal		168	the trial and judgement of the sea,/Or whatever event, this is your real destination.'/So
196	FQ: Little		194	/And are folded in a single party./Whatever we inherit from the fortunate/We
221	Old Deut		41	gastronomy/Must never be broken, whatever befall:/And the Oldest Inhabitant
227	Macavity		38	an alibi, and one or two to spare:/At whatever time the deed took place —
593	Grad 8		2	we are grown/Gray-haired and old, whatever be our lot,/We shall desire to see again
245	MC	Priest2	8	at least can be cooked and eaten./Whatever you are afraid of, in your craven
266	MC	Thomas	7	KNIGHTS]./{T} You are welcome, whatever your business may be./You say, from
277	MC	Knight3	2	It is this: in what we have done, and whatever/you may think of it, we have been
279	MC	Knight2	2	applause; and if there is any guilt whatever in the matter, you/must share it with
294	FR	Harry	37	I went/That she would be with me; whatever I did/That she was unkillable. It was
308	FR	Harry	18	/Or you would not have come./{H} Whatever I hoped for/Now that I am here I
318	FR	Harry	1	to mother;/What was wrong was whatever made her suffer,/And whatever made
318	FR	Harry	2	was whatever made her suffer,/And whatever made her happy was what was
327	FR	Agatha	1	asking for, I expect the worst./{Ag} Whatever you have learned, Harry, you must
329	FR	Chorus	2	waiting for the future to hear it./And whatever happens began in the past, and presses
346	FR	Downing	23	hardly credit it,/I've always said, whatever happened to his Lordship/Was just a
381	CP	Celia	20	/And, Edward, please believe that whatever happens/I shall not loathe you. I shall
404	CP	Edward	33	my wife/To have my things sent on: whatever I shall need./But of course you
425	CP	Lavinia	31	at that stage/There's nothing whatever you can do about it:/And everyone
473	CC	Colby	40	have two lives/Which have nothing whatever to do with each other —/Well, they're
496	CC	Lady E	11	Guzzard tells us,/If it satisfies Colby. Whatever happens/He shall be *our* son. {}/[*A*
511	CC	Lady E	6	my mother .../{LE} There is no doubt whatever about it, Barnabas./I am your mother.
533	ES	Gomez	14	homesickness,/Curiosity, restlessness, whatever you like./But I've been a pretty hard

537 ES	Ld Clav	34	admit no responsibility,/None whatever, for what happened to you later./{G}
549 ES	Carghil	9	/The turning point of all my life!/Now whatever were the names of those friends of
552 ES	Carghil	34	negligible. And you look the part./Whatever part you've played, I must say you've
562 ES	Monica	5	Michael has behaved, Father,/Whatever Father has said, Michael,/You must
570 ES	Ld Clav	15	her/And completely indifferent to whatever lay ahead of her./{M} It is time to
571 ES	Ld Clav	15	our vices as well as our virtues —/Or whatever the qualities for which they did admire
571 ES	Ld Clav	17	with./And Maisie loved me, with whatever capacity/For loving she had —

WHATSOEVER (1)

593 Grad 8		4	desire to see again the spot/Which, whatsoever we have been or done/Or to what

WHEAT (1)

150 Rock 1		114	*live?/When the field is tilled/And the wheat is bread/They shall not die in a shortened*

WHEEL (13)

62 WL: Burial		51	man with three staves, and here the Wheel,/And here is the one-eyed merchant, and
71 WL: Burial		53	/Gentile or Jew/O you who turn the wheel and look to windward,/Consider Phlebas,
243 MC	Priest3	7	welcome!/{P3} For good or ill, let the wheel turn./The wheel has been still, these seven
243 MC	Priest3	8	good or ill, let the wheel turn./The wheel has been still, these seven years, and no
243 MC	Priest3	9	and no good./For ill or good, let the wheel turn./For who knows the end of good or
245 MC	Thomas	21	the action/And the suffering, that the wheel may turn and still/Be forever still./{P2} O
247 MC	Thomas	21	his folly, may think/He can turn the wheel on which he turns./{T1} My Lord, a nod
254 MC	Tempt4	30	scorning./That nothing lasts, but the wheel turns,/The nest is rifled, and the bird
256 MC	Tempt4	3	That the pattern may subsist, that the wheel may turn and still/Be forever still./{C}
256 MC	Tempts	12	or disappointing:/The Catherine wheel, the pantomime cat,/The prizes given at
294 FR	Harry	31	For a momentary rest on the burning wheel/That cloudless night in the mid-Atlantic/
331 FR	Harry	30	strong,/The liberated from the human wheel./So I looked to you for strength. Now I
335 FR	Harry	29	chain breaks./The chain breaks,/The wheel stops, and the noise of machinery,/And

WHEELS (1)

160 Rock 7		15	that has died of starvation./Prayer wheels, worship of the dead, denial of this

WHEEZE (1)

223 Pekes Pols		30	together they started to grumble and wheeze/In their huffery-snuffery Heathen

WHELK (1)

270 MC	Chorus	2	living lobster, the crab, the oyster, the whelk and the prawn; and they live and spawn

WHEN (519)

WHENCE (3)

154 Rock 3		29	from the West and from the South/Whence thousands travel daily to the timekept
167 Rock 10		34	water./We see the light but see not whence it comes./O Light Invisible, we glorify
193 FQ: Little		87	sound was/Between three districts whence the smoke arose/I met one walking,

WHENE'ER (1)

587 Fable		20	rate, he sometimes came to dinner,/Whene'er the monks were having merry times./

WHENEVER (5)

228 Gus		11	famous, he says, in its time./And whenever he joins his friends at their club/
587 Fable		11	orchard, and a vineyard, and a dairy;/Whenever some old villainous baron died,/He
260 MC	Thomas	6	of our masses of Christmas Day. For whenever/Mass is said, we re-enact the Passion
449 CC	Eggers	22	Miss Angel;/She becomes abstracted, whenever I mention her./{SC} But she knew
532 ES	Ld Clav	28	/That we both want to see you, whenever you can come/If you're in the vicinity.

WHERE (214)

WHERE'S (4)

387 CP	Peter	13	door]/{E} Peter! {}/[*Enter* PETER]/{P} Where's Lavinia?/{E} Don't tell me that Lavinia
431 CP	Peter	1	cinema in Kinkanja./{P} Kinkanja? Where's that? They don't have pictures?/
445 CC	Eggers	20	lunch, and cheap, for nowadays./But where's Mr. Simpkins? Will he be here?/{SC} I
504 CC	Claude	8	/{SC} It's Parkman's day off. But where's the parlourmaid?/{L} I thought I heard

WHEREAS (1)

544 ES	Ld Clav	30	/Without knowing that they enjoy it. Whereas I've often known/That I didn't enjoy

WHEREIN (2)

181 FQ: ECoker		139	you are not,/You must go by a way wherein there is no ecstasy./In order to arrive at
181 FQ: ECoker		161	/Endowed by the ruined millionaire,/Wherein, if we do well, we shall/Die of the

WHEREVER (6)

189 FQ: DrySal		186	throat which will not reject them/Or wherever cannot reach them the sound of the
222 Pekes Pols		3	passionate foes;/It is always the same, wherever one goes./And the Pugs and the Poms,
281 MC	Chorus	19	shall create the holy places./For wherever a saint has dwelt, wherever a martyr
281 MC	Chorus	19	/For wherever a saint has dwelt, wherever a martyr has given his blood for the
294 FR	Harry	36	so quickly./I had always supposed, wherever I went/That she would be with me;
308 FR	Harry	32	near me,/Here and here and here — wherever I am not looking,/Always flickering at

WHEREWITH (1)

205 de la Mare		30	/By you; by those deceptive cadences/Wherewith the common measure is refined;/By

193 FQ: Little	85	below the horizon of his homing/While the dead leaves still rattled on like tin/
197 FQ: Little	237	is a pattern/Of timeless moments. So, while the light fails/On a winter's afternoon, in
220 Old Deut	4	proverb and famous in rhyme/A long while before Queen Victoria's accession./Old
225 Mr Mistoff	53	/Him in from the garden for hours,/While he was asleep in the hall./And not long
231 Bust Jones	40	and it shall be Spring in Pall Mall/While Bustopher Jones wears white spats!/
233 Skimble	53	of tea/With perhaps a drop of Scotch while he's keeping on the watch,/Only stopping
233 Skimble	57	the station;/You were sleeping all the while he was busy at Carlisle,/Where he greets
590 Space Time	5	lived as long as we./But let us live while yet we may,/While love and life are free,/
590 Space Time	6	we./But let us live while yet we may,/While love and life are free,/For time is time,
597 Before Mor	1	leaves were brown./Before Morning/While all the East was weaving red with gray,/
601 Nocturne	13	'Love forever?' — 'Love next week?')/While female readers all in tears are drowned:
604 Ode	3	years,/In thy shadow we wait, while thy presence dispels/Our vain hesitations
239 MC Chorus	12	breathes, waits, whispers in darkness./While the labourer kicks off a muddy boot and
258 MC Thomas	25	manners matched their finger-nails./While I ate out of the King's dish/To become
270 MC Chorus	9	a hellish sweet scent in the woodpath, while the ground heaved. I have seen/Rings of
272 MC m	10	vespers! Hurry. { }/[*They drag him off. While the* CHORUS *speak, the scene is changed*
272 MC m	11	*scene is changed to the cathedral.*]/[*while a* Dies Iræ *is sung in Latin by a choir in the*
275 MC m	21	my cause and that of the Church. { }/*While the* KNIGHTS *kill him, we hear the*
279 MC Knight4	18	ground traversed by the last speaker. While the late Archbishop/was Chancellor, no
279 MC Knight4	36	did not wish to happen; he/insisted, while we were still inflamed with wrath, that the
279 MC Knight4	38	render a verdict of Suicide while of/Unsound Mind. It is the only
281 MC m	7	us another Saint in Canterbury. { }/[*while a* Te Deum *is sung in Latin by a choir in the*
294 FR Harry	23	observation of one's own automatism/While the slow stain sinks deeper through the
300 FR Downing	33	a moon, but I was sure it was him./While I took my turn about, for near half an
303 FR Agatha	19	only thought of asking him a little while ago./{M} Well, there's something to be
308 FR Mary	15	springing/In an unexpected place, while we are unconscious of it./You hoped for
309 FR Mary	28	the man who believes that he is blind/While he still sees the sunlight. I know that this
328 FR Charles	17	a car for the/next twelve months./While trying to extricate his car from the
330 FR Harry	23	of eternity,/Because it feels eternal while it lasts. That is one hell./Then the
338 FR Harry	21	a flight/And phantoms fed upon me while I fled. Now I know/That the last apparent
343 FR m	31	Let the wind and rain do that. { }/[*While* AMY *has been speaking,* HARRY *has*
346 FR Mary	12	promise never to leave his Lordship/While you are away?/{Do} Oh, certainly, Miss;/
356 CP Celia	37	time./{C} And how will you manage while she is away?/{E} I really don't know. I
370 CP Edward	33	know/How lucky you are. In a little while/This might have become an ordinary
374 CP Edward	4	I could:/And I tried to get you a short while ago./{C} If there had happened to be
375 CP Edward	29	forgotten./He made his way in, a little while ago,/And insisted on cooking me
379 CP Celia	37	who betrayed my own dream/All the while; and to find I wanted/This world as well
410 CP Reilly	13	the bond which holds you together./While still in a state of unenlightenment,/*You*
414 CP Celia	13	know —/It no longer seems worth while to *speak* to anyone!/{R} And what about
435 CP Peter	24	better,/And that seemed possible, while Celia was alive./I wanted it, believed in it,
436 CP Lavinia	21	is something I want to say to you./While Alex was telling us what had happened to
446 CC Eggers	22	basis./{E} No doubt that's best. While he's still living/With his aunt in
465 CC Colby	31	sometimes./{C} Indeed, I have felt, while you've been talking,/That it's my own
466 CC Colby	36	/I was struck by what you said, a little while ago,/When you spoke of never having
467 CC Claude	35	pay.— I shall go now, and sit for a while with my china./{C} Excuse me, but I must
476 CC Lucasta	9	/{L} In one way, it matters. A little while ago/You said, very cleverly, that when we
485 CC Lady E	13	of the East/And believed, for a while, in reincarnation./That seemed to explain
494 CC Lady E	6	he is — then you never had a son;/While, if he were yours ... he could still take the
508 CC Guzzard	21	little boy./I was happy to have him while the payments were made;/But we could
535 ES Gomez	19	someone/You must make it worth his while to be trustworthy'. { }/[*During this*
537 ES Ld Clav	5	do you propose/To make it worth my while to be trustworthy?/{G} It's done already,
544 ES Monica	24	let's make the most of this weather while it lasts./I never remember you as other
565 ES Gomez	26	got to obey our doctors' orders./But while we're here, we must have some good talks
568 ES Ld Clav	35	one's child one can't reveal oneself/While she is a child. And by the time she's
572 ES Ld Clav	15	father prevented that:/Made it worth while for her not to marry me —/That was his
572 ES Ld Clav	17	it — and of course/Made it worth while for me not to marry her./In fact, we were
582 ES Ld Clav	5	no one, I begin to live./It is worth while dying, to find out what life is./And I love
582 ES Ld Clav	12	is something./I shall leave you for a while./This is your first visit to us at Badgley

WHIMPER (1)

86 Hollow Men	98	*the world ends/Not with a bang but a whimper.*/Ash-Wednesday/Because I do not hope

WHINE (1)

185 FQ: DrySal	30	voices/Often together heard: the whine in the rigging,/The menace and caress of

WHINING (1)

69 WL: Fire S	261	Lower Thames Street,/The pleasant whining of a mandoline/And a clatter and a

WHIPPING (1)
143 Lines OM   3   /Is not more irritable than I./The whipping tail is not more still/Than when I
WHIPSNADE (1)
151 Rock 2   16   saints,/Apostles, martyrs, in a kind of Whipsnade,/Then they could set about imperial
WHIRLED (4)
39 Gerontion   67   De Bailhache, Fresca, Mrs. Cammel, whirled/Beyond the circuit of the shuddering
96 Ash-Wed 5   8   the Word the unstilled world still whirled/About the centre of the silent Word./O
174 FQ: BurntN 107   concentration/Men and bits of paper, whirled by the cold wind/That blows before and
179 FQ: ECoker 66   fly/Hunt the heavens and the plains/Whirled in a vortex that shall bring/The world
WHIRLING (1)
98 Ash-Wed 6   16   to recover/The cry of quail and the whirling plover/And the blind eye creates/The
WHIRLPOOL (1)
71 WL: DWater 318   of his age and youth/Entering the whirlpool./Gentile or Jew/O you who turn the
WHISKERS (2)
209 NamingCats   16   tail perpendicular,/Or spread out his whiskers, or cherish his pride?/Of names of this
226 Macavity   14   /His coat is dusty from neglect, his whiskers are uncombed./He sways his head
WHISKY (10)
286 FR   m 29   {}/[*Enter* DENMAN *with sherry and whisky.* CHARLES *takes sherry and* GERALD
286 FR   m 29   *takes sherry and* GERALD *whisky.*]/{C} That's what it comes to. {}/[*Lights*
359 CP Edward   9   cocktails./Or would you rather have whisky?/{UG} Gin./{E} Anything in it?/{UG} A
360 CP Edward   10   /May I take another drink?/{E} Whisky?/{UG} Gin./{E} Anything in it?/{UG}
363 CP Edward   5   I'm sorry. What were you drinking?/Whisky?/{UG} Gin./{E} Anything with it?/{UG}
534 ES Gomez   38   don't tell me that there isn't any whisky in the house?/{LC} I can provide whisky.
534 ES Ld Clav   39   in the house?/{LC} I can provide whisky. {}/[*Presses the bell*]/{LC} But why have
535 ES Ld Clav   6   /{LC} Lambert, will you bring in the whisky. And soda./{L} Very good, my Lord./
535 ES   m 34   name. {}/[*Gets up and helps himself to whisky*]/{G} But of course you know!/Just enough
539 ES   m 22   to be thirsty again. {}/[*Pours himself whisky*]/{LC} An interesting historical epitome./
WHISPER (6)
73 WL: Thund 378   long black hair out tight/And fiddled whisper music on those strings/And bats with
83 Hollow Men   6   Alas!/Our dried voices, when/We whisper together/Are quiet and meaningless/As
180 FQ: ECoker 130   light, and the stillness the dancing./Whisper of running streams, and winter
232 Skimble   1   the Railway Cat/There's a whisper down the line at 11.39/When the Night
272 MC Thomas   5   a tremor of bliss, a wink of heaven, a whisper,/And I would no longer be denied; all
329 FR Chorus   14   /And the season of stifled sorrow/The whisper, the transparent deception/The keeping
WHISPERED (2)
205 de la Mare   27   what means, was this designed?/The whispered incantation which allows/Free
572 ES Ld Clav   6   waking and sleeping,/A voice that whispered, 'you didn't stop!'/I knew the voice: it
WHISPERING (7)
24 Rhapsody   4   of the street/Held in a lunar synthesis,/Whispering lunar incantations/Dissolve the
38 Gerontion   35   corridors/And issues, deceives with whispering ambitions,/Guides us by vanities.
164 Rock 9   5   empty walls, quavering lowly, whispering faintly,/Among a few flickering
246 MC Tempt1   39   on the water,/Singing at nightfall, whispering in chambers,/Fires devouring the
257 MC Tempts   2   may pass unseen unheard./{4T} Come whispering through the ear, or a sudden shock
308 FR Harry   34   at the corner of my eye,/Almost whispering just out of earshot —/And inside
319 FR Harry   9   was only a vacuum/Surrounded by whispering aunts: Ivy and Violet —/Agatha
WHISPERS (9)
37 Gerontion   23   to be divided, to be drunk/Among whispers; by Mr. Silvero/With caressing hands,
52 Whispers   t   jadis un bel homme, de haute taille./Whispers of Immortality/Webster was much
71 WL: DWater 316   current under sea/Picked his bones in whispers. As he rose and fell/He passed the
95 Ash-Wed 4   28   /Till the wind shake a thousand whispers from the yew/And after this our exile/
109 Marina   20   than stars and nearer than the eye/Whispers and small laughter between leaves and
239 MC Chorus   11   /The New Year waits, breathes, waits, whispers in darkness./While the labourer kicks
244 MC Chorus   9   of streets,/Talked not always in whispers,/Living and partly living./We have
542 ES Gomez   32   I'm out of sight. You'll be afraid of whispers,/The reflection in the mirror of the
572 ES Charles   31   miserable stories,/Confide them in whispers. They cannot harm you./{LC} Your
WHISTLE (3)
118 SP   m 15   court cards?/The Knave of Hearts! {}/(*Whistle outside of the window.*)/{Du} Well I
118 SP   m 17   a co*i*ncidence! Cards are queer! {}/(*Whistle again.*)/{Do} Is that Sam?/{Du} Of
142 Cape Ann   6   warbler, the shy one. Hail/With shrill whistle the note of the quail, the bob-white/
WHISTLED (1)
73 WL: Thund 380   bats with baby faces in the violet light/Whistled, and beat their wings/And crawled
WHISTLING (1)
248 MC Thomas   10   fancy,/So one thought goes whistling down the wind./The impossible is still

WHITE (38)

15 Prufrock	63	all —/Arms that are braceleted and white and bare/(But in the lamplight, downed
16 Prufrock	123	Do I dare to eat a peach?/I shall wear white flannel trousers, and walk upon the
17 Prufrock	127	seaward on the waves/Combing the white hair of the waves blown back/When the
17 Prufrock	128	back/When the wind blows the water white and black./We have lingered in the
24 Rhapsody	29	up/The secret of its skeleton,/Stiff and white./A broken spring in a factory yard,/Rust
32 Hysteria	6	/was hurriedly spreading a pink and white checked cloth over the rusty/green iron
39 Gerontion	71	Of Belle Isle, or running on the Horn./White feathers in the snow, the Gulf claims,/
50 Hippopot	33	a harp of gold./He shall be washed as white as snow,/By all the martyr'd virgins kist,/
67 WL: Fire S	193	king my father's death before him./White bodies naked on the low damp ground/
69 WL: Fire S	265	hold/Inexplicable splendour of Ionian white and gold./The river sweats/Oil and tar/
70 WL: Fire S	289	down stream/The peal of bells/White towers/Weialala leia/Wallala leialala/
73 WL: Thund	361	/But when I look ahead up the white road/There is always another one walking
91 Ash-Wed 2	1	at the hour of our death./Lady, three white leopards sat under a juniper-tree/In the
91 Ash-Wed 2	17	reject. The Lady is withdrawn/In a white gown, to contemplation, in a white gown./
91 Ash-Wed 2	17	a white gown, to contemplation, in a white gown./Let the whiteness of bones atone to
94 Ash-Wed 4	4	ranks of varied green/Going in white and blue, in Mary's colour,/Talking of
94 Ash-Wed 4	15	between sleep and waking, wearing/White light folded, sheathed about her, folded./
94 Ash-Wed 4	22	hearse./The silent sister veiled in white and blue/Between the yews, behind the
98 Ash-Wed 6	9	towards the granite shore/The white sails still fly seaward, seaward flying/
103 Journ Magi	25	trees on the low sky./And an old white horse galloped away in the meadow./Then
121 SA Sweeney	13	convert *you*!/Into a stew./A nice little, white little, missionary stew./{Do} You wouldn't
121 SA Sweeney	16	/{S} Yes I'd eat you!/In a nice little, white little, soft little, tender little,/Juicy little,
139 Virginia	8	hills/Wait. Gates wait. Purple trees,/White trees, wait, wait,/Delay, decay. Living,
140 Usk	3	the branch, or/Hope to find/The white hart behind the white well./Glance aside,
140 Usk	3	to find/The white hart behind the white well./Glance aside, not for lance, do not
173 FQ: BurntN	75	yet surrounded/By a grace of sense, a white light still and moving,/*Erhebung* without
191 FQ: Little	25	may time, you would find the hedges/White again, in May, with voluptuary
216 Jellicles	5	*Ball.*/Jellicle Cats are black and white,/Jellicle Cats are rather small;/Jellicle Cats
216 Jellicles	21	between their toes./Jellicle Cats are white and black,/Jellicle Cats are of moderate
216 Jellicles	29	Moon./Jellicle Cats are black and white,/Jellicle Cats (as I said) are small;/If it
230 Bust Jones	12	or bowed to/By Bustopher Jones in white spats!/His visits are occasional to the
231 Bust Jones	40	Mall/While Bustopher Jones wears white spats!/Skimbleshanks: the Railway Cat/
600 Moonflower	3	/The mist crawls in from sea;/A great white bird, a snowy owl,/Slips from the alder
600 Moonflower	6	the flowers, Love, you hold,/Than the white mist on the sea;/Have you no brighter
605 Narcissus	25	that he had been a fish/With slippery white belly held tight in his own fingers,/
606 Narcissus	37	came./As he embraced them his white skin surrendered itself to the redness of
244 MC Chorus	30	France. Thomas Archbishop, set the white sail between the grey sky and the bitter
272 MC Chorus	22	unmemorable; only is here/The white flat face of Death, God's silent servant,/

WHITE-HEADED (1)

478 CC Lucasta	1	prospects/Now that you're Claude's white-headed boy./Perhaps he'll adopt you, and

WHITENESS (2)

91 Ash-Wed 2	18	in a white gown./Let the whiteness of bones atone to forgetfulness./There
606 Narcissus	30	at the end the taste of his own whiteness/The horror of his own smoothness,/

WHITER (1)

600 Moonflower	5	snowy owl,/Slips from the alder tree./Whiter the flowers, Love, you hold,/Than the

WHITTINGTON'S (1)

228 Gus	32	flat,/And I once understudied Dick Whittington's Cat./But my grandest creation, as

WHO (423)

WHO'D (2)

558 ES Michael	8	couldn't retain any man on his staff/Who'd taken to gambling. Called me a gambler!
574 ES Michael	35	in London? With another Sir Alfred/Who'd constitute himself custodian of my

WHO'S (12)

232 Skimble	17	say that by and large it is Skimble who's in charge/Of the Sleeping Car Express./
323 FR Amy	6	to your mother .../{A} Harry! Harry!/Who's there with you? Is it Arthur or John? {}/
386 CP Celia	32	laughing./You look like a little boy who's been sent for/To the headmaster's study;
388 CP Lavinia	22	going away! {}/[*Enter* LAVINIA]/{L} Who's going away? Well, Celia. Well, Peter./I
425 CP Lavinia	14	That's never satisfactory./Everyone who's asked to either party/Suspects that the
452 CC Lucasta	23	I'm sure, so why bother?/But who's this, Eggy? Is it Colby Simpkins?/
486 CC Lady E	32	... {}/[*A knock on the door*]/{LE} Who's that? {}/[*Enter* SIR CLAUDE]/{SC}
524 ES Monica	20	the girl/That she's not the only one who's been there with him./{C} Well, tease me if
540 ES Gomez	38	what a preposterous suggestion!/Who's going to accept the unsupported
546 ES Piggott	20	/Though we never accept any guest who's incurable./You know, we've been deluged
562 ES Carghil	36	Richard./There's no denying it. But who's this coming?/It's another new guest here.
570 ES Ld Clav	27	the Central American,/A man who's made a fortune by his own peculiar

WHO-THE-DEVIL-ARE-YOU (1)

602 Humoresque	11	/Mouth twisted to the latest tune;/His	who-the-devil-are-you stare;/Translated, maybe,

WHOEVER (3)

386 CP	Reilly	7	/{E} Visitors? What visitors?/{UG} Whoever comes. The strangers./As for myself, I
552 ES	Carghil	38	be playing a part/In your obituary, whoever writes it./{LC} Considering how long
579 ES	Monica	4	will you be/When I see you again? Whoever you are then/I shall always pretend

WHOLE (24)

91 Ash-Wed 2	27	/Calm and distressed/Torn and most	whole/Rose of memory/Rose of forgetfulness/
161 Rock 7	37	/What does the world say, does the	whole world stray in high-powered cars on a
163 Rock 8	34	could have done what was good of it;/	Whole faith of a few,/Part faith of many./Not
181 FQ: ECoker	159	our sickness must grow worse./The	whole earth is our hospital/Endowed by the
213 Growltiger	55	on the strand./Rats were roasted	whole at Brentford, and at Victoria Dock,/And
230 Bust Jones	9	/Or such an impeccable back./In the	whole of St. James's the smartest of names is/
234 Ad-dress	22	seldom bite;/But yet a Dog is, on the	whole,/What you would call a simple soul./Of
248 MC Thomas	14	world,/So that the mind may not be	whole in the present. { }/[*Enter* SECOND
260 MC Thomas	11	and satisfaction/for the sins of the	whole world. It was in this same night that has/
274 MC Thomas	4	If you call that decision/To which my	whole being gives entire consent./I give my life/
320 FR Warburt	11	/At the present moment. The	whole machine is weak/And running down. Her
332 FR Agatha	31	is another kind,/I believe, across a	whole Thibet of broken stones/That lie, fang up,
403 CP Edward	28	perhaps, for the first time,/The	whole oppression, the unreality/Of the role she
426 CP Edward	10	/{E} This is the best moment/Of the	whole party./{L} Oh no, Edward./The best
429 CP Alex	16	/Even among pagans!/{A} Not on the	*whole* story./{E} And have any of the English
464 CC Claude	38	makes it real./That's not the	whole story. My father knew I hated it:/That
505 CC Claude	4	... in the country. But he knows the	whole story:/He's been in my confidence — and
524 ES Monica	6	When you said you could give me the	whole afternoon./{C} But I couldn't say what I
525 ES Charles	2	father:/I arranged to be free for the	whole afternoon/On the plain understanding .../
525 ES Charles	5	When I said that I was free for the	whole afternoon,/That meant you were to give
525 ES Charles	6	/That meant you were to give *me* the	whole afternoon./I couldn't say what I wanted
556 ES Ld Clav	23	/Are you staying there long? For the	whole of this holiday?/{Mi} Well, this isn't a
559 ES Ld Clav	25	your family,/To throw away the	whole of your inheritance?/{Mi} What is my
578 ES Ld Clav	6	many mistakes I have made/My	whole life through, mistake upon mistake,/The

WHOLLY (7)

182 FQ: ECoker	177	to use words, and every attempt/Is a	wholly new start, and a different kind of failure/
195 FQ: Little	172	of this place,/And of people, not	wholly commendable,/Of no immediate kin or
276 MC Chorus	16	that is defiled,/But the world that is	wholly foul./Clear the air! clean the sky! wash
307 FR Mary	25	/At the very moment when you are	wholly conscious/Of being a misfit, of being
465 CC Claude	17	by the craving/To create, when one is	wholly uncreative?/I don't think so. For I came
512 CC Guzzard	5	That your suspicions of me were	wholly unfounded./{LE} Oh, Mrs. Guzzard, I
572 ES Ld Clav	18	me not to marry her./In fact, we were	wholly unsuited to each other,/Yet she had a

WHOM (75)

68 WL: Fire S	233	one bold stare,/One of the low on	whom assurance sits/As a silk hat on a
111 Xmas Trees	6	— which is not that of the child/For	whom the candle is a star, and the gilded angel/
148 Rock 1	45	The Stranger./The God-shaken, in	whom is the truth inborn./*Enter the* ROCK, *led*
152 Rock 2	42	anchorite who meditates alone,/For	whom the days and nights repeat the praise of
182 FQ: ECoker	186	or twice, or several times, by men	whom one cannot hope/To emulate — but there
193 FQ: Little	95	the sudden look of some dead master/	Whom I had known, forgotten, half recalled/
196 FQ: Little	191	those who opposed them/And those	whom they opposed/Accept the constitution of
201 Def Island	18	but the weapons/and those again for	whom the paths of glory are/the lanes and the
205 de la Mare	26	face peers from an empty house;/By	whom, and by what means, was this designed?/
206 To my Wife	1	sound./A Dedication to my Wife/To	whom I owe the leaping delight/That quickens
211 Old Gumbie	38	let us now give three cheers —/On	whom well-ordered households depend, it
212 Growltiger	16	ships,/And woe to any Cat with	whom Growltiger came to grips!/But most to
234 Ad-dress	7	like you and me/And other people	whom we find/Possessed of various types of
235 Ad-dress	47	CAT!/But if he is the Cat next door,/	Whom I have often met before/(He comes to see
589 Fable	68	do surely —/That ghosts are fellows	whom you *can't* keep out;/It is a thing to be
598 Circe	14	they look at us with the eyes/Of men	whom we knew long ago./On a Portrait/Among
242 MC Mess	13	Lord, he said, I leave you as a man/	Whom in this life I shall not see again./I have
248 MC Tempt2	22	late ones rise! You, master of policy/	Whom all acknowledged, should guide the state
249 MC Thomas	33	decorum./{T} You forget the bishops/	Whom I have laid under excommunication./
259 MC Thomas	6	sword's end./Now my good Angel,	whom God appoints/To be my guardian, hover
266 MC Knights	15	who was made by the King;	whom he set in your place to carry out his
267 MC Thomas	9	as loyal subjects./{T} Loyal? to	whom?/{K1} To the King!/{K2} The King!/{K3}
268 MC Thomas	31	me. But it is not I/Who can loose	whom the Pope has bound./Let them go to him,
268 MC Thomas	32	has bound./Let them go to him, upon	whom redounds/Their contempt towards me,
269 MC Knight1	7	gross indignity;/Insolent madman,	whom nothing deters/From attainting his

281 MC	Chorus	13	the worm in the belly./Therefore man, whom Thou hast made to be conscious of Thee,
293 FR	Harry	28	what has happened./And people to whom nothing has ever happened/Cannot
293 FR	Harry	37	me, either./{H} You are all people/To whom nothing has happened, at most a
310 FR	Harry	13	the ghosts of the dead/Those whom the winter drowned/Do not the ghosts of
332 FR	Agatha	7	tell me nothing./{Ag} The dead man whom you have assumed to be your father,/And
332 FR	Agatha	8	to be your father,/And my sister whom you acknowledge as your mother:/There
357 CP	Edward	7	Aunt Laura?/{E} No; another aunt/Whom you wouldn't know. Her mother's sister/
360 CP	Reilly	30	of./{UG} Or another woman/Of whom she thought she had cause to be jealous?/
379 CP	Celia	1	promise me to see a very great doctor/Whom I have heard of — and his name *is*
380 CP	Celia	6	feel degraded to find that a man/With whom they thought they had shared something
382 CP	Celia	27	another person,/I see you as a person whom I never saw before./The man I saw
383 CP	Edward	18	me./{C} What should we drink to?/{E} Whom shall we drink to?/{C} To the Guardians.
387 CP	Edward	24	and bring me with her./{E} I wonder whom else Lavinia has invited./{P} Why, I got
394 CP	Lavinia	15	when somebody was coming/Whom I particularly wanted you to meet,/You
394 CP	Edward	35	life. You wished to be a hostess/For whom my career would be a support./Well, I
395 CP	Lavinia	13	for me, I'm rather a different person/Whom you must get to know./{E} This is very
397 CP	Edward	19	make my own choice;/Not take one whom you choose. How do I know/That you
401 CP	Reilly	22	/But I knew you would be there, and whom I should find with you./{E} But you had
402 CP	Reilly	30	And there are also patients/For whom a sanatorium is the worst place possible./
408 CP	Reilly	8	with someone,/And with someone of whom you had reason to be jealous./{E} Really,
417 CP	Celia	14	not know/When awake. But what, or whom I loved,/Or what in me was loving, I do
417 CP	Reilly	36	each other,/Breeding children whom they do not understand/And who will
419 CP	Reilly	20	to this sanatorium./I am very careful whom I send there:/Those who go do not come
422 CP	Reilly	29	{}/[*They drink*]/{R} There is one for whom the words cannot be spoken./{A} They
427 CP	Alex	18	the unexpected guest/Is the one to whom they give the warmest welcome./I know
447 CC	Claude	6	you ought to give her warning/Of whom she is to meet on her arrival./{E} How
459 CC	Lady E	38	I'd no sooner got to Lausanne/Than whom should I meet but Mildred Deverell./She
470 CC	Colby	13	I can't forget/That it's only myself to whom I'm playing./But with you, it was neither
481 CC	Lady E	22	has been lived in/By the person for whom it was designed./So I have to see you in
497 CC	Claude	15	is the name of the person/To whom her own child was entrusted./{E} What
498 CC	Claude	32	of *him*. It's your child, Elizabeth,/Whom we must try to trace./{E} If there was
503 CC	Lucasta	29	him,/And good-bye to the Lucasta whom Colby knew./We've changed since then:
504 CC	Lucasta	7	let someone in. It's the Mrs. Guzzard/Whom you are expecting. She looks rather
505 CC	Eggers	37	a child .../{LE} A son./{E} Had a son/Whom she could not, in the circumstances,
506 CC	Eggers	33	a Mrs. Guzzard of Teddington/To whom her new-born child was confided./Of
507 CC	Guzzard	17	to me by a third party,/Through whom the monthly payments were made./{E}
510 CC	Eggers	38	as a child, from Mrs. Guzzard,/To whom, it seems, you had first been entrusted./
513 CC	Colby	26	just come to me. I should like a father/Whom I have never known and couldn't know
513 CC	Colby	28	born/Or before I could remember; whom I could get to know/Only by report, by
522 ES	dedic	1	STATESMAN/TO MY WIFE/*To whom I owe the leaping delight*/*That quickens my*
533 ES	Gomez	33	heavily;/But I learnt by experience whom to pay;/And a little money laid out in the
536 ES	Gomez	39	/No, I need one old friend, a friend whom I can trust —/And one who will accept
541 ES	Gomez	9	—/But you'd never know to whom I'd told it,/Or who knew the story and
547 ES	Piggott	29	about the other guests/To know whom *not* to play with. I'll mention no names,/
555 ES	Ld Clav	32	or other. I'm sure he has friends/Whom he wouldn't care for you or me to know
557 ES	Ld Clav	22	pulled it off./{LC} Borrowed? From whom?/Not ... from the firm?/{Mi} I went to a
557 ES	Michael	25	firm?/{Mi} I went to a lender,/A man whom a friend of mine recommended./He gave
568 ES	Ld Clav	24	has one person, just one in his life,/To whom he is willing to confess everything —/And
575 ES	Michael	1	/The limey remittance man for whom a job was made./No! I want to go where
581 ES	Ld Clav	29	Monica, that you have found a man/Whom you can love for the man he really is./

WHORES (1)
254 MC	Tempt4	35	/Swept into the laps of parasites and whores./When miracles cease, and the faithful

WHOSE (23)
94 Ash-Wed	4	24	the yews, behind the garden god,/Whose flute is breathless, bent her head and
181 FQ: ECoker	156		the disease/If we obey the dying nurse/Whose constant care is not to please/But to
188 FQ: DrySal	166		/You who come to port, and you whose bodies/Will suffer the trial and
189 FQ: DrySal	173		/But fare forward, voyagers./Lady, whose shrine stands on the promontory,/Pray
189 FQ: DrySal	175		for all those who are in ships, those/Whose business has to do with fish, and/Those
204 de la Mare	11		drawn/Demand some poetry, please. Whose shall it be,/At not quite time for bed? .../
206 To my Wife	5		/The breathing in unison/Of lovers whose bodies smell of each other/Who think the
227 Macavity	39		/And they say that all the Cats whose wicked deeds are widely known/(I might
258 MC Thomas	24		most contemptible,/The raw nobility, whose manners matched their finger-nails./
277 MC Knight2	39		play. Now the worthy Archbishop,/whose good qualities I very much admired, has
280 MC Priest1	38		of you./{P1} O my lord/The glory of whose new state is hidden from us,/Pray for us
333 FR Agatha	28		known what sin/You shall expiate, or whose, or why. It is certain/That the knowledge

409 CP   Reilly   9   when you thought your wife had left you,/You discovered, to your
409 CP   Reilly   16   lover./Then you realised, what your wife has justly remarked,/That you had never
445 CC   Claude   4   an errand like this./But you know my wife wouldn't like anyone to meet her/At
448 CC   Claude   37   Eggerson,/Than for you and your wife, to have had a son/Lost in action, and his
449 CC   Claude   38   a lot I don't understand about my wife./There's always something one's ignorant
450 CC   Eggers   11   lot that *I* don't understand/About my wife./{SC} And just as much/She doesn't know
461 CC   Claude   26   But after two months —/And as my wife insists upon your being Mr. Colby —/I
468 CC   Claude   2   them here./{SC} Much depends on my wife. Be patient with her, Colby./— Oh yes, that
499 CC   Claude   7   putting the questions on behalf of my wife./{E} I understand, Sir Claude: I understand
500 CC   Claude   7   been some misunderstanding./My wife believes that Colby is *her* son./That is the
504 CC   Claude   30   First, let me introduce you to my wife./Lady Elizabeth Mulhammer./{LE} Good
507 CC   Claude   38   his?/{SC} That is just the point. My wife has convinced herself/That Colby is her
512 CC   Claude   11   any confusion now:/I'm sure that my wife is perfectly convinced;/And Mr. Kaghan's
512 CC   Guzzard 14   my interest as anyone's./But will your wife be satisfied,/When she has the evidence the
513 CC   Guzzard   4   whether you are satisfied/To be the wife of Barnabas Kaghan,/The daughter-in-law
518 CC   Guzzard 25   with you,/Having been, myself, the wife of an organist;/But you too, I think, have
522 ES   dedic   t   ELDER STATESMAN/TO MY WIFE/*To whom I owe the leaping delight/That*
WIFE'S (5)
203 Indians   2   his own village,/His own fire, and his wife's cooking;/To sit in front of his own door
466 CC   Claude   15   takes the place of religion:/Just as my wife's investigations/Into what she calls the life
533 ES   Gomez   3   when you married, you took your wife's name/And became Mr. Richard
533 ES   Gomez   8   change their names;/And besides, my wife's name is a good deal more normal/In my
538 ES   Gomez   13   with your father's money/And your wife's family influence, you got on in politics./
WILD (7)
180 FQ: ECoker 131   streams, and winter lightning./The wild thyme unseen and the wild strawberry,/The
180 FQ: ECoker 131   /The wild thyme unseen and the wild strawberry,/The laughter in the garden,
190 FQ: DrySal 213   fit, lost in a shaft of sunlight,/The wild thyme unseen, or the winter lightning/Or
590 Time Space   11   on the vine,/Were withered ere the wild bee flew/To suck the eglantine./So let us
590 Space Time   11   on the vine/Were withered ere the wild bee flew/To suck the eglantine./But let us
596 When we   7   withered petals lay beneath;/But the wild roses in your wreath/Were faded, and the
446 CC   Eggers   38   day/I read a letter in *The Times* about wild birds seen in London:/And I'm sure Mr.
WILDERNESS (5)
 38 Gerontion   65   pungent sauces, multiply variety/In a wilderness of mirrors. What will the spider do,/
 54 Mr E Sun   12   The nimbus of the Baptized God./The wilderness is cracked and browned/But through
307 FR   Mary   1   The hollow tree in what we called the wilderness/{H} Down near the river. That was
307 FR   Harry   15   /To find the old hiding place. The wilderness was gone,/The tree had been felled,
335 FR   Harry   24   /Among inner shadows in the smoky wilderness,/Trying to avoid the clasping
WILL (454)
WILLED (2)
245 MC   Thomas   18   which all must consent that it may be willed/And which all must suffer that they may
256 MC   Tempt4   1   which all must consent that it may be willed/And which all must suffer that they may
WILLIAM (3)
 62 WL: Burial   66   /Flowed up the hill and down King William Street,/To where Saint Mary Woolnoth
276 MC   Knight1   32   my neighbour in/the country: Baron William de Traci./{K3} I am afraid I am not
277 MC   Knight1   28   say./{K1} I think we will all agree that William de Traci has/spoken well and has made
WILLING (6)
261 MC   Thomas   26   will to/become a Saint, as a man by willing and contriving may become a ruler/of
304 FR   Mary   29   almost believed it — had killed her by willing./Doesn't that sound awful? I know that
382 CP   Edward   1   indomitable spirit of mediocrity./The willing self can contrive the disaster/Of this
436 CP   Lavinia   29   of mind in which they died?/{L} I'm willing to grant that. What struck me, though,/
558 ES   Ld Clav   33   it had gone further than you're willing to admit./{Mi} Well, after all, she was
568 ES   Ld Clav   24   just one in his life,/To whom he is willing to confess everything —/And that
WILLOW-HERB (1)
474 CP   Lucasta   26   a devastated area —/A bomb-site ... willow-herb ... a dirty public square./But I can't
WILLS (1)
381 CP   Edward   34   this — or want that' —/The self that wills — he is a feeble creature;/He has to come
WIN (1)
331 FR   Agatha   21   /{Ag} I had to fight for many years to win my dispossession,/And many years to keep
WINCHELL (16)
284 FR   m   9   /DR. WARBURTON/SERGEANT WINCHELL/THE EUMENIDES/*The scene is*
321 FR   Denman   9   /[*Enter* DENMAN]/{D} It's Sergeant Winchell is here, my Lord,/And wants to see
321 FR   Harry   18   Nothing can happen —/If Sergeant Winchell is real. But Denman saw him./But
321 FR   m   24   to one of your brothers. {}/[*Enter* WINCHELL]/{Wi} Good evening, my Lord.
321 FR   m   28   /{H} Her Ladyship's! {}/[*He darts at* WINCHELL *and seizes him by the shoulders*]/
321 FR   Harry   30   the conversation. You, and I/And Winchell. Sit down, Winchell,/And have a glass

321 FR	Harry	30	You, and I/And Winchell. Sit down, Winchell,/And have a glass of port. We were
321 FR	Warburt	36	the rheumatism./{W} For God's sake, Winchell, tell us your business./His Lordship
322 FR	Warburt	20	come about./{W} For Heaven's sake, Winchell,/Tell us your business./{Wi} It's about
323 FR	Amy	7	GERALD *and* CHARLES.]/{A} Winchell! what are you here for?/{Wi} I'm sorry,
323 FR	Warburt	11	the accident, Lady Monchensey;/And Winchell tells me Dr. Owen has seen him/And
324 FR	Warburt	6	the time to begin to doubt me./Come, Winchell. We can put your bicycle/On the back
324 FR	m	7	car. {}/[*Exeunt* WARBURTON *and* WINCHELL]/{V} Well, Harry,/I think that you
324 FR	Harry	12	of course I'm sorry. But from what Winchell says/I don't think the matter can be
325 FR	Charles	12	Warburton can't./If he's worse than Winchell said, then he'll let us know at once./
347 FR	Warburt	35	on nicely;/It wasn't so serious as Winchell made out,/And we'll have him up here

WIND (56)

17 Prufrock		128	of the waves blown back/When the wind blows the water white and black./We have
28 Boston ET		2	*Evening Transcript*/Sway in the wind like a field of ripe corn./When evening
38 Gerontion		30	the door. Vacant shuttles/Weave the wind. I have no ghosts,/An old man in a
39 Gerontion		69	/In fractured atoms. Gull against the wind, in the windy straits/Of Belle Isle, or
65 WL: Chess		118	their bones./'What is that noise?'/The wind under the door.'What is that noise now?
65 WL: Chess		119	/'What is that noise now? What is the wind doing?'/Nothing again nothing./'Do/'You
67 WL: Fire S		174	and sink into the wet bank. The wind/Crosses the brown land, unheard. The
70 WL: Fire S		286	swell/Rippled both shores/Southwest wind/Carried down stream/The peal of bells/
83 Hollow Men		8	/Are quiet and meaningless/As wind in dry grass/Or rats' feet over broken glass
84 Hollow Men		35	staves/In a field/Behaving as the wind behaves/No nearer —/Not that final
91 Ash-Wed 2		22	And God said/Prophesy to the wind, to the wind only for only/The wind will
91 Ash-Wed 2		22	said/Prophesy to the wind, to the wind only for only/The wind will listen. And the
91 Ash-Wed 2		23	wind, to the wind only for only/The wind will listen. And the bones sang chirping/
95 Ash-Wed 4		28	the word unheard, unspoken/Till the wind shake a thousand whispers from the yew/
105 Song Sime		4	/My life is light, waiting for the death wind,/Like a feather on the back of my hand./
105 Song Sime		7	and memory in corners/Wait for the wind that chills towards the dead land./Grant us
107 Animula		10	of the Christmas tree,/Pleasure in the wind, the sunlight and the sea;/Studies the sunlit
109 Marina		14	become unsubstantial, reduced by a wind,/A breath of pine, and the woodsong fog/
129 Cor2 State		34	the breast feather stirred by the small wind after noon/There the cyclamen spreads its
129 Cor2 State		39	bear them/Noses strong to break the wind/Mother/May we not be some time, almost
134 Wind		t	the tears/And hold us in derision./The wind sprang up at four o'clock/The wind sprang
134 Wind		1	wind sprang up at four o'clock/The wind sprang up at four o'clock/The wind sprang
134 Wind		2	wind sprang up at four o'clock/The wind sprang up and broke the bells/Swinging
149 Rock 1		99	/*And shiver in unlit rooms./Only the wind moves/Over empty fields, untilled/Where the*
155 Rock 3		34	flourish on the gravel court,/And the wind shall say: 'Here were decent godless
160 Rock 7		3	man without GOD is a seed upon the wind: driven this way and that, and finding no
160 Rock 7		16	sand, or the hills where the wind will not let the snow rest./Waste and void.
174 FQ: BurntN		107	and bits of paper, whirled by the cold wind/That blows before and after time,/Wind in
174 FQ: BurntN		109	/That blows before and after time,/Wind in and out of unwholesome lungs/Time
174 FQ: BurntN		113	faded air, the torpid/Driven on the wind that sweeps the gloomy hills of London./
177 FQ: ECoker		11	and for generation/And a time for the wind to break the loosened pane/And to shake
178 FQ: ECoker		49	heat and silence. Out at sea the dawn wind/Wrinkles and slides. I am here/Or there,
183 FQ: ECoker		210	empty desolation,/The wave cry, the wind cry, the vast waters/Of the petrel and the
191 FQ: Little		10	or brazier,/Stirs the dumb spirit: no wind, but pentecostal fire/In the dark time of
193 FQ: Little		90	metal leaves/Before the urban dawn wind unresisting./And as I fixed upon the
194 FQ: Little		105	/And so, compliant to the common wind,/Too strange to each other for
206 To my Wife		8	need of meaning./No peevish winter wind shall chill/No sullen tropic sun shall wither
210 Old Gumbie		26	/The curtain-cord she likes to wind, and tie it into sailor-knots./She sits upon
605 Narcissus		9	the sea and the high cliffs/When the wind made him aware of his limbs smoothly
243 MC Chorus		15	city, here is no abiding stay./Ill the wind, ill the time, uncertain the profit, certain
243 MC Chorus		17	too late, and rotten the year;/Evil the wind, and bitter the sea, and grey the sky, grey
248 MC Thomas		10	one thought goes whistling down the wind./The impossible is still temptation./The
253 MC Tempt4		40	broken teeth./You hold the skein: wind, Thomas, wind/The thread of eternal life
253 MC Tempt4		40	/You hold the skein: wind, Thomas, wind/The thread of eternal life and death./You
256 MC Priests		25	tide,/Do not sail the irresistible wind; in the storm,/Should we not wait for the
256 MC Tempts		31	Is it rain that taps at the window, is it wind that pokes at the door?/{C} Does the torch
263 MC Chorus		7	night./Still and stifling the air: but a wind is stored up in the East./The starved crow
263 MC Chorus		11	/What signs of a bitter spring?/The wind stored up in the East./What, at the time of
272 MC Chorus		21	shrink and dissolve/Into dust on the wind, forgotten, unmemorable; only is here/The
275 MC Chorus		21	Clear the air! clean the sky! wash the wind! take stone from stone and wash them./
276 MC Chorus		17	/Clear the air! clean the sky! wash the wind! take the stone from the stone, take the
281 MC Chorus		8	earth,/In the snow, in the rain, in the wind, in the storm; in all of Thy creatures, both
303 FR	Mary	8	belong here, which do not know/The wind and rain, as I know them./{Ag} I wonder
332 FR	Agatha	35	soon, not soon enough./The rain and wind had not shaken your father/Awake yet. I

343 FR   Amy   25   the endless weather,/Resist the wind? fight with increasing taxes/And unpaid
343 FR   Amy   30   /To bother about the upkeep. Let the wind and rain do that. {}/[*While* AMY *has been*

WIND (1) [*Foreign word*]
61 WL: Burial   31   in a handful of dust./*Frisch weht der Wind/Der Heimat zu/Mein Irisch Kind/Wo*

WIND'S (4)
73 WL: Thund   388   /There is the empty chapel, only the wind's home./It has no windows, and the door
84 Hollow Men   26   a tree swinging/And voices are/In the wind's singing/More distant and more solemn/
186 FQ: DrySal   70   them, the fishermen sailing/Into the wind's tail, where the fog cowers?/We cannot
290 FR   Agatha   32   the world around the corner/The wind's talk in the dry holly-tree/The inclination

WIND-WHIPPED (1)
160 Rock 7   16   forgotten meanings/In the restless wind-whipped sand, or the hills where the wind

WINDBLOWN (1)
303 FR   Mary   5   is, here./{M} I had rather wait for our windblown blossoms,/Such as they are, than

WINDING (1)
72 WL: Thund   333   water and the sandy road/The road winding above among the mountains/Which are

WINDINGS (1)
19 Portrait   29   — life, what *cauchemar!*/Among the windings of the violins/And the ariettes/Of

WINDLESS (1)
191 FQ: Little   6   the ice, on pond and ditches,/In windless cold that is the heart's heat,/Reflecting

WINDOW (30)
16 Prufrock   108   off a shawl,/And turning toward the window, should say:/'That is not it at all,/That
27 Morning   t   last twist of the knife./Morning at the Window/They are rattling breakfast plates in
37 Gerontion   8   house,/And the Jew squats on the window sill, the owner,/Spawned in some
57 Swee Night   30   the room and reappears/Outside the window, leaning in,/Branches of wistaria/
64 WL: Chess   90   by the air/That freshened from the window, these ascended/In fattening the
64 WL: Chess   98   mantel was displayed/As though a window gave upon the sylvan scene/The change
68 WL: Fire S   224   and lays out food in tins./Out of the window perilously spread/Her drying
92 Ash-Wed 3   13   of the third stair/Was a slotted window bellied like the fig's fruit/And beyond
98 Ash-Wed 6   8   to wish these things/From the wide window towards the granite shore/The white
107 Animula   22   dreams/Curl up the small soul in the window seat/Behind the *Encyclopaedia*
118 SP   m 15   of Hearts! {}/(*Whistle outside of the window.*)/{Du} Well I *never*/What a coincidence!
118 SP   Dusty 21   *is* Sam!/{Du} (*leaning out of the window*): Hello Sam!/{W} Hello dear/How
218 Mung Rump   7   of cats can very well bear./If the area window was found ajar/And the basement
223 Pekes Pols   28   heard the uproar,/Some came to the window, some came to the door;/There were
233 Skimble   40   your face in/And a crank to shut the window if you sneeze./Then the guard looks in
597 Before Mor   2   red with gray,/The flowers at the window turned toward dawn,/Petal on petal,
256 MC Tempts   31   bolt?/{4T} Is it rain that taps at the window, is it wind that pokes at the door?/{C}
282 MC Chorus   10   of God;/Who fear the hand at the window, the fire in the thatch, the fist in the
291 FR   Amy   7   I thought I saw someone pass the window./What time is it?/{C} Nearly twenty to
291 FR   m 14   *suddenly at the door and stares at the window*]/{I} Welcome, Harry!/{G} Well done!/{V}
291 FR   Harry 20   looked, when I saw you through the window!/Do you like to be stared at by eyes
291 FR   Harry 21   like to be stared at by eyes through a window?/{A} You forget, Harry, that you are at
302 FR   Chorus 6 About the noises in the cellar/And the window that should not have been open./Why
311 FR   m 27   *part, revealing the Eumenides in the window embrasure.*]/{H} Why do you show
311 FR   m 38   is no one here. {}/[*She goes to the window and pulls the curtains across*]/{H} They
336 FR   1m 23   *curtains close.* AGATHA *goes to the window, in a somnambular fashion,/and opens the*
348 FR   Chorus 6   do not like to look out of the same window, and see quite a different landscape./We
446 CC   Eggers 30   /But if I might make a suggestion: window boxes!/He's expressed such an interest
446 CC   Eggers 32   garden/That I think he ought to have window boxes./Some day, he'll want a garden of
457 CC   m 23   she's gone out again. {}/[*Goes to the window and looks down on the street*]/{SC} She's

WINDOW-BAR (1)
256 MC Priests   30   a signal between the trees?/{3P} Is the window-bar made fast, is the door under lock

WINDOW-PANES (4)
13 Prufrock   15   yellow fog that rubs its back upon the window-panes,/The yellow smoke that rubs its
13 Prufrock   16   smoke that rubs its muzzle on the window-panes,/Licked its tongue into the
14 Prufrock   25   the street/Rubbing its back upon the window-panes;/There will be time, there will be
54 Mr E Sun   3   sutlers of the Lord/Drift across the window-panes./In the beginning was the Word./

WINDOW-SILL (2)
56 Swee Night   18   man in mocha brown/Sprawls at the window-sill and gapes;/The waiter brings in
211 Old Gumbie   27   it into sailor-knots./She sits upon the window-sill, or anything that's smooth and flat:

WINDOWS (5)
15 Prufrock   72   men in shirt-sleeves, leaning out of windows?.../I should have been a pair of ragged
74 WL: Thund   389   only the wind's home./It has no windows, and the door swings,/Dry bones can
167 Rock 10   29   through the coloured panes of windows/And light reflected from the polished
263 MC Chorus   23   is clear and high,/And voices trill at windows, and children tumble in front of the

335 FR Agatha   21   straight ahead, passing barred windows./Up and down. Until the chain breaks.
WINDS (1)
141 Rannoch   5   /Moon cold or moon hot. The road winds in/Listlessness of ancient war,/Languor of
WINDWARD (1)
71 WL: DWater 320   you who turn the wheel and look to windward,/Consider Phlebas, who was once
WINDY (4)
24 Rhapsody   t   fuel in vacant lots./Rhapsody on a Windy Night/Twelve o'clock./Along the reaches
37 Gerontion   16   /I an old man,/A dull head among windy spaces./Signs are taken for wonders. 'We
38 Gerontion   32 old man in a draughty house/Under a windy knob./After such knowledge, what
39 Gerontion   69 atoms. Gull against the wind, in the windy straits/Of Belle Isle, or running on the
WINE (6)
136 5FingerEx3   7   shine,/I have had the Bread and Wine,/Let the feathered mortals take/That
157 Rock 4   6   in the month Nisan,/He served the wine to the king Artaxerxes,/And he grieved for
588 Fable   40   /And watered everything except the wine./So when all preparations had been made,/
247 MC Tempt1   2 /Eating up the darkness, with wit and wine and wisdom!/Now that the King and you
260 MC Thomas   30   gains, the swept hearth, his best wine for a friend/at the table, his wife singing to
292 FR Charles   31 of new hunters./{C} And I've a new wine merchant to recommend you;/Your cellar
WINE-PRESS (1)
162 Rock 8   7   from Edom?/He has trodden the wine-press alone./There came one who spoke of
WINE-SKINS (1)
103 Journ Magi   28   of silver,/And feet kicking the empty wine-skins./But there was no information, so we
WINEPRESS (1)
148 Rock 1   49   is not pleasant./I have trodden the winepress alone, and I know/That it is hard to
WING (11)
50 Hippopot   25 feed at once./I saw the 'potamus take wing/Ascending from the damp savannas,/And
64 WL: Chess   81 out/(Another hid his eyes behind his wing)/Doubled the flames of sevenbranched
127 Cor1 March   32   /O hidden under the dove's wing, hidden in the turtle's breast,/Under the
129 Cor2 State   47   with the sweep of the little bat's wing, with the small flare of the firefly or
138 New Hamp   5   the green tip and the root./Black wing, brown wing, hover over;/Twenty years
138 New Hamp   5   tip and the root./Black wing, brown wing, hover over;/Twenty years and the spring
138 New Hamp   9   light-in-leaves;/Golden head, black wing,/Cling, swing,/Spring, sing,/Swing up into
175 FQ: BurntN 137   /Down on us? After the kingfisher's wing/Has answered light to light, and is silent,
257 MC Chorus   32 round you, lie at your feet, swing and wing through the dark air./O Thomas
288 FR Agatha   39 nursery, round the corner/Of the new wing, he will have to face him —/And it will not
581 ES Ld Clav 27 of reason,/I have been brushed by the wing of happiness./And I am happy, Monica,
WINGS (12)
41 Burb Blei   29   /Klein. Who clipped the lion's wings/And flea'd his rump and pared his claws?/
73 WL: Thund   380   violet light/Whistled, and beat their wings/And crawled head downward down a
89 Ash-Wed 1   6 (Why should the agèd eagle stretch its wings?)/Why should I mourn/The vanished
90 Ash-Wed 1   34   be too heavy upon us/Because these wings are no longer wings to fly/But merely
90 Ash-Wed 1   34 us/Because these wings are no longer wings to fly/But merely vans to beat the air/The
98 Ash-Wed 6   10   seaward, seaward flying/Unbroken wings/And the lost heart stiffens and rejoices/In
111 Xmas Trees   7   and the gilded angel/Spreading its wings at the summit of the tree/Is not only a
129 Cor2 State   35 noon/There the cyclamen spreads its wings, there the clematis droops over the lintel/
180 FQ: ECoker 116   be changed/With a hollow rumble of wings, with a movement of darkness on
269 MC Chorus   30   and owls, have seen at noon/Scaly wings slanting over, huge and ridiculous. I have
310 FR   Mary   28   /To rise toward the violent sun/Wet wings into the rain cloud/Harefoot over the
315 FR Chorus   33 future was long since settled./And the wings of the future darken the past, the beak
WINK (2)
247 MC Tempt1   22 /{T1} My Lord, a nod is as good as a wink./A man will often love what he spurns./
272 MC Thomas   5 spared./I have had a tremor of bliss, a wink of heaven, a whisper,/And I would no
WINKING (1)
232 Skimble   25   occurred./He will watch you without winking and he sees what you are thinking/And
WINKLES (1)
230 Bust Jones   20 *Stage and Screen*/Which is famous for winkles and shrimps./In the season of venison
WINKS (1)
24 Rhapsody   52 La lune ne garde aucune rancune,/She winks a feeble eye,/She smiles into corners./She
WINTER (31)
22 Preludes   1 have the right to smile?/Preludes/The winter evening settles down/With smell of steaks
61 WL: Burial   5 stirring/Dull roots with spring rain./Winter kept us warm, covering/Earth in
61 WL: Burial   18   of the night, and go south in the winter./What are the roots that clutch, what
62 WL: Burial   61   City,/Under the brown fog of a winter dawn,/A crowd flowed over London
67 WL: Fire S   190   I was fishing in the dull canal/On a winter evening round behind the gashouse/
68 WL: Fire S   208   City/Under the brown fog of a winter noon/Mr. Eugenides, the Smyrna
103 Journ Magi   5   the weather sharp,/The very dead of winter.'/And the camels galled, sore-footed,

105 Song Sime	2	are blooming in bowls and/The winter sun creeps by the snow hills;/The
163 Rock 8	32	more than the tales/Of old men on winter evenings./Only the faith could have done
180 FQ: ECoker	130	/Whisper of running streams, and winter lightning./The wild thyme unseen and the
184 FQ: DrySal	14	table,/And the evening circle in the winter gaslight./The river is within us, the sea is
190 FQ: DrySal	213	/The wild thyme unseen, or the winter lightning/Or the waterfall, or music
206 To my Wife	8	without need of meaning./No peevish winter wind shall chill/No sullen tropic sun shall
218 Mung Rump	12	/And you couldn't find one of your winter vests,/Or after supper one of the girls/
240 MC Chorus	6	fear disturbance of the quiet seasons:/Winter shall come bringing death from the sea,/
240 MC Chorus	12	consolation/For autumn fires and winter fogs?/What shall we do in the heat of
244 MC Chorus	6	and cider,/Gathered wood against the winter,/Talked at the corner of the fire,/Talked
247 MC Templ1	1	in chambers,/Fires devouring the winter season,/Eating up the darkness, with wit
247 MC Templ1	9	of the new season./Spring has come in winter. Snow in the branches/Shall float as
257 MC Chorus	11	disease,/The old without fire in winter,/The child without milk in summer,/Our
263 MC Chorus	16	And the world must be cleaned in the winter, or we shall have only/A sour spring, a
281 MC Chorus	16	us the voices of seasons, the snuffle of winter, the song of spring, the drone of summer,
285 FR Ivy	14	told Amy she should go south in the winter./Were I in Amy's position, I would go
285 FR Ivy	15	position, I would go south in the winter./I would follow the sun, not wait for the
285 FR Ivy	17	to come here./I would go south in the winter, if I could afford it,/Not freeze, as I do,
286 FR Charles	1	/Ever to want to leave England in the winter./But a single man like me is better off in
286 FR Charles	4	cosy at his club/Even in an English winter./{G} Well, as for me,/I'd just as soon be a
310 FR Harry	13	ghosts of the dead/Those whom the winter drowned/Do not the ghosts of the
315 FR Violet	19	that she can't get about now in winter/You wouldn't think that she was a day
445 CC Eggers	15	to lose a moment at the end of the winter/And I matched some material for Mrs.
528 ES Monica	37	Charles./It's almost certain that the winter in Jamaica/Will never take place. 'Make

WINTER'S (1)

| 197 FQ: Little | 238 | So, while the light fails/On a winter's afternoon, in a secluded chapel/History |

WIPE (1)

| 23 Preludes | 52 | gentle/Infinitely suffering thing./Wipe your hand across your mouth, and laugh;/ |

WIPED (1)

| 29 Aunt Helen | 6 | were drawn and the undertaker wiped his feet —/He was aware that this sort of |

WIPES (1)

| 42 Swee Erect | 24 | /Knows the female temperament/And wipes the suds around his face./(The lengthened |

WIRE (3)

172 FQ: BurntN	51	Clot the bedded axle-tree./The trilling wire in the blood/Sings below inveterate scars/
229 Gus	43	once crossed the stage on a telegraph wire,/To rescue a child when a house was on
349 FR Violet	10	for the will to be read. I shall send a wire in the morning./{C} I fear that my mind is

WIRES (1)

| 181 FQ: ECoker | 165 | to knees,/The fever sings in mental wires./If to be warmed, then I must freeze/And |

WISDOM (9)

147 Rock 1	15	we have lost in living?/Where is the wisdom we have lost in knowledge?/Where is
179 FQ: ECoker	76	calm, the autumnal serenity/And the wisdom of age? Had they deceived us,/Or
179 FQ: ECoker	80	only a deliberate hebetude,/The wisdom only the knowledge of dead secrets/
179 FQ: ECoker	95	Do not let me hear/Of the wisdom of old men, but rather of their folly,/
179 FQ: ECoker	98	or to others, or to God./The only wisdom we can hope to acquire/Is the wisdom
179 FQ: ECoker	99	wisdom we can hope to acquire/Is the wisdom of humility: humility is endless./The
247 MC Templ1	2	the darkness, with wit and wine and wisdom!/Now that the King and you are in
448 CC Claude	10	And the Book of Revelation? And the Wisdom of Atlantis?/{E} Well, to tell the truth,
485 CC Lady E	12	myself to be/And then I took up the Wisdom of the East/And believed, for a while,

WISE (4)

21 Portrait	120	to feel or if I understand/Or whether wise or foolish, tardy or too soon .../Would she
588 Fable	38	lengthy story shorter,/He left no wise precaution incomplete;/He doused the
309 FR Mary	13	of this conversation./{M} I am not a wise person,/And in the ordinary sense I don't
501 CC Lady E	3	sure too, Lucasta, you have made a wise decision./{L} And I know very well why

WISER (1)

| 482 CC Lady E | 20 | older than you are,/And a good deal wiser in the ways of the world./{C} But, Lady |

WISEST (2)

| 62 WL: Burial | 45 | cold, nevertheless/Is known to be the wisest woman in Europe,/With a wicked pack of |
| 513 CC Guzzard | 2 | judge, with you./Perhaps you are the wisest wisher here:/I shall not ask you whether |

WISH (72)

32 Hysteria	7	saying: 'If the lady and gentleman wish to take their/tea in the garden, if the lady
32 Hysteria	8	the garden, if the lady and gentleman wish to take their tea in the/garden ...' I decided
98 Ash-Wed 6	7	/(Bless me father) though I do not wish to wish these things/From the wide
98 Ash-Wed 6	7	me father) though I do not wish to wish these things/From the wide window
165 Rock 9	29	senses?/The LORD who created must wish us to create/And employ our creation
243 MC Chorus	22	a doom on the world./We do not wish anything to happen./Seven years we have

258 MC Thomas	26	become servant of God was never my	wish./Servant of God has chance of greater sin/
260 MC Thomas	5	morning will be a/very short one. I	wish only that you should meditate in your
268 MC Thomas	16	were we sent./{T} Never was it my	wish/To uncrown the King's son, or to diminish
268 MC Thomas	18	honour and power. Why should he	wish/To deprive my people of me and keep me
268 MC Thomas	21	me sit in Canterbury, alone?/I would	wish him three crowns rather than one,/And as
275 MC Chorus	28	a curtain of falling blood?/We did not	wish anything to happen./We understood the
279 MC Knight4	35	to cool. That was just what he did not	wish to happen; he/insisted, while we were still
289 FR Amy	19	/But I don't believe he will. He will	wish to forget it./I do not mince matters in front
296 FR Charles	26	talk to./I suspect it is simply that the	wish to get rid of her/Makes him believe he did.
297 FR Violet	33	Amy would disapprove of —/I only	wish to express my emphatic protest/Both
298 FR Ivy	6	the means./{V} I do object./{I} And I	wish to associate myself with my sister/In her
298 FR Violet	15	witnesses. I intend to remain./And I	wish to be present to hear what Downing says./I
304 FR Mary	6	you any differently now;/But I really	wish that I'd taken your advice/And tried for a
305 FR Harry	33	the same as when you left it./{H} I	wish she had not done that. It's very unnatural,/
332 FR Harry	39	of murderer./{H} In what way did he	wish to murder her?/{Ag} Oh, a dozen foolish
334 FR Harry	19	frightened! I can hardly imagine it./I	wish I had known — but that was impossible./I
337 FR Amy	34	/I think I know well enough why you	wish him to go./{Ag} I wish nothing. I only say
337 FR Agatha	35	why you wish him to go./{Ag} I	wish nothing. I only say what I know must
356 CP Julia	24	She agreed with me./She said: 'I	wish you'd try.' And this is the first time/I've
387 CP Edward	7	way too, and laugh about it?/{E} I	wish I could. I wish I understood anything./I'm
387 CP Edward	7	laugh about it?/{E} I wish I could. I	wish I understood anything./I'm completely in
411 CP Lavinia	21	/But it's difficult to say./{L} But I	wish you would say it./At least, there is
417 CP Reilly	22	choose for you. If that is what you	wish,/I can reconcile you to the human
418 CP Celia	16	give anyone the kind of love —/I	wish I could — which belongs to that life./Oh,
439 CP Peter	16	go there .../{P} I see what you mean./I	wish I didn't have to. But the car will be
439 CP Lavinia	40	/How I could face my guests. I	wish it was over./I mean ... I am glad you came
440 CP Lavinia	35	party./{E} It will soon be over./{L} I	wish it would begin./{E} There's the doorbell./
451 CC Eggers	38	choir/And at the carol service. But I	wish I was musical./{C} I still don't feel very
461 CC Eggers	8	you want me./In fact, Mrs. E. said: 'I	wish he'd ring us up!/I'm sure he has a very
467 CC Colby	4	son/And he is still your father. I only	wish/That I had something to atone for!/There's
469 CC Lucasta	4	But I'd like to learn about music./I	wish you would teach me how to appreciate it./
471 CC Lucasta	19	something quite simple./{L} Then I	wish you'd tell me./Because I don't know./{C}
479 CC Kaghan	14	the new bachelor quarters,/And to	wish Colby luck. I've always been lucky,/And I
490 CC Colby	12	than it can be even to ... us./{C} I only	wish it was more acute agony:/I don't know
491 CC Colby	2	Now, you have made me think,/And I	wish that I could have had a father and a
494 CC Lady E	2	the night. I hardly slept at all./I	wish that Colby, somehow, might prove to be
494 CC Lady E	30	anything,/And perhaps I don't. But I	wish you would talk/Sometimes to me as if I did
499 CC Eggers	2	/Will you sit at the desk?/{E} If you	wish, Sir Claude./I do feel more at ease when
501 CC Eggers	28	of all I must take the occasion/To	wish Miss Angel every happiness./And I'm sure
504 CC Claude	19	B. do it. {}/[Exit LUCASTA]/{SC} I	wish you could arrange the servants' time-table
505 CC Guzzard	13	Sir Claude, if that is what you	wish./But is the subject of this meeting —/I
510 CC Eggers	33	it seems you are my son./{E} You will	wish to obtain confirmation/Of this interesting
511 CC Lady E	23	easier, certainly./{LE} And I shall	wish to meet them./Claude, we must invite the
512 CC Guzzard	25	of us have to adapt ourselves/To the	wish that is granted. That can be a painful
512 CC Eggers	36	great friends./{E} I'm sure we all	wish for nothing better./{MG} Wishes, when
513 CC Guzzard	10	ask you now, have you had your	wish?/{SC} Colby only wanted to be sure of the
513 CC Guzzard	39	to do./{MG} Whose son would you	wish to be, Colby:/Sir Claude's — or the son of
514 CC Guzzard	5	man./{MG} You shall have your	wish. And when you have your wish/You will
514 CC Guzzard	5	your wish. And when you have your	wish/You will have to come to terms with it.
514 CC Guzzard	16	be your aunt./So you may have your	wish, and have no mother./{SC} Mrs. Guzzard,
516 CC Colby	15	Colby, not very successful./{C} And I	wish to follow my father./{SC} But, Colby:/
518 CC Guzzard	26	/But you too, I think, have had a	wish realised./— I believe that this interview can
518 CC Guzzard	38	say goodbye. You have all had your	wish/In one form or another. You and I, Sir
542 ES Gomez	27	and almost convincing:/Don't you	wish you could believe it?/{LC} And what if I
543 ES Ld Clav	16	/{LC} Yes, I'll go and rest now. I	wish Charles was dining with us./I wish we were
543 ES Ld Clav	17	I wish Charles was dining with us./I	wish we were having a dinner party./{M}
549 ES Carghil	2	everybody knows you. But still,/I	wish you could have paid me that compliment,
556 ES Monica	26	/Oh. I said that before, didn't I?/{M} I	wish you'd stop being so polite to each other./
568 ES Ld Clav	12	life, Charles Hemington,/Which you	wish to forget? Which you wish to keep
568 ES Ld Clav	12	Which you wish to forget? Which you	wish to keep unknown?/{C} There are certainly
568 ES Charles	14	gladly forget, Sir,/Or rather, which I	wish had never happened./I can think of things
568 ES Charles	16	/But there's nothing I would ever	wish to conceal from you./{LC} If there's
571 ES Monica	27	they already know./Why should you	wish to conceal from those who love you/What
574 ES Michael	31	/{Mi} When I spoke, Father, of my	wish to get abroad,/You couldn't see my point
577 ES Carghil	28	Mr. Carghill, was a business man —/I	wish you could have known him, Señor Gomez!

578 ES　Monica　39　which inspired your decision:/If you wish to renounce your father and your family/

WISHED (7)
289 FR　　Amy　39　been one of the family,/She never wished to be one of the family,/She only wanted
337 FR　Agatha　14　not understand love./What you have wished to know, what you have learned/Mean
394 CP　Edward　34　/For your kind of public life. You wished to be a hostess/For whom my career
477 CC　Lucasta　9　there's no doubt of that./I'm sure he wished there had been. He's been good to me/In
512 CC　Guzzard　23　... I shall be very happy./{MG} You wished for your son, and now you have your
513 CC　　Colby　14　strange answer./Sir Claude is right: I wished to know the truth./What it is, doesn't
559 ES　Michael　30　/Being no longer wanted. And you wished to be Lord Claverton/Also, to hold your

WISHER
513 CC　Guzzard　2　with you./Perhaps you are the wisest wisher here:/I shall not ask you whether you are

WISHES (7)
278 MC　Knight2　15　Becket concurred/with the King's wishes, we should have had an almost ideal
405 CP　　Reilly　32　Mrs. Chamberlayne,/Your husband wishes to enter a sanatorium,/And that is a
496 CC　　Eggers　19　nowadays to bring me;/But Mrs. E. wishes I'd come up oftener!/Isn't that like the
512 CC　Guzzard　21　/I should like to gratify everyone's wishes./{LE} Oh, of course ... Yes, I'm sure ... I
512 CC　Guzzard　37　we all wish for nothing better./{MG} Wishes, when realised, sometimes turn/Against
519 CC　Guzzard　1　You and I, Sir Claude,/Had *our* wishes twenty-five years ago;/But we failed to
519 CC　Guzzard　2　failed to observe, when we had our wishes,/That there was a time-limit clause in the

WISHING (2)
242 MC　Priest1　28　power given by temporal devolution,/Wishing subjection to God alone./Had the King
381 CP　Edward　16　is left to be desired;/And you go on wishing that you could desire/What desire has

WISHT (1)
588 Fable　　　60　feet upon the table superposed/Each wisht he had not eaten so much goose./The

WISHWOOD (42)
285 FR　Agatha　13　spring never come? I am cold./{Ag} Wishwood was always a cold place, Amy./{I} I
287 FR　　Amy　25　you want to know why I never leave Wishwood/That is the reason. I keep Wishwood
287 FR　　Amy　26　Wishwood/That is the reason. I keep Wishwood alive/To keep the family alive, to
288 FR　Agatha　15　that has happened/To come back to Wishwood./{G} Why, painful?/{V} Gerald! you
288 FR　Agatha　23　/Harry must often have remembered Wishwood —/The nursery tea, the school
288 FR　Agatha　27　the little door./He will find a new Wishwood. Adaptation is hard./{A} Nothing is
288 FR　　Amy　28　/{A} Nothing is changed, Agatha, at Wishwood./Everything is kept as it was when he
288 FR　Agatha　33　seen to that./{Ag} Yes. I mean that at Wishwood he will find another Harry./The man
289 FR　Gerald　9　/Let him marry again and carry on at Wishwood./{A} Thank you, Gerald. Though
290 FR　　Amy　15　future:/Harry is to take command at Wishwood/And I hope we can contrive his
291 FR　　Violet　16　{G} Well done!/{V} Welcome home to Wishwood!/{C} Why, what's the matter?/{A}
291 FR　　Amy　22　You forget, Harry, that you are at Wishwood,/Not in town, where you have to
292 FR　　Harry　10　should they wait until I came back to Wishwood?/There were a thousand places where
293 FR　　Violet　3　needs a man in charge of things at Wishwood./{A} You see your aunts and uncles
293 FR　　Amy　7　/I have only struggled to keep Wishwood going/And to make no changes
295 FR　　Amy　36　the northern country. When you see Wishwood/Again by day, all will be the same
296 FR　　Amy　31　/I prefer to believe that a few days at Wishwood/Among his own family, is all that he
306 FR　　Harry　23　you ever happy here, as a child at Wishwood?/{M} Happy? not really, though I
308 FR　　Mary　16　for something, in coming back to Wishwood,/Or you would not have come./{H}
308 FR　　Mary　25　say/Only proves that you expected Wishwood/To be your real self, to do something
309 FR　　Mary　20　not know I knew./Even if, as you say, Wishwood is a cheat,/Your family a delusion —
315 FR Warburt　14　grown up/I haven't a patient left at Wishwood./Wishwood was always a cold place,
315 FR Warburt　15　/I haven't a patient left at Wishwood./Wishwood was always a cold place, but healthy.
320 FR Warburt　19　/She has only lived for your return to Wishwood,/For you to take command at
320 FR Warburt　20　/For you to take command at Wishwood,/And for that reason, it is most
320 FR Warburt　29　/The other is yourself: the future of Wishwood/Depends on you. I don't like to say
326 FR　　Harry　30　I came home, a few hours ago, to Wishwood./{V} I will make no observations on
330 FR　　Harry　4　be in the routine of normal life at Wishwood./John is the only one of us I can
330 FR　　Harry　6　down to make himself at home at Wishwood,/Make a dull marriage, marry some
330 FR　　Harry　9　himself. He can resist the influence/Of Wishwood, being unconscious, living in gentle
331 FR　　Harry　7　foolishly/That when I got back to Wishwood, as I had left it,/Everything would
332 FR　Agatha　13　she succeeded in making terms with Wishwood,/Until she took your father's place,
332 FR　Agatha　15　place, and reached the point where/Wishwood supported her, and she supported
332 FR　Agatha　15　supported her, and she supported Wishwood./At first it was a vacancy. A man
336 FR　　Harry　17　that you are ready,/Ready to leave Wishwood, and I am going with you./You
340 FR　　Amy　1　/{A} I was a fool, to ask you again to Wishwood;/But I thought, thirty-five years is
340 FR　Agatha　10　suppose that I wanted to return to Wishwood?/{A} The more rapacious, to take
340 FR　　Amy　26　/I forced myself to the purposes of Wishwood;/I even asked you back, for visits,
341 FR　　Amy　14　when he had been a happy boy at Wishwood;/For his future success./{Ag} Success
341 FR　　Amy　33　Eight years watching, without him, at Wishwood,/Years of bitterness and

341 FR   Amy   39   you take my son./You take him from Wishwood, you take him from me,/You take
343 FR   Harry 33   destined and the perfect master of Wishwood,/The satisfactory son. And as for me,
WISTARIA (1)
57 Swee Night   31   the window, leaning in,/Branches of wistaria/Circumscribe a golden grin;/The host
WISTFUL (1)
187 FQ: DrySal 129 a Royal Rose or a lavender spray/Of wistful regret for those who are not yet here to
WISTFULNESS (2)
529 ES   Charles 10 of his disappointments./{C} Is that wistfulness,/Compassion, or ... envy?/{M} Envy
529 ES   Monica   15 /It's all we can ask if compassion and wistfulness .../And tenderness, Charles! are
WIT (2)
143 Lines OM   7   tree./When I lay bare the tooth of wit/The hissing over the archèd tongue/Is more
247 MC Tempt1   2   season,/Eating up the darkness, with wit and wine and wisdom!/Now that the King
WITCHES' (1)
204 de la Mare   22 cower, flitter bats, and owls range/At witches' sabbath of the maiden aunts;/When the
WITH (794)
WITHDRAWN (3)
91 Ash-Wed 2   16   the leopards reject. The Lady is withdrawn/In a white gown, to contemplation,
188 FQ: DrySal 155   and the farther shore/While time is withdrawn, consider the future/And the past
363 CP   Reilly 3   of you is your body/And the 'you' is withdrawn. May I replenish?/{E} Oh, I'm sorry.
WITHDRAWS (1)
56 Swee Night   22 in brown/Contracts and concentrates, withdraws;/Rachel *née* Rabinovitch/Tears at the
WITHDREW (1)
538 ES   Gomez   37 led you to the very top!/And yet you withdrew from the world of politics/And went
WITHER (1)
206 To my Wife   9   shall chill/No sullen tropic sun shall wither/The roses in the rose-garden which is
WITHERED (14)
22 Preludes   7   shower wraps/The grimy scraps/Of withered leaves about your feet/And
42 Swee Erect   13   /Rises from the sheets in steam./This withered root of knots of hair/Slitted below and
64 WL: Chess   104   /'Jug Jug' to dirty ears./And other withered stumps of time/Were told upon the
97 Ash-Wed 5   35   drouth, spitting from the mouth the withered apple-seed./O my people./Although I
160 Rock 7   14 a flicker of life,/And they came to the withered ancient look of a child that has died of
186 FQ: DrySal 82   wailing,/No end to the withering of withered flowers,/To the movement of pain that
590 Time Space 11   dew/Was trembling on the vine,/Were withered ere the wild bee flew/To suck the
590 Space Time 11   dew/Was trembling on the vine,/Were withered ere the wild bee flew/To suck the
596 When we   6   bloomed with flowers still,/No withered petals lay beneath;/But the wild roses
597 Before Mor   4   waiting for the day,/Fresh flowers, withered flowers, flowers of dawn./This
597 Before Mor   8   fragrance of decay,/Fresh flowers, withered flowers, flowers of dawn./Circe's
256 MC Chorus   8 the dark green light from a cloud on a withered tree? The earth is heaving to
292 FR   Harry 26 nothing is changed?/You all look so withered and young./{G} We must have a ride
382 CP   Celia 11 every contour; and as I looked/It withered, as if I had unwrapped a mummy./I
WITHERING (2)
185 FQ: DrySal 52   of it, the soundless wailing,/The silent withering of autumn flowers/Dropping their
186 FQ: DrySal 82   the voiceless wailing,/No end to the withering of withered flowers,/To the movement
WITHIN (19)
37 Gerontion   18   'We would see a sign!'/The word within a word, unable to speak a word,/
57 Swee Night   37   of the Sacred Heart,/And sang within the bloody wood/When Agamemnon
69 WL: Fire S 262   /And a clatter and a chatter from within/Where fishmen lounge at noon: where
96 Ash-Wed 5   5 /The Word without a word, the Word within/The world and for the world;/And the
152 Rock 2   35   building, for it is forever decaying within and attacked from without;/For this is
157 Rock 4   16   him,/And spies and self-seekers within,/When he and his men laid their hands to
159 Rock 6   22   /From the darkness outside and within/By dreaming of systems so perfect that
184 FQ: DrySal 15   in the winter gaslight./The river is within us, the sea is all about us;/The sea is the
213 Growltiger 44   down the hatches on the crew within their bunks./Then Griddlebone she gave
253 MC Tempt4   36   pacts;/To be master or servant within an hour,/This is the course of temporal
280 MC Priest3 30 Aquitaine./In the small circle of pain within the skull/You still shall tramp and tread
375 CP   Edward 31 for supper;/And he said I must eat it within ten minutes./I suppose it's still cooking./
403 CP   Reilly 11 doing such amount of mischief/As lay within your power — until you came to grief./
403 CP   Reilly 21   like to think:/Only, shall we say, within your modest capacity./Try to explain
451 CC   Eggers 23 he began addressing her as Muriel —/Within the first ten minutes! I was horrified./
545 ES   Ld Clav   2   /With myself, I suspect, very deep within myself/Has impelled me all my life to
561 ES   Monica   37   But there's no vocabulary/For love within a family, love that's lived in/But not
561 ES   Monica   38   that's lived in/But not looked at, love within the light of which/All else is seen, the
561 ES   Monica   39 light of which/All else is seen, the love within which/All other love finds speech./This

WITHOUT (86)

18 Portrait		28	it means that I say this to you —/Without these friendships — life, what
72 WL: Thund		334	/Which are mountains of rock without water/If there were water we should
72 WL: Thund		342	the mountains/But dry sterile thunder without rain/There is not even solitude in the
83 Hollow Men		11	broken glass/In our dry cellar/Shape without form, shade without colour,/Paralysed
83 Hollow Men		11	dry cellar/Shape without form, shade without colour,/Paralysed force, gesture without
83 Hollow Men		12	colour,/Paralysed force, gesture without motion;/Those who have crossed/With
92 Ash-Wed 2		43	of all that/Is inconclusible/Speech without word and/Word of no speech/Grace to
96 Ash-Wed 5		5	word, the Word unheard,/The Word without a word, the Word within/The world
150 Rock 1		118	no peace and no end/But noise *without speech, food without taste./Without*
150 Rock 1		118	*no end/But noise without speech, food without taste./Without delay, without haste/We*
150 Rock 1		119	*without speech, food without taste./Without delay, without haste/We would build the*
150 Rock 1		119	*food without taste./Without delay, without haste/We would build the beginning and*
152 Rock 2		35	decaying within and attacked from without;/For this is the law of life; and you
155 Rock 3		42	/Build better than they that build without the LORD./Shall we lift up our feet
157 Rock 4		15	a beast to pass./There were enemies without to destroy him,/And spies and
160 Rock 7		3	for man is a vain thing, and man without GOD is a seed upon the wind: driven
160 Rock 7		20	was made through that moment: for without the meaning there is no time, and that
165 Rock 9		39	/For the work of creation is never without travail;/The formed stone, the visible
171 FQ: BurntN		26	were, dignified, invisible,/Moving without pressure, over the dead leaves,/In the
173 FQ: BurntN		76	light still and moving,/*Erhebung* without motion, concentration/Without
173 FQ: BurntN		77	without motion, concentration/Without elimination, both a new world/And the
180 FQ: ECoker		124	—/I said to my soul, be still, and wait without hope/For hope would be hope for the
180 FQ: ECoker		125	be hope for the wrong thing; wait without love/For love would be love of the
180 FQ: ECoker		128	the hope are all in the waiting./Wait without thought, for you are not ready for
193 FQ: Little		70	/Gapes at the vanity of toil,/Laughs without mirth./This is the death of earth./Water
194 FQ: Little		134	the cold friction of expiring sense/Without enchantment, offering no promise/But
197 FQ: Little		223	the new,/The common word exact without vulgarity,/The formal word precise but
197 FQ: Little		235	/Are of equal duration. A people without history/Is not redeemed from time, for
206 To my Wife		6	other/Who think the same thoughts without need of speech/And babble the same
206 To my Wife		7	speech/And babble the same speech without need of meaning./No peevish winter
210 Old Gumbie		21	/And believing that nothing is done without trying,/She sets to work with her
221 Old Deut		39	uproar' —/And out they all shuffle, without a word spoken./The digestive repose of
232 Skimble		25	anything occurred./He will watch you without winking and he sees what you are
233 Skimble		65	says: 'I'll see you again!/You'll meet without fail on the Midnight Mail/The Cat of
589 Fable		93	/Spirits from that time forth they did without,/And lived the admiration of the shire.
241 MC	Mess	12	the temple,/I am here to inform you, without circumlocution:/The Archbishop is in
255 MC	Thomas	35	sinful? Can I neither act nor suffer/Without perdition?/{T4} Well you act and do not
257 MC	Chorus	11	/Destitution, disease,/The old without fire in winter,/The child without milk in
257 MC	Chorus	12	old without fire in winter,/The child without milk in summer,/Our labour taken
267 MC	Knight2	19	command./Shall we say it now?/{K2} Without delay,/Before the old fox is off and
268 MC	Thomas	37	/To say: seven years were my people without/My presence; seven years of misery and
274 MC	Thomas	29	man who/Like a bold lion, should be without fear./I am here./No traitor to the King.
276 MC	Knight1	24	and therefore will not judge anybody without/hearing both sides of the case. And that
280 MC	Priest1	13	shall build on the ruins,/Their world without God. I see it. I see it./{P3} No. For the
294 FR	Agatha	13	you can:/Talk in your own language, without stopping to debate/Whether it may be
294 FR	Harry	17	thick smoke, many creatures moving/Without direction, for no direction/Leads
294 FR	Harry	19	round and round in that vapour —/Without purpose, and without principle of
294 FR	Harry	19	that vapour —/Without purpose, and without principle of conduct/In flickering
294 FR	Harry	21	/The partial anstheria of suffering without feeling/And partial observation of one's
314 FR	Harry	18	never get well./{H} Not, I think, without some justification:/For what you call
317 FR	Warburt	18	/{W} That is in a sense true,/But without your knowing it, and what you know/
336 FR	Agatha	27	the incredible/Becomes the actual/Without our intention/Knowing what is
341 FR	Amy	33	his life,/Eight years watching, without him, at Wishwood,/Years of bitterness
355 CP	Julia	21	but he's such a strain —/Edward without Lavinia! He's quite impossible!/Leaving
356 CP	Julia	25	this is the first time/I've ever seen you without Lavinia/Except for the time she got
358 CP	Julia	10	dine with you alone./{J} Yes, alone!/Without Lavinia! You'll like the other people —
360 CP	Edward	3	me./{UG} Your wife has left you?/{E} Without warning, of course;/Just when she'd
361 CP	Reilly	38	your life becoming cosier and cosier/Without the consistent critic, the patient
362 CP	Edward	13	her going away/At a moment's notice, without explanation,/Only a note to say that she
364 CP	Julia	33	here,/And I simply can't see a thing without them./I've been dragging Peter all over
401 CP	m	1	— { }/[*Stops and stares at* REILLY]/[*without looking up from his papers*]./{R} Good
401 CP	Edward	38	to persuade me/That I was better off without her. But didn't you realise/That I was in
403 CP	Edward	31	strength/That some women have. Without her, it was vacancy./When I thought
403 CP	Edward	35	that is now intolerable;/I cannot live without her, for she has made me incapable/Of

406 CP	Edward	23	I incline to the second explanation/Without the qualification 'lunatic'./Why should
417 CP	Celia	12	/In the spirit, a vibration of delight/Without desire, for desire is fulfilled/In the
418 CP	Celia	11	it./I want to live with it. I could do without everything,/Put up with anything, if I
425 CP	Lavinia	10	offended/To hear we'd given a party without asking them./{E} Perhaps we ought to
437 CP	Reilly	26	the way of life/To lead to death, and, without knowing the end/Yet choose the form
440 CP	Julia	15	party begins./They will get on better without us. You too, Alex./{L} We don't *want*
490 CC	Colby	20	understand/That when one has lived without parents, as a child,/There's a gap that
495 CC	Lady E	39	is the first time/I have talked to you, without feeling very stupid./You always made
506 CC	Eggers	13	/So, for many years, she has been without a clue/Until the other day. This son,
507 CC	Guzzard	25	was informed that the father had died/Without making a will./{LE} He was very
517 CC	Colby	11	you too much./You've become a man without illusions/About himself, and without
517 CC	Colby	12	without illusions/About himself, and without ambitions./Now that I've abandoned
522 ES	dedic	6	*lovers .../Who think the same thoughts without need of speech/And babble the same*
522 ES	dedic	7	*of speech/And babble the same speech without need of meaning:/To you I dedicate this*
529 ES	Monica	13	/{M} Envy is everywhere./Who is without envy? And most people/Are unaware or
531 ES	Lambert	38	/If you heard that he'd gone away without your seeing him./{LC} What sort of a
539 ES	Gomez	20	followed your undergraduate career/Without the protection of that prudent devil/Of
544 ES	Ld Clav	30	people. At least, as they seem to do/Without knowing that they enjoy it. Whereas
559 ES	Michael	29	/Of retiring from politics, not without dignity,/Being no longer wanted. And
569 ES	Ld Clav	6	actor/If she saw him, off the stage, without his costume and makeup/And without
569 ES	Ld Clav	7	his costume and makeup/And without his stage words. Monica!/I've had your
570 ES	Ld Clav	14	when she lay dying:/Completely without interest in the life that lay behind her/

WITNESS (8)

43 Swee Erect	35	themselves involved, disgraced,/Call witness to their principles/And deprecate the
148 Rock 1	44	And who sees what is to happen./The Witness. The Critic. The Stranger./The
239 MC Chorus	7	act/Which our eyes are compelled to witness, has forced our feet/Towards the
239 MC Chorus	8	the cathedral. We are forced to bear witness./Since golden October declined into
240 MC Chorus	25	is no action,/But only to wait and to witness. {}/[*Enter* PRIESTS]/{P1} Seven years
264 MC Priest1	2	/*Princes moreover did sit, and did witness falsely against me.*/A day that was always
493 CC Claude	15	barristers/Ready to cross-examine a witness./It's very awkward. We don't want to
576 ES Gomez	36	/Here's Mrs. Carghill, a reliable witness./{C} I know enough about the law of

WITNESSES (3)

279 MC Knight4	27	in the/presence of numerous witnesses, that he had not long to live, and/that
298 FR Violet	14	do not agree./I think there should be witnesses. I intend to remain./And I wish to be
361 CP Edward	13	often used these terms in examining witnesses,/So I don't like them. May I put it to

WIVES (1)

220 Old Deut	5	/Old Deuteronomy's buried nine wives/And more — I am tempted to say,

WIZARD (1)

539 ES Gomez	14	the great economist/And financial wizard that you're supposed to be./And I've

WO (1)

62 WL: Burial	34	*Wind/Der Heimat zu/Mein Irisch Kind/Wo weilest du?*/'You gave me hyacinths first a

WOE (4)

212 Growltiger	13	ON THE LOOSE!/Woe to the weak canary, that fluttered from its
212 Growltiger	14	canary, that fluttered from its cage;/Woe to the pampered Pekinese, that faced
212 Growltiger	15	that faced Growltiger's rage;/Woe to the bristly Bandicoot, that lurks on
212 Growltiger	16	that lurks on foreign ships,/And woe to any Cat with whom Growltiger came to

WOKEN (3)

221 Old Deut	37	/For Old Deuteronomy mustn't be woken —/I'll have the police if there's any
293 FR Harry	39	have gone through life in sleep,/Never woken to the nightmare. I tell you, life would be
536 ES Gomez	8	slowly and sweetly, that you've never woken up/To the fact that Dick Ferry died long

WOLF (3)

252 MC Thomas	20	over doves/Now take the shape of a wolf among wolves?/Pursue your treacheries as
273 MC Priests	27	/Against the lion, the leopard, the wolf or the boar,/Why not more/Against beasts
281 MC Chorus	12	finch; the beast on the earth, both the wolf and the lamb; the worm in the soil and the

WOLVES (1)

252 MC Thomas	20	/Now take the shape of a wolf among wolves?/Pursue your treacheries as you have

WOMAN (43)

24 Rhapsody	16	/The street-lamp said, 'Regard that woman/Who hesitates towards you in the light
37 Gerontion	13	moss, stonecrop, iron, merds./The woman keeps the kitchen, makes tea,/Sneezes at
62 WL: Burial	45	nevertheless/Is known to be the wisest woman in Europe,/With a wicked pack of cards.
69 WL: Fire S	253	and I'm glad it's over.'/When lovely woman stoops to folly and/Paces about her
73 WL: Thund	364	/I do not know whether a man or a woman/— But who is that on the other side of
73 WL: Thund	377	Alexandria/Vienna London/Unreal/A woman drew her long black hair out tight/And
124 SA Doris	9	/I don't care for such conversation/A woman runs a terrible risk./{Sn} Let Mr.
124 SA Doris	24	all get pinched in the end./{Do} A woman runs a terrible risk./{Sn} Let Mr.

177 FQ:	ECoker	29	bonfire/The association of man and woman/In daunsinge, signifying matrimonie —/
178 FQ:	ECoker	45	/The time of the coupling of man and woman/And that of beasts. Feet rising and
293 FR	Amy	9	it's for you to manage. I am an old woman./They can give me no further advice
320 FR	Warburt	16	any moment./If she had been another woman/She would not have lived until now./
330 FR	Harry	7	/Make a dull marriage, marry some woman stupider —/Stupider than himself. He
332 FR	Agatha	16	first it was a vacancy. A man and a woman/Married, alone in a lonely country
342 FR	Amy	5	car out./What is the matter?/{A} That woman there,/She has persuaded him: I do not
342 FR	· Amy	9	/In the hands of any unscrupulous woman./*I* have no influence over him; *you* can
343 FR	Amy	22	/{A} So you will all leave me!/An old woman alone in a damned house./I will let the
355 CP	Julia	25	a cocktail party/For a gluttonous old woman like me/Is a really nice tit-bit. I can
356 CP	Julia	28	/I know you think I'm a silly old woman/But I'm really very serious. Lavinia
359 CP	Edward	20	invited./But it's only that dreadful old woman who mattered —/I shouldn't have
360 CP	Reilly	29	that I know of./{UG} Or another woman/Of whom she thought she had cause to
360 CP	Reilly	34	want to come back to you. If another woman,/She might decide to be forgiving/And
360 CP	Reilly	36	gain an advantage. If there's no other woman/And no other man, then the reason may
361 CP	Reilly	1	somebody wanted you;/If another woman, you might have to marry her —/You
370 CP	Edward	36	have found that she was another woman/And that you were another man. I
389 CP	Lavinia	28	in so far as a girl *can* be a friend/Of a woman so much older than herself./{C} Lavinia,
392 CP	Lavinia	22	know./But I'm puzzled by Julia. That woman is the devil./She knows by instinct when
410 CP	Reilly	9	himself incapable of loving/And a woman who finds that no man can love her./{L}
410 CP	Reilly	14	always say: 'he could not love any woman;'/*You* could always say: 'no man could
437 CP	Reilly	22	So it was obvious/That here was a woman under sentence of death./That was her
440 CP	Lavinia	23	/{L} Oh, Edward, that spoils it. No woman can believe/That she always looks her
470 CC	Lucasta	31	think it's any compliment/To invite a woman to something she would like/When she
535 ES	Gomez	14	that mean? One trusts a man/Or a woman — in this respect or that./*A* won't let me
546 ES	Piggott	2	don't simply mean that I'm a married woman —/A widow in fact. But I was a Trained
550 ES	Carghil	36	'he doesn't understand women./Any woman who trusted *him* would soon find that
551 ES	Carghil	1	all the women/He has loved. But a woman doesn't want to forget/A single one of
551 ES	Carghil	5	women live on memories./Besides a woman has nothing to be ashamed of:/A man is
555 ES	Ld Clav	31	Perhaps he's in trouble/With some woman or other. I'm sure he has friends/Whom
560 ES	Ld Clav	24	driver./{LC} What then? That young woman?/{Mi} I'm not such a fool/As to get
569 ES	Ld Clav	29	He's a very rich man. And she's a rich woman./If people merely blackmail you to get
572 ES	Ld Clav	20	physical attraction/Which no other woman has had. And she knows it./And she
572 ES	Ld Clav	22	I was/Still clings to the ghost of the woman who was Maisie./We should have been
572 ES	Charles	26	forgiven me./{C} This man, and this woman, who are so vindictive:/Don't you see

WOMB (2)

189 FQ:	DrySal	198	terrors —/To explore the womb, or tomb, or dreams; all these are usual/
333 FR	Agatha	11	death through lifetime, death in my womb./I felt that you were in some way mine!/

WOMEN (28)

13 Prufrock		13	and make our visit./In the room the women come and go/Talking of Michelangelo./
14 Prufrock		35	of a toast and tea./In the room the women come and go/Talking of Michelangelo./
23 Preludes		53	laugh;/The worlds revolve like ancient women/Gathering fuel in vacant lots./Rhapsody
103 Journ Magi		12	away, and wanting their liquor and women,/And the night-fires going out, and the
150 Rock 1		104	*be one cigarette to two men,/To two women one half pint of bitter/Ale. In this land/No*
159 Rock 6		15	your teeth on rising and retiring;/Women! polish your fingernails:/You polish the
161 Rock 7		35	*be one cigarette to two men,/To two women one half pint of bitter/Ale..../CHORUS:/*
185 FQ:	DrySal	41	time counted by anxious worried women/Lying awake, calculating the future,/
189 FQ:	DrySal	179	/Repeat a prayer also on behalf of/Women who have seen their sons or husbands/
238 MC	m	3	Characters/PART I/A CHORUS OF WOMEN OF CANTERBURY/THREE
238 MC	m	14	THOMAS BECKET/CHORUS OF WOMEN OF CANTERBURY/
239 MC	Chorus	4	can be/For us, the poor, the poor women of Canterbury? what tribulation/With
245 MC	Priest2	2	are foolish, immodest and babbling women./Do you not know that the good
245 MC	Priest2	24	by the chatter of these foolish women./Forgive us, my Lord, you would have
257 MC	Chorus	7	been too happy./We are not ignorant women, we know what we must expect and not
270 MC	Chorus	21	of living worms/In the guts of the women of Canterbury./I have smelt them, the
282 MC	Chorus	7	of the common man,/Of the men and women who shut the door and sit by the fire;/
300 FRDowning		19	can go/For a quiet smoke, where the women can't follow him./She wouldn't leave
340 FR	Agatha	8	thirty years of solitude,/Alone, among women, in a women's college,/Trying not to
340 FR	Agatha	9	women's college,/Trying not to dislike women. Thirty years in which to think./Do you
357 CP	Julia	22	again./I understand these tough old women —/I'm one myself. I feel as if I knew/All
380 CP	Celia	4	To humiliate me. I suppose that most women/Would feel degraded to find that a man/
403 CP	Edward	31	sub-human strength/That some women have. Without her, it was vacancy./
449 CC	Claude	25	others./For one, they're both of them women./{E} True./{SC} But I don't think she
479 CC	Kaghan	4	to mix cocktails,/If you don't want women always dropping in on you./And
550 ES	Carghil	35	she was! — 'he doesn't understand women./Any woman who trusted *him* would

550 ES	Carghil	37	/A man may prefer to forget all the women/He has loved. But a woman doesn't
551 ES	Carghil	4	testimonial./Men live by forgetting — women live on memories./Besides a woman has

WOMEN'S (2)

331 FR	Agatha	23	me as,/The efficient principal of a women's college —/That is the surface. There is
340 FR	Agatha	8	solitude,/Alone, among women, in a women's college,/Trying not to dislike women.

WON (2)

255 MC	Thomas	5	/Is there no enduring crown to be won?/{T4} Yes, Thomas, yes; you have thought
533 ES	Ld Clav	25	/{LC} Do you mean that you've won respect out there/By the sort of activity

WON'T (70)

66 WL:	Chess	155	you can't./But if Albert makes off, it won't be for lack of telling./You ought to be
66 WL:	Chess	163	a proper fool, I said./Well, if Albert won't leave you alone, there it is, I said,/What
116 SP	Doris	3	/Sam's all right/{Do} But Pereira won't do./We can't have Pereira/{Du} Well
119 SP	Klip	25	first time/{Kl} And I certainly hope it won't be the last time./{Do} You like London,
123 SA	Kl & Kr	16	girl/I'm going to stay with you/And we won't worry what to do/We won't have to catch
123 SA	Kl & Kr	17	/And we won't worry what to do/We won't have to catch any trains/And we won't go
123 SA	Kl & Kr	18	won't have to catch any trains/And we won't go home when it rains/We'll gather hibiscus
123 SA	Kl & Kr	20	/We'll gather hibiscus flowers/For it won't be minutes but hours/For it won't be hours
123 SA	Kl & Kr	21	it won't be minutes but hours/For it won't be hours but years {}/diminuendo/{Kl&Kr}
214 RT	Tugger	26	/When there isn't any fish then he won't eat rabbit./If you offer him cream then he
233	Skimble	44	ready to remind him./For Skimble won't let anything go wrong./And when you
233	Skimble	48	that it's very nice/To know that you won't be bothered by mice —/You can leave all
246 MC	Templ	29	all the good time past./Your Lordship won't despise an old friend out of favour?/Old
246 MC	Templ	31	Becket of London,/Your Lordship won't forget that evening on the river/When the
266 MC	Knight2	34	Saving your insolence and greed./Won't you ask us to pray to God for you, in
277 MC	Knight3	24	show he put up at the end —/they won't give *us* any glory. No, we have done for
298 FR	Charles	30	I'd like to put to you,/I'm sure you won't mind, it's about his Lordship./You've
319 FR	Harry	35	kissed me,/I felt the trap close. If you won't tell me,/I must ask Agatha. I never dared
320 FR	Warburt	1	/And your brothers will be here. Won't you let me tell you/What I had to say?/
346 FR	Downing	20	a kind of feeling that his Lordship won't need me/Very long now. I can't give you
346 FR	Downing	32	I say now, I have a feeling/That he won't want me long, and he won't want
346 FR	Downing	32	/That he won't want me long, and he won't want anybody./{Ag} And, Downing, if his
357 CP	Julia	34	In the *depths* of Essex./{J} Well, we won't probe into it./You have the address, and
358 CP	Peter	14	/{E} Must you be going?/{P} But won't you tell the story about Lady Klootz?/{J}
360 CP	Reilly	38	/And you've ground for hope that she won't come back at all./If another man, then
366 CP	Peter	14	/Come along, Peter./{P} I hope you won't mind/If I don't come with you, Julia? On
367 CP	Peter	16	/What arts do you practise?/{P} You won't have seen my novel,/Though it had some
377 CP	Edward	27	to propose?/{E} No, I can't. But I won't drink to Alex's./{J} Oh, it isn't Alex's.
378 CP	Celia	22	unpleasant!/No, it can't be that. I won't think it's that./I think it is just a moment
382 CP	Celia	24	/Tread on me, if you like./{C} No, I won't tread on you./That is not what you are. It
386 CP	Edward	26	there is nothing to do but wait./Won't you sit down?/{C} Thank you. {}/[Pause]/
392 CP	Lavinia	11	It's about that party./I suppose you won't believe I forgot all about it!/I let you
398 CP	Lavinia	3	would burst out laughing. But you won't./{E} O God, O God, if I could return to
401 CP	Reilly	2	Mr. Chamberlayne./Please sit down. I won't keep you a moment./— Now, Mr.
404 CP	Edward	30	go home again. And at my club/They won't let you keep a room for more than seven
411 CP	Edward	9	you stop at your club?/{E} No, they won't let me./I must leave tomorrow — but how
412 CP	Reilly	24	/{R} Miss Celia Coplestone? ... Won't you sit down?/I believe you are a friend
414 CP	Celia	18	it's been in the family so long, they won't leave it./{R} And you live in London?/{C}
425 CP	Lavinia	18	think that you need worry:/They won't all come, out of those who accepted./You
425 CP	Lavinia	29	get at the cocktails,/And the man won't be able to take the tray about,/So they'll
427 CP	Alex	8	Kinkanja —/An island that you won't have heard of/Yet. Got back this
432 CP	Julia	6	Then if you know him already, you won't be afraid of him./You know, I was afraid
446 CC	Claude	13	/In a different form. He won't forget/That his great ambition was to be
446 CC	Claude	36	fond of bird watching./{SC} But there won't be any birds — none worth watching./{E}
455 CC	Eggers	17	/Always losing her jobs, because she won't stick to them./He gives her an allowance
456 CC	Colby	39	out of her difficulties./{C} Perhaps she won't even arrive by this plane./{E} Oh, that
470 CC	Colby	19	you learn about music —/And that won't take you long — and hear good
481 CC	Kaghan	1	live on a desert island./But I hope you won't do that. We need you where you are./{C}
482 CC	Lady E	8	altogether./But, Colby, I hope you won't mind a gentle hint./I feared it was
491 CC	Lady E	9	Let us regard him as being *our* son:/It won't be the same as what we had wanted —/
493 CC	Lady E	8	side, with the light behind me:/But won't you be sitting at the desk yourself?/{SC}
493 CC	Lady E	25	that in the corner/For Colby. He won't want to be conspicuous,/Poor boy!/{SC}
499 CC	Claude	14	not involved in this meeting, Lucasta./Won't it do another time?/{L} I came to
499 CC	Lucasta	21	But we haven't much time./{L} It won't take much time. I'm going to marry B./
518 CC	Eggers	3	because, Mr. Simpkins —/I hope you won't take this as an impertinence —/I don't see
525 ES	Charles	16	I will stop to tea,/But you know I won't get a chance to talk to you./You know

525 ES	Monica	30	to be buried in the library/And he won't think of leaving it until he's called for tea.
527 ES	Charles	10	Such things have happened./{C} That won't happen to me. {}/[*Knock. Enter*
527 ES	Lambert	14	/{L} He's busy at the moment. But he won't be very long. {}/[*Exit*]/{C} Don't you
529 ES	Monica	26	about nothing. Though I know that won't be easy./{LC} That is just what I was
531 ES	Ld Clav	26	filled/Are inwardly delighted. They won't want my ghost/Walking in the City or
535 ES	Gomez	15	a woman — in this respect or that./*A* won't let me down in this relationship,/*B* won't
535 ES	Gomez	16	let me down in this relationship,/*B* won't let me down in some other connection./
535 ES	Ld Clav	20	*silently, deposits tray and exit*]/{LC} Won't you help yourself? {}/[GOMEZ *does so,*
546 ES	Piggott	30	/Always to call me Mrs. Piggott, won't you?/{M} Yes, Mrs. Piggott, but please
547 ES	Piggott	37	You must learn the best walks./I won't apologise for the lack of excitement:/
548 ES	Monica	3	to enjoy it. {}/[*Exit*]/{M} I hope she won't remember anything else./{LC} She'll come
551 ES	Carghil	32	a breach of promise suit/Some people won't want to appear as his supporters.'/He
556 ES	Monica	3	want you to be free from worry./He won't make a scene. But I can see he's
558 ES	Michael	1	/{Mi} It's their own fault./They won't send in their bills, and then I forget them.

WONDER (31)

14 Prufrock		38	/And indeed there will be time/To wonder, 'Do I dare?' and, 'Do I dare?'/Time to
34 Figlia		21	and her arms full of flowers./And I wonder how they should have been together!/I
111 Xmas Trees		10	Tree:/Let him continue in the spirit of wonder/At the Feast as an event not accepted as
151 Rock 2		7	framed together, you sit ashamed and wonder whether and how you may be builded
187 FQ: DrySal		126	is what it always was./I sometimes wonder if that is what Krishna meant —/
194 FQ: Little		110	in a dead patrol./I said: 'The wonder that I feel is easy,/Yet ease is cause of
194 FQ: Little		111	that I feel is easy,/Yet ease is cause of wonder. Therefore speak:/I may not
226 Macavity		26	trellis past repair —/Ay, there's the wonder of the thing! *Macavity's not there!*/And
256 MC Tempts		22	grandeur to final illusion,/Lost in the wonder of his own greatness,/The enemy of
303 FR	Agatha	9	wind and rain, as I know them./{Ag} I wonder how many we shall be for dinner./{M}
321 FR	Warburt	14	see him. {}/[*Exit* DENMAN]/{W} I wonder what he wants. I hope nothing has
326 FR	Gerald	7	But I do think he is reckless./{G} I wonder how much Amy knows about Arthur?/
347 FR	Ivy	16	/[*Enter* GERALD *and* VIOLET]/{I} I wonder why he sent it, after telephoning./Shall I
354 CP	Alex	15	were several very lovely daughters:/I wonder what's become of them now./{J} Lady
356 CP	Julia	7	a film./{J} Oh, what film was it? I wonder if I've seen it./{P} No, you wouldn't
362 CP	Reilly	3	turning the past over and over,/You'll wonder only that you endured it for so long./
387 CP	Edward	24	to come and bring me with her./{E} I wonder whom else Lavinia has invited./{P}
396 CP	Lavinia	12	/And then it never happened./I wonder now/How you could have thought you
404 CP	Edward	5	Yes, you could be alone there./{E} I wonder/If you have understood a word of what
407 CP	Lavinia	37	of people to let me know about it./I wonder if there was anyone who didn't know./
408 CP	Edward	11	at concealment/Than I was. Now I wonder who it could have been./{L} Well, tell
455 CC	Colby	3	/Before you know it!/{C} I shouldn't wonder./I nearly did, a moment ago./Then I'd
484 CC	Lady E	32	obsessions, and I never told anyone./I wonder if *you* had the same obsessions?/{C}
539 ES	Gomez	6	yes, the usual euphemism./And yet I wonder. It *is* surprising:/You should have been
539 ES	Gomez	12	Yes. You might have another./But I wonder what brought about this ... stroke;/And
539 ES	Gomez	13	brought about this ... stroke;/And I wonder whether you're the great economist/And
539 ES	Gomez	32	/What would have happened to me, I wonder,/If I had never met you? I should have
558 ES	Michael	27	the office boys began to sneer at me./I wonder I stood it as long as I did./{LC} And
559 ES	Michael	39	upon me?/And what satisfaction, I wonder, will it give you/In the grave? If you're
561 ES	Michael	15	well: if you like, call me a coward./I wonder whether you would play the hero/If you
561 ES	Michael	21	made so much of, for my benefit:/I wonder whether *you* have always lived up to

WONDERED (12)

301 FR	Gerald	3	order:/I see to that./{G} I only wondered/Why you've been busy about it
347 FR	Downing	5	You mean them ghosts, Miss!/I wondered when his Lordship would get round
375 CP	Edward	15	/Yes, that's very interesting. But I just wondered/Whether it mightn't be rather
396 CP	Edward	7	we had to be alone./{E} I've often wondered why you married me./{L} Well, you
429 CP	Julia	12	native is not, I fear, very logical./{J} I wondered where you were taking us, with your
475 CC	Lucasta	20	little more about me./You must have wondered./{C} Must have wondered?/No, I
475 CC	Colby	21	must have wondered./{C} Must have wondered?/No, I haven't wondered. It's all a
475 CC	Colby	22	Must have wondered?/No, I haven't wondered. It's all a strange world/To me, you
475 CC	Colby	24	which I find myself./But if you mean, wondered about your ... background?/No. I've
528 ES	Charles	16	so well preserved/That I've sometimes wondered whether there was any .../Private self
537 ES	Gomez	19	at Oxford/I've no doubt your friends wondered what you found in me —/A
567 ES	Charles	12	admitted that you loved me,/But I wondered ... I'm sorry, I couldn't help

WONDERFUL (13)

19 Portrait		55	at peace, and find the world/To be wonderful and youthful, after all.'/The voice
219 Mung Rump		30	Mungojerrie and Rumpelteazer had a wonderful way of working together./And some
379 CP	Edward	13	you./{E} No, Celia./It has been very wonderful, and I'm very grateful,/And I think
380 CP	Celia	6	thought they had shared something wonderful/Had taken them only as a passing
388 CP	Peter	5	everything this morning./Alex is a wonderful person to know,/Because, you see, he

389 CP	Lavinia	14	go to California?/Everyone says it's a wonderful climate:/The people who go there
396 CP	Lavinia	11	I seemed always on the verge of some wonderful experience/And then it never
431 CP	Julia	37	typical./{J} Peter, I've thought of a wonderful idea!/I've always wanted to go to
460 CC	Lady E	1	she said: 'Come to Zürich!/There's a wonderful doctor who teaches mind control.'/So
475 CC	Lucasta	28	just accepted you./{L} Oh, that's so wonderful, to be accepted!/No one has ever 'just
478 CC	Lucasta	16	thought, when I tell him, it will be so wonderful/All in a moment. And now there's
487 CC	Colby	12	Colby, how's the piano?/{C} It's a wonderful piano. I've never played/On such an
579 ES	Carghil	12	in getting reservations./{MC} It's wonderful, Señor Gomez, how you manage

WONDERING (7)

20 Portrait		96	is as I had reckoned./'I have been wondering frequently of late/(But our
347 FR	Agatha	13	keep you;/His Lordship will be wondering why you've been so long. {}/[*Exit*
347 FR	Ivy	17	/Shall I read it to you? I was wondering/Whether to show it to Amy or not. {}
486 CC	Colby	27	I was told about him./But I can't help wondering why you are so interested:/There's
530 ES	Ld Clav	4	say, and no one to say it to./I've been wondering ... how many more empty pages?/
560 ES	Michael	4	reckoning up its profit and loss/And wondering why it bothered about such trifles./
567 ES	Charles	12	... I'm sorry, I couldn't help wondering/How much your words meant. You

WONDERS (3)

37 Gerontion		17	windy spaces./Signs are taken for wonders. 'We would see a sign!'/The word
111 Xmas Trees		9	a decoration, but an angel./The child wonders at the Christmas Tree:/Let him
455 CC	Eggers	31	to her, Mr. Simpkins./Time works wonders, that's what I always say./But I don't

WOOD (10)

57 Swee Night		37	Heart,/And sang within the bloody wood/When Agamemnon cried aloud/And let
123 SAWa & Ho		1	tree./*Tell me in what part of the wood/Do you want to flirt with me?/Under the*
123 SAWa & Ho		6	*/Any old tree will do for me/Any old wood is just as good/Any old isle is just my style/*
167 Rock 10		31	the polished stone,/The gilded carven wood, the coloured fresco./Our gaze is
179 FQ: ECoker		91	of the way/But all the way, in a dark wood, in a bramble,/On the edge of a grimpen,
244 MC	Chorus	6	have brewed beer and cider,/Gathered wood against the winter,/Talked at the corner
263 MC	Chorus	8	sits in the field, attentive; and in the wood/The owl rehearses the hollow note of
307 FR	Harry	19	freedom/Should be a hollow tree in a wood by the river./{M} But when I was a child I
310 FR	Mary	8	snowdrop crying for a moment in the wood./{H} Spring is an issue of blood/A season
329 FR	Chorus	9	the wail of little pain/The chopping of wood in autumn/And the singing in the kitchen/

WOOD-RETREAT (1)

599 On a Port		7	should meet/A pensive lamia in some wood-retreat,/An immaterial fancy of one's

WOODPATH (2)

270 MC	Chorus	9	incense, the smell of sweet soap in the woodpath, a hellish sweet scent in the
270 MC	Chorus	9	woodpath, a hellish sweet scent in the woodpath, while the ground heaved. I have seen

WOODS (1)

605 Narcissus		29	had been a young girl/Caught in the woods by a drunken old man/Knowing at the

WOODSONG (1)

109 Marina		15	by a wind,/A breath of pine, and the woodsong fog/By this grace dissolved in place/

WOODTHRUSH (2)

109 Marina		3	the bow/And scent of pine and the woodthrush singing through the fog/What
110 Marina		34	islands towards my timbers/And woodthrush calling through the fog/My

WOOLLY (1)

135 5FingerEx1		5	sharp desires/And the quick eyes of Woolly Bear./There is no relief but in grief./O

WOOLNOTH (1)

62 WL: Burial		67	William Street,/To where Saint Mary Woolnoth kept the hours/With a dead sound on

WOOLWORTH (1)

218 Mung Rump		14	one of the girls/Suddenly missed her Woolworth pearls:/Then the family would say:

WOPSICAL (1)

137 5FingerEx5		12	of fur/And a porpentine cat/And a wopsical hat:/How unpleasant to meet Mr.

WORD (67)

37 Gerontion		18	wonders. 'We would see a sign!'/The word within a word, unable to speak a word,/
37 Gerontion		18	would see a sign!'/The word within a word, unable to speak a word,/Swaddled with
37 Gerontion		18	within a word, unable to speak a word,/Swaddled with darkness. In the
54 Mr E Sun		4	/In the beginning was the Word./In the beginning was the Word./
54 Mr E Sun		5	the Word./In the beginning was the Word./Superfetation of τὸ ἕν,/And at the
92 Ash-Wed 2		43	that/Is inconclusible/Speech without word and/Word of no speech/Grace to the
92 Ash-Wed 2		44	/Speech without word and/Word of no speech/Grace to the Mother/For
92 Ash-Wed 3		24	/Lord, I am not worthy/but speak the word only./Who walked between the violet and
94 Ash-Wed 4		24	her head and signed but spoke no word/But the fountain sprang up and the bird
95 Ash-Wed 4		27	redeem the dream/The token of the word unheard, unspoken/Till the wind shake a
96 Ash-Wed 5		1	/And after this our exile/If the lost word is lost, if the spent word is spent/If the
96 Ash-Wed 5		1	/If the lost word is lost, if the spent word is spent/If the unheard, unspoken/Word is
96 Ash-Wed 5		3	is spent/If the unheard, unspoken/Word is unspoken, unheard;/Still is the

96 Ash-Wed 5	4	unheard;/Still is the unspoken word, the Word unheard,/The Word without a
96 Ash-Wed 5	4	/Still is the unspoken word, the Word unheard,/The Word without a word, the
96 Ash-Wed 5	5	word, the Word unheard,/The Word without a word, the Word within/The
96 Ash-Wed 5	5	Word unheard,/The Word without a word, the Word within/The world and for the
96 Ash-Wed 5	5	/The Word without a word, the Word within/The world and for the world;/And
96 Ash-Wed 5	8	shone in darkness and/Against the Word the unstilled world still whirled/About the
96 Ash-Wed 5	9	whirled/About the centre of the silent Word./O my people, what have I done unto
96 Ash-Wed 5	11	I done unto thee./Where shall the word be found, where will the word/Resound?
96 Ash-Wed 5	11	the word be found, where will the word/Resound? Not here, there is not enough
96 Ash-Wed 5	23	and time, between/Hour and hour, word and word, power and power, those who
96 Ash-Wed 5	23	between/Hour and hour, word and word, power and power, those who wait/In
105 Song Sime	22	the still unspeaking and unspoken Word,/Grant Israel's consolation/To one who
105 Song Sime	25	and no to-morrow./According to thy word./They shall praise Thee and suffer in every
136 5FingerEx4	5	Baskerville Hound/Which, just at a word from his master/Will follow you faster and
147 Rock 1	10	of words, and ignorance of the Word./All our knowledge brings us nearer to
149 Rock 1	88	*will build with new timbers/Where the word is unspoken/We will build with new speech/*
152 Rock 2	22	capital/And several versions of the Word of GOD:/The British race assured of a
152 Rock 2	28	for avarice, gluttony, neglect of the Word of GOD,/For pride, for lechery,
154 Rock 3	1	fire not be quenched in the forge./The Word of the LORD came unto me, saying:/O
154 Rock 3	16	/Much is your reading, but not the Word of GOD,/Much is your building, but not
154 Rock 3	27	where the goat climbs,/Where My Word is unspoken./2ND MALE VOICE:/A
155 Rock 3	30	daily to the timekept City;/Where My Word is unspoken,/In the land of lobelias and
161 Rock 7	21	from light to light, in the light of the Word,/Through the Passion and Sacrifice saved
175 FQ: BurntN	158	chattering,/Always assail them. The Word in the desert/Is most attacked by voices of
197 FQ: Little	219	sentence that is right (where every word is at home,/Taking its place to support the
197 FQ: Little	221	its place to support the others,/The word neither diffident nor ostentatious,/An easy
197 FQ: Little	223	of the old and the new,/The common word exact without vulgarity,/The formal word
197 FQ: Little	224	exact without vulgarity,/The formal word precise but not pedantic,/The complete
221 Old Deut	39	—/And out they all shuffle, without a word spoken./The digestive repose of that
231 Bust Jones	38	'I shall last out my time'/Is the word for this stoutest of Cats./It must and it
595 Grad 13	6	serene,/Still as the years pass by, the word 'Progress!'/So we are done; we may no
595 Grad 14	3	is the end of every tale: 'Farewell',/A word that echoes like a funeral bell/And one
260 MC Thomas	21	a moment about the meaning of this word 'peace'. Does/it seem strange to you that
264 MC Priest2	11	and our hands have handled/Of the word of life; that which we have seen and heard/
279 MC Knight1	5	to me that he has said almost the last word, for those who/have been able to follow
281 MC Chorus	13	praise Thee, in thought and in word and in deed./Even with the hand to the
296 FR Gerald	37	/When they were children. I'll have a word with him./He can talk to Harry, and
297 FR Charles	29	car./{C} Tell him I'd like to have a word with him, please. {}/[Exit DENMAN]/{V}
322 FR Winch	25	I'm sorry./I thought I'd better have a word with you quiet,/Rather than phone and
334 FR Agatha	13	just now?/{Ag} What does the word mean?/There's relief from a burden that I
368 CP Alex	27	make half a dozen dishes. Don't say a word./I shall begin at once. {}/[*Exit to kitchen*]/
379 CP Celia	25	a private world of *ours*,/Where the word 'happiness' had a different meaning/Or so
404 CP Edward	6	I wonder/If you have understood a word of what I have been saying./{R} You must
407 CP Reilly	27	/{R} You have come where the word 'insult' has no meaning;/And you must
414 CP Celia	35	/It sounds ridiculous — but the only word for it/That I can find, is a sense of sin./{R}
415 CP Celia	35	sinful!/And yet I can't find any other word for it./It must be some kind of
416 CP Celia	5	I feel I must ... *atone* — is that the word?/Can you treat a patient for such a state
453 CC Eggers	12	gas ring .../{E} You mustn't believe a word she says./{L} *Mr.* Simpkins is going to
514 CC Eggers	29	Sir Claude./Not that we doubt your word, Mrs. Guzzard:/But in a matter of such
531 ES Monica	5	a blaze of glory —/You've read every word about you in the papers./{C} And the
536 ES Gomez	10	/I married a girl who didn't know a word of English,/Didn't want to learn English,
536 ES Gomez	20	/Homesickness is a sickly word./You don't understand such isolation/As
569 ES Ld Clav	25	/{LC} Blackmail? Yes, I've heard that word before,/Not so very long ago. When I
578 ES Monica	34	you haven't understood a single word/Of what I said. You must make your own

WORDS (56)

65 WL: Chess	110	out in fiery points/Glowed into words, then would be savagely still./'My nerves
65 WL: Chess	140	I said —/I didn't mince my words, I said to her myself,/HURRY UP
90 Ash-Wed 1	31	I do not hope to turn again/Let these words answer/For what is done, not to be done
125 SA Sweeney	2	that don't apply/But I've gotta use words when I talk to you./But here's what I was
125 SA Sweeney	21	is life and life is death/I gotta use words when I talk to you/But if you understand
147 Rock 1	10	but not of silence;/Knowledge of words, and ignorance of the Word./All our
158 Rock 5	4	something to lose./Remembering the words of Nehemiah the Prophet: 'The trowel in
162 Rock 8	1	Power./O Father we welcome your words,/And we will take heart for the future,/
162 Rock 8	10	/Peter the Hermit, scourging with words./And among his hearers were a few good
164 Rock 9	22	life of music,/Out of the slimy mud of words, out of the sleet and hail of verbal

164 Rock 9	23	/Approximate thoughts and feelings, words that have taken the place of thoughts and
171 FQ: BurntN	14	opened/Into the rose-garden. My words echo/Thus, in your mind./But to what
175 FQ: BurntN	140	At the still point of the turning world./Words move, music moves/Only in time; but
175 FQ: BurntN	142	that which is only living/Can only die. Words, after speech, reach/Into the silence.
175 FQ: BurntN	144	Only by the form, the pattern,/Can words or music reach/The stillness, as a Chinese
175 FQ: BurntN	152	after the end./And all is always now. Words strain,/Crack and sometimes break,
179 FQ: ECoker	72	still with the intolerable wrestle/With words and meanings. The poetry does not
182 FQ: ECoker	176	*deux guerres* —/Trying to learn to use words, and every attempt/Is a wholly new start,
182 FQ: ECoker	178	has only learnt to get the better of words/For the thing one no longer has to say,
192 FQ: Little	49	And prayer is more/Than an order of words, the conscious occupation/Of the praying
193 FQ: Little	103	—/And he a face still forming; yet the words sufficed/To compel the recognition they
194 FQ: Little	120	kick the empty pail./For last year's words belong to last year's language/And next
194 FQ: Little	121	last year's language/And next year's words await another voice./But, as the passage
194 FQ: Little	125	much like each other,/So I find words I never thought to speak/In streets I
206 To my Wife	12	for others to read:/These are private words addressed to you in public./OLD
594 Grad 12	3	increase/Forever, and may stronger words than these/Proclaim the glory so that all
262 MC Thomas	4	have you keep in your hearts/these words that I say, and think of them at another
269 MC Knight2	25	with your bodies./{K2} Enough of words./{4K} We come for the King's justice, we
276 MC Knight1	27	you. I am a man of action and not of words. For that/reason I shall do no more than
305 FR Agatha	10	I can tell you, more than there are words for./At this moment, there is no decision
327 FR Harry	16	on me./But this is too real for your words to alter./Oh, there *must* be another way
337 FR Harry	25	that I made a decision/Which your words echo. I am still befouled,/But I know
338 FR Harry	6	it to anyone:/I do not know the words in which to explain it —/That is what
349 FR 6m	13	*out a few candles, so that their last/words are spoken in the dark.*]/{Ag} A curse is
402 CP Edward	15	me recently,/Almost in the same words, that I ought to see a doctor./They said
402 CP Edward	16	said — again, in almost the same words —/That I was on the edge of a nervous
422 CP Alex	12	to proceed to the libation./{A} The words for the building of the hearth. {}/[*They*
422 CP Alex	18	the bed. {}/[*They drink*]/{A} The words for those who go upon a journey./{R}
422 CP Reilly	29	*drink*]/{R} There is one for whom the words cannot be spoken./{A} They can not be
422 CP Reilly	32	{R} He has not yet come to where the words are valid./{J} Shall we ever speak them?/
438 CP Reilly	28	to the consequences/Of all our words and deeds, beyond the intention/And
457 CC note 16&	25	*voice off.**/* *Lady Elizabeth's words off stage are not intended to be heard*
478 CC Colby	6	...{C} You mustn't use such words! You don't know how it's hurting./{L} I
478 CC Lucasta	7	know how it's hurting./{L} I could use words much stronger than that,/And I will, if I
522 ES dedic	9	*this book, to return as best I can/With words a little part of what you have given me./*
522 ES dedic	10	*part of what you have given me./The words mean what they say, but some have a*
525 ES Charles	21	you to himself,/Before I've said two words he'll come ambling in .../{M} You've said
525 ES Monica	22	said a good deal more than two words already./And besides, my father doesn't
526 ES Charles	12	/Before I felt its presence./{C} Your words seem to come/From very far away. Yet
526 ES Charles	19	as a moment ago./What do the words mean now — *I* and *you*?/{M} In our
533 ES Ld Clav	37	/I assure you it does./{LC} In other words/You have been engaged in systematic
549 ES Carghil	29	be throwing yourself away./Mark my words' Effie said, 'if you chose to follow *that*
567 ES Charles	13	help wondering/How much your words meant. You didn't seem to need me then.
569 ES Ld Clav	7	and makeup/And without his stage words. Monica!/I've had your love under false
583 ES Charles	5	speech, and beyond./It's strange that words are so inadequate./Yet, like the asthmatic
583 ES Charles	7	breath,/So the lover must struggle for words./{M} I've loved you from the beginning

WORE (3)

588 Fable	33	off by force.'/He drencht the gown he wore with holy water,/The turkeys, capons,
266 MC Knights	17	servant, his tool, and his jack,/You wore his favours on your back,/You had your
528 ES Monica	12	public personage./In politics Father wore a public label./And later, as chairman of

WORK (35)

147 Rock 1	24	the Church/In the place where they work, but where they spend their Sundays./In
149 Rock 1	78	your will./Let me show you the work of the humble. Listen./*The lights fade; in*
149 Rock 1	90	*We will build with new speech/There is* work *together/A Church for all/And a job for*
149 Rock 1	93	/*And a job for each/Every man to his* work./*Now a group of* WORKMEN *is*
150 Rock 1	124	*all/And a job for each/Each man to his* work./Thus your fathers were made/Fellow
153 Rock 2	53	to build, much to restore;/Let the work not delay, time and the arm not waste;/Let
165 Rock 9	39	after many obstacles;/For the work of creation is never without travail;/The
167 Rock 10	37	rocket is fired; and the day is long for work or play./We tire of distraction or
210 Old Gumbie	6	is done,/Then the Gumbie Cat's work is but hardly begun./And when all the
210 Old Gumbie	18	is done,/Then the Gumbie Cat's work is but hardly begun./As she finds that the
210 Old Gumbie	22	is done without trying,/She sets to work with her baking and frying./She makes
211 Old Gumbie	30	is done,/Then the Gumbie Cat's work is but hardly begun./She thinks that the
234 Ad-dress	13	in verse./You've seen them both at work and games,/And learnt about their proper
252 MC Thomas	10	King,/How can he trust those who work for King's undoing?/{T3} Kings will allow

263	MC	Chorus	18	/Between Christmas and Easter what work shall be done?/The ploughman shall go
263	MC	Chorus	24	tumble in front of the door,/What work shall have been done, what wrong/Shall
277	MC	Knight3	15	our duty,/but all the same we had to work ourselves up to it. And, as I said,/*we* are
348	FR	Chorus	12	business of living,/We know how to work the machine,/We can usually avoid
373	CP	Alex	2	ten minutes,/Twenty minutes, and my work will be ruined. {}/[*Exeunt* ALEX *and*
393	CP	Lavinia	33	/You know it was I who made you work at the Bar .../{E} You nagged me because I
393	CP	Edward	34	me because I didn't get enough work/And said that I ought to meet more
411	CP	Reilly	36	you my account./Go in peace. And work out your salvation with diligence. {}/
413	CP	Celia	16	an active life — if there's anything to work for;/I don't imagine that I am being
420	CP	Reilly	18	kind./{R} Go in peace, my daughter./Work out your salvation with diligence. {}/
421	CP	Reilly	35	/{R} And when I say to one like her/'Work out your salvation with diligence', I do
462	CC	Claude	27	for asking —/How do you like your work? You don't find it uncongenial?/I'm not
463	CC	Colby	9	started by asking me how I found this work./{SC} Yes, how do you find it?/{C} In a
463	CC	Colby	16	rather disturbing. I don't mean the work:/I mean, about myself. As if I was
467	CC	Colby	26	best to justify your kindness/By the work I do./{SC} As my confidential clerk./{C}
467	CC	Colby	28	clerk./{C} I'm really interested by the work I'm doing/And eager for more. I don't
483	CC	Colby	14	/You see, I shall do a good deal of my work here./{LE} And what is that shrouded
483	CC	Colby	18	is a typewriter./I've already begun to work here. At the moment/I'm working on a
492	CC	Colby	19	/Tomorrow night. I must get to work on it./{SC} Tomorrow night. Must I go to
530	ES	Ld Clav	16	before me./If I had the energy to work myself to death/How gladly would I face
559	ES	Michael	1	only I'd been given some interesting work!/{LC} And what do you now propose to

WORKED (5)

446	CC	Eggers	1	feet, very quickly,/During the time we worked together./All he needs is confidence./
450	CC	Claude	6	/About you, Eggerson, although we worked together/For nearly thirty years./{E}
518	CC	Eggers	6	to find you've another vocation./We worked together every day, you know,/For
537	ES	Gomez	30	that you came to?/{G} This is how it worked out, Dick. You liked to play the rake,/
550	ES	Carghil	21	/{MC} He had a weak heart./And he worked too hard. Have you never heard/Of

WORKER (1)

533	ES	Gomez	15	you like./But I've been a pretty hard worker all these years/And I thought, now's the

WORKING (7)

156	Rock 3		67	the perfect refrigerator,/Engaged in working out a rational morality,/Engaged in
219	Mung Rump		30	had a wonderful way of working together./And some of the time you
391	CP	Lavinia	19	/I started some machine, that goes on working,/And I cannot stop it; no, it's not like a
430	CP	Peter	31	a leg-pull, Julia:/But you all know I'm working for Pan-Am-Eagle?/{E} No. Tell us,
453	CC	Lucasta	9	/You may take me out to dinner. A working girl like me/Is often very hungry —
483	CC	Colby	19	to work here. At the moment/I'm working on a company report./{LE} I hadn't
558	ES	Michael	20	/You don't know what I suffered, working in that office./In the first place, they all

WORKMEN (3)

149	Rock 1 m		79	*in the semi-darkness the voices of* WORKMEN *are heard chanting./In the vacant*
149	Rock 1 m		94	*man to his work./Now a group of* WORKMEN *is silhouetted against the dim sky.*
150	Rock 1 m		109	*in 'The Times'./Chant of* WORKMEN *again./The river flows, the*

WORKS (6)

14	Prufrock		29	and create,/And time for all the works and days of hands/That lift and drop a
49	Hippopot		23	in sleep; at night he hunts;/God works in a mysterious way —/The Church can
129	Cor2 State		19	commission is appointed/For Public Works, chiefly the question of rebuilding the
342	FR	Amy	12	not succeed: she has some spell/That works from generation to generation./{M} Is
455	CC	Eggers	31	get used to her, Mr. Simpkins./Time works wonders, that's what I always say./But I
517	CC	Colby	7	relation of father and son/Unless it works both ways. For you to regard me —/As

WORLD (137)

19	Portrait		54	immeasurably at peace, and find the world/To be wonderful and youthful, after all.'/
23	Preludes		30	against the ceiling./And when all the world came back/And the light crept up
23	Preludes		47	street/Impatient to assume the world./I am moved by fancies that are curled/
24	Rhapsody		27	/Eaten smooth, and polished/As if the world gave up/The secret of its skeleton,/Stiff
45	Cook Egg		25	conduct me./But where is the penny world I bought/To eat with Pipit behind the
64	WL: Chess		102	voice/And still she cried, and still the world pursues,/'Jug Jug' to dirty ears./And
86	Hollow Men		95	is/For Thine is the/*This is the way the* world ends/*This is the way the world ends/This is*
86	Hollow Men		96	*way the world ends/This is the way the* world ends/*This is the way the world ends/Not*
86	Hollow Men		97	*way the world ends/This is the way the* world ends/*Not with a bang but a whimper.*/
96	Ash-Wed 5		6	without a word, the Word within/The world and for the world;/And the light shone in
96	Ash-Wed 5		6	Word within/The world and for the world;/And the light shone in darkness and/
96	Ash-Wed 5		8	and/Against the Word the unstilled world still whirled/About the centre of the silent
97	Ash-Wed 5		32	surrender/And affirm before the world and deny between the rocks/In the last
107	Animula		2	of God, the simple soul'/To a flat world of changing lights and noise,/To light,
110	Marina		30	this face, this life/Living to live in a world of time beyond me; let me/Resign my life
119	SP	Klip	17	our bit, as you folks say,/I'll tell the world we got the Hun on the run/{Kr} What

326 FR	Harry	28	and aberration/Of all men, of the world, which I cannot put in order./If you only
330 FR	Harry	31	loathing/Diffused, I not a person, in a world not of persons/But only of contaminating
338 FR	Agatha	34	/{A} So you *will* run away./{Ag} In a world of fugitives/The person taking the
339 FR	Harry	6	directions./Where does one go from a world of insanity?/Somewhere on the other side
342 FR	Agatha	16	have only watched and waited. In this world/It is inexplicable, the resolution is in
342 FR	Agatha	34	privilege./For those who live in this world, this world only,/Do you think that I
342 FR	Agatha	34	/For those who live in this world, this world only,/Do you think that I would take the
346 FR	Agatha	36	bit as sane as you or I,/He sees the world as clearly as you or I see it,/It is only that
349 FR	Mary	27	Not in the day time/And in the hither world/Where we know what we are doing/There
350 FR	Agatha	4	in the night time/And in the nether world/Where the meshes we have woven/Bind
360 CP	Reilly	40	want to re-marry/To prove to the world that somebody wanted you;/If another
378 CP	Celia	27	of vanity:/That you think the world will laugh at you/Because your wife has
379 CP	Celia	24	time was meaningless, a private world of *ours,*/Where the word 'happiness' had
379 CP	Celia	38	the while; and to find I wanted/This world as well as that ... well, it's humiliating./
403 CP	Reilly	12	/Half of the harm that is done in this world/Is due to people who want to feel
403 CP	Edward	38	five years together!/She has made the world a place I cannot live in/Except on her
404 CP	Edward	1	I must be alone,/But not in the same world. So I want you to put me/Into your
413 CP	Celia	19	have no delusions —/Except that the world I live in seems all a delusion!/But
413 CP	Celia	31	from what it seemed to be,/With the world itself — and that's much more
418 CP	Reilly	2	/You have read once, and lost. In a world of lunacy,/Violence, stupidity, greed ... it
419 CP	Reilly	4	/Of solitude in the phantasmal world/Of imagination, shuffling memories and
419 CP	Reilly	31	very active lives/Very often, in the world./{C} How soon will you send me there?/
430 CP	Julia	28	your news;/Give us your news of the world, Peter./We lead such a quiet life, here in
438 CP	Reilly	9	labyrinths, Minotaur terrors./But that world does not take the place of this one./Do
449 CC	Claude	18	matters./You know she thinks the world of your opinion./{E} Well, I believe that
462 CC	Claude	18	being mine./She has always lived in a world of make-believe,/And the best one can do
462 CC	Colby	22	honest./If we all have to live in a world of make-believe,/Is that good for us? Or a
464 CC	Claude	13	into living,/Escape from a sordid world to a pure one./Sculpture and painting — I
464 CC	Claude	16	I have always longed for./I want a world where the form is the reality,/Of which
465 CC	Claude	30	through the private door/Into the real world, as I do, sometimes./{C} Indeed, I have
472 CC	Lucasta	39	on, I'm sure:/But it's only the outer world that you've lost:/You've still got your
472 CC	Lucasta	40	lost:/You've still got your inner world — a world that's more real./That's why
472 CC	Lucasta	40	You've still got your inner world — a world that's more real./That's why you're
473 CC	Colby	23	/Although it's as real to me as ... this world./But that's just the trouble. They seem so
473 CC	Colby	39	no less unreal to me/Than the world outside it. If you have two lives/Which
474 CC	Colby	2	/His garden is a part of one single world./{L} But what do you want?/{C} Not to
474 CC	Colby	6	my garden/And that would make the world outside it real/And acceptable, I think./
474 CC	Lucasta	38	I see it as a means of contact with a world/More real than any *I've* ever lived in./
475 CC	Colby	22	I haven't wondered. It's all a strange world/To me, you know, in which I find myself.
482 CC	Lady E	20	a good deal wiser in the ways of the world./{C} But, Lady Elizabeth, what is it you
495 CC	Lady E	25	/I thought I was escaping from a world that I loathed/In Tony — and then, too
495 CC	Lady E	27	late, I discovered/He belonged to the world I wanted to escape from./He was so
500 CC	Lucasta	29	he's undependable. He has his own world,/And he might vanish into it at any
526 ES	Monica	20	now — *I* and *you*?/{M} In our private world — now we have our private world —/The
526 ES	Monica	20	world — now we have our private world —/The meanings are different. Look!
526 ES	Monica	31	/{M} — Now we're in the public world./{C} And your father will come. With his
538 ES	Gomez	37	top!/And yet you withdrew from the world of politics/And went into the City.
545 ES	Ld Clav	4	find justification/Not so much to the world — first of all to myself./What is this self
549 ES	Carghil	26	a man I could follow round the world!'/But Effie it was — you know, Effie was
552 ES	Carghil	29	You wanted to pose:/As a man of the world. And now you're posing/As what? I
568 ES	Ld Clav	10	/Episodes we try to conceal from the world./Has there been nothing in your life,
568 ES	Ld Clav	22	it/To conceal from the rest of the world — your soul is safe./If a man has one
574 ES	Carghil	17	abroad!/And find his own way in the world. That's very natural./So I thought, why
574 ES	Michael	33	the use of chasing/Half round the world, for the same sort of job/You got me here
577 ES	Gomez	22	Hemington .../{G} As two men of the world, we discussed things very frankly;/And I
583 ES	Monica	8	loved you from the beginning of the world./Before you and I were born, the love was

WORLD'S (2)

192 FQ: Little		37	are other places/Which also are the world's end, some at the sea jaws,/Or over a
261 MC Thomas		23	mourning nor our rejoicing is as the world's is./A Christian martyrdom is never an

WORLDLY (5)

250 MC Thomas		11	order./Those who put their faith in worldly order/Not controlled by the order of
301 FR	Ivy	21	his confident vulgarity, acquired from worldly associates./{G} Ivy is only concerned for
482 CC	Lady E	25	suggestions:/But they are rather worldly and materialistic,/And ... well, rather
539 ES	Gomez	39	consider yourself a success .../{G} A worldly success, Dick. In another sense/We're
540 ES	Ld Clav	10	/In trying to persuade me of your ... worldly success?/{G} No, because I know the

WORLDS (10)

23 Preludes	53	across your mouth, and laugh;/The worlds revolve like ancient women/Gathering
165 Rock 9	34	and body./Visible and invisible, two worlds meet in Man;/Visible and invisible must
194 FQ: Little	124	and peregrine/Between two worlds become much like each other,/So I find
204 de la Mare	19	is what we have yet to learn,/And two worlds meet, and intersect, and change;/When
311 FR Harry	8	before, a vapour dissolving/All other worlds, and me into it. O Mary!/Don't look at
327 FR Agatha	4	try to penetrate the other private worlds/Of make-believe and fear. To rest in our
343 FR Agatha	9	in the neutral territory/Between two worlds./{M} Then you *will* help me!/You
369 CP Edward	18	ambition/To establish herself in two worlds at once —/But she herself had to be the
437 CP Reilly	8	*men, he saw./For know there are two worlds of life and death:/One that which thou*
466 CC Claude	22	to me, who have at best to live/In two worlds — each a kind of make-believe./That's

WORM (5)

136 5FingerEx3	11	finger too,/Easier had than squirming worm;/For I know, and so should you/That
136 5FingerEx3	13	should you/That soon the enquiring worm shall try/Our well-preserved complacency.
270 MC Chorus	5	have lain in the soil and criticised the worm. In the air/Flirted with the passage of the
281 MC Chorus	12	earth, both the wolf and the lamb; the worm in the soil and the worm in the belly./
281 MC Chorus	12	the lamb; the worm in the soil and the worm in the belly./Therefore man, whom Thou

WORMS (1)

270 MC Chorus	20	/Is woven like a pattern of living worms/In the guts of the women of Canterbury.

WORN (3)

267 MC Thomas	14	Then let your new coat of loyalty be worn/Carefully, so it get not soiled or torn./
390 CP Julia	33	wants us./I can see that she is quite worn out/After her anxiety about her aunt —/
543 ES Monica	14	money./{M} Father, this interview has worn you out./You must go and rest now,

WORN-OUT (2)

20 Portrait	80	mechanical and tired/Reiterates some worn-out common song/With the smell of
179 FQ: ECoker	70	satisfactory:/A periphrastic study in a worn-out poetical fashion,/Leaving one still

WORRIED (8)

31 Apollinax	11	/Hidden under coral islands/Where worried bodies of drowned men drift down in
91 Ash-Wed 2	31	/Exhausted and life-giving/Worried reposeful/The single Rose/Is now the
185 FQ: DrySal	41	older/Than time counted by anxious worried women/Lying awake, calculating the
298 FR Charles	37	that we've seen him,/We're a little worried about his health./He doesn't seem to be
325 FR Ivy	16	/Is not to let her see that anyone is worried./We must carry on as if nothing had
325 FR Gerald	19	the cake and presents./{G} But *I*'m worried about Arthur:/He's much more apt
420 CP Reilly	23	/{R} It's the other ones I am worried about./{J} Nonsense, Henry. *I* shall
567 ES Monica	3	I'm so glad you've come!/I've been so worried, and rather frightened./It was

WORRY (12)

123 SA Kl & Kr	16	*going to stay with you/And we won't worry what to do/We won't have to catch any*
343 FR Amy	23	let the walls crumble. Why should I worry/To keep the tiles on the roof, combat the
343 FR Harry	32	will always have Arthur and John/To worry about: not that John is any worry —/The
343 FR Harry	32	/To worry about: not that John is any worry —/The destined and the perfect master of
343 FR Harry	35	as for me,/I am the last you need to worry about;/I have my course to pursue, and I
346 FR Agatha	34	unaccountable/At times, you mustn't worry about that./He is every bit as sane as you
372 CP Alex	25	what about my breakfast?/{A} Don't worry about breakfast./All you should want is a
415 CP Celia	26	one knew disapproved of it./I don't worry much about form, myself —/But when
425 CP Lavinia	17	know, I don't think that you need worry:/They won't all come, out of those who
455 CC Eggers	19	she's always in debt. But you needn't worry/About her, Mr. Simpkins. She'll marry
556 ES Monica	2	the doctors want you to be free from worry./He won't make a scene. But I can see
560 ES Michael	27	somebody's divorce. No, you needn't worry/About that girl — or any other./But I

WORRYING (2)

348 FR Warburt	2	I hope Lady Monchensey hasn't been worrying?/I'm anxious to relieve her mind.
424 CP Edward	11	time, I think. I hope you've not been worrying./{L} Oh no. I did in fact ring up your

WORSE (22)

181 FQ: ECoker	158	be restored, our sickness must grow worse./The whole earth is our hospital/
234 Ad-dress	11	bad/And some are better, some are worse —/But all may be described in verse./
587 Fable	16	fairy visited their host,/Oh, no; much worse than that, they had a ghost./Some wicked
602 Humoresque	19	nose),/'Your damned thin moonlight, worse than gas —/'Now in New York' — and
254 MC Tempt4	38	their best to forget you./And later is worse, when men will not hate you/Enough to
303 FR Mary	26	between Arthur and John./Which is worse, thinking of what to say to John,/Or
309 FR Harry	2	/Explaining would only make a worse misunderstanding;/Explaining would only
321 FR Harry	20	yet he was not real?/That would be worse than anything that has happened./What if
325 FR Charles	12	do that Warburton can't./If he's worse than Winchell said, then he'll let us know
394 CP Lavinia	18	Everything I tried only made matters worse,/And the moment you were offered
402 CP Edward	3	know, I'm sure. They could hardly be worse./{R} They might be much worse. You
402 CP Reilly	4	be worse./{R} They might be much worse. You might have ruined three lives/By
404 CP Edward	12	/And now I know there is suffering worse than that./It is surprising, if one had time

432 CP	Julia	19	my interruptions:/That's really worse than interrupting./Now my head's fairly
436 CP	Edward	4	/That some men have to learn much worse things/About themselves, and learn them
447 CC	Claude	22	'guidance'./{SC} Guidance. That's worse than believing in her judgment:/We could
448 CC	Claude	36	you've never had children./{SC} No worse, Eggerson,/Than for you and your wife,
478 CC	Lucasta	18	nothing,/Nothing at all. It's far worse than ever./Just when you think you're on
496 CC	Eggers	32	I notice the traffic/Has got so much worse./{SC} Yes, it's always getting worse./{LE}
496 CC	Claude	33	worse./{SC} Yes, it's always getting worse./{LE} — I hope Mrs. Eggerson is well?/
547 ES	Ld Clav	13	not going to say/Nothing could be worse. Where there's a Mrs. Piggott/There may
547 ES	Ld Clav	14	may be, among the guests, something worse than Mrs. Piggott./{M} Let's hope this

WORSHIP (5)

154 Rock 3		6	given you hands which you turn from worship,/I have given you speech, for endless
160 Rock 7		15	has died of starvation./Prayer wheels, worship of the dead, denial of this world,
161 Rock 7		28	before/That men both deny gods and worship gods, professing first Reason,/And then
166 Rock 10		25	on a grassblade./O Light Invisible, we worship Thee!/We thank Thee for the lights that
339 FR	Harry	8	on the other side of despair./To the worship in the desert, the thirst and deprivation,

WORSHIPPED (2)

136 5FingerEx4		9	to meet Mr. Hodgson!/Who is worshipped by all waitresses/(They regard him
569 ES	Ld Clav	4	I'd become an idol/To Monica. She worshipped the part I played:/How could I be

WORSHIPPERS (2)

166 Rock 10		11	prize the serpent's golden eyes,/The worshippers, self-given sacrifice of the snake.
184 FQ: DrySal		10	Unhonoured, unpropitiated/By worshippers of the machine, but waiting,

WORSHIPPING (2)

160 Rock 7		5	and the shadow led them to darkness,/Worshipping snakes or trees, worshipping devils
160 Rock 7		5	/Worshipping snakes or trees, worshipping devils rather than nothing: crying

WORST (9)

103 Journ Magi		2	/'A cold coming we had of it,/Just the worst time of the year/For a journey, and such a
326 FR	Violet	37	Ivy that he's asking for, I expect the worst./{Ag} Whatever you have learned, Harry,
381 CP	Edward	12	know what it is to feel old./That is the worst moment, when you feel that you have lost
402 CP	Reilly	30	/For whom a sanatorium is the worst place possible./We must first find out
428 CP	Alex	17	/But characteristic. And that's not the worst of it./Some of the tribes are Christian
440 CP	Lavinia	26	look my best can only mean the worst./{E} I never shall learn how to pay a
450 CC	Claude	4	person/That you're liable to make the worst mistake about him./As a matter of fact,
538 ES	Gomez	23	make quite the same mistake./At the worst, you go into opposition/And let the other
540 ES	Gomez	5	/{G} What do I call failure?/The worst kind of failure, in my opinion,/Is the man

WORTH (21)

15 Prufrock		87	I was afraid./And would it have been worth it, after all,/After the cups, the
15 Prufrock		90	of you and me,/Would it have been worth while,/To have bitten off the matter with
16 Prufrock		99	not it, at all.'/And would it have been worth it, after all,/Would it have been worth
16 Prufrock		100	worth it, after all,/Would it have been worth while,/After the sunsets and the
16 Prufrock		106	on a screen:/Would it have been worth while/If one, settling a pillow or throwing
236 Cat Morgan		18	Faber —/I'll give you this tip, and it's worth a lot more:/You'll save yourself time, and
247 MC Thomas		7	that are past. I remember/Not worth forgetting./{T1} And of the new season./
299 FRDowning		36	high spirits./For what my judgment's worth, I always said his Lordship/Suffered from
364 CP	Reilly	19	she is?/{UG} That question is not worth the trouble of an answer./But if I bring
395 CP	Lavinia	36	your placid assumption/That I wasn't worth the trouble of understanding./{E} So here
414 CP	Celia	13	Do you know —/It no longer seems worth while to *speak* to anyone!/{R} And what
446 CC	Claude	36	But there won't be any birds — none worth watching./{E} I don't know, Sir Claude.
463 CC	Colby	31	never excel in,/Seems the one thing worth doing, the one thing/That I want to do. I
496 CC	Lady E	1	always made me feel that I wasn't worth talking to./{SC} And you always made
535 ES	Gomez	19	to trust someone/You must make it worth his while to be trustworthy'. {}/[*During*
537 ES	Ld Clav	5	how do you propose/To make it worth my while to be trustworthy?/{G} It's done
553 ES	Carghil	22	/Oh, not very many. Only a few worth keeping./Only a few. But very beautiful!/
553 ES	Carghil	25	when the break came,/'They'll be worth a fortune to you, Maisie.'/They would
572 ES	Ld Clav	15	but my father prevented that:/Made it worth while for her not to marry me —/That
572 ES	Ld Clav	17	of putting it — and of course/Made it worth while for me not to marry her./In fact, we
582 ES	Ld Clav	5	becoming no one, I begin to live./It is worth while dying, to find out what life is./And

WORTHIER (1)

594 Grad 12		5	the glory so that all may hear;/May worthier sons be thine, from far and near/To

WORTHLESS (4)

255 MC Thomas		25	/{T} Others offered real goods, worthless/But real. You only offer/Dreams to
435 CP	Peter	28	that Celia was alive./And now it's all worthless. Celia's not alive./{L} No, it's not all
435 CP	Lavinia	29	Celia's not alive./{L} No, it's not all worthless, Peter. You've only just begun./I
532 ES	Ld Clav	18	money. Or to sell me something worthless./{M} You ought not to bother with

WORTHY (6)

92 Ash-Wed 3	22	the third stair./Lord, I am not worthy/Lord, I am not worthy/but speak the
92 Ash-Wed 3	23	I am not worthy/Lord, I am not worthy/but speak the word only./Who walked
271 MC Thomas	23	Death will come only when I am worthy,/And if I am worthy, there is no danger.
271 MC Thomas	24	only when I am worthy,/And if I am worthy, there is no danger./I have therefore
277 MC Knight2	38	English spirit of fair play. Now the worthy Archbishop,/whose good qualities I very
368 CP Edward	21	Alex,/There'll be nothing in the larder worthy of your cooking./I couldn't think of it./

WOULD (311)

WOULDN'T (44)

115 SP	Doris	17	what he's going to do./{Do} No it wouldn't do to be too nice to Pereira./{Du}
121 SA	Doris	14	little, missionary stew./{Do} You wouldn't eat me!/{S} Yes I'd eat you!/In a nice
218 Mung Rump		22	/With their minds made up that they wouldn't get thinner/On Argentine joint,
300 FRDowning		15	of the usual opinion,/I dare say. She wouldn't leave him alone./And there's my
300 FRDowning		20	the women can't follow him./She wouldn't leave him out of her sight./{C} During
314 FR Warburt		35	My first patient, now —/You wouldn't believe it, ladies — was a murderer,/
315 FR Violet		20	can't get about now in winter/You wouldn't think that she was a day older/Than
321 FR Denman		12	He says it's very urgent/Or he wouldn't have troubled you./{H} I'll see him. {}/
326 FR Denman		35	me? why, who can want me?/{D} He wouldn't give his name, Miss; but it's Mr.
354 CP	Alex	32	/{A} No, there were three, but you wouldn't know the third one:/They kept him
356 CP	Peter	8	I wonder if I've seen it./{P} No, you wouldn't have seen it. As a matter of fact/It was
357 CP	Edward	7	/{E} No; another aunt/Whom you wouldn't know. Her mother's sister/And rather
369 CP	Peter	1	successes/For a time at least./{P} I wouldn't say that./But Lavinia was awfully kind
397 CP	Edward	20	choose. How do I know/That you wouldn't see him first, and tell him all about me
409 CP	Lavinia	5	began! and I never noticed it./{L} You wouldn't notice anything. You never noticed
430 CP	Peter	14	country this evening,/So I knew you wouldn't mind my looking in so early./It does
445 CC	Claude	4	like this./But you know my wife wouldn't like anyone to meet her/At Northolt,
447 CC	Eggers	19	of character than I am./{E} Oh, I wouldn't say that, Sir Claude!/She has too much
461 CC	Eggers	1	nothing./{E} Oh, not for nothing! I wouldn't have missed it./And besides, as I told
462 CC	Claude	16	in her eyes. She's like that./Why, it wouldn't surprise me if she came to believe/That
470 CC	Lucasta	32	she would like/When she knows *you* wouldn't like it? That's not a compliment:/
471 CC	Lucasta	12	as you/Yet knowing so much that one wouldn't suspect./Perhaps that's why I like you.
476 CC	Lucasta	24	a thing!/There are not many men who wouldn't have thought it./I don't know about
476 CC	Lucasta	38	money, a regular allowance;/But it wouldn't have mattered how much he'd given
478 CC	Lucasta	12	when I told you all I did,/That you wouldn't mind at all. That you might be sorry
484 CC	Lady E	13	loathe her? No, of course not./Or you wouldn't have her portrait. If you never knew
498 CC	Claude	31	child was Mrs. Guzzard's sister./She wouldn't dispose of *him*. It's your child,
499 CC	Lucasta	30	marry B./Made me determined that I wouldn't. Just to spite you,/I dare say. That was
502 CC	Lucasta	12	have misunderstood your reaction./It wouldn't have been like you — the way I
504 CC	Claude	1	visit./She ought to be here. It wouldn't be like her/To be late for an
508 CC	Eggers	7	had lost your son, in a similar way,/Wouldn't you grasp at any straw/That offered
509 CC	Claude	35	be out in my calculations./{SC} That wouldn't surprise me./{LE} Yes, what year was
511 CC	Kaghan	34	Kaghan — it sounds rather flashy:/It wouldn't make the right impression in the City./
517 CC	Eggers	20	/Do try to help him, Eggerson./{E} I wouldn't venture./Mr. Simpkins is a man who
534 ES	Gomez	10	enough,/Except for a false inference. I wouldn't dream/Of carrying on such business if
534 ES	Gomez	23	happens? You have to move on./That wouldn't do for me. I'm too domestic./And by
534 ES	Gomez	26	up, doing well for themselves./I wouldn't allow either of my sons/To go into
536 ES	Gomez	38	/Were ever told the story. *They* wouldn't want to see me./No, I need one old
540 ES	Gomez	26	'Dick, you've run over somebody'/Wouldn't you have shown it, if only for a
541 ES	Gomez	3	/What damages you'd get! The Press wouldn't look at it./Besides, you can't think I've
551 ES	Carghil	38	ended your career,/And then you wouldn't have become Lord Claverton./So
554 ES	Piggott	32	Mrs. Carghill had caught you./You wouldn't know that name, but you might
555 ES	Ld Clav	30	a man. But it can't be that,/Or he wouldn't be at large. Perhaps he's in trouble/
555 ES	Ld Clav	32	I'm sure he has friends/Whom he wouldn't care for you or me to know about./

WOUND (1)

515 CC Guzzard	30	the knife deeper and twists it in the wound?/I had very much rather that the facts

WOUNDED (2)

181 FQ: ECoker	149	you are is where you are not./The wounded surgeon plies the steel/That questions
334 FR Harry	34	not like that. Now I see/I have been wounded in a war of phantoms,/Not by human

WOVE (2)

196 FQ: Little	211	Name/Behind the hands that wove/The intolerable shirt of flame/Which
205 de la Mare	32	/By the delicate, invisible web you wove —/The inexplicable mystery of sound./A

WOVEN (8)

173 FQ: BurntN	82	the enchainment of past and future/Woven in the weakness of the changing body,/
177 FQ: ECoker	13	trots/And to shake the tattered arras woven with a silent motto./In my beginning is
270 MC Chorus	17	the consultations of powers./What is woven on the loom of fate/What is woven in the

270 MC Chorus 18 is woven on the loom of fate/What is woven in the councils of princes/Is woven also
270 MC Chorus 19 is woven in the councils of princes/Is woven also in our veins, our brains,/Is woven
270 MC Chorus 20 also in our veins, our brains,/Is woven like a pattern of living worms/In the guts
350 FR Agatha 5 world/Where the meshes we have woven/Bind us to each other/Follow follow/{M}
568 ES Ld Clav 36 And by the time she's grown/You've woven such a web of fiction about you!/I've

WRANGLING (2)
353 CP   Celia 12 there were no tigers./{C} Oh do stop wrangling,/Both of you. It's your turn, Julia./
525 ES Monica 28 with me/Which you've wasted in wrangling. But seriously, Charles,/Father's sure

WRAP (3)
15 Prufrock   67 /Arms that lie along a table, or wrap about a shawl./And should I then
251 MC Thomas 9 accord./{T} For a countryman/You wrap your meaning in as dark generality/As any
371 CP Edward 32 /{E} There's no memory you can wrap in camphor/But the moths will get in. So

WRAPPING (1)
397 CP Edward 28 on our honeymoon,/You were always wrapping things up in tissue paper/And then

WRAPS (1)
22 Preludes   5 smoky days./And now a gusty shower wraps/The grimy scraps/Of withered leaves

WRAPT (2)
50 Hippopot   36 the True Church remains below/Wrapt in the old miasmal mist./Dans le
73 WL: Thund 363 one walking beside you/Gliding wrapt in a brown mantle, hooded/I do not

WRATH (1)
279 MC Knight4 36 while we were still inflamed with wrath, that the doors/should be opened. Need I

WRATH-BEARING (1)
38 Gerontion   47 /These tears are shaken from the wrath-bearing tree./The tiger springs in the new

WREATH (1)
596 When we   7 beneath;/But the wild roses in your wreath/Were faded, and the leaves were brown./

WREATHED (1)
17 Prufrock   130 the chambers of the sea/By sea-girls wreathed with seaweed red and brown/Till

WRECK (1)
67 WL: Fire S 191 /Musing upon the king my brother's wreck/And on the king my father's death before

WRECKAGE (2)
185 FQ: DrySal 54 /Where is there an end to the drifting wreckage,/The prayer of the bone on the beach,
186 FQ: DrySal 84 To the drift of the sea and the drifting wreckage,/The bone's prayer to Death its God.

WREN (1)
270 MC Chorus 6 with the kite and cowered with the wren. I have felt/The horn of the beetle, the

WRESTLE (1)
179 FQ: ECoker 71 /Leaving one still with the intolerable wrestle/With words and meanings. The poetry

WRETCHED (1)
154 Rock 3   3 miserable cities of designing men,/O wretched generation of enlightened men,/

WRETCHEDNESS (1)
331 FR   Harry 13 meagre childhood,/Some origin of wretchedness. Is that what they would show me?

WRIGGLING (1)
14 Prufrock   58 on a pin,/When I am pinned and wriggling on the wall,/Then how should I begin/

WRINKLED (2)
68 WL: Fire S 219 between two lives,/Old man with wrinkled female breasts, can see/At the violet
68 WL: Fire S 228 and stays./I Tiresias, old man with wrinkled dugs/Perceived the scene, and foretold

WRINKLES (2)
178 FQ: ECoker 50 and silence. Out at sea the dawn wind/Wrinkles and slides. I am here/Or there, or
189 FQ: DrySal 192 signatures, evoke/Biography from the wrinkles of the palm/And tragedy from fingers;

WRITE (7)
20 Portrait   93 the bric-à-brac./'Perhaps you can write to me.'/My self-possession flares up for a
21 Portrait   106 must leave it now to fate./You will write, at any rate./Perhaps it is not too late./I
158 Rock 5   8 not justified, nor the others./And they write innumerable books; being too vain and
487 CC Claude 10 /I couldn't have asked Eggerson to write a speech for me./Oh, by the way, Colby,
580 ES Monica 1 Good-bye Michael. Will you let me write to you?/{G} Oh, I'm glad you reminded
580 ES Monica 5 mail./{M} Take the card, Charles. If I write to you, Michael,/Will you ever answer?/
580 ES Ld Clav 11 you know I'm flourishing./{LC} Yes, write to Monica./{G} Well, good-bye Dick. And

WRITES (2)
419 CP   m 36 for you to give your friends; {}/[*Writes on a slip of paper*]/{R} You had better let
552 ES Carghil 38 a part/In your obituary, whoever writes it./{LC} Considering how long ago it was

WRITHING (3)
143 Lines OM   5 still/Than when I smell the enemy/Writhing in the essential blood/Or dangling
178 FQ: ECoker 55 of the summer heat,/And snowdrops writhing under feet/And hollyhocks that aim
605 Narcissus   26 belly held tight in his own fingers,/Writhing in his own clutch, his ancient beauty/

WRITING (3)

154 Rock 3	13	action./Many are engaged in	writing books and printing them,/Many desire
445 CC	3m	1 *house. Early afternoon.* SIR CLAUDE	*writing at desk. Enter*/EGGERSON./{SC} Ah,
460 CC Claude	9	you know that I can't decipher your	writing./I like to have the cards, just to know

WRITING-TABLE (2)

483 CC Lady E	10	/And most of the furniture. But, that	writing-table!/Where did that writing-table
483 CC Lady E	11	that writing-table!/Where did that	writing-table come from?/{C} It's an office desk.

WRITTEN (7)

233 Skimble	34	found your little den/With your name	written up on the door./And the berth is very
585	t	at the door./MORGAN./POEMS	WRITTEN IN EARLY YOUTH/A Fable for
333 FR Agatha	25	supposed. What of it?/What we have	written is not a story of detection,/Of crime and
350 FR Mary	8	other/Follow follow/{M} A curse is	written/On the under side of things/Behind the
431 CP Peter	28	decaying houses?/{P} Oh dear no! I've	written the script of this film,/And Bela is very
465 CC Colby	38	/I hear the music I should like to have	written,/As the composer heard it when it came
487 CC Claude	1	know that I'll have to have my speech	written out/And then memorise it. I can't use

WRONG (48)

20 Portrait	83	have desired./Are these ideas right or	wrong?/The October night comes down;
141 Rannoch	8	of broken steel,/Clamour of confused	wrong, apt/In silence. Memory is strong/Beyond
180 FQ: ECoker	125	hope/For hope would be hope for the	wrong thing; wait without love/For love would
180 FQ: ECoker	126	love/For love would be love of the	wrong thing; there is yet faith/But the faith and
187 FQ: DrySal	108	/Having hopes for the	wrong things or dreaded the wrong things,/Is
187 FQ: DrySal	108	for the wrong things or dreaded the	wrong things,/Is not the question) are likewise
195 FQ: Little	146	stings, and honour stains./From	wrong to wrong the exasperated spirit/Proceeds,
195 FQ: Little	146	and honour stains./From wrong to	wrong the exasperated spirit/Proceeds, unless
214 RTTugger	14	wants to be out;/He's always on the	wrong side of every door,/And as soon as he's
232 Skimble	31	cannot be ignored;/So nothing goes	wrong on the Northern Mail/When
233 Skimble	44	/For Skimble won't let anything go	wrong./And when you creep into your cosy
602 Humoresque	21	so it goes./Logic a marionette's, all	wrong/Of premises; yet in some star/A hero! —
258 MC Thomas	6	treason:/To do the right deed for the	wrong reason./The natural vigour in the venial
259 MC Thomas	2	for every evil, every sacrilege,/Crime,	wrong, oppression and the axe's edge,/
263 MC Chorus	24	work shall have been done, what	wrong/Shall the bird's song cover, the green tree
263 MC Chorus	25	song cover, the green tree cover, what	wrong/Shall the fresh earth cover? We wait, and
276 MC Chorus	13	time,/An instant eternity of evil and	wrong./We are soiled by a filth that we cannot
290 FR Chorus	38	different play, or having rehearsed the	wrong parts,/Waiting for the rustling in the
297 FR Charles	35	/{C} My purpose is, to find out what's	wrong with Harry:/Until we know that, we can
300 FR Gerald	40	/{G} Oh, Downing,/Is there anything	wrong with his Lordship's car?/{Do} Oh no, Sir,
301 FRDowning	5	busy about it tonight./{Do} Nothing	wrong, Sir:/Only I like to have her always
302 FR Amy	16	not understand what could have gone	wrong/With both of them, coming from
309 FR Mary	25	do to loving: an infatuation/That's	wrong, a good that's misdirected. You deceive
318 FR Harry	1	being unkind to mother;/What was	wrong was whatever made her suffer,/And
322 FR Winch	39	looked him over;/Says there's nothing	wrong but some nasty cuts/And a bad
344 FR Gerald	17	tropical climate!/{G} There's nothing	wrong with a tropical climate —/But you have
370 CP Peter	26	interest in you?/{P} You put it just	wrong. I think of it differently./It is not her
402 CP Reilly	31	/We must first find out what is	wrong with you/Before we decide what to do
413 CP Celia	28	really *like* to think there's something	wrong with me —/Because, if there isn't, then
413 CP Celia	29	if there isn't, then there's something	wrong,/Or at least, very different from what it
413 CP Celia	33	I'd rather believe/There is something	wrong with me, that could be put right./I'd do
415 CP Celia	22	it was ever mentioned!/But anything	wrong, from our point of view,/Was either bad
418 CP Reilly	29	/Of what you have sought for in the	wrong place./{C} That sounds like what I want.
438 CP Edward	16	must be something else that is terribly	wrong,/And the rest of us are somehow
438 CP Edward	17	of us are somehow involved in the	wrong,/I should only speak for myself. I'm sure
438 CP Reilly	33	—/And sometimes I have made the	wrong decision./As for Miss Coplestone,
452 CC Lucasta	15	persistently unpunctual./{L} You're	wrong, Eggy. It's rank injustice./Two months
459 CC Lady E	19	mews done over./{LE} But all in the	wrong colours, I'm sure. My husband/Does not
464 CC Claude	33	And yet I was in awe of him./I was	wrong, in both. I loathed this occupation/Until
469 CC Lucasta	11	it./{L} But suppose I only like the	wrong things?/{C} No, I'm sure you'll prefer the
480 CC Kaghan	7	a good guesser. But I sometimes guess	wrong./I make decisions on the spur of the
487 CC Lady E	28	not to believe it yet,/Perhaps it is	wrong of me to feel so sure,/But it seems that
500 CC Lucasta	37	thought so too, Claude, but for the	wrong reasons,/And that put me off. So I'm
501 CC Lucasta	2	the reasons why you think so are the	wrong ones./{LE} And I'm sure too, Lucasta,
550 ES Carghil	34	to leave buried./{MC} There you're	wrong, Richard. Effie always said —/What a
551 ES Carghil	16	come and talk about the past./You're	wrong, you know. It's both pain and pleasure/
559 ES Michael	20	ideas of good and bad,/Of right and	wrong. I want to go far away/To some country
570 ES Ld Clav	8	one's heart/When one is sure of the	wrong response?/How make a confession with

WROTE (7)

289 FR	Charles	13	say that I agree with you./{C} I never wrote to him when he lost his wife —/That was
356 CP	Julia	11	scenario./{J} Not the one you wrote?/{P} Not the one I wrote:/But I had a
356 CP	Peter	12	the one you wrote?/{P} Not the one I wrote:/But I had a very enjoyable time./{C} Go
400 CP	Reilly	29	at his club./{R} Yes, that is where he wrote from. {}/[*The house-telephone rings*]/{R}
460 CC	Lady E	7	matter:/It's more advanced. But I wrote you all about it./{SC} It's true, you did
495 CC	Lady E	21	thought Tony was a poet./Because he wrote me poems. And he was so beautiful./I
553 ES	Carghil	21	/{MC} Have you forgotten that you wrote me letters?/Oh, not very many. Only a

WROUGHT (2)

64 WL: Chess		79	where the glass/Held up by standards wrought with fruited vines/From which a
549 ES	Carghil	36	I do remember you./{MC} Time has wrought sad changes in me, Richard./I was very

YARD (3)

24 Rhapsody	30	white./A broken spring in a factory yard,/Rust that clings to the form that the
212 Growltiger	28	he too had stol'n away —/In the yard behind the Lion he was prowling for his
226 Macavity	3	Law./He's the bafflement of Scotland Yard, the Flying Squad's despair:/For when

YARD'S (1)

226 Macavity	22	are not found in any file of Scotland Yard's./And when the larder's looted, or the

YAWN (1)

223 Pekes Pols	53	fearfully blazing,/He gave a great yawn, and his jaws were amazing;/And when he

YAWNING (2)

129 Cor2 State	31	by the flare/Of a sweaty torchbearer, yawning./O hidden under the... Hidden under
223 Pekes Pols	56	what with the glare of his eyes and his yawning,/The Pekes and the Pollicles quickly

YAWNS (1)

56 Swee Night	16	/Reorganised upon the floor/She yawns and draws a stocking up;/The silent man

YE (4)

92 Ash-Wed 2	52	of the desert. This is the land which ye/Shall divide by lot. And neither division nor
166 Rock 10	10	deep for mortal eyes to plumb. Come/Ye out from among those who prize the
166 Rock 10	12	of the snake. Take/Your way and be ye separate./Be not too curious of Good and
166 Rock 10	15	the future waves of Time;/But be ye satisfied that you have light/Enough to take

YEAR (41)

37 Gerontion	19	darkness. In the juvescence of the year/Came Christ the tiger/In depraved May,
38 Gerontion	48	tree./The tiger springs in the new year. Us he devours. Think at last/We have not
62 WL: Burial	35	*du*?/'You gave me hyacinths first a year ago;/'They called me the hyacinth girl.'/—
63 WL: Burial	71	Mylae!/'That corpse you planted last year in your garden,/'Has it begun to sprout?
63 WL: Burial	72	it begun to sprout? Will it bloom this year?/'Or has the sudden frost disturbed its bed?
67 WL: Fire S	195	garret,/Rattled by the rat's foot only, year to year./But at my back from time to time I
67 WL: Fire S	195	Rattled by the rat's foot only, year to year./But at my back from time to time I hear/
103 Journ Magi	2	had of it,/Just the worst time of the year/For a journey, and such a long journey:/
129 Cor2 State	15	at Christmas/And one week's leave a year./A committee has been appointed to
191 FQ: Little	11	fire/In the dark time of the year. Between melting and freezing/The soul's
594 Grad 12	1	dost not die — for each succeeding year/Thy honor and thy fame shall but increase/
239 MC Chorus	11	a waste of water and mud,/The New Year waits, breathes, waits, whispers in
239 MC Chorus	13	his hand to the fire,/The New Year waits, destiny waits for the coming./Who
243 MC Chorus	16	the time, late too late, and rotten the year;/Evil the wind, and bitter the sea, and grey
243 MC Chorus	33	/Sometimes the harvest is good,/One year is a year of rain,/Another a year of dryness,
243 MC Chorus	33	the harvest is good,/One year is a year of rain,/Another a year of dryness,/One
243 MC Chorus	34	/One year is a year of rain,/Another a year of dryness,/One year the apples are
243 MC Chorus	35	rain,/Another a year of dryness,/One year the apples are abundant,/Another year the
244 MC Chorus	1	the apples are abundant,/Another year the plums are lacking./Yet we have gone
260 MC Thomas	14	good will'; at this same time of all the year that we/celebrate at once the Birth of Our
263 MC Chorus	3	storm./What sign of the spring of the year?/Only the death of the old: not a stir, not a
265 MC Priest1	1	but another day, the dusk of the year./{P2} To-day, what is to-day? Another
289 FR Charles	14	lost his wife —/That was just about a year ago, wasn't it?/Do you think that I ought
315 FR Warburt	29	Monchensey,/And I hope that next year will bring me the same honour. {}/[*Exeunt*
321 FR Winch	32	at your jokes, I see. You don't look a year older/Than when I saw you last, my Lord.
325 FR Violet	31	— and always on his head./{V} But a year ago, Arthur took me out in his car,/And I
330 FR Harry	28	only as an eye, seeing./All this last year, I could not fit myself together:/When I
338 FR Harry	17	/It was not I who told her ... All this year,/This last year, I have been in flight/But
338 FR Harry	18	who told her ... All this year,/This last year, I have been in flight/But always in
356 CP Peter	2	him at Oxford:/I came across him last year in California./{J} I've always wanted to go
368 CP Peter	31	know Celia./I met her here, about a year ago./{E} At one of Lavinia's amateur
429 CP Alex	28	publication./{E} But when?/{A} In a year or two./{E} And meanwhile?/{A}
456 CC Eggers	34	Park in the evening,/And once a year our holiday at Dawlish'./And to think that
461 CC Eggers	17	way to Joshua Park, at this time of year!'/I said: 'Let's think about it in the Spring/
509 CC Lady E	36	wouldn't surprise me./{LE} Yes, what year was it?/I'm getting so confused. What with
529 ES Ld Clav	30	Just remember:/Every day, year after year, over my breakfast,/I have
529 ES Ld Clav	30	Just remember:/Every day, year after year, over my breakfast,/I have looked at this
547 ES Piggott	5	must be very careful at this time of year;/This early warm weather can be very
552 ES Ld Clav	2	/I seem to remember, it was only a year or so/Before your name appeared in very
553 ES Carghil	5	/{MC} I've followed your progress year by year, Richard./And although it's true
553 ES Carghil	5	I've followed your progress year by year, Richard./And although it's true that our

YEAR'S (3)

194 FQ: Little	120	shall kick the empty pail./For last year's words belong to last year's language/And
194 FQ: Little	120	/For last year's words belong to last year's language/And next year's words await
194 FQ: Little	121	to last year's language/And next year's words await another voice./But, as the

YEARN (1)
204 de la Mare   16   /The sad intangible who grieve and yearn;/When the familiar scene is suddenly
YEARNING (1)
567 ES   Monica   7 /And I couldn't, just when I had been yearning/For the sound of it, for the caress that
YEARS (137)
66 WL: Chess   148   Albert,/He's been in the army four years, he wants a good time,/And if you don't
94 Ash-Wed 4   12   colour,/Sovegna vos/Here are the years that walk between, bearing/Away the
94 Ash-Wed 4   16   sheathed about her, folded./The new years walk, restoring/Through a bright cloud of
94 Ash-Wed 4   17   /Through a bright cloud of tears, the years, restoring/With a new verse the ancient
105 Song Sime   9   us thy peace./I have walked many years in this city,/Kept faith and fast, provided
105 Song Sime   24   consolation/To one who has eighty years and no to-morrow./According to thy
123 SA Kl & Kr   21   *but hours/For it won't be hours but years {}/diminuendo/*{Kl&Kr} *And the morning/*
138 New Hamp   6   brown wing, hover over;/Twenty years and the spring is over;/To-day grieves,
148 Rock 1   62   thing does not change./In all of my years, one thing does not change./However you
182 FQ: ECoker   174   in the middle way, having had twenty years —/Twenty years largely wasted, the years
182 FQ: ECoker   175   having had twenty years —/Twenty years largely wasted, the years of *l'entre deux*
182 FQ: ECoker   175   —/Twenty years largely wasted, the years of *l'entre deux guerres* —/Trying to learn
185 FQ: DrySal   60   takes to itself the emotionless/Years of living among the breakage/Of what
593 Grad 4   6 /Would we might look into the future years./Great duties call — the twentieth century
593 Grad 5   4   store,/Or what great deeds the distant years may see,/What conquest over pain and
593 Grad 7   2   of benefits — may we/In future years be found with those who try/To labor for
593 Grad 8   1   is raised on high./Sometime in distant years when we are grown/Gray-haired and old,
593 Grad 8   6   we may have gone,/Through all the years will ne'er have been forgot./For in the
594 Grad 9   4   purity,/O school of ours! The passing years that roll/Between, as we press onward to
595 Grad 13   6   be, proud and serene,/Still as the years pass by, the word 'Progress!'/So we are
604 Ode   2   thee,/Ere we face the importunate years,/In thy shadow we wait, while thy
604 Ode   9   the past as we go./Yet for all of these years that to-morrow has lost/We are still the
604 Ode   13   of the life that we leave./And only the years that efface and destroy/Give us also the
239 MC Chorus   18   the fire, and deny his master?/Seven years and the summer is over/Seven years since
239 MC Chorus   19   years and the summer is over/Seven years since the Archbishop left us,/He who was
240 MC Priest1   26   {}/[*Enter* PRIESTS]/{P1} Seven years and the summer is over./Seven years since
240 MC Priest1   27   years and the summer is over./Seven years since the Archbishop left us./{P2} What
243 MC Priest3   8   /The wheel has been still, these seven years, and no good./For ill or good, let the
243 MC Chorus   23   not wish anything to happen./Seven years we have lived quietly,/Succeeded in
245 MC Priest2   27   /But your Lordship knows that seven years of waiting,/Seven years of prayer, seven
245 MC Priest2   28   that seven years of waiting,/Seven years of prayer, seven years of emptiness,/Have
245 MC Priest2   28   waiting,/Seven years of prayer, seven years of emptiness,/Have better prepared our
247 MC Thomas   39   to the bone./{T} You come twenty years too late./{T1} Then I leave you to your
258 MC Thomas   9   way in which our lives begin./Thirty years ago, I searched all the ways/That lead to
268 MC Thomas   37   I will be bold/To say: seven years were my people without/My presence;
268 MC Thomas   38   people without/My presence; seven years of misery and pain./Seven years a
268 MC Thomas   39   seven years of misery and pain./Seven years a mendicant on foreign charity/I lingered
269 MC Thomas   1   charity/I lingered abroad: seven years is no brevity./I shall not get those seven
269 MC Thomas   2   no brevity./I shall not get those seven years back again./Never again, you must make
278 MC Knight2   25   the King's servant, had/for so many years striven to establish; and that — God
288 FR   Amy   12   It will be the first time/For eight years that we have all been together./{Ag} It is
288 FR   Agatha   14   rather painful for Harry/After eight years and all that has happened/To come back
290 FR   Amy   18   had somewhere in the last eight years./{G} That will be a little difficult./{V}
297 FR   Charles   11   Downing?/He's been with Harry ten years, he's absolutely discreet./He was with
298 FR   Charles   25   good to see you again, after all these years./You're well, I hope?/{Do} Thank you,
298 FR   Charles   31   looked after his Lordship for over ten years .../{Do} Eleven years, Sir, next Lady Day./
298 FRDowning   32   for over ten years .../{Do} Eleven years, Sir, next Lady Day./{C} Eleven years, and
298 FR   Charles   33   years, Sir, next Lady Day./{C} Eleven years, and you know him pretty well./And I'm
298 FR   Charles   35   /We haven't seen him for nearly eight years;/And to tell the truth, now that we've seen
304 FR   Mary   7   /And tried for a fellowship, seven years ago./Now I want your advice, because
304 FR   Agatha   11   I want to get away./{Ag} After seven years?/{M} Oh, you don't understand!/But you
306 FR   Harry   12   ask you. I don't know yet./All these years I'd been longing to get back/Because I
309 FR   Harry   29   this is true./{H} I have spent many years in useless travel;/You have staid in
314 FR   Ivy   32   very rich experience, Doctor,/In forty years. {W} Indeed, yes./Even in a country
315 FR   Violet   21   a day older/Than on her birthday ten years ago./{G} Is there any use in waiting for
320 FR Warburt   14   all excitement/She may live several years. A sudden shock/Might send her off at
322 FR   Winch   6   her soul,/She's been dead these ten years. How is her Ladyship,/If I may ask, my
324 FR Warburt   4   You have trusted me a good many years, Lady Monchensey;/This is not the time to
326 FR   Harry   29   put in order./If you only knew the years that I have had to live/Since I came home,
330 FR   Harry   19   meaning is./At the beginning, eight years ago,/I felt, at first, that sense of

331 FR	Agatha	21	much./{Ag} I had to fight for many years to win my dispossession,/And many years
331 FR	Agatha	22	to win my dispossession,/And many years to keep it. What people know me as,/The
332 FR	Agatha	12	was not always so. There were many years/Before she succeeded in making terms
332 FR	Agatha	18	country house together,/For three years childless, learning the meaning/Of
334 FR	Agatha	9	It is as if/I had been living all these years upon my capital,/Instead of earning my
334 FR	Harry	24	training, I could endure, these ten years,/Playing a part that had been imposed
340 FR	Amy	2	Wishwood;/But I thought, thirty-five years is long, and death is an end,/And I
340 FR	Amy	4	It has made enough in *me*. Thirty-five years ago/You took my husband from me. Now
340 FR	Agatha	7	you ever had./What did I get? thirty years of solitude,/Alone, among women, in a
340 FR	Agatha	9	/Trying not to dislike women. Thirty years in which to think./Do you suppose that I
340 FR	Amy	17	/What I could plant here. Seven years I kept him,/For the sake of the future, a
341 FR	Amy	14	nothing except to remind him/Of the years when he had been a happy boy at
341 FR	Amy	21	/Is only the stronger for all these years of abstinence./Thirty-five years ago you
341 FR	Amy	22	these years of abstinence./Thirty-five years ago you took my husband from me/And
341 FR	Amy	32	his good? is it you or I?/Thirty-five years designing his life,/Eight years watching,
341 FR	Amy	33	years designing his life,/Eight years watching, without him, at Wishwood,/
341 FR	Amy	34	watching, without him, at Wishwood,/Years of bitterness and disappointment./What
343 FR	Mary	17	I deceived myself. It takes so many years/To learn that one is dead! So you must
346 FR	Downing	18	you come to look at it:/After all these years that I've been with him/I think I
355 CP	Julia	30	the Vincewell wedding. Oh, so many years ago! {}/[*To the* UNIDENTIFIED
360 CP	Edward	20	/How long married?/{E} Five years./{UG} Children?/{E} No./{UG} Then look
364 CP	Edward	7	what has happened/During the five years that we've been married. I must find out
385 CP	Reilly	14	those who enfolded/Your childhood years in comfort, mirth, security —/If they
385 CP	Edward	21	expect me to obliterate/The last five years./{UG} I ask you to forget nothing./To try
393 CP	Lavinia	5	/Finding that you've spent five years of your life/With a man who has no sense
403 CP	Edward	37	is what she has done to me in five years together!/She has made the world a place I
424 CP	2m	1	*the Chamberlaynes' London flat. Two years later./A late afternoon in July.*
424 CP	Lavinia	18	given *several* parties/In the last two years. And I've attended *all* of them./I hope
434 CP	Peter	35	all. But then I've been away/For two years, and I don't know what happened/To
434 CP	Peter	36	happened/To Celia, during those two years./Two years! Thinking about Celia./{E} It's
434 CP	Peter	37	Celia, during those two years./Two years! Thinking about Celia./{E} It's the waste
435 CP	Peter	1	everything else that's a waste./Two years! And it was all a mistake./Julia! Why
435 CP	Julia	3	anything?/{J} You gave her those two years, as best you could./{P} When did she ...
435 CP	Julia	5	did she ... take up this career?/{J} Two years ago./{P} Two years ago! I tried to forget
435 CP	Peter	6	career?/{J} Two years ago./{P} Two years ago! I tried to forget about her,/Until I
438 CP	Lavinia	4	— I know nothing of her last two years./{R} That shows some insight on your
439 CP	Lavinia	2	/When she said good-bye to us, two years ago./{E} Your responsibility is nothing to
450 CC	Claude	7	we worked together/For nearly thirty years./{E} Nearly thirty-one./But now you put it
463 CC	Claude	6	no doubts at the time — that's five years;/And then your school, and your military
467 CC	Colby	11	—/The father who was missing in the years of childhood./Those years have gone
467 CC	Colby	12	in the years of childhood./Those years have gone forever. The empty years./Oh,
467 CC	Colby	12	years have gone forever. The empty years./Oh, I'm terribly sorry to be saying this;/
477 CC	Lucasta	3	in a cupboard!/I was only eight years old/When she died of an 'accidental
487 CC	Lady E	39	name I've been hunting for all these years —/That, and the other name, *Teddington*:
489 CC	Claude	2	isn't Colby./I ought to have told you, years ago./I told you about Lucasta, and you
494 CC	Lady E	37	to have lived with you, all these years,/And now you tell me, you'd have liked to
505 CC	Claude	6	may say, my friend —/For very many years. So I asked him to be present./I hope you
505 CC	Eggers	29	/And now we must go back, many years:/Well, not so many years — when you get
505 CC	Eggers	30	back, many years:/Well, not so many years — when you get to my age/The past and
506 CC	Eggers	13	instituted enquiries./So, for many years, she has been without a clue/Until the
514 CC	Claude	19	out such a deception/Over all these years. And why *should* you have deceived me?/
514 CC	Claude	35	out a deception/For twenty-five years? It's quite impossible./{MG} I had no
519 CC	Guzzard	1	Claude,/Had *our* wishes twenty-five years ago;/But we failed to observe, when we
529 ES	Ld Clav	34	find out what I was doing/Twenty years ago, to-day, at this hour of the afternoon./
531 ES	Ld Clav	15	With an inset, a portrait taken twenty years ago./In five years' time, it will be the half
533 ES	Gomez	15	been a pretty hard worker all these years/And I thought, now's the time to take a
535 ES	Gomez	26	back to England/After thirty-five years. Can you imagine/What it would be like
535 ES	Gomez	28	been away from home/For thirty-five years? I was twenty-five —/The same age as you
537 ES	Gomez	6	It's done already, Dick; done many years ago:/Adoption tried, and grappled to my
539 ES	Gomez	7	have been good for another few years/At least. Why did they let you retire?/{LC}
541 ES	Gomez	2	something that happened so many years ago?/What damages you'd get! The Press
542 ES	Ld Clav	19	I gave you my friendship/So many years ago, I only gained in return/Your envy,
548 ES	Carghil	30	me, it's astonishing, after all these years;/And you don't even recognise me! I'd
550 ES	Ld Clav	11	/{LC} You married, I suppose, many years ago?/{MC} Many years ago, the first time.
550 ES	Carghil	12	many years ago?/{MC} Many years ago, the first time. That didn't last long./

300 FR	Charles	37	or else he'd have known it./{C} Oh yes ... quite so. Thank you, Downing,/I don't
305 FR	Mary	38	of people/All the more manifest./{M} Yes, nothing changes here,/And we just go on ...
314 FR	Warburt	33	Doctor,/In forty years./{W} Indeed, yes./Even in a country practice. My first patient,
315 FR	Violet	18	/That I ever see your mother./{V} Yes, look at your mother!/Except that she can't
318 FR	Warburt	37	you remember my father?/{W} Why, yes, of course, Harry, but I really don't see/
319 FR	Harry	34	Scandal? who said scandal? I did not./Yes, I see now. That night, when she kissed me,/
321 FR	Warburt	1	at about my present age?/{W} Why, yes, Harry, of course I did./{H} What did he
322 FR	Winch	24	It's about Mr. John./{H} John!/{Wi} Yes, my Lord, I'm sorry./I thought I'd better
328 FR	Charles	7	CHARLES, *with a newspaper*]/{C} Yes, there is a paragraph ... I'm glad to say/It's
345 FR	Harry	8	taking Downing with you?/{H} Oh, yes, I'm taking Downing./You need not fear
355 CP	Julia	36	the parents of Tony Vincewell?/{J} Yes. Tony was the product, but not the
358 CP	Julia	9	asked me to dine with you alone./{J} Yes, alone!/Without Lavinia! You'll like the
359 CP	Edward	5	news of Lavinia's aunt./{E} Oh ... yes ... thank you. Good-bye, Alex,/It was nice
362 CP	Reilly	18	a mystery:/It's so ... unfinished./{UG} Yes, it's unfinished;/And nobody likes to be left
367 CP	Edward	26	/Though she had her poetry./{E} Yes, I've seen her poetry —/Interesting if one is
371 CP	Edward	24	/{E} Hello! ... I can't talk now .../Yes, there is ... Well then, I'll ring you/As soon
372 CP	Peter	5	much older./{E} So much older?/{P} Yes, I'm sure that she would listen to you/As
374 CP	Edward	17	simple./Lavinia has left you./{E} Yes, that *was* the situation./I suppose it was
375 CP	Edward	12	it./Hello ... oh, hello! ... No. I mean yes, Alex;/Yes, of course ... it was marvellous.
375 CP	Edward	13	... oh, hello! ... No. I mean yes, Alex;/Yes, of course ... it was marvellous./I've never
375 CP	Edward	15	/I've never tasted anything like it .../Yes, that's very interesting. But I just wondered/
377 CP	Celia	7	it. That man who was here —/{C} Yes, who was that man? I was rather afraid of
382 CP	Celia	36	{E} You ... ask me to forgive *you*!/{C} Yes, for two things. First ... {}/[*The telephone*
382 CP	Celia	39	/I suppose I had better answer it./{C} Yes, better answer it./{E} Hello! ... Oh, Julia:
383 CP	Celia	8	you like;/We ... I'll look for them./{C} Yes, you look for them./I shall never go into
383 CP	Edward	30	hunt for them ... No, I found them./... Yes, she's bringing them now ... Good night. {}/
385 CP	Reilly	37	like you to bring her yourself./{UG} Yes, I know you would. And for definite
388 CP	Peter	1	/{C} You're going to California!/{P} Yes, I have a new job./{E} And how did that
388 CP	Peter	33	mischief./And is *she* coming?/{P} Yes, and Alex./{L} Then I shall ask *them* for an
388 CP	Peter	38	/{E} Peter's going to America./{P} Yes, and I would have rung you up tomorrow/
389 CP	Peter	12	where you are going, yourself?/{P} Yes, of course, I'm going to California./{L}
390 CP	Edward	19	ALEX]/{A} Has Lavinia arrived?/{E} Yes./{A} Welcome back, Lavinia!/When I got
392 CP	Lavinia	1	But of course I'm glad to see you./{L} Yes, that was a silly thing to say./Like a
392 CP	Lavinia	21	he was,/But *you* ought to know./{L} Yes, I think I know./But I'm puzzled by Julia.
393 CP	Lavinia	4	... how many? ... thirty-two hours./{L} Yes, a very important discovery,/Finding that
396 CP	Lavinia	23	of people being sorry for me./{L} Yes, because they can never be so sorry for you/
398 CP	Lavinia	1	/{E} Celia? Going to California?/{L} Yes, with Peter./Really, Edward, if you were
400 CP	Alex	11	is,/Does he trust your judgement?/{A} Yes, implicitly./It's not that he regards me as
400 CP	Reilly	29	her./{A} He is staying at his club./{R} Yes, that is where he wrote from. {}/[*The*
400 CP	Reilly	30	*house-telephone rings*]/{R} Hello! Yes, show him up./{A} You will have a busy
400 CP	Reilly	34	come back when they've gone./{R} Yes, when they've gone. {}/[*Exit* ALEX *by side*
401 CP	Reilly	24	But you had seen my wife?/{R} Oh yes, I had seen her./{E} So this *is* a trap!/{R}
402 CP	Reilly	35	in my own personality./{R} Oh, dear yes; this is serious. A very common malady./
404 CP	Reilly	3	*rings*]/[*into telephone*]/{R} Yes. {}/[*To* EDWARD]/{R} Yes, you could be
404 CP	Reilly	4	/{R} Yes. {}/[*To* EDWARD]/{R} Yes, you could be alone there./{E} I wonder/If
411 CP	Edward	19	else to ask him/Before we go?/{E} Yes, I have./But it's difficult to say./{L} But I
412 CP	Reilly	1	*rings. He/gets up and answers it.*]/{R} Yes? ... Yes. Come in. {}/[*Enter* JULIA *by side*
412 CP	Reilly	1	/*gets up and answers it.*]/{R} Yes? ... Yes. Come in. {}/[*Enter* JULIA *by side door*]/
412 CP	Reilly	21	/And come back when she's gone./{J} Yes, when she's gone./{J} Will Alex be here?/{R}
412 CP	Reilly	23	she's gone./{J} Will Alex be here?/{R} Yes, he'll be here. {}/[*Exit* JULIA *by side door*]
412 CP	Celia	26	a friend of Mrs. Shuttlethwaite./{C} Yes, it was Julia ... Mrs. Shuttlethwaite/Who
421 CP	Julia	15	go far, you agreed with me./{J} Oh yes, she will go far. And we know where she is
425 CP	Edward	35	a success. Is that picture straight?/{E} Yes, it is./{L} No, it isn't. Do please straighten
426 CP	Julia	35	What can Parkinson's do for me?/Oh yes, I know this is a Parkinson party;/I
428 CP	Alex	25	/When you cooked them?/{A} Oh yes, indeed./I invented for the natives several
429 CP	Alex	18	English residents been murdered?/{A} Yes, but they are not usually eaten./When these
430 CP	Peter	18	you've just come from New York./{P} Yes, from New York./The Bologolomskys saw
431 CP	Alex	10	connection in California, Alex?/{A} Yes, we have sometimes obliged each other./{P}
432 CP	Alex	30	Mr. MacColgie Gibbs./{A} Indeed, yes, we have met./{R} On several commissions./
433 CP	Lavinia	40	had experience of nursing .../{L} Yes, she had been a V.A.D. I remember./{A}
434 CP	Alex	29	/Who would have died anyway./{A} Yes, the patients died anyway;/Being tainted
446 CC	Claude	11	you told me./{SC} About his music./Yes, I think so. I understand his feelings./He's
446 CC	Eggers	28	him a really good piano./{E} A piano? Yes, I'm sure he'll feel at home/When he has a
446 CC	Eggers	33	he'll want a garden of his own. And yes, a bird bath!/{SC} A bird bath? In the mews?
449 CC	Claude	3	*she* lost./{SC} In a very different way, yes. You might say *mislaid*,/Since the father is

449	CC	Claude	5	dead, and there's no way of tracing it./Yes, I was thinking of her missing child:/In the
449	CC	Eggers	13	us to adopt him./{E} Adopt him! Yes, indeed,/That would be the solution. Yes,
449	CC	Eggers	14	indeed,/That would be the solution. Yes, quite ideal./{SC} I'm glad you agree. Your
451	CC	Eggers	17	company apart from business./{E} Oh yes, Mr. Kaghan is very good company./He
452	CC	Lucasta	13	my job!/{E} Again, Miss Angel?/{L} Yes, again! And serve them right!/{E} You have
453	CC	Lucasta	29	let's cope with the financial crisis./{L} Yes, Eggy, will you break the sad news to
454	CC	Eggers	18	/{C} Egg ... Mr. Eggerson!/{E} Yes, Mr. Simpkins?/{C} You seem to me sane.
455	CC	Eggers	27	/{C} But you have Mrs. Eggerson./{E} Yes, she's a great protection. And I have my
455	CC	Eggers	37	quite so unusual as Miss Angel./{E} O yes, Mr. Simpkins, much more unusual./{C} Oh!
456	CC	Eggers	13	way, besides being a lady?/{E} Why, yes, indeed, I must admit she is./Most of her
458	CC	Eggers	15	say that you changed your ticket?/{E} Yes, how did you manage to change your
458	CC	Claude	19	a very experienced traveller./{SC} Oh yes, of course we know that, Elizabeth./But why
460	CC	Claude	24	that was Mr. Colby./{SC} Oh, I see./Yes, now I am beginning to remember./I must
460	CC	Claude	31	/I must go and rest now./{SC} Yes, you go and rest./I'm in the middle of some
463	CC	Claude	10	me how I found this work./{SC} Yes, how do you find it?/{C} In a way,
463	CC	Claude	37	/{C} Your own experience?/{SC} Yes, I did not want to be a financier./{C} What
468	CC	Claude	3	Be patient with her, Colby./— Oh yes, that meeting. We must run through the
470	CC	Colby	17	again/And teach me about music?/{C} Yes, of course I will./But I'm sure that when
477	CC	Colby	13	Are you shocked?/{C} Shocked? No. Yes. You don't understand./I want to explain.
479	CC	Kaghan	17	Will you have a glass of sherry?/{K} Yes, I'll have a glass of sherry,/To drink success
479	CC	Kaghan	30	she's never wanted to pursue you./{K} Yes, I made a bad impression at the start:/I saw
485	CC	Lady E	39	The name means something to me./Yes. Guzzard. *That* is the name I've been
486	CC	Lady E	10	... I was an illegitimate child./{LE} Oh yes. An illegitimate child./So that the only
486	CC	Claude	38	tomorrow night, I believe./{SC} Yes it is./But you know that I'll have to have
490	CC	Claude	1	*did* care for the girl, didn't you?/{SC} Yes, I did care. Very much. I had never/Been in
490	CC	Claude	9	doesn't your instinct tell you?/{SC} Yes, tell us everything that's in your mind./I
492	CC	Claude	29	I feel in a reminiscent mood' —/Oh yes. To say something of my early ambitions/To
496	CC	Claude	33	traffic/Has got so much worse./{SC} Yes, it's always getting worse./{LE} — I hope
499	CC	Lucasta	23	But I thought that was all settled./{L} Yes, of course, Claude. You thought everything
500	CC	Claude	2	/{E} Half-brother, Miss Angel./{SC} Yes, half-brother./{L} What do you mean?/{SC}
503	CC	Lucasta	32	be brother and sister —/Or so I hope. Yes, in any event,/Good-bye, Colby. {}/[*Exit*
504	CC	Lady E	36	I suppose you mean Colby?/{LE} Yes. To do with Colby./{SC} Elizabeth, you
505	CC	Eggers	16	Colby — so very confidential?/{E} Yes, that is what I should call it, Mrs. Guzzard.
507	CC	Guzzard	8	you —/Under such conditions?/{MG} Yes, I did take in a child./My husband and I
508	CC	Guzzard	30	/{E} But you know their name?/{MG} Yes, I know their name:/Like mine, a somewhat
509	CC	Guzzard	17	a little cousin/Who had died?/{MG} Yes, Colby, that is what I told you./{LE} So my
509	CC	Claude	26	Kaghan./{LE} Barnabas?/{SC} Yes, Elizabeth. He sometimes has to sign his full
509	CC	Lady E	36	{SC} That wouldn't surprise me./{LE} Yes, what year was it?/I'm getting so confused.
510	CC	Kaghan	17	Is your name Barnabas?/{K} Why, yes, it is. Did you tell her, Sir Claude?/{SC} No,
510	CC	Kaghan	23	Alfred Kaghan your parents?/{K} Yes. They are. My adoptive parents./{MG} And
512	CC	Lady E	22	wishes./{LE} Oh, of course ... Yes, I'm sure ... I shall be very happy./{MG}
512	CC	Kaghan	30	—/If I can live up to it. And ... yes, of course,/If I can make it right with my
517	CC	Lady E	18	/Can't you persuade her?/{LE} Yes. My poor Claude!/Do try to help him,
518	CC	Claude	29	me, Sir Claude .../{SC} Excuse me? Yes./{MG} I shall return to Teddington. Colby,/
518	CC	Colby	32	go to Waterloo?/{C} Get you a taxi? Yes, Aunt Sarah;/But I should see you home./
526	ES	Lambert	28	lordship know that tea is waiting'./{L} Yes, Miss Monica./{M} I'm very glad, Charles,/
527	ES	Monica	7	sure that you want to marry me?/{M} Yes, Charles. I'm sure that I want to marry you/
529	ES	Ld Clav	23	{M} It's your engagement book./{LC} Yes, I've been brooding over it./{M} But what a
532	ES	Monica	9	I take the trolley, Miss Monica?/{M} Yes, thank you, Lambert. {}/[*Exit* LAMBERT]/
532	ES	Monica	30	the vicinity. Don't we, Monica?/{M} Yes, Father. {}/[*To* CHARLES]/{M} We *both*
535	ES	Lambert	9	my Lord./{G} And some ice./{L} Ice? Yes, my Lord. {}/[*Exit*]/{G} I began to say: when
538	ES	Gomez	8	when you were released./{G} Yes, and paid my passage out. I know the
539	ES	Gomez	5	the insistence of my doctors./{G} Oh yes, the usual euphemism./And yet I wonder. It
539	ES	Gomez	11	/And I might have another./{G} Yes. You might have another./But I wonder
543	ES	Ld Clav	11	/{M} Oh, so you knew him?/{LC} Yes. He'd changed his name./{M} Then I
543	ES	Ld Clav	16	go and rest now, before dinner./{LC} Yes, I'll go and rest now. I wish Charles was
545	ES	Ld Clav	14	dominating,/Has left us alone./{LC} Yes, but remember/What she said. She said:
546	ES	Monica	31	call me Mrs. Piggott, won't you?/{M} Yes, Mrs. Piggott, but please tell me one thing./
546	ES	Piggott	35	we address her as 'Nurse'?/{MP} Oh yes, that's different./She is a real nurse, you
550	ES	Carghill	6	Well, then, Maisie Montjoy./{MC} Yes. Maisie Montjoy./I was Maisie Montjoy
550	ES	Carghill	27	have sent me *here*/If I wasn't well off. Yes, I'm provided for./But isn't it strange that
552	ES	Carghill	5	letters/In Shaftesbury Avenue./{MC} Yes, I had my art./Don't you remember what a
552	ES	Ld Clav	10	Did you hear me sing it?/{LC} Yes, I heard you sing it./{MC} And what did
554	ES	Carghill	1	could have these letters auctioned.'/Yes, I'll bring the photostats tomorrow
555	ES	Ld Clav	28	been./He only ran into a tree./{LC} Yes, a tree./It might have been a man. But it

562 ES	Michael	18	Michael./I'm right, aren't I?/{Mi} Yes, you're right./But .../{MC} How did I
565 ES	Ld Clav	8	in the morning? After breakfast?/{LC} Yes, come tomorrow morning./{Mi} Well, I'll
569 ES	Ld Clav	25	man to advise you./{LC} Blackmail? Yes, I've heard that word before,/Not so very
571 ES	Ld Clav	12	responsible for that weakness in him?/Yes, I was./How easily we ignore the fact that
573 ES	Carghil	25	news for you!/But I suspect ... Dare I? Yes, I'm sure of it, Monica!/I can tell by the
575 ES	Ld Clav	6	job which is just what I wanted./{LC} Yes, I see the advantage of a job created for you
575 ES	Gomez	11	/And he thinks I'm just the man./{G} Yes, wasn't it extraordinary./{LC} Of course
577 ES	Gomez	10	/No doubt gives you pleasure?/{G} Yes, it's always pleasant/To repay an old debt.
579 ES	Ld Clav	22	at once and be done with it./{LC} Yes, if you're going, and I see no way to stop
579 ES	Gomez	30	Then we might as well be going./{G} Yes, we might as well be going./You'll be
580 ES	Ld Clav	11	to let you know I'm flourishing./{LC} Yes, write to Monica./{G} Well, good-bye Dick.
581 ES	Ld Clav	34	more/Because I love Charles./{LC} Yes, my dear./Your love is for the real Charles,
582 ES	Ld Clav	23	this season. It's chilly at dusk./{LC} Yes, it's chilly at dusk. But I'll be warm enough.
582 ES	Monica	31	to leave us alone together!/{M} Yes, he wanted to leave us alone together./And

YESTERDAY (12)

597 Before Mor	5	This morning's flowers and flowers of yesterday/Their fragrance drifts across the room
265 MC Knight1	14	France. We rode hard,/Took ship yesterday, landed last night,/Having business
384 CP Reilly	17	free./Your moment of freedom was yesterday./You made a decision. You set in
384 CP Edward	25	somewhat ... dramatic,/As it was only yesterday that my wife left me./{UG} Ah, but
387 CP Celia	1	/I couldn't have laughed at anything, yesterday;/But I've learnt a lot in twenty-four
387 CP Peter	30	— you remember our conversation yesterday?/{E} Of course./{P} I hope you've
391 CP Lavinia	18	know why. But it seems to me that yesterday/I started some machine, that goes on
396 CP Lavinia	40	into the kind of life we led/Until yesterday morning./{E} There was a door/And I
397 CP Edward	11	/To think about *me*?/{E} It was only yesterday/That damnation took place. And now
398 CP Edward	4	O God, O God, if I could return to yesterday/Before I thought that I had made a
452 CC Lucasta	17	no one ever wanted — at least, not till yesterday./Then, just by bad luck, the boss did
470 CC Lucasta	3	this week/And you had it tuned yesterday. Still, I'm flattered/To be your first

YESTERDAY'S (1)

| 387 CP Peter | 26 | that Lavinia intended/To have yesterday's cocktail party to-day./So I don't |

YET (135)

14 Prufrock	32	for you and time for me,/And time yet for a hundred indecisions,/And for a
19 Portrait	52	of course,/And go on drinking tea./'Yet with these April sunsets, that somehow
62 WL: Burial	37	/'They called me the hyacinth girl.'/— Yet when we came back, late, from the hyacinth
64 WL: Chess	100	the barbarous king/So rudely forced; yet there the nightingale/Filled all the desert
127 Cor1 March	8	a day?/Are they coming? No, not yet. You can see some eagles. And hear the
135 5FingerEx2	8	warm/Under a cretonne eiderdown,/Yet the field was cracked and brown/And the
161 Rock 7	24	selfish and purblind as ever before,/Yet always struggling, always reaffirming,
161 Rock 7	25	straying, delaying, returning, yet following no other way./But it seems that
163 Rock 8	46	/Because they will never assume it./Yet nothing is impossible, nothing,/To men of
164 Rock 9	9	they go about their daily occasions./Yet they walk in the street proudnecked, like
173 FQ: BurntN	74	the inner/And the outer compulsion, yet surrounded/By a grace of sense, a white light
173 FQ: BurntN	81	/The resolution of its partial horror./Yet the enchainment of past and future/Woven
180 FQ: ECoker	126	be love of the wrong thing; there is yet faith/But the faith and the love and the hope
187 FQ: DrySal	129	wistful regret for those who are not yet here to regret,/Pressed between yellow leaves
193 FQ: Little	102	I was still the same,/Knowing myself yet being someone other —/And he a face still
193 FQ: Little	103	other —/And he a face still forming; yet the words sufficed/To compel the
194 FQ: Little	111	I said: 'The wonder that I feel is easy,/Yet ease is cause of wonder. Therefore speak:/I
195 FQ: Little	153	conditions which often look alike/Yet differ completely, flourish in the same
204 de la Mare	18	/Or the well known is what we have yet to learn,/And two worlds meet, and
213 Growltiger	38	the sampans circled round,/And yet from all the enemy there was not heard a
222 Pekes Pols	5	say/That they do not like fighting, yet once in a way,/Or now and again, they join
228 Gus	7	from palsy that makes his paw shake./Yet he was, in his youth, quite the smartest of
234 Ad-dress	22	often bark, more seldom bite;/But yet a Dog is, on the whole,/What you would call
236 Cat Morgan	15	ain't no sich melliferous horgan;/But yet I can state, and I'm not one to boast,/That
590 Time Space	16	/And though our days of love be few/Yet let them be divine./Song/If space and time,
590 Space Time	5	as long as we./But let us live while yet we may,/While love and life are free,/For
590 Space Time	16	/And though the flowers of life be few/Yet let them be divine./Standing upon the shore
592 Grad 1	6	of rocks which lie below,/But let us yet put forth courageously./As colonists
602 Humoresque	2	my marionettes is dead,/Though not yet tired of the game —/But weak in body as in
602 Humoresque	22	a marionette's, all wrong/Of premises; yet in some star/A hero! — Where would he
604 Ode	9	/To the thoughts of the past as we go./Yet for all of these years that to-morrow has
242 MC Mess	7	the man to cherish any illusions,/Or yet to diminish the least of his pretensions./If
242 MC Priest2	31	been different for Thomas./{P2} Yet our lord is returned. Our lord has come
243 MC Chorus	29	/There has been minor injustice./Yet we have gone on living,/Living and partly
244 MC Chorus	2	/Another year the plums are lacking./Yet we have gone on living,/Living and partly

257	MC	Chorus	3	may walk with a lamp at night, and yet be drowned in a ditch./{3P} A man may
258	MC	Thomas	33	/But by what they are. I know/What yet remains to show you of my history/Will
262	MC	Thomas	2	that in a short time you may have yet another martyr,/and that one perhaps not
267	MC	Knight2	37	up against him false opinions./{K2} Yet the King, out of his charity,/And urged by
268	MC	Knight3	6	/All was granted for which you sued:/Yet how, I repeat, did you show your gratitude?
285	FR	Amy	1	*enters to draw the curtains*]/{A} Not yet! I will ring for you. It is still quite light./I
289	FR	Ivy	23	relief./{V} *I* call it providential./{I} Yet it must have been shocking,/Especially to
291	FR	Chorus	6	at the Vicar's American Tea./{Ch} Yet we are here at Amy's command, to play an
293	FR	Harry	16	talk as if nothing had happened,/And yet you are talking of nothing else. Why not get
296	FR	Agatha	1	{Ag} There are certain points I do not yet understand:/They will be clear later. I am
302	FR	Amy	11	Ivy! Violet! has Arthur or John come yet?/{I} There is no news of Arthur or John. {}/
306	FR	Harry	8	to that extent./{H} No, don't go just yet./{M} Are you glad to be at home?/{H} There
306	FR	Harry	11	/I wanted to ask you. I don't know yet./All these years I'd been longing to get back/
309	FR	Harry	30	travel;/You have staid in England, yet you seem/Like someone who comes from a
312	FR	Harry	9	/How can one fight with stupidity?/Yet I must speak to them. {}/[*He rushes forward*
313	FR	Violet	1	evening, Mary: aren't you dressed yet?/How do you think that Harry is looking?/
313	FR	Amy	25	/{A} Violet! Has Arthur or John come yet?/{V} Neither of them is here yet, Amy. {}/
313	FR	Violet	26	come yet?/{V} Neither of them is here yet, Amy. {}/[*Enter* AMY, *with* DR.
321	FR	Harry	19	/But what if Denman saw him, and yet he was not real?/That would be worse than
323	FR	Winch	24	/Of course, he hasn't come round yet./Dr. Owen was there, by a bit of luck./{G}
325	FR	Ivy	25	brilliant driver, but more reckless./{I} Yet I remember, when they were boys,/Arthur
332	FR	Agatha	36	had not shaken your father/Awake yet. I found him thinking/How to get rid of
336	FR	Harry	4	/You have a long journey./{H} Not yet! not yet! this is the first time that I have been
336	FR	Harry	4	have a long journey./{H} Not yet! not yet! this is the first time that I have been free/
338	FR	Harry	39	has just recovered sanity,/And not yet assured in possession, that is when/One
339	FR	Harry	5	That is still unsettled./I have not yet had the precise directions./Where does one
349	FR	Charles	11	is not what it was — or was it? — and yet I think that I might understand./{all} But we
357	CP	Julia	19	/{J} So it's very unselfish of Lavinia/Yet very like her. But really, Edward,/Lavinia
359	CP	Edward	7	GUEST]/{E} Don't go yet./Don't go yet. We'll finish the cocktails./Or
359	CP	Edward	8	GUEST]/{E} Don't go yet./Don't go yet. We'll finish the cocktails./Or would you
359	CP	Edward	33	I ought to be going./{E} Don't go yet./I very much want to talk to somebody;/
362	CP	Edward	7	advantage./{E} It might turn out so, yet .../{UG} Are you going to say, you love her?
364	CP	Edward	5	wearing/When I saw her last. And yet I want her back./And I *must* get her back, to
364	CP	Edward	24	been./{E} I will not ask them./And yet — it seems to me — when we began to talk/I
364	CP	Reilly	27	suggestion?/{UG} We do not know yet. In twenty-four hours/She will come to you
366	CP	Julia	23	and talk to Edward. I'm not helpless yet./And besides, I like to manage the machine
378	CP	Edward	17	that I ought to be thankful./And yet, the effect of all his argument/Was to make
382	CP	Celia	5	Edward, that I understand you;/And yet I understand as I never did before./I think
391	CP	Lavinia	23	interfering .../I don't feel free ... and yet I started it .../{J} Alex, do you think we
392	CP	Lavinia	7	And I am to ask no questions. And yet ... why not?/{E} I don't know why not. So
394	CP	Lavinia	25	know. I was warned of the danger,/Yet something, or somebody, compelled me to
395	CP	Edward	16	all the changing —/Though I haven't yet found it a change for the better./But doesn't
401	CP	Edward	9	of a man who did not know you./Yet Alex is so plausible. And his
407	CP	Reilly	20	pains, exhausting their energy,/Yet never quite successful. You have both of
414	CP	Reilly	40	seemed to *me* abnormal./{R} We have yet to find what would be normal/For *you,*
415	CP	Celia	35	should make one feel sinful!/And yet I can't find any other word for it./It must be
415	CP	Celia	37	must be some kind of hallucination;/Yet, at the same time, I'm frightened by the fear
418	CP	Celia	5	to accept that/If I might still have it. Yet it leaves me cold./Perhaps that's just a part
421	CP	Julia	28	an errand/In eagerness and patience. Yet she must suffer./{R} When I express
422	CP	Alex	30	spoken./{A} They can not be spoken yet./{J} You mean Peter Quilpe./{R} He has not
422	CP	Reilly	32	mean Peter Quilpe./{R} He has not yet come to where the words are valid./{J} Shall
424	CP	Lavinia	23	who should be tired./{L} I'm not tired yet. But I know that I'll be glad/When it's all
427	CP	Alex	9	island that you won't have heard of/Yet. Got back this morning. I heard about your
436	CP	Lavinia	33	did. In any case you knew *about* her./Yet I thought your expression was one of ...
437	CP	Reilly	27	death, and, without knowing the end/Yet choose the form of death. We know the
438	CP	Lavinia	39	for her death as you are./{L} Yet I know I shall go on blaming myself/For
440	CP	Edward	6	Oh, it isn't much/That I understand yet! But Sir Henry has been saying,/I think, that
448	CC	Claude	28	clear. But beyond that point/I haven't yet explained my plans to you./Why I've never
450	CC	Colby	33	I'm glad you don't have to leave just yet./I'm rather nervous about this meeting./
457	CC	Lady E	28	it. No, I forgot:/You haven't learned yet how to make tea properly./A cup of black
461	CC	Claude	32	go quite the way I'd intended;/And yet I believe that it's all for the best./It went off
462	CC	Colby	36	/And nothing about it is real to me yet./{SC} But now I want it to be different. It's
463	CC	Colby	15	self-confidence/I've never had before. Yet at the same time/It's rather disturbing. I
463	CC	Colby	24	— though he fascinates me./And yet from time to time, when I least expect it,/
464	CC	Claude	32	despised him/When I was young. And yet I was in awe of him./I was wrong, in both. I

467 CC	Claude	19	/My father made with me. And yet I seem/To have made a greater mistake than
471 CC	Lucasta	12	never met a man so ignorant as you/Yet knowing so much that one wouldn't
471 CC	Lucasta	31	there's one thing you haven't learnt yet,/And that is, to know when you're paying a
472 CC	Lucasta	35	— or the facts as you saw them./And yet, all the time, I found I *envied* you/And I
473 CC	Colby	22	You may be right, up to a point./And yet, you know, it's not quite real to me —/
476 CC	Colby	2	thing I can't tell you./At least, not yet. I'm not allowed to tell./And that's about
477 CC	Colby	14	/I want to explain. But I can't, just yet./Oh, why did I ever come into this house!/
478 CC	Colby	24	I'll be going./{C} You mustn't go yet!/There's something else that I want to
481 CC	Kaghan	9	hungry./{K} You can't want dinner yet./It's only six o'clock. We can't dine till eight;
481 CC	Lady E	33	I don't believe that you've been there yet./{K} Why no, as a matter of fact, I haven't./
484 CC	Lady E	19	understand what loathing really is./Yet we must have *some* similarity of
484 CC	Lady E	24	killing things and eating them./And yet our childhood must have been similar./
484 CC	Lady E	29	/They made me feel an outcast. And yet they were so commonplace./Do you know,
487 CC	Lady E	25	incredible, doesn't it, Claude?/And yet it would be still more incredible/If it were
487 CC	Lady E	27	/Perhaps I ought not to believe it yet,/Perhaps it is wrong of me to feel so sure,/
488 CC	Claude	29	like what one had planned for,/And yet such a travesty of all one's plans —/I'd
490 CC	Colby	16	agony/Which I can't begin to feel yet. I'm simply indifferent./And all the time that
491 CC	Colby	19	say what I feel at the moment:/And yet I believe I shall always feel the same./{SC}
497 CC	Eggers	1	the news. We don't often speak of it;/Yet I know what's on her mind, for days
507 CC	Claude	32	Colby?/{SC} Don't be certain yet, Elizabeth./{LE} There is no doubt about it./
526 ES	Charles	13	seem to come/From very far away. Yet very near. You are changing me/And I am
527 ES	Monica	2	the second place, we're not engaged yet./{C} Aren't we? We're agreed that we're in
530 ES	Ld Clav	18	simply waiting,/With no desire to act, yet a loathing of inaction./A fear of the vacuum,
530 ES	Monica	27	grate?/For no one. For nothing./{M} Yet you've been looking forward/To this very
538 ES	Gomez	37	have led you to the very top!/And yet you withdrew from the world of politics/
539 ES	Gomez	6	Oh yes, the usual euphemism./And yet I wonder. It *is* surprising/You should have
546 ES	Monica	32	me one thing./We haven't seen her yet, but the chambermaid/Referred to a nurse.
549 ES	Carghil	4	What!/{MC} Don't you know me yet?/{LC} I'm afraid not./{MC} There were the
562 ES	Carghil	31	I knew him ever so many years ago,/Yet you're the image of what he was then./Your
567 ES	Charles	14	/And you said we weren't engaged yet .../{M} We're engaged now./At least *I'm*
568 ES	Charles	15	/I can think of things you don't yet know about me, Monica,/But there's
570 ES	Ld Clav	20	stand for in your life?/{LC} ... yet they've both done better for themselves/In
572 ES	Ld Clav	19	were wholly unsuited to each other,/Yet she had a peculiar physical attraction/
582 ES	Monica	32	to leave us alone together./And yet, Charles, though we've been alone to-day/
583 ES	Charles	6	strange that words are so inadequate./Yet, like the asthmatic struggling for breath,/So

YEW (5)

95 Ash-Wed 4	28	shake a thousand whispers from the yew/And after this our exile/If the lost word is
97 Ash-Wed 5	30	the veiled sister between the slender/Yew trees pray for those who offend her/And
98 Ash-Wed 6	24	the yew-tree drift away/Let the other yew be shaken and reply./Blessèd sister, holy
108 Animula	36	by the boarhound slain between the yew trees,/Pray for us now and at the hour of
175 FQ: BurntN 136		/Clutch and cling?/Chill/Fingers of yew be curled/Down on us? After the

YEW-TREE (3)

98 Ash-Wed 6	23	/But when the voices shaken from the yew-tree drift away/Let the other yew be shaken
190 FQ: DrySal 236		nourish/(Not too far from the yew-tree)/The life of significant soil./Little
197 FQ: Little 234		of the rose and the moment of the yew-tree/Are of equal duration. A people

YEWS (1)

94 Ash-Wed 4	23	veiled in white and blue/Between the yews, behind the garden god,/Whose flute is

YIELD (1)

252 MC Thomas	18	/And in the tilt-yard I made many yield./Shall I who ruled like an eagle over doves

YIELDED (1)

332 FR Agatha	2	recognised your mother's power,/And yielded to it./{H} There was no ecstasy./Tell me

YOKE (1)

268 MC Thomas	22	/And as for the bishops, it is not my yoke/That is laid upon them, or mine to revoke.

YORE (1)

593 Grad 5	6	What heroes greater than were e'er of yore!/But if this century is to be more great/

YORK (6)

602 Humoresque	20	worse than gas —/'Now in New York' — and so it goes./Logic a marionette's,
246 MC Thomas	2	restless about us./Rebellious bishops, York, London, Salisbury,/Would have
299 FR Charles	5	with them on the voyage from New York —/We didn't learn very much about the
430 CP Peter	5	you arrive?/{P} I flew over from New York last night —/I left Los Angeles three days
430 CP Lavinia	17	/{L} So you've just come from New York./{P} Yes, from New York./The
430 CP Peter	18	from New York./{P} Yes, from New York./The Bologolomskys saw me off./You

YORKSHIRE (3)

47	Mél	Adult	5 Que vous suivrez à peine ma piste./En Yorkshire, conférencier;/A Londres, un peu
135	5FingerEx2		t /*When* will Time flow away?/*Lines to a Yorkshire Terrier*/In a brown field stood a tree/
223	Pekes	Pols	33 like,/For your Pollicle Dog is a dour Yorkshire tyke,/And his braw Scottish cousins

YOU (3813)

YOU'D (40)

122	SA	Sweeney	5 and death./{Do} I'd be bored./{S} You'd be bored./Birth, and copulation, and
122	SA	Sweeney	8 and death./{Do} I'd be bored./{S} You'd be bored./Birth, and copulation, and
304	FR	Mary	1 at college./{M} I might have known you'd throw that up against me./I know I
322	FR	Winch	30 they told me he was here, and that you'd arrived./Mr. John's had a bit of an
328	FR	Gerald	10 have been more in the later editions./You'd better read it to us. {}/[*reads*]./{C} '*Peer's*
346	FRDowning		22 But to show you what I mean, though you'd hardly credit it,/I've always said,
356	CP	Julia	24 She agreed with me./She said: 'I wish you'd try.' And this is the first time/I've ever
360	CP	Reilly	39 back at all./If another man, then you'd want to re-marry/To prove to the world
376	CP	Celia	2 *Re-enter* CELIA, *in an apron*.]/{C} You'd better answer the door, Edward./It's the
391	CP	Julia	30 *When* shall we see you?/{J} Did I say you'd see me?/Good-bye. I believe ... I haven't
393	CP	Edward	10 in to you./{E} I was unaware that you'd always given in to me./It struck me very
393	CP	Lavinia	23 in desperation/I said: 'I suppose you'd as soon go to Peacehaven' —And you
416	CP	Celia	8 your relations with this man?/{C} Oh, you'd guessed that, had you? That's clever of
433	CP	Peter	12 of seeing California./{P} You know you'd never come if we invited you./But there's
471	CC	Lucasta	19 quite simple./{L} Then I wish you'd tell me./Because *I* don't know./{C} The
472	CC	Lucasta	23 was in your life/When you found that you'd never be a good musician —/Of course, *I*
472	CC	Lucasta	27 musician:/But that's not the point. You'd convinced yourself;/And you felt that
477	CC	Lucasta	22 *you're* ashamed of me. I thought you'd understand./Little you know what it's like
477	CC	Lucasta	29 like that person either,/And I thought you'd come to see me as the real kind of person/
479	CC	Lucasta	9 I'm concerned, B. And as for Lizzie,/You'd better not get in *her* way when she's
480	CC	Kaghan	9 on the spur of the moment,/But you'd never take a leap in the dark;/You'd keep
480	CC	Kaghan	10 you'd never take a leap in the dark;/You'd keep me on the rails./{C} That's just
480	CC	Lucasta	20 is a good judge of character./{L} You'd need to be a better judge of character/
488	CC	Claude	32 you got to know him first — and that you'd want to adopt him./{LE} But of course I
494	CC	Lady E	38 all these years,/And now you tell me, you'd have liked to be a potter!/You really
518	CC	Eggers	16 point:/If you took the position, you'd want to find your feet/In Joshua Park,
519	CC	Kaghan	20 like to mean something to you ... if you'd let us;/And we'd take the responsibility of
531	ES	Lambert	37 it/You would want to see him. Said you'd be very angry/If you heard that he'd gone
537	ES	Gomez	16 could be/From the sort of men you'd been at school with —/I didn't fit into
537	ES	Gomez	26 a First./I suppose your tutor thought you'd be sent down./It went the other way. You
541	ES	Gomez	3 so many years ago?/What damages you'd get! The Press wouldn't look at it./
541	ES	Gomez	9 of some of your acquaintance —/But you'd never know to whom I'd told it,/Or who
549	ES	Carghil	28 was very shrewd —/Effie it was said 'you'd be throwing yourself away./Mark my
551	ES	Carghil	34 settlement/Is twice as much as I think you'd be awarded.'/Effie was against it — she
556	ES	Ld Clav	18 /It would be the sort of place that you'd choose for a holiday./{Mi} Well, this isn't
556	ES	Monica	26 I said that before, didn't I?/{M} I wish you'd stop being so polite to each other./
561	ES	Michael	19 rich, but was no one in particular,/So you'd nothing to live up to. Those standards of
562	ES	Carghil	12 /{MC} Richard! I didn't think you'd still be here./I came back to have a quiet
563	ES	Gomez	12 of a rest cure too./And when I heard you'd chosen to come to Badgley Court/I said
580	ES	Carghil	24 /We must always keep in touch. But you'd better rest now./You're looking rather

YOU'LL (70)

116	SP	Dusty	35 mustard and water/All right, Monday you'll phone through./Yes I'll tell her. Good
121	SA	Doris	3 carry you off/To a cannibal isle./{Do} You'll be the cannibal!/{S} You'll be the
121	SA	Sweeney	4 isle./{Do} You'll be the cannibal!/{S} You'll be the missionary!/You'll be my little
121	SA	Sweeney	5 /{S} You'll be the missionary!/You'll be my little seven stone missionary!/I'll
121	SA	Doris	7 you up. I'll be the cannibal./{Do} You'll carry me off? To a cannibal isle?/{S} I'll
214	RTTugger		29 likes what he finds for himself;/So you'll catch him in it right up to the ears,/If you
225	Mr Mistoff		36 one moment, and then it is *gawn*!/But you'll find it next week lying out on the lawn./
227	Macavity		33 Macavity!' — but he's a mile away./You'll be sure to find him resting, or a-licking
233	Skimble		65 tail/Which says: 'I'll see you again!/You'll meet without fail on the Midnight Mail/
236	Cat Morgan		19 this tip, and it's worth a lot more:/You'll save yourself time, and you'll spare
236	Cat Morgan		19 more:/You'll save yourself time, and you'll spare yourself labour/If jist you make
292	FR	Gerald	28 /{G} We must have a ride tomorrow./You'll find you know the country as well as
292	FR	Gerald	30 an inch of it you didn't know./But you'll have to see about a couple of new
292	FR	Ivy	33 do with a little attention./{I} And you'll really have to find a successor to old
313	FR	Charles	20 want Arthur and John/I'm glad that you'll all be together, Harry;/They need the
344	FR	Gerald	23 occasionally troublesome. But you'll have to learn the language/And several
344	FR	Gerald	28 vicar .../{G} And don't forget/That you'll need various inoculations —/That
353	CP	Peter	7 You haven't been listening./{P} You'll have to tell us all over again, Alex./{A} I

YOU'RE (177)

312	FR	Harry	6	your nonsense. Can't you help me?/You're of no use to me. I must face them./I
313	FR	Charles	24	a sobering effect upon him./After all, you're the head of the family./{A} Violet! Has
315	FR	Warburt	13	/I really don't know. — But now you're all grown up/I haven't a patient left at
318	FR	Warburt	18	what they are told./{W} Stop, Harry, you're mistaken./I mean, you don't know what
325	FR	Violet	35	I think an open car/Is so undignified: you're blown about so,/And you feel so
328	FR	Ivy	31	Amy./{I} Poor Arthur! I'm sure that you're being much too hard on him./{C} In my
344	FR	Gerald	29	—/That depends on where you're going./{C} Such a thing/Has never
345	FR	Gerald	7	night, and you will have to be careful./You're taking Downing with you?/{H} Oh, yes,
356	CP	Julia	16	do sit down for a moment./I know you're always the perfect host,/But just try to
356	CP	Julia	17	perfect host,/But just try to pretend you're another guest/At Lavinia's party. There
356	CP	Julia	27	/And couldn't get out. I know what you're thinking!/I know you think I'm a silly
358	CP	Julia	7	/I've already chosen the people you're to meet./{E} But you asked me to dine
358	CP	Julia	11	You'll like the other people —/But you're to talk to me. So that's all settled./And
361	CP	Reilly	34	you experience some relief/Of which you're not aware. It will come to you slowly:/
362	CP	Reilly	23	You no longer feel quite human./You're suddenly reduced to the status of an
367	CP	Peter	21	young people together./{P} Now you're only being sarcastic:/Celia was interested
368	CP	Alex	3	shut it when you go out./{A} Ah, but you're coming with me, Edward./I thought,
368	CP	Alex	6	hates to spend an evening alone,/So you're going to come out and have dinner with
378	CP	Julia	10	quickly. And take a taxi./You know, you're looking absolutely famished./Good
378	CP	Celia	37	I think you are mad —/I mean, you're on the edge of a nervous breakdown./
381	CP	Celia	3	/Now, in *my* future. I only hope you're competent/To manage your own. But if
383	CP	Edward	5	... Well, don't snap my head off .../You're sure, in the kitchen? Beside the
383	CP	Edward	6	Beside the champagne bottle?/You're quite sure? ... Very well, hold on if you
387	CP	Celia	37	no use. I'm going to California./{C} You're going to California!/{P} Yes, I have a
388	CP	Peter	19	*lets herself in with a latch-key*]/{P} You're going abroad?/{C} I don't know.
388	CP	Edward	21	/{C} I don't know. Perhaps./{E} You're both going away! {}/[*Enter* LAVINIA]/
389	CP	Lavinia	6	/At last, to realise your ambitions./You're going together?/{P} We're not going
396	CP	Edward	35	not want you to explain me to myself./You're still trying to invent a personality for me
396	CP	Lavinia	37	only keep me away from myself./{L} You're complicating what is in fact very simple.
397	CP	Lavinia	14	by hour, for ever and ever./{L} I think you're on the edge of a nervous breakdown!/{E}
397	CP	Lavinia	33	well, then, I shall not try to press you./You're much too divided to know what you
406	CP	Edward	27	fewer mental complications than you;/You're stronger than a ... battleship. That's
415	CP	Celia	14	to hurt other people/If you know that you're hurting them. I haven't hurt *her*./I wasn't
424	CP	Lavinia	19	And I've attended *all* of them./I hope you're not too tired?/{E} Oh no, a quiet day./
424	CP	Edward	25	/When it's all over./{E} I like the dress you're wearing:/I'm glad you put on that one./
432	CP	Julia	16	of trying to interrupt Julia .../{J} But you're both interrupting!/{R} Who is
433	CP	Julia	4	not the way we do it./{J} But, Peter;/If you're taking Boltwell to California/Why can't
433	CP	Julia	10	much cheaper./Oh, dear, I can see you're determined not to have me:/So good-bye
435	CP	Peter	36	being unkind .../{P} No, I don't think you're being unkind, Lavinia;/And I know that
435	CP	Peter	37	unkind, Lavinia;/And I know that you're right./{L} And perhaps what I've been
436	CP	Edward	7	beginning./It's not so hard for you. You're naturally good./{P} I'm sorry. I don't
436	CP	Julia	16	an eye for the films:/That is, when you're not concerned with yourself/But just
440	CP	Lavinia	24	/That she always looks her best. You're rather transparent,/You know, when
440	CP	Lavinia	25	rather transparent,/You know, when you're trying to cheer me up./To say I always
445	CC	Claude	25	came./{SC} Well, of course, Eggerson, you're irreplaceable .../{E} Oh, Sir Claude, you
447	CC	Claude	3	car will be ready —/Let's think what you're to say to Lady Elizabeth,/Coming back
449	CC	Eggers	1	and his grave unknown./{E} And you're thinking no doubt that Lady Elizabeth/
450	CC	Claude	3	of the greatest importance./It's when you're sure you understand a person/That
450	CC	Claude	4	sure you understand a person/That you're liable to make the worst mistake about
450	CC	Eggers	20	perhaps./{E} And do I infer/That you're not sure you understand Mr. Simpkins,
451	CC	Eggers	29	very different./She'll see at once that you're a man of culture;/And besides, she's very
452	CC	Kaghan	9	to ease the shock for Colby./But as you're here, Eggers, I can just relax./I'm going
452	CC	Lucasta	15	presume, persistently unpunctual./{L} You're wrong, Eggy. It's rank injustice./Two
453	CC	Lucasta	15	And I know he'll be nice to me/When you're out of the way. Why don't you let him
453	CC	Lucasta	33	to keep her fed between meals./{L} B., you're a beast. I've a very small appetite./But
453	CC	Lucasta	36	in lieu of notice./{L} B., remember you're only my fiancé on approval./Can I have
454	CC	Lucasta	3	/When I return from Northolt./{L} You're going to meet Lizzie?/{E} I am meeting
458	CC	Lady E	17	to change it./I can't understand why you're both so surprised./You know I'm a very
463	CC	Colby	21	to be/Rather a different person when you're talking it./I'm not at all sure that I like
471	CC	Lucasta	32	learnt yet,/And that is, to know when you're paying a compliment./*That* was a
472	CC	Colby	2	couldn't wait to see what happened./You're afraid of what would happen if you left
472	CC	Colby	3	to themselves./You jump — because you're afraid of being pushed./I think that
472	CC	Colby	4	afraid of being pushed./I think that you're brave — and I think that you're
472	CC	Colby	4	that you're brave — and I think that you're frightened./Perhaps you've been very
473	CC	Lucasta	1	a world that's more real./That's why you're different from the rest of us:/You have

473 CC   Colby   15   Canal./Floating, that's it./{C} You're very much a person./I'm sure that there

475 CC   Lucasta   4   to understand anyone?/{L} I think you're being very discouraging:/Are you doing

477 CC   Lucasta   19   /I suppose that's all. I believe you're more shocked/Than if I'd told you I *was*

477 CC   Lucasta   22 has always been ashamed of me:/Now *you're* ashamed of me. I thought you'd

477 CC   Lucasta   24 /And wanted by nobody. I know why you're shocked:/Claude has just accepted me

478 CC   Lucasta   1   be bad for your prospects/Now that you're Claude's white-headed boy./Perhaps he'll

478 CC   Lucasta   19 worse than ever./Just when you think you're on the point of release/From loneliness,

478 CC   Lucasta   21   down upon you;/When you think you're getting out, you're getting further in,/

478 CC   Lucasta   21 /When you think you're getting out, you're getting further in,/And you know at last

479 CC   Lucasta   1   to protect you from Lucasta./{L} You're *my* guardian angel at the moment, B./

479 CC   Lucasta   2 *my* guardian angel at the moment, B./You're to take me out to dinner. And I'm dying

479 CC   Lucasta   40   of changing my condition./{L} You're always free to think again./{K} Marriage

480 CC   Colby   12 just nonsense./You only pretend that you're a gambler./You've got as level a head as

480 CC   Colby   16   like to pretend to other people/That you're a gambler. I don't believe you ever

481 CC   Kaghan   5   very sound head for business./Maybe you're a better financier than I am!/That's why

481 CC   Lucasta   7   ought to be in business together./{L} You're both very good at paying compliments;/

481 CC   Lady E   30   salads!/And I told you, Mr. Kaghan, you're the type of person/Who needs to eat a

482 CC   Lady E   13   a good deal of attention./You see, you're rather a curiosity/To both of them —

482 CC   Lady E   14 rather a curiosity/To both of them — you're not the sort of person/They ever meet in

493 CC   Claude   28 /On this ... investigation. But perhaps you're right./{LE} Claude, I've been thinking

496 CC   Eggers   22 or six days a week:/But now she says: 'You're becoming such a countryman!/You're

496 CC   Eggers   23   becoming such a countryman!/You're losing touch with public affairs.'/The

498 CC   Claude   15   it's perfectly respectable./{SC} You're suggesting that she ran a baby farm./

499 CC   Claude   13   sorry./{SC} Colby will be here./But you're not involved in this meeting, Lucasta./

499 CC   Lucasta   17   It'll do another time./Oh, I'm glad you're here, Eggy! You're such a support./In

499 CC   Lucasta   17 time./Oh, I'm glad you're here, Eggy! You're such a support./In any case, I've an

502 CC   Lucasta   13   like you — the way I thought it was./You're much too ... detached, ever to be

502 CC   Lucasta   20   /{C} I don't care enough?/{L} No. You're either above caring,/Or else you're

502 CC   Lucasta   21   You're either above caring,/Or else you're insensible — I don't mean insensitive!/

502 CC   Lucasta   22   — I don't mean insensitive!/But you're terribly cold. Or else you've some fire/To

502 CC   Lucasta   24 kind of fire/That warms other people. You're either an egotist/Or something so

502 CC   Lucasta   31   are,/In the sense I've been told that you're my brother;/Which makes it more

511 CC   Lucasta   3   that language any longer:/Just say you're embarrassed./{K} Well, I am

511 CC   Lucasta   35   impression in the City./{L} When you're an alderman, you'll be Sir Barney

511 CC   Lady E   36   Kaghan!/{LE} And I'm very glad you're announcing your engagement./Lucasta, I

516 CC   Colby   4   future./{C} Thank you, Sir Claude./You're a very generous man. But now I know

524 ES   Charles   14 known/And get well served. And when *you're* with me!/It must be a perfect lunch./{M} It

525 ES   Charles   1   that I have a grievance./On Monday you're leaving London, with your father:/I

525 ES   Charles   18 retired/He's at home every day. And you're leaving London./And because your

525 ES   Monica   24   besides, my father doesn't amble./You're not at all respectful./{C} I try to be

525 ES   Charles   34 more, that I'm in love with you. Well, you're right./But I've something else to say that

525 ES   Monica   38   you are!/Really, you must imagine you're a hypnotist./{C} Is this a time to torment

526 ES   Charles   1   saying that, because I think —/I think you're tormenting yourself as well./{M} You're

526 ES   Monica   2   tormenting yourself as well./{M} You're right. I am. Because *I am* in love with

526 ES   Charles   7 need so much assurance! Are you sure you're not mistaken?/{M} How did this come,

526 ES   Monica   37   care for any company but his!/{M} You're not to assume that anything I've said to

527 ES   Charles   15 /[*Exit*]/{C} Don't you understand that you're torturing me?/How long will you be

527 ES   Charles   18   hotel for convalescents/To which you're taking him? And what after that?/{M}

528 ES   Monica   9   It's one thing meeting people/When you're in authority, with authority's costume,/

532 ES   Ld Clav   29 to see you, whenever you can come/If you're in the vicinity. Don't we, Monica?/{M}

532 ES   Ld Clav   31   /{LC} Good evening, Mr. ... Gomez. You're a friend of Mr. Culverwell?/{G} We're as

535 ES   Gomez   3   see you, Dick. A natural desire!/For you're the only old friend I can trust./{LC} You

535 ES   Gomez   5   the compliment./{G} Which you're sure you deserve. But when I say 'trust'

536 ES   Gomez   28   — so cosy, warm and padded:/You're not isolated — merely insulated./It's

539 ES   Gomez   13 this ... stroke;/And I wonder whether you're the great economist/And financial wizard

539 ES   Gomez   14 economist/And financial wizard that you're supposed to be./And I've learned

540 ES   Ld Clav   9   Isn't that the kind of pretence that you're maintaining/In trying to persuade me of

541 ES   Gomez   26 /Blackmail! On the contrary/Any time you're in a tight corner/My entire resources are

545 ES   Piggott   29   /He's led a busy life, too.' But I hope you're happy?/Is there anything you need that

545 ES   Monica   35 have the privilege of helping you!/{M} You're very kind ... Oh, I'm sorry,/We don't

548 ES   Monica   11   over your face/And pretend you're pretending to be asleep./If they think you

548 ES   Monica   13   to wake you,/But if they see you're shamming they'll have to take the hint. {}

550 ES   Carghil   3 Maisie Batterson./{MC} Oh, Richard, you're only saying that to tease me./You know I

550 ES   Carghil   14   say: 'Make one mistake in love,/You're more than likely to make another'./How

550 ES   Carghil   34 preferred to leave buried./{MC} There you're wrong, Richard. Effie always said —/

551 ES	Carghil	16	to come and talk about the past./You're wrong, you know. It's both pain and
552 ES	Carghil	27	was clear./At bottom, I believe you're still the same silly Richard/You always
552 ES	Carghil	29	/As a man of the world. And now you're posing/As what? I presume, as an elder
553 ES	Ld Clav	3	the brevity of our acquaintance,/You're surprisingly confident, I must say,/
554 ES	Carghil	17	do look after us well, Mrs. Piggott:/You're so considerate — and so understanding./
554 ES	Piggott	23	with talking./What he needs is *rest*! You're not going, Mrs. Carghill?/{MC} Oh, I
556 ES	Michael	13	/{Mi} What a lovely day!/I'm glad you're here, to enjoy such weather./{LC} You're
556 ES	Ld Clav	14	here, to enjoy such weather./{LC} You're glad I'm here? Did you drive down from
557 ES	Ld Clav	3	for stealing./But come to the point. You're in trouble again./We'll ignore, if you
557 ES	Michael	33	/Time passes pretty quickly, when you're in debt./{LC} And have you other debts?/
558 ES	Ld Clav	33	{LC} Perhaps it had gone further than you're willing to admit./{Mi} Well, after all, she
560 ES	Michael	1	will it give you/In the grave? If you're still conscious after death,/I bet it will be
561 ES	Ld Clav	10	failures waiting there to greet you./You're all I have to live for, Michael —/You
562 ES	Carghil	15	family party!/I know who you are! You're Monica, of course:/And this must be
562 ES	Michael	18	/I'm right, aren't I?/{Mi} Yes, you're right./But .../{MC} How did I know?
562 ES	Carghil	20	.../{MC} How did I know? Because you're so like your father/When he was your
562 ES	Carghil	22	of you, Richard,/As you were once. You're not to introduce us,/I'll introduce
562 ES	Carghil	31	him ever so many years ago,/Yet you're the image of what he was then./Your
563 ES	Gomez	10	me to join you here, were you?/You're here for a rest cure. I persuaded my
564 ES	Gomez	13	Señor Gomez./{G} My dear lady, you're not old enough/To have known Dick
564 ES	Carghil	29	San Marco./Señor Gomez, if it's true you're staying at Badgley Court,/I warn you —
565 ES	Monica	6	enough talk for to-day./Michael, as you're staying so close at hand/Will you come
565 ES	Gomez	19	I'm sure./{G} Taking a holiday?/You're in business in London, aren't you?/{Mi}
568 ES	Ld Clav	18	tell Monica/Then all is well with you. You're in love with each other —/I don't need
573 ES	Carghil	33	congratulate *you*, Mr. Hemington./You're a very lucky man, to get a girl like
575 ES	Ld Clav	12	it extraordinary./{LC} Of course you're just the man that Señor Gomez wants,/
575 ES	Gomez	18	is Culverwell .../{G} My dear Dick,/You're wasting your time, rehearsing ancient
575 ES	Ld Clav	28	than I did./{LC} On that point, Fred, you're wasting *your* time:/My daughter and my
576 ES	Gomez	4	lovely then./{G} We are sure of that! You're so lovely now/That we can well imagine
577 ES	Carghil	29	have known him, Señor Gomez!/You're very much alike in some ways —/So I
578 ES	Monica	17	/{M} Oh Michael, remember, you're my only brother/And I'm your only
579 ES	Ld Clav	22	once and be done with it./{LC} Yes, if you're going, and I see no way to stop you,/
580 ES	Carghil	25	in touch. But you'd better rest now./You're looking rather tired. I'll run and see
582 ES	Monica	21	not go far, will you?/You know you're not allowed to stop out late/At this
582 ES	Charles	34	felt all the time .../{C} I know what you're going to say!/We *were* alone together, in

YOU'VE (107)

117 SP	Doris	19	/It just depends on what comes next./You've got to *think* when you read the cards,/
117 SP	Dusty	21	that anyone can do./{Du} Yes I know you've a touch with the cards/What comes next?
118 SP	Dusty	7	they'll tell you nothing at all/{Du} You've got to know what you want to ask them
118 SP	Doris	8	what you want to ask them/{Do} You've got to know what you want to know/
125 SA	Chorus	35	like someone hit you in the head/You've had a cream of a nightmare dream and/
125 SA	Chorus	36	a cream of a nightmare dream and/you've got the hoo-ha's coming to you./Hoo
234 Ad-dress		1	Train.'/The Ad-dressing of Cats/You've read of several kinds of Cat,/And my
234 Ad-dress		13	—/But all may be described in verse./You've seen them both at work and games,/And
287 FR	Gerald	3	/Charles, as I remember. Besides, you've got to make allowances:/We haven't left
298 FR	Charles	31	won't mind, it's about his Lordship./You've looked after his Lordship for over ten
298 FR	Charles	34	him pretty well./And I'm sure that you've been a good friend to him, too./*We*
301 FR	Gerald	4	see to that./{G} I only wondered/Why you've been busy about it tonight./{Do}
313 FR	Gerald	14	authority./{G} Good evening, Mary. You've seen Harry, I see./It's good to have him
321 FR	Warburt	8	{W} What I want to know is, whether you've been sleeping ... {}/[*Enter* DENMAN]/
326 FR	Harry	13	have looked when she was a child./You've been holding a meeting — the usual
347 FR	Downing	1	Miss. And if I may say so,/Now that you've raised the subject, I'm most relieved —/
347 FR	Downing	6	get round to seeing them —/And so you've seen them too! They must have given
347 FR	Agatha	13	/His Lordship will be wondering why you've been so long. {}/[*Exit* DOWNING. *Enter*
353 CP	Alex	1	*an* UNIDENTIFIED GUEST./{A} You've missed the point completely, Julia:/
360 CP	Reilly	38	then the reason may be deeper/And you've ground for hope that she won't come
362 CP	Reilly	21	a loss of personality;/Or rather, you've lost touch with the person/You thought
362 CP	Reilly	27	about it/As quickly as we can. When you've dressed for a party/And are going
363 CP	Edward	37	/{E} Stop! I agree that much of what you've said/Is true enough. But that is not all./
365 CP	Julia	17	call an adventure!/Tell me about him. You've been *drinking* together!/So this is the
368 CP	Alex	9	to be alone, this evening./{A} But you've got to have some dinner. Are you going
376 CP	Julia	17	I know how to cook./{J} Celia! I see you've had the same inspiration/That I had.
387 CP	Peter	32	yesterday?/{E} Of course./{P} I hope you've done nothing about it./{E} No, I've done
390 CP	Julia	10	{L} And why from Essex?/{J} Because you've been in Essex./{L} Because I've been in
390 CP	Julia	12	been in Essex!/{J} Lavinia! Don't say you've had a lapse of memory!/Then that

393 CP	Lavinia	5	important discovery,/Finding that you've spent five years of your life/With a man
395 CP	Edward	15	/But you seem to assume that you've done all the changing —/Though I
400 CP	Alex	21	he's stolen a march on her./And when you've sent him to a sanatorium/Where she
407 CP	Edward	1	You do know that./{E} Only because you've told me so often./I'd like to see *you*
424 CP	Edward	11	/{E} I'm in good time, I think. I hope you've not been worrying./{L} Oh no. I did in
425 CP	Lavinia	3	/Do you know it's the first time you've paid me a compliment/*Before* a party?
430 CP	Lavinia	17	you, Alex? And dear old Julia!/{L} So you've just come from New York./{P} Yes, from
435 CP	Lavinia	29	/{L} No, it's not all worthless, Peter. You've only just begun./I mean, this only brings
435 CP	Lavinia	33	knew Celia. We none of us did./What you've been living on is an image of Celia/
436 CP	Peter	9	I don't believe I've taken in/All that you've been saying. But I'm grateful all the
436 CP	Peter	10	the same./You know, all the time that you've been talking,/One thought has been
448 CC	Eggers	35	it's been a grief to both of you/That you've never had children./{SC} No worse,
450 CC	Colby	35	rather nervous about this meeting./You've told me very little about Lady Elizabeth,
460 CC	Lady E	13	But Claude, I'm glad to find/That you've taken my advice./{SC} Your advice?
462 CC	Colby	7	able to feel very settled./And what you've had in mind still seems to me/Like
464 CC	Colby	22	music?/{C} Just the same./All the time you've been speaking, I've been translating/Into
465 CC	Colby	7	understand him, he was not there./{C} You've still not explained why you came to
465 CC	Colby	31	/{C} Indeed, I have felt, while you've been talking,/That it's my own feelings
467 CC	Colby	24	of that./{C} I'm very grateful for all you've done for me;/And I want to do my best
472 CC	Colby	5	think that you're frightened./Perhaps you've been very badly hurt, at some time./Or
472 CC	Lucasta	39	/But it's only the outer world that you've lost:/You've still got your inner world —
472 CC	Lucasta	40	only the outer world that you've lost:/You've still got your inner world — a world
474 CC	Lucasta	32	/{C} That's quite untrue./{L} But you've something else, that I haven't got:/
479 CC	Lucasta	11	matters now is, that I'm hungry,/And you've got to give me a very good dinner./{K}
479 CC	Kaghan	21	{L} You know I don't like sherry./{K} You've got to drink it,/To Colby, and a happy
479 CC	Kaghan	33	down./— I must say, I like the way you've had the place done up./{C} It was Lady
480 CC	Colby	13	only pretend that you're a gambler./You've got as level a head as anyone,/And you
481 CC	Colby	2	you are./{C} I'm beginning to believe you've a pretty shrewd insight/Into things that
481 CC	Lady E	19	to have a look at the flat/Now that you've moved in. Because you can't tell/
481 CC	Lady E	33	the address;/And I don't believe that you've been there yet./{K} Why no, as a matter
482 CC	Lady E	11	Kaghan and Miss Angel./I can see you've lived a rather sheltered life,/And I've
488 CC	Claude	6	beginning now to piece it together./You've been asking Colby about his family .../
490 CC	Colby	17	indifferent./And all the time that you've been talking/I've only been thinking:
494 CC	Lady E	27	I had done what I wanted to do./{LE} You've never talked like this to me before!/Why
499 CC	Lucasta	27	hands./Oh, I know what a nuisance you've always found me!/And I haven't made it
502 CC	Lucasta	22	/But you're terribly cold. Or else you've some fire/To warm you, that isn't the
517 CC	Colby	11	towards you. I like you too much./You've become a man without illusions/About
517 CC	Eggers	33	Don't say that, Mr. Simpkins, until you've tried our organ!/{C} Well, if you could
518 CC	Eggers	5	organist./I think you'll come to find you've another vocation./We worked together
524 ES	Charles	25	{M} We're getting off the point .../{C} You've got me off *my* point .../I was trying to
525 ES	Monica	22	words he'll come ambling in .../{M} You've said a good deal more than two words
525 ES	Monica	27	have a minute alone with you./{M} You've already had several minutes alone with
525 ES	Monica	28	several minutes alone with me/Which you've wasted in wrangling. But seriously,
526 ES	Charles	6	I've made you say so!/But now that you've said so, you must say it again,/For I
528 ES	Charles	20	self, Charles./I'm sure of that./{C} You've given two reasons,/One the
529 ES	Monica	19	{}/[*Enter* LORD CLAVERTON]/{M} You've been very long in coming, Father. What
530 ES	Monica	27	/For no one. For nothing./{M} Yet you've been looking forward/To this very time!
531 ES	Monica	4	want to revel in gloom!/You know you've retired in a blaze of glory —/You've read
531 ES	Monica	5	you've retired in a blaze of glory —/You've read every word about you in the
533 ES	Gomez	1	come back with another name?/{G} You've changed your name too, since I knew
533 ES	Ld Clav	25	reasons./{LC} Do you mean that you've won respect out there/By the sort of
534 ES	Ld Clav	16	at least, to be thankful for./I trust you've no need to engage in forgery./{G}
535 ES	Gomez	1	/{LC} But why have you come?/{G} You've asked me that already!/To see you,
536 ES	Gomez	2	to think you know more than you do./You've changed your name twice — by easy
536 ES	Gomez	8	/You, so slowly and sweetly, that you've never woken up/To the fact that Dick
539 ES	Gomez	2	an impressive figurehead./But again, you've retired at sixty. Why at sixty?/{LC}
540 ES	Ld Clav	14	interesting!/I still don't know why you've come to see me/Or what you mean by
540 ES	Gomez	25	been surprised/When I said 'Dick, you've run over somebody'/Wouldn't you have
550 ES	Ld Clav	8	And you didn't recognise me./{LC} You've changed your name, no doubt. And I've
552 ES	Carghil	34	you look the part./Whatever part you've played, I must say you've always looked
552 ES	Carghil	34	part you've played, I must say you've always looked it./{LC} I've no longer
554 ES	Piggott	18	/{MP} But I ought to introduce you. You've been talking to Lord Claverton,/The
556 ES	Monica	27	each other./Michael, you know what you've come to ask of Father/And Father
556 ES	Michael	31	awfully hard to explain things to *you*./You've always made up your mind that I was to
557 ES	Ld Clav	14	speculative business./{LC} I dare say you've tried a little private speculation./{Mi}

560 ES Ld Clav 21   for your wanting to go/Beyond what you've told me? It isn't ... manslaughter?/{Mi}
561 ES Michael 20   up to. Those standards of conduct/You've always made so much of, for my benefit:
562 ES Carghil 34   Did he really look like me?/{MC} You've his voice! and his way of moving! It's
563 ES Carghil 16   have?'/So he sent me here./{MC} Oh, you've seen each other lately?/Richard, I think
564 ES Carghil 11   How do you do./{MC} I don't believe you've known Lord Claverton/As long as I
564 ES Carghil 36   {MC} Secret for secret, Señor Gomez!/You've got to be the first to put your cards on
565 ES Monica   5   afternoon, Michael./{M} No, I think you've had enough talk for to-day./Michael, as
567 ES Monica   2   Charles, Charles, Charles, I'm so glad you've come!/I've been so worried, and rather
568 ES Ld Clav 33   to be quite honest with your child/If you've never been honest with anyone older,/On
568 ES Ld Clav 36   a child. And by the time she's grown/You've woven such a web of fiction about you!/
570 ES Monica   2   did the ghosts mean? All these years/You've kept them to yourself. Did Mother
574 ES Carghil 11   /{MC} He's told me all his story./You've cruelly misunderstood him, Richard./
574 ES Carghil 13   So I put on my thinking cap./I know you've always thought me utterly brainless,/But

YOUNG (40)

54 Mr E Sun   19   /The avenue of penitence;/The young are red and pustular/Clutching
66 WL: Chess 160   had five already, and nearly died of young George.)/The chemist said it would be all
68 WL: Fire S 231   awaited the expected guest./He, the young man carbuncular, arrives,/A small house
128 Cor1 March 44   didn't get to the country,/So we took young Cyril to church. And they rang a bell/
143 Lines OM   11   love of youth,/And inaccessible by the young./Reflected from my golden eye/The
202 War Poetry 15   that a poem might happen/To a very young man: but a poem is not poetry —/That is
605 Narcissus 28   his new beauty./Then he had been a young girl/Caught in the woods by a drunken
257 MC Chorus 15   heavier upon us./We have seen the young man mutilated,/The torn girl trembling
268 MC Knight1   7   those who had crowned the young prince,/Denying the legality of his
285 FR   Amy   7   was taken for granted/When I was young and strong, and sun and light unsought
286 FR   Charles 23   nothing on earth so bad for the young./All that a civilised person needs/Is a
286 FR   Charles 26   or two before dinner./The modern young people don't know what they're drinking,
286 FR   Charles 27   know what they're drinking,/Modern young people don't care what they're eating;/
292 FR   Harry   26   /You all look so withered and young./{G} We must have a ride tomorrow./
319 FR   Harry   20   Not Arthur or John,/They were too young. But now I remember/A summer day of
334 FR   Agatha   7   very tired, as only the old feel./The young feel tired at the end of an action —/The
367 CP   Edward 20   moving pictures/Frequently brings young people together./{P} Now you're only
408 CP   Reilly 13   /{L} Well, tell him if you like./{R} A young man named Peter./{E} Peter? Peter who?/
409 CP   Reilly 26   /When you discovered that your young friend/(Though you knew, in your heart,
409 CP   Reilly 30   When, I say, you discovered that your young friend/Had actually fallen in love with
428 CP   Alex   21   the monkeys. And they eat them./The young monkeys are extremely palatable:/I've
446 CC   Claude   4   /{SC} And experience./With a young man, some readjustment is necessary./
448 CC   Claude 23   finally retired/And that you have a young successor,/A Mr. Colby Simpkins./{E}
458 CC   Lady E 25   the Channel crossing./But who is this young man? His face is familiar./{SC} This
458 CC   Claude 26   man? His face is familiar./{SC} This young man is Eggerson's successor./You know
458 CC   Lady E 38   musical./{LE} Musical?/Isn't this the young man I interviewed/And recommended to
460 CC   Lady E 21   guidance for once, and engage that young man?'/Well, that was Mr. Colby./{SC}
464 CC   Claude 32   I thought I despised him/When I was young. And yet I was in awe of him./I was
465 CC   Claude   5   I never understood him./I was too young. And when I was mature enough/To
482 CC   Lady E   3   *and* LUCASTA]/{LE} Were those young people here by appointment?/Or did they
482 CC   Lady E   6   to her./{LE} You call her Lucasta? Young people nowadays/Seem to have dropped
486 CC   Colby   25   little boy/Who died when I was very young indeed./I don't remember him. I was told
501 CC   Eggers 30   Kaghan/Is one of the most promising young men in the City,/And he has a heart of
509 CC   Claude 22   Guzzard./I have a very promising young colleague —/In fact, the young man who
509 CC   Claude 23   young colleague —/In fact, the young man who showed you upstairs —/Whose
511 CC   Lady E 10   a fatal accident/When you were very young. That is why you were adopted./{K} But
544 ES   Ld Clav 17   It's often with us/When we are young, but then it's not noticed;/And by the
547 ES   Piggott 23   generation./When there are enough young people among us/We dance in the
560 ES   Ld Clav 24   good a driver./{LC} What then? That young woman?/{Mi} I'm not such a fool/As to
564 ES   Gomez   4   late. Don't you agree, Dick?/— This young lady I take to be your daughter?/And this

YOUNGER (11)

284 FR   m   2   IVY, VIOLET, *and* AGATHA, *her younger sisters*/COL. THE HON. GERALD
286 FR   Ivy   31   to. {}/[*Lights a cigarette*]/{I} The younger generation/Are undoubtedly decadent./
286 FR   Charles 33   /Are undoubtedly decadent./{C} The younger generation/Are not what we were.
286 FR   Gerald 36   /{G} You're being very hard on the younger generation./I don't come across them
287 FR   Gerald   5   such an easy world to live in./Let the younger generation speak for itself:/It's Mary's
287 FR   Mary   8   if you want information/About the younger generation, you must ask someone else.
314 FR Warburt   8   /A country practitioner doesn't get younger./It takes me back longer than you can
321 FR   Winch   34   But a country sergeant/Doesn't get younger. Thank you, no, my Lord;/I don't find
328 FR   Charles 12   Hon. Arthur Gerald Charles Piper, younger brother of Lord/Monchensey, who ran
547 ES   Piggott 22   Court/Can offer to guests of the younger generation./When there are enough

554 ES   Piggott 35   her name/Means nothing at all to the younger generation,/But you and I should
YOUNGEST (1)
332 FR   Agatha   20   wanted a sister here/Always. I was the youngest: I was then/An undergraduate at
YOUNGSTER (1)
293 FR   Gerald   31   has happened to *me*./I started as a youngster on the North-West Frontier —/Been
YOUR (801)
YOURS (22)
117 SP   Dusty   31   a party too!/{Du} Well it needn't be yours, it may mean a friend./{Do} No it's mine.
309 FR   Harry   6   clever/To admit you into *our* world. Yours is no better./They have seen to that: it is
324 FR   Harry   38   I choose to be talking. I will not talk yours./{A} You looked like your father/When
334 FR   Agatha   16   at the moment of relief./The burden's yours now, yours/The burden of all the family.
334 FR   Agatha   16   of relief./The burden's yours now, yours/The burden of all the family. And I am a
355 CP   Julia   34   to know./If they'd been friends of yours, I couldn't tell the story./{P} Were they
419 CP   Reilly   1   their loneliness. You will not forget yours./Each way means loneliness — and
420 CP   Reilly   14   no fee./{C} But .../{R} For a case like yours/There is no fee. {}/[*Presses button*]/{C}
489 CC   Claude   7   /That seemed fair enough — though yours had been lost,/And mine I couldn't lose.
491 CC   Lady E   5   from you/The son you thought was yours. And I know from what you said,/That
491 CC   Lady E   6 you would rather he was *ours* than only *yours*./Why should we make any further
494 CC   Lady E   6   never had a son;/While, if he were yours ... he could still take the place/Of my son:
494 CC   Lady E   9   mine,/But for you to believe that he is yours!/So I hope Mrs. Guzzard will say he is
507 CC   Guzzard 36   you suggesting that I kept a child of yours/And deceived Sir Claude by pretending it
515 CC   Guzzard   7   the child. You assumed that it was yours;/And you were so pleased, I shrank, at the
515 CC   Guzzard 11   you continue to think the child was yours,/My son was assured of a proper start in
515 CC   Guzzard 16 /Though I had never said 'this child is yours',/I feared you would ask for the birth
539 ES   Gomez   21   protection of that prudent devil/Of yours, to tell him not to go too far./Well, now,
540 ES   Gomez   2   /I'd rather be my kind of failure than yours./{LC} And what do you call failure?/{G}
549 ES   Carghil   9   were the names of those friends of yours/And which one was it invited us to lunch?
551 ES   Ld Clav 10 I learned my lesson/And you learned yours, if you needed the lesson./{MC} You
553 ES   Carghil 14   touch still lingers./And I've touched yours./It's frightening to think that we're still
YOURSELF (76)
65 WL: Chess   142   /Now Albert's coming back, make yourself a bit smart./He'll want to know what
66 WL: Chess   144   with that money he gave you/To get yourself some teeth. He did, I was there./You
192 FQ: Little   46   You are not here to verify,/Instruct yourself, or inform curiosity/Or carry report.
236 Cat Morgan   19 and it's worth a lot more:/You'll save yourself time, and you'll spare yourself labour/
236 Cat Morgan   19   save yourself time, and you'll spare yourself labour/If jist you make friends with the
243 MC   Chorus   21   /A doom on the house, a doom on yourself, a doom on the world./We do not wish
255 MC   Tempt4   12   /Seek the way of martyrdom, make yourself the lowest/On earth, to be high in
258 MC   Chorus   1   Archbishop, save us, save us, save yourself that we may be saved;/Destroy yourself
258 MC   Chorus   2   that we may be saved;/Destroy yourself and we are destroyed./{T} Now is my
290 FR   Violet   21   Nonsense, Gerald!/You must see for yourself it's the only thing to do./{Ag} Thus
295 FR   Charles   8   only doing harm to your mother and yourself./Of course we know what really
295 FR   Charles 15   /But *you* have no reason to reproach yourself./Your conscience may be clear./{H} I
308 FR   Mary   10   other. And in a way you contradict yourself:/That sudden comprehension of the
308 FR   Mary   27   for you/That you can only do for yourself./What you need to alter is something
309 FR   Mary   23   think,/But what you feel. You attach yourself to loathing/As others do to loving: an
309 FR   Mary   25 good that's misdirected. You deceive yourself/Like the man convinced that he is
320 FR   Warburt 29   the time she has to live./The other is yourself: the future of Wishwood/Depends on
321 FR   Warburt   6 you./And now, Harry, let's talk about yourself./{H} I never saw a photograph. There is
321 FR   Warburt 22   *you* saw him, and .../{W} Harry! Pull yourself together./Something may have
345 FR   Mary   18 /{M} Good-bye, Harry. Take care of yourself. {}/[*Exit* HARRY]/{A} At my age, I
356 CP   Celia   39   I may go away myself./{C} Go away yourself!/{J} Have you an aunt too?/{E} No, I
361 CP   Reilly   40   not quite the same friends as yourself,/Or making your friends like her better
363 CP   Reilly   23 /{UG} It will do you no harm to find yourself ridiculous./Resign yourself to be the
363 CP   Reilly   24   to find yourself ridiculous./Resign yourself to be the fool you are./That's the best
367 CP   Edward   10 /{E} Why, what could there be about yourself and Celia?/Have you anything in
380 CP   Celia   8   /Oh, I dare say that you deceived yourself:/But that's what it was, no doubt./{E} I
380 CP   Celia   18   too crude a subterfuge/To justify yourself. There was never anything/Between me
382 CP   Celia   6 /I think — I believe — you are being yourself/As you never were before, with me./
385 CP   Reilly   28   must also be a stranger./{UG} And to yourself as well. But remember,/When you see
385 CP   Edward   36 I think I should like you to bring her yourself./{UG} Yes, I know you would. And for
389 CP   Lavinia 11   do you know where you are going, yourself?/{P} Yes, of course, I'm going to
393 CP   Lavinia 15 decisions/That you should have made yourself. I remember —/Oh, I ought to have
393 CP   Lavinia 32   To what?/{L} To think well of yourself./You know it was I who made you
395 CP   Lavinia 20 boy,/I'm sure you were always getting yourself measured/To prove how you had
395 CP   Lavinia 22   were always intensely concerned with yourself;/And if other people grow, well, you

395 CP	Lavinia	29	mind, you'll soon get over it/And find yourself another little part to play,/With
396 CP	Lavinia	10	/I believe you were trying to persuade yourself you were./I seemed always on the verge
396 CP	Lavinia	24	be so sorry for you/As you are for yourself. And that's hard to bear./I thought that
396 CP	Edward	32	a child./{E} I don't want you to make yourself responsible for me:/It's only another
397 CP	Lavinia	9	*are* you talking about?/Talking to yourself. Could you bear, for a moment,/To
404 CP	Reilly	37	/But before I treat a patient like yourself/I need to know a great deal more about
409 CP	Reilly	15	your vanity./You liked to think of yourself as a passionate lover./Then you
409 CP	Reilly	34	it/Before he did. You pretended to yourself,/I suspect, and for as long as you could,
435 CP	Lavinia	34	image of Celia/Which you made for yourself, to meet your own needs./Peter, please
436 CP	Edward	2	you find out now, Peter, things about yourself/That you don't like to face: well, just
436 CP	Julia	16	is, when you're not concerned with yourself/But just being an eye. You will come to
438 CP	Reilly	20	impediment:/You must try to detach yourself from what you still feel/As your
461 CC	Eggers	5	turn up unexpected/And you find yourself non-plussed, you must get me on the
462 CC	Claude	33	formal relationship/In adapting yourself to a new situation./{C} I'm very
463 CC	Colby	20	So that you can think in it — you feel yourself to be/Rather a different person when
466 CC	Claude	7	play to myself./{SC} You shall play to yourself. And as for me,/I keep my pieces in a
471 CC	Lucasta	2	...{L} The next that you want to go to *yourself.*/{C} And perhaps you'll let me tell you
471 CC	Lucasta	7	/{L} I'd rather you played me bits yourself, and explained them./We'll begin my
472 CC	Lucasta	27	that's not the point. You'd convinced yourself;/And you felt that your life had all
474 CC	Lucasta	25	be broken./And you would find yourself in a devastated area —/A bomb-site ...
475 CC	Lucasta	38	for B. —/I'd much rather hear it from yourself./{C} There's only one thing I can't tell
477 CC	Lucasta	36	you think. It's to do with myself./{L} Yourself, indeed! Your precious self!/Why don't
477 CC	Lucasta	37	precious self!/Why don't you shut yourself up in that garden/Where you like to be
477 CC	Lucasta	38	/Where you like to be alone with yourself?/Or perhaps you think it would be bad
480 CC	Lucasta	21	need to be a better judge of character/Yourself, before you said that of Colby./{K}
493 CC	Lady E	8	/But won't you be sitting at the desk yourself?/{SC} No, that would look too formal.
508 CC	Eggers	5	against hope/To find her son. Put yourself in her position./If you had lost your
512 CC	Guzzard	27	Kaghan,/Are you satisfied to find yourself the son/Of Lady Elizabeth
514 CC	Guzzard	37	you, Sir Claude,/Till you deceived yourself. When you went to Canada/My sister
526 ES	Charles	1	I think —/I think you're tormenting yourself as well./{M} You're right. I am.
535 ES	Ld Clav	20	*tray and exit*]/{LC} Won't you help yourself? {}/[GOMEZ *does so, liberally*]/{G}
536 ES	Gomez	29	you come to see that you have lost *yourself*/That you are quite alone./{LC} I'm
538 ES	Gomez	14	Shall we say that you did very well by yourself?/Though not, I suspect, as well as you
539 ES	Ld Clav	38	in England./{LC} So, as you consider yourself a success .../{G} A worldly success,
544 ES	Monica	27	I want to see you learning to enjoy yourself!/{LC} Perhaps I've never really enjoyed
549 ES	Carghil	28	/Effie it was said 'you'd be throwing yourself away./Mark my words' Effie said, 'if
554 ES	Carghil	13	never sit still:/You simply sacrifice yourself for us./{MP} It's the breath of life to
559 ES	Ld Clav	2	what do you now propose to do with yourself?/{Mi} I want to go abroad./{LC} You
560 ES	Ld Clav	17	in any business/You may find for yourself — if, on investigation,/I am satisfied
570 ES	Monica	2	All these years/You've kept them to yourself. Did Mother know of them?/{LC} Your
577 ES	Charles	15	your father?/Remember, you put yourself completely in the power/Of a man you

YOURSELVES (5)

280 MC	Priest3	32	/Of thought, to justify your action to yourselves,/Weaving a fiction which unravels as
311 FR	Harry	27	*embrasure.*]/{H} Why do you show yourselves now for the first time?/When I knew
407 CP	Reilly	23	your own cure./But when you put yourselves into hands like mine/You surrender a
438 CP	Reilly	35	think her death was waste/You blame yourselves, and because you blame yourselves/
438 CP	Reilly	35	yourselves, and because you blame yourselves/You think her life was wasted. It was

YOUTH (6)

19 Portrait		48	it flow from you, you let it flow,/And youth is cruel, and has no more remorse/And
71 WL: DWater		317	/He passed the stages of his age and youth/Entering the whirlpool./Gentile or Jew/O
143 Lines OM		10	hate,/More bitter than the love of youth,/And inaccessible by the young./Reflected
228 Gus		7	his paw shake./Yet he was, in his youth, quite the smartest of Cats —/But no
585		t	/POEMS WRITTEN IN EARLY YOUTH/A Fable for Feasters/In England, long
592 Grad 4		3	a thousand fears,/To hopeful eye of youth it still appears/A lane by which the rose

YOUTHFUL (1)

| 19 Portrait | | 55 | find the world/To be wonderful and youthful, after all.'/The voice returns like the |

ZEAL (1)
158 Rock 5   2   doubtless men of public spirit and zeal./Preserve me from the enemy who has
ZEALAND (1)
559 ES Ld Clav 12 /Or what about sheep farming in New Zealand?/{Mi} Sheep farming? Good Lord, no./
ZEBRA (1)
 56 Swee Night   3   his arms hang down to laugh,/The zebra stripes along his jaw/Swelling to maculate
ZERO (1)
191 FQ: Little   20   is the summer, the unimaginable/Zero summer?/If you came this way,/Taking the
ZOROASTER (1)
437 CP   Reilly 5 /{R} *Ere Babylon was dust/The magus Zoroaster, my dead child,/Met his own image*
ZU (1)
 61 WL: Burial   32 */Frisch weht der Wind/Der Heimat zu/Mein Irisch Kind/Wo weilest du?/*'You gave
ZÜRICH (9)
459 CC   Lady E 34 Leroux is in Lausanne./I have been in Zürich, under Dr. Rebmann./{SC} But you were
459 CC   Claude 36 /In Lausanne. What made you go to Zürich?/{LE} Why, I'd no sooner got to
459 CC   Lady E 39   Deverell./She was going on to Zürich. So she said: 'Come to Zürich!/There's a
459 CC   Lady E 39   on to Zürich. So she said: 'Come to Zürich!/There's a wonderful doctor who teaches
460 CC   Lady E 2   mind control.'/So on I went to Zürich./{SC} So on you went to Zürich./But I
460 CC   Claude 3   to Zürich./{SC} So on you went to Zürich./But I thought that the doctor in
460 CC   Claude 8 true, you did send me postcards from Zürich;/But you know that I can't decipher
460 CC   Claude 37   it!/{SC} If this is what the doctor in Zürich has done for her,/I give him full marks.
541 ES   Gomez 22 /My current account in Stockholm or Zürich/Would keep me in comfort for the rest

Reverse Index of Word Forms

This list contains the complete vocabulary of Eliot's texts, with the words alphabetized starting from their right-hand end. For convenience, the list of words is right-justified, so that the word-endings are clear.

Such a list has several uses. First of all, it enables the reader to find word forms that are similar in meaning but have been spelled differently, such as *organ* and *horgan*. Second, it brings together words with the same grammatical ending, so that, for example, all the present participles ending with *-ing* are found together, as well as all words ending in *'s* and *-tion*. Third, it helps with the study of Eliot's rhymes. No attempt has been made in this book to produce a proper rhyming index—such a task is a research project in its own right—but with the help of the Reverse Index one can study all the *possible* rhyming words that Eliot uses. Naturally, care must be taken to ensure that rhyming sounds that use different word-endings are not missed, for example *sneers* and *ears*.

Reverse Index

bungled	settled	designed	dawned	shuddered
failed	unsettled	resigned	spawned	considered
blue-nailed	mauled	assigned	downed	reconsidered
sailed	befouled	gained	renowned ·	unconsidered
detailed	ruled	regained	browned	bewildered
prevailed	crawled	complained	crowned	wandered
reconciled	scowled	explained	drowned	rendered
veiled	puzzled	pained	disowned	surrendered
filed	screamed	drained	echoed	wondered
defiled	shamed	trained	escaped	well-ordered
boiled	ashamed	strained	scraped	disordered
soiled	unashamed	obtained	draped	murdered
piled	blamed	contained	peeped	powdered
reviled	inflamed	entertained	wiped	skeered
exiled	named	curtained	helped	peered
tickled	roamed	stained	cramped	offered
sprinkled	framed	sustained	humped	coffered
wrinkled	untamed	cabined	hoped	suffered
tinkled	redeemed	combined	developed	foresuffered
called	seemed	dined	enveloped	staggered
recalled	aimed	fined	galloped	lingered
galled	palmed	refined	snapped	deciphered
signalled	hummed	confined	unwrapped	feathered
metalled	welcomed	imagined	stepped	fathered
walled	domed	lined	worshipped	gathered
felled	bloomed	declined	wind-whipped	withered
impelled	accustomed	inclined	clipped	bothered
compelled	broadbottomed	well-disciplined	slipped	flickered
dispelled	armed	undisciplined	gripped	pampered
expelled	alarmed	underlined	stripped	distempered
quarrelled	warmed	determined	cropped	unstoppered
travelled	swarmed	predetermined	dropped	whispered
jewelled	affirmed	undetermined	topped	watered
towelled	confirmed	joined	stopped	slaughtered
filled	formed	conjoined	clasped	altered
fulfilled	half-formed	destined	grasped	sheltered
unfulfilled	reformed	ruined	red	entered
chilled	informed	twined	cared	mastered
killed	performed	damned	dared	festered
drilled	consumed	condemned	feared	blistered
thrilled	assumed	planned	unfeared	bolstered
tilled	leaned	unskinned	cleared	fostered
untilled	cleaned	pinned	smeared	battered
unstilled	maddened	abandoned	appeared	scattered
willed	hardened	telephoned	disappeared	shattered
rolled	freshened	pensioned	beggared	flattered
controlled	lengthened	auctioned	shared	mattered
pulled	awakened	mentioned	declared	tattered
cooled	blackened	unmentioned	glared	embittered
trampled	quickened	questioned	pared	littered
sawdust-trampled	darkened	reckoned	prepared	glittered
templed	opened	postponed	compared	frittered
dappled	happened	imprisoned	spared	buttered
grappled	loosened	learned	stared	shuttered
rippled	threatened	warned	bred	fluttered
snarled	straightened	concerned	well-bred	muttered
whirled	enlightened	adorned	ill-bred	sputtered
curled	frightened	hornèd	country-bred	conquered
sled	shortened	burned	sacred	fevered
entitled	listened	turned	mildred	delivered
whistled	battened	down-turned	hundred	covered
jostled	reigned	returned	remembered	recovered
rattled	maligned	upturned	first-remembered	discovered
nettled	signed	tuned	numbered	cowered

dowered	abased	self-possessed	elevated	wanted
lowered	ceased	guessed	cultivated	lamented
high-powered	deceased	kissed	undoubted	supplemented
answered	deceasèd	missed	acted	tormented
fred	released	dismissed	enacted	rented
alfred	pleased	crossed	refracted	presented
shred	unappeased	dreamcrossed	abstracted	consented
gray-haired	diseased	uncrossed	distracted	contented
repaired	purchased	engrossed	attracted	discontented
fired	raised	tossed	perfected	prevented
hired	criticised	discussed	rejected	invented
admired	exercised	non-plussed	projected	painted
aspired	exorcised	used	reflected	tainted
inspired	realised	accused	collected	acquainted
conspired	civilised	refused	connected	hinted
desired	promised	diffused	respected	pointed
undesired	surmised	confused	suspected	appointed
tired	reorganised	amused	expected	disappointed
retired	transhumanised	unused	unexpected	haunted
acquired	recognised	doused	erected	hunted
required	unrecognised	roused	directed	counted
enquired	despised	aroused	misdirected	mounted
bored	etherised	paralysed	resurrected	noted
underscored	surprised	dedicated	predicted	sore-footed
shored	practised	implicated	afflicted	looted
explored	hypnotised	complicated	inflicted	devoted
ignored	baptised	excommunicated	restricted	accepted
stored	bruised	educated	abducted	intercepted
restored	advised	defeated	pocketed	tempted
barred	devised	undefeated	braceleted	adopted
scarred	dispensed	cheated	completed	interrupted
marred	closed	repeated	interpreted	corrupted
referred	enclosed	created	uncorseted	cold-hearted
preferred	disclosed	seated	lifted	kind-hearted
conferred	imposed	arrogated	lighted	broken-hearted
stirred	composed	corrugated	delighted	parted
occurred	proposed	hated	baited	departed
concurred	opposed	humiliated	waited	started
purred	supposed	appropriated	awaited	thwarted
hatred	superposed	unpropitiated	inhabited	half-deserted
centred	disposed	unrelated	prohibited	asserted
self-centred	exposed	mutilated	excited	diverted
cured	collapsed	constellated	discredited	flirted
secured	rehearsed	violated	conceited	supported
endured	dispersed	desolated	limited	unsupported
figured	traversed	isolated	united	transported
configured	reversed	translated	reunited	distorted
disfigured	cursed	formulated	inherited	fasted
transfigured	passed	accumulated	low-spirited	roasted
injured	encompassed	insulated	visited	pasted
perjured	embarrassed	dominated	fruited	tasted
coloured	confessed	terminated	suited	wasted
unhonoured	blessed	separated	well-suited	suggested
dishonoured	blessèd	desecrated	unsuited	unmolested
poured	dressed	liberated	invited	rested
devoured	addressed	exasperated	uninvited	interested
measured	pressed	adulterated	exalted	disinterested
insured	depressed	concentrated	melted	arrested
assured	impressed	prostrated	bolted	insisted
reassured	oppressed	illustrated	insulted	persisted
fractured	expressed	precipitated	enchanted	twisted
enraptured	distressed	stated	planted	existed
martyred	obsessed	devastated	granted	exhausted
based	possessed	attenuated	unwarranted	trusted

portable	cycle	principle	slime	dine
incontestable	bicycle	trample	pantomime	keine
inscrutable	fiddle	example	crime	peine
conceivable	firefrorefiddle	temple	prime	seine
unlovable	middle	simple	time	fine
unobservable	riddle	people	kissing-time	imagine
unpayable	cuddle	apple	night-time	engine
prayable	huddle	ripple	fruit-time	machine
unprayable	muddle	tipple	teatime	shine
enjoyable	idle	supple	lifetime	moonshine
employable	candle	purple	sometime	sunshine
babble	handle	couple	wakingtime	thine
gobble	shuffle	isle	sleepingtime	whine
bubble	snuffle	carlisle	springtime	line
feeble	rifle	subtle	noontime	decline
treble	eagle	beetle	maytime	incline
incredible	pan-am-eagle	title	programme	feline
illegible	struggle	mantle	comme	mandoline
negligible	angle	gentle	homme	discipline
tangible	strangle	turtle	come	masculine
intangible	tangle	castle	become	mine
pénible	single	wrestle	welcome	examine
terrible	jungle	whistle	unwelcome	cross-examine
horrible	ile	bristle	income	nine
visible	mobile	apostle	home	ninety-nine
invisible	reconcile	bustle	nursing-home	canine
sensible	crocodile	hustle	rome	pine
insensible	file	battle	some	repine
responsible	while	rattle	handsome	volupine
irresponsible	meanwhile	nettle	troublesome	supine
inaccessible	mile	settle	unwholesome	submarine
possible	smile	little	toothsome	catherine
impossible	pile	belittle	epitome	peregrine
plausible	compile	bottle	forme	shrine
inconclusible	sterile	half-bottle	perfume	latrine
incompatible	tile	épaule	resume	doctrine
susceptible	volatile	coule	presume	usine
contemptible	subtile	houle	assume	eglantine
corruptible	gentile	rule	costume	argentine
indigestible	hostile	style	rhyme	porpentine
irresistible	futile	muzzle	thyme	routine
inexhaustible	exile	puzzle	ne	vine
inflexible	sickle	me	hurricane	divine
amble	chuckle	[foreign] me	lane	wine
gamble	twinkle	came	plane	lausanne
bramble	elle	became	aeroplane	chienne
thimble	belle	dame	inane	warenne
skimble	appelle	madame	pane	ravenne
nimble	taille	fame	counterpane	donne
humble	cornouaille	defame	membrane	cretonne
rumble	vieille	game	crâne	lynne
crumble	fille	shame	sane	one
grumble	baskerville	lame	insane	thirty-one
tumble	morville	blame	cène	bone
stumble	hole	flame	epicene	griddlebone
noble	whole	name	scene	backbone
marble	pole	frame	serene	done
double	metropole	same	allemagne	undone
trouble	coupole	tame	champagne	someone
jellicle	role	scheme	cologne	gone
pollicle	rôle	polypheme	againe	undergone
uncle	sole	supreme	maine	phone
circle	stole	extreme	aquitaine	telephone
muscle	steeple	lime	medicine	house-telephone

russin	television	education	vibration	relaxation
cousin	prevision	degradation	liberation	action
tin	division	recommendation	reverberation	reaction
latin	compulsion	foundation	laceration	satisfaction
satin	mansion	accommodation	consideration	dissatisfaction
martin	expansion	creation	generation	inaction
penguin	comprehension	congregation	veneration	abstraction
gauguin	apprehension	obligation	operation	distraction
ruin	dimension	investigation	desperation	attraction
angevin	dissension	prolongation	admiration	defection
win	tension	interrogation	inspiration	affection
damn	pretension	expurgation	decoration	disaffection
condemn	explosion	renunciation	exploration	objection
solemn	version	annunciation	restoration	subjection
column	reversion	association	aberration	dejection
autumn	diversion	reconciliation	concentration	projection
ann	passion	humiliation	registration	election
rebmann	compassion	expiation	administration	selection
inn	accession	deviation	frustration	reflection
on	succession	oblation	duration	collection
[foreign] on	procession	elation	organisation	recollection
ribbon	intercession	relation	dispensation	connection
bacon	confession	revelation	sensation	inspection
garçon	profession	constellation	malversation	retrospection
chelidon	digression	desolation	conversation	direction
cupidon	repression	isolation	expectation	insurrection
abandon	impression	consolation	eructation	intersection
clarendon	oppression	contemplation	superfetation	detection
london	expression	tribulation	vegetation	protection
pardon	possession	speculation	habitation	contradiction
guerdon	self-possession	calculation	concitation	valediction
surgeon	dispossession	circulation	meditation	jurisdiction
luncheon	mission	stipulation	prestidigitation	fiction
napoleon	submission	copulation	ingurgitation	affliction
simeon	commission	consummation	limitation	friction
thereon	concussion	affirmation	exploitation	conviction
agon	discussion	confirmation	levitation	distinction
python	confusion	information	invitation	extinction
suspicion	profusion	nation	exaltation	coniunction
contagion	conclusion	explanation	consultation	compunction
legion	delusion	indignation	incantation	concoction
religion	allusion	hallucination	plantation	reduction
fashion	illusion	subordination	lamentation	introduction
cushion	disillusion	imagination	presentation	obstruction
lion	intrusion	inclination	rotation	destruction
fragilion	libation	contamination	adaptation	self-destruction
rebellion	incubation	examination	temptation	completion
housekeeper-	vacation	elimination	flirtation	discretion
companion	desiccation	germination	station	ambition
opinion	dedication	determination	salutation	addition
onion	qualification	illumination	reputation	edition
union	simplification	destination	imputation	expedition
reunion	purification	divination	evacuation	condition
communion	identification	damnation	valuation	perdition
scorpion	justification	coronation	insinuation	coalition
orion	self-justification	incarnation	infatuation	self-demolition
occasion	publication	reincarnation	habituation	volition
evasion	supplication	consternation	situation	recognition
decision	communication	participation	elevation	definition
indecision	excommunication	occupation	deprivation	ammunition
imprecision	defalcation	exhilaration	cultivation	apparition
collision	suffocation	preparation	salvation	contrition
derision	vocation	separation	starvation	attrition
vision	provocation	celebration	observation	parturition

inquisition	sermon	halcyon	shown	to
position	mormon	horizon	blown	plato
opposition	agamemnon	barn	windblown	potato
repetition	cannon	learn	clown	brito
competition	loon	yearn	known	rialto
fruition	balloon	warn	well-known	into
intuition	moon	concern	unknown	onto
mention	honeymoon	modern	brown	unto
intention	noon	northern	crown	presto
abstention	afternoon	southern	uncrown	canaletto
attention	spoon	subaltern	drown	motto
inattention	macaroon	lantern	grown	tuo
invention	soon	stern	overthrown	bravo
convention	swoon	eastern	town	wo
intervention	upon	western	o	two
gerontion	baron	pattern	tambo	thirty-two
motion	saffron	tavern	co co rico	quaxo
emotion	iron	born	tobacco	alonzo
notion	apron	new-born	federico	cap
devotion	matron	stubborn	foco	ice-cap
deception	patron	reborn	marco	handicap
reception	son	inborn	fresco	heap
conception	[foreign] son	corn	do	cheap
perception	ben'son	scorn	waldo	leap
exception	reason	horn	quando	gap
description	treason	thorn	diminuendo	chap
prescription	season	hawthorn	overdo	lap
redemption	grandson	morn	romeo	slap
assumption	hodgson	torn	go	map
adoption	cargaison	worn	ago	snap
absorption	raison	unworn	lumbago	soap
interruption	venison	sworn	chicago	scrap
irruption	unison	urn	ego	drap
corruption	prison	burn	mango	trap
assertion	samson	mourn	cargo	clap-trap
extortion	crimson	turn	undergo	munkustrap
suggestion	parkinson	return	ho	wrap
question	eggerson	un	echo	unwrap
exhaustion	emerson	fun	who	sap
precaution	person	gun	figlio	deep
persecution	batterson	begun	scenario	snow-deep
circumlocution	lesson	hun	bucko	sheep
solution	stetson	run	buffalo	keep
absolution	ton	sun	michelangelo	upkeep
resolution	skeleton	bosun	hello	sleep
dissolution	teddington	dawn	hullo	asleep
evolution	wellington	gawn	no	peep
devolution	burlington	lawn	piano	creep
revolution	hemington	spawn	street-piano	weep
destitution	kensington	drawn	boo	sweep
constitution	wanton	longdrawn	bamboo	prep
oblivion	hampton	withdrawn	hoo	step
reckon	northampton	undrawn	cuckoo	doorstep
salon	claverton	prawn	waterloo	dip
talon	norton	yawn	too	hip
gallon	warburton	sea-strewn	tattoo	ship
babylon	launceston	own	hero	friendship
mon	boston	down	silvero	lordship
lemon	cotton	broken-down	zero	battleship
salmon	button	show-down	fro	clerkship
gammon	glutton	breakdown	montenegro	penmanship
common	mutton	sundown	so	citizenship
uncommon	von	eiderdown	also	companionship
summon	won	gown	gesso	relationship

scholarship	bear	o'er	meer	bother
partnership	dear	faber	sneer	mother
chancellorship	fear	chamber	peer	foster-mother
precentorship	gear	december	career	grandmother
worship	hear	member	queer	another
fellowship	clear	remember	safer	brother
ladyship	near	september	defer	half-brother
ker-flip	pear	november	refer	farther
philip	appear	timber	prefer	further
klip	reappear	number	differ	fancier
slip	disappear	sober	offer	financier
cowslip	rear	october	proffer	conférencier
drip	tear	cancer	suffer	worthier
trip	wear	dancer	infer	luckier
sip	swear	fiercer	confer	lonelier
gossip	year	der	eager	earlier
tip	far	leader	dowager	punier
help	afar	ladder	tugger	copier
yelp	gar	shudder	tiger	happier
kulp	cigar	cider	growltiger	hairier
camp	vulgar	spider	anger	terrier
damp	familiar	stupider	danger	easier
lamp	unfamiliar	consider	stranger	cosier
street-lamp	peculiar	outsider	messenger	métier
tramp	briar	provider	harbinger	weightier
limp	jar	alder	finger	frontier
hump	ajar	elder	five-finger	courtier
jump	similar	builder	ginger	banquier
lump	cellar	older	linger	heavier
rump	interstellar	colder	longer	brazier
shop	collar	householder	prolonger	speaker
bishop	dollar	shoulder	stronger	weaker
archbishop	somnambular	slander	hunger	maker
develop	secular	misunderstander	younger	undertaker
ker-flop	perpendicular	wander	forger	krumpacker
hoop	particular	alexander	her	flicker
loop	carbuncular	lender	cher	snicker
droop	circular	slender	preacher	baedeker
troop	regular	render	pencher	walker
stonecrop	irregular	surrender	watcher	coker
drop	singular	self-surrender	higher	joker
snowdrop	popular	tender	tougher	poker
top	pustular	lavender	photographer	broker
stop	cauchemar	reminder	decipher	darker
harp	grammar	verinder	bustopher	parker
sharp	lunar	fonder	britisher	worker
antwerp	oar	wonder	wisher	healer
chirp	boar	under	feather	gambler
clasp	uproar	thunder	heather	warbler
grasp	soar	blunder	weather	trifler
up	par	bounder	father	boiler
filled-up	spar	pounder	grandfather	caller
cup	tar	asunder	gather	smaller
coffee-cup	guitar	harder	rather	crueller
makeup	altar	larder	ether	traveller
loup	tartar	order	together	iller
group	mortar	border	altogether	simpler
bar	star	disorder	whether	butler
window-bar	jaguar	murder	nether	ruler
unbar	war	cruder	either	trawler
car	er	powder	neither	sous-mer
sleeping-car	e'er	beer	hither	dreamer
vicar	ne'er	cheer	wither	hammer
ear	whene'er	leer	other	mulhammer

summer	demeter	latter	flower	stupor
newcomer	peter	clatter	moonflower	emperor
former	interpreter	flatter	sunflower	error
groaner	after	platter	power	terror
gardener	hereafter	matter	tower	mirror
oftener	brighter	gratter	answer	horror
listener	daughter	better	layer	successor
foreigner	step-daughter	letter	prayer	predecessor
égratigner	laughter	setter	shyer	professor
liner	slaughter	bitter	destroyer	refrigerator
banner	self-slaughter	litter	dryer	accelerator
manner	manslaughter	flitter	lawyer	operator
inner	waiter	glitter	rumpelteazer	administrator
dinner	whiter	titter	air	actor
beginner	loiter	otter	[foreign] air	rent-collector
thinner	typewriter	potter	fair	director
sinner	alter	décrotter	affair	protector
practitioner	walter	utter	unfair	victor
sooner	shelter	butter	hair	doctor
corner	defaulter	gutter	chair	proprietor
turner	decanter	outer	deck-chair	traitor
partner	pleasanter	exchequer	deckchair	solicitor
owner	enter	conquer	armchair	visitor
per	re-enter	truer	flair	motor
caper	painter	palaver	pair	sculptor
cheaper	winter	ever	repair	tutor
paper	midwinter	fever	despair	languor
newspaper	saunter	whichever	stair	liquor
deeper	hunter	clever	waterstair	mayor
sleeper	encounter	never	heir	conveyor
piper	peloter	whenever	their	razor
viper	chapter	whoever	fir	err
temper	tempter	whatsoever	fakir	puss-purr
whimper	quarter	wherever	choir	minotaur
proper	shorter	forever	noir	cur
slipper	porter	sever	revoir	occur
copper	[prop. n.] porter	whatever	sir	recur
grasshopper	easter	however	stir	concur
upper	faster	receiver	elixir	dur
supper	plaster	shiver	or	grandeur
usurper	master	liver	labor	odeur
whisper	headmaster	deliver	harbor	chauffeur
prosper	schoolmaster	river	corridor	malheur
torchbearer	stationmaster	driver	for	monsieur
clearer	zoroaster	salver	camphor	peur
nearer	disaster	silver	senior	professeur
rarer	webster	over	junior	amateur
blunderer	lobster	cover	inferior	spectateur
murderer	leicester	recover	superior	conservateur
fairer	colchester	discover	prior	lecteur
admirer	prester	dover	bachelor	directeur
labourer	youngster	moreover	sailor	sueur
wiser	register	hover	chancellor	fur
closer	banister	lover	tremor	arthur
composer	cloister	plover	nor	murmur
purser	barrister	observer	señor	our
lesser	sister	preserver	minor	labour
guesser	holster	drawer	honor	neighbour
greater	minster	fewer	governor	arbour
later	monster	sewer	door	harbour
water	oyster	cower	outdoor	dour
bayswater	fatter	widower	floor	splendour
character	hatter	shower	moor	ardour
sweeter	chatter	lower	poor	four

pasties	bottles	shoes	creatures	creates
duties	half-bottles	heroes	signatures	gates
exequies	shuttles	negroes	fractures	propagates
cavies	saules	toes	pictures	hates
movies	hercules	potatoes	adventures	associates
cakes	rules	capes	ses	plates
shakes	dames	landscapes	cases	simulates
makes	games	escapes	ceases	mates
snakes	thames	gapes	pleases	intimates
takes	james	shapes	diseases	fascinates
mistakes	flames	grapes	phrases	separates
pekes	candle-flames	étapes	punaises	reiterates
likes	names	recipes	raises	concentrates
strikes	surnames	pipes	exercises	meditates
jokes	frames	stripes	premises	hesitates
pokes	schemes	wipes	noises	potentates
les	themes	trempés	rises	states
gales	chimes	hopes	enterprises	estates
nightingales	crimes	slopes	surprises	bites
tales	times	gropes	disguises	excites
tables	sometimes	types	impulses	kites
stables	pastimes	daguerreotypes	cleanses	unites
resembles	comes	cares	expenses	rites
crumbles	becomes	shares	senses	writes
troubles	homes	declares	responses	parasites
barnacles	perfumes	flares	loses	appetites
miracles	resumes	prepares	noses	invites
spectacles	costumes	stares	chooses	écroulantes
obstacles	fanes	acres	imposes	brûlantes
jellicles	lanes	londres	composes	côtes
pollicles	planes	spheres	purposes	anecdotes
articles	aeroplanes	misères	roses	notes
uncles	panes	primevères	lapses	pertes
circles	window-panes	actionnaires	rehearses	tastes
muscles	scenes	réactionnaires	verses	agonistes
cycles	centaines	fires	converses	ariettes
fiddles	carbines	night-fires	horses	marionettes
candles	engines	sapphires	nurses	cigarettes
handles	machines	admires	glasses	silhouettes
angeles	lines	pourboires	masses	mouettes
rifles	declines	spires	passes	tributes
trifles	sidelines	desires	successes	flutes
eagles	mines	retires	messes	minutes
angles	examines	requires	witnesses	routes
defiles	shrines	wires	eye-witnesses	disputes
miles	vines	shores	caresses	tongues
smiles	omnes	whores	addresses	cheques
piles	ones	stores	presses	ensues
tiles	bones	restores	waitresses	pursues
projectiles	scones	près	guesses	issues
wrinkles	telephones	pierres	kisses	virtues
winkles	gramophones	guerres	misses	leaves
marseilles	jones	très	losses	vine-leaves
guenilles	drones	spectres	crosses	rose-leaves
molles	tones	cures	tosses	light-in-leaves
soles	stones	epicures	causes	oakleaves
camisoles	prunes	heures	excuses	behaves
principles	fortunes	figures	fuses	graves
disciples	chamberlaynes	failures	amuses	saves
apples	does	pleasures	houses	staves
charles	foes	measures	chop-houses	waves
measles	goes	morsures	choruses	shirt-sleeves
apostles	mangoes	reassures	indicates	shirtsleeves
settles	echoes	features	implicates	thieves

briars	cavaliers	sisters	persecutors	faithless
friars	courtiers	monsters	tutors	worthless
jars	speakers	fosters	leurs	ruthless
cat-burglars	javelin-makers	oysters	amateurs	penniless
particulars	undertakers	matters	furs	reckless
mars	self-seekers	letters	lemurs	aimless
oars	walkers	potters	ours	realmless
boars	bankers	gutters	neighbours	harmless
roars	whiskers	shutters	odours	formless
soars	travelers	presbyters	hours	oceanless
altars	travellers	pursuers	jours	painless
mortars	dwellers	divers	toujours	brainless
stars	sutlers	self-deceivers	colours	erosionless
wars	rulers	rivers	rumours	motionless
scrubbers	performers	quivers	honours	emotionless
chambers	campaigners	covers	pours	devotionless
members	liners	recovers	tours	unless
remembers	banners	discovers	endeavours	sunless
timbers	manners	hovers	favours	sleepless
plumbers	dinners	lovers	devours	lipless
numbers	sinners	drawers	yours	helpless
tubers	corners	cowers	martyrs	powerless
dancers	papers	showers	jackass	doubtless
readers	newspapers	lowers	class	tactless
considers	keepers	flowers	first-class	sightless
elders	sweepers	garden-flowers	glass	spotless
landholders	pipers	powers	cutlass	effortless
shoulders	snappers	towers	mass	breastless
flanders	worshippers	answers	pass	restless
surrenders	slippers	layers	by-pass	honeyless
grinders	grasshoppers	prayers	trespass	mess
wonders	vespers	lawyers	brass	numbness
orders	whispers	airs	grass	gladness
cheers	prospers	affairs	success	madness
engineers	hearers	chairs	princess	sadness
sneers	admirers	lairs	process	wretchedness
peers	explorers	stairs	goddess	redness
sightseers	composers	backstairs	confess	kindness
offers	mousers	downstairs	chess	blindness
suffers	trousers	upstairs	less	goodness
villagers	two-seaters	heirs	bless	likeness
cottagers	six-seaters	souvenirs	lidless	idleness
voyagers	waters	stirs	childless	awareness
[abbrev.] eggers	characters	corridors	endless	obtuseness
tigers	deters	alors	windless	whiteness
dangers	chronometers	doors	soundless	remoteness
strangers	fighters	indoors	godless	forgiveness
passengers	daughters	floors	cloudless	nothingness
scavengers	waiters	moors	voiceless	richness
fingers	biters	blackamoors	lifeless	smoothness
lingers	typewriters	errors	nevertheless	filthiness
malingers	shelters	terrors	timeless	loneliness
death-bringers	enters	mirrors	homeless	loveliness
hers	re-enters	possessors	hopeless	holiness
watchers	hunters	conspirators	careless	happiness
fletchers	tempters	spectators	lustreless	unhappiness
feathers	quarters	agitators	futureless	weariness
fathers	porters	actors	ceaseless	business
gathers	supporters	contractors	senseless	drowsiness
panthers	feasters	directors	useless	emptiness
others	masters	doctors	meaningless	weakness
bothers	songsters	solicitors	speechless	sickness
brothers	ministers	visitors	fleshless	homesickness
financiers	barristers	motors	breathless	darkness

semi-darkness	discuss	drifts	moments	coasts
illness	fuss	doigts	equipments	chests
stillness	bats	fights	enchantments	priests
forgetfulness	acrobats	lights	appointments	rests
deceitfulness	cats	nights	disappointments	interests
sportfulness	soldats	knights	investments	tests
wistfulness	eats	rights	documents	guests
firmness	beats	insights	monuments	vests
meanness	feats	thoughts	instruments	nonconformists
wantonness	cheats	its	payments	organists
nearness	threats	portraits	enjoyments	colonists
harness	treats	straits	serpents	communists
wilderness	retreats	waits	rents	insists
tenderness	sweats	bits	parents	artists
eagerness	hats	habits	foster-parents	twists
bitterness	pats	benefits	currents	exists
governess	spats	profits	resents	costs
hopelessness	rats	[foreign] profits	presents	ghosts
tastelessness	photostats	misfits	portents	bursts
selflessness	squats	limits	events	busts
restlessness	debts	exploits	prevents	adjusts
listlessness	doubts	merits	saints	lusts
consciousness	acts	spirits	hints	trusts
unconsciousness	facts	sits	points	cuts
heinousness	pacts	visits	appoints	guts
cantankerousness	contracts	deposits	footprints	nuts
greatness	transacts	biscuits	aunts	chestnuts
sweetness	perfects	fruits	hunts	scouts
brightness	objects	suits	counts	boy-scouts
witness	subjects	faults	accounts	louts
bluntness	rejects	assaults	jennyanydots	puts
dryness	projects	results	faggots	us
caress	dialects	decants	shots	aus
dress	inspects	attendants	lots	nimbus
ad-dress	prospects	enfants	plots	phlaccus
address	suspects	slants	marmots	hibiscus
peeress	expects	tenants	knots	gus
digress	protects	currants	sailor-knots	magus
progress	districts	restaurants	roots	asparagus
press	instincts	peasants	chimney-pots	thus
wine-press	sheets	inhabitants	spots	ailanthus
winepress	meets	servants	trots	genius
express	greets	wants	accepts	angelus
waitress	streets	accents	attempts	allus
fortress	gets	innocents	arts	aeolus
distress	forgets	convalescents	darts	plus
mistress	prophets	accidents	hearts	stimulus
headmistress	pockets	incidents	parts	'potamus
possess	sockets	residents	starts	hippopotamus
countess	lets	correspondents	swarts	coriolanus
hostess	comets	students	concerts	menus
guess	bonnets	agents	experts	magnus
kiss	cornets	clients	deserts	terminus
bliss	poets	patients	converts	bonus
miss	crumpets	arrangements	shirts	tremendous
[prop. n.] miss	trumpets	increments	skirts	hideous
dismiss	secrets	basements	efforts	spontaneous
boss	frets	movements	reports	righteous
loss	regrets	fragments	sorts	courteous
moss	sets	compliments	courts	sagacious
cross	sunsets	sentiments	beasts	rapacious
across	quartets	ailments	feasts	veracious
gross	gifts	comments	breasts	voracious
toss	shifts	attainments	lasts	precious

organist	lout	threw	dix	railway
typist	knout	stew	fix	doorway
christ	spout	yew	crucifix	sway
humorist	sprout	bow	mix	straightway
tourist	tout	meadow	voix	anyway
subsist	devout	shadow	six	by
resist	put	widow	box	passer-by
insist	next	window	money-box	baby
consist	pretext	shop-window	fox	shabby
persist	au	somehow	smallpox	tabby
egotist	eau	show	aux	thereby
hypnotist	peau	low	bordeaux	selby
baptist	bureau	blow	chapitaux	colby
artist	du	below	deux	nearby
tornquist	dieu	flow	mieux	slingsby
twist	lieu	glow	sérieux	legacy
exist	milieu	allow	vieux	fallacy
against	peu	shallow	pluvieux	intimacy
dost	tereu	swallow	gueux	lunacy
host	[abbrev.] lu	bellow	baveux	conspiracy
ghost	venu	fellow	genoux	privacy
lost	où	yellow	leroux	icy
long-lost	thou	pillow	ay	policy
most	kinkajou	follow	decay	juicy
almost	anjou	hollow	day	vacancy
uttermost	lou	slow	to-day	fancy
post	you	now	birthday	chiromancy
frost	who-the-devil-are-you	know	holiday	nancy
first	tu	snow	friday	inoperancy
thirst	vêtu	[prop. n.] snow	monday	complacency
worst	vu	row	sunday	agency
burst	zu	brow	today	urgency
bust	jackdaw	highbrow	yesterday	clemency
dust	guffaw	crow	ash-wednesday	appetency
sawdust	jaw	hedgerow	thursday	potency
gust	law	grow	everyday	constituency
august	son-in-law	throw	gay	mercy
just	brother-in-law	arrow	hay	lucy
adjust	daughter-in-law	marrow	lay	ready
unjust	gnaw	narrow	clay	already
lust	paw	sparrow	delay	steady
must	raw	song-sparrow	play	lady
rust	braw	swamp-sparrow	display	malady
trust	draw	vesper-sparrow	may	landlady
distrust	straw	fox-sparrow	[prop. n.] may	freddy
ellicott	saw	borrow	dismay	muddy
piggott	dew	to-morrow	pay	seedy
but	few	tomorrow	repay	tragedy
cut	curfew	sorrow	fray	comedy
well-cut	matthew	burrow	gray	handy
fut	view	furrow	pray	brandy
shut	interview	bestow	spray	sandy
chestnut	jew	relax	tray	windy
out	kew	climax	betray	body
washed-out	flew	anti-climax	stray	somebody
worn-out	new	apollinax	astray	nobody
burnt-out	anew	tax	say	anybody
about	renew	income-tax	essay	everybody
roundabout	knew	wax	stay	szogody
knockabout	crew	alex	quay	bloody
égout	screw	complex	way	rhapsody
throughout	drew	essex	away	tardy
shout	withdrew	vortex	cuscuscaraway	study
without	grew		barraway	rowdy

levity
brevity
passivity
activity
festivity
perplexity
fixity
penalty
admiralty
loyalty
cruelty
novelty
guilty
difficulty
plenty
seventy
twenty
sovereignty
certainty
county
empty
hearty
party
liberty
property
poverty
dirty
thirty
forty
sty
pig-sty
nasty
majesty
honesty
travesty
frosty
thirsty
dusty
dusty
gusty
rusty
petty
pretty
beauty
duty
sixty
buy
guy
heavy
levy
ivy
envy
shadowy
showy
snowy
frenzy
chez
guiterriez
gomez
paierez
figurez
suivrez
fitz
klootz

Statistical Ranking List
of Word Forms

Statistical Ranking List of Word Forms

Each block in the list contains the following information:

R.

A (B) C

(D) E

WORDS

A (F) G

R is the ranking position of each WORD of the block within the list of word forms.

A is the total frequency of all WORDS in the block.

B is the relative % frequency of all WORDS in the block (**A/TOTAL**)% where **TOTAL** is the total number of words in the text.

C is the number of WORDS with frequency **A**.

D is the relative % frequency of all the words up to and including any one of the WORDS in the block.

E is the cumulative frequency of all the words up to and including any one of the WORDS in the block.

F is the cumulative % frequency of all the words up to the end of this block.

G is the cumulative frequency of all the words up to the end of this block.

If **C** = 1, the last line is omitted, since **F** = **D** and **G** = **E**.

To save space, the actual word forms are not shown for frequencies less than eleven. The statistical information for such word forms is, however, included.

1.
6940 (5.02) 1
     (5.02) 6940
the

2.
4123 (2.98) 1
     (8.00) 11063
i

3.
3926 (2.84) 1
     (10.84) 14989
and

4.
3838 (2.78) 1
     (13.62) 18827
to

5.
3813 (2.76) 1
     (16.38) 22640
you

6.
3114 (2.25) 1
     (18.63) 25754
of

7.
2665 (1.93) 1
     (20.56) 28419
a

8.
2154 (1.56) 1
     (22.12) 30573
in

9.
2085 (1.51) 1
     (23.63) 32658
that

10.
1756 (1.27) 1
     (24.90) 34414
is

11.
1440 (1.04) 1
     (25.94) 35854
it

12.
1248 (0.90) 1
     (26.84) 37102
but

13.
1161 (0.84) 1
     (27.68) 38263
have

14.
1122 (0.81) 1
     (28.49) 39385
for

15.
1114 (0.81) 1
     (29.30) 40499
not

16.
1014 (0.73) 1
     (30.03) 41513
be

17.
967 (0.70) 1
    (30.73) 42480
what

18.
908 (0.66) 1
    (31.39) 43388
me

19.
883 (0.64) 1
    (32.03) 44271
was

20.
874 (0.63) 1
    (32.66) 45145
we

21.
801 (0.58) 2
    (33.24) 45946
my
your
801 (33.82) 46747

23.
794 (0.57) 1
    (34.39) 47541
with

24.
751 (0.54) 1
    (34.94) 48292
at

25.
749 (0.54) 1
    (35.48) 49041
he

26.
699 (0.51) 1
    (35.98) 49740
as

27.
677 (0.49) 1
    (36.47) 50417
know

28.
665 (0.48) 1
    (36.96) 51082
are

29.
627 (0.45) 1
    (37.41) 51709
no

30.
595 (0.43) 1
    (37.84) 52304
all

31.
563 (0.41) 1
    (38.25) 52867
on

32.
547 (0.40) 1
    (38.64) 53414
do

33.
545 (0.39) 1
    (39.04) 53959
so

34.
540 (0.39) 1
    (39.43) 54499
or

35.
538 (0.39) 1
    (39.82) 55037
this

36.
528 (0.38) 1
    (40.20) 55565
if

37.
519 (0.38) 1
    (40.57) 56084
when

38.
485 (0.35) 1
    (40.92) 56569
his

39.
478 (0.35) 1
    (41.27) 57047
there

40.
477 (0.35) 1
    (41.62) 57524
from

41.
465 (0.34) 1
    (41.95) 57989
had

42.
454 (0.33) 1
    (42.28) 58443
will

43.
451 (0.33) 1
    (42.61) 58894
they

44.
446 (0.32) 1
    (42.93) 59340
she

45.
443 (0.32) 1
    (43.25) 59783
her

46.
439 (0.32) 1
    (43.57) 60222
very

47.
431 (0.31) 1
    (43.88) 60653
one

48.
423 (0.31) 1
    (44.19) 61076
who

49.
417 (0.30) 2
    (44.49) 61493
now
only
417 (44.79) 61910

51.
406 (0.29) 1
    (45.08) 62316
been

52.
405 (0.29) 1
    (45.38) 62721
him

53.
404 (0.29) 1
    (45.67) 63125
i'm

54.
395 (0.29) 1
    (45.95) 63520
don't

55.
386 (0.28) 1
    (46.23) 63906
about

56.
378 (0.27) 1
    (46.51) 64284
think

57.
374 (0.27) 1
    (46.78) 64658
by

58.
360 (0.26) 1
    (47.04) 65018
can

59.
357 (0.26) 1
    (47.30) 65375
time

60.
353 (0.26) 1
    (47.55) 65728
it's

61.
352 (0.25) 1
    (47.81) 66080
must

62.
346 (0.25) 1
    (48.06) 66426
like

63.
332 (0.24) 1
   (48.30) 66758
well

64.
329 (0.24) 1
   (48.53) 67087
us

65.
323 (0.23) 2
   (48.77) 67410
has
were
323 (49.00) 67733

67.
322 (0.23) 1
   (49.23) 68055
which

68.
321 (0.23) 1
   (49.47) 68376
see

69.
320 (0.23) 1
   (49.70) 68696
them

70.
317 (0.23) 1
   (49.93) 69013
shall

71.
314 (0.23) 2
   (50.15) 69327
an
say
314 (50.38) 69641

73.
311 (0.22) 1
   (50.61) 69952
would

74.
309 (0.22) 1
   (50.83) 70261
never

75.
290 (0.21) 1
   (51.04) 70551
come

76.
277 (0.20) 1
   (51.24) 70828
then

77.
263 (0.19) 1
   (51.43) 71091
always

78.
261 (0.19) 1
   (51.62) 71352
our

79.
256 (0.19) 1
   (51.80) 71608
want

80.
254 (0.18) 1
   (51.99) 71862
go

81.
252 (0.18) 1
   (52.17) 72114
how

82.
250 (0.18) 2
   (52.35) 72364
i've
why
250 (52.53) 72614

84.
248 (0.18) 1
   (52.71) 72862
here

85.
245 (0.18) 1
   (52.89) 73107
should

86.
241 (0.17) 1
   (53.06) 73348
am

87.
238 (0.17) 1
   (53.24) 73586
more

88.
233 (0.17) 1
   (53.40) 73819
good

89.
232 (0.17) 1
   (53.57) 74051
out

90.
230 (0.17) 1
   (53.74) 74281
did

91.
228 (0.16) 1
   (53.90) 74509
man

92.
222 (0.16) 1
   (54.06) 74731
oh

93.
221 (0.16) 2
   (54.22) 74952
may
some
221 (54.38) 75173

95.
220 (0.16) 1
   (54.54) 75393
could

96.
217 (0.16) 1
   (54.70) 75610
just

97.
216 (0.16) 1
   (54.86) 75826
than

98.
214 (0.15) 1
   (55.01) 76040
where

99.
209 (0.15) 1
   (55.16) 76249
other

100.
203 (0.15) 1
   (55.31) 76452
that's

101.
200 (0.14) 1
   (55.45) 76652
much

102.
195 (0.14) 1
   (55.59) 76847
nothing

103.
193 (0.14) 2
   (55.73) 77040
thought
up
193 (55.87) 77233

105.
189 (0.14) 1
   (56.01) 77422
life

106.
188 (0.14) 1
   (56.15) 77610
way

107.
186 (0.13) 1
   (56.28) 77796
make

108.
182 (0.13) 1
   (56.41) 77978
before

109.
179 (0.13) 1
   (56.54) 78157
their

110.
177 (0.13) 4
   (56.67) 78334
any
tell
yes
you're
177 (57.05) 78865

114.
174 (0.13) 2
   (57.18) 79039
said
too
174 (57.31) 79213

116.
171 (0.12) 1
   (57.43) 79384
let

117.
166 (0.12) 1
   (57.55) 79550
mrs.

118.
165 (0.12) 1
   (57.67) 79715
made

119.
160 (0.12) 2
   (57.79) 79875
he's
understand
160 (57.90) 80035

121.
159 (0.12) 1
   (58.02) 80194
people

122.
158 (0.11) 1
   (58.13) 80352
colby

123.
156 (0.11) 1
   (58.24) 80508
something

124.
154 (0.11) 1
   (58.35) 80662
over

125.
152 (0.11) 2
   (58.46) 80814
back
take
152 (58.57) 80966

127.
151 (0.11) 1
   (58.68) 81117
find

128.
150 (0.11) 2
   (58.79) 81267
father
mr.
150 (58.90) 81417

130.
148 (0.11) 1
   (59.01) 81565
going

131.
144 (0.10) 1
   (59.11) 81709
might

132.
140 (0.10) 1
   (59.21) 81849
still

133.
139 (0.10) 1
(59.31) 81988
another

134.
138 (0.10) 1
(59.41) 82126
first

135.
137 (0.10) 3
(59.51) 82263
get
world
years
137 (59.71) 82537

138.
135 (0.10) 1
(59.81) 82672
yet

139.
134 (0.10) 2
(59.91) 82806
because
really
134 (60.00) 82940

141.
132 (0.10) 1
(60.10) 83072
sure

142.
131 (0.09) 3
(60.19) 83203
again
into
own
131 (60.38) 83465

145.
130 (0.09) 1
(60.48) 83595
can't

146.
128 (0.09) 1
(60.57) 83723
there's

147.
127 (0.09) 2
(60.66) 83850
believe
mean
127 (60.75) 83977

149.
126 (0.09) 1
(60.84) 84103
those

150.
125 (0.09) 2
(60.93) 84228
moment
name
125 (61.02) 84353

152.
124 (0.09) 2
(61.11) 84477
death
such
124 (61.20) 84601

154.
123 (0.09) 1
(61.29) 84724
love

155.
122 (0.09) 1
(61.38) 84846
knew

156.
121 (0.09) 1
(61.47) 84967
these

157.
120 (0.09) 1
(61.56) 85087
came

158.
119 (0.09) 1
(61.64) 85206
men

159.
118 (0.09) 5
(61.73) 85324
after
down
edward
old
upon
118 (62.07) 85796

164.
114 (0.08) 1
(62.15) 85910
things

165.
113 (0.08) 3
(62.23) 86023
feel
right
same
113 (62.40) 86249

168.
112 (0.08) 4
(62.48) 86361
alone
lord
mind
perhaps
112 (62.72) 86697

172.
111 (0.08) 2
(62.80) 86808
better
day
111 (62.88) 86919

174.
110 (0.08) 1
(62.96) 87029
remember

175.
109 (0.08) 2
(63.04) 87138
myself
sir
109 (63.12) 87247

177.
108 (0.08) 1
(63.20) 87355
leave

178.
107 (0.08) 3
(63.27) 87462
left
once
you've
107 (63.43) 87676

181.
106 (0.08) 2
(63.51) 87782
long
wanted
106 (63.58) 87888

183.
104 (0.08) 2
(63.66) 87992
being
course
104 (63.73) 88096

185.
103 (0.07) 3
(63.81) 88199
lady
little
two
103 (63.96) 88405

188.
102 (0.07) 5
(64.03) 88507
claude
didn't
god
told
under
102 (64.33) 88915

193.
101 (0.07) 1
(64.40) 89016
enter

194.
100 (0.07) 2
(64.47) 89116
i'll
son
100 (64.54) 89216

196.
98 (0.07) 1
(64.61) 89314
give

197.
97 (0.07) 1
(64.68) 89411
light

198.
96 (0.07) 1
(64.75) 89507
harry

199.
95 (0.07) 1
(64.82) 89602
both

200.
93 (0.07) 2
(64.89) 89695
mother
need
93 (64.96) 89788

202.
92 (0.07) 4
(65.02) 89880
cannot
i'd
last
place
92 (65.22) 90156

206.
91 (0.07) 2
(65.29) 90247
anything
most
91 (65.35) 90338

208.
90 (0.07) 2
(65.42) 90428
away
night
90 (65.49) 90518

210.
89 (0.06) 7
(65.55) 90607
door
each
end
even
got
hope
many
89 (65.94) 91141

217.
88 (0.06) 1
(66.00) 91229
together

218.
87 (0.06) 1
(66.06) 91316
thing

219.
86 (0.06) 2
(66.12) 91402
rather
without
86 (66.19) 91488

221.
85 (0.06) 3
(66.25) 91573
between
lavinia
look
85 (66.37) 91743

224.
84 (0.06) 2
(66.43) 91827
quite
while
84 (66.49) 91911

226.
83 (0.06) 2
(66.55) 91994
elizabeth
though
83 (66.61) 92077

228.
82 (0.06) 3
(66.67) 92159
ask
celia
o
82 (66.79) 92323

231.
81 (0.06) 2
(66.85) 92404
happened
through
81 (66.91) 92485

233.
80 (0.06) 1
(66.97) 92565
done

234.
79 (0.06) 2
(67.02) 92644
ever
king
79 (67.08) 92723

236.
78 (0.06) 1
(67.14) 92801
seen

237.
77 (0.06) 3
(67.19) 92878
coming
guzzard
heard
77 (67.30) 93032

240.
76 (0.05) 2
(67.36) 93108
dead
yourself
76 (67.41) 93184

242.
75 (0.05) 4
(67.47) 93259
child
does
talk
whom
75 (67.63) 93484

246.
74 (0.05) 2
(67.68) 93558
living
past
74 (67.74) 93632

248.
73 (0.05) 2
(67.79) 93705
keep
morning
73 (67.84) 93778

250.
72 (0.05) 1
(67.90) 93850
wish

251.
71 (0.05) 3
(67.95) 93921
afraid
evening
its
71 (68.05) 94063

254.
70 (0.05) 5
(68.10) 94133
call
different
new
won't
you'll
70 (68.30) 94413

259.
69 (0.05) 2
(68.35) 94482
found
live
69 (68.40) 94551

261.
68 (0.05) 2
(68.45) 94619
cat
put
68 (68.50) 94687

263.
67 (0.05) 3
(68.55) 94754
every
suppose
word
67 (68.65) 94888

266.
66 (0.05) 6
(68.69) 94954
business
hear
julia
meet
michael
person
66 (68.93) 95284

272.
65 (0.05) 3
(68.98) 95349
exit
future
point
65 (69.07) 95479

275.
64 (0.05) 6
(69.12) 95543
house
kind
known
lost
miss
she's
64 (69.35) 95863

281.
63 (0.05) 4
(69.40) 95926
eggerson
least
ought
wait
63 (69.53) 96115

285.
62 (0.04) 2
(69.58) 96177
eyes
off
62 (69.62) 96239

287.
61 (0.04) 3
(69.67) 96300
enough
great
seem
61 (69.76) 96422

290.
60 (0.04) 1
(69.80) 96482
isn't

291.
59 (0.04) 2
(69.84) 96541
alex
saw
59 (69.89) 96600

293.
58 (0.04) 4
(69.93) 96658
late
matter
peter
simply
58 (70.05) 96832

297.
57 (0.04) 3
(70.09) 96889
among
family
london
57 (70.18) 97003

300.
56 (0.04) 9
(70.22) 97059
ago
charles
else
home
real
sorry
took
wind
words
56 (70.54) 97507

309.
55 (0.04) 3
(70.58) 97562
against
face
waiting
55 (70.66) 97672

312.
54 (0.04) 4
(70.70) 97726
aunt
happy
seems
until
54 (70.82) 97888

316.
53 (0.04) 4
(70.86) 97941
fact
far
glad
turn
53 (70.97) 98100

320.
52 (0.04) 6
(71.01) 98152
bring
feet
lucasta
power
room
speak
52 (71.20) 98412

326.
51 (0.04) 3
(71.23) 98463
archbishop
knows
reason
51 (71.31) 98565

329.
50 (0.04) 2
(71.34) 98615
gone
john
50 (71.38) 98665

331.
49 (0.04) 3
(71.41) 98714
dinner
peace
water
49 (71.49) 98812

334.
48 (0.03) 6
(71.52) 98860
fire
friends
sense
simpkins
try
wrong
48 (71.69) 99100

340.
47 (0.03) 7
  (71.73) 99147
become
beginning
behind
church
fear
good-bye
kaghan
47 (71.93) 99429

347.
46 (0.03) 7
  (71.96) 99475
already
best
dark
everything
friend
monica
part
46 (72.16) 99751

354.
45 (0.03) 8
  (72.20) 99796
doesn't
explain
forget
gomez
himself
sea
thank
three
45 (72.43) 100111

362.
44 (0.03) 9
  (72.46) 100155
also
country
garden
given
rest
sit
tree
went
wouldn't
44 (72.71) 100507

371.
43 (0.03) 8
  (72.74) 100550
couldn't
hands
haven't
help
music
street
use
woman
43 (72.96) 100851

379.
42 (0.03) 12
  (72.99) 100893
comes
de
england
experience
hand
others
return
since
sometimes
taken
we're
wishwood
42 (73.33) 101355

391.
41 (0.03) 10
  (73.35) 101396
air
b.
dick
indeed
longer
meaning
someone
soon
tea
year
41 (73.62) 101765

401.
40 (0.03) 10
  (73.65) 101805
action
anyone
dear
died
earth
forgotten
order
wife
you'd
young
40 (73.91) 102165

411.
39 (0.03) 3
  (73.94) 102204
party
show
true
39 (74.00) 102282

414.
38 (0.03) 12
  (74.02) 102320
blood
broken
children
few
having
neither
please
seemed
voice
wasn't
what's
white
38 (74.33) 102738

426.
37 (0.03) 9
  (74.35) 102775
amy
learn
makes
memory
often
question
saying
stop
used
37 (74.57) 103071

435.
36 (0.03) 14
  (74.59) 103107
arthur
asked
care
change
doing
either
eye
nor
present
ready
round
sent
several
thinking
36 (74.93) 103575

449.
35 (0.03) 11
  (74.96) 103610
beyond
days
doubt
escape
hour
mine
play
quiet
small
trying
work
35 (75.21) 103960

460.
34 (0.02) 14
  (75.23) 103994
act
afternoon
agatha
cats
empty
felt
happen
hard
heart
met
set
spring
stone
talking
34 (75.55) 104436

474.
33 (0.02) 8
  (75.58) 104469
changed
city
doctor
looking
richard
story
thee
thy
33 (75.74) 104700

482.
32 (0.02) 12
  (75.77) 104732
birth
dry
gave
head
knock
lordship
shadow
sort
stay
suffer
trust
whatever
32 (76.02) 105084

494.
31 (0.02) 14
  (76.05) 105115
bad
brought
common
flowers
follow
hold
land
less
next
strange
till
ways
winter
wonder
31 (76.34) 105518

508.
30 (0.02) 10
  (76.36) 105548
except
half
henry
lived
means
merely
public
voices
whether
window
30 (76.55) 105818

518.
29 (0.02) 12
    (76.57) 105847
carghill
deal
dream
goes
ill
later
looked
meeting
patient
silence
soul
wants
29 (76.81) 106166

530.
28 (0.02) 14
    (76.83) 106194
begin
darkness
decision
desert
downing
hardly
kept
money
scene
seven
sister
spirit
sun
women
28 (77.09) 106558

544.
27 (0.02) 12
    (77.11) 106585
case
chamberlayne
form
matters
open
perfectly
river
rock
sound
towards
walk
we'll
27 (77.32) 106882

556.
26 (0.02) 18
    (77.34) 106908
accept
answer
certain
conversation
expected
getting
king's
la
moon
pray
says
second
señor
speech
taking
thomas
trouble
waste
26 (77.66) 107350

574.
25 (0.02) 25
    (77.68) 107375
across
almost
along
bark
bear
build
claverton
desire
dr.
drink
dying
early
exeunt
flat
four
he'll
making
mary
possible
sudden
summer
times
tired
tomorrow
we've
25 (78.11) 107975

599.
24 (0.02) 23
    (78.13) 107999
able
barnabas
cold
court
girl
glory
hair
husband
important
knowledge
leaving
lives
married
parents
poor
read
run
side
sits
start
they're
to-day
whole
24 (78.51) 108527

622.
23 (0.02) 18
    (78.53) 108550
angel
besides
certainly
clear
faces
jellicle
mustn't
near
ring
sanatorium
season
send
sin
smell
surprise
telephone
themselves
whose
23 (78.81) 108941

640.
22 (0.02) 25
    (78.83) 108963
cry
dare
daughter
difficult
dust
everyone
free
ghosts
heaven
knowing
loved
meant
monkeys
needs
none
ourselves
papers
saints
table
teddington
touch
truth
warburton
worse
yours
22 (79.21) 109491

665.
21 (0.02) 19
    (79.23) 109512
age
brown
english
expect
five
gerald
he'd
human
lot
minutes
mistake
oxford
prepared
private
silent
sleep
song
terms
worth
21 (79.50) 109890

684.
20 (0.01) 15
    (79.51) 109910
abroad
accident
cause
corner
gives
history
itself
law
looks
nice
places
shouldn't
situation
state
success
20 (79.72) 110190

699.
19 (0.01) 25
    (79.73) 110209
aware
became
bed
believed
body
born
car
danger
eat
excuse
generation
imagine
impossible
interesting
likely
names
news
pride
reasons
rings
singing
strong
therefore
understanding
within
19 (80.07) 110665

724.
18 (0.01) 37
    (80.09) 110683
although
anybody
bird
bit
black
break
christmas
dawn
deep
dog
et
finding
forever
forward
guest
guests
high
job
journey
lambert
lay
lead
led
maisie
natural
pain
pattern
perfect
piggott
road
self
simple
stranger
strength
suffering
ten
tried
18 (80.54) 111331
─────────────

761.
17 (0.01) 36
    (80.56) 111348
alive
arrived
began
boy
california
drop
dull
engaged
facts
field
foreign
full
giving
hell
hidden
interest
laughter
leaves
let's
lights
liked
nobody
o'clock
pretty
purpose
rain
rejoice
school
seeing
shan't
started
trees
turning
understood
unless
wash
17 (80.99) 111943
─────────────

797.
16 (0.01) 43
    (81.00) 111959
à
asking
bell
bones
called
cards
chance
changing
choose
company
consider
denman
evil
failure
faith
frightened
happens
happiness
hello
idea
marry
mention
mouth
older
one's
opinion
outside
pass
played
pretend
rose
safe
somewhere
spoken
st.
stair
stand
suddenly
takes
telling
weak
welcome
winchell
16 (81.48) 112631
─────────────

840.
15 (0.01) 59
    (81.49) 112646
advice
agony
arrive
avoid
badgley
book
completely
compliment
conscious
convinced
coplestone
cousin
dance
die
during
easy
ends
feeling
fight
flesh
fog
further
ghost
granted
ground
herself
hours
impression
introduce
ivy
le
meanwhile
movement
moving
notice
offer
opportunity
pereira
position
practical
promise
questions
reality
red
rule
satisfied
settled
share
somebody
stage
staying
sunlight
sweeney
sweet
twenty
usual
violet
war
warm
15 (82.12) 113516
─────────────

899.
14 (0.01) 48
    (82.13) 113530
account
ah
anyway
arms
becket
belong
bright
brother
canterbury
chose
christian
culverwell
curtain
difference
endless
eternal
everybody
france
greater
harm
holy
horror
hotel
kingdom
kitchen
laugh
lie
lunch
master
nature
nearer
noticed
ordinary
park
persuade
piano
prayer
sam
secret
single
telegram
terror
turned
unreal
walking
watch
week
withered
14 (82.61) 114188
─────────────

947.
13 (0.01) 53
  (82.62) 114201
accepted
address
ambitions
beast
below
close
distant
dogs
ease
easier
east
exactly
film
final
fingers
friendship
gate
glass
green
grey
health
heat
however
interested
invited
keeping
les
lose
lucky
mystery
nearly
occasion
organist
playing
quick
quickly
reach
realise
regard
returns
saint
san
servants
sky
spoke
temple
thinks
third
thoughts
train
unusual
wheel
wonderful
13 (83.11) 114877
——————————

1000.
12 (0.01) 77
  (83.12) 114889
above
agree
around
barons
brain
breakfast
careful
cathedral
chorus
chosen
clever
curtains
d'
desk
doom
drawn
ecstasy
explained
fall
fault
feelings
fit
force
forgot
game
grow
guess
hearts
here's
hollow
instead
invisible
judge
laid
letters
macavity
marco
martyr
martyrs
memories
noise
note
office
ones
passing
passion
potter
priest
protect
remind
responsibility
servant
service
shown
sitting
snow
sons
sorrow
step
straight
subject

suggestion
surprising
taxi
tonight
torn
twice
vision
void
walked
wall
weather
who's
wings
wondered
worry
yesterday
12 (83.78) 115801
——————————

1077.
11 (0.01) 87
  (83.78) 115812
admit
adopt
appear
art
asleep
awfully
beat
behaviour
beneath
beside
bitter
blame
bone
brothers
cease
chair
coat
colour
command
condition
cross
crossed
curse
deceived
dine
eating
ended
essex
expression
fell
floor
fond
fool
forced
forgive
grateful
gumbie
hall
hurry
influence
inside
kinkanja
language
low
minor
mistaken
moved
odd
passage
perpetual
powers
prefer
priests
problem
propose
ran
reading
reilly
respect
running
sacrifice

sake
seas
shadows
shock
short
six
slow
smoke
south
streets
successful
suffered
suspect
talked
thine
town
traitor
trap
unexpected
unknown
various
view
waking
wedding
wing
younger
11 (84.47) 116758
——————————

1164.
10 (0.01) 104
   (84.48) 116768
10 (85.22) 117798

1268.
9 (0.01) 129
   (85.23) 117807
9 (86.06) 118959

1397.
8 (0.01) 162
   (86.07) 118967
8 (87.00) 120255

1559.
7 (0.01) 202
   (87.00) 120262
7 (88.02) 121669

1761.
6 (0.00) 259
   (88.03) 121675
6 (89.15) 123223

2020.
5 (0.00) 309
   (89.15) 123228
5 (90.26) 124768

2329.
4 (0.00) 504
   (90.27) 124772
4 (91.72) 126784

2833.
3 (0.00) 856
   (91.72) 126787
3 (93.58) 129352

3689.
2 (0.00) 1619
   (93.58) 129354
2 (95.92) 132590

5308.
1 (0.00) 5636
   (95.92) 132591
1 (100.00) 138226

Lines Containing Numbers

127 Cor1 March	13	5,800,000 rifles and carbines,
127 Cor1 March	14	102,000 machine guns,
127 Cor1 March	15	28,000 trench mortars,
127 Cor1 March	16	53,000 field and heavy guns,
127 Cor1 March	18	13,000 aeroplanes,
127 Cor1 March	19	24,000 aeroplane engines,
127 Cor1 March	20	50,000 ammunition waggons,
127 Cor1 March	21	now 55,000 army waggons,
127 Cor1 March	22	11,000 field kitchens,
127 Cor1 March	23	1,150 field bakeries.
129 Cor2 State	5	The Order of the Black Eagle (1st and 2nd class),
136 5FingerEx4	15	He has 999 canaries
154 Rock 3	m20	1ST MALE VOICE:
154 Rock 3	m28	2ND MALE VOICE:
232 Skimble	1	There's a whisper down the line at 11.39
232 Skimble	9	At 11.42 then the signal's overdue
238 MC	m 9	*The scene is the Archbishop's Hall, on December 2nd*, 1170
238 MC	m17	*the second scene is in the Cathedral, on December 29th*, 1170
260 MC	3m 1	*preaches in the Cathedral on Christmas Morning*, 1170
328 FR Charles	14	cart in Ebury Street early on the morning of January 1st, was
328 FR Charles	15	fined £50 and costs to-day, and forbidden to drive a car for the
328 FR Charles	23	travelling at the rate of 66 miles an hour. When asked why he
353 CP	1m 1	Act One. Scene 1
374 CP	1m 1	Act One. Scene 2
384 CP	1m 1	Act One. Scene 3
493 CC	2m 1	*The Business Room, as in Act 1. Several mornings later.*

Index of Words Containing
Hyphen or Apostrophe

Each part of every word that contains a hyphen or an apostrophe is sorted alphabetically and printed in capitals, followed (in alphabetical order) by all the words that contain that part in any position. Forms containing apostrophes are expanded (e.g., *hasn't* expands to the words *HAS* and *NOT*).

In cases of uncertainty, alternative expansions are given. For example, *he's* is expanded both to *HE IS* and to *HE HAS*. Cross-references are given for forms that may end in *'s*; these may be found by looking at the section of *'s* endings in the Reverse Index of Word Forms.

Certain hyphenated forms should be noted in particular because they occur in the text also in their unhyphenated form. For example, *to-day* is referred back to *TODAY*, which exists as a word in its own right.